Stanley Gibbons
SIMPLIFIED
CATALOGUE

Stamps of the World

2000 Edition

An illustrated and priced three-volume guide to the postage stamps of the whole world, excluding changes of paper, perforation, shade and watermark

VOLUME 3

COMMONWEALTH COUNTRIES

STANLEY GIBBONS LTD
London and Ringwood

By Appointment to
Her Majesty the Queen
Stanley Gibbons Limited
London
Philatelists

65th Edition

Published in Great Britain by
Stanley Gibbons Ltd
Publications Editorial, Sales Offices and Distribution Centre
5, Parkside, Christchurch Road,
Ringwood, Hampshire BH24 3SH
Telephone 01425 472363

ISBN: 085259-478-X

Published as Stanley Gibbons Simplified Stamp Catalogue from 1934 to 1970, renamed Stamps of the World in 1971, and produced in two (1982–88) or three (from 1989) volumes as Stanley Gibbons Simplified Catalogue of Stamps of the World.
This volume published November 1999

S.G. Item No. 2883 (00)

Origination by Polestar Whitefriars Ltd, Tunbridge Wells, Kent
Printed in Great Britain by Bemrose Security Printing, London & Derby

Stanley Gibbons

SIMPLIFIED CATALOGUE

Stamps of the World

This popular catalogue is a straightforward three-volume listing of the stamps that have been issued everywhere in the world since the very first–Great Britain's famous Penny Black in 1840.

This edition continues the three-volume format. Volume 1 (Foreign countries A–J) appeared in September, Volume 2 (Foreign countries K–Z) in October, and Volume 3 covering Commonwealth countries completes the trio.

Readers are reminded that the Catalogue Supplements, published in each issue of **Gibbons Stamp Monthly,** can be used to update the listings in **Stamps of the World** as well as our twenty-two part standard catalogue. To make the supplement even more useful the Type numbers given to the illustrations are the same in the Stamps of the World as in the standard catalogues. The first Catalogue Supplement to this Volume appeared in the October 1999 issue of **Gibbons Stamp Monthly.**

Gibbons Stamp Monthly can be obtained through newsagents or on postal subscription from Stanley Gibbons Publications, 5, Parkside, Christchurch Road, Ringwood, Hants BH24 3SH.

The catalogue has many important features:

- As an indication of current values virtually every stamp is priced. Thousands of alterations have been made since the last edition.
- By being set out on a simplified basis that excludes changes of paper, perforation, shade, watermark, gum or printer's and date imprints it is particularly easy to use. (For its exact scope see "Information for users" pages following.)
- The thousands of illustrations and helpful descriptions of stamp designs make it of maximum appeal to collectors with thematic interests.
- Its catalogue numbers are the world-recognised Stanley Gibbons numbers throughout.
- Helpful introductory notes for the collector are included, backed by much historical, geographical and currency information.
- A very detailed index gives instant location of countries in this volume, and a cross-reference to those included in the other volumes.

Over 9,275 stamps and 2,500 new illustrations have been added to the 2000 edition. The three volumes contain over 361,220 stamps and 87,170 illustrations.

The listings in this edition are based on the standard catalogues: Part 1 (British Commonwealth) (2000 edition), Part 2 (Austria & Hungary) (5th edition), Part 3 (Balkans) (4th edition), Part 4 (Benelux) (4th edition), Part 5 (Czechoslovakia & Poland) (5th edition), Part 6 (France) (4th edition), Part 7 (Germany) (5th edition), Part 8 (Italy & Switzerland) (5th edition), Part 9 (Portugal & Spain) (4th edition), Part 10 (Russia) (5th edition), Part 11 (Scandinavia) (4th edition), Part 12 (Africa since Independence A-E) (2nd edition), Part 13 (Africa since Independence F-M) (1st edition), Part 14 (Africa since Independence N-Z) (1st edition), Part 15 (Central America (2nd edition), Part 16 (Central Asia) (3rd edition), Part 17 (China) (6th edition), Part 18 (Japan & Korea) (4th edition), Part 19 (Middle East) (5th edition), Part 20 (South America) (3rd editon), Part 21 (South-East Asia) (3rd edition), and Part 22 (United States) (4th edition).

Stanley Gibbons Stamp Catalogue
Complete List of Parts

1 British Commonwealth
(Annual in two volumes)

Foreign Countries

2 Austria & Hungary (5th edition, 1994)
Austria · Bosnia & Herzegovina · U.N. (Vienna) · Hungary

3 Balkans (4th edition, 1998)
Albania · Bulgaria · Greece & Islands · Rumania · Yugoslavia

4 Benelux (4th edition, 1993)
Belgium & Colonies · Netherlands & Colonies · Luxembourg

5 Czechoslovakia & Poland (5th edition, 1995)
Czechoslovakia · Bohemia & Moravia · Slovakia · Poland

6 France (4th edition, 1993)
France · Colonies · Post Offices · Andorra · Monaco

7 Germany (5th edition, 1996)
Germany · States · Colonies · Post Offices

8 Italy & Switzerland (5th edition, 1997)
Italy & Colonies · Fiume · San Marino · Vatican City · Trieste · Liechtenstein · Switzerland · U.N. (Geneva)

9 Portugal & Spain (4th edition, 1996)
Andorra · Portugal & Colonies · Spain & Colonies

10 Russia (5th edition, 1999)
Russia · Baltic States · Mongolia · Tuva

11 Scandinavia (4th edition, 1994)
Aland Islands · Denmark · Faroe Islands · Finland · Greenland · Iceland · Norway · Sweden

12 Africa since Independence A-E (2nd edition, 1983)
Algeria · Angola · Benin · Bophuthatswana · Burundi · Cameroun · Cape Verde · Central African Republic · Chad · Comoro Islands · Congo · Djibouti · Equatorial Guinea · Ethiopia

13 Africa since Independence F-M (1st edition, 1981)
Gabon · Guinea · Guinea-Bissau · Ivory Coast · Liberia · Libya · Malagasy Republic · Mali · Mauritania · Morocco · Mozambique

14 Africa since Independence N-Z (1st edition, 1981)
Niger Republic · Rwanda · St. Thomas & Prince · Senegal · Somalia · Sudan · Togo · Transkei · Tunisia · Upper Volta · Venda · Zaire

15 Central America (2nd edition, 1984)
Costa Rica · Cuba · Dominican Republic · El Salvador · Guatemala · Haiti · Honduras · Mexico · Nicaragua · Panama

16 Central Asia (3rd edition, 1992)
Afghanistan · Iran · Turkey

17 China (6th edition, 1998)
China · Taiwan · Tibet · Foreign P.O.s

18 Japan & Korea (4th edition, 1997)
Japan · Ryukyus · Korean Empire · South Korea · North Korea

19 Middle East (5th edition, 1996)
Bahrain · Egypt · Iraq · Israel · Jordan · Kuwait · Lebanon · Oman · Qatar · Saudi Arabia · Syria · U.A.E. · Yemen

20 South America (3rd edition, 1989)
Argentina · Bolivia · Brazil · Chile · Colombia · Ecuador · Paraguay · Peru · Surinam · Uruguay · Venezuela

21 South-East Asia (3rd edition, 1995)
Bhutan · Indonesia · Kampuchea · Laos · Myanmar · Nepal · Philippines · Thailand · Vietnam

22 United States (4th edition, 1994)
U.S. & Possessions · Canal Zone · Marshall Islands · Micronesia · Palau · U.N. (New York, Geneva, Vienna)

Thematic Catalogues

Stanley Gibbons Catalogues for use with **Stamps of the World.**
Collect Aircraft on Stamps (1st edition, 1994)
Collect Birds on Stamps (4th edition, 1996)
Collect Chess on Stamps (2nd edition, 1999)
Collect Fish on Stamps (1st edition, 1999)
Collect Fungi on Stamps (2nd edition, 1997)
Collect Railways on Stamps (3rd edition, 1999)
Collect Shells on Stamps (1st edition, 1995)
Collect Ships on Stamps (new edition early 2000)

Information for users

Aim

The aim of this catalogue is to provide a straightforward illustrated and priced guide to the postage stamps of the whole world to help you to enjoy the greatest hobby of the present day.

Arrangement

The catalogue lists countries in alphabetical order and there is a complete index at the end of each volume. For ease of reference country names are also printed at the head of each page.

Within each country, postage stamps are listed first. They are followed by separate sections for such other categories as postage due stamps, parcel post stamps, express stamps, official stamps, etc.

All catalogue lists are set out according to dates of issue of the stamps, starting from the earliest and working through to the most recent. New issues received too late for inclusion in the main lists will be found as "Addenda" at the end of each volume.

Scope of the Catalogue

The *Simplified Catalogue of Stamps of the World* contains listings of postage stamps only. Apart from the ordinary definitive, commemorative and air-mail stamps of each country – which appear first in each list – there are sections for the following where appropriate:

- postage due stamps
- parcel post stamps
- official stamps
- express and special delivery stamps
- charity and compulsory tax stamps
- newspaper and journal stamps
- printed matter stamps
- registration stamps
- acknowledgement of receipt stamps
- late fee and too late stamps
- military post stamps
- recorded message stamps
- personal delivery stamps

We receive numerous enquiries from collectors about other items which do not fall within the categories set out above and which consequently do not appear in the catalogue lists. It may be helpful, therefore, to summarise the other kinds of stamp that exist but which we deliberately exclude from this postage stamp catalogue.

We do *not* list the following:

Fiscal or revenue stamps: stamps used solely in collecting taxes or fees for non-postal purposes. Examples would be stamps which pay a tax on a receipt, represent the stamp duty on a contract or frank a customs document. Common inscriptions found include: Documentary, Proprietary, Inter. Revenue, Contract Note.

Local stamps: postage stamps whose validity and use are limited in area, say to a single town or city, though in some cases they provided, with official sanction, services in parts of countries not covered by the respective government.

Local carriage labels and Private local issues: many labels exist ostensibly to cover the cost of ferrying mail from one of Great Britain's offshore islands to the nearest mainland post office. They are not recognised as valid for national or international mail. Examples: Calf of Man, Davaar, Herm, Lundy, Pabay, Stroma. Items from some other places have only the status of tourist souvenir labels.

Telegraph stamps: stamps intended solely for the prepayment of telegraphic communication.

Bogus or "phantom" stamps: labels from mythical places or non-existent administrations. Examples in the classical period were Sedang, Counani, Clipperton Island and in modern times Thomond and Monte Bello Islands. Numerous labels have also appeared since the War from dissident groups as propaganda for their claims and without authority from the home governments. Common examples are labels for "Free Albania", "Free Rumania" and "Free Croatia" and numerous issues for Nagaland, Indonesia and the South Moluccas ("Republik Maluku Selatan").

Railway letter fee stamps: special stamps issued by railway companies for the conveyance of letters by rail. Example: Talyllyn Railway. Similar services are now offered by some bus companies and the labels they issue likewise do not qualify for inclusion in the catalogue.

Perfins ("perforated initials"): numerous postage stamps may be found with initial letters or designs punctured through them by tiny holes. These are applied by private and public concerns as a precaution against theft and do not qualify for separate mention.

Information for users

Labels: innumerable items exist resembling stamps but – as they do not prepay postage – they are classified as labels. The commonest categories are:

— propaganda and publicity labels: designed to further a cause or campaign;

— exhibition labels: particularly souvenirs from philatelic events;

— testing labels: stamp-size labels used in testing stamp-vending machines;

— Post Office training school stamps: British stamps overprinted with two thick vertical bars or SCHOOL SPECIMEN are produced by the Post Office for training purposes;

— seals and stickers: numerous charities produce stamp-like labels, particularly at Christmas and Easter, as a means of raising funds and these have no postal validity.

Cut-outs: items of postal stationery, such as envelopes, cards and wrappers, often have stamps impressed or imprinted on them. They may usually be cut out and affixed to envelopes, etc., for postal use if desired, but such items are not listed in this catalogue.

Collectors wanting further information about exact definitions are referred to *Philatelic Terms Illustrated,* published by Stanley Gibbons and containing many illustrations in colour (new edition in preparation).

There is also a priced listing of the postal fiscals of Great Britain in our Part 1 *(British Commonwealth)* Catalogue and in Volume 1 of the *Great Britain Specialised* Catalogue (5th and later editions).

Catalogue Numbers

Stanley Gibbons catalogue numbers are recognised universally and any individual stamp can be identified by quoting the catalogue number (the one at the left of the column) prefixed by the name of the country and the letters "S.G.". Do not confuse the catalogue number with the type numbers which refer to illustrations.

Prices

Prices in the left-hand column are for unused stamps and those in the right-hand column for used. Prices are given in pence and pounds:

100 pence (p) = 1 pound (£1).

Prices are shown as follows:

10 means 10p (10 pence);
1.75 means £1.75 (1 pound and 75 pence);
For £100 and above, prices are in whole pounds.

Our prices are for stamps in fine average condition, and in issues where condition varies we may ask more for the superb and less for the sub-standard.

The minimum catalogue price quoted is 10p. For individual stamps prices between 10p and 30p are provided as a guide for catalogue users. The lowest price charged for individual stamps purchased from Stanley Gibbons is 30p.

The prices quoted are generally for the cheapest variety of stamps but it is worth noting that differences of watermark, perforation, or other details, outside the scope of this catalogue, may often increase the value of the stamp.

Prices quoted for mint issues are for single examples. Those in se-tenant pairs, strips, blocks or sheets may be worth more.

Where prices are not given in either column it is either because the stamps are not known to exist in that particular condition, or, more usually, because there is no reliable information as to value.

All prices are subject to change without prior notice and we give no guarantee to supply all stamps priced. Prices quoted for albums, publications, etc. advertised in this catalogue are also subject to change without prior notice.

Due to different production methods it is sometimes possible for new editions of Parts 2 to 22 to appear showing revised prices which are not included in that year's *Stamps of the World.*

Unused Stamps

In the case of stamps from *Great Britain* and the *Commonwealth,* prices for unused stamps of Queen Victoria to King George V are for lightly hinged examples; unused prices of King Edward VIII to Queen Elizabeth II issues are for unmounted mint. The prices of unused *Foreign* stamps are for lightly hinged examples for those issued before 1946, thereafter for examples unmounted mint.

Used Stamps

Prices for used stamps generally refer to postally used examples, though for certain issues they are for cancelled-to-order.

Information for users

Guarantee

All stamps supplied by us are guaranteed originals in the following terms:

If not as described, and returned by the purchaser, we undertake to refund the price paid to us in the original transaction. If any stamp is certified as genuine by the Expert Committee of the Royal Philatelic Society, London, or by B.P.A. Expertising Ltd., the purchaser shall not be entitled to make any claim against us for any error, omission or mistake in such certificate.

Consumers' statutory rights are not affected by the above guarantee.

Currency

At the beginning of each country brief details give the currencies in which the values of the stamps are expressed. The dates, where given, are those of the earliest stamp issues in the particular currency. Where the currency is obvious, e.g. where the colony has the same currency as the mother country, no details are given.

Illustrations

Illustrations of any surcharges and overprints which are shown and not described are actual size; stamp illustrations are reduced to $\frac{3}{4}$ linear, *unless otherwise stated.*

"Key-Types"

A number of standard designs occur so frequently in the stamps of the French, German, Portuguese and Spanish colonies that it would be a waste of space to repeat them. Instead these are all illustrated on page xii together with the descriptive names and letters by which they are referred to in the lists.

Type Numbers

These are the bold figures found below each illustration. References to "Type **6**", for example, in the lists of a country should therefore be understood to refer to the illustration below which the number **"6"** appears. These type numbers are also given in the second column of figures alongside each list of stamps, thus indicating clearly the design of each stamp. In the case of Key-Types – see above – letters take the place of the type numbers.

Where an issue comprises stamps of similar design, represented in this catalogue by one illustration, the corresponding type numbers should be taken as indicating this general design.

Where there are blanks in the type number column it means that the type of the corresponding stamps is that shown by the last number above in the type column of the same issue.

A dash (–) in the type column means that no illustration of the stamp is shown.

Where type numbers refer to stamps of another country, e.g. where stamps of one country are overprinted for use in another, this is always made clear in the text.

Stamp Designs

Brief descriptions of the subjects of the stamp designs are given either below or beside the illustrations, at the foot of the list of the issue concerned, or in the actual lists. Where a particular subject, e.g. the portrait of a well-known monarch, recurs frequently the description is not repeated, nor are obvious designs described.

Generally, the unillustrated designs are in the same shape and size as the one illustrated, except where otherwise indicated.

Surcharges and Overprints

Surcharges and overprints are usually described in the headings to the issues concerned. Where the actual wording of a surcharge or overprint is given it is shown in bold type.

Some stamps are described as being "Surcharged in words", e.g. **TWO CENTS,** and others "Surcharged in figures and words", e.g. **20 CENTS,** although of course many surcharges are in foreign languages and combinations of words and figures are numerous. There are often bars, etc., obliterating old values or inscriptions but in general these are only mentioned where it is necessary to avoid confusion.

No attention is paid in this catalogue to colours of overprints and surcharges so that stamps with the same overprints in different colours are not listed separately.

Numbers in brackets after the descriptions of overprinted or surcharged stamps are the catalogue numbers of the unoverprinted stamps.

Note – the words "inscribed" or "inscription" always refer to wording incorporated in the design of a stamp and not surcharges or overprints.

Coloured Papers

Where stamps are printed on coloured paper the description is given as e.g. "4c. black on blue" – a stamp printed in black on blue paper. No attention is paid in this catalogue to differences in the texture of paper, e.g. laid, wove.

Information for users

Watermarks

Stamps having different watermarks, but otherwise the same, are not listed separately. No reference is therefore made to watermarks in this volume.

Stamp Colours

Colour names are only required for the identification of stamps, therefore they have been made as simple as possible. Thus "scarlet", "vermilion", "carmine" are all usually called red. Qualifying colour names have been introduced only where necessary for the sake of clearness.

Where stamps are printed in two or more colours the central portion of the design is in the first colour given, unless otherwise stated.

Perforations

All stamps are perforated unless otherwise stated. No distinction is made between the various gauges of perforation but early stamp issues which exist both imperforate and perforated are usually listed separately.

Where a heading states "Imperf. or perf." or "Perf. or rouletted" this does not necessarily mean that all values of the issue are found in both conditions.

Dates of Issue

The date given at the head of each issue is that of the appearance of the earliest stamp in the series. As stamps of the same design or issue are usually grouped together a list of King George VI stamps, for example, headed "1938" may include stamps issued from 1938 to the end of the reign.

Se-tenant Pairs

Many modern issues are printed in sheets containing different designs or face values. Such pairs, blocks, strips or sheets are described as being "se-tenant" and they are outside the scope of this catalogue, although reference to them may occur in instances where they form a composite design.

Miniature Sheets

These are outside the scope of this catalogue but are listed in all other Stanley Gibbons catalogues.

"Appendix" Countries

We regret that, since 1968, it has been necessary to establish an Appendix (at the end of each country as appropriate) to which numerous stamps have had to be consigned. Several countries imagine that by issuing huge quantities of unnecessary stamps they will have a ready source of income from stamp collectors – and particularly from the less-experienced ones. Stanley Gibbons refuse to encourage this exploitation of the hobby and we do not stock the stamps concerned.

Two kinds of stamp are therefore given the briefest of mentions in the Appendix, purely for the sake of record. Administrations issuing stamps greatly in excess of true postal needs have the offending issues placed there. Likewise it contains stamps which have not fulfilled all the normal conditions for full catalogue listing.

These conditions are that the stamps must be issued by a legitimate postal authority, recognised by the government concerned, and are adhesives, valid for proper postal use in the class of service for which they are inscribed. Stamps, with the exception of such categories as postage dues and officials, must be available to the general public at face value with no artificial restrictions being imposed on their distribution.

The publishers of this catalogue have observed, with concern, the proliferation of 'artificial' stamp-issuing territories. On several occasions this has resulted in separately inscribed issues for various component parts of otherwise united states or territories.

Stanley Gibbons Publications have decided that where such circumstances occur, they will not, in the future, list these items in the SG catalogue without first satisfying themselves that the stamps represent a genuine political, historical or postal division within the country concerned. Any such issues which do not fulfil this stipulation will be recorded in the Catalogue Appendix only.

Stamps in the Appendix are kept under review in the light of any newly acquired information about them. If we are satisfied that a stamp qualifies for proper listing in the body of the catalogue it is moved there.

"Undesirable Issues"

The rules governing many competitive exhibitions – including the Melville Competition – are set by the Fédération Internationale de Philatelie and stipulate a downgrading of marks for stamps classed as "undesirable issues".

This catalogue can be taken as a guide to status. All stamps in the main listings and Addenda are acceptable. Stamps in the Appendix should not be entered for competition as these are the "undesirable issues".

Information for users

Particular care is advised with Aden Protectorate States, Ajman, Bhutan, Chad, Fujeira, Khor Fakkan, Manama, Ras al Khaima, Sharjah, Umm al Qiwain and Yemen. Totally bogus stamps exist (as explained in Appendix notes) and these are to be avoided also for competition. As distinct from "undesirable stamps" certain categories are not covered in this catalogue purely by reason of its scope (see page v). Consult the particular competition rules to see if such are admissible even though not listed by us.

Where to Look for More Detailed Listings

The present work deliberately omits details of paper, perforation, shade and watermark. But as you become more absorbed in stamp collecting and wish to get greater enjoyment from the hobby you may well want to study these matters.

All the information you require about any particular postage stamp will be found in the main Stanley Gibbons Catalogues.

Commonwealth countries in Volume 3 are covered by the Part 1 (British Commonwealth) Catalogue published annually in two volumes.

For foreign countries you can easily find which catalogue to consult by looking at the country headings in the present book.

To the right of each country name are code letters specifying which volume of our main catalogues contains that country's listing.

The code letters are as follows:

Pt. 2 Part 2

Pt. 3 Part 3 etc.

(See page iv for complete list of Parts.)

So, for example, if you want to know more about Chinese stamps than is contained in the *Simplified Catalogue of Stamps of the World* the reference to

CHINA Pt. 17

guides you to the Gibbons Part 17 *(China)* Catalogue listing for the details you require.

New editions of Parts 2 to 22 appear at irregular intervals.

Correspondence

Whilst we welcome information and suggestions we must ask correspondents to include the cost of postage for the return of any stamps submitted plus registration where appropriate. Letters should be addressed to The Catalogue Editor at Ringwood.

Where information is solicited purely for the benefit of the enquirer we regret we cannot undertake to reply unless stamps or reply coupons are sent to cover the postage.

Identification of Stamps

We regret we do not give opinions as to the genuineness of stamps, nor do we identify stamps or number them by our Catalogue.

Users of this catalogue are referred to our companion booklet entitled *Stamp Collecting — How to Identify Stamps.* It explains how to look up stamps in this catalogue, contains a full checklist of stamp inscriptions and gives help in dealing with unfamiliar scripts. It is available from Stanley Gibbons at £2.95, postage extra.

Stanley Gibbons would like to complement your collection

At Stanley Gibbons we offer a range of services which are designed to complement your collection.

Our modern stamp shop, the largest in Europe, together with our rare stamp department has one of the most comprehensive stocks of Great Britain in the world, so whether you are a beginner or an experienced philatelist you are certain to find something to suit your special requirements.

Alternatively through our Mail Order services you can control the growth of your collection from the comfort of your own home. Our Postal Sales Department regularly sends out mailings of Special Offers. We can also help with your wants list—so why not ask us for those elusive items?

And don't forget Stanley Gibbons Auctions which holds regular sales each year. Come along in person or send in a written bid for the items you require. For details of current subscription rates for Auction catalogues write to Stanley Gibbons Auctions, 399 Strand, London WC2R 0LX.

Why not take advantage of the many services we have to offer? Visit our premises in the Strand or, for more information, write to the appropriate address on page x.

Stanley Gibbons Holdings Plc Addresses

Stanley Gibbons Limited, Stanley Gibbons Auctions

399 Strand, London WC2R 0LX

Telephone 0171 (020 7 from 22nd April 2000) 836 8444 Fax 0171 (020 7) 836 7342 for all departments.

Auction Room and Specialist Stamp Departments. Open Monday–Friday 9.30 a.m. to 5 p.m.

Shop. Open Monday–Friday 8.30 a.m. to 6 p.m. and Saturday 9.30 a.m. to 5.30 p.m.

Fraser's

Autographs, photographs, letters and documents
399 Strand, London WC2 0LX
Telephone 0171 (020 7 from 22nd April 2000) 836 8444 Fax 0171 (020 7) 7342

Monday–Friday 9 a.m. to 5.30 p.m. and Saturday 10 a.m. to 4 p.m.

Stanley Gibbons Publications

5 Parkside, Christchurch Road, Ringwood, Hants BH24 3SH.
Telephone 01425 472363 (24 hour answerphone service) Fax 01425 470247.
E-mail: info@stangib.demon.co.uk

Publication Showroom (at above address). Open Monday–Friday 9 a.m. to 3 p.m.

Publications Mail Order. FREEPHONE 0800 611622. Monday–Friday 8.30 a.m. to 5 p.m.

Stanley Gibbons Publications Overseas Representation

Stanley Gibbons Publications are represented overseas by the following sole distributors (*), distributors (**) or licensees (***).

Australia*
Lighthouse Philatelic (Aust.) Pty. Ltd., P.O. Box 763, Strawberry Hills, New South Wales, 2012 Australia.

Stanley Gibbons (Australia) Pty. Ltd.***
Level 6, 36 Clarence Street, Sydney, New South Wales 2000, Australia.

Belgium and Luxembourg**
Davo c/o Philac, Rue du Midi 48, Bruxelles, 1000 Belgium.

Canada*
Lighthouse Publications (Canada) Ltd., 255 Duke Street, Montreal Quebec, Canada H3C 2M2.

Denmark**
Davo/Samlerforum, Ostergade 3, DK 7470 Karup, Denmark.

Finland**
Davo c/o Suomen Postimerkkeily Ludvingkatu 5 SF-00130 Helsinki, Finland.

France*
Davo France (Casteilla), 10, Rue Leon Foucault, 78184 St. Quentin Yvelines Cesex, France.

Germany and Austria*
Leuchtturm Albenverlag Gmbh u.Co. Am Spakenberg 45, Postfach 1340, D-21495 Geesthacht, Germany.

Hong Kong**
Po-on Stamp Service, G.P.O. Box 2498, Hong Kong.

Israel**
Capital Stamps, P.O. Box 3769, Jerusalem 91036, Israel.

Italy*
Ernesto Marini SRL, Via Struppa 300, I-16165, Genova GE, Italy.

Japan**
Japan Philatelic Co. Ltd., P.O. Box 2, Suginami-Minami, Tokyo, Japan.

Netherlands*
Davo Publications, P.O. Box 411, 7400 AK Deventer, Netherlands.

New Zealand***
Stanley Gibbons (New Zealand) Ltd., P.O. Box 80, Wellington, New Zealand.

Norway**
Davo Norge A/S, P.O. Box 738 Sentrum, N-0105, Oslo, Norway.

Singapore***
Stanley Gibbons (Singapore) Pte Ltd., Raffles City P.O. Box 1689, Singapore 9117.

South Africa**
Republic Coin and Stamp Accessories (Pty) Ltd., Republic House, 54A Silverwood Road, Bramley 2090, Gauteng, South Africa.

Sweden*
Chr Winther Soerensen AB, Box 43, S-310 Knaered, Sweden.

Switzerland**
Phila Service, Burgstrasse 160, CH 4125, Riehen, Switzerland.

West Indies/Caribbean**
Hugh Dunphy, P.O. Box 413, Kingston 10, Jamaica, West Indies.

Abbreviations

Anniv.	denotes	Anniversary
Assn.	,,	Association
Bis.	,,	Bistre
Bl.	,,	Blue
Bldg.	,,	Building
Blk.	,,	Black
Br.	,,	British *or* Bridge
Brn.	,,	Brown
B.W.I.	,,	British West Indies
C.A.R.I.F.T.A.	,,	Caribbean Free Trade Area
Cent.	,,	Centenary
Chest.	,,	Chestnut
Choc.	,,	Chocolate
Clar.	,,	Claret
Coll.	,,	College
Commem.	,,	Commemoration
Conf.	,,	Conference
Diag.	,,	Diagonally
E.C.A.F.E.	,,	Economic Commission for Asia and Far East
Emer.	,,	Emerald
E.P.T. Conference	,,	European Postal and Telecommunications Conference
Exn.	,,	Exhibition
F.A.O.	,,	Food and Agriculture Organization
Fig.	,,	Figure
G.A.T.T.	,,	General Agreement on Tariffs and Trade
G.B.	,,	Great Britain
Gen.	,,	General
Govt.	,,	Government
Grn.	,,	Green
Horiz.	,,	Horizontal
H.Q.	,,	Headquarters
Imperf.	,,	Imperforate
Inaug.	,,	Inauguration
Ind.	,,	Indigo
Inscr.	,,	Inscribed or inscription
Int.	,,	International
I.A.T.A.	,,	International Air Transport Association
I.C.A.O.	,,	International Civil Aviation Organization
I.C.Y.	,,	International Co-operation Year
I.G.Y.	,,	International Geophysical Year
I.L.O.	,,	International Labour Office (or later, Organization)
I.M.C.O.	,,	Inter-Governmental Maritime Consultative Organization
I.T.U.	,,	International Telecommunication Union
Is.	,,	Islands
Lav.	,,	Lavender
Mar.	,,	Maroon
mm.	,,	Millimetres
Mult.	,,	Multicoloured

Mve.	denotes	Mauve
Nat.	,,	National
N.A.T.O.	,,	North Atlantic Treaty Organization
O.D.E.C.A.	,,	Organization of Central American States
Ol.	,,	Olive
Optd.	,,	Overprinted
Orge. *or* oran.	,,	Orange
P.A.T.A.	,,	Pacific Area Travel Association
Perf.	,,	Perforated
Post.	,,	Postage
Pres.	,,	President
P.U.	,,	Postal Union
Pur.	,,	Purple
R.	,,	River
R.S.A.	,,	Republic of South Africa
Roul.	,,	Rouletted
Sep.	,,	Sepia
S.E.A.T.O.	,,	South East Asia Treaty Organization
Surch.	,,	Surcharged
T.	,,	Type
T.U.C.	,,	Trades Union Congress
Turq.	,,	Turquoise
Ultram.	,,	Ultramarine
U.N.E.S.C.O.	,,	United Nations Educational, Scientific & Cultural Organization
U.N.I.C.E.F.	,,	United Nations Children's Fund
U.N.O.	,,	United Nations Organization
U.N.R.W.A.	,,	United Nations Relief and Works Agency for Palestine Refugees in the Near East
U.N.T.E.A.	,,	United Nations Temporary Executive Authority
U.N.R.R.A.	,,	United Nations Relief and Rehabilitation Administration
U.P.U.	,,	Universal Postal Union
Verm.	,,	Vermilion
Vert.	,,	Vertical
Vio.	,,	Violet
W.F.T.U.	,,	World Federation of Trade Unions
W.H.O.	,,	World Health Organization
Yell.	,,	Yellow

Arabic Numerals

As in the case of European figures, the details of the Arabic numerals vary in different stamp designs, but they should be readily recognised with the aid of this illustration:

٠	١	٢	٣	٤
0	1	2	3	4
٥	٦	٧	٨	٩
5	6	7	8	9

Key-Types

(see note on page vii)

French Group

A. " Blanc."

B. " Mouchon."

C. " Merson."

D. " Tablet."

E.

F.

G.

H.

" International Colonial Exhibition."

I. " Faidherbe."

J. " Palms."

K. " Balay."

L. " Natives."

M. " Figure."

German Group

N. " Yacht."

O. " Yacht."

Spanish Group

X. " Alfonso XII."

Y. " Baby."

Z. "Curly Head"

Portuguese Group

P. " Crown."

Q. " Embossed."

R. " Figures."

S. " Carlos."

T. " Manoel."

U. " Ceres."

V. " Newspaper."

W. " Due."

STANLEY GIBBONS SIMPLIFIED CATALOGUE OF STAMPS OF THE WORLD—VOLUME 3 COMMONWEALTH COUNTRIES

ABU DHABI

The largest of the Trucial States in the Persian Gulf. Treaty relations with Great Britain expired on 31 December 1966, when the Abu Dhabi Post Office took over the postal services.

1964. 100 naye paise = 1 rupee.
1966. 1,000 fils = 1 dinar.

1 Shaikh Shakhbut bin Sultan

3 Ruler's Palace

1964.

1	1	5 n.p. green	1·50	1·75
2		15 n.p. brown	2·00	1·25
3		20 n.p. blue	2·00	85
4		30 n.p. orange	3·00	1·50
5	–	40 n.p. violet	3·25	60
6	–	50 n.p. bistre	3·50	1·75
7	–	75 n.p. black	3·50	3·00
8	3	1 r. green	4·00	1·25
9		2 r. black	7·50	3·25
10	–	5 r. red	16·00	8·50
11	–	10 r. blue	23·00	14·00

DESIGNS: As Type **1**: 40 to 75 n.p. Mountain gazelle; As Type **3**: 5, 10 r. Oil rig and camels.

5 Saker Falcon

1965. Falconry.

12	5	20 n.p. brown and blue	10·00	1·75
13	–	40 n.p. brown and blue	13·00	2·75
14	–	2 r. sepia and turquoise	22·00	13·00

DESIGNS: 40 n.p., 2 r. Other types of Saker falcon on gloved hand.

1966. Nos. 1/11 surch in new currency ("Fils" only on Nos. 5/7) and ruler's portrait obliterated with bars.

15	1	5 f. on 5 n.p. green	8·00	5·50
16		15 f. on 15 n.p. brown	8·00	4·50
17		20 f. on 20 n.p. blue	9·50	6·50
18		30 f. on 30 n.p. orange	9·00	13·00
19	–	40 f. on 40 n.p. violet	13·00	85
20	–	50 f. on 50 n.p. bistre	20·00	20·00
21	–	75 f. on 75 n.p. black	20·00	17·00
22	3	100 f. on 1 r. green	16·00	3·50
23		200 f. on 2 r. black	18·00	12·00
24	–	500 f. on 5 r. red	30·00	38·00
25	–	1 d. on 10 r. blue	40·00	65·00

Independent Postal Administration issues are listed in Volume 1.

ADEN

Peninsula on southern coast of Arabia. Formerly part of the Indian Empire. A Crown Colony from 1 April 1937 to 18 January 1963, when Aden joined the South Arabian Federation, whose stamps it then used.

1937. 16 annas = 1 rupee.
1951. 100 cents = 1 shilling.

1 Dhow

1937.

1	1	½ a. green	3·50	1·40
2		9 p. green	3·50	1·60
3		1 a. brown	3·50	70
4		2 a. red	3·50	2·00
5		2½ a. blue	3·25	80
6		3 a. red	9·00	6·50
7		3½ a. blue	7·00	2·00
8		8 a. purple	19·00	5·50
9		1 r. brown	28·00	6·00
10		2 r. yellow	48·00	16·00
11		5 r. purple	90·00	65·00
12		10 r. olive	£225	£275

2 King George VI and Queen Elizabeth

1937. Coronation.

13	2	1 a. brown	65	80
14		2½ a. blue	75	1·40
15		3½ a. blue	1·00	2·50

3 Aidrus Mosque, Crater

1939.

16	3	½ a. green	50	60
17	–	¾ a. brown	1·25	1·25
18	–	1 a. blue	20	25
19	–	1½ a. red	55	60
20	3	2 a. brown	20	25
21	–	2½ a. blue	40	30
22	–	3 a. brown and red	60	25
23	–	8 a. orange	55	40
23a	–	14 a. brown and blue	2·25	1·00
24	–	1 r. green	2·25	1·75
25	–	2 r. blue and mauve	4·75	2·00
26	–	5 r. brown and olive	11·00	7·00
27	–	10 r. brown and violet	29·00	11·00

DESIGNS: ¾ a., 5 r. Adenese Camel Corps; 1 a., 2 r. Harbour; 1½ a., 1 r. Adenese dhow; 2½, 8 a. Mukalla; 3, 14 a., 10 r. "Capture of Aden, 1839" (Capt. Rundle).

9 Houses of Parliament, London

1946. Victory.

28	9	1½ a. red	15	80
29		2½ a. blue	15	30

10 King George VI and Queen Elizabeth 11

1949. Royal Silver Wedding.

30	10	1½ a. red	40	80
31	11	10 r. purple	27·00	30·00

1949. 75th Anniv of U.P.U. As T **20/23** of Antigua surch with new values.

32	2½ a. on 20 c. blue	75	1·50
33	3 a. on 30 c. red	1·75	1·50
34	8 a. on 50 c. orange	1·60	1·50
35	1 r. on 1 s. blue	2·10	2·75

1951. Stamps of 1939 surch in cents or shillings.

36	5 c. on 1 a. blue	15	40
37	10 c. on 2 a. brown	15	45
38	15 c. on 2½ a. blue	20	1·25
39	20 c. on 3 a. brown and red	30	40
40	30 c. on 8 a. orange	30	65
41	50 c. on 8 a. orange	30	35
42	70 c. on 14 a. brown and blue	1·75	1·50
43	1 s. on 1 r. green	35	30
44	2 s. on 2 r. blue and mauve	7·00	2·75
45	5 s. on 5 r. brown and olive	16·00	8·50
46	10 s. on 10 r. brown and violet	24·00	11·00

13 Queen Elizabeth II

14 Minaret

15 Camel Transport

1953. Coronation.

47	13	15 c. black and green	70	1·25

1953.

48	14	5 c. green	20	10
49a		5 c. turquoise	10	40
50	15	10 c. orange	40	10
51		10 c. red	10	30
52	–	15 c. turquoise	1·25	60
79	–	15 c. grey	30	3·50
80	–	25 c. red	30	40
56	–	35 c. blue	2·50	2·00
58	–	50 c. blue	20	10
60	–	70 c. grey	20	10
61a	–	70 c. black	90	20
62	–	1 s. brown and violet	30	10
63	–	1 s. black and violet	1·50	10
64	–	1 s. 25 blue and black	2·25	60
65	–	2 s. brown and red	1·25	50
66	–	2 s. black and red	7·50	50
67	–	5 s. brown and blue	1·50	60
68	–	5 s. black and blue	5·00	80
69	–	10 s. brown and green	1·75	8·00
70	–	10 s. black and bronze	13·00	1·25
71	–	20 s. brown and lilac	6·50	10·00
72	–	20 s. black and lilac	40·00	14·00

DESIGNS—HORIZ: 15 c. Crater; 25 c. Mosque; 1 s. Dhow building; 20 s. (38 × 27 mm); Aden in 1572. VERT: 35 c. Dhow; 50 c. Map; 70 c. Salt works; 1 s. 25, Colony's badge; 2 s. Aden Protectorate Levy; 5 s. Crater Pass; 10 s. Tribesmen.

1954. Royal Visit. As No. 62 but inscribed "ROYAL VISIT 1954".

73	1 s. sepia and violet	30	45

1959. Revised Constitution. Optd **REVISED CONSTITUTION 1959** (in Arabic on No 74).

74	15 green (No. 53)	30	2·00
75	1 s. 25 blue and black (No. 64)	1·00	1·00

28 Protein Foods

1963. Freedom from Hunger.

76	28	1 s. 25 green	1·75	1·60

For later issues see **SOUTH ARABIAN FEDERATION**.

ADEN PROTECTORATE STATES

The states of the Eastern Aden Protectorate commonly known as the Hadhramaut.

The National Liberation Front took control on 1 October 1967, and full independence was granted by Great Britain on 30 November 1967 when the People's Republic of Southern Yemen (comprising the Protectorate States and the South Arabian Federation) was declared.

1937. 16 annas = 1 rupee.
1951. 100 cents = 1 shilling.
1966. 1,000 fils = 1 dinar.

SEIYUN

1 Sultan of Seiyun

2 Seiyun

1942.

1	1	½ a. green	20	35
2		¾ a. brown	30	55
3		1 a. blue	40	35
4	2	1½ a. red	40	40
5	–	2 a. sepia	30	70
6		2½ a. blue	75	1·00
7	–	3 a. sepia and red	1·25	1·75
8	–	8 a. red	60	50
9	–	1 r. green	2·00	75
10	–	2 r. blue and purple	7·00	10·00
11	–	5 r. brown and green	18·00	13·00

DESIGNS—VERT: 2 a. Tarim; 2½ a. Mosque at Seiyun; 1 r. South Gate, Tarim; 5 r. Mosque entrance, Tarim. HORIZ: 3 a. Fortress at Tarim; 8 a. Mosque at Seiyun; 2 r. A Kathiri house.

1946. Victory. Optd **VICTORY ISSUE 8TH JUNE 1946.**

12	2	1½ a. red	10	30
13	–	2½ a. blue (No. 6)	10	10

1949. Silver Wedding. As T **10/11** of Aden.

14	1½ a. red	30	2·00
15	5 r. green	13·00	9·00

1949. 75th Anniv of U.P.U. As T **20/23** of Antigua surch with new values.

16	2½ a. on 20 c. blue	25	50
17	3 a. on 30 c. red	1·00	65
18	8 a. on 50 c. orange	40	75
19	1 r. on 1 s. blue	60	90

1951. 1942 stamps surch in cents or shillings.

20	1	5 c. on 1 a. blue	15	20
21	–	10 c. on 2 a. sepia	30	20
22	–	15 c. on 2½ a. blue	15	20
23	–	20 c. on 3 a. sepia and red	15	65
24	–	50 c. on 8 a. red	15	20
25	–	1s. on 1 r. green	20	65
26	–	2s. on 2 r. blue and purple	2·50	15·00
27	–	5s. on 5 r. brown and green	15·00	30·00

1953. Coronation. As T **13** of Aden.

28	15 c. black and green	30	1·60

14 Sultan Hussein

29 "Telstar"

1954. As 1942 issue and new designs, but with portrait of Sultan Hussein as in T **14**.

29	14	5 c. brown	10	10
30		10 c. blue	15	10
31	2	15 c. green	15	10
32	–	25 c. red	15	10
33	–	35 c. blue	15	10
34	–	50 c. brown and red	15	10
39	–	70 c. black	2·00	75
35	–	1 s. orange	15	10
40	–	1 s. 25 green	2·00	6·50
41	–	1 s. 50 violet	2·00	6·50
36	–	2 s. green	4·00	2·00
37	–	5 s. blue and violet	6·50	3·50
38	–	10 s. brown and violet	6·00	6·50

DESIGNS—VERT: 35 c. Mosque at Seiyun; 70 c. Qarn Adh Dhabi; 2 s. South Gate, Tarim; 10 s. Mosque entrance, Tarim. HORIZ: 50 c. Fortress at Tarim; 1 s. Mosque at Seiyun; 1 s. 25, Seiyun; 1 s. 50, Gheil Omer; 5 s. Kathiri house.

1966. Nos. 29 etc surch **SOUTH ARABIA** in English and Arabic, with value and bar.

42	14	5 f. on 5 c.	15	10
43		5 f. on 10 c.	15	30
44	2	10 f. on 15 c.	15	30
45	–	15 f. on 25 c.	20	40
46	–	20 f. on 35 c.	15	30
47	–	25 f. on 50 c.	15	50
61	–	35 f. on 70 c.	1·25	40
49	–	50 f. on 1 s.	20	15
50	–	65 f. on 1 s. 25	20	15
51	–	75 f. on 1 s. 50	20	30
65	–	100 f. on 2 s.	2·75	2·00
53	–	250 f. on 5 s.	1·40	3·75
54	–	500 f. on 10 s.	1·75	3·75

Each value has two similar surcharges.

1966. Nos. 57, 59, 61/7 variously optd as given below, together with Olympic "rings".

68 10 f. on 15 c. (**LOS ANGELES 1932**) . . . 35 25
69 20 f. on 35 c. (**BERLIN 1936**) . . 45 35
70 35 f. on 70 c. (**INTERNATIONAL COOPERATION**, etc) . . . 45 35
71 50 f. on 1 s. (**LONDON 1948**) . . 50 40
72 65 f. on 1 s. 25 (**HELSINKI 1952**) 65 1·00
73 75 f. on 1 s. 50 (**MELBOURNE 1956**) . . . 80 1·50
74 100 f. on 2 s. (**ROME 1960**) . . 90 1·60
75 250 f. on 5 s. (**TOKYO 1964**) . 1·40 3·25
76 500 f. on 10 s. (**MEXICO CITY 1968**) . . . 1·75 3·75

1966. World Cup Football Championships. Nos. 57, 59, 61/2, 65/7 optd **CHAMPIONS ENGLAND** (10 f., 50 f. and 250 f.) or **FOOTBALL 1966** (others). Both with football symbol.

77 10 f. on 15 c. . . . 70 30
78 20 f. on 35 c. . . . 90 40
79 35 f. on 70 c. . . . 1·25 40
80 50 f. on 1 s. . . . 1·40 40
81 100 f. on 2 s. . . . 3·75 2·00
82 250 f. on 5 s. . . . 7·50 5·00
83 500 f. on 10 s. . . . 9·50 8·00

1966. Centenary of I.T.U. (1965).

84 **29** 5 f. green, black and violet . 1·25 25
85 – 10 f. purple, black and green 1·40 30
86 – 15 f. blue, black and orange 1·75 40
87 **29** 25 f. green, black and red . 2·50 50
88 – 35 f. purple, black and yellow 2·75 70
89 – 50 f. blue, black and brown . 3·25 1·10
90 **29** 65 f. green, black and yellow 3·75 1·25

DESIGNS: 10, 35 f. "Relay"; 15, 50 f. "Ranger".

32 Churchill at Easel

1966. Sir Winston Churchill's Paintings. Multicoloured.

91 5 f. Type **32** . . . 1·50 15
92 10 f. "Antibes" . . . 1·75 15
93 15 f. "Flowers" . . . 1·75 20
94 20 f. "Tapestries" . . . 1·75 35
95 25 f. "Village, Lake Lugano" . 1·75 35
96 35 f. "Church, Lake Como" . . 2·00 40
97 50 f. "Flowers at Chartwell" . 2·25 65
98 65 f. Type **32** . . . 2·75 90

The 15, 35 and 50 f. are vert.

1967. "World Peace". Nos. 57, 59, 61/7 optd **WORLD PEACE** and names as given below.

99 10 f. on 15 c. (**PANDIT NEHRU**) 1·25 85
100 20 f. on 35 c. (**WINSTON CHURCHILL**) . . . 4·50 2·25
101 35 f. on 70 c. (**DAG HAMMARSKJOLD**) . . . 50 80
102 50 f. on 1 s. (**JOHN F. KENNEDY**) . . . 60 90
103 65 f. on 1 s. 25 (**LUDWIG ERHARD**) . . . 70 1·10
104 75 f. on 1 s. 50 (**LYNDON JOHNSON**) . . . 80 1·25
105 100 f. on 2 s. (**ELEANOR ROOSEVELT**) . . . 1·00 1·75
106 250 f. on 5 s. (**WINSTON CHURCHILL**) . . . 13·00 9·50
107 500 f. on 10 s. (**JOHN F. KENNEDY**) . . . 5·00 10·00

40 "Master Crewe as Henry VIII" (Sir Joshua Reynolds)

1967. Paintings. Multicoloured.

108 5 f. Type **40** . . . 30 25
109 10 f. "The Dancer" (Degas) . 35 30
110 15 f. "The Fifer" (Manet) . 40 35
111 20 f. "Stag at Sharkey's" (boxing match, G. Bellows) . . 45 40
112 25 f. "Don Manuel Osorio" (Goya) . . . 50 45
113 35 f. "St Martin distributing his Cloak" (A. van Dyck) . . 70 65
114 50 f. "The Blue Boy" (Gainsborough) . . . 85 75
115 65 f. "The White Horse" (Gauguin) . . . 1·10 1·00
116 75 f. "Mona Lisa" (Da Vinci) (45×62 mm) . . . 1·40 1·25

1967. American Astronauts. Nos. 57, 59, 61/2 and 65/6 optd as below, all with space capsule.

117 10 f. on 15 c. (**ALAN SHEPARD JR.**) . . . 55 1·00
118 20 f. on 35 c. (**VIRGIL GRISSOM**) . . . 70 1·25
119 35 f. on 70 c. (**JOHN GLENN JR.**) . . . 95 1·50
120 50 f. on 1 s. (**SCOTT CARPENTER**) . . . 95 1·50
121 100 f. on 2 s. (**WALTER SCHIRRA JR.**) . . . 2·25 3·50
122 250 f. on 5 s. (**GORDON COOPER JR.**) . . . 3·50 6·50

50 Churchill Crown

1967. Churchill Commemoration.

123 **50** 75 f. multicoloured . . . 9·00 6·50

HADHRAMAUT

(a) Issues inscribed "SHIHR and MUKALLA"

1 Sultan of Shihr and Mukalla

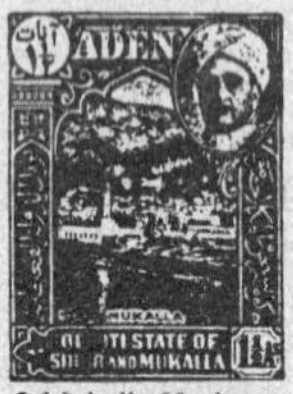

2 Mukalla Harbour

1942.

1 **1** ½ a. green . . . 50 40
2 ¾ a. brown . . . 50 30
3 1 a. blue . . . 60 70
4 **2** 1½ a. red . . . 70 40
5 – 2 a. sepia . . . 90 80
6 – 2½ a. blue . . . 40 30
7 – 3 a. sepia and red . . 80 40
8 – 8 a. red . . . 50 40
9 – 1 r. green . . . 2·25 1·75
10 – 2 r. blue and purple . . 10·00 8·00
11 – 5 r. brown and green . . 14·00 11·00

DESIGNS—VERT: 2 a. Gateway of Shihr; 3 a. Outpost of Mukalla; 1 r. Du'an. HORIZ: 2½ a. Shibam; 8 a. 'Einat; 2 r. Mosque in Hureidha; 5 r. Meshhed.

1946. Victory. Optd **VICTORY ISSUE 8TH JUNE 1946**.

12 **2** 1½ a. red . . . 10 30
13 – 2½ a. blue . . . 10 10

1949. Silver Wedding. As T **10/11** of Aden.

14 1½ a. red . . . 50 2·00
15 5 r. green . . . 13·00 9·00

1949. U.P.U. As T **20/23** of Antigua surch.

16 2½ a. on 20 c. blue . . . 20 20
17 3 a. on 30 c. red . . . 1·10 50
18 8 a. on 50 c. orange . . . 55 60
19 1 r. on 1 s. blue . . . 60 50

1951. Stamps of 1942 surch in cents or shillings.

20 5 c. on 1 a. blue . . . 15 15
21 10 c. on 2 a. sepia . . . 15 15
22 15 c. on 2½ a. blue . . . 15 15
23 20 c. on 3 a. sepia and red . . 30 20
24 50 c. on 8 a. red . . . 20 40
25 1 s. on 1 r. green . . . 65 25
26 2 s. on 2 r. blue and purple . . 6·00 9·00
27 5 s. on 5 r. brown and green . 9·00 14·00

1953. Coronation. As T **13** of Aden.

28 15 c. black and blue . . . 75 55

(b) Issues inscribed "HADHRAMAUT"

11

Metal Work. **22**

1955. Occupations. Portrait as in T **11**.

29 **11** 5 c. blue . . . 30 10
30 – 10 c. black (Mat-making) . 40 10
31 – 15 c. green (Weaving) . . 30 10
32 – 25 c. red (Pottery) . . 40 10
33 – 35 c. blue (Building) . . 50 10
34 – 50 c. orange (Date cultivation) 40 10
35 – 90 c. brown (Agriculture) . 50 15
36 – 1 s. black and orange (Fisheries) . . . 50 10
37 – 1 s. 25 black and orange (Lime-burning) . . . 55 55
38 – 2 s. black and blue (Dhow building) . . . 4·00 60
39 – 5 s. black and green (Agriculture) . . . 5·00 1·50
40 – 10 s. black and red (as No. 37) 5·50 6·50

Nos. 36/40 are horiz.

1963. Occupations. As Nos. 29/40 but with inset portrait of Sultan Awadh bin Saleh el Qu'aiti, as in T **22**.

41 **22** 5 c. blue . . . 10 30
42 – 10 c. black . . . 10 40
43 – 15 c. green . . . 10 40
44 – 25 c. red . . . 10 30
45 – 35 c. blue . . . 10 65
46 – 50 c. orange . . . 10 30
47 – 70 c. brown (As No. 35) . . 15 30
48 – 1 s. black and lilac . . . 20 20
49 – 1 s. 25 black and orange . . 45 2·50
50 – 2 s. black and blue . . . 3·25 1·00
51 – 5 s. black and green . . . 13·00 18·00
52 – 10 s. black and red . . . 16·00 18·00

1966. Nos. 41/52 surch **SOUTH ARABIA** in English and Arabic, with value and bar.

53 **5** 5 f. on 5 c. . . . 10 50
54 – 5 f. on 10 c. . . . 10 50
55 – 10 f. on 15 c. . . . 10 30
56 – 15 f. on 25 c. . . . 10 50
57 – 20 f. on 35 c. . . . 10 1·25
58 – 25 f. on 50 c. . . . 10 50
59 – 35 f. on 70 c. . . . 10 50
60 – 50 f. on 1 s. . . . 10 30
61 – 65 f. on 1 s. 25 . . . 55 30
62 – 100 f. on 2 s. . . . 90 75
63 – 250 f. on 5 s. . . . 1·25 1·50
64 – 500 f. on 10 s. . . . 18·00 3·00

1966. Churchill Commemoration. Nos. 54/6 optd **1874-1965 WINSTON CHURCHILL**.

65 5 f. on 10 c. . . . 5·50 7·50
66 10 f. on 15 c. . . . 6·50 8·50
67 15 f. on 25 c. . . . 8·50 11·00

1966. President Kennedy Commemoration. Nos. 57/9 optd **1917-63 JOHN F. KENNEDY**.

68 20 f. on 35 c. . . . 2·00 6·00
69 25 f. on 50 c. . . . 2·50 6·50
70 35 f. on 70 c. . . . 3·50 7·50

25 World Cup Emblem

1966. World Cup Football Championships.

71 **25** 5 f. purple and orange . . 1·75 25
72 – 10 f. violet and green . . 2·00 25
73 – 15 f. purple and orange . . 2·25 30
74 – 20 f. violet and green . . 2·50 40
75 **25** 25 f. green and red . . . 2·75 55
76 – 35 f. blue and yellow . . 3·25 80
77 – 50 f. green and red . . . 3·75 1·10
78 **25** 65 f. blue and yellow . . 4·50 1·40

DESIGNS: 10, 35 f. Wembley Stadium; 15, 50 f. Footballers; 20 f. Jules Rimet Cup and football.

29 Mexican Hat and Blanket

1966. Pre-Olympic Games, Mexico (1968).

79 **29** 75 f. sepia and green . . . 1·25 75

30 Telecommunications Satellite

1966. International Co-operation Year.

80 **30** 5 f. mauve, purple and green 2·25 35
81 – 10 f. multicoloured . . . 2·50 35
82 – 15 f. purple, blue and red . 2·75 40
83 **30** 20 f. blue, purple and red . 3·00 45
84 – 25 f. multicoloured . . . 3·00 50
85 **30** 35 f. purple, red and blue . 3·50 80
86 – 50 f. purple, green and red . 4·50 1·25
87 **30** 65 f. brown, violet and red . 5·00 1·75

DESIGNS: 10 f. Olympic runner (inscr "ROME 1960"); 15 f. Fishes; 25 f. Olympic runner (inscr "TOKIO 1964"); 50 f. Tobacco plant.

MAHRA SULTANATE OF QISHN AND SOCOTRA

The National Liberation Front took control on 1 October 1967, and full independence was granted by Great Britain on 30 November 1967. Subsequently part of Southern Yemen.

1 Mahra Flag

1967.

1 **1** 5 f. multicoloured . . . 1·50 30
2 10 f. multicoloured . . . 1·50 30
3 15 f. multicoloured . . . 1·50 30
4 20 f. multicoloured . . . 1·50 30
5 25 f. multicoloured . . . 1·50 30
6 35 f. multicoloured . . . 1·50 30
7 50 f. multicoloured . . . 1·50 30
8 65 f. multicoloured . . . 1·50 30
9 100 f. multicoloured . . . 1·50 30
10 250 f. multicoloured . . . 1·50 35
11 500 f. multicoloured . . . 1·50 50

APPENDIX

The following stamps have either been issued in excess of postal needs or have not been made available to the public in reasonable quantities at face value.

SEIYUN

1967.

Hunting. 20 f.

Olympic Games, Grenoble. Postage 10, 25, 35, 50, 75 f.; Air 100, 200 f.

Scout Jamboree, Idaho. Air 150 f.

Paintings—Renoir. Postage 10, 35, 50, 65, 75 f.; Air 100, 200, 250 f.

Paintings—Toulouse-Lautrec. Postage 10, 35, 50, 65, 75.; Air 100, 200, 250 f.

Stated to have been occupied by the N.L.F. on 1 October, 1967.

HADHRAMAUT

1967.

Stampex, London. Postage 5, 10, 15, 20, 25 f.; Air 50, 65 f.

Amphilex International Stamp Exhibition,

Amsterdam. Air 75 f.

Olympic Games, Mexico (1968). 75 f.

Paintings. Postage 5, 10, 15, 20, 25 f.; Air 50, 65 f.

Scout Jamboree, Idaho. Air 35 f.

Space Research. Postage 10, 25, 35, 50, 75 f.; Air 100, 250 f.

Stated to have been occupied by the N.L.F. on 17 September, 1967.

MAHRA

1967.

Scout Jamboree, Idaho. 15, 75, 100, 150 f.

President Kennedy Commemoration. Postage 10, 15, 25, 50, 75, 100, 150 f.; Air 250, 500 f.

Olympic Games, Mexico (1968). Postage 10, 25, 50 f.; Air 250, 500 f.

Stated to have been occupied by the N.L.F. on 1 October 1967.

For later issues see **SOUTHERN YEMEN** and **YEMEN PEOPLE'S DEMOCRATIC REPUBLIC** in Volume 2.

AITUTAKI

Island in the South Pacific.

1903. 12 pence = 1 shilling;
20 shillings = 1 pound.
1967. 100 cents = 1 dollar.

A. NEW ZEALAND DEPENDENCY.

The British Government, who had exercised a protectorate over the Cook Islands group since the 1880s handed the islands, including Aitutaki, to New Zealand administration in 1901. Cook Islands stamps were used from 1932 to 1972.

1903. Pictorial stamps of New Zealand surch **AITUTAKI.** and value in native language.

1 **23** ½d. green . . . 4·25 6·50
2 **42** 1d. red . . . 4·75 5·50
4 **26** 2½d. blue . . . 11·00 12·00
5 **28** 3d. brown . . . 15·00 15·00
6 **31** 6d. red . . . 28·00 25·00
7 **34** 1s. red . . . 55·00 85·00

1911. King Edward VII stamps of New Zealand surch **AITUTAKI.** and value in native language.

9	51	½d. green	1·00	2·75
10	53	1d. red	3·00	9·50
11	51	6d. red	40·00	90·00
12		1s. red	55·00	£140

1916. King George V stamps of New Zealand surch **AITUTAKI.** and value in native language.

13a	62	6d. red	7·50	25·00
14		1s. red	28·00	90·00

1917. King George V stamps of New Zealand optd **AITUTAKI.**

19	62	½d. green	1·00	5·50
20	53	1d. red	3·25	20·00
21	62	1½d. grey	3·75	30·00
22		1½d. brown	80	7·00
15a		2½d. blue	1·75	15·00
16a		3d. brown	1·50	18·00
17a		6d. red	4·75	20·00
18a		1s. red	12·00	27·00

1920. As 1920 pictorial stamps of Cook Islands but inscr "AITUTAKI".

30	½d. black and green	2·00	9·00
31	1d. black and red	6·00	6·50
26	1½d. black and brown	6·00	12·00
32	2½d. black and blue	7·50	50·00
27	3d. black and blue	2·00	14·00
28	6d. brown and grey	5·00	14·00
29	1s. black and purple	9·50	16·00

B. PART OF COOK ISLANDS.

On 9 August 1972. Aitutaki became a Port of Entry into the Cook Islands. Whilst remaining part of the Cook Islands, Aitutaki has a separate postal service.

1972. Nos. 227/8, 230, 233/4, 238, 240/1, 243 and 244 of Cook Islands optd **Aitutaki.**

33	79	½ c. multicoloured	30	80
34	–	1 c. multicoloured	70	1·40
35	–	2½ c. multicoloured	2·25	7·00
36	–	4 c. multicoloured	70	85
37	–	5 c. multicoloured	2·50	7·50
38	–	10 c. multicoloured	2·50	5·50
39	–	20 c. multicoloured	1·25	1·00
40	–	25 c. multicoloured	70	1·00
41	–	50 c. multicoloured	2·75	2·75
42	–	$1 multicoloured	4·00	5·50

1972. Christmas. Nos. 406/8 of Cook Islands optd **Aitutaki.**

43	130	1 c. multicoloured	10	10
44	–	5 c. multicoloured	15	15
45	–	10 c. multicoloured	15	25

1972. Royal Silver Wedding. As Nos. 413 and 415 of Cook Islands, but inscr "COOK ISLANDS Aitutaki".

46	131	5 c. black and silver	3·50	2·75
47	–	15 c. black and silver	1·50	1·50

1972. No. 245 of Cook Islands optd **AITUTAKI.**

48	$2 multicoloured	50	1·75

1972. Nos. 227/8, 230, 233, 234, 238, 240, 241, 243 and 244 of Cook Islands optd **AITUTAKI** within ornamental oval.

49	79	½ c. multicoloured	15	10
50	–	1 c. multicoloured	15	10
51	–	2½ c. multicoloured	20	10
52	–	4 c. multicoloured	25	15
53	–	5 c. multicoloured	25	15
54	–	10 c. multicoloured	35	25
55	–	20 c. multicoloured	1·00	50
56	–	25 c. multicoloured	50	55
57	–	50 c. multicoloured	75	90
58	–	$1 multicoloured	1·25	1·75

13 "Christ Mocked" (Grunewald)

16 Red Hibiscus and Princess Anne

1973. Easter. Multicoloured.

59	1 c. Type **13**	15	10
60	1 c. "St. Veronica" (Van der Weyden)	15	10
61	1 c. "The Crucified Christ with Virgin Mary, Saints and Angels" (Raphael)	15	10
62	1 c. "Resurrection" (Piero della Francesca)	15	10
63	5 c. "The Last Supper" (Master of Amiens)	20	15
64	5 c. "Condemnation" (Holbein)	20	15
65	5 c. "Christ on the Cross" (Rubens)	20	15
66	5 c. "Resurrection" (El Greco)	20	15
67	10 c. "Disrobing of Christ" (El Greco)	25	15
68	10 c. "St. Veronica" (Van Oostsanen)	25	15
69	10 c. "Christ on the Cross" (Rubens)	25	15
70	10 c. "Resurrection" (Bouts)	25	15

1973. Silver Wedding Coinage. Nos. 417/23 of Cook Islands optd **AITUTAKI.**

71	132	1 c. black, red and gold	10	10
72	–	2 c. black, blue and gold	10	10
73	–	5 c. black, green and silver	15	10
74	–	10 c. black, blue and silver	20	10
75	–	20 c. black, green and silver	30	15
76	–	50 c. black, red and silver	50	30
77	–	$1 black, blue and silver	70	45

1973. 10th Anniv of Treaty Banning Nuclear Testing. Nos. 236, 238, 240 and 243 of Cook Islands optd **AITUTAKI** within ornamental oval and **TENTH ANNIVERSARY CESSATION OF NUCLEAR TESTING TREATY.**

78	8 c. multicoloured	15	15
79	10 c. multicoloured	15	16
80	20 c. multicoloured	30	20
81	50 c. multicoloured	70	50

1973. Royal Wedding. Multicoloured.

82	25 c. Type **16**	25	10
83	30 c. Capt. Mark Phillips and blue hibiscus	25	10

17 "Virgin and Child" (Montagna)

1973. Christmas. "Virgin and Child" paintings by artists listed below. Multicoloured.

85	1 c. Type **17**	10	10
86	1 c. Crivelli	10	10
87	1 c. Van Dyck	10	10
88	1 c. Perugino	10	10
89	5 c. Veronese (child at shoulder)	25	10
90	5 c. Veronese (child on lap)	25	10
91	5 c. Cima	25	10
92	5 c. Memling	25	10
93	10 c. Memling	25	10
94	10 c. Del Colle	25	10
95	10 c. Raphael	25	10
96	10 c. Lotto	25	10

18 Rose-branch Murex

1974. Sea Shells. Multicoloured.

97	½ c. Type **18**	90	80
98	1 c. New Caledonia nautilus	90	80
99	2 c. Common or major harp	90	80
100	3 c. Striped bonnet	90	80
101	4 c. Mole cowrie	90	80
102	5 c. Pontifical mitre	90	80
103	8 c. Trumpet triton	90	80
104	10 c. Venus comb murex	90	80
105	20 c. Red-mouth olive	1·25	80
106	25 c. Ruddy frog shell	1·25	80
107	60 c. Widest pacific conch	3·00	1·25
108	$1 Maple-leaf triton or winged frog shell	2·50	1·40
109	$2 Queen Elizabeth II and Marlin-spike auger	6·00	9·00
110	$5 Queen Elizabeth II and Tiger cowrie	27·00	10·00

The $2 and $5 are larger, 53 × 25 mm.

19 Bligh and H.M.S. "Bounty"

1974. William Bligh's Discovery of Aitutaki. Multicoloured.

114	1 c. Type **19**	25	35
115	1 c. H.M.S. "Bounty"	25	35
116	5 c. Bligh, and H.M.S. "Bounty" at Aitutaki	55	45
117	5 c. Aitutaki chart of 1856	55	45
118	8 c. Captain Cook and H.M.S. "Resolution"	85	60
119	8 c. Map of Aitutaki and inset location map	85	60

See also Nos. 123/8.

20 Aitutaki Stamps of 1903, and Map

1974. Centenary of U.P.U. Multicoloured.

120	25 c. Type **20**	65	50
121	50 c. Stamps of 1903 and 1920, and map	85	75

1974. Air. As Nos. 114/119 in larger size (46 × 26 mm), additionally inscr "AIR MAIL".

123	10 c. Type **19**	60	40
124	10 c. H.M.S. "Bounty"	60	40
125	25 c. Bligh, and H.M.S. "Bounty" at Aitutaki	70	50
126	25 c. Aitutaki chart of 1856	70	50
127	30 c. Capt Cook and H.M.S. "Resolution"	80	50
128	30 c. Map of Aitutaki and inset location map	80	50

21 "Virgin and Child" (Hugo van der Goes)

22 Churchill as Schoolboy

1974. Christmas. "Virgin and Child" paintings by artists named. Multicoloured.

129	1 c. Type **21**	10	10
130	5 c. Bellini	10	10
131	8 c. Gerard David	10	10
132	10 c. Antonello da Messina	10	10
133	25 c. Joos van Cleve	20	20
134	30 c. Master of the Life of St. Catherine	20	20

1974. Birth Centenary of Sir Winston Churchill. Multicoloured.

136	10 c. Type **22**	25	25
137	25 c. Churchill as young man	30	40
138	30 c. Churchill with troops	35	45
139	50 c. Churchill painting	45	60
140	$1 Giving "V" sign	85	1·10

1974. Children's Christmas Fund. Nos. 129/34 surch.

142	21	1 c. + 1 c. multicoloured	10	10
143	–	5 c. + 1 c. multicoloured	10	10
144	–	8 c. + 1 c. multicoloured	10	10
145	–	10 c. + 1 c. multicoloured	10	10
146	–	25 c. + 1 c. multicoloured	20	20
147	–	30 c. + 1 c. multicoloured	20	20

24 Soviet and U.S. Flags

1975. "Apollo–Soyuz" Space Project. Multicoloured.

148	25 c. Type **24**	30	20
149	50 c. Daedalus with space capsule	40	30

25 St. Francis

26 "The Descent" (detail, 15th-century Flemish School)

1975. Christmas. Multicoloured.

151	6 c. Type **25**	10	10
152	6 c. Madonna and Child	10	10
153	6 c. St. John	10	10
154	7 c. King and donkey	10	10
155	7 c. Madonna, Child and King	10	10
156	7 c. Kings with gifts	10	10
157	15 c. Madonna and Child	15	15
158	15 c. St. Onufrius	15	15
159	15 c. John the Baptist	15	15
160	20 c. Shepherd and cattle	20	15
161	20 c. Madonna and Child	20	15
162	20 c. Shepherds	20	15

Stamps of the same value were printed together, se-tenant, each strip forming a composite design of a complete painting as follows: Nos. 151/3, "Madonna and Child with Saints Francis and John" (Lorenzetti); 154/6, "Adoration of the Kings" (Van der Weyden); 157/9, "Madonna and Child Enthroneth with Saints Onufrius and John the Baptist" (Montagna); 160/2, "Adoration of the Shepherds" (Reni).

1975. Children's Christmas Fund. Nos. 151/62 surch.

164	25	6 c. + 1 c. multicoloured	10	10
165	–	6 c. + 1 c. multicoloured	10	10
166	–	6 c. + 1 c. multicoloured	10	10
167	–	7 c. + 1 c. multicoloured	10	10
168	–	7 c. + 1 c. multicoloured	10	10
169	–	7 c. + 1 c. multicoloured	10	10
170	–	15 c. + 1 c. multicoloured	15	15
171	–	15 c. + 1 c. multicoloured	15	15
172	–	15 c. + 1 c. multicoloured	15	15
173	–	20 c. + 1 c. multicoloured	20	20
174	–	20 c. + 1 c. multicoloured	20	20
175	–	20 c. + 1 c. multicoloured	20	20

1976. Easter. Multicoloured.

176	15 c. Type **26**	15	10
177	30 c. "The Descent" (detail)	20	15
178	35 c. "The Descent" (detail)	25	20

27 Left Detail

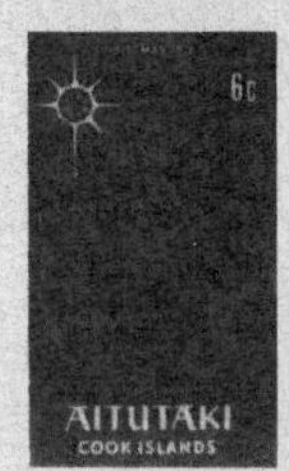

30 "The Visitation"

28 Cycling

1976. Bicentenary of American Revolution. Paintings by John Turnbull.

180	27	30 c. multicoloured	30	15
181	–	30 c. multicoloured	30	15
182	–	30 c. multicoloured	30	15
183	–	35 c. multicoloured	35	15
184	–	35 c. multicoloured	35	15
185	–	35 c. multicoloured	35	15
186	–	50 c. multicoloured	40	20
187	–	50 c. multicoloured	40	20
188	–	50 c. multicoloured	40	20

PAINTINGS: Nos. 180/2, "The Declaration of Independence"; 183/5, "The Surrender of Lord Cornwallis at Yorktown"; 186/8, "The Resignation of General Washington".

Stamps of the same value were printed together, se-tenant, each strip forming a composite design of the whole painting.

1976. Olympic Games, Montreal. Multicoloured.

190	15 c. Type **28**	30	15
191	35 c. Sailing	45	20
192	60 c. Hockey	70	25
193	70 c. Sprinting	70	30

1976. Royal Visit to the U.S.A. Nos. 190/3 optd **ROYAL VISIT JULY 1976.**

195	28	15 c. multicoloured	35	15
196	–	35 c. multicoloured	45	25
197	–	60 c. multicoloured	70	40
198	–	70 c. multicoloured	70	45

1976. Christmas.

200	30	6 c. gold and green	10	10
201	–	6 c. gold and green	10	10
202	–	7 c. gold and purple	10	10
203	–	7 c. gold and purple	10	10
204	–	15 c. gold and blue	10	10
205	–	15 c. gold and blue	10	10
206	–	20 c. gold and violet	15	15
207	–	20 c. gold and violet	15	15

DESIGNS: No. 201, Angel; 202, Angel; 203, Shepherds; 204, Joseph; 205, Mary and the Child; 206, Wise Man; 207, Two Wise Men.

Stamps of the same value were printed together, se-tenant, each pair forming a composite design.

1976. Children's Christmas Fund. Nos. 200/7 surch.

209	30	6 c. + 1 c. gold and green	10	10
210	–	6 c. + 1 c. gold and green	10	10
211	–	7 c. + 1 c. gold and purple	10	10
212	–	7 c. + 1 c. gold and purple	10	10
213	–	15 c. + 1 c. gold and blue	15	15
214	–	15 c. + 1 c. gold and blue	15	15
215	–	20 c. + 1 c. gold and violet	15	15
216	–	20 c. + 1 c. gold and violet	15	15

32 Alexander Graham Bell and First Telephone

1977. Centenary (1976) of Telephone.

218	32	25 c. black, gold and red	20	15
219	–	70 c. black, gold and lilac	40	40

DESIGN: 70 c. Satellite and Earth station.

33 "Christ on the Cross" (detail)

1977. Easter. 400th Birth Anniv of Rubens. Mult.

221	15 c. Type **33**	45	15
222	20 c. "Lamentation for Christ"	60	20
223	35 c. "Christ with Straw"	75	25

34 Captain Bligh, George III and H.M.S. "Bounty"

1977. Silver Jubilee. Multicoloured.

225	25 c. Type **34**	35	35
226	35 c. Rev. Williams, George IV and Aitutaki Church	40	40
227	50 c. Union Jack, Queen Victoria and island map	45	45
228	$1 Balcony scene, 1953	50	50

35 The Shepherds 37 Hawaiian Goddess

1977. Christmas. Multicoloured

230	6 c. Type **35**	10	10
231	6 c. Angel	10	10
232	7 c. Mary, Jesus and ox	10	10
233	7 c. Joseph and donkey	10	10
234	15 c. Three Kings	10	10
235	15 c. Virgin and Child	10	10
236	20 c. Joseph	10	10
237	20 c. Mary and Jesus on donkey	10	10

Stamps of the same value were printed together, se-tenant, forming composite designs.

1977. Children's Christmas Fund. Nos. 230/7 surch +1 c.

239	6 c.+1 c. Type **35**	10	10
240	6 c.+1 c. Angel	10	10
241	7 c.+1 c. Mary, Jesus and ox	10	10
242	7 c.+1 c. Joseph and donkey	10	10
243	15 c.+1 c. Three Kings	15	10
244	15 c.+1 c. Virgin and Child	15	10
245	20 c.+1 c. Joseph	15	10
246	20 c.+1 c. Mary and Jesus on donkey	15	10

1978. Bicentenary of Discovery of Hawaii. Mult.

248	35 c. Type **37**	35	25
249	50 c. Figurehead of H.M.S. "Resolution" (horiz)	60	40
250	$1 Hawaiian temple figure	70	70

38 "Christ on the Way to Calvary" (Martini) 39 The Yale of Beaufort

1978. Easter. Paintings from the Louvre, Paris. Mult.

252	15 c. Type **38**	15	10
253	20 c. "Pieta of Avignon" (E. Quarton)	20	10
254	35 c. "The Pilgrims at Emmaus" (Rembrandt)	25	10

1978. 25th Anniv of Coronation. Multicoloured.

257	$1 Type **39**	30	50
258	$1 Queen Elizabeth II	30	50
259	$1 Aitutaki ancestral statue	30	50

40 "Adoration of the Infant Jesus" 41 "Captain Cook" (Nathaniel Dance)

1978. Christmas. 450th Death Anniv of Durer. Multicoloured.

261	15 c. Type **40**	35	15
262	17 c. "The Madonna with Child"	40	15
263	30 c. "The Madonna with the Iris"	55	20
264	35 c. "The Madonna of the Siskin"	60	25

1979. Death Bicent of Captain Cook. Mult.

266	50 c. Type **41**	1·00	80
267	75 c. "H.M.S. "Resolution" and "Adventure" at Matavai Bay, Tahiti" (W. Hodges)	1·75	95

42 Girl with Flowers 43 "Man writing a Letter" (painting by Gabriel Metsu)

1979. International Year of the Child. Multicoloured.

269	30 c. Type **42**	15	15
270	35 c. Boy playing guitar	20	20
271	65 c. Children in canoe	30	30

1979. Death Centenary of Sir Rowland Hill. Multicoloured.

273	50 c. Type **43**	45	45
274	50 c. Sir Rowland Hill with Penny Black, 1903 ½d. and 1911 1d. stamps	45	45
275	50 c. "Girl in Blue reading a Letter" (Jan Vermeer)	45	45
276	65 c. "Woman writing a Letter" (Gerard Terborch)	50	50
277	65 c. Sir Rowland Hill, with Penny Black, 1903 3d. and 1920 ½d. stamps	50	50
278	65 c. "Lady reading a Letter" (Jan Vermeer)	50	50

44 "The Burial of Christ (left detail) (Quentin Metsys) 45 Einstein as a Young Man

1980. Easter. Multicoloured.

280	20 c. Type **44**	40	25
281	30 c. "The Burial of Christ" (centre detail)	50	35
282	35 c. "The Burial of Christ" (right detail)	65	45

1980. 25th Death Anniv of Albert Einstein (physicist). Multicoloured.

284	12 c. Type **45**	50	50
285	12 c. Atom and "$E=mc^2$" equation	50	50
286	15 c. Einstein in middle-age	55	55
287	15 c. Cross over nuclear explosion (Test Ban Treaty, 1963)	55	55
288	20 c. Einstein as an old man	65	65
289	20 c. Hand preventing atomic explosion	65	65

46 Ancestor Figure, Aitutaki 47 "Virgin and Child" (13th century)

1980. 3rd South Pacific Festival of Arts. Mult.

291	6 c. Type **46**	10	10
292	6 c. Staff god image, Rarotonga	10	10
293	6 c. Trade adze, Mangaia	10	10
294	6 c. Carved image of Tangaroa, Rarotonga	10	10
295	12 c. Wooden image Aitutaki	10	10
296	12 c. Hand club, Rarotonga	10	10
297	12 c. Carved mace "god", Mangaia	10	10
298	12 c. Fisherman's god, Rarotonga	10	10
299	15 c. Ti'i image, Aitutaki	15	15
300	15 c. Fisherman's god, Rarotonga (different)	15	15
301	15 c. Carved mace "god", Cook Islands	15	15
302	15 c. Carved image of Tangaroa, Rarotonga (different)	15	15
303	20 c. Chief's headdress, Aitutaki	15	15
304	20 c. Carved mace "god", Cook Islands (different)	15	15
305	20 c. Staff god image, Rarotonga (different)	15	15
306	20 c. Carved image of Tangaroa, Rarotonga (different)	15	15

1980. Christmas. Sculptures of "The Virgin and Child". Multicoloured.

308	15 c. Type **47**	20	15
309	20 c. 14th century	20	15
310	25 c. 15th century	20	15
311	35 c. 15th century (different)	30	20

48 "Mourning Virgin" 49 Gouldian Finch

1981. Easter. Details of Sculpture "Burial of Christ" by Pedro Roldan.

313	**48**	30 c. gold and green	25	25
314	–	40 c. gold and lilac	30	30
315	–	50 c. gold and blue	30	30

DESIGNS: 40 c. "Christ"; 50 c. "Saint John".

1981. Birds (1st series). Multicoloured.

317	1 c. Type **49**	45	30
318	1 c. Common starling	45	30
319	2 c. Golden whistler	50	30
320	2 c. Scarlet robin	50	30
321	3 c. Rufous fantail	60	30
322	3 c. Peregrine falcon	60	30
323	4 c. Java sparrow	70	30
324	4 c. Barn owl	70	30
325	5 c. Tahitian lory	70	30
326	5 c. White-breasted wood swallow	70	30
327	6 c. Purple swamphen	70	30
328	6 c. Rock dove	70	30
329	10 c. Chestnut-breasted mannikin	90	30
330	10 c. Zebra dove	90	30
331	12 c. Eastern reef heron	1·00	40
332	12 c. Common mynah	1·00	40
333	15 c. Whimbrel (horiz)	1·25	40
334	15 c. Black-browed albatross (horiz)	1·25	40
335	20 c. American golden plover (horiz)	1·50	55
336	20 c. White tern (horiz)	1·50	55
337	25 c. Spotbill duck (horiz)	1·75	70
338	25 c. Brown booby (horiz)	1·75	70
339	30 c. Great frigate bird (horiz)	2·00	85
340	30 c. Pintail (horiz)	2·00	85
341	35 c. Long-billed reed warbler	2·25	1·00
342	35 c. Pomarine skua	2·25	1·00
343	40 c. Banded rail	2·75	1·25
344	40 c. Spotted triller	2·75	1·25
345	50 c. Royal albatross	3·00	1·50
346	50 c. Stephen's lory	3·00	1·50
347	70 c. Red-headed parrot-finch	5·50	3·00
348	70 c. Orange dove	5·50	3·00
349	$1 Blue-headed flycatcher	5·50	3·75
350	$2 Red-bellied flycatcher	8·00	8·00
351	$4 Red munia	14·00	14·00
352	$5 Flat-billed kingfisher	15·00	16·00

See also Nos. 475/94.

50 Prince Charles 52 Footballers

1981. Royal Wedding. Multicoloured.

391	60 c. Type **50**	30	40
392	80 c. Lady Diana Spencer	40	55
393	$1.40 Prince Charles and Lady Diana (87×70 mm)	60	80

1981. International Year for Disabled Persons. Nos. 391/3 surch +5c.

394	60 c.+5 c. Type **50**	70	1·00
395	80 c.+5 c. Lady Diana Spencer	1·00	1·50
396	$1.40+5 c. Prince Charles and Lady Diana	1·75	2·75

1981. World Cup Football Championship, Spain (1982). Football Scenes. Multicoloured.

397	12 c. Ball to left of stamp	50	35
398	12 c. Ball to right	50	35
399	15 c. Ball to right	55	40
400	15 c. Ball to left	55	40
401	20 c. Ball to left	55	50
402	20 c. Ball to right	55	50
403	25 c. Type **52**	60	55
404	25 c. "ESPANA 82" inscription	60	55

53 "The Holy Family" 54 Princess of Wales

1981. Christmas. Etchings by Rembrandt.

406	**53**	15 c. brown and gold	45	45
407	–	30 c. brown and gold	70	70
408	–	40 c. brown and gold	95	95
409	–	50 c. brown and gold	1·25	1·25

DESIGNS—VERT: 30 c. "Virgin with Child". HORIZ: 40 c. "Adoration of the Shepherds"; 50 c. "The Holy Family".

1982. 21st Birthday of Princess of Wales Mult.

411	70 c. Type **54**	1·00	60
412	$1 Prince and Princess of Wales	1·25	75
413	$2 Princess Diana (different)	2·75	1·50

1982. Birth of Prince William of Wales (1st issue). Nos. 391/3 optd.

415	60 c. Type **50**	1·25	1·00
416	60 c. Type **50**	1·25	1·00
417	80 c. Lady Diana Spencer	1·40	1·10
418	80 c. Lady Diana Spencer	1·40	1·10
419	$1.40 Prince Charles and Lady Diana	1·75	1·40
420	$1.40 Prince Charles and Lady Diana	1·75	1·40

OPTS: Nos. 415, 417 and 419, **21 JUNE 1982. PRINCE WILLIAM OF WALES**. Nos. 416, 418 and 420, **COMMEMORATING THE ROYAL BIRTH**.

1982. Birth of Prince William of Wales (2nd issue). As Nos. 411/13 but inscr "ROYAL BIRTH 21 JUNE 1982 PRINCE WILLIAM OF WALES".

421	70 c. Type **54**	70	60
422	$1 Prince and Princess of Wales	80	75
423	$2 Princess Diana (different)	1·60	1·50

56 "Virgin and Child" (12th-century sculpture) 57 Aitutaki Bananas

1982. Christmas. Religious Sculptures. Multicoloured.

425	18 c. Type **56**	60	60
426	36 c. "Virgin and Child" (12th-century)	75	75
427	48 c. "Virgin and Child" (13th-century)	90	90
428	60 c. "Virgin and Child" (15th-century)	1·25	1·25

1983. Commonwealth Day. Multicoloured.

430	48 c. Type **57**	1·10	50
431	48 c. Ancient Ti'i image	1·10	50
432	48 c. Tourist canoeing	1·10	50
433	48 c. Captain William Bligh and chart	1·10	50

58 Scouts around Campfire 60 Modern Sport Balloon

1983. 75th Anniv of Boy Scout Movement. Mult.

434	36 c. Type **58**	55	55
435	48 c. Scout saluting	70	70
436	60 c. Scouts hiking	75	75

1983. 15th World Scout Jamboree, Alberta, Canada. Nos. 434/6 optd **15TH WORLD SCOUT JAMBOREE**.
438 36 c. Type **58** 80 45
439 48 c. Scout saluting . . . . . 1·00 55
440 60 c. Scouts hiking . . . . . . 1·25 75

1983. Bicentenary of Manned Flight.
442 **60** 18 c. multicoloured 55 30
443 – 36 c. multicoloured 75 50
444 – 48 c. multicoloured 90 60
445 – 60 c. multicoloured . . . . 1·00 80
DESIGNS: 36 c. to 60 c. Showing different modern sports balloons.

1983. Various stamps surch (a) Nos. 335/48 and 352.
447 18 c. on 20 c. American golden plover . . . . 2·50 75
448 18 c. on 20 c. White tern . . . 2·50 75
449 36 c. on 25 c. Spotbill duck . 3·50 1·00
450 36 c. on 25 c. Brown booby . 3·50 1·00
451 36 c. on 30 c. Great frigate bird 3·50 1·00
452 36 c. on 30 c. Pintail . . . . . 3·50 1·00
453 36 c. on 35 c. Long-billed reed warbler . . . . 3·50 1·00
454 36 c. on 35 c. Pomarine skua . 3·50 1·00
455 48 c. on 49 c. Banded rail . . 4·00 1·25
456 48 c. on 40 c. Spotted triller . 4·00 1·25
457 48 c. on 50 c. Royal albatross 4·00 1·25
458 48 c. on 50 c. Stephen's lory . 4·00 1·25
459 72 c. on 70 c. Red-headed parrot finch . . . . 7·00 2·00
460 72 c. on 70 c. Orange dove . . 7·00 2·00
461 $5.60 on $5 Flat-billed kingfisher (vert) . . . . 20·00 8·50

(b) Nos. 392/3 and 412/3.
462 96 c. on 80 c. Lady Diana Spencer . . . . 3·00 2·50
463 96 c. on $1 Prince and Princess of Wales . . . . 2·75 2·00
464 $1.20 on $1.40 Prince Charles and Lady Diana . . . . . . 3·00 2·50
465 $1.20 on $2 Princess Diana . . 2·75 2·00

63 International Mail **64** "Madonna of the Chair"

1983. World Communications Year. Multicoloured.
466 48 c. Type **63** 65 50
467 60 c. Telecommunications . . 95 70
468 96 c. Space satellite . . . . . 1·40 1·00

1983. Christmas. 500th Birth Anniv of Raphael. Multicoloured.
470 36 c. Type **64** 65 30
471 48 c. "The Alba Madonna" . 80 40
472 60 c. "Conestabile Madonna" 1·10 55

65 Gouldian Finch **66** Javelin throwing

1984. Birds (2nd series). Multicoloured.
475 2 c. Type **65** . . . . 1·25 1·00
476 3 c. Common starling . . . . 1·25 1·00
477 5 c. Scarlet robin . . . . . . 1·50 1·10
478 10 c. Golden whistler . . . . 1·50 1·10
479 12 c. Rufous fantail . . . . . 1·50 1·10
480 18 c. Peregrine falcon . . . . 2·00 1·50
481 24 c. Barn owl . . . . 2·00 1·50
482 30 c. Java sparrow . . . . . . 2·00 1·50
483 36 c. White-breasted wood swallow . . . . 2·00 1·50
484 48 c. Tahitian lory . . . . . . 2·00 1·50
485 50 c. Rock dove . . . . 2·50 2·00
486 60 c. Purple swamphen . . . . 2·50 2·00
487 72 c. Zebra dove . . . . . . 2·50 2·00
488 96 c. Chestnut-breasted mannikin . . . . 2·50 2·00
489 $1.20 Common mynah . . . . 2·50 2·75
490 $2.10 Eastern reef heron . . . 3·50 3·75
491 $3 Blue-headed flycatcher . . 6·50 6·00
492 $4.20 Red-bellied flycatcher . 3·75 6·00
493 $5.60 Red munia . . . . . . 4·50 7·00
494 $9.60 Flat-billed kingfisher . . 7·50 10·00

1984. Olympic Games. Los Angeles. Multicoloured.
495 36 c. Type **66** 35 35
496 48 c. Shot-putting 40 45
497 60 c. Hurdling 45 55
498 $2 Basketball . . . . 1·75 1·50
DESIGNS: 48 c. to $2, show Memorial Coliseum and various events.

1984. Olympic Gold Medal Winners. Nos. 495/8 optd
500 36 c. Type **66** (optd **Javelin Throw Tessa Sanderson Great Britain**) 35 35
501 48 c. Shot-putting (optd **Shot Put Claudia Losch Germany**) . . 40 45
502 60 c. Hurdling (optd **Heptathlon Glynis Nunn Australia**) . . 45 55
503 $2 Basketball (optd **Team Basketball United States**) . 1·10 1·50

67 Captain William Bligh and Chart

1984. "Ausipex" International Stamp Exhibition, Melbourne. Multicoloured.
504 60 c. Type **67** . . . . 3·25 3·25
505 96 c. H.M.S. "Bounty" and map 3·50 3·50
506 $1.40 Aitutaki stamps of 1974, 1979 and 1981 with map . 3·50 3·50

1984. Birth of Prince Henry (1st issue). No. 391 optd "**15-9-84 Birth Prince Henry**" and surcharge also.
508 $3 on 60 c. Type **50** . . . . . 2·75 3·25

69 The Annunciation **70** Princess Diana with Prince Henry

1984. Christmas. Details from Altarpiece, St Paul's Church, Palencia, Spain. Multicoloured.
509 36 c. Type **69** 30 35
510 48 c. The Nativity 40 45
511 60 c. The Epiphany 45 50
512 96 c. The Flight into Egypt . 75 80

1984. Birth of Prince Henry (2nd issue). Mult.
514 48 c. Type **70** . . . . 1·50 1·25
515 60 c. Prince William with Prince Henry . . . . 1·50 1·50
516 $2.10 Prince and Princess of Wales with children . . . . 3·00 3·00

71 Grey Kingbird

1985. Birth Bicentenary of John J. Audubon (ornithologist). Designs showing original paintings. Multicoloured.
518 55 c. Type **71** . . . . 1·10 1·10
519 65 c. Bohemian waxwing . . 1·25 1·25
520 75 c. Summer tanager . . . . 1·40 1·40
521 95 c. Common cardinal . . . 1·50 1·50
522 $1.15 White-winged cross-bill 1·90 1·90

72 The Queen Mother, aged Seven

1985. Life and Times of Queen Elizabeth the Queen Mother. Multicoloured.
523 55 c. Type **72** 45 50
524 65 c. Engagement photograph, 1922 . . . . 50 55
525 75 c. With young Princess Elizabeth 60 65
526 $1.30 With baby Prince Charles 1·00 1·10

73 "The Calmady Children" (T. Lawrence)

1985. International Youth Year. Multicoloured.
528 75 c. Type **73** . . . . 2·00 1·40
529 90 c. "Madame Charpentier's Children" (Renoir) . . . . 2·00 1·75
530 $1.40 "Young Girls at Piano" (Renoir) . . . . 2·50 2·75

74 "Adoration of the Magi" (Giotto) and "Giotto" Spacecraft

1985. Christmas. Appearance of Halley's Comet (1st issue). Multicoloured.
532 95 c. Type **74** . . . . 1·50 1·50
533 95 c. As Type **74** but showing "Planet A" spacecraft . . . 1·50 1·50
534 $1.15 Type **74** . . . . 1·50 1·50
535 $1.15 As No. 533 . . . . . . 1·50 1·50

75 Halley's Comet A.D. 684 (from "Nuremberg Chronicle")

1986. Appearance of Halley's Comet (2nd issue). Multicoloured.
537 90 c. Type **75** 90 90
538 $1.25 Halley's Comet, 1066 (from Bayeux Tapestry) . . . . . 1·10 1·10
539 $1.75 Halley's Comet, 1456 (from "Lucerne Chronicles") . . . 1·50 1·50

76 Queen Elizabeth II on Coronation Day (from photo by Cecil Beaton) **78** Prince Andrew and Miss Sarah Ferguson

77 Head of Statue of Liberty

1986. 60th Birthday of Queen Elizabeth II.
542 **76** 95 c. multicoloured . . . . 85 1·00

1986. Centenary of Statue of Liberty. Multicoloured.
544 $1 Type **77** . . . . 1·25 1·25
545 $2.75 Statue of Liberty at sunset 2·75 2·75

1986. Royal Wedding.
547 **78** $2 multicoloured . . . . . 2·00 2·00

79 "St. Anne with Virgin and Child" **83** Angels

1986. Christmas. Paintings by Durer. Multicoloured.
551 75 c. Type **79** . . . . 1·25 1·25
552 $1.35 "Virgin and Child" . . . 1·75 1·75
553 $1.95 "The Adoration of the Magi" . . . . 2·25 2·25
554 $2.75 "Madonna of the Rosary" 3·00 3·00

1986. Visit of Pope John Paul II to South Pacific. Nos. 551/4 optd **NOVEMBER 21–24 1986 FIRST VISIT TO SOUTH PACIFIC** and surch also.
556 75 c. + 10 c. Type **79** . . . . 2·50 2·50
557 $1.35 + 10 c. "Virgin and Child" 3·00 3·00
558 $1.95 + 10 c. "The Adoration of the Magi" . . . . 3·50 3·50
559 $2.75 + 10 c. "Madonna of the Rosary" . . . . 5·00 5·00

1987. Hurricane Relief Fund. Nos. 544/5, 547, 551/4 and 556/9 surch **HURRICANE RELIEF + 50c**.
561 75 c. + 50 c. Type **79** . . . . . 2·00 2·00
562 75 c. + 10 c. + 50 c. Type **79** . 2·25 2·25
563 $1 + 50 c. Type **77** . . . . . . 2·50 2·50
564 $1.35 + 50 c. "Virgin and Child" (Durer) . . . . 2·75 2·75
565 $1.35 + 10 c. + 50 c. "Virgin and Child" (Durer) . . . . . . 2·75 2·75
566 $1.95 + 50 c. "The Adoration of the Magi" (Durer) . . . . 3·25 3·25
567 $1.95 + 10 c. + 50 c. "The Adoration of the Magi" (Durer) . . . . 3·25 3·25
568 $2 + 50 c. Type **78** . . . . . . 3·25 3·25
569 $2.75 + 50 c. Statue of Liberty at sunset . . . . 3·75 3·75
570 $2.75 + 50 c. "Madonna of the Rosary" (Durer) . . . . . 3·75 3·75
571 $2.75 + 10 c. + 50 c. "Madonna of the Rosary" (Durer) . . . . 3·75 3·75

1987. Royal Ruby Wedding. Nos. 391/3 surch **2.50 Royal Wedding 40th Anniv**.
572 $2.50 on 60 c. Type **50** . . . 2·50 2·50
573 $2.50 on 80 c. Lady Diana Spencer . . . . 2·50 2·50
574 $2.50 on $1.40 Prince Charles and Lady Diana (87 × 70 mm) 2·50 2·50

1987. Christmas. Details of angels from "Virgin with Garland" by Rubens.
575 **83** 70 c. multicoloured . . . . 1·50 1·50
576 – 85 c. multicoloured . . . . 1·50 1·50
577 – $1.50 multicoloured . . . 2·50 2·50
578 – $1.85 multicoloured . . . 2·75 2·75

84 Chariot Racing and Athletics

1988. Olympic Games, Seoul. Ancient and modern Olympic sports. Multicoloured.
581 70 c. Type **84** . . . . 1·50 1·50
582 85 c. Greek runners and football 1·60 1·60
583 95 c. Greek wrestling and handball . . . . 1·75 1·75
584 $1.40 Greek hoplites and tennis 2·50 2·50

1988. Olympic Medal Winners, Los Angeles. Nos. 581/4 optd.
586 70 c. Type **84** (optd **FLORENCE GRIFFTH JOYNER UNITED STATES 100 M AND 200 M**) . . . . 1·10 1·25
587 85 c. Greek runners and football (optd **GELINDO BORDIN ITALY MARATHON**) . . 1·25 1·40
588 95 c. Greek wrestling and handball (optd **HITOSHI SAITO JAPAN JUDO**) . . 1·40 1·60
589 $1.40 Greek hoplites and tennis (optd **STEFFI GRAF WEST GERMANY WOMEN'S TENNIS**) . . . . 2·00 2·25

85 "Adoration of the Shepherds" (detail)

1988. Christmas. Paintings by Rembrandt. Mult.
590 55 c. Type **85** . . . . 1·25 1·25
591 70 c. "The Holy Family" . . 1·50 1·50
592 85 c. "Presentation in the Temple" . . . . 1·60 1·60
593 95 c. "The Holy Family" (different) . . . . 1·75 1·75
594 $1.15 "Presentation in the Temple" (different) . . . . 1·90 1·90

86 H.M.S. "Bounty" leaving Spithead and Captain Bligh

1989. Bicentenary of Discovery of Aitutaki by Captain Bligh. Multicoloured.
596 55 c. Type **86** . . . . 1·75 1·75
597 65 c. Breadfruit plants . . . . 2·00 2·00
598 75 c. Old chart showing Aitutaki and Captain Bligh . . . . . 2·25 2·25
599 95 c. Native outrigger and H.M.S. "Bounty" off Aitutaki 2·50 2·50
600 $1.65 Fletcher Christian confronting Bligh . . . . . 3·00 3·00

87 "Apollo 11" Astronaut on Moon

1989. 20th Anniv of First Manned Landing on Moon. Multicoloured.

602	75 c. Type **87**	1·50	1·50
603	$1.15 Conducting experiment on Moon	2·00	2·00
604	$1.80 Astronaut on Moon carrying equipment	3·00	3·00

88 Virgin Mary

91 "Madonna of the Basket" (Correggio)

89 Human Comet striking Earth

1989. Christmas. Details from "Virgin in the Glory" by Titian. Multicoloured.

606	70 c. Type **88**	1·75	1·75
607	85 c. Christ Child	2·25	2·25
608	95 c. Angel	2·50	2·50
609	$1.25 Cherubs	3·00	3·00

1990. Protection of the Environment. Multicoloured.

611	$1.75 Type **89**	2·25	2·25
612	$1.75 Comet's tail	2·25	2·25

Nos. 611/12 were printed together, se-tenant, forming a composite design.

1990. Christmas. Religious Paintings. Multicoloured.

615	70 c. Type **91**	1·25	1·25
616	85 c. "Virgin and Child" (Morando)	1·40	1·40
617	95 c. "Adoration of the Child" (Tiepolo)	1·50	1·50
618	$1.75 "Mystic Marriage of St Catherine" (Memling)	2·25	2·25

1990. "Birdpex '90" Stamp Exhibition, Christchurch, New Zealand. Nos. 349/50 optd **Birdpex '90** and bird's head.

620	$1 Blue-headed flycatcher	3·00	3·00
621	$2 Red-bellied flycatcher	4·00	4·00

1991. 65th Birthday of Queen Elizabeth II. No. 352 optd **COMMEMORATING 65th BIRTHDAY OF H.M. QUEEN ELIZABETH II.**

622	$5 Flat-billed kingfisher	7·50	8·50

93 "The Holy Family" (A. Mengs)

1991. Christmas. Religious Paintings. Multicoloured.

623	80 c. Type **93**	1·25	1·25
624	90 c. "Virgin and the Child" (Lippi)	1·40	1·40
625	$1.05 "Virgin and Child" (A. Durer)	1·60	1·60
626	$1.75 "Adoration of the Shepherds" (G. De La Tour)	2·25	2·25

94 Hurdling

1992. Olympic Games, Barcelona. Mult.

628	95 c. Type **94**	1·50	1·50
629	$1.25 Weightlifting	1·75	1·75
630	$1.50 Judo	2·25	2·25
631	$1.95 Football	2·75	2·75

95 Vaka Motu Canoe

1992. 6th Festival of Pacific Arts, Rarotonga. Sailing canoes. Multicoloured.

632	30 c. Type **95**	65	65
633	50 c. Hamatafua	80	80
634	95 c. Alia Kalia Ndrua	1·50	1·50
635	$1.75 Hokule'a Hawaiian	2·25	2·50
636	$1.95 Tuamotu Pahi	2·50	2·75

1992. Royal Visit by Prince Edward. Nos. 632/6 optd **ROYAL VISIT**.

637	30 c. Type **95**	75	75
638	50 c. Hamatafua	1·00	1·00
639	95 c. Alia Kalia Ndrua	1·75	1·75
640	$1.75 Hokule'a Hawaiian	2·50	2·75
641	$1.95 Tuamotu Pahi	2·50	2·75

96 "Virgin's Nativity" (detail) (Reni)

1992. Christmas. Different details from "Virgin's Nativity" by Guido Reni.

642	**96**	80 c. multicoloured	1·25	1·25
643	–	90 c. multicoloured	1·40	1·40
644	–	$1.05 multicoloured	1·60	1·60
645	–	$1.75 multicoloured	2·25	2·25

97 The Departure from Palos

1992. 500th Anniv of Discovery of America by Columbus. Multicoloured.

647	$1.25 Type **97**	2·25	2·50
648	$1.75 Map of voyages	2·75	3·00
649	$1.95 Columbus and crew in New World	3·25	3·50

98 Queen Victoria and King Edward VII

1993. 40th Anniv of Coronation. Mult.

650	$1.75 Type **98**	2·25	2·25
651	$1.75 King George V and King George VI	2·25	2·25
652	$1.75 Queen Elizabeth II in 1953 and 1986	2·25	2·25

99 "Madonna and Child" (Nino Pisano)

1993. Christmas. Religious Sculptures. Mult.

653	80 c. Type **99**	80	80
654	90 c. "Virgin on Rosebush" (Luca della Robbia)	85	85
655	$1.15 "Virgin with Child and St. John" (Juan Francisco Rustici)	1·25	1·25
656	$1.95 "Virgin with Child" (Miguel Angel)	2·00	2·00
657	$3 "Madonna and Child" (Jacopo della Quercia) (32 × 47 mm)	3·00	3·00

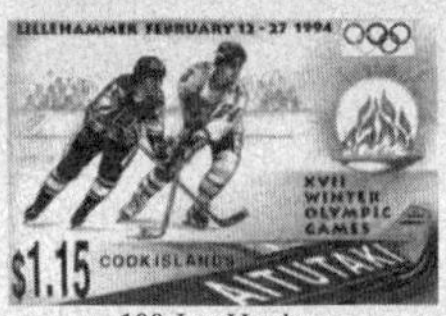

100 Ice Hockey

1994. Winter Olympic Games, Lillehammer. Multicoloured.

658	$1.15 Type **100**	2·00	2·00
659	$1.15 Ski-jumping	2·00	2·00
660	$1.15 Cross-country skiing	2·00	2·00

101 "Ipomoea pes-caprae"

103 "The Madonna of the Basket" (Correggio)

102 Cook Islands and U.S.A. Flags with Astronauts Collins, Armstrong and Aldrin

1994. Flowers. Multicoloured.

661	5 c. Type **101**	10	10
662	10 c. "Plumeria alba"	10	10
663	15 c. "Hibiscus rosa-sinensis"	10	15
664	20 c. "Allamanda cathartica"	15	20
665	25 c. "Delonix regia"	15	20
666	30 c. "Gardenia taitensis"	20	25
667	50 c. "Plumeria rubra"	30	35
668	80 c. "Ipomoea littoralis"	50	55
669	85 c. "Hibiscus tiliaceus"	55	60
670	90 c. "Erythrina variegata"	55	60
671	$1 "Solandra nitida"	65	70
672	$2 "Cordia subcordata"	1·25	1·40
673	$3 "Hibiscus rosa-sinensis" (different)	1·90	2·00
674	$5 As $3	3·25	3·50
675	$8 As $3 (34 × 47 mm)	5·00	5·25

Nos. 671/5 include a portrait of Queen Elizabeth II at top right.

1994. 25th Anniv of First Manned Moon Landing. Multicoloured.

676	$2 Type **102**	4·00	4·00
677	$2 "Apollo 11" re-entering atmosphere and landing in sea	4·00	4·00

1994. Christmas. Religious Paintings. Multicoloured.

678	85 c. Type **103**	1·00	1·10
679	85 c. "The Virgin and Child with Saints" (Memling)	1·00	1·10
680	85 c. "The Virgin and Child with Flowers" (Dolci)	1·00	1·10
681	85 c. "The Virgin and Child with Angels" (Bergognone)	1·00	1·10
682	90 c. "Adoration of the Kings" (Dosso)	1·00	1·10
683	90 c. "The Virgin and Child" (Bellini)	1·00	1·10
684	90 c. "The Virgin and Child" (Schiavone)	1·00	1·10
685	90 c. "Adoration of the Kings" (Dolci)	1·00	1·10

No. 678 is inscribed "Corregio" in error.

104 Battle of Britain

1995. 50th Anniv of End of Second World War. Multicoloured.

686	$4 Type **104**	5·50	6·00
687	$4 Battle of Midway	5·50	6·00

105 Queen Elizabeth the Queen Mother

1995. 95th Birthday of Queen Elizabeth the Queen Mother.

688	**105**	$4 multicoloured	5·50	6·00

106 Globe, Doves, United Nations Emblem and Headquarters

1995. 50th Anniv of United Nations.

689	**106**	$4.25 multicoloured	4·50	5·00

107 Green Turtle

1995. Year of the Sea Turtle. Multicoloured.

690	95 c. Type **107**	1·50	1·50
691	$1.15 Leatherback turtle	1·75	1·75
692	$1.50 Olive Ridley turtle	2·00	2·00
693	$1.75 Loggerhead turtle	2·50	2·50

108 Queen Elizabeth II

1996. 70th Birthday of Queen Elizabeth II.

694	**108**	$4.50 multicoloured	6·00	6·50

109 Baron Pierre de Coubertin, Torch and Opening of 1896 Olympic Games

1996. Centenary of Modern Olympic Games. Multicoloured.

695	$2 Type **109**	2·75	3·00
696	$2 Athletes and American flag, 1996	2·75	3·00

110 Princess Elizabeth, and Lieut. Philip Mountbatten with King George VI and Queen Elizabeth, 1947

1997. Golden Wedding of Queen Elizabeth and Prince Philip.

697	**110**	$2.50 multicoloured	2·00	2·25

111 Diana, Princess of Wales

1998. Diana, Princess of Wales Commemoration.

699	111	$1 multicoloured	65	70

OFFICIAL STAMPS

1978. Nos. 98/105, 107/10 and 227/8 optd **O.H.M.S.** or surch also.

O 1	1 c. multicoloured	90	10
O 2	2 c. multicoloured	1·00	10
O 3	3 c. multicoloured	1·00	10
O 4	4 c. multicoloured	1·00	10
O 5	5 c. multicoloured	1·00	10
O 6	8 c. multicoloured	1·25	10
O 7	10 c. multicoloured	1·50	15
O 8	15 c. on 60 c. multicoloured	2·50	20
O 9	18 c. on 60 c. multicoloured	2·50	20
O10	20 c. multicoloured	2·50	20
O11	50 c. multicoloured	1·00	55
O12	62 c. multicoloured	10·00	70
O13	$1 multicoloured (No. 108)	10·00	85
O14	$2 multicoloured	9·00	1·00
O15	$4 on $1 mult (No. 228)	2·50	1·00
O16	$5 multicoloured	11·00	1·75

1985. Nos. 351/2, 430/3, 475 and 477/94 optd **O.H.M.S.** or surch also.

O17	2 c. Type **65**	35	35
O18	5 c. Scarlet robin	45	45
O19	10 c. Golden whistler	50	50
O20	12 c. Rufous fantail	55	55
O21	18 c. Peregrine falcon	1·00	1·00
O22	20 c. on 24 c Barn owl	1·00	1·00
O23	30 c. Java sparrow	75	75
O24	40 c. on 36 c. White-breasted wood swallow	90	90
O25	50 c. Rock dove	1·00	1·00
O26	55 c. on 48 c. Tahitian lory	1·00	1·00
O27	60 c. Purple swamphen	1·25	1·25
O28	65 c. on 72 c. Zebra dove	1·25	1·25
O38	75 c. on 48 c. Type **57**	80	80
O39	75 c. on 48 c. Ancient Ti'i image	80	80
O40	75 c. on 48 c. Tourist canoeing	80	80
O41	75 c. on 48 c. Captain William Bligh and chart	80	80
O29	80 c. on 96 c. Chestnut-breasted mannikin	1·25	1·25
O30	$1.20 Common mynah	1·75	1·75
O31	$2.10 Eastern reef heron	2·75	2·75
O32	$3 Blue-headed flycatcher	3·50	3·50
O33	$4.20 Red-bellied flycatcher	5·00	5·00
O34	$5.60 Red munia	6·00	6·00
O35	$9.60 Flat-billed kingfisher	9·00	9·00
O36	$14 on $4 Red munia (35 × 48 mm)	12·00	12·00
O37	$18 on $5 Flat-billed kingfisher (35 × 48 mm)	14·00	14·00

ALWAR

A state of Rajputana N. India. Now uses Indian stamps.

12 pies = 1 anna; 16 annas = 1 rupee

1 Native Dagger

1877. Roul or perf.

1c	1	¼ a. blue	2·75	70
5		¼ a. green	2·75	2·00
2c		1 a. brown	2·00	80

ANGUILLA

St. Christopher, Nevis and Anguilla were granted Associated Statehood on 27 February 1967, but following a referendum Anguilla declared her independence and the St Christopher authorities withdrew. On 7 July 1969, the Anguilla post office was officially recognised by the Government of St. Christopher, Nevis and Anguilla and normal postal communications via St. Christopher were resumed.

By the Anguilla Act of 27 July 1971, the island was restored to direct British control.

100 cents = 1 West Indian dollar

1967. Nos. 129/44 of St Kitts-Nevis optd **Independent Anguilla** and bar.

1	–	½ c. sepia and blue	26·00	20·00
2	33	1 c. multicoloured	27·00	6·50
3	–	2 c. multicoloured	28·00	1·25
4	–	3 c. multicoloured	28·00	4·50
5	–	4 c. multicoloured	28·00	5·50
6	–	5 c. multicoloured	£100	18·00
7	–	6 c. multicoloured	50·00	9·00
8	–	10 c. multicoloured	28·00	6·50
9	–	15 c. multicoloured	60·00	11·00
10	–	20 c. multicoloured	95·00	13·00
11	–	25 c. multicoloured	85·00	22·00
12	–	50 c. multicoloured	£1800	£450
13	–	60 c. multicoloured	£2000	£850
14	–	$1 yellow and blue	£1600	£400
15	–	$2.50 multicoloured	£1500	£300
16	–	$5 multicoloured	£1500	£300
		Set of 16	£8000	£2250

Owing to the limited stocks available for overprinting, the sale of the stamps were personally controlled by the Postmaster and no orders from the trade were accepted.

2 Mahogany Tree, The Quarter

1967.

17	2	1 c. green, brown and orange	10	20
18	–	2 c. turquoise and black	10	20
19	–	3 c. black and green	10	10
20	–	4 c. blue and black	10	10
21	–	5 c. multicoloured	10	10
22	–	6 c. red and black	10	10
23	–	10 c. multicoloured	15	10
24	–	15 c. multicoloured	60	20
25	–	20 c. multicoloured	80	55
26	–	25 c. multicoloured	60	20
27	–	40 c. green, blue and black	80	25
28	–	60 c. multicoloured	3·00	2·50
29	–	$1 multicoloured	1·75	3·00
30	–	$2.50 multicoloured	2·00	3·25
31	–	$5 multicoloured	3·00	4·25

DESIGNS: 2 c. Sombrero Lighthouse; 3 c. St Mary's Church; 4 c. Valley Police Station; 5 c. Old Plantation House, Mt. Fortune; 6 c. Valley Post Office; 10 c. Methodist Church, West End; 15 c. Wall Blake Airport; 20 c. Beech A90 King Air aircraft over Sandy Ground; 25 c. Island harbour; 40 c. Map of Anguilla; 60 c. Hermit crab and starfish; $1, Hibiscus; $2.50, Local scene; $5, Spiny lobster.

On 9 January 1969, Anguilla reaffirmed her independence from St Kitts and issued Nos. 17/31 optd **INDEPENDENCE JANUARY, 1969.** These are outside the scope of this catalogue.

17 Yachts in Lagoon

1968. Anguillan Ships. Multicoloured.

32	10 c. Type **17**	30	10
33	15 c. Boat on beach	35	10
34	25 c. Schooner "Warspite"	50	15
35	40 c. Schooner "Atlantic Star"	60	20

18 Purple-throated Carib

1968. Anguillan Birds. Multicoloured.

36	10 c. Type **18**	85	15
37	15 c. Bananaquit	1·10	20
38	25 c. Black-necked stilt (horiz)	1·40	20
39	40 c. Royal tern (horiz)	1·60	30

19 Guides' Badge and Anniversary Years

1968. 35th Anniv of Anguillan Girl Guides. Multicoloured.

40	10 c. Type **19**	10	10
41	15 c. Badge and silhouettes of guides (vert)	15	10
42	25 c. Guides' badge and Headquarters	20	15
43	40 c. Association and proficiency badges (vert)	25	15

20 The Three Kings

1968. Christmas.

44	20	1 c. black and red	10	10
45	–	10 c. black and blue	10	10
46	–	15 c. black and brown	15	10
47	–	40 c. black and blue	15	10
48	–	50 c. black and green	20	15

DESIGNS—VERT: 10 c. The Wise Men; 15 c. Holy Family and manger. HORIZ: 40 c. The Shepherds; 50 c. Holy Family and donkey.

21 Bagging Salt

1969. Anguillan Salt Industry. Multicoloured.

49	10 c. Type **21**	25	10
50	15 c. Packing salt	30	10
51	40 c. Salt pond	35	10
52	50 c. Loading salt	35	10

22 "The Crucifixion" (Studio of Massys)

1969. Easter Commemoration. Multicoloured.

53	25 c. Type **22**	25	15
54	40 c. "The Last Supper" (ascr to Roberti)	35	15

23 Amaryllis

1969 Flowers of the Caribbean. Multicoloured.

55	10 c. Type **23**	20	20
56	15 c. Bougainvillea	25	20
57	40 c. Hibiscus	50	40
58	50 c. "Cattleya" orchid	1·50	1·00

24 Superb Gaza, Channelled Turban, Chestnut Turban and Carved Star Shell

1969. Sea Shells. Multicoloured.

59	10 c. Type **24**	20	15
60	15 c. American thorny oysters	20	15
61	40 c. Scotch, royal and smooth scotch bonnets	30	25
62	50 c. Atlantic trumpet triton	40	30

1969. Christmas. Nos. 17, 25/8 optd with different seasonal emblems.

63	1 c. green, brown and orange	10	10
64	20 c. multicoloured	20	10
65	25 c. multicoloured	20	10
66	40 c. green, blue and black	25	15
67	60 c. multicoloured	40	20

30 Spotted Goatfish

1969. Fishes. Multicoloured.

68	10 c. Type **30**	30	15
69	15 c. Blue-striped grunt	45	15
70	40 c. Nassau grouper	55	20
71	50 c. Banded butterflyfish	65	20

31 "Morning Glory" 32 "The Crucifixion" (Masaccio)

1970. Flowers. Multicoloured.

72	10 c. Type **31**	30	10
73	15 c. Blue petrea	45	10
74	40 c. Hibiscus	70	20
75	50 c. "Flame Tree"	80	25

1970. Easter. Multicoloured.

76	10 c. "The Ascent to Calvary" (Tiepolo) (horiz)	15	10
77	20 c. Type **32**	20	10
78	40 c. "Deposition" (Rosso Fiorentino)	25	15
79	60 c. "The Ascent to Calvary" (Murillo) (horiz)	25	15

33 Scout Badge and Map

1970. 40th Anniv of Scouting in Anguilla. Multicoloured.

80	10 c. Type **33**	15	15
81	15 c. Scout camp, and cubs practising first aid	20	15
82	40 c. Monkey bridge	25	25
83	50 c. Scout H.Q. building and Lord Baden-Powell	35	25

34 Boatbuilding

1970. Multicoloured.

84	1 c. Type **34**	30	30
85	2 c. Road construction	30	30
86	3 c. Quay, Blowing Point	30	20
87	4 c. Broadcaster, Radio Anguilla	30	40
88	5 c. Cottage Hospital extension	40	40
89	6 c. Valley Secondary School	30	40
90	10 c. Hotel extension	30	30
91	15 c. Sandy Ground	30	30
92	20 c. Supermarket and cinema	55	30
93	25 c. Bananas and mangoes	35	80
94	40 c. Wall Blake Airport	2·50	2·25
95	60 c. Sandy Ground jetty	65	2·25
96	$1 Administration buildings	1·25	1·40

97	$2.50 Livestock	1·50	3·75
98	$5 Sandy Hill Bay	2·75	3·75

35 "The Adoration of the Shepherds" (Reni)

1970. Christmas. Multicoloured.

99	1 c. Type **35**	10	10
100	20 c. "The Virgin and Child" (Gozzoli)	30	20
101	25 c. "Mystic Nativity" (detail, Botticelli)	30	20
102	40 c. "The Santa Margherita Madonna" (detail, Mazzola)	40	25
103	50 c. "The Adoration of the Magi" (detail, Tiepolo)	40	25

36 "Ecce Homo" (detail, Correggio)

1971. Easter. Paintings. Multicoloured.

104	10 c. Type **36**	15	10
105	15 c. "Christ appearing to St Peter" (detail, Carracci)	25	10
106	40 c. "Angels weeping over the Dead Christ" (detail, Guercino) (horiz)	30	10
107	50 c. "The Supper at Emmaus" (detail, Caravaggio) (horiz)	30	15

37 "Hypolimnas misippus"

1971. Butterflies. Multicoloured.

108	10 c. Type **37**	1·25	70
109	15 c. "Junonia evarete"	1·40	80
110	40 c. "Agraulis vanillae"	2·00	1·25
111	50 c. "Danaus plexippus"	2·00	1·50

38 "Magnanime" and "Aimable" in Battle

39 "The Ansidei Madonna" (detail, Raphael)

1971. Sea-battles of the West Indies. Multicoloured.

112	10 c. Type **38**	85	95
113	15 c. H.M.S. "Duke", "Glorieux" and H.M.S. "Agamemnon"	1·00	1·10
114	25 c. H.M.S. "Formidable" and H.M.S. "Namur" against "Ville de Paris"	1·40	1·50
115	40 c. H.M.S. "Canada"	1·50	1·60
116	50 c. H.M.S. "St. Albans" and wreck of "Hector"	1·75	1·90

Nos. 112/116 were issued together, se-tenant, forming a composite design.

1971. Christmas. Multicoloured.

117	20 c. Type **39**	20	25
118	25 c. "Mystic Nativity" (detail, Botticelli)	20	25
119	40 c. "Adoration of the Shepherds" (detail, ascr to Murillo)	30	35
120	50 c. "The Madonna of the Iris" (detail, ascr to Durer)	35	40

40 Map of Anguilla and St. Martin by Thomas Jefferys, 1775

41 "Jesus Buffeted"

1972. Caribbean Maps depicting Anguilla. Multicoloured.

121	10 c. Type **40**	25	10
122	15 c. Samuel Fahlberg's Map, 1814	35	15
123	40 c. Thomas Jefferys' Map, 1775 (horiz)	50	25
124	50 c. Captain E. Barnett's Map, 1847 (horiz)	60	25

1972. Easter. Multicoloured.

125	10 c. Type **41**	25	25
126	15 c. "The Way of Sorrows"	30	30
127	25 c. "The Crucifixion"	30	30
128	40 c. "Descent from the Cross"	35	35
129	50 c. "The Burial"	40	40

42 Loblolly Tree

44 Flight into Egypt

1972. Multicoloured.

130	1 c. Spear fishing	10	40
131	2 c. Type **42**	10	40
132	3 c. Sandy Ground	10	40
133	4 c. Ferry at Blowing Point	75	20
134	5 c. Agriculture	15	50
135	6 c. St. Mary's Church	25	20
136	10 c. St. Gerard's Church	25	40
137	15 c. Cottage hospital extension	25	30
138	20 c. Public library	30	35
139	25 c. Sunset at Blowing Point	40	1·25
140	40 c. Boat building	3·25	1·50
141	60 c. Hibiscus	4·00	3·50
142	$1 Magnificent frigate bird	8·50	7·00
143	$2.50 Frangipani	6·00	8·00
144	$5 Brown pelican	15·00	14·00
144a	$10 Green-back turtle	15·00	18·00

1972. Royal Silver Wedding. As T **52** of Ascension, but with Schooner and Common dolphin in background.

145	25 c. green	55	75
146	40 c. brown	55	75

1972. Christmas. Multicoloured.

147	1 c. Type **44**	10	10
148	20 c. Star of Bethlehem	20	20
149	25 c. Holy Family	20	20
150	40 c. Arrival of the Magi	20	25
151	50 c. Adoration of the Magi	25	25

45 "The Betrayal of Christ"

1973. Easter. Multicoloured.

152	1 c. Type **45**	10	10
153	10 c. "The Man of Sorrows"	10	10
154	20 c. "Christ bearing the Cross"	10	15
155	25 c. "The Crucifixion"	15	15
156	40 c. "The Descent from the Cross"	15	15
157	50 c. "The Resurrection"	15	20

46 "Santa Maria"

1973. Columbus Discovers the West Indies. Multicoloured.

159	1 c. Type **46**	10	10
160	20 c. Early map	1·25	1·25
161	40 c. Map of voyages	1·40	1·40
162	70 c. Sighting land	1·75	1·75
163	$1.20 Landing of Columbus	2·25	2·25

47 Princess Anne and Captain Mark Phillips

49 "The Crucifixion" (Raphael)

48 "The Adoration of the Shepherds" (Reni)

1973. Royal Wedding. Multicoloured. Background colours given.

165 **47**	60 c. green	20	15
166	$1.20 mauve	30	15

1973. Christmas. Multicoloured.

167	1 c. Type **48**	10	10
168	10 c. "The Madonna and Child with Saints Jerome and Dominic" (Filippino Lippi)	10	10
169	20 c. "The Nativity" (Master of Brunswick)	15	15
170	25 c. "Madonna of the Meadow" (Bellini)	15	15
171	40 c. "Virgin and Child" (Cima)	20	20
172	50 c. "Adoration of the Kings" (Geertgen)	20	20

1974. Easter. Details of Raphael's "Crucifixion".

174 **49**	1 c. multicoloured	10	10
175 –	15 c. multicoloured	10	10
176 –	20 c. multicoloured	15	15
177 –	25 c. multicoloured	15	15
178 –	40 c. multicoloured	15	15
179 –	$1 multicoloured	20	25

50 Churchill Making "Victory" Sign

1974. Birth Centenary of Sir Winston Churchill. Multicoloured.

181	1 c. Type **50**	10	10
182	20 c. Churchill with Roosevelt	20	20
183	25 c. Wartime broadcast	20	20
184	40 c. Birthplace, Blenheim Palace	30	30
185	60 c. Churchill's statue	40	35
186	$1.20 Country residence, Chartwell	60	55

51 U.P.U. Emblem

1974. Centenary of U.P.U.

188 **51**	1 c. black and blue	10	10
189	20 c. black and orange	15	15
190	25 c. black and yellow	15	15
191	40 c. black and mauve	20	25
192	60 c. black and green	30	40
193	$1.20 black and blue	50	60

52 Anguillan pointing to Star

1974. Christmas. Multicoloured.

195	1 c. Type **52**	10	10
196	20 c. Child in Manger	10	15
197	25 c. King's offering	10	15
198	40 c. Star over map of Anguilla	15	15
199	60 c. Family looking at star	15	20
200	$1.20 Angels of Peace	20	30

53 "Mary, John and Mary Magdalene" (Matthias Grunewald)

55 "Madonna, Child and the Infant John the Baptist" (Raphael)

54 Statue of Liberty

1975. Easter. Details from Isenheim Altarpiece, Colmar Museum. Multicoloured.

202	1 c. Type **53**	10	10
203	10 c. "The Crucifixion"	15	15
204	15 c. "St. John the Baptist"	15	15
205	20 c. "St. Sebastian and Angels"	20	20
206	$1 "The Entombment" (horiz)	25	35
207	$1.50 "St. Anthony the Hermit"	35	45

1975. Bicentenary of American Revolution. Mult.

209	1 c. Type **54**	10	10
210	10 c. The Capitol	20	10
211	15 c. "Congress voting for Independence" (Pine and Savage)	30	15
212	20 c. Washington and map	30	15
213	$1 Boston Tea Party	45	40
214	$1.50 Bicentenary logo	50	60

1975. Christmas. "Madonna and Child" paintings by artists named. Multicoloured.

216	1 c. Type **55**	10	10
217	10 c. Cima	15	10
218	15 c. Dolci	20	15
219	20 c. Durer	20	15
220	$1 Bellini	35	25
221	$1.50 Botticelli	45	35

1976. New Constitution. Nos. 130 etc optd **NEW CONSTITUTION 1976** or surch also.

223	1 c. Spear fishing	30	40
224	2 c. on 1 c. Spear fishing	30	40
225	2 c. Type **42**	4·50	1·75
226	3 c. on 40 c. Boat building	75	70
227	4 c. Ferry at Blowing Point	1·00	1·00
228	5 c. on 40 c. Boat building	30	50
229	6 c. St. Mary's Church	30	50
230	10 c. on 20 c. Public library	30	50
231	10 c. St. Gerard's Church	4·50	3·50
232	15 c. Cottage Hospital extension	30	90
233	20 c. Public library	30	50
234	25 c. Sunset at Blowing Point	30	50
235	40 c. Boat building	1·00	70
236	60 c. Hibiscus	70	70
237	$1 Magnificent frigate bird	6·00	2·25
238	$2.50 Frangipani	2·25	2·25
239	$5 Brown pelican	7·50	6·50
240	$10 Green-back turtle	4·00	6·00

57 Almond

1976. Flowering Trees. Multicoloured.

241	1 c. Type **57**	10	10
242	10 c. Autograph	20	20
243	15 c. Calabash	20	20
244	20 c. Cordia	20	20
245	$1 Papaya	30	45
246	$1.50 Flamboyant	35	55

58 The Three Marys

1976. Easter. Showing portions of the Altar Frontal Tapestry, Rheinau. Multicoloured.

248	1 c. Type **58**	10	10
249	10 c. The Crucifixion	10	10
250	15 c. Two Soldiers	15	15
251	20 c. The Annunciation	15	15
252	$1 The complete tapestry (horiz)	65	65
253	$1.50 The Risen Christ	80	80

59 French Ships approaching Anguilla

1976. Bicentenary of Battle of Anguilla. Mult.

255	1 c. Type **59**	10	10
256	3 c. "Margaret" (sloop) leaving Anguilla	90	35
257	15 c. Capture of "Le Desius"	1·25	55
258	25 c. "La Vaillante" forced aground	1·50	80
259	$1 H.M.S. "Lapwing"	2·00	1·25
260	$1.50 "Le Desius" burning	2·25	1·75

60 "Christmas Carnival" (A. Richardson)

1976. Christmas. Children's Paintings. Multicoloured.

262	1 c. Type **60**	10	10
263	3 c. "Dreams of Christmas Gifts" (J. Connor)	10	10
264	15 c. "Carolling" (P. Richardson)	15	15
265	25 c. "Candle-light Procession" (A. Mussington)	20	20
266	$1 "Going to Church" (B. Franklin)	30	30
267	$1.50 "Coming Home for Christmas" (E. Gumbs)	40	40

61 Prince Charles and H.M.S. "Minerva" (frigate)

1977. Silver Jubilee. Multicoloured.

269	25 c. Type **61**	15	10
270	40 c. Prince Philip landing by launch at Road Bay, 1964	15	10
271	$1.20 Coronation scene	20	20
272	$2.50 Coronation regalia and map of Anguilla	25	30

62 Yellow-crowned Night Heron

1977. Multicoloured.

274	1 c. Type **62**	30	70
275	2 c. Great barracuda	30	1·10
276	3 c. Queen or pink conch	90	1·50
277	4 c. Spanish bayonet (flower)	40	30
278	5 c. Honeycomb trunkfish	1·50	30
279	6 c. Cable and Wireless building	30	30
280	10 c. American kestrel	3·75	1·75
281	15 c. Ground orchid	2·75	1·75
282	20 c. Stop-light Parrotfish	2·00	75
283	22 c. Lobster fishing boat	45	60
284	35 c. Boat race	1·40	70
285	50 c. Sea bean	90	45
286	$1 Sandy Island	60	45
287	$2.50 Manchineel	1·00	1·00
288	$5 Ground lizard	2·00	1·75
289	$10 Red-billed tropic bird	9·00	4·25

63 "The Crucifixion" (Massys)

1977. Easter. Paintings by Castagno ($1.50) or Ugolino (others). Multicoloured.

291	1 c. Type **63**	10	10
292	3 c. "The Betrayal"	10	10
293	22 c. "The Way to Calvary"	20	20
294	30 c. "The Deposition"	25	25
295	$1 "The Resurrection"	50	50
296	$1.50 "The Crucifixion"	65	65

1977. Royal Visit. Nos. 269/72 optd **ROYAL VISIT TO WEST INDIES**.

298	25 c. Type **61**	10	10
299	40 c. Prince Philip landing at Road Bay, 1964	10	20
300	$1.20 Coronation scene	20	30
301	$1.50 Coronation regalia and map of Anguilla	25	50

65 "Le Chapeau de Paille"

1977. 400th Birth Anniv of Rubens. Multicoloured.

303	25 c. Type **65**	15	15
304	40 c. "Helene Fourment and her Two Children"	20	25
305	$1.20 "Rubens and his Wife"	60	65
306	$2.50 "Marchesa Brigida Spinola-Doria"	75	95

1977. Christmas. Nos. 262/7 with old date blocked out and additionally inscr "1977", some also surch.

308	1 c. Type **60**	10	10
309	5 c. on 3 c. "Dreams of Christmas Gifts"	10	10
310	12 c. on 15 c. "Carolling"	15	15
311	18 c. on 25 c. "Candle-light Procession"	20	20
312	$1 "Going to Church"	45	45
313	$2.50 on $1.50 "Coming Home for Christmas"	90	90

1978. Easter. Nos. 303/6 optd **EASTER 1978**.

315	25 c. Type **65**	15	20
316	40 c. "Helene Fourment with her Two Children"	15	20
317	$1.20 "Rubens and his Wife"	30	40
318	$2.50 "Marchesa Brigida Spinola-Doria"	40	60

68 Coronation Coach at Admiralty Arch

1978. 25th Anniv of Coronation. Multicoloured.

320	22 c. Buckingham Palace	10	10
321	50 c. Type **68**	10	10
322	$1.50 Balcony scene	15	15
323	$2.50 Royal coat of arms	25	25

1978. Anniversaries. Nos. 283/4 and 287 optd **VALLEY SECONDARY SCHOOL 1953-1978** and Nos. 285/6 and 288 optd **ROAD METHODIST CHURCH 1878-1978**, or surch also.

325	22 c. Lobster fishing boat	20	15
326	35 c. Boat race	30	20
327	50 c. Sea bean	30	30
328	$1 Sandy Island	40	40
329	$1.20 on $5 Ground lizard	45	45
330	$1.50 on $2.50 Manchineel	60	55

71 Mother and Child

1978. Christmas. Children's Paintings. Multicoloured.

331	5 c. Type **71**	10	10
332	12 c. Christmas masquerade	15	10
333	18 c. Christmas dinner	15	10
334	22 c. Serenading	15	10
335	$1 Child in manger	45	20
336	$2.50 Family going to church	90	40

1979. International Year of the Child. As Nos. 331/6, but additionally inscr "1979 INTERNATIONAL YEAR OF THE CHILD" and emblem. Borders in different colours.

338	5 c. Type **71**	10	10
339	12 c. Christmas masquerade	10	10
340	18 c. Christmas dinner	10	10
341	22 c. Serenading	10	10
342	$1 Child in manger	30	30
343	$2.50 Family going to church	50	50

1979. Nos. 274/7 and 279/80 surch.

345	12 c. on 2 c. Great barracuda	50	50
346	14 c. on 4 c. Spanish bayonet	40	50
347	18 c. on 3 c. Queen conch	80	55
348	25 c. on 6 c. Cable and Wireless building	55	50
349	38 c. on 10 c. American kestrel	2·00	70
350	40 c. on 1 c. Type **62**	2·00	70

73 Valley Methodist Church

1979. Easter. Church Interiors. Multicoloured.

351	5 c. Type **73**	10	10
352	12 c. St. Mary's Anglican Church, The Valley	10	10
353	18 c. St. Gerard's Roman Catholic Church, The Valley	15	15
354	22 c. Road Methodist Church	15	15
355	$1.50 St. Augustine's Anglican Church, East End	60	60
356	$2.50 West End Methodist Church	75	75

74 Cape of Good Hope 1d. "Woodblock" of 1881

1979. Death Centenary of Sir Rowland Hill. Multicoloured.

358	1 c. Type **74**	10	10
359	1 c. U.S.A. "inverted Jenny" of 1918	10	10
360	22 c. Penny Black ("V.R." Official)	15	15
361	35 c. Germany 2 m. "Graf Zeppelin" of 1928	20	20
362	$1.50 U.S.A. $5 "Columbus" of 1893	45	60
363	$2.50 Great Britain £5 orange of 1882	75	95

75 Wright "Flyer I" (1st powered Flight, 1903)

1979. History of Powered Fight. Multicoloured.

365	5 c. Type **75**	15	10
366	12 c. Louis Bleriot at Dover after Channel crossing, 1909	20	10
367	18 c. Vickers FB-27 Vimy (1st non-stop crossing of Atlantic, 1919)	25	15
368	22 c. Ryan NYP Special "Spirit of St Louis" (1st solo Atlantic flight by Charles Lindbergh, 1927)	25	20
369	$1.50 Airship LZ 127 "Graf Zeppelin", 1928	60	60
370	$2.50 Concorde, 1979	2·00	90

76 Sombrero Island

1979. Outer Islands. Multicoloured.

372	5 c. Type **76**	10	10
373	12 c. Anguillita Island	10	10
374	18 c. Sandy Island	15	15
375	25 c. Prickly Pear Cays	15	15
376	$1 Dog Island	30	40
377	$2.50 Scrub Island	50	70

77 Red Poinsettia

1979. Christmas. Multicoloured.

379	22 c. Type **77**	15	20
380	35 c. Kalanchoe	20	30
381	$1.50 Cream poinsettia	40	50
382	$2.50 White poinsettia	60	70

78 Exhibition Scene

1979. "London 1980" International Stamp Exhibition (1st issue). Multicoloured.

384	35 c. Type **78**	15	20
385	50 c. Earls Court Exhibition Centre	15	25
386	$1.50 Penny Black and Two-penny Blue stamps	25	60
387	$2.50 Exhibition Logo	45	95

See also Nos. 407/9.

79 Games Site

1980. Winter Olympic Games, Lake Placid, U.S.A. Multicoloured.

389	5 c. Type **79**	10	10
390	18 c. Ice hockey	10	10
391	35 c. Ice skating	15	20
392	50 c. Bobsleighing	15	20
393	$1 Skiing	20	35
394	$2.50 Luge-tobogganing	40	80

80 Salt ready for "Reaping"

1980. Salt Industry. Multicoloured.

396	5 c. Type **80**	10	10
397	12 c. Tallying salt	10	10
398	18 c. Unloading salt flats	15	15
399	22 c. Salt storage heap	15	15
400	$1 Salt for bagging and grinding	30	40
401	$2.50 Loading salt for export	50	70

1980. Anniversaries. Nos. 280, 282 and 287/8 optd **50th Anniversary Scouting 1980** (10 c., $2.50) or **75th Anniversary Rotary 1980** (others).

403	10 c. American kestrel	1·00	15
404	20 c. Stop-light parrotfish	80	20
405	$2.50 Manchineel	1·75	1·25
406	$5 Ground lizard	2·50	1·90

83 Palace of Westminster and Great Britain 1970 9d. "Philympia" Commemoration

1980. "London 1980" International Stamp Exhibition (2nd issue). Multicoloured.

407	50 c. Type **83**	55	65
408	$1.50 City Hall, Toronto and "Capex 1978" stamp of Canada	85	1·00
409	$2.50 Statue of Liberty and 1976 "Interphil" stamp of U.S.A.	1·10	1·40

84 Queen Elizabeth the Queen Mother

85 Brown Pelicans

1980. 80th Birthday of The Queen Mother.

411	84 35 c. multicoloured	30	30
412	50 c. multicoloured	45	40
413	$1.50 multicoloured	90	1·00
414	$3 multicoloured	2·25	2·00

1980. Christmas. Birds. Multicoloured.

416	5 c. Type **85**	30	10
417	22 c. Great blue heron	75	20
418	$1.50 Barn swallow	1·75	60
419	$3 Ruby-throated hummingbird	2·25	1·40

1980. Separation from St Kitts. Nos. 274, 277, 280/9, 334 and 418/9 optd **SEPARATION 1980** or surch also.

421	1 c. Type **62**	10	40
422	2 c. on 4 c. Spanish bayonet	10	40
423	5 c. on 15 c. Ground orchid	15	45
424	5 c. on $1.50 Barn swallow	15	45
425	5 c. on $3 Ruby-throated hummingbird	15	45
426	10 c. American kestrel	20	60
427	12 c. on $1 Sandy Island	20	60
428	14 c. on $2.50 Manchineel	20	60
429	15 c. Ground orchid	25	60
430	18 c. on $5 Ground lizard	25	60
431	20 c. Stop-light parrotfish	25	60
432	22 c. Lobster fishing boat	25	60
433	25 c. on 15 c. Ground orchid	30	65
434	35 c. Boat race	30	65
435	38 c. on 22 c. Serenading	30	65
436	40 c. on 1 c. Type **62**	30	65
437	50 c. Sea bean	35	75
438	$1 Sandy Island	50	1·00
439	$2.50 Manchineel	1·00	2·25
440	$5 Ground lizard	2·25	3·75
441	$10 Red-billed tropic bird	5·00	6·00
442	$10 on 6 c. Cable and Wireless Building	5·00	6·00

87 First Petition for Separation, 1825

1980. Separation from St Kitts. Multicoloured.

443	18 c. Type **87**	10	10
444	22 c. Referendum ballot paper, 1967	15	10
445	35 c. Airport blockade, 1967	15	15
446	50 c. Anguillan flag	20	20
447	$1 Separation celebration, 1980	30	35

88 "Nelson's Dockyard" (R. Granger Barrett)

1981. 175th Death Anniv of Lord Nelson. Mult.

449	22 c. Type **88**	1·25	30
450	35 c. "Ships in which Nelson Served" (Nicholas Pocock)	1·50	50
451	50 c. "H.M.S. Victory" (Monamy Swaine)	1·75	65
452	$3 "Battle of Trafalgar" (Clarkson Stanfield)	2·25	2·25

89 Minnie Mouse being chased by Bees

1981. Easter. Walt Disney Cartoon Characters. Multicoloured.

454	1 c. Type **89**	10	10
455	2 c. Pluto laughing at Mickey Mouse	10	10
456	3 c. Minnie Mouse tying ribbon round Pluto's neck	10	10
457	5 c. Minnie Mouse confronted by love-struck bird who fancies her bonnet	10	10
458	7 c. Dewey and Huey admiring themselves in mirror	10	10
459	9 c. Horace Horsecollar and Clarabelle Cow out for a stroll	10	10
460	10 c. Daisy Duck with hat full of Easter eggs	10	10
461	$2 Goofy unwrapping Easter hat	1·40	1·40
462	$3 Donald Duck in his Easter finery	1·60	1·60

90 Prince Charles, Lady Diana Spencer and St. Paul's Cathedral

1981. Royal Wedding. Multicoloured.

464	50 c. Type **90**	15	20
465	$2.50 Althorp	30	50
466	$3 Windsor Castle	35	60

91 Children playing in Tree

1981. 35th Anniv of U.N.I.C.E.F. Multicoloured.

470	5 c. Type **91**	20	30
471	10 c. Children playing by pool	20	30
472	15 c. Children playing musical instruments	20	30
473	$3 Children playing with pets	2·50	3·00

1981. Christmas. Designs as T **89** showing scenes from Walt Disney's cartoon film "The Night before Christmas".

475	1 c. multicoloured	10	10
476	2 c. multicoloured	10	10
477	3 c. multicoloured	10	10
478	5 c. multicoloured	10	10
479	7 c. multicoloured	10	10
480	10 c. multicoloured	10	10
481	12 c. multicoloured	10	10
482	$2 multicoloured	3·00	1·25
483	$3 multicoloured	3·00	1·60

92 Red Grouper

1982. Multicoloured.

485	1 c. Type **92**	15	60
486	5 c. Ferry service, Blowing Point	30	60
487	10 c. Island dinghies	20	60
488	15 c. Majorettes	20	60
489	20 c. Launching boat, Sandy Hill	40	60
490	25 c. Corals	1·25	60
491	30 c. Little Bay cliffs	30	75
492	35 c. Fountain Cave interior	1·25	80
493	40 c. Sunset over Sandy Island	30	75
494	45 c. Landing at Sombrero	50	80
495	60 c. Seine fishing	3·00	2·25
496	75 c. Boat race at sunset, Sandy Ground	80	1·75
497	$1 Bagging lobster at Island Harbour	2·25	1·75
498	$5 Brown pelicans	14·00	10·00
499	$7.50 Hibiscus	11·00	11·00
500	$10 Queen triggerfish	14·00	12·00

1982. No. 494 surch **50c.**

501	50 c. on 45 c. Landing at Sombrero	50	35

94 Anthurium and "Heliconius charithonia"

95 Lady Diana Spencer in 1961

1982. Easter. Flowers and Butterflies. Multicoloured.

502	10 c. Type **94**	45	10
503	35 c. Bird of paradise and "Junonia evarete"	1·10	40
504	75 c. Allamanda and "Danaus plexippus"	1·50	70
505	$3 Orchid tree and "Biblis hyperia"	2·25	2·25

1982. 21st Birthday of Princess of Wales. Mult.

507	10 c. Type **95**	30	20
508	30 c. Lady Diana Spencer in 1968	50	25
509	40 c. Lady Diana in 1970	50	30
510	60 c. Lady Diana in 1974	55	35
511	$2 Lady Diana in 1981	80	1·10
512	$3 Lady Diana in 1981 (different)	2·25	1·40

96 Pitching Tent

1982. 75th Anniv of Boy Scout Movement. Multicoloured.

515	10 c. Type **96**	45	20
516	35 c. Scout band	85	50
517	75 c. Yachting	1·25	90
518	$3 On parade	3·00	2·75

1982. World Cup Football Championship, Spain. Horiz designs as T **89** showing scenes from Walt Disney's cartoon film "Bedknobs and Broomsticks".

520	1 c. multicoloured	10	10
521	3 c. multicoloured	10	10
522	4 c. multicoloured	10	10
523	5 c. multicoloured	10	10
524	7 c. multicoloured	10	10
525	9 c. multicoloured	10	10
526	10 c. multicoloured	10	10
527	$2.50 multicoloured	2·25	1·75
528	$3 multicoloured	2·25	2·00

1982. Commonwealth Games, Brisbane. Nos. 487, 495/6 and 498 optd **COMMONWEALTH GAMES 1982.**

530	10 c. Island dinghies	15	25
531	60 c. Seine fishing	45	60
532	75 c. Boat race at sunset, Sandy Ground	60	80
533	$5 Brown pelicans	3·25	3·75

1982. Birth Cent of A. A. Milne (author). As T **89**.

534	1 c. multicoloured	10	10
535	2 c. multicoloured	15	10
536	3 c. multicoloured	20	10
537	5 c. multicoloured	25	15
538	7 c. multicoloured	25	20
539	10 c. multicoloured	25	15
540	12 c. multicoloured	35	20
541	20 c. multicoloured	55	25
542	$5 multicoloured	5·50	6·50

DESIGNS—HORIZ: 1 c. to $5 Scenes from various "Winnie the Pooh" stories.

98 Culture

1983. Commonwealth Day. Multicoloured.

544	10 c. Type **98**	10	15
545	35 c. Anguilla and British flags	30	30
546	75 c. Economic co-operation	60	80
547	$2.50 Salt industry (salt pond)	3·75	4·25

99 "I am the Lord Thy God"

101 Montgolfier Hot Air Balloon, 1783

100 Leatherback Turtle

1983. Easter. The Ten Commandments. Mult.

549	1 c. Type **99**	10	10
550	2 c. "Thou shalt not make any graven image"	10	10
551	3 c. "Thou shalt not take My Name in vain"	10	10
552	10 c. "Remember the Sabbath Day"	20	10
553	35 c. "Honour thy father and mother"	45	20
554	60 c. "Thou shalt not kill"	80	40
555	75 c. "Thou shalt not commit adultery"	90	50
556	$2 "Thou shalt not steal"	2·25	1·50
557	$2.50 "Thou shalt not bear false witness"	2·50	1·50
558	$5 "Thou shalt not covet"	3·75	2·75

1983. Endangered Species. Turtles. Multicoloured.

560	10 c. Type **100**	1·00	40
561	35 c. Hawksbill turtle	2·00	85
562	75 c. Green turtle	2·75	2·00
563	$1 Loggerhead turtle	3·25	3·50

1983. Bicentenary of Manned Flight. Multicoloured.

565	10 c. Type **101**	30	20
566	60 c. Blanchard and Jefferies crossing English Channel by balloon, 1785	85	55
567	$1 Henri Giffard's steam-powered dirigible airship, 1852	1·25	75
568	$2.50 Otto Lillienthal and biplane glider, 1890–96	2·00	1·50

102 Boys' Brigade Band and Flag

1983. Centenary of Boys' Brigade. Multicoloured.

570	10 c. Type **102**	25	15
571	$5 Brigade members marching	3·00	2·75

1983. 150th Anniv of Abolition of Slavery (1st issue). Nos. 487, 493 and 497/8 optd **150TH ANNIVERSARY ABOLITION OF SLAVERY ACT.**

573	10 c. Island dinghies	10	10
574	40 c. Sunset over Sandy Island	25	25
575	$1 Bagging lobster at Island Harbour	60	50
576	$5 Brown pelicans	4·75	2·75

See also Nos. 616/23.

104 Jiminy on Clock ("Cricket on the Hearth")

1983. Christmas. Walt Disney Cartoon Characters. Multicoloured.

577	1 c. Type **104**	10	10
578	2 c. Jiminy with fiddle ("Cricket on the Hearth")	10	10
579	3 c. Jiminy among toys ("Cricket on the Hearth")	10	10
580	4 c. Mickey as Bob Cratchit ("A Christmas Carol")	10	10
581	5 c. Donald Duck as Scrooge ("A Christmas Carol")	10	10
582	6 c. Mini and Goofy in "The Chimes"	10	10
583	10 c. Goofy sees an imp appearing from bells ("The Chimes")	10	10
584	$2 Donald Duck as Mr. Pickwick ("The Pickwick Papers")	3·00	2·00
585	$3 Disney characters as Pickwickians ("The Pickwick Papers")	3·25	2·25

105 100 Metres Race

1984. Olympic Games, Los Angeles. Multicoloured.
A. Inscr "1984 Los Angeles".
B. Inscr "1984 Olympics Los Angeles" and Olympic emblem.

		A		B	
587	1 c. Type **105**	10	10	10	10
588	2 c. Long jumping	10	10	10	10
589	3 c. Shot-putting	10	10	10	10
590	4 c. High jumping	10	10	10	10
591	5 c. 400 metres race	10	10	10	10
592	6 c. Hurdling	10	10	10	10
593	10 c. Discus-throwing	10	10	10	10
594	$1 Pole-vaulting	3·00	1·25	3·50	2·75
595	$4 Javelin-throwing	5·50	3·50	7·00	7·00

106 "Justice"

1984. Easter. Multicoloured.

597	10 c. Type **106**	15	10
598	25 c. "Poetry"	20	20
599	35 c. "Philosophy"	30	30
600	40 c. "Theology"	30	30
601	$1 "Abraham and Paul"	85	95
602	$2 "Moses and Matthew"	1·60	2·00
603	$3 "John and David"	2·25	2·75
604	$4 "Peter and Adam"	2·50	3·00

Nos. 597/604 show details from "La Stanza della Segnatura" by Raphael.

1984. Nos. 485, 491, 498/500 surch.

606	25 c. on $7.50 Hibiscus	45	35
607	35 c. on 30 c. Little Bay cliffs	50	40
608	60 c. on 1 c. Type **92**	55	45
609	$2.50 on $5 Brown pelicans	2·25	1·50
610	$2.50 on $10 Queen triggerfish	1·75	1·50

108 1913 1d. Kangaroo Stamp

1984. "Ausipex 84" International Stamp Exhibition. Multicoloured.

611	10 c. Type **108**	40	20
612	75 c. 1914 6d. Laughing Kookaburra	1·25	85
613	$1 1932 2d. Sydney Harbour Bridge	1·75	1·25
614	$2.50 1938 10s. King George VI	2·25	2·25

109 Thomas Fowell Buxton

1984. 150th Anniv of Abolition of Slavery (2nd issue). Multicoloured.

616	10 c. Type **109**	10	10
617	25 c. Abraham Lincoln	25	25
618	35 c. Henri Christophe	35	35
619	60 c. Thomas Clarkson	50	50
620	75 c. William Wilberforce	60	60
621	$1 Olaudah Equiano	70	70
622	$2.50 General Charles Gordon	1·60	1·60
623	$5 Granville Sharp	3·00	3·00

1984. Universal Postal Union Congress, Hamburg. Nos. 486/7 and 498 optd **U.P.U. CONGRESS HAMBURG 1984** or surch also (No 626).

625	5 c. Ferry service, Blowing Point	20	10
626	20 c. on 10 c. Island dinghies	30	15
627	$5 Brown pelicans	4·50	3·50

1984. Birth of Prince Henry. Nos. 507/12 optd **PRINCE HENRY BIRTH 15.9.84.**

628	10 c. Type **95**	10	10
629	30 c. Lady Diana Spencer in 1968	20	25
630	40 c. Lady Diana in 1970	25	30
631	60 c. Lady Diana in 1974	40	45
632	$2 Lady Diana in 1981	1·00	1·25
633	$3 Lady Diana in 1981 (different)	1·10	1·75

112 Christmas in Sweden

1984. Christmas. Walt Disney Cartoon Characters. National Scenes. Multicoloured.

636	1 c. Type **112**	10	10
637	2 c. Italy	10	10
638	3 c. Holland	10	10
639	4 c. Mexico	10	10
640	5 c. Spain	10	10
641	10 c. Disneyland, U.S.A.	10	10
642	$1 Japan	2·75	2·00
643	$2 Anguilla	3·50	4·00
644	$4 Germany	5·50	6·50

113 Icarus in Flight

1984. 40th Anniv of International Civil Aviation Authority. Multicoloured.

646	60 c. Type **113**	60	75
647	75 c. "Solar Princess" (abstract)	80	90
648	$2.50 I.C.A.O. emblem (vert)	2·25	3·00

114 Barn Swallow

115 The Queen Mother visiting King's College Hospital, London

1985. Birth Bicentenary of John J. Audubon (ornithologist). Multicoloured.

650	10 c. Type **114**	70	45
651	60 c. American wood stork	1·25	90
652	75 c. Roseate tern	1·25	1·00
653	$5 Osprey	4·50	4·50

1985. Life and Times of Queen Elizabeth the Queen Mother. Multicoloured.

655	10 c. Type **115**	10	10
656	$2 The Queen Mother inspecting Royal Marine Volunteer Cadets, Deal	80	1·25
657	$3 The Queen Mother outside Clarence House	1·10	1·50

116 White-tailed Tropic Bird

1985. Birds. Multicoloured.

659	5 c. Brown pelican	1·25	1·25
660	10 c. Mourning dove	1·25	1·25
661	15 c. Magnificent frigate bird (inscr "Man-o-War")	1·25	1·25
662	20 c. Antillean crested hummingbird	1·25	1·25
663	25 c. Type **116**	1·25	1·25
664	30 c. Caribbean elaenia	1·25	1·25
665	35 c. Black-whiskered vireo	5·50	5·00
665a	35 c. Lesser Antillean bullfinch	1·25	1·25
666	40 c. Yellow-crowned night heron	1·25	1·25
667	45 c. Pearly-eyed thrasher	1·25	1·25
668	50 c. Laughing gull	1·25	1·25
669	65 c. Brown booby	1·25	1·25
670	80 c. Grey kingbird	2·00	2·75
671	$1 Audubon's shearwater	2·00	2·75
672	$1.35 Roseate tern	1·50	2·75
673	$2.50 Bananaquit	4·50	6·00
674	$5 Belted kingfisher	3·75	7·00
675	$10 Green heron	6·50	9·00

1985. 75th Anniv of Girl Guide Movement. Nos. 486, 491, 496 and 498 optd **GIRL GUIDES 75TH ANNIVERSARY 1910–1985** and anniversary emblem.

676	5 c. Ferry service, Blowing Point	20	20
677	30 c. Little Bay cliffs	40	35
678	75 c. Boat race at sunset, Sandy Ground	60	85
679	$5 Brown pelicans	6·00	5·25

118 Goofy as Huckleberry Finn Fishing

1985. 150th Birth Anniv of Mark Twain (author). Walt Disney cartoon characters in scenes from "Huckleberry Finn". Multicoloured.

680	10 c. Type **118**	25	15
681	60 c. Pete as Pap surprising Huck	1·00	85
682	$1 "Multiplication tables"	1·60	1·25
683	$3 The Duke reciting Shakespeare	3·00	3·50

119 Hansel and Gretel (Mickey and Minnie Mouse) awakening in Forest

1985. Birth Bicentenaries of Grimm Brothers (folklorists). Designs showing Walt Disney cartoon characters in scenes from "Hansel and Gretel". Multicoloured.

685	5 c. Type **119**	10	10
686	50 c. Hansel and Gretel find the gingerbread house	55	40
687	90 c. Hansel and Gretel meeting the Witch	90	75
688	$4 Hansel and Gretel captured by the Witch	3·00	3·00

120 Statue of Liberty and "Danmark" (Denmark)

1985. Centenary of the Statue of Liberty (1986). The Statue of Liberty and Cadet ships.

690	10 c. Type **120**	50	50
691	20 c. "Eagle" (U.S.A.)	70	70
692	60c. "Amerigo Vespucci" (Italy)	1·25	1·50
693	75 c. "Sir Winston Churchill" (Great Britain)	1·25	1·75
694	$2 "Nippon Maru" (Japan)	1·75	2·50
695	$2.50 "Gorch Fock" (West Germany)	2·00	2·50

1985. 80th Anniv of Rotary (10, 35 c.) and International Youth Year (others). Nos 487, 491 and 497 optd or surch **80TH ANNIVERSARY ROTARY 1985** and emblem (10, 35 c.) or **INTERNATIONAL YOUTH YEAR** and emblem ($1, $5).

697	10 c. Island dinghies	10	10
698	35 c. on 30 c. Little Bay cliffs	25	25
699	$1 Bagging lobster at Island Harbour	70	70
700	$5 on 30 c. Little Bay cliffs	3·50	3·50

123 Johannes Hevelius (astronomer) and Mayan Temple Observatory

1986. Appearance of Halley's Comet. Multicoloured.

701	5 c. Type **123**	25	25
702	10 c. "Viking Lander" space vehicle on Mars, 1976	25	25
703	60 c. Comet in 1664 (from "Theatri Cosmicum", 1668)	85	85
704	$4 Comet over Mississippi riverboat, 1835 (150th birth anniv of Mark Twain)	3·50	3·50

124 "The Crucifixion"

125 Princess Elizabeth inspecting Guards, 1946

1986. Easter.

706	**124**	10 c. multicoloured	20	20
707	–	25 c. multicoloured	35	35
708	–	45 c. multicoloured	65	65
709	–	$4 multicoloured	3·25	3·75

DESIGNS: 25 c. to $4 Different stained glass windows from Chartres Cathedral.

1986. 60th Birthday of Queen Elizabeth II.

711	**125**	20 c. black and yellow	15	15
712	–	$2 multicoloured	1·25	1·25
713	–	$3 multicoloured	1·75	1·75

DESIGNS: $2 Queen at Garter ceremony; $3 At Trooping the Colour.

1986. "Ameripex" International Stamp Exhibition, Chicago. Nos. 659, 667, 671, 673 and 675 optd **AMERIPEX 1986.**

715	5 c. Brown pelican	40	40
716	45 c. Pearly-eyed thrasher	70	45
717	$1 Audubon's shearwater	1·25	85
718	$2.50 Bananaquit	2·25	2·50
719	$10 Green heron	6·00	7·50

127 Prince Andrew and Miss Sarah Ferguson

130 Christopher Columbus with Astrolabe

129 Trading Sloop

1986. Royal Wedding. Multicoloured.

720a	10 c. Type **127**	15	15
721a	35 c. Prince Andrew	35	35
722	$2 Miss Sarah Ferguson	1·50	1·50
723	$3 Prince Andrew and Miss Sarah Ferguson (diffferent)	2·00	2·00

1986. International Peace Year. Nos. 616/23 optd **INTERNATIONAL YEAR OF PEACE.**

725	10 c. Type **109**	25	25
726	25 c. Abraham Lincoln	45	45
727	35 c. Henri Christophe	55	55
728	60 c. Thomas Clarkson	80	80
729	75 c. William Wilberforce	90	90
730	$1 Olaudah Equiano	1·00	1·00
731	$2.50 General Gordon	2.00	2·00
732	$5 Granville Sharp	3·00	3·00

1986. Christmas. Ships. Multicoloured.

734	10 c. Type **129**	90	50
735	45 c. "Lady Rodney" (cargo liner)	1·75	1·10
736	80 c. "West Derby" (19th-century sailing ship)	2·50	2·50
737	$3 "Warspite" (local sloop)	4·75	5·50

1986. 500th Anniv (1992) of Discovery of America by Columbus (1st issue). Multicoloured.

739	5 c. Type **130**	30	30
740	10 c. Columbus on board ship	50	35
741	35 c. "Santa Maria"	1·25	90
742	80 c. King Ferdinand and Queen Isabella of Spain (horiz)	1·50	1·60
743	$4 Caribbean Indians smoking tobacco (horiz)	3·25	4·25

See also Nos. 902/5.

131 "Danaus plexippus"

1987. Easter. Butterflies. Multicoloured.

745	10 c. Type **131**	75	40
746	80 c. "Anartia jatrophae"	2·25	2·25
747	$1 "Heliconius charithonia"	2·50	2·50
748	$2 "Junonia evarete"	4·00	4·50

132 Old Goose Iron and Modern Electric Iron

1987. 20th Anniv of Separation from St. Kitts-Nevis. Multicoloured.

750	10 c. Type **132**	15	20
751	35 c. Old East End School and Albena Lake-Hodge Comprehensive College	20	20
752	45 c. Past and present markets	25	25
753	80 c. Previous sailing ferry and new motor ferry, Blowing Point	45	55
754	$1 Original mobile office and new telephone exchange	55	75

755 $2 Open-air meeting, Burrowes Park and House of Assembly in session . . . . 1·10 1·75

1987. "Capex '87" International Stamp Exhibition, Toronto. Nos. 665a, 667, 670 and 675 optd **CAPEX'87**.

757 35 c. Lesser Antillean bullfinch 70 60
758 45 c. Pearly-eyed thrasher . . 80 60
759 80 c. Grey kingbird . . . . . 1·25 1·25
760 $10 Green heron . . . . . 6·75 8·00

1987. 20th Anniv of Independence. Nos. 659, 661/4 and 665a/75 optd **20 YEARS OF PROGRESS 1967 – 1987**, No. 762 surch also.

761 5 c. Brown pelican . . . . . . 1·00 1·00
762 10 c. on 15 c. Magnificent frigate bird . . . . 1·00 1·00
763 15 c. Magnificent frigate bird . 1·25 1·25
764 20 c. Antillean crested hummingbird . . . . 1·25 1·25
765 25 c. Type **116** . . . . 1·25 1·25
766 30 c. Caribbean elaenia . . . 1·25 1·25
767 35 c. Lesser Antillean bullfinch 1·25 1·25
768 40 c. Yellow-crowned night heron . . . . 1·25 1·25
769 45 c. Pearly-eyed thrasher . . 1·25 1·25
770 50 c. Laughing gull . . . . . 1·25 1·25
771 65 c. Brown booby . . . . . 1·50 1·75
772 80 c. Grey kingbird . . . . . 1·50 1·75
773 $1 Audubon's shearwater . . 1·50 1·75
774 $1.35 Roseate tern . . . . . . 2·00 2·25
775 $2.50 Bananaquit . . . . . . 2·25 3·50
776 $5 Belted kingfisher . . . . . 3·50 5·00
777 $10 Green heron . . . . . . 6·00 8·50

135 Wicket Keeper and Game in Progress

1987. Cricket World Cup. Multicoloured.

778 10 c. Type **135** 65 50
779 35 c. Batsman and local Anguilla team . . . . 1·10 60
780 45 c. Batsman and game in progress . . . . 1·25 70
781 $2.50 Bowler and game in progress . . . . 3·00 4·00

136 West Indian Top Shell

1987. Christmas. Sea Shells and Crabs. Mult.

783 10 c. Type **136** 65 40
784 35 c. Ghost crab . . . . . . 1·00 60
785 50 c. Spiny Caribbean vase . . 1·75 1·25
786 $2 Great land crab . . . . . 3·00 4·25

1987. Royal Ruby Wedding. Nos. 665a, 671/2 and 675 optd **40TH WEDDING ANNIVERSARY H.M. QUEEN ELIZABETH II H.R.H. THE DUKE OF EDINBURGH**.

788 35 c. Lesser Antillean bullfinch 40 30
789 $1 Audubon's shearwater . . 1·00 80
790 $1.35 Roseate tern . . . . . . 1·10 90
791 $10 Green heron . . . . . . 5·25 6·00

138 "Crinum erubescens" **139** Relay Racing

1988. Easter. Lilies. Multicoloured.

792 30 c. Type **138** 20 15
793 45 c. Spider lily 30 25
794 $1 "Crinum macowanii" . . . 75 60
795 $2.50 Day lily . . . . 1·25 2·00

1988. Olympic Games, Seoul. Multicoloured.

797 35 c. Type **139** 40 30
798 45 c. Windsurfing 55 45
799 50 c. Tennis . . . . 1·25 1·00
800 80 c. Basketball . . . . 2·50 2·50

140 Common Sea Fan

1988. Christmas. Marine Life. Multicoloured.

802 35 c. Type **140** 30 30
803 80 c. Coral crab 70 70
804 $1 Grooved brain coral . . . 85 85
805 $1.60 Queen triggerfish . . . 1·40 2·00

1988. Visit of Princess Alexandra. Nos. 665a, 670/1 and 673 optd **H.R.H. PRINCESS ALEXANDRA'S VISIT NOVEMBER 1988**.

807 35 c. Lesser Antillean bullfinch 80 60
808 80 c. Grey kingbird . . . . . 1·40 1·40
809 $1 Audubon's shearwater . . 1·60 1·60
810 $2.50 Bananaquit . . . . . . 2·75 3·75

142 Wood Slave

1989. Lizards. Multicoloured.

811 45 c. Type **142** 45 35
812 80 c. Slippery back 70 70
813 $2.50 "Iguana delicatissima" . 2·00 2·75

143 "Christ Crowned with Thorns" (detail) (Bosch) **144** University Arms

1989. Easter. Religious Paintings. Multicoloured.

815 35 c. Type **143** 20 20
816 80 c. "Christ bearing the Cross" (detail) (Gerard David) . . 45 55
817 $1 "The Deposition" (detail) (Gerard David) 50 60
818 $1.60 "Pieta" (detail) (Rogier van der Weyden) . . . . . 85 1·40

1989. 40th Anniv of University of the West Indies.

820 **144** $5 multicoloured . . . . 2·40 3·00

1989. 20th Anniv of First Manned Landing on Moon. Nos. 670/2 and 674 optd **20TH ANNIVERSARY MOON LANDING**.

821 80 c. Grey kingbird 80 80
822 $1 Audubon's shearwater . . 90 90
823 $1.35 Roseate tern . . . . . 1·10 1·25
824 $5 Belted kingfisher . . . . . 3·75 4·25

146 Lone Star (house), 1930

1989. Christmas. Historic Houses. Multicoloured.

825 5 c. Type **146** 15 15
826 35 c. Whitehouse, 1906 . . . 35 35
827 45 c. Hodges House 45 45
828 80 c. Warden's Place . . . . 80 1·25

147 Bigeye ("Blear Eye")

1990. Fishes. Multicoloured.

830B 5 c. Type **147** 30 30
831B 10 c. Long-spined squirrelfish ("Redman") 30 30
832A 15 c. Stop-light parrotfish ("Speckletail") 30 40
833A 25 c. Blue-striped grunt . . . 40 50
834A 30 c. Yellow jack 50 60
835B 35 c. Red hind 40 40
836A 40 c. Spotted goatfish . . . 40 40
837A 45 c. Queen triggerfish ("Old wife") 40 40
838A 50 c. Coney ("Butter fish") . 40 40
839A 65 c. Smooth trunkfish ("Shell fish") 45 45
840A 80 c. Yellow-tailed snapper . 50 55
841A $1 Banded butterflyfish ("Katy") 55 60
842A $1.35 Nassau grouper . . . 70 80
843A $2.50 Blue tang ("Doctor fish") . . . . 1·10 1·40
844A $5 Queen angelfish . . . . 2·25 3·00
845A $10 Great barracuda . . . 4·50 5·50

148 The Last Supper **149** G.B. 1840 Penny Black

1990. Easter. Multicoloured.

846 35 c. Type **148** 55 20
847 45 c. The Trial 55 25
848 $1.35 The Crucifixion . . . . 1·50 1·60
849 $2.50 The Empty Tomb . . . 2·00 3·00

1990. "Stamp World London 90" International Stamp Exhibition. Multicoloured.

851 25 c. Type **149** 40 25
852 50 c. G.B. 1840 Twopenny Blue 70 50
853 $1.50 Cape of Good Hope 1861 1d. "woodblock" (horiz) . . 1·50 1·75
854 $2.50 G.B. 1882 £5 (horiz) . . 2·00 2·50

1990. Anniversaries and Events. Nos. 841/4 optd.

856 $1 Banded butterflyfish (optd **EXPO '90**) . . . . 1·00 1·00
857 $1.35 Nassau grouper (optd **1990 INTERNATIONAL LITERACY YEAR**) . . . . 1·25 1·25
858 $2.50 Blue tang (optd **WORLD CUP FOOTBALL CHAMPIONSHIPS 1990**) . 2·50 3·00
859 $5 Queen angelfish (optd **90TH BIRTHDAY H.M. THE QUEEN MOTHER**) . . . . 4·00 4·50

151 Mermaid Flag

1990. Island Flags. Multicoloured.

860 50 c. Type **151** 70 40
861 80 c. New Anguilla official flag 1·00 90
862 $1 Three Dolphins flag . . . 1·10 95
863 $5 Governor's official flag . . 3·75 5·00

152 Laughing Gulls

1990. Christmas. Sea Birds. Multicoloured.

864 10 c. Type **152** 50 30
865 35 c. Brown booby 85 50
866 $1.50 Bridled tern . . . . . . 1·75 1·75
867 $3.50 Brown pelican . . . . . 3·00 3·50

1991. Easter. Nos. 846/9 optd **1991**.

869 35 c. Type **148** 45 35
870 45 c. The Trial 55 45
871 $1.35 The Crucifixion . . . . 1·25 1·50
872 $2.50 The Empty Tomb . . . 2·00 3·00

154 Angel **155** Angels with Palm Branches outside St. Gerard's Church

1991. Christmas.

874 **154** 5 c. violet, brown & black 20 20
875 – 35 c. multicoloured 65 45
876 – 80 c. multicoloured . . . . 1·40 1·40
877 – $1 multicoloured . . . . . 1·50 1·50

DESIGNS—VERT: 35 c. Father Christmas. HORIZ: 80 c. Church and house; $1 Palm trees at night.

1992. Easter. Multicoloured.

879 30 c. Type **155** 35 25
880 45 c. Angels singing outside Methodist Church 45 35
881 80 c. Village (horiz) 90 90
882 $1 Congregation going to St. Mary's Church . . . . . . 1·00 1·00
883 $5 Dinghy regatta (horiz) . . . 3·75 5·00

1992. No. 834 surch **$1.60**.

884 $1.60 on 30 c. Yellow jack . . 1·10 1·10

157 Anguillan Flags

1992. 25th Anniv of Separation from St. Kitts-Nevis. Multicoloured.

885 80 c. Type **157** 90 90
886 $1 Present official seal . . . . 1·10 1·10
887 $1.60 Anguillan flags at airport 2·00 2·00
888 $2 Royal Commissioner's official seal . . . . 2·00 2·00

158 Dinghy Race

1992. Sailing Dinghy Racing.

890 **158** 20 c. multicoloured . . . 60 45
891 – 35 c. multicoloured . . . 80 50
892 – 45 c. multicoloured . . . 85 50
893 – 80 c. multicoloured . . . 1·50 2·00
894 – 80 c. black and blue . . . 1·50 2·00
895 – $1 multicoloured . . . . 1·50 1·75

DESIGNS—VERT: 35 c. Stylized poster; 80 c. (No. 893) "Blue Bird" in race; 80 c. (No. 894) Construction drawings of "Blue Bird" by Douglas Pyle; $1 Stylized poster (different). HORIZ: 45 c. Dinghies on beach.

159 Mucka Jumbie on Stilts

1992. Christmas. Local Traditions. Mult.

897 20 c. Type **159** 15 15
898 70 c. Masqueraders 45 50
899 $1.05 Baking in old style oven 65 80
900 $2.40 Collecting presents from Christmas tree . . . . . . 1·25 1·90

160 Columbus landing in New World

1992. 500th Anniv of Discovery of America by Columbus (2nd issue).

902 **160** 80 c. multicoloured . . . 1·10 1·10
903 – $1 black and brown . . . 1·10 1·10
904 – $2 multicoloured . . . . 2·00 2·50
905 – $3 multicoloured . . . . 2·50 3·00

DESIGNS—VERT: $1 Christopher Columbus. HORIZ: $2 Fleet of Columbus; $3 "Pinta".

161 "Kite Flying" (Kyle Brooks) **163** Lord Great Chamberlain presenting Spurs of Charity to Queen

162 Salt Picking

1993. Easter. Children's Paintings. Mult.

907 20 c. Type **161** 55 30
908 45 c. "Clifftop Village Service" (Kara Connor) 75 45
909 80 c. "Morning Devotion on Sombrero" (Junior Carty) . 1·40 1·40
910 $1.50 "Hill Top Church Service" (Leana Harris) . . . . . . 2·00 2·75

1993. Traditional Industries. Mult.

912	20 c. Type **162**	75	40
913	80 c. Tobacco growing	90	90
914	$1 Cotton picking	1·00	1·00
915	$2 Harvesting sugar cane	1·75	2·50

1993. 40th Anniv of Coronation. Mult.

917	80 c. Type **163**	60	50
918	$1 The Benediction	75	70
919	$2 Queen Elizabeth II in Coronation robes	1·25	1·40
920	$3 St. Edward's Crown	1·75	2·00

164 Carnival Pan Player

1993. Anguilla Carnival. Multicoloured.

922	20 c. Type **164**	20	15
923	45 c. Revellers dressed as pirates	40	30
924	80 c. Revellers dressed as stars	65	65
925	$1 Mas dancing	75	75
926	$2 Masked couple	1·50	2·00
927	$3 Revellers dressed as commandos	2·00	2·50

165 Mucka Jumbies Carnival Characters

167 Princess Alexandra, 1988

166 Travelling Branch Mail Van at Sandy Ground

1993. Christmas. Multicoloured.

929	20 c. Type **165**	15	20
930	35 c. Local carol singers	25	25
931	45 c. Christmas home baking	35	35
932	$3 Decorating Christmas tree	1·90	2·75

1994. Delivering the Mail. Multicoloured.

934	20 c. Type **166**	60	45
935	45 c. "Betsy R" (mail schooner) at The Forest (vert)	85	50
936	80 c. Mail van at old Post Office	1·25	1·25
937	$1 Jeep on beach, Island Harbour (vert)	1·25	1·25
938	$4 New Post Office	3·50	4·50

1994. Royal Visitors. Multicoloured.

939	45 c. Type **167**	45	35
940	50 c. Princess Alice, 1960	50	45
941	80 c. Prince Philip, 1993	75	75
942	$1 Prince Charles, 1973	85	85
943	$2 Queen Elizabeth II, 1994	1·50	2·00

168 "The Crucifixion"

170 "The Nativity" (Gustave Dore)

169 Cameroun Player and Pontiac Silverdome, Detroit

1994. Easter. Stained-glass Windows. Multicoloured.

945	20 c. Type **168**	30	30
946	45 c. "The Empty Tomb"	45	45
947	80 c. "The Resurrection"	80	90
948	$3 "Risen Christ with Disciples"	2·75	3·25

1994. World Cup Football Championship, U.S.A. Multicoloured.

949	20 c. Type **169**	30	20
950	70 c. Argentine player and Foxboro Stadium, Boston	70	65
951	$1.80 Italian player and RFK Memorial Stadium, Washington	1·50	1·75
952	$2.40 German player and Soldier Field, Chicago	1·90	2·50

1994. Christmas. Religious Paintings. Multicoloured.

954	20 c. Type **170**	30	20
955	30 c. "The Wise Men guided by the Star" (Dore)	40	30
956	35 c. "The Annunciation" (Dore)	45	35
957	45 c. "Adoration of the Shepherds" (detail) (Poussin)	50	45
958	$2.40 "The Flight into Egypt" (Dore)	1·50	2·50

171 Pair of Zenaida Doves

1995. Easter. Zenaida Doves. Multicoloured.

959	20 c. Type **171**	30	20
960	45 c. Dove on branch	50	40
961	50 c. Guarding nest	60	45
962	$5 With chicks	4·50	5·50

172 Trygve Lie (first Secretary-General) and General Assembly

1995. 50th Anniv of United Nations. Multicoloured.

963	20 c. Type **172**	20	20
964	80 c. Flag and building showing "50"	60	60
965	$1 Dag Hammarskjold and U. Thant (former Secretary-Generals) and U.N. Charter	70	70
966	$5 U.N. Building (vert)	4·00	5·00

173 Anniversary Emblem and Map of Anguilla

1995. 25th Anniv of Caribbean Development Bank. Multicoloured.

967	45 c. Type **173**	1·50	1·75
968	$5 Bank building and launches	3·00	3·75

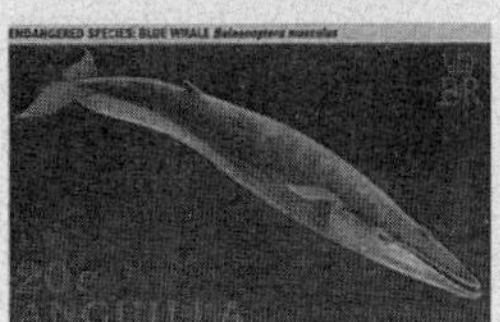

174 Blue Whale

1995. Endangered Species. Whales. Multicoloured.

969	20 c. Type **174**	55	40
970	45 c. Right whale (vert)	90	50
971	$1 Sperm whale	1·50	1·50
972	$5 Humpback whale	5·50	6·50

175 Palm Tree

1995. Christmas. Multicoloured.

973	10 c. Type **175**	25	20
974	25 c. Balloons and fishes	40	30
975	45 c. Shells	55	30
976	$5 Fishes in shape of Christmas tree	5·50	6·50

176 Deep Water Gorgonia

177 Running

1996. Corals. Multicoloured.

977	20 c. Type **176**	50	30
978	80 c. Common sea fan	1·10	90
979	$5 Venus sea fern	4·50	5·50

1996. Olympic Games, Atlanta. Multicoloured.

980	20 c. Type **177**	30	20
981	80 c. Javelin throwing and wheelchair basketball	80	70
982	$1 High jumping and hurdles	85	85
983	$3.50 Olympic rings and torch with Greek and American flags	2·75	3·25

178 Siege of Sandy Hill Fort

1996. Bicentenary of the Battle for Anguilla. Multicoloured.

984	60 c. Type **178**	60	60
985	75 c. French troops destroying church (horiz)	70	70
986	$1.50 Naval battle (horiz)	1·40	1·60
987	$4 French troops landing at Rendezvous Bay	2·75	3·50

179 Gooseberry

1997. Fruit. Multicoloured.

988	10 c. Type **179**	10	10
989	20 c. West Indian cherry	10	10
990	40 c. Tamarind	15	20
991	50 c. Pomme-surette	20	25
992	60 c. Sea almond	25	30
993	75 c. Sea grape	35	40
994	80 c. Banana	35	40
995	$1 Genip	45	50
996	$1.10 Coco plum	50	55
997	$1.25 Pope	55	60
998	$1.50 Pawpaw	65	70
999	$2 Sugar apple	85	90
1000	$3 Soursop	1·25	1·40
1001	$4 Pomegranate	1·75	1·90
1002	$5 Cashew	2·10	2·25
1003	$10 Mango	4·25	4·50

180 West Indian Iguanas hatching

1997. Endangered Species. West Indian Iguanas. Multicoloured.

1004	20 c. Type **180**	35	40
1005	50 c. On rock	55	60
1006	75 c. On branch	60	70
1007	$3 Head of West Indian iguana	1·50	1·75

181 "Juluca, Rainbow Deity"

1997. Ancient Stone Carvings from Fountain Cavern. Multicoloured.

1008	30 c. Type **181**	30	35
1009	$1.25 "Lizard with front legs extended"	75	80
1010	$2.25 "Chief"	1·40	1·60
1011	$2.75 "Jocahu, the Creator"	1·75	2·00

182 Diana, Princess of Wales

1998. Diana, Princess of Wales Commemoration. Multicoloured.

1012	15 c. Type **182**	30	35
1013	$1 Wearing yellow blouse	80	85
1014	$1.90 Wearing tiara	1·25	1·40
1015	$2.25 Wearing blue short-sleeved Red Cross blouse	1·40	1·60

183 "Treasure Island" (Valarie Alix)

1998. International Arts Festival. Multicoloured.

1016	15 c. Type **183**	25	30
1017	30 c. "Posing in the Light" (Melsadis Fleming) (vert)	35	40
1018	$1 "Pescadores de Anguilla" (Juan Garcia) (vert)	70	80
1019	$1.50 "Fresh Catch" (Verna Hart)	1·00	1·25
1020	$1.90 "The Bell Tower of St. Mary's" (Ricky Racardo Edwards) (vert)	1·25	1·50

184 Roasting Corn-cobs on Fire

1998. Christmas. "Hidden Beauty of Anguilla". Children's Paintings. Multicoloured.

1021	15 c. Type **184**	10	10
1022	$1 Fresh fruit and market stallholder	45	50
1023	$1.50 Underwater scene	65	70
1024	$3 Cacti and view of sea	1·25	1·40

185 University of West Indies Centre, Anguilla

1998. 50th Anniv of University of West Indies. Multicoloured.

1025	$1.50 Type **185**	65	70
1026	$1.90 Man with torch and University arms	80	85

186 Sopwith Camel and Bristol F2B Fighters

1998. 80th Anniv of Royal Air Force. Multicoloured.

1027	30 c. Type **186**	15	20
1028	$1 Supermarine Spitfire Mk II and Hawker Hurricane Mk I	45	50
1029	$1.50 Avro Lancaster	65	70
1030	$1.90 Panavia Tornado F3 and Harrier GR7	80	85

ANTIGUA

One of the Leeward Islands, Br. W. Indies. Used general issues for Leeward Islands, concurrently with Antiguan stamps until 1 July 1956. Ministerial Government introduced on 1 January 1960. Achieved Associated Statehood on 3 March 1967 and Independence within the Commonwealth on 1 November 1981.

Nos 718/22 and 733 onwards are inscribed "Antigua and Barbuda".

1862. 12 pence = 1 shilling;
20 shillings = 1 pound.
1951. 100 cents = 1 West Indian dollar.

1

3

1862.

5	1	1d. mauve	£110	42·00
25		1d. red	1·40	2·50
29		6d. green	60·00	£120

1879.

21	3	½d. green	2·25	10·00
22		2½d. brown	£130	55·00
27		2½d. blue	6·00	11·00
23		4d. blue	£275	15·00
28		4d. brown	1·50	2·25
30		1s. mauve	£160	£120

4

5

8

1903.

31	4	½d. black and green	3·25	5·00
41		½d. green	2·25	3·75
32		1d. black and red	5·00	80
43		1d. red	4·50	1·75
45		2d. purple and brown	3·75	25·00
34		2½d. black and blue	8·00	14·00
46		2½d. blue	9·50	15·00
47		3d. green and brown	6·50	18·00
48		6d. purple and black	7·50	35·00
49		1s. blue and purple	15·00	65·00
50		2s. green and violet	65·00	80·00
39		2s. 6d. black and purple	17·00	48·00
40	5	5s. green and violet	70·00	90·00

1913. Head of King George V.

51	5	5s. green and violet	70·00	£110

1916. Optd **WAR STAMP**.

52	4	½d. green	65	1·50
54		1½d. orange	65	85

1921.

62	8	½d. green	1·25	20
63		1d. red	1·00	20
64		1d. violet	2·25	1·50
67		1½d. orange	2·00	7·00
68		1½d. red	3·50	1·75
69		1½d. brown	2·00	60
70		2d. grey	1·50	75
72		2½d. yellow	1·50	17·00
73		2½d. blue	3·25	5·50
74		3d. purple on yellow	4·00	8·50
56		4d. black and red on yellow	1·50	5·00
75		6d. purple	2·75	6·50
57		1s. black on green	3·75	7·50
58		2s. purple and blue on blue	11·00	19·00
78		2s. 6d. black and red on blue	18·00	24·00
79		3s. green and violet	24·00	75·00
80		4s. black and red	48·00	60·00
60		5s. green and red on yellow	8·00	42·00
61		£1 purple and black on red	£170	£275

9 Old Dockyard, English Harbour

12 Sir Thomas Warner and "Concepcion"

1932. Tercentenary. Designs with medallion portrait of King George V.

81	9	½d. green	1·75	5·50
82		1d. red	2·50	4·25
83		1½d. brown	3·00	4·25
84	–	2d. grey	3·75	15·00
85	–	2½d. blue	3·75	8·50
86	–	3d. orange	3·75	12·00
87	–	6d. violet	13·00	12·00
88	–	1s. olive	18·00	25·00
89	–	2s. 6d. purple	38·00	48·00
90	12	5s. black and brown	75·00	£110

DESIGNS—HORIZ: 2d. to 3d. Government House, St John's; 6d. to 2s. 6d. Nelson's "Victory".

13 Windsor Castle

1935. Silver Jubilee.

91	13	1d. blue and red	2·00	2·25
92		1½d. blue and grey	2·75	45
93		2½d. brown and blue	5·50	1·00
94		1s. grey and purple	8·50	12·00

1937. Coronation. As T 2 of Aden.

95		1d. red	50	80
96		1½d. brown	60	90
97		2½d. blue	1·25	1·60

15 English Harbour

16 Nelson's Dockyard

1938.

98	15	½d. green	30	90
99	16	1d. red	2·75	1·75
100a		1½d. brown	2·25	1·25
101	15	2d. grey	50	50
102	16	2½d. blue	70	80
103	–	3d. orange	60	80
104	–	6d. violet	1·40	80
105	–	1s. black and brown	3·00	95
106a	–	2s. 6d. purple	22·00	8·00
107	–	5s. olive	14·00	7·00
108	16	10s. mauve	16·00	25·00
109	–	£1 green	25·00	35·00

DESIGNS—HORIZ: 3d., 2s. 6d., £1, Fort James. VERT: 6d., 1s., 5s., St. John's Harbour.

1946. Victory. As T 9 of Aden.

110		1½d. brown	15	10
111		3d. orange	15	30

1949. Silver Wedding. As T **10/11** of Aden.

112		2½d. blue	40	1·00
113		5s. green	8·00	5·50

20 Hermes, Globe and Forms of Transport

21 Hemispheres, Jet-powered Vickers Viking Airliner and Steamer

22 Hermes and Globe

23 U.P.U. Monument

1949. 75th Anniv of U.P.U.

114	20	2½d. blue	40	50
115	21	3d. orange	1·50	1·75
116	22	6d. purple	45	1·25
117	23	1s. brown	45	75

24 Arms of University

25 Princess Alice

1951. Inauguration of B.W.I. University College.

118	24	3 c. black and brown	45	50
119	25	12 c. black and violet	45	80

1953. Coronation. As T **13** of Aden.

120		2 c. black and green	30	60

27 Martello Tower

1953. Designs as 1938 issues but with portrait of Queen Elizabeth II as in T **27**.

120a	–	½ c. brown	20	30
121	15	1 c. grey	30	70
122	16	2 c. green	30	10
123		3 c. black and yellow	40	20
153	15	4 c. red	30	20
154	16	5 c. black and lilac	20	10
155	–	6 c. yellow	60	30
156	27	8 c. blue	30	20
157	–	12 c. violet	40	20
129	–	24 c. black and brown	2·50	15
130	27	48 c. purple and blue	7·00	2·50
131	–	60 c. purple	7·50	80
132a	–	$1.20 olive	2·25	70
133	16	$2.40 purple	10·00	12·00
134	–	$4.80 slate	15·00	23·00

DESIGNS—HORIZ: ½, 6, 60 c., $4.80, Fort James. VERT: 12, 24 c., $1.20, St John's Harbour.

28 Federation Map

1958. Inaug of British Caribbean Federation.

135	28	3 c. green	1·00	30
136		6 c. blue	1·40	2·25
137		12 c. red	1·60	70

1960. New Constitution. Nos. 123 and 157 optd **COMMEMORATION ANTIGUA CONSTITUTION**.

138	16	3 c. black and yellow	15	15
139	–	12 c. violet	15	15

30 Nelson's Dockyard and Admiral Nelson

1961. Restoration of Nelson's Dockyard.

140	30	20 c. purple and brown	90	1·00
141		30 c. green and blue	1·10	1·25

31 Stamp of 1862 and R.M.S.P. "Solent I" at English Harbour

1962. Stamp Centenary.

142	31	3 c. purple and green	60	10
143		10 c. blue and green	70	10
144		12 c. sepia and green	80	10
145		50 c. brown and green	1·50	1·75

1963. Freedom from Hunger. As T **28** of Aden.

146		12 c. green	15	15

33 Red Cross Emblem

1963. Centenary of Red Cross.

147	33	3 c. red and black	40	50
148		12 c. red and blue	60	1·00

34 Shakespeare and Memorial Theatre, Stratford-upon-Avon

1964. 400th Birth Anniv of Shakespeare.

164	34	12 c. brown	20	10

1965. No. 157 surch **15c.**

165		15 c. on 12 c. violet	10	10

36 I.T.U. Emblem

1965. Centenary of I.T.U.

166	36	2 c. blue and red	20	15
167		50 c. yellow and blue	90	80

37 I.C.Y. Emblem

1965. International Co-operation Year.

168	37	4 c. purple and turquoise	15	10
169		15 c. green and lavender	25	20

38 Sir Winston Churchill, and St. Paul's Cathedral in Wartime

1966. Churchill Commemoration. Designs in black, red and gold with background in colours given.

170	38	½ c. blue	10	1·50
171		4 c. green	30	10
172		25 c. brown	75	45
173		35 c. violet	85	55

39 Queen Elizabeth II and Duke of Edinburgh

1966. Royal Visit.

174	39	6 c. black and blue	1·75	1·10
175		15 c. black and mauve	1·75	1·40

40 Footballer's Legs, Ball and Jules Rimet Cup

1966. World Cup Football Championships.

176	40	6 c. multicoloured	20	25
177		35 c. multicoloured	60	25

41 W.H.O. Building

1966. Inaug of W.H.O. Headquarters, Geneva.
178 **41** 2 c. black, green and blue . . 15 15
179 15 c. black, purple and brown 70 25

42 Nelson's Dockyard

1966.
180 **42** ½ c. green and blue 10 40
181 – 1 c. purple and mauve . . 10 30
182 – 2 c. blue and orange . . . 10 20
183a – 3 c. red and black 15 15
184a – 4 c. violet and brown . . 15 15
185 – 5 c. blue and green . . . 10 10
186 – 6 c. orange and purple . . 15 10
187 – 10 c. green and red . . . 15 10
188a – 15 c. brown and blue . . 55 10
189 – 25 c. blue and brown . . 35 20
190a – 35 c. mauve and brown . 60 1·00
191a – 50 c. green and black . . 70 2·25
192 – 75 c. blue and ultramarine 1·50 2·50
193b – $1 mauve and green . . . 1·25 4·50
194 – $2.50 black and mauve . . 3·50 5·50
195 – $5 green and violet . . . 5·50 6·50
DESIGNS: 1 c. Old Post Office, St John's; 2 c. Health Centre; 3 c. Teachers' Training College; 4 c. Martello Tower, Barbuda; 5 c. Ruins of Officers' Quarters, Shirley Heights; 6 c. Government House, Barbuda; 10 c. Princess Margaret School. 15 c. Air terminal building; 25 c. General Post Office; 35 c. Clarence House; 50 c. Government House, St John's; 75 c. Administration building; $1 Courthouse, St. John's; $2.50, Magistrates' Court; $5 St. John's Cathedral.

54 "Education"

55 "Science"

56 "Culture"

1966. 20th Anniv of U.N.E.S.C.O.
196 **54** 4 c. violet, yellow and orange 15 10
197 **55** 25 c. yellow, violet and olive 35 10
198 **56** $1 black, purple and orange 1·10 2·25

57 State Flag and Maps

1967. Statehood. Multicoloured.
199 4 c. Type **57** 10 10
200 15 c. State Flag 10 20
201 25 c. Premier's Office and State Flag 10 25
202 35 c. As 15 c. 15 25

60 Gilbert Memorial Church

1967. Attainment of Autonomy by the Methodist Church.
203 **60** 4 c. black and red 10 10
204 – 25 c. black and green . . . 15 15
205 – 35 c. black and blue . . . 15 15
DESIGNS: 25 c. Nathaniel Gilbert's House; 35 c. Caribbean and Central American map.

63 Coat of Arms 66 Tracking Station

64 "Susan Constant" (settlers' ship)

1967. 300th Anniv of Treaty of Breda and Grant of New Arms.
206 **63** 15 c. multicoloured . . . 15 10
207 35 c. multicoloured . . . 15 10

1967. 300th Anniv of Barbuda Settlement.
208 **64** 4 c. blue 30 10
209 – 6 c. purple 30 90
210 **64** 25 c. green 40 20
211 – 35 c. black 40 25
DESIGN: 6, 35 c. Blaeu's Map of 1665.

1968. N.A.S.A. Apollo Project. Inauguration of Dow Hill Tracking Station.
212 **66** 4 c. blue, yellow and black 10 10
213 – 15 c. blue, yellow and black 20 10
214 – 25 c. blue, yellow and black 20 10
215 – 50 c. blue, yellow and black 30 30
DESIGNS: 15 c. Antenna and spacecraft taking off; 25 c. Spacecraft approaching Moon; 50 c. Re-entry of space capsule.

70 Limbo-dancing

1968. Tourism. Multicoloured.
216 ½ c. Type **70** 10 10
217 15 c. Water-skier and bathers 30 10
218 25 c. Yachts and beach . . . 40 10
219 35 c. Underwater swimming . 40 10
220 50 c. Type **70** 60 85

74 Old Harbour in 1768

1968. Opening of St. John's Deep Water Harbour.
221 **74** 2 c. blue and red 10 30
222 – 15 c. green and sepia . . . 35 10
223 – 25 c. yellow and blue . . . 40 10
224 – 35 c. salmon and emerald . 50 10
225 **74** $1 black . . . . 90 1·75
DESIGNS: 15 c. Old harbour in 1829; 25 c. Freighter and chart of new harbour; 35 c. New harbour.

78 Parliament Buildings

1969. Tercentenary of Parliament. Multicoloured.
226 4 c. Type **78** 10 10
227 15 c. Antigua Mace and bearer 20 10
228 25 c. House of Representative's Room 20 10
229 50 c. Coat of arms and Seal of Antigua . . . . 30 1·10

82 Freight Transport

1969. 1st Anniv of Caribbean Free Trade Area.
230 **82** 4 c. black and purple . . . 10 10
231 15 c. black and blue 20 30
232 – 25 c. brown, black and ochre 25 30
233 – 35 c. chocolate, black & brn 25 30
DESIGN—VERT: 25, 35 c. Crate of cargo.

84 Island of Redonda (Chart)

1969. Centenary of Redonda Phosphate Industry. Multicoloured.
249 15 c. Type **84** 20 10
250 25 c. View of Redonda from the sea 20 10
251 50 c. Type **84** 45 75

86 "The Adoration of the Magi" (Marcillat)

1969. Christmas. Stained Glass Windows. Mult.
252 6 c. Type **86** 10 10
253 10 c. "The Nativity" (unknown German artist, 15th century) 10 10
254 35 c. Type **86** 25 10
255 50 c. As 10 c. 50 40

1970. Surch **20c** and bars.
256 20 c. on 25c. (No. 189) 10 10

89 Coat of Arms 90 Sikorsky S-38 Flying Boat

1970. Coil Stamps.
257 **89** 5 c. blue 10 10
258 10 c. green 10 15
259 25 c. red 20 25

1970. 40th Anniv of Antiguan Air Services. Multicoloured.
260 5 c. Type **90** 50 10
261 20 c. Dornier Do-X flying boat 1·25 10
262 35 c. Hawker Siddeley H.S.748 1·50 10
263 50 c. Douglas C-124C Globemaster II . . . . . . 1·60 1·50
264 75 c. Vickers Super VC-10 . . 1·75 2·00

91 Dickens and Scene from "Nicholas Nickleby"

1970. Death Centenary of Charles Dickens.
265 **91** 5 c. bistre, sepia and black . 10 10
266 – 20 c. turquoise, sepia & blk 20 10
267 – 35 c. blue, sepia and black 30 10
268 – $1 red, sepia and black . . 75 60
DESIGNS: All stamps show Dickens and scene from: 20 c. "Pickwick Papers"; 35 c. "Oliver Twist"; $1 "David Copperfield".

92 Carib Indian and War Canoe

1970. Multicoloured.
323 ½ c. Type **92** 20 40
270 1 c. Columbus and "Nina" . 30 70
271 2 c. Sir Thomas Warner's emblem and "Concepcion" . 40 1·25
325 3 c. Viscount Hood and H.M.S. "Barfleur" 35 70
273 4 c. Sir George Rodney and H.M.S. "Formidable" . . . 40 1·25
327 5 c. Nelson and H.M.S. "Boreas" 50 40
275 6 c. William IV and H.M.S. "Pegasus" . . . . 50 1·50
276 10 c. "Blackbeard" and pirate ketch 65 20
277 15 c. Collingwood and H.M.S. "Pelican" . . . . 3·50 1·00
278 20 c. Nelson and H.M.S. "Victory" . . . . 1·25 40
279 25 c. "Solent I" (paddle-steamer) 1·25 40
280 35 c. George V (when Prince George) and H.M.S. "Canada" (screw corvette) . 1·75 80
281 50 c. H.M.S. "Renown" (battle cruiser) . . . . 5·00 3·25
331 75 c. "Federal Maple" (freighter) 7·50 3·00
332 $1 "Sol Quest" (yacht) and class emblem . . . . 3·00 1·75
333 $2.50 H.M.S. "London" (destroyer) . . . . 2·75 6·50
285 $5 "Pathfinder" (tug) . . . . 7·00 7·50

93 "The Small Passion" (detail) (Durer) 94 4th King's Own Regiment, 1759

1970. Christmas.
286 **93** 3 c. black and blue 10 10
287 – 10 c. purple and pink . . . 10 10
288 **93** 35 c. black and red 30 10
289 – 50 c. black and lilac 45 50
DESIGN: 10, 50 c. "Adoration of the Magi" (detail) (Durer).

1970. Military Uniforms (1st series). Mult.
290 ½ c. Type **94** 10 10
291 10 c. 4th West India Regiment, 1804 . . . . 50 10
292 20 c. 60th Regiment, The Royal American, 1809 . . . . . . 1·00 10
293 35 c. 93rd Regiment, Sutherland Highlanders, 1826–34 . . . 1·40 15
294 75 c. 3rd West India Regiment, 1851 . . . . 2·25 2·50
See also Nos. 303/7, 313/17, 353/7 and 380/4.

95 Market Woman casting Vote 96 "The Last Supper"

1971. 20th Anniv of Adult Suffrage.
296 **95** 5 c. brown 10 10
297 – 20 c. olive 10 10
298 – 35 c. purple 10 10
299 – 50 c. blue 15 30
DESIGNS: People voting: 20 c. Executive; 35 c. Housewife; 50 c. Artisan.

1971. Easter. Works by Durer.
300 **96** 5 c. black grey and red . . 10 10
301 – 35 c. black, grey and violet 10 10
302 – 75 c. black, grey and gold . 20 30
DESIGNS: 35 c. "The Crucifixion"; 75 c. "The Resurrection".

1971. Military Uniforms (2nd series). As T **94**. Multicoloured.
303 ½ c. Private, 12th Regiment, The Suffolk (1704) 10 10
304 10 c. Grenadier, 38th Regiment, South Staffordshire (1751) . . 35 15
305 20 c. Light Company, 5th Regiment, Royal Northumberland Fusiliers (1778) 65 20
306 35 c. Private, 48th Regiment, The Northamptonshire (1793) . 1·10 25
307 75 c. Private, 15th Regiment, East Yorks (1805) . . . . . 2·25 4·00

97 "Madonna and Child" (detail, Veronese)

1971. Christmas. Multicoloured.

309	3 c. Type **97**	10	10
310	5 c. "Adoration of the Shepherds" (detail, Veronese)	10	10
311	35 c. Type **97**	25	10
312	50 c. As 5 c.	40	30

1972. Military Uniforms (3rd series). As T **94**. Multicoloured.

313	½ c. Battalion Company Officer, 25th Foot, 1815	10	10
314	10 c. Sergeant, 14th Foot, 1837	85	10
315	20 c. Private, 67th Foot, 1853	1·60	15
316	35 c. Officer, Royal Artillery 1854	1·90	20
317	75 c. Private, 29th Foot, 1870	2·25	3·75

98 Reticulated Cowrie Helmet

1972. Shells. Multicoloured.

319	3 c. Type **98**	50	10
320	5 c. Measled cowrie	50	10
321	35 c. West Indian fighting conch	1·40	15
322	50 c. Hawk-wing conch	1·60	2·75

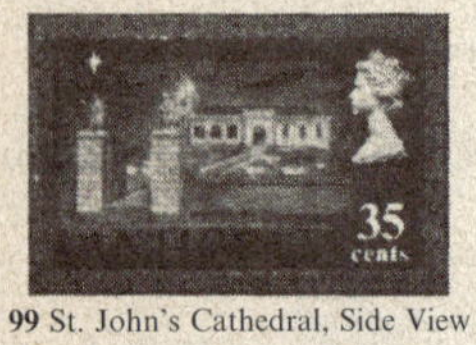

99 St. John's Cathedral, Side View

1972. Christmas and 125th Anniv of St. John's Cathedral. Multicoloured.

335	35 c. Type **99**	20	10
336	50 c. Cathedral interior	25	25
337	75 c. St. John's Cathedral	30	60

1972. Royal Silver Wedding. As T **52** of Ascension, but with floral background.

339	20 c. blue	15	15
340	35 c. blue	15	15

101 Batsman and Map

1972. 50th Anniv of Rising Sun Cricket Club. Multicoloured.

341	5 c. Type **101**	55	15
342	35 c. Batsman and wicket-keeper	1·25	40
343	$1 Club badge	2·25	3·00

102 Yacht and Map 103 "Episcopal Coat of Arms"

1972. Inauguration of Antigua and Barbuda Tourist Office in New York. Multicoloured.

345	35 c. Type **102**	15	10
346	50 c. Yachts	20	15
347	75 c. St. John's G.P.O.	25	25
348	$1 Statue of Liberty	25	25

1973. Easter. Multicoloured.

350	**103**	5 c. Type **103**	10	10
351	–	35 c. "The Crucifixion"	15	10
352	–	75 c. "Arms of 1st Bishop of Antigua"	25	30

Nos. 350/2 show different stained-glass windows from St. John's Cathedral.

1973. Military Uniforms (4th series). As T **94**. Multicoloured.

353	½ c. Private, Zachariah Tiffin's Regiment, of Foot, 1701	10	10
354	10 c. Private, 63rd Regiment of Foot, 1759	40	10
355	20 c. Light Company Officer, 35th Regiment of Foot, 1828	60	15
356	35 c. Private, 2nd West India Regiment, 1853	85	15
357	75 c. Sergeant, 49th Regiment, 1858	1·50	1·25

104 Butterfly Costumes

1973. Carnival. Multicoloured.

359	5 c. Type **104**	10	10
360	20 c. Carnival street scene	15	10
361	35 c. Carnival troupe	20	10
362	75 c. Carnival Queen	30	30

105 "Virgin of the Milk Porridge" (Gerard David)

1973. Christmas. Multicoloured.

364	3 c. Type **105**	10	10
365	5 c. "Adoration of the Magi" (Stomer)	10	10
366	20 c. "The Granducal Madonna" (Raphael)	15	10
367	35 c. "Nativity with God the Father and Holy Ghost" (Battista)	20	10
368	$1 "Madonna and Child" (Murillo)	40	60

106 Princess Anne and Captain Mark Phillips

1973. Royal Wedding.

370	**106**	35 c. multicoloured	10	10
371	–	$2 multicoloured	25	25

The $2 is as Type **106** but has a different border.

1973. Nos. 370/1 optd **HONEYMOON VISIT DECEMBER 16TH 1973**.

373	**106**	35 c. multicoloured	15	10
374	–	$2 multicoloured	30	30

108 Coat of Arms of Antigua and University

1974. 25th Anniv of University of West Indies. Multicoloured.

376	5 c. Type **108**	10	10
377	20 c. Extra-mural art	15	10
378	35 c. Antigua campus	20	10
379	75 c. Antigua chancellor	25	35

1974. Military Uniforms (5th series). As T **94**. Multicoloured.

380	½ c. Officer, 59th Foot, 1797	10	10
381	10 c. Gunner, Royal Artillery, 1800	45	10
382	20 c. Private, 1st West India Regiment, 1830	70	10
383	35 c. Officer, 92nd Foot, 1843	85	10
384	75 c. Private, 23rd Foot, 1846	1·25	2·00

109 English Postman, Mailcoach and Westland Dragonfly Helicopter

1974. Centenary of U.P.U. Multicoloured.

386	½ c. Type **109**	10	10
387	1 c. Bellman, mail steamer "Orinoco" and satellite	10	10
388	2 c. Train guard, post-bus and hydrofoil	10	10
389	5 c. Swiss messenger, Wells Fargo coach and Concorde	60	30
390	20 c. Postilion, Japanese postmen and carrier pigeon	35	10
391	35 c. Antiguan postman, Sikorsky S-88 flying boat and tracking station	45	15
392	$1 Medieval courier, American express train and Boeing 747-100	1·75	1·60

On the ½ c. English is spelt "Enlish" and on the 2 c. Postal is spelt "Fostal".

110 Traditional Player 111 Footballers

1974. Antiguan Steel Bands.

394	**110**	5 c. dp red, red and black	10	10
395	–	20 c. brown, lt brn & blk	10	10
396	–	35 c. lt green, grn & blk	10	10
397	–	75 c. blue, dp bl & blk	20	50

DESIGNS—HORIZ: 20 c. Traditional band; 35 c. Modern band. VERT: 75 c. Modern player.

1974. World Cup Football Championships.

399	**111**	5 c. multicoloured	10	10
400	–	35 c. multicoloured	15	10
401	–	75 c. multicoloured	30	30
402	–	$1 multicoloured	35	40

Nos. 400/2 show various footballing designs similar to Type **111**.

1974. Earthquake Relief Fund. Nos. 400/2 and 397 optd or surch **EARTHQUAKE RELIEF**.

404	35 c. multicoloured	20	10
405	75 c. multicoloured	30	25
406	$1 multicoloured	40	30
407	$5 on 75 c. deep blue, blue and black	1·25	2·00

113 Churchill as Schoolboy and School College Building, Harrow 114 "Madonna of the Trees" (Bellini)

1974. Birth Centenary of Sir Winston Churchill. Multicoloured.

408	5 c. Type **113**	15	10
409	35 c. Churchill and St. Paul's Cathedral	20	10
410	75 c. Coat of arms and catafalque	25	55
411	$1 Churchill, "reward" notice and South African escape route	40	90

1974. Christmas. "Madonna and Child" paintings by named artists. Multicoloured.

413	½ c. Type **114**	10	10
414	1 c. Raphael	10	10
415	2 c. Van der Weyden	10	10
416	3 c. Giorgione	10	10
417	5 c. Mantegna	10	10
418	20 c. Vivarini	20	10
419	35 c. Montagna	30	10
420	75 c. Lorenzo Costa	55	85

1975. Nos. 390/2 and 331 surch.

422	50 c. on 20 c. multicoloured	1·25	1·75
423	$2.50 on 35 c. multicoloured	3·00	5·00
424	$5 on $1 multicoloured	5·00	7·00
425	$10 on 75 c. multicoloured	4·00	7·50

MINIMUM PRICE

The minimum price quoted is 10p which represents a handling charge rather than a basis for valuing common stamps. For further notes about prices see introductory pages.

116 Carib War Canoe, English Harbour, 1300

1975. Nelson's Dockyard. Multicoloured.

427	5 c. Type **116**	20	10
428	15 c. Ship of the line, English Harbour, 1770	80	10
429	35 c. H.M.S "Boreas" at anchor, and Lord Nelson, 1787	1·25	15
430	50 c. Yachts during "Sailing Week", 1974	1·25	1·25
431	$1 Yacht Anchorage, Old Dockyard, 1970	1·50	2·00

117 Lady of the Valley Church

1975. Antiguan Churches. Multicoloured.

433	5 c. Type **117**	10	10
434	20 c. Gilbert Memorial	10	10
435	35 c. Grace Hill Moravian	15	10
436	50 c. St. Phillips	20	20
437	$1 Ebenezer Methodist	35	50

118 Map of 1721 and Sextant of 1640

1975. Maps of Antigua. Multicoloured.

439	5 c. Type **118**	30	15
440	20 c. Map of 1775 and galleon	55	15
441	35 c. Maps of 1775 and 1955	70	15
442	$1 1973 maps of Antigua and English Harbour	1·40	2·00

119 Scout Bugler

1975. World Scout Jamboree, Norway. Mult.

444	15 c. Type **119**	25	15
445	20 c. Scouts in camp	30	15
446	35 c. "Lord Baden-Powell" (D. Jagger)	50	20
447	$2 Scout dancers from Dahomey	1·50	2·00

120 "Eurema elathea"

1975. Butterflies. Multicoloured.

449	½ c. Type **120**	10	10
450	1 c. "Danaus plexippus"	10	10
451	2 c. "Phoebis philea"	10	10
452	5 c. "Hypolimnas misippus"	20	10
453	20 c. "Eurema proterpia"	75	60
454	35 c. "Battus polydamas"	1·40	90
455	$2 "Cynthia cardui"	4·00	7·50

No. 452 is incorrectly captioned "Marpesia petreus thetys".

121 "Madonna and Child" (Correggio) 122 Vivian Richards

1975. Christmas. "Madonna and Child" paintings by artists named. Multicoloured.

457	½ c. Type **121**	10	10
458	1 c. El Greco	10	10
459	2 c. Durer	10	10
460	3 c. Antonello	10	10
461	5 c. Bellini	10	10
462	10 c. Durer (different)	10	10
463	35 c. Bellini (different)	40	10
464	$2 Durer (different again)	1·00	1·00

1975. World Cricket Cup Winners. Multicoloured.

466	5 c. Type **122**	1·25	20
467	35 c. Andy Roberts	2·25	60
468	$2 West Indies team (horiz)	4·25	8·00

123 Antillean Crested Hummingbird

1976. Multicoloured.

469A	½ c. Type **123**	20	50
470A	1 c. Imperial amazon	30	50
471A	2 c. Zenaida dove	30	50
472A	3 c. Loggerhead kingbird	30	60
473A	4 c. Red-necked pigeon	30	60
474A	5 c. Rufous-throated solitaire	1·40	10
475A	6 c. Orchid tree	30	60
476A	10 c. Bougainvillea	30	10
477A	15 c. Geiger tree	35	10
478A	20 c. Flamboyant	35	35
479A	25 c. Hibiscus	40	15
480A	35 c. Flame of the wood	40	40
481A	50 c. Cannon at Fort James	55	60
482A	75 c. Premier's Office	60	75
483A	$1 Potworks Dam	75	90
484A	$2.50 Diamond irrigation scheme	1·50	3·50
485B	$5 Government House	3·00	5·50
486A	$10 Coolidge International Airport	3·50	6·50

Nos. 484/6 are larger, 44 × 28 mm.

124 Privates, Clark's Illinois Regiment

1976. Bicentenary of American Revolution. Mult.

487	½ c. Type **124**	10	10
488	1 c. Rifleman, Pennsylvania Militia	10	10
489	2 c. Powder horn	10	10
490	5 c. Water bottle	10	10
491	35 c. American flags	50	10
492	$1 "Montgomery" (American brig)	1·25	40
493	$5 "Ranger" (privateer sloop)	2·50	2·75

125 High Jump

1976. Olympic Games, Montreal.

495	**125** ½ c. brown, yellow and black	10	10
496	– 1 c. violet, blue and black	10	10
497	– 2 c. green and black	10	10
498	– 15 c. blue and black	15	10
499	– 30 c. brown, yell & blk	20	15
500	– $1 orange, red and black	40	40
501	– $2 red and black	60	80

DESIGNS: 1 c. Boxing; 2 c. Pole vault; 15 c. Swimming; 30 c. Running; $1 Cycling; $2 Shot put.

126 Water Skiing

1976. Water Sports. Multicoloured.

503	½ c. Type **126**	10	10
504	1 c. Sailing	10	10
505	2 c. Snorkeling	10	10
506	20 c. Deep sea fishing	15	10
507	50 c. Scuba diving	35	35
508	$2 Swimming	1·00	1·25

127 French Angelfish

1976. Fish. Multicoloured.

510	15 c. Type **127**	50	15
511	30 c. Yellow-finned grouper	75	30
512	50 c. Yellow-tailed snapper	95	50
513	90 c. Shy hamlet	1·25	80

128 The Annunciation

130 Royal Family

129 Mercury and U.P.U. Emblem

1976. Christmas. Multicoloured.

514	8 c. Type **128**	10	10
515	10 c. The Holy Family	10	10
516	15 c. The Magi	10	10
517	50 c. The Shepherds	20	25
518	$1 Epiphany scene	30	50

1976. Special Events, 1976. Multicoloured.

519	½ c. Type **129**	10	10
520	1 c. Alfred Nobel	10	10
521	10 c. Space satellite	30	10
522	50 c. Viv Richards and Andy Roberts	3·50	1·75
523	$1 Bell and telephones	1·00	2·00
524	$2 Yacht "Freelance"	2·25	4·00

1977. Silver Jubilee. Multicoloured. (a) Perf.

526	10 c. Type **130**	10	10
527	30 c. Royal Visit, 1966	10	10
528	50 c. The Queen enthroned	15	15
529	90 c. The Queen after Coronation	15	25
530	$2.50 Queen and Prince Charles	30	55

(b) Roul × imperf. Self-adhesive.

532	50 c. As 90 c.	35	60
533	$5 The Queen and Prince Philip	2·00	3·50

Nos. 532/3 come from booklets.

131 Making Camp

1977. Caribbean Scout Jamboree, Jamaica. Mult.

534	½ c. Type **131**	10	10
535	1 c. Hiking	10	10
536	2 c. Rock-climbing	10	10
537	10 c. Cutting logs	15	10
538	30 c. Map and sign reading	40	10
539	50 c. First aid	65	25
540	$2 Rafting	1·75	2·25

132 Carnival Costume

134 "Virgin and Child Enthroned" (Tura)

1977. 21st Anniv of Carnival. Multicoloured.

542	10 c. Type **132**	10	10
543	30 c. Carnival Queen	20	10
544	50 c. Butterfly costume	25	15
545	90 c. Queen of the band	35	25
546	$1 Calypso King and Queen	35	30

1977. Royal Visit. Nos. 526/30 optd **ROYAL VISIT 28TH OCTOBER 1977**.

548	10 c. Type **130**	10	10
549	30 c. Royal Visit, 1966	10	10
550	50 c. The Queen enthroned	15	10
551	90 c. The Queen after Coronation	25	20
552	$2.50 Queen and Prince Charles	45	35

1977. Christmas. Paintings by artists listed. Mult.

554	½ c. Type **134**	10	10
555	1 c. Crivelli	10	10
556	2 c. Lotto	10	10
557	8 c. Pontormo	15	10
558	10 c. Tura (different)	15	10
559	25 c. Lotto (different)	30	10
560	$2 Crivelli (different)	85	60

135 Pineapple

1977. 10th Anniv of Statehood. Multicoloured.

562	10 c. Type **135**	10	10
563	15 c. State flag	10	10
564	50 c. Police band	2·00	80
565	90 c. Premier V. C. Bird	55	80
566	$2 State Coat of Arms	90	1·40

136 Wright Glider III, 1902

1978. 75th Anniv of Powered Flight. Mult.

568	½ c. Type **136**	10	10
569	1 c. Wright Flyer I, 1903	10	10
570	2 c. Launch system and engine	10	10
571	10 c. Orville Wright (vert)	20	10
572	50 c. Wright Flyer III, 1905	50	15
573	90 c. Wilbur Wright (vert)	75	30
574	$2 Wright Type B, 1910	1·00	80

137 Sunfish Regatta

138 Queen Elizabeth and Prince Philip

1978. Sailing Week. Multicoloured.

576	10 c. Type **137**	20	10
577	50 c. Fishing and work boat race	35	20
578	90 c. Curtain Bluff race	60	35
579	$2 Power boat rally	1·10	1·25

1978. 25th Anniv. of Coronation. Mult. (a) Perf.

581	10 c. Type **138**	10	10
582	30 c. Crowning	10	10
583	50 c. Coronation procession	15	10
584	90 c. Queen seated in St. Edward's Chair	20	15
585	$2.50 Queen wearing Imperial State Crown	40	40

(b) Roul × imperf. Self-adhesive. Horiz designs as Type **138**

587	25 c. Glass Coach	15	30
588	50 c. Irish State Coach	25	50
589	$5 Coronation Coach	1·75	3·00

Nos. 587/9 come from booklets.

140 Player running with Ball

141 Petrea

1978. World Cup Football Championship, Argentina. Multicoloured.

590	10 c. Type **140**	15	10
591	15 c. Players in front of goal	15	10
592	$3 Referee and player	2·00	1·75

1978. Flowers. Multicoloured.

594	25 c. Type **141**	25	10
595	50 c. Sunflower	35	20
596	90 c. Frangipani	60	30
597	$2 Passion flower	1·25	1·10

142 "St. Ildefonso receiving the Chasuble from the Virgin" (Rubens)

1978. Christmas. Multicoloured.

599	8 c. Type **142**	10	10
600	25 c. "The Flight of St. Barbara" (Rubens)	20	10
601	$2 "Madonna and child, with St. Joseph, John the Baptist and Donor"	65	55

The painting shown on No. 601 is incorrectly attributed to Rubens on the stamp. The artist was Sebastiano del Piombo.

143 1d. Stamp of 1863

144 "The Deposition from the Cross" (painting)

1979. Death Centenary of Sir Rowland Hill. Multicoloured.

603	25 c. Type **143**	10	10
604	50 c. 1840 Penny Black	20	15
605	$1 Mail coach and woman posting letter, c. 1840	30	20
606	$2 Modern transport	1·10	60

1979. Easter. Works by Durer.

608	**144** 10 c. multicoloured	10	10
609	– 50 c. multicoloured	35	20
610	– $4 black, mauve and yellow	1·25	90

DESIGNS: 50 c. "Christ on the Cross–The Passion" (wood engraving); $4 "Man of Sorrows with Hands Raised" (wood engraving).

145 Toy Yacht and Child's Hand

147 Cook's Birthplace, Marton

146 Yellow Jack

1979. International Year of the Child. Mult.

612	25 c. Type **145**	10	10
613	50 c. Rocket	25	15
614	90 c. Car	40	25
615	$2 Toy train	1·00	90

Nos. 612/15 also show the hands of children of different races.

1979. Fish. Multicoloured.

617	30 c. Type **146**	40	15
618	50 c. Blue-finned tuna	50	25
619	90 c. Sailfish	75	40
620	$3 Wahoo	2·25	1·75

1979. Death Bicentenary of Captain Cook. Multicoloured.

622	25 c. Type **147**	55	25
623	50 c. H.M.S. "Endeavour"	75	60
624	90 c. Marine chronometer	75	80
625	$3 Landing at Botany Bay	1·60	2·75

148 The Holy Family

149 Javelin Throwing

1979. Christmas. Multicoloured.
627 8 c. Type **148** 10 10
628 25 c. Virgin and Child on ass 15 10
629 50 c. Shepherd and star 30 35
630 $4 Wise Men with gifts 1·10 2·25

1980. Olympic Games, Moscow. Multicoloured.
632 10 c. Type **149** 20 10
633 25 c. Running 25 10
634 $1 Pole vault 60 50
635 $2 Hurdles 90 1·50

150 Mickey Mouse and Aeroplane

1980. International Year of the Child. Walt Disney Cartoon Characters. Multicoloured.
637 ½ c. Type **150** 10 10
638 1 c. Donald Duck driving car (vert) 10 10
639 2 c. Goofy driving taxi 10 10
640 3 c. Mickey and Minnie Mouse on motorcycle 10 10
641 4 c. Huey, Dewey and Louie on a bicycle for three 10 10
642 5 c. Grandma Duck and truck of roosters 10 10
643 10 c. Mickey Mouse in jeep (vert) 10 10
644 $1 Chip and Dale in yacht 1·75 2·00
645 $4 Donald Duck riding toy train (vert) 3·75 6·00

1980. "London 1980" International Stamp Exhibition. Nos. 603/6 optd **LONDON 1980**.
647 25 c. Type **143** 20 15
648 50 c. Penny Black 30 35
649 $1 Stage-coach and woman posting letter, c. 1840 55 60
650 $2 Modern mail transport 2·50 2·75

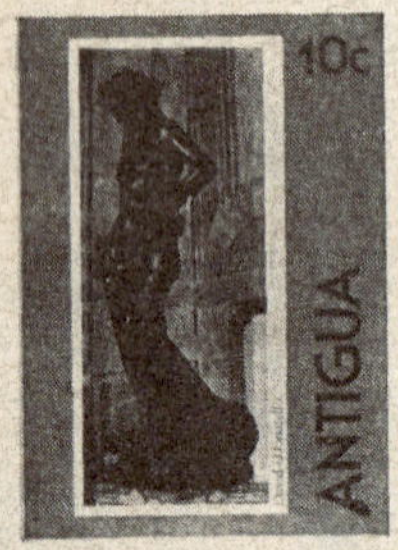

152 "David" (statue, Donatello)

1980. Famous Works of Art. Multicoloured.
651 10 c. Type **152** 10 10
652 30 c. "The Birth of Venus" (painting, Botticelli) (horiz) 30 15
653 50 c. "Reclining Couple" (sarcophagus), Cerveteri (horiz) 45 40
654 90 c. "The Garden of Earthly Delights" (painting by Bosch) (horiz) 65 65
655 $1 "Portinari Altarpiece" (painting, van der Goes) (horiz) 75 75
656 $4 "Eleanora of Toledo and her Son, Giovanni de'Medici" (painting, Bronzino) 2·25 3·00

153 Anniversary Emblem and Headquarters, U.S.A.

1980. 75th Anniv of Rotary International. Mult.
658 30 c. Type **153** 30 30
659 50 c. Rotary anniversary emblem and Antigua Rotary Club banner 40 50
660 90 c. Map of Antigua and Rotary emblem 60 70
661 $3 Paul P. Harris (founder) and Rotary emblem 2·00 3·25

154 Queen Elizabeth the Queen Mother

155 Ringed Kingfisher

1980. 80th Birthday of The Queen Mother.
663 **154** 10 c. multicoloured 20 10
664 $2.50 multicoloured 1·10 1·75

1980. Birds. Multicoloured.
666 10 c. Type **155** 60 25
667 30 c. Plain pigeon 90 50
668 $1 Green-throated carib 1·50 1·50
669 $2 Black-necked stilt 2·00 3·25

1980. Christmas. Walt Disney's "Sleeping Beauty". As T **150**. Multicoloured.
671 ½ c. The Bad Fairy with her raven 10 10
672 1 c. The good fairies 10 10
673 2 c. Aurora 10 10
674 4 c. Aurora pricks her finger 10 10
675 8 c. The prince 10 10
676 10 c. The prince fights the dragon 15 10
677 25 c. The prince awakens Aurora with a kiss 20 20
678 $2 The prince and Aurora's betrothal 2·25 2·25
679 $2.50 The prince and princess 2·50 2·50

156 Diesel Locomotive No. 15

158 "Pipes of Pan"

1981. Suger Cane Railway Locomotives. Mult.
681 25 c. Type **156** 15 15
682 50 c. Narrow-gauge steam locomotive 30 30
683 90 c. Diesel locomotives Nos. 1 and 10 55 60
684 $3 Steam locomotive hauling suger cane 2·00 2·25

1981. Independence. Nos. 475/6 and 478/86 optd **"INDEPENDENCE 1981"**.
686B 6 c. Orchid tree 10 10
687B 10 c. Bougainvillea 10 10
688B 20 c. Flamboyant 10 10
689B 25 c. Hibiscus 15 15
690B 35 c. Flame of the wood 20 20
691B 50 c. Cannon at Fort James 35 35
692B 75 c. Premier's Office 40 40
693B $1 Potworks Dam 55 55
694B $2.50 Irrigation scheme, Diamond Estate 1·25 1·25
695B $5 Government House 2·50 2·50
696B $10 Coolidge International Airport 3·50 5·00

1981. Birth Centenary of Picasso. Multicoloured.
697 10 c. Type **158** 10 10
698 50 c. "Seated Harlequin" 30 30
699 90 c. "Paulo as Harlequin" 55 55
700 $4 "Mother and Child" 2·50 2·50

159 Prince Charles and Lady Diana Spencer

160 Prince of Wales at Investiture, 1969

1981. Royal Wedding (1st issue). Multicoloured.
702 25 c. Type **159** 10 10
703 50 c. Glamis Castle 10 10
704 $4 Prince Charles skiing 80 80

1981. Royal Wedding (2nd issue). Multicoloured. Roul × imperf. Self-adhesive.
706 25 c. Type **160** 15 25
707 25 c. Prince Charles as baby, 1948 15 25
708 $1 Prince Charles at R.A.F. College, Cranwell, 1971 25 50
709 $1 Prince Charles attending Hill House School, 1956 25 50
710 $2 Prince Charles and Lady Diana Spencer 50 75
711 $2 Prince Charles at Trinity College, 1967 50 75
712 $5 Prince Charles and Lady Diana (different) 1·00 1·50

161 Irene Joshua (founder)

1981. 50th Anniv of Antigua Girl Guide Movement. Multicoloured.
713 10 c. Type **161** 15 10
714 50 c. Campfire sing-song 45 35
715 90 c. Sailing 75 65
716 $2.50 Animal tending 1·75 2·00

162 Antigua and Barbuda Coat of Arms

163 "Holy Night" (Jacques Stella)

1981. Independence. Multicoloured.
718 10 c. Type **162** 20 10
719 50 c. Pineapple, with Antigua and Barbuda flag and map 45 20
720 90 c. Prime Minister Vere Bird 55 55
721 $2.50 St. John's Cathedral (38 × 25 mm) 1·50 2·50

1981. Christmas. Paintings. Multicoloured.
723 8 c. Type **163** 15 10
724 30 c. "Mary with Child" (Julius Schnorr von Carolfeld) 40 15
725 $1 "Virgin and Child" (Alonso Cano) 80 90
726 $3 "Virgin and Child" (Lorenzo di Credi) 1·40 3·75

164 Swimming

1981. International Year of Disabled People. Sports for the Disabled. Multicoloured.
728 10 c. Type **164** 10 10
729 50 c. Discus-throwing 20 30
730 90 c. Archery 40 55
731 $2 Baseball 1·25 1·40

165 Scene from Football Match

1982. World Cup Football Championship, Spain.
733 **165** 10 c. multicoloured 20 10
734 – 50 c. multicoloured 50 35
735 – 90 c. multicoloured 80 70
736 – $4 multicoloured 3·50 3·50
DESIGNS: 50 c. to $4 Scenes from various matches.

166 Airbus Industrie A300

167 Cordia

1982. Coolidge International Airport. Mult.
738 10 c. Type **166** 10 10
739 50 c. Hawker-Siddeley H.S.748 30 30
740 90 c. De Havilland D.H.C.6 Twin Otter 60 60
741 $2.50 Britten Norman Islander 1·75 1·75

1982. Death Centenary of Charles Darwin. Fauna and Flora. Multicoloured.
743 10 c. Type **167** 15 10
744 50 c. Small Indian mongoose (horiz) 45 40
745 90 c. Corallita 75 75
746 $2 Mexican bulldog bat (horiz) 2·00 3·25

168 Queen's House, Greenwich

1982. 21st Birthday of Princess of Wales. Mult.
748 90 c. Type **168** 45 45
749 $1 Prince and Princess of Wales 50 50
750 $4 Princess Diana 2·00 2·00

170 Boy Scouts decorating Streets for Independence Parade

1982. 75th Anniv of Boy Scout Movement. Multicoloured.
752 10 c. Type **170** 20 10
753 50 c. Boy Scout giving helping hand during street parade 50 40
754 90 c. Boy Scouts attending H.R.H. Princess Margaret at Independence Ceremony 85 75
755 $2.20 Cub Scout giving directions to tourists 1·75 2·75

1982. Birth of Prince William of Wales. Nos. 748/50 optd **ROYAL BABY 21.6.82**.
757 90 c. Type **168** 45 45
758 $1 Prince and Princess of Wales 50 50
759 $4 Princess Diana 2·00 1·50

172 Roosevelt in 1940

1982. Birth Centenary of Franklin D. Roosevelt. (Nos. 761, 763 and 765/6) and 250th Birth Anniv of George Washington (others). Multicoloured.
761 10 c. Type **172** 20 10
762 25 c. Washington as blacksmith 45 15
763 45 c. Churchill, Roosevelt and Stalin at Yalta Conference 1·00 40
764 60 c. Washington crossing the Delaware (vert) 1·00 40
765 $1 "Roosevelt Special" train (vert) 1·25 90
766 $3 Portrait of Roosevelt (vert) 1·40 2·40

173 "Annunciation"

1982. Christmas. Religious Paintings by Raphael. Multicoloured.
769 10 c. Type **173** 10 10
770 30 c. "Adoration of the Magi" 15 15
771 $1 "Presentation at the Temple" 50 50
772 $4 "Coronation of the Virgin" 2·10 2·25

174 Tritons and Dolphins

175 Pineapple Produce

1983. 500th Birth Anniv of Raphael. Details from "Galatea" Fresco. Multicoloured.
774 45 c. Type **174** 20 25
775 50 c. Sea nymph carried off by Triton 25 30
776 60 c. Winged angel steering dolphins (horiz) 30 35
777 $4 Cupids shooting arrows (horiz) 1·90 2·00

1983. Commonwealth Day. Multicoloured.
779 25 c. Type **175** 15 15
780 45 c. Carnival 20 25
781 60 c. Tourism 30 35
782 $3 Airport 1·00 1·50

176 T.V. Satellite Coverage of Royal Wedding

1983. World Communications Year. Multicoloured.

783	15 c. Type **176**	40	20
784	50 c. Police communications	2·25	1·50
785	60 c. House-to-train telephone call	2·25	1·50
786	$3 Satellite earth station with planets Jupiter and Saturn	4·75	5·00

177 Bottle-nosed Dolphin

1983. Whales. Multicoloured.

788	15 c. Type **177**	85	20
789	50 c. Fin whale	1·75	1·25
790	60 c. Bowhead whale	2·00	1·25
791	$3 Spectacled porpoise	3·75	4·25

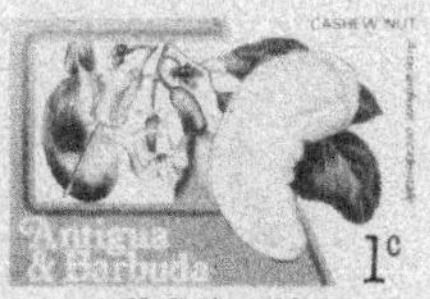

178 Cashew Nut

1983. Fruits and Flowers. Multicoloured.

793	1 c. Type **178**	15	50
794	2 c. Passion fruit	15	50
795	3 c. Mango	15	50
796	5 c. Grapefruit	20	30
797a	10 c. Pawpaw	30	20
798	15 c. Breadfruit	50	20
799	20 c. Coconut	50	20
800a	25 c. Oleander	60	20
801	30 c. Banana	60	40
802a	40 c. Pineapple	75	30
803a	45 c. Cordia	85	40
804	50 c. Cassia	90	60
805a	60 c. Poui	1·25	1·10
806a	$1 Frangipani	2·25	1·25
807a	$2 Flamboyant	3·25	3·75
808a	$2.50 Lemon	3·75	4·50
809a	$5 Linum vitae	6·00	10·00
810a	$10 National flag and coat of arms	9·50	15·00

179 Dornier Do-X Flying Boat

1983. Bicentenary of Manned Flight. Mult.

811	30 c. Type **179**	75	30
812	50 c. Supermarine S.6B seaplane	90	60
813	60 c. Curtiss F-9C Sparrowhawk biplane and airship U.S.S. "Akron"	1·00	85
814	$4 Hot-air balloon "Pro Juventute"	3·00	5·00

180 "Sibyls and Angels" (detail) (Raphael)

1983. Christmas. 500th Birth Anniv of Raphael.

816	**180**	10 c. multicoloured	30	20
817	–	30 c. multicoloured	65	35
818	–	$1 multicoloured	1·50	1·25
819	–	$4 multicoloured	4·00	5·00

DESIGNS—HORIZ: 10 c. to $4, Different details from "Sibyls and Angels".

181 John Wesley (founder)

182 Discus

1983. Bicentenary of Methodist Church (1984). Multicoloured.

821	15 c. Type **181**	25	15
822	50 c. Nathaniel Gilbert (founder in Antigua)	70	50
823	60 c. St. John Methodist Church steeple	75	65
824	$3 Ebenezer Methodist Church, St. John's	2·00	4·00

1984. Olympic Games, Los Angeles. Multicoloured.

825	25 c. Type **182**	20	15
826	50 c. Gymnastics	35	30
827	90 c. Hurdling	65	70
828	$3 Cycling	2·25	3·50

183 "Booker Vanguard" (freighter)

1984. Ships. Multicoloured.

830	45 c. Type **183**	1·00	55
831	50 c. S.S. "Canberra" (liner)	1·25	80
832	60 c. Sailing boats	1·50	1·00
833	$4 "Fairwind" (cargo liner)	3·00	7·00

184 Chenille

187 Abraham Lincoln

1984. Universal Postal Union Congress, Hamburg. Multicoloured.

835	15 c. Type **184**	40	15
836	50 c. Shell flower	1·00	70
837	60 c. Anthurium	1·10	1·10
838	$3 Angels trumpet	4·00	6·50

1984. Various stamps surch. (a) Nos. 702/4

840	$2 on 25 c. Type **159**	3·00	3·00
841	$2 on 50 c. Glamis Castle	3·00	3·00
842	$2 on $4 Prince Charles skiing	3·00	3·00
	(b) Nos. 748/50		
844	$2 on 90 c. Type **168**	2·40	2·25
845	$2 on $1 Prince and Princess of Wales	2·40	2·25
846	$2 on $4 Princess Diana	2·40	2·25
	(c) Nos. 757/9		
848	$2 on 90 c. Type **168**	2·40	2·25
849	$2 on $1 Prince and Princess of Wales	2·40	2·25
850	$2 on $4 Princess Diana	2·40	2·25
	(d) Nos. 779/82		
852	$2 on 25 c. Type **175**	2·00	1·25
853	$2 on 45 c. Carnival	2·00	1·25
854	$2 on 60 c. Tourism	2·00	1·25
855	$2 on $3 Airport	2·00	1·25

1984. Presidents of the United States of America. Multicoloured.

856	10 c. Type **187**	15	10
857	20 c. Harry S. Truman	20	15
858	30 c. Dwight D. Eisenhower	30	25
859	40 c. Ronald W. Reagan	50	30
860	90 c. Gettysburg Address, 1863	90	75
861	$1.10 Formation of N.A.T.O. 1949	1·25	1·25
862	$1.50 Eisenhower during the war	1·60	1·75
863	$2 Reagan and Caribbean Basin Initiative	1·75	2·00

188 View of Moravian Mission

1984. 150th Anniv of Abolition of Slavery. Multicoloured.

864	40 c. Type **188**	80	50
865	50 c. Antigua Courthouse, 1823	90	65
866	60 c. Planting suger-cane, Monks Hill	95	75
867	$3 Boiling house, Delaps' estate	4·00	4·75

189 Rufous-sided Towhee

190 Grass-skiing

1984. Songbirds. Multicoloured.

869	40 c. Type **189**	1·25	85
870	50 c. Parula warbler	1·40	1·10
871	60 c. House wren	1·50	1·50
872	$2 Ruby-crowned kinglet	2·00	3·75
873	$3 Common flicker	2·75	5·00

1984. "Ausipex" International Stamp Exhibition, Melbourne, Australian Sports. Multicoloured.

875	$1 Type **190**	1·50	1·50
876	$5 Australian football	4·25	5·50

191 "The Virgin and Infant with Angels and Cherubs"

192 "The Blue Dancers"

1984. 450th Death Anniv of Correggio (painter). Multicoloured.

878	25 c. Type **191**	40	20
879	60 c. "The Four Saints"	80	50
880	90 c. "St. Catherine"	1·10	90
881	$3 "The Campori Madonna"	2·75	4·25

1984. 150th Birth Anniv of Edgar Degas (painter). Multicoloured.

883	15 c. Type **192**	35	15
884	50 c. "The Pink Dancers"	80	60
885	70 c. "Two Dancers"	1·10	85
886	$4 "Dancers at the Bar"	3·00	4·75

193 Sir Winston Churchill

194 Donald Duck fishing

1984. Famous People. Multicoloured.

888	60 c. Type **193**	1·10	1·50
889	60 c. Mahatma Gandhi	1·10	1·50
890	60 c. John F. Kennedy	1·10	1·50
891	60 c. Mao Tse-tung	1·10	1·50
892	$1 Churchill with General De Gaulle, Paris, 1944 (horiz)	1·25	1·75
893	$1 Gandhi leaving London by train, 1931 (horiz)	1·25	1·75
894	$1 Kennedy with Chancellor Adenauer and Mayor Brandt, Berlin, 1963 (horiz)	1·25	1·75
895	$1 Mao Tse-tung with Lin Piao, Peking, 1969 (horiz)	1·25	1·75

1984. Christmas. 50th Birthday of Donald Duck. Walt Disney Cartoon Characters. Multicoloured.

897	1 c. Type **194**	10	10
898	2 c. Donald Duck lying on beach	10	10
899	3 c. Donald Duck and nephews with fishing rods and fishes	10	10
900	4 c. Donald Duck and nephews in boat	10	10
901	5 c. Wearing diving masks	10	10
902	10 c. In deckchairs reading books	10	10
903	$1 With toy shark's fin	2·00	1·25
904	$2 In sailing boat	3·00	3·00
905	$5 Attempting to propel boat	5·00	6·00

195 Torch from Statue in Madison Square Park, 1885

1985. Centenary (1986) of Statue of Liberty. Mult.

907	25 c. Type **195**	20	20
908	30 c. Statue of Liberty and scaffolding ("Restoration and Renewal") (vert)	20	20
909	50 c. Frederic Bartholdi (sculptor) supervising construction, 1876	30	30
910	90 c. Close-up of statue	55	55
911	$1 Statue and cadet ship ("Operation Sail", 1976) (vert)	90	90
912	$3 Dedication ceremony, 1886	1·75	2·00

196 Arawak Pot Sherd and Indians making Clay Utensils

1985. Native American Artefacts. Multicoloured.

914	15 c. Type **196**	15	10
915	50 c. Arawak body design and Arawak Indians tattooing	30	40
916	60 c. Head of the god "Yocahu" and Indians harvesting manioc	40	50
917	$3 Carib war club and Carib Indians going into battle	1·75	2·50

197 Triumph 2hp "Jap", 1903

1985. Centenary of the Motorcycle. Multicoloured.

919	10 c. Type **197**	65	15
920	30 c. "Indian Arrow", 1949	1·10	40
921	60 c. BMW "R100RS" 1976	1·60	1·25
922	$4 Harley-Davidson "Model II", 1916	5·50	7·00

198 Slavonian Grebe

1985. Birth Bicentenary of John J. Audubon (ornithologist) (1st issue). Multicoloured. Designs showing original paintings.

924	90 c. Type **198**	1·75	1·25
925	$1 British storm petrel	2·00	1·25
926	$1.50 Great blue heron	2·50	3·25
927	$3 Double-crested cormorant	3·75	6·00

See also Nos. 990/3.

199 "Anaea cyanea"

1985. Butterflies. Multicoloured.

929	25 c. Type **199**	1·00	30
930	60 c. "Leodonta dysoni"	2·25	1·25
931	90 c. "Junea doraete"	2·75	1·50
932	$4 "Prepona pylene"	7·50	10·50

200 Cessna 172D Skyhawk

201 Maimonides

1985. 40th Anniv of International Civil Aviation Organization. Multicoloured.

934	30 c. Type **200**	1·25	30
935	90 c. Fokker D.VII	2·75	1·25
936	$1.50 SPAD VII	3·75	3·25
937	$3 Boeing 747-100	5·50	7·50

1985. 850th Birth Anniv of Maimonides (physician, philosopher and scholar).

939	**201**	$2 green	4·00	3·25

202 Young Farmers with Produce

1985. International Youth Year. Multicoloured.

941	25 c. Type **202**	20	20
942	50 c. Hotel management trainees	30	40
943	60 c. Girls with goat and boys with football ("Environment")	40	60
944	$3 Windsurfing ("Leisure")	1·75	3·00

203 The Queen Mother attending Church

204 Magnificent Frigate Bird

1985. Life and Times of Queen Elizabeth the Queen Mother. Multicoloured.
946 $1 Type **203** 45 60
947 $1.50 Watching children playing in London garden 60 85
948 $2.50 The Queen Mother in 1979 90 1·40
Stamps as Nos. 946/8, but with face values of 90 c., $1 and $3 exists from additional sheetlets with changed background colours.

1985. Marine Life. Multicoloured.
950 15 c. Type **204** . . . . 1·00 30
951 45 c. Brain coral . . . . . . 2·00 95
952 60 c. Cushion star . . . . . . 2·25 1·75
953 $3 Spotted moray . . . . . . 7·00 9·00

205 Girl Guides Nursing **206** Bass Trombone

1985. 75th Anniv of Girl Guide Movement. Multicoloured.
955 15 c. Type **205** 75 20
956 45 c. Open-air Girl Guide meeting . . . . 1·40 60
957 60 c. Lord and Lady Baden-Powell . . . . 1·75 90
958 $3 Girl Guides gathering flowers 4·25 4·50

1985. 300th Birth Anniv of Johann Sebastian Bach (composer). Multicoloured.
960 25 c. Type **206** . . . . 1·40 55
961 50 c. English horn . . . . . . 1·75 1·10
962 $1 Violino piccolo . . . . . . 3·25 1·75
963 $3 Bass rackett . . . . 6·00 7·00

207 Flags of Great Britain and Antigua

1985. Royal Visit. Multicoloured.
965 60 c. Type **207** . . . . 1·00 65
966 $1 Queen Elizabeth II (vert) . 1·50 1·25
967 $4 Royal Yacht "Britannia" . . 3·25 6·00

1985. 150th Birth Anniv of Mark Twain (author). As T **118** of Anguilla showing Walt Disney cartoon characters in scenes from "Roughing It" Multicoloured.
969 25 c. Donald Duck and Mickey Mouse meeting Indians . . 50 20
970 50 c. Mickey Mouse, Donald Duck and Goofy canoeing . 75 55
971 $1.10 Goofy as Pony Express rider . . . . 1·25 1·50
972 $1.50 Donald Duck and Goofy hunting buffalo . . . . . 1·75 2·50
973 $2 Mickey Mouse and silver mine 2·50 3·50

1985. Birth Bicentenaries of Grimm Brothers (folklorists). As T **119** of Anguilla showing Walt Disney cartoon characters in scenes from "Spindle, Shuttle and Needle". Multicoloured.
975 30 c. The Prince (Mickey Mouse) searches for a bride . . . 80 40
976 60 c. The Prince finds the Orphan Girl (Minnie Mouse) . . . 1·10 80
977 70 c. The Spindle finds the Prince 1·40 90
978 $1 The Needle tidies the Girl's house . . . . 1·90 1·75
979 $3 The Prince proposes . . . 4·00 5·50

208 Benjamin Franklin and U.N. (New York) 1953 U.P.U. 5 c. Stamp

1985. 40th Anniv of United Nations Organization. Multicoloured.
981 40 c. Type **208** . . . . 1·00 70
982 $1 George Washington Carver (agricultural chemist) and 1982 Nature Conservation 28 c. stamp . . . . 2·00 2·00
983 $3 Charles Lindbergh (aviator) and 1978 I.C.A.O. 25 c. stamp 4·25 6·00
Nos. 981/3 each include a United Nations (New York) stamp design.

209 "Madonna and Child" (De Landi) **211** Tug

210 Football, Boots and Trophy

1985. Christmas. Religious Paintings. Mult.
985 10 c. Type **209** 30 15
986 25 c. "Madonna and Child" (Berlinghiero) 55 25
987 60 c. "The Nativity" (Fra Angelico) 70 60
988 $4 "Presentation in the Temple" (Giovanni di Paolo) . . . . 1·75 4·25

1986. Birth Bicentenary of John J. Audubon (ornithologist) (2nd issue). As T **198** showing original paintings. Multicoloured.
990 60 c. Mallard . . . . 2·00 1·50
991 90 c. North American black duck 2·50 2·00
992 $1.50 Pintail . . . . 3·25 4·50
993 $3 American wigeon . . . . 4·50 6·50

1986. World Cup Football Championship, Mexico. Multicoloured.
995 30 c. Type **210** . . . . 1·00 40
996 60 c. Goalkeeper (vert) . . . 1·50 85
997 $1 Referee blowing whistle (vert) 2·00 1·60
998 $4 Ball in net . . . . 5·50 7·50

1986. Appearance of Halley's Comet (1st issue). As T **123** of Anguilla. Multicoloured.
1000 5 c. Edmond Halley and Old Greenwich Observatory . . . 30 15
1001 10 c. Messerschmitt Me 163B Komet (fighter aircraft), 1944 30 15
1002 60 c. Montezuma (Aztec emperor) and Comet in 1517 (from "Historias de las Indias de Neuva Espana") . . . 1·50 70
1003 $4 Pocahontas saving Capt. John Smith and Comet in 1607 . . . . 4·50 5·00
See also Nos. 1047/50.

1986. 60th Birthday of Queen Elizabeth II. As T **125** of Anguilla.
1005 60 c. black and yellow . . . 30 35
1006 $1 multicoloured 50 55
1007 $4 multicoloured . . . . . 1·40 1·90
DESIGNS: 60 c. Wedding photograph, 1947; $1 Queen at Trooping the Colour; $4 In Scotland.

1986. Local Boats. Multicoloured.
1009 30 c. Type **211** 25 20
1010 60 c. Game fishing boat . . 45 35
1011 $1 Yacht 75 60
1012 $4 Lugger with auxiliary sail 2·50 3·25

212 "Hiawatha" express

1986. "Ameripex '86" International Stamp Exhibition, Chicago. Famous American Trains. Multicoloured.
1014 25 c. Type **212** . . . . . . 1·00 40
1015 50 c. "Grand Canyon" express 1·25 75
1016 $1 "Powhattan Arrow" express 1·50 1·75
1017 $3 "Empire State" express . 3·00 6·00

213 Prince Andrew and Miss Sarah Ferguson **214** Fly-specked Cerith

1986. Royal Wedding. Multicoloured.
1019 45 c. Type **213** 35 35
1020 60 c. Prince Andrew 40 45
1021 $4 Prince Andrew with Prince Philip . . . . 2·00 3·00

1986. Sea Shells. Multicoloured.
1023 15 c. Type **214** 75 50
1024 45 c. Smooth Scotch bonnet . 1·75 1·25
1025 60 c. West Indian crown conch 2·00 2·00
1026 $3 Ciboney murex . . . . . 6·50 10·00

215 Water Lily

1986. Flowers. Multicoloured.
1028 10 c. Type **215** 20 15
1029 15 c. Queen of the night . . . 20 15
1030 50 c. Cup of gold 55 55
1031 60 c. Beach morning glory . . 70 70
1032 70 c. Golden trumpet 80 80
1033 $1 Air plant . . . . 90 1·10
1034 $4 Purple wreath . . . . . . 1·75 3·00
1035 $4 Zephyr lily . . . . 2·00 3·75

1986. World Cup Football Championship Winners, Mexico. Nos. 995/8 optd **WINNERS Argentina 3 W.Germany 2**.
1037 30 c. Type **210** 65 40
1038 60 c. Goalkeeper (vert) . . . 1·00 75
1039 $1 Referee blowing whistle (vert) . . . . 1·40 1·10
1040 $4 Ball in net . . . . 4·50 4·50

217 "Hygrocybe occidentalis var. scarletina" **(218)**

1986. Mushrooms. Multicoloured.
1042 10 c. Type **217** 30 20
1043 50 c. "Trogia buccinalis" . . 70 55
1044 $1 "Collybia subpruinosa" . . 1·25 1·00
1045 $4 "Leucocoprinus brebissonii" 3·00 4·00

1986. Appearance of Halley's Comet (2nd issue). Nos. 1000/3 optd with T **218**.
1047 5 c. Edmond Halley and Old Greenwich Observatory . . 15 10
1048 10 c. Messerschmitt Me 163B Komet (fighter aircraft), 1944 20 10
1049 60 c. Montezuma (Aztec emperor) and Comet in 1517 (from "Historias de las Indias de Neuva Espana" . . . 1·00 65
1050 $4 Pocahontas saving Capt. John Smith and Comet in 1607 . . . . 4·50 4·00

219 Auburn "Speedster" (1933)

1986. Centenary of First Benz Motor Car. Mult.
1052 10 c. Type **219** 15 10
1053 15 c. Mercury "Sable" (1986) 20 10
1054 50 c. Cadillac (1959) 55 30
1055 60 c. Studebaker (1950) . . . 70 45
1056 70 c. Lagonda "V-12" (1939) 80 55
1057 $1 Adler "Standard" (1930) . 1·10 75
1058 $3 DKW (1956) . . . . . . 2·50 2·50
1059 $4 Mercedes "500K" (1936) . 3·00 3·00

220 Young Mickey Mouse playing Santa Claus

1986. Christmas. Designs showing Walt Disney cartoon characters as babies. Multicoloured.
1061 25 c. Type **220** 45 35
1062 30 c. Mickey and Minnie Mouse building snowman 50 40
1063 40 c. Aunt Matilda and Goofy baking 55 45
1064 60 c. Goofy and Pluto . . . 80 85
1065 70 c. Pluto, Donald and Daisy Duck carol singing . . . . 95 1·00
1066 $1.50 Donald Duck, Mickey Mouse and Pluto stringing popcorn . . . . 1·60 2·50
1067 $3 Grandma Duck and Minnie Mouse . . . . 3·00 4·50
1068 $4 Donald Duck and Pete . . 3·25 4·50

221 Arms of Antigua **222** "Canada I" (1981)

1986.
1070 **221** 10 c. blue 50 50
1071 – 25 c. red 75 75
DESIGN: 25 c. Flag of Antigua.

1987. America's Cup Yachting Championship. Multicoloured.
1072 30 c. Type **222** 30 20
1073 60 c. "Gretel II" (1970) . . . 45 50
1074 $1 "Sceptre" (1958) . . . . 85 1·00
1075 $3 "Vigilant" (1893) . . . . 2·25 3·00

223 Bridled Burrfish

1987. Marine Life. Multicoloured.
1077 15 c. Type **223** . . . . . . 1·50 30
1078 30 c. Common noddy . . . . 2·75 60
1079 40 c. Nassau grouper . . . . 2·00 70
1080 50 c. Laughing gull . . . . . 4·00 1·50
1081 60 c. French angelfish . . . 2·75 1·50
1082 $1 Porkfish . . . . 2·75 1·75
1083 $2 Royal tern . . . . 5·50 5·00
1084 $3 Sooty tern . . . . 6·00 6·00
Nos. 1078, 1080 and 1083/4 are without the World Wildlife Fund logo shown on Type **223**.

224 Handball

1987. Olympic Games, Seoul (1988) (1st issue). Multicoloured.
1086 10 c. Type **224** 30 10
1087 60 c. Fencing 55 35
1088 $1 Gymnastics 75 75
1089 $3 Football . . . . 2·00 3·00
See also Nos. 1222/5.

225 "The Profile"

1987. Birth Centenary of Marc Chagall (artist). Multicoloured.
1091 10 c. Type **225** 20 15
1092 30 c. "Portrait of the Artist's Sister" 35 30
1093 40 c. "Bride with Fan" 40 40
1094 60 c. "David in Profile" . . . 45 45
1095 90 c. "Fiancee with Bouquet" 60 60
1096 $1 "Self Portrait with Brushes" 65 65
1097 $3 "The Walk" . . . . 1·75 2·00
1098 $4 "Three Candles" . . . . . 2·00 2·25

226 "Spirit of Australia" (fastest powerboat), 1978

1987. Milestones of Transportation. Multicoloured.
1100 10 c. Type **226** 40 30
1101 15 c. Werner von Siemens's electric locomotive, 1879 . 60 40
1102 30 c. U.S.S. "Triton" (first submerged circum-navigation), 1960 . . . . . 60 45
1103 50 c. Trevithick's steam carriage (first passenger-carrying vehicle), 1801 . . . . . . 70 60
1104 60 c. U.S.S. "New Jersey" (battleship), 1942 . . . . . 80 70
1105 70 c. Draisaine bicycle 1818 . 80 80
1106 90 c. "United States" (liner) (holder of Blue Riband), 1952 1·00 1·00
1107 $1.50 Cierva C.4 (first autogyro), 1923 . . . . . 1·40 2·00
1108 $2 Curtiss NC-4 flying boat (first transatlantic flight), 1919 . . . . 1·50 2·25
1109 $3 "Queen Elizabeth 2" (liner), 1969 . . . . 2·50 3·00

227 Lee Iacocca at Unveiling of Restored Statue

228 Grace Kelly

1987. Centenary of Statue of Liberty (1986) (2nd issue). Multicoloured.
1110 15 c. Type **227** 15 15
1111 30 c. Statue at sunset (side view) 20 20
1112 45 c. Aerial view of head . . 30 30
1113 50 c. Lee Iacocca and torch . 35 35
1114 60 c. Workmen inside head of Statue (horiz) 35 35
1115 90 c. Restoration work (horiz) 50 50
1116 $1 Head of Statue 55 55
1117 $2 Statue at sunset (front view) 1·00 1·25
1118 $3 Inspecting restoration work (horiz) . . . . 1·25 1·75
1119 $5 Statue at night . . . . . 2·00 3·00

1987. Entertainers. Multicoloured.
1120 15 c. Type **228** 90 40
1121 30 c. Marilyn Monroe . . . . 1·75 65
1122 45 c. Orson Welles 90 60
1123 50 c. Judy Garland 90 65
1124 60 c. John Lennon . . . . . 2·25 1·10
1125 $1 Rock Hudson . . . . . . 1·40 1·10
1126 $2 John Wayne . . . . . . 2·25 2·00
1127 $3 Elvis Presley . . . . . . 6·00 3·50

229 Scouts around Camp Fire and Red Kangaroo

1987. 16th World Scout Jamboree, Australia. Mult.
1128 10 c. Type **229** 50 20
1129 60 c. Scouts canoeing and blue-winged kookaburra . . . . 1·25 70
1130 $1 Scouts on assault course and ring-tailed rock wallaby . . 1·25 85
1131 $3 Field kitchen and koala . 2·00 4·00

230 Whistling Frog

1987. "Capex '87" International Stamp Exhibition, Toronto. Reptiles and Amphibians. Mult.
1133 30 c. Type **230** 35 20
1134 60 c. Croaking lizard 45 40
1135 $1 Antiguan anole 70 60
1136 $3 Red-footed tortoise . . . 1·75 2·50

1987. 10th Death Anniv of Elvis Presley (entertainer). No. 1127 optd **10th ANNIVERSARY 16th AUGUST 1987.**
1138 $3 Elvis Presley . . . . . . 4·75 3·50

232 House of Burgesses, Virginia ("Freedom of Speech")

1987. Bicentenary of U.S. Constitution. Mult.
1139 15 c. Type **232** 10 10
1140 45 c. State Seal, Connecticut 20 25
1141 60 c. State Seal, Delaware . 25 35
1142 $4 Governor Morris (Pennsylvania delegate) (vert) 1·75 2·25

233 "Madonna and Child" (Bernardo Daddi)

234 Wedding Photograph, 1947

1987. Christmas. Religious Paintings. Mult.
1144 45 c. Type **233** 30 15
1145 60 c. St. Joseph (detail, "The Nativity" (Sano di Pietro)) 40 30
1146 $1 Virgin Mary (detail, "The Nativity" (Sano di Pietro)) 60 55
1147 $4 "Music-making Angel" (Melozzo da Forli) . . . . 2·00 3·00

1988. Royal Ruby Wedding.
1149 **234** 25 c. brown, black and blue 15 15
1150 – 60 c. multicoloured . . . 30 40
1151 – $2 brown, black and green 90 1·10
1152 – $3 multicoloured . . . . 1·40 1·60
DESIGNS: 60 c. Queen Elizabeth II; $2 Princess Elizabeth and Prince Philip with Prince Charles at his christening, 1948; $3 Queen Elizabeth (from photo by Tim Graham), 1980.

235 Great Blue Heron

1988. Birds of Antigua. Multicoloured.
1154 10 c. Type **235** 35 30
1155 15 c. Ringed kingfisher (horiz) 35 30
1156 50 c. Bananaquit (horiz) . . 70 50
1157 60 c. Purple gallinule (horiz) 70 50
1158 70 c. Blue-hooded euphonia (horiz) 80 55
1159 $1 Brown-throated conure ("Caribbean Parakeet") . 1·00 75
1160 $3 Troupial (horiz) . . . . 2·50 3·25
1161 $4 Purple-throated carib (horiz) 2·50 3·25

236 First Aid at Daycare Centre, Antigua

1988. Salvation Army's Community Service. Multicoloured.
1163 25 c. Type **236** 65 55
1164 30 c. Giving penicillin injection, Indonesia 65 55
1165 40 c. Children at daycare centre, Bolivia 75 65
1166 45 c. Rehabilitation of the handicapped, India . . . 75 65
1167 50 c. Training blind man, Kenya 90 1·00
1168 60 c. Weighing baby, Ghana 90 1·00
1169 $1 Training typist, Zambia . 1·40 1·75
1170 $2 Emergency food kitchen, Sri Lanka . . . . 2·00 3·25

237 Columbus's Second Fleet, 1493

1988. 500th Anniv (1992) of Discovery of America by Columbus (1st issue). Multicoloured.
1172 10 c. Type **237** 50 30
1173 30 c. Painos Indian village and fleet 50 35
1174 45 c. "Santa Mariagalante" (flagship) and Painos village 60 35
1175 60 c. Painos Indians offering Columbus fruit and vegetables 60 50
1176 90 c. Painos Indian and Columbus with scarlet macaw 1·00 80
1177 $1 Columbus landing on island 1·00 1·00
1178 £3 Spanish soldier and fleet . 2·00 2·75
1179 $4 Fleet under sail . . . . . 2·25 2·75
See also Nos. 1267/70, 1360/7, 1503/10, 1654/9 and 1670/1.

238 "Bust of Christ"

1988. Easter. 500th Birth Anniv of Titian (artist). Multicoloured.
1181 30 c. Type **238** 25 20
1182 40 c. "Scourging of Christ" . 30 25
1183 45 c. "Madonna in Glory with Saints" 30 25
1184 50 c. "The Averoldi Polyptych" (detail) 35 35
1185 $1 "Christ Crowned with Thorns" 55 55
1186 $2 "Christ Mocked" . . . . 90 1·25
1187 $3 "Christ and Simon of Cyrene" . . . . 1·50 1·75
1188 $4 "Crucifixion with Virgin and Saints" . . . . 1·75 2·25

239 Two Yachts rounding Buoy

1988. Sailing Week. Multicoloured.
1190 30 c. Type **239** 20 20
1191 60 c. Three yachts 35 40
1192 $1 British yacht under way . 50 55
1193 $3 Three yachts (different) . . 1·10 2·50

240 Mickey Mouse and Diver with Porpoise

1988. Disney EPCOT Centre, Orlando, Florida. Designs showing cartoon characters and exhibits. Multicoloured.
1195 1 c. Type **240** 10 10
1196 2 c. Goofy and Mickey Mouse with futuristic car (vert) . . 10 10
1197 3 c. Mickey Mouse and Goofy as Atlas (vert) 10 10
1198 4 c. Mickey Mouse and "Edaphosaurus" (prehistoric reptile) 10 10
1199 5 c. Mickey Mouse at Journey into Imagination exhibit . 10 10
1200 10 c. Mickey Mouse collecting vegetables (vert) 10 10
1201 25 c. Type **240** 25 25
1202 30 c. As 2 c. 25 25
1203 40 c. As 3 c. 30 30
1204 60 c. As 4 c. 50 50
1205 70 c. As 5 c. 60 60
1206 $1.50 As 10 c. . . . . . . 1·25 1·25
1207 $3 Goofy and Mickey Mouse with robot (vert) . . . . . 2·00 2·00
1208 $4 Mickey Mouse and Clarabelle at Horizons exhibit 2·25 2·25

1988. Stamp Exhibitions. Nos. 1083/4 optd.
1210 $2 Royal tern (optd **Praga '88**, Prague) . . . . 1·75 1·75
1211 $3 Sooty tern (optd **INDEPENDENCE 40**, Israel) 2·25 2·25

242 Jacaranda

243 Gymnastics

1988. Flowering Trees. Multicoloured.
1213 10 c. Type **242** 20 15
1214 30 c. Cordia 25 20
1215 50 c. Orchid tree 40 40
1216 90 c. Flamboyant 50 50
1217 $1 African tulip tree 55 55
1218 $2 Potato tree . . . . 1·10 1·25
1219 $3 Crepe myrtle . . . . . . 1·40 1·75
1220 $4 Pitch apple . . . . 1·75 2·50

1988. Olympic Games, Seoul (2nd issue). Mult.
1222 40 c. Type **243** 20 25
1223 60 c. Weightlifting 25 30
1224 $1 Water polo (horiz) . . . 45 50
1225 $3 Boxing (horiz) . . . . . 1·40 2·00

244 "Danaus plexippus"

1988. Caribbean Butterflies. Multicoloured.
1227 1 c. Type **244** 20 20
1228 2 c. "Greta diaphanus" . . . 30 30
1229 3 c. "Calisto archebates" . . 30 30
1230 5 c. "Hamadryas feronia" . . 40 40
1231 10 c. "Mestra dorcas" 50 30
1232 15 c. "Hypolimnas misippus" 60 30
1233 20 c. "Dione juno" 70 30
1234 25 c. "Heliconius charithonia" 70 30
1235 30 c. "Eurema pyro" 70 30
1236 40 c. "Papilio androgeus" . . 75 30
1237 45 c. "Anteos maerula" . . . 75 30
1238 50 c. "Aphrissa orbis" . . . 90 45
1239 60 c. "Astraptes xagua" . . 1·00 60
1240 $1 "Heliopetes arsalte" . . . 1·50 1·00
1241 $2 "Polites baracoa" . . . . 2·50 3·25
1242 $2.50 "Phocides pigmalion" . 3·00 3·75
1243 $5 "Prepona amphitoe" . . . 4·50 5·50
1244 $10 "Oarisma nanus" . . . . 7·00 8·00
1244a $20 "Parides lycimenes" . . 13·00 15·00

245 President Kennedy and Family

1988. 25th Death Anniv of John F. Kennedy (American statesman). Muticoloured.
1245 1 c. Type **245** 10 10
1246 2 c. Kennedy commanding "PT109" 10 10
1247 3 c. Funeral cortege 10 10
1248 4 c. In motorcade, Mexico City 10 10
1249 30 c. As 1 c. 25 15
1250 60 c. As 4 c. 35 30
1251 $1 As 3 c. 60 60
1252 $4 As 2 c. . . . . 1·75 2·50

246 Minnie Mouse carol singing

1988. Christmas. "Mickey's Christmas Chorale". Design showing Walt Disney cartoon characters. Multicoloured.
1254 10 c. Type **246** 30 30
1255 25 c. Pluto 45 45
1256 30 c. Mickey Mouse playing ukelele 45 45
1257 70 c. Donald Duck and nephew 80 80
1258 $1 Mordie and Ferdie carol singing . . . . 80 1·00
1259 $1 Goofy carol singing . . . 80 1·00
1260 $1 Chip n'Dale sliding off roof 80 1·00
1261 $1 Two of Donald Duck's nephews at window . . . 80 1·00
1262 $1 As 10 c. . . . . 80 1·00
1263 $1 As 25 c. . . . . 80 1·00
1264 $1 As 30 c. . . . . 80 1·00
1265 $1 As 70 c. . . . . 80 1·00
Nos. 1258/65 were printed together, se-tenant, forming a composite design.

247 Arawak Warriors

1989. 500th Anniv of Discovery of America by Columbus (1992) (2nd issue). Pre-Columbian Arawak Society. Multicoloured.
1267 $1.50 Type **247** . . . . 1·00 1·25
1268 $1.50 Whip dancers . . . . . 1·00 1·25
1269 $1.50 Whip dancers and chief with pineapple . . . . 1·00 1·25
1270 $1.50 Family and camp fire . 1·00 1·25
Nos. 1267/70 were printed together, se-tenant, forming a composite design.

248 De Havilland Comet 4 Airliner

1989. 50th Anniv of First Jet Flight. Mult.
1272 10 c. Type **248** 35 35
1273 30 c. Messerschmitt Me 262 fighter 55 45
1274 40 c. Boeing 707 airliner . . 60 45
1275 60 c. Canadair CL-13 Sabre (inscr "F-86") fighter . . . 75 55
1276 $1 Lockheed F-104 Starfighters 1·00 90
1277 $2 McDonnell Douglas DC-10 airliner . . . . 2·00 2·25
1278 $3 Boeing 747-300/400 airliner 2·50 2·75
1279 $4 McDonnell Douglas F-4 Phantom II fighter . . . . 2·50 2·75

249 "Festivale"

1989. Caribbean Cruise Ships. Multicoloured.
1281 25 c. Type **249** 55 30
1282 45 c. "Southward" 80 30
1283 50 c. "Sagafjord" 80 30
1284 60 c. "Daphne" 80 50
1285 75 c. "Cunard Countess" . . 90 70
1286 90c. "Song of America" . . . 1·00 90
1287 $3 "Island Princess" . . . . 2·50 3·50
1288 $4 "Galileo" . . . . 2·50 3·50

250 "Fish swimming by Duck half-submerged in Stream"

1989. Japanese Art. Paintings by Hiroshige. Mult.
1290 25 c. Type **250** 55 30
1291 45 c. "Crane and Wave" . . 65 40
1292 50 c. "Sparrows and Morning Glories" 70 40
1293 60 c. "Crested Blackbird and Flowering Cherry" 80 50
1294 $1 "Great Knot sitting among Water Grass" . . . . . . 1·00 70
1295 $2 "Goose on a Bank of Water" 2·00 2·00
1296 $3 "Black Paradise Flycatcher and Blossoms" . . . . . 2·50 2·50
1297 $4 "Sleepy Owl perched on a Pine Branch" . . . . . . 2·50 2·50

251 Mickey and Minnie Mouse in Helicopter over River Seine

1989. "Philexfrance 89" International Stamp Exhibition, Paris. Walt Disney cartoon characters in Paris. Multicoloured.
1299 1 c. Type **251** 10 10
1300 2 c. Goofy and Mickey Mouse passing Arc de Triomphe . 10 10
1301 3 c. Mickey Mouse painting picture of Notre Dame . . 10 10
1302 4 c. Mickey and Minnie Mouse with Pluto leaving Metro station 10 10
1303 5 c. Minnie Mouse as model in fashion show 10 10
1304 10 c. Daisy Duck, Minnie Mouse and Clarabelle as Folies Bergere dancers . . 10 10
1305 $5 Mickey and Minnie Mouse shopping in street market . 4·75 5·50
1306 $6 Mickey and Minnie Mouse, Jose Carioca and Donald Duck at pavement cafe . . 4·75 5·50

252 Goalkeeper

1989. World Cup Football Championship, Italy (1990). Multicoloured.
1308 15 c. Type **252** 65 15
1309 25 c. Goalkeeper moving towards ball 75 15
1310 $1 Goalkeeper reaching for ball 1·50 1·25
1311 $4 Goalkeeper saving goal . 3·00 4·25

253 "Mycena pura"

1989. Fungi. Multicoloured.
1313 10 c. Type **253** 50 40
1314 25 c. "Psathyrella tuberculata" (vert) 75 40
1315 50 c. "Psilocybe cubensis" . 1·00 60
1316 60 c. "Leptonia caeruleocapitata" (vert) . 1·00 70
1317 75 c. "Xeromphalina tenuipes" (vert) . . . . 1·25 90
1318 $1 "Chlorophyllum molybdites" (vert) . . . . 1·40 1·10
1319 $3 "Marasmius haematocephalus" . . . . 2·75 3·25
1320 $4 "Cantharellus cinnabarinus" 2·75 3·25

254 Desmarest's Hutia

1989. Local Fauna. Multicoloured.
1322 25 c. Type **254** 60 45
1323 45 c. Caribbean monk seal . 1·50 80
1324 80 c. Mustache bat (vert) . . 1·00 85
1325 $4 American manatee (vert) 3·00 4·50

255 Goofy and Old Printing Press

258 Launch of "Apollo II"

256 Mickey Mouse and Donald Duck with Camden and Amboy Locomotive "John Bull", 1831

1989. "American Philately". Walt Disney cartoon characters with stamps and the logo of the American Philatelic Society. Multicoloured.
1327 1 c. Type **255** 10 10
1328 2 c. Donald Duck cancelling first day cover for Mickey Mouse 10 10
1329 3 c. Donald Duck's nephews reading recruiting poster for Pony Express riders 10 10
1330 4 c. Morty and Ferdie as early radio broadcasters 10 10
1331 5 c. Donald Duck and water buffalo watching television . 10 10
1332 10 c. Donald Duck with stamp album 10 10
1333 $4 Daisy Duck with computer system . . . . 3·50 4·00
1334 $6 Donald's nephews with stereo radio, trumpet and guitar . . . . 4·50 5·00

1989. "World Stamp Expo '89" International Stamp Exhibition. Washington. Walt Disney cartoon characters and locomotives. Mult.
1336 25 c. Type **256** 50 50
1337 45 c. Mickey Mouse and friends with "Atlantic", 1832 . . . 60 50
1338 50 c. Mickey Mouse and Goofy with "William Crooks", 1861 60 50
1339 60 c. Mickey Mouse and Goofy with "Minnetonka", 1869 . 70 65
1340 $1 Chip n'Dale with "Thatcher Perkins", 1863 . . . . . 75 75
1341 $2 Mickey and Minnie Mouse with "Pioneer", 1848 . . . 1·50 2·00
1342 $3 Mickey Mouse and Donald Duck with cog railway locomotive "Peppersass", 1869 . . . . 1·75 2·50
1343 $4 Mickey Mouse with Huey, Dewey and Louie aboard N.Y. World's Fair "Gimbels Flyer", 1939 . . . . 2·00 2·50

1989. 20th Anniv of First Manned Landing on Moon. Multicoloured.
1346 10 c. Type **258** 30 20
1347 45 c. Aldrin on Moon 70 30
1348 $1 Module "Eagle" over Moon (horiz) . . . . 1·25 1·00
1349 $4 Recovery of "Apollo II" crew after splashdown (horiz) . . . . 2·75 3·75

259 "The Small Cowper Madonna" (Raphael)

260 Star-eyed Hermit Crab

1989. Christmas. Paintings by Raphael and Giotto. Multicoloured.
1351 10 c. Type **259** 10 10
1352 25 c. "Madonna of the Goldfinch" (Raphael) . . . 20 15
1353 30 c. "The Alba Madonna" (Raphael) 20 15
1354 50 c. Saint (detail, "Bologna Altarpiece") (Giotto) . . . 40 30
1355 60 c. Angel (detail, "Bologna Altarpiece") (Giotto) . . . 45 35
1356 70 c. Angel slaying serpent (detail, "Bologna Altarpiece") (Giotto) . . . 50 40
1357 $4 Evangelist (detail, "Bologna Altarpiece") (Giotto) . . . 2·50 3·00
1358 $5 "Madonna of Foligno" (detail) (Raphael) . . . . . 3·00 3·75

1990. 500th Anniv (1992) of Discovery of America by Columbus (3rd issue). New World Natural History—Marine Life. Multicoloured.
1360 10 c. Type **260** 15 15
1361 20 c. Spiny lobster 20 20
1362 25 c. Magnificent banded fanworm 25 25
1363 45 c. Cannonball jellyfish . . 40 40
1364 60 c. Red-spiny sea star . . . 60 60
1365 $2 Peppermint shrimp . . . . 1·50 2·00
1366 $3 Coral crab . . . . 1·75 2·25
1367 $4 Branching fire coral . . . 2·25 2·50

261 "Vanilla mexicana"

ANTIGUA & BARBUDA
262 Queen Victoria and Queen Elizabeth II

1990. "Expo '90" International Garden and Greenery Exhibition, Osaka. Orchids. Multicoloured.
1369 15 c. Type **261** 50 40
1370 45 c. "Epidendrum ibaguense" . 70 40
1371 50 c. "Epidendrum secundum" . 75 45
1372 60 c. "Maxillaria conferta" . . 80 50
1373 $1 "Oncidium altissimum" . . 1·10 85
1374 $2 "Spiranthes lanceolata" . 1·75 2·00
1375 $3 "Tonopsis utricularioides" 2·25 2·75
1376 $5 "Epidendrum nocturnum" 3·25 3·75

1990. 150th Anniv of the Penny Black.
1378 **262** 45 c. green 60 30
1379 – 60 c. mauve 70 55
1380 – $5 blue . . . . 3·25 4·50
DESIGNS: 60 c., $5 As Type **262**, but with different backgrounds.

ANTIGUA & BARBUDA
263 "Britannia" (mail paddle-steamer), 1840

1990. "Stamp World London '90" International Stamp Exhibition.
1382 **263** 50 c. green and red . . . 65 35
1383 – 75 c. brown and red . . 85 80
1384 – $4 blue and red . . . . 3·25 4·50
DESIGNS: 75 c. Travelling Post Office sorting van, 1892; $4 Short S.23 Empire "C" Class flying boat "Centaurus", 1938.

264 Flamefish

1990. Reef Fishes. Multicoloured.
1386 10 c. Type **264** 45 45
1387 15 c. Coney 55 45
1388 50 c. Long-spined squirrelfish 80 60
1389 60 c. Sergeant major 80 60
1390 $1 Yellow-tailed snapper . . 1·10 85
1391 $2 Rock beauty . . . . . . 2·00 2·50
1392 $3 Spanish hogfish . . . . . 2·50 3·00
1393 $4 Striped parrotfish . . . . 2·50 3·00

265 "Voyager 2" passing Saturn

266 Queen Mother in Evening Dress

1990. Achievement in Space. Multicoloured.
1395 45 c. Type **265** 50 50
1396 45 c. "Pioneer 11" photographing Saturn . . 50 50
1397 45 c. Astronaut in transporter 50 50
1398 45 c. Space shuttle "Columbia" 50 50
1399 45 c. "Apollo 10" command module on parachutes . . 50 50
1400 45 c. "Skylab" space station 50 50
1401 45 c. Astronaut Edward White in space 50 50
1402 45 c. "Apollo" spacecraft on joint mission 50 50
1403 45 c. "Soyuz" spacecraft on joint mission 50 50
1404 45 c. "Mariner 1" passing Venus 50 50
1405 45 c. "Gemini 4" capsule . . 50 50
1406 45 c. "Sputnik 1" 50 50
1407 45 c. Hubble space telescope 50 50
1408 45 c. North American X-15 rocket plane 50 50
1409 45 c. Bell XS-1 airplane . . . 50 50
1410 45 c. "Apollo 17" astronaut and lunar rock formation . . . 50 50
1411 45 c. Lunar Rover 50 50
1412 45 c. "Apollo 14" lunar module 50 50
1413 45 c. Astronaut Buzz Aldrin on Moon 50 50
1414 45 c. Soviet "Lunokhod" lunar vehicle 50 50

1990. 90th Birthday of Queen Elizabeth the Queen Mother.
1415 **266** 15 c. multicoloured . . . 30 15
1416 – 35 c. multicoloured . . . 40 25
1417 – 75 c. multicoloured . . . 70 70
1418 – $3 multicoloured . . . . 2·25 3·00
DESIGNS: Nos. 1416/18, Recent photographs of the Queen Mother.

267 Mickey Mouse as Animator

1990. Mickey Mouse in Hollywood. Walt Disney cartoon characters. Multicoloured.

1420	25 c. Type **267**	35	25
1421	45 c. Minnie Mouse learning lines while being dressed	50	25
1422	50 c. Mickey Mouse with clapper board	60	30
1423	60 c. Daisy Duck making-up Mickey Mouse	65	35
1424	$1 Clarabelle Cow as Cleopatra	90	70
1425	$2 Mickey Mouse directing Goofy and Donald Duck	1·60	2·00
1426	$3 Mickey Mouse directing Goofy as birdman	2·25	2·50
1427	$4 Donald Duck and Mickey Mouse editing film	2·25	2·50

268 Men's 20 Kilometres Walk

269 Huey and Dewey asleep ("Christmas Stories")

1990. Olympic Games, Barcelona (1992) (1st issue). Multicoloured.

1429	50 c. Type **268**	55	30
1430	75 c. Triple jump	70	65
1431	$1 Men's 10,000 metres	90	85
1432	$5 Javelin	3·00	4·25

See also Nos. 1553/60 and 1609/16.

1990. International Literacy Year. Walt Disney cartoon characters illustrating works by Charles Dickens. Multicoloured.

1434	15 c. Type **269**	25	25
1435	45 c. Donald Duck as Poor Jo looking at grave ("Bleak House")	45	45
1436	50 c. Dewey as Oliver asking for more ("Oliver Twist")	50	50
1437	60 c. Daisy Duck as The Marchioness ("Old Curiosity Shop")	55	55
1438	$1 Little Nell giving nosegay to her grandfather ("Little Nell")	85	85
1439	$2 Scrooge McDuck as Mr. Pickwick ("Pickwick Papers")	1·50	2·00
1440	$3 Minnie Mouse as Florence and Mickey Mouse as Paul ("Dombey and Son")	2·00	2·50
1441	$5 Minnie Mouse as Jenny Wren ("Our Mutual Friend")	2·75	3·25

1990. World Cup Football Championship Winners, Italy. Nos. 1308/11 optd **Winners West Germany 1 Argentina 0**.

1443	15 c. Type **252**	55	20
1444	25 c. Goalkeeper moving towards ball	55	20
1445	$1 Goalkeeper reaching for ball	1·40	1·40
1446	$4 Goalkeeper saving goal	3·25	4·50

271 Pearly-eyed Thrasher

1990. Birds. Multicoloured.

1448	10 c. Type **271**	30	30
1449	25 c. Purple-throated carib	35	35
1450	50 c. Yellowthroat	40	40
1451	60 c. American kestrel	70	70
1452	$1 Yellow-bellied sapsucker	80	80
1453	$2 Purple gallinule	1·75	2·00
1454	$3 Yellow-crowned night heron	2·10	2·50
1455	$4 Blue-hooded euphonia	2·10	2·50

272 "Madonna and Child with Saints" (detail, Sebastiano del Piombo)

1990. Christmas. Paintings by Renaissance Masters. Multicoloured.

1457	25 c. Type **272**	25	20
1458	30 c. "Virgin and Child with Angels" (detail, Grunewald) (vert)	30	20
1459	40 c. "The Holy Family and a Shepherd" (detail, Titian)	40	25
1460	60 c. "Virgin and Child" (detail, Lippi) (vert)	50	35
1461	$1 "Jesus, St. John and Two Angels" (Rubens)	70	60
1462	$2 "Adoration of the Shepherds" (detail, Vincenzo Catena)	1·40	1·60
1463	$4 "Adoration of the Magi" (detail, Giorgione)	2·50	3·00
1464	$5 "Virgin and Child adored by Warrior" (detail, Vincenzo Catena)	2·50	3·00

273 "Rape of the Daughters of Leucippus" (detail)

1991. 350th Death Anniv of Rubens. Mult.

1466	25 c. Type **273**	45	30
1467	45 c. "Bacchanal" (detail)	65	45
1468	50 c. "Rape of the Sabine Women" (detail)	70	50
1469	60 c. "Battle of the Amazons" (detail)	75	65
1470	$1 "Rape of the Sabine Women" (different detail)	1·00	1·00
1471	$2 "Bacchanal" (different detail)	1·50	1·75
1472	$3 "Rape of the Sabine Women" (different detail)	2·00	2·50
1473	$4 "Bacchanal" (different detail)	2·50	2·75

274 U.S. Troops cross into Germany, 1944

1991. 50th Anniv of Second World War. Mult.

1475	10 c. Type **274**	30	30
1476	15 c. Axis surrender in North Africa, 1943	35	25
1477	25 c. U.S. tanks invade Kwalajalein, 1944	40	40
1478	45 c. Roosevelt and Churchill meet at Casablanca, 1943	70	50
1479	50 c. Marshal Badoglio, Prime Minister of Italian anti-fascist government, 1943	60	50
1480	$1 Lord Mountbatten, Supreme Allied Commander South-east Asia, 1943	1·00	85
1481	$2 Greek victory at Koritza, 1940	1·75	2·00
1482	$4 Anglo-Soviet mutual assistance pact, 1941	2·50	2·75
1483	$5 Operation Torch landings, 1942	2·50	2·75

275 Locomotive "Prince Regent", Middleton Colliery, 1812

1991. Cog Railways. Multicoloured.

1485	25 c. Type **275**	60	30
1486	30 c. Snowdon Mountain Railway	60	35
1487	40 c. First railcar at Hell Gate, Manitou & Pike's Peak Railway, U.S.A.	65	45
1488	60 c. P.N.K.A. rack railway, Java	85	65
1489	$1 Green Mountain Railway, Maine, 1883	1·25	1·00
1490	$2 Rack locomotive "Pike's Peak", 1891	2·00	2·50
1491	$4 Vitznau–Rigi Railway, Switzerland, and Mt Rigi hotel local post stamp	3·25	3·50
1492	$5 Leopoldina Railway, Brazil	3·25	3·50

276 "Heliconius charithonia"

1991. Butterflies. Multicoloured.

1494	10 c. Type **276**	45	40
1495	35 c. "Marpesia petreus"	75	50
1496	50 c. "Anartia amathea"	80	60
1497	75 c. "Siproeta stelenes"	1·10	85
1498	$1 "Battus polydamas"	1·25	95
1499	$2 "Historis odius"	2·00	2·50
1500	$4 "Hypolimnas misippus"	3·25	3·50
1501	$5 "Hamadryas feronia"	3·25	3·50

277 Hanno the Phoenician, 450 B.C.

1991. 500th Anniv (1992) of Discovery of America by Columbus (4th issue). History of Exploration.

1503	10 c. Type **277**	30	30
1504	15 c. Pytheas the Greek, 325 B.C.	40	40
1505	45 c. Erik the Red discovering Greenland, 985 A.D.	70	50
1506	60 c. Leif Eriksson reaching Vinland, 1000 A.D.	75	60
1507	$1 Scylax the Greek in the Indian Ocean, 518 A.D.	1·00	75
1508	$2 Marco Polo sailing to the Orient, 1259 A.D.	1·75	2·00
1509	$4 Ship of Queen Hatshepsut of Egypt, 1493 B.C.	2·75	3·00
1510	$5 St. Brendan's coracle, 500 A.D.	2·75	3·00

278 "Camille Roulin" (Van Gogh)

1991. Death Centenary (1990) of Vincent van Gogh (artist). Multicoloured.

1512	5 c. Type **278**	20	20
1513	10 c. "Armand Roulin"	20	20
1514	15 c. "Young Peasant Woman with Straw Hat sitting in the Wheat"	30	30
1515	25 c. "Adeline Ravoux"	40	30
1516	30 c. "The Schoolboy"	40	40
1517	40 c. "Doctor Gachet"	45	40
1518	50 c. "Portrait of a Man"	55	40
1519	75 c. "Two Children"	75	60
1520	$2 "The Postman Joseph Roulin"	1·75	2·00
1521	$3 "The Seated Zouave"	2·25	2·50
1522	$4 "L'Arlesienne"	2·75	3·00
1523	"Self-Portrait, November/December 1888"	3·00	3·25

279 Mickey Mouse as Champion Sumo Wrestler

1991. "Philanippon '91" International Stamp Exhibition, Tokyo. Walt Disney cartoon characters participating in martial arts. Multicoloured.

1525	10 c. Type **279**	30	20
1526	15 c. Goofy using the tonfa (horiz)	40	25
1527	45 c. Donald Duck as a Ninja (horiz)	70	50
1528	60 c. Mickey armed for Kung fu	85	65
1529	$1 Goofy with Kendo sword	1·25	1·25
1530	$2 Mickey and Donald demonstrating Aikido (horiz)	1·75	2·00
1531	$4 Mickey and Donald in Judo bout (horiz)	2·75	3·00
1532	$5 Mickey performing Yabusame (mounted archery)	3·00	3·25

280 Queen Elizabeth and Prince Philip in 1976

1991. 65th Birthday of Queen Elizabeth II. Multicoloured.

1534	15 c. Type **280**	15	10
1535	20 c. The Queen and Prince Philip in Portugal, 1985	15	10
1536	$2 Queen Elizabeth II	1·25	1·50
1537	$4 The Queen and Prince Philip at Ascot, 1986	2·50	2·75

1991. 10th Wedding Anniv of Prince and Princess of Wales. As T **280**. Multicoloured.

1539	10 c. Prince and Princess of Wales at party, 1986	20	10
1540	40 c. Separate portraits of Prince, Princess and sons	40	25
1541	$1 Prince Henry and Prince William	80	70
1542	$5 Princess Diana in Australia and Prince Charles in Hungary	3·25	3·75

281 Daisy Duck teeing-off

1991. Golf. Walt Disney cartoon characters. Mult.

1544	10 c. Type **281**	40	40
1545	15 c. Goofy playing ball from under trees	50	40
1546	45 c. Mickey Mouse playing deflected shot	80	50
1547	60 c. Mickey hacking divot out of fairway	1·00	65
1548	$1 Donald Duck playing ball out of pond	1·25	1·10
1549	$2 Minnie Mouse hitting ball over pond	2·25	2·50
1550	$4 Donald in a bunker	3·00	3·25
1551	$5 Goofy trying snooker shot into hole	3·00	3·25

282 Moose receiving Gold Medal

1991. 50th Anniv of Archie Comics, and Olympic Games, Barcelona (1992) (2nd issue). Multicoloured.

1553	10 c. Type **282**	30	30
1554	25 c. Archie playing polo on a motorcycle (horiz)	40	30
1555	40 c. Archie and Betty at fencing class	70	45
1556	60 c. Archie joining girls' volleyball team	80	65
1557	$1 Archie with tennis ball in his mouth	1·00	1·00
1558	$2 Archie running marathon	2·00	2·25
1559	$4 Archie judging women's gymnastics (horiz)	3·50	3·75
1560	$5 Archie watching the cheer-leaders	3·50	3·75

283 Presidents De Gaulle and Kennedy, 1961

1991. Birth Centenary of Charles de Gaulle (French statesman). Multicoloured.

1562 10 c. Type **283** 40 30
1563 15 c. General De Gaulle with President Roosevelt, 1945 (vert) 40 30
1564 45 c. President De Gaulle with Chancellor Adenauer, 1962 (vert) 70 40
1565 60 c. De Gaulle at Arc de Triomphe, Liberation of Paris, 1944 (vert) 80 65
1566 $1 General De Gaulle crossing the Rhine, 1945 . . . . . 1·00 1·00
1567 $2 General De Gaulle in Algiers, 1944 . . . . . 1·75 2·00
1568 $4 Presidents De Gaulle and Eisenhower, 1960 . . . . . 2·75 3·00
1569 $5 De Gaulle returning from Germany, 1968 (vert) . . . 3·00 3·25

284 Parliament Building and Map

1991. 10th Anniv of Independence.

1571 **284** 10 c. multicoloured . . . 40 40

300th ANNIVERSARY OF BRANDENBURG GATE
285 Germans celebrating Reunification

1991. Anniversaries and Events. Multicoloured.

1573 25 c. Type **285** 30 30
1574 75 c. Cubs erecting tent . . . 50 50
1575 $1.50 "Don Giovanni" and Mozart . . . . 1·75 1·75
1576 $2 Chariot driver and Gate at night . . . . 1·10 1·10
1577 $2 Lord Baden-Powell and members of 3rd Antigua Methodist cub pack (vert) . 1·25 1·25
1578 $2 Lilienthal's signature and glider "Flugzeug Nr. 5" . 2·25 2·25
1579 $2.50 Driver in Class P36 steam locomotive (vert) . . . . . 2·25 2·25
1580 $3 Statues from podium . . . 1·75 1·75
1581 $3.50 Cubs and camp fire . . 1·90 1·90
1582 $4 St. Peter's Cathedral, Salzburg . . . . 2·75 2·75

ANNIVERSARIES AND EVENTS: Nos. 1573, 1576, 1580, Bicentenary of Brandenburg Gate, Germany; 1574, 1577, 1581, 17th World Scout Jamboree, Korea; 1575, 1582, Death bicentenary of Mozart (composer); 1578, Centenary of Otto Lilienthal's gliding experiments; 1579, Centenary of Trans-Siberian Railway.

286 "Nimitz" Class Carrier and "Ticonderoga" Class Cruiser

1991. 50th Anniv of Japanese Attack on Pearl Harbor. Multicoloured.

1585 $1 Type **286** . . . . 1·00 1·00
1586 $1 Tourist launch . . . . . 1·00 1·00
1587 $1 U.S.S. "Arizona" memorial 1·00 1·00
1588 $1 Wreaths on water and aircraft . . . . 1·00 1·00
1589 $1 White tern . . . . 1·00 1·00
1590 $1 Mitsubishi A6M Zero-Sen fighters over Pearl City . 1·00 1·00
1591 $1 Mitsubishi A6M Zero-Sen fighters attacking . . . . 1·00 1·00
1592 $1 Battleship Row in flames . 1·00 1·00
1593 $1 U.S.S. "Nevada" (battleship) underway . . . . 1·00 1·00
1594 $1 Mitsubishi A6M Zero-Sen fighters returning to carriers 1·00 1·00

287 "The Annunciation"

1991. Christmas. Religious Paintings by Fra Angelico. Multicoloured.

1595 10 c. Type **287** 20 20
1596 30 c. "Nativity" 35 25
1597 40 c. "Adoration of the Magi" 40 30
1598 60 c. "Presentation in the Temple" 55 45
1599 $1 "Circumcision" 75 65
1600 $3 "Flight into Egypt" . . . 2·25 2·75
1601 $4 "Massacre of the Innocents" 2·50 3·00
1602 $5 "Christ teaching in the Temple" . . . . 2·50 3·00

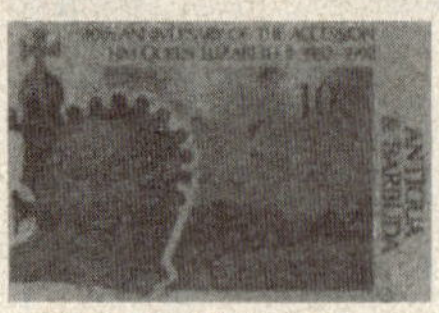
288 Queen Elizabeth II and Bird Sanctuary

1992. 40th Anniv of Queen Elizabeth II's Accession. Multicoloured.

1604 10 c. Type **288** 40 30
1605 30 c. Nelson's Dockyard . . 50 30
1606 $1 Ruins on Shirley Heights 80 70
1607 $5 Beach and palm trees . . 2·50 3·50

289 Mickey Mouse awarding Swimming Gold Medal to Mermaid

1992. Olympic Games, Barcelona (3rd issue). Walt Disney cartoon characters. Multicoloured.

1609 10 c. Type **289** 20 20
1610 15 c. Huey, Dewey and Louie with kayak 25 25
1611 30 c. Donald Duck and Uncle Scrooge in yacht 35 35
1612 50 c. Donald and horse playing water polo 50 50
1613 $1 Big Pete weightlifting . . . 80 80
1614 $2 Donald and Goofy fencing 1·40 1·40
1615 $4 Mickey and Donald playing volleyball . . . . 2·50 2·50
1616 $5 Goofy vaulting . . . . . 2·50 2·50

290 Pteranodon

1992. Prehistoric Animals. Mult.

1618 10 c. Type **290** 40 30
1619 15 c. Brachiosaurus 45 30
1620 30 c. Tyrannosaurus Rex . . . 55 35
1621 50 c. Parasaurolophus . . . 65 50
1622 $1 Deinonychus (horiz) . . . 1·00 1·00
1623 $2 Triceratops (horiz) . . . 1·75 1·75
1624 $4 Protoceratops hatching (horiz) . . . . 2·25 2·50
1625 $5 Stegosaurus (horiz) . . . 2·25 2·50

291 "Supper at Emmaus" (Caravaggio)

1992. Easter. Religious Paintings. Multicoloured.

1627 10 c. Type **291** 25 25
1628 15 c. "The Vision of St. Peter" (Zurbaran) 35 25
1629 30 c. "Christ driving the Money-changers from the Temple" (Tiepolo) 55 40
1630 40 c. "Martyrdom of St. Bartholomew" (detail) (Ribera) 65 50
1631 $1 "Christ driving the Money-changers from the Temple" (detail) (Tiepolo) . . . . 1·00 1·00
1632 $2 "Crucifixion" (detail" (Altdorfer) . . . . 2·00 2·25
1633 $4 "The Deposition" (detail) (Fra Angelico) . . . . . 3·00 3·25
1634 $5 "The Deposition" (different detail) (Fra Angelico) . . 3·00 3·25

292 "The Miracle at the Well" (Alonso Cano)

1992. "Granada '92" International Stamp Exhibition, Spain. Spanish Paintings. Multicoloured.

1636 10 c. Type **292** 30 30
1637 15 c. "The Poet Luis de Goingora y Argote" (Velazquez) 40 30
1638 30 c. "The Painter Francisco Goya" (Vicente Lopez Portana) 55 40
1639 40 c. "Maria de las Nieves Michaela Fourdinier" (Luis Paret y Alcazar) 65 50
1640 $1 "Carlos III eating before his Court" (Alcazar) (horiz) . . 1·00 1·00
1641 $2 "Rain Shower in Granada" (Antonio Munoz Degrain) (horiz) . . . . 1·50 1·75
1642 $4 "Sarah Bernhardt" (Santiago Rusinol i Prats) . . . . . 2·50 2·75
1643 $5 "The Hermitage Garden" (Joaquim Mir Trinxet) . . 2·75 3·00

293 "Amanita caesarea"

1992. Fungi. Multicoloured.

1645 10 c. Type **293** 50 40
1646 15 c. "Collybia fusipes" . . . 60 40
1647 30 c. "Boletus aereus" . . . 80 40
1648 40 c. "Laccaria amethystina" 90 50
1649 $1 "Russula virescens" . . . 1·50 1·25
1650 $2 "Tricholoma equestre" ("Tricholoma auratum") . 2·25 2·50
1651 $4 "Calocybe gambosa" . . . 3·25 3·50
1652 $5 "Lentinus tigrinus" ("Panus tigrinus") . . . . 3·25 3·50

294 Memorial Cross and Huts, San Salvador

1992. 500th Anniv of Discovery of America by Columbus (5th issue). World Columbian Stamp "Expo '92", Chicago. Multicoloured.

1654 15 c. Type **294** 20 20
1655 30 c. Martin Pinzon with telescope 35 25
1656 40 c. Christopher Columbus . 45 35
1657 $1 "Pinta" . . . . 1·00 1·00
1658 $2 "Nina" . . . . 1·60 1·75
1659 $4 "Santa Maria" . . . . . . 2·50 2·75

295 Antillean Crested Hummingbird and Wild Plantain

1992. "Genova '92" International Thematic Stamp Exhibition. Hummingbirds and Plants. Multicoloured.

1661 10 c. Type **295** 20 20
1662 25 c. Green mango and parrot's plantain 30 30
1663 45 c. Purple-throated carib and lobster claws 45 45
1664 60 c. Antillean mango and coral plant 55 55
1665 $1 Vervain hummingbird and cardinal's guard 85 85
1666 $2 Rufous-breasted hermit and heliconia . . . . 1·50 1·50
1667 $4 Blue-headed hummingbird and red ginger . . . . . . 2·75 2·75
1668 $5 Green-throated carib and ornamental banana . . . . 3·00 3·00

296 Columbus meeting Amerindians

1992. 500th Anniv of Discovery of America by Columbus (6th issue). Organization of East Caribbean States. Multicoloured.

1670 $1 Type **296** 65 65
1671 $2 Ships approaching island . 1·25 1·25

297 Ts'ai Lun and Paper

1992. Inventors and Inventions. Mult.

1672 10 c. Type **297** 15 15
1673 25 c. Igor Sikorsky and "Bolshoi Baltiskii" (first four-engined airplane) 40 40
1674 30 c. Alexander Graham Bell and early telephone 45 45
1675 40 c. Johannes Gutenberg and early printing press 45 45
1676 60 c. James Watt and stationary steam engine . . . . 1·00 1·00
1677 $1 Anton van Leeuwenhoek and early microscope . . . . . 1·10 1·10
1678 $4 Louis Braille and hands reading braille . . . . . . 3·00 3·00
1679 $5 Galileo and telescope . . 3·25 3·25

298 Elvis looking Pensive

1992. 15th Death Anniv of Elvis Presley. Multicoloured.

1681 $1 Type **298** 95 95
1682 $1 Wearing black and yellow striped shirt 95 95
1683 $1 Singing into microphone . 95 95
1684 $1 Wearing wide-brimmed hat 95 95
1685 $1 With microphone in right hand 95 95
1686 $1 In Army uniform 95 95
1687 $1 Wearing pink shirt . . . 95 95
1688 $1 In yellow shirt 95 95
1689 $1 In jacket and bow tie . . 95 95

300 "Virgin and Child with Angels" (detail) (School of Piero della Francesca)

301 Russian Cosmonauts

1992. Christmas. Details of the Holy Child from various paintings. Multicoloured.

1691 10 c. Type **300** 15 15
1692 25 c. "Madonna degli Alberelli" (Giovanni Bellini) 20 15
1693 30 c. "Madonna and Child with St. Anthony Abbot and St. Sigismund" (Neroccio) . 30 20
1694 40 c. "Madonna and the Grand Duke" (Raphael) 40 30
1695 60 c. "The Nativity" (Georges de la Tour) 60 60
1696 $1 "Holy Family" (Jacob Jordaens) 85 85
1697 $4 "Madonna and Child Enthroned" (Magaritone) . 3·00 3·25
1698 $5 "Madonna and Child on a Curved Throne" (Byzantine school) . . . . 3·25 3·50

1992. Anniversaries and Events. Mult.

1700	10 c. Type **301**	40	40
1701	40 c. "Graf Zeppelin" (airship), 1929	70	55
1702	45 c. Bishop Daniel Davis	50	40
1703	75 c. Konrad Adenauer making speech	65	65
1704	$1 Bus Mosbacher and "Weatherly" (yacht)	1·00	1·00
1705	$1.50 Rain forest	1·10	1·10
1706	$2 Tiger	3·00	3·00
1707	$2 National flag, plant and emblem (horiz)	1·75	1·75
1708	$2 Members of Community Players company (horiz)	1·75	1·75
1709	$2.25 Women carrying pots	1·75	1·75
1710	$3 Lions Club emblem	2·00	2·00
1711	$4 Chinese rocket on launch tower	2·00	2·00
1712	$4 West German and N.A.T.O. flags	2·00	2·00
1713	$6 Hugo Eckener (airship pioneer)	3·00	3·00

ANNIVERSARIES AND EVENTS: Nos. 1700, 1711, International Space Year; Nos. 1701, 1713, 75th death anniv of Count Ferdinand von Zeppelin; No. 1702, 150th anniv of Anglican Diocese of North-eastern Caribbean and Aruba; Nos. 1703, 1712, 25th death anniv of Konrad Adenauer (German statesman); No. 1704, Americas Cup yachting championship; Nos. 1705/6, Earth Summit '92, Rio; No. 1707, 50th anniv of Inter-American Institute for Agricultural Co-operation; No. 1708, 40th anniv of Cultural Development; No. 1709, United Nations World Health Organization Projects; No. 1710, 75th anniv of International Association of Lions Clubs.

302 Boy Hiker resting

304 Cardinal's Guard

303 Goofy playing Golf

1993. Hummel Figurines. Multicoloured.

1715	15 c. Type **302**	15	15
1716	30 c. Girl sitting on fence	25	25
1717	40 c. Boy hunter	35	35
1718	50 c. Boy with umbrella	45	45
1719	$1 Hikers at signpost	75	75
1720	$2 Boy hiker with pack and stick	1·40	1·40
1721	$4 Girl with young child and goat	2·50	2·50
1722	$5 Boy whistling	2·75	2·75

1993. Opening of Euro-Disney Resort, Paris. Multicoloured.

1724	10 c. Type **303**	40	30
1725	25 c. Chip and Dale at Davy Crockett's campground	50	30
1726	30 c. Donald Duck at the Cheyenne Hotel	50	35
1727	40 c. Goofy at the Santa Fe Hotel	55	35
1728	$1 Mickey and Minnie Mouse at the New York Hotel	90	80
1729	$2 Mickey, Minnie and Goofy in car	1·60	1·75
1730	$4 Goofy at Pirates of the Caribbean	2·75	3·25
1731	$5 Donald at Adventureland	2·75	3·25

1993. Flowers. Multicoloured.

1733	15 c. Type **304**	35	30
1734	25 c. Giant granadilla	40	30
1735	30 c. Spider flower	40	35
1736	40 c. Gold vine	45	35
1737	$1 Frangipani	80	80
1738	$2 Bougainvillea	1·40	1·40
1739	$4 Yellow oleander	2·50	2·50
1740	$5 Spicy jatropha	2·50	2·50

305 "The Destiny of Marie de' Medici" (upper detail)

1993. Bicentenary of the Louvre, Paris. Paintings by Peter Paul Rubens. Mult.

1742	$1 Type **305**	60	60
1743	$1 "The Birth of Marie de' Medici"	60	60
1744	$1 "The Education of Marie de' Medici"	60	60
1745	$1 "The Destiny of Marie de' Medici" (lower detail)	60	60
1746	$1 "Henry VI receiving the Portrait of Marie"	60	60
1747	$1 "The Meeting of the King and Marie at Lyons"	60	60
1748	$1 "The Marriage by Proxy"	60	60
1749	$1 "The Birth of Louis XIII"	60	60
1750	$1 "The Capture of Juliers"	60	60
1751	$1 "The Exchange of the Princesses"	60	60
1752	$1 "The Regency"	60	60
1753	$1 "The Majority of Louis XIII"	60	60
1754	$1 "The Flight from Blois"	60	60
1755	$1 "The Treaty of Angouleme"	60	60
1756	$1 "The Peace of Angers"	60	60
1757	$1 "The Reconciliation of Louis and Marie de' Medici"	60	60

Nos. 1742/57 depict details from "The Story of Marie de' Medici".

306 St. Lucia Amazon

1993. Endangered Species. Multicoloured.

1759	$1 Type **306**	70	70
1760	$1 Cahow	70	70
1761	$1 Swallow-tailed kite	70	70
1762	$1 Everglade kite	70	70
1763	$1 Imperial amazon	70	70
1764	$1 Humpback whale	70	70
1765	$1 Plain pigeon	70	70
1766	$1 St. Vincent amazon	70	70
1767	$1 Puerto Rican amazon	70	70
1768	$1 Leatherback turtle	70	70
1769	$1 American crocodile	70	70
1770	$1 Hawksbill turtle	70	70

Nos. 1759/70 were printed together, se-tenant, with the background forming a composite design.

307 Queen Elizabeth II at Coronation (photograph by Cecil Beaton)

1993. 40th Anniv of Coronation (1st issue).

1772	**307**	30 c. multicoloured	50	50
1773	–	40 c. multicoloured	60	60
1774	–	$2 blue and black	1·50	1·75
1775	–	$4 multicoloured	1·90	2·00

DESIGNS: 40 c. Queen Elizabeth the Queen Mother's Crown, 1937; $2 Procession of heralds; $4 Queen Elizabeth II and Prince Edward.

308 Princess Margaret and Antony Armstrong-Jones

1993. 40th Anniv of Coronation (2nd issue).

1777/1808	$1 x 32 either grey and black or multicoloured	18·00	20·00

DESIGNS: Various views as T **308** from each decade of the reign.

309 Edward Stanley Gibbons and Catalogue of 1865

1993. Famous Professional Philatelists (1st series).

1809	**309**	$1.50 brown, blk & grn	1·10	1·10
1810	–	$1.50 multicoloured	1·10	1·10
1811	–	$1.50 multicoloured	1·10	1·10
1812	–	$1.50 multicoloured	1·10	1·10
1813	–	$1.50 multicoloured	1·10	1·10
1814	–	$1.50 multicoloured	1·10	1·10

DESIGNS: No. 1810, Theodore Champion and France 1849 1 f. stamp; No. 1811, J. Walter Scott and U.S.A. 1918 24 c. "Inverted Jenny" error; No. 1812, Hugo Michel and Bavaria 1849 1 k. stamp; No. 1813, Alberto and Giulio Bolaffi with Sardinia 1851 5 c. stamp; No. 1814, Richard Borek and Brunswick 1865 1 gr. stamp.

See also No. 1957.

310 Paul Gascoigne

311 Grand Inspector W. Heath

1993. World Cup Football Championship, U.S.A. (1st issue). English Players. Multicoloured.

1816	$2 Type **310**	1·40	1·40
1817	$2 David Platt	1·40	1·40
1818	$2 Martin Peters	1·40	1·40
1819	$2 John Barnes	1·40	1·40
1820	$2 Gary Lineker	1·40	1·40
1821	$2 Geoff Hurst	1·40	1·40
1822	$2 Bobby Charlton	1·40	1·40
1823	$2 Bryan Robson	1·40	1·40
1824	$2 Bobby Moore	1·40	1·40
1825	$2 Nobby Stiles	1·40	1·40
1826	$2 Gordon Banks	1·40	1·40
1827	$2 Peter Shilton	1·40	1·40

See also Nos. 2039/44.

1993. Anniversaries and Events. Mult.

1829	10 c. Type **311**	30	30
1830	15 c. Rodnina and Oulanov (U.S.S.R.) (pairs figure skating) (horiz)	30	30
1831	30 c. Present Masonic Hall, St. John's (horiz)	50	50
1832	30 c. Willy Brandt with Helmut Schmidt and George Leber (horiz)	30	30
1833	30 c. "Cat and Bird" (Picasso) (horiz)	40	40
1834	40 c. Previous Masonic Hall, St. John's (horiz)	50	50
1835	40 c. "Fish on a Newspaper" (Picasso) (horiz)	40	40
1836	40 c. Early astronomical equipment	40	40
1837	40 c. Prince Naruhito and engagement photographs (horiz)	40	40
1838	60 c. Grand Inspector J. Jeffery	60	60
1839	$1 "Woman combing her Hair" (W. Slewinski) (horiz)	70	70
1840	$3 Masako Owada and engagement photographs (horiz)	1·75	1·75
1841	$3 "Artist's Wife with Cat" (Konrad Kryzanowski) (horiz)	1·75	1·75
1842	$4 Willy Brandt and protest march (horiz)	2·25	2·40
1843	$4 Galaxy	2·25	2·40
1844	$5 Alberto Tomba (Italy) (giant slalom) (horiz)	2·25	2·40
1845	$5 "Dying Bull" (Picasso) (horiz)	2·25	2·40
1846	$5 Pres. Clinton and family (horiz)	2·25	2·40

ANNIVERSARIES AND EVENTS: Nos. 1829, 1831, 1834, 1838, 150th anniv of St. John's Masonic Lodge No. 492; Nos. 1830, 1844, Winter Olympic Games '94, Lillehammer; Nos. 1832, 1842, 80th birth anniv of Willy Brandt (German politician); Nos. 1833, 1835, 1845, 20th death anniv of Picasso (artist); Nos. 1836, 1843, 450th death anniv of Copernicus (astronomer); Nos. 1837, 1840, Marriage of Crown Prince Naruhito of Japan; Nos. 1839, 1841, "Polska '93" International Stamp Exhibition, Poznan; No. 1846 Inauguration of U.S. President William Clinton.

312 Hugo Eckener and Dr. W. Beckers with Airship "Graf Zeppelin" over Lake George, New York

1993. Aviation Anniversaries. Multicoloured.

1848	30 c. Type **312**	55	55
1849	40 c. Chicago World's Fair from "Graf Zeppelin"	65	65
1850	40 c. Gloster Whittle E.28/39, 1941	65	65
1851	40 c. George Washington writing balloon mail letter (vert)	65	65
1852	$4 Pres. Wilson and Curtiss JN-4 Jenny	3·00	3·00
1853	$5 Airship "Hindenburg" over Ebbets Field baseball stadium, 1937	3·00	3·00
1854	$5 Gloster Meteor in dogfight	3·00	3·00

ANNIVERSARIES: Nos. 1848/9, 1853, 125th birth anniv of Hugo Eckener (airship commander); Nos. 1850, 1854, 75th anniv of Royal Air Force; Nos. 1851/2, Bicentenary of first airmail flight.

313 Lincoln Continental

1993. Centenaries of Henry Ford's First Petrol Engine (Nos. 1856, 1858,) and Karl Benz's First Four-wheeled Car (others). Multicoloured.

1856	30 c. Type **313**	60	60
1857	40 c. Mercedes racing car, 1914	65	65
1858	$4 Ford "GT40", 1966	3·25	3·25
1859	$5 Mercedes Benz "gull-wing" coupe, 1954	3·25	3·25

314 "The Musical Farmer", 1932

1993. Mickey Mouse Film Posters. Mult.

1861	10 c. Type **314**	40	30
1862	15 c. "Little Whirlwind", 1941	45	35
1863	30 c. "Pluto's Dream House", 1940	55	40
1864	40 c. "Gulliver Mickey", 1934	55	40
1865	50 c. "Alpine Climbers", 1936	55	45
1866	$1 "Mr. Mouse Takes a Trip", 1940	90	80
1867	$2 "The Nifty Nineties", 1941	1·50	1·75
1868	$4 "Mickey Down Under", 1948	2·25	2·75
1869	$5 "The Pointer", 1939	2·25	2·75

315 Marie and Fritz with Christmas Tree

1993. Christmas. Mickey's Nutcracker. Walt Disney cartoon characters in scenes from "The Nutcracker". Multicoloured.

1871	10 c. Type **315**	40	30
1872	15 c. Marie receives Nutcracker from Godfather Drosselmeir	40	30
1873	20 c. Fritz breaks Nutcracker	45	30
1874	30 c. Nutcracker with sword	50	30
1875	40 c. Nutcracker and Marie in the snow	55	30
1876	50 c. Marie and the Prince meet Sugar Plum Fairy	60	40
1877	60 c. Marie and Prince in Crystal Hall	60	50
1878	$3 Huey, Dewey and Louie as Cossack dancers	2·25	2·50
1879	$6 Mother Ginger and her puppets	3·50	4·00

316 "Hannah and Samuel" (Rembrandt)

1993. Famous Paintings by Rembrandt and Matisse. Multicoloured.

1881	15 c. Type **316**	30	30
1882	15 c. "Guitarist" (Matisse)	30	30
1883	30 c. "The Jewish Bride" (Rembrandt)	40	30
1884	40 c. "Jacob wrestling with the Angel" (Rembrandt)	50	30
1885	60 c. "Interior with a Goldfish Bowl" (Matisse)	70	50
1886	$1 "Mlle Yvonne Landsberg" (Matisse)	1·00	80
1887	$4 "The Toboggan" (Matisse)	2·75	3·25
1888	$5 "Moses with the Tablets of the Law" (Rembrandt)	2·75	3·25

317 Hong Kong 1981 $1 Golden Threadfin Bream Stamp and Fishing Boats, Shau Kei Wan

1994. "Hong Kong '94" International Stamp Exhibition (1st issue). Multicoloured.

1890	40 c. Type **317**	35	45
1891	40 c. Antigua 1990 $2 Rock beauty stamp and fishing boats, Shau Kei Wan	35	45

Nos. 1890/1 were printed together, se-tenant, forming a composite design.

See also Nos. 1892/7 and 1898/1905.

318 Terracotta Warriors

1994. "Hong Kong '94" International Stamp Exhibition (2nd issue). Qin Dynasty Terracotta Figures. Multicoloured.

1892	40 c. Type **318**	40	40
1893	40 c. Cavalryman and horse	40	40
1894	40 c. Warriors in armour	40	40
1895	40 c. Painted bronze chariot and team	40	40
1896	40 c. Pekingese dog	40	40
1897	40 c. Warriors with horses	40	40

319 Mickey Mouse in Junk

320 Sumatran Rhinoceros lying down

1994. "Hong Kong '94" International Stamp Exhibition (3rd issue). Walt Disney cartoon characters. Multicoloured.

1898	10 c. Type **319**	30	30
1899	15 c. Minnie Mouse as mandarin	35	35
1900	30 c. Donald and Daisy Duck on house boat	45	45
1901	50 c. Mickey holding bird in cage	60	60
1902	$1 Pluto and ornamental dog	90	90
1903	$2 Minnie and Daisy celebrating Bun Festival	1·50	1·75
1904	$4 Goofy making noodles	2·50	2·75
1905	$5 Goofy pulling Mickey in rickshaw	2·50	2·75

1994. Centenary (1992) of Sierra Club (environmental protection society). Endangered Species. Multicoloured.

1907	$1.50 Type **320**	1·00	1·00
1908	$1.50 Sumatran rhinoceros feeding	1·00	1·00
1909	$1.50 Ring-tailed lemur on ground	1·00	1·00
1910	$1.50 Ring-tailed lemur on branch	1·00	1·00
1911	$1.50 Red-fronted brown lemur on branch	1·00	1·00
1912	$1.50 Head of red-fronted brown lemur	1·00	1·00
1913	$1.50 Head of red-fronted brown lemur in front of trunk	1·00	1·00
1914	$1.50 Sierra Club Centennial emblem	80	80
1915	$1.50 Head of Bactrian camel	1·00	1·00
1916	$1.50 Bactrian camel	1·00	1·00
1917	$1.50 African elephant drinking	1·00	1·00
1918	$1.50 Head of African elephant	1·00	1·00
1919	$1.50 Leopard sitting upright	1·00	1·00
1920	$1.50 Leopard in grass (emblem at right)	1·00	1·00
1921	$1.50 Leopard in grass (emblem at left)	1·00	1·00

321 West Highland White Terrier

1994. Dogs of the World. Chinese New Year ("Year of the Dog"). Multicoloured.

1923	50 c. Type **321**	40	40
1924	50 c. Beagle	40	40
1925	50 c. Scottish terrier	40	40
1926	50 c. Pekingese	40	40
1927	50 c. Dachshund	40	40
1928	50 c. Yorkshire terrier	40	40
1929	50 c. Pomeranian	40	40
1930	50 c. Poodle	40	40
1931	50 c. Shetland sheepdog	40	40
1932	50 c. Pug	40	40
1933	50 c. Shih Tzu	40	40
1934	50 c. Chihuahua	40	40
1935	75 c. Mastiff	45	45
1936	75 c. Border collie	45	45
1937	75 c. Samoyed	45	45
1938	75 c. Airedale terrier	45	45
1939	75 c. English setter	45	45
1940	75 c. Rough collie	45	45
1941	75 c. Newfoundland	45	45
1942	75 c. Weimarana	45	45
1943	75 c. English springer spaniel	45	45
1944	75 c. Dalmatian	45	45
1945	75 c. Boxer	45	45
1946	75 c. Old English sheepdog	45	45

322 "Spiranthes lanceolata"

323 Hermann E. Sieger, Germany 1931 1 m. Zeppelin Stamp and Airship LZ-127 "Graf Zeppelin"

1994. Orchids. Multicoloured.

1948	10 c. Type **322**	30	30
1949	20 c. "Ionopsis utricularioides"	40	40
1950	30 c. "Tetramicra canaliculata"	50	50
1951	50 c. "Oncidium picturatum"	65	65
1952	$1 "Epidendrum difforme"	90	90
1953	$2 "Epidendrum ciliare"	1·50	1·75
1954	$4 "Epidendrum ibaguense"	2·50	2·75
1955	$5 "Epidendrum nocturnum"	2·50	2·75

1994. Famous Professional Philatelists (2nd series).

1957	**323**	$1.50 multicoloured	90	90

324 "Danaus plexippus"

325 Bottlenose Dolphin

1994. Butterflies. Multicoloured.

1958	10 c. Type **324**	30	30
1959	15 c. "Appias drusilla"	35	35
1960	30 c. "Eurema lisa"	50	50
1961	40 c. "Anaea troglodyta"	60	60
1962	$1 "Urbanus proteus"	90	90
1963	$2 "Junonia evarete"	1·50	1·75
1964	$4 "Battus polydamas"	2·50	2·75
1965	$5 "Heliconius charitonia"	2·50	2·75

No. 1959 is inscribed "Appisa drusilla" and No. 1965 "Heliconius charitonius", both in error.

1994. Marine Life. Multicoloured.

1967	50 c. Type **325**	45	45
1968	50 c. Killer whale	45	45
1969	50 c. Spinner dolphin	45	45
1970	50 c. Oceanic sunfish	45	45
1971	50 c. Caribbean reef shark and short fin pilot whale	45	45
1972	50 c. Copper-banded butterflyfish	45	45
1973	50 c. Mosaic moray	45	45
1974	50 c. Clown triggerfish	45	45
1975	50 c. Red lobster	45	45

326 Edwin Aldrin (astronaut)

1994. 25th Anniv of First Manned Moon Landing. Multicoloured.

1977	$1.50 Type **326**	1·25	1·25
1978	$1.50 First lunar footprint	1·25	1·25
1979	$1.50 Neil Armstrong (astronaut)	1·25	1·25
1980	$1.50 Aldrin stepping onto Moon	1·25	1·25
1981	$1.50 Aldrin and equipment	1·25	1·25
1982	$1.50 Aldrin and U.S.A. flag	1·25	1·25
1983	$1.50 Aldrin at Tranquility Base	1·25	1·25
1984	$1.50 Moon plaque	1·25	1·25
1985	$1.50 "Eagle" leaving Moon	1·25	1·25
1986	$1.50 Command module in lunar orbit	1·25	1·25
1987	$1.50 First day cover of U.S.A. 1969 10 c. First Man on Moon stamp	1·25	1·25
1988	$1.50 Pres. Nixon and astronauts	1·25	1·25

327 Edwin Moses (U.S.A.) (400 metres hurdles, 1984)

1994. Centenary of International Olympic Committee. Gold Medal Winners. Multicoloured.

1990	50 c. Type **327**	30	30
1991	$1.50 Steffi Graf (Germany) (tennis, 1988)	1·10	1·10

328 Antiguan Family

1994. International Year of the Family.

1993	**328**	90 c. multicoloured	40	45

329 Mike Atherton (England) and Wisden Trophy

1994. Centenary (1995) of First English Cricket Tour to the West Indies. Multicoloured.

1994	35 c. Type **329**	40	30
1995	75 c. Viv Richards (West Indies) (vert)	70	60
1996	$1.20 Richie Richardson (West Indies) and Wisden Trophy	1·00	1·25

330 Entrance Bridge, Songgwangsa Temple

1994. "Philakorea '94" International Stamp Exhibition, Seoul. Multicoloured.

1998	40 c. Type **330**	30	30
1999	75 c. Long-necked bottle	50	50
2000	75 c. Punch'ong ware jar with floral decoration	50	50
2001	75 c. Punch'ong ware jar with blue dragon pattern	50	50
2002	75 c. Ewer in shape of bamboo shoot	50	50
2003	75 c. Punch'ong ware green jar	50	50
2004	75 c. Pear-shaped bottle	50	50
2005	75 c. Porcelain jar with brown dragon pattern	50	50
2006	75 c. Porcelain jar with floral pattern	50	50
2007	90 c. Song-op Folk Village, Cheju	50	55
2008	$3 Port Sogwipo	1·75	2·00

331 Short S.25 Sunderland (flying boat)

1994. 50th Anniv of D-Day. Multicoloured.

2010	40 c. Type **331**	40	30
2011	$2 Lockheed P-38 Lightnings fighters attacking train	1·40	1·60
2012	$3 Martin B-26 Marauders bombers	1·90	2·00

332 Travis Tritt

1994. Stars of Country and Western Music. Multicoloured.

2014	75 c. Type **332**	40	40
2015	75 c. Dwight Yoakam	40	40
2016	75 c. Billy Ray Cyrus	40	40
2017	75 c. Alan Jackson	40	40
2018	75 c. Garth Brooks	40	40
2019	75 c. Vince Gill	40	40
2020	75 c. Clint Black	40	40
2021	75 c. Eddie Rabbit	40	40
2022	75 c. Patsy Cline	40	40
2023	75 c. Tanya Tucker	40	40
2024	75 c. Dolly Parton	40	40
2025	75 c. Anne Murray	40	40
2026	75 c. Tammy Wynette	40	40
2027	75 c. Loretta Lynn	40	40
2028	75 c. Reba McEntire	40	40
2029	75 c. Skeeter Davis	40	40
2030	75 c. Hank Snow	40	40
2031	75 c. Gene Autry	40	40
2032	75 c. Jimmie Rodgers	40	40
2033	75 c. Ernest Tubb	40	40
2034	75 c. Eddy Arnold	40	40
2035	75 c. Willie Nelson	40	40
2036	75 c. Johnny Cash	40	40
2037	75 c. George Jones	40	40

333 Hugo Sanchez (Mexico)

1994. World Cup Football Championship, U.S.A. (2nd issue). Multicoloured.

2039	15 c. Type **333**	40	30
2040	35 c. Jurgen Klinsmann (Germany)	60	30
2041	65 c. Antiguan player	80	55
2042	$1.20 Cobi Jones (U.S.A.)	1·25	1·25
2043	$4 Roberto Baggio (Italy)	2·50	2·75
2044	$5 Bwalya Kalusha (Zambia)	2·50	2·75

No. 2040 is inscribed "Klinsman" in error.

334 Sir Shridath Ramphal

1994. 1st Recipients of Order of the Caribbean Community. Multicoloured.

2046	65 c. Type **334**	50	40
2047	90 c. William Demas	65	60
2048	$1.20 Derek Walcott	85	90

335 Pair of Magnificent Frigate Birds

1994. Birds. Multicoloured.

2049	10 c. Type **335**	30	30
2050	15 c. Bridled quail dove	35	35
2051	30 c. Magnificent frigate bird chick hatching	55	55
2052	40 c. Purple-throated carib (vert)	55	55
2053	$1 Male magnificent frigate bird in courtship display (vert)	90	90
2054	$1 Broad-winged hawk (vert)	90	90
2055	$3 Young magnificent frigate bird	2·00	2·50
2056	$4 Yellow warbler	2·00	2·50

Nos. 2049, 2051, 2053 and 2055 also show the W.W.F. Panda emblem.

336 "The Virgin and Child by the Fireside" (Robert Campin)

337 Magnificent Frigate Bird

1994. Christmas. Religious Paintings. Multicoloured.

2058	15 c. Type **336**	30	20
2059	35 c. "The Reading Madonna" (Giorgione)	45	25
2060	40 c. "Madonna and Child" (Giovanni Bellini)	50	30
2061	45 c. "The Litta Madonna" (Da Vinci)	50	30
2062	65 c. "The Virgin and Child under the Apple Tree" (Lucas Cranach the Elder)	65	40
2063	75 c. "Madonna and Child" (Master of the Female Half-lengths)	75	50
2064	$1.20 "An Allegory of the Church" (Alessandro Allori)	1·00	1·00
2065	$5 "Madonna and Child wreathed with Flowers" (Jacob Jordaens)	2·50	3·00

1995. Birds. Multicoloured.

2067	15 c. Type **337**	10	10
2068	25 c. Blue-hooded euphonia	15	20
2069	35 c. Eastern meadowlark	15	20
2070	40 c. Red-billed tropic bird	15	20
2071	45 c. Greater flamingo	20	25
2072	60 c. Yellow-faced grassquit	25	30
2073	65 c. Yellow-billed cuckoo	30	35
2074	70 c. Purple-throated carib	30	35
2075	75 c. Bananaquit	35	40
2076	90 c. Painted bunting	40	45
2077	$1.20 Red-legged honeycreeper	50	55
2078	$2 Northern jacana	85	90
2079	$5 Greater Antillean bullfinch	2·10	2·25
2080	$10 Caribbean elaenia	4·25	4·50
2081	$20 Brown trembler	8·75	9·00

338 Head of Pachycephalosaurus

1995. Prehistoric Animals. Multicoloured.

2082	15 c. Type **338**	10	10
2083	20 c. Head of afrovenator	10	10
2084	65 c. Centrosaurus	30	35
2085	75 c. Kronosaurus (horiz)	35	40
2086	75 c. Ichthyosaurus (horiz)	35	40
2087	75 c. Plesiosaurus (horiz)	35	40
2088	75 c. Archelon (horiz)	35	40
2089	75 c. Pair of tyrannosaurus (horiz)	35	40
2090	75 c. Tyrannosaurus (horiz)	35	40
2091	75 c. Parasaurolophus (horiz)	35	40
2092	75 c. Pair of parasaurolophus (horiz)	35	40
2093	75 c. Oviraptor (horiz)	35	40
2094	75 c. Protoceratops with eggs (horiz)	35	40
2095	75 c. Pteranodon and protoceratops (horiz)	35	40
2096	75 c. Pair of protoceratops (horiz)	35	40
2097	90 c. Pentaceratops drinking	40	45
2098	$1.20 Head of tarbosaurus	50	55
2099	$5 Head of styracosaurus	2·10	2·25

339 Al Oerter (U.S.A.) (discus – 1956, 1960, 1964, 1968)

1995. Olympic Games, Atlanta (1996). Previous Gold Medal Winners (1st issue). Multicoloured.

2101	15 c. Type **339**	10	10
2102	20 c. Greg Louganis (U.S.A.) (diving – 1984, 1988)	10	10
2103	65 c. Naim Suleymanoglu (Turkey) (weightlifting – 1988)	30	35
2104	90 c. Louise Ritter (U.S.A.) (high jump – 1988)	40	45
2105	$1.20 Nadia Comaneci (Rumania) (gymnastics – 1976)	50	55
2106	$5 Olga Bondarenko (Russia) (10,000 metres – 1988)	2·10	2·25

No. 2106 is inscribed "BOLDARENKO" in error.

See also Nos. 2302/23.

340 Map of Berlin showing Russian Advance

1995. 50th Anniv of End of Second World War in Europe. Multicoloured.

2108	$1.20 Type **340**	50	55
2109	$1.20 Russian tank and infantry	50	55
2110	$1.20 Street fighting in Berlin	50	55
2111	$1.20 German tank exploding	50	55
2112	$1.20 Russian air raid	50	55
2113	$1.20 German troops surrendering	50	55
2114	$1.20 Hoisting the Soviet flag on the Reichstag	50	55
2115	$1.20 Captured German standards	50	55

See also Nos. 2132/7.

341 Signatures and Earl of Halifax

342 Woman buying Produce from Market

1995. 50th Anniv of United Nations. Multicoloured.

2117	75 c. Type **341**	35	40
2118	90 c. Virginia Gildersleeve	40	45
2119	$1.20 Harold Stassen	50	55

Nos. 2117/19 were printed together, se-tenant, forming a composite design.

1995. 50th Anniv of F.A.O. Multicoloured.

2121	75 c. Type **342**	35	40
2122	90 c. Women shopping	40	45
2123	$1.20 Women talking	50	55

Nos. 2121/3 were printed together, se-tenant, forming a composite design.

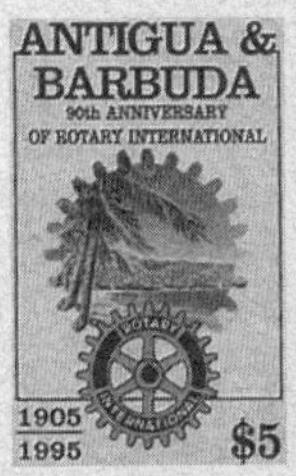

343 Beach and Rotary Emblem

344 Queen Elizabeth the Queen Mother

1995. 90th Anniv of Rotary International.

2125	**343** $5 multicoloured	2·10	2·25

1995. 95th Birthday of Queen Elizabeth the Queen Mother.

2127	– $1.50 brown, light brown and black	65	70
2128	**344** $1.50 multicoloured	65	70
2129	– $1.50 multicoloured	65	70
2130	– $1.50 multicoloured	65	70

DESIGNS: No. 2127, Queen Elizabeth the Queen Mother (pastel drawing); 2129, At desk (oil painting); 2130, Wearing green dress.

1995. 50th Anniv of End of Second World War in the Pacific. As T **340**. Multicoloured.

2132	$1.20 Gen. Chang Kai-Shek and Chinese guerrillas	50	55
2133	$1.20 Gen. Douglas MacArthur and beach landing	50	55
2134	$1.20 Gen. Claire Chennault and U.S. fighter aircraft	50	55
2135	$1.20 Brig. Orde Wingate and supply drop	50	55
2136	$1.20 Gen. Joseph Stilwell and U.S. supply plane	50	55
2137	$1.20 Field-Marshal Bill Slim and loading cow into plane	50	55

346 Purple-throated Carib

347 Original Church, 1845

1995. Birds. Multicoloured.

2140	75 c. Type **346**	35	40
2141	75 c. Antillean crested hummingbird	35	40
2142	75 c. Bananaquit	35	40
2143	75 c. Mangrove cuckoo	35	40
2144	75 c. Troupial	35	40
2145	75 c. Green-throated carib	35	40
2146	75 c. Yellow warbler	35	40
2147	75 c. Blue-hooded euphonia	35	40
2148	75 c. Scaly-breasted thrasher	35	40
2149	75 c. Burrowing owl	35	40
2150	75 c. Carib grackle	35	40
2151	75 c. Adelaide's warbler	35	40
2152	75 c. Ring-necked duck	35	40
2153	75 c. Ruddy duck	35	40
2154	75 c. Green-winged teal	35	40
2155	75 c. Wood duck	35	40
2156	75 c. Hooded merganser	35	40
2157	75 c. Lesser scaup	35	40
2158	75 c. Black-billed whistling duck ("West Indian Tree Duck")	35	40
2159	75 c. Fulvous whistling duck	35	40
2160	75 c. Bahama pintail	35	40
2161	75 c. Shoveler	35	40
2162	75 c. Masked duck	35	40
2163	75 c. American wigeon	35	40

Nos. 2140/51 and 2152/63 respectively were printed together, se-tenant, forming composite designs.

1995. 150th Anniv of Greenbay Moravian Church. Multicoloured.

2165	20 c. Type **347**	10	10
2166	60 c. Church in 1967	25	30
2167	75 c. Present church	35	40
2168	90 c. Revd. John Buckley (first minister of African descent)	40	45
2169	$1.20 Bishop John Ephraim Knight (longest-serving minister)	50	55
2170	$2 As 75 c.	85	90

348 Mining Bees

1995. Bees. Multicoloured.

2172	90 c. Type **348**	40	45
2173	$1.20 Solitary bee	50	55
2174	$1.65 Leaf-cutter bee	85	90
2175	$1.75 Honey bees	85	90

349 Narcissus

1995. Flowers. Multicoloured.

2177	75 c. Type **349**	35	40
2178	75 c. Camellia	35	40
2179	75 c. Iris	35	40
2180	75 c. Tulip	35	40
2181	75 c. Poppy	35	40
2182	75 c. Peony	35	40
2183	75 c. Magnolia	35	40
2184	75 c. Oriental lily	35	40
2185	75 c. Rose	35	40
2186	75 c. Pansy	35	40
2187	75 c. Hydrangea	35	40
2188	75 c. Azaleas	35	40

No. 2186 is inscribed "Pansie" in error.

350 Somali

1995. Cats. Multicoloured.

2190	45 c. Type **350**	20	25
2191	45 c. Persian and butterflies	20	25
2192	45 c. Devon rex	20	25
2193	45 c. Turkish angora	20	25
2194	45 c. Himalayan	20	25
2195	45 c. Maine coon	20	25
2196	45 c. Ginger non-pedigree	20	25
2197	45 c. American wirehair	20	25
2198	45 c. British shorthair	20	25
2199	45 c. American curl	20	25
2200	45 c. Black non-pedigree and butterfly	20	25
2201	45 c. Birman	20	25

Nos. 2190/2201 were printed together, se-tenant, forming a composite design.

351 The Explorer Tent

1995. 18th World Scout Jamboree, Netherlands. Tents. Multicoloured.

2203	$1.20 Type **351**	50	55
2204	$1.20 Camper tent	50	55
2205	$1.20 Wall tent	50	55
2206	$1.20 Trail tarp	50	55
2207	$1.20 Miner's tent	50	55
2208	$1.20 Voyager tent	50	55

352 Trans-Gabon Diesel-electric Train

1995. Trains of the World. Multicoloured.

2210	35 c. Type **352**	15	20
2211	65 c. Canadian Pacific diesel-electric locomotive	30	35
2212	75 c. Santa Fe Railway diesel-electric locomotive, U.S.A.	35	40
2213	90 c. High Speed Train, Great Britain	40	45
2214	$1.20 TGV express train, France	50	55
2215	$1.20 Diesel-electric locomotive, Australia	50	55
2216	$1.20 Pendolino "ETR 450" electric train, Italy	50	55
2217	$1.20 Diesel-electric locomotive, Thailand	50	55
2218	$1.20 Pennsylvania Railroad Type K4 steam locomotive, U.S.A.	50	55
2219	$1.20 Beyer-Garratt steam locomotive, East African Railways	50	55
2220	$1.20 Natal Govt steam locomotive	50	55
2221	$1.20 Rail gun, American Civil War	50	55
2222	$1.20 Locomotive "Lion" (red livery), Great Britain	50	55
2223	$1.20 William Hedley's "Puffing Billy" (green livery), Great Britain	50	55
2224	$6 Amtrak high speed diesel locomotive, U.S.A.	2·50	2·75

353 Dag Hammarskjold (1961 Peace)

1995. Cent of Nobel Prize Trust Fund. Mult.

2226	$1 Type **353**	45	50
2227	$1 Georg Wittig (1979 Chemistry)	45	50
2228	$1 Wilhelm Ostwald (1909 Chemistry)	45	50
2229	$1 Robert Koch (1905 Medicine)	45	50
2230	$1 Karl Ziegler (1963 Chemistry)	45	50
2231	$1 Alexander Fleming (1945 Medicine)	15	50
2232	$1 Hermann Staudinger (1953 Chemistry)	45	50
2233	$1 Manfred Eigen (1967 Chemistry)	45	50
2234	$1 Arno Penzias (1978 Physics)	45	50
2235	$1 Shmuel Agnon (1966 Literature)	45	50
2236	$1 Rudyard Kipling (1907 Literature)	45	50
2237	$1 Aleksandr Solzhenitsyn (1970 Literature)	45	50
2238	$1 Jack Steinberger (1988 Physics)	45	50
2239	$1 Andrei Sakharov (1975 Peace)	45	50
2240	$1 Otto Stern (1943 Physics)	45	50
2241	$1 John Steinbeck (1962 Literature)	45	50
2242	$1 Nadine Gordimer (1991 Literature)	45	50
2243	$1 William Faulkner (1949 Literature)	45	50

354 Elvis Presley

1995. 60th Birth Anniv of Elvis Presley. Mult.

2245	$1 Type **354**	45	50
2246	$1 Holding microphone in right hand	45	50
2247	$1 In blue shirt and with neck of guitar	45	50
2248	$1 Wearing blue shirt and smiling	45	50
2249	$1 On wedding day	45	50
2250	$1 In army uniform	45	50
2251	$1 Wearing red shirt	45	50
2252	$1 Wearing white shirt	45	50
2253	$1 In white shirt with microphone	45	50

355 John Lennon and Signature

357 "Rest on the Flight into Egypt" (Paolo Veronese)

1995. 15th Death Anniv of John Lennon (entertainer). Multicoloured.

2255	45 c. Type **355**	50	40
2256	50 c. In beard and spectacles	50	50
2257	65 c. Wearing sunglasses	55	55
2258	75 c. In cap with heart badge	65	65

1995. Hurricane Relief. Nos. 2203/8 optd **"Hurricane Relief"**.

2260	$1.20 Type **351**	50	55
2261	$1.20 Camper tent	50	55
2262	$1.20 Wall tent	50	55
2263	$1.20 Trail tarp	50	55
2264	$1.20 Miner's tent	50	55
2265	$1.20 Voyager tent	50	55

1995. Christmas. Religious Paintings. Multicoloured.

2267	15 c. Type **357**	10	10
2268	35 c. "Madonna and Child" (Van Dyck)	15	20
2269	65 c. "Sacred Conversation Piece" (Veronese)	30	35
2270	75 c. "Vision of St. Anthony" (Van Dyck)	35	40
2271	90 c. "Virgin and Child" (Van Eyck)	40	45
2272	$6 "The Immaculate Conception" (Giovanni Tiepolo)	2·50	2·75

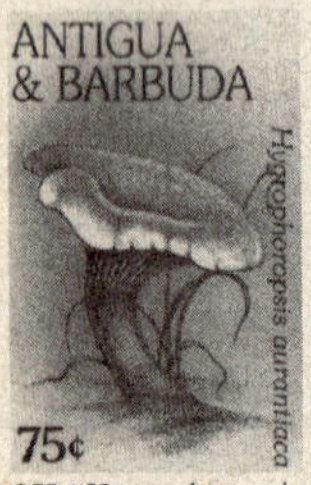

358 "Hygrophoropsis aurantiaca"

360 Florence Griffith Joyner (U.S.A.) (Gold – track, 1988)

359 H.M.S. "Resolution" (Cook)

1996. Fungi. Multicoloured.

2274	75 c. Type **358**	35	40
2275	75 c. "Hygrophorus bakerensis"	35	40
2276	75 c. "Hygrophorus conicus"	35	40
2277	75 c. "Hygrophorus miniatus" ("Hygrocybe miniata")	35	40
2278	75 c. "Suillus brevipes"	35	40
2279	75 c. "Suillus luteus"	35	40
2280	75 c. "Suillus granulatus"	35	40
2281	75 c. "Suillus caerulescens"	35	40

1996. Sailing Ships. Multicoloured.

2283	15 c. Type **359**	10	10
2284	25 c. "Mayflower" (Pilgrim Fathers)	10	15
2285	45 c. "Santa Maria" (Columbus)	20	25
2286	75 c. "Aemilia" (Dutch galleon)	35	40
2287	75 c. "Sovereign of the Seas" (English galleon)	35	40
2288	90 c. H.M.S. "Victory" (ship of the line, 1765)	40	45
2289	$1.20 As No. 2286	50	55
2290	$1.20 As No. 2287	50	55
2291	$1.20 "Royal Louis" (French galleon)	50	55
2292	$1.20 H.M.S. "Royal George" (ship of the line)	50	55
2293	$1.20 "Le Protecteur" (French frigate)	50	55
2294	$1.20 As No. 2288	50	55
2295	$1.50 As No. 2285	65	70
2296	$1.50 "Vitoria" (Magellan)	65	70
2297	$1.50 "Golden Hind" (Drake)	65	70
2298	$1.50 As No. 2284	65	70
2299	$1.50 "Griffin" (La Salle)	65	70
2300	$1.50 Type **359**	65	70

1996. Olympic Games, Atlanta. Previous Medal Winners (2nd issue). Multicoloured.

2302	65 c. Type **360**	30	35
2303	75 c. Olympic Stadium, Seoul (1988) (horiz)	35	40
2304	90 c. Allison Jolly and Lynne Jewell (U.S.A.) (Gold – yachting, 1988) (horiz)	40	45
2305	90 c. Wolfgang Nordwig (Germany) (Gold – pole vaulting, 1972)	40	45
2306	90 c. Shirley Strong (Great Britain) (Silver – 100 metres hurdles, 1984)	40	45
2307	90 c. Sergei Bubka (Russia) (Gold – pole vault, 1988)	40	45
2308	90 c. Filbert Bayi (Tanzania) (Silver – 3000 metres steeplechase, 1980)	40	45
2309	90 c. Victor Saneyev (Russia) (Gold – triple jump, 1968, 1972, 1976)	40	45
2310	90 c. Silke Renk (Germany) (Gold – javelin, 1992)	40	45
2311	90 c. Daley Thompson (Great Britain) (Gold – decathlon, 1980, 1984)	40	45
2312	90 c. Robert Richards (U.S.A.) (Gold – pole vault, 1952, 1956)	40	45
2313	90 c. Parry O'Brien (U.S.A.) (Gold – shot put, 1952, 1956)	40	45
2314	90 c. Ingrid Kramer (Germany) (Gold – women's platform diving, 1960)	40	45
2315	90 c. Kelly McCormick (U.S.A.) (Siver – women's springboard diving, 1984)	40	45
2316	90 c. Gary Tobian (U.S.A.) (Gold – men's springboard diving, 1960)	40	45
2317	90 c. Greg Louganis (U.S.A.) (Gold – men's diving, 1984 and 1988)	40	45
2318	90 c. Michelle Mitchell (U.S.A.) (Silver – women's platform diving, 1984 and 1988)	40	45
2319	90 c. Zhou Jihong (China) (Gold – women's platform diving, 1984)	40	45
2320	90 c. Wendy Wyland (U.S.A.) (Bronze – women's platform diving, 1984)	40	45
2321	90 c. Xu Yanmei (China) (Gold – women's platform diving, 1988)	40	45
2322	90 c. Fu Mingxia (China) (Gold – women's platform diving, 1992)	40	45
2323	$1.20 2000 metre tandem cycle race (horiz)	50	55

Nos. 2305/13 and 2314/22 were respectively printed together, se-tenant, with the background forming a composite design.

361 Black Skimmer

1996. Sea Birds. Multicoloured.

2325	75 c. Type **361**	35	40
2326	75 c. Black-capped petrel	35	40
2327	75 c. Sooty tern	35	40
2328	75 c. Royal tern	35	40
2329	75 c. Pomarine skua ("Pomarine Jaeger")	35	40
2330	75 c. White-tailed tropic bird	35	40
2331	75 c. Northern gannet	35	40
2332	75 c. Laughing gull	35	40

362 Mickey and Goofy on Elephant ("Around the World in Eighty Days")

1996. Novels of Jules Verne. Walt Disney cartoon characters in scenes from the books. Multicoloured.

2334	1 c. Type **362**	10	10
2335	2 c. Mickey, Donald and Goofy entering cave (A Journey to the Centre of the Earth)	10	10
2336	5 c. Mickey and Minnie driving postcart ("Michel Strogoff")	10	10
2337	10 c. Mickey, Donald and Goofy in space rocket ("From the Earth to the Moon")	10	10
2338	15 c. Mickey and Goofy in balloon ("Five Weeks in a Balloon")	10	10
2339	20 c. Mickey and Goofy in China ("Around the World in Eighty Days")	10	10
2340	$1 Mickey, Goofy and Pluto on island ("The Mysterious Island")	45	50
2341	$2 Mickey, Pluto, Goofy and Donald on Moon ("From the Earth to the Moon")	85	90
2342	$3 Mickey being lifted by bird ("Captain Grant's Children")	1·25	1·40
2343	$5 Mickey with seal and squid ("Twenty Thousand Leagues Under the Sea")	2·10	2·25

363 Bruce Lee

1996. "CHINA '96" 9th Asian International Stamp Exhibition, Peking. Bruce Lee (actor). Multicoloured.

2345	75 c. Type **363**	35	40
2346	75 c. Bruce Lee in white shirt and red tie	35	40
2347	75 c. In plaid jacket and tie	35	40
2348	75 c. In mask and uniform	35	40
2349	75 c. Bare-chested	35	40
2350	75 c. In mandarin jacket	35	40
2351	75 c. In brown jumper	35	40
2352	75 c. In fawn shirt	35	40
2353	75 c. Shouting	35	40

364 Queen Elizabeth II

1996. 70th Birthday of Queen Elizabeth II. Multicoloured.

2355	$2 Type **364**	85	90
2356	$2 With bouquet	85	90
2357	$2 In garter robes	85	90

365 Ancient Egyptian Cavalryman

1996. Cavalry through the Ages. Multicoloured.

2359	60 c. Type **365**	25	30
2360	60 c. 13th-century English knight	25	30
2361	60 c. 16th-century Spanish lancer	25	30
2362	60 c. 18th-century Chinese cavalryman	25	30

366 Girl in Red Sari

367 Tomb of Zachariah and "Verbascum sinuatum"

1996. 50th Anniv of U.N.I.C.E.F. Multicoloured.

2364	75 c. Type **366**	35	40
2365	90 c. South American mother and child	40	45
2366	$1.20 Nurse with child	50	55

1996. 3000th Anniv of Jerusalem. Multicoloured.

2368	75 c. Type **367**	35	40
2369	90 c. Pool of Siloam and "Hyacinthus orientalis"	40	45
2370	$1.20 Hurva Synagogue and "Ranunculus asiaticus"	50	55

368 Kate Smith

1996. Cent of Radio. Entertainers. Mult.

2372	65 c. Type **368**	30	35
2373	75 c. Dinah Shore	35	40
2374	90 c. Rudy Vallee	40	45
2375	$1.20 Bing Crosby	50	55

369 "Madonna Enthroned"

1996. Christmas. Religious Paintings by Filippo Lippi. Multicoloured.

2377	60 c. Type **369**	25	30
2378	90 c. "Adoration of the Child and Saints"	40	45
2379	$1 "The Annunciation"	45	50
2380	$1.20 "Birth of the Virgin"	50	55
2381	$1.60 "Adoration of the Child"	70	75
2382	$1.75 "Madonna and Child"	70	75

370 Robert Preston ("The Music Man")

1997. Broadway Musical Stars. Multicoloured.

2384	$1 Type **370**	45	50
2385	$1 Michael Crawford ("Phantom of the Opera")	45	50
2386	$1 Zero Mostel ("Fiddler on the Roof")	45	50
2387	$1 Patti Lupone ("Evita")	45	50
2388	$1 Raul Julia ("Threepenny Opera")	45	50
2389	$1 Mary Martin ("South Pacific")	45	50
2390	$1 Carol Channing ("Hello Dolly")	45	50
2391	$1 Yul Brynner ("The King and I")	45	50
2392	$1 Julie Andrews ("My Fair Lady")	45	50

371 Goofy and Wilbur

1997. Walt Disney Cartoon Characters. Mult.

2394	1 c. Type **371**	10	10
2395	2 c. Donald and Goofy in boxing ring	10	10
2396	5 c. Donald, Panchito and Jose Carioca	10	10
2397	10 c. Mickey and Goofy playing chess	10	10
2398	15 c. Chip and Dale with acorns	10	10
2399	20 c. Pluto and Mickey	10	15
2400	$1 Daisy and Minnie eating ice-cream	45	50
2401	$2 Daisy and Minnie at dressing table	85	90
2402	$3 Gus Goose and Donald	1·25	1·40

372 Charlie Chaplin as Young Man

1997. 20th Death Anniv of Charlie Chaplin (film star). Multicoloured.

2404	$1 Type **372**	45	50
2405	$1 Pulling face	45	50
2406	$1 Looking over shoulder	45	50
2407	$1 In cap	45	50
2408	$1 In front of star	45	50
2409	$1 In "The Great Dictator"	45	50
2410	$1 With movie camera and megaphone	45	50
2411	$1 Standing in front of camera lens	45	50
2412	$1 Putting on make-up	45	50

Nos. 2404/12 were printed together, se-tenant, with the backgrounds forming a composite design.

373 "Charaxes porthos"

1997. Butterflies. Multicoloured.

2414	90 c. Type **373**	40	45
2415	$1.10 "Charaxes protoclea protoclea"	50	55
2416	$1.10 "Byblia ilithyia"	50	55
2417	$1.10 Black-headed bush shrike ("Tchagra") (bird)	50	55
2418	$1.10 "Charaxes nobilis"	50	55
2419	$1.10 "Pseudacraea boisduvali trimeni"	50	55
2420	$1.10 "Charaxes smaragdalis"	50	55
2421	$1.10 "Charaxes lasti"	50	55
2422	$1.10 "Pseudacrea poggei"	50	55
2423	$1.10 "Graphium colonna"	50	55
2424	$1.10 Carmine bee eater (bird)	50	55
2425	$1.10 "Pseudacraea eurytus"	50	55
2426	$1.10 "Hypolimnas monteironis"	50	55
2427	$1.10 "Charaxes anticlea"	50	55
2428	$1.10 "Graphium leonidas"	50	55
2429	$1.10 "Graphium illyris"	50	55
2430	$1.10 "Nephronia argia"	50	55
2431	$1.10 "Graphium policenes"	50	55
2432	$1.10 "Papilio dardanus"	50	55
2433	$1.20 "Aethiopana honorius"	50	55
2434	$1.60 "Charaxes hadrianus"	70	75
2435	$1.75 "Precis westermanni"	85	90

Nos. 2415/23 and 2424/32 respectively were printed together, se-tenant, with the backgrounds forming a composite design.

No. 2430 is inscribed "Nepheronia argia" in error.

374 Convent of The Companions of Jesus, Morelia, Mexico

1997. 50th Anniv of U.N.E.S.C.O. Multicoloured.

2437	60 c. Type **374**	25	30
2438	90 c. Fortress at San Lorenzo, Panama (vert)	40	45
2439	$1 Canaima National Park, Venezuela (vert)	45	50
2440	$1.10 Aerial view of church with tower, Guanajuato, Mexico (vert)	50	55
2441	$1.10 Church facade, Guanajuato, Mexico (vert)	50	55
2442	$1.10 Aerial view of churches with domes, Guanajuato, Mexico (vert)	50	55
2443	$1.10 Jesuit Missions of the Chiquitos, Bolivia (vert)	50	55
2444	$1.10 Huascaran National Park, Peru (vert)	50	55
2445	$1.10 Jesuit Missions of La Santisima, Paraguay (vert)	50	55
2446	$1.10 Cartagena, Colombia (vert)	50	55
2447	$1.10 Fortification, Havana, Cuba (vert)	50	55
2448	$1.20 As No. 2444 (vert)	50	55
2449	$1.60 Church of San Fransisco, Guatemala (vert)	70	75
2450	$1.65 Tikal National Park, Guatemala	70	75
2451	$1.65 Rio Platano Reserve, Honduras	70	75
2452	$1.65 Ruins of Copan, Honduras	70	75
2453	$1.65 Antigua ruins, Guatemala	70	75
2454	$1.65 Teotihuacan, Mexico	70	75
2455	$1.75 Santo Domingo, Dominican Republic (vert)	70	75

No. 2446 is inscribed "Columbia" in error.

375 Red Bishop

1997. Endangered Species. Multicoloured.

2457	$1.20 Type **375**	50	55
2458	$1.20 Yellow baboon	50	55
2459	$1.20 Superb starling	50	55
2460	$1.20 Ratel	50	55
2461	$1.20 Hunting dog	50	55
2462	$1.20 Serval	50	55
2463	$1.65 Okapi	70	75
2464	$1.65 Giant forest squirrel	70	75
2465	$1.65 Lesser masked weaver	70	75
2466	$1.65 Small-spotted genet	70	75
2467	$1.65 Yellow-billed stork	70	75
2468	$1.65 Red-headed agama	70	75

Nos. 2457/62 and 2463/8 respectively were printed together, se-tenant, with the backgrounds forming composite designs.

376 Child's Face and U.N.E.S.C.O. Emblem

1997. 10th Anniv of Chernobyl Nuclear Disaster. Multicoloured.

2470	$1.65 Type **376**	70	75
2471	$2 As Type **376**, but inscribed "CHABAD'S CHILDREN OF CHERNOBYL" at foot	85	90

377 Paul Harris and James Grant

1997. 50th Death Anniv of Paul Harris (founder of Rotary International).

2472	**377** $1.75 multicoloured	70	75

378 Queen Elizabeth II

1997. Golden Wedding of Queen Elizabeth and Prince Philip. Multicoloured.

2474	$1 Type **378**	45	50
2475	$1 Royal coat of arms	45	50
2476	$1 Queen Elizabeth and Prince Philip at reception	45	50
2477	$1 Queen Elizabeth and Prince Philip in landau	45	50
2478	$1 Balmoral	45	50
2479	$1 Prince Philip	45	50

379 Kaiser Wilhelm I and Heinrich von Stephan

1997. "Pacific '97" International Stamp Exhibition, San Francisco. Death Centenary of Heinrich von Stephan (founder of the U.P.U.).

2481	**379** $1.75 blue	70	75
2482	– $1.75 brown	70	75
2483	– $1.75 mauve	70	75

DESIGNS: No. 2482, Von Stephan and Mercury; 2483, Carrier pigeon and loft.

380 The Three Ugly Sisters and their Mother

1997. 175th Anniv of Brothers Grimm's Third Collection of Fairy Tales. Cinderella. Multicoloured.

2485	$1.75 Type **380**	70	75
2486	$1.75 Cinderella and her Fairy Godmother	70	75
2487	$1.75 Cinderella and the Prince	70	75

381 "Marasmius rotula"

1997. Fungi. Multicoloured.

2489	45 c. Type **381**	20	25
2490	65 c. "Cantharellus cibarius"	30	35
2491	70 c. "Lepiota cristata"	30	35
2492	90 c. "Auricularia mesenteric"	40	45
2493	$1 "Pholiota alnicola"	45	50
2494	$1.65 "Leccinum aurantiacum"	70	75
2495	$1.75 "Entoloma serrulatum"	70	75
2496	$1.75 "Panaeolus sphinctrinus"	70	75
2497	$1.75 "Volvariella bombycina"	70	75
2498	$1.75 "Conocybe percincta"	70	75
2499	$1.75 "Pluteus cervinus"	70	75
2500	$1.75 "Russula foetens"	70	75

382 "Odontoglossum cervantesii"

1997. Orchids of the World. Multicoloured.

2502	45 c. Type **382**	20	25
2503	65 c. "Phalaenopsis" Medford Star	30	35
2504	75 c. "Vanda Motes" Resplendent	35	40
2505	90 c. "Odontonia" Debutante	40	45
2506	$1 "Iwanagaara" Apple Blossom	45	50
2507	$1.65 "Cattleya" Sophia Martin	70	75
2508	$1.65 Dogface Butterfly	70	75
2509	$1.65 "Laeliocattleya" Mini Purple	70	75
2510	$1.65 "Cymbidium" Showgirl	70	75
2511	$1.65 "Brassolaeliocattleya" Dorothy Bertsch	70	75
2512	$1.65 "Disa Blackii"	70	75
2513	$1.65 "Paphiopedilum leeanum"	70	75
2514	$1.65 "Paphiopedilum macranthum"	70	75
2515	$1.65 "Brassocattleya" Angel Lace	70	75
2516	$1.65 "Saphrolae liocattleya" Precious Stones	70	75
2517	$1.65 Orange Theope Butterfly	70	75
2518	$1.65 "Promenaea xanthina"	70	75
2519	$1.65 "Lycasle macrobulbon"	70	75
2520	$1.65 "Amestella philippinensis"	70	75
2521	$1.65 "Masdevallia" Machu Picchu	70	75
2522	$1.65 "Phalaenopsis" Zuma Urchin	70	75
2523	$2 "Dendrobium victoria-reginae"	85	90

Nos. 2507/14 and 2515/22 respectively were printed together, se-tenant, with the backgrounds forming composite designs.

MORE DETAILED LISTS
are given in the Stanley Gibbons Catalogues referred to in the country headings.
For lists of current volumes see Introduction.

383 Maradona holding World Cup Trophy, 1986

1997. World Cup Football Championship, France (1998).

2525	**383** 60 c. multicoloured	25	30
2526	– 75 c. brown	35	40
2527	– 90 c. multicoloured	40	45
2528	– $1 brown	45	50
2529	– $1 brown	45	50
2530	– $1 brown	45	50
2531	– $1 black	45	50
2532	– $1 brown	45	50
2533	– $1 brown	45	50
2534	– $1 brown	45	50
2535	– $1 brown	45	50
2536	– $1.20 multicoloured	50	55
2537	– $1.65 multicoloured	70	75
2538	– $1.75 multicoloured	70	75

DESIGNS—HORIZ: No. 2526, Fritzwalter, West Germany, 1954; 2527, Zoff, Italy, 1982; 2536, Moore, England, 1966; 2537, Alberto, Brazil, 1970; 2538, Matthaus, West Germany, 1990. VERT: No. 2528, Ademir, Brazil, 1950; 2529, Eusebio, Portugal, 1966; 2530, Fontaine, France, 1958; 2531, Schillaci, Italy, 1990; 2532, Leonidas, Brazil, 1938; 2533, Stabile, Argentina, 1930; 2534, Nejedly, Czechoslovakia, 1934; 2535, Muller, West Germany, 1970.

384 Scottish Fold Kitten

1997. Cats and Dogs. Multicoloured.

2540	$1.65 Type **384**	70	75
2541	$1.65 Japanese bobtail	70	75
2542	$1.65 Tabby manx	70	75
2543	$1.65 Bicolor American shorthair	70	75
2544	$1.65 Sorrel Abyssinian	70	75
2545	$1.65 Himalayan blue point	70	75
2546	$1.65 Dachshund	70	75
2547	$1.65 Staffordshire terrier	70	75
2548	$1.65 Shar-pei	70	75
2549	$1.65 Beagle	70	75
2550	$1.65 Norfolk terrier	70	75
2551	$1.65 Golden retriever	70	75

385 Original Drawing by Trevithick, 1803

1997. Railway Locomotives of the World. Multicoloured.

2553	$1.65 Type **385**	70	75
2554	$1.65 William Hedley's "Puffing Billy", (1813–14)	70	75
2555	$1.65 Crampton locomotive of French Nord Railway, 1858	70	75
2556	$1.65 Lawrence Machine Shop locomotive, U.S.A., 1860	70	75
2557	$1.65 Natchez and Hamburg Railway steam locomotive "Mississippi", U.S.A., 1834	70	75
2558	$1.65 Bury "Coppernob" locomotive, Furness Railway, 1846	70	75
2559	$1.65 David Joy's "Jenny Lind", 1847	70	75
2560	$1.65 Schenectady Atlantic locomotive, U.S.A., 1899	70	75
2561	$1.65 Kitsons Class 1800 tank locomotive, Japan, 1881	70	75
2562	$1.65 Pennsylvania Railroad express frieght	70	75
2563	$1.65 Karl Golsdorf's 4 cylinder locomotive, Austria	70	75
2564	$1.65 Series "E" locomotive, Russia, 1930	70	75

No. 2554 is dated "1860" in error.

386 "The Angel leaving Tobias and his Family" (Rembrandt)

1997. Christmas. Religious Paintings. Multicoloured.

2566	15 c. Type **386**	10	10
2567	25 c. "The Resurrection" (Martin Knoller)	10	15
2568	60 c. "Astronomy" (Raphael)	25	30
2569	75 c. "Music-making Angel" (Melozzo da Forli)	35	40
2570	90 c. "Amor" (Parmigianino)	40	45
2571	$1.20 "Madonna and Child with Saints" (Rosso Fiorentino)	50	55

387 Diana, Princess of Wales

1998. Diana, Princess of Wales Commemoration. Multicoloured (except Nos. 2574 and 2581/2).

2573	$1.65 Type **387**	70	75
2574	$1.65 Wearing hoop earrings (red and black)	70	75
2575	$1.65 Carrying bouquet	70	75
2576	$1.65 Wearing floral hat	70	75
2577	$1.65 With Prince Harry	70	75
2578	$1.65 Wearing white jacket	70	75
2579	$1.65 In kitchen	70	75
2580	$1.65 Wearing black and white dress	70	75
2581	$1.65 Wearing hat (brown and black)	70	75
2582	$1.65 Wearing floral print dress (brown and black)	70	75
2583	$1.65 Dancing with John Travolta	70	75
2584	$1.65 Wearing white hat and jacket	70	75

388 Yellow Damselfish

1998. Fishes. Multicoloured.

2586	75 c. Type **388**	35	40
2587	90 c. Barred hamlet	40	45
2588	$1 Yellow-tailed damselfish ("Jewelfish")	45	50
2589	$1.20 Blue-headed wrasse	55	60
2590	$1.50 Queen angelfish	70	75
2591	$1.65 Jackknife-fish	70	75
2592	$1.65 Spot-finned hogfish	70	75
2593	$1.65 Sergeant major	70	75
2594	$1.65 Neon goby	70	75
2595	$1.65 Jawfish	70	75
2596	$1.65 Flamefish	70	75
2597	$1.65 Rock beauty	70	75
2598	$1.65 Yellow-tailed snapper	70	75
2599	$1.65 Creole wrasse	70	75
2600	$1.65 Slender filefish	70	75
2601	$1.65 Long-spined squirrelfish	70	75
2602	$1.65 Royal gramma ("Fairy Basslet")	70	75
2603	$1.75 Queen triggerfish	75	80

Nos. 2591/6 and 2597/2602 respectively were printed together, se-tenant, with the backgrounds forming composite designs.

389 First Church and Manse, 1822–40

1998. 175th Anniv of Cedar Hall Moravian Church. Multicoloured.

2605	20 c. Type **389**	15	20
2606	45 c. Cedar Hall School, 1840	20	25
2607	75 c. Hugh A. King, minister 1945–53	35	40
2608	90 c. Present Church building	40	45
2609	$1.20 Water tank, 1822	50	55
2610	$2 Former Manse, demolished 1978	85	90

390 Europa Point Lighthouse, Gibraltar

391 Pooh and Tigger (January)

1998. Lighthouses of the World. Multicoloured.

2612	45 c. Type **390**	20	25
2613	65 c. Tierra del Fuego, Argentina (horiz)	30	35
2614	75 c. Point Loma, California, U.S.A. (horiz)	35	40
2615	90 c. Groenpoint, Cape Town, South Africa	40	45
2616	$1 Youghal, Cork, Ireland	45	50
2617	$1.20 Launceston, Tasmania, Australia	50	55
2618	$1.65 Point Abino, Ontario, Canada (horiz)	70	75
2619	$1.75 Great Inagua, Bahamas	75	80

No. 2613 is inscribed "Terra Del Fuego" in error.

1998. Through the Year with Winnie the Pooh. Multicoloured.

2621	$1 Type **391**	45	50
2622	$1 Pooh and Piglet indoors (February)	45	50
2623	$1 Piglet hang-gliding with scarf (March)	45	50
2624	$1 Tigger, Pooh and Piglet on pond (April)	45	50
2625	$1 Kanga and Roo with posy of flowers (May)	45	50
2626	$1 Pooh on balloon and Owl (June)	45	50
2627	$1 Pooh, Eeyore, Tigger and Piglet gazing at stars (July)	45	50
2628	$1 Pooh and Piglet by stream (August)	45	50
2629	$1 Christopher Robin going to school (September)	45	50
2630	$1 Eeyore in fallen leaves (October)	45	50
2631	$1 Pooh and Rabbit gathering pumpkins (November)	45	50
2632	$1 Pooh and Piglet skiing (December)	45	50

392 Miss Nellie Robinson (founder)

394 "Savannah" (paddle-steamer)

393 Spotted Eagle Ray

1998. Centenary of Thomas Oliver Robinson Memorial School.

2634	**392**	20 c. green and black	10	15
2635	–	45 c. multicoloured	20	25
2636	–	65 c. green and black	30	35
2637	–	75 c. multicoloured	35	40
2638	–	90 c. multicoloured	40	45
2639	–	$1.20 brown, green and black	50	55

DESIGNS—HORIZ: 45 c. School photo, 1985; 65 c. Former school building, 1930–49; 75 c. Children with Mrs. Natalie Hurst (present headmistress); $1.20 Present school building, 1950. VERT: 90 c. Miss Ina Loving (former teacher).

1998. International Year of the Ocean. Multicoloured.

2641/65	40 c. x 25 Type **393**; Manta ray; Hawksbill turtle; Jellyfish; Queen angelfish; Octopus; Emperor angelfish; Regal angelfish; Porkfish; Racoon butterflyfish; Atlantic barracuda; Sea horse; Nautilus; Trumpetfish; White tip shark; Sunken Spanish galleon; Black-tip shark; Long-nosed butterflyfish; Green moray eel; Captain Nemo; Treasure chest; Hammerhead shark; Divers; Lionfish; Clownfish		
2666/77	75 c. x 12 Maroon-tailed conure; Cocoi heron; Common tern; Rainbow lorikeet; Saddleback butterflyfish; Goatfish and cat shark; Blue shark and stingray; Majestic snapper; Nassau grouper; Black-cap gramma and blue tang; Stingrays; Stingrays and giant starfish		
2641/77	Set of 37	8·00	8·25

Nos. 2641/65 and 2666/77 respectively were printed together, se-tenant, with the backgrounds forming composite designs.

1998. Ships of the World. Multicoloured.

2679	$1.75 Type **394**	75	80
2680	$1.75 Viking longship	75	80
2681	$1.75 Greek galley	75	80
2682	$1.75 Sailing clipper	75	80
2683	$1.75 Dhow	75	80
2684	$1.75 Fishing catboat	75	80

395 Flags of Antigua and CARICOM

1998. 25th Anniv of Caribbean Community.

2686	**395**	$1 multicoloured	45	50

396 Ford, 1896

1998. Classic Cars. Multicoloured.

2687	$1.65 Type **396**	70	75
2688	$1.65 Ford A, 1903	70	75
2689	$1.65 Ford T, 1928	70	75
2690	$1.65 Ford T, 1922	70	75
2691	$1.65 Ford Blackhawk, 1929	70	75
2692	$1.65 Ford Sedan, 1934	70	75
2693	$1.65 Torpedo, 1911	70	75
2694	$1.65 Mercedes 22, 1913	70	75
2695	$1.65 Rover, 1920	70	75
2696	$1.65 Mercedes-Benz, 1956	70	75
2697	$1.65 Packard V-12, 1934	70	75
2698	$1.65 Opel, 1924	70	75

397 Lockheed-Boeing General Dynamics Yf-22

1998. Modern Aircraft. Multicoloured.

2700	$1.65 Type **397**	70	75
2701	$1.65 Dassault-Breguet Rafale BO 1	70	75
2702	$1.65 MiG 29	70	75
2703	$1.65 Dassault-Breguet Mirage 2000D	70	75
2704	$1.65 Rockwell B-1B "Lancer"	70	75
2705	$1.65 McDonnell-Douglas C-17A	70	75
2706	$1.65 Space shuttle	70	75
2707	$1.65 SAAB "Grippen"	70	75
2708	$1.65 Eurofighter EF-2000	70	75
2709	$1.65 Sukhoi SU 27	70	75
2710	$1.65 Northrop B-2	70	75
2711	$1.65 Lockheed F-117 "Nighthawk"	70	75

398 Karl Benz (internal-combustion engine)

399 Stylised Americas

1998. Millennium Series. Famous People of the Twentieth Century. Inventors. Multicoloured.

2713	$1 Type **398**	45	50
2714	$1 Early Benz car and Mercedes-Benz racing car (53 × 38 mm)	45	50
2715	$1 Atom bomb mushroom cloud (53 × 38 mm)	45	50
2716	$1 Albert Einstein (theory of relativity)	45	50
2717	$1 Leopold Godowsky Jr. and Leopold Damrosch Mannes (Kodachrome film)	45	50
2718	$1 Camera and transparencies (53 × 38 mm)	45	50
2719	$1 Heinkel He 178 (first turbo jet plane) (53 × 38 mm)	45	50
2720	$1 Dr. Hans Pabst von Ohain (jet turbine engine)	45	50
2721	$1 Rudolf Diesel (diesel engine)	45	50
2722	$1 Early Diesel engine and forms of transport (53 × 38 mm)	45	50
2723	$1 Zeppelin airship (53 × 38 mm)	45	50
2724	$1 Count Ferdinand von Zeppelin (airship pioneer)	45	50
2725	$1 Wilhelm Conrad Rontgen (X-rays)	45	50
2726	$1 X-ray of hand (53 × 38 mm)	45	50
2727	$1 Launch of Saturn rocket (53 × 38 mm)	45	50
2728	$1 Wernher von Braun (rocket research)	45	50

No. 2713 is inscribed "CARL BENZ" in error.

1998. 50th Anniv of Organization of American States.

2730	**399**	$1 multicoloured	45	50

400 "Figures on the Seashore"

1998. 25th Death Anniv of Pablo Picasso (painter). Multicoloured.

2731	$1.20 Type **400**	50	45
2732	$1.65 "Three Figures under a Tree" (vert)	70	75
2733	$1.75 "Two Women running on the Beach"	75	80

401 Dino 246 GT-GTS

1998. Birth Centenary of Enzo Ferrari (car manufacturer). Multicoloured.

2735	$1.75 Type **401**	75	80
2736	$1.75 Front view of Dino 246 GT-GTS	75	80
2737	$1.75 365 GT4 BB	75	80

402 Scout Handshake

1998. 19th World Scout Jamboree, Chile. Multicoloured.

2739	90 c. Type **402**	40	45
2740	$1 Scouts hiking	45	50
2741	$1.20 Scout salute	50	55

403 Mahatma Gandhi

1998. 50th Death Anniv of Mahatma Gandhi. Multicoloured.

2743	90 c. Type **403**	40	45
2744	$1 Gandhi seated	45	50
2745	$1.20 As young man	55	55
2746	$1.65 At primary school in Rajkot, aged 7	70	75

404 McDonnell Douglas Phantom F-GR1

1998. 80th Anniv of Royal Air Force. Multicoloured.

2748	$1.75 Type **404**	75	80
2749	$1.75 Two Sepecat Jaguar GR1As	75	80
2750	$1.75 Panavia Tornado F3	75	80
2751	$1.75 McDonnell Douglas Phantom F-GR2	75	80

405 Brown Pelican

1998. Sea Birds of the World. Multicoloured.

2753	15 c. Type **405**	10	10
2754	25 c. Dunlin	10	15
2755	45 c. Atlantic puffin	20	25
2756	75 c. King eider	35	40
2757	75 c. Inca tern	35	40
2758	75 c. Little auk ("Dovekie")	35	40
2759	75 c. Ross's gull	35	40
2760	75 c. Common noddy ("Brown Noddy")	35	40
2761	75 c. Marbled murrelet	35	40
2762	75 c. Northern gannet	35	40
2763	75 c. Razorbill	35	40
2764	75 c. Long-tailed skua ("Long-tailed Jaeger")	35	40

2765 75 c. Black guillemot 35 40
2766 75 c. Whimbrel 35 40
2767 75 c. Oystercatcher 35 40
2768 90 c. Pied cormorant 40 45
Nos. 2756/67 were printed together, se-tenant, with the backgrounds forming a composite design.
No. 2759 is inscribed "ROSS' BULL" in error.

406 Diana, Princess of Wales

1998. 1st Death Anniv of Diana, Princess of Wales.
2770 **406** $1.20 multicoloured . . . 50 55

407 Border Collie

1998. Christmas. Dogs. Multicoloured.
2771 15 c. Type **407** 10 10
2772 25 c. Dalmatian 10 15
2773 65 c. Weimaraner 30 35
2774 75 c. Scottish terrier 35 40
2775 90 c. Long-haired dachshund 40 45
2776 $1.20 Golden retriever . . . 50 55
2777 $2 Pekingese 85 90

408 Mickey Mouse Sailing

1999. 70th Birthday of Mickey Mouse. Walt Disney characters participating in water sports. Multicoloured.
2779 $1 Type **408** 45 50
2780 $1 Mickey and Goofy sailing 45 50
2781 $1 Goofy windsurfing 45 50
2782 $1 Mickey sailing and seagull 45 50
2783 $1 Goofy sailing 45 50
2784 $1 Mickey windsurfing . . . 45 50
2785 $1 Goofy running with surfboard 45 50
2786 $1 Mickey surfing 45 50
2787 $1 Donald Duck holding surfboard 45 50
2788 $1 Donald on surfboard (face value at right) 45 50
2789 $1 Minnie Mouse surfing in green shorts 45 50
2790 $1 Goofy surfing 45 50
2791 $1 Goofy in purple shorts waterskiing 45 50
2792 $1 Mickey waterskiing . . . 45 50
2793 $1 Goofy waterskiing with Mickey 45 50
2794 $1 Donald on surfboard (face value at left) 45 50
2795 $1 Goofy in yellow shorts waterskiing 45 50
2796 $1 Minnie in pink shorts surfing 45 50

409 Hell's Gate Steel Orchestra, 1996

1999. 50th Anniv of Hell's Gate Steel Orchestra. Multicoloured.
2798 20 c. Type **409** 10 10
2799 60 c. Orchestra members, New York, 1992 . . . . 25 30
2800 75 c. Orchestra members with steel drums, 1950 . . . . 35 40
2801 90 c. Eustace Henry, 1964 . . 40 45
2802 $1.20 Alston Henry playing double tenor 50 55

ASCENSION

An island in South Atlantic. A dependency of St. Helena.

1922. 12 pence = 1 shilling;
20 shillings = 1 pound.
1971. 100 pence = 1 pound.

1922. Stamps of St. Helena of 1912 optd **ASCENSION.**
1 ½d. black and green . . . . . 3·75 11·00
2 1d. green . . . . 3·75 11·00
3 1½d. red . . . . 14·00 48·00
4 2d. black and slate . . . . . 13·00 12·00
5 3d. blue . . . . 12·00 15·00
6 8d. black and purple . . . . 25·00 45·00
9 1s. black on green . . . . . 27·00 45·00
7 2s. black and blue on blue . . . 80·00 £120
8 3s. black and violet £120 £160

2 Badge of St. Helena

1924.
10 **2** ½d. black . . . . 3·00 11·00
11 1d. black and green . . . . 4·75 6·50
12 1½d. red . . . . 7·00 26·00
13 2d. black and grey . . . . 10·00 5·50
14 3d. blue . . . . 7·00 11·00
15 4d. black on yellow . . . . 45·00 75·00
15d 5d. purple and green . . . 10·00 20·00
16 6d. black and purple . . . 48·00 80·00
17 8d black and violet . . . . 13·00 40·00
18 1s. black and brown . . . . 19·00 45·00
19 2s. black and blue on blue . 55·00 85·00
20 3s. black on blue . . . . . 80·00 85·00

3 Georgetown

4 Ascension Island

1934. Medallion portrait of King George V. (except 1s.).
21 **3** ½d. black and violet 90 80
22 **4** 1d. black and green . . . . 1·75 1·25
23 – 1½d. black and red . . . . 1·75 2·25
24 **4** 2d. black and orange . . . . 1·75 2·50
25 – 3d. black and blue . . . . 1·75 1·50
26 – 5d. black and blue . . . . 2·25 3·25
27 **4** 8d. black and brown . . . . 4·25 4·75
28 – 1s. black and red . . . . . 18·00 6·50
29 **4** 2s. 6d. black and purple . . . 35·00 32·00
30 – 5s. black and brown . . . . 45·00 55·00
DESIGNS—HORIZ: 1½d. The Pier; 3d. Long Beach; 5d. Three Sisters; 1s. Sooty tern; 5s. Green mountain

1935. Silver Jubilee. As T **13** of Antigua.
31 1½d. blue and red . . . . . 3·50 6·50
32 2d. blue and grey . . . . . 11·00 22·00
33 5d. green and blue . . . . . 17·00 24·00
34 1s. grey and purple . . . . . 23·00 27·00

1937. Coronation. As T **2** of Aden.
35 1d. green 50 50
36 2d. orange . . . . 1·00 40
37 3d. blue . . . . 1·00 50

10 The Pier

1938.
38b A ½d. black and violet . . . 70 1·75
39 B 1d. black and green . . . 40·00 7·50
39b 1d. black and orange . . . 45 60
39d C 1d. black and green . . . 45 40
40b **10** 1½d. black and red . . . 85 80
40d 1½d. black and pink . . . 55 80
41a B 2d. black and orange . . . 80 40
41c 2d. black and red . . . 75 75
42 D 3d. black and blue . . . £100 26·00
42b 3d. black and grey . . . 70 80
42d B 4d. black and blue . . . 4·50 3·00
43 C 6d. black and blue . . . 9·00 1·25
44a A 1s black and brown . . . 4·75 2·00
45 **10** 2s. 6d. black and red . . . 40·00 7·50
46a D 5s. black and brown . . . 48·00 26·00
47a C 10s black and purple . . . 65·00 55·00
DESIGNS: A, Georgetown; B, Green Mountain; C, Three Sisters; D, Long Beach.

1946. Victory. As T **9** of Aden.
48 2d. orange 40 50
49 4d. blue 40 30

1948. Silver Wedding. As T **10/11** of Aden.
50 3d. black 50 30
51 10s. mauve . . . . 45·00 40·00

1949. U.P.U. As T **20/23** of Antigua.
52 3d. red . . . . 1·40 1·00
53 4d. blue . . . . 3·50 1·10
54 6d. olive . . . . 3·75 2·50
55 1s. black . . . . 3·75 1·50

1953. Coronation. As T **13** of Aden.
56 3d. black and grey . . . . . 1·00 1·50

15 Water Catchment

1956.
57 **15** ½d. black and brown 10 30
58 – 1d. black and mauve . . . . 1·75 60
59 – 1½d. black and orange . . . 30 60
60 – 2d. black and red . . . . . 1·25 50
61 – 2½d. black and brown 85 80
62 – 3d. black and blue . . . . . 2·75 1·00
63 – 4d. black and turquoise . . . 1·25 1·40
64 – 6d. black and blue . . . . . 1·25 90
65 – 7d. black and olive . . . . . 1·00 1·00
66 – 1s. black and red . . . . . 1·00 90
67 – 2s. 6d. black and purple . . 27·00 6·50
68 – 5s. black and green . . . . 35·00 17·00
69 – 10s. black and purple . . . . 48·00 35·00
DESIGNS: 1d. Map of Ascension; 1½d. Georgetown; 2d. Map showing Atlantic cables; 2½d. Mountain road; 3d. White-tailed tropic bird; 4d. Yellow-finned tuna; 6d. Rollers on seashore; 7d. Turtles; 1s. Land crab; 2s. 6d. Sooty tern; 5s. Perfect Crater; 10s. View of Ascension from north-west.

28 Brown Booby

1963. Birds. Multicoloured.
70 1d. Type **28** 90 30
71 1½d. White-capped noddy . . . 1·25 60
72 2d. White tern . . . . 1·25 30
73 3d. Red-billed tropic bird . . . 1·25 30
74 4½d. Common noddy . . . . . 1·25 30
75 6d. Sooty tern . . . . 1·25 30
76 7d. Ascension frigate-bird . . 1·25 30
77 10d. Blue-faced booby . . . . 1·25 30
78 1s. White-tailed tropic bird . . 1·25 30
79 1s. 6d. Red-billed tropic bird . . 4·50 1·75
80 2s. 6d. Madeiran storm petrel . 6·00 7·00
81 5s. Red-footed booby (brown phase) . . . . 7·00 6·00
82 10s. Ascension frigate-birds . 13·00 7·00
83 £1 Red-footed booby (white phase) . . . . 20·00 9·00

1963. Freedom from Hunger. As T **28** of Aden.
84 1s. 6d. red . . . . 1·40 40

1963. Centenary of Red Cross. As T **33** of Antigua.
85 3d. red and black . . . . . . 3·50 1·00
86 1s. 6d. red and blue . . . . . 7·50 2·25

1965. Centenary of I.T.U. As T **36** of Antigua.
87 3d. mauve and violet . . . . . 1·00 50
88 6d. turquoise and brown . . . . 1·25 50

1965. I.C.Y. As T **37** of Antigua.
89 1d. purple and turquoise 50 50
90 6d. green and lavender . . . . 1·00 75

1966. Churchill Commemoration. As T **38** of Antigua.
91 1d. blue 50 60
92 3d. green . . . . 2·75 1·25
93 6d. brown . . . . 3·50 1·50
94 1s. 6d. violet . . . . 4·50 2·00

1966. World Cup Football Championship. As T **40** of Antigua.
95 3d. multicoloured . . . . 1·25 50
96 6d. multicoloured . . . . 1·50 60

1966. Inauguration of W.H.O. Headquarters, Geneva. As T **41** of Antigua.
97 3d. black, green and blue . . . 1·75 75
98 1s. 6d. black, purple and ochre . 4·25 1·50

42 Satellite Station

44 Human Rights Emblem and Chain Links

43 B.B.C. Emblem

1966. Opening of Apollo Communication Satellite Earth Station.
99 **42** 4d. black and violet . . . 15 20
100 8d. black and green . . . 15 20
101 1s. 3d. black and brown . 20 25
102 2s. 6d. black and blue . . 25 35

1966. Opening of B.B.C. Relay Station.
103 **43** 1d. gold and blue 10 15
104 3d. gold and green 15 20
105 6d. gold and violet 15 20
106 1s. 6d. gold and red . . . 15 25

1967. 20th Anniv of U.N.E.S.C.O. As T **54/56** of Antigua.
107 3d. multicoloured . . . . . . 2·50 1·25
108 6d. yellow, violet and olive . . 3·75 1·50
109 1s. 6d. black, purple and orange 6·00 2·00

1968. Human Rights Year.
110 **44** 6d. orange, red and black . 25 25
111 1s. 6d. blue, red and black 35 35
112 2s. 6d. green, red and black 40 40

45 Black Durgon ("Ascension Black-Fish")

1968. Fishes (1st series).
113 **45** 4d. black, grey and blue . 40 35
114 – 8d. multicoloured 50 60
115 – 1s. 9d. multicoloured . . . 60 70
116 – 2s. 3d. multicoloured . . . 70 75
DESIGNS: 8d. Scribbled filefish ("Leather-jacket"); 1s. 9d. Yellow-finned tuna; 2s. 3d. Short-finned mako.
See also Nos. 117/20 and 126/9.

1969. Fishes (2nd series). As T **45**. Multicoloured.
117 4d. Sailfish . . . . 1·00 90
118 6d. White seabream ("Old wife") . . . . 1·25 1·25
119 1s. 6d. Yellowtail . . . . . . 2·00 2·25
120 2s. 11d. Rock hind ("Jack") . . 3·00 2·75

46 H.M.S. "Rattlesnake"

1969. Royal Navy Crests (1st series).
121 **46** 4d. multicoloured 70 25
122 – 9d. multicoloured 90 25
123 – 1s. 9d. blue and gold . . . 1·40 35
124 – 2s. 3d. multicoloured . . . 1·60 45
DESIGNS: 9d. H.M.S. "Weston"; 1s. 9d. H.M.S. "Undaunted"; 2s. 3d. H.M.S. "Eagle".
See also Nos. 130/3, 149/52, 154/7 and 166/9.

1970. Fishes (3rd series). As T **45**. Multicoloured.
126 4d. Wahoo . . . . 4·50 2·50
127w 9d. Ascension jack ("Coalfish") . . . . . . 5·00 1·75
128 1s. 9d. Pompouno dolphin . 5·00 3·25
129w 2s. 3d. Squirrelfish ("Soldier") . 5·00 2·50

1970. Royal Navy Crests (2nd series). As T **46**. Multicoloured.
130 4d. H.M.S. "Penelope" . . . 1·75 85
131 9d. H.M.S. "Carlisle" . . . . 2·25 1·25
132 1s. 6d. H.M.S. "Amphion" . . 2·75 1·75
133 2s. 6d. H.M.S. "Magpie" . . . 3·25 1·75

50 Early Chinese Rocket

51 Course of the "Quest"

1971. Decimal Currency. Evolution of Space Travel. Multicoloured.

135 ½p. Type **50** 15 20
136 1p. Medieval Arab astronomers 20 20
137 1½p. Tycho Brahe's observatory, quadrant and supernova . . 30 30
138 2p. Galileo, Moon and telescope 40 30
139 2½p. Isaac Newton, instruments and apple . . . . 1·00 70
140 3½p. Harrison's chronometer and ship . . . . 1·75 70
141 4½p. Space rocket taking off . 1·25 60
142 5p. World's largest telescope, Palomar . . . . 1·00 60
143 7½p. World's largest radio telescope, Jodrell Bank . . . 4·00 1·40
144 10p. "Mariner VII" and Mars 3·50 1·75
145 12½p. "Sputnik II" and Space dog, Laika . . . . 6·00 2·00
146 25p. Walking in Space . . . . 7·00 2·25
147 50p. "Apollo XI" crew on Moon 6·00 2·50
148 £1 Future Space Research station 6·00 4·50
Nos. 137/40, 142/5 and 147/8 are horiz.

1971. Royal Navy Crests (3rd series). As T **46**. Mult.

149 2p. H.M.S. "Phoenix" . . . . 1·50 30
150 4p. H.M.S. "Milford" . . . . 1·75 55
151 9p. H.M.S. "Pelican" . . . . 2·25 80
152 15p. H.M.S. "Oberon" . . . . 2·50 1·00

1972. Royal Navy Crests (4th series). As T **46**. Mult.

154 1½p. H.M.S. "Lowestoft" . . . 60 50
155 3p. H.M.S. "Auckland" . . . 65 75
156 6p. H.M.S. "Nigeria" . . . . 70 1·25
157 17½p. H.M.S. "Bermuda" . . 1·50 2·50

1972. 50th Anniv of Shackleton's Death. Mult.

159 2½p. Type **51** 55 60
160 4p. Shackleton and "Quest" (horiz) 60 70
161 7½p. Shackleton's cabin and "Quest" (horiz) 65 75
162 11p. Shackleton statue and memorial . . . . 75 1·00

52 Land Crab and Short-finned Mako

1972. Royal Silver Wedding. Multicoloured.

164 **52** 2p. violet 15 10
165 16p. red 35 30

1973. Royal Naval Crests (5th series). As T **46**. Multicoloured.

166 2p. H.M.S. "Birmingham" . . 2·50 1·00
167 4p. H.M.S. "Cardiff" . . . . 3·00 1·00
168 9p. H.M.S. "Penzance" . . . . 4·00 1·25
169 13p. H.M.S. "Rochester" . . 4·50 1·50

53 Green Turtle

1973. Turtles. Multicoloured.

171 4p. Type **53** . . . . 3·75 1·25
172 9p. Loggerhead turtle . . . . 4·00 1·50
173 12p. Hawksbill turtle . . . . 4·25 1·75

54 Sergeant, R.M. Light Infantry, 1900

1973. 50th Anniv of Departure of Royal Marines from Ascension. Multicoloured.

174 2p. Type **54** . . . . 2·00 1·25
175 6p. R.M. Private, 1816 . . . . 3·00 1·75
176 12p. R.M. Light Infantry Officer, 1880 . . . . 3·50 2·25
177 20p. R.M. Artillery Colour Sergeant, 1910 . . . . . 4·00 2·50

1973. Royal Wedding. As T **47** of Anguilla. Multicoloured. Background colours given.

178 2p. brown 15 10
179 18p. green 25 15

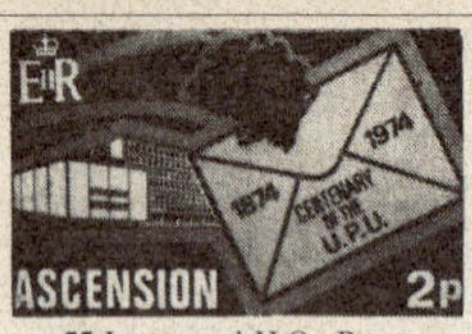

55 Letter and H.Q., Berne

1974. Centenary of Universal Postal Union. Mult.

180 2p. Type **55** 25 30
181 9p. Hermes and U.P.U. monument 40 45

56 Churchill as a Boy, and Birthplace, Blenheim Palace

1974. Birth Centenary of Sir Winston Churchill. Multicoloured.

182 5p. Type **56** 25 35
183 25p. Churchill as statesman, and U.N. Building 40 75

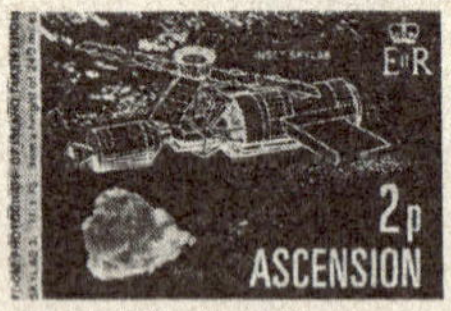

57 "Skylab 3" and Photograph of Ascension

1975. Space Satellites. Multicoloured.

185 2p. Type **57** 30 30
186 18p. "Skylab 4" Command module and photograph . . 35 40

58 U.S.A.F. Lockheed C-141A Starfighter

1975. Wideawake Airfield. Multicoloured.

187 2p. Type **58** . . . . 1·75 65
188 5p. R.A.F. Lockheed C-130 Hercules . . . . 2·00 85
189 9p. Vickers Super VC-10 . . 2·25 1·40
190 24p. U.S.A.F. Lockheed C-5A Galaxy . . . . 4·00 3·00

1975. "Apollo-Soyuz" Space Link. Nos. 141 and 145/6 optd **APOLLO-SOYUZ LINK 1975**.

192 4½p. multicoloured 15 15
193 12½p. multicoloured 20 20
194 25p. multicoloured 30 35

60 Arrival of Royal Navy, 1815

1975. 160th Anniv of Occupation. Multicoloured.

195 2p. Type **60** 30 25
196 5p. Water supply, Dampiers Drip 40 40
197 9p. First landing, 1815 . . . 45 60
198 15p. The garden on Green Mountain 60 85

61 Yellow Canaries

1976. Multicoloured.

199 1p. Type **61** . . . . 40 1·25
200 2p. White tern (vert) . . . . 45 1·25
201 3p. Common waxbill . . . . 45 1·25
202 4p. White-capped noddy (vert) 50 1·25
203 5p. Common noddy . . . . . 70 1·50
204 6p. Common mynah . . . . 70 1·50
205 7p. Madeiran storm petrel (vert) 70 1·50
206 8p. Sooty tern . . . . 70 1·50
207 9p. Blue-faced booby (vert) . 70 1·50
208 10p. Red-footed booby . . . . 70 1·50
209 15p. Bare-throated francolin (vert) . . . . 1·25 1·75
210 18p. Brown booby (vert) . . . 1·25 1·75
211 25p. Red-billed bo'sun bird . . 1·40 1·75
212 50p. Yellow-billed tropic bird . 2·25 2·50
213 £1 Ascension frigate-bird (vert) 2·75 3·25
214 £2 Boatswain Bird Island Sanctuary (50 x 38 mm) . . 5·50 7·50

63 G.B. Penny Red with Ascension Postmark

1976. Festival of Stamps, London.

215 **63** 5p. red, black and brown . 20 15
216 – 9p. green, black and brown 30 20
217 – 25p. multicoloured 50 45
DESIGNS—VERT: 9p. ½d. stamp of 1922. HORIZ: 25p. "Southampton Castle" (liner).

64 U.S. Base, Ascension

1976. Bicentenary of American Revolution. Multicoloured.

219 8p. Type **64** 75 40
220 9p. NASA Station at Devils Ashpit 75 45
221 25p. "Viking" landing on Mars 1·25 80

65 Visit of Prince Philip, 1957 66 Tunnel carrying Water Pipe

1977. Silver Jubilee. Multicoloured.

222 8p. Type **65** 15 15
223 12p. Coronation Coach leaving Buckingham Palace (horiz) . 20 20
224 25p. Coronation Coach (horiz) 35 40

1977. Water Supplies. Multicoloured.

225 3p. Type **66** 15 15
226 5p. Breakneck Valley wells . . 20 20
227 12p. Break tank (horiz) 35 35
228 25p. Water catchment (horiz) . 55 65

67 Mars Bay Location, 1877

1977. Centenary of Visit of Professor Gill (astronomer). Multicoloured.

229 3p. Type **67** 15 20
230 8p. Instrument sites, Mars Bay 20 25
231 12p. Sir David and Lady Gill . 30 40
232 25p. Maps of Ascension . . . 60 70

68 Lion of England 70 Flank of Sisters, Sisters' Red Hill and East Crater

1978. 25th Anniv of Coronation.

233 **68** 25p. yellow, brown and silver 35 50
234 – 25p. multicoloured 35 50
235 – 25p. yellow, brown and silver 35 50
DESIGNS: No. 234, Queen Elizabeth II; No 235, Green turtle.

1978. Ascension Island Volcanic Rock Formations. Multicoloured.

236 3p. Type **70** 15 20
237 5p. Holland's Crater (Hollow Tooth) 20 30
238 12p. Street Crater, Lower Valley Crater and Bear's Back . . 25 40
239 15p. Butt Crater, Weather Post and Green Mountain . . . 30 45
240 25p. Flank of Sisters, Thistle Hill and Two Boats Village . . 35 50
Nos. 236/40 were issued as a se-tenant strip within the sheet, forming a composite design.

71 "The Resolution" (H. Roberts) 72 St. Mary's Church, Georgetown

1979. Bicentenary of Captain Cook's Voyages, 1768–79. Multicoloured.

242 3p. Type **71** 40 25
243 8p. Cook's chronometer . . . 40 40
244 12p. Green turtle 45 50
245 25p. Flaxman/Wedgwood medallion of Cook 55 70

1979. Ascension Day. Multicoloured.

246 8p. Type **72** 15 20
247 12p. Map of Ascension . . . 20 30
248 50p. "The Ascension" (painting by Rembrandt) 55 90

73 Landing Cable, Comfortless Cove

1979. 80th Anniv of Eastern Telegraph Company's Arrival on Ascension.

249 **73** 3p. black and red 15 10
250 – 8p. black and green . . . 20 20
251 – 12p. black and yellow . . 25 25
252 – 15p. black and violet . . . 25 35
253 – 25p. black and brown . . 35 50
DESIGNS—HORIZ: 8p. C.S. "Anglia"; 15p. C.S. "Seine"; 25p. Cable and Wireless earth station. VERT: 12p. Map of Atlantic cable network.

74 1938 6d. Stamp

1979. Death Centenary of Sir Rowland Hill.

254 **74** 3p. black and blue 15 10
255 – 8p. black, green and pale green 15 20
256 – 12p. black, blue and pale blue 20 25
257 – 50p. black and red 60 90
DESIGNS—HORIZ: 8 p. 1956 5s. definitive. VERT: 12p. 1924 3s. stamp; 50p. Sir Rowland Hill.

75 "Anogramma ascensionis"

1980. Ferns and Grasses. Multicoloured.

258 3p. Type **75** 10 10
259 6p. "Xiphopteris ascensionense" 15 15
260 8p. "Sporobolus caespitosus" 15 15
261 12p. "Sporobolus durus" (vert) 15 25
262 18p. "Dryopteris ascensionis" (vert) 20 35
263 24p. "Marattia purpurascens" (vert) 30 50

76 17th-Century Bottle Post

1980. "London 1980" International Stamp Exhibition. Multicoloured.

264	8p. Type **76**	15	20
265	12p. 19th-century chance calling ship	20	25
266	15p. "Garth Castle" (regular mail service from 1863)	20	30
267	50p. "St. Helena" (mail services, 1980)	60	90

77 H.M. Queen Elizabeth the Queen Mother

1980. 80th Birthday of The Queen Mother.

269 **77**	15p. multicoloured	40	40

78 Lubbock's Yellowtail

1980. Fishes. Multicoloured.

270	3p. Type **78**	30	15
271	10p. Resplendent angelfish	45	25
272	25p. Bicoloured butterflyfish	75	50
273	40p. Marmalade razorfish	1·00	65

79 H.M.S. "Tortoise"

1980. 150th Anniv of Royal Geographical Society. Multicoloured.

274	10p. Type **79**	35	40
275	15p. "Wideawake Fair"	45	45
276	60p. Mid-Atlantic Ridge (38 × 48 mm)	80	1·25

80 Green Mountain Farm, 1881

1981. Green Mountain Farm. Multicoloured.

277	12p. Type **80**	15	35
278	15p. Two Boats, 1881	20	40
279	20p. Green Mountain and Two Boats, 1981	25	50
280	30p. Green Mountain Farm, 1981	35	70

81 Cable and Wireless Earth Station

1981. "Space Shuttle" Mission and Opening of 2nd Earth Station.

281 **81**	15p. black, blue and pale blue	30	35

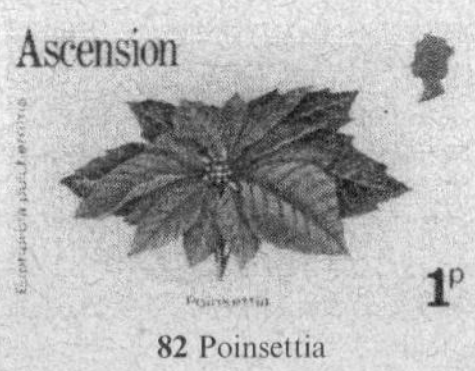

82 Poinsettia

83 Solanum

1981. Flowers. Multicoloured.

282A	1p. Type **82**	70	70
283B	2p. Clustered wax flower	50	75
284B	3p. Kolanchoe (vert)	50	75
285A	4p. Yellow pops	80	75
286A	5p. Camels foot creeper	80	75
287A	8p. White oleander	80	80
288B	10p. Ascension lily (vert)	45	75
289A	12p. Coral plant (vert)	1·50	85
290B	15p. Yellow allamanda	50	75
291B	20p. Ascension euphorbia	1·00	75
292A	30p. Flame of the forest (vert)	1·25	1·25
293A	40p. Bougainvillea "King Leopold"	1·25	2·00
294A	50p. Type **83**	1·25	2·50
295B	£1 Ladies petticoat	2·00	2·75
296A	£2 Red hibiscus	3·75	5·50

Nos. 294/6 are as Type **83**.

84 Map by Maxwell, 1793

1981. Early Maps of Ascension.

297 **84**	10p. black, gold and blue	25	35
298 –	12p. black, gold and green	25	35
299 –	15p. black, gold and stone	25	35
300 –	40p. black, gold and yellow	55	70

DESIGNS: 12p. Maxwell, 1793 (different); 15p. Ekeberg and Chapman, 1811; 40p. Campbell, 1819.

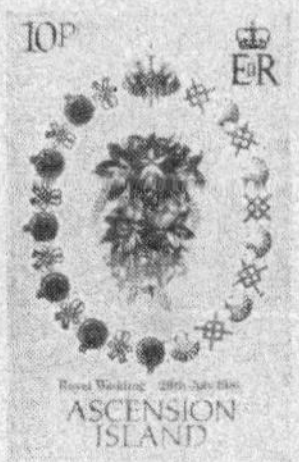

85 Wedding Bouquet from Ascension

87 "Interest"

1981. Royal Wedding. Multicoloured.

302	10p. Type **85**	15	15
303	15p. Prince Charles in Fleet Air Arm flying kit	25	25
304	50p. Prince Charles and Lady Diana Spencer	65	75

1981. 25th Anniv of Duke of Edinburgh Award Scheme. Multicoloured.

305	5p. Type **87**	15	15
306	10p. "Physical activities"	15	15
307	15p. "Service"	20	20
308	40p. Duke of Edinburgh	45	45

88 Scout crossing Rope Bridge

1982. 75th Anniv of Boy Scout Movement.

309 **88**	10p. black, blue and light blue	15	35
310 –	15p. black, brown and yellow	20	50
311 –	25p. black, mve & lt mve	30	60
312 –	40p. black, red and orange	50	85

DESIGNS: 15p. 1st Ascension Scout Group flag; 25p. Scouts learning to use radio; 40p. Lord Baden-Powell.

89 Charles Darwin

1982. 150th Anniv of Charles Darwin's Voyage. Multicoloured.

314	10p. Type **89**	25	40
315	12p. Darwin's pistols	30	50
316	15p. Rock crab	35	55
317	40p. H.M.S. "Beagle"	75	95

90 Fairey Swordfish Torpedo Bomber

1982. 40th Anniv of Wideawake Airfield. Multicoloured.

318	5p. Type **90**	1·00	35
319	10p. North American B-25C Mitchell	1·25	40
320	15p. Boeing EC-135N Aria	1·50	55
321	50p. Lockheed C-130 Hercules	2·25	1·10

91 Ascension Coat of Arms

1982. 21st Birthday of Princess of Wales. Mult.

322	12p. Type **91**	25	25
323	15p. Lady Diana Spencer in Music Room, Buckingham Palace	25	25
324	25p. Bride and Earl Spencer leaving Clarence House	40	40
325	50p. Formal portrait	75	75

1982. Commonwealth Games, Brisbane. Nos. 290/1 optd **1st PARTICIPATION COMMON-WEALTH GAMES 1982**.

326	15p. Yellow allamanda	30	40
327	20p. Ascension euphorbia	40	45

94 Bush House, London

1982. Christmas. 50th Anniv of B.B.C. External Broadcasting. Multicoloured.

328	5p. Type **94**	15	20
329	10p. Atlantic relay station	15	30
330	25p. Lord Reith, first Director-General	30	60
331	40p. King George V making his first Christmas broadcast, 1932	45	75

95 "Marasmius echinosphaerus"

1983. Fungi. Multicoloured.

332	7p. Type **95**	55	30
333	12p. "Chlorophyllum molybdites"	75	45
334	15p. "Leucocoprinus cepaestripes"	90	50
335	20p. "Lycoperdon marginatum"	1·10	65
336	50p. "Marasmiellus distantifolius"	1·75	1·25

96 Aerial View of Georgetown

1983. Island Views (1st series). Multicoloured.

337	12p. Type **96**	20	25
338	15p. Green Mountain farm	20	25
339	20p. Boatswain Bird Island	35	40
340	60p. Telemetry Hill by night	70	80

See also Nos. 367/70.

97 Westland Wessex 5 Helicopter of No. 845 Naval Air Squadron

1983. Bicentenary of Manned Flight. British Military Aircraft. Multicoloured.

341	12p. Type **97**	80	65
342	15p. Avro Vulcan B.2 of No. 44 Squadron	95	75
343	20p. Hawker Siddeley Nimrod M.R.2P of No. 20 Squadron	1·10	85
344	60p. Handey Page Victor K2 of No. 55 Squadron	2·00	2·00

98 Iguanid

1983. Introduced Species. Multicoloured.

345	12p. Type **98**	30	30
346	15p. Common rabbit	35	35
347	20p. Cat	45	45
348	60p. Donkey	1·40	1·40

99 Speckled Tellin

1983. Sea Shells. Multicoloured.

349	7p. Type **99**	20	20
350	12p. Lion's paw scallop	30	30
351	15p. Lurid cowrie	30	35
352	20p. Ascension nerite	40	45
353	50p. Miniature melo	75	1·10

100 1922 1½d. Stamp

102 Naval Semaphore

1984. 150th Anniv of St. Helena as a British Colony. Multicoloured.

354	12p. Type **100**	30	45
355	15p. 1922 2d. stamp	35	50
356	20p. 1922 8d. stamp	40	55
357	60p. 1922 1s. stamp	90	1·40

1984. 250th Anniv of "Lloyd's List" (newspaper). Multicoloured.

359	12p. Type **102**	40	30
360	15p. "Southampton Castle" (liner)	45	35
361	20p. Pier head	55	45
362	70p. "Dane" (screw steamer)	1·60	1·50

103 Penny Coin and Yellow-finned Tuna

1984. New Coinage. Multicoloured.

363	12p Type **103**	65	35
364	15p. Twopenny coin and donkey	75	40
365	20p. Fifty pence coin and green turtle	90	50
366	70p. Pound coin and sooty tern	2·25	1·75

1984. Island Views (2nd series). As T **96**. Mult.

367	12p. The Devil's Riding-school	30	30
368	15p. St. Mary's Church	35	35
369	20p. Two Boats Village	45	45
370	70p. Ascension from the sea	1·10	1·50

104 Bermuda Cypress

105 The Queen Mother with Prince Andrew at Silver Jubilee Service

1985. Trees. Multicoloured.

371 7p. Type **104** 55 20
372 12p. Norfolk Island pine 65 30
373 15p. Screwpine 75 35
374 20p. Eucalyptus 90 45
375 65p. Spore tree 2·25 1·40

1985. Life and Times of Queen Elizabeth the Queen Mother. Multicoloured.

376 12p. With the Duke of York at Balmoral, 1924 25 35
377 15p. Type **105** 25 40
378 20p. The Queen Mother at Ascot 30 55
379 70p. With Prince Henry at his christening (from photo by Lord Snowdon) 80 1·75

106 32 Pdr. Smooth Bore Muzzle-loader, c. 1820, and Royal Marine Artillery Hat Plate, c. 1816

1985. Guns on Ascension Island. Multicoloured.

381 12p. Type **106** 70 90
382 15p. 7 inch rifled muzzle-loader, c. 1866, and Royal Cypher on barrel 80 1·00
383 20p. 7 pdr rifled muzzle-loader, c. 1877, and Royal Artillery Badge 90 1·25
384 70p. 5.5 inch gun, 1941, and crest from H.M.S. "Hood" 2·50 3·50

107 Guide Flag

108 "Clerodendrum fragrans"

1985. 75th Anniv of Girl Guide Movement and International Youth Year. Multicoloured.

385 12p. Type **107** 75 60
386 15p. Practising first aid 85 75
387 20p. Camping 95 85
388 70p. Lady Baden-Powell 2·75 2·00

1985. Wild Flowers. Multicoloured.

389 12p. Type **108** 45 75
390 15p. Shell ginger 55 90
391 20p. Cape daisy 65 90
392 70p. Ginger lily 2·00 2·50

109 Newton's Reflector Telescope

110 Princess Elizabeth in 1926

1986. Appearance of Halley's Comet. Multicoloured.

393 12p. Type **109** 75 1·10
394 15p. Edmond Halley and Old Greenwich Observatory 85 1·25
395 20p. Short's Gregorian telescope and comet, 1759 95 1·25
396 70p. Ascension satellite tracking station and ICE spacecraft 2·75 3·50

1986. 60th Birthday of Queen Elizabeth II. Multicoloured.

397 7p. Type **110** 15 25
398 15p. Queen making Christmas broadcast, 1952 20 40
399 20p. At Garter ceremony, Windsor Castle, 1983 25 50
400 35p. In Auckland, New Zealand, 1981 35 80
401 £1 At Crown Agents' Head Office, London, 1983 1·00 2·25

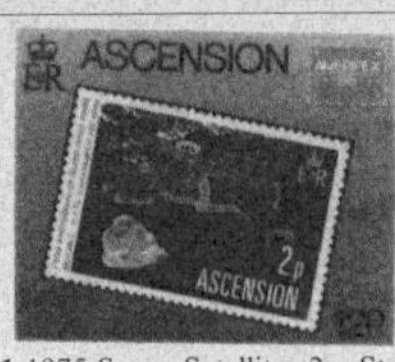

111 1975 Space Satellites 2p. Stamp

1986. "Ameripex '86" International Stamp Exhibition, Chicago. Designs showing previous Ascension stamps. Multicoloured.

402 12p. Type **111** 40 60
403 15p. 1980 "London 1980" International Stamp Exhibition 50p. 45 70
404 20p. 1976 Bicentenary of American Revolution 8p. 55 90
405 70p. 1982 40th anniv of Wideawake Airfield 10p. 1·25 2·00

112 Prince Andrew and Miss Sarah Ferguson

1986. Royal Wedding. Multicoloured.

407 15p. Type **112** 25 35
408 35p. Prince Andrew aboard H.M.S. "Brazen" 50 75

113 H.M.S. "Ganymede" (c. 1811)

1986. Ships of the Royal Navy. Multicoloured.

409 1p. Type **113** 55 1·25
410 2p. H.M.S. "Kangaroo" (c. 1811) 60 1·25
411 4p. H.M.S. "Trinculo" (c. 1811) 60 1·25
412 5p. H.M.S. "Daring" (c. 1811) 60 1·25
413 9p. H.M.S. "Thais" (c. 1811) 70 1·25
414 10p. H.M.S. "Pheasant" (1819) 70 1·25
415 15p. H.M.S. "Myrmidon" (1819) 80 1·50
416 18p. H.M.S. "Atholl" (1825) 90 1·50
417 20p. H.M.S. "Medina" (1830) 90 1·50
418 25p. H.M.S. "Saracen" (1840) 1·00 1·75
419 30p. H.M.S. "Hydra" (c. 1845) 1·00 1·75
420 50p. H.M.S. "Sealark" (1849) 1·25 2·25
421 70p. H.M.S. "Rattlesnake" (1868) 1·75 2·75
422 £1 H.M.S. "Penelope" (1889) 2·40 3·50
423 £2 H.M.S. "Monarch" (1897) 5·00 6·50

114 Cape Gooseberry

1987. Edible Bush Fruits. Multicoloured.

424 12p. Type **114** 65 90
425 15p. Prickly pear 75 1·00
426 20p. Guava 85 1·10
427 70p. Loquat 2·00 2·75

115 Ignition of Rocket Motors

116 Captains in Full Dress raising Red Ensign

1987. 25th Anniv of First American Manned Earth Orbit. Multicoloured.

428 15p. Type **115** 55 75
429 18p. Lift-off 60 80
430 25p. Re-entry 75 95
431 £1 Splashdown 2·50 5·25

1987. 19th-century Uniforms (1st series). Royal Navy, 1815–20. Multicoloured.

433 25p. Type **116** 60 60
434 25p. Surgeon and seamen 60 60
435 25p. Seaman with water-carrying donkey 60 60
436 25p. Midshipman and gun 60 60
437 25p. Commander in undress uniform surveying 60 60

See also Nos. 478/82.

117 "Cynthia cardui"

1987. Insects (1st series). Multicoloured.

438 15p. Type **117** 65 65
439 18p. "Danaus chrysippus" 70 75
440 25p. "Hypolimnas misippus" 85 85
441 £1 "Lampides boeticus" 2·25 2·50

See also Nos. 452/5 and 483/6.

118 Male Ascension Frigate Birds

1987. Sea Birds (1st series). Multicoloured.

442 25p. Type **118** 1·50 1·75
443 25p. Juvenile Ascension frigate bird, brown booby and blue-faced boobies 1·50 1·75
444 25p. Male Ascension frigate bird and blue-faced boobies 1·50 1·75
445 25p. Female Ascension frigate bird 1·50 1·75
446 25p. Adult male feeding juvenile Ascension frigate bird 1·50 1·75

Nos. 442/6 were printed together, se-tenant, forming a composite design.

See also Nos. 469/73.

1987. Royal Ruby Wedding. Nos. 397/401 optd **40TH WEDDING ANNIVERSARY.**

447 7p. Type **110** 15 15
448 15p. Queen making Christmas broadcast, 1952 25 30
449 20p. At Garter ceremony, Windsor Castle, 1983 30 40
450 35p. In Auckland, New Zealand, 1981 50 60
451 £1 At Crown Agents' Head Office, London, 1983 1·25 1·40

1988. Insects (2nd series). As T **117**. Multicoloured.

452 15p. "Gryllus bimaculatus" (field cricket) 50 50
453 18p. "Ruspolia differeus" (bush cricket) 55 55
454 25p. "Chilomenus lunata" (ladybird) 70 70
455 £1 "Diachrysia orichalcea" (moth) 2·25 2·25

120 Bate's Memorial, St. Mary's Church

1988. 150th Death Anniv of Captain William Bate (garrison commander, 1828–38). Multicoloured.

456 9p. Type **120** 35 35
457 15p. Commodore's Cottage 45 45
458 18p. North East Cottage 50 50
459 25p. Map of Ascension 70 70
460 70p. Captain Bate and marines 1·75 1·75

121 H.M.S. "Resolution" (ship of the line), 1667

1988. Bicentenary of Australian Settlement. Ships of the Royal Navy. Multicoloured.

461 9p. Type **121** 65 35
462 18p. H.M.S. "Resolution" (Captain Cook), 1772 90 55
463 25p. H.M.S. "Resolution" (battleship), 1892 1·25 75
464 65p. H.M.S. "Resolution" (battleship), 1916 2·25 1·50

1988. "Sydpex '88" National Stamp Exhibition, Sydney. Nos. 461/4 optd **SYDPEX 88 30.7.88 - 7.8.88.**

465 9p. Type **121** 40 25
466 18p. H.M.S. "Resolution" (Captain Cook), 1772 60 40
467 25p. H.M.S. "Resolution" (battleship), 1892 75 55
468 65p. H.M.S. "Resolution" (battleship), 1916 1·60 1·40

1988. Sea Birds (2nd series). Sooty Tern. As T **118**. Multicoloured.

469 25p. Pair displaying 1·00 1·00
470 25p. Turning egg 1·00 1·00
471 25p. Incubating egg 1·00 1·00
472 25p. Feeding chick 1·00 1·00
473 25p. Immature sooty tern 1·00 1·00

Nos. 469/73 were printed together, se-tenant, forming a composite design of a nesting colony.

123 Lloyd's Coffee House, London, 1688

124 Two Land Crabs

1988. 300th Anniv of Lloyd's of London. Mult.

474 8p. Type **123** 25 35
475 18p. "Alert IV" (cable ship) (horiz) 65 70
476 25p. Satellite recovery in space (horiz) 80 90
477 65p. "Good Hope Castle" (cargo liner) on fire off Ascension, 1973 1·75 2·00

1988. 19th-century Uniforms (2nd series). Royal Marines 1821–34. As T **116**. Multicoloured.

478 25p. Marines landing on Ascension, 1821 1·10 1·60
479 25p. Officer and Marine at semaphore station, 1829 1·10 1·60
480 25p. Sergeant and Marine at Octagonal Tank, 1831 1·10 1·60
481 25p. Officers at water pipe tunnel, 1833 1·10 1·60
482 25p. Officer supervising construction of barracks, 1834 1·10 1·60

1989. Insects (3rd series). As T **117**. Multicoloured.

483 15p. "Trichoptilus wahlbergi" (moth) 75 50
484 18p. "Lucilia sericata" (fly) 80 55
485 25p. "Alceis ornatus" (weevil) 1·10 70
486 £1 "Polistes fuscatus" (wasp) 3·00 2·40

1989. Ascension Land Crabs. Multicoloured.

487 15p. Type **124** 40 45
488 18p. Crab with claws raised 45 50
489 25p. Crab on rock 60 70
490 £1 Crab in surf 2·25 2·50

126 "Apollo 7" Tracking Station, Ascension

127 "Queen Elizabeth 2" (liner) and U.S.S. "John F. Kennedy" (aircraft carrier) in New York Harbour

1989. 20th Anniv of First Manned Landing on Moon. Multicoloured.

493 15p. Type **126** 65 45
494 18p. Launch of "Apollo 7" (30 × 30 mm) 70 50
495 25p. "Apollo 7" emblem (30 × 30 mm) 90 70
496 70p. "Apollo 7" jettisoning expended Saturn rocket 1·75 1·75

1989. "Philexfrance 89" International Stamp Exhibition, Paris, and "World Stamp Expo '89", Washington. Designs showing Statue of Liberty and Centenary celebrations. Mult.

498 15p. Type **127** 35 35
499 15p. Cleaning statue 35 35
500 15p. Statue of Liberty 35 35
501 15p. Crown of statue 35 35
502 15p. Warships and New York skyline 35 35
503 15p. "Jean de Vienne" (French destroyer) and skyscrapers 35 35

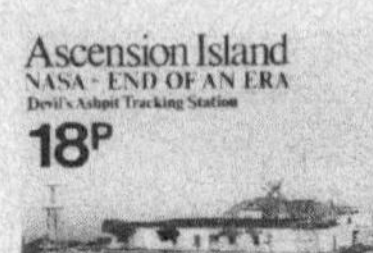

128 Devil's Ashpit Tracking Station

1989. Closure of Devil's Ashpit Tracking Station, Ascension. Multicoloured.

504 18p. Type **128** 80 50
505 25p. Launch of shuttle "Atlantis" 80 55

129 Bubonian Conch

1989. Sea Shells. Multicoloured.

506	8p. Type **129**	40	30
507	18p. Giant tun	70	50
508	25p. Doris loup	90	65
509	£1 Atlantic trumpet triton	2·75	2·50

130 Donkeys 131 Seaman's Pistol, Hat and Cutlass

1989. Ascension Wildlife. Multicoloured.

510	18p. Type **130**	35	40
511	25p. Green turtle	50	55

1990. Royal Navy Equipment, 1815–20. Mult.

512	25p. Type **131**	65	65
513	25p. Midshipman's belt plate, button, sword and hat	65	65
514	25p. Surgeon's hat, sword and instrument chest	65	65
515	25p. Captain's hat, telescope and sword	65	65
516	25p. Admiral's epaulette, megaphone, hat and pocket	65	65

See also Nos. 541/5.

132 Pair of Ascension Frigate Birds with Young 134 "Queen Elizabeth, 1940" (Sir Gerald Kelly)

133 Penny Black and Twopence Blue

1990. Ascension Frigate Bird. Multicoloured.

517	9p. Type **132**	1·25	1·00
518	10p. Fledgeling	1·25	1·00
519	11p. Adult male in flight	1·25	1·00
520	15p. Female and immature birds in flight	1·40	1·25

1990. "Stamp World London 90" International Stamp Exhibition. Multicoloured.

521	9p. Type **133**	50	30
522	18p. Ascension postmarks used on G.B. stamps	70	50
523	25p. Unloading mail at Wideawake Airfield	95	75
524	£1 Mail van and Main Post Office	2·25	2·25

1990. 90th Birthday of Queen Elizabeth the Queen Mother.

525	**134** 25p. multicoloured	75	75
526	– £1 black and lilac	2·25	2·25

DESIGN—29×37mm: £1 King George VI and Queen Elizabeth with Bren-gun carrier.

136 "Madonna and Child" (sculpture, Dino Felici) 137 "Garth Castle" (mail steamer), 1910

1990. Christmas. Works of Art. Multicoloured.

527	8p. Type **136**	70	70
528	18p. "Madonna and Child" (anon)	1·25	1·25
529	25p. "Madonna and Child with St. John" (Johann Gebhard)	1·75	1·75
530	65p. "Madonna and Child" (Giacomo Gritti)	3·00	3·50

1990. Maiden Voyage of "St. Helena II". Mult.

531	9p. Type **137**	90	75
532	18p. "St. Helena I" during Falkland Islands campaign, 1982	1·25	1·25
533	25p. Launch of "St. Helena II"	1·75	1·75
534	70p. Duke of York launching "St. Helena II"	3·00	3·50

1991. 175th Anniv of Occupation. Nos. 418, 420 and 422 optd **BRITISH FOR 175 YEARS**.

536	25p. H.M.S. "Saracen" (1840)	1·50	1·75
537	50p. H.M.S. "Sealark" (1849)	2·00	2·25
538	£1 H.M.S. "Penelope" (1889)	3·00	3·75

139 Queen Elizabeth II at Trooping the Colour

1991. 65th Birthday of Queen Elizabeth II and 70th Birthday of Prince Philip. Multicoloured.

539	25p. Type **139**	90	1·25
540	25p. Prince Philip in naval uniform	90	1·25

1991. Royal Marines Equipment, 1821–44. As T **131**. Multicoloured.

541	25p. Officer's shako, epaulettes, belt plate and button	1·10	1·40
542	25p. Officer's cap, sword, epaulettes and belt plate	1·10	1·40
543	25p. Drum major's shako and staff	1·10	1·40
544	25p. Sergeant's shako, chevrons, belt plate and canteen	1·10	1·40
545	25p. Drummer's shako and side-drum	1·10	1·40

140 B.B.C. World Service Relay Station

1991. 25th Anniv of B.B.C. Atlantic Relay Station. Multicoloured.

546	15p. Type **140**	90	1·00
547	18p. Transmitters at English Bay	1·00	1·10
548	25p. Satellite receiving station (vert)	1·25	1·40
549	70p. Antenna support tower (vert)	2·50	3·00

141 St. Mary's Church

1991. Christmas. Ascension Churches. Multicoloured.

550	8p. Type **141**	55	55
551	18p. Interior of St. Mary's Church	1·00	1·00
552	25p. Our Lady of Ascension Grotto	1·25	1·25
553	65p. Interior of Our Lady of Ascension Grotto	2·75	3·75

142 Black Durgon ("Blackfish")

1991. Fishes. Multicoloured.

554	1p. Type **142**	40	60
555	2p. Sergeant major ("Five finger")	50	60
556	4p. Resplendent angelfish	60	70
557	5p. Derbio ("Silver fish")	60	70
558	9p. Spotted scorpionfish ("Gurnard")	70	80
559	10p. St. Helena parrotfish ("Blue dad")	70	80
560	15p. St. Helena butterflyfish ("Cunning fish")	90	1·00
561	18p. Rock hind ("Grouper")	1·00	1·00
562	20p. Spotted moray	1·00	1·25
563	25p. Squirrelfish ("Hardback soldierfish")	1·00	1·25
564	30p. Blue marlin	1·25	1·40
565	50p. Wahoo	1·75	2·00
566	70p. Yellow-finned tuna	2·25	2·75
567	£1 Blue shark	2·75	3·50
568	£2.50 Bottlenose dolphin	6·00	7·00

143 Holland's Crater

1992. 40th Anniv of Queen Elizabeth II's Accession. Multicoloured.

569	9p. Type **143**	30	30
570	15p. Green Mountain	50	50
571	18p. Boatswain Bird Island	60	60
572	25p. Three portraits of Queen Elizabeth	80	80
573	70p. Queen Elizabeth II	2·00	2·00

The portraits shown on the 25p. are repeated from the three lower values of the set.

144 Compass Rose and "Eye of the Wind" (cadet brig)

1992. 500th Anniv of Discovery of America by Columbus and Re-enactment Voyages. Multicoloured.

574	9p. Type **144**	75	70
575	18p. Map of re-enactment voyages and "Soren Larsen" (cadet brigantine)	1·25	1·00
576	25p. "Santa Maria", "Pinta" and "Nina"	1·50	1·25
577	70p. Columbus and "Santa Maria"	2·75	2·75

145 Control Tower, Wideawake Airfield 146 Hawker Siddeley Nimrod

1992. 50th Anniv of Wideawake Airfield. Multicoloured.

578	15p. Type **145**	65	65
579	18p. Nose hangar	70	70
580	25p. Site preparation by U.S. Army engineers	90	90
581	70p. Laying fuel pipeline	2·25	2·25

1992. 10th Anniv of Liberation of Falkland Islands. Aircraft. Multicoloured.

582	15p. Type **146**	1·00	1·00
583	18p. Vickers VC-10 landing at Ascension	1·10	1·10
584	25p. Westland Wessex HU Mk 5 helicopter lifting supplies	1·40	1·25
585	65p. Avro Vulcan B.2 over Ascension	2·75	3·00

147 "Christmas in Great Britain and Ascension"

1992. Christmas. Children's Paintings. Mult.

587	8p. Type **147**	60	50
588	18p. "Santa Claus riding turtle"	1·00	80
589	25p. "Nativity"	1·25	1·10
590	65p. "Nativity with rabbit"	2·75	3·25

148 Male Canary Singing

1993 Yellow Canary. Multicoloured.

591	15p. Type **148**	75	60
592	18p. Adult male and female	85	70
593	25p. Young birds calling for food	95	90
594	70p. Adults and young birds on the wing	2·50	3·00

149 Sopwith Snipe

1993. 75th Anniv of Royal Air Force. Multicoloured.

595	20p. Type **149**	1·00	75
596	25p. Supermarine Southampton	1·10	85
597	30p. Avro Type 652 Anson	1·25	95
598	70p. Vickers-Armstrong Wellington	2·25	2·50

150 Map of South Atlantic Cable

1993. 25th Anniv of South Atlantic Cable Company. Multicoloured.

600	20p. Type **150**	80	80
601	25p. "Vercors" laying cable	90	90
602	30p. Map of Ascension	1·00	1·00
603	70p. "Vercors" (cable ship) off Ascension	2·25	2·25

151 Lanatana Camara

1993. Local Flowers. Multicoloured.

604	20p. Type **151**	80	70
605	25p. Moonflower	90	75
606	30p. Hibiscus	1·00	85
607	70p. Frangipani	2·25	2·00

152 Posting Christmas Card to Ascension 153 Ichthyosaurus

1993. Christmas. Multicoloured.

608	12p. Type **152**	45	35
609	20p. Loading mail onto R.A.F. Lockheed TriStar at Brize Norton	75	55
610	25p. TriStar over South Atlantic	85	65
611	30p. Unloading mail at Wideawake Airfield	1·10	75
612	65p. Receiving card and Georgetown Post Office	1·60	1·60

1994. Prehistoric Aquatic Reptiles. Mult.

614	12p. Type **153**	55	55
615	20p. Metriorhynchus	75	75
616	25p. Mosasaurus	80	80
617	30p. Elasmosaurus	90	90
618	65p. Plesiosaurus	1·75	2·00

1994. "Hong Kong '94" International Stamp Exhibition. Nos. 614/18 optd **HONG KONG '94** and emblem.

619	12p. Type **153**	65	70
620	20p. Metriorhynchus	85	90
621	25p. Mosasaurus	90	1·00
622	30p. Elasmosaurus	1·00	1·10
623	65p. Plesiosaurus	1·90	2·25

155 Young Green Turtles heading towards Sea

1994. Green Turtles. Multicoloured.

624	20p. Type **155**	1·10	80
625	25p. Turtle digging nest	1·25	90
626	30p. Turtle leaving sea	1·40	1·10
627	65p. Turtle swimming	2·25	2·50

156 "Yorkshireman" (tug)

1994. Civilian Ships used in Liberation of Falkland Islands, 1982. Multicoloured.

629	20p. Type **156**	1·10	80
630	25p. "St. Helena I" (minesweeper support ship)	1·25	90
631	30p. "British Esk" (tanker)	1·40	1·10
632	65p. "Uganda" (hospital ship)	2·25	2·50

157 Sooty Tern Chick

1994. Sooty Tern. Multicoloured.

633	20p. Type **157**	80	90
634	25p. Juvenile bird	85	95
635	30p. Brooding adult	95	1·10
636	65p. Adult male performing courting display	1·75	2·25

158 Donkey Mare with Foal

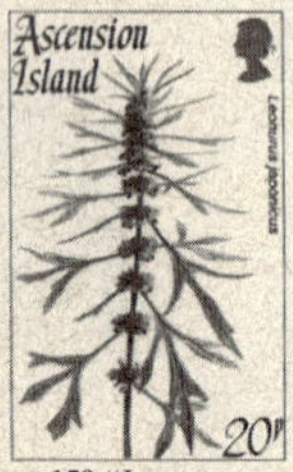

159 "Leonurus japonicus"

1994. Christmas. Donkeys. Multicoloured.

638	12p. Type **158**	55	55
639	20p. Juvenile	75	75
640	25p. Foal	80	80
641	30p. Adult and cattle egrets	95	95
642	65p. Adult	1·90	2·50

1995. Flowers. Multicoloured.

643	20p. Type **159**	1·00	85
644	25p. "Catharanthus roseus" (horiz)	1·10	95
645	30p. "Mirabilis jalapa"	1·25	1·10
646	65p. "Asclepias curassavica" (horiz)	2·25	2·50

ASCENSION ISLAND
160 Two Boats and Green Mountain

1995. Late 19th-century Scenes. Each in cinnamon and brown.

647	12p. Type **160**	50	50
648	20p. Island Stewards' Store	70	70
649	25p. Navy headquarters and barracks	80	80
650	30p. Police office	1·50	1·25
651	65p. Pierhead	1·75	2·25

161 5.5-inch Coastal Battery

1995. 50th Anniv of End of Second World War. Multicoloured.

652	20p. Type **161**	75	75
653	25p. Fairey Swordfish aircraft	1·00	1·00
654	30p. H.M.S. "Dorsetshire" (cruiser)	1·25	1·25
655	65p. H.M.S. "Devonshire" (cruiser)	2·25	2·50

162 Male and Female "Lampides boeticus"

1995. Butterflies. Multicoloured.

657	20p. Type **162**	80	65
658	25p. "Vanessa cardui"	90	75
659	30p. Male "Hypolimnas misippus"	1·10	85
660	65p. "Danaus chrysippus"	2·00	1·90

163 "Santa Claus on Boat" (Phillip Stephens)

1995. Christmas. Children's Drawings. Multicoloured.

662	12p. Type **163**	50	50
663	20p. "Santa sitting on Wall" (Kelly Lemon)	75	75
664	25p. "Santa in Chimney" (Mario Anthony)	80	80
665	30p. "Santa riding Dolphin" (Verena Benjamin)	90	1·00
666	65p. "Santa in Sleigh over Ascension" (Tom Butler)	1·75	2·50

164 "Cypraea lurida oceanica"

1996. Molluscs. Multicoloured.

667	12p. Type **164**	65	65
668	25p. "Cypraea spurca sanctaehelenae"	1·00	1·00
669	30p. "Harpa doris"	1·00	1·00
670	65p. "Umbraculum umbraculum"	1·75	1·75

Nos. 667/70 were printed together, se-tenant, forming a composite design.

165 Queen Elizabeth II and St. Mary's Church

1996 70th Birthday of Queen Elizabeth II. Mult.

671	20p. Type **165**	55	60
672	25p. The Residency	60	60
673	30p. The Roman Catholic Grotto	70	70
674	65p. The Exiles' Club	1·75	1·75

166 American Army Jeep

1996. "CAPEX '96" International Stamp Exhibition, Toronto. Island Transport. Multicoloured.

675	20p. Type **166**	65	65
676	25p. Citroen 7.5hp two-seater car, 1924	70	70
677	30p. Austin ten tourer car, 1930	80	80
678	65p. Series 1 Land Rover	1·75	1·75

MORE DETAILED LISTS

are given in the Stanley Gibbons Catalogues referred to in the country headings.
For lists of current volumes see Introduction.

167 Madeiran Storm Petrel

168 Pylons

1996. Birds and their Young. Multicoloured.

679	1p. Type **167**	10	10
680	2p. Red-billed tropic bird	10	10
681	4p. Common mynah	10	10
682	5p. House sparrow	10	15
683	7p. Common waxbill	15	20
684	10p. White tern	20	25
685	12p. Bare-throated francolin	25	30
686	15p. Common noddy	30	35
687	20p. Yellow canary	40	45
688	25p. Lesser noddy	50	55
689	30p. Red-footed booby	60	65
690	40p. White-tailed tropic bird	80	85
691	65p. Brown booby	1·25	1·40
692	£1 Blue-faced booby	2·00	2·10
693	£2 Sooty tern	4·00	4·25
694	£3 Ascension frigate bird	6·00	6·25

See also Nos. 726/7.

1996. 30th Anniv of B.B.C. Atlantic Relay Station. Multicoloured.

695	20p. Type **168**	65	65
696	25p. Pylons (different)	70	70
697	30p. Pylons and station buildings	80	80
698	65p. Dish aerial, pylon and beach	1·75	1·75

169 Santa Claus on Dish Aerial

1996. Christmas. Santa Claus. Multicoloured.

699	12p. Type **169**	35	35
700	20p. Playing golf	65	65
701	25p. In deck chair	65	65
702	30p. On top of aircraft	75	75
703	65p. On funnel of "St. Helena II" (mail ship)	1·75	2·00

170 Date Palm

171 Red Ensign and "Maersk Ascension" (tanker)

1997. "Hong Kong '97" International Stamp Exhibition. Trees. Multicoloured.

704	20p. Type **170**	55	55
705	25p. Mauritius hemp	65	65
706	30p. Norfolk Island pine	75	75
707	65p. Dwarf palm	1·50	1·60

1997. Flags. Multicoloured.

709	12p. Type **171**	45	45
710	25p. R.A.F. flag and Tristar airliner	75	75
711	30p. N.A.S.A. emblem and Space Shuttle "Atlantis" landing	85	85
712	65p. White Ensign and H.M.S. "Northumberland" (frigate)	1·60	1·60

172 "Solanum sodomaeum"

1997. Wild Herbs. Multicoloured.

713	30p. Type **172**	90	1·00
714	30p. "Ageratum conyzoides"	90	1·00
715	30p. "Leonurus sibiricus"	90	1·00
716	30p. "Cerastium vulgatum"	90	1·00
717	30p. "Commelina diffusa"	90	1·00

Nos. 713/17 were printed together, se-tenant, with the backgrounds forming a composite design.

173 Queen Elizabeth II

1997. Golden Wedding of Queen Elizabeth and Prince Philip. Multicoloured.

719	20p. Type **173**	65	65
720	20p. Prince Philip on horseback	65	65
721	25p. Queen Elizabeth with polo pony	75	75
722	25p. Prince Philip in Montserrat	75	75
723	30p. Queen Elizabeth and Prince Philip	80	80
724	30p. Prince William and Prince Harry on horseback	80	80

Nos. 719/20, 721/2 and 723/4 respectively were printed together, se-tenant, with the backgrounds forming composite designs.

1997. Birds and their Young. As Nos. 683 and 687, but smaller, size 20 × 24 mm. Multicoloured.

726	15p. Common waxbill	30	35
727	35p. Yellow canary	70	75

174 Black Marlin

1997. Gamefish. Multicoloured.

728	12p. Type **174**	40	40
729	20p. Atlantic sailfish	65	65
730	25p. Swordfish	75	75
731	30p. Wahoo	85	85
732	£1 Yellowfin tuna	2·25	2·25

175 Interior of St. Mary's Church

176 "Cactoblastis cactorum" (caterpillar and moth)

1997. Christmas. Multicoloured.

733	15p. Type **175**	35	40
734	35p. Falklands memorial window showing Virgin and child	75	80
735	40p. Falklands memorial window showing Archangel	85	95
736	50p. Pair of stained glass windows	1·10	1·25

1998. Biological Control using Insects. Multicoloured.

737	15p. Type **176**	40	40
738	35p. "Teleonemia scrupulosa" (lace-bug)	80	80
739	40p. "Neltumius arizonensis" (beetle)	90	90
740	50p. "Algarobius prosopis" (beetle)	1·25	1·25

178 Fairey Fawn

1998. 80th Anniv of Royal Air Force. Multicoloured.

742	15p. Type **178**	50	50
743	35p. Vickers Vernon	1·00	1·00
744	40p. Supermarine Spitfire F.22	1·25	1·25
745	50p. Bristol Britannia C.2	1·40	1·40

179 Barn Swallow

180 Cricket

1998. Migratory Birds. Multicoloured.

747	15p. Type **179**	45	45
748	25p. House martin	70	75
749	35p. Cattle egret	90	95
750	40p. Common swift	1·00	1·10
751	50p. Allen's gallinule	1·10	1·25

1998. Sporting Activities. Multicoloured.

752	15p. Type **180**	55	50
753	35p. Golf	1·00	90
754	40p. Football	1·00	95
755	50p. Shooting	1·10	1·25

181 Children in Nativity Play

1998. Christmas. Multicoloured.

756	15p. Type **181**	45	40
757	35p. Santa Claus arriving on Ascension	1·00	1·00
758	40p. Santa Claus on carnival float	1·10	1·10
759	50p. Carol singers	1·10	1·25

182 Curtiss C-46 Commando

1999. Aircraft. Multicoloured.

760	15p. Type **182**	30	35
761	35p. Douglas C-47 Dakota	70	75
762	40p. Douglas C-54 Skymaster	80	85
763	50p. Consolidated Liberator Mk. V	1·00	1·10

183 "Glengorm Castle" (mail ship), 1929

1999. "Australia '99" World Stamp Exhibition, Melbourne. Ships. Multicoloured.

765	15p. Type **183**	30	35
766	35p. "Gloucester Castle" (mail ship), 1930	70	75
767	40p. "Durham Castle" (mail ship), 1930	80	85
768	50p. "Garth Castle" (mail ship), 1930	1·00	1·10

184 Pair of White Terns ("Fairy Terns")

1999. Endangered Species. White Tern ("Fairy Tern"). Multicoloured.

[illegible]	0p. Type **184**	20	25
[illegible]	0p. On branch	20	25
[illegible]	0p. Adult and fledgling	20	25
[illegible]	0p. In flight	20	25

185 Prince Edward and Miss Sophie Rhys-Jones

1999. Royal Wedding. Multicoloured.

0p. Type **185**	1·00	1·10
1 Engagement photograph	2·00	2·10

POSTAGE DUE STAMPS

D 1 Outline Map of Ascension

1986.

D1	D 1	1p. deep brown and brown	10	10
D2		2p. brown and orange	10	10
D3		5p. brown and orange	10	10
D4		7p. black and violet	15	20
D5		10p. black and blue	20	25
D6		25p. black and green	50	55

AUSTRALIA

An island continent to the S.E. of Asia. A Commonwealth consisting of the states of New S. Wales, Queensland, S. Australia, Tasmania, Victoria and W. Australia.

1913. 12 pence = 1 shilling; 20 shillings = 1 pound.
1966. 100 cents = 1 dollar.

1 Eastern Grey Kangaroo

3

1913.

1	1	½d. green	6·00	2·75
2		1d. red	8·50	85
35		2d. grey	25·00	5·50
36		2½d. blue	22·00	9·50
37		3d. green	27·00	3·50
6		4d. orange	50·00	22·00
8		5d. brown	40·00	32·00
38		6d. blue	50·00	6·00
73		6d. brown	24·00	1·50
133		9d. violet	26·00	1·00
40		1s. green	35·00	3·00
41		2s. brown	£150	11·00
134		2s. purple	5·00	45
135		5s. grey and yellow	£110	12·00
136		10s. grey and pink	£250	£100
44		£1 brown and blue	£1300	£700
137		£1 grey	£425	£150
138		£2 black and pink	£1600	£325

1913.

20	3	½d. green	3·75	80
94		½d. orange	2·25	1·25
17		1d. red	2·50	4·50
57		1d. violet	7·00	1·25
125		1d. green	1·75	10
59		1½d. brown	6·50	40
61		1½d. green	4·00	55
77		1½d. red	2·25	30
62		2d. orange	15·00	70
127		2d. red	1·75	10
98		2d. brown	8·00	8·00
128		3d. blue	18·00	90
22		4d. orange	27·00	2·50
64		4d. violet	13·00	14·00
65		4d. blue	48·00	7·00
129		4d. green	18·00	1·00
92		4½d. violet	18·00	3·75
130		5d. brown	15·00	15
131		1s. 4d. blue	60·00	3·50

4 Laughing Kookaburra

8 Parliament House, Canberra

1913.

19	4	6d. purple	70·00	38·00

1927. Opening of Parliament House.

105	8	1½d. red	50	50

1928. National Stamp Exhibition, Melbourne.

106	4	3d. blue	4·25	4·75

9 De Havilland Hercules and Pastoral Scene

10 Black Swan

1929. Air.

115	9	3d. green	10·00	3·75

1929. Centenary of Western Australia.

116	10	1½d. red	1·25	1·60

11 "Capt. Chas Sturt" (J.H. Crossland)

13 The "Southern Cross" above Hemispheres

1930. Centenary of Sturt's Exploration of River Murray.

117	11	1½d. red	1·00	75
118		3d. blue	4·00	6·00

1930. Surch in words.

119	3	2d. on 1½d. red	1·25	50
120		5d. on 4½d. violet	7·50	8·00

1931. Kingsford Smith's Flights.

121	13	2d. red (postage)	75	75
122		3d. blue	4·50	4·50
123		6d. purple (air)	9·00	11·00

1931. Air. As T 13 but inscr "AIR MAIL SERVICE".

139	–	6d. brown	16·00	12·00

1931. Air. No. 139 optd O S.

139a	–	6d. brown	35·00	48·00

17 Superb Lyrebird

18 Sydney Harbour Bridge

1932.

140	17	1s. green	42·00	1·50

1932. Opening of Sydney Harbour Bridge.

144	18	2d. red	2·00	1·40
142		3d. blue	4·25	7·00
143		5s. green	£375	£180

19 Laughing Kookaburra

20 Melbourne and River Yarra

1932.

146	19	6d. red	25·00	55

1934. Centenary of Victoria.

147	20	2d. red	2·50	1·75
148		3d. blue	6·00	5·50
149		1s. black	45·00	19·00

21 Merino Ram

22 Hermes

1934. Death Centenary of Capt. John Macarthur.

150	21	2d. red	4·00	1·50
151		3d. blue	10·00	8·50
152		9d. purple	38·00	40·00

1934.

153b	22	1s. 6d. purple	4·75	1·25

23 Cenotaph, Whitehall

24 King George V on "Anzac"

1935. 20th. Anniv of Gallipoli Landing.

154	23	2d. red	80	30
155		1s. black	48·00	38·00

1935. Silver Jubilee.

156	24	2d. red	1·50	30
157		3d. blue	7·00	7·50
158		2s. violet	45·00	40·00

25 Amphitrite and Telephone Cable

26 Site of Adelaide, 1836; Old Gum Tree, Glenelg; King William Street, Adelaide

1936. Opening of Submarine Telephone Cable to Tasmania.

159	25	2d. red	75	50
160		3d. blue	2·75	2·75

1936. Centenary of South Australia.

161	26	2d. red	1·25	40
162		3d. blue	4·00	3·50
163		1s. green	10·00	8·50

27 Wallaroo

28 Queen Elizabeth

29 King George VI 30

31 King George VI

33 Merino Ram

38 Queen Elizabeth

40 King George VI and Queen Elizabeth

1937.

228	27	½d. orange	20	10
165	28	1d. green	40	10
180	–	1d. green	2·50	10
181	–	1d. purple	1·25	10
182	29	1½d. purple	4·00	7·50
183	–	1½d. green	1·00	70
167	30	2d. red	40	10
184	–	2d. red	2·50	10
185	30	2d. purple	50	80
186	31	3d. blue	45·00	2·25
187		3d. brown	30	10
188	–	4d. green	1·00	10
189	33	5d. purple	45	1·50
190a	–	6d. brown	1·75	10
191	–	9d. brown	1·00	20
192	–	1s. green	1·00	10
175	31	1s. 4d. mauve	1·50	1·50
176a	38	5s. purple	5·00	2·00
177	–	10s. purple	38·00	12·00
178	40	£1 slate	65·00	30·00

DESIGNS—As Type 28: 4d. Koala; 6d. Kookaburra; 1s. Lyrebird. As Type 33: 9d. Platypus. As Type 38: 10s. King George VI.

Nos. 180 and 184 are as Types 28 and 30 but with completely shaded background.

41 Governor Phillip at Sydney Cove (J. Allcot)

42 A.I.F. and Nurse

1937. 150th Anniv of New South Wales.

193	41	2d. red	2·25	15
194		3d. blue	7·50	2·75
195		9d. purple	15·00	9·50

1940. Australian Imperial Forces.

196	42	1d. green	1·75	1·25
197		2d. red	1·75	50
198		3d. blue	12·00	7·50
199		6d. purple	22·00	13·00

1941. Surch with figures and bars.

200	30	2½d. on 2d. red	60	40
201	31	3½d. on 3d. blue	75	1·50
202	33	5½d. on 5d. purple	3·50	4·00

46a Queen Elizabeth 47 King George VI 48

49 King George VI

50 Emu

1942.

203	46a	1d. purple	50	10
204		1½d. green	40	10
205	47	2d. purple	55	50
206	48	2½d. red	30	10
207	49	3½d. blue	40	20
208	50	5½d. grey	65	10

52 Duke and Duchess of Gloucester

53 Star and Wreath

1945. Royal Visit.

209	52	2½d. red	10	10
210		3½d. blue	15	55
211		5½d. grey	20	55

1946. Victory. Inscr "PEACE 1945".

213	53	2½d. red	10	10
214	–	3½d. blue	25	75
215	–	5½d. green	30	50

DESIGNS—HORIZ: 3½d. Flag and dove. VERT: 5½d. Angel.

56 Sir Thomas Mitchell and Queensland

1946. Centenary of Mitchell's Central Queensland Exploration.

216	56	2½d. red	10	10
217		3½d. blue	25	80
218		1s. green	30	30

57 Lt. John Shortland, R.N.

58 Steel Foundry

1947. 150th Anniv of City of Newcastle.

219	57	2½d. lake	10	10
220	58	3½d. blue	35	65
221	–	5½d. green	35	45

DESIGNS—As Type 58: HORIZ: 5½d. Coal carrier cranes.

60 Queen Elizabeth II when Princess

1947. Wedding of Princess Elizabeth.

222a	60	1d. purple	10	10

61 Hereford Bull

61a Hermes and Globe

62 Aboriginal Art

62a Commonwealth Coat of Arms

1948.

223	61	1s. 3d. brown	1·75	95
223a	61a	1s. 6d. brown	90	10
224	62	2s. brown	2·00	10
224a	62a	5s. red	3·25	10
224b		10s. purple	17·00	70
224c		£1 blue	35·00	3·50
224d		£2 green	£110	14·00

63 William J. Farrer   64 Ferdinand von Mueller

1948. W. J. Farrer (wheat research) Commem.
225 **63** 2½d. red 10 10

1948. Sir Ferdinand von Mueller (botanist) Commemoration.
226 **64** 2½d. red 10 10

65 Boy Scout   66 "Henry Lawson" (Sir Lionel Lindsay)

1948. Pan-Pacific Scout Jamboree, Wonga Park.
227 **65** 2½d. lake 10 10
For 3½d. value dates "1952–53", see No. 254.

1949. Henry Lawson (poet) Commemoration.
231 **66** 2½d. purple 15 10

67 Mounted Postman and Convair CV 240 Aircraft   68 John, Lord Forrest of Bunbury

1949. 75th Anniv of U.P.U.
232 **67** 3½d. blue 30 40

1949. John, Lord Forrest (explorer and politician) Commemoration.
233 **68** 2½d. red 15 10

69 King George VI   70 Queen Elizabeth

81 King George VI 80

71 Aborigine   82 King George VI

1950.
236 **70** 1½d. green 15 10
237 2d. green 15 10
234 **69** 2½d. red 10 10
237c 2½d. brown 15 15
235 3d. red 15 10
237d 3d. green 15 10
247 **81** 3½d. purple 10 10
248 4½d. red 15 70
249 6½d. brown 15 60
250 6½d. green 10 15
251 **80** 7½d. blue 15 45
238 **71** 8½d. brown 15 45
252 **82** 1s. 0½d. blue 35 30
253 **71** 2s. 6d. brown (21 × 25½ mm) 1·50 35

72 73
Reproduction of First Stamps of N.S.W. and Victoria

1950. Centenary of Australian States Stamps.
239 **72** 2½d. purple 15 10
240 **73** 2½d. purple 15 10

75 Sir Henry Parkes   77 Federal Parliament House, Canberra

1951. 50th Anniv of Commonwealth. Inscr as in T 75 and 77.
241 **75** 3d. lake 30 10
242 – 3d. lake 30 10
243 – 5½d. blue . . . . 20 2·00
244 **77** 1s. 6d. brown 35 50
DESIGNS—As Type **70**: No. 242, Sir Edmund Barton. As Type **77**: No. 243, Opening first Federal Parliament.

78 E. H. Hargraves   79 C. J. Latrobe

1951. Centenaries. Discovery of Gold in Australia and of Responsible Government in Victoria.
245 **78** 3d. purple 30 10
246 **79** 3d. purple 30 10

1952. Pan-Pacific Scout Jamboree, Greystanes. As T **65** but dated "1952–53".
254 **65** 3½d. lake 10 10

83 Butter   86 Queen Elizabeth II

1953. Food Production. Inscr "PRODUCE FOOD!".
255 **83** 3d. green 30 10
256 – 3d. green (Wheat) 30 10
257 – 3d. green (Beef) 30 10
258 **83** 3½d. red 30 10
259 – 3½d. red (Wheat) 30 10
260 – 3½d. red (Beef) 30 10

1953.
261 **86** 1d. purple 15 10
261a 2½d. blue 20 10
262 3d. green 20 10
263 3½d. red 20 10
263a 6½d. orange . . . . 1·50 10

87 Queen Elizabeth II   88 Young Farmers and Calf

1953. Coronation.
264 **87** 3½d. red 35 10
265 7½d. violet . . . . 75 1·10
266 2s. turquoise . . . . 2·50 1·10

1953. 25th Anniv of Australian Young Farmers' Clubs.
267 **88** 3½d. brown and green . . 10 10

89 Lt.-Gov. D. Collins   90 Lt.-Gov. W. Paterson

91 Sullivan Cove, Hobart, 1804   92 Stamp of 1853

1953. 150th Anniv of Settlement in Tasmania.
268 **89** 3½d. purple 30 10
269 **90** 3½d purple 30 10
270 **91** 2s. green . . . . 1·50 2·75

1953. 1st Centenary of Tasmania Postage Stamps.
271 **92** 3d. red 10 30

93 Queen Elizabeth II and Duke of Edinburgh

94 Queen Elizabeth II   95 "Telegraphic Communications"

1954. Royal Visit.
272 **93** 3½d. red 20 10
273 **94** 7½d. purple . . . . 35 1·25
274 **93** 2s. green 85 65

1954. Centenary of Telegraph.
275 **95** 3½d. brown 10 10

96 Red Cross and Globe   97 Mute Swan

1954. 40th Anniv of Australian Red Cross Society.
276 **96** 3½d. blue and red 10 10

1954. Centenary of Western Australian Stamps.
277 **97** 3½d. black 20 10

98 Locomotives of 1854 and 1954

1954. Centenary of Australian Railways.
278 **98** 3½d. purple 30 10

99 Territory Badge   100 Olympic Games Symbol

1954. Australian Antarctic Research.
279 **99** 3½d. black 15 10

1954. Olympic Games Propaganda.
280 **100** 2s. blue 70 80
280a 2s. green . . . . 1·75 1·50

101 Rotary Symbol, Globe and Flags   103 American Memorial, Canberra

1955. 50th Anniv of Rotary International.
281 **101** 3½d. red 10 10

1955. Australian-American Friendship.
283 **103** 3½d. blue 10 10

101a Queen Elizabeth II 102

1955.
282a **101a** 4d. lake 20 10
282b 7½d. violet . . . . 60 1·25
282c 10d. blue 60 75
282 **102** 1s. 0½d. blue . . . . . 2·00 75
282d 1s. 7d. brown . . . . . 2·00 30

104 Cobb & Co. Coach (from dry-print by Sir Lionel Lindsay)

1955. Mail-coach Pioneers Commemoration.
284 **104** 3½d. sepia 25 10
285 2s. brown . . . . 75 1·40

105 Y.M.C.A. Emblem and Map of the World

1955. World Centenary of Y.M.C.A.
286 **105** 3½d. green and red 10 10

106 Florence Nightingale and Young Nurse   107 Queen Victoria

1955. Nursing Profession Commemoration.
287 **106** 3½d. lilac 10 10

1955. Centenary of South Australian Postage Stamps.
288 **107** 3½d. green 10 10

108 Badges of N.S.W., Victoria and Tasmania

1956. Centenary of Responsible Government in N.S.W., Victoria and Tasmania.
289 **108** 3½d. lake 10 10

109 Arms of Melbourne   110 Olympic Torch and Symbol

111 Collins Street, Melbourne

1956. Olympic Games, Melbourne.
290 **109** 4d. red 25 10
291 **110** 7½d. blue . . . . 50 1·25
292 **111** 1s. multicoloured 50 30
293 – 2s. multicoloured . . . . 70 1·25
DESIGN—As Type **111**: 2s. Melbourne across River Yarra.

115 South Australia Coat of Arms   116 Map of Australia and Caduceus

1957. Centenary of Responsible Government in South Australia.
296 115 4d. brown 10 10

1957. Royal Flying Doctor Service of Australia.
297 116 7d. blue 15 10

117 "The Spirit of Christmas" (after Sir Joshua Reynolds)

1957. Christmas.
298 117 3½d. red 10 20
299 4d. purple 10 10

118 Lockheed Super Constellation Airliner

1958. Inaug of Australian "Round-the-World" Air Service.
301 118 2s. blue 60 1·00

119 Hall of Memory, Sailor and Airman

1958.
302 119 5½d. lake 40 30
303 – 5½d. lake 40 30
No. 303 shows a soldier and servicewoman instead of the sailor and airman.

120 Sir Charles Kingsford Smith and the "Southern Cross"

122 The Nativity

121 Silver Mine, Broken Hill

1958. 30th Anniv of 1st Air Crossing of the Tasman Sea.
304 120 8d. blue 60 95

1958. 75th Anniv of Founding of Broken Hill.
305 121 4d. brown 30 10

1958. Christmas Issue.
306 122 3½d. red 20 10
307 4d. violet 20 10

124 Queen Elizabeth II 126

127 128 129
Queen Elizabeth II

1959.
308 – 1d. purple 10 10
309 124 2d. brown 50 15
311 126 3d. turquoise 15 10
312 127 3½d. green 15 15
313 128 4d. red 1·75 10
314 129 5d. blue 90 10
No. 308 shows a head and shoulders portrait as in Type 128 and is vert.

131 Numbat

137 Christmas Bells

142 Aboriginal Stockman

1959.
316 131 6d. brown 2·00 10
317 – 8d. red 75 10
318 – 9d. sepia 1·75 45
319 – 11d. blue 1·25 15
320 – 1s. green 4·00 40
321 – 1s. 2d. purple 1·25 15
322 137 1s. 6d. red on yellow 2·50 80
323 – 2s. blue 1·25 10
324 – 2s. 3d. green on yellow 1·75 10
324a – 2s. 3d. green 6·00 1·50
325 – 2s. 5d. brown on yellow 7·00 55
326 – 3s. red 2·00 10
327 142 5s. brown 20·00 85
DESIGNS—As Type 131: VERT: 8d. Tiger Cat; 9d. Eastern grey kangaroo; 11d. Common rabbit bandicoot; 1s. Platypus. HORIZ: 1s. 2d. Thylacine. As Type 137: 2s. Flannel flower; 2s. 3d. Wattle; 2s. 5d. Banksia (plant); 3s. Waratah.

143 Postmaster Isaac Nichols boarding the Brig "Experiment"

1959. 150th Anniv of Australian P.O.
331 143 4d. slate 15 10

144 Parliament House, Brisbane, and Arms of Queensland

145 "The Approach of the Magi"

1959. Centenary of Queensland Self-Government.
332 144 4d. lilac and green 10 10

1959. Christmas.
333 145 5d. violet 10 10

146 Girl Guide and Lord Baden-Powell

147 "The Overlanders" (after Sir Daryl Lindsay)

1960. 50th Anniv of Girl Guide Movement.
334 146 5d. blue 30 15

1960. Centenary of Northern Territory Exploration.
335 147 5d. mauve 30 15

148 "Archer" and Melbourne Cup

149 Queen Victoria

1960. 100th Melbourne Cup Race Commemoration.
336 148 5d. sepia 20 10

1960. Centenary of Queensland Stamps.
337 149 5d. green 25 10

MORE DETAILED LISTS
are given in the Stanley Gibbons Catalogues referred to in the country headings.
For lists of current volumes see Introduction.

150 Open Bible and Candle

151 Colombo Plan Bureau Emblem

1960. Christmas Issue.
338 150 5d. lake 10 10

1961. Colombo Plan.
339 151 1s brown 10 10

152 Melba (after bust by Sir Bertram Mackennal)

153 Open Prayer Book and Text

1961. Birth Centenary of Dame Nellie Melba (singer).
340 152 5d. blue 30 15

1961. Christmas Issue.
341 153 5d. brown 10 10

154 J. M. Stuart

155 Flynn's Grave and Nursing Sister

1962. Centenary of Stuart's South to North Crossing of Australia.
342 154 5d. red 15 10

1962. 50th Anniv of Australian Inland Mission.
343 155 5d. multicoloured 30 15

156 "Woman"

157 "Madonna and Child"

1962. "Associated Country Women of the World" Conference, Melbourne.
344 156 5d. green 10 10

1962. Christmas.
345 157 5d. violet 15 10

158 Perth and Kangaroo Paw (plant)

160 Queen Elizabeth II

1962. British Empire and Commonwealth Games, Perth. Multicoloured.
346 5d. Type 158 40 10
347 2s. 3d. Arms of Perth and running track 3·25 2·75

1963. Royal Visit.
348 160 5d. green 35 10
349 – 2s. 3d. lake 2·00 3·50
DESIGN: 2s. 3d. Queen Elizabeth II and Duke of Edinburgh.

162 Arms of Canberra and W. B. Griffin (architect)

163 Centenary Emblem

1963. 50th Anniv of Canberra.
350 162 5d. green 15 10

1963. Centenary of Red Cross.
351 163 5d. red, grey and blue 30 10

164 Blaxland, Lawson and Wentworth on Mount York

1963. 150th Anniv of First Crossing of Blue Mountains.
352 164 5d. blue 15 10

165 "Export"

1963. Export Campaign.
353 165 5d. red 10 10

1963. As T 160 but smaller 17½×21½ mm "5D" at top right replacing "ROYAL VISIT 1963" and oak leaves omitted.
354 5d. green 65 10
354c 5d. red 55 10

167 Tasman and "Heemskerk"

173 "Peace on Earth ..."

1963. Navigators.
355 167 4s. blue 3·75 55
356 – 5s. brown 5·00 1·00
357 – 7s. 6d. olive 19·00 16·00
358 – 10s. purple 35·00 4·50
359 – £1 violet 35·00 15·00
360 – £2 sepia 75·00 75·00
DESIGNS—As Type 167: 7s. 6d. Captain Cook; 10s. Flinders and "Investigator". 20½×25½ mm: 5s. Dampier and "Roebuck"; £1 Bass and whale boat; £2 Admiral King and "Mermaid" (survey cutter).

1963. Christmas.
361 173 5d. blue 10 10

174 "Commonwealth Cable"

176 Black-backed Magpie

1963. Opening of COMPAC (Trans-Pacific Telephone Cable).
362 174 2s. 3d. multicoloured 2·00 3·50

1964. Birds.
363 – 6d. multicoloured 80 25
364 176 9d. black, grey and green 1·00 2·75
365 – 1s. 6d. multicoloured 75 1·40
366 – 2s. yellow, black and pink 1·75 50
367 – 2s. 5d. multicoloured 2·50 3·50
368 – 2s. 6d. multicoloured 5·00 3·25
369 – 3s. multicoloured 5·00 1·75
BIRDS—HORIZ: 6d. Yellow-tailed thornbill; 2s. 6d. Scarlet robin. VERT: 1s. 6d. Galah (cockatoo); 2s. Golden whistler (Thickhead); 2s. 5d. Blue wren; 3s. Straw-necked ibis.

182 Bleriot XI Aircraft (type flown by M. Guillaux, 1914)

1964. 50th Anniv of 1st Australian Airmail Flight.
370 182 5d. green 40 10
371 2s. 3d. red 3·50 2·50

183 Child looking at Nativity Scene

184 "Simpson and his Donkey"

1964. Christmas.
372 **183** 5d. red, blue, buff and black . . . 10 10

1965. 50th Anniv of Gallipoli Landing.
373 **184** 5d. brown 65 10
374 8d. blue . . . . 1·00 2·50
375 2s. 3d. purple . . . . . . 1·75 2·50

185 "Telecommunications"

186 Sir Winston Churchill

1965. Centenary of I.T.U.
376 **185** 5d. black, brown and blue . . 40 10

1965. Churchill Commemoration.
377 **186** 5d. multicoloured 15 10

187 General Monash

188 Hargrave and "Multiplane" Seaplane (1902)

1965. Birth Centenary of General Sir John Monash (engineer and soldier).
378 **187** 5d. multicoloured 15 10

1965. 50th Death Anniv of Lawrence Hargrave (aviation pioneer).
379 **188** 5d. multicoloured 15 10

189 I.C.Y. Emblem

190 "Nativity Scene"

1965. International Co-operation Year.
380 **189** 2s. 3d. green and blue . . 90 2·00

1965. Christmas.
381 **190** 5d. multicoloured 15 10

191 Queen Elizabeth II

192 Blue-faced Honeyeater

1966. Decimal currency. As earlier issues but with values in cents and dollars as in T **191/2**. Also some new designs.
382 **191** 1 c. brown 25 10
383 2 c. green 70 10
384 3 c. green 70 10
404 3 c. black, pink and green . . 30 60
385 4 c. red 20 10
405 4 c. black, brown and red . . 35 20
405a 5 c. black, brown and blue . . 40 10
386 – 5 c. multicoloured (as 363) . . 25 10
386c **191** 5 c. blue 70 10
387 **192** 6 c. multicoloured . . . 70 45
387a **191** 6 c. orange 55 10
388 – 7 c. multicoloured . . . 85 10
388a **191** 7 c. purple . . . . . . 1·10 10
389 – 8 c. multicoloured . . . 85 30
390 – 9 c. multicoloured . . . 85 15
391 – 10 c. multicoloured . . . 85 10
392 – 13 c. multicoloured . . . 2·25 25
393 – 15 c. multicoloured (as 365) 2·00 80
394 – 20 c. yellow, black and pink (as 366) . . . . 4·00 15
395 – 24 c. multicoloured . . . 90 95
396 – 25 c. multicoloured (as 368) 4·50 30
397 – 30 c. multicoloured (as 369) 16·00 65
398 **167** 40 c. blue . . . . . . 6·50 10
399 – 50 c. brown (as 356) . . . 8·00 10
400 – 75 c. olive (as 357) . . . 1·00 1·00
401 – $1 purple (as 358) . . . 2·25 15
402 – $2 violet (as 359) . . . 7·50 50
403 – $4 brown (as 360) . . . 6·50 5·50
DESIGNS—VERT: 7 c. White-tailed Dascyllus ("Humbug fish"); 8 c. Copper-banded butterflyfish ("Coral fish"); 9 c. Hermit crab; 10 c. Orange clownfish ("Anemone fish"); 13 c. Red-necked avocet. HORIZ: 24 c. Azure kingfisher.

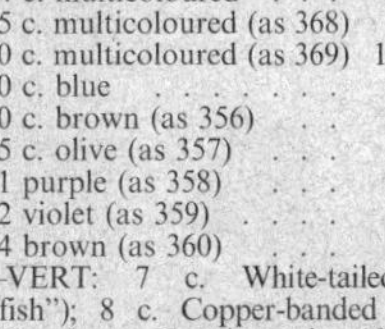

200 "Saving Life"

1966. 75th Anniv of Royal Life Saving Society.
406 **200** 4 c. black, lt bl & bl . . . 15 10

201 "Adoration of the Shepherds"

202 "Eendracht"

1966. Christmas.
407 **201** 4 c. black and olive . . . 10 10

1966. 350th Anniv of Dirk Hartog's Landing in Australia.
408 **202** 4 c. multicoloured 10 10

203 Open Bible

204 Ancient Keys and Modern Lock

1967. 150th Anniv of British and Foreign Bible Society in Australia.
409 **203** 4 c. multicoloured 10 10

1967. 150th Anniv of Australian Banking.
410 **204** 4 c. black, blue and green . . 10 10

205 Lions Badge and 50 Stars

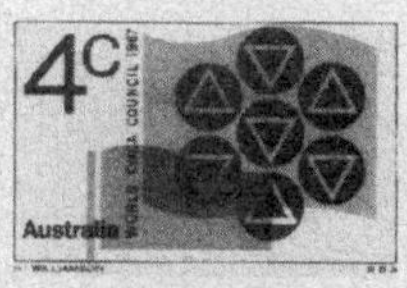

206 Y.W.C.A. Emblem

1967. 50th Anniv of Lions International.
411 **205** 4 c. black, gold and blue . . 10 10

1967. World Y.W.C.A. Council Meeting, Monash University, Melbourne.
412 **206** 4 c. multicoloured 10 10

207 Anatomical Figures

1967. 5th World Gynaecology and Obstetrics Congress, Sydney.
413 **207** 4 c. black, blue and violet . . 10 10

1967. No. 385 surch.
414 **191** 5 c. on 4 c. red 45 10

209 Christmas Bells and Gothic Arches

211 Satellite in Orbit

1967. Christmas. Multicoloured.
415 5 c. Type **209** 20 10
416 25 c. Religious symbols (vert) . . 1·40 2·00

1968. World Weather Watch. Multicoloured.
417 5 c. Type **211** 30 10
418 20 c. World weather map . . 1·40 3·25

213 Radar Antenna

214 Kangaroo Paw (Western Australia)

1968. World Telecommunications via Intelsat II.
419 **213** 25 c. blue, black and green 1·75 3·00

1968. State Floral Emblems. Multicoloured.
420 6 c. Type **214** 55 80
421 13 c. Pink Heath (Victoria) . . 65 50
422 15 c. Tasmanian Blue Gum (Tasmania) 90 20
423 20 c. Sturt's Desert Pea (South Australia) . . . . 3·00 50
424 25 c. Cooktown Orchid (Queensland) . . . . 2·50 50
425 30 c. Waratah (New South Wales) 80 10

220 Soil Sample Analysis

1968. International Soil Science Congress and World Medical Association Assembly. Mult.
426 5 c. Type **220** 10 10
427 5 c. Rubber-gloved hands, syringe and head of Hippocrates 10 10

222 Athlete carrying Torch and Sunstone Symbol

224 Houses and Dollar Signs

1968. Olympic Games, Mexico City. Multicoloured.
428 5 c. Type **222** 30 10
429 25 c. Sunstone symbol and Mexican flag . . . . 60 1·50

1968. Building and Savings Societies Congress.
430 **224** 5 c. multicoloured 10 40

225 Church Window and View of Bethlehem

226 Edgeworth David (geologist)

1968. Christmas.
431 **225** 5 c. multicoloured 10 10

1968. Famous Australians (1st series).
432 **226** 5 c. green on myrtle . . . 45 20
433 – 5 c. black on blue 45 20
434 – 5 c. brown on buff 45 20
435 – 5 c. violet on lilac 45 20
DESIGNS: No. 433, A. B. Paterson (poet); No. 434, Albert Namatjira (artist); No. 435, Caroline Chrisholm (social worker).
Nos. 432/5 were only issued in booklets and exist with one or two sides imperf.
See also Nos. 446/9, 479/82, 505/8, 537/40, 590/5, 602/7 and 637/40.

230 Macquarie Lighthouse

231 Pioneers and Modern Building, Darwin

1968. 150th Anniv of Macquarie Lighthouse.
436 **230** 5 c. black and yellow . . . 20 50

1969. Centenary of Northern Territory Settlement.
437 **231** 5 c. brown, olive and ochre . . 10 10

232 Melbourne Harbour

1969. 6th Biennial Conference of International Association of Ports and Harbours, Melbourne.
438 **232** 5 c. multicoloured 15 10

233 Concentric Circles (symbolising Management, Labour and Government)

1969. 50th Anniv of I.L.O.
439 **233** 5 c. multicoloured 15 10

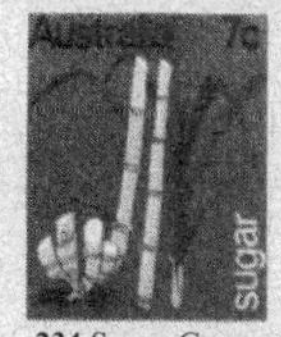

234 Sugar Cane

238 "The Nativity" (stained glass window)

1969. Primary Industries. Multicoloured.
440 7 c. Type **234** . . . . 80 1·50
441 15 c. Timber . . . . 1·75 3·50
442 20 c. Wheat 65 80
443 25 c. Wool . . . . 1·25 2·00

1969. Christmas. Multicoloured.
444 5 c. Type **238** 20 10
445 25 c. "Tree of Life", Christ in crib and Christmas Star (abstract) . . . . 1·00 2·00

240 Edmund Barton

244 Capt. Ross Smith's Vickers Vimy, 1919

1969. Famous Australians (2nd series). Prime Ministers.
446 **240** 5 c. black on green . . . 50 20
447 – 5 c. black on green . . . 50 20
448 – 5 c. black on green . . . 50 20
449 – 5 c. black on green . . . 50 20
DESIGNS: No. 447, Alfred Deakin; No. 448, J. C. Watson; No. 449, G. H. Reid.
Nos. 446/9 were only issued in booklets and only exist with one or two adjacent sides imperf.

1969. 50th Anniv of 1st England–Australia Flight.
450 **244** 5 c. multicoloured 15 10
451 – 5 c. red, black and green . . 15 10
452 – 5 c. multicoloured 15 10
DESIGNS: No. 451, Lt. H. Fysh and Lt. P. McGinness on 1919 survey with Ford car; No. 452, Capt. Wrigley and Sgt. Murphy in Royal Aircraft Factory B.E.2E taking off to meet the Smiths.

247 Symbolic Track and Diesel Locomotive

1970. Sydney–Perth Standard Gauge Railway Link.
453 **247** 5 c. multicoloured 15 10

248 Australian Pavilion, Osaka

1970. World Fair, Osaka.
454 **248** 5 c. multicoloured 15 10
455 – 20 c. red and black . . . 35 65
DESIGN: 20 c., "Southern Cross" and "from the Country of the south with warm feelings" (message).

251 Australian Flag

1970. Royal Visit.
456 – 5 c. black and ochre . . . 35 15
457 **251** 30 c. multicoloured . . . 1·00 2·25
DESIGN: 5 c. Queen Elizabeth II and Duke of Edinburgh.

252 Lucerne Plant, Bull and Sun

1970. 11th International Grasslands Congress, Queensland.
458 252 5 c. multicoloured 10 40

253 Captain Cook and H.M.S. "Endeavour"
259 Sturt's Desert Rose

1970. Bicentenary of Captain Cook's Discovery of Australia's East Coast. Multicoloured.
459 5 c. Type **253** 50 10
460 5 c. Sextant and H.M.S. "Endeavour" 50 10
461 5 c. Landing at Botany Bay . . 50 10
462 5 c. Charting and exploring . . 50 10
463 5 c. Claiming possession . . . 50 10
464 30 c. Captain Cook, H.M.S. "Endeavour", sextant, aborigines and kangaroo (63 × 30 mm) . . . . 1·75 2·50
Nos. 459/63 were issued together, se-tenant in horizontal strips of five, forming a composite design.

1970. Coil Stamps. Multicoloured.
465a 2 c. Type **259** 40 20
466 4 c. Type **259** . . . . 70 1·25
467 5 c. Golden wattle 20 10
468 6 c. Type **259** . . . . 1·25 1·00
468b 7 c. Sturt's desert pea 40 40
468d 10 c. As 7 c. 40 40

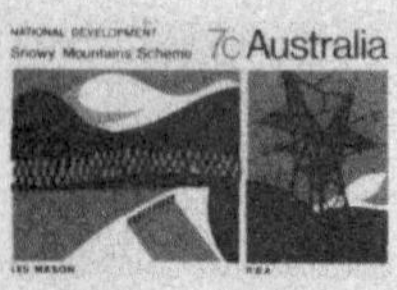

264 Snowy Mountains Scheme
265 Rising Flames

1970. National Development (1st series). Mult.
469 7 c. Type **264** 30 80
470 8 c. Ord River scheme 15 15
471 9 c. Bauxite to aluminium . . 15 15
472 10 c. Oil and natural gas . . . 40 10
See also Nos. 541/4.

1970. 16th Commonwealth Parliamentary Association Conference, Canberra.
473 265 6 c. multicoloured 10 10

266 Milk Analysis and Dairy Herd
267 "The Nativity"

1970. 18th International Dairy Congress, Sydney.
474 266 6 c. multicoloured 10 10

1970. Christmas.
475 267 6 c. multicoloured 10 10

268 U.N. "Plant" and Dove of Peace
269 Boeing 707 and Avro 504

1970. 25th Anniv of United Nations.
476 268 6 c. multicoloured 15 10

1970. 50th Anniv of QANTAS Airline.
477 269 6 c. multicoloured 30 10
478 – 30 c. multicoloured . . . 95 1·50
DESIGN: 30 c. Avro 504 and Boeing 707.

1970. Famous Australians (3rd series). As T **226**.
479 6 c. blue 85 20
480 6 c. black on brown 85 20
481 6 c. purple on pink 85 20
482 6 c. red on pink 85 20
DESIGNS: No. 479, The Duigan brothers (pioneer aviators); 480, Lachlan Macquarie (Governor of New South Wales); 481, Adam Lindsay Gordon (poet); 482, E. J. Eyre (explorer).

271 "Theatre"

1971. "Australia-Asia". 28th International Congress of Orientalists, Canberra. Multicoloured.
483 7 c. Type **271** 45 60
484 15 c. "Music" . . . . 70 1·00
485 20 c. "Sea Craft" 65 90

272 The Southern Cross
273 Market "Graph"

1971. Centenary of Australian Natives' Association.
486 272 6 c. black, red and blue . . 10 10

1971. Centenary of Sydney Stock Exchange.
487 273 6 c. multicoloured 10 10

274 Rotary Emblem
275 Dassault Mirage Jets and De Havilland D.H.9A Biplane

1971. 50th Anniv of Rotary International in Australia.
488 274 6 c. multicoloured 15 10

1971. 50th Anniv of R.A.A.F.
489 275 6 c. multicoloured 20 10

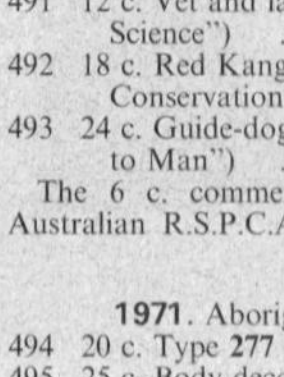

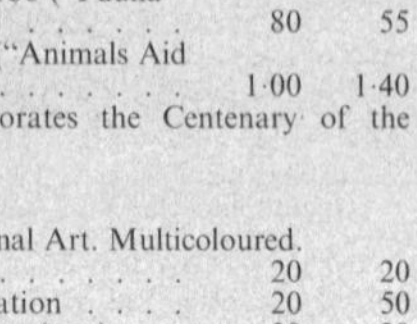

276 Draught-horse, Cat and Dog
277 Bark Painting

1971. Animals. Multicoloured.
490 6 c. Type **276** 20 10
491 12 c. Vet and lamb ("Animal Science") 45 35
492 18 c. Red Kangaroo ("Fauna Conservation") 80 55
493 24 c. Guide-dog ("Animals Aid to Man") . . . . 1·00 1·40
The 6 c. commemorates the Centenary of the Australian R.S.P.C.A.

1971. Aboriginal Art. Multicoloured.
494 20 c. Type **277** 20 20
495 25 c. Body decoration 20 50
496 30 c. Cave painting (vert) . . 30 20
497 35 c. Grave posts (vert) . . . 30 15

278 The Three Kings and the Star
280 Cameo Brooch

1971. Christmas. Colours of star and colour of "AUSTRALIA" given.
498 278 7 c. blue, mauve and brown 70 15
499 7 c. mauve, brown and white 70 15
500 7 c. mauve, white and black 4·50 80
501 7 c. black, green and black 70 15
502 7 c. lilac, green and mauve 70 15
503 7 c. black, brown and white 70 15
504 7 c. blue, mauve and green 20·00 2·25

1972. Famous Australians. (4th series). As T **240**. Prime Ministers.
505 7 c. blue 30 20
506 7 c. blue 30 20
507 7 c. red 30 20
508 7 c. red 30 20
DESIGNS: No. 505, Andrew Fisher; No. 506, W. M. Hughes; No. 507, Joseph Cook; No. 508, S. M. Bruce.

1972. 50th Anniv of Country Women's Association.
509 280 7 c. multicoloured 20 10

281 Fruit
282 Worker in Wheelchair

1972. Primary Industries. Multicoloured.
510 20 c. Type **281** . . . . 1·50 3·00
511 25 c. Rice . . . . 1·50 5·00
512 30 c. Fish . . . . 1·50 2·00
513 35 c. Beef . . . . 3·50 1·00

1972. Rehabilitation of the Disabled.
514 282 12 c. brown and green . . 10 10
515 – 18 c. green and orange . . 70 35
516 – 24 c. blue and brown . . . 15 10
DESIGNS—HORIZ: 18 c. Patient and teacher. VERT: 24 c. Boy playing with ball.

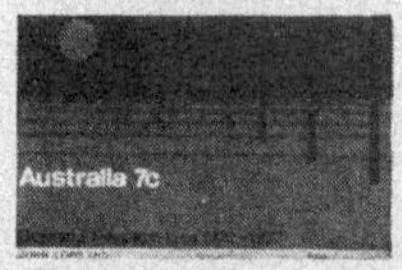

283 Telegraph Line
284 Athletics

1972. Centenary of Overland Telegraph Line.
517 283 7 c. multicoloured 15 15

1972. Olympic Games, Munich. Multicoloured.
518 7 c. Type **284** 25 25
519 7 c. Rowing 25 25
520 7 c. Swimming 25 25
521 35 c. Equestrian . . . . . . 1·50 3·50

285 Numerals and Computer Circuit

1972. 10th Int Congress of Accountants, Sydney.
522 285 7 c. multicoloured 15 15

286 Australian-built Harvester

1972. Pioneer Life. Multicoloured.
523 5 c. Pioneer family (vert) . . . 15 10
524 10 c. Water-pump (vert) . . . 40 10
525 15 c. Type **286** 15 10
526 40 c. House 30 60
527 50 c. Stage-coach 80 20
528 60 c. Morse key (vert) . . . . 60 1·00
529 80 c. "Gem" (paddle-steamer) . 60 1·00

287 Jesus with Children
288 "Length"

1972. Christmas. Multicoloured.
530 7 c. Type **287** 30 10
531 35 c. Dove and spectrum motif (vert) . . . . 4·00 6·00

1973. Metric Conversion. Multicoloured.
532 7 c. Type **288** 30 40
533 7 c. "Volume" 30 40
534 7 c. "Mass" 30 40
535 7 c. "Temperature" (horiz) . . 30 40

289 Caduceus and Laurel Wreath
291 Shipping

1973. 25th Anniv of World Health Organization.
536 289 7 c. multicoloured 30 15

1973. Famous Australians (5th series). As T **226**.
537 7 c. brown and black 35 35
538 7 c. lilac and black 35 35
539 7 c. brown and black 35 35
540 7 c. lilac and black 35 35
PORTRAITS: No. 537, William Wentworth (statesman and explorer); No. 538, Isaac Issacs (1st Australian-born Governor-General); No. 539, Mary Gilmore (writer); No. 540, Marcus Clarke (author).

1973. National Development (2nd series). Mult.
541 20 c. Type **291** . . . . 2·00 3·25
542 25 c. Iron ore and steel . . . 2·00 3·25
543 30 c. Beef roads . . . . . . 2·00 3·25
544 35 c. Mapping . . . . 2·50 3·25

292 Banded Coral Shrimp
293 Children at Play

1973. Marine Life and Gemstones. Multicoloured.
545 1 c. Type **292** 10 10
546 2 c. Fiddler crab 10 10
547 3 c. Coral crab 10 10
548 4 c. Mauve stinger 30 55
549 6 c. Chrysoprase (vert) . . . 30 10
550 7 c. Agate (vert) 30 10
551 8 c. Opal (vert) 30 10
552 9 c. Rhodonite (vert) 60 15
552a 10 c. Star sapphire (vert) . . 40 10

1973. 50th Anniv of Legacy (welfare organization).
553 293 7 c. brown, red and green 30 10

294 John baptising Jesus
295 Sydney Opera House

1973. Christmas. Multicoloured.
554 7 c. Type **294** 35 10
555 30 c. The Good Shepherd . . . 1·75 2·00

1973. Architecture.
556 295 7 c. blue and pale blue . . 30 15
557 – 10 c. ochre and brown . . . 80 70
558 – 40 c. grey, brown and black 1·25 2·00
559 – 50 c. multicoloured . . . 1·25 2·50
DESIGNS—HORIZ: 10 c. Buchanan's Hotel, Townsville; 40 c. Como House, Melbourne. VERT: 50 c. St. James' Church, Sydney.

296 Wireless Receiver and Speaker
297 Common Wombat

1973. 50th Anniv of Regular Radio Broadcasting.
560 296 7 c. blue, red and black . . 15 10

1974. Animals. Multicoloured.
561 20 c. Type **297** 35 10
562 25 c. Short-nosed echidna (inscr "Spiny Anteater") 75 60
563 30 c. Brush-tailed possum . . . 50 15
564 75 c. Pygmy (inscr "Feather-tailed") glider . . . . 1·00 85

298 "Sergeant of Light Horse" (G. Lambert)

299 Supreme Court Judge

1974. Australian Paintings. Multicoloured.

565		$1 Type **298**	1·00	10
566		$2 "Red Gums of the Far North" (H. Heysen)	1·50	25
566a		$4 "Shearing the Rams" (Tom Roberts)	3·00	2·25
567		$5 "McMahon's Point" (Sir Arthur Streeton)	6·00	2·25
567a		$10 "Coming South" (Tom Roberts)	8·50	3·50

The $2 and $4 are horiz.

1974. 150th Anniv of Australia's Third Charter of Justice.

568	**299**	7 c. multicoloured	20	10

300 Rugby Football

1974. Non-Olympic Sports. Multicoloured.

569		7 c. Type **300**	40	40
570		7 c. Bowls	40	40
571		7 c. Australian football (vert)	40	40
572		7 c. Cricket (vert)	40	40
573		7 c. Golf (vert)	40	40
574		7 c. Surfing (vert)	40	40
575		7 c. Tennis (vert)	40	40

301 "Transport of Mails"

302 Letter "A" and W. C. Wentworth (co-founder)

1974. Centenary of U.P.U. Multicoloured.

576		7 c. Type **301**	40	20
577		30 c. Three-part version of T **301** (vert)	85	1·90

1974. 150th Anniv of First Independent Newspaper. "The Australian".

578	**302**	7 c. black and brown	30	30

1974. No. 551 surch.

579		9 c. on 8 c. multicoloured	15	15

304 "The Adoration of the Magi"

305 "Pre-school Education"

1974. Christmas. Woodcuts by Durer.

580	**304**	10 c. black on cream	25	10
581	–	35 c. black on cream	80	1·00

DESIGN: 35 c. "The Flight into Egypt".

1974. Education in Australia. Multicoloured.

582		5 c. Type **305**	25	40
583		11 c. "Correspondence Schools"	25	25
584		15 c. "Science Education"	40	40
585		60 c. "Advanced Education" (vert)	75	2·50

306 "Road Safety"

307 Australian Women's Year Emblem

1975. Environment Dangers. Multicoloured.

586		10 c. Type **306**	50	50
587		10 c. "Pollution" (horiz)	50	50
588		10 c. "Bush Fires" (horiz)	50	50

1975. International Women's Year.

589	**307**	10 c. blue, green and violet	20	15

308 J. H. Scullin

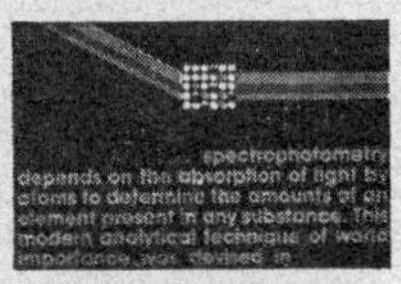

309 Atomic Absorption Spectrophotometry

1975. Famous Australians (6th series). Prime Ministers. Multicoloured.

590		10 c. Type **308**	25	35
591		10 c. J. A. Lyons	25	35
592		10 c. Earle Page	25	35
593		10 c. Arthur Fadden	25	35
594		10 c. John Curtin	25	35
595		10 c. J. B. Chifley	25	35

1975. Scientfic Development. Multicoloured.

596		11 c. Type **309**	60	40
597		24 c. Radio astronomy	1·40	1·90
598		33 c. Immunology	1·75	2·50
599		48 c. Oceanography	2·50	2·75

310 Logo of Australian Postal Commission

1975. Inauguration of Australian Postal and Telecommunications Commissions.

600	**310**	10 c. black, red and grey	25	10
601	–	10 c. black, orange and grey	25	10

DESIGN: No. 601, Logo of Australian Telecommunications Commission.

311 Edith Cowan

312 "Helichrysum thomsonii"

1975. Famous Australians (7th series). Australian Women. Multicoloured.

602		10 c. Type **311**	35	55
603		10 c. Louisa Lawson	35	55
604		10 c. "Henry Richardson" (pen-name of Ethel Richardson)	35	55
605		10 c. Catherine Spence	35	55
606a		10 c. Constance Stone	35	55
607		10 c. Truganini	35	55

1975. Wild Flowers. Multicoloured.

608		18 c. Type **312**	25	10
609		45 c. "Callistemon teretifolius" (horiz)	50	10

313 "Tambaran" House and Sydney Opera House

314 Epiphany Scene

1975. Independence of Papua New Guinea. Mult.

610		18 c. Type **313**	20	10
611		25 c. "Freedom" (bird in flight) (horiz)	50	1·25

1975. Christmas.

612	**314**	15 c. multicoloured	25	10
613	–	45 c. violet, blue and silver	75	2·40

DESIGN—HORIZ: 45 c. "Shining Star".

315 Australian Coat of Arms

1976. 75th Anniv of Nationhood.

614	**315**	18 c. multicoloured	40	20

316 Telephone-user, circa 1878

1976. Centenary of Telephone.

615	**316**	18 c. multicoloured	20	15

317 John Oxley

1976. 19th Century Explorers. Multicoloured.

616		18 c. Type **317**	35	40
617		18 c. Hume and Hovell	35	40
618		18 c. John Forrest	35	40
619		18 c. Ernest Giles	35	40
620		18 c. William Gosse	35	40
621		18 c. Peter Warburton	35	40

318 Measuring Stick, Graph and Computer Tape

1976. 50th Anniv of Commonwealth Scientific and Industrial Research Organization.

622	**318**	18 c. multicoloured	20	15

319 Football

1976. Olympic Games, Montreal. Multicoloured.

623		18 c. Type **319**	35	20
624		18 c. Gymnastics (vert)	35	20
625		25 c. Diving (vert)	60	80
626		40 c. Cycling	90	1·00

320 Richmond Bridge, Tasmania

321 Blamire Young (designer of first Australian stamp)

1976. Australian Scenes. Multicoloured.

627		5 c. Type **320**	20	10
628		25 c. Broken Bay, N.S.W.	55	20
629		35 c. Wittenoom Gorge, W.A.	45	20
630		50 c. Mt. Buffalo, Victoria (vert)	90	30
631		70 c. Barrier Reef	1·25	1·25
632		85 c. Ayers Rock, N.T.	1·25	1·75

1976. National Stamp Week.

633	**321**	18 c. multicoloured	15	15

322 "Virgin and Child" (detail, Simone Contarini)

1976. Christmas.

635	**322**	15 c. mauve and blue	25	10
636	–	45 c. multicoloured	70	90

DESIGN: 45 c. Toy koala bear and decorations.

323 John Gould

1976. Famous Australians. (8th series). Scientists. Multicoloured.

637		18 c. Type **323**	35	45
638		18 c. Thomas Laby	35	45
639		18 c. Sir Baldwin Spencer	35	45
640		18 c. Griffith Taylor	35	45

324 "Music"

325 Queen Elizabeth II

1977. Performing Arts. Multicoloured.

641		20 c. Type **324**	25	25
642		30 c. Drama	40	35
643		40 c. Dance	55	40
644		60 c. Opera	1·25	1·75

1977. Silver Jubilee. Multicoloured.

645		18 c. Type **325**	20	10
646		45 c. The Queen and Duke of Edinburgh	50	80

326 Fielder and Wicket Keeper

327 Parliament House

1977. Centenary of Australia–England Test Cricket.

647		18 c. Type **326**	55	55
648		18 c. Umpire and batsman	55	55
649		18 c. Fielders	55	55
650		18 c. Batsman and umpire	55	55
651		18 c. Bowler and fielder	55	55
652		45 c. Batsman facing bowler	1·00	1·50

1977. 50th Anniv of Opening of Parliament House, Canberra.

653	**327**	18 c. multicoloured	15	10

328 Trade Union Workers

329 Surfing Santa

1977. 50th Anniv of Australian Council of Trade Unions.

654	**328**	18 c. multicoloured	15	10

1977. Christmas. Multicoloured.

655		15 c. Type **329**	25	10
656		45 c. Madonna and Child	75	1·25

330 National Flag

1978. Australian Day.

657	**330**	18 c. multicoloured	20	15

331 Harry Hawker and Sopwith Atlantic

1978. Early Australian Aviators. Multicoloured.
658 18 c. Type **331** 40 45
659 18 c. Bert Hinkler and Avro Type 581 Avian 40 45
660 18 c. Sir Charles Kingsford Smith and "Southern Cross" 40 45
661 18 c. Charles Ulm and "Southern Cross" 40 45

332 Piper PA31 Navajo landing at Station Airstrip

1978. 50th Anniv of Royal Flying Doctor Service.
663 **332** 18 c. multicoloured . . . 20 15

333 Illawarra Flame Tree
334 Sturt's Desert Rose and Map

1978. Trees. Multicoloured.
664 18 c. Type **333** 20 15
665 25 c. Ghost gum . . . . . . 35 1·10
666 40 c. Grass tree . . . . 45 1·75
667 45 c. Cootamundra wattle . . 45 70

1978. Establishment of State Government for the Northern Territory.
668 **334** 18 c. multicoloured . . . 20 15

335 Hooded Plover
336 1928 3d. National Stamp Exhibition Commemorative

1978. Birds (1st series). Multicoloured.
669 1 c. Spotted-sided (inscr "Zebra") finch 10 20
670 2 c. Crimson finch 10 20
671 5 c. Type **335** 40 10
672 15 c. Forest kingfisher (vert) . 20 20
673 20 c. Australian dabchick (inscr "Little Grebe") 70 10
674 20 c. Eastern yellow robin . . 20 10
675 22 c. White-tailed kingfisher (22 × 29 mm) 30 10
676 25 c. Masked (inscr "Spur-wing") plover 90 35
677 30 c. Oystercatcher . . . . . 1·00 25
678 40 c. Variegated (inscr "Lovely") wren (vert) 30 45
679 50 c. Flame robin (vert) . . . 40 50
680 55 c. Comb-crested jacana (inscr "Lotus-Bird") 85 60
See also Nos. 734/40.

1978. 50th Anniv of National Stamp Week, and National Stamp Exhibition.
694 **336** 20 c. multicoloured . . . 15 15

337 "The Madonna and the Child" (after van Eyck)
338 "Tulloch"

1978. Christmas. Multicoloured.
696 15 c. Type **337** 30 10
697 25 c. "The Virgin and Child" (Marmion) 45 55
698 55 c. "The Holy Family" (del Vaga) 70 90

1978. Horse-racing. Multicoloured.
699 20 c. Type **338** 35 10
700 35 c. "Bernborough" (vert) . . 60 85
701 50 c. "Phar Lap" (vert) . . . 85 1·25
702 55 c. "Peter Pan" . . . . . . 90 1·10

339 Raising the Flag, Sydney Cove, 26th January, 1788
340 "Canberra" (paddle-steamer)

1979. Australia Day.
703 **339** 20 c. multicoloured . . . 15 15

1979. Ferries and Murray River Steamers. Mult.
704 20 c. Type **340** 35 10
705 35 c. "Lady Denman" . . . . 60 1·00
706 50 c. "Murray River Queen" (paddle-steamer) . . . . . . 80 1·40
707 55 c. "Curl Curl" (hydrofoil) . . 90 1·25

341 Port Campbell, Victoria

1979. National Parks. Multicoloured.
708 20 c. Type **341** 25 25
709 20 c. Uluru, Northern Territory 25 25
710 20 c. Royal, New South Wales 25 25
711 20 c. Flinders Ranges, South Australia 25 25
712 20 c. Nambung, Western Australia 25 25
713 20 c. Girraween, Queensland (vert) 25 25
714 20 c. Mount Field, Tasmania (vert) 25 25

342 "Double Fairlie" Type Locomotive, Western Australia

1979. Steam Railways. Multicoloured.
715 20 c. Type **342** 30 10
716 35 c. Locomotive, Puffing Billy Line, Victoria 60 70
717 50 c. Locomotive, Pichi Richi Line, South Australia . . . 70 1·50
718 55 c. Locomotive, Zig Zag Railway, New South Wales 80 1·40

343 Symbolic Swan

1979. 150th Anniv of Western Australia.
719 **343** 20 c. multicoloured . . . 15 15

344 Children playing on Slide
345 Letters and Parcels

1979. International Year of the Child.
720 **344** 20 c. multicoloured . . . 15 10

1979. Christmas. Multicoloured.
721 15 c. "Christ's Nativity" (Eastern European icon) 15 10
722 25 c. Type **345** 25 50
723 55 c. "Madonna and Child" (Buglioni) 40 75

346 Fly-fishing
347 Matthew Flinders

1979. Fishing.
724 **346** 20 c. multicoloured 20 10
725 – 35 c. blue and violet . . . 35 70
726 – 50 c. multicoloured 40 90
727 – 55 c. multicoloured 45 85
DESIGNS: 35 c. Spinning; 50 c. Deep sea game-fishing; 55 c. Surf-fishing.

1980. Australia Day.
728 **347** 20 c. multicoloured 20 10

348 Dingo

1980. Dogs. Multicoloured.
729 20 c. Type **348** 35 10
730 25 c. Border collie 35 50
731 35 c. Australian terrier 50 90
732 50 c. Australian cattle dog . . 1·10 1·75
733 55 c. Australian kelpie . . . . 1·00 1·40

1980. Birds (2nd series). As T **335**. Multicoloured.
734 10 c. Golden-shouldered parrot (vert) 40 10
734b 18 c. Spotted catbird (vert) . 70 1·25
735 28 c. Australian bee eater (inscr "Rainbow Bird") (vert) . . . 50 20
736 35 c. Regent bower bird (vert) . 35 10
737 45 c. Masked wood swallow . 40 10
738 60 c. Australian king parrot (vert) 50 15
739 80 c. Rainbow pitta . . . . . 1·00 75
740 $1 Black-backed (inscr "Weston") magpie (vert) . 1·00 10

349 Queen Elizabeth II
350 "Once a jolly Swagman camp'd by a Billabong"

1980. Birthday of Queen Elizabeth II.
741 **349** 22 c. multicoloured 30 20

1980. Folklore. "Waltzing Matilda". Multicoloured.
742 22 c. Type **350** 30 10
743 22 c. "And he sang as he shoved that jumbuck in his tuckerbag" 30 10
744 22 c. "Up rode the squatter mounted on his thoroughbred" 30 10
745 22 c. "Down came the troopers one, two, three" 30 10
746 22 c. "And his ghost may be heard as you pass by that billabong" 30 10

351 High Court Building, Canberra
352 Salvation Army

1980. Opening of High Court Building.
747 **351** 22 c. multicoloured 20 20

1980. Community Welfare. Multicoloured.
748 22 c. Type **352** 40 40
749 22 c. St. Vincent de Paul Society (vert) 40 40
750 22 c. Meals on Wheels (vert) . 40 40
751 22 c. "Life. Be in it" 40 40

353 Postbox, c. 1900
354 "Holy Family" (painting, Prospero Fontana)

1980. National Stamp Week. Multicoloured.
752 22 c. Type **353** 30 10
753 22 c. Postman, facing left . . . 30 10
754 22 c. Mail van 30 10
755 22 c. Postman, facing right . . 30 10
756 22 c. Postman and postbox . . 30 10

1980. Christmas. Multicoloured.
758 15 c. "The Virgin Enthroned" (Justin O'Brien) (detail) . . 15 10
759 28 c. Type **354** 25 40
760 60 c. "Madonna and Child" (sculpture by School of M. Zuern) . . . . 50 1·10

355 Commonwealth Aircraft Factory Wackett, 1941

1980. Australian Aircraft. Multicoloured.
761 22 c. Type **355** 35 10
762 40 c. Commonwealth Aircraft Factory Winjeel, 1955 . . . 70 90
763 45 c. Commonwealth Aircraft Factory Boomerang, 1944 . 70 1·00
764 60 c. Government Aircraft Factory Nomad, 1975 . . . 80 1·60

356 Flag in shape of Australia

1981. Australia Day.
765 **356** 22 c. multicoloured . . . 20 20

357 Caricature of Darby Munro (jockey)
358 1931 Kingsford Smith's Flights 6d. Commemorative

1981. Sporting Personalities. Caricatures. Mult.
766 22 c. Type **357** 30 10
767 35 c. Victor Trumper (cricket) 65 80
768 55 c. Sir Norman Brookes (tennis) . . . . 85 1·25
769 60 c. Walter Lindrum (billiards) 90 1·50

1981. 50th Anniversary of Official Australia–U.K. Airmail Service.
770 **358** 22 c. lilac, red and blue . . 20 10
771 – 60 c. lilac, red and blue . . 60 90
DESIGN—HORIZ: 60 c. As T **358**, but format changed.

359 Apex Emblem and Map of Australia

1981. 50th Anniv of Apex (young men's service club).
772 **359** 22 c. multicoloured . . . 20 20

360 Queen's Personal Standard for Australia
361 "Licence Inspected"

1981. Birthday of Queen Elizabeth II.
773 **360** 22 c. multicoloured . . . 20 20

1981. Gold Rush Era. Sketches by S. T. Gill. Mult.
774 22 c. Type **361** 20 25
775 22 c. "Puddling" 20 25
776 22 c. "Quality of washing stuff" 20 25
777 22 c. "On route to deposit gold" 20 25

MORE DETAILED LISTS
are given in the Stanley Gibbons Catalogues referred to in the country headings.
For lists of current volumes see Introduction.

362 "On the Wallaby Track" (Fred McCubbin)

1981. Paintings. Multicoloured.
778 $2 Type **362** . . . . 1·50 30
779 $5 "A Holiday at Mentone, 1888" (Charles Conder) . . 4·75 1·25

363 Thylacine **363a** Blue Mountain Tree Frog

363b "Papilio ulysses" (butterfly)

1981. Wildlife. Multicoloured.
781 1 c. Lace monitor 10 20
782 3 c. Corroboree frog 10 10
783 4 c. Regent skipper (butterfly) (vert) 55 55
784 5 c. Queensland hairy-nosed wombat (vert) 10 10
785 10 c. Cairns birdwing (butterfly) (vert) 60 10
786 15 c. Eastern snake-necked tortoise 40 30
787 20 c. MacLeay's swallowtail (butterfly) (vert) 80 35
788 24 c. Type **363** 45 10
789 25 c. Common rabbit-bandicoot (inscr "Greater Bilby") (vert) 35 30
790 27 c. Type **363a** 45 20
791 27 c. Type **363b** 90 30
792 30 c. Bridle nail-tailed wallaby (vert) 55 15
792a 30 c. Chlorinda hairstreak (butterfly) (vert) . . . . . 1·00 20
793 35 c. Blue tiger (butterfly) (vert) 1·00 30
794 40 c. Smooth knob-tailed gecko 45 30
795 45 c. Big greasy (butterfly) (vert) 1·00 30
796 50 c. Leadbeater's possum . . 50 10
797 55 c. Stick-nest rat (vert) . . 50 30
798 60 c. Wood white (butterfly) (vert) . . . . 1·10 30
799 65 c. Yellow-faced whip snake 80 30
800 70 c. Crucifix toad . . . . . 65 1·00
801 75 c. Eastern water dragon . . 1·25 40
802 80 c. Amaryllis azure (butterfly) (vert) . . . . 1·40 1·25
803 85 c. Centralian blue-tongued lizard . . . . 1·10 1·25
804 90 c. Freshwater crocodile . . 1·60 1·25
805 95 c. Thorny devil . . . . . 1·00 1·60
806 $1 Sword-grass brown (butterfly) (vert) . . . . . 1·40 30

364 Prince Charles and Lady Diana Spencer **365** "Cortinarius cinnabarinus"

1981. Royal Wedding.
821 **364** 24 c. multicoloured . . . 20 10
822 60 c. multicoloured . . . 55 1·00

1981. Australian Fungi. Multicoloured.
823 24 c. Type **365** 35 10
824 35 c. "Coprinus comatus" . . 60 90
825 55 c. "Armillaria luteobubalina" 80 1·25
826 60 c. "Cortinarius austro-venetus" . . . . 90 1·40

366 Disabled People playing Basketball **367** "Christmas Bush for His Adorning"

1981. International Year for Disabled Persons.
827 **366** 24 c. multicoloured . . . 20 20

1981. Christmas. Scenes and Verses from Carols by W. James and J. Wheeler. Multicoloured.
828 18 c. Type **367** 25 10
829 30 c. "The Silver Stars are in the Sky" 35 25
830 60 c. "Noeltime" 60 70

368 Globe depicting Australia **369** Ocean Racing Yacht

1981. Commonwealth Heads of Government Meeting, Melbourne.
831 **368** 24 c. black, blue and gold 20 10
832 60 c. black, blue and silver 65 75

1981. Yachts. Multicoloured.
833 24 c. Type **369** 35 10
834 35 c. "Sharpie" 50 50
835 55 c. "12 Metre" 75 85
836 60 c. "Sabot" . . . . 1·00 1·00

370 Aborigine, Governor Phillip (founder of N.S.W., 1788) and Post World War II Migrant

1982. Australia Day. "Three Great Waves of Migration".
837 **370** 24 c. multicoloured . . . 35 25

371 Humpback Whale **372** Queen Elizabeth II

1982. Whales. Multicoloured.
838 24 c. Sperm whale 40 10
839 35 c. Black (inscr "Southern") right whale (vert) 60 70
840 55 c. Blue whale (vert) . . . 1·10 1·75
841 60 c. Type **371** . . . . 1·25 1·75

1982. Birthday of Queen Elizabeth II.
842 **372** 27 c. multicoloured . . . 35 15

373 "Marjorie Atherton" **374** Radio Announcer and 1930-style Microphone

1982. Roses. Multicoloured.
843 27 c. Type **373** 40 15
844 40 c. "Imp" 75 75
845 65 c. "Minnie Watson" . . . 1·25 2·00
846 75 c. "Satellite" . . . . . . 1·25 1·60

1982. 50th Anniv of ABC (Australian Broadcasting Commission). Multicoloured.
847 27 c. Type **374** 40 45
848 27 c. ABC logo 40 45

375 Forbes Post Office **376** Early Australian Christmas Card

1982. Historic Australian Post Offices. Multicoloured.
849 27 c. Type **375** 40 40
850 27 c. Flemington Post Office . 40 40
851 27 c. Rockhampton Post Office 40 40
852 27 c. Kingston S. E. Post Office (horiz) 40 40
853 27 c. York Post Office (horiz) . 40 40
854 27 c. Launceston Post Office . 40 40
855 27 c. Old Post and Telegraph Station, Alice Springs (horiz) 40 40

1982. Christmas. Multicoloured.
856 21 c. Bushman's Hotel with Cobb's coach arriving (horiz) 30 10
857 35 c. Type **376** 50 60
858 75 c. Little girl offering Christmas pudding to swagman . . . . 75 1·40

377 Boxing

1982. Commonwealth Games, Brisbane.
859 **377** 27 c. stone, yellow and red 30 20
860 – 27 c. yellow, stone and green 30 20
861 – 27 c. stone, yellow and brown 30 20
862 – 75 c. multicoloured 90 90
DESIGNS: No. 860, Archery; No. 861, Weight-lifting; No. 862, Pole-vaulting.

378 Sydney Harbour Bridge 5s. Stamp of 1932 **379** "Yirawala" Bark Painting

1982. National Stamp Week.
864 **378** 27 c. multicoloured 35 30

1982. Opening of Australian National Gallery.
865 **379** 27 c. multicoloured 30 25

380 Mimi Spirits Dancing **381** "Eucalyptus calophylla" "Rosea"

1982. Aboriginal Culture, Music and Dance.
866 **380** 27 c. multicoloured 25 10
867 – 40 c. multicoloured 40 70
868 – 65 c. multicoloured . . . . 60 1·25
869 – 75 c. multicoloured . . . . 65 1·25
DESIGN: 40 c. to 75 c. Aboriginal bark paintings of Mimi Spirits.

1982. Eucalyptus Flowers. Multicoloured.
870 1 c. Type **381** 10 30
871 2 c. "Eucalyptus casia" 10 30
872 3 c. "Eucalyptus ficifolia" . . 90 1·40
873 10 c. "Eucalyptus globulus" . . 90 1·40
874 27 c. "Eucalyptus forrestiana" 30 40

382 Shand Mason Steam Fire Engine, 1891

1983. Historic Fire Engines. Multicoloured.
875 27 c. Type **382** 40 10
876 40 c. Hotchkiss fire engine, 1914 60 75
877 65 c. Ahrens-Fox PS2 fire engine, 1929 . . . . 1·00 1·50
878 75 c. Merryweather manual fire appliance, 1851 . . . . . 1·00 1·40

383 H.M.S. "Sirius" **384** Stylised Kangaroo and Kiwi

1983. Australia Day. Multicoloured.
879 27 c. Type **383** 40 50
880 27 c. H.M.S. "Supply" . . . 40 50

1983. Closer Economic Relationship Agreement with New Zealand.
881 **384** 27 c. multicoloured . . . 30 30

385 Equality and Dignity **386** R.Y. "Britannia" passing Sydney Opera House

1983. Commonwealth Day. Multicoloured.
882 27 c. Type **385** 20 25
883 27 c. Liberty and Freedom . . 20 25
884 27 c. Social Justice and Co-operation 20 25
885 75 c. Peace and Harmony . . 50 1·50

1983. Birthday of Queen Elizabeth II.
886 **386** 27 c. multicoloured . . . 45 30

387 "Postal and Telecommunications Services" **388** Badge of the Order of St. John

1983. World Communications Year.
887 **387** 27 c. multicoloured . . . 30 30

1983. Centenary of St. John Ambulance in Australia.
888 **388** 27 c. black and blue . . . 35 30

389 Jaycee Members and Badge **390** "The Bloke"

1983. 50th Anniv of Australian Jaycees.
889 **389** 27 c. multicoloured . . . 30 30

1983. Folklore. "The Sentimental Bloke" (humorous poem by C. J. Dennis). Multicoloured.
890 27 c. Type **390** 40 50
891 27 c. "Doreen–The Intro" . . . 40 50
892 27 c. "The Stror' at Coot" . . 40 50
893 27 c. "Hitched" 40 50
894 27 c. "The Mooch o' Life" . . 40 50

391 Nativity Scene **392** Sir Paul Edmund de Strzelecki

1983. Christmas. Children's Paintings. Mult.
895 24 c. Type **391** 20 10
896 35 c. Kookaburra 35 45
897 85 c. Father Christmas in sleigh over beach . . . . 90 1·40

1983. Explorers of Australia. Multicoloured.
898 30 c. Type **392** 35 40
899 30 c. Ludwig Leichhardt . . . 35 40
900 30 c. William John Wills and Robert O'Hara Burke . . . 35 40
901 30 c. Alexander Forrest . . . 35 40

393 Cook Family Cottage, Melbourne

1984. Australia Day.
902 **393** 30 c. black and stone . . 30 35

394 Charles Ulm, "Faith in Australia" and Trans-Tasman Cover

1984. 50th Anniv of First Official Airmail Flights. New Zealand—Australia and Australia—Papua New Guinea. Multicoloured.

903 45 c. Type **394** . . . . 1·00 1·25
904 45 c. As Type **394** but showing flown cover to Papua New Guinea . . . . 1·00 1·25

395 Thomson "Steamer", 1898

1984. Veteran and Vintage Cars. Multicoloured.

905 30 c. Type **395** 50 60
906 30 c. Tarrant, 1906 . . . . . 50 60
907 30 c. Gordon & Co "Australian Six", 1919 . . . . 50 60
908 30 c. Summit, 1923 . . . . . 50 60
909 30 c. Chic, 1924 . . . . . . 50 60

396 Queen Elizabeth II 397 "Cutty Sark"

1984. Birthday of Queen Elizabeth II.

910 **396** 30 c. multicoloured . . . 30 35

1984. Clipper Ships. Multicoloured.

911 30 c. Type **397** 40 25
912 45 c. "Orient" (horiz) 70 80
913 75 c. "Sobraon" (horiz) . . . 1·25 1·75
914 85 c. "Thermopylae" . . . . 1·25 1·50

398 Freestyle 399 Coral Hopper

1984. Skiing. Multicoloured.

915 30 c. Type **398** 40 45
916 30 c. Downhill racer 40 45
917 30 c. Slalom (horiz) 40 45
918 30 c. Nordic (horiz) 40 45

1984. Marine Life. Multicoloured.

919 2 c. Type **399** 10 20
920 3 c. Jimble 20 20
921 5 c. Tasselled frogfish ("Anglerfish") 15 10
922 10 c. Rough stonefish 20 10
923 20 c. Red handfish 65 30
924 25 c. Orange-lipped cowrie . . 45 40
925 30 c. Choat's wrasse 45 40
926 33 c. Leafy seadragon 65 10
927 40 c. Red velvetfish 85 60
928 45 c. Textile or cloth of gold cone 80 50
929 50 c. Clown surgeonfish . . . 80 50
930 55 c. Bennet's nudibranch . . 80 50
931 60 c. Zebra lionfish 90 70
932 65 c. Banded stingray 90 70
933 70 c. Southern blue-ringed octopus 90 65
934 80 c. Pineconefish ("Pineapple fish") . . . . 1·25 70
935 85 c. Royal angelfish 90 70
936 90 c. Crab-eyed goby . . . . 1·60 75
937 $1 Crown of thorns starfish . 1·50 80

400 Before the Event 401 Australian 1913 1d. Kangaroo Stamp

1984. Olympic Games, Los Angeles. Multicoloured.

941 30 c. Type **400** 35 35
942 30 c. During the event . . . 35 35
943 30 c. After the event (vert) . . 35 35

1984. "Ausipex '84" International Stamp Exhibition, Melbourne.

944 **401** 30 c. multicoloured . . . 35 30

402 "Angel" (stained-glass window St. Francis's Church, Melbourne) 403 "Stick Figures" (Cobar Region)

1984. Christmas. Stained-glass Windows. Mult.

946 24 c. "Angel and Child" (Holy Trinity Church, Sydney) . . 25 20
947 30 c. "Veiled Virgin and Child" (St. Mary's Catholic Church, Geelong) 35 30
948 40 c. Type **402** 50 60
949 50 c. "Three Kings" (St. Mary's Cathedral, Sydney) 65 80
950 85 c. "Madonna and Child" (St. Bartholomew's Church, Norwood) . . . . 80 1·25

1984. Bicentenary (1988) of Australian Settlement. (1st issue). The First Australians. Multicoloured.

951 30 c. Type **403** 35 45
952 30 c. "Bunjil" (large figure), Grampians 35 45
953 30 c. "Quikans" (tall figures), Cape York 35 45
954 30 c. "Wandjina Spirit and Baby Snakes" (Gibb River) . . . 35 45
955 30 c. "Rock Python" (Gibb River) 35 45
956 30 c. "Silver Barramundi" (fish) (Kakadu National Park) . 35 45
957 30 c. Bicentenary emblem . . 35 45
958 85 c. "Rock Possum" (Kakadu National Park) . . . . . . 80 1·40

See also Nos. 972/5, 993/6, 1002/7, 1019/22, 1059/63, 1064/6, 1077/81, 1090/2, 1110, 1137/41, 1145/8 and 1149.

404 Yellow-tufted Honeyeater 405 "Musgrave Ranges" (Sidney Nolan)

1984. 150th Anniv of Victoria.

959 30 c. Type **404** 40 65
960 30 c. Leadbeater's possum . . 40 65

1985. Australia Day. Birth Bicentenary of Dorothea Mackellar (author of poem "My Country"). Multicoloured.

961 30 c. Type **405** 45 70
962 30 c. "The Walls of China" (Russell Drysdale) 45 70

406 Young People of Different Races and Sun 407 Royal Victorian Volunteer Artillery

1985. International Youth Year.

963 **406** 30 c. multicoloured . . . 40 30

1985. 19th-Century Australian Military Uniforms. Multicoloured.

964 33 c. Type **407** 60 65
965 33 c. Western Australian Pinjarrah Cavalry 60 65
966 33 c. New South Wales Lancers 60 65
967 33 c. New South Wales Contingent to the Sudan . 60 65
968 33 c. Victorian Mounted Rifles 60 65

MINIMUM PRICE

The minimum price quoted is 10p which represents a handling charge rather than a basis for valuing common stamps. For further notes about prices see introductory pages.

408 District Nurse of early 1900s 410 Abel Tasman and Journal Entry

409 Sulphur-crested Cockatoos

1985. Centenary of District Nursing Services.

969 **408** 33 c. multicoloured 45 35

1985. Multicoloured, background colour given.

970 **409** 1 c. flesh . . . . 1·50 2·25
971 33 c. turquoise 45 55

1985. Bicentenary (1988) of Australian Settlement (2nd issue). Navigators. Multicoloured.

972 33 c. Type **410** 60 35
973 33 c. Dirk Hartog's "Eendracht" (detail, Aert Anthonisz) . . 60 35
974 33 c. "William Dampier" (detail, T. Murray) 60 35
975 90 c. Globe and hand with extract from Dampier's journal 1·40 1·75

411 Sovereign's Badge of Order of Australia 412 Tree, and Soil running through Hourglass ("Soil")

1985. Queen Elizabeth II's Birthday.

977 **411** 33 c. multicoloured 40 30

1985. Conservation. Multicoloured.

978 33 c. Type **412** 45 20
979 50 c. Washing on line and smog ("air") 80 85
980 80 c. Tap and flower ("water") 1·25 1·50
981 90 c. Chain encircling flames ("energy") . . . . 1·40 2·00

413 "Elves and Fairies" (Annie Rentoul and Ida Rentoul Outhwaite) 414 Dish Aerials

1985. Classic Australian Children's Books. Mult.

982 33 c. Type **413** 50 65
983 33 c. "The Magic Pudding" (Norman Lindsay) 50 65
984 33 c. "Ginger Meggs" (James Charles Bancks) . . 50 65
985 33 c. "Blinky Bill" (Dorothy Wall) 50 65
986 33 c. "Snugglepot and Cuddlepie" (May Gibbs) . . 50 65

1985. Electronic Mail Service.

987 **414** 33 c. multicoloured 35 30

415 Angel in Sailing Ship

1985. Christmas. Multicoloured.

988 27 c. Angel with holly wings . 35 15
989 33 c. Angel with bells 40 15
990 45 c. Type **415** 60 50
991 55 c. Angel with star 75 80
992 90 c. Angel with Christmas tree bauble . . . . 1·40 1·50

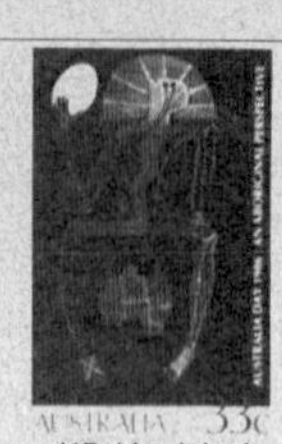

416 Astrolabe ("Batavia", 1629) 417 Aboriginal Wandjina Spirit, Map of Australia and Egg

1985. Bicentenary (1988) of Australian Settlement (3rd issue). Relics from Early Shipwrecks. Multicoloured.

993 33 c. Type **416** 40 15
994 50 c. German beardman jug ("Vergulde Draeck", 1656) . 80 90
995 90 c. Wooden bobbins ("Batavia", 1629) and encrusted scissors ("Zeewijk", 1727) . . . . 1·75 2·25
996 $1 Silver and brass buckle ("Zeewijk", 1727) . . . . 1·75 2·25

1986. Australia Day.

997 **417** 33 c. multicoloured . . . 40 30

418 AUSSAT Satellite, Moon and Earth's Surface 419 H.M.S. "Buffalo"

1986. AUSSAT National Communications Satellite System. Multicoloured.

998 33 c. Type **418** 50 15
999 80 c. AUSSAT satellite in orbit 1·50 2·25

1986. 150th Anniv of South Australia. Mult.

1000 33 c. Type **419** 70 90
1001 33 c. "City Sign" sculpture (Otto Hajek), Adelaide . . 70 90

Nos. 1000/1 were printed together se-tenant, the background of each horiz pair showing an extract from the colony's Letters Patent of 1836.

420 "Banksia serrata" 421 Radio Telescope, Parkes, and Diagram of Comet's Orbit

1986. Bicentenary of Australian Settlement (1988) (4th issue). Cook's Voyage to New Holland. Multicoloured.

1002 33 c. Type **420** 60 35
1003 33 c. "Hibiscus meraukensis" 60 35
1004 50 c. "Dillenia alata" . . . . 90 1·10
1005 80 c. "Correa reflexa" . . . 1·60 2·50
1006 90 c. "Joseph Banks" (botanist) (Reynolds) and Banks with Dr. Solander . . . . . . 2·00 2·00
1007 90 c. "Sydney Parkinson" (self-portrait) and Parkinson drawing . . . . 2·00 2·00

1986. Appearance of Halley's Comet.

1008 **421** 33 c. multicoloured . . . 50 35

422 Queen Elizabeth II 423 Brumbies (wild horses)

1986. 60th Birthday of Queen Elizabeth.

1009 **422** 33 c. multicoloured . . . 45 35

1986. Australian Horses. Multicoloured.

1010 33 c. Type **423** 60 15
1011 80 c. Mustering . . . . . . 1·50 2·00
1012 90 c. Show-jumping . . . . 1·75 2·25
1013 $1 Child on pony . . . . . 2·00 2·25

424 "The Old Shearer stands"

425 "King George III" (A. Ramsay) and Convicts

1986. Folklore. Scenes and Verses from the Folksong "Click go the Shears" Multicoloured.

1014 33 c. Type **424** 70 75
1015 33 c. "The ringer looks around" 70 75
1016 33 c. "The boss of the board" 70 75
1017 33 c. "The tar-boy is there" . 70 75
1018 33 c. "Shearing is all over" . . 70 75
Nos. 1014/18 were printed together, se-tenant, forming a composite design.

1986. Bicentenary of Australian Settlement (1988) (5th issue). Convict Settlement in New South Wales. Multicoloured.

1019 33 c. Type **425** 80 50
1020 33 c. "Lord Sydney" (Gilbert Stuart) and convicts . . . 80 50
1021 33 c. "Captain Arthur Phillip" (F. Wheatley) and ship . . 80 50
1022 $1 "Captain John Hunter" (W. B. Bennett) and aborigines . . . . 3·25 4·25

426 Red Kangaroo

427 Royal Bluebell

1986. Australian Wildlife (1st series). Multicoloured.

1023 36 c. Type **426** 55 70
1024 36 c. Emu 55 70
1025 36 c. Koala 55 70
1026 36 c. Laughing kookaburra . 55 70
1027 36 c. Platypus 55 70
See also Nos. 1072/6.

1986. Alpine Wildflowers. Multicoloured.

1028 3 c. Type **427** 35 35
1029 5 c. Alpine marsh marigold . 1·60 2·50
1030 25 c. Mount Buffalo sunray . 1·60 2·50
1031 36 c. Silver snow daisy . . . 45 30

428 Pink Enamel Orchid

429 "Australia II" crossing Finishing Line

1986. Native Orchids. Multicoloured.

1032 36 c. Type **428** 70 20
1033 55 c. "Dendrobium nindii" . 1·25 1·00
1034 90 c. Duck orchid . . . . . 2·00 2·00
1035 $1 Queen of Sheba orchid . 2·00 2·00

1986. Australian Victory in America's Cup, 1983. Multicoloured.

1036 36 c. Type **429** 75 75
1037 36 c. Boxing kangaroo flag of winning syndicate 75 75
1038 36 c. America's Cup trophy . 75 75

430 Dove with Olive Branch and Sun

431 Mary and Joseph

1986. International Peace Year.

1039 **430** 36 c. multicoloured . . . 65 40

1986. Christmas. Scenes from children's nativity play. Multicoloured.

1040 30 c. Type **431** 40 30
1041 36 c. Three Wise Men leaving gifts 50 45
1042 60 c. Angels (horiz) . . . . . 90 1·50

432 Australian Flag on Printed Circuit Board

433 Aerial View of Yacht

1987. Australia Day. Multicoloured.

1044 36 c. Type **432** 55 35
1045 36 c. "Australian Made" Campaign logos 55 35

1987. America's Cup Yachting Championship. Multicoloured.

1046 36 c. Type **433** 40 20
1047 55 c. Two yachts tacking . . 90 1·00
1048 90 c. Two yachts turning . . 1·40 2·00
1049 $1 Two yachts under full sail 1·50 1·75

434 Grapes and Melons

435 Livestock

1987. Australian Fruit. Multicoloured.

1050 36 c. Type **434** 40 20
1051 65 c. Tropical and sub-tropical fruits . . . . 1·00 1·25
1052 90 c. Citrus fruit, apples and pears . . . . 1·40 1·90
1053 $1 Stone and berry fruits . . 1·40 1·60

1987. Agricultural Shows. Multicoloured.

1054 36 c. Type **435** 60 20
1055 65 c. Produce . . . . 1·25 1·75
1056 90 c. Sideshows . . . . . . 1·75 2·40
1057 $1 Competitions . . . . . . 1·90 2·40

436 Queen Elizabeth in Australia, 1986

1987. Queen Elizabeth II's Birthday.

1058 **436** 36 c. multicoloured . . 55 50

437 Convicts on Quay

438 "At the Station"

1987. Bicentenary of Australian Settlement (1988) (6th issue). Departure of the First Fleet. Multicoloured.

1059 36 c. Type **437** 80 90
1060 36 c. Royal Marines officer and wife 80 90
1061 36 c. Sailors loading supplies 80 90
1062 36 c. Officers being ferried to ships 80 90
1063 36 c. Fleet in English Channel 80 90
See also Nos. 1064/6, 1077/81 and 1090/2.

1987. Bicentenary of Australian Settlement (1988) (7th issue). First Fleet at Tenerife. As T **437**. Multicoloured.

1064 36 c. Ferrying supplies, Santa Cruz 80 90
1065 36 c. Canary Islands fishermen and departing fleet 80 90
1066 $1 Fleet arriving at Tenerife 2·00 2·00
Nos. 1064/5 were printed together, se-tenant, forming a composite design.

1987. Folklore. Scenes and Verses from Poem "The Man from Snowy River". Multicoloured.

1067 36 c. Type **438** 70 90
1068 36 c. "Mountain bred" . . . 70 90
1069 36 c. "That terrible descent" 70 90
1070 36 c. "At their heels" . . . 70 90
1071 36 c. "Brought them back" . 70 90
Nos. 1067/71 were printed together, se-tenant, forming a composite background design of mountain scenery.

1987. Australian Wildlife (2nd series). As T **426**. Multicoloured.

1072 37 c. Common brushtail possum 55 65
1073 37 c. Sulphur-crested cockatoo 55 65
1074 37 c. Common wombat . . . 55 65
1075 37 c. Crimson rosella . . . 55 65
1076 37 c. Echidna 55 65

1987. Bicentenary of Australian Settlement (1988) (8th issue). First Fleet at Rio de Janeiro. As T **437**. Multicoloured.

1077 37 c. Sperm whale and fleet . 80 85
1078 37 c. Brazilian coast 80 85
1079 37 c. British officers in market 80 85
1080 37 c. Religious procession . . 80 85
1081 37 c. Fleet leaving Rio . . . 80 85
Nos. 1077/81 were printed together, se-tenant, forming a composite design.

439 Bionic Ear

440 Catching Crayfish

1987. Australian Achievements in Technology. Mult.

1082 37 c. Type **439** 40 35
1083 53 c. Microchips 75 60
1084 63 c. Robotics 85 70
1085 68 c. Ceramics 95 75

1987. "Aussie Kids". Multicoloured.

1086 37 c. Type **440** 40 35
1087 55 c. Playing cat's cradle . . 1·00 75
1088 90 c. Young football supporters 1·40 1·25
1089 $1 Children with kangaroo . 1·60 1·25

1987. Bicentenary of Australian Settlement (1988) (9th issue). First Fleet at Cape of Good Hope. As T **437**. Multicoloured.

1090 37 c. Marine checking list of livestock 75 90
1091 37 c. Loading livestock . . . 75 90
1092 $1 First Fleet at Cape Town . 1·75 2·00
Nos. 1090/1 were printed together, se-tenant, forming a composite design.

441 Detail of Spearthrower, Western Australia

1987. Aboriginal Crafts. Multicoloured.

1093 3 c. Type **441** . . . . . . 1·00 1·50
1094 15 c. Shield pattern, New South Wales . . . . 3·75 4·75
1095 37 c. Basket weave, Queensland 1·00 1·50
1096 37 c. Bowl design, Central Australia . . . . 90 1·25
1097 37 c. Belt pattern, Northern Territory . . . . 1·00 1·50

442 Grandmother and Granddaughters with Candles

443 Koala with Stockman's Hat and Eagle dressed as Uncle Sam

1987. Christmas. Designs showing carol singing by candlelight. Multicoloured.

1098 30 c. Type **442** 55 55
1099 30 c. Father and daughters . 55 55
1100 30 c. Four children 55 55
1101 30 c. Family 55 55
1102 30 c. Six teenagers 55 55
1103 37 c. Choir (horiz) 55 40
1104 63 c. Father and two children (horiz) . . . . 1·00 1·00

1988. Bicentenary of Australian Settlement (10th issue). Arrival of First Fleet. As T **437**. Mult.

1105 37 c. Aborigines watching arrival of Fleet, Botany Bay 80 85
1106 37 c. Aborigine family and anchored ships 80 85
1107 37 c. Fleet arriving at Sydney Cove 80 85
1108 37 c. Ship's boat 80 85
1109 37 c. Raising the flag, Sydney Cove, 26 January 1788 . . 80 85
Nos. 1105/9 were printed together, se-tenant, forming a composite design.

1988. Bicentenary of Australian Settlement (11th issue). Joint issue with U.S.A.

1110 **443** 37 c. multicoloured . . . 60 35

444 "Religion" (A. Horner)

445 "Government House, Sydney, 1790" (George Raper)

1988. "Living Together". Designs showing cartoons. Multicoloured (except 30 c.).

1111 1 c. Type **444** 50 30
1112 2 c. "Industry" (P. Nicholson) 50 30
1113 3 c. "Local Government" (A. Collette) 50 30
1114 4 c. "Trade Unions" (Liz Honey) 10 10
1115 5 c. "Parliament" (Bronwyn Halls) 50 30
1116 10 c. "Transport" (Meg Williams) 30 30
1117 15 c. "Sport" (G. Cook) . . 40 40
1118 20 c. "Commerce" (M. Atcherson) 70 30
1119 25 c. "Housing" (C. Smith) 45 30
1120 30 c. "Welfare" (R. Tandberg) (black and lilac) 55 40
1121 37 c. "Postal Services" (P. Viska) 60 50
1121b 39 c. "Tourism" (J. Spooner) 60 50
1122 40 c. "Recreation" (R. Harvey) 70 40
1123 45 c. "Health" (Jenny Coopes) 70 50
1124 50 c. "Mining" (G. Haddon) 70 50
1125 53 c. "Primary Industry" (S. Leahy) . . . . 1·75 1·00
1126 55 c. "Education" (Victoria Roberts) . . . . 1·50 55
1127 60 c. "Armed Forces" (B. Green) . . . . . . 1·50 70
1128 63 c. "Police" (J. Russell) . 2·00 85
1129 65 c. "Telecommunications" (B. Petty) . . . . 1·50 75
1130 68 c. "The Media" (A. Langoulant) . . . . 2·00 1·50
1131 70 c. "Science and Technology" (J. Hook) . 1·75 1·00
1132 75 c. "Visual Arts" (G. Dazeley) . . . . . . 1·00 1·00
1133 80 c. "Performing Arts" (A. Stitt) . . . . 1·25 1·00
1134 90 c. "Banking" (S. Billington) 1·50 90
1135 95 c. "Law" (C. Aslanis) . . 1·00 1·00
1136 $1 "Rescue and Emergency" (M. Leunig) . . . . . . 1·10 90

1988. Bicentenary of Australian Settlement (12th issue). "The Early Years, 1788–1809". Mult.

1137 37 c. Type **445** 75 75
1138 37 c. "Government Farm, Parramatta, 1791" ("The Port Jackson Painter") 75 75
1139 37 c. "Parramatta Road, 1796" (attr Thomas Watling) . . 75 75
1140 37 c. "View of Sydney Cove, c. 1800" (detail) (Edward Dayes) 75 75
1141 37 c. "Sydney Hospital, 1803", (detail) (George William Evans) 75 75
Nos. 1137/41 were printed together, se-tenant, forming a composite background design from the painting, "View of Sydney from the East Side of the Cove, c. 1808" by John Eyre.

446 Queen Elizabeth II (from photo by Tim Graham)

1988. Queen Elizabeth II's Birthday.

1142 **446** 37 c. multicoloured . . . 50 40

447 Expo '88 Logo

1988. "Expo '88" World Fair, Brisbane.

1143 **447** 37 c. multicoloured . . . 50 40

MINIMUM PRICE

The minimum price quoted is 10p which represents a handling charge rather than a basis for valuing common stamps. For further notes about prices see introductory pages.

448 New Parliament House

1988. Opening of New Parliament House, Canberra.
1144 **448** 37 c. multicoloured . . . 50 40

449 Early Settler and Sailing Clipper

1988. Bicentenary of Australian Settlement (13th issue). Multicoloured.
1145 37 c. Type **449** . . . . 75 1·00
1146 37 c. Queen Elizabeth II with British and Australian Parliament Buildings . . . 75 1·00
1147 $1 W. G. Grace (cricketer) and tennis racquet . . . . . . 1·50 2·25
1148 $1 Shakespeare, John Lennon (entertainer) and Sydney Opera House . . . . 1·50 2·25
Stamps in similar designs were also issued by Great Britain.

450 Kiwi and Koala at Campfire

1988. Bicentenary of Australian Settlement (14th issue).
1149 **450** 37c. multicoloured . . . 65 40
A stamp in a similar design was also issued by New Zealand.

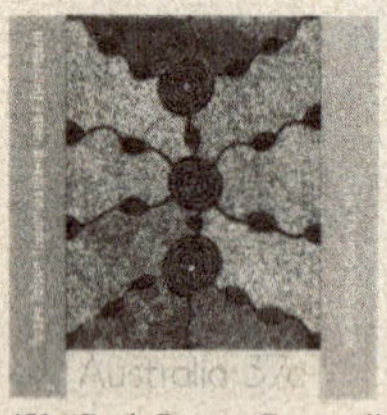

451 "Bush Potato Country" (Turkey Tolsen Tjupurrula and David Corby Tjapaltjarri)

1988. Art of the Desert. Aboriginal Paintings from Central Australia. Multicoloured.
1150 37 c. Type **451** 40 40
1151 55 c. "Courtship Rejected" (Limpi Puntungka Tjapangati) 80 60
1152 90 c. "Medicine Story" (artist unknown) . . . . 1·00 1·50
1153 $1 "Ancestor Dreaming" (Tim Leura Tjapaltjarri) . 1·25 1·40

452 Basketball

1988. Olympic Games, Seoul. Multicoloured.
1154 37 c. Type **452** 40 40
1155 65 c. Athlete crossing finish line 80 1·10
1156 $1 Gymnast with hoop . . . 1·25 1·50

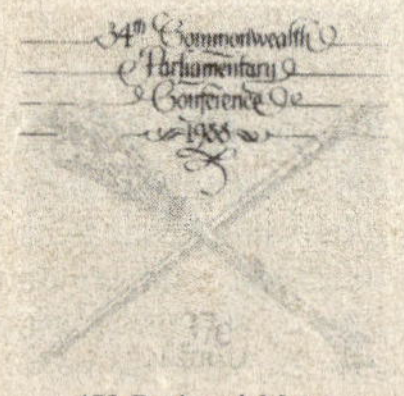

453 Rod and Mace

1988. 34th Commonwealth Parliamentary Conference, Canberra.
1157 **453** 37 c. multicoloured . . 50 60

454 Necklace by Peter Tully

1988. Australian Crafts. Multicoloured.
1158 2 c. Type **454** . . . . 3·00 4·00
1159 5 c. Vase by Colin Levy . . 3·00 4·00
1160 39 c. Teapot by Frank Bauer 50 35

455 Pinnacles Desert

1988. Panorama of Australia. Multicoloured.
1161 39 c. Type **455** 60 40
1162 55 c. Flooded landscape, Arnhem Land 85 85
1163 65 c. Twelve Apostles, Victoria 1·10 1·25
1164 70 c. Mountain Ash wood . 1·25 1·75

456 "The Nativity" (Danielle Hush)

1988. Christmas. Multicoloured.
1165 32 c. Type **456** 50 35
1166 39 c. "Koala as Father Christmas" (Kylie Courtney) 55 40
1167 63 c. "Christmas Cockatoo" (Benjamin Stevenson) . . 1·10 1·40

457 Sir Henry Parkes 458 Bowls

1989. Australia Day. Centenary of Federation Speech by Sir Henry Parkes (N.S.W. Prime Minister).
1168 **457** 39 c. multicoloured . . 45 40

1989. Sports. Multicoloured.
1169 1 c. Type **458** 10 10
1170a 2 c. Tenpin-bowling . . . 10 10
1171 3 c. Australian football . . 10 10
1172a 5 c. Kayaking and canoeing 10 10
1174a 10 c. Sailboarding 10 10
1176 20 c. Tennis 20 25
1179 39 c. Fishing 35 40
1180 41 c. Cycling 40 35
1181 43 c. Skateboarding 35 40
1184 55 c. Kite-flying 40 45
1186a 65 c. Rock-climbing 50 55
1187 70 c. Cricket 85 80
1188 75 c. Netball 55 60
1189 80 c. Squash 60 65
1190 85 c. Diving . . . . 1·75 80
1191 90 c. Soccer . . . . 1·75 80
1192 $1 Fun-run . . . . 1·00 95
1193 $1.10 Golf 85 90
1194 $1.20 Hang-gliding . . . . 1·75 1·10

459 Merino

1989. Sheep in Australia. Multicoloured.
1195 39 c. Type **459** 70 40
1196 39 c. Poll Dorset 70 40
1197 85 c. Polwarth . . . . . . 1·40 1·75
1198 $1 Corriedale . . . . . . 1·40 1·40

460 Adelaide Botanic Garden

1989. Botanic Gardens. Multicoloured.
1199 $2 Noroo, New South Wales 1·50 80
1200 $5 Mawarra, Victoria . . . . 4·25 1·25
1201 $10 Type **460** . . . . 7·50 2·00
1201a $20 "A View of the Artist's House and Garden in Mills Plains, Van Diemen's Land" (John Glover) . . . . . . 15·00 11·00

461 "Queen Elizabeth II" (sculpture, John Dowie) 462 Arrival of Immigrant Ship, 1830's

1989. Queen Elizabeth II's Birthday.
1202 **461** 39 c. multicoloured . . . 55 50

1989. Colonial Development (1st issue). Pastoral Era 1810–1850. Multicoloured.
1203 39 c. Type **462** 55 55
1204 39 c. Pioneer cottage and wool dray 55 55
1205 39 c. Squatter's homestead . . 55 55
1206 39 c. Shepherd with flock (from Joseph Lycett's "Views of Australia") 55 55
1207 39 c. Explorer in desert (after watercolour by Edward Frome) 55 55
See also Nos. 1254/8 and 1264/8.

463 Gladys Moncrieff and Roy Rene 464 "Impression" (Tom Roberts)

1989. Australian Stage and Screen Personalities. Multicoloured.
1208 39 c. Type **463** 45 40
1209 85 c. Charles Chauvel and Chips Rafferty . . . . 1·25 1·40
1210 $1 Nellie Stewart and J. C. Williamson . . . . 1·25 1·10
1211 $1.10 Lottie Lyell and Raymond Longford . . . . 1·25 1·25

1989. Australian Impressionist Paintings. Mult.
1212 41 c. Type **464** 55 50
1213 41 c. "Impression for Golden Summer" (Sir Arthur Streeton) 55 50
1214 41 c. "All on a Summer's Day" (Charles Conder) (vert) . . 55 50
1215 41 c. "Petit Dejeuner" (Frederick McCubbin) . . . 55 50

465 Freeways

1989. The Urban Environment.
1216 **465** 41 c. black, purple and green 65 90
1217 – 41 c. black, purple and mauve 65 90
1218 – 41 c. black, purple and blue 65 90
DESIGNS: No. 1217, City buildings, Melbourne; No. 1218, Commuter train at platform.

466 Hikers outside Youth Hostel

1989. 50th Anniv of Australian Youth Hostels.
1219 **466** 41 c. multicoloured . . . 55 50

467 Horse Tram, Adelaide, 1878

1989. Historic Trams. Multicoloured.
1220 41 c. Type **467** 60 60
1221 41 c. Steam tram, Sydney, 1884 60 60
1222 41 c. Cable tram, Melbourne, 1886 . . . . 60 60
1223 41 c. Double-deck electric tram, Hobart, 1893 . . . . . . 60 60
1224 41 c. Combination electric tram, Brisbane, 1901 . . . . . . 60 60

468 "Annunciation" (15th-century Book of Hours) 469 Radio Waves and Globe

1989. Christmas. Illuminated Manuscripts. Multicoloured.
1225 36 c. Type **468** 40 40
1226 41 c. "Annunciation to the Shepherds" (Wharncliffe Book of Hours, c. 1475) 50 45
1227 80 c. "Adoration of the Magi" (15th-century Parisian Book of Hours) . . . . 1·25 1·40

1989. 50th Anniv of Radio Australia.
1228 **469** 41 c. multicoloured . . . 55 50

470 Golden Wattle 471 Australian Wildflowers

1990. Australia Day.
1229 **470** 41 c. multicoloured . . . 55 50

1990. Greetings Stamps.
1230 **471** 41 c. multicoloured . . . 45 45
1231 43 c. multicoloured . . . 35 40

472 Dr. Constance Stone (first Australian woman doctor), Modern Doctor and Nurses

1990. Centenary of Women in Medical Practice.
1232 **472** 41 c. multicoloured . . . 50 45

473 Greater Glider 474 "Stop Smoking"

1990. Animals of the High Country. Multicoloured.
1233 41 c. Type **473** 60 45
1234 65 c. Tiger cat ("Spotted-tailed Quoll") 90 85
1235 70 c. Mountain pygmy-possum 95 90
1236 80 c. Brush-tailed rock-wallaby 1·10 1·00

1990. Community Health. Multicoloured.
1237 41 c. Type **474** 55 55
1238 41 c. "Drinking and driving don't mix" 55 55
1239 41 c. "No junk food, please" 55 55
1240 41 c. "Guess who's just had a check up?" 55 55

475 Soldiers from Two World Wars

476 Queen at Australian Ballet Gala Performance, London, 1988

1990. "The Anzac Tradition". Multicoloured.

1241 41 c. Type **475** 50 40
1242 41 c. Fighter pilots and munitions worker 50 40
1243 65 c. Veterans and Anzac Day parade 85 90
1244 $1 Casualty evacuation, Vietnam, and disabled veteran 1·25 1·40
1245 $1.10 Letters from home and returning troopships 1·40 1·50

1990. Queen Elizabeth II's Birthday.

1246 **476** 41 c. multicoloured 65 45

477 New South Wales 1861 5s. Stamp

1990. 150th Anniv of the Penny Black. Designs showing stamps. Multicoloured.

1247 41 c. Type **477** 60 75
1248 41 c. South Australia 1855 unissued 1s. 60 75
1249 41 c. Tasmania 1853 4d. 60 75
1250 41 c. Victoria 1867 5s. 60 75
1251 41 c. Queensland 1897 unissued 6d. 60 75
1252 41 c. Western Australia 1855 4d. with inverted frame 60 75

478 Gold Miners on Way to Diggings

1990. Colonial Development (2nd issue). Gold Fever. Multicoloured.

1254 41 c. Type **478** 60 60
1255 41 c. Mining camp 60 60
1256 41 c. Panning and washing for gold 60 60
1257 41 c. Gold Commissioner's tent 60 60
1258 41 c. Moving gold under escort 60 60

479 Glaciology Research

1990. Australian-Soviet Scientific Co-operation in Antarctica. Multicoloured.

1261 41 c. Type **479** 55 40
1262 $1.10 Krill (marine biology research) 1·40 1·50

Stamps in similar designs were also issued by Russia.

480 Auctioning Building Plots

1990. Colonial Development (3rd series). Boomtime. Multicoloured.

1264 41 c. Type **480** 55 55
1265 41 c. Colonial mansion 55 55
1266 41 c. Stock exchange 55 55
1267 41 c. Fashionable society 55 55
1268 41 c. Factories 55 55

481 "Salmon Gums" (Robert Juniper)

482 "Adelaide Town Hall" (Edmund Gouldsmith)

1990. "Heidelberg and Heritage" Art Exhibition. Multicoloured.

1269 28 c. Type **481** 1·75 2·25
1270 43 c. "The Blue Dress" (Brian Dunlop) 35 45

1990. 150th Anniv of Local Government.

1271 **482** 43 c. multicoloured 65 50

483 Laughing Kookaburras and Gifts

1990. Christmas. Multicoloured.

1272 38 c. Type **483** 50 40
1273 43 c. Baby Jesus with koalas and wallaby (vert) 50 40
1274 80 c. Possum on Christmas tree 1·50 1·25

484 National Flag

485 Black-necked Stork

1991. Australia Day. 90th Anniv of Australian Flag.

1275 **484** 43 c. blue, red and grey 50 40
1276 – 90 c. multicoloured 1·10 1·25
1277 – $1 multicoloured 1·25 1·40
1278 – $1.20 red, blue and grey 1·60 1·75

DESIGNS: 90 c. Royal Australian Navy ensign; $1 Royal Australian Air Force standard; $1.20, Australian merchant marine ensign.

1991. Waterbirds. Multicoloured.

1279 43 c. Type **485** 75 40
1280 43 c. Black swan (horiz) 75 40
1281 85 c. Cereopsis (inscr "Cape Barren") goose 1·75 2·25
1282 $1 Chestnut-breasted teal (horiz) 1·90 1·75

486 Recruitment Poster (Women's Services)

1991. Anzac Day. 50th Anniversaries.

1283 **486** 43 c. multicoloured 60 40
1284 – 43 c. black, green & brn 60 40
1285 – $1.20 multicoloured 2·25 2·00

DESIGNS: 43 c. (No. 1284) Patrol (Defence of Tobruk); $1.20, "V-P Day Canberra" (Harold Abbot) (Australian War Memorial).

487 Queen Elizabeth at Royal Albert Hall, London

489 "Bondi" (Max Dupain)

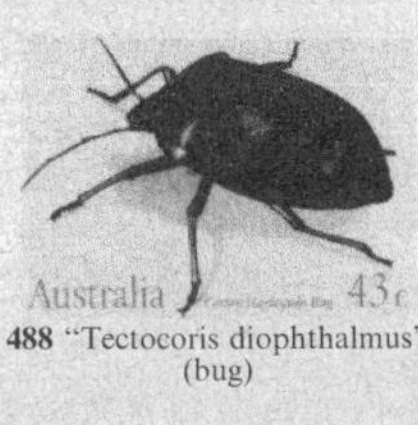

488 "Tectocoris diophthalmus" (bug)

1991. Queen Elizabeth II's Birthday.

1286 **487** 43 c. multicoloured 80 50

1991. Insects. Multicoloured.

1287 43 c. Type **488** 75 45
1288 43 c. "Cizara ardeniae" (hawk moth) 75 45
1289 80 c. "Petasida ephippigera" (grasshopper) 2·00 2·00
1290 $1 "Castiarina producta" (beetle) 2·00 1·50

1991. 150 Years of Photography in Australia.

1291 **489** 43 c. black, brown and blue 75 65
1292 – 43 c. black, green & brown 75 65
1293 – 70 c. black, green & brown 1·25 1·10
1294 – $1.20 black, brown & green 1·75 1·50

DESIGNS: No. 1292, "Gears for the Mining Industry, Vickers Ruwolt, Melbourne" (Wolfgang Sievers): 1293, "The Wheel of Youth" (Harold Cazneaux): 1294, "Teacup Ballet" (Olive Cotton).

490 Singing Group

491 Puppy

1991. Australian Radio Broadcasting. Designs showing listeners and scenes from radio programmes. Multicoloured.

1295 43 c. Type **490** 60 45
1296 43 c. "Blue Hills" serial 60 45
1297 85 c. "The Quiz Kids" 1·25 1·25
1298 $1 "Argonauts' Club" children's programme 1·50 1·40

1991. Domestic Pets. Multicoloured.

1299 43 c. Type **491** 70 45
1300 43 c. Kitten 70 45
1301 70 c. Pony 1·40 1·10
1302 $1 Sulphur-crested cockatoo 1·90 1·40

492 George Vancouver (1791) and Edward Eyre (1841)

493 "Seven Little Australians" (Ethel Turner)

1991. Exploration of Western Australia.

1303 **492** $1.05 multicoloured 1·00 1·10

1991. Australian Writers of the 1890s. Multicoloured.

1305 43 c. Type **493** 50 45
1306 75 c. "On Our Selection" (Steele Rudd) 80 75
1307 $1 "Clancy of the Overflow" (poem, A. B. Paterson) (vert) 1·10 95
1308 $1.20 "The Drover's Wife" (short story, Henry Lawson) (vert) 1·25 1·40

494 Shepherd

1991. Christmas. Multicoloured.

1309 38 c. Type **494** 40 40
1310 43 c. Infant Jesus 45 45
1311 90 c. Wise Man 1·50 1·25

495 Parma Wallaby

1992. Threatened Species. Multicoloured.

1312 45 c. Type **495** 65 60
1313 45 c. Ghost bat 65 60
1314 45 c. Long-tailed dunnart 65 60
1315 45 c. Little pygmy-possum 65 60
1316 45 c. Dusky hopping-mouse 65 60
1317 45 c. Squirrel glider 65 60

496 Basket of Wild Flowers

1992. Greetings Stamp.

1318 **496** 45 c. multicoloured 40 45

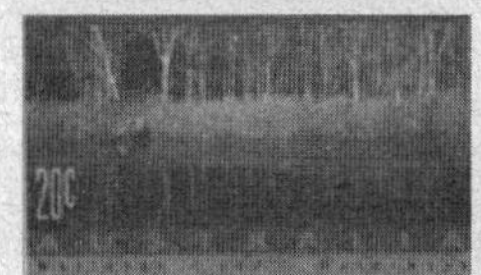

497 Noosa River, Queensland

1992. Wetlands and Waterways. Multicoloured.

1319 20 c. Type **497** 1·75 2·00
1320 45 c. Lake Eildon, Victoria 40 45

498 "Young Endeavour" (brigantine)

1992. Australia Day. Sailing Ships. Multicoloured.

1333 45 c. Type **498** 80 50
1334 45 c. "Britannia" (yacht) (vert) 80 50
1335 $1.05 "Akarana" (cutter) (vert) 1·75 2·00
1336 $1.20 "John Louis" (pearling lugger) 2·00 1·75

499 Bombing of Darwin

1992. 50th Anniv of Second World War Battles. Multicoloured.

1338 45 c. Type **499** 70 45
1339 75 c. Anti-aircraft gun and fighters, Milne Bay 1·25 1·00
1340 75 c. Infantry on Kokoda Trail 1·25 1·00
1341 $1.05 H.M.A.S. "Australia" (cruiser) and American carrier, Coral Sea 1·50 1·50
1342 $1.20 Australians advancing, El Alamein 1·75 1·60

500 "Helix Nebula"

1992. International Space Year. Multicoloured.

1343 45 c. Type **500** 60 45
1344 $1.05 "The Pleiades" 1·50 1·25
1345 $1.20 "Spiral Galaxy, NGC 2997" 1·75 1·50

501 Hunter Valley, New South Wales

1992. Vineyard Regions. Multicoloured.

1347 45 c. Type **501** 60 50
1348 45 c. North-east Victoria 60 50
1349 45 c. Barossa Valley, South Australia 60 50
1350 45 c. Coonawarra, South Australia 60 50
1351 45 c. Margaret River, Western Australia 60 50

502 3½d. Stamp of 1953

503 Salt Action

1992. Queen Elizabeth II's Birthday.

1352 **502** 45 c. multicoloured 70 50

1992. Land Conservation. Multicoloured.
1353 45 c. Type **503** 85 85
1354 45 c. Farm planning 85 85
1355 45 c. Erosion control 85 85
1356 45 c. Tree planting 85 85
1357 45 c. Dune care 85 85

504 Cycling

1992. Olympic Games and Paralympic Games (No. 1359), Barcelona. Multicoloured.
1358 45 c. Type **504** 60 45
1359 $1.20 High jumping . . . . . 1·50 1·60
1360 $1.20 Weightlifting . . . . . 1·50 1·60

505 Echidna

506 Sydney Harbour Tunnel (value at left)

1992. Australian Wildlife (1st series). Multicoloured.
1361 30 c. Saltwater crocodile . . 25 20
1362 35 c. Type **505** 25 20
1363 40 c. Platypus 30 25
1364 50 c. Koala 40 35
1365 60 c. Common bushtail possum 45 40
1366 70 c. Laughing kookaburra . 80 85
1367 85 c. Australian pelican . . . 65 70
1368 90 c. Eastern grey kangaroo . 1·00 85
1369 95 c. Common wombat . . . 75 80
1370 $1.20 Major Mitchell's cockatoo 90 95
1371 $1.35 Emu . . . . 1·00 1·10
See also Nos. 1453/8.

1992. Opening of Sydney Harbour Tunnel. Mult.
1375b 45 c. Type **506** . . . . . . 1·75 1·75
1376b 45 c. Sydney Harbour Tunnel (value at right) . . . . . 1·75 1·75
Nos. 1375/6 were printed together, se-tenant, forming a composite design.

507 Warden's Courthouse, Coolgardie

508 Bowler of 1892

1992. Centenary of Discovery of Gold at Coolgardie and Kalgoorlie. Multicoloured.
1377 45 c. Type **507** 60 45
1378 45 c. Post Office, Kalgoorlie . 60 45
1379 $1.05 York Hotel, Kalgoorlie 1·50 1·60
1380 $1.20 Town Hall, Kalgoorlie 1·75 1·90

1992. Centenary of Sheffield Shield Cricket Tournament. Multicoloured.
1381 45 c. Type **508** 85 50
1382 $1.20 Batsman and wicket-keeper . . . . 1·90 2·00

509 Children's Nativity Play

1992. Christmas. Multicoloured.
1383 40 c. Type **509** 55 40
1384 45 c. Child waking on Christmas Day 60 45
1385 $1 Children carol singing . . 1·90 1·60

510 "Ghost Gum, Central Australia" (Namatjira)

1993. Australia Day. Paintings by Albert Namatjira. Multicoloured.
1386 45 c. Type **510** . . . . . . 75 1·00
1387 45 c. "Across the Plain to Mount Giles" . . . . . . 75 1·00

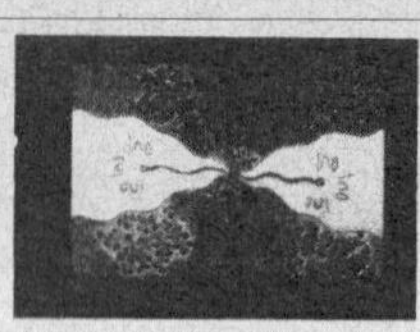
511 "Wild Onion Dreaming" (Pauline Nakamarra Woods)

1993. "Dreamings". Paintings by Aboriginal Artists. Multicoloured.
1388 45 c. Type **511** 60 45
1389 75 c. "Yam Plants" (Jack Wunuwun) (vert) . . . . 1·10 95
1390 85 c. "Goose Egg Hunt" (George Milpurrurru) (vert) 1·25 1·25
1391 $1 "Kalumpiwarra-Ngulalintji" (Rover Thomas) . . . . . 1·40 1·40

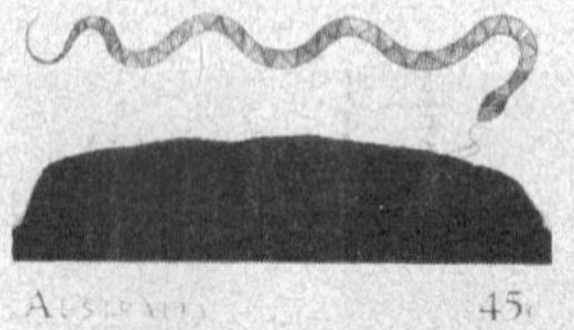

512 Uluru (Ayers Rock) National Park

1993. World Heritage Sites (1st series). Multicoloured.
1392 45 c. Type **512** 75 45
1393 85 c. Rain forest, Fraser Island 1·75 1·60
1394 95 c. Beach, Shark Bay . . . 1·75 1·60
1395 $2 Waterfall, Kakadu . . . 2·00 1·90
See also Nos. 1582/5.

513 Queen Elizabeth II on Royal Visit, 1992

514 H.M.A.S. "Sydney" (cruiser, launched 1934) in Action

1993. Queen Elizabeth II's Birthday.
1396 **513** 45 c. multicoloured . . 60 60

1993. Second World War Naval Vessels. Mult.
1397 45 c. Type **514** 80 45
1398 85 c. H.M.A.S. "Bathurst" (mine-sweeper) . . . . . 1·60 1·75
1399 $1.05 H.M.A.S. "Arunta" (destroyer) . . . . 1·75 2·10
1400 $1.20 "Centaur" (hospital ship) and tug . . . . 2·00 2·10

515 "Work in the Home"

516 "Centenary Special", Tasmania, 1971

1993. Working Life in the 1890s. Mult.
1401 45 c. Type **515** 55 45
1402 45 c. "Work in the Cities" . 55 45
1403 $1 "Work in the Country" . 1·10 1·10
1404 $1.20 Trade Union banner . 1·50 1·75

1993. Australian Trains. Multicoloured.
1405 45 c. Type **516** 65 70
1406 45 c. "Spirit of Progress", Victoria 65 70
1407 45 c. "Western Endeavour", Western Australia, 1970 . 65 70
1408 45 c. "Silver City Comet", New South Wales 65 70
1409 45 c. Cairns–Kuranda tourist train, Queensland 65 70
1410 45 c. "The Ghan", Northern Territory 65 70
Nos. 1405/10 also come self-adhesive.

517 "Black Cockatoo Feather" (Fiona Foley)

518 Conference Emblem

1993. International Year of Indigenous Peoples. Aboriginal Art. Multicoloured.
1417 45 c. Type **517** 55 45
1418 75 c. "Ngarrgooroon Country" (Hector Jandany) (horiz) . 1·10 1·25
1419 $1 "Ngak Ngak" (Ginger Riley Munduwalawala) (horiz) . . 1·25 1·40
1420 $1.05 "Untitled" (Robert Cole) 1·50 1·75

1993. Inter-Parliamentary Union Conference and 50th Anniv of Women in Federal Parliament. Multicoloured.
1421 45 c. Type **518** . . . . . . 1·00 1·25
1422 45 c. Dame Enid Lyons and Senator Dorothy Tangney . 1·00 1·25

519 Ornithocheirus

520 "Goodwill"

1993. Prehistoric Animals. Multicoloured.
1423 45 c. Type **519** 60 50
1424 45 c. Leaellynasaura (25 × 30 mm) 60 50
1425 45 c. Timimus (26 × 33 mm) . 60 50
1426 45 c. Allosaurus (26 × 33 mm) 60 50
1427 75 c. Muttaburrasaurus (30 × 50 mm) . . . . 1·00 90
1428 $1.05 Minmi (50 × 30 mm) . . 1·50 1·50
Nos. 1423/4 also come self-adhesive.

1993. Christmas. Multicoloured.
1432 40 c. Type **520** 50 45
1433 45 c. "Joy" 55 45
1434 $1 "Peace" . . . . 1·90 1·60

521 "Shoalhaven River Bank—Dawn" (Arthur Boyd)

1994. Australia Day. Landscape Paintings. Mult.
1435 45 c. Type **521** 60 45
1436 85 c. "Wimmera" (Sir Sidney Nolan) . . . . 1·40 1·40
1437 $1.05 "Lagoon, Wimmera" (Nolan) . . . . 1·60 1·60
1438 $2 "White Cockatoos with Flame Trees" (Boyd) (vert) 2·50 2·50

522 Teaching Lifesaving Techniques

1994. Centenary of Organised Life Saving in Australia. Multicoloured.
1439 45 c. Type **522** 60 45
1440 45 c. Lifeguard on watch . . 60 45
1441 95 c. Lifeguard team . . . . 1·25 1·40
1442 $1.20 Lifeguards on surf boards 1·60 1·75
Nos. 1439/40 also come self-adhesive.

523 Rose

524 Bridge and National Flags

1994. Greetings Stamps. Flower photographs by Lariane Fonseca. Multicoloured.
1445 45 c. Type **523** 40 45
1446 45 c. Tulips 40 45
1447 45 c. Poppies 40 45

1994. Opening of Friendship Bridge between Thailand and Laos.
1448 **524** 95 c. multicoloured . . . 1·25 1·40

525 "Queen Elizabeth II" (Sir William Dargie)

526 "Family in Field" (Bobbie-Lea Blackmore)

1994. Queen Elizabeth II's Birthday.
1449 **525** 45 c. multicoloured . . . 70 70

1994. International Year of the Family. Children's Paintings. Multicoloured.
1450 45 c. Type **526** 55 45
1451 75 c. "Family on Beach" (Kathryn Teoh) . . . . . 1·00 1·10
1452 $1 "Family around Fire" (Maree McCarthy) . . . . 1·25 1·50

1994. Australian Wildlife (2nd series). As T **505**. Multicoloured. Ordinary or self-adhesive gum.
1453 45 c. Kangaroo 60 50
1454 45 c. Female kangaroo with young 60 50
1455 45 c. Two kangaroos 60 50
1456 45 c. Family of koalas on branch 60 50
1457 45 c. Koala on ground . . . 60 50
1458 45 c. Koala asleep in tree . . 60 50

527 Suffragettes

1994. Centenary of Women's Emancipation in South Australia.
1465 **527** 45 c. multicoloured . . . 60 60

528 Bunyip from Aboriginal Legend

1994. The Bunyip (mythological monster). Mult.
1466 45 c. Type **528** 60 60
1467 45 c. Nature spirit bunyip . . 60 60
1468 90 c. "The Bunyip of Berkeley's Creek" (book illustration) . 1·50 1·50
1469 $1.35 Bunyip as natural history 1·90 1·90

529 "Robert Menzies" (Sir Ivor Hele)

530 Lawrence Hargrave and Box Kites

1994. Wartime Prime Ministers. Multicoloured.
1470 45 c. Type **529** 85 85
1471 45 c. "Arthur Fadden" (William Dargie) 85 85
1472 45 c. "John Curtin" (Anthony Dattilo-Rubbo) 85 85
1473 45 c. "Francis Forde" (Joshua Smith) 85 85
1474 45 c. "Joseph Chifley" (A. D. Colquhoun) 85 85

1994. Aviation Pioneers.
1475 **530** 45 c. brown, green and cinnamon 70 45
1476 – 45 c. brown, red and lilac 70 45
1477 – $1.35 brown, violet and blue . . . . 2·25 2·50
1478 – $1.80 brown, deep green and green . . . . . 2·50 2·75
DESIGNS: No. 1476, Ross and Keith Smith with Vickers Vimy (first England–Australia flight); 1477, Ivor McIntyre, Stanley Goble and Fairey IIID seaplane (first aerial circumnavigation of Australia); 1478, Freda Thompson and De Havilland Moth Major "Christopher Robin" (first Australian woman to fly solo from England to Australia).

531 Scarlet Macaw

532 "Madonna and Child" (detail)

1994. Australian Zoos. Endangered Species. Mult.
1479 45 c. Type **531** 65 55
1480 45 c. Cheetah (25 × 30 mm) . . 65 55
1481 45 c. Orang-utan (26 × 37 mm) . 65 55
1482 45 c. Fijian crested iguana (26 × 37 mm) 65 55
1483 $1 Asian elephants (49 × 28 mm) 1·75 1·60
Nos. 1479/80 also come self-adhesive.

1994. Christmas. "The Adoration of the Magi" by Giovanni Toscani. Multicoloured.
1487 40 c. Type **532** 60 40
1488 45 c. "Wise Man and Horse" (detail) (horiz) 60 45
1489 $1 "Wise Man and St. Joseph" (detail) (horiz) . . . . . . 1·50 1·40
1490 $1.80 Complete painting (49 × 29 mm) . . . . 2·00 2·50

533 Yachts outside Sydney Harbour

534 Symbolic Kangaroo

1994. 50th Sydney to Hobart Yacht Race. Mult.
1491 45 c. Type **533** 50 55
1492 45 c. Yachts passing Tasmania coastline 50 55
Nos. 1491/92 also comes self-adhesive.

1994. Self-adhesive. Automatic Cash Machine Stamps.
1495 **534** 45 c. gold, emerald and green 50 50
1496 45 c. gold, green and blue 50 50
1497 45 c. gold, green and lilac 50 50
1498 45 c. gold, emerald and green 50 50
1499 45 c. gold, emerald and green 50 50
1500 45 c. gold, green and pink 50 50
1501 45 c. gold, green and red 50 50
1502 45 c. gold, green and brown 50 50

535 "Back Verandah" (Russell Drysdale)

1995. Australia Day. Paintings. Multicoloured.
1503 45 c. Type **535** 50 45
1504 45 c. "Skull Springs Country" (Guy Grey-Smith) 50 45
1505 $1.05 "Outcamp" (Robert Juniper) . . . . . 1·40 1·50
1506 $1.20 "Kite Flying" (Ian Fairweather) . . . . . 1·50 1·50

536 Red Heart and Rose

537 "Endeavour" Replica at Sea

1995. St. Valentine's Day. Multicoloured.
1507 45 c. Type **536** 45 55
1508 45 c. Gold and red heart with rose 45 55
1509 45 c. Gold heart and roses . . 45 55

1995. Completion of "Endeavour" Replica. Mult.
1510 45 c. Type **537** 75 75
1511 45 c. "Captain Cook's Endeavour" (detail) (Oswald Brett) 75 75

538 Coalport Plate and Bracket Clock, Old Government House, Parramatta

1995. 50th Anniv of Australian National Trusts.
1514 **538** 45 c. blue and brown . . 45 45
1515 – 45 c. green and brown . 45 45
1516 – $1 red and blue . . . . 1·00 95
1517 – $2 green and blue . . . 1·90 1·90
DESIGNS: No. 1515, Steiner doll and Italian-style chair, Ayers House, Adelaide; 1516, "Advance Australia" teapot and parian-ware statuette, Victoria; 1517, Silver bowl and china urn, Old Observatory, Perth.

539 Light Opal (hologram)

1995. Opals. Mulitcoloured.
1518 $1.20 Type **539** . . . . . . 1·75 1·25
1519 $2.50 Black opal (hologram) . 3·25 3·25

540 Queen Elizabeth II at Gala Concert, 1992

541 Sir Edward Dunlop and P.O.W. Association Badge

1995. Queen Elizabeth II's Birthday.
1520 **540** 45 c. multicoloured . . 65 75

1995. Australian Second World War Heroes (1st series). Mult. Ordinary or self-adhesive gum.
1521 45 c. Type **541** 60 60
1522 45 c. Mrs. Jessie Vasey and War Widows' Guild badge . . 60 60
1523 45 c. Sgt. Tom Derrick and Victoria Cross 60 60
1524 45 c. Flt. Sgt. Rawdon Middleton and Victoria Cross 60 60
See also Nos. 1545/8.

542 Children and Globe of Flags

543 "The Story of the Kelly Gang"

1995. 50th Anniv of United Nations.
1529 **542** 45 c. multicoloured . . 75 75

1995. Centenary of Cinema. Scenes from Films. Multicoloured. (a) Size 23 × 35 mm.
1530 45 c. Type **543** 60 60
1531 45 c. "On Our Selection" . . 60 60
1532 45 c. "Jedda" 60 60
1533 45 c. "Picnic at Hanging Rock" 60 60
1534 45 c. "Strictly Ballroom" . . 60 60

(b) Self-adhesive. Size 19 × 30½ mm.
1535 45 c. Type **543** 60 60
1536 45 c. "On Our Selection" . . 60 60
1537 45 c. "Jedda" 60 60
1538 45 c. "Picnic at Hanging Rock" 60 60
1539 45 c. "Strictly Ballroom" . . 60 60

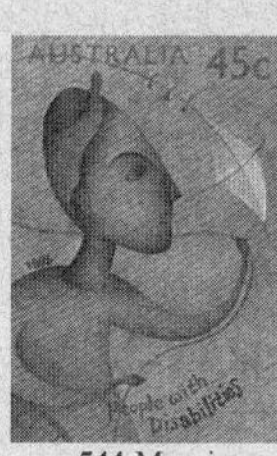

544 Man in Wheelchair flying Kite

545 Koala with Cub

1995. People with Disabilities. Multicoloured.
1540 45 c. Type **544** 65 65
1541 45 c. Blind woman playing violin 65 65

1995. 50th Anniv of Peace in the Pacific. Designs as 1946 Victory Commemoration (Nos. 213/15) redrawn with new face values.
1542 **53** 45 c. red 75 60
1543 – 45 c. green 75 60
1544 – $1.50 blue . . . . 1·90 2·25
DESIGNS—VERT: No. 1543, Angel. HORIZ: No. 1544, Flag and dove.

1995. Australian Second World War Heroes (2nd series). As T **541**. Multicoloured.
1545 45 c. Sister Ellen Savage and George Medal 60 60
1546 45 c. Chief Petty Officer Percy Collins and Distinguished Service Medal and Bar . . 60 60
1547 45 c. Lt-Comm. Leon Goldsworthy and George Cross 60 60
1548 45 c. Warrant Officer Len Waters and R.A.A.F. wings 60 60

1995. Australia–China Joint Issue. Endangered Species. Multicoloured.
1549 45 c. Type **545** 70 90
1550 45 c. Giant panda with cubs . 70 90

546 Father Joseph Slattery, Thomas Lyle and Walter Filmer (Radiology)

1995. Medical Scientists. Multicoloured.
1552 45 c. Type **546** 60 70
1553 45 c. Dame Jean Macnamara and Sir Macfarlane Burnet (viruses) 60 70
1554 45 c. Fred Hollows (ophthalmology) (vert) . . 60 60
1555 $2.50 Sir Howard Florey (antibiotics) (vert) . . . . . 3·75 4·50

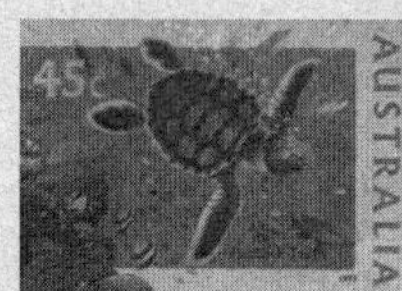

547 Flatback Turtle

548 "Madonna and Child"

1995. Marine Life. Multicoloured. Ordinary of Self-adhesive gum.
1556 45 c. Type **547** 55 55
1557 45 c. Flame angelfish and nudibranch 55 55
1558 45 c. Potato grouper ("Potato cod") and hump-headed wrasse ("Maori wrasse") . 55 55
1559 45 c. Giant trevally 55 55
1560 45 c. Black marlin 55 55
1561 45 c. Mako and tiger sharks . 55 55

1995. Christmas. Stained-glass Windows from Our Lady Help of Christians Church, Melbourne. Multicoloured.
1569 40 c. Type **548** 45 45
1570 45 c. "Angel carrying the Gloria banner" 45 45
1571 $1 "Rejoicing Angels" . . . . 1·10 1·50
No. 1569 also comes self-adhesive.

549 "West Australian Banksia" (Margaret Preston)

1996. Australia Day. Paintings. Multicoloured.
1573 45 c. Type **549** 60 45
1574 85 c. "The Babe is Wise" (Lina Bryans . . . . 1·40 1·25
1575 $1 "The Bridge in Curve" (Grace Cossington Smith) (horiz) . . . . 1·50 1·25
1576 $1.20 "Beach Umbrellas" (Vida Lahey) (horiz) . . . . . . 1·75 1·50

550 Gold Heart and Rose

1996. St. Valentine's Day.
1577 **550** 45 c. multicoloured . . . 50 50

551 Bristol Type 156 Beaufighter and Curtiss P-40E Kittyhawk I

1996. Military Aviation. Multicoloured.
1578 45 c. Type **551** 75 90
1579 45 c. Hawker Sea Fury and Fairey Firefly 75 90
1580 45 c. Bell Kiowa helicopters . 75 90
1581 45 c. Government Aircraft Factory Hornets 75 90

552 Tasmanian Wilderness

1996. World Heritage Sites (2nd series). Multicoloured.
1582 45 c. Type **552** 50 45
1583 75 c. Willandra Lakes . . . 90 90
1584 95 c. Naracoorte Fossil Cave 1·25 1·25
1585 $1 Lord Howe Island . . . . 1·50 1·60

553 Australian Spotted Cuscus

555 North Melbourne Players

554 Head of Queen Elizabeth II

1996. Australia–Indonesia Joint Issue. Multicoloured.
1586 45 c. Type **553** 70 70
1587 45 c. Indonesian bear cuscus 70 70

1996. Queen Elizabeth II's Birthday.
1589 **554** 45 c. multicoloured . . 55 55

1996. Centenary of Australian Football League. Players from different teams. Multicoloured. Ordinary or self-adhesive gum.
1590 45 c. Type **555** 60 65
1591 45 c. Brisbane (red and yellow shirt) 60 65
1592 45 c. Sydney (red and white shirt) 60 65
1593 45 c. Carlton (black shirt with white emblem) 60 65
1594 45 c. Adelaide (black, red and yellow shirt) 60 65
1595 45 c. Fitzroy (yellow, red and blue shirt) 60 65
1596 45 c. Richmond (black shirt with yellow diagonal stripe) 60 65
1597 45 c. St. Kilda (red, white and black shirt) 60 65
1598 45 c. Melbourne (black shirt with red top) 60 65
1599 45 c. Collingwood (black and white vertical striped shirt) 60 65
1600 45 c. Fremantle (green, red, white and blue shirt) . . . 60 65
1601 45 c. Footscray (blue, white and red shirt) 60 65
1602 45 c. West Coast (deep blue shirt with yellow stripes) . 60 65
1603 45 c. Essendon (black shirt with red stripe) 60 65
1604 45 c. Geelong (black and white horizontal striped shirt) . . 60 65
1605 45 c. Hawthorn (black and yellow vertical striped shirt) 60 65

556 Leadbeater's Possum

1996. Fauna and Flora. Multicoloured.
1622 5 c. Type **556** 10 10
1623 10 c. Powerful owl 10 15
1624 20 c. Saltwater crocodile . . 15 20
1625 25 c. Northern dwarf tree frog 20 25
1626 45 c. Comb-crested jacana . 35 40
1627 45 c. Little kingfisher 35 40

1628 45 c. Brolga 35 40
1629 45 c. Black-necked stork ("Jabiru") 35 40
1630 $1 "Cressida cressida" (butterfly) 75 80
1631 $2 Blackwood wattle . . . . 1·50 1·60
1632 $5 Soft tree fern and mountain ash (30 × 50 mm) . . . . . 3·75 4·00
1633 $10 Kakadu Wetlands (50 × 30 mm) . . . . 8·75 9·00

Nos. 1626/9 exist with ordinary or self-adhesive gum.

557 Edwin Flack (800 and 1500 metres gold medal winner, 1896)

1996. Centennial Olympic Games and 10th Paralympic Games, Atlanta. Multicoloured.

1639 45 c. Type **557** 70 70
1640 45 c. Fanny Durack (100 metres freestyle swimming gold medal winner, 1912) . . . 70 70
1641 $1.05 Wheelchair athletes . . . 1·60 1·60

558 "Animalia" (Graeme Base)

1996. 50th Anniv of Children's Book Council Awards. Designs taken from book covers. Ordinary or self-adhesive gum. Multicoloured.

1642 45 c. Type **558** 60 60
1643 45 c. "Greetings from Sandy Beach" (Bob Graham) . . 60 60
1644 45 c. "Who Sank the Boat?" (Pamela Allen) 60 60
1645 45 c. "John Brown, Rose and the Midnight Cat" (Jenny Wagner, illustrated by Ron Brooks) 60 60

559 American Bald Eagle, Kangaroo and Olympic Flame

560 Margaret Windeyer

1996. Passing of Olympic Flag to Sydney.
1650 **559** 45 c. multicoloured . . 55 50

1996. Centenary of the National Council of Women.
1651 **560** 45 c. purple and yellow . 50 50
1652 – $1 blue and yellow . . 1·25 1·25
DESIGN: $1 Rose Scott.

561 Pearl

1996. Pearls and Diamonds. Multicoloured.
1653 45 c. Type **561** 60 50
1654 $1.20 Diamond . . . . 1·40 1·50

The pearl on the 45 c. is shown as an exelgram (holographic printing on ultra thin plastic film) and the diamond on the $1.20 as a hologram, each embossed on to the stamp.

562 Silhouettes of Female Dancer and Musician on Rural Landscape

1996. 50th Anniv of Arts Councils. Multicoloured.
1655 20 c. Type **562** . . . . 60 1·00
1656 45 c. Silhouettes of musician and male dancer on landscape 35 40

563 Ginger Cats

1996. Australian Pets. Multicoloured.
1657 45 c. Type **563** 60 60
1658 45 c. Blue heeler dogs . . . 60 60
1659 45 c. Cockatoo (30 × 25 mm) . . 60 60
1660 45 c. Duck with ducklings (25 × 30 mm) 60 60
1661 45 c. Dog and cat (25 × 30 mm) . 60 60
1662 45 c. Ponies (30 × 50 mm) . . 60 60

Nos. 1657/8 also come self-adhesive.

564 Ferdinand von Mueller

1996 Australia–Germany Joint Issue. Death Centenary of Ferdinand von Mueller (botanist).
1666 **564** $1.20 multicoloured . . 1·25 1·40

565 Willem de Vlamingh

566 Madonna and Child

1996. 300th Anniv of the Visit of Willem de Vlamingh to Western Australia.
1667 **565** 45 c. multicoloured . . 75 75

1996. Christmas. Multicoloured.
1668 40 c. Type **566** 55 45
1669 45 c. Wise man with gift . . 55 50
1670 $1 Shepherd boy with lamb . 1·25 1·40

No. 1668 also comes self-adhesive.

567 "Landscape '74" (Fred Williams)

1997. Australia Day. Contemporary Paintings. Multicoloured.
1672 85 c. Type **567** . . . . . . 1·10 1·10
1673 90 c. "The Balcony 2" (Brett Whiteley) . . . . 1·10 1·10
1674 $1.20 "Fire Haze at Gerringong" (Lloyd Rees) . 1·40 1·40

568 Sir Donald Bradman

569 Red Roses

1997. Australian Legends (1st series). Sir Donald Bradman (cricketer). Multicoloured.
1675 45 c. Type **568** 55 55
1676 45 c. Bradman playing stroke . 55 55

See also Nos. 1731/42 and 1838/9.

1997. St. Valentine's Day. Ordinary or self-adhesive gum.
1677 **569** 45 c. multicoloured . . 50 50

570 Ford Coupe Utility, 1934

571 May Wirth and Horse

1997. Classic Cars. Multicoloured. Ordinary or self-adhesive gum.
1679 45 c. Type **570** 55 60
1680 45 c. GMH Holden 48-215 (FX), 1948 . . . . 55 60
1681 45 c. Austin Lancer, 1958 . . 55 60
1682 45 c. Chrysler Valiant "R" Series, 1962 . . . . 55 60

1997. 150th Anniv of the Circus in Australia. Multicoloured.
1687 45 c. Type **571** 50 55
1688 45 c. Con Colleano on tightrope 50 55
1689 45 c. Clowns 50 55
1690 45 c. Acrobats 50 55

572 Royal Wedding 1d. Stamp of 1947

573 Hand holding Globe and Lion's Emblem

1997. Queen Elizabeth II's Birthday.
1691 **572** 45 c. purple 50 50

1997. 50th Anniv of First Australian Lions Club.
1692 **573** 45 c. blue, brown and purple 50 50

574 Doll holding Teddy Bear (Kaye Wiggs)

575 Police Rescue Helicopter

1997. Dolls and Teddy Bears. Multicoloured.
1693 45 c. Type **574** 45 50
1694 45 c. Teddy bear standing (Jennifer Laing) 45 50
1695 45 c. Doll wearing white dress with teddy bear (Susie McMahon) 45 50
1696 45 c. Doll in brown dress and bonnet (Lynda Jacobson) . 45 50
1697 45 c. Teddy bear sitting (Helen Williams) 45 50

1997. Emergency Services. Multicoloured.
1698 45 c. Type **575** 40 45
1699 45 c. Emergency Service volunteers carrying victim . 40 45
1700 $1.05 Fire service at fire . . . 90 95
1701 $1.20 Loading casualty into ambulance . . . . 1·00 1·10

576 George Peppin Jnr (breeder) and Merino Sheep

1997. Bicentenary of Arrival of Merino Sheep in Australia. Multicoloured.
1702 45 c. Type **576** 40 45
1703 45 c. Pepe chair, cloth and wool logo 40 45

577 Dumbi the Owl

1997. "The Dreaming". Cartoons from Aboriginal Stories. Multicoloured.
1704 45 c. Type **577** 40 45
1705 $1 The Two Willy-Willies . . 90 95
1706 $1.20 How Brolga became a Bird . . . . 1·00 1·10
1707 $1.80 Tuggan-Tuggan . . . 1·50 1·60

578 "Rhoetosaurus brownei"

579 Spotted-tailed Quoll

1997. Prehistoric Animals. Multicoloured.
1708 45 c. Type **578** 40 45
1709 45 c. "Mcnamaraspis kaprios" 40 45
1710 45 c. "Ninjemys oweni" . . 40 45
1711 45 c. "Paracyclotosaurus davidi" 40 45
1712 45 c. "Woolungasaurus glendowerensis" 40 45

1997. Nocturnal Animals. Multicoloured.
1713 45 c. Type **579** 50 50
1714 45 c. Barking owl 50 50
1715 45 c. Platypus (30 × 25 mm) . . 50 50
1716 45 c. Brown antechinus (30 × 25 mm) 50 50
1717 45 c. Dingo (30 × 25 mm) . . 50 50
1718 45 c. Yellow-bellied glider (50 × 30 mm) 50 50

Nos. 1713/14 also come self-adhesive.

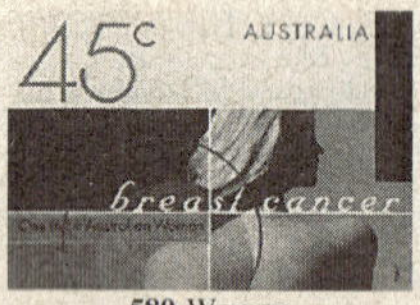

580 Woman

1997. Breast Cancer Awareness Campaign.
1722 **580** 45 c. multicoloured . . . 40 45

581 Two Angels

1997. Christmas. Children's Nativity Play. Multicoloured.
1723 40 c. Type **581** 35 40
1724 45 c. Mary 40 45
1725 $1 Three Kings 90 95

No. 1723 also comes self-adhesive.

582 "Flying Cloud" (clipper) (J. Scott)

1998. Ship Paintings. Multicoloured.
1727 45 c. Type **582** 40 45
1728 85 c. "Marco Polo" (full-rigged ship) (T. Robertson) . . . 75 80
1729 $1 "Chusan" (steamship) (C. Gregory) 90 95
1730 $1.20 "Heather Belle" (clipper) 1·00 1·10

583 Betty Cuthbert (1956)

584 "Champagne" Rose

1998. Australian Legends (2nd series). Olympic Gold Medal Winners. Multicoloured. Ordinary or self-adhesive gum.
1731 45 c. Type **583** 45 50
1732 45 c. Betty Cuthbert running . 45 50
1733 45 c. Herb Elliot (1960) . . . 45 50
1734 45 c. Herb Elliot running . . . 45 50
1735 45 c. Dawn Fraser (1956, 1960 and 1964) 45 50
1736 45 c. Dawn Fraser swimming . 45 50
1737 45 c. Marjorie Jackson (1952) . 45 50
1738 45 c. Marjorie Jackson running . 45 50

1739 45 c. Murray Rose (1956) . . 45 50
1740 45 c. Murray Rose swimming 45 50
1741 45 c. Shirley Strickland (1952 and 1956) 45 50
1742 45 c. Shirley Strickland hurdling 45 50

1998. Greeting Stamp. Ordinary or self-adhesive gum.
1755 **584** 45 c. multicoloured . . . 40 45

585 Queen Elizabeth II

1998. Queen Elizabeth II's Birthday.
1757 **585** 45 c. multicoloured . . 40 40

586 Sea Hawk (helicopter) landing on Frigate

1998. 50th Anniv of Royal Australian Navy Fleet Air Arm.
1758 **586** 45 c. multicoloured . . 40 40

587 Sheep Shearer and Sheep

1998. Farming. Multicoloured. Ordinary or self-adhesive gum.
1759 45 c. Type **587** 45 45
1760 45 c. Barley and silo 45 45
1761 45 c. Farmers herding beef cattle 45 45
1762 45 c. Sugar cane harvesting . 45 45
1763 45 c. Two dairy cows 45 45

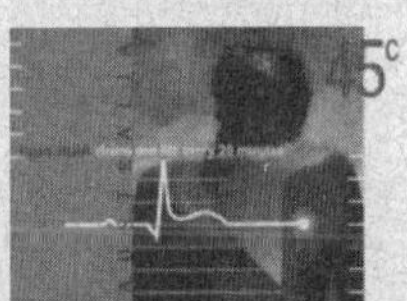
588 Cardiograph Trace and Heart

1998. Heart Disease Awareness.
1769 **588** 45 c. multicoloured . . 40 45

589 Johnny O'Keefe ("The Wild One", 1958)

1998. Australian Rock and Roll. Multicoloured. Ordinary or self-adhesive gum.
1770 45 c. Type **589** 35 40
1771 45 c. Col Joye ("Oh Yeah Uh Huh", 1959) 35 40
1772 45 c. Little Pattie ("He's My Blonde Headed Stompie Wompie Real Gone Surfer Boy", 1963) 35 40
1773 45 c. Normie Rowe ("Shakin all Over", 1965) 35 40
1774 45 c. Easybeats ("She's so Fine", 1965) 35 40
1775 45 c. Russell Morris ("The Real Thing", 1969) 35 40
1776 45 c. Masters Apprentices ("Turn Up Your Radio", 1970) 35 40
1777 45 c. Daddy Cool ("Eagle Rock", 1971) 35 40
1778 45 c. Billy Thorpe and the Aztecs ("Most People I know think I'm Crazy", 1972) . . 35 40
1779 45 c. Skyhooks ("Horror Movie", 1974) 35 40
1780 45 c. AC/DC ("It's a Long Way to the Top", 1975) 35 40
1781 45 c. Sherbet ("Howzat", 1976) 35 40

HAVE YOU READ THE NOTES AT THE BEGINNING OF THIS CATALOGUE?
These often provide answers to the enquiries we receive.

590 Helmeted Honeyeater (Yellow-tufted Honeyeater subspecies)

1998. Endangered Species. Multicoloured.
1794 5 c. Type **590** 20 20
1795 5 c. Orange-bellied parrot . 20 20
1796 45 c. Red-tailed black-cockatoo 45 45
1797 45 c. Gouldian finch 45 45

591 French Horn and Cello Players

1998. Youth Arts, Australia. Multicoloured.
1798 45 c. Type **591** 40 40
1799 45 c. Dancers 40 40

592 "Phalaenopsis rosenstromii"

1998. Australia–Singapore Joint Issue. Orchids. Multicoloured.
1800 45 c. Type **592** 45 40
1801 85 c. "Arundina graminifolia" 80 80
1802 $1 "Grammatophyllum speciosum" 90 90
1803 $1.20 "Dendrobium phalaenopsis" . . . . . . 1·10 1·25

593 Flying Angel with Teapot (cartoon by Michael Leunig)

1998. "The Teapot of Truth" (cartoons by Michael Leunig). Multicoloured.
1805 45 c. Type **593** 35 40
1806 45 c. Two birds in heart-shaped tree 35 40
1807 45 c Pouring tea 35 40
1808 $1 Mother and child (29 × 24 mm) 75 80
1809 $1.20 Cat with smiling face (29 × 24 mm) 90 95

594 Red Lacewing

595 Flinders' Telescope and Map of Tasmania

1998. Butterflies. Multicoloured. Ordinary or self-adhesive gum.
1810 45 c. Type **594** 35 40
1811 45 c. Dull oakblue 35 40
1812 45 c. Meadow argus 35 40
1813 45 c. Ulysses butterfly . . . 35 40
1814 45 c. Common red-eye . . . 35 40

1998. Bicentenary of the Circumnavigation of Tasmania by George Bass and Matthew Flinders. Multicoloured.
1820 45 c. Type **595** 35 40
1821 45 c. Sextant and letter from Bass 35 40

596 Weedy Seadragon

597 Rose of Freedom

1998. International Year of the Ocean. Multicoloured.
1822 45 c. Type **596** 35 40
1823 45 c. Bottlenose dolphin . . . 35 40
1824 45 c. Fiery squid (24 × 29 mm) 35 40
1825 45 c. Manta ray (29 × 24 mm) 35 40
1826 45 c. White pointer shark (29 × 49 mm) 35 40
1827 45 c. Southern right whale (49 × 29 mm) 35 40
Nos. 1822/3 also come self-adhesive.

1998. 50th Anniv of Universal Declaration of Human Rights.
1831 **597** 45 c. multicoloured . . . 35 40

598 Three Kings

1998. Christmas. Multicoloured.
1832 40 c. Type **598** 30 35
1833 45 c. Nativity scene 35 40
1834 $1 Mary and Joseph 75 80
No. 1832 also comes self-adhesive.

599 Australian Coat of Arms

1999. 50th Anniv of Australian Citizenship. Ordinary or self-adhesive gum.
1836 **599** 45 c. multicoloured . . . 35 40

600 Arthur Boyd

1999. Australian Legends (3rd series). Arthur Boyd (painter). Multicoloured. Ordinary or self-adhesive gum.
1838 45 c. Type **600** 35 40
1839 45 c. "Nebuchadnezzer on fire falling over Waterfall" (Arthur Boyd) 35 40

601 Red Roses

1999. Greetings Stamp. Romance. Ordinary or self-adhesive gum.
1842 **601** 45 c. multicoloured . . . 35 40

602 Elderly Man and Grandmother with Boy

1999. International Year of Older Persons. Mult.
1844 45 c. Type **602** 35 40
1845 45 c. Elderly woman and grandfather with boy . . . 35 40

603 "Polly Woodside" (barque)

604 Olympic Torch and 1956 $7\frac{1}{2}$d. Stamp

1999. Sailing Ships. Multicoloured.
1846 45 c. Type **603** 35 40
1847 85 c. "Alma Doepel" (topsail schooner) 65 70
1848 $1 "Enterprize" replica (topsail schooner) 75 80
1849 $1.05 "Lady Nelson" replica (topsail schooner) 80 85

1999. Olympic Torch Commemoration.
1853 **604** $1.20 multicoloured . . 90 95

605 "Correa reflexa" (native fuschia)

1999. Coastal Environment. Multicoloured. Ordinary or self-adhesive gum.
1854 45 c. Type **605** 35 40
1855 45 c. "Hibbertia scandens" (guinea flower) 35 40
1856 45 c. "Ipomoea pre-caprae" (beach morning glory) . . 35 40
1857 45 c. "Wahlenbergia stricta" (Australian bluebells) . . . 35 40

OFFICIAL STAMPS

1931. Optd **O.S.**
(a) Kangaroo issue.
O133 **1** 6d. brown . . . . 20·00 20·00

(b) King George V issue.
O128 **3** $\frac{1}{2}$d. orange . . . . 4·75 1·50
O129 1d. green . . . . 3·25 45
O130 2d. red . . . . 6·50 55
O131 3d. blue . . . . 7·50 4·00
O126 4d. olive . . . . 16·00 5·00
O132 5d. brown . . . . 35·00 27·00

(c) Various issues.
O123 **13** 2d. red . . . . 55·00 16·00
O134 **18** 2d. red . . . . 5·00 2·00
O124 **13** 3d. blue . . . . £200 32·00
O135 **18** 3d. blue . . . . 14·00 7·00
O136 **17** 1s. green . . . . 40·00 35·00

POSTAGE DUE STAMPS

D 1

D 3

1902. White space below value at foot.
D1 **D 1** $\frac{1}{2}$d. green . . . . 3·00 3·75
D2 1d. green . . . . 12·00 5·50
D3 2d. green . . . . 28·00 6·50
D4 3d. green . . . . 28·00 18·00
D5 4d. green . . . . 42·00 11·00
D6 6d. green . . . . 55·00 9·00
D7 8d. green . . . . 95·00 70·00
D8 5s. green . . . . £180 70·00

1902. White space filled in.
D22 **D 3** $\frac{1}{2}$d. green . . . . 6·00 5·00
D23 1d. green . . . . 6·00 2·50
D24 2d. green . . . . 20·00 2·75
D25 3d. green . . . . 60·00 7·50
D26 4d. green . . . . 50·00 8·50
D17 5d. green . . . . 40·00 9·50
D28 6d. green . . . . 50·00 9·50
D29 8d. green . . . . £120 40·00
D18 10d. green . . . . 70·00 17·00
D19 1s. green . . . . 55·00 10·00
D20 2s. green . . . . £100 16·00
D33 5s. green . . . . £180 21·00
D43 10s. green £1600 £1300
D44 20s. green £3250 £2250

1908. As Type D 3, but stroke after figure of value, thus "5/-".
D58 **D 3** 1s. green . . . . 75·00 8·00
D60 2s. green £850 £1200
D59 5s. green . . . . £200 48·00
D61 10s. green £2000 £2250
D62 20s. green £5000 £6000

D 7

D 10

1909.
D132 **D 7** $\frac{1}{2}$d. red and green . . . 1·60 1·75
D133a 1d. red and green . . . 1·00 65
D93 $1\frac{1}{2}$d. red and green . . 1·50 9·00
D121 2d. red and green . . . 4·50 1·25
D134 3d. red and green . . . 1·75 2·75
D109 4d. red and green . . . 3·75 2·25
D124 5d. red and green . . . 12·00 3·00
D137 6d. red and green . . . 2·75 3·00
D126 7d. red and green . . . 4·25 8·50
D127 8d. red and green . . . 10·00 25·00
D139 10d. red and green . . . 4·50 3·25
D128 1s. red and green . . . 18·00 1·60
D70 2s. red and green . . . 70·00 13·00
D71 5s. red and green . . . 90·00 15·00
D72 10s. red and green . . . £250 £150
D73 £1 red and green . . . £475 £275

1953.
D140 **D 10** 1s. red and green . . 5·00 2·75
D130 2s. red and green . . 18·00 12·00
D131a 5s. red and green . . 12·00 70

AUSTRALIAN ANTARCTIC TERRITORY

By an Order in Council of 7 February 1933, the territory S. of latitude 60°S. between 160th and 145th meridians of East longitude (excepting Adelie Land) was placed under Australian administration. Until 1957 stamps of Australia were used from the base

1957. 12 pence = 1 shilling;
20 shillings = 1 pound.
1966. 100 cents = 1 dollar.

1 1954 Expedition at Vestfold Hills and Map

1957.

1	1	2s. blue	1·25	50

2 Members of Shackleton Expedition at S. Magnetic Pole, 1909

3 Weazel and Team

1959.

2	2	5d. on 4d. black and sepia	60	15
3	3	8d. on 7d. black and blue	4·00	2·25
4	–	1s. myrtle	3·00	2·00
5	–	2s. 3d. green	8·00	4·00

DESIGNS—VERT (as Type 3): 1s. Dog-team and iceberg; 2s. 3d. Map of Antarctica and emperor penguins.

6

7 Sir Douglas Mawson (Expedition leader)

1961.

6	6	5d. blue	1·25	20

1961. 50th Anniv of 1911–14 Australian Antarctic Expedition.

7	7	5d. myrtle	35	20

8 Aurora and Camera Dome

11 Sastrugi (Snow Ridges)

1966. Multicoloured.

8	1 c. Type **8**	70	30
9	2 c. Emperor penguins	3·00	80
10	4 c. Ship and iceberg	90	90
11	5 c. Banding southern elephant-seals	2·75	1·75
12	7 c. Measuring snow strata	80	80
13	10 c. Wind gauges	1·00	90
14	15 c. Weather balloon	5·00	2·00
15	20 c. Bell Trooper helicopter (horiz)	6·00	2·50
16	25 c. Radio operator (horiz)	3·00	3·00
17	50 c. Ice-compression tests (horiz)	4·50	5·50
18	$1 Parahelion ("mock sun") (horiz)	26·00	14·00

1971. 10th Anniv of Antarctic Treaty.

19	11	6 c. blue and black	75	1·00
20	–	30 c. multicoloured	3·25	6·00

DESIGN: 30 c. Pancake ice.

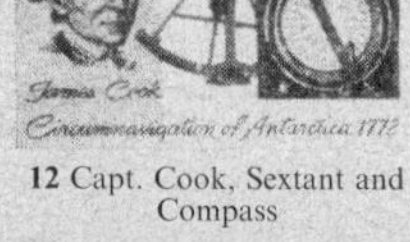

12 Capt. Cook, Sextant and Compass

13 Plankton

1972. Bicentenary of Cook's Circumnavigation of Antarctica. Multicoloured.

21	7 c. Type **12**	1·25	75
22	35 c. Chart and H.M.S. "Resolution"	4·75	6·00

1973. Multicoloured.

23	1 c. Type **13**	30	15
24	5 c. Mawson's De Havilland Gipsy Moth, 1931	70	70
25	7 c. Adelie penguin	2·25	70
26	8 c. De Havilland Fox Moth, 1934–37	75	90
27	9 c. Leopard seal (horiz)	40	90
28	10 c. Killer whale (horiz)	5·50	2·00
29	20 c. Wandering albatross (horiz)	1·25	1·00
30	25 c. Wilkins's Lockheed Vega "San Francisco", 1928 (horiz)	90	1·00
31	30 c. Ellsworth's Northrop Gamma "Polar Star", 1935	90	1·00
32	35 c. Christensen's Avro Type 581 Avian, 1934 (horiz)	90	1·00
33	50 c. Byrd's Ford Trimotor "Floyd Bennett", 1929	90	1·00
34	$1 Sperm whale	1·25	1·40

14 Admiral Byrd (expedition leader), Ford Trimotor "Floyd Bennett" and Map of South Pole

15 "Thala Dan" (supply ship)

1979. 50th Anniv of First Flight over South Pole. Multicoloured.

35	20 c. Type **14**	30	50
36	55 c. Admiral Byrd, aircraft and Antarctic terrain	80	1·50

1979. Ships. Multicoloured.

37	1 c. "Aurora" (horiz)	15	10
38	2 c. "Penola" (Rymill's ship)	40	10
39	5 c. Type **15**	30	40
40	10 c. H.M.S. "Challenger" (survey ship) (horiz)	50	55
41	15 c. "Morning" (bow view) (whaling ship) (horiz)	2·00	3·00
42	15 c. "Nimrod" (stern view) (Shackleton's ship) (horiz)	1·40	60
43	20 c. "Discovery II" (supply ship) (horiz)	1·25	1·50
44	22 c. "Terra Nova" (Scott's ship)	90	1·25
45	25 c. "Endurance" (Shackleton's ship)	60	1·00
46	30 c. "Fram" (Amundsen's ship) (horiz)	60	1·50
47	35 c. "Nella Dan" (supply ship) (horiz)	80	1·50
48	40 c. "Kista Dan" (supply ship)	1·25	1·50
49	45 c. "L'Astrolabe" (D'Urville's ship) (horiz)	70	1·00
50	50 c. "Norvegia" (supply ship) (horiz)	70	70
51	55 c. "Discovery" (Scott's ship)	85	2·00
52	$1 H.M.S. "Resolution" (Cook's ship)	1·75	2·50

No. 41 is incorrectly inscr "S.Y. Nimrod".

16 Sir Douglas Mawson in Antarctic Terrain

17 Light-mantled Sooty Albatross

1982. Birth Centenary of Sir Douglas Mawson (Antarctic explorer). Multicoloured.

53	27 c. Type **16**	35	30
54	75 c. Sir Douglas Mawson and map of Australian Antarctic Territory	1·25	2·00

1983. Regional Wildlife. Multicoloured.

55	27 c. Type **17**	85	90
56	27 c. King cormorant	85	90
57	27 c. Southern elephant seal	85	90
58	27 c. Royal penguin	85	90
59	27 c. Dove prion	85	90

18 Antarctic Scientist

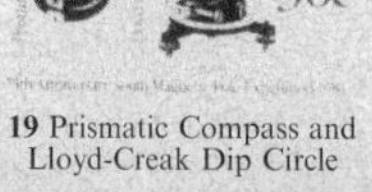

19 Prismatic Compass and Lloyd-Creak Dip Circle

1983. 12th Antarctic Treaty Consultative Meeting. Canberra.

60	18	27 c. multicoloured	55	55

1984. 75th Anniv of Magnetic Pole Expedition. Multicoloured.

61	30c. Type **19**	50	50
62	85 c. Aneroid barometer and theodolite	1·25	1·50

20 Dog Team pulling Sledge

21 Prince Charles Mountains near Mawson Station

1984. Antarctic Scenes. Multicoloured.

63	2 c. Summer afternoon Mawson station	10	30
64	5 c. Type **20**	15	15
65	10 c. Late summer evening, MacRobertson Land	15	15
66	15 c. Prince Charles Mountains	15	20
67	20 c. Summer morning Wilkesland	15	20
68	25 c. Sea-ice and iceberg	60	60
69	30 c. Mount Coates	25	30
70	33 c. "Iceberg Alley", Mawson	25	30
71	36 c. Early winter evening, Casey Station	30	35
72	45 c. Brash ice (vert)	70	1·00
73	60 c. Midwinter shadows, Casey Station	50	55
74	75 c. Coastline	2·25	2·75
75	85 c. Landing strip	2·50	3·00
76	90 c. Pancake ice (vert)	75	80
77	$1 Emperor penguins	2·25	1·25

1986. 25th Anniv of Antarctic Treaty.

78	21	36 c. multicoloured	1·25	85

22 Hourglass Dolphins and "Nella Dan"

23 "Antarctica"

1988. Environment, Conservation and Technology. Multicoloured.

79	37 c. Type **22**	1·10	1·10
80	37 c. Emperor penguins and Davis Station	1·10	1·10
81	37 c. Crabeater seal and Hughes 500D helicopters	1·10	1·10
82	37 c. Adelie penguins and tracked vehicle	1·10	1·10
83	37 c. Grey-headed albatross and photographer	1·10	1·10

1989. Antarctic Landscape Paintings by Sir Sidney Nolan. Multicoloured.

84	39 c. Type **23**	1·00	70
85	39 c. "Iceberg Alley"	1·00	70
86	60 c. "Glacial Flow"	1·75	1·25
87	80 c. "Frozen Sea"	2·25	1·40

24 "Aurora Australis"

1991. 30th Anniv of Antarctic Treaty (43 c.) and maiden voyage of "Aurora Australis" (research ship) ($1.20). Multicoloured.

88	43 c. Type **24**	75	50
89	$1.20 "Aurora Australis" off Heard Island	2·75	2·50

25 Adelie Penguin and Chick

26 Head of Husky

1992. Antarctic Wildlife. Multicoloured.

90	45 c. Type **25**	35	40
91	75 c. Elephant seal with pup	55	60
92	85 c. Northern giant petrel on nest with fledgeling	65	70
93	95 c. Weddell seal and pup	75	80
94	$1 Royal penguin	75	80
95	$1.20 Emperor penguins with chicks (vert)	90	95
96	$1.40 Fur seal	1·10	1·25
97	$1.50 King penguin (vert)	1·10	1·25

1994. Departure of Huskies from Antarctica. Multicoloured.

104	45 c. Type **26**	60	50
105	75 c. Dogs pulling sledge (horiz)	1·00	1·10
106	85 c. Husky in harness	1·25	1·40
107	$1.05 Dogs on leads (horiz)	1·40	1·50

27 Humpback Whale with Calf

1995. Whales and Dolphins. Multicoloured.

108	45 c. Type **27**	75	65
109	45 c. Pair of hourglass dolphins (vert)	75	65
110	45 c. Pair of minke whales (vert)	75	65
111	$1 Killer whale	1·50	1·50

Nos. 109/10 were printed together, se-tenant, forming a composite design.

28 "Rafting Sea Ice" (Christian Clare Robertson)

29 Apple Huts

1996. Paintings by Christian Clare Robertson. Multicoloured.

113	45 c. Type **28**	70	55
114	45 c. "Shadow on the Plateau"	70	55
115	$1 "Ice Cave"	1·60	1·40
116	$1.20 "Twelve Lake"	1·75	1·60

1997. 50th Anniv of Australian National Antarctic Research Expeditions (A.N.A.R.E.). Multicoloured.

117	45 c. Type **29**	50	55
118	45 c. Tuning a radio receiver	50	55
119	95 c. Summer surveying	90	1·10
120	$1.05 Scientists in cage above sea ice	80	85
121	$1.20 Scientists and tents	1·10	1·40

30 "Aurora Australis" (research ship)

1998. Antarctic Transport. Multicoloured.

122	45 c. Type **30**	65	65
123	45 c. "Skidoo"	65	65
124	$1 Helicopter lifting quad-bike (vert)	1·40	1·40
125	$2 Hagglunds tractor and trailer (vert)	2·00	2·00

BAHAMAS

A group of islands in the Br. W. Indies, S.E. of Florida. Self-Government introduced on 7 January 1964. The islands became an independent member of the British Commonwealth on 10 July 1973.

1859. 12 pence = 1 shilling;
20 shillings = 1 pound.
1966. 100 cents = 1 dollar.

1

2

3

1859. Imperf.

2	1	1d. red	50·00	£1500

1860. Perf.

33	1	1d. red	40·00	15·00
27	2	4d. red	£250	60·00
31		6d. violet	£160	60·00
39b	3	1s. green	7·50	7·00

1883. Surch **FOURPENCE**.

45	2	4d. on 6d. violet	£550	£400

5

6 Queen's Staircase, Nassau

1884.

48	5	1d. red	6·00	2·00
52		2½d. blue	9·00	2·00
53		4d. yellow	9·00	4·00
54		6d. mauve	4·50	26·00
56		5s. green	65·00	75·00
57		£1 red	£275	£225

1901.

111	6	1d. black and red	80	1·00
76a		3d. purple on buff	4·50	4·50
77		3d. black and brown	1·50	2·25
59		5d. black and orange	8·00	45·00
78		5d. black and mauve	2·75	5·50
113		2s. black and blue	15·00	22·00
61		3s. black and green	29·00	55·00

7

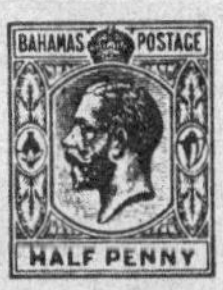

8

1902.

71	7	½d. green	4·50	2·00
62		1d. red	1·50	2·50
63		2½d. blue	6·50	1·25
64		4d. yellow	14·00	48·00
66		6d. brown	3·50	16·00
67		1s. black and red	18·00	48·00
69		5s. purple and blue	55·00	75·00
70		£1 green and black	£250	£325

1912.

115	8	½d. green	45	40
116		1d. red	1·00	15
117		1½d. red	2·00	1·00
118		2d. grey	95	2·75
119		2½d. blue	80	2·75
120a		3d. purple on yellow	5·50	15·00
121		4d. yellow	1·00	5·00
122		6d. brown	70	1·25
123		1s. black and red	2·50	5·50
124		5s. purple and blue	30·00	55·00
125		£1 green and black	£160	£300

1917. Optd **1.1.17.** and Red Cross.

90	6	1d. black and red	40	1·60

1918. Optd **WAR TAX** in one line.

96	8	½d. green	1·50	1·60
97		1d. red	55	35
93	6	1d. black and red	3·50	3·25
98		3d. purple on yellow	50	1·50
100		3d. black and brown	45	4·00
99	8	1s. black and red	7·50	2·75

1919. Optd **WAR CHARITY 3.6.18.**

101	6	1d. black and red	30	2·50

1919. Optd **WAR TAX** in two lines.

102	8	½d. green	30	1·25
103		1d. red	1·00	1·50
105	6	3d. black and brown	55	6·00
104	8	1s. black and red	10·00	26·00

16

17 Seal of the Colony

1920. Peace Celebration.

106	16	½d. green	1·00	4·50
107		1d. red	2·75	90
108		2d. grey	2·75	7·00
109		3d. brown	2·75	9·00
110		1s. green	11·00	32·00

1930. Tercentenary of the Colony.

126	17	1d. black and red	2·00	2·75
127		3d. black and brown	3·75	14·00
128		5d. black and violet	3·75	14·00
129		2s. black and blue	18·00	42·00
130		3s. black and green	40·00	75·00

1931. As T **17**, but without dates at top.

131b		2s. black and blue	5·50	2·50
132b		3s. black and green	5·00	2·00

1935. Silver Jubilee. As T **13** of Antigua.

141		1½d. blue and red	1·00	2·25
142		2½d. brown and blue	4·50	7·00
143		6d. blue and olive	7·00	10·00
144		1s. grey and purple	7·00	8·00

19 Greater Flamingo (in flight)

1935.

145	19	8d. blue and red	5·50	2·75

1937. Coronation. As T **2** of Aden.

146		½d. green	15	15
147		1½d. brown	30	75
148		2½d. blue	50	75

20 King George VI

21 Sea Garden, Nassau

1938.

149	20	½d. green	15	90
149e		½d. purple	85	2·50
150		1d. red	8·50	4·75
150ab		1d. grey	50	50
151		1½d. brown	1·25	1·00
152		2d. grey	18·00	6·00
152b		2d. red	75	55
152c		2d. green	90	80
153		2½d. blue	3·25	2·00
153a		2½d. violet	1·25	70
154		3d. violet	16·00	4·00
154a		3d. blue	60	90
154b		3d. red	50	3·00
158	21	4d. blue and orange	1·00	80
159	–	6d. green and blue	60	80
160	–	8d. blue and red	5·00	2·00
154c	20	10d. orange	2·00	20
155c		1s. black and red	8·00	50
156e		5s. purple and blue	23·00	11·00
157a		£1 green and black	60·00	45·00

DESIGNS—As Type **21**: 6d. Fort Charlotte; 8d. Flamingoes.

1940. Surch **3d.**

161	20	3d. on 2½d. blue	65	40

1942. 450th Anniv of Landing of Columbus. Optd **1492 LANDFALL OF COLUMBUS 1942.**

162	20	½d. green	30	60
163		1d. grey	30	60
164		1½d. brown	40	60
165		2d. red	30	65
166		2½d. blue	30	65
167		3d. blue	30	65
168	21	4d. blue and orange	40	90
169	–	6d. green & blue (No. 159)	40	1·75
170	–	8d. blue and red (No. 160)	90	70
171a	20	1s. black and red	4·25	3·25
172a	17	2s. black and blue	8·00	10·00
173		3s. black and green	5·00	6·50
174a	20	5s. purple and blue	18·00	12·00
175a		£1 green and black	30·00	25·00

1946. Victory. As T **9** of Aden.

176		1½d. brown	10	30
177		3d. blue	10	30

MORE DETAILED LISTS
are given in the Stanley Gibbons Catalogues referred to in the country headings. For lists of current volumes see Introduction.

26 Infant Welfare Clinic

1948. Tercentenary of Settlement of Island of Eleuthera. Inscr as in T **26**.

178	26	½d. orange	30	70
179	–	1d. olive	30	35
180	–	1½d yellow	30	80
181	–	2d. red	30	40
182	–	2½d. brown	45	75
183	–	3d. blue	65	85
184	–	4d. black	60	70
185	–	6d. green	1·75	80
186	–	8d. violet	60	70
187	–	10d. red	60	35
188	–	1s. brown	90	50
189	–	2s. purple	4·00	8·50
190	–	3s. blue	7·50	8·50
191	–	5s. mauve	7·50	4·50
192	–	10s. grey	9·50	9·00
193	–	£1 red	11·00	14·00

DESIGNS: 1d. Agriculture; 1½d., Sisal; 2d. Straw work; 2½d. Dairy; 3d. Fishing fleet; 4d. Island settlement; 6d. Tuna fishing; 8d. Paradise Beach; 10d. Modern hotels; 1s. Yacht racing; 2s. Water sports—skiing; 3s. Shipbuilding; 5s. Transportation; 10s. Salt production; £1 Parliament Buildings.

1948. Silver Wedding. As T **10/11** of Aden.

194		1½d. brown	20	25
195		£1 grey	32·00	32·00

1949. 75th Anniv of U.P.U. As T **20/23** of Antigua.

196		2½d. violet	35	40
197		3d. blue	2·00	2·00
198		6d. blue	55	2·00
199		1s. red	55	75

1953. Coronation. As T **13** of Aden.

200		6d. black and blue	40	35

42 Infant Welfare Clinic

43 Queen Elizabeth II

1954. Designs as Nos. 178/93 but with portrait of Queen Elizabeth II and without commemorative inscr as in T **42**.

201	42	½d. black and red	10	1·25
202	–	1d. olive and brown	10	10
203	–	1½d. blue and black	15	40
204	–	2d. brown and green	15	15
205	–	3d. black and red	55	65
206	–	4d. turquoise and purple	30	30
207	–	5d. brown and blue	1·40	2·25
208	–	6d. blue and black	1·25	10
209	–	8d. black and lilac	70	40
210	–	10d. black and blue	30	10
211	–	1s. blue and brown	70	10
212	–	2s. orange and black	2·00	70
213	–	2s. 6d. black and blue	3·50	2·00
214	–	5s. green and orange	18·00	75
215	–	10s. black and slate	20·00	2·00
216	–	£1 black and violet	20·00	6·00

DESIGNS: 1½d., Island settlement; 4d. Water sports—skiing; 5d. Dairy; 6d. Transportation; 2s. Sisal; 2s. 6d. Shipbuilding; 5s. Tuna fishing. Other values the same as for the corresponding values in Nos. 178/93.

1959. Centenary of Bahamas Stamp.

217	43	1d. black and red	35	20
218		2d. black and green	35	80
219		6d. black and blue	45	30
220		10d. black and brown	50	90

44 Christ Church Cathedral

1962. Centenary of Nassau

221	44	8d. green	45	55
222	–	10d. violet	45	25

DESIGN: 10d. Nassau Public Library.

1963. Freedom from Hunger. As T **28** of Aden.

223		8d. sepia	40	40

1963. Bahamas Talks. Nos. 209/10 optd **BAHAMAS TALKS 1962.**

224		8d. black and lilac	40	60
225		10d. black and blue	50	65

1963. Centenary of Red Cross. As T **33** of Antigua.

226		1d. red and black	50	50
227		10d. red and blue	1·75	2·50

1964. New Constitution. Nos. 201/16 optd **NEW CONSTITUTION 1964.**

228	42	½d. black and red	15	80
229	–	1d. olive and brown	15	15
230	–	1½d. blue and black	70	80
231	–	2d. brown and green	15	20
232	–	3d. black and red	1·25	90
233	–	4d. turquoise and purple	40	45
234	–	5d. brown and blue	40	1·25
235	–	6d. blue and black	1·50	30
236	–	8d. black and lilac	70	30
237	–	10d. black and blue	30	15
238	–	1s. blue and brown	1·00	15
239	–	2s. brown and black	1·50	1·75
240	–	2s. 6d. black and blue	2·50	2·50
241	–	5s. green and orange	6·00	3·25
242	–	10s. black and slate	6·00	5·50
243	–	£1 black and violet	8·50	17·00

1964. 400th Birth Anniv of Shakespeare. As T **34** of Antigua.

244		6d. turquoise	10	10

1964. Olympic Games, Tokyo. No. 211 surch **8d.** and Olympic rings.

245		8d. on 1s. blue and brown	45	15

49 Colony's Badge

1965.

247	49	½d. multicoloured	15	90
248	–	1d. slate, blue and orange	30	50
249	–	1½d. red, green and brown	15	1·25
250	–	2d. slate, green and blue	15	10
251	–	3d. red, blue and purple	1·25	20
252	–	4d. green, blue and brown	1·75	1·60
253	–	6d. green, blue and red	30	10
254	–	8d. purple, blue and bronze	50	30
255	–	10d. brown, green and violet	25	10
256a	–	1s. multicoloured	30	10
257	–	2s. brown, blue and green	1·00	1·25
258	–	2s. 6d. olive, blue and red	2·25	3·00
259	–	5s. brown, blue and green	2·25	1·00
260	–	10s. red, blue and brown	14·00	3·00
261	–	£1 brown, blue and red	14·00	8·00

DESIGNS: 1d. Out Island regatta; 1½d. Hospital; 2d. High School; 3d. Greater flamingo; 4d. R.M.S. "Queen Elizabeth"; 6d. "Development"; 8d. Yachting; 10d. Public square; 1s. Sea garden; 2s. Old cannons at Fort Charlotte; 2s. 6d. Sikorsky S-38 flying boat, 1929, and Boeing 707 airliner; 5s. Williamson film project, 1914, and undersea post office, 1939; 10s. Queen or pink conch; £1 Columbus's flagship.

1965. Centenary of I.T.U. As T **36** of Antigua.

262		1d. green and orange	15	10
263		2s. purple and olive	65	45

1965. No. 254 surch **9d.**

264	–	9d. on 8d. purple, blue and bronze	30	15

1965. I.C.Y. As T **37** of Antigua.

265		½d. purple and turquoise	10	85
266		1s. green and lavender	30	40

1966. Churchill Commemoration. As T **38** of Antigua.

267		½d. blue	10	40
268		2d. green	30	30
269		10d. brown	65	85
270		1s. violet	75	1·40

1966. Royal Visit. As T **39** of Antigua but inscr "to the Caribbean" omitted.

271		6d. black and blue	90	50
272		1s. black and mauve	1·60	1·25

1966. Decimal currency. Nos. 247/61 surch.

273	49	1 c. on ½d. multicoloured	10	30
274	–	2 c. on 1d. slate, blue and orange	60	30
275	–	3 c. on 2d. slate, green and blue	10	10
276	–	4 c. on 3d. red, blue and purple	85	10
277	–	5 c. on 4d. green, blue and brown	70	2·50
278	–	8 c. on 6d. green, blue and red	20	20
279	–	10 c. on 8d. purple, blue and bronze	30	75
280	–	11 c. on 1½d. red, green and brown	15	30
281	–	12 c. on 10d. brown, green and violet	15	10
282	–	15 c. on 1s. multicoloured	25	10
283	–	22 c. on 2s. brown, blue and green	60	80
284	–	50 c. on 2s. 6d. olive, blue and red	90	1·40
285	–	$1 on 5s. brown, blue and green	1·50	1·50
286	–	$2 on 10s. red, blue and brown	6·50	4·25
287	–	$3 on £1 brown, blue and red	6·50	4·25

1966. World Cup Football Championships. As T **36** of Antigua.

288		8 c. multicoloured	25	15
289		15 c. multicoloured	30	25

1966. Inauguration of W.H.O. Headquarters, Geneva. As T **41** of Antigua.

290		11 c. black, green and blue	40	40
291		15 c. black, purple and ochre	45	50

1966. 20th Anniv of U.N.E.S.C.O. As T **54/6** of Antigua.

292	3 c. multicoloured	10	10
293	15 c. yellow, violet and olive	25	35
294	$1 black, purple and orange	1·00	2·50

1967. As Nos. 247/51, 253/9 and 261 but values in decimal currency, and new designs for 5 c. and $2.

295	**49**	1 c. multicoloured	10	2·00
296	–	2 c. slate, blue and green	20	60
297	–	3 c. slate, green and violet	10	10
298	–	4 c. red, light blue and blue	4·25	50
299	–	5 c. black, blue and purple	75	2·00
300	–	8 c. green, blue and brown	25	10
301	–	10 c. purple, blue and red	30	70
302	–	11 c. red, green and blue	25	80
303	–	12 c. brown, green and olive	25	10
304	–	15 c. multicoloured	55	10
305	–	22 c. brown, blue and red	70	65
306	–	50 c. olive, blue and green	2·00	75
307	–	$1 maroon, blue and purple	2·00	60
308	–	$2 multicoloured	10·00	3·00
309	–	$3 brown, blue and purple	3·75	2·00

NEW DESIGNS: 5 c. "Oceanic"; $2 Conch shell (different).

69 Bahamas Crest

1967. Diamond Jubilee of World Scouting. Mult.

310	3 c. Type **69**	35	15
311	15 c. Scout badge	40	15

71 Globe and Emblem

1968. Human Rights Year. Multicoloured.

312	3 c. Type **71**	10	10
313	12 c. Scales of Justice and emblem	20	10
314	$1 Bahamas Crest and emblem	70	80

74 Golf

1968. Tourism. Multicoloured.

315	5 c. Type **74**	1·75	1·25
316	11 c. Yachting	1·25	40
317	15 c. Horse-racing	1·75	45
318	50 c. Water-skiing	2·50	5·50

78 Racing Yacht and Olympic Monument

1968. Olympic Games, Mexico City.

319	**78**	5 c. brown, yellow and green	30	40
320	–	11 c. multicoloured	40	25
321	–	50 c. multicoloured	80	1·40
322	**78**	$1 grey, blue and violet	2·25	3·50

DESIGNS: 11 c. Long jumping and Olympic Monument; 50 c. Running and Olympic Monument.

81 Legislative Building

1968. 14th Commonwealth Parliamentary Conference. Multicoloured.

323	3 c. Type **81**	10	20
324	10 c. Bahamas Mace and Westminster Clock Tower	15	25
325	12 c. Local straw market	15	25
326	15 c. Horse-drawn surrey	20	30

Nos. 324/5 are vert.

85 Obverse and reverse of $100 Gold Coin

1968. Gold Coins commemorating the first General Election under the New Constitution.

327	**85**	3 c. red on gold	40	25
328	–	12 c. green on gold	60	50
329	–	15 c. purple on gold	70	60
330	–	$1 black on gold	1·75	2·50

OBVERSE AND REVERSE OF: 12 c. $50 gold coin; 15 c. $20 gold coins; $1, $10 gold coin.

89 First Flight Postcard of 1919

1969. 50th Anniv of Bahamas Airmail Services.

331	**89**	12 c. multicoloured	50	50
332	–	15 c. multicoloured	60	1·25

DESIGN: 15 c. Sikorsky S-38 flying boat of 1929.

91 Game-fishing Boats

1969. Tourism. One Millionth Visitor to Bahamas. Multicoloured.

333	3 c. Type **91**	25	10
334	11 c. Paradise Beach	35	15
335	12 c. "Sunfish" sailing boats	35	15
336	15 c. Rawson Square and parade	45	25

92 "The Adoration of the Shepherds" (Louis le Nain)

1969. Christmas. Multicoloured.

338	3 c. Type **92**	10	10
339	11 c. "The Adoration of the Shepherds" (Poussin)	15	15
340	12 c. "The Adoration of the Kings" (Gerard David)	15	20
341	15 c. "The Adoration of the Kings" (Vincenzo Foppa)	20	40

93 Badge of Girl Guides

1970. Diamond Jubilee of Girl Guides' Association. Multicoloured.

342	3 c. Type **93**	30	10
343	12 c. Badge of Brownies	45	20
344	15 c. Badge of Rangers	50	35

94 New U.P.U. Headquarters and Emblem

1970. New U.P.U. Headquarters Building.

345	**94**	3 c. multicoloured	10	10
346		15 c. multicoloured	20	30

95 Coach and Globe

1970. "Goodwill Caravan". Multicoloured.

347	3 c. Type **95**	75	15
348	11 c. Diesel train and globe	2·00	30
349	12 c. "Canberra" (liner), yacht and globe	2·00	40
350	15 c. B.A.C. One Eleven airliner and globe	2·00	1·25

96 Nurse, Patients and Greater Flamingo

1970. Centenary of British Red Cross. Multicoloured.

352	3 c. Type **96**	1·00	50
353	15 c. Hospital and blue marlin	1·00	1·50

97 "The Nativity" (detail, Pittoni)

1970. Christmas. Multicoloured.

354	3 c. Type **97**	15	10
355	11 c. "The Holy Family" (detail, Anton Raphael Mengs)	20	20
356	12 c. "The Adoration of the Shepherds" (detail, Giorgione)	20	20
357	15 c. "The Adoration of the Shepherds" (detail, School of Seville)	30	55

98 International Airport

1971. Multicoloured.

359	1 c. Type **98**	10	30
360	2 c. Breadfruit	15	35
361	3 c. Straw market	15	30
362	4 c. Hawksbill turtle	1·75	7·00
363	5 c. Nassau grouper	60	60
364	6 c. As 4 c.	45	1·25
365	7 c. Hibiscus	2·00	3·25
366	8 c. Yellow elder	60	1·50
367	10 c. Bahamian sponge boat	55	30
368	11 c. Greater flamingoes	2·50	2·25
369	12 c. As 7 c.	2·00	3·00
370	15 c. Bonefish	40	55
466	16 c. As 7 c.	70	35
371	18 c. Royal poinciana	65	65
467a	21 c. As 2 c.	80	1·25
372	22 c. As 18 c.	2·75	11·00
468	25 c. As 4 c.	90	40
469	40 c. As 10 c.	3·25	75
470	50 c. Post Office, Nassau	1·75	1·75
471	$1 Pineapple (vert)	2·00	2·50
472	$2 Crawfish (vert)	3·00	7·00
525	$3 Junkanoo (vert)	4·50	8·00

99 Snowflake

101 Shepherd

100 High Jumping

1971. Christmas.

377	**99**	3 c. purple, orange and gold	10	10
378	–	11 c. blue and gold	20	15
379	–	15 c. multicoloured	20	20
380	–	18 c. blue, ultram and gold	25	25

DESIGNS: 11 c. "Peace on Earth" (doves); 15 c. Arms of Bahamas and holly; 18 c. Starlit lagoon

1972. Olympic Games, Munich. Multicoloured.

382	10 c. Type **100**	35	60
383	11 c. Cycling	1·50	75
384	15 c. Running	60	75
385	18 c. Sailing	95	1·25

1972. Christmas. Multicoloured.

387	3 c. Type **101**	10	10
388	6 c. Bells	10	10
389	15 c. Holly and Cross	15	20
390	20 c. Poinsettia	25	45

1972. Royal Silver Wedding. As T **52** of Ascension, but with mace and galleon in background.

393	11 c. pink	15	15
394	18 c. violet	15	20

104 Weather Satellite

1973. Centenary of I.M.O./W.M.O. Multicoloured.

410	15 c. Type **104**	50	25
411	18 c. Weather radar	60	35

105 C. A. Bain (national hero)

106 "The Virgin in Prayer" (Sassoferrato)

1973. Independence. Multicoloured.

412	3 c. Type **105**	10	10
413	11 c. Coat of arms	15	10
414	15 c. Bahamas flag	20	15
415	$1 Governor-General, M. B. Butler	65	1·00

1973. Christmas. Multicoloured.

417	3 c. Type **106**	10	10
418	11 c. "Virgin and Child with St. John" (Filippino Lippi)	15	15
419	15 c. "A Choir of Angels" (Simon Marmion)	15	15
420	18 c. "The Two Trinities" (Murillo)	25	25

107 "Agriculture and Sciences"

1974. 25th Anniv of University of West Indies. Multicoloured.

422	15 c. Type **107**	20	25
423	18 c. "Arts, Engineering and General Studies"	25	30

108 U.P.U. Monument, Berne

1974. Centenary of U.P.U.

424	**108**	3 c. multicoloured	10	10
425	–	13 c. multicoloured (vert)	20	25
426	–	14 c. multicoloured	20	30
427	–	18 c. multicoloured (vert)	25	35

DESIGNS: As Type **108** but showing different arrangements of the U.P.U. Monument.

HAVE YOU READ THE NOTES AT THE BEGINNING OF THIS CATALOGUE?
These often provide answers to the enquiries we receive.

109 Roseate Spoonbills

1974. 15th Anniv of Bahamas National Trust. Mult.

429	13 c. Type **109**	1·40	85
430	14 c. White-crowned pigeon	1·40	75
431	21 c. White-tailed tropic birds	1·75	1·25
432	36 c. Cuban amazon	2·25	3·75

110 "The Holy Family" (Jacques de Stella)

1974. Christmas. Multicoloured.

434	8 c. Type **110**	10	10
435	10 c. "Madonna and Child" (16th-century Brescian School)	15	15
436	12 c. "Virgin and Child with St. John the Baptist and St. Catherine" (Previtali)	15	15
437	21 c. "Virgin and Child with Angels" (Previtali)	25	30

111 "Anteos maerula"

1975. Butterflies. Multicoloured.

439	3 c. Type **111**	25	15
440	14 c. "Eurema nicippe"	80	50
441	18 c. "Papilio andraemon"	95	65
442	21 c. "Euptoieta hegesia"	1·10	85

112 Sheep Husbandry

1975. Economic Diversification. Multicoloured.

444	3 c. Type **112**	10	10
445	14 c. Electric-reel fishing (vert)	20	15
446	18 c. Farming	25	20
447	21 c. Oil refinery (vert)	45	35

113 Rowena Rand (evangelist)

1975. International Women's Year.

449	**113**	14 c. brown, lt blue & bl	20	40
450	–	18 c. yellow, grn & brn	25	45

DESIGN: 18 c. I.W.Y. symbol and harvest symbol.

114 "Adoration of the Shepherds" (Perugino)

1975. Christmas. Multicoloured.

451	3 c. Type **114**	15	50
452	8 c. "Adoration of the Magi" (Ghirlandaio)	20	10
453	18 c. As 8 c.	55	80
454	21 c. Type **114**	60	85

115 Telephones, 1876 and 1976

1976. Centenary of Telephone. Multicoloured.

456	3 c. Type **115**	15	30
457	16 c. Radio-telephone link, Deleporte	30	40
458	21 c. Alexander Graham Bell	40	55
459	25 c. Satellite	50	70

116 Map of North America

1976. Bicentenary of American Revolution. Mult.

475	16 c. Type **116**	30	30
476	$1 John Murray, Earl of Dunmore	1·50	1·75

117 Cycling **118** "Virgin and Child" (detail, Lippi)

1976. Olympic Games, Montreal.

478	**117**	8 c. mauve, blue and light blue	60	10
479	–	16 c. orange, brown and light blue	35	25
480	–	25 c. blue, mauve and light blue	45	45
481	–	40 c. brown, orange and blue	55	1·25

DESIGNS: 16 c. Jumping; 25 c. Sailing; 40 c. Boxing.

1976. Christmas. Multicoloured.

483	3 c. Type **118**	10	10
484	21 c. "Adoration of the Shepherds" (School of Seville)	20	15
485	25 c. "Adoration of the Kings" (detail, Foppa)	20	20
486	40 c. "Virgin and Child" (detail, Vivarini)	35	40

119 Queen beneath Cloth of Gold Canopy

1977. Silver Jubilee. Multicoloured.

488	8 c. Type **119**	10	10
489	16 c. The Crowning	15	15
490	21 c. Taking the Oath	15	15
491	40 c. Queen with sceptre and orb	25	30

120 Featherduster

1977. Marine Life. Multicoloured.

493	3 c. Type **120**	30	15
494	8 c. Porkfish and cave	45	20
495	16 c. Elkhorn coral	70	40
496	21 c. Soft coral and sponge	80	55

121 Scouts around Campfire and Home-made Shower

1977. 6th Caribbean Scout Jamboree. Multicoloured.

498	16 c. Type **121**	75	30
499	21 c. Boating scenes	85	35

1977. Royal Visit. Nos. 488/91 optd **Royal Visit October 1977.**

500	8 c. Type **119**	15	10
501	16 c. The Crowning	20	15
502	21 c. Taking the Oath	25	25
503	40 c. Queen with sceptre and orb	30	40

123 Virgin and Child **124** Public Library, Nassau (Colonial)

1977. Christmas. Multicoloured.

505	3 c. Type **123**	10	10
506	16 c. The Magi	20	25
507	21 c. Nativity scene	25	40
508	25 c. The Magi and star	30	45

1978. Architectural Heritage.

510	**124**	3 c. black and green	10	10
511	–	8 c. black and blue	15	10
512	–	16 c. black and mauve	20	20
513	–	18 c. black and pink	25	30

DESIGNS: 8 c. St. Matthew's Church; 16 c. Government House; 18 c. The Hermitage, Cat Island.

125 Sceptre, St. Edward's Crown and Orb **127** Child reaching for Adult

126 Coat of Arms within Wreath and Three Ships

1978. 25th Anniv of Coronation. Multicoloured.

515	16 c. Type **125**	15	10
516	$1 Queen in Coronation regalia	50	65

1978. Christmas.

532	**126**	5 c. gold, lake and red	20	10
533	–	21 c. gold, deep blue and blue	55	25

DESIGN: 21 c. Three angels with trumpets.

1979. International Year of the Child. Multicoloured.

535	5 c. Type **127**	20	15
536	16 c. Boys playing leapfrog	40	45
537	21 c. Girls skipping	50	60
538	25 c. Bricks with I.Y.C. emblem	50	75

128 Sir Rowland Hill and Penny Black

1979. Death Centenary of Sir Rowland Hill. Multicoloured.

540	10 c. Type **128**	30	10
541	21 c. Printing press, 1840, and 6d. stamp of 1862	40	30
542	25 c. Great Britain 1856 6d. with "A 05" (Nassau) cancellation, and 1840 2d. Blue	40	50
543	40 c. Early mailboat and 1d. stamp of 1859	45	70

129 Commemorative Plaque and Map of Bahamas

1979. 250th Anniv of Parliament. Multicoloured.

545	16 c. Type **129**	25	10
546	21 c. Parliament buildings	30	15
547	25 c. Legislative Chamber	30	15
548	$1 Senate Chamber	80	80

130 Goombay Carnival Headdress **132** Virgin and Child

131 Landfall of Columbus, 1492

1979. Christmas.

550	**130**	5 c. multicoloured	10	10
551	–	10 c. multicoloured	10	10
552	–	16 c. multicoloured	15	10
553	–	21 c. multicoloured	20	20
554	–	25 c. multicoloured	20	20
555	–	40 c. multicoloured	30	35

DESIGNS: 10 c. to 40 c. Various Carnival costumes.

1980. Multicoloured.

557	1 c. Type **131**	85	2·00
558	3 c. Blackbeard the pirate	30	2·00
559	5 c. Eleutheran Adventurers (Articles and Orders, 1647)	30	60
560	10 c. Ceremonial mace	20	30
561	12 c. The Loyalists, 1783–1788	30	1·50
562	15 c. Slave trading, Vendue House	5·50	75
563	16 c. Wrecking in the 1800s	80	75
564	18 c. Blockade running (American Civil War)	90	1·75
565	21 c. Bootlegging, 1919–1929	40	1·75
566	25 c. Pineapple cultivation	40	1·75
567	40 c. Sponge clipping	70	1·50
568	50 c. Tourist development	75	1·50
569	$1 Modern agriculture	1·10	4·00
570	$2 Modern air and sea transport	4·00	4·25
571	$3 Banking (Central Bank)	1·50	4·00
572	$5 Indpendence, 10 July 1973	1·75	6·00

1980. Christmas Straw-work. Multicoloured.

573	5 c. Three kings	10	10
574	21 c. Type **132**	25	10
575	25 c. Angel	25	15
576	$1 Christmas tree	75	70

133 Disabled Persons with Walking Stick

1981. International Year of Disabled People. Mult.

578	5 c. Type **133**	10	10
579	$1 Disabled person in wheel-chair	1·25	1·25

134 Grand Bahama Tracking Site

1981. Space Exploration. Multicoloured.

581	10 c. Type **134**	25	15
582	20 c. Satellite view of Bahamas (vert)	55	50
583	25 c. Satellite view of Eleuthera	60	60
584	50 c. Satellite view of Andros and New Province (vert)	85	1·25

135 Prince Charles and Lady Diana Spencer

1981. Royal Wedding. Multicoloured.

586	30 c. Type **135**	1·00	30
587	$2 Prince Charles and Prime Minister Pindling	1·50	1·25

136 Bahamas Pintail

1981. Wildlife (1st series). Birds. Multicoloured.

589	5 c. Type **136**	90	30
590	20 c. Reddish egret	1·75	50
591	25 c. Brown booby	1·75	55
592	$1 Black-billed whistling duck	3·50	5·00

See also Nos. 626/9, 653/6 and 690/3.

1981. Commonwealth Finance Ministers' Meeting. Nos. 559/60, 566 and 568 optd **COMMONWEALTH FINANCE MINISTERS' MEETING 21–23 SEPTEMBER 1981.**

594	5 c. Eleutheran Adventures (Articles and Orders, 1647)	15	15
595	10 c. Ceremonial mace	20	20
596	25 c. Pineapple cultivation	50	60
597	50 c. Tourist development	85	1·50

138 Poultry

1981. World Food Day. Multicoloured.

598	5 c. Type **138**	10	10
599	20 c. Sheep	30	35
600	30 c. Lobsters	40	50
601	50 c. Pigs	75	1·50

139 Father Christmas

141 Greater Flamingo (male)

140 Robert Koch

1981. Christmas. Multicoloured.

603	5 c. Type **139**	35	60
604	5 c. Mother and child	35	60
605	5 c. St. Nicholas, Holland	35	60
606	25 c. Lussibruden, Sweden	50	85
607	25 c. Mother and child (different)	50	85
608	25 c. King Wenceslas, Czechoslovakia	50	85
609	30 c. Mother with child on knee	50	85
610	30 c. Mother carrying child	50	85
611	$1 Christkindl Angel, Germany	1·00	1·50

1982. Centenary of Discovery of Tubercle Bacillus by Robert Koch.

612	**140**	5 c. black, brown and lilac	70	40
613	–	16 c. black, brown & orge	1·25	50
614	–	21 c. multicoloured	1·40	55
615	–	$1 multicoloured	3·00	6·50

DESIGNS: 16 c. Stylised infected person; 21 c. Early and modern microscopes; $1 Mantoux test.

1982. Greater Flamingoes. Multicoloured.

617	25 c. Type **141**	1·40	1·00
618	25 c. Female	1·40	1·00
619	25 c. Female with nestling	1·40	1·00
620	25 c. Juvenile	1·40	1·00
621	25 c. Immature bird	1·40	1·00

142 Lady Diana Spencer at Ascot, June 1981

143 House of Assembly Plaque

1982. 21st Birthday of Princess of Wales. Mult.

622	16 c. Bahamas coat of arms	20	10
623	25 c. Type **142**	45	15
624	40 c. Bride and Earl Spencer arriving at St. Paul's	60	20
625	$1 Formal portrait	1·00	1·25

1982. Wildlife (2nd series). Mammals. As T **136**. Multicoloured.

626	10 c. Buffy flower bat	70	15
627	16 c. Bahamian hutia	90	25
628	21 c. Common racoon	1·10	55
629	$1 Common dolphin	2·75	1·75

1982. 28th Commonwealth Parliamentary Association Conference. Multicoloured.

631	5 c. Type **143**	15	10
632	25 c. Association coat of arms	50	35
633	40 c. Coat of arms	80	60
634	50 c. House of Assembly	1·10	75

144 Wesley Methodist Church, Baillou Hill Road

1982. Christmas. Churches. Multicoloured.

635	5 c. Type **144**	10	10
636	12 c. Centreville Seventh Day Adventist Church	15	20
637	15 c. The Church of God of Prophecy, East Street	20	30
638	21 c. Bethel Baptist Church, Meeting Street	25	30
639	25 c. St. Francis Xavier Catholic Church, Highbury Park	25	50
640	$1 Holy Cross Anglican Church, Highbury Park	75	2·75

145 Prime Minister Lyndon O. Pindling

1983. Commonwealth Day. Multicoloured.

641	5 c. Type **145**	10	10
642	25 c. Bahamian and Commonwealth flags	30	40
643	35 c. Map showing position of Bahamas	40	50
644	$1 Ocean liner	1·10	1·40

1983. Nos. 562/5 surch.

645	20 c. on 15 c. Slave, Trading Vendue House	50	35
646	31 c. on 21 c. Bootlegging, 1919–29	60	55
647	35 c. on 16 c. Wrecking in the 1800s	1·25	60
648	80 c. on 18 c. Blockade running (American Civil War)	1·50	1·40

147 Customs Officers and Liner

148 Raising the National Flag

1983. 30th Anniv of Customs Co-operation Council. Multicoloured.

649	31 c. Type **147**	1·50	45
650	$1 Customs officers and Lockheed JetStar airliner	3·50	2·75

1983. 10th Anniv of Independence.

651	**148**	$1 multicoloured	1·00	1·40

1983. Wildlife (3rd series). Butterflies. As T **136**.

653	5 c. multicoloured	90	20
654	25 c. multicoloured	1·60	40
655	31 c. black, yellow and red	1·60	55
656	50 c. multicoloured	1·75	85

DESIGNS: 5 c. "Atalopedes carteri"; 25 c. "Ascia monuste"; 31 c. "Phoebis agarithe"; 50 c. "Dryas julia".

149 "Loyalist Dreams"

151 "Christmas Bells" (Monica Pinder)

150 Consolidated Catalina

1983. Bicentenary of Arrival of American Loyalists in the Bahamas. Multicoloured.

658	5 c. Type **149**	10	10
659	31 c. New Plymouth, Abaco (horiz)	45	50
660	35 c. New Plymouth Hotel (horiz)	50	70
661	50 c. "Island Hope"	65	90

1983. Air. Bicentenary of Manned Flight. Mult.

663	10 c. Type **150**	55	15
664	25 c. Avro Tudor IV	75	30
665	31 c. Avro Lancastrian	85	45
666	35 c. Consolidated Commodore	1·00	50

For these stamps without the Manned Flight logo, see Nos. 699/702.

1983. Christmas. Children's Paintings. Multicoloured.

667	5 c. Type **151**	10	10
668	20 c. "Flamingo" (Cory Bullard)	25	30
669	25 c. "Yellow Hibiscus with Christmas Candle" (Monique Bailey)	35	40
670	31 c. "Santa goes-a-sailing" (Sabrina Seiler) (horiz)	40	45
671	35 c. "Silhouette scene with Palm Trees" (James Blake)	45	50
672	50 c. "Silhouette scene with Pelicans" (Erik Russell) (horiz)	65	70

152 1861 4d. Stamp

153 "Trent I" (paddle-steamer)

1984. 125th Anniv of First Bahamas Postage Stamp. Multicoloured.

673	5 c. Type **152**	25	10
674	$1 1859 1d. stamp	1·75	1·50

1984. 250th Anniv of "Lloyd's List" (newspaper). Multicoloured.

675	5 c. Type **153**	30	10
676	31 c. "Orinoco II" (mail ship), 1886	80	60
677	35 c. Cruise liners in Nassau harbour	90	75
678	50 c. "Oropesa" (container ship)	1·40	1·60

154 Running

155 Bahamas and Caribbean Community Flags

1984. Olympic Games, Los Angeles.

679	**154**	5 c. green, black and gold	15	15
680	–	25 c. blue, black and gold	50	50
681	–	31 c. red, black and gold	55	60
682	–	$1 brown, black and gold	3·75	4·25

DESIGNS: 25 c. Shot-putting; 31 c. Boxing; $1 Basketball.

1984. 5th Conference of Caribbean Community Heads of Government.

684	**155**	50 c. multicoloured	90	95

156 Bahama Woodstar

157 "The Holy Virgin with Jesus and Johannes" (19th-century porcelain plaque after Titian)

1984. 25th Anniv of National Trust. Multicoloured.

685	31 c. Type **156**	2·75	2·75
686	31 c. Belted kingfishers, greater flamingos and "Eleutherodactylus planirostris" (frog)	2·75	2·75
687	31 c. Black-necked stilts, greater flamingos and "Phoebis sennae" (butterfly)	2·75	2·75
688	31 c. "Urbanus proteus" (butterfly) and "Chelonia mydas" (turtle)	2·75	2·75
689	31 c. Osprey and greater flamingos	2·75	2·75

Nos. 685/9 were printed together in horiz strips of 5 forming a composite design.

1984. Wildlife (4th series). Reptiles and Amphibians. As T **136**.

690	5 c. Allens' Cay iguana	30	20
691	25 c. Curly-tailed lizard	85	60
692	35 c. Greenhouse frog	1·00	85
693	50 c. Atlantic green turtle	1·60	2·25

1984. Christmas. Religious Paintings. Multicoloured.

695	5 c. Type **157**	20	10
696	31 c. "Madonna with Child in Tropical Landscape" (aquarelle, Anais Colin)	75	60
697	35 c. "The Holy Virgin with the Child" (miniature on ivory, Elena Caula)	80	65

1985. Air. As Nos. 663/6, but without Manned Flight Logo.

699	10 c. Type **150**	70	30
700	25 c. Avro Tudor IV	85	40
701	31 c. Avro Lancastrian	85	55
702	35 c. Consolidated Commodore	1·25	85

158 Brownie Emblem and Queen or Pink Conch

1985. International Youth Year. 75th Anniv of Girl Guide Movement. Multicoloured.

703	5 c. Type **158**	50	40
704	25 c. Tents and coconut palm	1·25	90
705	31 c. Guide salute and greater flamingos	1·50	90
706	35 c. Ranger emblem and marlin	1·75	1·40

159 Killdeer

1985. Birth Bicent of John J. Audubon (ornithologist). Multicoloured.

708	5 c. Type **159**	1·00	30
709	31 c. Mourning dove (vert)	2·25	55
710	35 c. "Mourning dove" (John J. Audubon) (vert)	2·25	60
711	$1 "Killdeer" (John J. Audubon)	3·50	3·25

160 The Queen Mother at Christening of Peter Phillips, 1977

162 Queen Elizabeth II

161 Ears of Wheat and Emblems

1985. Life and Times of Queen Elizabeth the Queen Mother. Multicoloured.
712 5 c. Visiting Auckland, New Zealand, 1927 . . . . . . 10 10
713 25 c. Type **160** 40 40
714 35 c. The Queen Mother attending church 55 55
715 50 c. With Prince Henry at his christening (from photo by Lord Snowdon) 75 75

1985. 40th Anniv of U.N.O. and F.A.O.
717 **161** 25 c. multicoloured . . . 85 60

1985. Commonwealth Heads of Government Meeting, Nassau. Multicoloured.
718 31 c. Type **162** . . . . . . 2·00 2·25
719 35 c. Bahamas Prime Minister's flag and Commonwealth emblem . . . . 2·00 2·75

163 "Grandma's Christmas Bouquet" (Alton Roland Lowe)

1985. Christmas. Paintings by Alton Roland Lowe. Multicoloured.
736 5 c. Type **163** 25 10
737 25 c. "Junkanoo Romeo and Juliet" (vert) 85 75
738 31 c. "Bunce Gal" (vert) . . . 1·10 1·25
739 35 c. "Home for Christmas" . . 1·40 1·50

1986. 60th Birthday of Queen Elizabeth II. As T **110** of Ascension. Multicoloured.
741 10 c. Princess Elizabeth aged one, 1927 . . . . 15 15
742 25 c. The Coronation, 1953 . . 30 30
743 35 c. Queen making speech at Commonwealth Banquet, Bahamas, 1985 . . . . . . 35 40
744 40 c. In Djakova, Yugoslavia, 1972 . . . . 35 45
745 $1 At Crown Agents Head Office, London, 1983 . . . 80 1·40

164 1980 1 c. and 18 c. Definitive Stamps

1986. "Ameripex '86" International Stamp Exhib., Chicago.
746 **164** 5 c. multicoloured 40 30
747 – 25 c. multicoloured . . . 1·00 50
748 – 31 c. multicoloured . . . 1·25 60
749 – 50 c. multicoloured . . . 1·75 2·75
750 – $1 black, green and blue . 2·00 3·25
DESIGNS—HORIZ: (showing Bahamas stamps)—25 c. 1969 50th Anniv of Bahamas Airmail Service pair; 31 c. 1976 Bicentenary of American Revolution; 16 c., 50 c. 1981 Space Exploration miniature sheet. VERT: $1 Statue of Liberty.
No. 750 also commemorates the Centenary of the Statue of Liberty.

1986. Royal Wedding. As T **112** of Ascension. Mult.
756 10 c. Prince Andrew and Miss Sarah Ferguson 20 20
757 $1 Prince Andrew . . . . . . 1·25 2·10

165 Rock Beauty (juvenile)

1986. Fishes. Multicoloured.
758A 5 c. Type **165** 75 75
759A 10 c. Stoplight parrotfish . . 80 90
760A 15 c. Jackknife-fish . . . . 1·50 1·50
761A 20 c. Flamefish . . . . . . 1·25 1·25
762A 25 c. Peppermint basslet ("Swissguard basslet") . . 1·50 1·50
763A 30 c. Spot-finned butterflyfish 1·10 1·50
764A 35 c. Queen triggerfish . . . 1·10 1·50
765B 40 c. Four-eyed butterflyfish 1·10 1·60
766A 45 c. Royal gramma ("Fairy basslet") . . . . 1·50 1·25
767A 50 c. Queen angelfish . . . 2·00 2·25
797 60 c. Blue chromis . . . . . 2·00 4·00
769B $1 Spanish hogfish . . . . 2·75 3·00
799 $2 Harlequin bass . . . . . 2·75 6·50
771A $3 Black-barred soldierfish . 6·00 7·00
772A $5 Cherub angelfish ("Pygmy angelfish") . . . . 6·50 8·00
773A $10 Red hind . . . . 15·00 20·00

166 Christ Church Cathedral, Nassau, 1861

167 Man and Boy looking at Crib

1986. 125th Anniv of City of Nassau, Diocese and Cathedral. Multicoloured.
774 10 c. Type **166** 20 20
775 40 c. Christ Church Cathedral, 1986 . . . . 65 80

1986. Christmas. International Peace Year. Mult.
777 10 c. Type **167** 35 20
778 40 c. Mary and Joseph journeying to Bethlehem . 85 75
779 45 c. Children praying and Star of Bethlehem . . . . . . 95 1·00
780 50 c. Children exchanging gifts 1·00 2·00

168 Great Isaac Lighthouse

169 Anne Bonney

1987. Lighthouses. Multicoloured.
782 10 c. Type **168** . . . . . . 1·50 60
783 40 c. Bird Rock lighthouse . . 3·50 1·50
784 45 c. Castle Island lighthouse . 3·50 1·50
785 $1 "Hole in the Wall" lighthouse 5·00 8·50

1987. Pirates and Privateers of the Caribbean. Multicoloured.
786 10 c. Type **169** . . . . . . 1·50 75
787 40 c. Edward Teach ("Blackbeard") . . . . . 3·50 2·50
788 45 c. Captain Edward England 3·50 2·50
789 50 c. Captain Woodes Rogers 4·00 3·75

170 Boeing 737

1987. Air. Aircraft. Multicoloured.
800 15 c. Type **170** . . . . . . 1·25 70
801 40 c. Boeing 757-200 . . . . 2·00 1·25
802 45 c. Airbus Industrie A300 B4-200 . . . . 2·00 1·25
803 50 c. Boeing 747-200 . . . . 2·00 2·00

171 "Norway" (liner) and Catamaran

172 "Cattleyopsis lindenii"

1987. Tourist Transport. Multicoloured.
804 40 c. Type **171** . . . . . . 1·50 1·50
805 40 c. Liners and speedboat . . 1·50 1·50
806 40 c. Game fishing boat and cruising yacht . . . . . . 1·50 1·50
807 40 c. Game fishing boat and racing yachts . . . . . . 1·50 1·50
808 40 c. Fishing boat and schooner 1·50 1·50
809 40 c. Hawker Siddeley H.S.748 airliner . . . . 1·50 1·50
810 40 c. Boeing 737 and Boeing 727-200 airliners . . . . 1·50 1·50
811 40 c. Beech 200 Super King Air aircraft and radio beacon . 1·50 1·50
812 40 c. Aircraft and Nassau control tower . . . . 1·50 1·50
813 40 c. Helicopter and parked aircraft . . . . 1·50 1·50
Nos. 804/8 and 809/13 were each printed together, se-tenant, forming composite design.

1987. Christmas. Orchids. Multicoloured.
814 10 c. Type **172** . . . . . . 1·00 30
815 40 c. "Encyclia lucayana" . . 2·25 1·00
816 45 c. "Encyclia hodgeana" . . 2·25 1·00
817 50 c. "Encyclia lleidae" . . . 2·25 2·25

173 King Ferdinand and Queen Isabella of Spain

174 Whistling Ducks in Flight

1988. 500th Anniv (1992) of Discovery of America by Columbus (1st issue). Multicoloured.
819 10 c. Type **173** 75 30
820 40 c. Columbus before Talavera Committee . . . . 1·60 1·60
821 45 c. Lucayan village . . . . 1·75 1·75
822 50 c. Lucayan potters . . . . 1·90 2·25
See also Nos. 844/7, 870/3, 908/11 and 933/6.

1988. Black-billed Whistling Duck. Multicoloured.
824 5 c. Type **174** . . . . . . 1·90 80
825 10 c. Whistling duck in reeds . 1·90 80
826 20 c. Pair with brood . . . . 3·50 1·75
827 45 c. Pair wading . . . . . . 5·50 2·25

175 Grantstown Cabin, c. 1820

177 "Oh Little Town of Bethlehem"

176 Olympic Flame, High Jumping, Hammer throwing, Basketball and Gymnastics

1988. 150th Anniv of Abolition of Slavery. Multicoloured.
828 10 c. Type **175** 50 30
829 40 c. Basket-making Grantstown 1·25 95

1988. Olympic Games, Seoul. Designs taken from painting by James Martin. Multicoloured.
830 10 c. Type **176** 50 20
831 40 c. Athletics, archery, swimming, long jumping, weightlifting and boxing . . 70 60
832 45 c. Javelin throwing, gymnastics, hurdling and shot put 70 60
833 $1 Athletics, hurdling, gymnastics and cycling . . . 2·50 2·75

1988. 300th Anniv of Lloyd's of London. As T **123** of Ascension. Multicoloured.
835 10 c. "Lloyd's List" of 1740 . 30 15
836 40 c. Freeport Harbour (horiz) 1·25 60
837 45 c. Space shuttle over Bahamas (horiz) . . . . 1·25 60
838 $1 "Yarmouth Castle" (freighter) on fire . . . . 2·25 1·90

1988. Christmas. Carols. Multicoloured.
839 10 c. Type **177** 35 20
840 40 c. "Little Donkey" . . . . 1·00 75
841 45 c. "Silent Night" . . . . 1·10 90
842 50 c. "Hark the Herald Angels Sing" . . . . 1·25 1·50

1989. 500th Anniv of (1992) of Discovery of America by Columbus (2nd issue). As T **173**. Multicoloured.
844 10 c. Columbus drawing chart 1·10 40
845 40 c. Types of caravel . . . 2·50 1·25
846 45 c. Early navigational instruments . . . . 2·50 1·25
847 50 c. Arawak artefacts . . . 2·50 2·75

178 Cuban Emerald

179 Teaching Water Safety

1989. Hummingbirds. Multicoloured.
849 10 c. Type **178** . . . . . . 1·50 75
850 40 c. Ruby-throated hummingbird . . . . . . 2·75 2·00
851 45 c. Bahama woodstar . . . . 2·75 2·00
852 50 c. Rufous hummingbird . . 3·00 3·00

1989. 125th Anniv of Int Red Cross. Mult.
853 10 c. Type **179** 75 25
854 $1 Henri Dunant (founder) and Battle of Solferino . . . . 3·00 2·50

1989. 20th Anniv of First Manned Landing on Moon. As T **126** of Ascension. Multicoloured.
855 10 c. "Apollo 8" Communications Station, Grand Bahama 35 30
856 40 c. Crew of "Apollo 8" (30×30 mm) 80 55
857 45 c. "Apollo 8" emblem (30×30 mm) 80 60
858 $1 The Earth seen from "Apollo 8" . . . . 1·50 2·75

180 Church of the Nativity, Bethlehem

1989. Christmas. Churches of the Holy Land. Multicoloured.
860 10 c. Type **180** 40 20
861 40 c. Basilica of the Annunciation, Nazareth . . 1·10 60
862 45 c. Tabgha Church, Galilee 1·10 60
863 $1 Church of the Holy Sepulchre, Jerusalem . . . . 2·25 3·00

181 1974 U.P.U.Centenary 13 c. Stamp and Globe

1989. "World Stamp Expo '89" International Stamp Exhibition, Washington. Multicoloured.
865 10 c. Type **181** 60 30
866 40 c. 1970 New U.P.U. Headquarters Building 3 c. and building . . . . 1·25 75
867 45 c. 1986 "Ameripex '86" $1 and Capitol, Washington . . . 1·25 80
868 $1 1949 75th anniv of U.P.U. 2½d. and Boeing 737 airliner 4·25 5·50

1990. 500th Anniv (1992) of Discovery of America by Columbus (3rd issue). As T **173**. Multicoloured.
870 10 c. Launching caravel . . . 1·25 60
871 40 c. Provisional ship . . . . 2·25 2·00
872 45 c. Shortening sail . . . . 2·25 2·00
873 50 c. Lucayan fisherman . . . 2·25 3·00

182 Bahamas Flag, O.A.S. Headquarters and Centenary Logo

1990. Centenary of Organization of American States.
875 **182** 40 c. multicoloured . . . 1·75 1·75

184 Teacher with Boy

1990. International Literacy Year. Multicoloured.
877 10 c. Type **184** 75 50
878 40 c. Three boys in class . . 1·60 1·25
879 50 c. Teacher and children with books . . . . 1·60 2·25

1990. 90th Birthday of Queen Elizabeth the Queen Mother. As T **134** of Ascension.
880 40 c. multicoloured . . . . . 1·00 50
881 $1.50 black and ochre . . . 2·25 3·00
DESIGNS—21×36 mm: 40 c. "Queen Elizabeth 1938" (Sir Gerald Kelly); 29×37 mm. $1.50, Queen Elizabeth at garden party, France, 1938.

HAVE YOU READ THE NOTES AT THE BEGINNING OF THIS CATALOGUE?
These often provide answers to the enquiries we receive.

185 Cuban Amazon preening

186 The Annunciation

1990. Cuban Amazon (Bahamian Parrot). Mult.

882	10 c. Type **185**	1·00	55
883	40 c. Pair in flight	2·00	1·00
884	45 c. Cuban amazon's head	2·00	1·00
885	50 c. Perched on branch	2·25	2·50

1990. Christmas. Multicoloured.

887	10 c. Type **186**	40	20
888	40 c. The Nativity	90	55
889	45 c. Angel appearing to Shepherds	90	65
890	$1 The Three Kings	2·50	3·50

187 Green Heron

189 The Annunciation

188 Radar Plot of Hurricane Hugo

1991. Birds. Multicoloured.

892	5 c. Type **187**	70	50
893	10 c. Turkey vulture	80	60
976	15 c. Osprey	70	70
895	20 c. Clapper rail	1·00	70
978	25 c. Royal tern	60	70
979	30 c. Key West quail dove	1·00	80
898	40 c. Smooth-billed ani	1·50	55
899	45 c. Burrowing owl	2·25	80
900	50 c. Hairy woodpecker	2·00	70
901	55 c. Mangrove cuckoo	2·00	75
902	60 c. Bahama mockingbird	2·00	1·40
903	70 c. Red-winged blackbird	2·00	1·50
904	$1 Thick-billed vireo	2·50	1·50
905	$2 Bahama yellowthroat	5·00	4·50
988	$5 Stripe-headed tanager	6·50	8·50
907	$10 Greater Antillean bullfinch	13·00	15·00

1991. 500th Anniv (1992) of Discovery of America by Columbus (4th issue). As T **173**. Multicoloured.

908	15 c. Columbus navigating by stars	1·25	65
909	40 c. Fleet in mid-Atlantic	2·00	1·75
910	55 c. Lucayan family worshipping at night	2·00	2·00
911	60 c. Map of First Voyage	2·50	3·50

1991. 65th Birthday of Queen Elizabeth II and 70th Birthday of Prince Philip. As T **139** of Ascension. Multicoloured.

913	15 c. Prince Philip	1·00	1·50
914	$1 Queen Elizabeth II	1·75	2·00

1991. International Decade for Natural Disaster Reduction. Multicoloured.

915	15 c. Type **188**	75	30
916	40 c. Diagram of hurricane	1·25	1·10
917	55 c. Flooding caused by Hurricane David, 1979	1·50	1·75
918	60 c. U.S. Dept of Commerce weather reconnaissance Lockhead WP-3D Orion	2·25	3·00

1991. Christmas. Multicoloured.

919	15 c. Type **189**	40	25
920	55 c. Mary and Joseph travelling to Bethlehem	1·00	1·00
921	60 c. Angel appearing to the shepherds	1·10	1·40
922	$1 Adoration of the kings	2·00	3·25

190 First Progressive Liberal Party Cabinet

1992. 25th Anniv of Majority Rule. Multicoloured.

924	15 c. Type **190**	60	40
925	40 c. Signing of Independence Constitution	1·40	1·10
926	55 c. Prince of Wales handing over Constitutional Instrument (vert)	1·50	1·50
927	60 c. First Bahamian Governor-General, Sir Milo Butler (vert)	1·75	2·75

1992. 40th Anniv of Queen Elizabeth II's Accession. As T **143** of Ascension. Multicoloured.

928	15 c. Queen Elizabeth with bouquet	50	30
929	40 c. Queen Elizabeth with flags	1·00	70
930	55 c. Queen Elizabeth at display	1·00	90
931	60 c. Three portraits of Queen Elizabeth	1·10	1·25
932	$1 Queen Elizabeth II	1·50	2·25

1992. 500th Anniv of Discovery of America by Columbus (5th issue). As T **173**. Multicoloured.

933	15 c. Lucayans sighting fleet	1·00	60
934	40 c. "Santa Maria" and dolphins	1·75	1·50
935	55 c. Lucayan canoes approaching ships	1·75	1·75
936	60 c. Columbus giving thanks for landfall	2·25	3·00

191 Templeton, Galbraith and Hansberger Ltd Building

1992. 20th Anniv of Templeton Prize for Religion.

938	**191** 55 c. multicoloured	1·50	1·50

192 Pole Vaulting

194 Mary visiting Elizabeth

193 Arid Landscape and Starving Child

1992. Olympic Games, Barcelona. Mutlicoloured.

939	15 c. Type **192**	50	35
940	40 c. Javelin	90	90
941	55 c. Hurdling	1·10	1·25
942	60 c. Basketball	3·50	3·75

1992 International Conference on Nutrition, Rome. Multicoloured.

944	15 c. Type **193**	75	50
945	55 c. Seedling, cornfield and child	1·75	2·00

1992. Christmas. Multicoloured.

947	15 c. Type **194**	40	20
948	55 c. The Nativity	1·10	1·00
949	60 c. Angel and shepherds	1·25	1·50
950	70 c. Wise Men and star	1·40	2·50

196 Flags of Bahamas and U.S.A. with Agricultural Worker

1993. 50th Anniv of The Contract (U.S.A.–Bahamas farm labour programme). Each including national flags. Multicoloured.

953	15 c. Type **196**	75	60
954	55 c. Onions	1·75	1·50
955	60 c. Citrus fruit	1·75	2·00
956	70 c. Apples	2·00	2·25

1993. 75th Anniv of Royal Air Force. As T **149** of Ascension. Multicoloured.

957	15 c. Westland Wapiti IIA	80	65
958	40 c. Gloster Gladiator I	1·50	1·00
959	55 c. De Havilland Vampire F.3	1·75	1·50
960	70 c. English Electric Lightning F.3	2·00	2·75

197 1978 Coronation Anniversary Stamps

198 "Lignum vitae" (national tree)

1993. 40th Anniv of Coronation. Mult.

962	15 c. Type **197**	70	50
963	55 c. Two examples of 1953 Coronation stamp	1·75	1·75
964	60 c. 1977 Silver Jubilee 8 c. and 16 c. stamps	1·75	2·00
965	70 c. 1977 Silver Jubilee 21 c. and 40 c. stamps	2·00	2·75

1993. 20th Anniv of Independence. Mult.

966	15 c. Type **198**	20	20
967	55 c. Yellow elder (national flower)	90	90
968	60 c. Blue marlin (national fish)	1·00	1·25
969	70 c. Greater flamingo (national bird)	1·40	1·90

199 Cordia

200 The Annunciation

1993. Environment Protection (1st issue). Wild-flowers. Multicoloured.

970	15 c. Type **199**	50	40
971	55 c. Seaside morning glory	1·50	1·25
972	60 c. Poinciana	1·75	1·75
973	70 c. Spider lily	1·75	2·50

See also Nos. 1017/21, 1035/8, 1084/7, 1121/4 and 1149/53.

1993. Christmas. Multicoloured.

990	15 c. Type **200**	55	30
991	55 c. Angel and shepherds	1·75	1·75
992	60 c. Holy Family	1·75	2·00
993	70 c. Three Kings	2·00	2·50

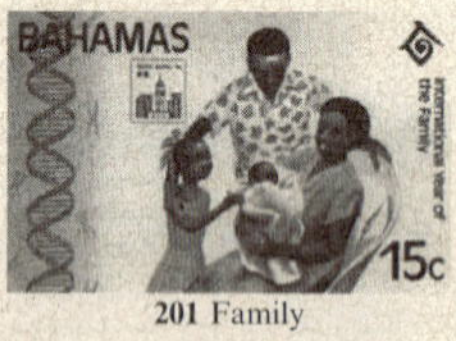

201 Family

1994. "Hong Kong '94" International Stamp Exhibition. International Year of the Family. Multicoloured.

995	15 c. Type **201**	50	30
996	55 c. Children doing homework	1·25	1·25
997	60 c. Grandfather and grandson fishing	1·40	1·40
998	70 c. Grandmother teaching grandchildren the Lord's Prayer	2·00	2·50

202 Flags of Bahamas and Great Britain

1994. Royal Visit. Multicoloured.

999	15 c. Type **202**	55	40
1000	55 c. Royal Yacht "Britannia"	1·75	1·25
1001	60 c. Queen Elizabeth II	1·75	1·75
1002	70 c. Queen Elizabeth and Prince Philip	1·75	2·50

203 Yachts

1994. 40th Anniv of National Family Island Regatta. Multicoloured.

1003	15 c. Type **203**	60	40
1004	55 c. Dinghy racing	1·40	1·10
1005	60 c. Working boats	1·50	1·75
1006	70 c. Sailing sloop	2·00	3·00

204 Logo and Bahamas 1968 Olympic Games Stamp

1994. Centenary of International Olympic Committee. Multicoloured.

1008	15 c. Type **204**	80	40
1009	55 c. 1976 Olympic Games stamps (vert)	1·75	1·25
1010	60 c. 1984 Olympic Games stamps	1·75	2·00
1011	70 c. 1992 Olympic Games stamps (vert)	2·25	2·75

206 "Calpodes ethlius" and Canna

207 Spot-finned Hogfish and Spanish Hogfish

1994. Butterflies and Flowers. Multicoloured.

1013	15 c. Type **206**	1·10	55
1014	55 c. "Phoebis sennae" and cassia	2·00	1·50
1015	60 c. "Anartia jatrophae" and passion flower	2·25	2·25
1016	70 c. "Battus devilliersi" and calico flower	2·25	2·75

1994. Environment Protection (2nd issue). Marine Life. Multicoloured.

1017	40 c. Type **207**	90	1·10
1018	40 c. Tomate and long-spined squirrelfish	90	1·10
1019	40 c. French angelfish	90	1·10
1020	40 c. Queen angelfish	90	1·10
1021	40 c. Rock beauty	90	1·10

Nos. 1017/21 were printed together, se-tenant, with the backgrounds forming a composite design.

208 Angel

1994. Christmas. Multicoloured.

1023	15 c. Type **208**	30	30
1024	55 c. Holy Family	90	1·10
1025	60 c. Shepherds	1·10	1·40
1026	70 c. Wise Men	1·25	2·00

209 Lion and Emblem

210 Kirtland's Warbler on Nest

1995. 20th Anniv of the College of the Bahamas. Multicoloured.

1028	15 c. Type **209**	30	30
1029	70 c. Queen Elizabeth II and College building	1·25	1·75

1995. 50th Anniv of End of Second World War. As T **161** of Ascension. Multicoloured..

1030	15 c. Bahamian infantry drilling	60	40
1031	55 c. Consolidated PBY-5A Catalina flying boat	1·75	1·25
1032	60 c. Bahamian women in naval operations room	1·75	1·75
1033	70 c. Consolidated B-24 Liberator bomber	2·00	2·50

1995. Environment Protection (3rd issue). Endangered Species. Kirtland's Warbler. Multicoloured.

1035	15 c. Type **210**	55	60
1036	15 c. Singing on branch	55	60
1037	25 c. Feeding chicks	55	60
1038	25 c. Catching insects	55	60

211 Eleuthera Cliffs

1995. Tourism. Multicoloured.

1040	15 c. Type **211**	55	40
1041	55 c. Clarence Town, Long Island	1·40	1·25
1042	60 c. Albert Lowe Museum	1·50	1·75
1043	70 c. Yachts	1·75	2·00

212 Pigs and Chick

1995. 50th Anniv of F.A.O. Multicoloured.

1044	15 c. Type **212**	50	35
1045	55 c. Seedling and hand holding seed	1·25	1·10
1046	60 c. Family with fruit and vegetables	1·40	1·60
1047	70 c. Fishes and crustaceans	1·75	2·00

213 Sikorsky S-55 Helicopter, Sinai, 1957

1995. 50th Anniv of United Nations. Multicoloured.

1048	15 c. Type **213**	50	40
1049	55 c. Ferret armoured car, Sinai, 1957	1·25	1·25
1050	60 c. Fokker F.27 Friendship (airliner), Cambodia, 1991–93	1·25	1·50
1051	70 c. Lockheed C-130 Hercules (transport)	1·50	2·00

214 St. Agnes Anglican Church

1995. Christmas. Churches. Multicoloured.

1052	15 c. Type **214**	30	25
1053	55 c. Church of God, East Street	90	90
1054	60 c. Sacred Heart Roman Catholic Church	95	1·25
1055	70 c. Salem Union Baptist Church	1·10	1·75

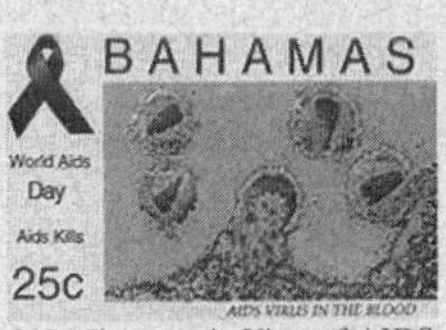

215 Microscopic View of AIDS Virus

1995. World AIDS Day. Multicoloured.

1056	25 c. Type **215**	60	50
1057	70 c. Research into AIDS	1·00	1·50

216 Sunrise Tellin

1996. Sea Shells. Multicoloured.

1098	5 c. Type **216**	10	10
1099	10 c. Queen conch	10	15
1100	15 c. Angular triton	20	25
1101	20 c. True tulip	25	30
1102	25 c. Reticulated cowrie-helmet	30	35
1103	30 c. Sand dollar	35	40
1104	40 c. Lace short-frond murex	50	55
1105	45 c. Inflated sea biscuit	55	60
1106	50 c. West Indian top shell	60	65
1107	55 c. Spiny oyster	65	70
1108	60 c. King helmet	70	75
1109	70 c. Lion's paw	85	90
1110	$1 Crown cone	1·25	1·40
1111	$2 Atlantic partridge tun	2·40	2·50
1112	$5 Wide-mouthed purpura	6·00	6·25
1113	$10 Atlantic trumpet triton	12·00	12·50

217 East Goodwin Lightship with Marconi Apparatus on Mast

1996. Centenary of Radio. Multicoloured.

1074	15 c. Type **217**	60	45
1075	55 c. Newspaper headline concerning Dr. Crippen	1·40	1·25
1076	60 c. "Philadelphia" (liner) and first readable transatlantic message	1·50	1·75
1077	70 c. Guglielmo Marconi and "Elettra" (yacht)	1·75	2·00

218 Swimming

219 Green Anole

1996. Centenary of Modern Olympic Games. Multicoloured.

1079	15 c. Type **218**	40	25
1080	55 c. Running	90	90
1081	60 c. Basketball	1·40	1·60
1082	70 c. Long jumping	1·40	2·00

1996. Environment Protection (4th issue). Reptiles. Multicoloured.

1084	15 c. Type **219**	55	40
1085	55 c. Little Bahama bank boa	1·10	1·00
1086	60 c. Inagua freshwater turtle	1·50	1·75
1087	70 c. Acklins rock iguana	1·75	2·25

220 The Annunciation

221 Department of Archives Building

1996. Christmas. Multicoloured.

1089	15 c. Type **220**	40	25
1090	55 c. Joseph and Mary travelling to Bethlehem	1·00	85
1091	60 c. Shepherds and angel	1·25	1·50
1092	70 c. Adoration of the Magi	1·40	2·00

1996. 25th Anniv of Archives Department.

1094	**221** 55 c. multicoloured	1·00	1·00

1997. Golden Wedding of Queen Elizabeth and Prince Philip. As T **173** of Ascension. Multicoloured.

1114	50 c. Queen Elizabeth II in Bonn, 1992	1·00	1·10
1115	50 c. Prince Philip and Prince Charles at Trooping the Colour	1·00	1·10
1116	60 c. Prince Philip	1·10	1·25
1117	60 c. Queen at Trooping the Colour	1·10	1·25
1118	70 c. Queen Elizabeth and Prince Philip at polo, 1970	1·40	1·50
1119	70 c. Prince Charles playing polo	1·40	1·50

222 Underwater Scene

1997. Environment Protection (5th issue). International Year of the Reefs.

1121	**222** 15 c. multicoloured	45	30
1122	– 55 c. multicoloured	1·10	1·00
1123	– 60 c. multicoloured	1·25	1·40
1124	– 70 c. multicoloured	1·50	1·75

DESIGNS: 55 c. to 70 c. Different children's paintings of underwater scenes.

223 Angel

1997. Christmas. Multicoloured.

1125	15 c. Type **223**	30	25
1126	55 c. Mary and Baby Jesus	80	70
1127	60 c. Shepherd	90	90
1128	70 c. King	1·10	1·25

1998. Diana, Princess of Wales Commemoration. As T **91** of Kiribati Multicoloured.

1130	15 c. Wearing grey jacket, 1988	40	40

1998. 80th Anniv of the Royal Air Force. As T **178** of Ascension. Multicoloured.

1132	15 c. Handley Page Hyderabad	40	30
1133	55 c. Hawker Demon	85	80
1134	60 c. Gloster Meteor F.8	95	95
1135	70 c. Lockheed Neptune MR.1	1·25	1·40

224 Newsletters

1998. 50th Anniv of Organisation of American States. Multicoloured.

1137	15 c. Type **224**	30	30
1138	55 c. Headquarters building and flags, Washington	70	80

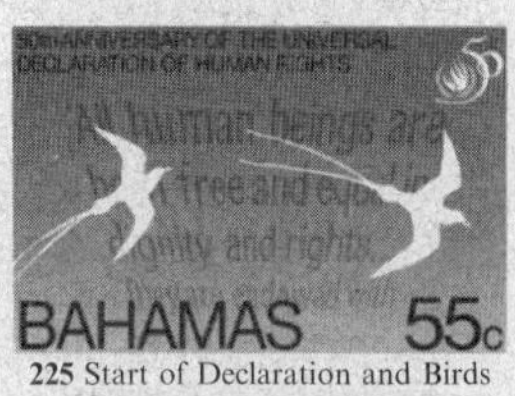

225 Start of Declaration and Birds

1998. 50th Anniv of Universal Declaration of Human Rights.

1139	**225** 55 c. blue and black	80	80

226 University Arms and Graduates

1998. 50th Anniv of University of the West Indies.

1140	**226** 55 c. multicoloured	80	80

227 Supreme Court Building

1998. 25th Anniv of Independence. Multicoloured.

1141	15 c. Type **227**	30	25
1142	55 c. Nassau Library	75	75
1143	60 c. Government House	80	85
1144	70 c. Gregory Arch	90	1·00

228 Cruise Liner at Night

1998. Disney Cruise Line's Castaway Cay Holiday Development. Multicoloured.

1146	55 c. Type **228**	75	80
1147	55 c. Cruise liner by day	75	80

229 "Ryndam" (cruise liner)

1998. Holland America Line's Half Moon Cay Holiday Development.

1148	**229** 55 c. multicoloured	80	80

230 Barrel Pink Rose

1998. Environment Protection (6th issue). Roses. Multicoloured.

1149	55 c. Type **230**	65	70
1150	55 c. Yellow cream	65	70
1151	55 c. Seven sisters	65	70
1152	55 c. Big red	65	70
1153	55 c. Island beauty	65	70

231 The Annunciation

1998. Christmas. Multicoloured.

1155	15 c. Type **231**	20	25
1156	55 c. Shepherds	65	70
1157	60 c. Three Kings	70	75
1158	70 c. The Flight into Egypt	85	90

232 Killer Whale and other Marine Life

1998. International Year of the Ocean. Multicoloured.

1160	15 c. Type **232**	30	30
1161	55 c. Tropical fish	70	80

233 Timothy Gibson (composer)

1998. 25th Anniv of "March on Bahamaland" (national anthem).

1162	**233** 60 c. multicoloured	70	75

234 Head of Greater Flamingo and Chick

1999. 40th Anniv of National Trust (1st issue). Inagua National Park. Multicoloured.

1163	55 c. Type **234**	65	70
1164	55 c. Pair with two chicks	65	70
1165	55 c. Greater flamingos asleep or stretching wings	65	70
1166	55 c. Greater flamingos feeding	65	70
1167	55 c. Greater flamingos in flight	65	70

Nos. 1163/7 were printed together, se-tenant, with the backgrounds forming a composite design.

See also Nos. 1173/9.

235 Arawak Indian Canoe

236 Dolphin

1999. "Australia '99" World Stamp Exhibition, Melbourne. Maritime History. Multicoloured.

1168	15 c. Type **235**	20	25
1169	55 c. "Santa Maria" (Columbus), 1492	65	70
1170	60 c. "Queen Anne's Revenge" (Blackbeard), 1716	70	75
1171	70 c. "The Banshee" (Confederate paddle-steamer) running blockade	85	90

1999. 40th Anniv of National Trust (2nd issue). Exuma Cays Land and Sea Park. Multicoloured.

1173	55 c. Type **236**	65	70
1174	55 c. Angelfish and parrotfish	65	70
1175	55 c. Queen triggerfish	65	70
1176	55 c. Turtle	65	70
1177	55 c. Lobster	65	70

Nos. 1173/7 were printed together, se-tenant, with the backgrounds forming a composite design.

SPECIAL DELIVERY STAMPS

1916. Optd **SPECIAL DELIVERY.**

S2	**6** 5d. black and orange	45	4·75
S3	5d. black and mauve	30	1·75

BAHAWALPUR

A former state of Pakistan.

12 pies = 1 anna, 16 annas = 1 rupee

(1)

2 Amir Muhammad Bahawal Khan I Abbasi

1947. Nos. 265/8, 269a/77 and 259/62 of India optd with Type **1**.

No.	Type	Description	Unused	Used
1	100a	3 p. slate	13·00	
2		½ a. purple	13·00	
3		9 p. green	13·00	
4		1 a. red	13·00	
5	101	1½ a. violet	13·00	
6		2 a. red	13·00	
7		3 a. violet	13·00	
8		3½ a. blue	13·00	
9	102	4 a. brown	13·00	
10		6 a. green	13·00	
11		8 a. violet	13·00	
12		12 a. lake	13·00	
13	–	14 a. purple	48·00	
14	93	1 r. grey and brown	19·00	
15		2 r. purple and brown	£850	
16		5 r. green and blue	£850	
17		10 r. purple and red	£850	

1948. Bicentenary Commemoration.

No.	Type	Description	Unused	Used
18	2	½ a. black and red	1·00	1·25

4 H. H. the Amir of Bahawalpur

5 The Tombs of the Amirs

1948.

No.	Type	Description	Unused	Used
19	4	3 p. black and blue	65	15·00
20		½ a. black and red	65	15·00
21		9 p. black and green	65	15·00
22		1 a. black and red	65	15·00
23		1½ a. black and violet	65	12·00
24	5	2 a. green and red	90	60·00
25	–	4 a. orange and brown	1·00	16·00
26	–	6 a. violet and blue	1·00	16·00
27	–	8 a. red and violet	1·00	16·00
28	–	12 a. green and red	1·25	22·00
29	–	1 r. violet and brown	16·00	32·00
35	–	1 r. green and orange	60	15·00
30	–	2 r. green and red	32·00	50·00
36	–	2 r. black and red	70	18·00
31	–	5 r. black and violet	32·00	65·00
37	–	5 r brown and blue	80	32·00
32	–	10 r. red and black	32·00	80·00
38	–	10 r. brown and green	90	38·00

DESIGNS—HORIZ: 6 a. Fort Derawar from the lake; 8 a. Nur-Mahal Palace; 12 a. Sadiq-Garh Palace. 46 × 32 mm: 10 r. Three generations of Rulers. VERT (As Type **5**): 4 a. Mosque in Sadiq-Garh; 1, 2, 5 r. H.H. the Amir of Bahawalpur.

12 H.H. the Amir of Bahawalpur and Mohammed Ali Jinnah

1948. 1st Anniv of Union with Pakistan.

No.	Type	Description	Unused	Used
33	12	1½ a. red and green	60	1·25

13 Soldiers of 1848 and 1948

14 Irrigation

1948. Centenary of Multan Campaign.

No.	Type	Description	Unused	Used
34	13	1½ a. black and red	70	7·50

1949. Silver Jubilee of Accesion of H.H. the Amir of Bahawalpur.

No.	Type	Description	Unused	Used
39	14	3 p. black and blue	10	8·00
40	–	½ a. black and orange	10	8·00
41	–	9 p. black and green	10	8·00
42	–	1 a. black and red	10	8·00

DESIGNS: ½ a. Wheat; 9 p. Cotton; 1 a. Sahiwal bull.

17 U.P.U. Monument, Berne

1949. 75th Anniv of U.P.U.

No.	Type	Description	Unused	Used
43	17	9 p. black and green	20	2·00
44		1 a. black and mauve	20	2·00
45		1½ a. black and orange	20	2·00
46		2½ a. black and blue	20	2·00

OFFICIAL STAMPS

O 4 Eastern White Pelicans

1945. As Type **O 4** with Arabic opt.

No.	Type	Description	Unused	Used
O1	–	½ a. black and green	2·75	9·50
O2	–	1 a. black and red	3·75	6·00
O7	–	1 a. black and brown	27·00	48·00
O3	–	2 a. black and violet	3·25	9·00
O4	O 4	4 a. black and olive	7·50	20·00
O5	–	8 a. black and brown	18·00	11·00
O6	–	1 r. black and orange	18·00	11·00

DESIGNS: ½ a. Panjnad Weir; 1 a. (No. O2), Camel and calf; 1 a. (No. O7), Baggage camels; 2 a. Blackbuck antelopes; 8 a. Friday Mosque, Fort Derawar; 1 r. Temple at Pattan Munara.

(O 8)

1945. Types as Nos. O1, etc., in new colours and without Arabic opt (a) Surch as Type **O 8**.

No.	Type	Description	Unused	Used
O11		½ a. on 8 a. black and purple (as No. O5)	4·25	3·50
O12		1½ a. on 5 r. black and orange (as No. O6)	30·00	9·00
O13		1½ a. on 2 r. black and blue (as No. O1)	£110	10·00

(b) Optd **SERVICE** and Arabic inscription.

No.	Type	Description	Unused	Used
O14		½ a. black and red (as No. O1)	1·25	10·00
O15		1 a. black and red (as No. O2)	2·00	13·00
O16		2 a. black and orange (as No. O3)	3·25	38·00

1945. As Type **4** but inscr "SERVICE" at left.

No.	Type	Description	Unused	Used
O17		3 p. black and blue	2·50	7·00
O18		1½ a. black and violet	13·00	7·00

O 11 Allied Banners

1946. Victory.

No.	Type	Description	Unused	Used
O19	O 11	1½ a. green and grey	2·00	3·00

1948. Stamps of 1948 with Arabic opt as in Type **O 4**.

No.	Type	Description	Unused	Used
O20	4	3 p. black and blue	60	10·00
O21		1 a. black and red	60	9·00
O22	5	2 a. green and red	60	10·00
O23	–	4 a. orange and brown	60	14·00
O24	–	1 r. green and orange	60	16·00
O25	–	2 r. black and red	60	18·00
O26	–	5 r. chocolate and blue	60	35·00
O27	–	10 r. brown and green	60	35·00

1949. 75th Anniv of U.P.U. optd as in Type **O 4**.

No.	Type	Description	Unused	Used
O28	17	9 p. black and green	15	4·50
O29		1 a. black and mauve	15	4·50
O30		1½ a. black and orange	15	4·50
O31		2½ a. black and blue	15	4·50

BAHRAIN

An archipelago in the Persian Gulf on the Arabian coast. An independent shaikhdom with Indian and later British postal administration. The latter was closed on 1 January 1966, when the Bahrain Post Office took over.

1933. 12 pies = 1 anna; 16 annas = 1 rupee.
1957. 100 naya paise = 1 rupee.

Stamps of India optd **BAHRAIN**.

1933. King George V.

No.	Type	Description	Unused	Used
1	55	3 p. grey	3·00	45
2	56	½ a. green	7·50	3·25
15	79	½ a. green	4·50	55
3	80	9 p. green	3·75	90
4	57	1 a. brown	7·00	2·50
16	81	1 a. brown	9·00	40
5	82	1 a. 3 p. mauve	4·00	70
6	70	2 a. orange	10·00	7·50
17	59	2 a. orange	38·00	7·50
7	62	3 a. blue	19·00	40·00
18		3 a. red	4·75	40
8	83	3 a. 6 p. blue	3·75	30
9	71	4 a. green	18·00	40·00
19	63	4 a. olive	3·50	40
10	65	8 a. mauve	6·00	30
11	66	12 a. red	7·50	1·00
12	67	1 r. brown and green	16·00	7·50
13		2 r. red and orange	32·00	38·00
14		5 r. blue and violet	90·00	£120

1938. King George VI.

No.	Type	Description	Unused	Used
20	91	3 p. slate	7·50	3·25
21		½ a. brown	3·75	10
22		9 p. green	3·00	3·00
23		1 a. red	2·50	10
24	92	2 a. red	6·50	1·50
26	–	3 a. green (No. 253)	10·00	5·00
27	–	3 a. 6 p. blue (No. 254)	4·25	3·00
28	–	4 a. brown (No. 255)	£120	60·00
30	–	8 a. violet (No. 257)	£140	35·00
31	–	12 a. red (No. 258)	£100	45·00
32	93	1 r. slate and brown	2·75	1·75
33		2 r. purple and brown	13·00	2·75
34		5 r. green and blue	15·00	13·00
35		10 r. purple and red	65·00	28·00
36		15 r. brown and green	45·00	45·00
37		25 r. slate and purple	95·00	80·00

1942. King George VI.

No.	Type	Description	Unused	Used
38	100a	3 p. slate	1·50	60
39		½ a. mauve	4·00	90
40		9 p. green	12·00	12·00
41		1 a. red	3·50	50
42	101	1 a. 3 p. bistre	8·00	13·00
43		1½ a. violet	4·75	4·25
44		2 a. red	4·00	1·50
45		3 a. violet	14·00	4·00
46		3½ a. blue	3·50	13·00
47	102	4 a. brown	2·00	1·50
48		6 a. green	9·50	9·00
49		8 a. violet	3·25	2·50
50		12 a. purple	5·00	4·00

Stamps of Great Britain surch **BAHRAIN** and new value in Indian currency.

1948. King George VI.

No.	Type	Description	Unused	Used
51	128	½ a. on ½d. green	40	85
71		½ a. on ½d. orange	80	90
52		1 a. on 1d. red	40	1·25
72		1 a. on 1d. blue	1·75	10
53		1½ a. on 1½d. brown	40	1·25
73		1½ a. on 1½d. green	1·75	9·00
54		2 a. on 2d. orange	40	20
74		2 a. on 2d. brown	80	30
55		2½ a. on 2½d. blue	50	2·25
75		2½ a. on 2½d. red	1·75	9·00
56		3 a. on 3d. violet	40	10
76	129	4 a. on 4d. blue	1·75	1·50
57		6 a. on 6d. purple	40	10
58	130	1 r. on 1s. brown	1·25	10
59	131	2 r. on 2s. 6d. green	5·00	4·50
60		5 r. on 5s. red	5·50	4·50
60a	–	10 r. on 10s. blue (No. 478a)	60·00	50·00

1948. Silver Wedding.

No.	Type	Description	Unused	Used
61	137	2½ a. on 2½d. blue	75	30
62	138	15 r. on £1 blue	40·00	48·00

1948. Olympic Games.

No.	Type	Description	Unused	Used
63	139	2½ a. on 2½d. blue	55	1·25
64	140	3 a. on 3d. violet	55	2·00
65	–	6 a. on 6d. purple	1·50	2·50
66	–	1 r. on 1s. brown	1·50	2·50

1949. U.P.U.

No.	Type	Description	Unused	Used
67	143	2½ a. on 2½d. blue	55	2·00
68	144	3 a. on 3d. violet	85	2·75
69	–	6 a. on 6d. purple	75	3·00
70	–	1 r. on 1s. brown	1·60	1·75

1951. Pictorial stamps (Nos. 509/11).

No.	Type	Description	Unused	Used
77	147	2 r. on 2s. 6d. green	21·00	5·50
78	–	5 r. on 5s. red	13·00	3·75
79	–	10 r. on 10s. blue	26·00	7·00

1952. Queen Elizabeth II.

No.	Type	Description	Unused	Used
97	154	½ a. on ½d. orange	10	15
81		1 a. on 1d. blue	10	10
82		1½ a. on 1½d. green	10	10
83		2 a. on 2d. brown	20	10
84	155	2½ a. on 2½d. red	20	1·25
85		3 a. on 3d. lilac	1·00	10
86		4 a. on 4d. blue	8·00	20
99	157	6 a. on 6d. purple	50	50
88	160	12 a. on 1s. 3d. green	3·00	20
89		1 r. on 1s. 6d. blue	3·25	10

1953. Coronation.

No.	Type	Description	Unused	Used
90	161	2½ a. on 2½d. red	1·25	75
91	–	4 a. on 4 d. blue	2·25	3·25
92	163	12 a. on 1s. 3d. green	3·25	3·25
93	–	1 r. on 1s. 6d. blue	7·50	50

1955. Pictorial stamps (Nos. 595a/598a).

No.	Type	Description	Unused	Used
94	166	2 r. on 2s. 6d. brown	5·50	1·60
95	–	5 r. on 5s. red	11·00	2·75
96	–	10 r. on 10s. blue	20·00	2·75

1957. Queen Elizabeth II.

No.	Type	Description	Unused	Used
102	157	1 n.p. on 5d. brown	10	10
103	154	3 n.p. on ½d. orange	30	1·50
104		6 n.p. on 1d. blue	30	1·50
105		9 n.p. on 1½d. green	30	1·50
106		12 n.p. on 2d. pale brown	30	60
107	155	15 n.p. on 2½d. red	30	15
108		20 n.p. on 3d. lilac	30	10
109		25 n.p. on 4d. blue	75	1·75
110	157	40 n.p. on 6d. purple	40	10
111		50 n.p. on 9d. olive	3·75	4·50
112		75 n.p. on 1s. 3d. green	2·25	50

1957. World Scout Jubilee Jamboree.

No.	Type	Description	Unused	Used
113	170	15 n.p. on 2½d. red	25	35
114	171	25 n.p. on 4d. blue	30	35
115	–	75 n.p. on 1s. 3d. green	40	45

16 Shaikh Sulman bin Hamed al-Khalifa

1960.

No.	Type	Description	Unused	Used
117	16	5 n.p. blue	10	10
118		15 n.p. orange	10	10
119		20 n.p. violet	10	10
120		30 n.p. bistre	10	10
121		40 n.p. grey	15	10
122		50 n.p. green	15	10
123		75 n.p. brown	30	15
124	–	1 r. black	1·50	30
125	–	2 r. red	2·75	1·50
126	–	5 r. blue	4·50	2·25
127	–	10 r. green	12·00	3·75

The rupee values are larger 27 × 32½ mm.

18 Shaikh Isa bin Sulman al-Khalifa

19 Air Terminal, Muharraq

1964.

No.	Type	Description	Unused	Used
128	18	5 n.p. blue	10	10
129		15 n.p. orange	10	10
130		20 n.p. violet	10	10
131		30 n.p. bistre	10	10
132		40 n.p. slate	15	10
133		50 n.p. green	15	10
134		75 n.p. brown	25	10
135	19	1 r. black	5·50	1·25
136		2 r. red	8·50	1·25
137	–	5 r. blue	9·50	8·50
138	–	10 r. myrtle	13·00	8·50

DESIGNS: As Type **19**. 5 r., 10 r. Deep water harbour.

For later issues see Volume 1.

BAMRA

A state in India. Now uses Indian stamps.

12 pies = 1 anna; 16 annas = 1 rupee

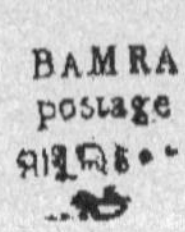

1

8

1888.

No.	Type	Description	Unused	Used
1	1	¼ a. black on yellow	£200	
2		½ a. black on red	70·00	
3		1 a. black on blue	42·00	
4		2 a. black on green	65·00	£200
5		4 a. black on yellow	48·00	£190
6		8 a. black on red	38·00	

1890. Imperf.

No.	Type	Description	Unused	Used
27	8	¼ a. black on red	1·25	1·60
11		½ a. black on green	1·60	1·90
13		1 a. black on yellow	2·25	1·75
16		2 a. black on red	2·75	3·25
19		4 a. black on red	6·00	3·75
22		8 a. black on red	9·00	12·00
25		1 r. black on red	15·00	18·00

BANGLADESH

Formerly the Eastern wing of Pakistan. Following a landslide victory at the Pakistan General Election in December 1970 by the Awami League party the National Assembly was suspended. Unrest spread throughout the eastern province culminating in the intervention of India on the side of the East Bengalis. The new state became effective after the surrender of the Pakistan army in December 1971.

1971. 100 paisa = 1 rupee.
1972. 100 paisa = 1 taka.

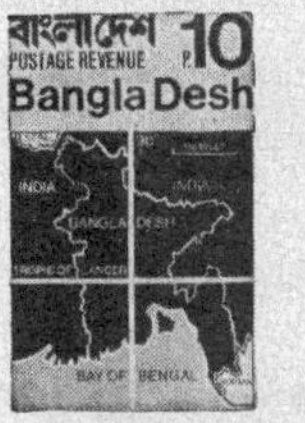

1 Map of Bangladesh

3 "Martyrdom"

1971.

1	1	10 p. indigo, orange and blue	10	10
2	–	20 p. multicoloured	10	10
3	–	50 p. multicoloured	10	10
4	–	1 r. multicoloured	10	10
5	–	2 r. turquoise, blue and red	25	35
6	–	3 r. light green, green and blue	30	55
7	–	5 r. multicoloured	50	90
8	–	10 r. gold, red and blue	1·00	1·75

DESIGNS: 20 p. "Dacca University Massacre"; 50 p. "75 Million People"; 1 r. Flag of Independence; 2 r. Ballot box; 3 r. Broken chain; 5 r. Shaikh Majibur Rahman; 10 r. "Support Bangla Desh" and map.

1971. Liberation. Nos. 1 and 7/8 optd BANGLADESH LIBERATED.

9		10 p. indigo, orange and blue	10	10
10		5 r. multicoloured	1·50	1·75
11		10 r. gold, red and blue	2·00	2·50

The remaining values of the original issue were also overprinted and placed on sale in Great Britian but were not issued in Bangladesh.

On the 1 February 1972 the Agency placed on sale a further issue in the flag, map and Sheikh Mujib designs in new colours and new currency (100 paisa = 1 taka). This issue proved to be unacceptable to the Bangladesh authorities who declared them to be invalid for postal purposes, no supplies being sold within Bangladesh. The values comprise 1, 2, 3, 5, 7, 10, 15, 20, 25, 40, 50, 75 p., 1, 2 and 5 t.

1972. In Memory of the Martyrs.

12	3	20p. green and red	30	50

4 Flames of Independence

5 Doves of Peace

1972. 1st Anniv of Independence.

13	4	20p. lake and red	20	10
14		60p. blue and red	25	45
15		75p. violet and red	30	55

1972. Victory Day.

16	5	20 p. multicoloured	15	10
17		60 p. multicoloured	20	55
18		75 p. multicoloured	20	55

6 "Homage to Martyrs"

7 Embroidered Quilt

8 Court of Justice

9 Flame Emblem

1973. In Memory of the Martyrs.

19	6	20 p. multicoloured	15	10
20		60 p. multicoloured	30	40
21		1 t. 35 multicoloured	65	1·75

1973.

22	7	2 p. black	10	40
23	–	3 p. green	20	30
24	–	5 p. brown	20	10
25	–	10 p. black	20	10
26	–	20 p. green	50	10
27	–	25 p. mauve	2·75	10
28	–	50 p. purple	1·50	30
29	–	60 p. grey	75	50
30	–	75 p. orange	80	50
31	–	90 p. brown	90	70
32	8	1 t. violet	4·00	30
33	–	2 t. green	4·00	55
34	–	5 t. blue	5·50	1·50
35	–	10 t. pink	5·50	3·25

DESIGNS—As Type 7: 3 p. Jute field; 5 p. Jack fruit; 10 p. Bullocks ploughing; 20 p. Rakta jaba (flower); 25 p. Tiger; 60 p. Bamboo grove; 75 p. Plucking tea; 90 p. Handicrafts. (28 × 22 mm): 50 p. Hilsa (fish). As Type 8. VERT: 2 t. Date tree. HORIZ: 5 t. Fishing boat; 10 t. Sixty-dome mosque, Bagerhat.

See also Nos. 49/51a and 64 etc.

1973. 25th Anniv of Declaration of Human Rights.

36	9	10 p. multicoloured	10	10
37		1 t. 25 multicoloured	20	20

10 Family, Map and Graph

11 Copernicus and Heliocentric System

1974. First Population Census.

38	10	20 p. multicoloured	10	10
39		25 p. multicoloured	10	10
40		75 p. multicoloured	20	20

1974. 500th Birth Anniv of Copernicus.

41	11	25 p. orange, violet and black	10	10
42		75 p. orange, green and black	25	50

12 U.N. H.Q. and Bangladesh Flag

13 U.P.U. Emblem

1974. Bangladesh's Admission to the U.N.

43	12	25 p. multicoloured	10	10
44		1 t. multicoloured	35	40

1974. Centenary of Universal Postal Union. Mult.

45		25 p. Type 13	10	10
46		1 t. 25 Mail runner	20	15
47		1 t. 75 Type 13	25	25
48		5 t. As 1 t. 25	80	1·60

14 Courts of Justice

1974. As Nos. 32/5 with revised inscriptions.

49	14	1 t. violet	1·50	10
50	–	2 t. olive	2·00	80
51	–	5 t. blue	5·50	70
51a	–	10 t. pink	12·00	8·00

15 Tiger

16 Symbolic Family

1974. Wildlife Preservation. Multicoloured.

52		25 p. Type 15	70	10
53		50 p. Tiger cub	1·25	70
54		2 t. Tiger in stream	2·75	3·50

1974. World Population Year. "Family Planning for All". Multicoloured.

55		25 p. Type 16	15	10
56		70 p. Village family	25	50
57		1 t. 25 Heads of family (horiz)	40	1·10

17 Radar Antenna

19 Telephones of 1876 and 1976

18 Woman's Head

1975. Inauguration of Betbunia Satellite Earth Station.

58	17	25 p. black, silver and red	10	10
59		1 t. black, silver and blue	20	60

1975. International Women's Year.

60	18	50 p. multicoloured	10	10
61		2 t. multicoloured	25	85

1976. As Nos. 24/31 and 49/51a but redrawn in smaller size.

64	–	5 p. green	20	10
65	–	10 p. black	20	10
66	–	20 p. green	70	10
67	–	25 p. mauve	2·25	10
68	–	50 p. purple	1·75	10
69	–	60 p. grey	40	20
70	–	75 p. green	1·25	2·00
71	–	90 p. brown	40	20
72	14	1 t. violet	2·00	10
73	–	2 t. green	6·00	10
74	–	5 t. blue	3·25	1·75
75	–	10 t. red	8·50	1·75

Nos. 64/71 are 23 × 18 mm (50 p.) or 18 × 23 mm (others) and Nos. 72/75 are 20 × 32 mm (2 t.) or 32 × 20 mm (others).

1976. Centenary of Telephone.

76	19	2 t. 25 multicoloured	25	20
77	–	5 t. red, green and black	55	65

DESIGN: 5 t. Alexander Graham Bell.

20 Eye and Nutriments

1976. Prevention of Blindness.

78	20	30 p. multicoloured	50	10
79		2 t. 25 multicoloured	1·40	2·25

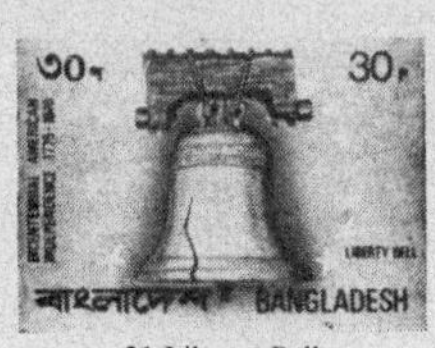

21 Liberty Bell

1976. Bicentenary of American Revolution. Mult.

80		30 p. Type 21	10	10
81		2 t. 25 Statue of Liberty	30	25
82		5 t. "Mayflower"	80	50
83		10 t. Mount Rushmore	80	80

22 Industry, Science, Agriculture and Education

23 Hurdling

1976. 25th Anniv of Colombo Plan.

85	22	30 p. multicoloured	15	10
86		2 t. 25 multicoloured	35	35

1976. Olympic Games, Montreal. Multicoloured.

87		25 p. Type 23	10	10
88		30 p. Running (horiz)	10	10
89		1 t. Pole vaulting	15	10
90		2 t. 25 Swimming (horiz)	40	45
91		3 t. 50 Gymnastics	75	1·25
92		5 t. Football	1·40	2·00

24 The Blessing

25 Qazi Nazrul Islam (poet)

1977. Silver Jubilee. Multicoloured.

93		30 p. Type 24	10	10
94		2 t. 25 Queen Elizabeth II	20	25
95		10 t. Queen Elizabeth and Prince Philip	70	85

1977. Qazi Nazrul Islam Commemoration.

97	25	40 p. green and black	10	10
98	–	2 t. 25 brown, red & lt brn	30	30

DESIGN—HORIZ: 2 t. 25, Head and shoulders portrait.

26 Bird with Letter

1977. 15th Anniv of Asian–Oceanic Postal Union.

99	26	30 p. red, blue and grey	10	10
100		2 t. 25 red, blue and grey	20	25

27 Sloth Bear

28 Campfire and Tent

1977. Animals. Multicoloured.

101		40 p. Type 27	20	10
102		1 t. Spotted deer	30	10
103		2 t. 25 Leopard (horiz)	85	20
104		3 t. 50 Gaur (horiz)	90	35
105		4 t. Indian elephant (horiz)	1·75	50
106		5 t. Tiger (horiz)	2·00	75

The Bengali numerals on the 40 p. resemble "80", and that on the 4 t. resembles "8".

1978. First National Scout Jamboree.

107	28	40 p. red, blue and pale blue	30	10
108	–	3 t. 50 lilac, green and blue	1·25	30
109	–	5 t. green, blue and red	1·40	45

DESIGNS—HORIZ: 3 t. 50, Scout stretcher-team. VERT: 5 t. Scout salute.

29 "Michelia champaca"

1978. Flowers. Multicoloured.

110		40 p. Type 29	30	10
111		1 t. "Cassia fistula"	55	15
112		2 t. 25 "Delonix regia"	85	30
113		3 t. 50 "Nymphaea nouchali"	1·00	60
114		4 t. "Butea monosperma"	1·10	80
115		5 t. "Anthocephalus indicus"	1·25	85

30 St. Edward's Crown and Sceptres

32 Fenchuganj Fertiliser Factory

31 Sir Alan Cobham's De Havilland D.H.50

1978. 25th Anniv of Coronation. Multicoloured.

116		40 p. Type **30**	10	10
117		3 t. 50 Balcony scene	15	30
118		5 t. Queen Elizabeth and Prince Philip	25	50
119		10 t. Coronation portrait by Cecil Beaton	45	80

1978. 75th Anniv of Powered Flight.

121	**31**	40 p. multicoloured	15	10
122	–	2 t. 25 brown and blue	50	45
123	–	3 t. 50 brown and yellow	65	65
124	–	5 t. multicoloured	4·00	3·50

DESIGNS: 2 t. 25, Captain Hans Bertram's seaplane "Atlantis"; 3 t. 50, Wright brothers' "Flyer III"; 5 t. Concorde.

1978.

125	–	5 p. brown	10	10
126	**32**	10 p. blue	10	10
127	–	15 p. orange	10	10
128	–	20 p. red	10	10
129	–	25 p. blue	15	10
130	–	30 p. green	1·25	10
131	–	40 p. purple	30	10
132	–	50 p. black	3·25	1·50
134	–	80 p. brown	20	10
136	–	1 t. violet	4·00	10
137	–	2 t. blue	50	1·75

DESIGNS—HORIZ: 5 p. Lalbag Fort; 25 p. Jute on a boat; 40, 50 p. Baitul Mukarram Mosque; 1 t. Dotara (musical instrument); 2 t. Karnaphuli Dam. VERT: 15 p. Pineapple; 20 p. Bangladesh gas; 30 p. Banana tree; 80 p. Mohastan Garh.

33 Tawaf-E-Ka'aba, Mecca

35 Moulana Abdul Hamid Khan Bhashani

34 Jasim Uddin

1978. Pilgrimage to Mecca. Multicoloured.

140		40 p. Type **33**	20	10
141		3 t. Pilgrims in Wuquf, Arafat (horiz)	60	45

1979. 3rd Death Anniv of Jasim Uddin (poet).

142	**34**	40 p. multicoloured	20	40

1979. 3rd Death Anniv of Moulana Abdul Hamid Khan Bhashani (national leader).

143	**35**	40 p. multicoloured	40	30

36 Sir Rowland Hill

37 Children with Hoops

1979. Death Centenary of Sir Rowland Hill.

144	**36**	40 p. blue, red and light blue	10	10
145	–	3 t. 50 multicoloured	35	30
146	–	10 t. multicoloured	80	1·00

DESIGNS: 3 t. 50, Sir Rowland Hill and first Bangladesh stamp; 10 t. Sir Rowland Hill and Bangladesh U.P.U. stamp.

1979. International Year of the Child. Multicoloured.

148		40 p. Type **37**	10	10
149		3 t. 50 Boy with kite	35	35
150		5 t. Children jumping	50	50

38 Rotary International Emblem

40 A. K. Fazlul Huq

39 Canal Digging

1980. 75th Anniv of Rotary International.

152	**38**	40 p. black, red and yellow	20	10
153	–	5 t. gold and blue	65	45

DESIGN: 5 t. Rotary emblem (different).

1980. Mass Participation in Canal Digging.

154	**39**	40 p. multicoloured	40	30

1980. 18th Death Anniv of A. K. Fazlul Huq (national leader).

155	**40**	40 p. multicoloured	30	30

41 Early Forms of Mail Transport

1980. "London 1980" International Stamp Exhibition. Multicoloured.

156		1 t. Type **41**	15	10
157		10 t. Modern forms of mail transport	1·25	85

42 Dome of the Rock

43 Outdoor Class

1980. Palestinian Welfare.

159	**42**	50 p. lilac	70	30

1980. Education.

160	**43**	50 p. multicoloured	40	30

44 Beach Scene

1980. World Tourism Conference, Manila. Mult.

161		50 p. Type **44**	30	30
162		5 t. Beach scene (different)	60	70

MINIMUM PRICE

The minimum price quoted is 10p which represents a handling charge rather than a basis for valuing common stamps. For further notes about prices see introductory pages.

45 Mecca

46 Begum Roquiah

1980. Moslem Year 1400 A. H. Commemoration.

164	**45**	50 p. multicoloured	20	20

1980. Birth Centenary of Begum Roquiah (campaigner for women's rights).

165	**46**	50 p. multicoloured	10	10
166		2 t. multicoloured	35	20

47 Spotted Deer and Scout Emblem

49 Queen Elizabeth the Queen Mother

1981. 5th Asia–Pacific and 2nd Bangladesh Scout Jamboree.

167	**47**	50 p. multicoloured	40	15
168		5 t. multicoloured	1·25	2·00

1981. 2nd Population Census. Nos. 38/40 optd **2nd. CENSUS 1981**.

169	**10**	20 p. multicoloured	10	10
170		25 p. multicoloured	10	10
171		75 p. multicoloured	20	30

1981. 80th Birthday of the Queen Mother.

172	**49**	1 t. multicoloured	15	15
173		15 t. multicoloured	1·75	2·50

50 Revolutionary with Flag and Submachine-gun

52 Kemal Ataturk in Civilian Dress

51 Bangladesh Village and Farm Scenes

1981. 10th Anniv of Independence. Mult.

175		50 p. Type **50**	15	10
176		2 t. Figures on map symbolising Bangladesh life style	25	45

1981. U.N. Conference on Least Developed Countries, Paris.

177	**51**	50 p. multicoloured	35	15

1981. Birth Centenary of Kemal Ataturk (Turkish statesman).

178		50 p. Type **52**	45	30
179		1 t. Kemal Ataturk in uniform	80	80

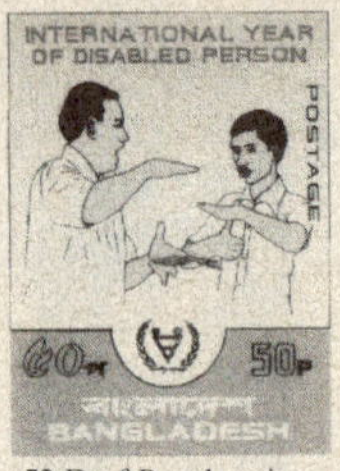

53 Deaf People using Sign Language

54 Farm Scene and Wheat Ear

1981. Int Year for Disabled Persons. Mult.

180		50 p. Type **53**	40	20
181		2 t. Disabled person writing (horiz)	1·25	2·00

1981. World Food Day.

182	**54**	50 p. multicoloured	50	80

55 River Scene

56 Dr. M. Hussain

1982. 10th Anniv of Human Environment Conference.

183	**55**	50 p. multicoloured	50	80

1982. 1st Death Anniv of Dr. Motahar Hussain (educationist).

184	**56**	50 p. multicoloured	50	80

57 Knotted Rope surrounding Bengali "75"

1982. 75th Anniv of Boy Scout Movement and 125th Birth Anniv of Lord Baden-Powell. Multicoloured.

185		50 p. Type **57**	1·00	30
186		2 t. Lord Baden-Powell (vert)	3·25	4·50

সম্মিলিত
সশস্ত্র বাহিনী দিবস
২১ নভেম্বর,৮২

(58)

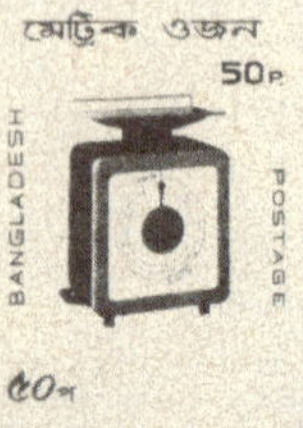

60 Metric Scales

59 Captain Mohiuddin Jahangir

1982. Armed Forces' Day. No. 175 optd with T **58**.

187		50 p. Type **50**	2·25	2·25

1983. Heroes and Martyrs of the Liberation. Multicoloured, background colour of commemorative plaque given.

188		50 p. Type **59** (orange)	30	45
189		50 p. Sepoy Hamidur Rahman (green)	30	45
190		50 p. Sepoy Mohammed Mustafa Kamal (red)	30	45
191		50 p. Muhammed Ruhul Amin (yellow)	30	45
192		50 p. Flt. Lt. M. Matiur Rahman (brown)	30	45
193		50 p. Lance-Naik Munshi Abdur Rob (brown)	30	45
194		50 p. Lance-Naik Nur Mouhammad (green)	30	45

1983. Introduction of Metric Weights and Measures. Multicoloured.

195		50 p. Type **60**	40	30
196		2 t. Weights, jug and tape measure (horiz)	1·75	2·50

61 Dr. Robert Koch

63 Dr. Muhammed Shahidulla

62 Open Stage Theatre

1983. Centenary (1982) of Robert Koch's Discovery of Tubercle Bacillus. Multicoloured.

197	50 p. Type **61**	1·00	40
198	1 t. Microscope, slide and X-ray	2·25	3·25

1983. Commonwealth Day. Multicoloured.

199	1 t. Type **62**	10	15
200	3 t. Boat race	20	30
201	10 t. Snake dance	50	90
202	15 t. Picking tea	60	1·50

1983. Dr. Muhammed Shahidulla (Bengali scholar) Commemoration.

203 **63**	50 p. multicoloured	75	1·00

64 Magpie Robin

1983. Birds of Bangladesh. Multicoloured.

204	50 p. Type **64**	1·25	40
205	2 t. White-breasted kingfisher (vert)	2·25	2·25
206	3 t. 75 Lesser golden-backed woodpecker (vert)	3·00	3·00
207	5 t. White-winged wood duck	3·50	3·50

65 "Macrobrachium rosenbergii"

1984. Marine Life. Multicoloured.

209	50 p. Type **65**	80	30
210	2 t. White pomfret	2·00	1·60
211	3 t. 75 Rohu	2·50	2·00
212	5 t. Climbing perch	3·00	2·75

1983. Visit of Queen Elizabeth II, No. 95 optd **Nov. '83 Visit of Queen**.

214	10 t. Queen Elizabeth and Prince Philip	3·00	4·00

67 Conference Hall, Dhaka

1983. 14th Islamic Foreign Ministers' Conference, Dhaka. Multicoloured.

215	50 p. Type **67**	50	30
216	5 t. Old Fort, Dhaka	1·75	2·75

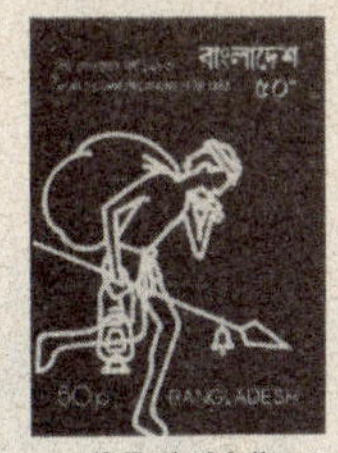

68 Early Mail Runner

69 Carrying Mail by Boat

1983. World Communications Year. Multicoloured.

217	50 p. Type **68**	30	15
218	5 t. Sailing ship, steam train and Boeing 707 airliner	2·00	1·50
219	10 t. Mail runner and dish aerial (horiz)	2·75	2·50

1983. Postal Communications.

220	**69**	5 p. blue	10	10
221	–	10 p. purple	10	10
222	–	15 p. blue	30	10
223	–	20 p. black	45	10
224	–	25 p. grey	15	10
225	–	30 p. brown	15	10
226	–	50 p. brown	30	10
227	–	1 t. blue	50	10
228	–	2 t. green	50	10
228a	–	3 t. brown	85	50
229	–	5 t. purple	90	60

DESIGNS—HORIZ (22 × 17 mm): 10 p. Counter, Dhaka G.P.O.; 15 p. I.W.T.A. Terminal, Dhaka; 20 p. Inside railway travelling post office; 30 p. Emptying pillar box; 50 p. Mobile post office van. (30 × 19 mm): 1 t. Kamalapur Railway Station, Dhaka; 2 t. Zia International Airport; 3 t. Sorting mail by machine; 5 t. Khulna G.P.O. VERT (17 × 22 mm): 25 p. Delivering a letter.

(70)

1984. 1st National Stamp Exhibition (1st issue). Nos. 161/2 optd with T **70** (5 t.) or "First Bangladesh National Philatelic Exhibition—1984" (50 p.)

230	**44**	50 p. multicoloured	80	1·00
231	–	5 t. multicoloured	1·10	1·75

71 Girl with Stamp Album (½-size illustration)

1984. 1st National Stamp Exhibition (2nd issue). Multicoloured.

232	50 p. Type **71**	65	1·25
233	7 t. 50 Boy with stamp album	1·10	1·60

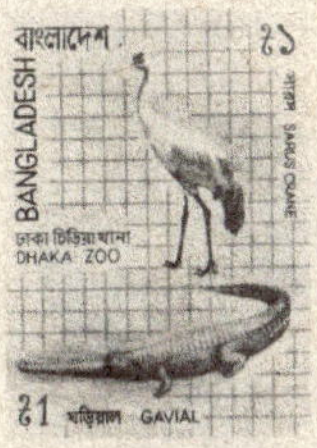

72 Sarus Crane and Gavial

73 Eagle attacking Hen with Chicks

1984. Dhaka Zoo. Multicoloured.

235	1 t. Type **72**	1·75	85
236	2 t. Common peafowl and tiger	2·50	3·50

1984. Centenary of Postal Life Insurance. Mult.

237	1 t. Type **73**	50	20
238	5 t. Bangladesh family and postman's hand with insurance cheque	1·50	1·50

74 Abbasuddin Ahmad

খুলনাপেক্স—৮৪

(75)

1984. Abbasuddin Ahmad (singer) Commemoration.

239	**74**	3 t. multicoloured	70	40

1984. "Khulnapex-84" Stamp Exhibition. No. 86 optd with T **75**.

240	**22**	2 t. 25 multicoloured	70	60

76 Cycling

1984. Olympic Games, Los Angeles. Multicoloured.

241	1 t. Type **76**	1·25	30
242	5 t. Hockey	2·50	2·25
243	10 t. Volleyball	2·75	3·00

77 Farmer with Rice and Sickle

1985. 9th Annual Meeting of Islamic Development Bank, Dhaka. Multicoloured.

244	1 t. Type **77**	35	15
245	5 t. Citizens of four races	1·25	1·25

78 Mother and Baby

80 Women working at Traditional Crafts

উপজেলা নির্বাচন ১৯৮৫

(79)

1985. Child Survival Campaign. Multicoloured.

246	1 t. Type **78**	30	10
247	10 t. Young child and growth graph	2·50	2·00

1985. Local Elections. Nos. 110/15 optd with T **79**.

248	40 p. Type **29**	10	15
249	1 t. "Cassia fistula"	10	20
250	2 t. 25 "Delonix regia"	15	35
251	3 t. 50 "Nymphaea nouchali"	20	45
252	4 t. "Butea monosperma"	20	45
253	5 t. "Anthocephalus indicus"	30	55

1985. U. N. Decade for Women. Multicoloured.

254	1 t. Type **80**	25	10
255	10 t. Women with microscope, computer terminal and in classroom	1·25	85

81 U.N. Building, New York, Peace Doves and Flags

1985. 40th Anniv of United Nations Organization and 11th Anniv of Bangladesh Membership. Multicoloured.

256	1 t. Type **81**	10	10
257	10 t. Map of world and Bangladesh flag	80	90

82 Head of Youth, Flowers and Symbols of Commerce and Agriculture

83 Emblem and Seven Doves

1985. International Youth Year. Multicoloured.

258	1 t. Type **82**	10	10
259	5 t. Head of youth, flowers and symbols of industry	40	60

1985. 1st Summit Meeting of South Asian Association for Regional Co-operation, Dhaka. Multicoloured.

260	1 t. Type **83**	10	10
261	5 t. Flags of member nations and lotus blossom	40	60

84 Zainul Abedin

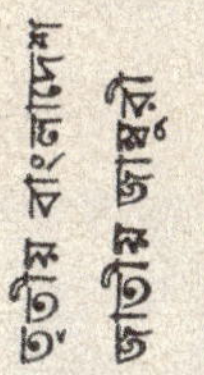

(85)

1985. 10th Death Anniv of Zainul Abedin (artist).

262	**84**	3 t. multicoloured	75	30

1985. 3rd National Scout Jamboree. No. 109 optd with T **85**.

263	5 t. green, blue and red	2·25	1·25

86 "Fishing Net" (Safiuddin Ahmed)

1986. Bangladesh Paintings. Multicoloured.

264	1 t. Type **86**	15	10
265	5 t. "Happy Return" (Quamrul Hassan)	40	50
266	10 t. "Levelling the Ploughed Field (Zainul Abedin)	70	80

87 Two Players competing for Ball

1986. World Cup Football Championship, Mexico. Multicoloured.

267	1 t. Type **87**	50	10
268	10 t. Goalkeeper and ball in net	2·25	2·50

88 General M. A. G. Osmani

90 Butterflies and Nuclear Explosion

1986. General M. A. G. Osmani (army commander-in-chief) Commemoration.

270	**88**	3 t. multicoloured	1·00	75

1986. South Asian Association for Regional Co-operation Seminar. No. 183 optd **SAARC SEMINAR '86**.

271	**55**	50 p. multicoloured	1·75	2·25

1986. International Peace Year. Multicoloured.

272	1 t. Type **90**	50	25
273	10 t. Flowers and ruined buildings	2·75	3·00

1987. Conference for Development. Nos. 152/3 optd **CONFERENCE FOR DEVELOPMENT '87**. No. 275 also surch **TK. 1.00**.

275	**38**	1 t. on 40 p. black, red and yellow	10	15
276	–	5 t. gold and blue	30	60

92 Demonstrators with Placards

1987. 35th Anniv of Bangla Language Movement. Multicoloured.

277	3 t. Type **92**	1·00	1·50
278	3 t. Martyrs' Memorial	1·00	1·50

Nos. 277/8 were printed together, se-tenant, forming a composite design.

93 Nurse giving Injection

94 Pattern and Bengali Script

1987. World Health Day.

279	**93**	1 t. black and blue	1·75	1·50

See also No. 295.

1987. Bengali New Year Day. Multicoloured.

280	1 t. Type **94**	10	10
281	10 t. Bengali woman	40	60

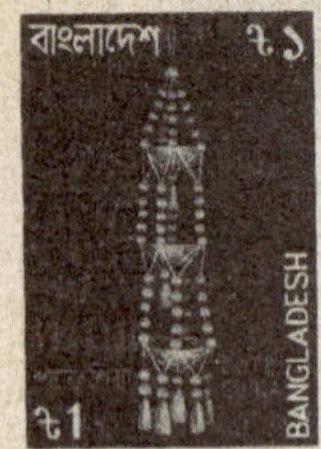
95 Jute Shika

96 Ustad Ayet Ali Khan and Surbahar

1987. Export Products. Multicoloured.
282 1 t. Type **95** 10 10
283 5 t. Jute carpet (horiz) 30 35
284 10 t. Cane table lamp 45 70

1987. 20th Death Anniv of Ustad Ayet Ali Khan (musician and composer).
285 **96** 5 t. multicoloured 55 40

97 Palanquin

1987. Transport. Multicoloured.
286 2 t. Type **97** 20 15
287 3 t. Bicycle rickshaw 30 20
288 5 t. River steamer 70 35
289 7 t. Express diesel train . . . 1·40 50
290 10 t. Bullock cart 50 75

98 H. S. Suhrawardy

1987. Hossain Shadid Suhrawardy (politician) Commemoration.
291 **98** 3 t. multicoloured 20 30

99 Villagers fleeing from Typhoon

1987. International Year of Shelter for the Homeless. Multicoloured.
292 5 t. Type **99** 20 30
293 5 t. Villagers and modern houses 20 30

100 President Ershad addressing Parliament

1987. 1st Anniv of Return to Democracy.
294 **100** 10 t. multicoloured . . . 40 60

1988. World Health Day. As T **93**.
295 25 p. brown 30 20
DESIGN: 25 p. Oral rehydration.

101 Woman planting Palm Saplings

1988. I.F.A.D. Seminar on Agricultural Loans for Rural Women. Multicoloured.
296 3 t. Type **101** 15 20
297 5 t. Village woman milking cow 20 40

102 Basketball

1988. Olympic Games, Seoul. Multicoloured.
298 5 t. Type **102** 40 30
299 5 t. Weightlifting 40 30
300 5 t. Tennis 40 30
301 5 t. Rifle-shooting 40 30
302 5 t. Boxing 40 30

103 Interior of Shait Gumbaz Mosque, Bagerhat

1988. Historical Buildings. Multicoloured.
303 1 t. Type **103** 10 10
304 4 t. Paharpur Monastery . . . 10 10
305 5 t. Kantanagar Temple, Dinajpur 10 10
306 10 t. Lalbag Fort, Dhaka . . . 15 15

104 Henri Dunant (founder), Red Cross and Crescent

105 Dr. Qudrat-i-Khuda in Laboratory

1988. 125th Anniv of International Red Cross and Red Crescent. Multicoloured.
307 5 t. Type **104** 25 25
308 10 t. Red Cross workers with patient 45 45

1988. Dr. Qudrat-i-Khuda (scientist) Commem.
309 **105** 5 t. multicoloured 20 25

106 Wicket-keeper

107 Labourers, Factory and Technician

1988. Asia Cup Cricket. Multicoloured.
310 1 t. Type **106** 70 90
311 5 t. Batsman . . . . 90 1·00
312 10 t. Bowler . . . . 1·10 1·40

1988. 32nd Meeting of Colombo Plan Consultative Committee, Dhaka.
313 **107** 3 t. multicoloured 10 10
314 10 t. multicoloured . . . 40 45

108 Dhaka G.P.O. Building

1988. 25th Anniv of Dhaka G.P.O. Building. Multicoloured.
315 1 t. Type **108** 10 10
316 5 t. Post Office counter . . . 20 25

৫ম জাতীয় রোভার মুট
১৯৮৮-৮৯
(109)

1988. 5th National Rover Scout Moot. No. 168 optd with T **109**.
317 **47** 5 t. multicoloured . . . . . 1·25 1·25

110 Bangladesh Airport

1989. Bangladesh Landmarks.
318 **110** 3 t. black and blue . . . 10 10
318a – 4 t. blue 15 20
319 – 5 t. black and brown . . 15 20
320 – 10 t. red 30 35
321 – 20 t. multicoloured 65 70
DESIGNS—VERT (22 × 33 mm): 5 t. Curzon Hall. ($19\frac{1}{2} \times 31\frac{1}{2}$ mm): 10 t. Fertiliser factory, Chittagong. HORIZ (33 × 23 mm): 4 t. Chittagong port; 20 t. Postal Academy, Rajshahi.

চতুর্থ দ্বিবার্ষিক এশীয়
চারুকলা প্রদর্শনী
বাংলাদেশ ১৯৮৯
(111)

1989. 4th Biennial Asian Art Exhibition. No. 266 optd with T **111**.
322 10 t. "Levelling the Ploughed Field" (Zainul Abedin) . . . 40 45

112 Irrigation Methods and Student with Telescope

113 Academy Logo

1989. 12th National Science and Technology Week.
323 **112** 10 t. multicoloured 40 45

1989. 75th Anniv of Police Academy, Sardah.
324 **113** 10 t. multicoloured 40 45

114 Rejoicing Crowds, Paris, 1789

1989. Bicentenary of French Revolution. Mult.
325 17 t. Type **114** 70 75
326 17 t. Storming the Bastille, 1789 70 75

115 Sowing and Harvesting

1989. 10th Anniv of Asia-Pacific Integrated Rural Development Centre. Multicoloured.
329 5 t. Type **115** 45 45
330 10 t. Rural activities 50 50
Nos. 329/30 were printed together, se-tenant, forming a composite design.

116 Helper and Child playing with Baby

1989. 40th Anniv of S.O.S. International Children's Village. Multicoloured.
331 1 t. Type **116** 15 10
332 10 t. Foster mother with children 55 55

HAVE YOU READ THE NOTES AT THE BEGINNING OF THIS CATALOGUE?
These often provide answers to the enquiries we receive.

117 U.N. Soldier on Watch

118 Festival Emblem

1989. 1st Anniv of Bangladesh Participation in U.N. Peace-keeping Force. Multicoloured.
333 4 t. Type **117** 50 30
334 10 t. Two soldiers checking positions . . . . 1·00 70

1989. 2nd Asian Poetry Festival, Dhaka.
335 **118** 2 t. red, deep red and green 15 10
336 – 10 t. multicoloured 60 65
DESIGN: 10 t. Festival emblem and hall.

119 State Security Printing Press

1989. Inauguration of State Security Printing Press, Gazipur.
337 **119** 10 t. multicoloured 65 65

120 Water Lilies and T.V. Emblem

1989. 25th Anniv of Bangladesh Television. Multicoloured.
338 5 t. Type **120** 30 30
339 10 t. Central emblem and water lilies 65 80

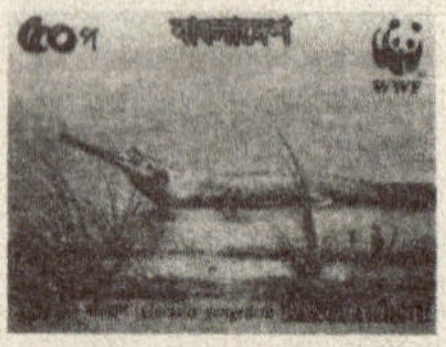
121 Gharial in Shallow Water

1990. Endangered Wildlife. Gharial. Multicoloured.
340 50 p. Type **121** 80 45
341 2 t. Gharial feeding . . . . . 1·00 60
342 4 t. Gharials basking on sand bank . . . . 1·40 70
343 10 t. Two gharials resting . . 1·75 95

122 Symbolic Family

124 Boy learning Alphabet

123 Justice S. M. Murshed

1990. Population Day.
344 **122** 6 t. multicoloured 55 35

1990. 10th Death Anniv of Justice Syed Mahbub Murshed.
345 **123** 5 t. multicoloured . . . . 1·25 35

1990. International Literacy Year. Multicoloured.
346 6 t. Type **124** 1·00 50
347 10 t. Boy teaching girl to write 1·50 1·00

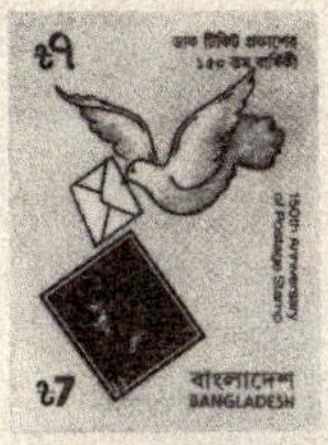
125 Penny Black with "Stamp World London 90" Exhibition Emblem

127 Mango

126 Goalkeeper and Ball

1990. 150th Anniv of the Penny Black. Multicoloured.
348 7 t. Type **125** 1·50 60
349 10 t. Penny Black, 1983 World Communications Year stamp and Bengali mail runner 1·75 1·00

1990. World Cup Football Championship, Italy. Multicoloured.
350 8 t. Type **126** 1·75 90
351 10 t. Footballer with ball 2·00 1·00

1990. Fruit. Multicoloured.
353 1 t. Type **127** 30 10
354 2 t. Guava 30 10
355 3 t. Water melon 35 15
356 4 t. Papaya 40 25
357 5 t. Bread fruit 65 50
358 10 t. Carambola 1·25 1·25

128 Man gathering Wheat

1990. U.N. Conference on Least Developed Countries, Paris.
359 **128** 10 t. multicoloured 1·25 90

129 Map of Asia with Stream of Letters

131 Lalan Shah

130 Canoe Racing

1990. 20th Anniv of Asia-Pacific Postal Training Centre. Multicoloured.
360 2 t. Type **129** 75 50
361 6 t. Map of Pacific with stream of letters 75 50
Nos. 360/1 were printed together, se-tenant, forming a composite map design.

1990. Asian Games, Beijing. Multicoloured.
362 2 t. Type **130** 60 10
363 4 t. Kabaddi 75 25
364 8 t. Wrestling 1·25 75
365 10 t. Badminton 2·00 1·50

1990. 1st Death Anniv of Lalan Shah (poet).
366 **131** 6 t. multicoloured 1·00 35

132 U.N. Logo and "40"

1990. 40th Anniv of United Nations Development Programme.
367 **132** 6 t. multicoloured 80 35

133 Baby

134 "Danaus chrysippus"

1990. Immunization.
368 **133** 1 t. green 10 10
369 2 t. brown 10 10

1990. Butterflies. Multicoloured.
370 6 t. Type **134** 1·60 1·60
371 6 t. "Precis almana" 1·60 1·60
372 10 t. "Ixias pyrene" 1·75 1·75
373 10 t. "Danaus plexippus" 1·75 1·75

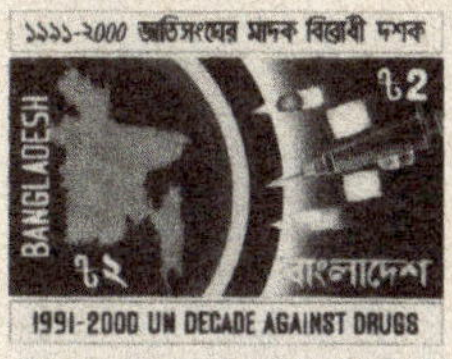
135 Drugs attacking Bangladesh

1991. U.N. Anti-Drugs Decade. Multicoloured.
374 2 t. Type **135** 1·00 50
375 4 t. "Drug" snake around globe 1·25 1·25

136 Salimullah Hall

1991.
376 **136** 6 t. blue and yellow 20 25

137 Silhouetted People on Map

138 "Invincible Bangla" (statue)

1991. 3rd National Census.
382 **137** 4 t. multicoloured 65 60

1991. 20th Anniv of Independence. Multicoloured.
383 4 t. Type **138** 55 65
384 4 t. "Freedom Fighter" (statue) 55 65
385 4 t. Mujibnagar Memorial 55 65
386 4 t. Eternal flame 55 65
387 4 t. National Martyrs' Memorial 55 65
Nos. 383/7 were issued together, se-tenant, forming a composite design.

139 President Rahman Seated

141 Kaikobad

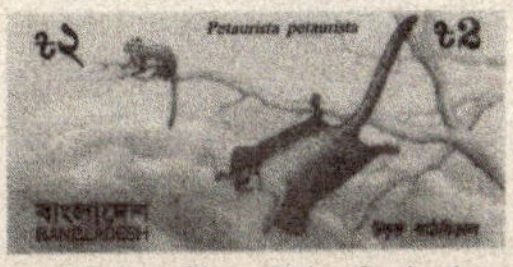
140 Red Giant Flying Squirrel

1991. 10th Death Anniv of President Ziaur Rahman. Multicoloured.
388 50 p. Type **139** 20 15
389 2 t. President Rahman's head in circular decoration 65 85

1991. Endangered Species. Multicoloured.
391 2 t. Type **140** 1·00 1·25
392 4 t. Black-faced monkey (vert) 1·00 1·25
393 6 t. Great Indian hornbill (vert) 1·00 1·25
394 10 t. Armoured pangolin 1·10 1·25

1991. 40th Death Anniv of Kaikobad (poet).
395 **141** 6 t. multicoloured 60 60

142 Rabindranath Tagore and Temple

1991. 50th Death Anniv of Rabindranath Tagore (poet).
396 **142** 4 t. multicoloured 70 55

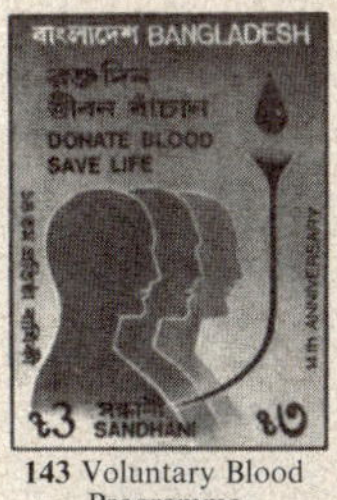
143 Voluntary Blood Programme

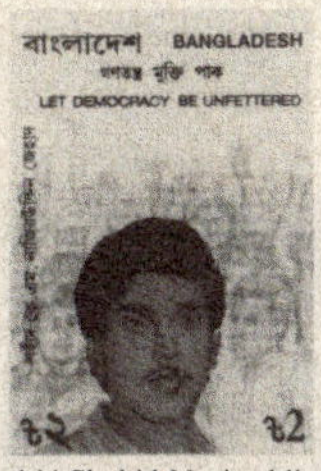
144 Shahid Naziruddin and Crowd

1991. 14th Anniv of "Sandhani" (medical students' association).
397 **143** 3 t. black and red 75 50
398 – 5 t. multicoloured 1·25 1·50
DESIGN: 5 t. Blind man and eye.

1991. 1st Death Anniv of Shahid Naziruddin Jahad (democrat).
399 **144** 2 t. black, green and brown 55 50

145 Shaheed Noor Hossain with Slogan on Chest

1991. 4th Death Anniv of Shaheed Noor Hossain (democrat).
400 **145** 2 t. multicoloured 45 40

146 Bronze Stupa

1991. Archaeological Relics from Mainamati. Multicoloured.
401 4 t. Type **146** 90 1·00
402 4 t. Earthenware and bronze pitchers 90 1·00
403 4 t. Remains of Salban Vihara Monastery 90 1·00
404 4 t. Gold coins 90 1·00
405 4 t. Terracotta plaque 90 1·00

147 Demonstrators

1991. 1st Anniv of Mass Uprising.
406 **147** 4 t. multicoloured 65 50

148 Munier Chowdhury

1991. 20th Anniv of Independence. Martyred Intellectuals (1st series). Each black and brown.
407 2 t. Type **148** 30 30
408 2 t. Ghyasuddin Ahmad 30 30
409 2 t. Rashidul Hasan 30 30
410 2 t. Muhammad Anwar Pasha 30 30
411 2 t. Dr. Muhammad Mortaza 30 30
412 2 t. Shahid Saber 30 30
413 2 t. Fazlur Rahman Khan 30 30
414 2 t. Ranada Prasad Saha 30 30
415 2 t. Adhyaksha Joges Chandra Ghose 30 30
416 2 t. Santosh Chandra Bhattacharyya 30 30
417 2 t. Dr. Gobinda Chandra Deb 30 30
418 2 t. A. Muniruzzaman 30 30
419 2 t. Mufazzal Haider Chaudhury 30 30
420 2 t. Dr. Abdul Alim Choudhury 30 30
421 2 t. Sirajuddin Hossain 30 30
422 2 t. Shahidulla Kaiser 30 30
423 2 t. Altaf Mahmud 30 30
424 2 t. Dr. Jyotirmay Guha Thakurta 30 30
425 2 t. Dr. Muhammad Abul Khair 30 30
426 2 t. Dr. Serajul Haque Khan 30 30
427 2 t. Dr. Mohammad Fazle Rabbi 30 30
428 2 t. Mir Abdul Quyyum 30 30
429 2 t. Golam Mostafa 30 30
430 2 t. Dhirendranath Dutta 30 30
431 2 t. S. Mannan 30 30
432 2 t. Nizamuddin Ahmad 30 30
433 2 t. Abul Bashar Chowdhury 30 30
434 2 t. Selina Parveen 30 30
435 2 t. Dr. Abul Kalam Azad 30 30
436 2 t. Saidul Hassan 30 30
See also Nos. 483/92, 525/40, 568/83, 620/35, 656/71 and 691/706.

149 "Penaeus monodon"

1991. Shrimps. Multicoloured.
437 6 t. Type **149** 1·25 1·50
438 6 t. "Metapenaeus monoceros" 1·25 1·50

150 Death of Raihan Jaglu

1992. 5th Death Anniv of Shaheed Mirze Abu Raihan Jaglu.
439 **150** 2 t. multicoloured 60 50

151 Rural and Urban Scenes

152 Nawab Sirajuddaulah

1992. World Environment Day. Multicoloured.
440 4 t. Type **151** 50 15
441 10 t. World Environment Day logo (horiz) 1·25 1·75

1992. 235th Death Anniv of Nawab Sirajuddaulah of Bengal
442 **152** 10 t. multicoloured 80 80

153 Syed Ismail Hossain Sirajee

1992. 61st Death Anniv of Syed Ismail Hossain Sirajee.
443 153 4 t. multicoloured 60 40

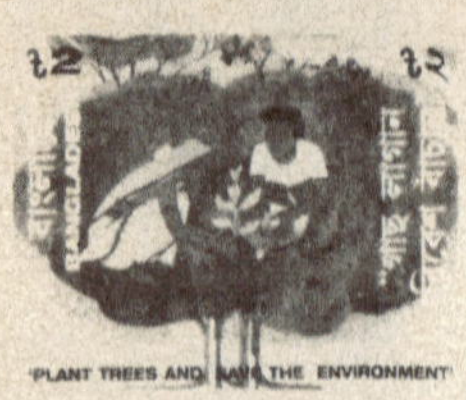
154 Couple planting Seedling

1992. Plant Week. Multicoloured.
444 2 t. Type **154** 85 70
445 4 t. Birds on tree (vert) . . . 85 70

155 Canoe Racing

1992. Olympic Games, Barcelona. Multicoloured.
446 4 t. Type **155** . . . . 90 1·00
447 6 t. Hands holding torch with Olympic rings . . . . 90 1·00
448 10 t. Olympic rings and doves 90 1·00
449 10 t. Olympic rings and multiracial handshake . . . 90 1·00

1992. "Banglapex '92", National Philatelic Exhibition (1st issue). No. 290 optd **Banglapex '92** in English and Bengali.
450 10 t. Bullock cart . . . . . . 1·00 1·25
See also Nos.452/3.

157 Masnad-e-Ala Isa Khan

1992. 393rd Death Anniv of Masnad-e-Ala Isa Khan.
451 157 4 t. multicoloured. 60 40

158 Ceremonial Elephant (19th-century ivory carving)

1992. "Banglapex '92" National Philatelic Exhibition (2nd issue). Multicoloured.
452 10 t. Type **158** . . . . 1·00 1·25
453 10 t. Victorian pillarbox between early and modern postmen . 1·00 1·25

159 Star Mosque

1992. Star Mosque, Dhaka.
455 159 10 t. mutlicoloured . . . 90 90

160 Meer Nisar Ali Titumeer and Fort

1992. 161st Death Anniv of Meer Nisar Ali Titumeer.
456 160 10 t. multicoloured . . . 90 90

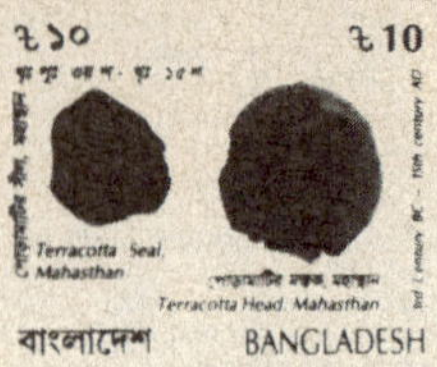

161 Terracotta Head and Seal

1992. Archaeological Relics from Mahasthangarh. Multicoloured.
457 10 t. Type **161** . . . . 1·10 1·25
458 10 t. Terracotta panel showing swan . . . . 1·10 1·25
459 10 t. Terracotta statue of Surya 1·10 1·25
460 10 t. Gupta stone column . . 1·10 1·25

162 Young Child and Food

1992. Int Conference on Nutrition, Rome.
461 162 4 t. multicoloured 60 40

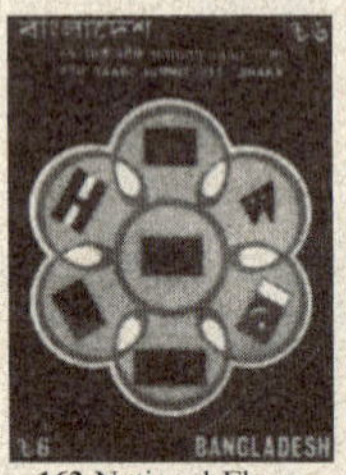

163 National Flags 164 Syed Abdus Samad

1992. 7th South Asian Association for Regional Co-operation Summit Conference, Dhaka. Mult.
462 6 t. Type **163** 60 60
463 10 t. S.A.A.R.C. emblem . . 80 90

1993. Syed Abdus Samad (footballer) Commem.
464 164 2 t. multicoloured 70 50

165 Haji Shariat Ullah

1993. Haji Shariat Ullah Commemoration.
465 165 2 t. multicoloured 50 40

166 People digging Canal

1993. Irrigation Canals Construction Project. Mult.
466 2 t. Type **166** 45 55
467 2 t. Completed canal and paddy-fields 45 55

167 Accident Prevention

1993. World Health Day. Multicoloured.
468 6 t. Type **167** . . . . 1·25 75
469 10 t. Satellite photograph and symbols of trauma (vert) . 1·50 1·75

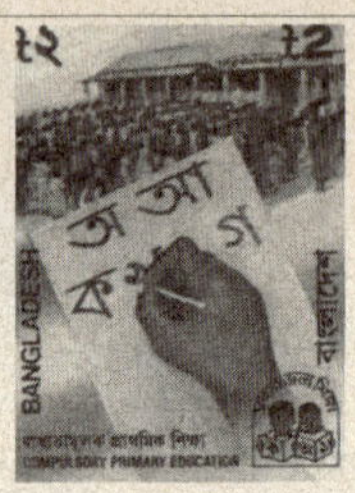

168 National Images 169 Schoolchildren and Bengali Script

1993. 1400th Year of Bengali Solar Calendar.
470 168 2 t. multicoloured 55 40

1993. Compulsory Primary Education. Mult.
471 2 t. Type **169** 40 50
472 2 t. Books and slate (horiz) . . 40 50

170 Nawab Sir Salimullah and Palace

1993. 122nd Birth Anniv of Nawab Sir Salimullah.
473 170 4 t. multicoloured 55 40

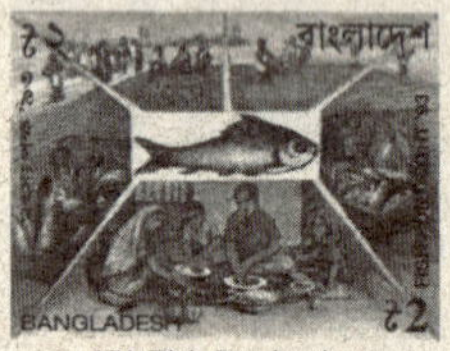

171 Fish Production

1993. Fish Fortnight.
474 171 2 t. multicoloured 30 30

172 Sunderban

1993. Natural Beauty of Bangladesh. Mult.
475 10 t. Type **172** 60 80
476 10 t. Kuakata beach 60 80
477 10 t. Madhabkunda waterfall (vert) 60 80
478 10 t. River Piyain, Jaflang (vert) 60 80

173 Exhibition Emblem 175 Burdwan House

174 Foy's Lake

1993. 6th Asian Art Biennale.
480 173 10 t. multicoloured 60 80

1993. Tourism Month.
481 174 10 t. multicoloured 70 80

1993. Foundation Day, Bangla Academy.
482 175 2 t. brown and green . . . 20 20

1993. Martyred Intellectuals (2nd series). As T **148**. Each black and brown.
483 2 t. Lt. Cdr. Moazzam Hussain 15 20
484 2 t. Muhammad Habibur Rahman 15 20
485 2 t. Khandoker Abu Taleb . . 15 20
486 2 t. Moshiur Rahman 15 20
487 2 t. Md Abdul Muktadir . . . 15 20
488 2 t. Nutan Chandra Sinha . . 15 20
489 2 t. Syed Nazmul Haque . . . 15 20
490 2 t. Dr. Mohammed Amin Uddin 15 20
491 2 t. Dr. Faizul Mohee 15 20
492 2 t. Sukha Ranjan Somaddar . 15 20

176 Throwing the Discus

1993. 6th South Asian Federation Games, Dhaka. Multicoloured.
493 2 t. Type **176** 15 15
494 4 t. Running (vert) 25 25

177 Tomb of Sultan Ghiyasuddin Azam Shah

1993. Muslim Monuments.
495 177 10 t. multicoloured . . . 60 70

178 Scouting Activities and Jamboree Emblem 179 Emblem and Mother giving Solution to Child

1994. 14th Asian-Pacific and 5th Bangladesh National Scout Jamboree.
496 178 2 t. multicoloured 30 30

1994. 25th Anniv of Oral Rehydration.
497 179 2 t. multicoloured 30 30

180 Interior of Chhota Sona Mosque, Nawabgonj

1994. Ancient Mosques. Multicoloured.
498 4 t. Type **180** 15 15
499 6 t. Exterior of Chhota Sona Mosque 30 40
500 6 t. Exterior of Baba Adam's Mosque, Munshigonj . . . 30 40

181 Agricultural Workers and Emblem

1994. 75th Anniv of I.L.O. Multicoloured.
501 4 t. Type **181** 15 15
502 10 t. Worker turning cog (vert) 60 85

182 Priest releasing Peace Doves 184 Family, Globe and Logo

183 Scenes from Baishakhi Festival

1994. 1500th Year of Bengali Solar Calendar.
503 **182** 2 t. multicoloured 15 15

1994. Folk Festivals. Multicoloured.
504 4 t. Type **183** 25 25
505 4 t. Scenes from Nabanna and Paush Parvana Festivals . . 25 25

1994. International Year of the Family.
506 **184** 10 t. multicoloured . . . 80 1·00

185 People planting Saplings

186 Player kicking Ball

1994. Tree Planting Campaign. Multicoloured.
507 4 t. Type **185** 25 15
508 6 t. Hands holding saplings . . 40 50

1994. World Cup Football Championship, U.S.A. Multicoloured.
509 20 t. Type **186** . . . . 1·50 2·00
510 20 t. Player heading ball . . . 1·50 2·00

187 Traffic on Bridge

1994. Inauguration of Jamuna Multi-purpose Bridge Project.
511 **187** 4 t. multicoloured 40 30

188 Asian Black-headed Oriole

190 Nawab Faizunnessa Chowdhurani

189 Dr. Mohammad Ibrahim and Hospital

1994. Birds. Multicoloured.
512 4 t. Type **188** 40 40
513 6 t. Greater racquet-tailed drongo 60 80
514 6 t. Indian tree pie 60 80
515 6 t. Red junglefowl 60 80

1994. 5th Death Anniv of Dr. Mohammad Ibrahim (diabetes treatment pioneer).
517 **189** 2 t. multicoloured 30 20

1994. 160th Birth Anniv of Nawab Faizunnessa Chowdhurani (social reformer).
518 **190** 2 t. muticoloured 20 20

191 Boxing

1994. Asian Games, Hiroshima, Japan.
519 **191** 4 t. multicoloured 50 30

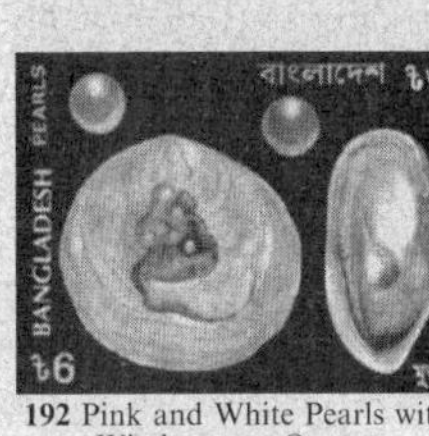

192 Pink and White Pearls with Windowpane Oysters

1994. Sea Shells. Multicoloured.
520 6 t. Type **192** 60 70
521 6 t. Tranquelous scallop and other shells 60 70
522 6 t. Lister's conch, Asiatic Arabian cowrie, bladder moon and woodcock murex . . . 60 70
523 6 t. Spotted tun, spiny frog shell, spiral melongena and gibbous olive (vert) 60 70

193 Dr. Milon and Demonstrators

1994. 4th Death Anniv of Dr. Shamsul Alam Khan Milon (medical reformer).
524 **193** 2 t. multicoloured 15 15

1994. Martyred Intellectuals (3rd series). As T **148**. Each black and brown.
525 2 t. Dr. Harinath Dey 15 15
526 2 t. Dr. A. F. Ziaur Rahman 15 15
527 2 t. Mamun Mahmud 15 15
528 2 t. Mohsin Ali Dewan . . . 15 15
529 2 t. Dr. N. A. M. Jahangir . . 15 15
530 2 t. Shah Abdul Majid . . . 15 15
531 2 t. Muhammad Akhter . . . 15 15
532 2 t. Meherunnesa 15 15
533 2 t. Dr. Kasiruddin Talukder 15 15
534 2 t. Fazlul Haque Choudhury 15 15
535 2 t. Md. Shamsuzzaman . . . 15 15
536 2 t. A. K. M. Shamsuddin . . 15 15
537 2 t. Lt. Mohammad Anwarul Azim 15 15
538 2 t. Nurul Amin Khan . . . 15 15
539 2 t. Mohammad Sadeque . . 15 15
540 2 t. Md. Araz Ali 15 15

194 "Diplazium esculentum"

1994. Vegetables. Multicoloured.
541 4 t. Type **194** 30 20
542 4 t. "Momordica charantia" . . 30 20
543 6 t. "Lagenaria siceraria" . . 50 40
544 6 t. "Trichosanthes dioica" . . 50 40
545 10 t. "Solanum melongena" . . 80 1·10
546 10 t. "Cucurbita maxima" (horiz) 80 1·10

195 Sonargaon

1995. 20th Anniv of World Tourism Organization.
547 **195** 10 t. multicoloured . . . 65 75

196 Exports

1995. Dhaka International Trade Fair '95. Mult.
548 4 t. Type **196** 20 20
549 6 t. Symbols of industry . . . 45 55

197 Soldiers of Ramgarh Battalion (1795) and of Bangladesh Rifles (1995)

1995. Bicentenary of Bangladesh Rifles. Mult.
550 2 t. Type **197** 15 15
551 4 t. Riflemen on patrol 25 30

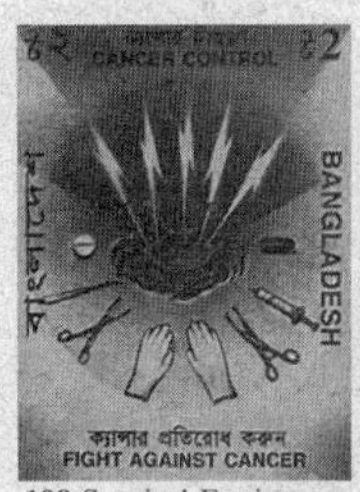

198 Surgical Equipment and Lightning attacking Crab (cancer)

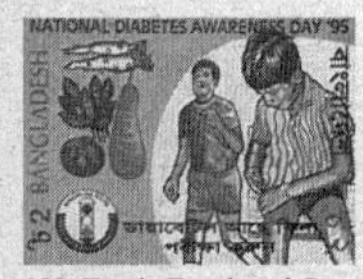

199 Fresh Food and Boy injecting Insulin

1995. Campaign against Cancer.
552 **198** 2 t. multicoloured 20 20

1995. National Diabetes Awareness Day.
553 **199** 2 t. multicoloured 20 20

200 Munshi Mohammad Meherullah

1995. Munshi Mohammad Meherullah (Islamic educator) Commemoration.
554 **200** 2 t. multicoloured 20 20

রাজশাহীপেক্স-৯৫
(**201**)

1995. "Rajshahipex '95" National Philatelic Exhibition. No. 499 optd with T **201**.
555 6 t. Exterior of Chhota Sona Mosque 60 60

202 "Lagerstroemia speciosa"

203 Aspects of Farming

1995. Flowers. Multicoloured.
556 6 t. Type **202** 50 50
557 6 t. "Bombax ceiba" (horiz) . . 50 50
558 10 t. "Passiflora incarnata" . . 75 75
559 10 t. "Bauhina purpurea" . . 75 75
560 10 t. "Canna indica" 75 75
561 10 t. "Gloriosa superba" . . . 75 75

1995. 50th Anniv of F.A.O.
562 **203** 10 t. multicoloured . . . 45 55

204 Anniversary Emblem, Peace Dove and U.N. Headquarters

1995. 50th Anniv of United Nations. Multicoloured.
563 2 t. Type **204** 15 15
564 10 t. Peace doves circling dates and Globe 65 75
565 10 t. Clasped hands and U.N. Headquarters 65 75

205 Diseased Lungs, Microscope, Family and Map

1995. 18th Eastern Regional Conference on Tuberculosis, Dhaka.
566 **205** 6 t. multicoloured 40 40

206 Peace Doves, Emblem and National Flags

1995. 10th Anniv of South Asian Association for Regional Co-operation.
567 **206** 2 t. multicoloured 15 15

1995. Martyred Intellectuals (4th series). As T **148**. Each black and brown.
568 2 t. Abdul Ahad 15 15
569 2 t. Lt. Col. Mohammad Qadir 15 15
570 2 t. Mozammel Hoque Chowdhury 15 15
571 2 t. Rafiqul Haider Chowdhury 15 15
572 2 t. Dr. Azharul Haque . . . 15 15
573 2 t. A. K. Shamsuddin . . . 15 15
574 2 t. Anudwaipayan Bhattacharjee 15 15
575 2 t. Lutfunnahar Helena . . . 15 15
576 2 t. Shaikh Habibur Rahman 15 15
577 2 t. Major Naimul Islam . . . 15 15
578 2 t. Md. Shahidullah 15 15
579 2 t. Ataur Rahman Khan Khadim 15 15
580 2 t. A. B. M. Ashraful Islam Bhuiyan 15 15
581 2 t. Dr. Md. Sadat Ali 15 15
582 2 t. Sarafat Ali 15 15
583 2 t. M. A. Sayeed 15 15

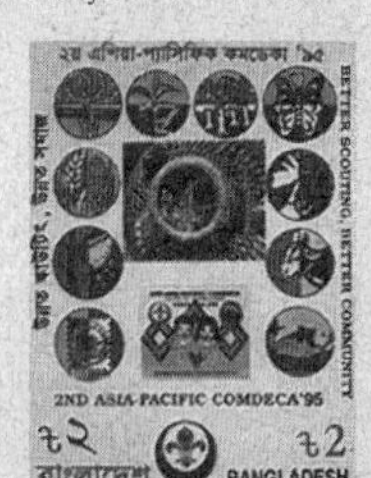

207 Aspects of COMDECA Projects

1995. 2nd Asia-Pacific Community Development Scout Camp.
584 **207** 2 t. multicoloured 15 15

208 Volleyball Players

1995. Centenary of Volleyball.
585 **208** 6 t. multicoloured 40 40

209 Man in Punjabi and Lungi

1995. Traditional Costumes. Multicoloured.
586 6 t. Type **209** 40 40
587 6 t. Woman in sari 40 40
588 10 t. Christian bride and groom 65 75
589 10 t. Muslim bride and groom 65 75
590 10 t. Buddhist bride and groom (horiz) 65 75
591 10 t. Hindu bride and groom (horiz) 65 75

210 Shaheed Amanullah Mohammad Asaduzzaman

1996. 27th Death Anniv of Shaheed Amanullah Mohammad Asaduzzaman (student leader).

592 **210** 2 t. multicoloured 20 20

211 Bowler and Map

1996. World Cup Cricket Championship. Multicoloured.

593 4 t. Type **211** 45 20
594 6 t. Batsman and wicket keeper 55 40
595 10 t. Match in progress (horiz) 95 1·10

212 Liberation Struggle, 1971

1996. 25th Anniv of Independence. Multicoloured.

596 4 t. Type **212** 15 20
597 4 t. National Martyrs Memorial 15 20
598 4 t. Education 15 20
599 4 t. Health 15 20
600 4 t. Communications 15 20
601 4 t. Industry 15 20

213 Michael Madhusudan Dutt

214 Gymnastics

1996. Michael Madhusudan Dutt (poet) Commemoration.

602 **213** 4 t. multicoloured 15 15

1996. Olympic Games, Atlanta. Multicoloured.

603 4 t. Type **214** 15 20
604 6 t. Judo 20 25
605 10 t. Athletics (horiz) 30 35
606 10 t. High jumping (horiz) . . 30 35

215 Bangabandhu Sheikh Mujibur Rahman

1996. 21st Death Anniv of Bangabandhu Sheikh Mujibur Rahman.

609 **215** 4 t. multicoloured 20 20

216 Maulana Mohammad Akrum Khan

1996. 28th Death Anniv of Maulana Mohammad Akrum Khan.

610 **216** 4 t. multicoloured 20 20

217 Ustad Alauddin Khan

1996. 24th Death Anniv of Ustad Alauddin Khan (musician).

611 **217** 4 t. multicoloured 20 20

218 "Kingfisher" (Mayeesha Robbani)

1996. Children's Paintings. Multicoloured.

612 2 t. Type **218** 15 10
613 4 t. "River Crossing" (Iffat Panchlais) (horiz) 15 20

219 Syed Nazrul Islam

1996. 21st Death Anniv of Jail Martyrs. Multicoloured.

614 4 t. Type **219** 15 20
615 4 t. Tajuddin Ahmad 15 20
616 4 t. M. Monsoor Ali 15 20
617 4 t. A. H. M. Quamaruzzaman 15 20

220 Children receiving Medicine

1996. 50th Anniv of U.N.I.C.E.F. Multicoloured.

618 4 t. Type **220** 25 20
619 10 t. Mother and child . . . 45 45

1996. Martyred Intellectuals (5th series). As T **148**. Each black and brown.

620 2 t. Dr. Jekrul Haque 15 15
621 2 t. Munshi Kabiruddin Ahmed 15 15
622 2 t. Md. Abdul Jabbar . . . 15 15
623 2 t. Mohammad Amir 15 15
624 2 t. A.K.M. Shamsul Huq Khan 15 15
625 2 t. Dr. Siddique Ahmed . . 15 15
626 2 t. Dr. Soleman Khan . . . 15 15
627 2 t. S.B.M. Mizanur Rahman 15 15
628 2 t. Aminuddin 15 15
629 2 t. Md. Nazrul Islam 15 15
630 2 t. Zahirul Islam 15 15
631 2 t. A.K. Lutfor Rahman . . 15 15
632 2 t. Afsar Hossain 15 15
633 2 t. Abul Hashem Mian . . . 15 15
634 2 t. A.T.M. Alamgir 15 15
635 2 t. Baser Ali 15 15

221 Celebrating Crowds

1996. 25th Anniv of Victory Day. Multicoloured.

636 4 t. Type **221** 15 20
637 6 t. Soldiers and statue (vert) . 20 25

222 Paul P. Harris

1997. 50th Death Anniv of Paul Harris (founder of Rotary International).

638 **222** 4 t. multicoloured 15 20

223 Shaikh Mujibur Rahman making Speech

1997. 25th Anniv of Shaikh Mujibur's Speech of 7 March (1996).

639 **223** 4 t. multicoloured 15 20

224 Sheikh Mujibur Rahman

226 Heinrich von Stephan

225 Sheikh Mujibur Rahman and Crowd with Banners

1997. 77th Birth Anniv of Sheikh Mujibur Rahman (first President).

640 **224** 4 t. multicoloured 30 20

1997. 25th Anniv (1996) of Independence.

641 **225** 4 t. multicoloured 15 20

1997. Death Centenary of Heinrich von Stephan (founder of U.P.U.).

642 **226** 4 t. multicoloured 15 20

227 Sheep

1997. Livestock. Multicoloured.

643 4 t. Type **227** 15 20
644 4 t. Goat 15 20
645 6 t. Buffalo bull 20 25
646 6 t. Cow 20 25

228 "Tilling the Field - 2" (S. Sultan)

1997. Bangladesh Paintings. Multicoloured.

647 6 t. Type **228** 20 25
648 10 t. "Three Women" (Quamrul Hassan) 30 35

229 Trophy, Flag and Cricket Ball

1997. 6th International Cricket Council Trophy Championship, Malaysia.

649 **229** 10 t. multicoloured . . . 55 55

230 Kusumba Mosque, Naogaon

1997. Historic Mosques. Multicoloured.

650 4 t. Type **230** 15 20
651 6 t. Atiya Mosque, Tangail . 20 25
652 10 t. Bagha Mosque, Rajshahi 30 35

231 Adul Karim Sahitya Vishard

232 Rover Moot Emblem and Scouts standing on top of World

1997. 126th Birth Anniv of Abdul Karim Sahitya Vishard (scholar).

653 **231** 4 t. multicoloured 15 20

1997. 9th Asia-Pacific and 7th Bangladesh Rover Moot, Lakkatura.

654 **232** 2 t. multicoloured 10 10

233 Officers and Flag

1997. 25th Anniv of Armed Forces.

655 **233** 2 t. multicoloured 10 10

1997. Martyred Intellectuals (6th series). As T **148**. Each black and brown.

656 2 t. Dr. Shamsuddin Ahmed . 10 10
657 2 t. Mohammad Salimullah . 10 10
658 2 t. Mohiuddin Haider . . . 10 10
659 2 t. Abdur Rahin 10 10
660 2 t. Nitya Nanda Paul . . . 10 10
661 2 t. Abdel Jabber 10 10
662 2 t. Dr. Humayun Kabir . . . 10 10
663 2 t. Khaja Nizamuddin Bhuiyan 10 10
664 2 t. Gulam Hossain 10 10
665 2 t. Ali Karim 10 10
666 2 t. Md. Moazzem Hossain . 10 10
667 2 t. Rafiqul Islam 10 10
668 2 t. M. Nur Husain 10 10
669 2 t. Captain Mahmood Hossain Akonda 10 10
670 2 t. Abdul Wahab Talukder . 10 10
671 2 t. Dr. Hasimoy Hazra . . . 10 10

234 Mohammad Mansooruddin

1998. Professor Mohammad Mansooruddin (folklorist) Commemoration.
672 **234** 4 t. multicoloured 15 20

235 Standard-bearer and Soldiers

1998. 50th Anniv of East Bengal Regiment.
673 **235** 2 t. multicoloured 10 10

236 Bulbul Chowdhury

1998. Bulbul Chowdhury (traditional dancer) Commemoration.
674 **236** 4 t. multicoloured 15 20

237 World Cup Trophy

1998. World Cup Football Championship, France. Multicoloured.
675 6 t. Type **237** 20 25
676 18 t. Footballer and trophy . . 60 65

238 Eastern Approach Road, Bangabandhu Bridge

1998. Opening of Bangabandhu Bridge. Mult.
677 4 t. Type **238** 15 20
678 6 t. Western approach road . 20 25
679 8 t. Embankment 30 35
680 10 t. Main span, Bangabandhu Bridge 30 35

239 Diana, Princess of Wales

1998. Diana, Princess of Wales Commemoration. Multicoloured.
681 8 t. Type **239** 30 35
682 18 t. Wearing pearl choker . . 60 65
683 22 t. Wearing pendant necklace 70 75

240 Means of collecting Solar Energy

1998. World Solar Energy Programme Summit.
684 **240** 10 t. multicoloured . . . 30 35

241 World Habitat Day Emblem and City Scene

1998. World Habitat Day.
685 **241** 4 t. multicoloured 15 20

242 Farmworkers, Sunflower and "20"

1998. 20th Anniv of International Fund for Agricultural Development. Multicoloured.
686 6 t. Type **242** 20 25
687 10 t. Farmworker with baskets and harvested crops 30 35

243 Batsman

1998. Wills International Cricket Cup, Dhaka.
688 **243** 6 t. multicoloured 20 25

244 Begum Rokeya

1998. Begum Rokeya (campaigner for women's education) Commemoration.
689 **244** 8 t. multicoloured 30 35

245 Anniversary Logo

1998. 50th Anniv of Universal Declaration of Human Rights.
690 **245** 10 t. multicoloured . . . 30 35

1998. Martyred Intellectuals (7th series). As T **148**. Each black and brown.
691 2 t. Md. Khorshed Ali Sarker 10 15
692 2 t. Abu Yakub Mahfuz Ali . 10 15
693 2 t. S.M. Nural Huda 10 15
694 2 t. Nazmul Hoque Sarker . . 10 15
695 2 t. Md. Taslim Uddin 10 15
696 2 t. Gulam Mostafa 10 15
697 2 t. A.H. Nural Alam 10 15
698 2 t. Timir Kanti Dev 10 15
699 2 t. Altaf Hossain 10 15
700 2 t. Aminul Hoque 10 15
701 2 t. S.M. Fazlul Hoque 10 15
702 2 t. Mozammel Ali 10 15
703 2 t. Syed Akbar Hossain . . . 10 15
704 2 t. Sk. Abdus Salam 10 15
705 2 t. Abdur Rahman 10 15
706 2 t. Dr. Shyamal Kanti Lala . 10 15

246 Dove of Peace and U.N. Symbols

1998. 50th Anniv of U.N. Peace-keeping Operations.
707 **246** 10 t. multicoloured 30 35

247 Kazi Nazrul Islam

1998. Birth Centenary (1999) of Kazi Nazrul Islam (poet).
708 **247** 6 t. multicoloured 20 25

248 Jamboree Emblem and Scout Activities

1999. 6th Bangladesh National Scout Jamboree.
709 **248** 2 t. multicoloured 10 10

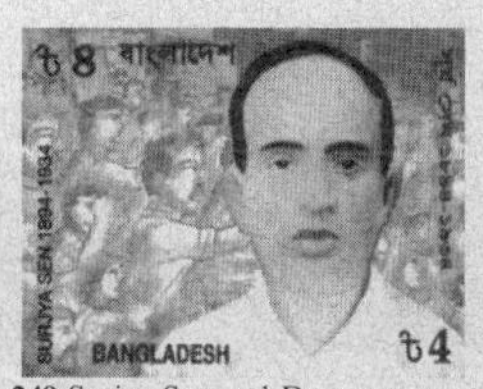

249 Surjya Sen and Demonstrators

1999. Surjya Sen (revolutionary) Commemoration.
710 **249** 4 t. multicoloured 15 20

250 Dr. Fazlur Rahman Khan and Sears Tower

1999. 70th Birth Anniv of Dr. Fazlur Rahman Khan (architect).
711 **250** 4 t. multicoloured 15 20

OFFICIAL STAMPS

1973. Nos. 22, etc. optd **SERVICE.**
O 1 **7** 2 p. black 10 60
O 2 – 3 p. green 10 60
O 3 – 5 p. brown 20 10
O 4 – 10 p. black 20 10
O 5 – 20 p. green . . . . 1·25 10
O 6 – 25 p. mauve . . . . 3·25 10
O 7 – 60 p. grey . . . . 3·25 1·50
O 8 – 75 p. orange . . . . 1·25 30
O 9 **8** 1 t. violet . . . . 11·00 4·25
O10 – 5 t. blue . . . . 5·00 7·50

1974. Nos. 49/51 optd **SERVICE.**
O11 **14** 1 t. violet . . . . 4·00 30
O12 – 2 t. olive . . . . 5·00 1·75
O13 – 5 t. blue . . . . 10·00 8·00

1976. Nos. 64/70 and 72/4 optd **SERVICE.**
O14 – 5 p. green . . . . 1·00 30
O15 – 10 p. black . . . . 1·50 30
O16 – 20 p. green . . . . 1·75 30
O17 – 25 p. mauve . . . . 3·00 30
O18 – 50 p. purple . . . . 3·00 30
O19 – 60 p. grey . . . . 30 1·50
O20 – 75 p. olive . . . . 30 2·00
O21 **14** 1 t. blue . . . . 2·50 40
O22 – 2 t. green . . . . 35 1·25
O23 – 5 t. blue . . . . 30 1·25

1981. Nos. 125/9 and 131/17 optd **SERVICE.**
O24 – 5 p. brown . . . . 90 1·25
O25 **32** 10 p. blue . . . . 90 1·25
O26 – 15 p. orange . . . . 1·00 1·50
O27 – 20 p. red . . . . 80 1·00
O28 – 25 p. blue . . . . 80 1·75
O29 – 30 p. green . . . . 2·00 1·75
O30 – 40 p. purple . . . . 2·00 15
O31 – 50 p. black 30 10
O32 – 80 p. brown 70 15
O33 – 1 t. violet 30 10
O34 – 2 t. blue . . . . 35 1·75

1983. Nos. 220/9 and 318a/19 optd **Service.**
O35 **69** 5 p. blue 10 10
O36 – 10 p. purple 10 10
O37 – 15 p. blue 10 10
O38 – 20 p. black 10 10
O39 – 25 p. grey 10 10
O40 – 30 p. brown 10 10
O41 – 50 p. brown 10 10
O42 – 1 t. blue 75 10
O43 – 2 t. green 75 10
O44 – 3 t. black and blue 10 10
O45 – 4 t. blue 15 20
O46 – 5 t. purple 15 20

সার্ভিস (O 5) সার্ভিস (O **6**)

1989. Nos. 227 and 319 optd with Type O **5**.
O47 1 t. blue 10 10
O48 5 t. black and brown 15 20

1990. Nos. 368/9 (Immunization) optd with Type O **6**.
O49 **133** 1 t. green 10 10
O50 2 t. brown 10 10

1992. No. 376 optd as Type O **6** but horiz.
O51 **136** 6 t. blue and yellow . . 20 25

1995. No. 553 (National Diabetes Awareness Day) optd as Type O **6** but horiz.
O52 **199** 2 t. multicoloured . . . 15 15

BARBADOS

An island in the Br. West Indies, E. of the Windward Islands, attained self-government on 16th October, 1961 and achieved independence within the Commonwealth on 30 November 1966.

1852. 12 pence = 1 shilling;
20 shillings = 1 pound.
1950. 100 cents = 1 West Indian, later Barbados, dollar.

1 Britannia 2

1852. Imperf.

8	1	(½d.) green	90·00	£200
10		(1d.) blue	22·00	55·00
4a		(2d.) slate	£200	£1100
5		(4d.) red	65·00	£250
11	2	6d. red	£700	£110
12a		1s. black	£170	70·00

1860. Perf.

21	1	(½d.) green	11·00	8·50
24		(1d.) blue	23·00	3·00
25		(4d.) red	65·00	28·00
31	2	6d. red	60·00	16·00
33		6d. orange	80·00	24·00
35		1s. black	40·00	6·00

1873. Perf.

72	2	½d. green	7·00	50
74		1d. blue	40·00	30
63		3d. brown	£325	£110
75		3d. mauve	80·00	4·50
76		4d. red	80·00	7·00
79		6d. yellow	90·00	1·00
81		1s. purple	£100	2·75

3 4

1873.

64	3	5s. red	£950	£300

1878. Half of No. 64 surch **1D.**

86	3	1d. on half 5s. red	£3500	£600

1882.

90	4	½d. green	10·00	1·00
92		1d. red	10·00	50
93		2½d. blue	70·00	1·00
96		3d. purple	3·50	12·00
97		4d. grey	£190	2·25
99		4d. brown	4·00	1·00
100		6d. brown	65·00	32·00
102		1s. brown	24·00	21·00
103		5s. bistre	£140	£180

1892. Surch **HALF-PENNY.**

104	4	½d. on 4d. brown	1·60	2·75

6 Seal of Colony 7

1892.

105	6	½d. grey and red	2·00	10
163		½d. brown	2·50	30
106		½d. green	1·50	10
107		1d. red	3·50	10
108		2d. black and orange	7·00	65
166		2d. grey	6·00	9·50
139		2½d. blue	6·50	15
110		5d. olive	6·00	4·50
111		6d. mauve and red	9·00	2·00
168		6d. deep purple and purple	8·00	14·00
112		8d. orange and blue	3·25	18·00
113		10d. green and red	7·00	6·50
169		1s. black on green	8·50	14·00
114		2s. 6d. black and orange	45·00	48·00
144		2s. 6d. violet and green	32·00	75·00

1897. Diamond Jubilee.

116	7	½d. grey and red	2·50	50
117		½d. green	2·50	50
118		1d. red	2·50	50
119		2½d. blue	5·50	75
120		5d. brown	13·00	13·00
121		6d. mauve and red	17·00	18·00
122		8d. orange and blue	6·50	20·00
123		10d. green and red	45·00	50·00
124		2s. 6d. black and orange	48·00	50·00

8 Nelson Monument 9 "Olive Blossom", 1650

1906. Death Centenary of Nelson.

145	8	¼d. black and grey	6·00	1·50
146		½d. black and green	8·50	15
147		1d. black and red	9·50	15
148		2d. black and yellow	1·75	4·50
149		2½d. black and blue	3·75	1·25
150		6d. black and mauve	18·00	25·00
151		1s. black and red	19·00	45·00

1906. Tercentenary of Annexation of Barbados.

152	9	1d. black, blue and green	10·00	25

1907. Surch **Kingston Relief Fund. 1d.**

153	6	1d. on 2d. black and orange	1·75	4·25

11 14

1912.

170a	11	¼d. brown	65	2·00
171		½d. green	2·75	10
172		1d. red	5·50	10
173		2d. grey	2·00	12·00
174		2½d. blue	1·25	30
175		3d. purple on yellow	1·25	11·00
176		4d. red and black on yellow	1·25	15·00
177		6d. deep purple and purple	9·50	11·00

Larger type, with portrait at top centre.

178		1s. black on green	7·00	9·00
179		2s. blue and purple on blue	38·00	40·00
180		3s. violet and green	70·00	80·00

1916.

181	14	¼d. brown	75	40
182		½d. green	1·10	15
183a		1d. red	2·50	15
184		2d. grey	3·50	15·00
185		2½d. blue	2·50	1·50
186		3d. purple on yellow	1·75	4·50
187		4d. red on yellow	70	14·00
199		4d. black and red	80	3·50
188		6d. purple	2·50	3·50
189		1s. black on green	7·00	7·00
190		2s. purple on blue	16·00	7·50
191		3s. violet	45·00	85·00
200		3s. green and violet	16·00	48·00

1917. Optd **WAR TAX.**

197	11	1d. red	15	15

16 18

1920. Victory. Inscr "VICTORY 1919".

201	16	¼d. black and brown	30	70
202		½d. black and green	90	15
203		1d. black and red	2·75	10
204		2d. black and grey	2·00	6·50
205		2½d. indigo and blue	2·75	10·00
206		3d. black and purple	2·75	5·00
207		4d. black and green	2·75	5·50
208		6d. black and orange	3·50	10·00
209	–	1s. black and green	9·00	22·00
210	–	2s. black and brown	21·00	28·00
211	–	3s. black and orange	24·00	35·00

The 1s. to 3s. show Victory full-face.

1921.

217	18	¼d. brown	15	10
219		½d. green	80	10
220		1d. red	80	10
221		2d. grey	1·60	20
222		2½d. blue	1·50	5·50
213		3d. purple on yellow	2·00	6·00
214		4d. red on yellow	1·75	12·00
225		6d. purple	3·50	5·50
215		1s. black on green	4·50	11·00
227		2s. purple on blue	10·00	19·00
228		3s. violet	13·00	45·00

19 21 Badge of the Colony

20 King Charles I and King George V

1925. Inscr "POSTAGE & REVENUE".

229	19	¼d. brown	15	10
230		½d. green	30	10
231		1d. red	50	10
231ba		1½d. orange	2·00	1·00
232		2d. grey	50	2·75
233		2½d. blue	50	80
234		3d. purple on yellow	60	45
235		4d. red on yellow	75	95
236		6d. purple	75	50
237		1s. black on green	1·50	5·50
238		2s. purple on blue	7·00	6·50
238a		2s. 6d. red on blue	22·00	24·00
239		3s. violet	11·00	13·00

1927. Tercentenary of Settlement of Barbados.

240	20	1d. red	75	60

1935. Silver Jubilee. As T **13** of Antigua.

241		1d. blue and red	30	20
242		1½d. blue and grey	3·00	5·00
243		2½d. brown and blue	2·25	3·25
244		1s. grey and purple	15·00	16·00

1937. Coronation. As T **2** of Aden.

245		1d. red	30	15
246		1½d. brown	40	45
247		2½d. blue	70	45

1938. "POSTAGE & REVENUE" omitted.

248	21	½d. green	6·00	15
248c		½d. bistre	15	30
249a		1d. red	16·00	10
249c		1d. green	15	10
250		1½d. orange	15	40
250c		2d. purple	40	1·75
250d		2d. red	15	40
251		2½d. blue	50	40
252b		3d. brown	20	40
252c		3d. blue	20	1·25
253		4d. black	20	10
254		6d. violet	80	10
254a		8d. mauve	55	1·75
255a		1s. green	1·00	10
256		2s. 6d. purple	6·50	1·50
256a		5s. blue	3·25	5·50

22 Kings Charles I, George VI, Assembly Chamber and Mace

1939. Tercentenary of General Assembly.

257	22	½d. green	2·00	30
258		1d. red	2·00	30
259		1½d. orange	2·00	60
260		2½d. blue	2·00	3·25
261		3d. brown	2·00	2·25

1946. Victory. As T **9** of Aden.

262		1½d. orange	15	15
263		3d. brown	15	15

1947. Surch **ONE PENNY.**

264	17	1d. on 2d. red	1·00	2·00

1948. Silver Wedding. As T **10/11** of Aden.

265		1½d. orange	30	10
266		5s. blue	9·50	6·00

1949. U.P.U. As T **20/23** of Antigua.

267		1½d. orange	30	35
268		3d. blue	1·50	1·25
269		4d. grey	35	1·75
270		1s. olive	35	60

24 Dover Fort

35 Seal of Barbados

1950.

271	24	1 c. blue	15	2·00
272	–	2 c. green	15	1·50
273	–	3 c. brown and green	75	2·00
274	–	4 c. red	15	30
275	–	6 c. blue	15	1·75
276	–	8 c. blue and purple	65	1·50
277	–	12 c. blue and olive	90	90
278	–	24 c. red and black	90	30
279	–	48 c. violet	8·00	5·00
280	–	60 c. green and lake	6·00	7·50
281	–	$1.20 red and olive	8·50	3·25
282	35	$2.40 black	15·00	12·00

DESIGNS—As Type **24**: HORIZ: 2 c. Sugar cane breeding; 3 c. Public buildings; 6 c. Casting net; 8 c. "Frances W. Smith" (schooner); 12 c. Four-winged flyingfish; 24 c. Old Main Guard Garrison; 60 c. Careenage. VERT: 4 c. Statue of Nelson; 48 c. St. Michael's Cathedral; $1.20, Map and wireless mast.

1951. Inauguration of B.W.I. University College. As T **24/25** of Antigua.

283		3 c. brown and blue	30	30
284		12 c. blue and olive	55	1·10

36 King George VI and Stamp of 1852

1952. Centenary of Barbados Stamps.

285	36	3 c. green and slate	15	40
286		4 c. blue and red	15	90
287		12 c. slate and green	15	90
288		24 c. brown and sepia	15	40

37 Harbour Police

1953. As 1950 issue but with portrait or cypher (No. 301) of Queen Elizabeth II as in T **37**.

289	24	1 c. blue	10	70
290	–	2 c. orange and turquoise	15	40
291	–	3 c. black and green	1·00	50
292	–	4 c. black and orange	20	20
293	37	5 c. blue and red	90	40
294	–	6 c. brown	50	40
314	–	8 c. black and blue	60	35
296	–	12 c. blue and olive	1·00	10
297	–	24 c. red and black	45	10
298	–	48 c. violet	5·00	1·00
318	–	60 c. green and purple	12·00	4·00
300	–	$1.20 red and olive	19·00	2·50
319	35	$2.40 black	1·75	2·25

1953. Coronation. As T **13** of Aden.

302		4 c. black and orange	40	10

1958. British Caribbean Federation. As T **28** of Antigua.

303		3 c. green	45	20
304		6 c. blue	60	2·00
305		12 c. red	60	30

38 Deep Water Harbour, Bridgetown

1961. Opening of Deep Water Harbour.

306	38	4 c. black and orange	25	40
307		8 c. black and blue	25	50
308		24 c. red and black	25	50

39 Scout Badge and Map of Barbados

1962. Golden Jubilee of Barbados Boy Scout Association.

309	39	4 c. black and orange	40	10
310		12 c. blue and brown	80	15
311		$1.20 red and green	1·25	3·00

1965. Centenary of I.T.U. As T **36** of Antigua.

320		2 c. lilac and red	20	40
321		48 c. yellow and drab	70	1·50

40 Deep Sea Coral

1965.

342	40	1 c. black, pink and blue	10	20
323	–	2 c. brown, yell and mve	20	15
324	–	3 c. brown and orange	45	60
344	–	3 c. brown and orange	30	2·00

325	– 4 c. blue and green	15	10
326	– 5 c. sepia, red and lilac	30	20
327	– 6 c. multicoloured	45	20
328	– 8 c. multicoloured	25	10
329	– 12 c. multicoloured	35	10
330	– 15 c. black, yellow and red	80	80
331	– 25 c. blue and ochre	95	75
332	– 35 c. red and green	1·50	15
333	– 50 c. blue and green	2·00	40
334	– $1 multicoloured	2·75	1·25
335	– $2.50 multicoloured	2·75	1·75
355a	– $5 multicoloured	12·00	7·00

DESIGNS:—Horiz: 2 c. Lobster; 3 c. (No. 324) Lined seahorse (wrongly inscribed "Hippocanpus"); 3 c. (No. 344) (correctly inscribed "Hippocampus"); 4 c. Sea urchin; 5 c. Staghorn coral; 6 c. Spot-finned butterflyfish; 8 c. Rough file shell; 12 c. Porcupinefish ("Balloon fish"); 15 c. Grey angelfish; 25 c. Brain coral; 35 c. Brittle star; 50 c. Four-winged flyingfish; $1 Queen or pink conch shell; $2.50, Fiddler crab. VERT: $5 Dolphin.

1966. Churchill Commemoration. As T **38** of Antigua.

336	1 c. blue	10	1·50
337	4 c. green	30	10
338	25 c. brown	70	50
339	35 c. violet	80	60

1966. Royal Visit. As T **39** of Antigua.

340	3 c. black and blue	50	25
341	35 c. black and mauve	1·75	80

54 Arms of Barbados

58 Policeman and Anchor

1966. Independence. Multicoloured.

356	4 c. Type **54**	10	10
357	25 c. Hilton Hotel (horiz)	15	10
358	35 c. G. Sobers (Test cricketer)	1·50	55
359	50 c. Pine Hill Dairy (horiz)	70	75

1967. 20th Anniv of U.N.E.S.C.O. As T **54/56** of Antigua.

360	4 c. multicoloured	30	10
361	12 c. yellow, violet and olive	70	65
362	25 c. black, purple and orange	1·00	1·50

1967. Centenary of Harbour Police. Multicoloured.

363	4 c. Type **58**	25	10
364	25 c. Policeman and telescope	40	15
365	35 c. "BPI" (police launch) (horiz)	45	15
366	50 c. Policeman outside H.Q.	60	1·25

62 Governor-General Sir Winston Scott G.C.M.G

67 Radar Antenna

66 U.N. Building, Santiago, Chile

1967. 1st Anniv of Independence. Multicoloured.

367	4 c. Type **62**	10	10
368	25 c. Independence Arch	20	10
369	35 c. Treasury Building	25	10
370	50 c. Parliament Building	35	60

Nos. 368/70 are horizontal.

1968. 20th Anniv of Economic Commission for Latin America.

371	**66** 15 c. multicoloured	10	10

1968. World Meteorological Day. Multicoloured.

372	3 c. Type **67**	10	10
373	25 c. Meteorological Institute (horiz)	25	10
374	50 c. Harp Gun and Coat of Arms	30	70

70 Lady Baden-Powell and Guide at Campfire

1968. Golden Jubilee of Girl Guiding in Barbados.

375	**70** 3 c. blue, black and gold	25	50
376	– 25 c. blue, black and gold	50	50
377	– 35 c. yellow, black and gold	65	50

DESIGNS: 25 c. Lady Baden-Powell and Pax Hill; 35 c. Lady Baden-Powell and Guides' Badge.

73 Hands breaking Chain, and Human Rights Emblem

1968. Human Rights Year.

378	**73** 4 c. violet, brown and green	10	15
379	– 25 c. black, blue and yellow	10	20
380	– 35 c. multicoloured	15	20

DESIGNS: 25 c. Human Rights emblem and family enchained; 35 c. Shadows of refugees beyond opening fence.

76 Racehorses in the Paddock

1969. Horse Racing. Multicoloured.

381	4 c. Type **76**	20	15
382	25 c. Starting-gate	25	15
383	35 c. On the flat	25	15
384	50 c. The Winning-post	35	1·75

80 Map showing "CARIFTA" Countries

1969. 1st Anniv of "CARIFTA". Multicoloured.

386	5 c. Type **80**	10	10
387	12 c. "Strength in Unity" (horiz)	10	10
388	25 c. Type **80**	10	10
389	50 c. As 12 c.	15	20

82 I.L.O. Emblem and "1919–1969"

1969. 50th Anniv of I.L.O.

390	**82** 4 c. black, green and blue	10	10
391	25 c. black, mauve and red	20	10

1969. No. 363 surch **ONE CENT**.

392	**58** 1 c. on 4 c. multicoloured	10	10

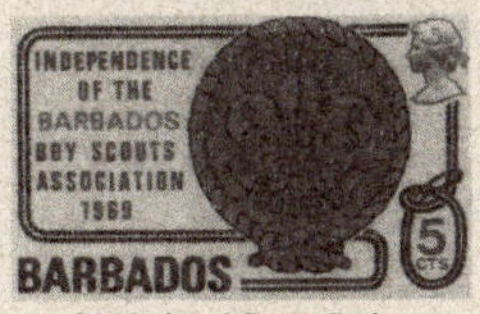

84 National Scout Badge

1969. Independence of Barbados Boy Scouts Association and 50th Anniv of Barbados Sea Scouts. Multicoloured.

393	5 c. Type **84**	15	10
394	25 c. Sea Scouts rowing	45	10
395	35 c. Scouts around campfire	55	10
396	50 c. Scouts and National Scout H.Q.	80	90

1970. No. 346 surch **4**.

398	4 c. on 5 c. sepia, red and lilac	10	10

89 Lion at Gun Hill

1970. Multicoloured.

399	1 c. Type **89**	10	50
400	2 c. Trafalgar Fountain	30	60
401	3 c. Montefiore Drinking Fountain	10	60
402a	4 c. St. James' Monument	10	10
403	5 c. St. Ann's Fort	10	10
404	6 c. Old Sugar Mill, Morgan Lewis	35	2·50
405	8 c. The Cenotaph	10	10
406a	10 c. South Point Lighthouse	85	15
407	12 c. Barbados Museum	60	10
408	15 c. Sharon Moravian Church	30	15
409	25 c. George Washington House	25	15
410	35 c. Nicholas Abbey	30	85
411	50 c. Bowmanston Pumping Station	40	95
412	$1 Queen Elizabeth Hospital	70	2·50
413	$2.50 Suger Factory	1·50	4·00
467	$5 Seawell International Airport	4·00	5·50

The 12 c. to $5 are horiz.

105 Primary Schoolgirl

1970. 25th Anniv of U.N. Multicoloured.

415	4 c. Type **105**	10	10
416	5 c. Secondary schoolboy	10	10
417	25 c. Technical student	35	10
418	50 c. University building	55	1·25

106 Minnie Root

1970. Flowers of Barbados. Multicoloured.

419	1 c. Barbados Easter lily	10	1·50
420	5 c. Type **106**	40	10
421	10 c. Eyelash orchid	1·75	20
422	25 c. Pride of Barbados	1·25	75
423	35 c. Christmas hope	1·25	85

The 1 c. and 25 c. are vertical.

107 "Via Dolorosa" Window, St. Margaret's Church, St. John

109 S. J. Prescod (politician)

108 "Sailfish" Craft

1971. Easter. Multicoloured.

425	4 c. Type **107**	10	10
426	10 c. "The Resurrection" (Benjamin West)	10	10
427	35 c. Type **107**	15	10
428	50c. As 10 c.	30	1·25

1971. Tourism. Multicoloured.

429	1 c. Type **108**	10	20
430	5 c. Tennis	30	10
431	12 c. Horse-riding	40	10
432	25 c. Water-skiing	40	20
433	50 c. Scuba-diving	50	80

1971. Death Centenary of Samuel Jackman Prescod.

434	**109** 3 c. multicoloured	10	15
435	35 c. multicoloured	15	15

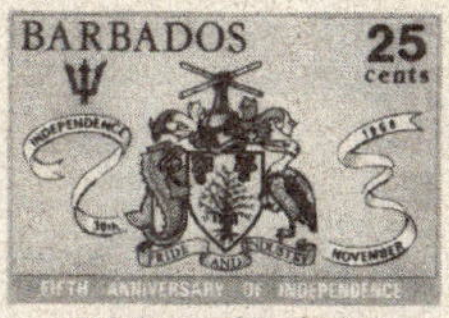

110 Arms of Barbados

1971. 5th Anniv of Independence. Multicoloured.

436	4 c. Type **110**	20	10
437	15 c. National flag and map	45	10
438	25 c. Type **110**	45	10
439	50 c. As 15 c.	90	1·25

111 Transmitting "Then and Now"

1972. Centenary of Cable Link. Mult.

440	4 c. Type **111**	10	10
441	10 c. Cable Ship "Stanley Angwin"	15	10
442	35 c. Barbados Earth Station and "Intelsat 4"	35	20
443	50 c. Mt. Misery and Tropospheric Scatter Station	50	1·10

112 Map and Badge

1972. Diamond Jubilee of Scouts. Multicoloured.

444	5 c. Type **112**	10	10
445	15 c. Pioneers of scouting	15	10
446	25 c. Scouts	30	15
447	50 c. Flags	50	75

Nos. 445/7 are horiz.

113 Mobile Library

1972. Int Book Year. Multicoloured.

448	4 c. Type **113**	20	10
449	15 c. Visual-aids van	25	10
450	25 c. Public library	30	10
451	$1 Codrington College	1·25	1·50

114 Potter's Wheel

1973. Pottery in Barbados. Multicoloured.

468	5 c. Type **114**	10	10
469	15 c. Kilns	20	10
470	25 c. Finished products	25	10
471	$1 Market scene	90	1·10

115 First Flight, 1911

1973. Aviation.

472	**115** 5 c. multicoloured	30	10
473	– 15 c. multicoloured	90	10
474	– 25 c. blue, blk & cobalt	1·25	20
475	– 50 c. multicoloured	2·00	1·90

DESIGNS: 15 c. De Havilland Cirrus Moth on first flight to Barbados, 1928; 25 c. Lockheed Super Electra, 1939; 50 c. Vickers Super VC-10 airliner, 1973.

116 University Chancellor

1973. 25th Anniv of University of West Indies. Multicoloured.

476	5 c. Type **116**	10	10
477	25 c. Sherlock Hall	25	15
478	35 c. Cave Hill Campus	30	25

1974. No. 462 surch **4c.**

479	4 c. on 25 c. multicoloured	15	15

118 Old Sail Boat

1974. Fishing Boats of Barbados. Multicoloured.
480 15 c. Type **118** 30 15
481 35 c. Rowing-boat 55 25
482 50 c. Motor fishing-boat 70 70
483 $1 "Calamar" (fishing boat) . 1·10 1·40

119 "Cattleya gaskelliana alba"

1974. Orchids. Multicoloured.
510 1 c. Type **119** . . . . 15 1·00
511 2 c. "Renanthera storiei" . . 15 1·00
512 3 c. "Dendrobium" "Rose Marie" . . . . 15 1·00
488 4 c. "Epidendrum ibaguense" 1·75 90
514 5 c. "Schomburgkia humboldtii" 35 15
490 8 c. "Oncidium ampliatum" . 1·00 90
515 10 c. "Arachnis maggie oei" . 35 10
492 12 c. "Dendrobium aggregatum" . . . . . . 45 1·75
517 15 c. "Paphiopedilum puddle" 70 15
493b 20 c. "Spathoglottis" "The Gold" . . . . 4·75 4·75
518 25 c. "Epidendrum ciliare" (Eyelash) 70 10
550 35 c. "Bletia patula" . . . . 2·00 1·75
519 45 c. "Phalaenopsis schilleriana" "Sunset Glow" 60 15
496 50 c. As 45 c. . . . . 4·50 3·50
497 $1 "Ascocenda" "Red Gem" 5·50 3·25
498 $2.50 "Brassolaeliocattleya" "Nugget" . . . . 3·50 5·50
499 $5 "Caularthron bicornutum" 3·50 6·00
500 $10 "Vanda" "Josephine Black" . . . . 4·00 13·00
The 1, 20, 25 c., $2.50 and $5 are horiz, the rest are vert.

120 4d. Stamp of 1882, and U.P.U. Emblem

1974. Centenary of Universal Postal Union.
501 **120** 8 c. mauve, orange & grn . 10 10
502 – 35 c. red, orge & brown . 20 10
503 – 50 c. ultram, bl & silver . 25 30
504 – $1 blue, brown & black . 55 80
DESIGNS: 35 c. Letters encircling the globe; 50 c. U.P.U. emblem and arms of Barbados; $1 Map of Barbados, sailing ship and Boeing 747 airliner.

121 Royal Yacht "Britannia"

1975. Royal Visit. Multicoloured.
506 8 c. Type **121** 55 20
507 25 c. Type **121** 90 30
508 35 c. Sunset and palms 60 35
509 $1 As 35 c. . . . . 1·75 2·50

122 St. Michael's Cathedral

1975. 150th Anniv of Anglican Diocese. Mult.
526 5 c. Type **122** 10 10
527 15 c. Bishop Coleridge 15 10
528 50 c. All Saints' Church . . . 45 50
529 $1 "Archangel Michael and Satan" (stained glass window, St. Michael's Cathedral, Bridgetown) 70 80

123 Pony Float

1975. Crop-over Festival. Multicoloured.
531 8 c. Type **123** 10 10
532 25 c. Man on stilts 10 10
533 35 c. Maypole dancing . . . 15 10
534 50 c. Cuban dancers 30 45

124 Barbados Coat of Arms

125 17th-Century Sailing Ship

1975. Coil Definitives.
536 **124** 5 c. blue 15 80
537 25 c. violet . . . . 25 1·10

1975. 350th Anniv of First Settlement. Multicoloured.
538 4 c. Type **125** 50 10
539 10 c. Bearded fig tree and fruit 40 15
540 25 c. Ogilvy's 17th-century map 1·00 30
541 $1 Captain John Powell . . . 2·00 5·00

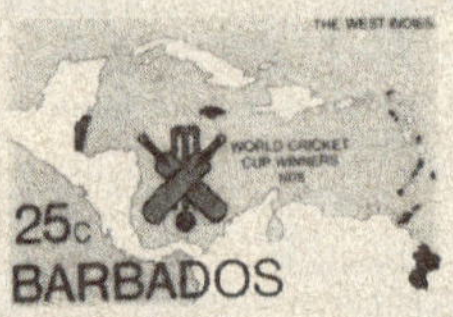
126 Map of Caribbean

1976. West Indian Victory in World Cricket Cup.
559 **126** 25 c. multicoloured . . . 1·25 1·00
560 – 45 c. black and purple . . 1·25 2·00
DESIGN—VERT: 45 c. The Prudential Cup.

127 Flag and Map of South Carolina

1976. Bicentenary of American Revolution. Mult.
561 15 c. Type **127** 55 15
562 25 c. George Washington and map of Bridgetown 55 15
563 50 c. Independence Declaration 70 1·00
564 $1 Prince Hall . . . . 1·00 3·00

128 Early Postman

1976. 125th Anniv of Post Office Act. Multicoloured.
565 8 c. Type **128** 10 10
566 35 c. Modern postman 25 10
567 50 c. Early letter 30 50
568 $1 Delivery van . . . . . . 50 1·40

129 Coast Guard Launches

1976. 10th Anniv of Independence. Multicoloured.
569 5 c. Type **129** 25 10
570 15 c. Reverse of currency note 25 10
571 25 c. Barbados national anthem 25 20
572 $1 Independence Day parade 90 2·25

130 Arrival of Coronation Coach at Westminster Abbey

132 Maces of the House of Commons

131 Underwater Park

1977. Silver Jubilee. Multicoloured.
574 15 c. Queen knighting Garfield Sobers 1975 . . . . 30 25
575 50 c. Type **130** 30 40
576 $1 Queen entering Abbey . . . 30 70

1977. Natural Beauty of Barbados. Multicoloured.
577 5 c. Type **131** 15 10
578 35 c. Royal palms (vert) . . . 30 10
579 50 c. Underwater caves 40 50
580 $1 Stalagmite in Harrison's Cave (vert) . . . . 70 1·10

1977. 13th Regional Conference of Commonwealth Parliamentary Association.
582 **132** 10 c. orange, yellow & brn 10 10
583 – 25 c. green, orge & dp grn 10 10
584 – 50 c. multicoloured 20 20
585 – $1 blue, orange and dp bl . 55 75
DESIGNS—VERT: 25 c. Speaker's Chair. 50 c. Senate Chamber. HORIZ: $1 Sam Lord's Castle.

133 The Charter Scroll

135 Brown Pelican

134 Gibson's Map of Bridgtown, 1766

1977. 350th Anniv of Granting of Charter to Earl of Carlisle. Multicoloured.
586 12 c. Type **133** 15 10
587 25 c. The earl receiving charter 15 10
588 45 c. The earl and Charles I (horiz) 30 35
589 $1 Ligon's map, 1657 (horiz) . 50 1·00

1977. Royal Visit. As Nos. 574/6 but inscr "SILVER JUBILEE ROYAL VISIT".
590 15 c. Garfield Sobers being knighted, 1975 . . . . 30 40
591 50 c. Type **130** 35 60
592 $1 Queen entering Abbey . . . 45 1·00

1978. 350th Anniv of Founding of Bridgetown.
593 **134** 12 c. multicoloured 15 10
594 – 25 c. black, green & gold . 20 10
595 – 45 c. multicoloured 25 15
596 – $1 multicoloured 40 60
DESIGNS: 25 c. "A Prospect of Bridgetown in Barbados" (engraving by S. Copens, 1695); 45 c. "Trafalgar Square, Bridgetown" (drawing by J. M. Carter, 1835); $1 The Bridges, 1978.

1978. 25th Anniv of Coronation.
597 – 50 c. olive, black & blue . 25 50
598 – 50 c. multicoloured 25 50
599 **135** 50 c. olive, black & blue . 25 50
DESIGNS: No. 597, Griffin of Edward III. No. 598, Queen Elizabeth II.

136 Barbados Bridge League Logo

1978. 7th Regional Bridge Tournament, Barbados. Multicoloured.
600 5 c. Type **136** 10 10
601 10 c. Emblem of World Bridge Federation 15 10
602 45 c. Central American and Caribbean Bridge Federation emblem 25 10
603 $1 Playing cards on map of Caribbean 40 60

137 Camp Scene

1978. Diamond Jubilee of Guiding. Multicoloured.
605 12 c. Type **137** 25 15
606 28 c. Community work 40 15
607 50 c. Badge and "60" (vert) . 55 30
608 $1 Guide badge (vert) . . . . 75 1·00

138 Garment Industry

1978. Industries of Barbados. Multicoloured.
609 12 c. Type **138** 15 10
610 28 c. Cooper (vert) 25 25
611 45 c. Blacksmith (vert) 35 80
612 50 c. Wrought iron working . 40 80

139 Early Mail Steamer

1979. Ships. Multicoloured.
613 12 c. Type **139** 35 10
614 25 c. "Queen Elizabeth 2" in Deep Water Harbour . . . 55 15
615 50 c. "Ra II" nearing Barbados 75 1·00
616 $1 Early mail steamer (different) 1·00 2·50

140 1953 1 c. Definitive Stamp

1979. Death Cent of Sir Rowland Hill. Mult.
617 12 c. Type **140** 15 15
618 28 c. 1975 350th anniv of first settlement 25 c. commemorative (vert) . . . 20 30
619 45 c. Penny Black with Maltese Cross postmark (vert) . . . 30 45

1979. St. Vincent Relief Fund. No. 495 surch **28c+4c ST. VINCENT RELIEF FUND.**
621 28 c. + 4 c. on 35 c. "Bletia patula" 50 60

142 Grassland Yellow Finch

1979. Birds. Multicoloured.
622 1 c. Type **142** 10 70
623 2 c. Grey kingbird 10 70
624 5 c. Lesser Antillean bullfinch 10 70
625 8 c. Magnificent frigate bird . 10 1·25
626 10 c. Cattle egret 10 40
627 12 c. Green heron 15 60
627a 15 c. Carib grackle . . . . . 4·50 5·00
628 20 c. Antillean crested hummingbird 20 55
629 25 c. Scaly-breasted ground dove 20 60
630 28 c. As 15 c. . . . . 75 1·25

631	35 c. Green-throated carib	30	70
631b	40 c. Red-necked pigeon	4·50	5·00
632	45 c. Zenaida dove	35	70
633	50 c. As 40 c.	55	1·00
633a	55 c. American golden plover	3·50	3·00
633b	60 c. Bananaquit	4·50	6·00
634	70 c. As 60 c.	55	2·00
635	$1 Caribbean elaenia	1·00	1·50
636	$2.50 American redstart	2·00	5·00
637	$5 Belted kingfisher	3·25	8·00
638	$10 Moorhen	6·50	14·00

143 Unloading H.A.R.P. Gun on Railway Wagon at Foul Bay

1979. Space Projects Commemorations. Multicoloured.

639	10 c. Type **143**	15	10
640	12 c. H.A.R.P. gun on railway wagon under tow (vert)	15	15
641	20 c. Firing launcher (vert)	15	20
642	28 c. Bath Earth Station and "Intelsat"	15	30
643	45 c. "Intelsat" over Caribbean	25	50
644	50 c. "Intelsat" over Atlantic (vert)	25	60

144 Family

146 Private, Artillery Company, Barbados Volunteer Force, circa 1909

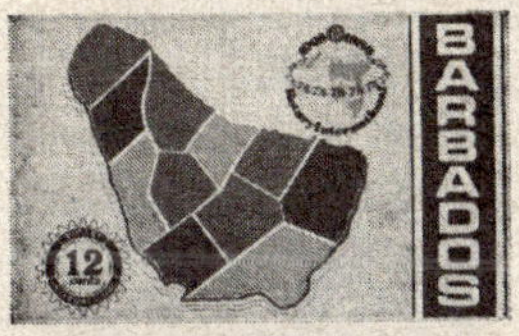

145 Map of Barbados

1979. International Year of the Child. Multicoloured.

646	12 c. Type **144**	10	10
647	28 c. Ring of children and map of Barbados	15	15
648	45 c. Child with teacher	20	20
649	50 c. Children playing	20	20
650	$1 Children and kite	35	45

1980. 75th Anniv of Rotary International. Multicoloured.

651	12 c. Type **145**	15	10
652	28 c. Map of Caribbean	20	15
653	50 c. Rotary anniversary emblem	25	35
654	$1 Paul P. Harris (founder)	40	95

1980. Barbados Regiment. Multicoloured.

655	12 c. Type **146**	25	10
656	35 c. Drum Major, Zouave uniform	35	15
657	50 c. Sovereign's and Regimental Colours	40	30
658	$1 Barbados Regiment Women's Corps	55	70

148 Yellow-tailed Snapper

1980. Underwater Scenery. Multicoloured

660	12 c. Type **148**	20	10
661	28 c. Banded butterflyfish	35	15
662	50 c. Male and Female blue-headed wrasse and princess parrotfish	45	25
663	$1 French grunt and French angelfish	70	70

149 Bathsheba Railway Station

1981. Early Transport. Multicoloured.

665	12 c. Type **149**	30	10
666	28 c. Cab stand at The Green	20	15
667	45 c. Animal-drawn tram	30	30
668	70 c. Horse-drawn bus	45	60
669	$1 Railway Station, Fairchild Street	70	95

150 The Blind at Work

1981. Int Year for Disabled Persons. Mult.

670	10 c. Type **150**	20	10
671	25 c. Sign Language (vert)	25	15
672	45 c. "Be alert to the white cane" (vert)	40	25
673	$2.50 Children at play	1·25	3·00

151 Prince Charles dressed for Polo

152 Landship Manoeuvre

1981. Royal Wedding. Multicoloured.

674	28 c. Wedding bouquet from Barbados	15	10
675	50 c. Type **151**	20	15
676	$2.50 Prince Charles and Lady Diana Spencer	55	1·25

1981. Carifesta (Caribbean Festival of Arts), Barbados. Multicoloured.

677	15 c. Type **152**	15	15
678	20 c. Yoruba dancers	15	15
679	40 c. Tuk band	20	25
680	55 c. Sculpture by Frank Collymore	25	35
681	$1 Harbour scene	50	75

1981. Nos. 630, 632 and 634 surch.

682	15 c. on 28 c. Carib grackle	30	15
683	40 c. on 45 c. Zenaida dove	30	35
684	60 c. on 70 c. Bananaquit	30	45

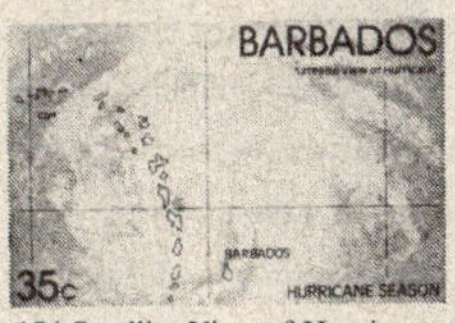

154 Satellite View of Hurricane

1981. Hurricane Season.

685 **154**	35 c. black and blue	35	20
686 –	50 c. multicoloured	45	35
687 –	60 c. multicoloured	70	50
688 –	$1 multicoloured	85	90

DESIGNS: 50 c. Hurricane "Gladys" from "Apollo 7"; 60 c. Police Department on hurricane watch; $1 McDonnell Banshee "hurricane chaser" aircraft.

155 Twin Falls

1981. Harrison's Cave. Multicoloured.

689	10 c. Type **155**	10	10
690	20 c. Stream in Rotunda Room	20	15
691	55 c. Formations in Rotunda Room	30	50
692	$2.50 Cascade Pool	80	2·25

156 Black Belly Ram

1982. Black Belly Sheep. Multicoloured.

693	40 c. Type **156**	20	30
694	50 c. Black belly ewe	20	35
695	60 c. Ewe with lambs	30	60
696	$1 Ram and ewe, with map of Barbados	50	1·50

157 Barbados Coat of Arms and Flag

1982. President Reagan's Visit. Multicoloured.

697	20 c. Type **157**	40	1·25
698	20 c. U.S.A. coat of arms and flag	40	1·25
699	55 c. Type **157**	50	1·50
700	55 c. As No. 698	50	1·50

158 Lighter

1982. Early Marine Transport. Multicoloured.

701	20 c. Type **158**	20	15
702	35 c. Rowing boat	35	25
703	55 c. Speightstown schooner	50	40
704	$2.50 Inter-colonial schooner	1·75	2·50

159 Bride and Earl Spencer Proceeding up the Aisle

160 "To Help other People"

1982. 21st Birthday of Princess of Wales. Mult.

705	20 c. Barbados coat of arms	20	15
706	60 c. Princess at Llanelwedd, October, 1981	45	50
707	$1.20 Type **159**	75	1·10
708	$2.50 Formal portrait	1·25	1·90

1982. 75th Anniv of Boy Scout Movement. Mult.

709	15 c. Type **160**	50	10
710	40 c. "I Promise to do my Best" (horiz)	80	30
711	55 c. "To do my Duty to God, the Queen and my Country" (horiz)	90	65
712	$1 National and Troop flags	1·40	1·75

161 Arms of George Washington

1982. 250th Birth Anniv of George Washington. Multicoloured.

714	10 c. Type **161**	10	10
715	55 c. Washington House, Barbados	45	45
716	60 c. Washington with troops	50	50
717	$2.50 Washington taking Oath	1·60	1·60

162 "Agraulis vanillae"

1983. Butterflies. Multicoloured.

718	20 c. Type **162**	1·00	30
719	40 c. "Danaus plexippus"	1·50	40
720	55 c. "Hypolimnas misippus"	1·50	45
721	$2.50 "Hemiargus hanno"	3·25	2·50

163 Map of Barbados and Satellite View

1983. Commonwealth Day. Multicoloured.

722	15 c. Type **163**	20	10
723	40 c. Tourist beach	25	20
724	60 c. Suger cane harvesting	35	40
725	$1 Cricket match	1·25	1·10

164 U.S. Navy "M" Class Airship M-20

1983. Bicentenary of Manned Flight.

726	20 c. Type **164**	60	15
727	40 c. Douglas DC-3	80	40
728	55 c. Vickers Viscount 837	90	80
729	$1 Lockheed TriStar 500	1·50	2·50

165 Nash "600", 1941

1983. Classic Cars. Multicoloured.

730	25 c. Type **165**	60	20
731	45 c. Dodge, 1938	75	30
732	75 c. Ford "Model AA", 1930	95	1·50
733	$2.50 Dodge "Four", 1918	2·50	4·00

166 Game in Progress

167 Angel playing Lute (detail "The Virgin and Child") (Masaccio)

1983. Table Tennis World Cup Competition. Multicoloured.

734	20 c. Type **166**	25	20
735	65 c. Map of Barbados	50	55
736	$1 World Table Tennis Cup	75	1·00

1983. Christmas. 50th Anniv of Barbados Museum.

737 **167**	10 c. multicoloured	30	10
738 –	25 c. multicoloured	60	20
739 –	45 c. multicoloured	90	40
740 –	75 c. black and gold	1·40	1·60
741 –	$2.50 multicoloured	4·50	5·50

DESIGNS—HORIZ: 45 c. "The Barbados Museum" (Richard Day); 75 c. "St. Ann's Garrison" (W. S. Hedges); $2.50, Needham's Point, Carlisle Bay. VERT: 25 c., $2 Different details from "The Virgin and Child" (Masaccio).

168 Track and Field Events

1984. Olympic Games, Los Angeles.

745 **168**	50 c. green, black and brown	60	45
746 –	65 c. orange, blk & brn	80	60
747 –	75 c. blue, black & dp bl	1·00	85
748 –	$1 brown, black and yellow	2·50	1·75

DESIGNS: 65 c. Shooting; 75 c. Sailing; $1 Cycling.

169 Global Coverage

171 Local Junior Match

1984. 250th Anniv of "Lloyd's List" (newspaper). Multicoloured.

750	45 c. Type **169**	70	40
751	50 c. Bridgetown harbour	80	50
752	75 c. "Philosopher" (full-rigged ship), 1857	1·10	90
753	$1 "Sea Princess" (liner), 1984	1·25	1·25

1984. 60th Anniv of International Chess Federation. Multicoloured.

755	25 c. Type **171**	1·25	30
756	45 c. Staunton and 19th-century knights	1·60	50
757	65 c. Staunton queen and 18th-century queen from Macao	1·75	1·60
758	$2 Staunton and 17th-century rooks	3·50	5·00

172 Poinsettia

174 The Queen Mother at Docks

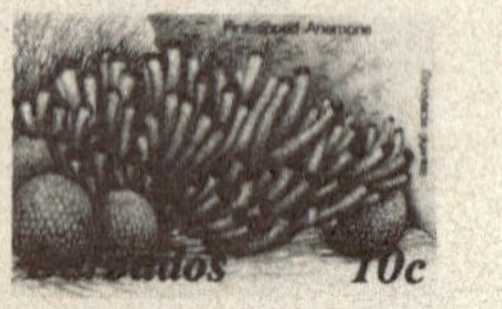

173 Pink-tipped Anemone

1984. Christmas. Flowers. Multicoloured.

759	50 c. Type **172**	1·50	80
760	65 c. Snow-on-the-Mountain	1·75	1·50
761	75 c. Christmas Candle	2·00	3·00
762	$1 Christmas Hope	2·25	3·50

1985. Marine Life. Multicoloured.

794B	1 c. Bristle worm	20	1·00
795B	2 c. Spotted trunkfish	20	1·00
796A	5 c. Coney	50	50
797B	10 c. Type **173**	30	30
798B	20 c. Christmas tree worm	30	40
799B	25 c. Hermit crab	40	40
800A	35 c. Animal flower	1·00	85
801B	40 c. Vase sponge	50	50
802B	45 c. Spotted moray	60	50
803B	50 c. Ghost crab	60	60
804B	65 c. Flamingo tongue snail	65	70
805B	75 c. Sergeant major	70	75
806B	$1 Caribbean warty anemone	85	85
807B	$2.50 Green turtle	2·00	3·50
808B	$5 Rock beauty (fish)	2·50	5·50
809B	$10 Elkhorn coral	4·25	8·00

1985. Life and Times of Queen Elizabeth the Queen Mother. Multicoloured.

779	25 c. In the White Drawing Room, Buckingham Palace, 1930s	15	20
780	65 c. With Lady Diana Spencer at Trooping the Colour, 1981	70	50
781	75 c. Type **174**	55	60
782	$1 With Prince Henry at his christening (from photo by Lord Snowdon)	70	75

175 Peregrine Falcon

1985. Birth Bicentenary of John J. Audubon (ornithologist). Designs showing original paintings. Multicoloured.

784	45 c. Type **175**	2·00	70
785	65 c. Prairie warbler (vert)	2·25	2·00
786	75 c. Great blue heron (vert)	2·50	2·75
787	$1 Yellow warbler (vert)	2·75	3·75

176 Intelsat Satellite orbiting Earth

1985. 20th Anniv of Intelsat Satellite System.

788	**176**	75 c. multicoloured	75	60

177 Traffic Policeman

1985. 150th Anniv of Royal Barbados Police. Multicoloured.

789	25 c. Type **177**	80	20
790	50 c. Police band on bandstand	1·40	80
791	65 c. Dog handler	2·10	1·40
792	$1 Mounted policeman in ceremonial uniform	2·25	2·00

1986. 60th Birthday of Queen Elizabeth II. As T **110** of Ascension. Multicoloured.

810	25 c. Princess Elizabeth aged two, 1928	15	20
811	50 c. At University College of West Indies, Jamaica, 1953	30	40
812	65 c. With Duke of Edinburgh, Barbados, 1985	40	50
813	75 c. At banquet in Sao Paulo, Brazil, 1968	45	60
814	$2 At Crown Agents Head Office, London, 1983	1·00	1·50

178 Canadair DC-4M2 North Star of Trans-Canada Airlines

1986. "Expo '86" World Fair, Vancouver. Mult.

815	50 c. Type **178**	75	50
816	$2.50 "Lady Nelson" (cargo liner)	2·00	2·50

1986. "Ameripex '86" International Stamp Exhibition, Chicago. As T **164** of Bahamas, showing Barbados stamps. Multicoloured.

817	45 c. 1976 Bicentenary of American Revolution 25 c.	85	35
818	50 c. 1976 Bicentenary of American Revolution 50 c.	95	55
819	65 c. 1981 Hurricane Season $1	1·10	1·00
820	$1 1982 Visit of President Reagan 55 c.	1·25	1·75

1986. Royal Wedding. As T **112** of Ascension. Multicoloured.

822	45 c. Prince Andrew and Miss Sarah Ferguson	60	35
823	$1 Prince Andrew in midshipman's uniform	1·00	75

179 Transporting Electricity Poles, 1923

180 "Alpinia purpurata" and Church Window

1986. 75th Anniv of Electricity in Barbados. Multicoloured.

824	10 c. Type **179**	15	10
825	25 c. Heathman Ladder, 1935 (vert)	25	20
826	65 c. Transport fleet, 1941	60	60
827	$2 Bucket truck, 1986 (vert)	1·60	2·00

1986. Christmas. Multicoloured.

828	25 c. Type **180**	20	20
829	50 c. "Anthurium andraeanum"	45	45
830	75 c. "Heliconia rostrata"	75	80
831	$2 "Heliconia × psittacorum"	1·50	2·50

181 Shot Putting

1987. 10th Anniv of Special Olympics. Multicoloured.

832	15 c. Type **181**	25	15
833	45 c. Wheelchair racing	45	30
834	65 c. Long jumping	60	65
835	$2 Logo and slogan	1·25	2·50

182 Barn Swallow

183 Sea Scout saluting

1987. "Capex '87" International Exhibition, Toronto. Birds. Multicoloured.

836	25 c. Type **182**	1·75	40
837	50 c. Yellow warbler	2·00	1·50
838	65 c. Audubon's shearwater	2·00	2·50
839	75 c. Black-whiskered vireo	2·25	3·00
840	$1 Scarlet tanager	2·50	3·75

1987. 75th Anniv of Scouting in Barbados. Multicoloured.

841	10 c. Type **183**	20	10
842	25 c. Scout jamboree	30	20
843	65 c. Scout badges	65	45
844	$2 Scout band	1·60	1·75

184 Bridgetown Synagogue

1987. Restoration of Bridgetown Synagogue. Multicoloured.

845	50 c. Type **184**	1·40	1·40
846	65 c. Interior of Synagogue	1·60	1·60
847	75 c. Ten Commandments (vert)	1·90	1·90
848	$1 Marble laver (vert)	2·25	2·75

185 Arms and Colonial Seal

1987. 21st Anniv of Independence. Mult.

849	29 c. Type **185**	30	20
850	45 c. Flags of Barbados and Great Britain	40	30
851	65 c. Silver dollar and one penny coins	70	45
852	$2 Colours of Barbados Regiment	1·50	1·40

186 Herman C. Griffith

1988. West Indian Cricket. Each showing portrait, cricket equipment and early belt buckle. Multicoloured.

854	15 c. E. A. (Manny) Martindale	1·75	50
855	45 c. George Challenor	2·50	75
856	50 c. Type **186**	2·75	2·00
857	75 c. Harold Austin	3·25	3·25
858	$2 Frank Worrell	4·25	8·00

187 "Kentropyx borckianus"

188 Cycling

1988. Lizards of Barbados. Multicoloured.

859	10 c. Type **187**	1·00	30
860	50 c. "Hemidactylus mabouia"	2·25	60
861	65 c. "Anolis extremus"	2·25	1·00
862	$2 "Gymnophthalmus underwoodii"	4·50	6·00

1988. Olympic Games, Seoul. Multicoloured.

863	25 c. Type **188**	50	20
864	45 c. Athletics	50	30
865	75 c. Relay swimming	65	55
866	$2 Yachting	1·50	1·75

1988. 300th Anniv of Lloyd's of London. As T **123** of Ascension.

868	40 c. multicoloured	55	30
869	50 c. multicoloured	65	35
870	65 c. multicoloured	1·25	45
871	$2 blue and red	2·50	2·00

DESIGNS—VERT: 40 c. Royal Exchange, 1774; $2 Sinking of "Titanic", 1912. HORIZ: 50 c. Early sugar mill; 65 c. "Author" (container ship).

189 Harry Bayley and Observatory

1988. 25th Anniv of Harry Bayley Observatory. Multicoloured.

872	25 c. Type **189**	60	20
873	65 c. Observatory with North Star and Southern Cross constellations	1·00	55
874	75 c. Andromeda galaxy	1·25	70
875	$2 Orion constellation	2·75	3·25

190 L.I.A.T. Hawker Siddeley H.S.748

1989. 50th Anniv of Commercial Aviation in Barbados. Multicoloured.

876	25 c. Type **190**	1·50	30
877	65 c. Pan Am Douglas DC-8-62	2·50	80
878	75 c. British Airways Concorde at Grantley Adams Aiport	2·50	90
879	$2 Caribbean Air Cargo Boeing 707-351C	4·00	3·50

191 Assembly Chamber

1989. 350th Anniv of Parliament.

880	**191**	25 c. multicoloured	40	20
881	–	50 c. multicoloured	60	35
882	–	75 c. blue and black	1·00	50
883	–	$2.50 multicoloured	2·50	2·00

DESIGNS: 50 c. The Speaker; 75 c. Parliament Buildings, c. 1882; $2.50 Queen Elizabeth II and Prince Philip in Parliament.

192 Brown Hare

193 Bread 'n Cheese

1989. Wildlife Preservation. Multicoloured.

884	10 c. Type **192**	55	20
885	50 c. Red-footed tortoise (horiz)	1·25	60
886	65 c. Savanna ("Green") monkey	1·40	1·10
887	$2 "Bufo marinus" (toad) (horiz)	2·75	4·25

1989. Wild Plants. Multicoloured.

921	2 c. Type **193**	20	90
891	5 c. Scarlet cordia	30	50
892	10 c. Columnar cactus	30	30
893	20 c. Spiderlily	40	30
925	25 c. Rock balsam	30	20
895	30 c. Hollyhock	50	25
895a	35 c. Red sage	1·00	1·00
927	45 c. Yellow shak-shak	45	35
928	50 c. Whitewood	50	40
898	55 c. Bluebell	70	55
930	65 c. Prickly sage	60	55
900	70 c. Seaside samphire	80	70
901	80 c. Flat-hand dildo	90	80
901a	90 c. Herringbone	1·50	2·00
902	$1.10 Lent tree	1·25	2·00
934	$2.50 Rodwood	1·90	4·00
935	$5 Cowitch	3·25	6·00
936	$10 Maypole	6·50	9·00

194 Water Skiing

195 Barbados 1852 1d. Stamp

1989. "World Stamp Expo '89" International Stamp Exn. Washington. Watersports. Mult.

906	25 c. Type **194**	80	30
907	50 c. Yachting	1·50	1·00
908	65 c. Scuba diving	1·60	1·60
909	$2.50 Surfing	4·75	6·50

1990. 150th Anniv of the Penny Black and "Stamp World London '90" International Stamp Exn.

910	**195** 25 c. green, black and yellow	1·00	30
911	– 50 c. multicoloured	1·50	1·00
912	– 65 c. multicoloured	1·60	1·25
913	– $2.50 multicoloured	3·75	5·50

DESIGNS: 50 c. 1d. 1882 Queen Victoria stamp; 65 c. 1899 2d. stamp; $2.50, 1912 3d. stamp.

196 Bugler and Jockeys

1990. Horse Racing. Multicoloured.

915	25 c. Type **196**	45	30
916	45 c. Horse and jockey in parade ring	70	50
917	75 c. At the finish	90	85
918	$2 Leading in the winner (vert)	2·50	4·00

1990. 90th Birthday of Queen Elizabeth the Queen Mother. As T **134** of Ascension.

919	75 c. multicoloured	75	60
920	$2.50 black and green	2·25	2·75

DESIGNS—21 × 36 mm: 75 c. Lady Elizabeth Bowes-Lyon, April 1923 (from painting by John Lander). 29 × 37 mm: $2.50, Lady Elizabeth Bowes-Lyon on her engagement, January 1923.

197 "Orthemis ferruginea" (dragonfly)

1990. Insects. Multicoloured.

937	50 c. Type **197**	1·25	70
938	65 c. "Ligyrus tumulosus" (beetle)	1·50	1·00
939	75 c. "Neoconocephalus sp." (grasshopper)	1·75	1·25
940	$2 "Bostra maxwelli" (stick-insect)	3·25	4·25

1990. Visit of the Princess Royal. Nos. 925, 901 and 903 optd **VISIT OF HRH THE PRINCESS ROYAL OCTOBER 1990**.

941	25 c. Rock balsam	65	20
942	80 c. Flat-hand dildo	1·40	1·40
943	$2.50 Rodwood	3·50	4·50

199 Star

201 Sorting Daily Catch

200 Adult Male Yellow Warbler

1990. Christmas. Multicoloured.

944	20 c. Type **199**	55	15
945	50 c. Figures from crib	85	50
946	$1 Stained glass window	1·75	1·25
947	$2 Angel (statue)	2·50	4·00

1991. Endangered Species. Yellow Warbler. Multicoloured.

948	10 c. Type **200**	1·10	55
949	20 c. Pair feeding chicks in nest	1·75	55
950	45 c. Female feeding chicks in nest	2·00	60
951	$1 Male with fledgeling	3·50	4·25

1991. Fishing in Barbados. Multicoloured.

952	5 c. Type **201**	40	40
953	50 c. Line fishing (horiz)	1·50	90
954	75 c. Fish cleaning (horiz)	2·00	1·25
955	$2.50 Game fishing	4·00	5·50

202 Masonic Building, Bridgetown

1991. 250th Anniv of Freemasonry in Barbados (1990).

956	**202** 25 c. multicoloured	1·00	40
957	– 65 c. multicoloured	1·75	1·00
958	– 75 c. black, yellow & brn	1·75	1·00
959	– $2.50 multicoloured	4·25	6·00

DESIGNS: 65 c. Compass and square (masonic symbols); 75 c. Royal Arch jewel; $2.50, Ceremonial apron, columns and badge.

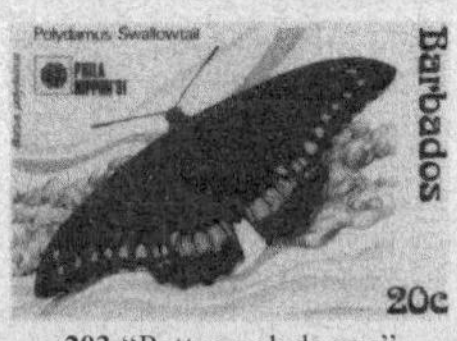

203 "Battus polydamus"

1991. "Phila Nippon '91" International Stamp Exhibition, Tokyo. Butterflies. Multicoloured.

960	20 c. Type **203**	75	30
961	50 c. "Urbanus proteus" (vert)	1·25	65
962	65 c. "Phoebis sennae"	1·40	95
963	$2.50 "Junonia evarete" (vert)	3·50	5·00

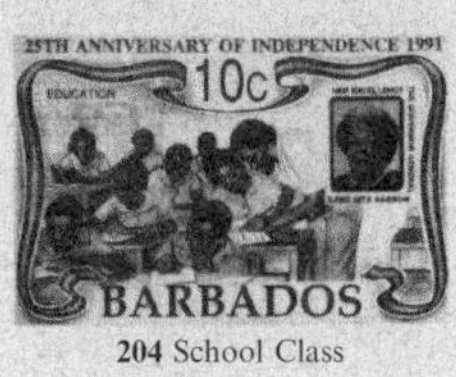

204 School Class

1991. 25th Anniv of Independence. Multicoloured.

965	10 c. Type **204**	15	15
966	25 c. Barbados Workers' Union Labour College	25	25
967	65 c. Building a house	60	80
968	75 c. Suger cane harvesting	70	90
969	$1 Health clinic	90	1·75

205 Jesus carrying Cross

1992. Easter. Multicoloured.

971	35 c. Type **205**	70	30
972	70 c. Crucifixion	1·25	90
973	90 c. Descent from the Cross	1·40	1·25
974	$3 Risen Christ	3·75	5·00

206 Cannon Ball

1992. Conservation. Flowering Trees. Multicoloured.

975	10 c. Type **206**	50	30
976	30 c. Golden shower tree	90	40
977	80 c. Frangipani	2·00	2·25
978	$1.10 Flamboyant	2·25	2·25

207 "Epidendrum Costa Rica"

1992. Orchids. Multicoloured.

979	55 c. Type **207**	75	55
980	65 c. "Cattleya guttaca"	90	90
981	70 c. "Laeliacattleya" "Splashing Around"	90	90
982	$1.40 "Phalaenopsis" "Kathy Saegert"	1·40	2·50

208 Mini Moke and Gun Hill Signal Station, St. George

1992. Transport and Tourism. Multicoloured.

983	5 c. Type **208**	40	40
984	35 c. Tour bus and Bathsheba Beach, St. Joseph	85	30
985	90 c. B.W.I.A. McDonnell Douglas MD-83 over Grantley Adams Airport	2·25	2·00
986	$2 "Festivale" (liner) and Bridgetown harbour	3·25	4·00

209 Barbados Gooseberry

212 Sailor's Shell-work Valentine and Carved Amerindian

211 18 pdr Culverin of 1625, Denmark Fort

1993. Cacti and Succulents. Multicoloured.

987	10 c. Type **209**	45	30
988	35 c. Night-blooming cereus	1·00	35
989	$1.40 Aloe	2·75	3·25
990	$2 Scrunchineel	3·25	4·00

1993. 75th Anniv of Royal Air Force. As T **149** of Ascension. Multicoloured.

991	10 c. Hawker Hunter F.6	50	30
992	30 c. Handley Page Victor K2	75	35
993	70 c. Hawker Typhoon IB	1·25	1·25
994	$3 Hawker Hurricane Mk I	3·00	4·00

1993. 14th World Orchid Conference, Glasgow. Nos. 979/82 optd **WORLD ORCHID CONFERENCE 1993**.

996	55 c. Type **207**	1·10	1·10
997	65 c. "Cattleya guttaca"	1·25	1·25
998	70 c. "Laeliacattleya" "Splashing Around"	1·25	1·25
999	$1.40 "Phalaenopsis" "Kathy Saegert"	2·00	2·50

1993. 17th-century English Cannon. Mult.

1000	5 c. Type **211**	30	40
1001	45 c. 6 pdr of 1649–60, St. Ann's Fort	85	50
1002	$1 9 pdr demi-culverin of 1691, The Main Guard	1·75	2·00
1003	$2.50 32 pdr demi-cannon of 1693–94, Charles Fort	2·75	3·75

1993. 60th Anniv of Barbados Museum. Mult.

1004	10 c. Type **212**	35	30
1005	75 c. "Barbados Mulatto Girl" (Agostino Brunias)	1·25	1·25
1006	90 c. Morris Cup and soldier of West India Regiment, 1858	1·50	1·60
1007	$1.10 Ogilby's map of Barbados, 1679, and Ashanti gold weights	1·75	2·25

213 Plesiosaurus

214 Cricket

1993. Prehistoric Aquatic Animals. Mult.

1008	90 c. Type **213**	1·40	1·60
1009	90 c. Ichthyosaurus	1·40	1·60
1010	90 c. Elasmosaurus	1·40	1·60
1011	90 c. Mosasaurus	1·40	1·60
1012	90 c. Archelon	1·40	1·60

Nos. 1008/12 were printed together, se-tenant, with the background forming a composite design.

1994. Sports and Tourism. Multicoloured.

1013	10 c. Type **214**	85	50
1014	35 c. Rally driving	1·00	40
1015	50 c. Golf	1·75	1·25
1016	70 c. Long distance running	1·50	1·75
1017	$1.40 Swimming	1·75	2·50

215 Whimbrel

1994. "Hong Kong '94" Int Stamp Exhibition. Migratory Birds. Mult.

1018	10 c. Type **215**	40	40
1019	35 c. American golden plover	75	40
1020	70 c. Turnstone	1·25	1·25
1021	$3 Louisiana heron ("Tricoloured Heron")	3·25	4·00

216 Bathsheba Beach and Logo

1994. 1st United Nations Conference of Small Island Developing States. Multicoloured.

1022	10 c. Type **216**	15	15
1023	65 c. Pico Tenneriffe	60	60
1024	90 c. Ragged Point Lighthouse	1·25	1·25
1025	$2.50 Consett Bay	2·25	3·50

217 William Demas

219 Private, 2nd West India Regt, 1860

218 Dutch Flyut, 1695

1994. First Recipients of Order of the Caribbean Community. Multicoloured.

1026	70 c. Type **217**	70	95
1027	70 c. Sir Shridath Ramphal	70	95
1028	70 c. Derek Walcott	70	95

1994. Ships. Multicoloured.

1029B	5 c. Type **218**	10	10
1030B	10 c. "Geestport" (container ship), 1994	10	10
1031A	25 c. H.M.S. "Victory" (ship of the line), 1805	15	20
1078	30 c. "Royal Viking Queen" (liner), 1994	20	25
1079	35 c. H.M.S. "Barbados" (frigate), 1945	20	25

1080	45 c. "Faraday" (cable ship), 1924	30	35
1081	50 c. U.S.C.G. "Hamilton" (coastguard cutter), 1974	30	35
1082	65 c. H.M.C.S. "Saguenay" (destroyer), 1939	40	45
1083	70 c. "Inanda" (cargo liner), 1928	40	45
1084	80 c. H.M.S. "Rodney" (battleship), 1944	50	55
1085	90 c. U.S.S. "John F. Kennedy" (aircraft carrier), 1982	55	60
1086	$1.10 "William and John" (immigrant ship), 1627	65	70
1087	$5 U.S.C.G. "Champlain" (coastguard cutter), 1931	3·00	3·25
1042A	$10 "Artist" (full-rigged ship), 1877	6·25	6·50

1995. Bicentenary of Formation of West India Regiment. Multicoloured.

1043	30 c. Type **219**	35	35
1044	50 c. Light Company private, 4th West India Regt, 1795	50	55
1045	70 c. Drum Major, 3rd West India Regt, 1860	65	85
1046	$1 Privates in undress and working dress, 5th West India Regt, 1815	90	1·25
1047	$1.10 Troops from 1st and 2nd West India Regts in Review Order, 1874	95	1·40

1995. 50th Anniv of End of Second World War. As T **161** of Ascension. Multicoloured.

1048	10 c. Barbadian Bren gun crew	50	40
1049	35 c. Avro Type 683 Lancaster bomber	75	40
1050	55 c. Supermarine Spitfire	1·00	65
1051	$2.50 "Davisian" (cargo liner)	2·75	3·50

220 Member of 1st Barbados Combermere Scout Troop, 1912

1995. 300th Anniv of Combermere School. Mult.

1053	5 c. Type **220**	20	30
1054	20 c. Violin and sheet of music	30	30
1055	35 c. Sir Frank Worrell (cricketer) (vert)	90	55
1056	$3 Painting by pupil	2·25	3·50

1995. 50th Anniv of United Nations. As T **213** of Bahamas. Multicoloured.

1058	30 c. Douglas C-124 Globemaster (transport), Korea, 1950–53	60	40
1059	45 c. Royal Navy Sea King helicopter	80	50
1060	$1.40 Westland Wessex helicopter, Cyprus, 1964	1·25	2·00
1061	$2 Sud Aviation SA 341 Gazelle helicopter, Cyprus, 1964	1·50	2·50

221 Blue Beauty

223 Football

222 Magnifying Glass, Tweezers and 1896 Colony Seal ¼d. Stamp

1995. Water Lilies. Multicoloured.

1062	10 c. Type **221**	30	30
1063	65 c. White water lily	75	60
1064	70 c. Sacred lotus	75	60
1065	$3 Water hyacinth	2·50	3·50

1996. Centenary of Barbados Philatelic Society. Each showing magnifying glass, tweezers and stamp. Multicoloured.

1066	10 c. Type **222**	30	30
1067	55 c. 1906 Tercentenary of Annexation 1d.	55	45
1068	$1.10 1920 Victory 1s.	1·10	1·25
1069	$1.40 1937 Coronation 2½d.	1·40	2·00

1996. Cent of Modern Olympic Games. Mult.

1070	20 c. Type **223**	30	30
1071	30 c. Relay running	35	30
1072	55 c. Basketball	85	60
1073	$3 Rhythmic gymnastics	2·25	3·00

224 Douglas DC-10 of Canadian Airlines

1996. "CAPEX '96" International Stamp Exhibition, Toronto. Aircraft. Multicoloured.

1089	10 c. Type **224**	30	20
1090	90 c. Boeing 767 of Air Canada	80	80
1091	$1 Airbus Industrie A320 of Air Canada	85	90
1092	$1.40 Boeing 767 of Canadian Airlines	1·10	1·50

225 Chattel House

1996. Chattel Houses.

1093	**225**	35 c. multicoloured	30	25
1094	–	70 c. multicoloured	55	55
1095	–	$1.10 multicoloured	80	1·10
1096	–	$2 multicoloured	1·60	2·25

DESIGNS: 70 c. to $2, Different houses.

226 "Going to Church"

1996. Christmas. 50th Anniv of U.N.I.C.E.F. Children's Paintings. Multicoloured.

1097	10 c. Type **226**	20	15
1098	30 c. "The Tuk Band"	35	25
1099	55 c. "Singing carols"	50	40
1100	$2.50 "Decorated house"	1·75	2·50

227 Doberman Pinscher

1997. "HONG KONG '97" International Stamp Exhibition. Dogs. Multicoloured.

1101	10 c. Type **227**	30	20
1102	30 c. German shepherd	50	35
1103	90 c. Japanese akita	1·10	1·10
1104	$3 Irish red setter	3·00	3·75

228 Barbados Flag and State Arms

1997. Visit of President Clinton of U.S.A. Multicoloured.

1105	35 c. Type **228**	50	65
1106	90 c. American flag and arms	70	85

229 Measled Cowrie

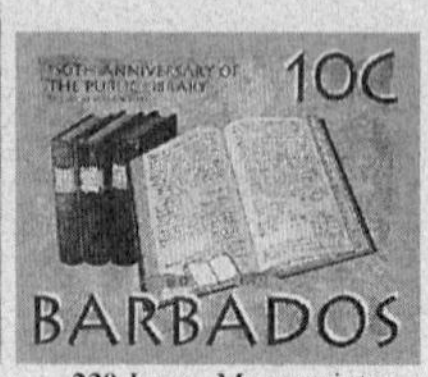

230 Lucas Manuscripts

1997. Shells. Multicoloured.

1107	5 c. Type **229**	15	15
1108	35 c. Trumpet triton	35	25
1109	90 c. Scotch bonnet	75	75
1110	$2 West Indian murex	1·50	2·00

1997. 150th Anniv of the Public Library Service. Multicoloured.

1112	10 c. Type **230**	15	15
1113	30 c. Librarian reading to children	30	25
1114	70 c. Mobile library van	60	60
1115	$3 Man using computer	2·25	3·00

231 Barbados Cherry

1997. Local Fruits. Multicoloured.

1116	35 c. Type **231**	30	25
1117	40 c. Sugar apple	35	30
1118	$1.15 Soursop	85	90
1119	$1.70 Pawpaw	1·25	1·50

233 Environment Regeneration

1998. 50th Anniv of Organization of American States. Multicoloured.

1122	15 c. Type **233**	10	10
1123	$1 Stilt dancing	60	65
1124	$2.50 Judge and figure of Justice	1·50	1·60

234 Frank Worrell Hall

1998. 50th Anniv of University of West Indies. Multicoloured.

1125	40 c. Type **234**	25	30
1126	$1.15 Student graduating	80	85
1127	$1.40 50th anniversary plaque	1·10	1·25
1128	$1.75 Quadrangle	2·50	2·75

235 Catamaran

1998. Tourism. Multicoloured.

1129	10 c. Type **235**	10	10
1130	45 c. "Jolly Roger" (tourist schooner) (horiz)	30	35
1131	70 c. "Atlantis" (submarine) (horiz)	40	45
1132	$2 "Harbour Master" (ferry)	1·25	1·40

237 Juvenile Piping Plover in Shallow Water

1999. Endangered Species. Piping Plover. Mult.

1134	10 c. Type **237**	10	10
1135	45 c. Female with eggs	30	35
1136	50 c. Male and female with fledglings	30	35
1137	70 c. Male in shallow water	40	45

POSTAGE DUE STAMPS

D 1

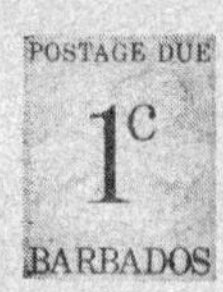

D 2

1934.

D1	D 1	½d. green	1·00	6·50
D2		1d. black	1·00	1·00
D3		3d. red	19·00	17·00

1950. Values in cents.

D4a	D 1	1 c. green	30	3·00
D8		2 c. black	30	3·50
D9		6 c. red	50	5·00

1976.

D14a	D 2	1 c. mauve and pink	10	10
D15a	–	2 c. blue and light blue	10	10
D16a	–	5 c. brown and yellow	10	15
D17a	–	10 c. blue and lilac	15	20
D18a	–	25 c. deep green and green	20	30
D19	–	$1 red and deep red	75	1·10

DESIGNS: Nos. D15/19 show different floral backgrounds.

BARBUDA

One of the Leeward Is., Br. W. Indies. Dependency of Antigua. Used stamps of Antigua and Leeward Is. concurrently. The issues from 1968 are also valid for use in Antigua. From 1971 to 1973 the stamps of Antigua were again used.

1922. 12 pence = 1 shilling;
20 shillings = 1 pound.
1951. 100 cents = 1 West Indian dollar.

1922. Stamps of Leeward Islands optd **BARBUDA**.

1	**11**	$\frac{1}{2}$d. green	1·00	8·00
2		1d. red	1·00	8·00
3		2d. grey	1·00	7·50
4		$2\frac{1}{2}$d. blue	1·00	7·50
9		3d. purple on yellow	1·00	9·00
5		6d. purple	1·75	16·00
10		1s. black on green	1·50	8·00
6		2s. purple and blue on blue	12·00	48·00
7		3s. green and violet	30·00	75·00
8		4s. black and red	38·00	75·00
11		5s. green and red on yellow	65·00	£130

2 Map of Barbuda

3 Greater Amberjack

1968.

12	**2**	$\frac{1}{2}$ c. brown, black and pink	20	30
13		1 c. orange, black and flesh	30	10
14		2 c. brown, red and rose	30	10
15		3 c. brown, yellow and lemon	30	10
16		4 c. black, green and light green	30	30
17		5 c. turquoise and black	30	10
18		6 c. black, purple and lilac	40	10
19		10 c. black, blue and colbalt	30	10
20		15 c. black, green and turquoise	30	55
20a	–	20 c. multicoloured	1·50	2·00
21	**3**	25 c. multicoloured	60	25
22	–	35 c. multicoloured	60	75
23	–	50 c. multicoloured	60	55
24	–	75 c. multicoloured	70	80
25	–	$1 multicoloured	85	2·00
26	–	$2.50 multicoloured	1·50	5·00
27	–	$5 multicoloured	3·75	7·50

DESIGNS: As T **3**—20 c. Great barracuda; 35 c. French angelfish; 50 c. Porkfish; 75 c. Princess parrotfish; $1, Long-spined squirrelfish; $2.50, Bigeye; $5, Blue chromis.

10 Sprinting and Aztec Sun-stone

1968. Olympic Games. Mexico. Muticoloured.

28	25 c. Type **10**	35	25
29	35 c. High-jumping and Aztec statue	40	25
30	75 c. Yachting and Aztec lion mask	55	45

14 "The Ascension" (Orcagna)"

18 "Sistine Madonna" (Raphael)

15 Scout Enrolment Ceremony

1969. Easter Commemoration.

32	**14**	25 c. black and blue	15	45
33		35 c. black and red	15	50
34		75 c. black and lilac	15	55

1969. 3rd Caribbean Scout Jamboree. Multicoloured.

35	25 c. Type **15**	45	55
36	35 c. Scouts around camp fire	60	65
37	75 c. Sea Scouts rowing boat	75	85

1969. Christmas.

38	**18**	$\frac{1}{2}$ c. multicoloured	10	10
39		25 c. multicoloured	10	15
40		35 c. multicoloured	10	20
41		35 c. multicoloured	20	35

19 William I (1066-87)

21 "The Way to Calvary" (Ugolino)

1970. English Monarchs. Multicoloured.

42	35 c. Type **19**	30	15
43	35 c. William II (1087–1100)	10	15
44	35 c. Henry I (1100–35)	10	15
45	35 c. Stephen (1135–54)	10	15
46	35 c. Henry II (1154–89)	10	15
47	35 c. Richard I (1189–99)	10	15
48	35 c. John (1199–1216)	10	15
49	35 c. Henry III (1216–72)	10	15
50	35 c. Edward I (1272–1307)	10	15
51	35 c. Edward II (1307–27)	10	15
52	35 c. Edward III (1327–77)	10	15
53	35 c. Richard II (1377–99)	10	15
54	35 c. Henry IV (1399–1413)	10	15
55	35 c. Henry V (1413–22)	10	15
56	35 c. Henry VI (1422–61)	10	15
57	35 c. Edward IV (1462–83)	10	15
58	35 c. Edward V (April–June 1483)	10	15
59	35 c. Richard III (1483–85)	10	15
60	35 c. Henry VII (1485–1509)	10	15
61	35 c. Henry VIII (1509–47)	10	15
62	35 c. Edward VI (1547–53)	10	15
63	35 c. Lady Jane Grey (1553)	10	15
64	35 c. Mary I (1553–8)	10	15
65	35 c. Elizabeth I (1558–1603)	10	15
66	35 c. James I (1603–25)	10	15
67	35 c. Charles I (1625–49)	10	15
68	35 c. Charles II (1649–1685)	10	15
69	35 c. James II (1685–1688)	10	15
70	35 c. William III (1689–1702)	10	15
71	35 c. Mary II (1689–1694)	10	15
72	35 c. Anne (1702–1714)	15	15
73	35 c. George I (1714–1727)	15	15
74	35 c. George II (1727–1760)	15	15
75	35 c. George III (1760–1820)	15	15
76	35 c. George IV (1820–1830)	15	15
77	35 c. William IV (1830–1837)	15	60
78	35 c. Victoria (1837–1901)	15	60

See also Nos. 710/5.

1970. No. 12 surch **20c**.

79	**2**	20 c. on $\frac{1}{2}$ c. brn, blk & pink	10	20

1970. Easter. Paintings. Multicoloured.

80	25 c. Type **21**	15	30
81	35 c. "The Deposition from the Cross" (Ugolino)	15	30
82	75 c. Crucifix (The Master of St Francis)	15	35

22 Oliver is introduced to Fagin ("Oliver Twist")

1970. Death Centenary of Charles Dickens. Mult.

83	20 c. Type **22**	10	15
84	75 c. Dickens and scene from "The Old Curiosity Shop"	20	40

23 "Madonna of the Meadows" (G. Bellini)

1970. Christmas. Multicoloured.

85	20 c. Type **23**	10	25
86	50 c. "Madonna, Child and Angels" (from Wilton diptych)	15	30
87	75 c. "The Nativity" (della Francesca)	15	35

24 Nurse with Patient in Wheelchair

25 "Angel with Vases"

1970. Centenary of British Red Cross. Multicoloured.

88	20 c. Type **24**	15	30
89	35 c. Nurse giving patient magazines (horiz)	20	40
90	75 c. Nurse and mother weighing baby (horiz)	25	70

1971. Easter. "Mond" Crucifixion by Raphael. Multicoloured.

91	35 c. Type **25**	15	75
92	50 c. "Christ crucified"	15	85
93	75 c. "Angel with vase"	15	90

26 Martello Tower

1971. Tourism. Multicoloured.

94	20 c. Type **26**	15	25
95	25 c. Sailing boats	25	30
96	50 c. Hotel bungalows	25	35
97	75 c. Government House and Mystery Stone	25	40

27 "The Granducal Madonna" (Raphael)

1971. Christmas. Multicoloured.

98	$\frac{1}{2}$ c. Type **27**	10	10
99	35 c. "The Ansidei Madonna" (Raphael)	10	20
100	50 c. "The Madonna and Child" (Botticelli)	15	25
101	75 c. "The Madonna of the Trees" (Bellini)	15	30

Four stamps to commemorate the 500th Birth Anniv of Durer were prepared in late 1971, but their issue was not authorised by the Antigua Government.

1973. Royal Wedding. Nos. 370/1 of Antigua optd **BARBUDA** twice.

102	**106**	25 c. multicoloured	4·50	2·75
103		$2 multicoloured	1·50	1·50

1973. Ships. Nos. 269/85 of Antigua optd **BARBUDA**.

116	**92**	$\frac{1}{2}$ c. multicoloured	15	20
104	–	1 c. multicoloured	15	30
105	–	2 c. multicoloured	25	30
117	–	3 c. multicoloured	25	25
106	–	4 c. multicoloured	30	30
107	–	5 c. multicoloured	40	40
108	–	6 c. multicoloured	40	40
109	–	10 c. multicoloured	45	45
118	–	15 c. multicoloured	45	50
110	–	20 c. multicoloured	55	60
111	–	25 c. multicoloured	55	60
112	–	35 c. multicoloured	55	70
113	–	50 c. multicoloured	55	70
114	–	75 c. multicoloured	55	70
119	–	$1 multicoloured	55	70
115	–	$2.50 multicoloured	1·25	1·50
121	–	$5 multicoloured	1·10	2·50

1973. Military Uniforms. Nos. 353, 355 and 357 of Antigua optd **BARBUDA**.

122	$\frac{1}{2}$ c. multicoloured	10	10
123	20 c. multicoloured	15	10
124	75 c. multicoloured	40	15

1973. Carnival. Nos. 360/2 of Antigua optd **BARBUDA**.

126	20 c. multicoloured	10	10
127	35 c. multicoloured	10	10
128	75 c. multicoloured	20	25

1973. Christmas. Nos. 364/68 of Antigua optd **BARBUDA**.

130	**105**	3 c. multicoloured	10	10
131	–	5 c. multicoloured	10	10
132	–	20 c. multicoloured	10	10
133	–	35 c. multicoloured	15	15
134	–	$1 multicoloured	30	30

1973. Honeymoon Visit. Nos. 373/4 of Antigua additionally optd **BARBUDA**.

136	35 c. multicoloured	30	20
137	$2 multicoloured	70	60

1974. University of West Indies. Nos. 376/9 of Antigua optd **BARBUDA**.

139	5 c. multicoloured	10	10
140	20 c. multicoloured	10	10
141	35 c. multicoloured	15	15
142	75 c. multicoloured	15	15

1974. Military Uniforms. Nos. 380/4 of Antigua optd **BARBUDA**.

143	$\frac{1}{2}$ c. multicoloured	10	10
144	10 c. multicoloured	10	10
145	20 c. multicoloured	20	10
146	35 c. multicoloured	25	10
147	75 c. multicoloured	45	25

1974. Centenary of U.P.U. (1st issue). Nos. 386/92 of Antigua optd with either a or b. (a) **BARBUDA 13 JULY 1922**.

148	$\frac{1}{2}$ c. multicoloured	10	10
150	1 c. multicoloured	10	10
152	2 c. multicoloured	20	15
154	5 c. multicoloured	50	15
156	20 c. multicoloured	40	70
158	35 c. multicoloured	80	1·50
160	$1 multicoloured	2·25	4·00

(b) **BARBUDA 15 SEPT. 1874 G.P.U.** ("General Postal Union").

149	$\frac{1}{2}$ c. multicoloured	10	10
151	1 c. multicoloured	10	10
153	2 c. multicoloured	20	15
155	5 c. multicoloured	50	15
157	20 c. multicoloured	40	70
159	35 c. multicoloured	80	1·50
161	$1 multicoloured	2·25	4·00

1974. Antiguan Steel Bands. Nos. 394/97 of Antigua optd **BARBUDA**.

163	5 c. deep red, red and black	10	10
164	20 c. brown, lt brown & blk	10	10
165	35 c. light green, green and black	10	10
166	75 c. deep blue, blue and black	20	20

39 Footballers

1974. World Cup Football Championships (1st issue).

168	**39**	35 c. multicoloured	10	10
169	–	$1.20 multicoloured	25	35
170	–	$2.50 multicoloured	35	50

DESIGNS: $1.20, $2.50, Footballers in action similar to Type **39**.

1974. World Cup Football Championships (2nd issue). Nos. 399/402 of Antigua optd **BARBUDA**.

172	**111**	5 c. multicoloured	10	10
173	–	35 c. multicoloured	10	10
174	–	75 c. multicoloured	15	15
175	–	$1 multicoloured	20	25

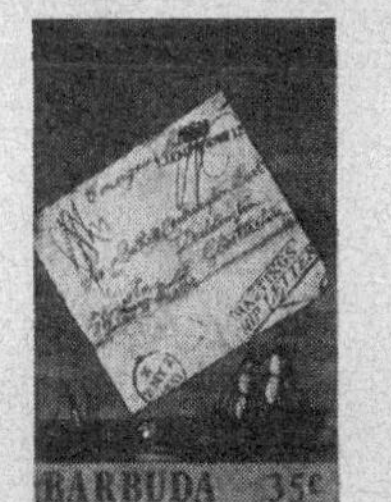

41 Ship Letter of 1833

1974. Cent of Universal Postal Union. (2nd issue). Multicoloured.

177	35 c. Type **41**	10	10
178	$1.20 Stamps and postmarks of 1922	30	50
179	$2.50 Britten Norman Islander mailplane over map of Barbuda	55	75

42 Greater Amberjack

1974. Multicoloured.

181	$\frac{1}{2}$ c. Oleander, Rose Bay	10	40
182	1 c. Blue petrea	15	40
183	2 c. Poinsettia	15	40
184	3 c. Cassia tree	15	40
185	4 c. Type **42**	1·40	40
186	5 c. Holy Trinity School	15	15
187	6 c. Snorkeling	15	30
188	10 c. Pilgrim Holiness Church	15	20
189	15 c. New Cottage Hospital	15	20
190	20 c. Post Office and Treasury	15	20
191	25 c. Island jetty and boats	30	30
192	35 c. Martello Tower	30	30
193	50 c. Warden's House	30	30
194	75 c. Britten Norman Islander aircraft	75	1·00
195	$1 Tortoise	70	80
196	$2.50 Spiny lobster	80	1·75

197		$5 Magnificent frigate bird	4·00	2·50
197b		$10 Hibiscus	2·50	4·50

The 50 c. to $1 are 39 × 25 mm., $2.50 and $5 45 × 29 mm., $10 34 × 48 mm. The ½ to 3 c., 25 c. and $10 are vertical.

1974. Birth Centenary of Sir Winston Churchill. (1st issue). Nos. 408/11 of Antigua optd **BARBUDA**.

198	**113**	5 c. multicoloured	15	10
199	–	35 c. multicoloured	25	15
200	–	75 c. multicoloured	40	45
201	–	$1 multicoloured	75	70

43 Churchill making Broadcast

1974. Birth Centenary of Sir Winston Churchill (2nd issue). Multicoloured.

203		5 c. Type **43**	10	10
204		35 c. Churchill and Chartwell	10	10
205		75 c. Churchill painting	20	20
206		$1 Churchill making "V" sign	25	30

1974. Christmas. Nos. 413/20 of Antigua optd **BARBUDA**.

208	**114**	½ c. multicoloured	10	10
209	–	1 c. multicoloured	10	10
210	–	2 c. multicoloured	10	10
211	–	3 c. multicoloured	10	10
212	–	5 c. multicoloured	10	10
213	–	20 c. multicoloured	10	10
214	–	35 c. multicoloured	15	15
215	–	75 c. multicoloured	30	30

1975. Nelson's Dockyard. Nos. 427/31 of Antigua optd **BARBUDA**.

217	**116**	5 c. multicoloured	15	15
218	–	15 c. multicoloured	40	25
219	–	35 c. multicoloured	55	35
220	–	50 c. multicoloured	60	50
221	–	$1 multicoloured	65	80

45 Ships of the Line

1975. Sea Battles. Battle of the Saints, 1782. Mult.

223		35 c. Type **45**	75	65
224		50 c. H.M.S. "Ramillies"	75	75
225		75 c. Ships firing broadsides	90	90
226		95 c. Sailors fleeing burning ship	1·00	1·25

1975. "Apollo-Soyuz" Space Project. No. 197 optd **U.S.A.-U.S.S.R SPACE COOPERATION 1975** with **APOLLO** (No. 227) or **SOYUZ** (No. 228).

227		$5 multicoloured	4·00	7·50
228		$5 multicoloured	4·00	7·50

47 Officer, 65th Foot, 1763

1975. Military Uniforms. Multicoloured.

229		35 c. Type **47**	75	75
230		50 c. Grenadier, 27th Foot 1701–10	90	90
231		75 c. Officer, 21st Foot, 1793–6	1·00	1·00
232		95 c. Officer, Royal Regiment of Artillery, 1800	1·25	1·25

1975. 25th Anniv of United Nations. Nos. 203/6 optd **30TH ANNIVERSARY UNITED NATIONS 1945–1975**.

233	**43**	5 c. multicoloured	10	10
234	–	35 c. multicoloured	10	15
235	–	75 c. multicoloured	15	20
236	–	$1 multicoloured	20	30

1975. Christmas. Nos. 457/64 of Antigua optd **BARBUDA**.

237	**121**	½ c. multicoloured	10	10
238	–	1 c. multicoloured	10	10
239	–	2 c. multicoloured	10	10
240	–	3 c. multicoloured	10	10
241	–	5 c. multicoloured	10	10
242	–	10 c. multicoloured	10	10
243	–	35 c. multicoloured	15	20
244	–	$2 multicoloured	60	1·00

1975. World Cup Cricket Winners. Nos. 466/8 of Antigua optd **BARBUDA**.

246	**122**	5 c. multicoloured	90	1·00
247	–	35 c. multicoloured	1·75	2·00
248	–	$2 multicoloured	3·25	4·25

51 Surrender of Cornwallis at Yorktown (Trumbull)

1976. Bicentenary of American Revolution.

249	**51**	15 c. multicoloured	10	15
250	–	15 c. multicoloured	10	15
251	–	15 c. multicoloured	10	15
252	–	35 c. multicoloured	10	15
253	–	35 c. multicoloured	10	15
254	–	35 c. multicoloured	10	15
255	–	$1 multicoloured	15	25
256	–	$1 multicoloured	15	25
257	–	$1 multicoloured	15	25
258	–	$2 multicoloured	25	40
259	–	$2 multicoloured	25	40
260	–	$2 multicoloured	25	40

DESIGNS—As Type **51**: Nos. 249/51; 252/4, The Battle of Princeton; 255/7, Surrender of General Burgoyne at Saratoga; 258/60, Jefferson presenting Declaration of Independence.

Type **51** shows the left-hand stamp of the 15 c. design.

52 Bananaquits

1976. Birds. Multicoloured.

262		35 c. Type **52**	1·00	50
263		50 c. Blue-hooded euphonia	1·25	60
264		75 c. Royal tern	1·25	80
265		95 c. Killdeer	1·75	85
266		$1.25 Common cowbird	1·75	1·00
267		$2 Purple gallinule	2·00	1·25

1976. Royal Visit to the U.S.A. Nos. 249/60 additionally inscr "H.M. QUEEN ELIZABETH ROYAL VISIT 6TH JULY 1976 H.R.H. DUKE OF EDINBURGH".

268		15 c. multicoloured	10	15
269		15 c. multicoloured	10	15
270		15 c. multicoloured	10	15
271		35 c. multicoloured	10	20
272		35 c. multicoloured	10	20
273		35 c. multicoloured	10	20
274		$1 multicoloured	15	50
275		$1 multicoloured	15	50
276		$1 multicoloured	15	50
277		$2 multicoloured	25	70
278		$2 multicoloured	25	70
279		$2 multicoloured	25	70

1976. Christmas. Nos. 514/8 of Antigua optd **BARBUDA**.

281	**128**	8 c. multicoloured	10	10
282	–	10 c. multicoloured	10	10
283	–	15 c. multicoloured	10	10
284	–	50 c. multicoloured	15	15
285	–	$1 multicoloured	25	30

1976. Olympic Games, Montreal. Nos. 495/501 of Antigua optd **BARBUDA**.

286	**125**	½ c. brown, yellow and black	10	10
287	–	1 c. violet and black	10	10
288	–	2 c. green and black	10	10
289	–	15 c. blue and black	10	10
290	–	30 c. brown, yellow & blk	10	10
291	–	$1 orange, red and black	20	20
292	–	$2 red and black	35	35

55 P.O. Tower, Telephones and Alexander Graham Bell

1977. Cent of First Telephone Transmission. Mult.

294		75 c. Type **55**	15	35
295		$1.25 T.V. transmission by satellite	20	55
296		$2 Globe showing satellite transmission scheme	30	75

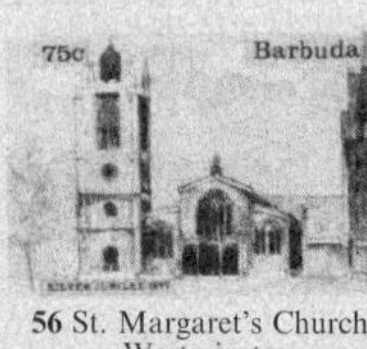

56 St. Margaret's Church, Westminster

1977. Silver Jubilee (1st issue). Multicoloured.

298		75 c. Type **56**	10	15
299		75 c. Street decorations	10	15
300		75 c. Westminster Abbey	10	15
301		$1.25 Household Cavalry	15	20
302		$1.25 Coronation Coach	15	20
303		$1.25 Postillions	15	20

1977. Nos. 469/86 of Antigua optd **BARBUDA**.

305		½ c. Antillean crested hummingbird	20	20
306		1 c. Imperial amazon	30	20
307		2 c. Zenaida dove	30	20
308		3 c. Loggerhead kingbird	30	20
309		4 c. Red-necked pigeon	30	20
310		5 c. Rufous throated solitaire	30	20
311		6 c. Orchid tree	30	20
312		10 c. Bougainvillea	30	20
313		15 c. Geiger tree	30	25
314		20 c. Flamboyant	30	25
315		25 c. Hibiscus	30	25
316		35 c. Flame of the Wood	35	30
317		50 c. Cannon at Fort James	40	40
318		75 c. Premier's Office	40	40
319		$1 Potworks Dam	50	60
320		$2.50 Irrigation scheme	1·25	1·60
321		$5 Government House	2·25	3·25
322		$10 Coolidge Airport	4·00	7·50

1977. Silver Jubilee (2nd issue). Nos. 526/30 of Antigua optd **BARBUDA**. (a) Ordinary gum.

323		10 c. Royal Family	10	15
324		30 c. Royal visit, 1966	15	20
325		50 c. The Queen enthroned	20	30
326		90 c. The Queen after Coronation	25	40
327		$2.50 The Queen and Prince Charles	75	1·25

(b) Self-adhesive.

329		50 c. Queen after Coronation	40	70
330		$5 The Queen and Prince Philip	5·50	13·00

1977. Caribbean Scout Jamboree, Jamaica. Nos. 534/40 of Antigua optd **BARBUDA**.

331		½ c. Type **131**	10	10
332		1 c. Hiking	10	10
333		2 c. Rock-climbing	10	10
334		10 c. Cutting logs	10	10
335		30 c. Map and sign reading	40	40
336		50 c. First aid	55	65
337		$2 Rafting	1·50	2·25

1977. 21st Anniv of Carnival. Nos. 542/46 of Antigua optd **BARBUDA**.

339		10 c. Type **312**	10	10
340		30 c. Carnival Queen	10	10
341		50 c. Butterfly costume	15	20
342		90 c. Queen of the Band	20	30
343		$1 Calypso King and Queen	25	40

61 Royal Yacht "Britannia"

1977. Royal Visit (1st issue). Multicoloured.

345		50 c. Type **61**	10	15
346		$1.50 Jubilee emblem	25	35
347		$2.50 Union Jack and flag of Antigua	35	55

1977. Royal Visit (2nd issue). Nos. 548/52 of Antigua optd **BARBUDA**.

349A		10 c. Royal Family	10	10
350B		30 c. Queen Elizabeth and Prince Philip in car	15	15
351B		50 c. Queen enthroned	20	20
352B		90 c. Queen after Coronation	30	30
353B		$2.50 The Queen and Prince Charles	60	80

1977. Christmas. Nos. 554/60 of Antigua optd **BARBUDA**.

355		½ c. Type **134**	10	10
356		1 c. Crivelli	10	10
357		2 c. Lotto	10	10
358		8 c. Pontormo	10	10
359		10 c. Tura (different)	10	10
360		25 c. Lotto (different)	15	10
361		$2 Crivelli (different)	45	45

64 Airship LZ-1

1977. Special Events, 1977. Multicoloured.

363		75 c. Type **64**	30	30
364		75 c. German battleship and German Navy airship L-31	30	30
365		75 c. "Graf Zeppelin" in hangar	30	30
366		75 c. Gondola of military airship	30	30
367		95 c. Sputnik 1	35	35
368		95 c. Vostok rocket	35	35
369		95 c. Voskhod rocket	35	35
370		95 c. Space walk	35	35
371		$1.25 Fuelling for flight	40	45
372		$1.25 Leaving New York	40	45
373		$1.25 "Spirit of St. Louis"	40	45
374		$1.25 Welcome to England	40	45
375		$2 Lion of England	50	70
376		$2 Unicorn of Scotland	50	70
377		$2 Yale of Beaufort	50	70
378		$2 Falcon of Plantagenets	50	70
379		$5 "Daniel in the Lion's Den" (Rubens)	50	1·25
380		$5 Different detail of painting	50	1·25
381		$5 Different detail of painting	50	1·25
382		$5 Different detail of painting	50	1·25

EVENTS: 75 c. 75th anniv of navigable airships; 95 c. 20th anniv of U.S.S.R. space programme; $1.25, 50th anniv of Lindbergh's transatlantic flight; $2 Silver Jubilee of Queen Elizabeth II; $5 400th birth anniv of Rubens.

Nos. 379/82 form a composite design.

1978. 10th Anniv of Statehood. Nos. 562/6 of Antigua optd **BARBUDA**.

384		10 c. Type **135**	10	10
385		15 c. State flag	15	10
386		50 c. Police band	1·25	70
387		90 c. Premier V. C. Bird	20	40
388		$2 State Coat of Arms	40	80

66 "Pieta" (sculpture) (detail)

1978. Easter. Paintings and Sculptures by Michelangelo. Multicoloured.

390		75 c. Type **66**	15	15
391		95 c. "The Holy Family"	20	20
392		$1.25 "Libyan sibyl" (from the Sistine Chapel)	25	25
393		$2 "The Flood" (from the Sistine Chapel)	30	35

1978. 75th Anniv of Powered Flight. Nos. 568/74 of Antigua optd **BARBUDA**.

395		½ c. Wright Glider No. III, 1902	10	10
396		1 c. Wright Flyer I, 1903	10	10
397		2 c. Launch system and engine	10	10
398		10 c. Orville Wright (vert)	10	10
399		50 c. Wright Flyer III, 1905	25	15
400		90 c. Wilbur Wright (vert)	35	15
401		$2 Wright Type B, 1910	60	45

1978. Sailing Week. Nos. 576/79 of Antigua optd **BARBUDA**.

403		10 c. Sunfish regatta	20	10
404		50 c. Fishing and work boat race	40	25
405		90 c. Curtain Bluff race	55	35
406		$2 Power boat rally	85	75

68 St. Edward's Crown

1978. 25th Anniv of Coronation (1st issue). Multicoloured.

408		75 c. Type **68**	15	15
409		75 c. Imperial State Crown	15	15
410		$1.50 Queen Mary's Crown	20	25
411		$1.50 Queen Mother's Crown	20	25
412		$2.50 Queen Consort's Crown	35	45
413		$2.50 Queen Victoria's Crown	35	45

1978. 25th Anniv of Coronation (2nd issue). Nos. 581/5 of Antigua optd **BARBUDA**.

415		10 c. Queen Elizabeth and Prince Philip	10	10
416		30 c. The Crowning	10	10
417		50 c. Coronation procession	10	15
418		90 c. Queen seated in St. Edward's Chair	15	20
419		$2.50 Queen wearing Imperial State Crown	30	60

1978. 25th Anniv of Coronation (3rd issue). As Nos. 587/9 of Antigua additionally inscr "BARBUDA".

421		25 c. Glass Coach	30	70
422		50 c. Irish State Coach	30	70
423		$5 Coronation Coach	1·00	2·25

1978. World Cup Football Championship, Argentina. Nos. 590/2 of Antigua optd **BARBUDA**.

424		10 c. Player running with ball	10	10
425		15 c. Players in front of goal	10	10
426		$3 Referee and player	1·00	1·25

1978. Flowers. As Nos. 594/7 of Antigua optd **BARBUDA**.

428		25 c. Petrea	20	30
429		50 c. Sunflower	30	50
430		90 c. Frangipani	50	60
431		$2 Passion flower	75	1·25

1978. Christmas. As Nos. 599/601 of Antigua optd **BARBUDA**.

433		8 c. "St. Ildefonso receiving the Chasuble from the Virgin"	10	10
434		25 c. "The Flight of St. Barbara"	15	15
435		$2 "Madonna and Child, with St. Joseph, John the Baptist and Donor"	60	1·25

70 Black-barred Soldierfish

1978. Flora and Fauna. Multicoloured.

437		25 c. Type **70**	1·25	1·50
438		50 c. "Cynthia cardui" (butterfly)	2·00	2·25
439		75 c. Dwarf poinciana	1·50	2·25
440		95 c. "Heliconius charithonia" (butterfly)	2·00	2·50
441		$1.25 Bougainvillea	1·50	2·50

71 Footballers and World Cup

72 Sir Rowland Hill

1978. Anniversaries and Events.
442 75 c. Type **71** 30 40
443 95 c. Wright Brothers and Flyer I (horiz) . . . 40 50
444 $1.25 Balloon "Double Eagle II" and map of Atlantic (horiz) 50 60
445 $2 Prince Philip paying homage to the Queen . . . 60 90
EVENTS: 75 c. Argentina—Winners of World Cup Football Championship; 95 c. 75th anniv of powered flight; $1.25, First Atlantic crossing by balloon; $2 25th anniv of Coronation.

1979. Death Centenary of Sir Rowland Hill (1st issue). Multicoloured.
447 75 c. Type **72** 25 45
448 95 c. Mail coach, 1840 (horiz) 25 50
449 $1.25 London's first pillar box, 1855 (horiz) . . . 30 60
450 $2 Mail leaving St. Martin's Le Grand Post Office, London 45 85

1979. Death Centenary of Sir Rowland Hill (2nd issue). Nos. 603/6 of Antigua optd **BARBUDA**.
452 25 c. 1d. Stamp of 1863 . . 15 15
453 50 c. Penny Black . . . 20 20
454 $1 Stage-coach and woman posting letter, c. 1840 . . 35 30
455 $2 Modern mail transport . . 80 60

1979. Easter. Works of Durer. Nos. 608/10 of Antigua optd **BARBUDA**.
457 10 c. multicoloured . . . 10 10
458 50 c. multicoloured . . . 20 20
459 $4 black, mauve and yellow . 90 1·10

74 Passengers alighting from British Airways Boeing 747

1979. 30th Anniv of International Civil Aviation Organization. Multicoloured.
461 75 c. Type **74** 25 50
462 95 c. Air traffic control . . 25 50
463 $1.25 Ground crew-man directing Douglas DC-8 on runway 25 50

1979. International Year of the Child (1st issue). Nos. 612/15 of Antigua optd **BARBUDA**.
464 25 c. Yacht 20 15
465 50 c. Rocket 30 25
466 90 c. Car 40 35
467 $2 Toy train 80 60

1979. Fishes. Nos. 617/20 of Antigua optd **BARBUDA**.
469 30 c. Yellow jack . . . 20 15
470 50 c. Blue-finned tuna . . 30 20
471 90 c. Sailfish 40 30
472 $3 Wahoo . . . . 1·10 1·10

1979. Death Bicentenary of Captain Cook. Nos. 622/5 of Antigua optd **BARBUDA**.
474 25 c. Cook's Birthplace, Marton 30 30
475 50 c. H.M.S. "Endeavour" . . 85 45
476 90 c. Marine chronometer . . 90 60
477 $3 Landing at Botany Bay . . 1·75 1·50

77 "Virgin with the Pear"

1979. International Year of the Child (2nd issue). Paintings by Durer. Multicoloured.
479 25 c. Type **77** 15 15
480 50 c. "Virgin with the Pink" (detail) 25 25
481 75 c. "Virgin with the Pear" (different detail) . . . 30 30
482 $1.25 "Nativity" (detail) . . 40 40

1979. Christmas. Nos. 627/630 of Antigua optd **BARBUDA**.
484 8 c. The Holy Family . . . 10 10
485 25 c. Mary and Jesus on donkey 15 10
486 50 c. Shepherd looking at star 25 15
487 $4 The Three Kings . . . 85 80

1980. Olympic Games, Moscow. Nos. 632/5 of Antigua optd **BARBUDA**.
489 10 c. Javelin 10 10
490 25 c. Running 10 10
491 $1 Pole vault 30 20
492 $2 Hurdles 55 40

1980. "London 1980" International Stamp Exhibition. Nos. 452/5 optd **LONDON 1980**.
494 25 c. 1d. stamp of 1863 . . 35 20
495 50 c. Penny Black . . . 45 40
496 $1 Stage-coach and woman posting letter, c. 1840 . . 85 65
497 $2 Modern mail transport . . 2·75 1·50

80 "Apollo II" Crew Badge

1980. 10th Anniv of "Apollo II" Moon Landing. Multicoloured.
498 75 c. Type **80** 30 25
499 95 c. Plaque left on Moon . . 35 30
500 $1.25 Rejoining the mother-ship 45 50
501 $2 Lunar module 70 75

81 American Wigeon

1980. Birds. Multicoloured.
503 1 c. Type **81** 70 70
504 2 c. Snowy plover . . . 70 70
505 4 c. Rose-breasted grosbeak . 75 70
506 6 c. Mangrove cuckoo . . 75 70
507 10 c. Adelaide's warbler . . 75 70
508 15 c. Scaly-breasted thrasher . 80 70
509 20 c. Yellow-crowned night heron 80 70
510 25 c. Bridled quail dove . . 80 70
511 35 c. Carib grackle . . . 85 70
512 50 c. Northern pintail . . 90 55
513 75 c. Black-whispered vireo . 1·00 55
514 $1 Blue-winged teal . . . 1·25 80
515 $1.50 Green-throated carib (vert) 1·50 80
516 $2 Red-necked pigeon (vert) . 2·25 1·25
517 $2.50 Wied's crested flycatcher (vert) . . . . 2·75 1·50
518 $5 Yellow-bellied sapsucker (vert) . . . . 3·50 2·50
519 $7.50 Caribbean elaenia (vert) 4·50 5·00
520 $10 Great egret (vert) . . . 5·00 5·00

1980. Famous Works of Art. Nos. 651/7 of Antigua optd **BARBUDA**.
521 10 c. "David" (statue, Donatello) 10 10
522 30 c. "The Birth of Venus" (painting, Sandro Botticelli) 15 15
523 50 c. "Reclining Couple" (sarcophagus), Cerveteri . . 20 20
524 90 c. "The Garden of Earthly Delights" (painting, Hieronymus Bosch) . . . 25 25
525 $1 "Portinari Altarpiece" (painting, Hugo van der Goes) 25 25
526 $4 "Eleanora of Toledo and her Son Giovanni de'Medici" painting, Agnolo Bronzino) 80 80

1980. 75th Anniv of Rotary International. Nos. 651/4 of Antigua optd **BARBUDA**.
528 30 c. Rotary Headquarters . 15 15
529 50 c. Antigua Rotary banner . 20 20
530 90 c. Map of Antigua . . . 25 25
531 $3 Paul P. Harris (founder) . 65 65

1980. 80th Birthday of the Queen Mother. Nos. 663/4 of Antigua optd **BARBUDA**.
533 10 c. multicoloured . . . 50 15
534 $2.50 multicoloured . . . 1·50 1·50

1980. Birds. Nos. 666/9 of Antigua optd **BARBUDA**.
536 10 c. Ringed kingfisher . . 1·50 75
537 30 c. Plain pigeon . . . 2·00 1·00
538 $1 Green-throated carib . . 3·25 2·25
539 $2 Black necked stilt . . . 3·75 4·25

1981. Sugar Cane Railway Locomotives. Nos. 681/4 of Antigua optd **BARBUDA**.
541 25 c. Diesel locomotive No. 15 1·00 25
542 50 c. Narrow-gauge steam locomotive . . . . 1·25 35
543 90 c. Diesel locomotive Nos. 1 and 10 . . . . 1·75 45
544 $3 Steam locomotive hauling sugar cane . . . . 3·25 1·40

84 Florence Nightingale

1981. Famous Women.
546 **84** 50 c. multicoloured . . . 15 30
547 – 90 c. multicoloured . . . 40 55
548 – $1 multicoloured . . . 35 60
549 – $4 black, brown and lilac . 50 1·75
DESIGNS: 90 c. Marie Curie; $1 Amy Johnson; $4 Eleanor Roosevelt.

85 Goofy in Motor-boat

1981. Walt Disney Cartoon Characters. Multicoloured.
550 10 c. Type **85** 55 15
551 20 c. Donald Duck reversing car into sea 65 20
552 25 c. Mickey Mouse asking tug-boat to take on more than it can handle . . . 80 30
553 30 c. Porpoise turning tables on Goofy 80 35
554 35 c. Goofy in sailing boat . . 80 35
555 40 c. Mickey Mouse and boat being lifted out of water by fish 90 40
556 75 c. Donald Duck fishing for flying-fish with butterfly net 1·00 60
557 $1 Minnie Mouse in brightly decorated sailing boat . . 1·10 80
558 $2 Chip and Dale on floating ship-in-bottle . . . 1·75 1·40

1981. Birth Centenary of Picasso. Nos. 697/700 of Antigua optd with **BARBUDA**.
560 10 c. "Pipes of Pan" . . . 10 10
561 50 c. "Seated Harlequin" . . 25 25
562 90 c. "Paulo as Harlequin" . . 45 45
563 $4 "Mother and Child" . . 1·60 1·60

87 Buckingham Palace **88**
(½-size illustration)

1981. Royal Wedding (1st issue). Buildings. Each printed in black on either pink, green or lilac backgrounds.
565 $1 Type **87** 25 40
566 $1 Type **88** 25 40
567 $1.50 Caernarvon Castle (right) 30 50
568 $1.50 Caernarvon Castle (left) . 30 50
569 $4 Highgrove House (right) . 55 90
570 $4 Highgrove House (left) . . 55 90
Same prices for any background colour. The two versions of each value form composite designs.

1981. Royal Wedding (2nd issue). Nos. 702/5 of Antigua optd **BARBUDA**.
572 25 c. Prince Charles and Lady Diana Spencer . . . 15 15
573 50 c. Glamis Castle . . . 25 25
574 $4 Prince Charles skiing . . 75 1·00

89 "Integration and Travel"

1981. International Year of Disabled Persons (1st issue).
576 **89** 50 c. multicoloured . . . 30 20
577 – 90 c. black, orange and green 35 30
578 – $1 black, blue and green . . 40 35
579 – $4 black, yellow and brown 60 1·25
DESIGNS: 90 c. Braille and sign language; $1 "Helping hands"; $4 "Mobility aids for disabled". See also Nos. 603/6.

1981. Royal Wedding (3rd issue). Nos. 706/12 of Antigua optd **BARBUDA**.
580 25 c. Prince of Wales at Investiture, 1969 . . . 35 55
581 25 c. Prince Charles as baby, 1948 . . . . 35 55
582 $1 Prince Charles at R.A.F. College, Cranwell, 1971 . . 40 60
583 $1 Prince Charles attending Hill House School, 1956 . . . 40 60
584 $2 Prince Charles and Lady Diana Spencer . . . 65 80
585 $2 Prince Charles at Trinity College, 1967 . . . 65 80
586 $5 Prince Charles and Lady Diana . . . . 2·50 3·50

1981. Independence. No. 686/96 of Antigua additionally optd **BARBUDA**.
587 6 c. Orchid tree 50 15
588 10 c. Bougainvillea . . . 55 15
589 20 c. Flamboyant 70 20
590 25 c. Hibiscus 80 25
591 35 c. Flame of the wood . . 90 30
592 50 c. Cannon at Fort James . 1·10 45
593 75 c. Premier's Office . . . 1·25 75
594 $1 Potworks Dam . . . . 1·50 80
595 $2.50 Irrigation scheme, Diamond Estate . . . 2·50 2·75
596 $5 Government House and Gardens . . . . 2·75 3·75
597 $10 Coolidge International Airport . . . . 4·50 6·00

1981. 50th Anniv of Antigua Girl Guide Movement. Nos. 713/16 of Antigua optd **BARBUDA**.
598 10 c. Irene Joshua (founder) . 55 10
599 50 c. Campfire sing-song . . 1·25 30
600 90 c. Sailing . . . . 1·75 45
601 $2.50 Animal tending . . . 3·00 1·40

1981. International Year of Disabled Persons (2nd issue). Sport for the Disabled. Nos. 728/31 of Antigua optd **BARBUDA**.
603 10 c. Swimming 20 15
604 50 c. Discus throwing . . . 30 25
605 90 c. Archery 70 45
606 $2 Baseball . . . . 1·75 1·50

1981. Christmas. Paintings. No. 726/6 of Antigua optd **BARBUDA**.
608 8 c. "Holy Night" (Jacques Stella) 10 10
609 30 c. "Mary with Child" (Julius Schnorr von Carolfeld) . . 20 20
610 $1 "Virgin and Child" (Alsono Cano) 40 40
611 $3 "Virgin and Child" (Lorenzo di Credi) . . . . 1·10 1·10

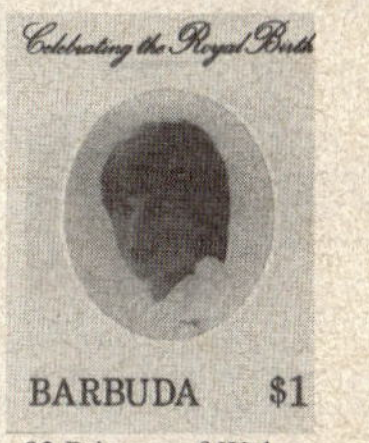

93 Princess of Wales

1982. Birth of Prince William of Wales (1st issue).
613 **93** $1 multicoloured . . . 50 50
614 $2.50 multicoloured . . . 90 1·10
615 $5 multicoloured . . . 2·00 2·25

1982. South Atlantic Fund. Nos. 580/6 surch **S. Atlantic Fund + 50 c.**
617 25 c. + 50 c. Prince of Wales at Investiture, 1969 . . . 20 20
618 25 c. + 50 c. Prince Charles as baby, 1948 . . . . 20 20
619 $1 + 50 c. Prince Charles at R.A.F. College, Cranwell, 1971 . . . . 45 45
620 $1 + 50 c. Prince Charles attending Hill House School, 1956 . . . . 45 45
621 $2 + 50 c. Prince Charles and Lady Diana Spencer . . 75 75
622 $2 + 50 c. Prince Charles at Trinity College, 1967 . . 75 75
623 $5 + 50 c. Prince Charles and Lady Diana Spencer . . . 2·00 2·00

1982. 21st Birthday of Princess of Wales (1st issue). As Nos. 613/16 but inscr "Twenty First Birthday Greetings to H.R.H. The Princess of Wales."
624 $1 multicoloured 75 45
625 $2.50 multicoloured . . . 1·40 1·25
626 $5 multicoloured . . . . 2·75 2·40

1982. 21st Birthday of Princess of Wales (2nd issue). Nos. 748/51 of Antigua optd **BARBUDA MAIL**.
628 90 c. Queen's House, Greenwich 65 45
629 $1 Prince and Princess of Wales 75 50
630 $4 Princess of Wales . . . 1·60 1·50

1982. Birth of Prince William of Wales (2nd issue). Nos. 757/9 of Antigua further optd **BARBUDA MAIL**.
632 90 c. Queen's House, Greenwich 55 45
633 $1 Prince and Princess of Wales 60 50
634 $4 Princess of Wales . . . 2·25 2·00

1982. Birth Centenary of Franklin D. Roosevelt and 250th Birth Anniv of George Washington. Nos. 761/6 of Antigua optd **BARBUDA MAIL**.
636 10 c. Roosevelt in 1940 . . . 10 10
637 25 c. Washington as blacksmith 15 15
638 45 c. Churchill, Roosevelt and Stalin at Yalta Conference . 35 25
639 60 c. Washington crossing Delaware 20 25
640 $1 "Roosevelt Special" train . 50 40
641 $3 Portrait of Roosevelt . . 60 90

1982. Christmas. Religious Paintings by Raphael. Nos. 769/72 of Antigua optd **BARBUDA MAIL**.
644 10 c. "Annunciation" . . . 10 10
645 30 c. "Adoration of the Magi" . 15 15
646 $1 "Presentation at the Temple" 40 40
647 $4 "Coronation of the Virgin" 1·25 1·25

1983. 500th Birth Anniv of Raphael. Details from "Galatea" Fresco. Nos. 774/7 of Antigua optd **BARBUDA MAIL**.
649 45 c. Tritons and dolphins . . 20 20
650 50 c. Sea Nymph carried off by Triton 25 25
651 60 c. Winged angel steering dolphins (horiz) . . . 30 30
652 $4 Cupids shooting arrows . . 1·25 1·25

1983. Commonwealth Day. Nos. 779/82 of Antigua optd **BARBUDA MAIL**.
654 25 c. Pineapple produce . . . 50 70
655 45 c. Carnival 80 90
656 60 c. Tourism . . . . . 1·25 1·60
657 $3 Airport . . . . . 2·75 4·00

1983. World Communications Year. Nos. 783/6 of Antigua optd **BARBUDA MAIL**.
658 15 c. T.V. satellite coverage of Royal Wedding 55 20
659 50 c. Police communications . 1·75 90
660 60 c. House-to-diesel train telephone call . . . . 1·75 90
661 $3 Satellite earth station with planets Jupiter and Saturn . 3·50 2·50

97 Vincenzo Lunardi's Balloon Flight, London, 1785

1983. Bicent of Manned Flight (1st issue). Mult.
663 $1 Type **97** 25 35
664 $1.50, Montgolfier brothers' balloon flight, Paris, 1783 . 40 55
665 $2.50, Blanchard and Jeffries' Cross Channel balloon flight, 1785 . . . . . 60 90
See also Nos. 672/5.

1983. Whales. Nos. 788/92 of Antigua optd **BARBUDA MAIL**.
667 15 c. Bottlenose dolphin . . . 1·25 40
668 50 c. Finback whale . . . . 4·00 1·60
669 60 c. Bowhead whale . . . . 4·50 1·75
670 $3 Spectacled porpoise . . . 5·50 4·25

1983. Bicentenary of Manned Flight (2nd issue). Nos. 811/15 of Antigua optd **BARBUDA MAIL**.
672 30 c. Dornier Do-X flying boat 85 35
673 50 c. Supermarine S6B seaplane 1·10 60
674 60 c. Curtiss Sparrowhawk biplane and airship U.S.S. "Akron" . . . . . 1·25 70
675 $4 Hot-air balloon "Pro-Juventute" . . . . . 4·50 4·00

1983. Nos. 565/70 surch.
677 45 c. on $1 Type **87** 35 50
678 45 c. on $1 Type **88** 35 50
679 50 c. on $1.50 Caernarvon Castle (right) 35 55
680 50 c. on $1.50 Caernarvon Castle (left) 35 55
681 60 c. on $4 Highgrove House (left) 35 60
682 60 c. on $4 Highgrove House (right) 35 60

1983. Nos. 793/810 of Antigua optd **BARBUDA MAIL**.
683 1 c. Cashew nut 10 10
684 2 c. Passion fruit 15 10
685 3 c. Mango 15 10
686 5 c. Grapefruit 15 10
687 10 c. Pawpaw 20 10
688 15 c. Breadfruit 40 10
689 20 c. Coconut 50 15
690 25 c. Oleander 50 15
691 30 c. Banana 55 20
692 40 c. Pineapple 65 25
693 45 c. Cordia 70 30
694 50 c. Cassia 80 30
695 60 c. Poui 80 30
696 $1 Frangipani . . . . . 1·10 50
697 $2 Flamboyant . . . . . 2·00 1·25
698 $2.50 Lemon . . . . . 2·25 1·75
699 $5 Lignum vitae . . . . . 3·50 2·75
700 $10 National Flag and coat of arms . . . . . 5·50 5·50

1983. Christmas. 500th Birth Anniv of Raphael. Nos. 816/20 of Antigua optd **BARBUDA MAIL**.
701 10 c. multicoloured 10 10
702 30 c. multicoloured 15 20
703 $1 multicoloured 40 50
704 $4 multicoloured . . . . 1·25 1·75

1983. Bicentenary (1984) of Methodist Church. Nos. 821/4 of Antigua optd **BARBUDA MAIL**.
706 15 c. Type **181** 25 15
707 50 c. Nathaniel Gilbert (founder in Antigua) 40 25
708 60 c. St. John Methodist Church steeple 40 30
709 $3 Ebenezer Methodist Church, St John's . . . . . 90 1·25

100 Edward VIII

1984. Members of British Royal Family. Mult.
710 $1 Type **100** . . . . . 50 1·10
711 $1 George V . . . . . 50 1·10
712 $1 George VI . . . . . 50 1·10
713 $1 Elizabeth II . . . . . 50 1·10
714 $1 Charles Prince of Wales . 50 1·10
715 $1 Prince William of Wales . 50 1·10

1984. Olympic Games, Los Angeles (1st issue). Nos. 825/8 of Antigua optd **BARBUDA MAIL**.
716 25 c. Discus 15 20
717 50 c. Gymnastics 35 40
718 90 c. Hurdling 50 60
719 $3 Cycling . . . . . 1·25 1·50

1984. Ships. Nos. 830/3 of Antigua optd **BARBUDA MAIL**.
721 45 c. "Booker Vanguard" (freighter) . . . . . 1·50 45
722 50 c. "Canberra" (liner) . . . 1·50 50
723 60 c. Sailing boats . . . . 1·75 60
724 $4 "Fairwind" (cargo liner) . 4·25 2·75

1984. Universal Postal Union Congress, Hamburg. Nos. 835/8 of Antigua optd **BARBUDA MAIL**.
726 15 c. Chenille 30 15
727 50 c. Shell flower 50 40
728 60 c. Anthurium 60 50
729 $3 Angels trumpet . . . . 1·25 1·50

101 Olympic Stadium, Athens, 1896

1984. Olympic Games, Los Angeles (2nd issue). Multicoloured.
731 $1.50 Type **101** . . . . . 80 1·10
732 $2.50 Olympic stadium, Los Angeles, 1984 . . . . . 1·25 1·75
733 $5 Athlete carrying Olympic torch . . . . . 2·25 2·75

1984. Presidents of the United States of America. Nos. 856/63 of Antigua optd **BARBUDA MAIL**.
735 10 c. Abraham Lincoln . . . 10 10
736 20 c. Harry Truman 15 15
737 30 c. Dwight Eisenhower . . . 20 25
738 40 c. Ronald Reagan 25 30
739 90 c. Gettysburg Address, 1863 50 55
740 $1.10 Formation of N.A.T.O., 1949 . . . . . 60 65
741 $1.50, Eisenhower during Second World War 80 85
742 $2 Reagan and Caribbean Basin Initiative . . . . . 1·00 1·25

1984. Abolition of Slavery. Nos. 864/7 of Antigua optd **BARBUDA MAIL**.
743 40 c. View of Moravian Mission 30 30
744 50 c. Antigua Courthouse, 1823 40 40
745 60 c. Planting suger-cane, Monks Hill 45 45
746 $3 Boiling house, Delaps' Estate 1·90 1·90

1984. Songbirds. Nos. 869/73 of Antigua optd **BARBUDA MAIL**.
748 40 c. Rufous-sided towhee . . 1·25 45
749 50 c. Parula warbler . . . . 1·40 50
750 60 c. House wren . . . . . 1·50 55
751 $2 Ruby-crowned kinglet . . 2·75 1·50
752 $3 Common flicker . . . . 3·25 2·25

1984. 450th Death Anniv of Correggio (painter). Nos. 878/81 of Antigua optd **BARBUDA MAIL**.
754 25 c. "The Virgin and Infant with Angels and Cherubs" . . . 15 20
755 60 c. "The Four Saints" . . . 40 45
756 90 c. "St. Catherine" 60 65
757 $3 "The Campori Madonna" . 1·75 2·25

1984. "Ausipex" International Stamp Exhibition Melbourne. Australian Sports. Nos. 875/6 of Antigua optd **BARBUDA MAIL**.
759 $1 Grass-skiing 70 75
760 $5 Australian Football . . . 3·00 3·75

1984. 150th Birth Anniv of Edgar Degas (painter). Nos. 883/6 of Antigua optd **BARBUDA MAIL**.
762 15 c. "The Blue Dancers" . . 10 10
763 50 c. "The Pink Dancers" . . 30 40
764 70 c. "Two Dancers" . . . 45 55
765 $4 "Dancers at the Bar" . . 2·40 3·50

1985. Famous People. Nos. 888/96 of Antigua optd **BARBUDA MAIL**.
767 60 c. Winston Churchill . . . 2·00 80
768 60 c. Mahatma Gandhi . . . 2·00 80
769 60 c. John F. Kennedy . . . 2·00 80
770 60 c. Mao Tse-tung . . . . 2·00 80
771 $1 Churchill with General De Gaulle, Paris, 1944 (horiz) . 2·25 1·00
772 $1 Gandhi leaving London by train, 1931 (horiz) . . . 2·25 1·00
773 $1 Kennedy with Chancellor Adenauer and Mayor Brandt, Berlin, 1963 (horiz) . . . 2·25 1·00
774 $1 Mao Tse-tung with Lin Piao, Peking, 1969 (horiz) . . . 2·25 1·00

HAVE YOU READ THE NOTES AT THE BEGINNING OF THIS CATALOGUE?
These often provide answers to the enquiries we receive.

103 Lady Elizabeth Bowes-Lyon, 1907, and Camellias

104 Roseate Tern

1985. Life and Times of Queen Elizabeth the Queen Mother. Multicoloured.
776 15 c. Type **103** 10 10
777 45 c. Duchess of York, 1926, and "Elizabeth of Glamis" roses 20 25
778 50 c. The Queen Mother after the Coronation, 1937 . . . . 20 25
779 60 c. In Garter robes, 1971, and dog roses 20 30
780 90 c. Attending Royal Variety Show, 1967, and red Hibiscus 30 45
781 $1 The Queen Mother in 1982, and blue plumbago . . . . 60 1·10
782 $3 Receiving 82nd birthday gifts from children, and morning glory . . . . . 90 1·60

1985. Birth Bicentenary of John J. Audubon (ornithologist) (1st issue). Designs showing original paintings. Multicoloured.
783 45 c. Type **104** 25 30
784 50 c. Mangrove cuckoo . . . 25 30
785 60 c. Yellow-crowned night heron 30 40
786 $5 Brown pelican . . . . . 2·25 3·50
See also Nos. 794/7 and 914/17.

1985. Centenary (1986) of Statue of Liberty (1st issue). Nos. 907/13 of Antigua optd **BARBUDA MAIL**.
787 25 c. Torch from statue in Madison Square Park, 1885 . 20 20
788 30 c. Statue of Liberty and scaffolding ("Restoration and Renewal") (vert) 20 20
789 50 c. Frederic Bartholdi (sculpture) supervising construction, 1876 . . . . 30 30
790 90 c. Close-up of Statue . . . 55 55
791 $1 Statue and sailing ship ("Operation Sail", 1976) (vert) 60 60
792 $3 Dedication ceremony, 1886 (vert . . . . . 1·75 1·75
See also Nos. 987/96.

1985. Birth Bicentenary of John J. Audubon (ornithologist) (2nd issue). Nos. 924/8 of Antigua optd **BARBUDA MAIL**.
794 90 c. Slavonian grebe . . . . 4·00 3·50
795 $1 British storm petrel . . . 4·25 3·75
796 $1.50 Great blue heron . . . 5·00 4·25
797 $3 Double-crested cormorant . 8·00 6·50

1985. Butterflies. Nos. 929/33 of Antigua optd **BARBUDA MAIL**.
799 25 c. "Anaea cyanea" . . . . 2·50 1·00
800 60 c. "Leodonta dysoni" . . . 4·00 1·75
801 90 c. "Junea doraete" . . . . 5·00 2·25
802 $4 "Prepona pylene" . . . . 10·00 10·00

1985. Centenary of Motorcycle. Nos. 919/23 of Antigua optd **BARBUDA MAIL**.
804 10 c. Triumph 2hp "Jap", 1903 40 10
805 30 c. Indian "Arrow", 1949 . . 70 20
806 60 c. BMW "R100RS", 1976 . 1·10 40
807 $4 Harely Davidson "Model II", 1916 . . . . . 3·50 2·75

1985. 85th Birthday of Queen Elizabeth the Queen Mother. Nos. 776/82 optd **4th Aug 1900–1985**.
809 15 c. Type **103** 60 30
810 45 c. Duchess of York, 1926 and "Elizabeth of Glamis" roses 90 50
811 50 c. The Queen Mother after the Coronation, 1937 . . . . 90 50
812 60 c. In Garter robes, 1971, and dog roses . . . . . 1·00 80
813 90 c. Attending Royal Variey Show, 1967, and red hibiscus 1·10 1·10
814 $2 The Queen Mother in 1982, and blue plumbago . . . . 1·40 2·75
815 $3 Receiving 82nd birthday gifts from children, and morning glory . . . . . 1·50 3·00

1985. Native American Artefacts. Nos. 914/18 of Antigua optd **BARBUDA MAIL**.
816 15 c. Arawak pot sherd and Indians making clay utensils 15 10
817 50 c. Arawak body design and Arawak Indians tattooing . 30 30
818 60 c. Head of the god "Yocahu" and Indians harvesting manioc 40 40
819 $3 Carib war club and Carib Indians going into battle . . 1·60 1·75

1985. 40th Anniv of International Civil Aviation Organization. Nos. 934/8 of Antigua optd **BARBUDA MAIL**.
821 30 c. Cessna Skyhawk 80 50
822 90 c. Fokker D.VII . . . . . 1·50 1·00
823 $1.50 SPAD VII . . . . . 2·25 3·00
824 $3 Boeing 747 . . . . . 3·50 4·25

1985. Life and Times of Queen Elizabeth the Queen Mother (2nd series). Nos. 946/8 of Antigua optd **BARBUDA MAIL**.
826 $1 The Queen Mother attending church . . . . . 2·50 2·50
827 $1.50 Watching children playing in London garden . . . . 3·00 3·00
828 $2.50 The Queen Mother in 1979 3·50 3·50

1985. 850th Birth Anniv of Maimonides (physician philosopher and scholar). No. 939 of Antigua optd **BARBUDA MAIL**.
830 $2 green . . . . . 4·50 3·75

1985. Marine Life. Nos. 950/3 of Antigua optd **BARBUDA MAIL**.
832 15 c. Magnificent frigate bird 3·00 75
833 45 c. Brain coral . . . . . 3·00 70
834 60 c. Cushion star . . . . . 3·00 90
835 $3 Spotted moray . . . . . 6·50 4·25

1986. International Youth Year. Nos. 941/5 of Antigua optd **BARBUDA MAIL**.
837 25 c. Young farmers with produce 15 15
838 50 c. Hotel management trainees 25 30
839 60 c. Girls with goat and boys with football ("Environment") 30 35
840 $3 Windsurfing ("Leisure") . 1·50 1·60

1986. Royal Visit. Nos. 965/8 of Antigua optd **BARBUDA MAIL**.
842 60 c. Flags of Great Britain and Antigua . . . . . 1·25 35
843 $1 Queen Elizabeth II (vert) . 1·40 55
844 $4 Royal Yacht "Britannia" . 3·75 2·10

1986. 75th Anniv of Girl Guide Movement. Nos. 955/8 of Antigua optd **BARBUDA MAIL**.
846 15 c. Girl Guides nursing . . 1·25 80
847 45 c. Open-air Girl Guide meeting . . . . . 2·50 1·75
848 60 c. Lord and Lady Baden-Powell . . . . . 2·75 2·50
849 $3 Girl Guides gathering flowers 7·00 8·50

1986. 300th Birth Anniv of Johann Sebastian Bach (composer). Nos. 960/3 of Antigua optd **BARBUDA MAIL**.
851 25 c. multicoloured . . . . 1·75 70
852 50 c. multicoloured . . . . 2·25 1·40
853 $1 multicoloured . . . . . 3·00 2·00
854 $3 multicoloured . . . . . 6·00 8·00

1986. Christmas. Religious Paintings. Nos. 985/8 of Antigua optd **BARBUDA MAIL**.
856 10 c. "Madonna and Child" (De Landi) 40 20
857 25 c. "Madonna and Child" (Berlinghiero) 80 50
858 60 c. "The Nativity" (Fra Angelico) . . . . . 1·50 1·00
859 $4 "Presentation in the Temple" (Giovanni di Paolo) . . . 4·00 6·50

108 Queen Elizabeth II meeting Members of Legislature

1986. 60th Birthday of Queen Elizabeth II (1st issue). Multicoloured.
861 $1 Type **108** . . . . . 50 1·00
862 $2 Queen with Headmistress of Liberta School . . . . . 60 1·10
863 $2.50 Queen greeted by Governor-General of Antigua 60 1·25
See also Nos. 872/4.

109 Halley's Comet over Barbuda Beach

1986. Appearance of Halley's Comet (1st issue). Multicoloured.
865 $1 Type **109** . . . . . 80 1·25
866 $2.50 Early telescope and dish aerial (vert) . . . . . 1·50 2·25
867 $5 Comet and world map . . 2·50 3·75
See also Nos. 886/9.

1986. 40th Anniv of United Nations Organization. Nos. 981/3 of Antigua optd **BARBUDA MAIL**.
868 40 c. Benjamin Franklin and U.N. (New York) 1953 U.P.U. 5 c. stamp . . . . . 1·50 1·00
869 $1 George Washington Carver (agricultural chemist) and 1982 Nature Conservation 28 c. stamp . . . . . 2·25 2·25
870 $3 Charles Lindbergh (aviator) and 1978 I.C.A.O. 25 c. stamp 4·00 5·00

1986. 60th Birthday of Queen Elizabeth II (2nd issue). Nos. 1005/7 of Antigua optd **BARBUDA MAIL**.
872 60 c. black and yellow . . . 1·50 1·25
873 $1 multicoloured . . . . . 2·00 1·75
874 $4 muticoloured . . . . . 3·75 4·25

1986. World Cup Football Championship, Mexico. Nos. 995/8 of Antigua optd **BARBUDA MAIL**.
876 30 c. Football, boots and trophy 2·00 1·00
877 60 c. Goalkeeper (vert) . . . 3·00 2·00
878 $1 Referee blowing whistle (vert) 3·25 2·25
879 $4 Ball in net . . . . . 7·50 7·00

1986. "Ameripex '86" International Stamp Exhibition, Chicago. Famous American Trains. Nos. 1014/17 of Antigua optd **BARBUDA MAIL**.
881 25 c. "Hiawatha" express . . 2·00 1·50
882 50 c. "Grand Canyon" express 2·75 2·25
883 $1 "Powhattan Arrow" express 3·50 3·00
884 $3 "Empire State" express . . 6·00 6·50

1986. Appearance of Halley's Comet (2nd issue). Nos. 1000/3 of Antigua optd **BARBUDA MAIL**.
886 5 c. Edmond Halley and Old Greenwich Observatory 75 55
887 10 c. Messerschmitt Me 163B Komet (fighter aircraft), 1944 75 55
888 60 c. Montezuma (Aztec Emperor) and Comet in 1517 (from "Historias de las Indias de Neuva Espana") 2·50 2·00
889 $4 Pocahontas saving Capt. John Smith and Comet in 1607 7·50 7·00

1986. Royal Wedding. Nos. 1019/21 of Antigua optd **BARBUDA MAIL**.
891 45 c. Prince Andrew and Miss Sarah Ferguson 75 50
892 60 c. Prince Andrew 90 65
893 $4 Prince Andrew with Prince Philip 3·50 4·00

1986. Sea Shells. Nos. 1023/6 of Antigua optd **BARBUDA MAIL**.
895 15 c. Fly-specked cerith 2·50 1·75
896 45 c. Smooth Scotch bonnet 2·75 2·25
897 60 c. West Indian crown conch 3·50 2·75
898 $3 Criboney murex 8·00 9·50

1986. Flowers. Nos. 1028/35 of Antigua optd **BARBUDA MAIL**.
900 10 c. "Nymphaea ampla" (water lily) 20 20
901 15 c. Queen of the night 30 30
902 50 c. Cup of gold 50 65
903 60 c. Beach morning glory 55 70
904 70 c. Golden trumpet 70 85
905 $1 Air plant 85 90
906 $3 Purple wreath 2·25 2·75
907 $4 Zephyr lily 2·75 3·25

1986. Mushrooms. Nos. 1042/5 of Antigua optd **BARBUDA MAIL**.
909 10 c. "Hygrocybe occidentalis var scarletina" 90 50
910 50 c. "Trogia buccinalis" 3·25 1·75
911 $1 "Collybia subpruinosa" 4·75 2·75
912 $4 "Leucocoprinus brebissonii" 9·50 8·00

1986. Birth Bicentenary of John J. Audubon (ornithologist) (3rd issue). Nos. 990/3 of Antigua optd **BARBUDA MAIL**.
914 60 c. Mallard 3·00 1·75
915 90 c. North American black duck 3·75 2·25
916 $1.50 American pintail 5·00 4·75
917 $3 Wigeon 8·00 8·50

1987. Local Boats. Nos. 1009/12 of Antigua optd **BARBUDA MAIL**.
918 30 c. Tugboat 60 50
919 60 c. Game fishing boat 80 80
920 $1 Yacht 1·25 1·25
921 $4 Lugger with auxiliary sail 3·25 4·00

1987. Centenary of First Benz Motor Car. Nos. 1052/9 of Antigua optd **BARBUDA MAIL**.
923 10 c. Auburn "Speedster" (1933) 45 30
924 15 c. Mercury "Sable" (1986) 55 40
925 50 c. Cadillac (1959) 1·10 60
926 60 c. Studebaker (1950) 1·10 70
927 70 c. Lagonda "V-12" (1939) 1·25 1·00
928 $1 Adler "Standard" (1930) 1·50 1·00
929 $3 DKW (1956) 2·75 2·75
930 $4 Mercedes "500K" (1936) 2·75 2·75

1987. World Cup Football Championship Winners, Mexico. Nos. 1037/40 of Antigua optd **BARBUDA MAIL**.
932 30 c. Football, boots and trophy 1·10 70
933 60 c. Goalkeeper (vert) 1·50 1·00
934 $1 Referee blowing whistle (vert) 2·00 1·75
935 $4 Ball in net 4·75 5·00

1987. America's Cup Yachting Championship. Nos. 1072/5 of Antigua optd **BARBUDA MAIL**.
936 30 c. "Canada I" (1981) 20 30
937 60 c. "Gretel II" (1970) 35 50
938 $1 "Sceptre" (1958) 60 80
939 $3 "Vigilant" (1893) 1·75 2·50

1987. Marine Life. Nos. 1077/84 of Antigua optd **BARBUDA MAIL**.
941 15 c. Bridled burrfish 3·25 70
942 30 c. Common noddy 3·50 85
943 40 c. Nassau grouper 3·50 90
944 50 c. Laughing gull 5·00 1·50
945 60 c. French angelfish 5·00 1·50
946 $1 Porkfish 5·00 1·75
947 $2 Royal tern 11·00 5·00
948 $3 Sooty tern 11·00 6·00

1987. Milestones of Transportation. Nos. 1100/9 of Antigua optd **BARBUDA MAIL**.
950 10 c. "Spirit of Australia" (fastest powerboat), 1978 1·00 60
951 15 c. Werner von Siemens's electric locomotive, 1879 1·50 80
952 30 c. U.S.S. "Triton" (first submerged circumnavigation), 1960 1·75 90
953 50 c. Trevithick's steam carriage (first passenger-carrying vehicle), 1801 2·00 1·25
954 60 c. U.S.S. "New Jersey" (battleship), 1942 2·25 1·25
955 70 c. Draisine bicycle, 1818 2·25 1·40
956 90 c. "United States" (liner) (holder of the Blue Riband), 1952 2·25 1·50
957 $1.50 Cierva C.4 (first autogyro), 1923 2·50 2·50
958 $2 Curtiss NC-4 flying boat (first transatlantic flight), 1919 3·50 3·50
959 $3 "Queen Elizabeth 2" (liner), 1969 4·25 4·25

110 Shore Crab

1987. Marine Life. Multicoloured.
960 5 c. Type **110** 10 20
961 10 c. Sea cucumber 15 20
962 15 c. Stop-light parrotfish 15 20
963 25 c. Banded coral shrimp 15 20
964 35 c. Spotted drum 15 20
965 60 c. Thorny starfish 25 40
966 75 c. Atlantic trumpet triton 35 60
967 90 c. Feather star and yellow beaker sponge 40 65
968 $1 Blue gorgonian (vert) 65 65
969 $1.25 Slender filefish (vert) 55 85
970 $5 Barred hamlet (vert) 1·25 4·00
971 $7.50 Royal gramma ("Fairy basslet") (vert) 1·75 5·50
972 $10 Fire coral and banded butterflyfish (vert) 2·25 6·50

1987. Olympic Games, Seoul (1988). Nos. 1086/9 of Antigua optd **BARBUDA MAIL**.
973 10 c. Handball 65 45
974 60 c. Fencing 90 70
975 $1 Gymnastics 1·25 1·25
976 $3 Football 2·50 3·50

1987. Birth Centenary of Marc Chagall (artist). Nos. 1091/8 of Antigua optd **BARBUDA MAIL**.
978 10 c. "The Profile" 10 10
979 30 c. "Portrait of the Artist's Sister" 15 15
980 40 c. "Bride with Fan" 20 25
981 60 c. "David in Profile" 25 30
982 90 c. "Fiancee with Bouquet" 40 50
983 $1 "Self Portrait with Brushes" 45 55
984 $3 "The Walk" 1·40 1·60
985 $4 "Three Candles" 1·75 2·00

1987. Centenary (1986) of Statue of Liberty (2nd issue). Nos. 1110/19 of Antigua optd **BARBUDA MAIL**.
987 15 c. Lee Iacocoa at unveiling of restored statue 10 10
988 30 c. Statue at sunset (side view) 15 15
989 45 c. Aerial view of head 20 25
990 50 c. Lee Iacocoa and torch 25 30
991 60 c. Workmen inside head of statue (horiz) 25 30
992 90 c. Restoration work (horiz) 40 50
993 $1 Head of statue 45 55
994 $2 Statue at sunset (front view) 90 1·40
995 $3 Inspecting restoration work (horiz) 1·40 2·00
996 $5 Statue at night 2·25 3·00

1987. Entertainers. Nos. 1120/7 of Antigua optd **BARBUDA MAIL**.
997 15 c. Grace Kelly 80 50
998 30 c. Marilyn Monroe 1·75 1·00
999 45 c. Orson Welles 90 75
1000 50 c. Judy Garland 95 85
1001 60 c. John Lennon 2·75 1·75
1002 $1 Rock Hudson 1·75 1·50
1003 $1 John Wayne 2·75 2·75
1004 $3 Elvis Presley 6·00 5·00

1987. "Capex '87" Internationl Stamp Exhibition, Toronto. Reptiles and Amphibians. Nos. 1133/6 of Antigua optd **BARBUDA MAIL**.
1005 30 c. Whistling frog 1·75 85
1006 60 c. Croaking lizard 2·25 1·25
1007 $1 Antiguan anole 2·50 1·40
1008 $3 Red-footed tortoise 6·00 7·00

1988. Christmas. Religious Paintings. Nos. 1144/7 of Antigua optd **BARBUDA MAIL**.
1010 45 c. "Madonna and Child" (Bernardo Daddi) 60 25
1011 60 c. St. Joseph (detail, "The Nativity" (Sano di Pietro) 75 45
1012 $1 Virgin Mary (detail, "The Nativity" (Sano di Pietro) 1·00 85
1013 $4 "Music-making Angel" (Melozzo da Forli) 3·00 4·25

1988. Salvation Army's Community Service. Nos. 1163/70 of Antigua optd **BARBUDA MAIL**.
1015 25 c. First aid at daycare centre, Antigua 80 80
1016 30 c. Giving penicillin injection, Indonesia 80 80
1017 40 c. Children at daycare centre, Bolivia 85 85
1018 45 c. Rehabilitation of the handicapped, India 85 85
1019 50 c. Training blind man, Kenya 1·25 1·25
1020 60 c. Weighing baby, Ghana 1·25 1·25
1021 $1 Training typist, Zambia 1·75 1·75
1022 $2 Emergency food kitchen, Sri Lanka 2·25 2·75

1988. Bicentenary of U.S. Constitution. Nos. 1139/42 of Antigua optd **BARBUDA MAIL**.
1024 15 c. House of Burgesses, Virginia ("Freedom of Speech") 10 10
1025 45 c. State Seal, Connecticut 20 25
1026 60 c. State Seal, Delaware 25 35
1027 $4 Gouverneur Morris (Pennsylvania delegate) (vert) 1·75 3·00

1988. Royal Ruby Wedding. Nos. 1149/52 of Antigua optd **BARBUDA MAIL**.
1029 25 c. brown, black and blue 60 30
1030 60 c. multicoloured 1·00 65
1031 $2 brown, black and green 2·25 2·25
1032 $3 multicoloured 2·50 2·75

1988. Birds of Antigua. Nos. 1154/61 of Antigua optd **BARBUDA MAIL**.
1034 10 c. Great blue heron 1·50 80
1035 15 c. Ringed kingfisher (horiz) 1·75 80
1036 50 c. Bananaquit (horiz) 2·50 1·50
1037 60 c. Purple gallinule (horiz) 2·50 1·50
1038 70 c. Blue-hooded euphonia (horiz) 2·75 2·00
1039 $1 Brown-throated concure ("Caribbean Parakeet") 3·00 2·00
1040 $3 Troupial (horiz) 4·50 5·00
1041 $4 Purple-throated carib (horiz) 4·50 5·00

1988. 500th Anniv (1992) of Discovery of America by Columbus (1st issue). Nos. 1172/9 of Antigua optd **BARBUDA MAIL**.
1043 10 c. Columbus's second fleet, 1493 75 75
1044 30 c. Painos Indian village and fleet 1·00 80
1045 45 c. "Santa Mariagalante" (flagship) and Painos village 1·00 80
1046 60 c. Painos Indians offering Columbus fruit and vegetables 1·00 85
1047 90 c. Painos Indian and Columbus with scarlet macaw 2·00 1·25
1048 $1 Columbus landing on island 2·00 1·25
1049 $3 Spanish soldier and fleet 2·75 3·00
1050 $4 Fleet under sail 2·75 3·25
See also Nos. 1112/15, 1177/84, 1285/92, 1374/9 and 1381/2.

1988. 500th Birth Anniv of Titian. Nos. 1181/8 of Antigua optd **BARBUDA MAIL**.
1052 30 c. "Bust of Christ" 15 15
1053 40 c. "Scourging of Christ" 20 25
1054 45 c. "Madonna in Glory with Saints" 20 25
1055 50 c. "The Averoldi Polyptych" (detail) 25 30
1056 $1 "Christ Crowned with Thorns" 45 50
1057 $2 "Christ Mocked" 90 1·10
1058 $3 "Christ and Simon of Cyrene" 1·40 1·75
1059 $4 "Crucifixion with Virgin and Saints" 1·75 2·25

1988. 16th World Scout Jamboree, Australia. Nos. 1128/31 of Antigua optd **BARBUDA MAIL**.
1061 10 c. Scouts around campfire and red kangaroo 75 60
1062 60 c. Scouts canoeing and blue-winged kookaburra 2·00 95
1063 $1 Scouts on assault course and ring-tailed rock wallaby 1·75 1·25
1064 $3 Field kitchen and koala 3·50 4·50

1988. Sailing Week. Nos. 1190/3 of Antigua optd **BARBUDA MAIL**.
1066 30 c. Two yachts rounding buoy 20 20
1067 60 c. Three yachts 45 55
1068 $1 British yacht under way 70 85
1069 $3 Three yachts (different) 1·60 2·25

1988. Flowering Trees. Nos. 1213/20 of Antigua optd **BARBUDA MAIL**.
1071 10 c. Jacaranda 10 10
1072 30 c. Cordia 15 15
1073 50 c. Orchid tree 20 25
1074 90 c. Flamboyant 40 45
1075 $1 African tulip tree 45 50
1076 $2 Potato tree 80 1·25
1077 $3 Crepe myrtle 1·25 1·75
1078 $4 Pitch apple 1·60 2·25

1988. Olympic Games, Seoul. Nos. 1222/5 of Antigua optd **BARBUDA MAIL**.
1080 40 c. Gymnastics 40 30
1081 60 c. Weightlifting 50 35
1082 $1 Water polo (horiz) 70 70
1083 $3 Boxing (horiz) 1·50 2·00

1988. Caribbean Butterflies. Nos. 1227/44 of Antigua optd **BARBUDA MAIL**.
1085 1 c. "Danaus plexippus" 30 60
1086 2 c. "Greta diaphanus" 30 60
1087 3 c. "Calisto archebates" 40 60
1088 5 c. "Hamadryas feronia" 40 60
1089 10 c. "Mestra dorcas" 50 50
1090 15 c. "Hypolimnas misippus" 60 40
1091 20 c. "Dione juno" 70 50
1092 25 c. "Heliconius charithonia" 75 50
1093 30 c. "Eurema pyro" 85 50
1094 40 c. "Papilio androgeus" 90 50
1095 45 c. "Anteos maerula" 90 50
1096 50 c. "Aphrissa orbis" 1·10 75
1097 60 c. "Astraptes xagua" 1·10 60
1098 $1 "Heliopetes arsalte" 1·40 1·00
1099 $2 "Polites baracoa" 3·00 3·50
1100 $2.50 "Phocides pigmalion" 3·25 4·00
1101 $5 "Prepona amphitoe" 4·50 5·50
1102 $10 "Oarisma nanus" 7·50 8·50
1102a $20 "Parides lycimenes" 12·00 13·00

1989. 25th Death Anniv of John F. Kennedy (American statesman). Nos. 1245/52 of Antigua optd **BARBUDA MAIL**.
1103 1 c. President Kennedy and family 10 10
1104 2 c. Kennedy commanding "PT109" 10 10
1105 3 c. Funeral cortege 10 10
1106 4 c. In motorcade, Mexico 10 10
1107 30 c. As 1 c. 60 30
1108 60 c. As 4 c. 80 55
1109 $1 As 3 c. 95 90
1110 $4 As 2 c. 3·25 4·50

1989. 500th Anniv (1992) of Discovery of America by Columbus (2nd issue). Pre-Columbian Arawak Society. Nos. 1267/70 of Antigua optd **BARBUDA MAIL**.
1112 $1.50 Arawak warriors 1·50 2·00
1113 $1.50 Whip dancers 1·50 2·00
1114 $1.50 Whip dancers and chief with pineapple 1·50 2·00
1115 $1.50 Family and camp fire 1·50 2·00

1989. 50th Anniv of First Jet Flight. Nos. 1272/9 of Antigua optd **BARBUDA MAIL**.
1117 10 c. Hawker Siddeley Comet 4 airliner 1·00 85
1118 30 c. Messerschmitt Me 262 fighter 1·40 90
1119 40 c. Boeing 707 airliner 1·60 90
1120 60 c. Canadair CL-13 Sabre fighter 1·75 1·00
1121 $1 Lockheed Starfighters 2·00 1·25
1122 $2 Douglas DC-10 airliner 3·25 3·50
1123 $3 Boeing 747-300/400 airliner 3·75 4·00
1124 $4 McDonnell Douglas Phantom II fighter 3·75 4·00

1989. Caribbean Cruise Ships. Nos. 1281/8 of Antigua optd **BARBUDA MAIL**.
1126 25 c. "Festivale" 60 60
1127 45 c. "Southward" 80 60
1128 50 c. "Sagafjord" 90 70
1129 60 c. "Daphne" 1·00 80
1130 75 c. "Cunard Countess" 1·10 1·40
1131 90 c. "Song of America" 1·25 1·40
1132 $3 "Island Princess" 3·25 4·25
1133 $4 "Galileo" 3·25 4·25

1989. Japanese Art. Paintings by Hiroshige. Nos. 1290/7 of Antigua optd **BARBUDA MAIL**.
1135 25 c. "Fish swimming by Duck half-submerged in Stream" 80 55
1136 45 c. "Crane and Wave" 1·25 60
1137 50 c. "Sparrows and Morning Glories" 1·40 80
1138 60 c. "Crested Blackbird and Flowering Cherry" 1·50 85
1139 $1 "Great Knot sitting among Water Grass" 1·75 1·25
1140 $2 "Goose on a Bank of Water" 2·50 2·75
1141 $3 "Black Paradise Fly-catcher and Blossoms" 2·75 3·00
1142 $4 "Sleepy Owl perched on a Pine Branch" 3·00 3·00

1989. World Cup Football Championship, Italy (1990). Nos. 1308/11 of Antigua optd **BARBUDA MAIL**.
1144 15 c. Goalkeeper 60 40
1145 25 c. Goalkeeper moving towards ball 70 40
1146 $1 Goalkeeper reaching for ball 1·25 1·25
1147 $4 Goalkeeper saving goal 3·25 4·00

1989. Christmas. Paintings by Raphael and Giotto. Nos. 1351/8 of Antigua optd **BARBUDA MAIL**.
1149 10 c. "The Small Cowper Madonna" (Raphael) 10 10
1150 25 c. "Madonna of the Goldfinch" (Raphael) 10 15
1151 30 c. "The Alba Madonna" (Raphael) 15 20
1152 50 c. Saint (detail, "Bologna Altarpiece") (Giotto) 25 30
1153 60 c. Angel (detail, "Bologna Altarpiece") (Giotto) 30 45
1154 70 c. Angel slaying serpent (detail, "Bologna Altarpiece") (Giotto) 35 50
1155 $4 Evangelist (detail, "Bologna Altarpiece") (Giotto) 1·90 2·50
1156 $5 "Madonna of Foligno" (Raphael) 2·40 3·00

1990. Fungi. Nos. 1313/20 of Antigua optd **BARBUDA MAIL**.
1158 10 c. "Mycena pura" 1·00 55
1159 25 c. Psathyrella turberculata" (vert) 1·25 55
1160 50 c. "Psilocybe cubenis" 1·75 90
1161 60 c. "Leptonia caeruleocapitata" (vert) 2·00 1·00
1162 75 c. "Xeromphalina tenuipes" (vert) 2·00 1·40
1163 $1 "Chlorophyllum molybdites" (vert) 2·00 1·40
1164 $4 "Marasmius haematocephalus" 4·00 4·25
1165 $4 "Cantharellus cinnabarinus" 4·00 4·50

1990. Local Fauna. Nos. 1322/5 optd **BARBUDA MAIL**.
1167 25 c. Desmarest's hutia 40 35
1168 45 c. Caribbean monk seal 85 70
1169 60 c. Mustache bat (vert) 90 80
1170 $4 American manatee (vert) 2·75 4·00

1990. 20th Anniv of First Manned Landing on Moon. Nos. 1346/9 optd **BARBUDA MAIL**.
1172 10 c. Launch of "Apollo 11" 75 55
1173 45 c. Aldrin on Moon 1·50 70
1174 $1 Module "Eagle" over Moon (horiz) 2·25 1·75
1175 $4 Recovery of "Apollo 11" crew after splashdown (horiz) 5·00 6·50

1990. 500th Anniv (1992) of Discovery of America by Columbus (3rd issue). New World Natural History—Marine Life. Nos. 1360/7 of Antigua optd **BARBUDA MAIL**.
1177 10 c. Star-eyed hermit crab 55 50
1178 20c. Spiny lobster 75 60
1179 25 c. Magnificent banded fanworm 75 60
1180 45 c. Cannonball jellyfish 1·00 60
1181 60 c. Red-spiny sea star 1·25 75
1182 $2 Peppermint shrimp 2·25 2·50
1183 $3 Coral crab 2·50 3·00
1184 $4 Branching fire coral 2·50 3·00

1990. "EXPO 90" International Gardens and Greenery Exhibition, Osaka. Orchids. Nos. 1369/76 of Antigua optd **BARBUDA MAIL**.

1186 15 c. "Vanilla mexicana" 1·25 70

1187 45 c. "Epidendrum ibaguense" 1·75 70

1188 50 c. "Epidendrum secundum" 1·75 80

1189 60 c. "Maxillaria conferta" 2·00 1·10

1190 $1 "Onicidium altissimum" 2·25 1·75

1191 $2 "Spiranthes lanceolata" 3·75 4·00

1192 $3 "Tonopsis utricularioides" 4·50 5·00

1193 $5 "Epidendrum nocturnum" 5·50 6·50

1990. Reef Fishes. Nos. 1386/93 of Antigua optd **BARBUDA MAIL**.

1195 10 c. Flamefish 50 50

1196 15 c. Coney 65 55

1197 50 c. Long-spined squirrelfish 1·00 85

1198 60 c. Sergeant major 1·25 1·00

1199 $1 Yellow-tailed snapper 1·75 1·75

1200 $2 Rock beauty 2·75 3·25

1201 $3 Spanish hogfish 3·00 3·50

1202 $4 Striped parrotfish 3·00 3·50

1990. 1st Anniv of Hurricane Hugo. Nos. 971/2 surch **1st Anniversary Hurricane Hugo 16th September, 1989–1990** and new value.

1204 $5 on $7.50 Fairy basslet (vert) 5·00 5·50

1205 $7.50 on $10 Fire coral and butterfly fish (vert) 6·00 6·50

1990. 90th Birthday of Queen Elizabeth the Queen Mother. Nos. 1415/18 of Antigua optd **BARBUDA MAIL**.

1206 15 c. multicoloured 90 55

1207 35 c. multicoloured 1·40 65

1208 75 c. multicoloured 2·25 1·50

1209 $3 multicoloured 5·00 4·50

1990. Achievements in Space. Nos. 1395/1414 of Antigua optd **BARBUDA MAIL**.

1211 45 c. "Voyager 2" passing Saturn 90 90

1212 45 c. "Pioneer 11" photographing Saturn 90 90

1213 45 c. Astronaut in transporter 90 90

1214 45 c. Space shuttle "Columbia" 90 90

1215 45 c. "Apollo 10" command module on parachutes 90 90

1216 45 c. "Skylab" space station 90 90

1217 45 c. Astronaut Edward White in space 90 90

1218 45 c. "Apollo" spacecraft on joint mission 90 90

1219 45 c. "Soyuz" spacecraft on joint mission 90 90

1220 45 c. "Mariner 1" passing Venus 90 90

1221 45 c. "Gemini 4" capsule 90 90

1222 45 c. "Sputnik 1" 90 90

1223 45 c. Hubble space telescope 90 90

1224 45 c. North American X-15 rocket plane 90 90

1225 45 c. Bell XS-1 airplane 90 90

1226 45 c. "Apollo 17" astronaut and lunar rock formation 90 90

1227 45 c. Lunar rover 90 90

1228 45 c. "Apollo 14" lunar module 90 90

1229 45 c. Astronaut Buzz Aldrin on Moon 90 90

1230 45 c. Soviet "Lunokhod" lunar vehicle 90 90

1990. Christmas. Paintings by Renaissance Masters. Nos. 1457/64 of Antigua optd **BARBUDA MAIL**.

1231 25 c. "Madonna and Child with Saints (detail, Sebastiano del Piombo) 60 35

1232 30 c. "Virgin and Child with Angels" (detail, Grunewald) (vert) 70 35

1233 40 c. "The Holy Family and a Shepherd" (detail, Titian) 80 35

1234 60 c. "Virgin and Child" (detail, Lippi) (vert) 1·25 50

1235 $1 "Jesus, St. John and Two Angels" (Rubens) 1·40 90

1236 $2 "Adoration of the Shepherds" (detail, Vincenzo Catena) 2·25 2·75

1237 $4 "Adoration of the Magi" (detail, Giorgione) 3·00 3·75

1238 $5 "Virgin and Child adored by Warriors" (detail, Vincenzo Catena) 3·00 3·75

1991. 150th Anniv of the Penny Black. Nos. 1378/80 of Antigua optd **BARBUDA MAIL**.

1240 45 c. green 1·40 60

1241 60 c. mauve 1·50 75

1242 $5 blue 6·00 7·00

1991. "Stamp World London 90" International Stamp Exhibition. Nos. 1382/4 of Antigua optd **BARBUDA MAIL**.

1244 50 c. green and red 1·50 75

1245 75 c. brown and red 1·75 1·10

1246 $4 blue and red 5·75 6·50

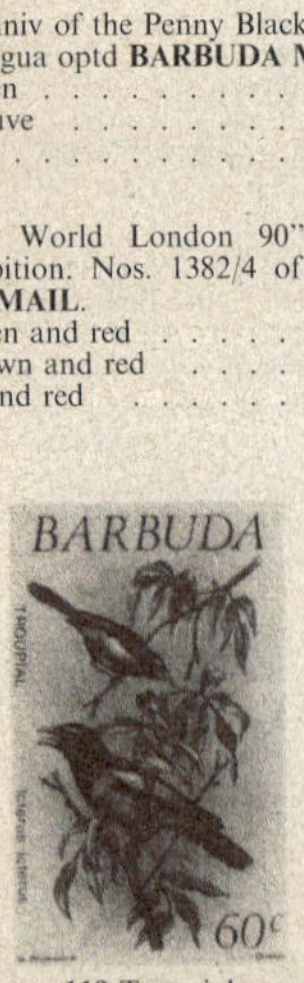

119 Troupial

1991. Wild Birds. Multicoloured.

1248 60 c. Type **119** 70 55

1249 $2 Adelaide's warbler ("Christmas Bird") 1·50 2·00

1250 $4 Rose-breasted grosbeak 3·00 3·50

1251 $7 Wied's crested flycatcher 4·75 6·00

1991. Olympic Games, Barcelona (1992). Nos. 1429/32 of Antigua optd **BARBUDA MAIL**.

1252 50 c. Men's 20 kilometres walk 75 60

1253 75 c. Triple jump 90 75

1254 $1 Men's 10,000 metres 1·25 1·00

1255 $5 Javelin 4·25 5·00

1991. Birds. Nos. 1448/55 of Antigua optd **BARBUDA MAIL**.

1257 10 c. Pearly-eyed thrasher 80 70

1258 25 c. Purple-throated carib 1·40 80

1259 50 c. Yellowthroat 1·75 1·00

1260 60 c. American kestrel 1·75 1·10

1261 $1 Yellow-bellied sapsucker 2·25 1·50

1262 $2 Purple gallinule 3·25 3·50

1263 $3 Yellow-crowned night heron 3·50 4·00

1264 $4 Blue-hooded euphonia 3·50 4·00

1991. 350th Death Anniv of Rubens. Nos. 1466/73 of Antigua optd **BARBUDA MAIL**.

1266 25 c. "Rape of the Daughters of Leucippus" (detail) 60 55

1267 45 c. "Bacchanal" (detail) 80 60

1268 50 c. "Rape of the Sabine Women" (detail) 90 75

1269 60 c. "Battle of the Amazons" (detail) 95 85

1270 $1 "Rape of the Sabine Women" (different detail) 1·50 1·25

1271 $2 "Bacchanal" (different detail) 2·50 2·50

1272 $3 "Rape of the Sabine Women" (different detail) 2·75 3·00

1273 $4 "Bacchanal" (different detail) 2·75 3·00

1991. 50th Anniv of Second World War. Nos. 1475/83 of Antigua optd **BARBUDA MAIL**.

1275 10 c. U.S. troops cross into Germany, 1944 80 75

1276 15 c. Axis surrender in North Africa, 1943 1·10 85

1277 25 c. U.S. tanks invade Kwalajalein, 1944 1·50 1·00

1278 45 c. Roosevelt and Churchill meet at Casablanca, 1943 2·00 1·50

1279 50 c. Marshall Badoglio, Prime Minister of Italian anti-facist government, 1943 1·50 1·50

1280 $1 Lord Mountbatten, Supreme Allied Commander South-east Asia, 1943 2·75 2·25

1281 $2 Greek victory at Koritza, 1940 3·75 4·00

1282 $4 Anglo-Soviet mutual assistance pact, 1941 5·00 5·50

1283 $5 Operation Torch landings, 1942 5·00 5·50

1991. 500th Anniv (1992) Discovery of America by Columbus (4th issue). History of Exploration. Nos. 1503/10 of Antigua optd **BARBUDA MAIL**.

1285 10 c. multicoloured 55 50

1286 15 c. multicoloured 70 60

1287 45 c. multicoloured 85 70

1288 60 c. multicoloured 1·00 1·00

1289 $1 multicoloured 1·40 1·40

1290 $2 multicoloured 2·25 2·50

1291 $4 multicoloured 3·50 4·00

1292 $5 multicoloured 3·75 4·00

1991. Butterflies. Nos. 1494/1501 of Antigua optd **BARBUDA MAIL**.

1294 10 c. "Heliconius charithonia" 90 85

1295 35 c. "Marpesia petreus" 1·40 1·10

1296 50 c. "Anartia amathea" 1·75 1·40

1297 75 c. "Siproeta stelenes" 2·00 1·60

1298 $1 "Battus polydamas" 2·25 1·75

1299 $2 "Historis odius" 3·00 3·25

1300 $4 "Hypolimnas misippus" 4·50 5·00

1301 $5 "Hamadryas feronia" 4·50 5·00

1991. 65th Birthday of Queen Elizabeth II. Nos. 1534/7 of Antigua optd **BARBUDA MAIL**.

1303 15 c. Queen Elizabeth and Prince Philip in 1976 80 60

1304 20 c. The Queen and Prince Philip in Portugal, 1985 80 60

1305 $2 Queen Elizabeth II 2·00 2·00

1306 $4 The Queen and Prince Philip at Ascot, 1986 3·50 4·00

1991. 10th Wedding Anniv of Prince and Princess of Wales. Nos. 1539/42 of Antigua optd **BARBUDA MAIL**.

1308 10 c. Prince and Princess of Wales at party, 1986 60 50

1309 40 c. Separate portraits of Prince, Princess and sons 1·00 60

1310 $1 Prince Henry and Prince William 1·40 1·25

1311 $5 Princess Diana in Australia and Prince Charles in Hungary 4·50 5·00

1991. Christmas. Religious Paintings by Fra Angelico. Nos. 1595/1602 of Antigua optd **BARBUDA MAIL**.

1313 10 c. "The Annunciation" 50 45

1314 30 c. "Nativity" 70 45

1315 40 c. "Adoration of the Magi" 70 45

1316 60 c. "Presentation in the Temple" 90 50

1317 $1 "Circumcision" 1·25 80

1318 $3 "Flight into Egypt" 3·00 3·50

1319 $4 "Massacre of the Innocents" 3·25 3·75

1320 $5 "Christ teaching in the Temple" 3·50 4·00

1992. Death Centenary (1990) of Vincent van Gogh (artist). Nos. 1512/23 of Antigua optd **BARBUDA MAIL**.

1321 5 c. "Camille Roulin" 40 40

1322 10 c. "Armand Roulin" 50 50

1323 15 c. "Young Peasant Woman with Straw Hat sitting in the Wheat" 60 60

1324 25 c. "Adeline Ravoux" 70 70

1325 30 c. "The Schoolboy" 70 70

1326 40 c. "Doctor Gachet" 75 75

1327 50 c. "Portrait of a Man" 75 75

1328 75 c. "Two Children" 1·10 1·10

1329 $2 "The Postman Joseph Roulin" 2·50 2·75

1330 $3 "The Seated Zouave" 2·75 3·00

1331 $4 "L'Arlesienne" 3·00 3·25

1332 $5 "Self-Portrait, November/December 1888" 3·25 3·50

1992. Birth Centenary of Charles de Gaulle (French statesman). Nos. 1562/9 of Antigua optd **BARBUDA MAIL**.

1334 10 c. Pres. De Gaulle and Kennedy, 1961 70 60

1335 15 c. General De Gaulle with Pres. Roosevelt, 1945 (vert) 75 65

1336 45 c. President De Gaulle with Chancellor Adenauer, 1962 (vert) 1·10 75

1337 60 c. De Gaulle at Arc de Triomphe, Liberation of Paris, 1944 (vert) 1·40 1·00

1338 $1 General De Gaulle crossing the Rhine, 1945 1·75 1·50

1339 $2 General De Gaulle in Algiers, 1944 2·75 3·00

1340 $4 Presidents De Gaulle and Eisenhower, 1960 3·75 4·00

1341 $5 De Gaulle returning from Germany, 1968 (vert) 3·75 4·00

1992. Easter. Religious Paintings. Nos. 1627/34 of Antigua optd **BARBUDA MAIL**.

1343 10 c. "Supper at Emmaus" (Caravaggio) 50 45

1344 15 c. "The Vision of St Peter" (Zurbaran) 60 50

1345 30 c. "Christ driving the Money-changers from the Temple" (Tiepolo) 75 55

1346 40 c. "Martyrdom of St Bartholomew" (detail) (Ribera) 80 60

1347 $1 "Christ driving the Money-changers from the Temple" (detail) (Tiepolo) 1·50 1·25

1348 $2 "Crucifixion" (detail) (Altdorfer) 2·50 3·00

1349 $4 "The Deposition" (detail) (Fra Angelico) 3·75 4·00

1350 $5 "The Deposition" (different detail) (Fra Angelico) 3·75 4·00

1992. Anniversaries and Events. Nos. 1573/82 of Antigua optd **BARBUDA MAIL**.

1352 25 c. Germans celebrating Reunification 60 60

1353 75 c. Cubs erecting tent 1·25 1·25

1354 $1.50 "Don Giovanni" and Mozart 2·25 2·25

1355 $2 Chariot driver and Gate at night 2·25 2·25

1356 $2 Lord Baden-Powell and members of the 3rd Antigua Methodist cub pack (vert) 2·25 2·25

1357 $2 Lilienthal's signature and glider "Flugzeug Nr. 5" 2·25 2·25

1358 $2.50 Driver in Class P36 steam locomotive (vert) 2·50 2·50

1359 $3 Statues from podium 2·50 2·50

1360 $3.50 Cubs and campfire 3·00 3·00

1361 $4 St. Peter's Cathedral, Salzburg 3·00 3·00

1992. 50th Anniv of Japanese Attack on Pearl Harbor. Nos. 1585/94 of Antigua optd **BARBUDA MAIL**.

1364 $1 "Nimitz" class carrier and "Ticonderoga" class cruiser 1·75 1·75

1365 $1 Tourist launch 1·75 1·75

1366 $1 U.S.S. "Arizona" memorial 1·75 1·75

1367 $1 Wreaths on water and aircraft 1·75 1·75

1368 $1 White tern 1·75 1·75

1369 $1 Japanese torpedo bombers over Pearl City 1·75 1·75

13790 $1 Zeros attacking 1·75 1·75

1371 $1 Battleship Row in flames 1·75 1·75

1372 $1 U.S.S. "Nevada" (battleship) underway 1·75 1·75

1373 $1 Zeros returning to carriers 1·75 1·75

1992. 500th Anniv of Discovery of America by Columbus (5th issue). World Columbian Stamp "Expo '92", Chicago. Nos. 1654/9 of Antigua optd **BARBUDA MAIL**.

1374 15 c. Memorial cross and huts, San Salvador 50 50

1375 30 c. Martin Pinzon with telescope 60 60

1376 40 c. Christopher Columbus 70 70

1377 $1 "Pinta" 2·25 2·00

1378 $2 "Nina" 3·00 3·00

1379 $4 "Santa Maria" 4·00 4·25

1992. 500th Anniv of Discovery of America by Columbus (6th issue). Organization of East Caribbean States. Nos. 1670/1 of Antigua optd **BARBUDA MAIL**.

1381 $1 Columbus meeting Amerindians 1·50 1·50

1382 $2 Ships approaching island 3·00 3·00

1992. 40th Anniv of Queen Elizabeth II's Accession. Nos. 1604/7 of Antigua optd **BARBUDA MAIL**.

1384 10 c. Queen Elizabeth II and bird sanctuary 90 70

1385 30 c. Nelson's Dockyard 1·50 85

1386 $1 Ruins on Shirley Heights 2·25 2·00

1387 $5 Beach and palm trees 5·50 6·50

1992. Prehistoric Animals. Nos. 1618/25 of Antigua optd **BARBUDA MAIL**.

1389 10 c. Pteranodon 90 90

1390 15 c. Brachiosaurus 1·00 1·00

1391 30 c. Tyrannosaurus Rex 1·25 1·25

1392 50 c. Parasaurolophus 1·50 1·50

1393 $1 Deinonychus (horiz) 2·00 2·00

1394 $2 Triceratops (horiz) 3·00 3·00

1395 $4 Protoceratops hatching (horiz) 3·75 3·75

1396 $5 Stegosaurus (horiz) 3·75 3·75

1992. Christmas. Nos. 1691/8 of Antigua optd **BARBUDA MAIL**.

1398 10 c. "Virgin and Child with Angels" (School of Piero della Francesca) 60 55

1399 25 c. "Madonna degli Alberelli" (Giovanni Bellini) 85 55

1400 30 c. "Madonna and Child with St. Anthony Abbot and St. Sigismund" (Neroccio) 90 55

1401 40 c. "Madonna and the Grand Duke" (Raphael) 1·00 55

1402 60 c. "The Nativity" (Georges de la Tour) 1·40 70

1403 $1 "Holy Family" (Jacob Jordaens) 2·00 1·40

1404 $4 "Madonna and Child Enthroned" (Magaritone) 5·00 5·50

1405 $5 "Madonna and Child on a Curved Throne" (Byzantine school) 5·00 5·50

1993. Fungi. Nos. 1645/52 of Antigua optd **BARBUDA MAIL**.

1407 10 c. "Amanita caesarea" 1·00 1·00

1408 15 c. "Collybia fusipes" 1·25 1·25

1409 30 c. "Boletus aereus" 1·50 1 50

1410 40 c. "Laccaria amethystina" 1·50 1·50

1411 $1 "Russula virescens" 2·00 2·00

1412 $2 "Tricholoma equestre" ("Tricholoma auratum") 3·00 3·00

1413 $4 "Calocybe gambosa" 3·75 3·75

1414 $5 "Lentinus tigrinus" ("Panus tigrinus") 3·75 3·75

1993. "Granada '92" International Stamp Exhibition, Spain. Spanish Paintings. Nos. 1636/43 of Antigua optd **BARBUDA MAIL**.

1416 10 c. "The Miracle at the Well" (Alonzo Cano) 60 60

1417 15 c. "The Poet Luis de Goingora y Argote" (Velazquez) 75 75

1418 30 c. "The Painter Francisco Goya" (Vincente Lopez Portana) 1·00 1·00

1419 40 c. "Maria de las Nieves Michaela Fourdinier" (Luis Paret y Alcazar) 1·00 1·00

1420 $1 "Carlos III eating before his Court" (Alcazar) (horiz) 2·00 2·00

1421 $2 "Rain Shower in Granada" (Antonio Munoz Degrain) (horiz) 3·00 3·00

1422 $4 "Sarah Bernhardt" (Santiago Ruisnol i Prats) 4·50 4·50

1423 $5 "The Hermitage Garden" (Joaquim Mir Trinxet) 4·50 4·50

1993. "Genova '92" International Thematic Stamp Exhibition. Hummingbirds and Plants. Nos. 1661/8 of Antigua optd **BARBUDA MAIL**.

1425 10 c. Antillean crested hummingbird and wild plantain 75 75

1426 25 c. Green mango and parrot's plantain 1·00 1·00

1427 45 c. Purple-throated carib and lobster claws 1·25 1·25

1428 60 c. Antillean mango and coral plant 1·50 1·50

1429 $1 Vervain hummingbird and cardinal's guard 1·75 1·75

1430 $2 Rufous-breasted hermit and heliconia 2·50 2·50

1431 $4 Blue-headed hummingbird and reed ginger 3·50 3·50

1432 $5 Green-throated carib and ornamental banana 3·50 3·50

1993. Inventors and Inventions. Nos. 1672/9 of Antigua optd **BARBUDA MAIL**.

1434 10 c. Ts'ai Lun and paper 25 25

1435 25 c. Igor Sikorsky and "Bolshoi Baltiskii" (first four-engined airplane) 60 60

1436 30 c. Alexander Graham Bell and early telephone 60 60

1437 40 c. Johannes Gutenberg and early printing press 60 60

1438 60 c. James Watt and stationary steam engine 1·50 1·25

1439 $1 Anton van Leeuwenhoek and early microscope 1·50 1·50

1440 $4 Louis Braille and hands reading braille 3·50 3·75

1441 $5 Galileo and telescope 3·50 3·75

1993. Anniversaries and Events. Nos. 900/13 of Antigua optd **BARBUDA MAIL**.

1443 10 c. Russian cosmonauts 60 60

1444 40 c. "Graf Zeppelin" (airship), 1929 1·00 1·00

1445 45 c. Bishop Daniel Davis 50 50

1446 75 c. Konrad Adenauer making speech 70 70

1447 $1 Bus Mosbacher and "Weatherly" (yacht) 1·25 1·25

1448 $1.50 Rain forest 1·50 1·50

1449 $2 Tiger 3·50 3·50

1450 $2 National flag, plant and emblem (horiz) 1·75 1·75

1451 $2 Members of Community Players company (horiz) 1·75 1·75

1452 $2.25 Women carrying pots 1·75 1·75

1453 $3 Lions Club emblem 2·75 2·75

1454 $4 Chinese rocket on launch tower 3·00 3·00
1455 $4 West German and N.A.T.O. flags 3·00 3·00
1456 $6 Hugo Eckener (airship pioneer) 4·50 4·50

1993. Flowers. Nos. 1733/40 of Antigua optd **BARBUDA MAIL.**
1458 15 c. Cardinal's guard 85 85
1459 25 c. Giant granadilla 1·10 1·10
1460 30 c. Spider flower 1·25 1·25
1461 40 c. Gold vine 1·40 1·40
1462 $1 Frangipani 2·00 2·00
1463 $2 Bougainvillea 2·75 2·75
1464 $4 Yellow oleander 3·75 3·75
1465 $5 Spicy jatropha 3·75 3·75

1993. World Bird Watch. Nos. 1248/51 optd **WORLD BIRDWATCH 9-10 OCTOBER 1993.**
1467 60 c. Type **119** 2·25 1·75
1468 $2 Adelaide's warbler 4·00 4·00
1469 $4 Rose-breasted grosbeak 5·50 6·00
1470 $7 Wied's crested flycatcher 7·00 8·50

1993. Endangered Species. Nos. 1759/70 of Antigua optd **BARBUDA MAIL.**
1471 $1 St. Lucia amazon 1·75 1·75
1472 $1 Cahow 1·75 1·75
1473 $1 Swallow-tailed kite 1·75 1·75
1474 $1 Everglade kite 1·75 1·75
1475 $1 Imperial amazon 1·75 1·75
1476 $1 Humpback whale 1·75 1·75
1477 $1 Plain pigeon 1·75 1·75
1478 $1 St. Vincent amazon 1·75 1·75
1479 $1 Puerto Rican amazon 1·75 1·75
1480 $1 Leatherback turtle 1·75 1·75
1481 $1 American crocodile 1·75 1·75
1482 $1 Hawksbill turtle 1·75 1·75

1994. Bicentenary of the Louvre, Paris. Paintings by Peter Paul Rubens. Nos. 1742/9 of Antigua optd **BARBUDA MAIL.**
1484 $1 "The Destiny of Marie de' Medici" (upper detail) 1·40 1·40
1485 $1 "The Birth of Marie de' Medici" 1·40 1·40
1486 $1 "The Education of Marie de' Medici" 1·40 1·40
1487 $1 "The Destiny of Marie de' Medici" (lower detail) 1·40 1·40
1488 $1 "Henry VI receiving the Portrait of Marie" 1·40 1·40
1489 $1 "The Meeting of the King and Marie at Lyons" 1·40 1·40
1490 $1 "The Marriage by Proxy" 1·40 1·40
1491 $1 "The Birth of Louis XIII" 1·40 1·40

1994. World Cup Football Championship, 1994, U.S.A. (1st Issue). Nos. 1816/27 of Antigua optd **BARBUDA MAIL.**
1493 $2 Paul Gascoigne 2·25 2·25
1494 $2 David Platt 2·25 2·25
1495 $2 Martin Peters 2·25 2·25
1496 $2 John Barnes 2·25 2·25
1497 $2 Gary Lineker 2·25 2·25
1498 $2 Geoff Hurst 2·25 2·25
1499 $2 Bobby Charlton 2·25 2·25
1500 $2 Bryan Robson 2·25 2·25
1501 $2 Bobby Moore 2·25 2·25
1502 $2 Nobby Stiles 2·25 2·25
1503 $2 Gordon Banks 2·25 2·25
1504 $2 Peter Shilton 2·25 2·25
See also Nos. 1573/8.

1994. Anniversaries and Events. Nos. 1829/38, 1840 and 1842/6 of Antigua optd **BARBUDA MAIL.**
1506 10 c. Grand Inspector W. Heath 45 45
1507 15 c. Rodnina and Oulanov (U.S.S.R.) (pairs figure skating) (horiz) 50 50
1508 30 c. Present Masonic Hall, St. John's (horiz) 70 70
1509 30 c. Willy Brandt with Helmut Schmidt and George Leber (horiz) 70 70
1510 30 c. "Cat and Bird" (Picasso) (horiz) 70 70
1511 40 c. Previous Masonic Hall, St. John's (horiz) 70 70
1512 40 c. "Fish on a Newspaper" (Picasso) (horiz) 70 70
1513 40 c. Early astronomical equipment 70 70
1514 40 c. Prince Naruhito and engagement photographs (horiz) 70 70
1515 60 c. Grand Inspector J. Jeffery 75 75
1516 $3 Masako Owada and engagement photographs (horiz) 2·00 2·00
1517 $4 Willy Brandt and protest march (horiz) 2·75 2·75
1518 $4 Galaxy 2·75 2·75
1519 $5 Alberto Tomba (Italy) (giant slalom) (horiz) 2·75 2·75
1520 $5 "Dying Bull" (Picasso) (horiz) 2·75 2·75
1521 $5 Pres. Clinton and family (horiz) 2·75 2·75

1994. Aviation Anniversaries. Nos. 1848/54 of Antigua optd **BARBUDA MAIL.**
1523 30 c. Hugo Eckener and Dr. W. Beckers with airship "Graf Zeppelin" over Lake George, New York 90 90
1524 40 c. Chicago World's Fair from "Graf Zeppelin" 90 90
1525 40 c. Gloster Whittle E28/39, 1941 90 90
1526 40 c. George Washington writing balloon mail letter (vert) 90 90
1527 $4 Pres. Wilson and Curtiss "Jenny" 3·75 3·75
1528 $5 Airship LZ-129 "Hindenburg" over Ebbets Field baseball stadium, 1937 3·75 3·75
1529 $5 Gloster Meteor in dogfight 3·75 3·75

1994. Centenaries of Henry Ford's First Petrol Engine (Nos. 1531, 1533) and Karl Benz's First Four-wheeled Car (others). Nos. 1856/9 of Antigua optd **BARBUDA MAIL.**
1531 30 c. Lincoln Continental 85 85
1532 40 c. Mercedes racing car, 1914 90 90
1533 $4 Ford "GT40", 1966 3·75 3·75
1534 $5 Mercedes Benz "gull-wing" coupe, 1954 3·75 3·75

1994. Famous Paintings by Rembrandt and Matisse. Nos. 1881/8 of Antigua optd **BARBUDA MAIL.**
1536 15 c. "Hannah and Samuel" (Rembrandt) 60 60
1537 15 c. "Guitarist" (Matisse) 60 60
1538 30 c. "The Jewish Bride" (Rembrandt) 90 90
1539 40 c. "Jacob wrestling with the Angel" (Rembrandt) 90 90
1540 60 c. "Interior with a Goldfish Bowl" (Matisse) 1·10 1·10
1541 $1 "Mlle. Yvonne Landsberg" (Matisse) 1·40 1·40
1542 $4 "The Toboggan" (Matisse) 3·75 3·75
1543 $5 "Moses with the Tablets of the Law" (Rembrandt) 3·75 3·75

1994. "Polska '93" International Stamp Exhibition, Poznan. Nos. 1839 and 1841 of Antigua optd **BARBUDA MAIL.**
1545 $1 "Woman Combing her Hair" (W. Slewinski) (horiz) 1·75 1·75
1546 $3 "Artist's Wife with Cat" (Konrad Kryzanowski) (horiz) 3·50 3·50

1994. Orchids. Nos. 1949/56 of Antigua optd **BARBUDA MAIL.**
1548 10 c. "Spiranthes lanceolata" 75 75
1549 20 c. "Ionopsis utricularioides" 1·00 1·00
1550 30 c. "Tetramicra canaliculata" 1·25 1·25
1551 50 c. "Oncidium picturatum" 1·50 1·50
1552 $1 "Epidendrum difforme" 2·00 2·00
1553 $2 "Epidendrum ciliare" 3·00 3·00
1554 $4 "Epidendrum ibaguense" 4·50 4·50
1555 $5 "Epidendrum nocturnum" 4·50 4·50

1994. Centenary of Sierra Club (environmental protection society) (1992). Endangered Species. Nos. 1907/21 of Antigua optd **BARBUDA MAIL.**
1557 $1.50 Sumatran rhinoceros lying down 2·00 2·00
1558 $1.50 Sumatran rhinoceros feeding 2·00 2·00
1559 $1.50 Ring-tailed lemur on ground 2·00 2·00
1560 $1.50 Ring-tailed lemur on branch 2·00 2·00
1561 $1.50 Red-fronted brown lemur on branch 2·00 2·00
1562 $1.50 Head of red-fronted brown lemur 2·00 2·00
1563 $1.50 Head of red-fronted brown lemur in front of trunk 2·00 2·00
1564 $1.50 Sierra Club Centennial emblem 1·25 1·25
1565 $1.50 Head of bactrian camel 2·00 2·00
1566 $1.50 Bactrian camel 2·00 2·00
1567 $1.50 African elephant drinking 2·00 2·00
1568 $1.50 Head of African elephant 2·00 2·00
1569 $1.50 Leopard sitting upright 2·00 2·00
1570 $1.50 Leopard in grass (emblem at right) 2·00 2·00
1571 $1.50 Leopard in grass (emblem at left) 2·00 2·00

1995. World Cup Football Championship, U.S.A. (2nd issue). Nos. 2039/44 of Antigua optd **BARBUDA MAIL.**
1573 15 c. Hugo Sanchez (Mexico) 60 60
1574 35 c. Jurgen Klinsmann (Germany) 90 90
1575 65 c. Antiguan player 1·25 1·25
1576 $1.20 Cobi Jones (U.S.A.) 1·75 1·75
1577 $4 Roberto Baggio (Italy) 3·50 3·50
1578 $5 Bwalya Kalusha (Zambia) 3·50 3·50

1995. Christmas. Religious Paintings. Nos. 2058/65 of Antigua optd **BARBUDA MAIL.**
1580 15 c. "Virgin and Child by the Fireside" (Robert Campin) 50 35
1581 35 c. "The Reading Madonna" (Giorgione) 65 40
1582 40 c. "Madonna and Child" (Giovanni Bellini) 65 40
1583 45 c. "The Little Madonna" (Da Vinci) 65 45
1584 65 c. "The Virgin and Child under the Apple Tree" (Lucas Cranach the Elder) 90 90
1585 75 c. "Madonna and Child" (Master of the Female Half-lengths) 1·00 1·00
1586 $1.20 "An Allegory of the Church" (Alessandro Allori) 1·60 2·00
1587 $5 "Madonna and Child wreathed with Flowers" (Jacob Jordaens) 3·75 4·50

1995. "Hong Kong '94" International Stamp Exhibition (1st issue). Nos. 1890/1 of Antigua optd **BARBUDA MAIL.**
1589 40 c. Hong Kong 1981 $1 Fish stamp and fishing boats, Shau Kei Wan 80 80
1590 40 c. Antigua 1990 $2 Reef fish stamp and fishing boats, Shau Kei Wan 80 80
See also Nos. 1591/6.

1995. "Hong Kong '94" International Stamp Exhibition (2nd issue). Nos. 1892/7 of Antigua optd **BARBUDA MAIL.**
1591 40 c. Terracotta warriors 30 30
1592 40 c. Cavalryman and horse 30 30
1593 40 c. Warriors in armour 30 30
1594 40 c. Painted bronze chariot and team 30 30
1595 40 c. Pekingese dog 30 30
1596 40 c. Warriors with horses 30 30

1995. Centenary of International Olympic Committee. Nos. 1990/1 of Antigua optd **BARBUDA MAIL.**
1597 50 c. Edwin Moses (U.S.A.) (400 metres hurdles), 1984 75 75
1598 $1.50 Steffi Graf (Germany) (tennis), 1988 3·00 3·00

1995. Dogs of the World. Chinese New Year ("Year of the Dog"). Nos. 1923/46 of Antigua optd **BARBUDA MAIL.**
1600 50 c. West Highland white terrier 50 50
1601 50 c. Beagle 50 50
1602 50 c. Scottish terrier 50 50
1603 50 c. Pekingese 50 50
1604 50 c. Dachshund 50 50
1605 50 c. Yorkshire terrier 50 50
1606 50 c. Pomeranian 50 50
1607 50 c. Poodle 50 50
1608 50 c. Shetland sheepdog 50 50
1609 50 c. Pug 50 50
1610 50 c. Shih tzu 50 50
1611 50 c. Chihuahua 50 50
1612 50 c. Mastiff 50 50
1613 50 c. Border collie 50 50
1614 50 c. Samoyed 50 50
1615 50 c. Airedale terrier 50 50
1616 50 c. English setter 50 50
1617 50 c. Rough collie 50 50
1618 50 c. Newfoundland 50 50
1619 50 c. Weimarana 50 50
1620 50 c. English springer spaniel 50 50
1621 50 c. Dalmatian 50 50
1622 50 c. Boxer 50 50
1623 50 c. Old English sheepdog 50 50

1995. Centenary of First English Cricket Tour to the West Indies (1995). Nos. 1994/6 of Antigua optd **BARBUDA MAIL.**
1625 35 c. Mike Atherton (England) and Wisden Trophy 60 45
1626 75 c. Viv Richards (West Indies) (vert) 1·25 1·25
1627 $1.20 Richie Richardson (West Indies) and Wisden Trophy 1·50 1·75

1995. "Philakorea '94" International Stamp Exhibition (1st issue). Nos. 1998/2008 of Antigua optd **BARBUDA MAIL.**
1629 40 c. Entrance bridge, Songgwangsa Temple 60 60
1630 75 c. Long-necked bottle 90 90
1631 75 c. Punch'ong ware jar with floral decoration 90 90
1632 75 c. Punch'ong ware jar with blue dragon pattern 90 90
1633 75 c. Ewer in shape of bamboo shoot 90 90
1634 75 c. Punch'ong ware green jar 90 90
1635 75 c. Pear-shaped bottle 90 90
1636 75 c. Porcelain jar with brown dragon pattern 90 90
1637 75 c. Porcelain jar with floral pattern 90 90
1638 90 c. Song-op Folk Village, Cheju 90 90
1639 $3 Port Sogwipo 2·50 2·50

1995. 1st Recipients of Order of the Caribbean Community. Nos. 2046/8 of Antigua optd **BARBUDA MAIL.**
1641 65 c. Sir Shridath Ramphal 45 50
1642 90 c. William Demas 55 60
1643 $1.20 Derek Walcott 75 85

1995. 25th Anniv of First Moon Landing. Nos. 1977/88 of Antigua optd **BARBUDA MAIL.**
1644 $1.50 Edwin Aldrin (astronaut) 1·50 1·50
1645 $1.50 First lunar footprint 1·50 1·50
1646 $1.50 Neil Armstrong (astronaut) 1·50 1·50
1647 $1.50 Aldrin stepping onto Moon 1·50 1·50
1648 $1.50 Aldrin and equipment 1·50 1·50
1649 $1.50 Aldrin and U.S.A. flag 1·50 1·50
1650 $1.50 Aldrin at Tranquility Base 1·50 1·50
1651 $1.50 Moon plaque 1·50 1·50
1652 $1.50 "Eagle" leaving Moon 1·50 1·50
1653 $1.50 Command module in lunar orbit 1·50 1·50
1654 $1.50 First day cover of U.S.A. 1969 10 c. First Man on Moon stamp 1·50 1·50
1655 $1.50 Pres. Nixon and astronauts 1·50 1·50

1995. International Year of the Family. No. 1993 of Antigua optd **BARBUDA MAIL.**
1656 90 c. Antiguan family 80 80

1995. 50th Anniv of D-Day. Nos. 2010/12 of Antigua optd **BARBUDA MAIL.**
1658 40 c. Short S.25 Sunderland flying boat 80 65
1659 $2 Lockheed P-38 Lightning fighters attacking train 2·50 2·50
1660 $3 Martin B-26 Marauder bombers 2·75 3·00

122 Queen Elizabeth the Queen Mother (90th birthday)

1995. Anniversaries. Multicoloured.
1662 $7.50 Type **122** 6·50 6·50
1663 $8 German bombers over St. Paul's Cathedral, London (horiz) (50th anniv of end of Second World War) 7·00 7·00
1664 $8 New York skyline with U.N. and national flags (horiz) (50th anniv of United Nations) 6·50 6·50

1995. Hurricane Relief. Nos. 1662/4 surch **HURRICANE RELIEF** and premium.
1665 $7.50 + $1 Type **122** (90th birthday) 5·00 5·50
1666 $8 + $1 German bombers over St. Paul's Cathedral, London (horiz) (50th anniv of end of Second World War) 5·00 5·50
1667 $8 + $1 New York skyline with U.N. and national flags (horiz) (50th anniv of United Nations) 5·00 5·50

1996. Marine Life. Nos. 1967/75 of Antigua optd **BARBUDA MAIL.**
1668 50 c. Bottlenose dolphin 50 50
1669 50 c. Killer whale 50 50
1670 50 c. Spinner dolphin 50 50
1671 50 c. Oceanic sunfish 50 50
1672 50 c. Caribbean reef shark and short fin pilot whale 50 50
1673 50 c. Copper-banded butterflyfish 50 50
1674 50 c. Mosaic moray 50 50
1675 50 c. Clown triggerfish 50 50
1676 50 c. Red lobster 50 50

1996. Christmas. Religious Paintings. Nos. 2267/72 of Antigua optd **BARBUDA MAIL.**
1678 15 c. "Rest on the Flight into Egypt" (Paolo Veronese) 40 30
1679 35 c. "Madonna and Child" (Van Dyck) 50 35
1680 65 c. "Sacred Conversation Piece" (Veronese) 70 55
1681 75 c. "Vision of St. Anthony" (Van Dyck) 80 60
1682 90 c. "Virgin and Child" (Van Eyck) 90 75
1683 $6 "The Immaculate Conception" (Giovanni Tiepolo) 3·75 4·50

1996. Stars of Country and Western Music. Nos. 2014/37 of Antigua optd **BARBUDA MAIL.**
1685 75 c. Travis Tritt 50 50
1686 75 c. Dwight Yoakam 50 50
1687 75 c. Billy Ray Cyrus 50 50
1688 75 c. Alan Jackson 50 50
1689 75 c. Garth Brooks 50 50
1690 75 c. Vince Gill 50 50
1691 75 c. Clint Black 50 50
1692 75 c. Eddie Rabbit 50 50
1693 75 c. Patsy Cline 50 50
1694 75 c. Tanya Tucker 50 50
1695 75 c. Dolly Parton 50 50
1696 75 c. Anne Murray 50 50
1697 75 c. Tammy Wynette 50 50
1698 75 c. Loretta Lynn 50 50
1699 75 c. Reba McEntire 50 50
1700 75 c. Skeeter Davis 50 50
1701 75 c. Hank Snow 50 50
1702 75 c. Gene Autry 50 50
1703 75 c. Jimmie Rodgers 50 50
1704 75 c. Ernest Tubb 50 50
1705 75 c. Eddy Arnold 50 50
1706 75 c. Willie Nelson 50 50
1707 75 c. Johnny Cash 50 50
1708 75 c. George Jones 50 50

1996. Birds. Nos. 2067/81 of Antigua optd **BARBUDA MAIL.**
1710 15 c. Magnificent frigate bird 10 10
1711 25 c. Blue-hooded euphonia 10 10
1712 35 c. Eastern meadowlark 15 20
1713 40 c. Red-billed tropic bird 15 20
1714 45 c. Greater flamingo 20 25
1715 60 c. Yellow-faced grassquit 25 30
1716 65 c. Yellow-billed cuckoo 30 35
1717 70 c. Purple-throated carib 30 35
1718 75 c. Bananaquit 35 40
1719 90 c. Painted bunting 40 45
1720 $1.20 Red-legged honeycreeper 50 55
1721 $2 Northern jacana 80 90
1722 $5 Greater Antillean bullfinch 2·10 2·25
1723 $10 Caribbean elaenia 4·25 4·50
1724 $20 Brown trembler 8·75 9·00

1996. Birds. Nos. 2050, 2052 and 2054/6 of Antigua optd **BARBUDA MAIL.**
1725 15 c. Bridled quail dove 40 30
1726 40 c. Purple-throated carib (vert) 60 40
1727 $1 Broad-winged hawk (vert) 1·25 1·00
1728 $4 Yellow warbler 2·50 3·00

1996. Prehistoric Animals. Nos. 2082/99 of Antigua optd **BARBUDA MAIL.**
1730 15 c. Head of pachycephalosaurus 30 30
1731 20 c. Head of afrovenator 30 30
1732 65 c. Centrosaurus 45 45
1733 75 c. Kronosaurus (horiz) 50 50
1734 75 c. Ichthyosaurus (horiz) 50 50
1735 75 c. Plesiosaurus (horiz) 50 50
1736 75 c. Archelon (horiz) 50 50
1737 75 c. Pair of tyrannosaurus (horiz) 50 50
1738 75 c. Tyrannosaurus (horiz) 50 50
1739 75 c. Parasaurolophus (horiz) 50 50
1740 75 c. Pair of parasaurolophus (horiz) 50 50
1741 75 c. Oviraptor (horiz) 50 50
1742 75 c. Protoceratops with eggs (horiz) 50 50

1743 75 c. Pteranodon and protoceratops (horiz) . . . 50 50
1744 75 c. Pair of protoceratops (horiz) . . . 50 50
1745 90 c. Pentaceratops drinking . 60 60
1746 $1.20 Head of tarbosaurus . 75 75
1747 $5 Head of styracosaurus . . 2·75 2·75

1996. Olympic Games, Atlanta (1st issue). Previous Gold Medal Winners. Nos. 2101/6 of Antigua optd **BARBUDA MAIL.**
1749 15 c. Al Oerter (U.S.A.) (discus – 1956, 1960, 1964, 1968) . 25 25
1750 20 c. Greg Louganis (U.S.A.) (diving – 1984, 1988) . . . 25 25
1751 65 c. Naim Suleymanoglu (Turkey) (weightlifting – 1988) . . . 55 55
1752 90 c. Louise Ritter (U.S.A.) (high jump – 1988) . . . 70 70
1753 $1.20 Nadia Comaneci (Rumania) (gymnastics – 1976) . . . 85 85
1754 $5 Olga Bondarenko (Russia) (10,000 metres – 1988) . . 2·50 3·00
See also Nos. 1922/43.

1996. 18th World Scout Jamboree, Netherlands. Tents. Nos. 2203/8 of Antigua optd **BARBUDA MAIL.**
1756 $1.20 The Explorer Tent . . 1·00 1·00
1757 $1.20 Camper tent . . . . 1·00 1·00
1758 $1.20 Wall tent . . . . 1·00 1·00
1759 $1.20 Trail tent . . . . 1·00 1·00
1760 $1.20 Miner's tent . . . . 1·00 1·00
1761 $1.20 Voyager tent . . . . 1·00 1·00

1996. Centenary of Nobel Prize Trust Fund. Nos. 2226/43 of Antigua optd **BARBUDA MAIL.**
1763 $1 Dag Hammarskjold (1961 Peace) . . . 60 60
1764 $1 Georg Wittig (1979 Chemistry) . . . 60 60
1765 $1 Wilhelm Ostwold (1909 Chemistry) . . . 60 60
1766 $1 Robert Koch (1905 Medicine) . . . 60 60
1767 $1 Karl Ziegler (1963 Chemistry) . . . 60 60
1768 $1 Alexander Fleming (1945 Medicine) . . . 60 60
1769 $1 Hermann Staudinger (1953 Chemistry) . . . 60 60
1770 $1 Manfred Eigen (1967 Chemistry) . . . 60 60
1771 $1 Arno Penzias (1978 Physics) . . . 60 60
1772 $1 Shumal Agnon (1966 Literature) . . . 60 60
1773 $1 Rudyard Kipling (1907 Literature) . . . 60 60
1774 $1 Aleksandr Solzhenitsyn (1970 Literature) . . . 60 60
1775 $1 Jack Steinburger (1988 Physics) . . . 60 60
1776 $1 Andrei Sakharov (1975 Peace) . . . 60 60
1777 $1 Otto Stern (1943 Physics) . . . 60 60
1778 $1 John Steinbeck (1962 Literature) . . . 60 60
1779 $1 Nadine Gordimer (1991 Literature) . . . 60 60
1780 $1 William Faulkner (1949 Literature) . . . 60 60

1996. 70th Birthday of Queen Elizabeth II. Nos. 2355/7 of Antigua optd **BARBUDA MAIL.**
1782 $2 Queen Elizabeth II in blue dress . . . 1·10 1·10
1783 $2 With bouquet . . . . 1·10 1·10
1784 $2 In Garter robes . . . . 1·10 1·10

1997. Christmas. Religious Paintings by Filippo Lippi. Nos. 2377/82 of Antigua optd **BARBUDA MAIL.**
1786 60 c. "Madonna Enthroned" 35 35
1787 90 c. "Adoration of the Child and Saints" . . . 55 55
1788 $1 "The Annunciation" . . 60 60
1789 $1.20 "Birth of the Virgin" . 75 75
1790 $1.60 "Adoration of the Child" 90 90
1791 $1.75 "Madonna and Child" 1·00 1·00

1997. 50th Anniv of F.A.O. Nos. 2121/3 of Antigua optd **BARBUDA MAIL.**
1793 75 c. Woman buying produce from market . . . 50 50
1794 90 c. Women shopping . . . 60 60
1795 $1.20 Women talking . . . 70 70

1997. 90th Anniv of Rotary International (1995). No. 2125 of Antigua optd **BARBUDA MAIL.**
1797 $5 Beach and rotary emblem 2·75 3·00

1997. 50th Anniv of End of Second World War in Europe and the Pacific. Nos. 2108/15 and 2132/7 of Antigua optd **BARBUDA MAIL.**
1799 $1.20 Map of Berlin showing Russian advance . . . 55 60
1800 $1.20 Russian tank and infantry 55 60
1801 $1.20 Street fighting in Berlin 55 60
1802 $1.20 German tank exploding 55 60
1803 $1.20 Russian air raid . . . 55 60
1804 $1.20 German troops surrendering . . . 55 60
1805 $1.20 Hoisting the Soviet flag on the Reichstag . . . 55 60
1806 $1.20 Captured German standards . . . 55 60
1807 $1.20 Gen. Chiang Kai-shek and Chinese guerrillas . . 55 60
1808 $1.20 Gen. Douglas MacArthur and beach landing . . . 55 60
1809 $1.20 Gen. Claire Chennault and U.S. fighter aircraft . . 55 60
1810 $1.20 Brig. Orde Wingate and supply drop . . . 55 60
1811 $1.20 Gen. Joseph Stilwell and U.S. supply plane . . . 55 60
1812 $1.20 Field-Marshal Bill Slim and loading cow onto plane 55 60

1997. 95th Birthday of Queen Elizabeth the Queen Mother. Nos. 2127/30 of Antigua optd **BARBUDA MAIL.**
1814 $1.50 brown, light brown and black . . . 70 75
1815 $1.50 multicoloured . . . 70 75
1816 $1.50 multicoloured . . . 70 75
1817 $1.50 multicoloured . . . 70 75

1997. 50th Anniv of United Nations. Nos. 2117/9 of Antigua optd **BARBUDA MAIL.**
1819 75 c. Signatures and Earl of Halifax . . . 35 40
1820 90 c. Virginia Gildersleeve . 40 45
1821 $1.20 Harold Stassen . . . 55 60

1997. Trains of the World. Nos. 2210/24 of Antigua optd **BARBUDA MAIL.**
1823 35 c. Trans-Gabon diesel-electric train . . . 15 20
1824 65 c. Canadian Pacific diesel-electric locomotive . . 30 35
1825 75 c. Santa Fe Railway diesel-electric locomotive, U.S.A. 35 40
1826 90 c. High Speed Train, Great Britain . . . 40 45
1827 $1.20 TGV express train, France . . . 55 60
1828 $1.20 Diesel-electric locomotive, Australia . . . 55 60
1829 $1.20 Pendolino "ETR 450" electric train, Italy . . 55 60
1830 $1.20 Diesel-electric locomotive, Thailand . . . 55 60
1831 $1.20 Pennsylvania Railroad Type 4 steam locomotive, U.S.A. . . . 55 60
1832 $1.20 Beyer-Garratt steam locomotive, East African Railways . . . 55 60
1833 $1.20 Natal Govt steam locomotive . . . 55 60
1834 $1.20 Rail gun, American Civil War . . . 55 60
1835 $1.20 Locomotive "Lion" (red livery), Great Britain . . 55 60
1836 $1.20 William Hedley's "Puffing Billy" (green livery), Great Britain . . . 55 60
1837 $6 Amtrak high speed diesel locomotive, U.S.A. . . . 2·75 3·00

1997. Golden Wedding of Queen Elizabeth II and Prince Philip (1st issue). Nos. 1662/3 optd **Golden Wedding of H.M. Queen Elizabth II and Prince Philip 1947–1997.**
1839 $7.50 Type **122** . . . . 3·50 3·75
1840 $8 German bombers over St. Pauls Cathedral, London (horiz) . . . 3·75 4·00
See also Nos. 1894/9.

1997. Fungi. Nos. 2274/81 of Antigua optd **BARBUDA MAIL.**
1841 75 c. "Hygrophoropsis aurantiaca" . . . 35 40
1842 75 c. "Hygrophorus bakerensis" 35 40
1843 75 c. "Hygrophorus conicus" 35 40
1844 75 c. "Hygrophorus miniatus" ("Hygrocybe miniata") . . 35 40
1845 75 c. "Suillus brevipes" . . 35 40
1846 75 c. "Suillus luteus" . . . 35 40
1847 75 c. "Suillus granulatus" . 35 40
1848 75 c. "Suillus caerulescens" . 35 40

1997. Birds. Nos. 2140/63 of Antigua optd **BARBUDA MAIL.**
1850 75 c. Purple-throated carib . 35 40
1851 75 c. Antillean crested hummingbird . . . 35 40
1852 75 c. Bananaquit 35 40
1853 75 c. Mangrove cuckoo . . 35 40
1854 75 c. Troupial 35 40
1855 75 c. Green-throated carib . 35 40
1856 75 c. Yellow warbler . . . 35 40
1857 75 c. Blue-hooded euphonia . 35 40
1858 75 c. Scaly-breasted thrasher 35 40
1859 75 c. Burrowing owl . . . 35 40
1860 75 c. Carib grackle . . . 35 40
1861 75 c. Adelaide's warbler . . 35 40
1862 75 c. Ring-necked duck . . 35 40
1863 75 c. Ruddy duck 35 40
1864 75 c. Green-winged teal . . 35 40
1865 75 c. Wood duck 35 40
1866 75 c. Hooded merganser . . 35 40
1867 75 c. Lesser scaup . . . 35 40
1868 75 c. Black-billed whistling duck 35 40
1869 75 c. Fulvous whistling duck 35 40
1870 75 c. Bahama pintail . . . 35 40
1871 75 c. Shoveler 35 40
1872 75 c. Masked duck 35 40
1873 75 c. American wigeon . . 35 40

1997. Sailing Ships. Nos. 2283/2300 of Antigua optd **BARBUDA MAIL.**
1875 15 c. H.M.S. "Resolution" (Cook) . . . 10 10
1876 25 c. "Mayflower" (Pilgrim Fathers) . . . 10 15
1877 45 c. "Santa Maria" (Columbus) . . . 20 25
1878 75 c. "Aemilia" (Dutch galleon) 35 40
1879 75 c. "Sovereign of the Seas" (English galleon) . . . 35 40
1880 90 c. H.M.S. "Victory" (ship of the line, 1765) . . . 40 45
1881 $1.20 As No. 1878 . . . 55 60
1882 $1.20 As No. 1879 . . . 55 60
1883 $1.20 "Royal Louis" (French galleon) . . . 55 60
1884 $1.20 H.M.S. "Royal George" (ship of the line) . . . 55 60
1885 $1.20 "Le Protecteur" (French frigate) . . . 55 60
1886 $1.20 As No. 1880 . . . 55 60
1887 $1.50 As No. 1877 . . . 70 75
1888 $1.50 "Victoria" (Magellan) 70 75
1889 $1.50 "Golden Hind" (Drake) 70 75
1890 $1.50 As No. 1876 . . . 70 75
1891 $1.50 "Griffin" (La Salle) . 70 75
1892 $1.50 As No. 1875 . . . 70 75

1997. Golden Wedding of Queen Elizabeth and Prince Philip (2nd issue). Nos. 2474/9 of Antigua optd **BARBUDA MAIL.**
1894 $1 Queen Elizabeth II . . 45 50
1895 $1 Royal coat of arms . . 45 50
1896 $1 Queen Elizabeth and Prince Philip at reception . . . 45 50
1897 $1 Queen Elizabeth and Prince Philip in landau . . . 45 50
1898 $1 Balmoral 45 50
1899 $1 Prince Philip 45 50

1997. Christmas. Religious Paintings. Nos. 2566/71 of Antigua optd **BARBUDA MAIL.**
1901 15 c. "The Angel leaving Tobias and his Family" (Rembrandt) 10 10
1902 25 c. "The Resurrection" (Martin Knoller) . . . 10 15
1903 60 c. "Astronomy" (Raphael) 25 30
1904 75 c. "Music-making Angel" (Melozzo da Forli) . . . 35 40
1905 90 c. "Amor" (Parmigianino) 40 45
1906 $1.20 "Madonna and Child with Saints" (Rosso Fiorentino) . . . 50 55

1998. Sea Birds. Nos. 2325/32 of Antigua optd **BARBUDA MAIL.**
1908 75 c. Black skimmer . . . 35 40
1909 75 c. Black-capped petrel . . 35 40
1910 75 c. Sooty tern 35 40
1911 75 c. Royal tern 35 40
1912 75 c. Pomarine skua ("Pomarine Jaeger") . . . 35 40
1913 75 c. White-tailed tropic bird . 35 40
1914 75 c. Northern gannet . . . 35 40
1915 75 c. Laughing gull . . . 35 40

1998. Centenary of Radio. Entertainers. Nos. 2372/5 of Antigua optd **BARBUDA MAIL.**
1917 65 c. Kate Smith 30 35
1918 75 c. Dinah Shore 35 40
1919 90 c. Rudy Vallee 40 45
1920 $1.20 Bing Crosby 50 55

1998. Olympic Games, Atlanta (2nd issue). Previous Medal Winners. Nos. 2302/23 of Antigua optd **BARBUDA MAIL.**
1922 65 c. Florence Griffith Joyner (U.S.A.) (Gold - track, 1988) 30 35
1923 75 c. Olympic Stadium, Seoul (1988) (horiz) . . . 35 40
1924 90 c. Allison Jolly and Lynne Jewell (U.S.A.) (Gold - yachting, 1988) (horiz) . . 40 45
1925 90 c. Wolfgang Nordwig (Germany) (Gold - pole vaulting, 1972) . . . 40 45
1926 90 c. Shirley Strong (Great Britain) (Silver - 100 metres hurdles, 1984) . . . 40 45
1927 90 c. Sergei Bubka (Russia) (Gold - pole vault, 1988) . 40 45
1928 90 c. Filbert Bayi (Tanzania) (Silver - 3000 metres steeple-chase, 1980) . . . 40 45
1929 90 c. Victor Saneyev (Russia) (Gold - triple jump, 1968, 1972, 1976) . . . 40 45
1930 90 c. Silke Renk (Germany) (Gold - javelin, 1992) . . 40 45
1931 90 c. Daley Thompson (Great Britain) (Gold - decathlon, 1980, 1984) . . . 40 45
1932 90 c. Robert Richards (U.S.A.) (Gold - pole vault, 1952, 1956) . . . 40 45
1933 90 c. Parry O'Brien (U.S.A) (Gold - shot put, 1952, 1956) 40 45
1934 90 c. Ingrid Kramer (Germany) (Gold - Women's platform diving, 1960) . . . 40 45
1935 90 c. Kelly McCormick (U.S.A.) (Silver - Women's springboard diving, 1984) 40 45
1936 90 c. Gary Tobian (U.S.A.) (Gold - Men's springboard diving, 1960) . . . 40 45
1937 90 c. Greg Louganis (U.S.A.) (Gold - Men's diving, 1984 and 1988) . . . 40 45
1938 90 c. Michelle Mitchell (U.S.A.) (Silver - Women's platform diving, 1984 and 1988) . . 40 45
1939 90 c. Zhou Jihong (China) (Gold - Women's platform diving, 1984) . . . 40 45
1940 90 c. Wendy Wyland (U.S.A.) (Bronze - Women's platform diving, 1984) . . . 40 45
1941 90 c. Xu Yanmei (China) (Gold - Women's platform diving, 1988) . . . 40 45
1942 90 c. Fu Mingxia (China) (Gold - Women's platform diving, 1992) . . . 40 45
1943 $1.20 2000 metre tandem cycle race (horiz) . . . 50 55

1998. World Cup Football Championship, France. Nos. 2525/38 of Antigua optd **BARBUDA MAIL.**
1945 60 c. multicoloured . . . 25 30
1946 75 c. brown 35 40
1947 90 c. multicoloured . . . 40 45
1948 $1 brown 45 50
1949 $1 brown 45 50
1950 $1 brown 45 50
1951 $1 black 45 50
1952 $1 brown 45 50
1953 $1 brown 45 50
1954 $1 brown 45 50
1955 $1 brown 45 50
1956 $1.20 multicoloured . . . 50 55
1957 $1.65 multicoloured . . . 75 80
1958 $1.75 multicoloured . . . 80 85

1998. Cavalry through the Ages. Nos. 2359/62 of Antigua optd **BARBUDA MAIL.**
1960 60 c. Ancient Egyptian cavalryman . . . 25 30
1961 60 c. 13th-century English knight . . . 25 30
1962 60 c. 16th-century Spanish lancer . . . 25 30
1963 60 c. 18th-century Chinese cavalryman . . . 25 30

1998. 50th Anniv of U.N.I.C.E.F. Nos. 2364/6 of Antigua optd **BARBUDA MAIL.**
1965 75 c. Girl in red sari . . . 35 40
1966 90 c. South American mother and child . . . 40 45
1967 $1.20 Nurse with child . . 50 55

1998. 3000th Anniv of Jerusalem. Nos. 2368/70 of Antigua optd **BARBUDA MAIL.**
1969 75 c. Tomb of Zachariah and "Verbascum sinuatum" . . 35 40
1970 90 c. Pool of Siloam and "Hyacinthus orientalis" . . 40 45
1971 $1.20 Hurva Synagogue and "Ranunculus asiaticus" . . 50 55

1998. Diana, Princess of Wales Commemoration. Nos. 2573/84 of Antigua optd **BARBUDA MAIL.**
1973 $1.65 Diana, Princess of Wales 75 80
1974 $1.65 Wearing hoop earrings (red and black) . . . 75 80
1975 $1.65 Carrying bouquet . . 75 80
1976 $1.65 Wearing floral hat . . 75 80
1977 $1.65 With Prince Harry . . 75 80
1978 $1.65 Wearing white jacket . 75 80
1979 $1.65 In kitchen 75 80
1980 $1.65 Wearing black and white dress . . . 75 80
1981 $1.65 Wearing hat (brown and black) . . . 75 80
1982 $1.65 Wearing floral print dress (brown and black) . . . 75 80
1983 $1.65 Dancing with John Travolta . . . 75 80
1984 $1.65 Wearing white hat and jacket . . . 75 80

1998. Broadway Musical Stars. Nos. 2384/92 of Antigua optd **BARBUDA MAIL.**
1986 $1 Robert Preston ("The Music Man") . . . 45 50
1987 $1 Michael Crawford ("Phantom of the Opera") 45 50
1988 $1 Zero Mostel ("Fiddler on the Roof") . . . 45 50
1989 $1 Patti Lupone ("Evita") . 45 50
1990 $1 Raul Julia ("Threepenny Opera") . . . 45 50
1991 $1 Mary Martin ("South Pacific") . . . 45 50
1992 $1 Carol Channing ("Hello Dolly") . . . 45 50
1993 $1 Yul Brynner ("The King and I") . . . 45 50
1994 $1 Julie Andrews ("My Fair Lady") . . . 45 50

1998. 20th Death Anniv of Charlie Chaplin (film star). Nos. 2404/12 of Antigua optd **BARBUDA MAIL.**
1996 $1 Charlie Chaplin as young man . . . 45 50
1997 $1 Pulling face 45 50
1998 $1 Looking over shoulder . . 45 50
1999 $1 In cap 45 50
2000 $1 In front of star . . . 45 50
2001 $1 In "The Great Dictator" . 45 50
2002 $1 With movie camera and megaphone . . . 45 50
2003 $1 Standing in front of camera lens . . . 45 50
2004 $1 Putting on make-up . . 45 50

1998. Butterflies. Nos. 2414/35 of Antigua optd **BARBUDA MAIL.**
2006 90 c. "Charaxes porthos" . . 40 45
2007 $1.10 "Charaxes protoclea protoclea" . . . 50 55
2008 $1.10 "Byblia ilithyia" . . 50 55
2009 $1.10 Black-headed bush shrike ("Tchagra") (bird) . . 50 55
2010 $1.10 "Charaxes nobilis" . . 50 55
2011 $1.10 "Pseudacraea boisduvali trimeni" . . . 50 55
2012 $1.10 "Charaxes smaragdalis" 50 55
2013 $1.10 "Charaxes lasti" . . 50 55
2014 $1.10 "Pseudacraea poggei" . 50 55
2015 $1.10 "Graphium colonna" . 50 55
2016 $1.10 Carmine bee eater (bird) 50 55
2017 $1.10 "Pseudacraea eurytus" 50 55
2018 $1.10 "Hypolimnas monteironis" . . . 50 55
2019 $1.10 "Charaxes anticlea" . 50 55
2020 $1.10 "Graphium leonidas" . 50 55
2021 $1.10 "Graphium illyris" . . 50 55
2022 $1.10 "Nephronia argia" . . 50 55
2023 $1.10 "Graphium policenes" . 50 55
2024 $1.10 "Papilio dardanus" . . 50 55
2025 $1.20 "Aethiopana honorius" 50 55
2026 $1.60 "Charaxes hadrianus" 70 75
2027 $1.75 "Precis westermanni" 75 80

1998. Christmas. Dogs. Nos. 2771/7 of Antigua optd **BARBUDA MAIL.**
2029 15 c. Border collie . . . 10 10
2030 25 c. Dalmatian 10 15
2031 65 c. Weimaraner . . . 30 35
2032 75 c. Scottish terrier . . . 35 40
2033 90 c. Long-haired dachshund 40 45
2034 $1.20 Golden retriever . . 50 55
2035 $2 Pekingese 85 90

1999. Lighthouses of the World. Nos. 2612/19 of Antigua optd **BARBUDA MAIL.**
2037 45 c. Europa Point Lighthouse, Gibraltar . . . 20 25
2038 65 c. Tierra del Fuego, Argentina (horiz) . . . 30 35
2039 75 c. Point Loma, California, U.S.A. (horiz) . . . 35 40
2040 90 c. Groenpoint, Cape Town, South Africa . . . 40 45
2041 $1 Youghal, Cork, Ireland . 45 50

2042	$1.20 Launceston, Tasmania, Australia	50	55
2043	$1.65 Point Abino, Ontario, Canada (horiz)	75	80
2044	$1.75 Great Inagua, Bahamas (horiz)	75	80

BARWANI

A State of Central India. Now uses Indian stamps.

12 pies = 1 anna; 16 annas = 1 rupee

1 Rana Ranjit Singh 2

1921.

3	1	¼ a. green	17·00	75·00
19		¼ a. blue	90	9·00
37B		¼ a. black	2·75	23·00
18		¼ a. pink	90	9·00
4		½ a. blue	17·00	£100
29		½ a. green	2·75	9·50
10	2	1 a. red	1·60	16·00
39B		1 a. brown	10·00	19·00
11		2 a. purple	1·90	17·00
41B		2 a. red	22·00	85·00
31		4 a. orange	50·00	£120
42Ba	–	4 a. green	10·00	30·00

DESIGN: 4 a. Another portrait of Rana Ranjit Singh.

4 Rana Devi Singh 5

1932.

32A	4	¼ a. slate	1·25	14·00
33A		½ a. green	1·75	14·00
34A		1 a. brown	1·75	13·00
35A		2 a. purple	3·25	22·00
36A		4 a. olive	6·00	26·00

1938.

43	5	1 a. brown	25·00	50·00

BASUTOLAND

An African territory under British protection, N.E. of Cape Province. Self-Government introduced on 1 April 1965. Attained independence on 4 October 1966, when the country was renamed Lesotho.

1933. 12 pence = 1 shilling;
20 shillings = 1 pound.
100 cents = 1 rand.

1 King George V, Nile Crocodile and Mountains

1933.

1	1	½d. green	70	1·75
2		1d. red	60	1·00
3		2d. purple	80	55
4		3d. blue	70	60
5		4d. grey	2·00	7·00
6		6d. yellow	2·25	1·50
7		1s. orange	2·25	4·50
8		2s. 6d. brown	20·00	45·00
9		5s. violet	42·00	60·00
10		10s. olive	£110	£120

1935. Silver Jubilee. As T **13** of Antigua.

11	1d. blue and red	55	25
12	2d. blue and grey	65	75
13	3d. brown and blue	3·75	2·75
14	6d. grey and purple	3·75	2·75

1937. Coronation. As T **2** of Aden.

15	1d. red	35	30
16	2d. purple	50	85
17	3d. blue	60	85

1938. As T **1**, but portrait of King George VI.

18	½d. green	30	85
19	1d. red	50	50
20	1½d. blue	40	50
21	2d. purple	30	50
22	3d. blue	30	75
23	4d. grey	1·50	3·00
24	6d. yellow	50	75
25	1s. orange	50	90
26	2s. 6d. brown	8·00	7·00
27	5s. violet	22·00	8·50
28	10s. olive	22·00	16·00

1945. Victory. Stamps of South Africa optd **Basutoland**. Alternate stamps inscr in English or Afrikaans.

29	55	1d. brown and red	40	40
30		2d. blue and violet	40	40
31		3d. blue	40	70

Prices are for bi-lingual pairs.

5 King George VI and Queen Elizabeth

1947. Royal Visit.

32	–	1d. red	10	10
33	5	2d. green	10	10
34	–	3d. blue	10	10
35	–	1s. mauve	15	10

DESIGNS—VERT: 1d. King George VI. HORIZ: 3d. Queen Elizabeth II as Princess and Princess Margaret; 1s. The Royal Family.

1948. Silver Wedding. As T **10/11** of Aden.

36	1½d. blue	20	10
37	10s. green	30·00	27·00

1949. U.P.U. As T **20/23** of Antigua.

38	1½d. blue	30	60
39	3d. blue	1·75	1·50
40	6d. orange	1·50	1·50
41	1s. brown	1·00	90

1953. Coronation. As T **13** of Aden.

42	2d. black and purple	40	50

8 Qiloane

9 Mohair (Shearing Goats)

1954.

43	8	½d. black and sepia	10	10
44	–	1d. black and green	10	10
45	–	2d. blue and orange	60	10
46	–	3d. sage and red	80	30
47	–	4½d. indigo and blue	70	15
48	–	6d. brown and green	1·25	15
49	–	1s. bronze and purple	1·25	30
50	–	1s. 3d. brown and turquoise	15·00	4·50
51	–	2s. 6d. blue and red	12·00	6·00
52	–	5s. black and red	5·00	8·50
53	9	10s. black and purple	18·00	23·00

DESIGNS—HORIZ: 1d. Orange River; 2d. Mosuto horseman; 3d. Basuto household; 4½d. Maletsunyane Falls; 6d. Herd-boy with lesiba; 1s. Pastoral scene; 1s. 3d. De Havilland Comet 1 airplane over Lancers' Gap; 2s. 6d. Old Fort, Leribe; 5s. Mission cave house.

1959. Surch ½d. and bar.

54	½ on 2d. blue and orange (No. 45)	10	15

20 "Chief Moshoeshoe I" (engraving by Delangle)

26 Basuto Household

1959. Inauguration of National Council.

55	20	3d. black and olive	30	10
56	–	1s. red and green	30	10
57	–	1s. 3d. blue and orange	45	45

DESIGNS: 1s. Council house; 1s. 3d. Mosuto horseman.

1961. Nos. 43/53 surch.

58	8	½ c. on ½d. black and sepia	10	10
59	–	1 c. on 1d. black and green	10	10
60	–	2 c. on 2d. blue and orange	10	10
61	–	2½ c. on 3d. green and red	10	10
62	–	3½ c. on 4½d. indigo and blue	10	10
63	–	5 c. on 6d. brown and green	10	10
64	–	10 c. on 1s. green and purple	10	10
65	–	12½ c. on 1s. 3d. brown and turquoise	75	20
66	–	25 c. on 2s. 6d. blue and red	30	30
67a	–	50 c. on 5s. black and red	90	1·40
68b	9	1 r. on 10s. black and purple	6·00	6·50

1961. As 1954 but value in new currency as in T **26**.

69	8	½ c. black and brown	10	20
70	–	1 c. black and green (as 1d.)	10	40
71	–	2 c. blue and orange (as 2d.)	50	1·40
86	26	2½ c. green and red	15	15
73	–	3½ c. indigo and blue (as 4½d.)	30	1·50
88	–	5 c. brown and green (as 6d.)	30	40
75	–	10 c. green and purple (as 1s.)	30	40
90	–	12½ c. brown & grn (as 1s. 3d.)	2·75	1·50
77	–	25 c. blue and red (as 2s. 6d.)	6·50	6·50
78	–	50 c. black and red (as 5s.)	13·00	14·00
79	9	1 r. black and purple	23·00	12·00

1963. Freedom from Hunger. As T **28** of Aden.

80	12½ c. violet	40	15

1963. Centenary of Red Cross. As T **33** of Antigua.

81	2½ c. red and black	20	10
82	12½ c. red and blue	60	60

27 Mosotho Woman and Child

1965. New Constitution. Inscr "SELF GOVERNMENT 1965". Multicoloured.

94	2½ c. Type **27**	20	10
95	3½ c. Maseru border post	25	20
96	5 c. Mountain scene	25	20
97	12½ c. Legislative Buildings	45	70

1965. Centenary of I.T.U. As T **36** of Antigua.

98	1 c. red and purple	15	10
99	20 c. blue and brown	35	30

1965. I.C.Y. As T **37** of Antigua.

100	½ c. purple and turquoise	10	10
101	12½ c. green and lavender	45	35

1966. Churchill Commemoration. As T **38** of Antigua.

102	1 c. blue	15	30
103	2½ c. green	35	10
104	10 c. brown	45	30
105	22½ c. violet	70	60

OFFICIAL STAMPS

1934. Nos. 1/3 and 6 optd **OFFICIAL**.

O1	1	½d. green	£3000	£3000
O2		1d. red	£1300	£1000
O3		2d. purple	£750	£550
O4		6d. yellow	£9500	£4500

POSTAGE DUE STAMPS

1933. As Type **D 1** of Barbados.

D1b	1d. red	55	1·50
D2a	2d. violet	30	6·00

D 2

1956.

D3	D 2	1d. red	30	2·75
D4		2d. violet	30	4·50

1961. Surch.

D5	D 2	1 c. on 1d. red	10	30
D6		1 c. on 2d. violet	10	30
D7		5 c. on 2d. violet	15	30
D8	–	5 c. on 2d. violet (No. D2a)	1·50	6·50

1964. As Type **D 2**, but value in decimal currency.

D 9	1 c. red	1·90	10·00
D10	5 c. violet	1·90	10·00

For later issues see **LESOTHO**.

BATUM

Batum, a Russian port on the Black Sea, had been taken by Turkish troops during the First World War. Following the Armistice British Forces occupied the town on 1 December 1918. Batum was handed over to the National Republic of Georgia on 7 July 1920.

100 kopeks = 1 rouble

1 Aloe Tree

БАТУМ. ОБ.

Руб 10 Руб

(2)

1919. Imperf.

1	1	5 k. green	5·00	6·50
2		10 k. blue	5·00	6·50
3		50 k. yellow	1·75	2·25
4		1 r. brown	2·25	2·75
5		3 r. violet	7·50	9·00
6		5 r. brown	8·50	11·00

1919. Arms types of Russia surch as T **2**. Imperf (Nos. 7/8), perf (Nos. 9/10).

7	10 r. on 1 k. orange	28·00	30·00
8	10 r. on 3 k. red	15·00	17·00
9	10 r. on 5 k. purple	£275	£275
10	10 r. on 10 on 7 k. blue	£225	£225

1919. T **1** optd **BRITISH OCCUPATION**.

11	1	5 k. green	7·00	7·00
12		10 k. blue	7·00	7·00
13		25 k. yellow	7·00	7·00
14		1 r blue	3·25	6·00
15		2 r. pink	1·00	1·25
16		3 r. violet	1·00	1·25
17		5 r. brown	1·25	1·40
18		7 r. red	2·75	4·00

1919. Arms types of Russia surch with Russian inscr, **BRITISH OCCUPATION** and new value.

19		10 r. on 3 k. red	11·00	13·00
20a		15 r. on 1 k. orange	30·00	30·00
29		25 r. on 5 k. purple	30·00	30·00
30a		25 r. on 10 on 7 k. blue	48·00	48·00
31a		25 r. on 20 on 14 k. red and blue	48·00	48·00
32a		25 r. on 25 k. purple and green	70·00	70·00
33		25 r. on 50 k. green and purple	48·00	48·00
21		50 r. on 1 k. orange	£275	£275
34		50 r. on 2 k. green	75·00	75·00
35		50 r. on 3 k. red	75·00	75·00
36		50 r. on 4 k. red	65·00	65·00
37		50 r. on 5 k. purple	48·00	48·00
27		50 r. on 10 k. blue	£950	£950
28		50 r. on 15 k. blue and brown	£375	£375

1920. Romanov type of Russia surch with Russian inscr, **BRITISH OCCUPATION** and new value.

41		50 r. on 4 k. red	38·00	42·00

1920. Nos. 11, 13 and 3 surch with new value (50 r. with **BRITISH OCCUPATION** also).

42	1	25 r. on 5 k. green	22·00	22·00
43		25 r. on 25 k. yellow	17·00	17·00
44a		50 r. on 50 k. yellow	10·00	10·00

1920. T **1** optd **BRITISH OCCUPATION.**

45	1	1 r. brown	60	3·00
46		2 r. blue	70	3·00
47		3 r. pink	70	3·00
48		5 r. black	70	3·00
49		7 r. yellow	70	3·00
50		10 r. green	60	3·00
51		15 r. violet	90	4·25
52		25 r. red	80	3·75
53		50 r. blue	1·00	6·00

BECHUANALAND

A colony and protectorate in Central S. Africa. British Bechuanaland (colony) was annexed to Cape of Good Hope in 1895. Internal Self-Government in the protectorate was introduced on 1st March, 1965. Attained independence on 30th September, 1966, when the country was renamed Botswana.

1885. 12 pence = 1 shilling;
20 shillings = 1 pound.
1961. 100 cents = 1 rand.

A. BRITISH BECHUANALAND

1885. Stamps of Cape of Good Hope ("Hope" seated) optd with **British Bechuanaland.**

4	6	½d. black	7·00	11·00
38		1d. red	2·25	2·25
32		2d. bistre	3·25	2·25
2		3d. red	32·00	35·00
3		4d. blue	55·00	60·00
7		6d. purple	75·00	38·00
8		1s. green	£200	£140

1887. Stamp of Great Britain (Queen Victoria) optd **BRITISH BECHUANALAND.**

9	71	½d. red	1·00	1·25

3

4

1887.

10	3	1d. lilac and black	13·00	1·50
11a		2d. lilac and black	38·00	22·00
12		3d. lilac and black	3·25	4·75
13		4d. lilac and black	40·00	2·25
14		6d. lilac and black	50·00	2·50
15	4	1s. green and black	28·00	5·00
16		2s. green and black	48·00	35·00
17		2s. 6d. green and black	60·00	42·00
18		5s. green and black	80·00	£140
19		10s. green and black	£170	£325
20	–	£1 lilac and black	£900	£800
21	–	£5 lilac and black	£2750	£1300

Nos. 20/1 are as Type **4** but larger, 23 × 39½ mm.

1888. Surch.

22	3	"1d." on 1d. lilac and black	7·50	5·50
23		"2d." on 2d. lilac and black	15·00	2·50
25		"4d." on 4d. lilac and black	£180	£250
26		"6d." on 6d. lilac and black	75·00	10·00
28	4	"1s." on 1s. green and black	£100	65·00

1888. Surch **ONE HALF PENNY** and bars.

29	3	½d. on 3d. lilac and black	£130	£140

1891. Stamps of Great Britain (Queen Victoria) optd **BRITISH BECHUANALAND.**

33	57	1d. lilac	6·00	85
34	73	2d. green and red	4·50	3·25
35	76	4d. green and brown	2·50	50
36	79	6d. purple on red	3·00	2·00
37	82	1s. green	13·00	16·00

B. BECHUANALAND PROTECTORATE.

1888. No. 9 to 19 optd **Protectorate** or surch also.

40	71	½d. red	3·00	22·00
41	3	1d. on 1d. lilac and black	6·50	12·00
42		2d. on 2d. lilac and black	19·00	17·00
43		3d. on 3d. lilac and black	95·00	£140
51		4d. on 4d. lilac and black	60·00	32·00
45		6d. on 6d. lilac and black	65·00	40·00
46	4	1s. green and black	65·00	50·00
47		2s. green and black	£500	£750
48		2s. 6s. green and black	£500	£650
49		5s. green and black	£1100	£1700
50		10s. green and black	£3000	£4500

1889. Stamp of Cape of Good Hope ("Hope" seated) optd **Bechuanaland Protectorate.**

52	6	½d. black	2·75	28·00

1889. No. 9 surch **Protectorate Fourpence.**

53	71	4d. on ½d. red	16·00	3·25

1897. Stamp of Cape of Good Hope ("Hope" seated) optd **BRITISH BECHUANALAND.**

56	6	½d. green	2·50	7·00

1897. Queen Victoria stamps of Great Britain optd **BECHUANALAND PROTECTORATE.**

59	71	½d. red	1·00	1·75
60		½d. green	1·40	2·50
61	57	1d. lilac	4·00	55
62	73	2d. green and red	2·50	4·50
63	75	3d. purple on yellow	5·50	8·50
64	76	4d. green and brown	11·00	11·00
65	79	6d. purple on red	21·00	11·00

1904. King Edward VII stamps of Great Britain optd **BECHUANALAND PROTECTORATE.**

66	83	½d. turquoise	1·25	1·25
68		1d. red	5·50	25
69		2½d. blue	5·00	5·00
70	–	1s. green and red (No 314)	35·00	90·00

1912. King George V stamps of Great Britain optd **BECHUANALAND PROTECTORATE.**

91	105	½d. green	1·00	1·75
72	102	1d. red	1·00	60
92	104	1d. red	1·50	70
75	105	1½d. brown	2·25	3·00
93	106	2d. orange	1·50	1·00
78	104	2½d. blue	3·50	16·00
79	106	3d. violet	5·50	12·00
80		4d. grey	6·00	14·00
81	107	6d. purple	6·50	16·00
82	108	1s. brown	9·00	18·00
88	109	2s. 6d. brown	80·00	£150
89		5s. red	£110	£225

22 King George V, Baobab Tree and Cattle drinking

1932.

99	22	½d. green	1·00	30
100		1d. red	1·00	25
101		2d. brown	1·00	30
102		3d. blue	1·00	70
103		4d. orange	1·25	4·50
104		6d. purple	2·50	2·25
105		1s. black and olive	3·00	7·00
106		2s. black and orange	24·00	38·00
107		2s. 6d. black and red	19·00	30·00
108		3s. black and purple	35·00	42·00
109		5s. black and blue	48·00	50·00
110		10s. black and brown	£100	£110

1935. Silver Jubilee. As T **13** of Antigua.

111		1d. blue and red	30	2·00
112		2d. blue and black	1·00	2·00
113		3d. brown and blue	1·75	2·00
114		6d. grey and purple	3·50	2·00

1937. Coronation. As T **2** of Aden.

115		1d. red	45	40
116		2d. brown	60	80
117		3d. blue	60	1·00

1938. As T **22**, but portrait of King George VI.

118		½d. green	2·00	2·25
119		1d. red	40	40
120a		1½d. blue	40	70
121		2d. brown	40	40
122		3d. blue	40	1·75
123		4d. orange	1·40	2·50
124a		6d. purple	3·00	2·50
125		1s. black and olive	3·00	2·75
126		2s. 6d. black and red	14·00	9·50
127		5s. black and blue	30·00	9·50
128		10s. black and brown	14·00	17·00

1945. Victory. Stamps of South Africa optd **Bechuanaland**. Alternate stamps inscr in English or Afrikaans.

129	55	1d. brown and red	50	45
130		2d. blue and violet (No. 109)	50	80
131		3d. blue (No. 110)	50	80

Prices for bi-lingual pairs.

1947. Royal Visit. As Nos. 32/5 of Basutoland.

132		1d. red	10	10
133		2d. green	10	10
134		3d. blue	10	10
135		1s. mauve	10	10

1948. Silver Wedding. As T **10/11** of Aden.

136		1½d. blue	30	10
137		10s. grey	27·00	35·00

1949. U.P.U. As T **20/23** of Antigua.

138		1½d. blue	45	65
139		3d. blue	1·25	1·75
140		6d. mauve	90	80
141		1s. olive	95	80

1953. Coronation. As T **13** of Aden.

142		2d. black and brown	30	30

1955. As T **22** but portrait of Queen Elizabeth II, facing right.

143		½d. green	50	30
144		1d. red	80	10
145		2d. brown	1·25	30
146		3d. blue	3·00	70
146b		4d. orange	6·50	7·00
147		4½d. blue	1·50	35
148		6d. purple	1·25	60
149		1s. black and olive	1·25	80
150		1s. 3d. black and lilac	13·00	9·50
151		2s. 6d. black and red	10·00	9·50
152		5s. black and blue	15·00	6·50
153		10s. black and brown	20·00	15·00

26 Queen Victoria. Queen Elizabeth II and Landscape

28 African Golden Oriole

1960. 75th Anniv of Protectorate.

154	26	1d. sepia and black	40	50
155		3d. mauve and black	40	30
156		6d. blue and black	40	50

1961. Stamps of 1955 surch.

157		1 c. on 1d. red	30	10
158		2 c. on 2d. brown	20	10
159		2½ c. on 2d. brown	30	10
160		2½ c. on 3d. blue	2·00	3·00
161d		3½ c. on 4d. orange	20	20
162a		5 c. on 6d. purple	20	10
163		10 c. on 1s. black and olive	20	10
164		12½ c. on 1s. 3d. black and lilac	65	20
165		25 c. on 2s. 6d. black and red	2·00	50
166		50 c. on 5s. black and blue	3·00	2·00
167b		1 r. on 10s. black and brown	7·00	2·25

1961.

168	28	1 c. multicoloured	1·25	40
169	–	2 c orange, black and olive	1·50	2·25
170	–	2½ c multicoloured	1·50	10
171	–	3½ c. multicoloured	1·75	1·25
172	–	5 c. multicoloured	3·00	1·00
173	–	7½ c. multicoloured	1·75	1·75
174	–	10 c. multicoloured	1·75	60
175	–	12½ c. multicoloured	18·00	5·00
176	–	20 c. brown and drab	80	70
177	–	25 c. sepia and lemon	1·00	85
178	–	35 c. blue and orange	1·00	1·75
179	–	50 c. sepia and olive	1·00	2·25
180	–	1 r. black and brown	3·00	2·50
181	–	2 r. brown and turquoise	18·00	9·00

DESIGNS—VERT: 2 c. Hoopoe; 2½ c. Scarlet-chested sunbird; 3½ c. Yellow-rumped bishop; 5 c. Swallow-tailed bee eater; 7½ c. African grey hornbill; 10 c. Red-headed weaver; 12½ c. Brown-hooded kingfisher; 20 c. Woman musician; 35 c. Woman grinding maize; 1 r. Lion; 2 r. Police camel patrol. HORIZ: 25 c. Baobab tree; 50 c. Bechuana ox.

1963. Freedom from Hunger. As T **28** of Aden.

182		12½ c. green	30	15

1963. Centenary of Red Cross. As T **33** of Antigua.

183		2½ c. red and black	20	10
184		12½ c. red and blue	40	50

1964. 400th Birth Anniv of Shakespeare. As T **34** of Antigua.

185		12½ c. brown	15	15

C. BECHUANALAND

42 Map and Gaberones Dam

1965. New Constitution.

186	42	2½ c. red and gold	10	10
187		5 c. blue and gold	15	40
188		12½ c. brown and gold	20	40
189		25 c. green and gold	20	55

1965. Centenary of I.T.U. As T **36** of Antigua.

190		2½ c. red and yellow	20	10
191		12½ c. mauve and brown	45	30

1965. I.C.Y. As T **37** of Antigua.

192		1 c. purple and turquoise	10	10
193		12½ c. green and lavender	60	55

1966. Churchill Commemoration. As T **38** of Antigua.

194		1 c. blue	15	30
195		2½ c. green	35	10
196		12½ c. brown	70	30
197		20 c. violet	75	40

43 Haslar Smoke Generator

1966. Bechuanaland Royal Pioneer Corps.

198	43	2½ c. blue, red and green	20	10
199	–	5 c. brown and blue	20	20
200	–	15 c. blue, red and green	30	25
201	–	35 c. multicoloured	30	80

DESIGNS: 5 c. Bugler; 15 c. Gun-site; 35 c. Regimental cap badge.

POSTAGE DUE STAMPS

1926. Postage Due stamps of Great Britain optd **BECHUANALAND PROTECTORATE.**

D1	D 1	½d. green	3·25	60·00
D2		1d. red	3·25	45·00
D3		2d. black	6·00	80·00

D 3

1932.

D4	D 3	½d. green	6·00	30·00
D5a		1d. red	1·00	12·00
D6b		2d. violet	1·50	17·00

1961. Surch.

D7	D 3	1 c. on 1d. red	25	50
D8		2 c. on 2d. violet	25	1·50
D9		5 c. on ½d. green	20	60

1961. As Type D **3** but value in decimal currency.

D10		1 c. red	15	1·50
D11		2 c. violet	15	1·50
D12		5 c. green	30	1·75

For later issues see **BOTSWANA**.

BELIZE

British Honduras was renamed Belize on the 1st June 1973 and the country became independent within the Commonwealth on 21 September 1981.

100 cents = 1 dollar

1973. Nos. 256/66 and 277/8 of British Honduras optd **BELIZE** and two stars.

347	–	½ c. multicoloured	10	20
348	63	1 c. black, brown and yellow	10	20
349	–	2 c. black, green and yellow	10	20
350	–	3 c. black, brown and lilac	10	10
351	–	4 c. multicoloured	10	20
352	–	5 c. black and red	10	20
353	–	10 c. multicoloured	15	15
354	–	15 c. multicoloured	20	20
355	–	25 c. multicoloured	35	35
356	–	50 c. multicoloured	65	75
357	–	$1 multicoloured	1·10	1·50
358	–	$2 multicoloured	2·00	2·75
359	–	$5 multicoloured	2·50	4·75

1973. Royal Wedding. As T **47** of Anguilla. Background colours given. Multicoloured.

360		26 c. blue	15	10
361		50 c. brown	15	20

82 Mozambique Mouthbrooder

1974. As Nos. 256/66 and 276/78 of British Honduras. Multicoloured.

362		½ c. Type **82**	10	20
363		1 c. Spotted jewfish	10	20
364		2 c. White-lipped peccary ("Waree")	10	20
365		3 c. Misty grouper	10	10
366		4 c. Collared anteater	10	20
367		5 c. Bonefish	10	20

368 10 c. Paca ("Gibnut") 15 15
369 15 c. Dolphin 20 20
370 25 c. Kinkajou ("Night Walker") 35 35
371 50 c. Mutton snapper 60 70
372 $1 Tayra ("Bush Dog") . . . 1·00 1·50
373 $2 Great barracuda . . . . . 1·50 2·25
374 $5 Puma . . . . 3·50 5·50

83 Deer

1974. Mayan Artefacts (1st series). Pottery Motifs. Multicoloured.
375 3 c. Type **83** 10 10
376 6 c. Jaguar deity 10 10
377 16 c. Sea monster 15 10
378 26 c. Cormorant 25 10
379 50 c. Scarlet macaw 40 40
See also Nos 398/402.

84 "Parides arcas"

1974. Butterflies of Belize. Multicoloured.
380 ½ c. Type **84** . . . . 90 2·50
381 1 c. "Evenus regalis" . . . . 90 1·75
405 2 c. "Colobura dirce" 50 70
406 3 c. "Catonephele numilia" . . 1·25 70
407 4 c. "Battus belus" . . . . . 3·00 30
408 5 c. "Callicore patelina" . . . 3·25 30
386 10 c. "Diaethria astala" . . . 1·50 70
410 15 c. "Nessaea aglaura" . . . 75 70
388 16 c. "Prepona pseudojoiceyi" . 4·00 5·00
412 25 c. "Papilio thoas" . . . . 2·75 40
390 26 c. "Hamadryas arethusa" . 2·50 4·25
413 35 c. Type **84** . . . . 11·00 4·50
391 50 c. "Panthiades bathildis" . 2·75 65
392 $1 "Caligo uranus" . . . . . 6·50 4·00
393 $2 "Heliconius sapho" . . . . 4·00 1·25
394 $5 "Eurytides philolaus" . . . 4·75 4·00
395 $10 "Philaethria dido" . . . . 10·00 4·00

85 Churchill when Prime Minister, and Coronation Scene

1974. Birth Centenary of Sir Winston Churchill. Multicoloured.
396 50 c. Type **85** 20 20
397 $1 Churchill in stetson, and Williamsburg Liberty Bell . 30 30

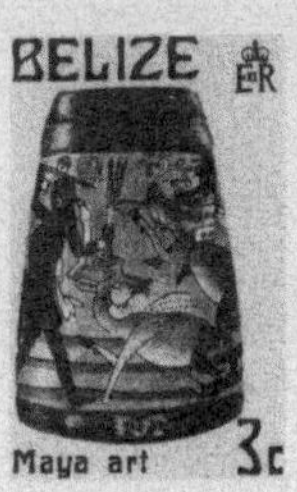

86 The Actun Balam Vase

1975. Mayan Artefacts (2nd series). Multicoloured.
398 3 c. Type **86** 10 10
399 6 c. Seated figure 10 10
400 16 c. Costumed priest 25 15
401 26 c. Head with headdress . . 35 20
402 50 c. Layman and priest . . . 45 1·40

87 Musicians

1975. Christmas. Multicoloured.
435 6 c. Type **87** 10 10
436 26 c. Children and "crib" . . 20 10
437 50 c. Dancer and drummers (vert) 30 45
438 $1 Family and map (vert) . . 55 1·40

88 William Wrigley Jr. and Chicle Tapping

1976. Bicent of American Revolution. Mult.
439 10 c. Type **88** 10 10
440 35 c. Charles Lindbergh . . . 20 40
441 $1 J. L. Stephens (archaeologist) 50 1·00

89 Cycling

1976. Olympic Games, Montreal. Multicoloured.
442 35 c. Type **89** 15 10
443 45 c. Running 20 15
444 $1 Shooting 35 80

1976. No. 390 surch **20c**.
445 20 c. on 26 c. multicoloured . 1·50 80

1976. West Indian Victory in World Cricket Cup. As Nos. 559/60 of Barbados.
446 35 c. multicoloured 50 50
447 $1 black and purple . . . . . 1·10 2·00

1976. No. 426 surch **5c**.
448 5 c. on 15 c. multicoloured . 1·50 2·25

92 Queen and Bishops

1977. Silver Jubilee. Multicoloured.
449 10 c. Royal Visit, 1975 . . . 10 10
450 35 c. Queen and Rose Window 15 15
451 $2 Type **92** 45 90

93 Red-capped Manakin **94** Laboratory Workers

1977. Birds (1st series). Multicoloured.
452 8 c. Type **93** 75 40
453 10 c. Hooded oriole 90 30
454 25 c. Blue-crowned motmot . 1·25 55
455 35 c. Slaty-breasted tinamou . 1·50 75
456 45 c. Ocellated turkey . . . . 1·75 1·25
457 $1 White hawk . . . . 3·00 5·00
See also Nos. 467/72, 486/91 and 561/6.

1977. 75th Anniv of Pan-American Health Organization. Multicoloured.
459 35 c. Type **94** 20 20
460 $1 Mobile medical unit . . . 40 65

1978. Nos. 386 and 413 optd **BELIZE DEFENCE FORCE 1ST JANUARY 1978**.
462 10 c. "Diaethria astala" . . . 75 75
463 35 c. Type **84** . . . . 1·50 1·75

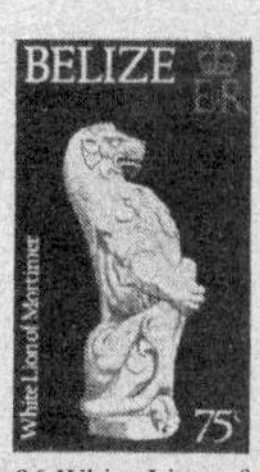

96 White Lion of Mortimer **97** "Russelia sarmentosa"

1978. 25th Anniv of Coronation.
464 **96** 75 c. brown, red and silver . 20 30
465 – 75 c. multicoloured 20 30
466 – 75 c. brown, red and silver . 20 30
DESIGNS: No. 465, Queen Elizabeth II. No. 466, Jaguar (Maya god of Day and Night).

1978. Birds (2nd series). As T **93**. Multicoloured.
467 10 c. White-capped parrot . . 55 30
468 25 c. Crimson-collared tanager 1·00 45
469 35 c. Citreoline trogon . . . 1·40 55
470 45 c. American finfoot . . . . 1·60 1·75
471 50 c. Muscovy duck . . . . . 1·75 2·50
472 $1 King vulture . . . . 2·50 5·00

1978. Christmas. Wild Flowers and Ferns. Mult.
474 10 c. Type **97** 15 10
475 15 c. "Lygodium polymorphum" 20 15
476 35 c. "Heliconia aurantiaca" . 25 20
477 45 c. "Adiantum tetraphyllum" 30 40
478 50 c. "Angelonia ciliaris" . . . 30 50
479 $1 "Thelypteris obliterata" . . 50 1·00

98 Fairchild Monoplane of Internal Airmail Service, 1937

1979. Centenary of U.P.U. Membership. Mult.
480 5 c. Type **98** 25 20
481 10 c. "Heron H" (mail boat), 1949 . . . . 25 10
482 35 c. Internal mail service, 1920 (canoe) 30 20
483 45 c. Steam Creek Railway mail, 1910 . . . . 60 55
484 50 c. Mounted mail courier, 1882 60 60
485 $1 "Eagle" (mail boat), 1856 . 1·10 2·25

1979. No. 413 surch **15c**.
487 **84** 15 c. on 35 c. multicoloured 1·50 1·75

1979. Birds (3rd series). As T **93**. Multicoloured.
488 10 c. Boat-billed heron . . . 50 20
489 25 c. grey-necked wood rail . 75 30
490 35 c. Lineated woodpecker . . 85 55
491 45 c. Blue-grey tanager . . . 90 70
492 50 c. Laughing falcon . . . . 90 1·25
493 $1 Long-tailed hermit . . . . 1·40 3·00

101 Paslow Building, Belize G.P.O.

1979. 25th Anniv of Coronation. Multicoloured.
495 25 c. Type **101** 80 10
496 50 c. Houses of Parliament . . 1·25 10
497 75 c. Coronation State Coach . 1·75 15
498 $1 Queen on horseback (vert) . 2·25 15
499 $2 Prince of Wales (vert) . . . 2·75 25
500 $3 Queen and Duke of Edinburgh (vert) . . . . . . 2·75 25
501 $4 Portrait of Queen (vert) . . 3·00 30
502 $5 St. Edward's Crown (vert) . 3·50 30

102 Mortimer and Vaughan "Safety" Airplane, 1910

1979. Death Centenary of Sir Rowland Hill. 60th Anniv of I.C.A.O. (International Civil Aviation Organization), previously Int Commission for Air Navigation. Multicoloured.
504 4 c. Type **102** 40 10
505 25 c. Boeing 720 . . . . 1·25 20
506 50 c. Concorde . . . . 3·00 30
507 75 c. Handley Page H.P.18 W.8b (1922) . . . . 1·75 30
508 $1 Avro Type F (1912) . . . . 1·75 30
509 $1.50 Samuel Cody's biplane (1910) . . . . 2·50 30
510 $2 A.V. Roe Triplane I (1909) 2·50 40
511 $3 Santos Dumont's biplane "14 bis" (1906) . . . . 2·50 45
512 $4 Wright Type A . . . . . . 3·00 65

103 Handball **104** Olympic Torch

1979. Olympic Games, Moscow (1980). Multicoloured.
514 25 c. Type **103** 45 10
515 50 c. Weightlifting 65 10
516 75 c. Athletics 90 15
517 $1 Football . . . . 1·25 20
518 $2 Yachting . . . . 1·75 25
519 $3 Swimming . . . . 2·00 30
520 $4 Boxing . . . . 2·50 30
521 $5 Cycling . . . . 4·00 50

1979. Winter Olympic Games, Lake Placid (1980). Multicoloured.
523 25 c. Type **104** 20 10
524 50 c. Giant slalom 45 15
525 75 c. Figure-skating 65 15
526 $1 Slalom skiing 80 15
527 $2 Speed-skating . . . . . . 1·60 20
528 $3 Cross-country skiing . . . 2·50 30
529 $4 Shooting . . . . 3·00 40
530 $5 Gold, Silver and Bronze medals . . . . 3·50 45

105 Measled Cowrie

1980. Shells. Multicoloured.
532 1 c. Type **105** 55 10
533 2 c. Callico clam 70 10
534 3 c. Altantic turkey wing (vert) 80 10
535 4 c. Leafy jewel box (vert) . . 80 10
536 5 c. Trochlear latirus 80 10
537 10 c. Alphabet cone (vert) . . 1·00 10
538 15 c. Cabrits murex (vert) . . 1·40 10
539 20 c. Stiff pen shell . . . . . 1·50 10
540 25 c. Little knotted scallop (vert) 1·50 10
541 35 c. Glory of the Altantic cone (vert) . . . . 1·75 10
542 45 c. Sunrise tellin (vert) . . . 2·00 10
543 50 c. "Leucozonia nassa leucozonalis" . . . . . . 2·00 10
544 85 c. Triangular typhis . . . 3·00 10
545 $1 Queen or pink conch (vert) 3·25 10
546 $2 Rooster-tail conch (vert) . 5·00 30
547 $5 True tulip . . . . 7·50 75
548 $10 Star arene . . . . 9·50 1·25

106 Girl and Flower Arrangement **108** Jabiru

1980. International Year of the Child (1st issue). Multicoloured.
550 25 c. Type **106** 45 10
551 50 c. Boy holding football . . 70 10
552 75 c. Boy with butterfly . . . 1·00 10
553 $1 Girl holding doll . . . . . 1·00 10
554 $1.50 Boy carrying basket of fruit 1·50 15
555 $2 Boy holding reticulated cowrie-helmet shell . . . . 1·75 20
556 $3 Girl holding posy . . . . 2·25 25
557 $4 Boy and girl wrapped in blanket . . . . 2·50 30
See also Nos. 583/90.

1980. No. 412 surch **10c**.
560 10 c. on 25 c. "Papilio thoas" . 75 1·00

1980. Birds (4th series). Multicoloured.
561 10 c. Type **108** . . . . 5·00 2·75
562 25 c. Barred antshrike . . . . 5·50 2·75
563 35 c. Northern royal flycatcher 5·50 2·75
564 45 c. White-necked puffbird . . 6·00 3·00
565 50 c. Ornate hawk-eagle . . . 6·00 3·00
566 $1 Golden-masked tanager . . 6·50 3·75

109 Speed Skating

111 Witch in Sky

1980. Winter Olympic Games, Lake Placid. Medal Winners. Multicoloured.
568 25 c. Type **109** 30 15
569 50 c. Ice-hockey 50 15
570 75 c. Figure-skating 60 15
571 $1 Alpine-skiing 85 15
572 $1.50 Giant slalom (women) 1·25 25
573 $2 Speed-skating (women) 1·50 30
574 $3 Cross-country skiing 2·25 40
575 $5 Giant slalom 3·50 55

1980. "ESPAMER" International Stamp Exhibition, Madrid. Nos. 560/5 optd **BELIZE ESPAMER '80 MADRID 3-12 OCT 1980** and emblem (Nos. 577/9) or surch also.
577 10 c. Type **107** 4·75 2·50
578 25 c. Barred antshrike 5·00 2·75
579 35 c. Northern royal flycatcher 5·00 2·75
580 40 c. on 45 c. White-necked puffbird 5·50 3·00
581 40c. on 50 c. Ornate hawk-eagle 5·50 3·00
582 40 c. on $1 Golden-masked tanager 5·50 3·00

1980. International Year of the Child (2nd issue). "Sleeping Beauty".
583 **111** 25 c. multicoloured 90 15
584 – 40 c. multicoloured 1·00 15
585 – 50 c. multicoloured 1·25 15
586 – 75 c. multicoloured 1·40 15
587 – $1 multicoloured 1·50 20
588 – $1.50 multicoloured 2·25 30
589 – $3 multicoloured 3·25 35
590 – $4 multicoloured 3·25 45
DESIGNS: 40 c. to $4, Illustrations from the story.

112 H.M. Queen Elizabeth the Queen Mother

1980. 80th Birthday of H.M. Queen Elizabeth the Queen Mother.
592 **112** $1 multicoloured 1·25 40

113 The Annunciation

115 Paul Harris (founder)

1980. Christmas. Multicoloured.
594 25 c. Type **113** 45 10
595 50 c. Bethlehem 75 10
596 75 c. The Holy Family 1·00 10
597 $1 The Nativity 1·10 10
598 $1.50 The Flight into Egypt 1·50 15
599 $2 Shepherds following the Star 1·75 20
600 $3 Virgin, Child and Angel 2·25 25
601 $4 Adoration of the Kings 2·25 30

1981. "WIPA" International Stamp Exhibition, Vienna. Nos. 598 and 601 surch.
603 $1 on $1.50 The Flight into Egypt 2·00 65
604 $2 on $4 Adoration of the Kings 2·50 1·40

1981. 75th Anniv of Rotary International. Mult.
606 25 c. Type **115** 80 25
607 50 c. Emblems of Rotary activities 1·25 35
608 $1 75th Anniversary emblem 1·75 65
609 $1.50 Educational scholarship programme (horiz) 2·50 1·00
610 $2 "Project Hippocrates" 3·00 1·40
611 $3 Emblems 3·50 2·00
612 $5 Emblems and handshake (horiz) 4·50 3·25

116 Coat of Arms of Prince of Wales

118 Athletics

1981. Royal Wedding. Mult. (a) Size 22 × 38 mm.
614 50 c. Type **116** 35 40
615 $1 Prince Charles in military uniform 70 75
616 $1.50 Royal couple 1·10 1·25

(b) Size 25 × 42 mm. with gold borders.
617 50 c. Type **116** 35 15
618 $1 As No. 615 70 35
619 $1.50 As No. 616 1·10 45

1981. No. 538 surch **10c**.
621 10 c. on 15 c. "Murex cabritii" 2·25 2·25

1981. History of the Olympics. Multicoloured.
622 85 c. Type **118** 1·50 30
623 $1 Cycling 3·00 30
624 $1.50 Boxing 2·50 30
625 $2 1984 Games–Los Angeles and Sarajevo 3·00 30
626 $3 Baron de Coubertin 3·50 45
627 $5 Olympic Flame 4·50 60

1981. Independence Commemoration (1st issue). Optd **Independence 21 Sept., 1981**. (a) On Nos. 532/44 and 546/8.
629 1 c. Type **105** 50 10
630 2 c. Callico clam 50 10
631 3 c. Atlantic turkey wing (vert) 60 10
632 4 c. Leafy jewel box (vert) 60 10
633 5 c. Trochlear latirus 60 10
634 10 c. Alphabet cone (vert) 75 10
635 15 c. Cabrits murex (vert) 1·25 10
636 20 c. Stiff pen shell 1·40 15
637 25 c. Little knobbed scallop (vert) 1·50 25
638 35 c. Glory of the Atlantic cone 1·50 30
639 45 c. Sunrise tellin (vert) 2·00 40
640 50 c. "Leucozonia nassa leucozonalis" 2·00 40
641 85 c. Triangular typhis 3·00 90
642 $2 Rooster-tail conch (vert) 6·00 2·50
643 $5 True tulip 8·00 5·50
644 $10 Star arene 12·00 9·50

(b) On Nos. 606/12.
646 25 c. Type **115** 1·00 25
647 50 c. Emblems of Rotary activities 1·50 35
648 $1 75th Anniversary emblem 1·75 65
649 $1.50 Educational scholarship programme 2·50 1·00
650 $2 "Project Hippocrates" 3·25 1·40
651 $3 Emblems 3·75 2·00
652 $5 Emblems and hand-shake 5·00 3·25
See also Nos. 657/62.

1981. "ESPAMER" International Stamp Exhibition, Buenos Aires. No. 609 surch **$1 ESPAMER 81 BUENOS AIRES 13-22 NOV** and emblem.
654 $1 on $1.50 Educational scholarship programme 3·25 1·75

122 Black Orchid

123 Uruguayan Footballer

1981. Independence Commemoration (2nd issue). Multicoloured.
657 10 c. Belize Coat of Arms (horiz) 70 10
658 35 c. Map of Belize 1·75 30
659 50 c. Type **122** 5·00 80
660 85 c. Baird's tapir (horiz) 2·00 1·00
661 $1 Mahogany tree 2·00 1·10
662 $2 Keel-billed toucan (horiz) 7·00 2·75

1981. World Cup Football Championship, Spain (1st issue). Multicoloured.
664 10c. Type **123** 1·40 20
665 25 c. Italian footballer 2·25 20
666 50 c. German footballer 3·00 30
667 $1 Brazilian footballer 4·00 40
668 $1.50 Argentinian footballer 4·50 70
669 $2 English footballer 5·00 80
See also Nos. 721/6.

124 British 19th-century Warship

1981. Sailing Ships. Multicoloured.
671 10 c. Type **124** 2·00 35
672 25 c. "Madagascar" (1837) 3·00 45
673 35 c. Brig "Whitby" (1838) 3·50 50
674 55 c. "China" (1838) 4·00 75
675 85 c. "Swiftsure" (1850) 4·75 1·10
676 $2 "Windsor Castle" (1857) 7·50 2·00

1982. "ESSEN '82" Int Stamp Exn, West Germany. Nos. 662 and 669 surch **$1 ESSEN 82**.
678 $1 on $2 Keel-billed toucan 3·75 1·00
679 $1 on $2 English footballer 3·75 1·00

126 Princess Diana

1982. 21st Birthday of Princess of Wales. (a) Size 22 × 38 mm.
680 **126** 50 c. multicoloured 70 45
681 – $1 multicoloured 80 75
682 – $1.50 multicoloured 1·00 1·25

(b) Size 25 × 43 mm.
683 **126** 50 c. multicoloured 70 30
684 – $1 multicoloured 80 50
685 – $1.50 multicoloured 1·00 75
DESIGNS: Portraits of Princess of Wales with different backgrounds.

127 Lighting Campfire

1982. 125th Birth Anniv of Lord Baden-Powell. Multicoloured.
687 10 c. Type **127** 1·00 20
668 25 c. Bird watching 1·75 25
689 35 c. Three scouts, one playing guitar 1·75 30
690 50 c. Hiking 2·00 55
691 85 c. Scouts with flag 2·50 90
692 $2 Saluting 3·50 2·25

128 "Gorgonia ventalina"

1982. 1st Anniv of Independence. Marine Life. Mult.
694 10 c. Type **128** 1·40 20
695 35 c. "Carpiuis corallinus" 2·50 20
696 50 c. "Plexaura flexuasa" 3·00 35
697 85 c. "Candylactis gigantea" 3·25 50
698 $1 "Stenopus hispidus" 3·75 70
699 $2 Sergeant major 4·50 1·25

1982. "BELGICA 82" International Stamp Exhibition, Brussels. Nos. 687/92 optd **BELGICA 82 INT. YEAR OF THE CHILD SIR ROWLAND HILL 1795 1879 Picasso CENTENARY OF BIRTH** and emblems.
701 10 c. Type **127** 1·50 30
702 25 c. Bird watching 2·50 75
703 35 c. Three scouts, one playing guitar 2·50 1·00
704 50 c. Hiking 3·00 1·50
705 85 c. Scouts with flag 4·50 2·50
706 $2 Saluting 9·00 6·50

1982. Birth of Prince William of Wales (1st issue). Nos. 680/5 optd **BIRTH OF H.R.H. PRINCE WILLIAM ARTHUR PHILIP LOUIS 21ST JUNE 1982**.

(a) Size 22 × 38 mm.
707 50 c. multicoloured 35 35
708 $1 multicoloured 45 50
709 $1.50 multicoloured 65 75

(b) Size 25 × 43 mm.
710 50 c. multicoloured 35 35
711 $1 multicoloured 45 50
712 $1.50 multicoloured 65 75

1982. Birth of Prince William of Wales (2nd issue). Nos. 614/19 optd **BIRTH OF H.R.H. PRINCE WILLIAM ARTHUR PHILIP LOUIS 21ST JUNE 1982.**

(a) Size 22 × 38 mm.
714 50 c. Type **116** 2·50 1·00
715 $1 Prince Charles in military uniform 5·00 2·00
716 $1.50 Royal couple 7·50 3·00

(b) Size 25 × 42 mm.
717 50 c. Type **116** 35 35
718 $1 As No. 715 70 70
719 $1.50 As No. 716 1·10 1·10

131 Scotland v New Zealand

1982. World Cup Football Championship, Spain (2nd issue). Multicoloured.
721 20 c. + 10 c. Type **131** 1·25 65
722 30 c. + 15 c. Scotland v New Zealand (different) 1·25 65
723 40 c. + 20 c. Kuwait v France 1·50 65
724 60 c. + 50 c. Italy v Brazil 2·00 85
725 $1 + 50 c. France v Northern Ireland 2·50 1·10
726 $1.50 + 75 c. Austria v Chile 3·00 1·40

133 Belize Cathedral

1983. Visit of Pope John Paul II.
729 **133** 50 c. multicoloured 2·25 90

134 Map of Belize

1983. Commonwealth Day. Multicoloured.
731 35 c. Type **134** 35 35
732 50 c. "Maya Stella" from Lamanai Indian church (horiz) 50 50
733 85 c. Supreme Court Building (horiz) 60 75
734 $2 University Centre, Belize (horiz) 1·25 2·00

1983. No. 658 surch **10c**.
735 10 c. on 35 c. Map of Belize

136 De Lana-Terzi's "Aerial Ship", 1670

1983. Bicentenary of Manned Flight. Multicoloured.
736 10 c. Type **136** 1·40 30
737 25 c. De Gusmao's "La Passarole", 1709 2·00 40
738 50 c. Guyton de Morveau's balloon with oars, 1784 2·25 70
739 85 c. Airship 2·75 1·10
740 $1 Airship "Clement Bayard" 3·00 1·50
741 $1.50 Beardmore airship R-34 3·25 2·25

1983. Nos. 662 and 699 surch **$1.25**.
743 $1.25 on $2 Keel-billed toucan 6·00 6·00
744 $1.25 on $2 Sergeant major 6·00 7·00

1983. No. 541 surch **10c**.
746 10 c. on 35 c. Glory of the Atlantic cone 27·00

141 Altun Ha

1983. Maya Monuments. Multicoloured.

747	10 c. Type **141**	10	10
748	15 c. Xunantunich	10	10
749	75 c. Cerros	30	40
750	$3 Lamanal	70	1·25

142 Belmopan Earth Station

1983. World Communications Year. Multicoloured.

752	10 c. Type **142**	30	10
753	15 c. "Telstar 2"	40	25
754	75 c. U.P.U. logo	1·25	1·75
755	$2 M.V. "Heron H" mail service	2·75	4·50

143 Jaguar Cub

1983. The Jaguar. Multicoloured.

756	5 c. Type **143**	30	30
757	10 c. Adult jaguar	35	20
758	85 c. Jaguar in river	1·75	2·25
759	$1 Jaguar on rock	2·00	2·75

144 Pope John Paul II

1983. Christmas.

761	**144** 10 c. multicoloured	25	10
762	15 c. multicoloured	25	10
763	75 c. multicoloured	60	60
764	$2 multicoloured	1·25	1·40

145 Four-eyed Butterflyfish

1984. Marine Life from the Belize Coral Reef. Multicoloured.

766	1 c. Type **145**	15	20
767	2 c. Cushion star	20	30
768	3 c. Flower coral	25	30
769	4 c. Royal gramma ("Fairy basslet")	25	30
770	5 c. Spanish hogfish	30	30
771	6 c. Star-eyed hermit crab	30	30
772a	10 c. Sea fans and fire sponge	35	35
773a	15 c. Blue-headed wrasse	50	60
774a	25 c. Blue-striped grunt	70	80
775a	50 c. Coral crab	1·25	1·75
776a	60 c. Tube sponge	1·25	1·75
777	75 c. Brain coral	1·00	1·00
778	$1 Yellow-tailed snapper	1·25	1·25
779	$2 Common lettuce slug	1·75	1·25
780	$5 Three-spotted damselfish	2·00	1·75
781	$10 Rock beauty	3·00	5·00

1984. Visit of the Archbishop of Canterbury. Nos. 772 and 775 optd **VISIT OF THE LORD ARCHBISHOP OF CANTERBURY 8th-11th MARCH 1984.**

782	10 c. Sea fans and fire sponge	75	40
783	50 c. Coral crab	1·50	1·00

147 Shooting

1984. Olympic Games, Los Angeles. Multicoloured. (a) As T **147**.

784	25 c. Type **147**	30	25
785	75 c. Boxing	70	70
786	$1 Marathon	90	90
787	$2 Cycling	1·75	2·00

(b) Similar designs to T **147** but Royal cypher replaced by Queen's Head.

789	5 c. Marathon	15	30
790	20 c. Sprinting	25	50
791	25 c. Shot-putting	25	50
792	$2 Olympic torch	35	80

148 British Honduras 1866 1s. Stamp

1984. "Ausipex" International Stamp Exhibition, Melbourne. Multicoloured.

793	15 c. Type **148**	15	15
794	30 c. British mail coach, 1784	25	25
795	65 c. Sir Rowland Hill and Penny Black	55	65
796	75 c. British Honduras railway locomotive, 1910	65	75
797	$2 Royal Exhibition Buildings, Melbourne (46 × 28 mm)	1·50	2·00

149 Prince Albert **150** White-fronted Amazon

1984. 500th Anniv (1985) of British Royal House of Tudor. Multicoloured.

799	50 c. Type **149**	25	35
800	50 c. Queen Victoria	25	35
801	75 c. King George VI	35	45
802	75 c. Queen Elizabeth the Queen Mother	35	45
803	$1 Princess of Wales	50	70
804	$1 Prince of Wales	50	70

1984. Parrots. Multicoloured.

806	$1 Type **150**	1·50	1·50
807	$1 White-capped parrot (horiz)	1·50	1·50
808	$1 Mealy amazon (horiz)	1·50	1·50
809	$1 Red-lored amazon	1·50	1·50

Nos. 806/9 were issued together, se-tenant, forming a composite design.

151 Effigy Censer, 1450 (Santa Rita Site) **153** White-tailed Kite

152 Governor-General inspecting Girl Guides

1984. Maya Artefacts. Multicoloured.

811	25 c. Type **151**	25	25
812	75 c. Vase, 675 (Actun Chapat)	50	70
813	$1 Tripod vase, 500 (Santa Rita site)	65	90
814	$2 Sun god Kinich Ahau, 600 (Altun Ha site)	1·40	2·25

1985. Internationl Youth Year and 75th Anniv of Girl Guides Movement. Multicoloured.

815	25 c. Type **152**	30	30
816	50 c. Girl Guides camping	45	45
817	90 c. Checking map on hike	60	65
818	$1.25 Students in laboratory	70	80
819	$2 Lady Baden-Powell (founder)	90	1·10

1985. Birth Bicentenary of John J. Audubon (ornithologist). Designs showing original paintings. Multicoloured.

820	10 c. Type **153**	70	40
821	15 c. Cuvier's kinglet (horiz)	90	40
822	25 c. Painted bunting	1·25	40
822a	60 c. As 25 c.	8·50	5·50
823	75 c. Belted kingfisher	1·75	1·40
824	$1 Northern cardinal	1·75	2·25
825	$3 Long-billed curlew (horiz)	3·00	4·00

154 The Queen Mother with Princess Elizabeth, 1928

1985. Life and Times of Queen Elizabeth the Queen Mother. Multicoloured.

827	10 c. Type **154**	10	10
828	15 c. The Queen Mother, 1980	10	10
829	75 c. Waving to the crowd, 1982	40	40
830	$5 Four generations of Royal Family at Prince William's Christening	1·50	2·75

1985. Inauguration of New Government. Nos. 772/3 and 775 optd **INAUGURATION OF NEW GOVERNMENT – 21st. DECEMBER 1984.**

832	10 c. Sea fans and fire sponge	65	30
833	15 c. Blue-headed wrasse	85	45
834	50 c. Coral crab	1·50	2·25

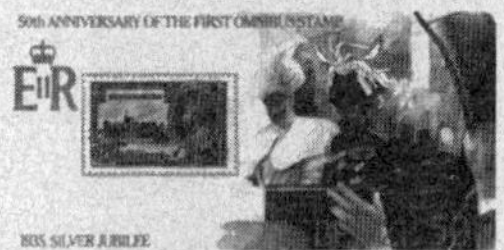

156 British Honduras 1935 Silver Jubilee 25 c. stamp and King George V with Queen Mary in Carriage (½-size illustration)

1985. 50th Anniv of First Commonwealth Omnibus Issue. Designs showing British Honduras/Belize stamps. Multicoloured.

835	50 c. Type **156**	40	50
836	50 c. 1937 Coronation 3 c., and King George VI and Queen Elizabeth in Coronation robes	40	50
837	50 c. 1946 Victory 3 c. and Victory celebrations	40	50
838	50 c. 1948 Royal Silver Wedding 4 c. and King George VI and Queen Elizabeth at Westminster Abbey service	40	50
839	50 c. 1953 Coronation 4 c. and Queen Elizabeth II in Coronation robes	40	50
840	50 c. 1966 Churchill 25 c., Sir Winston Churchill and fighter aircraft	40	50
841	50 c. 1972 Royal Silver Wedding 50 c. and 1948 Wedding photograph	40	50
842	50 c. 1973 Royal Wedding 50 c. and Princess Anne and Capt. Mark Phillips at their Wedding	40	50
843	50 c. 1977 Silver Jubilee $2 and Queen Elizabeth II during tour	40	50
844	50 c. 1978 25th anniversary of Coronation 75 c. and Imperial Crown	40	50

157 Mounted Postboy and Early Letter to Belize

1985. 350th Anniv of British Post Office. Mult.

846	10 c. Type **157**	40	15
847	15 c. "Hinchinbrook II" (sailing packet) engaging "Grand Turk" (American privateer)	55	25
848	25 c. "Duke of Marlborough II" (sailing packet)	70	30
849	75 c. "Diana" (packet)	1·25	1·50
850	$1 Falmouth packet ship	1·50	1·75
851	$3 "Conway" (mail paddle-steamer)	3·75	4·50

1985. Commonwealth Heads of Government Meeting, Nassau, Bahamas. Nos. 827/30 optd **COMMONWEALTH SUMMIT CONFERENCE, BAHAMAS 16th-22nd OCTOBER 1985.**

852	10 c. Type **154**	30	30
853	15 c. The Queen Mother, 1980	40	35
854	75 c. Waving to the crowd, 1982	80	80
855	$4 Four generations of Royal Family at Prince William's christening	2·75	3·75

1985. 80th Anniv of Rotary International. Nos. 815/19 optd **80TH ANNIVERSARY OF ROTARY INTERNATIONAL.**

857	25 c. Type **152**	50	30
858	50 c. Girl Guides camping	80	75
859	90 c. Checking map on hike	1·25	1·60
860	$1.25 Students in laboratory	1·75	2·25
861	$2 Lady Baden-Powell (founder)	2·25	2·75

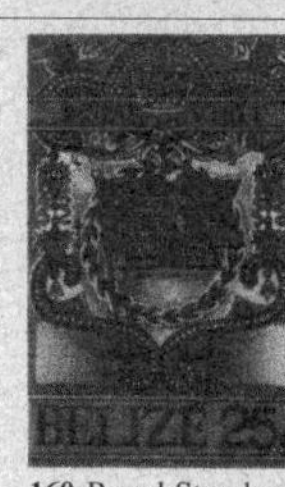

160 Royal Standard and Belize Flag

1985. Royal Visit. Multicoloured.

862	25 c. Type **160**	55	95
863	75 c. Queen Elizabeth II	1·25	2·00
864	$4 Royal Yacht "Britannia" (81 × 39 mm)	3·00	3·25

161 Mountie in Canoe (Canada)

1985. Christmas. 30th Anniv of Disneyland, U.S.A. Designs showing dolls from "It's a Small World" exhibition. Multicoloured.

866	1 c. Type **161**	10	10
867	2 c. Indian chief and squaw (U.S.A.)	10	10
868	3 c. Incas climbing Andes (South America)	10	10
869	4 c. Africans beating drums (Africa)	10	10
870	5 c. Snake-charmer and dancer (India and Far East)	10	10
871	6 c. Boy and girl with donkey (Belize)	10	10
872	50 c. Musician and dancer (Balkans)	1·00	1·25
873	$1.50, Boys with camel (Egypt and Saudi Arabia)	2·25	2·75
874	$3 Woman and girls playing with kite (Japan)	3·25	4·25

1985. World Cup Football Championship, Mexico (1986) (1st issue). Nos. 835/44 optd **PRE "WORLD CUP FOOTBALL" MEXICO 1986** and trophy.

876	50 c. Type **156**	65	65
877	50 c. 1937 Coronation 3 c., and King George VI and Queen Elizabeth in Coronation robes	65	65
878	50 c. Victory 3 c., and Victory celebrations	65	65
879	50 c. 1948 Royal Silver Wedding 4 c., and King George VI and Queen Elizabeth at Westminster Abbey service	65	65
880	50 c. 1953 Coronation 4 c., and Queen Elizabeth II in Coronation robes	65	65
881	50 c. 1966 Churchill 25 c., Sir Winston Churchill and fighter aircraft	65	65
882	50 c. 1972 Royal Silver Wedding 50 c. and 1948 wedding photograph	65	65
883	50 c. 1973 Royal Wedding 5 c., and Princess Anne and Capt. Mark Phillips at their Wedding	65	65
884	50 c. 1977 Silver Jubilee $2 and Queen Elizabeth II during tour	65	65
885	50 c. 1978 25th anniv of Coronation 75 c. and Imperial Crown	65	65

See also Nos. 936/9.

163 Indian Costume **165** Princess Elizabeth aged Three

164 Pope Pius X

1986. Costumes of Belize. Multicoloured.

887	5 c. Type **163**	75	30
888	10 c. Maya	80	30
889	15 c. Garifuna	1·00	35
890	25 c. Creole	1·25	35
891	50 c. Chinese	1·75	1·25
892	75 c. Lebanese	2·00	2·00
893	$1 European c 1900	2·00	2·50
894	$2 Latin	2·75	3·75

1986. Easter. 20th-century Popes. Multicoloured.

896	50 c. Type **164**	1·00	1·10
897	50 c. Benedict XV	1·00	1·10
898	50 c. Pius XI	1·00	1·10
899	50 c. Pius XII	1·00	1·10
900	50 c. John XXIII	1·00	1·10
901	50 c. Paul VI	1·00	1·10
902	50 c. John Paul I	1·00	1·10
903	50 c. John Paul II	1·00	1·10

1986. 60th Birthday of Queen Elizabeth II. Mult.

905	25 c. Type **165**	15	20
906	50 c. Queen wearing Imperial State Crown	35	40
907	75 c. At Trooping the Colour	50	55
908	$3 Queen wearing diadem	1·25	2·25

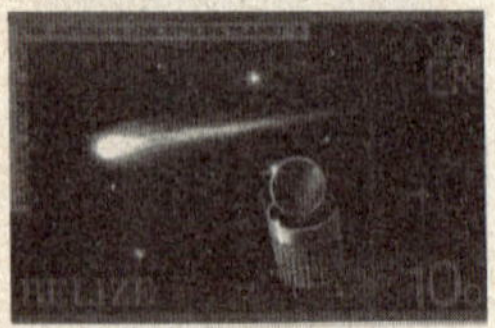

166 Halley's Comet and Japanese "Planet A" Spacecraft

1986. Appearance of Halley's Comet. Multicoloured.

910	10 c. Type **166**	20	35
911	15 c. Halley's Comet, 1910	30	50
912	50 c. Comet and European "Giotto" spacecraft	40	60
913	75 c. Belize Weather Bureau	70	80
914	$1 Comet and U.S.A. space telescope	95	1·10
915	$2 Edmond Halley	1·50	1·60

167 George Washington

1986. United States Presidents. Multicoloured.

917	10 c. Type **167**	35	45
918	20 c. John Adams	35	55
916	30 c. Thomas Jefferson	40	60
920	50 c. James Madison	50	60
921	$1.50 James Monroe	80	1·25
922	$2 John Quincy Adams	1·00	1·50

168 Auguste Bartholdi (sculptor) and Statue's Head

1986. Centenary of Statue of Liberty. Multicoloured.

924	25 c. Type **168**	50	65
925	50 c. Statue's head at U.S. Centennial Celebration, Philadelphia, 1876	60	85
926	75 c. Unveiling ceremony, 1886	65	90
927	£4 Statue of Liberty and flags of Belize and U.S.A.	1·40	2·00

169 British Honduras 1866 1s. Stamp

1986. "Ameripex" International Stamp Exhibition, Chicago. Multicoloured.

929	10 c. Type **169**	40	55
930	15 c. 1981 Royal Wedding $1.50 stamps	55	75
931	50 c. U.S.A. 1918 24 c. airmail inverted centre error	75	80
932	75 c. U.S.S. "Constitution" (frigate)	90	1·10
933	$1 Liberty Bell	1·00	1·40
934	$2 White House	1·40	1·60

170 English and Brazilian Players

1986. World Cup Football Championship, Mexico (2nd issue). Multicoloured.

936	25 c. Type **170**	1·00	1·25
937	50 c. Mexican player and Maya statues	1·40	1·60
938	75 c. Two Belizean players	1·75	2·00
939	$3 Aztec stone calendar	3·00	3·50

171 Miss Sarah Ferguson

1986. Royal Wedding. Multicoloured.

941	25 c. Type **171**	40	40
942	75 c. Prince Andrew	70	90
943	$3 Prince Andrew and Miss Sarah Ferguson (92 × 41 mm)	1·40	2·25

1986. World Cup Football Championship Winners, Mexico. Nos. 936/9 optd **ARGENTINA–WINNERS 1986**.

945	25 c. Type **170**	1·00	1·00
946	50 c. Mexican player and Maya statues	1·40	1·40
947	75 c. Two Belizean players	1·75	1·75
948	$3 Aztec stone calendar	3·00	3·00

1986. "Stockholmia '86" International Stamp Exhibition, Sweden. Nos. 929/34 optd **STOCKHOLMIA 86** and emblem.

950	10 c. Type **169**	40	50
951	15 c. 1981 Royal Wedding $1.50 stamp	50	60
952	50 c. U.S.A. 1918 24 c. airmail inverted centre error	70	80
953	75 c. U.S.S. "Constitution"	90	1·10
954	$1 Liberty Bell	1·10	1·25
955	$2 White House	1·60	1·60

174 Amerindian Girl

1986. International Peace Year. Multicoloured.

957	25 c. Type **174**	45	60
958	50 c. European boy and girl	70	85
959	75 c. Japanese girl	1·00	1·25
960	$3 Indian boy and European girl	1·75	2·25

175 "Amanita lilloi" 176 Jose Carioca

1986. Fungi and Toucans. Multicoloured.

962	5 c. Type **175**	75	75
963	10 c. Keel-billed toucan	90	90
964	20 c. "Boletellus cubensis"	1·25	1·25
965	25 c. Collared aracari	1·25	1·25
966	75 c. "Psilocybe caerulescens"	1·50	1·50
967	$1 Emerald toucanet	1·50	1·50
968	$1.25 Crimson-rumped toucanet	1·50	1·50
969	$2 "Russula puiggarii"	2·00	2·00

1986. Christmas. Designs showing Walt Disney cartoon characters in scenes from "Saludos Amigos". Multicoloured.

970	2 c. Type **176**	20	10
971	3 c. Jose Carioca, Panchito and Donald Duck	20	10
972	4 c. Daisy Duck as Rio Carnival dancer	20	10
973	5 c. Mickey and Minnie Mouse as musician and dancer	20	10
974	6 c. Jose Carioca using umbrella as flute	20	10
975	50 c. Donald Duck and Panchito	1·00	1·25
976	65 c. Joe Carioca and Donald Duck playing hide and seek	1·25	1·50
977	$1.35 Donald Duck playing maracas	2·00	3·00
978	$2 Goofy as matador	2·75	3·50

177 Princess Elizabeth in Wedding Dress, 1947 179 "Mother and Child"

178 "America II", 1983

1987. Royal Ruby Wedding. Multicoloured.

980	25 c. Type **177**	20	20
981	75 c. Queen and Duke of Edinburgh, 1972	35	40
982	$1 Queen on her 60th birthday	40	50
983	$4 In Garter robes	1·00	1·50

1987. America's Cup Yachting Championship. Multicoloured.

985	25 c. Type **178**	20	25
986	75 c. "Stars and Stripes", 1987	35	50
987	$1 "Australia II", 1983	40	60
988	$4 "White Crusader"	1·00	1·60

1987. Wood Carvings by George Gabb. Mult.

990	25 c. Type **179**	15	25
991	75 c. "Standing Form"	35	50
992	$1 "Love-doves"	40	60
993	$4 "Depiction of Music"	1·10	1·60

180 Black-handed Spider Monkey

1987. Primates. Multicoloured.

995	25 c. Type **180**	25	20
996	75 c. Black howler monkey	40	55
997	$1 Spider monkeys with baby	45	65
998	$4 Two black howler monkeys	1·10	2·00

181 Guides on Parade

1987. 50th Anniv of Girl Guide Movement in Belize. Multicoloured.

1000	25 c. Type **181**	45	20
1001	75 c. Brownie camp	80	90
1002	$1 Guide camp	1·00	1·25
1003	$4 Olave, Lady Baden-Powell	3·00	4·25

182 Indian Refugee Camp

1987. Int Year of Shelter for the Homeless. Mult.

1005	25 c. Type **182**	50	25
1006	75 c. Filipino family and slum	90	90
1007	$1 Family in Middle East shanty town	1·00	1·25
1008	$4 Building modern house in Belize	3·00	4·25

183 "Laelia euspatha"

1987. Christmas. Orchids. Illustrations from Sander's "Reichenbachia". Multicoloured.

1009	1 c. Type **183**	60	50
1010	2 c. "Cattleya citrina"	60	50
1011	3 c. "Masdevallia backhousiana"	60	50
1012	4 c. "Cypripedium tautzianum"	60	50
1013	5 c. "Trichopilia suavis alba"	60	50
1014	6 c. "Odontoglossum hebraicum"	60	50
1015	7 c. "Cattleya trianaei schroederiana"	60	50
1016	10 c. "Saccolabium giganteum"	75	65
1017	30 c. "Cattleya warscewiczii"	90	80
1018	50 c. "Chysis bractescens"	1·25	1·00
1019	70 c. "Cattleya rochellensis"	1·40	1·10
1020	$1 "Laelia elegans schilleriana"	1·50	1·10
1021	$1.50 "Laelia anceps percivaliana"	1·60	1·40
1022	$3 "Laelia gouldiana"	2·25	1·90

184 Christ condemned to Death

1988. Easter. The Stations of the Cross. Mult.

1024	40 c. Type **184**	35	45
1025	40 c. Christ carrying the Cross	35	45
1026	40 c. Falling for the first time	35	45
1027	40 c. Christ meets Mary	35	45
1028	40 c. Simon of Cyrene helping to carry the Cross	35	45
1029	40 c. Veronica wiping the face of Christ	35	45
1030	40 c. Christ falling a second time	35	45
1031	40 c. Consoling the women of Jerusalem	35	45
1032	40 c. Falling for the third time	35	45
1033	40 c. Christ being stripped	35	45
1034	40 c. Christ nailed to the Cross	35	45
1035	40 c. Dying on the Cross	35	45
1036	40 c. Christ taken down from the Cross	35	45
1037	40 c. Christ being laid in the sepulchre	35	45

185 Basketball

1988. Olympic Games, Seoul. Multicoloured.

1038	10 c. Type **185**	70	30
1039	25 c. Volleyball	75	30
1040	60 c. Table tennis	80	60
1041	75 c. Diving	80	70
1042	$1 Judo	90	85
1043	$2 Hockey	3·00	3·25

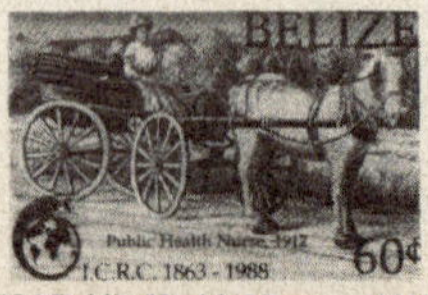

186 Public Health Nurse, c. 1912

1988. 125th Anniv of Int Red Cross. Mult.

1045 60 c. Type **186** 1·50 1·25
1046 75 c. Hospital ship and ambulance launch, 1937 1·75 1·50
1047 $1 Ambulance at hospital tent, 1956 2·25 1·75
1048 $2 Auster ambulance plane, 1940 3·00 4·00

187 Collared Anteater ("Ants Bear")

1989. Small Animals of Belize. Multicoloured.

1049 10 c. Paca ("Gibnut") 1·50 1·50
1050 25 c. Four-eyed opossum (vert) 1·50 1·50
1051 50 c. Type **187** 2·00 2·00
1052 60 c. As 10 c. 2·00 2·00
1053 75 c. Red brocket 2·00 2·00
1054 $1 Collared peccary 3·50 4·50

1989. 20th Anniv of First Manned Landing on Moon. As T **126** of Ascension. Multicoloured.

1055 25 c. Docking of "Apollo 9" modules 45 25
1056 50 c. "Apollo 9" command service module in Space (30×30 mm) 65 65
1057 75 c. "Apollo 9" emblem (30 x 30 mm) 90 1·00
1058 $1 "Apollo 9" lunar module in space 1·25 1·40

1989. No. 771 surch **5c**.

1060 5 c. on 6 c. Star-eyed hermit crab 12·00 1·50

190 Wesley Church

191 White-winged Tanager and "Catonephele numilia"

1989. Christmas. Belize Churches.

1062 **190** 10 c. black, pink and brown 20 10
1063 – 25 c. black, lilac and mauve 25 20
1064 – 60 c. black, turq & bl 50 60
1065 – 75 c. black, grn & lt grn 65 80
1066 – $1 black, lt yell and yell 80 1·10

DESIGNS: 25 c. Baptist Church; 60 c. St. John's Anglican Cathedral; 75 c. St. Andrew's Presbyterian Church; $1 Holy Redeemer Roman Catholic Cathedral.

1990. Birds and Butterflies. Multicoloured.

1067A 5 c. Type **191** 40 40
1068B 10 c. Reel-billed toucan and "Nessaea aglaura" 50 50
1069A 15 c. Magnificent frigate bird and "Eurytides philolaus" 60 30
1070A 25 c. Jabiru and "Heliconius sapho" 60 40
1071A 30 c. Great blue heron and "Colobura dirce" 60 40
1072A 50 c. Northern oriole and "Hamadyras arethusia" 70 60
1073A 60 c. Scarlet macaw and "Evenus regalis" 80 70
1074A 75 c. Red-legged honey-creeper and "Callicore patelina" 90 75
1075A $1 Spectacled owl and "Caligo uranus" 1·75 1·25
1076A $1 Green jay and "Philaethria dido" 2·25 3·00
1077A $5 Turkey vulture and "Battus belus" 4·00 5·00
1078A $10 Osprey and "Papilio thoas" 8·00 9·00

1990. First Belize Dollar Coin. No. 1075 optd **FIRST DOLLAR COIN 1990**.

1079 $1 Spectacled owl and "Caligo uranus" 3·50 2·50

193 Green Turtle

1990. Turtles. Multicoloured.

1080 10 c. Type **193** 55 30
1081 25 c. Hawksbill turtle 85 30
1082 60 c. Saltwater loggerhead turtle 1·25 1·25
1083 75 c. Freshwater loggerhead turtle 1·40 1·40
1084 $1 Bocatora turtle 1·75 1·75
1085 $2 Hicatee turtle 2·50 4·00

194 Fairey Battle

1990. 50th Anniv of the Battle of Britain. Multicoloured.

1086 10 c. Type **194** 60 40
1087 25 c. Bristol Type 152 Beaufort 1·10 40
1088 60 c. Bristol Type 142 Blenheim Mk IV 1·75 1·75
1089 75 c. Armstrong-Whitworth Whitley 1·75 1·75
1090 $1 Vickers-Armstrong Wellington Mk 1c 1·75 1·75
1091 $1 Handley Page Hampden 2·25 3·25

195 "Cattleya bowringiana"

1990. Christmas. Orchids. Multicoloured.

1092 25 c. Type **195** 70 20
1093 50 c. "Rhyncholaelia digbyana" 1·00 50
1094 60 c. "Sobralia macrantha" 1·25 1·00
1095 75 c. "Chysis bractescens" 1·25 1·00
1096 $1 "Vanilla planifolia" 1·50 1·50
1097 $2 "Epidendrum polyanthum" 2·25 3·00

196 Common Iguana

1991. Reptiles and Mammals. Multicoloured

1098 25 c. Type **196** 80 35
1099 50 c. Morelet's crocodile 1·25 90
1100 60 c. American manatee 1·50 1·50
1101 75 c. Boa constrictor 1·75 1·75
1102 $1 Baird's tapir 2·00 2·00
1103 $2 Jaguar 2·75 3·75

1991. 65th Birthday of Queen Elizabeth II and 70th Birthday of Prince Philip. As T **139** of Ascension. Multicoloured.

1104 $1 Queen Elizabeth II wearing tiara 1·00 1·25
1105 $1 Prince Philip wearing panama 1·00 1·25

197 Weather Radar

1991. International Decade for Natural Disaster Reduction.

1106 **197** 60 c. multicoloured 1·25 1·25
1107 – 75 c. multicoloured 1·40 1·40
1108 – $1 blue and black 1·50 1·50
1109 – $2 multicoloured 2·25 2·75

DESIGNS: 75 c. Weather station; $1 Floods in Belize after Hurricane Hattie, 1961; $2 Satellite image of Hurricane Gilbert.

198 Thomas Ramos and Demonstration

1991. 10th Anniv of Independence. Famous Belizians (1st series). Multicoloured.

1110 25 c. Type **198** 60 30
1111 60 c. Sir Isaiah Morter and palm trees 1·25 1·25
1112 75 c. Antonio Soberanis and political meeting 1·25 1·50
1113 $1 Santiago Ricalde and cutting suger-cane 1·50 1·75

See also Nos. 1126/9 and 1148/51.

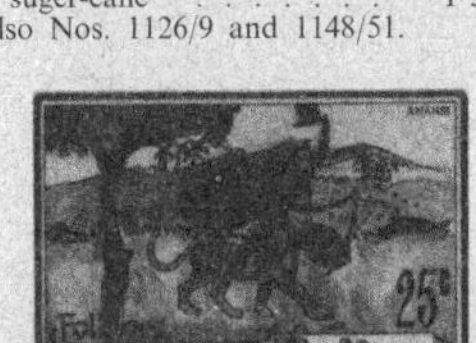

199 "Anansi the Spider"

1991. Christmas. Folklore. Multicoloured.

1114 25 c. Type **199** 70 20
1115 60 c. "Jack-o-Lantern" 1·00 55
1116 60 c. "Tata Duende" (vert) 1·25 1·25
1117 75 c. "Xtabai" 1·25 1·25
1118 $1 "Warrie Massa" (vert) 1·50 1·50
1119 $2 "Old Heg" 2·50 3·50

200 "Gongora quinquenervis"

1992. Easter. Orchids. Multicoloured.

1120 25 c. Type **200** 90 20
1121 50 c. "Oncidium sphacelatum" 1·50 75
1122 60 c. "Encyclia bratescens" 1·75 1·75
1123 75 c. "Epidendrum ciliare" 1·75 1·75
1124 $1 "Psygmorchis pusilla" 2·00 2·00
1125 $2 "Galeandra batemanii" 2·75 4·00

1992. Famous Belizeans (2nd series). As T **198**, but inscr "EMINENT BELIZEANS" at top. Multicoloured.

1126 25 c. Gwendolyn Lizarraga (politician) and High School 55 30
1127 60 c. Rafael Fonseca (civil servant) and Government Offices, Belize 90 1·00
1128 75 c. Vivian Seay (health worker) and nurses 1·10 1·25
1129 $1 Samuel Haynes (U.N.I.A. worker) and words of National Anthem 1·40 1·75

201 Xunantunich and National Assembly

1992. 500th Anniv of Discovery of America by Columbus. Mayan sites and modern buildings. Multicoloured.

1130 25 c. Type **201** 70 25
1131 60 c. Altun Ha and Supreme Court 1·00 1·00
1132 75 c. Santa Rita and Tower Hill Sugar Factory 1·25 1·25
1133 $5 Lamanai and Citrus Company works 6·00 7·50

202 Hashishi Pampi

1992. Christmas. Folklore. Multicoloured.

1134 25 c. Type **202** 30 20
1135 60 c. Cadejo 60 60
1136 $1 La Sucia (vert) 90 1·00
1137 $5 Sisimito 4·00 6·00

1993. 75th Anniv of Royal Air Force. As T **149** of Ascension. Multicoloured.

1138 25 c. Sud Aviation SA 330L Puma helicopter 70 40
1139 50 c. Hawker Siddeley Harrier GR3 90 65
1140 60 c. De Havilland DH98 Mosquito Mk XVIII 1·10 1·10
1141 75 c. Avro Type 683 Lancaster 1·10 1·10
1142 $1 Consolidated Liberator I 1·25 1·25
1143 $3 Short Stirling Mk I 3·00 4·50

203 "Lycaste aromatica"

1993. 14th World Orchid Conference, Glasgow. Mult.

1144 25 c. Type **203** 40 25
1145 60 c. "Sobralia decora" 75 80
1146 $1 "Maxillaria alba" 1·00 1·10
1147 $2 "Brassavola nodosa" 1·75 2·50

1993. Famous Belizeans (3rd series). As T **198**, but inscr "EMINENT BELIZEANS" at top. Multicoloured.

1148 25 c. Herbert Watkin Beaumont, Post Office and postmark 40 25
1149 60 c. Dr. Selvyn Walford Young and score of National Anthem 75 85
1150 75 c. Cleopatra White and health centre 90 1·25
1151 $1 Dr. Karl Heusner and early car 1·10 1·40

204 Boom and Chime Band

1993. Christmas. Local Customs. Mult.

1152 25 c. Type **204** 30 20
1153 60 c. John Canoe dance 70 70
1154 75 c. Cortez dance 80 80
1155 $2 Maya musical group 2·00 3·25

1994. "Hong Kong '94" International Stamp Exhibition. No. 1075 optd **HONG KONG '94** and emblem.

1156 $1 Spectacled owl and "Caligo uranus" 1·40 1·75

1994. Royal Visit. As T **202** of Bahamas. Mult.

1157 25 c. Flags of Belize and Great Britain 35 20
1158 60 c. Queen Elizabeth II in yellow coat and hat 65 65
1159 75 c. Queen Elizabeth in evening dress 85 85
1160 $1 Queen Elizabeth, Prince Philip and Yeomen of the Guard 1·25 1·40

205 "Lonchorhina aurita" (bat)

1994. Bats. Multicoloured.

1161 25 c. Type **205** 35 20
1162 60 c. "Vampyrodes caraccioli" 65 65
1163 75 c. "Noctilio leporinus" 80 80
1164 $2 "Desmodus rotundus" 2·00 3·00

1994. 75th Anniv of I.L.O. No. 1074 surch **10c** and anniversary emblem.

1165 10 c. on 75 c. multicoloured 50 50

207 "Cycnoches chlorochilon"

1994. Christmas. Orchids. Multicoloured.

1166 25 c. Type **207** 35 20
1167 60 c. "Brassavola cucullata" 65 70
1168 75 c. "Sobralia mucronata" 80 90
1169 $1 "Nidema boothii" 1·10 1·25

208 Ground Beetle (209)

1995. Insects. Multicoloured.

1170B 5 c. Type **208** 10 10
1171B 10 c. Harlequin beetle 10 10
1172B 15 c. Giant water bug 10 10
1173B 25 c. Peanut-head bug 15 20
1174B 30 c. Coconut weevil 15 20
1175B 50 c. Mantis 30 35
1176B 60 c. Tarantula wasp 35 40
1177B 75 c. Rhinoceros beetle 45 50
1178B $1 Metallic wood borer 60 65
1179B $2 Dobson fly 1·25 1·40
1180B $5 Click beetle 3·00 3·25
1181B $10 Long-horned beetle 6·00 6·50

1995. 50th Anniv of End of Second World War. As T **161** of Ascension. Multicoloured.

1182 25 c. War memorial 30 25
1183 60 c. Remembrance Day parade 65 70
1184 75 c. British Honduras forestry unit 80 90
1185 $1 Vickers-Armstrong Wellington bomber 95 1·10

1995. "Singapore '95" International Stamp Exhibition. Nos. 1166/9 optd with **T 209**.

1186	25 c. Type **207**	30	20
1187	60 c. "Brassavola cucullata"	65	80
1188	75 c. "Sobralia mucronata"	80	95
1189	$1 "Nidema boothii"	1·00	1·25

1995. 50th Anniv of United Nations. As T **213** of Bahamas. Multicoloured.

1190	25 c. M113-light reconnaisance vehicle	25	20
1191	60 c. Sultan armoured command vehicle	60	65
1192	75 c. Leyland-Daf 8 × 4 drops lorry	75	80
1193	$2 Warrior infantry combat vehicle	1·50	2·25

210 Male and Female Blue Ground Dove

1995. Christmas. Doves. Multicoloured.

1194	25 c. Type **210**	35	20
1195	60 c. White-fronted doves	70	70
1196	75 c. Pair of ruddy ground doves	85	90
1197	$1 White-winged doves	1·25	1·25

1996. "CHINA '96" 9th Asian International Stamp Exhibition, Peking. Nos. 1172, 1174/5 and 1179 optd **'96 CHINA** and emblem.

1198	15 c. Giant water bug	15	15
1199	30 c. Coconut weevil	30	30
1200	50 c. Mantis	45	50
1201	$2 Dobson fly	1·60	2·00

212 Unloading Banana Train, Commerce Bight Pier

1996. "CAPEX '96" International Stamp Exhibition, Toronto. Railways. Multicoloured8

1202	25 c. Type **212**	35	20
1203	60 c. Locomotive No. 1 Stann Creek station	65	55
1204	75 c. Locomotive No. 4 pulling mahogany log train	80	70
1205	$3 L.M.S. No. 5602 "British Honduras" locomotive	2·50	3·50

213 "Epidendrum stamfordianum"

214 Red Poll

1996. Christmas. Orchids. Multicoloured.

1206	25 c. Type **213**	40	20
1207	60 c. "Oncidium carthagenense"	70	70
1208	75 c. "Oerstedella verrucosa"	80	90
1209	$1 "Coryanthes speciosa"	1·10	1·25

1997. "HONG KONG '97" International Stamp Exhibition. Chinese New Year ("Year of the Ox"). Cattle Breeds. Multicoloured.

1210	25 c. Type **214**	30	20
1211	60 c. Brahman	60	70
1212	75 c. Longhorn	70	80
1213	$1 Charbray	95	1·10

215 Coral Snake

216 Adult Male Howler Monkey

1997. Snakes. Multicoloured.

1214	25 c. Type **215**	25	20
1215	60 c. Green vine snake	50	50
1216	75 c. Yellow-jawed tommygoff	60	60
1217	$1 Speckled racer	75	80

1997. Endangered Species. Howler Monkey. Multicoloured.

1218	10 c. Type **216**	15	10
1219	25 c. Female feeding	25	20
1220	60 c. Female with young	55	55
1221	75 c. Juvenile monkey feeding	65	75

217 "Maxillaria elatior"

1997. Christmas. Orchids. Multicoloured.

1222	25 c. Type **217**	25	20
1223	60 c. "Dimmerandra emarginata"	50	50
1224	75 c. "Macradenia brassavolae"	60	60
1225	$1 "Ornithocephalus gladiatus"	75	80

218 School Children using the Internet

1998. 50th Anniv of Organization of American States. Multicoloured.

1227	25 c. Type **218**	25	20
1228	$1 Map of Central America	75	80

219 University Arms

1998. 50th Anniv of University of West Indies.

1229	**219**	$1 multicoloured	75	75

220 Baymen Gun Flats

1998. Bicentenary of Battle of St. George's Cay. Multicoloured.

1230	10 c. Boat moored at quayside (vert)	20	20
1231	10 c. Three sentries and cannon (vert)	20	20
1232	10 c. Cannon and rowing boats (vert)	20	20
1233	25 c. Type **220**	30	20
1234	60 c. Baymen sloops	50	50
1235	75 c. British schooners	55	55
1236	$1 H.M.S. "Merlin" (sloop)	70	70
1237	$2 Spanish flagship	1·25	1·60

221 "Brassia maculata"

222 "Eucharis grandiflora"

1998. Christmas. Orchids. Multicoloured.

1238	25 c. Type **221**	15	20
1239	60 c. "Encyclia radiata"	35	40
1240	75 c. "Stanhopea ecornuta"	45	50
1241	$1 "Isochilus carnosiflorus"	60	65

1999. Easter. Flowers. Multicoloured.

1242	10 c. Type **222**	10	10
1243	25 c. "Hippeastrum puniceum"	15	20
1244	60 c. "Zephyranthes citrina"	35	40
1245	$1 "Hymenocallis littoralis"	60	65

POSTAGE DUE STAMPS

D 2

1976.

D 6	D 2	1 c. red and green	10	80
D 7	–	2 c. purple and violet	10	80
D 8	–	5 c. green and brown	15	1·00
D 9	–	15 c. green and red	25	1·25
D10	–	25 c. orange and green	40	1·40

DESIGNS: Nos. D7/10 as Type D **2** but with different frames.

BERMUDA

A group of islands in the W. Atlantic, E. of N. Carolina. Usually regarded by collectors as part of the Br. W. Indies group, though this is not strictly correct.

1865. 12 pence = 1 shilling;
20 shillings = 1 pound.
1970. 100 cents = 1 dollar (U.S.).

9 Queen Victoria

13 Dry Dock

1865. Portrait. Various frames.

19	**9**	½d. stone	2·50	3·75
21a		½d. green	2·50	80
24a		1d. red	8·50	20
25		2d. blue	50·00	3·50
26a		2d. purple	3·25	1·50
27a		2½d. blue	5·00	40
10		3d. yellow	£170	60·00
28		3d. grey	22·00	6·00
20		4d. red	16·00	1·75
34		4d. brown	27·00	48·00
7		6d. mauve	22·00	12·00
11		1s. green	11·00	£120
29b		1s. brown	13·00	15·00

1874. Surch in words.

15	**9**	1d. on 2d. blue	£700	£350
16		1d. on 3d. yellow	£450	£350
17		1d. on 1s. green	£500	£250
12		3d. on 1d. red	£10000	
14		3d. on 1s. green	£1200	£650

1901. Surch **ONE FARTHING** and bar.

30	**9**	¼d. on 1s. grey	90	50

1902.

34b	**13**	¼d. brown and violet	1·50	1·50
31		½d. black and green	9·50	1·25
41		½d. green	11·00	2·50
32		1d. brown and red	8·00	10
42		1d. red	18·00	10
37		2d. grey and orange	7·50	11·00
38		2½d. brown and blue	14·00	7·00
43		2½d. blue	12·00	5·75
33		3d. mauve and green	2·50	1·75
39		4d. blue and brown	3·00	15·00

14 Badge of the Colony

15

1910.

44a	**14**	¼d. brown	60	1·50
77		½d. green	90	15
78d		1d. red	9·00	80
79b		1½d. brown	8·00	35
80		2d. grey	1·50	1·50
82b		2½d. blue	1·75	50
81a		2½d. green	1·50	1·50
84		3d. purple on yellow	3·50	1·00
83		3d. blue	16·00	26·00
85		4d. red on yellow	1·75	1·00
86		6d. purple	1·00	80
51		1s. black on green	3·75	4·00
51b	**15**	2s. purple and blue on blue	17·00	48·00
52		2s. 6d. black and red on blue	27·00	70·00
52b		4s. black and red	60·00	£130
53c		5s. green and red on yellow	40·00	80·00
92		10s. green and red on green	£120	£250
93		12s. 6d. black and orange	£250	£350
55		£1 purple and black on red	£350	£550

1918 Optd **WAR TAX**.

56	**14**	1d. red	45	60

18

1920. Tercentenary of Representative Institutions. (a) 1st Issue.

59	**18**	¼d. brown	2·75	14·00
60		½d. green	2·75	7·50
65		1d. red	2·75	30
61		2d. grey	9·50	28·00
66		2½d. blue	8·50	9·50
62		3d. purple on yellow	8·50	26·00
63		4d. black and red on yellow	9·50	26·00
67		6d. purple	21·00	60·00
64		1s. black on green	16·00	48·00

19

(b) 2nd Issue.

74	19	½d. brown	80	2·75
75		½d. green	2·75	6·00
76		1d. red	2·50	35
68		2d. grey	4·50	23·00
69		2½d. blue	9·00	3·00
70		3d. purple on yellow	4·00	14·00
71		4d. red on yellow	14·00	18·00
72		6d. purple	9·00	40·00
73		1s. black on green	21·00	48·00

1935. Silver Jubilee. As T **13** of Antigua.

94	1d. blue and red	45	55
95	1½d. blue and grey	70	2·00
96	2½d. brown and blue	1·40	90
97	1s. grey and purple	13·00	22·00

20 Hamilton Harbour — 22 "Lucie" (yacht)

1936.

98	20	½d. green	10	10
99	–	1d. black and red	20	20
100	–	1½d. black and brown	90	30
101	22	2d. black and blue	4·50	2·00
102	–	2½d. blue	80	25
103	–	3d. black and red	2·50	90
104	–	6d. red and violet	80	10
105	–	1s. green	4·00	7·00
106	20	1s. 6d. brown	50	10

DESIGNS—HORIZ: 1d., 1½d. South Shore, near Spanish Rock; 3d. Point House, Warwick Parish. VERT: 2½d., 1s. Grape Bay, Paget Parish; 6d. House at Par-la-Ville, Hamilton.

The 1d., 1½d., 2½d. and 1s. values include a portrait of King George V.

1937. Coronation. As T 2 of Aden.

107	1d. red	50	50
108	1½d. brown	60	1·40
109	2½d. blue	70	1·50

26 Ships in Hamilton Harbour — 28 White-tailed Tropic Bird, Arms of Bermuda and Native Flower

1938.

110	26	1d. black and red	65	20
111b		1½d. blue and brown	2·25	35
112	22	2d. blue and brown	42·00	8·50
112a		2d. blue and red	1·50	80
113	–	2½d. blue and deep blue	11·00	1·25
113b	–	2½d. blue and black	2·75	1·25
114	–	3d. black and red	15·00	1·75
114a	–	3d. black and blue	1·75	40
114c	28	7½d. black, blue and green	4·50	2·25
115	–	1s. green	2·00	50

DESIGNS—VERT: 3d. St. David's Lighthouse. The 2½d. and 1s. are as 1935, but with King George VI portrait.

1938. As T **15**, but King George VI portrait.

116c	2s. purple and blue on blue	7·00	1·50
117d	2s. 6d. black and red on blue	16·00	12·00
118f	5s. green and red on yellow	21·00	16·00
119e	10s. green and red on green	32·00	40·00
120b	12s. 6d. grey and orange	90·00	50·00
121c	£1 purple and black on red	48·00	75·00

1940. Surch **HALF PENNY**.

122	26	½d. on 1d. black and red	40	45

1946. Victory. As T **9** of Aden.

123	1½d. brown	15	15
124	3d. blue	15	15

1948. Silver Wedding. As T **10/11** of Aden.

125	1½d. brown	30	50
126	£1 red	40·00	48·00

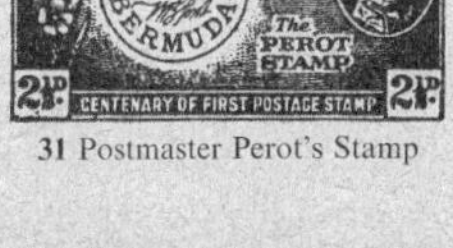

31 Postmaster Perot's Stamp

1949. Centenary of Postmaster Perot's Stamp.

127	31	2½d. blue and brown	15	15
128		3d. black and blue	15	15
129		6d. violet and green	15	15

1949. U.P.U. As T **20/23** of Antigua.

130	2½d. black	60	75
131	3d. blue	1·75	85
132	6d. purple	60	75
133	1s. green	60	75

1953. Coronation. As T **13** of Aden.

134	1½d. black and blue	60	15

34 Easter Lily — 43 Hog Coin

1953.

135a	–	½d. olive	40	60
136	–	1d. black and red	1·25	50
137	34	1½d. green	30	10
138	–	2d. blue and red	50	40
139	–	2½d. red	2·00	50
140	–	3d. purple	30	10
141	–	4d. black and blue	30	40
142	–	4½d. green	45	1·00
143	–	6d. black and turquoise	5·00	60
156	–	6d. black and mauve	70	15
143a	–	8d. black and red	2·50	30
143b	–	9d. violet	7·00	2·50
144	–	1s. orange	50	15
145	–	1s. 3d. blue	3·50	30
146	–	2s. brown	4·00	85
147	–	2s. 6d. red	4·50	45
148	43	5s. red	19·00	85
149	–	10s. blue	13·00	5·00
150	–	£1 multicoloured	24·00	21·00

DESIGNS—HORIZ: ½d. Easter lilies; 1d., 4d. Postmaster Perot's stamp; 2d. "Victory II" (racing dinghy); 2½d. Sir George Somers and "Sea Venture"; 3d., 1s. 3d. Map of Bermuda; 4½d. 9d. "Sea Venture" (galleon), coin and Perot stamp; 6d. (No. 143), 8d. White-tailed tropic bird; 6d. (No. 156), Perot's Post Office; 1s. Early Bermuda coins; 2s. Arms of St. George's 10s. Obverse and reverse of hog coin; £1 Arms of Bermuda. VERT: 2s. 6d. Warwick Fort; No. 156 commemorates the restoration and reopening of Perot's Post Office.

1953. Royal Visit. As No. 143a but inscr "ROYAL VISIT 1953".

151	6d. black and turquoise	30	20

1953. Three Power Talks. Nos. 140 and 145 optd **Three Power Talks December, 1953.**

152	3d. purple	10	10
153	1s. 3d. blue	10	10

1956. 50th Anniv of United States–Bermuda Yacht Race. Nos. 143a and 145 optd **50th ANNIVERSARY US–BERMUDA OCEAN RACE 1956.**

154	8d. black and red	20	40
155	1s. 3d. blue	20	55

49 Arms of King James I and Queen Elizabeth II

1959. 350th Anniv of Settlement. Arms in red, yellow and blue. Frame colours given.

157	49	1½d. blue	25	10
158		3d. grey	30	50
159		4d. purple	35	55
160		8d. violet	35	15
161		9d. olive	35	1·25
162		1s. 3d. brown	35	30

50 The Old Rectory, St George's, c. 1730

1962.

163	50	1d. purple, black and orange	10	45
164	–	2d. multicoloured	10	15
165	–	3d. brown and blue	10	10
166	–	4d. brown and mauve	20	40
167	–	5d. blue and red	1·50	2·50
168	–	6d. blue, green & lt blue	20	30
169	–	8d. blue, green and orange	30	35
170	–	9d. blue and brown	25	30
197	–	10d. violet and ochre	75	60
171	–	1s. multicoloured	20	10
172	–	1s. 3d. lake, grey and bistre	75	15
173	–	1s. 6d. violet and ochre	1·75	1·75
199	–	1s. 6d. blue and red	2·75	1·25
174	–	2s. brown and orange	3·00	1·25
175	–	2s. 3d. sepia and green	2·00	6·00
176	–	2s. 6d. sepia, green & yell	55	50
177	–	5s. purple and green	1·25	1·50
178	–	10s. mauve, green and buff	4·00	5·00
179	–	£1 black, olive and orange	14·00	14·00

DESIGNS: 2d. Church of St. Peter, St. George's; 3d. Government House, 1892; 4d. The Cathedral. Hamilton, 1894; 5d., 1s. 6d. (No. 199) H.M. Dockyard, 1811; 6d. Perot's Post Office, 1848; 8d. G.P.O., Hamilton, 1869; 9d. Library, Par-la-Ville; 10d., 1s. 6d. (No. 173) Bermuda cottage, c. 1705; 1s. Christ Church, Warwick, 1719; 1s. 3d. City Hall, Hamilton, 1960; 2s. Town of St. George; 2s. 3d. Bermuda house, c. 1710; 2s. 6d. Bermuda house, early 18th century; 5s. Colonial Secretariat, 1833; 10s. Old Post Office, Somerset, 1890; £1 The House of Assembly, 1815.

1963. Freedom from Hunger. As T **28** of Aden.

180	1s. 3d. sepia	80	40

1963. Centenary of Red Cross. As T **33** of Antigua.

181	3d. red and black	75	25
182	1s. 3d. red and blue	2·00	2·75

67 "Tsotsi in the Bundu" (Finn class yacht)

1964. Olympic Games, Tokyo.

183	67	3d. red, violet and blue	10	10

1965. Centenary of I.T.U. As T **36** of Antigua.

184	3d. blue and green	50	25
185	2s. yellow and blue	1·00	1·25

68 Scout Badge and St. Edward's Crown

1965. 50th Anniversary of Bermuda Boy Scouts Association.

186	68	2s. multicoloured	50	50

1965. I.C.Y. As T **37** of Antigua.

187	4d. purple and turquoise	50	20
188	2s. 6d. green and lavender	1·10	80

1966. Churchill Commemoration. As T **38** of Antigua.

189	3d. blue	45	20
190	6d. green	70	45
191	10d. brown	90	75
192	1s. 3d. violet	1·25	2·00

1966. World Cup Football Championship. As T **40** of Antigua.

193	10d. multicoloured	50	15
194	2s. 6d. multicoloured	75	65

1966. 20th Anniv of U.N.E.S.C.O. As T **54/56** of Antigua.

201	4d. multicoloured	60	15
202	1s. 3d. yellow, violet and olive	1·00	50
203	2s. black, purple and orange	1·25	1·25

69 G.P.O. Building

1967. Opening of New General Post Office.

204	69	3d. multicoloured	10	10
205		1s. multicoloured	10	10
206		1s. 6d. multicoloured	15	20
207		2s. 6d. multicoloured	15	40

70 "Mercury" (cable ship) and Chain Links

1967. Inauguration of Bermuda–Tortola Telephone Service. Multicoloured.

208	3d. Type **70**	15	10
209	1s. Map, telephone and microphone	20	10
210	1s. 6d. Telecommunications media	25	25
211	2s. 6d. "Mercury" (cable ship) and marine fauna	35	40

74 Human Rights Emblem and Doves

1968. Human Rights Year.

212	74	3d. indigo, blue and green	10	10
213		1s. brown, blue and light blue	10	10
214		1s. 6d. black, blue and red	10	10
215		2s. 6d. green, blue and yellow	15	15

75 Mace and Queen's Profile

1968. New Constitution.

216	75	3d. multicoloured	10	10
217		1s. multicoloured	10	10
218	–	1s. 6d. yellow, black and blue	10	20
219	–	2s. 6d. lilac, black and yellow	15	30

DESIGNS: 1s. 6d., 2s. 6d., Houses of Parliament, and House of Assembly, Bermuda.

77 Football, Athletics and Yachting

1968. Olympic Games, Mexico.

220	77	3d. multicoloured	15	10
221		1s. multicoloured	25	10
222		1s. 6d. multicoloured	50	25
223		2s. 6d. multicoloured	50	1·10

78 Brownie and Guide

1969. 50th Anniv of Girl Guides. Multicoloured.

224	3d. Type **78**	10	10
225	1s. Type **78**	20	10
226	1s. 6d. Guides and Badge	25	40
227	2s. 6d. As 1s. 6d.	35	1·10

80 Emerald-studded Gold Cross and Seaweed

1969. Underwater Treasure. Multicoloured.

228	4d. Type **80**	20	10
229	1s. 3d. Emerald-studded gold cross and sea-bed	35	15
230	2s. As Type **80**	45	80
231	2s. 6d. As 1s. 3d.	45	1·50

1970. Decimal Currency. Nos. 163/79 surch.

232	1 c. on 1d. purple, black & orge	10	1·50
233	2 c. on 2d. multicoloured	10	10
234	3 c. on 3d. brown and blue	10	10
235	4 c. on 4d. brown and mauve	10	10
236	5 c. on 8d. blue, green & orge	15	1·50
237	6 c. on 6d. blue, green & lt blue	15	70
238	9 c. on 9d. blue and brown	30	1·75
239	10 c. on 10d. violet and ochre	30	25
240	12 c. on 1s. multicoloured	30	50
241	15 c on 1s. 3d. lake, grey & bis	1·50	1·00
242	18 c. on 1s. 6d. blue and red	80	65
243	24 c. on 2s. brown and orange	85	85
244	30 c. on 2s. 6d. sepia, grn & yell	1·00	2·00
245	36 c. on 2s. 3d. sepia and green	1·75	5·00
246	60c. on 5s. purple and green	2·25	3·00
247	$1.20 on 10s. mauve, green and buff	4·00	15·00
248	$2.40 on £1 black, olive and orange	7·00	19·00

83 Spathiphyllum

1970. Flowers. Multicoloured.

249	1 c. Type **83**	10	20
250	2 c. Bottlebrush	20	25
251	3 c. Oleander (vert)	15	10
252	4 c. Bermudiana	15	10
253	5 c. Poinsettia	30	20
254	6 c. Hibiscus	30	30
255	9 c. Cereus	20	45
256	10c. Bougainvillea (vert)	20	15
257	12 c. Jacaranda	80	60
258	15 c. Passion flower	90	1·40
258a	17 c. As 15 c.	2·75	3·50
259	18 c. Coralita	2·25	2·25
259a	20 c. As 18 c.	2·75	3·25
260	24 c. Morning glory	1·50	3·50
260a	25 c. As 24 c.	2·75	4·50
261	30 c. Tecoma	1·00	1·25
262	36 c. Angel's trumpet	1·25	2·25
262a	40 c. As 36 c.	2·75	5·00
263	60 c. Plumbago	1·75	1·75
263a	$1 As 60 c.	3·25	6·50
264	$1.20 Bird of paradise flower	2·75	3·00
264a	$2 As $1.20	5·50	8·50
265	$2.40 Chalice cup	5·50	6·00
265a	$3 As $2.40	10·00	11·00

84 The State House, St. George's

1970. 350th Anniv of Bermuda Parliament. Multicoloured.

266	4 c. Type **84**	10	10
267	15 c. The Sessions House, Hamilton	25	15
268	18 c. St. Peter's Church, St. George's	25	20
269	24 c. Town Hall, Hamilton	35	45

85 Street Scene, St. George's

1971. "Keep Bermuda Beautiful". Multicoloured.

271	4 c. Type **85**	20	10
272	15 c. Horseshoe Bay	65	55
273	18 c. Gibbs Hill Lighthouse	1·25	1·75
274	24 c. Hamilton Harbour	1·25	2·25

86 Building of the "Deliverance"

1971. Voyage of the "Deliverance". Multicoloured.

275	4 c. Type **86**	50	20
276	15 c. "Deliverance" and "Patience" at Jamestown (vert)	1·50	1·75
277	18 c. Wreck of the "Sea Venture" (vert)	1·75	2·25
278	24 c. "Deliverance" and "Patience" on high seas	1·90	2·50

87 Green overlooking Ocean View

1971. Golfing in Bermuda. Multicoloured.

279	4 c. Type **87**	75	10
280	15 c. Golfers at Port Royal	1·50	70
281	18 c. Castle Harbour	1·60	1·00
282	24 c. Belmont	1·75	1·75

1971. Anglo-American Talks. Nos. 252, 258, 259 and 260 optd **HEATH-NIXON DECEMBER 1971**.

283	4 c. Bermudiana	10	10
284	15 c. Passion flower	10	20
285	18 c. Coralita	15	65
286	24 c. Morning glory	20	80

89 Bonefish

1972. World Fishing Records. Multicoloured.

287	4 c. Type **89**	35	10
288	15 c. Wahoo	40	50
289	18 c. Yellow-finned tuna	45	65
290	24 c. Greater amberjack	60	90

1972. Silver Wedding. As T **52** of Ascension, but with "Admiralty Oar" and Mace in background.

291	4 c. violet	15	10
292	15 c. red	15	50

91 Palmetto

1973. Tree Planting Year. Multicoloured.

293	4 c. Type **91**	30	10
294	15 c. Olivewood bark	90	75
295	18 c. Bermuda cedar	1·00	1·25
296	24 c. Mahogany	1·10	1·60

1973. Royal Wedding. As T **47** of Anguilla, background colour given. Mult.

297	15 c. mauve	15	15
298	18 c. blue	15	15

92 Bernard Park, Pembroke, 1973

1973. Centenary of Lawn Tennis. Multicoloured.

299	4 c. Type **92**	30	10
300	15 c. Clermont Court, 1873	60	65
301	18 c. Leamington Spa Court, 1872	70	1·25
302	24 c. Staten Island Courts, 1874	85	2·00

93 Weather Vane, City Hall

1974. 50th Anniv of Rotary in Bermuda. Mult.

320	5 c. Type **93**	15	10
321	17 c. St. Peter's Church, St. George's	45	35
322	20 c. Somerset Bridge	50	1·50
323	25 c. Map of Bermuda, 1626	60	2·00

94 Jack of Clubs and "good bridge hand"

1975. World Bridge Championships, Bermuda. Multicoloured.

324	5 c. Type **94**	20	10
325	17 c. Queen of Diamonds and Bermuda Bowl	35	50
326	20 c. King of Hearts and Bermuda Bowl	40	1·75
327	25 c. Ace of Spades and Bermuda Bowl	40	2·25

95 Queen Elizabeth II and the Duke of Edinburgh

1975. Royal Visit.

328	**95** 17 c. multicoloured	60	65
329	20 c. multicoloured	65	2·10

96 Short S.23 Flying Boat "Cavalier", 1937

1975. 50th Anniv of Air-mail Service to Bermuda. Multicoloured.

330	5 c. Type **96**	40	10
331	17 c. U.S. Navy airship "Los Angeles", 1925	1·25	85
332	20 c. Lockheed Constellation, 1946	1·40	2·75
333	25 c. Boeing 747-100, 1970	1·50	3·50

97 Supporters of American Army raiding Royal Magazine

1975. Bicentenary of Gunpowder Plot, St George's. Multicoloured.

335	5 c. Type **97**	20	10
336	17 c. Setting off for raid	40	30
337	20 c. Loading gunpowder aboard American ship	45	1·25
338	25 c. Gunpowder on beach	50	1·40

98 Launching "Ready" (bathysphere)

1976. 50th Anniv of Bermuda Biological Station. Multicoloured.

357	5 c. Type **98**	30	10
358	17 c. View from the sea (horiz)	60	60
359	20 c. H.M.S. "Challenger", 1873 (horiz)	65	2·25
360	25 c. Beebe's Bathysphere descent, 1934	70	2·75

99 "Christian Radich" (cadet ship)

1976. Tall Ships Race. Multicoloured.

361	5 c. Type **99**	75	20
362	12 c. "Juan Sebastian de Elcano" (Spanish cadet schooner)	1·00	2·00
363	17 c. "Eagle" (U.S. coastguard cadet ship)	1·10	1·75
364	20 c. "Sir Winston Churchill" (cadet schooner)	1·25	2·50
365	40 c. "Kruzenshtern" (Russian cadet barque)	1·40	3·25
366	$1 "Cutty Sark" trophy	2·25	8·00

100 Silver Trophy and Club Flags

1976. 75th Anniv of St. George's v. Somerset Cricket Cup Match. Multicoloured.

367	5 c. Type **100**	35	10
368	17 c. Badge and pavilion, St. George's Club	65	65
369	20 c. Badge and pavilion, Somerset Club	80	2·75
370	25 c. Somerset playing field	1·25	3·75

HAVE YOU READ THE NOTES AT THE BEGINNING OF THIS CATALOGUE?
These often provide answers to the enquiries we receive.

101 Royal Visit, 1975

1977. Silver Jubilee. Multicoloured.

371	5 c. Type **101**	10	10
372	20 c. St. Edward's Crown	15	20
373	$1 The Queen in Chair of Estate	40	1·25

102 Stockdale House, St. George's, 1784–1812

1977. Centenary of U.P.U. Membership. Mult.

374	5 c. Type **102**	15	10
375	15 c. Perot Post Office and stamp	30	50
376	17 c. St. George's P.O. c. 1860	30	50
377	20 c. Old G.P.O., Hamilton, c. 1935	35	60
378	40 c. New G.P.O., Hamilton, 1967	60	1·10

103 17th-Century Ship approaching Castle Island

1977. Piloting. Multicoloured.

379	5 c. Type **103**	35	10
380	15 c. Pilot leaving ship, 1795	65	50
381	17 c. Pilots rowing out to paddle-steamer	75	50
382	20 c. Pilot gig and brig "Harvest Queen"	80	2·25
383	40 c. Modern pilot cutter and R.M.S. "Queen Elizabeth 2"	1·25	3·25

104 Great Seal of Queen Elizabeth I

1978. 25th Anniv of Coronation. Multicoloured.

384	8 c. Type **104**	10	10
385	50 c. Great Seal of Queen Elizabeth II	30	30
386	$1 Queen Elizabeth II	60	75

105 White-tailed Tropic Bird

1978. Wildlife. Multicoloured.

387	3 c. Type **105**	1·75	2·00
388	4 c. White-eyed vireo	1·50	2·00
389	5 c. Eastern bluebird	1·25	1·75
390	7 c. Whistling frog	50	1·50
391	8 c. Common cardinal (Redbird)	1·25	55
392	10 c. Spiny lobster	20	10
393	12 c. Land crab	30	70
394	15 c. Lizard (Skink)	30	15
395	20 c. Four-eyed butterflyfish	30	30
396	25 c. Red hind	30	20
397	30 c. "Danaus plexippus" (butterfly)	2·25	2·50
398	40 c. Rock beauty	45	1·50
399	50 c. Banded butterflyfish	55	85
400	$1 Blue angelfish	1·25	1·75
401	$2 Humpback whale	2·00	2·75
402	$3 Green turtle	2·75	3·00
403	$5 Cahow	6·50	6·00

106 Map by Sir George Somers, 1609

1979. Antigue Maps. Multicoloured.

404	8 c. Type **106**	15	10
405	15 c. Map by John Seller, 1685	20	15
406	20 c. Map by H. Moll, 1729–40 (vert)	25	25
407	25 c. Map by Desbruslins, 1740	30	30
408	50 c. Map by Speed, 1626	45	80

107 Policeman and Policewoman

1979. Centenary of Police Force. Multicoloured.

409	8 c. Type **107**	30	10
410	20 c. Policeman directing traffic (horiz)	55	55
411	25 c. "Blue Heron" (police launch) (horiz)	65	65
412	50 c. Police car and motor cycle	1·00	1·50

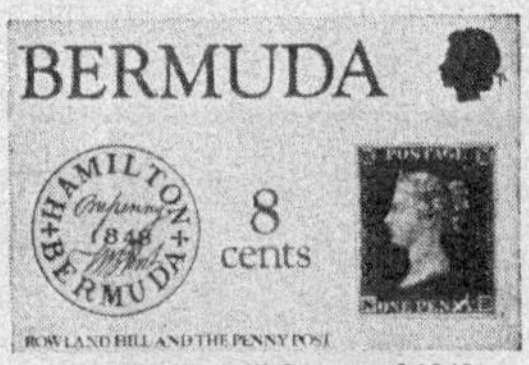

108 1d. "Perot" Stamp of 1848 and 1840 Penny Black

1980. Death Cent of Sir Rowland Hill. Mult.

413	8 c. Type **108**	15	10
414	20 c. "Perot" and Sir Rowland Hill	25	25
415	25 c. "Perot" and early letter	25	30
416	50 c. "Perot" and "Paid 1" cancellation	35	70

109 Lockheed TriStar 500 approaching Bermuda

1980. "London 1980" International Stamp Exhibition. Multicoloured.

417	25 c. Type **109**	30	15
418	50c. "Orduna I" (liner) at Grassy Bay, 1926	45	35
419	$1 "Delta" (screw steamer) at St. George's Harbour, 1856	85	1·00
420	$2 "Lord Sidmouth" (sailing packet) in Old Ship Channel, St. George's	1·40	2·00

110 Gina Swainson ("Miss World 1979–80")

1980. "Miss World 1979–80" Commem. Mult.

421	8 c. Type **110**	15	10
422	20 c. Miss Swainson after crowning ceremony	20	20
423	50 c. Miss Swainson on Peacock Throne	35	35
424	$1 Miss Swainson in Bermuda carriage	70	90

111 Queen Elizabeth the Queen Mother

1980. 80th Birthday of The Queen Mother.

425	**111** 25 c. multicoloured	30	70

112 Bermuda from Satellite

1980. Commonwealth Finance Ministers Meeting. Multicoloured.

426	8 c. Type **112**	10	10
427	20 c. "Camden"	20	40
428	25 c. Princess Hotel, Hamilton	20	50
429	50 c. Government House	35	1·25

113 Kitchen, 18th-century

1981. Heritage Week. Multicoloured.

430	8 c. Type **113**	15	10
431	25 c. Gathering Easter lilies, 20th-century	40	50
432	30 c. Fishing, 20th-century	50	70
433	40 c. Stone cutting, 19th-century	55	1·00
434	50 c. Onion shipping, 19th-century	75	1·25
435	$1 Privateering, 17th-century	1·60	2·75

114 Wedding Bouquet from Bermuda

115 "Service", Hamilton

1981. Royal Wedding. Multicoloured.

436	30 c. Type **114**	20	20
437	50 c. Prince Charles as Royal Navy Commander	35	40
438	$1 Prince Charles and Lady Diana Spencer	55	80

1981. 25th Anniv of Duke of Edinburgh Award Scheme. Multicoloured.

439	10 c. Type **115**	15	10
440	25 c. "Outward Bound", Paget Island	20	20
441	30 c. "Expedition", St. David's Island	20	30
442	$1 Duke of Edinburgh	55	1·25

116 Lightbourne's Cone

1982. Sea Shells. Multicoloured.

443	10 c. Type **116**	40	10
444	25 c. Finlay's frog shell	80	75
445	30 c. Royal bonnet	85	85
446	$1 Lightbourne's murex	2·25	3·25

117 Regimental Colours and Colour Party

1982. Bermuda Regiment. Multicoloured.

447	10 c. Type **117**	45	10
448	25 c. Queen's Birthday Parade	90	80
449	30 c. Governor inspecting Guard of Honour	1·00	1·40
450	40 c. Beating the Retreat	1·25	1·75
451	50 c. Ceremonial gunners	1·40	2·00
452	$1 Guard of Honour, Royal visit, 1975	2·25	3·50

118 Charles Fort

119 Arms of Sir Edwin Sandys

1982. Historic Bermuda Forts. Multicoloured.

453	10 c. Type **118**	20	20
454	25 c. Pembroks Fort	50	85
455	30 c. Southampton Fort (horiz)	60	1·25
456	$1 Smiths Fort and Pagets Fort (horiz)	1·75	4·25

1983. Coat of Arms (1st series). Multicoloured.

457	10 c. Type **119**	45	15
458	25 c. Arms of the Bermuda Company	1·40	1·00
459	50 c. Arms of William Herbert, Earl of Pembroke	2·25	3·25
460	$1 Arms of Sir George Somers	3·00	5·00

See also Nos. 482/5 and 499/502.

120 Early Fitted Dinghy

122 Joseph Stockdale

121 Curtiss N-9 Seaplane

1983. Fitted Dinghies. Multicoloured.

461	12 c. Type **120**	45	15
462	30 c. Modern dinghy inshore	75	75
463	40 c. Early dinghy (different)	90	90
464	$1 Modern dinghy with red and white spinnaker	1·75	3·25

1983. Bicentenary of Manned Flight. Multicoloured.

465	12 c. Type **121** (First flight over Bermuda)	60	20
466	30 c. Stinson Pilot Radio seaplane (First completed flight between U.S. and Bermuda)	1·25	1·25
467	40 c. S.23 Flying boat "Cavalier" (First scheduled passenger flight)	1·50	1·75
468	$1 U.S.N. "Los Angeles" (airship) moored to U.S.S. "Patoka"	2·50	5·00

1984. Bicentenary of Bermuda's First Newspaper and Postal Service. Multicoloured

469	12 c. Type **122**	30	15
470	30 c. "The Bermuda Gazette"	60	80
471	40 c. Stockdale's postal service (horiz)	80	1·10
472	$1 "Lady Hammond" (mail boat) (horiz)	2·50	3·25

123 Sir Thomas Gates and Sir George Somers

1984. 375th Anniv of First Settlement. Mult.

473	12 c. Type **123**	20	15
474	30 c. Jamestown, Virginia	50	1·25
475	40 c. Wreck of "Sea Venture"	90	1·25
476	$1 Fleet leaving Plymouth, Devon	2·00	5·00

124 Swimming

125 Buttery

1984. Olympic Games, Los Angeles. Multicoloured.

478	12 c. Type **124**	40	15
479	30 c. Track and field events (horiz)	70	75
480	40 c. Equestrian	1·25	1·25
481	$1 Sailing (horiz)	2·50	5·00

1984. Coat of Arms (2nd series). As T **119**. Mult.

482	12 c. Arms of Henry Wriothesley, Earl of Southampton	50	15
483	30 c. Arms of Sir Thomas Smith	1·00	85
484	40 c. Arms of William Cavendish, Earl of Devonshire	1·25	1·50
485	$1 Town arms of St. George	2·75	4·00

1985. Bermuda Architecture. Multicoloured.

486	12 c. Type **125**	35	15
487	30 c. Limestone rooftops (horiz)	80	70
488	40 c. Chimneys (horiz)	95	1·00
489	$1.50 Entrance archway	3·00	3·75

126 Osprey

127 The Queen Mother with Grandchildren, 1980

1985. Birth Bicentenary of John J. Audubon (ornithologist). Designs showing original drawings. Multicoloured.

490	12 c. Type **126**	2·00	65
491	30 c. Yellow-crowned night heron	2·00	95
492	40 c. Great egret (horiz)	2·25	1·25
493	$1.50 Eastern bluebird	3·75	5·50

1985. Life and Times of Queen Elizabeth the Queen Mother. Multicoloured.

494	12 c. Queen Consort, 1937	25	15
495	30 c. Type **127**	40	50
496	40 c. At Clarence House on 83rd birthday	50	60
497	$1.50 With Prince Henry at his christening (from photo by Lord Snowdon)	2·00	2·75

1985. Coats of Arms (3rd series). As T **119**. Mult.

499	12 c. Hamilton	75	15
500	30 c. Paget	1·40	80
501	40 c. Warwick	1·60	1·40
502	$1.50 City of Hamilton	3·75	4·25

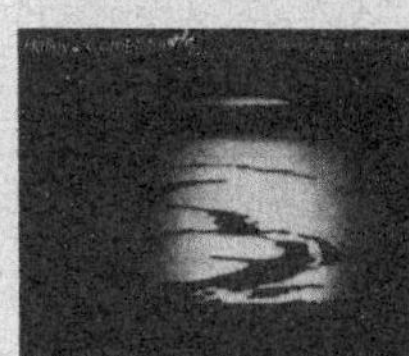

128 Halley's Comet and Bermuda Archipelago

1985. Appearance of Halley's Comet. Multicoloured.

503	15 c. Type **128**	85	25
504	40 c. Halley's Comet, A.D. 684 (from Nuremberg Chronicles, 1493)	1·60	1·75
505	50 c. "Halley's Comet, 1531" (from Peter Apian woodcut, 1532)	1·90	2·50
506	$1.50 "Halley's Comet, 1759" (Samuel Scott)	3·50	5·00

129 "Constellation" (schooner) (1943)

1986. Ships Wrecked on Bermuda. Multicoloured.

507A	3 c. Type **129**	70	1·00
508A	5 c. "Early Riser" (pilot boat), 1876	20	20
509A	7 c. "Madiana" (screw steamer), 1903	65	85
510A	10 c. "Curlew" (sail/steamer), 1856	30	30
511A	12 c. "Warwick" (galleon), 1619	60	80

512A 15 c. H.M.S. "Vixen" (gun-boat), 1890 . . . . 40 60
512cA 18 c. As 7 c. . . . . 4·50 2·75
513A 20 c. "San Pedro" (Spanish galleon), 1594 . . . . . 1·10 80
514A 25 c. "Alert" (fishing sloop), 1877 . . . . 60 1·50
515A 40 c. "North Carolina" (barque), 1880 . . . . 65 1·25
516A 50 c. "Mark Antonie" (Spanish privateer), 1777 1·50 1·75
517A 60 c. "Mary Celestia" (Confederate paddle-steamer), 1864 . . . . 1·50 1·75
517cA 70 c. "Caesar" (brig), 1818 5·00 4·50
518B $1 "L'Herminie" (French frigate), 1839 . . . . . . 1·50 1·60
519A $1.50 As 70 c. . . . . . . 4·50 4·50
520B $2 "Lord Amherst" (transport), 1778 . . . 2·50 3·50
521B $3 "Minerva" (sailing ship), 1849 . . . . 4·25 5·50
522A $5 "Caraquet" (cargo liner), 1923 . . . . 6·50 10·00
523A $8 H.M.S. "Pallas" (frigate), 1783 . . . . 8·00 12·00

1986. 60th Birthday of Queen Elizabeth II. As T **110** of Ascension. Multicoloured.
524 15 c. Princess Elizabeth aged three, 1929 . . . . 30 30
525 40 c. With Earl of Rosebery at Oaks May Meeting, Epsom, 1954 . . . . 50 60
526 50 c. With Duke of Edinburgh, Bermuda, 1975 . . . . . 65 75
527 60 c. At British Embassy, Paris, 1972 . . . . 80 90
528 $1.50 At Crown Agents Head Office, London, 1983 . . . 2·00 2·50

1986. "Ameripex '86" International Stamp Exhibition, Chicago. As T **164** of Bahamas, showing Bermuda stamps. Multicoloured.
529 15 c. 1984 375th Anniv of Settlement miniature sheet . 85 30
530 40 c. 1973 Lawn Tennis Centenary, 24 c. . . . . . 1·50 70
531 50 c. 1983 Bicentenary of Manned Flight 12 c. . . . . 1·75 1·00
532 $1 1976 Tall Ships Race 17 c. . 3·00 2·50

1986. 25th Anniv of World Wildlife Fund. No. 402 surch **90c**.
534 90 c. on $3 Green turtle . . . 2·25 3·25

131 Train in Front Street, Hamilton, 1940

1987. Transport (1st series). Bermuda Railway. Multicoloured.
535 15 c. Type **131** . . . . 1·25 25
536 40 c. Train crossing Springfield Trestle . . . . 1·75 90
537 50 c. "St. George Special" at Bailey's Bay Station . . . . 1·90 1·50
538 $1.50 Boat train at St. George 3·25 3·50
See also Nos. 557/60, 574/7 and 624/9.

132 "Bermuda Settlers", 1901

1987. Bermuda Paintings (1st series). Works by Winslow Homer. Multicoloured.
539 15 c. Type **132** 60 25
540 30 c. "Bermuda", 1900 . . . . 85 45
541 40 c. "Bermuda Landscape", 1901 (buff frame) 95 55
544 40 c. Type **132** . . . . . . 90 1·50
545 40 c. As No. 540 . . . . . . 90 1·50
546 40 c. As No. 541 (grey frame) 90 1·50
547 40 c. As No. 542 . . . . . . 90 1·50
548 40 c. As No. 543 . . . . . . 90 1·50
542 50 c. "Inland Water", 1901 . . 1·10 70
543 $1.50 "Salt Kettle", 1899 . . . 2·50 2·50
See also Nos. 607/10 and 630/3.

133 Sikorsky S-42B Flying Boat "Bermuda Clipper"

1987. 50th Anniv of Inauguration of Bermuda–U.S.A. Air Service. Multicoloured.
549 15 c. Type **133** . . . . . . 1·25 15
550 40 c. Short S.23 flying boat "Cavalier" . . . . 2·25 70
551 50 c. "Bermuda Clipper" in flight over signpost . . . . . . 2·50 80
552 $1.50 "Cavalier" on apron and "Bermuda Clipper" in flight 5·00 3·50

134 19th-century Wagon carrying Telephone Poles

1987. Centenary of Bermuda Telephone Company. Multicoloured.
553 15 c. Type **134** 75 15
554 40 c. Early telephone exchange 1·40 60
555 50 c. Early and modern telephones . . . . 1·75 70
556 $1.50 Communications satellite orbiting Earth . . . . . . 2·75 3·50

135 Mail Wagon, c. 1869

1988. Transport (2nd series). Horse-drawn Carts and Wagons. Multicoloured.
557 15 c. Type **135** 25 15
558 40 c. Open cart, c. 1823 . . . 55 55
559 50 c. Closed cart, c. 1823 . . 65 65
560 $1.50 Two-wheeled wagon, c. 1930 . . . . 2·00 2·50

136 "Old Blush"

1988. Old Garden Roses (1st series). Multicoloured.
561 15 c. Type **136** 45 25
562 30 c. "Anna Olivier" 60 40
563 40 c. "Rosa chinensis semperflorens" (vert) . . . 75 65
564 50 c. "Archduke Charles" . . . 85 85
565 $1.50 "Rosa chinensis viridiflora" (vert) . . . . . 2·25 2·75
See also Nos. 584/8 and, for designs with the royal cypher instead of the Queen's head, Nos. 589/98 and 683/6.

1988. 300th Anniv of Lloyd's of London. As T **123** of Ascension. Multicoloured.
566 18 c. Loss of H.M.S. "Lutine" (frigate), 1799 . . . . . . 45 25
567 50 c. "Sentinel" (cable ship) (horiz) . . . . 1·00 65
568 60 c. "Bermuda" (liner), Hamilton, 1931 (horiz) . . 1·10 75
569 $2 Loss of H.M.S. "Valerian" (sloop) in hurricane, 1926 . 3·00 3·25

137 Devonshire Parish Militia, 1812

1988. Military Uniforms. Multicoloured.
570 18 c. Type **137** 75 25
571 50 c. 71st (Highland) Regiment, 1831-34 . . . . 1·40 85
572 60 c. Cameron Highlanders, 1942 1·50 95
573 $2 Troop of horse, 1774 . . . 4·00 4·50

138 "Corona" (ferry)

1989. Transport (3rd series). Ferry Services. Mult.
574 18 c. Type **138** 25 25
575 50 c. Rowing boat ferry . . . 65 65
576 60 c. St. George's barge ferry 75 75
577 $2 "Laconia" . . . . 2·50 2·75

139 Morgan's Island

1989. 150 Years of Photography. Multicoloured.
578 18 c. Type **139** 45 25
579 30 c. Front Street, Hamilton . 65 45
580 50 c. Waterfront, Front Street, Hamilton . . . . 1·00 90
581 60 c. Crow Lane from Hamilton Harbour . . . . 1·10 1·25
582 70 c. Shipbuilding, Hamilton Harbour . . . . 1·25 1·40
583 $1 Dockyard . . . . 1·75 2·50

1989. Old Garden Roses (2nd series). As T **136**. Multicoloured.
584 18 c. "Agrippina" (vert) . . . 40 25
585 30 c. "Smith's Parish" (vert) . 55 60
586 50 c. "Champney's Pink Cluster" 90 1·25
587 60 c. "Rosette Delizy" . . . . 1·00 1·60
588 $1.50 "Rosa bracteata" . . . . 2·00 3·50

1989. Old Garden Roses (3rd series). Designs as Nos. 561/5 and 584/8, but with royal cypher at top left instead of Queen's head. Multicoloured.
589 50 c. As No. 565 (vert) . . . . 1·40 1·60
590 50 c. As No. 563 (vert) . . . . 1·40 1·60
591 50 c. Type **136** . . . . 1·40 1·60
592 50 c. As No. 562 . . . . . . 1·40 1·60
593 50 c. As No. 564 . . . . . . 1·40 1·60
594 50 c. As No. 585 (vert) . . . . 1·40 1·60
595 50 c. As No. 584 (vert) . . . . 1·40 1·60
596 50 c. As No. 586 . . . . . . 1·40 1·60
597 50 c. As No. 587 . . . . . . 1·40 1·60
598 50 c. As No. 588 . . . . . . 1·40 1·60

140 Main Library, Hamilton

1989. 150th Anniv of Bermuda Library. Mult.
599 18 c. Type **140** 30 25
600 50 c. The Old Rectory, St. George's 70 65
601 60 c. Somerset Library, Springfield 80 75
602 $2 Cabinet Building, Hamilton 2·75 2·75

141 1865 1d. Rose

1989. Commonwealth Postal Conference. Mult.
603 **141** 18 c. grey, pink and red . 70 25
604 – 50 c. grey, blue & lt blue . 1·25 65
605 – 60 c. grey, purple and mauve 1·40 1·00
606 – $2 grey, green and emerald 2·75 3·50
DESIGNS: 50 c. 1866 2d. blue; 60 c. 1865 6d. purple; $2 1865 1s. green.

142 "Fairylands, c. 1890" (Ross Turner)

1990. Bermuda Paintings (2nd series). Multicoloured.
607 18 c. Type **142** 40 25
608 50 c. "Shinebone Alley, c. 1953" (Ogden Pleissner) . . . . 85 1·10
609 60 c. "Salt Kettle, 1916" (Prosper Senat) . . . . 90 1·50
610 $2 "St. George's, 1934" (Jack Bush) . . . . 2·75 5·00

1990. "Stamp World London 90" International Stamp Exhibition. Nos. 603/6 optd **Stamp World London 90** and logo.
611 18 c. grey, pink and red . . . 75 25
612 50 c. grey, blue and light blue . 1·25 1·25
613 60 c. grey, purple and mauve . 1·40 1·50
614 $2 grey, green and emerald . . 3·25 5·00

1990. Nos. 511, 516 and 519 surch.
615 30 c. on 12 c. "Warwick" (galleon), (1619) 65 65
616 55 c. on 50 c. "Mark Antonie" (Spanish privateer), 1777 . . 1·00 1·00
617 80 c. on $1.50 "Caesar" (brig), 1818 . . . . 1·75 3·00

145 The Halifax and Bermudas Cable Company Office, Hamilton

1990. Centenary of Cable and Wireless in Bermuda.
618 **145** 20 c. brown and black . . 60 25
619 – 55 c. brown and black . . 1·75 1·25
620 – 70 c. multicoloured . . . 1·75 2·00
621 – $2 multicoloured . . . . 4·00 5·00
DESIGNS: 55 c. "Westmeath" (cable ship), 1890; 70 c. Wireless transmitter station, St. George's, 1928; $2 "Sir Eric Sharp" (cable ship).

1991. President Bush–Prime Minister Major Talks, Bermuda. Nos. 618/9 optd **BUSH-MAJOR 16 MARCH 1991**.
622 **145** 20 c. brown and black . . 1·25 75
623 – 55 c. brown and black . . 2·25 2·75

147 Two-seater Pony Cart, 1805

1991. Transport (4th series). Horse-drawn Carriages. Multicoloured.
624 20 c. Type **147** 70 30
625 30 c. Varnished rockaway, 1830 80 50
626 55 c. Vis-a-Vis victoria, 1895 . 1·40 1·10
627 70 c. Semi-formal phaeton, 1900 2·00 2·00
628 80 c. Pony runabout, 1905 . . 2·25 2·25
629 $1 Ladies phaeton, 1910 . . . 2·50 2·50

148 "Bermuda, 1916" (Prosper Senat)

1991. Bermuda Paintings (3rd series). Multicoloured.
630 20 c. Type **148** 80 30
631 55 c. "Bermuda Cottage" 1930 (Frank Allison) (horiz) . . 1·75 1·40
632 70 c. "Old Maid's Lane", 1934 (Jack Bush) . . . . 2·25 2·75
633 $2 "St. George's", 1953 (Ogden Pleissner) (horiz) . . . . . 4·00 6·00

1991. 65th Birthday of Queen Elizabeth II and 70th Birthday of Prince Philip. As T **139** of Ascension. Multicoloured.
634 55 c. Prince Philip in tropical naval uniform . . . . . . 90 1·25
635 70 c. Queen Elizabeth II in Bermuda . . . . 1·10 1·25

149 H.M.S. "Argonaut" (cruiser) in Floating Dock

1991. 50th Anniv of Second World War. Mult.
636 20 c. Type **149** . . . . 1·25 40
637 55 c. Kindley Airfield . . . . 2·00 1·40
638 70 c. Boeing 314A flying boat and map of Atlantic route . . 2·50 2·75
639 $2 Censored trans-Atlantic mail 4·25 6·00

1992. 40th Anniv of Queen Elizabeth II's Accession. As T **143** of Ascension. Multicoloured.
640 20 c. Old fort on beach . . . 50 30
641 30 c. Public gardens 65 55
642 55 c. Cottage garden . . . . 1·00 90
643 70 c. Beach and hotels . . . . 1·40 1·60
644 $1 Queen Elizabeth II . . . . 1·75 2·25

150 Rings and Medallion

1992. 500th Anniv of Discovery of America by Columbus. Spanish Artifacts. Multicoloured.
645 25 c. Type **150** 80 35
646 35 c. Ink wells . . . . 1·00 75
647 60 c. Gold ornaments . . . . 1·75 2·00
648 75 c. Bishop buttons and crucifix 2·00 2·75

649 85 c. Earrings and pearl buttons 2·25 3·00
650 $1 Jug and bowls 2·50 3·25

151 "Wreck of 'Sea Venture' "

1992. Stained Glass Windows. Multicoloured.
651 25 c. Type **151** 90 40
652 60 c. "Birds in tree" 2·00 2·00
653 75 c. "St. Francis feeding bird" 2·50 2·75
654 $2 "Shells" 5·25 6·00

152 German Shepherd

1992. 7th World Congress of Kennel Clubs. Mult.
655 25 c. Type **152** 1·00 40
656 35 c. Irish setter 1·25 70
657 60 c. Whippet (vert) 2·00 2·25
658 75 c. Border terrier (vert) 2·00 2·75
659 85 c. Pomeranian (vert) 2·25 3·25
660 $1 Schipperke (vert) 2·50 3·50

153 Policeman, Cyclist and Cruise Liner
154 "Duchesse de Brabant" and Bee

1993. Tourism Posters by Adolph Treidler. Mult.
679 25 c. Type **153** 1·00 60
680 60 c. Seaside golf course 2·00 2·25
681 75 c. Deserted beach 2·00 2·50
682 $2 Dancers in evening dress and cruise liner 4·00 5·50

1993. Garden Roses (4th series).
683 **154** 10 c. multicoloured 50 75
684 25 c. multicoloured 30 40
685 50 c. multicoloured 80 1·25
686 60 c. multicoloured 75 95

1993. 75th Anniv of Royal Air Force. As T **149** of Ascension. Multicoloured.
687 25 c. Consolidated PBY-5 Catalina 75 35
688 60 c. Supermarine Spitfire Mk IX 1·75 2·00
689 75 c. Bristol Type 156 Beaufighter Mk X 1·90 2·25
690 $2 Handley Page Halifax Mk III 3·50 4·50

155 Hamilton from the Sea

1993. Bicentenary of Hamilton. Mult.
691 25 c. Type **155** 75 35
692 60 c. Waterfront 1·75 2·00
693 75 c. Barrel warehouse 2·00 2·50
694 $2 Sailing ships off Hamilton 4·00 5·00

156 "Queen of Bermuda" (liner) at Hamilton
157 Queen Elizabeth II in Bermuda

1994. 75th Anniv of Furness Line's Bermuda Cruises. Adolphe Treidler Posters. Multicoloured.
695 25 c. Type **156** 45 35
696 60 c. "Monarch of Bermuda" entering port (horiz) 1·25 1·60
697 75 c. "Queen of Bermuda" and "Ocean Monarch" (liners) (horiz) 1·40 1·75
698 $2 Passengers on promenade deck at night 3·50 4·50

1994. Royal Visit. Multicoloured.
699 25 c. Type **157** 65 35
700 60 c. Queen Elizabeth and Prince Philip in open carriage 1·25 1·75
701 75 c. Royal Yacht "Britannia" 2·50 2·75

158 Peach

1994. Flowering Fruits. Multicoloured.
702A 5 c. Type **158** 10 10
703A 7 c. Fig 10 10
704A 10 c. Calabash (vert) 10 15
705A 15 c. Natal plum 20 25
706A 18 c. Locust and wild honey 25 30
707A 20 c. Pomegranate 25 30
708A 25 c. Mulberry (vert) 30 35
709A 35 c. Grape (vert) 40 45
710A 55 c. Orange (vert) 65 70
711A 60 c. Surinam cherry 70 75
712A 75 c. Loquat 90 95
713A 90 c. Sugar apple 1·10 1·25
714A $1 Prickly pear (vert) 1·25 1·40
715A $2 Paw paw 2·40 2·50
716A $3 Bay grape 3·50 3·75
717A $5 Banana (vert) 6·00 6·25
718A $8 Lemon 10·00 10·50

159 Nurse with Mother and Baby

1994. Centenary of Hospital Care. Multicoloured.
719 25 c. Type **159** 80 35
720 60 c. Patient on dialysis machine 1·75 1·90
721 75 c. Casualty on emergency trolley 2·00 2·25
722 $2 Elderly patient in wheelchair with physiotherapists 4·25 5·00

160 Gombey Dancers

1994. Cultural Heritage (1st series). Multicoloured.
723 25 c. Type **160** 55 35
724 60 c. Christmas carol singers 1·10 1·25
725 75 c. Marching band 1·40 2·00
726 $2 National Dance Group performers 3·50 4·75
See also Nos. 731/4.

161 Bermuda 1970 Flower 1 c. Stamps and 1 c. Coin
162 Bermuda Coat of Arms

1995. 25th Anniv of Decimal Currency. Mult.
727 25 c. Type **161** 45 35
728 60 c. 1970 5 c. stamps and coin 1·00 1·25
729 75 c. 1970 10 c. stamps and coin 1·25 1·75
730 $2 1970 25 c. stamps and coin 3·50 4·25

1995. Cultural Heritage (2nd series). As T **160**. Multicoloured.
731 25 c. Kite flying 55 35
732 60 c. Majorettes 1·50 1·50
733 75 c. Portuguese dancers 1·75 2·00
734 $2 Floral float 3·75 4·75

1995. 375th Anniv of Bermuda Parliament.
735 **162** 25 c. multicoloured 50 35
736 $1 multicoloured 1·75 2·25

For design as No. 736 but inscr "Commonwealth Finance Ministers Meeting", see No. 765.

163 U.S. Navy Ordnance Island Submarine Base

1995. Military Bases. Multicoloured.
737 20 c. Type **163** 50 30
738 25 c. Royal Naval Dockyard 60 35
739 60 c. U.S.A.F. Fort Bell and Kindley Field 1·25 1·25
740 75 c. R.A.F. Darrell's Island flying boat base 1·50 1·75
741 90 c. U.S. Navy operating base 1·50 2·25
742 $1 Canadian Forces Communications Station, Daniel's Head 1·60 2·25

164 Triple Jump

1996. Olympic Games, Atlanta. Multicoloured.
743 25 c. Type **164** 45 35
744 30 c. Cycling 75 60
745 65 c. Yachting 1·25 1·60
746 80 c. Show jumping 1·50 1·90

165 Jetty and Islets, Hamilton

1996. Panoramic Paintings of Hamilton (Nos. 747/51) and St. George's (Nos. 752/6) by E. J. Holland. Multicoloured.
747 60 c. Type **165** 70 75
748 60 c. End of island and buildings 70 75
749 60 c. Yachts and hotel 70 75
750 60 c. Islet, hotel and cathedral 70 75
751 60 c. Cliff and houses by shore 70 75
752 60 c. Islet and end of main island 70 75
753 60 c. Yacht and houses on hillside 70 75
754 60 c. Yacht and St. George's Hotel on hilltop 70 75
755 60 c. Shoreline and fishing boats 70 75
756 60 c. Entrance to harbour channel 70 75

166 Somerset Express Mail Cart, c. 1900

1996. "CAPEX '96" International Stamp Exhibition, Toronto. Local Transport. Multicoloured.
757 25 c. Type **166** 70 35
758 60 c. Victoria carriage and railcar, 1930s 1·75 1·75
759 75 c. First bus, 1946 1·75 2·00
760 $2 Sightseeing bus, c. 1947 4·00 4·50

167 Hog Fish Beacon

1996. Lighthouses. Multicoloured.
761 30 c. Type **167** 70 45
762 65 c. Gibbs Hill Lighthouse 1·25 1·25
763 80 c. St. David's Lighthouse 1·75 2·00
764 $2 North Rock Beacon 3·50 4·50
See also Nos. 770/3.

1996. Commonwealth Finance Ministers' Meeting. As No. 736, but inscr "Commonwealth Finance Ministers Meeting" at top and with wider gold frame.
765 $1 multicoloured 1·50 2·00

168 Waterville

1996. Architectural Heritage. Multicoloured.
766 30 c. Type **168** 60 45
767 65 c. Bridge House 1·10 1·25
768 80 c. Fannie Fox's Cottage 1·40 2·00
769 $2.50 Palmetto House 3·50 4·50

1997. "HONG KONG '97" International Stamp Exhibition. Designs as Nos. 761/4, but incorporating "HONG KONG '97" logo and with some values changed.
770 30 c. As Type **167** 60 45
771 65 c. Gibbs Hill Lighthouse 1·25 1·25
772 80 c. St David's Lighthouse 1·40 1·50
773 $2.50 North Rock Beacon 3·75 4·25

169 White-tailed Tropic Bird

1997. Birds Conservation. Multicoloured.
774 30 c. Type **169** 60 65
775 60 c. White-tailed tropic bird and chick (vert) 1·25 1·25
776 80 c. Cahow and chick (vert) 1·75 2·00
777 $2.50 Cahow 4·00 4·50

170 Queen Elizabeth II with Crowd

1997. Golden Wedding of Queen Elizabeth and Prince Philip. Multicoloured.
778 30 c. Type **170** 50 40
779 $2 Queen Elizabeth and Prince Philip 2·75 3·25

171 Father playing with Children

1997. Education. Multicoloured.
781 30 c. Type **171** 50 40
782 40 c. Teacher and children with map 60 55
783 60 c. Boys holding sports trophy 85 90
784 65 c. Pupils outside Berkeley Institute 90 1·00
785 80 c. Scientific experiments 1·25 1·40
786 90 c. New graduates 1·40 1·60

172 "Fox's Cottage, St. David's" (Ethel Tucker)

1998. Paintings by Catherine and Ethel Tucker. Multicoloured.
788 30 c. Type **172** 45 40
789 40 c. "East Side, Somerset" 60 60
790 65 c. "Long Bay Road, Somerset" 1·00 1·10
791 $2 "Flatts Village" 2·75 3·00

INDEX

Countries can be quickly located by referring to the index at the end of this volume.

173 Horse and Carriage

1998. Hospitality in Bermuda. Multicoloured.

809	25 c. Type **173**	30	35
810	30 c. Golf club desk	35	40
811	65 c. Chambermaid preparing room	80	85
812	75 c. Kitchen staff under training	90	95
813	80 c. Waiter at beach hotel	1·00	1·10
814	90 c. Nightclub bar	1·10	1·25

174 "Agave attenuata"

1998. Centenary of Botanical Gardens. Multicoloured.

815	30 c. Type **174**	35	40
816	65 c. Bermuda palmetto tree	80	85
817	$1 Banyan tree	1·25	1·40
818	$2 Cedar tree	2·40	2·50

175 Lizard with Fairy Lights (Claire Critchley)

1998. Christmas. Children's Paintings. Multicoloured.

819	25 c. Type **175**	30	35
820	40 c. "Christmas stairway" (Cameron Rowling) (horiz)	50	55

176 Shelly Bay

1999. Bermuda Beaches. Multicoloured.

821	30 c. Type **176**	35	40
822	60 c. Catherine's Bay	70	75
823	65 c. Jobson's Cove	80	85
824	$2 Warwick Long Bay	2·40	2·50

EXPRESS LETTER STAMP

E 1 Queen Elizabeth II

1996.

E1	**E 1**	$22 orange and blue	25·00	26·00

BHOPAL

A state of C. India. Now uses Indian stamps.

12 pies = 1 anna; 16 annas = 1 rupee

3

4

1876. Imperf.

5	**3**	¼ a. black	4·50	8·00
2		½ a. red	13·00	27·00

1878. Imperf or perf.

7	**4**	¼ a. green	7·00	10·00
15		¼ a. red	3·25	1·10
8		½ a. red	4·50	9·00
9		½ a. brown	20·00	30·00

1881. As T **3**, but larger. Imperf or perf.

29	¼ a. black	1·10	75
37	½ a. red	1·10	2·00
47	½ a. black	1·10	1·25
30	1 a. brown	1·00	3·25
31	2 a. blue	75	1·25
32	4 a. yellow	1·25	2·00

13

15

1884. Perf.

49	**13**	¼ a. green	2·75	8·00
76		¼ a. black	70	70

1884. Imperf or perf.

63	**15**	¼ a. green	40	40
65		¼ a. black	30	30
52		½ a. black	1·50	1·00
59		½ a. red	75	55

17

1890. Imperf or perf.

71	**17**	8 a. greenish black	15·00	15·00

19

20 State Arms

1902. Imperf.

90	**19**	¼ a. red	65	2·50
91		½ a. black	60	3·25
92		1 a. brown	1·00	4·25
94		2 a. blue	2·50	16·00
96		4 a. yellow	14·00	40·00
97		8 a. lilac	35·00	90·00
98		1 r. red	50·00	£120

1908. Perf.

100	**20**	1 a. green	2·50	2·50

OFFICIAL STAMPS

1908. As T **20** but inscr "H.H. BEGUM'S SERVICE" optd **SERVICE**.

O301	½ a. green	1·75	10
O302	1 a. red	3·00	35
O307	2 a. blue	3·00	40
O304	4 a. brown	8·50	15

O 4

1930. Type O **4** optd **SERVICE**.

O309	**4**	½ a. green	6·00	75
O310		1 a. red	7·50	15
O311		2 a. blue	7·00	40
O312		4 a. brown	6·00	50

1932. As T **20**, but inscr "POSTAGE" at left and "BHOPAL STATE" at right, optd **SERVICE**.

O313	–	¼ a. orange	2·50	45

1932. As T **20**, but inscr "POSTAGE" at left and "BHOPAL GOVT" at right, optd **SERVICE**.

O314	–	½ a. green	3·50	10
O315	–	1 a. red	6·50	15
O316	–	2 a. blue	6·50	45
O317	–	4 a. brown	5·00	70

1935. Nos O314, etc, surch.

O318	–	¼ a. on ½ a. green	18·00	10·00
O319	–	3 p. on ½ a. green	2·50	2·50
O320	–	¼ a. on 2 a. blue	18·00	12·00
O321	–	3 p. on 2 a. blue	2·75	2·75
O323	–	¼ a. on 4 a. brown	48·00	17·00
O325	–	3 p. on 4 a. brown	2·50	2·25
O326	–	1 a. on ½ a. green	2·50	1·50
O328	–	1 a. on 2 a. blue	70	1·00
O329	–	1 a. on 4 a. brown	3·00	3·25

O 8

1935.

O330	**O 8**	1 a. 3 p. blue and red	2·00	30
O331		1 a. 6 p. blue and red	1·25	30
O332		1 a. 6 p. red	3·50	65

Nos. O331/2 are similar to Type O **8**, but inscr "BHOPAL STATE POSTAGE".

O 9

1936. Type O **9** optd **SERVICE**.

O333	**O 9**	¼ a. yellow	90	20
O335		1 a. red	1·25	10

O 10 The Moti Mahal

1936. As Type O **4** optd **SERVICE**.

O336	**O 10**	½ a. purple and green	70	50
O337	–	2 a. brown and blue	1·25	25
O338	–	2 a. green and violet	5·50	25
O339	–	4 a. blue and brown	2·50	50
O340	–	8 a. purple and blue	3·50	65
O341	–	1 r. blue and purple	10·00	4·75

DESIGNS: 2 a. The Moti Masjid; 4 a. Taj Mahal and Be-Nazir Palaces; 8 a. Ahmadabad Palace; 1 r. Rait Ghat.

Nos. O336 is inscr "BHOPAL GOVT" below the arms, other values have "BHOPAL STATE".

1940. Animal designs, as Type O **10** but inscr "SERVICE" in bottom panel.

O344	–	¼ a. blue (Tiger)	2·50	70
O345	–	1 a. purple (Spotted deer)	14·00	80

1941. As Type O **8** but "SERVICE" inscr instead of optd.

O346	**O 8**	1 a. 3 p. green	70	70

1944. Palaces as Type O **10** but smaller.

O347	½ a. green (Moti Mahal)	85	40
O348	2 a. violet (Moti Masjid)	5·00	2·25
O348c	2 a. purple (Moti Masjid)	1·60	2·00
O349	4 a. brown (Be-Nazir)	3·50	1·10

The 2 a. and 4 a. are inscr "BHOPAL STATE", and the other "BHOPAL GOVT".

O 14 Arms of Bhopal

1944.

O350	**O 14**	3 p. blue	65	20
O351b		9 p. brown	2·00	2·50
O352		1 a. purple	3·25	80
O352b		1 a. violet	6·00	1·75
O353		1½ a. red	1·25	40
O354		3 a. yellow	6·50	7·50
O354d		3 a. brown	65·00	60·00
O355		6 a. red	10·00	28·00

1949. Surch **2 As.** and bars.

O356	**O 14**	2 a. on 1½ a. red	2·25	4·75

1949. Surch **2 As.** and ornaments.

O357	**O 14**	2 a. on 1½ a. red	£475	£500

BHOR

A state of W. India, Bombay district. Now uses Indian stamps.

12 pies = 1 anna; 16 annas = 1 rupee

1

3 Pandit Shankar Rao

1879. Imperf.

1	**1**	½ a. red	1·75	3·50

Similar to T **1**, but rectangular.

2		1 a. red	3·00	5·00

1901. Imperf.

3	**3**	½ a. red	8·00	30·00

BIAFRA

The following stamps were issued by Biafra (the Eastern Region of Nigeria) during the civil war with the Federal Government, 1967–70.

They were in regular use within Biafra from the time when supplies of Nigerian stamps were exhausted, and towards the end of the conflict they began to be used on external mail carried by air via Libreville.

Biafra was overrun by Federal troops on 10 January, 1970, and surrender took place on 15 January.

12 pence = 1 shilling;
20 shillings = 1 pound

1 Map of Republic

5 Weapon Maintenance

1968. Independence. Multicoloured.

1	2d. Type **1**	10	65
2	4d. Arms, flag and date of Independence	10	65
3	1s. Mother and child (17 × 22 mm)	15	1·75

1968. Nos. 172/5 and 177/85 of Nigeria optd **SOVEREIGN BIAFRA** and arms.

4	½d. multicoloured (No. 172)	1·50	3·00
5	1d. multicoloured (No. 173)	1·50	4·50
6	1½d. multicoloured (No. 174)	6·00	9·50
7	2d. multicoloured (No. 175)	20·00	45·00
8	4d. multicoloured (No. 177)	17·00	45·00
9	6d. multicoloured (No. 178)	5·00	9·50
10	9d. blue and red (No. 179)	3·00	2·50
11	1s. multicoloured (No. 180)	60·00	£110
12	1s. 3d. multicoloured (No. 181)	35·00	50·00
13	2s. 6d. multicoloured (No. 182)	1·75	10·00
14	5s. multicoloured (No. 183)	2·25	9·00
15	10s. multicoloured (No. 184)	10·00	32·00
16	£1 multicoloured (No. 185)	10·00	32·00

The overprint on No. 15 does not include **SOVEREIGN**.

1968. 1st Anniv of Independence. Multicoloured.

17	4d. Type **5**	15	10
18	1s. Victim of atrocity	20	20
19	2s. 6d. Nurse and refugees	45	2·50
20	5s. Biafran arms and banknote	60	3·00
21	10s. Orphaned child	1·00	3·50

16 Child in Chains, and Globe

17 Pope Paul VI, Africa, and Papal Arms

1969. 2nd Anniv of Independence. Multicoloured; frame colours given.

35	**16**	2d. orange	1·25	3·75
36		4d. red	1·25	3·75
37		1s. blue	1·75	6·00
38		2s. 6d. green	2·00	12·00

1969. Visit of Pope Paul to Africa. Multicoloured; background colours given.

39	**17**	4d. orange	40	2·50
40	–	6d. blue	55	5·50
41	–	9d. green	75	7·50
42	–	3s. mauve	2·25	12·00

DESIGNS: Pope Paul VI, map of Africa and— 6d. Arms of Vatican; 9d. St. Peter's Basilica; 3s. Statue of St. Peter.

BIJAWAR

A state of Central India. Now uses Indian stamps

12 pies = 1 anna; 16 annas = 1 rupee

1 Maharaja Sarwant Singh 2

1935.

6	1	3 p. brown	2·50	2·75
2		6 p. red	4·00	2·75
3		9 p. violet	4·25	3·25
4		1 a. blue	4·75	3·75
5		2 a. green	5·00	4·75

1937.

11	2	4 a. orange	7·50	55·00
12		6 a. lemon	8·00	55·00
13		8 a. green	8·00	70·00
14		12 a. blue	8·00	70·00
15		1 r. violet	29·00	£110

BOPHUTHATSWANA

The republic of Bophuthatswana was established on 6 December 1977 as one of the "black homelands" constructed from the territory of the Republic of South Africa.

Although this independence did not receive international political recognition we are satisfied that the stamps had "de facto" acceptance as valid for the carriage of mail outside Bophuthatswana.

Bophuthatswana was formally re-incorporated into South Africa on 27 April 1994.

100 cents = 1 rand

1 Hand releasing Dove

1977. Independence. Multicoloured.

1		4 c. Type 1	50	45
2		10 c. Leopard (national emblem)	1·00	70
3		15 c. Coat of arms	1·75	1·00
4		20 c. National flag	2·00	1·40

2 African Buffalo

1977. Tribal Totems. Multicoloured.

5a	1 c. Type 2	20	15
6a	2 c. Bush pig	20	15
7a	3 c. Chacma baboon	20	15
8a	4 c. Leopard	20	10
9a	5 c. Crocodile	20	10
10	6 c. Savanna monkey	20	10
11a	7 c. Lion	30	15
12a	8 c. Spotted hyena	20	15
13	9 c. Cape porcupine	25	15
14	10 c. Aardvark	25	10
15	15 c. Tilapia (fish)	30	15
16	20 c. Hunting dog	25	20
17	25 c. Common duiker	40	30
18	30 c. African elephant	60	35
19	50 c. Python	70	40
20	1 r. Hippopotamus	1·40	1·00
21	2 r. Greater kudu	1·75	2·25

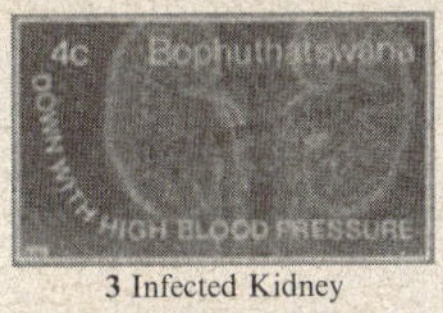

3 Infected Kidney

1978. World Hypertension Month. Multicoloured.

22	4 c. Type 3	50	25
23	10 c. Heart and spoon of salt	70	70
24	15 c. Spoon reflecting skull, knife and fork	1·25	1·25

4 Skull behind Wheel of Car

1978. Road Safety. Multicoloured.

25	4 c. Type 4	70	40
26	10 c. Child knocked off tricycle	1·10	80
27	15 c. Pedestrian stepping in front of car	1·25	1·10
28	20 c. Cyclist ignoring stop sign	1·75	1·75

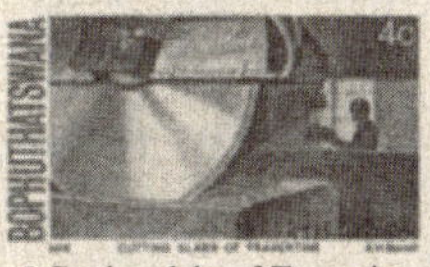

5 Cutting slabs of Travertine

1978. Semi-precious stones. Multicoloured.

29	4 c. Type 5	65	25
30	10 c. Polishing travertine	1·25	85
31	15 c. Sorting semi-precious stones	1·50	1·25
32	20 c. Factory at Taung	2·25	1·60

6 Wright Flyer I

1978. 75th Anniv of First Powered Flight by Wright Brothers.

33	6	10 c. black, blue and red	1·25	1·00
34	–	15 c. black, blue and red	1·75	1·50

DESIGN: 15 c. Orville and Wilbur Wright.

7 Pres. Lucas M. Mangope

9 Kallie Knoetze (South Africa)

8 Drying Germinated Wheat Sorghum

1978. 1st Anniv of Independence. Multicoloured.

35	4 c. Type 7	20	20
36	15 c. Full face portrait of President	60	60

1978. Sorghum Beer-making. Multicoloured.

37	4 c. Type 8	35	20
38	15 c. Cooking the ground grain	95	75
39	20 c. Sieving the liquid	1·10	85
40	25 c. Drinking the beer	1·50	1·25

1979. Knoetze–Tate Boxing Match. Multicoloured.

41	15 c. Type 9	75	75
42	15 c. John Tate (U.S.A.)	75	75

10 Emblem and Drawing of Local Fable (Hendrick Sebapo)

1979. International Year of the Child. Children's Drawings of Local Fables. Multicoloured.

43	4 c. Type 10	25	20
44	15 c. Family with animals (Daisy Morapedi)	35	35
45	20 c. Man's head and landscape (Peter Tladi)	45	45
46	25 c. Old man, boy and donkey (Hendrick Sebapo)	60	60

11 Miner and Molten Platinum

1979. Platinum Industry.

47	11	4 c. multicoloured	25	10
48	–	15 c. multicoloured	35	30
49	–	20 c. multicoloured	45	45
50	–	25 c. black and grey	60	65

DESIGNS: 15 c. Platinum granules and industrial use; 20 c. Telecommunications satellite; 25 c. Jewellery.

12 Cattle

13 Cigarettes forming Cross

1979. Agriculture. Multicoloured.

51	5 c. Type 12	20	20
52	15 c. Picking cotton	25	25
53	20 c. Scientist examining maize	30	30
54	25 c. Catch of fish	35	35

1979. Anti-smoking Campaign.

55	13	5 c. multicoloured	40	20

14 "Landolphia capensis"

15 Pied Babbler

1980. Edible Wild Fruits. Mutlicoloured.

56	5 c. Type 14	15	15
57	10 c. "Vangueria infausta"	30	30
58	15 c. "Bequaertiodendron magalismontanum"	40	40
59	20 c. "Sclerocarya caffra"	55	55

1980. Birds. Multicoloured.

60	5 c. Type 15	30	20
61	10 c. Carmine bee eater	40	35
62	15 c. Shaft-tailed whydah	60	60
63	20 c. Meyer's parrot	70	65

16 Sun City Hotel

17 Deaf Child

1980. Tourism. Sun City. Multicoloured.

64	5 c. Type 16	10	15
65	10 c. Gary Player Country Club	40	30
66	15 c. Casino	45	50
67	20 c. Extravaganza	50	70

1981. Int Year of Disabled Persons. Mult.

68	5 c. Type 17	15	10
69	15 c. Blind child	30	20
70	20 c. Archer in wheelchair	45	35
71	25 c. Tuberculosis X-ray	60	60

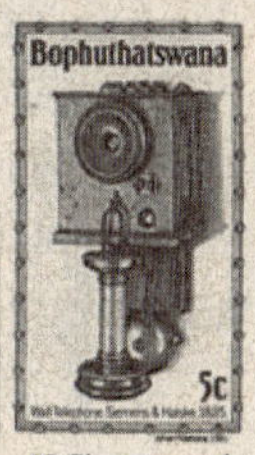

18 "Behold the Lamb of God . . ."

19 Siemens and Halske Wall Telephone, 1885

1981. Easter. Multicoloured.

72	5 c. Type 18	10	10
73	15 c. Bread ("I am the bread of life")	25	25
74	20 c. Shepherd ("I am the good shepherd")	35	35
75	25 c. Wheatfield ("Unless a grain of wheat falls into the earth and dies . . .")	45	45

1981. History of the Telephone (1st series). Multicoloured.

76	5 c. Type 19	10	10
77	15 c. Ericsson telephone, 1895	25	25
78	20 c. Hasler telephone, 1900	35	35
79	25 c. Mix and Genest wall telephone, 1904	45	45

See also Nos. 92/5, 108/11 and 146/9.

20 "Themeda triandra"

21 Boy Scout

1981. Indigenous Grasses (1st series). Multicoloured.

80	5 c. Type 20	10	10
81	15 c. "Rhynchelytrum repens"	25	25
82	20 c. "Eragrostis capensis"	30	30
83	25 c. "Monocymbium ceresiiforme"	40	40

See also Nos. 116/19.

1982. 75th Anniv of Boy Scout Movement. Multicoloured.

84	5 c. Type 21	15	10
85	15 c. Mafeking siege stamps	35	35
86	20 c. Original cadet	40	40
87	25 c. Lord Baden-Powell	45	45

22 Jesus arriving at Bethany (John 12:1)

23 Ericsson Telephone, 1878

1982. Easter. Multicoloured.

88	15 c. Type 22	25	25
89	20 c. Jesus sending disciples for donkey (Matthew 21:1,2)	30	30
90	25 c. Disciples taking donkey (Mark 11:5,6)	40	40
91	30 c. Disciples with donkey and foal (Matthew 21:7)	45	45

1982. History of the Telephone (2nd series). Multicoloured.

92	8 c. Type 23	15	10
93	15 c. Ericsson telephone, 1885	20	20
94	20 c. Ericsson telephone, 1893	20	20
95	25 c. Siemens and Halske telephone, 1898	30	30

24 Old Parliament Building

1982. 5th Anniv of Independence. Multicoloured.

96	8 c. Type 24	10	10
97	15 c. New government offices	20	20
98	20 c. University, Mmabatho	25	25
99	25 c. Civic Centre, Mmabatho	30	30

25 White Rhinoceros

1983. Pilanesberg Nature Reserve. Multicoloured.

100	8 c. Type 25	30	10
101	20 c. Common zebras	40	30
102	25 c. Sable antelope	40	35
103	40 c. Hartebeest	60	60

26 Disciples bringing Donkeys to Jesus (Matthew 21:7)

1983. Easter. Palm Sunday. Multicoloured.

104	8 c. Type 26	10	10
105	20 c. Jesus stroking colt (Mark 11:7)	30	30
106	25 c. Jesus enters Jerusalem on donkey (Matthew 21:8)	35	35
107	40 c. Crowd welcoming Jesus (Mark 11:9)	60	60

1983. History of the Telephone (3rd series). Multicoloured.

108	10 c. A.T.M. table telephone c. 1920	15	10
109	20 c. A/S Elektrisk wall telephone, c. 1900	30	30
110	25 c. Ericsson wall telephone c. 1900	35	35
111	40 c. Ericsson wall telephone c. 1900 (different)	60	60

27 Kori Bustard

1983. Birds of the Veld. Multicoloured.

112	10 c. Type **27**	30	20
113	20 c. Little black bustard	45	45
114	25 c. Crested bustard	55	55
115	40 c. Barrow's bustard	70	80

1984. Indigenous Grasses (2nd series). As T **20**. Multicoloured.

116	10 c. "Panicum maximum"	15	10
117	20 c. "Hyparrhenia dregeana"	25	20
118	25 c. "Cenchrus ciliaris"	35	35
119	40 c. "Urochloa brachyura"	60	70

28 Money-lenders in the Temple (Mark 11:11)

1984. Easter. Multicoloured.

120	10 c. Type **28**	15	10
121	20 c. Jesus driving the money-lenders from the Temple (Mark 11:15)	25	20
122	25 c. Jesus and fig tree (Matthew 21:9)	35	35
123	40 c. The withering of the fig tree (Matthew 21:9)	60	70

29 Car Upholstery, Ga-Rankuwa

1984. Industries. Multicoloured.

124	1 c. Textile mill	10	10
125	2 c. Sewing sacks, Selosesha	10	10
126	3 c. Ceramic tiles, Babelegi	10	10
127	4 c. Sheepskin car seat covers	10	10
128	5 c. Crossbow manufacture	15	10
129	6 c. Automobile parts, Babelegi	15	10
130	7 c. Hosiery, Babelegi	15	10
131	8 c. Specialised bicycle factory, Babelegi	30	10
132	9 c. Lawn mower assembly line	30	15
133	10 c. Dress factory, Thaba 'Nchu	20	10
134	11 c. Molten platinum	60	20
135	12 c. Type **29**	40	15
136	14 c. Maize mill, Mafeking	50	15
137	15 c. Plastic bags, Babelegi	25	15
137b	16 c. Brick factory, Mmabatho	60	15
137c	18 c. Cutlery manufacturing, Mogwase	60	15
138	20 c. Men's clothing, Babelegi	25	15
138b	21 c. Welding bus chassis	50	50
138c	21 c. Fitting engine to bus chassis	50	50
138d	21 c. Bus body construction	50	50
138e	21 c. Spraying and finishing bus	50	50
138f	21 c. Finished bus	50	50
139	25 c. Chromium plating pram parts	30	20
140	30 c. Spray painting metal beds	40	25
141	50 c. Milk processing plant	65	40
142	1 r. Modern printing works	1·25	75
143	2 r. Industrial complex, Babelegi	3·00	2·75

1984. History of the Telephone (4th series). As T **19**. Multicoloured.

146	11 c. Schuchhardt table telephone, 1905	15	10
147	20 c. Siemens wall telephone, 1925	25	20
148	25 c. Ericsson table telephone, 1900	30	30
149	30 c. Oki table telephone, 1930	40	50

MINIMUM PRICE

The minimum price quoted is 10p which represents a handling charge rather than a basis for valuing common stamps. For further notes about prices see introductory pages.

30 Yellow-throated Plated Lizard

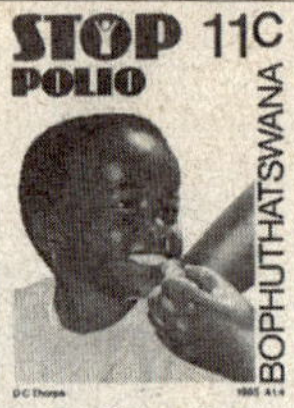

31 Giving Oral Vaccine against Polio

1984. Lizards. Multicoloured.

150	11 c. Type **30**	20	10
151	25 c. Transvaal girdled lizard	40	30
152	30 c. Ocellated sand lizard	45	40
153	45 c. Bibron's thick-toed gecko	65	60

1985. Health. Multicoloured.

154	11 c. Type **31**	35	10
155	25 c. Vaccinating against measles	45	30
156	30 c. Examining child for diphtheria	50	40
157	50 c. Examining child for whooping cough	70	65

32 Chief Montshiwa of Barolong booRatshidi

34 "Faurea saligna" and planting Sapling

33 The Sick flock to Jesus in the Temple (Matthew, 21:41)

1985. Centenary of Mafeking.

158 **32**	11 c. black, grey and orange	20	10
159 –	25 c. black, grey and blue	40	30

DESIGN: 25 c. Sir Charles Warren.

1985. Easter. Multicoloured.

160	12 c. Type **33**	20	10
161	25 c. Jesus cures the sick (Matthew 21:14)	30	20
162	30 c. Children praising Jesus (Matthew 21:15)	35	30
163	50 c. Community leaders discussing Jesus's acceptance of praise (Matthew 21:15, 16)	50	60

1985. Tree Conservation. Multicoloured.

164	12 c. Type **34**	20	10
165	25 c. "Boscia albitrunca" and kudu	25	20
166	30 c. "Erythrina lysistemon" and mariqua sunbird	35	30
167	50 c. "Bequaertiondendron magalismontanum" and bee	55	55

35 Jesus at Mary and Martha's, Bethany (John 12:2)

1986. Easter. Multicoloured.

168	12 c. Type **35**	25	10
169	20 c. Mary anointing Jesus's feet (John 12:3)	30	20
170	25 c. Mary drying Jesus's feet with her hair (John 12:3)	35	25
171	30 c. Disciple condemns Mary for anointing Jesus's head with oil (Matthew 26:7)	45	50

36 "Wesleyan Mission Station and Residence of Moroka, Chief of the Barolong, 1834" (C. D. Bell)

1986. Paintings of Thaba 'Nchu. Multicoloured.

172	14 c. Type **36**	20	15
173	20 c. "James Archbell's Congregation, 1834" (Charles Davidson Bell)	30	25
174	25 c. "Mission Station at Thaba 'Nchu, 1850" (Thomas Baines)	40	40

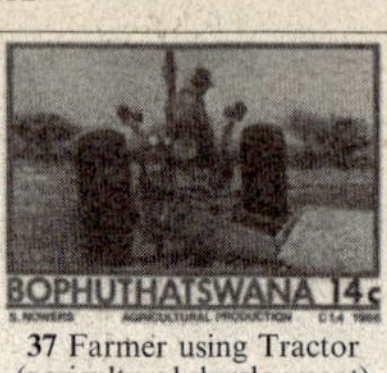

37 Farmer using Tractor (agricultural development)

1986. Temisano Development Project. Mult.

175	14 c. Type **37**	20	10
176	20 c. Children at school (community development)	30	20
177	25 c. Repairing engine (training)	35	30
178	30 c. Grain elevator (secondary industries)	50	50

38 Stewardesses and Cessna Citation II

1986. "B.O.P." Airways. Multicoloured.

179	14 c. Type **38**	25	10
180	20 c. Passengers disembarking from Boeing 707	40	20
181	25 c. Mmabatho International Airport	50	35
182	30 c. Cessna Citation II	60	50

39 Netball

40 "Berkheya zeyheri"

1987. Sports. Multicoloured.

183	14 c. Type **39**	20	15
184	20 c. Tennis	30	30
185	25 c. Football	30	30
186	30 c. Athletics	45	50

1987. Wild Flowers. Multicoloured.

187	16 c. Type **40**	25	15
188	20 c. "Plumbago auriculata"	35	35
189	25 c. "Pterodiscus speciosus"	35	35
190	30 c. "Gazania krebsiana"	40	50

41 E. M. Mokgoko Farmer Training Centre

1987. Tertiary Education. Multicoloured.

191	16 c. Type **41**	20	15
192	20 c. Main lecture block, University of Bophuthatswana	30	35
193	25 c. Manpower Centre	30	35
194	30 c. Hotel Training School	30	50

42 Posts

1987. 10th Anniv of Independence. Communications. Multicoloured.

195	16 c. Type **42**	25	15
196	30 c. Telephone	35	35
197	40 c. Radio	35	35
198	50 c. Television	40	50

43 Jesus entering Jerusalem on Donkey (John 12:12–14)

1988. Easter. Multicoloured.

199	16 c. Type **43**	25	15
200	30 c. Judas negotiating with chief priests (Mark 14:10–11)	35	35
201	40 c. Jesus washing the disciples' feet (John 13:5)	35	35
202	50 c. Jesus handing bread to Judas (John 13:26)	40	50

44 Environment Education

1988. National Parks Board. Multicoloured.

203	16 c. Type **44**	25	15
204	30 c. Rhinoceros (Conservation)	40	40
205	40 c. Catering workers	40	40
206	50 c. Cheetahs (Tourism)	55	65

45 Sunflowers

1988. Crops. Multicoloured.

207	16 c. Type **45**	25	15
208	30 c. Peanuts	35	35
209	40 c. Cotton	45	45
210	50 c. Cabbages	60	60

46 Ngotwane Dam

1988. Dams. Multicoloured.

211	16 c. Type **46**	30	20
212	30 c. Groothoek Dam	50	50
213	40 c. Sehujwane Dam	50	50
214	50 c. Molatedi Dam	70	70

47 The Last Supper (Matthew 26:26)

1989. Easter. Multicoloured.

215	16 c. Type **47**	35	20
216	30 c. Jesus praying in Garden of Gethsemane (Matthew 26:39)	50	50
217	40 c. Judas kissing Jesus (Mark 14:45)	60	60
218	50 c. Peter severing ear of High Priest's slave (John 18:10)	75	90

48 Cock (Thembi Atong)

49 Black-shouldered Kite

1989. Children's Art. Designs depicting winning entries in National Children's Day Art Competition.

219	18 c. Type **48**	30	20
220	30 c. Traditional thatched hut (Muhammad Mahri)	40	40
221	40 c. Airplane, telephone wires and houses (Tshepo Mashokwi)	45	45
222	50 c. City scene (Miles Brown)	50	60

1989. Birds of Prey. Paintings by Claude Finch-Davies. Multicoloured.

223	18 c. Type **49**	70	30
224	30 c. Pale chanting goshawk	90	75
225	40 c. Lesser kestrel	1·25	1·10
226	50 c. Short-toed eagle	1·60	1·50

50 Bilobial House

1989. Traditional Houses. Multicoloured.

227	18 c. Type **50**	25	20
228	30 c. House with courtyards at front and side	35	35
229	40 c. House with conical roof	35	35
230	50 c. House with rounded roof	40	50

51 Early Learning Schemes

1990. Community Services. Multicoloured.
231 18 c. Type **51** 25 20
232 30 c. Clinics 35 35
233 40 c. Libraries 35 35
234 50 c. Hospitals 40 45

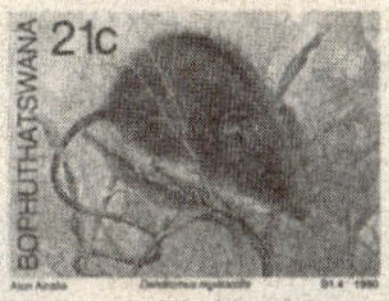

52 Lesser Climbing Mouse

1990. Small Mammals. Multicoloured.
235 21 c. Type **52** 30 20
236 30 c. Zorilla 40 40
237 40 c. Transvaal elephant shrew . . 60 60
238 50 c. Large-toothed rock hyrax . . 80 85

53 Variegated Sandgrouse 54 Basketry

1990. Sandgrouse. Paintings by Claude Finch-Davies. Multicoloured.
239 21 c. Type **53** 80 30
240 35 c. Double-banded sandgrouse . . 90 75
241 40 c. Namaqua sandgrouse . . . 1·10 90
242 50 c. Yellow-throated sand-grouse . . . . 1·40 1·40

1990. Traditional Crafts. Multicoloured.
243 21 c. Type **54** 35 20
244 35 c. Training 50 50
245 40 c. Beer making 55 55
246 50 c. Pottery 60 70

55 Sud Aviation Alouette II Helicopter 56 Wild Custard Apple

1990. Bophuthatswana Air Force. Multicoloured.
247 21 c. Type **55** 80 80
248 21 c. MBB-Kawasaki BK-117 helicopter 80 80
249 21 c. Pilatus PC-7 turbo trainer . . 80 80
250 21 c. Pilatus PC-6 . . . . 80 80
251 21 c. CASA C-212 Aviocar . . . 80 80

1991. Edible Wild Fruit. Multicoloured.
252 21 c. Type **56** 35 25
253 35 c. Spine-leaved monkey orange 50 50
254 40 c. Sycamore fig 55 55
255 50 c. Kei apple 60 70

57 Arrest of Jesus (Mark 14:46)

1991. Easter. Multicoloured.
256 21 c. Type **57** 35 25
257 35 c. First trial by the Sanhedrin (Mark 14:53) 50 50
258 40 c. Assault and derision of Jesus after sentence (Mark 14:65) 55 55
259 50 c. Servant girl recognizing Peter (Mark 14:67) 60 70

58 Class 7A Locomotive No. 350, 1897 59 Caneiro Chart, 1502

1991. Steam Locomotives. Multicoloured.
260 25 c. Class 6A locomotive No. 194, 1897, trucks and caboose (71 × 25 mm) 65 55
261 40 c. Type **58** 85 75
262 50 c. Double-boiler Class 6Z locomotives pulling Cecil Rhodes's funeral train (71 × 25 mm) 95 95
263 60 c. Class 8 locomotive at Mafeking station, 1904 . . 1·25 1·25

1991. Old Maps (1st series). Multicoloured.
264 25 c. Type **59** 65 40
265 40 c. Cantino Chart, 1502 . . 95 85
266 50 c. Giovanni Contarini's map, 1506 . . . . 1·00 1·00
267 60 c. Martin Waldseemuller's map, 1507 . . . . 1·10 1·25
See also Nos. 268/71 and 297/300.

60 Fracanzano Map, 1508

1992. Old Maps (2nd series). Multicoloured.
268 27 c. Type **60** 65 40
269 45 c. Martin Waldseemuller's map (from edition of Ptolemy), 1513 . . . . 90 85
270 65 c. Section of Waldseemuller's woodcut "Carta Marina Navigatora Portugallan Navigationes", 1516 . . . 1·00 1·00
271 85 c. Map from Laurent Fries's "Geographia", 1522 . . . 1·10 1·25

61 Delivery of Jesus to Pilate (Mark 15:1)

1992. Easter. Multicoloured.
272 27 c. Type **61** 25 20
273 45 c. Scourging of Jesus (Mark 15:15) 40 40
274 65 c. Placing crown of thorns on Jesus's head (Mark 15:17–18) 50 60
275 85 c. Soldiers mocking Jesus (Mark 15:19) 60 70

62 Sweet Thorn

1992. Acacia Trees. Multicoloured.
276 35 c. Type **62** 30 25
277 70 c. Camel thorn 50 50
278 90 c. Umbrella thorn 60 70
279 1 r. 05 Black thorn 70 85

63 View of Palace across Lake 64 Light Sussex

1992. The Lost City Complex, Sun City. Mult.
280 35 c. Type **63** 35 40
281 35 c. Palace facade 35 40
282 35 c. Palace porte cochere . . 35 40
283 35 c. Palace lobby 35 40
284 35 c. Tusk Bar, Palace . . . 35 40

1993. Chickens. Multicoloured.
285 35 c. Type **64** 30 25
286 70 c. Rhode Island red . . . 50 50
287 90 c. Brown leghorn 60 70
288 1 r. 05 White leghorn 70 85

65 Pilate offering Release of Barabbas (Luke 23:25)

1993. Easter. Multicoloured.
289 35 c. Type **65** 45 25
290 70 c. Jesus falling under cross (John 19:17) 75 75
291 90 c. Simon of Cyrene carrying cross (Mark 15:21) . . . . . 90 1·00
292 1 r. 05 Jesus being nailed to cross (Mark 15:23) . . . . 1·10 1·25

66 Mafeking Locomotive Shed, 1933 (½-size illustration)

1993. Steam Locomotives (2nd series). Multicoloured.
293 45 c. Type **66** 55 55
294 65 c. Rhodesian Railways steam locomotive No. 5, 1901 (34 × 25 mm) 65 65
295 85 c. Class 16B locomotive pulling "White Train" during visit of Prince George, 1934 . 85 85
296 1 r. 05 Class 19D locomotive, 1923 (34 × 25 mm) . . . . . 1·10 1·25

67 Sebastian Munster's Map (from edition of Ptolemy), 1540

1993. Old Maps (3rd series). Multicoloured.
298 45 c. Type **67** 50 40
299 65 c. Jacopo Gastaldi's map, 1564 . . . . 65 65
300 85 c. Map from Mercator's "Atlas", 1595 . . . . 75 75
301 1 r. 05 Map from Ortelius's "Theatrum Orbis Terrarum", 1570 . . . . 90 1·00

68 Crucifixion (Luke 23:33)

1994. Easter. Multicoloured.
302 35 c. Type **68** 45 45
303 65 c. Soldiers and Jews mocking Jesus (Luke 23:35–36) . . . 75 75
304 85 c. Soldier offering Jesus vinegar (Luke 23:36) 85 85
305 1 r. 05 Jesus on cross and charge notice (Luke 23:38) . . . . 1·25 1·25

BOTSWANA

Formerly Bechuanaland Protectorate, attained independence on 30 September 1966, and changed its name to Botswana.

1966. 100 cents = 1 rand.
1976. 100 thebe = 1 pula.

47 National Assembly Building

1966. Independence. Multicoloured.
202 2½ c. Type **47** 15 10
203 5 c. Abattoir, Lobatsi 20 10
204 15 c. National Airways Douglas DC-3 . . . . 65 20
205 35 c. State House, Gaberones . . 40 30

INDEX
Countries can be quickly located by referring to the index at the end of this volume.

1966. Nos. 168/81 of Bechuanaland optd **REPUBLIC OF BOTSWANA.**
206 **28** 1 c. multicoloured 25 10
207 – 2 c. orange, black and olive 30 40
208 – 2½ c. multicoloured 30 10
209 – 3½ c. multicoloured 40 15
210 – 5 c. multicoloured . . . . 40 1·00
211 – 7½ c. multicoloured . . . . 40 1·25
212 – 10 c. multicoloured 60 20
213 – 12½ c. multicoloured . . . 2·75 2·50
214 – 20 c. brown and drab . . . 75 1·00
215 – 25 c. sepia and lemon . . . 75 1·75
216 – 35 c. blue and orange . . . 85 2·00
217 – 50 c. sepia and olive . . . 50 70
218 – 1 r. black and brown . . . 75 1·25
219 – 2 r. brown and turquoise . 1·25 2·50

52 Golden Oriole

1967. Multicoloured.
220 1 c. Type **52** 30 15
221 2 c. Hoopoe 40 70
222 3 c. Groundscraper thrush . . 55 10
223 4 c. Cordon-bleu ("Blue Waxbill") 55 10
224 5 c. Secretary bird 55 10
225 7 c. Yellow-billed hornbill . . 60 90
226 10 c. Burchell's gonolek ("Crimson-breasted Strike") 60 15
227 15 c. Malachite kingfisher . . 8·00 2·75
228 20 c. African fish eagle . . . 8·00 1·75
229 25 c. Go-away bird ("Grey Loerie") . . . . 4·50 1·25
230 35 c. Scimitar-bill . . . . . 7·00 2·00
231 50 c. Comb duck . . . . . . 3·25 2·50
232 1 r. Levaillant's barbet . . . 8·00 3·50
233 2 r. Didric cuckoo . . . . . 9·50 16·00

66 Students and University

1967. 1st Conferment of University Degrees.
234 **66** 3 c. sepia, blue and orange 10 10
235 7 c. sepia, blue and turquoise 10 10
236 15 c. sepia, blue and red . 10 10
237 35 c. sepia, blue and violet 20 20

67 Bushbuck

1967. Chobe Game Reserve. Multicoloured.
238 3 c. Type **67** 10 20
239 7 c. Sable Antelope 15 30
240 35 c. Fishing on the Chobe River 80 1·10

70 Arms of Botswana and Human Rights Emblem

1968. Human Rights Year.
241 **70** 3 c. multicoloured 10 10
242 – 15 c. multicoloured 25 40
243 – 25 c. multicoloured 25 50
The designs of Nos. 242/3 are similar, but are arranged differently.

73 Eland and Giraffe Rock Paintings, Tsodilo Hills

1968. Opening of National Museum and Art Gallery. Multicoloured.
244 3 c. Type **73** 20 20
245 7 c. Girl wearing ceremonial beads 35 20
246 10 c. "Baobab Trees" (Thomas Baines) 35 30
247 15 c. National Museum and art gallery (72 × 19 mm) . . . . 50 1·40
No. 245 is vert, and the size is 31 × 48 mm.

77 African Family, and Star over Village

1968. Christmas.

249	77	1 c. multicoloured	10	10
250		2 c. multicoloured	10	10
251		5 c. multicoloured	10	10
252		25 c. multicoloured	15	50

78 Scout, Lion and Badge in frame

1969. 22nd World Scout Conference, Helsinki. Mult.

253	3 c. Type **78**	50	30
254	15 c. Scouts cooking over open fire	75	1·25
255	25 c. Scouts around camp fire	75	1·25

The 15 c. is vert.

81 Woman, Child and Christmas Star

82 Diamond Treatment Plant, Orapa

1969. Christmas.

256	81	1 c. blue and brown	10	10
257		2 c. olive and brown	10	10
258		4 c. yellow and brown	10	10
259		35 c. brown and violet	20	20

1970. Developing Botswana. Multicoloured.

261	3 c. Type **82**	70	20
262	7 c. Copper-nickel mining	95	20
263	10 c. Copper-nickel mine, Selebi-Pikwe (horiz)	1·25	25
264	35 c. Orapa Diamond mine and diamonds (horiz)	2·75	1·60

83 Mr. Micawber ("David Copperfield")

1970. Death Centenary of Charles Dickens. Mult.

265	3 c. Type **83**	25	10
266	7 c. Scrooge ("A Christmas Carol")	35	10
267	15 c. Fagin ("Oliver Twist")	60	40
268	25 c. Bill Sykes ("Oliver Twist")	90	60

84 U.N. Building and Emblem

1970. 25th Anniv of United Nations.

270	84	15 c. blue, brown and silver	70	30

85 Crocodile

1970. Christmas. Multicoloured.

271	1 c. Type **85**	10	10
272	2 c. Giraffe	10	10
273	7 c. Elephant	15	10
274	25 c. Rhinoceros	60	80

86 Sorghum

1971. Important Crops. Multicoloured.

276	3 c. Type **86**	15	10
277	7 c. Millet	20	10
278	10 c. Maize	20	10
279	35 c. Groundnuts	70	40

87 Map and Head of Cow

88 King bringing Gift of Gold

1971. 5th Anniv of Independence.

280	87	3 c. black, brown and green	10	10
281	–	4 c. black, light blue and blue	10	10
282	–	7 c. black and orange	20	15
283	–	10 c. multicoloured	25	15
284	–	20 c. multicoloured	80	2·00

DESIGNS: 4 c. Map and cogs; 7 c. Map and common zebra; 10 c. Map and sorghum stalk crossed by tusk; 20 c. Arms and map of Botswana.

1971. Christmas. Multicoloured.

285	2 c. Type **88**	10	10
286	3 c. King bringing frankincense	10	10
287	7 c. King bringing myrrh	10	10
288	20 c. Three Kings behold the star	35	65

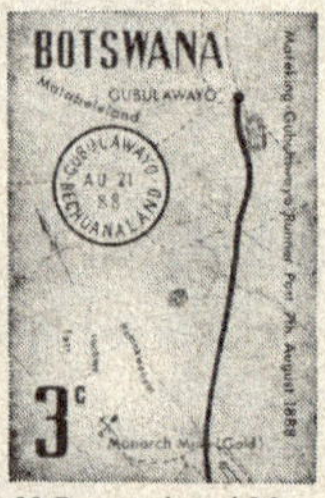

89 Orion

90 Postmark and Map

1972. "Night Sky".

290	89	3 c. blue, black and red	75	20
291	–	7 c. blue, black and yellow	1·10	60
292	–	10 c. green, black and orange	1·25	85
293	–	20 c. blue, black and green	1·75	2·75

CONSTELLATIONS: 7 c. The Scorpion; 10 c. The Centaur; 20 c. The Cross.

1972. Mafeking–Gubulawayo Runner Post. Mult.

294	3 c. Type **90**	30	10
295	4 c. Bechuanaland stamp and map	30	35
296	7 c. Runners and map	45	50
297	20 c. Mafeking postmark and map	1·10	1·25

For these designs with changed inscription see Nos. 652/5.

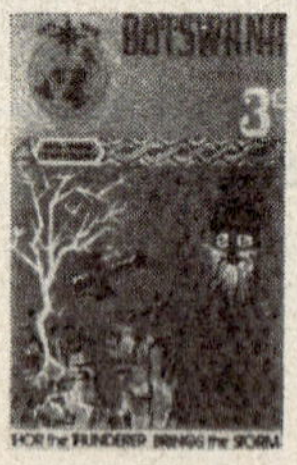

91 Cross, Map and Bells

92 Thor

1972. Christmas. Each with Cross and Map. Mult.

299	2 c. Type **91**	10	75
300	3 c. Cross, map and candle	10	10
301	7 c. Cross, map and Christmas tree	15	25
302	20 c. Cross, map, star and holly	40	85

1973. Centenary of I.M.O./W.M.O. Norse Myths. Multicoloured.

304	3 c. Type **92**	20	10
305	4 c. Sun God's chariot (horiz)	25	15
306	7 c. Ymir, the frost giant	30	15
307	20 c. Odin and Sleipnir (horiz)	75	70

93 Livingstone and River Scene

1973. Death Centenary of Dr. Livingstone. Mult.

308	3 c. Type **93**	20	10
309	20 c. Livingstone meeting Stanley	90	80

94 Donkey and Foal at Village Trough

1973. Christmas. Multicoloured.

310	3 c. Type **94**	10	10
311	4 c. Shepherd and flock (horiz)	10	10
312	7 c. Mother and Child	10	10
313	20 c. Kgotla meeting (horiz)	40	80

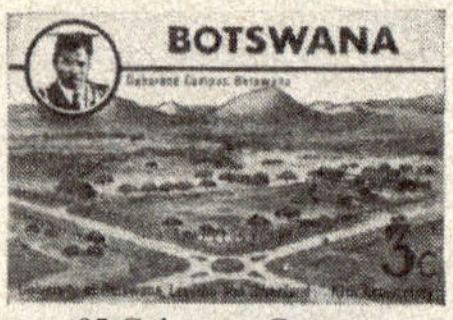

95 Gaborone Campus

1974. 10th Anniv of University of Botswana, Lesotho and Swaziland. Multicoloured.

314	3 c. Type **95**	10	10
315	7 c. Kwaluseni Campus	10	10
316	20 c. Roma Campus	15	20
317	35 c. Map and flags of the three countries	20	35

96 Methods of Mail Transport

1974. Centenary of U.P.U. Multicoloured.

318	2 c. Type **96**	55	35
319	3 c. Post Office, Palapye, circa 1889	55	35
320	7 c. Bechuanaland Police Camel Post, circa 1900	95	70
321	20 c. Hawker Siddeley H.S.748 and De Havilland D.H.9 mail planes of 1920 and 1974	2·75	2·50

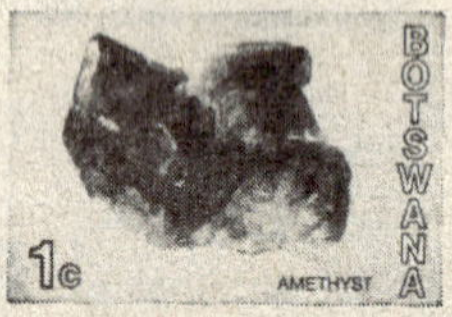

97 Amethyst

1974. Botswana Minerals. Multicoloured.

322	1 c. Type **97**	60	80
323	2 c. Agate–"Botswana Pink"	60	80
324	3 c. Quartz	65	80
325	4 c. Copper nickel	70	60
326	5 c. Moss agate	70	1·00
327	7 c. Agate	80	60
328	10 c. Stilbite	1·60	65
329	15 c. Moshaneng banded marble	2·00	3·00
330	20 c. Gem diamonds	4·00	3·25
331	25 c. Chrysotile	5·00	2·50
332	35 c. Jasper	5·00	3·75
333	50 c. Moss quartz	4·50	7·00
334	1 r. Citrine	7·50	10·00
335	2 r. Chalcopyrite	20·00	20·00

98 "Stapelia variegata"

99 President Sir Seretse Khama

1974. Christmas. Multicoloured.

336	2 c. Type **98**	20	40
337	7 c. "Hibiscus lunarifolius"	50	20
338	15 c. "Ceratotheca triloba"	80	1·50
339	20 c. "Nerine laticoma"	90	1·75

1975. 10th Anniv of Self-Government.

341	99	4 c. multicoloured	10	10
342		10 c. multicoloured	15	10
343		20 c. multicoloured	25	25
344		35 c. multicoloured	45	50

100 Ostrich

1975. Rock Paintings, Tsodilo Hills. Multicoloured.

346	4 c. Type **100**	80	10
347	10 c. White rhinoceros	1·40	10
348	25 c. Spotted hyena	2·75	55
349	35 c. Scorpion	2·75	1·10

101 Map of British Bechuanaland, 1885

102 "Aloe marlothii"

1975. Anniversaries. Multicoloured.

351	6 c. Type **101**	30	20
352	10 c. Chief Khama, 1875	40	15
353	25 c. Chiefs Sebele, Bathoen and Khama, 1895 (horiz)	80	75

EVENTS: 6 c. 90th anniv of Protectorate; 10 c. Centenary of Khama's accession; 25 c. 80th anniv of Chiefs' visit to London.

1975. Christmas. Aloes. Multicoloured.

354	3 c. Type **102**	30	10
355	10c. "Aloe lutescens"	75	20
356	15 c. "Aloe zebrina"	1·40	1·75
357	25 c. "Aloe littoralis"	1·60	3·00

103 Drum

1976. Traditional Musical Instruments. Mult.

358	4 c. Type **103**	15	10
359	10 c. Hand piano	20	10
360	15 c. Segankuru (violin)	25	50
361	25 c. Kudu signal horn	30	1·25

104 One Pula Note

1976. First National Currency. Multicoloured.

362	4 c. Type **104**	15	10
363	10 c. Two pula note	20	10
364	15 c. Five pula note	35	20
365	25 c. Ten pula note	45	45

1976. Nos. 322/35 surch in new currency.

367	1 t. on 1 c. multicoloured	2·00	70
368	2 t. on 2 c. multicoloured	2·00	80
369	3 t. on 3 c. multicoloured	1·50	60
370	4 t. on 4 c. multicoloured	2·50	40
371	5 t. on 5 c. multicoloured	2·50	40
372	7 t. on 7 c. multicoloured	1·25	2·00
373	10 t. on 10 c. multicoloured	1·25	80
374	15 t. on 15 c. multicoloured	4·25	1·50
375	20 t. on 20 c. multicoloured	7·50	80
376	25 t. on 25 c. multicoloured	5·00	1·25
377	35 t. on 35 c. multicoloured	4·50	3·50
378	50 t. on 50 c. multicoloured	7·00	8·50
379	1 p. on 1 r. multicoloured	8·00	9·00
380	2 p. on 2 r. multicoloured	11·00	11·00

106 Botswana Cattle

1976. 10th Anniv of Independence. Multicoloured.

381	4 t. Type **106**	15	10
382	10 t. Deer, Okavango Delta (vert)	30	10
383	15 t. School and pupils	40	40
384	25 t. Rural weaving (vert)	55	50
385	35 t. Miner (vert)	1·25	85

107 "Colophospermum mopane"

1976. Christmas. Trees. Multicoloured.

386	3 t. Type **107**	15	10
387	4 t. "Baikiaea plurijuga"	15	10
388	10 t. "Sterculia rogersii"	40	15
389	25 t. "Acacia nilotica"	80	50
390	40 t. "Kigelia africana"	1·25	1·25

108 Coronation Coach

1977. Silver Jubilee. Multicoloured.

391	4 t. The Queen and Sir Seretse Khama	10	10
392	25 t. Type **108**	20	15
393	40 t. The Recognition	35	80

109 African Clawless Otter

1977. Diminishing Species. Multicoloured.

394	3 t. Type **109**	2·00	30
395	4 t. Serval	2·00	30
396	10 t. Bat-eared fox	3·00	40
397	25 t. Temminck's ground pangolin	8·00	1·75
398	40 t. Brown hyena	9·50	5·50

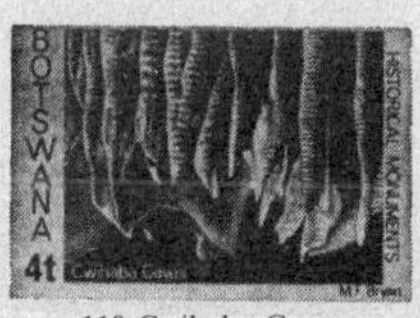

110 Cwihaba Caves

1977. Historical Monuments. Multicoloured.

399	4 t. Type **110**	25	10
400	5 t. Khama Memorial	25	10
401	15 t. Green's Tree	40	40
402	20 t. Mmajojo Ruins	40	45
403	25 t. Ancient morabaraba board	40	50
404	35 t. Matsieng's footprint	55	60

111 "Hypoxis nitida"

112 Little Black Bustard

1977. Christmas. Lilies. Multicoloured.

406	3 t. Type **111**	15	10
407	5 t. "Haemanthus magnificus"	15	10
408	10 t. "Boophane disticha"	20	10
409	25 t. "Vellozia retinervis"	40	55
410	40 t. "Ammocharis coranica"	55	1·25

1978. Birds. Multicoloured.

411	1 t. Type **112**	30	1·25
412	2 t. Marabou stork	30	1·25
413	3 t. Green wood hoopoe	30	85
414	4 t. Carmine bee eater	30	75
415	5 t. African jacana	30	40
416	7 t. African paradise flycatcher	40	2·00
417	10 t. Bennett's woodpecker	1·75	60
418	15 t. Red bishop	70	2·00
419	20 t. Crowned plover	1·00	2·00
420	25 t. Giant kingfisher	70	2·00
421	30 t. White-faced whistling duck	70	70
422	35 t. Green heron	70	2·75
423	45 t. Black-headed heron	70	2·25
424	50 t. Spotted eagle owl	6·00	4·50
425	1 p. Gabar goshawk	2·50	4·50
426	2 p. Martial eagle	3·25	8·00
427	5 p. Saddle-bill stork	12·00	16·00

113 Tawana making Kaross

1978. Okavango Delta. Multicoloured.

428	4 t. Type **113**	15	10
429	5 t. Tribe localities	15	10
430	15 t. Bushman collecting roots	35	40
431	20 t. Herero woman milking	40	55
432	25 t. Yei poling "mokoro" (canoe)	50	60
433	35 t. Mbukushu fishing	65	1·50

114 "Caralluma lutea"

115 Sip Well

1978. Christmas. Flowers. Multicoloured.

435	5 t. Type **114**	35	10
436	10 t. "Hoodia lugardii"	50	15
437	15 t. "Ipomoea transvaalensis"	90	55
438	25 t. "Ansellia gigantea"	1·10	70

1979. Water Development. Multicoloured.

439	3 t. Type **115**	10	10
440	5 t. Watering pit	15	10
441	10 t. Hand dug well	15	10
442	22 t. Windmill	30	30
443	50 t. Modern drilling rig	55	55

116 Pottery

1979. Handicrafts. Multicoloured.

444	5 t. Type **116**	10	10
445	10 t. Clay modelling	15	10
446	25 t. Basketry	30	25
447	40 t. Beadwork	50	50

117 British Bechuanaland 1885 1d. Stamp and Sir Rowland Hill

1979. Death Centenary of Sir Rowland Hill. Mult.

449	5 t. Type **117**	20	10
450	25 t. Bechuanaland Protectorate 1932 2d. stamp	45	50
451	45 t. 1967 Hoopoe 2 c. definitive stamp	55	1·10

118 Children Playing

1979. International Year of the Child. Multicoloured.

452	5 t. Type **118**	20	10
453	10 t. Child playing with doll (vert)	30	20

119 "Ximenia caffra"

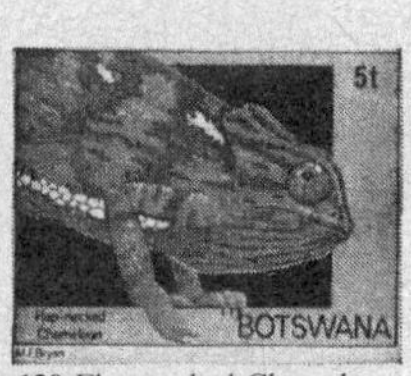

120 Flap-necked Chameleon

1979. Christmas. Flowers. Multicoloured.

454	5 t. Type **119**	10	10
455	10 t. "Sclerocarya caffra"	20	20
456	15 t. "Hexalobus monopetalus"	35	35
457	25 t. "Ficus soldanella"	45	45

1980. Reptiles. Multicoloured.

458	5 t. Type **120**	40	10
459	10 t. Leopard tortoise	40	15
460	25 t. Puff adder	1·10	65
461	40 t. White-throated monitor	1·25	2·50

121 Rock Breaking

1980. Early Mining. Multicoloured.

462	5 t. Type **121**	25	15
463	10 t. Ore hoisting	30	15
464	15 t. Ore transport	70	60
465	20 t. Ore crushing	75	70
466	25 t. Smelting	80	90
467	35 t. Tool and products	1·00	1·40

122 "Chiwele and the Giant"

1980. Folktales. Multicoloured.

468	5 t. Type **122**	10	10
469	10 t. "Kgori is not deceived" (vert)	15	10
470	30 t. "Nyambi's wife and Crocodile" (vert)	45	45
471	45 t. "Clever Hare" (horiz)	60	60

The 10 t. and 30 t. are 28 × 37 mm and the 45 t. 44 × 27 mm.

123 Game watching, Makgadikgadi Pans

1980. World Tourism Conference, Manila.

472	**123** 5 t. multicoloured	45	20

124 "Acacia gerrardii"

126 "Anax imperator" (dragonfly)

125 Heinrich von Stephan and Botswana 3d. and 3 c. U.P.U. Stamps

1980. Christmas. Multicoloured.

473	6 t. Type **124**	10	10
474	1 t. "Acacia nilotica"	20	10
475	25 t. "Acacia erubescens"	45	30
476	40 t. "Dichrostachys cinerea"	70	70

1981. 150th Birth Anniv of Heinrich von Stephan (founder of Universal Postal Union). Multicoloured.

477	6 t. Type **125**	75	30
478	20 t. 6d. and 7 c. U.P.U. stamps	1·75	2·25

1981. Insects. Multicoloured.

479	6 t. Type **126**	15	10
480	7 t. "Sphodromantis gastrica" (mantid)	15	20
481	10 t. "Zonocerus elegans" (grasshopper)	20	20
482	20 t. "Kheper nigroaeneus" (beetle)	35	50
483	30 t. "Papilio demodocus" (butterfly)	70	70
484	45 t. "Acanthocampa belina" (moth larva)	80	1·10

127 Camphill Community Rankoromane, Otse

1981. International Year for Disabled Persons. Multicoloured.

486	6 t. Type **127**	20	10
487	20 t. Resource Centre for the Blind, Mochudi	55	35
488	30 t. Tlamelong Rehabilitation Centre, Tlokweng	75	45

128 Woman reading Letter

1981. Literacy Programme. Multicoloured.

489	6 t. Type **128**	20	10
490	7 t. Man filling in form	20	15
491	20 t. Boy reading newspaper	60	35
492	30t. Child being taught to read	80	45

129 Sir Seretse Khama and Building

1981. 1st Death Anniv of Sir Seretse Khama (former President). Multicoloured.

493	6 t. Type **129**	15	10
494	10 t. Seretse Khama and building (different)	25	15
495	30 t. Seretse Khama and Botswana flag	40	45
496	45 t. Seretse Khama and building (different)	55	70

1981. Nos. 417 and 422 surch.

497	25 t. on 35 t. Green heron	2·75	2·00
498	30 t. on 10 t. Bennett's woodpecker	2·75	2·00

131 Traditional Ploughing

1981. Cattle Industry. Multicoloured.

499	6 t. Type **131**	10	10
500	20 t. Agricultural show	30	50
501	30 t. Botswana Meat Commission	35	60
502	45 t. Vaccine Institute, Botswana	50	1·00

132 "Nymphaea caerulea"

1981. Christmas. Flowers. Multicoloured.

503	6 t. Type **132**	20	10
504	10 t. "Nymphoides indica"	25	10
505	25 t. "Nymphaea lotus"	60	90
506	40 t. "Ottelia kunenensis"	80	2·25

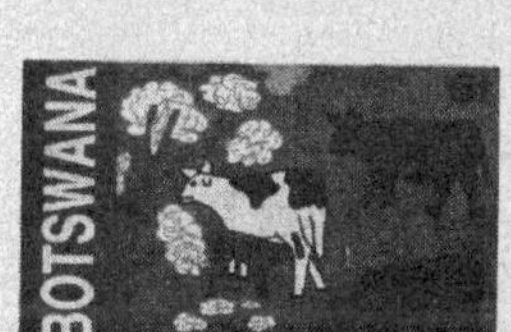

133 "Cattle Post Scene" (Boitumelo Golaakwena)

1982. Children's Art. Multicoloured.

507	6 t. Type **133**	40	10
508	10 t. "Kgotla Meeting" (Reginald Klinck)	50	15
509	30 t. "Village Water Supply" (Keronmemang Matswiri)	1·75	1·25
510	45 t. "With the Crops" (Kennedy Balemoge)	1·75	2·75

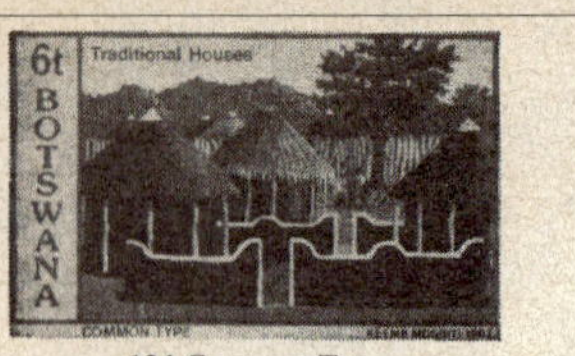

134 Common Type

1982. Traditional House. Multicoloured.
511 6 t. Type **134** 40 15
512 10 t. Kgatleng type 50 15
513 30 t. North Eastern type . . . 2·00 1·10
514 45 t. Sarwa type . . . . 2·00 3·00

135 African Masked Weaver 136 "Coprinus comatus"

1982. Birds. Multicoloured.
515 1 t. Type **135** . . . . 80 1·25
516 2 t. Lesser double-collared sunbird . . . . 90 1·40
517 3 t. Red-throated bee eater . . 1·00 1·40
518 4 t. Ostrich . . . . 1·00 1·40
519 5 t. Grey-headed gull . . . . 1·00 1·40
520 6 t. African pygmy goose . . . 1·00 40
521 7 t. Cattle egret . . . . 1·00 15
522 8 t. Lanner falcon . . . . . . 2·00 1·25
523 10 t. Yellow-billed stork . . . 1·00 20
524 15 t. Red-billed pintail (horiz) . 2·50 25
525 20 t. Barn owl (horiz) . . . . 5·00 3·50
526 25 t. Hammerkop (horiz) . . . 3·00 70
527 30 t. South African stilt (horiz) 3·50 90
528 35 t. Blacksmith plover (horiz) 3·50 80
529 45 t. Senegal wattled plover (horiz) . . . . 3·50 1·75
530 50 t. Helmet guineafowl (horiz) 4·50 2·50
531 1 p. Cape vulture (horiz) . . . 8·50 12·00
532 2 p. Augur buzzard (horiz) . . 10·00 16·00

1982. Christmas. Fungi. Multicoloured.
533 7 t. Type **136** . . . . 1·25 15
534 15 t. "Lactarius deliciosus" . . 2·25 55
535 35 t. "Amanita pantherina" . . 4·00 1·75
536 50 t. "Boletus edulis" . . . . 4·75 5·25

137 President Quett Masire

1983. Commonwealth Day. Multicoloured.
537 7 t. Type **137** 10 10
538 15 t. Native dancers 15 20
539 35 t. Melbourne conference centre 45 55
540 45 t. Meeting of Heads of State, Melbourne 55 80

138 Wattled Crane 139 Wooden Spoons

1983. Endangered Species. Multicoloured.
541 7 t. Type **138** . . . . 2·75 55
542 15 t. "Aloe lutescens" . . . . 2·25 80
543 35 t. Roan antelope . . . . . 2·50 3·00
544 50 t. Ivory palm . . . . 3·00 5·00

1983. Traditional Artifacts. Multicoloured.
545 7 t. Type **139** 25 10
546 15 t. Personal ornaments . . . 45 30
547 35 t. Ox-hide milk bag 75 65
548 50 t. Decorated knives . . . . 1·00 1·10

140 "Pantala flavescens"

1983. Christmas. Dragonflies. Multicoloured.
550 6 t. Type **140** 70 10
551 15 t. "Anax imperator" . . . 1·40 50
552 25 t. "Trithemis arteriosa" . . 1·75 85
553 45 t. "Chlorolestes elegans" . . 2·25 3·50

141 Sorting Diamonds 142 Riding Cattle

1984. Mining Industry. Multicoloured.
554 7 c. Type **141** . . . . 2·00 50
555 15 c. Lime kiln . . . . 2·00 75
556 35 c. Copper-nickel smelter plant (vert) . . . . 3·25 2·75
557 60 c. Stockpiled coal (vert) . 3·75 6·00

1984. Traditional Transport. Multicoloured.
558 7 t. Type **142** 20 10
559 25 t. Sledge 65 50
560 35 t. Wagon . . . . 85 1·25
561 50 t. Two-wheeled donkey cart 1·25 2·75

143 Avro 504 Aircraft 144 "Papilio demodocus"

1984. 40th Anniv of International Civil Aviation Organization. Multicoloured.
562 7 t. Type **143** 60 15
563 10 t. Westland Wessex trimotor 75 20
564 15 t. Junkers Ju 52/3m . . . 1·40 75
565 25 t. De Havilland Dominie . . 2·00 1·50
566 35 t. Douglas DC-3 "Wenala" . 2·25 2·75
567 50 t. Fokker Friendship . . . 2·50 4·25

1984. Christmas. Butterflies. Multicoloured.
568 7 t. Type **144** . . . . 1·75 30
569 25 t. "Byblia anvatara" . . . 3·00 1·50
570 35 t. "Danaus chrysippus" . . 3·25 2·75
571 50 t. "Graphium taboranus" . . 4·50 7·00
No. 570 is incorrectly inscr "Hypolimnas misippus".

145 Seswaa (meat dish) 146 1885 British Bechuanaland Overprint on Cape of Good Hope ½d.

1985. 5th Anniv of Southern African Development Co-ordination Conference. Traditional Foods. Multicoloured.
572 7 t. Type **145** 25 10
573 15 t. Bogobe (cereal porridge) . 45 35
574 25 t. Madila (soured coagulated cow's milk) 70 55
575 50 t. Phane (caterpillars) . . 1·10 1·75

1985. Centenary of First Bechuanaland Stamps.
577 **146** 7 t. black, grey and red . . 75 20
578 – 15 t. black, brown & yell . 1·25 50
579 – 25 t. black and red . . . 1·75 80
580 – 35 t. black, blue and gold 2·00 2·00
581 – 50 t. multicoloured . . . 2·25 3·25
DESIGNS—VERT: 15 t. 1897 Bechuanaland Protectorate overprint on G.B. 3d.; 25 t. Bechuanaland Protectorate 1932 1d. definitive. HORIZ: 35 t. Bechuanaland 1965 Internal Self-Government 5 c.; 50 t. Botswana 1966 Independence 2½ c.

147 Bechuanaland Border Police, 1885–95

1985. Centenary of Botswana Police. Multicoloured.
582 7 t. Type **147** . . . . 2·00 50
583 10 t. Bechuanaland Mounted Police, 1895–1902 . . . . . 2·25 50
584 25 t. Bechuanaland Protectorate Police, 1903–66 . . . . . . 3·25 2·00
585 50 t. Botswana Police, from 1966 4·50 6·00

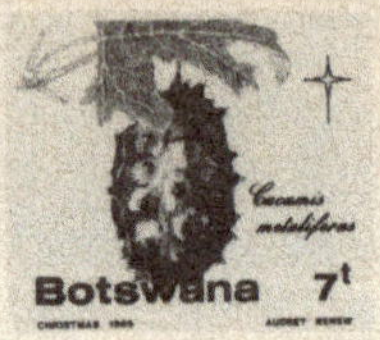

148 "Cucumis metuliferus"

1985. Christmas. Edible Wild Cucumbers. Mult.
586 7 t. Type **148** 75 10
587 15 t. "Acanthosicyos naudinianus" . . . . 1·25 70
588 25 t. "Coccinia sessifolia" . . 2·00 1·10
589 50 t. "Momordica balsamina" . 3·25 5·50

149 Mr. Shippard and Chief Gaseitsiwe of the Bangwaketse 150 Halley's Comet over Serowe

1985. Centenary of Declaration of Bechuanaland Protectorate. Multicoloured.
590 7 t. Type **149** 35 10
591 15 t. Sir Charles Warren and Chief Sechele of the Bakwena 70 45
592 25 t. Revd. Mackenzie and Chief Khama of the Bamangwato . 1·25 85
593 50 t. Map showing Protectorate 2·75 2·75

1986. Appearance of Halley's Comet. Multicoloured.
595 7 t. Type **150** 80 15
596 15 t. Comet over Bobonong at sunset . . . . 1·50 70
597 35 t. Comet over Gomare at dawn . . . . 2·00 1·50
598 50 t. Comet over Thamaga and Letlhakeng . . . . 2·25 3·50

151 Milk Bag 153 "Ludwigia stogonifera"

1986. Traditional Milk Containers. Multicoloured.
599 8 t. Type **151** 15 10
600 15 t. Clay pot and calabashes . 25 30
601 35 t. Wooden milk bucket . . 50 65
602 50 t. Milk churn . . . . . . 70 1·10

1986. Christmas. Flowers of Okavango. Mult.
604 8 t. Type **153** . . . . 1·25 10
605 15 t. "Sopubia mannii" . . . 2·25 1·10
606 35 t. "Commelina diffusa" . . 3·50 3·00
607 50 t. "Hibiscus diversifolius" . 4·00 8·50

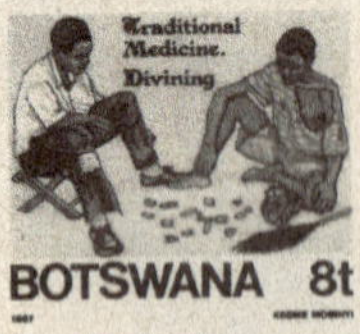

154 Divining 156 Oral Rehydration Therapy

1987. Traditional Medicine. Multicoloured.
608 8 t. Type **154** 80 10
609 15 t. Lightning prevention . . 1·50 80
610 35 t. Rain making . . . . . . 2·25 2·50
611 50 t. Blood letting . . . . . 2·75 5·50

1987. Nos. 520, 523 and 530 surch.
612 3 t. on 6 t. African pygmy goose 1·25 60
613 5 t. on 10 t. Yellow-billed stork 1·25 60
614 20 t. on 50 t. Helmet guineafowl (horiz) . . . . 2·75 1·40

1987. U.N.I.C.E.F. Child Survival Campaign. Multicoloured.
615 8 t. Type **156** 35 10
616 15 t. Growth monitoring . . . 60 55
617 35 t. Immunization . . . . . 1·25 1·75
618 50 t. Breast feeding . . . . 1·50 3·75

157 Cape Fox

1987. Animals of Botswana. Multicoloured.
619 1 t. Type **157** 10 50
620 2 t. Lechwe 10 50
621 3 t. Zebra 10 50
622 4 t. Duiker 10 70
623 5 t. Banded mongoose 15 70
624 6 t. Rusty-spotted genet . . . 15 70
625 8 t. Hedgehog 30 10
626 10 t. Scrub hare 25 10
627 12 t. Hippopotamus . . . . . 1·00 1·75
628 15 t. Suricate 60 15
629 20 t. Caracal 70 65
630 25 t. Steenbok 70 65
631 30 t. Gemsbok 85 50
632 35 t. Square-lipped rhinoceros 1·50 40
633 40 t. Mountain reedbuck . . . 1·10 65
634 50 t. Rock dassie . . . . . . 90 1·00
635 1 p. Giraffe . . . . 2·50 2·75
636 2 p. Tsessebe . . . . 2·50 3·50
637 3 p. Side-striped jackal . . . 3·75 6·50
638 5 p. Hartebeest . . . . 6·00 10·00

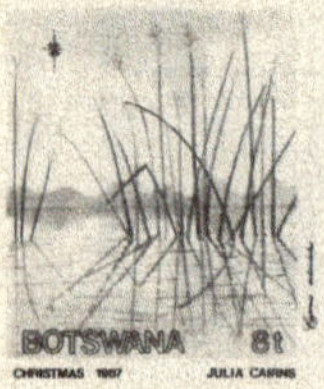

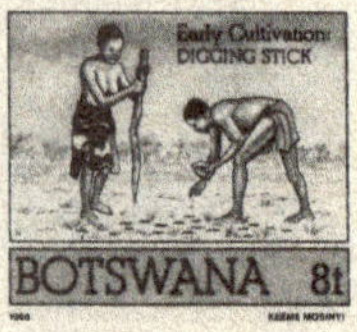

158 "Cyperus articulatus" 159 Planting Seeds with Digging Stick

1987. Christmas. Grasses and Sedges of Okavango. Multicoloured.
639 8 t. Type **158** 40 10
640 15 t. Broomgrass 60 40
641 30 t. "Cyperus alopurcides" . 1·25 75
642 1 p. Bulrush sedge . . . . . 2·50 4·00

1988. Early Cultivation. Multicoloured.
644 8 t. Type **159** 40 10
645 15 t. Using iron hoe 60 35
646 35 t. Wooden ox-drawn plough 1·00 1·00
647 50 t. Villagers using lesotlas . 1·40 2·00

160 Red Lechwe at Water-hole 161 Gubulawayo Postmark and Route Southwards to Tati

1988. Red Lechwe. Multicoloured.
648 10 t. Type **160** 65 15
649 15 t. Red lechwe and early morning sun . . . . 1·25 65
650 35 t. Female and calf . . . . 2·00 1·75
651 75 t. Herd on the move . . . 3·25 5·00

1988. Cent of Mafeking–Gubalawayo Runner Post. Designs as Nos. 294/7, but redrawn smaller with changed inscriptions as in T **161**. Multicoloured.
652 10 t. Type **161** 35 10
653 15 t. Bechuanaland 1888 6d. on 6d. stamp and route from Tati southwards 55 30
654 30 t. Runners and twin routes south from Shoshong . . . 95 75
655 60 t. Mafeking postmark and routes to Bechuanaland and Transvaal . . . . 1·60 2·75

162 Pope John Paul II and Outline Map of Botswana 163 National Museum and Art Gallery, Gaborone

1988. Visit of Pope John Paul II. Multicoloured.
657 10 t. Type **162** 70 10
658 15 t. Pope John Paul II . . . 90 30
659 30 t. Pope giving blessing and outline map . . . . 1·40 70
660 80 t. Pope John Paul II (different) 2·00 2·75

1988. 20th Anniv of National Museum and Art Gallery, Gaborone. Multicoloured.
661 8 t. Type **163** 15 10
662 15 t. Pottery 20 25
663 30 t. Blacksmith's buffalo bellows 35 40
664 60 c. Children and mobile museum van . . . . 70 1·00

164 "Grewia flava"

165 Basket Granary

1988. Flowering Plants of South-eastern Botswana. Multicoloured.
665 8 t. Type **164** 20 10
666 15 t. "Cienfuegosia digitata" 30 25
667 40 t. "Solanum seaforthianum" 60 55
668 75 t. "Carissa bispinosa" 1·00 1·40

1989. Traditional Grain Storage. Multicoloured.
669 8 t. Type **165** 30 10
670 15 t. Large letlole granary 60 40
671 30 t. Pot granary 1·00 60
672 60 t. Two types of serala 1·75 2·25

166 Female with Eggs

1989. Red-throated Heron ("Slaty Egret"). Mult.
673 8 t. Type **166** 45 15
674 15 t. Chicks in nest 65 40
675 30 t. In flight 90 75
676 60 t. Pair building nest 1·40 1·60

167 "My Work at Home" (Ephraim Seeletso)

1989. Children's Paintings. Multicoloured.
678 10 t. Type **167** 35 10
679 15 t. "My Favourite Game" (hopscotch) (Neelma Bhatia) (vert) 50 35
680 30 t. "My Favourite Toy" (clay animals) (Thabo Habana) 75 70
681 1 p. "My School Day" (Thabo Olesitse) 2·00 3·25

168 "Eulophia angolensis"

171 Telephone Engineer

169 Bechuanaland 1965 New Constitution 25 c. Stamp (25th anniv of Self-Government)

1989. Christmas. Orchids. Multicoloured.
682 8 t. Type **168** 60 10
683 15 t. "Eulophia hereroensis" 1·10 50
684 30 t. "Eulophia speciosa" 1·60 1·00
685 60 t. "Eulophia petersii" 2·25 4·50

1990. Anniversaries.
686 **169** 8 t. multicoloured 60 15
687 – 15 t. multicoloured 75 50
688 – 30 t. multicoloured 1·60 1·40
689 – 60 t. black, blue and yellow 2·25 3·50

DESIGNS: 15 t. Casting vote in ballot box (25th anniv of First Elections); 30 t. Outline map and flags of Southern Africa Development Co-ordination Conference countries (10th anniv); 60 t. Penny Black (150th anniv of first postage stamp).

1990. Nos. 619, 624 and 627 surch.
690 10 t. on 1 t. Type **157** 45 20
691 20 t. on 6 t. Rusty-spotted genet 60 70
692 50 t. on 12 t. Hippopotamus 1·75 2·50

1990. "Stamp World London 90" International Stamp Exhibition. Multicoloured.
693 8 t. Type **171** 35 10
694 15 t. Transmission pylon 65 40
695 30 t. Public telephone 1·00 75
696 2 p. Testing circuit board 3·00 5·00

172 Young Children

173 "Acacia nigrescens"

1990. Traditional Dress. Multicoloured.
697 8 t. Type **172** 35 10
698 15 t. Young woman 65 40
699 30 t. Adult man 1·00 70
700 2 p. Adult woman 3·00 5·00

1990. Christmas. Flowering Trees. Multicoloured.
702 8 t. Type **173** 40 10
703 15 t. "Peltophorum africanum" 75 30
704 30 t. "Burkea africana" 1·25 65
705 2 p. "Pterocarpus angolensis" 2·75 4·50

174 Children running in Front of Car

1990. 1st National Road Safety Day. Multicoloured.
706 8 t. Type **174** 1·00 25
707 15 t. Careless overtaking 1·50 85
708 30 t. Cattle on road 2·00 2·25

175 Cattle

176 Children

1991. Rock Paintings. Multicoloured.
709 8 t. Type **175** 75 30
710 15 t. Cattle, drying frames and tree 1·25 75
711 30 t. Animal hides 1·75 1·25
712 2 p. Family herding cattle 3·50 5·00

1991. National Census. Multicoloured.
713 8 t. Type **176** 40 10
714a 15 t. Village 75 55
715 30 t. School 85 75
716 2 p. Hospital 2·75 5·00

177 Tourists viewing Elephants

1991. African Tourism Year. Okavango Delta. Mult.
717 8 t. Type **177** 1·10 50
718 15 t. Crocodiles basking on river bank 1·50 70
719 35 t. Fish eagles and De Havilland D.H.C.7 Dash Seven aircraft 2·75 1·75
720 2 p. Okavango wildlife (26 × 44 mm) 4·50 6·00

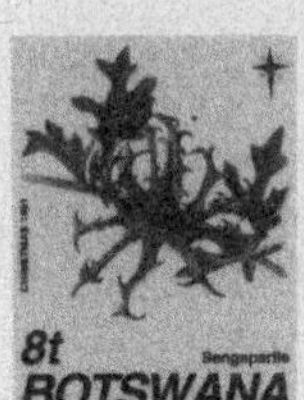

178 "Harpagophytum procumbens" **179** "Cacosternum boettgeri"

1991. Christmas. Seed Pods. Multicoloured.
721 8 t. Type **178** 60 10
722 15 t. "Tylosema esculentum" 90 40
723 30 t. "Abrus precatorius" 1·50 70
724 2 p. "Kigelia africana" 3·50 5·00

1992. Nos. 621, 624 and 627 surch.
725 8 t. on 12 t. Hippopotamus 90 40
726 10 t. on 12 t. Hippopotamus 90 40
727 25 t. on 6 t. Rusty-spotted genet 1·25 1·25
728 40 t. on 3 t. Zebra 2·00 2·50

1992. Climbing Frogs. Multicoloured.
729 8 t. Type **179** 45 20
730 10 t. "Hyperolius marmoratus angolensis" (vert) 45 20
731 40 t. "Bufo fenoulheti" 1·40 1·25
732 1 p. "Hyperolius sp." (vert) 2·00 3·50

180 Air-conditioned Carriages

1992. Deluxe Railway Service. Multicoloured.
733 10 t. Type **180** 75 30
734 25 t. Diesel locomotive No. BD001 (vert) 1·25 70
735 40 t. Carriage interior (vert) 1·75 1·00
736 2 p. Diesel locomotive No. BD028 3·50 5·00

181 Cheetah **182** Boxing

1992. Animals. Multicoloured.
738 1 t. Type **181** 20 50
739 2 t. Spring hare 20 50
740 4 t. Blackfooted cat 30 50
741 5 t. Striped mouse 30 50
742 10 t. Oribi 30 10
743 12 t. Pangolin 45 60
744 15 t. Aardwolf 45 30
745 20 t. Warthog 45 30
746 25 t. Ground squirrel 45 20
747 35 t. Honey badger 50 30
748 40 t. Common mole rat 50 30
749 45 t. Wild dog 50 30
750 50 t. Water mongoose 60 35
751 80 t. Klipspringer 90 1·00
752 1 p. Lesser bushbaby 1·00 1·00
753 2 p. Bushveld elephant shrew 1·75 2·00
754 5 p. Zorilla 3·50 4·25
755 10 p. Vervet monkey 5·50 7·00

1992. Olympic Games, Barcelona. Multicoloured.
756 10 t. Type **182** 30 10
757 50 t. Running 65 50
758 1 p. Boxing (different) 1·10 1·60
759 2 p. Running (different) 1·75 2·75

183 "Adiantum incisum" **184** Helping Blind Person (Lions Club International)

1992. Christmas. Ferns. Multicoloured.
761 10 t. Type **183** 30 10
762 25 t. "Actiniopteris radiata" 55 35
763 40 t. "Ceratopteris cornuta" 70 55
764 1 p. 50 "Pellaea calomelanos" 2·25 4·00

1993. Charitable Organizations in Botswana. Mult.
765 10 t. Type **184** 35 10
766 15 t. Nurse carrying child (Red Cross Society) (horiz) 45 25
767 25 t. Woman watering seedling (Ecumenical Decade) 55 40
768 35 t. Deaf children (Round Table) (horiz) 70 80
769 40 t. Crowd of people (Rotary International) 80 1·10
770 50 t. Hands at prayer (Botswana Christian Council) (horiz) 95 1·50

185 Bechuanaland Railways Class "6" Locomotive No. 1 **186** Long-crested Eagle

1993. Railway Centenary. Multicoloured.
771 10 t. Type **185** 50 20
772 40 t. Class "19" locomotive No. 317 90 60
773 50 t. Class "12" locomotive No. 256 95 70
774 1 p. 50 Class "7" locomotive No. 71 1·40 2·75

1993. Endangered Eagles. Multicoloured.
776 10 t. Type **186** 45 20
777 25 t. Snake eagle 80 60
778 50 t. Bateleur 1·25 1·50
779 1 p. 50 Secretary bird 2·50 3·75

187 "Aloe zebrina"

1993. Christmas. Flora. Multicoloured.
780 12 t. Type **187** 25 10
781 25 t. "Croton megalobotrys" 40 25
782 50 t. "Boophane disticha" 65 70
783 1 p. "Euphoria davyi" 1·10 2·00

188 Boy with String Puppet

1994. Traditional Toys. Multicoloured.
784 10 t. Type **188** 15 10
785 40 t. Boys with clay cattle 35 30
786 50 t. Boy with spinner 50 50
787 1 p. Girls playing in make-believe houses 90 1·60

189 Interior of Control Tower, Gaborone Airport

1994. 50th Anniv of I.C.A.O. Multicoloured.
788 10 t. Type **189** 20 10
789 25 t. Crash tender 35 25
790 40 t. Loading supplies onto airliner (vert) 50 60
791 50 t. Control tower, Gaborone (vert) 60 1·25

1994. No. 743 surch **10t.**
792 10 t. on 12 t. Pangolin 1·00 40

191 Lesser Flamingos at Sua Pan **192** "Ziziphus mucronata"

1994. Environment Protection. Makgadikgadi Pans. Multicoloured.
793 10 t. Type **191** 40 20
794 35 t. Baobab trees (horiz) 50 30
795 50 t. Zebra and palm trees 65 70
796 2 p. Map of area (horiz) 1·75 2·75

1994. Christmas. Edible Fruits. Multicoloured.
797 10 t. Type **192** 20 10
798 25 t. "Strychnos cocculoides" 30 25
799 40 t. "Bauhinia petersiana" 50 50
800 50 t. "Schinziphyton rautoneii" 60 70

193 Fisherman with Bow and Arrow

1995. Traditional Fishing. Multicoloured.
801 15 t. Type **193** 20 15
802 40 t. Men in canoe and boy with fishing rod 35 30
803 65 t. Fisherman with net 50 60
804 80 t. Fisherman with basket fish trap 65 1·25

194 Boys watering Horses (F.A.O.) **195** Brown Hyena

1995. 50th Anniv of United Nations. Multicoloured.

805	20 t. Type **194**	20	10
806	50 t. Schoolchildren queueing for soup (W.F.P.)	35	30
807	80 t. Letters and postman delivering to village (U.N.D.P.)	60	80
808	1 p. Weighing baby (U.N.I.C.E.F.)	70	1·00

1995. Endangered Species. Brown Hyena. Mult.

809	20 t. Type **195**	40	50
810	50 t. Pair of hyenas	55	65
811	80 t. Hyena stealing ostrich eggs	70	85
812	1 p. Adult hyena and cubs	75	90

196 "Adenia glauca"

198 Spears

1995. Christmas. Plants. Multicoloured.

813	20 t. Type **196**	20	10
814	50 t. "Pterodiscus ngamicus"	40	30
815	80 t. "Sesamothamnus lugardii"	65	80
816	1 p. "Fockea multiflora"	75	1·00

1996. Nos. 738/40 surch.

817	20 t. on 2 t. Spring hare	20	20
818	30 t. on 1 t. Type **181**	25	25
819	70 t. on 4 t. Blackfooted cat	50	70

1996. Traditional Weapons. Multicoloured.

820	20 t. Type **198**	15	10
821	50 t. Axes	30	30
822	80 t. Shield and knobkerries	45	60
823	1 p. Knives and sheaths	50	75

199 Child with Basic Radio

200 Olympic Flame, Rings and Wreath

1996. Centenary of Radio. Multicoloured.

824	20 t. Type **199**	20	10
825	50 t. Radio Botswana's mobile transmitter	35	30
826	80 t. Police radio control	50	65
827	1 p. Listening to radio	65	90

1996. Centenary of Modern Olympic Games. Multicoloured.

828	20 t. Type **200**	20	10
829	50 t. Pierre de Coubertin (founder of modern Olympics)	35	30
830	80 t. Map of Botswana with flags and athletes	50	70
831	1 p. Ruins of ancient stadium at Olympia	60	90

201 Family Planning Class (Botswana Family Welfare Association)

202 "Adansonia digitata" Leaf and Blossom

1996. Local Charities. Multicoloured.

832	20 t. Type **201**	15	10
833	30 t. Blind workers (Pudulogong Rehabilitation Centre)	15	15
834	50 t. Collecting seeds (Forestry Association of Botswana)	25	30
835	70 t. Secretarial class (Y.W.C.A.)	35	50
836	80 t. Children's day centre (Botswana Council of Women)	40	60
837	1 p. Children's village, Tlokweng (S.O.S. Children's village)	50	70

1996. Christmas. Parts of Life Cycle for "Adansonia digitata". Multicoloured.

838	20 t. Type **202**	15	10
839	50 t. Fruit	30	25
840	80 t. Tree in leaf	45	55
841	1 p. Tree with bare branches	50	70

203 Tati Hotel

204 Steam Locomotive, Bechuanaland Railway, 1897

1997. Francistown Centenary. Multicoloured.

842	20 t. Type **203**	15	10
843	50 t. Railway Station	30	25
844	80 t. Company Manager's House	40	50
845	1 p. Monarch Mine	50	75

1997. Railway Centenary. Multicoloured.

846	35 t. Type **204**	20	15
847	50 t. Elephants crossing railway line	30	25
848	80 t. First locomotive in Bechuanaland, 1897	40	40
849	1 p. Beyer-Garratt type steam locomotive No. 352	50	55
850	2 p. Diesel locomotive No. BD339	80	1·00
851	2 p. 50 Fantuzzi container stacker	90	1·25

205 Pel's Fishing Owl

206 "Combretum zeyheri"

1997. Birds. Multicoloured.

852	5 t. Type **205**	10	10
853	10 t. Gymnogene (horiz)	10	10
854	15 t. Meyer's parrot	10	10
855	20 t. Harlequin quail (horiz)	10	10
856	25 t. Marico sunbird (horiz)	10	10
857	30 t. Kurrichane thrush (horiz)	10	10
858	40 t. Redheaded finch	10	10
859	50 t. Buffalo weaver	15	20
860	60 t. Sacred ibis (horiz)	15	20
861	70 t. Cape shoveler (horiz)	20	25
862	80 t. Greater honeyguide (horiz)	20	25
863	1 p. Woodland kingfisher (horiz)	25	30
864	1 p. 25 Purple heron	25	30
865	1 p. 50 Yelllow-billed oxpecker (horiz)	25	30
866	2 p. Shaft-tailed whydah	55	60
867	2 p. 50 White stork	55	60
868	5 p. Sparrowhawk	1·40	1·50
869	10 p. Spotted crake	2·75	3·00

No. 861 is inscribed "Shoveller" in error.

1997. Golden Wedding of Queen Elizabeth and Prince Philip. As T **173** of Ascension. Multicoloured.

870	35 t. Prince Philip with carriage	20	20
871	35 t. Queen Elizabeth with binoculars	20	20
872	2 p. Queen Elizabeth with horse team	90	1·00
873	2 p. Prince Philip and horse	90	1·00
874	2 p. 50 Queen Elizabeth and Prince Philip	1·10	1·25
875	2 p. 50 Princess Anne and Prince Edward	1·10	1·25

1997. Christmas. Plants. Multicoloured.

877	35 t. Type **206**	20	10
878	1 p. "Combretum apiculatum"	50	35
879	2 p. "Combretum molle"	90	90
880	2 p. 50 "Combretum imberbe"	1·00	1·25

207 Baobab Trees

1998. Tourism (1st series). Multicoloured.

881	35 t. Type **207**	25	15
882	1 p. Crocodile	40	35
883	2 p. Stalactites (vert)	75	80
884	2 p. 50 Tourists and rock paintings (vert)	90	1·00

See also Nos. 899/902.

1998. Diana, Princess of Wales Commemoration. As T **177** of Ascension. Multicoloured.

885	35 t. Princess Diana, 1990	25	15
886	1 p. In green hat, 1992	40	35
887	2 p. In white blouse, 1993	75	80
888	2 p. 50 With crowd, Cambridge, 1993	90	1·00

208 "Village Life" (tapestry)

209 "Ficus ingens"

1998. Botswana Weavers. Multicoloured.

890	35 t. Type **208**	10	15
891	55 t. Weaver dyeing threads	15	20
892	1 p. "African wildlife" (tapestry)	25	30
893	2 p. Weaver at loom	55	60

1998. Christmas. Plants. Multicoloured.

895	35 t. Type **209**	10	10
896	55 t. "Ficus pygmaea"	15	20
897	1 p. "Ficus abutilifolia"	25	30
898	2 p. 50 "Ficus sycomorus"	65	70

1999. Tourism (2nd series). As T **207**. Multicoloured.

899	35 t. Rock painting of men and cattle	10	10
900	55 t. Expedition at Salt Pan	15	20
901	1 p. Rock painting of elephant and antelope (vert)	25	30
902	2p. Tourists under Baobab tree (vert)	55	60

POSTAGE DUE STAMPS

1967. Nos. D10/12 of Bechuanaland optd **REPUBLIC OF BOTSWANA.**

D13	D **1** 1 c. red	15	2·25
D14	2 c. violet	15	2·50
D15	5 c. green	20	2·50

D **5** African Elephant

D **6** Common Zebra

1971.

D16	D **5** 1 c. red	1·10	3·25
D17	2 c. violet	1·40	3·50
D18	6 c. brown	2·50	5·50
D19	14 c. green	2·75	7·50

1977.

D25a	D **6** 1 t. black and red	10	10
D26a	2 t. black and green	10	10
D27a	4 t. black and red	10	10
D28a	10 t. black and blue	10	10
D29a	16 t. black and brown	10	10

BRITISH ANTARCTIC TERRITORY

Constituted in 1962 comprising territories south of latitude 60°S., from the former Falkland Island Dependencies.

1963. 12 pence = 1 shilling;
20 shillings = 1 pound.
1971. 100 (new) pence = 1 pound.

1 M.V. "Kista Dan"

1963.

1	**1** ½d. blue	75	1·40
2	– 1d. brown	1·00	1·00
3	– 1½d. red and purple	1·00	80
4	– 2d. purple	1·25	80
5	– 2½d. myrtle	2·50	70
6	– 3d. turquoise	3·50	80
7	– 4d. sepia	2·50	1·25
8	– 6d. olive and blue	4·25	1·75
9	– 9d. green	3·50	1·50
10	– 1s. turquoise	3·75	70
11	– 2s. violet and brown	18·00	6·00
12	– 2s. 6d. blue	17·00	6·50
13	– 5s. orange and red	20·00	12·00
14	– 10s. blue and green	45·00	25·00
15	£1 black and blue	55·00	48·00
15a	– £1 red and black	£150	£120

DESIGNS: 1d. Manhauling; 1½d. Muskeg (tractor); 2d. Skiing; 2½d. De Havilland D.H.C.2 Beaver (aircraft); 3d. R.R.S. "John Biscoe II"; 4d. Camp scene; 6d. H.M.S. "Protector"; 9d. Sledging; 1s. De Havilland D.H.C.3 Otter (aircraft); 2s. Huskies; 2s. 6d. Westland Whirlwind helicopter; 5s. Snocat (tractor); 10s. R.R.S. "Shackleton"; £1 (No. 15), Antarctic map; £1 (No. 15a), H.M.S. "Endurance".

1966. Churchill Commemoration. As T **38** of Antigua.

16	½d. blue	80	3·25
17	1d. green	3·00	3·25
18	1s. brown	21·00	6·50
19	2s. violet	24·00	7·00

17 Lemaire Channel and Icebergs

1969. 25th Anniv of Continuous Scientific Work.

20	**17** 3½d. black, blue and ultram	4·00	3·00
21	– 6d. multicoloured	3·50	2·50
22	– 1s. black, blue and red	3·50	2·00
23	– 2s. black, orange and turquoise	3·75	3·00

DESIGNS: 6d. Radio Sonde balloon; 1s. Muskeg pulling tent equipment; 2s. Surveyors with theodolite.

1971. Decimal Currency. Nos. 1/14 surch.

24	½p. on ½d. blue	60	2·75
25	1p. on 1d. brown	1·00	75
26	1½p. on 1½d. red and purple	1·25	50
27	2p. on 2d. purple	1·25	30
28	2½p. on 2½d. green	2·25	1·25
29	3p. on 3d. blue	2·50	55
30	4p. on 4d. brown	2·25	55
31	5p. on 6d. green and blue	4·25	3·00
32	6p. on 9d. green	14·00	7·00
33	7½p. on 1s. blue	15·00	7·50
34	10p. on 2s. violet and brown	18·00	13·00
35	15p. on 2s. 6d. blue	18·00	14·00
36	25p. on 5s. orange and red	24·00	16·00
37	50p. on 10s. blue and green	42·00	30·00

19 Setting up Camp

21 James Cook and H.M.S. "Resolution"

1971. 10th Anniv of Antarctic Treaty. Muticoloured.

38	1½p. Type **19**	6·00	5·50
39	4p. Snow petrels	16·00	8·00
40	5p. Weddell seals	9·50	8·00
41	10p. Adelie penguins	22·00	9·00

Nos. 38/41 each include Antarctic map and Queen Elizabeth in their design.

1972. Royal Silver Wedding. As T **52** of Ascension, but with Kerguelen fur seals and Emperor penguins in background.

42	5p. brown	3·00	3·00
43	10p. green	3·00	3·00

1973. Multicoloured.

64a	½p. Type **21**	75	2·25
65	1p. Thaddeus von Bellingshausen and "Vostok"	60	2·00
66	1½p. James Weddell and "Jane"	60	1·50
67	2p. John Biscoe and "Tula"	1·50	2·00
68	2½p. J. S. C. Dumont d'Urville and "L'Astrolabe"	1·50	2·25
49	3p. James Clark Ross and H.M.S. "Erebus"	95	1·75
50	4p. C. A. Larsen and "Jason"	95	1·75
51	5p. Adrien de Gerlache and "Belgica"	1·00	1·75
52	6p. Otto Nordenskjold and "Antarctic"	1·25	1·75
53	7½p. W. S. Bruce and "Scotia"	1·50	2·25
74a	10p. Jean-Baptiste Charcot and "Pourquoi Pas?"	85	2·75
75	15p. Ernest Shackleton and "Endurance"	1·25	1·50
76	25p. Hubert Wilkins and Lockheed Vega "San Francisco"	1·25	1·50
77b	50p. Lincoln Ellsworth and Northrop Gamma "Polar Star"	85	2·75
78	£1 John Rymill and "Penola"	3·25	2·00

The 25p. and 50p. show aircraft; the rest show ships.

1973. Royal Wedding. As T **47** of Anguilla. Background colour given. Multicoloured.

59	5p. brown	40	20
60	15p. blue	70	30

22 Churchill and Churchill Peninsula, B.A.T.

1974. Birth Centenary of Sir Winston Churchill. Multicoloured.

61	5p. Type **22**	1·75	1·75
62	15p. Churchill and "Trepassey"	2·25	2·25

23 Sperm Whale

1977. Whale Conservation. Multicoloured.

79	2p. Type **23**	6·00	3·50
80	8p. Fin whale	7·00	4·00
81	11p. Humpback whale	7·50	4·00
82	25p. Blue whale	8·50	5·00

24 The Queen before Taking the Oath

1977. Silver Jubilee. Multicoloured.

83	6p. Prince Philip's visit, 1956/7	70	30
84	11p. The Coronation Oath	80	40
85	33p. Type **24**	1·25	50

25 Emperor Penguin

1978. 25th Anniv of Coronation.

86	– 25p. green, deep green and silver	80	1·00
87	– 25p. multicoloured	80	1·00
88 **25**	25p. green, deep green and silver	80	1·00

DESIGNS: No. 86, Black Bull of Clarence; No. 87, Queen Elizabeth II.

26 Macaroni Penguins

1979. Penguins. Multicoloured.

89	3p. Type **26**	11·00	11·00
90	8p. Gentoo penguins	3·00	3·00
91	11p. Adelie penguins	3·50	3·50
92	25p. Emperor penguins	4·50	4·50

27 Sir John Barrow and "Tula"

1980. 150th Anniv of Royal Geographical Society. Former Presidents. Multicoloured.

93	3p. Type **27**	20	15
94	7p. Sir Clement Markham and "Discovery"	25	25
95	11p. Lord Curzon and whaleboat "James Caird"	30	30
96	15p. Sir William Goodenough	35	35
97	22p. Sir James Wordie	50	55
98	30p. Sir Raymond Priestley	60	65

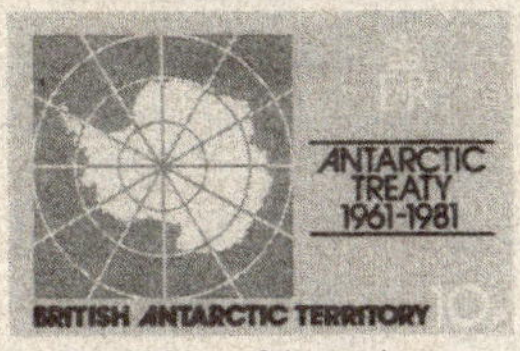

28 Map of Antarctic

1981. 20th Anniv of Antarctic Treaty.

99 **28**	10p. black, blue and light blue	40	80
100 –	13p. black, blue and green	45	90
101 –	25p. black, blue and mauve	55	1·00
102 –	26p. black, brown and red	55	1·00

DESIGNS: 13p. Conservation research ("scientific co-operation"); 25p. Satellite image mapping ("technical co-operation"); 26p. Global geophysics ("scientific co-operation").

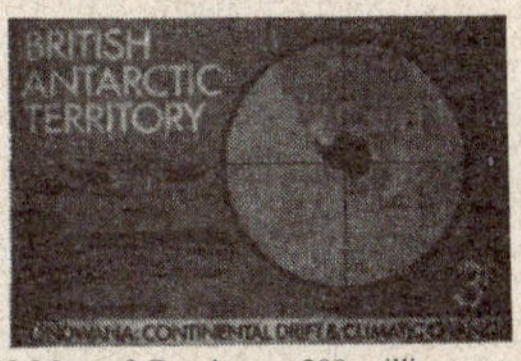

29 Map of Gondwana 280 million years ago and Contemporary Landscape Scene

1982. Gondwana — Continental Drift and Climatic Change. Maps of Gondwana showing position of continents, and contemporary landscapes. Mult.

103	3p. Type **29**	25	40
104	6p. 260 million years ago	30	50
105	10p. 230 million years ago	35	60
106	13p. 175 million years ago	45	70
107	25p. 50 million years ago	55	75
108	26p. Present day	55	75

30 British Antarctic Territory Coat of Arms

1982. 21st Birthday of Princess of Wales. Multicoloured.

109	5p. Type **30**	20	20
110	17p. Princess of Wales (detail of painting by Bryan Organ)	45	50
111	37p. Wedding ceremony	70	80
112	50p. Formal portrait	1·10	1·10

31 Leopard Seal

1983. 10th Anniv of Antarctic Seal Conservation Convention. Multicoloured.

113	5p. Type **31**	45	35
114	10p. Weddell seals	50	40
115	13p. Southern elephant seals	55	45
116	17p. Kerguelen fur seals	65	55
117	25p. Ross seals	75	65
118	34p. Crabeater seals	95	85

32 De Havilland Twin Otter 200/300

1983. Bicentenary of Manned Flight. Multicoloured.

119	5p. Type **32**	25	30
120	13p. De Havilland D.H.C.3 Otter	40	45
121	17p. Consolidated PBY-5A Canso amphibian	55	60
122	50p. Lockheed Vega "San Francisco"	1·10	1·25

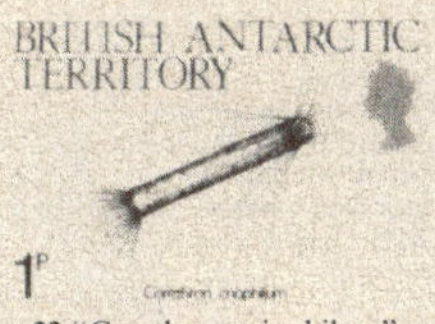

33 "Corethron criophilum"

1984. Marine Life. Multicoloured.

123	1p. Type **33**	60	1·40
124	2p. "Desmonema gaudichaudi"	65	1·40
125	3p. "Tomopteris carpenteri"	65	1·40
126	4p. "Pareuchaeta antarctica"	70	1·50
127	5p. "Antarctomysis maxima"	70	1·50
128	6p. "Antarcturus signiensis"	70	1·50
129	7p. "Serolis cornuta"	70	1·50
130	8p. "Parathemisto gaudichaudii"	70	1·50
131	9p. "Bovallia gigantea"	70	1·50
132	10p. "Euphausia superba"	70	1·50
133	15p. "Colossendeis australis"	70	1·75
134	20p. "Todarodes sagittatus"	75	1·75
135	25p. Antarctic rockcod	80	1·75
136	50p. Black-finned icefish	1·25	2·00
137	£1 Crabeater seal	1·75	2·50
138	£3 Antarctic marine food chain	5·00	6·50

34 M.Y. "Penola" in Stella Creek

1985. 50th Anniv of British Graham Land Expedition. Multicoloured.

139	7p. Type **34**	40	75
140	22p. Northern Base, Winter Island	70	1·40
141	27p. De Havilland Fox Moth at Southern Base, Barry Island	80	1·60
142	54p. Dog Team, near Ablation Point, George VI Sound	1·50	2·25

35 Robert McCormick and McCormick's Skua

36 Dr. Edmond Halley

1985. Early Naturalists. Multicoloured.

143	7p. Type **35**	1·25	1·50
144	22p. Sir Joseph Dalton Hooker and "Deschampsia antarctica"	1·75	2·75
145	27p. Jean Rene C. Quoy and hourglass dolphin	1·90	2·75
146	54p. James Weddell and Weddell seal	2·75	4·00

1986. Appearance of Halley's Comet. Multicoloured.

147	7p. Type **36**	1·00	1·25
148	22p. Halley Station, Antarctica	1·75	2·25
149	27p. "Halley's Comet, 1531" (from Peter Apian woodcut, 1532)	2·00	2·50
150	44p. "Giotto" spacecraft	3·50	4·50

37 Snow Crystal

38 Captain Scott, 1904

1986. 50th Anniv of International Glaciological Society. Snow Crystals.

151 **37**	10p. light blue and blue	60	75
152 –	24p. green and deep green	90	1·40
153 –	29p. mauve and deep mauve	1·00	1·50
154 –	58p. blue and violet	1·40	2·50

1987. 75th Anniv of Captain Scott's Arrival at South Pole. Multicoloured.

155	10p. Type **38**	85	95
156	24p. Hut Point and "Discovery" Ross Island, 1902–4	1·40	2·00
157	29p. Cape Evans Hut, 1911–13	1·75	2·25
158	58p. Scott's expedition at South Pole, 1912	2·25	3·00

39 I.G.Y. Logo

40 Aurora over South Ice Plateau Station

1987. 30th Anniv of International Geophysical Year.

159 **39**	10p. black and green	30	75
160 –	24p. multicoloured	60	1·40
161 –	29p. multicoloured	75	1·75
162 –	58p. multicoloured	1·40	2·50

DESIGNS: 24p. Port Lockroy; 29p. Argentine Islands; 58p. Halley Bay.

1988. 30th Anniv of Commonwealth Trans-Antarctic Expedition. Multicoloured.

163	10p. Type **40**	30	55
164	24p. "Otter" aircraft at Theron Mountains	60	90
165	29p. Seismic ice-depth sounding	70	1·10
166	58p. "Sno-cat" over crevasse	1·25	1·75

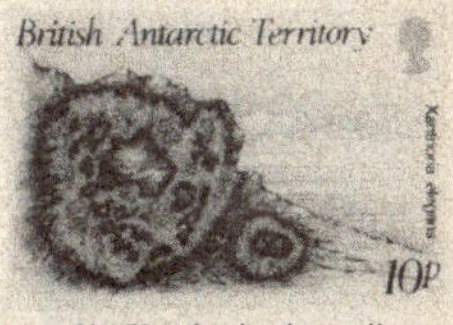

41 "Xanthoria elegans"

1989. Lichens. Multicoloured.

167	10p. Type **41**	90	90
168	24p. "Usnea aurantiaco-atra"	1·60	1·60
169	29p. "Cladonia chlorophaea"	1·75	1·75
170	58p. "Umbilicaria antarctica"	2·50	3·00

42 "Monocyathus" (archaeocyath)

1990. Fossils. Multicoloured.

171	1p. Type **42**	50	80
172	2p. "Lingulella" (brachiopod)	50	80
173	3p. "Triplagnoslus" (trilobite)	60	80
174	4p. "Lyriaspis" (trilobite)	60	80
175	5p. "Glossopteris" leaf (gymnosperm)	60	80
176	6p. "Gonatosorus" (fern)	70	90
177	7p. "Belemnopsis aucklandica" (belemnite)	70	90
178	8p. "Sanmartinoceras africanum insignicostatum" (ammonite)	70	90
179	9p. "Pinna antarctica" (mussel)	80	90
180	10p. "Aucellina andina" (mussel)	80	90
181	20p. "Pterotrigonia malagninoi" (mussel)	1·25	1·60
182	25p. "Perissoptera" (conch shell)	1·25	1·60
183	50p. "Ainoceras sp." (ammonite)	1·75	2·75
184	£1 "Gunnarites zinsmeisteri" (ammonite)	3·50	4·25
185	£4 "Hoploparia" (crayfish)	7·00	8·00

1990. 90th Birthday of Queen Elizabeth the Queen Mother. As T **134** of Ascension.

186	26p. multicoloured	1·75	2·25
187	£1 black and brown	3·95	4·25

DESIGNS: 29 × 36 mm: 26p. Wedding of Prince Albert and Lady Elizabeth Bowes-Lyon, 1923. 29- × 37 mm: £1 The Royal Family, 1940.

43 Late Cretaceous Forest and Southern Beech Fossil

1991. Age of the Dinosaurs. Multicoloured.

188	12p. Type **43**	1·25	1·25
189	26p. Hypsilophodont dinosaurs and skull	2·00	2·00
190	31p. Frilled sharks and tooth	2·25	2·25
191	62p. Mosasaur, plesiosaur, and mosasaur vertebra	3·50	3·50

44 Launching Meteorological Balloon, Halley IV Station

1991. Discovery of Antarctic Ozone Hole. Mult.

192	12p. Type **44**	90	90
193	26p. Measuring ozone with Dobson spectrophotometer	1·60	1·60
194	31p. Satellite map showing ozone hole	1·75	1·75
195	62p. Lockheed ER-2 aircraft and graph of chlorine monoxide and ozone levels	3·00	3·00

45 Researching Dry Valley

1991. 30th Anniv of Antarctic Treaty.

196	**45** 12p. multicoloured	90	90
197	– 26p. multicoloured	1·60	1·60
198	– 31p. black and green	1·75	1·75
199	– 62p. multicoloured	3·00	3·00

DESIGNS: 26p. Relief map of ice sheet; 31p. BIOMASS logo; 62p. Ross seal.

46 "H.M.S. 'Erebus' and H.M.S. 'Terror' in the Antarctic" (J. Carmichael)

1991. Maiden Voyage of "James Clark Ross" (research ship). Multicoloured.

200	12p. Type **46**	90	90
201	26p. Launch of "James Clark Ross"	1·60	1·60
202	31p. "James Clark Ross" in Antarctica	1·75	1·75
203	62p. Scientific research	3·00	3·00

1991. Birth Bicentenary of Michael Faraday (scientist). Nos. 200/3 additionally inscr "200th Anniversary M. Faraday 1791—1867".

204	12p. Type **46**	90	90
205	26p. Launch of "James Clark Ross"	1·60	1·60
206	31p. "James Clark Ross" in Antarctica	1·75	1·75
207	62p. Scientific research	3·00	3·00

47 Ross Seals

1992. Endangered Species. Seals and Penguins. Multicoloured.

208	4p. Type **47**	60	60
209	5p. Adelie penguins	60	60
210	7p. Weddell seal with pup	65	65
211	29p. Emperor penguins with chicks	1·75	1·75
212	34p. Crabeater seals with pup	1·75	1·75
213	68p. Chinstrap penguins with young	2·25	2·25

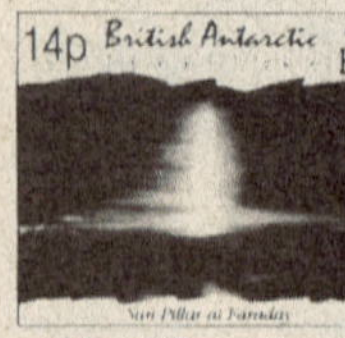

48 Sun Pillar at Faraday

1992. Lower Atmospheric Phenomena. Mult.

214	14p. Type **48**	80	70
215	29p. Halo over iceberg	1·40	1·00
216	34p. Lee Wave cloud	1·75	1·25
217	68p. Nacreous clouds	2·75	2·00

49 "Fitzroy" (mail and supply ship)

1993. Antarctic Ships. Multicoloured.

218	1p. Type **49**	10	10
219	2p. "William Scoresby" (research ship)	10	10
220	3p. "Eagle" (sealer)	10	10
221	4p. "Trepassey" (supply ship)	10	10
222	5p. "John Biscoe I" (research ship)	10	10
223	10p. "Norsel" (supply ship)	20	25
224	20p. H.M.S. "Protector" (ice patrol ship)	40	45
225	30p. "Oluf Sven" (supply ship)	60	65
226	50p. "John Biscoe II" and "Shackleton" (research ships)	1·00	1·10
227	£1 "Tottan" (supply ship)	2·00	2·10
228	£3 "Perla Dan" (supply ship)	6·00	6·25
229	£5 H.M.S. "Endurance I" (ice patrol ship)	10·00	10·50

1994. "Hong Kong '94", International Stamp Exhibition. Nos. 240/5 optd **HONG KONG '94** and emblem.

230	15p. Type **51**	85	90
231	24p. De Havilland Turbo Beaver III aircraft	1·25	1·50
232	31p. De Havilland Otter aircraft and dog team	1·50	1·60
233	36p. De Havilland Twin Otter 200/300 aircraft and dog team	1·60	1·75
234	62p. De Havilland Dash Seven aircraft over landing strip, Rothera Point	2·25	2·75
235	72p. De Havilland Dash Seven aircraft on runway	2·25	2·75

50 Bransfield House Post Office, Port Lockroy

1994. 50th Anniv of Operation Tabarin. Multicoloured.

236	15p. Type **50**	65	65
237	31p. Survey team, Hope Bay	1·10	1·10
238	36p. Dog team, Hope Bay	1·40	1·40
239	72p. "Fitzroy" (supply ship) and H.M.S. "William Scoresby" (minesweeper)	2·25	2·50

51 Huskies and Sledge

1994. Forms of Transportation. Multicoloured.

240	15p. Type **51**	60	70
241	24p. De Havilland Turbo Beaver III aircraft	80	90
242	31p. De Havilland Otter aircraft and dog team	90	1·00
243	36p. De Havilland Twin Otter 200/300 aircaft and dog team	1·00	1·25
244	62p. De Havilland Dash Seven aircraft over landing strip, Rothera Point	1·90	2·50
245	72p. De Havilland Dash Seven aircraft on runway	2·00	2·75

52 Capt. James Cook and H.M.S. "Resolution"

1994. Antarctic Heritage Fund. Multicoloured.

246	17p. + 3p. Type **52**	1·50	1·40
247	35p. + 15p. Sir James Clark Ross with H.M.S. "Erebus" and H.M.S. "Terror"	1·75	1·60
248	40p. + 10p. Capt. Robert Falcon Scott and interior of hut	1·75	1·60
249	76p. + 4p. Sir Ernest Shackleton and H.M.S. "Endurance"	2·50	2·25

53 Pair of Crabeater Seals

1994. Antarctic Food Chain. Multicoloured.

250	35p. Type **53**	95	1·25
251	35p. Blue whale	95	1·25
252	35p. Wandering albatross	95	1·25
253	35p. Mackerel icefish	95	1·25
254	35p. Krill	95	1·25
255	35p. Seven star flying squid	95	1·25

54 Hauberg Mountains

1995. Geological Structures. Multicoloured.

256	17p. Type **54**	65	60
257	35p. Arrowsmith Peninsula	1·25	1·10
258	40p. Colbert Mountains	1·50	1·40
259	76p. Succession Cliffs	2·25	2·25

55 World Map showing Member Countries

1996. 24th Meeting of Scientific Committee on Antarctic Research. Multicoloured.

260	17p. Type **55**	65	60
261	35p. Scientist analysing ice samples	1·25	1·10
262	40p. Releasing balloon	1·50	1·40
263	76p. Antarctic research ship catching marine life	2·25	2·00

56 Killer Whales

1996. Whales. Multicoloured.

265	17p. Type **56**	70	60
266	35p. Sperm whales	1·25	1·10
267	40p. Minke whales	1·50	1·40
268	76p. Blue whale and calf	2·25	2·00

1996. 70th Birthday of Queen Elizabeth II. As T **165** of Ascension, each incorporating a different photograph of the Queen. Mult.

270	17p. At premiere of "Chaplin", Leicester Square, 1992	50	60
271	35p. At Buckingham Palace dinner, 1991	95	1·10
272	40p. In Aberdeen, 1993	1·25	1·40
273	76p. At Royal Military School of Music, 1990	1·75	2·00

57 Chinstrap Penguins sledging

58 Chart of South Shetland Islands (Swedish South Polar Expedition, 1902–3)

1997. Christmas. Multicoloured.

276	17p. Type **57**	60	65
277	35p. Emperor penguins carol singing	1·10	1·25
278	40p. Adelie penguins throwing snowballs	1·40	1·50
279	76p. Gentoo penguins ice-skating	2·00	2·25

1998. History of Mapping in Antarctica. Multicoloured.

281	16p. Type **58**	55	65
282	30p. Map of Antarctic Peninsula (1949)	80	90
283	35p. Map of Antarctic Peninsula (1964)	1·00	1·10
284	40p. Map of Antarctic Peninsula from Landsat (1981)	1·10	1·25
285	65p. Map of Antarctic Peninsula from satellite (1995)	1·50	1·75

59 Antarctic Explorer, 1843

1998. Antarctic Clothing. Multicoloured.

286	30p. Type **59**	60	65
287	35p. Explorer with dog, 1900	70	75
288	40p. Surveyor, 1943	80	85
289	65p. Scientist with penguins, 1998	1·25	1·40

60 Snowy Sheathbill

1998. Antarctic Birds. Multicoloured.

290	1p. Type **60**	10	10
291	2p. Dove prion ("Antarctic Prion")	10	10
292	5p. Adelie penguin	10	10
293	10p. Emperor penguin	20	25
294	20p. Swallow-tailed tern ("Antarctic Tern")	40	45
295	30p. Black-bellied storm petrel	60	65
296	35p. Antarctic fulmar	70	75
297	40p. Blue-eyed shag	80	85
298	50p. McCormick's skua	1·00	1·10
299	£1 Southern black-backed gull ("Kelp Gull")	2·00	2·10
300	£3 Wilson's storm petrel	6·00	6·25
301	£5 Brown skua	10·00	10·50

BRITISH COLUMBIA AND VANCOUVER ISLAND

Former British colonies, now a Western province of the Dominion of Canada, whose stamps are now used.

1860. 12 pence = 1 shilling;
20 shillings = 1 pound.
1865. 100 cents = 1 dollar.

1

1860. Imperf or perf.

2	1	2½d. pink	£275	£180

VANCOUVER ISLAND

2

1865. Imperf or perf. Various frames.

13	2	5 c. red	£225	£140
14	–	10 c. blue	£200	£140

BRITISH COLUMBIA

4 Emblems of United Kingdom

1865.

21	4	3d. blue	75·00	60·00

1868. Surch in words or figures and words.

28	4	2 c. brown	90·00	90·00
29		5 c. red	£120	£120
24		10 c. red	£450	£425
31		25 c. yellow	£120	£120
26		50 c. mauve	£425	£375
27		$1 green	£650	£700

BRITISH COMMONWEALTH OCCUPATION OF JAPAN

Stamps used by British Commonwealth Occupation Forces, 1946–49.

12 pence = 1 shilling;
20 shillings = 1 pound

1946. Stamps of Australia optd **B.C.O.F. JAPAN 1946.**

J1	27	½d. orange	3·00	4·25
J2	46	1d. purple	2·50	1·75
J3	31	3d. brown	2·00	2·00
J4	–	6d. brown (No. 189a)	15·00	9·00
J5	–	1s. green (No. 191)	15·00	11·00
J6	1	2s. red	42·00	45·00
J7	38	5s. red	£120	£130

BRITISH EAST AFRICA

Now incorporated in Kenya and Uganda.

16 annas = 100 cents = 1 rupee

1890. Stamps of Great Britain (1881) surch **BRITISH EAST AFRICA COMPANY** and value in annas.

1	57	½ a. on 1d. lilac	£275	£200
2	73	1 a. on 2d. green and red	£450	£275
3	78	4 a. on 5d. purple and blue	£425	£275

3 Arms of the Company

11

1890. Nos. 16/19 are larger (24×25 mm).

4b	3	½ a. brown	70	3·25
5		1 a. green	3·25	4·50
6		2 a. red	2·75	3·50
7c		2½ a. black on yellow	4·25	5·00
8a		3 a. black on red	1·60	4·50
9		4 a. brown	2·50	4·75
11a		4½ a. purple	2·50	13·00
29		5 a. black on blue	1·25	9·50
30		7½ a. black	1·25	12·00
12	3	8 a. blue	5·50	8·50
13		8 a. grey	£275	£225
14		1 r. red	6·00	9·00
15		1 r. grey	£225	£225
16	–	2 r. red	13·00	25·00
17	–	3 r. purple	8·00	30·00
18	–	4 r. blue	12·00	30·00
19	–	5 r. green	30·00	65·00

1891. With handstamped or pen surcharges. Initialled in black.

23	3	½ a. on 2 a. red	£3500	£750
31		½ a. on 3 a. black on red	£375	48·00
32		1 a. on 3 a. black on red	£3750	£1800
26		1 a. on 4 a. brown	£3250	£1300

1894. Surch in words and figures.

27	3	5 a. on 8 a. blue	55·00	75·00
28		7½ a. on 1 r. red	55·00	75·00

1895. Optd **BRITISH EAST AFRICA.**

33	3	½ a. brown	60·00	23·00
34		1 a. green	80·00	80·00
35		2 a. red	£150	95·00
36		2½ a. black on yellow	£150	48·00
37		3 a. black on red	70·00	40·00
38		4 a. brown	40·00	35·00
39		4½ a. purple	£180	90·00
40		5 a. black on blue	£170	£110
41		7½ a. black	95·00	75·00
42		8 a. blue	90·00	75·00
43		1 r. red	55·00	42·00
44	–	2 r. red	£350	£200
45	–	3 r. purple	£180	£110
46	–	4 r. blue	£140	£130
47	–	5 r. green	£350	£250

1895. Surch with large 2½.

48	3	2½ a. on 4½ a. purple	£130	60·00

1895. Stamps of India (Queen Victoria) optd **British East Africa.**

49	23	½ a. turquoise	5·00	5·00
50	–	1 a. purple	4·25	4·75
51	–	1½ a. brown	3·75	4·00
52	–	2 a. blue	4·75	2·75
53	–	2 a. 6 p. green	5·50	2·50
54	–	3 a. orange	8·00	9·50
55a	–	4 a. green (No. 96)	27·00	24·00
56	–	6 a. brown (No. 80)	28·00	42·00
57c	–	8 a. mauve	28·00	48·00
58	–	12 a. purple on red	21·00	27·00
59	–	1 r. grey (No. 101)	70·00	65·00
60	37	1 r. green and red	42·00	85·00
61	38	2 r. red and orange	65·00	£100
62		3 r. brown and green	75·00	£120
63		5 r. blue and violet	95·00	£140

1895. No. 51 surch with small 2½.

64		2½ on 1½ a. brown	70·00	35·00

1896.

65	11	½ a. green	1·50	70
66		1 a. red	3·50	40
67		2 a. brown	2·50	4·25
68		2½ a. blue	6·50	1·60
69		3 a. grey	2·50	5·50
70		4 a. green	6·00	3·50
71		4½ a. yellow	5·00	14·00
72		5 a. brown	7·50	4·00
73		7½ a. mauve	5·00	22·00
74		8 a. grey	2·75	5·50
75		1 r. blue	38·00	23·00
76		2 r. orange	55·00	25·00
77		3 r. violet	55·00	29·00
78		4 r. red	55·00	55·00
79		5 r. brown	55·00	40·00

1897. Stamps of Zanzibar, 1896, optd **British East Africa.**

80	3	½ a. green and red	48·00	45·00
81		1 a. blue and red	90·00	85·00
82		2 a. brown and red	30·00	21·00
83		4½ a. orange and red	48·00	27·00
84		5 a. brown and red	48·00	32·00
85		7½ a. mauve and red	48·00	35·00

1897. As last, surch 2½.

86	3	2½ on 1 a. blue and red	85·00	55·00
89		2½ on 3 a. grey and red	80·00	48·00

1897. As Type **11**, but larger.

92a		1 r. blue	45·00	26·00
93		2 r. orange	70·00	70·00
94		3 r. violet	80·00	95·00
95		4 r. red	£200	£250
96		5 r. brown	£150	£200
97		10 r. brown	£225	£250
98		20 r. green	£550	£1200
99		50 r. mauve	£1600	£3750

BRITISH FORCES IN EGYPT

SPECIAL SEALS AND STAMPS FOR THE USE OF BRITISH FORCES IN EGYPT

A. SEALS

A 1

1932. (a) Inscr "POSTAL SEAL".

A1	A 1	1 p. blue and red	65·00	3·25

(b) Inscr "LETTER SEAL".

A2	A 1	1 p. blue and red	23·00	85

A 2

1932. Christmas Seals.

A3	A 2	3 m. black on blue	48·00	70·00
A4		3 m. lake	7·50	45·00
A5		3 m. blue	7·00	22·00
A6a		3 m. red	7·00	15·00

A 3

1934.

A9	A 3	1 p. red	2·00	2·00
A8		1 p. green	4·00	4·00

1935. Silver Jubilee. Optd **JUBILEE COMMEMORATION 1935.**

A10	A 3	1 p. blue	£200	£180

1935. Provisional Christmas Seal. Optd **Xmas 1935 3 Milliemes.**

A11	A 3	3 m. on 1 p. red	15·00	70·00

B. POSTAGE STAMPS

A 6 King Fuad I

A 7 King Farouk

1936.

A12	A 6	3 m. green	1·00	90
A13		10 m. red	2·50	10

1939.

A14	A 7	3 m. green	1·50	3·25
A15		10 m. red	2·25	10

BRITISH GUIANA

Situated on the N.E. coast of S. America. A British colony granted full internal self-government in August 1951. Attained independence on 26th May, 1966, when the country was renamed Guyana.

100 cents = 1 dollar

1

1850. Imperf.

				Used
1	1	2 c. black on red	—	£70000
2		4 c. black on orange	£25000	£4000
4		8 c. black on green	£15000	£3250
5		12 c. black on blue	£5500	£2000

Prices are for used stamps cut round. Stamps cut square are worth much more.

2

3 Seal of the Colony

1852. Imperf.

9	2	1 c. black on magenta	£8500	£4250
10		4 c. black on blue	£11000	£5500

1853. Imperf.

12	3	1 c. red	£2500	£900
20		4 c. blue	£850	£325

6

1856. Imperf.

23	6	1 c. black on magenta	†	—
24		4 c. black on magenta	†	£6000
25		4 c. black on blue	£20000	£8500

7

9

1860. Perf.

29	7	1 c. red	£1100	£200
40		1 c. brown	£300	90·00
85		1 c. black	8·50	3·50
87		2 c. orange	29·00	3·75
89		4 c. blue	65·00	12·00
92	9	6 c. blue	£100	27·00
95	7	8 c. red	£100	19·00
98		12 c. lilac	£150	13·00
99		12 c. grey	£140	16·00
64		24 c. green	£160	50·00
79	9	24 c. green	£120	8·00
82		48 c. red	£190	45·00

The prices quoted for Nos. 29/82 are for fine copies with four margins. Medium specimens can be supplied at much lower rates.

10

16

1862. Various borders. Roul.

116	10	1 c. black on red	£2000	£425
119		2 c. black on yellow	£2000	£275
122		4 c. black on blue	£2250	£450

The above prices are for stamps signed in the centre by the Postmaster. Unsigned stamps are worth considerably less.

1876.

126	16	1 c. grey	2·75	1·40
171		2 c. orange	20·00	15
172		4 c. blue	80·00	5·00
173		6 c. brown	5·00	6·50
174		8 c. red	85·00	40
131		12 c. violet	50·00	1·25
132		24 c. green	60·00	3·00
133		48 c. brown	£110	26·00
134		96 c. olive	£475	£250

1878. Optd with thick horiz or horiz and vert bars.

(a) On postage stamps.

137	16	1 c. on 6 c. brown	38·00	£100
141	9	1 c. on 6 c. blue	£130	75·00

(b) On official stamps of 1875 and 1877.

138	7	1 c. black	£160	70·00
139	16	1 c. grey	£120	55·00
140		2 c. orange	£250	65·00
144		4 c. blue	£190	90·00
145		6 c. brown	£250	90·00
146	7	8 c. red	£1000	£250
148	16	8 c. red	£250	95·00

1881. Surch with figure. Old value barred out in ink.

(a) On postage stamps.

152	9	"1" on 48 c. red	38·00	5·00
149	16	"1" on 96 c. olive	3·50	5·50
150		"2" on 96 c. olive	4·00	11·00

(b) On stamps optd **OFFICIAL.**

153	7	"1" on 12 c. lilac	£110	70·00
154	16	"1" on 48 c. brown	£120	90·00
155		"2" on 12 c. violet	60·00	24·00
157		"2" on 24 c. green	70·00	38·00

26

30

1882.

162	26	1 c. black on red	35·00	28·00
165		2 c. black on yellow	55·00	42·00

Each stamp is perforated with the word "SPECIMEN".

1888. T **16** without value in bottom tablet, surch **INLAND REVENUE** and value.

175	16	1 c. purple	1·25	20
176		2 c. purple	1·25	30
177		3 c. purple	70	20
178		4 c. purple	4·50	30
179		6 c. purple	4·50	3·25
180		8 c. purple	1·50	25
181		10 c. purple	6·00	2·50
182		20 c. purple	19·00	10·00
183		40 c. purple	20·00	17·00
184		72 c. purple	35·00	42·00
185		$1 green	£400	£400
186		$2 green	£180	£180
187		$3 green	£120	£120
188		$4 green	£375	£400
189		$5 green	£225	£200

1889. No. 176 surch with additional **2**.

192	16	"2" on 2 c. purple	1·25	15

1889.

193	30	1 c. purple and grey	2·50	1·50
213		1 c. green	40	10
194		2 c. purple and orange	1·50	10
234		2 c. purple and red	3·25	25
241a		2 c. purple & black on red	3·50	10
253a		2 c. red	8·50	10
195		4 c. purple and blue	4·50	1·50
254		4 c. brown and purple	2·25	60
214		5 c. blue	2·75	10
243a		5 c. purple & blue on blue	3·50	6·50
198		6 c. purple and brown	7·00	10·00
236		6 c. black and blue	6·50	11·00
256		6 c. grey and black	13·00	7·00
199		8 c. purple and red	12·00	60
215		8 c. purple and black	2·75	1·10
200a		12 c. purple and mauve	8·50	2·00
257		12 c. orange and purple	4·00	4·00
246a		24 c. purple and green	3·75	4·50
202		48 c. purple and red	15·00	9·00
247a		48 c. grey and brown	14·00	20·00
248a		60 c. green and red	14·00	85·00
203		72 c. purple and brown	28·00	38·00
205		96 c. purple and red	65·00	70·00
250		96 c. black & red on yellow	35·00	45·00

1890. Nos. 185/8 surch **ONE CENT.**

207	16	1 cent on $1 green	1·00	35
208		1 cent on $2 green	1·00	60
209		1 cent on $3 green	1·40	1·25
210		1 cent on $4 green	2·00	6·00

32 Mount Roraima

33 Kaieteur Falls

37

1898. Jubilee.

216	32	1 c. black and red	3·00	65
217	33	2 c. brown and blue	11·00	1·50
219	32	5 c. green and brown	35·00	3·00
220	33	10 c. black and red	16·00	20·00
221	32	15 c. brown and blue	26·00	16·00

1899. Nos. 219/21 surch **TWO CENTS.**

222	32	2 c. on 5 c. green and brown	2·25	1·75
223	33	2 c. on 10 c. black and red	1·75	1·75
224	32	2 c. on 15 c. brown and blue	1·25	1·25

1905. T **30** but inscr "REVENUE", optd **POSTAGE AND REVENUE.**

251	30	$2.40 green and violet	£160	£275

1913.

259a	37	1 c. green	1·50	25
260		2 c. red	70	10
274		2 c. violet	2·50	10
261b		4 c. brown and purple	3·50	25
262		5 c. blue	1·75	85
263		6 c. grey and black	1·75	85
276		6 c. blue	2·75	25
264		12 c. orange and violet	1·00	90
278		24 c. purple and green	2·00	4·50
279		48 c. grey and purple	9·50	3·50
280		60 c. green and red	9·50	48·00
281		72 c. purple and brown	17·00	45·00
269a		96 c. black and red on yellow	16·00	40·00

1918. Optd **WAR TAX.**

271	37	2 c. red	50	15

39 Ploughing a Rice Field

40 Indian shooting Fish

41 Kaieteur Falls

42 Public Buildings, Georgetown

1931. Centenary of County Union.

283	39	1 c. green	2·25	75
284	40	2 c. brown	1·75	10
285	41	4 c. red	1·75	45
286	42	6 c. blue	2·00	2·50
287	41	$1 violet	20·00	40·00

43 Ploughing a Rice Field

44 Gold Mining

53 South America

1934.

288	43	1 c. green	60	50
289	40	2 c. brown	1·50	40
290	44	3 c. red	30	10
291	41	4 c. violet	2·00	85
292	–	6 c. blue	2·50	2·75
293	–	12 c. orange	10	20
294	–	24 c. purple	2·75	4·00
295	–	48 c. black	7·00	8·50
296	41	50 c. green	10·00	16·00
297	–	60 c. brown	26·00	27·00
298	–	72 c. purple	1·25	2·00
299	–	96 c. black	20·00	30·00
300	–	$1 violet	32·00	28·00

DESIGNS—HORIZ: 6 c. Shooting logs over falls; 12 c. Stabroek Market; 24 c. Suger canes in punts; 48 c. Forest road; 60 c. Victoria Regia lilies; 72 c. Mount Roraima; $1 Botanical Gardens. VERT: 96 c. Sir Walter Raleigh and his son.

The 2 c., 4 c. and 50 c. are without the dates shown in Types **40/44** and the 12, 48, 72 and 96 c. have no portrait.

1935. Silver Jubilee. As T **13** of Antigua.

301	2 c. blue and grey	20	10
302	6 c. brown and blue	1·00	85
303	12 c. green and blue	2·50	7·00
304	24 c. grey and purple	4·75	7·00

1937. Coronation. As T **2** of Aden.

305	2 c. brown	15	10
306	4 c. grey	50	30
307	6 c. blue	60	1·00

1938. Designs as for same values of 1934 issue (except where indicated) but with portrait of King George VI (as in T **53**) where portrait of King George V previously appeared.

308aa	43	1 c. green	30	10
309a	–	2 c. violet (As 4 c.)	30	10
310b	53	4 c. red and black	45	15
311	–	6 c. blue (As 2 c.)	40	10
312a	–	24 c. green	1·25	10
313	–	36 c. violet (As 4 c.)	2·00	20
314	–	48 c. orange	60	40
315	–	60 c. brown (As 6 c.)	11·00	3·75
316	–	96 c. purple	2·50	2·75
317	–	$1 violet	11·00	35
318	–	$2 purple (As 72 c.)	4·50	14·00
319	–	$3 brown	27·00	25·00

DESIGN—HORIZ: $3 Victoria Regia lilies.

1946. Victory. As T **9** of Aden.

320	3 c. red	10	10
321	6 c. blue	30	40

1948. Silver Wedding. As T **10/11** of Aden.

322	3 c. red	10	40
323	$3 brown	12·00	23·00

1949. U.P.U. As T **20/23** of Antigua.

324	4 c. red	30	20
325	6 c. blue	90	65
326	12 c. orange	30	45
327	24 c. green	30	60

1951. Inauguration of B.W.I. University College. As T **24/25** of Antigua.

328	3 c. black and red	30	30
329	6 c. black and blue	30	60

1953. Coronation. As T **13** of Aden.

330	4 c. black and red	20	10

55 G.P.O., Georgetown

1954.

331	55	1 c. black	10	10
332	–	2 c. myrtle	10	10
333	–	3 c. olive and brown	3·00	10
334	–	4 c. violet	20	10
335	–	5 c. red and black	30	10
336	–	6 c. green	10	10
337	–	8 c. blue	10	10
338a	–	12 c. black and brown	15	10
360	–	24 c. black and orange	3·25	10
361	–	36 c. red and black	60	60
341a	–	48 c. blue and brown	40	40
342	–	72 c. red and green	12·00	2·75
364	–	$1 multicoloured	7·00	90
344	–	$2 mauve	16·00	5·50
345	–	$5 blue and black	12·00	20·00

DESIGNS—HORIZ: 2 c. Botanical Gardens; 3 c. Victoria Regia lilies; 5 c. Map of Caribbean; 6 c. Rice combine-harvester; 8 c. Sugar cane entering factory; 24 c. Bauxite mining; 36 c. Mount Roraima; $1 Channel-billed toucan; $2 Dredging gold. VERT: 4 c. Amerindian shooting fish; 12 c. Felling greenheart; 48 c. Kaieteur Falls; 72 c. Arapaima (fish); $5 Arms of British Guiana.

70

1961. History and Culture Week.

346	70	5 c. sepia and red	20	10
347		6 c. sepia and green	20	15
348		30 c. sepia and orange	45	45

1963. Freedom from Hunger. As T **28** of Aden.

349	20 c. violet	30	10

1963. Centenary of Red Cross. As T **33** of Antigua.

350	5 c. red and black	20	20
351	20 c. red and blue	55	35

71 Weightlifting

1964. Olympic Games, Tokyo.

367	71	5 c. orange	10	10
368		8 c. blue	15	25
369		25 c. mauve	25	40

1965. Centenary of I.T.U. As T **36** of Antigua.

370	5 c. green and olive	10	15
371	25 c. blue and mauve	20	15

1965. I.C.Y. As T **37** of Antigua.

372	5 c. purple and turquoise	10	10
373	25 c. green and lavender	25	20

72 St George's Cathedral, Georgetown

1966. Churchill Commemoration.

374	72	5 c. black, red and gold	50	10
375		25 c. black, blue and gold	1·40	50

1966. Royal Visit. As T **39** of Antigua.

376	3 c. black and blue	50	15
377	25 c. black and mauve	1·50	60

OFFICIAL STAMPS

1875. Optd **OFFICIAL.**

O1	7	1 c. black	40·00	14·00
O2		2 c. orange	£150	14·00
O3		8 c. red	£300	£120
O4		12 c. lilac	£1500	£475
O5	9	24 c. green	£850	£225

1877. Optd **OFFICIAL.**

O 6	16	1 c. grey	£200	55·00
O 7		2 c. orange	90·00	15·00
O 8		4 c. blue	80·00	20·00
O 9		6 c. brown	£2500	£600
O10		8 c. red	£1700	£450

POSTAGE DUE STAMPS

1940. As Type D 1 of Barbados, but inscr "BRITISH GUIANA".

D1a	1 c. green	1·50	8·00
D2a	2 c. black	1·50	3·50
D3	4 c. blue	30	8·00
D4	12 c. red	25·00	5·00

For later issues see **GUYANA.**

BRITISH HONDURAS

A British colony on the East coast of Central America. Self-government was granted on 1 January 1964. The country was renamed Belize from 1 June 1973.

1866. 12 pence = 1 shilling;
20 shillings = 1 pound.
1888. 100 cents = 1 dollar.

1

8

1866.

17	1	1d. blue	38·00	13·00
18		1d. red	20·00	12·00
13		3d. brown	95·00	16·00
20		4d. mauve	70·00	4·75
9		6d. red	£190	28·00
21		6d. yellow	£275	£180
16		1s. green	£160	11·00
22		1s. grey	£250	£150

1888. Surch as **2 CENTS.**

36	1	1 c. on 1d. green	40	1·25
37		2 c. on 1d. red	30	1·50
25		2 c. on 6d. red	85·00	75·00
38		3 c. on 3d. brown	2·25	1·40
39		6 c. on 3d. blue	2·25	10·00
40		10 c. on 4d. mauve	5·00	40
41		20 c. on 6d. yellow	11·00	14·00
42		50 c. on 1s. grey	27·00	70·00

1888. No. 42 surch **TWO.**

35	1	"TWO" on 50 c. on 1s. grey	42·00	80·00

1891. No. 40 surch **6** and bar.

43	1	6 c. on 10 c. on 4d. mauve	80	1·75

Nos. 38 and 39 surch.

49	1	"FIVE" on 3 c. on 3d. brown	80	1·40
50		"15" on 6 c. on 3d. blue	9·50	22·00

1891.

51	8	1 c. green	1·50	90
52		2 c. red	1·25	10
53		3 c. brown	4·75	2·25
54		5 c. blue	12·00	40
55		5 c. black and blue on blue	13·00	2·00
56		6 c. blue	4·75	1·75
57		10 c. mauve and green (A)	8·50	8·50
58		10 c. purple and green (B)	9·00	7·50
59a		12 c. mauve and green	2·50	2·00
60		24 c. yellow and blue	5·50	14·00
61		25 c. brown and green	50·00	90·00
62		50 c. green and red	21·00	50·00
63		$1 green and red	55·00	95·00
64		$2 green and blue	75·00	£110
65		$5 green and black	£225	£275

NOTE: 10 c. (A) inscr "POSTAGE POSTAGE"; (B) inscr "POSTAGE & REVENUE".

1899. Optd **REVENUE.**

66	8	5 c. blue	8·00	2·25
67		10 c. mauve and green	3·00	11·00
68		25 c. brown and green	2·75	30·00
69	1	50 c. on 1s. grey	£120	£275

14

16

1902.

84a	14	1 c. green	65	1·50
85a		2 c. purple and black on red	65	10
96		2 c. red	8·00	10
86		5 c. black and blue on blue	1·75	20
97		5 c. blue	1·75	10
87		10 c. purple and green	5·00	11·00
83		20 c. purple	4·25	17·00
89		25 c. purple and orange	7·00	40·00
100		25 c. black on green	2·75	45·00
90		50 c. green and red	15·00	65·00
91		$1 green and red	45·00	65·00
92		$2 green and blue	80·00	£140
93		$5 green and black	£180	£250

1913.

101	16	1 c. green	2·50	75
102		2 c. red	2·00	75
103		3 c. orange	40	20
104		5 c. blue	2·00	45
105		10 c. purple and green	2·75	6·50
106		25 c. black on green	1·25	11·00
107		50 c. purple and blue on blue	8·00	11·00
108		$1 black and red	16·00	35·00
109		$2 purple and green	60·00	70·00
110		$5 purple and black on red	£190	£225

1915. Optd with pattern of wavy lines.

111a	16	1 c. green	30	10·00
112		2 c. red	2·00	50
113		5 c. blue	30	4·50

1916. Optd **WAR**.

114	16	1 c. green (No. 111a)	10	50
119		1 c. green (No. 101)	10	25
120		3 c. orange (No. 103)	30	85

21

1921. Peace.

121	21	2 c. red	2·50	30

As last, but without word "PEACE"

123		4 c. grey	5·00	30

22

24 Maya figures

1922.

126	22	1 c. green	2·00	5·00
127		2 c. brown	75	80
128		2 c. red	1·25	80
129		3 c. orange	10·00	3·50
130		4 c. grey	2·75	65
131		5 c. blue	1·25	55
132		10 c. purple and olive	1·00	30
133		25 c. black on green	1·00	7·50
134		50 c. purple and blue on blue	4·75	14·00
136		$1 black and red	6·50	22·00
137		$2 green and purple	32·00	75·00
125		$5 purple and black on red	£170	£190

1932. Optd **BELIZE RELIEF FUND PLUS** and value.

138	22	1 c.+1 c. green	70	6·50
139		2 c.+2 c. red	75	6·50
140		3 c.+3 c. orange	85	12·00
141		4 c.+4 c. grey	7·00	17·00
142		5 c.+5 c. blue	6·00	13·00

1935. Silver Jubilee. As T **13** of Antigua.

143		3 c. blue and black	65	45
144		4 c. green and blue	1·50	2·75
145		5 c. brown and blue	1·50	60
146		25 c. grey and purple	2·50	2·75

1937. Coronation. As T **2** of Aden.

147		3 c. orange	30	30
148		4 c. grey	70	30
149		5 c. blue	80	1·10

1938.

150	24	1 c. purple and green	10	1·25
151	–	2 c. black and red	20	90
152	–	3 c. purple and brown	30	55
153	–	4 c. black and green	30	70
154	–	5 c. purple and blue	75	50
155	–	10 c. green and brown	75	60
156	–	15 c. brown and blue	2·00	70
157	–	25 c. blue and green	2·00	1·25
158	–	50 c. black and purple	11·00	3·00
159	–	$1 red and olive	20·00	9·00
160	–	$2 blue and purple	23·00	16·00
161	–	$5 red and brown	23·00	23·00

DESIGNS—VERT: 2 c. Chicle tapping; 3 c. Cohune palm; $1 Court House, Belize; $2 Mahogany felling; $5 Arms of Colony. HORIZ: 4 c. Local products; 5 c. Grapefruit; 10 c. Mahogany logs in river; 15 c. Sergeant's Cay; 25 c. Dorey; 50 c. Chicle industry.

1946. Victory. As T **9** of Aden.

162		3 c. brown	10	10
163		5 c. blue	10	10

1948. Silver Wedding. As T **10** and **11** of Aden.

164		4 c. green	15	20
165		$5 brown	15·00	35·00

36 Island of Saint George's Cay

1949. 150th Anniv of Battle of Saint George's Cay.

166	36	1 c. blue and green	10	50
167		3 c. blue and brown	10	1·00
168		4 c. olive and violet	10	50
169	–	5 c. brown and blue	70	20
170	–	10 c. green and brown	50	30
171	–	15 c. green and blue	50	30

DESIGNS: 5, 10 and 15 c. H.M.S. "Merlin".

1949. U.P.U. As T **20/23** of Antigua.

172		4 c. green	40	30
173		5 c. blue	1·50	30
174		10 c. brown	50	2·00
175		25 c. blue	60	50

1951. Inauguration of B.W.I. University College. As T **24/25** of Antigua.

176		3 c. violet and brown	45	1·00
177		10 c. green and brown	45	30

1953. Coronation. As T **13** of Aden.

178		4 c. black and green	40	30

39 Baird's Tapir

49 Mountain Orchid

1953.

179	–	1 c. green and black	10	40
180a	39	2 c. brown and black	50	10
181a	–	3 c. lilac and mauve	10	10
182	–	4 c. brown and green	40	30
183	–	5 c. olive and red	10	10
184	–	10 c. slate and blue	10	10
185	–	15 c. green and violet	15	10
186	–	25 c. blue and brown	6·00	2·00
187	–	50 c. brown and purple	6·00	1·75
188	–	$1 slate and brown	5·50	4·50
189	–	$2 red and grey	6·50	4·50
190	49	$5 purple and slate	42·00	17·00

DESIGNS—HORIZ: 1 c. Arms of British Honduras; 3 c. Mace and Legislative Council Chamber; 4 c. Pine industry; 5 c. Spiny lobster; 10 c. Stanley Field Airport; 15 c. Maya frieze; 25 c. "Morpho peleides (butterfly); $1 Nine-banded armadillo; $2 Hawkesworth Bridge. VERT: 50 c. Maya indian.

50 "Belize from Fort George, 1842" (C. J. Hullmandel)

1960. Post Office Centenary.

191	50	2 c. green	30	90
192	–	10 c. red	30	10
193	–	15 c. blue	35	35

DESIGNS: 10 c. Public seals, 1860 and 1960; 15 c. Tamarind tree, Newtown Barracks.

1961. New Constitution. Stamps of 1953 optd **NEW CONSTITUTION 1960**.

194	39	2 c. brown and black	25	10
195	–	3 c. lilac and mauve	30	10
196	–	10 c. slate and blue	30	10
197	–	15 c. green and violet	30	10

1962. Hurricane Hattie Relief Fund. Stamps of 1953 optd **HURRICANE HATTIE**.

198		1 c. green and black	10	50
199		10 c. slate and blue	30	10
200		25 c. blue and brown	1·40	70
201		50 c. brown and purple	50	90

55 Great Curassow

1962. Birds in natural colours; portrait and inscr in black; background colours given.

239	55	1 c. yellow	10	30
240	–	2 c. grey	30	50
204	–	3 c. green	2·00	1·75
241	–	4 c. grey	1·75	85
242	–	5 c. buff	40	10
243	–	10 c. stone	50	10
244	–	15 c. stone	60	10
209	–	25 c. slate	4·50	30
210	–	50 c. grey	6·00	35
211	–	$1 blue	9·00	75
212	–	$2 stone	13·00	3·00
213	–	$5 grey	25·00	14·00

BIRDS: 2 c. Red-legged honeycreeper; 3 c. Northern jacana; 4 c. Great kiskadee; 5 c. Scarlet-rumped tanager; 10 c. Scarlet macaw; 15 c. Slaty-tailed trogon; 25 c. Red-footed booby; 50 c. Keel-billed toucan; $1 Magnificent frigate bird; $2 Rufous-tailed jacamar; $5 Montezuma oropendola.

1963. Freedom from Hunger. As T **28** of Aden.

214		22 c. green	30	15

1963. Centenary of Red Cross. As T **33** of Antigua.

215		4 c. red and black	20	40
216		22 c. red and blue	40	85

1964. New Constitution. Nos. 202, 204, 205, 207 and 209 optd **SELF GOVERNMENT 1964**.

217	55	1 c. yellow	10	20
218	–	3 c. green	35	20
219	–	4 c. pale grey	35	20
220	–	10 c. stone	35	10
221	–	25 c. slate	55	30

1965. Centenary of I.T.U. As T **36** of Antigua.

222		2 c. red and green	10	10
223		50 c. yellow and purple	35	25

1965. I.C.Y. As T **37** of Antigua.

224		1 c. purple and turquoise	10	15
225		22 c. green and lavender	20	15

1966. Churchill Commemoration. As T **38** of Antigua.

226		1 c. blue	10	10
227		4 c. green	15	10
228		22 c. brown	40	10
229		25 c. violet	50	45

1966. Dedication of new Capital Site. Nos. 202, 204/5 207 and 209 optd **DEDICATION OF SITE NEW CAPITAL 9th OCTOBER 1965**.

230	55	1 c. yellow	10	30
231	–	3 c. green	35	30
232	–	4 c. grey	35	30
233	–	10 c. stone	35	10
234	–	25 c. slate	55	35

58 Citrus Grove

1966. Stamp Centenary. Multicoloured

235		5 c. Type **58**	10	10
236		10 c. Half Moon Cay	10	10
237		22 c. Hidden Valley Falls	10	10
238		25 c. Maya ruins, Xunantunich	15	30

59 Sailfish

1967. International Tourist Year.

246	59	5 c. blue, black and yellow	15	20
247	–	10 c. brown, black and red	15	10
248	–	22 c. orange, black and green	30	10
249	–	25 c. blue, black and yellow	30	45

DESIGNS: 10 c. Red brocket; 22 c. Jaguar; 25 c. Atlantic tarpon.

60 "Schomburgkia tibicinis"

61 Monument Belizean Patriots

1968. 20th Anniv of Economic Commission for Latin America. Orchids. Multicoloured.

250		5 c. Type **60**	20	15
251		10 c. "Maxillaria tenuifolia"	25	10
252		22 c. "Bletia purpurea"	30	10
253		25 c. "Sobralia macrantha"	40	20

1968. Human Rights Year. Multicoloured.

254		22 c. Type **61**	15	10
255		50 c. Monument at site of new capital	15	20

63 Spotted Jewfish

1968. Wildlife.

276	–	½ c. multicoloured and blue	10	10
277	–	½ c. multicoloured and yellow	1·75	1·00
256	63	1 c. black, brown and yellow	20	10
257	–	2 c. black, green and yellow	10	10
258	–	3 c. black, brown and lilac	20	10
259	–	4 c. multicoloured	10	60
260	–	5 c. black and red	10	60
261	–	10 c. multicoloured	15	10
262	–	15 c. multicoloured	40	20
263	–	25 c. multicoloured	30	20
264	–	50 c. multicoloured	70	1·25
265	–	$1 multicoloured	2·50	1·25
266	–	$2 multicoloured	2·50	2·00
278	–	$5 multicoloured	6·50	12·00

DESIGNS: ½ c. (Nos. 276 and 277) Mozambique mouthbrooder ("Crana"); 2 c. White-lipped peccary; 3 c. Misty grouper; 4 c. Collared anteater; 5 c. Bonefish; 10 c. Paca; 15 c. Dolphin; 25 c. Kinkajou; 50 c. Mutton snapper; $1 Tayra; $2 Great barracuda; $5 Puma.

64 "Rhyncholaelia digbyana"

65 Ziricote Tree

1969. Orchids of Belize (1st series). Multicoloured.

268		5 c. Type **64**	50	20
269		10 c. "Cattleya bowringiana"	55	15
270		22 c. "Lycaste cochleatum"	85	15
271		25 c. "Coryanthes speciosum"	1·10	1·10

See also Nos. 287/90.

1969. Indigenous Hardwoods (1st series). Mult.

272		5 c. Type **65**	10	20
273		10 c. Rosewood	10	10
274		22 c. Mayflower	20	10
275		25 c. Mahogany	20	45

See also Nos. 291/4, 315/8 and 333/7.

66 "The Virgin and Child" (Bellini)

69 Santa Maria

1969. Christmas. Paintings. Multicoloured.

279		5 c. Type **66**	10	10
280		15 c. Type **66**	10	10
281		22 c. "The Adoration of the Magi" (Veronese)	10	10
282		25 c. As No. 281	10	20

1970. Population Census. Nos. 260/3 optd **POPULATION CENSUS 1970**.

283		5 c. multicoloured	10	10
284		10 c. multicoloured	15	10
285		15 c. multicoloured	20	10
286		25 c. multicoloured	20	15

1970. Orchids of Belize (2nd series). As T **64**. Mult.

287		5 c. Black orchid	35	15
288		15 c. White butterfly orchid	50	10
289		22 c. Swan orchid	70	10
290		25 c. Butterfly orchid	70	40

1970. Indigenous Hardwoods (2nd series). Mult.

291		5 c. Type **69**	25	10
292		15 c. Nargusta	35	10
293		22 c. Cedar	40	10
294		25 c. Sapodilla	40	35

70 "The Nativity" (A. Hughes)

71 Legislative Assembly House

1970. Christmas. Multicoloured.

295		½ c. Type **70**	10	10
296		5 c. "The Mystic Nativity" (Botticelli)	10	10
297		10 c. Type **70**	10	10
298		15 c. As 5 c.	20	10
299		22 c. Type **70**	25	10
300		50 c. As 5 c.	40	60

1971. Establishment of New Capital, Belmopan. Multicoloured.

301		5 c. Old capital, Belize	10	10
302		10 c. Government Plaza	10	10
303		15 c. Type **71**	10	10
304		22 c. Magistrates' Court	15	10
305		25 c. Police H.Q.	15	15
306		50 c. New G.P.O.	25	40

The 5 c. and 10 c. are larger, 60 × 22 mm.

72 "Tabebuia chrysantha"

1971. Easter. Flowers. Multicoloured.

307		½ c. Type **72**	10	10
308		5 c. "Hymenocallis littoralis"	10	10
309		10 c. "Hippeastrum equestre"	10	10
310		15 c. Type **72**	20	10
311		22 c. As 5 c.	20	10
312		25 c. As 10 c.	20	30

1971. Racial Equality Year. Nos. 261 and 264 optd **RACIAL EQUALITY YEAR–1971**.

313		10 c. multicoloured	25	10
314		50 c. multicoloured	55	20

74 Tubroos

76 "Petrae volubis"

75 Hawksworth and Belcan Bridges

1971. Indigenous Hardwoods (3rd series). Mult.

315	5 c. Type **74**	50	10
316	15 c. Yemeri	70	30
317	26 c. Billywebb	95	35
318	50 c. Logwood	1·75	3·25

1971. Bridges of the World. Multicoloured.

320	½ c. Type **75**	10	10
321	5 c. Narrows Bridge, N.Y. and Quebec Bridge	20	10
322	26 c. London Bridge (1871) and reconstructed, Arizona (1971)	50	10
323	50 c. Belize Mexican Bridge and Swing Bridge	70	90

1972. Easter. Wild Flowers. Multicoloured.

324	6 c. Type **76**	15	10
325	15 c. Yemeri	25	30
326	26 c. Mayflower	50	45
327	50 c. Tiger's Claw	80	1·40

77 Seated Figure

78 Banak

1972. Mayan Artefacts. Multicoloured.

328	3 c. Type **77**	15	10
329	6 c. Priest in "dancing" pose	20	10
330	16 c. Sun God's head (horiz)	35	15
331	26 c. Priest and Sun God	50	20
332	50 c. Full-front figure	1·00	2·75

1972. Indigenous Hardwoods (4th series). Mult.

333	3 c. Type **78**	20	10
334	5 c. Quamwood	20	10
335	16 c. Waika Chewstick	55	15
336	26 c. Mamee-Apple	75	25
337	50 c. My Lady	1·60	3·25

1972. Royal Silver Wedding. As T **52** of Ascension, but with Orchids of Belize in background.

341	26 c. green	25	10
342	50 c. violet	40	55

80 Baron Bliss Day

1973. Festivals of Belize. Multicoloured.

343	3 c. Type **80**	15	10
344	10 c. Labour Day	15	10
345	26 c. Carib Settlement Day	30	10
346	50 c. Pan American Day	50	70

POSTAGE DUE STAMPS

D 1

1923.

D1	D **1**	1 c. black	2·00	12·00
D4		2 c. black	2·50	5·00
D5		4 c. black	75	5·50

For later issues see **BELIZE**.

BRITISH INDIAN OCEAN TERRITORY

A Crown Colony, established 8th November 1965, comprising the Chagos Archipelago (previously administered by Mauritius) and Aldabra, Farquhar and Desroches, previously administered by Seychelles to which country they were returned on 29th June 1976.

The Chagos Archipelago has no indigenous population, but stamps were provided from 1990 for use by civilian workers at the U.S. Navy base on Diego Garcia.

1968. 100 cents = 1 rupee.
1990. 100 pence = 1 pound.

1968. Nos 196/200, 202/4 and 206/12 of Seychelles optd **B.I.O.T.**

1	**24**	5 c. multicoloured	75	40
2	–	10 c. multicoloured	10	15
3	–	15 c. multicoloured	10	15
4	–	20 c. multicoloured	15	15
5	–	25 c. multicoloured	15	15
6	–	40 c. multicoloured	20	20
7	–	45 c. multicoloured	20	30
8	–	50 c. multicoloured	20	30
9	–	75 c. multicoloured	20	35
10	–	1 r. multicoloured	40	35
11	–	1 r. 50 multicoloured	1·75	1·50
12	–	2 r. 25 multicoloured	3·00	3·75
13	–	3 r. 50 multicoloured	3·00	4·50
14	–	5 r. multicoloured	6·50	7·50
15	–	10 r. multicoloured	17·00	20·00

2 Lascar

1968. Marine Life. Multicoloured.

16	5 c. Type **2**	30	1·50
17	10 c. Smooth hammerhead (vert)	30	1·25
18	15 c. Tiger shark	30	1·50
19	20 c. Spotted eagle ray ("Bat ray")	30	1·00
20	25 c. Yellow-finned butterflyfish and ear-spot angelfish (vert)	80	1·00
20a	30 c. Robber crab	3·50	2·75
21	40 c. Blue-finned trevalley ("Caranx")	40	40
22	45 c. Crocodile needlefish ("Garfish") (vert)	2·25	2·50
23	50 c. Pickhandle barracuda	45	30
23a	60 c. Spotted pebble crab	3·50	3·25
24	75 c. Indian Ocean steep-headed parrotfish	2·50	2·75
24a	85 c. Rainbow runner ("Dorade")	6·00	3·50
25	1 r. Giant hermit crab	1·50	35
26	1 r. 50 Parrotfish ("Humphead")	2·50	2·50
27	2 r. 25 Yellow-edged lyre-tail and Aredate grouper ("Rock cod")	8·00	8·50
28	3 r. 50 Black marlin	4·00	3·75
29	5 r. black, green and blue (Whale shark) (vert)	9·00	8·00
30	10 r. Lionfish	9·00	8·00

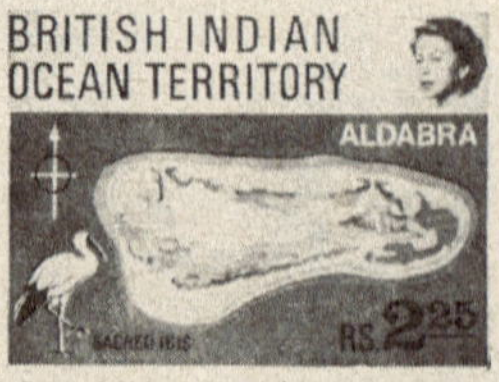

3 Sacred Ibis and Aldabra Coral Atoll

1969. Coral Atolls

31	**3**	2 r. 25 multicoloured	1·75	70

4 Outrigger Canoe

1969. Ships of the Islands. Multicoloured.

32	45 c. Type **4**	65	75
33	75 c. Pirogue	65	80
34	1 r. M.V. "Nordvaer"	70	90
35	1 r. 50 "Isle of Farquhar"	80	1·00

5 Giant Land Tortoise

1971. Aldabra Nature Reserve. Multicoloured.

36	45 c. Type **5**	2·50	2·25
37	75 c. Aldabra lily	3·00	2·50
38	1 r. Aldabra tree snail	3·50	2·75
39	1 r. 50 Western reef heron	12·00	9·00

6 Arms of Royal Society and White-throated Rail

1971. Opening of Royal Society Research Station, Aldabra.

40	**6**	3 r. 50 multicoloured	15·00	8·50

7 Staghorn Coral

1972. Coral. Multicoloured.

41	40 c. Type **7**	3·50	3·50
42	60 c. Brain coral	4·00	4·00
43	1 r. Mushroom coral	4·00	4·00
44	1 r. 75 Organ pipe coral	5·00	6·00

1972. Royal Silver Wedding. As T **52** of Ascension, but with White-throated rail and Sacred ibis in background.

45	95 c. green	75	40
46	1 r. 50 violet	75	40

9 "Christ on the Cross"

10 Upsidedown Jellyfish

1973. Easter. Multicoloured.

47	45 c. Type **9**	25	40
48	75 c. "Joseph and Nicodemus burying Jesus"	35	55
49	1 r. Type **9**	35	60
50	1 r. 50 As 75 c.	40	70

1973. Wildlife (1st series). Multicoloured.

53	50 c. Type **10**	3·50	3·00
54	1 r. "Hypolimnas misippus" and "Belenois aldabrensis" (butterflies)	4·00	3·00
55	1 r. 50 "Nephila madagascariensis" (spider)	4·25	3·00

See also Nos. 58/61, 77/80 and 86/9.

11 M.V. "Nordvaer"

13 Aldabra Drongo

12 Red-cloud Auger and Subulat Auger

1974. 5th Anniv of "Nordvaer" Travelling Post Office. Multicoloured.

56	85 c. Type **11**	85	75
57	2 r. 50 "Nordvaer" off shore	1·40	1·25

1974. Wildlife (2nd series). Shells. Multicoloured.

58	45 c. Type **12**	2·25	1·00
59	75 c. Great green turban	2·50	1·25
60	1 r. Strawberry drupe	2·75	1·50
61	1 r. 50 Bull-mouth helmet	3·00	1·75

1975. Birds. Multicoloured.

62	5 c. Type **13**	1·25	2·75
63	10 c. Black coucal	1·25	2·75
64	20 c. Mascarene fody	1·25	2·75
65	25 c. White tern	1·25	2·75
66	30 c. Crested tern	1·25	2·75
67	40 c. Brown booby	1·25	2·75
68	50 c. Common noddy (horiz)	1·25	3·00
69	60 c. Grey heron	1·25	3·00
70	65 c. Blue-faced booby (horiz)	1·25	3·00
71	95 c. Madagascar white eye (horiz)	1·25	3·00
72	1 r. Green heron (horiz)	1·25	3·00
73	1 r. 75 Lesser frigate bird (horiz)	2·00	4·75
74	3 r. 50 White-tailed tropic bird (horiz)	2·75	4·75
75	5 r. Souimanga sunbird (horiz)	4·00	5·00
76	10 r. Madagascar turtle dove (horiz)	8·00	9·00

14 "Grewia salicifolia"

1975. Wildlife (3rd series). Seashore Plants. Multicoloured.

77	50 c. Type **14**	60	1·25
78	65 c. "Cassia aldabrensis"	65	1·40
79	1 r. "Hypoestes aldabrensis"	80	1·50
80	1 r. 60 "Euphorbia pyrifolia"	1·10	1·60

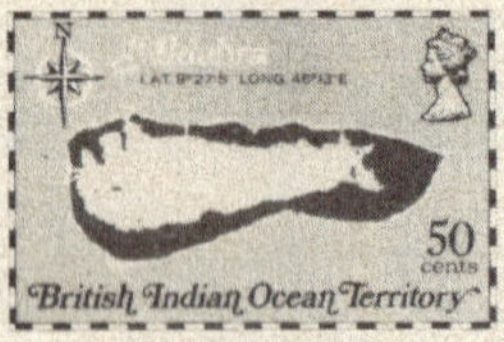

15 Map of Aldabra

1975. 10th Anniv of Territory. Maps. Multicoloured.

81	50 c. Type **15**	70	65
82	1 r. Desroches	85	85
83	1 r. 50 Farquhar	95	1·00
84	2 r. Diego Garcia	1·00	1·25

16 "Utetheisa pulchella" (moth)

1976. Wildlife (4th series). Multicoloured.

86	65 c. Type **16**	60	1·10
87	1 r. 20 "Dysdercus fasciatus" (bug)	75	1·25
88	1 r. 50 "Sphex torridus" (wasp)	80	1·40
89	2 r. "Oryctes rhinoceros" (beetle)	85	1·40

17 White-tailed Tropic Bird

19 Territory Flag

18 1974 Wildlife 1 r. 50 Stamp

1990. Birds. Multicoloured.
90 15p. Type **17** 1·10 1·50
91 20p. Madagascar turtle dove 1·25 1·60
92 24p. Great frigate bird 1·40 1·75
93 30p. Green heron 1·50 2·00
94 34p. Great sand plover 1·60 2·00
95 41p. Crab plover 1·75 2·25
96 45p. Crested tern 2·00 2·25
97 54p. Lesser crested tern 2·25 2·50
98 62p. White tern 2·25 2·50
99 71p. Red-footed booby 2·25 3·00
100 80p. Common mynah 2·50 3·25
101 £1 Madagascar red fody 2·50 3·50

1990. "Stamp World London 90" International Stamp Exhibition. Multicoloured.
102 15p. Type **18** 2·25 2·25
103 20p. 1976 Wildlife 2 r. stamp 2·50 2·50
104 34p. 1975 Diego Garcia map 2 r. stamp 4·00 4·00
105 54p. 1969 "Nordvaer" 1 r. stamp 5·75 5·75

1990. 90th Birthday of Queen Elizabeth the Queen Mother. As T **34** of Ascension.
106 24p. multicoloured 3·00 3·50
107 £1 black and ochre 5·00 5·50
DESIGNS—21 × 36 mm: Lady Elizabeth Bowes-Lyon, 1923. 29 × 37 mm: £1 Queen Elizabeth and her daughters, 1940.

1990. 25th Anniv of British Indian Ocean Territory. Multicoloured.
108 20p. Type **19** 4·00 4·50
109 24p. Coat of arms 4·00 4·50

20 Postman emptying Pillar Box

1991. British Indian Ocean Territory Administration. Multicoloured.
111 20p. Type **20** 2·00 2·50
112 24p. Commissioner inspecting guard of Royal Marines 2·25 2·50
113 34p. Policeman outside station 4·00 4·50
114 54p. Customs officers boarding yacht 5·50 6·00

21 "Experiment" (E.I.C. survey brig), 1786

1991. Visiting Ships. Multicoloured.
115 20p. Type **21** 2·75 3·00
116 24p. "Pickering" (American brig), 1819 3·00 3·25
117 34p. "Emden" (German cruiser), 1914 4·00 4·25
118 54p. H.M.S. "Edinburgh" (destroyer), 1988 5·00 5·50

1992. 40th Anniv of Queen Elizabeth II's Accession. As T **143** of Ascension. Multicoloured.
119 15p. Catholic chapel, Diego Garcia 1·00 1·25
120 20p. Planter's house, Diego Garcia 1·10 1·40
121 24p. Railway tracks on wharf, Diego Garcia 1·75 1·75
122 34p. Three portraits of Queen Elizabeth 1·75 1·90
123 54p. Queen Elizabeth II 2·00 2·40

22 R.A.F. Consolidated PBY-5 Catalina (flying boat)

1992. Visiting Aircraft. Multicoloured.
124 20p. Type **22** 2·00 2·50
125 24p. R.A.F. Hawker Siddeley Nimrod M.R.2 (maritime reconnaissance aircraft) 2·25 2·50
126 34p. Lockheed P-3 Orion (transport aircraft) 2·75 3·25
127 54p. U.S.A.A.F. Boeing B-52 Stratofortress (heavy bomber) 3·50 4·50

23 "The Mystical Marriage of St. Catherine" (Correggio)

1992. Christmas. Religious Paintings. Multicoloured.
128 5p. Type **23** 70 80
129 24p. "Madonna" (anon) 1·50 1·60
130 34p. "Madonna" (anon) (different) 1·75 2·25
131 54p. "The Birth of Jesus" (Kaspar Jele) 2·50 3·50

24 Coconut Crab and Rock

1993. Endangered Species. Coconut Crab. Multicoloured.
132 10p. Type **24** 1·25 1·25
133 10p. Crab on beach 1·25 1·25
134 10p. Two crabs 1·25 1·25
135 15p. Crab climbing coconut tree 1·50 1·50

1993. 75th Anniv of Royal Air Force. As T **149** of Ascension. Multicoloured.
136 20p. Vickers Virginia Mk X 1·25 1·50
137 24p. Bristol Bulldog IIA 1·40 1·50
138 34p. Short S.25 Sunderland Mk III 1·75 2·00
139 54p. Bristol Blenheim Mk IV 2·75 3·25

25 "Stachytarpheta urticifolia"

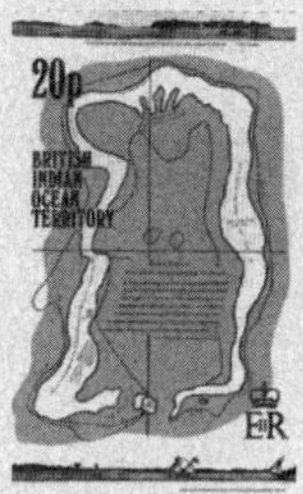
26 Forrest's Map of Diego Garcia, 1778

1993. Christmas. Flowers. Multicoloured.
141 20p. Type **25** 1·25 1·25
142 24p. "Ipomea pes-caprae" 1·25 1·25
143 34p. "Sida pusilla" 1·50 2·00
144 54p. "Catharanthus roseus" 2·50 3·00

1994. "Hong Kong '94" International Stamp Exhibition. Nos. 92 and 101 optd **HONG KONG '94** and emblem.
145 24p. Great frigate bird 1·25 1·50
146 £1 Madagascar red fody 3·00 4·00

1994. 18th-century Maps. Each black and blue.
147 20p. Type **26** 90 1·40
148 24p. Blair's plan of Diego Garcia harbour, 1786–87 1·00 1·50
149 34p. Blair's chart of Chagos Archipelago, 1786–87 1·10 1·60
150 44p. Plan of part of Diego Garcia, 1774 1·40 1·75
151 54p. Fontaine's plan of Diego Garcia, 1770 1·60 1·90

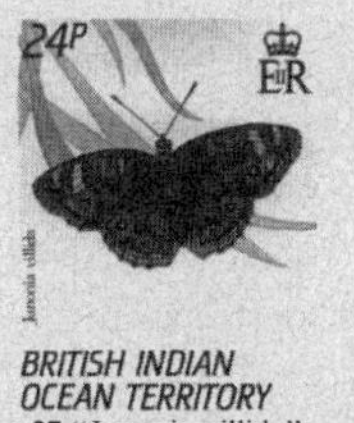
27 "Junonia villida"

1994. Butterflies. Multicoloured.
152 24p. Type **27** 1·50 1·50
153 30p. "Petrelaea dana" 2·00 2·25
154 56p. "Hypolimnas misippus" 3·00 3·75

28 Short-tailed Nurse Sharks

1994. Sharks. Multicoloured.
155 15p. Type **28** 30 35
156 20p. Silver-tipped sharks 40 45
157 24p. Black-finned reef shark 50 55
158 30p. Oceanic white-tipped sharks 60 65
159 35p. Black-tipped shark 70 75
160 41p. Smooth hammerhead 80 85
161 46p. Sickle-finned lemon shark 90 95
162 55p. White-tipped reef shark 1·10 1·25
163 65p. Tiger sharks 1·25 1·40
164 74p. Indian sand tiger 1·50 1·60
165 80p. Great hammerhead 1·60 1·75
166 £1 Great white shark 2·00 2·10

1995. 50th Anniv of End of Second World War. As T **161** of Ascension. Multicoloured.
167 20p. Military cemetery 1·25 1·50
168 24p. Rusty 6-inch naval gun at Cannon Point 1·40 1·50
169 30p. Short S.25 Sunderland flying boat 1·75 1·90
170 56p. H.M.I.S. "Clive"(sloop) 2·75 3·25

29 Dolphin (fish)

1995. Gamefish. Multicoloured.
172 20p. Type **29** 1·00 1·25
173 24p. Sailfish 1·10 1·25
174 30p. Wahoo 1·75 1·90
175 56p. Striped marlin 2·75 3·25

30 "Terebra crenulata"

1996. Sea Shells. Multicoloured.
176 20p. Type **30** 1·00 1·25
177 24p. "Bursa bufonia" 1·10 1·25
178 30p. "Nassarius papillosus" 1·75 1·90
179 56p. "Lopha cristagalli" 2·75 3·25

1996. 70th Birthday of Queen Elizabeth II. As T **165** of Ascension, each incorporating a different photograph of the Queen. Multicoloured.
180 20p. View of lagoon from south 60 80
181 24p. Manager's House, Peros Banhos 65 80
182 30p. Wireless hut, Peros Banhos 80 1·25
183 56p. Sunset 1·25 1·75

31 Loggerhead Turtle

1996. Turtles. Multicoloured.
185 20p. Type **31** 80 90
186 24p. Leatherback turtle 85 90
187 30p. Hawksbill turtle 1·25 1·50
188 56p. Green turtle 1·75 2·00

32 Commissioner's Representative (naval officer)

1996. Uniforms. Multicoloured.
189 20p. Type **32** 90 1·00
190 24p. Royal Marine officer 95 1·00
191 30p. Royal Marine in battle-dress 1·40 1·60
192 56p. Police officers 2·00 2·25

1997. Golden Wedding of Queen Elizabeth and Prince Philip. As T **173** of Ascension. Mult.
195 20p. Queen Elizabeth at Bristol, 1994 70 90
196 20p. Prince Philip competing in Royal Windsor Horse Show, 1996 70 90
197 24p. Queen Elizabeth in phaeton, Trooping the Colour, 1987 70 90
198 24p. Prince Philip 70 90
199 30p. Queen Elizabeth and Prince Philip with Land Rover 80 1·00
200 30p. Queen Elizabeth at Balmoral 80 1·00
Nos. 195/6, 197/8 and 199/20 respectively were printed together, se-tenant, with the backgrounds forming a compsite design.

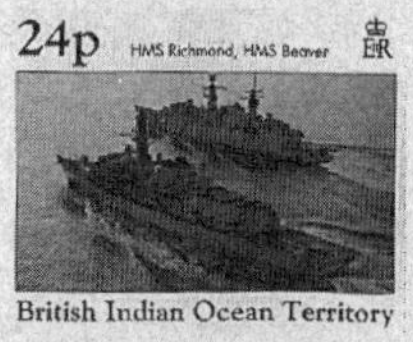
33 H.M.S. "Richmond" (frigate) and H.M.S. "Beaver" (frigate)

1997. Exercise Ocean Wave. Multicoloured.
202 24p. Type **33** 70 80
203 24p. H.M.S. "Illustrious" (aircraft carrier) launching aircraft 70 80
204 24p. H.M.S. "Beaver" 70 80
205 24p. R.Y. "Britannia", R.F.A. "Sir Percival" and H.M.S. "Beaver" 70 80
206 24p. R.Y. "Britannia" 70 80
207 24p. H.M.S. "Richmond", H.M.S. "Beaver" and H.M.S. "Gloucester" (destroyer) 70 80
208 24p. H.M.S. "Richmond" 70 80
209 24p. Aerial view of H.M.S. "Illustrious" 70 80
210 24p. H.M.S. "Gloucester" (wrongly inscr "Sheffield") 70 80
211 24p. H.M.S. "Trenchant" (submarine) and R.F.A. "Diligence" 70 80
212 24p. R.F.A. "Fort George" replenishing H.M.S. "Illustrious" and H.M.S. "Gloucester" 70 80
213 24p. Aerial view of H.M.S. "Richmond", H.M.S. "Beaver" and H.M.S. "Gloucester" 70 80

1998. 80th Anniv of the Royal Air Force. As T **178** of Ascension. Multicoloured.
215 26p. Blackburn Iris 75 80
216 34p. Gloster Gamecock 90 1·00
217 60p. North American Sabre F.4 1·75 2·00
218 80p. Avro Lincoln 2·25 2·50

34 Bryde's Whale

1998. International Year of the Ocean. Multicoloured.
220 26p. Type **34** 50 55
221 26p. Striped dolphin 50 55
222 34p. Pilot whale 70 75
223 34p. Spinner dolphin 70 75

35 "Westminster" (barque), 1837

1998. Ships. Multicoloured.
224 2p. Type **35** 10 10
225 15p. "Sao Cristovao" (Spanish galleon), 1589 30 35
226 20p. "Sea Witch" (U.S. clipper), 1849 40 45
227 26p. H.M.S. "Royal George" (ship of the line), 1778 55 60
228 34p. "Cutty Sark" (clipper), 1883 70 75
229 60p. "Mentor" (East Indiaman), 1789 1·25 1·40
230 80p. H.M.S. "Trinculo" (brig), 1809 1·60 1·70
231 £1 "Enterprise" (paddle-steamer), 1825 2·00 2·10
232 £1.15 "Confiance" (French privateer), 1800 2·25 2·40
233 £2 "Kent" (East Indiaman), 1820 4·00 4·25

BRITISH LEVANT

Stamps used at British post offices in the Turkish Empire. These offices closed in 1914. The stamps were again in use after 1918, during the British Occupation of Turkey.

Stamps of Great Britain surcharged or overprinted

A. BRITISH POST OFFICES IN TURKISH EMPIRE

I. TURKISH CURRENCY.

40 paras = 1 piastre

1885. Queen Victoria stamps surch in **PARAS** or **PIASTRES**.

7	**71**	40 pa. on ½d. red	£425	£100
1	**64**	40 pa. on 2½d. lilac	85·00	1·00
4	**74**	40 pa. on 2½d. purple on blue	1·75	10
2	**62**	80 pa. on 5d. green	£180	9·50
5	**78**	80 pa. on 5d. purple & blue	11·00	25
6	**81**	4 pi. on 10d. purple and red	35·00	8·00
3a	**58**	12 pi. on 2s. 6d. lilac	40·00	22·00

1902. King Edward VII stamps surch in **PARAS** or **PIASTRES**.

29	–	30 pa. on 1½d. purple & grn	4·25	55
8	**83**	40 pa. on 2½d. blue	9·00	10
9	–	80 pa. on 5d. purple and blue	3·25	2·00
13	**83**	1 pi. on 2½d. blue	8·00	10
30	–	2 pi. on 5d. purple and blue	6·50	1·50
10	–	4 pi. on 10d. purple and red	8·50	4·00
21	–	5 pi. on 1s. green and red	3·75	7·50
11	–	12 pi. on 2s. 6d. purple	32·00	35·00
12	–	24 pi. on 5s. red	32·00	40·00

1906. Surch **1 Piastre**.

15	–	1 pi. on 2d. green and red	£1300	£600

1909. King Edward VII stamps surch in **PIASTRE PARAS.**

17	–	1 pi. 10 pa. on 3d. pur on yell	11·00	26·00
18	–	1 pi. 30 pa. on 4d. grn & brn	5·00	15·00
19	–	1 pi. 30 pa. on 4d. orange	14·00	38·00
20	**83**	2 pi. 20 pa. on 6d. purple	15·00	48·00

1910. King Edward VII stamps surch in **PIASTRES**.

22	–	1¼ pi. on 3d. purple on yellow	40	1·00
23	–	1¾ pi. on 4d. orange	40	60
24	**83**	2½ pi. on 6d. purple	90	65

1913. King George V stamps surch.

41	**105**	30 pa. on ½d. green	40	8·00
35		30 pa. on 1½d. brown	3·00	11·00
36a	**104**	1 pi. on 2½d. blue	1·50	15
37	**106**	1¼ pi. on 3d. violet	3·00	4·25
42	**104**	1½ pi. on 1d. red	1·00	30
38b	**106**	1¾ pi. on 4d. grey-green	2·50	5·00
43	**104**	3¾ pi. on 2½d. blue	1·00	25
39	**108**	4 pi. on 10d. blue	6·00	14·00
44	**106**	4½ pi. on 3d. violet	1·50	3·25
40	**108**	5 pi. on 1s. brown	32·00	48·00
45	**107**	7½ pi. on 5d. brown	30	10
46	**108**	15 pi. on 10d. blue	55	15
47		18¾ pi. on 1s. brown	3·75	3·75
48	**109**	45 pi. on 2s. 6d. brown	20·00	42·00
49		90 pi. on 5s. red	25·00	30·00
50		180 pi. on 10s. blue	45·00	40·00

II. BRITISH CURRENCY.

1905. King Edward VII stamps optd **LEVANT**.

L 1	**83**	½d. green	5·50	15
L 2		1d. red	3·75	15
L 3	–	1½d. purple and green	4·50	1·50
L 4a	–	2d. green and red	2·00	6·00
L 5	**83**	2½d. blue	7·50	18·00
L 6	–	3d. purple and yellow	5·50	11·00
L 7	–	4d. green and brown	7·00	25·00
L 8	–	5d. purple and blue	14·00	25·00
L 9	**83**	6d. purple	11·00	25·00
L10		1s. green and red	30·00	40·00

1911. King George V stamps optd **LEVANT**.

L12	**98**	½d. green	40	90
L14	**101**	½d. green	25	10
L16	**105**	½d. green	15	30
L13	**99**	1d. red	40	3·75
L15	**102**	1d. red	25	85
L17	**104**	1d. red	15	3·25
L18	**106**	2d. orange	1·25	24·00
L19		3d. violet	7·50	10·00
L20		4d. green	4·50	13·00
L21	**107**	5d. brown	9·00	26·00
L22a		6d. purple	22·00	8·50
L23	**108**	1s. brown	11·00	7·50
L24	**109**	2s. 6d. brown	35·00	80·00

B. BRITISH FIELD OFFICE IN SALONICA

1916. King George V stamps of Great Britain optd **Levant**.

S1	**105**	½d. green	30·00	£160
S2	**104**	1d. red	30·00	£160
S3	**106**	2d. orange	£120	£300
S4		3d. violet	90·00	£300
S5		4d. green	£120	£300
S6	**107**	6d. purple	70·00	£250
S7	**108**	9d. black	£275	£500
S8		1s. brown	£225	£450

The above stamps were optd at Salonica during the war of 1914–18.

BRITISH OCCUPATION OF ITALIAN COLONIES

Issues for use in Italian colonies occupied by British Forces. Middle East Forces overprints were used in Cyrenaica, Dodecanese Islands, Eritrea, Italian Somaliland and Tripolitania.

MIDDLE EAST FORCES

12 pence = 1 shilling;
20 shillings = 1 pound

1942. Stamps of Great Britain optd **M.E.F.**

M11	**128**	1d. red	1·50	10
M12		2d. orange	1·50	90
M13		2½d. blue	45	10
M 4		3d. violet	30	10
M 5	**129**	5d. brown	30	15
M16		6d. purple	40	10
M17	**130**	9d. olive	85	10
M18		1s. brown	50	10
M19	**131**	2s. 6d. green	7·00	50
M20		5s. red	11·00	17·00
M21		10s. blue (No. 478a)	14·00	10·00

PRICES. Our prices for Nos. M1/21 in used condition are for stamps with identifiable postmarks of the territories in which they were issued. These stamps were also used in the United Kingdom with official sanction, from the summer of 1950 onwards, and with U.K. postmarks are worth about 25 per cent less.

POSTAGE DUE STAMPS.

1942. Postage Due stamps of Great Britain optd **M.E.F.**

MD1	**D 1**	½d. green	30	7·50
MD2		1d. red	30	1·50
MD3		2d. black	1·25	1·00
MD4		3d. violet	50	4·25
MD5		1s. blue	3·25	9·50

CYRENAICA

10 milliemes = 1 piastre; 100 piastres = 1 Egyptian pound

24 Mounted Warrior 25

1950.

136	**24**	1 m. brown	55	1·75
137		2 m. red	70	1·50
138		3 m. yellow	70	1·50
139		4 m. green	1·25	2·50
140		5 m. grey	60	70
141		8 m. orange	75	65
142		10 m. violet	75	65
143		12 m. red	75	65
144		20 m. blue	75	60
145	**25**	50 m. blue and brown	2·25	3·00
146		100 m. red and black	6·00	9·00
147		200 m. violet and blue	11·00	25·00
148		500 m. yellow and green	42·00	65·00

POSTAGE DUE STAMPS

D 26

1950.

D149	**D 26**	2 m. brown	45·00	90·00
D150		4 m. green	45·00	90·00
D151		8 m. red	45·00	90·00
D152		10 m. orange	45·00	90·00
D153		20 m. yellow	45·00	90·00
D154		40 m. blue	45·00	90·00
D155		100 m. brown	45·00	90·00

ERITREA

100 cents = 1 shilling

BRITISH MILITARY ADMINISTRATION

1948. Stamps of Great Britain surch **B.M.A. ERITREA** and value in cents or shillings.

E 1	**128**	5 c. on ½d. green	50	65
E 2		10 c. on 1d. red	65	2·00
E 3		20 c. on 2d. orange	45	2·25
E 4		25 c. on 2½d. blue	40	60
E 5		30 c. on 3d. violet	1·25	4·00
E 6	**129**	40 c. on 5d. brown	30	4·00
E 7		50 c. on 6d. purple	30	60
E 7a	**130**	65 c. on 8d. red	7·00	2·00
E 8		75 c. on 9d. olive	50	75
E 9		1 s. on 1s. brown	50	50
E10	**131**	2 s. 50 on 2s. 6d. green	6·50	10·00
E11		5 s. on 5s. red	6·50	16·00
E12	–	10 s. on 10s. blue (No. 478a)	18·00	21·00

BRITISH ADMINISTRATION

1950. Stamps of Great Britain surch **B.A. ERITREA** and value in cents or shillings.

E13	**128**	5 c. on ½d. green	50	6·00
E26		5 c. on ½d. orange	30	60
E14		10 c. on 1d. red	30	2·75
E27		10 c. on 1d. blue	30	60
E15		20 c. on 2d. orange	30	70
E28		20 c. on 2d. brown	30	30
E16	**128**	25 c. on 2½d. blue	30	60
E29		25 c. on 2½d. red	30	30
E17		30 c. on 3d. violet	30	1·00
E18	**129**	40 c. on 5d. brown	40	90
E19		50 c. on 6d. purple	30	20
E20	**130**	65 c. on 8d. red	40	1·00
E21		75 c. on 9d. olive	30	25
E22		1 s. on 1s. brown	30	15
E23	**131**	2 s. 50 on 2s. 6d. green	3·50	4·50
E24		5 s. on 5s. red	6·00	9·00
E25	–	10 s. on 10s. blue (No. 478a)	48·00	48·00

1951. Nos. 509/11 of Great Britain surch **B.A. ERITREA** and value in cents and shillings.

E30	**147**	2 s. 50 on 2s. 6d. green	6·00	17·00
E31	–	5 s. on 5s. red	18·00	17·00
E32	–	10 s. on 10s. blue	19·00	17·00

POSTAGE DUE STAMPS

1948. Postage Due stamps of Great Britain surch **B.M.A ERITREA** and new value in cents and shillings.

ED1	**D 1**	5 c. on ½d. green	9·00	18·00
ED2		10 c. on 1d. red	8·00	19·00
ED3		20 c. on 2d. black	7·00	14·00
ED4		30 c. on 3d. violet	8·00	13·00
ED5		1 s. on 1s. blue	15·00	24·00

1950. Postage Due stamps of Great Britain surch **B.A. ERITREA** and new value in cents or shillings.

ED 6	**D 1**	5 c. on ½d. green	11·00	35·00
ED 7		10 c. on 1d. red	9·00	15·00
ED 8		20 c. on 2d. black	9·50	13·00
ED 9		30 c. on 3d. violet	9·50	13·00
ED10		1 s. on 1s. blue	15·00	22·00

SOMALIA

BRITISH OCCUPATION

1943. Stamps of Great Britain optd **E.A.F.** (East African Forces).

S1	**128**	1d. red	60	40
S2		2d. orange	1·50	1·25
S3		2½d. blue	30	3·50
S4		3d. violet	50	15
S5	**129**	5d. brown	50	40
S6		6d. purple	30	90
S7	**130**	9d. olive	60	2·25
S8		1s. brown	1·25	15
S9	**131**	2s. 6d. green	6·00	6·50

PRICES. Our prices for Nos. S1/9 in used condition are for stamps with identifiable postmarks of the territories in which they were issued. These stamps were also used in the United Kingdom with official sanction, from the summer of 1950, and with U.K. postmarks are worth about 25 per cent less.

BRITISH MILITARY ADMINISTRATION.

1948. Stamps of Great Britain surch **B.M.A. SOMALIA** and new value in cents and shillings.

S10	**128**	5 c. on ½d. green	50	1·25
S11		15 c. on 1½d. brown	80	10·00
S12		20 c. on 2d. orange	1·50	3·25
S13		25 c. on 2½d. blue	1·00	4·00
S14		30 c. on 3d. violet	2·00	9·00
S15	**129**	40 c. on 5d. brown	40	20
S16		50 c. on 6d. purple	40	2·00
S17	**130**	75 c. on 9d. olive	2·00	14·00
S18		1 s. on 1s. brown	1·25	20
S19	**131**	2 s. 50 on 2s. 6d. green	3·25	22·00
S20		5 s. on 5s. red	8·00	29·00

BRITISH ADMINISTRATION

1950. Stamps of Great Britain surch **B.A. SOMALIA** and value in cents and shillings.

S21	**128**	5 c. on ½d. green	20	2·25
S22		15 c. on 1½d. brown	60	13·00
S23		20 c. on 2d. orange	60	3·50
S24		25 c. on 2½d. blue	40	4·50
S25		30 c. on 3d. violet	1·00	3·00
S26	**129**	40 c. on 5d. brown	55	85
S27		50 c. on 6d. purple	40	1·00
S28	**130**	75 c. on 9d. olive	1·00	5·50
S29		1 s. on 1s. brown	60	1·50
S30	**131**	2 s. 50 on 2s. 6d. green	4·00	22·00
S31		5 s. on 5s. red	8·50	27·00

TRIPOLITANIA

BRITISH MILITARY ADMINISTRATION

1948. Stamps of Great Britain surch **B.M.A. TRIPOLITANIA** and value in **M.A.L.** (Military Administration lire).

T 1	**128**	1 l. on ½d. green	30	80
T 2		2 l. on 1d. red	20	15
T 3		3 l. on 1½d. brown	20	50
T 4		4 l. on 2d. orange	25	50
T 5		5 l. on 2½d. blue	30	20
T 6		6 l. on 3d. violet	20	40
T 7	**129**	10 l. on 5d. brown	20	15
T 8		12 l. on 6d. purple	30	20
T 9	**130**	18 l. on 9d. olive	50	65
T10		24 l. on 1s. brown	50	65
T11	**131**	60 l. on 2s. 6d. green	2·00	6·00
T12		120 l. on 5 s. red	11·00	15·00
T13	–	240 l. on 10s. bright blue (No. 478a)	19·00	80·00

BRITISH ADMINISTRATION

1950. As Nos. T1/13 but surch **B.A. TRIPOLITANIA** and value in **M.A.L.**

T14	**128**	1 l. on ½d. green	90	8·50
T27		1 l. on ½d. orange	20	3·50
T15		2 l. on 1d. red	1·00	40
T28		2 l. on 1d. blue	20	90
T16		3 l. on 1½d. brown	35	8·00
T29		3 l. on 1½d. green	30	6·50
T17		4 l. on 2d. orange	25	4·50
T30		4 l. on 2d. brown	20	1·25
T18		5 l. on 2½d. blue	25	70
T31		5 l. on 2½d. red	30	6·50
T19		6 l. on 3d. violet	90	2·25
T20	**129**	10 l. on 5d. brown	30	2·75
T21		12 l. on 6d. purple	75	50
T22	**130**	18 l. on 9d. olive	75	1·60
T23		24 l. on 1s. brown	75	3·50
T24	**131**	60 l. on 2s. 6d. green	4·25	11·00
T25	**131**	120 l. on 5s. red	17·00	21·00
T26	–	240 l. on 10s. blue (No. 478a)	23·00	45·00

1951. Nos. 509/11 of Great Britain surch **B.A. TRIPOLITANIA** and value in **M.A.L.**

T32	**147**	60 l. on 2s. 6d. green	3·50	17·00
T33	–	120 l. on 5s. red	7·50	21·00
T34	–	240 l. on 10s. blue	26·00	35·00

POSTAGE DUE STAMPS

1948. Postage Due stamps of Great Britain surch **B.M.A. TRIPOLITANIA** and value in **M.A.L.**

TD1	**D 1**	1 l. on ½d. green	4·50	38·00
TD2		2 l. on 1d. red	2·50	28·00
TD3		4 l. on 2d. black	7·00	24·00
TD4		6 l. on 3d. violet	7·50	20·00
TD5		24 l. on 1s. blue	28·00	90·00

1950. As Nos. TD 1/5 but surch **B.A. TRIPOLITANIA** and value in **M.A.L.**

TD 6	**D 1**	1 l. on ½d. green	9·50	65·00
TD 7		2 l. on 1d. red	2·50	25·00
TD 8		4 l. on 2d. black	2·75	28·00
TD 9		6 l. on 3d. violet	17·00	60·00
TD10		24 l. on 1s. blue	40·00	£120

BRITISH POSTAL AGENCIES IN EASTERN ARABIA

British stamps surcharged for use in parts of the Persian Gulf.

The stamps were used in Muscat from 1st April 1948 to 29th April 1966; in Dubai from 1st April 1948 to 6th January 1961; In Qatar: Doha from August 1950, Umm Said from February 1956 to 31st March 1957; and in Abu Dhabi from 30th March 1963 (Das Island from December 1960) to 29th March 1964.

Nos. 21/2 were placed on sale in Kuwait Post Offices in 1951 and from February to November 1953 due to shortages of stamps with "KUWAIT" overprint. Isolated examples of other values can be found commercially used from Bahrain and Kuwait.

1948. 12 pies = 1 anna; 16 annas = 1 rupee.
1957. 100 naya paise = 1 rupee.

Stamps of Great Britain surch in Indian currency.

1948. King George VI.

16	**128**	½ a. on ½d. green	1·75	5·50
35		½ a. on ½d. orange	30	8·00
17		1 a. on 1d. red	1·75	20
36		1 a. on 1d. blue	30	5·50
18		1½ a. on 1½d. brown	4·00	60
37		1½ a. on 1½d. green	3·50	19·00
19		2 a. on 2d. orange	1·50	70
38		2 a. on 2d. brown	30	7·00
20		2½ a. on 2½d. blue	2·00	4·00
39		2½ a. on 2½d. red	30	15·00
21		3 a. on 3d. violet	2·00	10
40	**129**	4 a. on 4d. blue	30	2·50
22		6 a. on 6d. purple	2·00	10
23	**130**	1 r. on 1s. brown	3·00	50
24	**131**	2 r. on 2s. 6d. green	7·00	26·00

1948. Royal Silver Wedding.

25	**137**	2½ a. on 2½d. blue	1·25	75
26	**138**	15 r. on £1 blue	23·00	35·00

1948. Olympic Games.

27	**139**	2½ k on 2½d. blue	35	1·75
28	**140**	3 a. on 3d. violet	45	1·75
29	–	6 a. on 6d. purple	45	1·75
30	–	1 r. on 1s. brown	1·25	2·00

1949. 75th Anniv of U.P.U.

31	**143**	2½ a. on 2½d. blue	60	2·25
32	**144**	3 a. on 3d. violet	60	2·25
33	–	6 a. on 6d. purple	60	1·75
34	–	1 r. on 1s. brown	3·00	2·50

1951. Pictorial.

41	**147**	2 r. on 2s. 6d. green	22·00	6·00

1952. Queen Elizabeth.

42	**154**	½ a. on ½d. orange	10	1·50
43		1 a. on 1d. blue	10	1·50
44		1½ a. on 1½d. green	10	50
45		2 a. on 2d. brown	10	10
46	**155**	2½ a. on 2½d. red	10	10
47		3 a. on 3d. lilac	20	30
48		4 a. on 4d. blue	55	3·00
49	**157**	6 a. on 6d. purple	35	10
50	**160**	12 a. on 1s. 3d. green	2·00	30
51		1 r. on 1s. 6d. blue	2·00	10

1953. Coronation.

52	**161**	2½ a. on 2½d. red	1·75	95
53	–	4 a. on 4d. blue	1·75	95
54	**163**	12 a. on 1s. 3d. green	3·25	95
55	–	1 r. on 1s. 6d. blue	4·50	45

1955. Pictorials.

56	**166**	2 r. on 2s. 6d. brown	3·25	70
57	–	5 r. on 5s. red	9·00	2·00

1957. Value in naye paise. Queen Elizabeth II stamps surch **NP** twice (once only on 75 n.p.) and value.

79	**157**	1 n.p. on 5d. brown	10	20
80	**154**	3 n.p. on ½d. orange	55	80
81		5 n.p. on 1d. blue	80	55
67		6 n.p. on 1d. blue	20	1·75
68		9 n.p. on 1½d. green	20	75
83		10 n.p. on 1½d. green	50	1·00
69		12 n.p. on 2d. brown	30	1·00
85	**155**	15 n.p. on 2½d. red	25	10
71		20 n.p. on 3d. lilac	20	10
72		25 n.p. on 4d. blue	70	2·75
87		30 n.p. on 4½d. brown	40	40

73	**157**	40 n.p. on 6d. purple	30	10
89	**158**	50 n.p. on 9d. olive	1·00	1·25
75	**160**	75 n.p. on 1s. 3d. green	2·00	35

1957. World Scout Jubilee Jamboree.

76	**170**	15 n.p. on 2½d. red	25	85
77	**171**	25 n.p. on 4d. blue	30	85
78	–	75 n.p. on 3d. green	35	85

BRITISH POST OFFICES IN CHINA

Stamps for use in Wei Hai Wei, and the neighbouring islands, leased to Great Britain from 1898 to 1 October 1930, when they were returned to China. The stamps were also used in the Treaty Ports from 1917 until 1922.

100 cents = 1 dollar

1917. Stamps of Hong Kong (King George V) optd **CHINA**.

1	**24**	1 c. brown	2·50	1·50
2		2 c. green	2·50	30
3		4 c. red	3·25	30
4		6 c. orange	3·00	60
5		8 c. grey	8·00	1·25
6		10 c. blue	8·00	30
7		12 c. purple on yellow	4·50	2·50
8		20 c. purple and olive	10·00	60
9		25 c. purple	7·50	15·00
11		30 c. purple and orange	22·00	5·00
12b		50 c. black on green	20·00	5·50
13		$1 purple and blue on blue	55·00	2·25
14		$2 red and black	£170	45·00
15		$3 green and purple	£300	£150
16		$5 green and red on green	£300	£190
17		$10 purple and black on red	£750	£375

BRITISH POST OFFICES IN CRETE

40 paras = 1 piastre

B 1

B 2

1898.

B1	**B 1**	20 pa. violet	£425	£225

1898.

B2	**B 2**	10 pa. blue	8·00	15·00
B4		10 pa. brown	8·00	22·00
B3		20 pa. green	11·00	13·00
B5		20 pa. red	16·00	15·00

BRITISH POST OFFICE IN SIAM

Used at Bangkok.

100 cents = 1 dollar

1882. Stamps of Straits Settlements optd **B** on issue of 1867.

1	**19**	32 c. on 2 a. yellow	£35000	

On issues of 1867 to 1883.

14	**5**	2 c. brown	£450	£325
13	**9**	2 c. on 32 c. red (No. 60)	£2250	£2500
15	**5**	2 c. red	55·00	45·00
16		4 c. red	£500	£300
17		4 c. brown	75·00	70·00
4	**18**	5 c. brown	£250	£275
18		5 c. blue	£225	£160
5	**5**	6 c. lilac	£160	£110
20		8 c. orange	£140	65·00
21	**19**	10 c. grey	£150	85·00
8	**5**	12 c. blue	£900	£475
22		12 c. purple	£275	£150
9		24 c. green	£700	£150
10	**8**	30 c. red	£30000	£20000
11	**9**	96 c. grey	£4500	£2500

BRITISH VIRGIN ISLANDS

A group of the Leeward Islands, Br. W. Indies. Used general issues for Leeward Islands concurrently with Virgin Islands stamps until 1st July, 1956. A Crown Colony.

1951. 100 cents = 1 West Indian dollar.
1962. 100 cents = 1 U.S. dollar.

1 St. Ursula

2

3

4

1866.

1	**1**	1d. green	45·00	60·00
16	**3**	4d. red	40·00	60·00
7	**2**	6d. red	60·00	90·00
11	**4**	1s. black and red	£225	£300

No. 11 has a double-lined frame.

1867. With heavy coloured border.

18	**4**	1s. black and red	48·00	60·00

6

8

1880.

26	**6**	½d. yellow	80·00	80·00
27		½d. green	3·50	8·00
24		1d. green	65·00	85·00
29		1d. red	23·00	26·00
25		2½d. brown	90·00	£120
31		2½d. blue	2·50	13·00

1887.

32	**1**	1d. red	2·00	7·00
35	**3**	4d. brown	35·00	65·00
39	**2**	6d. violet	12·00	42·00
41	**4**	1s. brown	45·00	70·00

1888. No. 18 surch **4D**.

42	**4**	4d. on 1s. black and red	£110	£150

1899.

43	**8**	½d. green	75	55
44		1d. red	2·25	2·75
45		2½d. blue	12·00	4·00
46		4d. brown	4·00	17·00
47		6d. violet	4·50	4·50
48		7d. green	7·00	8·00
49		1s. yellow	20·00	32·00
50		5s. blue	65·00	80·00

9

11

1904.

54	**9**	½d. purple and green	60	40
55		1d. purple and red	1·50	35
56		2d. purple and brown	4·50	4·50
57		2½d. purple and blue	1·75	2·00
58		3d. purple and black	2·75	3·00
59		6d. purple and brown	2·75	3·00
60		1s. green and red	3·25	4·75
61		2s. 6d. green and black	22·00	48·00
62		5s. green and blue	48·00	65·00

1913.

69	**11**	½d. green	1·50	2·75
70a		1d. red	2·25	12·00
71		2d. grey	3·75	19·00
72		2½d. blue	4·50	7·00
73		3d. purple on yellow	2·25	5·00
74		6d. purple	4·00	7·00
75		1s. black on green	3·25	7·00
76		2s. 6d. black and red on blue	48·00	48·00
77		5s. green and red on yellow	32·00	£110

1917. Optd **WAR STAMP**.

78c	**11**	1d. red	20	3·25
79a		3d. purple on yellow	2·75	8·00

14

15 King George VI and Badge of Colony

1922.

86	**14**	½d. green	85	2·50
87		1d. red	60	60
88		1d. violet	1·00	3·50
91		1½d. red	1·75	2·00
92		2d. grey	60	5·50
95		2½d. blue	1·25	3·50
94		2½d. orange	1·25	1·25
96		3d. purple on yellow	2·00	9·00
97		5d. purple and olive	5·00	45·00
98		6d. purple	1·25	5·50
83		1s. black on green	75	12·00
84		2s. 6d. black and red on blue	4·00	9·00
101		5s. green and red on yellow	19·00	65·00

1935. Silver Jubilee. As T **13** of Antigua.

103	1d. blue and red	95	2·50
104	1½d. blue and grey	95	2·50
105	2½d. brown and blue	95	2·50
106	1s. grey and purple	5·50	12·50

1937. Coronation. As T **2** of Aden.

107	1d. red	20	1·00
108	1½d. brown	40	2·50
109	2½d. blue	45	1·00

1938.

110a	**15**	½d. green	30	90
111a		1d. red	30	60
112a		1½d. brown	65	95
113a		2d. grey	40	90
114a		2½d. blue	60	1·75
115a		3d. orange	40	80
116a		6d. mauve	1·50	80
117a		1s. brown	1·50	70
118a		2s. 6d. brown	14·00	3·00
119a		5s. red	13·00	4·00
120		10s. blue	7·00	8·00
121		£1 black	11·00	20·00

1946. Victory. As T **9** of Aden.

122	1½d. brown	10	10
123	3d. orange	10	10

1949. Silver Wedding. As T **10/11** of Aden.

124	2½d. blue	10	10
125	£1 grey	12·00	14·00

1949. 75th Anniv of U.P.U. As T **20/23** of Antigua.

126	2½d. blue	30	45
127	3d. orange	80	1·75
128	6d. mauve	50	40
129	1s. olive	50	40

1951. Inauguration of B.W.I. University College. As T **24/25** of Antigua.

130	3 c. black and red	40	60
131	12 c. black and violet	40	60

16 Map

1951. Restoration of Legislative Council.

132	**16**	6 c. orange	20	75
133		12 c. purple	20	50
134		24 c. olive	20	50
135		$1.20 red	45	75

18 Map of Jost Van Dyke

1952.

136	–	1 c. black	40	90
137	**18**	2 c. green	35	30
138	–	3 c. black and brown	30	80
139	–	4 c. red	35	90
140	–	5 c. red and black	90	50
141	–	8 c. blue	35	85
142	–	12 c. violet	45	1·00
143	–	24 c. brown	35	30
144	–	60 c. green and blue	2·50	11·00
145	–	$1.20 black and blue	3·75	12·00
146	–	$2.40 green and brown	10·00	13·00
147	–	$4.80 blue and red	11·00	14·00

DESIGNS—VERT: 1 c. Sombrero lighthouse; 24 c. Badge of Presidency. HORIZ—VIEWS: 3 c. Sheep industry; 5 c. Cattle industry; 60 c. Dead Man's Chest (Is); $1.20, Sir Francis Drake Channel; $2.40, Road Town. HORIZ—MAPS: 4 c. Anegada Island; 8 c. Virgin Gorda Island; 12 c. Tortola Island; $4.80, Virgin Islands.

1953. Coronation. As T **13** of Aden.

148	2 c. black and green	30	85

29 Map of Tortola

30 Brown Pelican

1956.

149	**29**	½ c. black and purple	40	20
150	–	1 c. turquoise and slate	1·50	75
151	–	2 c. red and black	30	10
152	–	3 c. blue and olive	30	30
153	–	4 c. brown and turquoise	35	30
154	–	5 c. black	45	10
155	–	8 c. orange and blue	60	40
156	–	12 c. blue and red	2·00	75
157	–	24 c. green and brown	1·00	65
158	–	60 c. blue and orange	8·00	8·00
159	–	$1.20 green and red	2·00	7·00
160	**30**	$2.40 yellow and purple	32·00	13·00
161	–	$4.80 sepia and turquoise	32·00	13·00

DESIGNS—HORIZ: As Type **13**: 1 c. Virgin Islands sloop; 2 c. Nelthrop Red Poll bull; 3 c. Road Harbour; 4 c. Mountain travel; 5 c. Badge of the Presidency; 8 c. Beach scene; 12 c. Boat launching; 24 c. White cedar tree; 60 c. Skipjack tuna ("Bonito"); $1.20, Treasury Square. As Type **30**: $4.80, Magnificent frigate bird.

1962. New Currency. Nos. 149/53, 155/61 surch in U.S. Currency.

162	**29**	1 c. on ½ c. black and purple	30	10
163	–	2 c. on 1 c. turq & vio	1·50	10
164	–	3 c. on 2 c. red and black	30	10
165	–	4 c. on 3 c. blue and olive	30	10
166	–	5 c. on 4 c. brown & turq	30	10
167	–	8 c. on 8 c. orange and blue	30	10
168	–	10 c. on 12 c. blue and red	40	10
169	–	12 c. on 24 c. green & brn	30	10
170	–	25 c. on 60 c. blue and orange	2·50	45
171	–	70 c. on $1.20 green and red	35	45
172	**30**	$1.40 on $2.40 yellow and purple	8·00	3·50
173	–	$2.80 on $4.80 sepia & turq	8·00	3·50

1963. Freedom from Hunger. As T **28** of Aden.

174	25 c. violet	20	10

1963. Centenary of Red Cross. As T **33** of Antigua.

175	2 c. red and black	15	20
176	25 c. red and blue	50	20

1964 400th Birth Anniv of Shakespeare. As T **34** of Antigua.

177	10 c. blue	20	10

43 Skipjack Tuna

44 Map of Tortola

1964.

178	**43**	1 c. blue and olive	30	1·25
179	–	2 c. olive and red	15	30
180	–	3 c. sepia and turquoise	3·00	1·25
181	–	4 c. black and red	80	1·25
182	–	5 c. black and green	65	1·25
183	–	6 c. black and orange	30	85
184	–	8 c. black and mauve	30	45
185	–	10 c. lake and lilac	1·25	30
186	–	12 c. green and blue	2·00	1·75
187	–	15 c. green and black	35	1·75
188	–	25 c. green and purple	11·00	1·60
189	**44**	70 c. black and brown	3·50	4·00
190	–	$1 green and brown	3·00	1·50
191	–	$1.40 blue and red	20·00	8·00
192	–	$2.80 black and purple	20·00	8·00

DESIGNS—HORIZ (As Type **43**): 2 c. Soper's Hole; 3 c. Brown pelican; 4 c. Dead Man's Chest; 5 c. Road Harbour; 6 c. Fallen Jerusalem; 8 c. The Baths, Virgin Gorda; 10 c. Map of Virgiin Islands; 12 c. "Youth of Tortola" (Tortola–St Thomas ferry); 15 c. The Towers, Tortola; 25 c. Beef Island Airfield. VERT (As Type **44**): $1 Virgin Gorda: $1.40, Yachts at anchor. ($27\frac{1}{2} \times 37\frac{1}{2}$ mm): $2.80, Badge of the Colony.

1965. Centenary of I.T.U. As T **36** of Antigua.

193	4 c. yellow and turquoise	20	10
194	25 c. blue and buff	45	20

1965. I.C.Y. As T **37** of Antigua.

195	1 c. purple and turquoise	10	15
196	25 c. green and lavender	30	15

1966. Churchill Commemoration. As T **38** of Antigua.

197	1 c. blue	10	10
198	2 c. green	15	10
199	10 c. brown	30	10
200	25 c. violet	60	25

1966. Royal Visit. As T **39** of Antigua.

201	4 c. black and blue	40	10
202	70 c. black and mauve	1·40	45

58 "Atrato I" (paddle-steamer), 1866

1966. Stamp Centenary. Multicoloured.

203	5 c. Type **58**	35	10
204	10 c. 1d. and 6d. stamps of 1866	35	10
205	25 c. Mail transport, Beef Island, and 6d. stamp of 1866	55	10
206	60 c. Landing mail at Roadtown, 1866 and 1d. stamp of 1866	1·00	2·25

1966. Nos. 189 and 191/2 surch.

207	**44**	50 c. on 70 c. blk & brn	1·00	90
208	–	$1.50 on $1.40 blue and red	2·75	2·00
209	–	$3 on $2.80 black and purple	2·75	2·75

1966. 20th Anniv of U.N.E.S.C.O. As T **54/6** of Antigua.

210	2 c. multicoloured	10	10
211	12 c. yellow, violet and olive	20	10
212	60 c. black, purple and orange	50	45

63 Map of Virgin Islands

1967. New Constitution.
213 63 2 c. multicoloured 10 10
214 10 c. multicoloured 15 10
215 25 c. multicoloured 15 10
216 $1 multicoloured 55 40

64 "Mercury" (cable ship) and Bermuda–Tortola Link

1967. Inauguration of Bermuda–Tortola Telephone Service. Multicoloured.
217 4 c. Type **64** 20 10
218 10 c. Chalwell Telecommunications Station 20 10
219 50c. "Mercury" (cable ship) . . 50 30

67 Blue Marlin

1968. Game Fishing. Multicoloured.
220 2 c. Type **67** 10 55
221 10 c. Cobia 25 10
222 25 c. Wahoo 55 10
223 40 c. Fishing launch and map . . 85 70

1968. Human Rights Year. Nos. 185 and 188 optd **1968 INTERNATIONAL YEAR FOR HUMAN RIGHTS.**
224 10 c. lake and lilac 20 10
225 25 c. green and purple 30 40

72 Dr. Martin Luther King, Bible, Sword and Armour Gauntlet

1968. Martin Luther King Commemoration.
226 72 4 c. multicoloured 20 20
227 25 c. multicoloured 30 40

73 De Havilland Twin Otter 100

1968. Opening of Beef Island Airport Extension. Multicoloured.
228 2 c. Type **73** 15 60
229 10 c. Hawker Siddeley H.S.748 airliner 20 10
230 25 c. De Havilland Heron 2 airplane 40 10
231 $1 Royal Engineers' cap badge . 50 2·00

77 Long John Silver and Jim Hawkins

1969. 75th Death Anniv of Robert Louis Stevenson. Scenes from "Treasure Island".
232 77 4 c. blue, yellow and red . . 25 15
233 – 10 c. multicoloured 25 10
234 – 40 c. brown, black and blue . 30 30
235 – $1 multicoloured . . . . 60 1·40
DESIGNS—HORIZ: 10 c. Jim Hawkins escaping from the pirates; $1 Treasure trove. VERT: 40 c. The fight with Israel Hands.

82 Yachts in Road Harbour, Tortola

1969. Tourism. Multicoloured.
236 2 c. Tourist and yellow-finned grouper (fish) 15 50
237 10 c. Type **82** 30 10
238 20 c. Sun-bathing at Virgin Gorda National Park . . . 40 20
239 $1 Tourist and Pipe Organ cactus at Virgin Gorda . . . . 90 1·50
Nos. 236 and 239 are vert.

85 Carib Canoe

1970.
240 85 ½ c. buff, brown and sepia 10 85
241 – 1 c. blue and green . . . 15 30
242 – 2 c. orange, brown and slate 40 1·00
243 – 3 c. red, blue and sepia . . 30 1·25
244 – 4 c. turquoise, blue & brn 30 50
245 – 5 c. green, pink and black 30 10
246 – 6 c. violet, mauve and green 40 1·75
247 – 8 c. green, yellow and sepia 50 2·25
248 – 10 c. blue and brown . . . 50 15
249 – 12 c. yellow, red and brown 65 1·00
250 – 15 c. green, orange and brown 6·00 85
251 – 25 c. green, blue and purple 6·00 1·75
252 – 50 c. mauve, green and brown 4·00 1·50
253 – $1 salmon, green and brown 4·50 4·75
254 – $2 buff, slate and grey . . 8·00 9·00
255 – $3 ochre, blue and sepia . 5·00 6·50
256 – $5 violet and grey . . . . 7·00 9·00
DESIGNS: 1 c. "Santa Maria" (Columbus's flagship); 2 c. "Elizabeth Bonaventure" (Drake's flagship); 3 c. Dutch buccaneer, c. 1660; 4 c. "Thetis", 1827 (after etching by E. W. Cooke); 5 c. Henry Morgan's ship (17th-century); 6 c. H.M.S. "Boreas" (Captain Nelson, 1784); 8 c. H.M.S. "Eclair", 1804; 10 c. H.M.S. "Formidable", 1782; 12 c. H.M.S. "Nymph", 1778; 15 c. "Windsor Castle" (sailing packet) engaging "Jeune Richard" (French brig), 1807; 25 c. H.M.S. "Astrea", 1808; 50 c. Wreck of R.M.S. "Rhone", 1867; $1 Tortola sloop; $2 H.M.S. "Frobisher"; $3 "Booker Viking" (cargo liner), 1967; $5 Hydrofoil "Sun Arrow".

102 "A Tale of Two Cities"

1970. Death Centenary of Charles Dickens.
257 102 5 c. black, red and grey . . 10 30
258 – 10 c. black, blue and green 20 10
259 – 25 c. black, green and yellow 30 40
DESIGNS: 10 c. "Oliver Twist"; 25 c. "Great Expectations".

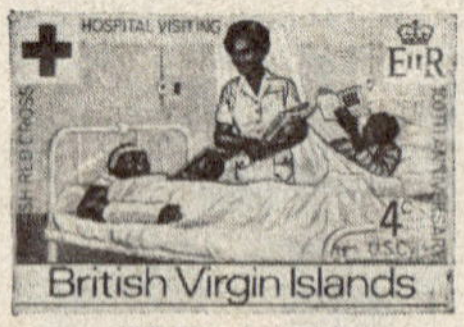

103 Hospital Visit

1970. Centenary of British Red Cross. Multicoloured.
260 4 c. Type **103** 25 10
261 10 c. First Aid class 35 10
262 25 c. Red Cross and coat of arms 80 55

104 Mary Read

105 Children and "UNICEF"

1970. Pirates. Multicoloured.
263 ½ c. Type **104** 10 15
264 10 c. George Lowther 35 10
265 30 c. Edward Teach (Blackbeard) 85 25
266 60 c. Henry Morgan . . . . 1·25 1·00

1971. 25th Anniv of U.N.I.C.E.F.
267 105 15 c. multicoloured 10 10
268 30 c. multicoloured 20 25

1972. Royal Visit of Princess Margaret. Nos 244 and 251 optd **VISIT OF H.R.H. THE PRINCESS MARGARET 1972 1972.**
269 4 c. blue, light blue and brown 20 15
270 25 c. green, blue and plum . . 30 45

107 Seaman of 1800

110 J. C. Lettsom

109 Blue Marlin

1972. "Interpex" Stamp Exhibition, New York. Naval Uniforms. Multicoloured.
271 ½ c. Type **107** 10 30
272 10 c. Boatswain, 1787–1807 . . 35 10
273 30 c. Captain, 1795–1812 . . . 85 55
274 60 c. Admiral, 1787–95 . . . 1·50 2·25

1972. Royal Silver Wedding. As T **52** of Ascension, but with sailfish and "Sir Winston Churchill" (cadet schooner) in background.
275 15 c. blue 20 15
276 25 c. blue 20 15

1972. Game Fish. Multicoloured.
277 ½ c. Type **109** 10 50
278 ½ c. Wahoo 15 50
279 15 c. Yellow-finned tuna ("Allison tuna") 55 25
280 25 c. White marlin 60 30
281 50 c. Sailfish . . . . 1·25 1·25
282 $1 Dolphin . . . . 2·00 2·50

1973. "Interpex 1973" (Quakers). Multicoloured.
284 ½ c. Type **110** 10 15
285 10 c. Lettsom House (horiz) . 15 10
286 15 c. Dr. W. Thornton 20 10
287 30 c. Dr. Thornton and Capitol, Washington (horiz) . . . 25 20
288 $1 William Penn (horiz) . . . 70 1·10

111 Green-throated Carib and Antillean Crested Hummingbird

1973. First Issue of Coinage. Coins and local scenery. Multicoloured.
289 1 c. Type **111** 10 30
290 5 c. "Zenaida Dove" (5 c. coin) 60 10
291 10 c. "Ringed Kingfisher" (10 c. coin) 75 10
292 25 c. "Mangrove Cuckoo" (25 c. coin) 95 15
293 50 c. "Brown Pelican" (50 c. coin) . . . . 1·10 1·00
294 $1 "Magnificent Frigate-bird ($1 coin) . . . . 1·40 2·00

1973. Royal Wedding. As T **47** of Anguilla. Multicoloured. Background colours given.
301 5 c. brown 10 10
302 50 c. blue 20 20

112 "Virgin and Child" (Pintoricchio)

113 Crest of the "Canopus" (French)

1973. Christmas. Multicoloured.
303 ½ c. Type **112** 10 10
304 3 c. "Virgin and Child" (Lorenzo di Credi) 10 10
305 25 c. "Virgin and Child" (Crivelli) 15 10
306 50 c. "Virgin and Child with St John" (Luini) 30 40

1974. "Interpex 1974". Naval Crests. Multicoloured.
307 5 c. Type **113** 20 10
308 18 c. U.S.S. "Saginaw" . . . 35 25
309 25 c. H.M.S. "Rothesay" . . 40 30
310 50 c. H.M.C.S. "Ottawa" . . 60 60

114 Christopher Columbus

1974. Historical Figures.
312 114 5 c. orange and black . . 20 10
313 – 10 c. blue and black . . . 30 10
314 – 25 c. violet and black . . 35 25
315 – 40 c. brown and deep brown 60 75
PORTRAITS: 10 c. Sir Walter Raleigh; 25 c. Sir Martin Frobisher; 40 c. Sir Francis Drake.

115 Atlantic Trumpet Triton

1974. Seashells. Multicoloured.
317 5 c. Type **115** 30 15
318 18 c. West Indian murex . . . 60 30
319 25 c. Bleeding tooth 75 35
320 75 c. Virgin Islands latirus . . 1·75 2·00

116 Churchill and St. Mary, Aldermanbury, London

1974. Birth Centenary of Sir Winston Churchill. Multicoloured.
322 10 c. Type **116** 15 10
323 50 c. St. Mary, Fulton, Missouri 35 50

117 H.M.S. "Boreas"

1975. "Interpex 1975" Stamp Exhibition, New York. Ships' Figure-heads. Multicoloured.
325 5 c. Type **117** 20 10
326 18 c. "Golden Hind" 50 15
327 40 c. H.M.S. "Superb" . . . 70 25
328 85 c. H.M.S. "Formidable" . . 1·50 1·50

118 Rock Beauty

1975. Fishes. Multicoloured.
330 ½ c. Type **118** 15 40
331 1 c. Long-spined squirrelfish . 40 1·25
332 3 c. Queen triggerfish . . . 90 1·25
333 5 c. Blue angelfish 30 20
334 8 c. Stoplight parrotfish . . . 30 25
335 10 c. Queen angelfish 30 25
336 12 c. Nassau grouper 40 30
337 13 c. Blue tang 40 30
338 15 c. Sergeant major 40 35
339 18 c. Spotted jewfish 70 80
340 20 c. Bluehead wrasse 60 80
341 25 c. Grey angelfish . . . . 1·00 60
342 60 c. Glass-eyed snapper . . 1·25 2·25
343 $1 Blue chromis . . . . 1·75 1·75
344 $2.50 French angelfish . . . 3·50 4·50
345 $3 Queen parrotfish . . . . 4·25 5·00
346 $5 Four-eyed butterflyfish . . 6·00 7·50

119 St George's Parish School (first meeting-place, 1950)

1975. 25th Anniv of Restoration of Legislative Council. Multicoloured.

347	5 c. Type **119**	10	10
348	25 c. Legislative Council Building	25	10
349	40 c. Mace and gavel	35	15
350	75 c. Commemorative scroll	55	65

120 Copper Mine Point

1976. Historic Sites. Multicoloured.

351	5 c. Type **120**	10	10
352	18 c. Pleasant Valley	20	10
353	50 c. Callwood Distillery	40	30
354	75 c. The Dungeon	60	65

121 Massachusetts Brig "Hazard"

1976. Bicentenary of American Revolution. Mult.

355	8 c. Type **121**	50	15
356	22 c. American privateer "Spy"	70	45
357	40 c. "Raleigh" (American frigate)	1·10	1·00
358	75 c. Frigate "Alliance" and H.M.S. "Trepassy"	1·25	1·90

122 Government House, Tortola

1976. 5th Anniv of Friendship Day with U.S. Virgin Islands. Multicoloured.

360	8 c. Type **122**	10	10
361	15 c. Government House, St. Croix (vert)	10	10
362	30 c. Flags (vert)	15	10
363	75 c. Government seals	30	40

123 Royal Visit, 1966

125 Divers checking Equipment

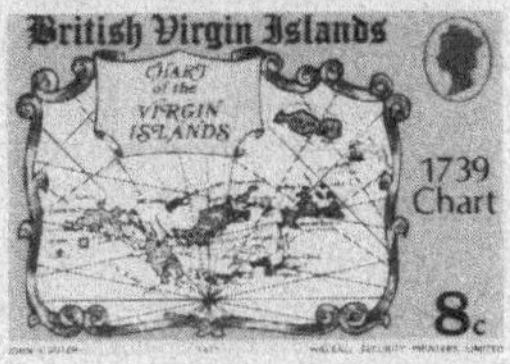

124 Chart of 1739

1977. Silver Jubilee. Multicoloured.

364	8 c. Type **123**	10	10
365	30 c. The Holy Bible	15	15
366	60 c. Presentation of Holy Bible	25	40

1977. 18th-century Maps. Multicoloured.

367	8 c. Type **124**	40	10
368	22 c. French map, 1758	65	30
369	30 c. Map from English and Danish surveys, 1775	80	65
370	75 c. Map of 1779	1·25	1·50

1977. Royal Visit. As Nos. 364/6 inscr "SILVER JUBILEE ROYAL VISIT".

371	5 c. Type **123**	10	10
372	25 c. The Holy Bible	20	10
373	50 c. Presentation of Holy Bible	35	25

1978. Tourism. Multicoloured.

374	½ c. Type **125**	10	10
375	5 c. Cup coral on wreck of "Rhone"	20	10
376	8 c. Sponge formation on wreck of "Rhone"	25	10
377	22 c. Cup coral and sponges	60	15
378	30 c. Sponges inside cave	75	20
379	75 c. Marine life	1·25	85

126 Fire Coral

127 Iguana

1978. Corals. Multicoloured.

380	8 c. Type **126**	25	15
381	15 c. Staghorn coral	40	30
382	40 c. Brain coral	75	85
383	75 c. Elkhorn coral	1·50	1·60

1978. 25th Anniv of Coronation.

384	– 50 c. brown, green and silver	20	40
385	– 50 c. multicoloured	20	40
386	**127** 50 c. brown, green and silver	20	40

DESIGNS: No. 384, Plantagenet Falcon; No. 385, Queen Elizabeth II.

128 Lignum Vitae

1978. Flowering Trees. Multicoloured.

387	8 c. Type **128**	15	10
388	22 c. Ginger Thomas	25	15
389	40 c. Dog almond	35	20
390	75 c. White cedar	60	70

129 "Eurema lisa"

1978. Butterflies. Multicoloured.

392	5 c. Type **129**	35	10
393	22 c. "Agraulis vanillae"	85	20
394	30 c. "Heliconius charithonia"	1·10	30
395	75 c. "Hemiargus hanno"	1·75	1·25

130 Spiny Lobster

1978. Wildlife Conservation. Multicoloured.

397	5 c. Type **130**	15	10
398	15 c. Large iguana (vert)	30	10
399	22 c. Hawksbill turtle	50	15
400	75 c. Black coral (vert)	1·10	90

131 Strawberry Cactus

132 West Indian Girl

1979. Native Cacti. Multicoloured.

402	½ c. Type **131**	10	10
403	5 c. Snowy cactus	15	10
404	13 c. Barrel cactus	20	20
405	22 c. Tree cactus	30	35
406	30 c. Prickly pear	35	40
407	75 c. Dildo cactus	60	1·00

1979. International Year of the Child. Multicoloured.

408	5 c. Type **132**	10	10
409	10 c. African boy	10	10
410	13 c. Asian girl	10	10
411	$1 European boy	50	85

133 1956 Road Harbour 3 c. Definitive Stamp

134 Pencil Urchin

1979. Death Centenary of Sir Rowland Hill.

413	**133** 5 c. dp blue, blue & grn	10	10
414	– 13 c. blue and mauve	10	10
415	– 75 c. blue and purple	45	50

DESIGNS—HORIZ: 13 c. 1880 2½d. red-brown; 75 c. Great Britain 1910 unissued 2d. Tyrian plum.

1979. Underwater Life. Multicoloured.

417	½ c. Calcified algae	40	1·50
418	1 c. Purple-tipped sea anemone	55	1·50
419	3 c. Common starfish	60	1·50
420	5 c. Type **134**	60	80
421	8 c. Atlantic trumpet triton	85	1·00
422	10 c. Christmas tree worms	30	85
423a	13 c. Flamingo tongue snail	1·50	75
424	15 c. Spider crab	40	60
425	18 c. Sea squirts	2·00	2·75
426	20 c. True tulip	55	85
427	25 c. Rooster-tail conch	1·25	2·75
428	30 c. West Indian fighting conch	1·75	1·25
429	60 c. Mangrove crab	1·75	2·50
430	$1 Coral polyps	2·00	3·50
431	$2.50 Peppermint shrimp	2·50	5·00
432	$3 West Indian murex	2·50	6·00
433	$5 Carpet anemone	3·25	7·50

135 Rotary Athletics Meeting, Tortola

1980. 75th Anniv of Rotary International. Mult.

434	8 c. Type **135**	10	10
435	22 c. Paul P. Harris (founder)	15	10
436	60 c. Mount Saga, Tortola ("Creation of National Park")	40	40
437	$1 Rotary anniversary emblem	70	75

136 Brown Booby

138 Sir Francis Drake

1980. "London 1980" International Stamp Exhibition. Birds. Multicoloured.

439	20 c. Type **136**	20	20
440	25 c. Magnificent frigate bird	25	25
441	50 c. White-tailed tropic bird	40	40
442	75 c. Brown pelican	55	55

1980. Caribbean Commonwealth Parliamentary Association Meeting, Tortola. Nos 414/15 optd **CARIBBEAN COMMONWEALTH PARLIAMENTARY ASSOCIATION MEETING TORTOLA 11–19 JULY 1980**.

444	13 c. blue and red	15	10
445	75 c. deep blue and blue	40	40

1980. Sir Francis Drake Commemoration. Mult.

446	8 c. Type **138**	50	10
447	15 c. Queen Elizabeth I	70	15
448	30 c. Drake receiving knighthood	90	30
449	75 c. "Golden Hind" and coat of arms	1·75	1·25

139 Jost Van Dyke

1980. Island Profiles. Multicoloured.

451	2 c. Type **139**	10	10
452	5 c. Peter Island	10	10
453	13 c. Virgin Gorda	15	10
454	22 c. Anegada	20	10
455	30 c. Norman Island	25	15
456	$1 Tortola	70	1·00

140 Dancing Lady

141 Wedding Bouquet from British Virgin Islands

1981. Flowers. Multicoloured.

458	5 c. Type **140**	15	10
459	20 c. Love in the mist	40	25
460	22 c. "Pitcairnia angustifolia"	40	25
461	75 c. Dutchman's pipe	75	1·10
462	$1 Maiden apple	90	1·40

1981. Royal Wedding. Multicoloured.

463	10 c. Type **141**	10	10
464	35 c. Prince Charles and Queen Elizabeth the Queen Mother in Garter robes	20	15
465	$1.25 Prince Charles and Lady Diana Spencer	60	80

142 Stamp Collecting

144 Detail from "The Adoration of the Shepherds" (Rubens)

143 "Development through Education"

1981. 25th Anniv of Duke of Edinburgh Award Scheme. Multicoloured.

466	10 c. Type **142**	10	10
467	15 c. Athletics	10	10
468	50 c. Camping	25	25
469	$1 Duke of Edinburgh	40	45

1981. International Year for Disabled Persons. Multicoloured.

470	15 c. Type **143**	15	15
471	20 c. Fort Charlotte Children's Centre	20	20
472	30 c. "Developing cultural awareness"	30	30
473	$1 Fort Charlotte Children's Centre (different)	85	1·25

1981. Christmas.

474	**144** 5 c. multicoloured	15	10
475	– 15 c. multicoloured	25	10
476	– 30 c. multicoloured	45	15
477	– $1 multicoloured	1·10	1·10

DESIGNS: 15 c. to $1 Further details from "The Adoration of the Shepherds" by Rubens.

145 Green-throated Caribs and Erythrina

147 Princess at Victoria and Albert Museum, November, 1981

146 "People caring for People"

1982. Hummingbirds. Multicoloured.

479	15 c. Type **145**	50	15
480	30 c. Green-throated carib and bougainvillea	75	45
481	35 c. Antillean crested hummingbirds and "granadilla passiflora"	85	55
482	$1.25 Antillean crested hummingbirds and hibiscus	2·50	3·00

1982. 10th Anniv of Lions Club of Tortola. Mult.

483	10 c. Type **146**	25	15
484	20 c. Tortola Headquarters	35	20
485	30 c. "We Serve"	45	30
486	$1.50 "Lions" symbol	1·25	1·75

1982. 21st Birthday of Princess of Wales. Mult.

488	10 c. British Virgin Islands coat of arms	15	10
489	35 c. Type **147**	30	25
490	50 c. Bride and groom proceeding into Vestry	45	45
491	$1.50 Formal portrait	1·10	1·40

148 Douglas DC-3

1982. 10th Anniv of Air BVI. Multicoloured.

492	10 c. Type **148**	45	15
493	15 c. Britten Norman Islander	60	20
494	60 c. Hawker Siddeley H.S.748	1·25	75
495	75 c. Runway scene	1·50	90

149 Scouts raising Flag

1982. 75th Anniv of Boy Scout Movement and 50th Anniv of Scouting in B.V.I. Multicoloured.

496	8 c. Type **149**	20	10
497	20 c. Cub Scout	45	25
498	50 c. Sea Scout	60	55
499	$1 First camp, Brownsea Island, and portrait of Lord Baden-Powell	1·00	1·50

150 Legislature in Session

1983. Commonwealth Day. Multicoloured.

500	10 c. Type **150**	10	10
501	30 c. Tourism	25	20
502	35 c. Satellite view of Earth showing Virgin Islands	25	25
503	75 c. B.V.I. and Commonwealth flags	70	90

151 Florence Nightingale

152 Frame Construction

1983. Nursing Week. Multicoloured.

504	10 c. Type **151**	50	15
505	30 c. Staff nurse and assistant nurse	90	45
506	60 c. Public Health nurses testing blood pressure (horiz)	1·75	1·25
507	75 c. Peebles Hospital (horiz)	1·90	1·75

1983. Traditional Boat-building. Multicoloured.

508	15 c. Type **152**	35	25
509	25 c. Planking	50	45
510	50 c. Launching	80	80
511	$1 Maiden voyage	1·25	1·75

153 Grumman Goose Amphibian

1983. Bicentenary of Manned Flight. Multicoloured.

513	10 c. Type **153**	20	15
514	30 c. Riley Turbo Skyliner	45	43
515	60 c. Embraer Bandeirante	85	85
516	$1.25 Hawker Siddeley H.S.748	1·50	1·60

154 "Madonna and Child with the Infant Baptist"

1983. Christmas. 500th Birth Anniv of Raphael. Multicoloured.

517	8 c. Type **154**	10	10
518	15 c. "La Belle Jardiniere"	20	25
519	50 c. "Madonna del Granduca"	65	70
520	$1 "The Terranuova Madonna"	1·25	1·40

155 Local Tournament

1984. 60th Anniv of International Chess Federation. Multicoloured.

522	10 c. Type **155**	1·00	40
523	35 c. Staunton king, rook and pawn (vert)	2·00	1·50
524	75 c. Karpov's winning position against Jakobsen in 1980 Olympiad (vert)	3·75	4·25
525	$1 B.V.I. Gold Medal won by Bill Hook at 1980 Chess Olympiad	4·25	5·50

156 Port Purcell

159 Steel Band

158 Running

1984. 250th Anniv of "Lloyd's List" (newspaper). Multicoloured.

526	15 c. Type **156**	25	30
527	25 c. Boeing 747-100	45	50
528	50 c. Wreck of "Rhone" (mail steamer), 1867	90	95
529	$1 "Booker Viking" (cargo liner)	1·50	1·60

1984. Olympic Games, Los Angeles. Multicoloured.

531	15 c. Type **158**	40	40
532	15 c. Runner	40	40
533	20 c. Wind-surfing	45	45
534	20 c. Surfer	45	45
535	30 c. Sailing	65	65
536	30 c. Yacht	65	65

1984. 150th Anniv of Abolition of Slavery. Mult.

538	10 c. Type **159**	30	35
539	10 c. Dancing girls	30	35
540	10 c. Men in traditional costumes	30	35
541	10 c. Girl in traditional costumes	30	35
542	10 c. Festival Queen	30	35
543	30 c. Green and yellow dinghies	45	50
544	30 c. Blue and red dinghies	45	50
545	30 c. White and blue dinghies	45	50
546	30 c. Red and yellow dinghies	45	50
547	30 c. Blue and white dinghies	45	50

DESIGNS: Various aspects of Emancipation Festival.

Nos. 543/7 form a composite design, the sail colours of the dinghies being described.

160 Sloop

1984. Boats. Multicoloured.

548	10 c. Type **160**	40	20
549	35 c. Fishing boat	1·00	65
550	60 c. Schooner	1·40	1·25
551	75 c. Cargo boat	1·40	1·60

161 One Cent Coin and Aerial View

1985. New Coinage. Coins and Local Scenery. Multicoloured.

553	1 c. Type **161**	10	10
554	5 c. Five cent coin and boulders on beach	10	10
555	10 c. Ten cent coin and scuba diving	20	20
556	25 c. Twenty-five cent coin and yachts	45	50
557	50 c. Fifty cent coin and jetty	90	1·25
558	$1 One dollar coin and beach at night	1·75	2·25

162 Red-billed Tropic Bird

163 The Queen Mother at Festival of Remembrance

1985. Birds of the British Virgin Islands. Multicoloured.

560	1 c. Type **162**	60	1·00
561	2 c. Yellow-crowned night heron	60	1·00
562	5 c. Mangrove cuckoo	70	90
563	8 c. Northern mockingbird	75	1·25
564	10 c. Grey kingbird	75	40
565	12 c. Red-necked pigeon	1·00	55
649	15 c. Least bittern	80	80
567	18 c. Smooth-billed ani	1·40	1·50
651	20 c. Clapper rail	80	70
652	25 c. American kestrel	90	75
570	30 c. Pearly-eyed thrasher	1·50	1·10
654	35 c. Bridled quail dove	90	85
572	40 c. Green heron	1·75	1·50
573	50 c. Scaly-breasted ground dove	2·00	2·25
574	60 c. Little blue heron	2·25	3·00
658	$1 Audubon's shearwater	2·00	3·25
576	$2 Blue-faced booby	3·50	6·00
577	$3 Cattle egret	4·75	7·50
578	$5 Zenaida dove	7·00	11·00

1985. Life and Times of Queen Elizabeth the Queen Mother. Multicoloured.

579A	10 c. Type **163**	10	20
580A	10 c. At Victoria Palace Theatre, 1984	10	20
581A	25 c. At the engagement of the Prince of Wales, 1981	15	40
582A	25 c. Opening Celia Johnson Theatre, 1985	15	40
583A	50 c. The Queen Mother on her 82nd birthday	20	70
584A	50 c. At the Tate Gallery, 1983	20	70
585A	75 c. At the Royal Smithfield Show, 1983	25	1·00
586A	75 c. Unveiling Mountbatten Statue, 1983	25	1·00

164 Seaside Sparrow

165 S.V. "Flying Cloud"

1985. Birth Bicentenary of John J. Audubon (ornithologist). Designs showing original paintings. Multicoloured.

588	5 c. Type **164**	40	20
589	30 c. Passenger pigeon	70	70
590	50 c. Yellow-breasted chat	80	1·75
591	$1 American kestrel	1·25	2·75

1986. Visiting Cruise Ships. Multicoloured.

592	35 c. Type **165**	80	85
593	50 c. M.V. "Newport Clipper"	1·10	1·50
594	75 c. M.V. "Cunard Countess"	1·40	2·50
595	$1 M.V. "Sea Goddess"	1·50	3·00

1986. Inaugural Flight of Miami–Beef Island Air Service. Nos 581/2 and 585/6 optd **MIAMI B.V.I. INAUGURAL FLIGHT**.

596A	25 c. At the engagement of the Prince of Wales, 1981	40	50
597A	25 c. Opening Celia Johnson Theatre, 1985	40	50
598A	75 c. At the Royal Smithfield Show, 1983	1·25	1·50
599A	75 c. Unveiling Mountbatten statue, 1983	1·25	1·50

167 Queen Elizabeth II in 1958

1986. 60th Birthday of Queen Elizabeth II. Multicoloured.

600	12 c. Type **167**	15	20
601	35 c. At a Maundy Service	20	45
602	$1.50 Queen Elizabeth	45	1·75
603	$2 During a visit to Canberra, 1982 (vert)	60	2·25

168 Miss Sarah Ferguson

1986. Royal Wedding. Multicoloured.

605	35 c. Type **168**	35	55
606	35 c. Prince Andrew and Miss Sarah Ferguson	25	55
607	$1 Prince Andrew in morning dress (horiz)	40	1·25
608	$1 Miss Sarah Ferguson (different) (horiz)	40	1·25

169 Harvesting Sugar Cane

1986. History of Rum Making. Multicoloured.

610	12 c. Type **169**	80	40
611	40 c. Bringing sugar cane to mill	1·50	1·25
612	60 c. Rum distillery	2·00	3·25
613	$1 Delivering barrels of rum to ship	3·25	4·00

170 "Sentinel"

1986. 20th Anniv of Cable and Wireless Caribbean Headquarters, Tortola. Cable Ships. Multicoloured.

615	35 c. Type **170**	60	80
616	35 c. "Retriever" (1961)	60	80
617	60 c. "Cable Enterprise" (1964)	1·00	1·50
618	60 c. "Mercury" (1962)	1·00	1·50
619	75 c. "Recorder" (1955)	1·10	1·75
620	75 c. "Pacific Guardian" (1984)	1·10	1·75
621	$1 "Great Eastern" (1860's)	1·25	2·00
622	$1 "Cable Venture" (1977)	1·25	2·00

172 18th-century Spanish Galleon

1987. Shipwrecks. Multicoloured.

625	12 c. Type **172**	1·50	45
626	35 c. H.M.S. "Astrea" (frigate), 1808	2·75	1·40
627	75 c. "Rhone" (mail steamer), 1867	4·25	4·00
628	$1.50 "Captain Rokos" (freighter), 1929	6·00	7·50

173 Outline Map and Flag of Montserrat

174 Spider Lily

1987. 11th Meeting of Organization of Eastern Caribbean States. Each showing map and flag. Multicoloured.

630	10 c. Type **173**	70	60
631	15 c. Grenada	80	60
632	20 c. Dominica	85	65
633	25 c. St. Kitts-Nevis	90	70
634	35 c. St. Vincent and Grenadines	1·40	1·00
635	50 c. British Virgin Islands	2·00	2·50
636	75 c. Antigua and Barbuda	2·25	3·00
637	$1 St. Lucia	2·75	3·25

1987. Opening of Botanical Gardens. Multicoloured.

638	12 c. Type **174**	80	35
639	35 c. Barrel cactus	1·75	1·00
640	$1 Wild plantain	2·75	3·25
641	$1.50 Little butterfly orchid	8·00	8·50

175 Early Mail Packet and 1867 1s. Stamp

1987. Bicentenary of Postal Services. Multicoloured.

662	10 c. Type **175**	1·00	55
663	20 c. Map and 1899 1d. stamp	1·50	95
664	35 c. Road Town Post Office and Customs House, c. 1913, and 1847 4d. stamp	2·00	1·50
665	$1.50 Piper Apache mail plane and 1964 25 c. definitive	6·00	9·00

1988. 500th Birth Anniv of Titian (artist). As T **238** of Antigua. Multicoloured.

667	10 c. "Salome"	55	55
668	12 c. "Man with the Glove"	60	60
669	20 c. "Fabrizio Salvaresio"	80	80
670	25 c. "Daughter of Roberto Strozzi"	90	90
671	40 c. "Pope Julius II"	1·40	2·00
672	50 c. "Bishop Ludovico Beccadelli"	1·60	2·00
673	60 c. "King Philip II"	1·75	2·50
674	$1 "Empress Isabella of Portugal"	2·25	2·75

176 De Havilland D.H.C.5 over Sir Francis Drake Channel and Staunton Pawn

1988. First British Virgin Islands Open Chess Tournament. Multicoloured.

676	35 c. Type **176**	4·00	1·50
677	$1 Jose Capablanca (former World Champion) and Staunton king	8·00	8·50

177 Hurdling

1988. Olympic Games, Seoul. Multicoloured.

679	12 c. Type **177**	30	25
680	20 c. Windsurfing	45	45
681	75 c. Basketball	3·00	3·25
682	$1 Tennis	3·50	3·75

178 Swimmer ("Don't Swim Alone")

1988. 125th Anniv of International Red Cross.

684	**178**	12 c. black, red and blue	85	40
685	–	30 c. black, red and blue	1·50	80
686	–	60 c. black, red and blue	2·75	3·00
687	–	$1 black, red and blue	3·25	4·00

DESIGNS: 30 c. Swimmers ("No swimming during electrical storms"); 60 c. Beach picnic ("Don't eat before swimming"); $1 Boat and equipment ("Proper equipment for boating").

179 Princess Alexandra

180 Brown Pelican in Flight

1988. Visit of Princess Alexandra. Designs showing different portraits.

689	**179**	40 c. multicoloured	1·75	75
690	–	$1.50 multicoloured	3·75	4·75

1988. Wildlife (1st series). Aquatic Birds. Multicoloured.

692	10 c. Type **180**	1·10	50
693	12 c. Brown pelican perched on post	1·25	55
694	15 c. Brown pelican	1·40	1·10
695	35 c. Brown pelican swallowing fish	2·75	3·00

181 Anegada Rock Iguana

1988. Wildlife (2nd series). Endangered Species. Multicoloured.

697	20 c. Type **181**	1·25	75
698	40 c. Virgin Gorda dwarf gecko	1·50	1·40
699	60 c. Hawksbill turtle	2·50	3·50
700	$1 Humpback whale	7·00	8·00

182 Yachts at Start

1989. Spring Regatta. Multicoloured.

702	12 c. Type **182**	45	40
703	40 c. Yacht tacking (horiz)	1·00	1·00
704	75 c. Yachts at sunset	1·60	2·50
705	$1 Yachts rounding buoy (horiz)	2·00	2·75

1989. 500th Anniv (1992) of Discovery of America by Columbus (1st issue). Pre-Columbian Arawak Society. As T **247** of Antigua. Multicoloured.

707	10 c. Arawak in hammock	60	45
708	20 c. Making fire	85	50
709	25 c. Making implements	90	60
710	$1.50 Arawak family	4·25	7·00

See also Nos. 741/4, 793/6 and 818/26.

183 "Apollo II" Emblem

1989. 20th Anniv of First Manned Landing on the Moon. Multicoloured.

712	15 c. Type **183**	90	50
713	30 c. Edwin Aldrin deploying scientific experiments	1·75	1·00
714	65 c. Aldrin and U.S. flag on Moon	2·50	3·50
715	$1 "Apollo II" capsule after splashdown	3·25	3·75

184 Black Harry and Nathaniel Gilbert preaching to Slaves

1989. Bicentenary of Methodist Church in British Virgin Islands. Multicoloured.

717	12 c. Type **184**	75	40
718	25 c. Methodist school exercise book	1·00	60
719	35 c. East End Methodist Church, 1810	1·10	75
720	$1.25 Reverend John Wesley (founder of Methodism) and church youth choir	3·25	5·00

185 Player tackling

1989. World Cup Football Championships, Italy, 1990. Multicoloured.

722	5 c. Type **185**	70	70
723	10 c. Player dribbling ball	70	70
724	20 c. Two players chasing ball	1·25	70
725	$1.75 Goalkeeper diving for ball	6·00	7·00

186 Princess Alexandra and Sunset House

1990 "Stamp World London 90" International Stamp Exhibition. Royal Visitors. Multicoloured.

727	50 c. Type **186**	1·50	1·75
728	50 c. Princess Margaret and Government House	1·50	1·75
729	50 c. Hon. Angus Ogilvy and Little Dix Bay Hotel	1·50	1·75
730	50 c. Princess Diana with Princes William and Henry and Necker Island Resort	1·50	1·75

187 Audubon's Shearwater

1990. Birds. Multicoloured.

732	5 c. Type **187**	40	60
733	12 c. Red-necked pigeon	60	40
734	20 c. Moorhen	70	50
735	25 c. Green heron	75	50
736	40 c. Yellow warbler	1·25	1·25
737	60 c. Smooth-billed ani	1·50	2·25
738	$1 Antillean crested hummingbird	1·75	2·25
739	$1.25 Black-faced grassquit	2·00	2·75

1990. 500th Anniv (1992) of Discovery of America by Columbus (2nd issue). New World Natural History–Fishes. As T **260** of Antigua. Mult.

741	10 c. Blue tang (horiz)	65	50
742	35 c. Glass-eyed snapper (horiz)	1·25	70
743	50 c. Slippery dick (horiz)	1·75	2·25
744	$1 Porkfish (horiz)	2·75	3·00

188 Queen Elizabeth the Queen Mother

189 Footballers

1990. 90th Birthday of Queen Elizabeth the Queen Mother.

746	**188**	12 c. multicoloured	35	20
747	–	25 c. multicoloured	65	45
748	–	60 c. multicoloured	1·40	2·00
749	–	$1 multicoloured	1·75	2·25

DESIGNS: 25, 60 c., $1 Recent photographs.

1990. World Cup Football Championships, Italy.

751	**189**	12 c. multicoloured	60	35
752	–	20 c. multicoloured	90	50
753	–	50 c. multicoloured	1·75	2·00
754	–	$1.25 multicoloured	2·50	3·00

DESIGNS: 20, 50 c., $1.25, Footballers.

190 Judo

1990. Olympic Games, Barcelona (1992). Mult.

756	12 c. Type **190**	70	35
757	40 c. Yachting	1·40	1·40
758	60 c. Hurdling	2·00	2·50
759	$1 Show jumping	2·50	3·00

191 Tree-fern, Sage Mountain National Park

192 Haiti Haiti

1991. 30th Anniv of National Parks Trust. Multicoloured.

761	10 c. Type **191**	50	50
762	25 c. Coppermine ruins, Virgin Gorda (horiz)	75	50
763	35 c. Ruined windmill, Mount Healthy	85	60
764	$2 The Baths (rock formation), Virgin Gorda (horiz)	5·50	7·00

1991. Flowers. Multicoloured.

765	1 c. Type **192**	20	40
766	2 c. Lobster claw	20	40
767	5 c. Frangipani	20	40
887	10 c. Autograph tree	40	60
769	12 c. Yellow allamanda	40	30
889	15 c. Lantana	55	35
771	20 c. Jerusalem thorn	50	30
772	25 c. Turk's cap	55	40
892	30 c. Swamp immortelle	70	50
893	35 c. White cedar	75	55
775	40 c. Mahoe tree	75	65
895	45 c. Pinguin	85	80
896	50 c. Christmas orchid	1·75	1·75
778	70 c. Lignum vitae	1·10	1·75
779	$1 African tulip tree	1·25	1·75
899	$2 Beach morning glory	2·75	4·00
781	$3 Organ pipe cactus	4·00	6·00
901	$5 Tall ground orchid	8·00	10·00
783	$10 Ground orchid	14·00	16·00

193 "Phoebis sennae"

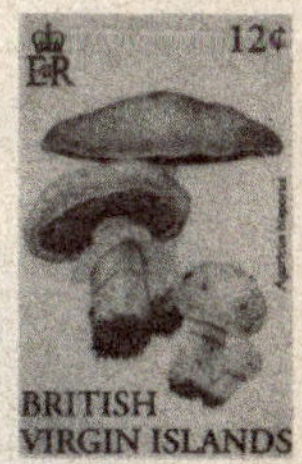

194 "Agaricus bisporus"

1991. Butterflies. Multicoloured.

784	5 c. Type **193**	60	70
785	10 c. "Dryas iulia"	65	70
786	15 c. "Junonia evarete"	80	70
787	20 c. "Dione vanillae"	90	75
788	25 c. "Battus polydamus"	1·00	85
789	30 c. "Eurema lisa"	1·10	95
790	35 c. "Heliconius charitonius"	1·25	1·10
791	$1.50 "Siproeta stelenes"	3·50	5·00

1991. 500th Anniv (1992) of Discovery of America by Columbus (3rd issue). History of Exploration. As T **277** of Antigua. Multicoloured.

793	12 c. "Vitoria" in Pacific (Magellan, 1519–21)	70	40
794	50 c. La Salle on the Mississippi, 1682	1·75	1·75
795	75 c. John Cabot landing in Nova Scotia, 1497–98	2·25	2·50
796	$1 Cartier discovering the St. Lawrence, 1534	2·75	3·25

1991. Death Centenary (1990) of Vincent Van Gogh (artist). As T **278** of Antigua. Multicoloured.

798	15 c. "Cottage with Decrepit Barn and Stooping Woman" (horiz)	65	40
799	30 c. "Paul Gauguin's Armchair"	1·10	80
800	75 c. "Breton Women" (horiz)	2·00	2·75
801	$1 "Vase with Red Gladioli"	2·50	3·25

1991. Christmas. Religious Paintings by Quinten Massys. As T **291** of Antigua. Multicoloured.

803	15 c. "The Virgin and Child Enthroned" (detail)	70	25
804	30 c. "The Virgin and Child Enthroned" (different detail)	1·25	50
805	60 c. "Adoration of the Magi" (detail)	2·75	3·50
806	$1 "Virgin in Adoration"	3·25	3·75

1992. Fungi. Multicoloured.

808	12 c. Type **194**	1·00	45
819	30 c. "Lentinula edodes" (horiz)	1·60	85
810	45 c. "Hygocybe acutoconica"	1·75	1·00
811	$1 "Gymnopilus chrysopellus" (horiz)	3·50	5·00

1992. 40th Anniv of Queen Elizabeth II Accession. As T **288** of Antigua. Multicoloured.

813	12 c. Little Dix Bay, Virgin Gorda	45	30
814	25 c. Deadchest Bay, Peter Island	1·10	90
815	60 c. Pond Bay, Virgin Gorda	1·40	2·00
816	$1 Cane Garden Bay, Tortola	1·75	2·50

195 Queen Isabella of Spain

196 Basketball

1992. 500th Anniv of Discovery of America by Columbus (4th issue). Multicoloured.

818	10 c. Type **195**	60	60
819	15 c. Fleet of Columbus (horiz)	80	80
820	20 c. Arms awarded to Columbus	80	80
821	30 c. Landing Monument, Watling Island and Columbus's signature (horiz)	90	90
822	45 c. Christopher Columbus	1·40	1·40
823	50 c. Landing in New World and Spanish royal standard (horiz)	1·40	1·50
824	70 c. Convent at La Rabida	2·25	3·00
825	$1.50 Replica of "Santa Maria" and Caribbean Pavilion, New York World's Fair (horiz)	3·50	4·25

1992. Olympic Games, Barcelona. Multicoloured.

827	15 c. Type **196**	1·25	65
828	30 c. Tennis	1·75	90
829	60 c. Volleyball	2·50	3·00
830	$1 Football	2·75	3·75

197 Issuing Social Security Cheque

1993. 25th Anniv of Ministerial Government. Multicoloured.

832	12 c. Type **197**	30	25
833	15 c. Map of British Virgin Islands	55	40
834	45 c. Administration building	70	70
835	$1.30 International currency abbreviations	2·00	3·25

198 Cruising Yacht and Swimmers, The Baths, Virgin Gorda

1993. Tourism. Multicoloured.

836	15 c. Type **198**	60	30
837	30 c. Cruising yacht under sail (vert)	85	60
838	60 c. Scuba diving	1·50	2·00
839	$1 Cruising yacht at anchor and snorklers (vert)	1·75	2·25

1993. 40th Anniv of Coronation. As T **307** of Antigua.

841	12 c. multicoloured	80	1·00
842	45 c. multicoloured	1·00	1·25
843	60 c. grey and black	1·10	1·40
844	$1 multicoloured	1·40	1·75

DESIGNS: 12 c. Queen Elizabeth II at Coronation (photograph by Cecil Beaton); 45 c. Orb; 60 c. Queen with Prince Philip, Queen Mother and Princess Margaret, 1953; $1 Queen Elizabeth II on official visit.

200 Columbus with King Ferdinand and Queen Isabella

1993. 500th Anniv of Discovery of Virgin Islands by Columbus. Multicoloured.

846	3 c. Type **200**	15	40
847	12 c. Columbus's ship leaving port	40	40
848	15 c. Blessing the fleet	45	45
849	25 c. Arms and flag of B.V.I.	60	60
850	30 c. Columbus and "Santa Maria"	70	70
851	45 c. Ships of second voyage	95	95
852	60 c. Columbus in ship's boat	1·50	2·25
853	$1 Landing of Columbus	2·00	2·50

201 Library Services Publications

1993. 50th Anniv of Secondary Education and Library Services. Multicoloured.

855	5 c. Type **201**	40	50
856	10 c. Secondary school sports	50	50
857	15 c. Stanley Nibbs (school teacher) (vert)	60	50
858	20 c. Mobile library	70	50
859	30 c. Dr. Norwell Harrigan (adminstrator and lecturer) (vert)	85	60
860	35 c. Children in library	90	65
861	70 c. Commemorative inscription on book	1·75	2·50
862	$1 B.V.I. High School	2·00	2·50

202 Anegada Ground Iguana

1994. Endangered Species. Anegada Ground Iguana.

863	**202**	5 c. multicoloured	30	40
864	–	10 c. multicoloured	30	40
865	–	15 c. multicoloured	40	40
866	–	45 c. multicoloured	1·10	1·25

DESIGNS: 10 c. to 45 c. Different iguanas.

203 Loading Disaster Relief Aircraft

1994. Centenary of Rotary International in B.V.I. Multicoloured.

868	15 c. Type **203**	35	35
869	45 c. Training children in marine safety	85	85
870	50 c. Donated operating table	90	1·00
871	90 c. Paul Harris (founder) and emblem	1·60	2·25

1994. 25th Anniv of First Manned Moon Landing. As T **326** of Antigua. Multicoloured.

872	50 c. Anniversary logo	1·75	2·00
873	50 c. Lunar landing training vehicle	1·75	2·00
874	50 c. Launch of "Apollo 11"	1·75	2·00
875	50 c. Lunar module "Eagle" in flight	1·75	2·00
876	50 c. Moon's surface	1·75	2·00
877	50 c. Neil Armstrong (astronaut) taking first step	1·75	2·00

204 Argentina v. Netherlands, 1978

205 Pair of Juvenile Flamingos

1994. World Cup Football Championship, U.S.A. Previous Winners. Multicoloured.

879	15 c. Type **204**	75	40
880	35 c. Italy v. West Germany, 1982	1·25	70
881	50 c. Argentina v. West Germany, 1986	2·00	2·00
882	$1.30 West Germany v. Argentina, 1990	4·00	5·00

1995. 50th Anniv of United Nations. As T **213** of Bahamas. Multicoloured.

903	15 c. Peugeot P4 all-purpose field cars	45	40
904	30 c. Foden medium road tanker	75	60
905	45 c. SISU all-terrain vehicle	1·00	90
906	$2 Westland Lynx AH7 helicopter	3·75	5·00

1995. Anegada Flamingos Restoration Project. Multicoloured.

907	15 c. Type **205**	60	40
908	20 c. Pair of adults	65	45
909	60 c. Adult feeding	1·25	1·75
910	$1.45 Adult feeding chick	2·25	3·25

206 "Tortola House with Christmas Tree" (Maureen Walters)

1995. Christmas. Children's Paintings. Multicoloured.

912	12 c. Type **206**	70	30
913	50 c. "Father Christmas in Rowing Boat" (Collin Collins)	1·75	1·40
914	70 c. "Christmas Tree and Gifts" (Clare Wassell)	2·00	2·25
915	$1.30 "Peace Dove" (Nicholas Scott)	3·00	3·50

207 Seine Fishing

1996. Island Profiles (1st series). Jost Van Dyke. Multicoloured.

916	15 c. Type **207**	60	35
917	35 c. Sandy Spit	80	55
918	90 c. Map	2·25	2·50
919	$1.50 Foxy's Regatta	2·75	3·50

See also Nos. 1003/6.

1996. 70th Birthday of Queen Elizabeth II. As T **165** of Ascension, each incorporating a different photograph of the Queen. Multicoloured.

920	10 c. Government House, Tortola	20	20
921	30 c. Legislative Council Building	55	55
922	45 c. Liner in Road Harbour	1·00	70
923	$1.50 Map of British Virgin Islands	2·75	3·50

208 Hurdling

1996. Centenary of Modern Olympic Games. Multicoloured.

925	20 c. Type **208**	35	30
926	35 c. Volley ball	60	60
927	50 c. Swimming	90	1·50
928	$1 Yachting	1·75	2·50

209 Mercedes-Benz "500 K A", 1934

1996. "CAPEX '96" International Stamp Exhibition, Toronto. Early Motor Cars. Multicoloured.

929	15 c. Type **209**	30	30
930	40 c. Citroen "12", 1934	70	70
931	60 c. Cadillac "V-8 Sport Phaeton", 1932	1·00	1·50
932	$1.35 Rolls Royce "Phantom II", 1934	2·25	3·00

210 Children with Computer

1996. 50th Anniv of U.N.I.C.E.F. Multicoloured.

934	10 c. Type **210**	30	30
935	15 c. Carnival costume	40	40
936	30 c. Children on Scales of Justice	70	70
937	45 c. Children on beach	1·00	1·00

211 Young Rainbows in Art Class

1996. 75th Anniv of Guiding in the British Virgin Islands. Multicoloured.

938	10 c. Type **211**	20	20
939	15 c. Brownies serving meals	30	25
940	30 c. Guides around campfire	50	45
941	45 c. Rangers on parade	65	60
942	$2 Lady Baden-Powell	2·75	3·50

212 Spanish Mackerel

1997. Game Fishes. Multicoloured.

943	1 c. Type **212**	10	10
944	10 c. Wahoo	10	15
945	15 c. Great barracuda	20	25
946	20 c. Tarpon	25	30
947	25 c. Tiger shark	30	35
948	35 c. Sailfish	40	45
949	40 c. Dolphin	50	55
950	50 c. Black-finned tuna	60	65
951	60 c. Yellow-finned tuna	75	80
952	75 c. King mackerel ("Kingfish")	90	95
953	$1.50 White marlin	1·75	1·90
954	$1.85 Amberjack	2·25	2·40
955	$2 Atlantic bonito	2·40	2·50
956	$5 Bonefish	6·00	6·25
957	$10 Blue marlin	12·00	12·50

1997. Golden Wedding of Queen Elizabeth and Prince Philip. As T **173** of Ascension. Multicoloured.

959	30 c. Prince Philip with horse	60	65
960	30 c. Queen Elizabeth at Windsor, 1989	60	65
961	45 c. Queen in phaeton, Trooping the Colour	80	90
962	45 c. Prince Philip in Scots Guards uniform	80	90
963	70 c. Queen Elizabeth and Prince Philip at the Derby, 1993	1·10	1·25
964	70 c. Prince Charles playing polo, Mexico, 1993	1·10	1·25

213 Fiddler Crab

1997. Crabs. Multicoloured.

966	12 c. Type **213**	30	25
967	15 c. Coral crab	35	30
968	35 c. Blue crab	70	60
969	$1 Giant hermit crab	1·50	2·00

214 "Psychilis macconnelliae"

1997. Orchids of the World. Multicoloured.

971	20 c. Type **214**	50	60
972	50 c. "Tolumnia prionochila"	80	90
973	60 c. "Tetramicra canaliculata"	85	1·00
974	75 c. "Liparis elata"	90	1·10

215 Sir Francis Drake and Signature

1997. 420th Anniv of Drake's Circumnavigation of the World. Multicoloured.

976	40 c. Type **215**	70	80
977	40 c. Drake's coat of arms	70	80
978	40 c. Queen Elizabeth I and signature	70	80
979	40 c. "Christopher" and "Marigold"	70	80
980	40 c. "Golden Hind"	70	80
981	40 c. "Swan"	70	80
982	40 c. "Cacafuego" (Spanish galleon)	70	80
983	40 c. "Elizabeth"	70	80
984	40 c. "Maria"	70	80
985	40 c. Drake's astrolabe	70	80
986	40 c. "Golden Hind's" figurehead	70	80
987	40 c. Compass rose	70	80

1998. 80th Anniv of Royal Air Force. As T **178** of Ascension. Multicoloured.

990	20 c. Fairey IIIF (seaplane)	45	35
991	35 c. Supermarine Scapa (flying boat)	65	50
992	50 c. Westland Sea King H.A.R.3 (helicopter)	90	90
993	$1.50 BAe Harrier GR7	2·25	2·50

216 Fingerprint Cyphoma

1998. Marine Life. Multicoloured.

995	15 c. Type **216**	40	30
996	30 c. Long-spined sea urchin	60	45
997	45 c. Split crown feather duster worm	80	65
998	$1 Upside down jelly	1·50	2·00

217 "Carnival Reveller" (Rebecca Peck)

1998. Festival. Children's Paintings. Multicoloured.

1000	30 c. Type **217**	35	40
1001	45 c. "Leader of a Troupe" (Jehiah Maduro)	55	60
1002	$1.30 "Steel Pans" (Rebecca McKenzie) (horiz)	1·50	1·60

218 Salt Pond

1998. Island Profiles (2nd series). Salt Island. Multicoloured.

1003	12 c. Type **218**	15	20
1004	30 c. Wreck of "Rhone" (mail steamer)	35	40
1005	70 c. Traditional house	85	90
1006	$1.45 Salt Island from the air	1·75	1·90

219 Business Studies, Woodwork and Technology Students

1998. Anniversaries. Multicoloured.

1008	5 c. Type **219**	10	10
1009	15 c. Comprehensive school band	20	25
1010	30 c. Chapel, Mona Campus, Jamaica	35	40
1011	45 c. Anniversary plaque and University arms	55	60
1012	50 c. Dr. John Coakley Lettsom and map of Little Jost Van Dyke	60	65
1013	$1 The Medical Society of London building and arms	1·25	1·40

EVENTS: 5, 15 c. 30th anniv of Comprehensive Education in B.V.I.; 30, 45 c. 50th anniv of University of West Indies; 50 c., $1 250th anniv of Medical Society of London.

220 Rock Iguana

1999. Lizards. Multicoloured.

1014	5 c. Type **220**	10	10
1015	35 c. Pygmy gecko	40	45
1016	60 c. Slippery back skink	70	75
1017	$1.50 Wood slave gecko	1·75	1·90

1999. Royal Wedding. As T **185** of Ascension. Multicoloured.

1019	20 t. Photographs of Prince Edward and Miss Sophie Rhys-Jones	25	30
1020	$3 Engagement photograph	3·50	3·75

OFFICIAL STAMPS

1985. Nos. 418/21 and 423/33 optd **OFFICIAL**.

O 1	1 c. Purple-tipped sea anemone	30	70
O 2	3 c. Common starfish	45	70
O 3	5 c. Type **134**	45	30
O 4	8 c. Triton's trumpet (shell)	55	30
O 5	13 c. Flamingo tongue snail	80	50
O 6	15 c. Spider crab	85	70
O 7	18 c. Sea squirts	90	1·00
O 8	20 c. True tulip (shell)	90	80
O 9	25 c. Rooster tail conch (shell)	1·25	1·25
O10	30 c. Fighting conch (shell)	1·40	1·00
O11	60 c. Mangrove crab	2·00	2·50
O12	$1 Coral polyps	3·00	3·75
O13	$2.50 Peppermint shrimp	4·50	9·00
O14	$3 West Indian murex (shell)	5·50	10·00
O15	$5 Carpet anemone	7·50	12·00

1986. Nos. 560/78 optd **OFFICIAL**.

O16	1 c. Type **162**	20	40
O17	2 c. Yellow-crowned night heron	20	40
O18	5 c. Mangrove cuckoo	30	50
O19	8 c. Northern mockingbird	30	60
O20	10 c. Grey kingbird	40	60
O21	12 c. Red-necked pigeon	40	40
O22	15 c. Least bittern	40	40
O23	18 c. Smooth-billed ani	45	60
O24	20 c. Clipper rail	70	70
O25	25 c. American kestrel	70	70
O26	30 c. Pearly-eyed thrasher	1·00	1·00
O27	35 c. Bridled quail dove	1·00	1·00
O28	40 c. Green heron	1·00	1·00
O29	50 c. Scaly-breasted ground dove	1·40	1·75
O30	60 c. Little blue heron	1·50	2·00
O31	$1 Audubon's shearwater	2·25	2·50
O32	$2 Blue-faced booby	2·50	3·50
O33	$3 Cattle egret	6·00	7·00
O34	$5 Zenaida dove	6·50	7·50

1991. Nos. 767/8, 771, 773/9 and 781 optd **OFFICIAL**.

O35	5 c. Frangipani	30	40
O36	10 c. Autograph tree	30	40
O37	20 c. Jerusalem thorn	35	40
O38	30 c. Swamp immortelle	50	50
O39	35 c. White cedar	55	55
O40	40 c. Mahoe tree	60	60
O41	45 c. Pinguin	70	65
O42	50 c. Christmas orchid	75	75
O43	70 c. Lignum vitae	1·00	1·75
O44	$1 African tulip tree	1·25	2·00
O45	$3 Organ pipe cactus	4·00	5·50

BRUNEI

A Sultanate on the North Coast of Borneo.

100 cents = 1 dollar

1 Star and Local Scene

1895.

1 **1**	½ c. brown	2·00	18·00
2	1 c. brown	2·50	13·00
3	2 c. black	3·75	13·00
4	3 c. blue	3·00	12·00
5	5 c. green	6·00	14·00
6	8 c. purple	6·00	23·00
7	10 c. red	7·50	23·00
8	25 c. green	45·00	65·00
9	50 c. green	18·00	80·00
10	$1 green	20·00	95·00

1906. Stamps of Labuan optd **BRUNEI.** or surch also.

11 **18**	1 c. black and purple	25·00	48·00
12	2 c. on 3 c. black and brown	2·00	7·50
13	2 c. on 8 c. black and orange	26·00	75·00
14	3 c. black and brown	27·00	75·00
15	4 c. on 12 c. black and yellow	2·50	5·00
16	5 c. on 16 c. green and brown	40·00	65·00
17	8 c. black and orange	8·50	28·00
18	10 c. on 16 c. green and brown	6·50	20·00
19	25 c. on 16 c. green and brown	95·00	£130
20	30 c. on 16 c. green and brown	85·00	£120
21	50 c. on 16 c. green and brown	85·00	£120
22	$1 on 8 c. black and orange	85·00	£120

5 View on Brunei River

1907.

23 **5**	1 c. black and green	2·25	10·00
24	2 c. black and red	2·50	4·50
25	3 c. black and brown	10·00	20·00
26	4 c. black and mauve	7·50	10·00
27	5 c. black and blue	50·00	90·00
28	8 c. black and orange	7·50	23·00
29	10 c. black and green	4·50	7·00
30	25 c. blue and brown	30·00	48·00
31	30 c. violet and black	20·00	22·00
32	50 c. green and brown	15·00	22·00
33	$1 red and grey	60·00	90·00

1908.

35 **5**	1 c. green	60	1·75
60	1 c. black	60	35
79	1 c. brown	50	1·50
36	2 c. black and brown	2·50	1·25
61	2 c. brown	90	5·00
62	2 c. green	60	30
80	2 c. grey	90	2·00
37	3 c. red	2·50	1·25
63	3 c. green	80	5·50
64	4 c. purple	1·50	75
65	4 c. orange	1·00	50
40	5 c. black and orange	7·00	7·00
82	5 c. orange	80	1·25
67	5 c. grey	9·00	9·00
68	5 c. brown	7·50	20
41	8 c. blue and indigo	7·00	11·00
71	8 c. blue	6·00	5·00
72	8 c. black	7·50	55
84	8 c. red	40	70
42	10 c. purple on yellow	1·50	1·25
85	10 c. violet	70	20
86	15 c. blue	50	60
87	25 c. purple	1·25	70
44	30 c. purple and yellow	8·50	12·00
88	30 c. black and orange	1·00	1·00
77	50 c. black on green	7·00	15·00
89	50 c. black	2·00	55
46	$1 black and red on blue	20·00	48·00
90	$1 black and red	4·50	75
47	$5 red on green	90·00	£150
91	$5 green and orange	16·00	17·00
92	$10 black and purple	48·00	30·00
48	$25 black on red	£450	£850

1922. Optd **MALAYA- BORNEO EXHIBITION. 1922.**

51 **5**	1 c. green	2·75	22·00
52	2 c. black and brown	3·75	27·00
53	3 c. red	6·00	35·00
54	4 c. red	6·00	42·00
55	5 c. orange	9·50	55·00
56	10 c. purple on yellow	6·50	55·00
57	25 c. lilac	14·00	80·00
58	50 c. black on green	45·00	£150
59	$1 black and red on blue	70·00	£190

7 Native Houses, Water Village

1924.

81 **7**	3 c. green	1·00	3·50
83	6 c. black	1·00	3·25
70	6 c. red	3·75	11·00
74	12 c. blue	4·50	9·00

8 Sultan Ahmed Tajudin and Water Village

1949. Silver Jubilee of H.H. the Sultan.

93 **8**	8 c. black and red	55	70
94	25 c. purple and orange	55	1·25
95	50 c. black and blue	70	1·25

1949. 75th Anniv of U.P.U. As T **20/23** of Antigua.

96	8 c. red	1·25	1·25
97	15 c. blue	3·00	1·50
98	25 c. mauve	1·25	1·50
99	50 c. black	1·75	1·25

9 Sultan Omar Ali Saifuddin

1952. Dollar values as T **8**, but with arms instead of portrait inset.

100 **9**	1 c. black	10	50
101	2 c. black and orange	10	50
102	3 c. black and brown	10	30
103	4 c. black and green	10	20
104	6 c. black and grey	10	10
123	8 c. black and red	60	10
106	10 c. black and sepia	15	10
125	12 c. black and violet	1·50	10
126	15 c. black and blue	55	10
109	25 c. black and purple	2·50	10
110	50 c. black and blue	1·50	10
111	$1 black and green	1·50	1·10
112	$2 black and red	4·50	2·25
113	$5 black and purple	12·00	6·00

11 Brunei Mosque and Sultan Omar

1958. Opening of the Brunei Mosque.

114 **11**	8 c. black and green	20	65
115	15 c. black and red	25	15
116	35 c. black and lilac	30	90

12 "Protein Foods"

1963. Freedom from Hunger.

117 **12**	12 c. sepia	2·75	90

13 I.T.U. Emblem

1965. Centenary of I.T.U.

132 **13**	4 c. mauve and brown	35	10
133	75 c. yellow and green	1·00	75

14 I.C.Y. Emblem

1965. International Co-operation Year.

134 **14**	4 c. purple and turquoise	20	10
135	15 c. green and lavender	55	35

15 Sir Winston Churchill and St. Paul's Cathedral in Wartime

1966. Churchill Commemoration. Designs in black, red and gold and with backgrounds in colours given.

136	15	3 c. blue	30	20
137		10 c. green	1·50	20
138		15 c. brown	1·75	35
139		75 c. violet	4·25	2·25

16 Footballer's Legs, Ball and Jules Rimet Cup

1966. World Cup Football Championships.

140	16	4 c. multicoloured	20	15
141		75 c. multicoloured	75	60

17 W.H.O. Building

1966. Inauguration of W.H.O. Headquarters, Geneva.

142	17	12 c. black, green and blue	35	40
143		25 c. black, purple and ochre	55	85

18 "Education"

1966. 20th Anniv of U.N.E.S.C.O.

144	18	4 c. multicoloured	35	10
145	–	15 c. yellow, violet and olive	75	50
146	–	75 c. black, purple and orange	2·50	5·50

DESIGNS: 15 c. "Science"; 75 c. "Culture".

21 Religious Headquarters Building

1967. 1400th Anniv of Revelation of the Koran.

147	21	4 c. multicoloured	10	10
148		10 c. multicoloured	15	10
149	–	25 c. multicoloured	20	30
150	–	50 c. multicoloured	35	1·50

Nos. 149/50 have sprigs of laurel flanking the main design (which has a smaller circle) in place of flagpoles.

22 Sultan of Brunei, Mosque and Flags

1968. Installation of Y.T.M. Seri Paduka Duli Pengiran Temenggong. Multicoloured.

151	4 c. Type **22**	15	30
152	12 c. Sultan of Brunei, Mosque and Flags (different) (horiz)	40	75
153	25 c. Type **22**	50	1·25

23 Sultan of Brunei

24 Sultan of Brunei

1968. Birthday of Sultan.

154	23	4 c. multicoloured	10	25
155		12 c. multicoloured	20	50
156		25 c. multicoloured	30	90

1968. Coronation of Sultan of Brunei.

157	24	4 c. multicoloured	15	25
158		12 c. multicoloured	25	50
159		25 c. multicoloured	40	75

25 New Building and Sultan's Portrait

1968. Opening of Hall of Language and Literature Bureau. Multicoloured.

160	10 c. Type **25**	20	1·50
161	15 c. New Building and Sultan's portrait (48½ × 22 mm)	20	35
162	30 c. As 15 c.	45	90

27 Human Rights Emblem and struggling Man

1968. Human Rights Year.

163	27	12 c. black, yellow and green	10	20
164		25 c. black, yellow and blue	15	25
165		75 c. black, yellow and purple	45	1·75

28 Sultan of Brunei and W.H.O. Emblem

1968. 20th Anniv of World Health Organization.

166	28	4 c. yellow, black and blue	30	30
167		15 c. yellow, black and violet	55	65
168		25 c. yellow, black and olive	65	1·25

29 Deep Sea Oil-Rig, Sultan of Brunei and inset portrait of Pengiran Di-Gadong

1969. Installation (9th May, 1968) of Pengiran Shar-bandar as Y.T.M. Seri Paduka Duli Pengiran Di-Gadong Sahibol Mal.

169	29	12 c. multicoloured	85	40
170		40 c. multicoloured	1·25	1·75
171		50 c. multicoloured	1·25	1·75

30 Aerial View of Parliament Buildings

1969. Opening of Royal Audience Hall and Legislative Council Chamber.

172	30	12 c. multicoloured	20	25
173		25 c. multicoloured	30	45
174	–	50 c. red and violet	60	1·50

DESIGN: 50 c. Elevation of new buildings.

32 Youth Centre and Sultan's Portrait

1969. Opening of New Youth Centre.

175	32	6 c. multicoloured	20	1·00
176		10 c. multicoloured	25	10
177		30 c. multicoloured	70	1·00

33 Soldier, Sultan and Badge

34 Badge, and Officer in Full-dress Uniform

1971. 10th Anniv of Royal Brunei Malay Regiment. Multicoloured.

178	10 c. Type **33**	70	30
179	15 c. Bell 205 Iroquois helicopter, Sultan and badge (horiz)	90	70
180	75 c. "Pahlawan" (patrol boat), Sultan and badge (horiz)	2·75	6·00

1971. 50th Anniv of Royal Brunei Police Force. Multicoloured.

181	10 c. Type **34**	50	30
182	15 c. Badge and Patrol Constable	60	80
183	50 c. Badge and Traffic Constable	1·75	5·50

35 Perdana Wazir, Sultan of Brunei and View of Water Village

1971. Installation of the Yang Teramat Mulia as the Perdana Wazir.

184	35	15 c. multicoloured	40	50
185	–	25 c. multicoloured	70	1·00
186	–	50 c. multicoloured	1·40	4·50

Nos. 185/6 show various views of Brunei Town.

36 Pottery

1972. Opening of Brunei Museum. Mult.

187	10 c. Type **36**	30	10
188	12 c. Straw-work	40	20
189	15 c. Leather-work	45	20
190	25 c. Gold-work	1·25	1·10
191	50 c. Museum Building (58 × 21 mm)	2·25	3·50

37 Modern Building, Queen Elizabeth and Sultan of Brunei

1972. Royal Visit. Each design with portrait of Queen and Sultan. Multicoloured.

192	10 c. Type **37**	70	20
193	15 c. Native houses	95	55
194	25 c. Mosque	2·00	1·60
195	50 c. Royal Assembly Hall	3·75	6·50

38 Secretariat Building

1972. Renaming of Brunei Town as Bandar Seri Begawan.

196	38	10 c. multicoloured	30	15
197	–	15 c. green, yellow and black	35	15
198	–	25 c. blue, yellow and black	60	50
199	–	50 c. red, blue and black	95	2·00

VIEWS: 15 c. Darul Hana Palace; 25 c. Old Brunei Town; 50 c. Town and Water Village.

39 Blackburn Beverley C1 parachuting Supplies

1972. Opening of R.A.F. Museum, Hendon. Multicoloured.

200	25 c. Type **39**	1·75	1·25
201	75 c. Blackburn Beverley C1 landing	3·25	3·75

1972. Royal Silver Wedding. As T **52** of Ascension, but with girl with traditional flower-pot, and boy with bowl and pipe in background.

210	12 c. red	10	10
211	75 c. green	20	50

41 Interpol H.Q., Paris

1973. 50th Anniv of Interpol.

212	41	25 c. green, purple and black	1·50	1·25
213	–	50 c. blue, ultram & red	1·50	1·25

DESIGN: 50 c. Different view of the H.Q.

42 Sultan, Princess Anne and Captain Phillips

1973. Royal Wedding.

214	42	25 c. multicoloured	15	10
215		50 c. multicoloured	15	25

43 Churchill Painting

44 Sultan Sir Hassanal Bolkiah Mu'izzaddin Waddaulah

1973. Opening of Churchill Memorial Building. Multicoloured.

216	12 c. Type **43**	10	20
217	50 c. Churchill statue	30	1·40

1975. Multicoloured. Background colours given.

218	44	4 c. green	20	20
219		5 c. blue	20	30
220		6 c. green	90	1·75
221		10 c. lilac	30	10
222		15 c. brown	75	10
223		20 c. stone	30	20
224		25 c. green	40	15
225		30 c. blue	40	15
226		35 c. grey	40	20
227		40 c. purple	40	20
228		50 c. brown	40	20
229		75 c. green	60	2·50
256		$1 orange	1·50	2·75
231		$2 yellow	2·25	8·50
232		$5 silver	4·50	17·00
233		$10 gold	7·00	28·00

INDEX

Countries can be quickly located by referring to the index at the end of this volume.

45 Aerial View of Airport

1974. Inauguration of Brunei International Airport. Multicoloured.
234 50 c. Type **45** . . . . 1·25 1·00
235 75 c. Sultan in Army uniform, and airport (48 × 36 mm) . . 1·50 1·50

46 U.P.U. Emblem and Sultan

1974. Centenary of Universal Postal Union.
236 **46** 12 c. multicoloured 20 20
237 50 c. multicoloured . . . . 40 1·40
238 75 c. multicoloured . . . . 50 1·75

47 Sir Winston Churchill

1974. Birth Centenary of Sir Winston Churchill.
239 **47** 12 c. black, blue and gold . . 25 20
240 – 75 c. black, green and gold . . 45 1·25
DESIGN: 75 c. Churchill smoking cigar (profile).

48 Boeing 737 and R.B.A. Crest

1975. Inauguration of Royal Brunei Airlines. Mult.
241 12 c. Type **48** . . . . 1·00 25
242 35 c. Boeing 737 over Bandar Seri Begawan Mosque . . . 1·75 1·25
243 75 c. Boeing 737 in flight . . . 2·25 2·50

1976. Surch **10 sen**.
263 **44** 10 c. on 6 c. brown . . . . 1·75 80

50 Royal Coat of Arms
51 The Moment of Crowning

1977. Silver Jubilee. Multicoloured.
264 10 c. Type **50** 15 15
265 20 c. Imperial State Crown . . . 20 20
266 75 c. Queen Elizabeth (portrait by Annigoni) 45 60

1978. 25th Anniv of Coronation. Multicoloured.
267 10 c. Type **51** 15 10
268 20 c. Queen in Coronation regalia 20 20
269 75 c. Queen's departure from Abbey 55 80

52 Royal Crest
53 Human Rights Emblem and Struggling Man

1978. 10th Anniv of Coronation of Sultan.
270 **52** 10 c. black, red and yellow . . 20 10
271 – 20 c. multicoloured 40 25
272 – 75 c. multicoloured . . . . 1·10 2·00
DESIGNS: 20 c. Coronation; 75 c. Sultan's Crown.

1978. Human Rights Year.
274 **53** 10 c. black, yellow and red . . 10 10
275 20 c. black, yellow and violet . . 20 35
276 75 c. black, yellow and bistre . . 50 1·75
Type **53** is similar to the design used for the previous Human Rights issue in 1968.

54 Smiling Children

1979. International Year of the Child.
277 **54** 10 c. multicoloured 20 10
278 – $1 black and green . . . . 1·25 2·50
DESIGN: $1 I.Y.C. emblem.

55 Earth Satellite Station

1979. Telisai Earth Satellite Station. Multicoloured.
279 10 c. Type **55** 20 15
280 20 c. Satellite and antenna . . 35 35
281 75 c. Television camera, telex machine and telephone . . . 75 2·25

56 Hegira Symbol
57 Installation Ceremony

1979. Moslem Year 1400 A.H. Commemoration.
282 **56** 10 c. black, yellow and green . . 10 15
283 20 c. black, yellow and blue . . 15 30
284 75 c. black, yellow and lilac . . 45 1·75

1980. 1st Anniv of Prince Sufri Bolkiah's Installation as First Wazir. Multicoloured. Blue borders.
286 10 c. Type **57** 15 10
287 75 c. Prince Sufri . . . . 85 1·75

1980. 1st Anniv of Prince Jefri Bolkiah's Installation as Second Wazir. Designs similar to T **57**. Multicoloured. Green borders.
288 10 c. Installation ceremony . . 15 10
289 75 c. Prince Jefri . . . . 45 1·75

58 Royal Umbrella and Sash
59 I.T.U. and W.H.O. Emblems

1981. Royal Regalia (1st series). Multicoloured.
290 10 c. Type **58** 20 15
291 15 c. Sword and Shield . . . 30 25
292 20 c. Lance and Sheath . . . 40 35
293 30 c. Betel Leaf Container . . 60 1·00
294 50 c. Coronation Crown (39 × 22 mm) . . . . 1·00 3·75
See Nos. 298/303, 314/19 and 320/5.

1981. World Telecommunications and Health Day.
296 **59** 10 c. black and red 50 25
297 75 c. black, blue and violet . . 2·25 4·25

60 Shield and Broadsword
61 Prince Charles as Colonel of the Welsh Guards

1981. Royal Regalia (2nd series). Multicoloured.
298 10 c. Type **60** 10 10
299 15 c. Blunderbuss and Pouch . . 20 20
300 20 c. Crossed Lances and Sash . . 30 30
301 30 c. Sword, Shield and Sash . . 40 65
302 50 c. Forked Lance . . . . . 60 2·00
303 75 c. Royal Drum (29 × 45 mm) . . 80 3·25

1981. Royal Wedding. Multicoloured.
304 10 c. Wedding bouquet from Brunei 15 15
305 $1 Type **61** . . . . 50 1·50
306 $2 Prince Charles and Lady Diana Spencer . . . . 70 2·50

62 Fishing
63 Blind Man and Braille Alphabet

1981. World Food Day. Multicoloured.
307 10 c. Type **62** 50 15
308 $1 Farm produce and machinery 4·50 6·00

1981. International Year for Disabled Persons. Multicoloured.
309 10 c. Type **63** 65 20
310 20 c. Deaf people and sign language . . . . 1·50 80
311 75 c. Disabled person and wheelchairs . . . . 3·00 5·50

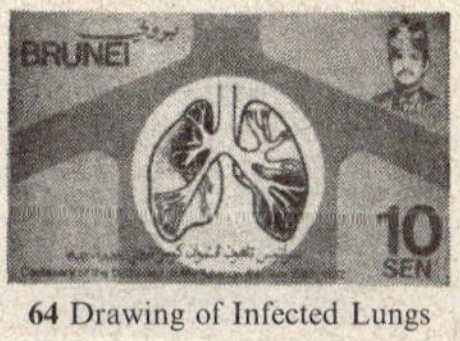

64 Drawing of Infected Lungs

1982. Centenary of Robert Koch's Discovery of Tubercle Bacillus. Multicoloured.
312 10 c. Type **64** 50 25
313 75 c. Magnified tubercle bacillus and microscope . . . . 3·00 4·50

1982. Royal Regalia (3rd series). As T **60**. Mult.
314 10 c. Ceremonial Ornament . . 10 10
315 15 c. Silver Betel Caddy . . . 20 20
316 20 c. Traditional Flowerpot . . . 25 25
317 30 c. Solitary Candle 50 70
318 50 c. Golden Pipe . . . . . . 70 2·00
319 75 c. Royal Chin Support (28 × 45 mm) . . . . 90 3·25

1982. Royal Regalia (4th series). As T **60**. Multicoloured.
320 10 c. Royal Mace 25 10
321 15 c. Ceremonial Shield and Spears 35 20
322 20 c. Embroidered Ornament . . 45 30
323 30 c. Golden-tasseled Cushion . . 75 1·25
324 50 c. Ceremonial Dagger and Sheath . . . . 1·25 3·00
325 75 c. Religious Mace (28 × 45 mm) . . . . 1·60 4·00

65 Brunei Flag
67 Football

66 "Postal Service"

1983. Commonwealth Day.
326 **65** 10 c. multicoloured 15 35
327 – 20 c. blue, black and buff . . 20 40
328 – 75 c. blue, black and green . . 45 75
329 – $2 blue, black and yellow . . 1·10 1·75
DESIGNS: 20 c. Brunei Mosque; 75 c. Machinery; $2 Sultan of Brunei.

1983. World Communications Year.
330 **66** 10 c. multicoloured 15 10
331 – 75 c. yellow, brown and black . . 60 75
332 – $2 multicoloured . . . . . 1·75 2·25
DESIGNS: 75 c. "Telephone Service"; $2 "Communications".

1983. Official Opening of the Negara Hassanal Bolkiah Stadium. Multicoloured.
333 10 c. Type **67** 55 15
334 75 c. Athletics . . . . 2·25 1·50
335 $1 View of stadium (44 × 27 mm) 2·75 3·00

68 Fishermen and Crustacea

1983. Fishery Resources. Multicoloured.
336 10 c. Type **68** 80 15
337 50 c. Fishermen with net . . . 2·00 1·25
338 75 c. Fishing trawler . . . . 2·50 2·25
339 $1 Fishing with hook and tackle 2·50 2·75

69 Royal Assembly Hall

1984. Independence.
340 **69** 10 c. brown and orange . . 20 10
341 – 20 c. pink and red 30 20
342 – 35 c. pink and purple . . . 60 60
343 – 50 c. light blue and blue . . 1·75 1·00
344 – 75 c. light green and green . . 1·75 2·00
345 – $1 grey and brown . . . . 2·00 2·50
346 – $3 multicoloured . . . . . 5·00 8·00
DESIGNS—34 × 25 mm: 20 c. Government Secretariat Building; 35 c. New Supreme Court; 50 c. Natural gas well; 75 c. Omar Ali Saifuddin Mosque; $1 Sultan's Palace. 68 × 24 mm: $3 Brunei flag and map of South-East Asia.

70 Natural Forests and Enrichment Planting

1984. Forestry Resources. Multicoloured.
349 10 c. Type **70** 90 25
350 50 c. Forests and water resources 2·00 2·25
351 75 c. Recreation forests . . . . 2·75 3·50
352 $1 Forests and wildlife . . . 4·00 4·50

71 Sultan Omar Saiffuddin 50 c. Stamp of 1952
72 United Nations Emblem

1984. "Philakorea" International Stamp Exhibition, Seoul. Multicoloured.
353 10 c. Type **71** 60 15
354 75 c. Brunei River view 10 c. stamp of 1907 . . . . . . 2·00 2·25
355 $2 Star and view ½ c. stamp of 1895 . . . . 3·00 5·00

1985. Admission of Brunei to World Organizations (1st issue).
357 **72** 50 c. black, gold and blue . . 50 70
358 – 50 c. multicoloured 50 70
359 – 50 c. multicoloured 50 70
360 – 50 c. multicoloured 50 70
DESIGNS: No. 358, Islamic Conference Organization logo; 359, Commonwealth logo; 360, A.S.E.A.N. emblem.
See also Nos. 383/6.

73 Young People and Brunei Flag

1985. International Youth Year. Multicoloured.

362	10 c. Type **73**	80	20
363	75 c. Young people at work	4·00	5·00
364	$1 Young people serving the community	4·50	5·50

74 Palestinian Emblem

1985. International Palestinian Solidarity Day.

365 **74**	10 c. multicoloured	1·00	20
366	50 c. multicoloured	3·00	1·50
367	$1 multicoloured	3·75	3·00

75 Early and Modern Scout Uniforms

76 Sultan Sir Hassanal Bolkiah Mu'izzaddin Waddaulah

1985. National Scout Jamboree. Multicoloured.

368	10 c. Type **75**	50	10
369	20 c. Scout on tower signalling with flag	80	40
370	$2 Jamboree emblem	2·50	3·25

1985.

371 **76**	10 c. multicoloured	10	10
372	15 c. multicoloured	10	10
373	20 c. multicoloured	15	10
374	25 c. multicoloured	20	15
375	35 c. multicoloured	25	20
376	40 c. multicoloured	30	25
377	50 c. multicoloured	40	35
378	75 c. multicoloured	55	50
379	$1 multicoloured	75	70
380	$2 multicoloured	1·50	1·60
381	$5 multicoloured	3·75	4·00
382	$10 multicoloured	7·50	7·75

Nos. 379/82 are larger, size 32 × 39 mm.

1986. Admission of Brunei to World Organizations (2nd issue). As T **72**.

383	50 c. black, gold and green	40	60
384	50 c. black, gold and mauve	40	60
385	50 c. black, gold and red	40	60
386	50 c. black, gold and blue	40	60

DESIGNS: No. 383, World Meteorological Organization emblem; 384, International Telecommunication Union emblem; 385, Universal Postal Union emblem; 386, International Civil Aviation Organization emblem.

78 Soldiers on Assault Course and Bell 205 Iroquois Helicopter

1986. 25th Anniv of Brunei Armed Forces. Multicoloured.

388	10 c. Type **78**	2·25	2·25
389	20 c. Operating computer	2·75	2·75
390	50 c. Anti-aircraft missile, MBB-Bolkow Bo 150L helicopter and missile boat	3·25	3·25
391	75 c. Army, commanders and parade	4·00	4·00

Nos. 388/91 were printed together, se-tenant, forming a composite design.

79 Tunggul Charok Buritan, Alam Bernaga (Alam Besar), Pisang-Pisang and Sandaran

80 Stylised Peace Doves

1986. Royal Ensigns (1st series).

392 **79**	10 c. black, yellow and red	30	10
393 –	75 c. multicoloured	1·10	1·10
394 –	$2 black, yellow and green	2·25	2·75

DESIGNS: 75 c. Ula-Ula Besar, Sumbu Layang and Payong Haram; $2 Panji-Panji, Chogan Istiadat (Chogan Di-Raja) and Chogan Ugama.

1986. Royal Ensigns (2nd series). As T **79**.

395	10 c. multicoloured	30	10
396	75 c. black, red and yellow	1·10	1·10
397	$2 multicoloured	2·25	2·75

DESIGNS: 10 c. Dadap, Tunggul Kawan, Ambal, Payong Ubor-Ubor, Sapu-Sapu Ayeng and Rawai Lidah; 75 c. Payong Tinggi and Payong Ubor-Ubor Tiga Ringkat; $2 Lambang Duli Yang Maha Mulia and Mahligai.

1986. International Peace Year. Multicoloured.

398	50 c. Type **80**	75	75
399	75 c. Stylised hands and "1986"	1·00	1·10
400	$1 International Peace Year emblem and arms of Brunei	1·25	1·50

81 Drug Addict in Cage and Syringe (poster by Othman bin Ramboh)

82 Cannon ("badil")

1987. National Anti-drug Campaign. Children's Posters. Multicoloured.

401	10 c. Type **81**	80	25
402	75 c. Drug addict and noose (Arman bin Mohd. Zaman)	2·25	3·00
403	$1 Blindfolded drug addict and noose (Abidin bin Hj. Rashid)	2·75	4·00

1987. Brassware (1st series). Multicoloured.

404	50 c. Type **82**	40	40
405	40 c. Lamp ("pelita")	40	40
406	40 c. Betel container ("langguai")	40	40
407	50 c. Water jug ("kiri")	40	40

See also Nos. 434/7.

83 Map showing Member Countries

1987. 20th Anniv of Association of South East Asian Nations. Multicoloured.

408	20 c. Type **83**	35	20
409	50 c. Dates and figures "20"	60	50
410	$1 Flags of member states	1·25	1·25

84 Brunei Citizens

1987. 25th Anniv (1986) of Language and Literature Bureau. Multicoloured.

411	10 c. Type **84**	10	10
412	50 c. Flame emblem and hands holding open book	40	40
413	$2 Scenes of village life	1·50	1·50

Nos. 411/13 were printed together, se-tenant, forming a composite design taken from a mural.

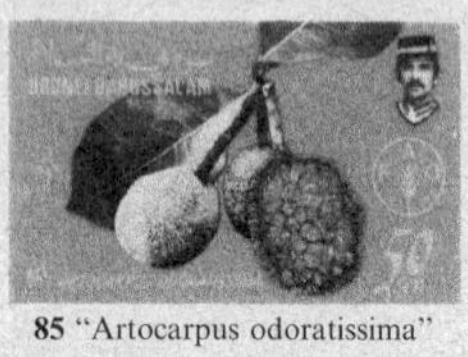

85 "Artocarpus odoratissima"

1987. Local Fruits (1st series). Multicoloured.

414	50 c. Type **85**	45	55
415	50 c. "Canarium odontophyllum mig"	45	55
416	50 c. "Litsea garciae"	45	55
417	50 c. "Mangifera foetida lour"	45	55

See also Nos. 421/4, 459/62, 480/2 and 525/8.

86 Modern House

1987. International Year of Shelter for the Homeless.

418 **86**	50 c. multicoloured	40	50
419 –	75 c. multicoloured	55	65
420 –	$1 multicoloured	80	90

DESIGNS: 75 c., $1 Modern Brunei housing projects.

1988. Local Fruits (2nd series). As T **85**. Mult.

421	50 c. "Durio spp"	50	50
422	50 c. "Durio oxleyanus"	50	50
423	50 c. "Durio graveolens" (blue background)	50	50
424	50 c. "Durio graveolens" (white background)	50	50

87 Wooden Lathe

89 Sultan reading Proclamation

88 Patterned Cloth

1988. Opening of Malay Technology Museum. Multicoloured.

425	10 c. Type **87**	15	10
426	75 c. Crushing sugar cane	55	70
427	$1 Bird scarer	70	85

1988. Handwoven Material (1st series). Mult.

428	10 c. Type **88**	10	10
429	20 c. Jong Sarat cloth	15	15
430	25 c. Si Pugut cloth	20	25
431	40 c. Si Pugut Bunga Berlapis cloth	30	35
432	75 c. Si Lobang Bangsi Bunga Belitang Kipas cloth	55	80

See also Nos. 442/6.

1988. Brassware (2nd series). As T **82**. Multicoloured.

434	50 c. Lidded two-handled pot ("periok")	40	50
435	50 c. Candlestick ("lampong")	40	50
436	50 c. Shallow circular dish with stand ("gangsa")	40	50
437	50 c. Repousse box with lid ("celapa")	40	50

1988. 20th Anniv of Sultan's Coronation. Mult.

438	20 c. Type **89**	15	15
439	75 c. Sultan reading from Koran	55	60
440	$2 In Coronation robes (26 × 63 mm)	1·50	1·60

1988. Handwoven Material (2nd series). As T **88**. Multicoloured.

442	10 c. Beragi cloth	10	10
443	20 c. Bertabur cloth	15	20
444	25 c. Sukma Indra cloth	20	25
445	40 c. Si Pugut Bunga cloth	30	35
446	75 c. Beragi Si Lobang Bangsi Bunga Cendera Kesuma cloth	55	60

90 Malaria-carrying Mosquito

1988. 40th Anniv of W.H.O. Multicoloured.

448	25 c. Type **90**	60	30
449	35 c. Man with insecticide spray and sample on slide	70	45
450	$2 Microscope and magnified malaria cells	2·25	2·00

91 Sultan and Council of Ministers

1989. 5th Anniv of National Day. Mult.

451	20 c. Type **91**	15	10
452	30 c. Guard of honour	20	15
453	60 c. Firework display (27 × 55 mm)	45	40
454	$2 Congregation in mosque	1·50	1·75

92 Dove escaping from Cage

1989. "Freedom of Palestine". Multicoloured.

456	20 c. Type **92**	30	20
457	75 c. Map and Palestinian flag	90	85
458	$1 Dome of the Rock, Jerusalem	1·10	1·25

1989. Local Fruits (3rd series). As T **85**. Mult.

459	60 c. "Daemonorops fissa"	1·60	1·75
460	60 c. "Eleiodoxa conferta"	1·60	1·75
461	60 c. "Salacca zalacca"	1·60	1·75
462	60 c. "Calamus ornatus"	1·60	1·75

93 Oil Pump

1989. 60th Anniv of Brunei Oil and Gas Industry. Multicoloured.

463	20 c. Type **93**	1·00	30
464	60 c. Loading tanker	2·00	2·00
465	90 c. Oil well at sunset	2·25	2·50
466	$1 Pipe laying	2·50	2·50
467	$2 Oil terminal	4·50	5·50

94 Museum Building and Exhibits

1990. 25th Anniv of Brunei Museum. Multicoloured.

468	30 c. Type **94**	1·00	60
469	60 c. Official opening, 1965	1·75	2·00
470	$1 Brunei Museum	2·25	2·50

95 Letters from Malay Alphabet

1990. International Literacy Year. Multicoloured.

471	15 c. Type **95**	60	20
472	90 c. English alphabet	2·25	2·75
473	$1 Literacy Year emblem and letters	2·25	3·00

96 Tarsier in Tree

97 Symbolic Family

1990. Endangered Species. Western Tarsier. Multicoloured.

474	20 c. Western Tarsier on branch	1·00	35
475	60 c. Western Tarsier feeding	2·00	2·50
476	90 c. Type **96**	3·00	3·50

1990. Worldwide Campaign against AIDS. Multicoloured.

477	20 c. Type **97**	1·00	60
478	30 c. Sources of infection	1·75	1·25
479	90 c. "AIDS" headstone surrounded by skulls	4·50	5·50

1990. Local Fruits (4th series). As T **85**. Mult.

480	60 c. "Willoughbea sp." (brown fruit)	2·50	2·75
481	60 c. Ripe "Willoughbea sp." (yellow fruit)	2·50	2·75
482	60 c. "Willoughbea angustifolia"	2·50	2·75

98 Proboscis Monkey on Ground

1991. Endangered Species. Proboscis Monkey. Multicoloured.

483	15 c. Type **98**	1·25	50
484	20 c. Head of monkey	1·40	60
485	50 c. Monkey sitting on branch	2·75	3·00
486	60 c. Female monkey with baby climbing tree	3·00	3·50

99 Junior School Classes

1991. Teachers' Day. Multicoloured.

487	60 c. Type **99**	2·00	2·25
488	90 c. Secondary school class	2·25	2·75

100 Young Brunei Beauty

1991. Fishes. Brunei Beauty. Multicoloured

489	30 c. Type **100**	1·50	85
490	60 c. Female fish	2·50	3·00
491	$1 Male fish	3·00	3·50

101 Graduate with Family
102 Symbolic Heart and Trace

1991. Happy Family Campaign. Multicoloured.

492	20 c. Type **101**	15	10
493	60 c. Mothers with children	45	50
494	90 c. Family	70	75

1992. World Health Day.

495	**102** 20 c. multicoloured	15	10
496	– 50 c. multicoloured	40	45
497	– 75 c. multicoloured	55	60

DESIGNS: 50 c., 70 c. (48×27 mm) Heart and heartbeat trace.

103 Map of Cable System

1992. Launching of Singapore–Borneo–Philippines Fibre Optic Submarine Cable System. Mult.

498	20 c. Type **103**	15	10
499	30 c. Diagram of Brunei connection	20	15
500	90 c. Submarine cable	70	75

104 Modern Sculptures

1992. Visit A.S.E.A.N. Year. Multicoloured.

501	20 c. Type **104**	15	20
502	60 c. Traditional martial arts	45	50
503	$1 Modern sculptures (different)	75	80

Nos. 501/3 were printed together, se-tenant, the backgrounds forming a composite design.

105 "A.S.E.A.N. 25" and Logo
106 Sultan in Procession

1992. 25th Anniv of A.S.E.A.N (Association of South East Asian Nations). Multicoloured.

504	20 c. Type **105**	85	50
505	60 c. Headquarters building	2·00	2·50
506	90 c. National landmarks	2·75	3·50

1992. 25th Anniv of Sultan's Accession. Mult.

507	25 c. Type **106**	20	25
508	25 c. Brunei International Airport	20	25
509	25 c. Sultan's Palace	20	25
510	25 c. Docks and Brunei University	20	25
511	25 c. Mosque	20	25

Nos. 507/11 were printed together, se-tenant, forming a composite design.

107 Crested Wood Partridge
108 National Flag and "10"

1992. Birds (1st series). Multicoloured.

512	30 c. Type **107**	65	50
513	60 c. Asiatic paradise flycatcher	1·50	2·00
514	$1 Great argus pheasant	1·75	2·75

See also Nos. 515/17, 518/20, 575/7 and 602/5.

1993. Birds (2nd series). As T **107**. Multicoloured.

515	30 c. Long-tailed parakeet	75	50
516	60 c. Magpie robin	1·50	2·00
517	$1 Blue-crowned hanging parrot	2·25	2·75

1993. Birds (3rd series). As T **107**. Multicoloured.

518	30 c. Chesnut-breasted malkoha	90	50
519	60 c. White-rumped shama	1·75	2·00
520	$1 Black and red broadbill (vert)	2·50	3·00

1994. 10th Anniv of National Day. Multicoloured.

521	10 c. Type **108**	10	10
522	20 c. Symbolic hands	15	20
523	30 c. Previous National Day symbols	20	25
524	60 c. Coat of arms	45	50

1994. Local Fruits (5th issue). As T **85**, but each 36×26 mm. Multicoloured.

525	60 c. "Nephelium mutabile"	45	50
526	60 c. "Nephelium xerospermoides"	45	50
527	60 c. "Nephelium spp"	45	50
528	60 c. "Nephelium macrophyllum"	45	50

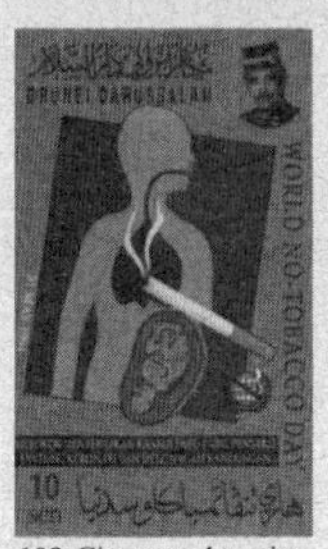

109 Cigarette burning Heart and Deformed Baby in Womb
110 Girl Guide

1994. World No Tobacco Day. Multicoloured.

529	10 c. Type **109**	10	10
530	15 c. Symbols of smoking over crowd of people	10	10
531	$2 Globe crushing cigarettes	1·50	1·60

1994. 40th Anniv of Brunei Girl Guides' Association. Multicoloured.

532	40 c. Type **110**	30	35
533	40 c. Guide receiving award	30	35
534	40 c. Guide reading	30	35
535	40 c. Group of guides	30	35
536	40 c. Guides erecting tent	30	35

111 Turbo-prop Airliner on Runway

1994. 20th Anniv of Royal Brunei Airlines. Multicoloured.

537	10 c. Type **111**	10	10
538	20 c. Jet airliner on runway	15	20
539	$1 Jet airliner in the air	75	80

112 Malay Family
113 Aerial View of City, 1970

1994. International Day against Drug Abuse and Trafficking. Multicoloured.

540	20 c. Type **112**	15	20
541	60 c. Chinese family	45	50
542	$1 Doctor, police officers and members of youth organizations	75	80

Nos. 540/2 were printed together, se-tenant, forming a composite design.

1995. 25th Anniv of Bandar Seri Begawan. Mult.

543	30 c. Type **113**	20	20
544	50 c. City in 1980	40	45
545	$1 City in 1990	75	80

114 United Nations General Assembly
115 Students in Laboratory

1995. 50th Anniv of United Nations. Multicoloured.

546	20 c. Type **114**	15	10
547	60 c. Security Council in session	45	50
548	90 c. United Nations Building, New York (27 × 44 mm)	70	75

1995. 10th Anniv of University of Brunei. Mult.

549	30 c. Type **115**	20	20
550	50 c. University building	40	45
551	90 c. Sultan visiting University	70	75

116 Police Officers
117 Telephones

1996. 25th Anniv of Royal Brunei Police Force. Multicoloured.

552	25 c. Type **116**	20	15
553	50 c. Aspects of police work	40	45
554	75 c. Sultan inspecting parade	55	60

1996. World Telecommunications Day. Children's Paintings. Multicoloured.

555	20 c. Type **117**	15	10
556	35 c. Telephone dial and aspects of telecommunications	25	30
557	$1 Globe and aspects of telecommunications	75	80

118 Sultan and Crowd
119 Sultan Hassanal Bolkiah Mu'izzaddin Waddaulah

1996. 50th Birthday of Sultan Hassanal Bolkiah Mu'izzaddin Waddaulah. Multicoloured.

558	50 c. Type **118**	40	45
559	50 c. Sultan in ceremonial dress	40	45
560	50 c. Sultan receiving dignitaries at mosque	40	45
561	50 c. Sultan with subjects	40	45

1996.

563	**119** 10 c. multicoloured	10	15
564	15 c. multicoloured	10	15
565	20 c. multicoloured	15	20
566	30 c. multicoloured	20	25
567	50 c. multicoloured	40	45
568	60 c. multicoloured	45	50
569	75 c. multicoloured	55	60
570	90 c. multicoloured	70	75
571	– $1 multicoloured	75	80
572	– $2 mulitcoloured	1·50	1·60
573	– $5 multicoloured	3·75	4·00
574	– $10 multicoloured	7·50	8·00

DESIGN—27 × 39 mm: $1 to $10 Sultan in ceremonial robes.

121 Black-naped Tern

1996. Birds (4th series). Sea Birds. Multicoloured.

575	20 c. Type **121**	15	10
576	30 c. Roseate tern	20	15
577	$1 Bridled tern	75	80

No. 576 is inscr "ROSLATE TERN" in error.

122 "Acanthus ebracteatus"

1997. Mangrove Flowers. Multicoloured.

578	20 c. Type **122**	15	20
579	30 c. "Lumnitzera littorea"	20	25
580	$1 "Nypa fruticans"	75	80

123 "Heterocentrotus mammillatus"

1997. Marine Life. Multicoloured.

581	60 c. Type **123**	45	50
582	60 c. "Linckia laevigata" (starfish)	45	50
583	60 c. "Oxycomanthus bennetti" (plant)	45	50
584	60 c. "Bohadschia argus" (sea slug)	45	50

124 Children and Sign Language

1998. Asian and Pacific Decade of Disabled Persons, 1993–2002. Multicoloured.

585	20 c. Type **124**	15	20
586	50 c. Woman typing and firework display	40	45
587	$1 Disabled athletes	75	80

125 Sultan performing Ceremonial Duties

1998. 30th Anniv of Coronation of Sultan Hassanal Bolkiah Mu'izzaddin Waddaulah. Multicoloured.

588	60 c. Type **125**	45	50
589	90 c. Sultan on Coronation throne	70	75
590	$1 Coronation parade	75	80

126 A.S.E.A.N. Architecture and Transport

127 Crown Prince at Desk

1998. 30th Anniv of Association of South-east Asian Nations. Multicoloured.

592	30 c. Type **126**	20	25
593	30 c. Map of Brunei and city scenes	20	25
594	30 c. Flags of member nations	20	25

1998. Proclamation of Prince Al-Muhtadee Billah as Crown Prince. Multicoloured.

595	$1 Type **127**	75	80
596	$2 Crown Prince in military uniform	1·50	1·60
597	$3 Crown Prince's emblem	2·25	2·40

128 Koran, Civil Servants and Handshake

129 Blue-eared Kingfisher

1998. 5th Anniv of Civil Service Day. Multicoloured.

599	30 c. Type **128**	20	25
600	60 c. Symbols of progress	45	50
601	90 c. Civil servants at work	70	75

1998. Birds (5th series). Kingfishers. Multicoloured.

602	20 c. Type **129**	15	20
603	30 c. Common kingfisher	20	25
604	60 c. White-collared kingfisher	45	50
605	$1 Stork-billed kingfisher	75	80

130 Water Village, Bandar Seri Begawan

1999. 15th Anniv of National Day. Multicoloured.

606	20 c. Type **130**	15	20
607	60 c. Mordern telecommunications and air travel	45	50
608	90 c. Aspects of modern Brunei	70	75

JAPANESE OCCUPATION OF BRUNEI

These stamps were valid throughout British Borneo (i.e. in Brunei, Labuan, North Borneo and Sarawak).

100 cents = 1 dollar

(**1**) ("Imperial Japanese Government")

(**2**) ("Imperial Japanese Postal Service $3")

1942. Stamps of Brunei optd with T **1**.

J 1	**5**	1 c. black	6·00	23·00
J 2		2 c. green	48·00	£100
J 3		2 c. orange	2·75	9·00
J 4		3 c. green	28·00	75·00
J 5		4 c. orange	3·00	13·00
J 6		5 c. brown	3·00	13·00
J 7	**7**	6 c. grey	50·00	£200
J 8		6 c. red	£550	£550
J 9	**5**	8 c. black	£650	£850
J10	**7**	8 c. red	3·75	12·00
J11	**5**	10 c. purple on yellow	8·50	26·00
J12	**7**	12 c. blue	22·00	26·00
J13		15 c. blue	13·00	26·00
J14	**5**	25 c. lilac	23·00	50·00
J15		30 c. purple and orange	90·00	£180
J16		50 c. black on green	38·00	60·00
J17		$1 black and red on blue	55·00	70·00
J18		$5 red on green	£800	£1600
J19		$25 black on red	£850	£1600

1944. No. J1 surch with T **2**.

J20	**5**	$3 on 1 c. black	£5500	£5000

BUNDI

A state of Rajasthan, India. Now uses Indian stamps.

12 pies = 1 anna; 16 annas = 1 rupee

3 Native Dagger

11 Raja protecting Sacred Cows

1894. Imperf.

12	**3**	$\frac{1}{2}$ a. grey	2·25	2·75
13		1 a. red	1·60	1·75
14		2 a. green	6·50	10·00
8		4 a. green	38·00	50·00
15		8 a. red	6·00	11·00
16a		1 r. yellow on blue	8·00	18·00

1898. As T **3**, but with dagger point to left.

17a	**3**	4 a. green	8·00	12·00

1914. Roul or perf.

26	**11**	$\frac{1}{4}$ a. blue	1·75	4·25
38		$\frac{1}{2}$ a. black	1·40	4·50
28		1 a. red	2·75	9·00
20a		2 a. green	1·60	9·00
30		2$\frac{1}{2}$ a. yellow	5·00	19·00
31		3 a. brown	4·50	25·00
32		4 a. green	3·50	27·00
33		6 a. blue	8·50	60·00
42		8 a. orange	9·00	48·00
43		10 a. olive	16·00	60·00
44		12 a. green	8·00	55·00
25		1 r. lilac	17·00	75·00
46		2 r. brown and black	50·00	£130
47		3 r. blue and brown	75·00	£170
48		4 r. green and red	£170	£275
49		5 r. red and green	£180	£300

20

21 Maharao Rajah Bahadur Singh

1941. Perf.

79	**20**	3 p. blue	85	3·00
80		6 p. blue	2·75	4·25
81		1 a. red	3·00	5·00
82		2 a. brown	4·25	11·00
83		4 a. green	8·00	32·00
84		8 a. green	10·00	£110
85		1 r. blue	28·00	£160

1947.

86	**21**	$\frac{1}{4}$ a. green	1·10	23·00
87		$\frac{1}{2}$ a. violet	1·10	23·00
88		1 a. green	1·10	23·00
89	–	2 a. red	1·10	42·00
90	–	4 a. orange	1·25	60·00
91	–	8 a. blue	2·25	
92	–	1 r. brown	13·00	

DESIGNS: 2, 4 a. Rajah in Indian dress; 8 a., 1 r. View of Bundi.

OFFICIAL STAMPS

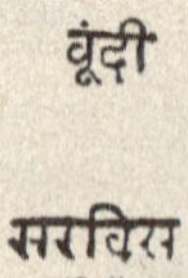

(O **1**)

(A). Type O **1**.

(B/C). Optd **BUNDI SERVICE**.

1918. Optd.

			A	B/C
O 6	**11**	$\frac{1}{4}$ a. blue	1·60	1·75
O16		$\frac{1}{2}$ a. black	6·00	3·00
O 8b		1 a. red	20·00	12·00
O18		2 a. green	4·50	12·00
O 2		2$\frac{1}{2}$ a. yellow	2·25	10·00
O 3		3 a. brown	2·50	16·00
O19		4 a. green	8·00	60·00
O11		6 a. blue	11·00	£140
O20		8 a. orange	14·00	24·00
O21		10 a. olive	40·00	65·00
O22		12 a. green	32·00	75·00
O 5		1 r. lilac	38·00	38·00
O24		2 r. brown and black	£300	£170
O25		3 r. blue and brown	£300	£200
O26		4 r. green and red	£275	£300
O27		5 r. red and green	£275	£300

Prices for Nos. O1/27 are for unused examples. Used examples are generally worth a small premium over the prices quoted.

1941. Optd **SERVICE**.

O53	**20**	3 p. blue	3·00	8·00
O54		6 p. blue	10·00	8·00
O55		1 a. red	9·00	7·00
O56		2 a.brown	7·00	8·50
O57		4 a. green	24·00	70·00
O58	**20**	8 a. green	95·00	£300
O59		1 r. blue	£120	£325

For later issues see **RAJASTHAN**.

BURMA

A territory in the east of India. Formerly part of the Indian Empire, but separated from it on 1 April 1937. Japanese forces were in occupation from 1942 to 1945 and Independence was established in 1948.

1937. 12 pies = 1 anna. 16 annas = 1 rupee.
1953. 100 pyas = 1 kyat (rupee).

1937. Stamps of India (King George V) optd **BURMA**.

1	**55**	3 p. grey	30	10
2	**79**	$\frac{1}{2}$ a. green	50	10
3	**80**	9 p. green	75	10
4	**81**	1 a. brown	40	10
5	**59**	2 a. red	40	10
6	**61**	2$\frac{1}{2}$ a. orange	30	10
7	**62**	3 a. red	75	30
8	**83**	3$\frac{1}{2}$ a. blue	65	10
9	**63**	4 a. olive	70	10
10	**64**	6 a. bistre	60	35
11	**65**	8 a. mauve	1·50	10
12	**66**	12 a. red	2·50	85
13	**67**	1 r. brown and green	16·00	2·00
14		2 r. red and orange	23·00	9·00
15		5 r. blue and violet	35·00	15·00
16		10 r. green and red	65·00	50·00
17		15 r. blue and olive	£200	90·00
18		25 r. orange and blue	£400	£190

2 King George VI and "Chinthes"

3 King George VI and "Nagas"

4 Royal Barge

8 King George VI and Peacock

1938. King George VI.

18a	**2**	1 p. orange	3·00	80
19		3 p. violet	20	30
20		6 p. blue	20	10
21		9 p. green	1·00	80
22	**3**	1 a. brown	20	10
23		1$\frac{1}{2}$ a. green	20	60
24		2 a. red	45	10
25	**4**	2 a. 6 p. red	14·00	90
26	–	3 a. mauve	14·00	1·50
27	–	3 a. 6 p. blue	1·25	3·75
28	**3**	4 a. blue	60	10
29	–	8 a. green	5·00	30
30	**8**	1 r. purple and blue	7·50	20
31		2 r. brown and purple	16·00	1·75
32	–	5 r. violet and red	48·00	20·00
33	–	10 r. brown and green	55·00	42·00

DESIGNS—HORIZ: As Type **4**: 3 a. Burma teak; 3 a. 6 p. Burma rice; 8 a. River Irrawaddy. VERT: As Type **3**: 5, 10 r. King George VI and "Nats".

1940. Cent of First Adhesive Postage Stamp. Surch **COMMEMORATION POSTAGE STAMP 6th MAY 1840 ONE ANNA 1A** and value in native characters.

34	**4**	1 a. on 2 a. 6 p. red	3·50	1·25

For Japanese issues see "Japanese Occupation of Burma".

1945. British Military Administration. Stamps of 1938 optd **MILY ADMN**.

35	**2**	1 p. orange	10	10
36		3 p. violet	10	30
37		6 p. blue	10	30
38		9 p. green	30	30
39	**3**	1 a. brown	10	10
40		1$\frac{1}{2}$ a. green	10	15
41		2 a. red	10	15
42	**4**	2 a. 6 p. red	2·00	60
43	–	3 a. mauve	1·50	20
44	–	3 a. 6 p. blue	10	70
45	**3**	4 a. blue	10	25
46	–	8 a. green	10	40
47	**8**	1 r. purple and blue	40	50
48		2 r. brown and purple	40	1·00
49	–	5 r. violet and red	40	1·00
50	–	10 r. brown and green	40	1·00

1946. British Civil Administration. As 1938, but colours changed.

51	**2**	3 p. brown	10	90
52		6 p. violet	10	30
53		9 p. green	15	1·60
54	**3**	1 a. blue	15	20
55		1½ a. orange	15	10
56		2 a. red	15	40
57	**4**	2 a. 6 p. blue	80	3·00
57a	–	3 a. blue	6·50	3·00
57b	–	3 a. 6 p. black and blue	30	1·25
58	**3**	4 a. purple	30	30
59	–	8 a. mauve	1·75	1·75
60	**8**	1 r. violet and mauve	1·00	40
61		2 r. brown and orange	6·00	2·00
62	–	5 r. green and brown	6·00	10·00
63	–	10 r. red and violet	6·00	16·00

14 Burman

ကြားဖြတ်
အစိုးရ။

(**18** Trans. "Interim Government")

1946. Victory.

64	**14**	9 p. green	20	20
65	–	1½ a. violet (Burmese woman)	20	10
66	–	2 a. red (Chinthe)	20	10
67	–	3 a. 6 p. (Elephant)	30	20

1947. Stamps of 1946 opt with T **18** or with larger opt on large stamps.

68	**2**	3 p. brown	70	70
69		6 p. violet	10	30
70		9 p. green	10	30
71	**3**	1 a. blue	10	30
72		1½ a. orange	90	10
73		2 a. red	30	15
74	**4**	2 a. 6 p. blue	1·75	95
75	–	3 a. blue	2·50	1·50
76	–	3 a. 6 p. black and blue	45	1·50
77	**3**	4 a. purple	1·75	30
78	–	8 a. mauve	1·75	90
79	**8**	1 r. violet and mauve	2·50	30
80		2 r. brown and orange	3·25	2·50
81	–	5 r. green and brown	3·25	3·25
82	–	10 r. red and violet	3·25	3·25

OFFICIAL STAMPS

1937. Stamps of India (King George V) optd **BURMA SERVICE**.

O 1	**55**	3 p. grey	1·00	10
O 2	**79**	½ a. green	5·50	10
O 3	**80**	9 p. green	3·25	30
O 4	**81**	1 a. brown	3·75	10
O 5	**59**	2 a. red	6·00	35
O 6	**61**	2½ a. orange	4·00	1·50
O 7	**63**	4 a. olive	3·75	10
O 8	**64**	6 a. bistre	4·00	5·50
O 9	**65**	8 a. mauve	3·00	80
O10	**66**	12 a. red	3·00	3·00
O11	**67**	1 r. brown and green	20·00	3·75
O12		2 r. red and orange	40·00	28·00
O13		5 r. blue and violet	85·00	42·00
O14		10 r. green and red	£250	£110

1939. Stamps of 1938 optd **SERVICE**.

O15	**2**	3 p. violet	15	20
O16		6 p. blue	15	20
O17		9 p. green	5·00	1·90
O18	**3**	1a. brown	15	15
O19		1½ a. green	4·50	1·25
O20		2 a. red	1·25	20
O21	**4**	2 a. 6 p. red	25·00	9·00
O22	**3**	4 a. blue	5·50	45
O23	–	8 a. green (No. 29)	25·00	3·75
O24	**8**	1 r. purple and blue	38·00	5·00
O25		2 r. brown and purple	45·00	10·00
O26	–	5 r. violet and red (No. 32)	42·00	28·00
O27	–	10 r. brown and green (No. 33)	£120	38·00

1946. Stamps of 1946 optd **SERVICE**.

O28	**2**	3 p. brown	60	2·25
O29		6 p. violet	60	1·75
O30		9 p. green	20	2·50
O31	**3**	1 a. blue	20	1·50
O32		1½ a. orange	20	20
O33		2 a. red	20	1·50
O34	**4**	2 a. 6 p. blue	1·40	4·00
O35	**3**	4 a. purple	20	70
O36	–	8 a. mauve (No. 59)	1·50	2·50
O37	**8**	1 r. violet and mauve	60	2·50
O38		2 r. brown and orange	7·00	32·00
O39	–	5 r. green and brown (No. 62)	9·00	38·00
O40	–	10 r. red and violet (No. 63)	17·00	48·00

1947. Interim Government. Nos. O28 etc., optd with T **18** or with large overprint on larger stamps.

O41	**2**	3 p. brown	15	40
O42		6 p. violet	70	10
O43		9 p. green	1·00	90
O44	**3**	1 a. blue	1·75	80
O45		1½ a. orange	3·25	20
O46		2 a. red	1·50	15
O47	**4**	2 a. 6 p. blue	19·00	7·00
O48	**3**	4 a. purple	5·50	40
O49	–	8 a. mauve	5·50	3·00
O50	**8**	1 r. violet and mauve	14·00	2·25
O51		2 r. brown and orange	14·00	17·00
O52	–	5 r. green and brown	14·00	18·00
O53	–	10 r. red and violet	14·00	28·00

For issues after Independence see Volume 1.

JAPANESE OCCUPATION OF BURMA

1942. 12 pies = 1 anna; 16 annas = 1 rupee.
1942. 100 cents = 1 rupee.

(1)

(3)

Note.—There are various types of the Peacock overprint. Our prices, as usual in this Catalogue, are for the cheapest type.

1942. Postage stamps of Burma of 1937 (India types) optd as T **1**.

J22	**55**	3 p. grey	3·00	17·00
J23	**80**	9 p. green	21·00	60·00
J24	**59**	2 a. red	£100	£180
J 2	**83**	3½ a. blue	48·00	

1942. Official stamp of Burma of 1937 (India type) optd as T **1**.

J3	**64**	6 a. bistre	70·00	

1942. Postage stamps of Burma, 1938, optd as T **1** or with T **3** (rupee values).

J25	**1**	1 p. orange	£180	£275
J12		3 p. violet	17·00	60·00
J27		6 p. blue	25·00	50·00
J14		9 p. green	17·00	55·00
J29	**3**	1 a. brown	9·00	38·00
J30		1½ a. green	21·00	65·00
J16		2 a. red	16·00	55·00
J17		4 a. blue	32·00	80·00
J18	**8**	1 r. purple and blue	£225	
J19		2 r. brown and purple	£140	

1942. Official stamps of Burma of 1939 optd with T **1**.

J 7	**1**	3 p. violet	20·00	70·00
J 8		6 p. blue	15·00	48·00
J 9	**3**	1 a. brown	14·00	40·00
J35		1½ a. green	£140	£200
J10		2 a. red	22·00	70·00
J11		4 a. blue	20·00	60·00

(**6a**) ("Yon Thon" = "Office use")

1942. Official stamp of Burma of 1939 optd with T **6a**.

J44	–	8 a. green (No. O23)	80·00	

7

8 Farmer

1942. Yano Seal.

J45	**7**	(1 a.) red	38·00	65·00

1942.

J46	**8**	1 a. red	15·00	15·00

1942. Stamps of Japan surch in annas or rupees.

J47	–	¼ a. on 1 s. brown (No. 314)	22·00	26·00
J48	**83**	½ a. on 2 s. red	22·00	26·00
J49	–	¾ a on 3 s. green (No. 316)	45·00	48·00
J50	–	1 a. on 5 s. purple (No. 396)	38·00	38·00
J51	–	3 a. on 7 s. green (No. 320)	75·00	85·00
J52	–	4 a. on 4 s. green (No. 317)	38·00	40·00
J53	–	8 a. on 8 s. violet (No. 321)	£140	£140
J54	–	1 r. on 10 s. red (No. 322)	15·00	24·00
J55	–	2 r. on 20 s. blue (No. 325)	42·00	42·00
J56	–	5 r. on 30 s. blue (No. 327)	12·00	27·00

1942. No. 386 of Japan commemorating the fall of Singapore, surch in figures.

J56g	–	4 a. on 4 s. + 2 s. green and red	£150	£160

1942. Handstamped **5 C**.

J57	**5**	5 c. on 1 a. red (No. J46)	11·00	15·00

1942. Nos. J47/53 with anna surcharges obliterated, and handstamped with new values in figures.

J58	–	1 c. on ¼ a. on 1 s. brown	40·00	40·00
J59	**84**	2 c. on ½ a. on 2 s. red	38·00	38·00
J60	–	3 c. on ¾ a. on 3 s. green	42·00	42·00
J61	–	5 c. on 1 a. on 5 s. red	65·00	65·00
J62	–	10 c. on 3 a. on 7 s. green	£100	95·00
J63	–	15 c. on 4 a. on 4 s. green	28·00	30·00
J64	–	20 c. on 8 a. on 8 s. violet	£325	£275

1942. Stamps of Japan surch in cents.

J65	–	1 c. on 1 s. brown (No. 314)	18·00	20·00
J66	**83**	2 c. on 2 s. red	35·00	32·00
J67	–	3 c. on 3 s. green (No. 316)	38·00	38·00
J68	–	5 c. on 5 s. purple (No. 396)	40·00	40·00
J69	–	10 c. on 7 s. green (No. 320)	48·00	50·00
J70	–	15 c. on 4 s. green (No. 317)	14·00	20·00
J71	–	20 c. on 8 s. violet (No. 321)	£120	85·00

14 Burma State Crest

15 Farmer

1943. Perf or Imperf.

J72	**14**	5 c. red	14·00	18·00

1943.

J73a	**15**	1 c. orange	70	3·75
J74		2 c. green	60	1·00
J75		3 c. blue	80	85
J77		5 c. red	1·50	3·00
J78		10 c. brown	3·00	3·25
J79		15 c. mauve	30	90
J80		20 c. lilac	30	65
J81		30 c. green	30	70

16 Soldier carving word "Independence"

17 Rejoicing Peasant

18 Boy with National Flag

1943. Independence Day. Perf or roul.

J85	**16**	1 c. orange	1·00	1·50
J86	**17**	3 c. blue	1·00	1·50
J87	**18**	5 c. red	1·00	1·50

19 Burmese Woman

20 Elephant carrying Log

21 Watch Tower Mandalay

1943.

J88	**19**	1 c. orange	20·00	15·00
J89		2 c. green	50	2·00
J90		3 c. violet	50	2·25
J91	**20**	5 c. red	55	60
J92		10 c. blue	65	95
J93		15 c. orange	65	2·00
J94		20 c. green	65	1·75
J95		30 c. brown	65	1·75
J96	**21**	1 r. orange	30	2·00
J97		2 r. violet	30	2·25

22 Bullock Cart

23 Shan Woman

1943. Shan States issue.

J 98	**22**	1 c. brown	22·00	28·00
J 99		2 c. green	20·00	30·00
J100		3 c. violet	2·75	10·00
J101		5 c. blue	2·00	5·50
J102	**23**	10 c. blue	8·00	17·00
J103		20 c. red	22·00	17·00
J104		30 c. brown	14·00	30·00

ဗမာနိုင်ငံတော်

၂၀ ဆင့်။

(**24** "Burma State" and value)

1944. Optd with T **24**.

J105	**22**	1 c. brown	2·50	6·00
J106		2 c. green	40	1·50
J107		3 c. violet	1·50	7·00
J108		5 c. blue	80	1·00
J109	**23**	10 c. blue	1·75	2·00
J110		20 c. red	40	1·50
J111		30 c. brown	40	1·75

BUSHIRE

An Iranian seaport. Stamps issued during the British Occupation in the 1914–18 War.

20 chahis = 1 kran, 10 krans = 1 toman

1915. Portrait stamps of Iran (1911) optd **BUSHIRE Under British Occupation**.

1	**57**	1 ch. orange and green	28·00	32·00
2		2 ch. brown and red	28·00	26·00
3		3 ch. green and grey	35·00	42·00
4		5 ch. red and brown	£250	£250
5		6 ch. lake and green	27·00	21·00
6		9 ch. lilac and brown	28·00	32·00
7		10 ch. brown and red	30·00	30·00
8		12 ch. blue and green	38·00	42·00
9		24 ch. green and purple	55·00	42·00
10		1 kr. red and blue	55·00	26·00
11		2 kr. red and green	£170	£120
12		3 kr. black and lilac	£150	£150
13		5 kr. blue and red	90·00	80·00
14		10 kr. red and brown	80·00	75·00

1915. Coronation issue of Iran optd **BUSHIRE Under British Occupation**.

15	**66**	1 ch. blue and red	£300	£300
16		2 ch. red and blue	£5000	£5500
17		3 ch. green	£375	£400
18		5 ch. red	£3750	£4000
19		6 ch. red and green	£3000	£3250
20		9 ch. violet and brown	£475	£500
21		10 ch. brown and green	£800	£850
22		12 ch. blue	£900	£1000
23		24 ch. black and brown	£375	£400
24	**67**	1 kr. black, brown and silver	£350	£375
25		2 kr. red, blue and silver	£300	£325
26		3 kr. black, lilac and silver	£425	£450
27		5 kr. slate, brown and silver	£400	£425
28	–	1 t. black, violet and gold	£350	£400
29	–	3 t. red, lake and gold	£2250	£2500

BUSSAHIR (BASHAHR)

A state in the Punjab, India. Now uses Indian stamps.

12 pies = 1 anna; 16 annas = 1 rupee

1

1895. Various frames. Imperf, perf or roul.

9	**1**	¼ a. pink	35·00	75·00
10		½ a. grey	15·00	85·00
11		1 a. red	16·00	75·00
12		2 a. yellow	24·00	75·00
13		4 a. violet	16·00	80·00
14		8 a. brown	17·00	85·00
15		12 a. green	50·00	£100
16		1 r. blue	28·00	85·00

1896. Similar types, but inscriptions on white ground and inscr "POSTAGE" instead of "STAMP".

27	**1**	¼ a. violet	12·00	11·00
37		¼ a. red	2·75	6·00
25		½ a. blue	4·50	11·00
26		1 a. olive	10·00	25·00
32		1 a. red	2·75	8·50
41		2 a. yellow	28·00	50·00
36		4 a. red	29·00	75·00

CAICOS ISLANDS

Separate issues for these islands, part of the Turks and Caicos Islands group, appeared from 1981 to 1985.

100 cents = 1 dollar

1981. Nos. 514, 518, 520, 523 and 525/7 of Turks and Caicos Islands optd **CAICOS ISLANDS**.

1	1 c. Indigo hamlet	15	15
2	5 c. Spanish grunt	20	20
3	8 c. Four-eyed butterflyfish	20	20
4	20 c. Queen angelfish	45	30
5	50 c. Royal gramma ("Fairy basslet")	85	1·00
6	$1 Fin-spot wrasse	1·50	1·75
7	$2 Stoplight parrotfish	2·50	3·25

1981. Royal Wedding. Nos. 653/6 of Turks and Caicos Islands optd A. **Caicos Islands**. B. **CAICOS ISLANDS**.

		A		B	
8	35 c. Prince Charles and Lady Diana Spencer	20	25	50	75
9	65 c. Kensington Palace	30	40	70	1·00
10	90 c. Prince Charles as Colonel of Welsh Guards	40	50	90	1·50

1981. Royal Wedding. Booklet stamps. As Nos. 657/9 of Turks and Caicos Islands, but each inscr "Caicos Islands". Mult. Self-adhesive.

12	20 c. Lady Diana Spencer	30	40
13	$1 Prince Charles	80	1·25
14	$2 Prince Charles and Lady Diana Spencer	5·50	5·50

4 Queen or Pink Conch and Lobster Fishing, South Caicos

1983. Multicoloured.

15	8 c. Type **4**	80	50
16	10 c. Hawksbill turtle, East Caicos	80	50
17	20 c. Arawak Indians and idol, Middle Caicos	80	50
18	35 c. Boat-building, North Caicos	1·25	85
19	50 c. Marine biologist at work, Pine Cay	2·00	90
20	95 c. Boeing 707 airliner at new airport, Providenciales	4·00	2·25
21	$1.10 Columbus's "Pinta", West Caicos	4·00	2·50
22	$2 Fort George Cay	3·50	3·75
23	$3 Pirates Anne Bonny and Calico Jack at Parrot Cay	6·00	4·75

5 Goofy and Patch

1983. Christmas. Multicoloured.

30	1 c. Type **5**	10	10
31	1 c. Chip and Dale	10	10
32	2 c. Morty	10	10
33	2 c. Morty and Ferdie	10	10
34	3 c. Goofy and Louie	10	10
35	3 c. Donald Duck, Huey, Dewey and Louie	10	10
36	50 c. Uncle Scrooge	2·75	2·25
37	70 c. Mickey Mouse and Ferdie	3·00	2·75
38	$1.10 Pinocchio, Jiminy Cricket and Figaro	3·50	3·50

6 "Leda and the Swan"

7 High Jumping

1984. 500th Birth Anniv of Raphael. Mult.

40	35 c. Type **6**	75	50
41	50 c. "Study of Apollo for Parnassus"	1·00	70
42	95 c. "Study of two figures for the battle of Ostia"	2·00	1·25
43	$1.10 "Study for the Madonna of the Goldfinch"	2·00	1·50

1984. Olympic Games, Los Angeles.

45	**7**	4 c. multicoloured	10	10
46	–	25 c. multicoloured	20	20
47	–	65 c. black, deep blue and blue	50	50
48	–	$1.10 multicoloured	85	85

DESIGNS: 25 c. Archery; 65 c. Cycling; $1.10, Football.

8 Horace Horsecollar and Clarabelle Cow

1984. Easter. Walt Disney Cartoon Characters. Multicoloured.

50	35 c. Type **8**	80	60
51	45 c. Mickey and Minnie Mouse, and Chip	95	75
52	75 c. Gyro Gearloose, Chip 'n Dale	1·60	1·25
53	85 c. Mickey Mouse, Chip 'n Dale	1·60	1·40

1984. Universal Postal Union Congress Hamburg. Nos. 20/1 optd **UNIVERSAL POSTAL UNION 1874-1984** and emblem.

55	95 c. Boeing 707 airliner at new airport, Providenciales	1·00	1·25
56	$1.10 Columbus's "Pinta", West Caicos	1·25	1·50

1984. "Ausipex" International Stamp Exhibition, Melbourne. No. 22 optd **AUSIPEX 1984**.

57	$2 Fort George Cay	2·40	2·50

11 Seamen sighting American Manatees

1984. 492nd Anniv of Columbus's First Landfall. Multicoloured.

58	10 c. Type **11**	85	60
59	70 c. Columbus's fleet	3·00	2·75
60	$1 First landing in the West Indies	3·50	3·25

12 Donald Duck and Mickey Mouse with Father Christmas

1984. Christmas. Walt Disney Cartoon Characters. Multicoloured.

62	20 c. Type **12**	1·00	75
63	35 c. Donald Duck opening refrigerator	1·40	1·00
64	50 c. Mickey Mouse, Donald Duck and toy train	1·90	1·50
65	75 c. Donald Duck and parcels	2·50	2·25
66	$1.10 Donald Duck and carol singers	2·75	2·75

13 Thick-billed Vireo

1985. Birth Bicentenary of John J. Audubon (ornithologist). Multicoloured.

68	20 c. Type **13**	1·60	50
69	35 c. Black-faced grassquit	1·90	75
70	50 c. Pearly-eyed thrasher	2·25	1·10
71	$1 Greater Antillean bullfinch	2·50	1·90

14 Two Children learning to Read and Write (Education)

16 The Queen Mother visiting Foundation for the Disabled, Leatherhead

15 Douglas DC-3 on Ground

1985. International Youth Year. 40th Anniv of United Nations. Multicoloured.

73	16 c. Type **14**	20	25
74	35 c. Two children on playground swings (Health)	50	55
75	70 c. Boy and girl (Love)	1·00	1·10
76	90 c. Three children (Peace)	1·25	1·40

1985. 40th Anniv of International Civil Aviation Organization. Multicoloured.

78	35 c. Type **15**	1·75	55
79	75 c. Convair CV 440 Metropolitan	3·00	1·25
80	90 c. Britten Norman Islander	3·00	1·40

1985. Life and Times of Queen Elizabeth the Queen Mother. Multicoloured.

82	35 c. Type **16**	50	55
83	65 c. With Princess Anne (horiz)	90	95
84	95 c. At Epsom, 1961	1·40	1·60

1985. 150th Birth Anniv of Mark Twain (author). Designs as T **118** of Anguilla, showing Walt Disney cartoon characters in scenes from "Tom Sawyer, Detective". Multicoloured.

86	8 c. Huckleberry Finn (Goofy) and Tom Sawyer (Mickey Mouse) reading reward notice	60	20
87	35 c. Huck and Tom meeting Jake Dunlap	1·75	65
88	95 c. Huck and Tom spying on Jubiter Dunlap	3·25	2·00
89	$1.10 Huck and Tom with hound (Pluto)	3·25	2·25

1985. Birth Bicentenaries of Grimm Brothers (folklorists). Designs as T **119** of Anguilla, showing Walt Disney cartoon characters in scenes from "Six Soldiers of Fortune". Multicoloured.

91	16 c. The Soldier (Donald Duck) with his meagre pay	1·00	30
92	25 c. The Soldier meeting the Strong Man (Horace Horsecollar)	1·25	45
93	65 c. The Soldier meeting the Marksman (Mickey Mouse)	2·50	1·25
94	$1.35 The Fast Runner (Goofy) winning the race against the Princess (Daisy Duck)	3·25	2·25

CAMEROON

12 pence = 1 shilling;
20 shillings = 1 pound

Former German colony occupied by British and French troops during 1914–16. The territory was divided between them and the two areas were administered under League of Nations mandates from 1922, converted into United Nations trusteeships in 1946.

The British section was administered as part of Nigeria until 1960, when a plebiscite was held. The northern area voted to join Nigeria and the southern part joined the newly-independent Cameroun Republic (formerly the French trust territory). In November 1995 this republic joined the Commonwealth.

For German and French issues and issues of the republic before November 1995, see Volume 1.

I. CAMEROONS EXPEDITIONARY FORCE

1915. "Yacht" key-types of German Kamerun surch **C.E.F.** and value in English currency.

B 1	N	½d. on 3 pf. brown	10·00	23·00
B 2		½d. on 5 pf. green	1·75	8·00
B 3		1d. on 10 pf. red	1·25	8·00
B 4		2d. on 20 pf. blue	3·50	17·00
B 5		2½d. on 25 pf. black and red on yellow	12·00	35·00
B 6		3d. on 30 pf. black and orange on buff	12·00	35·00
B 7		4d. on 40 pf. black and red	12·00	35·00
B 8		6d. on 50 pf. black and purple on buff	12·00	35·00
B 9		8d. on 80 pf. black and red on rose	12·00	35·00
B10	O	1s. on 1 m. red	£140	£500
B11		2s. on 2 m. blue	£140	£500
B12		3s. on 3 m. black	£140	£500
B13		5s. on 5 m. red and black	£170	£550

II. CAMEROONS TRUST TERRITORY

Issue used in the British trusteeship from October 1960 until June 1961 in the northern area and until September 1961 in the southern area, when they joined with Nigeria and the Cameroun Republic respectively.

1960. Stamps of Nigeria of 1953 optd **CAMEROONS U.K.T.T.**

T1	**18**	½d. black and orange	10	80
T2	–	1d. black and green	10	50
T3	–	1½d. green	10	20
T4	–	2d. grey	10	40
T5	–	3d. black and lilac	15	10
T6	–	4d. black and blue	10	80
T7	–	6d. brown and black	30	10
T8	–	1s. black and purple	15	10
T9	**26**	2s. 6d. black and green	1·10	80
T10	–	5s. black and orange	1·60	3·50
T11	–	10s. black and brown	2·50	5·00
T12	**29**	£1 black and violet	8·50	16·00

III. REPUBLIC OF CAMEROON

The Republic of Cameroon joined the Commonwealth on 1 November 1995 and issues from that date will be listed below when details and examples are received.

CANADA

A British dominion consisting of the former province of Canada with British Columbia, New Brunswick, Newfoundland, Nova Scotia and Prince Edward Island.

1851. 12 pence = 1 shilling (Canadian).
1859. 100 cents = 1 dollar.

COLONY OF CANADA

1 Beaver

2 Prince Albert

3

4

5

6 Jacques Cartier

1851. Imperf.

17	4	½d. red	£700	£400
5	1	3d. red	£1100	£160
2	2	6d. purple	£14000	£900
12	5	7½d. green	£7000	£1500
14	6	10d. blue	£6500	£1100
4	3	12d. black	£60000	£40000

1858. Perf.

25	4	½d. red	£1700	£600
26	1	3d. red	£2500	£300
27a	2	6d. purple	£6500	£2250

1859. Values in cents. Perf.

29	4	1 c. red	£225	24·00
44		2 c. red	£400	£140
31	1	5 c. red	£250	11·00
38	2	10 c. purple	£750	40·00
36		10 c. brown	£700	40·00
40	5	12½ c. green	£550	38·00
42	6	17 c. blue	£700	60·00

DOMINION OF CANADA

13

14

1868. Various frames.

54	13	½ c. black	45·00	45·00
55	14	1 c. brown	£300	40·00
56a		1 c. yellow	£650	60·00
57		2 c. green	£325	27·00
49		3 c. red	£600	20·00
63		5 c. green	£700	65·00
59b		6 c. brown	£650	35·00
60		12½ c. blue	£400	35·00
70		15 c. purple	60·00	16·00
69		15 c. blue	£130	27·00

27

21

28

1870. Various frames.

101	27	½ c. black	7·50	6·00
75	21	1 c. yellow	20·00	70
104		2 c. green	30·00	90
105		3 c. red	23·00	50
106		5 c. grey	60·00	1·25
107		6 c. brown	30·00	7·50
117	–	8 c. grey	80·00	3·50
120	–	8 c. purple	70·00	3·50
111	21	10 c. pink	£150	20·00

On 8 c. head is to left.

1893.

115	28	20 c. red	£160	42·00
116		50 c. blue	£225	24·00

30

31

1897. Jubilee.

121	30	½ c. black	48·00	48·00
122		1 c. orange	9·00	4·00
124		2 c. green	13·00	8·00
126		3 c. red	9·50	2·00
128		5 c. blue	35·00	13·00
129		6 c. brown	85·00	85·00
130		8 c. violet	32·00	29·00
131		10 c. purple	50·00	40·00
132		15 c. slate	85·00	85·00
133		20 c. red	85·00	85·00
134		50 c. blue	£120	95·00
136		$1 red	£400	£400
137		$2 violet	£700	£350
138		$3 bistre	£800	£650
139		$4 violet	£800	£600
140		$5 green	£800	£600

1897. Maple-leaves in four corners.

141	31	½ c. black	5·50	4·00
143		1 c. green	17·00	70
144		2 c. violet	17·00	1·00
145		3 c. red	22·00	40
146		5 c. blue	60·00	2·25
147		6 c. brown	55·00	18·00
148		8 c. orange	75·00	6·50
149		10 c. purple	£130	55·00

1898. As T **31** but figures in lower corners.

150	½ c. black	2·75	95
151	1 c. green	21·00	30
154	2 c. purple	22·00	30
155	2 c. red	28·00	30
156	3 c. red	38·00	70
157	5 c. blue	90·00	1·25
159	6 c. brown	85·00	48·00
160	7 c. yellow	50·00	11·00
162	8 c. orange	£100	23·00
163	10 c. purple	£160	13·00
165	20 c. green	£300	48·00

33

35 King Edward VII

1898. Imperial Penny Postage.

168	33	2 c. black, red and blue	23·00	4·75

1899. Surch **2 CENTS**.

171	2 c. on 3 c. red (No. 145)	11·00	7·00
172	2 c. on 3 c. red (No. 156)	16·00	3·50

1903.

175	35	1 c. green	18·00	30
176		2 c. red	18·00	20
178		5 c. blue	70·00	2·00
180		7 c. olive	55·00	2·25
182		10 c. purple	£110	7·50
185		20 c. olive	£200	22·00
187		50 c. violet	£350	75·00

36 King George V and Queen Mary, when Prince and Princess of Wales

44

1908. Tercentenary of Quebec. Dated "1608 1908".

188	36	½ c. brown	3·25	3·00
189	–	1 c. green	11·00	2·50
190	–	2 c. red	17·00	85
191	–	5 c. blue	45·00	16·00
192	–	7 c. olive	50·00	35·00
193	–	10 c. violet	55·00	45·00
194	–	15 c. orange	75·00	65·00
195	–	20 c. brown	£100	80·00

DESIGNS: 1 c. Cartier and Champlain; 2 c. King Edward VII and Queen Alexandra; 5 c. Champlain's House in Quebec; 7 c. Generals Montcalm and Wolfe; 10 c. Quebec in 1700; 15 c. Champlain's departure for the West; 20 c. Cartier's arrival before Quebec.

1912.

196	44	1 c. green	5·50	20
200		2 c. red	4·50	20
205		3 c. brown	5·00	20
205b		5 c. blue	60·00	50
209		7 c. yellow	20·00	2·50
210		10 c. purple	90·00	2·00
212		20 c. olive	28·00	1·25
215		50 c. brown	48·00	3·25

See also Nos. 246/55.

1915. Optd **WAR TAX** diagonally.

225	44	5 c. blue	£110	£180
226		20 c. olive	55·00	90·00
227		50 c. brown	£110	£140

46

47

1915.

228	46	1 c. green	7·50	20
229		2 c. red	9·00	30

1916.

233	47	2 c.+1 c. red	17·00	90
239		2 c.+1 c. brown	4·00	20

48 Quebec Conference, 1864, from painting "The Fathers of the Confederation" by Robert Harris

1917. 50th Anniv of Confederation.

244	48	3 c. brown	16·00	1·25

1922.

246	44	1 c. yellow	2·50	20
247		2 c. green	2·25	10
248		3 c. red	3·75	10
249		4 c. yellow	8·00	3·25
250		5 c. violet	5·00	1·00
251		7 c. brown	12·00	6·50
252		8 c. blue	19·00	9·00
253		10 c. blue	20·00	2·25
254a		10 c. brown	18·00	2·00
255		$1 orange	50·00	6·00

1926. Surch **2 CENTS** in one line.

264	44	2 c. on 3 c. red	38·00	48·00

1926. Surch **2 CENTS** in two lines.

265	44	2 c. on 3 c. red	14·00	18·00

51 Sir J. A. Macdonald

52 "The Fathers of the Confederation"

1927. 60th Anniv of Confederation. I. Commemoration Issue. Dated "1867–1927".

266	51	1 c. orange	2·00	95
267	52	2 c. green	2·00	10
268	–	3 c. red	6·50	3·75
269	–	5 c. violet	3·25	3·25
270	–	12 c. blue	20·00	4·50

DESIGNS—HORIZ: As Type **52**: 3 c. Parliament Buildings, Ottawa; 12 c. Map of Canada, 1867-1927. VERT: As Type **51**: 5 c. Sir W. Laurier.

56 Darcy McGee

57 Sir W. Laurier and Sir J. A. Macdonald

II. Historical Issue.

271	56	5 c. violet	3·00	2·00
272	57	12 c. green	14·00	4·00
273	–	20 c. red	14·00	11·00

DESIGN—As Type **57**: 20 c. R. Baldwin and L. H. Lafontaine.

59

1928. Air.

274	59	5 c. brown	3·75	2·50

60 King George V

61 Mount Hurd and Indian Totem Poles

1928.

275	60	1 c. orange	2·25	40
276		2 c. green	1·00	10
277		3 c. red	14·00	14·00
278		4 c. yellow	13·00	5·50
279		5 c. violet	5·50	2·50
280		8 c. blue	7·50	3·50
281	61	10 c. green	7·00	85
282	–	12 c. black	17·00	9·00
283	–	20 c. red	27·00	9·50
284	–	50 c. blue	£100	35·00
285	–	$1 olive	£110	55·00

DESIGNS—HORIZ: 12 c. Quebec Bridge; 20 c. Harvesting with horses; 50 c. "Bluenose" (fishing schooner); $1 Parliament Buildings, Ottawa.

66

67 Parliamentary Library, Ottawa

68 The Old Citadel, Quebec

1930.

288	66	1 c. orange	1·25	80
300		1 c. green	1·00	10
289		2 c. green	1·10	10
301		2 c. red	70	30
302b		2 c. brown	85	10
303		3 c. red	90	10
290		4 c. yellow	6·00	3·25
291		5 c. violet	2·50	3·50
304		5 c. blue	5·00	20
292		8 c. blue	7·00	13·00
305		8 c. red	6·50	4·75
293	67	10 c. olive	13·00	85
294	68	12 c. black	11·00	3·75
325		13 c. violet	32·00	2·00
295	–	20 c. red	22·00	60
296	–	50 c. blue	80·00	17·00
297	–	$1 olive	95·00	23·00

DESIGNS—HORIZ: 20 c. Harvesting with tractor; 50 c. Acadian Memorial Church, Grand Pre, Nova Scotia; $1 Mount Edith Cavell.

72 Mercury and Western Hemisphere

73 Sir Georges Etienne Cartier

1930. Air.

310	72	5 c. brown	15·00	17·00

1931

312	73	10 c. green	2·75	10

1932. Air. Surch **6** and bars.

313	59	6 c. on 5 c. brown	2·25	2·00

1932. Surch **3** between bars.

314a	66	3 c. on 2 c. red	1·00	40

76 King George V

77 Duke of Windsor when Prince of Wales

78 Allegory of British Empire

80 King George V

1932. Ottawa Conference (a) Postage.

315	76	3 c. red	70	60
316	77	5 c. blue	7·00	3·50
317	78	13 c. green	8·50	6·00

(b) Air. Surch **6 6 OTTAWA CONFERENCE 1932**.

318	72	6 c. on 5 c. brown	10·00	12·00

1932.

319	80	1 c. green	60	10
320		2 c. brown	70	10
321b		3 c. red	85	10
322		4 c. brown	35·00	7·50
323		5 c. blue	10·00	10
324		8 c. orange	22·00	3·50

81 Parliament Buildings, Ottawa

1933. U.P.U. Congress (Preliminary Meeting).

329	**81**	5 c. blue	5·00	2·50

1933. Optd **WORLD'S GRAIN EXHIBITION AND CONFERENCE REGINA 1933**.

330	–	20 c. red (No. 295)	16·00	6·50

83 S.S. "Royal William" (after S. Skillett)

1933. Cent of 1st Transatlantic Steamboat Crossing.

331	**83**	5 c. blue	8·00	2·75

84 Jacques Cartier approaching Land

1934. 4th Century of Discovery of Canada.

332	**84**	3 c. blue	2·00	1·25

85 U.E.L. Statue, Hamilton

1934. 150th Anniv of Arrival of United Empire Loyalists.

333	**85**	10 c. olive	8·50	4·50

86 Seal of New Brunswick

1934. 150th Anniv of New Brunswick.

334	**86**	2 c. brown	1·50	2·25

87 Queen Elizabeth II when Princess

88 King George VI when Duke of York

89 King George V and Queen Mary

1935. Silver Jubilee. Dated "1910–1935".

335	**87**	1 c. green	55	40
336	**88**	2 c. brown	60	30
337	**89**	3 c. red	1·75	30
338	–	5 c. blue	4·25	4·00
339	–	10 c. green	3·25	3·00
340	–	13 c. blue	6·50	4·50

DESIGNS—VERT: 5 c. Duke of Windsor when Prince of Wales. HORIZ: 10 c. Windsor Castle; 13 c. Royle Yacht "Britannia".

93 King George V

94 Royal Canadian Mounted Policeman

1935.

341	**93**	1 c. green	30	10
342		2 c. brown	50	10
343		3 c. red	60	10
344		4 c. yellow	2·50	90
345		5 c. blue	1·75	10
346		8 c. orange	2·50	2·50
347	**94**	10 c. red	5·00	30
348	–	13 c. violet	4·75	45
349	–	20 c. green	17·00	70
350	–	50 c. violet	25·00	4·25
351	–	$1 blue	40·00	10·00

DESIGNS—HORIZ: 13 c. Confederation, Charlottetown, 1864; 20 c. Niagara Falls; 50 c. Parliament Buildings, Victoria, B.C.; $1 Champlain Monument, Quebec.

99 Daedalus

1935. Air.

355	**99**	6 c. brown	2·50	60

100 King George VI and Queen Elizabeth

1937. Coronation.

356	**100**	3 c. red	85	30

101 King George VI

102 Memorial Chamber Parliament Buildings, Ottawa

104 Fort Garry Gate, Winnipeg

1937.

357	**101**	1 c. green	1·50	10
358		2 c. brown	1·75	10
359		3 c. red	2·25	10
360		4 c. yellow	3·75	1·50
361		5 c. blue	4·00	10
362		8 c. orange	3·75	1·50
363	**102**	10 c. red	5·00	10
364	–	13 c. blue	14·00	80
365	**104**	20 c. brown	22·00	50
366	–	50 c. green	45·00	6·50
367	–	$1 violet	60·00	8·00

DESIGNS—HORIZ: 13 c. Halifax Harbour; 50 c. Vancouver Harbour; $1 Chateau de Ramezay, Montreal.

107 Fairchild 45-80 Sekani Seaplane over "Distributor" on Mackenzie River

1938. Air.

371	**107**	6 c. blue	9·50	50

108 Queen Elizabeth II when Princess and Princess Margaret

1939. Royal Visit.

372	**108**	1 c. black and green	1·75	10
373	–	2 c. black and brown	60	40
374	–	3 c. black and red	60	10

DESIGNS—HORIZ: 3 c. King George VI and Queen Elizabeth. VERT: 2 c. National War Memorial, Ottawa.

111 King George VI in Naval Uniform

112 King George VI in Military Uniform

114 Grain Elevator

115 Farm Scene

121 Air Training Camp

1942. War Effort.

375	**111**	1 c. green (postage)	1·50	10
376	**112**	2 c. brown	1·75	10
377	–	3 c. red	1·25	60
378	–	3 c. purple	90	10
379	**114**	4 c. grey	5·50	90
380	**112**	4 c. red	70	10
381	**111**	5 c. blue	3·00	10
382	**115**	8 c. sepia	5·50	75
383	–	10 c. brown	5·00	10
384	–	13 c. green	6·00	6·00
385	–	14 c. green	14·00	75
386	–	20 c. brown	13·00	15
387	–	50 c. violet	25·00	2·25
388	–	$1 blue	42·00	4·75
399	**121**	6 c. blue (air)	14·00	4·00
400		7 c. blue	2·50	10

DESIGNS—As Type **112**: 3 c. King George VI. As Type **121**. VERT: 10 c. Parliament Buildings. HORIZ: 13, 14 c. Ram tank; 20 c. Corvette; 50 c. Munitions factory; $1 H.M.S. "Cossack" (destroyer).

122 Ontario Farm Scene

1946. Re-conversion to Peace.

401	**122**	8 c. brown (postage)	1·25	1·50
402	–	10 c. green	1·75	10
403	–	14 c. brown	4·00	80
404	–	20 c. grey	3·00	10
405	–	50 c. green	17·00	2·25
406	–	$1 purple	32·00	2·25
407	–	7 c. blue (air)	3·75	10

DESIGNS: 10 c. Great Bear Lake; 14 c. St. Maurice River power station; 20 c. Combine harvester; 50 c. Lumbering in British Columbia; $1 "Abegweit" (train ferry); 7 c. Canada geese in flight.

129 Alexander Graham Bell and "Fame"

130 "Canadian Citizenship"

1947. Birth Centenary of Graham Bell (inventor of the telephone).

408	**129**	4 c. blue	15	10

1947. Advent of Canadian Citizenship and 80th Anniv of Confederation.

409	**130**	4 c. blue	10	10

MORE DETAILED LISTS
are given in the Stanley Gibbons Catalogues referred to in the country headings.
For lists of current volumes see Introduction.

131 Queen Elizabeth II when Princess

132 Queen Victoria. Parliament Building, Ottawa, and King George VI

1948. Princess Elizabeth's Wedding.

410	**131**	4 c. blue	10	10

1948. Cent of Responsible Government.

411	**132**	4 c. grey	10	10

133 Cabot's Ship "Matthew"

1949. Entry of Newfoundland into Canadian Confederation.

412	**133**	4 c. green	30	10

134 "Founding of Halifax, 1749" (after C. W. Jeffries)

135 King George VI

1949. Halifax Bicentenary.

413	**134**	4 c. violet	20	10

1949. Portraits of King George VI.

414	**135**	1 c. green	10	10
415	–	2 c. brown	40	30
415a	–	2 c. green	30	10
416	–	3 c. purple	30	10
417	–	4 c. red	20	10
418	–	5 c. blue	1·75	10

1950. As Nos. 414 and 416/18 but without "POSTES POSTAGE".

424		1 c. green	10	50
425		2 c. brown	10	60
426		3 c. purple	10	90
427		4 c. red	10	20
428		5 c. blue	30	1·25

142 Drying Furs

141 Oil Wells in Alberta

145 Mackenzie King

1950.

432	**142**	10 c. purple	1·25	10
441	–	20 c. grey	1·25	10
431	**141**	50 c. green	7·50	1·00
433	–	$1 blue	38·00	5·00

DESIGNS: 20 c. Forestry products; $1 Fisherman.

1951. Canadian Prime Ministers.

434	–	3 c. green (Borden)	10	50
444	–	3 c. purple (Abbott)	15	20
435	**145**	4 c. red	10	10
445	–	4 c. red (A. Mackenzie)	15	10
475	–	4 c. violet (Thompson)	15	10
483	–	4 c. violet (Bennett)	10	20
476	–	5 c. blue (Bowell)	15	10
484	–	5 c. blue (Tupper)	10	10

146 Mail Trains, 1851 and 1951

149 Reproduction of 3d., 1851

1951. Centenary of First Canadian Postage Stamp. Dated "1851 1951".

436	**146**	4 c. black	35	10
437	–	5 c. violet	65	1·75
438	–	7 c. blue	35	1·00
439	**149**	15 c. red	1·10	10

DESIGNS—As Type **146**: 5 c. "City of Toronto" and S.S. "Prince George"; 7 c. Mail coach and Canadair DC-4M North Star airplane.

150 Queen Elizabeth II when Princess and Duke of Edinburgh

1951. Royal Visit.

440 **150** 4 c. violet 10 10

152 Red Cross Emblem

1952. 18th Int Red Cross Conf, Toronto.

442 **152** 4 c. red and blue 15 10

153 Canada Goose

1952.

443 **153** 7 c. blue 65 10

165 Eskimo Hunter **164** Northern Gannet

160 Textile Industry **154** Pacific Coast Indian House and Totem Pole

1953.

477 **165** 10 c. brown 20 10
474 **164** 15 c. black 60 10
488 – 20 c. green 40 10
489 – 25 c. red 45 10
462 **160** 50 c. green . . . . 1·25 10
446 **154** $1 black . . . . 5·50 20

DESIGNS (As Type **160**)—HORIZ: 20 c. Pulp and paper industry. VERT: 25 c. Chemical industry.

155 Polar Bear **158** Queen Elizabeth II

1953. National Wild Life Week.

447 **155** 2 c. blue 10 10
448 – 3 c. sepia (Elk) 10 20
449 – 4 c. slate (American bighorn) 15 10

1953.

450 **158** 1 c. brown 10 10
451 2 c. green 15 10
452 3 c. red 15 15
453 4 c. violet 20 10
454 5 c. blue 20 10

159 Queen Elizabeth II **161**

1953. Coronation.

461 **159** 4 c. violet 10 10

1954.

463 **161** 1 c. brown 10 10
464 2 c. green 20 10
465 3 c. red 60 10
466 4 c. violet 30 10
467 5 c. blue 30 10
468 6 c. orange . . . . 1·00 30

1954. National Wild Life Week. As T **155**.

472 4 c. slate (Walrus) 35 10
473 5 c. blue (Amerıean beaver) . 35 10

166 Musk-ox **168** Dove and Torch

167 Whooping Cranes

1955. National Wild Life Week.

478 **166** 4 c. violet 30 10
479 **167** 5 c. blue 90 10

1955. 10th Anniv of I.C.A.O.

480 **168** 5 c. blue 10 10

169 Pioneer Settlers

1955. 50th Anniv of Alberta and Saskatchewan Provinces.

481 **169** 5 c. blue 15 15

170 Scout Badge and Globe

1955. 8th World Scout Jamboree.

482 **170** 5 c. brown and green . . 20 10

173 Ice-hockey Players

1956. Ice-hockey Commemoration.

485 **173** 5 c. blue 15 15

1956. National Wild Life Week. As T **155**.

486 4 c. violet (Reindeer) 20 15
487 5 c. blue (Mountain goat) . . 20 10

178 **181** Hunting

1956. Fire Prevention Week.

490 **178** 5 c. red and black 30 10

1957. Outdoor Recreation.

491 – 5 c. blue (Fishing) . . . 25 10
492 – 5 c. blue (Swimming) . . 25 10
493 **181** 5 c. blue 25 10
494 – 5 c. blue (Skiing) 25 10

183 Great Northern Diver

1957. National Wild Life Week.

495 **183** 5 c. black 30 10

184 Thompson with Sextant, and North American Map **185** Parliament Buildings, Ottawa

1957. Death Cent of David Thompson (explorer).

496 **184** 5 c. blue 15 30

1957. 14th U.P.U. Congress, Ottawa.

497 **185** 5 c. slate 15 10
498 – 15 c. slate . . . . 45 1·50

DESIGNS—HORIZ ($33\frac{1}{2}\times22$ mm): 15 c. Globe within posthorn.

187 Miner **188** Queen Elizabeth II and Duke of Edinburgh

1957. Mining Industry.

499 **187** 5 c. black 35 10

1957. Royal Visit.

500 **188** 5 c. black 30 10

189 "A Free Press" **190** Microscope

1958. The Canadian Press.

501 **189** 5 c. black 15 30

1958. International Geophysical Year.

502 **190** 5 c. blue 20 10

191 Miner panning for Gold

1958. Centenary of British Columbia.

503 **191** 5 c. turquoise 20 10

192 La Verendrye statue

1958. La Verendrye (explorer) Commemoration.

504 **192** 5 c. blue 15 10

193 Samuel de Champlain and Heights of Quebec **194** Nurse

1958. 350th Anniv of Founding of Quebec by Samuel de Champlain.

505 **193** 5 c. brown and green . . . 30 10

1958. National Health.

506 **194** 5 c. purple 30 10

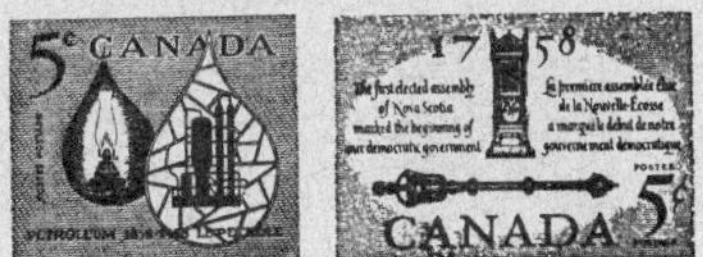

195 "Petroleum 1858–1958" **196** Speaker's Chair and Mace

1958. Centenary of Canadian Oil Industry.

507 **195** 5 c. red and olive 30 10

1958. Bicentenary of First Elected Assembly.

508 **196** 5 c. slate 30 10

197 John McCurdy's Biplane "Silver Dart" **198** Globe showing N.A.T.O. Countries

1959. 50th Anniv of First Flight of the "Silver Dart" in Canada.

509 **197** 5 c. black and blue 30 10

1959. 10th Anniv of N.A.T.O.

510 **198** 5 c. blue 40 10

199 **200**

1959. "Associated Country Women of the World" Commemoration.

511 **199** 5 c. black and olive . . . 15 10

1959. Royal Visit.

512 **200** 5 c. red 30 10

201 Maple Leaf Linked with American Eagle

1959. Opening of St. Lawrence Seaway.

513 **201** 5 c. blue and red 20 10

202 Maple Leaves **203** Girl Guides Badge

1959. Bicentenary of Battle of Quebec.

514 **202** 5 c. green and red 30 10

1960. Golden Jubilee of Canadian Girl Guides Movement.

515 **203** 5 c. blue and brown . . . 20 10

204 Dollard des Ormeaux **205** Surveyor, Bulldozer and Compass Rose

1960. Tercent of Battle of Long Sault.

516 **204** 5 c. blue and brown . . . 20 10

1961. Northern Development.

517 **205** 5 c. green and red 15 10

206 E. Pauline Johnson **207** Arthur Meighen (statesman)

1961. Birth Centenary of E. Pauline Johnson (Mohawk poetess).

518 **206** 5 c. green and red 15 10

1961. Arthur Meighen Commemoration.

519 **207** 5 c. blue 15 10

208 Engineers and Dam

1961. Colombo Plan.

520 **208** 5 c. brown and blue . . . 30 10

209 "Resources for Tomorrow" **210** "Education"

1961. Natural Resources.
521 **209** 5 c. green and brown . . 15 10

1962. Education Year.
522 **210** 5 c. black and brown . . 15 10

211 Lord Selkirk and Farmer **212** Talon bestowing gifts on Married Couple

1962. 150th Anniversary of Red River Settlement.
523 **211** 5 c. brown and green . . 20 10

1962. Jean Talon Commemoration.
524 **212** 5 c. blue 20 10

213 British Columbia and Vancouver Island 2½d. Stamp of 1860, and Parliament Buildings, B.C. **214** Highway (map version) and Provincial Arms

1962. Centenary of Victoria, B.C.
525 **213** 5 c. red and black 30 10

1962. Opening of Trans-Canada Highway.
526 **214** 5 c. black and brown . . 15 10

215 Queen Elizabeth II and Wheat (agriculture) Symbol **216** Sir Casimir Gzowski

1962. Different symbols in top left corner.
527 **215** 1 c. brown 10 10
528 2 c. green 15 10
529 3 c. violet 15 10
530 4 c. red 15 10
531 5 c. blue 15 10
SYMBOLS: 1 c. Crystals (Mining); 2 c. Tree (Forestry); 3 c. Fish (Fisheries); 4 c. Electricity pylon (Industrial power); 5 c. Wheat (Agriculture).

1963. 150th Birth Anniv of Sir Casimir Gzowski (engineer).
535 **216** 5 c. purple 10 10

217 "Export Trade" **218** Frobisher and barque "Gabriel"

1963.
536 **217** $1 red . . . . 4·75 2·00

1963. Sir Martin Frobisher Commemoration.
537 **218** 5 c. blue 20 10

219 Horseman and Map

1963. Bicent of Quebec—Trois-Rivieres—Montreal Postal Service.
538 **219** 5 c. brown and green . . 15 10

220 Canada Geese **221** Douglas DC-9 Airliner and Uplands Airport, Ottawa

1963.
540 **221** 7 c. blue 35 70
540a 8 c. blue 50 40
539 **220** 15 c. blue . . . . 1·25 10

222 "Peace on Earth" **223** Maple Leaves

1964 "Peace".
541 **222** 5 c. ochre, blue & turq . 15 10

1964. "Canadian Unity".
542 **223** 5 c. lake and blue 10 10

224 White Trillium and Arms of Ontario

1964. Provincial Badges.
543 **224** 5 c. green, brown and orange 40 20
544 – 5 c. green, brown and yellow 40 20
545 – 5 c. red, green and violet 30 20
546 – 5 c. blue, red and green . 30 20
547 – 5 c. purple, green and brown 30 20
548 – 5 c. brown, green and mauve 30 20
549 – 5 c. lilac, green and purple 50 20
550 – 5 c. green, yellow and red 30 20
551 – 5 c. sepia, orange and green 30 20
552 – 5 c. black, red and green 30 20
553 – 5 c. drab, green and yellow 30 20
554 – 5 c. blue, green and red . 30 20
555 – 5 c. red and blue 30 20
FLOWERS AND ARMS OF: No. 544, Madonna Lily, Quebec; No. 545, Purple Violet, New Brunswick; No. 546, Mayflower, Nova Scotia; No. 547, Dogwood, British Columbia; No. 548, Prairie Crocus, Manitoba; No. 549, Lady's Slipper, Prince Edward Island; No. 550, Wild Rose, Alberta; No. 551, Prairie Lily, Saskatchewan; No. 552, Pitcher Plant, Newfoundland; No. 553, Mountain Avens, Northwest Territories; No. 554, Fireweed, Yukon Territory; No. 555, Maple Leaf, Canada.

1964. Surch **8**.
556 **221** 8 c. on 7 c. blue 15 15

238 Fathers of the Confederation Memorial, Charlottetown

1964. Centenary of Charlottetown Conference.
557 **238** 5 c. black 10 10

239 Maple Leaf and Hand with Quill Pen

1964. Centenary of Quebec Conference.
558 **239** 5 c. red and brown . . . 15 10

240 Queen Elizabeth II **241** "Canadian Family"

1964. Royal Visit.
559 **240** 5 c. purple 15 10

1964. Christmas.
560 **241** 3 c. red 10 10
561 5 c. blue 10 10

242 Co-operation

1965. International Co-operation Year.
562 **242** 5 c. green 35 10

243 Sir W. Grenfell

1965. Birth Centenary of Sir Wilfred Grenfell (missionary).
563 **243** 5 c. green 20 10

244 National Flag

1965. Inauguration of National Flag.
564 **244** 5 c. red and blue 15 10

245 Sir Winston Churchill **246** Peace Tower, Parliament Buildings, Ottawa

1965. Churchill Commemoration.
565 **245** 5 c. brown 15 10

1965. Inter-Parliamentary Union Conference, Ottawa.
566 **246** 5 c. green 10 10

247 Parliament Buildings, Ottawa, 1865 **248** "Gold, Frankincense and Myrrh"

1965. Centenary of Proclamation of Ottawa as Capital.
567 **247** 5 c. brown 10 10

1965. Christmas.
568 **248** 3 c. green 10 10
569 5 c. blue 10 10

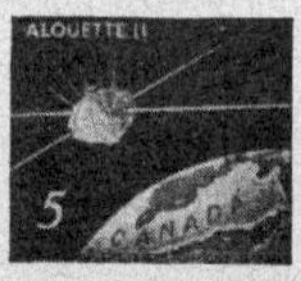

249 "Alouette 2" over Canada **250** La Salle

1966. Launching of Canadian Satellite, "Alouette 2".
570 **249** 5 c. blue 15 10

1966. 300th Anniv of La Salle's Arrival in Canada.
571 **250** 5 c. green 15 10

251 Road Signs **252** Canadian Delegation and Houses of Parliament

1966. Highway Safety.
572 **251** 5 c. yellow, blue and black 15 10

1966. Centenary of London Conference.
573 **252** 5 c. brown 10 10

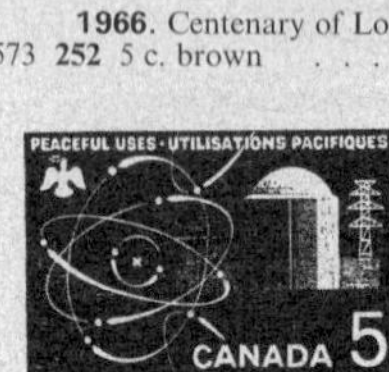

253 Douglas Point Nuclear Power Station **254** Parliamentary Library, Ottawa

1966. Peaceful Uses of Atomic Energy.
574 **253** 5 c. blue 10 10

1966. Commonwealth Parliamentary Association Conference, Ottawa.
575 **254** 5 c. purple 10 10

255 "Praying Hands", after Durer **256** Flags and Canada on Globe

1966. Christmas.
576 **255** 3 c. red 10 10
577 5 c. orange 10 10

1967. Canadian Centennial.
578 **256** 5 c. red and blue 10 10

257 Queen Elizabeth, Northern Lights and Dog-team **262** "Alaska Highway" (A. Y. Jackson)

1967.
579 **257** 1 c. brown 10 10
580 – 2 c. green 10 10
581 – 3 c. purple 30 10
582 – 4 c. red 20 10
583 – 5 c. blue 20 10
601 – 6 c. red 45 10
607 – 6 c. black 30 10
609 – 7 c. green 30 10
584 **262** 8 c. purple 35 30
610 – 8 c. black 30 10
585 – 10 c. olive 30 10
586 – 15 c. purple 30 10
587 – 20 c. blue 80 10
588 – 25 c. green . . . . 1·00 10
589 – 50 c. brown . . . . 1·75 10
590 – $1 red . . . . 2·50 65
DESIGNS—As Type **257**: Queen Elizabeth and 2 c. Totem pole; 3 c. Combine-harvester and Oil derrick; 4 c. Ship in lock; 5 c. (No. 583), Harbour scene; 6 c. (Nos 606/7), 7 c. "Transport"; 8 c. (No 610), Library of Parliament. As Type **262**: 10 c. "The Jack Pine" (T. Thomson); 15 c. "Bylot Island" (L. Harris); 2 c. "Quebec Ferry" (J. W. Morrice); 25 c. "The Solemn Land" (J. E. H. MacDonald); 50 c. "Summer's Stores" (Grain elevators, J. Ensor); $1 "Oilfield" (near Edmonton, H. G. Glyde).

269 Canadian Pavilion **270** Allegory of "Womanhood" on Ballot-box

1967. World Fair, Montreal.
611 **269** 5 c. blue and red 10 10

1967. 50th Anniv of Women's Franchise.
612 **270** 5 c. purple and black . . 10 10

271 Queen Elizabeth II and Centennial Emblem **272** Athlete

1967. Royal Visit.
613 **271** 5 c. plum and brown . . 15 10

1967. Pan-American Games, Winnipeg.
614 **272** 5 c. red 10 10

273 "World News"

1967. 50th Anniv of Canadian Press.
615 **273** 5 c. blue 10 10

274 Governor-General Vanier

1967. Vanier Commemoration.
616 **274** 5 c. black 10 10

275 People of 1867, and Toronto, 1967

276 Carol Singers

1967. Cent of Toronto as Capital City of Ontario.
617 **275** 5 c. green and red 10 10

1967. Christmas.
618 **276** 3 c. red 10 10
619 5 c. green 10 10

277 Grey Jays

278 Weather Map and Instruments

1968. Wild Life.
620 **277** 5 c. multicoloured 30 10
See also Nos. 638/40.

1968. 20th Anniv of First Meteorological Readings.
621 **278** 5 c. multicoloured 15 10

279 Narwhal

1968. Wild Life.
622 **279** 5 c. multicoloured 15 10

280 Globe, Maple Leaf and Rain Gauge

1968. International Hydrological Decade.
623 **280** 5 c. multicoloured 15 10

281 The "Nonsuch"

1968. 300th Anniv of Voyage of the "Nonsuch".
624 **281** 5 c. multicoloured 20 10

282 Lacrosse Players

283 Front Page of "The Globe", George Brown and Legislative Building

1968. Lacrosse.
625 **282** 5 c. multicoloured 15 10

1968. 150th Birth Anniv of George Brown (politician and journalist).
626 **283** 5 c. multicoloured 10 10

284 H. Bourassa (politician and journalist)

286 Armistice Monument, Vimy

285 John McCrae, Battlefield and First Lines of "In Flanders Fields"

1968. Birth Centenary of Henri Bourassa.
627 **284** 5 c. black, red and cream 10 10

1968. 50th Death Anniv of John McCrae (soldier and poet).
628 **285** 5 c. multicoloured 10 10

1968. 50th Anniv of 1918 Armistice.
629 **286** 15 c. black 30 40

287 Eskimo Family (carving)

289 Curling

1968. Christmas.
630 **287** 5 c. black and blue . . . 10 10
631 – 6 c. black and ochre . . . 10 10
DESIGN: 6 c. "Mother and Child" (carving).

1969. Curling.
632 **289** 6 c. black, blue and red . 15 10

290 Vincent Massey

292 Globe and Tools

291 "Return from the Harvest Field" (Suzor-Cote)

1969. Vincent Massey, First Canadian-born Governor-General.
633 **290** 6 c. sepia and ochre . . . 10 10

1969. Birth Centenary of Marc Aurele de Foy Suzor-Cote (painter).
634 **291** 50 c. multicoloured . . . 70 2·00

1969. 50th Anniv of I.L.O.
635 **292** 6 c. green 10 10

293 Vickers Vimy Aircraft over Atlantic Ocean

1969. 50th Anniv of 1st Non-stop Transatlantic Flight.
636 **293** 15 c. brown, green and blue 40 55

294 "Sir William Osler" (J. S. Sargent)

295 White-throated Sparrow

1969. 50th Death Anniv of Sir William Osler (physician).
637 **294** 6 c. blue and brown . . . 20 10

1969. Birds. Multicoloured.
638 6 c. Type **295** 25 10
639 10 c. Savannah sparrow . . . 50 1·10
640 25 c. Hermit thrush . . . . . 1·60 3·50
The 10 c. and 25 c. are horiz.

298 Flags of Winter and Summer Games

300 Sir Isaac Brock and Memorial Column

299 Outline of Prince Edward Island showing Charlottetown

1969. Canadian Games.
641 **298** 6 c. green, red and blue . . 10 10

1969. Bicentenary of Charlottetown as Capital of Prince Edward Island.
642 **299** 6 c. brown, black and blue 20 10

1969. Birth Bicentenary of Sir Isaac Brock.
643 **300** 6 c. orange, bistre and brown 10 10

301 Children of the World in Prayer

302 Stephen Butler Leacock, Mask and "Mariposa"

1969. Christmas.
644 **301** 5 c. multicoloured 10 10
645 6 c. multicoloured 10 10

1969. Birth Centenary of Stephen Butler Leacock (humorist).
646 **302** 6 c. multicoloured 10 10

303 Symbolic Cross-roads

1970. Centenary of Manitoba.
647 **303** 6 c. blue, yellow and red . 15 10

304 "Enchanted Owl" (Kenojuak)

1970. Centenary of Northwest Territories.
648 **304** 6 c. red and black 10 10

305 Microscopic View of Inside of Leaf

1970. International Biological Programme.
649 **305** 6 c. green, yellow and blue 15 10

306 Expo 67 Emblem and stylized Cherry Blossom

1970. World Fair, Osaka. Multicoloured.
650 25 c. Type **306** (red) . . . . . 1·50 2·00
651 25 c. Dogwood (violet) . . . . 1·50 2·00
652 25 c. White trillium (green) . . 1·50 2·00
653 25 c. White garden lily (blue) . 1·50 2·00
NOTE: Each stamp shows a stylized cherry blossom, in a different colour, given above in brackets.

310 Henry Kelsey

1970. 300th Birth Anniv of Henry Kelsey (explorer).
654 **310** 6 c. multicoloured 10 10

311 "Towards Unification"

1970. 25th Anniv of U.N.O.
655 **311** 10 c. blue 40 30
656 15 c. mauve and lilac . . 40 35

312 Louis Riel (Metis leader)

313 Mackenzie's Inscription, Dean Channel

1970. Louis Riel Commemoration.
657 **312** 6 c. blue and red 10 10

1970. Sir Alexander Mackenzie (explorer).
658 **313** 6 c. brown 15 10

314 Sir Oliver Mowat (statesman)

1970. Sir Oliver Mowat Commemoration.
659 **314** 6 c. red and black 10 10

315 "Isles of Spruce" (A. Lismer)

1970. 50th Anniv of "Group of Seven" (artists).
660 **315** 6 c. multicoloured 10 10

316 "Horse-drawn Sleigh" (D. Niskala)

328 Sir Donald A. Smith

1970. Christmas. Children's Drawings. Mult.
661 5 c. Type **316** 50 20
662 5 c. "Stable and Star of Bethlehem" (L. Wilson) . . 50 20
663 5 c. "Snowmen" (M. Lecompte) 50 20
664 5 c. "Skiing" (D. Durham) . . 50 20
665 5 c. "Santa Claus" (A. Martin) 50 20
666 6 c. "Santa Claus" (E. Bhattacharya) 50 20
667 6 c. "Christ in Manger" (J. McKinney) 50 20
668 6 c. "Toy Shop" (N. Whateley) 50 20
669 6 c. "Christmas Tree" (J. Pomperleau) 50 20
670 6 c. "Church" (J. McMillan) . 50 20
671 10 c. "Christ in Manger" (C. Fortier) (37×20 mm) . 30 30
672 15 c. "Trees and Sledge" (J. Dojcak) (37×20 mm). . . 45 60

1970. 150th Birth Anniv of Sir Donald Alexander Smith.
673 **328** 6 c. yellow, brown and green 15 10

329 "Big Raven" (E. Carr)

1971. Birth Centenary of Emily Carr (painter).
674 **329** 6 c. multicoloured 20 30

330 Laboratory Equipment **331** "The Atom"

1971. 50th Anniv of Discovery of Insulin.
675 **330** 6 c. multicoloured 30 30

1971. Birth Centenary of Lord Rutherford (scientist).
676 **331** 6 c. yellow, red and brown 20 20

332 Maple "Keys" **333** Louis Papineau

1971. "The Maple Leaf in Four Seasons". Mult.
677 6 c. Type **332** (spring) 20 20
678 6 c. Green leaves (summer) . . 20 20
679 7 c. Autumn leaves 20 20
680 7 c. Withered leaves and snow (winter) 20 20

1971. Death Centenary of Louis-Joseph Papineau (politician).
681 **333** 6 c. multicoloured 15 20

334 Chart of Coppermine River **335** "People" and Computer Tapes

1971. Bicentenary of Samuel Hearne's Expedition to the Coppermine River.
682 **334** 6 c. red, brown and buff . 40 40

1971. Centenary of 1st Canadian Census.
683 **335** 6 c. blue, red and black . 30 20

336 Maple Leaves

1971. Radio Canada International.
684 **336** 15 c. red, yellow and black 50 1·25

337 "B. C."

1971. Centenary of British Columbia's Entry into the Confederation.
685 **337** 7 c. multicoloured 15 10

338 "Indian Encampment on Lake Huron" (Kane) **339** "Snowflake"

1971. Death Centenary of Paul Kane (painter).
686 **338** 7 c. multicoloured 20 10

1971. Christmas.
687 **339** 6 c. blue 10 10
688 7 c. green 15 10
689 – 10 c. silver and red . . . 50 1·25
690 – 15 c. silver, purple and lavender . . . . 65 1·50
DESIGN: 10 c., 15 c. "Snowflake" design similar to Type **339** but square (26 × 26 mm).

340 Pierre Laporte (Quebec Cabinet Minister) **341** Skaters

1971. 1st Anniv of Assassination of Pierre Laporte.
691 **340** 7 c. black on buff 15 10

1972. World Figure Skating Championships, Calgary.
692 **341** 8 c. purple 15 10

342 J. A. MacDonald **343** Forest, Central Canada

344 Vancouver

1972.
693 **342** 1 c. orange 10 10
694 – 2 c. green 10 10
695 – 3 c. brown 10 30
696 – 4 c. black 10 10
697 – 5 c. mauve 10 10
698 – 6 c. red 10 10
699 – 7 c. brown 10 30
700 – 8 c. blue 15 10
701 – 10 c. red 40 10
702a **343** 10 c. green, turquoise and orange 40 15
703b – 15 c. blue and brown . . 60 10
704a – 20 c. orange, violet and blue 30 10
705b – 25 c. ultram and blue . . 90 10
706 – 50 c. green, blue and brown 45 30
709a **344** $1 multicoloured 85 70
708 – $2 multicoloured . . . . 1·50 2·00
DESIGNS—As Type **342** (1 to 7 c. show Canadian Prime Minister): 2 c. W. Laurier; 3 c. R. Borden; 4 c. W. L. Mackenzie King; 5 c. R. B. Bennett; 6 c. L. B. Pearson; 7 c. Louis St. Laurent; 8, 10 c. Queen Elizabeth II. As Type **343**: 15 c. American bighorn; 20 c. Prairie landscape from the air; 25 c. Polar bears; 50 c. Seashore, Eastern Canada. As Type **344**: $2 Quebec.

345 Heart

1972. World Health Day.
719 **345** 8 c. red 30 10

346 Frontenac and Fort Saint-Louis, Quebec

1972. 300th Anniv of Governor Frontenac's Appointment to New France.
720 **346** 8 c. red, brown and blue . 15 15

347 Plains Indians' Artefacts **347a** Buffalo Chase

348 Thunderbird and Tribal Pattern **348a** Dancer in Ceremonial Costume

1972. Canadian Indians. (a) Horiz designs showing Artefacts as T **347** or Scenes from Indian Life as T **347a**.
721 **347** 8 c. multicoloured 40 10
722 **347a** 8 c. brown, yellow & blk . 40 10
723 – 8 c. multicoloured 40 10
724 – 8 c. multicoloured 40 10
725 – 8 c. multicoloured 40 10
726 – 8 c. brown, yellow & blk . 40 10
727 – 8 c. multicoloured 40 10
728 – 8 c. multicoloured 40 10
729 – 10 c. multicoloured . . . 40 20
730 – 10 c. red, brown and black 40 20
TRIBES: Nos. 721/2, Plains Indians; Nos. 723/4, Algonkians; Nos. 725/6, Pacific Coast Indians; Nos. 727/8, Subarctic Indians; Nos. 729/30, Iroquoians.

(b) Vert designs showing Thunderbird and pattern as T **348** or Costumes as T **348a**.
731 **348** 8 c. orange, red and black 40 15
732 **348a** 8 c. multicoloured 40 15
733 – 8 c. red, violet and black . 40 10
734 – 8 c. green, brown and black 40 10
735 – 8 c. red and black 40 10
736 – 8 c. multicoloured 40 10
737 – 8 c. green, brown and black 40 10
738 – 8 c. multicoloured 40 10
739 – 10 c. brown, orange & blk 40 20
740 – 10 c. multicoloured . . . 40 20
TRIBES: Nos. 731/2, Plains Indians; Nos. 733/4, Algonkians; Nos. 735/6, Pacific Coast Indians; Nos. 737/8, Subarctic Indians; Nos. 739/40, Iroquoians.

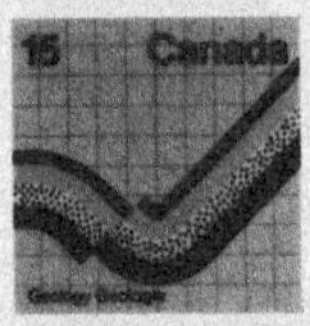

349 Earth's Crust **350** Candles

1972. Earth Sciences.
741 – 15 c. multicoloured . . . . 1·40 1·90
742 – 15 c. grey, blue and black . 1·40 1·90
743 **349** 15 c. multicoloured . . . . 1·40 1·90
744 – 15 c. green, orange and black 1·40 1·90
DESIGNS AND EVENTS: No. 741 Photo- grammetric surveying (12th Congress of International Society of Photogrammetry); No. 742 "Siegfried" lines (6th Conference of Int Cartographic Association); No. 743 (24th International Geological Congress); No. 744 Diagram of village at road-intersection (22nd Int Geographical Congress).

1972. Christmas. Multicoloured.
745 6 c. Type **350** 15 10
746 8 c. Type **350** 15 10
747 10 c. Candles with fruits and pine boughs (horiz) 50 85
748 15 c. Candles with prayerbook, caskets and vase (horiz) . . 60 1·25
Nos. 747/8 are size 36 × 20 mm.

351 "The Blacksmith's Shop" (Krieghoff) **352** F. de Montmorency-Laval

1972. Death Centenary of Cornelius Krieghoff (painter).
749 **351** 8 c. multicoloured 30 15

1973. 350th Birth Anniv of Monsignor de Laval (1st Bishop of Quebec).
750 **352** 8 c. blue, gold and silver . 20 40

353 Commissioner French and Route of the March West

1973. Centenary of Royal Canadian Mounted Police.
751 **353** 8 c. brown, orange and red 35 20
752 – 10 c. multicoloured . . . . 1·00 1·25
753 – 15 c. multicoloured . . . . 1·75 2·00
DESIGNS: 10 c. Spectrograph; 15 c. Mounted policeman.

354 Jeanne Mance

1973. 300th Death Anniv of Jeanne Mance (nurse).
754 **354** 8 c. multicoloured 20 40

355 Joseph Howe **356** "Mist Fantasy" (MacDonald)

1973. Death Centenary of Joseph Howe (Nova Scotian politician).
755 **355** 8 c. gold and black . . . 20 40

1973. Birth Cent of J. E. H. MacDonald (artist).
756 **356** 15 c. multicoloured . . . 30 55

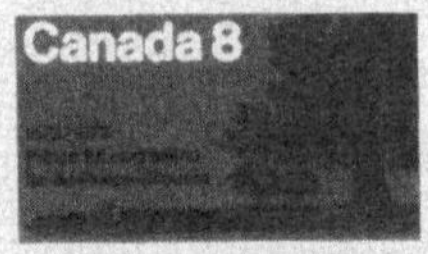

357 Oaks and Harbour

1973. Centenary of Prince Edward Island's Entry into the Confederation.
757 **357** 8 c. orange and red . . . 20 30

358 Scottish Settlers

1973. Bicentenary of Arrival of Scottish Settlers at Pictou, Nova Scotia.
758 **358** 8 c. multicoloured 25 20

359 Queen Elizabeth II

1973. Royal Visit and Commonwealth Heads of Government Meeting, Ottawa.
759 **359** 8 c. multicoloured 25 20
760 15 c. multicoloured . . . 80 1·50

360 Nellie McClung **361** Emblem of 1976 Olympics

1973. Birth Centenary of Nellie McClung (feminist).
761 **360** 8 c. multicoloured 20 50

1973. 1976 Olympic Games, Montreal (1st issue).
762 **361** 8 c. multicoloured 25 15
763 15 c. multicoloured . . . 45 1·25
See also Nos. 768/71, 772/4, 786/9, 798/802, 809/11, 814/16, 829/32, 833/7 and 842/4.

362 Ice-skate **363** Diving

1973. Christmas. Multicoloured.

764		6 c. Type **362**	15	10
765		8 c. Bird decoration	20	10
766		10 c. Santa Claus (20 × 36 mm)	70	1·40
767		15 c. Shepherd (20 × 36 mm)	80	1·75

1974. 1976 Olympic Games, Montreal. (2nd issue). "Summer Activities". Each blue.

768		8 c. Type **363**	25	50
769		8 c. "Jogging"	25	50
770		8 c. Cycling	25	50
771		8 c. Hiking	25	50

1974. 1976 Olympic Games, Montreal. (3rd issue). As T **361** but smaller (20 × 36½ mm).

772	**361**	8 c. + 2 c. multicoloured	25	45
773		10 c. + 5 c. multicoloured	35	1·00
774		15 c. + 5 c. multicoloured	40	1·40

364 Winnipeg Signpost, 1872

1974. Winnipeg Centennial.

775	**364**	8 c. multicoloured	20	15

365 Postmaster and Customer

366 "Canada's Contribution to Agriculture"

1974. Centenary of Canadian Letter Carrier Delivery Service. Multicoloured.

776		8 c. Type **365**	50	80
777		8 c. Postman collecting mail	50	80
778		8 c. Mail handler	50	80
779		8 c. Mail sorters	50	80
780		8 c. Postman making delivery	50	80
781		8 c. Rural delivery by car	50	80

1974. Centenary of "Agricultural Education". Ontario Agricultural College.

782	**366**	8 c. multicoloured	20	20

367 Telephone Development

1974. Centenary of Invention of Telephone by Alexander Graham Bell.

783	**367**	8 c. multicoloured	20	20

368 Bicycle Wheel

1974. World Cycling Championships, Montreal.

784	**368**	8 c. black, red and silver	20	30

369 Mennonite Settlers

1974. Centenary of Arrival of Mennonites in Manitoba.

785	**369**	8 c. multicoloured	20	20

1974. 1976 Olympic Games, Montreal (4th issue). "Winter Activities". As T **363**. Each red.

786		8 c. Snow-shoeing	50	60
787		8 c. Skiing	50	60
788		8 c. Skating	50	60
789		8 c. Curling	50	60

370 Mercury, Winged Horses and U.P.U. Emblem

1974. Centenary of U.P.U.

790	**370**	8 c. violet, red and blue	15	15
791		15 c. red, violet and blue	50	1·50

371 "The Nativity" (J. P. Lemieux)

1974. Christmas. Multicoloured.

792		6 c. Type **371**	10	10
793		8 c. "Skaters in Hull" (H. Masson) (34 × 31 mm)	10	10
794		10 c. "The Ice Cone, Montmorency Falls" (R. C. Todd)	20	75
795		15 c. "Village in the Laurentian Mountains" (C. A. Gagnon)	30	1·10

372 Marconi and St. John's Harbour, Newfoundland

1974. Birth Centenary of Guglielmo Marconi (radio pioneer).

796	**372**	8 c. multicoloured	20	20

373 Merritt and Welland Canal

1974. William Merritt Commemoration.

797	**373**	8 c. multicoloured	20	30

374 Swimming

376 "Anne of Green Gables" (Lucy Maud Montgomery)

375 "The Sprinter"

1975. 1976 Olympic Games, Montreal (5th issue). Multicoloured.

798		8 c. + 2 c. Type **374**	30	50
799		10 c. + 5 c. Rowing	40	90
800		15 c. + 5 c. Sailing	45	1·00

1975. 1976 Olympic Games, Montreal (6th issue). Multicoloured.

801		$1 Type **375**	2·00	2·75
802		$2 "The Diver" (vert)	2·75	4·75

1975. Canadian Writers (1st series). Multicoloured.

803		8 c. Type **376**	30	10
804		8 c. "Maria Chapdelaine" (Louis Hémon)	30	10

See also Nos. 846/7, 940/1 and 1085/6.

377 Marguerite Bourgeoys (founder of the Order of Notre Dame)

378 S. D. Chown (founder of United Church of Canada)

1975. Canadian Celebrities.

805	**377**	8 c. multicoloured	50	40
806	–	8 c. multicoloured	50	40
807	**378**	8 c. multicoloured	30	75
808	–	8 c. multicoloured	30	75

DESIGNS—As Type **377**: No. 806, Alphonse Desjardins (leader of Credit Union movement). As Type **378**: No. 808, Dr. J. Cook (first moderator of Presbyterian Church in Canada).

379 Pole-vaulting

380 "Untamed" (photo by Walt Petrigo)

1975. 1976 Olympics (7th issue). Multicoloured.

809		20 c. Type **379**	40	50
810		25 c. Marathon-running	55	80
811		50 c. Hurdling	70	1·25

1975. Centenary of Calgary.

812	**380**	8 c. multicoloured	20	30

381 I. W. Y. Symbol

382 Fencing

1975. International Women's Year.

813	**381**	8 c. grey, brown and black	20	30

1975. Olympic Games, Montreal (1976) (8th issue). Multicoloured.

814		8 c. + 2 c. Type **382**	30	45
815		10 c. + 5 c. Boxing	35	1·00
816		15 c. + 5 c. Judo	40	1·25

383 "Justice-Justitia" (statue by W. S. Allward)

385 "Santa Claus" (G. Kelly)

384 "William D. Lawrence" (full-rigged ship)

1975. Centenary of Canadian Supreme Court.

817	**383**	8 c. multicoloured	20	30

1975. Canadian Ships (1st series). Coastal Vessels.

818	**384**	8 c. brown and black	60	75
819	–	8 c. green and black	60	75
820	–	8 c. green and black	60	75
821	–	8 c. brown and black	60	75

DESIGNS: No. 819, "Neptune" (steamer); 820, "Beaver" (paddle-steamer); 821, "Quadra" (steamer).

See also Nos. 851/4, 902/5 and 931/4.

1975. Christmas. Multicoloured.

822		6 c. Type **385**	15	10
823		6 c. "Skater" (B. Cawsey)	15	10
824		8 c. "Child" (D. Hebert)	15	10
825		8 c. "Family" (L. Caldwell)	15	10
826		10 c. "Gift" (D. Lovely)	30	50
827		15 c. "Trees" (R. Kowalski) (horiz)	40	75

386 Text, Badge and Bugle

387 Basketball

1975. 50th Anniv of Royal Canadian Legion.

828	**386**	8 c. multicoloured	20	20

1976. Olympic Games, Montreal (9th issue). Mult.

829		8 c. + 2 c. Type **387**	50	55
830		10 c. + 5 c. Gymnastics	50	90
831		20 c. + 5 c. Soccer	65	1·25

388 Games Symbol and Snow Crystal

389 "Communications Arts"

1976. 12th Winter Olympic Games, Innsbruck.

832	**388**	20 c. multicoloured	20	40

1976. Olympic Games, Montreal (10th issue). Multicoloured.

833		20 c. Type **389**	30	25
834		25 c. Handicrafts	55	75
835		50 c. Performing Arts	70	1·60

390 Place Ville Marie and Notre-Dame Church

1976. Olympic Games, Montreal (11th issue). Multicoloured.

836		$1 Type **390**	2·00	4·50
837		$2 Olympic stadium and flags	2·50	5·50

391 Flower and Urban Sprawl

1976. HABITAT. U. N. Conference on Human Settlements, Vancouver.

838	**391**	20 c. multicoloured	20	30

392 Benjamin Franklin and Map

1976. Bicentenary of American Revolution.

839	**392**	10 c. multicoloured	20	35

393 Wing Parade before Mackenzie Building

394 Transfer of Olympic Flame by Satellite

1976. Centenary of Royal Military College. Multicoloured.

840	8 c. Colour party and Memorial Arch	15	20
841	8 c. Type **393**	15	20

1976. Olympic Games, Montreal (12th issue). Multicoloured.

842	8 c. Type **394**	15	10
843	20 c. Carrying the Olympic flag	40	60
844	25 c. Athletes with medals	40	85

395 Archer

1976. Disabled Olympics.

845	**395**	20 c. multicoloured	20	30

396 "Sam McGee" (Robert W. Service)

397 "Nativity" (F. Mayer)

1976. Canadian Writers (2nd series). Multicoloured.

846	8 c. Type **396**	15	30
847	8 c. "Le Survenant" (Germaine Guevremont)	15	30

1976. Christmas. Stained-glass Windows. Multicoloured.

848	8 c. Type **397**	10	10
849	10 c. "Nativity" (G. Maile & Son)	10	10
850	20 c. "Nativity" (Yvonne Williams)	20	60

398 "Northcote" (paddle-steamer)

1976. Canadian Ships (2nd series). Inland Vessels.

851	**398**	10 c. lt brown, brn & blk	40	55
852	–	10 c. blue and black	40	55
853	–	10 c. blue and black	40	55
854	–	10 c. lt green, grn & blk	40	55

DESIGNS: No. 852, "Passport" (paddle-steamer); 853, "Chicora" (paddle-steamer); 854, "Athabasca" (steamer).

399 Queen Elizabeth II

1977. Silver Jubilee.

855	**399**	25 c. multicoloured	30	50

400 Bottle Gentian

401 Queen Elizabeth II (bas-relief by J. Huta)

402 Houses of Parliament

403 Trembling Aspen

404 Prairie Town Main Street

405 Fundy National Park

1977.

856	**400**	1 c. multicoloured	10	10
870	**402**	1 c. blue	1·25	2·50
857	–	2 c. multicoloured	10	10
858	–	3 c. multicoloured	10	10
859	–	4 c. multicoloured	10	10
860	–	5 c. multicoloured	10	10
871	**402**	5 c. lilac	35	40
861	–	10 c. multicoloured	15	10
867	**401**	12 c. blue, grey and black	15	10
872	**402**	12 c. blue	30	10
866	–	12 c. multicoloured	15	40
868	**401**	14 c. red, grey and black	20	10
873	**402**	14 c. red	15	10
875	**403**	15 c. multicoloured	15	10
866a	–	15 c. multicoloured	15	15
869	**401**	17 c. black, grey and green	50	10
874	**402**	17 c. green	30	10
876	–	20 c. multicoloured	15	10
877	–	25 c. multicoloured	15	10
878	–	30 c. multicoloured	20	10
869b	**401**	30 c. dp pur, grey & pur	70	70
869c		32 c. black, grey and blue	45	60
879	–	35 c. multicoloured	25	10
883	**404**	50 c. multicoloured	85	60
883a	–	60 c. multicoloured	65	50
881	–	75 c. multicoloured	85	1·00
882	–	80 c. multicoloured	85	90
884	**405**	$1 multicoloured	90	50
884b	–	$1 multicoloured	85	45
884c	–	$1.50 multicoloured	2·50	2·50
885	–	$2 multicoloured	1·50	45
885c	–	$2 multicoloured	3·75	1·25
885d	–	$5 multicoloured	5·50	2·25
885e	–	$5 multicoloured	7·00	4·00

DESIGN—As Type **400**: 2 c. Red columbine; 3 c. Canada lily; 4 c. Hepatica; 5 c. Shooting star; 10 c. Franklin's lady's slipper orchid. 12 c. Jewel-weed; 15 c. (No. 866a) Canada violet. As Type **403**: 20 c. Douglas fir; 25 c. Sugar maple; 30 c. Red oak; 35 c. White pine. As Type **404**: 60 c. Ontario City street; 75 c. Eastern City street; 80 c. Maritimes street. As Type **405**: $1 Glacier; $1.50, Waterton Lakes; $2 (No. 885) Kluane; $2 (No. 885c) Banff; $5 (No. 885d) Point Pelee; $5 (-No. 885e) La Maurice.

406 Puma

407 "April in Algonquin Park"

1977. Endangered Wildlife (1st series).

886	**406**	12 c. multicoloured	20	20

See also Nos. 906, 936/7, 976/7 and 1006/7.

1977. Birth Centenary of Tom Thomson (painter). Multicoloured.

887	12 c. Type **407**	15	10
888	12 c. "Autumn Birches"	15	10

408 Crown and Lion

1977. Anniversaries. Multicoloured.

889	12 c. Type **408**	15	20
890	12 c. Order of Canada	15	20

EVENTS: No. 889, 25th anniv of First Canadian-born Governor-General; No. 890, 10th anniv of Order of Canada.

409 Peace Bridge, Niagara River

1977. 50th Anniv of Opening of Peace Bridge.

891	**409**	12 c. multicoloured	15	15

410 Sir Sandford Fleming (engineer)

1977. Famous Canadians.

892	**410**	12 c. blue	20	10
893	–	12 c. brown	20	10

DESIGN: No. 893, Joseph E. Bernier (explorer) and "Arctic" (survey ship).

411 Peace Tower, Parliament Buildings, Ottawa

1977. 23rd Commonwealth Parliamentary Conference

894	**411**	25 c. multicoloured	20	30

412 Hunter Braves following Star

1977. Christmas. Canada's first carol "Jesous Ahatonhia". Multicoloured.

895	10 c. Type **412**	10	10
896	12 c. Angelic choir	10	10
897	25 c. Christ Child and "Chiefs from afar"	20	45

413 Seal Hunter (soapstone sculpture)

1977. Canadian Eskimos "Inuits" (1st series). Hunting. Multicoloured.

898	12 c. Type **413**	25	25
899	12 c. Fishing with spear	25	25
900	12 c. Disguised archer	25	25
901	12 c. Walrus hunting	25	25

See also Nos. 924/7, 958/61 and 989/92.

414 Pinky (fishing boat)

1977. Canadian Ships (3rd series). Sailing Craft. Multicoloured.

902	12 c. Type **414**	20	30
903	12 c. "Malahat" (schooner)	20	30
904	12 c. Tern schooner	20	30
905	12 c. Mackinaw boat	20	30

415 Peregrine Falcon

1978. Endangered Wildlife (2nd series).

906	**415**	12 c. multicoloured	30	20

416 Pair of 1851 12 d. Black Stamps

1978. "CAPEX '78" International Philatelic Exhibition, Toronto.

907	**416**	12 c. black and sepia	10	10
914	–	14 c. blue, lt grey & grey	15	10
915	–	30 c. red, lt grey & grey	25	35
916	–	$1.25 violet, light grey & grey	1·00	1·40

DESIGNS: 14 c. Pair of 1855 10d. Cartier stamps; 30 c. Pair of 1857 ½d. red stamps; $1.25, Pair of 1851 6d. Prince Albert stamps.

417 Games Emblem

1978. 11th Commonwealth Games, Edmonton (1st issue). Multicoloured.

908	14 c. Type **417**	10	10
909	30 c. Badminton	20	50

See also Nos. 918/21.

418 "Captain Cook" (Nathaniel Dance)

419 Hardrock Silver Mine, Cobalt, Ontario

1978. Bicentenary of Cook's 3rd Voyage. Mult.

910	14 c. Type **418**	20	20
911	14 c. "Nootka Sound" (J. Webber)	20	20

1978. Resources Development. Multicoloured.

912	14 c. Type **419**	15	20
913	14 c. Giant excavators, Athabasca Tar Sands	15	20

1978. 11th Commonwealth Games, Edmonton (2nd issue). As T **417**. Multicoloured.

918	14 c. Games stadium	20	20
919	14 c. Running	20	20
920	30 c. Alberta legislature building	40	50
921	30 c. Bowls	40	50

420 Princes' Gate (Exhibition entrance)

421 Marguerite d'Youville

1978. Centenary of National Exhibition.

922	**420**	14 c. multicoloured	15	30

1978. Marguerite d'Youville (founder of Grey Nuns) Commemoration.

923	**421**	14 c. multicoloured	15	30

1978. Canadian Eskimos ("Inuits") (2nd series). Travel. As T **413**. Multicoloured.

924	14 c. Woman on foot (painting by Pitseolak)	20	15
925	14 c. "Migration" (soapstone sculpture of sailing umiak by Joe Talurinili)	20	15
926	14 c. Aeroplane (stonecut and stencil print by Pudlo)	20	15
927	14 c. Dogteam and dogsled (ivory sculpture by Abraham Kingmeatook)	20	15

422 "Madonna of the Flowering Pea" (Cologne School)

423 "Chief Justice Robinson" (paddle-steamer)

1978. Christmas. Paintings. Multicoloured.

928	12 c. Type **422**	10	10
929	14 c. "The Virgin and Child with St Anthony and Donor" (detail, Hans Memling)	10	10
930	30 c. "The Virgin and Child" (Jacopo di Cione)	25	75

1978. Canadian Ships (4th series). Ice Vessels. Multicoloured.

931	14 c. Type **423**	45	65
932	14 c. "St. Roch" (steamer)	45	65
933	14 c. "Northern Light" (steamer)	45	65
934	14 c. "Labrador" (steamer)	45	65

424 Carnival Revellers

425 Eastern Spiny Soft-shelled Turtle

1978. Quebec Carnival.

935	**424**	14 c. multicoloured	20	20

1979. Endangered Wildlife (3rd series). Multicoloured.
936 17 c. Type **425** 20 10
937 35 c. Bowhead whale 90 90

426 Knotted Ribbon round Woman's Finger
427 Scene from "Fruits of the Earth" by Frederick Philip Grove

1979. Postal Code Publicity. Multicoloured.
938 17 c. Type **426** 20 10
939 17 c. Knotted string around man's finger 20 10

1979. Canadian Writers (3rd series). Multicoloured.
940 17 c. Type **427** 15 15
941 17 c. Scene from "Le Vaisseau d'Or" by Emile Nelligan 15 15

428 Charles-Michel de Salaberry (military hero)
430 Paddling Kayak

1979. Famous Canadians. Multicoloured.
942 17 c. Type **428** 25 15
943 17 c. John By (engineer) 25 15

1979. Canoe-Kayak Championships.
956 **430** 17 c. multicoloured 15 30

431 Hockey Players

1979. Women's Field Hockey Championships, Vancouver.
957 **431** 17 c. black, yellow and green 15 30

1979. Canadian Eskimos (3rd series). Shelter and the Community. As T **413**. Multicoloured.
958 17 c. "Summer Tent" (print by Kiakshuk" 15 15
959 17 c. "Five Eskimos building an Igloo" (soapstone sculpture by Abraham) 15 15
960 17 c. "The Dance" (print by Kalvak) 15 15
961 17 c. "Inuit drum dance" (soapstone sculptures by Madeleine Isserkut and Jean Mapsalak) 15 15

432 Toy Train
433 Child watering Tree of Life (painting by Marie-Annick Viatour)

1979. Christmas. Multicoloured.
962 15 c. Type **432** 10 10
963 17 c. Hobby-horse 10 10
964 35 c. Rag doll (vert) 25 50

1979. International Year of the Child.
965 **433** 17 c. multicoloured 15 30

434 Canadair CL-215

1979. Canadian Aircraft (1st series). Flying Boats. Multicoloured.
966 17 c. Type **434** 20 15
967 17 c. Curtiss HS-2L 20 15
968 35 c. Vickers Vedette 50 55
969 35 c. Consolidated Canso 50 55
See also Nos. 996/9, 1050/3 and 1026/9.

435 Map of Arctic Islands
436 Skier

1980. Centenary of Arctic Islands Acquisition.
970 **435** 17 c. multicoloured 15 30

1980. Winter Olympic Games, Lake Placid.
971 **436** 35 c. multicoloured 55 75

437 "A Meeting of the School Trustees" (Robert Harris)

1980. Centenary of Royal Canadian Academy of Arts. Multicoloured.
972 17 c. Type **437** 25 15
973 17 c. "Inspiration" (Philippe Hebert) 25 15
974 35 c. "Sunrise on the Saguenay" (Lucius O'Brien) 50 35
975 35 c. Thomas Fuller's design sketch for the original Parliament Buildings 50 35

438 Canadian Whitefish
439 Garden Flowers

1980. Endangered Wildlife (4th series). Multicoloured.
976 17 c. Type **438** 25 15
977 17 c. Prairie chicken 25 15

1980. International Flower Show, Montreal.
978 **439** 17 c. multicoloured 15 20

440 "Helping Hand"
441 Opening Bars of "O Canada"

1980. Rehabilitation.
979 **440** 17 c. gold and blue 15 20

1980. Centenary of "O Canada" (national song). Multicoloured.
980 17 c. Type **441** 15 15
981 17 c. Calixa Lavallee (composer), Adolphe-Basile Routhier (original writer) and Robert Stanley Weir (writer of English version) 15 15

442 John G. Diefenbaker (statesman)
443 Emma Albani (singer)

1980. John G. Diefenbaker Commemoration.
982 **442** 17 c. blue 15 20

1980. Famous Canadians. Multicoloured.
983 17 c. Type **443** 15 25
984 17 c. Healey Willan (composer) 15 25
985 17 c. Ned Hanlan (oarsman) (horiz) 15 15

444 Alberta

1980. 75th Anniv of Alberta and Saskatchewan Provinces. Multicoloured.
986 17 c. Type **444** 15 15
987 17 c. Saskatchewan 15 15

445 Uraninite Molecular Structure
446 "Christmas Morning" (J. S. Hallam)

1980. Uranium Resources.
988 **445** 35 c. multicoloured 30 30

1980. Canadian Eskimos ("Inuits") (4th series). Spirits. As T **413**. Multicoloured.
989 17 c. "Return of the Sun" (print, Kenojouak) 20 15
990 17 c. "Sedna" (sculpture, Ashoona Kiawak) 20 15
991 35 c. "Shaman" (print, Simon Tookoome) 35 30
992 35 c. "Bird Spirit" (sculpture, Doris Hagiolok) 35 30

1980. Christmas. Multicoloured.
993 15 c. Type **446** 10 10
994 17 c. "Sleigh Ride" (Frank Hennessy) 15 10
995 35 c. "McGill Cab Stand" (Kathleen Morris) 30 1·25

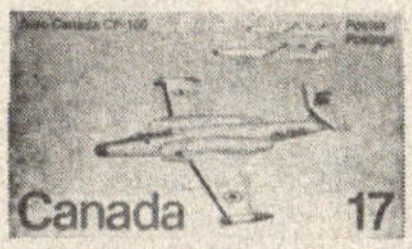

447 Avro (Canada) CF-100 Canuck Mk 5

1980. Canadian Aircraft (2nd series). Multicoloured.
996 17 c. Type **447** 15 15
997 17 c. Avro Type 683 Lancaster 15 15
998 35 c. Curtiss JN-4 Canuck biplane 30 50
999 35 c. Hawker Hurricane Mk I 30 50

448 Emmanuel-Persillier Lachapelle
449 Mandora (18th century)

1980. Dr. E.-P. Lachapelle (founder, Notre-Dame Hospital, Montreal) Commemoration.
1000 **448** 17 c. brown, deep brown and blue 15 15

1981. "The Look of Music" Exhibition, Vancouver.
1001 **449** 17 c. multicoloured 15 15

450 Henrietta Edwards

1981. Feminists. Multicoloured.
1002 17 c. Type **450** 20 15
1003 17 c. Louise McKinney 20 15
1004 17 c. Idola Saint-Jean 20 15
1005 17 c. Emily Stowe 20 15

451 Vancouver Marmot

1981. Endangered Wildlife (5th series). Multicoloured.
1006 17 c. Type **451** 15 10
1007 35 c. American bison 35 30

452 Kateri Tekakwitha
453 "Self Portrait" (Frederick H. Varley)

1981. 17th-century Canadian Women. Statues by Emile Brunet.
1008 **452** 17 c. brown and green 15 15
1009 – 17 c. deep blue and blue 15 15
DESIGN: No. 1009, Marie de I'Incarnation.

1981. Canadian Paintings. Multicoloured.
1010 17 c. Type **453** 15 10
1011 17c. "At Baie Saint-Paul" (Marc-Aurele Fortin) (horiz) 15 10
1012 35 c. "Untitled No 6" (Paul-Emile Borduas) 30 30

454 Canada in 1867

1981. Canada Day. Maps showing evolution of Canada from Confederation to present day. Multicoloured.
1013 17 c. Type **454** 15 20
1014 17 c. Canada in 1873 15 20
1015 17 c. Canada in 1905 15 20
1016 17 c. Canada since 1949 15 20

455 Frere Marie-Victorin
456 The Montreal Rose

1981. Canadian Botanists. Multicoloured.
1017 17 c. Type **455** 15 15
1018 17 c. John Macoun 15 15

1981. Montreal Flower Show.
1019 **456** 17 c. multicoloured 15 20

457 Drawing of Niagara-on-the-Lake
458 Acadian Community

1981. Bicentenary of Niagara-on-the-Lake (town).
1020 **457** 17 c. multicoloured 15 20

1981. Centenary of First Acadia (community) Convention.
1021 **458** 17 c. multicoloured 15 20

459 Aaron R. Mosher
460 Christmas Tree, 1781

1981. Birth Centenary of Aaron R. Mosher (founder of Canadian Labour Congress).
1022 **459** 17 c. multicoloured 15 20

1981. Christmas. Bicentenary of First Illuminated Christmas Tree in Canada.
1023 15 c. Type **460** 20 15
1024 15 c. Christmas Tree, 1881 20 15
1025 15 c. Christmas Tree, 1981 20 15

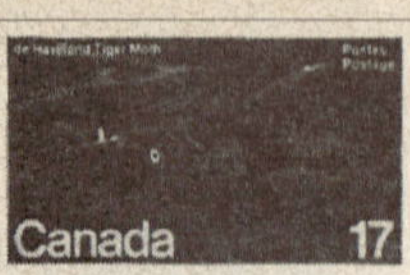

461 De Havilland Tiger Moth

462 Canadian Maple Leaf Emblem

1981. Canadian Aircraft (3rd series). Multicoloured.
1026 17 c. Type **461** 20 15
1027 17 c. Canadair CL-41 Tutor jet trainer 20 15
1028 35 c. Avro (Canada) CF-102 jet airliner 35 35
1029 35 c. De Havilland D.H.C.7 Dash 7 . . . . 35 35

1981.
1030a **462** A (30 c.) red 20 25
No. 1030a was printed before a new first class domestic letter rate had been agreed, "A" representing the face value of the stamp, later decided to be 30 c.

1982. As T **462** but including face values.
1033 **462** 5 c. purple 10 20
1033d 8 c. blue . . . . 1·25 1·75
1034 10 c. green . . . . . . 1·25 1·75
1036 30 c. red 35 30
1032 30 c. red, grey and blue 30 40
1036b 32 c. red . . . . 1·50 1·50
1032b 32 c. red, brown and stone 45 45

463 1851 3d. Stamp

1982. "Canada 82" International Philatelic Youth Exn, Toronto. Stamps on Stamps. Mult.
1037 30 c. Type **463** 30 25
1038 30 c. 1908 Centenary of Quebec 15 c. commemorative . . . 30 25
1039 35 c. 1935 10 c. 30 40
1040 35 c. 1928 10 c. 30 40
1041 60 c. 1929 50 c. 60 85

464 Jules Leger

465 Stylised drawing of Terry Fox

1982. Jules Leger (politician) Commemoration.
1043 **464** 30 c. multicoloured . . . 20 20

1982. Cancer victim Terry Fox's "Marathon of Hope" (Trans-Canada fund-raising run) Commemoration.
1044 **465** 30 c. multicoloured . . . 20 20

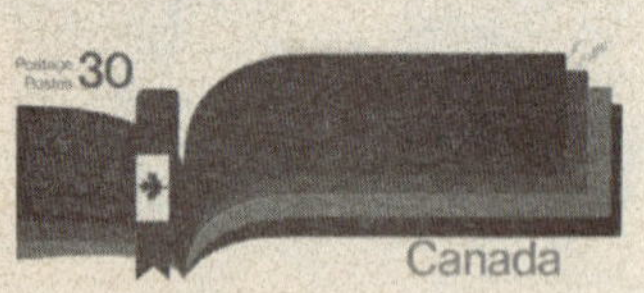

466 Stylised Open Book.

1982. Patriation of Constitution.
1045 **466** 30 c. multicoloured . . . 20 20

467 Male and Female Salvationists with Street Scene

1982. Centenary of Salvation Army in Canada.
1046 **467** 30 c. multicoloured . . . 20 20

469 Regina Legislative Building

1982. Centenary of Regina.
1048 **469** 30 c. multicoloured . . 20 20

470 Finish of Race

1982. Centenary of Royal Canadian Henley Regatta.
1049 **470** 30 c. multicoloured . . 20 25

471 Fairchild FC-2W1

1982. Canadian Aircraft (4th series) Bush Aircraft. Multicoloured.
1050 30 c. Type **471** 35 20
1051 30 c. De Havilland D.H.C.2 Beaver 35 20
1052 60 c. Fokker Super Universal 65 85
1053 60 c. Noorduyn Norseman . 65 85

472 Decoy

475 Mary, Joseph and Baby Jesus

1982. Heritage Artefacts.
1054 **472** 1 c. black, lt brn and brn 10 10
1055 – 2 c. black, blue and green 10 10
1056 – 3 c. black and deep blue 10 10
1057 – 5 c. black, pink and brown 10 10
1058 – 10 c. black, blue & turq 10 10
1059 – 20 c. black, lt brn & brn 20 10
1060 – 25 c. multicoloured . . 35 10
1061 – 37 c. black, grn & dp grn 50 40
1062 – 39 c. black, grey and violet 1·60 70
1063 – 42 c. multicoloured . . 50 15
1064 – 48 c. dp brn, brn & pink 70 40
1065 – 50 c. black, lt blue & blue 1·50 20
1066 – 55 c. multicoloured . . 65 30
1067 – 64 c. dp grey, blk & grey 80 35
1068 – 68 c. black, lt brn & brn 1·60 50
1069 – 72 c. multicoloured . . 85 35
DESIGNS—VERT: 2 c. Fishing spear; 3 c. Stable lantern; 5 c. Bucket; 10 c. Weathercock; 20 c. Skates; 25 c. Butter stamp. HORIZ: 37 c. Plough; 39 c. Settle-bed; 42 c. Linen chest; 48 c. Cradle; 50 c. Sleigh; 55 c. Iron kettle; 64 c. Kitchen stove; 68 c. Spinning wheel; 72 c. Hand-drawn cart.

1982. Christmas. Nativity Scenes.
1080 30 c. Type **475** 20 10
1081 35 c. The Shepherds 25 55
1082 60 c. The Three Wise Men . 45 1·10

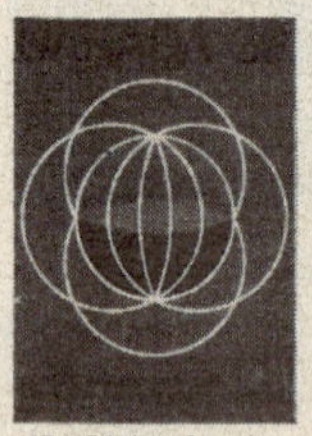
476 Globes forming Symbolic Designs

478 Scene from Novel "Angeline de Montbrun" by "Laure Conan" (Felicite Angers)

477 Map of World showing Canada

1983. World Communications Year.
1083 **476** 32 c. multicoloured . . 30 30

1983. Commonwealth Day.
1084 **477** $2 multicoloured . . . . 2·00 3·00

1983. Canadian Writers (4th series).
1085 32 c. Type **478** 40 75
1086 32 c. Woodcut illustrating "Sea-gulls" (poem by E. J. Pratt) 40 75

479 St. John Ambulance Badge and "100"

480 Victory Pictogram

1983. Centenary of St. John Ambulance in Canada.
1087 **479** 32 c. red, yellow and brown 30 30

1983. "Universiade 83" World University Games, Edmonton.
1088 **480** 32 c. multicoloured . . . 25 15
1089 64 c. multicoloured . . . 50 70

481 Fort William, Ontario

1983. Canada Day. Forts (1st series). Multicoloured.
1090 32 c. Fort Henry, Ontario (44 × 22 mm) 55 75
1091 32 c. Type **481** 55 75
1092 32 c. Fort Rodd Hill, British Columbia 55 75
1093 32 c. Fort Wellington, Ontario (28 × 22 mm) 55 75
1094 32 c. Fort Prince of Wales, Manitoba (28 × 22 mm) . . 55 75
1095 32 c. Halifax Citadel, Nova Scotia (44 × 22 mm) 55 75
1096 32 c. Fort Chambly, Quebec . 55 75
1097 32 c. Fort No. 1, Point Levis, Quebec 55 75
1098 32 c. Coteau-du-Lac Fort, Quebec (28 × 22 mm) . . . 55 75
1099 32 c. Fort Beausejour, New Brunswick (28 × 22 mm) . . 55 75
See also Nos. 1163/72.

482 Scouting Poster by Marc Fournier (aged 21)

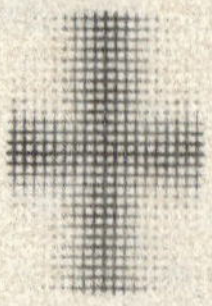
483 Cross Symbol

1983. Scouting in Canada (75th Anniv) and 15th World Scout Jamboree, Alberta.
1100 **482** 32 c. multicoloured . . . 30 30

1983. 6th Assembly of the World Council of Churches, Vancouver.
1101 **483** 32 c. green and lilac . . . 30 20

484 Sir Humphrey Gilbert (founder)

485 "NICKEL" Deposits

1983. 400th Anniv of Newfoundland.
1102 **484** 32 c. multicoloured . . . 30 20

1983. Cent of Discovery of Sudbury Nickel Deposits.
1103 **485** 32 c. multicoloured . . . 30 20

486 Josiah Henson and Escaping Slaves

1983. 19th-century Social Reformers. Multicoloured.
1104 32 c. Type **486** 35 25
1105 32 c. Father Antoine Labelle and rural village (32 × 26 mm) 35 25

487 Robert Stephenson's Locomotive "Dorchester", 1836

1983. Railway Locomotives (1st series). Mult.
1106 32 c. Type **487** 90 90
1107 32 c. Locomotive "Toronto", 1853 . . . . 90 90
1108 37 c. Timothy Hackworth's locomotive "Samson", 1838 90 1·00
1109 64 c. Western Canadian Railway locomotive "Adam Brown", 1855 . . . . . . 1·40 2·00
See also Nos. 1132/5, 1185/8 and 1223/6.

488 School Coat of Arms

1983. Centenary of Dalhousie Law School.
1110 **488** 32 c. multicoloured . . . 30 30

489 City Church

1983. Christmas. Churches. Multicoloured.
1111 32 c. Type **489** 40 10
1112 37 c. Family walking to church 55 70
1113 64 c. Country chapel . . . . 1·25 2·00

490 Royal Canadian Regiment and British Columbia Regiment

491 Gold Mine in Prospecting Pan

1983. Canadian Army Regiments. Multicoloured.
1114 32 c. Type **490** . . . . 75 1·00
1115 32 c. Royal Winnipeg Rifles and Royal Canadian Dragoons 75 1·00

1984. 50th Anniv of Yellowknife.
1116 **491** 32 c. multicoloured . . . 30 30

492 Montreal Symphony Orchestra

1984. 50th Anniv of Montreal Symphony Orchestra.
1117 **492** 32 c. multicoloured . . . 35 30

493 Jacques Cartier

494 U.S.C.S. "Eagle"

1984. 450th Anniv of Jacques Cartier's Voyage to Canada.
1118 **493** 32 c. multicoloured . . . 40 30

1984. Tall Ships Visit.
1119 **494** 32 c. multicoloured . . . 35 30

495 Service Medal

496 Oared Galleys

1984. 75th Anniv of Canadian Red Cross Society.
1120 **495** 32 c. multicoloured . . . 35 30

1984. Bicentenary of New Brunswick.
1121 **496** 32 c. multicoloured . . . 35 30

497 St. Lawrence Seaway

1984. 25th Anniv of St. Lawrence Seaway.

1122 **497** 32 c. multicoloured . . . 45 30

499 Loyalists of 1784

1984. Bicentenary of Arrival of United Empire Loyalists.

1124 **499** 32 c. multicoloured . . . 30 30

500 St. John's Basilica

501 Coat of Arms of Pope John Paul II

1984. Bicentenary of Roman Catholic Church in Newfoundland.

1125 **500** 32 c. multicoloured . . . 30 25

1984. Papal Visit.

1126 **501** 32 c. multicoloured . . . 40 20
1127 64 c. multicoloured . . . 85 1·10

502 Louisbourg Lighthouse, 1734

1984. Canadian Lighthouse (1st series). Mult.

1128 32 c. Type **502** . . . . 1·10 1·25
1129 32 c. Fisgard Lighthouse, 1860 1·10 1·25
1130 32 c. Ile Verte Lighthouse, 1809 1·10 1·25
1131 32 c. Gibraltar Point Lighthouse, 1808 . . . . . 1·10 1·25
See also Nos. 1176/9.

503 Great Western Railway Locomotive "Scotia", 1860

1984. Railway Locomotives (2nd series). Mult.

1132 32 c. Type **503** 90 90
1133 32 c. Northern Pacific Railroad locomotive "Countess of Dufferin", 1872 . . . . . 90 90
1134 37 c. Grand Trunk Railway Class E3 locomotive, 1886 90 1·40
1135 64 c. Canadian Pacific Class D10a steam locomotive . . 1·40 2·00
See also Nos. 1185/8 and 1223/6.

504 "The Annunciation" (Jean Dallaire)

505 Pilots of 1914–18, 1939–45 and 1984

1984. Christmas. Religious Paintings. Multicoloured.

1137 32 c. Type **504** 40 10
1138 37 c. "The Three Kings" (Simone Bouchard) 55 80
1139 64 c. "Snow in Bethlehem" (David Milne) . . . . . . 80 1·60

1984. 60th Anniv of Royal Canadian Air Force.

1140 **505** 32 c. multicoloured . . . 35 30

506 Treffle Berthiaume (editor)

508 Astronaut in Space, and Planet Earth

507 Heart and Arrow

1984. Centenary of "La Presse" (newspaper).

1141 **506** 32 c. brown, red & lt brn 35 30

1985. International Youth Year.

1142 **507** 32 c. multicoloured . . 30 30

1985. Canadian Space Programme.

1143 **508** 32 c. multicoloured . . 40 30

509 Emily Murphy

1985. Women's Rights Activists. Multicoloured.

1144 32 c. Type **509** 40 70
1145 32 c. Therese Casgrain . . . 40 70

510 Gabriel Dumont (Metis leader) and Battle of Batoche, 1885

1985. Centenary of the North-West Rebellion.

1146 **510** 32 c. blue red and grey . 30 30

511 Rear View, Parliament Building, Ottawa

512 Queen Elizabeth II

512a Queen Elizabeth II in 1984 (from photo by Karsh)

1985.

1147b	–	1 c. green	50	70
1148	–	2 c. green	20	40
1149	–	5 c. brown	40	50
1150a	–	6 c. brown	40	30
1150b	–	6 c. purple	65	95
1151	511	34 c. black	1·00	1·50
1155		34 c. multicoloured .	50	10
1158		34 c. brown	2·25	2·75
1161	512	34 c. black and blue .	45	30
1152	511	36 c. purple	2·50	3·00
1156		36 c. multicoloured .	30	30
1159		36 c. red	90	55
1162	512	36 c. purple	2·75	1·10
1153	511	37 c. blue	1·00	30
1157	–	37 c. multicoloured .	85	10
1162a	512a	37 c. multicoloured .	2·00	10
1154	511	38 c. blue	75	1·25
1157c	–	38 c. multicoloured .	35	10
1160b	511	38 c. green	40	30
1162b	512a	38 c. multicoloured .	35	20
1162c		39 c. multicoloured .	1·00	20
1162d		40 c. multicoloured .	80	20
1162e		42 c. multicoloured .	80	40
1162f		43 c. multicoloured .	80	55
1162g		45 c. multicoloured .	35	40
1162h		46 c. multicoloured .	35	40

DESIGNS: 1, 5, 6 c. (1150b) East Block, Parliament Building; 2, 6 c. (1150a) West Block, Parliament Building; 37 c. (1157) Front view, Parliament Building; 38 c. (1157c) Side view, Parliament Building.

1985. Canada Day. Forts (2nd series). As T **481**. Multicoloured.

1163 34 c. Lower Fort Garry, Manitoba 50 60
1164 34 c. Fort Anne, Nova Scotia 50 60
1165 34 c. Fort York, Ontario . . 50 60
1166 34 c. Castle Hill, Newfoundland 50 60
1167 34 c. Fort Whoop Up, Alberta 50 60
1168 34 c. Fort Erie, Ontario . . . 50 60
1169 34 c. Fort Walsh, Saskatchewan 50 60
1170 34 c. Fort Lennox, Quebec . 50 60
1171 34 c. York Redoubt, Nova Scotia 50 60
1172 34 c. Fort Frederick, Ontario 50 60
Nos. 1163 and 1168 measure 44 × 22 mm and Nos. 1166/7 and 1171/2 28 × 22 mm.

513 Louis Hebert (apothecary)

514 Parliament Buildings and Map of World

1985. 45th International Pharmaceutical Sciences Congress of Pharmaceutical Federation, Montreal.

1173 **513** 34 c. multicoloured . . . 45 35

1985. 74th Conference of Inter-Parliamentary Union, Ottawa.

1174 **514** 34 c. multicoloured . . . 45 35

515 Guide and Brownie Saluting

516 Sisters Islets Lighthouse

1985. 75th Anniv of Girl Guide Movement.

1175 **515** 34 c. multicoloured . . . 45 35

1985. Canadian Lighthouses (2nd series). Multicoloured.

1176 34 c. Type **516** . . . . 1·40 1·40
1177 34 c. Pelee Passage Lighthouse 1·40 1·40
1178 34 c. Haut-fond Prince Lighthouse . . . . 1·40 1·40
1179 34 c. Rose Blanche Lighthouse, Cains Island . . . . 1·40 1·40

517 Santa Claus in Reindeer-drawn Sleigh

518 Naval Personnel of 1910, 1939–45 and 1985

1985. Christmas. Santa Claus Parade. Multicoloured.

1181 32 c. Canada Post's parade float 70 70
1182 34 c. Type **517** 60 15
1183 39 c. Acrobats and horse-drawn carriage . . . . 70 1·00
1184 68 c. Christmas tree, pudding and goose on float . . . . 1·50 1·60

1985. Steam Railway Locomotives (3rd series). As T **503**. Multicoloured.

1185 34 c. Grand Trunk Railway Class K2 . . . . 80 80
1186 34 c. Canadian Pacific Class P2a 80 80
1187 39 c. Canadian Northern Class O10a . . . . 95 1·25
1188 68 c. Canadian Govt Railway Class H4D . . . . 1·60 1·75

1985. 75th Anniv of Royal Canadian Navy.

1189 **518** 34 c. multicoloured . . . 65 55

519 "The Old Holton House, Montreal" (James Wilson Morrice)

1985. 125th Anniv of Montreal Museum of Fine Arts.

1190 **519** 34 c. multicoloured . . . 40 35

520 Map of Alberta showing Olympic Sites

1986. Winter Olympic Games, Calgary (1988) (1st issue).

1191 **520** 34 c. multicoloured . . . 40 50
See also Nos. 1216/17, 1236/7, 1258/9 and 1281/4.

521 Canada Pavilion

1986. "Expo '86" World Fair, Vancouver (1st issue). Multicoloured.

1192 34p. Type **521** . . . . 1·00 50
1193 39p. Early telephone, dish aerial and satellite . . . . 1·25 2·00
See also Nos. 1196/7.

522 Molly Brant

523 Aubert de Gaspe and Scene from "Les Anciens Canadiens"

1986. 250th Birth Anniv of Molly Brant (Iroquois leader).

1194 **522** 34 c. multicoloured . . . 40 40

1986. Birth Bicentenary of Philippe Aubert de Gaspe (author).

1195 **523** 34 c. multicoloured . . . 40 40

1986. "Expo '86" World Fair, Vancouver (2nd issue). As T **521**. Multicoloured.

1196 34 c. Expo Centre, Vancouver (vert) 65 40
1197 68 c. Early and modern trains 1·25 2·00

524 Canadian Field Post Office and Cancellation, 1944

1986. 75th Anniv of Canadian Forces Postal Service.

1198 **524** 34 c. multicoloured . . . 75 40

525 Great Blue Heron

526 Railway Rotary Snowplough

1986. Birds of Canada. Multicoloured.

1199 34 c. Type **525** . . . . 1·40 1·40
1200 34 c. Snow goose . . . . . . 1·40 1·40
1201 34 c. Great horned owl . . . 1·40 1·40
1202 34 c. Spruce grouse . . . . 1·40 1·40

1986. Canada Day. Science and Technology. Canadian Inventions (1st series). Multicoloured.

1203 34 c. Type **526** . . . . 1·10 1·40
1204 34 c. Space shuttle "Challenger" launching satellite with Canadarm . . . . 1·10 1·40
1205 34 c. Pilot wearing antigravity flight suit and Supermarine Spitfire . . . . 1·10 1·40
1206 34 c. Variable-pitch propeller and Avro 504 airplane . . 1·10 1·40
See also Nos. 1241/4 and 1292/5.

527 C.B.C. Logos over Map of Canada

1986. 50th Anniv of Canadian Broadcasting Corporation.

1207 **527** 34 c. multicoloured . . . 40 45

528 Ice Age Artefacts, Tools and Settlement

1986. Exploration of Canada (1st series). Discoverers. Multicoloured.

1208 34 c. Type **528** 75 85
1209 34 c. Viking ships 75 85
1210 34 c. John Cabot's "Matthew", 1497, compass and Arctic char (fish) 75 85
1211 34 c. Henry Hudson cast adrift, 1611 . . . . 75 85

See also Nos. 1232/5, 1285/8 and 1319/22.

529 Crowfoot (Blackfoot Chief) and Indian Village

1986. Founders of the Canadian West. Multicoloured.

1213 34 c. Type **529** 35 55
1214 34 c. James Macleod of the North West Mounted Police and Fort Macleod 35 55

530 Peace Dove and Globe

1986. International Peace Year.

1215 **530** 34 c. multicoloured . . . 40 45

531 Ice Hockey **532** Angel with Crown

1986. Winter Olympic Games, Calgary (1988) (2nd issue). Multicoloured.

1216 34 c. Type **531** . . . . 1·25 1·40
1217 34 c. Biathlon . . . . 1·25 1·40

1986. Christmas. Multicoloured.

1218 29 c. Angel singing carol (36×22 mm) 65 30
1219 34 c. Type **532** 60 25
1220 39 c. Angel playing lute . . . 1·00 90
1221 68 c. Angel with ribbon . . . 1·50 2·25

533 John Molson with Theatre Royal, Montreal, "Accomodation" (paddle-steamer) and Railway Train

1966. 150th Death Anniv of John Molson (businessman).

1222 **533** 34 c. multicoloured . . . 50 50

1986. Railway Locomotives (4th series). As T **503** but size 60×22 mm. Multicoloured.

1223 34 c. Canadian National Class V-1-a steam locomotive No. 9000 . . . . 1·25 1·25
1224 34 c. Canadian Pacific Class T1a diesel locomotive No. 9000 . . . . 1·25 1·25
1225 39 c. Canadian National Class U-2-a steam locomotive . . 1·40 1·00
1226 68 c. Canadian Pacific Class H1c steam locomotive No. 2850 . . . . 2·25 2·75

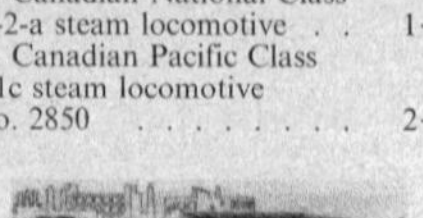

534 Toronto's First Post Office

1987. "Capex '87" International Stamp Exhibition, Toronto. Post Offices.

1227 34 c. Type **534** 60 20
1228 36 c. Nelson-Miramichi, New Brunswick 65 45
1229 42 c. Saint-Ours, Quebec . . . 70 65
1230 72 c. Battleford, Saskatchewan 1·00 1·25

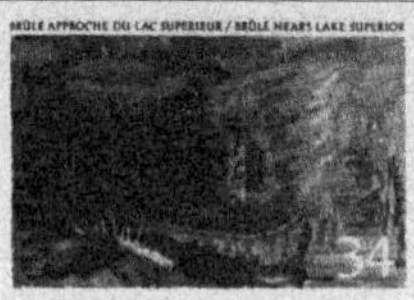

535 Etienne Brule exploring Lake Superior

1987. Exploration of Canada (2nd series). Pioneers of New France. Multicoloured.

1232 34 c. Type **535** . . . . . . 85 1·00
1233 34 c. Radisson and Des Groseilliers with British and French flags . . . . 85 1·00
1234 34 c. Jolliet and Father Marquette on the Mississippi 85 1·00
1235 34 c. Jesuit missionary preaching to Indians . . . 85 1·00

1987. Winter Olympic Games, Calgary (1988) (3rd issue). As T **531**. Multicoloured.

1236 36 c. Speed skating 50 40
1237 42 c. Bobsleighing 75 60

536 Volunteer Activities

1987. National Volunteer Week.

1238 **536** 36 c. multicoloured . . 30 35

537 Canadian Coat of Arms **539** R. A. Fessenden (AM Radio)

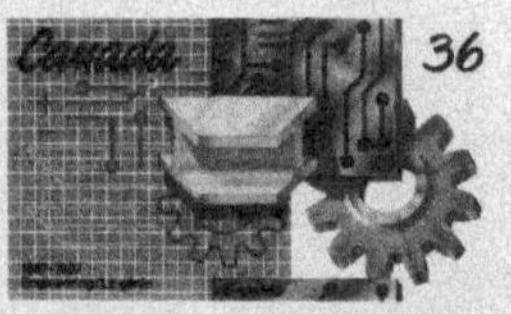

538 Steel Girder, Gear Wheel and Microchip

1987. 5th Anniv of Canadian Charter of Rights and Freedoms.

1239 **537** 36 c. multicoloured . . 35 35

1987. Centenary of Engineering Institute of Canada.

1240 **538** 36 c. multicoloured . . 35 40

1987. Canada Day. Science and Technology. Canadian Inventors (2nd series). Multicoloured.

1241 36 c. Type **539** 80 80
1242 36 c. C. Fenerty (newsprint pulp) 80 80
1243 36 c. G.-E. Desbarats and W. Leggo (half-tone engraving) 80 80
1244 36 c. F. N. Gisborne (first North American undersea telegraph) 80 80

540 "Segwun"

1987. Canadian Steamships. Multicoloured.

1245 36 c. Type **540** . . . . . . 1·25 1·75
1246 36 c. "Princess Marguerite" (52×22 mm) . . . . . . 1·25 1·75

541 Figurehead from "Hamilton", 1813

1987. Historic Shipwrecks. Multicoloured.

1247 36 c. Type **541** 70 85
1248 36 c. Hull of "San Juan", 1565 70 85
1249 36 c. Wheel from "Breadalbane", 1853 . . . 70 85
1250 36 c. Bell from "Ericsson", 1892 70 85

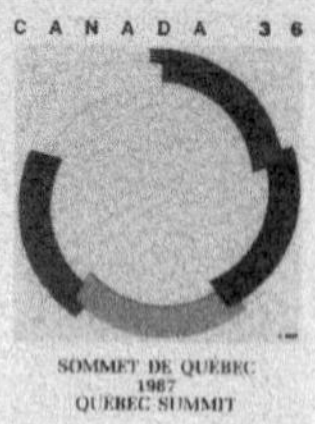

542 Air Canada Boeing 767-200 and Globe **543** Summit Symbol

1987. 50th Anniv of Air Canada.

1251 **542** 36 c. multicoloured . . . 55 35

1987. 2nd Int Francophone Summit, Quebec.

1252 **543** 36 c. multicoloured . . . 30 35

544 Commonwealth Symbol **545** Poinsettia

1987. Commonwealth Heads of Government Meeting, Vancouver.

1253 **544** 36 c. multicoloured . . . 35 40

1987. Christmas. Christmas Plants. Multicoloured.

1254 31 c. Decorated Christmas tree and presents (36×20 mm) . 50 35
1255 36 c. Type **545** 35 40
1256 42 c. Holly wreath 40 45
1257 72 c. Mistletoe and decorated tree 65 70

1987. Winter Olympic Games, Calgary (1988) (4th issue). As T **531**. Multicoloured.

1258 36 c. Cross-country skiing . . 50 40
1259 36 c. Ski-jumping 50 40

546 Football, Grey Cup and Spectators **547** Flying Squirrel

548a Runnymede Library, Toronto

1987. 75th Grey Cup Final (Canadian football championship), Vancouver.

1260 **546** 36 c. multicoloured . . . 35 40

1988. Canadian Mammals and Architecture. Multicoloured. (a) As T **547**.

1261 1 c. Type **547** 10 10
1262 2 c. Porcupine 10 10
1263 3 c. Muskrat 10 10
1264 5 c. Varying hare 10 10
1265 6 c. Red fox 10 10
1266 10 c. Striped skunk 10 10
1267 25 c. American beaver . . . 30 15
1268 43 c. Lynx (26×20 mm) . . 1·40 30
1269 44 c. Walrus (27×21 mm) . . 45 20
1270 45 c. Pronghorn (27×21 mm) 35 20
1270c 46 c. Wolverine (27×21 mm) 45 30
1271 57 c. Killer whale (26×20 mm) 2·00 55
1272 59 c. Musk ox (27×21 mm) 1·75 45
1273 61 c. Wolf (27×21 mm) . . 60 75
1273b 63 c. Harbour porpoise (27×21 mm) 65 45
1274 74 c. Wapiti (26×20 mm) . 1·60 50
1275 76 c. Brown bear (27×21 mm) 90 50
1276 78 c. White whale (27×21 mm) 90 55
1276c 80 c. Peary caribou (27×21 mm) 80 60

(b) As T **548a**.

1277 $1 Type **548a** . . . . 1·25 30
1278 $2 McAdam Railway Station, New Brunswick . . . . . 2·00 50
1279 $5 Bonsecours Market, Montreal . . . . 4·75 5·00

1988. Winter Olympic Games, Calgary (5th issue). As T **531**. Multicoloured.

1281 37 c. Slalom skiing 65 40
1282 37 c. Curling 65 40
1283 43 c. Figure skating 75 45
1284 74 c. Luge . . . . 1·25 70

549 Trade Goods, Blackfoot Encampment and Page from Anthony Henday's Journal

1988. Exploration of Canada (3rd series). Explorers of the West. Multicoloured.

1285 37 c. Type **549** 65 50
1286 37 c. Discovery and map of George Vancouver's voyage 65 50
1287 37 c. Simon Fraser's expedition portaging canoes 65 50
1288 37 c. John Palliser's surveying equipment and view of prairie 65 50

550 "The Young Reader" (Ozias Leduc)

1988. Canadian Art (1st series).

1289 **550** 50 c. multicoloured . . . 70 70

See also Nos. 1327, 1384, 1421, 1504, 1539, 1589, 1629, 1681, 1721 and 1825.

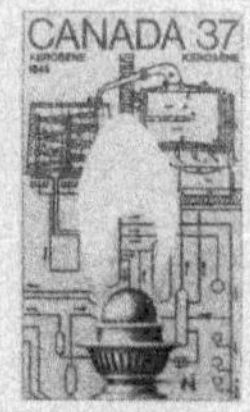

551 Mallard landing on Marsh **552** Kerosene Lamp and Diagram of Distillation Plant

1988. Wildlife and Habitat Conservation. Mult.

1290 37 c. Type **551** 75 40
1291 37 c. Moose feeding in marsh 75 40

1988. Canada Day. Science and Technology. Canadian Inventions (3rd series). Multicoloured.

1292 37 c. Type **552** 50 60
1293 37 c. Ears of Marquis wheat 50 60
1294 37 c. Electron microscope and magnified image 50 60
1295 37 c. Patient under "Cobalt 60" cancer therapy 50 60

553 "Papilio brevicauda"

1988. Canadian Butterflies. Multicoloured.

1296 37 c. Type **553** 70 60
1297 37 c. "Lycaeides idas" . . . 70 60
1298 37 c. "Oeneis macounii" . . 70 60
1299 37 c. "Papilio glaucus" . . . 70 60

554 St. John's Harbour Entrance and Skyline

1988. Centenary of Incorporation of St. John's, Newfoundland.

1300 **554** 37 c. multicoloured . . . 35 40

555 Club Members working on Forestry Project and Rural Scene

1988. 75th Anniv of 4-H Clubs.

1301 **555** 37 c. multicoloured . . . 35 40

556 Saint-Maurice Ironworks   **557** Tahltan Bear Dog

1988. 250th Anniv of Saint-Maurice Ironworks, Quebec.

1302 **556** 37 c. black, orge & brn . 35 40

1988. Canadian Dogs. Multicoloured.

1303 37 c. Type **557** 85 50
1304 37 c. Nova Scotia duck tolling retriever 85 50
1305 37 c. Canadian eskimo dog . 85 50
1306 37 c. Newfoundland 85 50

558 Baseball, Glove and Pitch   **559** Virgin with Inset of Holy Child

1988. 150th Anniv of Baseball in Canada. Multicoloured.

1307 **558** 37 c. multicoloured . . . 35 40

1988. Christmas. Icons. Multicoloured.

1308 32 c. Holy Family (36 × 21 mm) 35 35
1309 37 c. Type **559** 35 40
1310 43 c. Virgin and Child . . . 40 45
1311 74 c. Virgin and Child (different) 70 75

On No. 1308 the left-hand third of the design area is taken up by the bar code.

No. 1309 also commemorates the Millenium of Ukrainian Christianity.

560 Bishop Inglis and Nova Scotia Church

1988. Bicentenary of Consecration of Charles Inglis (first Canadian Anglican bishop) (1987).

1312 **560** 37 c. multicoloured . . . 35 40

561 Frances Ann Hopkins and "Canoe manned by Voyageurs"

1988. 150th Birth Anniv of Frances Anne Hopkins (artist).

1313 **561** 37 c. multicoloured . . . 35 40

562 Angus Walters and "Bluenose" (yacht)   **563** Chipewyan Canoe

1988. 20th Death Anniv of Angus Walters (yachtsman).

1314 **562** 37 c. multicoloured . . . 35 40

1989. Small Craft of Canada (1st series). Native Canoes. Multicoloured.

1315 38 c. Type **563** 70 50
1316 38 c. Haida canoe 70 50
1317 38 c. Inuit kayak 70 50
1318 38 c. Micmac canoe . . . 70 50

See also Nos. 1377/80 and 1428/31.

564 Matonabbee and Hearne's Expedition

1989. Exploration of Canada (4th issue). Explorers of the North. Multicoloured.

1319 38 c. Type **564** 65 65
1320 38 c. Relics of Franklin's expedition and White Ensign 65 65
1321 38 c. Joseph Tyrell's compass, hammer and fossil 65 65
1322 38 c. Vilhjalmur Stefansson, camera on tripod and sledge dog team 65 65

565 Construction of Victoria Bridge, Montreal and William Notman

1989. Canada Day. "150 Years of Canadian Photography". Designs showing early photograph and photographer. Multicoloured.

1323 38 c. Type **565** 50 50
1324 38 c. Plains Indian village and W. Hanson Boorne . . . 50 50
1325 38 c. Horse-drawn sleigh and Alexander Henderson . . 50 50
1326 38 c. Quebec street scene and Jules-Ernest Livernois . . 50 50

566 Tsimshian Ceremonial Frontlet, c. 1900

1989. Canadian Art (2nd series).

1327 **566** 50 c. multicoloured . . 55 60

567 Canadian Flag and Forest

1989. Self-adhesive. Multicoloured.

1328 38 c. Type **567** . . . . . . 90 1·40
1328b 39 c. Canadian flag and prairie 1·00 1·50
1328c 40 c. Canadian flag and sea 1·00 1·25
1328d 42 c. Canadian flag over mountains . . . . 1·00 1·50
1328e 43 c. Canadian flag over lake 80 1·10

568 Archibald Lampman   **569** "Clavulinopsis fusiformis"

1989. Canadian Poets. Multicoloured.

1329 38 c. Type **568** 40 45
1330 38 c. Louis-Honore Frechette 40 45

1989. Mushrooms. Multicoloured.

1331 38 c. Type **569** 70 60
1332 38 c. "Boletus mirabilis" . . 70 60
1333 38 c. "Cantharellus cinnabarinus" 70 60
1334 38 c. "Morchella esculenta" 70 60

570 Night Patrol, Korea

1989. 75th Anniv of Canadian Regiments. Multicoloured.

1335 38 c. Type **570** (Princess Patricia's Canadian Light Infantry) 70 70
1336 38 c. Trench raid, France, 1914–18 (Royal 22e Regiment) 70 70

571 Globe in Box   **572** Film Director

1989. Canada Export Trade Month.

1337 **571** 38 c. multicoloured . . . 40 45

1989. Arts and Entertainment.

1338 **572** 38 c. brown, dp brn & vio 40 45
1339 – 38 c. brown, dp brn & grn 40 45
1340 – 38 c. brown, dp brn & mve 40 45
1341 – 38 c. brown, dp brn & bl 40 45

DESIGNS: No. 1339, Actors; No. 1340, Dancers; No. 1341, Musicians.

573 "Snow II" (Lawren S. Harris)

1989. Christmas. Paintings of Winter Landscapes. Multicoloured.

1342 33 c. "Champ-de-Mars, Winter" (William Brymner) (35 × 21 mm) 80 55
1343 38 c. "Bend in the Gosselin River" (Marc-Aurele Suzor-Cote) (21 × 35 mm) 40 35
1344 44 c. Type **573** 45 50
1345 76 c. "Ste. Agnes" (A. H. Robinson) 80 85

On No. 1342 the left-hand third of the design area is taken up by a bar code.

574 Canadians listening to Declaration of War, 1939

1989. 50th Anniv of Outbreak of Second World War (1st issue).

1346 **574** 38 c. black, silver & pur . 55 55
1347 – 38 c. black, silver and grey 55 55
1348 – 38 c. black, silver and green 55 55
1349 – 38 c. black, silver and blue 55 55

DESIGNS: No. 1347, Army mobilization; No. 1348, British Commonwealth air crew training; No. 1349, North Atlantic convoy.

See also Nos. 1409/12, 1456/9, 1521/4, 1576/9, 1621/4, and 1625/8.

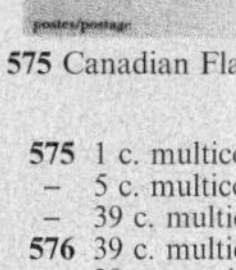

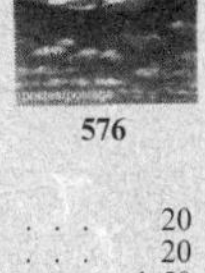

575 Canadian Flag   **576**

1989.

1350 **575** 1 c. multicoloured . . . 20 85
1351 – 5 c. multicoloured . . . 20 30
1352 – 39 c. multicoloured . . . 1·50 1·75
1354 **576** 39 c. multicoloured . . . 50 10
1360 – 39 c. purple 60 75
1353 – 40 c. multicoloured . . . 1·75 2·00
1355 – 40 c. multicoloured . . . 60 10
1361 – 40 c. blue 40 45
1356 – 42 c. multicoloured . . . 60 15
1362 – 42 c. red 40 45
1357 – 43 c. multicoloured . . . 60 60
1363 – 43 c. green 55 80
1358c – 45 c. multicoloured . . . 35 40
1364 – 45 c. green 35 40
1359 – 46 c. multicoloured . . . 35 40
1365 – 46 c. red 35 40

DESIGNS: Nos. 1351/3, 1360/5, As T **575** but different folds in flag. As T **576**: No. 1355, Flag over forest; 1356, Flag over mountains; 1357c, Flag over prairie; 1358, Flag and skyscraper; 1359, Flag and iceberg.

No. 1359 comes with ordinary or self-adhesive gum.

577 Norman Bethune in 1937 and performing Operation, Montreal

1990. Birth Centenary of Dr. Norman Bethune (surgeon). Multicoloured.

1375 39 c. Type **577** 45 65
1376 39 c. Bethune in 1939, and treating wounded Chinese soldiers 45 65

1990. Small Craft of Canada (2nd series). Early Work Boats. As T **563**. Multicoloured.

1377 39 c. Fishing dory 50 55
1378 39 c. Logging pointer 50 55
1379 39 c. York boat 50 55
1380 39 c. North canoe 50 55

578 Maple Leaf Mosaic

1990. Multiculturalism.

1381 **578** 39 c. multicoloured . . . 35 40

579 Mail Van (facing left)   **580** Amerindian and Inuit Dolls

1990. "Moving the Mail". Multicoloured.

1382 39 c. Type **579** 45 55
1383 39 c. Mail van (facing right) 45 55

1990. Canadian Art (3rd series). As T **550**. Multicoloured.

1384 50 c. "The West Wind" (Tom Thomson) 55 65

1990. Dolls. Multicoloured.

1385 39 c. Type **580** 65 60
1386 39 c. 19th-century settlers' dolls 65 60
1387 39 c. Commerical dolls, 1917–36 65 60
1388 39 c. Commercial dolls, 1940–60 65 60

581 Canadian Flag and Fireworks   **582** "Stromatolites" (fossil algae)

1990. Canada Day.

1389 **581** 39 c. multicoloured . . . 45 50

1990. Prehistoric Canada (1st series). Primitive Life. Multicoloured.

1390 39 c. Type **582** 60 70
1391 39 c. "Opabinia regalis" (soft invertebrate) 60 70
1392 39 c. "Paradoxides davidis" (trilobite) 60 70
1393 39 c. "Eurypterus remipes" (sea scorpion) 60 70

See also Nos. 1417/20, 1568/71 and 1613/16.

583 Acadian Forest

1990. Canadian Forests. Multicoloured.

1394 39 c. Type **583** 60 70
1395 39 c. Great Lake–St. Lawrence forest 60 70
1396 39 c. Pacific Coast forest . . 60 70
1397 39 c. Boreal forest 60 70

584 Clouds and Rainbow

1990. 150th Anniv of Weather Observing in Canada.
1398 **584** 39 c. multicoloured . . . 40 50

585 "Alphabet" Bird

586 Sasquatch

1990. International Literacy Year.
1399 **585** 39 c. multicoloured . . . 40 50

1990. Legendary Creatures. Multicoloured.
1400 39 c. Type **586** 70 70
1401 39 c. Kraken 70 70
1402 39 c. Werewolf 70 70
1403 39 c. Ogopogo 70 70

587 Agnes Macphail

588 "Virgin Mary with Christ Child and St. John the Baptist" (Norval Morrisseau)

1990. Birth Centenary of Agnes Macphail (first woman elected to Parliament).
1404 **587** 39 c. multicoloured . . . 40 50

1990. Christmas. Native Art.
1405 – 34 c. multicoloured . . . 40 35
1406 **588** 39 c. multicoloured . . . 40 40
1407 – 45 c. multicoloured . . . 40 45
1408 – 78 c. black, red and grey . . 70 75
DESIGNS—35 × 21 mm: 34 c. "Rebirth" (Jackson Beardy). As T **588**: 45 c. "Mother and Child" (Inuit sculpture, Cape Dorset); 78 c. "Children of the Raven" (Bill Reid).
No. 1405 includes a bar code in the design.

1990. 50th Anniv of Second World War (2nd issue). As T **574**.
1409 39 c. black, silver and green . 90 90
1410 39 c. black, silver and brown . 90 90
1411 39 c. black, silver and brown . 90 90
1412 39 c. black, silver and mauve . 90 90
DESIGNS: No. 1409, Canadian family at home, 1940; 1410, Packing parcels for the troops; 1411, Harvesting; 1412, Testing anti-gravity flying suit.

589 Jennie Trout (first woman physician) and Women's Medical College, Kingston

590 Blue Poppies and Butchart Gardens, Victoria

1991. Medical Pioneers. Multicoloured.
1413 40 c. Type **589** 90 90
1414 40 c. Wilder Penfield (neurosurgeon) and Montreal Neurological Institute . . . 90 90
1415 40 c. Frederick Banting (discoverer of insulin) and University of Toronto medical faculty 90 90
1416 40 c. Harold Griffith (anesthesiologist) and Queen Elizabeth Hospital, Montreal 90 90

1991. Prehistoric Canada (2nd series). Primitive Vertebrates. As T **582**. Multicoloured.
1417 40 c. Foord's crossopt ("Eusthenopteron foordi") (fish fossil) . . . . 1·25 1·40
1418 40 c. "Hylonomus lyelli" (land reptile) . . . . 1·25 1·40
1419 40 c. Fossil conodonts (fossil teeth) . . . . 1·25 1·40
1420 40 c. "Archaeopteris halliana" (early tree) . . . . . . 1·25 1·40

1991. Canadian Art (4th series). As T **550**. Multicoloured.
1421 50 c. "Forest, British Columbia" (Emily Carr) . 90 1·00

1991. Public Gardens. Multicoloured.
1422 40 c. Type **590** 55 55
1423 40 c. Marigolds and International Peace Garden, Boissevain 55 55
1424 40 c. Lilac and Royal Botanical Gardens, Hamilton 55 55
1425 40 c. Roses and Montreal Botanical Gardens 55 55
1426 40 c. Rhododendrons and Halifax Public Gardens . . 55 55

591 Maple Leaf

592 South Nahanni River

1991. Canada Day.
1427 **591** 40 c. multicoloured . . 50 60

1991. Small Craft of Canada (3rd series). As T **563**. Multicoloured.
1428 40 c. Verchere rowboat . . . 85 90
1429 40 c. Touring kayak 85 90
1430 40 c. Sailing dinghy 85 90
1431 40 c. Cedar strip canoe . . . 85 90

1991. Canadian Rivers (1st series). Multicoloured.
1432 40 c. Type **592** 80 90
1433 40 c. Athabasca River . . . 80 90
1434 40 c. Boundary Waters, Voyageur Waterway . . . 80 90
1435 40 c. Jacques-Cartier River . 80 90
1436 40 c. Main River 80 90
See also Nos. 1492/6, 1558/62 and 1584/8.

593 "Leaving Europe"

594 Ski Patrol rescuing Climber

1991. Centenary of Ukrainian Immigration. Panels from "The Ukrainian Pioneer" by William Kurelek. Multicoloured.
1437 40 c. Type **593** 80 85
1438 40 c. "Canadian Winter" . . 80 85
1439 40 c. "Clearing the Land" . . 80 85
1440 40 c. "Harvest" 80 85

1991. Emergency Services. Multicoloured.
1441 40 c. Type **594** . . . . . . 1·10 1·10
1442 40 c. Police at road traffic accident . . . . 1·10 1·10
1443 49 c. Firemen on extending ladder . . . . 1·10 1·10
1444 40 c. Boeing-Vertol Chinook rescue helicopter and lifeboat 1·10 1·10

595 "The Witched Canoe"

596 Grant Hall Tower

1991. Canadian Folktales. Multicoloured.
1445 40 c. Type **595** 95 95
1446 40 c. "The Orphan Boy" . . 95 95
1447 40 c. "Chinook" 95 95
1448 40 c. "Buried Treasure" . . 95 95

1991. 150th Anniv of Queen's University, Kingston.
1449 **596** 40 c. multicoloured . . 75 1·00

597 North American Santa Claus

598 Players jumping for Ball

1991. Christmas. Multicoloured.
1450 35 c. British Father Christmas (35 × 21 mm) 70 40
1451 40 c. Type **597** 70 20
1452 46 c. French Bonhomme Noel 75 90
1453 80 c. Dutch Sinterklaas . . 1·40 2·00

1991. Basketball Centenary. Multicoloured.
1454 **598** 40 c. multicoloured . . 90 75

1991. 50th Anniv of Second World War (3rd issue). As T **574**.
1456 40 c. black, silver and blue . . 1·10 1·10
1457 40 c. black, silver and brown . 1·10 1·10
1458 40 c. black, silver and lilac . . 1·10 1·10
1459 40 c. black, silver and brown . 1·10 1·10
DESIGNS: No. 1456, Women's services, 1941; 1457, Armament factory; 1458, Cadets and veterans, 1459, Defence of Hong Kong.

599 Blueberry

600 McIntosh Apple

600a Court House, Yorktown

1991. Multicoloured. (a) Edible Berries. As T **599**.
1460 1 c. Type **599** 10 10
1461 2 c. Wild strawberry 10 10
1462 3 c. Black crowberry 10 10
1463 5 c. Rose hip 10 10
1464 6 c. Black raspberry 10 10
1465 10 c. Kinnikinnick 10 10
1466 25 c. Saskatoon berry 20 25

(b) Fruit and Nut Trees. As T **600**
1467 48 c. Type **600** 50 35
1468 49 c. Delicious apple . . . . 1·00 1·00
1469 50 c. Snow apple . . . . . 1·00 1·00
1470b 52 c. Grauenstein apple . . 40 45
1471 65 c. Black walnut 70 50
1472 67 c. Beaked hazelnut . . . 1·00 1·25
1473 69 c. Shagbark hickory . . . 1·25 1·25
1474 71 c. American chestnut . . 80 1·00
1475 84 c. Stanley plum 90 75
1476 86 c. Bartlett pear . . . . 85 1·00
1477 88 c. Westcot apricot . . . 1·60 1·60
1478b 90 c. Elberta peach 70 75

(c) Architecture. As T **600a**
1479 $1 Type **600a** 90 95
1480a $2 Provincial Normal School, Truro . . . . 2·25 1·60
1481 $5 Public Library, Victoria . 4·00 4·25

601 Ski Jumping

1992. Winter Olympic Games, Albertville. Multicoloured.
1482 42 c. Type **601** 70 70
1483 42 c. Figure skating 70 70
1484 42 c. Ice hockey 70 70
1485 42 c. Bobsleighing 70 70
1486 42 c. Alpine skiing 70 70

602 Ville-Marie in 17th Century

1992. "CANADA 92" International Youth Stamp Exhibition, Montreal. Multicoloured.
1487 42 c. Type **602** 80 80
1488 42 c. Modern Montreal . . . 80 80
1489 48 c. Compass rose, snow shoe and crow's nest of Cartier's ship "Grande Hermine" . . 90 90
1490 84 c. Atlantic map, Aztec "calendar stone" and navigational instrument . . 1·75 2·00

1992. Canadian Rivers (2nd series). As T **592** but horiz. Multicoloured.
1492 42 c. Margaree River . . . . 80 1·00
1493 42 c. West (Eliot) River . . . 80 1·00
1494 42 c. Ottawa River . . . . . 80 1·00
1495 42 c. Niagara River . . . . . 80 1·00
1496 42 c. South Saskatchewan River 80 1·00

603 Road Bed Construction and Route Map

605 Jerry Potts (scout)

1992. 50th Anniv of Alaska Highway.
1497 **603** 42 c. multicoloured. . . 70 70

1992. Olympic Games, Barcelona. As T **601**. Multicoloured.
1498 42 c. Gymnastics . . . . . . 90 1·10
1499 42 c. Athletics . . . . 90 1·10
1500 42 c. Diving . . . . 90 1·10
1501 42 c. Cycling . . . . 90 1·10
1502 42 c. Swimming . . . . . . 90 1·10

1992. Canadian Art (5th series). As T **550**. Multicoloured.
1504 50 c. "Red Nasturtiums" (David Milne) 90 90

1992. Folk Heroes. Multicoloured.
1505 42 c. Type **605** . . . . . . 90 1·00
1506 42 c. Capt. William Jackman and wreck of "Sea Clipper", 1867 . . . . 90 1·00
1507 42 c. Laura Secord (messenger) 90 1·00
1508 42 c. Jos Montferrand (lumberjack) . . . . . . 90 1·00

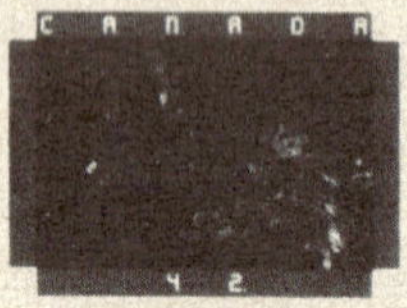

606 Copper

1992. 150th Anniv of Geological Survey of Canada. Minerals. Multicoloured.
1509 42 c. Type **606** . . . . . . 1·00 1·10
1510 42 c. Sodalite . . . . 1·00 1·10
1511 42 c. Gold . . . . 1·00 1·10
1512 42 c. Galena . . . . 1·00 1·10
1513 42 c. Grossular . . . . . . 1·00 1·10

607 Satellite and Photographs from Space

1992. Canadian Space Programme. Multicoloured.
1514 42 c. Type **607** . . . . . . 90 1·00
1515 42 c. Space shuttle over Canada (hologram) (32 × 26 mm) . 90 1·00

608 Babe Siebert, Skates and Stick

609 Companion of the Order of Canada Insignia

1992. 75th Anniv of National Ice Hockey League. Multicoloured.
1516 42 c. Type **608** . . . . . . 95 1·10
1517 42 c. Claude Provost, Terry Sawchuck and team badges 95 1·10
1518 42 c. Hockey mask, gloves and modern player . . . . . 95 1·10

1992. 25th Anniv of the Order of Canada and Daniel Roland Michener (former Governor-General) Commemoration. Multicoloured.
1519 42 c. Type **609** . . . . . . 90 1·00
1520 42 c. Daniel Roland Michener 90 1·00

1992. 50th Anniv of Second World War (4th issue). As T **574**.
1521 42 c. black, silver & brown . 90 1·00
1522 42 c. black, silver & green . . 90 1·00
1523 42 c. black, silver & brown . 90 1·00
1524 42 c. black, silver and blue . 90 1·00
DESIGNS: No. 1521, Reporters and soldier, 1942; 1522, Consolidated Liberator bombers over Newfoundland; 1523 Dieppe raid; 1524, U-boat sinking merchant ship.

610 Estonian Jouluvana

611 Adelaide Hoodless (women's movement pioneer)

1992. Christmas. Multicoloured.
1525 37 c. North American Santa Claus (35 × 21 mm) . . . 70 70
1526 42 c. Type **610** 40 20
1527 48 c. Italian La Befana . . 70 80
1528 84 c. German Weihnachtsmann 1·25 1·50

1993. Prominent Canadian Women. Multicoloured.

1529	43 c. Type **611**	85	85
1530	43 c. Marie-Josephine Gerin-Lajoie (social reformer)	85	85
1531	43 c. Pitseolak Ashoona (Inuit artist)	85	85
1532	43 c. Helen Kinnear (lawyer)	85	85

612 Ice Hockey Players with Cup

613 Coverlet, New Brunswick

1993. Centenary of Stanley Cup.

1533	**612** 43 c. multicoloured	75	60

1993. Hand-crafted Textiles. Multicoloured.

1534	43 c. Type **613**	75	90
1535	43 c. Pieced quilt, Ontario	75	90
1536	43 c. Doukhobor bedcover, Saskatchewan	75	90
1537	43 c. Ceremonial robe, Kwakwaka'wakw	75	90
1538	43 c. Boutonne coverlet, Quebec	75	90

1993. Canadian Art (6th series). As T **550**. Multicoloured.

1539	86 c. "The Owl" (Kenojuak Ashevak)	1·75	2·00

614 Empress Hotel, Victoria

1993. Historic Hotels. Multicoloured.

1540	43 c. Type **614**	60	80
1541	43 c. Banff Springs Hotel	60	80
1542	43 c. Royal York Hotel, Toronto	60	80
1543	43 c. Le Chateau Frontenac, Quebec	60	80
1544	43 c. Algonquin Hotel, St. Andrews	60	80

615 Algonquin Park, Ontario

616 Toronto Skyscrapers

1993. Canada Day. Provincial and Territorial Parks. Multicoloured.

1545	43 c. Type **615**	70	75
1546	43 c. De La Gaspesie Park, Quebec	70	75
1547	43 c. Cedar Dunes Park, Prince Edward Island	70	75
1548	43 c. Cape St. Mary's Seabird Reserve, Newfoundland	70	75
1549	43 c. Mount Robson Park, British Columbia	70	75
1550	43 c. Writing-on-Stone Park, Alberta	70	75
1551	43 c. Spruce Woods Park, Manitoba	70	75
1552	43 c. Herschel Island Park, Yukon	70	75
1553	43 c. Cypress Hills Park, Saskatchewan	70	75
1554	43 c. The Rocks Park, New Brunswick	70	75
1555	43 c. Blomidon Park, Nova Scotia	70	75
1556	43 c. Katannilik Park, Northwest Territories	70	75

1993. Bicentenary of Toronto.

1557	**616** 43 c. multicoloured	70	50

1993. Canadian Rivers (3rd series). As T **592**. Multicoloured.

1558	43 c. Fraser River	60	80
1559	43 c. Yukon River	60	80
1560	43 c. Red River	60	80
1561	43 c. St. Lawrence River	60	80
1562	43 c. St. John River	60	80

618 "The Alberta Homesteader"

1993. Folk Songs. Multicoloured.

1564	43 c. Type **618**	70	85
1565	43 c. "Les Raftmans" (Quebec)	70	85
1566	43 c. "I'se the B'y that Builds the Boat" (Newfoundland)	70	85
1567	43 c. "Onkwa:ri Tenhanonniahkwe" (Mohawk Indian)	70	85

1993. Prehistoric Canada (3rd series). Dinosaurs. As T **582** but 40 × 28 mm. Multicoloured.

1568	43 c. Massospondylus	60	60
1569	43 c. Stryacosaurus	60	60
1570	43 c. Albertosaurus	60	60
1571	43 c. Platecarpus	60	60

619 Polish Swiety Mikolaj

1993. Christmas. Multicoloured.

1572	38 c. North American Santa Claus (35 × 22 mm)	70	20
1573	43 c. Type **619**	50	20
1574	49 c. Russian Ded Moroz	70	70
1575	86 c. Australian Father Christmas	1·10	1·75

1993. 50th Anniv of Second World War (5th issue). As T **574**.

1576	43 c. black, silver and green	90	90
1577	43 c. black, silver and blue	90	90
1578	43 c. black, silver and blue	90	90
1579	43 c. black, silver and brown	90	90

DESIGNS: No. 1576, Loading munitions for Russia, 1943; No. 1577, Loading bombs on Avro Lancaster; No. 1578, Escorts attacking U-boat; No. 1579, Infantry advancing, Italy.

620 (face value at right)

1994. Self-adhesive Greetings stamps. Mult.

1580	43 c. Type **620**	60	70
1581	43 c. As Type **620** but face value at left	60	70

It was intended that the sender should insert an appropriate greetings label into the circular space on each stamp before use.

For 45 c. values in this design see Nos. 1654/5.

621 Jeanne Sauve

1994. Jeanne Sauve (former Governor-General) Commemoration.

1582	**621** 43 c. multicoloured	60	60

622 Timothy Eaton, Toronto Store of 1869 and Merchandise

1994. 125th Anniv of T. Eaton Company Ltd (department store group).

1583	**622** 43 c. multicoloured	55	75

1994. Canadian Rivers (4th series). As T **592**, but horiz. Multicoloured.

1584	43 c. Saguenay River	60	75
1585	43 c. French River	60	75
1586	43 c. Mackenzie River	60	75
1587	43 c. Churchill River	60	75
1588	43 c. Columbia River	60	75

1994. Canadian Art (7th series). As T **550**. Multicoloured.

1589	88 c. "Vera" (detail) (Frederick Varley)	1·25	1·60

623 Lawn Bowls

1994. 15th Commonwealth Games, Victoria. Multicoloured.

1590	43 c. Type **623**	40	50
1591	43 c. Lacrosse	40	50
1592	43 c. Wheelchair race	40	50
1593	43 c. High jumping	40	50
1594	50 c. Diving	45	60
1595	88 c. Cycling	80	95

625 Big Leaf Maple Tree

1994. Canada Day. Maple Trees. Multicoloured.

1597	43 c. Type **625**	60	65
1598	43 c. Sugar maple	60	65
1599	43 c. Silver maple	60	65
1600	43 c. Striped maple	60	65
1601	43 c. Norway maple	60	65
1602	43 c. Manitoba maple	60	65
1603	43 c. Black maple	60	65
1604	43 c. Douglas maple	60	65
1605	43 c. Mountain maple	60	65
1606	43 c. Vine maple	60	65
1607	43 c. Hedge maple	60	65
1608	43 c. Red maple	60	65

626 Billy Bishop (fighter ace) and Nieuport 17

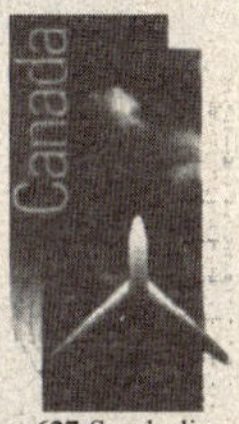

627 Symbolic Aircraft, Radar Screen and Clouds

1994. Birth Centenaries. Multicoloured.

1609	43 c. Type **626**	75	80
1610	43 c. Mary Travers ("La Bolduc") (singer) and musicians	75	80

1994. 50th Anniv of I.C.A.O.

1612	**627** 43 c. multicoloured	60	60

1994. Prehistoric Canada (4th series). Mammals. As T **582**, but 40 × 28 mm. Multicoloured.

1613	43 c. Coryphodon	90	1·00
1614	43 c. Megacerops	90	1·00
1615	43 c. Arctodus simus (bear)	90	1·00
1616	43 c. Mammuthus primigenius (mammoth)	90	1·00

628 Carol Singing around Christmas Tree

629 Flag and Lake

1994. Christmas. Multicoloured.

1617	(–) c. Carol singer (35 × 21 mm)	70	70
1618	43 c. Type **628**	45	20
1619	50 c. Choir (vert)	65	80
1620	88 c. Couple carol singing in snow (vert)	1·60	2·00

No. 1617 is without face value, but was intended for use as a 38 c. on internal greetings cards posted before 31 January 1995. The design shows a barcode at left.

1994. 50th Anniv of Second World War (6th issue). As T **574**.

1621	43 c. black, silver and green	85	85
1622	43 c. black, silver and red	85	85
1623	43 c. black, silver and blue	85	85
1624	43 c. black, silver and grey	85	85

DESIGNS: No. 1621, D-Day landings, Normandy; No. 1622, Canadian artillery, Normandy; No. 1623, Hawker Typhoons on patrol; No. 1624, Canadian infantry and disabled German self-propelled gun, Walcheren.

1995. 50th Anniv of Second World War (7th issue). As T **574**.

1625	43 c. black, silver and purple	90	90
1626	43 c. black, silver and brown	90	90
1627	43 c. black, silver and green	90	90
1628	43 c. black, silver and blue	90	90

DESIGNS: No. 1625, Returning troop ship; 1626, Canadian P.O.W.s celebrating freedom; 1627, Canadian tank liberating Dutch town; 1628, Parachute drop in support of Rhine Crossing.

1995. Canadian Art (8th series). As T **550**. Multicoloured

1629	88 c. "Floraison" (Alfred Pellan)	1·25	1·60

1995. 30th Anniv of National Flag. No face value.

1630	**629** (43 c.) multicoloured	50	50

630 Louisbourg Harbour

1995. 275th Anniv of Fortress of Louisbourg. Multicoloured.

1631	(43 c.) Type **630**	40	55
1632	(43 c.) Barracks (32 × 29 mm)	40	55
1633	(43 c.) King's Bastion (40 × 29 mm)	40	55
1634	(43 c.) Site of King's Garden, convent and hospital (56 × 29 mm)	40	55
1635	(43 c.) Site of coastal fortifications	40	55

631 Banff Springs Golf Club, Alberta

1995. Centenaries of Canadian Amateur Golf Championship and of the Royal Canadian Golf Association. Multicoloured.

1637	43 c. Type **631**	50	60
1638	43 c. Riverside Country Club, New Brunswick	50	60
1639	43 c. Glen Abbey Golf Club, Ontario	50	60
1640	43 c. Victoria Golf Club, British Columbia	50	60
1641	43 c. Royal Montreal Golf Club, Quebec	50	60

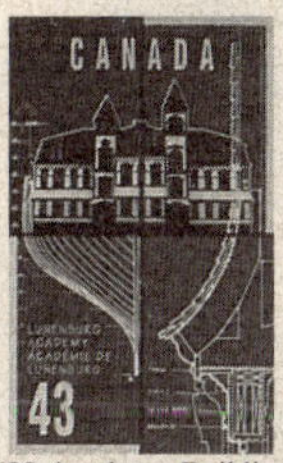

633 Academy Building and Ship Plan

634 Aspects of Manitoba

1995. Centenary of Lunenburg Academy.

1643	**633** 43 c. multicoloured	40	45

1995. 125th Anniv of Manitoba as Canadian Province.

1644	**634** 43 c. multicoloured	40	45

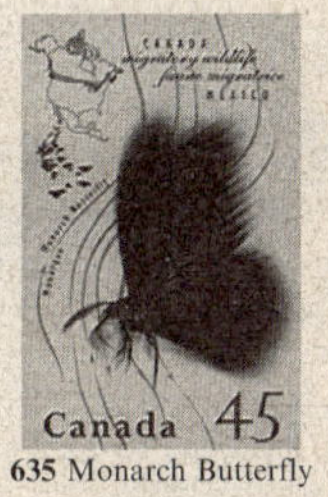

635 Monarch Butterfly

1995. Migratory Wildlife. Multicoloured.

1645	45 c. Type **635**	65	70
1646	45 c. Belted kingfisher*	65	70
1647	45 c. Belted kingfisher*	65	70
1648	45 c. Pintail	65	70
1649	45 c. Hoary bat	65	70

*No. 1646: Inscr "aune migratrice" in error. No. 1647: Inscr corrected to "faune migratrice".

636 Quebec Railway Bridge

1995. 20th World Road Congress, Montreal. Bridges. Multicoloured.

1650	45 c. Type **636**	90	90
1651	45 c. 401-403-410 Interchange, Mississauga	90	90
1652	45 c. Hartland Bridge, New Brunswick	90	90
1653	45 c. Alex Fraser Bridge, British Columbia	90	90

1995. Self-adhesive Greetings stamps. As T **620**. Multicoloured. Imperf.

1654 45 c. Face value at right . . 55 60
1655 45 c. Face value at left . . . 55 60

It is intended the sender should insert an appropriate greetings label into the circular space on each stamp before use.

637 Mountain, Baffin Island, Polar Bear and Caribou

1995. 50th Anniv of Arctic Institute of North America. Multicoloured.

1656 45 c. Type **637** 70 80
1657 45 c. Arctic poppy, Auyuittuq National Park and cargo canoe 70 80
1658 45 c. Inuk man and igloo . . . 70 80
1659 45 c. Ogilvie Mountains, dog team and ski-equipped airplane 70 80
1660 45 c. Inuit children 70 80

638 Superman

640 "The Nativity"

639 Prime Minister MacKenzie King signing U.N. Charter, 1945

1995. Comic Book Superheroes. Multicoloured.

1661 45 c. Type **638** 50 60
1662 45 c. Johnny Canuck 50 60
1663 45 c. Nelvana 50 60
1664 45 c. Captain Canuck 50 60
1665 45 c. Fleur de Lys 50 60

1995. 50th Anniv of United Nations.

1666 **639** 45 c. multicoloured . . . 50 50

1995. Christmas. Sculptured Capitals from Ste.-Anne-de-Beaupre Basilica designed by Emile Brunet (Nos. 1668/70). Multicoloured.

1667 40 c. Sprig of holly (35 × 22 mm) 65 65
1668 45 c. Type **640** 50 20
1669 52 c. "The Annunciation" . . 75 80
1670 90 c. "The Flight to Egypt" . 1·25 1·75

641 World Map and Emblem

1995. 25th Anniv of La Francophonie and The Agency for Cultural and Technical Co-operation.

1671 **641** 45 c. multicoloured . . . 50 50

642 Concentration Camp Victims, Uniform and Identity Card

1995. 50th Anniv of the End of The Holocaust.

1672 **642** 45 c. multicoloured . . . 50 50

643 American Kestrel

1996. Birds (1st series). Multicoloured.

1673 45 c. Type **643** 70 70
1674 45 c. Atlantic puffin 70 70
1675 45 c. Pileated woodpecker . . 70 70
1676 45 c. Ruby-throated hummingbird 70 70

See also Nos. 1717/20, 1779/82 and 1865/8.

644 "Louis R. Desmarais" (tanker), Three-dimensional Map and Radar Screen

1996. High Technology Industries. Multicoloured.

1677 45 c. Type **644** 65 70
1678 45 c. Canadair Challenger 601-3R, jet engine and navigational aid 65 70
1679 45 c. Map of North America and eye 65 70
1680 45 c. Genetic engineering experiment and Canola (plant) 65 70

1996. Canadian Art (9th series). As T **550**. Multicoloured.

1681 90 c. "The Spirit of Haida Gwaii" (sculpture) (Bill Reid) 1·40 1·75

645 "One World, One Hope" (Joe Average)

1996. 11th International Conference on AIDS, Vancouver.

1682 **645** 45 c. multicoloured . . 70 70

646 Skookum Jim Mason and Bonanza Creek

1996. Centenary of Yukon Gold Rush. Multicoloured.

1685 45 c. Type **646** 60 60
1686 45 c. Prospector and boats on Lake Laberge 60 60
1687 45 c. Superintendent Sam Steele (N.W.M.P.) and U.S.A.–Canada border 60 60
1688 45 c. Dawson saloon 60 60
1689 45 c. Miner with rocker box and sluice 60 60

647 Patchwork Quilt Maple Leaf

648 Ethel Catherwood (high jump), 1928

1996. Canada Day. Self-adhesive. Imperf.

1690 **647** 45 c. multicoloured . . . 50 50

1996. Canadian Olympic Gold Medal Winners. Multicoloured.

1691 45 c. Type **648** 55 60
1692 45 c. Etienne Desmarteau (56lb weight throw), 1904 . . . 55 60
1693 45 c. Fanny Rosenfeld (400 metres relay), 1928 . . . . 55 60
1694 45 c. Gerald Ouellette (small bore rifle, prone), 1956 . . 55 60
1695 45 c. Percy Williams (100 and 200 metres), 1928 . . . . 55 60

649 Indian Totems, City Skyline, Forest and Mountains

650 Canadian Heraldic Symbols

1996. 125th Anniv of British Columbia.

1696 **649** 45 c. multicoloured . . . 50 50

1996. 22nd International Congress of Genealogical and Heraldic Sciences, Ottawa.

1697 **650** 45 c. multicoloured . . . 50 50

652 Interlocking Jigsaw Pieces and Hands

1996. Literacy Campaign.

1699 **652** 45 c. + 5 c. mult . . . 60 65

653 Edouard Montpetit and Montreal University

1996. Edouard Montpetit (academic) Commem.

1700 **653** 45 c. multicoloured . . . 50 50

654 Winnie and Lt. Colebourn, 1914

1996. Stamp Collecting Month. Winnie the Pooh. Multicoloured.

1701 45 c. Type **654** 60 60
1702 45 c. Christopher Robin Milne and teddy bear, 1925 . . . 60 60
1703 45 c. Illustration from "Winnie the Pooh", 1926 . . . . . 60 60
1704 45 c. Winnie the Pooh at Walt Disney World, 1996 . . . 60 60

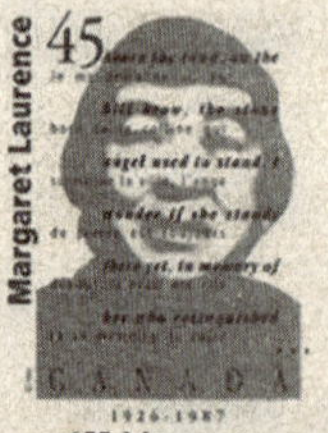

655 Margaret Laurence

656 Children tobogganing

1996. Canadian Authors.

1706 **655** 45 c. multicoloured . . . 60 65
1707 – 45 c. black, grey and red 60 65
1708 – 45 c. multicoloured . . . 60 65
1709 – 45 c. multicoloured . . . 60 65
1710 – 45 c. multicoloured . . . 60 65

DESIGNS: No. 1707, Donald G. Creighton; 1708, Gabrielle Roy; 1709, Felix-Antoine Savard; 1710, Thomas C. Haliburton.

1996. Christmas. 50th Anniv of U.N.I.C.E.F. Multicoloured.

1711 45 c. Type **656** 50 20
1712 52 c. Father Christmas skiing 60 70
1713 90 c. Couple ice-skating . . . 90 1·25

657 Head of Ox

659 Abbe Charles-Emile Gadbois

658 Man and Boy with Bike, and A. J. and J. W. Billes (company founders)

1997. Chinese New Year ("Year of the Ox").

1714 **657** 45 c. multicoloured . . . 85 90

1997. Birds (2nd series). As T **643**. Multicoloured.

1717 45 c. Mountain bluebird . . . 65 65
1718 45 c. Western grebe 65 65
1719 45 c. Northern gannet . . . 65 65
1720 45 c. Scarlet tanager 65 65

1997. Canadian Art (10th series). As T **550**. Multicoloured.

1721 90 c. "York Boat on Lake Winnipeg, 1930" (Walter Phillips) . . . . 1·00 1·25

1997. 75th Anniv of the Canadian Tire Corporation.

1722 **658** 45 c. multicoloured . . 50 50

1997. Abbe Charles-Emile Gadbois (musicologist) Commemoration.

1723 **659** 45 c. multicoloured . . 50 50

660 Blue Poppy

662 Osgoode Hall and Seal of Law School

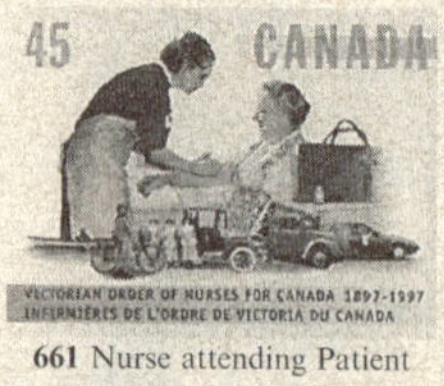

661 Nurse attending Patient

1997. "Quebec in Bloom" International Floral Festival.

1724 **660** 45 c. multicoloured . . 35 40

1997. Centenary of Victorian Order of Nurses.

1725 **661** 45 c. multicoloured . . 50 50

1997. Bicentenary of Law Society of Upper Canada.

1726 **662** 45 c. multicoloured . . 50 50

663 Great White Shark

1997. Ocean Fishes. Multicoloured.

1727 45 c. Type **663** 60 60
1728 45 c. Pacific halibut 60 60
1729 45 c. Common sturgeon . . . 60 60
1730 45 c. Blue-finned tuna . . . 60 60

664 Lighthouse and Confederation Bridge

1997. Opening of Confederation Bridge, Northumberland Strait. Multicoloured.

1731 45 c. Type **664** 65 65
1732 45 c. Confederation Bridge and great blue heron 65 65

665 Gilles Villeneuve in Ferrari T-3

1997. 15th Death Anniv of Gilles Villeneuve (racing car driver). Multicoloured.

1733 45 c. Type **665** 60 60
1734 90 c. Villeneuve in Ferrari T-4 1·25 1·25

666 Globe and the "Matthew"

1997. 500th Anniv of John Cabot's Discovery of North America.

1736 **666** 45 c. multicoloured . . 50 50

667 Sea to Sky Highway, British Columbia, and Skier

1997. Scenic Highways (1st series). Multicoloured.

1737 45 c. Type **667** 60 60
1738 45 c. Cabot Trail, Nova Scotia, and rug-making 60 60
1739 45 c. Wine route, Ontario, and glasses of wine 60 60
1740 45 c. Highway 34, Saskatchewan, and cowboy 60 60

See also Nos. 1810/13 and 1876/9.

668 Kettle, Ski-bike, Lounger and Plastic Cases

1997. 20th Congress of International Council of Societies for Industrial Design.

1741 **668** 45 c. multicoloured . . 50 50

669 Caber Thrower, Bagpiper, Drummer and Highland Dancer

1997. 50th Anniv of Glengarry Highland Games, Ontario.

1742 **669** 45 c. multicoloured . . 50 50

670 Knights of Columbus Emblem

1997. Centenary of Knights of Columbus (welfare charity) in Canada.

1743 **670** 45 c. multicoloured . . 50 50

671 Postal and Telephone Workers with P.T.T.I. Emblem

1997. 28th World Congress of Postal, Telegraph and Telephone International Staff Federation, Montreal.

1744 **671** 45 c. multicoloured . . 50 50

672 C.Y.A.P. Logo

1997. Canada's Year of Asia Pacific.

1745 **672** 45 c. multicoloured . . 50 50

673 Paul Henderson celebrating Goal

1997. 25th Anniv of Canada–U.S.S.R. Ice Hockey Series. Multicoloured.

1746 45 c. Type **673** 35 40
1747 45 c. Canadian team celebrating 35 40

674 Martha Black

1997. Federal Politicians. Multicoloured.

1748 45 c. Type **674** 35 40
1749 45 c. Lionel Chevrier 35 40
1750 45 c. Judy LaMarsh 35 40
1751 45 c. Real Caouette 35 40

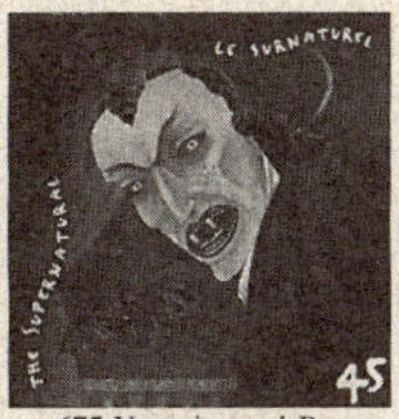

675 Vampire and Bat

1997. The Supernatural. Centenary of Publication of Bram Stoker's "Dracula". Multicoloured.

1752 45 c. Type **675** 35 40
1753 45 c. Werewolf 35 40
1754 45 c. Ghost 35 40
1755 45 c. Goblin 35 40

676 Grizzly Bear

1997. Mammals. Multicoloured.

1756 $1 Loon (47 × 39 mm) . . . 80 85
1757 $2 Polar bear (47 × 39 mm) . 1·60 1·75
1758 $3 Type **676** . . . . 6·50 6·75

677 "Our Lady of the Rosary" (detail, Holy Rosary Cathedral, Vancouver)

1997. Christmas. Stained Glass Windows. Multicoloured.

1763 45 c. Type **677** 30 40
1764 52 c. "Nativity" (detail, Leith United Church, Ontario) . 40 45
1765 90 c. "Life of the Blessed Virgin" (detail, St. Stephen's Ukrainian Catholic Church, Calgary) 75 80

678 Livestock and Produce

1997. 75th Anniv of Royal Agricultural Winter Fair, Toronto.

1766 **678** 45 c. multicoloured . . 35 40

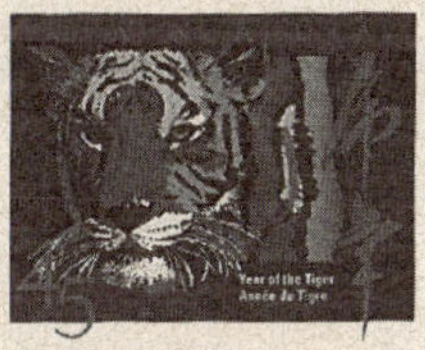

679 Tiger

1998. Chinese New Year ("Year of the Tiger").

1767 **679** 45 c. multicoloured . . 35 40

680 John Robarts (Ontario, 1961–71)

681 Maple Leaf

1998. Canadian Provincial Premiers. Multicoloured.

1769 45 c. Type **680** 35 40
1770 45 c. Jean Lesage (Quebec, 1960–66) 35 40
1771 45 c. John McNair (New Brunswick, 1940–52) . . . 35 40
1772 45 c. Tommy Douglas (Saskatchewan, 1944–61) . 35 40
1773 45 c. Joseph Smallwood (Newfoundland, 1949–72) . 35 40
1774 45 c. Angus MacDonald (Nova Scotia, 1933–40, 1945–54) 35 40
1775 45 c. W. A. C. Bennett (British Columbia, 1960–66) 35 40
1776 45 c. Ernest Manning (Alberta, 1943–68) 35 40
1777 45 c. John Bracken (Manitoba, 1922–43) 35 40
1778 45 c. J. Walter Jones (Prince Edward Island, 1943–53) . 35 40

1998. Birds (3rd series). As T **643**. Multicoloured.

1779 45 c. Hairy woodpecker . . . 35 40
1780 45 c. Great crested flycatcher 35 40
1781 45 c. Eastern screech-owl . . 35 40
1782 45 c. Gray-crowned rosy-finch 35 40

1998. Self-adhesive Automatic Cash Machine Stamps. Imperf.

1783 **681** 45 c. multicoloured . . . 35 40

For stamps in this design, but without "POSTAGE POSTES" at top left see Nos. 1836/40.

682 Coquihalla Orange Fly

1998. Fishing Flies. Multicoloured.

1784 45 c. Type **682** 35 40
1785 45 c. Steelhead Bee 35 40
1786 45 c. Dark Montreal 35 40
1787 45 c. Lady Amherst 35 40
1788 45 c. Coho Blue 35 40
1789 45 c. Cosseboom Special . . . 35 40

683 Mineral Excavation, Oil Rig and Pickaxe

684 1898 2 c. Imperial Penny Postage Stamp and Postmaster General Sir William Mulock

1998. Centenary of Canadian Institute of Mining, Metallurgy and Petoleum.

1790 **683** 45 c. multicoloured . . . 35 40

1998. Centenary of Imperial Penny Postage.

1791 **684** 45 c. multicoloured . . . 35 40

685 Two Sumo Wrestlers

1998. 1st Canadian Sumo Basho (tournament), Vancouver. Multicoloured.

1792 45 c. Type **685** 35 40
1793 45 c. Sumo wrestler in ceremonial ritual 35 40

686 St. Peters Canal, Nova Scotia

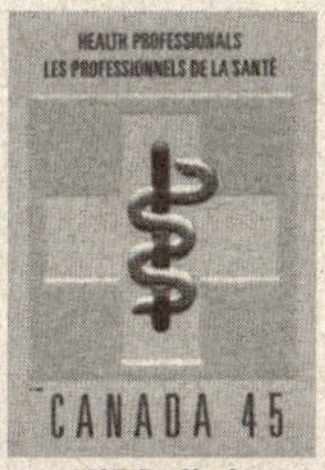

687 Staff of Aesculapius and Cross

1998. Canadian Canals. Multicoloured.

1795 45 c. Type **686** 35 40
1796 45 c. St. Ours Canal, Quebec 35 40
1797 45 c. Port Carling Lock, Ontario 35 40
1798 45 c. Lock on Rideau Canal, Ontario 35 40
1799 45 c. Towers and platform of Peterborough Lift Lock, Trent–Severn Waterway, Ontario 35 40
1800 45 c. Chambly Canal, Quebec 35 40
1801 45 c. Lachine Canal, Quebec 35 40
1802 45 c. Rideau Canal in winter, Ontario 35 40
1803 45 c. Boat on Big Chute incline railway, Trent–Severn Waterway, Ontario . . . 35 40
1804 45 c. Sault Ste. Marie Canal, Ontario 35 40

1998. Canadian Health Professionals.

1805 **687** 45 c. multicoloured . . 35 40

688 Policeman of 1873 and Visit to Indian Village

1998. 125th Anniv of Royal Canadian Mounted Police. Multicoloured.

1806 45 c. Type **688** 35 40
1807 45 c. Policewoman of 1998 and aspects of modern law enforcement 35 40

689 William J. Roue (designer) and "Bluenose" (schooner)

1998. William James Roue (naval architect) Commemoration.

1809 **689** 45 c. multicoloured . . 35 40

1998. Scenic Highways (2nd series). As T **667**. Multicoloured.

1810 45 c. Dempster Highway, Yukon, and caribou . . . 35 40
1811 45 c. Dinosaur Trail, Alberta, and skeleton 35 40
1812 45 c. River Valley Drive, New Brunswick, and fern . . . 35 40
1813 45 c. Blue Heron Route, Prince Edward Island, and lobster 35 40

690 "Painting" (Jean-Paul Riopelle)

691 Napoleon-Alexandre Comeau (naturalist)

1998. 50th Anniv of "Refus Global" (manifesto of The Automatistes group of artists). Multicoloured. Self-adhesive. Imperf.

1814 45 c. Type **690** 35 40
1815 45 c. "La derniere campagne de Napoleon" (Fernand Leduc) (37 × 31½ mm) 35 40
1816 45 c. "Jet fuligineux sur noir torture" (Jean-Paul Mousseau) 35 40
1817 45 c. "Le fond du garde-robe" (Pierre Gauvreau) (29½ × 42 mm) 35 40
1818 45 c. "Joie lacustre" (Paul-Emile Borduas) 35 40
1819 45 c. "Seafarers Union" (Marcelle Ferron) (36 × 34 mm) 35 40
1820 45 c. "Le tumulte a la machoire crispee" (Marcel Barbeau) (36 × 34 mm) 35 40

1998. Legendary Canadians. Multicoloured.

1821 45 c. Type **691** 35 40
1822 45 c. Phyllis Munday (mountaineer) 35 40
1823 45 c. Bill Mason (film-maker) 35 40
1824 45 c. Harry Red Foster (sports commentator) 35 40

1998. Canadian Art (11th series). As T **550**. Multicoloured.

1825 90 c. "The Farmer's Family" (Bruno Bobak) 70 75

692 Indian Wigwam

1998. Canadian Houses. Multicoloured.

1826	45 c. Type **692**	35	40
1827	45 c. Settler sod hut	35	40
1828	45 c. Maison Saint-Gabriel (17th-century farmhouse), Quebec	35	40
1829	45 c. Queen Anne style brick house, Ontario	35	40
1830	45 c. Terrace of town houses	35	40
1831	45 c. Prefabricated house	35	40
1832	45 c. Veterans' houses	35	40
1833	45 c. Modern bungalow	35	40
1834	45 c. Healthy House, Toronto	35	40

693 University of Ottawa

1998. 150th Anniv of University of Ottawa.

1835	**693**	45 c. multicoloured	35	40

1998. As T **681**, but without "POSTAGE POSTES" at top left. Self-adhesive gum, imperf (46 c.) or ordinary gum, perf (others).

1839	**681**	45 c. multicoloured	35	40
1840		46 c. multicoloured	35	40
1836		55 c. multicoloured	45	50
1837		73 c. multicoloured	60	65
1838		95 c. multicoloured	75	80

694 Performing Animals

1998. Canadian Circus. Multicoloured.

1851	45 c. Type **694**	35	40
1852	45 c. Flying trapeze and acrobat on horseback	35	40
1853	45 c. Lion tamer	35	40
1854	45 c. Acrobats and trapeze artists	35	40

695 John Peters Humphrey (author of original Declaration draft)

1998. 50th Anniv of Universal Declaration of Human Rights.

1856	**695**	45 c. multicoloured	35	40

696 H.M.C.S. "Sackville" (corvette)

1998. 75th Anniv of Canadian Naval Reserve. Multicoloured.

1857	45 c. Type **696**	35	40
1858	45 c. H.M.C.S. "Shawinigan" (coastal defence vessel)	35	40

697 Angel blowing Trumpet

698 Rabbit

1998. Christmas. Statues of Angels. Multicoloured.

1859	45 c. Type **697**	35	40
1860	52 c. Adoring Angel	40	45
1861	90 c. Angel at prayer	70	75

1999. Chinese New Year ("Year of the Rabbit").

1862	**698**	46 c. multicoloured	35	40

699 Stylised Mask and Curtain

701 "Marco Polo" (full-rigged ship)

700 "The Raven and the First Men" (B. Reid) and The Great Hall

1999. 50th Anniv of Le Theatre du Rideau Vert.

1864	**699**	46 c. multicoloured	35	40

1999. Birds (4th series). As T **643**. Multicoloured. Ordinary or self-adhesive gum.

1865	46 c. Northern goshawk	35	40
1866	46 c. Red-winged blackbird	35	40
1867	46 c. American goldfinch	35	40
1868	46 c. Sandhill crane	35	40

1999. 50th Anniv of University of British Columbia Museum of Anthropology.

1873	**700**	46 c. multicoloured	35	40

1999. Canada–Australia Joint Issue. "Marco Polo" (emigrant ship).

1874	**701**	46 c. multicoloured	35	40

1999. Scenic Highways (3rd series). As T **667**. Multicoloured.

1876	46 c. Route 132, Quebec, and hang-glider	35	40
1877	46 c. Yellowhead Highway, Manitoba, and bison	35	40
1878	46 c. Dempster Highway, Northwest Territories, and Indian village elder	35	40
1879	46 c. The Discovery Trail, Newfoundland, and whale's tailfin	35	40

702 Inuit Children and Landscape

1999. Creation of Nunavut Territory.

1880	**702**	46 c. multicoloured	35	40

703 Elderly Couple on Country Path

1999. International Year of Older Persons.

1881	**703**	46 c. multicoloured	35	40

OFFICIAL STAMPS

1949. Optd **O.H.M.S.**

O162	**111**	1 c. green (postage)	1·75	2·00
O163	**112**	2 c. brown	12·00	12·00
O164	–	3 c. purple (No. 378)	1·25	1·10
O165	**112**	4 c. red	2·00	80
O166	–	10 c. green (No. 402)	3·75	15
O167	–	14 c. brown (No. 403)	4·50	1·75
O168	–	20 c. grey (No. 404)	12·00	60
O169	–	50 c. green (No. 405)	£160	£120
O170	–	$1 purple (No. 406)	45·00	45·00
O171	–	7 c. blue (No. 407) (air)	24·00	7·00

1949. Optd **O.H.M.S.**

O172	**135**	1 c. green	85	85
O173	–	2 c. brown (No. 415)	1·75	1·50
O174	–	3 c. purple (No. 416)	1·00	70
O175	–	4 c. red (No. 417)	1·50	15
O176	–	5 c. blue (No. 418)	2·50	2·00
O177	**141**	50 c. green	32·00	28·00

1950. Optd **G.**

O178	**135**	1 c. green (postage)	70	10
O179	–	2 c. brown (No. 415)	1·50	1·60
O180	–	2 c. green (No. 415a)	1·75	10
O181	–	3 c. purple (No. 416)	1·50	10
O182	–	4 c. red (No. 417)	1·50	30
O184	–	5 c. blue (No. 418)	2·50	30
O193	**153**	7 c. blue	1·40	1·40
O185	–	10 c. green (No. 402)	3·00	10
O191	**142**	10 c. purple	2·25	10
O186	–	14 c. brown (No. 403)	11·00	2·25
O187	–	20 c. grey (No. 404)	15·00	20
O194	–	20 c. grey (No. 441)	1·60	10
O188	**141**	50 c. green	10·00	8·00
O189	–	$1 purple (No. 406)	60·00	55·00
O192	–	$1 blue (No. 433)	55·00	60·00
O190	–	7 c. blue (No. 407) (air)	24·00	12·00

1953. First Queen Elizabeth II stamps optd **G.**

O196	**158**	1 c. brown	15	10
O197		2 c. green	20	10
O198		3 c. red	20	10
O199		4 c. violet	30	10
O200		5 c. blue	30	10

1953. Pictorial stamps optd **G.**

O206	**165**	10 c. brown	40	10
O207	–	20 c. green (No. 488)	1·75	10
O201	**160**	50 c. green	3·00	1·75
O195	**154**	$1 black	10·00	11·00

1955. Second Queen Elizabeth II stamps optd **G.**

O202	**161**	1 c. brown	20	20
O203		2 c. green	15	10
O204		4 c. violet	40	10
O205		5 c. blue	15	10

1963. Third Queen Elizabeth II stamps optd **G.**

O208	**215**	1 c. brown	40	3·75
O209		2 c. green	40	3·50
O210		4 c. red	40	1·75
O211		5 c. blue	40	90

OFFICIAL SPECIAL DELIVERY STAMPS

1950. Optd **O.H.M.S.**

OS20	–	10 c. green (No. S15)	17·00	21·00

1950. Optd **G.**

OS21	–	10 c. green (No. S15)	26·00	27·00

POSTAGE DUE STAMPS

D 1

D 2

1906.

D1	**D 1**	1 c. violet	8·00	2·50
D4		2 c. violet	14·00	1·25
D5		4 c. violet	45·00	50·00
D7		5 c. violet	22·00	2·50
D8		10 c. violet	32·00	16·00

1930.

D 9	**D 2**	1 c. violet	8·50	10·00
D10		2 c. violet	7·50	1·60
D11		4 c. violet	15·00	6·50
D12		5 c. violet	15·00	25·00
D13		10 c. violet	65·00	26·00

D 3

D 4

1933.

D14	**D 3**	1 c. violet	9·00	13·00
D15		2 c. violet	6·50	4·00
D16		4 c. violet	11·00	12·00
D17		10 c. violet	23·00	27·00

1935.

D18	**D 4**	1 c. violet	60	10
D19		2 c. violet	60	10
D20		3 c. violet	3·50	5·00
D21		4 c. violet	1·50	10
D22		5 c. violet	3·00	65
D23		6 c. violet	1·50	3·00
D24		10 c. violet	60	10

D 5

1967. (a) Size 21 × 17 mm.

D25	**D 5**	1 c. red	1·75	3·50
D26		2 c. red	1·00	80
D27		3 c. red	1·00	4·00
D28		4 c. red	2·50	1·25
D29		5 c. red	3·75	3·25
D30		6 c. red	1·60	3·75
D31		10 c. red	2·00	2·50

(b) Size 20 × 15½ mm.

D32	**D 5**	1 c. red	30	30
D33		2 c. red	75	2·00
D34		3 c. red	2·50	3·00
D35		4 c. red	30	40
D36a		5 c. red	30	1·50
D37		6 c. red	2·75	3·50
D38		8 c. red	30	45
D39		10 c. red	30	45
D40		12 c. red	40	50
D41		16 c. red	80	2·75
D42		20 c. red	40	1·25
D43		24 c. red	40	1·75
D44		50 c. red	60	2·25

REGISTRATION STAMPS

R 1

1875.

R1	**R 1**	2 c. orange	60·00	1·00
R6		5 c. green	80·00	1·00
R8		8 c. blue	£325	£225

SPECIAL DELIVERY STAMPS

S 1

1898.

S2	**S 1**	10 c. green	45·00	5·50

S 2

1922.

S4	**S 2**	20 c. red	35·00	5·50

S 3 Mail-carrying, 1867 and 1927

1927. 60th Anniv of Confederation.

S5	**S 3**	20 c. orange	11·00	10·00

S 4

1930.

S6	**S 4**	20 c. red	40·00	7·00

1932. As Type **S 4**, but inscr "CENTS" instead of "TWENTY CENTS".

S7	–	20 c. red	45·00	12·00

S 5 Allegory of Progress

1935.

S8	S **5**	20 c. red	3·50	2·50

S **6** Canadian Coat of Arms

1938.

S 9	S **6**	10 c. green	18·00	3·00
S10		20 c. red	40·00	23·00

1939. Surch **10 10** and bars.

S11	S **6**	10 c. on 20 c. red	9·00	8·00

S **8** Coat of Arms and Flags

S **9** Lockheed Lodestar

1942.

S12	S **8**	10 c. green (postage)	4·25	30
S13	S **9**	16 c. blue (air)	4·00	45
S14		17 c. blue	4·00	55

1946.

S15	10 c. green (postage)	2·00	30
S16	17 c. blue (air)	4·00	3·50

DESIGNS: 10 c. As Type S **8** but with wreath of leaves; 17 c. As Type S **9** but with Canadair DC-4M North Star airplane.

CAPE OF GOOD HOPE

Formerly a British Colony, later the southernmost province of the Union of South Africa.

12 pence = 1 shilling;
20 shillings = 1 pound

1 "Hope"

1853. Imperf.

18	**1**	1d. red	£110	£225
19		4d. blue	£110	48·00
20		6d. lilac	£150	£450
8a		1s. green	£225	£500

3

1861. Imperf.

13	**3**	1d. red	£14000	£2250
14		4d. blue	£10000	£1600

4 "Hope" seated, with vine and ram (with outer frame-line)

6 (No outer frame-line)

1864. With outer frame line. Perf.

23a	**4**	1d. red	80·00	16·00
24		4d. blue	95·00	2·25
52a		6d. purple	5·00	15
53a		1s. green	48·00	30

1868. Surch.

32	**4**	1d. on 6d. violet	£375	70·00
33		1d. on 1s. green	55·00	30·00
34	**6**	3d. on 4d. blue	85·00	1·25
27	**4**	4d. on 6d. violet	£180	15·00

1880. No outer frame line.

48	**6**	½d. black	2·25	10
49		1d. red	2·25	10
36		3d. pink	£160	19·00
43		3d. purple	6·50	90
51		4d. blue	6·00	20
54		5s. orange	55·00	3·50

1880. Surch **THREEPENCE**.

35	**6**	3d. on 4d. pink	55·00	1·75

1880. Surch **3**.

37	**6**	"3" on 3d. pink	60·00	85

1882. Surch **One Half-penny.**

47	**6**	½d. on 3d. purple	17·00	2·25

1882.

61	**6**	½d. green	1·50	10
62		2d. brown	2·00	10
56		2½d. olive	4·25	10
63a		2½d. blue	3·00	10
64		3d. mauve	4·00	50
65		4d. olive	3·50	80
66		1s. green	45·00	2·25
67		1s. yellow	7·00	90

On the 2½d. stamps the value is in a white square at upper right-hand corner as well as at foot.

1891. Surch **2½d.**

55a	**6**	2½d. on 3d. mauve	2·75	20

1893. Surch **ONE PENNY.**

57a	**6**	1d. on 2d. brown	1·40	30

17 "Hope" standing. Table Bay in background

18 Table Mountain and Bay and Arms of the Colony

19

1893.

58	**17**	½d. green	90	10
59a		1d. red	55	10
60		3d. mauve	4·00	75

1900.

69	**18**	1d. red	1·50	10

1902. Various frames.

70	**19**	½d. green	1·25	10
71		1d. red	1·25	10
72		2d. brown	6·00	65
73		2½d. blue	2·75	6·00
74		3d. purple	6·00	30
75		4d. green	5·00	55
76		6d. mauve	10·00	30
77		1s. yellow	10·00	65
78		5s. orange	60·00	8·50

CAYES OF BELIZE

A chain of several hundred islands, coral atolls, reefs and sandbanks stretching along the eastern seaboard of Belize.

The following issues for the Cayes of Belize fall outside the criteria for full listing as detailed on page viii.

100 cents = 1 dollar

APPENDIX

1984.

Marine Life, Map and Views, 1, 2, 5, 10, 15, 25, 75 c., $3, $5.

250th Anniv of "Lloyd's List" (newspaper). 25, 75 c., $1, $2.

Olympic Games, Los Angeles. 10, 15, 75 c., $2.

90th Anniv of "Caye Service" Local Stamps. 10, 15, 75 c., $2.

1985.

Birth Bicent of John J. Audubon (ornithologist). 25, 75 c., $1, $3.

Shipwrecks. $1 × 4.

CAYMAN ISLANDS

A group of islands in the British West Indies. A dependency of Jamaica until August 1962, when it became a Crown Colony.

1900. 12 pence = 1 shilling;
20 shillings = 1 pound.
1969. 100 cents = 1 Jamaican dollar.

1

2

1900.

1a	**1**	½d. green	3·50	12·00
2		1d. red	2·50	1·75

1902.

8	**2**	½d. green	4·50	6·00
4		1d. red	8·50	7·50
10		2½d. blue	4·50	3·00
13		4d. brown and blue	27·00	48·00
11		6d. brown	16·00	35·00
14		6d. olive and red	27·00	55·00
12		1s. orange	32·00	48·00
15		1s. violet and green	45·00	65·00
16		5s. orange and green	£170	£275

1907. Surch **One Halfpenny.**

17	**2**	½d. on 1d. red	38·00	55·00

1907. Surch.

18	**2**	½d. on 5s. orange and green	£225	£300
19		1d. on 5s. orange and green	£225	£300
35		2½d. on 4d. brown and blue	£1500	£2250

11

8

1907.

38	**11**	¼d. brown	90	30
25	**8**	½d. green	1·50	3·50
26		1d. red	1·00	65
27		2½d. blue	2·75	3·50
28		3d. purple on yellow	2·75	6·50
29		4d. black and red on yellow	48·00	65·00
30		6d. purple	7·50	30·00
31		1s. black on green	5·50	18·00
32		5s. green and red on yellow	35·00	55·00
34		10s. green and red on green	£160	£225

12

19

1912.

40	**12**	¼d. brown	60	30
41		½d. green	2·50	4·25
42		1d. red	3·25	2·25
43		2d. grey	80	8·00
44		2½d. blue	7·00	9·00
45a		3d. purple on yellow	3·25	7·50
46		4d. black and red on yellow	75	8·00
47		6d. purple	3·50	6·50
48a		1s. black on green	2·75	3·00
49		2s. purple and blue on blue	9·50	45·00
50		3s. green and violet	19·00	60·00
51		5s. green and red on yellow	70·00	£140
52a		10s. green and red on green	80·00	£140

1917. Surch **1½d.** with **WAR STAMP.** in two lines.

54	**12**	1½d. on 2½d. blue	1·40	4·50

1917. Optd or surch as last, but with **WAR STAMP** in one line and without full point.

57	**12**	½d. green	20	1·75
58		1½d. on 2d. grey	1·25	6·50
56		1½d. on 2½d. blue	20	40
59		1½d. on 2½d. orange	60	80

1921.

69	**19**	¼d. brown	40	1·25
70		½d. green	50	30
71		1d. red	1·10	85
72		1½d. brown	1·75	30
73		2d. grey	1·75	3·50
74		2½d. blue	50	45
75		3d. purple on yellow	50	3·00
62		4d. red on yellow	80	3·75
76		4½d. green	1·75	3·00
77		6d. red	5·50	28·00
63		1s. black on green	1·25	8·50
80		2s. violet on blue	14·00	19·00
81		3s. violet	23·00	16·00
82		5s. green on yellow	24·00	42·00
83		10s. red on green	55·00	75·00

20 Kings William IV and George V

1932. Centenary of "Assembly of Justices and Vestry".

84	**20**	¼d. brown	1·25	90
85		½d. green	2·50	7·00
86		1d. red	2·50	5·50
87		1½d. orange	2·00	2·00
88		2d. grey	2·00	2·50
89		2½d. blue	2·00	1·25
90		3d. green	2·50	4·00
91		6d. purple	8·50	19·00
92		1s. black and brown	16·00	28·00
93		2s. black and blue	42·00	70·00
94		5s. black and green	80·00	£120
95		10s. black and red	£250	£350

21 Cayman Islands

1935.

96	**21**	¼d. black and brown	30	80
97	–	½d. blue and green	1·00	1·00
98	–	1d. blue and red	3·00	2·25
99	–	1½d. black and orange	1·50	1·75
100	–	2d. blue and purple	3·50	1·10
101	–	2½d. blue and black	3·00	1·25
102	**21**	3d. black and green	2·00	3·00
103	–	6d. purple and black	8·50	4·00
104	–	1s. blue and orange	6·00	6·50
105	–	2s. blue and black	45·00	32·00
106	–	5s. green and black	48·00	48·00
107	–	10s. black and red	70·00	85·00

DESIGNS—HORIZ: ½d., 2d., 1s. Cat boat; 1d., 2s. Red-footed Booby birds; 2½d., 6d., 5s. Hawksbill turtles. VERT: 1½d., 10s. Queen or pink conch shells and coconut palms.

1935. Silver Jubilee. As T **13** of Antigua.

108	½d. black and green	15	60
109	2½d. brown and blue	1·00	1·00
110	6d. blue and olive	1·00	3·00
111	1s. grey and purple	6·00	6·00

1937. Coronation. As T **2** of Aden.

112	½d. green	30	40
113	1d. red	50	20
114	2½d. blue	95	40

26 Beach View

30 Hawksbill Turtles

1938.

115a **26** ¼d. orange 10 55
116 – ½d. green 75 55
117 – 1d. red 30 75
118 **26** 1½d. black 30 10
119a **30** 2d. violet 60 30
120 – 2½d. blue 40 20
120a – 2½d. orange 1·75 50
121 – 3d. orange 40 15
121a – 3d. blue 1·75 30
122a **30** 6d. olive 2·00 1·25
123 – 1s. brown 4·50 1·50
124a **26** 2s. green 25·00 9·00
125 – 5s. red 32·00 15·00
126a **30** 10s. brown 21·00 9·00

DESIGNS—HORIZ: ½d., 1s. Caribbean dolphin; 1d., 3d. Map of Islands; 2½d., 5s. "Rembro" (schooner).

1946. Victory. As T **9** of Aden.

127 1½d. black 20 10
128 3d. yellow 20 10

1948. Silver Wedding. As T **10/11** of Aden.

129 ½d. green 10 10
130 10s. blue 13·00 10·00

1949. U.P.U. As T **20/25** of Antigua.

131 2½d. orange 30 30
132 3d. blue 1·50 1·25
133 6d. olive 60 1·25
134 1s. brown 60 30

31 Cat Boat

44 South Sound Lighthouse, Grand Cayman

1950.

135 **31** ¼d. blue and red 15 60
136 – ½d. violet and green 15 1·25
137 – 1d. olive and blue 60 75
138 – 1½d. green and brown 30 75
139 – 2d. violet and red 1·00 1·50
140 – 2½d. blue and black 50 60
141 – 3d. green and blue 1·40 1·50
142 – 6d. brown and blue 2·00 1·25
143 – 9d. red and green 4·00 2·00
144 – 1s. brown and orange 3·25 2·75
145 – 2s. violet and purple 7·50 8·50
146 – 5s. olive and violet 12·00 7·00
147 – 10s. black and red 14·00 13·00

DESIGNS: ½d. Coconut grove, Cayman Brac; 1d. Green turtle; 1½d. Making thatch rope; 2d. Cayman seamen; 2½d. Map; 3d. Parrotfish; 6d. Bluff, Cayman Brac; 9d. Georgetown Harbour. $1 Turtle in "crawl"; 2s. "Ziroma" (schooner); 5s. Boat-building; 10s. Government offices, Grand Cayman.

1953. As 1950 issue but with portrait of Queen Elizabeth II as in T **44**.

148 ¼d. blue and red 85 50
149 ½d. violet and green 20 50
150 1d. olive and blue 70 40
151 1½d. green and brown 50 20
152 2d. violet and red 3·00 85
153 2½d. blue and black 3·50 80
154 3d. green and blue 4·00 60
155 4d. black and blue 2·00 40
156 6d. brown and blue 1·75 30
157 9d. red and green 4·00 30
158 1s. brown and orange 3·25 20
159 2s. violet and purple 12·00 7·50
160 5s. olive and violet 14·00 4·50
161 10s. black and red 14·00 7·50
161a £1 blue 32·00 10·00

Portrait faces right on ¼d., 2d., 2½d., 4d., 1s and 10s. values and left on others. The £1 shows a larger portrait of the Queen (vert).

1953. Coronation. As T **13** of Aden.

162 1d. black and green 30 80

46 Arms of the Cayman Islands

1959. New Constitution.

163 **46** 2½d. black and blue 45 1·40
164 1s. black and orange 55 35

48 Cat Boat

1962. Portraits as in T **48**.

165 – ¼d. green and red 30 70
166 **48** 1d. black and olive 60 20
167 – 1½d. yellow and purple 2·75 80
168 – 2d. blue and brown 60 30
169 – 2½d. violet and turquoise 85 80
170 – 3d. blue and red 30 10
171 – 4d. green and purple 80 60
172 – 6d. turquoise and sepia 3·25 30
173 **48** 9d. blue and purple 1·25 40
174 – 1s. sepia and red 80 10
175 – 1s. 3d. turquoise and brown 3·50 1·75
176 – 1s. 9d. turquoise and violet 13·00 1·25
177 – 5s. plum and green 8·00 5·50
178 – 10s. olive and blue 14·00 8·00
179 – £1 red and black 19·00 15·00

DESIGNS—VERT: ¼d. Cuban amazon; 9d. Angler with king mackerel; 10s. Arms; £1 Queen Elizabeth II. HORIZ: 1½d. "Schomburgkia thomsoniana" (orchid); 2d. Cayman Islands map; 2½d. Fisherman casting net; 3d. West Bay Beach; 4d. Green turtle; 6d. "Lydia E. Wilson" (schooner), 1s. Iguana; 1s. 3d. Swimming pool, Cayman Brac; 1s. 9d. Water sports; 5s. Fort George.

1963. Freedom from Hunger. As T **28** of Aden.

180 1s. 9d. red 30 15

1963. Centenary of Red Cross. As T **33** of Antigua.

181 1d. red and black 20 65
182 1s. 9d. red and blue 1·10 1·60

1964. 400th Birth Anniv of Shakespeare. As T **34** of Antigua.

183 6d. purple 10 10

1965. Centenary of I.T.U. As T **36** of Antigua.

184 1d. blue and purple 15 10
185 1s. 3d. purple and green 40 35

1965. I.C.Y. As T **37** of Antigua.

186 1d. purple and turquoise 15 10
187 1s. green and lavender 50 25

1966. Churchill Commemoration. As T **38** of Antigua.

188 ¼d. blue 10 90
189 1d. green 20 10
190 1s. brown 60 10
191 1s. 9d. violet 70 65

1966. Royal Visit. As T **39** of Antigua.

192 1d. black and blue 60 25
193 1s. 9d. black and mauve 2·25 65

1966. World Cup Football Championships. As T **40** of Antigua.

194 1½d. multicoloured 15 10
195 1s. 9d. multicoloured 50 25

1966. Inauguration of W.H.O. Headquarters, Geneva. As T **41** of Antigua.

196 2d. black, green and blue 50 15
197 1s. 3d. black, purple and ochre 1·25 60

62 Telephone and Map

1966. International Telephone Links.

198 **62** 4d. multicoloured 20 20
199 9d. multicoloured 20 20

1966. 20th Anniv of U.N.E.S.C.O. As T **54/6** of Antigua.

200 1d. multicoloured 15 10
201 1s. 9d. yellow, violet and olive 45 10
202 5s. black, purple and orange 1·25 55

63 B.A.C One Eleven 200/400 Airliner over Cayman Schooner

1966. Opening of Cayman Jet Service.

203 **63** 1s. black, blue and green 50 30
204 1s. 9d. purple, blue and green 50 35

64 Water-skiing

1967. International Tourist Year. Multicoloured.

205 4d. Type **64** 50 10
206 6d. Skin diving 50 30
207 1s. Sport fishing 50 30
208 1s. 9d. Sailing 60 75

68 Former Slaves and Emblem

1968. Human Rights Year.

209 **68** 3d. green, black and gold 10 10
210 9d. brown, gold and green 10 10
211 5s. ultram, gold and green 30 70

69 Long-jumping

1968. Olympic Games, Mexico. Multicoloured.

212 1s. Type **69** 10 10
213 1s. 3d. High-jumping 15 25
214 2s. Pole-vaulting 15 40

72 "The Adoration of the Shepherds" (Fabritius)

1968. Christmas. Multicoloured.

215 ¼d. Type **72*** 10 20
221 ¼d. Type **72*** 10 20
216 1d. "The Adoration of the Shepherds" (Rembrandt) 10 10
217 6d. Type **72** 15 10
218 8d. As 1d. 15 15
219 1s. 3d. Type **72** 20 25
220 2s. As 1d. 25 35

*No. 215 has a brown background and No. 221 a bright purple one.

74 Grand Cayman Thrush

1969. Multicoloured.

222 ¼d. Type **74** 10 75
223 1d. Brahmin cattle 10 10
224 2d. Blowholes on the coast 10 10
225 2½d. Map of Grand Cayman 15 10
226 3d. Georgetown scene 15 10
227 4d. Royal "Poinciana" 30 10
228 6d. Cayman Brac and Little Cayman on chart 30 10
229 8d. Motor vessels at berth 40 10
230 1s. Basket-making 20 10
231 1s. 3d. Beach scene 35 1·50
232 1s. 6d. Straw-rope making 50 1·25
233 2s. Great barracuda 1·25 80
234 4s. Government House 50 80
235 10s. Arms of the Cayman Islands 1·00 2·25
236 £1 black, ochre and red (Queen Elizabeth II) 1·75 2·50

Nos. 235/6 are vert.

1969. Decimal Currency. Nos. 222/36 surch **C-DAY 8th September 1969**. Multicoloured.

238 **74** ¼ c. on ¼d. 10 75
239 – 1 c. on 1d. 10 10
240 – 2 c. on 2d. 10 10
241 – 3 c. on 4d. 10 10
242 – 4 c. on 2½d. 10 10
243 – 5 c. on 6d. 10 10
244 – 7 c. on 8d. 10 10
245 – 8 c. on 3d. 15 10
246 – 10 c. on 1s. 25 10
247 – 12 c. on 1s. 3d. 35 1·25
248 – 15 c. on 1s. 6d. 45 75
249 – 20 c. on 2s. 1·25 1·50
250 – 40 c. on 4s. 45 80
251 – $1 on 10s. 1·50 2·50
252 – $2 on £1 2·00 3·25

90 "Madonna and Child" (Vivarini)

92 "Noli me tangere" (Titian)

1969. Christmas. Multicoloured. Background colours given.

253 **90** ¼ c. red 10 10
254 ¼ c. mauve 10 10
255 ¼ c. green 10 10
256 ¼ c. blue 10 10
257 – 1 c. blue 10 10
258 **90** 5 c. red 10 10
259 – 7 c. green 10 10
260 **90** 12 c. green 15 15
261 – 20 c. purple 20 25

DESIGNS: 1 c., 7 c., 20 c. "The Adoration of the Kings" (Gossaert).

1970. Easter. Multicoloured; frame colours given.

262 **92** ¼ c. red 10 10
263 ¼ c. green 10 10
264 ¼ c. brown 10 10
265 ¼ c. violet 10 10
266 10 c. blue 25 10
267 12 c. brown 30 10
268 40 c. plum 40 45

93 Barnaby ("Barnaby Rudge")

1970. Death Centenary of Charles Dickens.

269 **93** 1 c. black, green and yellow 10 10
270 – 12 c. black, brown and red 25 10
271 – 20 c. black, brown and gold 30 10
272 – 40 c. black, ultram & blue 35 25

DESIGNS: 12 c. Sairey Gamp ("Martin Chuzzlewit"); 20 c. Mr. Micawber and David ("David Copperfield"); 40 c. The "Marchioness" ("The Old Curiosity Shop").

97 Grand Cayman Thrush

1970. Decimal Currency. Designs as Nos. 222/36, but with values inscribed in decimal currency as in T **97**.

273 ¼ c. multicoloured 10 10
274 1 c. multicoloured 10 10
275 2 c. multicoloured 10 10
276 3 c. multicoloured 20 10
277 4 c. multicoloured 20 10
278 5 c. multicoloured 35 10
279 7 c. multicoloured 30 10
280 8 c. multicoloured 30 10
281 10 c. multicoloured 30 10
282 12 c. multicoloured 90 45
283 15 c. multicoloured 1·25 2·50
284 20 c. multicoloured 2·50 1·25
285 40 c. multicoloured 85 75
286 $1 multicoloured 1·25 4·25
287 $2 black, ochre and red 2·00 4·75

98 The Three Wise Men

1970. Christmas.

288 **98** ¼ c. green, grey and emerald 10 10
289 – 1 c. black, yellow and green 10 10
290 **98** 5 c. grey, orange and red 10 10
291 – 10 c. black, yellow and red 10 10
292 **98** 12 c. grey, green and blue 15 10
293 – 20 c. black, yellow and green 20 15

DESIGN: 1, 10, 20 c. Nativity scene and Globe.

100 Grand Cayman Terrapin

1971. Turtles. Multicoloured.

294 5 c. Type **100** 30 25
295 7 c. Green turtle 35 25
296 12 c. Hawksbill turtle 55 30
297 20 c. Turtle farm 1·00 1·40

101 "Dendrophylax fawcettii"

102 "Adoration of the Kings" (French 15th century)

1971. Orchids. Multicoloured.

298	$\frac{1}{4}$ c. Type **101**	10	70
299	2 c. "Schomburgkia thomsoniana"	40	60
300	10 c. "Vanilla claviculata"	90	50
301	40 c. "Oncidium variegatum"	3·00	3·50

1971. Christmas. Multicoloured.

302	$\frac{1}{4}$ c. Type **102**	10	10
303	1 c. "The Nativity" (Parisian, 14th century)	10	10
304	5 c. "Adoration of the Magi" (Burgundian, 15th century)	10	10
305	12 c. Type **102**	20	15
306	15 c. As 1 c.	20	25
307	20 c. As 5 c.	25	35

103 Turtle and Telephone Cable

1972. Co-Axial Telephone Cable.

309 **103**	2 c. multicoloured	10	10
310	10 c. multicoloured	15	10
311	40 c. multicoloured	30	40

104 Court House Building

1972. New Government Buildings. Multicoloured.

312	5 c. Type **104**	10	10
313	15 c. Legislative Assembly Building	10	10
314	25 c. Type **104**	15	15
315	40 c. As 15 c.	20	30

1972. Royal Silver Wedding. As T **52** of Ascension but with Hawksbill Turtle and Queen or Pink Conch in background.

317	12 c. violet	15	10
318	30 c. green	15	20

106 $1 Coin and Note

107 "The Way of Sorrow"

1972. First Issue of Currency. Multicoloured.

319	3 c. Type **106**	20	10
320	6 c. $5 Coin and note	20	10
321	15 c. $10 Coin and note	60	20
322	25 c. $25 Coin and note	80	35

1973. Easter. Stained-glass Windows. Multicoloured.

324	10 c. Type **107**	15	10
325	12 c. "Christ Resurrected"	20	10
326	20 c. "The Last Supper" (horiz)	25	15
327	30 c. "Christ on the Cross" (horiz)	30	25

108 "The Nativity" (Sforza Book of Hours)

109 White-winged Dove

1973. Christmas.

329 **108**	3 c. multicoloured	10	10
330 –	5 c. multicoloured	10	10
331 **108**	9 c. multicoloured	15	10
332 –	12 c. multicoloured	15	10
333 **108**	15 c. multicoloured	15	15
334 –	25 c. multicoloured	20	25

DESIGN: 5, 12, 25 c. "The Adoration of the Magi" (Breviary of Queen Isabella).

1973. Royal Wedding. As T **47** of Anguilla. Background colour given. Multicoloured.

335	10 c. green	10	10
336	30 c. mauve	15	10

1974. Birds (1st series). Multicoloured.

337	3 c. Type **109**	2·00	20
338	10 c. Vitelline warbler	2·75	20
339	12 c. Antillean grackle	2·75	25
340	20 c. West Indian red-bellied woodpecker	4·25	65
341	30 c. Stripe-headed tanager	5·50	1·50
342	50 c. Yucatan vireo	7·00	3·25

See also Nos. 383/8.

110 Old School Building

1974. 25th Anniv of University of West Indies. Multicoloured.

343	12 c. Type **110**	10	10
344	20 c. New Comprehensive School	15	10
345	30 c. Creative Arts Centre, Mona	15	45

111 Hermit Crab and Staghorn Coral

1974. Size $41\frac{1}{2} \times 27$ mm or $27 \times 41\frac{1}{2}$ mm. Mult.

364	1 c. Type **111**	3·00	1·50
347	3 c. Treasure-chest and lion's paw	3·50	75
348	4 c. Treasure and spotted scorpionfish	50	70
349	5 c. Flintlock pistol and brain coral	3·00	75
350	6 c. Blackbeard and green turtle	35	2·25
415	8 c. As 9 c.	7·50	3·00
351	9 c. Jewelled pomander and porkfish	3·50	6·50
416	10 c. Spiny lobster and treasure	2·00	2·75
353	12 c. Jewelled sword and dagger and sea-fan	35	1·60
354	15 c. Cabrit's murex and treasure	45	1·25
417	20 c. Queen or pink conch and treasure	3·50	3·00
356	25 c. Hogfish and treasure	45	70
357	40 c. Gold chalice and seawhip	3·00	1·25
358	$1 Coat of arms (vert)	2·75	3·25
419	$2 Queen Elizabeth II (vert)	7·50	6·50

For smaller designs see Nos. 445/52.

112 Sea Captain and Ship (Shipbuilding)

1974. Local Industries. Multicoloured.

360	8 c. Type **112**	15	10
361	12 c. Thatcher and cottage	15	10
362	20 c. Farmer and plantation	25	20

113 Arms of Cinque Ports and Lord Warden's Flag

114 "The Crucifixion"

1974. Birth Centenary of Sir Winston Churchill. Multicoloured.

380	12 c. Type **113**	15	10
381	50 c. Churchill's coat of arms	45	70

1975. Birds (2nd series). As T **109**. Multicoloured.

383	3 c. Common flicker	70	45
384	10 c. Black-billed whistling duck	1·25	45
385	12 c. Yellow warbler	1·40	65
386	20 c. White-bellied dove	2·00	2·00
387	30 c. Magnificent frigate bird	3·25	4·25
388	50 c. Cuban amazon	3·75	10·00

1975. Easter. French Pastoral Staffs.

389 **114**	15 c. multicoloured	10	15
390 –	35 c. multicoloured	20	30

DESIGN: 35 c. Pastoral staff similar to Type **114**.

115 Israel Hands

1975. Pirates. Multicoloured.

392	10 c. Type **115**	20	10
393	12 c. John Fenn	20	10
394	20 c. Thomas Anstis	40	35
395	30 c. Edward Low	55	1·25

1975. Christmas. "Virgin and Child with Angels". As T **114**.

396	12 c. multicoloured	10	10
397	50 c. multicoloured	30	30

116 Registered Cover, Government House and Sub-Post Office

1975. 75th Anniv of First Cayman Islands Postage Stamp. Multicoloured.

399	10 c. Type **116**	15	10
400	20 c. $\frac{1}{2}$d. stamp and 1890–94 postmark	20	15
401	30 c. 1d. stamp and 1908 surcharge	30	25
402	50 c. $\frac{1}{2}$d. and 1d. stamps	45	50

117 Seals of Georgia, Delaware and New Hampshire

1976. Bicentenary of American Revolution. Mult.

404	10 c. Type **117**	50	15
405	15 c. Carolina, New Jersey and Maryland seals	65	20
406	20 c. Virginia, Rhode Island and Massachusetts seals	75	25
407	25 c. New York, Connecticut and North Carolina seals	75	35
408	30 c. Pennsylvania seal, Liberty Bell and U.S. Great Seal	90	40

118 Racing Dinghies

119 Queen Elizabeth II and Westminster Abbey

1976. Olympic Games, Montreal. Multicoloured.

410	20 c. Type **118**	40	10
411	50 c. Racing dinghy	70	50

1977. Silver Jubilee. Multicoloured.

427	8 c. The Prince of Wales' visit, 1973	10	20
428	30 c. Type **119**	15	40
429	50 c. Preparation for the Anointing (horiz)	30	75

120 Scuba Diving

1977. Tourism. Multicoloured.

430	5 c. Type **120**	10	10
431	10 c. Exploring a wreck	15	10
432	20 c. Royal gramma ("Fairy basslet") (fish)	45	20
433	25 c. Sergeant major (fish)	55	35

121 "Composia fidelissima" (moth)

1977. Butterflies and Moth. Multicoloured.

435	5 c. Type **121**	65	10
436	8 c. "Heliconius charithonia"	70	15
437	10 c. "Danaus gilippus"	70	15
438	15 c. "Agraulis vanillae"	90	40
439	20 c. "Junonia evarete"	1·00	45
440	30 c. "Anartia jatrophae"	1·25	70

122 Cruise Liner "Southward"

123 "The Crucifixion" (Durer)

1978. New Harbour and Cruise Ships. Multicoloured.

441	3 c. Type **122**	20	10
442	5 c. Cruise liner "Renaissance"	20	10
443	30 c. New harbour (vert)	80	25
444	50 c. Cruise liner "Daphne" (vert)	1·00	55

1978. As Nos. 346/59, 349, 352, 355 and 357/9, but designs smaller, 40×26 mm or 26×40 mm.

445	1 c. Type **111**	1·00	1·25
446	3 c. Treasure chest and lion's paw	80	50
447	5 c. Flintlock pistol and brain coral	2·00	2·50
448	10 c. Spiny lobster and treasure	1·60	60
449	20 c. Queen or pink conch and treasure	3·25	1·25
450	40 c. Gold chalice and seawhip	15·00	20·00
451	$1 Coat of arms (vert)	16·00	8·00
452	$2 Queen Elizabeth II (vert)	6·00	24·00

1978. Easter and 450th Death Anniv of Durer.

459 **123**	10 c. mauve and black	20	10
460 –	15 c. yellow and black	30	15
461 –	20 c. turquoise and black	40	20
462 –	30 c. lilac and black	55	35

DESIGNS: 15 c. "Christ at Emmaus"; 20 c. "The Entry into Jerusalem"; 30 c. "Christ washing Peter's Feet".

124 "Explorers" Singing Game

125 Yale of Beaufort

1978. 3rd International Council Meeting of Girls' Brigade. Multicoloured.

464	3 c. Type **124**	20	10
465	10 c. Colour party	30	10
466	20 c. Girls and Duke of Edinburgh Award interests	60	20
467	50 c. Girls using domestic skills	1·10	80

1978. 25th Anniv of Coronation.

468 **125**	30 c. green, mauve and silver	20	25
469 –	30 c. multicoloured	20	25
470 –	30 c. green, mauve and silver	20	25

DESIGNS: No. 469, Queen Elizabeth II; No. 470, Barn owl.

126 Four-eyed Butterflyfish

1978. Fish (1st series). Multicoloured.

471	3 c. Type **126**	25	10
472	5 c. Grey angelfish	30	10
473	10 c. Squirrelfish	45	10
474	15 c. Queen parrotfish	60	30
475	20 c. Spanish hogfish	70	35
476	30 c. Queen angelfish	80	50

127 Lockheed L.18 Lodestar

1979. 25th Anniv of Owen Roberts Airfield. Mult.

477	3 c. Type **127**	25	10
478	5 c. Consolidated PBY-5A Catalina amphibian	25	10
479	10 c. Vickers Viking 1B	30	10
480	15 c. B.A.C. One Eleven 455 on tarmac	55	20
481	20 c. Piper PA-31 Cheyenne II, Bell 47G Trooper helicopter and Hawker Siddeley H.S.125	65	30
482	30 c. B.A.C. One Eleven 475 over airfield	90	45

128 Trumpetfish

1979. Fishes (2nd series). Multicoloured.

483	1 c. Type **128**	10	10
484	3 c. Nassau grouper	25	10
485	5 c. French angelfish	25	10
486	10 c. Schoolmaster snapper	35	10
487	20 c. Banded butterflyfish	55	25
488	50 c. Black-barred soldierfish	1·00	70

129 1900 1d. Stamp

1979. Death Centenary of Sir Rowland Hill.

489 **129**	5 c. black, carmine and blue	10	10
490 –	10 c. multicoloured	15	10
491 –	20 c. multicoloured	20	25

DESIGNS: 10 c. Great Britain 1902 3d. purple on lemon; 20 c. 1955 £1 blue.

130 The Holy Family and Angels

1979. Christmas. Multicoloured.

493	10 c. Type **130**	15	10
494	20 c. Angels appearing to Shepherds	20	10
495	30 c. Nativity	30	20
496	40 c. The Magi	40	30

131 Local Rotary Project

1980. 75th Anniv of Rotary International.

497 **131**	20 c. blue, black and yellow	20	15
498 –	30 c. blue, black and yellow	25	20
499 –	50 c. blue, yellow and black	35	30

DESIGNS—VERT: 30 c. Paul P. Harris (founder); 50 c. Rotary anniversary emblem.

132 Walking Mail Carrier

1980. "London 1980" International Stamp Exhibition. Multicoloured.

500	5 c. Type **132**	10	10
501	10 c. Delivering mail by cat boat	15	10
502	15 c. Mounted mail carrier	20	10
503	30 c. Horse-drawn wagonette	30	15
504	40 c. Postman on bicycle	30	15
505	$1 Motor transport	65	55

133 Queen Elizabeth the Queen Mother at the Derby, 1976

1980. 80th Birthday of the Queen Mother.

506 **133**	20 c. multicoloured	20	25

134 American Thorny Oyster

1980. Shells. (1st series). Multicoloured.

507	5 c. Type **134**	50	10
508	10 c. West Indian murex	50	10
509	30 c. Angular triton	85	40
510	50 c. Caribbean vase	1·00	80

See also Nos. 565/8 and 582/5.

135 Lantana

1980. Flowers (1st series). Multicoloured.

511	5 c. Type **135**	10	10
512	15 c. "Bauhinia"	25	10
513	30 c. "Hibiscus Rosa"	35	10
514	$1 "Milk and Wine Lily"	1·00	75

See also Nos. 541/4.

136 Juvenile Tarpon and Fire Sponge

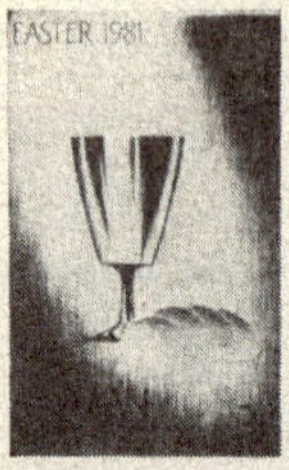

137 Eucharist

1980. Multicoloured.

515A	3 c. Type **136**	50	1·50
516A	5 c. Flat tree or mangrove-root oyster	60	1·00
517A	10 c. Mangrove crab	40	80
518A	15 c. Lizard and "Phyciodes phaon" (butterfly)	1·00	1·50
519A	20 c. Louisiana heron	1·50	2·00
520A	30 c. Red mangrove flower	70	1·00
521A	40 c. Red mangrove seeds	75	1·00
522A	50 c. Waterhouse's leaf-nosed bat	1·25	1·50
523A	$1 Black-crowned night heron	4·50	4·50
524A	$2 Coat of arms	1·50	3·75
525A	$4 Queen Elizabeth II	2·25	4·75

1981. Easter. Multicoloured.

526	3 c. Type **137**	10	10
527	10 c. Crown of thorns	10	10
528	20 c. Crucifix	20	10
529	$1 Lord Jesus Christ	70	80

138 Wood Slave

1981. Reptiles and Amphibians. Multicoloured.

530	20 c. Type **138**	30	20
531	30 c. Cayman iguana	45	35
532	40 c. Lion lizard	55	45
533	50 c. Terrapin ("Hickatee")	65	55

139 Prince Charles

1981. Royal Wedding. Multicoloured.

534	20 c. Wedding bouquet from Cayman Islands	15	10
535	30 c. Type **139**	20	10
536	$1 Prince Charles and Lady Diana Spencer	50	75

140 Disabled Scuba Divers

1981. Int Year for Disabled Persons. Mult.

537	5 c. Type **140**	10	10
538	15 c. Old school for the handicapped	25	20
539	20 c. New school for the handicapped	30	25
540	$1 Disabled people in wheelchairs by the sea	1·25	85

1981. Flowers (2nd series). As T **135**. Multicoloured.

541	3 c. Bougainvillea	10	10
542	10 c. Morning Glory	20	10
543	20 c. Wild amaryllis	45	25
544	$1 Cordia	1·75	1·75

141 Dr. Robert Koch and Microscope

1982. Centenary of Robert Koch's Discovery of Tubercle Bacillus. Multicoloured.

545	15 c. Type **141**	25	25
546	30 c. Koch looking through microscope (vert)	45	45
547	40 c. Microscope (vert)	70	70
548	50 c. Dr. Robert Koch (vert)	80	80

142 Bride and Groom walking down Aisle

144 "Madonna and Child with the Infant Baptist"

143 Pitching Tent

1982. 21st Birthday of Princess of Wales. Multicoloured.

549	20 c. Cayman Islands coat of arms	30	35
550	30 c. Lady Diana Spencer in London, June, 1981	60	45
551	40 c. Type **142**	60	65
552	50 c. Formal portrait	80	90

1982. 75th Anniv of Boy Scout Movement. Multicoloured.

553	3 c. Type **143**	15	10
554	20 c. Scouts camping	55	40
555	30 c. Cub Scouts and Leaders	70	55
556	50 c. Boating skills	1·10	85

1982. Christmas. Raphael Paintings. Multicoloured.

557	3 c. Type **144**	10	10
558	10 c. "Madonna of the Tower"	20	20
559	20 c. "Ansidei Madonna"	35	35
560	30 c. "Madonna and Child"	50	50

145 Mace

1982. 150th Anniv of Representative Government. Multicoloured.

561	3 c. Type **145**	10	20
562	10 c. Old Courthouse	20	20
563	20 c. Commonwealth Parliamentary Association coat of arms	35	45
564	30 c. Legislative Assembly building	50	90

1983. Shells (2nd series). As T **134**. Multicoloured.

565	5 c. Colourful Atlantic moon	15	10
566	10 c. King helmet	25	20
567	20 c. Rooster-tail conch	45	40
568	$1 Reticulated cowrie-helmet	1·75	3·50

146 Legislative Building, Cayman Brac

1983. Royal Visit. Multicoloured.

569	20 c. Type **146**	45	35
570	30 c. Legislative Building, Grand Cayman	60	50
571	50 c. Duke of Edinburgh (vert)	1·25	90
572	$1 Queen Elizabeth II (vert)	2·00	2·00

147 Satellite View of Earth

1983. Commonwealth Day. Multicoloured.

574	3 c. Type **147**	10	10
575	15 c. Cayman Islands and Commonwealth flags	25	30
576	20 c. Fishing	30	35
577	40 c. Portrait of Queen Elizabeth II	60	65

148 MRCU Cessna Ag Wagon

1983. Bicentenary of Manned Flight. Multicoloured.

578	3 c. Type **148**	50	30
579	10 c. Consolidated PBY-5A Catalina amphibian	70	30
580	20 c. Boeing 727-200	1·50	1·50
581	40 c. Hawker Siddeley H.S.748	2·00	3·00

1984. Shells (3rd series). As T **134**. Multicoloured.

582	3 c. Florida moon	60	25
583	10 c. Austin's cone	85	25
584	30 c. Leaning dwarf triton	2·25	2·50
585	50 c. Filose or threaded turban	2·50	3·50

149 "Song of Norway" (cruise liner)

152 Couple on Beach at Sunset

151 Snowy Egret

1984. 250th Anniv of "Lloyd's List" (newspaper). Multicoloured.

586	5 c. Type **149**	25	20
587	10 c. View of old harbour	35	25
588	25 c. Wreck of "Ridgefield" (freighter)	1·00	1·00
589	50 c. "Goldfield" (schooner)	1·60	2·25

1984. Universal Postal Union Congress, Hamburg. No. 589 optd **U.P.U. CONGRESS HAMBURG 1984.**

591	50 c. Schooner "Goldfield"	1·00	1·50

1984. Birds of the Cayman Islands (1st series). Multicoloured.

592	5 c. Type **151**	90	45
593	10 c. Bananaquit	90	45
594	35 c. Belted kingfisher	2·75	2·25
595	$1 Brown booby	5·50	7·50

See also Nos. 627/30.

1984. Christmas. Local Festivities. Multicoloured.

596	5 c. Type **152**	50	75
597	5 c. Family and schooner	50	75
598	5 c. Carol singers	50	75
599	5 c. East End bonfire	50	75
600	25 c. Yachts	70	85
601	25 c. Father Christmas in power-boat	70	85
602	25 c. Children on beach	70	85
603	25 c. Beach party	70	85

Nos. 596/9 and 600/3 were each printed together, se-tenant, the four designs of each value forming a composite picture of a beach scene at night (5 c.) or in the daytime (25 c.).

153 "Schomburgkia thomsoniana (var. minor)

154 Freighter Aground

1985. Orchids. Multicoloured.

605	5 c. Type **153**	80	20
606	10 c. "Schomburgkia thomsoniana"	90	20
607	25 c. "Encyclia plicata"	2·25	1·00
608	50 c. "Dendrophylax fawcettii"	3·00	2·75

1985. Shipwrecks. Multicoloured.

609	5 c. Type **154**	80	30
610	25 c. Submerged sailing ship	2·50	95
611	35 c. Wrecked trawler	2·75	2·25
612	40 c. Submerged wreck on its side	3·00	3·00

155 Athletics

156 Morse Key (1935)

1985. International Youth Year. Multicoloured.

613	5 c. Type **155**	20	20
614	15 c. Students in library	35	30
615	25 c. Football (vert)	65	55
616	50 c. Netball (vert)	1·25	2·00

1985. 50th Anniv of Telecommunications System. Multicoloured.

617	5 c. Type **156**	40	30
618	10 c. Hand cranked telephone	45	30
619	25 c. Tropospheric scatter dish (1966)	1·25	80
620	50 c. Earth station dish aerial (1979)	2·00	3·00

1986. 60th Birthday of Queen Elizabeth II. As T **110** of Ascension. Multicoloured.

621	5 c. Princess Elizabeth at wedding of Lady May Cambridge, 1931	10	20
622	10 c. In Norway, 1955	15	20
623	25 c. Queen inspecting Royal Cayman Islands Police, 1983	1·25	75
624	50 c. During Gulf tour, 1979	75	1·25
625	$1 At Crown Agents Head Office, London, 1983	1·10	2·25

157 Magnificent Frigate Bird

1986. Birds of the Cayman Islands (2nd series). Multicoloured.

627	10 c. Type **157**	1·25	50
628	25 c. Black-billed whistling duck (vert)	1·75	1·25
629	35 c. La Sagra's flycatcher (vert)	2·00	2·25
630	40 c. Yellow-faced grassquit	2·25	3·00

1986. Royal Wedding. As T **112** of Ascension. Multicoloured.

633	5 c. Prince Andrew and Miss Sarah Ferguson	25	10
634	50 c. Prince Andrew aboard H.M.S. "Brazen"	1·25	1·40

158 Red Coral Shrimp

159 Golf

1986. Marine Life. Multicoloured.

635	5 c. Type **158**	40	50
636	10 c. Yellow crinoid	40	50
637	15 c. Hermit crab	35	60
638	20 c. Tube dwelling anemone	35	80
639	25 c. Christmas tree worm	45	1·75
640	35 c. Porcupinefish	70	2·00
641	50 c. Orangeball anemone	80	3·50
642	60 c. Basket starfish	3·00	5·00
643	75 c. Flamingo tongue	5·50	6·50
644	$1 Sea anemone	1·40	2·50
645	$2 Diamond blenny	2·25	4·25
646	$4 Rough file shell	4·00	6·50

1987. Tourism. Multicoloured.

647	10 c. Type **159**	1·50	75
648	15 c. Sailing	1·75	85
649	25 c. Snorkelling	1·90	1·25
650	35 c. Paragliding	2·00	1·75
651	$1 Game fishing	3·50	6·00

160 Ackee

162 Poinsettia

161 Lion Lizard

1987. Cayman Islands Fruits. Multicoloured.

652	5 c. Type **160**	20	30
653	25 c. Breadfruit	55	45
654	35 c. Pawpaw	75	60
655	$1 Soursop	2·00	3·25

1987. Lizards. Multicoloured.

656	10 c. Type **161**	60	20
657	50 c. Iguana	1·75	1·40
658	$1 Anole	2·50	2·50

1987. Flowers. Multicoloured.

659	5 c. Type **162**	40	20
660	25 c. Periwinkle	1·25	60
661	35 c. Yellow allamanda	1·50	1·00
662	75 c. Blood lily	2·50	2·50

163 "Hemiargus ammon" and "Strymon martialis"

164 Green Heron

1988. Butterflies. Multicoloured.

663	5 c. Type **163**	1·00	50
664	25 c. "Phocides pigmalion"	2·25	75
665	50 c. "Anaea troglodyta"	3·50	3·25
666	$1 "Papilio andraemon"	4·25	4·25

1988. Herons. Multicoloured.

667	5 c. Type **164**	1·00	50
668	25 c. Louisiana heron	2·00	65
669	50 c. Yellow-crowned night heron	2·75	2·75
670	$1 Little blue heron	3·25	4·00

165 Cycling

166 Princess Alexandra

1988. Olympic Games, Seoul. Multicoloured.

671	10 c. Type **165**	90	45
672	50 c. Cayman Airways Boeing 727 airliner and national team	1·75	1·75
673	$1 Sailing	2·00	2·50

1988. Visit of Princess Alexandra. Multicoloured.

675	5 c. Type **166**	75	50
676	$1 Princess Alexandra in evening dress	4·00	3·50

167 George Town Post Office, and Cayman Postmark on Jamaica 1d., 1889

168 Captain Bligh ashore in West Indies

1989. Centenary of Cayman Islands Postal Service. Multicoloured.

677	**167** 5 c. multicoloured	55	40
678	– 25 c. green, black and blue	1·50	70
679	– 35 c. multicoloured	1·50	1·00
680	– $1 multicoloured	4·25	4·50

DESIGNS: 25 c. "Orinoco" (mail steamer) and 1900 ½d. stamp; 35 c. G.P.O., Grand Cayman and "London 1980" $1 stamp; $1 Cayman Airways B.A.C. One Eleven 200/400 airplane and 1966 1s. Jet Service stamp.

1989. Captain Bligh's Second Breadfruit Voyage, 1791–93. Multicoloured.

681	50 c. Type **168**	2·75	3·25
682	50 c. H.M.S. "Providence" (sloop) at anchor	2·75	3·25
683	50 c. Breadfruit in tubs and H.M.S. "Assistant" (transport)	2·75	3·25
684	50 c. Sailors moving tubs of breadfruit	2·75	3·25
685	50 c. Midshipman and stores	2·75	3·25

Nos. 681/5 were printed together, se-tenant, forming a composite design.

169 Panton House

170 Map of Grand Cayman, 1773, and Surveying Instruments

1989. Architecture. Designs showing George Town buildings. Multicoloured.

686	5 c. Type **169**	30	30
687	10 c. Town hall and clock tower	30	30
688	25 c. Old Court House	70	50
689	35 c. Elmslie Memorial Church	80	70
690	$1 Post Office	2·00	2·75

1989. Island Maps and Survey Ships. Multicoloured.

691	5 c. Type **170**	70	70
692	25 c. Map of Cayman Islands, 1956, and surveying instruments	2·00	1·25
693	50 c. H.M.S. "Mutine", 1914	3·00	3·50
694	$1 H.M.S. "Vidal", 1956	4·50	5·00

171 French Angelfish

1990. Angelfishes. Multicoloured.

707	10 c. Type **171**	1·00	50
708	25 c. Grey angelfish	2·00	90
709	50 c. Queen angelfish	3·00	3·50
710	$1 Rock beauty	4·50	5·00

1990. 90th Birthday of Queen Elizabeth the Queen Mother. As T **134** of Ascension.

711	50 c. multicoloured	1·25	2·00
712	$1 black and blue	2·50	3·25

DESIGNS—21 × 36 mm: 50 c. Silver Wedding photograph, 1948. 29 × 37 mm: $1 King George VI and Queen Elizabeth with Winston Churchill, 1940.

172 "Danaus eresimus"

1990. "Expo 90" International Garden and Greenery Exhibition, Osaka. Butterflies. Multicoloured.

713	5 c. Type **172**	65	50
714	25 c. "Brephidium exilis"	1·50	1·10
715	35 c. "Phyciodes phaon"	1·75	1·25
716	$1 "Agraulis vanillae"	4·00	6·00

173 Goes Weather Satellite

1991. International Decade for Natural Disaster Reduction. Multicoloured.

717	5 c. Type **173**	75	50
718	30 c. Meteorologist tracking hurricane	1·75	1·10
719	40 c. Damaged buildings	2·00	1·25
720	$1 U.S. Dept of Commerce weather reconnaisance Lockheed WP-3D Orion	4·50	6·50

174 Angels and "Datura candida"

1991. Christmas. Multicoloured.

721	5 c. Type **174**	40	40
722	30 c. Mary and Joseph going to Bethlehem and "Allamanda cathartica"	1·00	60
723	40 c. Adoration of the Kings and "Euphorbia pulcherrima"	1·40	90
724	60 c. Holy Family and "Guaiacum officinale"	2·00	3·00

175 Coconut Palm

177 Woman and Donkey with Panniers

176 Single Cyclist

1991. Island Scenes. Multicoloured.

725	5 c. Type **175**	40	30
726	15 c. Beach scene (horiz)	60	30
727	20 c. Poincianas in bloom (horiz)	60	35
728	30 c. Blowholes (horiz)	70	50
729	40 c. Police band (horiz)	2·50	1·40
730	50 c. "Song of Norway" (liner) at George Town	1·75	1·40
731	60 c. The Bluff, Cayman Brac (horiz)	1·75	1·75
732	80 c. Coat of arms	1·50	2·00
733	90 c. View of Hell (horiz)	1·60	2·00
734	$1 Game fishing (horiz)	2·00	2·00
735	$2 "Nieuw Amsterdam" (1983) and "Holiday" (liners) in harbour	4·25	4·50
736	$8 Queen Elizabeth II	13·00	15·00

1992. 40th Anniv of Queen Elizabeth II's Accession. As T **143** of Ascension. Multicoloured.

737	5 c. Caymans' house	30	30
738	20 c. Sunset over islands	80	50
739	30 c. Beach	90	65
740	40 c. Three portraits of Queen Elizabeth	1·00	1·00
741	$1 Queen Elizabeth II	2·00	3·50

1992. Olympic Games, Barcelona. Cycling. Multicoloured.

742	15 c. Type **176**	1·00	55
743	40 c. Two cyclists	1·75	1·50
744	60 c. Cyclist's legs	2·25	2·75
745	$1 Two pursuit cyclists	3·00	3·50

1992. Island Heritage. Multicoloured.

746	5 c. Type **177**	40	40
747	30 c. Fisherman weaving net	1·00	75
748	40 c. Maypole dancing	1·25	95
749	60 c. Basket making	2·25	3·00
750	$1 Cooking on caboose	2·75	3·50

178 Yellow Stingray

1993. Rays. Multicoloured.

751	5 c. Type **178**	60	50
752	30 c. Southern stingray	1·50	1·25
753	40 c. Spotted eagle-ray	1·75	1·50
754	$1 Manta	3·50	4·50

179 Turtle and Sailing Dinghies

180 Cuban Amazon with Wings spread

1993. Tourism. Multicoloured.

755	15 c. Type **179**	60	70
756	15 c. Tourist boat, fishing launch and scuba diver	60	70
757	15 c. Golf	60	70
758	15 c. Tennis	60	70
759	15 c. Pirates and ship	60	70
760	30 c. Liner, tourist launch and yacht	85	1·00
761	30 c. George Town street	85	1·00
762	30 c. Tourist submarine	85	1·00
763	30 c. Motor scooter riders and cyclist	85	1·00
764	30 c. Cayman Airways Boeing 737 airliners	85	1·00

1993. Endangered Species. Cuban Amazon ("Grand Cayman Parrot"). Multicoloured.

765	5 c. Type **180**	60	60
766	5 c. On branch with wings folded	60	60
767	30 c. Head of parrot	1·60	1·75
768	30 c. Pair of parrots	1·60	1·75

181 "Ionopsis utricularioides" and Manger

1993. Christmas. Orchids. Multicoloured.

769	5 c. Type **181**	60	45
770	40 c. "Encyclia cochleata" and shepherd	1·50	85
771	60 c. "Vanilla pompona" and wise men	2·00	3·00
772	$1 "Oncidium caymanense" and Virgin Mary	3·25	4·25

183 Flags of Great Britain and Cayman Islands

184 Black-billed Whistling Duck

1994. Royal Visit. Multicoloured.

774	5 c. Type **183**	40	35
775	15 c. Royal Yacht "Britannia"	1·00	70
776	30 c. Queen Elizabeth II	1·25	1·00
777	$2 Queen Elizabeth and Prince Philip disembarking	4·50	6·50

1994. Black-billed Whistling Duck ("West Indian Whistling Duck"). Multicoloured.

778	5 c. Type **184**	60	55
779	15 c. Duck landing on water (horiz)	1·00	60
780	20 c. Duck preening (horiz)	1·10	70
781	80 c. Duck flapping wings	2·75	3·50
782	$1 Adult and duckling	3·25	3·75

185 "Electrostrymon angelia"

186 H.M.S. "Convert" (frigate)

1994. Butterflies. Multicoloured.

784	10 c. Type **185**	50	75
785	10 c. "Eumaeus atala"	50	75
786	$1 "Eurema daira"	3·00	3·50
787	$1 "Urbanus dorantes"	3·00	3·50

1994. Bicentenary of Wreck of Ten Sail off Grand Cayman. Multicoloured.

788	10 c. Type **186**	35	35
789	10 c. Merchant brig and full-rigged ship	35	35
790	15 c. Full-rigged ship near rock	55	45
791	20 c. Long boat leaving full-rigged ship	65	55
792	$2 Merchant brig	4·00	6·00

187 Young Green Turtles

1995. Sea Turtles. Multicoloured.

793	10 c. Type **187**	45	40
794	20 c. Kemp's ridley turtle	70	45
795	25 c. Hawksbill turtle	80	50
796	30 c. Leatherback turtle	85	60
797	$1.30 Loggerhead turtle	3·25	3·75
798	$2 Pacific ridley turtles	4·25	5·00

188 Running

1995. C.A.R.I.F.T.A. and I.A.A.F. Games, George Town. Multicoloured.

800	10 c. Type **188**	50	40
801	20 c. High jumping	80	60
802	30 c. Javelin throwing	1·00	80
803	$1.30 Yachting	3·50	5·00

1995. 50th Anniv of End of Second World War. As T **161** of Ascension. Multicoloured.

805	10 c. Members of Cayman Home Guard	65	45
806	25 c. "Comayagua" (freighter)	1·50	80
807	40 c. U-boat "U125"	1·75	1·50
808	$1 U.S. Navy L-3 airship	3·25	4·75

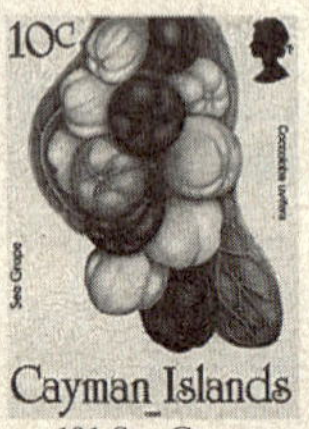

190 Ox and Christ Child

191 Sea Grape

1995. Christmas. Nativity Animals. Multicoloured.

811	10 c. Type **190**	45	30
812	20 c. Sheep and lamb	75	45
813	30 c. Donkey	90	60
814	$2 Camels	4·75	6·50

1996. Wild Fruit. Multicoloured.

816	10 c. Type **191**	30	30
817	25 c. Guava	65	50
818	40 c. West Indian cherry	90	70
819	$1 Tamarind	2·00	3·00

192 Dinghy Sailing

193 Guitar and Score of National Song

1996. Centenary of Modern Olympic Games. Multicoloured.

820	10 c. Type **192**	25	25
821	20 c. Sailboarding	50	55
822	30 c. Dinghy sailing (different)	70	80
823	$2 Running	3·75	5·00

1996. National Identity. Multicoloured.

824	10 c. Type **193**	15	20
825	20 c. Cayman Airways Boeing 737-200	30	35
826	25 c. Queen Elizabeth opening Legislative Assembly	35	40
827	30 c. Seven Mile Beach	40	45
828	40 c. Scuba diver and stingrays	60	65
829	60 c. Children at turtle farm	90	95
830	80 c. Cuban amazon ("Cayman Parrot") (national bird)	1·10	1·25
831	90 c. Silver thatch palm (national tree)	1·25	1·40
832	$1 Cayman Islands flag	1·50	1·60
833	$2 Wild Banana Orchid (national flower)	3·00	3·25
834	$4 Cayman Islands coat of arms	5·75	6·00
835	$6 Cayman Islands currency	8·75	9·00

194 "Christmas Time on North Church Street" (Joanne Sibley)

1996. Christmas. Paintings. Multicoloured.

836	10 c. Type **194**	25	25
837	25 c. "Gone Fishing" (Lois Brezinsky)	50	50
838	30 c. "Claus Encounters" (John Doak)	60	70
839	$2 "A Caymanian Christmas" (Debbie van der Bol)	3·75	5·50

1997. Golden Wedding of Queen Elizabeth and Prince Philip. As T **173** of Ascension. Multicoloured.

841	10 c. Queen Elizabeth	35	40
842	10 c. Prince Philip and Prince Charles at Trooping the Colour	35	40
843	30 c. Prince William horse riding, 1989	75	90
844	30 c. Queen Elizabeth and Prince Philip at Royal Ascot	75	90
845	40 c. Prince Philip at the Brighton Driving Trials	80	1·00
846	40 c. Queen Elizabeth at Windsor Horse Show, 1993	80	1·00

195 Children accessing Internet

196 Santa in Hammock

1997. Telecommunications. Multicoloured.

848	10 c. Type **195**	30	25
849	25 c. Cable & Wireless cable ship	60	45
850	30 c. New area code "345" on children's T-shirts	70	60
851	60 c. Satellite dish	1·25	1·75

1997. Christmas. Multicoloured.

852	10 c. Type **196**	20	20
853	30 c. Santa with children on the Bluff	40	45
854	40 c. Santa playing golf	80	70
855	$1 Santa scuba diving	1·40	2·00

1998. Diana, Princess of Wales Commemoration. As T **91** of Kiribati. Multicoloured.

856	10 c. Wearing gold earrings, 1997	25	25
857	20 c. Wearing black hat	45	45

1998. 80th Anniv of the Royal Air Force. As T **178** of Ascension. Multicoloured.

859	10 c. Hawker Horsley	30	30
860	20 c. Fairey Hendon	45	45
861	25 c. Hawker Siddeley Gnat	55	60
862	30 c. Hawker Siddeley Dominie	65	75

197 West Indian Whistling Duck

198 Santa at the Blowholes

1998. Birds. Multicoloured.

864	10 c. Type **197**	15	20
865	20 c. Magnificent frigate bird	30	35
866	60 c. Red-footed booby	90	95
867	$1 Grand cayman parrot	1·50	1·60

1998. Christmas. Multicoloured.

868	10 c. Type **198**	15	20
869	30 c. Santa diving on wreck of "Capt. Keith Tibbetts"	40	45
870	40 c. Santa at Pedro Castle	60	65
871	60 c. Santa arriving on Little Cayman	1·50	1·60

199 "They Rolled the Stone Away" (Miss Lassie)

1999. Easter. Paintings by Miss Lassie (Gladwyn Bush). Multicoloured.

872	10 c. Type **199**	15	20
873	20 c. "Ascension" (vert)	30	35
874	30 c. "The World Praying for Peace"	40	45
875	40 c. "Calvary" (vert)	60	65

CEYLON

An island to the south of India formerly under British administration, then a self-governing Dominion. The island became a Republic within the Commonwealth on 22 May 1972 and was renamed Sri Lanka (q.v.).

1857. 12 pence = 1 shilling;
20 shillings = 1 pound.
1872. 100 cents = 1 rupee.

1

2

4

8

1857. Imperf.

17	**4**	½d. lilac	£160	£160
2	**1**	1d. blue	£650	23·00
3		2d. green	£150	55·00
4	**2**	4d. red	£50000	£4500
5	**1**	5d. brown	£1500	£150
6		6d. brown	£1800	£130
7	**2**	8d. brown	£22000	£1500
8		9d. brown	£32000	£900
9	**1**	10d. orange	£800	£300
10		1s. violet	£4500	£200
11	**2**	1s. 9d. green	£700	£800
12		2s. blue	£5000	£1200

The prices of these imperf stamps vary greatly according to condition. The above prices are for fine copies with four margins. Poor to medium specimens are worth much less.

1861. Perf.

48c	**4**	½d. lilac	22·00	23·00
49	**1**	1d. blue	75·00	3·25
50		2d. green	50·00	7·50
64b		2d. yellow	38·00	7·00
65b	**2**	4d. red	40·00	13·00
22	**1**	5d. brown	75·00	8·00
66c		5d. green	24·00	38·00
67b		6d. brown	25·00	32·00
56	**2**	8d. brown	65·00	32·00
69b		9d. brown	30·00	6·00
70b	**1**	10d. orange	35·00	10·00
71b		1s. violet	65·00	5·50
72b	**2**	2s. blue	85·00	12·00

1866. The 3d. has portrait in circle.

61	**8**	1d. blue	16·00	6·00
62	–	3d. red	55·00	28·00

9

10

30

1872. Various frames.

256	**9**	2 c. brown	1·75	30
147		2 c. green	1·75	15
122	**10**	4 c. grey	28·00	1·50
148		4 c. purple	2·00	30
149		4 c. red	3·25	11·00
258		4 c. yellow	2·25	2·75
150a	–	8 c. yellow	3·00	7·00
126	–	16 c. violet	60·00	2·75
127	–	24 c. green	40·00	2·00
128	–	32 c. grey	£110	15·00
129	–	36 c. blue	£100	16·00
130	–	48 c. red	60·00	5·00
131	–	64 c. brown	£200	60·00
132	–	90 c. grey	£150	26·00
201	**30**	1 r. 12 red	22·00	19·00
138		2 r. 50 red	£450	£300
249		2 r. 50 purple on red	25·00	48·00

1882. Nos. 127 and 131 surch in words and figures.

142	–	16 c. on 24 c. green	21·00	6·50
143	–	20 c. on 64 c. brown	9·00	4·50

1885. As Nos. 148/132 surch **Postage & Revenue** and value in words.
178 5 c. on 4 c. red 17·00 3·50
179 5 c. on 8 c. yellow 50·00 6·50
180 5 c. on 16 c. violet 70·00 9·50
154 5 c. on 24 c. green £1700 £100
182 5 c. on 24 c. purple — £500
155 5 c. on 32 c. grey 55·00 15·00
156 5 c. on 36 c. blue £170 8·00
157 5 c. on 48 c. red £750 48·00
158 5 c. on 64 c. brown 75·00 4·50
159 5 c. on 96 c. grey £325 60·00

1885. As Nos. 126/249 surch with new value in words.
184 10 c. on 16 c. violet £3500 £800
162 10 c. on 24 c. green £350 £100
185 10 c. on 24 c. purple 10·00 5·50
163 10 c. on 36 c. blue £325 £160
174 10 c. on 64 c. brown 48·00 85·00
186 15 c. on 16 c. violet 8·50 6·50
165 20 c. on 24 c. green 45·00 18·00
166 20 c. on 32 c. grey 45·00 45·00
167 25 c. on 32 c. grey 13·00 4·50
168 28 c. on 48 c. red 30·00 6·00
169 30 c. on 36 c. blue 12·00 8·50
170 56 c. on 96 c. grey 18·00 15·00
176 1 r. 12 on 2 r. 50 red 75·00 42·00

1885. Surch **REVENUE AND POSTAGE 5 CENTS.**
187 – 5 c. on 8 c. lilac (as No. 150a) 11·00 14·00

1885. As Nos. 126/32 surch, in words and figures.
188 10 c. on 24 c. purple 8·50 6·00
189 15 c. on 16 c. yellow 45·00 7·00
190 28 c. on 32 c. grey 17·00 2·50
191 30 c. on 36 c. olive 28·00 14·00
192 56 c. on 96 c. grey 40·00 10·00

1885. Surch **1 R. 12 C.**
193 **30** 1 r. 12 on 2 r. 50 red 35·00 80·00

39

28

43

1886.
245 **39** 3 c. brown and green 2·50 45
257 3 c. green 1·75 55
195 **28** 5 c. purple 1·75 10
259 **39** 6 c. red and black 1·00 45
260 12 c. olive and red 3·00 6·50
196 15 c. olive 3·75 1·25
261 15 c. blue 4·75 1·25
198 25 c. brown 2·75 1·00
199 28 c. grey 13·00 1·40
247 30 c. mauve and brown 4·00 1·75
262 75 c. black and brown 4·25 5·00
263 **43** 1 r. 50 red 16·00 35·00
264 2 r. 25 blue 29·00 35·00

1887. Nos. 148/9 surch. A. Surch **TWO CENTS.**
202 **10** 2 c. on 4 c. purple 1·00 70
203 2 c. on 4 c. red 1·50 30

B. Surch **TWO.**
204 **10** 2 c. on 4 c. purple 60 30
205 2 c. on 4 c. red 3·75 20

C. Surch **2 Cents** and bar.
206 **10** 2 c. on 4 c. purple 45·00 28·00
207 2 c. on 4 c. red 2·25 75

D. Surch **Two Cents** and bar.
208 **10** 2 c. on 4 c. purple 42·00 16·00
209 2 c. on 4 c. red 2·00 1·10

E. Surch **2 Cents** without bar.
210 **10** 2 c. on 4 c. purple 40·00 24·00
211 2 c. on 4 c. red 8·00 60

1890. Surch **POSTAGE Five Cents REVENUE.**
233 **39** 5 c. on 15 c. olive 1·60 1·75

1891. Surch **FIFTEEN CENTS.**
239 **39** 15 c. on 25 c. brown 7·50 10·00
240 15 c. on 28 c. grey 11·00 8·50

1892. Surch **3 Cents** and bar.
241 **10** 3 c. on 4 c. purple 85 2·75
242 3 c. on 4 c. red 2·50 6·00
243 **39** 3 c. on 28 c. grey 2·75 3·00

1898. Surch **Six Cents.**
250 **39** 6 c. on 15 c. green 70 75

1898. Surch with new value.
254 **30** 1 r. 50 on 2 r. 50 grey 20·00 40·00
255 2 r. 25 on 2 r. 50 yellow 32·00 70·00

44

45

1903. Various frames.
277 **44** 2 c. brown 75 10
278 **45** 3 c. green (A) 75 15
293 3 c. green (B) 1·00 75
279 4 c. orange and blue 90 1·00
268 – 5 c. purple 1·50 50
289 – 5 c. purple 2·00 10
281 – 6 c. red 1·10 15
291 – 6 c. red 80 10
294 **45** 10 c. olive and red 2·25 1·40
282 12 c. olive and red 1·50 1·75
283 15 c. blue 1·00 60
284 25 c. brown 6·00 3·75
295 25 c. grey 2·50 90
285 30 c. violet and green 2·50 2·00
296 50 c. brown 4·00 7·50
286 75 c. blue and orange 5·25 8·00
297 1 r. purple on yellow 7·50 10·00
287 1 r. 50 grey 20·00 10·00
298 2 r. red on yellow 15·00 27·00
288 2 r. 25 brown and green 18·00 29·00
299 5 r. black on green 35·00 65·00
300 10 r. black on red 70·00 £170

(A) has value in shaded tablet; (B) in white tablet as in Type **45**.
Nos. 268 and 281 have the value in words; Nos. 289 and 291 in figures.

52

57

1912.
301 **52** 1 c. brown 90 10
307a 2 c. orange 30 20
339 3 c. green 2·25 75
340 3 c. grey 40 20
341 5 c. purple 40 15
342 6 c. red 1·50 75
343 6 c. violet 50 15
345 9 c. red on yellow 40 30
346 10 c. olive 80 40
347a 12 c. red 80 2·00
311a 15 c. blue 1·50 1·25
349a 15 c. green on yellow 1·25 1·00
350b 20 c. blue 2·50 45
351 25 c. yellow and blue 90 1·90
352b 30 c. green and violet 1·75 1·25
353 50 c. black and red 1·25 80
315a 1 r. purple on yellow 1·75 4·00
355 2 r. black and red on yellow 4·00 6·50
317 5 r. black on green 14·00 25·00
318 10 r. purple & blk on red 60·00 70·00
319 20 r. black and red on blue 85·00 £100

Large type, As Bermuda T **15**.
358 50 r. purple £350
359 100 r. black £1400
360 100 r. purple and blue £1300

1918. Optd **WAR STAMP**, No. 335 surch **ONE CENT** and bar also.
335 **52** 1 c. on 5 c. purple 50 30
330 2 c. orange 20 40
332 3 c. green 20 50
333 5 c. purple 30 30

1918. Surch **ONE CENT** and bar.
337 **52** 1 c. on 5 c. purple 15 25

1926. Surch with new value and bar.
361 **52** 2 c. on 3 c. grey 70 1·00
362 5 c. on 6 c. violet 50 40

1927.
363 **57** 1 r. purple 1·75 1·25
364 2 r. green and red 3·75 2·75
365 5 r. green and purple 12·00 18·00
366 10 r. green and orange 28·00 80·00
367 20 r. purple and blue 90·00 £180

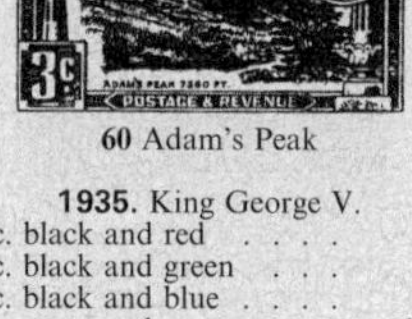

60 Adam's Peak

1935. King George V.
368 – 2 c. black and red 30 40
369 **60** 3 c. black and green 35 40
370 – 6 c. black and blue 30 30
371 – 9 c. green and orange 1·00 50
372 – 10 c. black and purple 1·25 2·00
373 – 15 c. brown and green 1·00 50
374 – 20 c. black and blue 1·75 2·00
375 – 25 c. blue and brown 1·40 1·25
376 – 30 c. red and green 3·00 2·00
377 – 50 c. black and violet 8·00 1·40
378 – 1 r. violet and brown 14·00 13·00

DESIGNS—VERT: 2 c. Tapping rubber; 6 c. Colombo Harbour; 9 c. Plucking tea; 20 c. Coconut palms. HORIZ: 10 c. Hill paddy (rice); 15 c. River scene; 25 c. Temple of the Tooth, Kandy; 30 c. Ancient irrigation tank; 50 c. Indian elephants; 1 r. Trincomalee.

1935. Silver Jubilee. As T **13** of Antigua.
379 6 c. blue and grey 55 30
380 9 c. green and blue 70 70
381 20 c. brown and blue 4·25 2·75
382 50 c. grey and purple 5·25 7·00

1937. Coronation. As T **2** of Aden.
383 6 c. red 65 15
384 9 c. green 2·50 2·75
385 20 c. blue 3·50 3·50

70 Sigiriya (Lion Rock)

1938. As 1935 issue but with portrait of King George VI and "POSTAGE & REVENUE" omitted.
386b – 2 c. black and red 1·50 10
387d **60** 3 c. black and green 70 10
387f – 5 c. green and orange 30 10
388 – 6 c. black and blue 30 10
389 **70** 10 c. black and blue 2·00 10
390 – 15 c. green and brown 1·50 10
391 – 20 c. black and blue 3·25 10
392a – 25 c. blue and brown 4·00 10
393 – 30 c. red and green 11·00 1·25
394e – 50 c. black and violet 3·75 20
395 – 1 r. blue and brown 15·00 75
396 – 2 r. black and red 13·00 2·00
396a – 2 r. black and violet 1·75 1·40

DESIGNS—VERT: 5 c. Coconut palms; 20 c. Plucking tea; 2 r. Ancient guard-stone, Anuradhapura; Others, same as for corresponding values of 1935 issue.

1938. As T **57**, but head of King George VI to right.
397a 5 r. green and purple 13·00 2·00

1940. Surch with new value and bars.
398 – 3 c. on 6 c. blk & bl (No. 388) 10 10
399 – 3 c. on 20 c. blk & bl (No. 391) 2·00 1·50

1946. Victory. As T **9** of Aden.
400 6 c. blue 10 10
401 15 c. brown 10 40

75 Parliament Building

1947. New Constitution.
402 **75** 6 c. black and blue 10 15
403 – 10 c. black, orange and red 10 20
404 – 15 c. green and purple 10 55
405 – 25 c. yellow and green 10 20

DESIGNS—VERT: 10 c. Adam's Peak; 25 c. Anuradhapura. HORIZ: 15 c. Temple of the Tooth.

79 Lion Flag of Dominion

80 D. S. Senanayake

1949. 1st Anniv of Independence.
406 **79** 4 c. red, yellow and brown 10 20
407 **80** 5 c. brown and green 10 10
408 **79** 15 c. red, yellow and orange 25 15
409 **80** 25 c. brown and blue 15 40

No. 408 is larger 28 × 22 mm.

82 Globe and Forms of Transport

1949. 75th Anniv of U.P.U. Inscr as in T **82**. Designs showing globe.
410 **82** 5 c. brown and green 75 10
411 – 15 c. black and red (horiz) 1·40 1·75
412 – 25 c. black and blue (vert) 1·40 1·10

85 Kandyan Dancer

88 Sigiriya (Lion Rock)

90 Ruins at Madirigiriya

1950.
413 **85** 4 c. purple and red 10 10
414 – 5 c. green 10 10
415 – 15 c. green and violet 1·50 30
416 **88** 30 c. red and yellow 30 40
417 – 75 c. blue and orange 3·00 10
418 **90** 1 r. blue and brown 1·75 30

DESIGNS—VERT (As Types **85** and **88**): 5 c. Kiri Vehera, Polonnaruwa; 15 c. Vesak orchid. (As Type **90**): 75 c. Octagon Library, Temple of the Tooth.

94 Coconut Trees

99 Tea Plantation

1951.
419 – 2 c. brown and turquoise 10 40
420 – 3 c. black and violet 10 50
421 – 6 c. sepia and green 10 20
422 **94** 10 c. green and grey 75 65
423 – 25 c. orange and blue 10 20
424 – 35 c. red and green 1·50 1·50
425 – 40 c. brown 4·50 80
426 – 50 c. slate 30 10
427 **99** 85 c. black and turquoise 50 10
428 – 2 r. blue and brown 6·50 90
429 – 5 r. brown and orange 4·75 1·00
430 – 10 r. brown and buff 30·00 8·50

DESIGNS— VERT (As Type **94**): 2 c. Sambars, Ruhuna National Park; 3 c. Ancient guardstone, Anuradhapura; 6 c. Harvesting rice; 25 c. Sigiriya fresco; 35 c. Star orchid. (As Type **99**): 5 r Bas-relief, Anuradhapura; 10 r. Harvesting rice. HORIZ (As Type **94**): 40 c. Rubber plantation; 50 c. Outrigger canoe. (As Type **99**): 2 r. River Gal Dam.

103 Ceylon, Mace and Symbols of Progress

104 Queen Elizabeth II

1952. Colombo Plan Exhibition.
431 **103** 5 c. green 10 10
432 15 c. blue 20 40

1953. Coronation.
433 **104** 5 c. green 90 10

105 Ceremonial Procession

106 King Coconuts

1954. Royal Visit.
434 **105** 10 c. blue 30 10

1954.
435 **106** 10 c. orange, brown and buff 10 10

107 Farm Produce

1955. Royal Agricultural and Food Exhibition.
436 **107** 10 c. brown and orange 10 10

108 Sir John Kotelawala and House of Representatives

1956. Prime Minister's 25 years of Public Service.
437 **108** 10 c. green 10 10

109 Arrival of Vijaya in Ceylon

110 Lampstand and Dharmachakra

1956. Buddha Jayanti. Inscr "2500".
438 **109** 3 c. blue and grey 15 15
439 **110** 4 c. + 2 c. yellow and blue 20 75
440 – 10 c. + 5 c. red, yell & grey 20 75
441 – 15 c. blue 25 10
DESIGNS—VERT: 10 c. Hand of Peace and Dharmachakra. HORIZ: 15 c. Dharmachakra encircling the globe.

113 Mail Transport

114 Stamp of 1857

1957. Stamp Centenary.
442 **113** 4 c. red and turquoise . . 75 40
443 10 c. red and blue 75 10
444 **114** 35 c. brown, yellow and blue 30 50
445 85 c. brown, yellow and green . . . . 80 1·60

1958. Nos. 439/40 with premium obliterated with bars.
446 **110** 4 c. yellow and blue . . . 10 10
447 – 10 c. red, yellow and grey 10 10

117 Kandyan Dancer

118 "Human Rights"

1958. As Nos. 413 and 419 etc., and 435, but with inscriptions changed as in T **117**.
448 2 c. brown and turquoise . . . 10 50
449 3 c. black and violet 10 70
450 4 c. purple and red 10 10
451 5 c. green 10 75
452 6 c. sepia and green 10 65
453 10 c. orange, brown and buff 10 10
454 15 c. green and violet . . . . 3·50 70
455 25 c. orange and blue 10 10
456 30 c. red and yellow 15 90
457 35 c. red and green . . . . . 6·50 30
459 50 c. slate 30 10
460a 75 c. blue and orange . . . . 9·00 1·50
461 85 c. black and turquoise . . . 3·75 3·75
462 1 r. blue and brown 60 10
463 2 r. blue and brown . . . . 1·00 30
464 5 r. brown and orange . . . 2·75 30
465 10 r. brown and buff . . . . 8·00 1·00

1958. 10th Anniv of Declaration of Human Rights.
466 **118** 10 c. red, brown and purple 10 10
467 85 c. red, turq & grn . . . 30 45

119 Portraits of Founders and University Buildings

1959. Institution of Pirivena Universities.
468 **119** 10 c. orange and blue . . 10 10

120 "Uprooted Tree"

121 S.W.R.D. Bandaranaike

1960. World Refugee Year.
469 **120** 4 c. brown and gold . . . 10 60
470 25 c. violet and gold . . . 10 15

1961. Prime Minister Bandaranaike Commemoration.
471 **121** 10 c. blue and turquoise . 10 10
See also Nos. 479 and 481.

122 Ceylon Scout Badge

123 Campaign Emblem

1962. Golden Jubilee of Ceylon Boy Scouts Association.
472 **122** 35 c. buff and blue . . . 15 10

1962. Malaria Eradication.
473 **123** 25 c. red and drab . . . 10 10

124 De Havilland Leopard Moth and Hawker Siddeley Comet 4

1963. 25th Anniv of Airmail Services.
474 **124** 50 c. black and blue . . . 40 50

125 "Produce" and Campaign Emblem

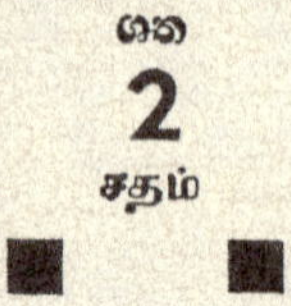

(**126**)

1963. Freedom from Hunger.
475 **125** 5 c. red and blue . . . . 30 1·75
476 25 c. brown and olive . . 1·50 30

1963. No. 450 surch with T **126**.
477 2 c. on 4 c. purple and red . . 10 10

127 "Rural Life"

131 Anagarika Dharmapala (Buddhist missionary)

129 Terrain, Indian Elephant and Tree

1963. Golden Jubilee of Ceylon Co-operative Movement (1962).
478 **127** 60 c. red and black . . . 70 60

1963. Design as T **121**, but smaller (21 × 26 mm) and with inscription rearranged at top.
479 10 c. blue 10 10
481 10 c. violet and grey 10 10
No. 481 has a decorative pattern at foot instead of the inscription.

1963. National Conservation Week.
480 **129** 5 c. sepia and blue . . . 60 40

1964. Birth Centenary of A. Dharmapala (founder of Maha Bodhi Society)
482 **131** 25 c. sepia and yellow . . 10 10

135 D. S. Senanayake

143 Ceylon Jungle Fowl

138 Ruins at Madirigiriya

1964.
485 – 5 c. multicoloured . . . . 1·40 1·50
486 **135** 10 c. green 50 10
487 – 10 c. green 10 10
488 – 15 c. multicoloured . . . . 2·25 30
489 **138** 20 c. purple and buff . . . 10 15
494 **143** 60 c. multicoloured . . . 3·25 80
495 – 75 c. multicoloured . . . 1·50 70
497 – 1 r. brown and green . . 1·00 30
499 – 5 r. multicoloured . . . . 5·00 3·25
500 – 10 r. multicoloured . . . 19·00 3·25
DESIGNS—HORIZ (As Type **143**): 5 c. Grackle; 15 c. Peacock; 75 c. Asian black-headed oriole. (As Type **138**): 5 r. Girls transplanting rice. VERT (As Type **135**): 10 c. (No. 487) Similar portrait, but large head and smaller inscriptions. (21 × 35 mm): 1 r. Tea plantation. (23 × 36 mm): 10 r. Map of Ceylon.

150 Exhibition Buildings and Cogwheels

1964. Industrial Exhibition.
501 – 5 c. multicoloured 10 75
502 **150** 5 c. multicoloured 10 75
No. 501 is inscribed "INDUSTRIAL EXHIBITION" in Sinhala and Tamil, No. 502 in Sinhala and English.

151 Trains of 1864 and 1964

1964. Centenary of Ceylon Railways.
503 – 60 c. blue, purple and green 2·75 40
504 **151** 60 c. blue, purple and green 2·75 40
No. 503 is inscribed "RAILWAY CENTENARY" in Sinhala and Tamil, No. 504 in Sinhala and English.

152 I.T.U. Emblem and Symbols

1965. Centenary of I.T.U.
505 **152** 2 c. blue and red . . . . . 50 1·10
506 30 c. brown and red . . . 2·75 45

153 I.C.Y. Emblem

1965. International Co-operation Year.
507 **153** 3 c. blue and red . . . . . 1·00 1·00
508 50 c. black, red and gold . 3·00 50

154 Town Hall, Colombo

1965. Centenary of Colombo Municipal Council.
509 **154** 25 c. green and sepia . . . 10 10

1965. No. 481 surch **5**.
510 5 c. on 10 c. violet and grey . . 10 30

157 Kandy and Council Crest

1966. Centenary of Kandy Municipal Council.
512 **157** 25 c. multicoloured 10 10

158 W.H.O. Building

159 Rice Paddy and Map of Ceylon

1966. Inauguration of W.H.O. Headquarters, Geneva.
513 **158** 4 c. multicoloured . . . . 1·75 2·50
514 1 r. multicoloured . . . . 6·75 1·50

1966. International Rice Year. Multicoloured.
515 6 c. Type **159** 20 75
516 30 c. Rice paddy and globe . . 30 15

161 U.N.E.S.C.O. Emblem

162 Water-resources Map

1966. 20th Anniv of U.N.E.S.C.O.
517 **161** 3 c. multicoloured . . . . 1·75 1·50
518 50 c. multicoloured . . . 5·25 30

1966. International Hydrological Decade.
519 **162** 2 c. brown, yellow and blue 30 85
520 2 r. multicoloured . . . . 95 2·25

163 Devotees at Buddhist Temple

1967. Poya Holiday System. Multicoloured.
521 5 c. Type **163** 10 40
522 20 c. Mihintale 10 10
523 35 c. Sacred Bo-tree Anuradhapura 10 15
524 60 c. Adam's Peak 10 10

167 Galle Fort and Clock Tower

1967. Centenary of Galle Municipal Council.
525 **167** 25 c. multicoloured . . . 60 20

168 Field Research

1967. Centenary of Ceylon Tea Industry. Mult.
526 4 c. Type **168** 40 80
527 40 c. Tea-tasting equipment . . 1·50 1·25
528 50 c. Leaves and bud . . . . 1·50 40
529 1 r. Shipping tea . . . . . . 1·50 10

172 Elephant Ride

1967. International Tourist Year.
530 **172** 45 c. multicoloured . . . 2·00 70

173 Ranger, Jubilee Emblem and Flag

1967. Golden Jubilee of Ceylon Girl Guides' Association.
532 **173** 3 c. multicoloured 30 20
533 25 c. multicoloured . . . 55 10

174 Colonel Olcott and Buddhist Flag

1967. 60th Death Anniv of Colonel Olcott (theosophist).
534 **174** 15 c. multicoloured . . . 30 20

175 Independence Hall

177 Sir D. B. Jayatilleke

1968. 20th Anniv of Independence. Multicoloured.
535 5 c. Type **175** 10 55
536 1 r. Lion flag and sceptre . . . 40 10

1968. Birth Centenary of Sir Baron Jayatilleke (scholar and statesman).
537 **177** 25 c. brown 10 10

178 Institute of Hygiene

1968. 20th Anniv of World Health Organization.
538 **178** 50 c. multicoloured . . . 10 10

179 Vickers Super VC-10 over Terminal Building

1968. Opening of Colombo Airport.
539 **179** 60 c. multicoloured . . . 30 10

181 Open Koran and "1400"

1968. 1400th Anniv of Koran.
541 **181** 25 c. multicoloured . . . 10 10

182 Human Rights Emblem

1968. Human Rights Year.
542 **182** 2 c. multicoloured 10 15
543 20 c. multicoloured . . . 10 10
544 40 c. multicoloured . . . 10 10
545 2 r. multicoloured . . . 70 3·00

183 All-Ceylon Buddhist Congress Headquarters

1968. Golden Jubilee of All-Ceylon Buddhist Congress.
546 **183** 5 c. multicoloured 10 40

184 E. W. Perera (patriot)

185 Symbols of Strength in Savings

1969. Perera Commemoration.
547 **184** 60 c. brown 10 30

1969. Silver Jubilee of National Savings Movement.
548 **185** 3 c. multicoloured 10 10

186 Seat of Enlightenment under Sacred Bodhi Tree

188 A. E. Goonesinghe

1969. Vesak Day. Inscribed "Wesak".
549 **186** 4 c. multicoloured 10 40
550 – 6 c. multicoloured 10 40
551 **186** 35 c. multicoloured . . . 10 10
DESIGN: 6 c. Buduresmala (six-fold Buddha-rays).

1969. Goonesinghe Commemoration.
552 **188** 15 c. multicoloured . . . 10 10

189 I.L.O. Emblem

1969. 50th Anniv of I.L.O.
553 **189** 5 c. black and blue . . . 10 10
554 25 c. black and red . . . 10 10

190 Convocation Hall, University of Ceylon

194 Ath Pana (Elephant Lamp)

1969. Educational Centenary. Multicoloured.
555 4 c. Type **190** 10 80
556 35 c. Lamp of learning, globe and flags (horiz) 15 10
557 50 c. Uranium atom 15 10
558 60 c. Symbols of scientific education 20 10

1969. Archaeological Centenary. Multicoloured.
559 6 c. Type **194** . . . . 15 1·25
560 1 r. Rock fortress of Sigiriya . 25 10

196 Leopard

1970. Wild Life Conservation. Multicoloured.
561 5 c. Water buffalo . . . . . 40 1·25
562 15 c. Slender loris 90 30
563 50 c. Spotted deer . . . . . 90 1·25
564 1 r. Type **196** . . . . 90 1·75

197 Emblem and Symbols

1970. Asian Productivity Year.
565 **197** 60 c. multicoloured . . . 10 10

198 New U.P.U. H.Q. Building

199 Oil Lamp and Caduceus

1970. New U.P.U. Headquarters Building.
566 **198** 50 c. orange, black and blue 20 10
567 1 r. 10 red, black and blue 2·00 30

1970. Centenary of Colombo Medical School.
568 **199** 5 c. multicoloured 40 80
569 45 c. multicoloured 40 60

200 Victory March and S.W.R.D. Bandaranaike

1970. Establishment of United Front Government.
570 **200** 10 c. multicoloured 10 10

201 U.N. Emblem and Dove of Peace

202 Keppetipola Dissawa

1970. 25th Anniv of United Nations.
571 **201** 2 r. multicoloured . . . . 2·00 2·50

1970. 152nd Death Anniv of Keppetipola Dissawa (Kandyan patriot).
572 **202** 25 c. multicoloured 10 10

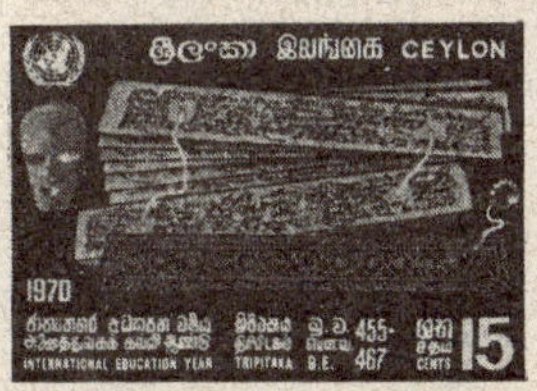

203 Ola Leaf Manuscript

1970. International Education Year.
573 **203** 15 c. multicoloured . . . . 1·50 1·25

204 C. H. de Soysa

205 D. E. H. Pedris (patriot)

1971. 135th Birth Anniv of C. H. de Soysa (philanthropist)
574 **204** 20 c. multicoloured 15 40

1971. D. E. H. Pedris Commemoration.
575 **205** 25 c. multicoloured 15 50

206 Lenin

207 Ananda Rajakaruna

1971. Lenin Commemoration.
576 **206** 40 c. multicoloured 15 40

1971. Poets and Philosophers.
577 **207** 5 c. blue 10 15
578 – 5 c. brown 10 15
579 – 5 c. orange 10 15
580 – 5 c. blue 10 15
581 – 5 c. brown 10 15
PORTRAITS: No. 578, Arumuga Navalar; No. 579, Rev. S. Mahinda; No. 580, Ananda Coomaraswamy; No. 581, Cumaratunga Munidasa.

1971. Surch in figures.
582 **186** 5 c. on 4 c. multicoloured . 4·50 1·75
583 **190** 5 c. on 4 c. multicoloured . 10 1·00
584 **200** 15 c. on 10 c. multicoloured 10 30
585 – 25 c. on 6 c. multicoloured (No. 550) 30 60
586 **194** 25 c. on 6 c. multicoloured 30 1·00

209 Colombo Plan Emblem and Ceylon

1971. 20th Anniv of Colombo Plan.
587 **209** 20 c. multicoloured 15 30

210 Globe and C.A.R.E. Package

1971. 20th Anniv of Co-operative for American Relief Everywhere.
588 **210** 50 c. blue, violet and lilac 35 30

211 W.H.O. Emblem and Heart

1972. World Health Day.
589 **211** 25 c. multicoloured . . . 1·75 60

212 Map of Asia and U.N. Emblem

1972. 25th Anniv of E.C.A.F.E.
590 **212** 85 c. multicoloured . . . 3·50 2·75

OFFICIAL STAMPS

1895. Stamps of Queen Victoria optd **On Service**.
O 1 **9** 2 c. green . . . . 7·00 45
O 8 2 c. brown . . . . 6·00 60
O 2 **39** 3 c. brown and green . . 10·00 55
O 9 3 c. green . . . . 8·00 1·75
O 3 **28** 5 c. purple . . . . 3·25 30
O 4 **39** 15 c. olive . . . . 12·00 50
O10 15 c. blue . . . . 16·00 60
O 5 25 c. brown . . . . 10·00 1·00
O 6 30 c. mauve and brown . 13·00 50
O11 75 c. black and brown . . 5·50 5·00
O 7 **30** 1 r. 12 red . . . . 70·00 55·00

1903. Stamps of King Edward VII optd **On Service**.
O12 **44** 2 c. brown . . . . 10·00 85
O13 **45** 3 c. green . . . . 6·50 2·00
O14 – 5 c. purple (No. 268) . . . 15·00 1·25
O15 **45** 15 c. blue . . . . 25·00 2·50
O16 25 c. brown . . . . 21·00 18·00
O17 30 c. violet and green . . 10·00 1·50

For later issues see **SRI LANKA**.

CHAMBA

An Indian "convention" state of the Punjab. Stamps of India overprinted.

12 pies = 1 anna; 16 annas = 1 rupee

1886. Queen Victoria. Optd **CHAMBA STATE** in two lines.
1 **23** ½ a. turquoise 10 35
2 – 1 a. purple 60 90
4 – 1 a. 6 p. brown . . . . . . 60 8·00
6 – 2 a. blue . . . . 90 1·10
7 – 2 a. 6 p. green . . . . . . 24·00 60·00
9 – 3 a. orange . . . . 60 3·25
11 – 4 a. green (No. 96) . . . . 3·00 4·00
12 – 6 a. brown (No. 80) . . . . 2·00 10·00
14 – 8 a. mauve . . . . 4·50 7·00
16 – 12 a. purple on red . . . . 3·75 8·00
17 – 1 r. grey (No. 101) . . . . 26·00 85·00
18 **37** 1 r. green and red . . . . . 4·25 9·00
19 **38** 2 r. red and brown . . . . 65·00 £190
20 3 r. brown and green . . . 65·00 £170
21 5 r. blue and violet . . . . 75·00 £300

1900. Queen Victoria. Optd **CHAMBA STATE** in two lines.
22 **40** 3 p. red 10 30
23 3 p. grey . . . . 15 1·50
25 **23** ½ a. green 10 60
26 – 1 a. red 10 30
27 – 2 a. lilac . . . . 5·00 19·00

1903. King Edward VII. Optd **CHAMBA STATE** in two lines.
28 **41** 3 p. grey 10 85
30 – ½ a. green (No. 122) 10 20
31 – 1 a. red (No. 123) 45 20
33 – 2 a. lilac . . . . 55 1·60
34 – 3 a. orange . . . . 2·00 3·00
35 – 4 a. olive . . . . 2·50 10·00
36 – 6 a. bistre . . . . 2·00 13·00
37 – 8 a. mauve . . . . 2·50 12·00
39 – 12 a. purple on red . . . . 3·50 16·00
40 – 1 r. green and red . . . . . 4·25 15·00

1907. King Edward VII. Optd **CHAMBA STATE** in two lines.
41 – ½ a. green (No. 149) . . . . 25 2·25
42 – 1 a. red (No. 150) . . . . . 35 2·25

1913. King George V. Optd **CHAMBA STATE** in two lines.
43 **55** 3 p. grey 10 40
44 **56** ½ a. green 20 45
46 **57** 1 a. red . . . . 35 1·50
55 1 a. brown . . . . 80 2·50
56 **58** 1½ a. brown (No. 163) . . . 16·00 75·00

57	**58**	$1\frac{1}{2}$ a. brown (No. 165)	60	3·50
58		$1\frac{1}{2}$ a. red	60	12·00
47	**59**	2 a. lilac	1·25	5·50
59	**61**	2 a. 6 p. blue	50	2·75
60		2 a. 6 p. orange	90	10·00
48	**62**	3 a. orange	1·50	4·50
61		3 a. blue	1·60	12·00
49	**63**	4 a. olive	1·00	3·00
50	**64**	6 a. bistre	90	2·75
51	**65**	8 a. mauve	1·90	6·50
52	**66**	12 a. red	1·60	9·00
53	**67**	1 r. brown and green	9·00	16·00

1921. No. 192 of India optd **CHAMBA**.

54	**57**	9 p. on 1 a. red	80	14·00

1927. Stamps of India (King George V) optd **CHAMBA STATE** in one line.

62	**55**	3 p. grey	10	65
63	**56**	$\frac{1}{2}$ a. green	20	1·00
76	**79**	$\frac{1}{2}$ a. green	55	5·50
64	**80**	9 p. green	1·25	7·50
65	**57**	1 a. brown	1·25	25
77	**81**	1 a. brown	60	45
66	**82**	1 a. 3 p. mauve	75	3·50
67	**58**	$1\frac{1}{2}$ a. red	3·25	3·25
68	**70**	2 a. lilac	75	1·00
78	**59**	2 a. red	45	16·00
69	**61**	2 a. 6 p. orange	90	11·00
70	**62**	3 a. blue	80	11·00
80		3 a. red	1·25	6·00
71	**71**	4 a. green	55	2·75
81	**63**	4 a. olive	1·10	8·50
72	**64**	6 a. bistre	25·00	£120
73	**65**	8 a. mauve	1·00	6·50
74	**66**	12 a. red	1·10	7·50
75	**67**	1 r. brown and green	3·50	16·00

1938. Stamps of India (King George VI Nos. 247/64) optd **CHAMBA STATE**.

82	**91**	3 p. slate	3·25	7·50
83		$\frac{1}{2}$ a. brown	90	4·25
84		9 p. green	4·25	20·00
85		1 a. red	90	1·25
86	**92**	2 a. red	2·75	6·50
87	–	2 a. 6 p. violet	3·25	14·00
88	–	3 a. green	4·00	15·00
89	–	3 a. 6 p. blue	4·00	17·00
90	–	4 a. brown	13·00	11·00
91	–	6 a. green	12·00	35·00
92	–	8 a. violet	13·00	30·00
93	–	12 a. red	8·00	35·00
94	**93**	1 r. slate and brown	27·00	42·00
95		2 r. purple and brown	42·00	£180
96		5 r. green and blue	65·00	£275
97		10 r. purple and red	£110	£425
98		15 r. brown and green	£200	£600
99		25 r. slate and purple	£225	£700

1942. Stamps of India (King George VI) optd **CHAMBA**. (a) On issue of 1938.

100	**91**	$\frac{1}{2}$ a. brown	23·00	15·00
101		1 a. red	26·00	16·00
102	**93**	1 r. slate and brown	21·00	42·00
103		2 r. purple and brown	28·00	£160
104		5 r. green and blue	60·00	£170
105		10 r. purple and red	85·00	£325
106		15 r. brown and green	£180	£500
107		25 r. slate and purple	£200	£550

(b) On issue of 1940.

108	**100a**	3 p. slate	60	3·00
109		$\frac{1}{2}$ a. mauve	70	2·00
110		9 p. green	70	8·00
111		1 a. red	90	2·00
112	**101**	$1\frac{1}{2}$ a. violet	90	5·50
113		2 a. red	1·90	6·00
114		3 a. violet	7·00	15·00
115		$3\frac{1}{2}$ a. blue	3·50	23·00
116	**102**	4 a. brown	5·00	7·00
117		6 a. green	14·00	35·00
118		8 a. violet	13·00	40·00
119		12 a. purple	26·00	50·00
120	–	14 a. purple (No. 277)	6·00	3·00

OFFICIAL STAMPS

Stamps of India optd

1886. Queen Victoria. Optd **SERVICE CHAMBA STATE**.

O 1	**23**	$\frac{1}{2}$ a. turquoise	10	10
O 3	–	1 a. purple	55	10
O 4	–	2 a. blue	1·00	80
O 7	–	3 a. orange	1·60	8·00
O 8	–	4 a. green (No. 96)	1·25	3·00
O10	–	6 a. brown (No. 80)	3·25	7·50
O13	–	8 a. mauve	90	1·60
O14	–	12 a. purple on red	7·00	27·00
O15	–	1 r. grey (No. 101)	12·00	80·00
O16	**37**	1 r. green and red	5·50	22·00

1902. Queen Victoria. Optd **SERVICE CHAMBA STATE**.

O17	**40**	3 p. grey	15	45
O18	**23**	$\frac{1}{2}$ a. green	20	2·50
O20	–	1 a. red	40	40
O21	–	2 a. lilac	8·00	21·00

1903. King Edward VII. Optd **SERVICE CHAMBA STATE**.

O22	**41**	3 p. grey	15	15
O24		$\frac{1}{2}$ a. green (No. 122)	15	10
O25		1 a. red (No. 123)	35	25
O27	–	2 a. lilac	50	50
O28	–	4 a. olive	2·50	11·00
O29	–	8 a. mauve	3·00	11·00
O31	–	1 r. green and red	1·40	6·50

1907. King Edward VII. Optd **SERVICE CHAMBA STATE**.

O32	–	$\frac{1}{2}$ a. green (No. 149)	25	75
O33	–	1 a. red (No. 150)	1·40	1·00

1913. King George V Official stamps optd **CHAMBA STATE**.

O35	**55**	3 p. grey	20	40
O36	**56**	$\frac{1}{2}$ a. green	10	10
O38	**57**	1 a. red	10	10
O47		1 a. brown	1·40	50
O40	**59**	2 a. lilac (No. O83)	1·00	8·50
O41	**63**	4 a. olive (No. O86)	1·10	10·00
O42	**65**	8 a. mauve	1·60	11·00
O43	**67**	1 r. brown and green	3·25	19·00

1914. King George Postage stamps optd **SERVICE CHAMBA STATE**.

O44	**59**	2 a. lilac (No. 166)	10·00	
O45	**63**	4 a. olive (No. 210)	9·00	

1921. No O97 of India optd **CHAMBA**.

O46	**57**	9 p. on 1 a. red	15	4·50

1927. King George V Postage stamps optd **CHAMBA STATE SERVICE**.

O48	**55**	3 p. grey	40	30
O49	**56**	$\frac{1}{2}$ a. green	30	15
O61	**79**	$\frac{1}{2}$ a. green	1·00	40
O50	**80**	9 p. green	1·25	6·00
O51	**57**	1 a. brown	20	10
O62	**81**	1 a. brown	1·75	45
O52	**82**	$1\frac{1}{4}$ a. mauve	4·50	50
O53	**70**	2 a. lilac	70	55
O63	**59**	2 a. red	2·75	85
O54	**71**	4 a. olive	70	90
O65	**63**	4 a. green	3·00	2·75
O55	**65**	8 a. mauve	3·00	6·50
O56	**66**	12 a. red	1·60	15·00
O57	**67**	1 r. brown and green	9·50	27·00
O58		2 r. red and orange	18·00	£160
O59		5 r. blue and violet	40·00	£225
O60		1 r. green and red	50·00	£200

1938. King George VI Postage stamps of India optd **CHAMBA STATE SERVICE**.

O66	**91**	9 p. green	7·50	32·00
O67		1 a. red	6·00	1·50
O68	**93**	1 r. slate and brown	£500	£750
O69		2 r. purple and brown	50·00	£250
O70		5 r. green and blue	80·00	£325
O71		10 r. purple and red	£120	£500

1940. Official stamps of India optd **CHAMBA**.

O72	O **20**	3 p. grey	60	50
O73		$\frac{1}{2}$ a. brown	11·00	1·25
O74		$\frac{1}{2}$ a. purple	60	1·40
O75		9 p. green	3·25	5·00
O76		1 a. red	60	1·10
O77		1 a. 3 p. brown	38·00	13·00
O78		$1\frac{1}{2}$ a. violet	3·75	4·25
O79		2 a. orange	3·00	3·50
O80		$2\frac{1}{2}$ a. violet	1·75	15·00
O81		4 a. brown	3·25	6·50
O82		8 a. violet	9·50	38·00

1942. King George VI Postage stamps of India optd **CHAMBA SERVICE**.

O83	**93**	1 r. slate and brown	32·00	£140
O84		2 r. purple and brown	50·00	£200
O85		5 r. green and blue	80·00	£300
O86		10 r. purple and red	£120	£500

CHARKHARI

A state of Central India. Now uses Indian stamps.

12 pies = 1 anna; 16 annas = 1 rupee

1

2

1894. Imperf. No gum.

10	**1**	$\frac{1}{4}$ a. purple	1·75	2·50
6a		$\frac{1}{2}$ a. purple	2·50	3·00
7a		1 a. green	4·00	4·50
8a		2 a. green	7·00	8·00
9a		4 a. green	6·00	9·00

1909. Perf or imperf.

15a	**2**	1 p. brown	2·50	38·00
16		1 p. blue	35	45
33		1 p. violet	13·00	£100
32		1 p. green	40·00	£140
25		$\frac{1}{2}$ a. red	90	1·10
35		$\frac{1}{2}$ a. brown	3·25	22·00
34		$\frac{1}{2}$ a. olive	70	11·00
36		$\frac{1}{2}$ a. black	45·00	£120
18a		1 a. green	1·60	1·25
40		1 a. brown	5·00	22·00
41		1 a. red	75·00	55·00
19		2 a. blue	2·50	3·25
43		2 a. grey	35·00	48·00
20		4 a. green	3·00	4·00
44		4 a. red	4·00	18·00
21		8 a. red	6·00	13·00
22		1 r. brown	10·00	26·00

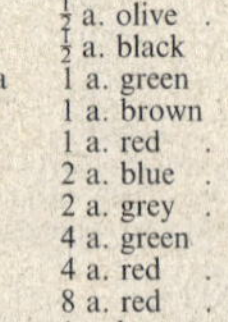

4

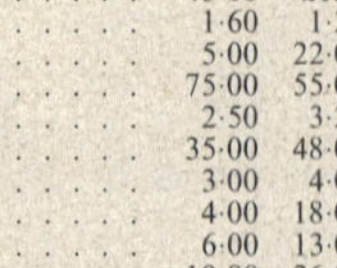

7 Imlia Palace

5

1912. Imperf.

28	**4**	1 p. violet	7·00	5·00

1922. Imperf.

29	**5**	1 a. violet	60·00	75·00

1931. Perf.

45	–	$\frac{1}{2}$ a. green	80	10
46	**7**	1 a. sepia	1·00	10
47	–	2 a. violet	60	10
48	–	4 a. olive	80	15
49	–	8 a. mauve	1·00	10
50	–	1 r. green and red	1·40	15
51	–	2 r. red and brown	2·25	20
52	–	3 r. brown and green	6·00	30
53	–	5 r. blue and lilac	7·00	45

DESIGNS—HORIZ: $\frac{1}{2}$ a. The Lake; 2 a. Industrial school; 4 a. Bird's-eye view of city; 8 a. Fort; 1 r. Guest House; 2 r. Palace Gate; 3 r. Temples at Rainpur; 5 r. Goverdhan Temple.

1940. Nos. 21/2 surch.

54	**2**	$\frac{1}{2}$ a. on 8 a. red	26·00	£110
55		1 a. on 1 r. brown	70·00	£275
56		"1 ANNA" on 1 r. brown	£500	£550

CHINA EXPEDITIONARY FORCE

Stamps used by Indian military forces in China.

12 pies = 1 anna; 16 annas = 1 rupee

Stamps of India optd **C.E.F.**

1900. Queen Victoria.

C 1	**40**	3 p. red	40	1·25
C 2	**23**	$\frac{1}{2}$ a. green	75	30
C 3	–	1 a. purple	4·00	1·50
C11	–	1 a. red	27·00	8·00
C 4	–	2 a. blue	3·00	9·00
C 5	–	2 a. 6 p. green	2·75	13·00
C 6	–	3 a. orange	2·75	16·00
C 7	–	4 a. green (No. 96)	2·75	7·50
C 8	–	8 a. mauve	2·75	15·00
C 9	–	12 a. purple on red	15·00	15·00
C10	**37**	1 r. green and red	16·00	16·00

1904. King Edward VII.

C12c	**41**	3 p. grey	3·50	6·50
C13	–	1 a. red (No. 123)	6·50	70
C14	–	2 a. lilac	14·00	2·00
C15	–	2 a. 6 p. blue	3·25	5·00
C16	–	3 a. orange	3·75	4·00
C17	–	4 a. olive	8·50	11·00
C18	–	8 a. mauve	8·00	7·50
C19	–	12 a. purple on red	11·00	19·00
C20	–	1 r. green and red	13·00	28·00

1909. King Edward VII.

C21		$\frac{1}{2}$ a. green (No. 149)	1·50	1·25
C22		1 a. red (No. 150)	1·50	30

1913. King George V.

C23	**55**	3 p. grey	3·75	22·00
C24	**56**	$\frac{1}{2}$ a. green	2·75	4·50
C25	**57**	1 a. red	3·25	3·25
C26	**58**	$1\frac{1}{2}$ a. brown (No. 163)	21·00	65·00
C27	**59**	2 a. lilac	10·00	48·00
C28	**61**	2 a. 6 p. blue	8·50	22·00
C29	**62**	3 a. orange	23·00	£180
C30	**63**	4 a. olive	19·00	£150
C32	**65**	8 a. mauve	20·00	£325
C33	**66**	12 a. red	19·00	£110
C34	**67**	1 r. brown and green	55·00	£250

BRITISH RAILWAY ADMINISTRATION

1901. No. 121 of China surch **B.R.A. 5 Five Cents**.

BR133b	**32**	5 c. on $\frac{1}{2}$ c. brown	£275	£140

CHRISTMAS ISLAND

Situated in the Indian Ocean about 600 miles south of Singapore. Formerly part of the Straits Settlements and then of the Crown Colony of Singapore, Christmas Island was occupied by the Japanese from 31 March 1942 until September 1945. It reverted to Singapore after liberation but subsequently became an Australian territory on 15 October 1958.

1958. 100 cents = 1 Malayan dollar.
1968. 100 cents = 1 Australian dollar.

1 Queen Elizabeth II

2 Map

1958. Type of Australia with opt and value in black.

1	**1**	2 c. orange	55	70
2		4 c. brown	60	30
3		5 c. mauve	60	30
4		6 c. blue	1·50	30
5		8 c. sepia	3·00	50
6		10 c. violet	2·00	30
7		12 c. red	3·25	1·75
8		20 c. blue	2·00	1·75
9		50 c. green	3·00	1·75
10		\$1 turquoise	3·75	1·75

1963.

11	**2**	2 c. orange	90	55
12	–	4 c. brown	50	20
13	–	5 c. purple	50	30
14	–	6 c. blue	40	50
15	–	8 c. black	3·25	60
16	–	10 c. violet	40	20
17	–	12 c. red	40	40
18	–	20 c. blue	1·00	35
19	–	50 c. green	1·50	35
20	–	\$1 yellow	3·50	60

DESIGNS—VERT: 4 c. Moonflower; 5 c. Robber crab; 8 c. Phosphate train; 10 c. Raising phosphate. HORIZ: 6 c. Island scene; 12 c. Flying Fish cove; 20 c. Loading cantilever; 50 c. Christmas Island frigate bird. LARGER (35 × 21 mm): \$1 White-tailed tropic bird.

1965. 50th Anniv of Gallipoli Landing. As T **184** of Australia, but slightly larger ($22 \times 34\frac{1}{2}$ mm).

21	10 c. brown, black and green	45	80

12 Golden-striped Grouper

1968. Fishes. Multicoloured.

22	1 c. Type **12**	45	45
23	2 c. Moorish idol	60	20
24	3 c. Long-nosed butterflyfish	60	30
25	4 c. Pink-tailed triggerfish	60	20
26	5 c. Regal angelfish	75	20
27	9 c. White-cheeked surgeonfish	1·25	40
28	10 c. Lionfish	1·00	20
28a	15 c. Saddle butterflyfish	10·00	5·50
29	20 c. Ornate butterflyfish	3·50	55
29a	30 c. Giant ghost pipefish	10·00	5·50
30	50 c. Clown surgeonfish	5·00	3·00
31	\$1 Meyer's butterflyfish	5·50	5·00

13 "Angel" (mosaic)

14 "The Ansidei Madonna" (Raphael)

1969. Christmas.

32	**13**	5 c. multicoloured	20	30

1970. Christmas. Paintings. Multicoloured.

33	3 c. Type **14**	20	15
34	5 c. "The Virgin and Child, St. John the Baptist and an Angel" (Morando)	20	15

15 "The Adoration of the Shepherds" (attr to the School of Seville)

16 H.M.S. "Flying Fish" (survey ship), 1887

1971. Christmas. Multicoloured.

35	6 c. Type **15**	30	50
36	20 c. "The Adoration of the Shepherds" (Reni)	70	1·00

1972. Ships. Multicoloured.

37	1 c. "Eagle" (merchant sailing ship), 1714	25	60
38	2 c. H.M.S. "Redpole" (gunboat), 1890	30	70
39	3 c. "Hoi Houw" (freighter), 1959	30	70
40	4 c. "Pigot" (sailing ship), 1771	40	75
41	5 c. "Valetta" (cargo-liner), 1968	40	75
42	6 c. Type **16**	40	75
43	7 c. "Asia" (sail merchantman), 1805	40	75
44	8 c. "Islander" (freighter), 1929–60	45	80
45	9 c. H.M.S. "Imperieuse" (armoured cruiser), 1888	65	70
46	10 c. H.M.S. "Cerberus" (coast defence turret ship), 1871	55	80
47	20 c. "Thomas" (galleon), 1615	70	90
48	25 c. Royal Navy sail sloop, 1864	80	1·50
49	30 c. "Cygnet" (flute), 1688	80	1·00
50	35 c. "Triadic" (freighter), 1958	80	1·00
51	50 c. H.M.S. "Amethyst" (frigate), 1857	80	1·50
52	\$1 "Royal Mary" (warship), 1643	1·10	1·75

No. 45 is inscribed "H.M.S. Imperious", No. 46 "H.M.S. Egeria" and No. 48 "H.M.S. Gordon", all in error.

17 Angel of Peace

19 Mary and Holy Child within Christmas Star

18 Virgin and Child, and Map

1972. Christmas. Multicoloured.

53		3 c. Type **17**	20	40
54		3 c. Angel of Joy	20	40
55		7 c. Type **17**	30	50
56		7 c. As No. 54	30	50

1973. Christmas.

57	**18**	7 c. multicoloured	35	35
58		25 c. multicoloured	1·25	1·25

1974. Christmas.

59	**19**	7 c. mauve and grey	35	75
60		30 c. orange, yellow and grey	1·25	2·75

20 "The Flight into Egypt"

21 Dove of Peace and Star of Bethlehem

1975. Christmas.

61	**20**	10 c. yellow, brown and gold	40	35
62		35 c. pink, blue and gold	1·10	1·75

1976. Christmas.

63	**21**	10 c. red, yellow and mauve	20	45
64	–	10 c. red, yellow and mauve	20	45
65	**21**	35 c. violet, blue and green	25	55
66	–	35 c. violet, blue and green	25	55

DESIGNS: Nos. 64 and 66 are "mirror-images" of Type **21**.

22 William Dampier (explorer)

1977. Famous Visitors. Multicoloured.

67		1 c. Type **22**	15	70
68		2 c. Captain de Vlamingh (explorer)	20	70
69		3 c. Vice-Admiral MacLear	30	70
70		4 c. Sir John Murray (oceanographer)	30	80
71		5 c. Admiral Aldrich	30	40
72		6 c. Andrew Clunies Ross (first settler)	30	60
73		7 c. J. J. Lister (naturalist)	30	40
74		8 c. Admiral of the Fleet Sir William May	35	70
75		9 c. Henry Ridley (botanist)	40	75
76		10 c. George Clunies Ross (phosphate miner)	55	55
77		20 c. Captain Joshua Slocum (yachtsman)	50	75
78		45 c. Charles Andrews (naturalist)	85	45
79		50 c. Richard Hanitsch (biologist)	95	60
80		75 c. Victor Purcell (scholar)	85	1·25
81		$1 Fam Choo Beng (educator)	85	1·25
82		$2 Sir Harold Spencer-Jones (astronomer)	1·00	2·25

23 Australian Coat of Arms on Map of Christmas Island

1977. Silver Jubilee.

83	**23**	45 c. multicoloured	45	55

24 "A Partridge in a Pear Tree"

25 Abbott's Booby

1977. Christmas. "The Twelve Days of Christmas". Multicoloured.

84A		10 c. Type **24**	10	20
85A		10 c. "Two turtle doves"	10	20
86A		10 c. "Three French hens"	10	20
87A		10 c. "Four calling birds"	10	20
88A		10 c. "Five gold rings"	10	20
89A		10 c. "Six geese a-laying"	10	20
90A		10 c. "Seven swans a-swimming"	10	20
91A		10 c. "Eight maids a-milking"	10	20
92A		10 c. "Nine ladies dancing"	10	20
93A		10 c. "Ten lords a-leaping"	10	20
94A		10 c. "Eleven pipers piping"	10	20
95A		10 c. "Twelve drummers drumming"	10	20

1978. 25th Anniv of Coronation.

96	–	45 c. black and blue	45	75
97	–	45 c. multicoloured	45	75
98	**25**	45 c. black and blue	45	75

DESIGNS: No. 96, White Swan of Bohun; No. 97, Queen Elizabeth II.

26 "Christ Child"

27 Chinese Children

1978. Christmas Scenes from "The Song of Christmas". Multicoloured.

99		10 c. Type **26**	15	20
100		10 c. "Herald Angels"	15	20
101		10 c. "Redeemer"	15	20
102		10 c. "Israel"	15	20
103		10 c. "Star"	15	20
104		10 c. "Three Wise Men"	15	20
105		10 c. "Manger"	15	20
106		10 c. "All He Stands For"	15	20
107		10 c. "Shepherds Come"	15	20

1979. International Year of the Child. Children of different races. Multicoloured, colours of inscr given.

108		20 c. green (Type **27**)	30	45
109		20 c. turquoise (Malay children)	30	45
110		20 c. lilac (Indian children)	30	45
111		20 c. red (European children)	30	45
112		20 c. yellow ("Oranges and Lemons")	30	45

28 1958 2 c. Definitive

1979. Death Centenary of Sir Rowland Hill. Multicoloured.

113		20 c. Type **28**	25	40
114		20 c. 1963 2 c. map definitive	25	40
115		20 c. 1965 50th Anniv of Gallipoli Landing 10 c. commemorative	25	40
116		20 c. 1964 4 c. Pink-tailed triggerfish definitive	25	40
117		20 c. 1969 Christmas 5 c. value	25	40

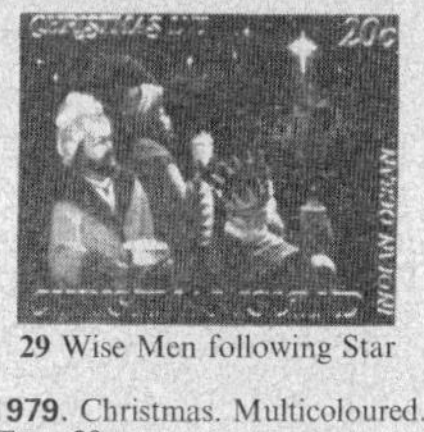

29 Wise Men following Star

1979. Christmas. Multicoloured.

118		20 c. Type **29**	20	30
119		55 c. Virgin and Child	45	70

30 9th Green

1980. 25th Anniv of Christmas Island Golf Club. Multicoloured.

120		20 c. Type **30**	35	50
121		55 c. Clubhouse	40	1·00

31 Surveying

1980. Phosphate Industry (1st series). Multicoloured.

122		15 c. Type **31**	15	25
123		22 c. Drilling for samples	20	30
124		40 c. Sample analysis	30	45
125		55 c. Mine planning	40	55

See also Nos. 126/9, 136/9 and 140/3.

1980. Phosphate Industry (2nd series). As T **31**. Multicoloured.

126		15 c. Jungle clearing	15	15
127		22 c. Overburden removal	20	20
128		40 c. Open cut mining	30	25
129		55 c. Restoration	35	30

32 Angel with Harp

33 "Cryptoblepharus egeriae"

1980. Christmas. Multicoloured.

130		15 c. Type **32**	15	25
131		15 c. Angel with wounded soldier	15	25
132		22 c. Virgin and Child	15	30
133		22 c. Kneeling couple	15	30
134		60 c. Angel with harp (different)	35	45
135		60 c. Angel with children	35	45

1981. Phosphate Industry (3rd series). As T **31**. Multicoloured.

136		22 c. Screening and Stockpiling	20	20
137		28 c. Train loading	25	25
138		40 c. Railing	40	40
139		60 c. Drying	55	55

1981. Phosphate Industry (4th series). As T **31**. Multicoloured.

140		22 c. Crushing	30	20
141		28 c. Conveying	40	25
142		40 c. Bulk storage	60	40
143		60 c. "Consolidated Venture" (bulk carrier) loading	70	55

1981. Reptiles. Multicoloured.

144		24 c. Type **33**	25	25
145		30 c. "Emoia nativitata"	30	30
146		40 c. "Lepidodactylus listeri"	45	45
147		60 c. "Cyrtodactylus sp. nov."	65	65

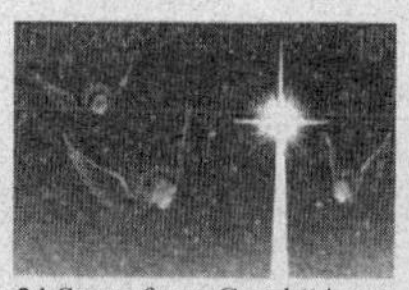
34 Scene from Carol "Away in a Manger"

1981. Christmas.

148	**34**	18 c. silver, dp blue & bl	35	50
149	–	24 c. multicoloured	40	55
150	–	40 c. multicoloured	45	65
151	–	60 c. multicoloured	50	75

DESIGNS: 24 c. to 60 c. show various scenes from carol "Away in a Manger".

35 Eastern Reef Heron

1982. Birds. Multicoloured.

152		1 c. Type **35**	70	30
153		2 c. Common noddy	70	30
154		3 c. White-bellied swiftlet	70	70
155		4 c. Christmas Island imperial pigeon	70	70
156		5 c. Christmas Island white eye	80	70
157		10 c. Island thrush	70	70
158		25 c. Red-tailed tropic bird	1·25	60
159		30 c. Emerald dove	80	70
160		40 c. Brown booby	80	55
161		50 c. Red-footed booby	80	55
162		65 c. Christmas Island frigate bird	80	55
163		75 c. White-tailed tropic bird	90	65
164		80 c. Australian kestrel (vert)	1·25	1·75
165		$1 Indonesian hawk-owl (vert)	2·50	2·00
166		$2 Australian goshawk	1·75	4·00
167		$4 Abbott's booby (vert)	3·00	3·25

36 Joseph

37 "Mirror" Dinghy and Club House

1982. Christmas. Origami Paper Sculptures. Mult.

168		27 c. Type **36**	30	30
169		50 c. Angel	45	45
170		75 c. Mary and baby Jesus	65	65

1983. 25th Anniv of Christmas Island Boat Club. Multicoloured.

171		27 c. Type **37**	30	35
172		35 c. Ocean-going yachts	35	40
173		50 c. Fishing launch and cargo ship (horiz)	40	50
174		75 c. Dinghy-racing and cantilever (horiz)	60	70

38 Maps of Christmas Island and Australia, Eastern Grey Kangaroo and White-tailed Tropic Bird

1983. 25th Anniv of Australian Territory. Multicoloured.

175		24 c. Type **38**	40	25
176		30 c. Christmas Island and Australian flag	45	45
177		85 c. Maps of Christmas Island and Australia, and Boeing 727	1·25	1·25

39 Candle and Holly

40 Feeding on Leaf

1983. Christmas. Candles. Multicoloured.

178		24 c. Type **39**	20	20
179		30 c. Six gold candles	30	40
180		85 c. Candles	70	1·00

1984. Red Land Crab. Multicoloured.

181		30 c. Type **40**	30	30
182		40 c. Migration	40	40
183		55 c. Development stages	50	50
184		85 c. Adult females and young	70	70

41 "Leucocoprinus fragilissimus"

42 Run-out

1984. Fungi. Multicoloured.

185		30 c. Type **41**	65	55
186		40 c. "Microporus xanthopus"	75	70
187		45 c. "Hydropus anthidepes" ("Trogia anthidepas")	85	80
188		55 c. "Haddowia longipes"	85	90
189		85 c. "Phillipsia domingensis"	1·10	1·25

1984. 25th Anniv of Cricket on Christmas Island. Multicoloured.

190		30 c. Type **42**	75	85
191		40 c. Bowled-out	85	1·10
192		50 c. Batsman in action	1·10	1·50
193		85 c. Fielder diving for catch	1·25	1·75

44 Robber Crab

45 "Once in Royal David's City"

1985. Crabs (1st series). Multicoloured.

195	30 c. Type **44**	1·00	70
196	40 c. Horn-eyed ghost crab	1·10	1·10
197	55 c. Purple hermit crab	1·50	1·60
198	85 c. Little nipper	2·25	2·50

1985. Crabs (2nd series). As T **44**. Multicoloured.

199	33 c. Blue crab	1·00	55
200	45 c. Tawny hermit crab	1·10	1·10
201	60 c. Red nipper	1·60	1·75
202	90 c. Smooth-handed ghost crab	2·25	2·50

1985. Crabs (3rd series). As T **44**. Multicoloured.

203	33 c. Red crab	1·10	60
204	45 c. Mottled crab	1·50	1·40
205	60 c. Rock hopper crab	2·25	2·50
206	90 c. Yellow nipper	2·75	3·50

1985. Christmas Carols. Multicoloured.

207	27 c. Type **45**	1·00	1·25
208	33 c. "While Shepherds Watched Their Flocks by Night"	1·10	1·40
209	45 c. "Away in a Manger"	1·40	1·60
210	60 c. "We Three Kings of Orient Are"	1·50	1·75
211	90 c. "Hark the Herald Angels Sing"	1·60	1·90

46 Halley's Comet over Christmas Island

47 Ridley's Orchid

1986. Appearance of Halley's Comet. Multicoloured.

212	33 c. Type **46**	65	80
213	45 c. Edmond Halley	80	1·10
214	60 c. Comet and "Consolidated Venture" (bulk carrier) loading phosphate	1·00	2·25
215	90 c. Comet over Flying Fish Cove	1·50	2·50

1986. Native Flowers. Multicoloured.

216	33 c. Type **47**	70	55
217	45 c. Hanging flower	65	85
218	60 c. Hoya	75	1·50
219	90 c. Sea hibiscus	90	2·00

1986. Royal Wedding. As T **112** of Ascension. Multicoloured.

220	33 c. Prince Andrew and Miss Sarah Ferguson	45	50
221	90 c. Prince Andrew piloting helicopter, Digby, Canada, 1985	95	1·75

48 Father Christmas and Reindeer in Speed Boat

1986. Christmas. Multicoloured.

222	30 c. Type **48**	75	50
223	36 c. Father Christmas and reindeer on beach	85	60
224	55 c. Father Christmas fishing	1·50	1·50
225	70 c. Playing golf	2·00	2·50
226	$1 Sleeping in hammock	2·25	3·25

49 H.M.S. "Flying Fish" and Outline Map of Christmas Island

1987. Centenary of Visits by H.M.S. "Flying Fish" and H.M.S. "Egeria". Multicoloured.

227	36 c. Type **49**	80	75
228	90 c. H.M.S. "Egeria" and outline map	1·60	3·00

50 Blind Snake

1987. Wildlife. Multicoloured.

229	1 c. Type **50**	40	80
230	2 c. Blue-tailed skink	40	80
231	3 c. Insectivorous bat	80	80
232	5 c. Grasshopper	80	80
233	10 c. Christmas Island fruit bat	80	80
234	25 c. Gecko	80	90
235	30 c. "Mantis religiosa" (mantid)	1·00	90
236	36 c. Indonesian hawk owl	2·75	1·60
237	40 c. Bull-mouth helmet	1·50	85
237a	41 c. Nudibranch ("Phidiana" sp.)	1·00	70
238	50 c. Textile or cloth of gold cone	1·40	1·00
239	65 c. Brittle stars	1·10	1·00
240	75 c. Regal angelfish	1·10	1·00
241	90 c. "Appias paulina" (butterfly)	3·50	2·50
242	$1 "Hypolimnas misippus" (butterfly)	3·50	2·50
243	$2 Shrew	3·50	5·50
244	$5 Green turtle	4·50	6·50

1988. Bicentenary of Australian Settlement. Arrival of First Fleet. As Nos. 1105/9 of Australia, but each inscribed "CHRISTMAS ISLAND Indian Ocean" and "AUSTRALIA BICENTENARY".

246	37 c. Aborigines watching arrival of Fleet, Botany Bay	1·40	1·60
247	37 c. Aboriginal family and anchored ships	1·40	1·60
248	37 c. Fleet arriving at Sydney Cove	1·40	1·60
249	37 c. Ship's boat	1·40	1·60
250	37 c. Raising the flag, Sydney Cove, 26 January 1788	1·40	1·60

Nos. 246/50 were printed together, se-tenant, forming a composite design.

52 Captain William May

53 Pony and Trap, 1910

1988. Cent of British Annexation. Mult.

251	37 c. Type **52**	35	40
252	53 c. Annexation ceremony	50	55
253	95 c. H.M.S. "Imperieuse" (armoured cruiser) firing salute	90	95
254	$1.50 Building commemorative cairn	1·40	1·50

1988. Cent of Permanent Settlement. Mult.

255	37 c. Type **53**	50	40
256	55 c. Phosphate mining, 1910	75	55
257	70 c. Steam locomotive, 1914	1·10	85
258	$1 Arrival of first aircraft, 1957	1·50	1·25

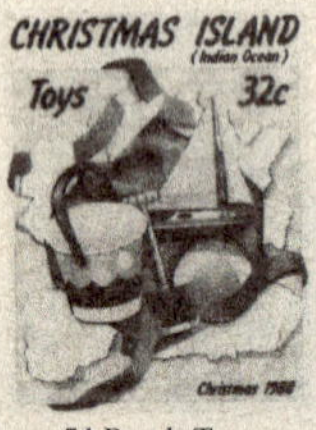

54 Beach Toys

55 Food on Table ("Good Harvesting")

1988. Christmas. Toys and Gifts. Multicoloured.

259	32 c. Type **54**	40	35
260	39 c. Flippers, snorkel and mask	50	40
261	90 c. Model soldier, doll and soft toys	1·10	1·10
262	$1 Models of racing car, lorry and jet aircraft	1·25	1·25

1989. Chinese New Year. Multicoloured.

263	39 c. Type **55**	45	40
264	70 c. Decorations ("Prosperity")	80	70
265	90 c. Chinese girls ("Good Fortune")	1·10	90
266	$1 Lion dance ("Progress Every Year")	1·25	1·00

56 Sir John Murray

1989. 75th Death Anniv of Sir John Murray (oceanographer). Multicoloured.

267	39 c. Type **56**	50	50
268	80 c. Map of Christmas Island showing Murray Hill	1·25	95
269	$1 Oceanographic equipment	1·50	1·25
270	$1.10 H.M.S. "Challenger" (survey ship), 1872	1·75	1·50

57 Four Children

58 "Huperzia phlegmaria"

1989. Malay Hari Raya Festival. Multicoloured.

271	39 c. Type **57**	55	50
272	55 c. Man playing tambourine	80	70
273	80 c. Girl in festival costume	1·25	1·00
274	$1.10 Christmas Island Mosque	1·60	1·40

1989. Ferns. Multicoloured.

275	41 c. Type **58**	75	60
276	65 c. "Asplenium polydon"	1·10	85
277	80 c. Common bracken	1·40	1·00
278	$1.10 Birds-nest fern	1·60	1·40

59 Virgin Mary and Star

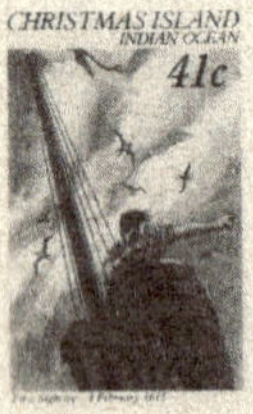

61 First Sighting, 1615

1989. Christmas. Multicoloured.

279	36 c. Type **59**	60	40
280	41 c. Christ Child in manger	60	45
281	80 c. Shepherds and star	1·40	80
282	$1.10 Three Wise Men following star	1·50	1·10

1989. "Melbourne Stampshow '89". Nos. 237a and 242 optd with Stampshow logo.

283	41 c. Nudibranch ("Phidiana sp.")	60	45
284	$1 "Hypolimnas misippus" (butterfly)	1·40	1·00

1990. 375th Anniv of Discovery of Christmas Island. Multicoloured.

285	41 c. Type **61**	1·00	50
286	$1.10 Second sighting and naming, 1643	2·00	1·40

62 Miniature Tractor pulling Phosphate

63 Male Abbott's Booby

1990. Christmas Island Transport. Multicoloured.

287	1 c. Type **62**	15	20
288	2 c. Phosphate train	40	40
289	3 c. Diesel railcar No. 8802 (vert)	20	20
290	5 c. Loading road train	40	40
291	10 c. Trishaw (vert)	30	30
292	15 c. Terex truck	65	65
293	25 c. Articulated bus	30	30
294	30 c. Cable passenger carriage (vert)	30	35
295	40 c. Passenger barge (vert)	35	40
296	50 c. Kolek (outrigger canoe)	55	55
297	65 c. Flying Doctor aircraft and ambulance	3·00	1·50
298	75 c. Commercial van	1·50	1·50
299	90 c. Vintage lorry	1·75	1·75
300	$1 Water tanker	1·75	1·75
301	$2 Traction engine	3·25	3·25
302	$5 Steam locomotive No. 1	4·50	4·75

1990. Abbott's Booby. Multicoloured.

303	10 c. Type **63**	85	30
304	20 c. Juvenile male	1·40	50
305	29 c. Female with egg	1·60	55
306	41 c. Pair with chick	2·25	70

64 1977 Famous Visitors 9 c. Stamp

1990. Centenary of Henry Ridley's Visit.

308	41 c. Type **64**	55	65
309	75 c. Ridley (botanist) in rainforest	85	1·75

65 "Corymborkus veratrifolia"

66 "Islander" (freighter), 1898

1990. Christmas. Flowers. Multicoloured.

311	38 c. Type **65**	1·00	60
312	43 c. "Hoya aldrichii"	1·10	65
313	80 c. "Quisqualis indica"	2·00	2·50
314	$1.20 "Barringtonia racemosa"	2·50	3·00

1991. Centenary of First Phosphate Mining Lease. Multicoloured.

316	43 c. Type **66**	90	90
317	43 c. Miners loading tipper wagons, 1908	90	90
318	85 c. Shay steam locomotive No. 4, 1925	1·25	1·25
319	$1.20 Extracting phosphate, 1951	1·60	1·60
320	$1.70 Land reclamation, 1990	1·90	1·90

Nos. 316/20 were printed together, se-tenant, forming a composite forest design.

67 Teaching Children Road Safety

68 Map of Christmas Island, 1991

1991. Christmas Island Police Force. Multicoloured.

321	43 c. Type **67**	1·25	60
322	43 c. Traffic control	1·25	60
323	90 c. Airport customs	2·00	1·75
324	$1.20 Police launch "Fregata Andrews" towing rescued boat	2·75	2·50

1991. Maps of Christmas Island. Multicoloured.

326	43 c. Type **68**	85	65
327	75 c. Goos Atlas, 1666	1·50	1·10
328	$1.10 De Manevillette, 1745	2·25	1·60
329	$1.20 Comberford, 1667	2·25	1·90

69 "Bruguiera gymnorrhiza"

1991. Local Trees. Multicoloured.

330	43 c. Type **69**	75	65
331	70 c. "Syzygium operculatum"	1·25	1·00
332	85 c. "Ficus microcarpa"	1·50	1·25
333	$1.20 "Arenga listeri"	1·75	1·60

70 "Family round Christmas Tree" (S'ng Yen Luiw)

1991. Christmas. Children's Paintings. Multicoloured.

334	38 c. Type **70**	65	55
335	38 c. "Opening Presents" (Liew Ann Nee)	65	55
336	38 c. "Beach Party" (Foo Pang Chuan)	65	55
337	38 c. "Christmas Walk" (Too Lai Peng)	65	55
338	38 c. "Santa Claus and Christmas Tree" (Jesamine Wheeler)	65	55
339	43 c. "Santa Claus fishing" (Ho Puay Ha)	70	60
340	$1 "Santa Claus in Boat" (Ng Hooi Hua)	1·50	1·25
341	$1.20 "Santa Claus surfing" (Yani Kawi)	1·75	1·50

71 Discussing Evacuation, 1942

72 Snake's-head Cowrie

1992. 50th Anniv of Partial Evacuation. Mult.

342 45 c. Type **71** 80 80
343 45 c. Families waiting to embark 80 80
344 $1.05 Ferrying evacuees to "Islander" . . . . 2·25 2·25
345 $1.20 Departure of "Islander" (freighter) . . . . 2·50 2·50

1992. Shells. Multicoloured.

346 5 c. Tiger cowrie 40 40
347 10 c. Type **72** 50 50
348 15 c. Scorpion conch 65 50
349 20 c. Royal oak scallop . . . 75 50
350 25 c. Striped engina 75 50
351 30 c. Prickly Pacific drupe . . . 90 50
352 40 c. Reticulate distorsio . . . 90 55
353 45 c. Tapestry turban . . . . 1·25 60
354 50 c. Beautiful goblet . . . . 1·25 55
355 60 c. Captain cone . . . . . . 1·50 65
356 70 c. Layonkaire's turban . . . 1·50 75
357 80 c. Chirage spider conch . . 1·75 85
358 90 c. Common delphinia . . . 1·75 1·10
359 $1 Ceramic vase . . . . . . 1·75 1·25
360 $2 Partridge tun . . . . . . 2·00 2·10
361 $5 Strawberry drupe . . . . . 5·00 5·25

73 Torpedoing of "Eidsvold"

1992. 50th Anniv of Sinkings of "Eidsvold" and "Nissa Maru". Multicoloured.

362 45 c. Type **73** . . . . 1·25 75
363 80 c. "Eidsvold" sinking . . . 2·00 1·75
364 $1.05 "Nissa Maru" under attack 2·50 2·75
365 $1.20 "Nissa Maru" beached . 2·50 3·00

1992. "Kuala Lumpur '92" International Philatelic Exhibition. No. 361 optd with exhibition symbol.

366 $5 Strawberry drupe . . . . . 8·50 7·00

75 Jungle

76 Abbott's Booby

1992. Christmas. Multicoloured.

367 40 c. Type **75** . . . . 90 1·00
368 40 c. Seabirds over rock . . . 90 1·00
369 45 c. Brown boobies on headland . . . . 90 1·00
370 $1.05 Seabirds and cliffs . . . 1·60 1·75
371 $1.20 Cliffs . . . . 1·60 1·75

Nos. 367/71 were printed together, se-tenant, forming a composite coastal design.

1993. Seabirds. Multicoloured.

372 45 c. Type **76** 60 80
373 45 c. Christmas Island frigate bird 60 80
374 45 c. Common noddy 60 80
375 45 c. White-tailed tropic bird ("Golden Bosunbird") . . . 60 80
376 45 c. Brown booby 60 80

Nos. 372/6 were printed together, se-tenant, forming a composite design.

77 Dolly Beach

1993. Scenic Views of Christmas Island. Multicoloured.

378 85 c. Type **77** . . . . 1·25 1·50
379 95 c. Blow Holes . . . . . . 1·50 1·75
380 $1.05 Merrial Beach . . . . . 1·60 1·90
381 $1.20 Rainforest . . . . 1·75 2·00

78 Turtle on Beach

1993. Christmas. Multicoloured.

382 40 c. Type **78** 80 50
383 45 c. Crabs and wave 80 50
384 $1 Christmas Island frigate bird and rainforest . . . . . . 2·00 2·50

79 Map of Christmas Island

1993. 350th Anniv of Naming of Christmas Island.

385 **79** $2 multicoloured . . . . . 3·00 3·25

80 Pekingese

1994. Chinese New Year ("Year of the Dog"). Multicoloured.

386 45 c. Type **80** . . . . 1·00 1·25
387 45 c. Mickey (Christmas Island dog) . . . . 1·00 1·25

81 Shay Locomotive No. 4

1994. Steam Locomotives. Multicoloured.

389 85 c. Type **81** . . . . 1·50 1·75
390 95 c. Locomotive No. 9 . . . 1·50 1·75
391 $1.20 Locomotive No. 1 . . . 1·75 2·25

82 "Brachypeza archytas"

83 Angel blowing Trumpet

1994. Orchids. Multicoloured.

392 45 c. Type **82** . . . . . . 1·00 1·10
393 45 c. "Thelasis capitata" . . 1·00 1·10
394 45 c. "Corymborkis veratrifolia" 1·00 1·10
395 45 c. "Flickingeria nativitatis" 1·00 1·10
396 45 c. "Dendrobium crumenatum" . . . . . . 1·00 1·10

1994. Christmas. Multicoloured.

397 40 c. Type **83** 80 50
398 45 c. Wise Man holding gift . 80 50
399 80 c. Star over Bethlehem . . 1·75 2·50

84 Pig

1995. Chinese New Year ("Year of the Pig").

400 **84** 45 c. multicoloured . . . 75 50
401 – 85 c. multicoloured . . . 1·25 1·60

DESIGN: 85 c. Pig (different).

85 Golfer playing Shot

1995. 40th Anniv of Christmas Island Golf Course.

403 **85** $2.50 multicoloured . . . . 3·50 3·75

86 Father Christmas with Map on Christmas Island Frigate Bird

1995. Christmas. Multicoloured.

404 40 c. Type **86** 80 50
405 45 c. Father Christmas distributing presents 80 50
406 80 c. Father Christmas waving goodbye . . . . 1·75 2·50

87 De Havilland D.H.98 Mosquito on Reconnaissance Mission

1995. 50th Anniv of End of Second World War. Each black, stone and red.

407 45 c. Type **87** 80 80
408 45 c. H.M.S. "Rother" (frigate) 80 80

88 Lemon-peel Angelfish

1995. Marine Life. Multicoloured.

412 20 c. Pink-tailed triggerfish . . 15 20
413 30 c. Japanese inflator-filefish ("Longnose filefish") 25 30
414 45 c. Princess anthias 30 35
415 75 c. Type **88** 55 60
416 85 c. Moon wrasse 65 70
417 90 c. Spotted boxfish 70 75
418 95 c. Moorish idol 75 80
419 $1 Emperor angelfish 75 80
420 $1.20 Glass-eyed snapper ("Glass bigeye") . . . . 1·00 1·10

89 Rat with Drum

1996. Chinese New Year ("Year of the Rat"). Multicoloured.

425 45 c. Type **89** 75 75
426 45 c. Rat with tambourine . . 75 75

90 Christmas Island White Eye

91 Three Ships approaching Island

1996. Christmas Island Land Birds. Multicoloured.

428 45 c. Type **90** 75 50
429 85 c. Christmas Island hawk owl . . . . 1·75 2·00

1996. Christmas. "I saw Three Ships" (carol). Multicoloured.

430 40 c. Type **91** 65 50
431 45 c. Madonna and Child with ships at anchor 65 50
432 80 c. Ships leaving . . . . . . 1·50 1·75

1996. 300th Anniv of Willem de Vlamingh's Discovery of Christmas Island. As No. 1667 of Australia.

433 45 c. multicoloured 75 75

92 Ox facing Right

1997. Chinese New Year ("Year of the Ox"). Multicoloured.

434 45 c. Type **92** 70 80
435 45 c. Ox facing left 70 80

93 Father Christmas reading Letter

1997. Christmas. Multicoloured.

437 40 c. Type **93** 55 45
438 45 c. Father Christmas carving wooden boat 55 45
439 80 c. Father Christmas in sleigh 1·10 1·40

94 Tiger

1998. Chinese New Year ("Year of the Tiger"). Multicoloured.

440 45 c. Type **94** 55 65
441 45 c. Tiger with head facing left 55 65

95 Christmas Island Frigate Bird

1998. Marine Life. Multicoloured.

443 5 c. Type **95** 15 20
444 5 c. Four ambon chromis . . 15 20
445 5 c. Three ambon chromis . . 15 20
446 5 c. One pink anemonefish . . 15 20
447 5 c. Three pink anemonefish . 15 20
448 10 c. Eastern reef egret . . . 20 25
449 10 c. Whitelined cod 20 25
450 10 c. Pyramid butterflyfish . . 20 25
451 10 c. Dusky parrotfish 20 25
452 10 c. Spotted garden eel . . . 20 25
453 25 c. Sooty tern 25 30
454 25 c. Stripe-tailed damselfish ("Scissortail sergeant") . . 25 30
455 25 c. Thicklip wrasse 25 30
456 25 c. Blackaxil chromis 25 30
457 25 c. Orange anthias 25 30
458 45 c. Brown booby 35 40
459 45 c. Green turtle 35 40
460 45 c. Pink anemonefish . . . 35 40
461 45 c. Blue sea star 35 40
462 45 c. Kunie's chromodoris . . 35 40

Nos. 443/62 were printed together, se-tenant, with the backgrounds forming a composie design.

96 Orchid Tree

1998. Christmas. Flowering Trees. Multicoloured.

463 40 c. Type **96** 40 35
464 80 c. Flame tree 80 90
465 95 c. Sea hibiscus 90 95

97 Leaping Rabbit

1999. Chinese New Year ("Year of the Rabbit"). Multicoloured.

466 45 c. Type **97** 35 40
467 45 c. Rabbit with pestle and mortar 35 40

CISKEI

The Republic of Ciskei was established on 4 December 1981, being constructed from tribal areas formerly part of the Republic of South Africa.

This independence did not receive international political recognition. We are satisfied, however, that the stamps had "de facto" acceptance for the carriage of mail outside Ciskei.

Ciskei was formerly re-incorporated into South Africa on 27 April 1994.

100 cents = 1 rand

1 Dr. Lennox Sebe, Chief Minister

2 Knysna Turaco

1981. Independence. Multicoloured.

1	5 c. Type **1**	10	10
2	15 c. Coat of arms	20	15
3	20 c. Flag	30	30
4	25 c. Mace	35	25

1981. Birds. Multicoloured.

5	1 c. Type **2**	20	15
6	2 c. Cape wagtail	20	15
7	3 c. White-browed coucal	30	15
8	4 c. Yellow-tufted malachite sunbird	20	15
9	5 c. Stanley crane	20	15
10	6 c. African red-winged starling	20	15
11	7 c. Giant kingfisher	20	15
12	8 c. Hadada ibis	30	15
13	9 c. Black cuckoo	30	15
14	10 c. Black-collared barbet	30	15
14a	11 c. African black-headed oriole	55	30
14b	12 c. Malachite kingfisher	70	30
14c	14 c. Hoopoe	1·00	30
15	15 c. African fish eagle	30	30
15a	16 c. Cape puff-back flycatcher	65	30
15b	18 c. Long-tailed whydah	1·00	30
16	20 c. Cape longclaw	40	30
16a	21 c. Lemon dove	1·50	60
17	25 c. Cape dikkop	30	30
18	30 c. African green pigeon	40	40
19	50 c. Cape parrot	60	60
20	1 r. Narina trogon	1·25	1·25
21	2 r. Cape eagle owl	2·50	2·50

3 Cecilia Makiwane (first Xhosa nurse)

4 Boom Sprayer

1982. Nursing. Multicoloured.

22	8 c. Type **3**	15	10
23	15 c. Operating theatre	30	30
24	20 c. Matron lighting nurse's lamp (horiz)	40	40
25	25 c. Nurses and patient (horiz)	50	50

1982. Pineapple Industry. Multicoloured.

26	8 c. Type **4**	10	10
27	15 c. Harvesting	20	25
28	20 c. Despatch to cannery	25	30
29	30 c. Packing for local market	30	35

5 Brown Hare

1982. Small Mammals. Multicoloured.

30	8 c. Type **5**	15	15
31	15 c. Cape fox	30	25
32	20 c. Cape ground squirrel	40	30
33	25 c. Caracal	50	35

6 Assegai

7 Dusky Shark

1983. Trees (1st series). Multicoloured.

34	8 c. Cabbage tree	15	10
35	20 c. Type **6**	30	30
36	25 c. Cape chestnut	35	35
37	40 c. Outeniqua yellowwood	50	55

See also Nos. 52/5.

1983. Sharks. Multicoloured.

38	8 c. Type **7**	15	15
39	20 c. Sand tiger ("Ragged-tooth shark")	40	40
40	25 c. Tiger shark (57 × 21 mm)	45	45
41	30 c. Scalloped hammerhead (57 × 21 mm)	50	50
42	40 c. Great white shark (57 × 21 mm)	70	70

8 Lovedale

9 White Drill Uniform

1983. Educational Institutions.

43 **8**	10 c. lt brown, brown & black	10	10
44 –	20 c. lt brown, brown & black	20	20
45 –	25 c. brown, red and black	25	25
46 –	40 c. lt brown, brown & black	40	45

DESIGNS: 20 c. Fort Hare; 25 c. Healdtown; 40 c. Lennox Sebe.

1983. British Military Uniforms (1st series). 6th Warwickshire Regiment of Foot, 1821–27. Multicoloured.

47	20 c. Type **9**	40	40
48	20 c. Light Company privates	40	40
49	20 c. Grenadier Company sergeants	40	40
50	20 c. Undress blue frock coats	40	40
51	20 c. Officer and field officer in parade order	40	40

See also Nos. 64/8 and 95/8.

1984. Trees (2nd series). As T **6**. Multicoloured.

52	10 c. "Rhus chirindensis"	20	15
53	20 c. "Phoenix reclinata"	35	35
54	25 c. "Ptaeroxyon obliquum"	40	40
55	40 c. "Apodytes dimidiata"	55	55

10 Sandprawn

1984. Fish-bait. Multicoloured.

56	11 c. Type **10**	20	15
57	20 c. Coral worm	30	30
58	25 c. Bloodworm	35	35
59	30 c. Red-bait	40	40

11 Banded Sand Martin

1984. Migratory Birds. Multicoloured.

60	11 c. Type **11**	25	20
61	25 c. House martin	50	50
62	30 c. Greater striped swallow	60	60
63	45 c. European swallow	80	85

1984. British Military Uniforms (2nd series). Cape Mounted Rifles. As T **9**. Multicoloured.

64	25 c. (1) Trooper in field and sergeant in undress uniforms, 1830	45	45
65	25 c. (2) Trooper and sergeant in full dress, 1835	45	45
66	25 c. (3) Officers in undress, 1830	45	45
67	25 c. (4) Officers in full dress, 1827–1834	45	45
68	25 c. (5) Officers in full dress, 1834	45	45

The stamps are numbered as indicated in brackets.

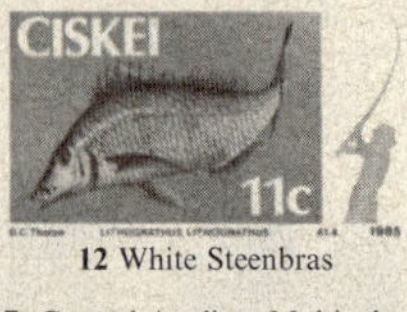

12 White Steenbras

1985. Coastal Angling. Multicoloured.

69	11 c. Type **12**	30	20
70	25 c. Bronze seabream	50	50
71	30 c. Kob	60	60
72	50 c. Spotted grunt	85	85

13 Brownies holding Handmade Doll

1985. International Youth Year. 75th Anniv of Girl Guide Movement. Multicoloured.

73	12 c. Type **13**	15	15
74	25 c. Rangers planting trees	25	25
75	30 c. Guides with flag	30	30
76	50 c. Guides building fire	60	65

14 Furniture making

1985. Small Businesses. Multicoloured.

77	12 c. Type **14**	15	10
78	25 c. Dressmaking	30	30
79	30 c. Welding	30	30
80	50 c. Basketry	60	65

15 "Antelope"

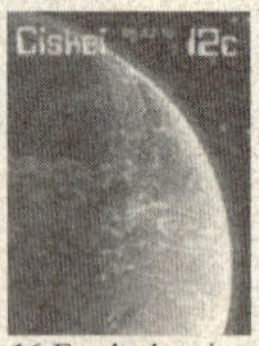

16 Earth showing Africa

1985. Sail Troopships. Multicoloured.

81	12 c. Type **15**	20	15
82	25 c. "Pilot"	45	45
83	30 c. "Salisbury"	45	45
84	50 c. "Olive Branch"	80	85

1986. Appearance of Halley's Comet. Mult.

85	12 c. (1) Earth showing South America	1·10	90
86	12 c. (2) Type **16**	1·10	90
87	12 c. (3) Stars and Moon	1·10	90
88	12 c. (4) Moon and Milky Way	1·10	90
89	12 c. (5) Milky Way and stars	1·10	90
90	12 c. (6) Earth showing Australia	1·10	90
91	12 c. (7) Earth and meteor	1·10	90
92	12 c. (8) Meteor, Moon and comet tail	1·10	90
93	12 c. (9) Comet head and Moon	1·10	90
94	12 c. (10) Sun	1·10	90

Nos. 85/94 were issued in sheetlets of 10 stamps forming a composite design of the southern skies in April. Each stamp is inscribed with a number from "A1-10" to "A10-10". The first number is given in brackets in the listing to aid identification.

17 Fifer in Winter Dress

18 Welding Bicycle Frame

1986. British Military Uniforms (3rd series). 98th Regiment of Foot. Multicoloured.

95	14 c. Type **17**	20	15
96	20 c. Private in summer dress	30	30
97	25 c. Grenadier in full summer dress	35	35
98	30 c. Sergeant-major in full winter dress	50	50

1986. Bicycle Factory, Dimbaza. Multicoloured.

99	14 c. Type **18**	20	15
100	20 c. Spray-painting frame	30	30
101	25 c. Installing wheelspokes	35	35
102	30 c. Final assembly	50	50

19 President Dr. Lennox Sebe

20 "Boletus edulis"

1986. 5th Anniv of Independence. Multicoloured.

103	14 c. Type **19**	15	15
104	20 c. National Shrine, Ntaba kaNdoda	20	30
105	25 c. Legislative Assembly, Bisho	25	35
106	30 c. Automatic telephone exchange, Bisho	35	50

1987. Edible Mushrooms. Multicoloured.

107	14 c. Type **20**	25	15
108	20 c. "Macrolepiota zeyheri"	40	40
109	25 c. "Termitomyces spp"	50	50
110	30 c. "Russula capensis"	60	60

21 Nkone Cow and Calf

22 Wire Windmill

1987. Nkone Cattle. Multicoloured.

111	16 c. Type **21**	20	15
112	20 c. Nkone cow	25	30
113	25 c. Nkone bull	30	35
114	30 c. Herd of Nkone	40	55

1987. Homemade Toys. Multicoloured.

115	16 c. Type **22**	20	15
116	20 c. Rag doll	25	30
117	25 c. Clay horse (horiz)	30	35
118	30 c. Wire car (horiz)	40	55

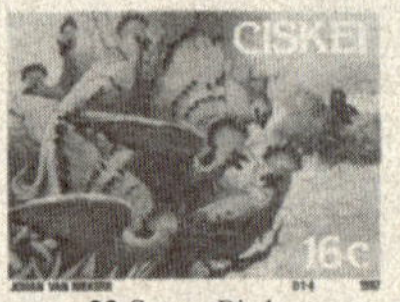

23 Seven Birds

24 Bush Lily

1987. Folklore (1st series). Sikulume. Mult.

119	16 c. Type **23**	20	15
120	20 c. Cannibals chasing Sikulume	25	30
121	25 c. Sikulume attacking the inabulele	30	35
122	30 c. Chief Mangangezulu chasing Sikulume and his bride	40	55

See also Nos. 127/36, 153/6 and 161/4.

1988. Protected Flowers. Multicoloured.

123	16 c. Type **24**	20	15
124	30 c. Harebell	35	35
125	40 c. Butterfly iris	40	40
126	50 c. Vlei lily	60	65

25 Numbakatali crying and Second Wife feeding Crows

1988. Folklore (2nd series). Mbulukazi. Mult.

127	16 c. Type **25**	30	35
128	16 c. Numbakatali telling doves of her childlessness	30	35
129	16 c. Numbakatali finding children in earthenware jars	30	35
130	16 c. Broad Breast sees Mbulukazi and brother at river	30	35
131	16 c. Broad Breast asking to marry Mbulukazi	30	35
132	16 c. Broad Breast and his two wives, Mbulukazi and her half-sister Mahlunguluza	30	35
133	16 c. Mahlunguluza pushing Mbulukazi from precipice to her death	30	35
134	16 c. Mbulukazi's ox tearing down Mahlunguluza's hut	30	35
135	16 c. Ox licking Mbulukazi back to life	30	35
136	16 c. Mahlunguluza being sent back to her father in disgrace	30	35

26 Oranges and Grafted Rootstocks in Nursery

1988. Citrus Farming. Multicoloured.

137	16 c. Type **26**	20	15
138	30 c. Lemons and inarching rootstock onto mature tree	40	40
139	40 c. Tangerines and fruit being hand-picked	50	50
140	50 c. Oranges and fruit being graded	60	65

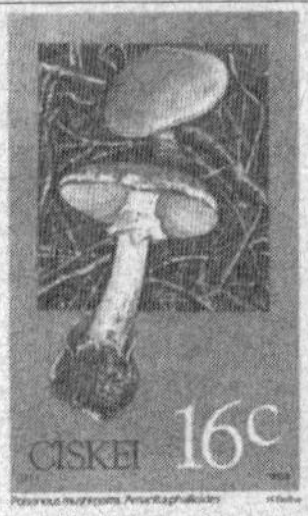

27 "Amanita phalloides"

28 Kat River Dam

1988. Poisonous Fungi. Multicoloured.

141	16 c. Type **27**	75	30
142	30 c. "Chlorophyllum molybdites"	1·10	75
143	40 c. "Amanita muscaria"	1·40	1·10
144	50 c. "Amanita pantherina"	1·60	1·25

1989. Dams. Multicoloured.

145	16 c. Type **28**	35	25
146	30 c. Cata dam	55	50
147	40 c. Binfield Park dam	65	65
148	50 c. Sandile dam	70	80

29 Taking Eggs from Rainbow Trout

1989. Trout Hatcheries. Multicoloured.

149	18 c. Type **29**	25	15
150	30 c. Fertilized eyed trout ova and alevins	45	45
151	40 c. Five-week-old fingerlings	55	55
152	50 c. Adult male	60	65

30 Lion and Little Jackal killing Eland

31 Cape Horse-cart

1989. Folklore (3rd series). Little Jackal and the Lion. Multicoloured.

153	18 c. Type **30**	20	15
154	30 c. Little Jackal's children carrying meat to clifftop home	35	35
155	40 c. Little Jackal pretending to be trapped	40	40
156	50 c. Lion falling down cliff face	45	50

1989. Animal-drawn Transport. Multicoloured.

157	18 c. Type **31**	20	15
158	30 c. Jubilee spider	35	35
159	40 c. Ballantine half-tent ox-drawn wagon	40	40
160	50 c. Voortrekker wagon	45	50

32 Mpunzikazi offering Food to Five Heads

33 Handweaving on Loom

1990. Folklore (4th series). The Story of Makanda Mahlanu (Five Heads). Multicoloured.

161	18 c. Type **32**	20	15
162	30 c. Five Heads killing Mpunzikazi with his tail	35	35
163	40 c. Mpunzanyana offering food to Five Heads	40	40
164	50 c. Five Heads transformed into a man	45	50

1990. Handmade Carpets. Multicoloured.

165	21 c. Type **33**	30	20
166	35 c. Spinning	50	50
167	40 c. Dyeing yarn	70	70
168	50 c. Knotting carpet	70	70

34 Wooden Beam Plough, 1855

1980. Ploughs. Multicoloured.

169	21 c. Type **34**	25	20
170	35 c. Triple disc plough, 1895	40	40
171	40 c. Reversible disc plough, 1895	50	50
172	50 c. "Het Volk" double furrow plough, 1910	60	65

35 Prickly Pear Vendor

1990. Prickly Pear. Multicoloured.

173	21 c. Type **35**	30	20
174	35 c. Prickly pear bushes	50	50
175	40 c. Whole and opened fruits	60	60
176	50 c. Bushes in bloom	70	80

36 African Marsh Owl

37 Sao Bras (now Mossel Bay) on Map, 1500

1991. Owls. Multicoloured.

177	21 c. Type **36**	75	40
178	35 c. African scops owl	1·00	80
179	40 c. Barn owl	1·25	1·00
180	50 c. African wood owl	1·50	1·40

1991. Stamp Day. D'Ataide's Letter of 1501. Multicoloured.

181	25 c. Type **37**	60	60
182	25 c. Bartolomeo Dias's ship foundering off Cabo Tormentoso (now Cape of Good Hope) during voyage to India, 1500	60	60
183	25 c. Captain Pedro d'Ataide landing at Sao Bras, 1601	60	60
184	25 c. D'Ataide leaving letter relating death of Dias on tree	60	60
185	25 c. Captain Joao da Nova finding letter, 1501	60	60

The inscriptions at the foot of Nos. 181 and 182 are transposed.

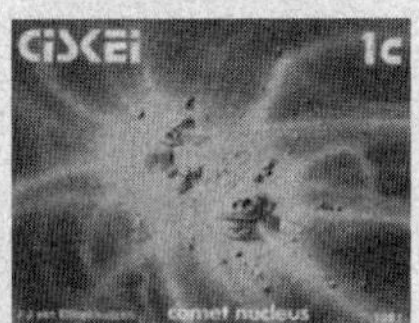

38 Comet Nucleus

1991. The Solar System. Multicoloured.

186	1 c. Type **38**	20	15
187	2 c. Trojan asteroids	20	15
188	5 c. Meteoroids	20	15
189	7 c. Pluto	30	15
190	10 c. Neptune	30	15
191	20 c. Uranus	50	20
192	25 c. Saturn	60	20
193	30 c. Jupiter	65	30
194	35 c. Planetoids in asteroid belt	65	40
195	40 c. Mars	80	50
196	50 c. The Moon	90	70
197	60 c. Earth	1·00	80
198	1 r. Venus	1·50	1·25
199	2 r. Mercury	2·50	2·25
200	5 r. The Sun	4·50	4·50

39 Fort Armstrong and Xhosa Warrior

1991. 19th-century Frontier Forts. Multicoloured.

202	27 c. Type **39**	40	30
203	45 c. Keiskamma Hoek Post and Sir George Grey (governor of Cape Colony, 1854–58)	55	55
204	65 c. Fort Hare and Xhosa Chief Sandile	70	70
205	85 c. Peddie Cavalry Barracks and cavalryman	1·10	1·25

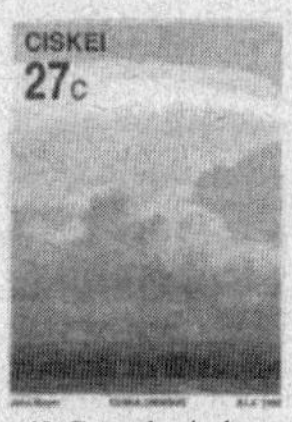

40 Cumulonimbus

1992. Cloud Formations. Multicoloured.

206	27 c. Type **40**	40	25
207	45 c. Altocumulus	65	65
208	65 c. Cirrus	80	80
209	85 c. Cumulus	1·00	1·10

41 "Intelsat VI" Communications Satellite

1992. International Space Year. Satellites over Southern Africa. Multicoloured.

210	35 c. Type **41**	40	25
211	70 c. "G P S Navstar" (navigation)	80	80
212	90 c. "Meteosat" (meteorology)	1·10	1·10
213	1 r. 05 "Landsat VI" (Earth resources survey)	1·25	1·40

42 Universal Disc-harrow, 1914

1992. Agricultural Tools. Multicoloured.

214	35 c. Type **42**	40	25
215	70 c. Clod crusher and pulveriser, 1914	80	70
216	90 c. Self-dump hay rake, 1910	1·10	95
217	1 r. 05 McCormick hay tedder, 1900	1·10	1·10

43 Mpekweni Sun Marine Resort

1992. Hotels. Multicoloured.

218	35 c. Type **43**	40	25
219	70 c. Katberg Protea Hotel	80	80
220	90 c. Fish River Sun Hotel	1·10	1·10
221	1 r. 05 Amatola Sun Hotel, Amatole Mountains	1·10	1·25

44 Vasco da Gama, "Sao Gabriel" and Voyage round Cape of Good Hope, 1497

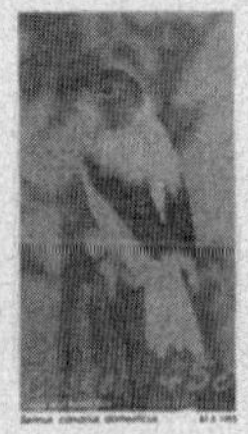

45 Canary

1993. Navigators. Multicoloured.

222	45 c. Type **44**	55	30
223	65 c. James Cook, H.M.S. "Endeavour" and first voyage, 1768–71	90	75
224	85 c. Ferdinand Magellan, "Vitoria" and circumnavigation, 1519	1·10	90
225	90 c. Sir Francis Drake, "Golden Hind" and circumnavigation, 1577–80	1·10	95
226	1 r. 05 Abel Tasman, "Heemskerk" and discovery of Tasmania, 1642	1·25	1·25

The ship on No. 222 is wrongly inscribed "San Gabriel", that on No. 224 "Victoria" and that on No. 226 "Heemskerck".

1993. Cage Birds. Multicoloured.

227	45 c. Type **45**	45	30
228	65 c. Budgerigar	70	60
229	85 c. Peach-faced lovebirds	90	80
230	90 c. Cockatiel	95	85
231	1 r. 05 Gouldian finch	1·00	1·10

46 Goshen Church (Moravian Mission), Whittlesea

1993. Churches and Missions.

232	**46**	45 c. stone, black and red	35	20
233	–	65 c. blue, black and red	60	60
234	–	85 c. brown, black and red	80	80
235	–	1 r. 05 yellow, black and red	90	1·00

DESIGNS: 65 c. Kamastone Mission Church; 85 c. Richie Thompson Memorial Church (Hertzog Mission), near Seymour; 1 r. 05, Bryce Ross Memorial Church (Pirie Mission), near Dimbaza.

47 Jointed Cactus

48 "Losna" (steamer) (near Fish River), 1921

1993. Invader Plants. Multicoloured.

236	45 c. Type **47**	40	30
237	65 c. Thorn apple	70	60
238	85 c. Coffee weed	90	80
239	1 r. 05 Poisonous wild tobacco	1·00	1·00

1994. Shipwrecks. Multicoloured.

241	45 c. Type **48**	55	30
242	65 c. "Catherine" (barque) (Waterloo Bay), 1846	90	60
243	85 c. "Bennebroek" (East Indiaman) (near Mtana River), 1713	1·10	90
244	1 r. 05 "Sao Joao Baptista" (galleon) (between Fish and Kei Rivers), 1622	1·25	1·25

49 "Herman Steyn"

1994. Hybrid Roses. Multicoloured.

245	45 c. Type **49**	35	30
246	70 c. "Esther Geldenhuys"	60	60
247	95 c. "Margaret Wasserfall"	80	80
248	1 r. 15 "Professor Fred Ziady"	1·00	1·00

COCHIN

A state of South West India. Now uses Indian stamps.

6 puttans = 5 annas
12 pies = 1 anna; 16 annas = 1 rupee

1 Emblems of State

1892. Value in "puttans".

5a	**1**	½ put. orange	1·50	1·10
2		1 put. purple	2·00	1·50
3		2 put. violet	1·50	1·60

3

5

1903. Value in "pies" or "puttans". With or without gum.

16	**3**	3 pies, blue	40	10
17		½ put. green (smaller)	75	20
18	**5**	1 put. red	1·40	10
19	**3**	2 put. violet	1·75	30

1909. Surch **2**. No gum.

22	**3**	2 on 3 pies, mauve	15	25

8 Raja Rama Varma I

10 Raja Rama Varma II

1911. Value in "pies" or "annas".

26	**8**	2 p. brown	30	10
27		3 p. blue	35	10
28		4 p. green	1·00	10
29		9 p. red	1·10	10
30		1 a. orange	1·90	10
31		1½ a. purple	4·75	45
32		2 a. grey	7·50	40
33		3 a. red	28·00	32·00

1918. Various frames.
35b 10 2 p. brown 1·00 10
36 4 p. green 95 10
37 6 p. brown 1·60 10
38 8 p. brown 1·40 10
39 9 p. red 13·00 15
40 10 p. blue 1·90 10
41a 1 a. orange 8·50 30
42 1½ a. purple 2·25 15
43 2 a. grey 4·00 10
44 2¼ a. green 3·75 2·25
45 3 a. red 11·00 35

1922. Surch with figure and words.
46 8 2 p. on 3 p. blue 40 30

1928. Surch **ONE ANNA ANCHAL & REVENUE** and value in native characters.
50 10 1 a. on 2¼ a. green 5·00 12·00

1932. Surch in figures and words both in English and in native characters.
51 10 3 p. on 4 p. green 1·00 80
52 3 p. on 8 p. brown 1·00 2·00
53 9 p. on 10 p. blue 1·50 2·50

18 Maharaja Rama Varma III

26 Maharaja Kerala Varma II

1933.
54 18 2 p. brown 60 20
55 4 p. green 60 10
56 6 p. red 70 10
57 1 a. orange 70 10
58 1 a. 8 p. red 3·00 3·75
59 2 a. grey 3·75 45
60 2¼ a. green 1·50 10
61 3 a. orange 3·50 1·25
62 3 a. 4 p. violet 1·50 1·40
63 6 a. 8 p. sepia 1·75 9·00
64 10 a. blue 3·00 10·00

1934. Surch with figure and words.
65 10 6 p. on 8 p. brown 75 50
66 6 p. on 10 p. blue 1·75 1·50

1939. Optd **ANCHAL.**
72 18 1 a. orange 1·60 45

1939. Surch in words only.
75 18 3 p. on 1 a. 8 p. red £160 70·00
77 6 p. on 1 a. 8 p. red 2·50 16·00

1943. Surch **SURCHARGED** and value in words.
79 18 3 p. on 4 p. green 5·00 3·00
76 3 p. on 1 a. 8 p. red 2·00 6·00
78 1 a. 3 p. on 1 a. 8 p. red 1·00 30

1943. Surch **ANCHAL SURCHARGED NINE PIES.**
84 18 9 p. on 1 a. orange 13·00 4·00

1943. Surch **ANCHAL** and value in words.
81a 18 6 p. on 1 a. orange 85·00 40·00
82 9 p. on 1 a. orange 95·00 £100

1943.
85 26 2 p. brown 1·00 1·60
87a 4 p. green 3·00 3·00
88 6 p. brown 1·25 10
89 9 p. blue 23·00 1·00
90a 1 a. orange 21·00 38·00
91 2¼ a. green 18·00 1·50

1944. Surch with value in words only.
93 26 2 p. on 6 p. brown 75 2·25
94 3 p. on 4 p. green 2·00 10
96 3 p. on 6 p. brown 85 20
97 4 p. on 6 p. brown 2·75 8·00

1944. Surch **SURCHARGED** and value in words.
95 26 3 p. on 4 p. green 3·00 10
92c 1 a. 3 p. on 1 a. orange — £2750

1944. Surch **ANCHAL NINE PIES.**
92a 26 9 p. on 1 a. orange 4·25 1·50

1944. Surch **ANCHAL SURCHARGED NINE PIES.**
92b 26 9 p. on 1 a. orange 3·25 1·75

28 Maharaja Ravi Varma

29 Maharaja Ravi Varma

1944.
98 28 9 p. blue 9·00 1·50
99 1 a. 3 p. mauve 5·00 7·50
100 1 a. 9 p. blue 8·00 10·00

1946. No gum.
101 29 2 p. brown 1·25 10
102 3 p. red 50 10
103 4 p. green £1600 80·00
104 6 p. brown 20·00 3·00
105 9 p. blue 50 10
106 1 a. orange 6·00 25·00
107 2 a. black 80·00 6·50
108 3 a. red 50·00 50
For No. 106, optd "U.S.T.C." or "T.-C." with or without surch, see Travancore-Cochin.

30 Maharaja Kerala Varma III

31 Chinese Nets

1948.
109 30 2 p. brown 1·00 15
110 3 p. red 75 15
111 4 p. green 8·50 1·00
112 6 p. brown 11·00 20
113 9 p. blue 1·75 15
114 2 a. black 38·00 40
115 3 a. orange 48·00 50
116 3 a. 4 p. violet 90·00 £350

1949.
117 31 2 a. black 3·00 4·75
118 – 2¼ a. green (Dutch palace) 2·25 4·25

SIX PIES

ആറു പൈ
(33)

1949. Surch as T 33.
121 29 3 p. on 9 p. blue 7·50 15·00
124a 30 3 p. on 9 p. blue 2·25 50
126 6 p. on 9 p. blue 75 40
119 28 6 p. on 1 a. 3 p. mauve 2·75 3·00
122 29 6 p. on 1 a. 3 p. mauve 9·50 11·00
120 1 a. on 1 a. 9 p. blue 75 90
123 1 a. on 1 a. 9 p. blue 3·00 1·50

1949. Surch **SIX PIES** or **NINE PIES** only.
127 29 6 p. on 1 a. orange 55·00 £120
128 9 p. on 1 a. orange 65·00 £110

OFFICIAL STAMPS

1913. Optd **ON C G S.**
O1 8 3 p. blue £120 10
O2 4 p. green 8·00 10
O3a 9 p. red 15·00 10
O4 1½ a. purple 32·00 10
O5 2 a. grey 13·00 10
O6 3 a. red 45·00 30
O7 6 a. violet 38·00 2·00
O8 12 a. blue 35·00 5·50
O9 1½ r. green 24·00 45·00

1919. Optd **ON C G S.**
O10 10 4 p. green 3·25 10
O11 6 p. brown 5·50 10
O26 8 p. brown 6·00 10
O13 9 p. red 45·00 10
O27 10 p. blue 6·00 10
O15 1½ a. purple 5·50 10
O28 2 a. grey 23·00 15
O17 2¼ a. green 11·00 10
O29 3 a. red 8·00 15
O19 6 a. violet 29·00 50
O19a 12 a. blue 15·00 2·75
O19b 1½ r. green 22·00 80·00

1923. Official stamps surch in figures and words.
O32 10 6 p. on 8 p. brown 2·00 10
O33 6 p. on 10 p. blue 4·00 10
O20b 8 8 p. on 9 p. red £130 20
O21 10 8 p. on 9 p. red 70·00 10
O23 8 10 p. on 9 p. red £750 7·50
O22 10 10 p. on 9 p. red 65·00 55

1933. Optd **ON C G S.**
O34 18 4 p. green 2·00 10
O35 6 p. red 2·25 10
O52 1 a. orange 1·00 10
O37 1 a. 8 p. red 1·50 20
O38 2 a. grey 9·50 10
O39 2¼ a. green 4·00 10
O53 3 a. orange 2·75 60
O41 3 a. 4 p. violet 1·50 15
O42 6 a. 8 p. sepia 1·50 20
O43 10 a. blue 1·50 70

1943. Official stamp surch **NINE PIES.**
O57 10 9 p. on 1½ a. purple £375 19·00

1943. Official stamps surch **SURCHARGED** and value in words.
O63 18 3 p. on 4 p. green 80·00 42·00
O58 3 p. on 1 a. 8 p. red 4·00 45
O66 1 a. 3 p. on 1 a. orange £225 90·00
O61 1 a. 9 p. on 1 a. 8 p. red 80 30

1943. Official stamps surch in words.
O62 18 3 p. on 4 p. green 18·00 4·50
O64 3 p. on 1 a. orange 1·75 2·00
O65 9 p. on 1 a. orange £180 45·00
O59 9 p. on 1 a. 8 p. red £100 26·00
O60 1 a. 9 p. on 1 a. 8 p. red 1·40 1·60

1944. Optd **ON C G S.**
O68 26 4 p. green 16·00 2·25
O69b 6 p. brown 90 10
O70 1 a. orange £1500 45·00
O71 2 a. black 2·75 40
O72 2¼ a. green 1·75 40
O73a 3 a. red 3·75 40

1944. Official stamps surch **SURCHARGED** and value in words.
O75 26 3 p. on 4 p. green 3·25 30
O78 9 p. on 6 p. brown 2·50 25
O80 1 a. 3 p. on 1 a. orange 2·75 10

1944. Official stamps surch in words.
O74 26 3 p. on 4 p. green 1·25 10
O76 3 p. on 1 a. orange 13·00 2·75
O77 9 p. on 6 p. brown 5·50 1·25
O79 1 a. 3 p. on 1 a. orange 4·50 75

1946. Optd **ON C G S.**
O81 28 9 p. blue 2·00 10
O82 1 a. 3 p. mauve 1·00 20
O83 1 a. 9 p. blue 40 60

1948. Optd **ON C G S.**
O84 29 3 p. red 40 10
O85 4 p. green 22·00 4·50
O86 6 p. brown 4·25 50
O87 9 p. blue 75 10
O88 1 a. 3 p. mauve 1·60 30
O89 1 a. 9 p. blue 1·40 40
O90 2 a. black 13·00 2·25
O91 2¼ a. green 15·00 2·25

1949. Optd **ON C G S.**
O92 30 3 p. red 60 15
O93 4 p. green 85 20
O94 6 p. brown 2·00 10
O95 9 p. blue 1·75 10
O96 2 a. black 85 15
O97 2¼ a. green 2·00 4·00
O98 3 a. orange 1·10 40
O99 3 a. 4 p. violet 26·00 24·00

1949. Official stamps surch as T 33.
O103 30 6 p. on 3 p. red 35 50
O104 9 p. on 4 p. green 55 1·40
O100 28 1 a. on 1 a. 9 p. blue 60 40
O101 29 1 a. on 1 a. 9 p. blue 15·00 11·00

1949. Optd **SERVICE.**
O105 30 3 p. on 9 p. (No. 125) 60 65

For later issues see under Travancore-Cochin.

COCOS (KEELING) ISLANDS

Islands in the Indian Ocean formerly administered by Singapore and transferred to Australian administration on 23 November 1955. From No. 296 issues were also valid for use in Australia.

1963. 12 pence = 1 shilling;
20 shillings = 1 pound.
1966. 100 cents = 1 dollar (Australia).

5 Jukong (sailboat)

6 White Tern

1963.
1 – 3d. brown 1·25 1·50
2 – 5d. blue 1·50 80
3 – 8d. red 1·75 2·25
4 – 1s. green 1·25 55
5 5 2s. purple 11·00 3·25
6 6 2s. 3d. green 35·00 3·25
DESIGNS—HORIZ (As Type 5): 3d. Copra industry; 1s. Palms. (As Type 6): 5d. Lockheed Super Constellation airliner. VERT (As Type 5): 8d. Map of islands.

1965. 50th Anniv of Gallipoli Landing. As T 184 of Australia, but slightly larger (22 × 34½ mm).
7 5d. brown, black and green 60 45

With the introduction of decimal currency on 14 February, 1966, Australian stamps were used in Cocos Islands until the 1969 issue.

7 Reef Clam

9 "Dragon", 1609

1969. Decimal Currency. Multicoloured.
8 1 c. Lajonkaines turbo shell (vert) 30 60
9 2 c. Elongate or small giant clam (vert) 1·00 80
10 3 c. Type 7 40 20
11 4 c. Floral blenny (fish) 30 50
12 5 c. "Porites cocosensis" (coral) 35 30
13 6 c. Atrisignis flyingfish 75 75
14 10 c. Banded rail 1·00 70
15 15 c. Java sparrow 1·00 30
16 20 c. Red-tailed tropic bird 1·00 30
17 30 c. Sooty tern 1·00 30
18 50 c. Eastern reef heron (vert) 1·00 30
19 $1 Great frigate bird (vert) 3·00 1·00

1976. Ships. Multicoloured.
20 1 c. Type 9 30 40
21 2 c. H.M.S. "Juno", 1857 (horiz) 30 40
22 5 c. H.M.S. "Beagle", 1836 (horiz) 30 40
23 10 c. H.M.A.S. "Sydney", 1914 (horiz) 35 40
24 15 c. S.M.S. "Emden", 1914 (horiz) 1·00 55
25 20 c. "Ayesha", 1907 (horiz) 1·00 65
26 25 T.S.S. "Islander", 1927 1·00 1·00
27 30 c. M.V. "Cheshire", 1951 1·00 1·00
28 35 c. Jukong (sailboat) (horiz) 1·00 1·00
29 40 c. C.S. "Scotia", 1900 (horiz) 1·00 1·00
30 50 c. R.M.S. "Orontes", 1929 1·40 1·10
31 $1 Royal Yacht "Gothic", 1954 2·00 1·40

10 Map of Cocos (Keeling) Islands, Union Flag, Stars and Trees

1979. Inauguration of Independent Postal Service and First Statutory Council. Multicoloured.
32 20 c. Type 10 25 30
33 50 c. Council seat and jukong (sailboat) 35 50

11 Forceps Fish

12 "Peace on Earth"

1979. Fishes. Multicoloured.
34 1 c. Type 11 30 80
35 2 c. Ornate butterflyfish 30 30
36 5 c. Barbier 50 90
37 10 c. Meyer's butterflyfish 30 55
38 15 c. Pink wrasse 30 30
39 20 c. Clark's anemonefish 45 30
39a 22 c. Undulate triggerfish 45 30
40 25 c. Red-breasted wrasse 45 60
40a 28 c. Guineafowl wrasse 35 35
41 30 c. Madagascar butterflyfish 65 45
42 35 c. Cocos-keeling angelfish 65 1·40
43 40 c. Coral hogfish 70 90
44 50 c. Clown wrasse 85 75
45 55 c. Yellow-tailed tamarin 75 1·00
45a 60 c. Greasy grouper 75 75
46 $1 Palette surgeonfish 1·75 3·50
47 $2 Melon butterflyfish 2·00 3·50

1979. Christmas. Multicoloured.
48 25 c. Type 12 25 35
49 55 c. Atoll seascape ("Goodwill") 40 55

13 Star, Map of Cocos (Keeling) Islands and Island Landscape

1980. Christmas. Multicoloured.
50 15 c. Type 13 10 10
51 28 c. The Three Kings 15 15
52 60 c. Adoration 40 40

14 "Administered by the British Government, 1857"

15 "Eye of the Wind" and Map of Cocos (Keeling) Islands

1980. 25th Anniv of Territorial Status under Australian Administration. Multicoloured.
53 22 c. Type 14 15 15
54 22 c. Arms of Ceylon 15 15
55 22 c. Arms of Straits Settlements 15 15
56 22 c. Arms of Singapore 15 15
57 22 c. Arms and flag of Australia 15 15

1980. "Operation Drake" (round the world expedition) and 400th Anniv of Sir Francis Drake's Circumnavigation of the World. Multicoloured.
58 22 c. Type 15 25 15
59 28 c. Routes map (horiz) 25 15
60 35 c. Sir Francis Drake and "Golden Hind" 25 15
61 60 c. Prince Charles (patron) and "Eye of the Wind" (brigantine) 45 30

16 Aerial View of Animal Quarantine Station

1981. Opening of Animal Quarantine Station. Multicoloured.

62 22 c. Type **16** 15 15
63 45 c. Unloading livestock . . . 30 30
64 60 c. Livestock in pen 35 35

17 Consolidated Catalina Flying Boat "Guba"

1981. Aircraft. Multicoloured.

65 22 c. Type **17** 25 25
66 22 c. Consolidated Liberator and Avro Lancastrian 25 25
67 22 c. Douglas DC-4 and Lockheed Constellation 25 25
68 22 c. Lockheed Electra 25 25
69 22 c. Boeing 727-100 airliners . . 25 25

18 Prince Charles and Lady Diana Spencer

1981. Royal Wedding.

70 **18** 24 c. multicoloured 30 20
71 60 c. multicoloured 50 60

19 "Angels we have heard on High"

1981. Christmas. Scenes and Lines from Carol "Angels we have heard on High". Multicoloured.

72 18 c. Type **19** 10 10
73 30 c. "Shepherds why this Jubilee?" 20 20
74 60 c. "Come to Bethlehem and see Him" 35 35

20 "Pachyseris speciosa" and "Heliofungia actiniformis" (corals)

1981. 150th Anniv of Charles Darwin's Voyage. Multicoloured.

75 24 c. Type **20** 35 15
76 45 c. Charles Darwin in 1853 and "Pavona cactus" (coral) . . . 55 30
77 60 c. H.M.S. "Beagle", 1832, and "Lobophyllia hemprichii" (coral) 70 35

21 Queen Victoria

1982. 125th Anniv of Annexation of Cocos (Keeling) Islands to British Empire. Multicoloured.

79 24 c. Type **21** 20 15
80 45 c. Union flag 35 25
81 60 c. Captain S. Fremantle (annexation visit, 1857) . . . 40 35

22 Lord Baden-Powell

1982. 75th Anniv of Boy Scout Movement. Multicoloured.

82 27 c. Type **22** 30 25
83 75 c. "75" and map of Cocos (Keeling) Islands (vert) . . . 1·10 1·50

23 "Precis villida"

24 "Call His Name Immanuel"

1982. Butterflies and Moths. Multicoloured.

84 1 c. Type **23** . . . . 1·00 60
85 2 c. "Cephonodes picus" (horiz) 40 40
86 5 c. "Macroglossom corythus" (horiz) . . . . 1·50 70
87 10 c. "Chasmina candida" . . 40 40
88 20 c. "Nagia linteola" (horiz) . 40 65
89 25 c. "Eublemma rivula" . . . 40 75
90 30 c. "Eurrhyparodes tricoloralis" 40 65
91 35 c. "Hippotion boerhaviae" (horiz) . . . . 1·50 75
92 40 c. "Euploea core" 40 80
93 45 c. "Psara hipponalis" (horiz) 50 80
94 50 c. "Danaus chrysippus" (horiz) 60 1·25
95 55 c. "Hypolimnas misippus" . . 60 70
96 60 c. "Spodoptera litura" . . . 65 1·75
97 $1 "Achaea janata" . . . . . 2·75 2·75
98 $2 "Panacra velox" (horiz) . . 2·00 2·75
99 $3 "Utetheisa pulchelloides" (horiz) . . . . 2·75 2·75

1982. Christmas. Multicoloured.

100 21 c. Type **24** 25 20
101 35 c. "I bring you good tidings" 40 35
102 75 c. "Arise and flee into Egypt" 1·00 1·00

25 "God will look after us" (Matt. 1:20)

26 Hari Raya Celebration

1983. Christmas. Extracts from New Testament. Multicoloured.

103 24 c. Type **25** 30 40
104 24 c. "Our baby King, Jesus" (Matthew. 2:2) 30 40
105 24 c. "Your Saviour is born" (Luke. 2:11) 30 40
106 24 c. "Wise men followed the Star" (Matthew. 2:9–10) . . 30 40
107 24 c. "And worship the Lord" (Matthew. 2:11) 30 40

1984. Cocos-Malaya Culture (1st series). Mult.

108 45 c. Type **26** 45 25
109 75 c. Melenggok dancing . . . 65 50
110 85 c. Cocos-Malay wedding . 75 55

See also Nos. 128/31

27 Unpacking Barrel

1984. 75th Anniv of Cocos Barrel Mail. Multicoloured.

111 35 c. Type **27** 40 25
112 55 c. Jukong awaiting mail ship 75 50
113 70 c. P & O mail ship "Morea" 85 55

28 Captain William Keeling

29 Malay Settlement, Home Island

1984. 375th Anniv of Discovery of Cocos (Keeling) Islands. Multicoloured.

115 30 c. Type **28** 60 40
116 65 c. "Hector" . . . . 1·25 90
117 95 c. Mariner's astrolabe . . 1·50 1·25
118 $1.10 Map circa 1666 . . . . 1·60 1·50

1984. "Ausipex" International Stamp Exhibition, Melbourne. Multicoloured.

119 45 c. Type **29** 75 50
120 55 c. Airstrip, West Island . . 85 60

30 "Rainbow" Fish

32 Jukong-building

1984. Christmas. Multicoloured.

122 24 c. Type **30** 50 50
123 35 c. "Rainbow" butterfly . . 1·10 1·25
124 55 c. "Rainbow" bird . . . . 1·25 1·60

1985. Cocos-Malay Culture (2nd series). Handicrafts. Multicoloured.

126 30 c. Type **32** 75 35
127 45 c. Blacksmithing . . . . . 1·00 55
128 55 c. Woodcarving . . . . . . 1·25 65

33 C.S. "Scotia"

1985. Cable-laying Ships. Multicoloured.

129 33 c. Type **33** . . . . 1·25 40
130 65 c. C.S. "Anglia" . . . . . 2·00 1·60
131 80 c. C.S. "Patrol" . . . . . 2·25 2·25

34 Red-footed Booby 35 Mantled Top

1985. Birds of Cocos (Keeling) Islands. Multicoloured.

132 33 c. Type **34** . . . . 1·75 1·75
133 60 c. Rufous night heron (juvenile) (horiz) . . . . . 2·00 2·00
134 $1 Banded rail (horiz) . . . . 2·25 2·25

Nos. 132/4 were issued together, se-tenant, forming a composite design.

1985. Shells and Molluscs. Multicoloured.

135 1 c. Type **35** 45 60
136 2 c. Rang's nerite 55 65
137 3 c. Jewel box 60 70
138 4 c. Money cowrie 60 70
139 5 c. Purple Pacific drupe . . . 60 70
140 10 c. Soldier cone 70 75
141 15 c. Merlin-spike auger . . . 1·25 1·00
142 20 c. Pacific strawberry cockle 1·25 1·10
143 30 c. Lajonkaire's turban . . 1·25 1·25
144 33 c. Reticulate mitre . . . . 1·40 1·25
145 40 c. Common spider conch . . 1·40 1·40
146 50 c. Fluted giant clam or scaled tridacna . . . . 1·40 1·50
147 60 c. Minstrel cowrie . . . . 1·75 2·00
148 $1 Varicose nudibranch . . . 2·75 3·00
149 $2 Tesselated nudibranch . . . 3·50 4·00
150 $3 Hamincea cymballum . . . 4·25 4·75

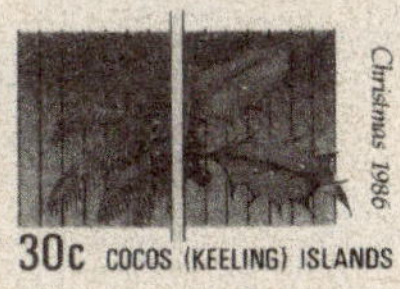

37 Charles Darwin, c 1840

38 Coconut Palm and Holly Sprigs

1986. 150th Anniv of Charles Darwin's Visit. Multicoloured.

152 33 c. Type **37** 70 50
153 60 c. Map of H.M.S. "Beagle's" route, Australia to Cocos Islands . . . . 1·25 2·00
154 $1 H.M.S. "Beagle" . . . . . 1·75 2·50

1986. Christmas. Multicoloured.

155 30 c. Type **38** 60 50
156 90 c. Nautilus shell and Christmas tree bauble . . . 2·00 2·50
157 $1 Tropical fish and bell . . . 2·00 2·50

39 Jukong

1987. Sailing Craft. Multicoloured.

158 36 c. Type **39** . . . . 1·10 1·25
159 36 c. Ocean racing yachts . . 1·10 1·25
160 36 c. "Sarimanok" (replica of early dhow) . . . . 1·10 1·25
161 36 c. "Ayesha" (schooner) . . 1·10 1·25

Nos. 158/61 were printed together, se-tenant, each strip forming a composite background design.

40 Beach, Direction Island

1987. Cocos Islands Scenes. Multicoloured.

162 70 c. Type **40** . . . . 1·40 1·40
163 90 c. Palm forest, West Island 1·75 2·00
164 $1 Golf course . . . . 2·75 3·00

41 Radio Transmitter and Palm Trees at Sunset

1987. Communications. Multicoloured.

165 70 c. Type **41** . . . . 1·25 1·50
166 75 c. Boeing 727-100 airliner at terminal . . . . 1·50 1·75
167 90 c. "Intelsat 5" satellite . . 1·75 2·25
168 $1 Airmail letter and globe . . 2·00 2·25

42 Batik Printing

1987. Cocos (Keeling) Islands Malay Industries. Multicoloured.

169 45 c. Type **42** . . . . 1·25 1·50
170 65 c. Jukong building . . . . 1·75 2·00
171 75 c. Copra production . . . 2·00 2·25

43 Hands releasing Peace Dove and Map of Islands

44 Coconut Flower

1987. Christmas. Multicoloured.

172 30 c. Type **43** 40 40
173 90 c. Local children at Christmas party . . . . 1·25 1·90
174 $1 Island family and Christmas star . . . . 1·50 1·90

1988. Bicentenary of Australian Settlement. Arrival of First Fleet. As Nos. 1105/9 of Australia but each inscribed "COCOS (KEELING) ISLANDS" and "AUSTRALIA BICENTENARY".

175 37 c. Aborigines watching arrival of Fleet, Botany Bay . . . 1·50 1·75
176 37 c. Aboriginal family and anchored ships . . . . . 1·50 1·75
177 37 c. Fleet arriving at Sydney Cove . . . . 1·50 1·75
178 37 c. Ship's boat . . . . . . 1·50 1·75
179 37c. Raising the flag, Sydney Cove, 26 January 1788 . . 1·50 1·75

Nos. 175/9 were printed together, se-tenant, forming a composite design.

1988. Life Cycle of the Coconut. Multicoloured.

180 37 c. Type **44** 50 40
181 65 c. Immature nuts . . . . . 75 1·00
182 90 c. Coconut palm and mature nuts . . . . 1·10 1·75
183 $1 Seedlings . . . . 1·25 1·75

45 Copra 3d. Stamp of 1963

46 "Pisonia grandis"

1988. 25th Anniv of First Cocos (Keeling) Islands Stamps. Each showing stamp from 1963 definitive set.

185	45	37 c. green, black and blue	1·25	85
186	–	55 c. green, black and brown	1·75	50
187	–	65 c. blue, black and lilac	1·90	2·00
188	–	70 c. red, black and grey	1·90	2·00
189	–	90 c. purple, black and grey	2·25	2·25
190	–	$1 green, black and brown	2·25	2·25

DESIGNS: 55 c. Palms 1s.; 65 c. Lockheed Super Constellation airplane 5d.; 70 c. Map 8d.; 90 c. "Jukong" (sailboat) 2s.; $1 White tern 2s. 3d.

1988. Flora. Multicoloured.

191	1 c. Type **46**	30	50
192	2 c. "Cocos nucifera"	40	60
193	5 c. "Morinda citrifolia"	65	70
194	10 c. "Cordia subcordata"	70	70
195	30 c. "Argusia argentea"	1·00	90
196	37 c. "Calophyllum inophyllum"	1·00	1·00
197	40 c. "Barringtonia asiatica"	1·00	1·25
198	50 c. "Caesalpinia bonduc"	1·25	1·50
199	90 c. "Terminalia catappa"	1·75	2·25
200	$1 "Pemphis acidula"	1·75	2·25
201	$2 "Scaevola sericea"	2·50	2·50
202	$3 "Hibiscus tiliaceus"	3·50	3·75

47 Beach at Sunset

1988. Christmas.

204	47	32 c. multicoloured	80	50
205		90 c. multicoloured	1·75	2·50
206		$1 multicoloured	2·00	2·50

48 Captain P. G. Taylor　49 Jukong and Star

1989. 50th Anniv of First Indian Ocean Aerial Survey.

207	48	40 c. multicoloured	80	65
208	–	70 c. multicoloured	1·75	2·00
209	–	$1 multicoloured	2·00	2·25
210	–	$1.10 blue, lilac and black	2·25	2·50

DESIGNS: 70 c. Consolidated Catalina flying boat "Guba I" and crew; $1 "Guba" over Direction Islands; $1.10, Unissued Australia 5s. stamp commemorating flight.

1989. Christmas.

211	49	35 c. multicoloured	75	50
212		80 c. multicoloured	2·25	2·50
213		$1.10 multicoloured	2·25	2·50

50 H.M.A.S. "Sydney" (cruiser)

1989. 75th Anniv of Destruction of German Cruiser "Emden". Multicoloured.

214	40 c. Type **50**	1·75	1·75
215	70c. "Emden"	2·00	2·00
216	$1 "Emden's" steam launch	2·25	2·25
217	$1.10 H.M.A.S. "Sydney" (1914) and crest	2·25	2·25

51 Xanthid Crab

1990. Cocos Islands Crabs. Multicoloured.

219	45 c. Type **51**	1·50	75
220	75 c. Ghost crab	2·00	2·00
221	$1 Red-backed mud crab	2·25	2·25
222	$1.30 Coconut crab (vert)	2·50	3·00

52 Captain Keeling and "Hector", 1609

1990. Navigators of the Pacific.

223	52	45 c. mauve	2·00	85
224	–	75 c. mauve and blue	2·25	2·50
225	–	$1 mauve and stone	2·75	3·00
226	–	$1.30 mauve and buff	3·50	4·25

DESIGNS: 75 c. Captain Fitzroy and H.M.S. "Beagle", 1836; $1 Captain Belcher and H.M.S. "Samarang", 1846; $1.30, Captain Fremantle and H.M.S. "Juno", 1857.

1990. "New Zealand 1990" International Stamp Exhibition, Auckland. No. 188 optd with logo and **NEW ZEALAND 1990 24 AUG 2 SEP AUCKLAND**.

228	70 c. red, black and grey	2·25	2·75

1990. No. 187 surch **$5**.

230	$5 on 65 c. blue, black and lilac	17·00	15·00

55 Cocos Atoll from West and Star　58 Beaded Sea Star

1990. Christmas. Multicoloured.

231	40 c. Type **55**	70	80
232	70 c. Cocos atoll from south	1·50	2·25
233	$1.30 Cocos atoll from east	2·50	2·75

1990. Nos. 140/1, 143 and 146/7 surch **POSTAGE PAID** plus additional words as indicated.

236	(1 c.) on 30 c. Lajonkaire's turban (**LOCAL**)	1·50	2·00
235	(43 c.) on 10 c. Soldier cone (**MAINLAND**)	1·40	1·75
237	70 c. on 60 c. Minstrel cowrie (**ZONE 1**)	1·50	2·25
238	80 c. on 50 c. Fluted giant clam or scaled tridacna (**ZONE 2**)	1·75	3·00
239	$1.20 on 15 c. Marlin-spike auger (**ZONE 5**)	2·00	3·25

1991. Starfish and Sea Urchins. Multicoloured.

240	45 c. Type **58**	1·00	65
241	75 c. Feather star	1·90	2·00
242	$1 Slate pencil urchin	2·00	2·25
243	$1.30 Globose sea urchin	2·50	3·00

59 Cocos Islands

1991. Malay Hari Raya Festival. Multicoloured.

244	45 c. Type **59**	1·00	65
245	75 c. Island house	1·75	2·00
246	$1.30 Islands scene	2·50	3·00

60 Child praying

1991. Christmas. Multicoloured.

247	38 c. Type **60**	80	55
248	43 c. Child dreaming of Christmas Day	85	60
249	$1 Child singing	2·00	2·25
250	$1.20 Child fascinated by decorations	2·50	3·25

61 "Lybia tessellata"

1992. Crustaceans. Multicoloured.

252	5 c. Type **61**	40	40
253	10 c. "Pilodius areolatus"	45	45
254	20 c. "Trizopagurus strigatus"	70	70
255	30 c. "Lophozozymus pulchellus"	1·00	1·00
256	40 c. "Thalamitoides quadridens"	1·00	1·00
257	45 c. "Calcinus elegans" (vert)	1·00	1·00
258	50 c. "Clibarius humilis"	1·25	1·25
259	60 c. "Trapezia rufopunctata" (vert)	1·50	1·50
260	80 c. "Pylopaguropsis magnimanus" (vert)	1·75	1·75
261	$1 "Trapezia ferruginea" (vert)	1·75	1·75
262	$2 "Trapezia guttata" (vert)	3·00	3·50
263	$3 "Trapezia cymodoce" (vert)	3·50	3·75

62 "Santa Maria"　64 R.A.F. Supermarine Spitfires on Island Airstrip

63 Banded Rail searching for Food

1992. 500th Anniv of Discovery of America by Columbus.

264	62	$1.05 multicoloured	2·25	2·50

1992. Endangered Species. Banded Rail. Mult.

265	10 c. Type **63**	50	60
266	15 c. Banded rail with chick	65	75
267	30 c. Two rails drinking	80	90
268	45 c. Rail and nest	90	1·10

1992. 50th Anniv of Second World War. Mult.

270	45 c. Type **64**	1·50	80
271	85 c. Mitsubishi A6M Zero-Sen aircraft bombing Kampong	2·25	2·50
272	$1.20 R.A.F. Short Sunderland flying boat	2·75	3·50

65 Waves breaking on Reef　66 "Lobophyllia hemprichii"

1992. Christmas. Multicoloured.

273	40 c. Type **65**	80	60
274	80 c. Direction Island	2·00	2·50
275	$1 Moorish idols (fish) and coral	2·00	2·50

1993. Corals. Multicoloured.

276	45 c. Type **66**	55	55
277	85 c. "Pocillopora eydouxi"	1·00	1·40
278	$1.05 "Fungia scutaria"	1·40	1·75
279	$1.20 "Sarcophyton sp"	1·50	2·00

67 Plastic 5 r. Token　68 Primary School Pupil

1993. Early Cocos (Keeling) Islands Currency. Multicoloured.

280	45 c. Type **67**	75	55
281	85 c. 1968 1 r. plastic token	1·25	1·75
282	$1.05 1977 150 r. commemorative gold coin	1·75	2·00
283	$1.20 1910 plastic token	1·75	2·25

1993. Education. Multicoloured.

284	5 c. Type **68**	30	50
285	45 c. Secondary school pupil	75	50
286	85 c. Learning traditional crafts	1·50	1·75
287	$1.05 Learning office skills	1·75	2·25
288	$1.20 Seaman training	2·25	2·75

69 Lifeboat and Crippled Yacht

1993. Air-Sea Rescue. Multicoloured.

289	45 c. Type **69**	1·25	75
290	85 c. Israeli Aircraft Industry Westwind Seascan (aircraft)	2·25	2·50
291	$1.05 "R.J. Hawke" (ferry)	2·50	3·25

70 Peace Doves　71 Rectangle Triggerfish and Coral

1993. Christmas.

293	70	40 c. multicoloured	80	60
294		80 c. multicoloured	2·00	2·50
295		$1 multicoloured	2·00	2·50

1994. Transfer of Postal Service to Australia Post. Multicoloured.

296	5 c. Type **71**	25	30
297	5 c. Three rectangle triggerfish and map section	25	30
298	5 c. Two rectangle triggerfish and map section	25	30
299	5 c. Two rectangle triggerfish, map section and red coral	25	30
300	5 c. Rectangle triggerfish with red and brown corals	25	30
301	10 c. Green turtles on beach	25	30
302	10 c. Two green turtles	25	30
303	10 c. Crowd of young green turtles	25	30
304	10 c. Green turtle and map section	25	30
305	10 c. Green turtle, pyramid butterflyfish and map section	25	30
306	20 c. Three pyramid butterflyfish and map section	40	45
307	20 c. Pyramid butterflyfish with brown coral	40	45
308	20 c. Two pyramid butterflyfish and coral	40	45
309	20 c. Three pyramid butterflyfish and coral	40	45
310	20 c. Coral, pyramid butterflyfish and map section	40	45
311	45 c. Jukongs with map of airport	50	55
312	45 c. Two jukongs with red or blue sails and map section	50	55
313	45 c. Jukong in shallows	50	55
314	45 c. Two jukongs with red or yellow sails and map section	50	55
315	45 c. Two jukongs, one with blue jib, and map section	50	55

Nos. 296/315 were printed together, se-tenant, with the backgrounds forming a composite map.

72 Prabu Abjasa Puppet　73 Angel playing Harp

1994. Shadow Puppets. Multicoloured.

316	45 c. Type **72**	65	50
317	90 c. Prabu Pandu	1·25	1·50
318	$1 Judistra	1·40	1·50
319	$1.35 Abimanju	1·50	2·00

1994. Seasonal Festivals. Multicoloured.

320	40 c. Type **73**	50	50
321	45 c. Wise Man holding gift	55	50
322	80 c. Mosque at night	1·00	1·75

74 White-tailed Tropic Bird and Blue-faced Booby

1995. Sea-birds of North Keeling Island. Multicoloured.

323	45 c. Type **74**	60	45
324	85 c. Great frigate bird and white tern	1·00	1·50

75 Yellow Crazy Ant　76 Saddle Butterflyfish

1995. Insects. Multicoloured.

326	45 c. Type **75**	70	80
327	45 c. Aedes mosquito	70	80
328	45 c. Hawk moth	70	80
329	45 c. Scarab beetle	70	80
330	45 c. Lauxaniid fly	70	80
331	$1.20 Common eggfly (butterfly)	1·25	1·50

Nos. 326/30 were printed together, se-tenant, forming a composite design.

1995. Marine Life. Multicoloured.

332	5 c. Redspot wrasse	10	10
333	30 c. Blue-throated triggerfish ("Gilded triggerfish")	25	30
334	40 c. Type **76**	30	35
335	45 c. Arc-eyed hawkfish	35	40
335a	70 c. Crowned squirrelfish	55	60
336	75 c. Orange-pine unicornfish	55	60
337	80 c. Blue tang	60	65
338	85 c. Juvenile twin-spotted wrasse ("Humpback wrasse")	65	70
339	90 c. Threadfin butterflyfish	70	75
339a	95 c. Sixstripe wrasse	75	80
340	$1 Bluestripe snapper	75	80
341	$1.05 Longnosed butterflyfish	80	85
342	$1.20 Freckled hawkfish	90	95
343	$2 Powder-blue surgeonfish	1·50	1·60
343a	$5 Goldback anthias	3·75	4·00

77 Members of Malay Community

78 Black Rhinoceros with Calf

1996. Hari Raya Puasa Festival. Multicoloured.

344	45 c. Type **77**	55	50
345	75 c. Beating drums	1·00	1·25
346	85 c. Preparing festival meal	1·10	1·50

1996. Cocos Quarantine Station. Multicoloured.

347	45 c. Type **78**	70	70
348	50 c. Alpacas	70	70
349	$1.05 Boran cattle	1·25	1·50
350	$1.20 Ostrich with chicks	1·50	1·75

79 Dancers and Tambourine

80 "Wrapped Present" (Lazina Brian)

1997. Hari Raya Puasa Festival. Multicoloured.

351	45 c. Type **79**	55	50
352	75 c. Girl clapping and sailing dinghies	90	1·25
353	85 c. Dancers on beach and food	1·00	1·25

1998. Hari Raya Puasa Festival. Paintings by children. Multicoloured.

354	45 c. Type **80**	40	45
355	45 c. "Mosque" (Azran Jim)	40	45
356	45 c. "Cocos Malay Woman" (Kate Gossage)	40	45
357	45 c. "Yacht" (Matt Harber)	40	45
358	45 c. "People dancing" (Rakin Chongkin)	40	45

81 Preparing Food on Beach

1999. Hari Raya Puasa Festival. Multicoloured.

359	45 c. Type **81**	35	40
360	45 c. Woman with child and jukongs on beach	35	40
361	45 c. Jukongs and palm fronds	35	40
362	45 c. Two men watching jukongs	35	40
363	45 c. Jukong and white flowers	35	40

OFFICIAL STAMPS

1991. No. 182 surch **OFFICIAL PAID MAINLAND.**

O1	(43 c.) on 90 c. Coconut palm and mature nuts	†	90·00

No. O1 was not sold to the public in unused condition.

COOK ISLANDS

A group of islands in the South Pacific under New Zealand control, including Aitutaki, Niue, Penrhyn and Rarotonga. Granted Self-Government in 1965.

See also issues for Aitutaki and Penrhyn Island.

1892. 12 pence = 1 shilling;
20 shillings = 1 pound.
1967. 100 cents = 1 dollar.

1

1892.

1b	**1**	1d. black	26·00	26·00
2		1½d. mauve	40·00	38·00
3		2½d. blue	40·00	38·00
4		10d. red	£140	£130

2 Queen Makea Takau

3 White Tern or Torea

1893.

11ba	**3**	½d. blue	4·00	4·75
28		½d. green	2·25	3·25
13	**2**	1d. brown	13·00	13·00
12		1d. blue	4·25	4·50
29		1d. red	4·00	3·00
43		1½d. mauve	7·50	3·75
15a	**3**	2d. brown	8·00	6·50
16a	**2**	2½d. red	14·00	9·00
32		2½d. blue	3·75	6·50
9		5d. black	15·00	13·00
18a	**3**	6d. purple	19·00	20·00
19	**2**	10d. green	17·00	42·00
46	**3**	1s. red	27·00	75·00

1899. Surch **ONE HALF PENNY.**

21	**2**	½d. on 1d. blue	32·00	40·00

1901. Optd with crown.

22	**2**	1d. brown	£180	£140

1919. New Zealand stamps (King George V) surch **RAROTONGA** and value in native language in words.

56	**62**	½d. green	40	80
47	**53**	1d. red	85	1·75
57	**62**	1½d. brown	40	75
58		2d. yellow	1·25	1·25
48a		2½d. blue	2·00	2·25
49a		3d. brown	2·25	1·50
50c		4d. violet	1·75	4·00
51a		4½d. green	1·75	6·50
52a		6d. red	1·75	5·00
53		7½d. brown	1·50	5·50
54a		9d. green	2·00	12·00
55a		1s. red	2·75	15·00

9 Captain Cook landing

17 Harbour, Rarotonga and Mount Ikurangi

1920. Inscr "RAROTONGA".

81	**9**	½d. black and green	4·50	7·50
82	–	1d. black and red	6·00	1·75
72	–	1½d. black and blue	8·00	8·50
83	–	2½d. brown and blue	5·00	20·00
73	–	3d. black and brown	2·25	5·50
84	**17**	4d. green and violet	8·00	15·00
74	–	6d. brown and orange	2·25	8·50
75	–	1s. black and violet	5·00	17·00

DESIGNS—VERT: 1d. Wharf at Avarua; 1½d. Captain Cook (Dance); 2½d. Te Po, Rarotongan chief; 3d. Palm tree. HORIZ: 6d. Huts at Arorangi; 1s. Avarua Harbour.

1921. New Zealand stamps optd **RAROTONGA.**

76	**F 4**	2s. blue	27·00	55·00
77		2s. 6d. brown	18·00	50·00
78		5s. green	27·00	65·00
79		10s. red	48·00	85·00
89		£1 red	80·00	£130

1926. "Admiral" type of New Zealand optd **RAROTONGA.**

90	**71**	2s. blue	10·00	40·00
92		3s. mauve	16·00	42·00

1931. No. 77 surch **TWO PENCE.**

93		2d. on 1½d. black and blue	9·00	2·75

1931. Arms type of New Zealand optd **RAROTONGA.**

95	**F 6**	2s. 6d. brown	9·50	20·00
96		5s. green	16·00	48·00
97		10s. red	35·00	80·00
98		£1 pink	80·00	£130

20 Captain Cook landing

22 Double Maori Canoe

1932. Inscribed "COOK ISLANDS".

106	**20**	½d. black and green	1·00	3·50
107	–	1d. black and red	1·00	1·75
108	**22**	2d. black and brown	1·25	40
140	–	2½d. black and blue	65	1·75
110	–	4d. black and blue	1·50	40
142	–	6d. black and orange	1·25	1·75
105	–	1s. black and violet	8·00	20·00

DESIGNS—VERT: 1d. Captain Cook. HORIZ: 2½d. Natives working cargo; 4d. Port of Avarua; 6d. R.M.S. "Monowai"; 1s. King George V.

1935. Jubilee. As 1932 optd **SILVER JUBILEE OF KING GEORGE V. 1910-1935.**

113	1d. red	60	1·10
114	2½d. blue	1·00	2·00
115	6d. green and orange	3·50	5·50

1936. Stamps of New Zealand optd **COOK ISLANDS.**

116	**71**	2s. blue	12·00	45·00
131w	**F 6**	2s. 6d. brown	13·00	17·00
117	**71**	3s. mauve	13·00	65·00
132	**F 6**	5s. green	7·50	18·00
133w		10s. red	40·00	65·00
134		£1 pink	45·00	70·00
135w		£3 green	55·00	£160
98b		£5 blue	£170	£300

1937. Coronation. T **106** of New Zealand optd **COOK IS'DS.**

124	**106**	1d. red	40	30
125		2½d. blue	80	30
126		6d. orange	80	30

29 King George VI

30 Native Village

1938.

143	**29**	1s. black and violet	1·25	2·25
128	**30**	2s. black and orange	18·00	10·00
145	–	3s. blue and green	28·00	25·00

DESIGN—HORIZ: 3s. Native canoe.

32 Tropical Landscape

34 Ngatangiia Channel, Rarotonga

1940.

130	**32**	3d. on 1½d. black and purple	40	50

1946. Peace. Peace stamps of New Zealand of 1946 optd **COOK ISLANDS.**

146	**132**	1d. green	30	10
147	–	2d. purple	30	40
148	–	6d. brown and red	30	40
149	**139**	8d. black and red	30	40

1949.

150	**34**	½d. violet and brown	10	1·00
151	–	1d. brown and green	3·50	2·00
152	–	2d. brown and red	1·00	2·00
153	–	3d. green and blue	1·25	2·00
154	–	5d. green and violet	4·00	1·50
155	–	6d. black and red	4·25	2·75
156	–	8d. olive and orange	55	3·75
157	–	1s. blue and brown	4·25	3·75
158	–	2s. brown and red	3·00	11·00
159	–	3s. blue and green	8·50	17·00

DESIGNS—HORIZ: 1d. Captain Cook and map of Hervey Is; 2d. Rarotonga and Rev. John Williams; 3d. Aitutaki and palm trees; 5d. Rarotonga Airfield; 6d. Penrhyn village; 8d. Native hut. VERT: 1s. Map and statue of Capt. Cook; 2s. Native hut and palms; 3s. "Matua" (inter-island freighter).

1953. Coronation. As Types of New Zealand but inscr "COOK ISLANDS".

160	**164**	3d. brown	1·00	75
161	**166**	6d. grey	1·25	1·25

1960. No 154 surch **1/6.**

162	1s. 6d. on 5d. green and violet	30	30

45 Tiare Maori

52 Queen Elizabeth II

55 Rarotonga

56 Eclipse and Palm

1963.

163	**45**	1d. green and yellow	45	40
164	–	2d. red and yellow	20	40
165	–	3d. yellow, green and violet	70	40
166	–	5d. blue and black	8·00	75
167	–	6d. red, yellow and green	1·00	30
168	–	8d. black and blue	3·50	1·25
169	–	1s. yellow and green	40	30
170	**52**	1s. 6d. violet	2·75	2·00
171	–	2s. brown and blue	1·00	75
172	–	3s. black and green	1·25	1·00
173	**55**	5s. brown and blue	10·00	3·25

DESIGNS—VERT (As Type **45**): 2d. Fishing god; 8d. Long-tailed tuna. HORIZ (As Type **45**): 3d. Frangipani (plant); 5d. Love tern; 6d. Hibiscus; 1s. Oranges. (As Type **55**): 2s. Island scene; 3s. Administration Centre, Mangaia.

1965. Solar Eclipse Observation, Manuae Island.

174	**56**	6d. black, yellow and blue	20	10

57 N.Z. Ensign and Map

1965. Internal Self-Government.

175	**57**	4d. red and blue	20	10
176	–	10d. multicoloured	20	15
177	–	1s. multicoloured	20	15
178	–	1s. 9d. multicoloured	50	1·00

DESIGNS: 10d. London Missionary Society Church; 1s. Proclamation of Cession, 1900; 1s. 9d. Nikao School.

1966. Churchill Commemoration. Nos. 171/3 and 175/7 optd **In Memoriam SIR WINSTON CHURCHILL 1874 – 1965.**

179	**57**	4d. red and blue	75	30
180	–	10d. multicoloured	1·50	45
181	–	1s. multicoloured	1·50	65
182	–	2s. brown and blue	1·50	1·25
183	–	3s. black and green	1·50	1·25
184	**55**	5s. brown and blue	2·00	1·75

1966. Air. Various stamps optd **Airmail** and Douglas DC-3 airplane or surch in addition.

185	–	6d. red, yell & grn (No. 167)	1·25	20
186	–	7d. on 8d. blk & bl (No. 168)	1·50	25
187	–	10d. on 3d. green and violet (No. 165)	1·00	15
188	–	1s. yellow and green (No. 169)	1·00	15
189	**52**	1s. 6d. violet	1·50	1·25
190	–	2s. 3d. on 3s. black and green (No. 172)	1·00	65
191	**55**	5s. brown and blue	1·75	1·50
192	–	10s. on 2s. brown and blue (No. 171)	1·75	10·00
193	–	£1 pink (No. 143)	12·00	17·00

63 "Adoration of the Magi" (Fra Angelico)

1966. Christmas. Multicoloured.

194a	1d. Type **63**	10	10
195a	2d. "The Nativity" (Memling)	20	10
196a	4d. "Adoration of the Wise Men" (Velazquez)	30	15
197a	10d. "Adoration of the Wise Men" (H. Bosch)	30	20
198a	1s. 6d. "Adoration of the Shepherds" (J. de Ribera)	40	35

68 Tennis and Queen Elizabeth II

1967. 2nd South Pacific Games, Noumea. Multicoloured.

199	½d. Type **68** (postage)	10	10
200	1d. Basketball and Games emblem	10	10
201	4d. Boxing and Cook Islands Team badge	10	10
202	7d. Football and Queen Elizabeth II	20	15

203		10d. Running and Games Emblem (air)	20	15
204		2s. 3d. Running and Cook Islands' Team badge	25	30

1967. Decimal currency. Various stamps surch.

205	45	1 c. on 1d.	45	1·25
206	–	2 c. on 2d. (No. 164)	10	10
207	–	2½ c. on 3d. (No. 165)	20	10
209	57	3 c. on 4d.	15	10
210	–	4 c. on 5d. (No. 166)	5·50	30
211	–	5 c. on 6d. (No. 167)	15	10
212	56	5 c. on 6d.	5·00	40
213	–	7 c. on 8d. (No. 168)	30	10
214	–	10 c. on 1s. (No. 169)	15	10
215	52	15 c. on 1s. 6d.	2·00	1·00
216	–	30 c. on 3s. (No. 172)	15·00	4·50
217	55	50 c. on 5s.	4·00	1·25
218	–	$1 and 10s. on 10d. (No. 176)	15·00	6·50
219	–	$2 on £1 (No. 134)	50·00	70·00
220	–	$6 on £3 (No. 135)	95·00	£110
221	–	$10 on £5 (No. 136)	£150	£170

75 Village Scene, Cook Islands 1d. Stamp of 1892 and Queen Victoria

1967. 75th Anniv of First Cook Island Stamps. Multicoloured.

222		1 c. (1d.) Type **75**	10	10
223		3 c. (4d.) Post Office, Avarua, Rarotonga and Queen Elizabeth II	15	10
224		8 c. (10d.) Avarua, Rarotonga, and Cook Islands 10d. stamp of 1892	30	10
225		18 c. (1s. 9d.) "Moana Roa", (inter-island ship), Douglas DC-3 aircraft, map and Captain Cook	1·40	25

The face values are expressed in decimal currency and in the sterling equivalent.

79 Hibiscus

81 Queen Elizabeth and Flowers

1967. Flowers. Multicoloured.

227A		½ c. Type **79**	10	10
228A		1 c. "Hibiscus syriacus"	10	10
229A		2 c. Frangipani	10	10
230A		2½ c. "Clitoria ternatea"	20	10
231B		3 c. "Suva Queen"	40	10
232A		4 c. Water lily (wrongly inscribed "Walter Lily")	70	1·00
233B		4 c. Water lily	2·50	10
234B		5 c. "Bauhinia bipinnata rosea"	30	10
235B		6 c. Yellow hibiscus	30	10
236B		8 c. "Allamanda cathartica"	30	10
237B		9 c. Stephanotis	30	10
238B		10 c. "Poinciana regia flamboyant"	30	10
239A		15 c. Frangipani	40	10
240B		20 c. Thunbergia	3·50	75
241A		25 c. Canna lily	80	30
242A		30 c. "Euphorbia pulcherrima poinsettia"	65	50
243A		50 c. "Gardinia taitensis"	1·00	55
244B		$1 Queen Elizabeth II	1·75	80
245B		$2 Queen Elizabeth II	3·50	1·50
246A		$4 Type **81**	2·00	4·00
247A		$6 Type **81**	2·50	5·50
247cA		$8 Type **81**	7·00	14·00
248A		$10 Type **81**	6·00	12·00

97 "Ia Orana Maria"

1967. Gauguin's Polynesian Paintings.

249	97	1 c. multicoloured	10	10
250	–	3 c. multicoloured	15	10
251	–	5 c. multicoloured	20	10
252	–	8 c. multicoloured	25	10
253	–	15 c. multicoloured	50	15
254	–	22 c. multicoloured	65	20

DESIGNS: 3 c. "Riders on the Beach"; 5 c. "Still Life with Flowers" and inset portrait of Queen Elizabeth; 8 c. "Whispered Words"; 15 c. "Maternity"; 22 c. "Why are you angry?".

98 "The Holy Family" (Rubens)

100 "Matavai Bay, Tahiti" (J. Barralet)

1967. Christmas. Renaissance Paintings.

256	98	1 c. multicoloured	10	10
257	–	3 c. multicoloured	10	10
258	–	4 c. multicoloured	10	10
259	–	8 c. multicoloured	15	10
260	–	15 c. multicoloured	30	10
261	–	25 c. multicoloured	35	10

DESIGNS: 3 c. "The Epiphany" (Durer); 4 c. "The Lucca Madonna" (J. van Eyck); 8 c. "The Adoration of the Shepherds" (J. da Bassano); 15 c. "The Nativity" (El Greco); 25 c. "The Madonna and Child" (Correggio).

1968. Hurricane Relief. Nos. 231, 233, 251, 238, 241 and 243/4 optd **HURRICANE RELIEF PLUS** and premium.

262		3 c.+1 c. multicoloured	15	10
263		4 c.+1 c. multicoloured	15	10
264		5 c.+2 c. multicoloured	20	10
265		10 c.+2 c. multicoloured	20	10
266		25 c.+5 c. multicoloured	25	10
267		50 c.+10 c. multicoloured	30	20
268		$1 +10 c. multicoloured	50	40

On No. 264 silver blocking obliterates the design area around the lettering.

1968. Bicentenary of Captain Cook's First Voyage of Discovery.

269	100	½ c. multicoloured (postage)	10	10
270	–	1 c. multicoloured	15	10
271	–	2 c. multicoloured	45	35
272	–	4 c. multicoloured	60	35
273	–	6 c. multicoloured (air)	1·00	65
274	–	10 c. multicoloured	1·00	75
275	–	15 c. multicoloured	1·25	90
276	–	25 c. multicoloured	1·50	1·25

DESIGNS—VERT: 1 c. "Island of Huaheine" (John Cleveley); 2 c. "Town of St. Peter and St. Paul, Kamchatka" (J. Webber); 4 c. "The Ice Islands" (Antarctica: W. Hodges). HORIZ: 6 c. "Resolution" and "Discovery" (J. Webber); 10 c. "The Island of Tahiti" (W. Hodges); 15 c. "Karakakooa, Hawaii" (J. Webber); 25 c. "The Landing at Middleburg" (J. Sherwin).

102 Sailing

1968. Olympic Games, Mexico. Multicoloured.

277		1 c. Type **102**	10	10
278		5 c. Gymnastics	10	10
279		15 c. High-jumping	20	10
280		20 c. High-diving	20	10
281		30 c. Cycling	40	20
282		50 c. Hurdling	40	25

103 "Madonna and Child" (Titian)

1968. Christmas. Multicoloured.

283		1 c. Type **103**	10	10
284		4 c. "The Holy Family of the Lamb" (Raphael)	15	10
285		10 c. "The Madonna of the Rosary" (Murillo)	25	10
286		20 c. "Adoration of the Magi" (Memling)	40	10
287		30 c. "Adoration of the Magi" (Ghirlandaio)	45	10

104 Campfire Cooking

1969. Diamond Jubilee of New Zealand Scout Movement and 5th National (New Zealand) Jamboree. Multicoloured.

289		½ c. Type **104**	10	10
290		1 c. Descent by rope	10	10
291		5 c. Semaphore	10	10
292		10 c. Tree-planting	15	10
293		20 c. Constructing a shelter	25	10
294		30 c. Lord Baden-Powell and island scene	40	15

105 High Jumping

1969. 3rd South Pacific Games, Port Moresby. Multicoloured.

295		½ c. Type **105**	10	30
296		½ c. Footballer	10	30
297		1 c. Basketball	50	40
298		1 c. Weightlifter	50	40
299		4 c. Tennis-player	50	50
300		4 c. Hurdler	50	50
301		10 c. Javelin-thrower	55	50
302		10 c. Runner	55	50
303		15 c. Golfer	1·75	1·50
304		15 c. Boxer	1·75	1·50

106 Flowers, Map and Captain Cook (½-size illustration)

1969. South Pacific Conf, Noumea. Mult.

306		5 c. Premier Albert Henry	50	20
307		10 c. Type **106**	1·00	75
308		25 c. Flowers, map and arms of New Zealand	1·00	95
309		30 c. Queen Elizabeth II, map and flowers	1·00	1·10

107 "Virgin and Child with Saints Jerome and Dominic" (Lippi)

1969. Christmas. Multicoloured.

310		1 c. Type **107**	10	10
311		4 c. "The Holy Family" (Fra Bartolomeo)	10	10
312		10 c. "The Adoration of the Shepherds" (A. Mengs)	15	10
313		20 c. "Madonna and Child with Saints" (Robert Campin)	25	20
314		30 c. "The Madonna of the Basket" (Correggio)	25	30

108 "The Resurrection of Christ" (Raphael)

115 Mary, Joseph, and Christ in Manger

MINIMUM PRICE

The minimum price quoted is 10p which represents a handling charge rather than a basis for valuing common stamps. For further notes about prices see introductory pages.

110 The Royal Family

1970. Easter.

316	108	4 c. multicoloured	10	10
317	–	8 c. multicoloured	10	10
318	–	20 c. multicoloured	15	10
319	–	25 c. multicoloured	20	10

DESIGNS: "The Resurrection of Christ" by Dirk Bouts (8 c.), Altdorfer (20 c.), Murillo (25 c.).

1970. "Apollo 13". Nos. 233, 236, 239/40, 242 and 245/6 optd **KIA ORANA APOLLO 13 ASTRONAUTS Te Atua to Tatou Irinakianga.**

321		4 c. multicoloured	10	10
322		8 c. multicoloured	10	10
323		15 c. multicoloured	10	10
324		20 c. multicoloured	15	15
325		30 c. multicoloured	20	20
326		$2 multicoloured	60	90
327a		$4 multicoloured	1·25	2·75

1970. Royal Visit to New Zealand. Multicoloured.

328		5 c. Type **110**	65	30
329		30 c. Captain Cook and H.M.S. "Endeavour"	2·75	1·75
330		$1 Royal Visit commemorative coin	4·00	3·00

1970. 5th Anniv of Self-Government. Nos. 328/30 optd **FIFTH ANNIVERSARY SELF-GOVERNMENT AUGUST 1970.**

332	110	5 c. multicoloured	40	15
333	–	30 c. multicoloured	1·25	35
334	–	$1 multicoloured	2·00	90

On No. 332, the opt is arranged in one line around the frame of the stamp.

1970. Surch **FOUR DOLLARS $4.00.**

335a	81	$4 on $8 multicoloured	2·50	3·00
336a		$4 on $10 multicoloured	1·50	1·75

1970. Christmas. Multicoloured.

337		1 c. Type **115**	10	10
338		4 c. Shepherds and Apparition of the Angel	10	10
339		10 c. Mary showing Child to Joseph	15	10
340		20 c. The Wise Men bearing Gifts	20	10
341		30 c. Parents wrapping Child in swaddling clothes	25	15

1971. Surch **PLUS 20c UNITED KINGDOM SPECIAL MAIL SERVICE.**

343		30 c.+20 c. (No. 242)	30	50
344		50 c.+20 c. (No. 243)	1·00	1·75

The premium of 20 c. was to prepay a private delivery service fee in Great Britain during the postal strike. The mail was sent by air to a forwarding address in the Netherlands. No. 343 was intended for ordinary airmail ½ oz. letters, and No. 344 included registration fee.

117 Wedding of Princess Elizabeth and Prince Philip

1971. Royal Visit of Duke of Edinburgh. Multicoloured.

345		1 c. Type **117**	20	50
346		4 c. Queen Elizabeth, Prince Philip, Prince Charles and Princess Anne at Windsor	60	1·10
347		10 c. Prince Philip sailing	80	1·25
348		15 c. Prince Philip in polo gear	80	1·25
349		25 c. Prince Philip in naval uniform, and Royal Yacht, "Britannia"	1·50	2·00

1971. 4th South Pacific Games, Tahiti. Nos. 238, 241 and 242 optd **Fourth South Pacific Games Papeete** and emblem or surch also.

351		10 c. multicoloured	10	10
352		10 c.+1 c. multicoloured	10	10
353		10 c.+3 c. multicoloured	10	10
354		25 c. multicoloured	15	10
355		25 c.+1 c. multicoloured	15	10
356		25 c.+3 c. multicoloured	15	10
357		30 c. multicoloured	15	10
358		30 c.+1 c. multicoloured	15	10
359		30 c.+3 c. multicoloured	15	10

The stamps additionally surch 1 c. or 3 c. helped to finance the Cook Islands' team at the games.

1971. Nos. 230, 233, 236/7 and 239 surch **10c.**

360		10 c. on 2½ c. multicoloured	15	25
361		10 c. on 4 c. multicoloured	15	25
362		10 c. on 8 c. multicoloured	15	25
363		10 c. on 9 c. multicoloured	15	25
364		10 c. on 15 c. multicoloured	15	25

121 "Virgin and Child" (Bellini)

123 St. John

1971. Christmas.

365	121	1 c. multicoloured	10	10
366	–	4 c. multicoloured	10	10
367	–	10 c. multicoloured	25	10
368	–	20 c. multicoloured	50	10
369	–	30 c. multicoloured	50	20

DESIGNS: Various paintings of the "Virgin and Child" by Bellini. Similar to Type **121**.

1972. 25th Anniv of South Pacific Commission. No. 244 optd **SOUTH PACIFIC COMMISSION FEB. 1947 – 1972.**

372	$1 multicoloured	40	75

1972. Easter. Multicoloured.

373	5 c. Type **123**	10	10
374	10 c. Christ on the Cross	10	10
375	30 c. Mary, Mother of Jesus	25	25

1972. Hurricane Relief. (a). Nos. 239, 241 and 243 optd **HURRICANE RELIEF PLUS** and premium.

379	15 c. + 5 c. multicoloured	20	20
380	25 c. + 5 c. multicoloured	20	20
382	50 c. + 10 c. multicoloured	25	25

(b). Nos. 373/5 optd **Hurricane Relief Plus** and premium.

377	5 c. + 2 c. multicoloured	10	10
378	10 c. + 2 c. multicoloured	15	15
381	30 c. + 5 c. multicoloured	20	20

126 Rocket heading for Moon 127

1972. Apollo Moon Exploration Flights. Mult.

383	5 c. Type **126**	20	10
384	5 c. Type **127**	20	10
385	10 c. Lunar module and astronaut	20	10
386	10 c. Astronaut and experiment	20	10
387	25 c. Command capsule and Earth	25	15
388	25 c. Lunar Rover	25	15
389	30 c. Sikorsky Sea King helicopter	45	15
390	30 c. Splashdown	45	15

These were issued in horizontal se-tenant pairs of each value, forming one composite design.

1972. Hurricane Relief. Nos. 383/390 surch **HURRICANE RELIEF Plus** and premium.

392	5 c. + 2 c. multicoloured	10	10
393	5 c. + 2 c. multicoloured	10	10
394	10 c. + 2 c. multicoloured	10	10
395	10 c. + 2 c. multicoloured	10	10
396	25 c. + 2 c. multicoloured	15	15
397	25 c. + 2 c. multicoloured	15	15
398	30 c. + 2 c. multicoloured	15	15
399	30 c. + 2 c. multicoloured	15	15

129 High-jumping

130 "The Rest on the Flight into Egypt" (Caravaggio)

1972. Olympic Games, Munich. Multicoloured.

401	10 c. Type **129**	20	10
402	25 c. Running	40	15
403	30 c. Boxing	40	20

1972. Christmas. Multicoloured.

406	1 c. Type **130**	10	10
407	5 c. "Madonna of the Swallow" (Guercino)	25	10
408	10 c. "Madonna of the Green Cushion" (Solario)	35	10
409	20 c. "Madonna and Child" (di Credi)	55	20
410	30 c. "Madonna and Child" (Bellini)	85	30

131 Marriage Ceremony

133 "Noli me Tangere" (Titian)

132 Taro Leaf

1972. Royal Silver Wedding. Each black and silver.

413	5 c. Type **131**	25	15
414	10 c. Leaving Westminster Abbey	35	40
415	15 c. Bride and Bridegroom (40 × 41 mm)	45	65
416	30 c. Family Group (67 × 40 mm)	55	90

1973. Silver Wedding Coinage.

417	132	1 c. gold, mauve and black	10	10
418	–	2 c. gold, blue and black	10	10
419	–	5 c. silver, green and black	10	10
420	–	10 c. silver, blue and black	20	10
421	–	20 c. silver, green and black	30	10
422	–	50 c. silver, mauve and black	50	15
423	–	$1 silver, blue and black	75	30

DESIGNS—HORIZ (37 × 24 mm): 2 c. Pineapple; 5 c. Hibiscus. (46 × 30 mm): 10 c. Oranges; 20 c. White tern; 50 c. Striped bonito. VERT: (32 × 55 mm): $1 Tangaroa.

1973. Easter. Multicoloured.

424	5 c. Type **133**	15	10
425	10 c. "The Descent from the Cross" (Rubens)	20	10
426	30 c. "The Lamentation of Christ" (Durer)	25	10

134 Queen Elizabeth II in Coronation Regalia

137 The Annunciation

136 Tipairua

1973. 20th Anniv of Queen Elizabeth's Coronation.

429	134	10 c. multicoloured	50	90

1973. 10th Anniv of Treaty Banning Nuclear Testing. Nos. 234, 236, 238 and 240/2 optd **TENTH ANNIVERSARY CESSATION OF NUCLEAR TESTING TREATY.**

431	5 c. multicoloured	10	10
432	8 c. multicoloured	10	10
433	10 c. multicoloured	10	10
434	20 c. multicoloured	15	15
435	25 c. multicoloured	20	15
436	30 c. multicoloured	20	15

1973. Maori Exploration of the Pacific, Sailing Craft. Multicoloured.

437	$\frac{1}{2}$ c. Type **136**	10	10
438	1 c. Wa'a Kaulua	10	10
439	$1\frac{1}{2}$ c. Tainui	15	10
440	5 c. War canoe	50	15
441	10 c. Pahi	70	15
442	15 c. Amatasi	1·25	65
443	25 c. Vaka	1·50	80

1973. Christmas. Scene from a 15th-century Flemish "Book of Hours". Multicoloured.

444	1 c. Type **137**	10	10
445	5 c. The Visitation	10	10
446	10 c. Annunciation to the Shepherds	10	10
447	20 c. Epiphany	15	10
448	30 c. The Slaughter of the Innocents	20	15

138 Princess Anne

140 "Jesus carrying the Cross" (Raphael)

139 Running

1973. Royal Wedding. Multicoloured.

450	25 c. Type **138**	20	10
451	30 c. Captain Mark Phillips	25	10
452	50 c. Princess Anne and Captain Phillips	30	15

1974. British Commonwealth Games, Christchurch. Multicoloured.

455	1 c. Diving (vert)	10	10
456	3 c. Boxing (vert)	10	10
457	5 c. Type **139**	10	10
458	10 c. Weightlifting	10	10
459	30 c. Cycling	20	25

1974. Easter. Multicoloured.

461	5 c. Type **140**	10	10
462	10 c. "The Holy Trinity" (El Greco)	15	10
463	30 c. "The Deposition of Christ" (Caravaggio)	25	20

141 Grey Bonnet

142 Queen Elizabeth II

1974. Sea Shells. Multicoloured.

466	$\frac{1}{2}$ c. Type **141**	30	10
467	1 c. Common Pacific vase	30	10
468	$1\frac{1}{2}$ c. True heart cockle	30	10
469	2 c. Terebellum conch	30	10
470	3 c. Bat volute	45	10
471	4 c. Gibbose conch	50	10
472	5 c. Common hairy triton	50	10
473	6 c. Serpent's head cowrie	50	90
474	8 c. Granulate frog shell	60	10
475	10 c. Fly-spotted auger	60	10
476	15 c. Episcopan mitre	70	20
477	20 c. Butterfly moon	1·00	20
478	25 c. Royal oak scallop	1·00	30
479	30 c. Soldier cone	1·00	30
480	50 c. Textile or cloth of gold cone	7·50	4·50
481	60 c. Red-mouth olive	7·50	4·50
482	$1 Type **142**	3·00	4·50
483	$2 Type **142**	2·50	2·25
484	$4 Queen Elizabeth II and sea shells	3·50	5·50
485	$6 As $4	14·00	7·00
486	$8 As $4	15·00	8·50
487	$10 As $4	18·00	9·00

Nos. 484/7 are larger, 60 × 39 mm.

143 Footballer and Australasian Map

1974. World Cup Football Championships, West Germany. Multicoloured.

488	25 c. Type **143**	20	10
489	50 c. Map and Munich Stadium	35	25
490	$1 Footballer, stadium and World Cup	55	45

144 Obverse and Reverse of Commemorative $2.50 Silver Coin

146 "Madonna of the Goldfinch" (Raphael)

145 Early Stamps of Cook Islands

1974. Bicentenary of Captain Cook's Second Voyage of Discovery.

492	144	$2.50 silver, black and violet	13·00	7·00
493	–	$7.50 silver, black and green	27·00	13·00

DESIGN: $7.50, As Type **144** but showing $7.50 coin.

1974. Centenary of U.P.U. Multicoloured.

495	10 c. Type **145**	20	15
496	25 c. Old landing strip, Rarotonga, and stamp of 1898	35	40
497	30 c. Post Office, Rarotonga, and stamp of 1920	40	40
498	50 c. U.P.U. emblem and stamps	45	65

1974. Christmas. Multicoloured.

500	1 c. Type **146**	10	10
501	5 c. "The Sacred Family" (Andrea del Sarto)	20	10
502	10 c. "The Virgin adoring the Child" (Correggio)	25	10
503	20 c. "The Holy Family" (Rembrandt)	40	20
504	30 c. "The Virgin and Child" (Rogier van der Weyden)	50	30

147 Churchill and Blenheim Palace

1974. Birth Centenary of Sir Winston Churchill. Multicoloured.

506	5 c. Type **147**	20	10
507	10 c. Churchill and Houses of Parliament	20	10
508	25 c. Churchill and Chartwell	30	20
509	30 c. Churchill and Buckingham Palace	30	25
510	50 c. Churchill and St. Paul's Cathedral	40	50

148 Vasco Nunez de Balboa and Discovery of Pacific Ocean (1513)

1975. Pacific Explorers. Multicoloured.

513	1 c. Type **148**	15	10
514	5 c. Fernando de Magellanes and map (1520)	65	20
515	10 c. Juan Sebastian del Cano and "Vitoria" (1520)	1·25	20
516	25 c. Friar Andres de Urdaneta and ship (1564–67)	2·25	75
517	30 c. Miguel Lopez de Legazpi and ship (1564–67)	2·25	80

149 "Apollo" Capsule

1975. "Apollo-Soyuz" Space Project. Multicoloured.

518	25 c. Type **149**	30	15
519	25 c. "Soyuz" capsule	30	15
520	30 c. "Soyuz" crew	35	15
521	30 c. "Apollo" crew	35	15
522	50 c. Cosmonaut within "Soyuz"	40	25
523	50 c. Astronauts within "Apollo"	40	25

These were issued in horizontal se-tenant pairs of each value, forming one composite design.

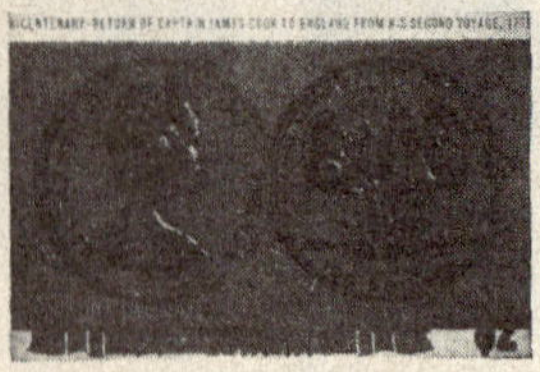

150 $100 Commemorative Gold Coin

1975. Bicentenary of Captain Cook's 2nd Voyage.

525 **150**	$2 brown, gold and violet	3·75	1·75

151 Cook Islands' Flag and Map

152 "Madonna by the Fireside" (R. Campin)

1975. 10th Anniv of Self-Government.

526	5 c. Type **151**	40	10
527	10 c. Premier Sir Albert Henry and flag (vert)	45	10
528	25 c. Rarotonga and flag	80	30

1975. Christmas. Multicoloured.

529	6 c. Type **152**	15	10
530	10 c. "Madonna in the Meadow" (Raphael)	20	10
531	15 c. "Madonna of the Oak" (att. Raphael)	25	10
532	20 c. "Adoration of the Shepherds" (J. B. Maino)	30	15
533	35 c. "The Annunciation" (Murillo)	45	20

153 "Entombment of Christ" (Raphael)

1976. Easter. Multicoloured.

536	7 c. Type **153**	30	10
537	15 c. "Pieta" (Veronese)	50	15
538	35 c. "Pieta" (El Greco)	75	25

154 Benjamin Franklin and H.M.S. "Resolution"

1976. Bicentenary of American Revolution. Multicoloured.

541	$1 Type **154**	7·50	1·50
542	$2 Captain Cook and H.M.S. "Resolution"	9·50	2·50

1976. Visit of Queen Elizabeth to U.S.A. Nos. 541/2 optd **Royal Visit July 1976.**

544 **154**	$1 multicoloured	5·00	1·50
545 –	$2 multicoloured	7·00	2·50

156 Hurdling

157 "The Visitation"

1976. Olympic Games, Montreal. Multicoloured.

547	7 c. Type **156**	20	10
548	7 c. Hurdling (value on left)	20	10
549	15 c. Hockey (value on right)	40	15
550	15 c. Hockey (value on left)	40	15
551	30 c. Fencing (value on right)	40	15
552	30 c. Fencing (value on left)	40	15
553	35 c. Football (value on right)	40	20
554	35 c. Football (value on left)	40	20

1976. Christmas. Renaissance Sculptures. Multicoloured.

556	6 c. Type **157**	10	10
557	10 c. "Adoration of the Shepherds"	10	10
558	15 c. "Adoration of the Shepherds" (different)	15	10
559	20 c. "The Epiphany"	20	20
560	35 c. "The Holy Family"	25	25

158 Obverse and Reverse of $5 Mangaia Kingfisher Coin

1976. National Wildlife and Conservation Day.

563 **158**	$1 multicoloured	2·25	1·25

159 Imperial State Crown

1977. Silver Jubilee. Multicoloured.

564	25 c. Type **159**	40	40
565	25 c. The Queen with regalia	40	40
566	50 c. Westminster Abbey	50	50
567	50 c. Coronation coach	50	50
568	$1 The Queen and Prince Philip	80	80
569	$1 Royal Visit, 1974	80	80

160 "Christ on the Cross"

161 "Virgin and Child" (Memling)

1977. Easter. 400th Birth Anniv of Rubens. Multicoloured.

571	7 c. Type **160**	35	10
572	15 c. "Christ on the Cross"	55	15
573	35 c. "The Deposition of Christ"	1·10	30

1977. Christmas. Multicoloured.

576	6 c. Type **161**	20	10
577	10 c. "Madonna and Child with Saints and Donors" (Memling)	20	10
578	15 c. "Adoration of the Kings" (Geertgen)	30	10
579	20 c. "Virgin and Child with Saints" (Crivelli)	40	15
580	35 c. "Adoration of the Magi" (16th century Flemish school)	50	20

162 Obverse and Reverse of $5 Cook Islands Swiftlet Coin

1977. National Wildlife and Conservation Day.

583 **162**	$1 multicoloured	2·00	1·25

163 Captain Cook and H.M.S. "Resolution" (from paintings by N. Dance and H. Roberts)

1978. Bicentenary of Discovery of Hawaii. Multicoloured.

584	50 c. Type **163**	1·50	60
585	$1 Earl of Sandwich and Cook landing at Owhyhee (from paintings by Thomas Gainsborough and J. Cleveley)	2·00	1·00
586	$2 Obverse and reverse of $200 coin and Cook monument, Hawaii	3·25	1·75

164 "Pieta" (Van der Weyden)

1978. Easter. Paintings from the National Gallery, London. Multicoloured.

588	15 c. Type **164**	40	15
589	35 c. "The Entombment" (Michelangelo)	50	30
590	75 c. "The Supper at Emmaus" (Caravaggio)	75	55

165 Queen Elizabeth II

169 "The Virgin and Child" (Van Der Weyden)

168 Obverse and Reverse of Pitcairn Warblers $5 Coin

1978. 25th Anniv of Coronation. Multicoloured.

593	50 c. Type **165**	25	30
594	50 c. The Lion of England	25	30
595	50 c. Imperial State Crown	25	30
596	50 c. Statue of Tangaroa (god)	25	30
597	70 c. Type **165**	25	30
598	70 c. Sceptre with Cross	25	30
599	70 c. St. Edward's Crown	25	30
600	70 c. Rarotongan staff god	25	30

1978. Nos. 466, 468, 473/4 and 478/82 surch.

602	5 c. on 1½ c. True heart cockle	40	10
603	7 c. on ½ c. Type **141**	45	15
604	10 c. on 6 c. Serpent's-head cowrie	50	15
605	10 c. on 8 c. Granulate frog shell	50	15
606	15 c. on ½ c. Type **141**	50	20
607	15 c. on 25 c. Royal oak scallop	50	20
608	15 c. on 30 c. Soldier cone	50	20
609	15 c. on 50 c. Textile or cloth of gold cone	50	20
610	15 c. on 60 c. Red-mouth olive	50	20
611	17 c. on ½ c. Type **141**	80	25
612	17 c. on 50 c. Textile or cloth of gold cone	80	25

1978. 250th Birth Anniv of Captain James Cook. Nos. 584/6 optd **1728 250th ANNIVERSARY OF COOK'S BIRTH 1978.**

613	50 c. Type **163**	2·00	75
614	$1 Earl of Sandwich and Cook landing at Owhyhee	2·25	1·00
615	$2, $200 commemorative coin and Cook monument, Hawaii	2·50	2·00

1978. National Wildlife and Conservation Day.

617 **168**	$1 multicoloured	1·60	1·00

1978. Christmas. Paintings. Multicoloured.

618	15 c. Type **169**	35	10
619	17 c. "The Virgin and Child" (Crivelli)	35	15
620	35 c. "The Virgin and Child" (Murillo)	65	30

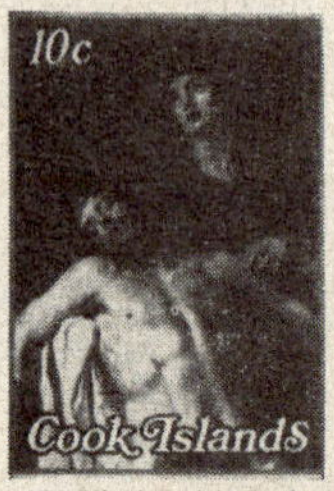

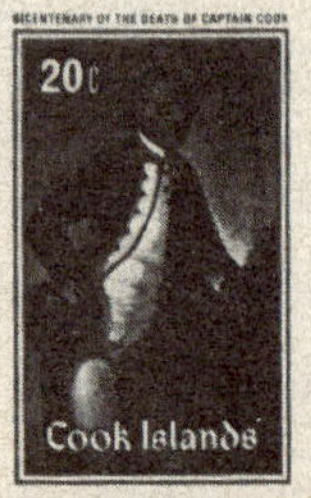

170 Virgin with Body of Christ

171 "Captain Cook" (James Weber)

1979. Easter. Details of Painting "Descent" by Gaspar de Crayar. Multicoloured.

623	10 c. Type **170**	25	10
624	12 c. St. John	30	20
625	15 c. Mary Magdalene	35	25
626	20 c. Weeping angels	45	30

1979. Death Bicent of Captain Cook. Mult.

628	20 c. Type **171**	40	20
629	30 c. H.M.S. "Resolution"	70	35
630	35 c. H.M.S. "Royal George" (ship of the line)	70	45
631	50 c. "Death of Captain Cook" (George Carter)	70	60

172 Post-Rider

174 Brother and Sister

1979. Death Centenary of Sir Rowland Hill. Mult.

633	30 c. Type **172**	25	20
634	30 c. Mail coach	25	20
635	30 c. Automobile	25	20
636	30 c. Diesel train	25	20
637	35 c. "Cap-Hornier" (full-rigged ship)	30	20
638	35 c. River steamer	30	20
639	35 c. "Deutschland" (liner)	30	20
640	35 c. "United States" (liner)	30	20
641	50 c. Balloon "Le Neptune"	40	25
642	50 c. Junkers F13 airplane	40	25
643	50 c. Airship "Graf Zeppelin"	40	25
644	50 c. Concorde	40	25

1979. Nos. 466, 468 and 481 surch.

646	6 c. on ½ c. Type **141**	20	30
647	10 c. on 1½ c. Cockle shell	25	20
648	15 c. on 60 c. Olive shell	40	40

1979. International Year of the Child. Multicoloured.

649	30 c. Type **174**	25	25
650	50 c. Boy with tree drum	40	40
651	65 c. Children dancing	50	50

175 "Apollo 11" Emblem

177 Glass Christmas Tree Ornaments

176 Obverse and reverse of $5 Rarotongan Fruit Dove Coin

1979. 10th Anniv of "Apollo 11" Moon Landing. Multicoloured.

653	30 c. Type **175**	40	50
654	50 c. "Apollo 11" crew	50	70
655	60 c. Neil Armstrong on the Moon	65	75
656	65 c. Splashdown recovery	70	85

1979. National Wildlife and Conservation Day.

658 **176**	$1 multicoloured	1·60	2·50

1979. Christmas. Multicoloured.

659	6 c. Type **177** (postage)	10	10
660	10 c. Hibiscus and star	10	10
661	12 c. Poinsettia, bells and candle	15	10
662	15 c. Poinsettia leaves and Tiki (god)	15	15
663	20 c. Type **177** (air)	20	15
664	25 c. As No. 660	25	20
665	30 c. As No. 661	30	25
666	35 c. As No. 662	35	30

1980. Christmas. As Nos. 659/66 but with charity premium.

667	6 c. + 2 c. Type **177** (postage)	10	10
668	10 c. + 2 c. Hibiscus and star	15	15
669	12 c. + 2 c. Poinsettia, bells and candle	15	20
670	15 c. + 2 c. Poinsettia leaves and Tiki (god)	15	20
671	20 c. + 4 c. Type **177** (air)	15	25
672	25 c. + 4 c. As No. 660	15	25
673	30 c. + 4 c. As No. 661	20	30
674	35 c. + 4 c. As No. 662	25	35

178 "Flagellation"

181 Queen Elizabeth the Queen Mother

179 Dove with Olive Twig

1980. Easter. Illustrations by Gustav Dore. Each gold and brown.
675 20 c. Type **178** 25 20
676 20 c. "Crown of Thorns" . . 25 20
677 30 c. "Jesus Insulted" 35 30
678 30 c. "Jesus Falls" 35 30
679 35 c. "The Crucifixion" . . . 40 30
680 35 c. "The Descent from the Cross" 40 30

1980. 75th Anniv of Rotary International. Mult.
683 30 c. Type **179** 35 35
684 35 c. Hibiscus flower 40 40
685 50 c. Ribbons 50 50

1980. "Zeapex 80" International Stamp Exhibition, Auckland. Nos. 633/44 optd **ZEAPEX STAMP EXHIBITION—AUCKLAND 1980** and New Zealand 1865 1s. Stamp.
687 30 c. Type **172** 30 25
688 30 c. Mail coach 30 25
689 30 c. Automobile 30 25
690 30 c. Diesel train 30 25
691 35 c. "Cap-Hornier" (full-rigged ship) 35 30
692 35 c. River steamer 35 30
693 35 c. "Deutschland" (liner) . . 35 30
694 35 c. "United States" (liner) . . 35 30
695 50 c. Balloon "Le Neptune" . . 50 35
696 50 c. Junkers "F13" airplane . . 50 35
697 50 c. Airship"Graf Zeppelin" . . 50 35
698 50 c. Concorde 50 35

1980. 80th Birthday of the Queen Mother.
701 **181** 50 c. multicoloured . . . 80 90

182 Satellites orbiting Moon

1980. 350th Death Anniv of Johannes Kepler (astronomer). Multicoloured.
703 12 c. Type **182** 50 35
704 12 c. Space-craft orbiting Moon 50 35
705 50 c. Space-craft orbiting Moon (different) . . . . 1·00 80
706 50 c. Astronaut and Moon vehicle . . . . 1·00 80

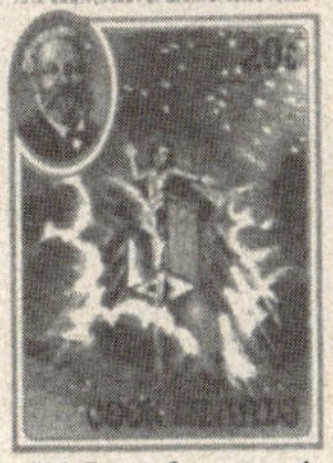
183 Scene from novel "From the Earth to the Moon"

184 "Siphonogorgia"

1980. 75th Death Anniv of Jules Verne (author).
708 **183** 20 c. multicoloured . . . 45 35
709 – 20 c. multicoloured . . . 45 35
710 – 30 c. multicoloured (mauve background) 55 45
711 – 30 c. multicoloured (blue background 55 45
DESIGNS: Showing scenes from the novel "From the Earth to the Moon".

1980. Corals (1st series). Multicoloured.
713 1 c. Type **184** 20 20
714 1 c. "Pavona praetorta" . . . 20 20
715 1 c. "Stylaster echinatus" . . 20 20
716 1 c. "Tubastraea" 20 20
717 3 c. "Millepora alcicornis" . . 25 20
718 3 c. "Junceella gemmacea" . . 25 20
719 3 c. "Fungia fungites" 25 20
720 3 c. "Heliofungia actiniformis" 25 20
721 4 c. "Distichopora violacea" . . 25 20
722 4 c. "Stylaster" 25 20
723 4 c. "Gonipora" 25 20
724 4 c. "Caulastraea echinulata" 25 20
725 5 c. "Ptilosarcus gurneyi" . . 25 20
726 5 c. "Stylophora pistillata" . . 25 20
727 5 c. "Melithaea squamata" . . 25 20
728 5 c. "Porites andrewsi" . . . 25 20
729 6 c. "Lobophyllia bemprichii" . 25 20
730 6 c. "Palauastrea ramosa" . . 25 20
731 6 c. "Bellonella indica" . . . 25 20
732 6 c. "Pectinia alcicornis" . . 25 20
733 8 c. "Sarcophyton digitatum" . 25 20
734 8 c. "Melithaea albitincta" . . 25 20
735 8 c. "Plerogyra sinuosa" . . 25 20
736 8 c. "Dendrophyllia gracilis" . 25 20
737 10 c. As Type **184** 30 20
738 10 c. As No. 714 . . . . . . 30 20
739 10 c. As No. 715 . . . . . . 30 20
740 10 c. As No. 716 . . . . . . 30 20
741 12 c. As No. 717 . . . . . . 30 20
742 12 c. As No. 718 . . . . . . 30 20
743 12 c. As No. 719 . . . . . . 30 20
744 12 c. As No. 720 . . . . . . 30 20
745 15 c. As No. 721 . . . . . . 30 20
746 15 c. As No. 722 . . . . . . 30 20
747 15 c. As No. 723 . . . . . . 30 20
748 15 c. As No. 724 . . . . . . 30 20
749 20 c. As No. 725 . . . . . . 35 30
750 20 c. As No. 726 . . . . . . 35 30
751 20 c. As No. 727 . . . . . . 35 30
752 20 c. As No. 728 . . . . . . 35 30
753 25 c. As No. 729 . . . . . . 35 30
754 25 c. As No. 730 . . . . . . 35 30
755 25 c. As No. 731 . . . . . . 35 30
756 25 c. As No. 732 . . . . . . 35 30
757 30 c. As No. 733 . . . . . . 40 30
758 30 c. As No. 734 . . . . . . 40 30
759 30 c. As No. 735 . . . . . . 40 30
760 30 c. As No. 736 . . . . . . 40 30
761 35 c. Type **184** 45 35
762 35 c. As No. 714 . . . . . . 45 35
763 35 c. As No. 715 . . . . . . 45 35
764 35 c. As No. 716 . . . . . . 45 35
765 50 c. As No. 717 . . . . . . 65 75
766 50 c. As No. 718 . . . . . . 65 75
767 50 c. As No. 719 . . . . . . 65 75
768 50 c. As No. 720 . . . . . . 65 75
769 60 c. As No. 721 . . . . . . 75 75
770 60 c. As No. 722 . . . . . . 75 75
771 60 c. As No. 723 . . . . . . 75 75
772 60 c. As No. 724 . . . . . . 75 75
773 70 c. As No. 725 . . . . . . 2·50 75
774 70 c. As No. 726 . . . . . . 2·50 75
775 70 c. As No. 727 . . . . . . 2·50 75
776 70 c. As No. 728 . . . . . . 2·50 75
777 80 c. As No. 729 . . . . . . 2·50 80
778 80 c. As No. 730 . . . . . . 2·50 80
779 80 c. As No. 731 . . . . . . 2·50 80
780 80 c. As No. 732 . . . . . . 2·50 80
781 £1 As No. 733 . . . . 3·75 1·00
782 $1 As No. 734 . . . . 3·75 1·00
783 $1 As No. 735 . . . . 3·75 1·00
784 $1 As No. 736 . . . . 3·75 1·00
785 $2 As No. 723 . . . . 12·00 3·00
786 $3 As No. 720 . . . . 12·00 3·00
787 $4 As No. 726 . . . . 4·50 10·00
788 $6 As No. 715 . . . . 6·00 13·00
789 $10 As No. 734 . . . . 27·00 32·00
Nos. 761/74 are 30×40 mm, and Nos. 785/9, which include a portrait of Queen Elizabeth II in each design, are 55×35 mm.
See also Nos. 966/94.

185 Annunciation

187 Prince Charles

186 "The Crucifixion" (from book of Saint-Amand)

1980. Christmas. Scenes from 13th-century French Prayerbooks. Multicoloured.
801 15 c. Type **185** 25 15
802 30 c. The Visitation 35 25
803 40 c. The Nativity 45 30
804 50 c. The Epiphany 60 40

1981. Easter. Illustrations from 12th-century French Prayer Books. Multicoloured.
807 15 c. Type **186** 20 20
808 25 c. "Placing in Tomb" (from book of Ingeburge) 30 30
809 40 c. "Mourning at the Sepulchre" (from book of Ingeburge) 40 40

1981. Royal Wedding. Multicoloured.
812 $1 Type **187** . . . . 50 1·10
813 $2 Prince Charles and Lady Diana Spencer . . . . . . 60 1·40

188 Footballers

1981. World Cup Football Championship, Spain (1982). Designs showing footballers. Multicoloured.
815 20 c. Type **188** 40 20
816 20 c. Figures to right of stamp 40 20
817 30 c. Figures to left 50 30
818 30 c. Figures to right 50 30
819 35 c. Figures to left 50 35
820 35 c. Figures to right 50 35
821 50 c. Figures to left 65 45
822 50 c. Figures to right 65 45
The two designs of each value were printed together, se-tenant, in horizontal pairs throughout the sheet, forming composite designs.

1981. International Year for Disabled Persons. Nos. 812/13 surch + **5 c.**
824 $1 + 5 c. Type **187** . . . . 1·00 2·00
825 $2 + 5 c. Prince Charles and Lady Diana Spencer . . . . . . 1·40 3·00

190 "Holy Virgin with Child"

1982. Christmas. Details of Paintings by Rubens. Multicoloured.
827 8 c. Type **190** 55 20
828 15 c. "Coronation of St. Catherine" 65 35
829 40 c. "Adoration of the Shepherds" 90 80
830 50 c. "Adoration of the Magi" 1·00 1·00

191 Princess of Wales (inscr "21st Birthday")

1982. 21st Birthday of Princess of Wales. Multicoloured.
833 $1.25 Type **191** . . . . . . 1·75 1·50
834 $1.25 As Type **191**, but inscr "1 July 1982" . . . . . . 1·75 1·50
835 $2.50 Princess (inscr "21st Birthday") (different) . . . . 2·50 2·25
836 $2.50 As No. 835, but inscr "1 July 1982" . . . . . . 2·50 2·25

1982. Birth of Prince William of Wales (1st issue). Nos. 812/13 optd.
838 $1 Type **187** . . . . 1·50 1·25
839 $1 Type **187** . . . . 1·50 1·25
840 $2 Prince Charles and Lady Diana Spencer . . . . . . 2·50 2·00
841 $2 Prince Charles and Lady Diana Spencer . . . . . . 2·50 2·00
OPTS: Nos. 838 and 840, **"ROYAL BIRTH 21 JUNE 1982"**. Nos. 839 and 841, **"PRINCE WILLIAM OF WALES"**.

1982. Birth of Prince William of Wales (2nd issue). As Nos. 833/6 but with changed inscriptions. Multicoloured.
843 $1.25 As Type **191**, inscribed "Royal Birth" . . . . . . 1·40 1·00
844 $1.25 As Type **191**, inscribed "21 June 1982" . . . . . . 1·40 1·00
845 $2.50 As No. 835, inscribed "Royal Birth" . . . . . . 2·00 1·50
846 $2.50 As No. 835, inscribed "21 June 1982" . . . . . . 2·00 1·50

193 "The Accordionist" (inscr "Serenade")

194 Franklin D. Roosevelt

1982. Norman Rockwell (painter) Commemoration. Multicoloured.
848 5 c. Type **193** 15 10
849 10 c. "Spring" (inscr "The Hikers") 20 15
850 20 c. "The Doctor and the Doll" 25 25
851 30 c. "Home from Camp" . . 25 30

1982. Air. American Anniversaries. Multicoloured.
852 60 c. Type **194** . . . . . . 1·50 80
853 80 c. Benjamin Franklin . . . 1·75 1·00
854 $1.40 George Washington . . 2·00 1·50
ANNIVERSARIES: 60 c. Roosevelt birth centenary; 80 c. "Articles of Peace" negotiations bicentenary; $1.40, Washington 250th birth anniv.

195 "Virgin with Garlands" (detail, Rubens) and Princess Diana with Prince William

1982. Christmas.
856 **195** 35 c. multicoloured . . . 95 60
857 – 48 c. multicoloured . . . 1·50 1·00
858 – 60 c. multicoloured . . . 1·75 1·75
859 – $1.70 multicoloured . . . 2·50 3·25
DESIGNS: 48 c. to $1.70, Different details from Ruben's painting "Virgin with Garlands".

197 Statue of Tangaroa

198 Scouts using Map and Compass

1983. Commonwealth Day. Multicoloured.
862 60 c. Type **197** 55 60
863 60 c. Rarotonga oranges . . . 55 60
864 60 c. Rarotonga Airport . . . 55 60
865 60 c. Prime Minister Sir Thomas Davis 55 60

1983. 75th Anniv of Boy Scout Movement and 125th Anniv of Lord Baden-Powell (founder). Multicoloured.
866 12 c. Type **198** 60 20
867 12 c. Hiking 60 20
868 36 c. Campfire cooking . . . 90 40
869 36 c. Erecting tent 90 40
870 48 c. Hauling on rope . . . . 1·10 55
871 48 c. Using bos'n's chair . . . 1·10 55
872 60 c. Digging hole for sapling 1·25 70
873 60 c. Planting sapling . . . . 1·25 70

1983. 15th World Scout Jamboree, Alberta, Canada. Nos. 866/73 optd **XV WORLD JAMBOREE** (Nos. 875, 877, 879, 881) or **ALBERTA, CANADA 1983** (others).
875 12 c. Type **198** 55 20
876 12 c. Hiking 55 20
877 36 c. Campfire cooking . . . 80 40
878 36 c. Erecting tent 80 40
879 48 c. Hauling on rope 95 55
880 48 c. Using bos'n's chair . . . 95 55
881 60 c. Digging hole for sapling 1·10 70
882 60 c. Planting sapling . . . . 1·10 70

1983. Various stamps surch.
884 – 18 c. on 8 c. mult (No. 733) 75 50
885 – 18 c. on 8 c. mult (No. 734) 75 50
886 – 18 c. on 8 c. mult (No. 735) 75 50
887 – 18 c. on 8 c. mult (No. 736) 75 50
888 – 36 c. on 15 c. multicoloured (No. 745) . . . . 1·25 85
889 – 36 c. on 15 c. multicoloured (No. 746) . . . . 1·25 85
890 – 36 c. on 15 c. multicoloured (No. 747) . . . . 1·25 85
891 – 36 c. on 15 c. multicoloured (No. 748) . . . . 1·25 85
892 – 36 c. on 30 c. multicoloured (No. 757) . . . . 1·25 85
893 – 36 c. on 30 c. multicoloured (No. 758) . . . . 1·25 85
894 – 36 c. on 30 c. multicoloured (No. 759) . . . . 1·25 85
895 – 36 c. on 30 c. multicoloured (No. 760) . . . . 1·25 85
896 **184** 36 c. on 35 c. multicoloured 1·25 85
897 – 36 c. on 35 c. multicoloured (No. 762) . . . . 1·25 85
898 – 36 c. on 35 c. multicoloured (No. 763) . . . . 1·25 85
899 – 36 c. on 35 c. multicoloured (No. 764) . . . . 1·25 85
900 – 48 c. on 25 c. multicoloured (No. 753) . . . . 1·50 1·25
901 – 48 c. on 25 c. multicoloured (No. 754) . . . . 1·50 1·25
902 – 48 c. on 25 c. multicoloured (No. 755) . . . . 1·50 1·25
903 – 48 c. on 25 c. multicoloured (No. 756) . . . . 1·50 1·25
904 – 72 c. on 70 c. multicoloured (No. 773) . . . . 2·50 1·75

905 – 72 c. on 70 c. multicoloured (No. 774) . . . . 2·50 1·75
906 – 72 c. on 70 c. multicoloured (No. 775) . . . . 2·50 1·75
907 – 72 c. on 70 c. multicoloured (No. 776) . . . . 2·50 1·75
908 – 96 c. on $1.40 multicoloured (No. 854) . . . . 2·00 2·00
909 – 96 c. on $2 mult (No. 813) 8·50 5·50
910 – 96 c. on $2.50 multicoloured (No. 835) . . . . 3·00 3·00
911 – 96 c. on $2.50 multicoloured (No. 836) . . . . 3·00 3·00
912 – $5.60 on $6 mult (No. 788) 23·00 18·00
913 – $5.60 on $10 multicoloured (No. 789) . . . . 23·00 18·00

202 Union Flag

1983. Cook Islands Flags and Ensigns. Multicoloured.
914 6 c. Type **202** (postage) . . . 35 25
915 6 c. Group Federal flag . . . 35 25
916 12 c. Rarotonga ensign . . . 50 30
917 12 c. Flag of New Zealand . . 50 30
918 15 c. Cook Islands' flag (1973–79) 50 30
919 15 c. Cook Islands' National flag 50 30
920 20 c. Type **202** (air) 60 40
921 20 c. Group Federal flag . . . 60 40
922 30 c. Rarotonga ensign . . . 70 45
923 30 c. Flag of New Zealand . . 70 45
924 35 c. Cook Islands' flag (1973–1979) 75 50
925 35 c. Cook Islands' National flag 75 50

203 Dish Aerial, Satellite Earth Station **204** "La Belle Jardiniere"

1983. World Communications Year.
927 – 36 c. multicoloured 50 50
928 – 48 c. multicoloured . . . 65 65
929 **203** 60 c. multicoloured . . . 85 1·00
930 – 96 c. multicoloured . . . 1·40 2·00
DESIGNS: 36, 48 and 96 c. Various satellites.

1983. Christmas. 500th Birth Anniv of Raphael. Multicoloured.
932 12 c. Type **204** 70 40
933 18 c. "Madonna and Child with five Saints" 95 60
934 36 c. "Madonna and Child with St. John" . . . . 1·60 1·60
935 48 c. "Madonna of the Fish" . 2·00 2·00
936 60 c. "Madonna of the Baldacchino" . . . . 2·50 3·50

205 Montgolfier Balloon, 1783

1984. Bicent (1983) of Manned Flight. Mult.
939 36 c. Type **205** 50 50
940 48 c. Ascent of Adorne, Strasbourg, 1784 . . . . . 60 60
941 60 c. Balloon driven by sails, 1785 . . . . 75 85
942 72 c. Ascent of man on horse, 1798 . . . . 90 1·00
943 96 c. Godard's aerial acrobatics, 1850 . . . . 1·00 1·25

206 Cuvier's Beaked Whale

1984. Save the Whale. Multicoloured.
946 10 c. Type **206** 50 50
947 18 c. Risso's dolphin 75 75
948 20 c. True's beaked whale . . 75 75
949 24 c. Long-finned pilot whale 80 80
950 30 c. Narwhal 90 90
951 36 c. White whale . . . . . 1·10 1·10
952 42 c. Common dolphin . . . 1·40 1·40
953 48 c. Commerson's dolphin . 1·60 1·60
954 60 c. Bottle-nosed dolphin . . 1·90 1·90
955 72 c. Sowerby's beaked whale 2·00 2·00
956 96 c. Common porpoise . . . 2·50 2·50
957 $2 Boutu . . . . 3·25 3·25

207 Athens, 1896 208 "Siphonogorgia"

1984. Olympic Games, Los Angeles. Multicoloured.
958 18 c. Type **207** 40 40
959 24 c. Paris, 1900 . . . . . . 45 45
960 36 c. St. Louis, 1904 . . . . 55 55
961 48 c. London, 1948 . . . . . 65 65
962 60 c. Tokyo, 1964 . . . . . 75 75
963 72 c. Berlin, 1936 . . . . . 90 90
964 96 c. Rome, 1960 . . . . . 1·00 1·00
965 $1.20 Los Angeles, 1930 . . . 1·25 1·25

1984. Corals (2nd series). New designs and Nos. 785/9 surch. Multicoloured.
966 1 c. Type **208** 30 10
967 2 c. "Millepora alcicornis" . 30 10
968 3 c. "Distichopora violacea" . 40 10
969 5 c. "Ptilosarcus gurneyi" . . 45 10
970 10 c. "Lobophyllia bemprichii" 50 10
971 12 c. "Sarcophyton digitatum" 60 15
972 14 c. "Pavona praetorta" . . 60 15
973 18 c. "Junceella gemmacea" . 70 20
974 20 c. "Stylaster" 70 20
975 24 c. "Stylophora pistillata" . 70 20
976 30 c. "Palauastrea ramosa" . 1·00 25
977 36 c. "Melithaea albitincta" . 1·25 30
978 40 c. "Stylaster echinatus" . 1·25 30
979 42 c. "Fungia fungites" . . . 1·25 35
980 48 c. "Gonipora" . . . . . . 1·25 35
981 50 c. "Melithaea squamata" . 1·75 45
982 52 c. "Bellonella indica" . . 1·75 60
983 55 c. "Plerogyra sinuosa" . . 1·75 65
984 60 c. "Tubastraea" . . . . . 1·90 70
985 70 c. "Heliofungia actiniformis" 2·00 85
986 85 c. "Caulastraea echinulata" 2·25 1·00
987 96 c. "Porites andrewsi" . . . 2·50 1·10
988 $1.10 "Pectinia alcicornis" . 2·50 1·40
989 $1.20 "Dendrophyllia gracilis" 2·50 1·50
990 $3.60 on $2 "Gonipora" (55 × 35mm) . . . . 5·50 4·00
991 $4.20 on $3 "Heliofungia actiniformis" (55 × 35 mm) 6·00 5·00
992 $5 on $4 "Stylophora pistillata" (55 × 35 mm) . . . . . 6·50 5·50
993 $7.20 on $6 "Stylaster echinatus" (55 × 35 mm) . . . . . 8·50 8·50
994 $9.60 on $10 "Melithaea albitincta" (55 × 35 mm) . . 10·00 10·00

1984. Olympic Gold Medal Winners. Nos. 963/5 optd.
995 72 c. Berlin, 1936 (optd **Equestrian Team Dressage Germany**) 60 65
996 96 c. Rome, 1960 (optd **Decathlon Daley Thompson Great Britain**) 80 85
997 $1.20 Los Angeles, 1930 (optd **Four Gold Medals Carl Lewis U.S.A.**) . . . . 1·00 1·10

211 Captain Cook's Cottage, Melbourne

1984. "Ausipex" International Stamp Exhibition, Melbourne. Multicoloured.
998 36 c. Type **211** . . . . 1·25 1·25
999 48 c. H.M.S. "Endeavour" careened for Repairs" (Sydney Parkinson) . . . 2·25 2·25
1000 60 c. "Cook's landing at Botany Bay" (E. Phillips Fox) . . 3·00 3·00
1001 $2 "Captain James Cook" (John Webber) . . . . . 3·50 3·50

1984. Birth of Prince Henry. Nos. 812 and 833/6 variously optd or surch also (No. 1007)
1003 $1.25 Optd **Commemorating - 15 Sept. 1984** (No. 833) . . . 1·50 1·10
1004 $1.25 Optd **Birth H.R.H. Prince Henry** (No. 834) . . . . 1·50 1·10
1005 $2.50 Optd **Commemorating - 15 Sept. 1984** (No. 835) . . . 2·25 2·00
1006 $2.50 Optd **Birth H.R.H. Prince Henry** (No. 836) . . . . 2·25 2·00
1007 $3 on $1 Optd **Royal Birth Prince Henry 15 Sept. 1984** (No. 812) . . . . 4·50 4·00

213 "Virgin on Throne with Child" (Giovanni Bellini) 214 Downy Woodpecker

1984. Christmas. Multicoloured.
1008 36 c. Type **213** . . . . 1·00 40
1009 48 c. "Virgin and Child" (anonymous, 15th century) . 1·10 60
1010 60 c. "Virgin and Child with Saints" (Alvise Vivarini) . . 1·40 80
1011 96 c. "Virgin and Child with Angels" (H. Memling) . . . 1·75 1·60
1012 $1.20 "Adoration of Magi" (G. Tiepolo) . . . . . . 2·00 2·00

1985. Birth Bicentenary of John J. Audubon (ornithologist). Designs showing original paintings. Multicoloured.
1015 30 c. Type **214** . . . . 2·25 1·25
1016 55 c. Black-throated blue warbler . . . . 2·50 1·75
1017 65 c. Yellow-throated warbler 2·75 2·25
1018 75 c. Chestnut-sided warbler . 3·00 2·75
1019 95 c. Dickcissel . . . . 3·25 3·00
1020 $1.15 White-crowned sparrow 3·25 3·50

215 "The Kingston Flyer" (New Zealand)

1985. Famous Trains. Multicoloured.
1022 20 c. Type **215** 50 50
1023 55 c. Class 625 locomotive (Italy) 65 85
1024 65 c. Gotthard electric locomotive (Switzerland) . 70 90
1025 75 c. Union Pacific diesel locomotive No. 6900 (U.S.A.) 90 1·10
1026 95 c. Canadian National "Super Continental" type diesel locomotive (Canada) . . . 90 1·25
1027 $1.15 TGV express train (France) . . . . 95 1·50
1028 $2.20 "The Flying Scotsman" (Great Britain) . . . . . . 1·00 2·50
1029 $3.40 "Orient Express" . . . 1·10 3·75
No. 1023 is inscribed "640" in error.

216 "Helena Fourment" (Peter Paul Rubens) 217 "Lady Elizabeth 1908" (Mabel Hankey)

1985. International Youth Year. Multicoloured.
1030 55 c. Type **216** . . . . 2·50 2·25
1031 65 c. "Vigee-Lebrun and Daughter" (E. Vigee-Lebrun) 2·75 2·75
1032 75 c. "On the Terrace" (Renoir) 3·00 3·00
1033 $1.30 "Young Mother Sewing" (M. Cassatt) . . . . . . 3·75 4·00

1985. Life and Times of Queen Elizabeth the Queen Mother. Designs showing paintings. Multicoloured.
1035 65 c. Type **217** 40 50
1036 75 c. "Duchess of York, 1923" (Savely Sorine) 45 60
1037 $1.15 "Duchess of York, 1925" (Philip de Laszlo) 55 85
1038 $2.80 "Queen Elizabeth, 1938" (Sir Gerald Kelly) . . . . 1·40 2·25

218 Albert Henry (Prime Minister, 1965–78) 219 Golf

1985. 20th Anniv of Self-Government. Mult.
1040 30 c. Type **218** 80 60
1041 50 c. Sir Thomas Davis (Prime Minister, 1978–April 1983 and from November 1983) 1·25 90
1042 65 c. Geoffrey Henry (Prime Minister, April–November 1983) . . . . 1·50 1·50

1985. South Pacific Mini Games, Rarotonga. Multicoloured.
1044 55 c. Type **219** . . . . 4·00 3·50
1045 65 c. Rugby . . . . 4·00 4·00
1046 75 c. Tennis . . . . 5·50 6·00

220 Sea Horse, Gearwheel and Leaves 221 "Madonna of the Magnificat"

1985. Pacific Conference, Rarotonga.
1048 **220** 55 c. black, gold and red 85 65
1049 – 65 c. black, gold and violet 95 80
1050 – 75 c. black, gold and green 1·25 1·10
No. 1048 shows the South Pacific Bureau for Economic Co-operation logo and is inscribed "S.P.E.C. Meeting, 30 July–1 August 1985, Rarotonga". No. 1049 also shows the S.P.E.C. logo, but is inscribed "South Pacific Forum, 4–6 August 1985, Rarotonga". No. 1050 shows the Pacific Islands Conference logo and the inscription "Pacific Islands Conference, 7–10 August 1985, Rarotonga".

1985. Christmas. Virgin and Child Paintings by Botticelli. Multicoloured.
1052 55 c. Type **221** . . . . 1·75 60
1053 65 c. "Madonna with Pomegranate" . . . . . 1·90 65
1054 75 c. "Madonna and Child with Six Angels" . . . . . . 2·25 1·00
1055 95 c. "Madonna and Child with St. John" . . . . 2·50 1·40

222 "The Eve of the Deluge" (John Martin) 223 Queen Elizabeth II

1986. Appearance of Halley's Comet. Paintings. Multicoloured.
1058 55 c. Type **222** . . . . 1·25 1·25
1059 65 c. "Lot and his Daughters" (Lucas van Leyden) . . . 1·40 1·40
1060 75 c. "Auspicious Comet" (from treatise c 1857) . . . . 1·50 1·50
1061 $1.25 "Events following Charles I" (Herman Saftleven) . . 2·25 2·25
1062 $2 "Ossian receiving Napoleonic Officers" (Anne Louis Girodet-Trioson) . . 3·00 3·00

1986. 60th Birthday of Queen Elizabeth II. Designs showing formal portraits.
1065 **223** 95 c. multicoloured . . . 1·10 1·50
1066 – $1.25 multicoloured . . . 1·40 1·75
1067 – $1.50 multicoloured . . 1·50 2·00

224 U.S.A. 1847 Franklin 5 c. Stamp and H.M.S. "Resolution" at Rarotonga

1986. "Ameripex '86" International Exhibition, Chicago. Multicoloured.
1069 $1 Type **224** . . . . 4·50 3·75
1070 $1.50 Chicago . . . . 3·50 4·25
1071 $2 1975 definitive $2, Benjamin Franklin and H.M.S. "Resolution" . . . . . . 5·50 5·50

225 Head of Statue of Liberty

226 Miss Sarah Ferguson

1986. Centenary of Statue of Liberty. Multicoloured.
1072 $1 Type **225** 75 85
1073 $1.25 Hand and torch of Statue 90 1·10
1074 $2.75 Statue of Liberty . . . 2·00 2·50

1986. Royal Wedding. Multicoloured.
1075 $1 Type **226** . . . . 1·00 1·25
1076 $2 Prince Andrew . . . . . . 1·75 2·25
1077 $3 Prince Andrew and Miss Sarah Ferguson (57 × 31 mm) 2·50 3·00

228 "Holy Family with St. John the Baptist and St. Elizabeth"

1986. Christmas. Paintings by Rubens. Multicoloured.
1080 55 c. Type **228** . . . . . . 1·25 90
1081 $1.30 "Virgin with the Garland" 2·25 2·00
1082 $2.75 "Adoration of the Magi" (detail) . . . . 4·25 4·00

1986. Visit of Pope John Paul II to South Pacific. Nos. 1080/2 surch **FIRST PAPAL VISIT TO SOUTH PACIFIC POPE JOHN PAUL II NOV 21–24 1986.**
1085 55 c. + 10 c. Type **228** . . . . 2·50 1·75
1086 $1.30 + 10 c. "Virgin with the Garland" . . . . 3·25 2·25
1087 $2.75 + 10 c. "Adoration of the Magi" (detail) . . . . . . 5·50 3·75

1987. Various stamps surch. (a) On Nos. 741/56, 761/76 and 787/8.
1090 10 c. on 15 c. "Distichopora violacea" 10 10
1091 10 c. on 15 c. "Stylaster" . . 10 10
1092 10 c. on 15 c. "Gonipora" . . 10 10
1093 10 c. on 15 c. "Caulastraea echinulata" 10 10
1094 10 c. on 25 c. "Lobophyllia bemprichii" 10 10
1095 10 c. on 25 c. "Palauastrea ramosa" 10 10
1096 10 c. on 25 c. "Bellonella indica" 10 10
1097 10 c. on 25 c. "Pectinia alcicornis" 10 10
1098 18 c. on 12 c. "Millepora alcicornis" 15 15
1099 18 c. on 12 c. "Junceella gemmacea" 15 15
1100 18 c. on 12 c. "Fungia fungites" 15 15
1101 18 c. on 12 c. "Heliofungia actiniformis" 15 15
1102 18 c. on 20 c. "Ptilosarcus gurneyi" 15 15
1103 18 c. on 20 c. "Stylophora pistillata" 15 15
1104 18 c. on 20 c. "Melithaea squamata" 15 15
1105 18 c. on 20 c. "Porites andrewsi" 15 15
1106 55 c. on 35 c. Type **184** . . . 40 45
1107 55 c. on 35 c. "Pavona praetorta" 40 45
1108 55 c. on 35 c. "Stylaster echinatus" 40 45
1109 55 c. on 35 c. "Tubastraea" . 40 45
1110 65 c. on 50 c. As No. 1098 . 45 50
1111 65 c. on 50 c. As No. 1099 . 45 50
1112 65 c. on 50 c. As No. 1100 . 45 50
1113 65 c. on 50 c. As No. 1101 . 45 50
1114 65 c. on 60 c. As No. 1090 . 45 50
1115 65 c. on 60 c. As No. 1091 . 45 50
1116 65 c. on 60 c. As No. 1092 . 45 50
1117 65 c. on 60 c. As No. 1093 . 45 50
1118 75 c. on 70 c. As No. 1102 . 55 60
1119 75 c. on 70 c. As No. 1103 . 55 60
1120 75 c. on 70 c. As No. 1104 . 55 60
1121 75 c. on 70 c. As No. 1105 . 55 60
1122 $6.40 on $4 "Stylophora pistillata" . . . . 4·50 4·75
1123 $7.20 on $6 "Stylaster echinatus" . . . . 5·00 5·25

(b) On Nos. 812/13.
1124 $9.40 on $1 Type **187** . . . . 15·00 16·00
1125 $9.40 on $2 Prince Charles and Lady Diana Spencer . . . 15·00 16·00

(c) On Nos. 835/6.
1126 $9.40 on $2.50 Princess of Wales (inscribed "21st Birthday") 15·00 16·00
1127 $9.40 on $2.50 As No. 1126, but inscribed "1 July 1982" . . 15·00 16·00

(d) On Nos. 966/8, 971/2, 975, 979/80, 982 and 987/9.
1128 5 c. on 1 c. Type **208** 10 10
1129 5 c. on 2 c. "Millepora alcicornis" 10 10
1130 5 c. on 3 c. "Distichopora violacea" 10 10
1131 5 c. on 12 c. "Sarcophyton digitatum" 10 10
1132 5 c. on 14 c. "Pavona praetorta" 10 10
1133 18 c. on 24 c. "Stylophora pistillata" 15 15
1134 55 c. on 52 c. "Bellonella indica" 40 45
1135 65 c. on 42 c. "Fungia fungites" 45 50
1136 75 c. on 48 c. "Gonipora" . 55 60
1137 95 c. on 96 c. "Porites andrewsi" 70 75
1138 95 c. on $1.10 "Pectinia alcicornis" 70 75
1139 95 c. on $1.20 "Dendrophyllia gracilis" 70 75

(e) On Nos. 998/1001.
1140 $1.30 on 36 c. Type **211** . . 1·40 1·50
1141 $1.30 on 48 c. "The "Endeavour" careened for Repairs" (Sydney Parkinson) 1·40 1·50
1142 $1.30 on 60 c. "Cook's landing at Botany Bay" (E. Phillips Fox) . . . . 1·40 1·50
1143 $1.30 on $2 "Captain James Cook" (John Webber) . . 1·40 1·50

(f) On Nos. 1065/7.
1144 **223** $2.30 on 95 c. mult . . 7·00 7·50
1145 – $2.80 on $1.25 mult . . 7·00 7·50
1146 – $2.80 on $1.50 mult . . 7·00 7·50

(g) On Nos. 1075/7.
1147 $2.80 on $1 Type **226** . . . 6·00 6·50
1148 $2.80 on $2 Prince Andrew . 6·00 6·50
1149 $2.80 on $3 Prince Andrew and Miss Sarah Ferguson (57 × 31 mm) . . . . 6·00 6·50

1987. Various stamps surch.
1150 $2.80 on $2 "Gonipora" (No. 785) . . . . 2·10 2·25
1151 $5 on $3 "Heliofungia actiniformis" (No. 786) . . 4·00 4·25
1152 $9.40 on $10 "Melithaea albitincta" (No. 789) . . . 7·50 7·75
1153 $9.40 on $1 Type **187** (No. 838) 7·50 7·75
1154 $9.40 on $1 Type **187** (No. 839) 7·50 7·75
1155 $9.40 on $2 Prince Charles and Lady Diana Spencer (No. 840) . . . . 7·50 7·75
1156 $9.40 on $2 Prince Charles and Lady Diana Spencer (No. 841) . . . . 7·50 7·75

1987. Hurricane Relief. Various stamps surch **HURRICANE RELIEF** and premium. (a) On Nos. 1035/8.
1158 65 c. + 50 c. Type **217** . . . 80 85
1159 75 c. + 50 c. "Duchess of York, 1923" (Savely Sorine) . . 85 1·00
1160 $1.15 + 50 c. "Duchess of York, 1925" (Philip de Laszlo) . 1·10 1·40
1161 $2.80 + 50 c. "Queen Elizabeth, 1938" (Sir Gerald Kelly) . 2·25 2·75

(b) On Nos. 1058/62.
1163 55 c. + 50 c. Type **222** . . . 75 80
1164 65 c. + 50 c. "Lot and his Daughters" (Lucas van Leyden) 80 85
1165 75 c. + 50 c. "Auspicious Comet" (from treatise c. 1587) 85 90
1166 $1.50 + 50 c. "Events following Charles I" (Herman Saftleven) . . . . 1·25 1·40
1167 $2 + 50 c. "Ossian receiving Napoleonic Officers" (Anne Louis Girodet-Trioson) . . 1·75 2·00

(c) On Nos. 1065/7.
1168 **223** 95 c. + 50 c. multicoloured 1·00 1·10
1169 – $1.25 + 50 c. multicoloured 1·25 1·40
1170 – $1.50 + 50 c. multicoloured 1·40 1·50

(d) On Nos. 1069/71.
1172 $1 + 50 c. Type **224** . . . . 2·00 2·00
1173 $1.50 + 50 c. Chicago . . . . 1·75 2·00
1174 $2 + 50 c. 1975 definitive $2, Benjamin Franklin and H.M.S. "Resolution" . . 2·75 2·75

(e) On Nos. 1072/4.
1175 $1 + 50 c. Type **225** . . . . 1·00 1·25
1176 $1.25 + 50 c. Hand and torch of Statue . . . . 1·25 1·50
1177 $2.75 + 50 c. Statue of Liberty 2·25 2·75

(f) On Nos. 1075/7.
1178 $1 + 50 c. Type **226** . . . . 1·00 1·25
1179 $2 + 50 c. Prince Andrew . . 1·75 2·00
1180 $3 + 50 c. Prince Andrew and Miss Sarah Ferguson (57 × 31 mm) . . . . . 2·40 2·75

(g) On Nos. 1080/2.
1181 55 c. + 50 c. Type **228** . . . 75 80
1182 $1.30 + 50 c. "Virgin with the Garland" . . . . 1·25 1·40
1183 $2.75 + 50 c. "The Adoration of the Magi" (detail) . . . . 2·25 2·40

(h) On Nos. 1122, 1134/7 and 1150/1.
1186 55 c. + 25 c. on 52 c. "Bellonella indica" 70 70
1187 65 c. + 25 c. on 42 c. "Fungia fungites" 80 80
1188 75 c. + 25 c. on 48 c. "Gonipora" 90 90
1189 95 c. + 25 c. on 96 c. "Porites andrewsi" . . . . 1·10 1·10
1190 $2.80 + 50 c. on $2 "Gonipora" 2·75 2·75
1191 $5 + 50 c. on $3 "Heliofungia actiniformis" . . . . . . 4·50 4·50
1192 $6.40 + 50 c. on $4 "Stylophora pistillata" . . . . 6·00 6·00

1987. Royal Ruby Wedding. Nos. 484 and 787 optd **ROYAL WEDDING FORTIETH ANNIVERSARY.**
1193 $4 Queen Elizabeth II and sea shells . . . . 4·50 4·50
1194 $4 Queen Elizabeth II and "Stylophora pistillata" . . 4·50 4·50

233 "The Holy Family" (Rembrandt)

1987. Christmas. Different paintings of the Holy Family by Rembrandt.
1195 **233** $1.25 multicoloured . . . 2·25 2·00
1196 – $1.50 multicoloured . . . 2·75 2·25
1197 – $1.95 multicoloured . . . 4·00 3·50

234 Olympic Commemorative $50 Coin

1988. Olympic Games, Seoul. Multicoloured.
1200 $1.50 Type **234** . . . . 2·75 2·25
1201 $1.50 Olympic torch and Seoul Olympic Park . . . . . . 2·75 2·25
1202 $1.50 Steffi Graf playing tennis and Olympic medal . . . 2·75 2·25
Nos. 1200/2 were printed together, se-tenant, forming a composite design.

1988. Olympic Tennis Medal Winners, Seoul. Nos. 1200/2 optd.
1204 $1.50 Type **234** (optd **MILOSLAV MECIR CZECHOSLOVAKIA GOLD MEDAL WINNER MEN'S TENNIS**) . . . . . 2·25 2·25
1205 $1.50 Olympic torch and Seoul Olympic Park (optd **TIM MAYOTTE UNITED STATES GABRIELA SABATINI ARGENTINA SILVER MEDAL WINNERS**) . . . . . . 2·25 2·25
1206 $1.50 Steffi Graf playing tennis and Olympic medal (optd **GOLD MEDAL WINNER STEFFI GRAF WEST GERMANY**) . . . . 2·25 2·25

236 "Virgin and Child"

1988. Christmas.
1208 **236** 70 c. multicoloured . . . 2·00 2·00
1209 – 85 c. multicoloured . . . 2·25 2·25
1210 – 95 c. multicoloured . . . 2·50 2·50
1221 – $1.25 multicoloured . . . 3·25 3·25
DESIGNS: 85 c., 95 c., $1.25, Various versions of the "Virgin and Child" by Durer.

237 "Apollo 11" leaving Earth

1989. 20th Anniv of First Manned Landing on Moon. Multicoloured.
1213 40 c. Type **237** . . . . 1·25 1·25
1214 40 c. Lunar module over Moon 1·25 1·25
1215 55 c. Aldrin stepping onto Moon . . . . 1·40 1·40
1216 55 c. Astronaut on Moon . . 1·40 1·40
1217 65 c. Working on lunar surface 1·75 1·75
1218 65 c. Conducting experiment . 1·75 1·75
1219 75 c. "Apollo 11" leaving Moon 1·75 1·75
1220 75 c. Splashdown in South Pacific . . . . 1·75 1·75

238 Rarotonga Flycatcher

1989. Endangered Birds of the Cook Islands. Multicoloured.
1222 15 c. Type **238** . . . . 1·75 1·75
1223 20 c. Pair of Rarotonga flycatchers . . . . 1·75 1·75
1224 65 c. Pair of Rarotongan fruit doves . . . . 2·75 2·75
1225 70 c. Rarotonga fruit dove . . 2·75 2·75

239 Villagers

1989. Christmas. Details from "Adoration of the Magi" by Rubens. Multicoloured.
1227 70 c. Type **239** . . . . 1·25 1·25
1228 85 c. Virgin Mary . . . . . 1·40 1·50
1229 95 c. Christ Child . . . . . 1·50 1·75
1230 $1.50 Boy with gift . . . . . 2·00 2·75

240 Reverend John Williams and L.M.S. Church

1990. Christianity in the Cook Islands. Multicoloured.
1232 70 c. Type **240** 75 80
1233 85 c. Mgr. Bernardine Castanie and Roman Catholic Church 90 1·10
1234 95 c. Elder Osborne Widstoe and Mormon Church . . . 1·00 1·40
1235 $1.60 Dr. J. E. Caldwell and Seventh Day Adventist Church . . . . 1·75 2·00

241 "Woman writing a Letter" (Terborch)

243 Queen Elizabeth the Queen Mother

242 Sprinting

1990. 150th Anniv of the Penny Black. Designs showing paintings. Multicoloured.
1237 85 c. Type **241** . . . . 1·10 1·25
1238 $1.15 "George Gisze" (Holbein the Younger) . . . . . . 1·50 1·75
1239 $1.55 "Mrs. John Douglas" (Gainsborough) . . . . . . 1·90 2·25
1240 $1.85 "Portrait of a Gentleman" (Durer) . . . . 2·25 2·50

1990. Olympic Games, Barcelona, and Winter Olympic Games, Albertville (1992) (1st issue). Multicoloured.
1242 $1.85 Type **242** . . . . 4·00 4·50
1243 $1.85 Cook Islands $50 commemorative coin . . . 4·00 4·50
1244 $1.85 Skiing . . . . 4·00 4·50
See also Nos. 1304/9.

1990. 90th Birthday of Queen Elizabeth the Queen Mother.
1246 **243** $1.85 multicoloured . . 3·75 4·25

244 "Adoration of the Magi" (Memling)

1990. Christmas. Religious Paintings. Multicoloured.

1248	70 c. Type **244**	1·10	1·10
1249	85 c. "Holy Family" (Lotto)	1·25	1·25
1250	95 c. "Madonna and Child with Saints John and Catherine" (Titian)	1·60	1·75
1251	$1.50 "Holy Family" (Titian)	2·75	3·25

246 Columbus (engraving by Theodoro de Bry)

249 Red-breasted Wrasse

248 "Adoration of the Child" (G. delle Notti)

1991. 500th Anniv (1992) of Discovery of America by Columbus (1st issue).

1254	**246** $1 multicoloured	2·00	2·25

See also No. 1302.

1991. 65th Birthday of Queen Elizabeth II. No. 789 optd **65TH BIRTHDAY**.

1255	$10 "Melithaea albitincta"	13·00	14·00

1991. Christmas. Religious Paintings. Multicoloured.

1256	70 c. Type **248**	1·50	1·50
1257	85 c. "The Birth of the Virgin" (B. Murillo)	1·75	1·75
1258	$1.15 "Adoration of the Shepherds" (Rembrandt)	2·25	2·25
1259	$1.50 "Adoration of the Shepherds" (L. le Nain)	3·25	3·75

1992. Reef Life (1st series). Multicoloured with white borders.

1261	5 c. Type **249**	40	40
1262	10 c. Blue sea star	40	40
1263	15 c. Bicoloured angelfish ("Black and gold angelfish")	55	55
1264	20 c. Spotted pebble crab	70	70
1265	25 c. Black-tipped grouper ("Black-tipped cod")	70	70
1266	30 c. Spanish dancer	70	70
1267	50 c. Regal angelfish	90	90
1268	80 c. Big-scaled soldierfish ("Squirrel fish")	1·25	1·25
1269	85 c. Red pencil sea urchin	2·50	2·50
1270	90 c. Red-spotted rainbowfish	2·50	2·50
1271	$1 Cheek-lined wrasse	2·50	2·50
1272	$2 Long-nosed butterflyfish	2·50	2·50
1273	$3 Red-spotted rainbowfish	2·25	2·50
1274	$5 Blue sea-star	3·75	4·25
1275	$7 "Pygoplites diacanthus"	7·00	8·00
1276	$10 Spotted pebble crab	7·25	8·00
1277	$15 Red pencil sea urchin	13·00	14·00

The 25, 50 c., $1 and $2 include a silhouette of the Queen's head.

For designs in a larger size, 40 × 30 mm, and with brown borders, see Nos. 1342/52.

250 Tiger

1992. Endangered Wildlife. Multicoloured.

1279	$1.15 Type **250**	1·25	1·25
1280	$1.15 Indian elephant	1·25	1·25
1281	$1.15 Brown bear	1·25	1·25
1282	$1.15 Black rhinoceros	1·25	1·25
1283	$1.15 Chimpanzee	1·25	1·25
1284	$1.15 Argali	1·25	1·25
1285	$1.15 Heaviside's dolphin	1·25	1·25
1286	$1.15 Eagle owl	1·25	1·25
1287	$1.15 Bee hummingbird	1·25	1·25
1288	$1.15 Puma	1·25	1·25
1289	$1.15 European otter	1·25	1·25
1290	$1.15 Red kangaroo	1·25	1·25
1291	$1.15 Jackass penguin	1·25	1·25
1292	$1.15 Asian lion	1·25	1·25
1293	$1.15 Peregrine falcon	1·25	1·25
1294	$1.15 Persian fallow deer	1·25	1·25
1295	$1.15 Key deer	1·25	1·25
1296	$1.15 Alpine ibex	1·25	1·25
1297	$1.15 Mandrill	1·25	1·25
1298	$1.15 Gorilla	1·25	1·25
1299	$1.15 "Vanessa atalanta" (butterfly)	1·25	1·25
1300	$1.15 Takin	1·25	1·25
1301	$1.15 Ring-tailed lemur	1·25	1·25

251 Columbus and Landing in New World

1992. 500th Anniv of Discovery of America by Columbus (2nd issue).

1302	**251** $6 multicoloured	6·50	7·50

252 Football and $50 Commemorative Coin

1992. Olympic Games, Barcelona (2nd issue). Multicoloured.

1304	$1.75 Type **252**	2·50	2·50
1305	$1.75 Olympic gold medal	2·50	2·50
1306	$1.75 Basketball and $10 coin	2·50	2·50
1307	$2.25 Running	3·50	3·50
1308	$2.25 $10 and $50 coins	3·50	3·50
1309	$2.25 Cycling	3·50	3·50

253 Festival Poster

255 "Worship of Shepherds" (Parmigianino)

1992. 6th Festival of Pacific Arts, Rarotonga. Multicoloured.

1311	80 c. Type **253**	1·00	1·10
1312	85 c. Seated Tangaroa carving	1·00	1·10
1313	$1 Seated Tangaroa carving (different)	1·10	1·25
1314	$1.75 Standing Tangaroa carving	2·00	2·50

1992. Royal Visit by Prince Edward. Nos. 1311/14 optd **ROYAL VISIT**.

1315	80 c. Type **253**	1·25	1·25
1316	85 c. Seated Tangaroa carving	1·25	1·25
1317	$1 Seated Tangaroa carving (different)	1·40	1·40
1318	$1.75 Standing Tangaroa carving	2·75	2·75

1992. Christmas. Religious Paintings by Parmigianino. Multicoloured.

1319	70 c. Type **255**	1·00	1·00
1320	85 c. "Virgin with Long Neck"	1·25	1·25
1321	$1.15 "Virgin with Rose"	1·50	1·75
1322	$1.90 "St. Margaret's Virgin"	2·75	3·75

256 Queen in Garter Robes

258 "Virgin with Child" (Filippo Lippi)

257 Coronation Ceremony

1992. 40th Anniv of Queen Elizabeth II's Accession. Multicoloured.

1324	80 c. Type **256**	1·50	1·50
1325	$1.15 Queen at Trooping the Colour	1·75	1·90
1326	$1.50 Queen in evening dress	2·50	2·75
1327	$1.95 Queen with bouquet	3·00	3·25

1993. 40th Anniv of Coronation. Mult.

1328	$1 Type **257**	1·75	1·75
1329	$2 Coronation photograph by Cecil Beaton	3·00	3·25
1330	$3 Royal family on balcony	4·25	4·50

1993. Christmas. Religious Paintings. Mult.

1331	70 c. Type **258**	80	80
1332	85 c. "Bargellini Madonna" (Lodovico Carracci)	95	95
1333	$1.15 "Virgin of the Curtain" (Rafael Sanzio)	1·40	1·60
1334	$2.50 "Holy Family" (Agnolo Bronzino)	3·25	3·75
1335	$4 "Saint Zachary Virgin" (Parmigianino) (32 × 47 mm)	4·00	5·00

259 Skiing, Flags and Ice Skating (½-size illustration)

1994. Winter Olympic Games, Lillehammer.

1336	**259** $5 multicoloured	6·00	7·00

260 Cup on Logo with German and Argentinian Players

1994. World Cup Football Championship, U.S.A.

1337	**260** $4.50 multicoloured	4·50	5·50

261 Neil Armstrong taking First Step on Moon

1994. 25th Anniv of First Manned Moon Landing. Multicoloured.

1338	$2.25 Type **261**	3·50	3·50
1339	$2.25 Astronaut on Moon and view of Earth	3·50	3·50
1340	$2.25 Astronaut and flag	3·50	3·50
1341	$2.25 Astronaut with reflection in helmet visor	3·50	3·50

1994. Reef Life (2nd series). As Nos. 1261 and 1263/71, but each 40 × 30 mm and with brown borders.

1342	5 c. Type **249**	30	30
1344	15 c. Bicoloured angelfish	40	40
1345	20 c. Spotted pebble crab	45	45
1346	25 c. Black-tipped grouper	50	50
1347	30 c. Spanish dancer	50	50
1348	50 c. Regal angelfish	60	60
1349	80 c. Big-scaled soldierfish	85	85
1350	85 c. Red pencil sea urchin	85	85
1351	90 c. Red-spotted rainbowfish	90	90
1352	$1 Cheek-lined wrasse	1·00	1·00

262 Actors in Outrigger Canoe

1994. Release of "The Return of Tommy Tricker" (film shot in Cook Islands). Scenes from film. Multicoloured.

1359	85 c. Type **262**	1·10	1·25
1360	85 c. Male and female dancers	1·10	1·25
1361	85 c. European couple on beach	1·10	1·25
1362	85 c. Aerial view of island	1·10	1·25
1363	85 c. Two female dancers	1·10	1·25
1364	85 c. Cook Islands couple on beach	1·10	1·25
1364a	90 c. Type **262**	65	70
1364b	90 c. As No. 1360	65	70
1364c	90 c. As No. 1361	65	70
1364d	90 c. As No. 1362	65	70
1364e	90 c. As No. 1363	65	70
1364f	90 c. As No. 1364	65	70

263 "The Virgin and Child" (Morales)

1994. Christmas. Religious Paintings. Multicoloured.

1365	85 c. Type **263**	1·10	1·25
1366	85 c. "Adoration of the Kings" (Gerard David)	1·10	1·25
1367	85 c. "Adoration of the Kings" (Foppa)	1·10	1·25
1368	85 c. "The Madonna and Child with St. Joseph and Infant Baptist" (Baroccio)	1·10	1·25
1369	$1 "Madonna with Iris" (Durer)	1·25	1·40
1370	$1 "Adoration of the Shepherds" (Le Nain)	1·25	1·40
1371	$1 "The Virgin and Child" (school of Leonardo)	1·25	1·40
1372	$1 "The Mystic Nativity" (Botticelli)	1·25	1·40

264 Pirates ("Treasure Island")

1994. Death Centenary of Robert Louis Stevenson (author). Multicoloured.

1373	$1.50 Type **264**	1·60	1·90
1374	$1.50 Duel ("David Balfour")	1·60	1·90
1375	$1.50 Mr. Hyde, ("Dr. Jekyll and Mr. Hyde")	1·60	1·90
1376	$1.50 Rowing boat and sailing ship ("Kidnapped")	1·60	1·90

265 U.N. and National Flags with Peace Doves

1995. 50th Anniv of United Nations.

1377	**265** $4.75 multicoloured	4·75	6·00

266 Queen Elizabeth the Queen Mother and Coat of Arms

1995. 95th Birthday of Queen Elizabeth the Queen Mother.

1378	**266** $5 multicoloured	6·00	7·00

267 German Delegation signing Unconditional Surrender at Rheims

1995. 50th Anniv of End of Second World War. Multicoloured.

1379	$3.50 Type **267**	4·75	5·50
1380	$3.50 Japanese delegation on U.S.S. "Missouri", Tokyo Bay	4·75	5·50

1995. 50th Anniv of F.A.O. As T **265**. Multicoloured.

1381	$4.50 F.A.O. and U.N. emblems	4·75	6·00

268 Green Turtle

1995. Year of the Sea Turtle. Multicoloured.

1382	85 c. Type **268**	1·60	1·60
1383	$1 Hawksbill turtle	1·75	1·75
1384	$1.75 Green turtle on beach	2·75	2·75
1385	$2.25 Young hawksbill turtles hatching	3·25	3·25

269 Emblem and Throwing the Discus

1996. Olympic Games, Atlanta. Multicoloured.

1386	85 c. Type **269**	1·10	1·10
1387	$1 Athlete with Olympic Torch	1·40	1·40
1388	$1.50 Running	1·90	1·90
1389	$1.85 Gymnastics	2·25	2·25
1390	$2.10 Ancient archery	2·50	2·50
1391	$2.50 Throwing the javelin	2·75	2·75

270 Queen Elizabeth II

1996. 70th Birthday of Queen Elizabeth II. Multicoloured.

1392	$1.90 Type **270**	2·25	2·25
1393	$2.25 Wearing tiara	2·75	2·75
1394	$2.75 In Garter robes	3·00	3·00

1997. 28th South Pacific Forum. Nos. 1364a/f optd **28th Pacific Forum** (Nos. 1396, 1399/1400) or **12–22 September 1997** (Nos. 1397/8 and 1401). Multicoloured.

1396	90 c. Type **262**	90	1·00
1397	90 c. As No. 1360	90	1·00
1398	90 c. As No. 1361	90	1·00
1399	90 c. As No. 1362	90	1·00
1400	90 c. As No. 1363	90	1·00
1401	90 c. As No. 1364	90	1·00

272 "Lampides boeticus" (female)

1997. Butterflies. Multicoloured.

1402	5 c. Type **272**	10	10
1403	10 c. "Vanessa atalanta"	10	10
1404	15 c. "Lampides boeticus" (male)	10	15
1405	20 c. "Papilio godeffroyi"	15	20
1406	25 c. "Danaus hamata"	15	20
1407	30 c. "Xois sesara"	20	25
1408	50 c. "Vagrans egista"	30	35
1409	70 c. "Parthenos sylvia"	45	50
1410	80 c. "Hyblaea sanguinea"	50	55
1411	85 c. "Melanitis leda"	55	60
1412	90 c. "Ascalapha odorata"	55	60
1413	$1 "Precis villida"	65	70
1414	$1.50 "Parthenos sylvia"	95	1·00
1415	$2 "Lampides boeticus" (female)	1·25	1·40
1416	$3 "Precis villida"	1·90	2·00
1417	$4 "Melanitis leda"	2·50	2·75
1418	$5 "Vagrans egista"	3·25	3·50
1419	$7 "Hyblaea sanguinea"	4·50	4·75
1420	$10 "Vanessa atalanta"	6·25	6·50
1421	$15 "Papilio godeffroyi"	9·00	9·50

The $1 includes an outline portrait of Queen Elizabeth II. Nos. 1414/21 are larger, 41 × 25 mm, with the Queen's portrait included on the $4 to $15.

273 Queen Elizabeth and Prince Philip

1997. Golden Wedding of Queen Elizabeth and Prince Philip.

1424	**273**	$2 multicoloured	1·75	2·00

274 Diana, Princess of Wales

1998. Diana, Princess of Wales Commemoration.

1426	**274**	$1.15 multicoloured	1·10	1·25

OFFICIAL STAMPS

1975. Nos. 228, etc., optd **O.H.M.S.** or surch also.

O 1	1 c. multicoloured		
O 2	2 c. multicoloured		
O 3	3 c. multicoloured		
O 4	4 c. multicoloured		
O 5	5 c. on 2$\frac{1}{2}$ c. multicoloured		
O 6	8 c. multicoloured		
O 7	10 c. on 6 c. multicoloured		
O 8	18 c. on 20 c. multicoloured		
O 9	25 c. on 9 c. multicoloured		
O10	30 c. on 15 c. multicoloured		
O11	50 c. multicoloured		
O12	$1 multicoloured		
O13	$2 multicoloured		
O14	$4 multicoloured		
O15	$6 multicoloured		
O1/15	Set of 15	†	15·00

These stamps were only sold to the public cancelled-to-order and not in unused condition.

1978. Nos. 466/7, 474, 478/81, 484/5, 542 and 568/9 optd **O.H.M.S.** or surch also.

O16	–	1 c. multicoloured (No. 467)	60	10
O17	**141**	2 c. on $\frac{1}{2}$ c. multicoloured	60	10
O18	–	5 c. on $\frac{1}{2}$ c. multicoloured	60	10
O19	–	10 c. on 8 c. multicoloured (No. 474)	65	10
O20	–	15 c. on 50 c. multicoloured (No. 480)	90	10
O21	–	18 c. on 60 c. multicoloured (No. 481)	90	15
O22	–	25 c. mult (No. 478)	1·00	20
O23	–	30 c. mult (No. 479)	1·00	25
O24	–	35 c. on 60 c. multicoloured (No. 481)	1·25	30
O25	–	50 c. mult (No. 480)	1·75	35
O26	–	60 c. mult (No. 481)	2·00	45
O27	–	$1 multicoloured (No. 568)	4·00	65
O28	–	$1 multicoloured (No. 569)	4·00	65
O29	–	$2 multicoloured (No. 542)	7·00	2·25
O30	–	$4 multicoloured (No. 484)	12·00	2·25
O31	–	$6 multicoloured (No. 485)	12·00	3·50

1985. Nos. 786/8, 862/5, 969/74, 976, 978, 981, 984/6 and 988/9 optd **O.H.M.S.** or surch also.

O32	5 c. "Ptilosarcus gurneyi"	50	50
O33	10 c. "Lobophyllia bemprichii"	50	50
O34	12 c. "Sarcophyton digitatum"	1·50	60
O35	14 c. "Pavona praetorta"	1·50	60
O36	18 c. "Junceella gemmacea"	1·50	60
O37	20 c. "Stylaster"	60	50
O38	30 c. "Palauastrea ramosa"	60	50
O39	40 c. "Stylaster echinatus"	60	50
O40	50 c. "Melithaea squamata"	2·25	70
O41	55 c. on 85 c. "Caulastraea echinulata"	70	50
O42	60 c. "Tubastraea"	70	60
O43	70 c. "Heliofungia actiniformis"	2·50	85
O46	75 c. on 60 c. Type **197**	2·75	1·00
O47	75 c. on 60 c. Rarotonga oranges	2·75	1·00
O48	75 c. on 60 c. Rarotonga Airport	2·75	1·00
O49	75 c. on 60 c. Prime Minister Sir Thomas Davis	2·75	1·00
O44	$1.10 "Pectinia alcicornis"	1·10	90
O45	$2 on $1.20 "Dendrophyllia gracilis"	2·00	1·75
O50	$5 on $3 "Heliofungia actiniformis"	7·00	4·75
O51	$9 on $4 "Stylophora pistillata"	8·00	8·25
O52	$14 on $6 "Stylaster echinatus"	12·50	13·00
O53	$18 on $10 "Melithaea albitincta"	17·00	17·00

1995. Nos. 1261/6 optd **O.H.M.S.**

O54	5 c. Type **249**	10	10
O55	10 c. Blue sea star	10	10
O56	15 c. Bicoloured angelfish	10	15
O57	20 c. Spotted pebble crab	15	20
O58	25 c. Black-tipped grouper	15	20
O59	30 c. Spanish dancer	20	25
O60	50 c. Regal angelfish	30	35
O61	80 c. Big-scaled soldierfish	50	55
O62	85 c. Red pencil sea urchin	55	60
O63	90 c. Red-spotted rainbowfish	55	60
O64	$1 Cheek-lined wrasse	65	70
O65	$2 Long-nosed butterflyfish	1·25	1·40
O66	$3 Red-spotted rainbowfish	1·90	2·00
O67	$5 Blue sea star	3·25	3·50
O68	$7 "Pygoplites diacanthus"	4·50	4·75
O69	$10 Spotted pebble crab	6·25	6·50

CYPRUS

An island in the East Mediterranean. A British colony which became a republic within the British Commonwealth in 1960.

1880. 12 pence = 1 shilling.
1881. 40 paras = 1 piastre;
180 piastres = 1 pound.
1955. 1000 mils = 1 pound.
1983. 100 cents = 1 pound.

1880. Stamps of Great Britain (Queen Victoria) optd **CYPRUS**.

1	**7**	$\frac{1}{2}$d. red	£100	£100
2	**5**	1d. red	9·00	28·00
3	**41**	2$\frac{1}{2}$d. mauve	2·00	6·50
4	–	4d. green (No. 153)	£120	£200
5	–	6d. grey (No. 161)	£500	£650
6	–	1s. green (No. 150)	£650	£450

1881. Stamps of Great Britain (Queen Victoria) surch with new values.

9	**5**	$\frac{1}{2}$d. on 1d. red	45·00	65·00
10		30 paras on 1d. red	£100	80·00

7

13

1881.

31	**7**	$\frac{1}{2}$ pi. green	3·25	50
40		$\frac{1}{2}$ pi. green and red	4·00	70
32		30 pa. mauve	3·50	3·50
41		30 pa. mauve and green	2·00	75
33		1 pi. red	8·50	1·00
42		1 pi. red and blue	4·00	80
34		2 pi. blue	11·00	1·00
43		2 pi. blue and purple	5·00	80
35a		4 pi. olive	16·00	22·00
44		4 pi. olive and purple	12·00	3·75
21		6 pi. grey	38·00	16·00
45		6 pi. brown and green	9·00	10·00
46		9 pi. brown and red	15·00	12·00
22		12 pi. brown	£160	32·00
47		12 pi. brown and black	14·00	50·00
48		18 pi. grey and brown	42·00	45·00
49		45 pi. purple and blue	90·00	£120

1882. Surch.

25	**7**	$\frac{1}{2}$ pi. on $\frac{1}{2}$ pi. green	£120	6·50
24		30 pa. on 1 pi. red	£1400	£100

1903. As T **7** but portrait of King Edward VII.

60	5 pa. brown and black	60	30
61	10 pa. orange and green	2·00	30
50	$\frac{1}{2}$ pi. green and red	3·25	60
51	30 pa. violet and green	4·50	2·00
64	1 pi. red and blue	3·25	70
65	2 pi. blue and purple	4·50	1·00
66	4 pi. brown and purple	9·00	6·00
67	6 pi. brown and green	9·50	11·00
68	9 pi. brown and red	23·00	7·50
69	12 pi. brown and black	21·00	30·00
70	18 pi. black and brown	27·00	9·50
71	45 pi. purple and blue	70·00	£130

1912. As T **7** but portrait of King George V.

74b	10 pa. orange and green	2·25	60
86	10 pa. grey and yellow	10·00	6·50
75	$\frac{1}{2}$ pi. green and red	1·75	20
76	30 pa. violet and green	2·00	50
88	30 pa. green	6·00	40
77	1 pi. red and blue	3·75	1·25
90	1 pi. violet and red	3·00	3·25
91	1$\frac{1}{2}$ pi. yellow and black	3·25	3·75
78	2 pi. blue and purple	6·50	1·25
93	2 pi. red and blue	9·00	22·00
94	2$\frac{3}{4}$ pi. blue and purple	7·00	9·00
79	4 pi. olive and purple	3·75	3·75
80	6 pi. brown and green	3·00	7·50
81	9 pi. brown and red	21·00	22·00
82	12 pi. brown and black	9·00	24·00
83	18 pi. black and brown	22·00	24·00
84	45 pi. purple and blue	65·00	£110
100	10s. green and red on yellow	£350	£650
101	£1 purple and black on red	£1000	£1400

1924.

103	**13**	$\frac{1}{4}$ pi. grey and brown	80	15
104		$\frac{1}{2}$ pi. black	2·00	5·50
118		$\frac{1}{2}$ pi. green	1·75	85
105		$\frac{3}{4}$ pi. green	1·75	90
119		$\frac{3}{4}$ pi. black	1·75	10
106		1 pi. purple and brown	1·50	50
107		1$\frac{1}{2}$ pi. orange and black	1·50	4·75
120		1$\frac{1}{2}$ pi. red	2·25	30
108		2 pi. red and green	1·75	8·00
121		2 pi. yellow and black	4·25	2·00
122		2$\frac{1}{2}$ pi. blue	1·75	30
109		2$\frac{3}{4}$ pi. blue and purple	2·75	2·25
110		4 pi. olive and purple	2·50	2·00
111		4$\frac{1}{2}$ pi. black and orange on green	3·00	3·00
112		6 pi. brown and green	3·00	4·50
113		9 pi. brown and purple	4·50	3·50
114		12 pi. brown and black	7·00	48·00
115		18 pi. black and orange	17·00	4·50
116		45 pi. purple and blue	28·00	35·00
117		90 pi. green and red on yellow	70·00	£150
102		£1 purple and black on red	£300	£550
117a		£5 black on yellow	£2750	£5500

14 Silver coin of Amathus, 6th-century BC

1928. 50th Anniv of British Rule. Dated "1878 1928".

123	**14**	$\frac{3}{4}$ pi. violet	2·50	80
124	–	1 pi. black and blue	2·75	1·00
125	–	1$\frac{1}{2}$ pi. red	4·00	2·00
126	–	2$\frac{1}{2}$ pi. blue	3·00	2·00
127	–	4 pi. brown	4·00	6·00
128	–	6 pi. blue	5·00	18·00
129	–	9 pi. purple	6·00	10·00
130	–	18 pi. black and brown	16·00	17·00
131	–	45 pi. violet and blue	32·00	45·00
132	–	£1 blue and brown	£200	£300

DESIGNS—VERT: 1 pi. Philosopher Zeno; 2$\frac{1}{2}$ pi. Discovery of body of St. Barnabas; 4 pi. Cloister, Abbey of Bella Paise; 9 pi. Tekke of Umm Haram; 18 pi. Statue of Richard I, Westminster; 45 pi. St. Nicholas Cathedral, Famagusta, (now Lala Mustafa Pasha Mosque); £1 King George V. HORIZ: 1$\frac{1}{2}$ pi. Map of Cyprus; 6 pi. Badge of Cyprus.

24 Ruins of Vouni Palace

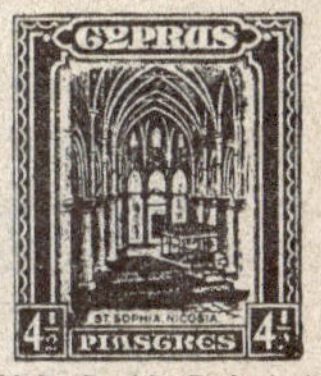

30 St. Sophia Cathedral, Nicosia (now Selimiye Mosque)

1934.

133	**24**	$\frac{1}{4}$ pi. blue and brown	75	50
134	–	$\frac{1}{2}$ pi. green	80	90
135	–	$\frac{3}{4}$ pi. black and violet	90	10
136	–	1 pi. black and brown	80	80
137	–	1$\frac{1}{2}$ pi. red	90	55
138	–	2$\frac{1}{2}$ pi. blue	1·25	1·50
139	**30**	4$\frac{1}{2}$ pi. black and red	3·00	3·25
140	–	6 pi. black and blue	7·00	12·00
141	–	9 pi. brown and violet	4·50	4·00
142	–	18 pi. black and green	40·00	27·00
143	–	45 pi. green and black	60·00	45·00

DESIGNS—HORIZ: $\frac{1}{2}$ pi. Small Marble Forum, Salamis; $\frac{3}{4}$ pi. Church of St. Barnabas and St. Hilarion, Peristerona; 1 pi. Roman theatre, Soli; 1$\frac{1}{2}$ pi. Kyrenia Harbour; 2$\frac{1}{2}$ pi. Kolossi Castle; 45 pi. Forest scene, Troodos. VERT: 6 pi. Bayraktar Mosque, Nicosia; 9 pi. Queen's Window, St. Hilarion Castle; 18 pi. Buyuk Khan, Nicosia.

The $\frac{1}{2}$ pi. to 2$\frac{1}{2}$ pi. values have a medallion portrait of King George V.

1935. Silver Jubilee. As T **13** of Antigua.

144	$\frac{3}{4}$ pi. blue and grey	1·75	40
145	1$\frac{1}{2}$ pi. blue and red	3·50	2·50
146	2$\frac{1}{2}$ pi. brown and blue	3·75	1·50
147	9 pi. grey and purple	13·00	11·00

1937. Coronation. As T **2** of Aden.

148	$\frac{3}{4}$ pi. grey	60	20
149	1$\frac{1}{2}$ pi. red	90	80
150	2$\frac{1}{2}$ pi. blue	2·00	1·25

36 Map of Cyprus

37 Othello's Tower, Famagusta

38 King George VI

1938.

151	–	$\frac{1}{4}$ pi. blue and brown	20	20
152	–	$\frac{1}{2}$ pi. green	30	10
152a	–	$\frac{1}{2}$ pi. violet	1·75	20
153	–	$\frac{3}{4}$ pi. black and violet	14·00	40
154	–	1 pi. orange	40	10
155	–	1$\frac{1}{2}$ pi. red	5·00	1·50
155a	–	1$\frac{1}{2}$ pi. violet	30	30
155ab	–	1$\frac{1}{2}$ pi. green	2·25	40
155b	–	2 pi. black and red	40	10
156	–	2$\frac{1}{2}$ pi. blue	17·00	2·50
156a	–	3 pi. blue	80	15
156b	–	4 pi. blue	3·00	30
157	**36**	4$\frac{1}{2}$ pi. grey	40	10
158	–	6 pi. black and blue	65	1·00
159	**37**	9 pi. black and purple	1·75	20
160	–	18 pi. black and olive	5·00	85
161	–	45 pi. green and black	14·00	2·50

162 38 90 pi. mauve and black . . 20·00 4·50
163 – £1 red and blue . . . . . 45·00 21·00
DESIGNS: 2 pi. Peristerona Church; 3 pi., 4 pi. Kolossi Castle. All other values except 4½ pi., 9 pi., 90 pi. and £1 have designs as 1934 issue but portrait of King George VI.

1946. Victory. As T **9** of Aden.
164 1½ pi. violet 15 10
165 3 pi. blue 15 15

1948. Silver Wedding. As T **10/11** of Aden.
166 1½ pi. violet 50 20
167 £1 blue . . . . 42·00 48·00

1949. U.P.U. As T **20/23** of Antigua.
168 1½ pi. violet 90 70
169 2 pi. red . . . . 2·00 1·50
170 3 pi. blue . . . . 1·25 1·00
171 9 pi. purple . . . . 1·50 1·10

1953. Coronation. As T **13** of Aden.
172 1½ pi. black and green 65 10

39 Carobs

42 Mavrovouni Copper Pyrites Mine

49 St. Hilarion Castle

53 Arms of Byzantium, Lusignan, Ottoman Empire and Venice

1955.
173 **39** 2 m. brown 10 40
174 – 3 m. violet 10 15
175 – 5 m. orange 50 10
176 **42** 10 m. brown and green . . 75 10
177 – 15 m. olive and blue . . . 2·50 45
178 – 20 m. brown and blue . . . 80 15
179 – 25 m. turquoise . . . . . 1·50 60
180 – 30 m. black and lake . . . 1·00 10
181 – 35 m. brown and turquoise 55 40
182 – 40 m. green and brown . . 1·00 60
183 **49** 50 m. blue and brown . . . 85 30
184 – 100 m. mauve and green . . 11·00 60
185 – 250 m. blue and brown . . 9·00 6·50
186 – 500 m. slate and purple . . 24·00 11·00
187 **53** £1 lake and slate . . . . . 24·00 28·00
DESIGNS—As Type **39**: 3 m. Grapes; 5 m. Oranges. As Type **42**: 15 m. Troodos Forest; 20 m. Beach of Aphrodite; 25 m. 5th-century B.C. coin of Paphos; 30 m. Kyrenia; 35 m. Harvest in Mesaoria; 40 m. Famagusta harbour. As Type **49**: 100 m. Hala Sultan Tekke; 250 m. Kanakaria Church. As Type **53**: 500 m. Coins of Salamis, Paphos, Citium and Idalium.

ΚΥΠΡΙΑΚΗ ΔΗΜΟΚΡΑΤΙΑ
KIBRIS CUMHURIYETI
(54)

55 Map of Cyprus

1960. Nos. 173/87 optd as T **54** ("CYPRUS REPUBLIC" in Greek and Turkish).
188 **39** 2 m. brown 20 40
189 – 3 m. violet 20 15
190 – 5 m. orange . . . . 1·00 10
191 **42** 10 m. brown and green . . 70 10
192 – 15 m. olive and blue . . . 75 10
193 – 20 m. brown and blue . . . 40 60
194 – 25 m. turquoise . . . . . 1·25 55
195 – 30 m. black and lake . . . 1·75 10
196 – 35 m. brown and turquoise 1·75 20
197 – 40 m. green and brown . . 2·00 1·25
198 **49** 50 m. blue and brown . . . 2·00 40
199 – 100 m. mauve and green . . 9·00 40
200 – 250 m. blue and brown . . 25·00 2·00
201 – 500 m. slate and purple . . 40·00 15·00
202 **53** £1 lake and slate . . . . . 60·00 48·00

1960. Constitution of Republic.
203 **55** 10 m. sepia and green . . . 30 10
204 30 m. blue and brown . . . 65 10
205 100 m. purple and slate . . 2·00 1·75

INDEX
Countries can be quickly located by referring to the index at the end of this volume.

56 Doves

1962. Europa.
206 **56** 10 m. purple and mauve . . 10 10
207 40 m. blue and cobalt . . 20 15
208 100 m. emerald and green 20 20

57 Campaign Emblem

1962. Malaria Eradication.
209 **57** 10 m. black and green . . 20 15
210 30 m. black and brown . . 40 15

63 St. Barnabas's Church

1962.
211 – 3 m. brown and orange . . 10 30
212 – 5 m. purple and green . . 10 10
213 – 10 m. black and green . . 15 10
214 – 15 m. black and purple . . 20 15
215 **63** 25 m. brown and chestnut 30 20
216 – 30 m. blue and light blue 20 10
217 – 35 m. green and blue . . . 35 10
218 – 40 m. black and blue . . . 1·25 1·50
219 – 50 m. bronze and bistre . . 50 10
220 – 100 m. brown and bistre . 3·50 30
221 – 250 m. black and brown . 8·00 2·25
222 – 500 m. brown and green . 15·00 10·00
223 – £1 bronze and grey . . . 16·00 26·00
DESIGNS—VERT: 3 m. Iron Age jug; 5 m. Grapes; 10 m. Bronze head of Apollo; 15 m. Selimiye Mosque, Nicosia; 35 m. Head of Aphrodite; 100 m. Hala Sultan Tekke; 500 m. Mouflon. HORIZ: 30 m. Temple of Apollo Hylates; 40 m. Skiing, Troodos; 50 m. Salamis Gymnasium; 250 m. Bella Paise Abbey; £1 St. Hilarion Castle.

72 Europa "Tree"

1963. Europa.
224 **72** 10 m. blue and black . . . 75 20
225 40 m. red and black . . . 3·00 2·00
226 150 m. green and black . . 12·00 6·00

73 Harvester

75 Wolf Cub in Camp

1963. Freedom from Hunger.
227 **73** 25 c. ochre, sepia and blue 30 25
228 – 75 m. grey, black and lake 1·75 1·00
DESIGN: 75 m. Demeter, Goddess of Corn.

1963. 50th Anniv of Cyprus Scout Movement and 3rd Commonwealth Scout Conference, Platres. Multicoloured.
229 3 m. Type **75** 10 20
230 20 m. Sea Scout 45 10
231 150 m. Scout with Mouflon . 1·50 2·25

79 Children's Centre, Kyrenia

1963. Centenary of Red Cross. Multicoloured.
232 10 m. Nurse tending child (vert) 50 15
233 100 m. Type **79** . . . . . . 2·50 3·50

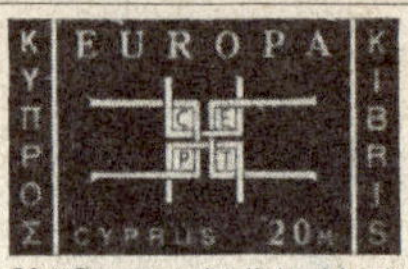

80 "Co-operation" (emblem)

1963. Europa.
234 **80** 20 m. buff, blue and violet . 1·25 40
235 30 m. grey, yellow and blue 1·75 40
236 150 m. buff, blue and brown 8·00 9·00

1964. U.N. Security Council's Cyprus Resolution, March, 1964. Nos. 213 etc optd with U.N. emblem and **1964**.
237 10 m. black and green 20 10
238 30 m. blue and light blue . . . 20 10
239 40 m. black and blue 20 20
240 50 m. bronze and bistre 20 10
241 100 m. brown and bistre . . . 25 50

82 Soli Theatre

1964. 400th Birth Anniv of Shakespeare. Multicoloured.
242 15 m. Type **82** 40 15
243 35 m. Curium Theatre 40 15
244 50 m. Salamis Theatre 40 15
245 100 m. Othello Tower, and scene from "Othello" . . . . . . 1·00 2·00

86 Running

89 Europa "Flower"

1964. Olympic Games, Tokyo.
246 **86** 10 m. brown, black and yellow 15 10
247 – 25 m. brown, black and slate 35 10
248 – 75 m. brown, black and chest 50 65
DESIGNS—HORIZ: 25 m. Boxing; 75 m. Chariot-eers.

1964. Europa.
249 **89** 20 m. brown and ochre . . 60 10
250 30 m. ultramarine and blue 75 10
251 150 m. olive and green . . 5·25 8·00

90 Dionysus and Acme

1964. Cyprus Wines. Multicoloured.
252 10 m. Type **90** 25 10
253 40 m. Silenus (satyr) 55 85
254 50 m. Commandaria wine . . 60 10
255 100 m. Wine factory . . . . . 2·00 1·75
Nos. 253/4 are vert.

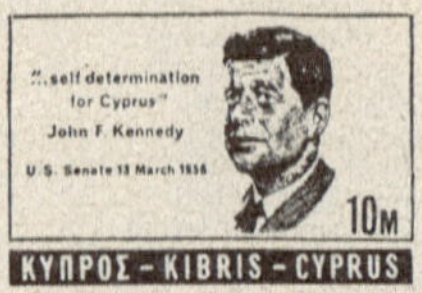

94 President Kennedy

1965. President Kennedy Commemoration.
256 **94** 10 m. blue 10 10
257 40 m. green 25 25
258 100 m. red 30 25

95 "Old Age"

98 I.T.U. Emblem and Symbols

1965. Introduction of Social Insurance Law.
259 **95** 30 m. drab and green . . . 20 10
260 – 45 m. green, blue and ultramarine 30 10
261 – 75 m. brown and flesh . . 1·50 2·25
DESIGNS—(As Type **95**): 45 m. "Accident". LARGER (23 × 48 mm): 75 m. "Maternity".

1965. Centenary of I.T.U.
262 **98** 15 m. black, brown and yellow 75 20
263 60 m. black, green and light green . . . . 4·75 2·50
264 75 m. black, indigo and blue 5·50 4·00

99 I.C.Y. Emblem

1965. International Co-operation Year.
265 **99** 50 m. brown and green . . 75 10
266 100 m. purple and green . 1·25 70

100 Europa "Sprig"

1965. Europa.
267 **100** 5 m. black, brown and orange 20 10
268 45 m. black, brown and green . . . . 1·25 1·50
269 150 m. black, brown and grey . . . . 3·00 3·75

1966. U.N. General Assembly's Cyprus Resolution. Nos. 211, 213, 216 and 221 optd **U.N. Resolution on Cyprus 18 Dec. 1965**.
270 3 m. brown and orange . . . 10 25
271 10 m. black and green 10 10
272 30 m. blue and light blue . . 10 15
273 250 m. black and brown . . . 55 1·75

102 Discovery of St. Barnabas's Body

1966. 1900th Death Anniv of St. Barnabas.
274 **102** 15 m. multicoloured . . . 10 10
275 – 25 m. drab, black and blue 20 10
276 – 100 m. multicoloured . . 65 1·75
DESIGNS—HORIZ: 25 m. St. Barnabas's Chapel. VERT: 100 m. St. Barnabas (icon).

1966. No. 211 surch **5M**.
278 – 5 m. on 3 m. brown and orange 10 10

107 General K. S. Thimayya and U. N. Emblem

1966. General Thimayya Commemoration.
279 **107** 50 m. black and brown . 30 10

108 Europa "Ship"

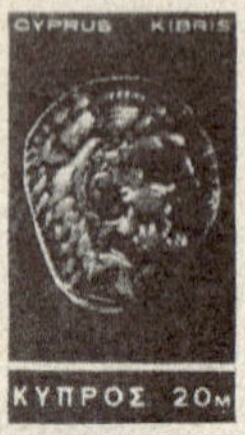

113 Silver Coin of Evagoras I

109 Stavrovouni Monastery

1966. Europa.
280 **108** 20 m. green and blue . . . 25 10
281 30 m. purple and blue . . 25 10
282 150 m. bistre and blue . . 1·75 3·00

1966. Multicoloured.
283 3 m. Type **109** 40 20
284 5 m. Church of St. James, Trikomo 10 10
285 10 m. Zeno of Citium (marble bust) 15 15
286 15 m. Minoan wine ship of 700 B.C. (painting) 15 10
287 20 m. Type **113** . . . . 1·25 90
288 25 m. Sleeping Eros (marble statue) 30 10
289 30 m. St Nicholas Cathedral, Famagusta 50 20
290 35 m. Gold sceptre from Curium 50 30
291 40 m. Silver dish from 7th century 70 30
292 50 m. Silver coin of Alexander the Great 90 10
293 100 m. Vase, 7th century B.C. 3·75 15
294 250 m. Bronze ingot-stand . . 1·50 40
295 500 m. "The Rape of Ganymede" (mosaic) . . . 2·25 70
296 £1 Aphrodite (marble statue) . 2·50 6·00
DESIGNS—VERT (As Type **109**): 5 m. and 10 m. HORIZ (As Type **113**): 15 m., 25 m. and 50 m. VERT (As Type **113**): 30 m., 35 m., 40 m. and 100 m. Nos. 294/6 are as Type **113** but larger, 28 × 40 mm.

123 Power Station, Limassol **124** Cogwheels

1967. First Development Programme. Multicoloured.
297 10 m. Type **123** 10 10
298 15 m. Arghaka-Maghounda Dam 15 10
299 35 m. Troodos Highway . . . 20 10
300 50 m. Hilton Hotel, Nicosia . 20 10
301 100 m. Famagusta Harbour . 20 90
Nos. 298/301 are vert.

1967. Europa.
302 **124** 20 m. olive, green and light green 25 10
303 30 m. violet, lilac and mauve 25 10
304 150 m. sepia, brn & chestnut 1·00 2·00

125 Throwing the Javelin

1967. Athletic Games, Nicosia. Multicoloured.
305 15 m. Type **125** 20 10
306 35 m. Running 20 35
307 100 m. High-jumping 30 85

127 Ancient Monuments

1967. International Tourist Year. Multicoloured.
309 10 m. Type **127** 10 10
310 40 m. Famagusta Beach . . . 15 70
311 50 m. Hawker Siddeley Comet-4 at Nicosia Airport 15 10
312 100 m. Skier and youth hostel 20 75

128 Saint Andrew Mosaic **129** "The Crucifixion" (icon)

1967. Centenary of St Andrew's Monastery.
313 **128** 25 m. multicoloured . . . 10 10

1967. Cyprus Art Exhibition, Paris.
314 **129** 50 m. multicoloured . . . 10 10

130 The Three Magi **131** Human Rights Emblem over Stars

1967. 20th Anniv of U.N.E.S.C.O.
315 **130** 75 m. multicoloured . . . 20 20

1968. Human Rights Year. Multicoloured.
316 50 m. Type **131** 10 10
317 90 m. Human Rights and U.N. emblems 30 70

134 Europa "Key"

1968. Europa.
319 **134** 20 m. multicoloured . . . 20 10
320 30 m. multicoloured . . . 20 10
321 150 m. multicoloured . . 60 2·00

135 U.N. Children's Fund Symbol and Boy drinking Milk

1968. 21st Anniv of U.N.I.C.E.F.
322 **135** 35 m. brown, red and black 10 10

136 Aesculapius **137** Throwing the Discus

1968. 20th Anniv of W.H.O.
323 **136** 50 m. black, green and olive 10 10

1968. Olympic Games, Mexico. Multicoloured.
324 10 m. Type **137** 10 10
325 25 m. Sprint finish 10 10
326 100 m. Olympic Stadium (horiz) 20 95

138 I.L.O. Emblem **141** Europa Emblem

139 Mercator's Map of Cyprus, 1554

1969. 50th Anniv of I.L.O.
327 **138** 50 m. brown and blue . . 15 10
328 90 m. brown, black and grey 15 40

1969. 1st International Congress of Cypriot Studies.
329 **139** 35 m. multicoloured . . . 20 30
330 – 50 m. multicoloured . . . 20 10
DESIGN: 50 m. Blaeu's map of Cyprus, 1635.

1969. Europa.
331 **141** 20 m. multicoloured . . . 20 10
332 30 m. multicoloured . . . 20 10
333 150 m. multicoloured . . 80 2·00

142 Common Roller

1969. Birds of Cyprus. Multicoloured.
334 5 m. Type **142** 40 15
335 15 m. Audouin's gull 60 15
336 20 m. Cyprus warbler 60 15
337 30 m. Jay 60 15
338 40 m. Hoopoe 65 30
339 90 m. Eleonora's falcon . . . 1·50 5·00
Nos. 337/339 are vert.

143 "The Nativity" (12th-century wall painting)

1969. Christmas. Multicoloured.
340 20 m. Type **143** 15 10
341 45 m. "The Nativity" (14th century wall painting) . . . 15 20

146 Mahatma Gandhi

1970. Birth Centenary of Mahatma Gandhi.
343 **146** 25 m. blue, drab and black 15 10
344 75 m. brown, drab and black 20 65

147 "Flaming Sun"

1970. Europa.
345 **147** 20 m. brown, yell & orge . 20 10
346 30 m. blue, yellow & orge . 20 10
347 150 m. purple, yell & orge 80 2·25

148 Gladioli **149** I.E.Y. Emblem

1970. Nature Conservation Year. Multicoloured.
348 10 m. Type **148** 10 10
349 50 m. Poppies 15 10
350 90m. Giant fennel . . . . . 50 1·40

1970. Anniversaries and Events.
351 **149** 5 m. black and brown . . . 10 10
352 – 15 m. multicoloured . . . 10 10
353 – 75 m. multicoloured . . . 15 60
DESIGNS AND EVENTS: 5 m. International Education Year. HORIZ: 15 m. Mosaic (50th General Assembly of International Vine and Wine Office); 75 m. Globe, dove and U.N. emblem (25th anniv of United Nations).

152 Virgin and Child **153** Cotton Napkin

1970. Christmas. Wall-painting from Church of Panayia Podhythou, Galata. Multicoloured.
354 25 m. Archangel (facing right) 15 20
355 25 m. Type **152** 15 20
356 25 m. Archangel (facing left) . 15 20
357 75 m. Virgin and Child between Archangels (42 × 30 mm) . . 15 30

1971. Multicoloured.
358 3 m. Type **153** 30 55
359 5 m. Saint George and Dragon (19th-century bas-relief) . . 10 10
360 10 m. Woman in festival costume 15 30
361 15 m. Archaic Bichrome Kylix (cup) (horiz) 20 10
362 20 m. A pair of donors (Saint Mamas Church) 35 50
363 25 m. "The Creation" (6th-century mosaic) 30 10
364 30 m. Athena and horse-drawn chariot (4th-century B.C. terracotta) (horiz) 30 10
365 40 m. Shepherd playing pipe (14th-century fresco) . . . 1·00 90
366 50 m. Hellenistic head (3rd-century B.C.) 80 10
367 75 m. "Angel" (mosaic detail), Kanakaria Church . . . . 1·75 1·00
368 90 m. Mycenaean silver bowl (horiz) . . . . 2·00 1·50
369 250 m. Moufflon (detail of 3rd-century mosaic) (horiz) . . 1·50 30
370 500 m. Ladies and sacred tree (detail 6th-century amphora) (horiz) 80 40
371 £1 Horned god from Enkomi (12th-century bronze statue) 1·50 60
SIZES: 24 × 37 mm or 37 × 24 mm 10 m. to 90 m, 41 × 28 mm or 28 × 41 mm 250 m. to £1.

154 Europa Chain

1971. Europa.
372 **154** 20 m. blue, ultram & blk . 20 10
373 30 m. grn, myrtle & blk . 20 10
374 150 m. yellow, grn & blk . 90 2·25

155 Archbishop Kyprianos

1971. 150th Anniv of Greek War of Independence. Multicoloured.
375 15 m. Type **155** 10 10
376 30 m. "Taking the Oath" (horiz) 10 10
377 100 m. Bishop Germanos, flag and freedom-fighters . . . 20 50

156 Kyrenia Castle

1971. Tourism. Multicoloured.
378 15 m. Type **156** 10 10
379 25 m. Gourd on sunny beach (vert) 10 10
380 60 m. Mountain scenery (vert) 20 60
381 100 m. Church of Saint Evlalios, Lambousa 20 65

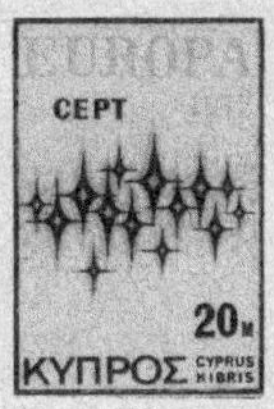

157 Madonna and Child in Stable **159** "Communications"

158 Heart

1971. Christmas. Multicoloured.
382 10 m. Type **157** 10 10
383 50 m. The Three Wise Men . 15 35
384 100 m. The Shepherds 20 35

1972. World Heart Month.
385 **158** 15 m. multicoloured . . . 10 10
386 50 m. multicoloured . . . 20 45

1972. Europa.
387 **159** 20 m. orge, sepia & brn . 20 15
388 30 m. orge, ultram & bl . 20 15
389 150 m. orge, myrtle & grn 1·60 3·25

160 Archery

1972. Olympic Games, Munich. Multicoloured.
390 10 m. Type **160** 10 10
391 40 m. Wrestling 15 15
392 100 m. Football . . . . 35 1·10

161 Stater of Marion **162** Bathing the Child Jesus

1972. Ancient Coins of Cyprus (1st series).
393 **161** 20 m. blue, black and silver 20 10
394 – 30 m. blue, black and silver 20 10
395 – 40 m. brown, blk & silver 20 20
396 – 100 m. pink, black and silver 60 1·00
COINS: 30 m. Stater of Paphos; 40 m. Stater of Lapithos; 100 m. Stater of Idalion.
See also Nos. 486/9.

1972. Christmas. Detail of mural in Holy Cross Church, Agiasmati. Multicoloured.
397 10 m. Type **162** 10 10
398 20 m. The Magi 10 10
399 100 m. The Nativity 15 30

163 Mount Olympus, Troodos

1973. 29th International Ski Federation Congress. Multicoloured.
401 20 m. Type **163** 10 10
402 100 m. Congress emblem . . . 25 35

164 Europa "Posthorn"

1973. Europa.
403 **164** 20 m. multicoloured . . . 15 10
404 30 m. multicoloured . . . 15 10
405 150 m. multicoloured . . 1·10 2·75

165 Archbishop's Palace, Nicosia

1973. Traditional Architecture. Multicoloured.
406 20 m. Type **165** 10 10
407 30 m. House of Hajigeorgajis Cornessios, Nicosia (vert) . 10 10
408 50 m. House at Gourri, 1850 (vert) 15 10
409 100 m. House at Rizokarpaso, 1772 . . . . 40 75

1973. No. 361 surch **20M**.
410 20 m. on 15 m. multicoloured 15 15

167 Scout Emblem **168** Archangel Gabriel

1973. Anniversaries and Events.
411 **167** 10 m. green and brown . 20 10
412 – 25 m. blue and lilac . . . 20 10
413 – 35 m. olive, stone and green 20 25
414 – 50 m. blue and indigo . . 20 10
415 – 100 m. brown and sepia . 50 80
DESIGNS AND EVENTS—VERT: 10 m. (60th anniv of Cyprus Boy Scouts); 50 m. Airline emblem (25th anniv of Cyprus Airways); 100 m. Interpol emblem (50th anniv of Interpol). HORIZ: 25 m. Outlines of Cyprus and the E.E.C. (Association of Cyprus with "Common Market"); 35 m. F.A.O. emblem (10th anniv of F.A.O.).

1973. Christmas. Murals from Araka Church. Multicoloured.
416 10 m. Type **168** 10 10
417 20 m. Madonna and Child . 10 10
418 100 m. Araka Church (horiz) 40 75

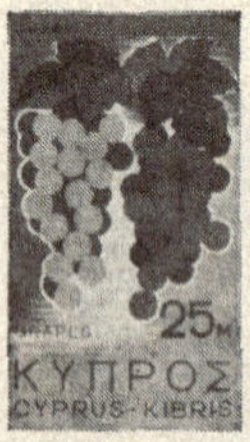

169 Grapes **170** "The Rape of Europa" (Silver Stater of Marion)

1974. Products of Cyprus. Multicoloured.
419 25 m. Type **169** 10 15
420 50 m. Grapefruit 20 50
421 50 m. Oranges 20 50
422 50 m. Lemons 20 50

1974. Europa.
423 **170** 10 m. multicoloured . . . 15 10
424 40 m. multicoloured . . . 35 30
425 150 m. multicoloured . . 1·10 2·75

171 Title Page of A. Kyprianos' "History of Cyprus" (1788) **174** "Refugees"

1974. 2nd International Congress of Cypriot Studies. Multicoloured.
426 10 m. Type **171** 10 10
427 25 m. Solon (philososopher) in mosaic (horiz) 15 10
428 100 m. "Saint Neophytos" (wall painting) 60 75

1974. Obligatory Tax. Refugee Fund. No. 359 surch **REFUGEE FUND** in English, Greek and Turkish and **10M**.
430 10 m. on 5 m. multicoloured . 10 10

1974. U.N. Security Council Resolution 353. Nos. 360, 365, 366 and 369 optd **SECURITY COUNCIL RESOLUTION 353 20 JULY 1974**.
431 10 m. multicoloured 20 10
432 40 m. multicoloured 25 50
433 50 m. multicoloured 25 10
434 250 m. multicoloured . . . . 60 2·50

1974. Obligatory Tax. Refugee Fund.
435 **174** 10 m. black and grey . . 10 10

175 "Virgin and Child between Two Angels", Stavros Church

1974. Christmas. Church Wall-paintings. Mult.
436 10 m. Type **175** 10 10
437 50 m. "Adoration of the Magi", Ayios Neophytos Monastery (vert) 20 10
438 100 m. "Flight into Egypt", Ayios Neophytos Monastery 25 45

176 Larnaca–Nicosia Mail-coach, 1878

1975. Anniversaries and Events.
439 **176** 20 m. multicoloured . . . 25 10
440 – 30 m. blue and orange . . 25 60
441 **176** 50 m. multicoloured . . . 25 10
442 – 100 m. multicoloured . . . 40 1·40
DESIGNS AND EVENTS—HORIZ: 20 m., 50 m. Centenary of Universal Postal Union. VERT: 30 m. "Disabled Persons" (8th European Meeting of International Society for the Rehabilitation of Disabled Persons); 100 m. Council flag (25th anniv of Council of Europe).

177 "The Distaff" (M. Kashalos) **178** Red Cross Flag over Map

1975. Europa. Multicoloured.
443 20 m. Type **177** 25 40
444 30 m. "Nature Morte" (C. Savva) 25 50
445 150 m. "Virgin and Child of Liopetri" (G. P. Georghiou) 40 80

1975. Anniversaries and Events. Multicoloured.
446 25 m. Type **178** 25 10
447 30 m. Nurse and lamp (horiz) 25 10
448 75 m. Woman's steatite idol (horiz) 35 90
EVENTS: 25 m. 25th anniv of Red Cross; 30 m. International Nurses' Day; 75 m. International Women's Year.

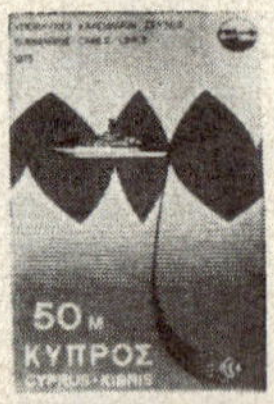

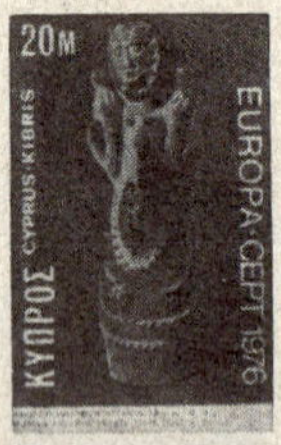

179 Submarine Cable Links **181** Human-figured Vessel, 19th-Century

1976. Telecommunications Achievements.
449 **179** 50 m. multicoloured . . . 40 10
450 – 100 m. yellow, vio & lilac . 50 90
DESIGN—HORIZ: 100 m. International subscriber dialling.

1976. Surch **10M**.
451 **153** 10 m. on 3 m. multicoloured 20 50

1976. Europa. Ceramics. Multicoloured.
452 20 m. Type **181** 20 10
453 60 m. Composite vessel, 2100–2000 B.C. 50 80
454 100 m. Byzantine goblet . . . 90 1·75

182 Self-help Housing

1976. Economic Reactivation. Multicoloured.
455 10 m. Type **182** 10 10
456 25 m. Handicrafts 20 20
457 30 m. Reafforestation 20 20
458 60 m. Air communications . . 35 55

183 Terracotta Statue of Youth **184** Olympic Symbol

1976. Cypriot Treasures.
459 **183** 5 m. multicoloured . . . 10 60
460 – 10 m. multicoloured . . . 15 40
461 – 20 m. red, yellow and black 30 40
462 – 25 m. multicoloured . . . 30 10
463 – 30 m. multicoloured . . . 30 10
464 – 40 m. green, brown & blk 45 45
465 – 50 m. lt brown, brn & blk 45 10
466 – 60 m. multicoloured . . . 45 20
467 – 100 m. multicoloured . . 50 40
468 – 250 m. blue, grey and black 80 1·50
469 – 500 m. black, brn & grn . 80 2·00
470 – £1 multicoloured . . . . 1·25 2·25
DESIGNS—VERT: 10 m. Limestone head (23 × 34 mm); 20 m. Gold necklace from Lambousa (24 × 37 mm); 25 m. Terracotta warrior (24 × 37 mm); 30 m. Statue of a priest of Aphrodite (24 × 37 mm); 250 m. Silver dish from Lambousa (28 × 41 mm); 500 m. Bronze stand (28 × 41 mm); £1 Statue of Artemis (28 × 41 mm). HORIZ: 40 m. Bronze tablet (37 × 24 mm); 50 m. Mycenaean crater (37 × 24 mm); 60 m. Limestone sarcophagus (37 × 24 mm); 100 m. Gold bracelet from Lambousa (As Type **183**).

1976. Olympic Games, Montreal.
471 **184** 20 m. red, black and yellow 10 10
472 – 60 m. multicoloured (horiz) 20 30
473 – 100 m. multicoloured (horiz) 30 35
DESIGNS: 60 m. and 100 m. Olympic symbols (different).

185 "George Washington" (G. Stuart) **186** Children in Library

1976. Bicentenary of American Revolution.
474 **185** 100 m. multicoloured . . 40 30

1976. Anniversaries and Events.
475 **186** 40 m. multicoloured . . . 20 15
476 – 50 m. brown and black . . 20 10
477 – 80 m. multicoloured . . . 45 60
DESIGNS AND EVENTS: 40 m. Type **186** (Promotion of Children's books); 50 m. Low-cost housing (HABITAT Conference, Vancouver); 80 m. Eye protected by hands (World Health Day).

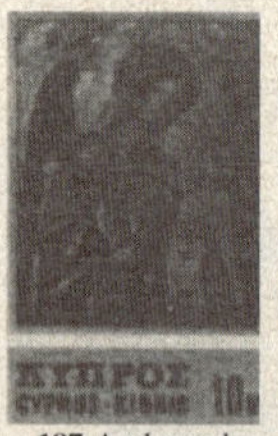

187 Archangel Michael **188** "Cyprus 74" (wood engraving by A. Tassos)

1976. Christmas. Multicoloured.
478 10 m. Type **187** 15 10
479 15 m. Archangel Gabriel . . . 15 10
480 150 m. The Nativity 60 80
Designs show icons from Ayios Neophytis Monastery.

1977. Refugee Fund.
481 **188** 10 m. black 20 10
See also Nos. 634 and 807 (after No. 728).

189 "View of Prodhromos" (A. Diamantis)

1977. Europa. Paintings. Multicoloured.
482 20 m. Type **189** 15 10
483 60 m. "Springtime at Monagroulli" (T. Kanthos) 30 55
484 120 m. "Old Port, Limassol" (V. Ioannides) . . . . . . 60 1·50

190 500 m. Stamp of 1960 **192** Archbishop Makarios in Ceremonial Robes

191 Bronze Coin of Emperor Trajan

1977. Silver Jubilee.
485 **190** 120 m. multicoloured . . 30 30

1977. Ancient Coins of Cyprus (2nd series).
486 **191** 10 m. black, gold and blue 15 10
487 – 40 m. black, silver and blue 30 30
488 – 60 m. blk, silver & orge . 35 35
489 – 100 m. black, gold and green 50 95
DESIGNS: 40 m. Silver tetradrachm of Demetrios Poliorcetes; 60 m. Silver tetradrachm of Ptolemy VIII; 100 m. Gold octadrachm of Arsinoe II.

1977. Death of Archbishop Makarios. Multicoloured.
490 20 m. Type **192** 15 10
491 60 m. Archbishop in doorway 20 10
492 250 m. Head and shoulders portrait . . . . 50 1·10

193 Embroidery, Pottery and Weaving

1977. Anniversaries and Events. Multicoloured.
493 20 m. Type **193** 10 10
494 40 m. Map of Mediterranean . 15 20
495 60 m. Gold medals 20 20
496 80 m. Sputnik 20 85
DESIGNS COMMEMORATE: 20 m. Revitalisation of handicrafts; 40 m. "Man and the Biosphere" Programme in the Mediterranean region; 60 m. Gold medals won by Cypriot students in the Orleans Gymnasiade; 80 m. 60th anniv of Russian Revolution.

194 "Nativity"

1977. Christmas. Children's Paintings Multicoloured.
497 10 m. Type **194** 10 10
498 40 m. "The Three Kings" . . 10 10
499 150 m. "Flight into Egypt" . . 25 80

195 Demetrios Libertis

1978. Cypriot Poets.
500 **195** 40 m. brown and bistre . 10 10
501 – 150 m. grey, black and red 30 80
DESIGN: 150 m. Vasilis Michaelides.

196 Chrysorrhogiatissa Monastery Courtyard

197 Archbishop of Cyprus, 1950–1977

1978. Europa. Architecture. Multicoloured.
502 25 m. Type **196** 15 10
503 75 m. Kolossi Castle 25 35
504 125 m. Municipal Library, Paphos . . . . 45 1·50

1978. Archbishop Makarios Commem. Mult.
505 15 m. Type **197** 15 20
506 25 m. Exiled in Seychelles, 9 March 1956–28 March 1957 15 20
507 50 m. President of the Republic 1960–1977 . . . . 20 25
508 75 m. "Soldier of Christ" . . 20 30
509 100 m. "Fighter for Freedom" 25 35

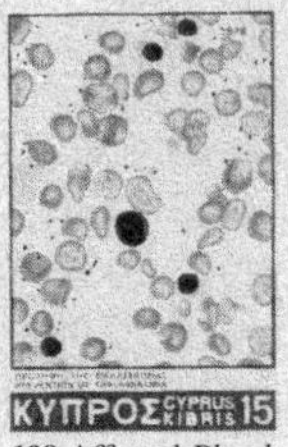

198 Affected Blood Corpuscles (Prevention of Thalassaemia)

199 Icon Stand

1978. Anniversaries and Events.
511 **198** 15 m. multicoloured . . . 10 10
512 – 35 m. multicoloured . . . 15 10
513 – 75 m. black and grey . . 20 30
514 – 125 m. multicoloured . . 35 80
DESIGNS—VERT: 35 m. Aristotle (sculpture) (2300th death anniv). HORIZ: 75 m. "Heads" (Human Rights); 125 m. Wright brothers and Wright Flyer I (75th anniv of Powered Flight).

1978. Christmas.
515 **199** 15 m. multicoloured . . . 10 10
516 – 35 m. multicoloured . . . 15 10
517 – 150 m. multicoloured . . 40 60
DESIGNS: 35 m., 150 m. Different icon stands.

200 Aphrodite (statue from Soli)

1979. Goddess Aphrodite (1st issue). Multicoloured.
518 75 m. Type **200** 25 10
519 125 m. Aphrodite on shell (detail from Botticelli's "Birth of Venus") 35 25
See also Nos. 584/5.

201 Van, Larnaca–Nicosia Mail-coach and Envelope

1979. Europa. Communications. Multicoloured.
520 25 m. Type **201** 15 10
521 75 m. Radar, satellite and early telephone 30 20
522 125 m. Aircraft, ship and envelopes 65 80

202 Peacock Wrasse

1979. Flora and Fauna. Multicoloured.
523 25 m. Type **202** 15 10
524 50 m. Black partridge (vert) . 45 40
525 75 m. Cedar (vert) 45 30
526 125 m. Mule . . . . 50 1·25

203 I.B.E. and U.N.E.S.C.O. Emblems

204 "Jesus" (from Church of the Virgin Mary of Arakas, Lagoudhera)

1979. Anniversaries and Events.
527 **203** 15 m. multicoloured . . . 10 10
528 – 25 m. multicoloured . . . 10 10
529 – 50 m. black, brown and ochre 20 15
530 – 75 m. multicoloured . . . 25 10
531 – 100 m. multicoloured . . 30 20
532 – 125 m. multicoloured . . 30 75
DESIGNS AND COMMEMORATIONS—VERT: 15 m. Type **203** (50th anniv of International Bureau of Education); 125 m. Rotary International emblem and "75" (75th anniv). HORIZ: 25 m. Graphic design of dove and stamp album (20th anniv of Cyprus Philatelic Society); 50 m. Lord Kitchener and map of Cyprus (Cyprus Survey Centenary); 75 m. Child's face (International Year of the Child); 100 m. Graphic design of footballers (25th anniv of U.E.F.A. European Football Association).

1979. Christmas. Icons. Multicoloured.
533 15 m. Type **204** 10 10
534 35 m. "Nativity" (Church of St Nicholas, Famagusta District) (29 × 41 mm) 10 10
535 150 m. "Holy Mary" (Church of the Virgin Mary of Arakas) . 25 30

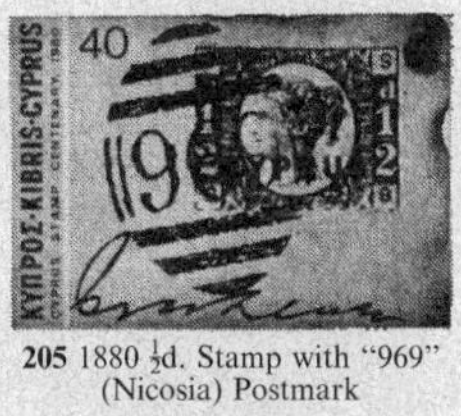

205 1880 $\frac{1}{2}$d. Stamp with "969" (Nicosia) Postmark

1980. Centenary of Cyprus Stamps. Multicoloured.
536 40 m. Type **205** 10 10
537 125 m. 1880 $2\frac{1}{2}$d. stamp with "974" (Kyrenia) postmark . 15 15
538 175 m. 1880 1s. stamp with "942" (Larnaca) postmark 15 20

206 St Barnabas (patron saint of Cyprus)

208 Gold Necklace, Arsos (7th-century B.C.)

207 Sailing

1980. Europa. Personalities. Multicoloured.
540 40 m. Type **206** 15 10
541 125 m. Zeno of Citium (founder of Stoic philosophy) 30 20

1980. Olympic Games, Moscow. Multicoloured.
542 40 m. Type **207** 10 10
543 125 m. Swimming 20 20
544 200 m. Gymnastics 25 25

1980. Archaeological Treasures.
545 **208** 10 m. multicoloured . . . 30 45
546 – 15 m. multicoloured . . . 30 45
547 – 25 m. multicoloured . . . 30 10
548 – 40 m. multicoloured . . . 40 30
549 50 m. multicoloured . . . 40 10
550 – 75 m. multicoloured . . . 80 70
551 – 100 m. multicoloured . . . 85 15
552 – 125 m. multicoloured . . . 85 15
553 – 150 m. multicoloured . . . 1·00 15
554 – 175 m. multicoloured . . . 1·00 55
555 – 200 m. multicoloured . . . 1·00 30
556 – 500 m. multicoloured . . . 1·00 1·00
557 – £1 multicoloured . . . . . 1·25 1·25
558 – £2 multicoloured . . . . . 2·50 2·00
DESIGNS—HORIZ: 15 m. Bronze cow, Vouni Palace (5th-cent B.C.); 40 m. Gold finger-ring, Enkomi (13th-cent B.C.); 500 m. Stone bowl, Khirokitia (6th-millennium B.C.). VERT: 25 m. Amphora, Salamis (6th-cent B.C.); 50 m. Bronze cauldron, Salamis (8th-cent B.C.); 75 m. Funerary stele, Marion (5th-cent B.C.). 100 m. Jug (15–14th-cent B.C.); 125 m. Warrior (terracotta) (6th–5th-cent B.C.); 150 m. Lions attacking bull (bronze relief), Vouni Palace (5th-cent B.C.); 175 m. Faience rhyton, Kition (13th-cent B.C.); 200 m. Bronze statue of Ingot God, Enkomi (12th-cent B.C.); £1 Ivory plaque, Salamis (7th-cent B.C.); £2 "Leda and the Swan" (mosaic), Kouklia (3rd-cent A.D.).

209 Cyprus Flag

1980. 20th Anniv of Republic of Cyprus. Multicoloured.
559 40 m. Type **209** 10 10
560 125 m. Signing Treaty of Establishment (41 × 29 mm) . 20 15
561 175 m. Archbishop Makarios . 35 25

210 Head and Peace Dove

1980. International Day of Solidarity with Palestinian People.
562 **210** 40 m. black and grey . . 20 20
563 – 125 m. black and grey . . 35 35
DESIGN: 125 m. Head and dove with olive branch.

211 Pulpit, Tripiotis Church, Nicosia

212 Folk Dancing

1980. Christmas. Multicoloured.
564 25 m. Type **211** 10 10
565 100 m. Holy Doors, Panayia Church Paralimni 15 15
565 125 m. Pulpit, Ayios Lazaros Church, Larnaca 15 15

1981. Europa. Folklore, showing folk-dancing from paintings by T. Photiades.
567 **212** 40 m. multicoloured . . . 30 10
568 – 175 m. multicoloured . . 60 50

213 Self-portrait

214 "Ophrys kotschyi"

1981. 500th Anniv of Leonardo da Vinci's Visit. Multicoloured.
569 50 m. Type **213** 40 10
570 125 m. "The Last Supper" (50 × 25 mm) 70 40
571 175 m. Cyprus lace and Milan Cathedral 95 60

1981. Cypriot Wild Orchids. Multicoloured.
572 25 m. Type **214** 50 60
573 50 m. "Orchis punctulata" . . 60 70
574 75 m. "Ophrys argolica elegans" 70 80
575 150 m. "Epipactis veratrifolia" 75 90

215 Heinrich von Stephan

1981. Anniversaries and Events.
576 **215** 25 m. dp green, grn & bl . 15 10
577 – 40 m. multicoloured . . . 15 10
578 – 125 m. black, red and green 30 25
579 – 150 m. multicoloured . . 35 30
580 – 200 m. multicoloured . . 40 35
DESIGNS AND COMMEMORATIONS: 25 m. Type **137** (150th birth anniv of Heinrich von Stephan (founder of U.P.U.); 40 m. Stylised man holding dish of food (World Food Day); 125 m. Stylised hands (International Year for Disabled People); 150 m. Stylised building and flower (European Campaign for Urban Renaissance); 200 m. Prince Charles, Lady Diana Spencer and St. Paul's Cathedral (Royal Wedding).

216 "The Lady of the Angels" (from Church of the Transfiguration of Christ, Palekhori)

217 "Louomene" (Aphrodite bathing) (statue, 250 B.C.)

1981. Christmas. Murals from Nicosia District Churches. Multicoloured.

581	25 m. Type **216**	20	10
582	100 m. "Christ Pantokrator" (Church of Madonna of Arakas, Lagoudera) (vert)	60	20
583	125 m. "Baptism of Christ" (Church of Our Lady of Assinou, Nikitari)	70	30

1982. Aphrodite (Greek goddess of love and beauty) Commemoration. (2nd issue). Multicoloured.

584	125 m. Type **217**	80	45
585	175 m. "Anadyomene" (Aphordite emerging from the waters) (Titian)	95	65

218 Naval Battle with Greek Fire, 985 A.D.

1982. Europa. Historic Events. Multicoloured.

586	40 m. Type **218**	60	10
587	175 m. Conversion of Roman Proconsul Sergius Paulus to Christianity, Paphos, 45 A.D.	1·00	2·50

219 "XP" (monogram of Christ) (mosaic)

1982. World Cultural Heritage. Multicoloured.

588	50 m. Type **219**	25	10
589	125 m. Head of priest-king of Paphos (sculpture) (24×37 mm)	50	25
590	225 m. Theseus (Greek god) (mosaic)	75	95

1982. No. 550 surch **100**.

591	100 m. on 75 m. Funerary stele, Marion (5th-century B.C.)	50	50

221 Cyprus and Stylised "75"

1982. 75th Anniv of Boy Scout Movement. Multicoloured.

592	100 m. Type **221**	40	20
593	125 m. Lord Baden-Powell	45	30
594	175 m. Camp-site	55	55

222 Holy Communion, The Bread

1982. Christmas.

595	**222** 25 m. multicoloured	10	10
596	– 100 m. gold and black	30	15
597	– 250 m. multicoloured	70	1·00

DESIGN—VERT: 100 m. Holy Chalice. HORIZ: 250 m. Holy Communion, The Wine.

223 Cyprus Forest Industries' Sawmill

1983. Commonwealth Day. Multicoloured.

598	50 m. Type **223**	10	10
599	125 m. "Ikarios and the Discovery of Wine" (3rd-century mosaic)	20	25
600	150 m. Folk-dancers, Commonwealth Film and Television Festival, 1980	25	35
601	175 m. Royal Exhibition Building, Melbourne (Commonwealth Heads of Government Meeting, 1981)	25	40

224 Cyprosyllabic Inscription (6th-century B.C.)

1983. Europa. Multicoloured.

602	50 m. Type **224**	40	10
603	200 m. Copper ore, ingot (Enkomi 1400–1250 B.C.) and bronze jug (2nd century A.D.)	1·10	2·40

225 "Pararge aegeria"

1983. Butterflies. Multicoloured.

604	60 m. Type **225**	25	20
605	130 m. "Aricia agestis"	45	25
606	250 m. "Glaucopsyche melanops"	85	2·00

1983. Nos. 545/56 surch.

607	1 c. on 10 m. Type **208**	35	40
608	2 c. on 15 m. Bronze cow, Vouni Palace (5th-century B.C.) (horiz)	35	40
609	3 c. on 25 m. Amphora, Salamis (6th-century B.C.)	35	20
610	4 c. on 40 m. Gold finger-ring, Enkomi (13th-century B.C.) (horiz)	40	20
611	5 c. on 50 m. Bronze cauldron, Salamis (8th-century B.C.)	50	50
612	6 c. on 75 m. Funerary stele, Marion (5th-century B.C.)	50	20
613	10 c. on 100 m. Jug (15th–14th-century B.C.)	50	40
614	13 c. on 125 m. Warrior (Terracotta) (6–5th-cent B.C.)	60	50
615	15 c. on 150 m. Lions attacking bull (bronze relief), Vouni Palace (5th-century B.C.) (horiz)	70	55
616	20 c. on 200 m. Bronze statue of Ingot God, Enkomi (12th-century B.C.)	70	65
617	25 c. on 175 m. Faience rhyton, Kition (13th-century B.C.)	80	1·10
618	50 c. on 500 m. Stone bowl, Khirokitia (6th-millenium B.C.) (horiz)	1·00	2·00

227 View of Power Station

228 St Lazaros Church, Larnaca

1983. Anniversaries and Events. Multicoloured.

619	3 c. Type **227**	10	20
620	6 c. W.C.Y. logo	20	15
621	13 c. "Sol Olympia" (liner) and "Polys" (tanker)	40	35
622	15 c. Human Rights emblem and map of Europe	40	25
623	20 c. Nicos Kazantzakis	45	75
624	25 c. Makarios in church	50	75

COMMEMORATIONS: 3 c. 30th anniv of Cyprus Electricity Authority; 6 c. World Communications Year; 13 c. 25th anniv of International Maritime Organization; 15 c. 35th anniv of Universal Declaration of Human Rights; 20 c. Birth centenary; 25 c. 70th birth anniv.

1983. Christmas. Church Towers. Multicoloured.

625	4 c. Type **228**	15	10
626	13 c. St. Varvara Church, Kaimakli, Nicosia	40	35
627	20 c. St. Ioannis Church, Larnaca	70	1·50

229 Waterside Cafe, Larnaca

1984. Old Engravings. Each brown and black.

628	6 c. Type **229**	15	15
629	20 c. Bazaar at Larnaca (39×25 mm)	40	85
630	30 c. Famagusta Gate, Nicosia (39×25 mm)	65	1·50

230 C.E.P.T. 25th Anniversary Logo

1984. Europa.

632	**230** 6 c. lt green, grn & blk	50	10
633	15 c. lt blue, blue & blk	1·10	2·50

1984. Obligatory Tax. Refugee Fund. As T **188** but new value and dated "1984".

634	1 c. black	10	10

231 Running

1984. Olympic Games, Los Angeles. Multicoloured.

635	3 c. Type **231**	20	10
636	4 c. Olympic column	20	20
637	13 c. Swimming	55	75
638	20 c. Gymnastics	80	1·50

232 Prisoners-of-War

1984. 10th Anniv of Turkish Landings in Cyprus. Multicoloured.

639	15 c. Type **232**	40	45
640	20 c. Map and burning buildings	50	55

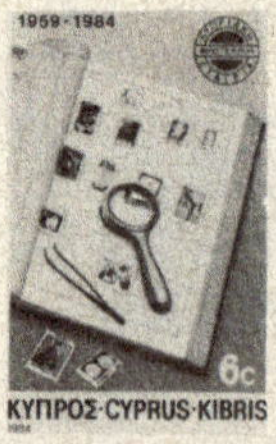

233 Open Stamp Album (25th Anniv of Cyprus Philatelic Society)

234 St. Mark (miniature from 11th-century Gospel)

1984. Anniversaries and Events. Multicoloured.

641	6 c. Type **233**	30	20
642	10 c. Football in motion (horiz) (50th anniv of Cyprus Football Association)	45	30
643	15 c. "Dr. George Papanicolaou" (medical scientist) (birth centenary)	60	50
644	25 c. Antique map of Cyprus and ikon (horiz) (International Symposia on Cartography and Medieval Paleography)	1·00	2·00

1984. Christmas. Illuminated Gospels. Multicoloured.

645	4 c. Type **234**	30	10
646	13 c. Beginning of St. Mark's Gospel	75	50
647	20 c. St. Luke (miniature from 11th-century Gospel)	1·25	2·00

235 Autumn at Platania, Troodos Mountains

1985. Cyprus Scenes and Landscapes. Multicoloured.

648	1 c. Type **235**	20	40
649	2 c. Ayia Napa Monastery	20	40
650	3 c. Phini Village—panoramic view	20	30
651	4 c. Kykko Monastery	20	30
652	5 c. Beach at Makronissos, Ayia Napa	20	20
653	6 c. Village street, Omodhos (vert)	30	20
654	10 c. Panoramic sea view	45	30
655	13 c. Windsurfing	55	25
656	15 c. Beach at Protaras	65	25
657	20 c. Forestry for development (vert)	80	50
658	25 c. Sunrise at Protaras (vert)	1·00	1·00
659	30 c. Village house, Pera	1·25	1·25
660	50 c. Apollo Hylates Sanctuary, Curium	2·00	1·75
661	£1 Snow on Troodos Mountains (vert)	3·50	3·00
662	£5 Personification of Autumn, House of Dionyssos, Paphos (vert)	13·00	15·00

236 Clay Idols of Musicians (7/6th century B.C.)

1985. Europa. European Music Year. Multicoloured.

663	6 c. Type **236**	85	35
664	15 c. Violin lute, flute and score from the "Cyprus Suite"	1·40	2·00

237 Cyprus Coat of Arms (25th Anniv of Republic)

238 "The Visit of the Madonna to Elizabeth" (Lambadistis Monastery, Kalopanayiotis)

1985. Anniversaries and Events.

665	**237** 4 c. multicoloured	30	15
666	– 6 c. multicoloured	35	15
667	– 13 c. multicoloured	75	1·25
668	– 15 c. black, olive-black and orange	1·25	1·25
669	– 20 c. multicoloured	80	2·00

DESIGNS—HORIZ (43×30 mm): 6 c. "Barn of Liopetri" (detail) (Pol Georghiou (30th anniv of EOKA Campaign); 13 c. Three profiles (International Youth Year); 15 c. Solon Michaelides (composer and conductor) (European Music Year). VERT—(as T **237**): 20 c. U.N. Building, New York, and flags (40th anniv of United Nations Organization).

1985. Christmas. Frescoes from Cypriot Churches. Multicoloured.

670	4 c. Type **238**	30	10
671	13 c. "The Nativity" (Lambadistis Monastery, Kalopanayiotis)	80	65
672	20 c. "Candlemas-day" (Asinou Church)	1·25	2·00

239 Figure from Hellenistic Spoon Handle

1986. New Archaeological Museum Fund. Multicoloured.

673	15 c. Type **239**	70	45
674	20 c. Pattern from early Ionian helmet and foot from statue	80	75
675	25 c. Roman statue of Eros and Psyche	1·00	95
676	30 c. Head of statue	1·25	1·10

No. 676 also commemorates the 50th anniv of the Department of Antiquities.

240 Cyprus Moufflon and Cedars

1986. Europa. Protection of Nature and the Environment. Multicoloured.

678	7 c. Type **240**	50	30
679	17 c. Greater flamingos at Larnaca Salt Lake	1·75	2·50

241 Cat's-paw Scallop

1986. Sea Shells. Multicoloured.

680	5 c. Type **241**	40	15
681	7 c. Atlantic trumpet triton	45	15
682	18 c. Purple dye murex	1·00	70
683	25 c. Yellow cowrie	1·50	2·00

1986. Nos. 653 and 655 surch.

684	7 c. on 6 c. Village street, Omodhos (vert)	40	30
685	18 c. on 13 c. Windsurfing	1·10	60

243 Globe Outline Map of Cyprus and Barn Swallows (Overseas Cypriots' Year)

1986. Anniversaries and Events. Multicoloured.

686	15 c. Type **243**	1·00	45
687	18 c. Halley's Comet over Cyprus beach (40 × 23 mm)	1·25	2·00
688	18 c. Comet's tail over sea and Edmond Halley (40 × 23 mm)	1·25	2·00

Nos. 687/8 were printed together, se-tenant, forming a composite design.

244 Pedestrian Crossing

1986. Road Safety Campaign. Multicoloured.

689	5 c. Type **244**	1·00	30
690	7 c. Motor cycle crash helmet	1·10	30
691	18 c. Hands fastening car seat belt	2·25	3·00

245 "The Nativity" (Church of Panayia tou Araka)

1986. Christmas. International Peace Year. Details of Nativity frescoes from Cypriot churches. Multicoloured.

692	5 c. Type **245**	40	15
693	15 c. Church of Panayia tou Moutoulla	1·00	30
694	17 c. Church of St. Nicholas tis Steyis	1·25	2·00

246 Church of Virgin Mary, Asinou

1987. Troodos Churches on the World Heritage List. Multicoloured.

695	15 c. Type **246**	1·00	1·10
696	15 c. Fresco of Virgin Mary, Moutoulla's Church	1·00	1·10
697	15 c. Church of Virgin Mary, Podithou	1·00	1·10
698	15 c. Fresco of Three Apostles, St. Ioannis Lampadistis Monastery	1·00	1·10
699	15 c. Annunciation fresco, Church of the Holy Cross, Pelentriou	1·00	1·10
700	15 c. Fresco of Saints, Church of the Cross, Ayiasmati	1·00	1·10
701	15 c. Fresco of Archangel Michael and Donor, Pedoula's Church of St. Michael	1·00	1·10
702	15 c. Church of St. Nicolaos, Steyis	1·00	1·10
703	15 c. Fresco of Prophets, Church of Virgin Mary, Araka	1·00	1·10

247 Proposed Central Bank of Cyprus Building

1987. Europa. Modern Architecture.

704 **247**	7 c. multicoloured	50	30
705 –	18 c. black, grey and green	1·10	2·00

DESIGN: 18 c. Headquarters complex, Cyprus Telecommunications Authority.

248 Remains of Ancient Ship and Kyrenia Castle

1987. Voyage of "Kyrenia II" (replica of ancient ship). Multicoloured.

706	2 c. Type **248**	30	20
707	3 c. "Kyrenia II" under construction, 1982–5	30	90
708	5 c. "Kyrenia II" at Paphos, 1986	55	20
709	17 c. "Kyrenia II" at New York, 1986	1·40	90

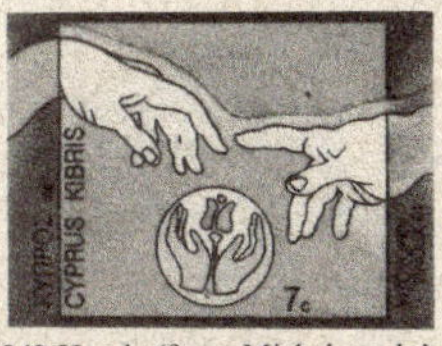

249 Hands (from Michelangelo's "Creation") and Emblem

1987. Anniversaries and Events. Multicoloured.

710	7 c. Type **249** (10th anniv of Blood Donation Co-ordinating Committee)	50	25
711	15 c. Snail with flowered shell and countryside (European Contryside Campaign)	1·10	40
712	20 c. Symbols of ocean bed and Earth's crust ("Troodos '87" Ophiolites and Oceanic Lithosphere Symposium)	1·40	3·00

250 Nativity Crib

1987. Christmas. Traditional Customs. Mult.

713	5 c. Type **250**	35	15
714	15 c. Door knocker decorated with foliage	1·10	35
715	17 c. Bowl of fruit and nuts	1·25	2·00

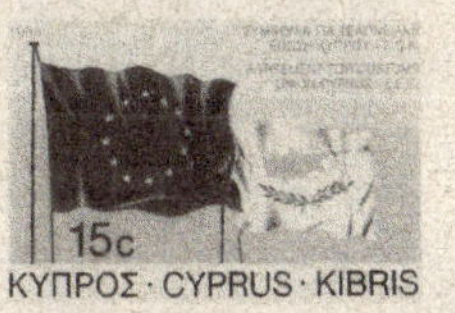

251 Flags of Cyprus and E.E.C

1988. Cypriot-E.E.C. Customs Union. Multicoloured.

716	15 c. Type **251**	80	1·50
717	18 c. Outline maps of Cyprus and E.E.C. countries	80	80

252 Intelpost Telefax Terminal

1988. Europa. Transport and Communications. Multicoloured.

718	7 c. Type **252**	65	75
719	7 c. Car driver using mobile telephone	65	75
720	18 c. Nose of Cyprus Airways airliner and greater flamingos	1·75	2·25
721	18 c. Boeing 739 airliner in flight and greater flamingos	1·75	2·25

253 Sailing

255 "Cyprus 74" (wood-engraving by A. Tassos)

254 Conference Emblem

1988. Olympic Games, Seoul. Multicoloured.

722	5 c. Type **253**	30	20
723	7 c. Athletes at start	35	40
724	10 c. Shooting	40	70
725	20 c. Judo	90	1·50

1988. Non-Aligned Foreign Ministers' Conference, Nicosia.

726 **254**	1 c. black, blue and green	10	10
727 –	10 c. multicoloured	45	70
728 –	50 c. multicoloured	2·25	2·50

DESIGNS: 10 c. Emblem of Republic of Cyprus; 50 c. Nehru, Tito, Nasser and Makarios.

1988. Obligatory Tax. Refugee Fund. Variously dated.

892 **255**	1 c. black and grey	10	10

1988. No. 651 surch **15c**.

730	15 c. on 4 c. Kykko Monastery	90	70

256 "Presentation of Christ at the Temple" (Church of Holy Cross tou Agiasmati)

257 Human Rights Logo

1988. Christmas. Designs showing frescoes from Cypriot churches. Multicoloured.

731	5 c. Type **256**	30	20
732	15 c. "Virgin and Child" (St. John Lampadistis Monastery)	70	25
733	17 c. "Adoration of the Magi" (St. John Lampadistis Monastery)	1·00	1·75

1988. 40th Anniv of Universal Declaration of Human Rights.

734 **257**	25 c. lt blue, dp blue & bl	90	1·25

258 Basketball

1989. 3rd Small European States' Games, Nicosia. Multicoloured.

735	1 c. Type **258**	10	15
736	5 c. Javelin	20	15
737	15 c. Wrestling	45	20
738	18 c. Athletics	60	1·00

259 Lingri Stick Game

1989. Europa. Children's Games. Multicoloured.

740	7 c. Type **259**	65	75
741	7 c. Ziziros	65	75
742	18 c. Sitsia	80	1·00
743	18 c. Leapfrog	80	1·00

260 "Universal Man"

1989. Bicentenary of the French Revolution.

744 **260**	18 c. multicoloured	60	60

261 Stylized Human Figures

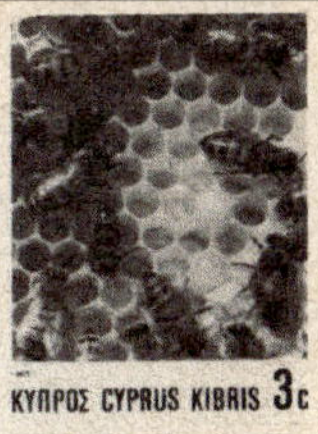

262 Worker Bees tending Larvae

1989. Centenary of Interparliamentary Union (15 c.) and 9th Non-Aligned Summit Conference, Belgrade (30 c.). Multicoloured.

745	15 c. Type **261**	50	40
746	30 c. Conference logo	1·00	1·10

1989. Bee-keeping. Multicoloured.

748	3 c. Type **262**	15	20
749	10 c. Bee on rock-rose flower	40	50
750	15 c. Bee on lemon flower	60	50
751	18 c. Queen and worker bees	65	90

263 Outstretched Hand and Profile (aid for Armenian earthquake victims)

264 Winter (detail from "Four Seasons")

1989. Anniversaries and Events. Multicoloured.

752	3 c. Type **263**	15	40
753	5 c. Airmail envelope (Cyprus Philatelic Society F.I.P. membership)	25	10
754	7 c. Crab symbol and daisy (European Cancer Year)	45	90
755	17 c. Vegetables and fish (World Food Day)	75	90

1989. Roman Mosaics from Paphos. Multicoloured.

756	1 c. Type **264**	10	10
757	2 c. Personification of Crete (32 × 24 mm)	10	10
758	3 c. Centaur and Maenad (24 × 32 mm)	10	10
759	4 c. Poseidon and Amymone (32 × 24 mm)	15	15
760	5 c. Leda	20	20
761	7 c. Apollon	25	25
762	10 c. Hermes and Dionysos (24 × 32 mm)	30	30
763	15 c. Cassiopeia	50	45
764	18 c. Orpheus (32 × 24 mm)	55	50
765	20 c. Nymphs (24 × 32 mm)	65	60
766	25 c. Amazon (24 × 32 mm)	75	70
767	40 c. Doris (32 × 24 mm)	1·40	1·25
768	50 c. Heracles and the Lion (39 × 27 mm)	1·60	1·50
769	£1 Apollon and Daphne (39 × 27 mm)	3·00	3·00
770	£3 Cupid (39 × 27 mm)	8·00	8·25

265 Hands and Open Book (International Literacy Year)

1990. Anniversaries and Events. Multicoloured.

771	15 c. Type **265**	55	50
772	17 c. Dove and profiles (83rd Inter-Parliamentary Conference, Nicosia)	65	90
773	18 c. Lions International emblem (Lions Europa Forum, Limassol)	75	90

266 District Post Office, Paphos

1990. Europa. Post Office Buildings. Multicoloured.

774	7 c. Type **266**	80	25
775	18 c. City Centre Post Office, Limassol	1·10	1·50

267 Symbolic Lips (25th anniv of Hotel and Catering Institute)

1990. European Tourism Year. Multicoloured.
776 5 c. Type **267** 25 20
777 7 c. Bell tower, St. Lazarus Church (1100th anniv) . . 30 25
778 15 c. Butterflies and woman . 1·25 40
779 18 c. Birds and man . . . . . 1·50 3·00

268 Sun (wood carving)

269 "Chionodoxa lochiae"

1990. 30th Anniv of Republic. Multicoloured.
780 15 c. Type **268** 55 45
781 17 c. Bulls (pottery design) . . 65 60
782 18 c. Fishes (pottery design) . 75 70
783 40 c. Tree and birds (wood carving) . . . . 1·40 2·75

1990. Endangered Wild Flowers. Book illustrations by Elektra Megaw. Multicoloured.
785 2 c. Type **269** 30 60
786 3 c. "Pancratium maritimum" 30 60
787 5 c. "Paeonia mascula" . . . 45 20
788 7 c. "Cyclamen cyprium" . . 50 25
789 15 c. "Tulipa cypria" 85 30
790 18 c. "Crocus cyprius" . . . . 1·10 2·50

270 "Nativity"

271 Archangel

1990. Christmas. 16th-century Icons. Multicoloured.
791 5 c. Type **270** 25 20
792 15 c. "Virgin Hodegetria" . . 65 30
793 17 c. "Nativity" (different) . . 90 2·25

1991. 6th-century Mosaics from Kanakaria Church. Multicoloured.
794 5 c. Type **271** 20 15
795 15 c. Christ Child 75 20
796 17 c. St. James . . . . 1·00 1·25
797 18 c. St. Matthew . . . . . . 1·00 1·75

272 "Ulysses" Spacecraft

1991. Europa. Europa in Space. Multicoloured.
798 7 c. Type **272** 60 20
799 18 c. "Giotto" and Halley's Comet . . . . 1·25 2·00

273 Young Pied Wheatear

1991. Pied ("Cyprus") Wheatear. Multicoloured.
800 5 c. Type **273** 35 30
801 7 c. Adult bird in autumn plumage 40 30
802 15 c. Adult male in breeding plumage 70 45
803 30 c. Adult female in breeding plumage . . . . 1·25 2·25

274 Mother and Child with Tents

1991. 40th Anniv of U.N. Commission for Refugees. Each deep brown, brown and silver.
804 5 c. Type **274** 25 15
805 15 c. Three pairs of legs . . . 90 65
806 18 c. Three children . . . . . 1·10 2·00

275 The Nativity

276 Swimming

1991. Christmas. Multicoloured.
808 5 c. Type **275** 20 15
809 15 c. Saint Basil 50 40
810 17 c. Baptism of Jesus . . . . 80 1·50

1992. Olympic Games, Barcelona. Multicoloured.
811 10 c. Type **276** 50 35
812 20 c. Long jump 85 70
813 30 c. Running . . . . 1·25 1·25
814 35 c. Discus . . . . 1·40 2·25

277 World Map and Emblem ("EXPO '92" Worlds Fair, Seville)

1992. Anniversaries and Events. Multicoloured
815 20 c. Type **277** . . . . 1·00 80
816 25 c. European map and football (10th under-16 European Football Championship) . 1·40 95
817 30 c. Symbols of learning (inauguration of University of Cyprus) . . . . 1·40 2·75

278 Compass Rose and Map of Voyage

1992. Europa. 500th Anniv of Discovery of America by Columbus. Multicoloured.
818 10 c. Type **278** . . . . 90 1·25
819 10 c. "Departure from Palos" (R. Balaga) . . . . 90 1·25
820 30 c. Fleet of Columbus . . . 1·40 1·75
821 30 c. Christopher Columbus . 1·40 1·75
Nos. 818/9 and 820/1 were each issued together, se-tenant, forming composite designs.

279 "Chamaeleo chamaeleon"

1992. Reptiles. Multicoloured.
822 7 c. Type **279** 55 30
823 10 c. "Lacerta laevis troodica" (lizard) 75 45
824 15 c. "Mauremys caspica" (turtle) 90 80
825 20 c. "Coluber cypriensis" (snake) . . . . 1·00 2·00

280 Minoan Wine Ship of 7th Century B.C. and Modern Tanker

1992. 7th International Maritime and Shipping Conference, Nicosia.
826 **280** 50 c. multicoloured . . . . 2·50 2·75

281 "Visitation of the Virgin Mary to Elizabeth", Church of the Holy Cross, Pelendri

282 School Building and Laurel Wreath

1992. Christmas. Church Fresco Paintings. Multicoloured.
827 7 c. Type **281** 40 25
828 15 c. "Virgin and Child Enthroned", Church of Panayia tou Araka 75 65
829 20 c. "Virgin and Child", Ayios Nicolaos tis Stegis Church . 1·10 1·90

1993. Centenary of Pancyprian Gymnasium (secondary school)
830 **282** 10 c. multicoloured 60 50

283 "Motherhood" (bronze sculpture, Nicos Dymiotis)

1993. Europa. Comtemporary Art. Multicoloured.
831 10 c. Type **283** 50 40
832 30 c. "Motherhood" (painting, Christoforos Savva) (horiz) . 1·25 2·00

284 Women Athletes (13th European Cup for Women)

1993. Anniversaries and Events. Multicoloured.
833 7 c. Type **284** 40 30
834 10 c. Scout symbols (80th anniv of Scouting in Cyprus) (vert) 55 40
835 20 c. Water-skier, dolphin and gull (Moufflon Encouragement Cup) (inscr "Mufflon") . . . . 10·00 10·00
835a 20 c. Water-skier, dolphin and seabird (inscr "Moufflon") . 95 95
836 25 c. Archbishop Makarios III and monastery (80th birth anniv) . . . . 1·40 1·75

285 Red Squirrelfish

1993. Fishes. Multicoloured.
837 7 c. Type **285** 40 25
838 15 c. Red scorpionfish 65 55
839 20 c. Painted comber 75 85
840 30 c. Grey triggerfish . . . . 1·40 2·00

286 Conference Emblem

1993. 12th Commonwealth Summit Conf.
841 **286** 35 c. brown and ochre . . 1·60 1·90
842 40 c. brown and ochre . . 1·90 2·40

287 Ancient Sailing Ship and Modern Coaster

1993. "Maritime Cyprus '93" International Shipping Conference, Nicosia.
843 **287** 25 c. multicoloured . . . 1·40 1·40

288 Cross from Stavrovouni Monastery

290 Symbols of Disability (Persons with Special Needs Campaign)

289 Copper Smelting

1993. Christmas. Church Crosses. Multicoloured.
844 7 c. Type **288** 30 25
845 20 c. Cross from Lefkara . . 75 75
846 25 c. Cross from Pedoulas (horiz) 1·00 1·75

1994. Europa. Discoveries. Ancient Copper Industry. Multicoloured.
847 10 c. Type **289** 50 35
848 30 c. Ingot, ancient ship and map of Cyprus . . . . 1·25 1·75

1994. Anniversaries and Events. Multicoloured.
849 7 c. Type **290** 40 25
850 15 c. Olympic rings in flame (Centenary of International Olympic Committee) . . . 65 55
851 20 c. Peace doves (World Gymnasiade, Nicosia) . . . 80 80
852 25 c. Adults and unborn baby in tulip (International Year of the Family) . . . . 1·10 1·75

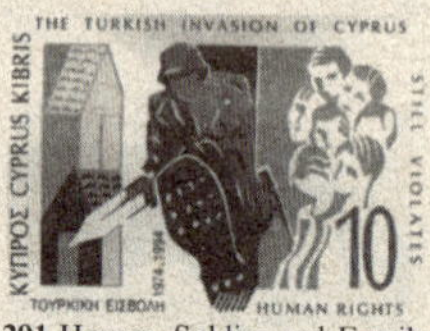

291 Houses, Soldier and Family

1994. 20th Anniv of Turkish Landings in Cyprus. Multicoloured.
853 10 c. Type **291** 50 40
854 50 c. Soldier and ancient columns . . . . 2·00 3·00

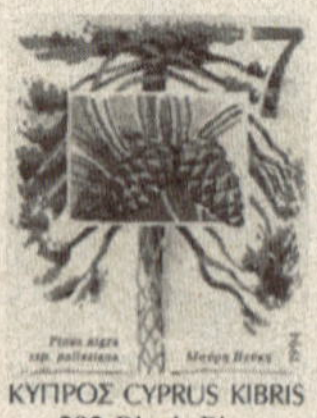

292 Black Pine

1994. Trees. Multicoloured.
855 7 c. Type **292** 30 25
856 15 c. Cyprus cedar 55 55
857 20 c. Golden oak 70 80
858 30 c. Strawberry tree . . . . 1·10 1·75

293 Airliner, Route Map and Emblem

1994. 50th Anniv of I.C.A.O.
859 **293** 30 c. multicoloured . . . 1·50 1·50

294 "Virgin Mary" (detail) (Philip Goul) 295 Woman from Paphos wearing Foustani

1994. Christmas. Church Paintings. Multicoloured.

860	7 c. Type **294**	35	25
861	20 c. "The Nativity" (detail) (Byzantine)	85	70
862	25 c. "Archangel Michael" (detail) (Goul)	1·10	1·90

1994. Traditional Costumes. Multicoloured.

863	1 c. Type **295**	10	10
864	2 c. Bride from Karpass	10	10
865	3 c. Woman from Paphos wearing sayia	10	10
866	5 c. Woman from Messaoria wearing foustani	10	10
867	7 c. Bridegroom	15	20
868	10 c. Shepherd from Messaoria	25	30
869	15 c. Woman from Nicosia in festive costume	35	40
870	20 c. Woman from Karpass wearing festive sayia	50	55
871	25 c. Woman from Pitsillia	60	65
872	30 c. Woman from Karpass wearing festive doupletti	70	75
873	35 c. Countryman	80	85
874	40 c. Man from Messaoria in festive costume	95	1·00
875	50 c. Townsman	1·25	1·40
876	£1 Townswoman wearing festive sarka	2·40	2·50

296 "Hearth Room" Excavation, Alassa, and Frieze 297 Statue of Liberty, Nicosia (left detail)

1995. 3rd International Congress of Cypriot Studies, Nicosia. Multicoloured.

877	20 c. Type **296**	75	75
878	30 c. Hypostyle hall, Kalavasos, and Mycenaean amphora	1·00	1·50

1995. 40th Anniv of Start of E.O.K.A. Campaign. Different details of the statue. Multicoloured.

880	20 c. Type **297**	90	1·10
881	20 c. Centre detail (face value at top right)	90	1·10
882	20 c. Right detail (face value at bottom right)	90	1·10

Nos. 880/2 were printed together, se-tenant, forming a composite design.

298 Nazi Heads on Peace Dove over Map of Europe 299 Symbolic Figure holding Healthy Food

1995. Europa. Peace and Freedom. Multicoloured.

883	10 c. Type **298**	50	35
884	30 c. Concentration camp prisoner and peace dove	1·25	1·75

1995. Healthy Living. Multicoloured.

885	7 c. Type **299**	25	25
886	10 c. "AIDS" and patients (horiz)	50	50
887	15 c. Drug addict (horiz)	55	55
888	20 c. Smoker and barbed wire	75	1·00

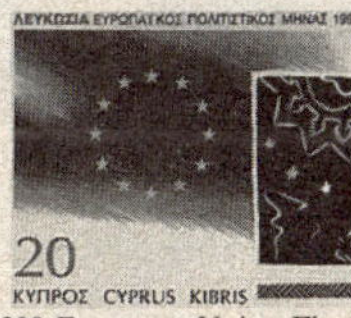

300 European Union Flag and European Culture Month Logo

1995. European Culture Month and "Europhilex '95" International Stamp Exhibition, Nicosia. Each blue, yellow and stone.

889	20 c. Type **300**	55	60
890	25 c. Map of Europe and Cypriot church	70	75

301 Peace Dove with Flags of Cyprus and United Nations

1995. Anniversaries and Events. Multicoloured.

893	10 c. Type **301** (50th anniv of United Nations)	30	35
894	15 c. Hand pushing ball over net (centenary of volleyball) (vert)	55	50
895	20 c. Safety pin on leaf (European Nature Conservation Year) (vert)	65	65
896	25 c. Clay pigeon contestant (World Clay Target Shooting Championship)	75	1·10

302 Reliquary from Kykko Monastery 303 Family (25th anniv of Pancyprian Organization of Large Families)

1995. Christmas.

897	**302** 7 c. multicoloured	20	25
898	– 20 c. multicoloured	60	60
899	– 25 c. multicoloured	75	1·10

DESIGNS: 20, 25 c. Different reliquaries of Virgin and Child from Kykko Monastery.

1996. Anniversaries and Events. Multicoloured.

900	10 c. Type **303**	45	35
901	20 c. Film camera (centenary of cinema)	75	70
902	35 c. Silhouette of parent and child in globe (50th anniv of U.N.I.C.E.F.)	1·40	1·40
903	40 c. "13" and Commonwealth emblem (13th Conference of Commonwealth Speakers and Presiding Officers)	1·50	2·00

304 Maria Synglitiki 306 Watermill

305 High Jump

1996. Europa. Famous Women. Multicoloured.

904	10 c. Type **304**	40	30
905	30 c. Queen Caterina Cornaro	1·00	1·25

1996. Centennial Olympic Games, Atlanta. Multicoloured.

906	10 c. Type **305**	40	30
907	20 c. Javelin	75	65
908	25 c. Wrestling	85	95
909	30 c. Swimming	95	1·40

1996. Mills. Multicoloured.

910	10 c. Type **306**	40	40
911	15 c. Olivemill	55	50
912	20 c. Windmill	70	80
913	25 c. Handmill	80	1·10

307 Icon of Our Lady of Iberia, Moscow

1996. Cyprus–Russia Joint Issue. Orthodox Religion. Multicoloured.

914	30 c. Type **307**	1·10	1·25
915	30 c. Stravrovouni Monastery, Cyprus	1·10	1·25
916	30 c. Icon of St. Nicholas, Cyprus	1·10	1·25
917	30 c. Iberia Gate, Moscow	1·10	1·25

308 "The Nativity" (detail)

1996. Christmas. Religious Murals from Church of The Virgin of Asinou. Multicoloured.

918	7 c. Type **308**	30	25
919	20 c. "Virgin Mary between the Archangels Gabriel and Michael"	75	60
920	25 c. "Christ bestowing Blessing" (vert)	1·10	1·40

309 Basketball

1997. Final of European Basketball Cup.

921	**309** 30 c. multicoloured	1·10	1·10

310 "The Last Supper"

1997. Easter. Religious Frescoes from Monastery of St. John Lambadestis. Multicoloured.

922	15 c. Type **310**	50	50
923	25 c. "The Crucifixion"	75	1·00

311 Kori Kourelleni and Prince

1997. Europa. Tales and Legends. Multicoloured.

924	15 c. Type **311**	50	40
925	30 c. Digenis and Charon	90	1·25

312 "Oedipoda miniata" (grasshopper)

1997. Insects. Multicoloured.

926	10 c. Type **312**	30	30
927	15 c. "Acherontia atropos" (hawk moth)	50	40
928	25 c. "Daphnis nerii" (hawk moth)	90	95
929	35 c. "Ascalaphus macaronius" (owl-fly)	1·10	1·50

313 Archbishop Makarios III and Chapel

1997. 20th Death Anniv of Archbishop Makarios III.

930	**313** 15 c. multicoloured	35	40

314 The Nativity

1997. Christmas. Byzantine Frescos from the Monastery of St. John Lambadestis. Multicoloured.

931	10 c. Type **314**	20	25
932	25 c. Three Kings following the star	65	65
933	30 c. Flight into Egypt	85	1·00

315 Green Jasper

1998. Minerals. Multicoloured.

934	10 c. Type **315**	25	30
935	15 c. Iron pyrite	35	45
936	25 c. Gypsum	60	70
937	30 c. Chalcedony	70	1·00

316 Players competing for Ball

1998. World Cup Football Championship, France.

938	**316** 35 c. multicoloured	80	85

317 Cataclysmos Festival, Larnaca

1998. Europa. Festivals. Multicoloured.

939	15 c. Type **317**	35	40
940	30 c. House of Representatives, Nicosia (Declaration of Independence)	70	75

318 Mouflon Family Group 319 Flames and Globe Emblem

1998. Endangered Species. Cyprus Mouflon. Multicoloured.

941	25 c. Type **318**	60	65
942	25 c. Mouflon herd	60	65
943	25 c. Head of ram	60	65
944	25 c. Ram on guard	60	65

1998. 50th Anniv of Universal Declaration of Human Rights.

959	**319** 50 c. multicoloured	1·25	1·40

320 World "Stamp" and Magnifying Glass

1998. World Stamp Day.

960	**320** 30 c. multicoloured	70	75

321 "The Annunciation"

322 "Pleurotus eryngii"

1998. Christmas. Multicoloured.

961	10 c. Type **321**	25	30
962	25 c. "The Nativity"	60	65
963	30 c. "The Baptism of Christ"	70	75

1999. Mushrooms of Cyprus. Multicoloured.

965	10 c. Type **322**	25	30
966	15 c. "Lactarius deliciosus"	35	40
967	25 c. "Sparassis crispa"	60	65
968	30 c. "Morchella elata"	70	75

323 Pair of Moufflons at Tripylos Reserve

1999. Europa. Parks and Gardens. Multicoloured.

969	15 c. Type **323**	35	40
970	30 c. Turtles on beach at Lara Reserve	70	75

324 Council of Europe Building, Emblem and Flags

1999. 50th Anniv of Council of Europe.

971	**324** 30 c. multicoloured	70	75

TURKISH CYPRIOT POSTS

After the inter-communal clashes during December 1963, a separate postal service was established on 6 January 1964, between some of the Turkish Cypriot areas, using handstamps inscribed "KIBRIS TURK POSTALARI". During 1964, however, an agreement was reached between representatives of the two communities for the restoration of postal services. This agreement to which the United Nations representatives were a party, was ratified in November 1966 by the Republic's Council of Ministers. Under the scheme postal servcies were provided for the Turkish Cypriot communities in Famagusta, Limassol, Lefka and Nicosia, staffed by Turkish Cypriot employees of the Cypriot Department of Posts.

On 8 April 1970, 5 m. and 15 m. locally produced labels, originally designated "Social Aid Stamps", were issued by the Turkish Cypriot community and these can be found on commercial covers. These local stamps are outside the scope of this catalogue.

On 29 October 1973 Nos. 1/7 were placed on sale, but were again used only on mail between the Turkish Cypriot areas.

Following the intervention by the Republic of Turkey in July 1974 these stamps replaced issues of the Republic of Cyprus in that part of the island, north and east of the Attila Line, controlled by the Autonomous Turkish Cypriot Administration.

1974. 1000 mils = 1 pound.
1978. 100 kurus = 1 lira.

1 50th Anniversary Emblem

1974. 50th Anniv of Republic of Turkey.

1	– 3 m. multicoloured	30·00	30·00
2	– 5 m. multicoloured	60	40
3	– 10 m. multicoloured	50	20
4	**1** 15 m. red and black	2·50	1·50
5	– 20 m. multicoloured	70	20
6	– 50 m. multicoloured	2·00	1·50
7	– 70 m. multicoloured	16·00	16·00

DESIGNS—VERT: 3 m. Woman sentry; 10 m. Man and woman with Turkish flags; 20 m. Ataturk statue, Kyrenia Gate, Nicosia; 50 m. "The Fallen". HORIZ: 5 m. Military parade, Nicosia; 70 m. Turkish flag and map of Cyprus.

1975. Proclamation of the Turkish Federated State of Cyprus. Nos. 3 and 5 surch **KIBRIS TURK FEDERE DEVLETI 13.2.1975** and value.

8	30 m. on 20 m. multicoloured	75	1·00
9	100 m. on 10 m. multicoloured	1·25	2·00

3 Namik Kemal's Bust, Famagusta

1975. Multicoloured.

10	3 m. Type **3**	15	40
11	10 m. Ataturk Statue, Nicosia	15	10
12	15 m. St. Hilarion Castle	25	20
13	20 m. Ataturk Square, Nicosia	35	20
14	25 m. Famagusta Beach	35	30
15	30 m. Kyrenia Harbour	45	10
16	50 m. Lala Mustafa Pasha Mosque, Famagusta (vert)	50	10
17	100 m. Interior, Kyrenia Castle	80	90
18	250 m. Castle walls, Kyrenia	1·25	2·75
19	500 m. Othello Tower, Famagusta (vert)	2·25	5·00

See also Nos. 36/8.

4 Map of Cyprus

1975. "Peace in Cyprus". Multicoloured.

20	30 m. Type **4**	30	15
21	50 m. Map, laurel and broken chain	35	20
22	150 m. Map and laurel-sprig on globe (vert)	90	1·00

5 "Pomegranates" (I. V. Guney)

1975. Europa. Paintings. Multicoloured.

23	90 m. Type **5**	80	60
24	100 m. "Harvest Time" (F. Direkoglu)	95	60

1976. Nos. 16/17 surch.

25	10 m. on 50 m. multicoloured	50	70
26	30 m. on 100 m. multicoloured	50	80

7 "Expectation" (ceramic statuette)

9 Olympic Symbol "Flower"

8 Carob

1976. Europa. Multicoloured.

27	60 m. Type **7**	40	80
28	120 m. "Man in Meditation"	60	90

1976. Export Products. Fruits. Multicoloured.

29	10 m. Type **8**	25	10
30	25 m. Mandarin	30	10
31	40 m. Strawberry	40	25
32	60 m. Orange	50	65
33	80 m. Lemon	55	1·75

1976. Olympic Games, Montreal. Multicoloured.

34	60 m. Type **9**	25	20
35	100 m. Olympic symbol and doves	35	25

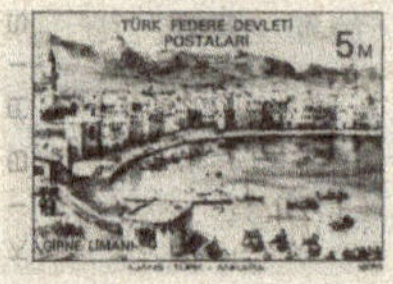

10 Kyrenia Harbour

11 Liberation Monument, Karaeglanoglu (Ay Georghios)

1976. Multicoloured.

36	5 m. Type **10**	40	15
37	15 m. St. Hilarion Castle	40	15
38	20 m. Ataturk Square, Nicosia	40	15

1976. Liberation Monument.

47	**11** 30 m. blue, pink and black	15	20
48	– 150 m. red, pink and black	35	45

DESIGN: 150 m. Liberation Monument (different view).

12 Hotel, Salamis Bay

1977. Europa. Multicoloured.

49	80 m. Type **12**	65	80
50	100 m. Kyrenia Port	75	80

13 Pottery

14 Arap Ahmet Pasha Mosque, Nicosia

1977. Handicrafts. Multicoloured.

51	15 m. Type **13**	10	10
52	30 m. Pottery (vert)	10	10
53	125 m. Basketware	30	50

1977. Turkish Buildings in Cyprus. Multicoloured.

54	20 m. Type **14**	10	10
55	40 m. Paphos Castle (horiz)	10	10
56	70 m. Bekir Pasha aqueduct (horiz)	15	20
57	80 m. Sultan Mahmut library (horiz)	15	25

15 Namik Kemal (bust) and House, Famagusta

1977. Namik Kemal (patriotic poet). Multicoloured.

58	30 m. Type **15**	15	15
59	140 m. Namik Kemal (portrait) (vert)	35	60

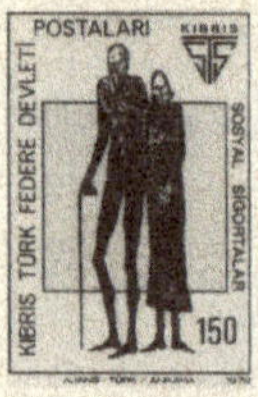

16 Old Man and Woman

17 Oratory in Buyuk Han, Nicosia

1978. Social Security.

60	**16** 150 k. black, yellow and blue	10	10
61	– 275 k. black, orange and green	15	15
62	– 375 k. black, blue and orange	25	20

DESIGNS: 275 k. Injured man with crutch; 375 k. Woman with family.

1978. Europa. Multicoloured.

63	225 k. Type **17**	30	30
64	450 k. Cistern in Selimiye Mosque, Nicosia	60	70

18 Motorway Junction

1978. Communications. Multicoloured.

65	75 k. Type **18**	15	10
66	100 k. Hydrofoil	15	10
67	650 k. Boeing 720 at Ercan Airport	50	35

19 Dove with Laurel Branch

20 Kemal Ataturk

1978. National Oath.

68	**19** 150 k. yellow, violet and black	10	10
69	– 225 k. black, red and yellow	10	10
70	– 725 k. black, blue and yellow	20	20

DESIGNS—VERT: 225 k. "Taking the Oath". HORIZ: 725 k. Symbolic dove.

1978. Ataturk Commemoration.

71	**20** 75 k. turquoise and deep turquoise	10	10
72	450 k. pink and brown	15	15
73	650 k. blue and light blue	20	25

1979. Nos. 30/3 surch.

74	50 k. on 25 k. Mandarin	10	10
75	1 l. on 40 m. Strawberry	15	10
76	3 l. on 60 m. Orange	15	10
77	5 l. on 80 m. Lemon	35	15

23 Postage Stamp and Map of Cyprus

24 Microwave Antenna

1979. Europa. Communications. Multicoloured.

79	2 l. Type **23**	10	10
80	3 l. Postage stamps, building and map	10	10
81	8 l. Telephones, Earth and satellite	20	30

1979. 50th Anniv of International Consultative Radio Committee.

82	**24** 2 l. multicoloured	20	10
83	5 l. multicoloured	20	10
84	6 l. multicoloured	25	15

25 School Children

26 Lala Mustafa Pasha Mosque, Magusa

1979. International Year of the Child. Multicoloured.

85	1½ l. Type **25**	25	15
86	4½ l. Children and globe (horiz)	40	20
87	6 l. College children	60	20

1980. Islamic Commemorations. Multicoloured.

88	2½ l. Type **26**	10	10
89	10 l. Arap Ahmet Pasha Mosque, Lefkosa	30	15
90	20 l. Mecca and Medina	50	20

COMMEMORATIONS: 2½ l. 1st Islamic Conference in Turkish Cyprus; 10 l. General Assembly of World Islam Congress; 20 l. Moslem Year 1400 AH.

27 Ebu-Su'ud Efendi (philosopher)

28 Omer's Shrine, Kyrenia

1980. Europa. Personalities. Multicoloured.

91	5 l. Type **27**	20	10
92	30 l. Sultan Selim II	70	40

1980. Ancient Monuments.

93	**28**	2½ l. blue and stone	10	10
94	–	3½ l. green and pink	10	10
95	–	5 l. brown on green	15	10
96	–	10 l. mauve and green	30	10
97	–	20 l. blue and yellow	50	25

DESIGNS: 3½ l. Entrance gate, Famagusta; 5 l. Funerary monuments (16th-century), Famagusta; 10 l. Bella Paise Abbey, Kyrenia; 20 l. Selimiye Mosque, Nicosia.

29 Cyprus 1880 6d. Stamp

30 Dome of the Rock

1980. Cyprus Stamp Centenary.

98	**29**	7½ l. black, brown and green	20	10
99	–	15 l. brown, dp blue & bl	25	10
100	–	50 l. black, red and grey	65	55

DESIGNS—HORIZ: 15 l. Cyprus 1960 Constitution of the Republic 30 m. commemorative stamp. VERT: 50 l. Social Aid local, 1970.

1980. Palestinian Solidarity. Multicoloured.

101	15 l. Type **30**	25	15
102	35 l. Dome of the Rock (horiz)	65	30

31 Extract from World Muslim Congress Statement in Turkish

32 "Ataturk" (F. Duran)

1981. Day of Solidarity with Islamic Countries.

103	**31**	1 l. buff, red and brown	15	15
104	–	35 l. light green, black & green	55	85

DESIGN: 35 l. Extract in English.

1981. Ataturk Stamp Exhibition, Lefkosa.

105	**32**	10 l. multicoloured	25	35

33 Folk-dancing

35 Wild Convolvulus

1981. Europa. Folklore. Multicoloured.

106	10 l. Type **33**	35	15
107	30 l. Folk-dancing (different)	60	35

1981. Flowers. Multicoloured.

109	1 l. Type **35**	10	10
110	5 l. Persian cyclamen (horiz)	10	10
111	10 l. Spring mandrake (horiz)	10	10
112	25 l. Corn poppy	15	10
113	30 l. Wild arum (horiz)	20	10
114	50 l. Sage-leaved rock rose	30	20
115	100 l. "Cistus salviaefolius L."	55	30
116	150 l. Giant fennel (horiz)	1·00	90

36 Stylised Disabled Person in Wheelchair

1981. Commemorations. Multicoloured.

117	7½ l. Type **36**	30	35
118	10 l. Heads of people of different races, peace dove and barbed wire (vert)	50	55
119	20 l. People of different races reaching out from globe, with dishes (vert)	75	85

COMMEMORATIONS: 7½ l. International Year for Disabled Persons; 10 l. Anti-apartheid publicity; 20 l. World Food Day.

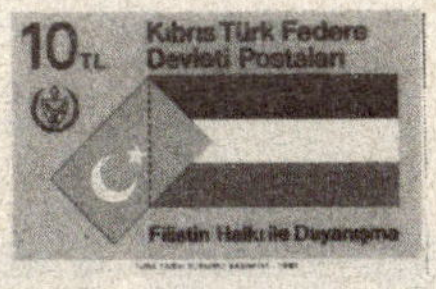

37 Turkish Cypriot and Palestinian Flags

1981. Palestinian Solidarity.

120	**37**	10 l. multicoloured	30	40

38 Prince Charles and Lady Diana Spencer

40 Buffavento Castle

1981. Royal Wedding.

121	**38**	50 l. multicoloured	1·00	85

1982. Tourism. Multicoloured.

123	5 l. Type **40**	10	10
124	10 l. Windsurfing	15	10
125	15 l. Kantara Castle	25	15
126	30 l. Shipwreck (300 B.C.)	50	40

Nos. 124/6 are horiz.

41 "Wedding" (A. Orek)

1982. Paintings (1st series). Multicoloured.

127	30 l. Type **41**	15	30
128	50 l. "Carob Pickers" (O. Nazim Selenge) (vert)	30	70

See also Nos. 132/3, 157/8, 176/7, 185/6, 208/9, 225/7, 248/50, 284/5, 315/16, 328/9, 369/70 and 436/7.

42 Cross of Lorraine, Koch and Bacillus (Centenary of Koch's Discovery of Tubercle Bacillus)

1982. Anniversaries and Events. Multicoloured.

129	10 l. Type **42**	1·00	40
130	30 l. Spectrum on football pitch (World Cup Football Championships, Spain)	1·75	1·00
131	70 l. "75" and Lord Baden-Powell (75th Anniv of Boy Scout movement and 125th birth anniv) (vert)	2·25	3·50

43 "Calloused Hands" (Salih Oral)

45 First Turkish Cypriot 10 m. Stamp

1983. Paintings (2nd series). Multicoloured.

132	30 l. Type **43**	90	1·40
133	35 l. "Malya-Limassol Bus" (Emin Cizenel)	90	1·40

1983. Anniversaries and Events. Multicoloured.

135	15 l. Type **45**	50	50
136	20 l. "Turkish Achievements in Cyprus" (horiz)	60	60
137	25 l. "Liberation Fighters"	70	70
138	30 l. Dish aerial and telegraph pole (horiz)	85	90
139	50 l. Dove and envelopes (horiz)	1·75	2·25

EVENTS: 15, 20, 25 l. T.M.T. (25th anniv of Turkish Cypriot Resistance Organization); 30, 50 l. World Communications Year.

46 European Bee Eater

1983. Birds of Cyprus. Multicoloured.

140	10 l. Type **46**	80	1·00
141	15 l. Goldfinch	1·00	1·10
142	50 l. European robin	1·25	1·40
143	65 l. Golden oriole	1·40	1·50

1983. Establishment of Republic. Nos. 109, 111/12 and 116 optd **Kuzey Kibris Turk Cumhuriyeti 15.11.1983**, or surch also.

144	10 l. Spring mandrake	20	15
145	15 l. on 1 l. Type **35**	30	15
146	25 l. Corn poppy	40	25
147	150 l. Giant fennel	2·25	3·25

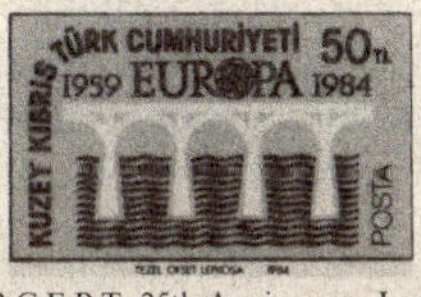

48 C.E.P.T. 25th Anniversary Logo

1984. Europa.

148	**48**	50 l. yellow, brown and black	2·25	3·00
149		100 l. lt blue, blue & blk	2·25	3·00

49 Olympic Flame

50 Ataturk Cultural Centre

1984. Olympic Games, Los Angeles. Multicoloured.

150	10 l. Type **49**	15	10
151	20 l. Olympic events within rings (horiz)	25	25
152	70 l. Martial arts event (horiz)	50	1·50

1984. Opening of Ataturk Cultural Centre, Lefkosa.

153	**50**	120 l. stone, black and brown	1·25	1·75

52 Turkish Cypriot Flag and Map

1984. 10th Anniv of Turkish Landings in Cyprus. Multicoloured.

154	20 l. Type **52**	50	25
155	70 l. Turkish Cypriot flag within book	1·00	2·00

53 Burnt and Replanted Forests

1984. World Forestry Resources.

156	**53**	90 l. multicoloured	1·25	1·75

54 "Old Turkish Houses, Nicosia" (Cevdet Cagdas)

1984. Paintings (3rd series). Multicoloured.

157	20 l. Type **54**	50	40
158	70 l. "Scenery" (Olga Rauf)	1·10	2·00

See also Nos. 176/7, 185/6, 208/9, 225/7, 248/50, 284/5, 315/16, 328/9 and 369/70.

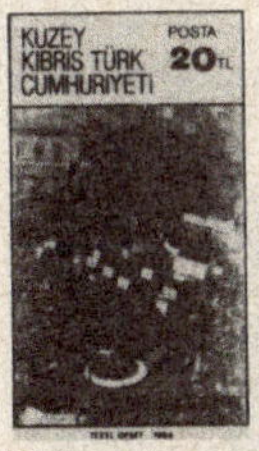

55 Kemal Ataturk, Flag and Crowd

56 Taekwondo Bout

1984. 1st Anniv of Turkish Republic of Northern Cyprus. Multicoloured.

159	20 l. Type **55**	50	40
160	70 l. Legislative Assembly voting for Republic (horiz)	1·10	2·00

1984. International Taekwondo Championship, Girne.

161	**56**	10 l. black, brown and grey	40	25
162	–	70 l. multicoloured	1·60	2·50

DESIGN: 70 l. Emblem and flags of competing nations.

57 "Le Regard"

58 Musical Instruments and Music

1984. Exhibition by Saulo Mercader (artist). Multicoloured.

163	20 l. Type **57**	30	25
164	70 l. "L'equilibre de L'esprit" (horiz)	1·10	2·25

1984. Visit of Nurnberg Chamber Orchestra.

165	**58**	70 l. multicoloured	1·50	2·25

59 Dr. Fazil Kucuk (politician)

61 George Frederick Handel

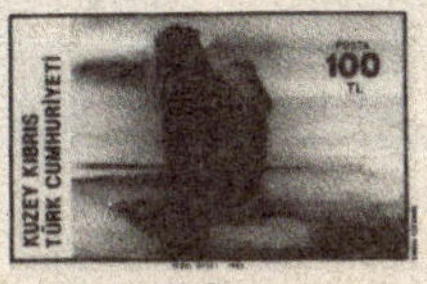

60 Goat

1985. 1st Death Anniv of Dr. Fazil Kucuk (politician). Multicoloured.
166 20 l. Type **59** 30 30
167 70 l. Dr. Fazil Kucuk reading newspaper 95 2·00

1985. Domestic Animals. Multicoloured.
168 100 l. Type **60** 55 30
169 200 l. Cow and calf 90 80
170 300 l. Ram 1·25 2·00
171 500 l. Donkey 2·00 3·25

1985. Europa. Composers.
172 **61** 20 l. purple, grn & lt grn 2·00 2·50
173 – 20 l. purple, brown and pink 2·00 2·50
174 – 100 l. purple, blue & lt bl 2·50 3·00
175 – 100 l. purple, brn & lt brn 2·50 3·00
DESIGNS: No. 173, Giuseppe Domenico Scarlatti; 174, Johann Sebastian Bach; 175, Buhurizade Mustafa Itri Efendi.

1985. Paintings (4th series). As T **54**. Multicoloured.
176 20 l. "Village Life" (Ali Atakan) 60 50
177 50 l. "Woman carrying Water" (Ismet V. Guney)) 1·40 2·50

62 Heads of Three Youths

1985. International Youth Year. Multicoloured.
178 20 l. Type **62** 75 40
179 100 l. Dove and globe 3·50 4·00

63 Parachutist (Aviation League)

65 Karagoz Show Puppets

1985. Anniversaries and Events.
180 **63** 20 l. multicoloured 1·00 30
181 – 50 l. black, brown and blue 1·50 1·00
182 – 100 l. brown 1·75 2·50
183 – 100 l. multicoloured 1·75 2·50
184 – 100 l. multicoloured 1·75 2·50
DESIGNS—VERT: No. 181, Louis Pasteur (Centenary of Discovery of Rabies vaccine); 182, Ismet Inonu (Turkish statesman) (birth centenary (1984)). HORIZ: 183, "40" in figures and symbolic flower (40th anniv of United Nations Organization); 184, Patient receiving blood transfusion (Prevention of Thalassaemia).

1986. Paintings (5th series). As T **54**. Multicoloured.
185 20 l. "House with Arches" (Gonen Atakol) 50 30
186 100 l. "Ataturk Square" (Yalkin Muhtaroglu) 1·75 1·75

1986. Karagoz Folk Puppets.
188 **65** 100 l. multicoloured 2·25 2·00

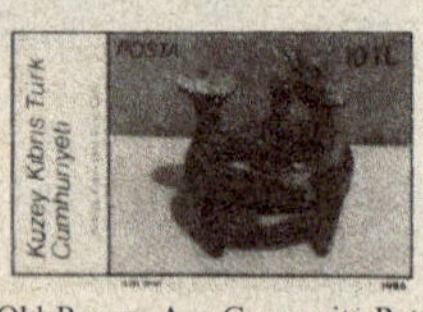

66 Old Bronze Age Composite Pottery

1986. Archaeological Artefacts. Cultural Links with Anatolia. Multicoloured.
189 10 l. Type **66** 55 20
190 20 l. Late Bronze Age bird jug (vert) 95 30
191 50 l. Neolithic earthenware pot 1·75 1·75
192 100 l. Roman statue of Artemis (vert) 2·25 3·25

67 Soldiers, Defence Force Badge and Ataturk (10th anniv of Defence Forces)

69 Prince Andrew and Miss Sarah Ferguson

68 Guzelyurt Dam and Power Station

1986. Anniversaries and Events. Multicoloured.
193 20 l. Type **67** 80 30
194 50 l. Woman and two children (40th anniv of F.A.O.) 1·40 1·40
195 100 l. Football and world map (World Cup Football Championship, Mexico) (horiz) 2·75 3·25
196 100 l. Orbit of Halley's Comet and "Giotto" space probe (horiz) 2·75 3·25

1986. Modern Development (1st series). Mult.
197 20 l. Type **68** 1·25 30
198 50 l. Low cost housing project, Lefkosa 1·40 1·25
199 100 l. Kyrenia Airport 3·25 3·50
See also Nos. 223/4 and 258/63.

1988. 60th Birthday of Queen Elizabeth II and Royal Wedding. Multicoloured.
200 100 l. Queen Elizabeth II 1·50 2·00
201 100 l. Type **69** 3·00 4·00

70 Locomotive No. 11 and Trakhoni Station

1986. Cyprus Railway. Multicoloured.
202 50 l. Type **70** 3·00 2·75
203 100 l. Locomotive No. 1 3·50 3·75

1987. Nos. 94, 96/7 and 113 optd **Kuzey Kibris Turk Cumhuriyeti** or surch also (No. 205).
204 10 l. mauve and green 50 70
205 15 l. on 3½ l. green and pink 50 70
206 20 l. blue and yellow 55 75
207 30 l. multicoloured 70 1·10

1987. Paintings (6th series). As T **54**. Multicoloured.
208 50 l. "Shepherd" (Feridun Isiman) 1·25 1·25
209 25 l. "Pear Woman" (Mehmet Uluhan) 1·75 2·75

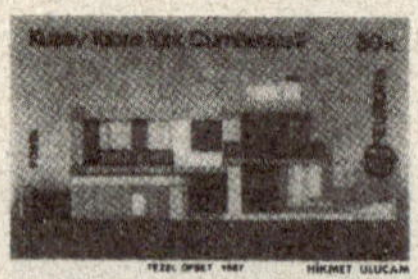

72 Modern House (architect A. Vural Behaeddin)

1987. Europa. Modern Architecture. Multicoloured.
210 50 l. Type **72** 1·00 30
211 200 l. Modern house (architect Necdet Turgay) 1·75 3·00

73 Kneeling Folk Dancer

74 Regimental Colour (1st anniv of Infantry Regiment)

1987. Folk Dancers. Multicoloured.
212 20 l. Type **73** 60 20
213 50 l. Standing male dancer 90 40
214 200 l. Standing female dancer 2·00 1·75
215 1000 l. Woman's headdress 4·75 6·50

1987. Anniversaries and Events. Multicoloured.
216 50 l. Type **74** 1·25 75
217 50 l. President Denktash and Turgut Ozal (1st anniv of Turkish Prime Minister's visit) (horiz) 1·25 75
218 200 l. Emblem and Crescent (5th Islamic Summit Conference, Kuwait) 2·25 3·25
219 200 l. Emblem and laurel leaves (Membership of Pharmaceutical Federation) (horiz) 2·25 3·25

75 Ahmet Belig Pasha (Egyptian judge)

76 Tourist Hotel, Girne

1987. Turkish Cypriot Personalities.
220 **75** 50 l. brown and yellow 65 40
221 – 50 l. multicoloured 65 40
222 – 125 l. multicoloured 1·50 3·00
DESIGNS: 50 l. (No. 221) Mehmet Emin Pasha (Ottoman Grand Vizier); 125 l. Mehmet Kamil Pasha (Ottoman Grand Vizier).

1987. Modern Development (2nd series). Mult.
223 150 l. Type **76** 1·50 1·50
224 200 l. Dogu Akdeniz University 1·75 2·25

1988. Paintings (7th series). As T **54**. Multicoloured.
225 20 l. "Woman making Pastry" (Ayhan Mentes) (vert) 50 20
226 50 l. "Chair Weaver" (Osman Guvenir) 75 75
227 150 l. "Woman weaving a Rug" (Zekai Yesiladali) (vert) 1·75 3·25

77 "Piyale Pasha" (tug)

1988. Europa. Transport and Communications. Multicoloured.
228 200 l. Type **77** 1·75 75
229 500 l. Dish aerial and antenna tower, Selvilitepe (vert) 2·50 4·00
No. 229 also commemorates the 25th anniv of Bayrak Radio and Television Corporation.

78 Lefkosa

79 Bulent Ecevit

1988. Tourism. Multicoloured.
230 150 l. Type **78** 80 80
231 100 l. Gazi-Magusa 90 1·00
232 300 l. Girne 1·50 2·00

1988. Turkish Prime Ministers. Multicoloured.
233 50 l. Type **79** 60 75
234 50 l. Bulent Ulusu 60 75
235 50 l. Turgut Ozal 60 75

80 Red Crescent Members on Exercise

1988. Civil Defence.
236 **80** 150 l. multicoloured 1·25 1·50

81 Hodori the Tiger (Games mascot) and Fireworks

1988. Olympic Games, Seoul. Multicoloured.
237 200 l. Type **81** 80 1·00
238 250 l. Athletics 1·00 1·25
239 400 l. Shot and running track with letters spelling "SEOUL" 1·50 2·00

82 Sedat Simavi (journalist)

85 Girl with Doll

1988. Anniversaries and Events.
240 **82** 50 l. green 25 25
241 – 100 l. multicoloured 50 45
242 – 300 l. multicoloured 70 1·00
243 – 400 l. multicoloured 1·50 1·75
244 – 400 l. multicoloured 1·00 1·75
245 – 600 l. multicoloured 2·00 2·50
DESIGNS—HORIZ: No. 241, Stylised figures around table and flags of participating countries (International Girne Conferences); 244, Presidents Gorbachev and Reagan signing treaty (Summit Meeting). VERT: No. 242, Cogwheels as flowers (North Cyprus Industrial Fair); 243, Globe (125th anniv of International Red Cross); 245, "Medical Services" (40th anniv of W.H.O.).

1989. Paintings (8th series). As T **54**. Multicoloured.
248 150 l. "Dervis Pasa Mansion, Lefkosa" (Inci Kansu) 90 60
249 400 l. "Gamblers' Inn, Lefkosa" (Osman Guvenir) 1·75 2·25
250 600 l. "Mosque, Paphos" (Hikmet Ulucam) (vert) 2·50 3·00

1989. Europa. Children's Games. Multicoloured.
251 600 l. Type **85** 1·75 1·25
252 1000 l. Boy with kite 2·00 3·25

86 Meeting of Presidents Vassiliou and Denktash

1989. Cyprus Peace Summit, Geneva, 1988.
253 **86** 500 l. red and black 1·25 1·25

87 Chukar Partridge

1989. Wildlife. Multicoloured.
254 100 l. Type **87** 65 25
255 200 l. Cyprus hare 70 35
256 700 l. Black partridge 2·50 2·00
257 2000 l. Red fox 3·00 3·50

88 Road Construction

1989. Modern Development (3rd series). Mult.
258 100 l. Type **88** 15 15
259 150 l. Laying water pipeline (vert) 20 20
260 200 l. Seedling trees (vert) 30 30
261 450 l. Modern telephone exchange (vert) 75 1·00
262 650 l. Steam turbine power station (vert) 1·00 1·50
263 700 l. Irrigation reservoir 1·25 1·75

89 Unloading Freighter at Quayside (15th anniv of Gazi Magusa Free Port)

1989. Anniversaries.
264 **89** 100 l. multicoloured 35 20
265 – 450 l. black, blue and red 80 80
266 – 500 l. black, yellow and grey 80 80
267 – 600 l. black, red and blue 1·10 1·50
268 – 1000 l. multicoloured 2·00 2·75
DESIGNS—VERT (26 × 47 mm): 450 l. Airmail letter and stylized bird (25th anniv of Turkish Cypriot postal service). HORIZ (as T **89**): 500 l. Newspaper and printing press (centenary of "Saded" newspaper); 600 l. Statue of Aphrodite, lifebelt and seabird (30th anniv of International Maritime Organization); 1000 l. Soldiers (25th anniv of Turkish Cypriot resistance).

90 Erdal Inonu

91 Mule-drawn Plough

1989. Visit of Professor Erdal Inonu (Turkish politician).
269 **90** 700 l. multicoloured 50 70

1989. Traditional Agricultural Implements. Multicoloured.

270	150 l. Type **91**	15	20
271	450 l. Ox-drawn threshing sledge	50	65
272	550 1l. Olive press (vert)	60	80

92 Smoking Ashtray and Drinks

1990. World Health Day. Multicoloured.

273	200 l. Type **92**	50	40
274	700 l. Smoking cigarette and heart	1·00	1·50

93 Yenierenkoy Post Office

1990. Europa. Post Office Buildings. Multicoloured.

275	1000 t. Type **93**	90	75
276	1500 t. Ataturk Meydani Post Office	1·60	2·25

94 Song Thrush **96** Amphitheatre, Soli

95 Two Football Teams

1990. World Environment Day. Birds. Multicoloured.

278	150 l. Type **94**	1·00	55
279	300 l. Blackcap	1·50	85
280	900 l. Black redstart	2·25	2·75
281	1000 l. Chiff-chaff	2·25	3·00

1990. World Cup Football Championship, Italy. Multicoloured.

282	300 l. Type **95**	75	50
283	1000 l. Championship symbol, globe and ball	2·50	3·00

1990. Paintings (9th series). As T **54**. Multicoloured.

284	300 l. "Abstract" (Filiz Ankacc)	25	25
285	1000 l. Wooden sculpture (S. Tekman) (vert)	85	1·50

1990. Tourism. Multicoloured.

286	150 l. Type **96**	40	20
287	10000 l. Swan mosaic, Soli	1·75	2·50

97 Kenan Evren and Rauf Denktas

1990. Visit of President Kenan Evren of Turkey.

288	**97** 500 l. multicoloured	1·00	1·00

98 Road Signs and Heart wearing Seat Belt

1990. Traffic Safety Campaign. Multicoloured.

289	150 l. Type **98**	50	25
290	300 l. Road signs, speeding car and spots of blood	75	50
291	1000 l. Traffic lights and road signs	2·25	2·75

99 Yildirim Akbulut **100** "Rosularia cypria"

1990. Visit of Turkish Prime Minister Yildrim Akbulut.

292	**99** 1000 l. multicoloured	1·10	1·10

1990. Plants. Multicoloured.

293	150 l. Type **100**	30	20
294	200 l. "Silene fraudratrix"	40	30
295	300 l. "Scutellaria sibthorpii"	45	35
296	600 l. "Sedum lampusae"	65	70
297	1000 l. "Onosma caespitosum"	90	1·25
298	1500 l. "Arabis cypria"	1·25	1·75

101 Kemal Ataturk at Easel (wood carving)

1990. International Literacy Year. Multicoloured.

299	300 l. Type **101**	40	35
300	750 l. Globe, letters and books	1·00	1·40

1991. Nos. 189, 212 and 293 surch.

301	**66** 250 l. on 10 l. multicoloured	50	50
302	**73** 250 l. on 20 l. multicoloured	50	50
303	**100** 500 l. on 150 l. multicoloured	75	75

103 "Ophrys lapethica" **106** Symbolic Roots (Year of Love to Yunus Emre)

105 Kucuk Medrese Fountain, Lefkosa

1991. Orchids (1st series). Multicoloured.

304	250 l. Type **103**	1·00	60
305	500 l. "Ophrys kotschyi"	1·75	2·00

See also Nos. 311/14.

1991. Fountains. Multicoloured.

307	250 l. Type **105**	30	15
308	500 l. Cafer Pasa fountain, Magusa	40	30
309	1500 l. Sarayonu Square fountain, Lefkosa	70	80
310	5000 l. Arabahmet Mosque fountain, Lefkosa	1·75	2·50

1991. Orchids (2nd series). As T **103**. Multicoloured.

311	100 l. "Serapias levantina"	30	20
312	500 l. "Dactylorhiza romana"	70	50
313	2000 l. "Orchis simia"	2·00	2·50
314	3000 l. "Orchis sancta"	2·50	3·00

1991. Paintings (10th series). As T **54**. Multicoloured.

315	250 l. "Hindiler" (S. Cizel) (vert)	50	35
316	500 l. "Dusme" (A. Mene) (vert)	1·00	1·25

1991. Anniversaries and Events.

317	**106** 250 l. yellow, black and mauve	25	25
318	– 500 l. multicoloured	45	50
319	– 500 l. multicoloured	45	50
320	– 1500 l. multicoloured	1·75	2·00

DESIGNS—VERT: No. 318, Mustafa Cagatay commemoration; 319, University building (5th anniv of Eastern Mediterranean University). HORIZ: No. 320, Mozart (death bicentenary).

107 Four Sources of Infection

1991. "AIDS" Day.

321	**107** 1000 l. multicoloured	1·10	1·10

108 Lighthouse, Gazimagusa

1991. Lighthouses. Multicoloured.

322	250 l. Type **108**	65	35
323	500 l. Ancient lighthouses, Girne harbour	1·00	80
324	1500 l. Modern lighthouse, Girne harbour	2·25	2·75

109 Elephant and Hippopotamus Fossils, Karaoglanoglu

1991. Tourism (1st series). Multicoloured.

325	250 l. Type **109**	50	30
326	500 l. Roman fish ponds, Lambusa	65	45
327	1500 l. Roman remains, Lambusa	1·50	2·25

See also Nos. 330/3 and 351/2.

1992. Paintings (11th series). As T **54**, but 31 × 49 mm. Multicoloured.

328	500 l. "Ebru" (A.Kandulu)	40	20
329	3500 l. "Street in Lefkosa" (I. Tatar)	1·60	2·25

1992. Tourism (2nd series). As T **109**. Multicoloured.

330	500 l. Bugday Camii, Gazimagusa	30	30
331	500 l. Clay pigeon shooting	30	30
332	1000 l. Salamis Bay Hotel, Gazimagusa	60	80
333	1500 l. Casino, Girne (vert)	90	1·50

112 Gymnastics **113** New Generating Station, Girne

1992. Olympic Games, Barcelona. Multicoloured.

336	500 l. Type **112**	45	55
337	500 l. Tennis	45	55
338	1000 l. High jumping (horiz)	70	80
339	1500 l. Cycling (horiz)	1·00	1·25

1992. Anniversaries and Events (1st series). Multicoloured.

340	500 l. Type **113**	30	20
341	500 l. Symbol of Housing Association (15th anniv)	30	20
342	1500 l. Domestic animals and birds (30th anniv of Veterinary Service)	1·50	1·75
343	1500 l. Cat (International Federation of Cat Societies Conference)	1·50	1·75

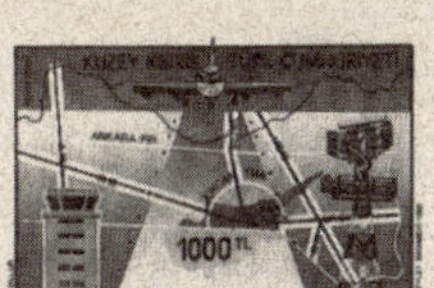

114 Airliner over Runway

1992. Anniversaries and Events (2nd series). Multicoloured.

344	1000 l. Type **114** (17th anniv of civil aviation)	80	80
345	1000 l. Meteorological instruments and weather (18th anniv of Meteorological Service)	80	80
346	1200 l. Surveying equipment and map (14th anniv of Survey Department)	1·00	1·25

115 Zubiye

1992. International Conference on Nutrition, Rome. Turkish Cypriot Cuisine. Multicoloured.

347	2000 l. Type **115**	50	80
348	2500 l. Cicek Dolmasi	80	90
349	3000 l. Tatar Boregi	90	1·00
350	4000 l. Seftali Kebabi	1·10	1·25

1993. Tourism (3rd series). As T **109**. Multicoloured.

351	500 l. St. Barnabas Church and Monastery, Salamis	30	15
352	10000 l. Ancient pot	2·25	2·50

117 Olive Tree, Girne **118** Traditional Houses

1993. Ancient Trees. Multicoloured.

354	500 l. Type **117**	15	15
355	1000 l. River red gum, Kyrenia Gate, Lefkosa	25	25
356	3000 l. Oriental plane, Lapta	70	90
357	4000 l. Calabrian pine, Cinarli	85	1·25

1993. Arabahmet District Conservation Project, Lefkosa. Multicoloured.

358	1000 l. Type **118**	50	40
359	3000 l. Arabahmet street	1·50	2·00

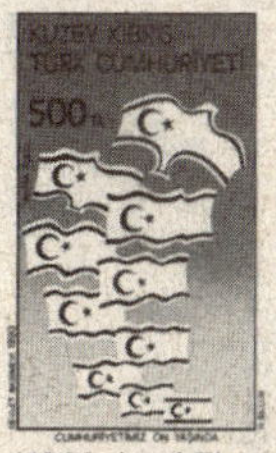

119 National Flags turning into Doves **120** Kemal Ataturk

1993. 10th Anniv of Proclamation of Turkish Republic of Northern Cyprus.

360	**119** 500 l. red, black and blue	20	15
361	– 500 l. red and blue	20	15
362	– 1000 l. red, black and blue	30	30
363	– 5000 l. multicoloured	1·40	2·00

DESIGNS—HORIZ: No. 361, National flag forming figure "10"; No. 362, Dove carrying national flag; No. 363, Map of Cyprus and figure "10" wreath.

1993. Anniversaries. Multicoloured.

364	500 l. Type **120** (55th death anniv)	20	20
365	500 l. Stage and emblem (30th anniv of Turkish Cypriot theatre) (horiz)	20	20
366	1500 l. Branch badges (35th anniv of T.M.T. organization) (horiz)	35	45
367	2000 l. World map and computer (20th anniv of Turkish Cypriot news agency) (horiz)	45	55
368	5000 l. Ballet dancers and Caykovski'nin (death centenary) (horiz)	1·40	2·00

121 "Soyle Falci" (Goral Ozkan)

1994. Art (12th series). Multicoloured.

369	1000 l. Type **121**	15	20
370	6500 l. "IV. Hareket" (sculpture) (Senol Ozdevrim)	85	1·40

See also Nos. 436/7.

122 Dr. Kucuk and Memorial

1994. 10th Death Anniv of Dr. Fazil Kucuk (politician).

371	**122** 1500 l. multicoloured	30	40

124 Peace Doves and Letters over Pillar Box

125 World Cup Trophy

1994. 30th Anniv of Turkish Cypriot Postal Service.
373 **124** 50000 l. multicoloured . . 2·75 3·50

1994. World Cup Football Championship, U.S.A. Multicoloured.
374 2500 l. Type **125** 30 20
375 10000 l. Footballs on map of U.S.A. (horiz) . . . . 1·25 1·50

126 Peace Emblem

1994. 20th Anniv of Turkish Landings in Cyprus.
376 **126** 2500 l. yellow, green and black 30 30
377 – 5000 l. multicoloured . . . 50 50
378 – 7000 l. multicoloured . . . 70 70
379 – 8500 l. multicoloured . . . 90 90
DESIGNS—HORIZ: 5000 l. Memorial; 7000 l. Sculpture; 8500 l. Peace doves forming map of Cyprus and flame.

127 Cyprus 1934 4½ pi. Stamp and Karpas Postmark

1994. Postal Centenary. Multicoloured.
380 1500 l. Type **127** 20 20
381 2500 l. Turkish Cypriot Posts 1979 Europa 2 l. and Gazimagusa postmark . . . 30 30
382 5000 l. Cyprus 1938 6 pi. and Bey Keuy postmark 50 50
383 7000 l. Cyprus 1955 100 m. and Aloa postmark 70 70
384 8500 l. Cyprus 1938 18 pi. and Pyla postmark 90 90

128 Trumpet Triton

1994. Sea Shells. Multicoloured.
385 2500 l. Type **128** 45 30
386 12500 l. Mole cowrie . . . . 1·25 1·50
387 12500 l. Giant tun . . . . . 1·25 1·50

1994. Nos. 280, 295, 315 and 317 surch.
388 1500 l. on 250 l. Type **106** . . 10 10
389 2000 l. on 900 l. Black redstart 50 50
390 2500 l. on 250 l. "Hindiler" (Sizel) 20 20
391 3500 l. on 300 l. "Scutellaria sibthorpii" 50 50

130 Donkeys on Mountain

1995. European Conservation Year. Multicoloured.
392 2000 l. Type **130** 20 20
393 3500 l. Coastline 30 30
394 15000 l. Donkeys in field . . 1·25 1·75

132 Sini Katmeri

1995. Turkish Cypriot Cuisine. Multicoloured.
396 3500 l. Type **132** 20 20
397 10000 l. Kolokas musakka and bullez kizartma 55 55
398 14000 l. Enginar dolmasi . . 90 1·10

133 "Papilio machaon"

1995. Butterflies. Multicoloured.
399 3500 l. Type **133** 30 15
400 4500 l. "Charaxes jasius" . . 35 20
401 15000 l. "Cynthia cardui" . . 1·00 1·10
402 30000 l. "Vanessa atalanta" . 1·75 2·00

134 Forest

1995. Obligatory Tax. Forest Regeneration Fund.
403 **134** 1000 l. green and black . 60 20

135 Beach, Girne

1995. Tourism. Multicoloured.
404 3500 l. Type **135** 15 15
405 7500 l. Sail boards 35 35
406 15000 l. Ruins of Salamis (vert) 70 80
407 20000 l. St. George's Cathedral, Gazimagusa (vert) . . . . 90 1·00

136 Suleyman Demirel and Rauf Denktas

1995. Visit of President Suleyman Demirel of Turkey.
408 **136** 5000 l. multicoloured . . 20 20

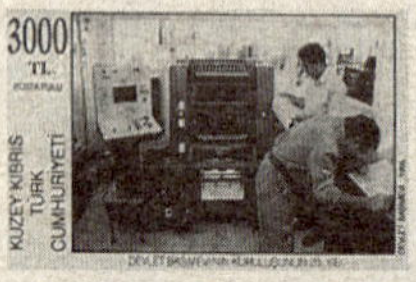
137 Stamp Printing Press

138 Kultegin Epitaph and Sculpture

1995. Anniversaries.
409 **137** 3000 l. multicoloured . . 40 40
410 – 3000 l. multicoloured . . 40 40
411 – 5000 l. multicoloured . . 70 70
412 – 22000 l. ultramarine, blue and black . . . . 1·00 1·25
413 – 30000 l. multicoloured . . 1·40 1·75
414 – 30000 l. multicoloured . . 1·40 1·75
DESIGNS—HORIZ: No. 409, Type **137** (20th anniv of State Printing Works); 410, Map of Turkey (75th anniv of Turkish National Assembly); 411, Louis Pasteur (chemist) and microscope (death centenary); 412, United Nations anniversary emblem (50th anniv); 413, Guglielmo Marconi (radio pioneer) and dial (centenary of first radio transmissions). VERT: No. 414, Stars and reel of film (centenary of cinema).

1995. Centenary of Deciphering of Orhon Epitaphs. Multicoloured.
415 5000 l. Type **138** 35 35
416 10000 l. Epitaph and tombstone 65 75

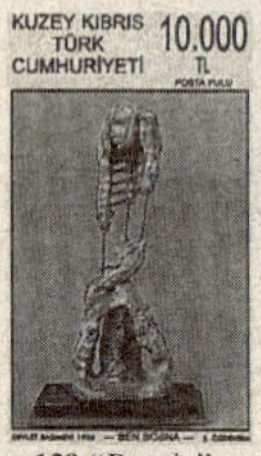

139 "Bosnia" (sculpture)

140 Striped Red Mullet

1996. Support for Moslems in Bosnia and Herzegovina.
417 **139** 10000 l. multicoloured . . 60 70

1996. Fishes. Multicoloured.
418 6000 l. Type **140** 40 30
419 10000 l. Peacock wrasse . . . 60 45
420 28000 l. Common two-banded seabream . . . . 1·00 1·25
421 40000 l. Dusky grouper . . . . 1·50 1·75

141 Palm Trees

142 Beria Remzi Ozoran

1996. Tourism. Multicoloured.
422 100000 l. Type **141** 40 45
423 150000 l. Pomegranate 60 65
424 250000 l. Ruins of Bella Paise Abbey (horiz) . . . . 1·00 1·10
425 500000 l. Traditional dancers (horiz) . . . . 2·00 2·10

1996. Europa. Famous Women. Multicoloured.
426 15000 l. Type **142** 50 25
427 50000 l. Kadriye Hulusi Hacibulgur . . . . 1·40 1·75

145 Symbolic Footballs

1996. European Football Championship, England. Multicoloured.
430 15000 l. Type **145** 55 55
431 35000 l. Football and flags of participating nations . . . . 1·00 1·00

146 Houses on Fire (Auxiliary Fire Service)

147 "Amanita phalloides"

1996. Anniversaries and Events. Multicoloured.
432 10000 l. Type **146** 30 30
433 20000 l. Colour party (20th anniv of Defence Forces) (vert) . . 40 40
434 50000 l. Children by lake (Nasreddin-Hoca Year) . . . 85 85
435 75000 l. Flowers (Children's Rights) . . . . 1·25 1·25

1997. Arts (13th series). As T **121**. Multicoloured.
436 25000 l. "City" (Lebibe Sonuc) (horiz) 50 30
437 70000 l. "Woman opening Letter" (Ruzen Atakan) (horiz) . . . . 1·40 1·60

1997. Fungi. Multicoloured.
438 15000 l. Type **147** 30 30
439 25000 l. "Morchella esculenta" 45 45
440 25000 l. "Pleurotus eryngii" . . 45 45
441 70000 l. "Amanita muscaria" . 1·25 1·25

148 Flag on Hillside

150 Prime Minister Necmettin Erbakan of Turkey

149 Mother and Children playing Leapfrog

1997. Besparmak Mountains Flag Sculpture.
442 **148** 60000 l. multicoloured . . 1·00 1·00

1997. Europa. Tales and Legends. Multicoloured.
443 25000 l. Type **149** 45 30
444 70000 l. Apple tree and well . 1·25 1·50

1997. Visit of the President and the Prime Minister of Turkey.
445 15000 l. Type **150** 30 20
446 80000 l. President Suleyman Demirel of Turkey (horiz) . 1·25 1·50

151 Golden Eagle

152 Coin of Sultan Abdulaziz, 1861–76

1997. Birds of Prey. Multicoloured.
447 40000 l. Type **151** 60 60
448 40000 l. Eleonora's falcon . . 60 60
449 75000 l. Common kestrel . . 1·00 1·10
450 100000 l. Honey buzzard . . 1·25 1·40

1997. Rare Coins. Multicoloured.
451 25000 l. Type **152** 15 20
452 40000 l. Coin of Sultan Mahmud II, 1808–39 . . . . 25 30
453 75000 l. Coin of Sultan Selim II, 1566–74 . . . . 45 50
454 100000 l. Coin of Sultan Mehmed V, 1909–18 . . . . 60 65

153 Open Book and Emblem

1997. Anniversaries.
455 **153** 25000 l. multicoloured . . 15 20
456 – 40000 l. multicoloured . . 25 30
457 – 100000 l. black, red and stone 60 65
458 – 150000 l. multicoloured . . 95 1·00
DESIGNS—HORIZ: 25000 l. Type **153** (centenary of Turkish Cypriot Scouts); 40000 l. Guides working in field (90th anniv of Turkish Cypriot Guides); 150000 l. Rudolph Diesel and first oil engine (centenary of the diesel engine). VERT: 100000 l. Couple and symbols (AIDS prevention campaign).

154 Ahmet and Ismet Sevki

1998. Ahmet and Ismet Sevki (photographers) Commemoration. Multicoloured.
459 40000 l. Type **154** 20 25
460 105000 l. Ahmet Sevki (vert) . 40 45

155 "Agrion splendens" (dragonfly)

156 Wooden Double Door

1998. Useful Insects. Multicoloured.
461 40000 l. Type **155** 20 25
462 65000 l. "Ascalaphus macaronius" (owl-fly) . . . 30 35
463 125000 l. "Podalonia hirsuta" 50 55
464 150000 l. "Rhyssa persuasoria" 60 65

1998. Old Doors.
465 **156** 115000 l. multicoloured . . 50 55
466 – 140000 l. multicoloured . 60 65
DESIGN: 140000 l. Different door.

157 Legislative Assembly Building (Republic Establishment Festival)

1998. Europa. Festivals. Multicoloured.
467 40000 l. Type **157** 20 25
468 150000 l. Globe, flags and map (Int Children's Folk Dance Festival) (vert) 60 65

158 Marine Life

1998. International Year of the Ocean.

469	158	40000 l. multicoloured	20	25
470	–	90000 l. multicoloured	35	40

DESIGN: 90000 l. Different underwater scene.

159 Prime Minister Mesut Yilmaz of Turkey

1998. Prime Minister Yilmaz's Visit to Northern Cyprus.

471	159	75000 l. multicoloured	30	35

160 Pres. Suleyman Demirel of Turkey
162 Deputy Prime Minister Bulent Ecevit

161 Victorious French Team

1998. President Demirel's "Water for Peace" Project.

472		75000 l. Type **160**	30	35
473		175000 l. Turkish and Turkish Cypriot leaders with inflatable water tank (horiz)	65	70

1998. World Cup Football Championship, France. Multicoloured.

474		75000 l. Type **161**	30	35
475		175000 l. World Cup trophy (vert)	65	70

1998. Visit of the Deputy Prime Minister of Turkey.

476	162	200000 l. multicoloured	80	85

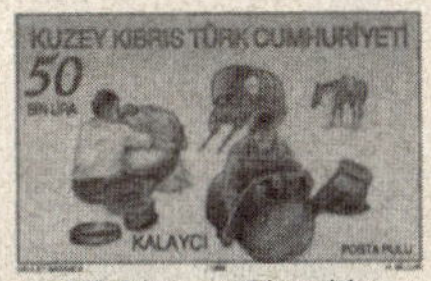

163 Itinerant Tinsmiths

1998. Local Crafts. Multicoloured.

477		50000 l. Type **163**	20	25
478		75000 l. Basket weaver (vert)	30	35
479		130000 l. Grinder sharpening knife (vert)	60	65
480		400000 l. Wood carver	1·90	2·00

164 Stylised Satellite Dish
165 Dr. Fazil Kucuk

1998. Anniversaries. Multicoloured (except No. 483).

481		50000 l. Type **164**	20	25
482		75000 l. Stylised birds and "15"	30	35
483		75000 l. "75" and Turkish flag (red, black and orange)	30	35
484		175000 l. Scroll, "50" and quill pen (vert)	75	80

ANNIVERSARIES: No. 481, 35th anniv of Bayrak Radio and Television; 482, 15th anniv of Turkish Republic of Northern Cyprus; 483, 75th anniv of Turkish Republic; 484, 50th anniv of Universal Declaration of Human Rights.

1999. 15th Death Anniv of Dr. Fazil Kucuk (politician).

486	165	75000 l. multicoloured	35	40

DHAR

A state of Central India. Now uses Indian stamps.

4 pice = 1 anna

1 2

1897. Imperf.

1	1	½ pice black on red	1·90	2·25
3		¼ a. black on orange	1·50	2·50
4		½ a. black on mauve	2·75	3·50
5		1 a. black on green	5·50	9·50
6		2 a. black on yellow	20·00	32·00

1898. Perf.

7b	2	½ a. red	2·25	4·50
8		1 a. purple	2·50	4·75
10		2 a. green	4·50	17·00

DOMINICA

Until 31 December, 1939, one of the Leeward Islands, but then transferred to the Windward Islands. Used Leeward Island stamps concurrently with Dominican issues from 1903 to above date.

1874. 12 pence = 1 shilling;
20 shillings = 1 pound.
1949. 100 cents = 1 West Indian dollar.

1

1874.

13	1	½d. yellow	2·00	8·50
20		½d. green	1·50	4·50
5		1d. lilac	4·50	1·75
22a		1d. red	2·75	4·50
15		2½d. brown	£140	2·00
23		2½d. blue	3·75	4·50
7		4d. blue	£110	2·50
24		4d. grey	2·00	3·75
8		6d. green	£150	20·00
25		6d. orange	6·00	32·00
9		1s. mauve	£120	48·00

1882. No. 5 bisected and surch with a small ½.

10	1	½ (d.) on half 1d. lilac	£140	35·00

1882. No. 5 bisected and surch with large ½.

11	1	½ (d.) on half 1d. lilac	28·00	13·00

1883. No. 5 bisected and surch **HALF PENNY** vert.

12	1	½d. on half 1d. lilac	48·00	20·00

1886. Nos. 8 and 9 surch in words and bar.

17	1	½d. on 6d. green	4·00	3·50
18		1d. on 6d. green	£20000	£11000
19		1d. on 1s. mauve	14·00	14·00

9 "Roseau from the Sea" (Lt. Caddy)
10

1903.

37	9	½d. green	1·50	2·50
38		1d. grey and red	2·00	30
29		2d. green and brown	2·50	4·50
30		2½d. grey and blue	4·50	3·75
31		3d. purple and black	8·00	3·00
32		6d. grey and brown	4·25	16·00
43		1s. mauve and green	3·75	48·00
34		2s. black and purple	24·00	27·00
45		2s. 6d. green and orange	22·00	55·00
46	10	5s. black and brown	60·00	60·00

1908.

48bw	9	1d. red	1·00	50
64		1½d. orange	2·75	9·50
65		2d. grey	2·75	3·25
66		2½d. blue	1·75	8·50
51		3d. purple on yellow	3·00	4·25
67		6d. purple	3·50	18·00
53		1s. black on green	2·75	2·75
53b		2s. purple and blue on blue	25·00	70·00
70		2s. 6d. black and red on blue	30·00	70·00

1914. As T **10**, but portrait of King George V.

54		5s. red and green on yellow	55·00	80·00

1916. No. 37 surch **WAR TAX ONE HALFPENNY.**

55	9	½d. on ½d. green	10	75

1918. Optd **WAR TAX.**

57	9	½d. green	10	30
58		3d. purple on yellow	65	3·50

1919. Surch **WAR TAX 1½D.**

59	9	1½d. on 2½d. orange	10	55

1920. Surch **1½D.**

60	9	1½d. on 2½d. orange	2·00	4·00

16

1923.

71	16	½d. black and green	1·50	30
72		1d. black and violet	1·75	1·25
73		1d. black and red	9·00	90
74		1½d. black and red	2·00	65
75		1½d. black and brown	9·00	60
76		2d. black and grey	1·75	40
77		2½d. black and yellow	1·00	8·50
78		2½d. black and blue	3·50	1·75
79		3d. black and blue	1·00	11·00
80		3d. black and red on yellow	1·25	1·00
81		4d. black and brown	2·00	4·50
82		6d. black and mauve	3·50	5·50
83		1s. black on green	2·00	2·75
84		2s. black and blue on blue	7·50	14·00
85		2s. 6d. black and red on blue	18·00	15·00
86		3s. black and purple on yellow	3·00	9·00
87		4s. black and red on green	9·50	17·00
90		5s. black and green on yellow	9·00	42·00
91		£1 black and purple on red	£225	£325

1935. Silver Jubilee. As T **13** of Antigua.

92		1d. blue and red	75	20
93		1½d. blue and grey	1·25	55
94		2½d. brown and blue	1·40	2·25
95		1s. grey and purple	1·50	3·25

1937. Coronation. As T **2** of Aden.

96		1d. red	40	10
97		1½d. brown	40	10
98		2½d. blue	60	1·25

17 Fresh Water Lake
21 King George VI

1938.

99	17	½d. brown and green	10	15
100	–	1d. black and red	20	20
101	–	1½d. green and purple	30	70
102	–	2d. red and black	50	90
103a	–	2½d. purple and blue	20	1·00
104	–	3d. olive and brown	30	40
104a	–	3½d. blue and mauve	1·50	1·25
105	17	6d. green and violet	1·75	90
105a		7d. green and brown	1·50	1·25
106	–	1s. violet and olive	2·25	80
106a	–	2s. grey and purple	4·50	8·00
107	17	2s. 6d. black and red	12·00	4·75
108	–	5s. blue and brown	7·50	8·00
108a	–	10s. black and orange	12·00	14·00

DESIGNS—As Type **17**: 1d., 3d., 2s., 5s. Layou River; 1½d., 2½d., 3½d. Picking Limes; 2d., 1s., 10s. Boiling Lake.

1940.

109a	21	¼d. brown	10	10

1946. Victory. As T **9** of Aden.

110		1d. red	20	10
111		3½d. blue	20	10

1948. Silver Wedding. As T **10/11** of Aden.

112		1d. red	15	10
113		10s. brown	7·50	20·00

1949. U.P.U. As T **20/23** of Antigua.

114		5 c. blue	15	15
115		6 c. brown	75	1·50
116		12 c. purple	30	80
117		24 c. olive	30	30

1951. Inauguration of B.W.I. University College. As T **24/25** of Antigua.

118		3 c. green and violet	50	45
119		12 c. green and red	50	30

23 Drying Cocoa
40 Seashore at Rosalie

1951. New Currency.

120	–	½ c. brown	10	15
121	23	1 c. black and red	10	30
122	–	2 c. brown and green	10	20
123	–	3 c. green and purple	15	70
124	–	4 c. orange and sepia	15	70
125	–	5 c. black and red	85	30
126	–	6 c. olive and brown	90	30
127	–	8 c. green and blue	60	60
128	–	12 c. black and green	45	1·25
129	–	14 c. blue and purple	95	1·25
130	–	24 c. purple and red	75	30
131	–	48 c. green and orange	2·50	6·50
132	–	60 c. red and black	2·50	5·00
133	–	$1.20 green and black	4·00	5·00
134	–	$2.40 orange and black	22·00	29·00

DESIGNS: ½ c. As Type **21**, but with portrait as Type **23**. HORIZ (as Type **23**): 2 c., 60 c. Carib baskets; 3 c., 48 c. Lime plantation; 4 c. Picking oranges; 5 c. Bananas; 6 c. Botanical Gardens; 8 c. Drying vanilla beans; 12 c., $1.20, Fresh Water Lake; 14 c. Layou River, 24 c. Boiling Lake. VERT: $2.40, Pickling oranges.

1951. New Constitution. Stamps of 1951 optd **NEW CONSTITUTION 1951.**

135		3 c. green and violet	15	70
136		5 c. black and red	15	70
137		8 c. green and blue	15	15
138		14 c. blue and violet	15	20

1953. Coronation. As T **13** of Aden.

139		2 c. black and green	20	10

1954. As Nos 120/34 but with portrait of Queen Elizabeth II.

140		½ c. brown	10	30
141		1 c. black and red	10	10
142		2 c. brown and green	55	90
143		3 c. green and purple	1·25	30
144		3 c. black and red	3·25	1·75
145		4 c. orange and brown	20	10
146		5 c. black and red	1·25	30
147		5 c. blue and brown	10·00	90
148		6 c. green and brown	40	10
149		8 c. green and blue	75	10
150		10 c. green and brown	5·00	1·75
151		12 c. black and green	50	10
152		14 c. blue and purple	30	10
153		24 c. purple and red	40	10
154		48 c. green and orange	1·25	6·00
155		48 c. brown and violet	1·25	80
156		60 c. red and black	1·00	1·50
157		$1.20 green and black	16·00	6·00
158		$2.40 orange and black	16·00	14·00

DESIGNS (New)—HORIZ: Nos. 144, 155, Mat making; No. 147, Canoe making; No. 150, Bananas.

1958. British Caribbean Federation. As T **25** of Antigua.

159		3 c. green	35	10
160		6 c. blue	50	90
161		12 c. red	70	10

1963.

162	40	1 c. green, blue and sepia	10	75
163	–	2 c. blue	30	10
164	–	3 c. brown and blue	90	90
165	–	4 c. green, sepia and violet	10	10
166	–	5 c. mauve	30	10
167	–	6 c. green, bistre and violet	10	10
168		8 c. green, sepia and black	10	10
169	–	10 c. sepia and pink	10	10
170	–	12 c. green, blue and sepia	45	10
171	–	14 c. multicoloured	70	10
204	–	15 c. yellow, green and brown	70	10
173	–	24 c. multicoloured	8·00	20
174	–	48 c. green, blue and black	75	40
175	–	60 c. orange, green and black	1·00	60
176	–	$1.20 multicoloured	6·50	80
177	–	$2.40 blue, turq & brn	3·25	2·00
178	–	$4.80 green, blue and brown	9·00	20·00

DESIGNS—VERT: 2 c., 5 c. Queen Elizabeth II (after Annigoni); 14 c. Traditional costume; 24 c. Imperial amazon; $2.40, Trafalgar Falls; $4.80, Coconut palm. HORIZ: 3 c. Sailing canoe; 4 c. Sulphur springs; 6 c. Road making; 8 c. Dug-out canoe; 10 c. Crapaud (frog); 12 c. Scott's Head; 15 c. Bananas; 48 c. Goodwill; 60 c. Cocoa tree; $1.20, Coat of Arms.

1963. Freedom from Hunger. As T **28** of Aden.

179		15 c. violet	15	10

1963. Centenary of Red Cross. As T **33** of Antigua.

180		5 c. red and black	15	30
181		15 c. red and blue	30	55

1964. 400th Birth Anniv of Shakespeare. As T **34** of Antigua.

182		15 c. purple	10	10

1965. Centenary of I.T.U. As T **36** of Antigua.

183		2 c. green and blue	10	10
184		48c. turquoise and grey	30	20

1965. I.C.Y. As T **37** of Antigua.

185		1 c. purple and turquoise	10	20
186		15 c. green and lavender	20	10

1966. Churchill Commemoration. As T **38** of Antigua.

187		1 c. blue	10	30
188		5 c. green	10	10
189		15 c. brown	20	10
190		24 c. violet	30	20

1966. Royal Visit. As T **39** of Antigua.

191		5 c. black and blue	1·00	20
192		15 c. black and mauve	1·50	30

1966. World Cup Football Championship. As T **40** of Antigua.

193		5 c. multicoloured	20	15
194		24 c. multicoloured	65	15

1966. Inauguration of W.H.O. Headquarters, Geneva. As T **41** of Antigua.

195		5 c. black, green and blue	10	15
196		24 c. black, purple and ochre	20	15

1966. 20th Anniv of U.N.E.S.C.O. As T **54/6** of Antigua.

197	5 c. red, yellow and orange	15	15
198	15 c. yellow, violet and olive	35	10
199	24 c. black, purple and orange	40	15

56 Children of Three Races

1967. National Day. Multicoloured.

205	5 c. Type **56**	10	10
206	10 c. The "Santa Maria" and motto	30	10
207	15 c. Hands holding motto ribbon	15	15
208	24 c. Belaire dancing	15	15

57 John F. Kennedy

1968. Human Rights Year. Multicoloured.

209	1 c. Type **57**	10	10
210	10 c. Cecil E. A. Rawle	10	10
211	12 c. Pope John XXIII	50	15
212	48 c. Florence Nightingale	35	20
213	60 c. Albert Schweitzer	35	20

1968. Associated Statehood. Nos. 162 etc, optd **ASSOCIATED STATEHOOD**.

214	1 c. green, blue and sepia	10	10
215	2 c. blue	10	10
216	3 c. brown and blue	10	10
217	4 c. green, sepia and violet	10	10
218	5 c. mauve	10	10
219	6 c. green, bistre and violet	10	10
220	8 c. green, sepia and black	10	10
221	10 c. sepia and pink	55	10
222	12 c. green, blue and brown	10	10
224	14 c. multicoloured	10	10
225	15 c. yellow, green and brown	10	10
226	24 c. multicoloured	3·50	10
227	48 c. green, blue and black	55	90
228	60 c. orange, green and black	90	70
229	$1.20 multicoloured	1·00	1·75
230	$2.40 blue, turquoise and brown	1·25	2·25
231	$4.80 green, blue and brown	1·25	4·50

1968. National Day. Nos. 162/4, 171 and 176 optd **NATIONAL DAY 3 NOVEMBER 1968**.

232	1 c. green, blue and sepia	10	10
233	2 c. blue	10	10
234	3 c. brown and blue	10	10
235	14 c. multicoloured	10	10
236	$1.20 multicoloured	55	40

60 Forward shooting at Goal

1968. Olympic Games, Mexico. Multicoloured.

237	1 c. Type **60**	10	10
238	1 c. Goalkeeper attempting to save ball	10	10
239	5 c. Swimmers preparing to dive	10	10
240	5 c. Swimmers diving	10	10
241	48 c. Javelin-throwing	15	15
242	48 c. Hurdling	15	15
243	60 c. Basketball	65	15
244	60 c. Basketball players	65	15

61 "The Small Cowper Madonna" (Raphael)

62 "Venus and Adonis" (Rubens)

1968. Christmas.

245	**61** 5 c. multicoloured	10	10

1969. 20th Anniv of World Health Organization.

246	**62** 5 c. multicoloured	20	10
247	– 15 c. multicoloured	30	10
248	– 24 c. multicoloured	30	10
249	– 50 c. multicoloured	50	40

DESIGNS: 15 c. "The Death of Socrates" (J.-L. David); 24 c. "Christ and the Pilgrims of Emmaus" (Velasquez); 50 c. "Pilate washing his Hands" (Rembrandt).

66 Picking Oranges

71 "Spinning" (J. Millet)

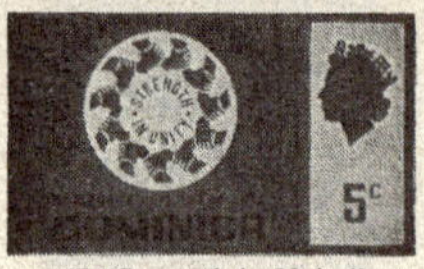

67 "Strength in Unity" Emblem and Fruit Trees

1969. Tourism. Multicoloured.

250	10 c. Type **66**	15	10
251	10 c. Woman, child and ocean scene	15	10
252	12 c. Fort Yeoung Hotel	30	10
253	12 c. Red-necked amazon	30	10
254	24 c. Calypso band	30	10
255	24 c. Women dancing	30	15
256	48 c. Underwater life	30	25
257	48 c. Skin-diver and turtle	30	25

1969. 1st Anniv of C.A.R.I.F.T.A. (Caribbean Free Trade Area). Multicoloured.

258	5 c. Type **67**	10	10
259	8 c. Hawker Siddeley H.S.748 aircraft, emblem and island	25	15
260	12 c. Chart of Caribbean Sea and emblem	25	20
261	24 c. Steamship unloading, tug and emblem	30	20

1969. 50th Anniv of International Labour Organization. Multicoloured.

262	15 c. Type **71**	10	10
263	30 c. "Threshing" (J. Millet)	15	15
264	38 c. "Flax-pulling" (J. Millet)	15	15

72 Mahatma Gandhi weaving and Clock Tower, Westminster

1969. Birth Cent of Mahatma Gandhi. Mult.

265	6 c. Type **72**	30	10
266	38 c. Gandhi, Nehru and Mausoleum	50	15
267	$1.20 Gandhi and Taj Mahal	1·00	75

All stamps are incorrectly inscribed "Ghandi".

75 "Saint Joseph"

1969. National Day. Multicoloured.

268	6 c. Type **75**	10	10
269	8 c. "Saint John"	10	10
270	12 c. "Saint Peter"	10	10
271	60 c. "Saint Paul"	30	50

79 Queen Elizabeth II

99 "Virgin and Child with St. John" (Perugino)

80 Purple-throated Carib and Flower

1969. Centres multicoloured; colours of "D" given.

272a	**79** ½ c. black and silver	30	70
273	**80** 1 c. black and yellow	30	1·50
274	– 2 c. black and yellow	15	10
275a	– 3 c. black and yellow	1·75	80
276a	– 4 c. black and yellow	1·75	70
277a	– 5 c. black and yellow	1·75	80
278a	– 6 c. black and brown	1·75	2·25
279	– 8 c. black and brown	20	10
280	– 10 c. black and yellow	20	10
281	– 12 c. black and yellow	20	10
282	– 15 c. black and blue	20	10
283	– 25 c. black and red	30	10
284a	– 30 c. black and olive	1·50	70
285	– 38 c. black and purple	8·00	1·75
286	– 50 c. black and brown	50	45
287	– 60 c. black and yellow	55	1·25
288	– $1.20 black and yellow	1·00	1·75
289	– $2.40 black and gold	1·00	3·50
290	– $4.80 black and gold	1·75	6·50

DESIGNS—HORIZ (As Type **80**): 2 c. Poinsettia; 3 c. Redneck pigeon; 4 c. Imperial amazon; 5 c. "Battus polydamas" (butterfly); 6 c. "Dryas julia" (butterfly); 8 c. Shipping bananas; 10 c. Portsmouth Harbour; 12 c. Copra processing plant; 15 c. Straw workers; 25 c. Timber plant; 30 c. Pumice mine; 38 c. Grammar school and playing fields; 50 c. Roseau Cathedral. (38 × 26½ mm): 60 c. Government Headquarters. (40 × 27 mm): $1.20, Melville Hall airport. (39½ × 26 mm): $2.40, Coat of arms. VERT: (26 × 39 mm): $4.80, As Type **79**, but larger.

1969. Christmas. Paintings. Multicoloured.

291	6 c. "Virgin and Child with St. John" (Lippi)	10	10
292	10 c. "Holy Family with Lamb" (Raphael)	10	10
293	15 c. Type **99**	10	10
294	$1.20 "Madonna of the Rose Hedge" (Botticelli)	35	40

101 Astronaut's First Step onto the Moon

1970. Moon Landing. Multicoloured.

296	½ c. Type **101**	10	10
297	5 c. Scientific experiment on the Moon and flag	15	10
298	8 c. Astronauts collecting rocks	15	10
299	30 c. Module over Moon	30	15
300	50 c. Moon plague	40	25
301	60 c. Astronauts	40	30

107 Giant Green Turtle

1970. Flora and Fauna. Multicoloured.

303	6 c. Type **107**	50	20
304	24 c. Atlantic flyingfish	60	45
305	38 c. Anthurium lily	70	65
306	60 c. Imperial and red-necked amazons	3·25	4·75

108 18th-Century National Costume

1970. National Day. Multicoloured.

308	5 c. Type **108**	10	10
309	8 c. Carib basketry	10	10
310	$1 Flag and chart of Dominica	30	40

109 Scrooge and Marley's Ghost

1970. Christmas and Death Centenary of Charles Dickens. Scenes from "A Christmas Carol". Multicoloured.

312	2 c. Type **109**	10	10
313	15 c. Fezziwig's Ball	20	10
314	24 c. Scrooge and his Nephew's Party	20	10
315	$1.20 Scrooge and the Ghost of Christmas Present	65	60

110 "The Doctor" (Sir Luke Fildes)

1970. Centenary of British Red Cross. Multicoloured.

317	8 c. Type **110**	10	10
318	10 c. Hands and Red Cross	10	10
319	15 c. Flag of Dominica and Red Cross emblem	15	10
320	50 c. "The Sick Child" (E. Munch)	50	35

111 Marigot School

1971. International Education Year. Multicoloured.

322	5 c. Type **111**	10	10
323	8 c. Goodwill Junior High School	10	10
324	14 c. University of West Indies (Jamaica)	10	10
325	$1 Trinity College, Cambridge	25	30

112 Waterfall

1971. Tourism. Multicoloured.

327	5 c. Type **112**	15	10
328	10 c. Boat-building	15	10
329	30 c. Sailing	25	10
330	50 c. Yacht and motor launch	40	30

113 U.N.I.C.E.F. Symbol in "D"

1971. 25th Anniv of U.N.I.C.E.F.

332	**113** 5 c. violet, black and gold	10	10
333	10 c. yellow, black and gold	10	10
334	38 c. green, black and gold	10	10
335	$1.20 orange, black and gold	30	45

114 German Boy Scout

1971. World Scout Jamboree, Asagiri, Japan. Various designs showing Boy Scouts from the nations listed. Multicoloured.

337	20 c. Type **114**	15	15
338	24 c. Great Britain	20	15
339	30 c. Japan	25	20
340	$1 Dominica	50	1·75

115 Groine at Portsmouth

1971. National Day. Multicoloured.

342	8 c. Type **115**	10	10
343	15 c. Carnival scene	10	10
344	20 c. Carifta Queen (vert)	10	10
345	50 c. Rock of Atkinson (vert)	20	25

116 Eight Reals Piece, 1761

1972. Coins.

347	**116** 10 c. black, silver and violet	10	10
348	– 30 c. black, silver and green	15	15
349	– 35 c. black, silver and blue	20	20
350	– 50 c. black, silver and red	40	1·40

DESIGNS—HORIZ: 30 c. Eleven and three bitt pieces, 1798. VERT: 35 c. Two reals and two bitt pieces, 1770; 50 c. Mocos, pieces-of-eight and eight reals-eleven bitts piece, 1798.

117 Common Opossum

1972. U.N. Conference on the Human Enviroment, Stockholm. Multicoloured.

352	½ c. Type **117**	10	10
353	35 c. Brazilian agouti (rodent)	40	15
354	60 c. Orchid	2·50	50
355	$1.20 Hibiscus	2·50	1·60

118 Sprinter

1972. Olympic Games, Munich. Multicoloured.

357	30 c. Type **118**	10	10
358	35 c. Hurdler	15	15
359	58 c. Hammer-thrower (vert)	20	20
360	72 c. Long-jumper (vert)	40	40

119 General Post Office

1972. National Day. Multicoloured.

362	10 c. Type **119**	10	10
363	20 c. Morne Diablotin	10	10
364	30 c. Rodney's Rock	15	15

1972. Royal Silver Wedding. As T **52** of Ascension, but with Bananas and Sisserou Parrot in background.

366	5 c. green	20	10
367	$1 green	60	40

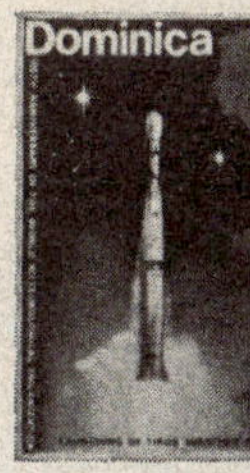

121 "The Adoration of the Shepherds" (Caravaggio)

122 Launching of Weather Satellite

1972. Christmas. Multicoloured.

368	8 c. Type **121**	10	10
369	14 c. "The Myosotis Virgin" (Rubens)	10	10
370	30 c. "Madonna and Child with St Francesca Romana" (Gentileschi)	15	10
371	$1 "Adoration of the Kings" (Mostaert)	50	90

1973. Centenary of I.M.O./W.H.O. Multicoloured.

373	½ c. Type **122**	10	10
374	1 c. Nimbus satellite	10	10
375	2 c. Radiosonde balloon	10	10
376	30 c. Radarscope (horiz)	15	15
377	35 c. Diagram of pressure zones (horiz)	20	20
378	50 c. Hurricane shown by satellite (horiz)	30	35
379	$1 Computer weather-map (horiz)	60	65

123 Going to Hospital

1973. 25th Anniv of W.H.O. Multicoloured.

381	½ c. Type **123**	10	10
382	1 c. Maternity care	10	10
383	2 c. Smallpox inoculation	10	10
384	30 c. Emergency service	30	15
385	35 c. Waiting for the doctor	35	15
386	50 c. Medical examination	45	25
387	$1 Travelling doctor	65	60

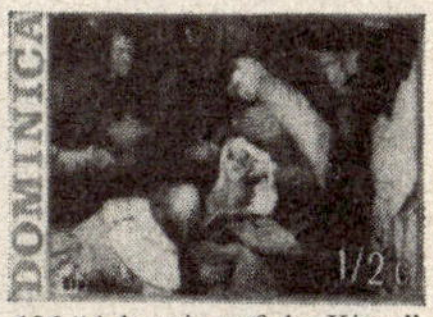

124 Cyrique Crab

126 "Adoration of the Kings" (Brueghel)

125 Princess Anne and Captain Mark Phillips

1973. Flora and Fauna. Multicoloured.

389	½ c. Type **124**	10	10
390	22 c. Blue land-crab	35	10
391	25 c. Bread fruit	35	15
392	$1.20 Sunflower	1·00	2·00

1973. Royal Wedding.

394	**125** 25 c. multicoloured	10	10
395	– $2 multicoloured	30	30

DESIGN: $2 As Type **125**, but with different frame.

1973. Christmas. Religious Paintings. Multicoloured.

397	½ c. Type **126**	10	10
398	1 c. "Adoration of the Magi" (Botticelli)	10	10
399	2 c. "Adoration of the Magi" (Durer)	10	10
400	12 c. "Mystic Nativity" (Botticelli)	20	10
401	22 c. "Adoration of the Magi" (Rubens)	25	10
402	35 c. "The Nativity" (Durer)	25	10
403	$1 "Adoration of the Shepherds" (Giorgione)	90	55

127 Carib Basket-weaving

1973. National Day. Multicoloured.

405	5 c. Type **127**	10	10
406	10 c. Staircase of the Snake	10	10
407	50 c. Miss Caribbean Queen	15	15
408	60 c. Miss Carifta Queen	15	15
409	$1 Dance group	25	30

Nos. 407/8 are vert.

128 University Centre, Dominica

1973. 25th Anniv of West Indies University. Multicoloured.

411	12 c. Type **128**	10	10
412	30 c. Graduation ceremony	10	10
413	$1 University coat of arms	25	35

129 Dominica 1d. Stamp of 1874 and Map

1974. Stamp Centenary. Multicoloured.

415	½ c. Type **129**	10	10
416	1 c. 6d. stamp of 1874 and posthorn	10	10
417	2 c. 1d. stamp of 1874 and arms	10	10
418	10 c. Type **129**	20	10
419	50 c. As 1 c.	60	30
420	$1.20 As 2 c.	75	70

130 Footballer and Flag of Brazil

1974. World Cup Football Championship, West Germany. Multicoloured.

422	½ c. Type **130**	10	10
423	1 c. West Germany	10	10
424	2 c. Italy	10	10
425	30 c. Scotland	50	10
426	40 c. Sweden	50	10
427	50 c. Netherlands	55	35
428	$1 Yugoslavia	90	90

131 Indian Hole

1974. National Day. Multicoloured.

430	10 c. Type **131**	10	10
431	40 c. Teachers' Training College	10	10
432	$1 Bay Oil distillery plant, Petite Savanne	50	45

132 Churchill with "Colonist"

1974. Birth Centenary of Sir Winston Churchill. Multicoloured.

434	½ c. Type **132**	10	10
435	1 c. Churchill and Eisenhower	10	10
436	2 c. Churchill and Roosevelt	10	10
437	20 c. Churchill and troops on assault-course	15	10
438	45 c. Painting at Marrakesh	25	10
439	$2 Giving the "V" sign	80	1·00

133 Mailboats "Orinoco" (1851) and "Geesthaven" (1974)

1974. Centenary of U.P.U. Multicoloured.

441	10 c. Type **133**	20	10
442	$2 De Havilland D.H.4 (1918) and Boeing 747-100 (1974)	80	1·00

134 "The Virgin and Child" (Tiso)

135 Queen Triggerfish

1974. Christmas. Multicoloured.

444	½ c. Type **134**	10	10
445	1 c. "Madonna and Child with Saints" (Costa)	10	10
446	2 c. "The Nativity" (school of Rimini, 14th-century)	10	10
447	10 c. "The Rest on the Flight into Egypt" (Romanelli)	20	10
448	25 c. "The Adoration of the Shepherds" (da Sermoneta)	35	10
449	45 c. "The Nativity" (Guido Reni)	45	10
450	$1 "The Adoration of the Magi" (Caselli)	65	40

1975. Fishes. Multicoloured.

452	½ c. Type **135**	10	10
453	1 c. Porkfish	10	10
454	2 c. Sailfish	10	10
455	3 c. Swordfish	10	10
456	20 c. Great barracuda	1·00	50
457	$2 Nassau grouper	4·25	2·75

136 "Myscelia antholia"

1975. Dominican Butterflies. Multicoloured.

459	½ c. Type **136**	10	40
460	1 c. "Lycorea ceres"	10	40
461	2 c. "Anaea marthesia" ("Siderone nemesis")	15	40
462	6 c. "Battus polydamas"	60	55
463	30 c. "Anartia lytrea"	1·75	70
464	40 c. "Morpho peleides"	2·00	75
465	$2 "Dryas julia"	3·75	7·50

137 "Yare" (cargo liner)

1975. "Ships tied to Dominica's History". Mult.

467	½ c. Type **137**	20	35
468	1 c. "Thames II" (liner), 1890	20	35
469	2 c. "Lady Nelson" (cargo liner)	20	35
470	20 c. "Lady Rodney" (cargo liner)	1·00	35
471	45 c. "Statesman" (freighter)	1·25	55
472	50 c. "Geestcape" (freighter)	1·25	80
473	$2 "Geeststar" (freighter)	3·25	4·50

138 "Women in Agriculture"

1975. International Women's Year. Multicoloured.

475	10 c. Type **138**	10	10
476	$2 "Women in Industry and Commerce"	40	60

139 Miss Caribbean Queen, 1975

140 "Virgin and Child" (Mantegna)

1975. National Day. Multicoloured.

477	5 c. Type **139**	10	10
478	10 c. Public library (horiz)	10	10
479	30 c. Citrus factory (horiz)	10	10
480	$1 National Day Trophy	25	50

1975. Christmas. "Virgin and Child" paintings by artists named. Multicoloured.

482	½ c. Type **140**	10	10
483	1 c. Fra Filippo Lippi	10	10
484	2 c. Bellini	10	10
485	10 c. Botticelli	15	10
486	25 c. Bellini	25	10
487	45 c. Correggio	30	10
488	$1 Durer	55	50

141 Hibiscus

1975. Multicoloured.

490	½ c. Type **141**	10	50
491	1 c. African tulip	15	50
492	2 c. Castor-oil tree	15	50
493	3 c. White cedar flower	15	50
494	4 c. Egg plant	15	50
495	5 c. Needlefish ("Gare")	20	50
496	6 c. Ochro	20	60
497	8 c. Zenaida dove	2·25	60
498	10 c. Screw pine	20	15
499	20 c. Mango longue	30	15

500	25 c. Crayfish	35	15
501	30 c. Common opossum	90	80
502	40 c. Bay leaf groves	90	80
503	50 c. Tomatoes	55	50
504	$1 Lime factory	75	65
505	$2 Rum distillery	1·75	3·50
506	$5 Bay Oil distillery	2·25	5·00
507	$10 Queen Elizabeth II (vert)	3·00	15·00

Nos. 502/7 are larger, 28 × 44 mm. ($10) or 44 × 28 (others).

142 American Infantry 143 Rowing

1976. Bicentenary of American Revolution. Mult.

508	½ c. Type **142**	10	10
509	1 c. British three-decker, 1782	10	10
510	2 c. George Washington	10	10
511	45 c. British sailors	55	10
512	75 c. British ensign	80	40
513	$2 Admiral Hood	1·25	1·25

1976. Olympic Games, Montreal. Multicoloured.

515	½ c. Type **143**	10	10
516	1 c. Shot putting	10	10
517	2 c. Swimming	10	10
518	40 c. Relay	15	10
519	45 c. Gymnastics	15	10
520	60 c. Sailing	20	20
521	$2 Archery	55	80

144 Ringed Kingfisher

1976. Wild Birds. Multicoloured.

523	½ c. Type **144**	10	50
524	1 c. Mourning dove	15	50
525	2 c. Green heron	15	50
526	15 c. Blue-winged hawk (vert)	1·25	45
527	30 c. Blue-headed hummingbird (vert)	1·75	80
528	45 c. Bananaquit (vert)	2·50	1·00
529	$2 Imperial amazon (vert)	9·00	14·00

1976. West Indian Victory in World Cricket Cup. As Nos. 559/60 of Barbados.

531	15 c. Map of the Caribbean	75	1·25
532	25 c. Prudential Cup	75	1·75

145 Viking Spacecraft System 146 "Virgin and Child with Saints Anthony of Padua and Roch" (Giorgione)

1976. Viking Space Mission. Multicoloured.

533	½ c. Type **145**	10	10
534	1 c. Landing pad (horiz)	10	10
535	2 c. Titan IIID and Centaur DII	10	10
536	3 c. Orbiter and lander capsule	10	10
537	45 c. Capsule, parachute unopened	30	15
538	75 c. Capsule, parachute opened	40	50
539	$1 Lander descending (horiz)	45	60
540	$2 Space vehicle on Mars (horiz)	60	1·60

1976. Christmas. "Virgin and Child" paintings by artists named. Multicoloured.

542	½ c. Type **146**	10	10
543	1 c. Bellini	10	10
544	2 c. Mantegna	10	10
545	6 c. Mantegna (different)	10	10
546	25 c. Memling	15	10
547	45 c. Correggio	20	10
548	$3 Raphael	1·00	1·00

147 Island Craft Co-operative

1976. National Day. Multicoloured.

550	10 c. Type **147**	10	10
551	50 c. Harvesting bananas	15	10
552	$1 Boxing plant	30	35

148 American Giant Sundial 150 Joseph Haydn

149 The Queen Crowned and Enthroned

1976. Shells. Multicoloured.

554	½ c. Type **148**	10	10
555	1 c. Flame helmet	10	10
556	2 c. Mouse cone	10	10
557	20 c. Caribbean vase	45	10
558	40 c. West Indian fighting conch	70	25
559	50 c. Short coral shell	70	25
560	$3 Apple murex	3·00	2·75

1977. Silver Jubilee. Multicoloured.

562	½ c. Type **149**	10	10
563	1 c. Imperial State Crown	10	10
564	45 c. The Queen and Princess Anne	15	10
565	$2 Coronation Ring	25	30
566	$2.50 Ampulla and Spoon	30	40

1977. 150th Death Anniv of Ludwig van Beethoven. Multicoloured.

568	½ c. Type **150**	10	10
569	1 c. Scene from "Fidelio"	10	10
570	2 c. Maria Casentini (dancer)	10	10
571	15 c. Beethoven and pastoral scene	25	10
572	30 c. "Wellington's Victory"	35	10
573	40 c. Henriette Sontag (singer)	35	10
574	$2 The young Beethoven	1·10	2·00

151 Hiking

1977. Caribbean Scout Jamboree, Jamaica. Multicoloured.

576	½ c. Type **151**	10	10
577	1 c. First-aid	10	10
578	2 c. Camping	10	10
579	45 c. Rock climbing	35	15
580	50 c. Canoeing	40	20
581	$3 Sailing	2·00	1·75

152 Holy Family

1977. Christmas. Multicoloured.

583	½ c. Type **152**	10	10
584	1 c. Angel and Shepherds	10	10
585	2 c. Holy Baptism	10	10
586	6 c. Flight into Egypt	15	10
587	15 c. Three Kings with gifts	15	10
588	45 c. Holy Family in the Temple	30	10
589	$3 Flight into Egypt (different)	1·25	1·10

1977. Royal Visit. Nos. 562/66 optd **ROYAL VISIT W.I. 1977.**

591	½ c. Type **149**	10	10
592	1 c. Imperial State Crown	10	10
593	45 c. The Queen and Princess Anne	15	10
594a	$2 Coronation Ring	30	30
595a	$2.50 Ampulla and Spoon	35	35

154 "Sousouelle Souris"

1978. "History of Carnival". Multicoloured.

597	½ c. Type **154**	10	10
598	1 c. Sensay costume	10	10
599	2 c. Street musicians	10	10
600	45 c. Douiette band	15	10
601	50 c. Pappy Show wedding	15	10
602	$2 Masquerade band	45	60

155 Colonel Charles Lindbergh and "Spirit of St. Louis"

1978. Aviation Anniversaries. Multicoloured.

604	6 c. Type **155**	20	10
605	10 c. "Spirit of St. Louis", New York, 20 May 1927	25	10
606	15 c. Lindbergh and map of Atlantic	35	10
607	20 c. Lindbergh reaches Paris, 21 May 1927	45	10
608	40 c. Airship LZ-1, Lake Constance, 1900	55	20
609	60 c. Count F. von Zeppelin and Airship LZ-2, 1906	65	30
610	$3 Airship "Graf Zeppelin", 1928	1·40	1·10

156 Queen receiving Homage 158 "Two Apostles"

157 Wright Flyer III

1978. 25th Anniv of Coronation. Multicoloured.

612	45 c. Type **156**	15	10
613	$2 Balcony scene	30	30
614	$2.50 Queen and Prince Philip	40	40

1978. 75th Anniv of First Powered Flight. Mult.

616	30 c. Type **157**	15	15
617	40 c. Wright Type A, 1908	20	20
618	60 c. Wright Flyer I	25	25
619	$2 Wright Flyer I (different)	85	85

1978. Christmas. Paintings by Rubens. Multicoloured.

621	20 c. Type **158**	10	10
622	45 c. "Descent from the Cross"	15	10
623	50 c. "St Ildefonso receiving the Chasuble"	15	10
624	$3 "Assumption of the Virgin"	35	80

159 Map showing Parishes 161 Sir Rowland Hill

1978. Independence. Multicoloured.

626	10 c. Type **159**	40	15
627	25 c. "Sabinea carinalis" (national flower)	45	15
628	45 c. New National flag	50	15
629	50 c. Coat of arms	50	30
630	$2 Prime Minister Patrick John	60	1·50

1978. Nos. 490/507 optd **INDEPENDENCE 3rd NOVEMBER 1978.**

632	½ c. Type **57**	40	10
633	1 c. African tulip	45	10
634	2 c. Castor-oil tree	45	10
635	3 c. White cedar flower	50	15
636	4 c. Egg plant	50	15
637	5 c. Needlefish ("Gare")	50	15
638	6 c. Ochro	50	15
639	8 c. Zenaida dove	2·25	20
640	10 c. Screw pine	50	15
641	20 c. Mango longue	60	15
642	25 c. Crayfish	70	20
643	30 c. Common opossum	70	20
644	40 c. Bay leaf groves	70	25
645	50 c. Tomatoes	80	30
646	$1 Lime factory	80	65
647	$2 Rum distillery	1·00	1·00
648	$5 Bay Oil distillery	1·50	2·25
649	$10 Queen Elizabeth II	2·00	4·50

1979. Death Centenary of Sir Rowland Hill. Multicoloured.

650	25 c. Type **161**	10	10
651	45 c. G.B. 1840 Twopenny Blue	15	10
652	50 c. Dominica 1874 1d. stamp	15	10
653	$2 Maltese Cross handstamps	35	65

162 Children and Canoe

1979. International Year of the Child. Multicoloured.

655	30 c. Type **162**	25	15
656	40 c. Children with bananas	25	15
657	50 c. Children playing cricket	1·25	80
658	$3 Child feeding rabbits	1·75	2·00

163 Nassau Grouper

1979. Marine Wildlife. Multicoloured.

660	10 c. Type **163**	40	15
661	30 c. Striped dolphin	70	35
662	50 c. White-tailed tropic-bird	2·25	65
663	60 c. Brown pelican	2·25	1·50
664	$1 Long-finned pilot whale	2·50	1·75
665	$2 Brown booby	3·00	4·50

No. 661 is inscribed "SPOTTED DOLPHIN" in error.

164 H.M.S. "Endeavour"

1979. Death Bicent of Captain Cook. Mult.

667	10 c. Type **164**	65	30
668	50 c. H.M.S. "Resolution" (Second Voyage)	1·10	1·00
669	60 c. H.M.S. "Discovery" (Third Voyage)	1·25	1·50
670	$2 Detail of Cook's chart of New Zealand, 1770	1·60	2·50

165 Cooking at Campfire

1979. 50th Anniv of Girl Guide Movement in Dominica. Multicoloured.

672	10 c. Type **165**	20	10
673	20 c. Pitching emergency rain tent	25	10
674	50 c. Raising Dominican flag	35	10
675	$2.50 Singing and dancing to accordion	90	80

166 Colvillea 169 Mickey Mouse and Octopus playing Xylophone

167 Cathedral of the Assumption, Roseau

1979. Flowering Trees. Multicoloured.
677 20 c. Type **166** 15 10
678 40 c. "Lignum vitae" 20 15
679 60 c. Dwarf poinciana 30 25
680 $2 Fern tree 70 90

1979. Christmas. Cathedrals. Multicoloured.
682 6 c. Type **167** 10 10
683 45 c. St. Paul's, London (vert) . . 15 10
684 60 c. St. Peter's, Rome 15 10
685 $3 Notre Dame, Paris (vert) . . 55 60

1979. Hurricane Relief. Nos. 495, 502 and 506/7 optd **HURRICANE RELIEF**.
687 5 c. Gare 10 10
688 40 c. Bay leaf groves 10 10
689 $5 Bay Oil distillery . . . . 1·00 1·25
690 $10 Queen Elizabeth II . . . . 1·25 1·75

1979. International Year of the Child. Walt Disney Characters. Multicoloured.
691 $\frac{1}{2}$ c. Type **169** 10 10
692 1 c. Goofy playing guitar on rocking-horse 10 10
693 2 c. Mickey Mouse playing violin and Goofy on bagpipes . . 10 10
694 3 c. Donald Duck playing drum with a pneumatic drill . . . 10 10
695 4 c. Minnie Mouse playing saxophone 10 10
696 5 c. Goofy one-man band . . . 10 10
697 10 c. Horace Horsecollar blowing Dale from french horn . . . 10 10
698 $2 Huey, Dewey and Louie playing bass . . . . 2·00 2·00
699 $2.50 Donald Duck at piano and Huey playing trumpet . . . 2·00 2·25

170 Hospital Ward

1980. 75th Anniv of Rotary International. Mult.
701 10 c. Type **170** 10 10
702 20 c. Electro-cardiogram 15 10
703 40 c. Mental hospital site . . . 20 15
704 $2.50 Paul Harris (founder) . . 55 90

1980. "London 1980" International Stamp Exhibition. Optd **LONDON 1980**.
706 **161** 25 c. multicoloured . . . 25 10
707 – 45 c. multicoloured . . . 30 15
708 – 50 c. brown, blue and red . . 30 15
709 – $2 brown, red and yellow . . 80 60

171 Shot Putting

1980. Olympic Games, Moscow. Multicoloured.
710 30 c. Type **171** 15 10
711 40 c. Basketball 60 15
712 60 c. Swimming 35 20
713 $2 Gymnastics 60 65

172 "Supper at Emmaus" (Caravaggio)

1980. Famous Paintings. Multicoloured.
715 20 c. Type **172** 20 10
716 25 c. "Portrait of Charles I Hunting" (Van Dyck) (vert) . . 20 10
717 30 c. "The Maids of Honour" (Velasquez) (vert) 25 10
718 45 c. "The Rape of the Sabine Women" (Poussin) 25 10
719 $1 "Embarkation for Cythera" (Watteau) 50 35
720 $5 "Girl before a Mirror" (Picasso) (vert) . . . . . . 1·40 1·50

173 Scene from "Peter Pan"

1980. Christmas. Scenes from "Peter Pan". Multicoloured.
722 $\frac{1}{2}$ c. Type **173** (Tinker Bell) . . . 10 10
723 1 c. Wendy sewing back Peter's shadow 10 10
724 2 c. Peter introduces the mermaids 10 10
725 3 c. Wendy and Peter with lost boys 10 10
726 4 c. Captain Hook, Pirate Smee and Tiger Lily 10 10
727 5 c. Peter with Tiger Lily and her father 10 10
728 10 c. Captain Hook captures Peter and Wendy 10 10
729 $2 Peter fights Captain Hook . 2·25 1·50
730 $2.50 Captain Hook in crocodile's jaws . . . . . . 2·25 1·75

174 Queen Elizabeth the Queen Mother in Doorway

1980. 80th Birthday of the Queen Mother.
732a **174** 40 c. multicoloured . . 15 15
733a $2.50 multicoloured . . 45 60

175 Douglas Bay

1981 "Dominica Safari". Multicoloured.
735 20 c. Type **175** 10 10
736 30 c. Valley of Desolation . . . 10 10
737 40 c. Emerald Pool (vert) . . . 10 10
738 $3 Indian River (vert) . . . . 75 1·10

1981. Walt Disney's Cartoon Character, Pluto. As T **169**. Multicoloured.
740 $2 Pluto and Fifi . . . . . . 1·25 1·50

176 Forest Thrush

1981. Birds. Multicoloured.
742 20 c. Type **176** 55 30
743 30 c. Wied's crested flycatcher . 65 35
744 40 c. Blue-hooded euphonia . . 75 45
745 $5 Lesser Antillean pewee . . 3·50 4·75

177 Windsor Castle 178 Lady Diana Spencer

1981. Royal Wedding. Multicoloured.
747 40 c. Prince Charles and Lady Diana Spencer 10 10
748 60 c. Type **177** 15 15
749a $4 Prince Charles flying helicopter 40 65

1981. Royal Wedding. Multicoloured.
751 25 c. Type **178** 20 35
752 $2 Prince Charles . . . . . . 70 1·00
753 $5 Prince Charles and Lady Diana Spencer . . . . . . 1·75 2·50

1981. Christmas. Scenes from Walt Disney's cartoon film "Santa's Workshop". As T **169**.
754 $\frac{1}{2}$ c. multicoloured 10 10
755 1 c. multicoloured 10 10
756 2 c. multicoloured 10 10
757 3 c. multicoloured 10 10
758 4 c. multicoloured 15 10
759 5 c. multicoloured 15 10
760 10 c. multicoloured 20 10
761 45 c. multicoloured . . . . . 1·50 30
762 $5 multicoloured . . . . . 4·25 4·50

179 Ixora 180 Curb Slope for Wheelchairs

1981. Plant Life. Multicoloured.
764A 1 c. Type **179** 10 50
765A 2 c. Flamboyant 10 50
766A 4 c. Poinsettia 15 40
767A 5 c. Bois caribe (national flower of Dominica) . . . 15 20
768A 8 c. Annatto or roucou . . . 20 20
769A 10 c. Passion fruit 30 10
770A 15 c. Breadfruit or yampain . 55 15
771A 20 c. Allamanda or buttercup . 40 15
772A 25 c. Cashew nut 40 15
773A 35 c. Soursop or couassol . . 45 30
774A 40 c. Bougainvillea 45 30
775A 45 c. Anthurium 50 35
776A 60 c. Cacao or cocoa . . . . 1·25 70
777A 90 c. Pawpaw tree or papay . . 70 1·00
778A $1 Coconut palm . . . . . 1·50 1·00
779A $2 Coffee tree or cafe . . . 1·00 2·75
780B $5 Heliconia or lobster claw . 3·25 5·50
781B $10 Banana fig . . . . . . 5·00 11·00
Nos. 769, 770, 776, 778, 780 and 781 come with or without imprint date.

1981. International Year for Disabled People. Multicoloured.
782 45 c. Type **180** 55 25
783 60 c. Bus with invalid step . . 60 35
784 75 c. Motor car controls adapted for handicapped 70 40
785 $4 Bus with wheelchair ramp . 2·00 2·50

181 "Olga Picasso in an Armchair" 182 "Gone Fishing"

1981. Birth Centenary of Picasso. Multicoloured.
787 45 c. Type **181** 65 25
788 60 c. "Bathers" 75 30
789 75 c. "Woman in Spanish Costume" 80 60
790 $4 "Detail of Dog and Cock" . 1·75 3·00

1982. World Cup Football Championship, Spain. Walt Disney Cartoon Characters. As T **169**. Multicoloured.
792 $\frac{1}{2}$ c. Goofy chasing ball with butterfly net 10 10
793 1 c. Donald Duck with ball in beak 10 10
794 2 c. Goofy as goalkeeper . . . 10 10
795 3 c. Goofy looking for ball . . 10 10
796 4 c. Goofy as park attendant puncturing ball with litter spike 10 10
797 5 c. Pete and Donald Duck playing 10 10
798 10 c. Donald Duck after kicking rock instead of ball . . . 15 10
799 60 c. Donald Duck feeling effects of a hard game and Daisy Duck dusting ball . . . . 1·50 1·25
800 $5 Goofy hiding ball under his jersey from Mickey Mouse . 5·50 6·50

1982. Norman Rockwell (painter) Commemoration. Multicoloured.
802 10 c. Type **182** 10 10
803 25 c. "Breakfast" 15 10
804 45 c. "The Marbles Champ" . . 30 30
805 $1 "Speeding Along" 55 55
No. 802 is inscribed "Golden Days" and No. 803 "The Morning News".

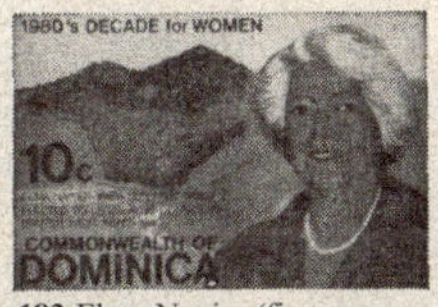
183 Elma Napier (first woman elected to B.W.I. Legislative Council)

1982. Decade for Women. Multicoloured.
806 10 c. Type **183** 10 10
807 45 c. Margaret Mead (anthropologist) 30 30
808 $1 Mabel (Cissy) Caudeiron (folk song composer and historian) 55 55
809 $4 Eleanor Roosevelt . . . . . 2·25 2·25

184 George Washington and Independence Hall, Philadelphia

1982. 250th Birth Anniv of George Washington and Birth Centenary of Franklin D. Roosevelt. Multicoloured.
811 45 c. Type **184** 40 25
812 60 c. Franklin D. Roosevelt and Capitol, Washington D.C. . . 45 35
813 90 c. Washington at Yorktown (detail "The Surrender of Cornwallis" by Trumbull) . . 60 55
814 $2 Construction of dam (from W. Groppers' mural commemorating Roosevelt's) "New Deal" . . . . 1·00 1·60

185 "Anaea dominicana" 186 Prince and Princess of Wales

1982. Butterflies. Multicoloured.
816 15 c. Type **185** . . . . 1·50 35
817 45 c. "Heliconius charithonia" . 2·50 65
818 60 c. "Hypolimnas misippus" . . 2·75 1·75
819 $3 "Biblis hyperia" . . . . . 5·50 6·00

1982. 21st Birthday of Princess of Wales. Multicoloured.
821 45 c. Buckingham Palace . . . 20 10
822 $2 Type **186** 50 70
823 $4 Princess of Wales . . . . 80 1·25

187 Scouts around Campfire

1982. 75th Anniv of Boy Scouts Movement. Mult.
825 45 c. Type **187** . . . . 1·25 50
826 60 c. Temperature study, Valley of Desolation . . . . . . 1·75 1·25
827 75 c. Learning about native birds 2·25 1·50
828 $3 Canoe trip along Indian River 4·25 5·50

1982. Birth of Prince William of Wales. Nos. 821/3 optd **ROYAL BABY 21.6.82**.
830 45 c. Buckingham Palace . . . 30 30
831 $2 Type **186** . . . . 80 1·10
832 $4 Princess of Wales . . . . 1·40 1·90

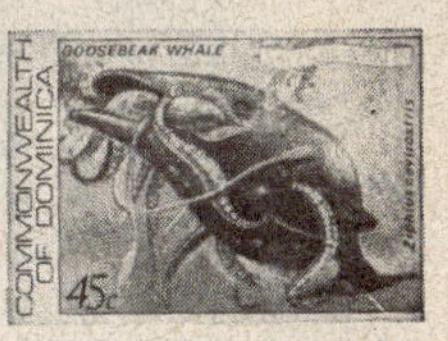
188 "Holy Family of Francis I" 189 Cuvier's Beaked Whale

1982. Christmas. Raphael Paintings. Multicoloured.
834 25 c. Type **188** 15 10
835 30 c. "Holy Family of the Pearl" 15 15
836 90 c. "Canigiani Holy Family" . 45 55
837 $4 "Holy Family of the Oak Tree" . . . . 1·50 1·50

1983. Save the Whales. Multicoloured.
839 45 c. Type **189** . . . . 2·00 65
840 60 c. Humpback whale . . . . 2·25 1·75
841 75 c. Black right whale . . . . 2·25 2·25
842 $3 Melon-headed whale . . . 4·50 6·50

190 Banana Export

1983. Commonwealth Day. Multicoloured.
844 25 c. Type **190** 15 15
845 30 c. Road building 15 20
846 90 c. Community nursing . . . 40 45
847 $3 Tourism–handicrafts . . . 1·00 1·50

191 Map and Satellite Picture of Hurricane

1983. World Communications Year. Multicoloured.
848 45 c. Type **191** 20 25
849 60 c. Aircraft-to-ship transmission 30 35
850 90 c. Satellite communications 40 45
851 $2 Shortwave radio 95 1·00

192 Short-Mayo Composite

1983. Bicentenary of Manned Flight. Multicoloured.
853 45 c. Type **192** 50 30
854 60 c. Macchi M.39 Schneider Trophy seaplane 75 85
855 90 c. Fairey Swordfish torpedo bomber 1·10 1·40
856 $4 Airship LZ-3 3·25 4·75

193 Duesenberg "SJ", 1935

1983. Classic Motor Cars. Multicoloured.
858 10 c. Type **193** 30 15
859 45 c. Studebaker "Avanti", 1962 50 25
860 60 c. Cord "812" 60 35
861 75 c. MG "TC", 1945 65 50
862 90 c. Camaro "350 SS", 1967 75 60
863 $3 Porsch "356", 1948 1·50 1·60

194 "Charity"

1983. Christmas. 500th Birth Anniv of Raphael. Multicoloured.
865 45 c. Type **194** 40 30
866 60 c. "Hope" 45 50
867 90 c. "Faith" 60 60
868 $4 "The Cardinal Virtues" 1·50 3·00

195 Plumbeous Warbler

1984. Birds. Multicoloured.
870 5 c. Type **195** 1·60 90
871 45 c. Imperial amazon 3·50 75
872 60 c. Blue-headed hummingbird 3·75 3·00
873 90 c. Red-necked amazon 5·00 5·50

196 Donald Duck **197** Gymnastics

1984. Easter. Multicoloured.
875 ½ c. Type **196** 10 10
876 1 c. Mickey Mouse 10 10
877 2 c. Tortoise and Hare 10 10
878 3 c. Brer Rabbit and Brer Bear 10 10
879 4 c. Donald Duck (different) 10 10
880 5 c. White Rabbit 10 10
881 10 c. Thumper 10 10
882 $2 Pluto 3·25 2·75
883 $4 Pluto (different) 4·50 4·00

1984. Olympic Games, Los Angeles. Multicoloured.
885 30 c. Type **197** 20 25
886 45 c. Javelin-throwing 30 35
887 60 c. High diving 40 45
888 $4 Fencing 2·00 2·50

198 "Atlantic Star"

1984. Shipping. Multicoloured.
890 45 c. Type **198** 1·75 75
891 60 c. "Atlantic" (liner) 2·00 1·75
892 90 c. Carib fishing boat 2·50 2·50
893 $4 "Norway" (liner) 6·00 8·00

1984. Universal Postal Union Congress, Hamburg. Nos. 769 and 780 optd **19th UPU CONGRESS HAMBURG**.
895 10 c. Passion fruit 10 10
896 $5 Heliconia or lobster claw 2·75 3·75

200 "Guzmania lingulata" **201** "The Virgin and Child with Young St. John" (Correggio)

1984. "Ausipex" International Stamp Exhibition, Melbourne. Bromeliads. Multicoloured.
897 45 c. Type **200** 30 35
898 60 c. "Pitcairnia angustifolia" 40 55
899 75 c. "Tillandsia fasciculata" 50 75
900 $3 "Aechmea smithiorum" 2·00 3·25

1984. 450th Death Anniv of Correggio (painter). Multicoloured.
902 25 c. Type **201** 45 20
903 60 c. "Christ bids Farewell to the Virgin Mary" 70 40
904 90 c. "Do not Touch Me" 90 80
905 $4 "The Mystical Marriage of St Catherine" 2·00 3·25

202 "Before the Start" (Edgar Degas)

1984. 150th Birth Anniv of Edgar Degas (painter). Multicoloured.
907 30 c. Type **202** 45 25
908 45 c. "Race on the Racecourse" 60 35
909 $1 "Jockeys at the Flagpole" 1·10 1·10
910 $3 "Racehorses at Longchamp" 2·50 3·50

203 Tabby

1984. Cats. Multicoloured.
912 10 c. Type **203** 20 15
913 15 c. Calico shorthair 25 15
914 20 c. Siamese 35 15
915 25 c. Manx 40 20
916 45 c. Abyssinian 65 30
917 60 c. Tortoise-shell longhair 80 65
918 $1 Cornish rex 1·40 1·00
919 $2 Persian 2·00 3·00
920 $3 Himalayan 2·75 4·00
921 $5 Burmese 3·75 7·00

204 Hawker Siddeley H.S.748 **205** Donald Duck, Mickey Mouse and Goofy with Father Christmas

1984. 40th Anniv of International Civil Aviation Organisation. Multicoloured.
923 30 c. Type **204** 1·25 35
924 60 c. De Havilland Twin Otter 100 2·00 80
925 $1 Britten Norman Islander 2·25 1·40
926 $3 De Havilland Twin Otter 100 (different) 4·00 4·50

1984. Christmas. Walt Disney Cartoon Characters. Multicoloured.
928 45 c. Type **205** 1·25 30
929 60 c. Donald Duck as Father Christmas with toy train 1·50 70
930 90 c. Donald Duck as Father Christmas in sleigh 2·00 1·75
931 $2 Donald Duck and nephews in sledge 3·25 3·75
932 $4 Donald Duck in snow with Christmas tree 4·25 5·50

206 Mrs. M. Bascom presenting Trefoil to Chief Guide Lady Baden-Powell

1985. 75th Anniv of Girl Guide Movement. Multicoloured.
934 35 c. Type **206** 60 30
935 45 c. Lady Baden-Powell inspecting Dominican brownies 80 35
936 60 c. Lady Baden-Powell with Mrs. M. Bascom and Mrs. A. Robinson (guide leaders) 1·00 65
937 $3 Lord and Lady Baden-Powell (vert) 2·50 3·50

1985. Birth Bicentenary of John J Audubon (ornithologist) (1st issue). As T **198** of Antigua. Multicoloured.
939 45 c. Clapper rail 1·10 30
940 $1 Black and white warbler (vert) 2·00 1·25
941 $2 Broad-winged hawk (vert) 2·75 2·75
942 $3 Ring-necked duck 3·50 3·25
See also Nos. 1013/16.

207 Student with Computer **208** The Queen Mother visiting Sadlers Wells Opera

1985. Duke of Edinburgh's Award Scheme. Multicoloured.
944 45 c. Type **207** 35 30
945 60 c. Assisting doctor in hospital 75 40
946 90 c. Two youths hiking 90 80
947 $4 Family jogging 2·75 3·75

1985. Life and Times of Queen Elizabeth the Queen Mother. Multicoloured.
949 60 c. Type **208** 75 50
950 $1 Fishing in Scotland 80 60
951 $3 On her 84th birthday 1·90 2·25

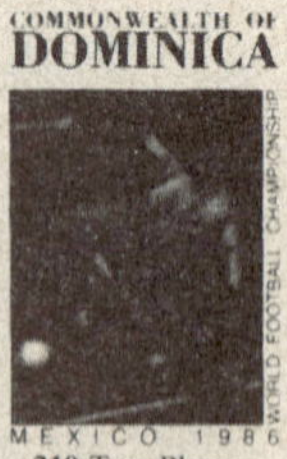

209 Cricket Match ("Sports") **210** Two Players competing for Ball

1985. International Youth Year. Multicoloured.
953 45 c. Type **209** 3·50 1·50
954 60 c. Bird-watching ("Environmental Study") 3·75 2·25
955 $1 Stamp collecting ("Education") 4·00 3·25
956 $3 Boating ("Leisure") 5·50 7·50

1985. 300th Birth Anniv of Johann Sebastian Bach (composer). As T **206** of Antigua. Multicoloured.
958 45 c. Cornet 1·50 40
959 60 c. Coiled trumpet 1·75 60
960 $1 Piccolo 2·25 1·00
961 $3 Violoncello piccolo 4·00 3·50

1985. Royal Visit. As T **207** of Antigua. Mult.
963 60 c. Flags of Great Britain and Dominica 1·00 70
964 $1 Queen Elizabeth II (vert) 1·25 1·75
965 $4 Royal Yacht "Britannia" 2·75 5·50

1985. 150th Birth Anniv of Mark Twain (author). As T **118** of Anguilla showing Walt Disney cartoon characters in scenes from "Tom Sawyer". Multicoloured.
967 20 c. "The glorius white-washer" 65 30
968 60 c. "Aunt Polly's home dentistry" 1·25 75
969 $1 "Aunt Polly's pain killer" 1·75 1·25
970 $1.50, Mickey Mouse balancing on fence 2·25 3·00
971 $2 "Lost in the cave with Becky" 2·75 3·50

1985. Birth Bicentenaries of Grimm Brothers (folklorists). Designs as T **119** of Anguilla showing Walt Disney cartoon characters in scenes from "Little Red Cap". Multicoloured.
973 10 c. Little Red Cap (Daisy Duck) meeting the Wolf 30 20
974 45 c. The Wolf at the door 85 30
975 90 c. The Wolf in Grandmother's bed 1·75 1·75
976 $1 The Wolf lunging at Little Red Cap 2·00 1·75
977 $3 The Woodsman (Donald Duck) chasing the Wolf 3·75 5·00

1985. 40th Anniv of United Nations Organization. Designs as T **208** of Antigua showing United Nations (New York) stamps. Multicoloured.
979 45 c. Lord Baden-Powell and 1984 International Youth Year 35 c. 70 50
980 $2 Maimonides (physician) and 1966 W.H.O. Building 11 c. 3·00 3·25
981 $3 Sir Rowland Hill (postal reformer) and 1976 25th anniv of U.N. Postal Administration 13 c. 3·00 3·50

1986. World Cup Football Championship, Mexico. Multicoloured.
983 45 c. Type **210** 1·75 40
984 60 c. Player heading ball 2·00 1·50
985 $1 Two players competing for ball (different) 2·25 1·75
986 $3 Player with ball 4·50 6·00

211 Police in Rowing Boat pursuing River Pirates, 1890

1986. Centenary of Statue of Liberty. Multicoloured.
988 15 c. Type **211** 1·50 65
989 25 c. Police patrol launch, 1986 2·00 85
990 45 c. Hoboken Ferry Terminal c. 1890 2·00 85
991 $4 Holland Tunnel entrance and staff, 1986 4·50 6·00

1986. Appearance of Halley's Comet (1st issue). As T **123** of Anguilla. Multicoloured.
993 5 c. Nasir al Din al Tusi (Persian astronomer) and Jantal Mantar Observatory, Delhi 15 15
994 10 c. Bell XS-1 Rocket Plane breaking sound barrier for first time, 1947 20 15
995 45 c. Halley's Comet of 1531 (from "Astronomicum Caesareum", 1540) 55 30
996 $4 Mark Twain and quotation, 1910 2·75 3·75
See also Nos. 1032/5.

1986. 60th Birthday of Queen Elizabeth II. As T **125** of Anguilla. Multicoloured.
998 2 c. Wedding photograph, 1947 10 15
999 $1 Queen meeting Pope John Paul II, 1982 70 80
1000 $4 Queen on Royal Visit, 1971 2·00 3·00

212 Mickey Mouse and Pluto mounting Stamps in Album

1986. "Ameripex" International Stamp Exhibition, Chicago. Showing Walt Disney cartoon characters. Multicoloured.
1002 25 c. Type **212** 60 40
1003 45 c. Donald Duck examining stamp under magnifying glass 80 65
1004 60 c. Chip n' Dale soaking and drying stamps 1·10 1·50
1005 $4 Donald Duck as scoutmaster awarding merit badges to Nephews 3·50 6·00

213 William I **214** "Virgin at Prayer"

1986. 500th Anniv (1985) of Succession of House of Tudor to English Throne. Multicoloured.

1007	10 c. Type **213**	40	40
1008	40 c. Richard II	80	80
1009	50 c. Henry VIII	90	90
1010	$1 Charles II	1·75	1·75
1011	$2 Queen Anne	2·75	3·00
1012	$4 Queen Victoria	3·75	4·50

1986. Birth Bicentenary (1985) of John J. Audubon (ornithologist) (2nd issue). As T **198** of Antigua showing original paintings. Multicoloured.

1013	25 c. Black-throated diver	1·50	50
1014	60 c. Great blue heron (vert)	2·00	1·50
1015	90 c. Yellow-crowned night heron (vert)	2·00	2·25
1016	$4 Common shoveler	4·50	6·50

1986. Royal Wedding. As T **213** of Antigua. Multicoloured.

1018	45 c. Prince Andrew and Miss Sarah Ferguson	35	30
1019	50 c. Prince Andrew	45	45
1020	$4 Prince Andrew climbing aboard aircraft	2·00	3·00

1986. World Cup Football Championship Winners, Mexico. Nos. 983/6 optd **WINNERS Argentina 3 W. Germany 2.**

1022	45 c. Type **210**	1·50	55
1023	60 c. Player heading ball	1·75	1·50
1024	$1 Two players competing for ball	2·25	2·50
1025	$3 Player with ball	5·00	7·00

1986. Christmas. Paintings by Durer. Multicoloured.

1027	45 c. Type **214**	1·00	35
1028	60 c. "Madonna and Child"	1·50	1·25
1029	$1 "Madonna of the Pear"	2·00	2·25
1030	$3 "Madonna and Child with St. Anne"	5·50	8·50

1986. Appearance of Halley's Comet (2nd issue). Nos. 993/6 optd as T **218** of Antigua.

1032	5 c. Nasir al Din al Tusi (Persian astronomer) and Jantal Mantar Observatory, Delhi	15	15
1033	10 c. Bell XS-1 Rocket Plane breaking sound barrier for first time, 1947	20	15
1034	45 c. Halley's Comet of 1531 (from "Astronomicum Caesareum", 1540)	55	30
1035	$4 Mark Twain and quotation, 1910	2·75	3·50

215 Broad-winged Hawk

216 Poulsen's Triton

1987. Birds of Dominica. Multicoloured.

1037	1 c. Type **215**	20	40
1038	2 c. Ruddy quail dove	20	40
1039	5 c. Red-necked pigeon	30	40
1040	10 c. Green heron	30	15
1041	15 c. Moorhen	40	20
1042	20 c. Ringed kingfisher	40	20
1043	25 c. Brown pelican	40	20
1044	35 c. White-tailed tropic bird	40	30
1045	45 c. Red-legged thrush	50	30
1046	60 c. Purple-throated carib	65	45
1047	90 c. Magnificent frigate bird	70	70
1048	$1 Brown trembler	80	80
1049	$2 Black-capped petrel	1·25	4·00
1050	$5 Brown owl	3·00	5·00
1051	$10 Imperial amazon	5·00	9·50

1987. America's Cup Yachting Championships. As T **222** of Antigua. Multicoloured.

1052	45 c. "Reliance", 1903	50	30
1053	60 c. "Freedom", 1980	60	55
1054	$1 "Mischief", 1881	80	90
1055	$3 "Australia", 1977	1·75	3·00

1987. Birth Centenary of Marc Chagall (artist). As T **225** of Antigua. Multicoloured.

1057	25 c. "Artist and His Model"	40	15
1058	35 c. "Midsummer Night's Dream"	40	25
1059	45 c. "Joseph the Shepherd"	50	25
1060	60 c. "The Cellist"	70	50
1061	90 c. "Woman with Pigs"	1·00	1·00
1062	$1 "The Blue Circus"	1·00	1·00
1063	$3 "For Vava"	2·25	3·00
1064	$4 "The Rider"	2·50	3·00

1987. Sea Shells.

1066	**216**	35 c. multicoloured	20	20
1067	–	45 c. violet, black and red	25	25
1068	–	60 c. multicoloured	30	40
1069	–	$5 multicoloured	2·40	4·00

DESIGNS: 45 c. Elongate janthina; 60 c. Banded tulip; $5 Deltoid rock shell.

No. 1066 is inscribed "TIRITON" in error.

217 "Cantharellus cinnabarinus"

1987. "Capex '87" International Stamp Exhibition, Toronto. Mushrooms of Dominica. Multicoloured.

1071	45 c. Type **217**	1·50	50
1072	60 c. "Boletellus cubensis"	2·00	1·25
1073	$2 "Eccilia cystiophorus"	4·25	4·50
1074	$3 "Xerocomus guadelupae"	4·50	5·00

218 Discovery of Dominica, 1493

1987. 500th Anniv (1992) of Discovery of America by Columbus (1st issue). Multicoloured.

1076	10 c. Type **218**	40	25
1077	15 c. Caribs greeting Columbus's fleet	50	30
1078	45 c. Claiming the New World for Spain	65	35
1079	60 c. Wreck of "Santa Maria"	80	60
1080	90 c. Fleet leaving Spain	1·00	1·00
1081	$1 Sighting the New World	1·10	1·25
1082	$3 Trading with Indians	2·25	3·00
1083	$5 Building settlement	3·25	4·00

See also Nos. 1221/5, 1355/62, 1406/13, 1547/53 and 1612/13.

1987. Milestone of Transportation. As T **226** of Antigua. Multicoloured.

1085	10 c. H.M.S. "Warrior" (first ironclad warship, 1860)	50	50
1086	15 c. "MAGLEV-MLU 001" (fastest train), 1979	60	60
1087	25 c. "Flying Cloud" (fastest clipper passage New York–San Francisco) (vert)	70	70
1088	35 c. First elevated railway, New York, 1868 (vert)	80	80
1089	45 c. Peter Cooper's locomotive "Tom Thumb" (first U.S. passenger locomotive), 1829	80	80
1090	60 c. "Spray" (Slocum's solo, circumnavigation), 1895–98 (vert)	90	90
1091	90 c. "Sea-Land Commerce" (fastest Pacific passage), 1973 (vert)	1·25	1·25
1092	$1 First cable cars, San Francisco, 1873	1·40	1·40
1093	$3 "Orient Express", 1883	3·00	3·00
1094	$4 "Clermont" (first commercial paddle-steamer), 1807	3·25	3·25

219 "Virgin and Child with St. Anne" (Durer)

220 Three Little Pigs in People Mover, Walt Disney World

1987. Christmas. Religious Paintings. Multicoloured.

1095	20 c. Type **219**	30	15
1096	25 c. "Virgin and Child" (Murillo)	30	15
1097	$2 "Madonna and Child" (Foppa)	1·50	2·25
1098	$4 "Madonna and Child" (Da Verona)	2·75	4·00

1987. 60th Anniv of Mickey Mouse (Walt Disney cartoon character). Cartoon characters in trains. Multicoloured.

1100	20 c. Type **220**	45	35
1101	25 c. Goofy driving horse tram, Disneyland	45	35
1102	45 c. Donald Duck in "Roger E. Broggie", Walt Disney World	75	65
1103	60 c. Goofy, Mickey Mouse, Donald Duck and Chip 'n Dale aboard "Big Thunder Mountain" train, Disneyland	85	75
1104	90 c. Mickey Mouse in "Walter E. Disney", Disneyland	1·40	1·25
1105	$1 Mickey and Minnie Mouse, Goofy, Donald and Daisy Duck in monorail, Walt Disney World	1·50	1·40
1106	$3 Dumbo flying over "Casey Jr"	3·25	3·75
1107	$4 Daisy Duck and Minnie Mouse in "Lilly Belle", Walt Disney World	3·75	4·50

1988. Royal Ruby Wedding. As T **234** of Antigua.

1109	45 c. multicoloured	85	30
1110	60 c. brown, black and green	1·00	70
1111	$1 multicoloured	1·25	1·00
1112	$3 multicoloured	2·50	3·50

DESIGNS: 45 c. Wedding portrait with attendants, 1947; 60 c. Princess Elizabeth with Prince Charles, c. 1950; $1 Princess Elizabeth and Prince Philip with Prince Charles and Princess Anne, 1950; $3 Queen Elizabeth.

221 Kayak Canoeing

222 Carib Indian

1988. Olympic Games, Seoul. Multicoloured.

1114	45 c. Type **221**	75	35
1115	60 c. Taekwon-do	1·00	1·00
1116	$1 High diving	1·10	1·25
1117	$3 Gymnastics on bars	2·25	4·00

1988. "Reunion '88" Tourism Programme. Multicoloured.

1119	10 c. Type **222**	10	10
1120	25 c. Mountainous interior (horiz)	10	15
1121	35 c. Indian River	10	15
1122	60 c. Belaire dancer and tourists	15	30
1123	90 c. Boiling Lake	20	60
1124	$3 Coral reef (horiz)	60	1·60

1988. Stamp Exhibitions. Nos. 1092/3 optd.

1126	$1 First cable cars, San Francisco, 1873 (optd **FINLANDIA 88**, Helsinki)	75	70
1127	$3 "Orient Express", 1883 (optd **INDEPENDENCE 40**, Israel)	1·75	2·00

223 White-tailed Tropic Bird)

225 Gary Cooper

224 Battery Hens

1988. Dominica Rain Forest Flora and Fauna. Multicoloured.

1129	45 c. Type **223**	50	50
1130	45 c. Blue-hooded euphonia	50	50
1131	45 c. Smooth-billed ani	50	50
1132	45 c. Scaly-breasted thrasher	50	50
1133	45 c. Purple-throated carib	50	50
1134	45 c. "Marpesia petreus" and "Strymon maesites" (butterflies)	50	50
1135	45 c. Brown trembler	50	50
1136	45 c. Imperial amazon	50	50
1137	45 c. Mangrove cuckoo	50	50
1138	45 c. "Dynastes hercules" (beetle)	50	50
1139	45 c. "Historis odius" (butterfly)	50	50
1140	45 c. Red-necked amazon	50	50
1141	45 c. Tillandsia (plant)	50	50
1142	45 c. Bananaquit and "Polystacha luteola" (plant)	50	50
1143	45 c. False chameleon	50	50
1144	45 c. Iguana	50	50
1145	45 c. "Hypolimnas misippus" (butterfly)	50	50
1146	45 c. Green-throated carib	50	50
1147	45 c. Heliconia (plant)	50	50
1148	45 c. Agouti	50	50

Nos. 1129/48 were printed together, se-tenant, forming a composite design.

1988. 10th Anniv of International Fund for Agricultural Development. Multicoloured.

1149	45 c. Type **224**	50	30
1150	60 c. Pig	70	65
1151	90 c. Cattle	95	1·25
1152	$3 Black belly sheep	2·25	4·00

1988. Entertainers. Multicoloured.

1154	10 c. Type **225**	40	20
1155	35 c. Josephine Baker	50	35
1156	45 c. Maurice Chevalier	55	35
1157	60 c. James Cagney	60	50
1158	$1 Clark Gable	80	70
1159	$2 Louis Armstrong	1·25	1·50
1160	$3 Liberace	1·75	2·25
1161	$4 Spencer Tracy	2·25	3·00

1988. Flowering Trees. As T **242** of Antigua. Multicoloured.

1163	15 c. Sapodilla	10	10
1164	20 c. Tangerine	10	10
1165	25 c. Avocado pear	10	10
1166	45 c. Amherstia	20	25
1167	90 c. Lipstick tree	40	55
1168	$1 Cannonball tree	45	55
1169	$3 Saman	1·25	1·75
1170	$4 Pineapple	1·60	2·00

1988. 500th Birth Anniv of Titian (artist). As T **238** of Antigua. Multicoloured.

1172	25 c. "Jacopo Strada"	15	15
1173	35 c. "Titian's Daughter Lavinia"	20	20
1174	45 c. "Andrea Navagero"	25	25
1175	60 c. "Judith with Head of Holoferenes"	30	30
1176	$1 "Emilia di Spilimbergo"	50	50
1177	$2 "Martyrdom of St. Lawrence"	1·00	1·25
1178	$3 "Salome"	1·60	2·00
1179	$4 "St. John the Baptist"	1·90	2·50

226 Imperial Amazon

227 President and Mrs. Kennedy

1988. 10th Anniv of Independence. Multicoloured.

1181	20 c. Type **226**	90	40
1182	45 c. Dominica 1874 1d. stamp and landscape (horiz)	90	30
1183	$2 1978 Independence 10 c. stamp and landscape (horiz)	1·50	2·75
1184	$3 Carib wood (national flower)	1·75	3·25

1988. 25th Death Anniv of John F. Kennedy (American statesman). Multicoloured.

1186	20 c. Type **227**	10	10
1187	25 c. Kennedy sailing	10	10
1188	$2 Outside Hyannis Port house	80	1·50
1189	$4 Speaking in Berlin (vert)	1·60	2·50

228 Donald Duck's Nephews decorating Christmas Tree

1988. Christmas. "Mickey's Christmas Mall". Walt Disney Cartoon Characters. Multicoloured.

1191	60 c. Type **228**	55	65
1192	60 c. Daisy Duck outside clothes shop	55	65
1193	60 c. Winnie the Pooh in shop window	55	65
1194	60 c. Goofy with parcels	55	65
1195	60 c. Donald Duck as Father Christmas	55	65
1196	60 c. Mickey Mouse contributing to collection	55	65
1197	60 c. Minnie Mouse	55	65
1198	60 c. Chip n' Dale with peanut	55	65

Nos. 1191/8 were printed together, se-tenant, forming a composite design.

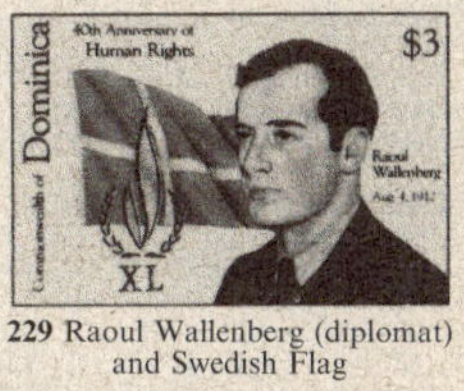

229 Raoul Wallenberg (diplomat) and Swedish Flag

1988. 40th Anniv of Universal Declaration of Human Rights.

1200	**229**	$3 multicoloured	2·00	2·50

230 Greater Amberjack

1988. Game Fishes. Multicoloured.

1202	10 c. Type **230**	20	15
1203	15 c. Blue marlin	20	15
1204	35 c. Cobia	35	30
1205	45 c. Dolphin (fish)	45	30
1206	60 c. Cero	60	55
1207	90 c. Mahogany snapper	85	95
1208	$3 Yellow-finned tuna	2·50	3·25
1209	$4 Rainbow parrotfish	3·00	3·75

231 Leatherback Turtle

1988. Insects and Reptiles. Multicoloured.
1211 10 c. Type **231** 45 35
1212 25 c. "Danaus plexippus" (butterfly) 1·25 75
1213 60 c. Green anole (lizard) 1·60 1·25
1214 $3 "Mantis religiosa" (mantid) 4·00 6·50

1989. Olympic Medal Winners, Seoul. Nos. 1114/17 optd.
1216 45 c. Type **221** (optd **Men's C-1, 500m O. Heukrodt DDR**) 20 25
1217 60 c. Taekwon-do (optd **Women's Flyweight N. Y. Choo S. Korea**) 25 35
1218 $1 High diving (optd **Women's Platform Y. Xu China**) 40 60
1219 $3 Gymnastics on bars (optd **V. Artemov USSR**) 1·25 1·75

1989. 500th Anniv (1992) of Discovery of America by Columbus (2nd issue). Pre-Columbian Carib Society. As T **247** of Antigua but horiz. Mult.
1221 20 c. Carib canoe 20 20
1222 35 c. Hunting with bows and arrows 30 20
1223 $1 Dugout canoe making 70 90
1224 $3 Shield contest 1·75 2·75

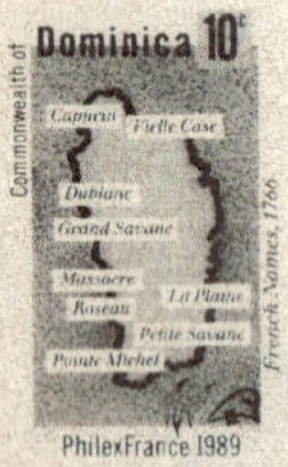

233 Map of Dominica, 1766

235 "Oncidium pusillum"

234 "Papilio homerus"

1989. "Philexfrance '89" International Stamp Exhibition, Paris. Multicoloured.
1226 10 c. Type **233** 45 30
1227 35 c. French coin of 1653 (horiz) 65 40
1228 $1 French warship, 1720 (horiz) 1·40 1·25
1229 $4 Coffee plant (horiz) 2·00 3·00

1989. Japanese Art. Paintings by Taikan. As T **250** of Antigua but vert Multicoloured.
1231 10 c. "Lao-tzu" (detail) 10 10
1232 20 c. "Red Maple Leaves" (panels 1 and 2) 10 10
1233 45 c. "King Wen Hui learns a Lesson from his Cook" (detail) 20 25
1234 60 c. "Red Maple Leaves" (panels 3 and 4) 25 35
1235 $1 "Wild Flowers" (detail) 40 50
1236 $2 "Red Maple Leaves" (panels 5 and 6) 85 1·00
1237 $3 "Red Maple Leaves" (panels 7 and 8) 1·25 1·60
1238 $4 "Indian Ceremony of Floating Lamps on the River" (detail) 1·75 2·10

1989. Butterflies. Multicoloured.
1255 10 c. Type **234** 40 30
1256 15 c. "Morpho peleides" 45 30
1257 25 c. "Dryas julia" 65 30
1258 35 c. "Parides gundlachianus" 70 30
1259 60 c. "Danaus plexippus" 1·00 75
1260 $1 "Agraulis vanillae" 1·25 1·25
1261 $3 "Phoebis avellaneda" 2·75 3·25
1262 $5 "Papilio andraemon" 3·75 5·00

1989. Orchids. Multicoloured.
1264 10 c. Type **235** 35 30
1265 35 c. "Epidendrum cochleata" 70 30
1266 45 c. "Epidendrum ciliare" 75 40
1267 60 c. "Cyrtopodium andersonii" 1·00 80
1268 $1 "Habenaria pauciflora" 1·25 1·25
1269 $2 "Maxillaria alba" 2·00 2·25
1270 $3 "Selenipedium palmifolium" 2·50 2·75
1271 $4 "Brassavola cucullata" 3·25 3·75

236 "Apollo II" Command Module in Lunar Orbit

1989. 20th Anniv of First Manned Landing on Moon. Multicoloured.
1273 10 c. Type **236** 30 30
1274 60 c. Neil Armstrong leaving lunar module 70 70
1275 $2 Edwin Aldrin at Sea of Tranquility 1·60 2·00
1276 $3 Astronauts Armstrong and Aldrin with U.S. flag 2·00 2·50

237 Brazil v Italy Final, 1970

1989. World Cup Football Championship, Italy (1st issue). Multicoloured.
1278 $1 Type **237** 1·50 1·75
1279 $1 England v West Germany, 1966 1·50 1·75
1280 $1 West Germany v Holland, 1974 1·50 1·75
1281 $1 Italy v West Germany, 1982 1·50 1·75
Nos. 1278/81 were printed together, se-tenant, forming a composite central design of a football surrounded by flags of competing nations.
See also Nos. 1383/6.

238 George Washington and Inauguration, 1789

1989. "World Stamp Expo '89" International Stamp Exhibition, Washington. Bicentenary of the U.S. Presidency. Multicoloured.
1283 60 c. Type **238** 50 50
1284 60 c. John Adams and Presidential Mansion, 1800 50 50
1285 60 c. Thomas Jefferson, Graff House, Philadelphia and Declaration of Independence 50 50
1286 60 c. James Madison and U.S.S. "Constitution" defeating H.M.S. "Guerriere", 1812 50 50
1287 60 c. James Monroe and freed slaves landing in Liberia 50 50
1288 60 c. John Quincy Adams and barge on Erie Canal 50 50
1289 60 c. Millard Fillmore and Perry's fleet off Japan 50 50
1290 60 c. Franklin Pierce, Jefferson Davis and San Xavier Mission, Tucson 50 50
1291 60 c. James Buchanan, "Buffalo Bill" Cody carrying mail and Wells Fargo Pony Express stamp 50 50
1292 60 c. Abraham Lincoln and U.P.U. Monument, Berne 50 50
1293 60 c. Andrew Johnson, polar bear and Mount McKinley, Alaska 50 50
1294 60 c. Ulysses S. Grant and Golden Spike Ceremony, 1869 50 50
1295 60 c. Theodore Roosevelt and steam shovel excavating Panama Canal 50 50
1296 60 c. William H. Taft and Admiral Peary at North Pole 50 50
1297 60 c. Woodrow Wilson and Curtis "Jenny" on first scheduled airmail flight, 1918 50 50
1298 60 c. Warren G. Harding and airship U.S.S. "Shenandoah" at Lakehurst 50 50
1299 60 c. Calvin Coolidge and Lindbergh's "Spirit of St Louis" on trans-Atlantic flight 50 50
1300 60 c. Mount Rushmore National Monument 50 50
1301 60 c. Lyndon B. Johnson and Earth from Moon as seen by "Apollo 8" crew 50 50
1302 60 c. Richard Nixon and visit to Great Wall of China 50 50
1303 60 c. Gerald Ford and "Gorch Fock" (German cadet barque) at Bicentenary of Revolution celebrations 50 50
1304 60 c. Jimmy Carter and President Sadat of Egypt with Prime Minister Begin of Israel 50 50
1305 60c. Ronald Reagan and space shuttle "Columbia" 50 50
1306 60 c. George Bush and Grumman TBF Avenger (fighter-bomber) 50 50

1989. Mickey Mouse in Hollywood (Walt Disney cartoon character). As T **267** of Antigua. Mult.
1308 20 c. Mickey Mouse reading script 40 40
1309 35 c. Mickey Mouse giving interview 55 55
1310 45 c. Mickey and Minnie Mouse with newspaper and magazines 65 65
1311 60 c. Mickey Mouse signing autographs 75 75
1312 $1 Trapped in dressing room 1·25 1·25
1313 $2 Mickey and Minnie Mouse with Pluto in limousine 2·00 2·50
1314 $3 Arriving at Awards ceremony 2·25 2·75
1315 $4 Mickey Mouse accepting award 2·40 2·75

1989. Christmas. Paintings by Botticelli. As T **259** of Antigua. Multicoloured.
1317 20 c. "Madonna in Glory with Seraphim" 40 30
1318 25 c. "The Annunciation" 40 30
1319 35 c. "Madonna of the Pomegranate" 55 40
1320 45 c. "Madonna of the Rosegarden" 65 45
1321 60 c. "Madonna of the Book" 80 60
1322 $1 "Madonna under a Baldachin" 1·00 90
1323 $4 "Madonna and Child with Angels" 3·00 4·50
1324 $4 "Bardi Madonna" 3·50 4·75

240 Lady Olave Baden-Powell and Agatha Robinson (Guide leaders)

241 Jawaharal Nehru

1989. 60th Anniv of Girl Guides in Dominica.
1326 **240** 60 c. multicoloured 1·00 1·00

1989. Birth Centenary of Jawaharal Nehru (Indian statesman).
1328 **241** 60 c. multicoloured 1·50 1·25

242 Cocoa Damselfish

1990. Tropical Fishes. Multicoloured.
1330 45 c. Type **242** 45 50
1331 45 c. Stinging jellyfish 45 50
1332 45 c. Dolphin (fish) 45 50
1333 45 c. Atlantic spadefish and queen angelfish 45 50
1334 45 c. French angelfish 45 50
1335 45 c. Blue-striped grunt 45 50
1336 45 c. Porkfish 45 50
1337 45 c. Great hammerhead 45 50
1338 45 c. Atlantic spadefish 45 50
1339 45 c. Great barracuda 45 50
1340 45 c. Southern stingray 45 50
1341 45 c. Black grunt 45 50
1342 45 c. Spot-finned butterflyfish 45 50
1343 45 c. Dog snapper 45 50
1344 45 c. Band-tailed puffer 45 50
1345 45 c. Four-eyed butterfly-fish 45 50
1346 45 c. Lane snapper 45 50
1347 45 c. Green moray 45 50
Nos. 1330/47 were printed together, se-tenant, forming a composite design.

243 St. Paul's Cathedral, London, c. 1840

244 Blue-headed Hummingbird

1990. 150th Anniv of the Penny Black and "Stamp World London 90" International Stamp Exhibition.
1348 **243** 45 c. green and black 50 25
1349 – 50 c. blue and black 55 35
1350 – 60 c. blue and black 65 45
1351 – 90 c. green and black 85 85
1352 – $3 blue and black 2·25 3·00
1353 – $4 blue and black 2·75 3·50
DESIGNS: 50 c. British Post Office "accelerator" carriage, 1830; 60 c. St. Paul's and City of London; 90 c. Travelling post office, 1838; $3 "Hen and chickens" delivery cycle, 1883; $4 London skyline.

1990. 500th Anniv (1992) of Discovery of America by Columbus (3rd issue). New World Natural History—Seashells. As T **260** of Antigua. Mult.
1355 10 c. Reticulated cowrie-helmet 30 30
1356 20 c. West Indian chank 40 40
1357 35 c. West Indian fighting conch 50 35
1358 60 c. True tulip 75 60
1359 $1 Sunrise tellin 1·00 1·00
1360 $2 Crown cone 1·75 2·50
1361 $3 Common dove shell 2·50 3·25
1362 $4 Common or Atlantic fig shell 2·75 3·25

1990. Birds. Multicoloured.
1364 10 c. Type **244** 35 35
1365 20 c. Black-capped petrel 45 45
1366 45 c. Red-necked amazon 65 40
1367 60 c. Black swift 80 70
1368 $1 Troupial 1·25 1·25
1369 $2 Common noddy 2·00 2·50
1370 $4 Lesser Antillean pewee 3·25 3·50
1371 $5 Little blue heron 3·75 4·25

1990. 90th Birthday of Queen Elizabeth the Queen Mother. As T **266** of Antigua.
1373 20 c. multicoloured 20 15
1374 45 c. multicoloured 35 25
1375 60 c. multicoloured 60 60
1376 $3 multicoloured 2·25 3·00
DESIGNS: 20 c. to $3, Recent photographs of Queen Mother.

1990. Olympic Games, Barcelona (1992) (1st issue). As T **268** of Antigua. Multicoloured.
1378 45 c. Tennis 75 40
1379 60 c. Fencing 75 50
1380 $2 Swimming 1·60 2·75
1381 $3 Yachting 2·25 3·00
See also Nos. 1603/11.

245 Barnes, England

1990. World Cup Football Championship, Italy (2nd issue). Multicoloured.
1383 15 c. Type **245** 40 30
1384 45 c. Romario, Brazil 70 30
1385 60 c. Franz Beckenbauer, West Germany manager 85 70
1386 $4 Lindenberger, Austria 3·25 5·00

246 Mickey Mouse riding Herschell-Spillman Frog

1990. Christmas. Walt Disney cartoon characters and American carousel animals. Multicoloured.
1388 10 c. Type **246** 30 20
1389 15 c. Huey, Ducy and Louie on Allan Herschell elephant 35 25
1390 25 c. Donald Duck on Allan Herschell polar bear 45 30
1391 45 c. Goofy on Dentzel goat 70 30
1392 $1 Donald Duck on Zalar giraffe 1·00 1·00
1393 $2 Daisy Duck on Herschell-Spillman stork 1·75 2·25
1394 $4 Goofy on Dentzel lion 3·00 3·75
1395 $5 Daisy Duck on Stein and Goldstein palomino stander 3·50 4·00

1991. Cog Railways. As T **275** of Antigua. Mult.
1397 10 c. Steam locomotive, Glion–Roches De Naye rack railway, 1890 30 30
1398 35 c. Electric railcar, Mt Pilatus rack railway 45 30
1399 45 c. Schynige Platte rack railway train 50 30
1400 60 c. Steam train on Bugnli Viaduct, Furka–Oberalp rack railway (vert) 75 75
1401 $1 Jungfrau rack railway train, 1910 1·00 1·25
1402 $2 Testing Pike's Peak railcar, Switzerland, 1983 1·75 2·25
1403 $4 Brienz–Rothorn railway locomotive, 1991 3·00 4·00
1404 $5 Steam locomotive, Arth–Rigi, 1890 3·50 4·25

1991. 500th Anniv (1992) of Discovery of America by Columbus (4th issue). History of Exploration. As T **277** of Antigua. Multicoloured.
1406 10 c. Gil Eannes sailing south of Cape Bojador, 1433–34 25 25
1407 25 c. Alfonso Baldaya sailing south to Cape Blanc, 1436 35 35
1408 45 c. Bartolomeu Dias in Table Bay, 1487 45 35
1409 60 c. Vasco da Gama on voyage to India, 1497–99 55 50
1410 $1 Vallarte the Dane off African coast 75 90
1411 $2 Aloisio Cadamosto in Cape Verde Islands, 1456–58 1·40 1·75
1412 $4 Diogo Gomes on River Gambia, 1457 2·75 3·50
1413 $5 Diogo Cao off African coast, 1482–85 3·25 3·75

1991. "Phila Nippon '91" International Stamp Exhibition, Tokyo. As T **279** of Antigua. Mult.
1415 10 c. Donald Duck as Shogun's guard (horiz) 20 20

1416 15 c. Mickey Mouse as Kabuki actor (horiz) 25 25
1417 25 c. Minnie and Mickey Mouse as bride and groom (horiz) 35 25
1418 45 c. Daisy Duck as geisha 45 25
1419 $1 Mickey Mouse in Sokutai court dress 85 85
1420 $2 Goofy as Mino farmer 1·60 2·00
1421 $4 Pete as Shogun 2·75 3·25
1422 $5 Donald Duck as Samurai (horiz) 3·25 3·75

247 "Craterellus cornucopioides"

248 Empire State Building, New York

1991. Fungi. Multicoloured.
1424 10 c. Type **247** 50 40
1425 15 c. "Coprinus comatus" 60 40
1426 45 c. "Morchella esculenta" 85 40
1427 60 c. "Cantharellus cibarius" 1·10 70
1428 $1 "Lepista nuda" 1·40 1·10
1429 $2 "Suillus luteus" 2·00 2·50
1430 $4 "Russula emetica" 3·25 3·75
1431 $5 "Armillaria mellea" 3·25 3·75

1991. 65th Birthday of Queen Elizabeth II. As T **280** of Antigua. Multicoloured.
1433 10 c. Queen and Prince William on Buckingham Palace Balcony, 1990 30 20
1434 60 c. The Queen at Westminster Abbey, 1988 75 50
1435 $2 The Queen and Prince Philip in Italy, 1990 1·60 2·00
1436 $5 The Queen at Ascot, 1986 2·50 3·00

1991. 10th Wedding Anniv of the Prince and Princess of Wales. As T **280** of Antigua. Multicoloured.
1438 15 c. Prince and Princess of Wales in West Germany, 1987 40 25
1439 40 c. Separate photographs of Prince, Princess and sons 70 25
1440 $1 Separate photographs of Prince William and Prince Henry 95 95
1441 $4 Prince Charles at Caister and Princess Diana in Thailand 3·50 4·50

1991. Death Centenary (1990) of Vincent van Gogh (artist). As T **278** of Antigua. Multicoloured.
1443 10 c. "Thatched Cottages" (horiz) 30 30
1444 25 c. "The House of Pere Eloi" (horiz) 45 30
1445 45 c. "The Midday Siesta" (horiz) 65 30
1446 60 c. "Portrait of a Young Peasant" 85 70
1447 $1 "Still Life: Vase with Irises against Yellow Background" 1·25 1·10
1448 $2 "Still Life: Vase with Irises" (horiz) 1·75 2·00
1449 $4 "Blossoming Almond Tree" (horiz) 3·00 3·75
1450 $5 "Irises" (horiz) 3·25 4·25

1991. International Literacy Year (1990). Scenes from Disney cartoon film "The Little Mermaid". As T **269** of Antigua. Multicoloured.
1452 10 c. Ariel, Flounder and Sebastian (horiz) 25 25
1453 25 c. King Triton (horiz) 35 30
1454 45 c. Sebastian playing drums (horiz) 50 30
1455 60 c. Flotsam and Jetsam taunting Ariel (horiz) 75 55
1456 $1 Scuttle, Flounder and Ariel with pipe (horiz) 1·00 1·00
1457 $2 Ariel and Flounder discovering book (horiz) 1·75 2·00
1458 $4 Prince Eric and crew (horiz) 3·00 3·50
1459 $5 Ursula the Sea Witch (horiz) 3·50 4·00

1991. World Landmarks. Multicoloured.
1461 10 c. Type **248** 40 30
1462 25 c. Kremlin, Moscow (horiz) 40 30
1463 45 c. Buckingham Palace, London (horiz) 60 30
1464 60 c. Eiffel Tower, Paris 75 60
1465 $1 Taj Mahal, Agra (horiz) 2·00 1·50
1466 $2 Opera House, Sydney (horiz) 3·00 3·00
1467 $4 Colosseum, Rome (horiz) 3·50 4·00
1468 $5 Pyramids, Giza (horiz) 3·75 4·50

249 Japanese Aircraft leaving Carrier "Akagi"

1991. 50th Anniv of Japanese Attack on Pearl Harbor. Multicoloured.
1470 10 c. Type **249** 25 25
1471 15 c. U.S.S. "Ward" (destroyer) and Consolidated Catalina flying boat attacking midget submarine 30 30
1472 45 c. Second wave of Mitsubishi A6M Zero-Sen aircraft leaving carriers 40 30
1473 60 c. Japanese Mitsubishi M6M Zero-Sen aircraft attacking Kaneche naval airfield 75 60
1474 $1 U.S.S. "Breeze", "Medusa" and "Curtiss" (destroyers) sinking midget submarine 1·00 1·00
1475 $2 U.S.S. "Nevada" (battleship) under attack 1·75 2·00
1476 $4 U.S.S. "Arizona" (battleship) sinking 3·00 3·50
1477 $5 Mitsubishi A6M Zero-Sen aircraft 3·50 4·00

250 "Eurema venusta"

251 Symbolic Cheque

1991. Butterflies. Multicoloured.
1479 1 c. Type **250** 30 60
1480 2 c. "Agraulis vanillae" 30 60
1481 5 c. "Danaus plexippus" 40 60
1482 10 c. "Biblis hyperia" 40 15
1483 15 c. "Dryas julia" 50 15
1484 20 c. "Phoebis agarithe" 50 20
1485 25 c. "Junonia genoveva" 50 20
1486 35 c. "Battus polydamas" 60 30
1487 45 c. "Leptotes cassius" 60 30
1487a 55 c. "Ascia monuste" 75 55
1488 60 c. "Anaea dominicana" 70 35
1488a 65 c. "Hemiargus hanno" 75 55
1489 90 c. "Hypolimnas misippus" 80 55
1490 $1 "Urbanus proteus" 80 60
1490a $1.20 "Historis odius" 1·00 1·25
1491 $2 "Phoebis sennae" 1·50 2·00
1492 $5 "Cynthia cardui" ("Vanessa cardui") 2·50 3·50
1493 $10 "Marpesia petreus" 4·75 6·00
1494 $20 "Anartia jatrophae" 9·50 12·00

1991. Birth Centenary (1990) of Charles De Gaulle (French statesman). As T **283** of Antigua.
1495 45 c. brown 75 75
DESIGNS—VERT: 45 c. De Gaulle in uniform.

1992. 40th Anniv of Credit Union Bank.
1497 **251** 10 c. grey and black 20 20
1498 – 60 c. multicoloured 80 80
DESIGNS—HORIZ: 60 c. Credit Union symbol.

252 "18th-Century Creole Dress" (detail) (Agostino Brunias)

254 Cricket Match

253 Island Beach

1991. Creole Week. Multicoloured.
1499 45 c. Type **252** 50 25
1500 60 c. Jing Ping band 70 60
1501 $1 Creole dancers 1·00 1·40

1991. Year of Environment and Shelter. Mult.
1503 15 c. Type **253** 15 15
1504 60 c. Imperial amazon 2·00 1·25

1991. Christmas. Religious Paintings by Jan van Eyck. As T **287** of Antigua. Multicoloured.
1506 10 c. "Virgin Enthroned with Child" (detail) 40 20
1507 20 c. "Madonna at the Fountain" 50 30
1508 35 c. "Virgin in a Church" 60 30
1509 45 c. "Madonna with Canon van der Paele" 70 30
1510 60 c. "Madonna with Canon van der Paele" (detail) 1·00 60
1511 $1 "Madonna in an Interior" 1·25 1·00
1512 $3 "The Annunciation" 2·50 3·50
1513 $5 "The Annunciation" (different) 3·50 5·50

1992. 40th Anniv of Queen Elizabeth II's Accession. As T **288** of Antigua. Multicoloured.
1515 10 c. Coastline 10 10
1516 15 c. Mountains overlooking small village 10 10
1517 $1 River estuary 45 60
1518 $5 Waterfall 2·25 3·00

1992. Centenary (1991) of Botanical Gardens. Multicoloured.
1520 10 c. Type **254** 20 20
1521 15 c. Scenic entrance 20 20
1522 45 c. Traveller's tree 30 25
1523 60 c. Bamboo House 40 30
1524 $1 The Old Pavilion 60 60
1525 $2 "Ficus benjamina" 1·10 1·50
1526 $4 Cricket match (different) 2·25 2·75
1527 $5 Thirty-five Steps 2·50 3·00

1992. Easter. Religious Paintings. As T **291** of Antigua. Multicoloured.
1529 10 c. "The Supper at Emmaus" (Van Honthorst) 20 20
1530 15 c. "Christ before Caiaphas" (Van Honthorst) (vert) 25 25
1531 45 c. "The Taking of Christ" (De Boulogne) 40 30
1532 60 c. "Pilate washing his Hands" (Preti) (vert) 55 45
1533 $1 "The Last Supper" (detail) (Master of the Church of S. Francisco d'Evora) 75 75
1534 $2 "The Three Marys at the Tomb" (detail) (Bouguereau) (vert) 1·50 1·75
1535 $3 "Denial of St. Peter" (Terbrugghen) 1·75 2·25
1536 $5 "Doubting Thomas" (Strozzi) 2·75 3·50

1992. "Granada '92" International Stamp Exhibition, Spain. Art of Diego Rodriguez Velasquez. As T **292** of Antigua. Mult.
1538 10 c. "Pope Innocent X" (detail) 20 15
1539 15 c. "The Forge of Vulcan" (detail) 20 15
1540 45 c. "The Forge of Vulcan" (different detail) 40 25
1541 60 c. "Queen Mariana of Austria" (detail) 55 40
1542 $1 "Pablo de Valladolid" 70 70
1543 $2 "Sebastian de Morra" 1·50 2·00
1544 $3 "King Felipe IV" (detail) 1·75 2·25
1545 $4 "King Felipe IV" 2·25 2·50

255 Columbus and "Dynastes hercules" (beetle)

1992. 500th Anniv of Discovery of America by Columbus (5th issue). World Columbian Stamp "Expo '92", Chicago. Multicoloured.
1547 10 c. Type **255** 15 15
1548 25 c. Columbus and "Leptodactylus fallax" (frog) 20 15
1549 75 c. Columbus and red-necked amazon (bird) 60 60
1550 $2 Columbus and "Ameiva fuscata" (lizard) 1·25 1·75
1551 $4 Columbus and royal gramma (fish) 2·25 2·75
1552 $5 Columbus and "Rosa sinensis" (flower) 2·50 3·00

1992. "Genova '92" International Thematic Stamp Exhibition. Hummingbirds. As T **295** of Antigua. Multicoloured.
1554 10 c. Female purple-throated carib 20 20
1555 15 c. Female rufous-breasted hermit 20 20
1556 45 c. Male Puerto Rican emerald 50 30
1557 60 c. Female Antillean mango 60 45
1558 $1 Male green-throated carib 95 85
1559 $2 Male blue-headed hummingbird 1·50 1·75
1560 $4 Female eastern streamertail 2·50 2·75
1561 $5 Female Antillean crested hummingbird 2·75 3·00

1992. Prehistoric Animals. As T **290** of Antigua, but horiz. Multicoloured.
1563 10 c. Head of Camptosaurus 20 20
1564 15 c. Edmontosaurus 20 20
1565 25 c. Corythosaurus 30 20
1566 60 c. Stegosaurus 60 45
1567 $1 Torosaurus 95 85
1568 $3 Euoplocephalus 2·00 2·25
1569 $4 Tyrannosaurus 2·50 2·75
1570 $5 Parasaurolophus 2·75 3·00

256 Trumpetfish and Blue Chromis

1992. Marine Life. Multicoloured.
1572/1601 65 c. × 30 As Type **256** 12·00 13·00

1992. Olympic Games, Barcelona (2nd issue). As T **268** of Antigua. Multicoloured.
1603 10 c. Archery 15 15
1604 15 c. Two-man canoeing 15 15
1605 25 c. Men's 110 metres hurdles 20 15
1606 60 c. Men's high jump 40 30
1607 $1 Greco-Roman wrestling 65 65
1608 $2 Men's gymnastics—rings 1·25 1·75
1609 $4 Men's gymnastics—parallel bars 2·50 3·00
1610 $5 Equestrian dressage 3·00 3·25

1992. 500th Anniv of Discovery of America by Columbus (6th issue). Organization of East Caribbean States. As Nos. 1670/1 of Antigua. Multicoloured.
1612 $1 Columbus meeting Amerindians 65 65
1613 $2 Ships approaching island 1·10 1·25

1992. Hummel Figurines. As T **302** of Antigua. Multicoloured.
1614 20 c. Angel playing violin 15 15
1615 25 c. Angel playing recorder 15 15
1616 55 c. Angel playing lute 35 35
1617 65 c. Seated angel playing trumpet 45 45
1618 90 c. Angel on cloud with lantern 60 60
1619 $1 Angel with candle 65 65
1620 $1.20 Flying angel with Christmas tree 75 1·00
1621 $6 Angel on cloud with candle 4·25 5·00

257 Brass "Reno" Locomotive, Japan (1963)

1992. Toy Trains from Far Eastern Manufacturers. Multicoloured.
1623 15 c. Type **257** 15 15
1624 25 c. Union Pacific "Golden Classic" locomotive, China (1992) 20 20
1625 55 c. L.M.S. third class brake carriage, Hong Kong (1970s) 40 40
1626 65 c. Brass Wabash locomotive, Japan (1958) 50 50
1627 75 c. Pennsylvania "Duplex" type locomotive, Korea (1991) 60 60
1628 $1 Streamlined locomotive, Japan (post 1945) 70 70
1629 $3 Japanese National Railways Class "C62" locomotive, Japan (1960) 2·00 2·50
1630 $5 Tinplate friction driven trains, Japan (1960s) 2·75 3·25

258 Goofy in "Two Weeks Vacation", 1952

1992. 60th Anniv of Goofy (Disney cartoon character). Designs showing sports from cartoon films. Multicoloured.
1632 10 c. Type **258** 35 15
1633 15 c. "Aquamania", 1961 45 15
1634 25 c. "Goofy Gymnastics", 1949 50 15
1635 45 c. "How to Ride a Horse", 1941 70 25
1636 $1 "Foul Hunting", 1947 1·00 65
1637 $2 "For Whom the Bulls Toil", 1953 1·75 2·00
1638 $4 "Tennis Racquet", 1949 2·25 2·75
1639 $5 "Double Dribble", 1946 2·50 3·00

259 "Graf Zeppelin", 1929

260 Elvis Presley

1992. Anniversaries and Events. Multicoloured.
1641 25 c. Type **259** 15 15
1642 45 c. Elderly man on bike 30 25
1643 45 c. Elderly man with seedling 30 25
1644 45 c. Elderly man and young boy fishing 30 25
1645 90 c. Space Shuttle "Atlantis" 60 60
1646 90 c. Konrad Adenauer (German statesman) 60 60
1647 $1.20 Sir Thomas Lipton and "Shamrock N" (yacht) 75 75
1648 $1.20 Snowy egret (bird) 75 75
1649 $1.20 Wolfgang Amadeus Mozart 75 75
1650 $2 Pulling fishing net ashore 1·25 1·25

1651 $3 Helen Keller (lecturer) 1·75 1·75
1652 $4 Eland (antelope) 2·50 2·50
1653 $4 Map of Allied Zones of Occupation, Germany, 1949 2·50 2·50
1654 $4 Earth resources satellite 2·50 2·50
1655 $5 Count von Zeppelin 2·75 3·00

ANNIVERSARIES AND EVENTS: Nos. 1641, 1655, 75th death anniv of Count Ferdinand von Zeppelin; Nos. 1642/4, International Day of the Elderly; Nos. 1645, 1654, International Space Year; Nos. 1646, 1653, 25th death anniv of Konrad Adenauer; No. 1647, Americas Cup Yachting Championship; Nos. 1648, 1652, Earth Summit '92, Rio; No. 1649, Death bicent of Mozart; No. 1650, International Conference on Nutrition, Rome; No. 1651, 75th anniv of International Association of Lions Clubs.

1993. Bicentenary of the Louvre, Paris. As T **305** of Antigua. Multicoloured.

1657 $1 "Madonna and Child with St. Catherine and a Rabbit" (left detail) (Titian) 65 70
1658 $1 "Madonna and Child with St. Catherine and a Rabbit" (right detail) (Titian) 65 70
1659 $1 "Woman at her Toilet" (Titian) 65 70
1660 $1 "The Supper at Emmaus" (left detail) (Titian) 65 70
1661 $1 "The Supper at Emmaus" (right detail) (Titian) 65 70
1662 $1 "The Pastoral Concert" (Titian) 65 70
1663 $1 "An Allegory, perhaps of Marriage" (detail) (Titian) 65 70
1664 $1 "An Allegory, perhaps of Marriage" (different detail) (Titian) 65 70

1993. 15th Death Anniv of Elvis Presley (singer). Multicoloured.

1666 $1 Type **260** 70 70
1667 $1 Elvis with guitar 70 70
1668 $1 Elvis with microphone 70 70

261 Plumbeous Warbler

1993. Birds. Multicoloured.

1669 90 c. Type **261** 70 80
1670 90 c. Black swift 70 80
1671 90 c. Blue-hooded euphonia 70 80
1672 90 c. Rufous-throated solitaire 70 80
1673 90 c. Ringed kingfisher 70 80
1674 90 c. Blue-headed hummingbird 70 80
1675 90 c. Bananaquit 70 80
1676 90 c. Brown trembler 70 80
1677 90 c. Forest thrush 70 80
1678 90 c. Purple-throated carib 70 80
1679 90 c. Ruddy quail dove 70 80
1680 90 c. Least bittern 70 80

Nos. 1669/80 were printed together, se-tenant, forming a composite design.

262 School Crest

1993. Cent of Dominica Grammar School. Mult.

1682 25 c. Type **262** 15 10
1683 30 c. V. Archer (first West Indian headmaster) 20 20
1684 65 c. Hubert Charles (first Dominican headmaster) 35 45
1685 90 c. Present school buildings 50 65

263 Leatherback Turtle on Beach

1993. Turtles. Multicoloured.

1686 25 c. Type **263** 50 15
1687 55 c. Hawksbill turtle swimming 70 40
1688 65 c. Atlantic ridley turtle 80 50
1689 90 c. Green turtle laying eggs 1·00 70
1690 $1 Green turtle swimming 1·00 70
1691 $2 Hawksbill turtle swimming (different) 1·50 2·00
1692 $4 Loggerhead turtle 2·25 2·75
1693 $5 Leatherback turtle swimming 2·25 2·75

264 Ford "Model A", 1928

1993. Centenaries of Henry Ford's First Petrol Engine (90 c., $5) and Karl Benz's First Four-wheeled Car (others). Multicoloured.

1695 90 c. Type **264** 70 50
1696 $1.20 Mercedes Benz car winning Swiss Grand Prix, 1936 1·00 1·00
1697 $4 Mercedes Benz car winning German Grand Prix, 1935 2·50 2·75
1698 $5 Ford "Model T", 1915 2·50 2·75

1993. 40th Anniv of Coronation. As T **307** of Antigua.

1700 20 c. multicoloured 10 10
1701 25 c. brown and black 10 10
1702 65 c. multicoloured 30 35
1703 $5 multicoloured 2·25 2·40

DESIGNS: 20 c. Queen Elizabeth II at Coronation (photograph by Cecil Beaton); 25 c. Queen wearing King Edward's Crown during Coronation ceremony; 65 c. Coronation coach; $5 Queen and Queen Mother in carriage.

265 New G.P.O. and Duke of Edinburgh

1993. Anniversaries and Events. Each brown, deep brown and black (Nos. 1707, 1717) or multicoloured (others).

1705 25 c. Type **265** 10 10
1706 25 c. "Bather with Beach Ball" (Picasso) (vert) 10 10
1707 65 c. Willy Brandt and Pres. Eisenhower, 1959 30 35
1708 90 c. As Type **265** but portrait of Queen Elizabeth II 40 45
1709 90 c. "Portrait of Leo Stein" (Picasso) (vert) 40 45
1710 90 c. Monika Holzner (Germany) (speed skating) (vert) 40 45
1711 90 c. "Self-portrait" (Marian Szczyrbula) (vert) 40 45
1712 90 c. Prince Naruhito and engagement photographs 40 45
1713 $1.20 16th-century telescope (vert) 55 60
1714 $3 "Bruno Jasienski" (Tytus Czyzewski) (vert) 1·40 1·50
1715 $3 Modern observatory (vert) 1·40 1·50
1716 $4 Ray Leblanc and Tim Sweeney (U.S.A.) (ice hockey) (vert) 1·90 2·00
1717 $5 "Wilhelm Unde" (Picasso) (vert) 2·25 2·40
1718 $5 Willy Brandt and N.K. Winston at World's Fair, 1964 2·25 2·40
1719 $5 Masako Owada and engagement photographs 2·25 2·40
1720 $5 Pres. Clinton and wife applauding 2·25 2·40

ANNIVERSARIES AND EVENTS: Nos. 1705, 1708, Opening of New General Post Office Building; Nos. 1706, 1709, 1717, 20th death anniv of Picasso (artist); Nos. 1707, 1718, 80th birth anniv of Willy Brandt (German politician); Nos. 1710, 1716, Winter Olympic Games '94, Lille-hammer; Nos. 1711, 1714, "Polska '93" International Stamp Exhibition, Poznan; Nos. 1712, 1719, Marriage of Crown Prince Naruhito of Japan; Nos. 1713, 1715, 450th death anniv of Copernicus (astronomer); No. 1720, Inauguration of U.S. President William Clinton.

No. 1714 is inscribed "Tyrus" in error.

266 Hugo Eckener in New York Parade, 1928

1993. Aviation Anniversaries. Multicoloured.

1722 25 c. Type **266** 30 15
1723 55 c. English Electric Lightning F.2 (fighter) 50 40
1724 65 c. Airship "Graf Zeppelin" over Egypt, 1929 60 55
1725 $1 Boeing 314A (flying boat) on transatlantic mail flight 80 75
1726 $2 Astronaut carrying mail to the Moon 1·50 1·75
1727 $4 Airship "Viktoria Luise" over Kiel harbour, 1912 2·50 3·00
1728 $5 Supermarine Spitfire (vert) 2·50 3·00

ANNIVERSARIES. Nos. 1722, 1724, 1727, 125th birth anniv of Hugo Eckener (airship commander); Nos. 1723, 1728, 75th anniv of Royal Air Force; Nos. 1725/6, Bicentenary of first airmail flight.

267 Maradona (Argentina) and Buchwald (Germany)

268 Ornate Chedi, Wat Phra Boromathat Chaiya

1993. World Cup Football Championship, U.S.A (1994) (1st issue). Multicoloured.

1730 25 c. Type **267** 30 15
1731 55 c. Ruud Gullit (Netherlands) 50 40
1732 65 c. Chavarria (Costa Rica) and Bliss (U.S.A.) 55 45
1733 90 c. Diego Maradona (Argentina) 70 60
1734 90 c. Leonel Alvares (Colombia) 70 60
1735 $1 Altobelli (Italy) and Yong-hwang (South Korea) 75 70
1736 $2 Stopyra (France) 1·25 1·50
1737 $5 Renquin (Belgium) and Yaremtchuk (Russia) 2·25 3·00

See also Nos. 1849/55.

1993. Asian International Stamp Exhibitions. Multicoloured. (a) "Indopex '93", Surabaya, Indonesia.

1739 25 c. Type **268** 40 15
1740 55 c. Temple ruins, Sukhothai 65 45
1741 90 c. Prasat Hin Phimai, Thailand 80 65
1742 $1.65 Arjuna and Prabu Gilling Wesi puppets 1·00 1·10
1743 $1.65 Loro Blonyo puppet 1·00 1·10
1744 $1.65 Yogyanese puppets 1·00 1·10
1745 $1.65 Wayang gedog puppet, Ng Setro 1·00 1·10
1746 $1.65 Wayang golek puppet 1·00 1·10
1747 $1.65 Wayang gedog puppet, Raden Damar Wulan 1·00 1·10
1748 $5 Main sanctuary, Prasat Phanom Rung, Thailand 3·25 3·50

(b) "Taipei '93", Taiwan

1750 25 c. Aw Boon Haw Gardens, Causeway Bay 40 15
1751 65 c. Observation building, Kenting Park 65 45
1752 90 c. Tzu-en pagoda on lakeshore, Taiwan 80 65
1753 $1.65 Chang E kite 1·00 1·10
1754 $1.65 Red Phoenix and Rising Sun kite 1·00 1·10
1755 $1.65 Heavenly Judge kite 1·00 1·10
1756 $1.65 Monkey King kite 1·00 1·10
1757 $1.65 Goddess of Luo River kite 1·00 1·10
1758 $1.65 Heavenly Maiden kite 1·00 1·10
1759 $5 Villa, Lantau Island 3·25 3·50

(c) "Bangkok '93", Thailand

1761 25 c. Tugu Monument, Java 40 15
1762 55 c. Candi Cangkuang mon, West Java 65 45
1763 90 c. Merus, Pura Taman Ayun, Mengwi 80 65
1764 $1.65 Hun Lek puppets of Rama and Sita 1·00 1·10
1765 $1.65 Burmese puppet 1·00 1·10
1766 $1.65 Burmese puppets 1·00 1·10
1767 $1.65 Demon puppet at Wat Phra Kaew 1·00 1·10
1768 $1.65 Hun Lek puppet performing Khun Chang 1·00 1·10
1769 $1.65 Hun Lek puppets performing Ramakien 1·00 1·10
1770 $5 Stone mosaic, Ceto 3·25 3·50

No. 1753 is inscribed "Chang E Rising Up th the Moon" in error.

269 Willie

1993. "Willie the Operatic Whale". Scenes from Walt Disney's cartoon film. Multicoloured.

1772 $1 Type **269** 75 80
1773 $1 Willie's pelican friend 75 80
1774 $1 Willie singing to seals 75 80
1775 $1 Willie singing "Lucia" 75 80
1776 $1 Willie in "Pagliacci" 75 80
1777 $1 Willie as Mephistopheles 75 80
1778 $1 Tetti Tatti searching for Willie 75 80
1779 $1 Whalers listening to Willie 75 80
1780 $1 Tetti Tatti with harpoon gun 75 80

270 "Adoration of the Magi" (detail) (Durer)

1993. Christmas. Religious Paintings. Each black, yellow and red (Nos. 1782/5) or multicoloured (others).

1782 25 c. Type **270** 35 10
1783 55 c. "Adoration of the Magi" (different detail) (Durer) 55 30
1784 65 c. "Adoration of the Magi" (different detail) (Durer) 65 35
1785 90 c. "Adoration of the Magi" (different detail) (Durer) 80 50
1786 90 c. "Madonna of Foligno" (detail) (Raphael) 80 50
1787 $1 "Madonna of Foligno" (different detail) (Raphael) 90 60
1788 $3 "Madonna of Foligno" (different detail) (Raphael) 2·00 2·75
1789 $5 "Madonna of Foligno" (different detail) (Raphael) 2·75 3·75

1994. "Hong Kong '94" International Stamp Exhibition (1st issue). As T **317** of Antigua. Multicoloured.

1791 65 c. Hong Kong 1988 Peak Tramway 50 c. stamp and skyscrapers 50 65
1792 65 c. Dominica 1991 Cog Railways $5 stamp and Hong Kong Peak tram 50 65

Nos. 1791/2 were printed together, se-tenant, forming a composite design.

See also Nos. 1793/8.

1994. "Hong Kong '94" International Stamp Exhibition (2nd issue). Tang Dynasty Jade. As T **318** of Antigua, but vert. Multicoloured.

1793 65 c. Horse 40 50
1794 65 c. Cup with handle 40 50
1795 65 c. Vase with birthday peaches 40 50
1796 65 c. Vase 40 50
1797 65 c. Fu Dog with puppy 40 50
1798 65 c. Drinking cup 40 50

271 Male "Dynastes hercules" (beetle)

1994. Endangered Species. Birds and Insects. Multicoloured.

1799 20 c. Type **271** 20 15
1800 25 c. Male "Dynastes hercules" (different) 20 15
1801 65 c. Male "Dynastes hercules" (different) 45 35
1802 90 c. Female "Dynastes hercules" 60 55
1803 $1 Imperial Amazon ("Imperial Parrot") 90 75
1804 $2 "Marpesia petreus" (butterfly) 1·50 2·00
1805 $3 "Hypolimnus misippus" (butterfly) 2·00 2·25
1806 $5 Purple-throated carib 2·75 3·25

Nos. 1803/7 do not carry the W.W.F. Panda emblem.

272 "Laelio-cattleya"

273 "Russula matoubensis"

1994. Orchids. Multicoloured.

1808 20 c. Type **272** 35 15
1809 25 c. "Sophrolaelio cattleya" 35 15
1810 65 c. "Odontocidium" 70 45
1811 90 c. "Laelio-cattleya" (different) 90 75
1812 $1 "Cattleya" 1·00 75
1813 $2 "Odontocidium" (different) 1·50 2·00
1814 $3 "Epiphronitis" 2·00 2·50
1815 $4 "Oncidium" 2·00 2·50

1994. Fungi. Multicoloured.

1817 20 c. Type **273** 35 15
1818 25 c. "Leptonia caeruleocapitata" 35 15
1819 65 c. "Inocybe littoralis" 70 45
1820 90 c. "Russula hygrophytica" 90 75

1821 $1 "Pyrrhoglossum lilaceipes" 1·00 75
1822 $2 "Hygrocybe konradii" 1·40 1·90
1823 $3 "Inopilus magnificus" 1·75 2·25
1824 $5 "Boletellus cubensis" 2·50 3·00

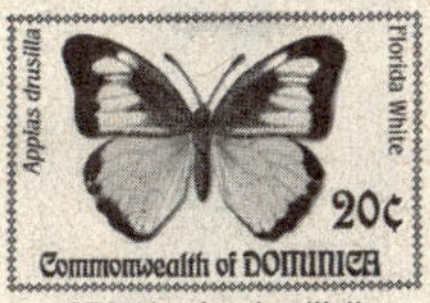

274 "Appias drusilla"

1994. Butterflies. Multicoloured.
1826 20 c. Type **274** 35 15
1827 25 c. "Didonis biblis" 35 15
1828 55 c. "Eurema daira" 70 45
1829 65 c. "Hypolimnas misippus" 75 45
1830 $1 "Phoebis agarithe" 1·00 75
1831 $2 "Marpesia petreus" 1·50 1·90
1832 $3 "Libytheana fulvescens" 1·75 2·50
1833 $5 "Precis evarete" 2·50 3·00

275 Dachshund

1994. Chinese New Year ("Year of the Dog"). Multicoloured.
1835 20 c. Type **275** 35 15
1836 25 c. Beagle 35 15
1837 55 c. Greyhound 65 45
1838 90 c. Jack Russell terrier 90 75
1839 $1 Pekingese 1·00 75
1840 $2 Wire fox terrier 1·50 1·75
1841 $4 English toy spaniel 2·25 2·50
1842 $5 Irish setter 2·25 2·50

1994. Royal Visit. Nos. 1700/4 optd **ROYAL VISIT FEBUARY 19, 1994.**
1844 20 c. multicoloured 50 55
1845 25 c. brown and black 50 55
1846 65 c. multicoloured 80 90
1847 $5 multicoloured 2·50 2·75

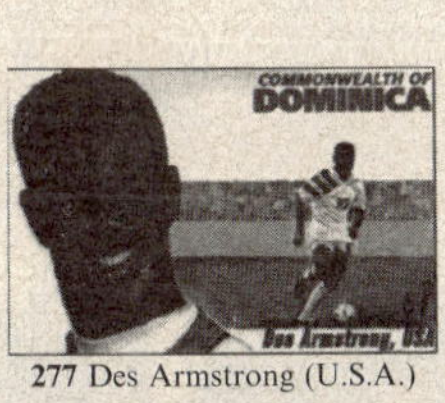

277 Des Armstrong (U.S.A.)

1994. World Cup Football Championship, U.S.A. (2nd issue). Multicoloured.
1849 25 c. Jefferey Edmund (Dominica) 10 10
1850 $1 Type **277** 45 50
1851 $1 Dennis Bergkamp (Netherlands) 45 50
1852 $1 Roberto Baggio (Italy) 45 50
1853 $1 Rai (Brazil) 45 50
1854 $1 Cafu (Brazil) 45 50
1855 $1 Marco van Basten (Netherlands) 45 50

278 Scout Backpacking

1994. 10th Caribbean Scout Jamboree. Multicoloured.
1857 20 c. Type **278** 35 15
1858 25 c. Cooking over campfire 35 15
1859 55 c. Erecting tent 60 30
1860 65 c. Serving soup 70 45
1861 $1 Corps of drums 1·00 75
1862 $2 Planting tree 1·50 2·00
1863 $4 Sailing dinghy 2·25 2·50
1864 $5 Saluting 2·25 2·50

1994. 25th Anniv of First Manned Moon Landing. As T **326** of Antigua. Multicoloured.
1866 $1 Crew of "Apollo 14" 70 80
1867 $1 "Apollo 14" mission logo 70 80
1868 $1 Lunar module "Antares" on Moon 70 80
1869 $1 Crew of "Apollo 15" 70 80
1870 $1 "Apollo 15" mission logo 70 80
1871 $1 Lunar crater on Mt. Hadley 70 80

1994. Centenary of International Olympic Committee. Gold Medal Winners. As T **327** of Antigua. Multicoloured.
1873 55 c. Ulrike Meyfarth (Germany) (high jump), 1984 35 30
1874 $1.45 Dieter Baumann (Germany) (5000 metres), 1992 90 1·25

1994. Centenary (1995) of First English Cricket Tour to the West Indies. As T **329** of Antigua. Mult.
1876 55 c. David Gower (England) (vert) 40 30
1877 90 c. Curtly Ambrose (West Indies) and Wisden Trophy 60 60
1878 $1 Graham Gooch (England) (vert) 70 80

1994. 50th Anniv of D-Day. As T **331** of Antigua. Multicoloured.
1880 65 c. American Waco gliders 50 35
1881 $2 British Horsa glider 1·40 1·60
1882 $3 British glider and troops attacking Pegasus Bridge 1·75 2·00

279 Pink Bird and Red Flowers Screen Painting

280 Dippy Dawg

1994. "Philakorea '94" International Stamp Exhibition, Seoul. Multicoloured.
1884 55 c. Type **279** 40 50
1885 55 c. Bird with yellow, pink and red flowers 40 50
1886 55 c. Pair of birds and yellow flowers 40 50
1887 55 c. Chickens and flowers 40 50
1888 55 c. Pair of birds and pink flowers 40 50
1889 55 c. Ducks and flowers 40 50
1890 55 c. Blue bird and red flowers 40 50
1891 55 c. Pheasant and flowers 40 50
1892 55 c. Stork and flowers 40 50
1893 55 c. Deer and flowers 40 50
1894 65 c. P'alsang-jon Hall (38 × 24 mm) 50 55
1895 90 c. Popchu-sa Temple (38 × 24 mm) 60 65
1896 $2 Uhwajong Pavillion (38 × 24 mm) 1·25 1·50

1994. 65th Anniv (1993) of Mickey Mouse. Walt Disney Cartoon Characters. Multicoloured.
1898 20 c. Type **280** 35 15
1899 25 c. Clarabelle Cow 35 15
1900 55 c. Horace Horsecollar 60 35
1901 65 c. Mortimer Mouse 70 45
1902 $1 Joe Piper 1·00 75
1903 $3 Mr. Casey 2·00 2·25
1904 $4 Chief O'Hara 2·25 2·50
1905 $5 Mickey and The Blot 2·25 2·50

281 Marilyn Monroe

284 Pig's Head facing Right

283 Wood Duck

1994. Entertainers. Multicoloured.
1907 20 c. Sonia Lloyd (folk singer) 20 20
1908 25 c. Ophelia Marie (singer) 20 20
1909 55 c. Edney Francis (accordion player) 50 40
1910 65 c. Norman Letang (saxophonist) 60 45
1911 90 c. Edie Andre (steel-band player) 70 70
1912 90 c. Type **281** 70 80
1913 90 c. Marilyn Monroe wearing necklace 70 80
1914 90 c. In yellow frilled dress 70 80
1915 90 c. In purple dress 70 80
1916 90 c. Looking over left shoulder 70 80
1917 90 c. Laughing 70 80
1918 90 c. In red dress 70 80
1919 90 c. Wearing gold cluster earrings 70 80
1920 90 c. In yellow dress 70 80
No. 1907 is inscribed "Llyod" in error.

1994. Christmas. Religious Paintings. As T **336** of Antigua. Multicoloured.
1922 20 c. "Madonna and Child" (Luis de Morales) 25 10
1923 25 c. "Madonna and Child with Yarn Winder" (De Morales) 25 10
1924 55 c. "Our Lady of the Rosary" (detail) (Zurbaran) 40 30
1925 65 c. "Dream of the Patrician" (detail) (Murillo) 50 55
1926 90 c. "Madonna of Charity" (El Greco) 70 45
1927 $1 "The Annunciation" (Zurbaran) 75 50
1928 $2 "Mystical Marriage of St. Catherine" (Jusepe de Ribera) 1·25 1·75
1929 $3 "The Holy Family with St. Bruno and Other Saints" (detail) (De Ribera) 1·50 2·00

1994. First Recipients of Order of the Caribbean Community. As Nos. 2046/8 of Antigua. Multicoloured.
1931 25 c. Sir Shridath Ramphal 20 10
1932 65 c. William Demas 50 50
1933 90 c. Derek Walcott 70 80

1995. 18th World Scout Jamboree, Netherlands. Nos. 1860 and 1863/4 optd **18th World Scout Jamboree Mondial, Holland, May 6, 1995.**
1934 65 c. Serving soup 30 35
1935 $4 Sailing dinghy 1·75 1·90
1936 $5 Saluting 2·10 2·25

1995. Water Birds. Multicoloured.
1938 25 c. Type **283** 10 10
1939 55 c. Mallard 25 30
1940 65 c. Blue-winged teal 30 35
1941 65 c. Cattle egret (vert) 30 35
1942 65 c. Snow goose (vert) 30 35
1943 65 c. Peregrine falcon (vert) 30 35
1944 65 c. Barn owl (vert) 30 35
1945 65 c. Black-crowned night heron (vert) 30 35
1946 65 c. Common grackle (vert) 30 35
1947 65 c. Brown pelican (vert) 30 35
1948 65 c. Great egret (vert) 30 35
1949 65 c. Ruby-throated hummingbird (vert) 30 35
1950 65 c. Laughing gull (vert) 30 35
1951 65 c. Greater flamingo (vert) 30 35
1952 65 c. Moorhen (vert) 30 35
1953 $5 Red-eared conure ("Blood eared parakeet") 2·10 2·25
Nos. 1941/5 were printed together, se-tenant, forming a composite design.
No. 1946 is inscribed "Common Gralkle" in error.

1995. Chinese New Year ("Year of the Pig"). Multicoloured.
1955 25 c. Type **284** 10 10
1956 65 c. Pig facing to the front 30 35
1957 $1 Pig facing left 45 50

1995. 50th Anniv of End of Second World War in Europe. As T **340** of Antigua. Multicoloured.
1960 $2 German Panther tank in the Ardennes 85 90
1961 $2 American fighter-bomber 85 90
1962 $2 American mechanized column crossing the Rhine 85 90
1963 $2 Messerschmitt Me 163B Komet and Allied bombers 85 90
1964 $2 V2 rocket on launcher 85 90
1965 $2 German U-boat surrendering 85 90
1966 $2 Heavy artillery in action 85 90
1967 $2 Soviet infantry in Berlin 85 90

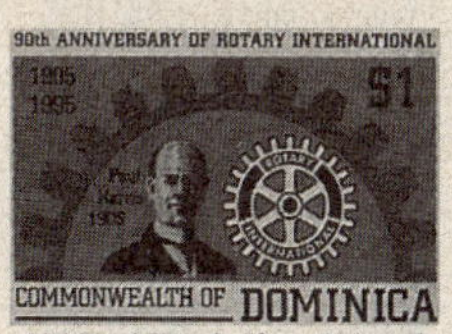

285 Paul Harris (founder) and Emblem

1995. 90th Anniv of Rotary International.
1969 **285** $1 brown, purple & blk 45 50

1995. 50th Anniv of End of Second World War in the Pacific. As T **340** of Antigua. Multicoloured.
1971 $2 Mitsubishi A6M Zero-Sen torpedo-bomber 85 90
1972 $2 Aichi D3A "Val" dive bomber 85 90
1973 $2 Nakajima B5N "Kate" bomber 85 90
1974 $2 "Zuikaku" (Japanese aircraft carrier) 85 90
1975 $2 "Akagi" (Japanese aircraft carrier) 85 90
1976 $2 "Ryuho" (Japanese aircraft carrier) 85 90

286 Boxing

1995. Olympic Games, Atlanta (1996). (1st Issue). Multicoloured.
1978 15 c. Type **286** 10 10
1979 20 c. Wrestling 10 10
1980 25 c. Judo 10 10
1981 55 c. Fencing 25 30
1982 65 c. Swimming 30 35
1983 $1 Gymnastics (vert) 45 50
1984 $2 Cycling (vert) 85 90
1985 $5 Volleyball 2·10 2·25
See also Nos. 2122/45 and 2213.

1995. 50th Anniv of United Nations. As T **341** of Antigua. Multicoloured.
1987 65 c. Signatures and U.S. delegate 30 35
1988 $1 U.S. delegate 45 50
1989 $2 Governor Stassen (U.S. delegate) 85 90
Nos. 1987/9 were printed together, se-tenant, forming a composite design.

1995. 95th Birthday of Queen Elizabeth the Queen Mother. As T **344** of Antigua.
1993 $1.65 brown, light brown and black 70 75
1994 $1.65 multicoloured 70 75
1995 $1.65 multicoloured 70 75
1996 $1.65 multicoloured 70 75
DESIGNS: No. 1993, Queen Elizabeth the Queen Mother (pastel drawing); 1994, Holding bouquet of flowers; 1995, At desk (oil painting); 1996, Wearing blue dress.

288 Monoclonius

1995. "Singapore '95" International Stamp Exhibition. Prehistoric Animals. Multicoloured.
1998 20 c. Type **288** 10 10
1999 25 c. Euoplocephalus 10 10
2000 55 c. Head of coelophysis 25 30
2001 65 c. Head of compsognathus 30 35
2002 90 c. Dimorphodon 40 45
2003 90 c. Ramphorynchus 40 45
2004 90 c. Head of giant alligator 40 45
2005 90 c. Pentaceratops 40 45
2006 $1 Ceratosaurus (vert) 45 50
2007 $1 Comptosaurus (vert) 45 50
2008 $1 Stegosaur (vert) 45 50
2009 $1 Camarasaurs (vert) 45 50
2010 $1 Baronyx (vert) 45 50
2011 $1 Dilophosaurus (vert) 45 50
2012 $1 Dromaeosaurids (vert) 45 50
2013 $1 Deinonychus (vert) 45 50
2014 $1 Dinichthys (terror fish) (vert) 45 50
2015 $1 Head of carcharodon (Giant-toothed shark) (vert) 45 50
2016 $1 Nautiloid (vert) 45 50
2017 $1 Trilobite (vert) 45 50
Nos. 2002/5 and 2006/17 were respectively printed together, se-tenant, forming composite designs.
Nos. 2002/5 do not carry the "Singapore '95" exhibition logo.

289 Oscar Sanchez (1987 Peace)

1995. Centenary of Nobel Prize Trust Fund. Mult.
2019 $2 Type **289** 85 90
2020 $2 Ernst Chain (1945 Medicine) 85 90
2021 $2 Aage Bohr (1975 Physics) 85 90
2022 $2 Jaroslav Seifert (1984 Literature) 85 90
2023 $2 Joseph Murray (1990 Medicine) 85 90
2024 $2 Jaroslav Heyrovsky (1959 Chemistry) 85 90
2025 $2 Adolf von Baeyer (1905 Chemistry) 85 90
2026 $2 Eduard Buchner (1907 Chemistry) 85 90
2027 $2 Carl Bosch (1931 Chemistry) 85 90
2028 $2 Otto Hahn (1944 Chemistry) 85 90
2029 $2 Otto Diels (1950 Chemistry) 85 90
2030 $2 Kurt Alder (1950 Chemistry) 85 90

1995. Christmas. Religious Paintings. As T **357** of Antigua. Multicoloured.

2032	20 c. "Madonna and Child with St. John" (Pontormo)	10	10
2033	25 c. "The Immaculate Conception" (Murillo)	10	10
2034	55 c. "The Adoration of the Magi" (Filippino Lippi)	25	30
2035	65 c. "Rest on the Flight into Egypt" (Van Dyck)	30	35
2036	90 c. "The Holy Family" (Van Dyck)	40	45
2037	$5 "The Annunciation" (Van Eyck)	2·10	2·25

1995. Centenary (1992) of Sierra Club (environmental protection society). Endangered Species. As T **320** of Antigua. Multicoloured.

2039	$1 Florida panther	45	50
2040	$1 Manatee	45	50
2041	$1 Sockeye salmon	45	50
2042	$1 Key deer facing left	45	50
2043	$1 Key deer doe	45	50
2044	$1 Key deer stag	45	50
2045	$1 Wallaby with young in pouch	45	50
2046	$1 Wallaby feeding young	45	50
2047	$1 Wallaby and young feeding	45	50
2048	$1 Florida panther showing teeth (horiz)	45	50
2049	$1 Head of Florida panther (horiz)	45	50
2050	$1 Manatee (horiz)	45	50
2051	$1 Pair of manatees (horiz)	45	50
2052	$1 Pair of sockeye salmon (horiz)	45	50
2053	$1 Sockeye salmon spawning (horiz)	45	50
2054	$1 Pair of southern sea otters (horiz)	45	50
2055	$1 Southern sea otter with front paws together (horiz)	45	50
2056	$1 Southern sea otter with front paws apart (horiz)	45	50

290 Street Scene

1995. "A City of Cathay" (Chinese scroll painting). Multicoloured.

2057	90 c. Type **290**	40	45
2058	90 c. Street scene and city wall	40	45
2059	90 c. City gate and bridge	40	45
2060	90 c. Landing stage and junk	40	45
2061	90 c. River bridge	40	45
2062	90 c. Moored junks	40	45
2063	90 c. Two rafts on river	40	45
2064	90 c. Two junks on river	40	45
2065	90 c. Roadside tea house	40	45
2066	90 c. Wedding party on the road	40	45

291 "Bindo Altoviti" (Raphael)

1995. Paintings by Raphael. Multicoloured.

2068	$2 Type **291**	85	90
2069	$2 "Pope Leo with Nephews"	85	90
2070	$2 "Agony in the Garden"	85	90

292 Rat

1996. Chinese New Year ("Year of the Rat").

2072	**292**	25 c. black, violet and brown	10	10
2073	–	65 c. black, red and green	30	35
2074	–	$1 black, mauve and blue	45	50

DESIGNS: 65 c., $1, Rats and Chinese symbols (different).

293 Mickey and Minnie Mouse (Year of the Rat)

1996. Chinese Lunar Calendar. Walt Disney Cartoon Characters. Multicoloured.

2077	55 c. Type **293**	25	30
2078	55 c. Casey Jones (Year of the Ox)	25	30
2079	55 c. Tigger, Pooh and Piglet (Year of the Tiger)	25	30
2080	55 c. White Rabbit (Year of the Rabbit)	25	30
2081	55 c. Dragon playing flute (Year of the Dragon)	25	30
2082	55 c. Snake looking in mirror (Year of the Snake)	25	30
2083	55 c. Horace Horsecollar and Clarabelle Cow (Year of the Horse)	25	30
2084	55 c. Black Lamb and blue birds (Year of the Ram)	25	30
2085	55 c. King Louis reading book (Year of the Monkey)	25	30
2086	55 c. Cock playing lute (Year of the Cock)	25	30
2087	55 c. Mickey and Pluto (Year of the Dog)	25	30
2088	55 c. Pig building bridge (Year of the Pig)	25	30

294 Steam Locomotive "Dragon", Hawaii

1996. Trains of the World. Multicoloured.

2090	$2 Type **294**	85	90
2091	$2 Class 685 steam locomotive "Regina", Italy	85	90
2092	$2 Class 745 steam locomotive, Calazo to Padua line, Italy	85	90
2093	$2 Mogul steam locomotive, Philippines	85	90
2094	$2 Class 23 and 24 steam locomotives, Germany	85	90
2095	$2 Class BB-15000 electric locomotive "Stanislaus", France	85	90
2096	$2 Class "Black Five" steam locomotive, Scotland	85	90
2097	$2 Diesel-electric locomotive, France	85	90
2098	$2 LNER class A4 steam locomotive "Sir Nigel Gresley", England	85	90
2099	$2 Class 9600 steam locomotive, Japan	85	90
2100	$2 "Peloponnese Express" train, Greece	85	90
2101	$2 Porter type steam locomotive, Hawaii	85	90
2102	$2 Steam locomotive "Holand", Norway	85	90
2103	$2 Class 220 diesel-hydraulic locomotive, Germany	85	90
2104	$2 Steam locomotive, India	85	90
2105	$2 East African Railways Class 29 steam locomotive	85	90
2106	$2 Electric trains, Russia	85	90
2107	$2 Steam locomotive, Austria	85	90

295 Horse-drawn Gig, 1965

1996. Traditional Island Transport. Multicoloured.

2109	65 c. Type **295**	30	35
2110	90 c. Early automobile, 1910	40	45
2111	$2 Lorry, 1950	85	90
2112	$3 Bus 1955	1·25	1·40

296 Giant Panda

1996. "CHINA '96" 9th Asian International Stamp Exhibition, Peking. Giant Pandas. Multicoloured.

2113	55 c. Type **296**	25	30
2114	55 c. Panda on rock	25	30
2115	55 c. Panda eating bamboo shoots	25	30
2116	55 c. Panda on all fours	25	30

1996. 70th Birthday of Queen Elizabeth II. As T **364** of Antigua. Multicoloured.

2118	$2 As Type **364** of Antigua	85	90
2119	$2 Queen in robes of Order of St. Michael and St. George	85	90
2120	$2 Queen in blue dress with floral brooch	85	90

297 Moscow Stadium, 1980

1996. Olympic Games, Atlanta (2nd issue). Multicoloured.

2122	20 c. Type **297**	10	15
2123	25 c. Hermine Joseph (running) (vert)	10	15
2124	55 c. Zimbabwe women's hockey team, 1980	25	30
2125	90 c. Jerome Romain (long jump) (vert)	40	45
2126	90 c. Sammy Lee (diving), 1948 and 1952 (vert)	40	45
2127	90 c. Bruce Jenner (decathalon), 1976 (vert)	40	45
2128	90 c. Olga Korbut (gymnastics), 1972 (vert)	40	45
2129	90 c. Steffi Graff (tennis), 1988 (vert)	40	45
2130	90 c. Florence Griffith-Joyner (track and field), 1988 (vert)	40	45
2131	90 c. Mark Spitz (swimming), 1968 and 1972 (vert)	40	45
2132	90 c. Li Ning (gymnastics), 1984 (vert)	40	45
2133	90 c. Erika Salumae (cycling), 1988 (vert)	40	45
2134	90 c. Abebe Bikila (marathon), 1960 and 1964 (vert)	40	45
2135	90 c. Ulrike Meyfarth (high jump), 1972 and 1984 (vert)	40	45
2136	90 c. Pat McCormick (diving), 1952 and 1956 (vert)	40	45
2137	90 c. Takeichi Nishi (equestrian), 1932 (vert)	40	45
2138	90 c. Peter Farkas (Greco-Roman wrestling), 1992 (vert)	40	45
2139	90 c. Carl Lewis (track and field), 1984, 1988 and 1992 (vert)	40	45
2140	90 c. Agnes Keleti (gymnastics), 1952 and 1956 (vert)	40	45
2141	90 c. Yasuhiro Yamashita (judo), 1984 (vert)	40	45
2142	90 c. John Kelly (single sculls), 1920 (vert)	40	45
2143	90 c. Naim Suleymanoglu (weightlifting), 1988 and 1992 (vert)	40	45
2144	$1 Polo (vert)	45	50
2145	$2 Greg Louganis (diving), 1976, 1984 and 1988	85	90

Nos. 2126/34 and 2135/43 respectively were printed together, se-tenant, the backgrounds forming composite designs.

1996. 50th Anniv of U.N.I.C.E.F. As T **366** of Antigua. Multicoloured.

2147	20 c. Child and globe (horiz)	10	10
2148	55 c. Child with syringe and stethoscope (horiz)	25	30
2149	$5 Doctor and child (horiz)	2·10	2·25

1996. Centenary of Radio. Entertainers. As T **368** of Antigua. Multicoloured.

2153	90 c. Artie Shaw	40	45
2154	$1 Benny Goodman	45	50
2155	$2 Duke Ellington	85	90
2156	$4 Harry James	1·75	1·90

298 Irene Peltier in National Dress

1996. Local Entertainers. Multicoloured.

2158	25 c. Type **298**	10	15
2159	55 c. Rupert Bartley (steel-band player)	25	30
2160	65 c. Rosemary Cools-Lartigue (pianist)	30	35
2161	90 c. Celestine 'Orion' Theophile (singer)	40	45
2162	$1 Cecil Bellot (band master)	45	50

299 Humphrey Bogart as Sam Spade

1996. Centenary of Cinema. Screen Detectives. Multicoloured.

2163	$1 Type **299**	45	50
2164	$1 Sean Connery as James Bond	45	50
2165	$1 Warren Beatty as Dick Tracy	45	50
2166	$1 Basil Rathbone as Sherlock Holmes	45	50
2167	$1 William Powell as the Thin Man	45	50
2168	$1 Sidney Toler as Charlie Chan	45	50
2169	$1 Peter Sellers as Inspector Clouseau	45	50
2170	$1 Robert Mitchum as Philip Marlowe	45	50
2171	$1 Peter Ustinov as Hercule Poirot	45	50

300 Scribbled Filefish

301 Anthony Trollope and Postal Scenes

1996. Fishes. Multicoloured.

2173	1 c. Type **300**	10	10
2174	2 c. Lionfish	10	10
2175	5 c. Porcupinefish	10	10
2176	10 c. Powder-blue surgeon fish	10	10
2177	15 c. Red hind	10	10
2178	20 c. Golden butterflyfish	10	10
2179	25 c. Copper-banded butterflyfish	10	15
2180	35 c. Pennant coralfish	15	20
2181	45 c. Spotted drum	20	25
2182	55 c. Blue-girdled angelfish	25	30
2183	60 c. Scorpionfish	25	30
2184	65 c. Harlequin sweetlips	30	35
2185	90 c. Flame angelfish	40	45
2186	$1 Queen triggerfish	45	50
2187	$1.20 Spotlight parrotfish	50	55
2188	$1.45 Black durgon	65	70
2189	$2 Glass-eyed snapper	85	90
2190	$5 Balloonfish	2·10	2·25
2191	$10 Creole wrasse	4·25	4·50
2192	$20 Sea bass	8·75	9·00

For these designs size 24 × 21 mm, see Nos. 2374/91.

1996. World Post Day. Multicoloured.

2193	10 c. Type **301**	10	10
2194	25 c. Anthony Trollope and Dominican postmen	10	15
2195	55 c. "Yare" (mail streamer)	25	30
2196	65 c. Rural post office	30	35
2197	90 c. Postmen carrying mail	40	45
2198	$1 Grumman Goose (seaplane) and 1958 Caribbean Federation 12 c. stamp	45	50
2199	$2 Old and new post offices and 1978 Independence 10 c. stamp	85	90

302 "Enthroned Madonna and Child" (S. Veneziano)

303 "Herdboy playing the Flute" (Li Keran)

1996. Christmas. Religious Paintings. Multicoloured.
2201 25 c. Type **302** 10 10
2202 55 c. "Noli Me Tangere" (Fra Angelico) 25 30
2203 65 c. "Madonna and Child Enthroned" (Angelico) 30 35
2204 90 c. "Madonna of Corneto Tarquinia" (F. Lippi) 40 45
2205 $2 "The Annunciation" and "The Adoration of the Magi" (School of Angelico) 85 90
2206 $5 "Madonna and Child of the Shade" (Angelico) 2·10 2·25

1997. Lunar New Year ("Year of the Ox"). Paintings by Li Keran. Multicoloured.
2208 90 c. Type **303** 40 45
2209 90 c. "Playing Cricket in the Autumn" 40 45
2210 90 c. "Listening to the Summer Cicada" 40 45
2211 90 c. "Grazing in the Spring" 40 45

304 Lee Lai-shan (Gold Medal - Wind Surfing, 1996)

1997. Olympic Games, Atlanta (3rd issue).
2213 **304** $2 multicoloured 85 95

305 "Meticella metis"

1997. Butterflies. Multicoloured.
2215 55 c. Type **305** 25 30
2216 55 c. "Coeliades forestan" 25 30
2217 55 c. "Papilio dardanus" 25 30
2218 55 c. "Mylothris chloris" 25 30
2219 55 c. "Poecilmitis thysbe" 25 30
2220 55 c. "Myrina silenus" 25 30
2221 55 c. "Bematistes aganice" 25 30
2222 55 c. "Euphaedra neophron" 25 30
2223 55 c. "Precis hierta" 25 30
2224 90 c. "Coeliades forestan" (vert) 40 45
2225 90 c. "Spialia spio" (vert) 40 45
2226 90 c. "Belenois aurota" (vert) 40 45
2227 90 c. "Dingana bowkom" (vert) 40 45
2228 90 c. "Charaxes jasius" (vert) 40 45
2229 90 c. "Catacroptera cloanthe" (vert) 40 45
2230 90 c. "Colias electo" (vert) 40 45
2231 90 c. "Junonia archesia" (vert) 40 45
No. 2230 is inscribed "Collas electo" in error.
Nos. 2215/23 and 2224/31 respectively were printed together, se-tenant, with the backgrounds forming a composite design.

1997. 50th Anniv of U.N.E.S.C.O. As T **374** of Antigua. Multicoloured.
2233 55 c. Temple roof, China 25 30
2234 65 c. The Palace of Diocletian, Split, Croatia 30 35
2235 90 c. St. Mary's Cathedral, Hildesheim, Germany 40 45
2236 $1 The Monastery of Rossanou, Mount Athos, Greece 45 50
2237 $1 Carved face, Copan, Honduras (vert) 45 50
2238 $1 Cuzco Cathedral, Peru (vert) 45 50
2239 $1 Church, Olinda, Brazil (vert) 45 50
2240 $1 Canaima National Park, Venezuela (vert) 45 50
2241 $1 Galapagos Islands National Park, Ecuador (vert) 45 50
2242 $1 Church ruins, La Santisima Jesuit Missions, Paraguay (vert) 45 50
2243 $1 San Lorenzo Fortress, Panama (vert) 45 50
2244 $1 Fortress, National Park, Haiti (vert) 45 50
2245 $2 Scandola Nature Reserve, France 85 90
2246 $4 Church of San Antao, Portugal 1·75 1·90
No. 2234 is inscribed "DICELECIAN" in error.

306 Tanglefoot and Minnie

1997. Disney Sweethearts. Multicoloured.
2248 25 c. Type **306** 10 15
2249 35 c. Mickey and Minnie kissing on ship's wheel 15 20
2250 55 c. Pluto and kitten 25 30
2251 65 c. Clarabelle Cow kissing Horace Horsecollar 30 35
2252 90 c. Elmer Elephant and tiger 40 45
2253 $1 Minnie kissing Mickey in period costume 45 50
2254 $2 Donald Duck and nephew 85 90
2255 $4 Dog kissing Pluto 1·75 1·90

307 Afghan Hound

308 "Oncidium altissimum"

1997. Cats and Dogs. Multicoloured.
2257 20 c. Type **307** 10 15
2258 25 c. Cream Burmese 10 15
2259 55 c. Cocker spaniel 25 30
2260 65 c. Smooth fox terrier 30 35
2261 90 c. West highland white terrier 40 45
2262 90 c. St. Bernard puppies 40 45
2263 90 c. Boy with grand basset 40 45
2264 90 c. Rough collie 40 45
2265 90 c. Golden retriever 40 45
2266 90 c. Golden retriever, Tibetan spaniel and smooth fox terrier 40 45
2267 90 c. Smooth fox terrier 40 45
2268 $1 Snowshoe 45 50
2269 $2 Sorrell Abyssinian 85 90
2270 $2 British bicolour shorthair 85 90
2271 $2 Maine coon and Somali kittens 85 90
2272 $2 Maine coon kitten 85 90
2273 $2 Lynx point Siamese 85 90
2274 $2 Blue Burmese kitten and white Persian 85 90
2275 $2 Persian kitten 85 90
2276 $5 Torbie Persian 2·10 2·25
Nos. 2262/7 and 2270/5 respectively were printed together, se-tenant, with the backgrounds forming composite designs.

1997. Orchids of the Caribbean. Multicoloured.
2278 20 c. Type **308** 10 10
2279 25 c. "Oncidium papilio" 10 15
2280 55 c. "Epidendrum fragrans" 25 30
2281 65 c. "Oncidium lanceanum" 30 35
2282 90 c. "Campylocentrum micranthum" 40 45
2283 $1 "Brassavola cucculata" (horiz) 40 45
2284 $1 "Epidendrum ibaguense" (horiz) 40 45
2285 $1 "Ionopsis utricularioides" (horiz) 40 45
2286 $1 "Rodriguezia lanceolata" (horiz) 40 45
2287 $1 "Oncidium cebolleta" (horiz) 40 45
2288 $1 "Epidendrum ciliare" (horiz) 40 45
2289 $4 "Pogonia rosea" 1·75 1·90
Nos. 2283/8 were printed together, se-tenant, with the backgrounds forming a composite design.

1997. 10th Anniv of Chernobyl Nuclear Disaster. As T **376** of Antigua. Multicoloured.
2292 $2 As Type **376** of Antigua 85 90
2293 $2 As Type **376** of Antigua but inscribed "CHABAD'S CHILDREN OF CHERNOBYL" at foot 85 90

1997. 50th Death Anniv of Paul Harris (founder of Rotary International). As T **377** of Antigua. Multicoloured.
2294 $2 Paul Harris and irrigation project, Honduras 85 90

1997. Golden Wedding of Queen Elizabeth and Prince Philip. As T **378** of Antigua. Multicoloured.
2296 $1 Queen Elizabeth II 45 50
2297 $1 Royal Coat of Arms 45 50
2298 $1 Queen Elizabeth and Prince Philip in shirt sleeves 45 50
2299 $1 Queen Elizabeth and Prince Philip in naval uniform 45 50
2300 $1 Buckingham Palace 45 50
2301 $1 Prince Philip 45 50

1997. "Pacific '97" International Stamp Exhibition, San Francisco. Death Centenary of Heinrich von Stephan (founder of the U.P.U.). As T **379** of Antigua.
2303 $2 violet 85 90
2304 $2 brown 85 90
2305 $2 brown 85 90
DESIGNS: No. 2303, Kaiser Wilhelm II and Heinrich von Stephan; 2304, Heinrich von Stephan and Mercury; 2305, Early Japanese postal messenger.

310 "Ichigaya Hachiman Shrine"

1997. Birth Centenary of Hiroshige (Japanese painter). "One Hundred Famous Views of Edo". Multicoloured.
2307 $1.55 Type **310** 65 70
2308 $1.55 "Blossoms on the Tama River Embankment" 65 70
2309 $1.55 "Kumano Junisha Shrine, Tsunohazu" 65 70
2310 $1.55 "Benkei Moat from Soto-Sakurada to Kojimachi" 65 70
2311 $1.55 "Kinokuni Hill and View of Akasak Tameike" 65 70
2312 $1.55 "Naito Shinjuku, Yotsuya" 65 70

1997. 175th Anniv of Brothers Grimm's Third Collection of Fairy Tales. The Goose Girl. As T **380** of Antigua. Multicoloured.
2314 $2 Goose girl with horse 85 90
2315 $2 Geese in front of castle 85 90
2316 $2 Goose girl 85 90

311 Hong Kong Skyline at Dusk

312 Yukto Kasaya (Japan) (ski jump), 1972

1997. Return of Hong Kong to China. Multicoloured.
2318 65 c. Type **311** 30 35
2319 90 c. Type **311** 40 45
2320 $1 Type **311** 45 50
2321 $1 Hong Kong at night 45 50
2322 $1.45 Hong Kong by day 65 70
2323 $2 Hong Kong at night (different) 85 90
2324 $3 Type **311** 1·25 1·40

1997. Winter Olympic Games, Nagano, Japan (1998). Multicoloured.
2325 20 c. Type **312** 10 15
2326 25 c. Jens Weissflog (Germany) (ski jump), 1994 10 15
2327 55 c. Anton Maier (Norway) (100m men's speed skating), 1968 25 30
2328 55 c. Ljubov Egorova (Russia) (women's 5km cross-country skiing), 1994 25 30
2329 65 c. Swedish ice hockey, 1994 30 35
2330 90 c. Bernhard Glass (Germany) (men's single luge), 1980 40 45
2331 $1 Type **312** 45 50
2332 $1 As No. 2326 45 50
2333 $1 As No. 2327 45 50
2334 $1 Christa Rethenburger (Germany) (women's 100m speed skating), 1988 45 50
2335 $4 Frank-Peter Roetsch (Germany) (men's biathlon), 1988 1·75 1·90

1997. World Cup Football Championship, France (1998). As T **383** of Antigua. Multicoloured (except Nos. 2343/4, 2348, 2350, 2353/4).
2337 20 c. Klinsmann, Germany (vert) 10 10
2338 55 c. Bergkamp, Holland (vert) 25 30
2339 65 c. Ravanelli, Italy (vert) 30 35
2340 65 c. Wembley Stadium, England 30 35
2341 65 c. Bernabeu Stadium, Spain 30 35
2342 65 c. Maracana Stadium, Brazil 30 35
2343 65 c. Stadio Torino, Italy (black) 30 35
2344 65 c. Centenary Stadium, Uruguay (black) 30 35
2345 65 c. Olympiastadion, Germany 30 35
2346 65 c. Rose Bowl, U.S.A. 30 35
2347 65 c. Azteca Stadium, Mexico 30 35
2348 65 c. Meazza, Italy (black) 30 35
2349 65 c. Matthaus, Germany 30 35
2350 65 c. Walter, West Germany (black) 30 35
2351 65 c. Maradona, Argentina 30 35
2352 65 c. Beckenbaur, Germany 30 35
2353 65 c. Moore, England (black) 30 35
2354 65 c. Dunga, Brazil (black) 30 35
2355 65 c. Zoff, Italy 30 35
2356 90 c. Klinkladze, Georgia 40 45
2357 $2 Shearer, England (vert) 85 90
2358 $4 Dani, Portugal (vert) 1·75 1·90

313 Joffre Robinson (former Credit Union President)

314 Louis Pasteur

1997. 40th Anniv of Co-operative Credit Union League.
2360 **313** 25 c. blue and black 10 10
2361 – 55 c. green and black 25 30
2362 – 65 c. purple and black 30 35
2363 – 90 c. multicoloured 40 45
DESIGNS—As T **313**: 55 c. Sister Alicia (founder); 65 c. Lorrel Bruce (first Credit Union President). 30 × 60 mm: $5 Sister Alicia, Joffre Robinson and Lorrel Bruce.

1997. Medical Pioneers.
2365 **314** 20 c. brown 10 10
2366 – 25 c. pink and red 10 15
2367 – 55 c. violet 25 30
2368 – 65 c. red and brown 30 35
2369 – 90 c. yellow and olive 40 45
2370 – $1 blue and ultramarine 45 50
2371 – $2 black 85 90
2372 – $3 red and brown 1·25 1·50
DESIGNS: 25 c. Christiaan Barnard (first heart transplant); 55 c. Sir Alexander Fleming (discovery of penicillin); 65 c. Camillo Golgi (neurologist); 90 c. Jonas Salk (discovery of polio vaccine); $1 Har Gobind Khorana (genetics); $2 Elizabeth Black (first woman doctor); $3 Sir Frank MacFarlane Burnet (immunologist).

1997. Fishes. As Nos. 2175/92, but smaller, 24 × 21 mm.
2374 5 c. Porcupinefish 10 10
2375 10 c. Powder-blue surgeonfish 10 10
2376 15 c. Red hind 10 10
2377 20 c. Golden butterflyfish 10 10
2378 25 c. Copper-banded butterflyfish 10 15
2379 35 c. Pennant coralfish 15 20
2380 45 c. Spotted drum 20 25
2381 55 c. Blue-girdled angelfish 25 30
2382 60 c. Scorpionfish 25 30
2383 65 c. Harlequin sweetlips 30 35
2384 90 c. Flame angelfish 40 45
2385 $1 Queen triggerfish 45 50
2386 $1.20 Spotlight parrotfish 50 55
2387 $1.45 Black durgon 65 70
2388 $2 Glass-eyed snapper 85 90
2389 $5 Balloonfish 2·10 2·25
2390 $10 Creole wrasse 4·25 4·50
2391 $20 Seabass 8·75 9·00

315 Diana, Princess of Wales

316 "Echo et Narcisse" (Toile)

1997. Diana, Princess of Wales Commemoration. Multicoloured.
2392 $2 Type **315** 85 90
2393 $2 Wearing diamond-drop earrings 85 90
2394 $2 Resting head on hand 85 90
2395 $2 Wearing tiara 85 90

1997. Christmas. Paintings.
2397 20 c. Type **316** 10 10
2398 55 c. "The Archangel Raphael leaving the Family of Tobias" (Rembrandt) 25 30
2399 65 c. "Seated Nymphs with Flute" (Francois Boucher) 30 35
2400 90 c. "Angel" (Rembrandt) 40 45
2401 $2 "Dispute" (Raphael) 85 90
2402 $4 "Holy Trinity" (Raphael) 1·75 1·90

317 "Tiger" (Gao Qifeng)

318 Akira Kurosawa

1998. Chinese New Year ("Year of the Tiger"). Multicoloured.
2404 55 c. Type **317** 25 30
2405 65 c. "Tiger" (Zhao Shao'ang) 30 35
2406 90 c. "Tiger" (Gao Jianfu) . . 40 45
2407 $1.20 "Tiger" (different) (Gao Jianfu) 50 55

1998. Millennium Series. Famous People of the Twentieth Century. Multicoloured (except Nos. 2410 and 2413/14). (a) Japanese Cinema Stars.
2409 $1 Type **318** 45 50
2410 $1 "Rashomon" directed by Kursawa (56 × 42 mm) . . 45 50
2411 $1 Toshiro Mifune in "Seven Samurai" (black and grey) (56 × 42 mm) 45 50
2412 $1 Toshiro Mifune 45 50
2413 $1 Yasujiro Ozu 45 50
2414 $1 "Late Spring" directed by Ozu (black and grey) (56 × 42 mm) 45 50
2415 $1 Sessue Hayakawa in "Bridge on the River Kwai" (brown, deep brown and black) (56 × 42 mm) 45 50
2416 $1 Sessue Hayakawa 45 50

(b) Sporting Record Holders. Multicoloured.
2418 $1 Jesse Owens (winner of four Olympic gold medals, Berlin, 1936) 45 50
2419 $1 Owens competing at Berlin (56 × 42 mm) 45 50
2420 $1 Isaac Berger competing (56 × 42 mm) 45 50
2421 $1 Isaac Berger (weightlifter) 45 50
2422 $1 Boris Becker (Wimbledon champion) 45 50
2423 $1 Boris Becker on court (56 × 42 mm) 45 50
2424 $1 Ashe with Wimbledon trophy (56 × 42 mm) 45 50
2425 $1 Arthur Ashe (1st African-American Wimbledon singles champion, 1975) 45 50

319 "Omphalotus illudens"

1998. Fungi of the World. Multicoloured.
2427 10 c. Type **319** 10 15
2428 15 c. "Inocybe fastigiata" . . 10 15
2429 20 c. "Marasmius plicatulus" 10 15
2430 50 c. "Mycena lilacifolia" . . 20 25
2431 55 c. "Armillaria straminea" and "Calastrina argiolus" (butterfly) 25 30
2432 90 c. "Tricholomopsis rutilans" and "Melitaea didyma" (butterfly) 45 50
2433 $1 "Lepiota naucina" 45 50
2434 $1 "Cortinarius violaceus" . 45 50
2435 $1 "Boletus aereus" 45 50
2436 $1 "Tricholoma aurantium" . 45 50
2437 $1 "Lepiota procera" 45 50
2438 $1 "Clitocybe geotropa" . . 45 50
2439 $1 "Lepiota acutesquamosa" . 45 50
2440 $1 "Tricholoma saponaceum" 45 50
2441 $1 "Lycoperdon gemmatum" 45 50
2442 $1 "Boletus ornatipes" . . . 45 50
2443 $1 "Russula xerampelina" . . 45 50
2444 $1 "Cortinarius collinitus" . 45 50
2445 $1 "Agaricus meleagris" . . 45 50
2446 $1 "Coprinus comatus" . . . 45 50
2447 $1 "Amanita caesarea" . . . 45 50
2448 $1 "Amanita brunnescens" . . 45 50
2449 $1 "Amanita muscaria" . . . 45 50
2450 $1 "Morchella esculenta" . . 45 50

Nos. 2433/41 and 2442/50 respectively were printed together, se-tenant, with the backgrounds forming composite designs.

INDEX

Countries can be quickly located by referring to the index at the end of this volume.

320 Topsail Schooner

1998. History of Sailing Ships. Multicoloured.
2452 55 c. Type **320** 25 30
2453 55 c. "Golden Hind" (Drake) 25 30
2454 55 c. "Moshulu" (barque) . 25 30
2455 55 c. "Bluenose" (schooner) 25 30
2456 55 c. Roman merchant ship . 25 30
2457 55 c. "Gazela Primiero" (barquentine) 25 30
2458 65 c. Greek war galley . . . 30 35
2459 90 c. Egyptian felucca . . . 40 45
2460 $1 Viking longship 45 50
2461 $2 Chinese junk 85 90

No. 2457 is inscribed "GAZELA PRIMERIRO", and both Nos. 2458/9 "EGPYTIAN FELUCCA", all in error.

321 "Steamboat Willie", 1928

1998. 70th Anniv of Mickey and Minnie Mouse. Multicoloured.
2463 25 c. Type **321** 10 15
2464 55 c. "The Brave Little Tailor", 1938 . . . . 25 30
2465 65 c. "Nifty Nineties", 1941 30 35
2466 90 c. "Mickey Mouse Club", 1955 . . . . 40 45
2467 $1 Mickey and Minnie at opening of Walt Disney World, 1971 . . . . 45 50
2468 $1.45 "Mousercise Mickey and Minnie", 1980 . . . . . . 65 70
2469 $5 "Runaway Brain", 1995 (97 × 110 mm) . . . . . . 2·10 2·25

322 Big-crested Penguin ("Erect Crested Penguin")

1998. Sea Birds. Multicoloured.
2471 25 c. Type **322** 10 15
2472 65 c. Humboldt penguin . . 30 35
2473 90 c. Knot 40 45
2474 90 c. Crested tern 40 45
2475 90 c. Franklin's gull 40 45
2476 90 c. Australian pelican . . 40 45
2477 90 c. Fairy prion 40 45
2478 90 c. Andean gull 40 45
2479 90 c. Blue-eyed cormorant ("Imperial Shag") 40 45
2480 90 c. Grey phalarope ("Red Phalarope") 40 45
2481 90 c. Hooded grebe 40 45
2482 90 c. Least aucklet 40 45
2483 90 c. Little grebe 40 45
2484 90 c. Pintado petrel ("Cape Petrel") 40 45
2485 90 c. Slavonian grebe ("Horned Grebe") 40 45
2486 $1 Audubon's shearwater . . 45 50

Nos. 2474/85 were printed together, se-tenant, with the backgrounds forming a composite design.

323 Jetstar II

1998. Modern Aircraft. Multicoloured.
2488 20 c. Type **323** 10 10
2489 25 c. AN 225 . . . . 10 15
2490 55 c. L.I.A.T. Dash-8 . . . 25 30
2491 65 c. Cardinal Airlines, Beech-99 . . . . 30 35
2492 90 c. American Airlines Eagle 40 45
2493 $1 SR 71 "Blackbird" spy plane 45 50
2494 $1 Stealth Bomber 45 50
2495 $1 Northrop YF23 . . . . . 45 50
2496 $1 F-14A Tomcat 45 50
2497 $1 F-15 Eagle S 45 50
2498 $1 MiG 29 Fulcrum 45 50
2499 $1 Europa X5 . . . . 45 50
2500 $1 Camion 45 50
2501 $1 E 400 . . . . 45 50
2502 $1 CL-215 C-GKDN amphibian 45 50
2503 $1 Piper Jet 45 50
2504 $1 Beech Hawker 45 50
2505 $1 Lockheed YF22 . . . . . 45 50
2506 $1 Piper Seneca V 45 50
2507 $1 CL-215 amphibian 45 50
2508 $1 Vantase 45 50
2509 $2 Itansa HFB 320 . . . . . 85 90

324 Stylised Americas

1998. 50th Anniv of Organization of American States.
2511 **324** $1 multicoloured 45 50

325 "The Painter and his Model"

1998. 25th Death Anniv of Pablo Picasso (painter). Multicoloured.
2512 90 c. Type **325** 40 45
2513 $1 "The Crucifixion" 45 50
2514 $2 "Nude with Raised Arms" (vert) 85 90

326 365 GT 2 + 2

1998. Birth Centenary of Enzo Ferrari (car manufacturer). Multicoloured.
2516 55 c. Type **326** 25 30
2517 90 c. Boano/Ellena 250 GT . 40 45
2518 $1 375 MM coupe 45 50

327 Mahatma Gandhi

329 Scout Saluting

328 H.S. 801 Nimrod MR2P (reconnaissance)

1998. 50th Death Anniv of Mahatma Gandhi. Multicoloured.
2520 **327** 90 c. multicoloured . . . 40 45

1998. 80th Anniv of Royal Air Force. Multicoloured.
2522 $2 Type **328** 85 90
2523 $2 Lockheed C-130 Hercules (transport) 85 90
2524 $2 Panavia Tornado GR1 . . 85 90
2525 $2 Lockheed C-130 Hercules landing 85 90

No. 2525 is inscribed "Panavia Tornado GR1" in error.

1998. 19th World Scout Jamboree, Chile. Multicoloured.
2527 65 c. Type **329** 30 35
2528 $1 Scout handshake 45 50
2529 $2 International scout flag . . 85 90

330 Fridman Fish

1998. International Year of the Ocean. Multicoloured.
2531 25 c. Type **330** 10 15
2532 55 c. Hydrocoral 25 30
2533 65 c. Feather-star 30 35
2534 90 c. Royal angelfish 40 45
2535 $1 Monk seal 45 50
2536 $1 Galapagos penguin . . . 45 50
2537 $1 Manta ray 45 50
2538 $1 Hawksbill turtle 45 50
2539 $1 Moorish idols 45 50
2540 $1 Nautilius 45 50
2541 $1 Giant clam 45 50
2542 $1 Tubeworms 45 50
2543 $1 Nudibranch 45 50
2544 $1 Spotted dolphins 45 50
2545 $1 Atlantic sailfish 45 50
2546 $1 Sailfin flying fish 45 50
2547 $1 Fairy basslet 45 50
2548 $1 Atlantic spadefish 45 50
2549 $1 Leatherback turtle 45 50
2550 $1 Blue tang 45 50
2551 $1 Coral-banded shrimp . . 45 50
2552 $1 Rock beauty 45 50

Nos. 2535/43 and 2544/52 respectively were printed together, se-tenant, with the backgrounds forming composite designs.

1998. Save the Turtles Campaign. Nos. 1686/7, 1689/90 and 1692 optd **Save the Turtles**.
2554 25 c. Type **263** 10 15
2555 55 c. Hawksbill turtle swimming 25 30
2556 90 c. Green turtle laying eggs 40 45
2557 $1 Green turtle swimming . . 45 50
2558 $4 Loggerhead turtle . . . . 1·75 1·90

332 Northern Cardinal

1998. Christmas. Birds. Multicoloured.
2559 25 c. Type **332** 10 15
2560 55 c. Eastern bluebird . . . 25 30
2561 65 c. Carolina wren 30 35
2562 90 c. Blue jay 40 45
2563 $1 Evening grosbeak 45 50
2564 $2 Bohemian waxwing . . . 85 90

333 "Magpies and Hare" (Ts'ui Pai)

1999. Chinese New Year ("Year of the Rabbit").
2566 **333** $1.50 multicoloured . . . 65 70

APPENDIX

The following stamps have either been issued in excess of postal needs, or have not been made available to the public in reasonable quantities at face value.

1978-79

History of Aviation. $16 × 30, each embossed on gold foil.

DUNGARPUR

A state of Rajasthan. Now uses Indian stamps.

12 pies = 1 anna; 16 annas = 1 rupee

1 State Arms

2 Maharawal Lakshman Singh

1933.

1	**1**	¼ a. yellow	—	£110
2		¼ a. red	—	£325
3		¼ a. brown	—	£200
4		1 a. blue	—	95·00
5		1 a. red	—	£1000
6		1 a. 3 p. violet	—	£150
7		2 a. green	—	£180
8		4 a. red	—	£350

1932. T **2** (various frames).

9	**2**	¼ a. orange	£350	48·00
10		½ a. red	£160	35·00
11		1 a. blue	£150	27·00
12		1 a. 3 p. mauve	£400	£140
13		1¼ a. violet	£425	£140
14		2 a. green	£475	£250
15		4 a. brown	£400	£110

DUTTIA (DATIA)

A state of Central India. Now uses Indian stamps.

12 pies = 1 anna; 16 annas = 1 rupee

2 (½ a.) Ganesh

3 (4 a.) Ganesh

1894?. Imperf.

1	**2**	½ a. black on green	£5500
2a		2 a. blue on yellow	£2250

Nos. 1/2a are as Type **2**, but have rosettes in lower corners.

1896. Imperf.

4	**3**	¼ a. black on orange	£2750
5		½ a. black on green	£3250
6		2 a. black on yellow	£1800
7		4 a. black on red	£1300

Stamps of Type **3** come with the circular handstamp as shown on Type **2**. Examples of Nos. 4/5 without handstamp are worth slightly less than the prices quoted.

1896. Imperf.

8b	**2**	½ a. black on green	15·00	£150
3		1 a. red	£1900	£2000
9		1 a. black	60·00	£170
10		2 a. black on yellow	20·00	£160
11		4 a. black on red	17·00	£130

4 (½ a.)

5 (¼ a.)

1897. Imperf.

12	**4**	½ a. black on green	55·00	£325
13		1 a. black	£120	
14		2 a. black on yellow	65·00	
15		4 a. black on red	60·00	

1899. Imperf roul or perf.

16c	**5**	¼ a. red	3·00	11·00
38		¼ a. blue	1·75	8·00
37		¼ a. black	3·50	15·00
17		½ a. black on green	1·60	11·00
30		½ a. green	4·00	17·00
35		½ a. blue	2·50	11·00
39		½ a. pink	2·00	12·00
18		1 a. black	1·90	11·00
31		1 a. purple	3·50	18·00
36		1 a. pink	2·25	13·00
19b		2 a. black on yellow	2·00	13·00
32		2 a. brown	10·00	22·00
33		2 a. lilac	5·00	22·00
20		4 a. black on red	2·50	12·00
34		4 a. brown	65·00	

FALKLAND ISLANDS

A British colony in the South Atlantic.

1878. 12 pence = 1 shilling;
20 shillings = 1 pound.
1971. 100 (new) pence = 1 pound.

3

6

1878.

17b	**3**	½d. green	2·00	2·50
23		1d. red to brown	5·00	2·00
26		2d. purple	5·00	11·00
30		2½d. blue	20·00	8·50
32		4d. black	10·00	21·00
3		6d. green	50·00	50·00
34		6d. yellow	27·00	35·00
35		9d. red	28·00	55·00
38		1s. brown	40·00	40·00
41	–	2s. 6d. blue	£200	£250
42	**6**	5s. red	£160	£200

DESIGN: 2s. 6d. As Type **6**, but different frame.

1891. No. 23 bisected diagonally and each half surch **½d.**

13	**3**	½d. on half of 1d. brown	£500	£300

7

8

1904.

43	**7**	½d. green	4·25	1·50
44b		1d. red	1·00	2·25
45		2d. purple	11·00	26·00
46		2½d. blue	29·00	7·50
47		6d. orange	38·00	48·00
48		1s. brown	40·00	32·00
49b	**8**	3s. green	£120	£120
50		5s. red	£140	£150

1912. As T **7/8** but portrait of King George V.

60	½d. green	2·75	3·50
74	1d. red	5·00	1·25
75	2d. purple	10·00	6·00
76b	2½d. blue	5·50	16·00
77a	2½d. purple on yellow	4·25	32·00
64	6d. orange	14·00	20·00
65	1s. brown	30·00	30·00
66	3s. green	70·00	80·00
67	5s. red	70·00	95·00
67b	5s. purple	70·00	95·00
68	10s. red on green	£150	£225
69	£1 black on red	£325	£375

1918. As 1912, optd **WAR STAMP**.

70b	½d. green	50	6·50
71c	1d. red	50	3·50
72a	1s. brown	4·00	42·00

1928. No. 75 surch **2½D**.

115	2½d. on 2d. purple	£650	£750

13 Fin Whale and Gentoo Penguins

15 Romney Marsh Ram

1929.

116	**13**	½d. green	80	3·00
117		1d. red	2·50	80
118		2d. grey	2·25	2·00
119		2½d. blue	2·50	2·25
120		4d. orange	12·00	13·00
121		6d. purple	13·00	13·00
122		1s. black on green	17·00	26·00
123		2s. 6d. red on blue	35·00	40·00
124		5s. green on yellow	60·00	75·00
125		10s. red on green	£100	£140
126		£1 black on red	£275	£375

1933. Centenary of British Administration. Inscr "1833–1933".

127	**15**	½d. black and green	1·50	5·00
128	–	1d. black and red	3·50	2·25
129	–	1½d. black and blue	10·00	13·00
130	–	2d. black and brown	9·00	21·00
131	–	3d. black and violet	11·00	14·00
132	–	4d. black and orange	11·00	15·00
133	–	6d. black and grey	48·00	55·00
134	–	1s. black and olive	38·00	55·00
135	–	2s. 6d. black and violet	£130	£150
136	–	5s. black and yellow	£500	£650
137	–	10s. black and brown	£500	£700
138	–	£1 black and red	£1300	£1800

DESIGNS—HORIZ: 1d. Iceberg; 1½d. Whale-catcher; 2d. Port Louis; 3d. Map of Falkland Islands; 4d. South Georgia; 6d. Fin whale; 1s. Government House, Stanley. VERT: 2s. 6d. Battle Memorial; 5s. King penguin; 10s. Arms; £1 King George V.

1935. Silver Jubilee. As T **13** of Antigua.

139	1d. blue and red	2·75	40
140	2½d. brown and blue	8·00	1·60
141	4d. green and blue	9·00	4·00
142	1s. grey and purple	8·00	3·25

1937. Coronation. As T **2** of Aden.

143	½d. green	30	10
144	1d. red	40	45
145	2½d. blue	80	55

27 Whales' Jaw Bones

1938.

146	**27**	½d. black and green	30	75
147a	A	1d. black and red	3·00	85
148	B	1d. black and violet	2·50	1·75
149		2d. black and violet	1·00	50
150	A	2d. black and red	75	2·25
151	C	2½d. black and blue	75	30
152	D	2½d. black and blue	5·50	6·50
153	C	3d. black and blue	6·50	2·25
154	D	4d. black and purple	2·75	50
155	E	6d. black and brown	3·25	1·50
156		6d. black	4·25	3·75
157	F	9d. black and blue	13·00	80
158a	G	1s. blue	16·00	2·50
159	H	1s. 3d. black and red	2·25	1·40
160	I	2s. 6d. black	55·00	10·00
161	J	5s. blue and orange	£110	55·00
162	K	10s. black and orange	55·00	27·00
163	L	£1 black and violet	£110	48·00

DESIGNS—HORIZ: A, Black-necked swan; B, Battle memorial; C, Flock of sheep; D, Magellan goose; E, "Discovery II" (polar supply vessel); F, "William Scoresby" (research ship); G, Mount Sugar Top; H. Turkey vultures; I, Gentoo penguins; J, Southern sealion; K, Deception Is.; L, Arms of Falkland Islands.

1946. Victory. As T **9** of Aden.

164	1d. mauve	30	15
165	3d. blue	45	15

1948. Silver Wedding. As T **10/11** of Aden.

166	2½d. blue	2·00	70
167	£1 mauve	90·00	55·00

1949. U.P.U. As T **20/23** of Antigua.

168	1d. violet	1·50	75
169	3d. blue	5·00	2·00
170	1s. 3d. green	4·00	2·25
171	2s. blue	4·00	7·50

39 Sheep

1952.

172	**39**	½d. green	70	70
173	–	1d. red	1·25	40
174	–	2d. violet	3·25	2·50
175	–	2½d. black and blue	95	50
176	–	3d. blue	1·00	1·00
177	–	4d. purple	7·50	1·50
178	–	6d. brown	12·00	1·00
179	–	9d. yellow	9·00	2·00
180	–	1s. black	20·00	80
181	–	1s. 3d. orange	12·00	5·00
182	–	2s. 6d. olive	16·00	7·00
183	–	5s. purple	8·50	6·00
184	–	10s. grey	20·00	17·00
185	–	£1 black	25·00	17·00

DESIGNS—HORIZ: 1d. "Fitzroy" (supply ship); 2d. Magellan goose; 2½d. Map; 4d. Auster Autocrat aircraft; 6d. "John Biscoe I" (research ship); 9d. View of the Two Sisters; 1s. 3d. Kelp goose and gander; 10s. Southern sealion and South American fur seal; £1 Hulk of "Great Britain". VERT: 3d. Arms; 1s. Gentoo penguins; 2s. 6d. Sheep shearing; 5s. Battle Memorial.

1953. Coronation. As T **13** of Aden.

186	1d. black and red	80	1·25

1955. As 1952 issue but with portrait of Queen Elizabeth II.

187	½d. green	70	1·25
188	1d. red	1·25	1·00
189	2d. violet	2·75	4·50
190	6d. brown	6·50	60
191	9d. yellow	17·00	17·00
192	1s. black	5·00	1·25

54 Austral Thrush

1960. Birds.

227	**54**	½d. black and green	30	40
194	–	1d. black and red	1·50	70
195	–	2d. black and blue	3·25	1·00
196	–	2½d. black and bistre	1·50	20
197	–	3d. black and olive	80	15
198	–	4d. black and red	1·25	60
199	–	5½d. black and violet	1·75	1·50
200	–	6d. black and sepia	2·00	15
201	–	9d. black and red	2·00	80
202	–	1s. black and purple	80	15
203	–	1s. 3d. black and blue	10·00	12·00
204	–	2s. black and brown	27·00	2·25
205	–	5s. black and turquoise	27·00	11·00
206	–	10s. black and purple	48·00	13·00
207	–	£1 black and yellow	48·00	27·00

BIRDS: 1d. Southern black-backed gull; 2d. Gentoo penguins; 2½d. Long-tailed meadow lark; 3d. Magellan goose; 4d. Falkland Island flightless steamer ducks; 5½d. Rock-hopper penguins; 6d. Black-browed albatross; 9d. Silver grebe; 1s. Magellanic oystercatcher; 1s. 3d. Chilean teal; 2s. Kelp geese; 5s. King cormorants; 10s. Common caracara; £1 Black-necked swan.

69 Morse Key

72 H.M.S. "Glasgow"

1962. 50th Anniv of Establishment of Radio Communications.

208	**69**	6d. red and orange	1·00	30
209	–	1s. green and olive	1·25	35
210	–	2s. violet and blue	1·25	1·50

DESIGNS: 1s. One-valve receiver; 2s. Rotary spark transmitter.

1963. Freedom from Hunger. As T **28** of Aden.

211	1s. blue	13·00	1·25

1963. Centenary of Red Cross. As T **33** of Antigua.

212	1d. red and black	5·00	50
213	1s. red and blue	20·00	6·00

1964. 400th Birth Anniv of Shakespeare. As T **34** of Antigua.

214	6d. black	1·00	40

1964. 50th Anniv of Battle of the Falkland Islands.

215	**72**	2½d. black and red	9·00	3·25
216	–	6d. black and blue	75	25
217	–	1s. black and red	75	75
218	–	2s. black and blue	50	75

DESIGNS—HORIZ: 6d. H.M.S. "Kent"; 1s. H.M.S. "Invincible". VERT: 2s. Battle Memorial.

1965. Centenary of I.T.U. As T **36** of Antigua.

219	1d. light blue and deep blue	75	20
220	2s. lilac and yellow	9·00	1·50

1965. I.C.Y. As T **37** of Antigua.

221	1d. purple and turquoise	2·00	20
222	1s. green and lavender	7·50	1·10

1966. Churchill Commemoration. As T **38** of Antigua.

223	½d. blue	65	50
224	1d. green	2·25	15
225	1s. brown	6·50	2·00
226	2s. violet	5·50	2·00

76 Globe and Human Rights Emblem

77 Dusty Miller

1968. Human Rights Year.

228	**76**	2d. multicoloured	60	20
229		6d. multicoloured	70	20
230		1s. multicoloured	70	20
231		2s. multicoloured	70	30

1968. Flowers. Multicoloured.

232	½d. Type **77**	15	1·60
233	1½d. Pig vine	30	15
234	2d. Pale maiden	40	15
235	3d. Dog orchid	4·75	65
236	3½d. Sea cabbage	30	15
237	4½d. Vanilla daisy	1·25	1·75
238	5½d. yellow, brown and green (Arrowleaf marigold)	1·25	1·75
239	6d. red, black and green (Diddle dee)	60	20
240	1s. Scurvy grass	60	1·00
241	1s. 6d. Prickly burr	4·50	11·00
242	2s. Fachine	5·50	6·50
243	3s. Lavender	8·00	7·00
244	5s. Felton's flower	27·00	13·00
245	£1 Yellow orchid	13·00	2·00

Nos. 233, 236, 238/40 and 244 are horiz.

91 De Havilland Beaver Seaplane

1969. 21st Anniv of Government Air Services. Multicoloured.

246	2d. Type **91**	35	30
247	6d. Noorduyn Norseman V	40	35
248	1s. Auster Autocrat	50	35
249	2s. Arms of the Falkland Islands	1·25	1·75

92 Holy Trinity Church, 1869

1969. Centenary of Bishop Stirling's Consecretation.

250	**92** 2d. black, grey and green	50	60
251	– 6d. black, grey and red	50	60
252	– 1s. black, grey and lilac	50	60
253	– 2s. multicoloured	70	75

DESIGNS: 6d. Christ Church Cathedral, 1969; 1s. Bishop Stirling; 2s. Bishop's Mitre.

96 Mounted Volunteer

1970. Golden Jubilee of Defence Force. Mult.

254	2d. Type **96**	1·90	70
255	6d. Defence Post	2·00	70
256	1s. Corporal in No. 1 Dress uniform	2·00	70
257	2s. Badge	3·00	75

Nos. 255 and 257 are horiz.

97 S.S. "Great Britain" (1843)

1970. S.S. "Great Britain" Restoration. Stamps show S.S. "Great Britain" in year given. Multicoloured.

258	2d. Type **97**	1·75	40
259	4d. 1845	2·00	1·00
260	9d. 1876	2·00	1·00
261	1s. 1886	2·00	1·00
262	2s. 1970	2·00	1·00

1971. Decimal Currency. Nos. 232/44 surch.

263	½p. on ½d. multicoloured	25	20
264	1p. on 1½d. multicoloured	30	15
265	1½p. on 2d. multicoloured	30	15
266	2p. on 3d. multicoloured	50	20
267	2½p. on 3½d. multicoloured	30	20
268	3p. on 4½d. multicoloured	30	20
269	4p. on 5½d. yellow, brn & grn	30	20
270	5p. on 6d. red, black and green	30	20
271	6p. on 1s. multicoloured	6·00	4·25
272	7½p. on 1s. 6d. multicoloured	8·00	5·50
273	10p. on 2s. multicoloured	8·50	3·00
274	15p. on 3s. multicoloured	6·50	2·75
275	25p. on 5s. multicoloured	7·00	3·25

1972. Decimal Currency. Nos. 232/44 inscr in decimal currency.

276	½p. multicoloured	35	4·00
277	1p. multicoloured	30	40
278	1½p. multicoloured	30	3·50
279	2p. multicoloured	13·00	1·25
280	2½p. multicoloured	35	3·50
281	3p. multicoloured	35	1·25
282	4p. yellow, brown and green	40	50
283	5p. red, black and green	40	55
295	6p. multicoloured	2·00	2·25
285	7½p. multicoloured	1·50	4·00
286	10p. multicoloured	8·00	4·50
287	15p. multicoloured	4·50	5·00
288	25p. multicoloured	4·50	6·00

1972. Royal Silver Wedding. As T **52** of Ascension but with Romney Marsh Sheep and Giant Sea Lions in background.

289	1p. green	40	40
290	10p. blue	85	85

1973. Royal Wedding. As T **47** of Anguilla. Background colour given. Multicoloured.

291	5p. mauve	25	10
292	15p. brown	35	20

101 South American Fur Seal

1974. Tourism. Multicoloured.

296	2p. Type **101**	2·25	1·00
297	4p. Trout-fishing	3·00	1·25
298	5p. Rockhopper penguins	9·50	2·50
299	15p. Long-tailed meadow lark	12·00	4·25

102 19th-century Mail-coach

1974. U.P.U. Multicoloured.

300	2p. Type **102**	25	25
301	5p. Packet ship, 1841	35	45
302	8p. First U.K. aerial post, 1911	40	55
303	16p. Ship's catapult mail, 1920s	60	75

103 Churchill and Houses of Parliament

1974. Birth Centenary of Sir Winston Churchill. Multicoloured.

304	16p. Type **103**	1·40	1·60
305	20p. Churchill with H.M.S. "Inflexible" and H.M.S. "Invincible", 1914	1·40	1·90

104 H.M.S. "Exeter"

1974. 35th Anniv of Battle of the River Plate. Multicoloured.

307	2p. Type **104**	3·00	1·60
308	6p. H.M.N.Z. "Achilles"	4·50	3·50
309	8p. "Admiral Graf Spee"	5·00	4·50
310	16p. H.M.S. "Ajax"	8·50	15·00

105 Seal and Flag Badge

1975. 50th Anniv of Heraldic Arms. Multicoloured.

311	2p. Type **105**	70	35
312	7½p. Coat of arms, 1925	1·40	1·40
313	10p. Coat of arms, 1948	1·60	1·60
314	16p. Arms of the Dependencies, 1952	2·25	3·25

106 ½p. Coin and Brown Trout

1975. New Coinage. Multicoloured.

316	2p. Type **106**	85	50
317	5½p. 1p. coin and Gentoo penguin	1·25	1·40
318	8p. 2p. coin and Magellan goose	1·60	1·60
319	10p. 5p. coin and Black-browed albatross	1·75	1·75
320	16p. 10p. coin and Southern sealion	1·90	2·25

107 Gathering Sheep

1976. Sheep Farming Industry. Multicoloured.

321	2p. Type **107**	55	40
322	7½p. Shearing	1·25	1·50
323	10p. Dipping	1·60	1·60
324	20p. Shipping	2·25	3·00

108 The Queen awaiting Anointment

1977. Silver Jubilee. Multicoloured.

325	6p. Visit of Prince Philip, 1957	2·00	1·25
326	11p. The Queen, ampulla and anointing spoon	30	75
327	33p. Type **108**	40	1·25

109 Map of Falkland Islands

1977. Telecommunications. Multicoloured.

328	3p. Type **109**	60	15
329	11p. Ship to shore communications	1·00	40
330	40p. Telex and telephone service	2·75	1·75

110 "A.E.S.", 1957–74

1978. Mail Ships. Multicoloured.

331A	1p. Type **110**	20	30
332A	2p. "Darwin", 1957–73	30	30
333A	3p. "Merak-N", 1951–52	25	80
334A	4p. "Fitzroy", 1936–57	30	40
335A	5p. "Lafonia", 1936–41	30	30
336A	6p. "Fleurus", 1924–33	30	40
337A	7p. "Falkland", 1914–34	30	1·50
338A	8p. "Oravia", 1900–12	35	50
339A	9p. "Memphis", 1890–97	35	50
340A	10p. "Black Hawk", 1873–80	35	50
341B	20p. "Foam", 1863–72	1·25	1·75
342B	25p. "Fairy", 1857–61	1·25	2·50
343B	50p. "Amelia", 1852–54	2·25	3·00
344B	£1 "Nautilus", 1846–48	2·50	4·50
345B	£3 "Hebe", 1842–46	5·50	9·50

Nos. 331/45 come with and without date imprint.

111 Short Hythe at Stanley

112 Red Dragon of Wales

1978. 26th Anniv of First Direct Flight, Southampton–Port Stanley. Multicoloured.

346	11p. Type **111**	2·75	2·50
347	33p. Route map and Short Hythe flying boat	3·25	3·00

1978. 25th Anniv of Coronation. Multicoloured.

348	**112** 25p. brown, blue and silver	60	1·00
349	– 25p. multicoloured	60	1·00
350	– 25p. brown, blue and silver	60	1·00

DESIGNS: No 349, Queen Elizabeth II; No. 350, Hornless ram.

113 First Fox Bay P.O. and 1d. Stamp of 1878

114 "Macrocystis pyrifera"

1978. Centenary of First Falkland Island Postage Stamp. Multicoloured.

351	3p. Type **113**	25	20
352	11p. Second Stanley P.O. and 4d. stamp of 1878	40	50
353	15p. New Island P.O. and 6d. stamp of 1878	50	60
354	22p. First Stanley P.O. and 1s. stamp of 1878	80	1·00

1979. Kelp and Seaweed. Multicoloured.

355	3p. Type **114**	30	25
356	7p. "Durvillea sp."	50	45
357	11p. "Lessonia sp." (horiz)	65	60
358	15p. "Callophyllis sp." (horiz)	85	80
359	25p. "Iradaea sp."	1·00	1·40

115 Britten Norman Islander over Falkland Islands

1979. Opening of Stanley Airport. Multicoloured.

360	3p. Type **115**	30	20
361	11p. Fokker F.27 Friendship over South Atlantic	70	60
362	15p. Fokker F.28 Fellowship over Airport	80	60
363	25p. Cessna 172 Skyhawk, Britten Norman Islander, Fokker F.27 Friendship and Fokker F.28 Fellowship over runway	1·50	80

116 Sir Rowland Hill and 1953 Coronation 1d. Commemorative

1979. Death Centenary of Sir Rowland Hill. Multicoloured.

364	3p. Type **116**	25	25
365	11p. 1878 1d. stamp (vert)	40	70
366	25p. Penny Black	60	85

117 Mail Drop by De Havilland Beaver Aircraft

1979. Centenary of U.P.U. Membership. Multicoloured.

368	3p. Type **117**	20	20
369	11p. Mail by horseback	45	55
370	25p. Mail by schooner "Gwendolin"	75	1·00

118 Peale's Porpoise

1980. Dolphins and Porpoises. Multicoloured.

371	3p. Type **118**	40	40
372	6p. Commerson's dolphin (horiz)	50	50
373	7p. Hour-glass dolphin (horiz)	50	50
374	11p. Spectacled porpoise	70	80
375	15p. Dusky dolphin (horiz)	80	1·00
376	25p. Killer whale (horiz)	1·00	1·60

119 1878 Falkland Islands Postmark

1980. "London 1980" International Stamp Exhibition.
377 **119** 11p. black, gold and blue . . 30 30
378 – 11p. black, gold and yellow 30 30
379 – 11p. black, gold and green 30 30
380 – 11p. black, gold and purple 30 30
381 – 11p. black, gold and red . 30 30
382 – 11p. black, gold and flesh 30 30
POSTMARKS: No. 378, 1915 New Island; No. 379, 1901 Falkland Islands; No. 380, 1935 Port Stanley; No. 381, 1952 Port Stanley first overseas airmail; No. 382, 1934 Fox Bay.

120 Queen Elizabeth the Queen Mother at Ascot, 1971

1980. 80th Birthday of Queen Mother.
383 **120** 11p. multicoloured 40 30

121 Forster's Caracara

1980. Birds of Prey. Multicoloured.
384 3p. Type **121** 50 25
385 11p. Red-backed buzzard . . 80 60
386 15p. Common caracara . . . 95 75
387 25p. Peregrine falcon . . . . 1·25 1·00

122 Stanley

1981. Early Settlements. Multicoloured.
388 3p. Type **122** 15 15
389 11p. Port Egmont 30 35
390 25p. Port Louis 60 65
391 33p. Mission House, Keppel Island 70 80

123 Sheep

1981. Farm Animals. Multicoloured.
392 3p. Type **123** 20 30
393 11p. Cattle 35 55
394 25p. Horse . . . . 70 1·25
395 33p. Dogs . . . . 1·00 1·50

124 Bowles and Carver, 1779

1981. Early Maps.
396 **124** 3p. multicoloured 25 30
397 – 10p. multicoloured 45 55
398 – 13p. multicoloured 55 75
399 – 15p. multicoloured 55 85
400 – 25p. multicoloured 65 90
401 – 26p. black, pink and stone 65 90
MAPS: 10p. J. Hawkesworth, 1773; 13p. Eman Bowen, 1747; 15p. T. Boutflower, 1768; 25p. Philippe de Pretot, 1771; 26p. Bellin "Petite Atlas Maritime", Paris, 1764.

125 Wedding Bouquet from Falkland Islands

126 "Handicrafts"

1981. Royal Wedding. Multicoloured.
402 10p. Type **125** 30 40
403 13p. Prince Charles riding . . 40 50
404 52p. Prince Charles and Lady Diana Spencer . . . . . . 70 1·00

1981. 25th Anniv of Duke of Edinburgh Award Scheme. Multicoloured.
405 10p. Type **126** 15 20
406 13p. "Camping" 20 30
407 15p. "Canoeing" 30 40
408 26p. Duke of Edinburgh . . 35 60

127 "The Adoration of the Holy Child" (16th-century Dutch Artist)

1981. Christmas. Paintings. Multicoloured.
409 3p. Type **127** 20 20
410 13p. "The Holy Family in an Italian Landscape" (17th-century Genoan artist) . . 35 45
411 26p. "The Holy Virgin" (Reni) 55 75

128 Patagonian Sprat

1981. Shelf Fishes. Multicoloured.
412 5p. Type **128** 20 20
413 13p. Gunther's rockcod (vert) 35 35
414 15p. Argentine hake . . . 40 40
415 25p. Southern blue whiting . 60 75
416 26p. Grey-tailed skate (vert) . 60 75

129 "Lady Elizabeth", 1913

1982. Shipwrecks. Multicoloured.
417 5p. Type **129** 30 50
418 13p. "Capricorn", 1882 . . . 35 70
419 15p. "Jhelum", 1870 . . . 40 85
420 25p. "Snowsquall", 1864 . . 55 1·10
421 26p. "St. Mary", 1890 . . . 55 1·10

130 Charles Darwin

1982. 150th Anniv of Charles Darwin's Voyage. Multicoloured.
422 5p. Type **130** 20 25
423 17p. Darwin's microscope . . 50 60
424 25p. Falkland Islands wolf . 65 80
425 34p. H.M.S. "Beagle" . . . 85 1·10

131 Falkland Islands Coat of Arms

134 Blackish Cinclodes

132 Map of Falkland Islands

1982. 21st Birthday of Princess of Wales. Multicoloured.
426 5p. Type **131** 15 20
427 17p. Princess at Royal Opera House, Covent Garden, November 1981 . . . . . . 30 40
428 37p. Bride and groom in doorway of St. Paul's . . . 50 70
429 50p. Formal portrait 65 90

1982. Rebuilding Fund.
430 **132** £1 + £1 multicoloured . . . 2·40 4·50

1982. Commonwealth Games, Brisbane. Nos. 335 and 342 optd **1st PARTICIPATION COMMONWEALTH GAMES 1982.**
431 5p. "Lafonia", 1936–41 . . . 15 30
432 25p. "Fairy", 1857–61 . . . 60 1·10

1982. Birds of the Passerine Family. Multicoloured.
433 5p. Type **134** 25 30
434 10p. Black-chinned siskin . . 35 40
435 13p. Short-billed marsh wren . 40 45
436 25p. Black-throated finch . . 45 55
437 25p. Correndera pipit . . . 55 75
438 34p. Dark-faced ground-tyrant 70 95

135 Raising Flag, Port Louis, 1833

1983. 150th Anniv of British Administration. Multicoloured.
439 1p. Type **135** 20 30
440 2p. Chelsea pensioners and barracks, 1849 (horiz) . . . 30 40
441 5p. Development of wool trade, 1874 . . . . 30 40
442 10p. Ship-repairing trade, 1850 1890 (horiz) 60 70
443 15p. Government House, early 20th century (horiz) . . . 70 80
444 20p. Battle of Falkland Islands, 1914 . . . . 90 1·25
445 25p. Whalebone Arch (horiz) . 90 1·25
446 40p. Contribution to War effort, 1939–45 . . . . 1·40 1·60
447 50p. Duke of Edinburgh's visit, 1957 (horiz) . . . . . . 1·50 2·00
448 £1 Royal Marine uniforms . . 2·00 3·00
449 £2 Queen Elizabeth II . . . 2·75 4·50

136 1933 British Administration Centenary 3d. Commemorative

1983. Commonwealth Day. Multicoloured.
450 5p. Type **136** 15 15
451 17p. 1933 British Administration Centenary ½d. commemorative 30 35
452 34p. 1933 British Administration Centenary 10s. commemorative (vert) 60 80
453 50p. 1983 British Administration 150th anniv £2 commemorative (vert) . . . . . . 75 1·00

137 British Army advancing across East Falkland

1983. 1st Anniv of Liberation. Multicoloured.
454 5p. Type **137** 25 30
455 13p. S.S. "Canberra" and M.V. "Norland" at San Carlos . . 40 60
456 17p. R.A.F. Siddeley Harrier fighter 45 70
457 50p. H.M.S. "Hermes" (aircraft carrier) . . . . 1·00 1·40

138 Diddle Dee

1983. Native Fruits. Multicoloured.
459 5p. Type **138** 20 20
460 17p. Tea berry 30 50
461 25p. Mountain berry . . . 45 65
462 34p. Native strawberry . . . 65 80

139 Britten Norman Islander

1983. Bicentenary of Manned Flight. Multicoloured.
463 5p. Type **139** 15 20
464 13p. De Havilland Beaver . . 35 45
465 17p. Noorduyn Norseman V . 40 50
466 50p. Auster Autocrat . . . 1·00 1·25

1984. Nos. 443 and 445 surch.
467 17p. on 15p. Government House, early 20th century 60 45
468 22p. on 25p. Whalebone Arch, 1933 . . . . 65 55

141 "Araneus cinnabarinus" (juvenile spider)

142 "Wavertree" (sail merchantman)

1984. Insects and Spiders. Multicoloured.
469A 1p. Type **141** 20 65
470A 2p. "Alopophion occidentalis" (fly) . . . . 2·00 1·50
471A 3p. "Pareuxoina falklandica (moth) 40 65
472A 4p. "Lissopterus quadrinotatus" (beetle) . . 30 65
473A 5p. "Issoria cytheris" (butterfly) 30 65
474A 6p. "Araneus cinnabarinus" (adult spider) 30 65
475A 7p. "Trachysphyrus penai" (fly) 30 65
476A 8p. "Caphornia ochricraspia" (moth) 30 65
477A 9p. "Caneorhinus biangulatus" (weevil) 30 65
478A 10p. "Syrphus octomaculatus" (fly) 30 65
479A 20p. "Malvinius compressiventris" (weevil) . . . . 2·25 75
480A 25p. "Metius blandus" (beetle) 75 90
481A 50p. "Parudenus falklandicus" (cricket) . . . . 1·00 1·50
482A £1 "Emmenomma beauchenieus" (spider) . . 1·75 2·25
483A £3 "Cynthia carye" (butterfly) 4·00 6·00
No. 470 comes with or without imprint date.

1984. 250th Anniv of "Lloyd's List" (newspaper). Multicoloured.
484 6p. Type **142** 55 40
485 17p. "Bjerk" (whale catcher) at Port Stanley . . . . . . 1·10 60
486 22p. "Oravia" (liner) stranded 1·10 65
487 52p. "Cunard Countess" (liner) 1·60 2·00

143 Ship, Lockheed Hecules Aircraft and U.P.U. Logo

1984. Universal Postal Union Congress, Hamburg.
488 **143** 22p. multicoloured . . . 55 75

144 Great Grebe

145 Black-browed Albatross

1984. Grebes. Multicoloured.

489	17p. Type **144**	1·25	1·25
490	22p. Silver grebe	1·40	1·40
491	52p. White-tufted grebe	3·00	4·75

1984. Nature Conservation. Multicoloured.

492	6p. Type **145**	1·25	80
493	17p. Tussock grass	1·25	1·10
494	22p. Dusky dolphin and Southern sea lion	1·40	1·40
495	52p. Rockcod (fish) and krill	2·00	3·00

146 Technical Drawing of Class "Wren" Locomotive

1985. 70th Anniv of Camber Railway. Each black, brown and light brown.

497	7p. Type **146**	35	30
498	22p. Sail-propelled trolley	60	90
499	27p. Class "Wren" locomotive at work	65	1·25
500	54p. "Falkland Islands Express" passenger train (76 × 25 mm)	1·10	2·00

147 Construction Workers' Camp

1985. Opening of Mount Pleasant Airport. Multicoloured.

501	7p. Type **147**	75	40
502	22p. Building construction	1·40	90
503	27p. Completed airport	1·60	1·10
504	54p. Lockheed TriStar 500 airliner over runway	2·00	2·50

148 The Queen Mother on 84th Birthday

149 Captain J. McBride and H.M.S. "Jason", 1765

1985. Life and Times of Queen Elizabeth the Queen Mother. Multicoloured.

505	7p. Attending reception at Lancaster House	25	20
506	22p. With Prince Charles, Mark Phillips and Princess Anne at Falklands Memorial Service	60	50
507	27p. Type **148**	70	60
508	54p. With Prince Henry at his christening (from photo by Lord Snowdon)	1·25	1·25

1985. Early Cartographers. Multicoloured.

510	7p. Type **149**	1·00	40
511	22p. Commodore J. Byron and H.M.S. "Dolphin" and "Tamar", 1765	1·40	80
512	27p. Vice-Admiral R. FitzRoy and H.M.S. "Beagle", 1831	1·50	85
513	54p. Admiral Sir B. J. Sullivan and H.M.S. "Philomel", 1842	2·00	1·75

1985. Early Naturalists. As T **35** of British Antarctic Territory. Multicoloured.

514	7p. Philibert Commerson and Commerson's dolphin	85	40
515	22p. Rene Primevere Lesson and "Lessonia sp." (kelp)	1·50	1·10
516	27p. Joseph Paul Gaimard and Common diving petrel	1·90	1·90
517	54p. Charles Darwin and "Calceolaria darwinii"	2·25	2·75

150 Painted Keyhole Limpet

1986. Seashells. Multicoloured.

518	7p. Type **150**	65	60
519	22p. "Provocator palliata"	1·25	1·40
520	27p. Patagonian or Falkland scallop	1·40	2·25
521	54p. Rough thorn drupe	2·25	3·50

1986. 60th Birthday of Queen Elizabeth II. As T **110** of Ascension. Multicoloured.

522	10p. With Princess Margaret at St. Paul's, Walden Bury, Welwyn, 1932	20	25
523	24p. Queen making Christmas television broadcast, 1958	35	50
524	29p. In robes of Order of the Thistle, St. Giles Cathedral, Edinburgh, 1962	35	60
525	45p. Aboard Royal Yacht "Britannia", U.S.A., 1976	1·00	1·25
526	58p. At Crown Agents Head Office, London, 1983	80	1·50

151 S.S. "Great Britain" crossing Atlantic, 1845

1986. "Ameripex '86" International Stamp Exhibition, Chicago. Centenary of Arrival of S.S. "Great Britain" in Falkland Islands. Multicoloured.

527	10p. Type **151**	40	50
528	24p. Beached at Sparrow Cove, 1937	50	70
529	29p. Refloated on pontoon, 1970	55	80
530	58p. Undergoing restoration, Bristol, 1986	80	2·00

152 Head of Rockhopper Penguin

153 Prince Andrew and Miss Sarah Ferguson presenting Polo Trophy, Windsor

1986. Rockhopper Penguins. Multicoloured.

532	10p. Type **152**	1·00	60
533	24p. Rockhopper penguins at sea	1·50	1·75
534	29p. Courtship display	1·75	2·00
535	58p. Adult with chick	2·25	4·00

1986. Royal Wedding. Multicoloured.

536	17p. Type **153**	75	50
537	22p. Prince Andrew and Duchess of York on wedding day	85	65
538	29p. Prince Andrew in battledress at opening of Fox Bay Mill	1·10	90

154 Survey Party, Sapper Hill

1987. Bicentenary of Royal Engineers' Royal Warrant. Multicoloured.

539	10p. Type **154**	1·25	80
540	24p. Mine clearance by robot	1·75	1·50
541	29p. Boxer Bridge, Stanley	2·00	2·50
542	58p. Unloading mail, Mount Pleasant Airport	2·75	4·00

155 Southern Sea Lion

1987. Seals. Multicoloured.

543	10p. Type **155**	70	55
544	24p. Falkland fur seal	1·50	90
545	29p. Southern elephant seal	1·60	1·50
546	58p. Leopard seal	2·25	2·50

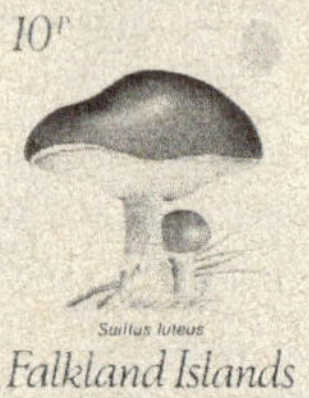

156 "Suillus luteus"

1987. Fungi. Multicoloured.

547	10p. Type **156**	1·40	75
548	24p. "Mycena sp."	2·25	1·75
549	29p. "Hygrophorus adonis" ("Camarophyllus adonis")	2·50	3·00
550	58p. "Gerronema schusteri"	3·50	4·50

157 Victoria Cottage Home, c. 1912

1987. Local Hospitals. Multicoloured.

551	10p. Type **157**	40	25
552	24p. King Edward VII Memorial Hospital, c. 1914	75	55
553	29p. Churchill Wing, King Edward VII Memorial Hospital, c. 1953	85	60
554	58p. Prince Andrew Wing, New Hospital, 1987	1·40	1·25

158 Morris Truck, Fitzroy, 1940

1988. Early Vehicles. Multicoloured.

555	10p. Type **158**	40	25
556	24p. Citroen "Kegresse" half-track, San Carlos, 1929	75	55
575	29p. Ford one ton truck, Port Stanley, 1933	85	60
558	58p. Ford "Model T" car, Darwin, 1935	1·40	1·25

159 Kelp Goose

1988. Falkland Islands Geese. Multicoloured.

559	10p. Type **159**	1·75	45
560	24p. Magellan ("Upland") goose	2·25	70
561	29p. Ruddy-headed goose	2·50	80
562	58p. Ashy-headed goose	3·50	2·00

1988. 300th Anniv of Lloyd's of London. Multicoloured. As T **123** of Ascension.

563	10p. Silver from Lloyd's Nelson Collection	40	30
564	24p. Falkland Islands hydroponic market garden (horiz)	75	65
565	29p. "A.E.S." (mail ship) (horiz)	1·00	75
566	58p. "Charles Cooper" (full-rigged ship), 1866	1·50	1·25

160 "Padua" (barque)

1989. Cape Horn Sailing Ships. Multicoloured.

567	1p. Type **160**	60	60
613	2p. "Priwall" (barque) (vert)	60	70
614	3p. "Passat" (barque)	60	70
570	4p. "Archibald Russell" (barque) (vert)	80	80
571	5p. "Pamir" (barque) (vert)	80	80
617	6p. "Mozart" (barquentine)	70	65
573	7p. "Pommern" (barque)	1·00	1·00
574	8p. "Preussen" (full-rigged ship)	1·00	1·00
620	9p. "Fennia" (barque)	80	80
576	10p. "Cassard" (barque)	1·00	1·00
577	20p. "Lawhill" (barque)	1·75	2·00
578	25p. "Garthpool" (barque)	1·75	2·00
579	50p. "Grace Harwar" (full-rigged ship)	2·75	3·00
625	£1 "Criccieth Castle" (full-rigged ship)	2·75	3·25
581	£3 "Cutty Sark" (full-rigged ship) (vert)	8·50	8·50
582	£5 "Flying Cloud" (full-rigged ship)	11·00	9·00

161 Southern Right Whale

1989. Baleen Whales. Multicoloured.

583	10p. Type **161**	90	40
584	24p. Minke whale	1·50	85
585	29p. Humpback whale	1·75	1·25
586	58p. Blue whale	2·50	2·50

162 "Gymkhana" (Sarah Gilding)

1989. Sports Associations' Activities. Children's Drawings. Multicoloured.

587	5p. Type **162**	20	20
588	10p. "Steer Riding" (Karen Steen)	30	30
589	17p. "Sheep Shearing" (Colin Shepherd)	45	45
590	24p. "Sheepdog Trials" (Rebecca Edwards)	60	70
591	29p. "Horse Racing" (Dilys Blakeley)	70	80
592	45p. "Sack Race" (Donna Newell)	1·00	1·10

163 Vice-Admiral Sturdee and H.M.S. "Invincible" (battle cruiser)

164 Southern Sea Lions on Kidney Island

1989. 75th Anniv of the Falkland Islands and 50th Anniv of Battle of the River Plate. Mult.

593	10p. Type **163**	30	30
594	24p. Vice-Admiral Graf von Spee and "Scharnhorst" (German cruiser)	70	75
595	29p. Commodore Harwood and H.M.S. "Ajax" (cruiser)	80	85
596	58p. Captain Langsdorff and "Admiral Graf Spee" (German pocket battleship)	1·50	2·00

1990. Nature Reserves and Sanctuaries. Mult.

597	12p. Type **164**	45	35
598	26p. Black-browed albatrosses on Beauchene Island	1·00	70
599	31p. Penguin colony on Bird Island	1·10	80
600	62p. Tussock grass on Elephant Jason Island	1·40	1·40

165 Supermarine Spitfire Mk. I "Falkland Islands I"

1990. "Stamp World London 90" International Stamp Exhibition, London. Presentation Spitfires. Multicoloured.

601	12p. Type **165**	50	35
602	26p. Supermarine Spitfire Mk. I "Falkland Islands VII"	90	70
603	31p. Cockpit and wing of "Falkland Islands I"	1·00	80
604	62p. Squadron scramble, 1940	1·40	1·40

1990. 90th Birthday of Queen Elizabeth the Queen Mother. As T **134** of Ascension.

606	26p. multicoloured	75	65
607	£1 black and red	2·50	2·75

DESIGNS: (21 × 36 mm): 26p. Queen Mother in Dover. (29 × 37 mm): £1 On bridge of liner "Queen Elizabeth", 1946.

166 Black-browed Albatrosses

1990. Black-browed Albatrosses. Multicoloured.

608	12p. Type **166**	60	50
609	26p. Female with egg	1·25	1·00
610	31p. Adult and chick	1·50	1·25
611	62p. Black-browed albatrosses in flight	2·50	3·00

167 "Gavilea australis"

168 Heads of Two King Penguins

1991. Orchids. Multicoloured.

629	12p. Type **167**	60	60
630	26p. Dog orchid	1·00	1·00
631	31p. "Chlorea gaudichaudii"	1·25	1·50
632	62p. Yellow orchid	2·25	3·25

1991. Endangered Species. King Penguin. Multicoloured.

633	2p. Type **168**	50	60
634	6p. Female incubating egg	70	70
635	12p. Female with two chicks	1·00	80
636	20p. Penguin underwater	1·25	1·25
637	31p. Parents feeding their chick	1·50	1·75
638	62p. Courtship dance	2·25	2·75

Nos. 637/8 do not include the W.W.F. panda emblem.

169 ½d. and 2½d. Stamps of September 1891

1991. Cent of Bisected Surcharges. Mult.

639	12p. Type **169**	60	50
640	26p. Cover of March 1891 franked with strip of five ½d. bisects	1·00	1·00
641	31p. Unsevered pair of ½d. surcharge	1·25	1·50
642	62p. "Isis" (mail ship)	2·00	3·25

1991. 500th Anniv of Discovery of America by Columbus. Re-enactment Voyages. As T **144** of Ascension. Multicoloured.

643	14p. Map of re-enactment voyages and "Eye of the Wind" (cadet brig)	60	60
644	29p. Compass rose and "Soren Larsen" (cadet brigantine)	1·25	1·40
645	34p. "Santa Maria", "Pinta" and "Nina"	1·50	1·75
646	68p. Columbus and "Santa Maria"	2·50	4·00

1992. 40th Anniv of Queen Elizabeth II's Accession. As T **143** of Ascension. Multicoloured.

647	7p. "Stanley through the Narrows" (A. Asprey)	35	35
648	14p. "Hill Cove" (A. Asprey)	60	60
649	29p. "San Carlos Water" (A. Asprey)	95	95
650	34p. Three portraits of Queen Elizabeth	1·25	1·25
651	68p. Queen Elizabeth II	1·75	2·00

170 Laying Foundation Stone, 1890

172 Private, Falkland Islands Volunteers, 1892

171 Captain John Davis and Backstaff

1992. Centenary of Christ Church Cathedral, Stanley. Multicoloured.

652	14p. Type **170**	65	55
653	29p. Interior of Cathedral, 1920	1·25	1·00
654	34p. Bishop's chair	1·50	1·25
655	68p. Cathedral in 1900 (horiz)	1·90	1·90

1992. 10th Anniv of Liberation. As T **146** of Ascension. Multicoloured.

656	14p. + 6p. San Carlos Cemetery	75	1·25
657	29p. + 11p. War Memorial, Port Stanley	1·40	1·75
658	34p. + 16p. South Atlantic medal	1·60	1·90
659	68p. + 32p. Government House, Port Stanley	2·75	3·00

The premiums on Nos. 656/9 were for the S.S.A.F.A.

1992. 400th Anniv of First Sighting of the Falkland Islands. Multicoloured.

661	22p. Type **171**	1·00	80
662	29p. Captain John Davis	1·25	1·10
663	34p. Queen Elizabeth I and Queen Elizabeth II	1·50	1·50
664	68p. "Desire" sighting Falkland Islands	2·25	3·00

1992. Centenary of Falkland Islands Defence Force and 50th Anniv of Affiliation to West Yorkshire Regiment. Multicoloured.

665	7p. Type **172**	30	30
666	14p. Officer, Falkland Islands Defence Corps, 1914	50	50
667	22p. Officer, Falkland Islands Defence Force, 1920	70	70
668	29p. Private, Falkland Islands Defence Force, 1939–45	90	90
669	34p. Officer, West Yorkshire Regiment, 1942	1·25	1·25
670	68p. Private, West Yorkshire Regiment, 1942	2·00	2·10

173 South American Tern

1993. Gulls and Terns. Multicoloured.

671	15p. Type **173**	75	65
672	31p. Brown-hooded gull ("Pink-breasted gull")	1·25	1·25
673	36p. Magellan gull	1·40	1·60
674	72p. Southern black-backed gull ("Dominican gull")	2·50	3·50

1993. 75th Anniv of Royal Air Force. As T **149** of Ascension. Multicoloured.

676	15p. Avro Vulcan B.1A	65	85
677	15p. Lockheed Hercules	65	85
678	15p. Boeing-Vertol Chinook	65	85
679	15p. Lockhead TriStar 500	65	85

175 Short-finned Squid

1993. Fisheries. Multicoloured.

681	15p. Type **175**	60	60
682	31p. Catch of whip-tailed hake	1·25	1·40
683	36p. "Falklands Protector" (fisheries patrol vessel)	1·50	1·75
684	72p. Britten Norman Islander patrol aircraft and fish factory ship	2·25	3·50

176 "Great Britain" in Drydock, Bristol

178 Pony

177 "Explorer" (liner)

1993. 150th Anniv of Launch of "Great Britain" (liner). Multicoloured.

685	8p. Type **176**	50	50
686	£1 "Great Britain" at sea	2·75	4·00

1993. Tourism. Multicoloured.

687	16p. Type **177**	75	60
688	34p. Rockhopper penguins	1·50	1·25
689	39p. "World Discoverer" (liner)	1·75	1·75
690	78p. "Columbus Caravelle" (liner)	2·25	2·75

1993. Pets. Multicoloured.

691	8p. Type **178**	50	50
692	16p. Lamb	65	65
693	34p. Puppy and cat	1·50	1·75
694	39p. Kitten (vert)	1·60	2·00
695	78p. Collie dog (vert)	2·50	3·50

1994. "Hong Kong '94" International Stamp Exhibition. Nos. 691/5 optd **HONG KONG '94** and emblem.

696	8p. Type **178**	50	50
697	16p. Lamb	65	65
698	34p. Puppy and cat	1·50	1·75
699	39p. Kitten (vert)	1·60	2·00
700	78p. Collie dog (vert)	2·50	3·50

179 Goose Barnacles

1994. Inshore Marine Life. Multicoloured.

701	1p. Type **179**	20	40
702	2p. Painted shrimp (horiz)	30	40
703	8p. Patagonian copper limpet (horiz)	50	50
704	9p. Eleginops ("Mullet") (horiz)	50	50
705	10p. Sea anemones (horiz)	50	50
706	20p. Flathead eelpout (horiz)	75	75
707	25p. Spider crab (horiz)	80	80
708	50p. Lobster krill	1·40	1·50
709	80p. Falkland skate (horiz)	2·00	2·25
710	£1 Centollon crab (horiz)	2·25	2·50
711	£3 Wilton's notothen ("Rock Cod") (horiz)	6·00	6·25
712	£5 Octopus	10·00	10·50

180 Dockyard Blacksmith's Shop and Sir James Clark Ross (explorer)

1994. 150th Anniv of Founding of Stanley. Multicoloured.

713	9p. Type **180**	50	50
714	17p. 21 Fitzroy Road (home of Chaplain James Moody)	75	60
715	30p. Stanley Cottage (built by Dr. Henry Hamblin)	1·25	1·25
716	35p. Pioneer Row and Sgt-maj Henry Felton	1·50	1·75
717	40p. Government House (designed by Governor R. Moody)	1·60	1·90
718	65p. View of Stanley and Edward Stanley, Earl of Derby (Secretary of State for Colonies)	2·25	3·00

181 Lockheed L-1011 TriStar over Gypsy Cove

1994. Falkland Beaches. Multicoloured.

719	17p. Type **181**	75	60
720	35p. Cruise ship off Sea Lion Island	1·40	1·25
721	40p. Britten Norman Islander aircraft at Pebble Island	1·75	1·75
722	65p. Landrover at Volunteer Beach	2·00	3·00

182 Mission House, Keppel Island

1994. 150th Anniv of South American Missionary Society. Multicoloured.

723	5p. Type **182**	20	30
724	17p. Thomas Bridges (compiler of Yahgan dictionary)	50	50
725	40p. Fuegian Indians	1·10	1·50
726	65p. Capt. Allen Gardiner and "Allen Gardiner" (schooner)	1·50	2·25

183 "Lupinus arboreus"

1995. Flowering Shrubs. Multicoloured.

727	9p. Type **183**	40	40
728	17p. "Hebe elliptica"	60	55
729	30p. "Fuschia magellanica"	85	85
730	35p. "Berberis ilicifolia"	90	1·00
731	40p. "Ulex europaeus"	95	1·10
732	65p. "Hebe × franciscana"	1·75	2·50

184 Magellanic Oystercatcher

1995. Shore Birds. Multicoloured.

733	17p. Type **184**	85	60
734	35p. Rufous-chested dotterel	1·40	1·25
735	40p. Blackish oystercatcher	1·50	1·50
736	65p. Two-banded plover	2·50	3·50

1995. 50th Anniv of End of Second World War. As T **161** of Ascension. Multicoloured.

737	17p. Falkland Islands contingent in Victory Parade	60	60
738	35p. Governor Sir Alan Cardinall on Bren gun-carrier	1·10	1·10
739	40p. H.M.A.S. "Esperance Bay" (troopship)	1·25	1·50
740	65p. H.M.S. "Exeter" (cruiser)	2·25	3·50

185 Ox and Cart

1995. Transporting Peat. Multicoloured.

742	17p. Type **185**	60	50
743	35p. Horse and cart	1·10	1·10
744	40p. Caterpillar tractor pulling sleigh	1·25	1·25
745	65p. Lorry	2·25	3·00

186 Kelp Geese

1995. Wildlife. Multicoloured.

746	35p. Type **186**	1·10	1·10
747	35p. Black-browed albatross	1·10	1·10
748	35p. Blue-eyed cormorants	1·10	1·10
749	35p. Magellanic penguins	1·10	1·10
750	35p. Fur seals	1·10	1·10
751	35p. Rockhopper penguins	1·10	1·10

Nos. 746/51 were printed together, se-tenant, forming a composite design.

187 Cottontail Rabbit

1995. Introduced Wild Animals. Multicoloured.

752	9p. Type **187**	45	45
753	17p. Brown hare	65	55
754	35p. Guanacos	1·10	1·25
755	40p. Fox	1·25	1·40
756	65p. Otter	1·90	2·50

188 Princess Anne and Government House

1996. Royal Visit. Multicoloured.

757	9p. Type **188**	45	45
758	19p. Falklands War Memorial, San Carlos Cemetery	75	65
759	30p. Christ Church Cathedral	1·10	1·10
760	73p. Helicopter over Goose Green	2·50	3·00

1996. 70th Birthday of Queen Elizabeth II. As T **165** of Ascension each incorporating a different photograph of the Queen. Multicoloured.

761	17p. Steeple Jason	60	50
762	40p. "Tamar" (container ship)	1·50	1·25
763	45p. New Island	1·50	1·40
764	65p. Falkland Islands Community School	1·60	1·60

189 Mounted Postman, c. 1890

1996. "CAPEX '96" International Stamp Exhibition. Mail Transport. Multicoloured.

766	9p. Type **189**	50	45
767	40p. Noorduyn Norseman V seaplane	1·50	1·25
768	45p. "Forrest" (freighter) at San Carlos	1·60	1·40
769	76p. De Havilland D.H.C.2 Beaver seaplane	2·50	2·50

190 Southern Bottlenose Whale

1996. Beaked Whales. Multicoloured.

771	9p. Type **190**	30	30
772	30p. Cuvier's beaked whale	80	80
773	35p. Straptoothed beaked whale	90	90
774	75p. Gray's beaked whale	1·90	1·90

191 Magellanic Penguins performing Courtship Dance

1997. Magellanic Penguins. Multicoloured.

775	17p. Type **191**	55	45
776	35p. Penguins in burrow	1·00	85
777	40p. Adult and chick	1·10	90
778	65p. Group of Penguins swimming	1·60	1·60

193 Coral Fern

1997. Ferns. Multicoloured.

780	17p. Type **193**	55	45
781	35p. Adder's tongue fern	1·00	1·00
782	40p. Fuegian tall fern	1·10	1·10
783	65p. Small fern	1·60	1·75

1997. Golden Wedding of Queen Elizabeth and Prince Philip. As T **173** of Ascension. Multicoloured.

785	9p. Queen Elizabeth holding bouquet, 1993	40	40
786	9p. Prince Philip and horse, 1995	40	40
787	17p. Queen Elizabeth in phaeton at Trooping the Colour, 1996	65	65
788	17p. Prince Philip in R.A.F. uniform	65	65
789	40p. Queen Elizabeth wearing red coat, 1986	1·00	1·00
790	40p. Prince William and Princess Beatrice on horseback	1·00	1·00

Nos. 785/6, 787/8 and 789/90 respectively were printed together, se-tenant, with the backgrounds forming composite designs.

194 Bull Point Lighthouse

1997. Lighthouses. Multicoloured.

792	9p. Type **194**	40	30
793	30p. Cape Pembroke Lighthouse	90	90
794	£1 Cape Meredith Lighthouse	2·40	2·75

195 Forster's Caracara

1997. Endangered Species. Multicoloured.

795	17p. Type **195**	70	55
796	19p. Southern sealion	70	60
797	40p. Felton's flower	1·25	1·25
798	73p. Trout	2·25	2·25

196 Merryweather and Son Greenwich Gem Fire Engine

1998. Centenary of Falkland Islands Fire Service. Multicoloured.

799	9p. Type **196**	40	35
800	17p. Merryweather's Hatfield trailer pump	60	50
801	40p. Coventry Climax Godiva trailer pump	1·25	1·00
802	65p. Carmichael Bedford "Type B" water tender	2·00	1·75

197 Tawny-throated Dotterel

1998. Rare Visiting Birds. Multicoloured. (a) Designs 39½ × 23½ mm.

804	1p. Type **197**	10	10
805	2p. Hudsonian godwit	10	10
806	5p. Eared dove	10	10
807	9p. Great grebe	20	25
808	10p. Chilian lapwing ("Southern Lapwing")	20	25
809	16p. Buff-necked ibis	30	35
810	30p. Ashy-headed goose	60	65
811	65p. Red-legged cormorant ("Red-legged Shag")	1·25	1·40
812	88p. Argentine shoveler ("Red Shoveler")	1·75	1·90
813	£1 Red-fronted coot	2·00	2·10
814	£3 Chilian flamingo	6·00	6·25
815	£5 Fork-tailed flycatcher	10·00	10·50

(b) Designs 35 × 22 mm.

816	9p. Roseate spoonbill	20	25
817	17p. Austral conure ("Austral Parakeet")	35	40
818	35p. American kestrel	70	75

198 "Penelope", 1926

200 Marine at Port Egmont, Saunders Island, 1766

199 First Medivac Air Ambulance Service

1998. Local Vessels. Multicoloured.

819	17p. Type **198**	55	45
820	35p. "Ilen", 1926	95	95
821	40p. "Weddell", 1940	1·10	1·10
822	65p. "Lively", 1940 (31 × 22 mm)	1·60	1·75

1998. 50th Anniv of Falkland Islands Government Air Service. Multicoloured.

823	17p. Type **199**	35	40
824	£1 F.I.G.A.S. aircraft over map	2·00	2·10

1998. Royal Marine Uniforms. Multicoloured.

825	17p. Type **200**	35	40
826	30p. Officer at Port Louis, East Falklands, 1833	60	65
827	35p. Corporal and H.M.S. "Kent" (cruiser), 1914	70	75
828	65p. Bugler at Government House, 1976	1·25	1·40

201 Altar, St. Mary's Church

1999. Centenary of St. Mary's Church. Multicoloured.

829	17p. Type **201**	35	40
830	40p. St. Mary's Church	80	85
831	75p. Laying of foundation stone, 1899	1·50	1·60

202 H.M.S. "Beagle" (Darwin)

1999. "Australia '99" World Stamp Exhibition, Melbourne. Maritime History. Multicoloured.

832	25p. Type **202**	50	55
833	35p. H.M.A.S. "Australia" (battle cruiser)	70	75
834	40p. "Canberra" (liner)	80	85
835	50p. "Great Britain" (steam/sail)	1·00	1·10
836	50p. All-England Cricket Team, 1861–62	1·00	1·10

203 Prince of Wales (from photo by Clive Arrowsmith)

1999. Royal Visit.

837	**203** £2 multicoloured	4·00	4·25

1999. Royal Wedding. As T **185** of Ascension. Multicoloured.

838	80p. Photographs of Prince Edward and Miss Sophie Rhys-Jones	1·60	1·75
839	£1.20 Engagement photograph	2·40	2·50

204 "Jeanne d'Arc" (French cruiser)

1999. "PHILEXFRANCE '99", International Stamp Exhibition, Paris. First Flight over Falkland Islands, 1931. Multicoloured.

840	35p. Type **204**	70	75
841	40p. CAMS 37 (flying boat) taking off	80	85

POSTAGE DUE STAMPS

D 1 King Penguin

1991.

D1	**D 1**	1p. red and mauve	10	10
D2		2p. orange and light orange	10	10
D3		3p. ochre and yellow	10	10
D4		4p. green and light green	10	10
D5		5p. blue and light blue	10	15
D6		10p. deep blue and blue	20	25
D7		20p. violet and lilac	40	45
D8		50p. green and light green	1·00	1·10

FALKLAND ISLANDS DEPENDENCIES

Four groups of Islands situated between the Falkland Is. and the South Pole. In 1946 the four groups ceased issuing separate issues which were replaced by a single general issue. From 1963 the stamps of British Antarctic Territory were used in all these islands except South Georgia and South Sandwich for which separate stamps were issued inscribed "SOUTH GEORGIA" from 1963 until 1980.

Under the new constitution effective on 3 October 1985, South Georgia and South Sandwich Islands ceased to be dependencies of the Falkland Islands.

1944. 12 pence = 1 shilling;
20 shillings = 1 pound.
1971. 100 (new) pence = 1 pound.

GRAHAM LAND

1944. Stamps of Falkland Islands of 1938 optd **GRAHAM LAND DEPENDENCY OF.**

A1	**27**	½d. black and green	30	1·75
A2	–	1d. black and violet	30	1·00
A3	–	2d. black and red	40	1·00
A4	–	3d. black and blue	30	1·00
A5	–	4d. black and purple	3·00	1·75
A6	–	6d. black and brown	13·00	2·25
A7	–	9d. black and blue	1·00	1·25
A8	–	1s. blue	1·00	1·25

SOUTH GEORGIA

1944. Stamps of Falkland Islands of 1938 optd **SOUTH GEORGIA DEPENDENCY OF.**

B1	**27**	½d. black and green	30	1·75
B2	–	1d. black and violet	30	1·00
B3	–	2d. black and red	40	1·00
B4	–	3d. black and blue	30	1·00
B5	–	4d. black and purple	3·00	1·75
B6	–	6d. black and brown	13·00	2·25
B7	–	9d. black and blue	1·00	1·25
B8	–	1s. blue	1·00	1·25

SOUTH ORKNEYS

1944. Stamps of Falkland Islands of 1938 optd **SOUTH ORKNEYS DEPENDENCY OF.**

C1	**27**	½d. black and green	30	1·75
C2	–	1d. black and violet	30	1·00
C3	–	2d. black and red	40	1·00
C4	–	3d. black and blue	30	1·00
C5	–	4d. black and purple	3·00	1·75
C6	–	6d. black and brown	13·00	2·25
C7	–	9d. black and blue	1·00	1·25
C8	–	1s. blue	1·00	1·25

SOUTH SHETLANDS

1944. Stamps of Falkland Islands of 1938 optd **SOUTH SHETLAND DEPENDENCY OF.**

D1	**27**	½d. black and green	30	1·75
D2	–	1d. black and violet	30	1·00
D3	–	2d. black and red	40	1·00
D4	–	3d. black and blue	30	1·00
D5	–	4d. black and purple	3·00	1·75
D6	–	6d. black and brown	13·00	2·25
D7	–	9d. black and blue	1·00	1·25
D8	–	1s. blue	1·00	1·25

GENERAL ISSUES

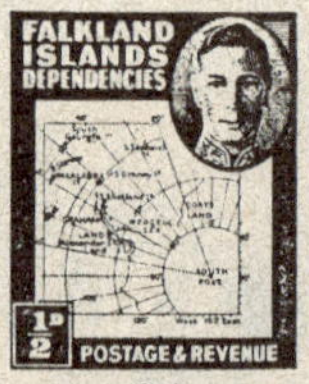

G 1

G 3 "Trepassey", 1945-47

1946.

G 1	**G 1**	½d. black and green	1·00	2·00
G 2		1d. black and violet	1·25	1·75
G 3		2d. black and red	1·25	2·50
G11a		2½d. black and blue	7·50	7·00
G 4		3d. black and blue	1·25	4·00
G 5		4d. black and red	2·25	4·75
G 6		6d. black and orange	3·25	4·75
G 7		9d. black and brown	2·00	3·25
G 8		1s. black and purple	2·00	4·25

1946. Victory. As T **9** of Aden.

G17	1d. violet	50	15
G18	3d. blue	75	15

1949. Silver Wedding. As T **10/11** of Aden.

G19	2½d. blue	1·25	1·00
G20	1s. blue	2·25	1·75

1949. U.P.U. As T **20/23** of Antigua.

G21	1d. violet	1·50	1·50
G22	2d. red	5·00	2·50
G23	3d. blue	4·00	1·25
G24	6d. orange	7·00	3·00

1953. Coronation. As T **13** of Aden.

G25	1d. black and violet	1·10	1·25

1954. Ships.

G26	–	½d. black and green	30	1·75
G27	**G 3**	1d. black and sepia	1·25	1·50
G28	–	1½d. black and olive	2·00	1·25
G29	–	2d. black and red	1·25	20
G30	–	2½d. black and yellow	1·25	15
G31	–	3d. black and blue	1·25	15
G32	–	4d. black and purple	3·25	55
G33	–	6d. black and lilac	3·25	55
G34	–	9d. black	3·25	1·00
G35	–	1s. black and brown	3·25	90
G36	–	2s. black and red	19·00	10·00

G37	–	2s. 6d. black and turquoise	19·00	6·00
G38	–	5s. black and violet	40·00	6·50
G39	–	10s. black and blue	55·00	18·00
G40	–	£1 black	90·00	48·00

SHIPS—VERT: 1½d. "John Biscoe"; 6d. "Discovery"; 9d. "Endurance"; 2s. 6d. "Francais"; 5s. "Scotia"; £1 "Belgica". HORIZ: 1½d. "Wyatt Earp"; 2d. "Eagle"; 2½d. "Penola"; 3d. "Discovery II"; 4d. "William Scoresby" 1s. "Deutschland"; 2s. "Pourquoi pas?"; 10s. "Antarctic".

1956. Trans-Atlantic Expedition. Nos. G27, G30/1 and G33 optd **TRANS-ANTARCTIC EXPEDITION 1955-1958.**

G41	G 3	1d. black and sepia	10	30
G42	–	2½d. black and yellow	55	50
G43	–	3d. black and blue	55	30
G44	–	6d. black and lilac	55	30

For later issues see **BRITISH ANTARCTIC TERRITORIES** and **SOUTH GEORGIA**.

ISSUES FOR SOUTH GEORGIA AND SOUTH SANDWICH ISLANDS.

In 1980 stamps were again inscribed "FALKLAND ISLANDS DEPENDENCIES" for use in the above area.

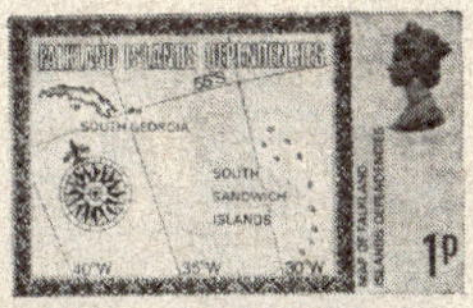

14 Map of Falkland Islands Dependencies

1980. Multicoloured.

74A	1p. Type **14**	30	30
75A	2p. Shag Rocks	30	30
76A	3p. Bird and Willis Islands	30	30
77A	4p. Gulbrandsen Lake	30	30
78A	5p. King Edward Point	30	30
79A	6p. Sir Ernest Shackleton's memorial cross, Hope Point	60	30
80A	7p. Sir Ernest Shackleton's grave, Grytviken	60	40
81A	8p. Grytviken Church	50	40
82A	9p. Coaling Hulk "Louise" at Grytviken	50	45
83A	10p. Clerke Rocks	50	45
84B	20p. Candlemas Island	2·00	1·50
85B	25p. Twitcher Rock and Cook Island, Southern Thule	2·00	2·25
86A	50p. R.R.S. "John Biscoe II" in Cumberland Bay	1·00	2·00
87A	£1 R.R.S. "Bransfield" in Cumberland Bay	1·25	2·75
88A	£3 H.M.S. "Endurance" in Cumberland Bay	3·00	6·50

These stamps come with or without date imprint.

15 Magellanic Clubmoss

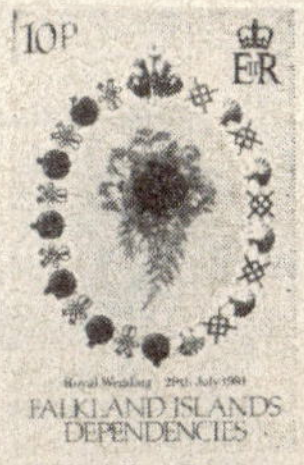

16 Wedding Bouquet from Falkland Islands Dependencies

1981. Plants. Multicoloured.

89	3p. Type **15**	20	25
90	6p. Alphine cat's-tail	20	30
91	7p. Greater burnet	20	30
92	11p. Antarctic bedstraw	20	35
93	15p. Brown rush	25	45
94	25p. Antarctic hair grass	35	75

1981. Royal Wedding. Multicoloured.

95	10p. Type **16**	15	30
96	13p. Prince Charles dressed for skiing	20	35
97	52p. Prince Charles and Lady Diana Spencer	65	85

17 Introduced Reindeer during Calving, Spring

1982. Reindeer. Multicoloured.

98	5p. Type **17**	25	65
99	13p. Bull at rut, Autumn	30	85
100	25p. Reindeer and mountains, Winter	40	1·40
101	26p. Reindeer feeding on tussock, late Winter	40	1·40

18 "Gamasellus racovitzai" (tick)

19 Lady Diana Spencer at Tidworth, Hampshire, July 1981

1982. Insects. Multicoloured.

102	5p. Type **18**	15	25
103	10p. "Alaskozetes antarcticus" (mite)	25	35
104	13p. "Cryptopygus antarcticus" (spring-tail)	25	40
105	15p. "Notiomaso australis" (spider)	30	45
106	25p. "Hydromedion sparsutum" (beetle)	50	70
107	26p. "Parochlus steinenii" (midge)	50	70

1982. 21st Birthday of Princess of Wales. Multicoloured.

108	5p. Falkland Islands Dependencies coat of arms	10	15
109	17p. Type **19**	40	35
110	37p. Bride and groom on steps of St Paul's	45	80
111	50p. Formal portrait	1·00	1·10

20 Map of South Georgia

1982. Rebuilding Fund.

112	**20**	£1+£1 multicoloured	2·40	4·00

21 Westland Whirlwind

1983. Bicentenary of Manned Flight. Multicoloured.

113	5p. Type **21**	30	30
114	13p. Westland Wasp helicopter	55	65
115	17p. Vickers Supermarine Walrus II	60	70
116	50p. Auster Autocrat	1·40	1·50

22 "Euphausia superba"

1983. Crustacea. Multicoloured.

117	5p. Type **22**	40	20
118	17p. "Glyptonotus antarcticus"	70	50
119	25p. "Epimeria monodon"	85	60
120	34p. "Serolis pagenstecheri"	1·10	80

23 Zavodovski Island

1984. Volcanoes of South Sandwich Islands. Multicoloured.

121	6p. Type **23**	80	80
122	17p. Mt. Michael, Saunders Island	2·00	1·60
123	22p. Bellingshausen Island	2·00	1·75
124	52p. Bristol Island	2·50	3·25

24 Grey-headed Albatross

1985. Albatrosses. Multicoloured.

125	7p. Type **24**	1·50	75
126	22p. Black-browed albatross	2·25	1·25
127	27p. Wandering albatross	2·50	1·40
128	54p. Light-mantled sooty albatross	3·25	2·25

25 The Queen Mother

1985. Life and Times of Queen Elizabeth the Queen Mother. Multicoloured.

129	7p. At Windsor Castle on Princess Elizabeth's 14th Birthday, 1940	30	30
130	22p. With Princess Anne, Lady Sarah Armstrong-Jones and Prince Edward at Trooping the Colour	60	70
131	27p. Type **25**	70	80
132	54p. With Prince Henry at his christening (from photo by Lord Snowdon)	1·25	1·40

1985. Early Naturalists. As T **35** of British Antarctic Territory. Multicoloured.

134	7p. Dumont d'Urville and "Durvillea antarctica" (kelp)	1·25	1·00
135	22p. Johann Reinhold Forster and king penguin	2·25	2·00
136	27p. Johann Georg Adam Forster and tussock grass	2·25	2·25
137	54p. Sir Joseph Banks and dove prion	3·00	3·50

For later issues see **SOUTH GEORGIA** and **SOUTH SANDWICH ISLANDS**.

FARIDKOT

A state of the Punjab, India. Now uses Indian stamps.

1879. 1 folus = 1 paisa = ¼ anna.
1886. 12 pies = 1 anna; 16 annas = 1 rupee.

N 1 (1 folus)

N 2 (1 paisa)

1879. Imperf.

N5	N 1	1 f. blue	1·50	2·75
N6	N 2	1 p. blue	2·50	6·50

1887. Stamps of India (Queen Victoria) optd **FARIDKOT STATE**.

17	**40**	3 p. red	50	30·00
1	**23**	½ a. turquoise	75	75
3	–	1 a. purple	90	1·00
4	–	2 a. blue	2·50	3·25
7	–	3 a. orange	1·40	2·50
8	–	4 a. green (No. 96)	4·50	12·00
11	–	6 a. brown (No. 80)	1·75	9·50
12	–	8 a. mauve	8·00	25·00
14	–	12 a. purple on red	29·00	£300
15	–	1 r. grey	28·00	£275
16	**37**	1 r. green and red	29·00	60·00

OFFICIAL STAMPS

1886. Stamps of India (Queen Victoria) optd **SERVICE FARIDKOT STATE**.

O 1	**23**	½ a. turquoise	15	50
O 3	–	1 a. purple	65	90
O 4	–	2 a. blue	1·40	6·00
O 6	–	3 a. orange	3·75	5·50
O 8	–	4 a. green (No. 96)	2·75	14·00
O11	–	6 a. brown (No. 80)	13·00	16·00
O12	–	8 a. mauve	4·00	16·00
O14	–	1 r. grey	38·00	£130
O15	**37**	1 r. green and red	70·00	£375

FEDERATED MALAY STATES

A British protectorate in South East Asia, comprising the States of Negri Sembilan (with Sungei Ujong), Pahang, Perak and Selangor.

Separate issues for each of these states appeared in 1936.

100 cents = $1 (Straits)

1900. Stamps of Negri Sembilan optd **FEDERATED MALAY STATES** and bar.

1	**3**	1 c. purple and green	2·00	4·25
2		2 c. purple and brown	24·00	48·00
3		3 c. purple and black	2·00	3·50
4		5 c. purple and yellow	65·00	£150
5		10 c. purple and orange	4·00	17·00
6		20 c. green and olive	70·00	90·00
7		25 c. green and red	£180	£300
8		50 c. green and black	75·00	£100

1900. Stamps of Perak optd **FEDERATED MALAY STATES** and bar.

9	**31**	5 c. purple and yellow	11·00	48·00
10		10 c. purple and orange	60·00	65·00
11	**32**	$1 green	£140	£180
12		$2 green and red	95·00	£170
13		$5 green and blue	£250	£400
14		$25 green and orange	£6000	

3

4

1900.

15a	**3**	1 c. black and green	2·25	30
29		1 c. green	2·00	20
30		1 c. brown	2·25	90
53		1 c. black	60	20
31		2 c. green	1·00	30
54		2 c. brown	4·25	3·75
16b		3 c. black and brown	2·25	20
58		3 c. brown	70	50
34		3 c. red	2·00	10
35		3 c. grey	1·25	20
57		3 c. green	1·25	1·50
36d		4 c. black and red	4·00	30
38		4 c. red	80	15
60		4 c. orange	65	10
18		5 c. green and red on yellow	1·75	2·00
61		5 c. mauve on yellow	85	20
62		5 c. brown	2·25	10
63		6 c. orange	55	45
64		6 c. red	90	10
41bb		8 c. black and blue	5·00	3·50
42		8 c. blue	13·00	90
43b		10 c. black and mauve	16·00	30
44a		10 c. blue	6·50	85
66		10 c. black and blue	2·00	75
67		10 c. purple and yellow	3·50	40
68		12 c. blue	1·25	10
69		20 c. mauve and black	4·00	35
70		25 c. purple and mauve	2·50	1·00
71		30 c. purple and orange	3·25	2·50
46		35 c. red on yellow	5·50	12·00
73		35 c. red and purple	13·00	14·00
74		50 c. black and orange	13·00	6·50
75		50 c. black on green	4·00	1·75
76a	**4**	$1 green	14·00	35·00
77	**3**	$1 black and red on blue	12·00	3·00
78	**4**	$2 green and red	17·00	70·00
79	**3**	$2 green and red on yellow	32·00	30·00
80	**4**	$5 green and blue	70·00	£150
81	**3**	$5 green and red on green	£140	£150
82	**4**	$25 green and orange	£800	£500

POSTAGE DUE STAMPS

D 1

1924.

D1	**D 1**	1 c. violet	4·50	17·00
D2		2 c. black	1·75	3·00
D3		4 c. green	2·25	4·75
D4		8 c. red	4·50	18·00
D5		10 c. orange	8·00	15·00
D6		12 c. blue	9·00	20·00

FIJI

A British colony in the South Pacific which became independent within the Commonwealth during October 1970. Following a military coup on 25 September 1987 Fiji was declared a republic on 7 October. The Governor-General resigned on 15 October 1987 and Fiji's Commonwealth membership lapsed until 1 October 1997 when the country was readmitted following further constitutional changes.

1870. 12 pence = 1 shilling;
20 shillings = 1 pound.
1969. 100 cents = 1 dollar.

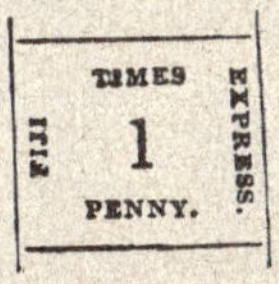

1

2

1870.

5	**1**	1d. black on pink	£900	£1800
6		3d. black on pink	£1500	£2750
7		6d. black on pink	£1100	£1800
8		9d. black on pink	£1700	£2750
9		1s. black on pink	£1000	£1400

1871.

10	**2**	1d. blue	50·00	£120
11		3d. green	£110	£350
12		6d. red	£120	£275

1872. Surch in words.

13a	**2**	2 c. on 1d. blue	28·00	48·00
14		6 c. on 3d. green	65·00	65·00
15		12 c. on 6d. red	85·00	75·00

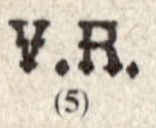
(5)

(8)

1874. Optd as T 5.

16	**2**	2 c. on 1d. blue	£800	£200
17		6 c. on 3d. green	£1200	£550
18		12 c. on 6d. red	£500	£170

1875. Nos. 17 and 18 surch **2d.**

22	**2**	2d. on 6 c. on 3d. green	£425	£150
27		2d. on 12 c. on 6d. red	£1200	£550

1876. Optd with T **8**, and the 3d. surch in words also.

31	**2**	1d. blue	13·00	24·00
29a		2d. on 3d. green	38·00	50·00
34		4d. on 3d. mauve	85·00	25·00
33		6d. red	48·00	27·00

10

12

1878. Surch on Nos. 36 and 41/2 in words.

35	**10**	1d. blue	6·50	6·50
40		2d. green	10·00	1·00
36		2d. on 3d. green	4·50	14·00
54		4d. mauve	8·50	9·00
41		4d. on 1d. mauve	30·00	20·00
42		4d. on 2d. mauve	70·00	9·00
59a		6d. red	7·00	3·75
67	**12**	1s. brown	32·00	9·00
69		5s. red and black	55·00	35·00

1891. Surch in figures or words.

72a	**10**	½d. on 1d. blue	38·00	60·00
70		2½d. on 2d. green	40·00	48·00
73		5d. on 4d. mauve	48·00	65·00
74a		5d. on 6d. red	55·00	60·00

20

21 Native Canoe

23

1891.

99	**20**	½d. grey	1·00	2·50
87	**21**	1d. black	3·00	3·00
101		1d. mauve	3·75	80
89		2d. green	4·75	80
103a	**10**	2½d. brown	5·00	5·00
85	**21**	5d. blue	9·50	7·50

1903.

104	**23**	½d. green	2·25	1·75
105		1d. purple and black on red	12·00	55
119		1d. red	5·00	10
106		2d. purple and orange	3·50	1·25
107		2½d. purple and blue on blue	14·00	8·00
120		2½d. blue	6·00	7·50
108		3d. purple	1·50	4·50
109		4d. purple and black	1·50	2·50
110		5d. purple and green	1·50	5·00
111		6d. purple and red	1·50	2·50
121		6d. purple	8·50	22·00
112		1s. green and red	10·00	45·00
122		1s. black on green	4·00	10·00
113		5s. green and black	42·00	95·00
123		5s. green and red on yellow	48·00	55·00
114		£1 black and blue	£300	£375
124		£1 purple and black on red	£300	£300

1912. As T **23**, but portrait of King George V.

125a	½d. brown	1·25	40
126b	½d. green	1·25	50
127	1d. red	2·00	10
231	1d. violet	1·25	10
232	1½d. red	4·00	3·25
233	2d. grey	1·25	10
129	2½d. blue	3·50	3·50
130	3d. purple on yellow	4·00	4·25
234	3d. blue	2·75	1·25
235	4d. black and red on yellow	5·00	7·00
236	5d. purple and olive	1·50	2·00
237	6d. purple	2·00	1·25
134a	1s. black on green	1·00	8·00
239	2s. purple and blue on blue	28·00	60·00
240	2s. 6d. black and red on blue	11·00	32·00
136	5s. green and red on yellow	32·00	40·00
137	£1 purple and black on red	£250	£275

1916. Nos. 126/7 optd **WAR STAMP**.

138b	½d. green	60	2·50
139a	1d. red	1·50	75

1935. Silver Jubilee. As T **13** of Antigua.

242	1½d. blue and red	80	5·00
243	2d. blue and grey	1·50	35
244	3d. brown and blue	2·50	3·00
245	1s. grey and purple	4·50	4·50

1937. Coronation. As T **2** of Aden.

246	1d. violet	60	45
247	2d. grey	60	1·25
248	3d. blue	60	1·25

28 Native Sailing Canoe

29 Native Village

32 Government Offices

1938.

249	**28**	½d. green	20	60
250	**29**	1d. brown and blue	40	20
252c	–	1½d. red	90	1·25
254	–	2d. brown and green	16·00	16·00
255	**32**	2d. green and mauve	40	60
256b	–	2½d. brown and green	80	50
257	–	3d. blue	1·00	30
258	–	5d. blue and red	42·00	10·00
259	–	5d. green and red	20	30
261b	–	6d. black	1·50	1·50
261c	–	8d. red	1·00	1·50
262	–	1s. black and yellow	75	60
263	–	1s. 5d. black and red	20	10
263a	–	1s. 6d. blue	3·50	2·75
264	–	2s. violet and orange	2·50	40
265	–	2s. 6d. green and brown	2·50	1·50
266	–	5s. green and purple	2·50	1·75
266a	–	10s. orange and green	32·00	40·00
266b	–	£1 blue and red	48·00	50·00

DESIGNS—HORIZ (As Type **32**): 1½d. Camakua (canoe); 2d. (No. 254), 2½d., 6d. Map of Fiji Is. HORIZ (As Type **29**): 3d. Canoe and arms; 8d., 1s. 5d., 1s. 6d. Arms; 2 s. Suva Harbour; 2s. 6d. River scene; 5s. Chief's hut. VERT (As Type **29**): 5d. (Nos. 258/9), Sugar cane; 1s. Spearing fish; 10s. Paw-paw tree; £1 Police bugler.

1941. No. 254 surch **2½d.**

267	–	2½d. on 2d. brown and green	55	20

1946. Victory. As T **9** of Aden.

268	2½d. green	10	75
269	3d. blue	10	10

1948. Silver Wedding. As T **10/11** of Aden.

270	2½d. green	40	75
271	5s. blue	14·00	6·50

1949. U.P.U. As T **20/23** of Antigua.

272	2d. purple	30	30
273	3d. blue	2·25	2·00
274	8d. red	45	1·25
275	1s. 6d. blue	45	1·00

43 Children Bathing

1951. Health stamps. Inscr "HEALTH".

276	**43**	1d. + 1d. brown	10	60
277	–	2d. + 1d. green	30	60

DESIGNS—VERT: 2d. Rugby footballer.

1953. Coronation. As T **13** of Aden.

278	2½d. black and green	50	30

1953. Royal Visit. As No. 261c, but with portrait of Queen Elizabeth II and inscr "ROYAL VISIT 1953".

279	8d. red	15	15

46 Queen Elizabeth II (after Annigoni)

48 Loading Copra

1954. Queen Elizabeth II. (I) inscr "FIJI". (II) inscribed "Fiji".

280	**28**	½d. green	15	1·00
298	**46**	½d. green	15	90
281		1d. turquoise (I)	70	10
299		1d. blue (II)	1·75	1·00
282		1½d. sepia (I)	70	30
300		1½d. sepia (II)	1·25	30
283	**32**	2d. green and mauve	1·25	30
312	**46**	2d. red (I)	45	10
284		2½d. violet (I)	1·25	10
302		2½d. brown (I)	1·50	2·25
285	**48**	3d. brown and purple	2·50	20
287	–	6d. black (As No. 261)	2·25	75
303	A	6d. red and black	1·25	10
288	–	8d. red (As No. 261d)	1·75	1·25
316	B	10d. brown and red	60	50
289	–	1s. black and yellow (As No. 262)	2·25	10
306	C	1s. blue	1·50	10
290	D	1s. 6d. blue and green	18·00	90
291	E	2s. black and red	5·50	30
292a	–	2s. 6d. green and brown (As No. 265)	1·25	10
320a	F	2s. 6d. black and purple	1·75	70
293	G	5s. ochre and blue	25·00	1·25
294	–	10s. orange and green (As No. 266a)	12·00	20·00
309	H	10s. green and sepia	6·50	3·00
295	–	£1 bl & red (As No. 266b)	42·00	18·00
325	I	£1 black and orange	18·00	11·00

DESIGNS—HORIZ (As Type **48**): A, Fijian beating lali; B, Yaqona ceremony; C, Location map; D, Sugar cane train; E, Preparing bananas for export; F, Nadi Airport; G, Gold industry; H, Cutting sugar-cane; I, Arms of Fiji.

52 River Scene

56 Hibiscus

1954. Health stamps.

296	**52**	1½d. + ½d. brown and green	10	50
297	–	2½d. + ½d. orange and black	10	10

DESIGN: 2½d. Queen's portrait and Cross of Lorraine inscribed "FIJI WAR MEMORIAL" and "ANTI-TUBERCULOSIS CAMPAIGN".

1959.

313	–	3d. multicoloured	25	10
304	**56**	8d. multicoloured	50	25
315	–	9d. multicoloured	90	65
318	–	1s. 6d. multicoloured	2·75	90
319	–	2s. yellow, green and copper	16·00	3·00
308	–	4s. multicoloured	1·75	1·75
323	–	5s. red, yellow and grey	14·00	35

DESIGNS—HORIZ: 1s. 6d. International date line; 4s. Red shining parrot; 5s. Orange dove. VERT: 2s. White orchid. 23 × 28 mm: 3d. Queen Elizabeth II.

1963 Royal Visit. Optd **ROYAL VISIT 1963**.

326	–	3d. mult (No. 313)	20	10
327	C	1s. blue (No. 306)	20	10

1963. Freedom from Hunger. As T **28** of Aden.

328	–	2s. blue	2·50	70

69 Running

1963. 1st South Pacific Games, Suva. Inscr as in T **69**.

329	**69**	3d. brown, yellow and black	25	10
330	–	9d. brown, violet and black	35	1·40
331	–	1s. brown, green and black	35	10
332	–	2s. 6d. brown, blue and black	90	1·00

DESIGNS—VERT: 9d. Throwing the discus; 1s. Hockey. HORIZ: 2s. 6d. High-jumping.

1963. Centenary of Red Cross. As T **33** of Antigua.

333	2d. red and black	50	10
334	2s. red and blue	2·25	2·50

1963. Opening of COMPAC (Trans-Pacific Telephone Cable). No. 306 optd **COMPAC CABLE IN SERVICE DECEMBER 1963** and ship.

335	C	1s. blue	40	10

74 Jamborette Emblem

76 Flying-boat "Aotearoa"

1964. 50th Anniv of Fijian Scout Movement.

336	**74**	3d. multicoloured	15	20
337	–	1s. violet and brown	15	25

DESIGN: 1s. Scouts of three races.

1964. 25th Anniv of 1st Fiji–Tonga Airmail Service.

338	**76**	3d. black and red	40	10
339	–	6d. red and blue	70	85
340	–	1s. black and turquoise	70	85

DESIGNS—VERT: 6d. De Havilland Heron 2. HORIZ (37½ × 25 mm): 1s. "Aotearoa" and map.

1965. Centenary of I.T.U. As T **36** of Antigua.

341	3d. blue and red	35	10
342	2s. yellow and bistre	80	25

1965. I.C.Y. As T **37** of Antigua.

343	2d. purple and turquoise	20	10
344	2s. 6d. green and lavender	60	25

1966. Churchill Commemoration. As T **38** of Antigua.

345	3d. blue	70	10
346	9d. green	90	40
347	1s. brown	90	10
348	2s. 6d. violet	1·00	50

1966. World Cup Football Championships. As T **40** of Antigua.

349	2d. multicoloured	20	10
350	2s. multicoloured	50	20

79 H.M.S. "Pandora" approaching Split Island, Rotuma

1966. 175th Anniv of Discovery of Rotuma. Mult.

351	3d. Type **79**	30	10
352	10d. Rotuma chiefs	30	10
353	1s. 6d. Rotumans welcoming H.M.S. "Pandora"	40	30

1966. Inauguration of W.H.O. Headquarters, Geneva. As T **41** of Antigua.

354	6d. black, green and blue	1·00	25
355	2s. 6d. black, purple and ochre	2·50	1·75

82 Running

1966. 2nd South Pacific Games.

356	**82**	3d. black, brown and green	10	10
357	–	9d. black, brown and blue	15	15
358	–	1s. multicoloured	15	15

DESIGNS—VERT: 9d. Putting the shot. HORIZ: 1s. Diving.

85 Military Forces Band

1967. International Tourist Year. Multicoloured.

360	3d. Type **85**	40	10
361	9d. Reef diving	20	10
362	1s. Beqa fire walkers	20	10
363	2s. "Oriana" (cruise liner) at Suva	55	15

89 Bligh (bust), H.M.S. "Providence" and Chart

1967. 150th Death Anniv of Admiral Bligh.

364	**89**	4d. multicoloured	10	10
365	–	1s. multicoloured	10	10
366	–	2s. 6d. multicoloured	15	15

DESIGNS (As Type **89**): 2s. 6d. Bligh's tomb. (54 × 20 mm): 1s. "Bounty's longboat being chased in Fiji waters".

92 Simmonds Spartan Seaplane

1968. 40th Anniv of Kingsford Smith's Pacific Flight via Fiji.

367	**92**	2d. black and green	15	10
368	–	6d. blue, black and lake	15	10
369	–	1s. violet and green	20	10
370	–	2s. brown and blue	30	15

DESIGNS: 6d. Hawker Siddeley H.S.748 and airline insignias; 1s. "Southern Cross" and crew; 2s. "Lady Southern Cross".

96 Bure Huts

1968.

371 96 ½d. multicoloured 10 10
372 – 1d. blue, red and yellow . . 10 10
373 – 2d. blue, brown and ochre . 10 10
374 – 3d. green, blue and ochre . 35 10
375 – 4d. multicoloured 80 50
376 – 6d. multicoloured 25 10
377 – 9d. multicoloured 15 50
378 – 10d. blue, orange and brown 1·25 20
379 – 1s. blue and red 20 10
380 – 1s. 6d. multicoloured . . . 3·25 4·00
381 – 2s. turquoise, black and red 75 2·00
382 – 2s. 6d. multicoloured . . . 75 75
383 – 3s. multicoloured . . . . . 2·75 6·00
384 – 4s. ochre, black and olive . 6·00 2·75
385 – 5s. multicoloured . . . . . 3·00 2·50
386 – 10s. brown, black and ochre 1·50 3·50
387 – £1 multicoloured . . . . . 1·50 6·00

DESIGNS—As T 96: 1d. Passion flowers; 2d. Chambered or pearly nautilus; 4d. "Psilogramma jordana" (moth); 6d. Pennant coralfish; 9d. Bamboo raft; 10d. "Asota woodfordi" (moth); 3s. Golden cowrie shell. 33×22 mm: 2s. Sea snake; 2s. 6d. Outrigger canoes; 5s. Bamboo orchids; £1 Queen Elizabeth and Arms of Fiji. 23×33 mm: 3d. Eastern reef heron; 1s. Black marlin; 1s. 6d. Orange-breasted honeyeaters; 4s. Mining industry; 10s. Ceremonial whale's tooth.

113 Map of Fiji, W.H.O. Emblem and Nurses

1968. 20th Anniv of W.H.O. Multicoloured.

388 3d. Type 113 . . . . 15 10
389 9d. Transferring patient to medical ship "Vuniwai" . . 20 10
390 3s. Recreation 25 20

116 Passion Flowers

120 Javelin Throwing

117 Fijian Soldiers overlooking the Solomon Islands

1969. Decimal Currency. Designs as T 96 etc, but with values inscr in decimal currency as in T 116.

391 116 1 c. blue, red and yellow . 10 10
392 – 2 c. blue, brown and ochre (As 373) 10 10
393 – 3 c. green, blue and ochre (As 374) 30 10
394 – 4 c. multicoloured (As 375) 1·50 10
395 – 5 c. multicoloured (As 376) 20 10
396 96 6 c. multicoloured 10 10
397 – 8 c. multicoloured (As 377) 10 10
398 – 9 c. blue, orange and brown (As 378) . . . . . . 1·50 1·50
399 – 10 c. blue and red (As 379) 20 10
400 – 15 c. multicoloured (As 380) 9·00 4·25
401 – 20 c. turquoise, black and red (As 381) . . . . 1·00 80
402 – 25 c. multicoloured (As 382) 1·00 30
403 – 30 c. multicoloured (As 383) 6·50 1·75
404 – 40 c. ochre, black and olive (As 384) . . . . . . 6·50 4·00
405 – 50 c. multicoloured (As 385) 4·50 30
406 – $1 brown, black and ochre (As 386) . . . . . . 1·50 60
407 – $2 multicoloured (As 387) 1·50 4·00

1969. 25th Anniv of Fijian Military Forces' Solomons Campaign.

408 117 3 c. multicoloured 20 10
409 – 10 c. multicoloured 25 10
410 – 25 c. multicoloured 35 20

DESIGNS: 10 c. Regimental flags and soldiers in full dress and battledress; 25 c. Sefanaia Sukanaivalu and Victoria Cross.

1969. 3rd South Pacific Games, Port Moresby.

411 120 4 c. black, brown and red 10 10
412 – 8 c. black, grey and blue . 10 10
413 – 20 c. multicoloured 20 20

DESIGNS: 8 c. Yachting; 20 c. Games medal and winner's rostrum.

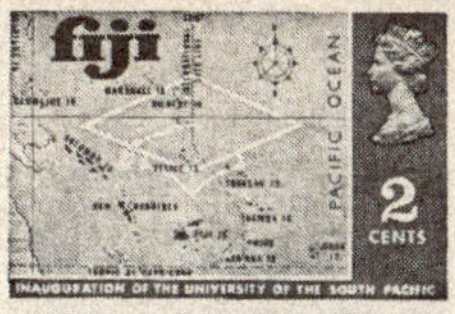

123 Map of South Pacific and "Mortar-board"

1969. Inauguration of University of the South Pacific. Multicoloured.

414 2 c. Type 123 . . . . 10 15
415 8 c. R.N.Z.A.F. Badge and Short S.25 Sunderland flying boat over Laucala Bay (site of University) 15 10
416 25 c. Science students at work 25 15

1970. Royal Visit. Nos. 392, 399 and 402 optd ROYAL VISIT 1970.

417 2 c. blue, brown and ochre . . 10 20
418 10 c. blue and red 10 10
419 25 c. multicoloured 20 10

127 Chaulmugra Tree, Makogai

1970. Closing of Leprosy Hospital, Makogai.

420 127 2 c. multicoloured 10 10
421 – 10 c. green and black . . 20 10
422 – 10 c. blue, black and mauve 20 10
423 – 30 c. multicoloured 35 50

DESIGNS: 10 c. (No. 421) "Cascade" (Semisi Maya); 10 c. (No. 422) "Sea Urchins" (Semisi Maya); 30 c. Makogai Hospital.
Nos. 421/2 are vert.

131 Abel Tasman and Log, 1643

1970. Explorers and Discoverers.

424 131 2 c. black, brown & turq 40 25
425 – 3 c. multicoloured 80 25
426 – 8 c. multicoloured 80 15
427 – 25 c. multicoloured 60 15

DESIGNS: 3 c. Captain Cook and H.M.S. "Endeavour", 1774; 8 c. Captain Bligh and longboat, 1789; 25 c. Fijian and ocean-going Canoe.

135 King Cakobau and Cession Stone

1970. Independence. Multicoloured.

428 2 c. Type 135 . . . . 10 10
429 3 c. Children of the world . . 10 10
430 10 c. Prime Minister and Fijian flag 10 10
431 25 c. Dancers in costume . . 20 20

139 1d. and 6d. Stamps of 1870

1970. Stamp Centenary. Multicoloured.

432 4 c. Type 139 . . . . 15 10
433 15 c. Fijian stamps of all reigns (61×21 mm) 40 15
434 20 c. "Fiji Times" office and modern G.P.O. 40 15

140 Grey-backed White-eye

142 Women's Basketball

1971. Birds and Flowers. Multicoloured.

435 1 c. "Cirrhopetalum umbellatum" 15 30
436 2 c. Cardinal honeyeater . . . 10 10
437 3 c. "Calanthe furcata" 85 20
438 4 c. "Bulbophyllum sp. nov." . . 75 60
439 5 c. Type 140 . . . . 35 10
510 6 c. "Phaius tancarvilliae" . . 2·75 20
441 8 c. Blue-headed flycatcher . . 35 10
442 10 c. "Acanthephippium vitiense" 40 10
513 15 c. "Dendrobium tokai" . . 2·50 60
444 20 c. Slaty flycatcher . . . . . 1·50 30
468 25 c. Yellow-faced honeyeater . . 1·75 90
516 30 c. "Dendrobium gordonii" . . 6·00 95
517 40 c. Masked shining parrot . . 3·50 60
448 50 c. White-throated pigeon . . 3·50 50
449 $1 Collared lory . . . . . . 4·00 1·25
520 $2 "Dendrobium platygastrium" 2·50 2·00

The 25 c. to $2 are larger 22½×35½ mm.

1971. 4th South Pacific Games, Tahiti.

451 142 8 c. multicoloured 10 10
452 – 10 c. blue, black and brown 10 10
453 – 25 c. green, black and brown 30 25

DESIGNS: 10 c. Running; 25 c. Weightlifting.

143 Community Education

144 "Native Canoe"

1972. 25th Anniv of South Pacific Commission. Multicoloured.

454 2 c. Type 143 . . . . 10 10
455 4 c. Public health 10 10
456 50 c. Economic growth 35 65

1972. South Pacific Festival of Arts, Suva.

457 144 10 c. black, orange and blue 10 10

145 Flowers, Conch and Ceremonial Whale's Tooth

1972. Royal Silver Wedding. Multicoloured. Background colours given.

474 145 10 c. green 20 15
475 25 c. purple 30 15

1972. Hurricane Relief. Nos. 400 and 403 surch HURRICANE RELIEF + and premium.

476 15 c. + 5 c. multicoloured . . . 15 15
477 30 c. + 10 c. multicoloured . . 15 15

147 Line Out

149 Christmas

148 Forestry Development

1973. Diamond Jubilee of Rugby Union. Mult.

478 2 c. Type 147 . . . . 30 1·40
479 8 c. Body tackle 45 10
480 25 c. Conversion . . . . . . 1·00 40

1973. Development Projects. Multicoloured.

481 5 c. Type 148 . . . . 10 10
482 8 c. Rice irrigation scheme . . 10 10
483 10 c. Low income housing . . 10 10
484 25 c. Highway construction . . 20 30

1973. Festivals of Joy. Multicoloured.

485 3 c. Type 149 . . . . 10 10
486 10 c. Diwali 10 10
487 20 c. Id-ul-Fitar 15 15
488 25 c. Chinese New Year . . . 15 15

150 Athletics

151 Bowler

1974. Commonwealth Games, Christchurch, New Zealand. Multicoloured.

489 3 c. Type 150 . . . . 15 10
490 8 c. Boxing 15 10
491 50 c. Bowling 50 75

1974. Centenary of Cricket. Multicoloured.

492 3 c. Type 151 . . . . 50 25
493 25 c. Batsman and wicket-keeper 1·00 35
494 40 c. Fielder (horiz) . . . . . 1·50 90

152 Fiji Postman

1974. Centenary of U.P.U. Multicoloured.

495 3 c. Type 152 . . . . 10 10
496 8 c. Loading mail onto "Fijian Princess" 10 10
497 30 c. Fijian post office and mailbus 20 25
498 50 c. B.A.C. One Eleven 200/400 modern aircraft . . . . . . 35 1·60

153 Cubs lighting Fire

1974. 1st National Scout Jamboree, Lautoka. Multicoloured.

499 3 c. Type 153 . . . . 15 10
500 10 c. Scouts reading map . . . 20 10
501 40 c. Scouts and Fijian flag (vert) 65 2·00

154 Cakobau Club and Flag

155 "Diwali" (Hindu Festival)

1974. Centenary of Deed of Cession and 4th Anniv of Independence. Multicoloured.

502 3 c. Type 154 . . . . 10 10
503 8 c. King Cakobau and Queen Victoria 10 10
504 50 c. Raising the Royal Standard at Nasova Ovalau 30 80

1975. "Festivals of Joy". Multicoloured.

521 3 c. Type 155 . . . . 10 10
522 15 c. "Id-Ul-Fitar" (Muslim Festival) 10 10
523 25 c. Chinese New Year . . . 15 15
524 30 c. Christmas 20 85

156 Steam Locomotive No. 21

1976. Sugar Trains. Multicoloured.

526 4 c. Type 156 . . . . 25 10
527 15 c. Diesel loco No. 8 . . . 75 40
528 20 c. Diesel loco No. 1 . . . 85 80
529 30 c. Free passenger train . . 1·10 2·00

157 Fiji Blind Society and Rotary Symbols

1976. 40th Anniv of Rotary in Fiji.

530	**157**	10 c blue, green and black	15	10
531	–	25 c. multicoloured	40	50

DESIGN: 25 c. Ambulance and Rotary Symbol.

158 De Havilland Drover 1

1976. 25th Anniv of Air Services. Multicoloured.

532	4 c. Type **158**	40	20
533	15 c. B.A.C. One Eleven 200/400	1·00	1·50
534	25 c. Hawker Siddeley H.S.748	1·25	1·75
535	30 c. Britten Norman "long nose" Trislander	1·25	3·75

159 The Queen's Visit to Fiji, 1970

1977. Silver Jubilee. Multicoloured.

536	10 c. Type **159**	10	10
537	25 c. King Edward's Chair	15	10
538	30 c. The Queen wearing cloth of gold supertunica	25	15

160 Map of the World

1977. E.E.C./A.C.P.* Council of Ministers Conference. Multicoloured.

539	4 c. Type **160**	10	10
540	30 c. Map of Fiji group	30	1·00

*A.C.P. = African, Caribbean, Pacific Group.

161 "Hibiscus rosa-sinensis"

1977. 21st Anniv of Fiji Hibiscus Festival.

541	**161**	4 c. multicoloured	10	10
542	–	15 c. multicoloured	15	15
543	–	30 c. multicoloured	25	25
544	–	35 c. multicoloured	40	50

Nos. 542/44 show different varieties of "Hibiscus rosa-sinensis".

162 Drua

1977. Canoes. Multicoloured.

545	4 c. Type **162**	15	10
546	15 c. Tabilai	30	20
547	25 c. Takai	35	25
548	40 c. Camakua	55	80

163 White Hart of Richard II

165 Shallow Wooden Oil Dish in Shape of Human Figure

164 Defence Force surrounding "Southern Cross", Suva

1978. 25th Anniv of Coronation. Multicoloured.

549	**163**	25 c. brown, green and silver	15	20
550	–	25 c. multicoloured	15	20
551	–	25 c. brown, green and silver	15	20

DESIGNS: No. 550, Queen Elizabeth II; No. 551, Banded iguana.

1978. Aviation Anniversaries. Multicoloured.

552	4 c. Type **164**	20	10
553	15 c. "Southern Cross" prior to leaving Naselai Beach	40	30
554	25 c. Wright Flyer I	55	60
555	30 c. Bristol F2B Brisfit	55	85

The 25 c. value commemorates the 75th anniv of Powered Flight, the 30 c. the 60th anniv of R.A.F. and the other values the 50th anniv of First Trans-Pacific Flight by Kingsford-Smith.

1978. Fijian Artifacts. Multicoloured.

556	4 c. Type **165**	10	10
557	15 c. Necklace of cachalot teeth (horiz)	10	10
558	25 c. Double water bottle (horiz)	15	10
559	30 c. Finely carved Ula or throwing club	15	15

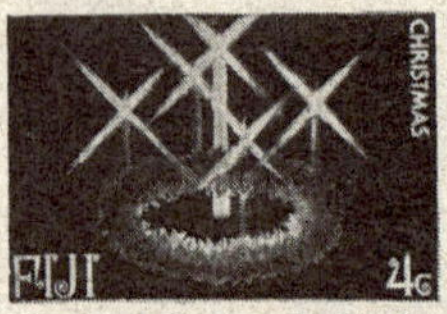

166 Advent Crown with Candles (Christmas)

1978. Festivals. Multicoloured.

560	4 c. Type **166**	10	10
561	15 c. Lamps (Diwali)	15	10
562	25 c. Coffee pot, cups and fruit (Id-Ul-Fitr)	20	10
563	40 c. Lion (Chinese New Year)	35	40

167 Banded Iguana

1979. Endangered Wildlife. Multicoloured.

564	4 c. Type **167**	50	10
565	15 c. Tree frog	1·00	15
566	25 c. Long-legged warbler	3·75	40
567	30 c. Pink-billed parrot finch	3·75	2·00

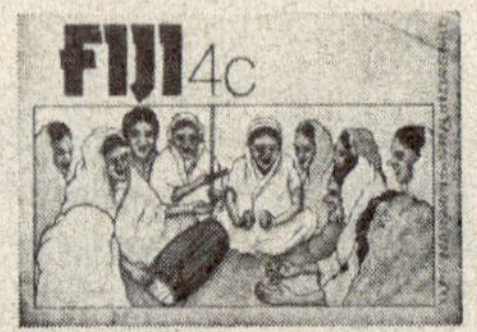

168 Women with Dholak

1979. Centenary of Arrival of Indians. Multicoloured.

568	4 c. Type **168**	10	10
569	15 c. Men sitting around tanoa	10	10
570	30 c. Farmer and suger cane plantation	15	10
571	40 c. Sailing ship "Leonidas"	40	25

169 Soccer

1979. 6th South Pacific Games. Multicoloured.

572	4 c. Type **169**	20	10
573	15 c. Rugby Union	40	20
574	30 c. Lawn tennis	80	80
575	40 c. Weightlifting	80	1·10

170 Indian Child and Map of Fiji

1979. International Year of the Child. Multicoloured.

576	4 c. + 1 c. Type **170**	10	10
577	15 c. + 2 c. European child	15	15
578	30 c. + 3 c. Chinese child	15	15
579	40 c. + 4 c. Fijian child	15	20

171 Old Town Hall, Suva

1979. Architecture. Multicoloured.

580A	1 c. Type **171**	15	60
581Bc	2 c. Dudley Church, Suva	30	20
721	3 c. Fiji International Telecommunications Building, Suva	30	30
722	4 c. Lautoka Mosque	30	30
583A	5 c. As 4 c.	15	10
584B	6 c. General Post Office, Suva	15	10
724	8 c. Public School, Levuka	1·50	1·50
585A	10 c. Fiji Visitors Bureau, Suva	20	10
586A	12 c. As 8 c.	20	90
726	15 c. Colonial War Memorial Hospital, Suva	30	20
588A	18 c. Labasa sugar mill	20	30
589A	20 c. Rewa Bridge, Nausori	55	30
590A	30 c. Sacred Heart Cathedral, Suva (vert)	65	50
591A	35 c. Grand Pacific Hotel, Suva	30	1·00
592A	45 c. Shiva Temple, Suva	40	45
593A	50 c. Serua Island Village	40	40
594A	$1 Solo Rock Lighthouse (30 × 46 mm)	2·50	1·75
595A	$2 Baker Memorial Hall, Nausori (46 × 30 mm)	1·40	1·90
595cA	$5 Government House (46 × 30 mm)	2·00	4·00

Most values come with or without date imprint.

172 "Southern Cross", 1873

1980. "London 1980" Int Stamp Exhibition. Mult.

596	6 c. Type **172**	30	10
597	20 c. "Levuka", 1910	40	10
598	45 c. "Matua", 1936	55	40
599	50 c. "Oronsay", 1951	55	55

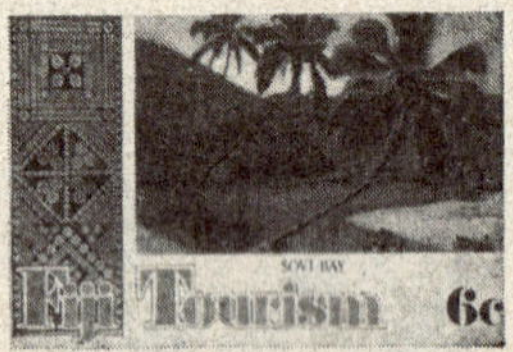

173 Sovi Bay

1980. Tourism. Multicoloured.

600	6 c. Type **173**	10	10
601	20 c. Evening scene, Yanuca Island	15	15
602	45 c. Dravuni Beach	20	40
603	50 c. Wakaya Island	20	45

174 Official Opening of Parliament, 1979

1980. 10th Anniv of Independence. Multicoloured.

604	6 c. Type **174**	10	10
605	20 c. Fiji coat of arms (vert)	15	10
606	45 c. Fiji flag	20	20
607	50 c. Queen Elizabeth II (vert)	25	35

175 "Coastal Scene" (painting, Semisi Maya)

1981. Int Year for Disabled Persons. Mult.

608	6 c. Type **175**	10	10
609	35 c. "Underwater Scene" (Semisi Maya)	35	30
610	50 c. Semisi Maya (disabled artist) at work (vert)	40	40
611	60 c. "Peacock" (Semisi Maya) (vert)	45	45

176 Prince Charles Sailing

1981. Royal Wedding. Multicoloured.

612	6 c. Wedding bouquet from Fiji	10	10
613	45 c. Type **176**	30	15
614	$1 Prince Charles and Lady Diana Spencer	50	60

177 Operator Assistance Centre

1981. Telecommunications. Multicoloured.

615	6 c. Type **177**	10	10
616	35 c. Microwave station	45	50
617	50 c. Satellite earth station	60	75
618	60 c. Cable ship "Retriever"	80	90

178 "Eat Fiji Foods"

1981. World Food Day.

619	**178**	20 c. multicoloured	30	10

179 Ratu Sir Lala Sukuna (first Speaker, Legislative Council)

1981. Commonwealth Parliamentary Association Conference, Suva.

620	**179**	6 c. black, buff and brown	10	10
621	–	35 c. multicoloured	30	30
622	–	50 c. multicoloured	45	45

DESIGNS: 35 c. Mace of the House of Representatives; 50 c. Suva Civic Centre.

180 Bell P-39 Airacobra

1981. World War II Aircraft. Multicoloured.

624	6 c. Type **180**	1·00	10
625	18 c. Consolidated PBY-5 Catalina	1·75	40
626	35 c. Curtiss P-40E Warhawk	2·00	95
627	60 c. Short Singapore III	2·50	5·00

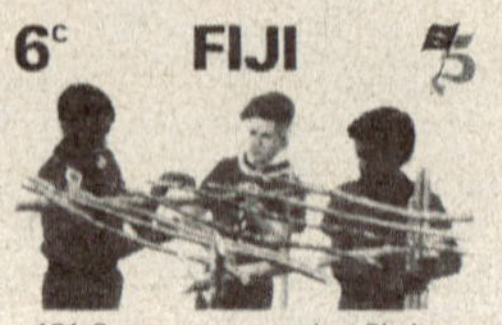

181 Scouts constructing Shelter

1982. 75th Anniv of Boy Scout Movement. Mult.

628	6 c. Type **181**	15	10
629	20 c. Scouts sailing (vert)	50	30
630	45 c. Scouts by campfire	85	50
631	60c. Lord Baden-Powell (vert)	1·00	1·00

182 Fiji Soldiers at U.N. Checkpoint

1982. Disciplined Forces. Multicoloured.
632 12 c. Type **182** 30 10
633 30 c. Soldiers engaged on rural development 60 45
634 40 c. Police patrol . . . . . . 1·50 1·25
635 70 c. "Kiro" (minesweeper) . . 1·50 3·00

183 Footballers and Fiji Football Association Logo

1982. World Cup Football Championship, Spain.
636 **183** 6 c. red, black and yellow . . 10 10
637 – 18 c. multicoloured . . . 25 20
638 – 50 c. multicoloured . . . 70 70
639 – 90 c. multicoloured . . . 1·10 2·00
DESIGNS: 18 c. Footballers and World Cup emblem; 50 c. Football and Bernabeu Stadium; 90 c. Footballers and Naranjito (mascot).

184 Bride and Groom leaving St. Paul's

185 Prince Philip

1982. 21st Birthday of Princess of Wales. Mult.
640 20 c. Fiji coat of arms 20 15
641 35 c. Lady Diana Spencer at Broadlands, May 1981 . . . 35 25
642 45 c. Type **184** 40 40
643 $1 Formal portrait . . . . . 1·00 2·25

1982. Royal Visit. Multicoloured.
644 6 c. Type **185** 30 15
645 45 c. Queen Elizabeth II . . . 80 2·25

186 Baby Jesus with Mary and Joseph

187 Red-throated Lorikeet

1982. Christmas. Multicoloured.
647 6 c. Type **186** 10 10
648 20 c. Three Wise Men presenting gifts 30 20
649 35 c. Carol-singing 45 35

1983. Parrots. Multicoloured.
651 20 c. Type **187** . . . . . . 1·25 15
652 40 c. Blue-crowned lory . . . 1·60 40
653 55 c. Masked shining parrot . . 1·75 1·00
654 60 c. Red shining parrot . . . 2·00 2·75

188 Bure in Traditional Village

1983. Commonwealth Day. Multicoloured.
655 8 c. Type **188** 10 10
656 25 c. Barefoot firewalkers . . . 20 15
657 50 c. Sugar industry 30 35
658 80 c. Kava "Yagona" ceremony . . 55 70

189 First Manned Balloon Flight, 1783

1983. Bicentenary of Manned Flight. Multicoloured.
659 8 c. Type **189** 25 10
660 20 c. Wright brothers' Flyer I . . 45 30
661 25 c. Douglas Super DC-3 . . . 50 40
662 40 c. De Havilland Comet 1 . . 75 60
663 50 c. Boeing 747 . . . . . . 90 70
664 58 c. Space shuttle . . . . . 1·00 80

190 Nawanawa

191 Fijian beating Lali and Earth Satellite Station

1983. Flowers (1st series). Multicoloured.
665 8 c. Type **190** 10 10
666 25 c. Rosawa 30 30
667 40 c. Warerega 40 50
668 $1 Saburo . . . . 80 1·40
See also Nos. 680/3.

1983. World Communications Year.
669 **191** 50 c. multicoloured . . . 50 80

192 "Dacryopinax spathularia"

193 "Tui Lau" (freighter) on Reef

1984. Fungi. Multicoloured.
670 8 c. Type **192** 85 15
671 15 c. "Podoscypha involuta" . . 1·25 25
672 40 c. "Lentinus squarrosulus" . . 2·25 1·00
673 50 c. "Scleroderma cepa" ("Scleroderma flavidum") (horiz) . . . . 2·25 1·25
674 $1 "Phillipsia domingensis" (horiz) . . . . 2·75 3·50

1984. 250th Anniv of "Lloyd's List" (newspaper). Multicoloured.
675 8 c. Type **193** 55 10
676 40 c. "Tofua" (cargo liner) . . 1·25 80
677 55 c. "Canberra" (liner) . . . 1·25 1·50
678 60 c. "Nedlloyd Madras" (freighter) at Suva wharf . 1·40 1·75

1984. Flowers (2nd series). As T **190**. Multicoloured.
680 15 c. Drividrivi 25 25
681 20 c. Vesida 35 40
682 50 c. Vuga 50 90
683 70 c. Qaiqi . . . . 60 1·40

195 Prize Bull, Yalavou Cattle Scheme

1984 "Ausipex" International Stamp Exhibition, Melbourne. Multicoloured.
684 8 c. Type **195** 25 10
685 25 c. Wailoa Power Station (vert) . 55 40
686 40 c. Air Pacific Boeing 737 airliner . . . . 1·40 1·10
687 $1 Container ship "Fua Kavenga" . . . . 1·40 2·75

196 The Stable at Bethlehem

1984. Christmas. Children's Paintings. Multicoloured.
688 8 c. Type **196** 10 10
689 20 c. Outrigger canoe 30 20
690 25 c. Father Christmas and Christmas tree 30 25
691 40 c. Going to church 40 70
692 $1 Decorating Christmas tree (vert) . . . . 70 1·75

197 "Danaus plexippus"

1985. Butterflies. Multicoloured.
693 8 c. Type **197** . . . . 1·25 15
694 25 c. "Hypolimnas bolina" . . 2·25 60
695 40 c. "Lampides boeticus" (vert) 3·00 2·00
696 $1 "Precis villida" (vert) . . . 4·00 6·50

198 Outrigger Canoe off Toberua Island

199 With Prince Charles at Garter Ceremony

1985 "Expo '85" World Fair, Japan. Multicoloured.
697 20 c. Type **198** 50 30
698 25 c. Wainivula Falls 85 40
699 50 c. Mana Island 95 90
700 $1 Sawa-I-Lau Caves . . . . 1·25 2·25

1985. Life and Times of Queen Elizabeth II the Queen Mother. Multicoloured.
701 8 c. With Prince Andrew on her 60th Birthday 10 10
702 25 c. Type **199** 35 40
703 40 c. The Queen Mother at Epsom Races 50 80
704 50 c. With Prince Henry at his christening (from photo by Lord Snowdon) . . . . . . 65 1·25

200 Horned Squirrelfish

1985. Shallow Water Marine Fishes. Multicoloured.
706 40 c. Type **200** . . . . . . 1·50 55
707 50 c. Yellow-banded goatfish . 1·75 1·10
708 55 c. Yellow-edged lyretail ("Fairy cod") . . . . . . 1·75 1·75
709 $1 Peacock hind . . . . . . 2·75 4·50

201 Collared Petrel

202 Children and "Peace for Fiji and the World" Slogan

1985. Seabirds. Multicoloured.
710 15 c. Type **201** . . . . . . 1·75 50
711 20 c. Lesser frigate bird . . . 2·00 50
712 50 c. Brown booby . . . . . 3·25 3·50
713 $1 Crested tern . . . . . . 5·00 7·00

1986. 60th Birthday of Queen Elizabeth II. As T **110** of Ascension. Multicoloured.
714 20 c. With Duke of York at Royal Tournament, 1936 . . 20 25
715 25 c. Royal Family on Palace balcony after Princess Margaret's wedding, 1960 . . 20 25
716 40 c. Queen inspecting guard of honour, Suva, 1982 . . . 25 45
717 50 c. In Luxembourg, 1976 . . 30 60
718 $1 At Crown Agents Head Office, London, 1983 . . . 45 1·60

1986. International Peace Year. Multicoloured.
736 8 c. Type **202** 25 10
737 40 c. Peace dove and houses . . 65 1·00

203 Halley's Comet in Centaurus Constellation and Newton's Reflector

1986. Appearance of Halley's Comet. Multicoloured.
738 25 c. Type **203** . . . . . . 1·25 40
739 40 c. Halley's Comet over Lomaiviti . . . . 1·50 85
740 $1 "Giotto" spacecraft photographing comet nucleus 2·50 4·75

204 Ground Frog

1986 Reptiles and Amphibians. Multicoloured.
741 8 c. Type **204** 55 10
742 20 c. Burrowing snake . . . . 1·00 30
743 25 c. Spotted gecko . . . . . 1·10 35
744 40 c. Crested iguana . . . . 1·25 90
745 50 c. Blotched skink . . . . 1·40 3·00
746 $1 Speckled skink . . . . . 1·75 5·00

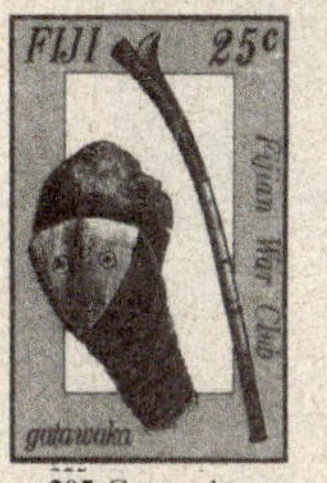

205 Gatawaka

206 Weasel Cone

1986. Ancient War Clubs. Multicoloured.
747 25 c. Type **205** 80 35
748 40 c. Siriti . . . . 1·00 60
749 50 c. Bulibuli . . . . 1·25 1·40
750 $1 Culacula . . . . 2·25 2·75

1987. Cone Shells of Fiji. Multicoloured.
751 15 c. Type **206** 80 25
752 20 c. Pertusus cone 90 35
753 25 c. Admiral cone . . . . . 1·10 40
754 40 c. Leaden cone . . . . . 1·40 1·25
755 50 c. Imperial cone . . . . . 1·50 2·50
756 $1 Geography cone . . . . . 2·00 4·25

209 Traditional Fijian House

1987. Int Year of Shelter for the Homeless. Mult.
759 55 c. Type **209** 45 50
760 70 c. Modern bungalows . . . 55 60

210 "Bulbogaster ctenostomoides" (stick insect)

1987. Fijian Insects. Multicoloured.
761 20 c. Type **210** . . . . . . 1·25 30
762 25 c. "Paracupta flaviventris" (beetle) . . . . 1·40 35
763 40 c. "Cerambyrhynchus schoenherri" (beetle) . . . 1·75 1·25
764 50 c. "Rhinoscapha lagopyga" (weevil) . . . . 1·75 2·25
765 $1 "Xixuthrus heros" (beetle) . 2·75 5·00

211 The Nativity

1987. Christmas. Multicoloured.
766 8 c. Type **211** 40 10
767 40 c. The Shepherds (horiz) . . 1·25 40
768 50 c. The Three Kings (horiz) . 1·75 90
769 $1 The Three Kings presenting gifts . . . . 2·25 2·50

212 Windsurfer and Beach

1988. "Expo '88" World Fair, Brisbane.
770 **212** 30 c. multicoloured . . . 1·00 50

213 Woman using Fiji "Nouna" (stove)

1988. Centenary of International Council of Women.
771 **213** 45 c. multicoloured . . . 75 60

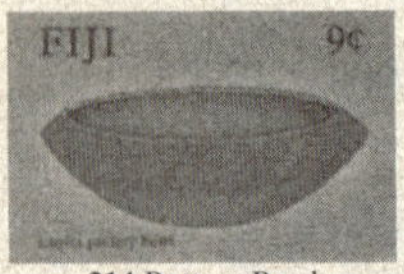
214 Pottery Bowl

1988. Ancient Fijian Pottery. Multicoloured.
772 9 c. Type **214** 15 10
773 23 c. Cooking pot 25 25
774 58 c. Priest's drinking vessel . 50 90
775 63 c. Drinking vessel . . . . 55 1·10
776 69 c. Earthenware oil lamp . . 60 1·25
777 75 c. Cooking pot with relief pattern (vert) . . . . 70 1·40

215 Fiji Tree Frog
216 "Dendrobium mohlianum"

1988. Fiji Tree Frog. Multicoloured.
778 18 c. Type **215** . . . . . . 1·60 50
779 23 c. Frog climbing grass stalks 1·75 1·10
780 30 c. On leaf . . . . 2·25 2·50
781 45 c. Moving from one leaf to another . . . . 3·00 4·00

1988. Native Flowers. Multicoloured.
782 9 c. Type **216** 45 15
783 30 c. "Dendrobium cattilare" . 70 45
784 45 c. "Degeneria vitiensis" . 70 70
785 $1 "Degeneria roseiflora" . . 1·25 2·00

217 Battle of Solferino, 1859

1989. 125th Anniv of International Red Cross.
786 **217** 58 c. multicoloured . . . 90 80
787 – 63 c. multicoloured . . . 1·00 1·00
788 – 69 c. multicoloured . . . 1·25 1·25
789 – $1 black and red . . . . 1·40 1·50
DESIGNS—VERT: 63 c. Henri Dunant (founder); $1 Anniversary logo. HORIZ: 69 c. Fijian Red Cross worker with blood donor.

218 Plan of "Bounty's" Launch

1989. Bicentenary of Captain Bligh's Boat Voyage. Multicoloured.
790 45 c. Type **218** . . . . . . 1·50 50
791 58 c. Cup, bowl and Bligh's journal . . . . 1·60 1·25
792 80 c. Bligh and extract from journal . . . . 2·00 2·75
793 $1 "Bounty's" launch and map of Fiji . . . . 2·75 3·00

219 "Platygyra daedalea"

1989. Corals. Multicoloured.
794 46 c. Type **219** . . . . . . 1·75 75
795 60 c. "Caulastrea furcata" . . 2·00 1·75
796 75 c. "Acropora echinata" (vert) 2·25 2·25
797 90 c. "Acropora humilis" (vert) 2·50 2·75

220 Goalkeeper

1989. World Cup Football Championship, Italy (1990). Multicoloured.
798 35 c. Type **220** . . . . . . 1·00 40
799 63 c. Goalkeeper catching ball 1·75 2·00
800 70 c. Player with ball . . . . 1·90 2·25
801 85 c. Tackling . . . . 2·00 2·75

221 Congregation in Church

1989. Christmas. Multicoloured.
802 9 c. Type **221** 25 10
803 45 c. "Delonix regia" (Christmas tree) 75 35
804 $1 The Nativity . . . . . . 1·50 2·00
805 $1.40 Fijian children under tree 1·75 3·00

222 River Snapper

1990. Freshwater Fishes. Multicoloured.
806 50 c. Type **222** . . . . . . 2·00 70
807 70 c. Kner's grunter ("Orange-spotted Therapon") . . . . 2·50 2·75
808 85 c. Spotted scat . . . . . 2·75 3·00
809 $1 Rock flagtail . . . . . . 3·25 3·75

224 Vertiver Grass Contours
225 "Dacrydium nidulum"

1990. Soil Conservation. Multicoloured.
811 50 c. Type **224** 85 50
812 70 c. Mulching . . . . 1·10 1·50
813 90 c. Hillside contour cultivation . . . . 1·40 1·90
814 $1 Land use rotation (vert) . 1·50 2·25

1990. Timber Trees. Multicoloured.
815 25 c. Type **225** 65 20
816 35 c. "Decussocarpus vitiensis" 75 30
817 $1 "Agathis vitiensis" . . . . 2·25 2·75
818 $1.55 "Santalum yasy" . . . 3·00 4·50

226 "Hark the Herald Angels sing"

1990. Christmas. Carols. Multicoloured.
819 10 c. Type **226** 25 10
820 35 c. "Still the Night, Holy the Night" 60 30
821 65 c. "Joy to the World!" . . 1·00 1·50
822 $1 "The Race that long in Darkness pined" . . . . . . 1·75 2·50

227 Sigatoka Sand Dunes

1991. Environmental Protection. Multicoloured.
823 35 c. Type **227** . . . . . . 1·00 30
824 50 c. Monu and Monuriki Islands . . . . 1·50 90
825 65 c. Ravilevu Nature Reserve, Taveuni . . . . 1·60 2·25
826 $1 Colo-I-Suva Forest Park . . 2·50 3·25

228 H.M.S. "Pandora" (frigate)

1991. Bicentenary of Discovery of Rotuma Island. Multicoloured.
827 54 c. Type **228** . . . . . . 1·75 85
828 70 c. Map of Rotuma . . . . 2·00 2·25
829 75 c. Natives welcoming H.M.S. "Pandora" . . . . 2·00 2·25
830 $1 Mount Soloroa and Uea Island . . . . 2·75 3·50

229 "Scylla serrata"

1991. Mangrove Crabs. Multicoloured.
831 38 c. Type **229** 70 35
832 54 c. "Metopograpsus messor" 95 85
833 96 c. "Parasesarma erythrodactyla" . . . . . . 1·75 2·50
834 $1.65 "Cardisoma carnifex" . . 2·50 3·75

230 Mary and Joseph travelling to Bethlehem

1991. Christmas. Multicoloured.
835 11 c. Type **230** 30 10
836 75 c. Manger scene . . . . . 1·25 1·25
837 96 c. Presentation in the Temple 1·50 2·50
838 $1 Infant Jesus with symbols . 1·60 2·50

231 De Havilland D.H.89 Dragon Rapide of Fiji Airways

1991. 40th Anniv of Air Pacific. Multicoloured.
839 54 c. Type **231** . . . . . . 1·50 1·00
840 75 c. Douglas DC-3 . . . . . 2·00 2·25
841 96 c. Aerospatial/Aeritalia ATR 42 . . . . 2·25 2·75
842 $1.40 Boeing 767 . . . . . 2·75 3·50

232 Ethnic Dancers

1992. "Expo 92" World's Fair, Seville, Spain. Multicoloured.
843 27 c. Type **232** 55 40
844 75 c. Peoples of Fiji . . . . . 1·25 1·75
845 96 c. Gold bars and sugar cane train . . . . 3·50 3·75
846 $1.40 "Queen Elizabeth 2" (cruise liner) at Suva . . . . 3·75 4·00

233 "Tabusoro"

1992. Inter-Islands Shipping. Multicoloured.
847 38 c. Type **233** . . . . . . 1·50 55
848 54 c. "Degei II" . . . . . . 2·00 1·40
849 $1.40 "Dausoko" . . . . . 3·25 3·75
850 $1.65 "Nivanga" . . . . . . 3·25 3·75

234 Running
235 European War Memorial, Levuka

1992. Olympic Games, Barcelona. Multicoloured.
851 20 c. Type **234** 65 20
852 86 c. Yachting . . . . 2·25 2·25
853 $1.34 Swimming . . . . . . 2·75 3·25
854 $1.50 Judo . . . . 2·75 3·25

1992. Historic Levuka (former capital). Mult.
855 30 c. Type **235** 30 30
856 42 c. Map of Fiji 45 55
857 59 c. Beach Street . . . . . 65 1·00
858 77 c. Sacred Heart Church (vert) 80 1·50
859 $2 Deed of Cession site (vert) 1·75 3·25

236 The Nativity

1992. Christmas. Multicoloured.
860 12 c. Type **236** 40 10
861 77 c. Shepherds and family giving presents . . . . 1·60 1·60
862 83 c. Shepherds at manger and giving presents to pensioners 1·75 1·75
863 $2 Wise Men and collecting Fiji produce . . . . 3·25 4·50

237 International Planned Parenthood Federation Logo

1992. 40th Anniv of International Planned Parenthood Federation. Multicoloured.
864 77 c. Type **237** 85 85
865 $2 Man weeping and pregnant mother with children . . . 2·50 3·25

238 Dove and Peace Corps Emblem

1993. 25th Anniv of Peace Corps in Fiji. Mult.
866 59 c. Type **238** 85 75
867 77 c. Handshake . . . . . . 1·10 1·40
868 $1 Educational symbols . . . 1·50 1·75
869 $2 Symbols of home businesses scheme . . . . 2·25 3·25

239 Fijian Players performing Cibi (traditional dance)

1993. Hong Kong Rugby Sevens Competition. Multicoloured.
870 77 c. Type **239** . . . . . . 1·25 1·40
871 $1.06 Players and map of Pacific 1·75 2·50
872 $2 Scrum and stadium . . . . 2·75 3·50

1993. 75th Anniv of Royal Air Force. As T **149** of Ascension. Multicoloured.
873 59 c. Gloster Gauntlet II . . . 90 75
874 77 c. Armstrong Whitworth Whitley Mk V . . . . . . 1·10 1·40
875 83 c. Bristol F2B "Brisfit" . . 1·25 1·60
876 $2 Hawker Tempest Mk V . . 1·90 3·00

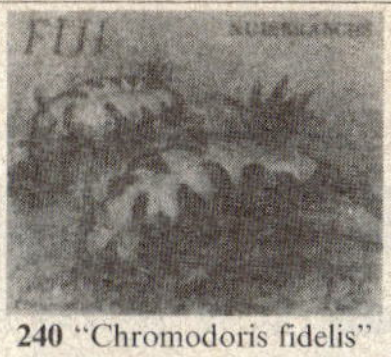
240 "Chromodoris fidelis"

1993. Nudibranchs. Multicoloured.
878 12 c. Type **240** 40 10
879 42 c. "Halgerda carlsoni" 90 55
880 53 c. "Chromodoris lochi" 1·25 1·00
881 83 c. Blue sea lizard 1·75 2·00
882 $1 "Phyllidia bourguini" 1·90 2·25
883 $2 Spanish dancer 3·00 3·75

241 Mango

1993. Tropical Fruits. Multicoloured.
884 30 c. Type **241** 85 45
885 42 c. Guava 1·10 80
886 $1 Lemon 2·25 2·25
887 $2 Soursop 4·00 4·50

243 The Last Supper

1994. Easter. Multicoloured.
890 59 c. Type **243** 80 60
891 77 c. The Crucifixion (vert) 1·00 1·25
892 $1 The Resurrection 1·60 2·00
893 $2 Examining Christ's wounds (vert) 2·75 4·00

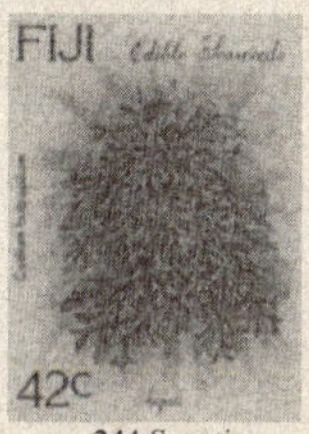
244 Sagati

247 Father Ioane Batita

1994. Edible Seaweeds. Multicoloured.
894 42 c. Type **244** 80 45
895 83 c. Nama 1·50 1·75
896 $1 Lumicevata 2·00 2·25
897 $2 Lumiwawa 3·25 4·50

1994. 150th Anniv of Arrival of Catholic Missionaries in Fiji. Multicoloured.
900 23 c. Type **247** 25 25
901 31 c. Local catechist 30 30
902 44 c. Sacred Heart Cathedral, Suva 40 60
903 63 c. Lomary Church 55 85
904 81 c. Pope Gregory XVI 90 1·25
905 $2 Pope John Paul II 2·00 2·75

1995. 50th Anniv of End of Second World War. As T **161** of Ascension. Multicoloured.
907 13 c. Fijian soldiers guarding crashed Japanese Mitsubishi A6M Zero-Sen aircraft 50 20
908 63 c. American spotter plane landing on Kameli Airstrip, Solomon Islands 1·40 1·25
909 87 c. Corporal Sukanaivalu and Victoria Cross 1·75 2·25
910 $1.12 H.M.S. "Fiji" (cruiser) 2·25 2·50

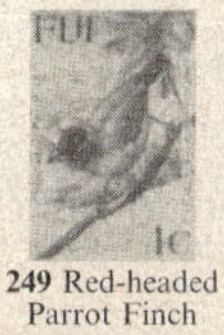
249 Red-headed Parrot Finch

251 Pres. Ratu Sir Kamisese Mara, Parliament Building and National Flag

1995. Birds. Multicoloured.
912 1 c. Type **249** 10 10
913 2 c. Golden whistler 10 10
914 3 c. Versicoloured flycatcher ("Ogea Flycatcher") 10 10
915 4 c. Peale's pigeon 10 10
916 6 c. Blue-headed flycatcher ("Blue-crested Broadbill") 10 10
917 13 c. Island thrush 10 10
918 23 c. Many-coloured fruit dove 15 20
919 31 c. Green heron ("Mangrove heron") 20 25
920 44 c. Purple swamphen 25 30
921 63 c. Fiji goshawk 40 45
922 81 c. Kandavu fantail ("Kadavu Fantail") 50 55
923 87 c. Collard lory 55 60
924 $1 Scarlet robin 60 65
925 $2 Peregrine falcon 1·25 1·40
926 $3 Barn owl 1·75 1·90
927 $5 Masked shining parrot ("Yellow-breasted musk parrot") 3·00 3·25

1995. 25th Anniv of Independence. Multicoloured.
930 81 c. Type **251** 90 1·00
931 87 c. Young citizens of Fiji 95 1·10
932 $1.06 Rugby players 1·25 1·60
933 $2 Boeing 747 "Island of Viti Levu" 2·25 2·75

252 "Praying Madonna with the Crown of Stars" (workshop of Correggio)

253 Trolling Lure

1995. Christmas. Multicoloured.
934 10 c. Type **252** 20 10
935 63 c. "Madonna and Child with Crowns" (on porcelain) 80 80
936 87 c. "The Holy Virgin with Holy Child and St. John" (after Titian) 1·10 1·25
937 $2 "The Holy Family and St. John" (workshop of Rubens) 2·50 3·50

1996. 50th Anniv of Resettlement of Banabans (inhabitants of Ocean Island) in Fiji. Multicoloured.
938 81 c. Type **253** 90 1·10
939 87 c. Banaban fishing canoes 95 1·10
940 $1.12 Banaban warrior (vert) 1·25 1·75
941 $2 Great frigate bird (vert) 3·25 3·75

254 L2B Portable Tape Recorder

255 Winged Monster and Ring (bronze), c. 450 B.C.

1996. Centenary of Radio. Multicoloured.
942 44 c. Type **254** 55 45
943 63 c. Broadcasting House, Fiji 75 70
944 81 c. Communications satellite 90 1·25
945 $3 Guglielmo Marconi 3·50 4·75

1996. "CHINA '96" 9th Asian International Stamp Exhibition, Peking. Multicoloured.
946 63 c. Type **255** 75 65
947 81 c. Archer (terracotta sculpture), 210 B.C. 90 1·10
948 $1 Dragon plate, 1426–35 1·25 1·50
949 $2 Central Asian horseman (sculpture), 706 2·75 3·50

256 Hurdling

1996. Cent of Modern Olympic Games. Mult.
951 31 c. Type **256** 45 30
952 63 c. Judo 85 70
953 87 c. Sailboarding 1·10 1·25
954 $1.12 Swimming 1·40 1·75

257 Computerised Telephone Exchange

1996. Innauguration of Independent Postal and Telecommunications Companies. Multicoloured.
956 31 c. Type **257** 35 30
957 44 c. Unloading mail from aircraft 60 55
958 81 c. Manual telephone exchange (vert) 90 1·25
959 $1 Postman on motorbike (vert) 1·25 1·75

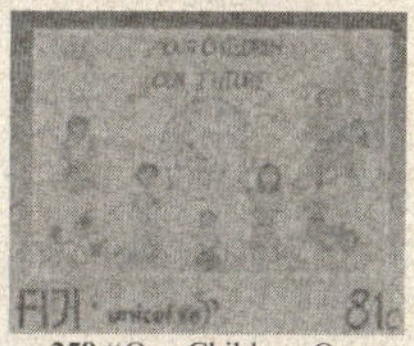
258 "Our Children Our Future"

1996. 50th Anniv of U.N.I.C.E.F. Children's Paintings. Multicoloured.
961 81 c. Type **258** 1·00 85
962 87 c. "Village Scene" 1·10 95
963 $1 "Living in Harmony the World over" 1·25 1·50
964 $2 "Their Future" 2·25 3·25

259 First Seaplane in Fiji, 1921

1996. 50th Anniv of Nadi International Airport. Multicoloured.
965 31 c. Type **259** 40 30
966 44 c. Nadi Airport in 1946 60 50
967 63 c. Arrival of first jet airliner, 1959 80 80
968 87 c. Airport entrance 1·10 1·25
969 $1 Control tower 1·40 1·75
970 $2 Diagram of Global Positioning System 2·25 3·50

260 The Annunciation and Fijian beating Lali (drum)

1996. Christmas. Multicoloured.
971 13 c. Type **260** 20 15
972 81 c. Shepherds with sheep, and canoe 90 85
973 $1 Wise men on camels, and people on cross 1·25 1·40
974 $3 The Nativity, and Fijian blowing conch 3·25 4·50

263 "Dendrobium biflorum"

1997. Orchids. Multicoloured.
977 81 c. Type **263** 90 90
978 87 c. "Dendrobium dactylodes" 95 95
979 $1.06 "Spathoglottis pacifica" 1·10 1·40
980 $2 "Dendrobium macropus" 2·25 2·75

265 Branching Hard Coral

1997. Year of the Coral Reef. Multicoloured.
982 63 c. Type **265** 70 55
983 87 c. Massive hard coral 1·00 1·00
984 $1 White soft coral 1·25 1·50
985 $3 Pink soft coral 3·50 4·25

266 Fijian Monkey-faced Bat

267 Waisale Serevi (Captain)

1997. Endangered Species. Fijian Monkey-faced Bat.
986 **266** 44 c. multicoloured 50 40
987 – 63 c. multicoloured 70 55
988 – 81 c. multicoloured 95 1·00
989 – $2 multicoloured 2·25 3·00
DESIGNS: 63 c. to $2 Showing different bats.

1997. Fiji Rugby Club's Victory in Hong Kong Rugby Sevens Competition. Multicoloured.
991 50 c. Type **267** 60 70
992 50 c. Taniela Qauqau 60 70
993 50 c. Jope Tuikabe 60 70
994 50 c. Leveni Duvuduvukula 60 70
995 50 c. Inoke Maraiwai 60 70
996 50 c. Aminiasi Naituyaga 60 70
997 50 c. Lemki Koroi 60 70
998 50 c. Marika Vunibaka 60 70
999 50 c. Luke Erenavula 60 70
1000 50 c. Manasa Bari 60 70
1001 $1 Fijian rugby team (56×42 mm) 80 85

268 Shepherd and Angel

1997. Christmas. Multicoloured.
1002 13 c. Type **268** 15 10
1003 31 c. Mary, Joseph and baby Jesus 35 30
1004 87 c. The Three Kings 90 90
1005 $3 Mary and baby Jesus 3·00 3·75

269 Chief in War Dress

1998. Traditional Chiefs' Costumes. Multicoloured.
1006 81 c. Type **269** 65 65
1007 87 c. Formal dress 75 1·25
1008 $1.12 Presentation dress 1·00 1·25
1009 $2 War dress of Highland chief 1·55 2·00

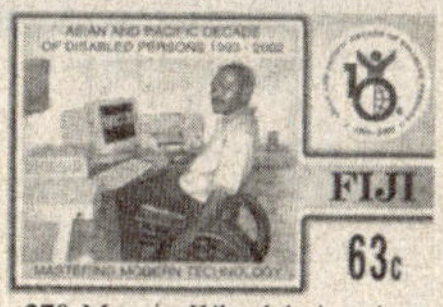
270 Man in Wheelchair using Computer

1998. Asian and Pacific Decade of Disabled People. Multicoloured.
1010 63 c. Type **270** 60 60
1011 87 c. Woman with child 80 80
1012 $1 Man at desk 90 1·00
1013 $2 Wheelchair race 1·60 2·00

1998. Diana, Princess of Wales Commemoration. As T **177** of Ascension. Multicoloured.
1014 81 c. Wearing tartan jacket, 1990 1·00 1·00

1998. 80th Anniv of Royal Air Force. As T **178** of Ascension. Multicoloured.
1016 44 c. R34 airship 40 30
1017 63 c. Handley Page Heyford 65 55
1018 87 c. Supermarine Swift FR.5 90 90
1019 $2 Westland Whirlwind 1·50 1·75

271 Pod of Sperm Whales Underwater

1998. Sperm Whales. Multicoloured.

1021	63 c. Type **271**	65	55
1022	81 c. Female and calf	80	80
1023	87 c. Pod on surface	90	90
1024	$2 Ceremonial whale tooth	1·60	1·75

272 Athletics

1998. 16th Commonwealth Games, Kuala Lumpur. Multicoloured.

1026	44 c. Type **272**	25	30
1027	63 c. Lawn bowls	40	45
1028	81 c. Throwing the javelin	50	55
1029	$1.12 Weightlifting	70	75

273 Takia (traditional raft)

1998. Maritime Past and Present (1st series). Multicoloured.

1031	13 c. Type **273**	10	10
1032	44 c. Camakau (outrigger canoe)	25	30
1033	87 c. Drua (outrigger canoe)	55	60
1034	$3 "Pioneer" (inter-island ship)	1·75	1·90

See also Nos. 1044/47.

274 "Jesus in a Manger" (Grace Lee)

1998. Christmas. Children's Paintings. Multicoloured.

1036	13 c. Type **274**	10	10
1037	50 c. "A Time with Family and Friends" (Brian Guevara)	30	35
1038	$1 "What Christmas Means to Me" (Naomi Tupou) (vert)	60	65
1039	$2 "The Joy of Christmas" (Lauretta Ah Sam) (vert)	1·25	1·40

275 Women's Sitting Dance

1999. Traditional Fijian Dances. Multicoloured.

1040	13 c. Type **275**	10	10
1041	81 c. Club dance	50	55
1042	87 c. Women's fan dance	55	60
1043	$3 Kava-serving dance	1·75	1·90

1999. Maritime Past and Present (2nd series). As T **273**. Multicoloured.

1044	63 c. "Tofua" (cargo liner)	40	45
1045	81 c. "Adi Beti" (government launch)	50	55
1046	$1 "Niagara" (liner)	60	65
1047	$2 "Royal Viking Sun" (liner)	1·25	1·40

POSTAGE DUE STAMPS

D 1

D 3

1917.

D5a	D 1 ½d. black	£450	£225
D2	1d. black	£275	70·00
D3	2d. black	£225	60·00
D4	3d. black	£275	75·00
D5	4d. black	£650	£350

1918.

D 6	D 3 ½d. black	3·00	14·00
D 7	1d. black	3·50	4·50
D 8	2d. black	2·75	7·50
D 9	3d. black	3·25	45·00
D10	4d. black	5·50	24·00

D 4

1940.

D11	D 4 1d. green	6·50	55·00
D12	2d. green	8·50	55·00
D13	3d. green	11·00	60·00
D14	4d. green	14·00	65·00
D15	5d. green	15·00	65·00
D16	6d. green	17·00	70·00
D17	1s. red	21·00	95·00
D18	1s. 6d. green	22·00	£140

GAMBIA

A British colony and protectorate on the West coast of Africa. Granted full internal self-government on 4 October 1963, and achieved indepedence on 18 February 1965. Became a republic within the Commonwealth on 24 April 1970.

1869. 12 pence = 1 shilling;
20 shillings = 1 pound.
1971. 100 bututs = 1 dalasy.

1

2

1869. Imperf.

5	1	4d. brown	£350	£180
8		6d. blue	£300	£180

1880. Perf.

11B	1	½d. orange	6·00	11·00
12B		1d. purple	3·50	5·00
13B		2d. pink	18·00	10·00
14cB		3d. blue	48·00	25·00
30		4d. brown	2·75	2·00
17B		6d. blue	75·00	45·00
19B		1s. green	£190	£110

1886.

21	1	½d. green	2·00	2·00
23		1d. red	3·75	5·00
25		2d. orange	1·40	7·00
27		2½d. blue	1·75	1·25
29		3d. grey	2·25	13·00
34		6d. green	10·00	42·00
35		1s. violet	3·25	15·00

1898.

37	2	½d. green	2·00	1·75
38		1d. red	1·25	75
39		2d. orange and mauve	4·50	3·50
40		2½d. blue	1·40	1·75
41		3d. purple and blue	13·00	12·00
42		4d. brown and blue	7·50	26·00
43		6d. green and red	9·00	21·00
44		1s. mauve and green	25·00	50·00

1902. As T **2**, but portrait of King Edward VII.

57	½d. green	3·50	25
46	1d. red	1·50	70
47	2d. orange and mauve	3·25	2·00
74	2d. grey	1·60	8·50
60	2½d. blue	4·00	4·25
61	3d. purple and blue	5·00	2·00
75	3d. purple on yellow	3·00	90
50	4d. brown and blue	3·00	22·00
76	4d. black and red on yellow	80	65
63	5d. grey and black	12·00	15·00
77	5d. orange and purple	1·50	1·25
51	6d. green and red	3·25	10·00
78	6d. purple	2·00	2·25
65	7½d. green and red	7·00	30·00
79	7½d. brown and blue	2·00	2·50
80	10d. green and red	2·50	6·50
67	1s. mauve and green	16·00	48·00
81	1s. black on green	3·00	16·00
53	1s. 6d. green and red on yellow	5·50	15·00
82	1s. 6d. violet and green	9·50	48·00
54	2s. grey and orange	42·00	55·00
83	2s. purple and blue on blue	14·00	19·00
55	2s. 6d. purple & brn on yell	15·00	55·00
84	2s. 6d. black and red on blue	21·00	19·00
56	3s. red and green on yellow	19·00	55·00
85	3s. yellow and green	22·00	48·00

1906. Surch in words.

69	½d. on 2s. 6d. (No. 55)	45·00	65·00
70	1d. on 3s. (No. 56)	55·00	30·00

1912. As T **2**, but portrait of King George V.

86	½d. green	1·00	1·25
87a	1d. red	1·50	30
88	1½d. olive and green	30	30
111	2d. grey	1·00	1·50
112	2½d. blue	50	4·25
91	3d. purple on yellow	30	30
92c	4d. black and red on yellow	1·50	6·00
93	5d. orange and purple	70	1·50
94	6d. purple	70	1·75
95	7½d. brown and blue	1·00	6·00
96a	10d. green and red	2·00	15·00
97	1s. black on green	1·50	1·00
98	1s. 6d. violet and green	8·00	10·00
99	2s. purple and blue on blue	2·50	6·00
100	2s. 6d. black and red on blue	2·75	13·00
101	3s. yellow and green	7·50	20·00
117	4s. black and red	55·00	90·00
102	5s. green and red on yellow	60·00	90·00

9

10

1922.

122	9	½d. black and green	55	40
124		1d. black and brown	70	10
125		1½d. black and red	80	10
126		2d. black and grey	1·00	2·00
127	9	2½d. black and orange	90	9·50
128		3d. black and blue	1·00	10
118		4d. black and red on yellow	1·75	1·75
130		5d. black and olive	2·00	10·00
131		6d. black and red	1·25	30
119		7½d. black & pur on yell	2·00	6·50
133		10d. black and blue	4·50	18·00
134	10	1s. black & pur on yell	2·25	80
135		1s. 6d. black and blue	9·50	12·00
136		2s. black and purple on blue	3·50	3·50
137		2s. 6d. black and green	4·00	9·50
138		3s. black and purple	11·00	40·00
140		4s. black and brown	4·25	16·00
141		5s. black and green on yellow	12·00	32·00
142		10s. black and olive	70·00	£100

1935. Silver Jubilee. As T **13** of Antigua.

143	1½d. blue and red	50	30
144	3d. brown and blue	55	70
145	6d. blue and olive	90	1·75
146	1s. grey and purple	2·50	4·75

1937. Coronation. As T **2** of Aden.

147	1d. brown	30	15
148	1½d. red	30	30
149	3d. blue	55	45

11 Elephant (from Colony Badge)

12 Tapping for Palm Wine

1938.

150	11	½d. black and green	15	50
151		1d. purple and brown	20	40
152b		1½d. pink and red	30	1·75
152c		1½d. blue and black	30	1·25
153		2d. blue and black	2·25	2·50
153a		2d. pink and red	60	1·75
154		3d. blue	30	10
154a		5d. green and purple	45	45
155		6d. olive and red	1·50	35
156		1s. blue and purple	2·00	10
156a		1s. 3d. purple and blue	2·00	2·00
157		2s. red and blue	4·50	3·25
158		2s. 6d. brown and green	12·00	2·00
159		4s. red and purple	21·00	2·50
160		5s. blue and red	21·00	4·00
161		10s. orange and black	21·00	7·00

1946. Victory. As T **9** of Aden.

162	1½d. black	10	10
163	3d. blue	10	10

1948. Silver Wedding. As T **10/11** of Aden.

164	1½d. black	25	10
165	£1 mauve	12·00	13·00

1949. U.P.U. As T **20/23** of Antigua.

166	1½d. black	40	30
167	3d. blue	1·50	60
168	6d. mauve	60	30
169	1s. violet	60	30

1953. Coronation. As T **13** of Aden.

170	1½d. black and blue	40	30

1953. Queen Elizabeth II.

171	12	½d. red and green	30	20
172	–	1d. blue and brown	40	30
173	–	1½d. brown and black	20	50
174	–	2½d. black and red	45	70
175	–	3d. blue and lilac	35	10
176	–	4d. black and blue	60	1·75
177	12	6d. brown and purple	35	15
178	–	1s. brown and green	60	40
179	–	1s. 3d. ultramarine and blue	10·00	50
180	–	2s. blue and red	7·00	3·50
181	–	2s. 6d. green and brown	4·00	1·50
182	–	4s. blue and brown	10·00	2·75
183	–	5s. brown and blue	2·50	1·50
184	–	10s. blue and green	19·00	7·00
185	–	£1 green and black	12·00	9·00

DESIGNS—HORIZ: 1d., 1s. 3d. Cutter (sailing ship); 1½d., 5s. Wollof woman; 2½d., 2s. Barra canoe; 3s., 10s. S.S. "Lady Wright"; 4d., 4s. James Island; 1s., 2s. 6d. Woman hoeing; £1 As Type **11**.

20 Queen Elizabeth II and Palm

22 Beautiful Sunbird

1961. Royal Visit.

186	20	2d. green and purple	30	15
187	–	3d. turquoise and sepia	65	15
188	–	6d. blue and red	65	50
189	20	1s. 3d. violet and green	65	1·75

DESIGN: 3d., 6d. Queen Elizabeth II and West African map.

1963. Freedom from Hunger. As T **28** of Aden.

190	1s. 3d. red	40	15

1963. Centenary of Red Cross. As T **33** of Antigua.

191	2d. red and black	25	10
192	1s. 3d. red and blue	65	45

1963. Queen Elizabeth II. Multicoloured.

193	½d. Type **22**	30	60
194	1d. Yellow-mantled whydah	30	30
195	1½d. Cattle egret	1·75	70
196	2d. Senegal parrot	1·75	70
197	3d. Rose-ringed parakeet	1·75	70
198	4d. Violet starling	1·75	80
199	6d. Village weaver	1·75	10
200	1s. Rufous-crowned roller	1·25	10
201	1s. 3d. Red-eyed dove	12·00	1·40
202	2s. 6d. Double-spurred francolin	9·00	2·50
203	5s. Palm-nut vulture	9·00	2·75
204	10s. Orange-checked waxbill	13·00	7·00
205	£1 African emerald cuckoo	28·00	14·00

1963. New Constitution. Nos. 194, 197 and 200/1 optd **SELF GOVERNMENT 1963.**

206	1d. multicoloured	10	30
207	3d. multicoloured	25	10
208	1s. multicoloured	25	10
209	1s. 3d. multicoloured	30	45

1964. 400th Birth Anniv of Shakespeare. As T **34** of Antigua.

210	6d. blue	10	10

36 Gambia Flag and River

1965. Independence. Multicoloured.

211	½d. Type **36**	10	20
212	2d. Arms	10	10
213	7½d. Type **36**	30	25
214	1s. 6d. Arms	35	25

1985. Nos 193/205 optd **INDEPENDENCE 1965.** Multicoloured.

215	½d. Type **22**	30	60
216	1d. Yellow-mantled whydah	30	20
217	1½d. Cattle egret	60	60
218	2d. Senegal parrot	70	30
219	3d. Rose-ringed parakeet	70	15
220	4d. Violet starling	70	70
221	6d. Village weaver	70	10
222	1s. Rufous-crowned roller	70	10
223	1s. 3d. Red-eyed dove	70	10
224	2s. 6d. Double-spurred francolin	70	50
225	5s. Palm-nut vulture	70	65
226	10s. Orange-checked waxbill	1·60	1·50
227	£1 African emerald cuckoo	6·00	7·00

39 I.T.U. Emblem and Symbols

1965. Centenary of I.T.U.

228	39	1d. silver and blue	20	10
229		1s 6d. gold and violet	80	80

40 Sir Winston Churchill and Houses of Parliament

1966. Churchill Commemoration.

230	40	1d. multicoloured	10	10
231		6d. multicoloured	20	10
232		1s. 6d. multicoloured	40	65

41 Red-cheeked Cordon-bleu

1966. Birds. Multicoloured.

233	½d. Type **41**	75	40
234	1d. White-faced whistling duck	30	40
235	1½d. Red-throated bee eater	30	40
236	2d. Lesser pied kingfisher	4·25	40
237	3d. Golden bishop	30	10
238	4d. African fish eagle	50	30
239	6d. Yellow-bellied green pigeon	40	10
240	1s. Blue-bellied roller	40	10
241	1s. 6d. African pygmy kingfisher	75	30
242	2s. 6d. Spur-winged goose	75	70
243	5s. Cardinal woodpecker	75	75
244	10s. Violet turaco	75	2·75
245	£1 Pin-tailed whydah (25 × 39½ mm)	1·00	6·50

54 Arms, Early Settlement and Modern Buildings

1966. 150th Anniv of Bathurst.

246	54	1d. silver, brown and orange	10	10
247		2d. silver, brown and blue	10	10
248		6d. silver, brown and green	10	10
249		1s. 6d. silver, brown & pur	15	15

55 I.T.Y. Emblem and Hotels

1967. International Tourist Year.

250	55	2d. silver, brown and green	10	10
251		1s. silver, brown and orange	10	10
252		1s. 6d. silver, brn & mve	15	15

56 Handcuffs

1968. Human Rights Year. Multicoloured.

253	1d. Type **56**	10	10
254	1s. Fort Bullen	10	10
255	5s. Methodist Church	30	50

59 Queen Victoria, Queen Elizabeth II and 4d. Stamp of 1869

1969. Gambia Stamp Centenary.

256	59	4d. sepia and ochre	20	10
257		6d. blue and green	20	10
258	–	2s. 6d. multicoloured	70	1·00

DESIGN: 2s. 6d. Queen Elizabeth II with 4d. and 6d. stamps of 1869.

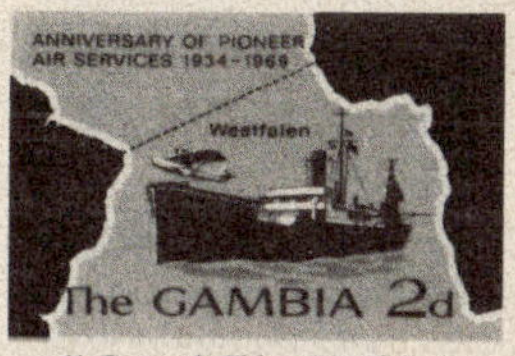

61 Catapult-Ship "Westfalen" launching Dornier Wal

1969. 35th Anniv of Pioneer Air Service. Mult.

259	2d. Type **61**	35	20
260	1s. Dornier Wal flying boat "Boreas"	45	20
261	1s. 6d. Airship "Graf Zeppelin"	55	1·40

63 Athlete and Gambian Flag

1970. 9th British Commonwealth Games, Edinburgh.

262	63	1d. multicoloured.	10	10
263		1s. multicoloured	10	10
264		5s. multicoloured	30	30

64 President Sir Dawda Kairaba Jawara and State House

1970. Republic Day. Multicoloured.

265	2d. Type **64**	10	10
266	1s. President Sir Dawda Jawara	15	10
267	1s. 6d. President and flag of Gambia	30	20

The 1s. and 1s. 6d. are both vertical designs.

65 Methodist Church, Georgetown

1971. 150th Anniv of Establishment of Methodist Mission. Multicoloured.

268		2d. Type **65**	10	10
269		1s. Map of Africa and Gambian flag (vert)	15	10
270		1s. 6d. John Wesley and scroll	15	20

66 Yellow-finned Tunny

1971. New Currency. Fishes. Multicoloured.

271		2 b. Type **66**	10	40
272		4 b. Peter's mormyrid	10	15
273		6 b. Four-winged flyingfish	15	40
274		8 b. African sleeper goby	15	40
275		10 b. Yellow-tailed snapper	20	15
276		13 b. Rock hind	20	40
277		25 b. West African eel catfish	35	40
278		38 b. Tiger shark	55	45
279		50 b. Electric catfish	70	55
280		63 b. Black swampeel	80	1·50
281		1 d. 25 Small-toothed sawfish	1·40	2·50
282		2 d. 50 Great barracuda	2·00	4·50
283		5 d. Brown bullhead	2·25	7·00

67 Mungo Park in Scotland

1971. Birth Centenary of Mungo Park (explorer). Multicoloured.

284		4 b. Type **67**	20	10
285		25 b. Dug-out canoe	45	30
286		37 b. Death of Mungo Park, Busa Rapids	75	1·25

68 Radio Gambia

1972. 10th Anniv of Radio Gambia.

287	**68**	4 b. brown and black	10	10
288	–	25 b. blue, orange and black	10	25
289	**68**	37 b. green and black	20	70

DESIGN: 25 b. Broadcast-area map.

69 High Jumping

1972. Olympic Games, Munich.

290	**69**	4 b. multicoloured	10	10
291		25 b. multicoloured	15	15
292		37 b. multicoloured	15	20

70 Manding Woman

72 Groundnuts

71 Children carrying Fanal

1972. International Conference on Manding Studies. Multicoloured.

293		2 b. Type **70**	10	10
294		25 b. Musician playing the Kora	15	15
295		37 b. Map of Mail Empire	25	25

1972. Fanals (Model Boats). Multicoloured.

296		2 b. Type **71**	10	10
297		1 d. 25 Fanal with lanterns	30	45

1973. Freedom from Hunger Campaign.

298	**72**	2 b. multicoloured	10	10
299		25 b. multicoloured	15	10
300		37 b. multicoloured	25	20

73 Planting and Drying Rice

74 Oil Palm

1973. Agriculture (1st series). Multicoloured.

301		2 b. Type **73**	10	10
302		25 b. Guinea corn	20	15
303		37 b. Rice	25	25

1973. Agriculture (2nd series). Multicoloured.

304		2 b. Type **74**	10	10
305		25 b. Limes	30	30
306		37 b. Oil palm (fruits)	40	40

75 Cassava

1973. Agriculture (3rd series). Multicoloured.

307		2 b. Type **75**	10	10
308		50 b. Cotton	40	25

76 O.A.U. Emblem

1973. 10th Anniv of O.A.U.

309	**76**	4 b. multicoloured	10	10
310		25 b. multicoloured	15	10
311		37 b. multicoloured	15	20

77 Red Cross

1973. 25th Anniv of Gambian Red Cross.

312	**77**	4 b. red and black	10	10
313		25 b. red, black and blue	15	15
314		37 b. red, black and green	20	20

78 Arms of Banjul

1973. Change of Bathurst's Name to Banjul.

315	**78**	4 b. multicoloured	10	10
316		25 b. multicoloured	15	15
317		37 b. multicoloured	15	20

79 U.P.U. Emblem

1974. Centenary of U.P.U.

318	**79**	4 b. multicoloured	10	10
319		37 b. multicoloured	20	30

80 Churchill as Harrow Schoolboy

1974. Birth Cent of Sir Winston Churchill. Mult.

320		4 b. Type **80**	10	10
321		37 b. Churchill as 4th Hussars officer	25	15
322		50 b. Churchill as Prime Minister	40	60

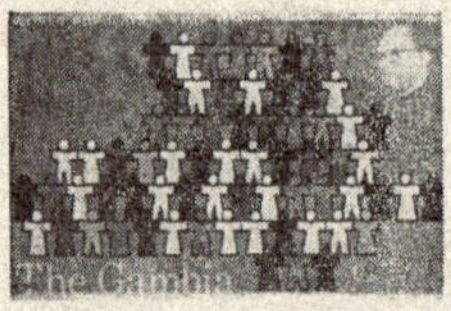
81 "Different Races"

1974. World Population Year. Multicoloured.

323		4 b. Type **81**	10	10
324		37 b. "Multiplication and Division of Races"	15	15
325		50 b. "World Population"	20	25

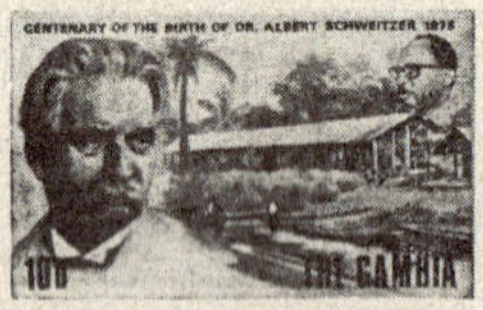

82 Dr. Schweitzer and River Scene

1975. Birth Centenary of Dr. Albert Schweitzer. Multicoloured.

326		10 b. Type **82**	20	10
327		50 b. Surgery scene	55	25
328		1 d. 25 River journey	1·00	55

83 Dove of Peace

1975. 10th Anniv of Independence. Multicoloured.

329		4 b. Type **83**	10	10
330		10 b. Gambian flag	10	10
331		50 b. Gambian arms	15	10
332		1 d. 25 Map of The Gambia	35	40

84 Development Graph

85 Statue of "David" (Michelangelo)

1975. 10th Anniv of African Development Bank. Multicoloured.

333		10 b. Type **84**	10	10
334		50 b. Symbolic plant	20	15
335		1 d. 25 Bank emblem and symbols	55	60

1975. 500th Birth Anniv of Michelangelo. Mult.

336		10 b. Type **85**	15	10
337		50 b. "Madonna of the Steps"	45	15
338		1 d. 25 "Battle of the Centaurs" (horiz)	75	1·25

86 School Building

1975. Centenary of Gambia High School. Mult.

339		10 b. Type **86**	10	10
340		50 b. Pupil with scientific apparatus	15	10
341		1 d. 50 School crest	35	35

87 "Teaching"

1975. International Women's Year. Multicoloured.

342		4 b. Type **87**	10	10
343		10 b. "Planting rice"	10	10
344		50 b. "Nursing"	35	15
345		1 d. 50 "Directing traffic"	85	35

88 Woman playing Golf

1975. 11th Anniv of Independence. Mult.

346		10 b. Type **88**	55	10
347		50 b. Man playing golf	1·50	20
348		1 d. 50 President playing golf	2·25	70

89 American Militiaman

90 Mother and Child

1976. Bicentenary of American Revolution. Mult.

349		25 b. Type **89**	20	10
350		50 b. Soldier of the Continental Army	30	20
351		1 d. 25 Independence Declaration	40	60

1976. Christmas.

353	**90**	10 b. multicoloured	10	10
354		50 b. multicoloured	15	10
355		1 d. 25 multicoloured	50	45

91 Serval Cat

1976. Abuko Nature Reserve (1st series). Mult.

356		10 b. Type **91**	2·25	20
357		20 b. Bushbuck	3·25	20
358		50 b. Sitatunga (deer)	4·50	40
359		1 d. 25 Leopard	10·00	2·00

See also Nos. 400/3, 431/4 and 460/3.

92 Festival Emblem and Gambian Weaver

1977. 2nd World Black and African Festival of Arts and Culture, Nigeria.

361	92	25 b. multicoloured	15	10
362		50 b. multicoloured	20	15
363		1 d. 25 multicoloured	50	70

93 The Spurs and Jewelled Sword

1977. Silver Jubilee. Multicoloured.

365	25 b. The Queen's visit, 1961	25	30
366	50 b. Type **93**	20	25
367	1 d. 25 Oblation of the Sword	30	35

94 Stone Circles, Kuntaur

1977. Tourism. Multicoloured.

368	25 b. Type **94**	10	10
369	50 b. Ruined Fort, James Island	20	20
370	1 d. 25 Mungo Park Monument	70	70

95 Widow of Last Year

1977. Flowers and Shrubs. Multicoloured.

371	2 b. Type **95**	10	15
372	4 b. White water-lily	10	30
373	6 b. Fireball lily	10	30
374	8 b. Cocks-comb	10	15
375	10 b. Broad leaved ground orchid	2·00	30
376	13 b. Fibre plant (yellow background)	15	40
376a	13 b. Fibre plant (grey background)	2·75	3·50
377	25 b. False kapok	15	15
378	38 b. Baobab	25	55
379	50 b. Coral tree	35	35
380	63 b. Gloriosa lily	40	70
381	1 d. 25 Bell-flowered mimosa	60	1·25
382	2 d. 50 Kindin dolo	65	1·25
383	5 d. African tulip tree	85	2·00

Nos. 373/78 and 381/2 are vert designs.

96 Endangered Animals

97 "Flight into Egypt"

1977. Banjul Declaration.

384	96	10 b. black and blue	25	10
385	–	25 b. multicoloured	40	10
386	–	50 b. multicoloured	65	20
387	–	1 d. 25 black and red	1·75	75

DESIGNS: 25 b. Extract from Declaration; 50 b. Declaration in full; 1 d. 25, Endangered insects and flowers.

1977. 400th Birth of Rubens. Multicoloured.

388	10 b. Type **97**	15	10
389	25 b. "The Education of the Virgin"	25	10
390	50 b. "Clara Serena Rubens"	50	30
391	1 d. "Madonna with Saints"	90	90

98 Dome of the Rock, Jerusalem

1978. Palestinian Welfare.

392	98	8 b. multicoloured	50	15
393		25 b. multicoloured	2·00	85

99 Walking on a Greasy Pole

100 Lion

1978. 13th Anniv of Independence. Multicoloured.

394	10 b. Type **99**	10	10
395	50 b. Pillow fighting	20	10
396	1 d. Long boat rowing	45	45

1978. 25th Anniv of Coronation.

397	–	1 d. black, brown and yellow	20	45
398	–	1 d. multicoloured	20	45
399	**100**	1 d. black, brown and yellow	20	45

DESIGNS: No. 397, White Greyhound of Richmond; No. 398, Queen Elizabeth II.

101 Verreaux's Eagle Owl

1978. Abuko Nature Reserve (2nd series). Multicoloured.

400	20 b. Type **101**	5·00	50
401	25 b. Lizard buzzard	5·00	50
402	50 b. African harrier hawk	8·00	2·00
403	1 d. 25 Long-crested eagle	12·00	8·00

102 M.V. "Lady Wright"

1978. Launching of River Vessel "Lady Chilel Jawara". Multicoloured.

404	8 b. Type **102**	15	10
405	25 b. Sectional view of "Lady Chilel Jawara"	40	25
406	1 d. "Lady Chilel Jawara"	1·25	1·10

103 Police Service

1979. 14th Anniv of Independence. Multicoloured.

407	10 b. Type **103**	60	10
408	50 b. Fire service	1·10	25
409	1 d. 25 Ambulance service	1·40	80

1979. Nos. 376 and 380/1 surch **25b**.

410	25 b. on 13 b. Fibre plant	20	35
411	25 b. on 63 b. Gloriosa lily	15	20
412	25 b. on 1 d. 25 Bell-flowered mimosa	15	20

105 "Ramsgate Sands" (detail showing children playing on beach)

1979. International Year of the Child. "Ramsgate Sands" (William Powell Frith). Multicoloured.

413	10 b. Type **105**	10	10
414	25 b. Detail showing child paddling (vert)	20	10
415	1 d. Complete painting (60 × 23 mm)	60	60

106 1883 2½d. Stamp

1979. Death Centenary of Sir Rowland Hill. Multicoloured.

416	10 b. Type **106**	10	10
417	25 b. 1869 4d. stamp	15	10
418	50 b. 1965 Independence 7½d. commemorative	20	20
419	1 d. 25 1935 Silver Jubilee 1½d. commemorative	40	50

107 Satellite Earth Station under Construction

1979. Abuko Satellite Earth Station. Multicoloured.

421	25 b. Type **107**	20	10
422	50 b. Satellite Earth Station (completed)	30	20
423	1 d. "Intelsat" satellite	65	60

108 "Apollo II" leaving Launch Pad

1979. 10th Anniv of Moon Landing. Multicoloured.

424	25 b. Type **108**	20	10
425	38 b. "Apollo II" in Moon orbit	25	20
426	50 b. Splashdown	30	40
430	2 d. Lunar module on Moon	1·50	2·25

Nos. 424/6 also exist self-adhesive from booklet panes. No. 430 only exists in this form.

109 "Acraea zetes"

1980. Abuko Nature Reserve (3rd series). Butterflies. Multicoloured.

431	25 b. Type **109**	2·50	20
432	50 b. "Precis hierta"	3·00	50
433	1 d. "Graphium leonidas"	5·00	1·00
434	1 d. 25 "Charaxes jasius"	5·00	1·10

110 Steam Launch "Vampire"

1980. "London 1980" International Stamp Exhibition. Multicoloured.

436	10 b. Type **110**	25	10
437	25 b. T.S.S. "Lady Denham"	35	10
438	50 b. T.S.C.M.Y. "Mansa Kila Ba"	40	20
439	1 d. 25 T.S.S. "Prince of Wales"	65	60

Nos. 438 and 439 are larger, 49 × 26 mm.

111 Queen Elizabeth the Queen Mother

1980. 80th Birthday of Queen Elizabeth The Queen Mother.

440	**111**	67 b. multicoloured	30	35

112 Phoenician Trading Vessel

1980. Early Sailing Vessels. Multicoloured.

441	8 b. Type **112**	10	10
442	67 b. Egyptian sea-going vessel	40	20
443	75 b. Portuguese caravel	50	30
444	1 d. Spanish galleon	70	50

113 "Madonna and Child" (Francesco de Mura)

1980. Christmas. Multicoloured.

445	8 b. Type **113**	10	10
446	67 b. "Praying Madonna with Crown of Stars" (workshop of Correggio)	25	25
447	75 b. "La Zingarella" (workshop replica of Correggio painting)	25	30

114 New Atlantic Hotel

1981. World Tourism Conference, Manila. Mult.

448	25 b. Type **114**	15	10
449	75 b. Ancient stone circles	30	40
450	85 b. Conference emblem	40	50

115 1979 Abuko Satellite Earth Station 50 b. Commemorative

1981. World Telecommunications Day.

451	**115**	50 b. multicoloured	30	20
452	–	50 b. multicoloured	30	20
453	–	85 b. black and brown	50	45

DESIGNS: No. 452, 1975 Birth centenary of Schweitzer 50 b. commemorative; No. 453 I.T.U. and W.H.O. emblems.

116 Prince Charles in Naval Uniform

1981. Royal Wedding. Multicoloured.

454	75 b. Wedding bouquet from Gambia	20	20
455	1 d. Type **116**	25	30
456	1 d. 25 Prince Charles and Lady Diana Spencer	30	35

117 Planting-out Seedlings

1981. 10th Anniv of West African Rice Development Association. Multicoloured.

457	10 b. Type **117**	10	10
458	50 b. Care of the crops	25	35
459	85 b. Winnowing and drying	40	55

118 Bosc's Monitor

1981. Abuko Nature Reserve (4th series). Reptiles. Multicoloured.

460	40 b. Type **118**	3·00	20
461	60 b. Dwarf crocodile	3·50	60
462	80 b. Royal python	4·50	1·00
463	85 b. Chameleon	4·50	1·00

119 Examination Room

1982. 30th Anniv of West African Examinations Council. Multicoloured.

464	60 b. Type **119**	50	30
465	85 b. First high school	65	45
466	1 d. 10 Council's office	85	55

1982. No. 454 surch **60B**.

467	60 b. on 75 b. Wedding bouquet from Gambia	75	1·60

121 Tree-planting ("Conservation")

1982. 75th Anniv of Boy Scout Movement. Multicoloured.

468	85 b. Type **121**	2·00	1·25
469	1 d. 25 Woodworking	2·25	2·50
470	1 d. 27 Lord Baden-Powell	2·50	3·25

122 Gambia Football Team

1982. World Cup Football Championship, Spain. Multicoloured.

471	10 b. Type **122**	20	10
472	1 d. 10 Gambian team practice	1·10	70
473	1 d. 25 Bernabeu Stadium, Madrid	1·10	75
474	1 d. 55 FIFA World Cup	1·25	80

123 Gambia Coat of Arms

1982. 21st Birthday of Princess of Wales. Multicoloured.

476	10 b. Type **123**	10	10
477	85 b. Princess at City Hall, Cardiff, October 1981	30	20
478	1 d. 10 Bride and groom returning to Buckingham Palace	35	35
479	2 d. 50 Formal portrait	1·25	1·00

124 Vegetable Garden at Yundum Experimental Farm

1982. Economic Community of West African States Development. Multicoloured.

480	10 b. Type **124**	30	15
481	60 b. Banjul/Kaolack microwave tower	2·00	2·25
482	90 b. Soap factory, Denton Bridge, Banjul	2·00	3·00
483	1 d. 25 Control tower, Yundum Airport	3·00	3·50

125 "Kassina cassinoides"

1982. Frogs. Multicoloured.

484	10 b. Type **125**	80	20
485	20 b. "Hylarana galamensis"	1·75	30
486	85 b. "Euphlyctis occipitalis"	2·75	2·00
487	2 d. "Kassina senegalensis"	4·25	7·50

126 Satellite View of Gambia

1983. Commonwealth Day. Multicoloured.

488	10 b. Type **126**	10	10
489	60 b. Batik cloth	20	45
490	1 d. 10 Bagging groundnuts	35	65
491	2 d. 10 Gambia flag	55	1·25

127 Blessed Anne Marie Javouhey (foundress of Order)

1983. Centenary of Sisters of St. Joseph of Cluny's Work in Gambia. Multicoloured.

492	10 b. Type **127**	10	10
493	85 b. Bathurst Hospital, nun and school children (horiz)	45	50

128 Canoes

1983. River Craft. Multicoloured.

494	1 b. Type **128**	15	40
495	2 b. Upstream ferry	20	40
496	3 b. Dredger	20	40
497	4 b. "Sir Dawda" (harbour launch)	30	40
498	5 b. Cargo liner	30	40
499	10 b. "Lady Dale" (60 ft. launch)	30	10
500	20 b. "Shonga" (container ship)	45	40
501	30 b. Large sailing canoe	45	40
502	40 b. "Lady Wright" (river steamer)	65	55
503	50 b. Container ship (different)	65	55
504	75 b. Fishing boats	75	60
505	1 d. Tug with groundnut barges	90	80
506	1 d. 25 Groundnut canoe	1·00	1·25
507	2 d. 50 "Banjul" (car ferry)	1·75	2·50
508	5 d. "Bintang Bolong" (freighter)	2·50	4·00
509	10 d. "Lady Chilel Jawara" (river vessel)	4·00	6·50

129 Osprey in Tree

1983. The Osprey. Multicoloured.

510	10 b. Type **129**	1·50	50
511	60 b. Osprey	2·50	2·50
512	85 b. Osprey with catch	3·00	3·00
513	1 d. 10 In flight	3·50	4·50

130 Local Ferry

1983. World Communications Year. Multicoloured.

514	10 b. Type **130**	10	10
515	85 b. Telex operator	45	50
516	90 b. Radio Gambia	45	50
517	1 d. 10 Loading mail onto Douglas DC-9-80 aircraft	1·00	65

131 "St. Paul preaching at Athens" (detail)

1983. 500th Birth Anniv of Raphael.

518	**131** 60 b. multicoloured	35	40
519	– 85 b. multicoloured	45	50
520	– 1 d. multicoloured	50	55

Nos. 519/20 show different details of "St. Paul preaching at Athens".

132 Montgolfier Balloon and Siege of Paris Cover

1983. Bicentenary of Manned Flight. Multicoloured.

522	60 b. Type **132**	35	40
523	85 b. Douglas DC-10 aircraft and flown cover	45	50
524	90 b. Junkers seaplane "Atlantis" and Hans Bertram cover	45	50
525	1 d. 25 Lunar module and H. E. Sieger's space cover	65	70
526	4 d. Airship "Graf Zeppelin"	2·00	3·00

133 Shot-putting

134 Goofy

1984. Olympic Games, Los Angeles (1st issue). Multicoloured.

527	60 b. Type **133**	25	30
528	85 b. High jumping (horiz)	35	40
529	90 b. Wrestling	35	40
530	1 d. Gymnastics	40	45
531	1 d. 25 Swimming (horiz)	50	55
532	2 d. Diving	80	85

See also Nos. 555/8.

1984. Easter. Multicoloured.

534	1 b. Type **134**	10	10
535	2 b. Mickey Mouse	10	10
536	3 b. Huey, Dewey and Louie	10	10
537	4 b. Goofy (different)	10	10
538	5 b. Donald Duck	10	10
539	10 b. Chip 'n' Dale	10	10
540	60 b. Pluto	35	40
541	90 b. Scrooge McDuck	50	60
542	5 d. Morty and Ferdie	2·25	2·75

Nos. 534/42 show Walt Disney cartoon characters painting eggs.

135 Young Crocodiles Hatching

1984. Endangered Species. The Nile Crocodile. Multicoloured.

544	4 b. Type **135**	45	45
545	6 b. Adult carrying young	45	45
546	90 b. Adult	4·00	2·75
547	1 d. 50 Crocodile at riverbank	5·00	6·50

136 Port Banjul

1984. 250th Anniv of "Lloyd's List" (newspaper). Multicoloured.

549	60 b. Type **136**	60	50
550	85 b. Bulk carrier	75	80
551	90 b. Sinking of the "Dagomba"	75	90
552	1 d. 25 19th century frigate	1·25	1·60

1984. Universal Postal Union Congress, Hamburg. Nos. 507/8 optd **19th UPU CONGRESS HAMBURG**.

553	2 d. 50 "Banjul" (car ferry)	1·00	1·50
554	5 d. "Bintang Bolong" (ferry)	1·75	2·50

138 Sprinting

1984. Olympic Games, Los Angeles (2nd issue). Multicoloured.

555	60 b. Type **138**	25	30
556	85 b. Long jumping	35	40
557	90 b. Long-distance running	35	40
558	1 d. 25 Triple jumping	50	55

139 Airship "Graf Zeppelin"

1984. 50th Anniv of Gambia-South America Trans-Atlantic Flights. Multicoloured.

559	60 b. Type **139**	1·10	1·00
560	85 b. Dornier Wal on S.S. "Westfalen"	1·60	1·75
561	90 b. Dornier DO-18	1·75	2·50
562	1 d. 25 Dornier Wal	1·75	2·75

140 Pink Shrimp

1984. Marine Life. Multicoloured.

563	55 b. Type **140**	35	30
564	75 b. Atlantic loggerhead turtle	55	40
565	1 d. 50 Portuguese man-of-war	90	1·00
566	2 d. 35 Fiddler crab	1·40	1·60

141 "Antanartia hippomene"

1984. Butterflies. Multicoloured.

568	10 b. Type **141**	30	20
569	85 b. "Pseudacraea eurytus"	80	90
570	90 b. "Charaxes lactitinctus"	80	90
571	3 d. "Graphium pylades"	2·00	3·75

142 Oral Re-hydration Therapy

1985. Campaign for Child Survival.

573	**142** 10 b. black, blue and brown	10	10
574	– 85 b. multicoloured	35	45
575	– 1 d. 10 multicoloured	45	65
576	– 1 d. 50 multicoloured	60	80

DESIGNS: 85 b. Growth monitoring; 1 d. 10, Health care worker with women and babies ("Promotion of breast feeding"); 1 d. 50, Universal immunisation.

143 Women at Market

1985. Women and Development. Multicoloured.

577	60 b. Type **143**	25	35
578	85 b. Type **143**	35	50
579	1 d. Woman office worker	40	60
580	1 d. 25 As 1 d.	50	90

144 Turkey Vulture

145 The Queen Mother

1985. Birth Bicentenary of John J. Audubon (ornithologist). Designs showing original paintings. Multicoloured.

581 60 b. Type **144** 1·40 75
582 85 b. American anhinga 1·60 1·50
583 1 d. 50 Green heron 2·00 3·25
584 5 d. Wood duck 3·25 5·50

1985. Life and Times of Queen Elizabeth the Queen Mother. Multicoloured.

586 85 b. The Queen Mother and King George VI reviewing Home Guard 25 30
587 3 d. Type **145** 80 1·00
588 5 d. The Queen Mother with posy 1·40 1·75

1985. 150th Birth Anniv of Mark Twain (author). Designs as T **118** of Anguilla showing Walt Disney cartoon characters in scenes from "Life on the Mississippi". Multicoloured.

590 1 d. 50 Mickey Mouse steering the "Calamity Jane" 90 90
591 2 d. Mickey and Minnie Mouse at antebellum mansion 1·25 1·25
592 2 d. 50 Donald Duck and Goofy heaving the lead 1·50 1·50
593 3 d. Poker game aboard the "Gold Dust" 1·60 1·60

1985. Birth Bicentenaries of Grimm Brothers (folklorists). As T **119** of Anguilla, but vertical, showing Walt Disney cartoon characters in scenes from "Faithful John". Multicoloured.

595 60 b. The King (Mickey Mouse) and portrait of the Princess (Minnie Mouse) 40 40
596 85 b. The King showing the Princess his treasures 50 50
597 2 d. 35 Faithful John (Goofy) playing trumpet 1·10 1·40
598 5 d. Faithful John turned to stone 2·25 2·50

1985. Olympic Gold Medal Winners, Los Angeles. Nos. 527/32 optd.

600 60 b. Type **133** (optd **GOLD MEDALLIST CLAUDIA LOCH WEST GERMANY**) 40 40
601 85 b. High jumping (optd **GOLD MEDALLIST ULRIKE MEYFARTH WEST GERMANY**) 50 50
602 90 b. Wrestling (optd **GOLD MEDALLIST PASQUALE PASSARELLI WEST GERMANY**) 50 50
603 1 d. Gymnastics (optd **GOLD MEDALLIST LI NING CHINA**) 55 55
604 1 d. 25 Swimming (optd **GOLD MEDALLIST MICHAEL GROSS WEST GERMANY**) 70 70
605 2 d. Diving (optd **GOLD MEDALLIST SYLVIE BERNIER CANADA**) 1·00 1·00

147 Inspecting Maize

1985. United Nations Anniversaries. Multicoloured.

607 60 b. Type **147** 40 35
608 85 b. Football match, Independence Stadium, Banjul 50 40
609 1 d. 10 Rice fields 60 60
610 2 d. Central Bank of The Gambia 85 1·00
611 3 d. Cow and calf 1·50 1·75
612 4 d. Banjul harbour 2·00 2·25
613 5 d. Gambian fruits 2·25 2·50
614 6 d. Oyster Creek Bridge 2·50 3·00

Nos. 607, 609, 611 and 613 commemorate the 40th anniv of the Food and Agriculture Organization and Nos. 608, 610, 612 and 614 the 40th anniv of the United Nations Organization.

148 Fishermen in Fotoba, Guinea

1985. 50th Anniv of Diocese of The Gambia and Guinea. Multicoloured.

615 60 b. Type **148** 30 30
616 85 b. St. Mary's Primary School, Banjul 30 40
617 1 d. 10 St. Mary's Cathedral, Banjul 35 65
618 1 d. 50 Mobile dispensary at Christy Kunda 50 85

149 "Virgin and Child" (Dieric Bouts)

1985. Christmas. Religious Paintings. Multicoloured.

619 60 b. Type **149** 20 25
620 85 b. "The Annunciation" (Robert Campin) 25 30
621 1 d. 50 "Adoration of the Shepherds" (Gerard David) 45 50
622 5 d. "The Nativity" (Gerard David) 1·60 1·75

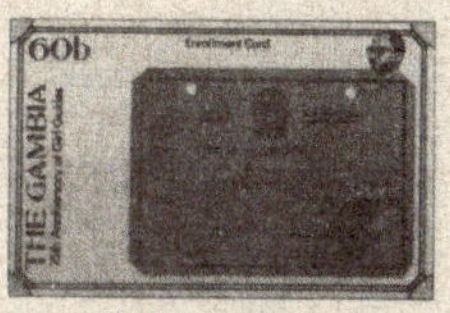

150 Enrolment Card

1985. 75th Anniv of Girl Guide Movement. Multicoloured.

624 60 b. Type **150** 40 30
625 85 b. 2nd Bathurst Company centre 50 35
626 1 d. 50 Lady Baden-Powell (vert) 70 1·00
627 5 d. Miss Rosamond Fowlis (Gambian Guide Association leader) (vert) 2·00 3·75

151 Girl and Village Scene

1985. International Youth Year. Multicoloured.

629 60 b. Type **151** 25 30
630 85 b. Youth and wrestling bout 30 35
631 1 d. 10 Girl and Griot storyteller 40 85
632 1 d. 50 Youth and crocodile pool 50 1·10

1986. Appearance of Halley's Comet. As T **123** of Anguilla. Multicoloured.

634 10 b. Maria Mitchell (astronomer) and Kitt Peak National Observatory, Arizona 40 20
635 20 b. Neil Armstrong, first man on Moon, 1969 55 25
636 75 b. "Skylab 4" and Comet Kohoutek, 1973 85 65
637 1 d. N.A.S.A.'s infra-red astronomical satellite and Halley's Comet 1·00 80
638 2 d. Comet of 1577 from Turkish painting 1·50 1·50
639 10 d. N.A.S.A.'s International Cometary Explorer 4·00 5·50

1986. 60th Birthday of Queen Elizabeth II. As T **125** of Anguilla.

641 1 d. black and yellow 25 30
642 2 d. 50 multicoloured 65 70
643 10 d. multicoloured 2·50 3·50

DESIGNS: Nos. 641, Duke of York and family, Royal Tournament, 1936; 642, Queen attending christening, 1983; 643, In West Germany, 1978.

152 Two Players competing for Ball

1986. World Cup Football Championship, Mexico. Multicoloured.

645 75 b. Type **152** 75 60
646 1 d. Player kicking ball 1·00 85
647 2 d. 50 Player kicking ball (different) 2·00 2·25
648 10 d. Player heading ball 5·00 6·00

153 Mercedes "500" (1986)

1986. "Ameripex" International Stamp Exhibition, Chicago. Centenary (1985) of First Benz Motor Car. Multicoloured.

650 25 b. Type **153** 20 10
651 75 b. Cord "810" (1935) 50 40
652 1 d. Borgward "Isabella Coupe" (1957) 70 60
653 1 d. 25 Lamborghini "Countach" (1985/6) 80 70
654 2 d. Ford "Thunderbird" (1955) 90 1·25
655 2 d. 25 Citroen "DS19" (1956) 90 1·60
656 5 d. Bugatti "Atlante" (1936) 1·25 3·00
657 10 d. Horch "853" (1936) 1·75 5·00

The 25 b. value is inscribed "MECEDES" and the 10 d. "LARL BENZ".

1986. Centenary of Statue of Liberty (1st issue). Multicoloured. As T **211** of Dominica, showing Statue of Liberty and immigrants to the U.S.A.

659 20 b. John Jacob Astor (financier) 10 10
660 1 d. Jacob Riis (journalist) 40 50
661 1 d. 25 Igor Sikorsky (aeronautics engineer) 60 60
662 5 d. Charles Boyer (actor) 2·50 2·50

See also Nos. 705/14.

1986. Royal Wedding. As T **213** of Antigua. Multicoloured.

664 1 d. Prince Andrew and Miss Sarah Ferguson 40 45
665 2 d. 50 Prince Andrew 1·00 1·40
666 4 d. Prince Andrew as helicopter pilot 1·60 2·00

1986. World Cup Football Championship Winners, Mexico. Nos. 645/8 optd **WINNERS Argentine 3 W. Germany 2**.

668 75 b. Type **152** 30 40
669 1 d. Player kicking ball 40 55
670 2 d. 50 Player kicking ball (different) 1·00 1·25
671 10 d. Player heading ball 4·25 4·75

154 Minnie Mouse (Great Britain)

1986. Christmas. Designs showing Walt Disney cartoon characters posting letters in various countries. Multicoloured.

673 1 d. Type **154** 75 60
674 1 d. 25 Huey (U.S.A.) 80 80
675 2 d. Huey, Dewey and Louie (France) 1·25 1·40
676 2 d. 35 Kanga and Roo (Australia) 1·40 1·75
677 5 d. Goofy (Germany) 2·25 3·00

Nos. 673/7 also show the "Stockholmia '86" International Stamp Exhibition emblem.

1986. Appearance of Halley's Comet (2nd issue). Nos. 634/9 optd as T **218** of Antigua.

679 10 b. Maria Mitchell (astronomer) and Kitt Peak National Observatory, Arizona 30 15
680 20 b. Neil Armstrong, first man on Moon, 1969 50 20
681 75 b. "Skylab 4" and Comet Kohoutek, 1973 75 50
682 1 d. N.A.S.A.'s infra-red astronomical satellite and Halley's Comet 85 60
683 2 d. Comet of 1577 from Turkish painting 1·40 1·75
684 10 d. N.A.S.A.'s International Cometary Explorer 3·75 6·00

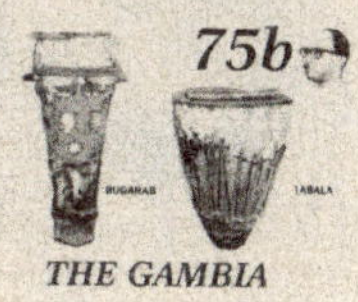

155 Bugarab and Tabala

1987. Manding Musical Instruments. Multicoloured.

686 75 b. Type **155** 15 20
687 1 d. Balaphong and fiddle 15 25
688 1 d. 25 Bolongbato and konting (vert) 20 35
689 10 d. Antique and modern koras (vert) 1·60 3·00

156 "Snowing"

1987. Birth Centenary of Marc Chagall (artist). Multicoloured.

691 75 b. Type **156** 40 40
692 85 b. "The Boat" 50 50
693 1 d. "Maternity" 65 65
694 1 d. 25 "The Flute Player" 75 75
695 2 d. 35 "Lovers and the Beast" 1·25 1·25
696 4 d. "Fishes at Saint Jean" 2·00 2·00
697 5 d. "Entering the Ring" 2·50 2·50
698 10 d. "Three Acrobats" 3·75 3·75

157 "America", 1851

1987. America's Cup Yachting Championship. Multicoloured.

700 20 b. Type **157** 20 15
701 1 d. "Courageous", 1974 35 35
702 2 d. 50 "Volunteer", 1887 75 1·10
703 10 d. "Intrepid", 1967 2·25 3·25

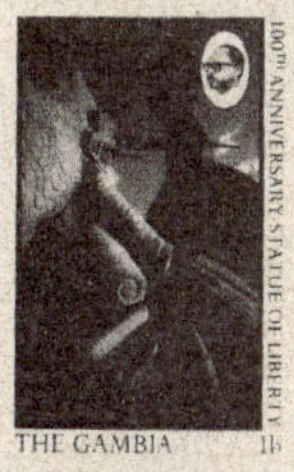

158 Arm of Statue of Liberty

159 "Lantana camara"

1987. Centenary of Statue of Liberty (1986) (2nd issue). Multicoloured.

705 1 b. Type **158** 10 10
706 2 b. Launch passing Statue (horiz) 10 10
707 3 b. Schooner passing Statue (horiz) 10 10
708 5 b. U.S.S. "John F. Kennedy" (aircraft carrier) and "Queen Elizabeth 2" (liner) (horiz) 10 10
709 50 b. Checking Statue for damage 40 40
710 75 b. Cleaning in progress 55 55
711 1 d. Working on Statue 70 70
712 1 d. 25 Statue and fireworks 80 80
713 10 d. Statue illuminated 4·25 4·25
714 12 d. Statue and fireworks (different) 4·50 4·50

1987. Flowers of Abuko Nature Reserve. Multicoloured.

715 75 b. Type **159** 15 15
716 1 d. "Clerodendrum thomsoniae" 15 20
717 1 d. 50 "Haemanthus multiflorus" 25 30
718 1 d. 70 "Gloriosa simplex" 25 35
719 1 d. 75 "Combretum microphyllum" 30 40
720 2 d. 25 "Eulophia quineensis" 35 45
721 5 d. "Erythrina senegalensis" 80 1·25
722 15 d. "Dichrostachys glomerata" 2·40 3·50

160 Front of Mail Bus

161 Basketball

1987. "Capex '87" International Stamp Exhibition, Toronto and 10th Anniv of Gambia Public Transport Corporation. Mail Buses. Mult.

724 20 b. Type **160** 40 20
725 75 b. Bus in Banjul (horiz) 70 45
726 1 d. Passengers queueing for bus (horiz) 70 45
727 10 d. Two buses on rural road 3·00 5·00

1987. Olympic Games, Seoul (1988) (1st issue). Multicoloured.
729 50 b. Type **161** 35 20
730 1 d. Volleyball 50 35
731 3 d. Hockey (horiz) . . . . . 1·10 85
732 10 d. Handball (horiz) . . . . 2·50 2·25
See also Nos. 779/82.

162 "A Partridge in a Pear Tree"

163 Campfire Singsong

1987. Christmas. Designs showing a Victorian couple in scenes from carol "The Twelve Days of Christmas". Multicoloured.
734 20 b. Type **162** 20 25
735 40 b. "Two turtle doves" . . . 20 25
736 60 b. "Three French hens" . . 20 25
737 75 b. "Four calling birds" . . 30 35
738 1 d. "Five golden rings" . . . 30 35
739 1 d. 25 "Six geese a-laying" . . 40 45
740 1 d. 50 "Seven swans a-swimming" 40 45
741 2 d. "Eight maids a-milking" . 50 55
742 3 d. "Nine ladies dancing" . . 70 75
743 5 d. "Ten lords a-leaping" . . 1·00 1·10
744 10 d. "Eleven pipers piping" . 1·60 1·75
745 12 d. "Twelve drummers drumming" . . . . 1·90 2·00

1987. World Scout Jamboree, Australia. Multicoloured.
747 75 b. Type **163** 50 30
748 1 d. Scouts examining African katydid 60 40
749 1 d. 25 Scouts watching Red-tailed tropic bird 75 75
750 12 d. Scouts helping bus passenger . . . . 2·75 3·75

1987. 60th Anniv of Mickey Mouse (Walt Disney cartoon character) (1st issue). As T **220** of Dominica. Multicoloured.
752 60 b. Morty and Ferdie examining Trevithick's locomotive, 1804 . . . . . . 25 25
753 75 b. Clarabelle Cow in "Empire State Express", 1893 . . . . 30 30
754 1 d. Donald Duck inspecting Stephenson's "Rocket", 1829 40 40
755 1 d. 25 Piglet and Winnie the Pooh with Santa Fe Railroad locomotive, 1920 . . . . . 45 45
756 2 d. Donald and Daisy Duck with Pennsylvania Railroad Class GG1 electric locomotive, 1933 . . . . 70 70
757 5 d. Mickey Mouse in "Stourbridge Lion", 1829 . . 1·60 1·75
758 10 d. Goofy in "Best Friend of Charleston", 1830 . . . . . 2·75 3·00
759 12 d. Brer Bear and Brer Rabbit with Union Pacific diesel locomotive No. M10001, 1934 3·00 3·25
See also Nos. 849/57.

164 Common Duiker and Acacia

165 Wedding Portrait, 1947

1988. Flora and Fauna. Multicoloured.
761 50 b. Type **164** 20 10
762 75 b. Red-billed hornbill and casuarina (vert) 30 15
763 90 b. West African dwarf crocodile and rice 30 20
764 1 d. Leopard and papyrus (vert) 30 20
765 1 d. 25 Crowned crane and millet 40 30
766 2 d. Waterbuck and baobab tree (vert) 40 60
767 3 d. Oribi and Senegal palm . . 50 1·10
768 5 d. Hippopotamus and papaya (vert) . . . . 80 1·60

1988. Royal Ruby Wedding.
770 **165** 75 b. brown, black & orange 30 15
771 – 1 d. brown, black and blue 40 20
772 – 3 d. multicoloured . . . . 90 1·00
773 – 10 d. multicoloured . . . 2·25 3·25
DESIGNS: 1 d. Engagement photograph; 3 d. Wedding portrait, 1947 (different); 10 d. Queen Elizabeth II and Prince Philip (photo by Karsh), 1986.

1988. Stamp Exhibitions. Nos. 689, 703, 722 and 726 optd.
775 1 d. Passengers queueing for bus (optd **Independence 40**, Israel) 25 25
776 10 d. Antique and modern koras (optd **FINLANDIA 88**, Helsinki) . . . . 2·00 2·50
777 10 d. "Intrepid" (yacht), 1967 (optd **Praga '88**, Prague) . . 2·00 2·50
778 15 d. "Dichrostachys glomerata" (optd **OLYMPHILEX '88**, Seoul) . . . . 2·75 3·00

1988. Olympic Games, Seoul (2nd issue). As T **161**. Multicoloured.
779 1 d. Archery 15 20
780 1 d. 25 Boxing 20 25
781 5 d. Gymnastics . . . . . . 80 1·10
782 10 d. Start of 100 metre race (horiz) . . . . 1·60 2·25

166 Red Cross Flag

1988. Anniversaries and Events. Multicoloured.
784 50 b. Type **166** (125th anniv) 55 55
785 75 b. "Friendship 7" spacecraft (25th anniv of first American manned Earth orbit) . . . 60 60
786 1 d. British Airways Concorde (10th anniv of Concorde London–New York service) 1·00 1·00
787 1 d. 25 "Spirit of St. Louis" (60th anniv of first solo transatlantic flight) . . . . 1·00 1·00
788 2 d. North American X-15 (20th anniv of fastest aircraft flight) 1·40 1·40
789 3 d. Bell "XS-1" rocket plane (40th anniv of first supersonic flight) . . . . 1·50 1·50
790 10 d. English and Spanish galleons (400th anniv of Spanish Armada) . . . . . 3·50 3·50
791 12 d. "Titanic" (75th anniv of sinking) . . . . 3·75 3·75

1988. 500th Birth Anniv of Titian (artist). As T **238** of Antigua. Multicoloured.
793 25 b. "Emperor Charles V" . . 20 20
794 50 b. "St. Margaret and the Dragon" 35 35
795 60 b. "Ranuccio Farnese" . . . 40 40
796 75 b. "Tarquin and Lucretia" . 55 55
797 1 d. "The Knight of Malta" . . 70 70
798 5 d. "Spain succouring Faith" 2·25 2·50
799 10 d. Doge Francesco Venier" 3·50 3·50
800 12 d. "Doge Grimani before the Faith" (detail) . . . . . . 3·75 3·75

167 John Kennedy sailing

1988. 25th Death Anniv of President John F. Kennedy. Multicoloured.
802 75 b. Type **167** 15 15
803 1 d. Kennedy signing Peace Corps legislation, 1962 . . 15 20
804 1 d. 25 Speaking at U.N., New York (vert) 20 25
805 12 d. Grave and eternal flame, Arlington National Cemetery (vert) . . . . 1·90 2·75

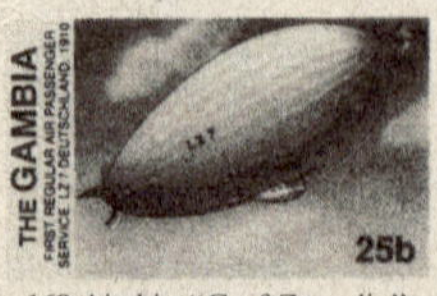

168 Airship "Graf Zeppelin" (first regular air passenger service), 1910

1988. Milestones of Transportation. Multicoloured.
807 25 b. Type **168** 45 35
808 50 b. Stephenson's "Locomotion" (first permanent public railway), 1825 . . . . 70 50
809 75 b. G.M. "Sun Racer" (first world solar challenge), 1987 80 65
810 1 d. Sprague's "Premiere" (first operational electric tramway), 1888 . . . . 1·00 80
811 1 d. 25 "Gold Rush" Bicycle (holder of man-powered land speed record), 1986 . . . . 1·00 85
812 2 d. 50 Robert Goddard and rocket launcher (first liquid fuel rocket), 1925 . . . . . 1·40 1·25
813 10 d. "Orukter Amphibolos" (first steam traction engine), 1805 . . . . 3·50 3·25
814 12 d. "Sovereign of the Seas" (largest cruise liner), 1988 . 3·50 3·50

169 Emmett Kelley

170 Prince Henry the Navigator and Caravel

1988. Entertainers. Multicoloured.
816 20 b. Type **169** 10 10
817 1 d. Gambia National Ensemble 25 25
818 1 d. 25 Jackie Gleason 30 30
819 1 d. 50 Laurel and Hardy . . . 40 40
820 2 d. 50 Yul Brynner 75 75
821 3 d. Cary Grant 95 95
822 10 d. Danny Kaye . . . . . . 3·00 3·00
823 20 d. Charlie Chaplin . . . . 5·50 5·50

1988. Exploration of West Africa. Multicoloured.
825 50 b. Type **170** 60 60
826 75 b. Jesse Ramsden's sextant, 1785 . . . . 70 70
827 1 d. 15th-century hourglass . . 80 80
828 1 d. 25 Prince Henry the Navigator and Vasco da Gama 95 95
829 2 d. 50 Vasco da Gama and ship 1·60 1·60
830 5 d. Mungo Park and map of Gambia River (horiz) . . . 2·50 2·50
831 10 d. Map of West Africa, 1563 (horiz) . . . . 3·75 3·75
832 12 d. Portuguese caravel (horiz) 4·00 4·00

171 Projected Space Plane and Ernst Mach (physicist)

1988. 350th Anniv of Publications of Galileo's "Discourses". Space Achievements. Mult.
834 50 b. Type **171** 30 30
835 75 b. OAO III astronomical satellite and Niels Bohr (physicist) 40 40
836 1 d. Space shuttle, projected space station and Robert Goddard (physicist) (horiz) 45 45
837 1 d. 25 Jupiter probe, 1979, and Edward Barnard (astronomer) (horiz) 60 60
838 2 d. Hubble Space Telescope and George Hale (astronomer) . 75 75
839 3 d. Earth-to-Moon laser measurement and Albert Michaelson (physicist) (horiz) 85 85
840 10 d. HEAO-2 "Einstein" orbital satellite and Albert Einstein "physicist" . . . . 2·50 2·50
841 20 d. "Voyager" (first non-stop round-the-world flight), 1987, and Wright Brothers (aviation pioneers) (horiz) . . . . . . 4·50 4·50

172 Passing Out Parade

1989. Army Day. Multicoloured.
843 75 b. Type **172** 25 25
844 1 d. Standards of The Gambia Regiment 25 25
845 1 d. 25 Side drummer in ceremonial uniform (vert) . . 30 30
846 10 d. Marksman with Atlantic Shooting Cup (vert) . . . . 2·00 2·00
847 15 d. Soldiers on assault course (vert) . . . . 2·75 2·75
848 20 d. Gunner with 105 mm field gun . . . . 3·00 3·00

173 Mickey Mouse, 1928

1989. 60th Birthday of Mickey Mouse (2nd issue). Multicoloured.
849 2 d. Type **173** 55 65
850 2 d. Mickey Mouse, 1931 . . 55 65
851 2 d. Mickey Mouse, 1936 . . 55 65
852 2 d. Mickey Mouse, 1955 . . 55 65
853 2 d. Mickey Mouse, 1947 . . 55 65
854 2 d. Mickey Mouse as magician, 1940 . . . . 55 65
855 2 d. Mickey Mouse with palette, 1960 . . . . 55 65
856 2 d. Mickey Mouse as Uncle Sam, 1976 . . . . 55 65
857 2 d. Mickey Mouse, 1988 . . . 55 65
Nos. 849/57 were printed together, se-tenant, forming a composite design.

174 "Le Coup de Lance" (detail)

176 "Druryia antimachus"

175 African Emerald Cuckoo

1989. Easter. Religious Paintings by Rubens. Multicoloured.
859 50 b. Type **174** 25 25
860 75 b. "Flagellation of Christ" . . 35 35
861 1 d. "Lamentation for Christ" . 35 35
862 1 d. 25 "Descent from the Cross" 40 40
863 2 d. "Holy Trinity" 60 70
864 5 d. "Doubting Thomas" . . . 1·25 1·50
865 10 d. "Lamentation over Christ" 2·00 2·50
866 12 d. "Lamentation with Virgin and St. John" . . . . . . 2·25 2·75

1989. West African Birds. Multicoloured.
868 20 b. Type **175** 60 30
869 60 b. Grey-headed bush shrike 85 50
870 75 b. South African crowned crane 90 55
871 1 d. Secretary bird . . . . . 1·00 60
872 2 d. Red-billed hornbill . . . 1·50 1·00
873 5 d. Superb sunbird . . . . . 2·00 2·75
874 10 d. Pearl-spotted owlet ("Little owl") . . . . 2·75 4·00
875 12 d. Bateleur . . . . 2·75 4·00

1989. Butterflies of Gambia. Multicoloured.
877 50 b. Type **176** 30 30
878 75 b. "Euphaedra neophron" . . 45 45
879 1 d. "Aterica rabena" 45 45
880 1 d. 25 "Salamis parhassus" . . 55 55
881 5 d. "Precis rhadama" . . . . 1·75 2·00
882 10 d. "Papilio demodocus" . . 2·25 2·50
883 12 d. "Charaxes etesipe" . . . 2·50 2·75
884 15 d. "Danaus formosa" . . . 2·50 2·75

177 Class "River" Steam Locomotive No. 021, 1959, Nigeria

1989. African Steam Locomotive. Multicoloured.
886 50 b. Type **177** 35 35
887 75 b. Class 14A steam locomotive, Rhodesia . . . 45 45
888 1 d. British-built steam locomotive No. 120, Sudan 55 55
889 1 d. 25 Steam locomotive, 1925, U.S.A. 65 65
890 5 d. North British steam locomotive, 1955 . . . . 1·75 1·75
891 7 d. Scottish-built steam locomotive No. 120, 1926 . 2·00 2·00
892 10 d. East African Railways Class 1T steam tank locomotive . . . . 2·25 2·25
893 12 d. American-built steam locomotive, Ghana . . . . 2·50 2·50

1989. "Philexfrance '89" Int Stamp Exhibition, Paris. Nos. 686/9 optd **PHILEXFRANCE '89**
895 75 b. Type **155** 10 10
896 1 d. Balaphong and fiddle . . 15 20
897 1 d. 25 Bolongbato and konting (vert) 20 25
898 10 d. Antique and modern koras (vert) . . . . 1·50 2·25

1989. Japanese Art. As T **250** of Antigua. Mult.

900	50 b. "Sparrow and Bamboo" (Hiroshige) (vert)	40	30
901	75 b. "Peonies and a Canary" (Hokusai) (vert)	50	40
902	1 d. "Crane and Marsh Grasses" (Hiroshige) (vert)	60	45
903	1 d. 25 "Crossbill and Thistle" (Hokusai) (vert)	70	60
904	2 d. "Cuckoo and Azalea" (Hokusai) (vert)	90	80
905	5 d. "Parrot on a Pine Branch" (Hiroshige) (vert)	1·50	1·75
906	10 d. "Mandarin Ducks in a Stream" (Hiroshige) (vert)	2·25	2·50
907	12 d. "Bullfinch and Drooping Cherry" (Hokusai) (vert)	2·25	2·50

179 Rialto Bridge, Venice

1989. World Cup Football Championship, Italy (1990) (1st issue). Designs showing landmarks and players. Multicoloured.

909	75 b. Type **179**	45	45
910	1 d. 25 The Baptistery, Pisa	60	60
911	7 d. Casino, San Remo	2·25	2·75
912	12 d. Colosseum, Rome	3·00	3·50

See also Nos. 1064/7.

180 "Vitex doniana"

1989. Medicinal Plants. Multicoloured.

914	20 b. Type **180**	20	20
915	50 b. "Ricinus communis"	30	30
916	75 b. "Palisota hirsuta"	45	45
917	1 d. "Smilax kraussiana"	55	55
918	1 d. 25 "Aspilia africana"	65	65
919	5 d. "Newbouldia laevis"	1·75	2·00
920	8 d. "Monodora tenuifolia"	1·90	2·50
921	10 d. "Gossypium arboreum"	2·00	2·50

181 Lookdown Fish

1989. Fishes. Multicoloured.

923	20 b. Type **181**	25	25
924	75 b. Boarfish	55	55
925	1 d. Grey triggerfish	65	65
926	1 d. 25 Skipjack tuna	75	75
927	2 d. Striped rudderfish	95	95
928	4 d. Atlantic manta	1·60	1·75
929	5 d. Flat-headed grey mullet	1·75	1·90
930	10 d. Ladyfish	2·75	3·25

1989. "World Stamp Expo '89" International Stamp Exhibition, Washington. As T **256** of Antigua, but showing Walt Disney cartoon characters and American carousel horses. Multicoloured.

932	20 b. Little Hiawatha on Daniel Muller Indian Pony	40	30
933	50 b. Morty on Herschell-Spillman stander	60	50
934	75 b. Goofy on Gustav Dentzel stander	75	65
935	1 d. Mickey Mouse on Daniel Muller armoured stander	80	70
936	1 d. 25 Minnie Mouse on jumper from Smithsonian Collection	90	80
937	2 d. Webby on Illion "American Beauty"	1·25	1·10
938	8 d. Donald Duck on Zalar jumper	3·00	3·50
939	10 d. Mickey Mouse on Parker bucking horse	3·00	3·50

183 Mickey and Minnie Mouse in Pierce-Arrow, 1922

1989. Christmas. Designs showing Walt Disney cartoon characters with cars. Multicoloured.

942	20 b. Type **183**	50	25
943	50 b. Goofy in Spyker, 1919	70	45
944	75 b. Donald and Grandma Duck with Packard, 1929	80	55
945	1 d. Mickey Mouse driving Daimler, 1920	85	65
946	1 d. 25 Mickey Mouse in Hispano "Suiza", 1924	90	90
947	2 d. Mickey and Minnie Mouse in Opel "Laubfrosch", 1924	1·25	1·25
948	10 d. Donald Duck driving Vauxhall "30/98", 1927	3·25	4·00
949	12 d. Goofy with Peerless, 1923	3·25	4·00

184 Charles Nicolle (typhus transmission) and Vaccination

1989. Great Medical Discoveries. Multicoloured.

951	20 b. Type **184**	40	20
952	50 b. Paul Ehrlich (immunization pioneer) and medical examination	50	30
953	75 b. Selman Waksman (discoverer of streptomycin) and T.B. clinic	65	40
954	1 d. Edward Jenner (smallpox vaccination), and Jenner conducting experiment, 1796	75	50
955	1 d. 25 Robert Koch (developer of tuberculin test) and Gambian using vaccination gun	90	75
956	5 d. Sir Alexander Fleming (discoverer of penicillin) and doctor giving injection	2·00	2·25
957	8 d. Max Theiler (developer of yellow fever vaccine) and child clinic	2·50	2·75
958	10 d. Louis Pasteur (bacteriologist) and health survey	2·50	2·75

185 "Bulbophyllum lepidum"

186 John Newcombe

1989. Orchids. Multicoloured.

960	20 b. Type **185**	30	30
961	75 b. "Tridactyle tridactylites"	55	55
962	1 d. "Vanilla imperialis"	70	70
963	1 d. 25 "Oeceoclades maculata"	80	90
964	2 d. "Polystachya affinis"	1·10	1·25
965	4 d. "Ancistrochilus rothschildianus"	1·90	2·25
966	5 d. "Angraecum distichum"	2·00	2·25
967	10 d. "Liparis guineensis"	3·50	4·00

1990. Wimbledon Tennis Champions. Multicoloured.

969	20 b. Type **186**	10	10
970	20 b. Mrs. G. W. Hillyard	10	10
971	50 b. Roy Emerson	20	20
972	50 b. Dorothy Chambers	20	20
973	75 b. Donald Budge	30	30
974	75 b. Suzanne Lenglen	30	30
975	1 d. Laurence Doherty	35	35
976	1 d. Helen Wills Moody	35	35
977	1 d. 25 Bjorn Borg	40	40
978	1 d. 25 Maureen Connolly	40	40
979	4 d. Jean Borotra	1·00	1·00
980	4 d. Maria Bueno	1·00	1·00
981	5 d. Anthony Wilding	1·00	1·00
982	5 d. Louise Brough	1·00	1·00
983	7 d. Fred Perry	1·40	1·40
984	7 d. Margaret Court	1·40	1·40
985	10 d. Bill Tilden	2·00	2·00
986	10 d. Billie Jean King	2·00	2·00
987	12 d. Rod Laver	2·25	2·25
988	12 d. Martina Navratilova	2·25	2·25

187 Lunar Module "Eagle"

1990. 20th Anniv (1989) of First Manned Landing on Moon. Multicoloured.

990	20 b. Type **187**	35	20
991	50 b. Lift-off of "Apollo 11" (vert)	45	30
992	75 b. Neil Armstrong stepping on to Moon	60	45
993	1 d. Buzz Aldrin and American flag	65	55
994	1 d. 25 "Apollo 11" emblem (vert)	75	60
995	1 d. 75 Crew of "Apollo 11"	90	90
996	8 d. Lunar Module "Eagle" on Moon	2·50	3·00
997	12 d. Recovery of "Apollo 11" after splashdown	2·75	3·25

188 Bristol Type 142 Blenheim Mk I

1990. R.A.F. Aircraft of Second World War. Multicoloured.

999	10 b. Type **188**	35	30
1000	20 b. Fairey Battle	45	30
1001	50 b. Bristol Type 142 Blenheim Mk IV	55	40
1002	60 b. Vickers-Armstrong Wellington Mk 1c	60	40
1003	75 b. Armstrong Whitworth Whitley Mk V	60	40
1004	1 d. Handley Page Hampden Mk I	70	45
1005	1 d. 25 Supermarine Spitfire Mk 1A and Hawker Hurricane Mk I	80	50
1006	2 d. Avro Manchester	1·00	80
1007	3 d. Short Stirling Mk I	1·25	1·25
1008	5 d. Handley Page Halifax Mk I	1·50	1·75
1009	10 d. Avro Lancaster Mk III	2·25	2·75
1010	12 d. De Havilland Mosquito Mk IV	2·25	2·75

189 White-faced Scops Owl

191 Flag and National Assembly Building

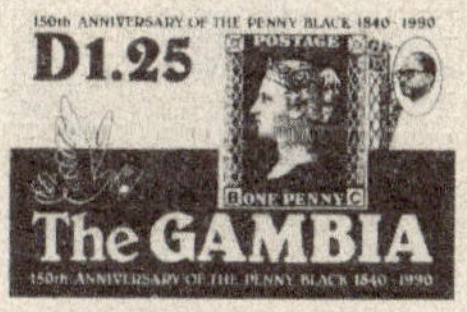

190 Penny Black

1990. African Birds. Multicoloured

1012	1 d. 25 Type **189**	50	55
1013	1 d. 25 Village weaver	50	55
1014	1 d. 25 Red-throated bee eater	50	55
1015	1 d. 25 Brown harrier eagle	50	55
1016	1 d. 25 Red bishop	50	55
1017	1 d. 25 Scarlet-chested sunbird	50	55
1018	1 d. 25 Red-billed hornbill	50	55
1019	1 d. 25 Mosque swallow	50	55
1020	1 d. 25 White-faced whistling duck	50	55
1021	1 d. 25 African fish eagle	50	55
1022	1 d. 25 Eastern white pelican	50	55
1023	1 d. 25 Carmine bee eater	50	55
1024	1 d. 25 Hadada ibis	50	55
1025	1 d. 25 Egyptian plover	50	55
1026	1 d. 25 Variable sunbird	50	55
1027	1 d. 25 African skimmer	50	55
1028	1 d. 25 Woodland kingfisher	50	55
1029	1 d. 25 African jacana	50	55
1030	1 d. 25 African pygmy goose	50	55
1031	1 d. 25 Hammerkop	50	55

Nos. 1012/31 were printed together, se-tenant, forming a composite design of birds at a lake.

1990. 150th Anniv of the Penny Black.

1032	**190** 1 d. 25 black and blue	75	50
1033	12 d. black and red	3·00	3·75

1990. 25th Anniv of Independence. Multicoloured.

1035	1 d. Type **191**	40	25
1036	3 d. President Sir Dawda Jawara	50	50
1037	12 d. Map of Yundum airport and Boeing 707 airliner	3·50	4·00

192 Baobab Tree

1990. Gambian Life. Multicoloured.

1039	5 b. Type **192**	10	30
1040	10 b. Woodcarving, Albert Market, Banjul	10	30
1041	20 b. President Jawara planting seedling (vert)	10	10
1042	50 b. Sailing canoe and map	40	10
1043	75 b. Batik fabric	20	10
1044	1 d. Hibiscus and Bakau beach	30	20
1045	1 d. 25 Bougainvillea and Tendaba Camp	30	20
1046	2 d. Shrimp fishing and sorting	45	35
1047	5 d. Groundnut oil mill, Denton Bridge	80	1·25
1048	10 d. Handicraft pot and kora (musical instrument)	1·50	2·25
1049	15 d. "Ansellia africana" (orchid) (vert)	3·75	4·00
1050	30 d. "Euriphene gambiae" (butterfly) and ancient stone ring near Georgetown	6·50	7·50

193 Daisy Duck at 10 Downing Street

1990. "Stamp World London 90" International Stamp Exhibition. Walt Disney cartoon characters in England. Multicoloured.

1051	20 b. Type **193**	30	30
1052	50 b. Goofy in Trafalgar Square	35	35
1053	75 b. Mickey Mouse on White Cliffs of Dover (horiz)	50	50
1054	1 d. Mickey Mouse at Tower of London	50	50
1055	5 d. Mickey Mouse and Goofy at Hampton Court Palace (horiz)	1·75	2·00
1056	8 d. Mickey Mouse by Magdalen Tower, Oxford	2·00	2·50
1057	10 d. Mickey Mouse on Old London Bridge (horiz)	2·25	2·75
1058	12 d. Scrooge McDuck and Rosetta Stone, British Museum (horiz)	2·25	2·75

194 Lady Elizabeth Bowes-Lyon in High Chair

195 Vialli, Italy

1990. 90th Birthday of Queen Elizabeth the Queen Mother.

1060	**194** 6 d. black, mauve & yell	1·25	1·60
1061	– 6 d. black, mauve & yell	1·25	1·60
1062	– 6 d. black, mauve & yell	1·25	1·60

DESIGNS: No. 1061, Lady Elizabeth Bowes-Lyon as a young girl; No. 1062, Lady Elizabeth Bowes-Lyon with wild flowers.

1990. World Cup Football Championships, Italy (2nd issue). Multicoloured.

1064	1 d. Type **195**	30	30
1065	1 d. 25 Cannegia, Argentina	35	35
1066	3 d. Marchena, Costa Rica	80	90
1067	5 d. Shaiba, United Arab Emirates	1·10	1·40

1990. Olympic Games, Barcelona (1992) (1st issue). As T **268** of Antigua. Multicoloured.

1069	20 b. Men's discus	35	15
1070	50 b. Men's 100 metres	45	20
1071	75 b. Women's 400 metres	55	30
1072	1 d. Men's 200 metres	60	40
1073	1 d. 25 Women's rhythmic gymnastics	65	50
1074	3 d. Football	1·25	1·50
1075	10 d. Men's marathon	2·50	3·25
1076	12 d. "Tornado" class yachting	2·50	3·25

See also Nos. 1289/96 and 1351/62.

1990. Christmas. Paintings by Renaissance Masters. As T **272** of Antigua. Multicoloured.

1078	20 b. "The Annunciation, with St. Emidius" (detail) (Crivelli) (vert)	20	10
1079	50 b. "The Annunciation" (detail) (Campin) (vert)	30	10
1080	75 b. "The Solly Madonna" (detail) (Raphael) (vert)	40	20
1081	1 d. 25 "The Tempi Madonna" (Raphael) (vert)	40	30
1082	2 d. "Madonna of the Linen Window" (detail) (Raphael) (vert)	55	50

1083 7 d. "The Annunciation, with St. Emidius" (different detail) (Crivelli) (vert) . . . . . . 1·75 2·50
1084 10 d. "The Orleans Madonna" (Raphael) (vert) . . . . . 2·00 2·50
1085 15 d. "Madonna and Child" (detail) (Crivelli) (vert) . . 2·50 3·25

1990. 350th Death Anniv of Rubens. As T **273** of Antigua. Multicoloured.
1087 20 b. "The Lion Hunt" (sketch) 15 15
1088 75 b. "The Lion Hunt" (detail) 25 25
1089 1 d. "The Tiger Hunt" (detail) 30 30
1090 1 d. 25 "The Tiger Hunt" (different detail) 35 35
1091 3 d. "The Tiger Hunt" (different detail) 75 80
1092 5 d. "The Boar Hunt" (detail) 1·10 1·25
1093 10 d. "The Lion Hunt" (different detail) . . . . . 1·75 2·25
1094 15 d. "The Tiger Hunt" (different detail) . . . . . 2·40 3·00

196 Summit Logo

1991. World Summit for Children, New York.
1096 **196** 1 d. multicoloured . . . 40 40

1991. International Literacy Year (1990). As T **269** of Antigua, but scenes from Disney cartoon film "The Sword in the Stone". Multicoloured.
1097 3 d. Sir Kay and Wart searching for lost arrow (horiz) . . . 1·00 1·10
1098 3 d. Merlin the Magician (horiz) 1·00 1·10
1099 3 d. Merlin teaching Wart (horiz) . . . . 1·00 1·10
1100 3 d. Wart writing on blackboard (horiz) . . . . 1·00 1·10
1101 3 d. Wart transformed into bird and Madame Mim (horiz) . 1·00 1·10
1102 3 d. Merlin and Madame Mim (horiz) . . . . 1·00 1·10
1103 3 d. Madame Mim transformed into dragon (horiz) . . . . 1·00 1·10
1104 3 d. Wart pulling sword from stone (horiz) . . . . 1·00 1·10
1105 3 d. King Arthur on throne (horiz) . . . . 1·00 1·10

197 "Bebearia senegalensis"

1991. Wildlife. Multicoloured.
1107 1 d. Type **197** 30 35
1108 1 d. "Graphium ridleyanus" (butterfly) 30 35
1109 1 d. "Precis antilope" (butterfly) 30 35
1110 1 d. "Charaxes ameliae" (butterfly) 30 35
1111 1 d. Addax 30 35
1112 1 d. Sassaby 30 35
1113 1 d. Civet 30 35
1114 1 d. Green monkey 30 35
1115 1 d. Spur-winged goose . . . 30 35
1116 1 d. Red-billed hornbill . . . 30 35
1117 1 d. Osprey 30 35
1118 1 d. Glossy ibis 30 35
1119 1 d. Egyptian plover 30 35
1120 1 d. Golden-tailed woodpecker 30 35
1121 1 d. Green wood hoopoe . . . 30 35
1122 1 d. Gaboon viper 30 35
1123 1 d. 50 Red-billed fire finch . 40 45
1124 1 d. 50 Leaf-love 40 45
1125 1 d. 50 Piapiac 40 45
1126 1 d. 50 African emerald cuckoo 40 45
1127 1 d. 50 Red colobus monkey 40 45
1128 1 d. 50 African elephant . . 40 45
1129 1 d. 50 Duiker 40 45
1130 1 d. 50 Giant eland 40 45
1131 1 d. 50 Oribi 40 45
1132 1 d. 50 Western African dwarf crocodile 40 45
1133 1 d. 50 Crowned crane . . . 40 45
1134 1 d. 50 Jackal 40 45
1135 1 d. 50 Yellow-throated longclaw 40 45
1136 1 d. 50 Abyssinian ground hornbill 40 45
1137 1 d. 50 "Papilio hesperus" . . 40 45
1138 1 d. 50 "Papilio antimachus" 40 45
1139 5 d. Martial eagle . . . . . 1·00 1·10
1140 5 d. Red-checked cordon-bleu 1·00 1·10
1141 5 d. Red bishop . . . . . . 1·00 1·10
1142 5 d. Eastern white pelican . . 1·00 1·10
1143 5 d. Patas monkey . . . . . 1·00 1·10
1144 5 d. Vervet monkey . . . . 1·00 1·10
1145 5 d. Roan antelope . . . . 1·00 1·10
1146 5 d. Western hartebeest . . 1·00 1·10
1147 5 d. Waterbuck . . . . . . 1·00 1·10
1148 5 d. Warthog . . . . 1·00 1·10
1149 5 d. Spotted hyena . . . . 1·00 1·10
1150 5 d. Olive baboon . . . . . 1·00 1·10
1151 5 d. "Palla decius" . . . . 1·00 1·10
1152 5 d. "Acraea pharsalus" . . 1·00 1·10
1153 5 d. "Neptidopsis ophione" . 1·00 1·10
1154 5 d. "Acraea caecilia" . . . 1·00 1·10

Nos. 1107/22, 1123/38 and 1139/54 respectively were issued together, se-tenant, forming composite designs.

198 "Papilio dardanus"

1991. Butterflies. Multicoloured.
1156 20 b. Type **198** 50 30
1157 50 b. "Bematistes poggei" . 70 40
1158 1 d. "Vanessa cardui" . . . 80 55
1159 1 d. 50 "Amphicallia tigris" 90 85
1160 3 d. "Hypolimnas dexithea" 1·50 1·25
1161 8 d. "Acraea egina" . . . . 2·00 2·75
1162 10 d. "Salamis temora" . . 2·00 2·75
1163 15 d. "Precis octavia" . . . 2·75 3·75

1991. 65th Birthday of Queen Elizabeth II. As T **280** of Antigua. Multicoloured.
1165 50 b. The Queen and Prince Charles at Windsor polo match 30 20
1166 1 d. The Queen and Princess Anne at the Derby, 1988 . 45 35
1167 1 d. 25 The Queen at the Royal London Hospital, 1970 . . 55 50
1168 12 d. The Queen and Prince Philip at Balmoral, 1976 . 3·00 3·50

1991. 10th Wedding Anniv of Prince and Princess of Wales. As T **280** of Antigua. Multicoloured.
1170 20 b. Prince and Princess with sons in June, 1989 . . . . 35 25
1171 75 b. Separate photographs of Prince, Princess and sons . 60 50
1172 1 d. 50 Prince Henry on first day of school, 1987, and Prince William at polo match . . 70 70
1173 15 d. Separate photographs of Prince and Princess of Wales 3·50 4·00

1991. "Phila Nippon '91" International Stamp Exhibition, Tokyo. As T **279** of Antigua showing Walt Disney cartoon characters playing Japanese sports and games. Multicoloured.
1175 50 b. Donald Duck and Mickey Mouse playing "go" (horiz) 40 30
1176 75 b. Morty, Ferdie and Pete as Sumo wrestlers (horiz) . . 55 40
1177 1 d. Minnie Mouse, Clarabelle Cow and Daisy Duck playing battledore and shuttlecock (horiz) 60 45
1178 1 d. 25 Goofy and Mickey at Okinawa bullfight 70 55
1179 5 d. Mickey flying hawk . . 1·75 1·75
1180 7 d. Mickey, Minnie and Donald playing "jan-ken-pon" . . . . 2·00 2·25
1181 10 d. Goofy as archer (horiz) 2·25 2·50
1182 15 d. Morty and Ferdie flying kites . . . . 2·75 3·00

1991. International Literacy Year (1990). As T **269** of Antigua showing Walt Disney cartoon characters in Kipling's "Just So" stories. Multicoloured.
1184 50 b. "How the Whale got his Throat" (horiz) 40 30
1185 75 b. "How the Camel got his Hump" (horiz) 55 40
1186 1 d. "How the Leopard got his Spots" (horiz) 60 45
1187 1 d. 25 "The Elephant's Child" (horiz) 70 55
1188 1 d. 50 "The Singsong of Old Man Kangaroo" (horiz) . . 85 70
1189 7 d. "The Crab that played with the Sea" (horiz) . . . . 2·00 2·25
1190 10 d. "The Cat that walked by Himself" (horiz) . . . . . 2·25 2·50
1191 15 d. "The Butterfly that Stamped" (horiz) . . . . 2·75 3·00

199 Canadian Pacific Steel Cupola Caboose

1991. Railway Brake-vans. Multicoloured.
1193 1 d. Type **199** 25 25
1194 1 d. Cumberland and Pennsylvania four-wheeled caboose, U.S.A. 25 25
1195 1 d. Ferrocarril Interoceanico caboose, Mexico 25 25
1196 1 d. Northern Pacific Railroad steel cupola caboose, U.S.A. 25 25
1197 1 d. Morristown and Erie Railroad four-wheeled caboose, U.S.A. 25 25
1198 1 d. Burlington Northern Railroad streamlined cupola caboose, U.S.A. 25 25
1199 1 d. McCloud River Railroad caboose-coach, U.S.A. . . 25 25
1200 1 d. Santa Fe Railroad wide-vision caboose, U.S.A. . . 25 25
1201 1 d. Frisco Railroad wide-vision caboose, U.S.A. 25 25
1202 1 d. 50 Colorado and Southern Railroad four-wheeled caboose, U.S.A. 35 40
1203 1 d. 50 Santa Fe Railroad transfer caboose, U.S.A. . 35 40
1204 1 d. 50 Canadian National wooden cupola caboose . . 35 40
1205 1 d. 50 Union Pacific steel transfer caboose, U.S.A. . . 35 40
1206 1 d. 50 Virginia and Truckee Railroad caboose-coach, U.S.A. 35 40
1207 1 d. 50 British Railways standard brake van 35 40
1208 1 d. 50 International Railways of Central America caboose 35 40
1209 1 d. 50 Northern Pacific Railroad steel cupola caboose, U.S.A. 35 40
1210 1 d. 50 Burlington Northern Railroad wooden caboose, U.S.A. 35 40
1211 2 d. Oahu Railway caboose, Hawaii 40 50
1212 2 d. British Railways standard brake van 40 50
1213 2 d. Union Pacific steel wide-view caboose, U.S.A. . . . 40 50
1214 2 d. Belt Railway of Chicago four-wheeled caboose, U.S.A. 40 50
1215 2 d. McCloud River Railroad four-wheeled caboose, U.S.A. 40 50
1216 2 d. Angelina County Lumber Co caboose, U.S.A. 40 50
1217 2 d. Coahuila & Zacateca caboose, Mexico 40 50
1218 2 d. United Railways of Yucatan caboose, Mexico . . 40 50
1219 2 d. Rio Grande Railroad steel cupola caboose, U.S.A. . . 40 50

200 Tiger Shark

1991. Fishes. Multicoloured.
1221 20 b. Type **200** 15 15
1222 25 b. Common jewelfish . . . 15 15
1223 50 b. Five-spotted cichlid . . 25 25
1224 75 b. Small-toothed sawfish . 25 25
1225 1 d. Spotted tilapia 30 30
1226 1 d. 25 Dwarf jewelfish . . . 35 35
1227 1 d. 50 Five-spotted jewelfish 40 40
1228 3 d. Lion-headed cichlid . . . 65 65
1229 10 d. Egyptian mouthbrooder 2·00 2·50
1230 15 d. Burton's mouthbrooder 2·75 3·50

1991. Hummel Figurines. As T **302** of Antigua. Multicoloured.
1232 20 b. Children waving . . . 10 10
1233 75 b. Children under umbrella 15 15
1234 1 d. Girl kissing friend . . . 20 20
1235 1 d. 50 Children at window . 30 30
1236 2 d. 50 Two girls in aprons . 45 45
1237 5 d. Two boys in bow ties . . 85 85
1238 10 d. Two girls sitting on fence with birds . . . . 1·75 2·00
1239 15 d. Boy and girl in Swiss costume . . . . 2·50 3·00

1991. Death Centenary of Vincent van Gogh (artist). As T **278** of Antigua. Multicoloured.
1241 20 b. "The Old Cemetery Tower at Nuenen in the Snow" (horiz) 15 15
1242 25 b. "Head of Peasant Woman with White Cap" 15 15
1243 50 b. "The Green Parrot" . . 20 20
1244 75 b. "Vase with Carnations" . 20 20
1245 1 d. "Vase with Red Gladioli" 25 25
1246 1 d. 25 "Beach at Scheveningen in Calm Weather" (horiz) . 30 30
1247 1 d. 50 "Boy cutting Grass with Sickle" (horiz) 35 35
1248 2 d. "Coleus Plant in a Flowerpot" (detail) 40 40
1249 3 d. "Self-portrait 1887" . . . 60 60
1250 4 d. "Self-portrait" (different) 70 70
1251 5 d. "Self-portrait" (different) 85 85
1252 6 d. "Self-portrait 1887" (different) . . . . 1·25 125
1253 8 d. "Still Life with Bottle, Two Glasses, Cheese and Bread" (detail) . . . . 1·75 1·75
1254 10 d. "Still Life with Cabbage, Clogs and Potatoes" (horiz) 2·25 2·25
1255 12 d. "Montmartre:The Street Lamps" . . . . 2·75 2·75
1256 15 d. "Head of Peasant Woman with Brownish Cap" . . . 3·00 3·00

1991. Christmas. Religious Paintings by Fra Angelico. As T **287** of Antigua. Multicoloured.
1258 20 b. "The Madonna of Humility" 10 10
1259 50 b. "Madonna and Child with Angels" 20 20
1260 75 b. "Virgin and Child with Angels" 25 25
1261 1 d. "The Annunciation" . . 30 30
1262 1 d. 25 "Presentation in the Temple" 35 35
1263 5 d. "The Annunciation" (different) . . . . 1·25 1·50
1264 10 d. "Madonna della Stella" 2·00 2·50
1265 15 d. "Naming of St. John the Baptist" . . . . 2·50 3·25

INDEX

Countries can be quickly located by referring to the index at the end of this volume.

201 Son House

202 Pope John Paul II

1992. Famous Blues Singers. Multicoloured.
1267 20 b. Type **201** 15 15
1268 25 b. W. C. Handy 15 15
1269 50 b. Muddy Waters 30 30
1270 75 b. Lightnin Hopkins . . . 40 40
1271 1 d. Ma Rainey 45 45
1272 1 d. 25 Mance Lipscomb . . 50 50
1273 1 d. 50 Mahalia Jackson . . 60 60
1274 2 d. Ella Fizgerald 70 70
1275 3 d. Howlin Wolf 85 85
1276 5 d. Bessie Smith . . . . . 1·25 1·25
1277 7 d. Leadbelly . . . . . . 1·50 1·50
1278 10 d. Joe Willie Wilkins . . 2·00 2·00

1992. Papal Visit. Multicoloured.
1280 1 d. Type **202** 40 40
1281 1 d. 25 Pope John Paul II and Pres. Sir Dawda Jawara . . 50 50
1282 20 d. Gambian and Papal flags 4·75 5·50

1992. 40th Anniv of Queen Elizabeth II's Accession. As T **288** of Antigua. Multicoloured.
1284 20 b. Pottery market 10 10
1285 50 b. Ruins of early fort . . 20 20
1286 1 d. Fishing boat 30 30
1287 15 d. Canoes on beach . . . 2·75 3·50

203 Nadia Comaneci (Rumania) (combined gymnastic events) and Map of Barcelona

1992. Olympic Games, Barcelona (2nd issue). Past Medal Winners. Multicoloured.
1289 20 b. Type **203** 10 10
1290 50 b. D. Moorcroft (G.B.) (5000 metres) and map 20 20
1291 75 b. M. Nemeth (Hungary) (javelin) and decorative tiles 25 25
1292 1 d. J. Pedraza (Mexico) (20k walk) and decorative plate 30 30
1293 1 d. 25 "Soling" class yachting (Brazil), state arms and flag 40 40
1294 1 d. 50 Women's hockey (G.D.R.) and Barcelona building 45 45
1295 12 d. M. Jordan (U.S.A.) (basketball) and map . . . 2·50 3·25
1296 15 d. V. Borzov (U.S.S.R.) (100 metres) and galleon . . . 3·00 3·50

204 Mickey Mouse as Christopher Columbus

1992. International Stamp Exhibitions. Walt Disney Cartoon Characters. Multicoloured. (a) "Granada '92", Spain. Voyage of Columbus.
1298 20 b. Type **204** 30 15
1299 75 b. Mickey's plans derided 45 25
1300 1 d. 50 Mickey lands in America 65 60
1301 15 d. Mickey presents treasure to Minnie . . . . 3·25 4·00

(b) World Columbian Stamp "Expo '92". Chicago Landmarks.
1303 50 b. Navy Pier 10 10
1304 1 d. Wrigley Building 20 25
1305 1 d. 25 University of Chicago 25 30
1306 12 d. Alder Planetarium . . 1·75 2·75

1992. Easter. Religious Paintings. As T **291** of Antigua but vert. Multicoloured.
1308 20 b. "Christ presented to the People" (Rembrandt) . . . 10 10
1309 50 b. "Christ carrying the Cross" (Grunewald) . . . 20 20
1310 75 b. "The Crucifixion" (Grunewald) 25 25
1311 1 d. "The Crucifixion" (Rubens) 30 30
1312 1 d. 25 "The Road to Calvary" (detail) (Tintoretto) . . . 35 35
1313 1 d. 50 "The Road to Calvary" (Tintoretto) (different) . . 40 40
1314 15 d. "The Crucifixion" (Masaccio) . . . . 2·75 3·25
1315 20 d. "The Descent from the Cross" (Rembrandt) . . . 3·50 4·00

205 "Hibiscus rosa-sinensis"

1992. Flowers. Multicoloured.
1317 20 b. Type **205** 10 10
1318 50 b. "Monodora myristica" 20 20
1319 75 b. "Bombax costatum" . . 25 25
1320 1 d. "Oncoba spinosa" . . . 30 30
1321 1 d. 25 "Combretum grandiflorum" 35 35
1322 1 d. 50 "Rothmannia longiflora" 40 40
1323 2 d. "Clerodendrum splendens" 55 55
1324 5 d. "Mussaenda erythrophylla" 1·10 1·25
1325 10 d. "Nauclea latifolia" . . 1·75 2·00
1326 12 d. "Clerodendrum capitatum" . . . . 1·90 2·25
1327 15 d. "Costus spectabilis" . . 2·50 2·75
1328 18 d. "Strophanthus preussii" 2·75 3·00

206 "Joven Antonia" (River Gambia)

1992. River Boats of the World. Multicoloured.
1330 20 b. Type **206** 10 10
1331 50 b. "Dresden" (River Elbe) 20 20
1332 75 b. "Medway Queen" (River Medway) 25 25
1333 1 d. "Lady Wright" (River Gambia) 30 30
1334 1 d. 25 "Devin" (River Vltava) 35 35
1335 1 d. 50 "Lady Chilel Jawara" (River Gambia) 40 50
1336 5 d. "Robert Fulton" (River Hudson) . . . . 1·10 1·25
1337 10 d. "Coonawarra" (River Murray) . . . . 1·75 2·00
1338 12 d. "Nakusp" (River Columbia) . . . . 2·00 2·25
1339 15 d. "Lucy Ashton" (Firth of Clyde) . . . . 2·50 2·75

1992. 50th Anniv of Japanese Attack on Pearl Harbor. As T **286** of Antigua. Multicoloured.
1341 2 d. U.S.S. "Pennsylvania" (battleship) 80 90
1342 2 d. Japanese Mitsubishi A6M Zero-Sen aircraft over Pearl Harbor 80 90
1343 2 d. U.S.S. "Ward" (destroyer) sinking midget submarine . 80 90
1344 2 d. Ford Naval Station under attack 80 90
1345 2 d. Agency report of Japanese attack 80 90
1346 2 d. Newspaper headline . . 80 90
1347 2 d. Japanese troops on Guam 80 90
1348 2 d. U.S. forces regaining Wake Island 80 90
1349 2 d. North American B-25B Mitchell bomber raid on Japan 80 90
1350 2 d. American Douglas Dauntless dive bomber attacking Japanese carrier, Midway 80 90

207 Women's Double Sculls

1992. Winter Olympic Games, Albertville, and Olympic Games, Barcelona (3rd issue). Multicoloured.
1351 20 b. Type **207** 10 10
1352 50 b. Men's kayak (vert) . . 20 20
1353 75 b. Women's rapid precision pistol shooting 25 25
1354 1 d. Judo (vert) 30 30
1355 1 d. 25 Men's javelin (vert) . 35 35
1356 1 d. 50 Men's vaulting horse (vert) 40 40
1357 2 d. Men's downhill skiing (vert) 55 55
1358 3 d. Windsurfing (vert) . . . 70 75
1359 5 d. Men's high jump . . . . 1·10 1·25
1360 10 d. Four-man bobsled (vert) 1·90 2·25
1361 12 d. 90 meter ski-jump (vert) 2·00 2·50
1362 15 d. Men's slalom skiing . . 2·40 2·75

1992. "Genova '92" International Thematic Stamp Exhibition. Dinosaurs. As T **290** of Antigua. Multicoloured.
1364 20 b. Dryosaurus 15 10
1365 25 b. Saurolophus 15 10
1366 50 b. Allosaurus 20 20
1367 75 b. Fabrosaurus 25 25
1368 1 d. Deinonychus 30 30
1369 1 d. 25 Cetiosaurus 35 35
1370 1 d. 50 Camptosaurus . . . 35 35
1371 2 d. Ornithosuchus 45 45
1372 3 d. Spinosaurus 60 60
1373 5 d. Ornithomimus . . . . . 1·00 1·00
1374 10 d. Kentrosaurus . . . . . 1·75 2·00
1375 12 d. Schlermochus . . . . . 1·90 2·25

1992. Christmas. Religious Paintings. As T **300** of Antigua. Multicoloured.
1378 50 b. "The Holy Family" (Raphael) 20 20
1379 75 b. "The Little Holy Family" (Raphael) 25 25
1380 1 d. "The Little Holy Family" (detail) (Raphael) 30 30
1381 1 d. 25 "Escape to Egypt" (Melchior Broederlam) . . 35 35
1382 1 d. 50 "Flight into Egypt" (Adriaen Isenbrant) . . . 35 35
1383 2 d. "The Holy Family" (El Greco) 45 45
1384 2 d. "Flight into Egypt" (detail) (Cosimo Tura) 45 45
1385 2 d. "Flight into Egypt" (detail) (Master of Hoogstraelen) . 45 45
1386 4 d. "The Holy Family" (Bernard van Orley) . . . 80 90
1387 5 d. "Holy Family with Infant Jesus Sleeping" (detail) (Charles Le Brun) . . . . 95 1·10
1388 10 d. "Rest on The Flight to Egypt" (Orazio Gentileschi) 1·75 2·25
1389 12 d. "Rest on The Flight to Egypt" (detail) (Orazio Gentileschi) . . . . 1·90 2·50

1992. 60th Anniv of Goofy (Disney cartoon character). As T **258** of Dominica. Multicoloured.
1391 50 b. Goofy in "Orphan's Benefit", 1934 . . . . . . 30 20
1392 75 b. Goofy and Donald Duck in "Moose Hunters", 1937 40 30
1393 1 d. Goofy in "Mickey's Amateurs", 1937 . . . . 50 40
1394 1 d. 25 Goofy, Donald and Mickey Mouse in "Lonesome Ghosts", 1937 . . . . . . 55 55
1395 5 d. Goofy, Donald and Mickey in "Boat Builders", 1938 . 1·40 1·40
1396 7 d. Goofy, Donald and Mickey in "The Whalers", 1938 . 1·75 2·00
1397 10 d. Goofy and Wilbur the grasshopper in "Goofy and Wilbur", 1939 . . . . . . 2·00 2·25
1398 15 d. Goofy in "Saludos Amigos", 1941 . . . . . 2·50 2·75

208 Pres. Jawara playing Golf and Map of Australia

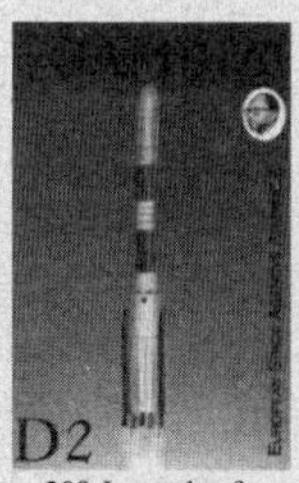

209 Launch of European "Ariane 4"

1992. Open Golf Championships. Multicoloured.
1400 20 b. Type **208** 15 15
1401 1 d. Pres. Jawara and Gambia Open trophy 45 45
1402 1 d. 50 Pres. Jawara (winner of Gambia Open, 1985) . . . 55 55
1403 2 d. Pres. Jawara and map of Japan 70 70
1404 3 d. Pres. Jawara and map of U.S.A. 80 90
1405 5 d. Gambia Open trophy . 1·40 1·60
1406 10 d. Pres. Jawara and map of Scotland . . . . 2·50 2·75
1407 12 d. Pres. Jawara and map of Italy . . . . 2·50 2·75

1993. Anniversaries and Events. Multicoloured.
1409 2 d. Type **209** 50 50
1410 2 d. Konrad Adenauer and Berlin Airlift (horiz) . . . 50 50
1411 2 d. Airship "Hindenburg", 1928 (horiz) 50 50
1412 5 d. "Santa Maria" (horiz) . 1·25 1·25
1413 6 d. Jentink's duiker (horiz) 1·40 1·40
1414 7 d. World map and emblem (horiz) . . . . 1·40 1·40
1415 9 d. Wolfgang Amadeus Mozart 1·75 1·75
1416 10 d. Lions Club emblem . . 1·75 1·75
1417 10 d. "Enterprise" (yacht), 1930 1·75 1·75
1418 10 d. Imperial amazon ("Sisserou Parrot") . . . 1·75 1·75
1419 12 d. American space shuttle 2·00 2·00
1420 12 d. Fleet of Columbus (horiz) 2·00 2·00
1421 15 d. Adenauer and returning prisoners of war (horiz) . 2·40 2·40
1422 18 d. Airship LZ-1, 1900 (horiz) 3·00 3·00

ANNIVERSARIES AND EVENTS: Nos. 1409, 1419, International Space Year; 1410, 1421, 25th death anniv of Konrad Adenauer (German statesman); Nos. 1411, 1422, 75th death anniv of Count Ferdinand von Zeppelin; 1412, 1420, 500th anniv of discovery of America by Columbus; 1413, 1418, Earth Summit '92, Rio; 1414, International Nutrition Conference, Rome; 1415, Death bicentenary of Mozart; 1416, 75th anniv of International Association of Lions Clubs; 1417, Americas Cup Yachting Championship.

1993. 15th Death Anniv (1992) of Elvis Presley (singer). As Nos. 1666/8 of Dominica. Mult.
1424 3 d. Elvis Presley 70 70
1425 3 d. Elvis with guitar 70 70
1426 3 d. Elvis with microphone . 70 70

1993. Bicentenary of the Louvre, Paris. Paintings. As T **305** of Antigua. Multicoloured.
1427 3 d. "St John the Baptist" (Da Vinci) 55 60
1428 3 d. "Virgin of the Rocks" (Da Vinci) 55 60
1429 3 d. "Bacchus" (Da Vinci) . 55 60
1430 3 d. "Lady of the Court, Milan" (Da Vinci) 55 60
1431 3 d. "Virgin of the Rocks" (detail) (Da Vinci) 55 60
1432 3 d. "Mona Lisa" (Da Vinci) 55 60
1433 3 d. "Mona Lisa" (detail) (Da Vinci) 55 60
1434 3 d. Sketches for "Two Horsemen" (Da Vinci) . . 55 60
1435 3 d. "The Oath of Horatii" (left detail) (David) 55 60
1436 3 d. "The Oath of Horatii" (right detail) (David) . . . 55 60
1437 3 d. "The Love of Paris and Helen" (detail) (David) . . 55 60
1438 3 d. "The Sabine Women" (detail) (David) 55 60
1439 3 d. "Leonidas at Thermopylae" (detail) (David) 55 60
1440 3 d. "The Coronation of Napoleon" (left detail) (David) 55 60
1441 3 d. "The Coronation of Napoleon" (centre detail) (David) 55 60
1442 3 d. "The Coronation of Napoleon" (right detail) (David) 55 60
1443 3 d. "Peasant Family at Home" (detail) (L. le Nain) . . . 55 60
1444 3 d. "Smoking Room" (left detail) (L. le Nain) 55 60
1445 3 d. "Smoking Room (right detail) (L. le Nain) 55 60
1446 3 d. "The Cart" (detail) (L. le Nain) 55 60
1447 3 d. "Peasants' Repast" (detail) (L. le Nain) 55 60
1448 3 d. "Portrait in an Interior" (detail) (L. le Nain) 55 60
1449 3 d. "Portrait in an Interior" (different detail) (L. le Nain) 55 60
1450 3 d. "The Forge" (L. le Nain) 55 60

Nos. 1432/3 are incorrectly inscribed "Monna Lisa".

210 Peace Corps and Gambian Flags

1993. 25th Anniv of U.S. Peace Corps.
1452 **210** 2 d. multicoloured . . . 60 60

211 Jackie Robinson and Ruby Dee ("The Jackie Robinson Story")

1993. Baseball Films. Multicoloured.
1453 3 d. Type **211** 60 70
1454 3 d. Robert DeNiro ("Bang the Drum Slowly") 60 70
1455 3 d. James Earl Jones and Billy Dee Williams ("The Bingo Long Travelling All-Stars and Motor Kings") 60 70
1456 3 d. Kevin Costner and Susan Sarandon ("Bull Durham") 60 70
1457 3 d. Cast photograph ("Eight Men Out") 60 70
1458 3 d. Ray Liotta ("Field of Dreams") 60 70
1459 3 d. Charlie Sheen ("Major League") 60 70
1460 3 d. Tom Selleck ("Mr. Baseball") 60 70
1461 3 d. Wallace Beery, 1927, and Elliott Gould, 1986 ("Casey at the Bat") 60 70
1462 3 d. Anna Nilsson and Babe Ruth ("Babe comes Home") 60 70
1463 3 d. Joe Brown ("Elmer the Great") 60 70
1464 3 d. Bud Abbott and Lou Costello ("The Naughty Nineties") 60 70
1465 3 d. Frank Sinatra, Gene Kelly and Esther Williams ("Take Me Out to the Ball Game") 60 70
1466 3 d. Tab Hunter and Gwen Verdon ("Damn Yankees") 60 70
1467 3 d. Dan Dailey ("The Pride of St. Louis") 60 70
1468 3 d. John Candy and Richard Pryor ("Brewster's Millions") 60 70

212 Giraffe

213 Long-tailed Pangolin hanging by Tail

1993. Animals of West Africa. Multicoloured.
1470 2 d. Type **212** 40 45
1471 2 d. Baboon 40 45
1472 2 d. Caracal 40 45
1473 2 d. Large-spotted genet . . 40 45
1474 2 d. Bushbuck 40 45
1475 2 d. Red-fronted gazelle . . 40 45
1476 2 d. Red-flanked duiker . . 40 45
1477 2 d. Cape buffalo 40 45
1478 2 d. African civet 40 45
1479 2 d. Side-striped jackal . . . 40 45
1480 2 d. Ratel 40 45
1481 2 d. Striped polecat 40 45
1482 5 d. Vervet 70 75
1483 5 d. Blackish-green guenon . 70 75
1484 5 d. Long-tailed pangolin . . 70 75
1485 5 d. Leopard 70 75
1486 5 d. Elephant 70 75
1487 5 d. Hunting dog 70 75
1488 5 d. Spotted hyena 70 75
1489 5 d. Lion 70 75
1490 5 d. Hippopotamus 70 75
1491 5 d. Nile crocodile 70 75
1492 5 d. Aardvark 70 75
1493 5 d. Warthog 70 75

Nos. 1470/81 and 1482/93 were each printed together, se-tenant, with the backgrounds forming composite designs.

1993. Endangered Species. Long-tailed Pangolin. Multicoloured.
1495 1 d. 25 Type **213** 45 25
1496 1 d. 50 Sitting on branch . . 55 40
1497 2 d. Climbing up branch . . 65 60
1498 5 d. Climbing down branch . 1·60 2·00

214 Osprey

215 Rose-ringed Parakeet

1993. Birds of Prey. Multicoloured.
1500 1 d. 25 Type **214** 80 50
1501 1 d. 50 Egyptian vulture (horiz) 90 50
1502 2 d. Martial eagle . . . . . 1·00 55
1503 3 d. Ruppell's griffon (horiz) 1·25 75
1504 5 d. Augur buzzard . . . . 1·50 1·25
1505 8 d. Greater kestrel . . . . 2·00 2·25
1506 10 d. Secretary bird . . . . 2·25 2·50
1507 15 d. Bateleur (horiz) . . . . 2·50 3·25

1993. African Birds. Multicoloured.
1509 2 d. Type **215** . . . . . . 1·00 1·10
1510 2 d. Variable sunbird . . . . 1·00 1·10
1511 2 d. Red-billed hornbill . . . 1·00 1·10
1512 2 d. Red-billed fire finch . . 1·00 1·10
1513 2 d. Go-away bird . . . . . 1·00 1·10
1514 2 d. Burchell's Gonolek ("Crimson-breasted shrike") 1·00 1·10
1515 2 d. Grey-headed bush shrike 1·00 1·10
1516 2 d. Western nicator . . . . 1·00 1·10
1517 2 d. Egyptian plover . . . . 1·00 1·10
1518 2 d. Congo peafowl . . . . 1·00 1·10
1519 2 d. Painted snipe . . . . . 1·00 1·10
1520 2 d. South African crowned crane . . . . 1·00 1·10

1993. 40th Anniv of Coronation. As T **307** of Antigua.
1521 2 d. multicoloured 60 75
1522 5 d. multicoloured . . . . . 1·00 1·25
1523 8 d. brown and black . . . . 1·25 1·50
1524 10 d. multicoloured . . . . 1·50 1·60

DESIGNS—(38×47 mm): 2 d. Queen Elizabeth II at Coronation (photograph by Cecil Beaton); 5 d. Orb and sceptre; 8 d. Sir Winston Churchill; 10 d. Queen Elizabeth II at Trooping the Colour.

216 Hugo Eckener and "Graf Zeppelin"

1993. Aviation Anniversaries. Multicoloured.
1526 2 d. Type **216** 55 50
1527 2 d. Guyot's balloon, 1785 (vert) 55 50
1528 5 d. Airship "Luftschiffe 3" and crowd . . . . 1·00 1·00
1529 5 d. Sopwith Snipe (fighter) . 1·00 1·00
1530 8 d. Eckener and "Graf Zeppelin" . . . . 1·60 1·75
1531 10 d. "Comte D'Artois" (hot air balloon), 1785 (vert) . . . 1·90 2·00
1532 15 d. Royal Aircraft Factory S.E.5 (fighter) . . . . . 2·40 2·50

ANNIVERSARIES: Nos. 1526, 1528, 1530, Birth anniv of Hugo Eckener (airship pioneer); Nos. 1527, 1531, Bicentenary of first airmail flight; Nos. 1529, 1532, 75th anniv of Royal Air Force.

217 Henry Ford and "Model T", 1910

1993. Centenaries of Henry Ford's First Petrol Engine (Nos. 1534/45) and Karl Benz's First Four-wheeled Car (Nos. 1546/57). Multicoloured.

1534	2 d. Type **217**	45	50
1535	2 d. Car of 1896	45	50
1536	2 d. Henry Ford with Barney Oldfield and "999", 1902	45	50
1537	2 d. Henry Ford, 1893, and car of 1896	45	50
1538	2 d. "Model A", 1903	45	50
1539	2 d. "Model T" with roof lowered, 1908	45	50
1540	2 d. "Model T" with roof raised, 1908	45	50
1541	2 d. "Model K", 1906	45	50
1542	2 d. "Model A", 1931	45	50
1543	2 d. "Model A", 1906	45	50
1544	2 d. "Model N", 1906	45	50
1545	2 d. "Model F", 1905	45	50
1546	2 d. Benz "Velo", 1894	45	50
1547	2 d. Car of 1894	45	50
1548	2 d. Three-wheeled car of 1885 from side	45	50
1549	2 d. "Mannheim", 1905	45	50
1550	2 d. Car of 1892	45	50
1551	2 d. Car of 1900 from front	45	50
1552	2 d. Racing car of 1911 from side	45	50
1553	2 d. "Velo", 1893	45	50
1554	2 d. Black car of 1900 from side	45	50
1555	2 d. Red car of 1900 from side	45	50
1556	2 d. Racing car of 1911 from front	45	50
1557	2 d. Three-wheeled car of 1885 from back	45	50

Nos. 1534/45 and 1546/57 were each printed together, se-tenant, with the backgrounds forming composite designs.

218 Marilyn Monroe

220 "Woman with a Comb" (Picasso)

219 Siamese

1993. Musical Entertainers.

1559/93	3d. × 35 multicoloured	14·50	15·00

Nos. 1559/93 were issued as four sheetlets, three of nine different designs (Nos. 1559/85) and one of eight (Nos. 1586/93), depicting Marilyn Monroe (Nos. 1559/67), Elvis Presley (Nos. 1568/76), Madonna (Nos. 1577/85) and Buddy Holly, Otis Redding, Bill Haley, Dinah Washington, musical instruments, Ritchie Valens, Clyde McPhatter, Elvis Presley (Nos. 1586/93).

1993. Oriental Cats. Multicoloured.

1594	2 d. Type **219**	75	75
1595	2 d. Colourpoint longhair sitting	75	75
1596	2 d. Burmese	75	75
1597	2 d. Birman	75	75
1598	2 d. Snowshoe	75	75
1599	2 d. Tonkinese	75	75
1600	2 d. Foreign shorthair stretching	75	75
1601	2 d. Balinese	75	75
1602	2 d. Oriental shorthair	75	75
1603	2 d. Foreign shorthair lying	75	75
1604	2 d. Colourpoint longhair with black face standing	75	75
1605	2 d. Colourpoint longhair with white face standing	75	75

Nos. 1594/1605 were printed together, se-tenant, with the background forming a composite design.

1993. Royal Dogs. As T **219**. Multicoloured.

1607	2 d. Shih tzu (Emperor of China)	70	75
1608	2 d. Skye terrier (Queen Victoria)	70	75
1609	2 d. Berner laufhund (King Louis XV, France)	70	75
1610	2 d. Boxer (King Francis I, France)	70	75
1611	2 d. Welsh corgi (Queen Elizabeth II)	70	75
1612	2 d. Dumfriesshire (Princess Anne)	70	75
1613	2 d. Lurcher (King George VI)	70	75
1614	2 d. Welsh corgi (Princess Anne)	70	75
1615	2 d. Pekinese (Empress Ts'Eu-Hi, China)	70	75
1616	2 d. Papillon (King Louis XIII, France)	70	75
1617	2 d. Otterhound (King John)	70	75
1618	2 d. Pug (Napoleon I, France)	70	75

Nos. 1607/18 were printed together, se-tenant, with the background forming a composite design.

1993. Asian International Stamp Exhibitions. As T **268** of Dominica. Multicoloured. (a) "Indopex '93", Surabaya, Indonesia.

1620	20 b. National Monument and statue, Jakarta	20	20
1621	20 b. Pura Taman Ayun Temple, Bali	20	20
1622	2 d. Guardian statue, Singosari Palace, Java	60	60
1623	2 d. Candi Jawi, Java	60	60
1624	5 d. Telek Luh mask	1·40	1·40
1625	5 d. Jero Gde mask	1·40	1·40
1626	5 d. Barong Macan mask	1·40	1·40
1627	5 d. Monkey mask	1·40	1·40
1628	5 d. Mata Gde mask	1·40	1·40
1629	5 d. Jauk Kras mask	1·40	1·40
1630	5 d. "Tree Mask" (Soedibio)	1·40	1·40
1631	5 d. "Dry Lizard" (Hendra Gunawan)	1·40	1·40
1632	5 d. "The Corn Eater" (Sudjana Kerton)	1·40	1·40
1633	5 d. "Night Watchman" (Djoko Pekik)	1·40	1·40
1634	5 d. "Hunger" (Kerton)	1·40	1·40
1635	5 d. "Arje Player" (Soedjojono)	1·40	1·40
1636	5 d. Central Temple, Lara Djonggrang	1·40	1·40
1637	5 d. Irian Jaya Monument, Jakarta	1·40	1·40
1638	15 d. Brahma and Siva Temples, Java	2·75	3·25
1639	15 d. Date of the Year Temple, Java	2·75	3·25

(b) "Taipei '93", Taiwan.

1641	20 b. Fawang Si Pagoda, Henan	20	20
1642	20 b. Wanshoubao Pagoda, Shashi	20	20
1643	2 d. Red Pavilion, Shibaozhai	60	60
1644	2 d. Songyue Si Pagoda, Henan	60	60
1645	5 d. Pottery camel (walking)	1·40	1·40
1646	5 d. Pottery horse and rider	1·40	1·40
1647	5 d. Pottery camel (standing with mouth closed)	1·40	1·40
1648	5 d. Yellow-glazed pottery horse	1·40	1·40
1649	5 d. Pottery camel (standing with mouth open)	1·40	1·40
1650	5 d. Pottery saddled horse	1·40	1·40
1651	5 d. Qianlong vase	1·40	1·40
1652	5 d. Small wine cup	1·40	1·40
1653	5 d. Mei-ping vase	1·40	1·40
1654	5 d. Urn vase	1·40	1·40
1655	5 d. Tureen	1·40	1·40
1656	5 d. Lidded potiche	1·40	1·40
1657	5 d. Tianning Si Pagoda, Beijing	1·40	1·40
1658	5 d. Bond Centre, Hong Kong	1·40	1·40
1659	15 d. Forbidden City pavilion, Beijing	2·75	3·25
1660	15 d. Xuanzhuang Pagoda, Shenxi	2·75	3·25

(c) "Bangkok '93", Thailand.

1662	20 b. Sanctuary of Prasat Phanom Wan	20	20
1663	20 b. Lai Kham Vihan, Chiang Mai	20	20
1664	2 d. Upmarket spirit shrine, Bangkok	60	60
1665	2 d. Walking Buddha statue, Wat Phra Si Ratana Mahathat	60	60
1666	5 d. "Early Fruit Stand"	1·40	1·40
1667	5 d. "Scene Rendered in Chinese Style"	1·40	1·40
1668	5 d. "Buddha descends from Tauatimsa"	1·40	1·40
1669	5 d. "Sang Thong Tales" (detail)	1·40	1·40
1670	5 d. "The Damned in Hell"	1·40	1·40
1671	5 d. "King Sanjaya travels on Elephant"	1·40	1·40
1672	5 d. U Thong C Buddha (bronze)	1·40	1·40
1673	5 d. Seated Buddha (bronze)	1·40	1·40
1674	5 d. Phra Chai Buddha (ivory and gold)	1·40	1·40
1675	5 d. Buddha (bronze)	1·40	1·40
1676	5 d. U Thong A Buddha (bronze)	1·40	1·40
1677	5 d. Crowned Buddha (bronze)	1·40	1·40
1678	5 d. Statue of Buddha, Wat Mahathat	1·40	1·40
1679	5 d. The Gopura of Prasat Phanom Rung	1·40	1·40
1680	15 d. Slender Chedis, Mongkon	2·75	3·25
1681	15 d. The Prang of Prasat Hin Phimai	2·75	3·25

1993. Anniversaries and Events. Mult.

1683	2 d. Type **220**	65	65
1684	2 d. "Niedzica Castle" (horiz)	65	65
1685	5 d. "The Mirror" (Picasso)	1·25	1·25
1686	5 d. Early astronomical instrument	1·25	1·25
1687	7 d. "Woman on a Pillow" (Picasso)	1·50	1·50
1688	10 d. "Pont-Neuf in Paris" (Hanna Rudza-Cybisowa (horiz)	2·00	2·25
1689	10 d. "Honegger's Liturgical Symphony" (Marian Bogusz) (horiz)	2·00	2·25
1690	10 d. Modern telescope	2·00	2·25

ANNIVERSARIES AND EVENTS: Nos. 1683, 1685, 1687, 20th death anniv of Picasso (artist); Nos. 1684, 1688/9, "Polska '93" International Stamp Exhibition, Poznan; Nos. 1686, 1690, 450th death anniv of Copernicus (astronomer).

The captions on Nos. 1684 and 1689 are transposed in error.

221 Mudville Player at the Plate

1993. "Casey at the Bat". Scenes from Walt Disney's cartoon film. Multicoloured.

1692	2 d. Type **221**	75	80
1693	2 d. Mudville player out	75	80
1694	2 d. Umpire and player arguing	75	80
1695	2 d. Fans applauding	75	80
1696	2 d. Casey reading newspaper at plate	75	80
1697	2 d. Casey letting second pitch go by	75	80
1698	2 d. Over-confident Casey	75	80
1699	2 d. Casey striking out	75	80
1700	2 d. Casey striking out at night	75	80

1993. World Cup Football Championship, 1994, U.S.A. (1st issue). As T **310** of Antigua. Mult.

1702	1 d. 25 Hannich (Hungary) and Stopyra (France)	65	40
1703	1 d. 50 Labd (Morocco) and Gary Lineker (England)	75	50
1704	2 d. Segota (Canada) and Morozov (Russia)	90	65
1705	3 d. Roger Milla (Cameroun)	1·10	1·10
1706	5 d. Rodax (Austria) and Weiss (Czechoslovakia)	1·40	1·50
1707	10 d. Claesen (Belgium), Bossis and Amoros (France)	2·00	2·25
1708	12 d. Candida (Brazil) and Ramirez (Costa Rica)	2·25	2·50
1709	15 d. Silva (Brazil) and Michel Platini (France)	2·50	2·75

See also Nos. 1882/9.

1993. Christmas. Religious Paintings. As T **270** of Dominica. Black, yellow and red (Nos. 1712/13 and 1715/17) or multicoloured (others).

1711	25 b. "The Adoration of the Magi" (detail) (Rubens)	20	20
1712	1 d. "The Holy Family with Joachim and Anna" (Durer)	45	20
1713	1 d. 50 "The Annunciation" (Durer)	60	30
1714	2 d. "The Adoration of the Magi" (different detail) (Rubens)	75	50
1715	2 d. "The Virgin Mary worshipped by Albrecht Bonstetten" (Durer)	75	50
1716	7 d. "The Holy Family with Two Angels in a Portico" (detail) (Durer)	2·00	2·50
1717	10 d. "Virgin on a Throne, crowned by an Angel" (Durer)	2·25	2·50
1718	15 d. "The Adoration of the Magi" (different detail) (Rubens)	2·50	3·25

1993. Famous Paintings by Rembrandt and Matisse. As T **316** of Antigua. Multicoloured.

1720	50 b. "A Man in a Cap" (Rembrandt)	40	20
1721	1 d. 50 "Pierre Matisse" (Matisse)	70	35
1722	2 d. "Man with a Gold Helmet" (Rembrandt)	75	55
1723	2 d. "Auguste Pellerin" (Matisse)	75	55
1724	5 d. "Andre Derain" (Matisse)	1·50	1·50
1725	7 d. "A Franciscan Monk" (Rembrandt)	2·00	2·50
1726	12 d. "The Young Sailor (II)" (Matisse)	2·50	3·25
1727	15 d. "The Apostle Paul" (Rembrandt)	2·50	3·25

222 Mickey Mouse performing Ski Ballet

1993. Winter Sports. Walt Disney cartoon characters. Multicoloured.

1729	50 b. Type **222**	30	15
1730	75 b. Clarabelle and Horace ice dancing	40	15
1731	1 d. Donald Duck and Dale speed skating	45	20
1732	1 d. 25 Donald in biathlon	50	20
1733	4 d. Donald and nephews in bob-sled	1·40	1·40
1734	5 d. Goofy on luge	1·50	1·50
1735	7 d. Minnie Mouse figure skating	2·00	2·50
1736	10 d. Goofy downhill skiing	2·25	2·50
1737	15 d. Goofy playing ice hockey	2·50	3·00

1994. "Hong Kong '94" International Stamp Exhibition (1st issue). As T **317** of Antigua. Multicoloured.

1739	1 d. 50 Hong Kong 1979 $2 Butterflies stamp and "Spring Garden" (M. Bruce) (left detail)	40	50
1740	1 d. 50 Gambia 1990 50 d. Gambian Life stamp and "Spring Garden" (M. Bruce) (right detail)	40	50

Nos. 1739/40 were printed together, se-tenant, forming the complete painting.

See also Nos. 1742/7.

1994. "Hong Kong '94" International Stamp Exhibition (2nd issue). Qin Dynasty Terracotta Figures. As T **318** of Antigua, but vert. Multicoloured.

1742	1 d. 50 Warriors and horses	40	50
1743	1 d. 50 Head of warrior	40	50
1744	1 d. 50 Kneeling warrior	40	50
1745	1 d. 50 Chariot driver	40	50
1746	1 d. 50 Dog	40	50
1747	1 d. 50 Warriors as excavated	40	50

223 Pluto the Racer, 1934–35

1994. Chinese New Year ("Year of the Dog"). Walt Disney cartoon dogs. Multicoloured.

1748	25 b. Type **223**	20	15
1749	50 b. Fifi, 1933	30	20
1750	75 b. Pluto Jnr, 1942	40	30
1751	1 d. 25 Goofy and Bowser	50	30
1752	1 d. 50 Butch, 1940	60	35
1753	2 d. Toliver, 1936	70	50
1754	3 d. Ronnie, 1946	90	90
1755	5 d. Primo, 1950	1·25	1·25
1756	8 d. Pluto's kid brother, 1946	1·75	2·00
1757	10 d. The army mascot, 1942	1·90	2·25
1758	12 d. Pluto and Fifi's puppies, 1937	2·00	2·50
1759	18 d. Bent Tail Jnr, 1949	2·75	3·25

No. 1758 is inscribed "DINAH'S PUPPIES" in error.

224 Ludwig von Drake and Easter Bunny

1994. Easter. Walt Disney cartoon characters. Multicoloured.

1761	25 b. Type **224**	20	10
1762	50 b. Minnie Mouse and Daisy Duck carrying banner	30	10
1763	3 d. Mickey Mouse wearing top hat	90	75
1764	4 d. Von Drake holding hatching egg	1·00	1·00
1765	5 d. Donald Duck pushing trolley full of eggs	1·25	1·25
1766	8 d. Bunny taking photograph of Von Drake	1·50	1·75
1767	10 d. Goofy dressed as Easter Bunny	1·75	2·25
1768	12 d. Von Drake holding dinosaur egg	2·00	2·50

1994. Centenary (1992) of Sierra Club (environmental protection society). Endangered Environments. As T **320** of Antigua. Mult.

1770	5 d. Briksdal Fjord	70	80
1771	5 d. Glacier, Briksdal Fjord	70	80
1772	5 d. Waterfall, Briksdal Fjord	70	80
1773	5 d. Frozen lake, Yosemite	70	80
1774	5 d. Cliffs and river, Yosemite	70	80
1775	5 d. Forest, Yosemite	70	80
1776	5 d. Mother and child, Tibetan Plateau	70	80
1777	5 d. Yellowstone in winter	70	80
1778	5 d. Ross Island	70	80
1779	5 d. Mount Erebus	70	80
1780	5 d. Tibetan Plateau	70	80
1781	5 d. Waterfall, Yellowstone	70	80
1782	5 d. Sunset on the Serengeti	70	80
1783	5 d. Dead trees, Ansel Adams Wilderness	70	80
1784	5 d. Ansel Adams Wilderness in winter (horiz)	70	80
1785	5 d. Ansel Adams Wilderness in summer (horiz)	70	80
1786	5 d. Ridge on Mount Erebus (horiz)	70	80
1787	5 d. Mount Erebus from a distance (horiz)	70	80

1788 5 d. Prince William Sound (horiz) . . . 70 80
1789 5 d. Geysers, Yellowstone (horiz) . . . 70 80
1790 5 d. Local dwelling, Tibetan Plateau (horiz) . . . 70 80
1791 5 d. Sierra Club Centennial emblem (horiz) . . . 70 80
1792 5 d. Frozen lake, Prince William Sound (horiz) . . . 70 80
1793 5 d. Forest, Prince William Sound (horiz) . . . 70 80
1794 5 d. Baobab Tree, Serengeti (horiz) . . . 70 80
1795 5 d. Plains, Serengeti (horiz) . 70 80
1796 5 d. Volcano, Ross Island (horiz) . . . 70 80
1797 5 d. Mountains, Ross Island (horiz) . . . 70 80

225 "Oeceoclades maculata"

226 "Girl with a Kitten" (Perronneau)

1994. Orchids. Multicoloured.

1798 1 d. Type **225** . . . 35 20
1799 1 d. 25 "Angraecum distichum" (horiz) . . . 45 30
1800 2 d. "Plectrelminthus caudatus" 60 35
1801 5 d. "Tridactyle tridactylites" (horiz) . . . 1·25 1·25
1802 8 d. "Bulbophyllum lepidum" (horiz) . . . 1·40 1·50
1803 10 d. "Angraecum eburneum" 1·60 1·90
1804 12 d. "Eulophia guineensis" . 1·75 2·00
1805 15 d. "Angraecum eichleranum" (horiz) . . . 2·00 2·50

1994. Cats. Paintings of Cats. Multicoloured.

1807 5 d. Type **226** . . . 90 90
1808 5 d. "Still Life with Cat and Fish" (Chardin) . . . 90 90
1809 5 d. "Tinkle a Cat" . . . 90 90
1810 5 d. "Naughty Puss!" (advertisement) . . . 90 90
1811 5 d. "Cats" (T.-A Steinlen) . 90 90
1812 5 d. "Girl in Red with Cat and Dog" (Phillips) . . . 90 90
1813 5 d. "Cat, Butterfly and Begonia" (Harunobu) . . . 90 90
1814 5 d. "Cat and Kitten" (Pamela Higgins) . . . 90 90
1815 5 d. "Woman with a Cat" (Renoir) . . . 90 90
1816 5 d. "Minnie from Outskirts of the Village" (Thrall) . . . 90 90
1817 5 d. "The Fisher" (Raphael Tuck postcard) . . . 90 90
1818 5 d. "Artist and His Family" (detail) (Vaenius) . . . 90 90
1819 5 d. "The Arena" (Harold Weston) (horiz) . . . 90 90
1820 5 d. "Cat killing a Bird" (Picasso) (horiz) . . . 90 90
1821 5 d. "Cat and Butterfly" (Hokusai) (horiz) . . . 90 90
1822 5 d. "Winter: Cat on a Cushion" (Steinlen) (horiz) 90 90
1823 5 d. "Rattown Tigers" (Prang) (horiz) . . . 90 90
1824 5 d. "Cat on the Floor" (Steinlen) (horiz) . . . 90 90
1825 5 d. "Cat and Kittens" (horiz) 90 90
1826 5 d. "Cats looking over Fence" (Prang) (horiz) . . . 90 90
1827 5 d. "Little White Kittens into Mischief" (Ives) (horiz) . . 90 90
1828 5 d. "Cat Bathing" (Hiroshige) (horiz) . . . 90 90
1829 5 d. "Playtime" (Tuck postcard) (horiz) . . . 90 90
1830 5 d. "Summer: Cat on a Balustrade" (Steinlen) (horiz) 90 90

227 Patas Monkey

229 Bobby Charlton (England)

228 "Mylothris rhodope"

1994. Monkeys. Multicoloured.

1832 1 d. Type **227** . . . 35 20
1833 1 d. 50 Collared mangabey . 55 30
1834 2 d. Black and white colobus 60 35
1835 5 d. Mona monkey . . . 1·10 1·10
1836 8 d. Kirk's colobus . . . 1·50 1·75
1837 10 d. Vervet . . . 1·75 2·00
1838 12 d. Red colobus . . . 2·00 2·25
1839 15 d. Guinea baboon . . . 2·25 2·50

1994. 25th Anniv of First Manned Moon Landing. As T **326** of Antigua. Multicoloured.

1841 2 d. Yuri Gagarin (first cosmonaut) . . . 50 55
1842 2 d. Valentina Tereshkova (first woman in Space) . . . 50 55
1843 2 d. Ham (first chimpanzee in Space) . . . 50 55
1844 2 d. Aleksei Leonov (first man to walk in Space) . . . 50 55
1845 2 d. Neil Armstrong (first man on Moon) . . . 50 55
1846 2 d. Svetlana Savitskaya (first woman to walk in Space) . 50 55
1847 2 d. Marc Garneau (first Canadian in Space) . . . 50 55
1848 2 d. Vladimir Komarov (first Soviet Space casualty) . . 50 55
1849 2 d. Ulf Merbold (first German in Space) . . . 50 55

1994. Centenary of International Olympic Committee. Gold Medal Winners. As T **327** of Antigua, but vert. Multicoloured.

1851 1 d. 50 Daley Thompson (Great Britain) (decathlon), 1980 and 1984 . . . 40 30
1852 5 d. Heide Marie Rosendohl (Germany) (long jump), 1972 1·10 1·25

1994. 50th Anniv of D-Day. As T **331** of Antigua. Multicoloured.

1854 50 b. "Soema" (Dutch sloop) 40 40
1855 75 b. H.M.S. "Belfast" (cruiser) 50 50
1856 1 d. U.S.S. "Texas" (battleship) 60 60
1857 2 d. "Georges Leygues" (French cruiser) . . . 1·00 1·00

1994. "Philakorea '94" International Stamp Exhibition, Seoul. Screen paintings of the "Sanguozhi". As T **281** of Dominica. Mult.

1859 50 b. Kungnakchon Hall (38 × 25 mm) . . . 20 20
1860 1 d. Soldiers on horses . . . 30 30
1861 1 d. Soldiers defending fort . 30 30
1862 1 d. Archers . . . 30 30
1863 1 d. General on horse . . . 30 30
1864 1 d. Three soldiers in battle . 30 30
1865 1 d. Army in retreat . . . 30 30
1866 1 d. Archers using fire arrows 30 30
1867 1 d. Horsemen attacking fort 30 30
1868 1 d. Women in summer house 30 30
1869 1 d. Old man, child and house 30 30
1870 2 d. Kettle of Popchusa (38 × 25 mm) . . . 50 50
1871 3 d. Pomun tourist resort (38 × 25 mm) . . . 55 55

1994. Butterflies. Multicoloured.

1873 1 d. Type **228** . . . 40 25
1874 1 d. 25 "Iolaphilus menas" . 55 35
1875 2 d. "Neptis nemetes" . . . 65 40
1876 5 d. "Antanartia delius" . . 1·10 1·10
1877 8 d. "Acraea caecilia" . . . 1·40 1·60
1878 10 d. "Papilio nireus" . . . 1·50 1·75
1879 12 d. "Papilio menestheus" . 1·75 2·25
1880 15 d. "Iolaphilus julus" . . 2·00 2·50

1994. World Cup Football Championship, U.S.A. (2nd issue). Multicoloured.

1882 50 b. Type **229** . . . 30 20
1883 75 b. Ferenc Puskas (Hungary) 35 25
1884 1 d. Paolo Rossi (Italy) . . 40 25
1885 2 d. Biri Biri (Spain) . . . 60 40
1886 3 d. Diego Maradona (Argentina) . . . 75 60
1887 8 d. Johann Cruyff (Netherlands) . . . 1·40 1·60
1888 10 d. Franz Beckenbauer (Germany) . . . 1·50 1·75
1889 15 d. Thomas Dooley (U.S.A.) 2·00 2·50

230 "Suillus luteus"

231 Marilyn Monroe

1994. Fungi. Multicoloured.

1891 5 d. Type **230** . . . 90 90
1892 5 d. "Bolbitius vitellinus" . 90 90
1893 5 d. "Clitocybe nebularis" . 90 90
1894 5 d. "Omphalotus olearius" . 90 90
1895 5 d. "Auricularia auricula" . 90 90
1896 5 d. "Macrolepiota rhacodes" 90 90
1897 5 d. "Volvariella volvacea" . 90 90
1898 5 d. "Psilocybe coprophila" . 90 90
1899 5 d. "Suillus granulatus" . . 90 90
1900 5 d. "Agaricus campestris" . 90 90
1901 5 d. "Lepista nuda" . . . 90 90
1902 5 d. "Podaxis pistillaris" . . 90 90
1903 5 d. "Oudemansiella radicata" 90 90
1904 5 d. "Schizophyllum commune" 90 90
1905 5 d. "Chlorophyllum molybdites" . . . 90 90
1906 5 d. "Hypholoma fasciculare" 90 90
1907 5 d. "Mycena pura" . . . 90 90
1908 5 d. "Ganoderma lucidum" . 90 90

1994. Christmas. Religious Paintings. As T **336** of Antigua. Multicoloured.

1910 50 b. "Expectant Madonna with St. Joseph" (French 15th-century) . . . 20 10
1911 75 b. "Rest of the Holy Family" (Louis le Nain) . . . 30 20
1912 1 d. "Rest on the Flight into Egypt" (Antoine Watteau) . 35 20
1913 2 d. "Rest on the Flight into Egypt" (Jean-Honore Fragonard) . . . 50 40
1914 2 d. "Rest on the Flight into Egypt" (Francois Boucher) 50 40
1915 2 d. "Noon" (Claude Lorrain) 50 40
1916 10 d. "The Holy Family" (Nicolas Poussin) . . . 2·00 2·50
1917 12 d. "Mystical Marriage of St. Catherine" (Pierre-Francois Mignard) . . . 2·00 2·50

1995. Marilyn Monroe (American entertainer) Commemoration. Multicoloured.

1919 4 d. Type **231** . . . 70 80
1920 4 d. Wearing pendant necklace 70 80
1921 4 d. In blue jacket . . . 70 80
1922 4 d. With sun-glasses on head 70 80
1923 4 d. Looking over right arm . 70 80
1924 4 d. Wearing gold beret and jacket . . . 70 80
1925 4 d. Wearing hooped earrings 70 80
1926 4 d. Smiling . . . 70 80
1927 4 d. Laughing . . . 70 80

232 Elvis as a Child

1995. 60th Birth Anniv of Elvis Presley (singer). Multicoloured.

1929 4 d. Type **232** . . . 70 80
1930 4 d. Wearing white shirt . . . 70 80
1931 4 d. With his mother Gladys . 70 80
1932 4 d. With his wife Priscilla . . 70 80
1933 4 d. With large gold medallion 70 80
1934 4 d. In army uniform . . . 70 80
1935 4 d. In purple shirt . . . 70 80
1936 4 d. Wearing stetson . . . 70 80
1937 4 d. With his daughter Lisa-Marie . . . 70 80

233 Pteranodon

1995. Prehistoric Animals. Multicoloured.

1938 2 d. Type **233** . . . 40 40
1939 2 d. Archaeopteryx . . . 40 40
1940 2 d. Rhamphorhynchus . . . 40 40
1941 2 d. Ornithomimus . . . 40 40
1942 2 d. Stegosaurus . . . 40 40
1943 2 d. Heterodontosaurus . . . 40 40
1944 2 d. Lystrosaurus . . . 40 40
1945 2 d. Euoplocephalus . . . 40 40
1946 2 d. Coelophysis . . . 40 40
1947 2 d. Staurikosaurus . . . 40 40
1948 2 d. Giantoperis . . . 40 40
1949 2 d. Diarthrognathus . . . 40 40
1950 3 d. Archaeopteryx . . . 50 50
1951 3 d. Vangehuanosaurus . . . 50 50
1952 3 d. Celophysis . . . 50 50
1953 3 d. Plateosaurus . . . 50 50
1954 3 d. Baryonyx . . . 50 50
1955 3 d. Ornitholestes . . . 50 50
1956 3 d. Dryosaurus . . . 50 50
1957 3 d. Estemmenosuchus . . . 50 50
1958 3 d. Macroplata . . . 50 50
1959 3 d. Shonisaurus . . . 50 50
1960 3 d. Muraeonosaurus . . . 50 50
1961 3 d. Archelon . . . 50 50

Nos. 1938/49 and 1950/61 respectively were printed together, se-tenant, forming composite designs.

234 Pig (Chinese characters in green)

236 Rural Road

235 Great White Egret

1995. Chinese New Year ("Year of the Pig").

1963 **234** 3 d. red, black and green 35 40
1964 – 3 d. multicoloured (characters in blue) . . 35 40
1965 – 3 d. orange, red and black (characters in white) . 35 40
1966 – 3 d. pink, red and black (characters in black) . 35 40

DESIGNS: Nos. 1964/6, Different symbolic pigs.

1995. Water Birds. Multicoloured.

1968 2 d. Type **235** . . . 20 25
1969 3 d. Pintails . . . 35 40
1970 3 d. Fulvous whistling duck . 35 40
1971 3 d. Garganey . . . 35 40
1972 3 d. White-faced whistling duck . . . 35 40
1973 3 d. White-backed duck . . 35 40
1974 3 d. Egyptian goose . . . 35 40
1975 3 d. African pygmy geese . . 35 40
1976 3 d. Little bitterns . . . 35 40
1977 3 d. Redshanks . . . 35 40
1978 3 d. Ringed plovers . . . 35 40
1979 3 d. Black-winged stilt . . . 35 40
1980 3 d. Squacco herons . . . 35 40
1981 8 d. Hammerkop . . . 90 95
1982 10 d. Common shovelers . . 1·10 1·25
1983 12 d. Crowned crane . . . 1·40 1·50

Nos. 1969/80 were printed together, se-tenant, forming a composite design.

1995. 20th Anniv of Economic Community of West African States (E.C.O.W.A.S.). Multicoloured.

1985 2 d. Type **236** . . . 20 25
1986 5 d. Pres. Yayah Jammeh . . 60 65

237 Leather Back Turtle

1995. Marine Life. Multicoloured.

1987 3 d. Type **237** . . . 35 40
1988 3 d. Tiger shark . . . 35 40
1989 3 d. Powder-blue surgeonfish 35 40
1990 3 d. Emperor angelfish . . . 35 40
1991 3 d. Blue parrotfish . . . 35 40
1992 3 d. Clown triggerfish . . . 35 40
1993 3 d. Sea horses . . . 35 40
1994 3 d. Lionfish . . . 35 40
1995 3 d. Moray eel . . . 35 40
1996 3 d. Melon butterflyfish . . 35 40
1997 3 d. Octopus . . . 35 40
1998 3 d. Common stingray . . . 35 40
1999 8 d. Stoplight parrotfish ("Multicoloured Parrot Fish") (vert) . . . 90 95
2000 8 d. Stoplight parrotfish ("Sparisoma Viride") (vert) 90 95
2001 8 d. Queen parrotfish (vert) . 90 95
2002 8 d. Bicoloured parrotfish (vert) . . . 90 95

Nos. 1987/98 and 1999/2002 respectively were printed together, se-tenant, forming composite designs.

No. 1991 is inscribed "BLUE PARRO FISH" in error.

1995. 50th Anniv of End of Second World War in Europe. Film Stars. As T **340** of Antigua. Black and red (Nos. 2008 and 2010) or multicoloured (others).

2006 3 d. Peter Lawford . . . 60 60
2007 3 d. Gene Tierney and Dana Andrews . . . 60 60
2008 3 d. Groucho and Harpo Marx 60 60
2009 3 d. James Stewart . . . 60 60
2010 3 d. Chico and Zeppo Marx 60 60
2011 3 d. Tyrone Power . . . 60 60
2012 3 d. Cary Grant and Ingrid Bergman . . . 60 60
2013 3 d. Veronica Lake . . . 60 60

No. 2012 is inscribed "BERMAN" in error.

1995. 50th Anniv of United Nations. As T **341** of Antigua. Multicoloured.

2015 3 d. Children in class . . . 35 40
2016 3 d. Teacher helping child . . 35 40
2017 3 d. Child writing on blackboard . . . 35 40

Nos. 2015/17 were printed together, se-tenant, forming a composite design.

1995. 50th Anniv of F.A.O. As T **342** of Antigua. Multicoloured.

2019 3 d. Woman carrying sack on head . . . 35 40
2020 3 d. Two men carrying sacks 35 40
2021 3 d. Man carrying sack . . . 35 40

Nos. 2019/21 were printed together, se-tenant, forming a composite design.

239 Paul Harris (founder) and Rotary Emblem

1995. 90th Anniv of Rotary International.

2023 **239**	15 d. multicoloured	1·75	1·90

1995. 95th Birthday of Queen Elizabeth the Queen Mother. As T **344** of Antigua.

2025	5 d. brown, light brown and black	60	65
2026	5 d. multicoloured	60	65
2027	5 d. multicoloured	60	65
2028	5 d. multicoloured	60	65

DESIGNS: No. 2025, Queen Elizabeth the Queen Mother (pastel drawing); 2026, Wearing blue hat and dress; 2027, At desk (oil painting); 2028, Wearing green hat and dress.

1995. 50th Anniv of End of Second World War in the Pacific. As T **340** of Antigua. Multicoloured.

2030	5 d. Fairey Firefly	60	65
2031	5 d. Fairey Barracuda Mk III	60	65
2032	5 d. Supermarine Seafire II	60	65
2033	5 d. H.M.S. "Repulse" (battle cruiser)	60	65
2034	5 d. H.M.S. "Illustrious" (aircraft carrier)	60	65
2035	5 d. H.M.S. "Exeter" (cruiser)	60	65

240 Kenichi Fukui (1981 Chemistry)

1995. Centenary of Nobel Prize Trust Fund. Past Prize Winners. Multicoloured.

2037	2 d. Type **240**	20	25
2038	3 d. Gustav Stresemann (1929 Peace)	35	40
2039	5 d. Thomas Mann (1929 Literature)	60	65
2040	5 d. Marie Curie (1911 Chemistry)	60	65
2041	5 d. Adolf Butenandt (1939 Chemistry)	60	65
2042	5 d. Susumu Tonegwa (1987 Medicine)	60	65
2043	5 d. Nelly Sachs (1966 Literature)	60	65
2044	5 d. Yasunari Kawabata (1968 Literature)	60	65
2045	5 d. Hideki Yukawa (1949 Physics)	60	65
2046	5 d. Paul Ehrlich (1908 Medicine)	60	65
2047	5 d. Bisaku Sato (1974 Peace)	60	65
2048	5 d. Carl von Ossietsky (1935 Peace)	60	65
2049	8 d. Albert Schweitzer (1952 Peace)	90	95
2050	12 d. Leo Esaki (1973 Physics)	1·40	1·50
2051	15 d. Lech Walesa (1983 Peace)	1·75	1·90

Nos. 2040/8 were printed together, se-tenant, forming a composite design.

No. 2048 is dated "1974" and No. 2051 inscribed "Lech Walsea", both in error.

241 Bruce Jenner (U.S.A.) (decathlon)

1995. Olympic Games, Atlanta (1996) (1st issue). Multicoloured.

2053	1 d. Type **241**	10	15
2054	1 d. 25 Greg Louganis (U.S.A.) (diving)	15	20
2055	1 d. 50 Michael Gross (Germany) (50 metre butterfly)	20	25
2056	2 d. Vasily Alexeev (Russia) (weightlifting)	20	25
2057	3 d. Ewing (U.S.A.) and Corbalan (Spain) (basketball)	35	40
2058	3 d. Stefano Cerioni (Italy) (fencing) (vert)	35	40
2059	3 d. Alberto Cova (Italy) (10000 metres) (vert)	35	40
2060	3 d. Mary Lou Retton (U.S.A.) (gymnastics) (vert)	35	40
2061	3 d. Vladimir Artemov (Russia) (gymnastics) (vert)	35	40
2062	3 d. Florence Griffith-Joyner (U.S.A.) (400 metre relay) (vert)	35	40
2063	3 d. Brazil (football) (vert)	35	40
2064	3 d. Nelson Vails (U.S.A.) (sprint cycling) (vert)	35	40
2065	3 d. Cheryl Miller (U.S.A.) (basketball) (vert)	35	40
2066	5 d. U.S.A. v Brazil (men's volleyball)	60	65
2067	10 d. Svenden (West Germany) and Fernandez (U.S.A.) (water polo)	1·10	1·25
2068	15 d. Pertii Karppinen (Finland) (single sculls)	1·75	1·90

No. 2059 is inscribed "Alberto Covo" and No. 2064 "Nelson Valis", both in error.

See also Nos. 2281/2302.

242 Rotary Emblem and Rotarians supporting School for the Deaf

1995. Local Rotary and Boy Scout Projects. Multicoloured.

2070	2 d. Type **242**	20	25
2071	5 d. Scout wood badge course, 1980	60	65
2072	5 d. Scout Commissioner M. J. E. Sambou (vert)	60	65

243 "Zantedeschia rehmannii"

1995. African Flowers. Multicoloured.

2073	2 d. Type **243**	20	25
2074	3 d. "Kigelia africana"	35	40
2075	3 d. "Hibiscus schizopelatus"	35	40
2076	3 d. "Dombeya mastersii"	35	40
2077	3 d. "Agapanthus orientalis"	35	40
2078	3 d. "Strelitzia reginae"	35	40
2079	3 d. "Spathodea companulata"	35	40
2080	3 d. "Rhodolaena bakeriana"	35	40
2081	3 d. "Gazania rigens"	35	40
2082	3 d. "Ixianthes retzioides"	35	40
2083	3 d. "Canarina abyssinica"	35	40
2084	3 d. "Nerine bowdenii"	35	40
2085	3 d. "Zantedeschia aethiopica"	35	40
2086	3 d. "Aframomum sceptrum"	35	40
2087	3 d. "Schotia brachypetala"	35	40
2088	3 d. "Catharanthus roseus"	35	40
2089	3 d. "Protea grandiceps"	35	40
2090	3 d. "Plumbago capensis"	35	40
2091	3 d. "Uncarina grandidieri"	35	40
2092	5 d. "Euadenia eminens"	60	65
2093	10 d. "Passiflora vitifolia"	1·10	1·25
2094	15 d. "Dietes grandiflora"	1·75	1·90

Nos. 2074/82 and 2083/91 respectively were printed together, se-tenant, forming composite background designs.

244 Children outside Huts

1995. Kinderdorf International S.O.S. Children's Villages. Multicoloured.

2096	2 d. Type **244**	20	25
2097	2 d. Charity worker with children (vert)	20	25
2098	5 d. Children at party	60	65

245 Roy Orbison

1995. History of Rock n' Roll Music. Multicoloured.

2099	3 d. Type **245**	35	40
2100	3 d. Mick Jagger	35	40
2101	3 d. Bruce Springsteen	35	40
2102	3 d. Jimi Hendrix	35	40
2103	3 d. Bill Hailey	35	40
2104	3 d. Gene Vincent	35	40
2105	3 d. Buddy Holly	35	40
2106	3 d. Jerry Lee Lewis	35	40
2107	3 d. Chuck Berry	35	40

Nos. 2099/2107 were printed together, se-tenant, forming a composite design.

1995. Centenary of Cinema. As T **245** depicting James Dean. Multicoloured.

2109	3 d. As a boy	35	40
2110	3 d. On motorbike	35	40
2111	3 d. With sports car and trophy	35	40
2112	3 d. Close-up portrait	35	40
2113	3 d. Facing left	35	40
2114	3 d. Holding girl	35	40
2115	3 d. "Rebel without a Cause" (film)	35	40
2116	3 d. "Giant" (film)	35	40
2117	3 d. "East of Eden" (film)	35	40

Nos. 2109/17 were printed together, se-tenant, forming a composite design.

1995. Christmas. Religious Paintings. As T **357** of Antigua. Multicoloured.

2119	75 b. "Madonna and Child" (Maria della Vallicella)	10	10
2120	1 d. "Madonna" (Giotto)	10	10
2121	2 d. "The Flight into Egypt" (Luca Giordano)	20	25
2122	5 d. "The Epiphany" (Bondone)	60	65
2123	8 d. "Virgin and Child" (Burgkmair)	90	95
2124	12 d. "Madonna" (Bellini)	1·40	1·50

246 Terminal Building

1995. Opening of New Terminal Building, Banjul International Airport.

2126 **246**	1 d. multicoloured	10	10
2127	2 d. multicoloured	20	25
2128	3 d. multicoloured	35	40
2129	5 d. multicoloured	60	65

247 U.P.U. Emblem

1995. 121st Anniv of Universal Postal Union.

2130 **247**	1 d. black and violet	10	10
2131	2 d. black and blue	20	25
2132	3 d. black and red	35	40
2133	7 d. black and green	80	85

248 Commerson's Dolphin

1995. Whales and Dolphins. Multicoloured.

2134	2 d. Type **248**	20	25
2135	3 d. Bryde's whale	35	40
2136	3 d. Sperm whale	35	40
2137	3 d. Humpback whale	35	40
2138	3 d. Sei whale	35	40
2139	3 d. Blue whale	35	40
2140	3 d. Grey whale	35	40
2141	3 d. Fin whale	35	40
2142	3 d. Killer whale	35	40
2143	3 d. Right whale	35	40
2144	3 d. Northern right whale dolphin	35	40
2145	3 d. Spotted dolphin	35	40
2146	3 d. Common dolphin	35	40
2147	3 d. Pacific white-sided dolphin	35	40
2148	3 d. Atlantic humpbacked dolphin	35	40
2149	3 d. Atlantic white-sided dolphin	35	40
2150	3 d. White-beaked dolphin	35	40
2151	3 d. Striped dolphin	35	40
2152	3 d. Risso's dolphin	35	40
2153	5 d. Narwhal	60	65
2154	8 d. True's beaked whale	90	95
2155	10 d. Rough-toothed dolphin	1·10	1·25

Nos. 2135/43 and 2144/52 respectively were printed together, se-tenant, forming composite designs.

249 Big Pete as Seminole with Alligator

1995. Disney Cowboys and Indians. Walt Disney Cartoon Characters. Multicoloured.

2157	15 b. Type **249**	10	10
2158	20 b. Donald Duck as Chinook fisherman	10	10
2159	25 b. Huey, Dewey and Louie as Blackfoot braves	10	10
2160	30 b. Minnie Mouse shooting bottles	10	10
2161	40 b. Donald riding bull	10	10
2162	50 b. Mickey Mouse branding steer	10	10
2163	2 d. Donald in Tlingit mask	20	25
2164	3 d. Mickey bronco-busting	35	40
2165	12 d. Grandma Duck with lasso	1·40	1·50
2166	15 d. Mickey in Pomo canoe	1·75	1·90
2167	15 d. Goofy as ranch hand	1·75	1·90
2168	20 d. Goofy and Minnie with Navaho weavin	2·25	2·50

250 Rat

1996. Chinese New Year ("Year of the Rat").

2170 **250**	63 b. multicoloured	10	10
2171 –	75 b. multicoloured	10	10
2172 –	1 d. 50 multicoloured	20	25
2173 –	4 d. multicoloured	45	50

DESIGNS: 75 b. to 4 d. Different stylised rats.

251 "Don Tiburcio Perez y Cuervo" (detail) (Goya)

1996. 125th Anniv of Metropolitan Museum of Art, New York. Multicoloured.

2176/83	4 d. × 8 (Type **251**; "Jean Antoine Moltedo" (Ingres); "The Letter" (Corot); "General Etienne Gerard" (David); "Portrait of the Artist" (Van Gogh); "Joseph Henri Altes" (Degas); "Princess de Broglie" (Ingres); "Lady at the Table" (Cassatt))		
2184/91	4 d. × 8 ("Broken Eggs" (Greuze); "Johann Joachim Winckleman" (Mengs); "Col. George Coussmaker" (Reynolds); "Self Portrait with Pupils" (Labille-Guiard); "Courtesan holding a Fan" (Utamaro); "The Woodgatherers" (Gainsborough); "Mrs Grace Elliott" (Gainsborough); "The Drummond Children" (Raeburn))		
2192/9	4 d. × 8 ("Sunflowers" (Monet); "Still Life with Pansies" (Fantin-Latour); "Parisians enjoying the Parc" (Monet); "La Mere Larcheveque" (Pissarro); "Rue de L'Epicerie, Rouen" (Pissarro); "The Abduction of Rebecca" (Delacroix); "Daughter, Abraham-Ben-Chimol" (Delacroix); "Christ on Lake of Gennesaret" (Delacroix))		
2200/7	4 d. × 8 ("Henry Prince of Wales" (Peake); "Saints Peter, Martha, Mary and Leonard" (Correggio); "Marriage Feast at Cana" (Juan de Flandes); "Portrait of One of Wedigh Family" (Holbein); "Guillaume Bude" (Clouet); "Portrait of a Cardinal" (El Greco); "St. Jerome as a Cardinal" (El Greco); "Portrait of a Man" (Titian))		
2176/2207	Set of 32	14·00	14·50

252 Fire-eater

253 Bruce Lee

1996. Fire-eating in the Gambia.

2209 **252**	1 d. multicoloured	10	10
2210 –	2 d. multicoloured	20	25
2211 –	3 d. multicoloured	35	40
2212 –	7 d. multicoloured	80	85

DESIGNS: 2 d. to 7 d. Various fire-eating scenes, the 2 d. and 7 d. being horiz.

1996. Bruce Lee (film star) Commemoration. Different portraits. Multicoloured.

2213	3 d. Wearing cap and mask	35	40
2214	3 d. Type **253**	35	40
2215	3 d. Facing left	35	40
2216	3 d. Wearing blue jumper and with hand to face	35	40
2217	3 d. Wearing buff jacket	35	40
2218	3 d. Wearing brown jacket (Chinese characters in brown)	35	40
2219	3 d. Wearing black shirt (Chinese characters in lilac)	35	40
2220	3 d. Wearing white shirt	35	40
2221	3 d. Bare-chested	35	40

254 Donald Duck and Big Pete giving Blood

1996. Voluntary Activities. Walt Disney Cartoon Characters. Multicoloured.

2223	1 d. Type **254**	10	10
2224	4 d. Daisy Duck and Minnie Mouse adopting pets	45	50
2225	5 d. Goofy as one-man band raising money for the needy	60	65
2226	10 d. Goofy teaching outdoor skills	1·10	1·25
2227	15 d. Minnie teaching reading	1·75	1·90
2228	20 d. Donald, Mickey and Goofy as volunteer fire fighters	2·25	2·50

255 Roan Antelope

1996. Wildlife. Multicoloured.

2230	3 d. Type **255**	35	40
2231	3 d. Lesser bushbaby	35	40
2232	3 d. Black leopard	35	40
2233	3 d. Guinea forest red colobus	35	40
2234	3 d. Kobs	35	40
2235	3 d. Common eland	35	40
2236	4 d. African buffalo	45	50
2237	4 d. Herd of topi	45	50
2238	4 d. Vervet	45	50
2239	4 d. Hippopotamuses	45	50
2240	4 d. Waterbuck	45	50
2241	4 d. Senegal chameleon	45	50
2242	4 d. Western green mamba	45	50
2243	4 d. Slender-snouted crocodile	45	50
2244	4 d. Adanson's mud turtle	45	50
2245	15 d. African civet	1·75	1·90

Nos. 2230/5 and 2236/44 respectively were printed together, se-tenant, Nos. 2236/44 forming a composite design.

1996. 70th Birthday of Queen Elizabeth II. As T **364** of Antigua showing different photographs. Multicoloured.

2247	8 d. As Type **364** of Antigua	90	95
2248	8 d. Wearing tiara facing right	90	95
2249	8 d. Wearing tiara facing left	90	95

256 Pumper Hose Cart, U.S.A. (1850)

1996. Classic Road Transport. Fire Engines (Nos. 2251/6) or Cars (Nos. 2257/62). Multicoloured.

2251	4 d. Type **256**	45	50
2252	4 d. Steam fire engine, U.S.A. (1891)	45	50
2253	4 d. Lausitzer engine, Germany (1864)	45	50
2254	4 d. Chemical engine, Great Britain (1902)	45	50
2255	4 d. Motor fire engine, Great Britain (1904)	45	50
2256	4 d. Colonia No. 5 engine, Germany (1860)	45	50
2257	4 d. Fiat Tipo 510, Italy (1912)	45	50
2258	4 d. Toyota Model 4B Phaeton, Japan (1936)	45	50
2259	4 d. Nag C4B, Germany (1924)	45	50
2260	4 d. Cadillac, U.S.A. (1903)	45	50
2261	4 d. Bentley, Great Britain (1925)	45	50
2262	4 d. Renault Model AX, France (1909)	45	50

257 Bulgarian Team

1996. European Football Championship, England. Multicoloured.

2264	2 d. Type **257**	20	25
2265	2 d. Croatian team	20	25
2266	2 d. Czech Republic team	20	25
2267	2 d. Danish team	20	25
2268	2 d. English team	20	25
2269	2 d. French team	20	25
2270	2 d. German team	20	25
2271	2 d. Dutch team	20	25
2272	2 d. Italian team	20	25
2273	2 d. Portuguese team	20	25
2274	2 d. Rumanian team	20	25
2275	2 d. Russian team	20	25
2276	2 d. Scottish team	20	25
2277	2 d. Spanish team	20	25
2278	2 d. Swiss team	20	25
2279	2 d. Turkish team	20	25

258 Ray Ewry (U.S.A.) (standing high jump), 1912

260 Jacqueline Kennedy Onassis in Wedding Dress

259 Roman Officer and Pillar of Absalom

1996. Olympic Games, Atlanta (2nd issue). Previous Gold Medal Winners. Multicoloured.

2281	1 d. Type **258**	10	10
2282	2 d. Fanny Durack (Australia) (100m freestyle swimming), 1912	20	25
2283	3 d. Fu Mingxia (China) (platform diving), 1992	30	35
2284	3 d. H. Henkel (Germany) (high jump), 1992	30	35
2285	3 d. Spanish team (soccer), 1992	30	35
2286	3 d. Jackie Joyner-Kersee (U.S.A.) (heptathlon), 1988 and 1992	30	35
2287	3 d. T. Gutsu (Russia) (gymnastics), 1992	30	35
2288	3 d. M. Johnson (U.S.A.) (400m running), 1992	30	35
2289	3 d. Lin Li (China) (200m medley swimming), 1992	30	35
2290	3 d. G. Devers (U.S.A.) (100m running), 1992	30	35
2291	3 d. Michael Powell (U.S.A.) (long jump), 1992	30	35
2292	3 d. Japanese volleyball team, 1964	30	35
2293	3 d. Li Neng (China) (floor exercises), 1984	30	35
2294	3 d. S. Bubka (U.S.S.R.) (pole vault), 1988	30	35
2295	3 d. Nadia Comaneci (Romania) (gymnastics), 1976	30	35
2296	3 d. Edwin Moses (U.S.A.) (400m hurdles), 1984	30	35
2297	3 d. Victor Scherbo (Russia) (gymnastics), 1992	30	35
2298	3 d. Evelyn Ashford (U.S.A.) (100m running), 1984	30	35
2299	3 d. Mohammed Ali (U.S.A.) (light heavyweight boxing), 1960	30	35
2300	3 d. Carl Lewis and C. Smith (U.S.A.) (400m relay), 1984	30	35
2301	5 d. Stockholm Olympic arena, 1912	60	65
2302	10 d. Jim Thorpe (U.S.A.) (decathalon and pentathlon), 1912	1·10	1·25

1996. 50th Anniv of U.N.I.C.E.F. As T **366** of Antigua. Multicoloured.

2304	63 b. Boy holding shoes	10	10
2305	3 d. Girl being inoculated	35	40
2306	8 d. Boy holding ladle	90	95
2307	10 d. Child with blanket	1·10	1·25

1996. 3000th Anniv of Jerusalem. Multicoloured.

2309	1 d. 50 Type **259**	20	25
2310	2 d. Turk and Gate of Mercy	20	25
2311	3 d. Ancient Greek and Church of the Holy Sepulchre	35	40
2312	10 d. Modern Hasidic Jew at Wailing Wall	1·10	1·25

1996. Centenary of Radio. Entertainers. As T **368** of Antigua. Multicoloured.

2314	1 d. Glenn Miller	10	10
2315	4 d. Louis Armstrong	45	50
2316	5 d. Nat "King" Cole	60	65
2317	10 d. The Andrew Sisters	1·10	1·25

No. 2314 is inscribed "Glen Miller" in error.

1996. Famous People of the 20th Century. Multicoloured.

2319	5 d. Type **260**	60	65
2320	5 d. Jaqueline Kennedy and White House	60	65
2321	5 d. Jaqueline Kennedy wearing pink hat	60	65
2322	5 d. Jaqueline Kennedy and motor yacht	60	65
2323	5 d. Jacqueline Kennedy wearing red jumper	60	65
2324	5 d. Jacqueline Kennedy and horse	60	65
2325	5 d. Jacqueline Kennedy on book	60	65
2326	5 d. Jacqueline Kennedy in blue dress and three rows of pearls	60	65
2327	5 d. Jacqueline Kennedy and corner of fountain	60	65
2328	5 d. President John Kennedy	60	65
2329	5 d. Jacqueline Kennedy (inscr in capitals)	60	65
2330	5 d. Willy Brandt	60	65
2331	5 d. Marilyn Monroe	60	65
2332	5 d. Mao Tse-tung	60	65
2333	5 d. Sung Ching Ling	60	65
2334	5 d. Charles De Gaulle	60	65
2335	5 d. Marlene Dietrich	60	65

No. 2330 is inscr "WILLIE BRANDT", No. 2331 "MARYLYN MONROE" and No. 2332 "MAO TSE TONG", all in error.

261 Richard Petty's 1969 Ford

1996. Richard Petty (stock car driver) Commem. Multicoloured.

2337	5 d. Type **261**	60	65
2338	5 d. Richard Petty	60	65
2339	5 d. Dodge Magnum, 1978	60	65
2340	5 d. Pontiac, 1987	60	65
2341	5 d. Pontiac, 1989	60	65
2342	5 d. Dodge Daytona, 1975	60	65

1996. Results of European Football Championships, England. As Nos. 2265/6, 2268, 2270, 2272 and 2275, but each additionally inscribed with date and match result. Multicoloured.

2344	2 d. Croatian team ("23/6/96 Germany 2, Croatia 1")	20	25
2345	2 d. Czech Republic team ("9/6/96 Germany 2, Czech Rep. 0")	20	25
2346	2 d. English team ("26/6/96 Germany 6, England 5")	20	25
2347	2 d. German team ("30/6/96 Germany 2, Czech Rep. 1")	20	25
2348	2 d. Italian team ("19/6/96 Germany 0, Italy 0")	20	25
2349	2 d. Russian team ("16/6/96 Germany 3, Russia 0")	20	25

262 Elvis Presley with Microphone

263 Bob Dylan

1996. Elvis Presley Commemoration. Different Portraits. Multicoloured.

2351	5 d. Type **262**	60	65
2352	5 d. In dinner jacket	60	65
2353	5 d. In Mexican outfit	60	65
2354	5 d. Wearing blue jumper	60	65
2355	5 d. In leather jacket	60	65
2356	5 d. Wearing lei	60	65

1996. Rock and Roll Legends. Bob Dylan.

2357	**263** 5 d. multicoloured	60	65

264 Supermarine Spitfire Prototype K5054

1996. 65th Anniv of Britain's Victory in Schneider Trophy Air Race. Multicoloured.

2358	4 d. Type **264**	45	50
2359	4 d. First production Spitfire K9787	45	50
2360	4 d. Spitfire Mk 1A in Battle of Britain	45	50
2361	4 d. Spitfire LFmk IXE with D-Day markings	45	50
2362	4 d. Spitfire Mk XII (first with "Griffon" engine)	45	50
2363	4 d. Spitfire Mk XIVC with jungle markings	45	50
2364	4 d. Spitfire XIX of Royal Swedish Air Force	45	50
2365	4 d. Spitfire Mk XIX	45	50
2366	4 d. Spitfire FMk 22/24 (final variant)	45	50
2367	4 d. Spitfire Mk XIX of Royal Swedish Air Force (from below)	45	50
2368	4 d. Spitfire Mk VB of United States Army Air Corps	45	50
2369	4 d. Spitfire Mk VC of French Air Force	45	50
2370	4 d. Spitfire Mk VB of Soviet Air Force	45	50
2371	4 d. Spitfire Mk IXE of Netherlands East Indies Air Force	45	50
2372	4 d. Spitfire Mk IXE of Israeli Air Force	45	50
2373	4 d. Spitfire Mk VIII of Royal Australian Air Force	45	50
2374	4 d. Spitfire Mk VB of Turkish Air Force	45	50
2375	4 d. Spitfire Mk XI of Royal Danish Air Force	45	50

265 Egyptian Plover

1996. Birds. Multicoloured.

2377	50 b. Type **265**	10	10
2378	63 b. Painted snipe	10	10
2379	75 b. Golden-breasted bunting	10	10
2380	1 d. Bateleur	10	10
2381	1 d. 50 Didric cuckoo	20	25
2382	2 d. Turtle dove	20	25
2383	3 d. Village weaver	35	40
2384	4 d. Common roller	45	50
2385	5 d. Cut-throat	60	65
2386	10 d. Hoopoe	1·10	1·25
2387	15 d. White-faced scops owl	1·75	1·90
2388	20 d. Narina trogon	2·25	2·40
2389	25 d. Lesser pied kingfisher	3·00	3·25
2390	30 d. Common kestrel	3·50	3·75
2391	40 d. Temminck's courser	4·75	5·00
2392	50 d. European bee-eater	5·75	6·00

No. 2388 is inscribed "TROGAN" in error.

1996. Christmas. Religious Paintings. As T **369** of Antigua.

2393	1 d. multicoloured	10	10
2394	1 d. 50 multicoloured	20	25
2395	2 d. multicoloured	20	25
2396	3 d. multicoloured	35	40
2397	10 d. multicoloured	1·10	1·25
2398	15 d. multicoloured	1·75	1·90

DESIGNS: 1 d. 50 to 15 d. Different details of "Assumption of the Madonna" (Tiziano Vecellio).

267 Ox

268 "Arch 22" Monument

1997. Chinese New Year ("Year of the Ox").

2401	**267**	63 b. multicoloured	10	10
2402	–	75 b. multicoloured	10	10
2403	–	1 d. 50 multicoloured	20	25
2404	–	4 d. multicoloured	45	50

DESIGNS: 75 b. to 4 d. Symbolic oxen.

1997. Economic Development. Multicoloured.

2407	63 b. Type **268**	10	10
2408	1 d. Tractor (horiz)	10	10
2409	1 d. 50 Man planting rice	20	25
2410	2 d. As Type **268**, but with white panel at top	20	25
2411	3 d. Model of Banjul International Airport terminal building (horiz)	35	40
2412	5 d. Chamoi Bridge (horiz)	60	65

269 Monkey King extinguishing Fire on Flame Mountain

1997. Mickey Mouse's Journey to the West. Disney Cartoon Characters. Multicoloured.

2414 2 d. Type **269** 20 25
2415 2 d. Demon Ox and Monkey King fighting 20 25
2416 2 d. Mickey, Donald, Monkey King and Master San Tsang 20 25
2417 2 d. Fighting the Spider Demon 20 25
2418 2 d. Fighting the White Skeleton Demon 20 25
2419 2 d. The real and the fake Monkey King 20 25
2420 3 d. Monkey King trapped in furnace 35 40
2421 3 d. Monkey King with magic weapon 35 40
2422 3 d. Type **269** 35 40
2423 3 d. At the Gate of South Heaven 35 40
2424 3 d. Tasting the celestial peaches 35 40
2425 3 d. Monkey King rescued from Five-Finger Mountain . . 35 40

270 Jackie Chan

1997. "HONG KONG '97" International Stamp Exhibition. Jackie Chan (film star). Multicoloured.

2427 4 d. Type **270** 45 50
2428 4 d. Wearing red jacket . . . 45 50
2429 4 d. In open-necked shirt . . 45 50
2430 4 d. Bare-chested 45 50
2431 4 d. Wearing black jacket . . 45 50
2432 4 d. Wearing black and white spotted shirt 45 50
2433 4 d. Wearing white T-shirt and red anorak 45 50
2434 4 d. Wearing white sleeveless T-shirt 45 50

271 Clouded Leopard

1997. Endangered Species. Multicoloured.

2436 1 d. 50 Type **271** 20 25
2437 1 d. 50 Audouin's gull . . . 20 25
2438 1 d. 50 Leatherback turtle . . 20 25
2439 1 d. 50 White-eared pheasant 20 25
2440 1 d. 50 Kakapo 20 25
2441 1 d. 50 Right whale 20 25
2442 1 d. 50 Black-footed ferret . . 20 25
2443 1 d. 50 Dwarf lemur 20 25
2444 1 d. 50 Peacock-pheasant . . 20 25
2445 1 d. 50 Brown hyena 20 25
2446 1 d. 50 Cougar 20 25
2447 1 d. 50 Gharial 20 25
2448 1 d. 50 Monk seal 20 25
2449 1 d. 50 Mountain gorilla . . . 20 25
2450 1 d. 50 Blyth's tragopan . . . 20 25
2451 1 d. 50 Malayan tapir 20 25
2452 1 d. 50 Black rhinoceros . . . 20 25
2453 1 d. 50 Polar bear 20 25
2454 1 d. 50 Red colobus 20 25
2455 1 d. 50 Tiger 20 25
2456 1 d. 50 Arabian oryx 20 25
2457 1 d. 50 Baiji 20 25
2458 1 d. 50 Ruffed lemur 20 25
2459 1 d. 50 California condor . . 20 25
2460 1 d. 50 Blue-headed quail dove 20 25
2461 1 d. 50 Numbat 20 25
2462 1 d. 50 Congo peacock . . . 20 25
2463 1 d. 50 White uakari 20 25
2464 1 d. 50 Eskimo curlew . . . 20 25
2465 1 d. 50 Gouldian finch . . . 20 25
2466 1 d. 50 Coelacanth 20 25
2467 1 d. 50 Toucan barbet . . . 20 25
2468 1 d. 50 Snow leopard 20 25
2469 1 d. 50 Queen Alexandra's birdwing 20 25
2470 1 d. 50 Dalmatian pelican . . 20 25
2471 1 d. 50 Chaco tortoise . . . 20 25
2472 1 d. 50 Mekong catfish . . . 20 25
2473 1 d. 50 Helmeted hornbill . . 20 25
2474 1 d. 50 White-eyed river martin 20 25
2475 1 d. 50 Fluminense swallowtail 20 25

272 Monkey

1997. "The Jungle Book" by Rudyard Kipling. Multicoloured.

2477 3 d. Type **272** 35 40
2478 3 d. Baloo (bear) 35 40
2479 3 d. Elephant 35 40
2480 3 d. Monkey and temple . . 35 40
2481 3 d. Bagheera (panther) . . 35 40
2482 3 d. Buffalo 35 40
2483 3 d. Mandrill 35 40
2484 3 d. Shere Khan (tiger) . . . 35 40
2485 3 d. Rama (wolf) 35 40
2486 3 d. Kaa (cobra) 35 40
2487 3 d. Mongoose 35 40
2488 3 d. Mowgli 35 40

Nos. 2477/88 were printed together, se-tenant, with the backgrounds forming a composite design.

273 "Polyporus squamosus"

1997. Fungi. Multicoloured.

2489 1 d. Type **273** 10 15
2490 3 d. "Armillaria tabescens" . 35 40
2491 4 d. "Amanita caesarea" (vert) 45 50
2492 4 d. "Lepiota procera" (vert) 45 50
2493 4 d. "Hygrophorus psittacinus" (vert) 45 50
2494 4 d. "Russula xerampelina" (vert) 45 50
2495 4 d. "Laccaria amethystina" (vert) 45 50
2496 4 d. "Coprinus micaceus" (vert) 45 50
2497 4 d. "Boletus edulis" (vert) . 45 50
2498 4 d. "Morchella esculenta" (vert) 45 50
2499 4 d. "Otidea auricula" (vert) 45 50
2500 5 d. "Collybia velutipes" . . 60 65
2501 10 d. "Sarcoscypha coccinea" 1·10 1·25

1997. 50th Anniv of U.N.E.S.C.O. As T **374** of Antigua. Multicoloured.

2503 1 d. Cloister, Horyu-ji, Japan 10 15
2504 2 d. Great Wall, China . . . 20 25
2505 3 d. Statues, Ayutthaya, Thailand 35 40
2506 4 d. Ascension Convent, Santa Maria, Philippines 45 50
2507 4 d. Mount Nimba Nature Reserve, Guinea (vert) . . 45 50
2508 4 d. Banc d'Argun National Park, Mauritania (vert) . . 45 50
2509 4 d. Doorway, Marrakesh, Morocco (vert) 45 50
2510 4 d. Ichkeul National Park, Tunisia (vert) 45 50
2511 4 d. Village pottery, Mali (vert) 45 50
2512 4 d. Hippopotamus, Salonga National Park, Zaire (vert) 45 50
2513 4 d. Timgad Roman Ruins, Algeria (vert) 45 50
2514 4 d. Wooden statue, Benin (vert) 45 50
2515 4 d. Temple, Magao Caves, China (vert) 45 50
2516 4 d. Statue, Magao Caves (vert) 45 50
2517 4 d. Domes, Magao Caves (vert) 45 50
2518 4 d. Great Wall from air, China (vert) 45 50
2519 4 d. Statue, Great Wall (vert) 45 50
2520 4 d. Bronze Bird, Imperial Palace, China (vert) . . . 45 50
2521 4 d. Temples, Imperial Palace, China (vert) 45 50
2522 4 d. Dragon statue, Imperial Palace (vert) 45 50
2523 4 d. Kyoto Gardens, Japan (vert) 45 50
2524 4 d. Himeji Castle, Japan (vert) 45 50
2525 4 d. Horyu-ji Temple, Japan (vert) 45 50
2526 4 d. Buddha, Horyu-ji, Japan (vert) 45 50
2527 4 d. Yakushima Forest, Japan (vert) 45 50
2528 4 d. Ancient tree, Yakushima Forest, Japan (vert) . . . 45 50
2529 4 d. Temple, Kyoto, Japan (vert) 45 50
2530 4 d. Pavilion, Kyoto, Japan (vert) 45 50
2531 5 d. Riverside houses, Inselstadt, Germany . . . 60 65
2532 5 d. Rosaleda Gardens, Bamberg, Germany . . . 60 65
2533 5 d. Bamberg Cathedral, Germany 60 65
2534 5 d. Timbered house, Maulbronn, Germany . . 60 65
2535 5 d. Maulbronn Monastry, Germany 60 65
2536 5 d. Ruins at Delphi, Greece 60 65
2537 5 d. Rhodes waterfront, Greece 60 65
2538 5 d. Knights' Hospital, Rhodes, Greece 60 65
2539 5 d. Temple, Delphi, Greece . 60 65
2540 5 d. Delphi from air, Greece . 60 65
2541 5 d. Foliage, Shirakami-Sanchi, Japan 60 65
2542 5 d. Notice board, Shirakami-Sanchi, Japan 60 65
2543 5 d. Tower, Himeji Castle, Japan 60 65
2544 5 d. Roof tops, Himeji Castle, Japan 60 65
2545 5 d. Gateway, Himeji Castle, Japan 60 65
2546 10 d. Komodo Dragons, Indonesia . . . . 1·10 1·40
2547 15 d. Ancient hut, Timbuktu, Mali . . . . 1·75 1·90

274 Minnie Mouse, 1928

1997. Minnie Mouse Through the Years. Designs showing Disney cartoon character in years stated. Multicoloured.

2549 4 d. Type **274** 45 50
2550 4 d. In 1933 . . . . 45 50
2551 4 d. In 1934 . . . . 45 50
2552 4 d. In 1937 . . . . 45 50
2553 4 d. In 1938 . . . . 45 50
2554 4 d. In 1941 . . . . 45 50
2555 4 d. In 1950 . . . . 45 50
2556 4 d. In 1990 . . . . 45 50
2557 4 d. In 1997 . . . . 45 50

275 Dipstick

1997. "101 Dalmatians". Disney cartoon characters. Multicoloured.

2559 50 b. Type **275** 10 10
2560 50 b. Fidget 10 10
2561 50 b. Jewel 10 10
2562 50 b. Lucky 10 10
2563 50 b. Two-Tone 10 10
2564 50 b. Wizzer 10 10
2565 2 d. Two puppies playing (horiz) 20 25
2566 2 d. Puppy and pig (horiz) . . 20 25
2567 2 d. Two puppies with butterfly (horiz) 20 25
2568 2 d. Puppy lying on back (horiz) 20 25
2569 2 d. Puppy with ball (horiz) 20 25
2570 2 d. Puppy with bone (horiz) . 20 25
2571 2 d. One puppy pulling another puppy's tail (horiz) . . . 20 25
2572 2 d. Two puppies pulling third puppy's ears (horiz) . . . 20 25
2573 2 d. Puppy with teddy bear (horiz) 20 25
2574 3 d. Puppy asleep on biscuit box (horiz) 35 40
2575 3 d. Puppy with hose (horiz) . 35 40
2576 3 d. Puppy and bottle (horiz) 35 40
2577 3 d. Puppy and biscuit bowl (horiz) 35 40
2578 3 d. Puppy wearing hat (horiz) 35 40
2579 3 d. Three puppies with lipstick (horiz) 35 40
2580 3 d. Puppy tying another up with string (horiz) 35 40
2581 3 d. Two puppies and lunch box (horiz) 35 40
2582 3 d. Three puppies and computer (horiz) 35 40

276 Juventus Team, 1897

1997. Centenary of Juventus Football Team. Multicoloured.

2584 5 d. Type **276** 60 65
2585 5 d. Centenary emblem and player 60 65
2586 5 d. Giampiero Boniperti . . 60 65
2587 5 d. Roberto Bettega 60 65
2588 5 d. Juventus team, 1996 . . 60 65
2589 5 d. Juventus '97 logo . . . 60 65

1997. 10th Anniv of Chernobyl Nuclear Disaster. As T **376** of Antigua. Multicoloured.

2591 15 d. As Type **376** of Antigua 1·75 1·90
2592 15 d. As No. 2591 but inscribed "CHABAD'S CHILDREN OF CHERNOBYL" . . . 1·75 1·90

1997. 50th Death Anniv of Paul Harris (founder of Rotary International). As T **377** of Antigua. Multicoloured.

2593 10 d. Rotary President Sydney Pascall planting tree of friendship . . . . 1·10 1·25

1997. Golden Wedding of Queen Elizabeth and Prince Philip. As T **378** of Antigua. Multicoloured.

2595 4 d. Queen Elizabeth II . . . 45 50
2596 4 d. Royal coat of arms . . 45 50
2597 4 d. Queen Elizabeth and Prince Philip applauding 45 50
2598 4 d. Queen Elizabeth and Prince Philip taking the salute . . 45 50
2599 4 d. Royal Yacht "Britannia" 45 50
2600 4 d. Prince Philip 45 50

1997. "Pacific '97" International Stamp Exhibition, San Francisco. Death Centenary of Henrich von Stephan (founder of U.P.U.). As T **379** of Antigua.

2602 5 d. mauve 60 65
2603 5 d. brown 60 65
2604 5 d. green and black . . . 60 65

DESIGNS: No. 2602, Von Stephan and Otto von Bismarck; 2603, Von Stephan and Mercury; 2604, Mail wagon, Boston, 1900.

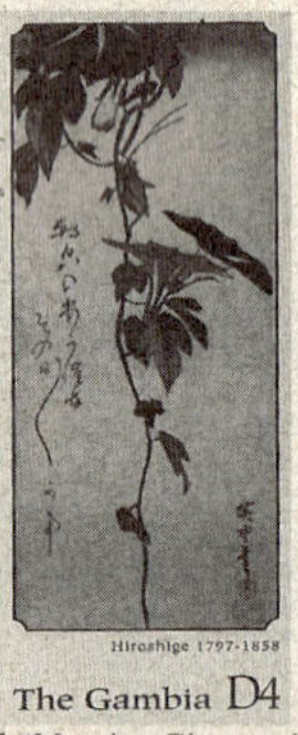

277 "Morning Glory and Cricket"

1997. Birth Bicentenary of Hiroshige (Japanese painter). Multicoloured.

2606/11 4 d. × 6 (Type **277**; "Dragonfly and Begonia"; "Two Ducks swimming among Reeds"; "A Black-naped Oriole perched on a Stem of Rose Mallow"; "A Pheasant on a Snow-covered Pine"; "A Cuckoo flying through the Rain")
2612/17 4 d. × 6 ("An Egret among Rushes"; "Peacock and Peonies"; "Three Wild Geese flying across the Moon"; "A Cock in the Snow"; "A Pheasant and Bracken"; "Peonies") .
2618/23 4 d. × 6 ("Sparrow and Bamboo"; "Mandarin Ducks on an Icy Pond with Brown Leaves falling"; "Blossoming Plum Tree"; "Java Sparrow and Magnolia"; "Chinese Bellflowers and Miscanthus"; "A Small Black Bird clinging to a Tendril of Ivy") . . . .
2624/9 5 d. × 6 ("Sparrows and Camellia in Snow", "Parrot on a Branch of Pine"; "A Long-tailed Blue Bird on a Branch of Flowering Plum"; "Sparrow and Bamboo"; "Bird in a Tree"; "A Wild Duck swimming beneath Snow-laden reeds") . . .
2630/5 5 d. × 6 ("Kingfisher above a Yellow-flowered Water Plant"; "Wagtail and Roses"; "A Mandarin Duck on a Snowy Bank"; "A Japanese White-eye on a Persimmon Branch"; "Sparrows and Camellia in Snow"; "Kingfisher and Moon above a Yellow-flowered Water Plant")
2636/41 5 d. × 6 ("Sparrow and Bamboo by Night"; "Birds Flying over Waves"; "Blossoming Plum Tree with Full Moon"; "Kingfisher and Iris"; "A Blue-and-White Flycatcher on a Hibiscus Flower"; "Mandarin Ducks in Snowfall") . .
2606/41 Set of 35 15·00 16·00

1997. 175th Anniv of Brothers Grimm's Third Collection of Fairy Tales. Little Red Riding Hood. As T **380** of Antigua. Multicoloured.

2643	10 d. Grandma's cottage	1·10	1·25
2644	10 d. Little Red Riding Hood	1·10	1·25
2645	10 d. The Wolf	1·10	1·25

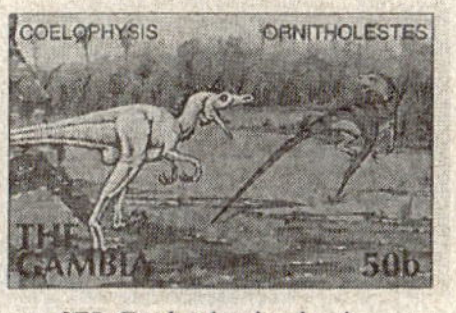

278 Coelophysis chasing Ornitholestes

1997. Dinosaurs. Multicoloured.

2647	50 b. Type **278**	10	10
2648	63 b. Spinosaurus	10	10
2649	75 b. Kentrosaurus	10	10
2650	1 d. Ceratosaurus	10	10
2651	1 d. 50 Stygimoloch	20	25
2652	2 d. Troodon	20	25
2653	3 d. Velociraptor	35	40
2654	4 d. Triceratops	45	50
2655	4 d. Anurognathus	45	50
2656	4 d. Pteranodon	45	50
2657	4 d. Pterosaurus	45	50
2658	4 d. Saltasaurus	45	50
2659	4 d. Agathaumus	45	50
2660	4 d. Stegosaurus	45	50
2661	4 d. Albertosaurus libratus	45	50
2662	4 d. Three Lesothosauruses running	45	50
2663	4 d. Five Lesothosauruses running	45	50
2664	4 d. Tarbosaurus bataar	45	50
2665	4 d. Brachiosaurus	45	50
2666	4 d. Styracosaurus	45	50
2667	4 d. Baryonyx	45	50
2668	4 d. Coelophysis	45	50
2669	4 d. Carnotaurus	45	50
2670	4 d. Compsognathus longipes	45	50
2671	4 d. Compsognathus "Elegant Jaw"	45	50
2672	4 d. Stenonychosaurus	45	50
2673	4 d. Protoceratops	60	65
2674	10 d. Ornithomimus	1·10	1·25
2675	15 d. Stegosaurus	1·75	1·90
2676	20 d. Ankylosaurus saichania	2·25	2·40

Nos. 2655/63 and 2664/72 respectively were printed together, se-tenant, with the backgrounds forming composite designs.

279 Margaret Thatcher and Deng Xiaoping toasting Joint Declaration, 1984

1997. Return of Hong Kong to China. Multicoloured.

2678	3 d. Type **279**	35	40
2679	3 d. Signing Joint Declaration on Hong Kong, 1984	35	40
2680	3 d. Signing Joint Declaration on Macao, 1987	35	40
2681	3 d. Deng Xiaoping toasting Prime Minister Anibal Silva of Portugal	35	40
2682	4 d. Hong Kong in 1843 and Governor Sir Henry Pottinger	45	50
2683	4 d. Kowloon in 1860 and Governor Sir Hercules Robinson	45	50
2684	4 d. Reception in New Territories, 1898, and Governor Sir Henry Blake	45	50
2685	5 d. Governor Sir Henry Pottinger and British warship	60	65
2686	5 d. Governor Christopher Patten and Lantau Bridge	60	65
2687	5 d. Chief Executive C.H. Tung and Hong Kong by night	60	65
2688	6 d. Signing the Treaty of Nanking, 1842	70	75
2689	6 d. Signing the Japanese Surrender of Hong Kong, 1945	70	75
2690	6 d. Signing of the Sino-British Joint Declaration, 1984	70	75

280 Great Mosque, Samarra, Iran

1997. Natural and Man-made Wonders of the World. Multicoloured.

2691	63 b. Type **280**	10	10
2692	75 b. Moai statues, Easter Island (horiz)	10	10
2693	1 d. Golden Gate Bridge, San Francisco (horiz)	10	10
2694	1 d. 50 The Statue of Liberty, New York	20	25
2695	2 d. The Parthenon, Athens (horiz)	20	25
2696	3 d. Pyramid of the Sun, Mexico (horiz)	35	40
2697	5 d. The Rock of Gibraltar (horiz)	60	65
2698	5 d. St. Peter's Basilica, Rome (horiz)	60	65
2699	5 d. Santa Sophia, Istanbul (horiz)	60	65
2700	5 d. "Gateway to the West" monument, St. Louis (horiz)	60	65
2701	5 d. Great Wall of China (horiz)	60	65
2702	5 d. City of Carcassonne, France (horiz)	60	65
2703	5 d. Stonehenge, England (horiz)	60	65
2704	5 d. Hughes HK-1 "Spruce Goose" flying boat (World's largest aircraft) (horiz)	60	65
2705	5 d. Hoverspeed "Seacat" catamaran (fastest Atlantic crossing by a commercial catamaran) (horiz)	60	65
2706	5 d. "Thrust 2" car (official land speed record) (horiz)	60	65
2707	5 d. Stepped Pyramid, Egypt (horiz)	60	65
2708	5 d. L.N.E.R. Clas A4 "Mallard" (fastest steam locomotive), 1938 (horiz)	60	65

No. 2702 is inscribed "CARCASSONNNE" in error.

281 Downhill Skiing

1997. Winter Olympic Games, Nagano (1998). Multicoloured.

2710	5 d. Type **281**	60	65
2711	5 d. Two-man bobsleigh (vert)	60	65
2712	5 d. Freestyle skiing (vert)	60	65
2713	5 d. Speed skating (vert)	60	65
2714	5 d. Downhill skiing (No. 8 on bib) (vert)	60	65
2715	5 d. Womens figure skating (vert)	60	65
2716	5 d. Downhill skiing (No. 4 on bib) (vert)	60	65
2717	5 d. Pairs figure skating (vert)	60	65
2718	5 d. Cross-country (vert)	60	65
2719	5 d. Ski jumping (vert)	60	65
2720	5 d. One-man luge	60	65
2721	5 d. Ice hockey	60	65
2722	5 d. Four-man bobsleigh	60	65
2723	5 d. Ski-jumping	60	65
2724	5 d. Curling	60	65
2725	5 d. Figure skating	60	65
2726	5 d. Speed skating	60	65
2727	5 d. Biathlon	60	65
2728	5 d. Downhill skiing (different)	60	65
2729	10 d. One-man luge	1·10	1·25
2730	15 d. Speed skating	1·75	1·90
2731	20 d. Ice hockey	2·25	2·40

282 Brown Pelican

1997. Sea Birds. Multicoloured.

2733	3 d. Type **282**	35	40
2734	3 d. Galapagos penguin	35	40
2735	3 d. Red-billed tropic bird	35	40
2736	3 d. Little tern	35	40
2737	3 d. Dunlin	35	40
2738	3 d. Kittiwake	35	40
2739	3 d. Atlantic puffin	35	40
2740	3 d. Wandering albatross	35	40
2741	3 d. Masked booby	35	40
2742	3 d. Galucous winged tern	35	40
2743	3 d. Arctic tern	35	40
2744	3 d. Piping plover	35	40
2745	5 d. Roseate tern	60	65
2746	10 d. Red-legged cormorant	1·10	1·25
2747	15 d. Blue-footed booby	1·75	1·90
2748	20 d. Sanderling	2·25	2·40

The captions on Nos. 2745/6 are transposed in error.

283 Scottish Fold Cat

1997. Cats and Dogs. Multicoloured.

2750	63 b. Type **283**	10	10
2751	75 b. Dalmatian	10	10
2752	1 d. Rottweiler	10	15
2753	1 d. 50 American curl cat	20	25
2754	2 d. British bi-colour cat	20	25
2755	3 d. Newfoundland	35	40
2756	3 d. Devon Rex cat	35	40
2757	4 d. Great Dane	45	50
2758	5 d. Burmilla cat	60	65
2759	5 d. Blue Burmese cat	60	65
2760	5 d. Korat cat	60	65
2761	5 d. British tabby cat	60	65
2762	5 d. Foreign white cat	60	65
2763	5 d. Somali cat	60	65
2764	5 d. Akita	60	65
2765	5 d. Welsh corgi	60	65
2766	5 d. German shepherd	60	65
2767	5 d. Saint Bernard	60	65
2768	5 d. Bullmastiff	60	65
2769	5 d. Malamute	60	65
2770	6 d. Silver tabby cat	70	75
2771	10 d. Old English sheepdog	1·10	1·25
2772	15 d. Queensland heeler cat	1·75	1·90
2773	20 d. Abyssinian cat	2·25	2·40

1997. World Cup Football Championship, France (1998). As T **383** of Antigua.

2775	1 d. black	10	10
2776	1 d. 50 black	20	25
2777	2 d. black	20	25
2778	3 d. black	35	40
2779/86	4 d. × 8 multicoloured or brown (Nos. 2782/3)	3·50	
2787/94	4 d. × 8 multicoloured or black (No. 2788)	3·50	
2795/2802	4 d. × 8 brown (Nos. 2795/6, 2800 and 2802) or multicoloured	3·50	
2803/10	4 d. × 8 multicoloured	3·50	
2811	5 d. black	60	65
2812	10 d. black	1·10	1·25

DESIGNS—HORIZ: No. 2775, Uruguay team, 1950; 2776, West German team, 1954; 2777, Brazilian team, 1970; 2778, Brazilian team, 1962; 2779, Brazilian team, 1994; 2780, Argentine team, 1986; 2781, Brazilian team, 1970; 2782, Italian team, 1934; 2783, Uruguay team, 1958; 2784, English team, 1966; 2785, Brazilian team, 1962; 2786, West German team, 1990; 2787, Mario Kempes, Argentina (1978); 2788, Joseph Gaetjens, U.S.A. (1950) (inscr "ADEMIR BRAZIL" in error); 2789, Muller, West Germany (1970); 2790, Lineker, England (1986); 2791, Eusebio, Portugal (1966); 2792, Schillaci, Italy (1990); 2793, Lato, Poland (1974); 2794, Rossi, Italy (1982); 2811, Italian team, 1938; 2812, Uruguay team, 1930. VERT: No. 2795, Moore, England (1966); 2796, Fritzwalter, West Germany (1954); 2797, Beckenbauer, West Germany (1974); 2798, Zoff, Italy (1982); 2799, Maradona, Argentina (1986); 2800, Passarella, Argentina (1978); 2801, Matthaus, West Germany (1990); 2802, Dunga, Brazil (1994); 2803, Kinkladze, Georgia; 2804, Shearer, England; 2805, Dani, Portugal; 2806, Weah, Portugal; 2807, Ravanelli, Italy; 2808, Raducioiu, Rumania; 2809, Schmeichel, Denmark; 2810, Bergkamp, Holland.

284 Diana, Princess of Wales

285 Tiger

1997. Diana, Princess of Wales Commemoration. Each brown and black.

2814	10 d. Type **284**	1·10	1·25
2815	10 d. Wearing open-necked shirt	1·10	1·25
2816	10 d. Wearing polo-neck jumper	1·10	1·25
2817	10 d. Wearing diamond-drop earrings	1·10	1·25

1997. Christmas. Paintings. As T **386** of Antigua. Multicoloured.

2819	1 d. "Angel" (Rembrandt)	10	15
2820	1 d. 50 "Initiation into the Rites of Dionysus" at Villa dei Misteri	20	25
2821	2 d. "Pair of Erotes with Purple Cloaks"	20	25
2822	3 d. "The Ecstasy of Saint Theresa" (Gianlorenzo Bernini)	35	40
2823	5 d. "Virgin and Child with Angels" (Matthias Grunewald)	60	65
2824	10 d. "Angel playing the Organ" (Stefan Lochner)	1·10	1·25

1998. Chinese New Year ("Year of the Tiger"). Multicoloured.

2826	3 d. Type **285** ("GAMBIA" in green)	35	40
2827	3 d. Tiger ("GAMBIA" in mauve)	35	40
2828	3 d. Tiger ("GAMBIA" in lilac)	35	40
2829	3 d. Tiger ("GAMBIA" in blue)	35	40

286 Class 91 Electric Train, Great Britian

1998. Trains of the World. Multicoloured.

2831	5 d. Type **286**	60	65
2832	5 d. Class 26 steam locomotive No. 3450 "Red Devil", South Africa	60	65
2833	5 d. TGV express train, France	60	65
2834	5 d. People Mover railcar, Great Britain	60	65
2835	5 d. ICE high speed train, Germany	60	65
2836	5 d. Montmartre funicular car, France	60	65
2837	5 d. Burlington Northern SD70 diesel locomotive No. 9716, U.S.A.	60	65
2838	5 d. L.N.E.R. Class A4 steam locomotive "Mallard", 1938	60	65
2839	5 d. Baldwin steam locomotive, Peru	60	65
2840	5 d. Amtrak Class ARM-7 electric locomotive, U.S.A.	60	65
2841	5 d. Rack steam locomotive No. B2503, Amberawa, Java	60	65
2842	5 d. Beyer-Peacock steam locomotive No. 3108, Pakistan	60	65

No. 2832 is inscribed "BEACONSFIELD CHINA", No. 2836 "MOUNTMAETRE FUNICULAR" and No. 2840 "SWEDEN RAIL 125 MPH", all in error.

287 Yellow Orchid

289 Mulan

288 Wright "Flyer I", 1903

1998. African Flowers. Multicoloured.

2844	75 b. Type **287**	10	10
2845	1 d. 50 Transvaal daisy	20	25
2846	3 d. Torch lily	35	40
2847	4 d. "Ancistrochilus rothschildianus"	45	50
2848	5 d. "Adenium multiflorum" (horiz)	60	65
2849	5 d. "Huernia namaquensis" (horiz)	60	65
2850	5 d. "Gloriosa superba" (horiz)	60	65
2851	5 d. "Strelitzia reginae" (horiz)	60	65
2852	5 d. "Passiflora mollissima" (horiz)	60	65
2853	5 d. "Bauhinia variegata" (horiz)	60	65
2854	10 d. "Polystachya vulcanica"	1·10	1·25
2855	15 d. Gladiolus	1·75	1·90

Nos. 2848/53 were printed together, se-tenant, forming a composite background design.

1998. History of Aviation. Multicoloured.

2857	5 d. Type **288**	60	65
2858	5 d. Curtiss A-1 seaplane, 1910	60	65
2859	5 d. Farman biplane, 1907	60	65
2860	5 d. Bristol monoplane, 1911	60	65
2861	5 d. Antoinette IV, 1908	60	65
2862	5 d. Sopwith "Bat Boat" amphibian, 1912	60	65
2863	5 d. Short Type 38, 1913	60	65
2864	5 d. Fokker F.VIIb/3m, 1925	60	65
2865	5 d. Junkers J.13, 1919	60	65
2866	5 d. Pitcairn "Mailwing", 1927	60	65
2867	5 d. Douglas, 1920	60	65
2868	5 d. Curtiss T-32 Condor II airliner, 1934	60	65

Nos. 2857/62 and 2863/8 respectively were printed together, se-tenant, forming composite background designs.

No. 2857 is dated "1902" in error.

1998. "Mulan" (film). Multicoloured.

2870	4 d. Type **289**	45	50
2871	4 d. Mushu	45	50
2872	4 d. Little Brother	45	50
2873	4 d. Cri-kee	45	50
2874	4 d. Grandmother Fa	45	50
2875	4 d. Fa Li	45	50
2876	4 d. Fa Zhou	45	50
2877	4 d. Mulan and Khan	45	50
2878	5 d. Mulan riding Khan	60	65
2879	5 d. Shang	60	65
2880	5 d. Chi-fu	60	65
2881	5 d. Chien-po	60	65
2882	5 d. Yao	60	65
2883	5 d. Ling	60	65
2884	5 d. Shan-yu	60	65
2885	5 d. Mulan, Shang and Mushu	60	65

1998. Millennium Series. Famous People of the Twentieth Century. As T **318** of Dominica. Multicoloured. (a) Famous Jazz Musicians.

2887	4 d. Sidney Bechet	45	50
2888	4 d. Sidney Bechet playing saxophone (53 × 38 mm)	45	50
2889	4 d. Duke Ellington conducting (53 × 38 mm)	45	50
2890	4 d. Duke Ellington	45	50
2891	4 d. Louis Armstrong	45	50
2892	4 d. Louis Armstrong playing trumpet (53 × 38 mm)	45	50

2893	4 d. Charlie "Bird" Parker playing saxophone (53 × 38 mm)	45	50
2894	4 d. Charlie "Bird" Parker	45	50
	(b) Famous Theatrical Composers.		
2895	4 d. Cole Porter	45	50
2896	4 d. "Born to Dance" (Cole Porter) (53 × 38 mm)	45	50
2897	4 d. "Porgy and Bess" (George Gershwin) (53 × 38 mm)	45	50
2898	4 d. George Gershwin	45	50
2899	4 d. Rogers and Hammerstein	45	50
2900	4 d. "The King and I" (Rogers and Hammerstein) (53 × 38 mm)	45	50
2901	4 d. "West Side Story" (Leonard Bernstein) (53 × 38 mm)	45	50
2902	4 d. Leonard Bernstein	45	50

290 Chinese Junk

291 Captain Edward Smith

1998. Ships. Multicoloured.

2904	2 d. Type **290**	20	25
2905	3 d. H.M.S. "Victory" (ship of the line, 1765)	35	40
2906	5 d. "Santa Maria" (Columbus)	60	65
2907	5 d. "Mary Rose" (galleon)	60	65
2908	5 d. "Mayflower" (Pilgrim Fathers)	60	65
2909	5 d. "Ark Royal" (galleon, 1587)	60	65
2910	5 d. H.M.S. "Beagle" (Darwin)	60	65
2911	5 d. H.M.S. "Bounty" (Bligh)	60	65
2912	5 d. H.M.S. "Dreadnought" (battleship)	60	65
2913	5 d. American Truxton Class cruiser	60	65
2914	5 d. "Queen Mary" (liner)	60	65
2915	5 d. "Canberra" (liner)	60	65
2916	5 d. "Queen Elizabeth" (liner)	60	65
2917	5 d. "Queen Elizabeth II" (liner)	60	65
2918	10 d. British County Class destroyer	1·10	1·25
2919	15 d. Viking longship	1·75	1·90

1998. "Titanic" Commemoration.

2921	**291** 5 d. brown, black and blue	60	65
2922	– 5 d. brown, black and blue	60	65
2923	– 5 d. brown and black	60	65
2924	– 5 d. blue and black	60	65
2925	– 5 d. mauve and black	60	65
2926	– 5 d. mauve and black	60	65

DESIGNS: No. 2922, Mrs. J. J. "Molly" Brown (passenger); 2923, Newspaper boy with placard; 2924, Benjamin Guggenheim (passenger); 2925, Isidor Strauss (passenger); 2926, Ida Strauss (passenger).

292 Mahatma Gandhi

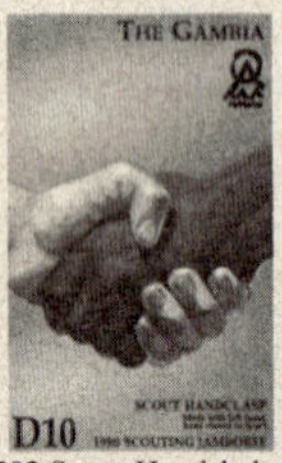

293 Scout Handshake

1998. 50th Death Anniv of Mahatma Gandhi. Multicoloured.

2928	10 d. Type **292**	1·10	1·25
2929	10 d. Gandhi on Salt March with Mrs. Sarojini Naidu (53 × 38 mm)	1·10	1·25
2930	10 d. Gandhi spinning yarn (53 × 38 mm)	1·10	1·25
2931	10 d. Gandhi in 1916	1·10	1·25

1998. 25th Death Anniv of Pablo Picasso (painter). As T **325** of Dominica. Multicoloured.

2933	3 d. "Death of Casagemas"	35	40
2934	5 d. "Seated Woman" (vert)	60	65
2935	10 d. "Mother and Child" (vert)	1·10	1·25

1998. 80th Anniv of Royal Air Force. As T **328** of Dominica. Multicoloured.

2937	5 d. Sepecat Jaguar GR1A (from above)	60	65
2938	5 d. Panavia Tornado GR1A	60	65
2939	5 d. Sepecat Jaguar GR1A (side view)	60	65
2940	5 d. BAe Hawk 200	60	65
2941	5 d. Sepecat Jaguar GR1A firing Sparrow missile	60	65
2942	5 d. BAe Harrier GR7 firing SNEB rockets	60	65
2943	5 d. Panavia Tornado GR1 firing AIM-9L missile	60	65
2944	5 d. Panavia Tornado GR1 in low level flight	60	65
2945	7 d. Panavia Tornado GR1 (facing left)	80	85
2946	7 d. BAe Hawk T1A	80	85
2947	7 d. Sepecat Jaguar GR1A	80	85
2948	7 d. Panavia Tornado GR1 (facing right)	80	85

1998. 19th World Scout Jamboree, Chile. Multicoloured.

2950	10 d. Type **293**	1·10	1·25
2951	10 d. Dinghy sailing	1·10	1·25
2952	10 d. Scout salute	1·10	1·25

294 "Mule-drivers from Tetuan"

1998. Birth Bicentenary of Eugene Delacroix (painter). Multicoloured.

2954	4 d. Type **294**	45	50
2955	4 d. "Encampment of Arab Mule-drivers"	45	50
2956	4 d. "An Orange Seller"	45	50
2957	4 d. "The Banks of the River"	45	50
2958	4 d. "View of Tangier from the Seashore"	45	50
2959	4 d. "Arab Horses fighting in a Stable"	45	50
2960	4 d. "Horses at the Trough"	45	50
2961	4 d. "The Combat of Giaour and Hassan"	45	50
2962	4 d. "Turk on a Sofa, Smoking"	45	50
2963	4 d. "View of Tangier"	45	50
2964	4 d. "The Spanish Coast at Salobrena"	45	50
2965	4 d. "The Aissaouas"	45	50
2966	4 d. "The Sea from the Cliffs of Dieppe"	45	50
2967	4 d. "The Fanatics of Tangier"	45	50
2968	4 d. "Arab Musicians"	45	50
2969	4 d. "An Arab Camp at Night"	45	50
2970	4 d. "Moroccan from Tangier, standing" (vert)	45	50
2971	4 d. "A Man of Tangier" (vert)	45	50
2972	4 d. "Young Arab standing with a Rifle" (vert)	45	50
2973	4 d. "Moroccan Chieftain" (vert)	45	50
2974	4 d. "Jewish Bride, Tangier" (vert)	45	50
2975	4 d. "Seated Jewess from Morocco" (vert)	45	50
2976	4 d. "Young Arab seated by a Wall" (vert)	45	50
2977	4 d. "Arab Dancer" (vert)	45	50

295 Puppy in Stocking

296 Rabbit

1998. Christmas. Multicoloured.

2979	1 d. Type **295**	10	15
2980	2 d. Giraffe in Christmas wreath	20	25
2981	3 d. Rainbow bee eater (bird) with bauble	35	40
2982	4 d. Deer	45	50
2983	5 d. Fawn	60	65
2984	10 d. Puppy in gift box	1·10	1·25

1999. Chinese New Year ("Year of the Rabbit"). Multicoloured.

2986	3 d. Type **296**	35	40
2987	3 d. Rabbit looking over shoulder	35	40
2988	3 d. Rabbit facing left	35	40
2989	3 d. Rabbit running	35	40

GHANA

Formerly the British Colony of Gold Coast. Attained Dominion status on 6 March 1957, and became a republic within the British Commonwealth in 1960.

1957. 12 pence = 1 shilling;
20 shillings = 1 pound.
1965. 100 pesewas = 1 cedi.
1967. 100 new pesewas = 1 new cedi.
1972. 100 pesewas = 1 cedi = 0.8 (1967) new cedi.

CANCELLED REMAINDERS. In 1961 remainders of some issues of 1957 to 1960 were put on the market cancelled-to-order in such a way as to be indistinguishable from genuine postally used copies. Our used quotations which are indicated by an asterisk are, therefore, for cancelled-to-order copies.

29 Dr. Kwame Nkrumah, Palm-nut Vulture and Map of Africa

1957. Independence Commemoration.

166	**29** 2d. red	10	10*
167	2½d. green	10	15*
168	4d. brown	10	15*
169	1s. 3d. blue	15	15*

1957. Queen Elizabeth stamps of 1952 of Gold Coast optd **GHANA INDEPENDENCE 6TH.. MARCH, 1957.**

170	½d. brown and red	10	10*
171	1d. blue	10	10*
172	1½d. green	10	10*
173	2d. brown	30	30
174	2½d. red	1·00	1·25
175	3d. mauve	30	10*
176	4d. blue	3·75	6·00
177	6d. black and orange	10	10*
178	1s. black and red	10	10*
179	2s. olive and red	60	10*
180	5s. purple and black	75	10*
181	10s. black and olive	75	60*

31 Viking Ship

1957. Inauguration of Black Star Shipping Line.

182	**31** 2½d. green	70	20
183	– 1s. 3d. blue	1·00	1·25
184	– 5s. purple	1·50	3·00

DESIGNS—HORIZ: 1s. 3d. Galleon; 5s. M.V. "Volta River".

34 Ambassador Hotel, Accra

1958. 1st Anniv of Independence. Flag and Coat of Arms in national colours.

185	**34** ½d. black and red	10	10
186	– 2½d. black, red and yellow	10	10
187	– 1s. 3d. black and blue	30	10
188	– 2s. yellow and black	45	35

DESIGNS—HORIZ: 2½d. State Opening of Parliament; 1s. 3d. National Monument. VERT: 2s. Ghana Coat of Arms.

38 Map showing the Independent African States

40 Palm-nut Vulture over Globe

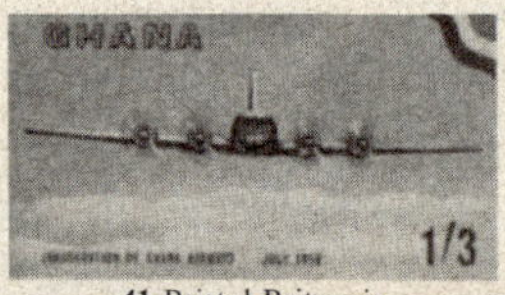

41 Bristol Britannia

1958. 1st Conference of Independent African States, Accra. Star in black and yellow.

189	**38** 2½d. red and yellow	10	10
190	3d. green and brown	10	10
191	– 1s. blue, yellow and orange	20	10
192	– 2s. 6d. purple, yell & orge	40	35

DESIGN—VERT: 1s., 2s. 6d. Map of Africa and flaming torch.

1958. Inauguration of Ghana Airways. Inscr as in T **40/41**.

193	**40** 2½d. black, bistre and red	45	10
194	**41** 1s. 3d. multicoloured	90	20
195	– 2s. multicoloured	1·00	55
196	– 2s. 6d. black and bistre	1·00	95

DESIGNS—(As Type **41**): 2s. Boeing Stratocruiser and yellow-nosed albatross. (As Type **40**): 2s. 6d. Palm-nut vulture and Vickers VC-10 aircraft.

1958. Prime Minister's Visit to United States and Canada. Optd **PRIME MINISTER'S VISIT, U.S.A. AND CANADA**.

197	**29** 2d. red	10	10
198	2½d. green	10	10
199	4d. brown	10	15
200	1s. 3d. blue	15	25

45

46 Dr. Nkrumah and Lincoln Statue, Washington

1958. United Nations Day.

201	**45** 2½d. brown, green and black	10	10
202	1s. 3d. brown, blue and black	20	10
203	2s. 6d. brown, violet & blk	25	35

1959. 150th Birth Anniv of Abraham Lincoln.

204	**46** 2½d. pink and purple	15	10
205	1s. 3d. light blue and blue	15	10
206	2s. 6d. yellow and olive	20	20

49 Talking Drums and Elephant-horn Blower

1959. Independence. Inscr "SECOND ANNIVERSARY OF INDEPENDENCE".

207	– ½d. multicoloured	10	10
208	**49** 2½d. multicoloured	10	10
209	– 1s. 3d. multicoloured	15	10
210	– 2s. multicoloured	30	1·00

DESIGNS—HORIZ: ½d. Kente cloth and traditional symbols; 2s. Map of Africa, Ghana flag and palms. VERT: 1s. 3d. "Symbols of Greeting".

52 Globe and Flags

1959. Africa Freedom Day.

211	**52** 2½d. multicoloured	15	10
212	8½d. multicoloured	15	20

54 Nkrumah Statue, Accra

55 Ghana Timber

65a Red-fronted Gazelle

1959. Multicoloured.
213 ½d. "God's Omnipotence" (postage) 10 10
213a ½d. "Gye Nyame" 30 10
214 1d. Type **54** 10 10
215 1½d. Type **55** 10 10
216 2d. Volta river 10 10
217 2½d. Cocoa bean 10 10
218 3d. "God's Omnipotence" . . 10 10
218a 3d. "Gye Nyame" 30 10
219 4d. Diamond and mine . . . 4·50 65
220 6d. Red-crowned bishop (bird) 50 10
221 11d. Golden-spider lily . . . 25 10
222 1s. Shell ginger 25 10
223 2s. 6d. Giant blue turaco . . 2·25 15
224 5s. Tiger orchid . . . . . . 5·50 50
225 10s. Jewel cichlid . . . . . . 1·50 70
225a £1 Type **65a** . . . . 12·00 4·75
226 1s. 3d. Pennant-winged nightjar (air) . . . . 2·50 10
227 2s. Crowned cranes . . . . . 1·75 10
SIZES—HORIZ (As Type **54**): ½d. (As Type **55**): 2d., 2½d., 3d., 4d., 6d., 1s. 3d., 2s. 6d. (As Type **65a**): 10s. VERT (As Type **55**): 11d., 1s., 2s., 5s. The 3d. is a different symbolic design from the ½d.

68 Gold Cup and West African Map

1959. West African Football Competition, 1959. Multicoloured.
228 ½d. Type **68** 10 10*
229 1d. Footballers 10 10*
230 3d. Goalkeeper saving ball . . 15 10*
231 8d. Forward attacking goal . . 70 15*
232 2s. 6d. "Kwame Nkrumah" Gold Cup . . . . 1·00 15*
Nos. 229 and 232 are vert and the rest horiz.

73 Duke of Edinburgh and Arms of Ghana

1959. Visit of the Duke of Edinburgh.
233 **73** 3d. black and mauve . . . 30 10*

74 Ghana Flag and Talking Drums

1959. U.N. Trusteeship Council. Multicoloured.
234 3d. Type **74** 10 10*
235 6d. Ghana flag and U.N. emblem 10 10*
236 1s. 3d. As 6d. but emblem above flag 30 15*
237 2s. 6d. "Totem pole" 40 15*
Nos. 235/7 are vert.

78 Eagles in Flight

85 Dr. Nkrumah

82 Flags and Map forming letter "A"

1960. 3rd Anniv of Independence. Mult.
238 ½d. Type **78** 10 10*
239 3d. Fireworks 10 10*
240 1s. 3d. "Third Anniversary" . 30 10*
241 2s. "Ship of State" 30 15*

1960. African Freedom Day. Multicoloured.
242 3d. Type **82** 10 10*
243 6d. Letter "f" 20 10*
244 1s. Letter "d" 20 10*

1960. Republic Day. Inscr "REPUBLIC DAY 1ST JULY 1960". Multicoloured.
245 3d. Type **85** 10 10
246 1s. 3d. Ghana flag 30 10
247 2s. Torch of Freedom 40 20
248 10s. Ghana arms . . . . . . 90 1·25
The 10s. is horiz and the rest vert.

90 Athlete

1960. Olympic Games.
249 – 3d. multicoloured 10 10
250 – 6d. multicoloured 15 10
251 **90** 1s. 3d. multicoloured . . . 25 10
252 2s. 6d. multicoloured . . . 35 45
DESIGN—VERT: 3d., 6d. Olympic torch.

91 President Nkrumah

1960. Founder's Day. Inscribed as in T **91**.
253 **91** 3d. multicoloured 10 10
254 – 6d. multicoloured 10 10
255 – 1s. 3d. multicoloured . . . 20 20
DESIGNS—VERT: 6d. President Nkumah within star; 1s. 3d. Map of Africa and column.

94 U.N. Emblem and Ghana Flag

97 Talking Drums

1960. Human Rights Day.
256 **94** 3d. multicoloured 10 10
257 – 6d. yellow, black and blue 20 10
258 – 1s. 3d. multicoloured . . . 40 30
DESIGNS: U.N. Emblem with torch (6d.) or within laurel (1s. 3d.).

1961. Africa Freedom Day. Inscr "15th APRIL 1961".
259 **97** 3d. multicoloured 10 10
260 – 6d. red, black and green . 20 10
261 – 2s. multicoloured 50 45
DESIGNS—VERT: 6d. Map of Africa. HORIZ: 2s. Flags and map.

100 Eagle on Column

103 Dove with Olive Branch

1961. 1st Anniv of Republic. Multicoloured.
262 3d. Type **100** 10 10
263 1s. 3d. "Flower" 10 10
264 2s. Ghana flags 20 70

1961. Belgrade Conference.
265 **103** 3d. green 10 10
266 – 1s. 3d. blue 15 10
267 – 5s. purple 60 50
DESIGNS—HORIZ: 1s. 3d. World map, chain and olive branch; 5s. Rostrum, Conference room.

106 President Nkrumah and Globe

1961. Founder's Day. Multicoloured.
268 3d. Type **106** 10 10
269 1s. 3d. President in Kente cloth 35 10
270 5s. President in national costume 1·25 2·50
Nos. 269/70 are vert.

109 Queen Elizabeth II and African Map

1961. Royal Visit.
271 **109** 3d. multicoloured 15 10
272 1s. 3d. multicoloured . . . 75 20
273 5s. multicoloured . . . . . 2·50 3·50

110 Ships in Tema Harbour

1962. Opening of Tema Harbour. Multicoloured.
274 **110** 3d. Type **110** (postage) . . 15 10
275 – 1s. 3d. Douglas DC-8 aircraft and ships at Tema (air) 80 15
276 – 2s. 6d. As No. 275 . . . . 1·00 1·50

112 Africa and Peace Dove

1962. 1st Anniv of Casablanca Conference.
277 **112** 3d. multicoloured (post) . . 10 10
278 1s. 3d. multicoloured (air) . 30 15
279 2s. 6d. multicoloured . . . 40 1·10

113 Compass over Africa

115 Atomic Bomb-burst "Skull"

1962. Africa Freedom Day.
280 **113** 3d. sepia, turquoise & pur 10 10
281 6d. sepia, turquoise & brn 10 15
282 1s. 3d. sepia, turq & red . 15 15

1962. The Accra Assembly.
283 – 3d. black and lake 10 10
284 **115** 6d. black and red 25 30
285 – 1s. 3d. turquoise 30 45
DESIGNS: 3d. Ghana Star over "five continents"; 1s. 3d. Dove of Peace.

117 Patrice Lumumba

1962. 1st Death Anniv of Lumumba.
286 **117** 3d. black and yellow . . . 10 10
287 6d. black, green and slate . 10 30
288 1s. 3d. black, pink and green 15 35

118 Star over Two Columns

121 President Nkrumah

1962. 2nd Anniv of Republic. Inscribed "1st JULY 1962". Multicoloured.
289 3d. Type **118** 10 10
290 6d. Flaming torch 20 30
291 1s. 3d. Eagle trailing flag . . 40 55
The 1s. 3d. is horiz.

1962. Founder's Day.
292 **121** 1d. multicoloured 10 10
293 – 3d. multicoloured 10 10
294 – 1s. 3d. black and blue . . . 30 15
295 – 2s. multicoloured 30 40
DESIGNS: 3d. Nkrumah medallion; 1s. 3d. President and Ghana Star; 2s. Laying "Ghana" brick.

125 Campaign Emblem

126 Campaign Emblem

1962. Malaria Eradication.
296 **125** 1d. red 15 10
297 4d. green . . . . 50 1·00
298 6d. bistre 50 30
299 1s. 3d. violet 60 90

1963. Freedom from Hunger.
300 **126** 1d. multicoloured 15 10
301 – 4d. sepia, yellow and orange 75 45
302 – 1s. 3d. ochre, blk & grn . . 1·60 80
DESIGNS—HORIZ: 4d. Emblem in hands; 1s. 3d. World map and emblem.

129 Map of Africa

133 Red Cross

1963. Africa Freedom Day.
303 **129** 1d. gold and red 10 10
304 – 4d. red, black and yellow . 10 10
305 – 1s. 3d. multicoloured . . 35 10
306 – 2s. 6d. multicoloured . . 50 1·25
DESIGNS—HORIZ: 4d. Carved stool. VERT: 1s. 3d. Map and bowl of fire; 2s. 6d. Topi (antelope) and flag.

1963. Centenary of Red Cross. Multicoloured.
307 1d. Type **133** 60 15
308 1½d. Centenary emblem . . . 90 1·25
309 4d. Nurses and child . . . . 2·25 20
310 1s. 3d. Emblem, globe and laurel 3·50 2·00
The 1½d. and 4d. are horiz.

137 "3rd Anniversary"

1963. 3rd Anniv of Republic. Multicoloured.
311 1d. Type **137** 10 10
312 4d. Three Ghanian flags . . . 10 10
313 1s. 3d. Map, flag and star (vert) 35 15
314 2s. 6d. Flag and torch (vert) . 55 1·50

141 President Nkrumah and Ghana Flag

145 Rameses II, Abu Simbel

1963. Founder's Day.

315	141	1d. multicoloured	10	10
316	–	4d. multicoloured	15	10
317	–	1s. 3d. multicoloured	30	10
318	–	5s. yellow and mauve	65	75

DESIGNS—VERT: 4d. Type 141 but with larger flag behind President Nkrumah. HORIZ: 1s. 3d. President Nkrumah and fireworks; 5s. Native symbol of wisdom.

1963. Preservation of Nubian Monuments. Multicoloured.

319	1d. Type 145	15	10
320	1½d. Rock paintings	20	65
321	2d. Queen Nefertari	20	10
322	4d. Sphinx, Sebua	35	15
323	1s. 3d. Rock Temple, Abu Simbel	80	90

The 1d. and 4d. are vert, the rest are horiz.

150 Class 248 Steam Locomotive and Diesel-electric Locomotive No. 1401

1963. 60th Anniv of Ghana Railway.

324	150	1d. multicoloured	10	10
325		6d. multicoloured	60	10
326		1s. 3d. multicoloured	1·25	60
327		2s. 6d. multicoloured	2·25	2·25

151 Eleanor Roosevelt and "Flame of Freedom"

154 Sun and Globe Emblem

1963. 5th Anniv of Declaration of Human Rights. Multicoloured.

328	1d. Type 151	10	10
329	4d. Type 151	10	10
330	6d. Eleanor Roosevelt	10	10
331	1s. 3d. Eleanor Roosevelt and emblems (horiz)	15	15

1964. International Quiet Sun Years.

332	154	3d. multicoloured	15	10
333		6d. multicoloured	25	10
334		1s. 3d. multicoloured	25	15

155 Harvesting Corn on State Farm

1964. 4th Anniv of Republic.

335	155	3d. olive, brown and yellow	10	10
336	–	6d. green, brown & turq	10	10
337	–	1s. 3d. red, brn & salmon	10	10
338	–	5s. multicoloured	40	70

DESIGNS: 6d. Oil refinery, Tema; 1s. 3d. "Communal Labour"; 5s. Procession headed by flag.

159 Globe and Dove

163 President Nkrumah and Hibiscus Flowers

1964. 1st Anniv of African Unity Charter.

339	159	3d. multicoloured	10	10
340	–	6d. green and red	10	10
341	–	1s. 3d. multicoloured	15	10
342	–	5s. multicoloured	45	70

DESIGNS—VERT: 6d. Map of Africa and quill pen; 5s. Planting flower. HORIZ: 1s. 3d. Hitched rope on map of Africa.

1964. Founder's Day.

343	163	3d. multicoloured	10	10
344		6d. multicoloured	15	10
345		1s. 3d. multicoloured	25	10
346		2s. 6d. multicoloured	40	60

164 Hurdling

1964. Olympic Games, Tokyo. Multicoloured.

347	1d. Type 164	10	10
348	2½d. Running	10	1·25
349	3d. Boxing	10	10
350	4d. Long-jumping	10	10
351	6d. Football	15	10
352	1s. 3d. Athlete holding Olympic Torch	20	10
353	5s. Olympic "Rings" and flags	85	3·25

Nos. 249/52 are vert.

171 G. Washington Carver (botanist) and Plant

1964. UNESCO Week.

354	171	6d. blue and green	15	10
355	–	1s. 3d. purple and blue	75	10
356	171	5s. sepia and red	2·10	4·00

DESIGN: 1s. 3d. Albert Einstein (scientist) and Atomic symbol.

173 African Elephant

181 I.C.Y. Emblem

1964. Multicoloured.

357	1d. Type 173	50	50
358	1½d. Secretary bird (horiz)	1·00	2·25
359	2½d. Purple wreath (flower)	60	2·25
360	3d. Grey parrot	1·50	50
361	4d. Blue-naped mousebird (horiz)	1·50	70
362	6d. African tulip tree (horiz)	60	30
363	1s. 3d. Violet starling (horiz)	1·75	1·25
364	2s. 6d. Hippopotamus (horiz)	1·75	5·50

1965. International Co-operation Year.

365	181	1d. multicoloured	35	60
366		4d. multicoloured	1·25	95
367		6d. multicoloured	1·50	60
368		1s. 3d. multicoloured	1·75	2·75

182 I.T.U. Emblem and Symbols

1965. Centenary of I.T.U.

369	182	1d. multicoloured	15	15
370		6d. multicoloured	55	15
371		1s. 3d. multicoloured	1·00	25
372		5s. multicoloured	2·25	2·75

183 Lincoln's Home

1965. Death Centenary of Abraham Lincoln.

373	183	6d. multicoloured	15	10
374	–	1s. 3d. black, red and blue	25	15
375	–	2s. black, brown and yellow	30	30
376	–	5s. black and red	70	1·50

DESIGNS: 1s. 3d. Lincoln's Inaugural Address; 2s. Abraham Lincoln; 5s. Adaption of U.S. 90 c. Lincoln stamp of 1869.

MORE DETAILED LISTS
are given in the Stanley Gibbons Catalogues referred to in the country headings.
For lists of current volumes see Introduction.

187 Obverse (President Nkrumah) and Reverse of 5 p. Coin

1965. Introduction of Decimal Currency. Multicoloured designs showing coins expressed in the same denominations as on the stamps.

377	5 p. Type 187	25	10
378	10 p. As Type 187	30	10
379	25 p. Size 63 × 39 mm	1·00	1·00
380	50 p. Size 71 × 43½ mm	2·00	2·25

1965. Nos. 214/27 surch **Ghana New Currency 19th July. 1965.** and value. Multicoloured.

381	54	1 p. on 1d. (postage)	10	10
382	–	2 p. on 2d.	10	10
383	–	3 p. on 3d. (No. 218a)	95	4·50
384	–	4 p. on 4d.	3·75	45
385	–	6 p. on 6d.	50	10
386	–	11 p. on 11d.	25	10
387	–	12 p. on 1s.	25	10
388	–	30 p. on 2s. 6d.	3·00	2·25
389	–	60 p. on 5s.	4·50	70
390	–	1 c. 20 on 10s.	75	2·25
391	65a	2 c. 40 on £1	1·00	6·00
392	–	15 p. on 1s. 3d. (air)	2·00	50
393	–	24 p. on 2s.	2·50	30

189 "OAU" and Flag

1965. O.A.U. Summit Conf, Accra. Mult.

394	1 p. Type 189	10	10
395	2 p. "OAU" heads and flag	10	10
396	5 p. OAU emblem and flag	10	10
397	6 p. African map and flag	10	10
398	15 p. "Sunburst" and flag	20	30
399	24 p. "O.A.U." on map, and flag	35	60

Nos. 397/9 are horiz, 37½ × 27½ mm.

195 Goalkeeper saving Ball

1965. African Soccer Cup Competition. Mult.

400	6 p. Type 195	20	10
401	15 p. Player with ball (vert)	35	25
402	24 p. Player, ball and Soccer Cup	45	50

198 President Kennedy and Grave Memorial

1965. 2nd Death Anniv of President Kennedy.

403	198	6 p. multicoloured	15	10
404	–	15 p. violet, red and green	25	35
405	–	24 p. black and purple	30	60
406	–	30 p. purple and black	40	75

DESIGNS: 15 p. President Kennedy and Eternal Flame; 24 p. President Kennedy and Memorial Inscription; 30 p. President Kennedy.

202 Section of Dam and Generators

1966. Volta River Project.

408	202	6 p. multicoloured	15	10
409	–	15 p. multicoloured	20	15
410	–	24 p. multicoloured	25	20
411	–	30 p. black and blue	35	50

DESIGNS: 15 p. Dam and Lake Volta; 24 p. Word "GHANA" as Dam; 30 p. "Fertility".

1966. "Black Stars" Victory in African Soccer Cup Competition. Optd **Black Stars Retain Africa Cup 21st Nov. 1965.**

412	195	6 p. multicoloured	20	10
413	–	15 p. multicoloured	35	20
414	–	24 p. multicoloured	45	35

207 W.H.O. Building and Ghana Flag

1966. Inaug of W.H.O. Headquarters, Geneva. Mult.

415	6 p. Type 207	50	10
416	15 p. Type 207	1·25	65
417	24 p. W.H.O. Building and emblem	1·40	1·25
418	30 p. W.H.O. Building and emblem	1·60	2·25

209 Atlantic Herring

1966. Freedom from Hunger. Multicoloured.

420	6 p. Type 209	15	10
421	15 p. Turbot	35	15
422	24 p. Spadefish	65	35
423	30 p. Red snapper	80	90
424	60 p. Blue-finned tuna	2·00	3·50

214 African "Links" and Ghana Flag

1966. 3rd Anniv of African Charter. Multicoloured.

426	6 p. Type 214	15	10
427	15 p. Flags as "Quill" and diamond (horiz)	35	45
428	24 p. Ship's wheel, map and cocoa bean (horiz)	40	60

217 Player heading Ball, and Jules Rimet Cup

1966. World Cup Football Championships. Multicoloured.

429	5 p. Type 217	30	10
430	15 p. Goalkeeper clearing ball	70	20
431	24 p. Player and Jules Rimet Cup (replica)	85	35
432	30 p. Players and Jules Rimet Cup (replica)	1·10	1·25
433	60 p. Players with ball	1·75	4·75

222 U.N.E.S.C.O. Emblem

1966. 20th Anniv of U.N.E.S.C.O.

435	222	5 p. multicoloured	25	15
436		15 p. multicoloured	60	40
437		24 p. multicoloured	90	85
438		30 p. multicoloured	1·25	2·25
439		60 p. multicoloured	2·25	4·75

223 Fair Emblem and Crates

1967. Ghana Trade Fair, Accra. Multicoloured.

441 5 p. Type **223** 10 10
442 15 p. Fair emblem and world map 15 20
443 24 p. Shipping and flags . . . 25 30
444 36 p. Fair emblem and hand-held hoist . . . . 40 1·90

1967. New Currency. Nos. 216/26 and 393 surch with new value.

445 1½ n.p. on 2d. (postage) . . . 3·50 4·00
446 3½ n.p. on 4d. . . . . 4·00 85
447 5 n.p. on 6d. . . . . 1·25 50
448 9 n.p. on 11d. 30 20
449 10 n.p. on 1s. 30 30
450 25 n.p. on 2s. 6d. . . . . . . 3·50 4·50
451 1 n.c. on 10s. . . . . 3·00 14·00
452 2 n.c. on £1 . . . . 6·00 24·00
453 12½ n.p. on 1 s. 3d. (air) . . . 4·00 2·00
454 20 n.p. on 24 p. on 2s. . . . . 4·00 3·00

229 Ghana Eagle and Flag

1967. 1st Anniv of 24 February Revolution.

455 **229** 1 n.p. multicoloured . . . 10 15
456 4 n.p. multicoloured . . . 10 10
457 12½ n.p. multicoloured . . 40 60
458 25 n.p. multicoloured . . 85 2·50

230 Maize 232 The Ghana Mace

1967. Multicoloured.

460 1 n.p. Type **230** 10 10
461 1½ n.p. Forest kingfisher . . . 90 1·75
462 2 n.p. Type **232** 10 10
463 2½ n.p. Commelina 35 10
464 3 n.p. West African lungfish . 20 40
465 4 n.p. Rufous-crowned roller . 1·50 10
466 6 n.p. Akosombo Dam 15 50
467 8 n.p. Adomi Bridge 15 10
468 9 n.p. Chameleon 75 10
469 10 n.p. Tema Harbour 15 10
470 20 n.p. Bush hare (blue) . . . 20 10
471 50 n.p. Black-winged stilt . . 4·50 1·50
472 1 n.c. Wooden stool . . . . . 2·25 75
473 2 n.c. Frangipani . . . . . . 2·00 3·50
474 2 n.c. 50 Seat of State . . . . 3·50 7·50

SIZES—VERT (As Type **230**): 4 n.p. (As Type **232**): 1½ n.p:, 2½ n.p., 20 n.p., 2 n.c., 2 n.c. 50. HORIZ (as Type **230**): 8 n.p. (As Type **232**): 3 n.p., 6 n.p., 9 n.p., 10 n.p., 50 n.p., 1 n.c.

245 Kumasi Fort

1967. Castles and Forts

475 **245** 4 n.p. multicoloured . . . 25 10
476 – 12½ n.p. multicoloured . . 1·00 1·00
477 – 20 n.p. multicoloured . . 1·40 2·75
478 – 25 n.p. multicoloured . . 1·75 3·50

DESIGNS: 12½ n.p. Christiansborg Castle and British galleon; 20 n.p. Elmina Castle and Portuguese galleon; 25 n.p. Cape Coast Castle and Spanish galleon.

249 "Luna 10" 255 U.N. Headquarters Building

252 Scouts and Campfire

1967. "Peaceful Use of Outer Space". Multicoloured.

479 4 n.p. Type **249** 10 10
480 10 n.p. "Orbiter 1" 10 35
481 12½ n.p. Man in Space . . . 20 70

1967. 50th Anniv of Ghanaian Scout Movement. Multicoloured.

483 4 n.p. Type **252** 20 10
484 10 n.p. Scout on march . . . 50 50
485 12½ n.p. Lord Baden-Powell . . 70 1·75

1967. United Nations Day (24 October).

487 **255** 4 n.p. multicoloured . . . 10 10
488 10 n.p. multicoloured . . 10 15
489 – 50 n.p. multicoloured . . 30 70
490 – 2 n.c. 50 multicoloured . 1·00 4·00

DESIGN: 50 n.p., 2 n.c. 50, General view of U.N. H.Q., Manhattan.

257 Leopard

1967. International Tourist Year. Multicoloured.

492 4 n.p. Type **257** . . . . 1·00 20
493 12½ n.p. "Papilio demodocus" (butterfly) . . . . 2·50 1·50
494 20 n.p. Carmine bee eater . . 3·00 3·50
495 50 n.p. Waterbuck . . . . . 3·00 7·00

261 Revolutionaries entering Accra

1968. 2nd Anniv of February Revolution. Mult.

497 4 n.p. Type **261** 10 10
498 12½ n.p. Marching troops . . 20 20
499 20 n.p. Cheering people . . . 30 40
500 40 n.p. Victory celebrations . . 50 1·25

265 Microscope and Cocoa Beans

1968. Cocoa Research.

501 **265** 2½ n.p. multicoloured . . 10 40
502 – 4 n.p. multicoloured . . 10 10
503 **265** 10 n.p. multicoloured . . 15 20
504 – 25 n.p. multicoloured . . 60 1·10

DESIGNS: 4 n.p. and 25 n.p. Microscope and cocoa tree, beans and pods.

267 Kotoka and Flowers

1968. 1st Death Anniv of Lt.-Gen. E. K. Kotoka. Multicoloured.

506 4 n.p. Type **267** 10 10
507 12½ n.p. Kotoka and wreath . . 20 30
508 20 n.p. Kotoka in civilian clothes 35 75
509 40 n.p. Lt.-Gen. Kotoka . . 50 1·60

271 Tobacco 277 Hurdling

276 Surgeons, Flag and W.H.O. Emblem

1968. Flora and Fauna. Multicoloured.

510 4 n.p. Type **271** 15 10
511 5 n.p. North African crested porcupine 15 60
512 12½ n.p. Rubber 50 75
513 20 n.p. "Cymothoe sangaris" (butterfly) . . . . 2·25 2·75
514 40 n.p. "Charaxes ameliae" (butterfly) . . . . 2·50 4·75

1968. 20th Anniv of W.H.O.

516 **276** 4 n.p. multicoloured . . . 25 10
517 12½ n.p. multicoloured . . 60 40
518 20 n.p. multicoloured . . 95 1·10
519 40 n.p. multicoloured . . . 1·50 3·00

1969. Olympic Games, Mexico (1968). Multicoloured.

521 4 n.p. Type **277** 10 10
522 12½ n.p. Boxing 20 30
523 20 n.p. Torch, Olympic Rings and flags 40 75
524 40 n.p. Football . . . . 70 2·50

281 U.N. Building 285 Dr. J. B. Danquah

1969. United Nations Day. Multicoloured.

526 4 n.p. Type **281** 10 10
527 12½ n.p. Native stool, staff and U.N. emblem 15 25
528 20 n.p. U.N. building and emblem over Ghanian Flag . 20 35
529 40 n.p. U.N. emblem encircled by flags . . . . 40 1·25

1969. Human Rights Year. Multicoloured.

531 4 n.p. Type **285** 10 10
532 12½ n.p. Dr. Martin Luther King 20 35
533 20 n.p. As 12½ n.p. 35 75
534 40 n.p. Type **285** . . . . 50 1·60

287 Constituent Assembly Building

1969. 3rd Anniv of Revolution. Multicoloured.

536 4 n.p. Type **287** 10 10
537 12½ n.p. Arms of Ghana . . . 10 10
538 20 n.p. Type **287** 15 15
539 40 n.p. As 12½ n.p. 20 35

1969. New Constitution. Nos. 460/74 optd **NEW CONSTITUTION 1969**.

541 **230** 1 n.p. multicoloured . . . 10 1·00
542 – 1½ n.p. multicoloured . . . 85 2·00
543 **232** 2 n.p. multicoloured . . . 10 1·50
544 – 2½ n.p. multicoloured . . . 10 1·25
545 – 3 n.p. multicoloured . . . 60 1·50
546 – 4 n.p. multicoloured . . . 2·25 30
547 – 6 n.p. multicoloured . . . 15 1·50
548 – 8 n.p. multicoloured . . . 15 1·00
549 – 9 n.p. multicoloured . . . 15 1·50
550 – 10 n.p. multicoloured . . . 20 85
551 – 20 n.p. multicoloured . . . 35 90
552 – 50 n.p. multicoloured . . . 5·00 5·50
553 – 1 n.c. multicoloured . . . 1·75 7·00
554 – 2 n.c. multicoloured . . . 2·75 8·00
555 – 2 n.c. 50 multicoloured . . 2·75 9·50

On Nos. 541, 545, 547/50 and 552/3 the opt is horiz. The rest are vert.

MINIMUM PRICE

The minimum price quoted is 10p which represents a handling charge rather than a basis for valuing common stamps. For further notes about prices see introductory pages.

290 Map of Africa and Flags 294 Red Cross and Globe

293 I.L.O. Emblem and Cogwheels

1969. Inauguration of 2nd Republic. Multicoloured.

556 4 n.p. Type **290** 10 10
557 12½ n.p. Figure "2", branch and Ghanaian colours 20 10
558 20 n.p. Hands receiving egg . . 35 30
559 40 n.p. Type **290** 60 70

1970. 50th Anniv of I.L.O.

560 **293** 4 n.p. multicoloured . . . 10 10
561 12½ n.p. multicoloured . . 20 25
562 20 n.p. multicoloured . . 30 45

1970. 50th Anniv of League of Red Cross Societies. Multicoloured.

564 4 n.p. Type **294** 30 10
565 12½ n.p. Henri Dunant and Red Cross emblem 40 20
566 20 n.p. Patient receiving medicine 50 55
567 40 n.p. Patient having arm bandaged . . . . 75 1·40

Nos. 565/7 are horiz.

298 General Kotoka, Vickers VC-10 and Airport 302 Lunar Module landing on Moon

1970. Inauguration of Kotoka Airport. Mult.

569 4 n.p. Type **298** 15 10
570 12½ n.p. Control tower and tail of Vickers VC-10 . . . . . . 25 15
571 20 n.p. Aerial view of airport . 40 30
572 40 n.p. Airport and flags . . . 75 80

1970. Moon Landing. Multicoloured.

573 4 n.p. Type **302** 30 10
574 12½ n.p. Astronaut's first step onto the Moon 85 60
575 20 n.p. Astronaut with equipment on Moon . . . 1·25 1·40
576 40 n.p. Astronauts . . . . . 2·25 3·00

Nos. 575/6 are horiz.

306 Adult Education

1970. International Education Year. Multicoloured.

578 4 n.p. Type **306** 10 10
579 12½ n.p. International education symbols 20 20
580 20 n.p. "Ntesie" and I.E.Y. symbols 35 30
581 40 n.p. Nursery schools 60 85

310 Saluting March-Past

1970. 1st Anniv of Second Republic. Multicoloured.

582 4 n.p. Type **310** 10 10
583 12½ n.p. Busia Declaration . . 15 15
584 20 n.p. Doves symbol 25 30
585 40 n.p. Opening of Parliament 50 65

314 "Crinum ornatum"

1970. Flora and Fauna. Multicoloured.

586	4 n.p. Type **314**	1·50	10
587	12½ n.p. Lioness	1·50	85
588	20 n.p. "Ansellia africana" (flower)	1·60	1·25
589	40 n.p. African elephant	4·75	5·50

315 Kuduo Brass Casket

1970. Monuments and Archaeological Sites in Ghana. Multicoloured.

590	4 n.p. Type **315**	15	10
591	12½ n.p. Akan traditional house	40	20
592	20 n.p. Larabanga Mosque	55	50
593	40 n.p. Funerary clay head	70	1·10

316 Trade Fair Building

1971. International Trade Fair, Accra. Multicoloured.

595	4 n.p. Type **316**	10	10
596	12½ n.p. Cosmetic and pharmaceutical goods	60	20
597	20 n.p. Vehicles	65	25
598	40 n.p. Construction equipment	95	95
599	50 n.p. Transport and packing case (vert)	1·10	1·10

317 Christ on the Cross

318 Corn Cob

1971. Easter. Multicoloured.

600	4 n.p. Type **317**	20	10
601	12½ n.p. Christ and Disciples	45	45
602	20 n.p. Christ blessing Disciples	65	1·10

1971. Freedom from Hunger Campaign.

603 **318**	4 n.p. multicoloured	10	10
604	12½ n.p. multicoloured	35	60
605	20 n.p. multicoloured	65	1·10

Remainder stocks of the above stamps were optd on the occasion of the death of Lord Boyd Orr and further surch 12½, 20 and 60 n.p.

It is understood that 8070 sets from the agency were overprinted locally and returned to New York. Limited remainders of these stamps (only 330 of 60 n.p.) were sold at the G.P.O. We do not list these as they were not freely on sale in Ghana.

319 Guides Emblem and Ghana Flag

1971. Golden Jubilee of Ghana Girl Guides. Each design includes Guides emblem. Mult.

606	4 n.p. Type **319**	20	10
607	12½ n.p. Mrs E. Ofuatey-Kodjoe (founder) and guides with flags	60	50
608	20 n.p. Guides laying stones	90	90
609	40 n.p. Camp-fire and tent	1·50	1·75
610	50 n.p. Signallers	1·75	2·00

320 Child-care Centre

1971. Y.W.C.A. World Council Meeting, Accra. Multicoloured.

612	4 n.p. Type **320**	10	10
613	12½ n.p. Council meeting	10	15
614	20 n.p. School typing class	15	30
615	40 n.p. Building Fund Day	30	60

321 Firework Display

322 Weighing Baby

1971. Christmas. Multicoloured.

617	1 n.p. Type **321**	10	60
618	3 n.p. African Nativity	15	70
619	6 n.p. The Flight into Egypt	15	70

1971. 25th Anniv of U.N.I.C.E.F. Multicoloured.

620	5 n.p. Type **322**	10	10
621	15 n.p. Mother and child (horiz)	20	30
622	30 n.p. Nurse	30	70
623	50 n.p. Young boy (horiz)	50	2·25

323 Unity Symbol and Trade Fair Emblem

1972. All African Trade Fair. Multicoloured.

625	5 n.p. Type **323**	10	10
626	15 n.p. Horn of Plenty	15	30
627	30 n.p. Fireworks on map of Africa	25	70
628	60 n.p. "Participating Nations"	35	2·00
629	1 n.c. As No. 628	50	2·50

On 24 June 1972, on the occasion of the Belgian International Philatelic Exhibition, Nos. 625/9 were issued optd **BELGICA 72**. Only very limited supplies were sent to Ghana (we understand not more than 900 sets), and for this reason we do not list them.

324 Books for the Blind

1972. International Book Year. Multicoloured.

630	5 p. Type **324**	20	10
631	15 p. Children's books	55	50
632	30 p. Books for recreation	1·00	1·25
633	50 p. Books for students	1·75	2·75
634	1 c. Book and flame of knowledge (vert)	2·50	3·75

325 "Hypoxis urceolata"

1972. Flora and Fauna. Multicoloured.

636	5 p. Type **325**	30	10
637	15 p. Mona monkey	65	65
638	30 p. "Crinum ornatum"	5·50	4·00
639	1 c. De Winton's tree squirrel	6·00	8·00

326 Football

1972. Olympic Games, Munich. Multicoloured.

640	5 p. Type **326**	15	10
641	15 p. Running	25	20
642	30 p. Boxing	50	65
643	50 p. Long-jumping	80	2·00
644	1 c. High-jumping	1·25	3·25

327 Senior Scout and Cub

1972. 65th Anniv of Boy Scouts. Multicoloured.

646	5 p. Type **327**	30	10
647	15 p. Scout and tent	65	45
648	30 p. Sea scouts	1·25	1·25
649	50 p. Leader with cubs	1·60	2·00
650	1 c. Training school	3·00	3·50

328 "The Holy Night" (Correggio)

330 Under 5's Clinic

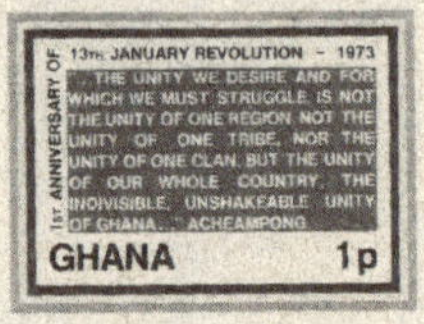

329 Extract from Speech

1972. Christmas. Multicoloured.

652	1 p. Type **328**	10	10
653	3 p. "Adoration of the Kings" (Holbein the Elder)	10	10
654	15 p. "Madonna of the Passion" (School of Ricco)	40	30
655	30 p. "King Melchior"	70	70
656	60 p. "King Gaspar, Mary and Jesus"	1·00	2·00
657	1 c. "King Balthasar"	1·50	3·00

1973. 1st Anniv of 13 January Revolution. Multicoloured.

659	1 p. Type **329**	10	10
660	3 p. Market scene	10	10
661	5 p. Selling bananas (vert)	10	10
662	15 p. Farmer with hoe and produce (vert)	20	25
663	30 p. Market traders	30	40
664	1 c. Farmer cutting palm-nuts	70	1·40

1973. 25th Anniv of W.H.O. Multicoloured.

666	5 p. Type **330**	10	10
667	15 p. Radiography	25	30
668	30 p. Immunisation	35	50
669	50 p. Starving child	50	1·25
670	1 c. W.H.O. H.Q., Geneva	75	2·25

1973. World Scouting Conference, Nairobi/Addis Ababa. Nos. 646/50 optd **1st WORLD SCOUTING CONFERENCE IN AFRICA.**

671 **327**	5 p. multicoloured	10	15
672 –	15 p. multicoloured	35	60
673 –	30 p. multicoloured	60	1·40
674 –	50 p. multicoloured	80	2·00
675 –	1 c. multicoloured	1·50	3·00

332 Poultry Farming

1973. 10th Anniv of World Food Programme. Multicoloured.

677	5 p. Type **332**	10	10
678	15 p. Mechanisation	15	15
679	50 p. Cocoa harvest	40	90
680	1 c. F.A.O. H.Q., Rome	60	1·90

333 "Green Alert"

1973. 50th Anniv of Interpol. Multicoloured.

682	5 p. Type **333**	15	10
683	30 p. "Red Alert"	75	80
684	50 p. "Blue Alert"	1·50	1·75
685	1 c. "Black Alert"	3·00	4·00

334 Handshake

1973. 10th Anniv of O.A.U. Multicoloured.

686	5 p. Type **334**	10	10
687	30 p. Africa Hall, Addis Ababa	15	30
688	50 p. O.A.U. emblem	20	1·00
689	1 c. "X" in colours of Ghana flag	35	1·50

335 Weather Balloon

1973. Centenary of I.M.O./W.M.O. Multicoloured.

690	5 p. Type **335**	10	10
691	15 p. Satellite "Tiros"	15	20
692	30 p. Computer weather map	30	65
693	1 c. Radar screen	60	2·25

336 Epiphany Scene

337 "Christ carrying the Cross" (Thomas de Kolozsvar)

1973. Christmas. Multicoloured.

695	1 p. Type **336**	10	10
696	3 p. Madonna and Child	10	10
697	30 p. "Madonna and Child" (Murillo)	30	75
698	50 p. "Adoration of the Magi" (Tiepolo)	45	1·00

1974. Easter.

700 **337**	5 p. multicoloured	10	10
701 –	30 p. blue, silver and brown	20	35
702 –	50 p. red, silver and brown	30	60
703 –	1 c. green, silver and brown	50	1·25

DESIGNS (from 15th-century English carved alabaster): 30 p. "The Betrayal"; 50 p. "The Deposition"; 1 c. "The Risen Christ and Mary Magdalene".

338 Letters

1974. Centenary of U.P.U. Multicoloured.

705	5 p. Type **338**	10	10
706	9 p. U.P.U. Monument and H.Q.	10	15
707	50 p. Airmail letter	35	1·00
708	1 c. U.P.U. Monument and Ghana stamp	60	1·75

1974. "Internaba 1974" Stamp Exhibition. As Nos. 705/8 additionally inscr "INTERNABA 1974".

710	5 p. multicoloured	10	10
711	9 p. multicoloured	10	15
712	50 p. multicoloured	30	1·00
713	1 c. multicoloured	45	1·75

339 Footballers

1974. World Cup Football Championships.

715 **339**	5 p. multicoloured	10	10
716 –	30 p. multicoloured	25	60
717 –	50 p. multicoloured	35	85
718 –	1 c. multicoloured	50	1·50

DESIGNS: As Type **339** showing footballers in action.

340 Roundabout

1974. Change to Driving on the Right.

720	340	5 p. green, red and black	10	10
721	–	15 p. purple, red and black	25	35
722	–	30 p. multicoloured	45	60
723	–	50 p. multicoloured	70	1·10
724	–	1 c. multicoloured	1·40	2·00

DESIGNS—HORIZ: 15 p. Warning triangle sign. VERT: 30 p. Highway arrow and slogan; 50 p. Warning hands; 1 c. Car on symbolic hands.

1974. West Germany's Victory in World Cup. Nos. 715/18 optd **WEST GERMANY WINNERS**.

725	5 p. multicoloured	10	10
726	30 p. multicoloured	35	40
727	50 p. multicoloured	50	55
728	1 c. multicoloured	90	1·25

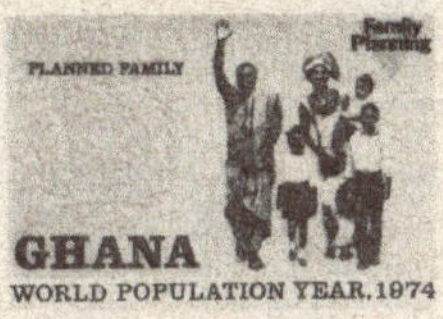

342 "Planned Family"

1974. World Population Year. Multicoloured.

730	5 p. Type 342	10	10
731	30 p. Family planning clinic	25	35
732	50 p. Immunization	35	60
733	1 c. Population census enumeration	60	1·40

343 Angel 346 Angel

345 Tractor Driver

1974. Christmas. Multicoloured.

734	5 p. Type 343	10	10
735	7 p. The Magi (diamond 47×47 mm)	10	10
736	9 p. The Nativity	10	10
737	1 c. The Annunciation	60	1·40

1975. "Apollo-Soyuz" Space Link. Nos. 715/18 optd **APOLLO SOYUZ JULY 15, 1975.**

739	339	5 p. multicoloured	10	10
740	–	30 p. multicoloured	25	25
741	–	50 p. multicoloured	45	55
742	–	1 c. multicoloured	70	80

1975. International Women's Year. Multicoloured.

744	7 p. Type 345	25	10
745	30 p. Motor mechanic	75	35
746	60 p. Factory workers	90	80
747	1 c. Cocoa research	1·10	1·40

1975. Christmas.

749	346	2 p. multicoloured	10	10
750	–	5 p. yellow and green	10	10
751	–	7 p. yellow and green	10	10
752	–	30 p. yellow and green	20	20
753	–	1 c. yellow and green	50	1·00

DESIGNS: 5 p. Angle with harp; 7 p. Angel with lute; 30 p. Angel with violin; 1 c. Angel with trumpet.

347 Map Reading

1976. 14th World Scout Jamboree, Norway. Multicoloured.

755	7 p. Type 347	20	10
756	30 p. Sailing	60	90
757	60 p. Hiking	90	2·25
758	1 c. Life-saving	1·10	2·50

348 Bottles (litre)

1976. Metrication Publicity. Multicoloured.

760	7 p. Type 348	15	10
761	30 p. Scales (kilogramme)	40	40
762	60 p. Tape measure and bale of cloth (metre)	80	1·00
763	1 c. Ice, thermometer and kettle (temperature)	1·25	1·75

349 Fair Site

1976. International Trade Fair, Accra.

764	349	7 p. multicoloured	10	10
765	–	30 p. multicoloured	20	20
766	–	60 p. multicoloured	35	60
767	–	1 c. multicoloured	55	1·00

DESIGNS: As Type 349 showing different views of the Fair.

1976. Interphil Stamp Exhibition. Nos. 755/8 optd **'INTERPHIL' 76 BICENTENNIAL EXHIBITION**.

768	347	7 p. multicoloured	15	15
769	–	30 p. multicoloured	35	50
770	–	60 p. multicoloured	55	75
771	–	1 c. multicoloured	80	1·25

351 Shot-put

1976. Olympic Games, Montreal. Multicoloured.

773	7 p. Type 351	15	10
774	30 p. Football	30	25
775	60 p. Women's 1500 metres	45	50
776	1 c. Boxing	60	80

352 Supreme Court

1976. Centenary of Supreme Court.

778	352	8 p. multicoloured	10	10
779	–	30 p. multicoloured	20	25
780	–	60 p. multicoloured	35	50
781	–	1 c. multicoloured	60	1·00

DESIGNS: As Type 352 showing different views of the Court Buildings.

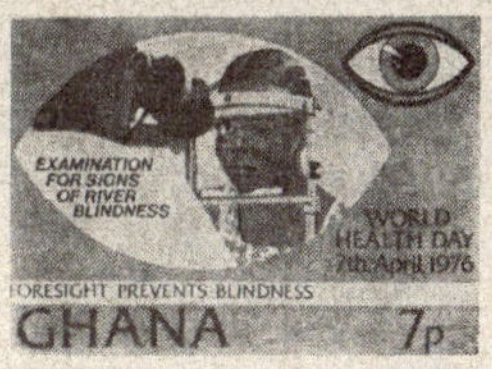

353 Examination for River Blindness

1976. Prevention of Blindness. Multicoloured.

782	7 p. Type 353	65	10
783	30 p. Entomologist	1·75	1·40
784	60 p. Normal vision	2·75	2·75
785	1 c. Blackfly eradication	4·25	4·50

354 Fireworks Party, Christmas Eve

1976. Christmas. Multicoloured.

786	6 p. Type 354	15	10
787	8 p. Children and gifts	15	10
788	30 p. Christmas feast	50	30
789	1 c. As 8 p.	1·10	1·75

355 "Gallows Frame" Telephone and Alexander Graham Bell

1976. Centenary of Telephone. Multicoloured.

791	8 p. Type 355	20	10
792	30 p. Bell and 1895 telephone	30	30
793	60 p. Bell and 1929 telephone	50	70
794	1 c. Bell and 1976 telephone	75	1·25

1977. Olympic Winners. Nos. 773/6 optd **WINNERS** and country name.

796	351	7 p. multicoloured	15	15
797	–	30 p. multicoloured	35	40
798	–	60 p. multicoloured	45	85
799	–	1 c. multicoloured	65	1·50

OPTD: 7 p., 30 p. **EAST GERMANY**; 60 p. **U.S.S.R.**; 1 c. **U.S.A.**

357 Dipo Dancers and Drum Ensemble

1977. Second World Black and African Festival of Arts and Culture, Nigeria. Multicoloured.

801	8 p. Type 357	15	15
802	30 p. Arts and crafts	30	60
803	60 p. Acon music and dancing priests	50	1·25
804	1 c. African huts	60	2·00

1977. Prince Charles's Visit to Ghana. Nos. 791/94 optd **PRINCE CHARLES VISITS GHANA 17th TO 25th MARCH, 1977.**

806	8 p. Type 355	50	55
807	30 p. 1895 telephone	1·25	1·00
808	60 p. 1929 telephone	1·75	2·00
809	1 c. 1976 telephone	2·25	2·50

359 Olive Colobus Monkey

1977. Wildlife. Multicoloured.

811	8 p. Type 359	45	15
812	20 p. Temminck's giant squirrel	1·25	80
813	30 p. Hunting dog	1·75	1·25
814	60 p. African manatee (sea cow)	3·00	2·75

360 "Le Chapeau de Paille" (Rubens—400th Birth Anniv) 361 The Magi, Madonna and Child

1977. Painters' Anniversaries. Multicoloured.

816	8 p. Type 360	25	10
817	30 p. "Isabella of Portugal" (Titian—500th birth anniv)	50	40
818	60 p. "Duke and Duchess of Cumberland" (Gainsborough—250th birth anniv)	65	65
819	1 c. "Rubens and Isabella Brandt"	85	1·25

1977. Christmas. Multicoloured.

821	1 p. Type 361	10	10
822	2 p. Choir, St. Andrew's Anglican Church, Abossey Okai	10	10
823	6 p. Methodist Church, Wesley, Accra	10	10
824	8 p. Madonna and Child	10	10
825	30 p. Holy Spirit Cathedral, Accra	40	50
826	1 c. Ebenezer Presbyterian Church, Accra	1·25	1·60

1978. Referendum. Nos. 821/26 optd **REFERENDUM 1978 VOTE EARLY**.

828	1 p. Type 361	10	10
829	2 p. Choir, St. Andrew's Anglican Church, Abossey Okai	10	10
830	6 p. Methodist Church, Wesley, Accra	10	10
831	8 p. Madonna and Child	10	10
832	30 p. Holy Spirit Cathedral, Accra	40	50
833	1 c. Ebenezer Presbyterian Church, Accra	1·25	1·50

363 Cutting Bananas

1978. Operation "Feed Yourself". Multicoloured.

835	2 p. Type 363	10	10
836	8 p. Home produce	10	10
837	30 p. Market	25	35
838	60 p. Fishing	60	60
839	1 c. Mechanisation	80	1·25

364 Wright Flyer III 367 "The Betrayal"

366 Players and African Cup Emblem

1978. 75th Anniv of Powered Flight.

840	364	8 p. black, brown and ochre	20	10
841	–	30 p. black, brown and green	40	30
842	–	60 p. black, brown and red	60	60
843	–	1 c. black, brown and blue	1·75	1·10

DESIGNS: 30 p. Handley Page H.P.42; 60 p. De Havilland Comet 1; 1 c. Concorde.

1978. "CAPEX 1978" International Stamp Exhibition, Toronto. Nos. 840/3 optd **"CAPEX 78 JUNE 9-18 1978"**.

845	364	8 p. black, brown and ochre	15	15
846	–	30 p. black, brown and green	25	25
847	–	60 p. black, brown and red	50	50
848	–	1 c. black, brown and blue	1·10	80

1978. Football Championships. Multicoloured.

850	8 p. Type 366	20	15
851	30 p. Players and African Cup emblem (different)	25	30
852	60 p. Players and World Cup emblem	40	60
853	1 c. Goalkeeper and World Cup emblem	55	1·00

1978. Easter. Drawings by Durer.

855	367	11 p. black and mauve	10	10
856	–	39 p. black and flesh	25	30
857	–	60 p. black and yellow	40	45
858	–	1 c. black and green	60	65

DESIGNS: 39 p. "The Crucifixion"; 60 p. "The Deposition"; 1 c. "The Resurrection".

1978. Football Victories of Ghana and Argentina. Nos. 850/3 optd **"GHANA WINNERS"** (8, 30 p.) or **"ARGENTINA WINS"** (others).

859	366	8 p. multicoloured	15	15
860	–	30 p. multicoloured	25	30
861	–	60 p. multicoloured	35	45
862	–	1 c. multicoloured	55	75

369 "Bauhinia purpurea"

1978. Flowers. Multicoloured.

864	11 p. Type **369**	15	10
865	39 p. "Cassia fistula"	30	55
866	60 p. "Plumeria acutifolia"	40	70
867	1 c. "Jacaranda mimosifolia"	45	1·00

370 Mail Van

1978. 75th Anniv of Ghana Railways. Multicoloured.

868	11 p. Type **370**	25	10
869	39 p. Pay and bank car	35	65
870	60 p. Steam locomotive No. 1 "Amanful", 1922	40	1·00
871	1 c. Diesel-electric locomotive No. 1651, 1960	40	1·40

371 "Orbiter" Spacecraft

1979. "Pioneer" Venus Space Project. Multicoloured.

872	11 p. Type **371**	15	10
873	39 p. "Multiprobe" space craft	25	30
874	60 p. "Orbiter" and "Multiprobe" spacecraft in Venus orbit	40	45
875	3 c. Radar chart of Venus	60	1·40

372 "O Come All Ye Faithful"

1979. Christmas. Lines and Scenes from Christmas Carols. Multicoloured.

877	8 p. Type **372**	10	10
878	10 p. "O Little Town of Bethlehem"	10	10
879	15 p. "We Three Kings of Orient Are"	10	10
880	20 p. "I Saw Three Ships come Sailing By"	10	15
881	2 c. "Away In a Manger"	40	80
882	4 c. "Ding Dong Merrily on High"	65	1·40

373 Dr. J. B. Danquah (lawyer and nationalist)

375 Children in Classroom

374 Tribesman ringing Clack Bells

1980. Famous Ghanaians. Multicoloured.

884	20 p. Type **373**	15	10
885	65 p. John Mensah Sarbah (nationalist)	20	20
886	80 p. Dr. J. E. K. Aggrey (educationalist)	25	30
887	2 c. Dr. Kwame Nkrumah (nationalist)	40	40
888	4 c. G. E. (Paa) Grant (lawyer)	70	1·10

1980. Death Centenary of Sir Rowland Hill (1979). Multicoloured.

889	20 p. Type **374**	15	15
893	25 p. Type **374**	15	20
894	50 p. Chieftain with Golden Elephant staff	30	40
890	65 p. As 50 p.	30	30
895	1 c. Signalling with drums	50	85
891	2 c. As 1 c.	50	1·00
892	4 c. Chieftain with ivory and gold staff	75	2·00
896	5 c. As 4 c.	1·25	3·00

1980. International Year of the Child (1979). Multicoloured.

898	20 p. Type **375**	15	15
899	65 p. Playing football	30	45
900	2 c. Playing in a boat	50	1·00
901	4 c. Mother and child	75	1·75

1980. "London 1980" International Stamp Exhibition. Nos. 889/96 optd **"LONDON 1980" 6th - 14th May 1980.**

903	**374**	20 p. multicoloured	15	15
907	–	25 p. multicoloured	60	1·00
908	–	50 p. multicoloured	90	1·50
904	–	65 p. multicoloured	25	50
909	–	1 c. multicoloured	1·50	2·25
905	–	2 c. multicoloured	50	1·25
906	–	4 c. multicoloured	75	2·25
910	–	5 c. multicoloured	3·50	4·50

1980. Papal Visit. Nos. 898/901 optd **"PAPAL VISIT" 8th - 9th May 1980.**

912	**375**	20 p. multicoloured	45	35
913	–	65 p. multicoloured	90	60
914	–	2 c. multicoloured	1·50	1·40
915	–	4 c. multicoloured	2·25	2·50

378 Parliament House

1980. 3rd Republic Commemoration. Multicoloured.

917	20 p. Type **378**	10	10
918	65 p. Supreme Court	20	25
919	2 c. The Castle	40	70

379 Boeing 737 Airliner and Map of West Africa

1980. 5th Anniv of Economic Community of West African States. Multicoloured.

921	20 p. Type **379**	10	10
922	65 p. Antenna and map	15	20
923	80 p. Cog-wheels and map	20	25
924	2 c. Corn and map	35	50

380 "OAU."

381 "The Adoration of the Magi"

1980. First Organization of African Unity Economic Summit Conference, Nigeria.

925	**380**	20 p. multicoloured	10	10
926	–	65 p. multicoloured	15	20
927	–	80 p. deep red, red and black	15	25
928	–	2 c. multicoloured	20	65

DESIGNS: 65 p. Maps of Africa and Ghana and banner; 80 p. Map of Africa; 2 c. Map of Africa, banner and Ghanaian flag.

1980. Christmas. Paintings by Fra Angelico. Multicoloured.

929	15 p. Type **381**	10	10
930	20 p. "The Virgin and Child, enthroned with Four Angels"	10	10
931	2 c. "The Virgin and Child enthroned with Eight Angels"	35	80
932	4 c. "The Annunciation"	60	1·60

382 "Health"

1980. 75th Anniv of Rotary International. Multicoloured.

934	20 p. Type **382**	10	10
935	65 p. Rotary emblem and motto with maps of World and Ghana	15	30
936	2 c. Rotary emblem, globe and outstretched hands	35	85
937	4 c. "Eradication of Hunger"	60	1·50

383 Narina Trogon

385 Royal Yacht "Britannia"

384 Pope John Paul II, Archbishop of Canterbury and President Limann during Papal Visit

1981. Birds. Multicoloured.

939	20 p. Type **383**	1·25	15
940	65 p. White-crowned robin chat	2·25	50
941	2 c. Swallow-tailed bee eater	2·75	1·75
942	4 c. Rose-ringed parakeet	4·25	3·25

1981. 1st Anniv of Papal Visit.

944	**384**	20 p. multicoloured	25	15
945		65 p. multicoloured	45	55
946		80 p. multicoloured	60	70
947		2 c. multicoloured	1·10	2·00

1981. Royal Wedding. Multicoloured.

948	20 p. Prince Charles and Lady Diana Spencer	10	10
952	65 p. As 20 p.	15	25
949	80 p. Prince Charles on visit to Ghana	15	20
953	1 c. As 80 p.	25	35
955	2 c. Type **385**	1·00	1·50
954	3 c. Type **385**	70	1·10
950	4 c. Type **385**	50	80
956	5 c. As 20 p.	1·00	2·75

386 Earth Satellite Station

388 "The Betrothal of St. Catherine of Alexandria" (Lucas Cranach)

387 Pounding Fufu

1981. Commissioning of Earth Satellite Station. Mult.

957	20 p. Type **386**	10	10
958	65 p. Satellites beaming signals to Earth	15	15
959	80 p. Satellite	15	20
960	4 c. Satellite orbiting Earth	1·00	1·50

1981. World Food Day. Multicoloured.

962	20 p. Type **387**	10	10
963	65 p. Plucking cocoa	25	35
964	80 p. Preparing banku	35	40
965	2 c. Garri processing	75	2·25

1981. Christmas. Details from Paintings. Multicoloured.

967	15 p. Type **388**	15	10
968	20 p. "Angelic Musicians play for Mary and Child" (Aachener Altares)	15	10
969	65 p. "Child Jesus embracing his Mother" (Gabriel Metsu)	20	15
970	80 p. "Madonna and Child" (Fra Filippo Lippi)	20	20
971	2 c. "The Madonna with Infant Jesus" (Barnaba da Modena)	40	70
972	4 c. "The Immaculate Conception" (Murillo)	45	1·10

389 Blind Person

1982. International Year for Disabled Persons. Multicoloured.

974	20 p. Type **389**	10	10
975	65 p. Disabled person with crutches	30	35
976	80 p. Blind child reading braille	40	45
977	4 c. Disabled people helping one another	1·75	2·25

390 African Clawless Otter

391 "Precis westermanni"

1982. Flora and Fauna. Multicoloured.

979	20 p. Type **390**	25	15
980	65 p. Bushbuck	60	40
981	80 p. Aardvark	70	50
982	1 c. Scarlet bell tree	85	60
983	2 c. Glory-lilies	1·60	1·25
984	4 c. Blue-pea	2·75	2·25

1982. Butterflies. Multicoloured.

986	20 p. Type **391**	70	15
987	65 p. "Papilio menestheus"	1·50	1·00
988	2 c. "Antanartia delius"	2·50	3·50
989	4 c. "Charaxes castor"	4·00	4·75

392 Scouts planting Tree

1982. 75th Anniv of Boy Scout Movement. Multicoloured.

991	20 p. Type **392**	35	15
992	65 p. Scouts cooking on campfire	90	65
993	80 p. Sea Scouts sailing	1·25	85
994	3 c. Scouts observing African elephant	2·50	3·25

393 Initial Stages of Construction

1982. Kpong Hydro-Electric Project. Multicoloured.

996	20 p. Type **393**	65	10
997	65 p. Truck removing rubble	1·40	45
998	80 p. Hydro-electric turbines	1·60	65
999	2 c. Aerial view of completed plant	3·00	1·60

394 Footballers

1982. World Cup Football Championship, Spain.

1000	**394**	20 p. multicoloured	10	10
1005		30 p. multicoloured	20	20
1001	–	65 p. multicoloured	30	35
1002	–	80 p. multicoloured (Heading)	40	45
1006	–	80 p. multicoloured (Three footballers)	35	45
1007	–	1 c. multicoloured	40	55
1008	–	3 c. multicoloured	1·00	1·60
1003	–	4 c. multicoloured	1·50	2·00

DESIGNS: 65 p. to 4 c. Scenes showing footballers.

395 The Fight against Tuberculosis

1982. Centenary of Robert Koch's Discovery of Tubercle Bacillus. Multicoloured.

1009	20 p. Type **395**	70	20
1010	65 p. Robert Koch	1·60	1·25
1011	80 p. Robert Koch in Africa	2·00	1·75
1012	1 c. Centenary of discovery of Tuberculosis	2·25	2·75
1013	2 c. Robert Koch and Nobel Prize, 1905	3·25	4·00

396 The Shepherds worship Jesus

397 Ghana and Commonwealth Flags with Coat of Arms

1982. Christmas. Multicoloured.

1014 15 p. Type **396** 10 10
1015 20 p. Mary, Joseph and baby Jesus 10 10
1016 65 p. The Three Kings sight star 25 30
1017 4 c. Winged Angel . . . . . 1·00 1·75

1983. Commonwealth Day. Multicoloured.

1019 20 p. Type **397** 25 15
1020 55 p. Satellite view of Ghana . . 45 65
1021 80 p. Minerals of Ghana . . 1·00 1·25
1022 3 c. African fish eagle . . . . 2·75 4·25

1983. Italy's Victory in World Cup Football Championships (1982). Nos. 1000/8 optd **WINNER ITALY 3-1.**

1023 20 p. multicoloured 10 10
1028 30 p. multicoloured 15 30
1024 65 p. multicoloured 15 15
1025 80 p. multicoloured 15 20
1029 80 p. multicoloured 50 80
1030 1 c. multicoloured 60 95
1031 3 c. multicoloured . . . . . 1·50 2·00
1026 4 c. multicoloured . . . . . 1·25 1·75

1983. No. 470 surch **C1.**

1031a 1 c. on 20 n.p. Bush hare (blue) 40 40

399 Short-finned Pilot Whale

1983. Coastal Marine Mammals. Multicoloured.

1032 1 c. Type **399** . . . . . . 1·00 1·00
1033 1 c. 40 Risso's dolphin . . . . 1·10 1·10
1034 2 c. False killer whale . . . 1·25 1·25
1035 3 c. Spinner dolphin . . . . 1·60 1·60
1036 4 c. Atlantic hump-backed dolphin . . . . 2·00 2·00

400 Banded Jewelfish

401 Communication Devices

1983.

1038 **400** 5 p. multicoloured . . . 30 20
1039 – 10 p. multicoloured . . . 30 20
1040 – 20 p. multicoloured . . . 40 20
1041 – 50 p. green, orange & blk 40 30
1042 – 1 c. orange, blue and black 50 20
1043 – 2 c. multicoloured . . . 50 30
1044 – 3 c. multicoloured . . . 80 30
1045 – 4 c. multicoloured . . . 40 40
1046 – 5 c. multicoloured . . . 50 40
1047 – 10 c. multicoloured . . . 65 1·00

DESIGNS—HORIZ: 10 p. Banded jewelfish (different); 2 c. Jet airliner. VERT: 20 p. "Haemanthus rupestris"; 50 p. Mounted warrior; 1 c. Scorpion; 3 c. White-collared mangabey; 4 c. Demidoff's galago; 5 c. "Kaemferia nigerica"; 10 c. Grey-backed camaroptera.

1983. World Communications Year. Multicoloured.

1048 1 c. Type **401** 15 25
1049 1 c. 40 Satellite dish aerial . . 20 30
1050 2 c. 30 Cable and cable-laying ship 35 55
1051 3 c. Switchboard operators . 40 65
1052 5 c. Aircraft cockpit and air traffic controllers 55 85

402 Children receiving Presents

1983. Christmas. Multicoloured.

1054 70 p. Type **402** 20 10
1055 1 c. Nativity and Star of Bethlehem (vert) 20 10
1056 1 c. 40 Children celebrating (vert) 35 55
1057 2 c. 30 Family praying together (vert) . . . . 45 1·00
1058 3 c. Dancing to bongo drum 55 1·25

403 Soldiers with Rifles

407 Cross and Crown of Thorns

1983. Namibia Day.

1060 **403** 50 p. green and black . . 10 10
1061 – 1 c. multicoloured . . . 10 10
1062 – 1 c. 40 blue, lt blue & blk 15 15
1063 – 2 c. 30 multicoloured . . 20 25
1064 – 3 c. multicoloured . . . 25 30

DESIGNS: 1 c. Soldiers supported by tank; 1 c. 40, Machete cutting chains; 2 c. 30, Peasant woman; 3 c. Soldiers and artillery support.

1984. (a) Nos. 948/50, 952 and 954 surch.

1065 1 c. on 20 p. Prince Charles and Lady Diana Spencer . . . 2·50 3·00
1066 9 c. on 65 p. Prince Charles and Lady Diana Spencer . . . 3·00 4·00
1067 9 c. on 80 p. Prince Charles on visit to Ghana . . . . . . 3·00 4·00
1068 20 c. on 3 c. Type **385** . . . 3·50 6·00
1069 20 c. on 4 c. Type **385** . . . 3·50 6·00

(b) Nos. 991/2 and 994 surch.

1071 10 c. on 20 p. Type **392** . . 40 45
1072 19 c. on 65 p. Scouts cooking on campfire 80 85
1073 30 c. on 3 c. Scouts observing African elephant . . . . . 1·50 1·50

(c) Nos. 1000/3, 1005/6 and 1008 surch.

1075 **394** 1 c. on 20 p. multicoloured 30 30
1076 – 9 c. on 65 p. multicoloured 70 70
1077 – 9 c. on 3 c. multicoloured 70 70
1078 **394** 10 c. on 30 p. multicoloured 70 70
1079 – 10 c. on 80 p. multicoloured 70 70
1080 – 20 c. on 80 p. multicoloured 1·50 1·50
1081 – 20 c. on 4 c. multicoloured 1·50 1·50

(d) Nos. 1019/22 surch.

1083 1 c. on 20 p. Type **397** . . . 10 10
1084 9 c. on 55 p. Satellite view of Ghana 40 45
1085 30 c. on 80 p. Minerals of Ghana . . . . 1·50 1·50
1086 50 c. on 3 c. African fish eagle 2·50 3·00

(e) Nos. 1023/6, 1028/9 and 1031 surch.

1087 **394** 1 c. on 20 p. multicoloured 10 10
1088 – 9 c. on 65 p. multicoloured 40 45
1089 – 9 c. on 3 c. multicoloured 40 45
1090 **394** 10 c. on 30 p. multicoloured 40 45
1091 – 10 c. on 80 p. multicoloured 40 45
1092 – 20 c. on 80 p. multicoloured 80 85
1093 – 20 c. on 4 c. multicoloured 80 85

1984. Universal Postal Union Congress, Hamburg. Nos. 1035/6 surch **19th U.P.U. CONGRESS – HAMBURG,** emblem and new value.

1095 10 c. on 3 c. Spinner dolphin 40 45
1096 50 c. on 5 c. Atlantic humpbacked dolphin . . . 2·10 2·25

1984. Easter. Multicoloured.

1098 1 c. Type **407** 10 10
1099 1 c. 40 Christ praying . . . 10 10
1100 2 c. 30 The Resurrection . . 10 10
1101 3 c. Palm Sunday 10 15
1102 50 c. Christ on the road to Emmaus . . . . 1·10 2·25

408 Women's 400 Metre Race

409 "Amorphophallus johnsonii"

1984. Olympic Games, Los Angeles. Multicoloured.

1104 1 c. Type **408** 10 10
1105 1 c. 40 Boxing 15 10
1106 2 c. 30 Hockey 20 15
1107 3 c. Men's 400 metre hurdles race 20 15
1108 50 c. Rhythmic gymnastics . 2·40 3·50

1984. Flowers. Multicoloured.

1110 1 c. Type **409** 10 10
1111 1 c. 40 "Pancratium trianthum" 10 10
1112 2 c. 30 "Eulophia cucullata" 15 15
1113 3 c. "Amorphophallus abyssinicus" 15 15
1114 50 c. "Chlorophytum togoense" 3·00 5·00

410 Young Bongo

1984. Endangered Antelopes. Multicoloured.

1116 1 c. Type **410** 30 20
1117 2 c. 30 Bongo bucks fighting . 55 55
1118 3 c. Bongo family 70 70
1119 20 c. Bongo herd in high grass 2·50 3·50

411 Dipo Girl

412 The Three Wise Men bringing Gifts

1984. Ghanaian Culture. Multicoloured.

1121 1 c. Type **411** 10 10
1122 1 c. 40 Adowa dancer . . . 10 10
1123 2 c. 30 Agbadza dancer . . . 10 15
1124 3 c. Damba dancer 10 15
1125 50 c. Dipo dancer . . . . . 1·75 3·00

1984. Christmas. Multicoloured.

1127 70 p. Type **412** 10 10
1128 1 c. Choir of angels 10 10
1129 1 c. 40 Mary and shepherds at manger 10 10
1130 2 c. 30 The flight into Egypt . 10 10
1131 3 c. Simeon blessing Jesus . . 10 15
1132 50 c. Holy Family and angels 1·75 3·00

1984. Olympic Winners. Nos. 1104/8 optd

1134 1 c. Type **408** (optd **VALERIE BRISCO-HOOKS U.S.A.**) 10 10
1135 1 c. 40 Boxing (optd **U.S. WINNERS**) 10 10
1136 2 c. 30 Hockey (optd **PAKISTAN (FIELD HOCKEY)**) 10 10
1137 3 c. Men's 400 metre hurdles race (optd **EDWIN MOSES U.S.A.**) 10 10
1138 50 c. Rhythmic gymnastics (optd **LAURI FUNG CANADA**) . . . . 1·50 1·60

414 The Queen Mother attending Church Service

415 Moslems going to Mosque

1985. Life and Times of Queen Elizabeth the Queen Mother. Multicoloured.

1140 5 c. Type **414** 10 15
1141 12 c. At Ascot Races 25 30
1142 100 c. At Clarence House on her 84th birthday . . . . 1·75 2·50

Stamps as Nos. 1140/2 but with face values of 8 c., 20 c. and 70 c. exist from additional sheetlets with changed background colours.

1985. Islamic Festival of Id-el-Fitr. Multicoloured.

1144 5 c. Type **415** 25 20
1145 8 c. Moslems at prayer . . . 35 30
1146 12 c. Pilgrims visiting the Dome of the Rock 55 45
1147 18 c. Preaching the Koran . . 70 60
1148 50 c. Banda Nkwanta Mosque, Accra, and map of Ghana . 1·75 1·60

416 Youths clearing Refuse ("Make Ghana Clean")

418 Fork-tailed Flycatcher

417 Honda "Interceptor", 1984

1985. International Youth Year. Multicoloured.

1149 5 c. Type **416** 10 10
1150 8 c. Planting sapling ("Make Ghana Green") 15 15
1151 12 c. Youth carrying bananas ("Feed Ghana") 20 25
1152 100 c. Open-air class ("Educate Ghana") . . . . 1·60 2·25

1985. Centenary of the Motorcycle. Multicoloured.

1154 5 c. Type **417** 55 55
1155 8 c. DKW, 1938 . . . . . . 65 75
1156 12 c. BMW "R 32", 1923 . . 1·00 1·00
1157 100 c. NSU, 1900 . . . . . 5·50 7·00

1985. Birth Bicentenary of John J. Audubon (ornithologist). Designs showing original paintings. Multicoloured.

1159 5 c. Type **418** . . . . . . 1·25 50
1160 8 c. Barred owl . . . . . . 2·25 2·00
1161 12 c. Black-throated mango . 2·25 2·00
1162 100 c. White-crowned pigeon 6·00 9·50

No. 1159 is inscribed "York-tailed fly catcher" in error

419 United Nations Building, New York

1985. 40th Anniv of U.N.O. Multicoloured.

1164 5 c. Type **419** 10 10
1165 8 c. Flags of member nations and U.N. Building 15 15
1166 12 c. Dove with olive branch . 15 25
1167 18 c. General Assembly . . . 25 35
1168 100 c. Flags of Ghana and United Nations . . . . . 1·25 1·75

420 Coffee

1985. 20th Anniv of United Nations Conference on Trade and Development. Designs showing export products. Multicoloured.

1170 5 c. Type **420** 10 10
1171 8 c. Cocoa 15 15
1172 12 c. Timber 25 25
1173 18 c. Bauxite . . . . 1·25 90
1174 100 c. Gold . . . . 6·50 8·50

421 Growth Monitoring

1985. U.N.I.C.E.F. Child Survival Campaign. Multicoloured.

1176 5 c. Type **421** 30 10
1177 8 c. Oral rehydration therapy 50 30
1178 12 c. Breast feeding 70 40
1179 100 c. Immunization . . . . 3·00 4·50

422 Airline Stewardess and Boys with Stamp Album

1986. "Ameripex" International Stamp Exhibition, Chicago. Multicoloured.

1181 5 c. Type **422** 15 15
1182 25 c. Globe and Douglas DC-10 airplane 60 45
1183 100 c. Ghana Airways stewardess (vert) . . . . . 2·25 3·00

MINIMUM PRICE

The minimum price quoted is 10p which represents a handling charge rather than a basis for valuing common stamps. For further notes about prices see introductory pages.

423 Kejetia Roundabout, Kumasi

1986. "Inter-Tourism '86" Conference. Mult.
1185 5 c. Type **423** 10 10
1186 15 c. Fort St. Jago, Elmina . 30 30
1187 25 c. Tribal warriors 45 45
1188 100 c. Chief holding audience 1·75 3·25

424 Tackling 425 Fertility Doll

1987. World Cup Football Championship, Mexico (1986). Multicoloured.
1190 5 c. Type **424** 15 10
1191 15 c. Player taking control of ball 25 15
1192 25 c. Player kicking ball . . . 40 25
1193 100 c. Player with ball . . . 1·40 1·25

1987. Ghanaian Fertility Dolls. Designs showing different dolls.
1195 **425** 5 c. multicoloured . . . 10 10
1196 – 15 c. multicoloured . . . 20 15
1197 – 25 c. multicoloured . . . 35 25
1198 – 100 c. multicoloured . . 1·25 1·50

426 Children of Different Races, Peace Doves and Sun

1987. International Peace Year (1986). Multicoloured.
1200 5 c. Type **426** 15 10
1201 25 c. Plough, peace dove and rising sun 75 25
1202 100 c. Peace dove, olive branch and globe (vert) . . . . . 2·50 3·00

427 Lumber and House under Construction

1987. "Gifex '87" International Forestry Exposition, Accra. Multicoloured.
1204 5 c. Type **427** 10 10
1205 15 c. Planks and furniture . . 15 15
1206 25 c. Felled trees 30 25
1207 200 c. Logs and wood carvings 1·90 2·25

1987. Appearance of Halley's Comet (1986). As T **123** of Anguilla. Multicoloured.
1208 5 c. Mikhail Lomonosov (scientist) and Chamber of Curiosities, St. Petersburg . 20 10
1209 25 c. Lunar probe "Surveyor 3", 1966 . . . . 70 30
1210 200 c. Wedgwood plaques for Isaac Newton, 1790 and "Apollo 11" Moon landing, 1968 . . . . 3·25 2·25

428 Demonstrator and Arms breaking Shackles

1987. Solidarity with the People of Southern Africa. Multicoloured.
1212 5 c. Type **428** 10 10
1213 15 c. Miner and gold bars . . 40 15
1214 25 c. Xhosa warriors 30 25
1215 100 c. Nelson Mandela and shackles . . . . 1·25 2·00

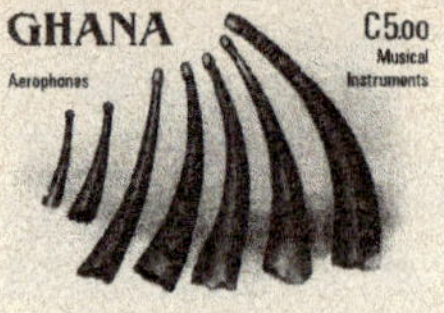

429 Aerophones

1987. Musical Instruments. Multicoloured.
1217 5 c. Type **429** 10 10
1218 15 c. Xylophone 15 15
1219 25 c. Chordophones 30 25
1220 100 c. Membranophones . . 1·00 1·25

430 Woman filling Water Pot at Pump

1987. Int Year of Shelter for the Homeless. Mult.
1222 5 c. Type **430** 10 10
1223 15 c. Building house from breeze blocks 15 15
1224 25 c. Modern village with stream 25 25
1225 100 c. Modern houses with verandahs . . . . 1·25 1·25

431 Ga Women preparing Kpokpoi for Homowo Festival

1988. Ghana Festivals. Multicoloured.
1226 5 c. Type **431** 10 10
1227 15 c. Efute hunters with deer, Aboakyir festival 15 15
1228 25 c. Fanti chief dancing at Odwira festival 25 25
1229 100 c. Chief in palanquin, Yam festival . . . . 1·25 1·25

432 Port Installation

1988. 5th Anniv (1987) of 31 December Revolution. Multicoloured.
1230 5 c. Type **432** . . . . 1·00 40
1231 15 c. Repairing railway line . 7·00 2·25
1232 25 c. Planting cocoa . . . . 1·25 55
1233 100 c. Miners with ore truck 7·50 7·50

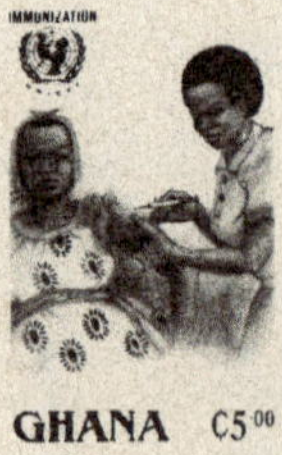

433 Nurse giving Injection 435 Akwadjan Men

434 Fishing

1988. U.N.I.C.E.F. Global Immunization Campaign. Multicoloured.
1234 5 c. Type **433** 20 10
1235 15 c. Girl receiving injection 25 20
1236 25 c. Schoolgirl crippled by polio 35 50
1237 100 c. Nurse giving oral vaccine to baby . . . . 60 2·25

1988. 10th Anniv of International Fund for Agricultural Development. Multicoloured.
1238 5 c. Type **434** 45 20
1239 15 c. Women harvesting crops 70 30
1240 25 c. Cattle 85 40
1241 100 c. Village granaries . . . 2·50 4·25

1988. Tribal Costumes. Multicoloured.
1242 5 c. Type **435** 15 10
1243 25 c. Banaa man 35 20
1244 250 c. Agwasen woman . . . 1·50 2·00

1988. Nos.. 460, 464/6, 469/70, 1031a, 1038/42, 1044 and 1046 surch.
1245 – 20 c. on 50 p. green, orange and black (No. 1041) . 30 15
1246 – 20 c. on 1 c. orange, blue and black (No. 1042) . 30 15
1247 – 50 c. on 10 n.p. mult (No. 469) 30 25
1248 – 50 c. on 20 n.p. deep blue and blue (No. 470) (surch **C50**) . . . . . 2·50 45
1249 – 50 c. on 20 n.p. deep blue and blue (No. 470) (surch **C50.00**) . . . . 2·50 45
1250 – 50 c. on 10 p. mult (No. 1039) 30 15
1251 – 50 c. on 1 c. on 20 n.p. deep blue and blue (No. 1031a) (surch **C50**) . . . . . . 2·50 45
1252 – 50 c. on 1 c. on 20 n.p. deep blue and blue (No. 1031a) (surch **C50.00**) . . . . 2·50 45
1254 – 50 c. on 1 c. orange, blue and black (No. 1042) . 2·50 45
1255 **230** 60 c. on 1 n.p. mult . . . 2·00 45
1256 – 60 c. on 4 n.p. mult (No. 465) . . . . . . 2·50 30
1257 – 60 c. on 3 c. mult (No. 1044) 50 30
1258 **400** 80 c. on 5 p. mult 55 35
1259 – 80 c. on 5 c. mult (No. 1046) 3·25 3·50
1260 – 100 c. on 3 n.p. mult (No. 464) . . . . 5·50 5·50
1261 – 100 c. on 20 n.p. deep blue and blue (No. 470) . . 50 55
1262 – 100 c. on 20 p. mult (No. 1040) 50 55
1263 – 100 c. on 3 c. mult (No. 1044) 50 55
1264 – 200 c. on 6 n.p. mult (No. 466) 50 65

440 Boxing

1988. Olympic Games, Seoul. Multicoloured.
1265 20 c. Type **440** 20 15
1266 60 c. Athletics 55 55
1267 80 c. Discus-throwing 60 80
1268 100 c. Javelin-throwing . . . 70 1·10
1269 350 c. Weightlifting . . . . . 1·75 3·00

441 Nutrition Lecture 443 "African Solidarity"

442 Tropical Forest

1988. 125th Anniv of Int Red Cross. Mult.
1271 20 c. Type **441** 40 15
1272 50 c. Red Cross volunteer with blind woman 90 90
1273 60 c. Distributing flood relief supplies . . . . 1·00 1·00
1274 200 c. Giving first aid . . . . 2·50 3·25

1988. Christmas. Multicoloured.
1275 20 c. Type **442** 15 10
1276 60 c. Christ Child (vert) . . . 35 35
1277 80 c. Virgin and Child with Star (vert) 50 50
1278 100 c. Three Wise Men following Star 60 70
1279 350 c. Symbolic Crucifixion (vert) . . . . 2·00 2·50

1989. 25th Anniv (1988) of Organization of African Unity. Multicoloured.
1281 20 c. Type **443** 10 10
1282 50 c. O.A.U. Headquarters Addis Ababa 15 20
1283 60 c. Emperor Haile Selassie and Ethiopian flag (horiz) 20 25
1284 200 c. Kwame Nkrumah (former Ghanaian President) and flag (horiz) 60 85

444 "Amor"

1989. 500th Birth Anniv of Titian (artist). Multicoloured.
1285 20 c. Type **444** 40 15
1286 60 c. "The Appeal" 90 65
1287 80 c. "Bacchus and Ariadne" (detail) . . . . 1·00 85
1288 100 c. "Portrait of a Musician" 1·10 1·60
1289 350 c. "Philip II seated" . . 2·75 4·50

1989. Olympic Medal Winners, Seoul. Nos. 1251/5 optd.
1291 20 c. Type **436** (optd **A. ZUELOW DDR 60 KG**) 10 10
1292 20 c. Athletics (optd **G. BORDIN ITALY MARATHON**) 20 25
1293 80 c. Discus-throwing (optd **J. SCHULT DDR**) 25 30
1294 100 c. Javelin-throwing (optd **T. KORJUS FINLAND**) . 30 35
1295 350 c. Weightlifting (optd **B. GUIDIKOV BULGARIA 75 KG**) . . . . 1·00 1·10

1989. Various stamps surch. (a) Nos. 949/50 and 952/4
1297 80 c. on 65 p. Prince Charles and Lady Diana Spencer . 35 40
1298 100 c. on 80 p. Prince Charles on visit to Ghana 45 50
1299 100 c. on 1 c. Prince Charles on visit to Ghana 45 50
1300 300 c. on 3 c. Type **385** . . . 1·25 1·60
1301 500 c. on 4 c. Type **385** . . . 2·25 2·75

(b) Nos. 1048/51
1302 60 c. on 1 c. Type **401** . . . 50 50
1303 80 c. on 1 c. 40 Satellite dish aerial 65 65
1304 200 c. on 2 c. 30 Cable and cable-laying ship . . . . . 1·75 2·00
1305 300 c. on 3 c. Switchboard operators . . . . 2·00 2·25

(c) Nos. 1104/7
1307 60 c. on 1 c. Type **408** . . . 30 30
1308 80 c. on 1 c. 40 Boxing . . . 40 40
1309 200 c. on 2 c. 30 Hockey . . 1·25 1·60
1310 300 c. on 3 c. Men's 400 metre hurdles race . . . . 1·40 1·75

(d) Nos. 1134/7
1312 60 c. on 1 c. Type **408** (optd **VALERIE BRISCO-HOOKS U.S.A.**) 85 90
1313 80 c. on 1 c. 40 Boxing (optd **U.S. WINNERS**) . . . . 1·10 1·25
1314 200 c. on 2 c. 30 Field hockey (optd **PAKISTAN (FIELD HOCKEY)**) . . . . 3·25 3·50
1315 300 c. on 3 c. Men's 400 metre hurdles race (optd **EDWIN MOSES U.S.A.**) . . . . . 3·50 3·75

(e) Nos. 1140/2
1317 80 c. on 5 c. Type **414** . . . 35 40
1318 250 c. on 12 c. At Ascot Races 1·10 1·75
1319 300 c. on 100 c. At Clarence House on her 84th birthday 1·25 1·75

(f) Nos. 1159/61
1321 80 c. on 5 c. Type **418** . . . 1·00 1·00
1322 100 c. on 8 c. Barred owl . . 2·25 2·25
1323 300 c. on 12 c. Black-throated mango . . . . 2·50 3·00

(g) Nos. 1190/2
1325 60 c. on 5 c. Type **424** . . . 45 45
1326 200 c. on 15 c. Player taking control of ball . . . . . . 1·50 2·00
1327 300 c. on 25 c. Player kicking ball . . . . 2·00 2·50

(h) As Nos. 1190/2 but with unissued opt **WINNERS Argentina 3 W. Germany 2**
1329 60 c. on 5 c. Type **424** . . . 30 30
1330 200 c. on 15 c. Player taking control of ball . . . . . . 1·00 1·50
1331 300 c. on 25 c. Player kicking ball . . . . 1·40 2·00

(i) Nos. 1208/10
1333 60 c. on 5 c. Mikhail Lomonosov (scientist) and Chamber of Curiosities, St. Petersburg 65 55
1334 80 c. on 25 c. Lunar probe "Surveyor 3", 1966 . . . . 85 70
1335 500 c. on 200 c. Wedgwood plaques for Isaac Newton, 1790, and "Apollo 11" Moon landing, 1968 . . . . . . 3·25 4·50

(j) As Nos. 1208/10 but with unissued logo opt as T **218** of Antigua
1337 60 c. on 5 c. Mikhail Lomonosov (scientist) and Chamber of Curiosities, St. Petersburg 35 40

1338 80 c. on 25 c. Lunar probe "Surveyor 3", 1966 . . . . 45 50
1339 500 c. on 200 c. Wedgwood plaques for Isaac Newton, 1790, and "Apollo 11" Moon landing, 1968 . . . . . . 2·50 4·00

448 French Royal Standard and Field Gun

449 Storming the Bastille

1989. "Philexfrance 89" International Stamp Exhibition, Paris. Multicoloured.
1341 20 c. Type **448** 50 25
1342 60 c. Regimental standard, 1789, and French infantryman . . . . 1·00 90
1343 80 c. Revolutionary standard, 1789, and pistol . . . . . 1·25 1·00
1344 350 c. Tricolour, 1794, and musket . . . . 3·25 5·00

1989. Japanese Art. Portraits. As T **250** of Antigua. Multicoloured.
1346 20 c. "Minamoto-no-Yoritomo" (Fujiwara-no-Takanobu) (vert) 20 20
1347 50 c. "Takami Senseki" (Watanabe Kazan) (vert) . 30 30
1348 60 c. "Ikkyu Sojun" (study) (Bokusai) (vert) 35 35
1349 75 c. "Nakamura Kuranosuka" (Ogata Korin) (vert) . . 40 40
1350 125 c. "Portrait of a Lady" (Kyoto branch, Kano School) (vert) 65 70
1351 150 c. "Portrait of Zemmui" (anon, 12th-century) (vert) 70 75
1352 200 c. "Ono no Komachi the Poetess" (Hokusai) (vert) . 90 1·00
1353 500 c. "Kobo Daisi as a Child" (anon) (vert) . . . . . . 2·25 3·00

1989. Bicentenary of the French Revolution. Multicoloured.
1355 20 c. Type **449** 35 20
1356 60 c. Declaration of Human Rights 60 50
1357 80 c. Storming the Bastille (horiz) 80 75
1358 200 c. Revolution monument (horiz) . . . . 1·75 2·00
1359 350 c. Tree of Liberty (horiz) . 2·50 3·25

450 "Collybia fusipes"

451 "The Curse of True Love....."

1989. Fungi (1st series). Multicoloured.
1360 20 c. Type **450** 25 25
1361 50 c. "Coprinus comatus" . . 40 40
1362 60 c. "Xerocomus subtomentosus" 45 45
1363 80 c. "Lepista nuda" 55 55
1364 150 c. "Suillus placidus" . . 95 95
1365 200 c. "Lepista nuda" (different) . . . . 1·25 1·25
1366 300 c. "Marasmius oreades" . 1·75 1·75
1367 500 c. "Agaricus campestris" 3·00 3·00
See also Nos. 1489/96.

1989. 425th Birth Anniv of Shakespeare. Verses and scenes from "A Mid-summer Night's Dream". Multicoloured.
1369 40 c. Type **451** 60 60
1370 40 c. "Love looks not with the eye but with the mind" . . 60 60
1371 40 c. "Nature here shows art" . 60 60
1372 40 c. "Things growing are not ripe till their season" . . . 60 60
1373 40 c. "He is defiled that draws a sword on thee" 60 60
1374 40 c. "It is not enough to speak, but to speak true" 60 60
1375 40 c. "Thou art as wise as thou are beautiful" 60 60
1376 40 c. Wildcat in wood (face value at left) 60 60
1377 40 c. Man 60 60
1378 40 c. Woman with flower . . 60 60
1379 40 c. King and queen 60 60
1380 40 c. Bottom 60 60
1381 40 c. Wildcat in wood (face value at right) 60 60
1382 40 c. Woman 60 60
1383 40 c. Leopard 60 60
1384 40 c. Tree trunk and man . . 60 60
1385 40 c. Meadow flowers . . . 60 60
1386 40 c. Mauve flowers 60 60
1387 40 c. Plants 60 60
1388 40 c. Lion 60 60
1389 40 c. Fern and flowers . . . 60 60
Nos. 1369/89 were printed together, forming a composite design.

1989. Birds. As T **244** of Dominica. Multicoloured.
1390 20 c. Bronze mannikin (horiz) 30 10
1391 50 c. African pied wagtail (horiz) 45 30
1392 60 c. African pygmy kingfisher (inscr "Halcyon malimbicus") (horiz) . . 1·25 1·75
1392a 60 c. African pygmy kingfisher (inscr "Ispidina picta") (horiz) . . . . 1·25 1·50
1393 80 c. Blue-breasted kingfisher (inscr "Ispidina picta") (horiz) . . . . 1·75 2·25
1393a 80 c. Blue-breasted kingfisher (inscr "Halcyon malimbicus") (horiz) . . 1·50 2·00
1394 150 c. Striped kingfisher . . 1·10 1·25
1395 200 c. Shikra . . . . 1·25 1·40
1396 300 c. Grey parrot . . . . 1·50 1·75
1397 500 c. Black kite . . . . . 2·50 3·25

452 Command Module "Columbia" orbiting Moon

1989. 20th Anniv of First Manned Landing on Moon. Multicoloured.
1399 20 c. Type **452** 30 15
1400 80 c. Neil Armstrong's footprint on Moon 50 60
1401 200 c. Edwin Aldrin on Moon 1·25 1·75
1402 300 c. "Apollo 11" capsule on parachutes . . . . 1·60 2·00

453 Desertification of Pasture

1989. World Environment Day. Multicoloured.
1404 20 c. Type **453** 50 15
1405 60 c. Wildlife fleeing bush fire 90 80
1406 400 c. Industrial pollution . 2·75 3·50
1407 500 c. Erosion . . . . . . 3·00 3·75

454 "Bebearia arcadius"

1990. Butterflies. Multicoloured.
1408 20 c. Type **454** 35 20
1409 60 c. "Charaxes laodice" . . 50 40
1410 80 c. "Euryphura porphyrion" 60 45
1411 100 c. "Neptis nicomedes" . 70 50
1412 150 c. "Citrinophila erastus" 90 90
1413 200 c. "Aethiopana honorius" 1·25 1·25
1414 300 c. "Precis westermanni" 1·50 1·75
1415 500 c. "Cymothoe hypatha" 2·00 2·50

455 Great Ribbed Cockle

1990. Seashells. Multicoloured.
1417 20 c. Type **455** 60 25
1418 60 c. Elephant's snout . . . 75 40
1419 80 c. Garter cone 85 80
1420 200 c. Tankerville's ancilla . 2·00 2·25
1421 350 c. Coronate prickly-winkle 2·75 3·50

456 Nehru welcoming President Nkrumah of Ghana

1990. Birth Centenary of Jawaharlal Nehru (Indian statesman). Multicoloured.
1422 20 c. Type **456** 60 25
1423 60 c. Nehru addressing Bandung Conference, 1955 . 75 30
1424 80 c. Nehru with garland and flowers (vert) 80 55
1425 200 c. Nehru releasing pigeon (vert) . . . . 1·25 1·50
1426 350 c. Nehru (vert) . . . . . 1·75 2·75

457 Wyon Medal, 1838

1990. 150th Anniv of the Penny Black.
1427 **457** 20 c. black and violet . . 30 20
1428 – 60 c. black and green . . 45 30
1429 – 80 c. black and violet . . 60 35
1430 – 200 c. black and green . . 1·25 1·25
1431 – 350 c. black and green . . 1·75 2·00
1432 – 400 c. black and red . . 1·75 2·00
DESIGNS: 60 c. Bath mail coach, 1840; 80 c. Leeds mail coach, 1840; 200 c. Proof of Queen's head engraved by Heath, 1840; 350 c. Master die, 1840; 400 c. London mail coach, 1840.

458 Anniversary Emblem

459 Map of Africa and Satellite Network

1990. 10th Anniv (1989) of 4 June Revolution. Multicoloured.
1434 20 c. Type **458** 15 15
1435 60 c. Foodstuffs 20 20
1436 80 c. Cocoa 25 30
1437 200 c. Mining . . . . 1·50 1·75
1438 350 c. Scales of Justice and sword . . . . 1·75 2·25

1990. 25th Anniv of Intelsat Satellite System. Multicoloured.
1439 20 c. Type **459** 20 20
1440 60 c. Map of Americas . . . 30 30
1441 80 c. Map of Asia and Pacific 35 35
1442 200 c. Map of South America and Africa . . . . 90 1·00
1443 350 c. Map of Indian Ocean and Pacific . . . . 1·50 2·00

460 Housewife using Telephone

1990. 2nd Anniv of Introduction of International Direct Dialling Service. Multicoloured.
1444 20 c. Type **460** 25 20
1445 60 c. Businessman using telephone 35 35
1446 80 c. Man using phonecard telephone 40 40
1447 200 c. Public telephones for internal and IDD services . 90 1·00
1448 350 c. Satellite station . . . 1·50 2·00

461 Blue Flycatcher

463 "Eulophia guineensis"

462 Jupiter

1990. African Tropical Rain Forest. Multicoloured.
1449 40 c. Type **461** 55 60
1450 40 c. Boomslang (snake) . . 55 60
1451 40 c. Superb sunbird 55 60
1452 40 c. Bateleur 55 60
1453 40 c. Yellow-casqued hornbill 55 60
1454 40 c. "Salamis temora" (butterfly) 55 60
1456 40 c. Leopard 55 60
1457 40 c. Bongo 55 60
1458 40 c. Grey parrot 55 60
1459 40 c. Okapi 55 60
1460 40 c. Gorilla 55 60
1461 40 c. Flap-necked chameleon 55 60
1462 40 c. West African dwarf crocodile 55 60
1463 40 c. Python 55 60
1464 40 c. Giant ground pangolin 55 60
1465 40 c. "Pseudacraea boisduvali" (butterfly) 55 60
1466 40 c. North African crested porcupine 55 60
1467 40 c. Rosy-columned aerangis (orchid) 55 60
1468 40 c. "Cymothoe sangaris" (butterfly) 55 60
Nos. 1449/68 were printed together, se-tenant, forming a composite design.

1990. Space Flight of "Voyager 2". Multicoloured.
1470 100 c. Type **462** 70 70
1471 100 c. Neptune and Triton . 70 70
1472 100 c. Ariel, moon of Uranus 70 70
1473 100 c. Saturn from Mimas . 70 70
1474 100 c. Saturn 70 70
1475 100 c. Rings of Saturn . . . 70 70
1476 100 c. Neptune 70 70
1477 100 c. Uranus from Miranda 70 70
1478 100 c. Volcano on Io 70 70

1990. Orchids. Multicoloured.
1480 20 c. Type **463** 45 45
1481 40 c. "Eurychone rothschildiana" 60 60
1482 60 c. "Bulbophyllum barbigerum" 80 80
1483 80 c. "Polystachya galeata" . 1·10 1·10
1484 200 c. "Diaphananthe kamerunensis" . . . . . . 1·75 1·75
1485 300 c. "Podangis dactyloceras" 2·00 2·00
1486 400 c. "Ancistrochilus rothschildianus" . . . . . 2·00 2·00
1487 500 c. "Rangaeris muscicola" 2·00 2·00

464 "Coprinus atramentarius"

1990. Fungi (2nd series). Multicoloured.
1489 20 c. Type **464** 60 45
1490 50 c. "Marasmius oreades" . 80 65
1491 60 c. "Oudemansiella radicata" 90 70
1492 80 c. "Boletus edulis" (Cep) . 1·10 90
1493 150 c. "Hebeloma crustuliniforme" . . . . 1·50 1·50
1494 200 c. "Coprinus micaceus" . 1·75 1·75
1495 300 c. "Macrolepiota procera" ("Lepiota procera") . . 2·00 2·00
1496 500 c. "Amanita phalloides" . 2·50 2·50

465 Italian and Swedish Players chasing Ball

1990. World Cup Football Championship, Italy. Multicoloured.
1498 20 c. Type **465** 35 20
1499 50 c. Egyptian player penetrating Irish defence . 45 30
1500 60 c. Cameroon players celebrating 50 30
1501 80 c. Rumanian player beating challenge 60 40
1502 100 c. Russian goalkeeper Dassayev 75 65
1503 150 c. Roger Milla of Cameroon (vert) . . . . 1·10 1·10
1504 400 c. South Korean player challenging opponent . . 2·00 2·25
1505 600 c. Klinsman of West Germany celebrating . . . 2·50 3·00

1990. 350th Death Anniv of Rubens. As T **273** of Antigua, but vert. Multicoloured.
1507 20 c. "Duke of Mantua" . . 20 20
1508 50 c. "Jan Brant" 30 30
1509 60 c. "Portraits of a Young Man" 30 30
1510 80 c. "Michel Ophovius" . . 40 40
1511 100 c. "Caspar Gevaerts" . . 55 55
1512 200 c. "Head of Warrior" (detail) . . . . 85 1·00
1513 300 c. "Study of a Bearded Man" . . . . 1·25 1·50
1514 400 c. "Paracelsus" . . . . 1·75 2·00

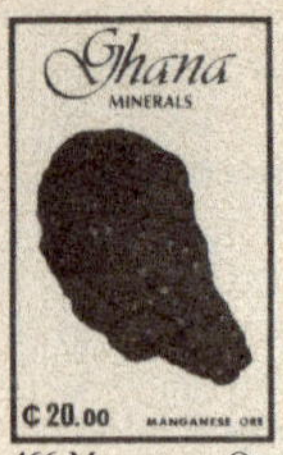

466 Manganese Ore

467 Dance Drums

1991. Minerals. Multicoloured.

1516	20 c. Type **466**	55	30
1517	60 c. Iron ore	70	60
1518	80 c. Bauxite ore	90	75
1519	200 c. Gold ore	2·00	2·00
1520	350 c. Diamond	3·00	4·00

1991. Tribal Drums. Multicoloured.

1522	20 c. Type **467**	20	20
1523	60 c. Message drums	50	40
1524	80 c. War drums	60	50
1525	200 c. Dance drums (different)	1·25	1·75
1526	350 c. Ceremonial drums	1·75	2·50

468 "Amorphophallus dracontioides"

469 Transport and Telecommunication Symbols

1991. Flowers (1st series). Multicoloured.

1528	20 c. Type **468**	55	25
1529	60 c. "Anchomanes difformis"	75	50
1530	80 c. "Kaemferia nigerica"	85	70
1531	200 c. "Aframomum sceptrum"	2·00	2·25
1532	350 c. "Amorphophallus flavovirens"	2·25	3·25

1991. Flowers (2nd series). As T **468** but inscr "GHANA" in capitals. Multicoloured.

1534	20 c. "Urginea indica"	55	25
1535	60 c. "Hymencallis littoralis"	75	50
1536	80 c. "Crinum jagus"	1·25	70
1537	200 c. "Dipcadi tacazzeanum"	2·00	2·25
1538	350 c. "Haemanthus rupestris"	2·25	3·25

1991. 40th Anniv of United Nations Development Programme. Multicoloured.

1540	20 c. Type **469**	30	20
1541	60 c. Agricultural research	50	40
1542	80 c. Literacy	60	55
1543	200 c. Advances in agricultural crop growth	1·25	1·50
1544	350 c. Industrial symbols	1·75	2·50

470 Drawing of Scout from First Handbook

471 Women sorting Fish

1991. 50th Death Anniv of Lord Baden-Powell.

1545	**470**	20 c. black and buff	50	20
1546	–	50 c. grey, blue and black	70	40
1547	–	60 c. multicoloured	70	45
1548	–	80 c. black and buff	80	55
1549	–	100 c. multicoloured	95	75
1550	–	200 c. multicoloured	1·75	1·75
1551	–	500 c. multicoloured	2·50	3·00
1552	–	600 c. multicoloured	2·75	3·50

DESIGNS—VERT: 50 c. Lord Baden-Powell; 80 c. Handbook illustrations by Norman Rockwell; 500 c. Scout at prayer. HORIZ: 60 c. Hands holding Boy Scout emblem; 100 c. Mafeking Siege 1d. Goodyear stamp and African runner; 200 c. Scouts with Blitz victim, London, 1944; 600 c. Mafeking Siege 1d. Goodyear stamp.

1991. Chorkor Smoker (fish smoking process). Multicoloured.

1554	20 c. Type **471**	30	20
1555	60 c. Cleaning the ovens	55	40
1556	80 c. Washing fish	65	55
1557	200 c. Laying fish on pallets	1·25	1·50
1558	350 c. Stacking pallets over ovens	1·75	2·50

472 African Hind

1991. Fishes. Multicoloured.

1559	20 c. Type **472**	25	25
1560	50 c. Shrew squeaker	40	40
1561	80 c. West African triggerfish	55	55
1562	100 c. Stonehead	70	70
1563	200 c. Lesser pipefish	1·50	1·50
1564	300 c. Aba	1·60	1·60
1565	400 c. Jewel cichlid	1·75	1·75
1566	500 c. Smooth hammerhead	1·90	1·90

1991. Death Centenary (1990) of Vincent van Gogh (artist). As T **278** of Antigua. Multicoloured.

1568	20 c. "Reaper with Sickle"	35	25
1569	50 c. "The Thresher"	55	40
1570	60 c. "The Sheaf-Binder"	60	50
1571	80 c. "The Sheep-Shearers"	70	65
1572	100 c. "Peasant Woman cutting Straw"	85	80
1573	200 c. "The Sower"	1·60	1·75
1574	500 c. "The Plough and the Harrow" (horiz)	2·25	2·50
1575	600 c. "The Woodcutter"	2·25	2·50

473 Gamal Nasser (Egypt) and Conference Hall

1991. 10th Non-Aligned Ministers' Conference, Accra. Statesmen. Multicoloured.

1577	20 c. Type **473**	50	30
1578	60 c. Josip Tito (Yugoslavia)	55	45
1579	80 c. Pandit Nehru (India)	1·75	1·25
1580	200 c. Kwame Nkrumah (Ghana)	1·75	2·25
1581	350 c. Achmad Sukarno (Indonesia)	1·90	3·00

474 Green-winged Pytilia

1991. Birds. As T **474**. Multicoloured.

1582/1629	80 c. × 16, 100 c. × 32 Set of 48	20·00	23·00

Nos. 1582/1629 were issued together, se-tenant, as three sheetlets of 16 forming composite designs. The 80 c. values show Green-winged pytilia, Orange-cheeked waxbill, African paradise flycatcher, Great blue turaco ("Blue plantain-eater"), Red bishop, Splendid glossy starling, Red-faced lovebird, African palm swift, Narina trogon, Tawny eagle, Bateleur, Hoopoe, Secretary bird, African white-backed vulture, White-necked bald crow ("Bare-headed rockfowl"), Abyssinian ground hornbill, and the 100 c. African open-bill stork, African spoonbill, Pink-backed pelican, Little bittern, Purple swamphen ("King reed-hen"), Saddle-bill stork, Glossy ibis, White-faced whistling duck, Black-headed heron, Hammerkop, African darter, Woolly-necked stork, Yellow-billed stork, Black-winged stilt, Goliath heron, African jacana ("Lily trotter"), Shikra, Abyssinian roller, Carmine bee eater, Pin-tailed whydah, Purple glossy starling, Yellow-mantled whydah, Pel's fishing owl, Crested touraco, Red-cheeked cordon-bleu, Olive-bellied sunbird, Red-billed hornbill, Red-billed quelea, South African crowned crane, Blue quail, Egyptian vulture and Helmet guineafowl.

475 "Nularda" (beetle)

476 Boti Falls

1991. Insects. Multicoloured.

1631	20 c. Type **475**	50	20
1632	50 c. "Zonocrus" (grasshopper)	65	30
1633	60 c. "Gryllotalpa africana" (mole cricket)	70	30
1634	80 c. Weevil	80	60
1635	100 c. "Coenagrion" (dragonfly)	90	70
1636	150 c. "Sahlbergella" (fly)	1·25	1·60
1637	200 c. "Anthia" (ant)	1·40	1·75
1638	350 c. "Megacephala" (beetle)	2·00	2·75

1991. Multicoloured.

1639a	20 c. Oil palm fruit	10	10
1640	50 c. Type **476**	15	10
1641	60 c. Larabanga Mosque (horiz)	10	10
1642	80 c. Fort Sebastian, Shama (horiz)	10	10
1643	100 c. Cape Coast Castle (horiz)	20	20
1644	200 c. White-toothed cowrie (horiz)	40	30
1645	400 c. True achatina (horiz)	70	55

1991. Christmas. Religious Paintings. As T **287** of Antigua. Multicoloured.

1646	20 c. "Adoration of the Magi" (Bosch)	35	20
1647	50 c. "The Annunciation" (Campin)	50	30
1648	60 c. "Virgin and Child" (detail) (Bouts)	55	30
1649	80 c. "Presentation in the Temple" (Memling)	65	50
1650	100 c. "Virgin and Child enthroned with Angel and Donor" (Memling)	85	65
1651	200 c. "Virgin and Child with Saints and Donor" (Van Eyck)	1·50	1·75
1652	400 c. "St. Luke painting the Virgin" (Van der Weyden)	2·50	3·00
1653	700 c. "Virgin and Child" (Bouts)	3·50	4·50

477 Women collecting Water from Bore Hole

1992. Decade of Revolutionary Progress. Multicoloured.

1655	20 c. Type **477**	15	10
1656	50 c. Miners	20	15
1657	60 c. Wood carver	20	15
1658	80 c. Forestry	25	20
1659	200 c. Cacao tree	50	75
1660	350 c. Village electrification	75	1·00

478 Mount Fuji and Flying Fish

1992. "Phila Nippon '91" International Stamp Exhibition, Tokyo. Multicoloured.

1661	20 c. Type **478**	35	30
1662	60 c. Itsukushima Jingu Shrine	45	40
1663	80 c. Geisha	60	50
1664	100 c. Samurai house	80	70
1665	200 c. Bonsai tree	1·50	1·50
1666	400 c. Olympic Sports Hall	2·00	2·25
1667	500 c. Great Buddha (statue)	2·25	2·50
1668	600 c. Nagoya Castle	2·40	2·75

479 East and West Germans celebrating

1992. Reunification of Germany. Multicoloured.

1670	20 c. Type **479**	30	20
1671	60 c. Signing Reunification Treaty	40	40
1672	80 c. Chariot on Brandenburg Gate and fireworks	45	45
1673	1000 c. Germans with unified currency	5·50	7·00

480 Steam Side-tank Locomotive, 1903

1992. Ghanaian Railways. Multicoloured.

1675	20 c. Type **480**	40	30
1676	50 c. A1A-A1A diesel locomotive	60	40
1677	60 c. First class coach, 1931	60	45
1678	80 c. Railway inspection coach No. 2212	70	70
1679	100 c. Steam locomotive No. 401 on Kumasi turntable	90	90
1680	200 c. Cocoa wagon, 1921	1·40	1·50
1681	500 c. Steam locomotive No. 223 "Prince of Wales"	2·25	2·50
1682	600 c. Cattle wagon	2·25	2·50

1992. Olympic Games, Albertville and Barcelona. Past Medal Winners. As T **204** of Gambia. Mutlcoloured.

1684	20 c. E. Blay (Ghana) (boxing) and windmill	30	20
1685	60 c. M. Ahey (Ghana) (athletics) and Catalan coat of arms	50	35
1686	80 c. T. Wilson (U.S.A.) (70 metres ski jump) and grapes	60	50
1687	100 c. Four-man bobsleighing (East Germany) and passport	75	75
1688	200 c. G. Louganis (U.S.A.) (platform diving) and decorative vase	1·25	1·25
1689	300 c. L. Visser (Netherlands) (5000 metres speed skating) and wine bottle cork	1·50	1·60
1690	350 c. J. Passler (Italy) (biathlon) and lily	1·60	1·75
1691	400 c. M. Retton (U.S.A.) (gymnastics) and silhouette of castle	1·75	2·00
1692	500 c. J. Hingsen (West Germany) (decathlon) and gold and silver coins	1·75	2·00
1693	600 c. R. Neubert (West Germany) (heptathlon) and leather work	1·75	2·00

481 "Angides lugubris"

1992. Reptiles. Multicoloured.

1695	20 c. Type **481**	20	20
1696	50 c. "Kinixys erosa" (tortoise)	30	30
1697	60 c. "Agama agama" (lizard)	30	30
1698	80 c. "Chameleo gracilis" (chameleon)	40	40
1699	100 c. "Naja melanleuca" (snake)	50	50
1700	200 c. "Crocodylus niloticus" (crocodile)	90	1·10
1701	400 c. "Chelonia mydas" (turtle)	1·75	2·00
1702	500 c. "Varanus exanthematicus" (lizard)	1·90	2·25

1992. Easter. Religious Paintings. As T **291** of Antigua but vert designs. Multicoloured.

1704	20 c. "The Four Apostles" (detail) (Durer)	25	20
1705	50 c. "The Last Judgement" (detail) (Rubens)	35	30
1706	60 c. "The Four Apostles" (different detail) (Durer)	35	30
1707	80 c. "The Last Judgement" (different detail) (Rubens)	50	40
1708	100 c. "Crucifixion" (Rubens)	60	50
1709	200 c. "The Last Judgement" (different detail) (Rubens)	1·10	1·25
1710	500 c. "Christum Videre" (Rubens)	2·00	2·50
1711	600 c. "The Last Judgement" (different detail) (Rubens)	2·25	2·75

1992. "Granada '92" International Stamp Exhibition, Spain. Spanish Paintings. As T **292** of Antigua. Multicoloured.

1713	20 c. "Two Men at Table" (Velazquez) (horiz)	20	20
1714	60 c. "Christ in the House of Mary and Martha" (detail) (Velazquez) (horiz)	30	30
1715	80 c. "The Supper at Emmaus" (Velazquez) (horiz)	40	40
1716	100 c. "Three Musicians" (Velazquez) (horiz)	50	50
1717	200 c. "Old Woman cooking Eggs" (Velazquez)	90	90
1718	400 c. "Old Woman cooking Eggs" (detail) (Velazquez)	1·60	1·60
1719	500 c. "The Surrender of Breda" (detail) (Velazquez)	1·75	1·75
1720	700 c. "The Surrender of Breda" (different detail) (Velazquez)	2·00	2·00

482 "Danaus chrysippus"

483 Martin Pinzon and "Pinta"

1992. "Genova '92" International Thematic Stamp Exhibition. Butterflies. Mult.

1722	20 c. Type **482**	50	30
1723	60 c. "Papilio dardanus"	80	45
1724	80 c. "Cynthia cardui"	90	60
1725	100 c. "Meneris tulbaghia"	1·00	75
1726	200 c. "Salamis temora"	1·50	1·60
1727	400 c. "Charaxes jasius"	2·00	2·50
1728	500 c. "Precis oenone"	2·25	2·50
1729	700 c. "Precis sophia"	2·50	2·75

1992. Prehistoric Animals. As T **290** of Antigua. Multicoloured.

1731	20 c. Iguanodon	35	25
1732	50 c. Anchisaurus	50	35
1733	60 c. Heterodontosaurus	55	35
1734	80 c. Ouranosaurus	60	45
1735	100 c. Anatosaurus	75	55
1736	200 c. Elaphrosaurus	1·25	1·50
1737	500 c. Coelophysis	2·25	2·75
1738	600 c. Rhamphorynchus	2·50	3·00

1992. World Columbian Stamp "Expo '92", Chicago. 500th Anniv of Discovery of America by Columbus. Multicoloured.

1740	200 c. Type **483**	90	90
1741	200 c. Vincente Pinzon and "Nina"	90	90
1742	200 c. Columbus and Father Marchena at La Rabida	90	90
1743	200 c. Columbus in his cabin	90	90

1744 200 c. Fleet sights land . . . 90 90
1745 200 c. Columbus on Samana Cay . . . 90 90
1746 200 c. Wreck of "Santa Maria" 90 90
1747 200 c. Amerindians at Spanish Court . . . 90 90

484 Olive-grey Ancilla

485 "Presentation in the Temple" (Master of the Braunschweiti)

1992. Shells. Multicoloured.
1749 20 c. Type **484** . . . 20 20
1750 20 c. Radula cerith . . . 20 20
1751 60 c. Rugose donex . . . 30 30
1752 60 c. Horned murex . . . 30 30
1753 80 c. Concave ear moon . . 40 40
1754 80 c. Triple twella . . . 40 40
1755 200 c. "Pila africana" . . . 90 90
1756 200 c. Rat cowrie . . . 90 90
1757 350 c. "Thais hiatula" . . . 1·60 1·60
1758 350 c. West African helmet . 1·60 1·60

1992. Christmas. Religious Paintings. Mult.
1760 20 c. Type **485** . . . 20 20
1761 50 c. "Presentation in the Temple" (detail) (Master of St. Severin) . . . 30 30
1762 60 c. "The Visitation" (Sebastiano del Piombo) . 30 30
1763 80 c. "The Visitation" (detail) (Giotto) . . . 40 40
1764 100 c. "The Circumcision" (detail) (Studio of Bellini) . 50 50
1765 200 c. "The Circumcision" (Studio of Garofalo) . . . 90 90
1766 500 c. "The Visitation" (Studio of Van der Weyden) . . . 1·60 1·60
1767 800 c. "The Visitation" (detail) (Studio of Van der Weyden) 1·90 1·90

486 "Calappa rubroguttata"

1993. Crabs. Multicoloured.
1769 20 c. Type **486** . . . 40 20
1770 60 c. "Cardisoma amatum" . 60 25
1771 80 c. "Maia squinado" . . . 70 25
1772 400 c. "Ocypoda cursor" . 1·40 1·60
1773 800 c. "Grapus grapus" . . . 2·00 2·50

487 "Clerodendrum thomsoniae"

1993. Flowers. Multicoloured.
1775 20 c. Type **487** . . . 20 15
1776 20 c. "Lagerstroemia flos-reginae" . . . 20 15
1777 60 c. "Cassia fistula" . . . 35 25
1778 60 c. "Spathodea campanulata" 35 25
1779 80 c. "Hildegardia barteri" . 40 25
1780 80 c. "Mellitea ferrugenea" . 40 25
1781 200 c. "Petrea volubilis" . . 60 75
1782 200 c. "Ipomoea asarifolia" . 60 75
1783 350 c. "Bryphyllum pinnatum" 90 1·00
1784 350 c. "Ritchiea reflexa" . . 90 1·00

488 Zeppelin "LZ-3" entering Floating Hangar, Lake Constance

1993. Anniversaries and Events. Multicoloured.
1786 20 c. Type **488** . . . 55 30
1787 100 c. Launch of European "Ariane 4" rocket (vert) . . 90 75
1788 200 c. Leopard . . . 1·60 1·75
1789 300 c. Colosseum and fruit . 1·75 2·00
1790 400 c. Mozart (vert) . . . 2·00 2·25
1791 600 c. Launch of Japanese "H-1" rocket (vert) . . . 2·50 2·75
1792 800 c. Zeppelin "LZ-10" "Schwaben" . . . 2·75 3·00

ANNIVERSARIES AND EVENTS: Nos. 1786, 1792, 75th death anniv of Count Ferdinand von Zeppelin; Nos. 1787, 1791, International Space Year; No. 1788, Earth Summit '92, Rio; No. 1789, International Conference on Nutrition, Rome; No. 1790, Death bicentenary of Mozart.

1993. Bicentenary of the Louvre, Paris. As T **305** of Antigua. Multicoloured.
1794 200 c. "Carnival Minuet" (left detail) (Giovanni Domenico Tiepolo) . . . 85 1·00
1795 200 c. "Carnival Minuet" (centre detail) (Giovanni Domenico Tiepolo) . . . 85 1·00
1796 200 c. "Carnival Minuet" (right detail) (Giovanni Domenico Tiepolo) . . . 85 1·00
1797 200 c. "The Tooth Puller" (left detail) (Giovanni Domenico Tiepolo) . . . 85 1·00
1798 200 c. "The Tooth Puller" (right detail) (Giovanni Domenico Tiepolo) . . . 85 1·00
1799 200 c. "Rebecca at the Well" (Giovanni Battista Tiepolo) 85 1·00
1800 200 c. "Presenting Christ to the People" (left detail) (Giovanni Battista Tiepolo) 85 1·00
1801 200 c. "Presenting Christ to the People" (right detail) (Giovanni Battista Tiepolo) 85 1·00

489 Energy Foods

1993. Int Conference on Nutrition, Rome. Mult.
1803 20 c. Type **489** . . . 20 15
1804 60 c. Body-building foods . 30 20
1805 80 c. Protective foods . . . 35 25
1806 200 c. Disease prevention equipment . . . 80 90
1807 400 c. Quality control and preservation of fish products 1·50 1·75

490 Kwame Nkrumah Mausoleum

1993. Proclamation of 4th Republic. Mult.
1808 50 c. Type **490** . . . 20 15
1809 100 c. Kwame Nkrumah Conference Centre . . . 35 25
1810 200 c. Book of Constitution (vert) . . . 80 80
1811 350 c. Independence Square (vert) . . . 1·60 1·75
1812 400 c. Christiansborg Castle (vert) . . . 1·75 2·00

491 Resurrection Egg

492 African Buffalo

1993. Easter. Faberge Eggs. Multicoloured.
1813 50 c. Type **491** . . . 40 15
1814 80 c. Imperial Red Cross egg with Resurrection triptych 65 25
1815 100 c. Imperial Uspensky Cathedral egg . . . 75 25
1816 150 c. Imperial Red Cross egg with portraits . . . 1·10 65
1817 200 c. Orange Tree egg . . . 1·25 1·25
1818 250 c. Rabbit egg . . . 1·25 1·50
1819 400 c. Imperial Coronation egg 2·00 2·50
1820 900 c. Silver-gilt enamel Easter egg . . . 3·25 4·00

1993. Centenaries of Henry Ford's First Petrol Engine (Nos. 1823/4) and Karl Benz's First Four-wheeled Car (others). As T **264** of Dominica. Multicoloured.
1822 150 c. Mercedes Benz "300 SLR", Mille Miglia, 1955 . 75 50
1823 400 c. Ford "Depot Wagon", 1920 . . . 1·75 1·75
1824 600 c. Ford "Mach 1 Mustang", 1970 . . . 2·25 2·50
1825 800 c. Mercedes Benz racing car, Monaco Grand Prix, 1937 3·50 4·00

1993. Aviation Anniversaries. As T **266** of Dominica. Multicoloured.
1827 50 c. Airship "Graf Zeppelin" over Alps (vert) . . . 50 30
1828 150 c. Airship "LZ-7" "Deutschland" . . . 85 55
1829 400 c. Avro Vulcan jet bomber 1·75 1·75
1830 400 c. U.S. Mail Ford Trimotor 1·75 1·75
1831 600 c. Nieuport 27 biplane (vert) 2·25 2·25
1832 600 c. Loading mail on "Graf Zeppelin" (vert) . . . 2·25 2·25
1833 800 c. Airship "LZ-10" "Schwaben" . . . 3·50 4·00

ANNIVERSARIES: Nos. 1827/28, 1833, 125th birth anniv of Hugo Eckener (airship commander); Nos. 1829, 1831, 75th anniv of Royal Air Force; Nos. 1830, 1832, Bicentenary of first airmail flight.

1993. Wild Animals. Multicoloured.
1835 20 c. Type **492** . . . 25 15
1836 50 c. Giant forest hog . . . 30 20
1837 60 c. Potto . . . 40 25
1838 80 c. Bay duiker . . . 50 30
1839 100 c. Royal antelope . . . 60 35
1840 200 c. Serval . . . 90 90
1841 500 c. Golden cat . . . 1·75 2·00
1842 800 c. "Megaloglossus woermanni" (bat) . . . 3·00 3·50

1993. 40th Anniv of Coronation. Nos. 1549/52 optd **40TH ANNIVERSARY OF CORONATION H.M. ELIZABETH II.**
1844 100 c. multicoloured . . . 50 25
1845 200 c. multicoloured . . . 90 70
1846 500 c. multicoloured . . . 2·50 2·75
1847 600 c. multicoloured . . . 2·75 3·00

1993. 35th Anniv of Rotary International and 60th Anniv of Ghana Red Cross Society (1992). Nos. 1562 and 1564/6 optd **35 YEARS OF ROTARY INTERNATIONAL GHANA 1958** (Nos. 1849, 1852) or **GHANA RED CROSS SOCIETY FOUNDED 1932** and cross (others).
1849 100 c. Stonehead . . . 50 25
1850 300 c. Aba . . . 1·50 1·50
1851 400 c. Jewel cichlid . . . 1·75 1·75
1852 500 c. Smooth hammerhead . 2·00 2·25

496 "Cantharellus cibarius"

1993. Mushrooms. Multicoloured.
1854 20 c. Type **496** . . . 40 25
1855 50 c. "Russula cyanoxantha" 50 30
1856 60 c. "Clitocybe rivulosa" . . 55 30
1857 80 c. "Cortinarius elatior" . . 60 33
1858 80 c. "Mycena galericulata" . 60 35
1859 200 c. "Tricholoma gambosum" 1·00 1·00
1860 200 c. "Boletus edulis" . . . 1·00 1·00
1861 200 c. "Lepista saeva" . . . 1·00 1·00
1862 250 c. "Gyroporus castaneus" 1·10 1·10
1863 300 c. "Boletus chrysenteron" 1·25 1·25
1864 350 c. "Nolanea sericea" . . 1·40 1·40
1865 350 c. "Hygrophorus punicea" ("Hygrophorus puiceus") 1·40 1·40
1866 500 c. "Gomphidius glutinosus" 1·60 1·75
1867 600 c. "Russula olivacea" . . 1·75 2·00
1868 1000 c. "Russula aurata" . . 2·25 2·75

497 "The Actor" (Picasso)

498 Abedi Pele (Ghana)

1993. Anniversaries and Events. Multicoloured.
1870 20 c. Type **497** . . . 30 20
1871 20 c. Early astronomical equipment . . . 30 20
1872 80 c. "Portrait of Allan Stein" (Picasso) . . . 40 25
1873 200 c. Modern telescope . . . 80 80
1874 200 c. "Tattoo" (Lesek Sobocki) . . . 80 80
1875 600 c. "Prison" (Sasza Blonder) 2·00 2·50
1876 800 c. "Seated Male Nude" (Picasso) . . . 2·75 3·25

ANNIVERSARIES AND EVENTS: Nos. 1870, 1872, 1876, 20th death anniv of Picasso (artist); Nos. 1871, 1873, 450th death anniv of Copernicus (astronomer); Nos. 1874/5, "Polska '93" International Stamp Exhibition, Poznan.

1993. World Cup Football Championship, U.S.A. (1st issue). Multicoloured.
1878 50 c. Type **498** . . . 50 25
1879 80 c. Pedro Troglio (Argentina) 60 30
1880 100 c. Fernando Alvez (Uruguay) . . . 70 40
1881 200 c. Franco Baresi (Italy) . 1·25 1·00
1882 250 c. Gomez (Colombia) and Katanec (Yugoslavia) . . . 1·25 1·25
1883 600 c. Diego Maradona (Argentina) . . . 2·50 2·75
1884 800 c. Hasek (Czechoslovakia) and Wynalda (U.S.A.) . . 3·00 3·25
1885 1000 c. Lothar Matthaeus (Germany) . . . 3·50 4·00

See also Nos. 2037/42.

499 Common Turkey

1993. Domestic Animals. Multicoloured.
1887 50 c. Type **499** . . . 50 25
1888 100 c. Goats . . . 70 40
1889 150 c. Muscovy ducks . . . 1·00 75
1890 200 c. Donkeys . . . 1·25 1·00
1891 250 c. Red junglefowl cock . 1·25 1·25
1892 300 c. Pigs . . . 1·40 1·40
1893 400 c. Helmet guineafowl . . 1·75 1·75
1894 600 c. Dog . . . 2·50 2·75
1895 800 c. Red junglefowl hen . 3·00 3·50
1896 1000 c. Sheep . . . 3·50 4·00

1993. Christmas. Religious Paintings. As T **270** of Dominica. Black, yellow and red (Nos. 1898, 1900/1 and 1905) or multicoloured (others).
1898 50 c. "Adoration of the Magi" (Durer) . . . 50 20
1899 100 c. "The Virgin and Child with St. John and an Angel" (Botticelli) . . . 70 25
1900 150 c. "Mary as Queen of Heaven" (Durer) . . . 90 45
1901 200 c. "Saint Anne" (Durer) 1·00 65
1902 250 c. "The Madonna of the Magnificat" (Botticelli) . . 1·10 75
1903 400 c. "The Madonna of the Goldfinch" (Botticelli) . . 1·75 1·75
1904 600 c. "The Virgin and Child with the young St. John the Baptist" (Botticelli) . . . 2·25 2·75
1905 1000 c. "Adoration of the Shepherds" (Durer) . . . 3·00 4·00

500 Doll

501 Mickey Mouse in "Steamboat Willie", 1928

1994. Traditional Crafts. Multicoloured.
1907 50 c. Type **500** . . . 25 15
1908 50 c. Pot with "head" lid . . 25 15
1909 200 c. Bead necklace . . . 60 60
1910 200 c. Snake charmers (statuette) . . . 60 60
1911 250 c. Hoe . . . 60 60
1912 250 c. Scabbard . . . 60 60
1913 600 c. Pipe . . . 1·50 1·75
1914 600 c. Deer (carving) . . . 1·50 1·75
1915 1000 c. Mask . . . 2·25 2·50
1916 1000 c. Doll (different) . . 2·25 2·50

1994. "Hong Kong '94" International Stamp Exhibition (1st issue). As T **317** of Antigua. Multicoloured.
1918 200 c. Hong Kong 1986 50 c. "Expo '86" stamp and tram 70 80
1919 200 c. Ghana 1992 20 c. Railways stamp and tram . 70 80

Nos. 1918/19 were printed together, se-tenant, forming a complete design.

See also Nos. 1920/25.

1994. "Hong Kong '94" International Stamp Exhibition (2nd issue). Imperial Palace Clocks. As T **318** of Antigua, but vert. Multicoloured.
1920 600 c. Windmill clock . . . 60 65
1921 600 c. Horse clock . . . 60 65
1922 600 c. Balloon clock . . . 60 65
1923 600 c. Zodiac clock . . . 60 65
1924 100 c. Shar-pei dog clock . . 60 65
1925 100 c. Cat clock . . . 60 65

1994. 65th Anniv (1993) of Mickey Mouse (Walt Disney cartoon character) (1993). Scenes from various cartoon films.
1926 50 c. Type **501** . . . 30 15
1927 100 c. "The Band Concert", 1935 . . . 40 20
1928 150 c. "Moose Hunters", 1937 45 35
1929 200 c. "Brave Little Tailor", 1938 . . . 55 50
1930 250 c. "Fantasia", 1940 . . . 60 60
1931 400 c. "The Nifty Nineties", 1941 . . . 1·25 1·50
1932 600 c. "Canine Caddy", 1941 1·50 1·75
1933 1000 c. "Mickey's Christmas Carol", 1983 . . . 2·25 2·50

No. 1929 is inscribed "TAYLOR" in error. The dates on Nos. 1927 and 1932 are incorrectly shown as "1937" and "1944".

1994. Easter. Hummel Figurines. As T **302** of Antigua. Multicoloured.

1935 50 c. Boy hiker 30 15
1936 100 c. Girl with basket behind back 40 20
1937 150 c. Boy with rabbits . . . 45 35
1938 200 c. Boy holding basket . . 55 50
1939 250 c. Girl with chicks . . . 60 60
1940 400 c. Girl with lamb . . . . 1·25 1·50
1941 600 c. Girl waving red handkerchief with lamb . . 1·50 1·75
1942 1000 c. Girl with basket and posy . . . . 2·25 2·50

502 Diana Monkey with Young

1994. Wildlife. Multicoloured.

1944 50 c. Type **502** 30 15
1945 100 c. Bushbuck (horiz) . . . 40 20
1946 150 c. Spotted hyena (horiz) . 45 35
1947 200 c. Diana monkey on branch facing left 50 40
1948 500 c. Diana monkey on branch facing right . . . . . 1·00 1·25
1949 800 c. Head of Diana monkey . 1·50 1·75
1950 1000 c. Aardvark (horiz) . . 1·75 2·00

Designs of Nos. 1944 and 1947/9 include the W.W.F. Panda emblem.

503 Norwegian Forest Cat

1994. Cats. Multicoloured.

1952 200 c. Type **503** 40 40
1953 200 c. Blue longhair 40 40
1954 200 c. Red self longhair . . . 40 40
1955 200 c. Black longhair 40 40
1956 200 c. Chinchilla 40 40
1957 200 c. Dilute calico longhair . 40 40
1958 200 c. Blue tabby and white longhair 40 40
1959 200 c. Ruby Somali 40 40
1960 200 c. Blue smoke longhair . 40 40
1961 200 c. Calico longhair . . . 40 40
1962 200 c. Brown tabby longhair . 40 40
1963 200 c. Balinese 40 40
1964 200 c. Sorrel Abyssinian . . 40 40
1965 200 c. Silver classic tabby . . 40 40
1966 200 c. Chocolate-point Siamese 40 40
1967 200 c. Brown tortie Burmese . 40 40
1968 200 c. Exotic shorthair . . . 40 40
1969 200 c. Havana brown 40 40
1970 200 c. Devon rex 40 40
1971 200 c. Black Manx 40 40
1972 200 c. British blue shorthair . 40 40
1973 200 c. Calico American wirehair 40 40
1974 200 c. Spotted oriental Siamese 40 40
1975 200 c. Red classic tabby . . . 40 40

No. 1957 is inscribed "Dilut" in error.

504 Red-bellied Paradise Flycatcher

1994. Birds. Multicoloured.

1977 200 c. Type **504** 50 50
1978 200 c. Many-coloured bush shrike 50 50
1979 200 c. Broad-tailed paradise whydah 50 50
1980 200 c. White-crowned robin chat 50 50
1981 200 c. Violet turaco ("Violet plantain-eater") 50 50
1982 200 c. Village weaver 50 50
1983 200 c. Red-crowned bishop . . 50 50
1984 200 c. Common shoveler . . 50 50
1985 200 c. Spur-winged goose . . 50 50
1986 200 c. African crake 50 50
1987 200 c. Purple swamphen ("King reed-hen") 50 50
1988 200 c. African tiger bittern . . 50 50
1989 200 c. Oriole warbler ("Moho") 50 50
1990 200 c. Superb sunbird 50 50
1991 200 c. Blue-breasted kingfisher 50 50
1992 200 c. African blue cuckoo shrike 50 50
1993 200 c. Great blue turaco ("Blue plantain-eater") 50 50
1994 200 c. Greater flamingo . . . 50 50
1995 200 c. African jacana (" Lily-trotter") 50 50
1996 200 c. Black-crowned night heron 50 50
1997 200 c. Black-winged stilt . . 50 50
1998 200 c. White-spotted crake . . 50 50
1999 200 c. African pygmy goose . 50 50
2000 200 c. African pitta 50 50

505 Women at Stand-pipe

1994. 1st Anniv of Fourth Republic. Multicoloured.

2002 50 c. Type **505** 25 15
2003 100 c. Presenting certificate to farmers 35 20
2004 200 c. Village electricity supply 50 35
2005 600 c. Bridge . . . . 1·25 1·50
2006 800 c. National Theatre . . . 1·50 1·75
2007 1000 c. Lighting perpetual flame 1·75 2·00

1994. 25th Anniv of First Manned Moon Landing. As T **326** of Antigua showing scientists. Mult.

2008 300 c. Sigmund Jahn 80 90
2009 300 c. Ulf Merbold 80 90
2010 300 c. Hans Wilhelm Schegal 80 90
2011 300 c. Ulrich Walter 80 90
2012 300 c. Reinhard Furrer . . . 80 90
2013 300 c. Ernst Messerschmid . 80 90
2014 300 c. Mamoru Mohri . . . 80 90
2015 300 c. Klaus-Dietrich Flade . 80 90
2016 300 c. Chaiki Naito-Mukai . 80 90

1994. Centenary of International Olympic Committee. Gold Medal Winners. As T **327** of Antigua, but vert. Multicoloured.

2018 300 c. Dieter Modenburg (Germany) (high jump), 1984 60 65
2019 400 c. Ruth Fuchs (Germany) (javelin), 1972 and 1976 . 80 85

1994. 50th Anniv of D-Day. As T **331** of Antigua. Multicoloured.

2021 60 c. H.M.S. "Roberts" (monitor) 50 50
2022 100 c. H.M.S. "Warspite" (battleship) 70 70
2023 200 c. U.S.S. "Augusta" (cruiser) . . . . 1·00 1·00

1994. "Philakorea '94" International Stamp Exn, Seoul. As T **279** of Dominica. Mult.

2025 20 c. Ch'unghak-dong village elder in traditional costume, ($24\frac{1}{2} \times 38$ mm) 15 15
2026 150 c. Stone Pagoda, Punhwangsa ($24\frac{1}{2} \times 38$ mm) 40 40
2027 250 c. Character with eggs . 45 50
2028 250 c. Character with pair of birds on house 45 50
2029 250 c. Character with cock . 45 50
2030 250 c. Character with dragon and pagoda 45 50
2031 250 c. Character with orange flowers 45 50
2032 250 c. Character with parrot and pagoda 45 50
2033 250 c. Character with plant . 45 50
2034 250 c. Character with fish . 45 50
2035 300 c. Traditional country house, Andong ($24\frac{1}{2} \times 34$ mm) 50 55

506 Dennis Bergkamp (Netherlands)

1994. World Cup Football Championship, U.S.A. (2nd issue). Multicoloured.

2037 200 c. Type **506** 45 50
2038 200 c. Lothar Matthaus (Germany) 45 50
2039 200 c. Giuseppe Signori (Italy) 45 50
2040 200 c. Carlos Valderama (Colombia) 45 50
2041 200 c. Jorge Campos (Mexico) 45 50
2042 200 c. Tony Meola (U.S.A.) . 45 50

507 Common ("Crowned") Duiker

1994. Duikers (antelopes). Multicoloured.

2044 50 c. Type **507** 30 15
2045 100 c. Red-flanked duiker . . 40 25
2046 200 c. Yellow-backed duiker . 60 40
2047 400 c. Ogilby's duiker . . . 1·00 1·25
2048 600 c. Bay duiker . . . . . 1·25 1·50
2049 800 c. Jentink's duiker . . . 1·50 1·75

1994. Christmas. Religious Paintings. As T **336** of Antigua. Multicoloured.

2051 100 c. "Madonna of the Annunciation" (Simone Martini) 30 15
2052 200 c. "Madonna and Child" (Niccolo di Pietro Gerini) 45 20
2053 250 c. "Virgin and Child on the Throne with Angels and Saints" (Raffaello Botticini) 55 45
2054 300 c. "Madonna and Child with Saints" (Antonio Fiorentino) 75 75
2055 400 c. "Adoration of the Magi" (Bartolo di Fredi) 90 90
2056 500 c. "The Annunciation" (Cima da Congeliano) . . . 1·00 1·00
2057 600 c. "Virgin and Child with the Young St. John the Baptist" (workshop of Botticelli) . . . . 1·25 1·50
2058 1000 c. "The Holy Family" (Giorgione) . . . . 1·75 2·25

508 Northern Region Dancer

510 Fertility Doll

509 Red Cross Stretcher-bearers

1994. Panafest '94 (2nd Pan-African Historical Theatre Festival). Multicoloured.

2060 50 c. Type **508** 20 15
2061 100 c. Traditional artefacts . . 35 25
2062 200 c. Chief with courtiers . . 65 60
2063 400 c. Woman in ceremonial costume . . . . 1·25 1·25
2064 600 c. Cape Coast Castle . . 1·75 2·00
2065 800 c. Clay figurines . . . . 2·25 2·75

1994. 75th Anniv of Red Cross. Multicoloured.

2066 50 c. Type **509** 30 15
2067 200 c. Worker with children . 50 35
2068 600 c. Workers erecting tents . 1·25 1·50

1994. Fertility Dolls.

2070 **510** 50 c. multicoloured . . . 15 10
2071 – 100 c. multicoloured . . . 20 15
2072 – 150 c. multicoloured . . . 30 25
2073 – 200 c. multicoloured . . . 35 30
2074 – 400 c. multicoloured . . . 60 60
2075 – 600 c. multicoloured . . . 75 80
2076 – 800 c. multicoloured . . . 90 1·00
2077 – 1000 c. multicoloured . . . 1·00 1·25

DESIGNS: 100 c. to 1000 c. Different dolls.

511 Ghanaian Family

1994. International Year of the Family. Mult.

2079 50 c. Type **511** 15 15
2080 100 c. Teaching carpentry . . 25 15
2081 200 c. Child care 40 25
2082 400 c. Care for the elderly . . 60 60
2083 600 c. Learning pottery . . . 85 95
2084 1000 c. Adult education students . . . . 1·25 1·50

512 Control Tower and Emblem

1995. 50th Anniv of I.C.A.O. Mult. (a) Inscr "50 Anniversary Of Ghana Civil Aviation Authority".

2085 100 c. Type **512** 30
2086 400 c. Communications equipment 80
2087 1000 c. Airliner taking off . . 1·60

(b) Inscr "50th Anniversary Of The International Civil Aviation Organisation (I.C.A.O.)."

2088 100 c. Type **512** 30 20
2089 400 c. Communications equipment 80 80
2090 1000 c. Airliner taking off . . 1·60 1·75

513 Pluto, Donald Duck and Chip n' Dale around Table

1995. 60th Anniv of Donald Duck. Walt Disney Cartoon Characters at Birthday Party. Mult.

2091 40 c. Type **513** 25 15
2092 50 c. Mickey Mouse and pup with banner 25 15
2093 60 c. Daisy Duck with balloons 25 20
2094 100 c. Goofy making cake . . 30 20
2095 150 c. Goofy on roller blades delivering cake 40 30
2096 250 c. Donald pinning donkey tail on Goofy 50 50
2097 400 c. Ludwig von Drake singing to Pluto 70 70
2098 500 c. Grandma Duck giving cake to puppies 80 80
2099 1000 c. Mickey and Minnie Mouse at piano . . . . . 1·40 1·75
2100 1500 c. Pluto with bone and ball . . . . 2·25 2·75

514 Fort Appolonia, Beyin

1995. Forts and Castles of Ghana. Multicoloured.

2102 50 c. Type **514** 10 10
2103 200 c. Fort Patience, Apam . 10 15
2104 250 c. Fort Amsterdam, Kormantin 15 20
2105 300 c. Fort St. Jago, Elmina . 15 20
2106 400 c. Fort William, Anomabo 20 25
2107 600 c. Kumasi Fort 30 35

515 Cochem Castle, Germany

1995. Castles of the World. Multicoloured.

2109 150 c. Type **515** 10 10
2110 500 c. Windsor Castle, England 25 30
2111 500 c. Osaka Castle, Japan . 25 30
2112 500 c. Vaj Dahunyad Castle, Hungary 25 30
2113 500 c. Karlstejn Castle, Czech Republic 25 30
2114 500 c. Kronborg Castle, Denmark 25 30
2115 500 c. Alcazar of Segovia, Spain 25 30
2116 500 c. Chambourd Castle, France 25 30
2117 500 c. Linderhof Castle, Germany 25 30
2118 500 c. Red Fort, Delhi, India 25 30
2119 600 c. Hohenzollern Castle, Germany 25 30
2120 800 c. Uwajima Castle, Japan 40 45
2121 1000 c. Hohenschwangau Castle, Germany 50 55

516 European Pochard ("Eurasian Pochard")

1995. Ducks. Multicoloured.

2123 200 c. Type **516** 10 15
2124 400 c. African pygmy goose . 20 25
2125 400 c. Southern pochard . . 20 25
2126 400 c. Cape teal 20 25
2127 400 c. Ruddy shelduck . . . 20 25
2128 400 c. Fulvous whistling duck 20 25
2129 400 c. White-faced whistling duck 20 25
2130 400 c. Ferruginous duck ("Ferruginous white-eye") 20 25
2131 400 c. Hottentot teal 20 25
2132 400 c. African black duck . . 20 25
2133 400 c. African yellow-bill . . 20 25
2134 400 c. Bahama pintail ("White-checked pintail duck") . . 20 25
2135 400 c. Hartlaub's duck . . . 20 25
2136 500 c. Maccoa duck 25 30
2137 800 c. Cape shoveler 40 45
2138 1000 c. Red-crested pochard 50 55

Nos. 2124/35 were printed together, se-tenant, forming a composite design.

No. 2128 is inscribed "Wistling" in error.

517 Cycling

518 "Cymothoe beckeri" (butterfly)

1995. Olympic Games, Atlanta (1996) (1st issue). Multicoloured.

2140	300 c. Type **517**	15	20
2141	300 c. Archery	15	20
2142	300 c. Diving	15	20
2143	300 c. Swimming	15	20
2144	300 c. Women's gymnastics	15	20
2145	300 c. Fencing	15	20
2146	300 c. Boxing	15	20
2147	300 c. Men's gymnastics	15	20
2148	300 c. Javelin	15	20
2149	300 c. Tennis	15	20
2150	300 c. Football	15	20
2151	300 c. Equestrian	15	20
2152	500 c. Carl Lewis (U.S.A.)	25	30
2153	800 c. Eric Liddell (Great Britain)	40	45
2154	900 c. Jesse Owens (U.S.A.)	45	50
2155	1000 c. Jim Thorpe (U.S.A.)	50	55

Nos. 2140/51 were printed together, se-tenant, forming a composite design.

See also Nos. 2334/55.

1995. Multicoloured.

2157	400 c. Type **518**	20	25
2158	500 c. "Graphium policenes" (butterfly)	25	30
2158a	550 c. Atumpan drums (vert)	25	30
2158b	800 c. "Cyrestis camillus" (butterfly) (vert)	40	45
2159	1000 c. African long-tailed hawk (vert)	50	55
2159a	1100 c. Kente cloth	55	60
2160	2000 c. Swordfish	1·00	1·10
2161	3000 c. Guinean fingerfish	1·50	1·60
2162	5000 c. Purple heron (vert)	2·50	2·75

519 Ghanaian Scouts

520 Trygve Lie (1946–52) and United Nations Building

1995. 18th World Scout Jamboree, Netherlands.

2163	**519** 400 c. multicoloured	20	25
2164	– 800 c. multicoloured	40	45
2165	– 1000 c. multicoloured	50	55

DESIGNS: 800 c. to 1000 c. Ghanaian scouts (different).

1995. 50th Anniv of End of Second World War in Europe. As T **340** of Antigua. Multicoloured.

2167	400 c. Winston Churchill	20	25
2168	400 c. Gen. Dwight D. Eisenhower	20	25
2169	400 c. Air Marshal Sir Arthur Tedder	20	25
2170	400 c. Field-Marshal Sir Bernard Montgomery	20	25
2171	400 c. Gen. Omar Bradley	20	25
2172	400 c. Gen. Charles de Gaulle	20	25
2173	400 c. French resistance fighters	20	25
2174	400 c. Gen. George S. Patton	20	25

1995. 50th Anniv of United Nations. Secretary-Generals. Multicoloured.

2176	200 c. Type **520**	10	15
2177	300 c. Dag Hammarskjold (1953–61)	15	20
2178	400 c. U. Thant (1961–71)	20	25
2179	500 c. Kurt Waldheim (1972–81)	25	30
2180	600 c. Javier Perez de Cuellar (1982–91)	30	35
2181	800 c. Boutrous Boutrous-Ghali (1992)	40	45

521 Preserving Fish

1995. 50th Anniv of F.A.O. Multicoloured.

2183	200 c. Type **521**	10	15
2184	300 c. Fishermen with fish traps	15	20
2185	400 c. Ox-drawn plough	20	25
2186	600 c. Harvesting bananas	30	35
2187	800 c. Planting saplings	40	45

522 National Flag and Rotary Emblem

1995. 90th Anniv of Rotary International.

2189	**522** 600 c. multicoloured	30	35

1995. 95th Birthday of Queen Elizabeth the Queen Mother. As T **344** of Antigua. Multicoloured.

2191	600 c. brown, light brown and black	30	35
2192	600 c. multicoloured	30	35
2193	600 c. multicoloured	30	35
2194	600 c. multicoloured	30	35

DESIGNS: No. 2191, Queen Elizabeth the Queen Mother (pastel drawing); 2192, Wearing light blue hat and floral dress; 2193, At desk (oil painting); 2194, Wearing red hat and dress.

1995. 50th Anniv of End of Second World War in the Pacific. Medals. As T **340** of Antigua. Mult.

2196	500 c. Navy Cross and Purple Heart, U.S.A.	25	30
2197	500 c. Air Force Cross and Distinguished Flying Cross, Great Britain	25	30
2198	500 c. Navy and Marine Corps Medal and Distinguished Service Cross, U.S.A.	25	30
2199	500 c. Distinguished Service Medal and Distinguished Conduct Medal, Great Britain	25	30
2200	500 c. Military Medal and Military Cross, Great Britain	25	30
2201	500 c. Distinguished Service Cross and Distinguished Service Order, Great Britain	25	30

523 Seismosaurus

524 Arms of Otumfuo Opoku Ware II

1995. "Singapore '95" International Stamp Exhibition. Prehistoric Animals. Multicoloured.

2203	400 c. Type **523**	20	25
2204	400 c. Supersaurus	20	25
2205	400 c. Ultrasaurus	20	25
2206	400 c. Saurolophus	20	25
2207	400 c. Lambeosaurus	20	25
2208	400 c. Parasaurolophus	20	25
2209	400 c. Triceratops	20	25
2210	400 c. Styracosaurus	20	25
2211	400 c. Pachyrhinosaurus	20	25
2212	400 c. Peteinosaurus	20	25
2213	400 c. Quetzalcoatlus	20	25
2214	400 c. Eudimorphodon	20	25
2215	400 c. Allosaurus	20	25
2216	400 c. Daspletosaurus	20	25
2217	400 c. Tarbosaurus bataar	20	25
2218	400 c. Velociraptor mongoliensis	20	25
2219	400 c. Herrerasaurus	20	25
2220	400 c. Coelophysis	20	25

Nos. 2203/11 and 2212/20 respectively were printed together, se-tenant, forming composite designs.

1995. Silver Jubilee of Otumfuo Opoku Ware II (King of Ashanti). Multicoloured.

2222	50 c. Type **524**	10	10
2223	100 c. Silver casket	10	10
2224	200 c. Golden stool	10	15
2225	400 c. Busummuru sword bearer	20	25
2226	600 c. Otumfuo Opoku Ware II	30	35
2227	800 c. Otumfuo Opoku Ware II under umbrella	40	45
2228	1000 c. Mponponsuo sword bearer	50	55

525 Nelson Mandela (1993 Peace)

1995. Centenary of Nobel Prize Trust Fund. Past Prize Winners. Multicoloured.

2229	400 c. Type **525**	20	25
2230	400 c. Albert Schweitzer (1952 Peace)	20	25
2231	400 c. Wole Soyinka (1986 Literature)	20	25
2232	400 c. Emil Fischer (1902 Chemistry)	20	25
2233	400 c. Rudolf Mossbauer (1961 Physics)	20	25
2234	400 c. Archbishop Desmond Tutu (1984 Peace)	20	25
2235	400 c. Max Born (1954 Physics)	20	25
2236	400 c. Max Planck (1918 Physics)	20	25
2237	400 c. Hermann Hesse (1946 Literature)	20	25

1995. Christmas. Religious Paintings. As T **357** of Antigua. Multicoloured.

2239	50 c. "The Child Jesus and the Young St. John" (Murillo)	10	10
2240	80 c. "Rest on the Flight into Egypt" (Memling)	10	10
2241	300 c. "Holy Family" (Van Dyck)	15	20
2242	600 c. "Enthroned Madonna and Child" (Uccello)	30	35
2243	800 c. "Madonna and Child" (Van Eyck)	40	45
2244	1000 c. "Head of Christ" (Rembrandt)	50	55

526 Ernemann Camera (1903)

1995. Centenary of Cinema. Multicoloured.

2246	400 c. Type **526**	20	25
2247	400 c. Charlie Chaplin	20	25
2248	400 c. Rudolph Valentino	20	25
2249	400 c. Will Rogers	20	25
2250	400 c. Greta Garbo	20	25
2251	400 c. Jackie Cooper	20	25
2252	400 c. Bette Davis	20	25
2253	400 c. John Barrymore	20	25
2254	400 c. Shirley Temple	20	25

No. 2246 is inscribed "ERNMANN" in error.

527 John Lennon

1995. John Lennon (musician) Commemoration. Multicoloured.

2256	400 c. Type **527**	1·10	1·10
2257	400 c. Full face portrait (green background)	1·10	1·10
2258	400 c. With guitar	1·10	1·10
2259	400 c. Wearing glasses and caftan	1·10	1·10
2260	400 c. Full face portrait (red background)	1·10	1·10
2261	400 c. Wearing headphones	1·10	1·10
2262	400 c. Wearing purple T-shirt	1·10	1·10
2263	400 c. Full face portrait (blue background)	1·10	1·10
2264	400 c. Facing right	1·10	1·10
2265	400 c. As No. 2263, but smaller (24 × 39 mm)	1·10	1·10

528 Louis Pasteur in Laboratory

529 Rat Musicians

1995. Death Centenary of Louis Pasteur (scientist). Multicoloured.

2267	600 c. Type **528**	30	35
2268	600 c. Pasteur injecting rabid dog	30	35
2269	600 c. Pasteur and microscope slide	30	35
2270	600 c. Laboratory equipment and birds	30	35
2271	600 c. Yeast vats	30	35

1996. Chinese New Year ("Year of the Rat").

2272	**529** 250 c. brown, violet and red	15	20
2273	– 250 c. brown, violet and red	15	20
2274	– 250 c. brown, violet and red	15	20
2275	– 250 c. brown, violet and red	15	20

DESIGNS: No. 2273, Rats carrying banners; 2274, Rats carrying palanquin; 2275, Rats with offerings.

1996. 125th Anniv of Metropolitan Museum of Art, New York. As T **251** of Gambia. Multicoloured.

2278	400 c. "Portrait of a Man" (Van der Goes)	20	25
2279	400 c. "Paradise" (detail) (Di Paolo)	20	25
2280	400 c. "Portrait of a Young Man" (Messina)	20	25
2281	400 c. "Tommaso Portinari" (detail) (Memling)	20	25
2282	400 c. "Maria Portinari" (detail) (Memling)	20	25
2283	400 c. "Portrait of a Lady" (detail) (Ghirlandaio)	20	25
2284	400 c. "St. Christopher and the Infant Christ" (Ghirlandaio)	20	25
2285	400 c. "Francesco D'Este" (detail) (Weyden)	20	25
2286	400 c. "The Interrupted Sleep" (Boucher)	20	25
2287	400 c. "Diana and Cupid" (detail) (Batoni)	20	25
2288	400 c. "Boy blowing Bubbles" (Chardin)	20	25
2289	400 c. "Ancient Rome" (detail) (Pannini)	20	25
2290	400 c. "Modern Rome" (detail) (Pannini)	20	25
2291	400 c. "The Calmady Children" (Lawrence)	20	25
2292	400 c. "The Triumph of Marius" (detail) (Tiepolo)	20	25
2293	400 c. "Garden at Vaucression" (detail) (Vuillard)	20	25

530 Toco Toucan

1996. Wildlife of the Rainforest. Multicoloured.

2295	400 c. Type **530**	20	25
2296	400 c. Two-toed sloth	20	25
2297	400 c. Orang-utan	20	25
2298	400 c. Crested hawk eagle	20	25
2299	400 c. Tiger	20	25
2300	400 c. Yellow-billed stork	20	25
2301	400 c. Green-winged macaw	20	25
2302	400 c. Common squirrel-monkey	20	25
2303	400 c. Crab-eating macaque	20	25
2304	400 c. "Cithaerias menander" and "Ithomiidae" (butterflies)	20	25
2305	400 c. "Coryptophanes cristatus" and "Gekkonidae" (lizards)	20	25
2306	400 c. Boa constrictor	20	25
2307	400 c. Hoatzin	20	25
2308	400 c. Western tarsier	20	25
2309	400 c. Golden Lion tamarin	20	25
2310	400 c. "Pteropus gouldii" (bat)	20	25
2311	400 c. Guianan cock of the rock	20	25
2312	400 c. Resplendent quetzal	20	25
2313	400 c. Tree frog and poison-arrow frog	20	25
2314	400 c. Ring-tailed lemur	20	25
2315	400 c. Iguana	20	25
2316	400 c. "Heliconius burneyi" (butterfly)	20	25
2317	400 c. Vervain hummingbird	20	25
2318	400 c. Verreauv's sifaka	20	25

531 Pagoda of Kaiyan Si Temple, Fujian

532 Serafim Todorow (Bulgaria)

1996. "CHINA '96" 9th Asian International Stamp Exhibition. Pagodas. Multicoloured.

2320	400 c. Type **531**	20	25
2321	400 c. Kaiyuan Si Temple, Hebei	20	25
2322	400 c. Fogong Si Temple, Shanxi	20	25
2323	400 c. Xiangshan, Beijing	20	25

1996. 70th Birthday of Queen Elizabeth II. As T **364** of Antigua showing different photographs. Multicoloured.

2325	1000 c. As Type **364** of Antigua	50	55
2326	1000 c. In blue hat and coat	50	55
2327	1000 c. Wearing straw hat and carrying bouquet	50	55

1996. 50th Anniv of International Amateur Boxing Association. Multicoloured.

2329	300 c. Type **532**	15	20
2330	400 c. Oscar de la Hoya (U.S.A.)	20	25
2331	800 c. Ariel Hernandez (Cuba)	40	45
2332	1500 c. Arnoldo Mesa (Cuba)	80	85

533 Ancient Greek Wrestlers

1996. Olympic Games, Atlanta (2nd issue). Previous Medal Winners. Multicoloured.

2334	300 c. Type **533**	15	20
2335	400 c. Aileen Riggin, 1920 (U.S.A.)	20	25
2336	400 c. Pat McCormick, 1952 (U.S.A.)	20	25
2337	400 c. Dawn Fraser, 1956 (Australia)	20	25
2338	400 c. Chris von Saltza, 1960 (U.S.A.)	20	25
2339	400 c. Anita Lonsbrough, 1960 (Great Britain)	20	25
2340	400 c. Debbie Meyer, 1968 (U.S.A.)	20	25
2341	400 c. Shane Gould, 1972 (Australia)	20	25
2342	400 c. Petra Thuemer, 1976 (Germany)	20	25
2343	400 c. Marjorie Gestring, 1936 (U.S.A.)	20	25
2344	400 c. Abedi Pele (Ghana) (vert)	20	25
2345	400 c. Quico Navarez (Spain) (vert)	20	25
2346	400 c. Heino Hanson (Denmark) (vert)	20	25
2347	400 c. Mostafa Ismail (Egypt) (vert)	20	25
2348	400 c. Anthony Yeboah (Ghana) (vert)	20	25
2349	400 c. Jurgen Klinsmann (Germany) (vert)	20	25
2350	400 c. Cobi Jones (U.S.A.) (vert)	20	25
2351	400 c. Franco Baresi (Italy) (vert)	20	25
2352	400 c. Igor Dobrovolski (Russia) (vert)	20	25
2353	500 c. Wilma Rudolph (U.S.A.) (track and field, 1960)	25	30
2354	600 c. Olympic Stadium, 1960, and Roman landmarks	30	35
2355	800 c. Ladies Kayak pairs, 1960 (Soviet Union)	40	45

Nos. 2335/43 (swimming and diving), and 2344/52 (football) respectively were printed together, se-tenant, with the backgrounds forming composite designs.

534 E. W. Agyare (35 years service with Ghana Broadcasting)

535 Fiddles

1996. Local Broadcasting.

2357	**534**	100 c. multicoloured	10	10

1996. 50th Anniv of U.N.I.C.E.F. As T **366** of Antigua. Multicoloured.

2358	400 c. Ghanaian child	20	25
2359	500 c. Mother and child	25	30
2360	600 c. Mother and child drinking	30	35

1996. 3000th Anniv of Jerusalem. As T **367** of Antigua. Multicoloured.

2362	400 c. St Stephen's Gate and "Jasminum mesnyi"	20	25
2363	600 c. The Citadel, Tower of David and "Nerium oleander"	30	35
2364	800 c. Chapel of the Ascension and "Romulea bulbocodium"	40	45

1996. Centenary of Radio. Entertainers. As T **368** of Antigua. Multicoloured.

2366	500 c. Frank Sinatra	25	30
2367	600 c. Judy Garland	30	35
2368	600 c. Bing Crosby	30	35
2369	800 c. Martin and Lewis	40	45

1996. 50th Anniv of U.N.E.S.C.O. As T **374** of Antigua. Multicoloured.

2371	400 c. The Citadel, Haiti (vert)	20	25
2372	800 c. Ait-Ben-Hadou (fortified village), Morocco (vert)	40	45
2373	1000 c. Spissky Hrad, Slovakia	50	55

1996. Musical Insruments. Multicoloured.

2375	500 c. Type **535**	45	50
2376	500 c. Proverbial drum	45	50
2377	500 c. Double clapless bell and castanet	45	50
2378	500 c. Gourd rattle	45	50
2379	500 c. Horns	45	50

536 Ariel, Flounder and Sebastian

1996. Disney Friends. Disney Cartoon Characters. Multicoloured.

2380	60 c. Type **536**	10	10
2381	60 c. Pinocchio and Jiminy Cricket	10	10
2382	60 c. Cogsworth and Lumiere	10	10
2383	60 c. Copper and Tod	10	10
2384	60 c. Pocahontas, Meeko and Flit	10	10
2385	60 c. Bambi, Flower and Thumper	10	10
2386	150 c. As No. 2373	10	10
2387	200 c. Type **537**	10	15
2388	200 c. As No. 2375	10	15
2389	300 c. As No. 2377	15	20
2390	350 c. As No. 2374	20	25
2391	450 c. As No. 2376	25	30
2392	600 c. Aladdin and Abu	30	35
2393	700 c. Penny and Rufus	35	40
2394	800 c. Mowgli and Baloo	40	45

537 Herd Boy and Ox

1997. Chinese New Year ("Year of the Ox"). "The Herd Boy and Weaver". Each brown, silver and black.

2397	500 c. Type **537**	25	30
2398	500 c. Ox and weaver in lake	25	30
2399	500 c. Weaver at work	25	30
2400	500 c. Herd boy with dying Ox	25	30
2401	500 c. Weaver flying out of window	25	30
2402	500 c. Herd boy carrying children	25	30
2403	500 c. Family separated by "river"	25	30
2404	500 c. Petitioning the emperor	25	30
2405	500 c. Family reunited	25	30

538 The Tomb of Dr. Hideyo Noguchi

539 Dipo Hairstyle

1997. 120th Birth Anniv of Dr. Hideyo Noguchi (bacteriologist). Multicoloured.

2406	1000 c. Type **538**	50	55
2407	1000 c. Dr. Hideyo Noguchi	50	55
2408	1000 c. Birthplace of Dr. Noguchi at Sanjogarta	50	55
2409	1000 c. Noguchi Institute, Legon	50	55
2410	1000 c. Noguchi Gardens, Accra	50	55

1997. Ghanaian Women's Hairstyle. Multicoloured.

2412	1000 c. Type **539**	50	55
2413	1000 c. Oduku with flowers	50	55
2414	1000 c. Dansinkran	50	55
2415	1000 c. Mbobom	50	55
2416	1000 c. Oduku with hair pins	50	55
2417	1000 c. African corn row	50	55
2418	1000 c. Chinese raster	50	55
2419	1000 c. Chinese raster with top knot	50	55
2420	1000 c. Corn row	50	55
2421	1000 c. Mbakaa	50	55

540 Independence Anniversary Emblem

1997. 40th Anniv of Independence. Multicoloured.

2422	200 c. Type **540**	10	10
2423	200 c. President J. J. Rawlings (vert)	1·50	1·50
2424	550 c. Dr. Kwane Nkrumah (first President) (vert)	30	35
2425	800 c. Children in class	40	45
2426	1100 c. Akosombo Dam	55	60

No. 2425 is inscribed "Acheivement" in error.

1997. 10th Anniv of Chernobyl Nuclear Disaster. As T **376** of Antigua. Multicoloured.

2428	800 c. Child's face and U.N.E.S.C.O. emblem	40	45
2429	1000 c. As No. 2428, but inscribed "CHABAD'S CHILDREN OF CHERNOBYL" at foot	50	55

541 Deng Xiaoping

1997. Deng Xiaoping (Chinese statesman) Commemoration. Different portraits. Multicoloured.

2430	300 c. Type **541**	15	20
2431	500 c. Looking thoughtful	25	30
2432	600 c. Wearing glasses	30	35
2433	600 c. Delivering speech	30	35
2434	800 c. As No. 2432	40	45
2435	800 c. As No. 2433	40	45
2436	1000 c. Type **541**	50	55
2437	1000 c. As No. 2431	50	55

1997. 50th Death Anniv of Paul Harris (founder of Rotary International). As T **377** of Antigua. Multicoloured.

2439	2000 c. Paul Harris and Egyptian patient receiving polio vaccination	1·00	1·10

1997. Golden Wedding of Queen Elizabeth and Prince Philip. As T **378** of Anitgua. Multicoloured.

2441	800 c. Queen Elizabeth II	40	45
2442	800 c. Royal coat of arms	40	45
2443	800 c. Queen Elizabeth and Prince Philip waving	40	45
2444	800 c. Queen Elizabeth and Prince Philip on official visit	40	45
2445	800 c. Queen in Irish State Coach	40	45
2446	800 c. Prince Philip in 1947	40	45

1997. "Pacific '97" International Stamp Exhibition, San Francisco. Death Centenary of Heinrich von Stephan (founder of the U.P.U.). As T **379** of Antigua.

2448	1000 c. blue	50	55
2449	1000 c. brown	50	55
2450	1000 c. red	50	55

DESIGNS: No. 2448, Early motor car; 2449, Von Stephan and Mercury; 2450, Blanchard's balloon flight, 1784.

1997. Birth Bicentenary of Hiroshige (Japanese painter). "One Hundred Famous Views of Edo". As T **310** of Dominica. Multicoloured.

2452	600 c. "Nihonbashi Bridge and Edobashi Bridge"	30	35
2453	600 c. "View of Nihonbashi Tori 1-chome"	30	35
2454	600 c. "Open Garden at Fukagawa Hachiman Shrine"	30	35
2455	600 c. "Inari Bridge and Minato Shrine, Teppozu"	30	35
2456	600 c. "Bamboo Yards, Kyobashi Bridge"	30	35
2457	600 c. "Hall of Thirty-Three Bays, Fukagawa"	30	35

542 Jackie Gleason

1997. Famous Comedians. Multicoloured.

2459	600 c. Type **542**	30	35
2460	600 c. Danny Kaye	30	35
2461	600 c. John Cleese	30	35
2462	600 c. Lucille Ball	30	35
2463	600 c. Jerry Lewis	30	35
2464	600 c. Sidney James	30	35
2465	600 c. Louis Defuenes	30	35
2466	600 c. Mae West	30	35
2467	600 c. Bob Hope	30	35

543 "Galerina calyptrata"

545 Ghanaian Players holding Trophy

544 African Pygmy Angelfish

1997. Fungi of the World. Multicoloured.

2469	200 c. Type **543**	10	15
2470	300 c. "Lepiota ignivolvata"	15	20
2471	400 c. "Omphalotus olearius"	20	25
2472	550 c. "Amanita phalloides"	30	35
2473	600 c. "Entoloma conferendum"	30	35
2474	800 c. "Entoloma nitidum"	40	45
2475	800 c. "Coprinus picaceus"	40	45
2476	800 c. "Stropharia aurantiaca"	40	45
2477	800 c. "Cortinarius splendens"	40	45
2478	800 c. "Gomphidius roseus"	40	45
2479	800 c. "Russula sardonia"	40	45
2480	800 c. "Geastrum schmidelia"	40	45

1997. World Football Championship, France (1998). As T **383** of Antigua. Multicoloured.

2482	200 c. Azteca Stadium, Mexico	10	10
2483	300 c. The Rose Bowl, U.S.A.	15	20
2484	400 c. Stadio Giuseppe Meazza, Italy	20	25
2485	500 c. Olympiastadion, Germany	25	30
2486	600 c. Patrick Kluivert, Netherlands	30	35
2487	600 c. Roy Keane, Republic of Ireland	30	35
2488	600 c. Abedi Ayew Pele, Ghana	30	35
2489	600 c. Peter Schmeichel, Denmark	30	35
2490	600 c. Roberto di Matteo, Italy	30	35
2491	600 c. Bebeto, Brazil	30	35
2492	600 c. Steve McManaman, England	30	35
2493	600 c. George Oppon Weah, Liberia	30	35
2494	1000 c. Maracana Stadium, Brazil	50	55
2495	2000 c. Bernabeu Stadium, Spain	1·00	1·10

1997. Marine Life. Multicoloured.

2497	400 c. Type **544**	20	25
2498	500 c. Violet-crested turaco	25	30
2499	500 c. Pied avocet	25	30
2500	500 c. Bottle-nosed dolphin	25	30
2501	500 c. Bottle-nosed dolphin and long-toed lapwing	25	30
2502	500 c. Longfinned spadefish	25	30
2503	500 c. Imperial angelfish and manta	25	30
2504	500 c. Racoon butterflyfish and African pompano	25	30
2505	500 c. Silvertip shark	25	30
2506	500 c. Longfin banner fish	25	30
2507	500 c. Longfin banner fish and manta	25	30
2508	500 c. Rust parrotfish	25	30
2509	500 c. Coral trout	25	30
2510	600 c. Angelfish	30	35
2511	800 c. Broomtail wrasse	40	45
2512	1000 c. Indian butterflyfish	50	55

Nos. 2498/2509 were printed together, se-tenant, with the backgrounds forming a composite design.

1997. J.V.C. Under-17 World Soccer Champions (1995). Multicoloured.
2514 200 c. + 50 c. Type **545** . . 15 20
2515 550 c. + 50 c. Ghana football team (horiz) 30 35
2516 800 c. + 50 c. Abu Iddrisu . 45 50
2517 1000 c. + 50 c. Emmanuel Bentil (captain) 60 65
2518 1500 c. + 50 c. Basiru Gambo 80 85

546 "Eurychone rothschildiana"

547 Goldfinch

1997. Flowers of the World. Multicoloured.
2519 200 c. Type **546** 10 10
2520 550 c. "Bulbophyllum lepidum" 30 35
2521 800 c. "Ansellia africana" . . 40 45
2522 800 c. "Strophanthus preusii" (vert) 40 45
2523 800 c. "Ancistrochilus rothschildlanus" (vert) . . 40 45
2524 800 c. "Mussaendra arcuata" (vert) 40 45
2525 800 c. "Microcoelia guyoniane" (vert) 40 45
2526 800 c. "Gloriosa simplex" (vert) 40 45
2527 800 c. "Brachycorythis kalbreyeri" (vert) 40 45
2528 800 c. "Aframomum sceptrum" (vert) 40 45
2529 800 c. "Thunbergia alata" (vert) 40 45
2530 800 c. "Clerodendrum thomsoniae" (vert) 40 45
2531 1100 c. "Combbretum grandiflorum" 60 65

Nos. 2522/30 were printed together, se-tenant, with the backgrounds forming a composite design.

1997. Birds of Africa. Multicoloured.
2533 200 c. Type **547** 10 10
2534 300 c. Cape puff-back flycatcher ("Batis") 15 20
2535 400 c. Red-headed barbet . . 20 25
2536 500 c. African white-necked raven 25 30
2537 600 c. Purple grenadier . . . 30 35
2538 800 c. Black bustard 40 45
2539 800 c. Lapwing 40 45
2540 800 c. Lichtenstein's sandgrouse 40 45
2541 800 c. Red-crested turaco . . 40 45
2542 800 c. White-browed coucal . 40 45
2543 800 c. Lilac-breasted roller . 40 45
2544 800 c. Golden pipit 40 45
2545 800 c. Burchell's gonolek . . 40 45
2546 800 c. Blackcap 40 45
2547 1000 c. Zebra waxbill 50 55

548 Havana Cat

1997. Cats and Dogs. Multicoloured.
2549 20 c. Type **548** 10 10
2550 50 c. Singapura cat 10 10
2551 80 c. Papillon 10 10
2552 100 c. Sphinx cat 10 10
2553 150 c. British white cat . . . 10 10
2554 200 c. Bulldog 10 15
2555 300 c. Snowshoe cat 15 20
2556 400 c. Shetland sheepdog . . 20 25
2557 500 c. Schnauzer 25 30
2558 600 c. Persian cat 30 35
2559 800 c. Shih tzu 40 45
2560 1000 c. Russian wolfhound . 50 55
2561 1000 c. Birman cat 50 55
2562 1000 c. Basset hound 50 55
2563 1000 c. Silver tabby cat . . . 50 55
2564 1000 c. Afghan 50 55
2565 1000 c. Burmilla cat 50 55
2566 1000 c. Abyssinian cat . . . 50 55
2567 1000 c. Border terrier 50 55
2568 1000 c. Scottish fold cat . . . 50 55
2569 1000 c. Boston terrier 50 55
2570 1000 c. Oriental cat 50 55
2571 1000 c. Keeshond 50 55
2572 2000 c. Chow Chow . . . . 1·00 1·10

549 "Landscape" (Huang Binhong)

550 Diana, Princess of Wales

1997. Return of Hong Kong to China.
2574 **549** 200 c. multicoloured . . 10 15
2575 – 300 c. multicoloured . . 15 20
2576 – 400 c. multicoloured . . 20 25
2577 – 500 c. multicoloured . . 25 30
2578 – 600 c. multicoloured . . 30 35
2579 – 800 c. multicoloured . . 40 45
2580 – 1000 c. multicoloured . 50 55
2581 – 2000 c. multicoloured . 1·00 1·10

DESIGNS: 300 c. to 2000 c. Landscape paintings by Huang Binhong.

1997. Christmas. Paintings. As T **386** of Antigua. Multicoloured.
2584 200 c. "Cupid" (Botticelli) . 10 15
2585 550 c. "Zephyr and Chloris" (Botticelli) 30 35
2586 800 c. "Triumphant Cupid" (Caravaggio) 40 45
2587 1100 c. "The Seven Works of Mercy" (Caravaggio) . . 55 60
2588 1500 c. "The Toilet of Venus" (Diego Velazquez) 80 85
2589 2000 c. "Freeing of St. Peter" (Raphael) . . . . 1·00 1·10

1997. Diana, Princess of Wales Commemoration. Multicoloured (except Nos. 2591, 2596, 2602).
2591 1200 c. Type **550** (red) . . . 60 65
2592 1200 c. Wearing blue suit and holding flowers 60 65
2593 1200 c. Looking right . . . 60 65
2594 1200 c. Sitting crossed-legged 60 65
2595 1200 c. With Prince William 60 65
2596 1200 c. Wearing spotted scarf (blue and black) 60 65
2597 1200 c. Wearing pink shirt . 60 65
2598 1200 c. Wearing red dress . 60 65
2599 1200 c. Carrying bouquet . . 60 65
2600 1200 c. Wearing sunglasses . 60 65
2601 1200 c. With children . . . 60 65
2602 1200 c. Wearing hat (brown and black) 60 65

551 Horse

1998. Animals of the Chinese Lunar Calendar. Multicoloured.
2604 400 c. Type **551** 20 25
2605 400 c. Monkey 20 25
2606 400 c. Ram 20 25
2607 400 c. Cock 20 25
2608 400 c. Dog 20 25
2609 400 c. Ox 20 25
2610 400 c. Rabbit 20 25
2611 400 c. Pig 20 25
2612 400 c. Snake 20 25
2613 400 c. Dragon 20 25
2614 400 c. Tiger 20 25
2615 400 c. Rat 20 25

552 Mortie and Ferdie (January)

554 Maya Agelou

553 Union Pacific SD60M Diesel Locomotive No. 6331, U.S.A.

1998. A Year in the Life of Mickey Mouse and Friends. Walt Disney cartoon characters. Multicoloured.
2616 1000 c. Type **552** 50 55
2617 1000 c. Minnie on Valentine's Day (February) 50 55
2618 1000 c. Goofy with kite (March) 50 55
2619 1000 c. Mickey, Minnie and Pluto in rain (April) 50 55
2620 1000 c. Minnie with flowers (May) 50 55
2621 1000 c. Daisy watering garden (June) 50 55
2622 1000 c. Donald at Independance Day celebrations (July) . . 50 55
2623 1000 c. Donald and Daisy on the beach (August) 50 55
2624 1000 c. Morty and Ferdie returning to school (September) 50 55
2625 1000 c. Hewey, Dewey and Louie at Hallowe'en (October) 50 55
2626 1000 c. Mickey on Thanksgiving Day (November) 50 55
2627 1000 c. Mickey and Minnie at Christmas (December) . . . 50 55

1998. Trains of the World. Multicoloured.
2629 300 c. Type **553** 15 20
2630 500 c. ETR 450 high-speed train, Italy 25 30
2631 800 c. X200 high-speed train, Sweden 40 45
2632 800 c. SPS steam locomotive, Pakistan 40 45
2633 800 c. Class WP steam locomotive, India 40 45
2634 800 c. Class QJ steam locomotive, China 40 45
2635 800 c. Type 12 steam locomotive, Belgium 40 45
2636 800 c. Class P8 steam locomotive, Germany . . . 40 45
2637 800 c. Class "Castle" steam locomotive, Great Britain . 40 45
2638 800 c. Tank locomotive, Austria 40 45
2639 800 c. Class P36 steam locomotive, Russia 40 45
2640 800 c. Steam locomotive "William Mason", U.S.A. . 40 45
2641 800 c. AVE high-speed train, Spain 40 45
2642 800 c. Diesel locomotive No. 1602, Luxembourg 40 45
2643 800 c. "Hikari" express train, Japan 40 45
2644 800 c. Santa Fe Railroad GM F7 "Warbonnet" diesel locomotive, U.S.A. 40 45
2645 800 c. Class E1500 diesel locomotive, Morocco . . . 40 45
2646 800 c. Class "Deltic" diesel locomotive, Great Britain . 40 45
2647 800 c. XPT high-speed train, Australia 40 45
2648 800 c. Channel Tunnel shuttle train, France and Great Britain 40 45
2649 800 c. Class 201 diesel locomotive, Ireland 40 45
2650 1000 c. TGV Duplex high-speed train, France 50 55
2651 2000 c. Class EL diesel locomotive, Australia . . . 1·00 1·10
2652 3000 c. Eurostar high-speed train, Great Britain . . . . 1·50 1·60

1998. Great Writers of the 20th Century. Mult.
2654 350 c. Type **554** 20 25
2655 350 c. Alex Haley 20 25
2656 350 c. Charles Johnson . . . 20 25
2657 350 c. Richard Wright 20 25
2658 350 c. Toni Cade Bambara . . 20 25
2659 350 c. Henri Louis Gates Jr . 20 25

555 Breguet Br 14 B2, France

1998. History of Aviation. Multicoloured.
2660 800 c. Type **555** 40 45
2661 800 c. Curtiss BF2C-1 Goshawk, U.S.A. 40 45
2662 800 c. Supermarine Spitfire Mk IX, Great Britain . . . 40 45
2663 800 c. Fiat G.50, Italy 40 45
2664 800 c. Douglas B-18A, U.S.A. 40 45
2665 800 c. Boeing FB-5, U.S.A. . 40 45
2666 800 c. Bristol F2B "Brisfit", Great Britain 40 45
2667 800 c. Hawker Fury 1, Great Britain 40 45
2668 800 c. Fiat CR-42, Italy . . 40 45
2669 800 c. Messerschmitt Bf 109 E-7, Germany 40 45
2670 800 c. Lockheed PV-2 Harpoon, U.S.A. 40 45
2671 800 c. Airspeed Oxford Mk 1, Great Britain 40 45
2672 800 c. Junkers Ju 87D-1, Germany 40 45
2673 800 c. Yakovlev Yak-9D, U.S.S.R. 40 45
2674 800 c. North American P-51D Mustang, U.S.A. 40 45
2675 800 c. Douglas A-206 Havoc, U.S.A. 40 45
2676 800 c. Supermarine Attacker F1, Great Britain 40 45
2677 800 c. Mikoyan Gurevich MiG-15, U.S.S.R. 40 45

556 "Empress of Ireland" (liner)

1998. Famous Ships. Multicoloured.
2679 800 c. Type **556** 40 45
2680 800 c. "Transylvania" (liner) 40 45
2681 800 c. "Mauretania I" (liner) 40 45
2682 800 c. "Reliance" (liner) . . 40 45
2683 800 c. "Aquitania" (liner) . . 40 45
2684 800 c. "Lapland" (liner) . . 40 45
2685 800 c. "Cap Polonio" (liner) 40 45
2686 800 c. "France I", 1910 (liner) 40 45
2687 800 c. "Imperator" (liner) . . 40 45
2688 800 c. H.M.S. "Rodney" (battleship) 40 45
2689 800 c. U.S.S. "Alabama" (battleship) 40 45
2690 800 c. H.M.S. "Nelson" (battleship) 40 45
2691 800 c. "Ormonde" (camouflaged liner) 40 45
2692 800 c. U.S.S. "Radford" (destroyer) 40 45
2693 800 c. "Empress of Russia" (camouflaged liner) 40 45
2694 800 c. Type XIV U-boat . . 40 45
2695 800 c. Japanese Type A midget submarine 40 45
2696 800 c. "Brin" (Italian submarine) 40 45

No. 2681 is inscribed "MAURITANIA" in error.

1998. "Israel 98" International Stamp Exhibition, Tel-Aviv. Nos. 2362/4 optd with Emblem.
2698 400 c. St. Stephen's Gate and "Jasminum mesnyi" . . . 20 25
2699 600 c. The Citadel, Tower of David and "Nerium oleander" 30 35
2700 800 c. Chapel of the Ascension and "Romulea bulbocodium" 40 45

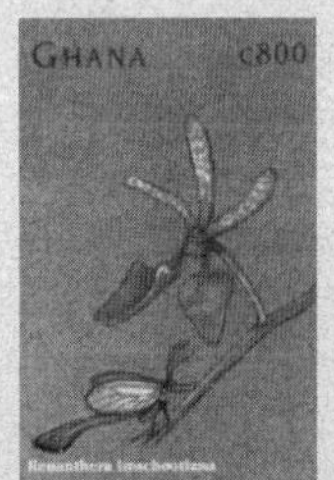

558 "Renanthera imschootiana"

1998. Orchids of the World. Multicoloured.
2702 800 c. Type **558** 40 45
2703 800 c. "Arachnis flos-aeris" . 40 45
2704 800 c. "Restrepia lansbergi" . 40 45
2705 800 c. "Paphiopedilum tonsum" 40 45
2706 800 c. "Phalaenopsis ebauche" 40 45
2707 800 c. "Pleione limprichti" . 40 45
2708 800 c. "Phragmipedium schroderae" 40 45
2709 800 c. "Zygopetalum clayii" . 40 45
2710 800 c. "Vanda coerulea" . . 40 45
2711 800 c. "Odontonia boussole" . 40 45
2712 800 c. "Disa uniflora" . . . 40 45
2713 800 c. "Dendrobium bigibbum" 40 45

559 Elvis Presley

1998. 30th Anniv of Elvis Presley's "68 Special" Television Programme. Multicoloured.
2715 800 c. Type **559** 40 45
2716 800 c. Elvis in white suit . . 40 45

2717	800 c. In leather jacket, holding microphone	40	45
2718	800 c. Wearing light blue jacket	40	45
2719	800 c. Elvis with silhouetted figures in background	40	45
2720	800 c. Elvis with guitar and microphone	40	45

560 Crest of Accra Metropolitan Assembly and Surf Boats

1998. Centenary of Accra Metropolitan Assembly. Multicoloured.

2721	200 c. Type **560**	10	15
2722	550 c. King Tackie Tawiah I	30	35
2723	800 c. Achimota School	40	45
2724	1100 c. Korle Bu Hospital	60	65
2725	1500 c. Christianborg Castle	80	85

561 Tetteh Quarshie (cocoa industry pioneer)

1998. 50th Anniv of Ghana Cocoa Board. Multicoloured.

2726	200 c. Type **561**	10	15
2727	550 c. Ripe hybrid cocoa pods	30	35
2728	800 c. Opening cocoa pods	40	45
2729	1100 c. Fermenting cocoa beans	60	65
2730	1500 c. Loading freighter with cocoa	80	85

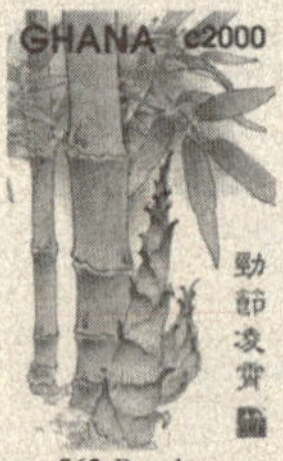

562 Bamboo

1998. Oriental Flowers. Multicoloured.

2731	2000 c. Type **562**	1·00	1·10
2732	2000 c. Cherry blossom	1·00	1·10
2733	2000 c. Yellow chrysanthemum	1·00	1·10
2734	2000 c. Orchid	1·00	1·10
2735	2000 c. Green peony	1·00	1·10
2736	2000 c. Red peony	1·00	1·10
2737	2000 c. Pink peony	1·00	1·10
2738	2000 c. White peony	1·00	1·10

563 Two Dolphins

1998. International Year of the Ocean. Multicoloured.

2740	500 c. Type **563**	25	30
2741	500 c. Dolphin	25	30
2742	500 c. Seagull	25	30
2743	500 c. Least tern	25	30
2744	500 c. Emperor angelfish	25	30
2745	500 c. White ear (juvenile)	25	30
2746	500 c. Blue shark and diver	25	30
2747	500 c. Parrotfish	25	30
2748	500 c. Dottyback	25	30
2749	500 c. Blue-spotted stingray	25	30
2750	500 c. Masked butterflyfish	25	30
2751	500 c. Jackknife-fish	25	30
2752	500 c. Octopus	25	30
2753	500 c. Lionfish	25	30
2754	500 c. Seadragon	25	30
2755	500 c. Rock cod	25	30

Nos. 2740/55 were printed together, se-tenant, with the backgrounds forming a composite design.

No. 2745 is inscribed "Whit Ear" in error.

POSTAGE DUE STAMPS

1958. Postage Due stamps of Gold Coast optd **GHANA** and bar.

D 9	D 1	1d. black	10	20
D10		2d. black	10	25
D11		3d. black	10	30
D12		6d. black	15	65
D13		1s. black	20	1·25

INDEX

Countries can be quickly located by referring to the index at the end of this volume.

D 3

1958.

D14	D 3	1d. red	10	30
D15		2d. green	10	30
D16		3d. orange	10	30
D17		6d. blue	10	50
D18		1s. violet	15	2·00

1965. Surch **Ghana New Currency 19th July, 1965.** and value.

D19	D 3	1 p. on 1d.	10	60
D20		2 p. on 2d.	10	60
D21		3 p. on 3d.	10	60
D22		6 p. on 6d.	10	1·50
D23		12 p. on 1s.	15	2·00

1968. Nos. D20/2 additionally surch.

D24	D 3	$1\frac{1}{2}$ n.p. on 2 p. on 2d.	5·50	4·25
D25		$2\frac{1}{2}$ n.p. on 3 p. on 3d.	1·00	4·50
D26		5 n.p. on 6 p. on 6d.	1·00	

1970. Inscr in new currency.

D27	D 3	1 n.p. red	80	3·25
D28		$1\frac{1}{2}$ n.p. green	80	3·75
D29		$2\frac{1}{2}$ n.p. orange	1·10	4·25
D30		5 n.p. blue	1·75	4·50
D31		10 n.p. violet	2·50	5·50

1980. Currency described as "p".

D32	D 3	2p. orange	90	2·75
D33		3 p. brown	90	2·75

GIBRALTAR

A British colony at the W. entrance to the Mediterranean.

1886. 12 pence = 1 shilling;
20 shillings = 1 pound.
1971. 100 (new) pence = 1 pound.

1886. Stamps of Bermuda (Queen Victoria) optd **GIBRALTAR**.

1	9	$\frac{1}{2}$d. green	9·00	6·00
2		1d. red	50·00	4·00
3		2d. purple	95·00	75·00
4		$2\frac{1}{2}$d. blue	£120	3·00
5		4d. orange	£120	85·00
6		6d. lilac	£200	£180
7		1s. brown	£400	£350

2

7

1886. Various frames.

39	2	$\frac{1}{2}$d. green	3·50	1·25
40		1d. red	5·00	35
10		2d. purple	30·00	17·00
42		$2\frac{1}{2}$d. blue	22·00	40
12		4d. brown	70·00	70·00
13		6d. lilac	95·00	95·00
14		1s. brown	£180	£180

1889. Surch with new value in **CENTIMOS**.

15	2	5 c. on $\frac{1}{2}$d. green	6·00	14·00
16		10 c. on 1d. red	10·00	6·50
17		25 c. on 2d. purple	4·25	5·00
18		25 c. on $2\frac{1}{2}$d. blue	25·00	2·00
19		40 c. on 4d. brown	60·00	80·00
20		50 c. on 6d. lilac	60·00	80·00
21		75 c. on 1s. brown	65·00	75·00

1889.

22	7	5 c. green	3·50	70
23		10 c. red	3·50	45
24		20 c. green and brown	35·00	17·00
25		20 c. green	9·00	48·00
26		25 c. blue	12·00	70
27		40 c. brown	2·75	2·25
28		50 c. lilac	2·25	1·50
29		75 c. green	32·00	32·00
30		1 p. brown	75·00	20·00
31		1 p. brown and blue	4·00	3·50
32		2 p. black and red	8·50	24·00
33		5 p. grey	42·00	95·00

1898. As 1886.

41	2	2d. purple and blue	17·00	1·50
43		4d. brown and green	16·00	6·50
44		6d. violet and red	38·00	20·00
45		1s. brown and red	32·00	16·00

8

9

1903.

66	8	$\frac{1}{2}$d. green	2·25	90
57c		1d. purple on red	2·25	70
58a		2d. green and red	7·00	3·50
49		$2\frac{1}{2}$d. purple and black on blue	3·50	60
60a		6d. purple and violet	18·00	8·00
61		1s. black and red	38·00	10·00
62	9	2s. green and blue	65·00	85·00
53		4s. purple and green	75·00	£140
54		8s. purple and black on blue	£110	£140
55		£1 purple and black on red	£450	£500

1907.

67	8	1d. red	4·25	45
68		2d. grey	6·50	9·00
69		$2\frac{1}{2}$d. blue	4·25	1·25
70		6d. purple	£120	£375
71		1s. black on green	21·00	19·00
72	9	2s. purple and blue on blue	48·00	45·00
73		4s. black and red	90·00	£130
74		8s. purple and green	£180	£180

1912. As T **8/9**, but portrait of King George V. (3d. A. Inscr "3 PENCE". B. Inscr "THREE PENCE").

89	$\frac{1}{2}$d. green	70	90
90	1d. red	1·50	70
91a	$1\frac{1}{2}$a. brown	1·25	30
93	2d. grey	1·25	85
79	$2\frac{1}{2}$d. blue	3·25	1·75
95a	3d. blue (A)	1·40	1·50
109	3d. blue (B)	7·50	2·00
97a	6d. purple	1·60	3·50
81	1s. black on green	7·00	3·25
102a	1s. olive and black	14·00	12·00
82	2s. purple and blue on blue	25·00	3·25
103	2s. brown and black	9·00	29·00
104	2s. 6d. green and black	9·00	17·00
83	4s. black and red	29·00	55·00
105	5s. red and black	13·00	48·00
84	8s. purple and green	70·00	85·00
106	10s. blue and black	32·00	65·00
85	£1 purple and black on red	£140	£190
107	£1 orange and black	£140	£180
108	£5 violet and black	£1400	£3500

1918 Optd **WAR TAX**.

86	$\frac{1}{2}$d. green (No. 89)	55	1·40

13 The Rock of Gibraltar

1931.

110	13	1d. red	1·75	2·25
111		$1\frac{1}{2}$d. brown	1·75	2·25
112		2d. grey	4·50	1·00
113		3d. blue	4·50	2·75

1935. Silver Jubilee. As T **13** of Antigua.

114	2d. blue and black	1·60	2·50
115	3d. brown and blue	3·25	3·50
116	6d. green and blue	8·50	12·00
117	1s. grey and purple	8·50	8·50

1937. Coronation. As T **2** of Aden.

118	$\frac{1}{2}$d. green	25	10
119	2d. grey	80	2·00
120	3d. blue	2·00	2·00

14 King George VI

15 Rock of Gibraltar

1938. King George VI.

121	14	$\frac{1}{2}$d. green	10	40
122b	15	1d. brown	50	55
123		$1\frac{1}{2}$d. red	35·00	75
123b	–	$1\frac{1}{2}$d. violet	30	1·00
124a	–	2d. grey	55	35
124c	–	2d. red	40	60
125b	–	3d. blue	30	30
125c	–	5d. orange	70	1·25
126b	–	6d. red and violet	2·00	1·60
127b	–	1s. black and green	3·00	4·00
128b	–	2s. black and brown	3·25	6·00
129b	–	5s. black and red	12·00	17·00
130a	–	10s. black and blue	35·00	25·00
131	14	£1 orange	38·00	45·00

DESIGNS—HORIZ: 2d. The Rock (North side); 3d., 5d. Europa Point; 6d. Moorish Castle; 1s. Southport Gate; 2s. Eliott Memorial; 5s. Government House; 10s. Catalan Bay.

1946. Victory. As T **9** of Aden.

132	$\frac{1}{2}$d. green	10	10
133	3d. blue	30	20

1948. Silver Wedding. As T **10/11** of Aden.

134	$\frac{1}{2}$d. green	70	85
135	£1 orange	50·00	60·00

1949. U.P.U. As T **20/23** of Antigua.

136	2d. red	1·00	1·10
137	3d. blue	2·50	1·10
138	6d. purple	2·00	1·10
139	1s. green	1·60	2·50

1950. Inauguration of Legislative Council. Optd **NEW CONSTITUTION 1950**.

140	2d. red (No. 124c)	30	1·00
141	3d. blue (No. 125b)	40	1·00
142	6d. red and violet (No. 126b)	50	1·40
143	1s. black and green (No. 127b)	50	1·40

1953. Coronation. As T **13** of Aden.

144	$\frac{1}{2}$d. black and green	30	75

24 Cargo and Passenger Wharves

1953.

145	24	$\frac{1}{2}$d. blue and green	15	30
146	–	1d. green	1·50	30
147	–	$1\frac{1}{2}$d. black	90	90
148	–	2d. brown	1·25	40
149a	–	$2\frac{1}{2}$d. red	2·75	70
150	–	3d. blue	3·25	10
151	–	4d. blue	2·25	1·50
152	–	5d. purple	60	70
153	–	6d. black and blue	40	50
154a	–	1s. blue and brown	30	60
155a	–	2s. orange and violet	19·00	3·50
156	–	5s. brown	24·00	12·00
157	–	10s. brown and blue	50·00	35·00
158	–	£1 red and yellow	50·00	38·00

DESIGNS—HORIZ: 1d. South view from Straits; $1\frac{1}{2}$d. Tuna fishing industry; 2d. Southport Gate; $2\frac{1}{2}$d. Sailing in the Bay; 3d. Liner; 4d. Coaling wharf; 5d. Airport; 6d. Europa Point; 1s. Straits from Buena Vista; 2s. Rosia Bay and Straits; 5s. Main entrance, Government House. VERT: 10s. Tower of Homage, Moorish Castle; £1 Arms of Gibraltar.

1954. Royal Visit. As No. 150, but inscr "ROYAL VISIT 1954".

159	3d. blue	15	20

38 Gibraltar Candytuft

40 Rock and Badge of Gibraltar Regiment

1960.
160 38 ½d. purple and green . . . 15 30
161 – 1d. black and green . . . 10 10
162 – 2d. blue and brown . . . 15 15
163a – 2½d. black and blue . . . 20 15
164 – 3d. blue and orange . . . 30 10
199 – 4d. brown and turquoise . 30 60
166 – 6d. brown and green . . . 70 50
167 – 7d. blue and red 70 75
168 – 9d. blue and turquoise . . 50 50
169 – 1s. brown and green . . . 90 40
170 – 2s. brown and blue . . . 13·00 2·25
171 – 5s. blue and green . . . . 8·00 5·50
172 – 10s. yellow and blue . . . 14·00 10·00
173 40 £1 black and brown . . . 17·00 11·00
DESIGNS (As Type **38**):—HORIZ: 1d. Moorish Castle; 2d. St George's Hall; 3d. The Rock by moonlight; 4d. Catalan Bay; 1s. Barbary ape; 2s. Barbary Partridge; 5s. Blue Rock Thrush. VERT: 2½d. The keys; 6d. Map of Gibraltar; 7d. Air terminal; 9d. American War Memorial; 10s. Rock lily.

1963. Freedom from Hunger. As T **28** of Aden.
174 9d. sepia . . . . 9·00 1·50

1963. Centenary of Red Cross. As T **33** of Antigua.
175 1d. red and black . . . . . . 1·50 1·50
176 9d. red and blue . . . . . . 14·00 3·00

1964. 400th Birth Anniv of Shakespeare. As T **34** of Antigua.
177 7d. bistre 40 20

1964. New Constitution. Nos. 164 and 166 optd **NEW CONSTITUTION 1964.**
178 3d. blue and orange 15 10
179 6d. sepia and green 15 20

1965. Centenary of I.T.U. As T **36** of Antigua.
180 4d. green and yellow . . . . . 4·00 50
181 2s. green and blue . . . . . . 11·00 3·00

1965. I.C.Y. As T **37** of Antigua.
182 ½d. green and lavender . . . . 20 1·25
183 4d. purple and turquoise . . . 1·00 80
The value of the ½d. stamp is shown as "1/2".

1966. Churchill Commemoration. As T **38** of Antigua.
184 ½d. blue . . . . 20 1·25
185 1d. green 30 10
186 4d. brown . . . . 1·25 10
187 9d. violet . . . . 1·25 2·00

1966. World Cup Football Championships. As T **40** of Antigua.
188 2½d. multicoloured 75 30
189 6d. multicoloured . . . . . . 1·00 50

53 Red Seabream

1966. European Sea Angling Championships. Gibraltar.
190 53 4d. red, blue and black . . 20 10
191 – 7d. red, green and black . . 30 30
192 – 1s. brown, green and black 30 30
DESIGNS—HORIZ: 7d. Red scorpionfish. VERT: 1s. Stone bass.

1966. Inauguration of W.H.O. Headquarters, Geneva. As T **41** of Antigua.
193 6d. black, green and blue . . . 2·50 1·50
194 9d. black, purple and ochre . 3·00 1·50

56 "Our Lady of Europa"

1966. Centenary of Re-enthronement of "Our Lady of Europe".
195 56 2s. blue and black 30 70

1966. 20th Anniv of U.N.E.S.C.O. As T **54/6** of Antigua.
196 2d. multicoloured 25 10
197 7d. yellow, violet and olive . . 60 10
198 5s. black, purple and orange . 2·50 2·50

57 H.M.S. "Victory"

1967. Multicoloured.
200 ½d. Type **57** 10 15
201 1d. "Arab" (early steamer) . 10 10
202 2d. H.M.S. "Carmania" (merchant cruiser) 15 10
203 2½d. "Mons Calpe" (ferry) . 30 30
204 3d. "Canberra" (liner) . . . 20 10
205 4d. H.M.S. "Hood" (battle cruiser) 30 10
205a 5d. "Mirror" (cable ship) . . 3·25 55
206 6d. Xebec (sailing vessel) . . 30 50
207 7d. "Amerigo Vespucci" (Italian cadet ship) 30 45
208 9d. "Raffaello" (liner) . . . 30 60
209 1s. "Royal Katherine" (galleon) 30 35
210 2s. H.M.S. "Ark Royal" (aircraft carrier, 1937) . . 3·50 2·50
211 5s. H.M.S. "Dreadnought" (nuclear submarine) . . . 3·50 6·50
212 10s. "Neuralia" (liner) . . . 14·00 22·00
213 £1 "Mary Celeste" (sailing vessel) . . . . 14·00 22·00

58 Aerial Ropeway

59 Mary, Joseph and Child Jesus

1967. International Tourist Year. Multicoloured.
214 7d. Type **58** 10 10
215 9d. Shark fishing (horiz) . . . 10 10
216 1s. Skin-diving (horiz) 15 15

1967. Christmas. Multicoloured.
217 2d. Type **59** 15 10
218 6d. Church window (vert) . . 15 10

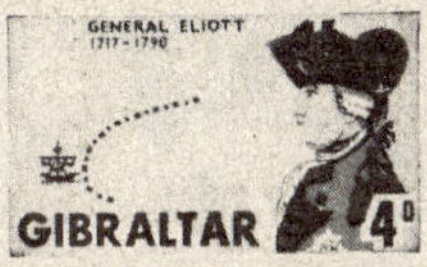

61 General Eliott and Route Map

1967. 250th Birth Anniv of General Eliott. Multicoloured.
219 4d. Type **61** 10 10
220 9d. Heathfield Tower and Monument, Sussex 15 10
221 1s. General Eliott (vert) . . . 15 10
222 2s. Eliott directing rescue operations 40 30
No. 222 is 55×21 mm.

65 Lord Baden-Powell

1968. 60th Anniv of Gibraltar Scout Association.
223 65 4d. buff and violet 15 10
224 – 7d. ochre and green . . . 15 10
225 – 9d. blue, orange and black 20 30
226 – 1s. yellow and green . . . 20 30
DESIGNS: 7d. Scout flag over the Rock; 9d. Tent, Scouts and salute; 1s. Scout badges.

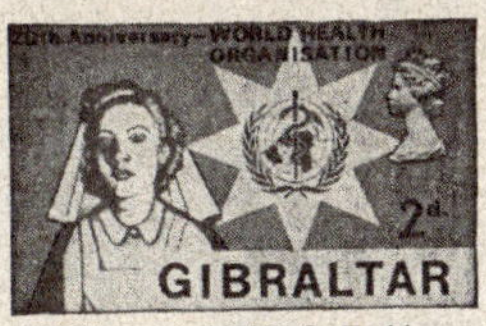

66 Nurse and W.H.O. Emblem

1968. 20th Anniv of W.H.O. Multicoloured.
227 2d. Type **66** 10 15
228 4d. Doctor and W.H.O. emblem 10 15

68 King John signing Magna Carta

70 Shepherd, Lamb and Star

1968. Human Rights Year.
229 68 1s. orange, brown and gold 15 10
230 – 2s. myrtle and gold 15 20
DESIGN: 2s. "Freedom" and Rock of Gibraltar.

1968. Christmas. Multicoloured.
231 4d. Type **70** 10 10
232 9d. Mary holding Holy Child . 10 10

72 Parliament Houses

1969. Commonwealth Parliamentary Association Conference.
233 72 4d. green and gold 10 10
234 – 9d. violet and gold 10 10
235 – 2s. red, gold and blue . . . 15 20
DESIGNS—HORIZ: 9d. Parliamentary emblem and outline of "The Rock". VERT: 2s. Clock Tower, Westminster (Big Ben) and Arms of Gibraltar.

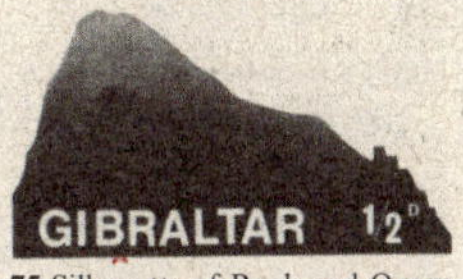

75 Silhouette of Rock and Queen Elizabeth II

1969. New Constitution.
236 75 ½d. gold and orange 10 10
237 5d. silver and green 20 10
238 7d. silver and purple . . . 20 10
239 5s. silver and blue 70 70

77 Soldier and Cap Badge, Royal Anglian Regiment, 1969

80 "Madonna of the Chair" (detail, Raphael)

1969. Military Uniforms (1st series). Multicoloured.
240 1d. Royal Artillery Officer, 1758, and modern cap badge . . . 20 10
241 6d. Type **77** 45 20
242 9d. Royal Engineers' Artificer, 1786, and modern cap badge 55 30
243 2s. Private, Fox's Marines, 1704, and modern Royal Marines' cap badge . . . . 2·00 1·25
See also Nos. 248/51, 290/3, 300/303, 313/16, 331/4, 340/3 and 363/6.

1969. Christmas. Multicoloured.
244 5d. Type **80** 10 10
245 7d. "Virgin and Child" (detail, Morales) 20 20
246 1s. "The Virgin of the Rocks" (detail, Leonardo da Vinci) . 20 20

83 Europa Point

88 Stamp and Rock of Gibraltar

1970. Europa Point.
247 83 2s. multicoloured 40 30

1970. Military Uniforms (2nd series). As T **77**. Multicoloured.
248 2d. Royal Scots Officer (1839) and cap badge 35 10
249 5d. South Wales Borderers Private (1763) and cap badge 70 10
250 7d. Queen's Royal Regiment Private (1742) and cap badge 70 15
251 2s. Royal Irish Rangers piper (1969) and cap badge . . . 2·75 1·25

1970. "Philympia 70" Stamp Exhibition, London.
252 88 1s. red and green 15 10
253 – 2s. blue and mauve 25 55
DESIGN: 2s. Stamp and Moorish Castle.
The stamps shown in the designs are well-known varieties with values omitted.

90 "The Virgin and Mary" (stained-glass window, Gabriel Loire)

1970. Christmas.
254 90 2s. multicoloured 30 30

91 Saluting Battery, Rosia

92 Saluting Battery, Rosia, Modern View

1971. Decimal Currency.
255 91 ½p. multicoloured 15 20
256 92 ½p. multicoloured 15 20
257 – 1p. multicoloured 80 30
258 – 1p. multicoloured 80 30
259 – 1½p. multicoloured 20 40
260 – 1½p. multicoloured 20 40
317 – 2p. multicoloured . . . . 1·10 1·75
318 – 2p. multicoloured . . . . 1·10 1·75
263 – 2½p. multicoloured 20 40
264 – 2½p. multicoloured 20 40
265 – 3p. multicoloured 20 20
266 – 3p. multicoloured 20 20
319 – 4p. multicoloured . . . . 1·25 1·75
320 – 4p. multicoloured . . . . 1·25 1·75
269 – 5p. multicoloured 30 30
270 – 5p. multicoloured 30 30
271 – 7p. multicoloured 65 65
272 – 7p. multicoloured 65 65
273 – 8p. multicoloured 70 80
274 – 8p. multicoloured 70 80
275 – 9p. multicoloured 70 70
276 – 9p. multicoloured 70 70
277 – 10p. multicoloured 80 80
278 – 10p. multicoloured 80 80
279 – 12½p. multicoloured . . . . 1·00 1·60
280 – 12½p. multicoloured . . . . 1·00 1·60
281 – 25p. multicoloured . . . . 1·10 1·60
282 – 25p. multicoloured . . . . 1·10 1·60
283 – 50p. multicoloured . . . . 1·25 2·50
284 – 50p. multicoloured . . . . 1·25 2·50
285 – £1 multicoloured . . . . . 2·00 4·00
286 – £1 multicoloured . . . . . 2·00 4·00
DESIGNS: (The two versions of each value show the same Gibraltar view taken from an early 19th-century print (first design) or modern photograph (second design)): HORIZ: 1p. Prince George of Cambridge Quarters and Trinity Church; 1½p. The Wellington Bust, Alameda Gardens; 2p. Gibraltar from the North Bastion; 2½p. Catalan Bay; 3p. Convent Garden; 4p. The Exchange and Spanish Chapel; 5p. Commercial Square and Library; 7p. South Barracks and Rosia Magazine; 8p. Moorish Mosque and Castle; 9p. Europa Pass Road; 10p. South Barracks from Rosia Bay; 12½p. Southport Gates; 25p. Trooping the Colour, The Alameda. VERT: 50p. Europa Pass Gorge; £1 Prince Edward's Gate.

93

94 Regimental Arms

1971. Coil Stamps.
287 93 ½p. orange 15 30
288 1p. blue 15 30
289 2p. green . . . . 50 1·10

1971. Military Uniforms (3rd series). As T **77**. Multicoloured.
290 1p. The Black Watch (1845) . . 35 30
291 2p. Royal Regimental of Fusiliers (1971) 65 30
292 4p. King's Own Royal Border Regiment (1704) . . . . . . 1·25 50
293 10p. Devonshire and Dorset Regiment (1801) . . . . . . 3·75 2·50

1971. Presentation of Colours to the Gibraltar Regiment.
294 **94** 3p. black, gold and red . . 30 30

95 Nativity Scene

1971. Christmas. Multicoloured.
295 3p. Type **95** 45 45
296 5p. Mary and Joseph going to Bethlehem 55 55

96 Soldier Artificer, 1773
97 "Our Lady of Europa"

1972. Bicentenary of Royal Engineers in Gibraltar. Multicoloured.
297 1p. Type **96** 50 30
298 3p. Modern tunneller 70 60
299 5p. Old and new uniforms and badge (horiz) 90 80

1972. Military Uniforms (4th series). As T **77**. Multicoloured.
300 1p. The Duke of Cornwall's Light Infantry, 1704 . . . . 60 20
301 3p. King's Royal Rifle Corps, 1830 . . . . 1·75 40
302 7p. 37th North Hampshire, Officer, 1825 . . . . 2·75 70
303 10p. Royal Navy, 1972 . . . . 3·25 1·50

1972. Christmas.
304 **97** 3p. multicoloured 10 10
305 5p. multicoloured 10 30

1972. Royal Silver Wedding. As T **52** of Ascension, but with Keys of Gibraltar and "Narcissus niveus" in background.
306 5p. red 20 20
307 7p. green 20 20

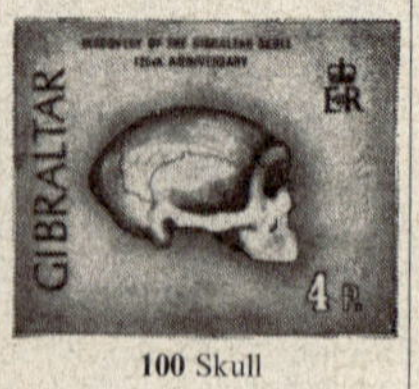

99 Flags of Member Nations and E.E.C. Symbol
100 Skull

1973. Britain's Entry into E.E.C.
308 **99** 5p. multicoloured 55 40
309 10p. multicoloured 70 60

1973. 125th Anniv of Gibraltar Skull Discovery. Multicoloured.
310 4p. Type **100** . . . . 1·25 50
311 6p. Prehistoric man . . . . . 1·25 70
312 10p. Prehistoric family . . . . 1·75 1·25
No. 312 is size 40 × 26 mm.

1973. Military Uniforms (5th series). As T **77**. Multicoloured.
313 1p. King's Own Scottish Borderers, 1770 . . . . . . 50 40
314 4p. Royal Welsh Fusiliers, 1800 1·50 1·00
315 60p. Royal Northumberland Fusiliers, 1736 . . . . 2·25 2·00
316 10p. Grenadier Guards, 1898 . 3·00 4·25

101 "Nativity" (Danckerts)

1973. Christmas.
321 **101** 4p. violet and red 35 15
322 6p. mauve and blue . . . 50 95

1973. Royal Wedding. As T **43** of Anguilla. Background colours given. Multicoloured.
323 6p. blue 10 10
324 14p. green 20 20

102 Victorian Pillar-box
103 "Madonna with the Green Cushion" (Solario)

1974. Centenary of U.P.U. Multicoloured.
325 2p. Type **102** 15 20
326 6p. Pillar-box of George VI . 25 30
327 14p. Pillar-box of Elizabeth II 40 65
Nos. 325/7 also come self-adhesive from booklet panes.

1974. Military Uniforms (6th series). As T **77**. Multicoloured.
331 4p. East Lancashire Regiment, 1742 . . . . 50 50
332 6p. Somerset Light Infantry, 1833 . . . . 70 70
333 10p. Royal Sussex Regiment, 1790 . . . . 1·00 1·40
334 16p. R.A.F. officer, 1974 . . 2·25 4·00

1974. Christmas. Multicoloured.
335 4p. Type **103** 40 30
336 6p. "Madonna of the Meadow" (Bellini) 60 95

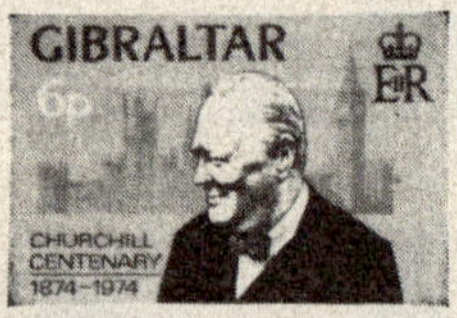

104 Churchill and Houses of Parliament

1974. Birth Centenary of Sir Winston Churchill. Multicoloured.
337 **104** 6p. black, purple and lavender 25 15
338 – 20p. black, brown and red 50 75
DESIGN: 20p. Churchill and "King George V" (battleship).

1975. Military Uniforms (7th series). As T **77**. Multicoloured.
340 4p. East Surrey Regiment, 1846 40 30
341 6p. Highland Light Infantry, 1777 . . . . 60 50
342 10 p. Coldstream Guards, 1704 80 90
343 20p. Gibraltar Regiment, 1974 1·50 2·50

105 Girl Guides' Badge

1975. 50th Anniversary of Gibraltar Girl Guides.
346 **105** 5p. gold, blue and violet . 30 45
347 7p. gold, brown and light brown 40 50
348 – 15p. silver, black and brown 65 1·00
No. 348 is as Type **105** but shows a different badge.

106 Child at Prayer
107 Bruges Madonna

1975. Christmas. Multicoloured.
349 6p. Type **106** 40 60
350 6p. Angel with lute 40 60
351 6p. Child singing carols . . . 40 60
352 6p. Three children 40 60
353 6p. Girl at prayer 40 60
354 6p. Boy and lamb 40 60

1975. 500th Birth Anniv of Michelangelo. Multicoloured.
355 6p. Type **107** 20 25
356 9p. Taddei Madonna 25 40
357 15p. Pieta 35 90
Nos. 355/7 also come self-adhesive from booklet panes.

108 Bicentennial Emblem and Arms of Gibraltar
109 The Holy Family

1976. Bicentenary of American Revolution.
361 **108** 25p. multicoloured 50 50

1976. Military Uniforms (8th series). As T **24**. Multicoloured.
363 1p. Suffolk Regiment, 1795 . . 25 15
364 6p. Northamptonshire Regiment, 1779 . . . . 50 30
365 12p. Lancashire Fusiliers, 1793 75 55
366 25p. Ordnance Corps, 1896 . . 1·25 1·10

1976. Christmas. Multicoloured.
367 6p. Type **109** 25 15
368 9p. Madonna and Child . . . 30 25
369 12p. St. Bernard 45 60
370 20p. Archangel Michael . . . 70 1·25
Nos. 367/70 show different stained-glass windows from St. Joseph's Church, Gibraltar.

110 Queen Elizabeth II, Royal Arms and Gibraltar Arms
111 Toothed Orchid

1977. Silver Jubilee. Multicoloured.
371 **110** 6p. red 25 20
372 £1 blue . . . . 1·40 2·25

1977. Birds, Flowers, Fish and Butterflies. Multicoloured.
374 ½p. Type **111** . . . . 60 1·75
375 1p. Red mullet (horiz) 15 10
376 2p. "Maculinea arion" (butterfly) (horiz) 30 50
377 2½p. Sardinian warbler . . . . 40 1·50
378 3p. Giant squill 20 10
379 4p. Grey wrasse (fish) . . . 30 10
380 5p. "Vanessa atalanta" (butterfly) (horiz) 50 70
381 6p. Black kite . . . . 1·25 30
382 9p. Shrubby scorpion-vetch . 70 70
383 10p. John dory (fish) (horiz) 40 20
384 12p. "Colias crocea" (butterfly) (horiz) . . . . 1·00 35
384b 15p. Winged asparagus pea . 3·25 55
385 20p. Audouin's gull . . . . . 1·25 2·00
386 25p. Barbary nut (iris) . . . . 1·25 2·00
387 50p. Swordfish (horiz) . . . . 2·00 95
388 £1 "Papilio machaon" (butterfly) (horiz) . . . . . 4·25 4·50
389 £2 Hoopoe . . . . 7·50 10·00
389a £5 Arms of Gibraltar . . . . 10·00 10·00

112 "Our Lady of Europa" Stamp

1977. "Amphilex '77" Stamp Exhibition, Amsterdam. Multicoloured.
390 6p. Type **112** 10 20
391 12p. "Europa Point" stamp . 15 30
392 25p. "E.E.C. Entry" stamp . 20 50

113 "The Annunciation" (Rubens)

1977. Christmas and 400th Birth Anniv of Rubens. Multicoloured.
393 3p. Type **113** 10 10
394 9p. "The Adoration of the Magi" 25 20
395 12p. "The Adoration of the Magi" (horiz) 30 30
396 15p. "The Holy Family under the Apple Tree" 30 40

114 Aerial View of Gibraltar

1978. Gibraltar from Space.
398 **114** 12p. multicoloured 25 40

115 Holyroodhouse

1978. 25th Anniv of Coronation. Multicoloured.
400 6p. Type **115** 20 15
401 9p. St. James's Palace . . . 25 15
402 12p. Sandringham 30 30
403 18p. Balmoral 40 55
406 25p. Windsor Castle . . . . 90 1·75
Nos. 402/3 also exist as self-adhesive stamps from booklet panes, No. 406 only coming in this form.

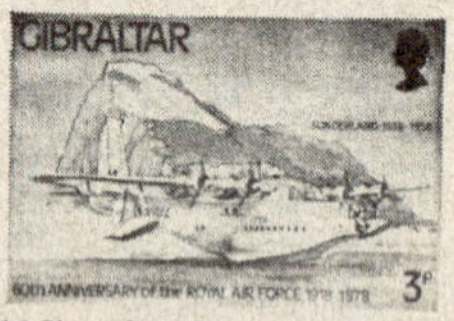

116 Short S.25 Sunderland, 1938–58

1978. 60th Anniv of Royal Air Force. Multicoloured.
407 3p. Type **116** 15 10
408 9p. Caudron G-3, 1918 . . . 35 40
409 12p. Avro Shackleton M.R.2, 1953–66 . . . . 40 55
410 16p. Hawker Hunter F.6, 1954–77 . . . . 45 80
411 18p. Hawker Siddeley Nimrod M.R.1, 1969–78 . . . . . . 50 90

117 "Madonna with Animals"

1978. Christmas. Paintings by Durer. Multicoloured.
412 5p. Type **117** 15 10
413 9p. "The Nativity" 20 15
414 12p. "Madonna of the Goldfinch" 25 40
415 15p. "Adoration of the Magi" 35 50

118 Sir Rowland Hill and 1d. Stamp of 1886

1979. Death Centenary of Sir Rowland Hill.
416 **118** 3p. multicoloured 10 10
417 – 9p. multicoloured 20 15
418 – 12p. multicoloured 25 20
419 – 25p. black, purple & yell . . 35 50
DESIGNS: 9p. 1971 1p. coil stamp; 12p. 1840 Post Office Regulations; 25p. "G" cancellation.

119 Posthorn, Dish Antenna and Early Telephone

1979. Europa. Communications.
420 **119** 3p. green and pale green . 15 10
421 9p. brown and ochre . . . 30 90
422 12p. blue and violet . . . 35 1·25

120 African Child

121 Early Policeman

1979. Christmas. International Year of the Child. Multicoloured.
423 12p. Type **120** 25 30
424 12p. Asian child 25 30
425 12p. Polynesian child 25 30
426 12p. American Indian child . . 25 30
427 12p. Nativity and children of different races 25 30
428 12p. European child 25 30

1980. 150th Anniv of Gibraltar Police Force. Multicoloured.
429 3p. Type **121** 20 10
430 6p. Policemen of 1895, early 1900s and 1980 . . . . . 20 15
431 12p. Police officer and police ambulance 25 20
432 37p. Policewoman and police motor-cyclist 55 90

122 Peter Amigo (Archbishop)

124 "Horatio Nelson" (J. F. Rigaud)

123 Queen Elizabeth the Queen Mother

1980. Europa. Personalities. Multicoloured.
433 12p. Type **122** 20 25
434 12p. Gustavo Bacarisas (artist) 20 25
435 12p. John Mackintosh (philanthropist) 20 25

1980. 80th Birthday of The Queen Mother.
436 **123** 15p. multicoloured 30 30

1980. 175th Death Anniv of Nelson. Paintings. Multicoloured.
437 3p. Type **124** 15 10
438 9p. "H.M.S. Victory' (horiz) . 25 25
439 15p. "Horatio Nelson" (Sir William Beechey) 35 35
440 40p. "'H.M.S. Victory' being towed into Gibraltar" (Clarkson Stanfield) (horiz) . 80 1·00

125 Three Kings

1980. Christmas.
442 **125** 15p. brown and yellow . 25 35
443 – 15p. brown and yellow . 25 35
DESIGN: No. 443, Nativity scene.

126 Hercules creating the Mediterranean

127 Dining-room

1981. Europa. Multicoloured.
444 9p. Type **126** 20 15
445 15p. Hercules and Pillars of Hercules 25 35

1981. 450th Anniv of The Convent (Govenor's Residence). Multicoloured.
446 4p. Type **127** 10 10
447 14p. King's Chapel 15 15
448 15p. The Convent 15 15
449 55p. Cloister 60 80

128 Prince Charles and Lady Diana Spencer

129

1981. Royal Wedding.
450 **128** £1 multicoloured . . . . 1·50 1·50

1981.
451 **129** 1p. black 30 30
452 4p. blue 30 30
453 15p. green 30 30

130 Paper Airplane

1981. 50th Anniv of Gibraltar Airmail Service. Multicoloured.
454 14p. Type **130** 15 15
455 15p. Airmail letters, post box and aircraft tail fin 15 15
456 55p. Jet airliner circling globe . 60 70

131 Carol Singers

1981. Christmas. Children's Drawings. Multicoloured.
457 15p. Type **131** 30 15
458 55p. Postbox (vert) . . . . . 1·00 85

132 I.Y.D.P. Emblem and Stylised Faces

1981. International Year for Disabled Persons.
459 **132** 14p. multicoloured . . . 30 30

133 Douglas DC-3

1982. Aircraft. Multicoloured.
460 1p. Type **133** . . . . 25 1·00
461 2p. Vickers Viking 1B . . . . 30 1·00
462 3p. Airspeed Ambassador AS.57 30 90
463 4p. Vickers Viscount 800 . . . 40 20
464 5p. Boeing 727-100 . . . . . 90 60
465 10p. Vickers Vanguard . . . . 1·50 50
466 14p. Short Solent 2 . . . . . 1·00 2·25
467 15p. Fokker F.27 Friendship . 2·25 1·75
468 17p. Boeing 737 . . . . . . 1·00 55
469 20p. B.A.C. One Eleven . . . 1·00 50
470 25p. Lockheed Constellation . 3·50 3·00
471 50p. Hawker Siddeley Comet 4B 4·00 2·25
472 £1 Saro Windhover . . . . . 5·50 2·25
473 £2 Hawker Siddeley Trident 2E 6·50 5·00
474 £5 De Havilland D.H.89A Dragon Rapide . . . . . 9·00 14·00

134 Crest, H.M.S. "Opossum"

136 Gibraltar Chamber of Commerce Centenary

135 Hawker Hurricane Mk I and Supermarine Spitfires at Gibraltar

1982. Naval Crests (1st series). Multicoloured.
475 ½p. Type **134** 10 10
476 15½p. H.M.S. "Norfolk" . . . 55 65
477 17p. H.M.S. "Fearless" . . . 60 70
478 60p. H.M.S. "Rooke" . . . . 1·40 2·75
See also Nos. 493/6, 510/13, 522/5, 541/4, 565/8, 592/5, 616/19 and 651/4.

1982. Europa. Operation Torch. Multicoloured.
479 14p. Type **135** 25 70
480 17p. General Giraud, General Eisenhower and Gibraltar . . 35 80

1982. Anniversaries. Multicoloured.
481 ½p. Type **136** 10 10
482 15½p. British Forces Postal Service centenary 30 25
483 60p. 75th anniv of Gibraltar Scout Association . . . . 1·10 1·25

137 Printed Circuit forming Map of World

1982. International Direct Dialling.
484 **137** 17p. black, blue and orange . 35 35

138 Gibraltar illuminated at Night and Holly

1982. Christmas. Multicoloured.
485 14p. Type **138** 45 30
486 17p. Gibraltar illuminated at night and mistletoe 50 35

139 Yacht Marina

1983. Commonwealth Day. Multicoloured.
487 4p. Type **139** 10 10
488 14p. Scouts and Guides Commonwealth Day Parade 20 15
489 17p. Flag of Gibraltar (vert) . 25 20
490 60p. Queen Elizabeth II (from photo by Tim Graham) (vert) 70 1·00

140 St. George's Hall Gallery

1983. Europa.
491 **140** 16p. black and brown . . 35 35
492 – 19p. black and blue . . . 40 40
DESIGN: 19p. Water catchment slope.

1983. Naval Crests (2nd series). As T **134**. Multicoloured.
493 4p. H.M.S. "Faulknor" . . . 30 10
494 14p. H.M.S. "Renown" . . . 70 35
495 17p. H.M.S. "Ark Royal" . . 75 40
496 60p. H.M.S. "Sheffield" . . . 1·75 1·50

141 Landport Gate, 1729

1983. Fortress Gibraltar in the 18th Century. Multicoloured.
497 4p. Type **141** 20 10
498 17p. Koehler Gun, 1782 . . . 50 40
499 77p. King's Bastion, 1779 . . 1·50 1·75

142 "Adoration of the Magi" (Raphael)

1983. Christmas. 500th Birth Anniv of Raphael. Multicoloured.
501 4p. Type **142** 25 10
502 17p. "Madonna of Foligno" (vert) 70 35
503 60p. "Sistine Madonna" (vert) 1·75 1·40

143 1932 2d. Stamp and Globe

1984. Europa, Posts and Telecommunications. Multicoloured.
504 17p. Type **143** 35 50
505 23p. Circuit board and globe . 45 1·00

144 Hockey

1984. Sports. Multicoloured.
506 20p. Type **144** 55 65
507 21p. Basketball 55 65
508 26p. Rowing . . . . 65 1·00
509 29p. Football . . . . 70 1·10

1984. Naval Crests (3rd series). As T **134**. Multicoloured.
510 20p. H.M.S. "Active" . . . . 1·60 1·75
511 21p. H.M.S. "Foxhound" . . 1·60 2·00
512 26p. H.M.S. "Valiant" . . . 1·75 2·00
513 29p. H.M.S. "Hood" . . . . 1·90 2·25

145 Mississippi River Boat Float

1984. Christmas. Epiphany Floats. Multicoloured.
514 20p. Type **145** 40 50
515 80p. Roman Temple float . . 1·60 2·00

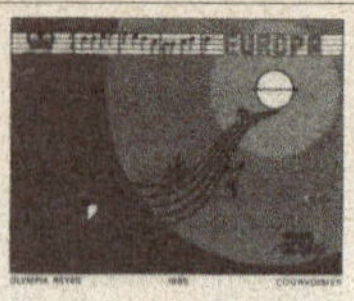

146 Musical Symbols, and Score from Beethoven's 9th (Choral) Symphony

1985. Europa. European Music Year. Multicoloured.

516	**146** 20p. multicoloured	60	50
517	– 29p. multicoloured	90	2·00

DESIGN: The 29p. is as T **146**, but shows different symbols.

147 Globe and Stop Polio Campaign Logo

1985. Stop Polio Campaign.

518	26p. multicoloured (Type **147**)	90	1·25
519	26p. multicoloured ("ST" visible)	90	1·25
520	26p. multicoloured ("STO" visible)	90	1·25
521	26p. multicoloured ("STOP" visible)	90	1·25

Each design differs in the position of the logo across the centre of the globe. On No. 518 only the letter "S" is fully visible, on No. 519 "ST", on No. 520 "STO" and on No. 521 "STOP". Other features of the design also differ, so that the word "Year" moves towards the top of the stamp and on No. 521 the upper logo is omitted.

1985. Naval Crests (4th series). As T **134**. Multicoloured.

522	4p. H.M.S. "Duncan"	60	10
523	9p. H.M.S. "Fury"	90	50
524	21p. H.M.S. "Firedrake"	2·00	2·00
525	80p. H.M.S. "Malaya"	4·00	6·00

148 I.Y.Y. Logo

149 St. Joseph

1985. International Youth Year. Multicoloured.

526	4p. Type **148**	25	10
527	20p. Hands passing diamond	95	1·10
528	80p. 75th anniv logo of Girl Guide Movement	2·50	3·25

1985. Christmas. Centenary of St. Joseph's Parish Church. Multicoloured.

529	4p. Type **149**	50	70
530	4p. St. Joseph's Parish Church	50	70
531	80p. Nativity crib	3·00	3·50

150 "Papilio machaon" (butterfly) and The Convent

1986. Europa. Nature and the Environment. Multicoloured.

532	22p. Type **150**	1·25	50
533	29p. Herring gull and Europa Point	1·75	4·25

151 1887 Queen Victoria 6d. Stamp

152 Queen Elizabeth II in Robes of Order of the Bath

1986. Centenary of First Gibraltar Postage Stamps. Designs showing stamps. Multicoloured.

534	4p. Type **151**	30	10
535	22p. 1903 Edward VII 2½d.	1·00	1·00
536	32p. 1912 George V 1d.	1·50	2·00
537	36p. 1938 George VI £1	1·60	2·50
538	44p. 1953 Coronation ½d. (29 × 46 mm)	2·00	3·00

1986. 60th Birthday of Queen Elizabeth II.

540	**152** £1 multicoloured	1·60	3·00

1986. Naval Crests (5th series). As T **134**. Multicoloured.

541	22p. H.M.S. "Lightning"	1·75	1·00
542	29p. H.M.S. "Hermione"	2·00	1·75
543	32p. H.M.S. "Laforey"	2·25	3·25
544	44p. H.M.S. "Nelson"	2·75	4·00

154 Three Kings and Cathedral of St. Mary the Crowned

155 Neptune House

1986. Christmas. International Peace Year. Multicoloured.

546	18p. Type **154**	1·00	50
547	32p. St. Andrew's Church	1·50	2·75

1987. Europa. Architecture. Multicoloured.

563	22p. Type **155**	1·50	50
564	29p. Ocean Heights	2·50	4·00

1987. Naval Crests (6th series). As T **134**. Multicoloured.

565	18p. H.M.S. "Wishart"	1·25	75
566	22p. H.M.S. "Charybdis"	1·40	1·10
567	32p. H.M.S. "Antelope"	1·90	3·00
568	44p. H.M.S. "Eagle"	2·50	4·00

156 13-inch Mortar, 1783

157 Victoria Stadium

1987. Guns. Multicoloured.

569	1p. Type **156**	20	50
570	2p. 6-inch coastal gun, 1909	30	50
571	3p. 8-inch howitzer, 1783	30	50
572	4p. Bofors "L40/70" AA gun, 1951	40	10
573	5p. 100 ton rifled muzzle-loader, 1882	40	50
574	10p. 5.25 inch heavy AA gun, 1953	40	55
575	18p. 25-pounder gun-how, 1943	65	80
576	19p. 64-pounder rifled muzzle-loader, 1873	70	90
577	22p. 12-pounder gun, 1758	70	50
578	50p. 10-inch rifled muzzle-loader, 1870	1·40	3·00
579	£1 Russian 24-pounder gun, 1854	2·50	3·50
580	£3 9.2 inch "Mk 10" coastal gun, 1935	6·50	14·00
581	£5 24-pounder gun, 1779	10·00	16·00

1987. Bicentenary of Royal Engineers' Royal Warrant. Multicoloured.

582	18p. Type **157**	1·25	65
583	32p. Freedom of Gibraltar scroll and casket	1·75	3·00
584	44p. Royal Engineers' badge	2·50	4·00

158 The Three Kings

1987. Christmas. Multicoloured.

585	4p. Type **158**	15	10
586	22p. The Holy Family	90	1·00
587	44p. The Shepherds	1·75	3·25

159 "Canberra" (liner) passing Gibraltar

1988. Europa. Transport and Communications. Multicoloured.

588	22p. Type **159**	1·50	2·25
589	22p. "Gibline I" (ferry), dish aerial and Boeing 737 airliner	1·50	2·25
590	32p. Horse-drawn carriage and modern coach	2·00	2·75
591	32p. Car, telephone and Rock of Gibraltar	2·00	2·75

1988. Naval Crests (7th series). As T **134**.

592	18p. multicoloured	1·50	65
593	22p. black, brown and gold	2·00	1·25
594	32p. multicoloured	2·25	3·25
595	44p. multicoloured	3·00	4·50

DESIGNS: 18p. H.M.S. "Clyde"; 22p. H.M.S. "Foresight"; 32p. H.M.S. "Severn"; 44p. H.M.S. "Rodney".

160 European Bee Eater

1988. Birds. Multicoloured.

596	4p. Type **160**	65	20
597	22p. Atlantic puffin	1·50	90
598	32p. Honey buzzard	2·00	3·00
599	44p. Blue rock thrush	2·50	4·25

161 "Zebu" (brigantine)

1989. Operation Raleigh. Multicoloured.

600	19p. Type **161**	65	60
601	22p. Miniature of Sir Walter Raleigh and logo	75	70
602	32p. "Sir Walter Raleigh" (expedition ship) and world map	1·10	1·50

162 "Snowman" (Rebecca Falero)

1988. Christmas. Children's Paintings. Multicoloured.

604	4p. Type **162**	15	10
605	22p. "The Nativity" (Dennis Penalver)	55	60
606	44p. "Father Christmas" (Gavin Key) (23 × 31 mm)	1·00	1·50

163 Soft Toys and Toy Train

1989. Europa. Children's Toys. Multicoloured.

607	25p. Type **163**	1·25	75
608	32p. Soft toys, toy boat and doll's house	1·75	2·75

164 Port Sergeant with Keys

165 Nurse and Baby

1989. 50th Anniv of Gibraltar Regiment. Mult.

609	4p. Type **164**	40	10
610	22p. Regimental badge and colours	1·25	95
611	32p. Drum major	1·75	2·25

1989. 125th Anniv of International Red Cross.

613	**165** 25p. black, red and brown	75	60
614	– 32p. black, red and brown	95	1·60
615	– 44p. black, red and brown	1·25	2·75

DESIGNS: 32p. Famine victims; 44p. Accident victims.

1989. Naval Crests (8th series). As T **134**.

616	22p. multicoloured	1·50	75
617	25p. black and gold	1·50	1·50
618	32p. gold, black and red	2·00	2·25
619	44p. multicoloured	3·00	3·50

DESIGNS: 22p. H.M.S. "Blankney"; 25p. H.M.S. "Deptford"; 32p. H.M.S. "Exmoor"; 44p. H.M.S. "Stork".

167 Father Christmas in Sleigh

1989. Christmas. Multicoloured.

622	4p. Type **167**	15	10
623	22p. Shepherds and sheep	70	70
624	32p. The Nativity	1·10	1·75
625	44p. The Three Wise Men	1·75	3·00

168 General Post Office Entrance

169 19th-century Firemen

1990. Europa. Post Office Buildings. Multicoloured.

626	22p. Type **168**	1·00	1·50
627	22p. Interior of General Post Office	1·00	1·50
628	32p. Interior of South District Post Office	1·50	2·25
629	32p. South District Post Office	1·50	2·25

1990. 125th Anniv of Gibraltar Fire Service. Multicoloured.

630	4p. Type **169**	60	15
631	20p. Early fire engine (horiz)	1·50	1·00
632	42p. Modern fire engine (horiz)	1·75	2·75
633	44p. Modern fireman in breathing apparatus	2·00	2·75

170 Henry Corbould (artist) and Penny Black

172 Candle and Holly

171 Model of Europort Development

1990. 150th Anniv of the Penny Black. Multicoloured.

634	19p. Type **170**	85	70
635	22p. Bath Royal Mail coach	95	80
636	32p. Sir Rowland Hill and Penny Black	2·00	3·25

1990. Naval Crests (9th series). As T **134**. Multicoloured.

638	22p. H.M.S. "Calpe"	1·50	70
639	25p. H.M.S. "Gallant"	1·60	1·75
640	32p. H.M.S. "Wrestler"	2·00	2·75
641	44p. H.M.S. "Greyhound"	2·50	3·75

1990. Development Projects. Multicoloured.

642	22p. Type **171**	75	80
643	23p. Construction of building material factory	75	1·40
644	25p. Land reclamation	95	1·40

1990. Christmas. Multicoloured.

645	4p. Type **172**	15	10
646	22p. Father Christmas	75	65
647	42p. Christmas tree	1·50	2·25
648	44p. Nativity crib	1·50	2·25

173 Space Laboratory and Spaceplane (Columbus Development Programme)

1991. Europa. Europe in Space. Multicoloured.

649 25p. Type **173** 75 75
650 32p. "ERS-1" earth resources remote sensing satellite . . . 1·00 2·00

1991. Naval Crests (10th series). As T **134**.

651 4p. black, blue and gold . . . 35 10
652 21p. multicoloured . . . . . 1·25 1·25
653 22p. multicoloured . . . . . 1·25 1·25
654 62p. multicoloured . . . . . 3·25 5·50

DESIGNS: 4p. H.M.S. "Hesperus"; 21p. H.M.S. "Forester"; 22p. H.M.S. "Furious"; 62p. H.M.S. "Scylla".

174 Shag

1991. Endangered Species. Birds. Multicoloured.

655 13p. Type **174** . . . . 85 1·10
656 13p. Barbary partridge . . . . 85 1·10
657 13p. Egyptian vulture . . . . 85 1·10
658 13p. Black stork . . . . 85 1·10

1991. No. 580 surch **£1.05**.

659 £1.05 on £3 9.2-inch "Mk.10" coastal gun, 1935 . . . . . 3·50 1·60

176 "North View of Gibraltar" (Gustavo Bacarisas)

1991. Local Paintings. Multicoloured.

660 22p. Type **176** 85 50
661 26p. "Parson's Lodge" (Elena Mifsud) . . . . 1·00 1·00
662 32p. "Governor's Parade" (Jacobo Azagury) . . . . . 1·50 2·25
663 42p. "Waterport Wharf" (Rudesindo Mannia) (vert) . 2·25 3·50

177 "Once in Royal David's City"

1991. Christmas. Carols. Multicoloured.

664 4p. Type **177** 20 10
665 24p. "Silent Night" . . . . . 1·00 70
666 25p. "Angels We Have Heard on High" . . . . 1·00 1·25
667 49p. "O Come All Ye Faithful" 1·75 3·00

179 Columbus and "Santa Maria"

1992. Europa. 500th Anniv of Discovery of America by Columbus. Multicoloured.

669 24p. Type **179** . . . . 1·00 1·50
670 24p. Map of Old World and "Nina" . . . . 1·00 1·50
671 34p. Map of New World and "Pinta" . . . . 1·25 1·75
672 34p. Map of Old World and look-out . . . . 1·25 1·75

Nos. 669/70 and 671/2 were issued together, se-tenant, each pair forming a composite design.

1992. 40th Anniv of Queen Elizabeth II's Accession. As T **143** of Ascension. Multicoloured.

673 4p. Gibraltar from north . . . 15 10
674 20p. H.M.S. "Arrow" (frigate) and Gibraltar from south . . 60 60
675 24p. Southport Gates 75 80
676 44p. Three portraits of Queen Elizabeth . . . . 1·25 1·60
677 54p. Queen Elizabeth II . . . 1·60 1·90

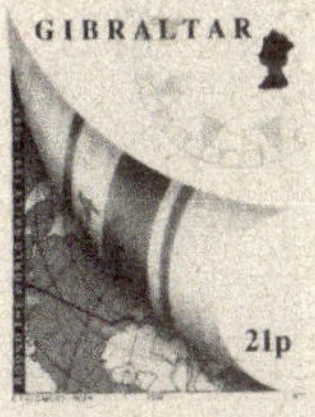

180 Compass Rose, Sail, and Atlantic Map

181 Holy Trinity Cathedral

1992. Round the World Yacht Rally. Multicoloured designs, each incorporating compass rose and sail.

678 21p. Type **180** 75 80
679 24p. Map of Indonesian Archipelago (horiz) . . . . 95 1·40
680 25p. Map of India Ocean (horiz) 95 1·75

1992. 150th Anniv of Anglican Diocese of Gibraltar-in-Europe. Multicoloured.

682 4p. Type **181** 20 10
683 24p. Diocesan crest and map (horiz) . . . . 1·00 65
684 44p. Construction of Cathedral and Sir George Don (horiz) 1·75 2·75
685 54p. Bishop Tomlinson . . . 2·00 3·00

182 Sacred Heart of Jesus Church

183 "Drama and Music"

1992. Christmas. Churches. Multicoloured.

686 4p. Type **182** 20 10
687 24p. Cathedral of St. Mary the Crowned . . . . 1·00 55
688 34p. St. Andrew's Church of Scotland . . . . 1·60 2·25
689 49p. St. Joseph's Church . . 2·25 3·75

1993. Europa. Contemporary Art. Multicoloured.

690 24p. Type **183** . . . . 1·25 1·50
691 24p. "Sculpture, Art and Pottery" . . . . 1·25 1·50
692 34p. "Architecture" . . . . . 1·75 2·25
693 34p. "Printing and Photography" . . . . 1·75 2·25

185 Landport Gate

186 £sd and Decimal British Coins (25th anniv of decimal currency)

1993. Architectural Heritage. Multicoloured.

695 1p. Type **185** 10 10
696 2p. St. Mary the Crowned Church (horiz) 10 10
697 3p. Parsons Lodge Battery (horiz) 10 10
698 4p. Moorish Castle (horiz) . . 10 10
699 5p. General Post Office . . . 10 10
699a 6p. House of Assembley . . 10 10
699b 7p. Bleak House (horiz) . . 15 10
699c 8p. General Eliott Memorial 15 20
699d 9p. Supreme Court Building (horiz) 20 25
700 10p. South Barracks (horiz) . 20 25
700a 20p. The Convent (horiz) . . 40 45
701 21p. American War Memorial 40 45
702 24p. Garrison Library (horiz) 50 55
703 25p. Southport Gates 50 55
704 26p. Casemates Gate (horiz) 50 55
704a 30p. St. Bernard's Hospital . 60 65
704b 40p. City Hall (horiz) . . . 80 85
705 50p. Central Police Station (horiz) . . . . 1·00 1·10
706 £1 Prince Edward's Gate . . 2·00 2·25
706a £2 Church of the Sacred Heart of Jesus . . . . 4·00 4·25
707 £3 Lighthouse, Europa Point 6·00 6·25
708 £5 Coat of Arms and fortress keys . . . . 10·00 10·50

1993. Anniversaries. Multicoloured.

709 21p. Type **186** 75 65
710 24p. R.A.F. crest with Handley Page 0/400 and Panavia Tornado F Mk 3 (75th anniv) 1·00 75
711 34p. Garrison Library badge and building (bicent) . . . . 1·40 2·00
712 49p. Sir Winston Churchill and air raid (50th anniv of visit) 2·00 3·00

187 Mice decorating Christmas Tree

1993. Christmas. Multicoloured.

713 5p. Type **187** 20 10
714 24p. Mice pulling cracker . . 90 70
715 44p. Mice singing carols . . . 1·75 2·25
716 49p. Mice building snowman 1·90 2·50

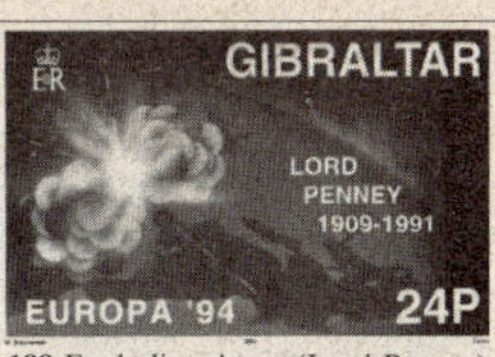

188 Exploding Atom (Lord Penney)

1994. Europa. Scientific Discoveries. Mult.

717 24p. Type **188** . . . . 1·00 1·25
718 24p. Polonium and radium experiment (Marie Curie) . . 1·00 1·25
719 34p. First oil engine (Rudolph Diesel) . . . . 1·25 1·75
720 34p. Early telescope (Galileo) . 1·25 1·75

189 World Cup and Map of U.S.A.

1994. World Cup Football Championship, U.S.A. Multicoloured.

721 26p. Type **189** 80 55
722 39p. Players and pitch in shape of U.S.A. . . . . 1·25 1·75
723 49p. Player's legs (vert) . . . . 1·60 2·50

191 Golden Star Coral

193 Great Tit

192 Throwing the Discus and Centenary Emblem

1994. Marine Life. Multicoloured.

726 21p. Type **191** 75 45
727 24p. Star fish 90 55
728 34p. Gorgonian sea-fan . . . . 1·50 2·25
729 49p. Peacock wrasse ("Turkish wrasse") . . . . 2·00 3·25

1994. Centenary of Int Olympic Committee. Mult.

730 49p. Type **192** . . . . 1·50 2·00
731 54p. Javelin throwing and emblem . . . . 1·75 2·50

1994. Christmas. Songbirds. Multicoloured.

732 5p. Type **193** 25 10
733 24p. European robin (horiz) . 90 70
734 34p. Blue tit (horiz) . . . . . 1·25 1·50
735 54p. Goldfinch . . . . 1·75 2·75

194 Austrian Flag, Hand and Star

1995. Expansion of European Union. Multicoloured.

736 24p. Type **194** 60 55
737 26p. Finnish flag, hand and star 60 60
738 34p. Swedish flag, hand and star 90 1·50
739 49p. Flags of new members and European Union emblem . . 1·60 2·50

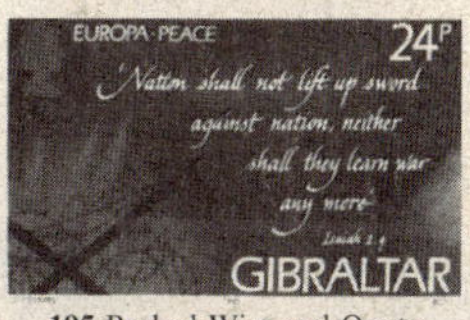

195 Barbed Wire and Quote from Isaiah Ch 2.4

1995. Europa. Peace and Freedom. Multicoloured.

740 24p. Type **195** . . . . 70 1·00
741 24p. Rainbow and hands releasing peace dove . . . . 70 1·00
742 34p. Shackles on wall and quote from Isaiah ch 61.1 . . . . 1·00 1·40
743 34p. Hands and sea birds . . . 1·00 1·40

197 Yachting

198 Bee Orchid

1995. Island Games '95. Multicoloured.

745 24p. Type **197** 50 60
746 44p. Athlete on starting blocks 1·50 2·25
747 49p. Swimmer at start of race 1·50 2·25

1995. "Singapore '95" International Stamp Exhibition. Orchids. Multicoloured.

749 22p. Type **198** 65 85
750 23p. Brown bee orchid . . . 65 85
751 24p. Pyramidal orchid 65 85
752 25p. Mirror orchid 65 85
753 26p. Sawfly orchid 65 85

199 Handshake and United Nations Emblem

1995. 50th Anniv of United Nations. Multicoloured.

754 34p. Type **199** . . . . 1·10 1·10
755 49p. Peace dove and U.N. emblem . . . . 1·40 2·00

201 Father Christmas

1995. Christmas. Multicoloured.

757 5p. Type **201** 15 10
758 24p. Toys in sack 65 55
759 34p. Reindeer . . . . 90 1·25
760 54p. Sleigh over houses . . . 1·25 1·75

202 Shih Tzu

1996. Puppies. Multicoloured.

761 5p. Type **202** 30 40
762 21p. Dalmatians 60 70
763 24p. Cocker spaniels 70 80
764 25p. West Highland white terriers 70 80
765 34p. Labrador 80 85
766 35p. Boxer 80 85

No. 762 is inscr "Dalmation" in error.

203 Princess Anne

1996. Europa. Famous Women.

767 **203** 24p. black and yellow . . 75 75
768 – 24p. black and green . . 75 75
769 – 34p. black and red . . . 1·00 1·50
770 – 34p. black and purple . . 1·00 1·50

DETAILS: No. 768, Princess Diana; 769, Queen Elizabeth II; 770, Queen Elizabeth the Queen Mother.

204 West German Player, 1980

205 Ancient Greek Athletes

1996. European Football Championship, England. Players from previous winning teams. Multicoloured.
771 21p. Type **204** 55 45
772 24p. French player, 1984 . . . 65 55
773 34p. Dutch player, 1988 . . . 95 1·10
774 £1.20 Danish player, 1992 . . 3·00 4·25

1996. Centenary of Modern Olympic Games.
776 **205** 34p. black, purple and orange 95 90
777 – 49p. black and brown . . 1·40 1·75
778 – £1.05 multicoloured . . . 2·75 3·50
DESIGNS: 49p. Start of early race; £1.05, Start of modern race

206 Asian Children

1996. 50th Anniv of U.N.I.C.E.F.
780 **206** 21p. multicoloured 60 80
781 – 24p. multicoloured 70 90
782 – 49p. multicoloured . . . . 1·25 1·40
783 – 54p. multicoloured . . . . 1·40 1·60
DESIGNS: 24p. to 54p. Children from different continents.

207 Red Kites in Flight

1996. Endangered Species. Red Kite. Multicoloured.
784 34p. Type **207** . . . . . . 90 1·10
785 34p. Red kite on ground . . . 90 1·10
786 34p. On rock . . . . . . 90 1·10
787 34p. Pair at nest . . . . . . 90 1·10

208 Christmas Pudding

1996. Christmas. Designs created from "Lego" Blocks. Multicoloured.
788 5p. Type **208** 15 15
789 21p. Snowman face 60 45
790 24p. Present 70 55
791 34p. Father Christmas face . . 90 1·25
792 54p. Candle . . . . 1·25 1·90

209 "Mary Celeste" passing Gibraltar
211 "Anthocharis belia euphenoides"

210 American Shorthair Silver Tabby

1997. Europa. Tales and Legends. "The Mary Celeste". Multicoloured.
793 28p. Type **209** 70 80
794 28p. Boarding the "Mary Celeste" 70 80
795 30p. Crew leaving "Mary Celeste" 80 95
796 30p. "Mary Celeste" found by "Dei Gratia" 80 95

1997. Kittens. Multicoloured.
797 5p. Type **210** 30 40
798 24p. Rumpy Manx red tabby . . 65 75
799 26p. Blue point birmans . . . 65 75
800 28p. Red self longhair . . . 70 85
801 30p. British shorthair tortoiseshell and white . . . 70 85
802 35p. British bicolour shorthairs 80 90

1997. Butterflies. Multicoloured.
804 23p. Type **211** 60 50
805 26p. "Charaxes jasius" . . . 75 60
806 30p. "Vanessa cardui" . . . 80 90
807 £1.20 "Iphiclides podalirius" . 3·00 3·75

212 Queen Elizabeth and Prince Philip at Carriage-driving Trials

1997. Golden Wedding of Queen Elizabeth and Prince Philip. Multicoloured.
810 £1.20 Type **212** . . . . . 3·00 3·50
811 £1.40 Queen Elizabeth in Trooping the Colour uniform 3·00 3·50

213 Christian Dior Evening Dress
214 "Our Lady and St. Bernard" (St. Joseph's Parish Church)

1997. Christian Dior Spring/Summer '97 Collection. Multicoloured.
812 30p. Type **213** 80 90
813 35p. Tunic top and skirt . . . 1·10 1·25
814 50p. Ballgown . . . . . . 1·25 1·40
815 62p. Two-piece suit . . . . 1·60 1·90

1997. Christmas. Stained Glass Windows. Mult.
817 5p. Type **214** 15 10
818 26p. "The Epiphany" (Our Lady of Sorrows Church) 65 60
819 38p. "St. Joseph" (Our Lady of Sorrows Church) 85 90
820 50p. "The Holy Family" (St. Joseph's Parish Church) . . 1·25 1·40
821 62p. "The Miraculous Medal" (St. Joseph's Parish Church) 1·50 2·00

215 Sir Joshua Hassan
216 Wales v Brazil (1958)

1997. Sir Joshua Hassan (former Chief Minister) Commemoration.
822 **215** 26p. black 55 60

1998. World Football Championship, France (1998). Multicoloured.
823 5p. Type **216** 15 10
824 26p. Northern Ireland v France (1958) 65 60
825 38p. Scotland v Holland (1978) 85 90
826 £1.20 England v West Germany (1966) . . . . 2·50 3·25

1998. 80th Anniv of Royal Air Force. As T **178** of Ascension. Multicoloured.
829 24p. Saro London (flying boat) 70 55
830 26p. Fairey Fox 75 60
831 38p. Handley Page Halifax GR.VI 95 95
832 50p. Hawker Siddeley Buccaneer S.2B . . . . 1·25 1·40

217 Miss Gibraltar saluting
219 Nileus (dog) with Hat and Telescope

1998. Europa. Festivals. National Day. Mult.
834 26p. Type **217** 70 70
835 26p. In black bodice and long red skirt 70 70
836 38p. In black bodice and short red skirt, with Gibraltar flag 95 1·10
837 38p. In Genoese-style costume 95 1·10

1998. Bicentenary of Battle of the Nile. Multicoloured.
839 12p. Type **219** 35 30
840 26p. Rear-Admiral Sir Horatio Nelson 65 55
841 28p. Frances Nisbet, Lady Nelson 75 75
842 35p. H.M.S. "Vanguard" (ship of the line) 95 95
843 50p. Battle of the Nile (47 × 29 mm) . . . . . . 1·25 1·50

220 "Love comforts like Sunshine after Rain" (William Shakespeare)
221 The Nativity

1998. Famous Quotations. Multicoloured.
844 26p. Type **220** 55 60
845 26p. "The price of greatness is responsibility" (Sir Winston Churchill) 55 60
846 38p. "Hate the sin, love the sinner" (Mahatma Gandhi) . 75 80
847 38p. "Imagination is more important than knowledge" (Albert Einstein) 75 80

1998. Christmas. Multicoloured.
848 5p. Type **221** 10 10
849 26p. Star and stable 55 60
850 30p. King with gold 60 65
851 35p. King with myrrh 70 75
852 50p. King with frankincense . 1·00 1·10

222 Barbary Macaque
223 Queen Elizabeth II

1999. Europa. Parks and Gardens. Upper Rock Nature Reserve. Multicoloured.
853 30p. Type **222** 60 65
854 30p. Dartford warbler 60 65
855 42p. Dusky grouper 85 90
856 42p. Common kingfisher . . . 85 90

1999. (a) Ordinary gum.
857 **223** 1p. purple 10 10
858 2p. brown 10 10
859 4p. blue 10 10
860 5p. green 10 10
861 10p. orange 20 25
862 12p. red 25 30
863 20p. green 40 45
864 28p. mauve 55 60
865 30p. orange 60 65
866 40p. grey 80 85
867 42p. green 85 90
868 50p. bistre . . . . 1·00 1·10
869 £1 black . . . . 2·00 2·10
870 £3 blue . . . . 6·00 6·25
(b) Self-adhesive.
871 **223** (1st) orange 55 60
Nos. 868/71 are larger, 25 × 30 mm.
No. 871 was initially sold at 26p.

224 Roman Marine and Galley
225 John Lennon (musician)

1999. Maritime Heritage. Multicoloured.
872 5p. Type **224** 10 10
873 30p. Arab sailor, medieval galley house and dhow 60 65
874 42p. Marine officer and British ship of the line (1779–83) . . 85 90
875 £1.20 Naval rating, Queen Alexandra Dry Dock and H.M.S. "Berwick" (cruiser) (1904) . . . . 2·40 2·50

1999. 30th Wedding Anniv of John Lennon and Yoko Ono. Designs showing John Lennon.
877 **225** 20p. multicoloured . . . 40 45
878 – 30p. black and blue . . . 60 65
879 – 40p. multicoloured . . . 80 85
DESIGNS: 20p. With flower over left eye; 40p. Wearing orange glasses.

POSTAGE DUE STAMPS

1956. As Type D **1** of Barbados
D1 1d. green . . . . 2·00 3·50
D2 2d. brown . . . . 2·50 3·75
D3 4d. blue . . . . 3·00 6·25

1971. As Nos. D1/3, but inscr in decimal currency.
D4 ½p. green 30 80
D5 1p. brown 30 70
D6 2p. blue 30 80

D **2**
D **3** Gibraltar Coat of Arms

1976.
D 7 D **2** 1p. orange 15 50
D 8 3p. blue 15 65
D 9 5p. red 20 75
D10 7p. violet 25 75
D11 10p. green 35 75
D12 20p. green . . . . . . 70 1·00

1984.
D13 D **3** 1p. black 25 40
D14 3p. red 35 40
D15 5p. blue 40 40
D16 10p. blue 50 40
D17 25p. mauve . . . . . . 90 1·00
D18 50p. orange . . . . . 1·40 1·50
D19 £1 green . . . . 2·25 2·50

D **4** Water Port Gates

1996. Gibraltar Landmarks.
D20 D **4** 1p. black, emerald and green 10 10
D21 – 10p. black and grey . . 20 25
D22 – 25p. black, brown and chestnut 50 55
D23 – 50p. black and lilac . . 1·00 1·10
D24 – £1 black, brown and chestnut . . . . . . 2·00 2·10
D25 – £2 black and blue . . . 4·00 4·25
DESIGNS: 10p. Naval Dockyard; 25p. Military Hospital; 50p. Governor's Cottage; £1 Swans on the Laguna; £2 Catalan Bay.

GILBERT AND ELLICE ISLANDS

A British colony in the South Pacific.

1911. 12 pence = 1 shilling;
20 shillings = 1 pound.
1966. 100 cents = $1 Australian.

1911. Stamps of Fiji (King Edward VII) optd **GILBERT & ELLICE PROTECTORATE.**

1	**23**	½d. green	4·50	38·00
2		1d. red	45·00	27·00
3		2d grey	8·00	13·00
4		2½d. blue	12·00	25·00
5		5d. purple and green	38·00	65·00
6		6d. purple	20·00	40·00
7		1s. black on green	20·00	45·00

2 Pandanus Pine **3**

1911

8	**2**	½d. green	4·25	11·00
9		1d. red	2·00	6·00
10		2d. grey	1·50	6·00
11		2½d. blue	3·50	9·00

1912.

27	**3**	½d. green	2·25	2·00
13		1d. red	1·75	4·00
28		1d. violet	3·50	3·75
29		1½d. red	3·50	1·50
30		2d. grey	5·50	20·00
15		2½d. blue	1·75	11·00
16		3d. purple on yellow	2·50	8·50
17		4d. black & red on yellow	60	5·50
18		5d. purple and green	1·50	7·00
19		6d. purple	1·25	7·50
20		1s. black on green	1·25	5·50
21		2s. purple & blue on blue	14·00	28·00
22		2s. 6d. black & red on blue	14·00	24·00
23		5s. green & red on yellow	32·00	55·00
35		10s. green & red on green	£180	£350
24		£1 purple and black on red	£600	£1400

1918. Optd **WAR TAX**.

26	**3**	1d. red	30	6·00

1935. Silver Jubilee. As T **13** of Antigua.

36	1d. blue and black	2·25	8·00
37	1½d. blue and red	1·75	3·50
38	3d. brown and blue	5·50	11·00
39	1s. grey and purple	35·00	24·00

1937. Coronation. As T **2** of Aden.

40	1d. violet	35	55
41	1½d. red	35	55
42	3d. blue	40	60

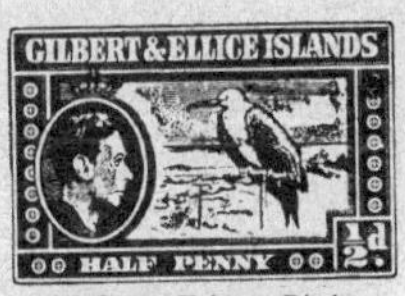

6 Great Frigate Bird

7 Pandanus Pine

1939

43	**6**	½d. blue and green	30	75
44	**7**	1d. green and purple	30	1·50
45	–	1½d. black and red	30	90
46	–	2d. brown and black	50	1·00
47	–	2½d. black and green	40	70
48	–	3d. black and blue	45	1·00
49	–	5d. blue and brown	4·25	1·25
50	–	6d. green and violet	40	50
51a	–	1s. black and turquoise	4·50	2·00
52	–	2s. blue and red	16·00	11·00
53	–	2s. 6d. blue and green	17·00	14·00
54	–	5s. red and blue	18·00	16·00

DESIGNS: 1½d. Canoe crossing reef; 2d. Canoe and boat-house; 2½d. Native house; 3d. Seascape; 5d. Ellice Is. canoe; 6d. Coconut palms; 1s. Jetty, Ocean Is.; 2s. H.M.C.S. "Nimanoa"; 2s. 6d. Gilbert Is. canoe; 5s. Coat of arms.

1946. Victory. At T **9** of Aden.

55	1d. purple	15	30
56	3d. blue	15	30

1949. Silver Wedding. As T **10/11** of Aden.

57	1d. violet	40	50
58	£1 red	15·00	18·00

1949. U.P.U. As T **20/23** of Antigua.

59	1d. purple	55	90
60	2d. black	2·25	2·25
61	3d. blue	1·00	2·00
62	1s. blue	1·25	2·00

1953. Coronation. As T **13** of Aden.

63	2d. black and grey	55	2·00

18 Great Frigate Bird

1956. As 1939 issue but with portrait of Queen Elizabeth II as in T **18** and colours changed.

64	**18**	½d. black and blue	35	1·00
65	**7**	1d. olive and violet	60	60
85	–	2d. green and purple	75	2·00
67	–	2½d. black and green	50	60
68	–	3d. black and red	50	60
69	–	5d. blue and orange	8·50	2·50
70	–	6d. brown and black	55	1·75
71	–	1s. black and olive	1·50	60
72	–	2s. blue and sepia	8·50	5·50
73	–	2s. 6d. red and blue	10·00	5·50
74	–	5s. blue and green	12·00	8·50
75	–	10s. black & turq (as 1½d.)	28·00	15·00

19 Loading Phosphate from Cantilever

1960. Diamond Jubilee of Phosphate Discovery at Ocean Is. Inscr "1900 1960".

76	**19**	2d. green and red	70	85
77	–	2½d. black and olive	70	85
78	–	1s. black and turquoise	70	85

DESIGNS: 2½d. Phosphate rock; 1s. Phosphate mining.

1963. Freedom from Hunger. As T **28** of Aden.

79	10d. blue	1·25	30

1963. Red Cross Cent. As T **33** of Antigua.

80	2d. red and black	1·00	50
81	10d. red and blue	2·00	2·50

23 Eastern Reef Heron in Flight

1964. First Air Service.

82	–	3d. blue, black & lt blue	70	30
83	**23**	1s. lt blue, black and blue	90	30
84	–	3s. 7d. green, black & emer	1·40	1·25

DESIGNS—VERT: 3d. De Havilland Heron 2 and route map; 3s. 7d. De Havilland Heron 2 over Tarawa lagoon.

1965. Cent of I.T.U. As T **36** of Antigua.

87	3d. orange and green	20	10
88	2s. 6d. turquoise and purple	80	20

26 Gilbertese Women's Dance

1965. Multicoloured.

89	½d. Maneaba and Gilbertese man blowing Bu shell	10	10
90	1d. Ellice Islanders Reef fishing by flare	10	10
91	2d. Gilbertese girl weaving head-garland	10	10
92	3d. Gilbertese woman performing Ruoia	10	10
93	4d. Gilbertese man performing Kamei	15	10
94	5d. Gilbertese girl drawing water	20	10
95	6d. Ellice Islander performing a Fatele	20	10
96	7d. Ellice youths performing spear dance	25	10
97	1s. Gilbertese girl tending Ikaroa Babai plant	50	10
98	1s. 6d. Ellice Islanders dancing a Fatele	1·00	65
99	2s. Ellice Islanders pounding Pulaka	1·00	1·25
100	3s. 7d. Type **26**	2·25	65
101	5s. Gilbertese boys playing a stick game	2·25	80
102	10s. Ellice youths beating the box for the Fatele	4·00	1·25
103	£1 Coat of arms	4·50	2·50

Nos. 89/99 are vert.

1965. I.C.Y. As T **37** of Antigua.

104	½d. purple and turquoise	10	10
105	3s. 7d. green and lavender	60	20

1966. Churchill Commem. As T **38** of Antigua.

106	½d. blue	10	10
107	3d. green	20	10
108	3s. brown	35	35
109	3s. 7d. violet	40	35

1966. Decimal Currency. Nos. 89/103 surch.

110	1 c. on 1d.	10	10
111	2 c. on 2d.	10	10
112	3 c. on 3d.	10	10
113	4 c. on ½d.	10	10
114	5 c. on 6d.	15	10
115	6 c. on 4d.	15	10
116	8 c. on 5d.	15	10
117	10 c. on 1s.	15	10
118	15 c. on 7d.	80	30
119	20 c. on 1s. 6d.	45	25
120	25 c. on 2s.	45	20
121	35 c. on 3s. 7d.	1·25	20
122	50 c. on 5s.	75	35
123	$1 on 10s.	75	40
124	$2 on £1	1·50	2·25

1966. World Cup Football Championship. As T **40** of Antigua.

125	3 c. multicoloured	15	10
126	35 c. multicoloured	45	20

1966. Inauguration of W.H.O. Headquarters, Geneva. As T **41** of Antigua.

127	3 c. black, green and blue	20	10
128	12 c. black, purple & ochre	45	40

1966. 20th Anniv of U.N.E.S.C.O. As T **54/6** of Antigua.

129	5 c. multicoloured	25	10
130	10 c. yellow, violet and olive	35	10
131	20 c. black, purple & orange	60	45

41 H.M.S. "Royalist"

1967. 75th Anniv of Protectorate.

132	**41**	3 c. red, blue and green	30	50
133	–	10 c. multicoloured	15	15
134	–	35 c. sepia, yellow & green	30	50

DESIGNS: 10 c. Trading post; 35 c. Island family.

1968. Decimal Currency. As Nos. 89/103, but with values inscr in decimal currency.

135	–	1 c. multicoloured (as 1d.)	10	15
136	–	2 c. multicoloured (as 2d.)	15	10
137	–	3 c. multicoloured (as 3d.)	15	10
138	–	4 c. multicoloured (as ½d.)	15	10
139	–	5 c. multicoloured (as 6d.)	15	10
140	–	6 c. multicoloured (as 4d.)	20	10
141	–	8 c. multicoloured (as 5d.)	20	10
142	–	10 c. multicoloured (as 1s.)	20	10
143	–	15 c. multicoloured (as 7d.)	50	20
144	–	20 c. multicoloured (as 1s. 6d.)	65	15
145	–	25 c. multicoloured (as 2s.)	1·25	20
146	**26**	35 c. multicoloured	1·50	20
147	–	50 c. multicoloured (as 5s.)	1·50	2·25
148	–	$1 multicoloured (as 10s.)	1·50	3·25
149	–	$2 multicoloured (as £1)	4·00	3·50

45 Map of Tarawa Atoll

1968. 25th Anniversary of Battle of Tarawa.

150	3 c. Type **45**	20	25
151	10 c. Marines landing	20	15
152	15 c. Beach-head assault	30	30
153	35 c. Raising U.S. and British flags	40	40

46 Young Pupil against Outline of Abemama Island

1969. End of Inaugural Year of South Pacific University.

154	**46**	3 c. multicoloured	10	15
155	–	10 c. multicoloured	10	10
156	–	35 c. black, brown & grn	15	30

DESIGNS: 10 c. Boy and girl students and Tarawa atoll; 35 c. University graduate and South Pacific islands.

47 "Virgin and Child" in Pacific Setting

1969. Christmas

157	–	2 c. multicoloured	15	20
158	**47**	10 c. multicoloured	15	10

DESIGN: 2 c. as Type **47**. but with grass foreground instead of sand.

48 "Kiss of Life"

1970. Centenary of British Red Cross.

159	**48**	10 c. multicoloured	20	10
160	–	15 c. multicoloured	30	35
161	–	35 c. multicoloured	60	70

Nos. 160/1 are as Type **48**, but arranged differently.

49 Foetus and Patients

1970. 25th Anniversary of U.N.

162	**49**	5 c. multicoloured	15	20
163	–	10 c. black, grey and red	15	15
164	–	15 c. multicoloured	20	25
165	–	35 c. blue, green, & black	30	35

DESIGNS: 10 c. Nurse and surgical instruments; 15 c. X-ray plate and technician; 35 c. U.N. emblem and map.

53 Map of Gilbert Islands **57** "Child with Halo" (T. Collis)

1970. Centenary of Landing in Gilbert islands by London Missionary Society.

166	**53**	2 c. multicoloured	15	70
167	–	10 c. black and green	25	15
168	–	25 c. brown and blue	20	20
169	–	35 c. blue, black and red	50	70

DESIGNS—VERT: 10 c. Sailing-ship "John Williams III"; 25 c. Rev. S. J. Whitmee. HORIZ: 35 c. M.V. "John Williams VII".

1970. Christmas. Sketches. Multicoloured.

170	2 c. Type **57**	10	15
171	10 c. "Sanctuary, Tarawa Cathedral" (Mrs A. Burroughs)	10	10
172	35 c. "Three Ships inside Star" (Mrs. C. Barnett)	20	20

60 Casting Nets

1971. Multicoloured.

173	1 c. Cutting toddy (vert)	10	10
174	2 c. Lagoon fishing	15	30
175	3 c. Cleaning pandanus leaves	15	15
176	4 c. Type **60**	20	25
177	5 c. Gilbertese canoe	35	15
178	6 c. De-husking coconuts (vert)	30	45
179	8 c. Weaving pandanus fronds (vert)	35	15
180	10 c. Weaving a basket (vert)	40	15
181	15 c. Tiger shark and fishermen (vert)	2·50	1·50
182	20 c. Beating rolled pandanus leaf	1·50	90
183	25 c. Loading copra	2·00	1·00
184	35 c. Fishing at night	2·25	50
185	50 c. Local handicrafts (vert)	1·50	1·50
186	$1 Weaving coconut screens (vert)	2·00	2·25
187	$2 Coat of arms (vert)	6·50	11·00

61 House of Representatives

1971. New Constitution. Multicoloured.
188 3 c. Type **61** 10 20
189 10 c. Maneaba Betio (Assembly hut) 20 10

62 Pacific Nativity Scene

1971. Christmas.
190 **62** 3 c. black, yellow and blue 10 15
191 – 10 c. black, gold and blue 10 10
192 – 35 c. black, gold and red 25 35
DESIGNS: 10 c. Star and palm leaves; 35 c. Outrigger canoe and star.

63 Emblem and Young Boys

1971. 25th Anniv of U.N.I.C.E.F. Multicoloured.
193 3 c. Type **63** 10 60
194 10 c. Young boy 15 15
195 35 c. Young boy's face 45 60
Nos. 193/5 include the UNICEF emblem within each design.

64 Flag and Map of South Pacific

1972. 25th Anniv of South Pacific Commission. Multicoloured.
196 3 c. Type **64** 10 65
197 10 c. Flag and native boats 15 20
198 35 c. Flags of member nations 15 95

65 "Alveopora"

1972. Coral. Multicoloured.
199 3 c. Type **65** 25 35
200 10 c. "Euphyllia" 30 15
201 15 c. "Melithea" 40 25
202 35 c. "Spongodes" 80 50

66 Star of Peace

69 Dancer

68 Funafuti ("The Land of Bananas")

1972. Christmas. Multicoloured.
208 3 c. Type **66** 10 10
209 10 c. "The Nativity" 10 10
210 35 c. Baby in "manger" (horiz) 20 20

1972. Royal Silver Wedding. As T **52** of Ascension, but with Floral Head-dresses in background
211 3 c. brown 10 15
212 35 c. brown 25 15

1973. Legends of Island Names (1st series). Mult.
213 3 c. Type **68** 10 40
214 10 c. Butaritari ("The Smell of the Sea") 20 20
215 25 c. Tarawa ("The Centre of the World") 30 45
216 35 c. Abemama ("The Land of the Moon") 35 50
See also Nos. 252/5.

1973. Christmas. Multicoloured.
217 3 c. Type **69** 10 15
218 10 c. Canoe and lagoon 10 10
219 35 c. Lagoon at evening 20 15
220 50 c. Map of Christmas Island 30 1·25

1973. Royal Wedding. As T **47** of Anguilla. Multicoloured, background colours given.
221 3 c. green 10 15
222 35 c. blue 20 15

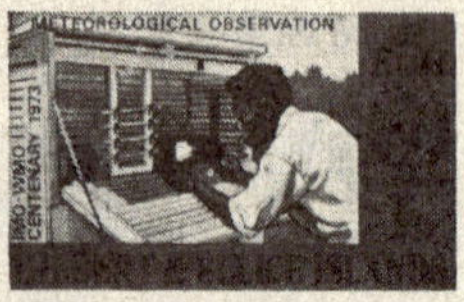

70 Meteorological Observation

1973. Centenary of I.M.O./W.M.O. Mult.
223 3 c. Type **70** 50 30
224 10 c. Island observing-station 50 20
225 35 c. Wind-finding radar 70 25
226 50 c. World weather watch stations 1·10 1·25

71 Te Mataaua Crest

1974. Canoe Crests. Multicoloured.
227 3 c. Type **71** 10 10
228 10 c. "Te Nimta-wawa" 15 10
229 35 c. "Tara-tara-venei-na" 25 10
230 50 c. "Te Bou-uoua" 35 50

72 £1 Stamp of 1924 and Te Koroba (canoe)

1974. Centenary of U.P.U.
232 **72** 4 c. multicoloured 20 15
233 – 10 c. multicoloured 20 10
234 – 25 c. multicoloured 25 25
235 – 35 c. multicoloured 30 25
DESIGNS: 10 c. 5s. stamp of 1939 and sailing vessel "Kiakia"; 25 c. $2 stamp of 1971 and B.A.C. One Eleven airplane; 35 c. U.P.U. emblem.

73 Toy Canoe

1974. Christmas. Multicoloured.
236 4 c. Type **73** 10 15
237 10 c. Toy windmill 15 10
238 25 c. Coconut "ball" 20 30
239 35 c. Canoes and constellation Pleiades 25 35

74 North Front Entrance, Blenheim Palace

1974. Birth Cent of Sir Winston Churchill. Mult.
240 4 c. Type **74** 10 25
241 10 c. Churchill painting 10 10
242 35 c. Churchill's statue, London 25 35

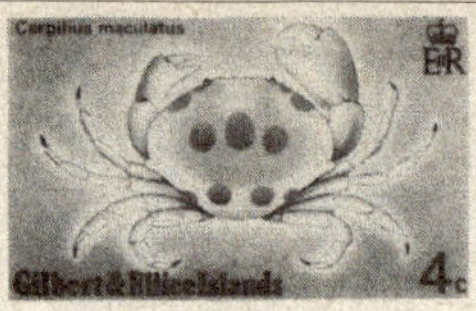

75 Barometer Crab

1975. Crabs. Multicoloured.
243 4 c. Type **75** 40 60
244 10 c. "Ranina ranina" 50 20
245 25 c. Pelagic swimmming crab 90 60
246 35 c. Ghost crab 1·00 1·00

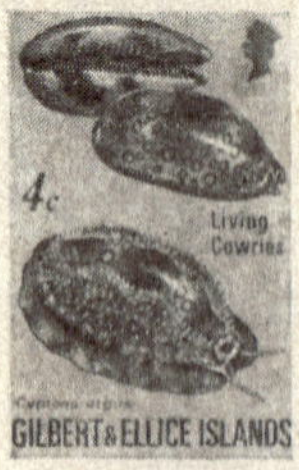

76 Eyed Cowrie

77 "Christ is Born"

1975. Cowrie Shells. Multicoloured.
247 4 c. Type **76** 55 50
248 10 c. Sieve cowrie 80 15
249 25 c. Mole cowrie 1·75 90
250 35 c. All-red map cowrie 2·00 1·75

1975. Legends of Island Names (2nd series). As T **68**. Multicoloured.
252 4 c. Beru ("The Bud") 10 20
253 10 c. Onotoa ("Six Giants") 10 10
254 25 c. Abaiang ("Land to the North") 20 25
255 35 c. Marakei ("Fish-trap floating on eaves") 30 40

1975. Christmas. Multicoloured.
256 4 c. Type **77** 20 50
257 10 c. Protestant Chapel, Tarawa 20 30
258 25 c. Catholic Church, Ocean Island 35 90
259 35 c. Fishermen and star 40 1·50

POSTAGE DUE STAMPS

D 1

1940
D1 **D 1** 1d. green 8·00 20·00
D2 2d. red 9·00 20·00
D3 3d. brown 13·00 21·00
D4 4d. blue 15·00 27·00
D5 4d. olive 20·00 27·00
D6 6d. purple 20·00 27·00
D7 1s. violet 22·00 38·00
D8 1s. 6d. green 42·00 75·00

GILBERT ISLANDS

On 1 January, 1976 the Gilbert Islands and Tuvalu (Ellice) Islands became separate Crown Colonies. The Islands became independent on 12 July 1979, under the name of Kiribati.

100 cents = $1

1 Charts of Gilbert Islands and Tuvalu (formerly Ellice) Islands

1976. Separation of the Islands. Multicoloured.
1 4 c. Type **1** 40 75
2 35 c. Maps of Tarawa and Funafuti 70 1·50

1976. Nos. 173/87 of Gilbert and Ellice Islands optd **THE GILBERT ISLANDS.**
3 1 c. Cutting toddy 25 30
5 2 c. Lagoon fishing 50 30
12 3 c. Cleaning pandanus leaves 40 70
7 4 c. Type **60** 30 80
13 5 c. Gilbertese canoe 50 60
14 6 c. De-husking coconuts 50 70
15 8 c. Weaving pandanus fronds 50 70
16 10 c. Weaving a basket 50 70
17 15 c. Tiger shark 2·00 1·25
18 20 c. Beating a pandanus leaf 1·50 1·25
19 25 c. Loading copra 2·00 1·25
20 35 c. Fishing at night 2·00 1·75
21 50 c. Local handicrafts 2·00 2·75
22 $1 Weaving coconut screens 4·00 9·00

3 "Teraaka" (training ship)

1978. Multicoloured.
23 1 c. Type **3** 40 60
24 3 c. "Tautunu" (inter-island freighter) 60 70
25 4 c. Moorish idol (fish) 30 60
26 5 c. Hibiscus 30 30
27 6 c. Eastern reef heron 1·25 85
28 7 c. Catholic Cathedral, Tarawa 30 30
29 8 c. Frangipani 30 30
30 10 c. Maneaba, Bikenibeu 30 30
31 12 c. Betio Harbour 45 45
32 15 c. Evening scene 55 45
33 20 c. Marakei Atoll 35 35
34 35 c. G.I.P.C. Chapel, Tangintebu 35 40
35 40 c. Flamboyant tree 40 45
36 50 c. "Hypolimnas bolina", (butterfly) 2·25 1·75
37 $1 "Tabakea" (Tarawa Lagoon ferry) 1·75 2·50
38 $2 National flag 1·75 2·50

4 Church

1976. Christmas. Children's Drawings. Mult.
39 5 c. Type **4** 25 15
40 15 c. Feasting (vert) 35 15
41 20 c. Maneaba (vert) 40 30
42 35 c. Dancing 55 45

5 Porcupine Fish Helmet

6 The Queen in Coronation Robes

1976. Artefacts. Multicoloured.
43 5 c. Type **5** 20 15
44 15 c. Shark's teeth dagger 30 35
45 20 c. Fighting gauntlet 30 40
46 35 c. Coconut body armour 45 55

1977. Silver Jubilee. Multicoloured.
48 8 c. Prince Charles' visit, 1970 10 10
49 20 c. Prince Philip's visit, 1959 15 15
50 40 c. Type **6** 20 35

7 Commodore Bryon and H.M.S. "Dolphin"

1977. Explorers. Multicoloured.
51 5 c. Type **7** 65 1·50
52 15 c. Capt. Fanning and "Betsey" 80 2·75
53 20 c. Admiral Bellingshausen and "Vostok" 80 2·75
54 35 c. Capt. Wilkes and U.S.S. "Vincennes" 1·10 4·00

8 H.M.S. "Resolution" and H.M.S. "Discovery"

9 Scout Emblem and Island Scene

1977. Christmas and Bicentenary of Capt. Cook's Discovery of Christmas Is. Mult.
55 8 c. Type **8** 30 10
56 15 c. Logbook entry (horiz) 30 15
57 20 c. Captain Cook 40 20
58 40 c. Landing party (horiz) 40 60

1977. 50th Anniv of Scouting in the Gilbert Is. Multicoloured.
60 8 c. Type **9** 25 10
61 15 c. Patrol meeting (horiz) 30 20

62		20 c. Scout making mat (horiz)	35	20
63		40 c. Canoeing	45	55

10 Taurus (The Bull)

11 Unicorn of Scotland

1978. The Night Sky over the Gilbert Islands.

64	**10**	10 c. black and blue	30	15
65	–	20 c. black and red	35	30
66	–	25 c. black and green	35	35
67	–	45 c. black and orange	55	60

DESIGNS: 20 c. Canis Major (the Great Dog); 25 c. Scorpio (the Scorpion); 45 c. Orion (the Giant Warrior).

1978. 25th Anniv of Coronation.

68	**11**	45 c. green, violet and silver	25	40
69	–	45 c. multicoloured	25	40
70	–	45 c. green, violet and silver	25	40

DESIGNS: No. 69, Queen Elizabeth II. No. 70, Great Frigate Bird.

12 Birds in Flight to Tarawa

1978. 25th Anniv of Return of George V School to Tarawa. Multicoloured.

71	10 c. Type **12**	10	10
72	20 c. Tarawa, Abemama and school badge	20	20
73	25 c. Rejoicing islanders	20	20
74	45 c. King George V School on Tarawa and Abemama	35	35

13 "Te Kaue ni Maie"

1978. Christmas. Kaue (traditional head decorations) Multicoloured.

75	10 c. Type **13**	10	10
76	20 c. "Te Itera"	15	15
77	25 c. "Te Bau"	20	20
78	45 c. "Te Tai"	25	30

14 H.M.S. "Endeavour"

1979. Bicentenary of Captain Cook's Voyages. 1768–79.

80	**14**	10 c. multicoloured	20	15
81	–	20 c. multicoloured	25	30
82	–	25 c. black, lilac and green	25	45
83	–	45 c. multicoloured	25	80

DESIGNS: 20 c. Green Turtle; 25 c. Quadrant; 45 c. Flaxman/Wedgwood medallion.

For later issues see **KIRIBATI**.

GOLD COAST

A British colony on the W. coast of Africa. For later issues after independence in 1957 see under Ghana.

12 pence = 1 shilling
20 shillings = 1 pound

1

4

1875.

4	**1**	½d. yellow	48·00	22·00
11a		½d. green	1·50	60
5		1d. blue	14·00	6·50
12a		1d. red	2·25	50
6		2d. green	60·00	9·00
13b		2d. grey	1·50	50
14		2½d. blue and orange	2·75	50
15a		3d. olive	5·50	4·25
16		4d. mauve	5·00	1·25
17		6d. orange	4·75	4·50
18a		1s. mauve	3·50	1·25
19a		2s. brown	32·00	15·00

1889. Surch **ONE PENNY.** and bar.

20	**1**	1d. on 6d. orange	£100	48·00

1889.

26	**4**	½d. mauve and green	1·75	75
27		1d. mauve and red	1·75	40
27b		2d. mauve and red	35·00	90·00
28		2½d. mauve and blue	4·25	4·00
29		3d. mauve and orange	4·50	1·25
30		6d. mauve and violet	5·50	1·25
31		1s. green and black	8·50	9·50
32		2s. green and red	9·00	17·00
22		5s. mauve and blue	60·00	12·00
33		5s. green and mauve	48·00	26·00
23		10s. mauve and red	75·00	15·00
34		10s. green and brown	£130	50·00
24		20s. green and red	£3250	
25		20s. mauve & black on red	£150	35·00

1901. Surch **ONE PENNY.** and bar.

35	**4**	1d. on 2½d. mauve and blue	1·75	3·00
36		1d. on 6d. mauve and violet	1·75	3·00

1902. As T **4**, but with portrait of King Edward VII.

38	½d. purple and green	75	40
39	1d. purple and red	1·00	15
51	2d. purple and orange	4·00	50
41	2½d. purple and blue	4·50	9·00
42	3d. purple and orange	2·75	1·50
43	6d. purple and violet	2·75	1·50
44	1s. green and black	9·00	3·00
45	2s. green and red	12·00	16·00
57	2s. 6d. green and yellow	27·00	95·00
46	5s. green and mauve	32·00	75·00
47	10s. green and brown	48·00	£120
48	20s. purple and black on red	£130	£170

1907. As last.

59	½d. green	2·00	30
60	1d. red	4·25	30
61	2d. grey	2·00	40
62	2½d. blue	3·50	1·75
63	3d. purple on yellow	6·00	55
64a	6d. purple	3·50	3·50
65	1s. black and green	6·50	50
66	2s. purple and blue on blue	5·00	16·00
67	2s. 6d. black and red on blue	25·00	65·00
68	5s. green and red on yellow	55·00	£130

8

13 King George V and Christiansborg Castle

1908.

69	**8**	1d. red	2·25	10

1913. As T **4** and **8** (1d.) but portraits of King George V.

86	½d. green	30	30
72	1d. red	60	10
87	1d. brown	30	10
88	1½d. red	90	10
89	2d. grey	90	30
76	2½d. blue	3·75	90
90	2½d. orange	50	8·00
77b	3d. purple on yellow	30	40
91	3d. blue	90	60
94	6d. purple	90	3·00
79	1s. black on green	1·25	1·25
96	2s. purple and blue on blue	2·50	3·25
97	2s. 6d. black and red on blue	5·50	15·00
98	5s. green and red on yellow	9·00	40·00
83a	10s. green and red on green	18·00	65·00
100a	15s. purple and green	£100	£250
84	20s. purple and black on red	£120	80·00
102	£2 green and orange	£350	£800

1918. Surch **WAR TAX ONE PENNY**.

85	1d. on red (No. 72)	30	40

1928.

103	**13**	½d. green	50	40
104		1d. brown	50	10
105		1½d. red.	50	1·50
106		2d. grey	50	20
107		2½d. orange	1·25	3·50
108		3d. blue	55	40
109		6d. black and purple	75	40
110		1s. black and orange	1·75	75
111		2s. black and violet	14·00	4·00
112		3s. red and olive	45·00	38·00

1935. Silver Jubilee. As T **13** of Antigua.

113	1d. blue and black	60	50
114	3d. brown and blue	3·00	6·00
115	6d. green and blue	4·25	9·50
116	1s. grey and purple	3·25	9·50

1937. Coronation. As T **2** of Aden.

117	1d. brown	1·00	1·25
118	2d. grey	1·10	2·75
119	3d. blue	1·25	1·25

14

15 King George VI and Christiansborg Castle, Accra

1938.

120a	**14**	½d. green	40	50
121a		1d. brown	40	10
122a		1½d. red	40	50
123a		2d. black	40	10
124a		3d. blue	40	35
125a		4d. mauve	70	1·25
126a		6d. purple	70	20
127a		9d. orange	90	55
128a	**15**	1s. black and olive	1·00	50
129		1s. 3d. brown and blue	2·00	40
130a		2s. blue and violet	4·50	8·00
131a		5s. olive and red	8·00	11·00
132		10s. black and violet	7·00	16·00

1946. Victory. As T **9** of Aden.

133a	2d. grey	10	10
134a	4d. mauve	75	2·75

16 Northern Territories Mounted Constabulary

1948.

135	**16**	½d. green	20	30
136	–	1d. blue	15	15
137	–	1½d. red	1·25	70
138	–	2d. brown	55	10
139	–	2½d. brown and red	2·00	2·50
140	–	3d. blue	4·00	45
141	–	4d. mauve	3·50	1·25
142	–	6d. black and orange	30	30
143	–	1s. black and red	60	30
144	–	2s. olive and red	3·00	2·00
145	–	5s. purple and black	20·00	4·50
146	–	10s. black and olive	8·00	4·50

DESIGNS—HORIZ: 1d. Christiansborg Castle; 1½d. Emblem of Joint Provincial Council; 2½d. Map showing position of Gold Coast; 3d. Nsuba manganese mine; 4d. Lake Bosumtwi; 1s. Breaking cocoa pods; 2s. Gold Coast Regt. trooping the Colour; 5s. Surfboats. VERT: 2d. Talking drums; 6d. Cocoa farmer; 10s. Forest.

1948. Silver Wedding. As T **10/11** of Aden.

147	1½d. red	30	30
148	10s. olive	12·00	17·00

1949. U.P.U. As T **20/23** of Antigua.

149	2d. brown	30	30
150	2½d. orange	2·00	1·75
151	3d. blue	50	70
152	1s. green	50	50

1952. As 1948 but portrait of Queen Elizabeth II. Designs as for corresponding values except where stated.

153	½d. brown and red (as 2½d.)	10	10
154	1d. blue	30	10
155	1½d. green	30	1·25
156	2d. brown	30	10
157	2½d. red (as ½d.)	35	35
158	3d. mauve	50	10
159	4d. blue	30	30
160	6d. black and orange	30	15
161	1s. black and red	30	15
162	2s. olive and red	11·00	85
163	5s. purple and black	17·00	5·00
164	10s. black and olive	14·00	12·00

1953. Coronation. As T **13** of Aden.

165	2d. black and brown	60	10

POSTAGE DUE STAMPS

D 1

1923.

D1	**D 1**	½d. black	14·00	£100
D2		1d. black	75	1·25
D5		2d. black	3·00	17·00
D6		3d. black	1·50	15·00
D7		6d. black	1·75	8·00
D8		1s. black	1·75	55·00

For later issues see **GHANA**.

GREAT BRITAIN

Consisting of England, Wales, Scotland and Northern Ireland, lying to the N.W. of the European continent.

1840. 12 pence = 1 shilling;
20 shillings = 1 pound sterling.
1971. 100 (new) pence = 1 pound sterling.

1

3

1840. Letters in lower corners. Imperf.

2	**1**	1d. black	£3250	£175
5		2d. blue	£6000	£350

1841. Imperf.

8	**1**	1d. brown	£150	6·00
14	**3**	2d. blue	£1300	55·00

In T **3** there are white lines below "POSTAGE" and above "TWO PENCE".

12

10

1847. Imperf.

59	**12**	6d. purple	£3000	£525
57	**10**	10d. brown	£2750	£700
54		1s. green	£3250	£475

1854. Perf.

29	**1**	1d. brown	£140	5·00
40		1d. red	35·00	7·00
34	**3**	2d. blue	£1300	40·00

14

18

19

1855. No letters in corners.

66a	**14**	4d. red	£700	50·00
70	**18**	6d. lilac	£575	60·00
72	**19**	1s. green	£725	£175

7

5

8

6

1858. Letters in four corners.

48	**7**	½d. red	60·00	12·00
43	**5**	1d. red	5·00	1·50
51	**8**	1½d. red	£200	30·00
45	**6**	2d. blue	£190	7·00

21

22

23

24

25

1862. Small white letters in corners.

76	**21**	3d. red	£850	£150
80	**22**	4d. red	£600	50·00
84	**23**	6d. lilac	£800	55·00
87	**24**	9d. bistre	£1600	£175
90	**25**	1s. green	£900	£100

30 32

1865. Designs as 1862 and T **30** and **32**, but large white letters in corners.

103	**21**	3d. red	£275	25·00
94	**22**	4d. red	£300	35·00
97	**23**	6d. lilac (with hyphen)	£425	50·00
109		6d. lilac (without hyphen)	£350	45·00
110	**24**	9d. straw	£725	£150
112	**30**	10d. brown	£1200	£200
117	**25**	1s. green	£400	22·00
118	**32**	2s. blue	£1200	90·00
121		2s. brown	£7500	£1600

35

38

1867.

126	**35**	5s. red	£3250	£375
128	–	10s. green	£22000	£1200
129	–	£1 brown	£27000	£1700
137	**38**	£5 orange	£5750	£1700

The 10s. and £1 are as Type **35**, but have different frames.

34

1872. Large white letters in corners.

122b	**34**	6d. brown	£400	32·00
125		6d. grey	£825	£150

41 46

1873. Large coloured letters in corners.

141	**41**	2½d. mauve	£300	30·00
157		2½d. blue	£250	15·00
143	**21**	3d. red	£250	25·00
152	**22**	4d. red	£825	£225
153		4d. green	£525	£150
160		4d. brown	£250	40·00
161	**34**	6d. grey	£225	45·00
156	**46**	8d. orange	£675	£190
150	**25**	1s. green	£350	45·00
163		1s. brown	£325	90·00

The 3d, 4d. and 1s. are as 1862, and the 6d. as Type **34**, but all with large coloured letters.

52 53

1880. Various frames.

164	**52**	½d. green	30·00	8·00
187		½d. blue	16·00	6·00
166	**53**	1d. brown	12·00	8·00
167	–	1½d. brown	£125	30·00
168	–	2d. red	£140	60·00
169	–	5d. blue	£425	75·00

57 58

61

1881.

173	**57**	1d. lilac	2·00	1·00

1883. Types, as 1873, surch **3d.** or **6d.**

159	**21**	3d. on 3d. lilac	£300	95·00
162	**34**	6d. on 6d. lilac	£250	95·00

1883.

178	**58**	2s. 6d. lilac	£300	90·00
180	–	5s. red	£500	£110
183	–	10s. blue	£1000	£325
185	**61**	£1 brown	£13500	£1300
212		£1 green	£2250	£400

The 5s. and 10s. are similar to Type **58**, but have different frames.

62 63

1883. Various frames.

188	**62**	1½d. purple	80·00	30·00
189	**63**	2d. purple	£125	60·00
190		2½d. purple	65·00	11·00
191	**62**	3d. purple	£150	80·00
192		4d. green	£375	£160
193		5d. green	£375	£160
194	**63**	6d. green	£400	£175
195		9d. green	£725	£350
196	**62**	1s. green	£525	£190

71 72

73 74

75 76

77 78

79 80

81 82

1887.

197	**71**	½d. red	1·50	1·00
213		½d. green*	1·50	1·25
198	**72**	1½d. purple and green	15·00	5·50
200	**73**	2d. green and red	22·00	10·00
201	**74**	2½d. purple on blue	15·00	2·50
202	**75**	3d. purple on yellow	20·00	3·00
205a	**76**	4d. green and brown	22·00	11·00
206	**77**	4½d. green and red	8·00	30·00
207a	**78**	5d. purple and blue	25·00	10·00
208	**79**	6d. purple on red	22·00	10·00
209	**80**	9d. purple and blue	50·00	32·00
210	**81**	10d. purple and red	40·00	32·00
211	**82**	1s. green	£190	55·00
214		1s. green and red	45·00	£110

*No. 213, in blue, has had the colour changed after issue.

83 90

1902. Designs not shown are as 1887 (2s. 6d. to £1 as 1883) but with portrait of King Edward VII.

217	**83**	½d. green	1·25	1·00
219		1d. red	1·25	1·00
221	–	1½d. purple and green	20·00	12·00
291	–	2d. green and red	18·00	10·00
231	**83**	2½d. blue	11·00	6·00
232	–	3d. purple on yellow	28·00	6·00
236a	–	4d. green and brown	28·00	12·00
240	–	4d. orange	15·00	12·00
294	–	5d. purple and blue	18·00	10·00
246	**83**	6d. purple	25·00	11·00
249	**90**	7d. grey	9·00	11·00
307	–	9d. purple and blue	40·00	32·00
311	–	10d. purple and red	50·00	32·00
314	–	1s. green and red	38·00	22·00
260	–	2s. 6d. purple	£140	65·00
263	–	5s. red	£140	90·00
265	–	10s. blue	£400	£275
266	–	£1 green	£1000	£400

98 (Hair heavy) 99 (Lion unshaded)

1911.

325	**98**	½d. green	4·50	1·50
327	**99**	1d. red	4·50	2·50

101 (Hair light) 102 (Lion shaded)

1912.

344	**101**	½d. green	6·00	2·00
341	**102**	1d. red	4·00	2·00

104 105

106 107

108 109

1912. Lined background.

418	**105**	½d. green	50	50
419	**104**	1d. red	50	40
420	**105**	1½d. brown	50	40
421	**106**	2d. orange	1·75	1·50
422	**104**	2½d. blue	3·50	1·75
375	**106**	3d. violet	4·00	3·00
379		4d. green	7·00	2·00
381	**107**	5d. brown	6·00	5·00
426a		6d. purple	2·25	1·00
387		7d. green	11·00	6·00
390		8d. black on yellow	24·00	10·00
392	**108**	9d. black	13·00	5·00
427		9d. green	75·00	2·75
394		10d. blue	15·00	15·00
395		1s. brown	13·00	3·00
450	**109**	2s. 6d. brown	60·00	30·00
451		5s. red	£125	75·00
452		10s. blue	£300	65·00
403		£1 green	£1250	£750

112

1924. British Empire Exn. Dated "1924".

430	**112**	1d. red	7·50	10·00
431		1½d. brown	11·00	14·00

1925. Dated "1925".

432	**112**	1d. red	12·00	22·00
433		1½d. brown	35·00	60·00

113 114

115 116 St. George and the Dragon

1929. 9th U.P.U. Congress, London.

434	**113**	½d. green	2·25	2·25
435	**114**	1d. red	2·25	2·25
436		1½d. brown	2·25	1·75
437	**115**	2½d. blue	10·00	10·00
438	**116**	£1 black	£750	£550

118 119

120 121

122 123

1934. Solid background.

439	**118**	½d. green	30	40
440	**119**	1d. red	30	40
441	**118**	1½d. brown	30	40
442	**120**	2d. orange	50	75
443	**119**	2½d. blue	1·50	1·25
444	**120**	3d. violet	1·50	1·25
445		4d. green	2·00	1·25
446	**121**	5d. brown	6·00	2·25
447	**122**	9d. olive	12·00	2·25
448		10d. blue	15·00	10·00
449		1s. brown	15·00	1·25

1935. Silver Jubilee.

453	**123**	½d. green	75	50
454		1d. red	1·25	1·50
455		1½d. brown	75	50
456		2½d. blue	4·50	5·50

Emblems at right differ.

124 King Edward VIII 126 King George VI and Queen Elizabeth

1936.

457	**124**	½d. green	30	30
458		1d. red	60	40
459		1½d. brown	30	30
460		2½d. blue	30	75

1937. Coronation.

461	**126**	1½d. brown	50	40

128 129

130 131 King George VI

1937.

462	128	½d. green	10	25
503		½d orange	30	30
463		1d. red	10	25
504		1d. blue	30	30
464		1½d. brown	20	25
505		1½d. green	50	60
465		2d. orange	75	50
506		2d. brown	50	40
466		2½d. blue	25	15
507		2½d. red	50	40
490		3d. violet	2·00	90
468	129	4d. green	60	60
508		4d. blue	2·50	1·75
469		5d. brown	2·50	75
470		6d. purple	1·25	60
471	130	7d. green	3·25	60
472		8d. red	3·50	70
473		9d. green	5·50	80
474		10d. blue	5·00	80
474a		11d. purple	2·00	2·00
475		1s. brown	5·75	75

1939.

476	131	2s. 6d. brown	38·00	6·50
476a		2s. 6d. green	7·00	1·25
477		5s. red	14·00	1·75
478a	–	10s. blue	30·00	5·50
478b	–	£1 brown	10·00	23·00

The 10s. and £1 values have the portrait in the centre in an ornamental frame.

134 Queen Victoria and King George VI

1940. Centenary of First Adhesive Postage Stamps.

479	134	½d. green	30	30
480		1d. red	1·00	50
481		1½d. brown	50	50
482		2d. orange	50	50
483		2½d. blue	2·25	1·00
484		3d. violet	3·00	3·25

135

1946. Victory Commemoration.

491	135	2½d. blue	30	30
492	–	3d. violet	30	30

DESIGN—HORIZ: 3d. Symbols of Peace and Reconstruction.

137

138 King George VI and Queen Elizabeth

1948. Royal Silver Wedding.

493	137	2½d. blue	30	30
494	138	£1 blue	38·00	35·00

139 Globe and Laurel Wreath

140 "Speed"

1948. Olympic Games. Inscr "OLYMPIC GAMES 1948".

495	139	2½d. blue	30	30
496	140	3d. violet	30	30
497	–	6d. purple	60	30
498	–	1s. brown	1·25	1·50

DESIGNS: 6d. Olympic symbol; 1s. Winged Victory.

143 Two Hemispheres

144 U.P.U. Monument, Berne

1949. 75th Anniv of U.P.U. Inscr as in T 143/4.

499	143	2½d. blue	30	30
500	144	3d. violet	30	40
501	–	6d. purple	60	75
502	–	1s. brown	1·25	1·50

DESIGNS: 6d. Goddess Concordia, globe and points of compass; 1s. Posthorn and globe.

147 H.M.S. "Victory"

1951.

509	147	2s. 6d. green	6·00	1·00
510	–	5s. red	32·00	1·50
511	–	10s. blue	21·00	8·50
512	–	£1 brown	32·00	20·00

DESIGNS: 5s. White Cliffs of Dover; 10s. St. George and dragon; £1 Royal Coat of Arms.

152 Festival Symbol

1951. Festival of Britain.

513	–	2½d. red	30	30
514	152	4d. blue	50	55

DESIGN: 2½d. Britannia, cornucopia and Mercury.

154

155

157

158

159 Queen Elizabeth II and National Emblems

1952.

570	154	½d. orange	10	10
571		1d. blue	10	10
517		1½d. green	10	15
573		2d. brown	10	10
574	155	2½d. red	10	10
575		3d. lilac	10	20
576a		4d. blue	15	10
577		4½d. brown	10	30
578	157	5d brown	25	40
579		6d. purple	40	30
617a		7d. green	60	30
617b	158	8d. mauve	30	30
617c		9d. green	60	30
617d		10d. blue	80	35
553		11d. plum	50	1·75
617e	159	1s. brown	40	40
585		1s. 3d. green	40	40
618a		1s. 6d. blue	2·00	1·25

The 4d., 4½d. and 1s. 3d. values are printed with colour tones reversed.

Stamps with either one or two vertical black lines on the back were issued in 1957 in connection with the Post Office automatic facing machine experiments in the Southampton area. Later the lines were replaced by almost invisible phosphor bands on the face, in the above and later issues. They are listed in the Stanley Gibbons British Commonwealth Catalogue.

161

163

1953. Coronation. Portraits of Queen Elizabeth II.

532	161	2½d. red	10	50
533	–	4d. blue	40	1·75
534	163	1s. 3d. green	3·50	3·00
535	–	1s. 6d. blue	7·00	3·75

DESIGNS: 4d. Coronation and National Emblems; 1s. 6d. Crowns and Sceptres dated "2 JUNE 1953".

166 Carrickfergus Castle

1955.

595a	166	2s. 6d. brown	50	30
596a	–	5s. red	1·00	60
597a	–	10s. blue	3·00	3·50
762	–	£1 black	4·50	6·00

CASTLES: 5s. Caernarvon; 10s. Edinburgh; £1 Windsor.

170 Scout Badge and "Rolling Hitch"

171 "Scouts coming to Britain"

1957. World Scout Jubilee Jamboree.

557	170	2½d. red	15	25
558	171	4d. blue	50	1·25
559	–	1s. 3d. green	5·00	4·75

DESIGN: 1s. 3d. Globe within a compass.

1957. Inter-Parliamentary Union Conference. As No. 576a but inscr "46th PARLIAMENTARY CONFERENCE".

560	4d. blue	1·00	1·25

176 Welsh Dragon

1958. 6th British Empire and Commonwealth Games, Cardiff. Inscr as in T 176.

567	176	3d. lilac	15	10
568	–	6d. mauve	25	45
569	–	1s. 3d. green	3·00	3·00

DESIGNS: 6d. Flag and Games emblem; 1s. 3d. Welsh Dragon.

180 Postboy of 1660

181 Posthorn of 1660

1960. Tercentenary of Establishment of General Letter Office.

619	180	3d. lilac	20	10
620	181	1s. 3d. green	4·00	4·00

182 Conference Emblem

1960. 1st Anniv of European Postal and Telecommunications Conference.

621	182	6d. green and purple	50	60
622		1s. 6d. brown and blue	7·00	5·50

184 "Growth of Savings"

1961. Centenary of Post Office Savings Bank. Inscr "POST OFFICE SAVINGS BANK".

623	–	2½d. black and red	20	20
624	184	3d. brown and violet	20	20
625	–	1s. 6d. red and blue	3·00	2·50

DESIGNS—VERT: 2½d. Thrift plant. HORIZ: 1s. 6d. Thrift plant.

186 C.E.P.T. Emblem

187 Doves and Emblem

1961. Europa.

626	186	2d. orange, pink & brown	25	20
627	187	4d. buff, mauve and blue	25	20
628	–	10d. turquoise, green & bl	60	75

DESIGN: 10d. As 4d. but arranged differently.

189 Hammer Beam Roof, Westminster Hall

1961. 7th Commonwealth Parliamentary Conference.

629	189	6d. purple and gold	25	25
630	–	1s. 3d. green & blue	2·75	2·75

DESIGN—VERT: 1s. 3d. Palace of Westminster.

191 "Units of Productivity"

1962. National Productivity Year.

631	191	2½d. green and red	20	10
632	–	3d. blue and violet	25	10
633	–	1s. 3d. red, blue & green	1·75	2·00

DESIGNS: 3d. Arrows over map; 1s. 3d. Arrows in formation.

194 Campaign Emblem and Family

1963. Freedom from Hunger.

634	194	2½d. red and pink	10	10
635	–	1s. 3d. brown and yellow	2·00	2·00

DESIGN: 1s. 3d. Children of three races.

196 "Paris Conference"

1963. Centenary of Paris Postal Conference.

636	196	6d. green and mauve	50	50

197 Posy of Flowers

1963. National Nature Week. Multicoloured.
637 3d. Type **197** 25 20
638 4½d. Woodland life 40 50

199 Rescue at Sea

1963. 9th International Lifeboat Conference, Edinburgh. Multicoloured.
639 2½d. Type **199** 10 10
640 4d. 19th-century lifeboat . . . 40 30
641 1s. 6d. Lifeboatmen . . . . . 2·75 3·00

202 Red Cross

1963. Red Cross Centenary Congress.
642 **202** 3d. red and lilac 10 10
643 – 1s. 3d. red, blue and grey . . 3·25 3·00
644 – 1s. 6d. red, blue and bistre . 3·00 3·00
DESIGNS: Nos. 643/4 are as Type **202** but differently arranged.

205 Commonwealth Cable

1963. COMPAC (Trans-Pacific Telephone Cable) Opening.
645 **205** 1s. 6d. blue and black . . 2·50 2·50

206 Puck and Bottom ("A Midsummer Night's Dream")

210 Hamlet contemplating Yorick's Skull ("Hamlet") and Queen Elizabeth II

1964. Shakespeare Festival.
646 **206** 3d. multicoloured 10 10
647 – 6d. multicoloured 20 30
648 – 1s. 3d. multicoloured . . . 90 1·00
649 – 1s. 6d. multicoloured . . . 1·25 1·00
650 **210** 2s. 6d. slate-purple . . . 2·00 2·25
DESIGNS—As Type **206**: 6d. Feste ("Twelfth Night"); 1s. 3d. Balcony scene ("Romeo and Juliet"); 1s. 6d. "Eve of Agincourt" ("Henry V").

211 Flats near Richmond Park

1964. 20th Int. Geographical Congress, London. Multicoloured.
651 2½d. Type **211** 10 10
652 4d. Shipbuilding yards, Belfast 25 25
653 8d. Beddgelert Forest Park, Snowdonia 60 50
654 1s. 6d. Nuclear reactor, Dounreay . . . . 3·25 3·25
The designs represent "Urban development", "Industrial activity", "Forestry" and "Technological development" respectively.

215 Spring Gentian

1964. 10th Int Botanical Congress, Edinburgh. Multicoloured.
655 3d. Type **215** 10 10
656 6d. Dog rose 20 20
657 9d. Honeysuckle . . . . . . 1·60 2·50
658 1s. 3d. Fringed water lily . . 2·50 1·90

219 Forth Road Bridge

1964. Opening of Forth Road Bridge.
659 **219** 3d. black, blue and violet 15 10
660 – 6d. lilac, blue and red . . 45 40
DESIGN: 6d. Forth Road and Railway Bridges.

221 Sir Winston Churchill

1965. Churchill Commemoration.
661 **221** 4d. black and drab . . . 15 10
662 – 1s. 3d. black and grey . . 45 40
The 1s. 3d. shows a closer view of Churchill's head.

222 Simon de Montfort's Seal

1965. 700th Anniv of Simon de Montfort's Parliament.
663 **222** 6d. olive 10 10
664 – 2s. 6d. blk, grey & drab . 1·25 1·25
DESIGN—(58½ × 21½ mm): 2s. 6d. Parliament buildings (after engraving by Hollar, 1647).

224 Bandsmen and Banner

1965. Centenary of Salvation Army. Mult.
665 3d. Type **224** 10 10
666 1s. 6d. Three Salvationists . . 1·00 1·00

226 Lister's Carbolic Spray

1965. Centenary of Joseph Lister's Discovery of Antiseptic Surgery.
667 **226** 4d. blue, brown & grey . . 10 10
668 – 1s. black, purple & blue . 1·00 1·50
DESIGN: 1s. Lister and chemical symbols.

228 Trinidad Carnival Dancers

1965. Commonwealth Arts Festival.
669 **228** 6d. black and orange . . . 10 10
670 – 1s. 6d. black and violet . 1·25 1·50
DESIGN: 1s. 6d. Canadian folk-dancers.

230 Flight of Supermarine Spitfires

234 Supermarine Spitfire attacking Junkers Ju 878 "Stuka"

1965. 25th Anniv of Battle of Britain. Inscr "Battle of Britain 1940".
671 **230** 4d. olive and black . . . 30 35
672 – 4d. olive and black . . . 30 35
673 – 4d. multicoloured 30 35
674 – 4d. olive and black . . . 30 35
675 **234** 4d. olive and black . . . 30 35
676 – 4d. multicoloured 30 35
677p – 9d. violet, orange and purple . . . . 1·25 80
678p – 1s. 3d. grey, black & bl . 1·25 80
DESIGNS: No. 672, Pilot in Hawker Hurricane Mk I; 673, Wing-tips of Supermarine Spitfire and Messerschmitt BF 109; 674, Supermarine Spitfires attacking Heinkel HE 111H bomber; 676, Hawker Hurricanes Mk I over wreck of Dornier DO-17Z bomber; 9d. Anti-aircraft artillery in action; 1s. 3d. Air battle over St. Paul's Cathedral.

239 Tower and "Nash" Terrace, Regent's Park

1965. Opening of Post Office Tower.
679 – 3d. yellow, blue & green . 10 10
680p **239** 1s. 3d. green and blue . . 50 60
DESIGN—VERT: 3d. Tower and Georgian buildings.

240 U.N. Emblem

1965. 20th Anniv of U.N.O. and International Co-operation Year.
681 **240** 3d. black, orange & blue . 15 20
682 – 1s. 6d. black, purple & bl . 1·10 1·25
DESIGN: 1s. 6d. I.C.Y. Emblem.

242 Telecommunications Network

1965. Centenary of I.T.U. Multicoloured.
683 9d. Type **242** 20 25
684 1s. 6d. Radio waves and switchboard . . . . 1·60 1·75

244 Robert Burns (after Skirving chalk drawing)

1966. Burns Commemoration.
685 **244** 4d. black, indigo and blue 15 15
686 – 1s. 3d. black, blue and orge 70 85
DESIGN: 1s. 3d. Robert Burns (after Nasmyth portrait).

246 Westminster Abbey

1966. 900th Anniv of Westminster Abbey.
687 **246** 3d. black, brown and blue 15 20
688 – 2s. 6d. black . . . . 85 1·25
DESIGN: 2s. 6d. Fan vaulting, Henry VII Chapel.

248 View near Hassocks, Sussex

1966. Landscapes.
689 **248** 4d. black, green and blue 15 15
690 – 6d. black, green and blue 25 25
691 – 1s. 3d. black, yellow & blue 40 45
692 – 1s. 6d. black, orange & blue 60 60
VIEWS: 6d. Antrim, Northern Ireland; 1s. 3d. Harlech Castle, Wales; 1s. 6d. Cairngorm Mountains, Scotland.

253 Goalmouth Melee

1966. World Cup Football Championship. Multicoloured.
693 4d. Players with ball (vert) . . 15 10
694 6d. Type **253** 20 30
695 1s. 3d. Goalkeeper saving goal 75 90

255 Black-headed Gull

1966. British Birds. Multicoloured.
696 4d. Type **255** 10 15
697 4d. Blue tit 10 15
698 4d. European robin 10 15
699 4d. Blackbird 10 15

1966. England's World Cup Football Victory. As No. 693 but inscr "ENGLAND WINNERS".
700 – 4d. multicoloured 30 30

260 Jodrell Bank Radio Telescope

1966. British Technology.
701 **260** 4d. black and lemon . . . 15 15
702 – 6d. red, blue and orange . 15 20
703 – 1s. 3d. multicoloured . . 30 50
704 – 1s. 6d. multicoloured . . 50 55
DESIGN: 6d. British motor-cars; 1s. 3d. SRN 6 hovercraft; 1s. 6d. Windscale reactor.

264

265

1966. 900th Anniv of Battle of Hastings. Mult.
705 4d. Type **264** 10 15
706 4d. Type **265** 10 15
707 4d. "Yellow" horse 10 15
708 4d. "Blue" horse 10 15
709 4d. "Purple" horse 10 15
710 4d. "Grey" horse 10 15
711 6d. Norman horsemen 10 10
712 1s. 3d. Norman horsemen attacking Harold's troops (59 × 22½ mm). 20 20

272 King of the Orient

274 Sea Freight

1966. Christmas. Multicoloured.
713 3d. Type **272** 10 10
714 1s. 6d. Snowman 40 40

1967. European Free Trade Assn (EFTA).
715 9d. Type **274** 20 20
716 1s. 6d. Air freight 30 30

276 Hawthorn and Bramble — 282

1967. British Wild Flowers. Multicoloured.

717p	4d. Type **276**	10	10
718p	4d. Larger bindweed and viper's bugloss	10	10
719p	4d. Ox-eye daisy, coltsfoot and buttercup	10	10
720p	4d. Bluebell, red campion and wood anemone	10	10
721p	9d. Dog violet	10	10
722	1s. 9d. Primroses	20	20

1967.

723	**282** ½d. brown	10	20
724	1d. olive	10	10
726	2d. brown	10	15
729	3d. violet	10	10
731	4d. sepia	10	10
733	4d. red	10	10
735	5d. blue	10	10
736	6d. purple	20	20
737	7d. green	50	30
738	8d. red	20	30
739	8d. turquoise	75	60
740	9d. green	60	30
741	10d. drab	55	50
742	1s. violet	50	30
743	1s. 6d. blue and indigo	60	30
744	1s. 9d. orange and black	50	30

For decimal issue, see Nos. X841 etc.

284 "Mares and Foals in a Landscape" (George Stubbs)

1967. British Paintings.

748	– 4d. multicoloured	10	10
749	**284** 9d. multicoloured	20	20
750	– 1s. 6d. multicoloured	60	60

PAINTINGS—VERT: 4d. "Master Lambton" (Sir Thomas Lawrence). HORIZ: 1s. 6d. "Children Coming Out of School" (L. S. Lowry).

286 "Gipsy Moth IV"

1967. Sir Francis Chichester's World Voyage.

751	**286** 1s. 9d. multicoloured	25	25

287 Radar Screen

1967. British Discovery and Invention. Mult.

752	4d. Type **287**	10	10
753	1s. "Penicillium notatum"	15	15
754	1s. 6d. Vickers VC-10 jet engines	35	35
755	1s. 9d. Television equipment	50	50

292 "Madonna and Child" (Murillo)

1967. Christmas.

756	– 3d. multicoloured	10	20
757	**292** 4d. multicoloured	10	20
758	– 1s. 6d. multicoloured	60	60

PAINTINGS—VERT: 3d. "The Adoration of the Shepherds" (School of Seville). HORIZ: 1s. 6d. "The Adoration of the Shepherds" (Louis le Nain).

294 Tarr Steps, Exmoor

1968. British Bridges. Multicoloured.

763	4d. Type **294**	10	10
764	9d. Aberfeldy Bridge	10	10
765	1s. 6d. Menai Bridge	40	40
766	1s. 9d. M4 viaduct	50	50

298 "T U C" and Trades Unionists

1968. British Annivs. Events described on stamps.

767	**298** 4d. multicoloured	10	10
768	– 9d. violet, grey and black	10	15
769	– 1s. multicoloured	40	35
770	– 1s. 9d. ochre and brown	50	50

DESIGNS: 9d. Mrs. Emmeline Pankhurst (statue); 1s. Sopwith Camel and English Electric Lightning fighters; 1s. 9d. Captain Cook's "Endeavour" and signature.

302 "Queen Elizabeth I" (unknown artist)

1968. British Paintings.

771	**302** 4d. multicoloured	10	10
772	– 1s. multicoloured	20	20
773	– 1s. 6d. multicoloured	30	30
774	– 1s. 9d. multicoloured	50	50

PAINTINGS—VERT: 1s. "Pinkie" (Lawrence); 1s. 6d. "Ruins of St. Mary Le Port" (Piper). HORIZ: 1s. 9d. "The Hay Wain" (Constable).

306 Boy and Girl with Rocking Horse

1968. Christmas. Multicoloured.

775	4d. Type **306**	10	10
776	9d. Girl with doll's house	30	30
777	1s. 6d. Boy with train set	45	45

Nos. 776/7 are vert.

310 Elizabethan Galleon

1969. British Ships. Multicoloured.

778	5d. "Queen Elizabeth 2"	10	10
779	9d. Type **310**	10	15
780	9d. East Indiaman	10	15
781	9d. "Cutty Sark"	10	15
782	1s. "Great Britain"	40	30
783	1s. "Mauretania I"	40	30

Nos. 778 and 782/3 are 58 × 23 mm.

315 Concorde in Flight

1969. 1st Flight of Concorde.

784	**315** 4d. multicoloured	10	10
785	– 9d. multicoloured	35	35
786	– 1s. 6d. indigo, grey and blue	50	50

DESIGNS: 9d. Plan and elevation views; 1s. 6d. Concorde's nose and tail.

318 Queen Elizabeth II

1969.

787	**318** 2s. 6d. brown	50	30
788	5s. lake	2·25	60
789	10s. blue	7·00	6·50
790	£1 black	3·00	2·00

For decimal issues see Nos. 829/31b.

No. 790 has an italic "£". For later version with roman "£" see No. 831b.

319 Page from "Daily Mail", and Vickers Vimy Biplane

1969. Anniversary Events described on stamps.

791	**319** 5d. multicoloured	10	10
792	– 9d. multicoloured	20	25
793	– 1s. claret, red and blue	25	25
794	– 1s. 6d. multicoloured	25	30
795	– 1s. 9d. turquoise, yell & sepia	30	35

DESIGNS: 9d. Europa and C.E.P.T. emblems; 1s. I.L.O. emblem; 1s. 6d. Flags of N.A.T.O. countries; 1s. 9d. Vickers Vimy biplane and globe showing flight route.

324 Durham Cathedral

1969. British Architecture (Cathedrals). Mult.

796	5d. Type **324**	10	10
797	5d. York Minster	10	10
798	5d. St. Giles' Cathedral, Edinburgh	10	10
799	5d. Canterbury Cathedral	10	10
800	9d. St. Paul's Cathedral	15	15
801	1s. 6d. Liverpool Metropolitan Cathedral	15	15

332 Queen Eleanor's Gate, Caernarvon Castle

1969. Investiture of H.R.H. The Prince of Wales.

802	– 5d. multicoloured	10	10
803	– 5d. multicoloured	10	10
804	**332** 5d. multicoloured	10	10
805	– 9d. multicoloured	20	10
806	– 1s. black and gold	20	10

DESIGNS: No. 802, The King's Gate, Caernarvon Castle; No. 803, The Eagle Tower, Caernarvon Castle; No. 805, Celtic Cross, Margam Abbey; No. 806, H.R.H. The Prince of Wales.

335 Mahatma Gandhi

1969. Gandhi Centenary Year.

807	**335** 1s. 6d. multicoloured	30	30

336 National Giro "G" Symbol

1969. Post Office Technology Commemoration.

808	**336** 5d. multicoloured	10	10
809	– 9d. green, blue and black	25	25
810	– 1s. green, lavender & black	25	25
811	– 1s. 6d. purple, blue & black	50	50

DESIGNS: 9d. International subscriber dialling (Telecommunications); 1s. Pulse code modulations (Telecommunications); 1s 6d. Automatic sorting (Postal Mechanisation).

340 Herald Angel

1969. Christmas. Multicoloured.

812	4d. Type **340**	10	15
813	5d. The Three Shepherds	25	20
814	1s. 6d. The Three Kings	50	50

343 Fife Harling

1970. British Rural Architecture. Multicoloured.

815	5d. Type **343**	10	15
816	9d. Cotswold limestone	30	25
817	1s. Welsh stucco	30	25
818	1s. 6d. Ulster thatch	40	45

The 1s. and 1s. 6d. are larger (38 × 27 mm).

347 Signing the Declaration of Arbroath

1970. Anniversaries. Events described on stamps. Multicoloured.

819	5d. Type **347**	10	10
820	9d. Florence Nightingale attending patients	15	15
821	1s. Signing of International Co-operative Alliance	25	35
822	1s. 6d. Pilgrims and "Mayflower"	30	40
823	1s. 9d. Sir William and Sir John Herschel, Francis Baily and Telescope	30	40

352 Mr Pickwick and Sam ("Pickwick Papers") — 357 Queen Elizabeth II

1970. Literary Annivs. Death Cent of Charles Dickens (novelist) (824/7) and Birth Bicent of William Wordsworth (poet) (828). Mult.

824	5d. Type **352**	10	10
825	5d. Mr. and Mrs. Micawber ("David Copperfield")	10	10
826	5d. David Copperfield and Betsy Trotwood ("David Copperfield")	10	10
827	5d. "Oliver asking for more" ("Oliver Twist")	10	10
828	1s. 6d. "Grasmere" (from engraving by J. Farrington, R.A.)	20	20

1970. Decimal Currency. Designs as T **318** but inscr in decimal currency as T **357**.

829	**357** 10p red	1·00	85
830	20p. green	1·00	30
831	50p. blue	2·00	60
831b	£1 black	4·00	1·00

On No. 831b the "£" is in roman type.

360 Cyclists

1970. 9th British Commonwealth Games. Mult.

832	5d. Runners	10	10
833	1s. 6d. Swimmers	50	55
834	1s. 9d. Type **360**	50	55

361 1d. Black (1840) — 364 Shepherds and Apparition of the Angel

1970. "Philympia 70" Stamp Exhibition. Mult.

835	5d. Type **361**	10	10
836	9d. 1s. green (1847)	50	50
837	1s. 6d. 4d. red (1855)	50	60

1970. Christmas. Multicoloured.

838	4d. Type **364**	15	15
839	5d. Mary, Joseph, and Christ in the manger	20	20
840	1s. 6d. The Wise Men bearing gifts	50	50

367

1971. Decimal currency. As Nos. 723, etc. but new colours and with decimal figures of value as in T **367**.

X841	½p. blue	10	10
X844	1p. red	10	10
X848	1½p. black	30	15
Y1668	2p. green	10	10
X1001	2p. light green and green	1·25	70
X851	2½p. mauve	25	10
X929	2½p. red	30	30
X855	3p. blue	30	10
X930	3p. mauve	30	30
X859	3½p. grey	40	15
X931	3½p. brown	60	60
X861	4p. brown	30	30
Y1669	4p. blue	10	10
X865	4½p. blue	30	25
X866	5p. violet	30	10
Y1670	5p. brown	10	10
X869	5½p. violet	30	20
Y1671	6p. green	10	15
X872	6½p. blue	40	15
X875	7p. brown	40	30
X937	7p. red	2·00	2·00
Y1671a	7p. grey	10	15
X877	7½p. brown	40	30
X879	8p. red	30	30
X881	8½p green	40	30
X882	9p. yellow and black	70	40
X883	9p. violet	50	30
X884	9½p. purple	50	40
X885	10p. brown and light brown	50	40
X939	10p. brown	50	30
Y1672	10p. orange	15	20
X890	10½p. yellow	60	40
X891	10½p. blue	80	50
X892	11p. red	70	40
X893	11½p. drab	60	40
X942	11½p. brown	60	50
X943	12p. green	60	60
X898	12½p. green	50	30
X900	13p. brown	50	40
X944	13p. grey	70	50
X945	13½p. brown	70	70
X903	14p. blue	70	50
X905	15p. blue	75	50
X948	15½p. violet	70	50
X949	16p. brown	70	40
X950	16½p. brown	90	80
X951	17p. green	80	50
X952	17p. blue	70	50
X953	17½p. brown	90	90
X954	18p. violet	90	80
X955	18p. grey	90	70
X913	18p. green	75	50
X956	19p. red	90	75
Y1673	19p. bistre	30	35
X957	19½p. grey	1·50	1·50
X958	20p. purple	1·00	40
Y1675	20p. green	30	35
X960	20p. black	1·00	50
X961	20½p. blue	1·40	1·25
X962	22p. blue	90	50
X963	22p. green	90	65
X964	22p. orange	90	60
X965	23p. red	1·10	70
X966	23p. green	1·25	70
X967	24p. violet	1·40	1·10
X968	24p. red	1·75	1·10
X969	24p. brown	1·00	60
X970	25p. purple	1·10	1·10
Y1677	25p. red	80	80
X971	26p. red	1·00	40
Y1678	26p. brown	40	45
X973	27p. brown	1·25	1·25
X974	27p. violet	1·25	1·25
X975	28p. violet	1·25	1·25
X976	28p. ochre	1·25	1·25
X977	28p. grey	1·25	1·25
X978	29p. brown	2·00	1·25
X979	29p. mauve	2·00	1·25
Y1679	29p. grey	1·00	1·00
Y1680	30p. grey	45	50
X981	31p. purple	1·50	1·50
X982	31p. blue	1·50	1·50
Y1681	31p. mauve	50	55
X983	32p. blue	1·50	1·50
X1057	33p. green	1·50	1·50
X985	34p. brown	1·50	1·50
X986	34p. grey	1·75	1·50
X987	34p. mauve	1·50	1·50
X988	35p. brown	1·75	1·50
Y1683	35p. yellow	1·00	1·00
Y1684	36p. blue	1·00	1·00
X990	37p. red	1·75	1·75
Y1685	37p. mauve	1·00	1·00
Y1686	38p. red	1·00	1·00
Y1686b	38p. blue	55	60
Y1687	39p. mauve	60	65
Y1688	41p. drab	1·25	1·25
Y1691	43p. brown	65	70
Y1691b	44p. brown	65	70
Y1692	50p. brown	75	80
Y1758	60p. grey	2·00	2·00
Y1693	63p. green	95	1·00
Y1693a	64p. green	95	1·00
X993	75p. black	2·50	2·50
X1024	75p. grey and black	10·00	9·00
Y1694	£1 violet	1·50	1·60
Y1800	£1.50 red	2·25	2·40
Y1801	£2 blue	3·00	3·25
Y1802	£3 violet	4·50	4·75
Y1803	£5 brown	7·50	7·75

For 26p. in gold see No. 1978.

368 "A Mountain Road" (T. P. Flanagan)

1971. "Ulster '71" Festival. Paintings. Mult.

881	3p. Type **368**	10	10
882	7½p. "Deer's Meadow" (Tom Carr)	50	50
883	9p. "Slieve na brock" (Colin Middleton)	50	50

371 John Keats (150th Death Anniv)

1971. Literary Anniversaries.

884	**371**	3p. black, gold and blue	10	10
885	–	5p. black, gold and green	50	50
886	–	7½p. black, gold and brown	50	50

DESIGNS AND ANNIVERSARIES: 5p. Thomas Gray (death bicentenary); 7½p. Sir Walter Scott (birth bicentenary).

374 Servicemen and Nurse of 1921

1971. British Anniversaries Events described on stamps. Multicoloured.

887	3p. Type **374**	10	10
888	7½p. Roman centurion	50	50
889	9p. Rugby football, 1871	50	50

377 Physical Sciences Building, University College of Wales, Aberystwyth

1971. British Architecture. Modern University Buildings.

890	**377**	3p. multicoloured	10	10
891	–	5p. multicoloured	20	20
892	–	7½p. ochre, black & brown	50	50
893	–	9p. multicoloured	90	90

DESIGNS: 5p. Faraday Building, Southampton University; 7½p. Engineering Department, Leicester University; 9p. Hexagon Restaurant, Essex University.

381 "Dream of the Wise Men"

1971. Christmas. Multicoloured.

894	2½p. Type **381**	10	10
895	3p. "Adoration of the Magi"	10	10
896	7½p. "Ride of the Magi"	90	90

384 Sir James Clark Ross

391 St. Andrew's Greensted-juxta-Ongar, Essex

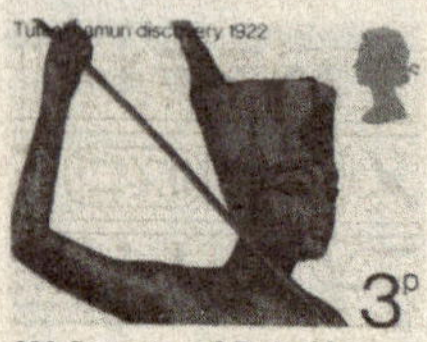

388 Statuette of Tutankhamun

1972. British Polar Explorers. Multicoloured.

897	3p. Type **384**	10	10
898	5p. Sir Martin Frobisher	20	20
899	7½p. Henry Hudson	50	50
900	9p. Capt. Robert Scott	90	90

See also Nos. 923/7.

1972. General Anniveraries. Multicoloured.

901	3p. Type **388**	10	10
902	7½p. 19th-century Coastguard	50	50
903	9p. Ralph Vaughan Williams (composer) and score	50	50

ANNIVERSARIES: 3p. 50th anniversary of discovery of Tutankhamun's tomb; 7½p. 150th anniversary of Formation of H.M. Coastguard: 9p. Birth centenary.

1972. British Architecture. Village Churches. Multicoloured.

904	3p. Type **391**	10	10
905	4p. All Saints, Earls Barton, Northants	20	20
906	5p. St. Andrew's, Letheringsett, Norfolk	30	25
907	7½p. St. Andrew's, Helpringham, Lincs.	75	80
908	9p. St. Mary the Virgin, Huish Episcopi, Somerset	85	90

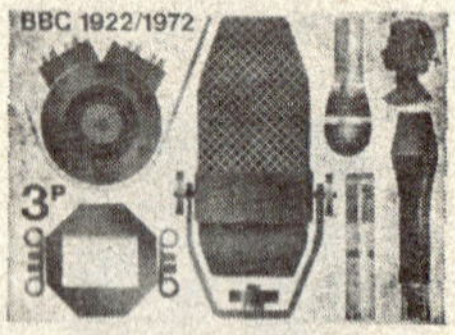

396 Microphones, 1924-69

1972. Broadcasting Anniversaries Multicoloured.

909	3p. Type **396**	10	10
910	5p. Horn loudspeaker	15	20
911	7½p. T.V. camera, 1972	75	75
912	9p. Oscillator and spark transmitter, 1897	75	75

ANNIVERSARIES: Nos. 909/11, 50th anniversary of daily broadcasting by the B.B.C.; No. 912, 75th anniversary of Marconi and Kemp's radio experiments.

400 Angel holding Trumpet

403 Queen Elizabeth and Duke of Edinburgh

1972. Christmas. Multicoloured.

913	2½p. Type **400**	10	15
914	3p. Angel playing lute	10	15
915	7½p. Angel playing harp	90	80

1972. Royal Silver Wedding.

916	**403**	3p. black, blue and silver	25	25
917		20p. black, purple & silver	1·00	1·00

404 "Europe"

411 W. G. Grace

405 Oak Tree

1973. Britain's Entry into European Communities.

919	**404**	3p. multicoloured	10	10
920		5p. mult (blue jig-saw)	25	50
921		5p. mult (green jig-saw)	25	50

1973. Tree Planting Year. British Trees (1st issue).

922	**405**	9p. multicoloured	50	50

See also No. 949.

1973. British Explorers. As T **384**. Mult.

923	3p. David Livingstone	25	20
924	3p. H. M. Stanley	25	20
925	5p. Sir Francis Drake	20	30
926	7½p. Sir Walter Raleigh	20	30
927	9p. Charles Sturt	25	40

1973. County Cricket 1873–1973. Designs as T **411** showing caricatures of W. G. Grace by Harry Furniss.

928	**411**	3p. black, brown & gold	10	10
929	–	7½p. black, green & gold	80	70
930	–	9p. black, blue and gold	1·00	90

414 "Self-portrait" (Reynolds)

418 Court Masque Costumes

1973. British Paintings. 250th Birth Anniv of Sir Joshua Reynolds, and 150th Death Anniv of Sir Henry Raeburn. Multicoloured.

931	3p. Type **414**	10	10
932	5p. "Self-portrait" (Raeburn)	20	25
933	7½p. "Nelly O' Brien" (Reynolds)	55	50
934	9p. "Rev. R. Walker (The Skater)" (Raeburn)	60	60

1973. 400th Birth Anniv of Inigo Jones (architect and designer). Multicoloured.

935	3p. Type **418**	10	15
936	3p. St. Paul's Church, Covent Garden	10	15
937	5p. Prince's Lodging, Newmarket	40	45
938	5p. Court Masque stage scene	40	45

422 Palace of Westminster, seen from Whitehall

1973. 19th Commonwealth Parliamentary Conf.

939	**422**	8p. stone, grey & black	50	60
940	–	10p. gold and black	50	40

DESIGN: 10p. Palace of Westminster, seen from Millbank.

424 Princess Anne and Capt. Mark Phillips

1973. Royal Wedding.

941	**424**	3½p. violet and silver	10	10
942		20p. brown and silver	90	90

425 "Good King Wenceslas looked out."

1973. Christmas. Multicoloured.

943	Type **425**	15	15
944	3p. King and page at window	15	15
945	3p. Leaving the palace	15	15
946	3p. Struggling against the wind	15	15
947	3p. Delivering gifts	15	15
948	3½p. King, page and peasant	15	15

431 Horse Chestnut

1974. British Trees (2nd issue).

949	**431**	10p. multicoloured	50	50

432 First Motor Fire-engine, 1904

1974. Bicentenary of Fire Prevention (Metropolis) Act. Multicoloured.

950	3½p. Type **432**	10	10
951	5½p. Prize-winning fire-engine, 1863	35	35
952	8p. First steam fire-engine, 1830	45	45
953	10p. Fire-engine, 1766	50	50

436 P. & O. Packet "Peninsular", 1888

1974. Cent of Universal Postal Union. Mult.

954		3½p. Type 436	10	10
955		5½p. Farman H.F.III biplane, 1911	30	35
956		8p. Airmail-blue van and postbox, 1930	40	45
957		10p. Short S.21 flying boat "Maia", 1937	60	50

440 Robert the Bruce

1974. Medieval Warriors. Multicoloured.

958		4½p. Type 440	10	10
959		5½p. Owain Glyndwr	20	30
960		8p. Henry the Fifth	50	50
961		10p. The Black Prince	55	50

444 Churchill in Royal Yacht Squadron Uniform

1974. Birth Centenary of Sir Winston Churchill.

962	444	4½p. silver, blue & green	15	15
963	–	5½p. silver, brown & grey	30	25
964	–	8p. silver, red & pink	60	50
965	–	10p. silver, brown & stone	65	50

DESIGNS: 5½p. Prime Minister, 1940; 8p. Secretary for War and Air, 1919; 10p. War correspondent, South Africa, 1899.

448 "Adoration of the Magi" (York Minster, c. 1355)

1974. Christmas. Church Roof Bosses. Multicoloured.

966		3½p. Type 448	10	10
967		4½p. "The Nativity" (St. Helen's Church, Norwich, c. 1480)	10	10
968		8p. "Virgin and Child" (Ottery St. Mary Church, c. 1350)	45	45
969		10p. "Virgin and Child" (Worcester Cathedral, c. 1224)	50	50

452 Invalid in Wheelchair

1975. Health and Handicap Funds.

970	452	4½p. + 1½p. blue and azure	25	25

453 "Peace—Burial at Sea"

1975. Birth Bicentenary of J. M. W. Turner (painter). Multicoloured.

971		4½p. Type 453	10	10
972		5½p. "Snowstorm—Steamer off a Harbour's Mouth"	15	15
973		8p. "The Arsenal, Venice"	40	40
974		10p. "St. Laurent"	45	45

457 Charlotte Square, Edinburgh

1975. European Architectural Heritage Year. Multicoloured.

975		7p. Type 457	50	55
976		7p. The Rows, Chester	50	55
977		8p. Royal Observatory, Greenwich	25	25
978		10p. St. George's Chapel, Windsor	25	25
979		12p. National Theatre, London	25	35

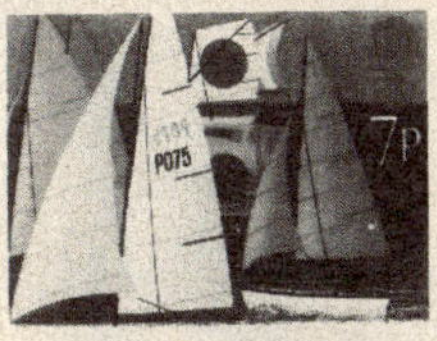

462 Sailing Dinghies

1975. Sailing. Multicoloured.

980		7p. Type 462	20	20
981		8p. Racing keel yachts	35	30
982		10p. Cruising Yachts	40	30
983		12p. Multihulls	45	35

466 Stephenson's "Locomotion", 1825

1975. 150th Anniv of Public Railways. Mult.

984		7p. Type 466	20	20
985		8p. "Abbotsford", 1876	45	35
986		10p. "Caerphilly Castle", 1923	50	40
987		12p. High Speed Train, 1975	55	45

470 Palace of Westminster

1975. 62nd Inter-Parliamentary Union Conference.

988	470	12p. multicoloured	50	50

471 Emma and Mr. Woodhouse ("Emma")

1975. Birth Bicentenary of Jane Austen (novelist). Multicoloured.

989		8½p. Type 471	20	20
990		10p. Catherine Morland ("Northanger Abbey")	25	25
991		11p. Mr. Darcy ("Pride and Prejudice")	30	30
992		13p. Mary and Henry Crawford ("Mansfield Park")	35	35

475 Angels with Harp and Lute

1975. Christmas. Multicoloured.

993		6½p. Type 475	20	15
994		8½p. Angel with mandolin	20	20
995		11p. Angel with horn	30	35
996		13p. Angel with trumpet	40	40

479 Housewife

1976. Centenary of Telephone. Multicoloured.

997		8½p. Type 479	20	20
998		10p. Policeman	25	25
999		11p. District Nurse	30	30
1000		13p. Industrialist	35	35

483 Hewing Coal (Thomas Hepburn)

1976. Industrial and Social Reformers. Mult.

1001		8½p. Type 483	20	20
1002		10p. Machinery (Robert Owen)	35	35
1003		11p. Chimney cleaning (Lord Shaftesbury)	40	40
1004		13p. Hands clutching prison bars (Elizabeth Fry)	45	45

487 Benjamin Franklin (bust by Jean-Jacques Caffieri)

488 "Elizabeth of Glamis"

1976. Bicentenary of American Revolution.

1005	487	11p. multicoloured	50	50

1976. Centenary of Royal National Rose Society. Multicoloured.

1006		8½p. Type 488	20	20
1007		10p. "Grandpa Dickson"	30	30
1008		11p. "Rosa Mundi"	55	55
1009		13p. "Sweet Briar"	60	60

492 Archdruid

496 Woodcut from "The Canterbury Tales"

1976. British Cultural Traditions. Multicoloured.

1010		8½p. Type 492	20	20
1011		10p. Morris dancing	35	35
1012		11p. Scots piper	40	40
1013		13p. Welsh harpist	45	45

The 8½p. and 13p. commemorate the 800th Anniv of the Royal National Eisteddfod.

1976. 500th Anniv of British Printing. Multicoloured.

1014		8½p. Type 496	20	20
1015		10p. Extract from "The Tretyse of Love"	35	35
1016		11p. Woodcut from "The Game and Playe of Chesse" by William Caxton	40	40
1017		13p. Early printing press	45	45

500 Virgin and Child

1976. Christmas. English Medieval Embroidery. Multicoloured.

1018		6½p. Type 500	15	15
1019		8½p. Angel with crown	20	20
1020		11p. Angel appearing to Shepherds	35	35
1021		13p. The Three Kings	40	40

504 Lawn Tennis

1977. Racket Sports. Multicoloured.

1022		8½p. Type 504	20	20
1023		10p. Table tennis	35	25
1024		11p. Squash	40	30
1025		13p. Badminton	45	35

508

1977.

1026	508	£1 green and olive	3·25	30
1026b		£1.30 brown and blue	5·75	5·25
1026c		£1.33 mauve and black	6·00	6·00
1026d		£1.41 brown and blue	7·00	6·00
1026e		£1.50 olive and black	5·75	4·00
1026f		£1.60 brown and blue	5·75	6·00
1027		£2 green and brown	5·75	1·00
1028		£5 pink and blue	14·00	2·25

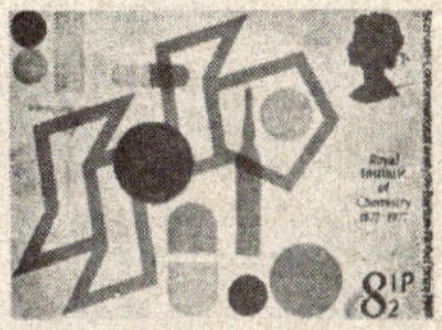

509 Steroids — Conformational Analysis

1977. Centenary of Royal Insitute of Chemistry. Multicoloured.

1029		8½p. Type 509	20	20
1030		10p. Vitamin C — synthesis	30	30
1031		11p. Starch — chromatography	30	30
1032		13p. Salt — crystallography	30	30

513

1977. Silver Jubilee. Multicoloured.

1033		8½p. Type 513	20	20
1034		9p. Type 513	25	25
1035		10p. "Leaf" initials	25	25
1036		11p. "Star" initials	30	30
1037		13p. "Oak" initials	40	40

517 "Gathering of Nations"

518 West European Hedgehog

1977. Commonwealth Heads of Government Meeting, London.

1038	517	13p. multicoloured	50	50

1977. British Wildlife. Multicoloured.

1039		9p. Type 518	40	45
1040		9p. Brown hare	40	45
1041		9p. Eurasian red squirrel	40	45
1042		9p. European otter	40	45
1043		9p. Eurasian badger	40	45

523 "Three French Hens, Two Turtle Doves and a Partridge in a Pear Tree"

1977. Christmas. "The Twelve Days of Christmas". Multicoloured.

1044		7p. Type 523	15	35
1045		7p. "Six Geese a-laying, Five Gold Rings, Four Colly Birds"	15	35
1046		7p. "Eight Maids a-milking, Seven Swans a-Swimming"	15	35
1047		7p. "Ten Pipers piping, Nine Drummers drumming"	15	35
1048		7p. "Twelve Lords a-leaping, Eleven Ladies dancing"	15	35
1049		9p. "A Partridge in a Pear Tree"	20	20

529 Oil — North Sea Production Platform

537 State Coach

533 The Tower of London

1978. Energy Resources. Multicoloured.

1050	9p. Type **529**	25	20
1051	10½p. Coal—modern pithead	25	30
1052	11p. Natural gas—flame rising from sea	30	30
1053	13p. Electricity—nuclear power station and uranium atom	30	30

1978. British Architecture. Historic Buildings. Multicoloured.

1054	9p. Type **533**	25	20
1055	10½p. Holyroodhouse	25	30
1056	11p. Caernarvon Castle	30	30
1057	13p. Hampton Court Palace	30	30

1978. 25th Anniv of Queen's Coronation.

1059	**537** 9p. gold and blue	20	20
1060	– 10½p. gold and red	25	30
1061	– 11p. gold and green	30	30
1062	– 13p. gold and violet	35	30

DESIGNS: 10½p. St. Edward's Crown; 11p. The Sovereign's Orb; 13p. Imperial State Crown.

541 Shire Horse

1978. Horses. Multicoloured.

1063	9p. Type **541**	20	20
1064	10½p. Shetland pony	35	25
1065	11p. Welsh pony	40	30
1066	13p. Thoroughbred	45	35

545 "Penny-farthing" and 1884 Safety Bicycle

1978. Centenaries of Cyclists' Touring Club and British Cycling Federation. Multicoloured.

1067	9p. Type **545**	20	20
1068	10½p. 1920 Touring bicycles	25	25
1069	11p. Modern small-wheeled bicycles	30	30
1070	13p. 1978 Road-racers	35	35

549 Singing Carols round the Christmas Tree

1978. Christmas. Carol-singing. Mult.

1071	7p. Type **549**	20	20
1072	9p. The Waits	25	25
1073	11p. 18th-century carol singers	30	30
1074	13p. "The Boar's Head Carol"	35	35

553 Old English Sheepdog

1979. Dogs. Multicoloured.

1075	9p. Type **553**	20	20
1076	10½p. Welsh springer spaniel	40	40
1077	11p. West Highland terrier	40	40
1078	13p. Irish setter	40	40

557 Primrose

1979. Spring Wild Flowers. Multicoloured.

1079	9p. Type **557**	20	20
1080	10½p. Daffodil	40	40
1081	11p. Bluebell	40	40
1082	13p. Snowdrop	40	40

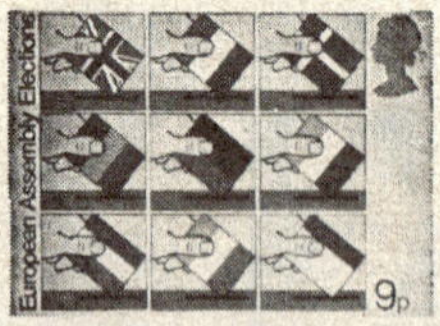

561 Hands placing National Flags into Ballot Boxes

1979. First Direct Elections to European Assembly.

1083	**561** 9p. multicoloured	20	20
1084	– 10½p. multicoloured	30	40
1085	– 11p. multicoloured	30	40
1086	– 13p. multicoloured	30	40

DESIGNS: Nos. 1084/6 differ from Type **561** in the position of the hands and flags.

565 "Saddling 'Mahmoud' for the Derby, 1936" (Sir Alfred Munnings)

1979. Horseracing Paintings. Bicentenary of the Derby (9p). Multicoloured.

1087	9p. Type **565**	25	25
1088	10½p. "The Liverpool Great National Steeple Chase, 1839" (aquatint, F. C. Turner)	30	30
1089	11p. "The First Spring Meeting, Newmarket, 1793" (J. N. Sartorius)	30	30
1090	13p. "Racing at Dorsett Ferry, Windsor, 1684" (Francis Barlow)	30	30

569 "The Tale of Peter Rabbit" (Beatrix Potter)

573 Sir Rowland Hill

1979. International Year of the Child. Multicoloured.

1091	9p. Type **569**	25	20
1092	10½p. "The Wind in the Willows" (Kenneth Grahame)	30	35
1093	11p. "Winnie-the-Pooh" (A. A. Milne)	35	40
1094	13p. "Alice's Adventures in Wonderland" (Lewis Carroll)	50	45

1979. Death Cent of Sir Rowland Hill. Mult.

1095	10p. Type **573**	25	25
1096	11½p. Postman, c. 1839	30	35
1097	13p. London postman, c. 1839	35	40
1098	15p. Woman and young girl with letters, 1840	50	40

577 Policeman on the Beat

1979. 150th Anniv of Metropolitan Police. Mult.

1100	10p. Type **577**	25	25
1101	11½p. Policeman directing traffic	30	35
1102	13p. Mounted policewoman	35	40
1103	15p. River patrol boat	50	40

581 The Three Kings

1979. Christmas. Multicoloured.

1104	8p. Type **581**	20	20
1105	10p. Angel appearing to the Shepherds	25	25
1106	11½p. The Nativity	30	35
1107	13p. Mary and Joseph travelling to Bethlehem	40	40
1108	15p. The Annunciation	50	45

586 Common Kingfisher

1980. Cent of Wild Bird Protection Act. Mult.

1109	10p. Type **586**	25	25
1110	11½p. Dipper	40	35
1111	13p. Moorhen	50	40
1112	15p. Yellow wagtails	55	45

590 "Rocket" approaching Moorish Arch, Liverpool

1980. 150th Anniv of Liverpool and Manchester Railway. Multicoloured.

1113	12p. Type **590**	25	40
1114	12p. First and Second Class carriages passing through Olive Mount cutting	25	40
1115	12p. Third Class carriage and sheep truck crosssing Chat Moss	25	40
1116	12p. Horsebox and carriage truck near Bridgewater Canal	25	40
1117	12p. Truck and mail coach at Manchester	25	40

595 Montage of London Buildings

1980. "London 1980" International Stamp Exn.

1118	**595** 50p. brown	1·50	1·50

596 Buckingham Palace

605 Queen Elizabeth the Queen Mother

601 Charlotte Bronte ("Jane Eyre")

1980. London Landmarks. Multicoloured.

1120	10½p. Type **596**	25	25
1121	12p. The Albert Memorial	30	30
1122	13½p. Royal Opera House	35	35
1123	15p. Hampton Court	40	40
1124	17½p. Kensington Palace	40	40

1980. Famous Authoresses. Multicoloured.

1125	12p. Type **601**	30	30
1126	13½p. George Eliot ("The Mill on the Floss")	35	35
1127	15p. Emily Bronte ("Wuthering Heights")	40	45
1128	17½p. Elizabeth Gaskell ("North and South")	60	60

1980. 80th Birthday of The Queen Mother.

1129	**605** 12p. multicoloured	75	75

606 Sir Henry Wood

610 Running

1980. British Conductors. Multicoloured.

1130	12p. Type **606**	30	30
1131	13½p. Sir Thomas Beecham	35	40
1132	15p. Sir Malcolm Sargent	45	45
1133	17½p. Sir John Barbirolli	55	50

1980. Sport Centenaries. Multicoloured.

1134	12p. Type **610**	30	30
1135	13½p. Rugby	35	40
1136	15p. Boxing	40	40
1137	17½p. Cricket	60	55

CENTENARIES: 12p. Amateur Athletics Association; 13½p. Welsh Rugby Union; 15p. Amateur Boxing Association; 17½p. First England–Australia Test Match.

614 Christmas Tree

1980. Christmas. Multicoloured.

1138	10p. Type **614**	25	25
1139	12p. Candles	30	35
1140	13½p. Mistletoe and apples	35	40
1141	15p. Crown, chains and bell	40	40
1142	17½p. Holly wreath	50	40

619 St. Valentine's Day

1981. Folklore. Multicoloured.

1143	14p. Type **619**	35	35
1144	18p. Morris dancers	45	50
1145	22p. Lammastide	60	60
1146	25p. Medieval mummers	75	70

623 Blind Man with Guide Dog

1981. Int Year of Disabled Persons. Mult.

1147	14p. Type **623**	35	35
1148	18p. Hands spelling "Deaf" in sign language	45	50
1149	22p. Disabled man in wheelchair	60	60
1150	25p. Disabled artist painting with foot	75	70

627 "Aglais urticae"

636 Prince Charles and Lady Diana Spencer

631 Glenfinnan, Scotland

1981. Butterflies. Multicoloured.

1151	14p. Type **627**	35	35
1152	18p. "Maculinea arion"	70	70
1153	22p. "Inachis io"	80	80
1154	25p. "Carterocephalus palaemon"	90	90

1981. 50th Anniv of National Trust for Scotland. British Landscapes. Multicoloured.

1155	14p. Type **631**	30	30
1156	18p. Derwentwater, England	40	40
1157	20p. Stackpole Head, Wales	60	60
1158	22p. Giant's Causeway, Northern Ireland	70	70
1159	25p. St. Kilda, Scotland	80	80

1981. Royal Wedding.

1160 **636**	14p. multicoloured	2·00	1·75
1161	25p. multicoloured	3·00	2·25

637 "Expeditions"

1981. 25th Anniv of Duke of Edinburgh Award Scheme. Multicoloured.

1162	14p. Type **637**	35	35
1163	18p. "Skills"	50	50
1164	22p. "Service"	60	60
1165	25p. "Recreation"	70	70

641 Cockle-dredging from "Linsey II"

1981. Fishing Industry. Multicoloured.

1166	14p. Type **641**	35	35
1167	18p. Hauling in trawl net	50	50
1168	22p. Lobster potting	60	60
1169	25p. Hoisting seine net	70	65

645 Father Christmas

1981. Christmas. Children's Pictures. Mult.

1170	11½p. Type **645**	30	30
1171	14p. Jesus Christ	40	40
1172	18p. Flying Angel	50	50
1173	22p. Joseph and Mary arriving at Bethlehem	60	60
1174	25p. Three Kings approaching Bethlehem	70	70

650 Charles Darwin and Giant Tortoises

1982. Death Cent of Charles Darwin. Mult.

1175	15½p. Type **650**	35	35
1176	19½p. Darwin and Marine iguanas	60	60
1177	26p. Darwin and cactus ground finch and large ground fish	70	70
1178	29p. Darwin and prehistoric skulls	75	75

654 Boys' Brigade

658 Ballerina

1982. Youth Organizations. Multicoloured.

1179	15½p. Type **654**	35	35
1180	19½p. Girls' Brigade	60	50
1181	26p. Boy Scout Movement	85	75
1182	29p. Girl Guides Movement	1·00	90

1982. Europa. British Theatre. Multicoloured.

1183	15½p. Type **658**	35	35
1184	19½p. Harlequin	60	50
1185	26p. Hamlet	90	75
1186	29p. Opera singer	1·25	90

662 Henry VIII and "Mary Rose"

1982. Maritime Heritage. Multicoloured.

1187	15½p. Type **662**	35	35
1188	19½p. Admiral Blake and "Triumph"	60	60
1189	24p. Lord Nelson and H.M.S. "Victory"	70	70
1190	26p. Lord Fisher and H.M.S. "Dreadnought"	80	80
1191	29p. Viscount Cunningham and H.M.S. "Warspite"	90	90

667 "Strawberry Thief" (William Morris)

1982. British Textiles. Multicoloured.

1192	15½p. Type **667**	35	35
1193	19½p. Untitled (Steiner and Co.)	65	65
1194	26p. "Cherry Orchard" (Paul Nash)	80	80
1195	29p. "Chevron" (Andrew Foster)	1·00	1·00

671 Development of Communications. (⅔-size illustration)

1982. Information Technology. Multicoloured.

1196	15½p. Type **671**	45	50
1197	26p. Modern technological aids	80	85

673 Austin "Seven" and "Metro"

1982. British Motor Industry. Multicoloured.

1198	15½p. Type **673**	50	50
1199	19½p. Ford "Model T" and "Escort"	70	70
1200	26p. Jaguar "SS1" and "XJ6"	90	90
1201	29p. Rolls-Royce "Silver Ghost" and "Silver Spirit"	1·25	1·25

677 "While Shepherds Watched"

1982. Christmas. Carols. Multicoloured.

1202	12½p. Type **677**	30	30
1203	15½p. "The Holly and the Ivy"	40	40
1204	19½p. "I saw Three Ships"	70	70
1205	26p. "We Three Kings"	80	80
1206	29p. "Good King Wenceslas"	90	90

682 Atlantic Salmon

1983. British River Fishes. Multicoloured.

1207	15½p. Type **682**	35	35
1208	19½p. Northern pike	65	65
1209	26p. Brown trout	80	80
1210	29p. Eurasian perch	1·00	1·00

686 Tropical Island

1983. Commonwealth Day. Geographical Regions. Multicoloured.

1211	15½p. Type **686**	35	35
1212	19½p. Desert	65	65
1213	26p. Temperate farmland	80	80
1214	29p. Mountain range	1·00	1·00

690 Humber Bridge

1983. Europa. Engineering Achievements. Multicoloured.

1215	16p. Type **690**	45	45
1216	20½p. Thames Flood Barrier	1·10	1·10
1217	28p. "Iolair" (oilfield emergency support vessel)	1·25	1·25

693 Musketeer and Pikeman, The Royal Scots (1633)

698 20th-century Garden, Sissinghurst

1983. British Army Uniforms. Multicoloured.

1218	16p. Type **693**	40	40
1219	20½p. Fusilier and Ensign, The Royal Welsh Fusiliers (mid-18th century)	70	70
1220	26p. Riflemen, 95th Rifles (The Royal Green Jackets) (1805)	85	85
1221	28p. Sergeant (khaki service uniform) and Guardsman (full dress), The Irish Guards (1900)	85	85
1222	31p. Paratroopers, The Parachute Regiment (1983)	1·10	1·10

1983. British Gardens. Multicoloured.

1223	16p. Type **698**	40	40
1224	20½p. 19th-century garden, Biddulph Grange	50	50
1225	28p. 18th-century garden, Blenheim	90	90
1226	31p. 17th-century garden, Pitmedden	1·00	1·00

702 Merry-go-round

1983. British Fairs. Multicoloured.

1227	16p. Type **702**	40	40
1228	20½p. Big wheel, helter-skelter and performing animals	65	65
1229	28p. Side shows	85	85
1230	31p. Early produce fair	90	90

706 "Christmas Post" (pillar-box)

1983. Christmas. Multicoloured.

1231	12½p. Type **706**	30	30
1232	16p. "The Three Kings" (chimney pots)	35	35
1233	20½p. "World at Peace" (dove and blackbird)	60	60
1234	28p. "Light of Christmas" (street lamp)	70	80
1235	31p. "Christmas Dove" (hedge sculpture)	85	1·00

711 Arms of College of Arms

1984. 500th Anniv of College of Arms. Mult.

1236	16p. Type **711**	40	40
1237	20½p. Arms of King Richard III (founder)	60	60
1238	28p. Arms of Earl Marshal of England	85	85
1239	31p. Arms of City of London	95	95

715 Highland Cow

1984. Cattle. Multicoloured.

1240	16p. Type **715**	40	40
1241	20½p. Chillingham wild bull	65	65
1242	26p. Hereford bull	70	70
1243	28p. Welsh black bull	70	70
1244	31p. Irish moiled cow	90	90

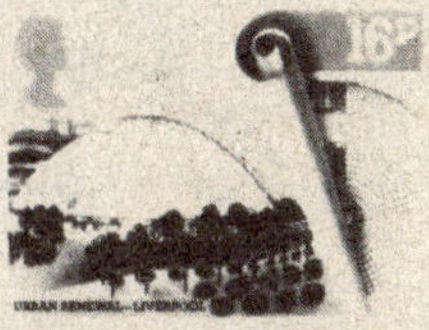

720 Garden Festival Hall, Liverpool

1984. Urban Renewal. Multicoloured.

1245	16p. Type **720**	40	40
1246	20½p. Milburngate Centre, Durham	60	60
1247	28p. Bush House, Bristol	90	90
1248	31p. Commercial Street development, Perth	90	90

725 Abduction of Europa

1984. 25th Anniv of C.E.P.T. (Europa) (Nos. 1249, 1251), and Second Election to European Parliament (others).

1249 –	16p. grey, blue & gold	90	90
1250 **725**	16p. grey, black, & gold	90	90
1251 –	20½p. red, purple & gold	1·60	1·60
1252 **725**	20½p. red, pur, blk, & gold	1·60	1·60

DESIGN: Nos. 1249 and 1251, Bridge (C.E.P.T. 25th anniv logo).

726 Lancaster House

727 View of Earth from "Apollo II"

1984. London Economic Summit Conference.

1253 **726**	31p. multicoloured	1·00	1·00

1984. Centenary of Greenwich Meridian. Mult.

1254	16p. Type **727**	40	40
1255	20½p. Navigational chart of the English Channel	65	65
1256	28p. Greenwich Observatory	85	90
1257	31p. Sir George Airey's Transit Telescope	90	1·10

731 Bath Mail Coach leaving London, 1784

1984. Bicentenary of First Mail Coach Run Bath and Bristol to London. Multicoloured.

1258	16p. Type **731**	65	65
1259	16p. Attack on Exeter Mail, 1816	65	65
1260	16p. Norwich Mail in thunderstorm, 1827	65	65
1261	16p. Holyhead and Liverpool Mails leaving London, 1828	65	65
1262	16p. Edinburgh Mail snowbound, 1831	65	65

736 Nigerian Clinic

1984. 50th Anniv of British Council. Mult.

1263	17p. Type **736**	50	50
1264	22p. Violinist and Acropolis, Athens	65	65
1265	31p. Building project, Sri Lanka	90	90
1266	34p. British Council library, Middle East	1·00	1·00

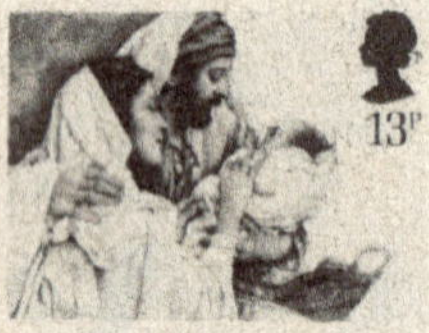

740 The Holy Family

1984. Christmas. Multicoloured.

1267	13p. Type **740**	30	30
1268	17p. Arrival in Bethlehem	50	50
1269	22p. Shepherd and Lamb	60	60
1270	31p. Virgin and Child	95	95
1271	34p. Offering of Frankincense	1·00	1·00

745 "Flying Scotsman"

1985. Famous Trains. Multicoloured.

1272	17p. Type **745**	50	50
1273	22p. "Golden Arrow"	85	70
1274	29p. "Cheltenham Flyer"	1·00	90
1275	31p. "Royal Scot"	1·25	1·00
1276	34p. "Cornish Riviera"	1·40	1·10

750 "Bombus terrestris" (bee)

755 "Water Music" (George Frideric Handel)

1985. Insects. Multicoloured.

1277	17p. Type **750**	40	40
1278	22p. "Coccinella septempunctata" (ladybird)	60	60
1279	29p. "Decticus verrucivorus" (bush-cricket)	80	80
1280	31p. "Lucanus cervus" (stag beetle)	90	90
1281	34p. "Anax imperator" (dragonfly)	90	90

1985. Europa. European Music Year. British Composers. Mutlicoloured.

1282	17p. Type **755**	65	65
1283	22p. "The Planets" Suite (Gustav Holst)	90	90
1284	31p. "The First Cuckoo" (Frederick Delius)	1·40	1·40
1285	34p. "Sea Pictures" (Edward Elgar)	1·50	1·50

759 R.N.L.I. Lifeboat and Signal Flags

1985. Safety at Sea. Multicoloured.

1286	17p. Type **759**	50	50
1287	22p. Beachy Head Lighthouse and chart	65	65
1288	31p. "Marecs A" communications satellite and dish aerials	1·10	1·10
1289	34p. Buoys	1·10	1·10

763 Datapost Motorcyclist, City of London

771 Peter Sellers (from photo by Bill Brandt)

767 King Arthur and Merlin

1985. 350 Years of Royal Mail Public Postal Service. Multicoloured.

1290	17p. Type **763**	50	50
1291	22p. Rural postbus	65	75
1292	31p. Parcel delivery in winter	1·10	1·10
1293	34p. Town letter delivery	1·10	1·10

1985. Arthurian Legends. Multicoloured.

1294	17p. Type **767**	50	50
1295	22p. Lady of the Lake	75	75
1296	31p. Queen Guinevere and Sir Lancelot	1·10	1·10
1297	34p. Sir Galahad	1·25	1·25

1985. British Film Year. Multicoloured.

1298	17p. Type **771**	50	50
1299	22p. David Niven (from photo by Cornell Lucas)	75	75
1300	29p. Charlie Chaplin (from photo by Lord Snowdon)	1·10	1·10
1301	31p. Vivien Leigh (from photo by Angus McBean)	1·25	1·25
1302	34p. Alfred Hitchcock (from photo by Howard Carter)	1·40	1·40

776 Principal Boy

1985. Christmas. Pantomime Characters. Mult.

1303	12p. Type **776**	35	30
1304	17p. Genie	45	40
1305	22p. Dame	70	80
1306	31p. Good fairy	95	1·00
1307	34p. Pantomime cat	1·00	1·10

781 Light Bulb and North Sea Oil Drilling Rig (Energy)

1986. Industry Year. Multicoloured.

1308	17p. Type **781**	45	45
1309	22p. Thermometer and pharmaceutical laboratory (Health)	60	60
1310	31p. Garden hoe and steelworks (Steel)	1·00	1·00
1311	34p. Loaf of bread and cornfield (Agriculture)	1·25	1·25

785 Dr. Edmond Halley as Comet

1986. Appearance of Halley's Comet. Multicoloured.

1312	17p. Type **785**	45	45
1313	22p. "Giotto" spacecraft approaching comet	70	70
1314	31p. "Twice in a lifetime"	1·10	1·10
1315	34p. Comet orbiting sun and planets	1·10	1·10

789 Queen Elizabeth II in 1928, 1942 and 1952

1986. 60th Birthday of Queen Elizabeth II. Multicoloured.

1316	17p. Type **789**	70	40
1317	17p. Queen Elizabeth II in 1958, 1973 and 1982	70	40
1318	34p. Type **789**	1·50	1·50
1319	34p. As No. 1317	1·50	1·50

791 Barn Owl

1986. Europa. Nature Conservation. Endangered Species. Multicoloured.

1320	17p. Type **791**	50	50
1321	22p. Pine marten	90	75
1322	31p. Wild cat	1·40	1·25
1323	34p. Natterjack toad	1·75	1·50

795 Peasants working in Fields

1986. 900th Anniv of Domesday Book. Mult.

1324	17p. Type **795**	50	50
1325	22p. Freemen working at town trades	75	75
1326	31p. Knights and retainers	1·10	1·10
1327	34p. Lord at banquet	1·25	1·25

799 Athletics

1986. 13th Commonwealth Games, Edinburgh, and World Hockey Cup for Men, London. Multicoloured.

1328	17p. Type **799**	50	50
1329	22p. Rowing	70	70
1330	29p. Weightlifting	90	90
1331	31p. Rifle shooting	1·10	1·10
1332	34p. Hockey	1·25	1·25

804 Prince Andrew and Miss Sarah Ferguson (from photo by Gene Nocon)

806 Stylized Cross on Ballot Paper

1986. Royal Wedding.

1333	**804**	12p. multicoloured	60	60
1334	–	17p. multicoloured	90	90

DESIGN: 17p. As Type **804** but with naval motif at foot.

1986. 32nd Commonwealth Parliamentary Association Conference.

1335	**806**	34p. multicoloured	1·25	1·25

807 Lord Dowding and Hawker Hurricane Mk I

1986. History of Royal Air Force. Multicoloured.

1336	17p. Type **807**	50	40
1337	22p. Lord Tedder and Hawker Typhoon IB	75	85
1338	29p. Lord Trenchard and De Havilland D.H.9A	1·00	1·00
1339	31p. Sir Arthur Harris and Avro Type 683 Lancaster	1·25	1·10
1340	34p. Lord Portal and De Havilland D.H.'98 Mosquito	1·50	1·25

Nos. 1336/40 were issued to celebrate 50th anniv of the first R.A.F. Commands.

812 The Glastonbury Thorn

1986. Christmas. Folk Customs. Multicoloured.

1341	12p. Type **812**	50	50
1342	13p. Type **812**	30	30
1343	18p. The Tanad Valley Plygain	45	45
1344	22p. The Hebrides Tribute	65	65
1345	31p. The Dewsbury Church Knell	80	80
1346	34p. The Hereford Boy Bishop	90	90

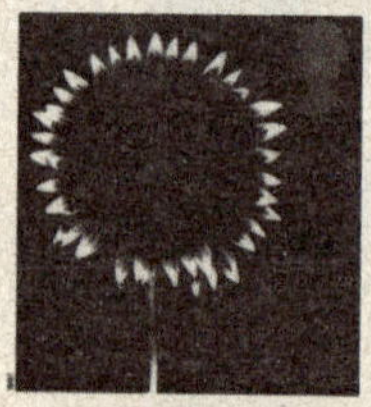
817 North American Blanket Flower

821 "Principia Mathematica"

1987. Flower Photographs by Alfred Lammer. Multicoloured.

1347	18p. Type **817**	50	50
1348	22p. Globe thistle	80	70
1349	31p. "Echeveria"	1·25	1·10
1350	34p. Autumn crocus	1·40	1·25

1987. 300th Anniv of "Principia Mathematica" by Sir Isaac Newton. Multicoloured.

1351	18p. Type **821**	50	50
1352	22p. "Motion of Bodies in Ellipses"	70	70
1353	31p. "Optick Treatise"	1·25	1·25
1354	34p. "The System of the World"	1·40	1·40

825 Willis Faber & Dumas Building, Ipswich

1987. Europa. British Architects in Europe.

1355	18p. Type **825**	50	50
1356	22p. Pompidou Centre, Paris	70	70
1357	31p. Staatsgalerie, Stuttgart	1·10	1·10
1358	34p. European Investment Bank, Luxembourg	1·25	1·25

829 Brigade Members with Ashford Litter, 1887

833 Arms of the Lord Lyon, King of Arms

1987. Centenary of St. John Ambulance Brigade. Multicoloured.

1359	18p. Type **829**	50	50
1360	22p. Bandaging blitz victim, 1940	65	65
1361	31p. Volunteer with fainting girl, 1965	1·10	1·10
1362	34p. Transport of transplant organ by Air Wing, 1987	1·10	1·10

1987. 300th Anniv of Revival of Order of the Thistle. Multicoloured.

1363	18p. Type **833**	50	50
1364	22p. Scottish heraldic banner of Prince Charles	65	65
1365	31p. Arms of Royal Scottish Academy of Painting, Sculpture and Architecture	1·25	1·25
1366	34p. Arms of Royal Society of Edinburgh	1·25	1·25

837 Crystal Palace, "Monarch of the Glen" (Landseer) and Grace Darling

1987. 150th Anniv of Queen Victoria's Accession. Multicoloured.

1367	18p. Type **837**	50	50
1368	22p. "Great Eastern", Beeton's "Book of Household Management" and Prince Albert	75	75
1369	31p. Albert Memorial, ballot box and Disraeli	1·10	1·10
1370	34p. Diamond Jubilee emblem, newspaper placard for Relief of Mafeking and morse key	1·25	1·25

841 Pot by Bernard Leach

1987. Studio Pottery. Multicoloured.

1371	18p. Type **841**	50	50
1372	26p. Pot by Elizabeth Fritsch	70	70
1373	31p. Pot by Lucie Rie	1·10	1·10
1374	34p. Pot by Hans Coper	1·25	1·25

845 Decorating the Christmas Tree

1987. Christmas. Multicoloured.

1375	13p. Type **845**	30	30
1376	18p. Waiting for Father Christmas	50	50
1377	26p. Sleeping child and Father Christmas in sleigh	75	75
1378	31p. Child reading	95	1·10
1379	34p. Child playing recorder and snowman	1·10	1·25

850 Short-spined Seascorpion ("Bull-rout") (Jonathan Couch)

1988. Bicentenary of Linnean Society. Archive Illustrations. Multicoloured.

1380	18p. Type **850**	60	45
1381	26p. Yellow Waterlily (Major Joshua Swatkin)	80	70
1382	31p. Whistling ("Bewick's") Swan (Edward Lear)	1·25	1·10
1383	34p. "Morchella esculenta" (James Sowerby)	1·25	1·10

INDEX

Countries can be quickly located by referring to the index at the end of this volume.

854 Revd. William Morgan (Bible translator, 1588)

1988. 400th Anniversary of Welsh Bible. Mult.

1384	18p. Type **854**	45	45
1385	26p. William Salesbury (New Testament translator, 1567)	70	70
1386	31p. Bishop Richard Davies (New Testament translator, 1567)	1·10	1·10
1387	34p. Bishop Richard Parry (editor of Revised Welsh Bible, 1620)	1·10	1·10

858 Gymnastics (Cent of British Amateur Gymnastics Association)

1988. Sports Organizations. Multicoloured.

1388	18p. Type **858**	45	45
1389	26p. Downhill skiing (Ski Club of Great Britain)	70	70
1390	31p. Tennis (centenary of Lawn Tennis Association)	1·10	1·10
1391	34p. Football (centenary of Football League)	1·10	1·10

862 "Mallard" and Mailbags on Pick-up Arms

1988. Europa. Transport and Mail Services in 1930s. Multicoloured.

1392	18p. Type **862**	50	50
1393	26p. Loading transatlantic mail on liner "Queen Elizabeth"	80	80
1394	31p. Glasgow tram No. 1173 and pillar box	1·10	1·10
1395	34p. Imperial Airways Handley Page "Horatius" and airmail van	1·25	1·25

866 Early Settler and Sailing Clipper

1988. Bicentenary of Australian Settlement. Mult.

1396	18p. Type **866**	60	60
1397	18p. Queen Elizabeth II with British and Australian Parliament Buildings	60	60
1398	34p. W. G. Grace (cricketer) and tennis racquet	1·10	1·10
1399	34p. Shakespeare, John Lennon (entertainer) and Sydney Opera House	1·10	1·10

Stamps in similar designs were also issued by Australia.

870 Spanish Galeasse off The Lizard

1988. 400th Anniv of Spanish Armada. Mult.

1400	18p. Type **870**	65	65
1401	18p. English Fleet leaving Plymouth	65	65
1402	18p. Engagement off Isle of Wight	65	65
1403	18p. Attack of English fire-ships, Calais	65	65
1404	18p. Armada in storm, North Sea	65	65

Nos. 1400/4 were printed together, se-tenant, forming a composite design.

875 "The Owl and the Pussy-cat"

1988. Death Centenary of Edward Lear (artist and author).

1405	**875** 19p. black, cream & red	50	50
1406	– 27p. black, cream & yellow	80	80
1407	– 32p. black, cream & green	1·10	1·10
1408	– 35p. black, cream & blue	1·25	1·25

DESIGNS: 27p. "Edward Lear as a Bird" (self-portrait); 32p. "Cat" (from alphabet book); 35p. "There was a Young Lady whose Bonnet..." (limerick).

879 Carrickfergus Castle

1988.

1410	**879** £1 green	3·00	50
1411	– £1.50 red	4·50	1·25
1412	– £2 blue	6·50	1·75
1413	– £5 brown	15·00	3·50

DESIGNS: £1.50, Caernarfon Castle; £2, Edinburgh Castle; £5, Windsor Castle.

For similar designs, but with silhouette of Queen's head, see Nos. 1611/14.

883 Journey to Bethlehem

1988. Christmas. Christmas Cards. Multicoloured.

1414	14p. Type **883**	35	35
1415	19p. Shepherds and Star	40	45
1416	27p. Three Wise Men	70	70
1417	32p. Nativity	80	1·00
1418	35p. The Annunciation	1·10	1·10

888 Atlantic Puffin

1989. Centenary of Royal Society for the Protection of Birds. Multicoloured.

1419	19p. Type **888**	45	45
1420	27p. Avocet	1·25	1·10
1421	32p. Oystercatcher	1·25	1·10
1422	35p. Northern gannet	1·50	1·25

892 Rose

1989. Greetings Stamps. Multicoloured.

1423	19p. Type **892**	6·25	4·50
1424	19p. Cupid	6·25	4·50
1425	19p. Yachts	6·25	4·50
1426	19p. Fruit	6·25	4·50
1427	19p. Teddy bear	6·25	4·50

897 Fruit and Vegetables

1989. Food and Farming Year. Multicoloured.

1428	19p. Type **897**	50	50
1429	27p. Meat products	80	80
1430	32p. Dairy produce	1·10	1·10
1431	35p. Cereal products	1·25	1·25

901 Mortar Board **905** Toy Train and Airplane

1989. Anniversaries. Multicoloured.

1432	19p. Type **901** (150th anniv of Public Education in England)	1·25	1·25
1433	19p. Cross on Ballot paper (3rd Direct Elections to European Parliament)	1·25	1·25
1434	35p. Posthorn (26th Postal, Telegraph and Telephone International Congress, Brighton)	1·75	1·75
1435	35p. Globe (Inter-Parliamentary Union Centenary Conference, London)	1·75	1·75

1989. Europa. Games and Toys. Multicoloured.

1436	19p. Type **905**	50	50
1437	27p. Building bricks	90	90
1438	32p. Dice and board games	1·25	1·25
1439	35p. Toy robot, boat and doll's house	1·40	1·40

909 Ironbridge, Shropshire **913**

1989. Industrial Archaeology. Multicoloured.

1440	19p. Type **909**	50	50
1441	27p. Tin Mine, St. Agnes Head, Cornwall	90	90
1442	32p. Cotton Mills, New Lanark, Strathclyde	1·10	1·10
1443	35p. Ponteysylte Aqueduct, Clwyd	1·10	1·10

1989.

1663a	**913** (2nd) blue	30	35
1447	(1st) black	1·75	60
1664a	(1st) red	40	45

The above were sold at the current rate for the day.

The 2nd blue and 1st red exist with ordinary or self-adhesive gum.

For 1st class in gold see No. 1979.

915 Snowflake (× 10) **919** Royal Mail Coach

1989. 150th Anniv of Royal Microscopical Society. Multicoloured.

1453	19p. Type **915**	50	50
1454	27p. "Calliphora erythrocephala" (fly) (× 5)	85	85
1455	32p. Blood cells (× 500)	1·25	1·25
1456	35p. Microchip (× 600)	1·40	1·40

1989. Lord Mayor's Show, London. Multicoloured.

1457	20p. Type **919**	80	80
1458	20p. Escort of Blues and Royals	80	80
1459	20p. Lord Mayor's Coach	80	80
1460	20p. Coach team passing St. Paul's	80	80
1461	20p. Blues and Royals drum horse	80	80

This issue commemorates the 800th anniv of the installation of the first Lord Mayor of London.

924 14th-century Peasants from Stained-glass Window

1989. Christmas. 800th Anniv of Ely Cathedral.

1462	**924** 15p. gold, silver & blue	35	35
1463	– 15p. + 1p. gold, silver and blue	50	40
1464	– 20p. + 1p. gold, silver and red	60	50

1465 – 34p. + 1p. gold, silver and green . . . . 1·25 1·40
1466 – 37p. + 1p. gold, silver and green . . . . 1·25 1·40
DESIGNS: 15p. + 1p. Arches and roundels, West Front; 20p. + 1p. Octagon Tower; 34p. + 1p. Arcade from West Transept; 37p. + 1p. Triple arch from West Front.

929 Queen Victoria and Queen Elizabeth II

930 Kitten

1990. 150th Anniv of the Penny Black.
1467 **929** 15p. blue 50 50
1469 20p. black and cream . . 75 75
1471 29p. mauve . . . . . . 1·25 1·25
1473 34p. grey . . . . 1·50 1·25
1474 37p. red . . . . 1·50 1·50

1990. 150th Anniv of Royal Society for Prevention of Cruelty to Animals. Multicoloured.
1479 20p. Type **930** 65 70
1480 29p. Rabbit . . . . 1·25 1·10
1481 34p. Duckling . . . . . . 1·50 1·25
1482 37p. Puppy . . . . 1·60 1·40

934 Teddy Bear

1990. Greetings Stamps. "Smiles". Multicoloured (except No. 1492).
1483 20p. Type **934** . . . . 3·25 2·50
1484 20p. Dennis the Menace . . . 3·25 2·50
1485 20p. Punch . . . . 3·25 2·50
1486 20p. Cheshire Cat . . . . . 3·25 2·50
1487 20p. The Man in the Moon . 3·25 2·50
1488 20p. The Laughing Policeman 3·25 2·50
1489 20p. Clown . . . . 3·25 2·50
1490 20p. Mona Lisa . . . . . . 3·25 2·50
1491 20p. Queen of Hearts . . . . 3·25 2·50
1492 20p. Stan Laurel (comedian) (gold and black) . . . . . 3·25 2·50
See also Nos. 1550/9.

944 Alexandra Palace ("Stamp World London 90" Exhibition)

948 Export Achievement Award

1990. Europa. (Nos. 1493 and 1495) and "Glasgow 1990 European City of Culture" (Nos. 1494 and 1496). Multicoloured.
1493 20p. Type **944** 50 50
1494 20p. Glasgow School of Art . 50 50
1495 29p. British Philatelic Bureau, Edinburgh . . . . 1·10 1·10
1496 37p. Templeton Carpet Factory, Glasgow . . . . 1·25 1·25

1990. 25th Anniv of Queen's Awards for Export and Technology. Multicoloured.
1497 20p. Type **948** 75 75
1498 20p. Technological Achievement Award . . . 75 75
1499 37p. Type **948** . . . . 1·40 1·40
1500 37p. As No. 1498 . . . . . . 1·40 1·40

950 Cycad and Sir Joseph Banks Building

954 Thomas Hardy and Clyffe Clump, Dorset

1990. 150th Anniv of Kew Gardens. Mult.
1502 20p. Type **950** 50 50
1503 29p. Stone pine and Princess of Wales Conservatory . . . 80 80
1504 34p. Willow tree and Palm House . . . . 1·25 1·25
1505 37p. Cedar tree and Pagoda . 1·40 1·40

1990. 150th Anniv of Thomas Hardy (author).
1506 **954** 20p. multicoloured . . . 75 75

955 Queen Elizabeth the Queen Mother

959 Victoria Cross

1990. 90th Birthday of Queen Elizabeth the Queen Mother. Multicoloured.
1507 20p. Type **955** 70 70
1508 29p. Queen Elizabeth . . . 1·10 1·10
1509 34p. Elizabeth, Duchess of York 1·75 1·75
1510 37p. Lady Elizabeth Bowes-Lyon . . . . 2·00 2·00

1990. Gallantry Awards. Multicoloured.
1517 20p. Type **959** 80 80
1518 20p. George Cross 80 80
1519 20p. Distinguished Service Cross and Distinguished Service Medal (horiz) . . 80 80
1520 20p. Military Cross and Military Medal (horiz) . . 80 80
1521 20p. Distinguished Flying Cross and Distinguished Flying Medal (horiz) 80 80

964 Armagh Observatory, Jodrell Bank Radio Telescope and La Palma Telescope

1990. Astronomy. Multicoloured.
1522 22p. Type **964** 50 40
1523 26p. Newton's moon and tides diagram with early telescopes 80 90
1524 31p. Greenwich Old Observatory and early astronomical equipment . 1·00 1·00
1525 37p. Stonehenge, gyroscope and navigating by stars . . . . 1·10 1·10
Nos. 1522/5 commemorate the Centenary of the British Astronomical Association and the Bicentenary of the Armagh Observatory.

968 Building a Snowman

1990. Christmas. Multicoloured.
1526 17p. Type **968** 45 35
1527 22p. Fetching the Christmas tree 55 65
1528 26p. Carol singing 80 80
1529 31p. Tobogganing . . . . . 1·00 1·00
1530 37p. Ice-skating . . . . . . 1·10 1·10

973 "King Charles Spaniel"

988 Michael Faraday, (inventor of electric motor) (birth bicentenary)

978 Thrush's Nest

1991. Dogs. Paintings by George Stubbs. Mult.
1531 22p. Type **973** 75 75
1532 26p. "A Pointer" 90 90
1533 31p. "Two Hounds in a Landscape" . . . . 1·00 1·00
1534 33p. "A Rough Dog" . . . . 1·10 1·10
1535 37p. "Fino and Tiny" . . . 1·25 1·25

1991. Greetings Stamps. "Good Luck". Mult.
1536 (1st) Type **978** . . . . 1·60 1·60
1537 (1st) Shooting star and rainbow 1·60 1·60
1538 (1st) Magpies and charm bracelet . . . . 1·60 1·60
1539 (1st) Black cat . . . . 1·60 1·60
1540 (1st) Common kingfisher with key . . . . 1·60 1·60
1541 (1st) Mallard and frog . . . . 1·60 1·60
1542 (1st) Four-leaf clover in boot and match box . . . . . . 1·60 1·60
1543 (1st) Pot of gold at end of rainbow . . . . 1·60 1·60
1544 (1st) Heart-shaped butterflies 1·60 1·60
1545 (1st) Wishing well and sixpence 1·60 1·60
The background of the stamps forms a composite design.
Nos. 1536/45 were sold at the current rate.

1991. Scientific Achievements. Multicoloured.
1546 22p. Type **988** 65 65
1547 22p. Charles Babbage (computer science pioneer) (birth bicentenary) 65 65
1548 31p. Radar sweep of East Anglia (50th anniv of operational radar network) 95 95
1549 37p. Gloster Whittle E28/39 airplane over East Anglia (50th anniv of first flight of Sir Frank Whittle's jet engine) 1·10 1·10

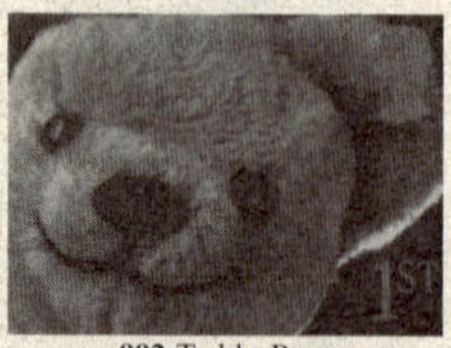

992 Teddy Bear

1991. Greetings Stamps. "Smiles". As Nos. 1483/92, but inscr "1st" as in T **992**. Multicoloured (except No. 1559).
1550 (1st) Type **992** . . . . 1·00 1·00
1551 (1st) Dennis the Menace . . . 1·00 1·00
1552 (1st) Punch . . . . 1·00 1·00
1553 (1st) Cheshire Cat . . . . . . 1·00 1·00
1554 (1st) The Man in the Moon . 1·00 1·00
1555 (1st) The Laughing Policeman 1·00 1·00
1556 (1st) Clown . . . . 1·00 1·00
1557 (1st) Mona Lisa . . . . 1·00 1·00
1558 (1st) Queen of Hearts . . . . 1·00 1·00
1559 (1st) Stan Laurel (comedian) (gold and black) . . . . . 1·00 1·00
Nos. 1550/9 were sold at the current rate.

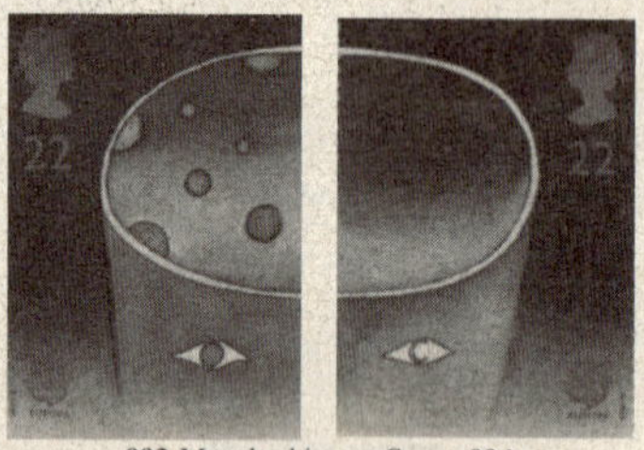

993 Man looking at Space 994

1991. Europa. Europe in Space. Multicoloured.
1560 22p. Type **993** 55 55
1561 22p. Type **994** 55 55
1562 37p. Space looking at Man (Queen's head on left) . . . 1·10 1·10
1563 37p. Similar to No. 1562 (Queen's head on right) . . 1·10 1·10
Stamps of the same value were printed together in horizontal pairs, each pair forming a composite design.

997 Fencing

1001 "Silver Jubilee"

1991. World Student Games, Sheffield (Nos. 1564/6) and World Cup Rugby Championship (No. 1567).
1564 22p. Type **997** 50 50
1565 26p. Hurdling 80 80
1566 31p. Diving 95 95
1567 37p. Rugby . . . . 1·10 1·10

1991. 9th World Congress of Roses, Belfast. Multicoloured.
1568 22p. Type **1001** 80 80
1569 26p. "Mme Alfred Carriere" . 1·00 1·00
1570 31p. "Rosa moyesii" . . . . 1·10 1·10
1571 33p. "Harvest Fayre" . . . . 1·25 1·25
1572 37p. "Mutabilis" . . . . . . 1·40 1·40

INDEX

Countries can be quickly located by referring to the index at the end of this volume.

1006 Iguanodon

1991. 150th Anniv of Dinosaurs' Identification by Owen. Multicoloured.
1573 22p. Type **1006** 75 60
1574 26p. Stegosaurus . . . . . . 90 1·10
1575 31p. Tyrannosaurus . . . . 1·10 1·10
1576 33p. Protoceratops . . . . . 1·40 1·25
1577 37p. Triceratops . . . . . . 1·50 1·50

1011 Map of 1816

1991. Bicentenary of Ordnance Survey. Maps of Hamstreet, Kent.
1578 **1011** 24p. black, mauve and cream 50 50
1579 – 28p. multicoloured . . 85 85
1580 – 33p. multicoloured . . 1·00 1·00
1581 – 39p. multicoloured . . 1·25 1·25
DESIGNS: 28p. Map of 1906; 33p. Map of 1959; 39p. Map of 1991.

1015 Adoration of the Magi

1991. Christmas. Illuminated Letters from "Acts of Mary and Jesus" Manuscript in Bodleian Library, Oxford. Multicoloured.
1582 18p. Type **1015** 70 40
1583 24p. Mary and Baby Jesus in the Stable 80 50
1584 28p. The Holy Family and Angel . . . . 85 1·00
1585 33p. The Annunciation . . . 95 1·10
1586 39p. The Flight into Egypt . 1·10 1·40

1020 Fallow Deer in Scottish Forest

1992. The Four Seasons. Wintertime. Multicoloured.
1587 18p. Type **1020** 50 50
1588 24p. Hare on North Yorkshire moors 70 70
1589 28p. Fox in the Fens . . . 90 90
1590 33p. Redwing and Home Counties village . . . . . 1·10 1·10
1591 39p. Welsh mountain sheep in Snowdonia . . . . . . 1·25 1·25

1025 Flower Spray

1992. Greetings Stamps. "Memories". Multicoloured.
1592 (1st) Type **1025** 90 90
1593 (1st) Double locket 90 90
1594 (1st) Key 90 90
1595 (1st) Model car and cigarette cards 90 90
1596 (1st) Compass and map . . . 90 90
1597 (1st) Pocket watch 90 90
1598 (1st) 1854 1d. Red stamp and pen 90 90
1599 (1st) Pearl necklace 90 90
1600 (1st) Marbles 90 90
1601 (1st) Bucket, spade and starfish 90 90
Nos. 1592/1601 were issued together, se-tenant, the backgrounds forming a composite design.

1035 Queen Elizabeth in Coronation Robes and Parliamentary Emblem

1992. 40th Anniversary of Accession. Multicoloured.

1602	24p. Type **1035**	1·40	1·40
1603	24p. Queen Elizabeth in Garter robes and archiepiscopal arms	1·40	1·40
1604	24p. Queen Elizabeth with baby Prince Andrew and Royal Arms	1·40	1·40
1605	24p. Queen Elizabeth at Trooping the Colour	1·40	1·40
1606	24p. Queen Elizabeth and Commonwealth emblem	1·40	1·40

1040 Tennyson in 1888 and "The Beguiling of Merlin" (Sir Edward Burne-Jones)

1992. Death Centenary of Alfred, Lord Tennyson (poet). Multicoloured.

1607	24p. Type **1040**	50	50
1608	28p. Tennyson in 1856 and "April Love" (Arthur Hughes)	75	75
1609	33p. Tennyson in 1864 and "I am Sick of the Shadows" (John Waterhouse)	1·25	1·25
1610	39p. Tennyson as a young man and "Mariana" (Dante Gabriel Rossetti)	1·40	1·40

1044 Carrickfergus Castle

1992. Designs as Nos. 1410/13, but showing Queen's head in silhouette as T **1044**.

1611	**1044**	£1 green and gold	5·00	1 50
1993	–	£1.50 purple & gold	2·25	2·40
1994	–	£2 blue and gold	3·00	3·25
1995	–	£3 violet and gold	4·50	4·75
1996	–	£5 brown and gold	7·50	7·75

The Queen's head on these stamps is printed in optically variable ink which changes colour from gold to green when viewed from different angles.

1045 British Olympic Association Logo (Olympic Games, Barcelona)

1992. Europa. International Events. Mult.

1615	24p. Type **1045**	75	75
1616	24p. British Paralympic Association symbol (Paralympics 92, Barcelona)	75	75
1617	24p. "Santa Maria" (500th anniv of discovery of America by Columbus)	75	75
1618	39p. "Kaisei" (Japanese cadet brigantine), (Grand Regatta Columbus, 1992)	1·10	1·10
1619	39p. British Pavilion, "EXPO '92", Seville	1·10	1·10

1050 Pikeman

1054 "The Yeomen of the Guard"

1992. 350th Anniversary of the Civil War. Mult.

1620	24p. Type **1050**	55	55
1621	28p. Drummer	70	70
1622	33p. Musketeer	1·25	1·25
1623	39p. Standard Bearer	1·40	1·40

1992. 150th Birth Anniv of Sir Arthur Sullivan (composer). Gilbert and Sullivan Operas. Multicoloured.

1624	18p. Type **1054**	45	45
1625	24p. "The Gondoliers"	60	60
1626	28p. "The Mikado"	75	75
1627	33p. "The Pirates of Penzance"	1·25	1·25
1628	39p. "Iolanthe"	1·40	1·40

1059 "Acid Rain Kills"

1992. Protection of the Environment. Children's Paintings. Multicoloured.

1629	24p. Type **1059**	60	60
1630	28p. "Ozone Layer"	90	90
1631	33p. "Greenhouse Effect"	1·00	1·00
1632	39p. "Bird of Hope"	1·10	1·10

1063 European Star

1992. Single European Market.

1633	**1063**	24p. multicoloured	75	75

1064 "Angel Gabriel", St. James's, Pangbourne

1992. Christmas. Stained Glass Windows. Multicoloured.

1634	18p. Type **1064**	40	40
1653	24p. "Madonna and Child", St. Mary's, Bibury	65	65
1636	28p. "King with Gold", Our Lady and St. Peter, Leatherhead	80	80
1637	33p. "Shepherds", All Saints, Porthcawl	95	95
1638	39p. "Kings with Frankincense and Myrrh", Our Lady and St. Peter, Leatherhead	1·10	1·10

1069 Mute Swan Cob and St. Catherine's Chapel, Abbotsbury

1993. 600th Anniv of Abbotsbury Swannery. Multicoloured.

1639	18p. Type **1069**	1·50	85
1640	24p. Cygnet and decoy	1·00	1·10
1641	28p. Swans and cygnet	1·25	1·60
1642	33p. Eggs in nest and tithe barn, Abbotsbury	2·00	1·75
1643	39p. Young swan and the Fleet	2·25	2·25

1074 Long John Silver and Parrot ("Treasure Island")

1993. Greetings Stamps. "Gift Giving". Gold, cream and black (No. 1645) or multicoloured (others).

1644	(1st) Type **1074**	95	85
1645	(1st) Tweedledum and Tweedledee ("Alice Through the Looking Glass")	95	85
1646	(1st) William ("William" books)	95	85
1647	(1st) Mole and Toad ("The Wind in the Willows")	95	85
1648	(1st) Teacher and Wilfrid ("The Bash Street Kids")	95	85
1649	(1st) Peter Rabbit and Mrs. Rabbit ("The Tale of Peter Rabbit")	95	85
1650	(1st) Snowman ("The Snowman") and Father Christmas ("Father Christmas")	95	85
1651	(1st) The Big Friendly Giant and Sophie ("The BFG")	95	85
1652	(1st) Bill Badger and Rupert Bear	95	85
1653	(1st) Aladdin and the Genie	95	85

1084 Decorated Enamel Dial

1993. 300th Birth Anniv of John Harrison (inventor of the marine chronometer). Details of "H4" Clock. Multicoloured.

1654	24p. Type **1084**	50	50
1655	28p. Escapement remontoire and fusee	85	85
1656	33p. Balance, spring and temperature compensator	1·10	1·10
1657	39p. Back of movement	1·25	1·25

1088 "Britannia"

1993.

1658	**1088**	£10 multicoloured	15·00	6·00

1089 "Dendrobium hellwigianum"

1993. 14th World Orchid Conference, Glasgow. Multicoloured.

1659	18p. Type **1089**	40	40
1660	24p. "Paphiopedilum" Maudiae "Magnificum"	65	65
1661	28p. "Cymbidium lowianum"	90	90
1662	33p. "Vanda" Rothschildiana	1·10	1·10
1663	39p. "Dendrobium vexillarius var albiviride"	1·40	1·40

1094 "Family Group" (bronze sculpture) (Henry Moore)

1993. Europa. Contemporary Art. Multicoloured.

1767	24p. Type **1094**	50	50
1768	28p. "Kew Gardens" (lithograph) (Edward Bawden)	80	80
1769	33p. "St. Francis and the Birds" (Stanley Spencer)	95	95
1770	39p. "Still Life: Odyssey I" (Ben Nicholson)	1·10	1·10

1098 Emperor Claudius (from gold coin)

1993. Roman Britain. Multicoloured.

1771	24p. Type **1098**	50	50
1772	28p. Emperor Hadrian (bronze head)	80	80
1773	33p. Goddess Roma (from gemstone)	95	95
1774	39p. Christ (Hinton St. Mary mosaic)	1·10	1·10

1102 "Midland Maid" and other Narrow Boats, Grand Junction Canal

1993. Inland Waterways. Multicoloured.

1775	24p. Type **1102**	50	50
1776	28p. "Yorkshire Lass" and other Humber keels, Stainforth and Keadby Canal	80	80
1777	35p. "Valley Princess" and other horse-drawn barges, Brecknock and Abergavenny Canal	95	95
1778	39p. Steam barges, including "Pride of Scotland", and fishing boats, Crinan Canal	1·10	1·10

Nos. 1775/8 commemorate the bicentenary of the Acts of Parliament authorising the canals depicted.

1106 Horse Chestnut

1993. The Four Seasons. Autumn. Fruits and Leaves. Multicoloured.

1779	18p. Type **1106**	40	40
1780	24p. Blackberry	65	65
1781	28p. Hazel	90	90
1782	33p. Rowan	1·10	1·10
1783	39p. Pear	1·40	1·40

1111 "The Reigate Squire"

1116

1993. Sherlock Holmes. Centenary of the Publication of "The Final Problem". Multicoloured.

1784	24p. Type **1111**	1·00	1·00
1785	24p. "The Hound of the Baskervilles"	1·00	1·00
1786	24p. "The Six Napoleons"	1·00	1·00
1787	24p. "The Greek Interpreter"	1·00	1·00
1788	24p. "The Final Problem"	1·00	1·00

1993. Self-adhesive.

1976	**1116**	(2nd) blue	1·00	1·00
1977		(1st) red	1·00	1·00

Nos. 1976/7 were sold at the current rates.

1117 Bob Cratchit and Tiny Tim

1993. Christmas. 150th Anniv of Publication of "A Christmas Carol" by Charles Dickens. Multicoloured.

1790	19p. Type **1117**	40	40
1791	25p. Mr. and Mrs. Fezziwig	70	70
1792	30p. Scrooge	1·00	1·00
1793	35p. The prize turkey	1·10	1·10
1794	41p. Mr. Scrooge's nephew	1·25	1·25

1122 Class 5 No. 44957 and Class B1 No. 61342 on West Highland Line

1994. The Age of Steam. Railway Photographs by Colin Gifford.

1795	**1122**	19p. green, grey & blk	45	40
1796	–	25p. lilac, grey & black	75	65
1797	–	30p. brown, grey & blk	1·00	90
1798	–	35p. purple, grey & blk	1·25	1·10
1799	–	41p. blue, grey & black	1·40	1·25

DESIGNS: 25p. Class A1 No. 60149 "Amadis" at Kings Cross; 30p. Class 4 No. 43000 on turntable at Blyth North; 35p. Class 4 No. 42455 near Wigan Central; 41p. Class "Castle" No. 7002 "Devizes Castle" on bridge crossing Worcester and Birmingham Canal.

1127 Dan Dare and the Mekon

1994. Greetings Stamps. "Messages". Mult.

1800	(1st) Type **1127**	90	90
1801	(1st) The Three Bears	90	90
1802	(1st) Rupert Bear	90	90
1803	(1st) Alice ("Alice in Wonderland")	90	90
1804	(1st) Noggin and The Ice Dragon	90	90
1805	(1st) Peter Rabbit posting a letter	90	90
1806	(1st) Red Riding Hood and wolf	90	90
1807	(1st) Orlando the Marmalade Cat	90	90
1808	(1st) Biggles	90	90
1809	(1st) Paddington Bear on station	90	90

Castell Y Waun/Chirk Castle, Clwyd, Cymru/Wales

1137 Castell Y Waun (Chirk Castle), Clwyd, Wales

1994. 25th Anniv of Investiture of the Prince of Wales. Paintings by Prince Charles. Multicoloured.

1810	19p. Type **1137**	40	40
1811	25p. Ben Arkle, Sutherland, Scotland	75	75
1812	30p. Mourne Mountains, County Down, Northern Ireland	1·00	1·00
1813	35p. Dersingham, Norfolk, England	1·10	1·10
1814	41p. Dolwyddelan, Gwynedd, Wales	1·25	1·25

1142 Bather at Blackpool

1994. Centenary of Picture Postcards. Mult.

1815	19p. Type **1142**	45	45
1816	25p. "Where's my Little Lad?"	75	75
1817	30p. "Wish You were Here!"	90	90
1818	35p. Punch and Judy show	1·10	1·10
1819	41p. "The Tower Crane" machine	1·25	1·25

1147 British Lion and French Cockerel over Tunnel

1994. Opening of Channel Tunnel. Multicoloured.

1820	25p. Type **1147**	75	75
1821	25p. Symbolic hands over train	75	75
1822	41p. Type **1147**	1·50	1·50
1823	41p. As No. 1821	1·50	1·50

1149 Groundcrew replacing Smoke Canisters on Douglas Boston of 88 Sqn

1994. 50th Anniv of D-Day. Multicoloured.

1824	25p. Type **1149**	1·00	1·00
1825	25p. H.M.S. "Warspite" (battleship) shelling enemy positions	1·00	1·00
1826	25p. Commandos landing on Gold Beach	1·00	1·00
1827	25p. Infantry regrouping on Sword Beach	1·00	1·00
1828	25p. Tank and infantry advancing, Ouistreham	1·00	1·00

1154 The Old Course, St. Andrews

1994. Scottish Golf Courses. Multicoloured.

1829	19p. Type **1154**	55	55
1830	25p. The 18th Hole, Muirfield	80	80
1831	30p. The 15th Hole ("Luckyslap"), Carnoustie	1·00	1·00
1832	35p. The 8th Hole ("The Postage Stamp"), Royal Troon	1·25	1·25
1833	41p. The 9th Hole, Turnberry	1·40	1·40

Nos. 1829/33 commemorate the 250th anniversary of golf's first set of rules produced by the Honourable Company of Edinburgh Golfers.

1159 Royal Welsh Show, Llanelwedd

1994. The Four Seasons. Summertime. Multicoloured.

1834	19p. Type **1159**	50	50
1835	25p. All England Tennis Championships, Wimbledon	75	75
1836	30p. Cowes Week	1·10	1·10
1837	35p. Test Match, Lord's	1·25	1·25
1838	41p. Braemar Gathering	1·40	1·40

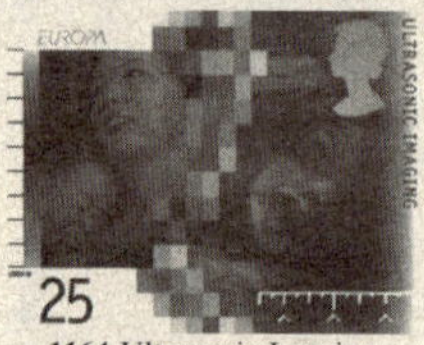

1164 Ultrasonic Imaging

1994. Europa. Medical Discoveries. Multicoloured.

1839	25p. Type **1164**	65	65
1840	30p. Scanning electron microscopy	85	85
1841	35p. Magnetic resonance imaging	90	90
1842	41p. Computed tomography	1·00	1·00

1168 Mary and Joseph

1994. Christmas. Children's Nativity Plays. Multicoloured.

1843	19p. Type **1168**	60	60
1844	25p. Three Wise Men	80	80
1845	30p. Mary with doll	90	90
1846	35p. Shepherds	1·00	1·00
1847	41p. Angels	1·10	1·10

1173 Sophie (black cat)

1995. Cats. Multicoloured.

1848	19p. Type **1173**	60	60
1849	25p. Puskas (Siamese) and Tigger (tabby)	75	75
1850	30p. Chloe (ginger cat)	1·00	1·00
1851	35p. Kikko (tortoiseshell) and Rosie (Abyssinian)	1·10	1·10
1852	41p. Fred (black and white cat)	1·25	1·25

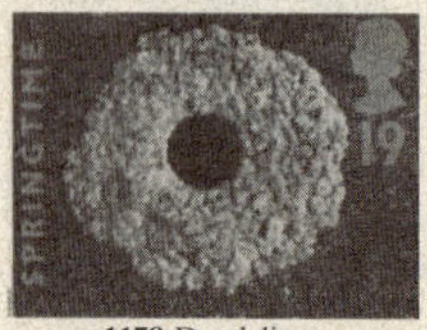

1178 Dandelions

1995. The Four Seasons. Springtime. Plant Sculptures by Andy Goldsworthy. Multicoloured.

1853	19p. Type **1178**	65	65
1854	25p. Sweet chestnut leaves	75	75
1855	30p. Garlic leaves	1·10	1·10
1856	35p. Hazel leaves	1·10	1·10
1857	41p. Spring grass	1·40	1·40

1183 "La Danse a la Campagne" (Renoir)

1995. Greetings Stamps. "Greetings in Art".

1858	**1183** (1st) multicoloured	40	45
1859	– (1st) multicoloured	40	45
1860	– (1st) multicoloured	40	45
1861	– (1st) multicoloured	40	45
1862	– (1st) multicoloured	40	45
1863	– (1st) multicoloured	40	45
1864	– (1st) brown and silver	40	45
1865	– (1st) multicoloured	40	45
1866	– (1st) multicoloured	40	45
1867	– (1st) black, yellow and silver	40	45

DESIGNS: No. 1859, "Troilus and Criseyde" (Peter Brookes); 1860, "The Kiss" (Rodin); 1861, "Girls on the Town" (Beryl Cook); 1862, "Jazz" (Andrew Mockett); 1863, "Girls performing a Kathak Dance" (Aurangzeb period); 1864, "Alice Keppel with her Daughter" (Alice Hughes); 1865, "Children Playing" (L. S. Lowry); 1866, "Circus Clowns" (Emily Firmin and Justin Mitchell); 1867, Decoration from "All the Love Poems of Shakespeare" (Eric Gill).

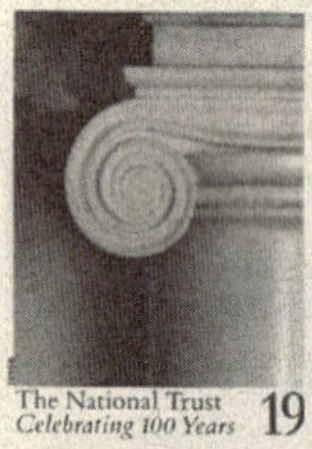

1193 Fireplace Decoration, Attingham Park, Shropshire

1198 British Troops and French Civilians celebrating

1995. Centenary of The National Trust. Multicoloured.

1868	19p. Type **1193**	55	55
1869	25p. Oak seedling	75	75
1870	30p. Carved table leg, Attingham Park	90	90
1871	35p. St. David's Head, Dyfed, Wales	1·00	1·00
1872	41p. Elizabethan window, Little Moreton Hall, Cheshire	1·25	1·25

1995. Europa. Peace and Freedom.

1873	**1198** 19p. silver, brown and black	60	60
1874	– 19p. multicoloured	60	60
1875	– 25p. silver, blue and black	85	85
1876	– 25p. multicoloured	85	85
1877	– 30p. multicoloured	1·00	1·00

DESIGNS: No. 1874, Symbolic hands and Red Cross; 1875, St. Paul's Cathedral and searchlights; 1876, Symbolic hand releasing peace dove; 1877, Symbolic hands.

Nos. 1873 and 1875 commemorate the 50th anniversary of the end of the Second World War, No. 1874 the 125th anniversary of the British Red Cross Society and Nos. 1876/7 the 50th anniversary of the United Nations.

Nos. 1876/7 include the "EUROPA" emblem.

1203 "The Time Machine"

1995. Science Fiction. Novels by H. G. Wells. Multicoloured.

1878	25p. Type **1203**	65	65
1879	30p. "The First Men in the Moon"	95	95
1880	35p. "The War of the Worlds"	1·00	1·00
1881	41p. "The Shape of Things to Come"	1·10	1·10

Nos. 1878/81 commemorate the centenary of publication of Wells's "The Time Machine".

1207 The Swan, 1595

1995. Reconstruction of Shakespeare's Globe Theatre. Multicoloured.

1882	25p. Type **1207**	80	80
1883	25p. The Rose, 1592	80	80
1884	25p. The Globe, 1599	80	80
1885	25p. The Hope, 1613	80	80
1886	25p. The Globe, 1614	80	80

Nos. 1882/6 were printed together, se-tenant, forming a composite design.

1212 Sir Rowland Hill and Uniform Penny Postage Petition

1995. Pioneers of Communications.

1887	**1212** 19p. silver, red and black	55	55
1888	– 25p. silver, brown and black	80	80
1889	– 41p. silver, green and black	1·10	1·10
1890	– 60p. silver, blue and black	1·50	1·50

DESIGNS: 25p. Hill and Penny Black; 41p. Guglielmo Marconi and early wireless; 60p. Marconi and sinking of "Titanic" (liner).

Nos. 1887/8 mark the birth bicentenary of Sir Rowland Hill and Nos. 1889/90 the centenary of the first radio transmissions.

1216 Harold Wagstaff

1995. Centenary of Rugby League. Multicoloured.

1891	19p. Type **1216**	55	55
1892	25p. Gus Risman	70	70
1893	30p. Jim Sullivan	80	80
1894	35p. Billy Batten	1·00	1·00
1895	41p. Brian Bevan	1·40	1·40

1221 European Robin in Mouth of Pillar Box

1995. Christmas. Christmas Robins. Multicoloured.

1896	19p. Type **1221**	45	45
1897	25p. European robin on railings and holly	60	60
1898	30p. European robin on snow-covered milk bottles	80	80
1899	41p. European robin on road sign	1·10	1·10
1900	60p. European robin on door knob and Christmas wreath	1·50	1·50

1226 Opening Lines of "To a Mouse" and Fieldmouse

1996. Death Bicentenary of Robert Burns (Scottish poet).

1901	**1226** 19p. cream, brown and black	55	55
1902	– 25p. multicoloured	80	80
1903	– 41p. multicoloured	1·10	1·10
1904	– 60p. multicoloured	1·50	1·50

DESIGNS: 25p. "O my Luve's like a red, red rose" and wild rose; 41p. "Scots, wha hae wi Wallace bled" and Sir William Wallace; 60p. "Auld Lang Syne" and highland dancers.

1230 "MORE! LOVE" (Mel Calman)

1996. Greetings Stamps. Cartoons.

1905	**1230** (1st) black and mauve	40	45
1906	– (1st) black and green	40	45
1907	– (1st) black and blue	40	45
1908	– (1st) black and violet	40	45
1909	– (1st) black and red	40	45

1910 – (1st) black and blue . . . 40 45
1911 – (1st) black and red . . . 40 45
1912 – (1st) black and violet . . 40 45
1913 – (1st) black and green . . 40 45
1914 – (1st) black and mauve . . 40 45

DESIGNS: No. 1906, "Sincerely" (Charles Barsotti); 1907, "Do you have something for the HUMAN CONDITION?" (Mel Calman); 1908, "MENTAL FLOSS" (Leo Cullum); 1909, "4.55 P.M." (Charles Barsotti); 1910, "Dear lottery prize winner" (Larry); 1911, "I'm writing to you because...." (Mel Calman); 1912, "FETCH THIS, FETCH THAT" (Charles Barsotti); 1913, "My day starts before I'm ready for it" (Mel Calman); 1914, "THE CHEQUE IN THE POST" (Jack Ziegler).

Nos. 1905/14 were sold at the current rate.

1240 "Muscovy Duck"

1996. 50th Anniv of the Wildfowl and Wetlands Trust. Bird paintings by C. F. Tunnicliffe. Multicoloured.
1915 19p. Type **1240** 50 50
1916 25p. "Lapwing" 70 70
1917 30p. "White-fronted Goose" . 80 80
1918 35p. "Bittern" . . . . 1·10 1·10
1919 41p. "Whooper Swan" . . . 1·40 1·40

1245 The Odeon, Harrogate

1996. Centenary of Cinema.
1920 **1245** 19p. multicoloured . . . 50 50
1921 – 25p. multicoloured . . . 70 70
1922 – 30p. multicoloured . . . 80 80
1923 – 35p. black, red and silver . . . . 1·10 1·10
1924 – 41p. multicoloured . . . 1·40 1·40

DESIGNS: 25p. Laurence Olivier and Vivien Leigh in "Lady Hamilton" (film); 30p. Old cinema ticket; 35p. Pathe News still; 41p. Cinema sign, The Odeon, Manchester.

1250 Dixie Dean

1996. European Football Championship. Multicoloured.
1925 19p. Type **1250** 40 40
1926 25p. Bobby Moore 70 70
1927 35p. Duncan Edwards . . . 1·25 1·25
1928 41p. Billy Wright . . . . . . 1·25 1·25
1929 60p. Danny Blanchflower . . 1·60 1 60

1255 Athlete on Starting Blocks

1996. Olympic and Paralympic Games, Atlanta. Multicoloured.
1930 26p. Type **1255** 90 90
1931 26p. Throwing the javelin . . 90 90
1932 26p. Basketball 90 90
1933 26p. Swimming 90 90
1934 26p. Athlete celebrating and Olympic Rings 90 90

1260 Prof. Dorothy Hodgkin (scientist)

1996. Europa. Famous Women.
1935 **1260** 20p. green, grey and black 50 50
1936 – 26p. mauve, grey & black 70 70
1937 – 31p. bronze, grey and black 90 90
1938 – 37p. silver, grey and black . . . . 1·10 1·10
1939 – 43p. gold, grey and black . . . . 1·25 1·25

DESIGNS: 26p. Dame Margot Fonteyn (ballerina); 31p. Dame Elisabeth Frink (sculptress); 37p. Dame Daphne du Maurier (novelist); 43p. Dame Marea Hartman (sports administrator).

Nos. 1936/7 include the "EUROPA" emblem.

1265 "Muffin the Mule"

1996. 50th Anniv of Children's Television. Multicoloured.
1940 20p. Type **1265** 55 55
1941 26p. "Sooty" 80 80
1942 31p. "Stingray" . . . . . . 1·00 1·00
1943 37p. "The Clangers" . . . . 1·25 1·25
1944 43p. "Dangermouse" . . . . 1·40 1·40

1270 Triumph TR3

1996. Classic Sports Cars. Multicoloured.
1945 20p. Type **1270** 60 60
1946 26p. MG TD 70 70
1947 37p. Austin-Healey 100 . . 1·00 1·00
1948 43p. Jaguar XK120 . . . . 1·10 1·10
1949 63p. Morgan Plus 4 . . . . 1·50 1·50

1275 The Three Kings

1996. Christmas. Multicoloured.
1950 (2nd) Type **1275** 60 60
1951 (1st) The Annunciation . . . 75 75
1952 31p. The Journey to Bethlehem 85 85
1953 43p. The Nativity . . . . . 1·10 1·10
1954 63p. The Shepherds . . . . 1·50 1·50

1280 "Gentiana acaulis" (Georg Ehret)

1997. Greeting Stamps. 19th-century Flower Paintings. Multicoloured.
1955 (1st) Type **1280** 40 45
1956 (1st) "Magnolia grandiflora" (Ehret) 40 45
1957 (1st) "Camellia japonica" (Alfred Chandler) 40 45
1958 (1st) "Tulipa" (Ehret) . . . 40 45
1959 (1st) "Fuchsia" "Princess of Wales" (Augusta Withers) 40 45
1960 (1st) "Tulipa gesneriana" (Ehret) 40 45
1961 (1st) "Guzmania splendens" (Charlotte Sowerby) . . . 40 45
1962 (1st) "Iris latifolia" (Ehret) . . 40 45
1963 (1st) "Hippeastrum rutilum" (Pierre-Joseph Redoute) . 40 45
1964 (1st) "Passiflora coerulea" (Ehret) 40 45

1290 "King Henry VIII"

1997. 450th Death Anniv of King Henry VIII. Multicoloured.
1965 26p. Type **1290** 75 75
1966 26p. "Catherine of Aragon" . . 75 75
1967 26p. "Anne Boleyn" 75 75
1968 26p. "Jane Seymour" 75 75
1969 26p. "Anne of Cleves" . . . 75 75
1970 26p. "Catherine Howard" . . 75 75
1971 26p. "Catherine Parr" . . . 75 75

1297 St. Columba in Boat

1303 "Dracula"

1997. Religious Anniversaries. Multicoloured.
1972 26p. Type **1297** 70 70
1973 37p. St. Columba on Iona . . 1·00 1·00
1974 43p. St. Augustine with King Ethelbert . . . . 1·25 1·25
1975 63p. St. Augustine with Model of Cathedral . . . . 1·75 1·75

Nos. 1972/3 commemorate the 1400th death anniversary of St. Columba and Nos. 1974/5 the 1400th anniversary of the arrival of St. Augustine of Canterbury in Kent.

1997. Royal Golden Wedding (1st issue). Designs as T **367** and **913** but colours changed.
1978 **367** 26p. gold 80 80
1979 **913** (1st) gold 80 80

See also Nos. 2011/14.

1997. Europa. Tales and Legends. Horror Stories. Multicoloured.
1980 26p. Type **1303** . . . . 1·00 1·00
1981 31p. "Frankenstein" . . . . 1·10 1·10
1982 37p. "Dr. Jekyll and Mr. Hyde" . . . . 1·25 1·25
1983 43p. "The Hound of the Baskervilles" . . . . 1·25 1·25

Nos. 1980/3 commemorate the birth bicentenary of Mary Shelley (creator of Frankenstein) with the 26p. and 31p. values incorporating the "EUROPA" emblem.

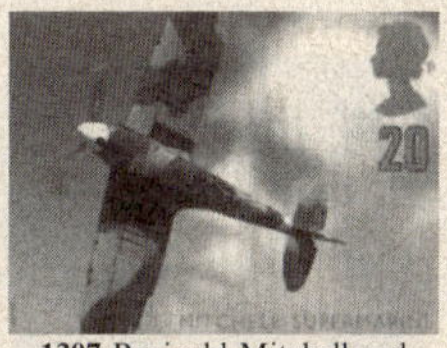
1307 Reginald Mitchell and Supermarine Spitfire MkIIA

1997. British Aircraft Designers. Multicoloured.
1984 20p. Type **1307** 55 55
1985 26p. Roy Chadwick and Avro Lancaster MkI 95 95
1986 37p. Ronald Bishop and De Havilland Mosquito B MkXVI . . . . 1·10 1·10
1987 43p. George Carter and Gloster Meteor T Mk7 . . . . . . 1·25 1·25
1988 63p. Sir Sidney Camm and Hawker Hunter FGA Mk9 1·75 1·75

1312 Carriage Horse and Coachman

1997. "All the Queen's Horses". 50th Anniv of the British Horse Society. Multicoloured.
1989 20p. Type **1312** 70 70
1990 26p. Lifeguards horse and trooper . . . . 1·00 1·00
1991 43p. Blues and Royals drum horse and drummer . . . . 1·25 1·25
1992 63p. Duke of Edinburgh's horse and groom . . . . 1·75 1·75

1316 Haroldswick, Shetland

1997. Sub-Post Offices. Multicoloured.
1997 20p. Type **1316** 65 65
1998 26p. Painswick, Gloucestershire 80 80
1999 43p. Beddgelert, Gwynedd . . 1·25 1·25
2000 63p. Ballyroney, County Down 1·75 1·75

Nos. 1997/2000 were issued on the occasion of the Centenary of the National Federation of Sub-Postmasters.

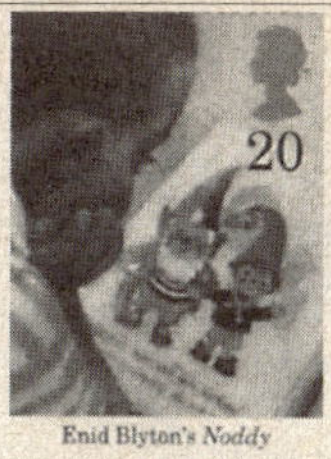

1320 "Noddy"

1997. Birth Centenary of Enid Blyton (children's author). Multicoloured.
2001 20p. Type **1320** 55 55
2002 26p. "Famous Five" 95 95
2003 37p. "Secret Seven" . . . . 1·10 1·10
2004 43p. "Faraway Tree" . . . . 1·25 1·25
2005 63p. "Malory Towers" . . . 1·75 1·75

1325 Children and Father Christmas pulling Cracker

1997. Christmas. 150th Anniv of the Christmas Cracker. Multicoloured.
2006 (2nd) Type **1325** 70 70
2007 (1st) Father Christmas with traditional cracker 80 80
2008 31p. Father Christmas riding cracker 90 90
2009 43p. Father Christmas on snowball . . . . 1·10 1·10
2010 63p. Father Christmas and chimney . . . . 1·50 1·50

1330 Wedding Photograph, 1947

1997. Royal Golden Wedding (2nd issue).
2011 **1330** 20p. gold, brown and black 65 65
2012 – 26p. multicoloured . . 80 80
2013 **1330** 43p. gold, green and black 1·25 1·25
2014 – 63p. multicoloured . . 1·75 1·75

DESIGNS: 26p. and 63p. Queen Elizabeth II and Prince Philip, 1997.

1332 Common Dormouse

1338 Diana, Princess of Wales (photo by Lord Snowdon)

1998. Endangered Species. Multicoloured.
2015 20p. Type **1332** 50 50
2016 26p. Lady's slipper orchid . 60 60
2017 31p. Song thrush 80 80
2018 37p. Shining ram's-horn snail 90 90
2019 43p. Mole cricket . . . . . 1·00 1·00
2020 63p. Devil's bolete . . . . 1·50 1·50

1998. Diana, Princess of Wales Commemoration. Multicoloured.
2021 26p. Type **1338** 40 45
2022 26p. At British Lung Foundation Function, April 1997 (photo by John Stillwell) 40 45
2023 26p. Wearing tiara, 1991 (photo by Lord Snowdon) 40 45
2024 26p. On visit to Birmingham, October 1995 (photo by Tim Graham) (checked suit) . . 40 45
2025 26p. In evening dress, 1987 (photo by Terence Donovan) 40 45

MINIMUM PRICE

The minimum price quoted is 10p which represents a handling charge rather than a basis for valuing common stamps. For further notes about prices see introductory pages.

1343 Lion of England and Griffin of Edward III

1348

1998. 650th Anniv of the Order of the Garter. The Queen's Beasts. Multicoloured.

2026	26p. Type **1343**	65	65
2027	26p. Falcon of Plantagenet and Bull of Clarence	65	65
2028	26p. Lion of Mortimer and Yale of Beaufort	65	65
2029	26p. Greyhound of Richmond and Dragon of Wales	65	65
2030	26p. Unicorn of Scotland and Horse of Hanover	65	65

1998. As Type **157** (Wilding definitive of 1952–54) but with face values in decimal currency as Type **1348**.

2031	**1348** 20p. green	60	60
2032	26p. brown	60	60
2033	37p. purple	1·10	1·10

1349 St. John's Point Lighthouse, County Down

1998. 300th Anniv of the 1st Lighthouse and Final Year of Manned Lighthouses. Multicoloured.

2034	20p. Type **1349**	50	50
2035	26p. Smalls Lighthouse, Pembrokeshire	70	70
2036	37p. Needles Rock Lighthouse, Isle of Wight, c.1900	1·00	1·00
2037	43p. Bell Rock Lighthouse, Arbroath, mid-19th century	1·10	1·10
2038	63p. Eddystone Lighthouse, Plymouth, 1698	1·75	1·75

1354 Tommy Cooper

1998. Comedians. Multicoloured.

2041	20p. Type **1354**	50	50
2042	26p. Eric Morecambe	70	70
2043	37p. Joyce Grenfell	1·00	1·00
2044	43p. Les Dawson	1·10	1·10
2045	63p. Peter Cook	1·75	1·75

1359 Hands forming Heart

1998. 50th Anniv of the National Health Service. Multicoloured.

2046	20p. Type **1359**	50	50
2047	26p. Adult and child holding hands	70	70
2048	43p. Hands forming cradle	1·10	1·10
2049	63p. Hand taking pulse	1·75	1·75

1363 "The Hobbit" (J.R.R. Tolkien)

1998. Famous Children's Fantasy Novels. Multicoloured.

2050	20p. Type **1363**	50	50
2051	26p. "The Lion, The Witch and the Wardrobe" (C.S. Lewis)	70	70
2052	37p. "The Phoenix and the Carpet" (E. Nesbit)	1·00	1·00
2053	43p. "The Borrowers" (Mary Norton	1·10	1·10
2054	63p. "Through the Looking Glass" (Lewis Carroll)	1·75	1·75

Nos. 2050/4 commemorate the birth centenary of C.S. Lewis and the death centenary of Lewis Carroll.

1368 Woman in Yellow Feathered Costume

1998. Europa. Festivals. Notting Hill Carnival. Multicoloured.

2055	20p. Type **1368**	30	35
2056	26p. Woman in blue costume and headdress	40	45
2057	43p. Group of children in white and gold robes	65	70
2058	63p. Child in "Tree" costume	95	1·00

The 20p. and 26p. incorporate the "EUROPA" emblem.

1372 Sir Malcolm Campbell's "Bluebird", 1925

1998. British Land Speed Record Holders. Multicoloured.

2059	20p. Type **1372**	30	35
2060	26p. Sir Henry Segrave's "Sunbeam", 1926	40	45
2061	30p. John G. Parry Thomas's "Babs", 1926	45	50
2062	43p. John R. Cobb's "Railton Mobil Special", 1947	65	70
2063	63p. Donald Campbell's "Bluebird CN7", 1964	95	1·00

Nos. 2059/63 commemorate the 50th death anniversary of Sir Malcolm Campbell.

1377 Angel with Hands raised in Blessing

1998. Christmas. Angels. Multicoloured.

2064	20p. Type **1377**	30	35
2065	26p. Angel praying	40	45
2066	30p. Angel plaing flute	45	50
2067	43p. Angel playing lute	65	70
2068	63p. Angel praying (different)	95	1·00

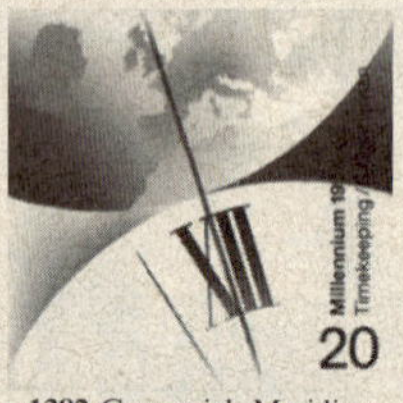

1382 Greenwich Meridian and Clock (John Harrison's chronometer)

1999. Millennium Series. The Inventors' Tale. Multicoloured.

2069	20p. Type **1382**	30	35
2070	26p. Industrial worker and blast furnace (James Watt's discovery of steam power)	40	45
2071	43p. Early photos of leaves (Henry Fox-Talbot's photographic experiments)	65	70
2072	63p. Computer inside human head (Alan Turing's work on computers)	95	1·00

1386 Airliner hugging Globe (International air travel)

1999. Millennium Series. The Travellers' Tale.

2073	**1386** 20p. multicoloured	30	35
2074	– 26p. multicoloured	40	45
2075	– 43p. black, stone and bronze	65	70
2076	– 63p. multicoloured	95	1·00

DESIGNS: 26p. Woman on bicycle (development of the bicycle); 43p. Victorian railway station (growth of public transport); 63p. Captain Cook and Maori (Captain James Cook's voyages).

1390

1999. (a) Self-adhesive.

2077	**1390** (1st) grey (face value) (Queen's head in colourless relief)	40	45

(b) Ordinary gum.

2078	**1390** (1st) black	40	45

1391 Vaccinating Child (pattern in cow markings) (Jenner's development of smallpox vaccine)

1999. Millennium Series. The Patients' Tale. Multicoloured.

2080	20p. Type **1391**	30	35
2081	26p. Patient on trolley (nursing care)	40	45
2082	43p. Penicillin mould (Fleming's discovery of penicillin)	65	70
2083	63p. Sculpture of test-tube baby (development of in vitro fertilization)	95	1·00

1395 Dove and Norman Settler (medieval migration to Scotland)

1999. Millennium Series. The Settlers' Tale. Multicoloured.

2084	20p. Type **1395**	30	35
2085	26p. Pilgrim Fathers and red indian (17th-century migration to America)	40	45
2086	43p. Sailing ship and aspects of settlement (19th-century migration to Australia)	65	70
2087	63p. Hummingbird and superimposed stylised face (20th-century migration to Great Britain)	95	1·00

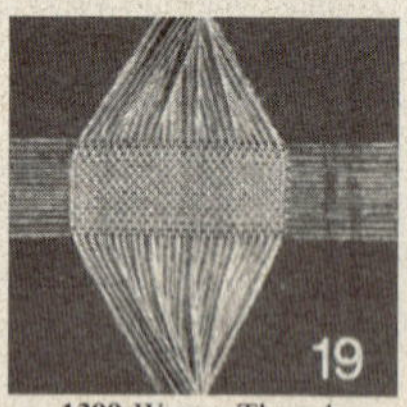

1399 Woven Threads (woollen industry)

1999. Millennium Series. The Workers' Tale. Multicoloured.

2088	19p. Type **1399**	30	35
2089	26p. Northern mill town (cotton industry)	40	45
2090	44p. Hull on slipway (shipbuilding)	70	75
2091	64p. Modern office block (City of London finance centre)	1·00	1·10

1403 Freddie Mercury (lead singer of pop group Queen) ("Popular Music")

1999. Millennium Series. The Entertainers' Tale. Multicoloured.

2092	19p. Type **1403**	30	35
2093	26p. Bobby Moore with World Cup, 1966 ("Sport")	40	45
2094	44p. Dalek from "Dr. Who" (science-fiction series) ("Television")	70	75
2095	64p. Charlie Chaplin (film star) ("Cinema")	1·00	1·10

1407 Prince Edward and Miss Sophie Rhys-Jones (from photo by John Swannell)

1999. Royal Wedding. Multicoloured.

2096	26p. Type **1407**	40	45
2097	64p. Couple in profile	1·00	1·10

1409 Suffragette behind Prison Window (Equal Rights for Women)

1999. Millennium Series. The Citizens' Tale. Multicoloured.

2098	19p. Type **1409**	30	35
2099	26p. Water tap (Right to Health)	40	45
2100	44p. Grenerations of school children (Right to Education)	70	75
2101	64p. "MAGNA CARTA" (Human Rights)	1·00	1·10

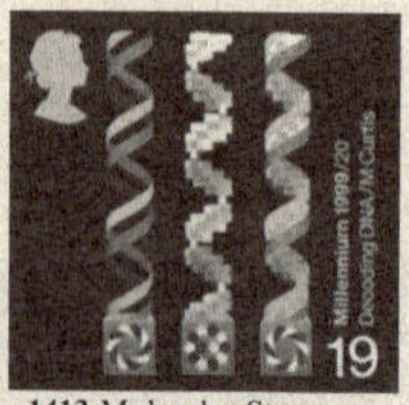

1413 Molecular Structures (DNA Decoding)

1999. Millennium Series. The Scientists' Tale. Multicoloured.

2102	19p. Type **1413**	30	35
2103	26p. Bird and Fossilized Skeleton (Darwin's Theory of Evolution)	40	45
2104	44p. Electrical Generator (Faraday's work on electricity)	70	75
2105	64p. Saturn (development of astronomical telescopes)	1·00	1·10

REGIONAL ISSUES

I. CHANNEL ISLANDS.

Islands in the English Channel off N.W. coast of France. Occupied by German forces from June, 1940 to May, 1945, when separate issues for both islands were made.

C 1 Gathering Vraic (seaweed)

1948. 3rd Anniversary of Liberation.

C1	**C 1**	1d. red	20	20
C2	–	2½d. blue	30	30

DESIGN: 2½d. Islanders gathering vraic.

II. GUERNSEY.

2

3

1958.

6	**2**	2½d. red	35	40
7p	**3**	3d. lilac	20	20
9		4d. blue	10	25
10		4d. sepia	15	20
11		4d. red	15	30
12		5d. blue	15	30

For War Occupation issues and issues of independent postal administration from 1967 see GUERNSEY.

III. ISLE OF MAN.

1

2

3

1958.

1	**1**	2½d. red	45	90
2	**2**	3d. lilac	20	10
3p		4d. blue	20	25
5		4d. sepia	20	30
6		4d. red	45	75
7		5d. blue	45	75

1971. Decimal Currency.

8	**3**	2½p. red	20	15
9		3p. blue	20	15
10		5p. violet	40	50
11		7½p. brown	40	65

For issues of independent postal administration from 1973 see ISLE OF MAN.

IV. JERSEY.

8

9

1958.

9	**8**	2½d. red	35	75
10p	**9**	3d. lilac	20	20
11p		4d. blue	20	25
12		4d. sepia	20	25
13		4d. red	20	35
14		5d. blue	20	50

For War Occupation issues and issues of independent postal administration from 1969 see JERSEY.

V. NORTHERN IRELAND.

N 1

N 2

N 3

N 4

1958.

NI1	**N 1**	3d. lilac	20	10
NI2		4d. blue	20	15
NI8		4d. sepia	20	15
NI9		4d. red	20	20
NI10		5d. blue	20	20
NI3	**N 2**	6d. purple	20	20
NI4		9d. green	30	70
NI5	**N 3**	1s. 3d. green	30	70
NI6		1s. 6d. blue	30	70

1971.

NI12	**N 4**	2½p. mauve	80	25
NI14		3p. blue	20	15
NI15		3½p. grey	20	20
NI17		4½p. blue	25	25
NI18		5p. violet	1·50	1·50
NI19		5½p. violet	20	20
NI21		6½p. blue	20	20
NI22		7p. brown	35	25
NI23		7½p. brown	2·25	2·25
NI24		8p. red	30	30
NI25		8½p. green	30	30
NI26		9p. violet	30	30
NI28		10p. brown	35	35
NI29		10½p. blue	50	50
NI30		11p. red	50	50
NI34		11½p. drab	70	70
NI31		12p. green	50	50
NI36		12½p. green	50	50
NI37		13p. brown	1·25	50
NI32		13½p. brown	70	80
NI39		14p. blue	70	60
NI40		15p. blue	70	60
NI41		15½p. violet	80	65
NI42		16p. brown	1·00	1·00
NI44		17p. blue	70	80
NI45		18p. violet	90	90
NI46		18p. grey	80	80
NI47		18p. green	70	70
NI49		19p. red	80	70
NI69		19p. bistre	50	50
NI50		19½p. grey	1·75	2·25
NI51		20p. black	80	70
NI78		20p. green	30	35
NI52		20½p. blue	4·00	4·00
NI53		22p. blue	1·00	1·10
NI54		22p. green	1·00	1·00
NI55		22p. red	1·00	85
NI56		23p. green	1·00	1·10
NI57		24p. red	1·00	1·10
NI58		24p. brown	90	75
NI72		25p. red	85	85
NI60		26p. red	1·10	1·40
NI61		26p. drab	1·00	1·00
NI79		26p. brown	40	45
NI62a		28p. blue	1·10	1·10
NI63		28p. grey	1·10	1·10
NI74		30p. grey	1·00	1·00
NI64		31p. purple	1·40	1·40
NI65		32p. blue	1·25	1·25
NI66		34p. grey	1·40	1·40
NI67		37p. red	1·40	1·40
NI80		37p. mauve	60	65
NI68		39p. mauve	1·40	1·40
NI76		41p. brown	1·25	1·25
NI81		63p. green	95	1·00

VI. SCOTLAND.

S 1

S 2

S 3

S 4

1958.

S7	**S 1**	3d. lilac	10	15
S8		4d. blue	10	15
S9		4d. sepia	10	10
S10		4d. red	10	10
S11		5d. blue	20	10
S3	**S 2**	6d. purple	20	15
S4		9d. green	30	30
S5	**S 3**	1s. 3d. green	30	30
S6		1s. 6d. blue	35	30

1971. Decimal Currency.

S14	**S 4**	2½p. mauve	25	15
S16		3p. blue	15	15
S17		3½p. grey	20	20
S19		4½p. blue	25	20
S20		5p. violet	1·00	1·00
S21		5½p violet	20	20
S23		6½p. blue	20	20
S24		7p. brown	25	25
S25		7½p. brown	1·25	1·25
S26		8p. red	30	40
S27		8½p. green	30	30
S28		9p. violet	30	30
S29		10p. brown	35	30
S31		10½p. blue	50	35
S32		11p. red	50	35
S36		11½p. drab	85	60
S33		12p. green	50	30
S38		12½p. green	60	50
S39		13p. brown	70	50
S34		13½p. brown	70	65
S54		14p. blue	50	50
S35		15p. blue	60	45
S41		15½p. violet	70	65
S42		16p. drab	70	55
S58	**S 4**	17p. blue	60	60
S44		18p. violet	80	80
S59		18p. grey	80	80
S60		18p. green	70	70
S62		19p. red	80	65
S81		19p. bistre	50	50
S45		19½p. grey	1·75	1·75
S64		20p. black	80	60
S90		20p. green	30	35
S46		20½p. blue	4·00	4·00
S47		22p. blue	90	1·25
S65		22p. green	90	90
S66		22p. red	1·00	75
S67		23p. green	1·00	1·10
S69		24p. red	1·00	1·00
S70		24p. brown	75	75
S84		25p. red	85	85
S49		26p. red	1·10	1·25
S73		26p. drab	1·00	1·00
S91		26p. brown	40	45
S74		28p. blue	1·10	1·10
S75		28p. grey	1·10	1·10
S86		30p. grey	1·00	1·00
S76		31p. purple	1·75	1·75
S77		32p. blue	1·25	1·25
S78		34p. grey	1·40	1·40
S79		37p. red	1·40	1·40
S92		37p. mauve	60	65
S80		39p. mauve	1·40	1·40
S88		41p. brown	1·25	1·25
S93		63p. green	95	1·00

VII. WALES.

W 1

W 2

W 3

W 4

1958.

W1	**W 1**	3d. lilac	20	10
W8		4d. blue	20	10
W9		4d. sepia	20	10
W10		4d. red.	20	20
W11		5d. blue	20	10
W3	**W 2**	6d. purple	40	20
W4		9d. green	40	40
W5	**W 3**	1s. 3d. green	30	30
W6		1s. 6d. blue	35	40

1971. Decimal Currency.

W13	**W 4**	2½p. mauve	20	15
W15		3p. blue	20	20
W16		3½p. grey	20	25
W18		4½p. blue	25	20
W19		5p. violet	1·00	1·00
W20		5½p. violet	20	25
W22		6½p. blue	20	20
W23		7p. brown	25	25
W24		7½p. brown	1·25	1·50
W25		8p. red	30	30
W26		8½p. green	30	30
W27		9p. violet	30	30
W29		10p. brown	35	30
W30		10½p. blue	50	50
W31		11p. red	50	50
W35		11½p. drab	85	60
W32		12p. green	50	45
W37		12½p. green	80	60
W38		13p. brown	50	35
W33		13½p. brown	60	70
W40		14p. blue	55	50
W41		15p. blue	50	50
W42		15½p. violet	80	65
W43		16p. drab	1·75	1·25
W45		17p. blue	70	55
W46		18p. violet	80	75
W47		18p. grey	80	70
W48		18p. green	55	55
W50		19p. red	85	60
W70		19p. bistre	50	50
W51		19½p. grey	2·00	2·00
W52		20p. black	80	80
W72		20p. green	70	70
W53		20½p. blue	4·00	4·00
W54		22p. blue	1·10	1·00
W55		22p. green	90	1·25
W56		22p. red	80	70
W57		23p. green	90	1·25
W58		24p. red	40	40
W59		24p. brown	90	90
W73		25p. red	85	85
W61		26p. red	1·10	1·40
W62		26p. drab	1·00	1·00
W74		26p. brown	90	90
W63a		28p. blue	1·10	1·00
W64		28p. grey	1·10	1·10
W75		30p. grey	1·00	1·00
W65		31p. purple	1·25	1·25
W66		32p. blue	1·25	1·25
W67		34p. grey	1·50	1·40
W68		37p. red	1·50	1·40
W76		37p. mauve	1·00	1·00
W69		39p. mauve	1·50	1·40
W77		41p. brown	1·25	1·25
W78		63p. green	1·75	1·75

W 5 Without "p"

1997.

W79	**W 5**	20p. green	30	35
W80		26p. brown	40	45
W81		37p. mauve	60	65
W82		63p. green	95	1·00

OFFICIAL STAMPS

(for Government Departments)

ADMIRALTY

Overprinted **ADMIRALTY OFFICIAL**.

1903. Stamps of King Edward VII.

O107	**83**	½d. turquoise	10·00	6·00
O102	–	1d. red	6·00	3·00
O103	–	1½d. purple and green	65·00	50·00
O104	–	2d. green and red	£125	60·00
O105	**83**	2½d. blue	£140	50·00
O106	–	3d. purple on yellow	£125	50·00

ARMY

Overprinted **ARMY OFFICIAL**.

1896. Stamps of Queen Victoria.

O41	**71**	½d. red	2·00	1·00
O42		½d. green	2·00	4·00
O43	**57**	1d. lilac	2·00	1·00
O44	**74**	2½d. purple on blue	5·00	3·00
O45	**79**	6d. purple on red	17·00	10·00

1902. Stamps of King Edward VII.

O48	**83**	½d. turquoise	2·50	1·00
O49		1d. red	2·00	1·00
O50		6d. purple	75·00	35·00

BOARD OF EDUCATION

Overprinted **BOARD OF EDUCATION**.

1902. Stamps of Queen Victoria.

O81	**78**	5d. purple on blue	£575	£120
O82	**82**	1s. green and red	£1000	£400

1902. Stamps of King Edward VII.

O83	**83**	½d. turquoise	20·00	8·00
O84		1d. red	20·00	7·00
O85		2½d. blue	£550	60·00
O86	–	5d. purple and blue	£2250	£1000
O87	–	1s. green and red	£40000	£30000

GOVERNMENT PARCELS

Overprinted **GOVT. PARCELS**.

1883. Stamps of Queen Victoria.

O61	**62**	1½d. purple	£125	30·00
O62	–	6d. green (No. 194)	£825	£300
O63	–	9d. green (No. 195)	£675	£190
O64	**25**	1s. brown (No. 163)	£450	80·00

1887. Stamps of Queen Victoria.

O69	**57**	1d. lilac	30·00	9·00
O65	**72**	1½d. purple and green	15·00	3·00
O70	**73**	2d. green and red	50·00	8·00
O71	**77**	4½d. green and red	£125	80·00
O66	**79**	6d. purple on red	30·00	12·00
O67	**80**	9d. purple and blue	60·00	16·00
O68	**82**	1s. green	£140	80·00
O72		1s. green and red	£175	55·00

1902. Stamps of King Edward VII.

O74	**83**	1d. red	17·00	6·00
O75	–	2d. green and red	70·00	18·00
O76	**83**	6d. purple	£100	18·00
O77	–	9d. purple and blue	£240	60·00
O78	–	1s. green and red	£375	90·00

INLAND REVENUE

Overprinted **I.R. OFFICIAL**.

1882. Stamps of Queen Victoria.

O 1	**52**	½d. green	15·00	5·00
O 5		½d. blue	30·00	20·00
O 3	**57**	1d. lilac	2·00	1·00
O 6	–	2½d. purple (No. 190)	£140	50·00
O 4	**34**	6d. grey (No. 161)	80·00	25·00
O 7	–	1s. green (No. 196)	£2600	£500
O 9	–	5s. red (No. 181)	£1500	£450
O10	–	10s. blue (No. 183)	£2750	£600
O11	**61**	£1 brown	£20000	

1888.

O13	**71**	½d. red	2·00	1·00
O17		½d. green	5·00	4·00
O14	**74**	2½d. purple on blue	60·00	5·00
O18	**79**	6d. purple on red	£125	25·00
O15	**89**	1s. green	£225	25·00
O19		1s. green and red	£800	£175
O16	**61**	£1 green	£3750	£500

1902. Stamps of King Edward VII.

O20	**83**	½d. turquoise	20·00	2·00
O21		1d. red	12·00	1·00
O22		2½d. blue	£450	90·00
O23		6d. purple	£85000	£65000
O24	–	1s. green and red	£550	95·00
O25	–	5s. red	£4000	£1500
O26	–	10s. blue	£16000	£9500
O27	–	£1 green	£13000	£7000

OFFICE OF WORKS

Overprinted **O.W. OFFICIAL**.

1896. Stamps of Queen Victoria.

O31	**71**	½d. red	£100	50·00
O32		½d. green	£175	85·00
O33	**57**	1d. lilac	£175	50·00
O34	**78**	5d. purple and blue	£850	£190
O35	**81**	10d. purple and red	£1400	£275

1902. Stamps of King Edward VII.

O36	**83**	½d. turquoise	£400	£100
O37	–	1d red	£400	£100
O38	–	2d. green and red	£700	£100
O39	**83**	2½d. blue	£800	£275
O40	–	10d. purple and red	£5250	£1750

ROYAL HOUSEHOLD

Overprinted **R.H. OFFICIAL**.

1902. Stamps of King Edward VII.

O91	**83**	½d. turquoise	£160	£100
O92		1d. red	£140	90·00

POSTAGE DUE STAMPS

D 1

D 4

1914.

D 1	D 1	½d. green	50	50
D56		½d. orange	10	1·00
D2		1d. red	50	50
D57		1d. blue	10	50
D3		1½d. brown	40·00	12·00
D58		1½d. green	90	2·75
D69		2d. black	20	60
D60		3d. violet	40	30
D15		4d. green	13·00	3·00
D61		4d. blue	40	30
D62		5d. brown	45	75
D63		6d. purple	60	30
D76		8d. red	1·00	1·25
D17		1s. blue	8·50	75
D64		1s. brown	1·40	30
D65		2s. 6d. purple on yellow	4·25	45
D66		5s. red on yellow	8·00	1·00
D67		10s. blue on yellow	10·00	5·50
D68		£1 black on yellow	45·00	8·50

On the 2s. 6d. to £1 the inscription reads "TO PAY".

1970. Decimal Currency.

D77	–	½p. blue	10	20
D78	–	1p. purple	10	15
D79	–	2p. green	10	15
D80	–	3p. blue	15	15
D81	–	4p. brown	15	15
D82	–	5p. violet	20	20
D83	–	7p. brown	35	45
D84	D 4	10p. red	30	20
D85		11p. green	60	60
D86		20p. brown	60	50
D87		50p. blue	1·50	50
D88		£1 black	3·50	75
D89		£5 yellow and black	35·00	2·00

DESIGN: ½p. to 7p. similar to Type D **4**, but with "TO PAY" reading vertically upwards at the left.

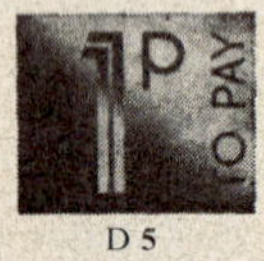

D 5

D 7

1982.

D 90	D 5	1p. red	10	10
D 91		2p. blue	20	10
D 92		3p. mauve	10	15
D 93		4p. blue	10	20
D 94		5p. brown	20	20
D 95	–	10p. brown	20	25
D 96	–	20p. green	40	30
D 97	–	25p. blue	50	70
D 98	–	50p. black	1·00	75
D 99	–	£1 red	2·00	50
D100	–	£2 blue	4·50	50
D101	–	£5 orange	12·00	50

DESIGNS: 10p. to £5, as Type D **5** but with "TO PAY" horizontal.

1994.

D102	D 7	1p. red, yellow & blk	10	10
D103		2p. mauve, pur & blk	10	10
D104		5p. yellow, brn & blk	10	10
D105		10p. yellow, grn & blk	15	20
D106		20p. green, vio & blk	30	35
D107		25p. mauve, red & blk	40	45
D108		£1 violet, mve & blk	1·50	1·60
D109		£1.20 blue, grn & blk	1·75	1·90
D110		£5 dp grn, grn & blk	7·50	7·75

GRENADA

One of the Windward Is., Br. W. Indies. Ministerial Government was introduced on 1 January 1960. Achieved Associated Statehood on 3 March 1967 and Independence on 7 February 1974.

1861. 12 pence = 1 shilling;
20 shillings = 1 pound.
1949. 100 cents = 1 West Indian dollar.

1

5

1861.

14	1	1d green	55·00	6·00
6		6d. red	£600	12·00

1875. Surch **POSTAGE** and value in words.

21	5	½d. mauve	11·00	5·50
22		2½d. lake	50·00	5·50
23		4d. blue	90·00	8·00
13		1s. mauve	£650	9·00

1883. Revenue stamp surch crown and value (in green) optd **POSTAGE**.

27	5	1d. orange	£250	48·00

1883. Revenue stamp as last but optd **POSTAGE** diagonally on each half.

29	5	Half of 1d. orange	£200	£110

13

21

1883.

30	13	½d. green	1·00	85
31		1d. red	65·00	3·25
32		2½d. blue	6·50	85
33		4d. grey	4·50	1·75
34		6d. mauve	3·00	3·75
35		8d. brown	8·50	12·00
36		1s. violet	£110	55·00

1886. Revenue stamps as No. 27 but surch **POSTAGE** and value in words or figures.

43	5	½d. on 2s. orange	12·00	17·00
37		1d. on 1½d. orange	35·00	29·00
39		1d. on 4d. orange	£140	90·00
38		1d. on 1s. orange	32·00	30·00
41		4d. on 2s. orange	35·00	17·00

1887. As T **13**, but inscr "GRENADA POSTAGE & REVENUE" at top.

40	13	1d. red	60	50

1890. Revenue stamp as No. 27 but surch **POSTAGE AND REVENUE 1d.**

45	5	1d. on 2s. orange	50·00	50·00

1891. Surch **POSTAGE AND REVENUE 1d.**

46	13	1d. on 8d. brown	9·00	11·00

1891. Surch **2½d.**

47	13	2½d. on 8d. brown	8·00	11·00

1895.

48	21	½d. mauve and green	2·50	1·25
49		1d. mauve and red	4·25	60
50		2d. mauve and brown	40·00	32·00
51		2½d. mauve and blue	5·00	1·25
52		3d. mauve and orange	6·50	16·00
53		6d. mauve and green	9·50	19·00
54		8d. mauve and black	12·00	35·00
55		1s. green and orange	17·00	30·00

23 Flagship of Columbus (Columbus named Grenada "La Concepcion")

1898. 400th Anniv of Discovery of Grenada by Columbus.

56	23	2½d. blue	13·00	5·50

1902. As T **21**, but portrait of King Edward VII.

57		½d. purple and green	3·00	50
58		1d. purple and red	3·50	20
59		2d. purple and brown	3·00	8·00
60		2½d. purple and blue	3·50	2·00
61		3d. purple and orange	3·50	7·00
72		6d. purple and green	4·50	8·50
63		1s. green and orange	3·25	22·00
64		2s. green and blue	18·00	55·00
65		5s. green and red	38·00	55·00
66		10s. green and purple	£100	£190

26 Badge of the Colony

28

1906.

77	26	½d. green	2·50	30
78		1d. red	3·50	10
79		2d. orange	2·00	3·00
80		2½d. blue	3·75	1·50
84		3d. purple on yellow	3·25	1·75
85		6d. purple	18·00	23·00
86		1s. black on green	5·00	4·00
87		2s. blue and purple on blue	18·00	12·00
88		5s. green and red on yellow	50·00	65·00
83		10s. green and red on green	80·00	£150

1913.

112	28	½d. green	1·25	15
113		1d red	80	50
114		1d. brown	1·50	20
115		1½d. red	1·50	1·50
116		2d. orange	1·25	15
117		2d. grey	2·50	2·00
94		2½d. blue	1·40	2·75
118		2½d. grey	75	8·00
96		3d. purple on yellow	65	85
121		3d. blue	1·25	8·50
123		4d. black & red on yell	1·00	3·50
124		5d. purple and green	1·50	3·75
97		6d. purple	1·25	8·00
126		6d. black and red	2·25	2·50
127		9d. purple and black	2·25	8·00
98a		1s. black on green	1·00	5·00
129		1s. brown	3·00	10·00
99		2s. purple & blue on blue	4·75	11·00
131		2s. 6d. black & red on bl	6·00	16·00
132		3s. green and violet	6·00	27·00
133		5s. green & red on yellow	12·00	32·00
101		10s. green & red on green	48·00	80·00

1916. Optd **WAR TAX**.

111	28	1d. red	30	20

31 Grand Anse Beach

32 Badge of the Colony

1934.

135	31	½d. green	15	80
136a	32	1d. black and brown	65	35
137a	–	1½d. black and red	90	55
138	32	2d. black and orange	90	40
139	–	2½d. blue	40	30
140	32	3d. black and olive	55	2·00
141		6d. black and purple	1·40	1·25
142		1s. black and brown	90	2·75
143		2s. 6d. black and blue	7·00	25·00
144		5s. black and violet	32·00	48·00

DESIGNS—VERT: 1½d. Grand Etang; 2½d. St. George's.

1935. Silver Jubilee. As T **13** of Antigua.

145		½d. black and green	50	75
146		1d. blue and grey	50	1·25
147		1½d. blue and red	50	1·25
148		1s. grey and purple	5·50	15·00

1937. Coronation. As T **2** of Aden.

149		1d. violet	40	20
150		1½d. red	40	20
151		2½d. blue	80	30

35 King George VI

40 Badge of the Colony

1937.

152b	35	¼d brown	20	60

1938. As 1934, but with portrait of King George VI.

153b	31	½d. green	60	1·25
154a	32	1d. black and brown	50	50
155	–	1½d. black and red	50	60
156	32	2d. black and orange	30	50
157	–	2½d. blue	30	30
158ab	32	3d. black and olive	30	80
159		6d. black and purple	1·25	40
160		1s. black and brown	2·25	30
161		2s. black and blue	16·00	1·50
162		5s. black and violet	3·50	1·50
163e	40	10s. blue and red	27·00	8·50

1946. Victory. As T **9** of Aden.

164		1½d. red	10	10
165		3½d. blue	10	10

1948. Silver Wedding. As T **10/11** of Aden.

166		1½d. red	15	10
167		10s. grey	8·00	16·00

1949. U.P.U. As T **20/23** of Antigua.

168		5 c. blue	20	10
169		6 c. olive	90	90
170		12 c. mauve	35	30
171		24 c. brown	35	30

41 King George VI

42 Badge of the Colony

1951.

172	41	½ c. black and brown	15	1·00
173		1 c. black and green	15	25
174		2 c. black and brown	15	30
175		3 c. black and red	15	10
176		4 c. black and orange	35	40
177		5 c. black and violet	20	10
178		6 c. black and olive	30	60
179		7 c. black and blue	1·75	10
180		12 c. black and purple	2·25	30
181	42	25 c. black and brown	2·25	50
182		50 c. black and blue	6·00	40
183		$1.50 black and orange	7·50	5·50
184		$2.50 slate and red	5·50	5·50

No. 184 is larger 24½×30½ mm.

1951. Inauguration of B.W.I. University College. As T **24/25** of Antigua.

185		3 c. black and red	45	20
186		6 c. black and olive	45	20

1951. New Constitution. Nos. 175/7 and 180 optd **NEW CONSTITUTION 1951.**

187	41	3 c. black and red	10	10
188		4 c. black and orange	10	10
189		5 c. black and violet	10	10
190		12 c. black and purple	10	15

1953. Coronation. As T **13** of Aden.

191		3 c. black and red	20	10

1953. As T **41**, but with portrait of Queen Elizabeth II, and T **42**, but Royal Cypher changed.

192	41	½ c. black and brown	10	10
193		1 c. black and green	10	10
214		2 c. black and brown	10	10
195		3 c. black and red	10	10
196		4 c. black and orange	10	10
197		5 c. black and violet	10	10
198		6 c. black and olive	45	70
199		7 c. black and blue	1·25	10
219		12 c. black and purple	20	10
201	42	25 c. black and brown	1·25	20
202		50 c. black and blue	5·50	40
203		$1.50 black and orange	11·00	12·00
204		$2.50 slate and red	18·00	10·00

No. 204 is larger 24½×30½ mm.

1958. British Caribbean Federation. As T **28** of Antigua.

205		3 c. green	35	10
206		6 c. blue	45	60
207		12 c. red	55	10

48 Queen Victoria, Queen Elizabeth II, Mail Van and Post Office, St. George's

1961. Grenada Stamp Centenary.

208	48	3 c. red and black	25	10
209	–	8 c. blue and orange	55	25
210	–	25 c. lake and blue	55	25

DESIGNS (incorporating Queen Victoria and Queen Elizabeth II): 8 c. Flagship of Columbus; 25 c. "Solent I" (paddle-steamer) and Douglas DC-3 aircraft.

1963. Freedom from Hunger. As T **28** of Aden.

211		8 c. green	30	15

1963. Centenary of Red Cross. As T **33** of Antigua.

212		3 c. red and black	15	15
213		25 c. red and blue	30	15

1965. Centenary of I.T.U. As T **36** of Antigua.

221		2 c. orange and olive	10	10
222		50 c. yellow and red	25	20

1965. I.C.Y. As T **37** of Antigua.

223		1 c. purple and turquoise	10	15
224		25 c. green and lavender	20	15

1966. Churchill Commen. As T **38** of Antigua.

225		1 c. blue	10	15
226		3 c. green	10	15
227		25 c. brown	15	10
228		35 c. violet	25	15

1966. Royal Visit. As T **39** of Antigua.

229		3 c. black and blue	25	15
230		35 c. black and mauve	65	15

52 Hillsborough, Carriacou

1966. Multicoloured.

231		1 c. Type **52**	20	40
232		2 c. Bougainvillea	20	10
233		3 c. Flamboyant plant	20	30
234		5 c. Levera Beach	50	10
235		6 c. Carenage, St. George's	50	10
236		8 c. Annandale Falls	50	10
237		10 c. Cocoa pods	30	10
238		12 c. Inner Harbour	30	50
239		15 c. Nutmeg	30	50
240		25 c. St. George's	30	10
241		35 c. Grand Anse beach	30	10
242		50 c. Bananas	1·00	1·25
243		$1 Badge of the Colony	7·00	2·75
244		$2 Queen Elizabeth II	4·50	5·00
245		$3 Map of Grenada	4·50	11·00

Nos. 243/5 are vert and larger, 25×39 mm.

1966. World Cup Football Championship. As T **40** of Antigua.

246		5 c. multicoloured	10	10
247		50 c. multicoloured	40	50

1966. Inauguration of W.H.O. Headquarters, Geneva. As T **41** of Antigua.

248		8 c. black, green and blue	10	10
249		25 c. black, purple & ochre	25	20

1966. 20th Anniv of U.N.E.S.C.O. As T **54/56** of Antigua.

250		2 c. multicoloured	10	10
251		15 c. yellow, violet & orange	15	10
252		50 c. black, purple & orange	30	60

1967. Statehood. Nos. 232/3, 236 and 240 optd **ASSOCIATED STATEHOOD 1967**.

253		2 c. multicoloured	10	15
254		3 c. multicoloured	10	15
255		8 c. multicoloured	15	10
256		25 c. multicoloured	15	15

1967. World Fair, Montreal. Nos. 232, 237, 239 and 243/4 surch or optd **expo67 MONTREAL CANADA** and emblem.

257		1 c. on 15 c. multicoloured	10	20
258		2 c. multicoloured	10	20
259		3 c. on 10 c. multicoloured	10	20
260		$1 multicoloured	30	25
261		$2 multicoloured	45	30

1967. Nos. 231/45 optd **ASSOCIATED STATEHOOD**.

262	52	1 c. multicoloured	10	10
263	–	2 c. multicoloured	10	10
264	–	3 c. multicoloured	10	10
265	–	5 c. multicoloured	10	10
266	–	6 c. multicoloured	10	10
267	–	8 c. multicoloured	10	10
268	–	10 c. multicoloured	10	10
269	–	12 c. multicoloured	10	10
270	–	15 c. multicoloured	15	10
271	–	25 c. multicoloured	20	10
272	–	35 c. multicoloured	55	10
273	–	50 c. multicoloured	70	20
274	–	$1 multicoloured	70	60
275	–	$2 multicoloured	1·25	3·25
276	–	$3 multicoloured	2·25	3·25

70 Kennedy and Local Flower

1968. 50th Birth Anniv of Pres. Kennedy. Multicoloured.

277		1 c. Type **70**	10	15
278		15 c. Type **70**	10	10
279		25 c. Kennedy and strelitzia	10	10
280		35 c. Kennedy and roses	10	10
281		50 c. As 25 c.	15	20
282		$1 As 35 c.	25	50

73 Scout Bugler

1968. World Scout Jamboree, Idaho. Mult.

283		1 c. Type **73**	10	10
284		2 c. Scouts camping	10	10
285		3 c. Lord Baden-Powell	10	10
286		35 c. Type **73**	20	10
287		50 c. As 2 c.	25	20
288		$1 As 3 c.	40	40

76 "Near Antibes"

1968. Paintings by Sir Winston Churchill. Multicoloured.

289	10 c. Type **76**	10	10
290	12 c. "The Mediterranean"	15	10
291	15 c. "St. Jean, Cap Ferratt"	15	10
292	25 c. Type **76**	20	10
293	35 c. As No. 291	25	10
294	50 c. Sir Winston painting	35	25

1968. No. 275 surch **$5**.

295	$5 on $2 multicoloured	1·50	2·25

1968. "Children Need Milk". Surch **CHILDREN NEED MILK** and value. (a) Nos. 244/5.

296	2 c. + 3 c. on $2 multicoloured	10	10
297	3 c. + 3 c. on $3 multicoloured	10	10

(b) Nos. 243/4.

298	1 c. + 3 c. on $1 multicoloured	10	40
299	2 c. + 3 c. on $2 multicoloured	13·00	45·00

83 Edith McGuire (U.S.A.)

1968. Olympic Games, Mexico.

300	**83**	1 c. brown, black & blue	10	10
301	–	2 c. multicoloured	10	10
302	–	3 c. scarlet, brown & green	10	10
303	**83**	10 c. multicoloured	15	10
304	–	50 c. multicoloured	55	65
305	–	60 c. red, brown & orange	60	80

DESIGNS: 2 c., 50 c. Arthur Wint (Jamaica); 3 c., 60 c. Ferreira da Silva (Brazil).

86 Hibiscus

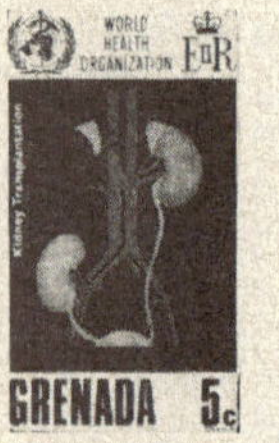

102 Kidney Transplant

1968. Multicoloured.

306	1 c. Type **86**	10	10
307	2 c. Strelitzia	10	10
308	3 c. Bougainvillea	10	10
309	5 c. Rock hind	10	10
310	6 c. Sailfish	10	10
311	8 c. Red snapper	10	30
312	10 c. Marine toad	10	10
313	12 c. Turtle	15	10
314	15 c. Tree boa	90	60
314a	15 c. Thunbergia	5·50	2·50
315	25 c. Greater Trinidadian murine opossum	30	10
316	35 c. Nine-banded armadillo	35	10
317	50 c. Mona monkey	45	25
317a	75 c. Yacht in St. George's Harbour	12·00	8·50
318	$1 Bananaquit	3·00	1·50
319	$2 Brown pelican	5·00	9·00
320	$3 Magnificent frigate bird	4·50	5·00
321	$5 Bare-eyed thrush	7·00	16·00

Nos. 309, 311/12, 314, 316 and 317a are horiz.
Nos. 318/21 are larger $25\frac{1}{2} \times 48$ mm.

1968. 20th Anniv of W.H.O. Multicoloured

322	5 c. Type **102**	20	10
323	25 c. Heart transplant	30	10
324	35 c. Lung transplant	30	10
325	50 c. Eye transplant	35	50

106 "The Adoration of the Kings" (Veronese)

114 Dame Hylda Bynoe

111 Dame Hylda Bynoe (Governor) and Island Scene

1968. Christmas.

326	**106**	5 c. multicoloured	10	10
327	–	15 c. multicoloured	10	10
328	–	35 c. multicoloured	10	10
329	–	$1 multicoloured	30	40

DESIGNS: 15 c. "Madonna and Child with Saints John and Catherine" (Titian); 35 c. "The Adoration of the Kings" (Botticelli); $1 "A Warrior Adoring" (Catena).

1969. Caribbean Free Trade Area Exhibition. Nos. 300/5 surch **VISIT CARIFTA EXPO '69 April 5-30** and value.

330	**83**	5 c. on 1 c.	10	10
331	–	8 c. on 2 c.	10	10
332	–	25 c. on 3 c.	10	10
333	**83**	35 c. on 10 c.	10	10
334	–	$1 on 50 c.	20	30
335	–	$2 on 60 c.	35	60

1969. Carifta Expo '69. Multicoloured.

336	5 c. Type **111**	10	10
337	15 c. Premier E. M. Gairy and island scene	10	10
338	50 c. Type **111**	10	25
339	60 c. Emblems of 1958 and 1967 World's Fairs	10	30

1969. Human Rights Year. Multicoloured.

340	5 c. Type **114**	10	10
341	25 c. Dr. Martin Luther King	15	10
342	35 c. As 5 c.	15	10
343	$1 "Balshazzar's Feast" (Rembrandt) (horiz)	30	45

117 Batsman and Wicket-keeper

1969. Cricket.

344	**117**	3 c. yellow, brown & bl	25	70
345	–	10 c. multicoloured	30	40
346	–	25 c. brown., ochre & grn	60	85
347	–	35 c. multicoloured	80	90

DESIGNS: 10 c. Batsman playing defensive stroke; 25 c. Batsman sweeping ball; 35 c. Batsman playing on-drive.

129 Astronaut handling Moon Rock

1969. First Man on the Moon. Multicoloured.

348	$\frac{1}{2}$ c. As Type **129** but larger (56 x 35 mm)	10	10
349	1 c. Moon rocket and moon	10	10
350	2 c. Module landing	10	10
351	3 c. Declaration left on the moon	10	10
352	8 c. Module leaving rocket	10	10
353	25 c. Rocket lifting-off	20	10
354	35 c. Spacecraft in orbit	20	10
355	50 c. Capsule with parachutes	30	30
356	$1 Type **129**	45	70

The 25, 35 and 50 c. are vert.

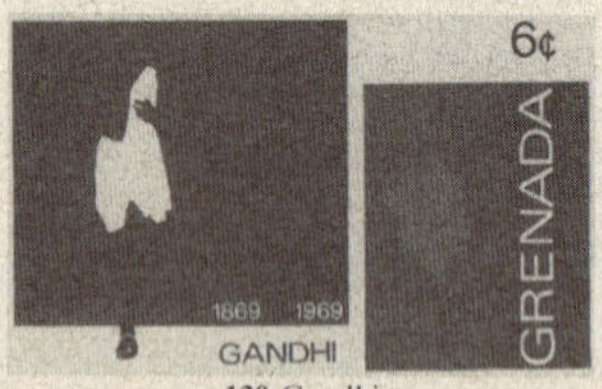

130 Gandhi

1969. Birth Cent of Mahatma Gandhi. Mult.

358	6 c. Type **130**	15	10
359	15 c. Gandhi standing	20	10
360	25 c. Gandhi walking	30	10
361	$1 Head of Gandhi	75	60

1969. Christmas. Nos. 326/9 optd **1969** and surch (No. 363).

363	–	2 c. on 15 c. multicoloured	10	10
364	**106**	5 c. multicoloured	10	10
365	–	35 c. multicoloured	20	10
366	–	$1 multicoloured	80	1·50

135 "Blackbeard" (Edward Teach)

1970. Pirates.

367	**135**	15 c. black	35	10
368	–	25 c. green	50	10
369	–	50 c. lilac	90	20
370	–	$1 carmine	1·50	75

DESIGNS: 25 c. Anne Bonney; 50 c. Jean Lafitte; $1 Mary Read.

1970. No. 348 surch **5c**.

371	5 c. on $\frac{1}{2}$ c. multicoloured	10	10

141/2 "The Last Supper" (detail, Del Sarto)

1970. Easter. Paintings.

372	**141**	5 c. multicoloured	10	15
373	**142**	5 c. multicoloured	10	15
374	–	15 c. multicoloured	20	20
375	–	15 c. multicoloured	20	25
376	–	25 c. multicoloured	25	30
377	–	25 c. multicoloured	25	30
378	–	60 c. multicoloured	40	55
379	–	60 c. multicoloured	40	55

DESIGNS: 15 c. "Christ crowned with Thorns" (detail, Van Dyck); 25 c. "The Passion of Christ" (detail, Memling); 60 c. "Christ in the Tomb" (detail, Rubens).

Each value was issued in sheets containing the two stamps se-tenant. Each design is spread over two stamps as in Type **141/2**.

149 Girl with Kittens in Pram

1970. Birth Bicentenary of Wordsworth. "Children and Pets". Multicoloured.

381	5 c. Type **149**	15	15
382	15 c. Girl with puppy and kitten	20	15
383	30 c. Boy with fishing-rod and cat	25	20
384	60 c. Boys and girls with cats and dogs	40	1·10

153 Parliament of India

1970. 7th Regional Conference of Commonwealth Parliamentary Association. Parliament Buildings. Multicoloured.

386	5 c. Type **153**	10	10
387	25 c. Great Britain	10	10
388	50 c. Canada	15	15
389	60 c. Grenada	15	15

157 Tower of the Sun

1970. World Fair, Osaka. Multicoloured.

391	1 c. Type **157**	10	10
392	2 c. Livelihood and Industry Pavilion (horiz)	10	10
393	3 c. Flower painting, 1634	10	10
394	10 c. "Adam and Eve" (Tintoretto) (horiz)	15	10
395	25 c. Organization For Economic Co-operation and Development (O.E.C.D.) Pavilion (horiz)	20	10
396	50 c. San Francisco Pavilion	45	1·25

164 Roosevelt and "Raising U.S. Flag on Iwo Jima"

1970. 25th Anniv of Ending of World War II. Multicoloured.

398	$\frac{1}{2}$ c. Type **164**	10	10
399	5 c. Zhukov and "Fall of Berlin"	70	15
400	15 c. Churchill and "Evacuation at Dunkirk"	1·50	45
401	25 c. De Gaulle and "Liberation of Paris"	1·50	45
402	50 c. Eisenhower and "D-Day Landing"	2·00	1·50
403	60 c. Montgomery and "Battle of Alamein"	2·00	2·75

1970. "Philympia 1970" Stamp Exhibition, London. Nos. 353/6 optd **PHILYMPIA LONDON 1970**.

405	–	25 c. multicoloured	10	10
406	–	35 c. multicoloured	10	10
407	–	50 c. multicoloured	15	15
408	**129**	$1 multicoloured	20	30

170 U.P.U. Headquarters Building and Transport

1970. New U.P.U. Headquarters Building. Multicoloured.

409	15 c. Type **170**	35	10
410	25 c. As Type **170**, but modern transport	35	10
411	50 c. Sir Rowland Hill and U.P.U. Building	35	30
412	$1 Abraham Lincoln and U.P.U. Building	40	1·25

The 50 c. and $1 are both vert.

171 "The Madonna of the Goldfinch" (Tiepolo)

1970. Christmas. Multicoloured.

414	$\frac{1}{2}$ c. Type **171**	10	10
415	$\frac{1}{2}$ c. "The Virgin and Child with St. Peter and St. Paul" (Bouts)	10	10
416	$\frac{1}{2}$ c. "The Virgin and Child" (Bellini)	10	10
417	2 c. "The Madonna of the Basket" (Correggio)	10	10
418	3 c. Type **171**	10	10
419	35 c. As No. 415	20	10
420	50 c. As 2 c.	30	35
421	$1 As No. 416	50	1·25

172 19th-Century Nursing

1970. Cent of British Red Cross. Multicoloured.

423	5 c. Type **172**	20	10
424	15 c. Military ambulance, 1918	25	10
425	25 c. First-Aid post, 1941	35	10
426	60 c. Red Cross transport, 1970	90	80

173 John Dewey and Art Lesson

1971. Int. Education Year. Multicoloured.

428	5 c. Type **173**	10	10
429	10 c. Jean-Jacques Rousseau and "Alphabetisation"	15	10
430	50 c. Maimonides and laboratory	50	15
431	$1 Bertrand Russell and mathematics class	95	40

174 Jennifer Hosten and Outline of Grenada

1971. Winner of "Miss World" Competition (1970).

433	**174** 5 c. multicoloured	10	10
434	10 c. multicoloured	10	10
435	15 c. multicoloured	15	10
436	25 c. multicoloured	15	10
437	35 c. multicoloured	15	10
438	50 c. multicoloured	35	55

175 French and Canadian Scouts

1971. 13th World Scout Jamboree, Asagiri, Japan. Multicoloured.

440	5 c. Type **175**	10	10
441	35 c. German and American scouts	30	25
442	50 c. Australian and Japanese scouts	40	50
443	75 c. Grenada and British scouts	50	75

176 "Napoleon reviewing the Guard" (E. Detaille)

1971. 150th Death Anniv of Napoleon Bonaparte. Paintings. Multicoloured.

445	5 c. Type **176**	15	15
446	15 c. "Napoleon before Madrid" (Vernet)	25	15
447	35 c. "Napoleon crossing Mt. St. Bernard" (David)	30	15
448	$2 "Napoleon in his Study" (David)	75	1·50

177 1d. Stamp of 1861 and Badge of Grenada

1971. 110th Anniv of the Postal Service. Mult.

450	5 c. Type **177**	20	20
451	15 c. 6d. stamp of 1861 and Queen Elizabeth II	25	15
452	35 c. 1d. and 6d. stamps of 1861 and badge of Grenada	50	20
453	50 c. Scroll and 1d. stamp of 1861	65	1·75

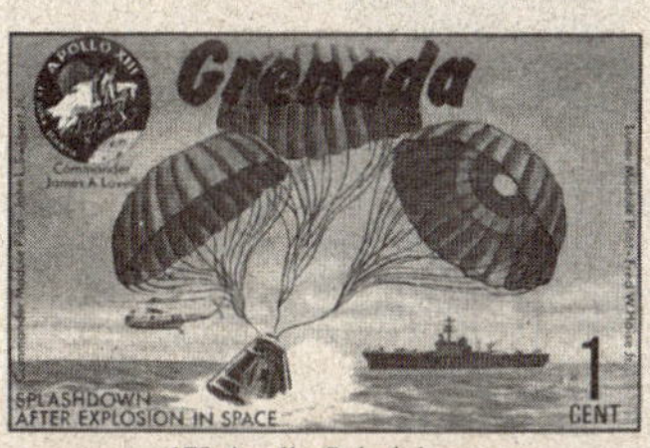

178 Apollo Splashdown

1971. Apollo Moon Exploration Series. Mult.

455	1 c. Type **178**	10	10
456	2 c. Recovery of "Apollo 13"	10	10
457	3 c. Separation of Lunar Module from "Apollo 14"	10	10
458	10 c. Shepard and Mitchell taking samples of moon rock	25	10
459	25 c. Moon Buggy	75	20
460	$1 "Apollo 15" blast-off (vert)	2·00	3·25

179 67th Regt of Foot, 1787

1971. Military Uniforms. Multicoloured.

462	½ c. Type **179**	10	10
463	1 c. 45th Regt of Foot, 1792	10	10
464	2 c. 29th Regt of Foot, 1794	10	10
465	10 c. 9th Regt of Foot, 1801	45	10
466	25 c. 2nd Regt of Foot, 1815	85	20
467	$1 70th Regt of Foot, 1764	2·50	2·00

180 "The Adoration of the Kings" (Memling)

1972. Christmas (1971). Multicoloured.

469	15 c. Type **180**	15	10
470	25 c. "Madonna and Child" (Michelangelo)	20	10
471	35 c. "Madonna and Child" (Murillo)	25	10
472	50 c. "The Virgin with the Apple" (Memling)	30	1·00

1972. Winter Olympic Games, Sapporo, Japan. Nos. 462/4 surch **WINTER OLYMPICS FEB. 3-13, 1972 SAPPORO, JAPAN**, Olympic rings and premium. Nos. 476/7 additionally optd **AIR MAIL**.

474	$2 on 2 c. mult (postage)	50	90
476	35 c. on ½ c. multicoloured (air)	15	25
477	50 c. on 1 c. multicoloured	15	35

1972. General Election. Nos. 307/8, 310 and 315 optd **VOTE FEB. 28 1972**.

478	2 c. multicoloured	10	10
479	3 c. multicoloured	10	10
480	6 c. multicoloured	10	15
481	25 c. multicoloured	15	30

183 King Arthur

1972. U.N.I.C.E.F. Multicoloured.

482	½ c. Type **183**	10	10
483	1 c. Robin Hood	10	10
484	2 c. Robinson Crusoe (vert)	10	10
485	25 c. Type **183**	10	10
486	50 c. As 1 c.	25	40
487	75 c. As 2 c.	30	80
488	$1 Mary and her little lamb (vert)	45	1·10

1972. "Interpex" Stamp Exhib., New York. Nos. 433/8 optd **INTERPEX 1972**.

490	**174** 5 c. multicoloured	10	10
491	10 c. multicoloured	10	10
492	15 c. multicoloured	10	10
493	25 c. multicoloured	10	10
494	35 c. multicoloured	15	15
495	50 c. multicoloured	25	30

1972. Nos. 306/8 and 433 surch **12c.**

497	– 12 c. on 1 c. multicoloured	40	55
498	– 12 c. on 2 c. multicoloured	40	55
499	– 12 c. on 3 c. multicoloured	40	55
500	**174** 12 c. on 5 c. multicoloured	40	55

1972. Air. Optd **AIR MAIL** or surch in addition.

501	– 5 c. mult (No. 309)	10	10
518	**175** 5 c. multicoloured	75	10
502	– 8 c. mult (No. 311)	15	10
503	– 10 c. mult (No. 312)	15	10
504	– 15 c. mult (No. 314a)	30	10
505	– 25 c. mult (No. 315)	35	20
506	– 30 c. on 1 c. mult (No. 306)	40	25
507	– 35 c. mult (No. 316)	40	25
519	– 35 c. mult (No. 441)	2·00	30
508	– 40 c. on 2 c. mult (No. 307)	50	25
509	– 45 c. on 3 c. mult (No. 308)	55	35
510	– 50 c. mult (No. 317)	55	35
520	– 50 c. mult (No. 442)	2·25	45
511	– 60 c. on 5 c. mult (No. 309)	60	40
512	– 70 c. on 6 c. mult (No. 310)	70	50
521	– 75 c. mult (No. 443)	3·00	1·00
513	– $1 mult (No. 318)	4·50	60
514	– $1.35 on 8 c. mult (No. 311)	3·25	1·50
515	– $2 mult (No. 319)	6·50	4·50
516	– $3 mult (No. 320)	7·00	4·50
517	– $5 mult (No. 321)	8·50	10·00

187 Yachting

1972. Olympic Games, Munich. Multicoloured.

522	½ c. Type **187** (postage)	10	10
523	1 c. Show-jumping	10	10
524	2 c. Running (vert)	10	10
525	35 c. As 2 c.	30	10
526	50 c. As 1 c.	40	40
527	25 c. Boxing (air)	25	10
528	$1 As 25 c.	65	85

1972. Royal Silver Wedding. As T **52** of Ascension, but with Badge of Grenada and Nutmegs in background.

530	8 c. brown	10	10
531	$1 blue	45	55

189 Boy Scout Saluting

1972. 65th Anniv of Boy Scouts. Multicoloured.

532	½ c. Type **189** (postage)	10	10
533	1 c. Scouts knotting ropes	10	10
534	2 c. Scouts shaking hands	10	10
535	3 c. Lord Baden-Powell	10	10
536	75 c. As 2 c.	1·10	2·75
537	$1 As 3 c.	1·25	2·75
538	25 c. Type **189** (air)	50	20
539	25 c. As 1 c.	70	20

190 Madonna and Child

1972. Christmas. Multicoloured.

541	1 c. Type **190**	10	10
542	3 c. The Three Kings	10	10
543	5 c. The Nativity	10	10
544	25 c. Type **190**	15	10
545	35 c. As 3 c.	20	10
546	$1 As 5 c.	60	75

191 Greater Flamingoes

1973. National Zoo. Multicoloured.

548	25 c. Type **191**	80	35
549	35 c. Brazilian tapir	80	35
550	60 c. Blue and yellow macaws	1·50	1·25
551	70 c. Ocelot	1·50	1·50

192 Class II Racing Yacht

1973. Yachting. Multicoloured.

552	25 c. Type **192**	25	10
553	35 c. Harbour, St. George's	30	10
554	60 c. Yacht "Bloodhound"	45	65
555	70 c. St. George's	50	75

193 Helios (Greek god) and Earth orbiting the Sun

1973. Centenary of I.M.O./W.M.O. Greek Gods. Multicoloured.

556	½ c. Type **193**	10	10
557	1 c. Poseidon and "Normad" storm detector	10	10
558	2 c. Zeus and radarscope	10	10
559	3 c. Iris and weather ballon	10	10
560	35 c. Hermes and "ATS-3" satellite	35	10
561	50 c. Zephyrus and diagram of pressure zones	50	30
562	75 c. Demeter and space photo	60	60
563	$1 Selene and rainfall diagram	65	1·00

194 Racing Class Yachts

1973. Carriacou Regatta. Multicoloured.

565	½ c. Type **194**	10	10
566	1 c. Cruising Class yacht	10	10
567	2 c. Open-decked sloops	10	10
568	35 c. "Mermaid" (sloop)	30	10
569	50 c. St. George's Harbour	35	25
570	75 c. Map of Carriacou	40	55
571	$1 Boat-building	55	70

195 Ignatius Semmelweis (obstetrician)

197 "Virgin and Child" (Maratti)

196 Princess Anne and Capt. Mark Phillips

1973. 25th Anniv of W.H.O. Multicoloured.

573	½ c. Type **195**	10	10
574	1 c. Louis Pasteur	10	10
575	2 c. Edward Jenner	10	10
576	3 c. Sigmund Freud	10	10
577	25 c. Emil von Behring (bacteriologist)	65	10
578	35 c. Carl Jung	75	20
579	50 c. Charles Calmette (bacteriologist)	1·10	80
580	$1 William Harvey	1·40	2·00

1973. Royal Wedding.

582	**196** 25 c. multicoloured	10	10
583	$2 multicoloured	30	45

1973. Christmas. Multicoloured.

585	½ c. Type **197**	10	10
586	1 c. "Madonna and Child" (Crivelli)	10	10
587	2 c. "Virgin and Child with two Angels" (Verrocchio)	10	10
588	3 c. "Adoration of the Shepherds" (Roberti)	10	10
589	25 c. "The Holy Family with the Infant Baptist" (Baroccio)	15	10
590	35 c. "The Holy Family" (Bronzino)	20	10
591	77 c. "Mystic Nativity" (Botticelli)	30	20
592	$1 "Adoration of the Kings" (Geertgen)	40	30

1974. Independence. Nos. 306/9, 311/13, 315/16 and 317a/21 optd INDEPENDENCE 7TH FEB. 1974.

594 86	1 c. multicoloured	10	10
595 –	2 c. multicoloured	10	10
596 –	3 c. multicoloured	10	10
597 –	5 c. multicoloured	10	10
598 –	8 c. multicoloured	15	10
599 –	10 c. multicoloured	20	15
600 –	12 c. multicoloured	20	15
601 –	25 c. multicoloured	45	35
602 –	35 c. multicoloured	75	50
603 –	75 c. multicoloured	2·00	1·25
604 –	$1 multicoloured	3·75	1·50
605 –	$2 multicoloured	6·00	5·00
606 –	$3 multicoloured	8·00	6·50
607 –	$5 multicoloured	12·00	14·00

199 Creative Arts Theatre, Jamaica Campus

1974. 25th Anniv of University of West Indies. Multicoloured.

608	10 c. Type **199**	10	10
609	25 c. Marryshow House	10	10
610	50 c. Chapel, Jamaica Campus (vert)	20	10
611	$1 University arms (vert)	30	30

200 Nutmeg Pods and Scarlet Mace

201 Footballers (West Germany v. Chile)

1974. Independence. Multicoloured.

613	3 c. Type **200**	10	10
614	8 c. Map of Grenada	10	10
615	25 c. Prime Minister Eric Gairy	15	10
616	35 c. Grand Anse Beach and flag	15	10
617	$1 Coat of arms	35	40

1974. World Cup Football Championships, West Germany. Multicoloured.

619	½ c. Type **201**	10	10
620	1 c. East Germany v. Australia	10	10
621	2 c. Yugoslavia v. Brazil	10	10
622	10 c. Scotland v. Zaire	10	10
623	25 c. Netherlands v. Uruguay	15	10
624	50 c. Sweden v. Bulgaria	20	10
625	75 c. Italy v. Haiti	35	15
626	$1 Poland v. Argentina	50	25

202 Early U.S. Mail-trains and Concorde

1974. Centenary of U.P.U. Multicoloured.

628	½ c. Type **202**	10	10
629	1 c. "Caesar" (snow) (1839) and Westland Wessex HU Mk 5 helicopter	10	10
630	2 c. Airmail transport	10	10
631	8 c. Pigeon post (1480) and telephone dial	15	10
632	15 c. 18th-century bellman and tracking antenna	30	10
633	25 c. Messenger (1450) and satellite	35	10
634	35 c. French pillar-box (1850) and mail-boat	50	10
635	$1 18th-century German postman and British Advanced Passenger train	1·50	1·25

203 Sir Winston Churchill

1974. Birth Centenary of Sir Winston Churchill.

637 203	35 c. multicoloured	15	10
638	$2 multicoloured	45	50

204 "Madonna and Child of the Eucharist" (Botticelli)

1974. Christmas. "Madonna and Child" paintings by named artists. Multicoloured.

640	½ c. Type **204**	10	10
641	1 c. Niccolo di Pietro	10	10
642	2 c. Van der Weyden	10	10
643	3 c. Bastiani	10	10
644	10 c. Giovanni	10	10
645	25 c. Van der Weyden	20	10
646	50 c. Botticelli	25	20
647	$1 Mantegna	35	50

205 Yachts, Point Saline

1975. Multicoloured.

649	½ c. Type **205**	10	40
650	1 c. Yacht Club race	10	10
651	2 c. Carenage taxi	10	10
652	3 c. Large working boats	10	10
653a	5 c. Deep-water dock	10	15
654	6 c. Cocoa beans in drying trays	10	10
655	8 c. Nutmegs	55	10
656	10 c. Rum distillery, River Antoine Estate, c. 1785	10	10
657	12 c. Cocoa tree	30	10
658	15 c. Fishermen at Fontenoy	10	10
659	20 c. Parliament Building	15	15
660	25 c. Fort George cannons	20	15
661	35 c. Pearls Airport	20	15
662	50 c. General Post Office	25	30
663	75 c. Carib's Leap, Sauteurs Bay	45	50
664	$1 Carenage, St. George's	50	70
665	$2 St. George's Harbour by night	65	1·50
666	$3 Grand Anse Beach	75	2·00
667	$5 Canoe Bay and Black Bay	1·10	3·00
668	$10 Sugar-loaf Island	2·50	6·50

Nos. 663/8 are size 45 × 28 mm.

206 Sailfish

1975. Big Game Fishing. Multicoloured.

669	½ c. Type **206**	10	10
670	1 c. Blue marlin	10	10
671	2 c. White marlin	10	10
672	10 c. Yellow-finned tuna	10	10
673	25 c. Wahoo	25	10
674	50 c. Dolphin (fish)	40	15
675	70 c. Giant grouper	60	20
676	$1 Great barracuda	80	35

207 Granadilla Barbadine

1975. Flowers. Multicoloured.

678	½ c. Type **207**	10	10
679	1 c. Bleeding Heart (Easter Lily)	10	10
680	2 c. Poinsettia	10	10
681	3 c. Cocoa flower	10	10
682	10 c. Gladioli	10	10
683	25 c. Redhead/Yellowhead	25	10
684	50 c. Plumbago	45	15
685	$1 Orange flower	70	25

208 Dove, Grenada Flag and U.N. Emblem

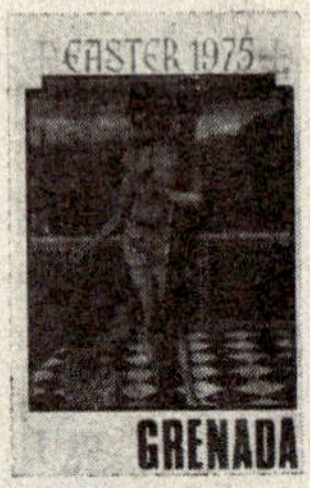

210 "Blood of the Redeemer" (G. Bellini)

209 Paul Revere's Midnight Ride

1975. Grenada's Admission to the U.N. (1974). Multicoloured.

687	½ c. Type **208**	10	10
688	1 c. Grenada and U.N. flags	10	10
689	2 c. Grenada coat of arms	10	10
690	35 c. U.N. emblem over map of Grenada	15	10
691	50 c. U.N. buildings and flags	20	15
692	$2 U.N. emblem and scroll	45	45

CANCELLED REMAINDERS*. Some of the following issues have been remaindered, cancelled to order, at a fraction of their face value. For all practical purposes these are indistinguishable from genuine postally used copies. Our used quotations which are indicated by an asterisk are the same for cancelled-to-order or postally used copies.

1975. Bicentenary of American Revolution (1st issue). Multicoloured.

694	½ c. Type **209** (postage)	10	10*
695	1 c. Crispus Attucks	10	10*
696	2 c. Patrick Henry	10	10*
697	3 c. Franklin visits Washington	10	10*
698	5 c. Rebel troops	10	10*
699	10 c. John Paul Jones	10	10*
700	40 c. "John Hancock" (Copley) (air)	35	10*
701	50 c. "Benjamin Franklin" (Roslin)	50	15*
702	75 c. "John Adams" (Copley)	70	15*
703	$1 "Lafayette" (Casanova)	80	20*

Nos. 700/3 are vert.

See also Nos. 785/91.

1975. Easter. Multicoloured.

705	½ c. Type **210**	10	10*
706	1 c. "Pieta" (Bellini)	10	10*
707	2 c. "The Entombment" (Van der Weyden)	10	10*
708	3 c. "Pieta" (Bellini)	10	10*
709	35 c. "Pieta" (Bellini)	25	10*
710	75 c. "The Dead Christ" (Bellini)	35	10*
711	$1 "The Dead Christ supported by Angels" (Procaccini)	50	10*

211 Wildlife Study

1975. 14th World Scout Jamboree, Norway. Multicoloured.

713	½ c. Type **211**	10	10*
714	1 c. Sailing	10	10*
715	2 c. Map-reading	10	10*
716	35 c. First-aid	40	10*
717	40 c. Physical training	45	10*
718	75 c. Mountaineering	60	10*
719	$2 Sing-song	1·25	20*

212 Leafy Jewel Box

213 "Lycorea ceres"

1975. Sea Shells. Multicoloured.

721	½ c. Type **212**	10	10*
722	1 c. Emerald nerite	10	10*
723	2 c. Yellow American cockle	10	10*
724	25 c. Common purple janthina	85	10*
725	50 c. Atlantic turkey wing	1·75	10*
726	75 c. West Indian fighting conch	2·25	15*
727	$1 Noble wentletrap	2·25	15*

1975. Butterflies. Multicoloured.

729	½ c. Type **213**	10	10*
730	1 c. "Adelpha cytherea"	10	10*
731	2 c. "Atlides polybe"	10	10*
732	35 c. "Anteos maerula"	80	10*
733	45 c. "Parides neophilus"	85	10*
734	75 c. "Nymula orestes"	1·25	15*
735	$2 "Euptychia cephus"	1·75	20*

MINIMUM PRICE

The minimum price quoted is 10p which represents a handling charge rather than a basis for valuing common stamps. For further notes about prices see introductory pages.

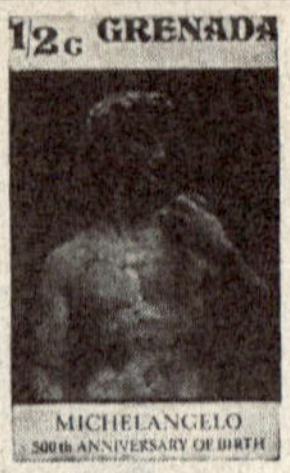

214 Rowing

215 "The Boy David" (Michelangelo)

1975. Pan-American Games, Mexico City. Multicoloured.

737	½ c. Type **214**	10	10*
738	1 c. Swimming	10	10*
739	2 c. Show-jumping	10	10*
740	35 c. Gymnastics	15	10*
741	45 c. Football	15	10*
742	75 c. Boxing	25	15*
743	$2 Cycling	65	20*

1975. 500th Birth Anniv of Michelangelo. Multicoloured.

745	½ c. Type **215**	10	10*
746	1 c. "Young Man" (detail)	10	10*
747	2 c. "Moses"	10	10*
748	40 c. "Prophet Zachariah"	40	10*
749	50 c. "St. John the Baptist"	40	15*
750	75 c. "Judith and Holofernes"	70	20*
751	$2 "Doni Madonna" (detail from "Holy Family")	1·25	25*

216 "Madonna and Child" (Filippino Lippi)

217 Bananaquit

1975. Christmas. "Virgin and Child" paintings by artists named. Multicoloured.

753	½ c. Type **216**	10	10*
754	1 c. Mantegna	10	10*
755	2 c. Luis de Morales	10	10*
756	35 c. G. M. Morandi	20	10*
757	50 c. Antonello da Messina	25	10*
758	75 c. Durer	30	10*
759	$1 Velasquez	40	10*

1976. Flora and Fauna. Multicoloured.

761	½ c. Type **217**	10	10*
762	1 c. Brazilian agouti	10	10*
763	2 c. Hawksbill turtle (horiz)	10	10*
764	5 c. Dwarf poinciana	10	10*
765	35 c. Black-finned tuna ("Albacore") (horiz)	90	10*
766	40 c. Cardinal's guard	95	10*
767	$2 Nine-banded armadillo (horiz)	2·50	30*

218 Carnival Time

1976. Tourism. Multicoloured.

769	½ c. Type **218**	10	10*
770	1 c. Scuba diving	10	10*
771	2 c. Liner "Southward" at St. George's	10	10*
772	35 c. Game fishing	65	10*
773	50 c. St. George's Golf Course	2·25	20*
774	75 c. Tennis	2·50	25*
775	$1 Ancient rock carvings at Mount Rich	2·75	25*

219 "Pieta" (Master of Okolicsno)

220 Sharpshooters

1976. Easter. Paintings by artists named. Multicoloured.

777	½ c. Type **219**	10	10*
778	1 c. Correggio	10	10*
779	2 c. Van der Weyden	10	10*
780	3 c. Durer	10	10*
781	35 c. Master of the Holy Spirit	20	10*
782	75 c. Raphael	45	15*
783	$1 Raphael	50	20*

1976. Bicentenary of American Revolution (2nd issue). Multicoloured.

785 ½ c. Type **220** 10 10*
786 1 c. Defending the Liberty Pole 10 10*
787 2 c. Loading muskets 10 10*
788 35 c. The Fight for Liberty 35 10*
789 50 c. Peace Treaty, 1783 40 10*
790 $1 Drummers 65 20*
791 $3 Gunboat 1·25 30*

221 Nature Study

222 Volleyball

1976. 50th Anniv of Girl Guides in Grenada. Multicoloured.

793 ½ c. Type **221** 10 10*
794 1 c. Campfire cooking 10 10*
795 2 c. First aid 10 10*
796 50 c. Camping 65 10*
797 75 c. Home economics 90 15*
798 $2 First aid 1·25 25*

1976. Olympic Games, Montreal. Multicoloured.

800 ½ c Type **222** 10 10*
801 1 c. Cycling 10 10*
802 2 c. Rowing 10 10*
803 35 c. Judo 30 10*
804 45 c. Hockey 60 10*
805 75 c. Gymnastics 60 20*
806 $1 High jump 60 20*

223 "Cha-U-Kao at the Moulin Rouge"

225 Satellite Assembly

224 Piper Apache 235

1976. 75th Death Anniv of Toulouse-Lautrec. Multicoloured.

808 ½ c. Type **223** 10 10*
809 1 c. "Quadrille of the Moulin Rouge" 10 10*
810 2 c. "Profile of a Woman" 10 10*
811 3 c. "Salon in the Rue des Moulins" 10 10*
812 40 c. "The Laundryman" 55 10*
813 50 c. "Marcelle Lender dancing the Bolero" 65 10*
814 $2 "Signor Boileau at the Cafe" 1·75 25*

1976. West Indian Victory in World Cricket Cup. As Nos. 559/60 of Barbados.

816 35 c. Map of the Caribbean 1·25 35
817 $1 The Prudential Cup 2·75 5·00

1976. Airplanes. Multicoloured.

818 ½ c. Type **224** 10 10*
819 1 c. Beech 50 Twin Bonanza 10 10*
820 2 c. De Havilland Twin Otter 100 10 10*
821 40 c. Britten Norman Islander 70 10*
822 50 c. De Havilland Heron 2 75 10*
823 $2 Hawker Siddeley H.S.748 2·50 50*

1976. Viking and Helios Space Missions. Multicoloured.

825 ½ c Type **225** 10 10*
826 1 c. Helios satellite 10 10*
827 2 c. Helios encapsulation 10 10*
828 15 c. Systems test 10 10*
829 45 c. Viking lander (horiz) 20 10*
830 75 c. Lander on Mars 35 15*
831 $2 Viking encapsulation 90 25*

226 S.S. "Geestland"

1976. Ships. Multicoloured.

833 ½ c. Type **226** 10 10*
834 1 c. M.V. "Federal Palm" 10 10*
835 2 c. H.M.S "Blake" 10 10*
836 25 c. M.V. "Vistafjord" 45 10*
837 75 c. S.S. "Canberra" 90 15*
838 $1 S.S. "Regina" 1·10 20*
839 $5 S.S. "Arandora Star" 2·75 40*

227 "San Barnaba Altarpiece" (Botticelli)

1976. Christmas. Multicoloured.

841 ½ c. Type **227** 10 10*
842 1 c. "Annunciation" (Botticelli) 10 10*
843 2 c. "Madonna of Chancellor Rolin" (Jan van Eyck) 10 10*
844 35 c. "Annunciation" (Fra Filippo Lippi) 15 10*
845 50 c. "Madonna of the Magnificat" (Botticelli) 20 10*
846 75 c. "Madonna of the Pomegranate" (Botticelli) 35 15*
847 $3 "Madonna with St. Cosmas and other Saints" (Botticelli) 1·00 25*

228 Alexander Graham Bell and Telephones

1976. Centenary of First Telephone. Multicoloured.

849 ½ c. Type **228** 10 10*
850 1 c. Telephone users within globe 10 10*
851 2 c. Telephone satellite 10 10*
852 18 c. Telephone viewer and console 20 10*
853 40 c. Satellite and tracking stations 35 10*
854 $1 Satellite transmitting to ships 50 15*
855 $2 Dish aerial and modern telephone 75 25*

229 Coronation Scene

1977. Silver Jubilee. Multicoloured. (a) Perf.

857 ½ c. Type **229** 10 10*
858 1 c. Sceptre and orb 10 10*
859 35 c. The Queen on horseback 10 10*
860 $2 Spoon and ampulla 25 15*
861 $2.50 The Queen and Prince Philip 25 15*

(b) Roul. Self-adhesive.

863 35 c. As $2.50 15 25
864 50 c. As $2 25 1·00
865 $1 As 1 c. 50 1·40
866 $3 As 35 c. 1·25 2·75

230 Water Skiing

1977. Easter Water Parade. Multicoloured.

867 ½ c. Type **230** 10 10*
868 1 c. Speedboat race 10 10*
869 2 c. Row boat race 10 10*
870 22 c. Swimming 15 10*
871 35 c. Work boat race 25 10*
872 75 c. Water polo 40 15*
873 $2 Game fishing 90 25*

231 Meeting Place, Grand Anse Beach

1977. 7th Meeting of Organization of American States.

875 **231** 35 c. multicoloured 10 10
876 $1 multicoloured 25 60
877 $2 multicoloured 40 1·75

232 Rafting

1977. Caribbean Scout Jamboree, Jamaica. Multicoloured.

878 ½ c. Type **232** 10 10*
879 1 c. Tug-of-war 10 10*
880 2 c. Sea Scouts regatta 10 10*
881 18 c. Camp fire 25 10*
882 40 c. Field kitchen 50 10*
883 $1 Scouts and sea scouts 1·00 15*
884 $2 Hiking and map reading 1·40 25*

233 Angel and Shepherd

1977. Christmas. Ceiling Panels from Church of St. Martin, Zillis. Multicoloured.

886 ½ c. Type **233** 10 10*
887 1 c. St. Joseph 10 10*
888 2 c. Virgin and Child fleeing to Egypt 10 10*
889 22 c. Angel 10 10*
890 35 c. Magus on horseback 15 10*
891 75 c. Three horses 20 15*
892 $2 Virgin and Child 50 25*

1977. Royal Visit. Nos. 857/61 optd **Royal Visit W. I. 1977.**

894 ½ c. Type **229** 10 10
895 1 c. Sceptre and Orb 10 10
896 35 c. Queen on horseback 10 10
897 $2 Spoon and ampulla 30 40
898 $2.50 The Queen and Prince Philip 35 45

235 Christjaan Eijkman (Medicine)

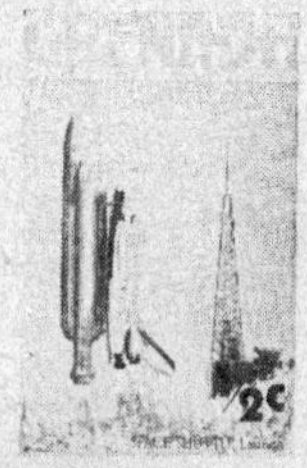

237 Rocket Launching

236 Count von Zeppelin and First Zeppelin Airship LZ-1

1978. Nobel Prize Winners. Multicoloured.

900 ½ c. Type **235** 10 10*
901 1 c. Sir Winston Churchill (Literature) 30 10*
902 2 c. Woodrow Wilson (Peace) 10 10*
903 35 c. Frederic Passy (Peace) 15 10*
904 $1 Albert Einstein (Physics) 1·00 15*
905 $3 Carl Bosch (Chemistry) 1·75 25*

1978. 75th Anniv of First Zeppelin Flight and 50th Anniv of Lindbergh's Transatlantic Flight. Multicoloured.

907 ½ c. Type **236** 10 10*
908 1 c. Lindbergh with "Spirit of St. Louis" 10 10*
909 2 c. Airship "Deutschland" 10 10*
910 22 c. Lindbergh's arrival in France 25 10*
911 75 c. Lindbergh and "Spirit of St. Louis" in flight 50 10*
912 $1 "Graf Zeppelin" over Alps 55 15*
913 $3 "Graf Zeppelin" over White House 1·25 25*

1978. Space Shuttle. Multicoloured.

915 ½ c. Type **237** 10 10*
916 1 c. Booster jettison 10 10*
917 2 c. External tank jettison 10 10*
918 18 c. Space Shuttle in orbit 25 10*
919 75 c. Satellite placement 55 10*
920 $2 Landing approach 1·25 20*

238 Black-headed Gull

239 "The Landing of Marie de Medici at Marseilles"

1978. Wild Birds of Grenada. Multicoloured.

922 ½ c. Type **238** 10 10*
923 1 c. Wilson's petrel 10 10*
924 2 c. Killdeer 10 10*
925 50 c. White-necked jacobin 1·50 10*
926 75 c. Blue-faced booby 2·00 15*
927 $1 Broad-winged hawk 3·00 20*
928 $2 Red-necked pigeon 4·00 30*

1978. 400th Birth Anniv of Peter Paul Rubens. Multicoloured.

930 5 c. Type **239** 10 10*
931 15 c. "Rubens and Isabella Brandt" 10 10*
932 18 c. "Marchesa Brigida Spindola-Doria" 10 10*
933 25 c. "Ludovicus Nonninus" 10 10*
934 45 c. "Helene Fourment and her Children" 15 10*
935 75 c. "Clara Serena Rubens" 25 10*
936 $3 "Le Chapeau de Paille" 60 20*

240 Ludwig van Beethoven

241 King Edward's Chair

1978. 150th Death Anniv of Beethoven. Mult.

938 5 c. Type **240** 10 10*
939 15 c. Woman violinist (horiz) 15 10*
940 18 c. Musical instruments (horiz) 20 10*
941 22 c. Piano (horiz) 20 10*
942 50 c. Violins 40 10*
943 75 c. Piano and sonata score 60 15*
944 $3 Beethoven's portrait and home (horiz) 2·25 25*

1978. 25th Anniv of Coronation. Mult. (a) Perf.

946 35 c. Type **241** 10 10
947 $2 Queen with regalia 30 35
948 $2.50 St. Edward's Crown 30 40

(b) Roul × imperf. Self-adhesive.

950 25 c. Queen Elizabeth II taking salute, Trooping the Colour 15 15
951 35 c. Queen at Maundy Thursday ceremony 15 25
952 $5 Queen and Prince Philip at Opening of Parliament 1·50 2·50

243 Goalkeeper reaching for Ball

244 Aerial Phenomena, Germany, 1561 and U.S.A., 1952

1978. World Cup Football Championships, Argentina.

953 **243** 40 c. multicoloured 10 10
954 – 60 c. multicoloured 15 20
955 – 90 c. multicoloured 25 30
956 – $2 multicoloured 60 60

DESIGNS: 60 c. to $2. Designs similar to Type **243** with goalkeeper reaching for ball.

1978. U.F.O. Research. Multicoloured.

958 5 c. Type **244** 15 10
959 35 c. Various aerial phenomena, 1950 35 25
960 $3 U.F.O.s, 1965 2·00 1·75

245 Wright Flyer III, 1902

1978. 75th Anniv of Powered Flight. Mult.

962 5 c. Type **245** 10 10
963 15 c. Wright Flyer I, 1903 10 10
964 18 c. Wright Type A 10 10
965 22 c. Wright Flyer I from above 15 10
966 50 c. Orville Wright and Wright Type A 20 20
967 75 c. Wright Type A, Pau, France, 1908 25 25
968 $3 Wilbur Wright and Wright glider No. IV 80 70

246 Cook and Hawaiian Feast

1978. 250th Birth Anniv of Captain James Cook and Bicentenary of Discovery of Hawaii. Multicoloured.

970	18 c. Type **246**	60	20
971	35 c. Cook and Hawaiian dance	80	25
972	75 c. Cook and Honolulu harbour	1·50	1·50
973	$3 Cook's statue and H.M.S. "Resolution"	3·00	6·00

247 "Paumgartner Altarpiece" (detail)

248 National Convention and Cultural Centre (interior)

1978. Christmas. Paintings by Durer. Multicoloured.

975	40 c. Type **247**	20	15
976	60 c. "The Adoration of the Magi"	25	20
977	90 c. "Virgin and Child"	30	20
978	$2 "Virgin and Child with St. Anne" (detail)	55	55

1979. 5th Anniv of Independence.

980	5 c. Type **248**	10	10
981	18 c. National Convention and Cultural Centre (exterior)	10	10
982	22 c. Easter Water Parade, 1978	10	10
983	35 c. Sir Eric M. Gairy (Prime Minister)	15	10
984	$3 The Cross, Fort Frederick	60	80

249 "Acalypha hispida"

250 Birds in Flight

1979. Flowers. Multicoloured.

985	18 c. Type **249**	10	10
986	50 c. "Hibiscus rosa sinensis"	25	15
987	$1 "Thunbergia grandiflora"	40	25
988	$3 "Nerium oleander"	1·10	1·10

1979. 30th Anniv of Declaration of Human Rights. Multicoloured.

990	15 c. Type **250**	10	10
991	$2 Bird in Flight	55	65

251 Children playing Cricket

1979. Int Year of the Child (1st issue). Mult.

992	18 c. Type **251**	40	30
993	22 c. Children playing baseball	40	30
994	$5 Children playing in a tree	3·75	6·00

See also Nos. 1006/7 and 1025/33.

252 "Around the World in 80 Days"

1979. 150th Birth Anniv of Jules Verne. Mult.

996	18 c. Type **252**	25	10
997	35 c. "20,000 Leagues under the Sea"	35	15
998	75 c. "From the Earth to the Moon"	50	50
999	$3 "Master of the World"	1·40	1·60

253 Mail Runner, Africa (early 19th-century)

1979. Death Cent of Sir Rowland Hill. Mult.

1001	20 c. Type **253**	10	10
1002	40 c. Pony Express, America (mid 19th-century)	10	10
1003	$1 Pigeon post	20	25
1004	$3 Mail coach, Europe (18–19th century)	50	80

254 "The Pistol of Peace" (vaccination gun), Map of Grenada and Children

1979. International Year of the Child (2nd issue). "Grenada—First Nation 100% Immunized"

1006	**254** 5 c. multicoloured	30	20
1007	$1 multicoloured	1·00	2·00

255 Reef Shark

1979. Marine Wildlife. Multicoloured.

1008	40 c. Type **255**	40	30
1009	45 c. Spotted eagle ray	40	30
1010	50 c. Many-toothed conger	45	40
1011	60 c. Golden olive (shell)	70	75
1012	70 c. West Indian murex (shell)	85	90
1013	75 c. Giant tun (shell)	90	1·00
1014	90 c. Brown booby	2·25	2·00
1015	$1 Magnificent frigate bird	2·25	2·00

256 The Flight into Egypt

1979. Christmas. Tapestries. Multicoloured.

1017	6 c. Type **256**	10	10
1018	25 c. The Flight into Egypt (detail)	10	10
1019	30 c. Angel (vert)	15	10
1020	40 c. (Doge Marino Grimani (detail) (vert)	15	10
1021	90 c. The Annunciation to the Shepherds (vert)	30	20
1022	$1 The Flight into Egypt (Rome) (vert)	30	25
1023	$2 The Virgin in Glory (vert)	40	50

257 Mickey Mouse playing Baseball

258 Paul Harris (founder)

1979. International Year of the Child (3rd issue). Disney Characters. Multicoloured.

1025	½ c. Type **257**	10	10
1026	1 c. Donald Duck high-jumping	10	10
1027	2 c. Goofy playing basketbal	10	10
1028	3 c. Goofy hurdling	10	10
1029	4 c. Donald Duck playing golf	10	10
1030	5 c. Mickey Mouse playing cricket	10	10
1031	10 c. Mickey Mouse playing football	10	10
1032	$2 Mickey Mouse playing tennis	2·75	3·00
1033	$2.50 Minnie Mouse riding horse	2·75	3·00

1980. 75th Anniv of Rotary International. Mult.

1035	6 c. Type **258**	10	10
1036	30 c. "Health"	20	15
1037	90 c. "Hunger"	40	30
1038	$2 "Humanity"	80	80

1980. 1st Anniv of Revolution (1st issue). Nos. 651/2, 654/7, 659/60 and 662/8 optd **PEOPLE'S REVOLUTION 13 MARCH 1979.**

1040	2 c. Carenage taxi	10	10
1041	3 c. Large working boats	10	10
1042	6 c. Cocoa beans in drying trays	10	10
1043	8 c. Nutmegs	10	10
1044	10 c. Rum distillery, River Antoine Estate, c. 1785	10	10
1045	12 c. Cocoa tree	10	10
1046	20 c. Parliament Building	10	15
1047	25 c. Fort George cannons	30	30
1048	50 c. General Post Office	30	30
1049	75 c. Carib's Leap, Sauteurs Bay	50	40
1050	$1 Carenage, St. George's	60	60
1051	$2 St. George's Harbour by night	1·25	2·00
1052	$3 Grand Anse Beach	1·50	3·25
1053	$5 Canoe Bay and Black Bay	2·50	5·00
1054	$10 Sugar-loaf Island	3·75	7·50

See also Nos. 1069/72.

260 Boxing

1980. Olympic Games, Moscow. Multicoloured.

1055	25 c. Type **260**	10	10
1056	40 c. Cycling	15	10
1057	90 c. Show-jumping	20	30
1058	$2 Running	40	1·00

261 Tropical Kingbird

1980. Wild Birds. Multicoloured.

1060	20 c. Type **261**	85	15
1061	40 c. Rufous-breasted hermit	1·25	25
1062	$1 Troupial	1·75	1·75
1063	$2 Ruddy quail dove	2·25	3·50

1980. "London 1980". International Stamp Exhibition. Nos. 1001/4 optd **LONDON 1980**.

1065	**253** 20 c. Mail runner, Africa	20	20
1066	– 40 c. Pony Express, America	30	30
1067	– $1 Pigeon post	60	60
1068	– $3 Mail coach, Europe	1·75	1·75

263 Free Hot Lunch at Schools

1980. 1st Anniv of Revolution (2nd issue). Multicoloured.

1069	10 c. Type **263**	10	10
1070	40 c. "From tree to can" (agro-industry)	15	20
1071	$1 National Health care	40	45
1072	$2 New housing projects	75	90

264 Jamb Statues, West Portal, Chartres Cathedral

1980. Famous Works of Art. Multicoloured.

1074	8 c. Type **264**	10	10
1075	10 c. "Les Demoiselles d' Avignon" (painting, Picasso)	10	10
1076	40 c. Winged Victory of Samothrace (statue)	20	20
1077	50 c. "The Night Watch" (painting, Rembrandt)	20	20
1078	$1 "Portrait of Edward VI as a Child" (painting, Holbein the Younger)	35	35
1079	$3 Portrait head of Queen Nefertiti (carving)	80	80

265 Carib Canoes

1980. Shipping. Multicoloured.

1081A	½ c. Type **265**	10	10
1082A	1 c. Boat building	10	10
1083A	2 c. Small working boat	15	10
1084A	4 c. Columbus's "Santa Maria"	40	10
1085A	5 c. West Indiaman barque, c. 1840	40	10
1086A	6 c. "Orinoco" (paddle-steamer), c. 1851	40	10
1087A	10 c. Working schooner	50	10
1088A	12 c. Trimaran at Grand Anse anchorage	50	10
1089A	15 c. Spice Island cruising yacht "Petite Amie"	50	10
1090A	20 c. Fishing pirogue	1·00	10
1091A	25 c. Harbour police launch	1·75	20
1092A	30 c. Grand Anse speedboat	1·50	20
1093A	40 c. "Seimstrand" (freighter)	1·50	25
1094B	50 c. "Ariadne" (cadet schooner)	50	50
1095A	90 c. "Geestide" (freighter)	1·75	50
1096A	$1 "Cunard Countess" (liner)	2·00	70
1097A	$3 Rum-runner	3·00	4·00
1098A	$5 "Statendam" (liner) off St. George's	4·50	7·00
1099B	$10 Coastguard patrol boat	7·00	8·50

Nos. 1081/99 come with and without date imprint.

1980. Christmas. Scenes from Walt Disney's "Snow White and the Seven Dwarfs". As T **257**. Multicoloured.

1100	½ c. Snow White at well	10	10
1101	1 c. The Wicked Queen	10	10
1102	2 c. Snow White singing to animals	10	10
1103	3 c. Snow White doing housework for Dwarfs	10	10
1104	4 c. The Seven Dwarfs	10	10
1105	5 c. Snow White with Dwarfs	10	10
1106	10 c. Witch offering Snow White apple	10	10
1107	$2.50 Snow White with Prince and Dwarfs	3·00	1·75
1108	$3 Snow White and Prince	3·50	2·00

1981. 50th Anniv of Walt Disney's Pluto (cartoon character). As T **257**. Multicoloured.

1110	$2 Pluto with birthday cake	1·25	1·50

266 Revolution and Grenada Flags

1981. Festival of the Revolution. Multicoloured.

1112	5 c. Type **266**	10	10
1113	10 c. Teacher, pupil, book and pencil ("education")	10	10
1114	15 c. Food processing plant ("industry")	10	10
1115	25 c. Selection of fruits and farm scene ("agriculture")	15	15
1116	40 c. Crawfish and boat ("fishing")	20	20
1117	90 c. "Cunard Countess" arriving at St. George's Harbour ("shipping")	50	50
1118	$1 Straw-work ("native handicrafts")	60	60
1119	$3 Map of Caribbean with expanded view of Grenada	1·75	1·75

1981. Easter. Walt Disney Cartoon Characters. As T **257**. Multicoloured.

1120	35 c. Mickey Mouse and Goofy	40	25
1121	40 c. Donald Duck, Chip and Daisy Duck	40	25
1122	$2 Minnie Mouse	1·40	1·50
1123	$2.50 Pluto and Mickey Mouse	1·60	1·75

267 "Woman-Flower"

268 Prince Charles playing Polo

1981. Birth Centenary of Picasso. Multicoloured.

1125	25 c. Type **267**	15	15
1126	30 c. "Portrait of Madame"	20	15
1127	90 c. "Cavalier with Pipe"	40	45
1128	$4 "Large Heads"	1·50	1·75

1991. Royal Wedding (1st issue). Multicoloured.

1134	30 c. Prince Charles and Lady Diana Spencer	20	20
1135	40 c. Holyrood House	30	30
1130	50 c. As 30 c.	10	10
1131	$2 As 40 c.	35	50
1132	$4 Type **268**	50	75

269 Lady Diana Spencer

270 "The Bath" (Mary Cassatt)

1981. Royal Wedding (2nd issue). Multicoloured. Self-adhesive.

1136	$1 Type **269**	30	65
1137	$2 Prince Charles	30	65
1138	$5 Prince Charles and Lady Diana Spencer	1·00	1·75

1981. "Decade for Women". Paintings. Mult.

1139	15 c. Type **270**	15	10
1140	40 c. "Mademoiselle Charlotte du Val d'Ognes" (Constance Marie Charpentier)	45	20
1141	60 c. "Self-portrait" (Mary Beale)	65	30
1142	$3 "Woman in White Stockings" (Suzanne Valadon)	2·00	1·25

1981. Christmas. As T **257** showing scenes from Walt Disney's cartoon film "Cinderella".

1144	½ c. multicoloured	10	10
1145	1 c. multicoloured	10	10
1146	2 c. multicoloured	10	10
1147	3 c. multicoloured	10	10
1148	4 c. multicoloured	10	10
1149	5 c. multicoloured	10	10
1150	10 c. multicoloured	15	10
1151	$2.50 multicoloured	3·50	2·25
1152	$3 multicoloured	3·50	2·50

271 Landing

273 General Post Office, St. George's

272 West German Footballer and Flag

1981. Space Shuttle Project. Multicoloured.

1154	30 c. Type **271**	20	15
1155	60 c. Working in space	40	30
1156	70 c. Lift off	45	35
1157	$3 Separation	1·40	1·25

1981. World Cup Football Championship, Spain (1982). Multicoloured.

1159	25 c. + 10 c. Type **272**	55	30
1160	40 c. + 20 c. Argentinian footballer and flag	70	40
1161	50 c. + 25 c. Brazilian footballer and flag	80	50
1162	$1 + 50 c. English footballer and flag	1·25	95

1981. Cent of U.P.U. Membership. Mult.

1164	25 c. Type **273**	20	15
1165	30 c. 1861 1d. stamp	25	20
1166	90 c. New U.P.U. Headquarters Building 25 c. commemorative	65	50
1167	$4 1961 Stamp Centenary 25 c. commemorative	1·75	2·00

274 Artist without Hands

276 "Dryas julia"

275 Tending Vegetable Patch

1982. International Year for the Disabled (1981). Multicoloured.

1169	30 c. Type **274**	45	15
1170	40 c. Computer operator without hands	50	15
1171	70 c. Blind schoolteacher teaching braille	75	25
1172	$3 Midget playing drums	1·75	1·10

1982. 75th Anniv of Boy Scout Movement and 125th Birth Anniv of Lord Baden-Powell. Multicoloured.

1174	70 c. Type **275**	50	45
1175	90 c. Map-reading	55	55
1176	$1 Bee-keeping	65	65
1177	$4 Hospital reading	2·25	2·75

1982. Butterflies. Multicoloured.

1179	10 c. Type **276**	75	30
1180	60 c. "Phoebis agarithe"	2·50	1·50
1181	$1 "Anartia amathea"	3·00	2·00
1182	$3 "Battus polydamas"	4·25	7·00

277 "Saying Grace"

278 Kensington Palace

1982. Norman Rockwell (painter) Commemoration. Multicoloured.

1184	15 c. Type **277**	35	10
1185	30 c. "Nothing Up His Sleeve" (inscr "Card Tricks")	60	15
1186	60 c. "Pharmacist"	75	25
1187	70 c. "Hobo" (inscr "Pals")	80	35

1982. 21st Birthday of Princess of Wales. Multicoloured.

1188	50 c. Type **278**	40	45
1189	60 c. Type **278**	80	45
1190	$1 Prince and Princess of Wales	90	1·00
1191	$2 As $1	1·75	1·25
1192	$3 Princess of Wales	2·00	2·25
1193	$4 As $3	2·25	2·25

279 Mary McLeod Bethune appointed Director of Negro Affairs, 1942

1982. Birth Centenary of Franklin D. Roosevelt. Multicoloured.

1195	10 c. Type **279**	10	10
1196	60 c. Huddie Ledbetter "Leadbelly" in concert (Works Progress administration)	35	20
1197	$1.10 Signing bill No. 8802, 1941 (Fair Employment committee)	65	40
1198	$3 Farm Security administration	1·00	80

1982. Birth of Prince William of Wales. Nos. 1188/93 optd **ROYAL BABY 21.6.82.**

1200	50 c. Type **278**	30	60
1201	60 c. Type **278**	35	35
1202	$1 Prince and Princess of Wales	55	85
1203	$2 As $1	1·00	1·00
1204	$3 Princess of Wales	1·75	1·90
1205	$4 As $3	1·90	1·90

280 Apostle and Tormentor

1982. Easter. Details from Painting "The Way to Calvary" by Raphael. Multicoloured.

1207	40 c. Type **280**	30	15
1208	70 c. Captain of the guards (vert)	40	25
1209	$1.10 Christ and apostle (vert)	60	35
1210	$4 Mourners (vert)	1·50	1·50

281 "Orient Express"

1982. Famous Trains of the World. Mult.

1212	30 c. Type **281**	50	35
1213	60 c. "Trans-Siberian Express"	60	70
1214	70 c. "Fleche d'Or"	70	80
1215	90 c. "Flying Scotsman"	85	1·00
1216	$1 German Federal Railways steam locomotive	1·00	1·25
1217	$3 German National Railways Class 05 steam locomotive	2·25	4·00

282 Footballers

1982. World Cup Football Championship Winners.

1219	**282** 60 c. multicoloured	35	35
1220	$4 multicoloured	2·00	2·00

1982. Christmas. Scenes from Walt Disney's cartoon film "Robin Hood". As T **257**, but horiz.

1222	½ c. multicoloured	10	10
1223	1 c. multicoloured	10	10
1224	2 c. multicoloured	10	10
1225	3 c. multicoloured	10	10
1226	4 c. multicoloured	10	10
1227	5 c. multicoloured	10	10
1228	10 c. multicoloured	10	10
1229	$2.50 multicoloured	2·00	2·75
1230	$3 multicoloured	2·25	2·75

283 Killer Whale

285 Dentistry at Health Centre

284 "Construction of Ark"

1983. Save the Whales. Multicoloured.

1232	15 c. Type **283**	1·00	30
1233	40 c. Sperm whale	2·25	90
1234	70 c. Blue whale	2·75	2·75
1235	$3 Common dolphin	3·50	6·50

1983. 500th Birth Anniv of Raphael. Mult.

1237	25 c. Type **284**	20	15
1238	30 c. "Jacob's Vision"	20	20
1239	90 c. "Joseph interprets the Dreams of his Brothers"	40	45
1240	$4 "Joseph interprets Pharaoh's dreams"	1·60	1·75

1983. Commonwealth Day. Multicoloured.

1242	10 c. Type **285**	10	10
1243	70 c. Airport runway construction	35	35
1244	$1.10 Tourism	40	55
1245	$3 Boat-building	80	1·40

286 Maritime Communications via Satellite

1983. World Communications Year. Multicoloured.

1246	30 c. Type **286**	15	15
1247	40 c. Rural telephone installation	20	20
1248	$2.50 Satellite weather map	1·25	1·25
1249	$4 Airport control room	1·40	1·40

287 Franklin Sport Sedan, 1928

1983. 75th Anniv of Model "T" Ford Car. Multicoloured.

1251	6 c. Type **287**	15	10
1252	10 c. Delage "D8", 1933	20	10
1253	40 c. Alvis, 1938	35	25
1254	60 c. Invicta "S-type" tourer, 1931	45	45
1255	70 c. Alfa-Romeo "1750 Gran Sport", 1930	55	55
1256	90 c. Isotta Fraschini, 1930	60	65
1257	$1 Bugatti "Royale Type 41"	70	65
1258	$2 BMW "328", 1938	1·40	1·50
1259	$3 Marmon "V16", 1931	1·60	2·25
1260	$4 Lincoln "K8" saloon, 1932	1·90	2·75

288 Airship N.1 "Norge"

1983. Bicentenary of Manned Flight. Multicoloured.

1262	30 c. Type **288**	60	30
1263	60 c. Gloster VI seaplane	1·00	1·00
1264	$1.10 Curtiss NC-4 flying boat	1·60	1·75
1265	$4 Dornier Do 18 flying boat "Aeolus"	3·50	4·50

289 Morty

291 William I

290 Daisy Duck on Pommel Horse

1983. Christmas. Multicoloured.

1267	½ c. Type **289**	10	10
1268	1 c. Ludwig von Drake	10	10
1269	2 c. Gyro Gearloose	10	10
1270	3 c. Pluto and Figaro	10	10
1271	4 c. Morty and Ferdie	10	10
1272	5 c. Mickey Mouse and Goofy	10	10
1273	10 c. Chip n'Dale	10	10
1274	$2.50 Mickey and Minnie Mouse	2·75	3·50
1275	$3 Donald and Grandma Duck	3·00	3·50

Nos. 1267/75 show Disney cartoon characters in scenes from "It's beginning to look a lot like Christmas" (song).

1984. Olympic Games. Los Angeles. Multicoloured.
A. Inscr "1984 LOS ANGELES"
B. Inscr "1984 OLYMPICS LOS ANGELES" and Olympic Emblem

		A		B	
1277	½ c. Type **290**	10	10	10	10
1278	1 c. Mickey Mouse boxing	10	10	10	10
1279	2 c. Daisy Duck in archery event	10	10	10	10
1280	3 c. Clarabelle Cow on uneven bars	10	10	10	10
1281	4 c. Mickey and Minnie Mouse in hurdles race	10	10	10	10
1282	5 c. Donald Duck with Chip'n'Dale weightlifting	10	10	10	10
1283	$1 Little Hiawatha in single kayak	1·75	2·00	1·75	2·00
1284	$2 The Tortoise and the Hare in marathon	2·25	3·00	2·25	3·00
1285	$3 Mickey Mouse polevaulting	2·75	3·25	2·75	3·25

1984. English Monarchs. Multicoloured.

1287	$4 Type **291**	3·00	3·25
1288	$4 William II	3·00	3·25
1289	$4 Henry I	3·00	3·25
1290	$4 Stephen	3·00	3·25
1291	$4 Henry II	3·00	3·25
1292	$4 Richard I	3·00	3·25
1293	$4 John	3·00	3·25
1294	$4 "Henry III"	3·00	3·25
1295	$4 Edward I	3·00	3·25
1296	$4 Edward II	3·00	3·25
1297	$4 Edward III	3·00	3·25
1298	$4 Richard II	3·00	3·25
1299	$4 Henry IV	3·00	3·25
1300	$4 Henry V	3·00	3·25
1301	$4 Henry VI	3·00	3·25
1302	$4 Edward IV	3·00	3·25
1303	$4 Edward V	3·00	3·25
1304	$4 Richard III	3·00	3·25
1305	$4 Henry VII	3·00	3·25
1306	$4 Henry VIII	3·00	3·25
1307	$4 Edward VI	3·00	3·25
1308	$4 Jane Grey	3·00	3·25

1309	$4 Mary I	3·00	3·25
1310	$4 Elizabeth I	3·00	3·25
1311	$4 James I	3·00	3·25
1312	$4 Charles I	3·00	3·25
1313	$4 Charles II	3·00	3·25
1314	$4 James II	3·00	3·25
1315	$4 William III	3·00	3·25
1316	$4 Mary II	3·00	3·25
1317	$4 Anne	3·00	3·25
1318	$4 George I	3·00	3·25
1319	$4 George II	3·00	3·25
1320	$4 George III	3·00	3·25
1321	$4 George IV	3·00	3·25
1322	$4 William IV	3·00	3·25
1323	$4 Victoria	3·00	3·25
1324	$4 Edward VII	3·00	3·25
1325	$4 George V	3·00	3·25
1326	$4 Edward VIII	3·00	3·25
1327	$4 George VI	3·00	3·25
1328	$4 Elizabeth II	3·00	3·25

Although inscribed "Henry III" the portrait on No. 1294 is actually of Edward II.

292 Lantana

1984. Flowers. Multicoloured.

1329	25 c. Type **292**	20	15
1330	30 c. Plumbago	25	20
1331	90 c. Spider lily	70	60
1332	$4 Giant alocasia	2·50	3·00

293 Blue Parrotfish

1984. Coral Reef Fishes. Multicoloured.

1334	10 c. Type **293**	1·40	45
1335	30 c. Flame-backed angelfish	2·75	1·10
1336	70 c. Painted wrasse	4·00	3·25
1337	90 c. Rosy razorfish	4·75	3·50

1984. Universal Postal Union Congress, Hamburg. Nos. 1331/2 optd **19th U.P.U. CONGRESS – HAMBURG**.

1339	90 c. Spider lily	60	65
1340	$4 Giant alocasia	2·00	2·50

295 Freighter

296 "The Night" (detail) (Correggio)

1984. Ships. Multicoloured.

1342	40 c. Type **295**	1·25	55
1343	70 c. "Queen Elizabeth 2"	1·50	1·50
1344	90 c. Sailing boats	1·90	2·00
1345	$4 "Amerikanis"	6·00	8·00

1984. 450th Death Anniv of Correggio (painter). Multicoloured.

1347	10 c. Type **296**	45	15
1348	30 c. "The Virgin adoring the Child"	80	50
1349	40 c. "The Mystical Marriage of St. Catherine with St. Sebastian"	2·00	1·75
1350	$4 "The Madonna and the Fruit Basket"	4·50	5·50

297 "L'Absinthe" (Degas)

298 Train on Puffing Billy Line, Victoria

1984. 150th Birth Anniv of Edgar Degas (painter). Multicoloured.

1352	25 c. Type **297**	80	30
1353	70 c. "Pouting" (horiz)	1·50	1·25
1354	$1.10 "The Millinery Shop"	2·00	2·00
1355	$3 "The Bellelli Family" (horiz)	3·75	4·25

1984. "Ausipex" International Stamp Exhibition, Melbourne. Multicoloured.

1357	$1.10 Type **298**	2·25	1·75
1358	$4 Yacht "Australia II" (winner of America's Cup)	4·75	5·25

299 George Stephenson's "Locomotion" (1825)

1984. Railway Locomotives. Multicoloured.

1360	30 c. Type **299**	80	35
1361	40 c. Braithwaite and Ericsson's "Novelty" (1829)	95	40
1362	60 c. William Norris's "Washington Farmer" (1836)	1·10	75
1363	70 c. French Crampton type (1859)	1·25	1·00
1364	90 c. Dutch State Railways (1873)	1·50	1·50
1365	$1.10 "Champion", U.S.A. (1882)	1·75	2·00
1366	$2 Webb Compound type (1893)	2·25	3·25
1367	$4 Berlin "No. 74" (1900)	3·75	5·50

1984. Opening of Point Saline International Airport (1st issue). Nos. 1247 and 1249 optd **OPENING OF POINT SALINE INT'L AIRPORT**.

1369	40 c. Rural telephone installation	30	30
1370	$3 Airport control room	2·00	2·00

See Nos. 1399/5.

301 Donald Duck as Father Christmas looking into Mirror

1984. Christmas. Walt Disney Cartoon Characters. Multicoloured.

1372	45 c. Type **301**	1·25	40
1373	60 c. Donald Duck filling stocking with presents	1·50	55
1374	90 c. As Father Christmas pulling a sleigh	2·00	1·10
1375	$2 As Father Christmas decorating Christmas tree	3·50	3·50
1376	$4 Donald Duck and nephews singing carols	5·00	5·50

1985. Birth Bicentenary of John J. Audubon (ornithologist) (1st issue). As T **198** of Antigua. Multicoloured.

1378	50 c. Clapper rail (vert)	2·00	75
1379	70 c. Hooded warbler (vert)	2·25	1·50
1380	90 c. Common flicker (vert)	2·75	1·75
1381	$4 Bohemian waxwing (vert)	5·50	8·00

See also Nos. 1480/3.

302 Honda "XL500R"

1985. Centenary of the Motor Cycle. Multicoloured.

1383	25 c. Type **302**	90	50
1384	50 c. Suzuki "GS1100ES"	1·40	1·00
1385	90 c. Kawasaki "KZ700"	2·00	2·00
1386	$4 BMW "K100"	5·50	6·50

303 "Explorer"

1985. 75th Anniv of Girl Guide Movement. Designs showing work for Guide badges. Multicoloured.

1388	25 c. Type **303**	55	30
1389	60 c. "Cook"	90	65
1390	90 c. "Musician"	1·50	1·10
1391	$3 "Home nurse"	3·00	3·50

304 Hawker Siddeley H.S.748 on Inaugural Flight from Barbados

1985. Opening of Point Saline International Airport (1984) (2nd issue). Multicoloured.

1393	70 c. Type **304**	2·50	1·00
1394	$1 Lockheed TriStar 500 on inaugural flight from New York	3·25	1·50
1395	$4 Lockheed TriStar 500 on inaugural flight to Miami	6·50	8·00

305 Douglas DC-8-61

1985. 40th Anniv of International Civil Aviation Organization. Multicoloured.

1397	10 c. Type **305**	40	20
1398	50 c. Lockheed Starliner (inscr "Super Constellation")	1·00	75
1399	60 c. Vickers 952 Cargoliner	1·25	85
1400	$4 De Havilland Twin Otter 200/300	4·50	6·00

306 Model Boat Racing

1985. Water Sports. Multicoloured.

1402	10 c. Type **306**	20	10
1403	50 c. Scuba diving, Carriacou	45	35
1404	$1.10 Windsurfers on Grand Anse Beach	75	1·25
1405	$4 Windsurfing	2·00	4·00

307 Bird of Paradise (flower)

1985. Native Flowers. Multicoloured.

1407a	½ c. Type **307**	30	40
1408a	1 c. Passion flower	40	40
1409a	2 c. Oleander	40	40
1410a	4 c. Bromeliad	45	40
1411a	5 c. Anthurium	45	40
1412a	6 c. Bougainvillea	45	50
1413a	10 c. Hibiscus	45	30
1414a	15 c. Ginger	65	30
1415a	25 c. Poinsettia	65	30
1425d	30 c. Mexican creeper	20	60
1417a	40 c. Angel's trumpet	75	50
1425e	50 c. Amaryllis	30	75
1425f	60 c. Prickly pear	30	1·00
1420a	70 c. Chenille plant	75	1·00
1420b	75 c. Cordia	1·25	1·75
1425g	$1 Periwinkle	35	1·25
1422a	$1.10 Ixora	1·75	2·25
1423a	$3 Shrimp plant	2·50	5·00
1424a	$5 Plumbago	2·50	6·00
1425a	$10 "Lantana camara"	4·00	9·00
1425b	$20 Peregrina	8·50	16·00

308 The Queen Mother at Royal Opera House, London

309 Youth Gardening (Horticulture)

1985. Life and Times of Queen Elizabeth the Queen Mother. Multicoloured.

1426	$1 Type **308**	40	60
1427	$1.50 The Queen Mother playing snooker at London Press Club (horiz)	55	85
1428	$2.50 At Epsom Races, 1960	95	1·50

Stamps as Nos. 1426/8 but with face values of 90 c., $1 and $3 exist from additional sheetlets with changed background colours.

1985. International Youth Year. Multicoloured.

1430	25 c. Type **309**	25	20
1431	50 c. Young people on beach (Leisure)	45	40
1432	$1.10 Girls in classroom (Education)	90	1·10
1433	$3 Nurse and young patient (Health Care)	2·25	2·50

1985. 300th Birth Anniv of Johann Sebastian Bach (composer). As T **206** of Antigua. Multicoloured.

1435	25 c. Crumhorn	80	20
1436	70 c. Oboe d'amore	1·50	85
1437	$1 Violin	2·00	1·25
1438	$3 Harpsichord	3·00	4·00

310 Cub Scouts Camping

1985. 4th Caribbean Cuboree. Multicoloured.

1440	10 c. Type **310**	30	15
1441	50 c. Cub scouts swimming ("Physical Fitness")	65	40
1442	$1 Stamp collecting	1·50	80
1443	$4 Birdwatching	3·50	3·00

1985. Royal Visit. As T **207** of Antigua. Multicoloured.

1445	50 c. Flags of Great Britain and Grenada	75	40
1446	$1 Queen Elizabeth II (vert)	1·00	1·25
1447	$4 Royal Yacht "Britannia"	2·50	5·00

1985. 150th Birth Anniv of Mark Twain (author). As T **118** of Anguilla. Design showing Walt Disney cartoon characters in scenes from "The Prince and the Pauper". Multicoloured.

1449	25 c. Mortie as Tom meeting the Prince (Ferdie)	50	20
1450	50 c. Tom and the Prince exchanging clothes	70	50
1451	$1.10 The Prince with John Cantry	1·60	1·60
1452	$1.50 The Prince knights Mike Hendon (Goofy)	2·00	2·50
1453	$2 Tom and the Whipping Boy	2·25	2·75

1985. Birth Bicentenaries of Grimm Brothers (folklorists). As T **119** of Anguilla, showing Walt Disney cartoon characters in scenes from "The Fisherman and his Wife". Multicoloured.

1455	30 c. The Fisherman (Goofy) catching enchanted fish	55	30
1456	60 c. The Fisherman scolded by his Wife (Clarabelle)	80	80
1457	70 c. The Fisherman's Wife with dream cottage	95	95
1458	$1 The Fisherman's Wife as King	1·50	1·50
1459	$3 The Fisherman and Wife in their original shack	3·00	3·75

311 Red-spotted Hawkfish

1985. Marine Life. Multicoloured.

1461	25 c. Type **311**	1·25	55
1462	50 c. Spot-finned butterflyfish	2·00	1·10
1463	$1.10 Fire coral and orange sponges	3·25	3·25
1464	$3 Pillar coral	6·00	7·50

1985. 40th Anniv of U.N.O. As T **208** of Antigua showing United Nations (New York) stamps. Multicoloured.

1466	50 c. Mary McLeod Bethune (educationist) and 1975 International Women's Year 10 c.	50	50
1467	$2 Maimonides (physician) and 1966 W.H.O. 5 c.	3·00	3·50
1468	$2.50 Alexander Graham Bell (telephone inventor) and 1956 I.T.U. 3 c.	3·00	3·75

312 "Adoration of the Shepherds" (Mantegna)

1985. Christmas. Religious Paintings. Multicoloured.

1470	25 c. Type **312**	20	15
1471	60 c. "Journey of the Magi" (Sassetta)	40	40
1472	90 c. "Madonna and Child enthroned with Saints" (Raphael)	50	70
1473	$4 "Nativity" (Monaco)	1·50	3·50

1986. Centenary of Statue of Liberty (1st issue). As T **211** of Dominica. Multicoloured.

1475	5 c. Columbus Monument, 1893 (vert)	15	20
1476	25 c. Columbus Monument, 1986 (vert)	40	20
1477	40 c. Mounted police, Central Park, 1895	1·75	1·10
1478	$4 Mounted police, 1986	6·50	8·00

See also Nos. 1644/52.

1986. Birth Bicentenary of John J. Audubon (ornithologist) (2nd issue). As T **198** of Antigua. Multicoloured.
1480 50 c. Snowy egret . . . . . 2·00 80
1481 90 c. Greater flamingo . . . 2·75 2·00
1482 $1.10 Canada goose . . . . 2·75 2·50
1483 $3 Smew . . . . 4·50 6·00

1986. Visit of President Reagan. Nos. 1418 and 1424 optd **VISIT OF PRES REAGAN 20 FEB. 1986.**
1485 50 c. Amaryllis 50 50
1486 $5 Plumbago . . . . 3·00 5·00

314 Methodist Church, St. George's

1986. Bicentenary of Methodist Church in Grenada.
1487 **314** 60 c. multicoloured . . . 70 1·00

315 Player with Ball **316** Brown-lined Latirus

1986. World Cup Football Championship, Mexico. Multicoloured.
1489 50 c. Type **315** 80 55
1490 70 c. Player heading ball . . 1·00 1·00
1491 90 c. Player controlling ball . 1·50 1·50
1492 $4 Player controlling ball with right foot . . . . 5·50 7·00

1986. Appearance of Halley's Comet (1st issue). As T **123** of Anguilla. Multicoloured.
1494 5 c. Clyde Tombaugh (astronomer) and Dudley Observatory, New York . . 40 40
1495 20 c. N.A.S.A — U.S.A.F. "X-24B" Space Shuttle prototype, 1973 . . . . . 50 30
1496 40 c. German comet medal, 1618 . . . . 70 45
1497 $4 Destruction of Sodom and Gomorrah, 1949 B.C. . . . 3·50 4·50
See also Nos. 1533/6 and 1980/3.

1986. 60th Birthday of Queen Elizabeth II. As T **125** of Anguilla.
1499 2 c. black and yellow 10 15
1500 $1.50 multicoloured 60 80
1501 $4 multicoloured . . . . . . 1·50 2·50
DESIGNS: 2 c. Princess Elizabeth in 1951, $1.50, Queen presenting trophy at polo match, Windsor, 1965. $4 at Epsom, Derby Day 1977.

1986. "Ameripex" International Stamp Exhibition, Chicago. As T **212** of Dominica, showing Walt Disney cartoon characters playing baseball. Multicoloured.
1503 1 c. Goofy as pitcher 10 10
1504 2 c. Goofy as catcher 10 10
1505 5 c. Mickey Mouse striking ball and Donald Duck as catcher 10 10
1506 4 c. Huey forcing out Dewey 10 10
1507 5 c. Chip n'Dale chasing flyball 10 10
1508 6 c. Mickey Mouse, Donald Duck and Clarabelle in argument 10 10
1509 $2 Minnie Mouse and Donald Duck reading baseball rules 1·75 2·50
1510 $3 Ludwig von Drake as umpire with Goofy and Pete colliding 2·25 3·00

1986. Royal Wedding. As T **213** of Antigua. Multicoloured.
1512 2 c. Prince Andrew and Miss Sarah Ferguson 10 15
1513 $1.10 Prince Andrew 70 80
1514 $4 Prince Andrew with H.M.S. "Brazen's" Westland Lynx helicopter . . . . 2·50 3·25

1986. Sea Shells. Multicoloured.
1516 25 c. Type **316** 45 25
1517 60 c. Lamellose wentletrap . 75 90
1518 70 c. Turkey wing . . . . . 85 1·00
1519 $4 Rooster tail conch . . . 2·75 5·00

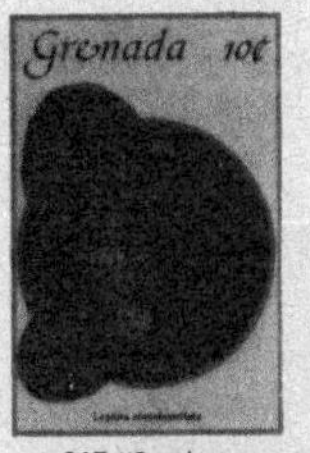

317 "Lepiota roseolamellata" **318** Dove on Rifles and Mahatma Gandhi (Disarmament Week)

1986. Mushrooms. Multicoloured.
1521 10 c. Type **317** 60 40
1522 60 c. "Lentinus bertieri" . . 1·75 1·75
1523 $1 "Lentinus retinervis" . . 2·50 2·50
1524 $4 "Eccilia cystiophorus" . . 5·75 7·50

1986. World Cup Football Championship Winners, Mexico. Nos. 1489/92 optd **WINNERS Argentina 3 W. Germany 2.**
1526 50 c. Type **315** 85 85
1527 70 c. Player heading ball . . 1·00 1·00
1528 90 c. Player controlling ball . 1·40 1·60
1529 $4 Player controlling ball with right foot . . . . 4·50 5·00

1986. International Events. Multicoloured.
1531 60 c. Type **318** 50 50
1532 $4 Hands passing olive branch and Martin Luther King (International Peace Year) (horiz) . . . . 1·50 3·00

1986. Appearance of Halley's Comet (2nd issue). Nos. 1494/7 optd with T **218** of Antigua.
1533 5 c. Clyde Tombaugh (astronomer) and Dudley Observatory, New York . 60 60
1534 20 c. N.A.S.A — U.S.A.F. "X-24B" Space Shuttle prototype, 1973 . . . . . 85 60
1535 40 c. German comet medal, 1618 . . . . 1·25 70
1536 $4 Destruction of Sodom and Gomorrah, 1949 B.C. . . 5·00 7·00

1986. Christmas. As T **220** of Antigua showing Walt Disney cartoon characters. Multicoloured.
1538 30 c. Mickey Mouse asleep in armchair (vert) 35 25
1539 45 c. Young Mickey Mouse with Father Christmas (vert) 45 30
1540 60 c. Donald Duck with toy telephone 60 50
1541 70 c. Pluto with pushcart . . 70 70
1542 $1.10 Daisy Duck with doll . 1·00 1·25
1543 $2 Goofy as Father Christmas (vert) . . . . 1·75 2·00
1544 $2.50 Goofy singing carols at piano (vert) . . . . 2·00 2·50
1545 $3 Mickey Mouse, Donald Duck and nephew riding toy train . . . . 2·25 3·00

319 Cockerel and Hen

1986. Fauna and Flora. Multicoloured.
1547 10 c. Type **319** 20 10
1548 30 c. Fish-eating bat 35 20
1549 60 c. Goat 55 45
1550 70 c. Cow 60 50
1551 $1 Anthurium . . . . 1·50 1·25
1552 $1.10 Royal poinciana . . . 1·50 1·25
1553 $2 Frangipani . . . . 2·50 3·25
1554 $4 Orchid . . . . 8·50 9·50

320 Maserati "Biturbo" (1984) **321** Pole Vaulting

1986. Centenary of Motoring. Multicoloured.
1556 10 c. Type **320** 25 25
1557 30 c. AC "Cobra" (1960) . . 40 40
1558 60 c. Corvette (1963) 60 60
1559 70 c. Dusenberg "SJ7" (1932) 70 70
1560 90 c. Porsche (1957) . . . . 85 1·00
1561 $1 Stoewer (1930) . . . . . 1·00 1·25
1562 $2 Volkswagen "Beetle" (1957) 1·60 2·00
1563 $3 Mercedes "600 Limo" (1963) 1·90 2·50

1986. Olympic Games, Seoul, South Korea (1988). Multicoloured.
1565 10 c. + 5 c. Type **321** . . . 10 30
1566 50 c. + 20 c. Gymnastics . . 35 60
1567 70 c. + 30 c. Putting the shot 50 85
1568 $2 + $1 High jumping . . . 1·00 2·25
The premiums on Nos. 1565/9 were to support the participation of the Grenada team.

1986. Birth Centenary of Marc Chagall (artist). As T **225** of Antigua, showing various paintings.
1570/1609 $1 × 40 multicoloured Set of 40 . . . . . . 24·00 26·00

1987. America's Cup Yachting Championship. As T **222** of Antigua. Multicoloured.
1611 10 c. "Columbia", 1958 . . 25 20
1612 60 c. "Resolute", 1920 . . . 55 60
1613 $1.10 "Endeavor", 1934 . . 1·00 1·25
1614 $4 "Rainbow", 1934 . . . . 2·25 3·50

322 Virgin Mary and Outline Map of Grenada **323** Black Grouper

1987. 500th Anniv (1992) of Discovery of America by Christopher Columbus (1st issue). Multicoloured.
1616 10 c. Type **322** 20 20
1617 30 c. "Santa Maria", "Pinta" and "Nina" (horiz) 60 35
1618 50 c. Columbus and outline map of Grenada 70 45
1619 60 c. Christopher Columbus . 70 55
1620 90 c. King Ferdinand and Queen Isabella of Spain (horiz) 70 80
1621 $1.10 Map of Antilles by Columbus . . . . 1·10 1·00
1622 $2 Caribs with sailing raft (horiz) . . . . 1·40 2·25
1623 $3 Columbus in the New World, 1493 (contemporary drawing) 1·75 2·25
See also Nos. 2051/4, 2091/8, 2222/9, 2389/94 and 2423/4.

1987. Milestones of Transportation. As T **226** of Antigua. Multicoloured.
1625 10 c. Cornu's first helicopter, 1907 . . . . 55 55
1626 15 c. "Monitor" and "Merrimack" (first battle between ironclad warships), 1862 . . . . 60 60
1627 30 c. LZ1 (first Zeppelin), 1900 80 80
1628 50 c. "Sirius" (first transatlantic paddle-steamer crossing), 1838 . . . . 85 85
1629 60 c. Steam locomotive on Trans-Siberian Railway (longest line) . . . . 1·00 1·00
1630 70 c. U.S.S "Enterprise" (largest aircraft carrier), 1960 . . . 1·25 1·25
1631 90 c. Blanchard and Jeffries' balloon (first balloon across English Channel), 1785 . . 1·40 1·40
1632 $1.50 U.S.S. "Holland I" (first steam-powered submarine), 1900 . . . . 2·00 2·00
1633 $2 "Oceanic I" (first luxury liner), 1871 . . . . 2·50 2·50
1634 $3 Lamborghini "Countach" (fastest commercial car), 1984 2·75 2·75

1987. "Capex '87" International Stamp Exhibition, Toronto. Game Fishes. Multicoloured.
1635 10 c. Type **323** 30 15
1636 30 c. Blue marlin (horiz) . . . 40 15
1637 60 c. White marlin 60 55
1638 70 c. Bigeye threshershark (horiz) 70 70
1639 $1 Bonefish (horiz) . . . . . 90 1·00
1640 $1.10 Wahoo (horiz) . . . . 1·00 1·25
1641 $2 Sailfish (horiz) . . . . . 1·75 2·25
1642 $4 Albacore (horiz) . . . . . 2·75 3·50

1987. Centenary of Statue of Liberty (2nd issue). As T **227** of Antigua. Multicoloured.
1644 10 c. Computer projections of Statue and base (horiz) . . 15 15
1645 25 c. Statue and fireworks (horiz) 20 15
1646 50 c. Statue and fireworks (different) (horiz) 35 35
1647 60 c. Statue and boats 45 45
1648 70 c. Computer projection of top of Statue (horiz) . . . 50 50
1649 $1 Rear view of Statue and fireworks 80 80
1650 $1.10 Aerial view of Statue . 95 1·25
1651 $2 Statue and flotilla . . . . 2·00 2·25
1652 $4 "Queen Elizabeth 2" in New York Harbour . . . . . . 3·50 4·00

324 Alice and the Rabbit Hole

1987. 50th Anniv of First Full-Length Disney Cartoon Film. Scenes from various films.
1653/1706 30 c. × 54 multicoloured Set of 54 . . . . . . 15·00 16·00

325 Isaac Newton holding Apple (Law of Gravity)

1987. Great Scientific Discoveries. Multicoloured.
1708 50 c. Type **325** 85 85
1709 $1.10 John Jacob Berzelius and symbols of chemical elements 1·75 1·75
1710 $2 Robert Boyle (law of Pressure and Volume) . . 2·50 3·00
1711 $3 James Watt and drawing of steam engine . . . . 3·75 4·25
No. 1711 is inscribed "RUDOLF DIESEL" in error.

1987. 60th Anniv of International Social Security Association. Nos. 1413, 1418 and 1423 optd **INTERNATIONAL SOCIAL SECURITY ASSOCIATION** and emblem.
1714 10 c. Hibiscus 10 15
1715 50 c. Amaryllis 25 35
1716 $3 Shrimp plant . . . . . . 1·40 2·25

1987. Bicentenary of U.S. Constitution. As T **232** of Antigua. Multicoloured.
1717 15 c. Independence Hall, Philadelphia (vert) 10 10
1718 50 c. Benjamin Franklin (Pennsylvania delegate) (vert) 25 35
1719 60 c. State Seal, Massachusetts 25 35
1720 $4 Robert Morris (Pennsylvania delegate) (vert) . . . . . . 1·75 2·75

328 Goofy in "The Shadow" **329** "The Annunciation" (Fra Angelico)

1987. "Hafnia '87" International Stamp Exhibition. Walt Disney cartoon characters in scenes from Hans Christian Andersen's fairy tales. Mult.
1722 25 c. Type **328** 50 30
1723 30 c. Mother Stork and brood in "The Storks" 50 30
1724 50 c. King Richard, Robin Hood and Little John (from Robin Hood) in "The Emperor's New Clothes" . 75 55
1725 60 c. Goofy and Pluto in "The Tinderbox" 75 55
1726 70 c. Daisy and Donald Duck in "The Shepherdess and the Chimney Sweep" 80 70
1727 $1.50 Mickey and Minnie Mouse in "The Little Mermaid" . . . . 1·60 1·75
1728 $3 Clarabelle and Goofy in "The Princess and the Pea" 2·50 3·50
1729 $4 Minnie Mouse and Pegleg Pete in "The Marsh King's Daughter" . . . . 2·50 3·50

1987. Christmas. Religious Paintings. Multicoloured.
1731 15 c. Type **329** 55 10
1732 30 c. "The Annunciation" (attr. Hubert van Eyck) 90 30
1733 60 c. "The Adoration of the Magi" (Januarius Zick) . . 1·75 1·40
1734 $4 "The Flight into Egypt" (Gerard David) . . . . . 5·50 7·00

330 T. Albert Marryshow

1988. Birth Centenary of T. Albert Marryshow (nationalist).
1736 **330** 25 c. brown, light brown and red 30 30

1988. Royal Ruby Wedding. As T **234** of Antigua. Multicoloured.
1737 15 c. brown, black and blue . 35 10
1738 50 c. multicoloured 70 50
1739 $1 brown and black . . . . 1·25 1·00
1740 $4 multicoloured . . . . . . 3·00 4·00
DESIGNS: 15 c. Wedding photograph, 1947; 50 c. Queen Elizabeth II with Prince Charles and Princess Anne, c. 1955; $1 Queen with Princess Anne, c. 1957; $4 Queen Elizabeth (from photo by Tim Graham), 1980.

331 Goofy and Daisy Duck lighting Olympic Torch, Olympia
332 Scout fishing from Boat

1988. Olympic Games, Seoul. Designs showing Walt Disney cartoon characters. Multicoloured.
1742 1 c. Type **331** 10 10
1743 2 c. Donald and Daisy Duck carrying Olympic torch 10 10
1744 3 c. Donald Duck, Goofy and Mickey Mouse carrying flags of U.S., Korea and Spain 10 10
1745 4 c. Donald Duck releasing doves 10 10
1746 5 c. Mickey Mouse flying with rocket belt 10 10
1747 10 c. Morty and Ferdie carrying banner with Olympic motto 10 10
1748 $6 Donald Duck, Minnie Mouse and Hodori the Tiger (mascot of Seoul Games) 4·75 5·00
1749 $7 Pluto, Hodori and old post office, Seoul 4·75 5·00

1988. Stamp Exhibitions. Nos. 1631/4 optd.
1751 90 c. Blanchard and Jeffries' balloon, 1785 (optd **OLYMPHILEX '88**, Seoul) 75 85
1752 $1.50 U.S.S "Holland I", 1900 (optd **INDEPENDENCE 40**, Israel) 1·00 1·25
1753 $2 "Oceanic I", 1871 (optd **FINLANDIA 88**, Helsinki) 1·40 1·75
1754 $3 Lamborghini "Countach", 1984 (optd **PRAGA 88**, Prague) 1·90 2·25

1988. World Scout Jamboree, Australia. Mult.
1755 20 c. Type **332** 40 15
1756 70 c. Scouts hiking through forest (horiz) 1·00 1·00
1757 90 c. Practising first aid (horiz) 1·40 1·40
1758 $3 Shooting rapids in inflatable canoe 3·00 3·75

333 "Santa Maria de Guia" (Columbus), 1498 and Map of Rotary District
334 Roseate Tern

1988. Rotary District 405 Conference, St. George's.
1760 **333** $2 multicoloured 80 1·00

1988. Birds. Multicoloured.
1762 10 c. Type **334** 50 20
1763 25 c. Laughing gull 65 25
1764 50 c. Osprey 1·00 60
1765 60 c. Rose-breasted grosbeak 1·00 60
1766 90 c. Purple gallinule 1·00 90
1767 $1.10 White-tailed tropic bird 1·00 1·00
1768 $3 Blue-faced booby 1·75 2·50
1769 $4 Common shoveler 1·90 2·75

335 Vauxhall Type "OE 30/98", 1925

1988. Cars. Multicoloured.
1771 $2 Type **335** 1·00 1·25
1772 $2 Wills "Sainte Claire", 1926 1·00 1·25
1773 $2 Bucciali, 1928 1·00 1·25
1774 $2 Irving Napier "Golden Arrow", 1929 1·00 1·25
1775 $2 Studebaker "President", 1930 1·00 1·25
1776 $2 Thomas "Flyer", 1907 1·00 1·25
1777 $2 Isotta-Franschini "Tipo J", 1908 1·00 1·25
1778 $2 Fiat 10/14HP, 1910 1·00 1·25
1779 $2 Mercer "Type 35 Raceabout", 1911 1·00 1·25
1780 $2 Marmon "Model 34 Cloverleaf", 1917 1·00 1·25
1781 $2 Tatra "Type 77", 1934 1·00 1·25
1782 $2 Rolls-Royce "Phantom III", 1938 1·00 1·25
1783 $2 Studebaker "Champion Starlight", 1947 1·00 1·25
1784 $2 Porsche "Gmund", 1948 1·00 1·25
1785 $2 Tucker, 1948 1·00 1·25
1786 $2 Peerless "V-16", 1931 1·00 1·25
1787 $2 Minerva "AL", 1931 1·00 1·25
1788 $2 Reo "Royale", 1953 1·00 1·25
1789 $2 Pierce Arrow "Silver Arrow", 1933 1·00 1·25
1790 $2 Hupmobile "Aerodynamic", 1934 1·00 1·25
1791 $2 Peugeot "404", 1965 1·00 1·25
1792 $2 Ford "Capri", 1969 1·00 1·25
1793 $2 Ferrari "312T", 1975 1·00 1·25
1794 $2 Lotus "T-79", 1978 1·00 1·25
1795 $2 Williams-Cosworth "FW07", 1979 1·00 1·25
1796 $2 H.R.G. "1500 Sports", 1948 1·00 1·25
1797 $2 Crosley "Hotshot", 1949 1·00 1·25
1798 $2 Volvo "PV444", 1955 1·00 1·25
1799 $2 Maserati "Tipo 61", 1960 1·00 1·25
1800 $2 Saab "96", 1963 1·00 1·25

1988. 500th Birth Anniv of Titian (artist). As T **238** of Antigua. Multicoloured.
1801 10 c. "Lavinia Vecellio" 10 10
1802 20 c. "Portrait of a Man" 10 10
1803 25 c. "Andrea de Franceschi" 10 15
1804 90 c. "Head of a Soldier" 40 45
1805 $1 "Man with a Flute" 45 50
1806 $2 "Lucrezia and Tarquinius" 80 1·00
1807 $3 "Duke of Mantua with Dog" 1·25 1·60
1808 $4 "La Bella di Tiziano" 1·60 2·00

336 "Graf Zeppelin" over Chicago World's Fair, 1933
338 Pineapple

337 Tasmanian Wolf, Mickey Mouse and Pluto

1988. Airships. Multicoloured.
1810 10 c. Type **336** 20 20
1811 15 c. LZ-1 over Lake Constance, 1901 (horiz) 25 25
1812 25 c. "Washington" (balloon) and "George Washington Curtis" (balloon barge), 1862 30 30
1813 45 c. "Hindenburg" and Maybach "Zeppelin" car (horiz) 40 40
1814 50 c. Goodyear Aerospace airship in Statue of Liberty Centenary Race, 1986 40 40
1815 60 c. "Hindenburg" over Statue of Liberty, 1937 (horiz) 50 50
1816 90 c. Heinkel biplane docking experiment with "Hindenburg", 1936 (horiz) 80 80
1817 $2 "Hindenburg" over Olympic Stadium, Berlin, 1936 1·60 1·60
1818 $3 "Hindenburg" over Christ of the Andes Monument, 1937 2·00 2·00
1819 $4 "Hindenburg" and "Bremen" (liner), 1936 (horiz) 2·25 2·25

1988. "Sydpex '88". National Stamp Exhibition, Sydney and 60th Birthday of Mickey Mouse. Multicoloured.
1821 1 c. Type **337** 10 10
1822 2 c. Mickey Mouse feeding wallabies 10 10
1823 3 c. Mickey Mouse and Goofy with kangaroo 10 10
1824 4 c. Mickey and Minnie Mouse riding emus 10 10
1825 5 c. Mickey and Minnie Mouse with wombat 10 10
1826 10 c. Mickey Mouse and Donald Duck watching platypus 10 10
1827 $5 Mickey Mouse and Goofy photographing blue-winged kookaburra 4·50 5·00
1828 $6 Mickey Mouse and Koala on map of Australia 4·50 5·00

1988. 10th Anniv of International Fund for Agricultural Development. Multicoloured.
1830 25 c. Type **338** 25 15
1831 75 c. Bananas 60 60
1832 $3 Mace and nutmeg (horiz) 2·00 2·75

339 Lignum Vitae

1988. Flowering Trees and Shrubs. Mult.
1833 15 c. Type **339** 15 15
1834 25 c. Saman 20 15
1835 35 c. Red frangipani 25 20
1836 45 c. Flowering maple 30 25
1837 60 c. Yellow poui 40 40
1838 $1 Wild chestnut 60 70
1839 $3 Mountain immortelle 1·50 2·25
1840 $4 Queen of flowers 1·75 2·50

340 Mickey Mantle (New York Yankees)

1988. Major League Baseball Players (1st series). Designs showing portraits or league emblems.
1842/1922 30 c. × 81 multicoloured Set of 81 8·75 9·50

1988. Christmas. "Mickey's Christmas Eve". As T **246** of Antigua showing Walt Disney cartoon characters. Multicoloured.
1923 $1 Donald Duck's nephew on mantelpiece 65 65
1924 $1 Goofy with string of popcorn 65 65
1925 $1 Chip'n'Dale decorating Christmas tree 65 65
1926 $1 Father Christmas in sleigh 65 65
1927 $1 Donald's nephew with stocking 65 65
1928 $1 Donald's nephew unpacking decorations 65 65
1929 $1 Donald Duck with present 65 65
1930 $1 Mickey Mouse with present 65 65

341 Tina Turner
342 Atlantic Railway No. 2, 1889, Canada

1988. Entertainers. Multicoloured.
1932 10 c. Type **341** 25 20
1933 25 c. Lionel Ritchie 25 20
1934 45 c. Whitney Houston 35 30
1935 60 c. Joan Armatrading 50 45
1936 75 c. Madonna 70 60
1937 $1 Elton John 1·00 80
1938 $3 Bruce Springsteen 2·00 2·75
1939 $4 Bob Marley 3·00 3·50

No. 1935 is incorrectly inscribed "JOAN AMMERTRADING".

1989. North American Railway Locomotives. Mult.
1941 $2 Type **342** 1·25 1·25
1942 $2 Virginia & Truckee Railroad "J. W Bowker" type, 1875, U.S.A. 1·25 1·25
1943 $2 Philadelphia & Reading Railway "Ariel", 1872, U.S.A. 1·25 1·25
1944 $2 Chicago & Rock Island Railroad "America" type, 1867, U.S.A. 1·25 1·25
1945 $2 Lehigh Valley Railroad Consolidation No. 63, 1866, U.S.A. 1·25 1·25
1946 $2 Great Western Railway "Scotia", 1860, Canada 1·25 1·25
1947 $2 Grand Trunk Railway Class "Birkenhead", 1854, Canada 1·25 1·25
1948 $2 Camden & Amboy Railroad "Monster", 1837, U.S.A. 1·25 1·25
1949 $2 Baltimore & Ohio Railroad Class "Grasshopper", 1834, U.S.A. 1·25 1·25
1950 $2 Peter Cooper's "Tom Thumb", 1829, Baltimore & Ohio Railroad, U.S.A. 1·25 1·25
1951 $2 United Railways of Yucatan "Yucatan", 1925, Mexico 1·25 1·25
1952 $2 Canadian National Railways Class T2, 1924 1·25 1·25
1953 $2 St. Louis-San Francisco Railroad Class "Light Mikado", 1919, U.S.A. 1·25 1·25
1954 $2 Atlantic Coast Line Railroad Class "Light Pacific", 1919, U.S.A. 1·25 1·25
1955 $2 Edaville Railroad No. 7, 1913, U.S.A. 1·25 1·25
1956 $2 Denver & Rio Grande Western Railroad Class K 27, 1903, U.S.A. 1·25 1·25
1957 $2 Pennsylvania Railroad Class E-2 No. 7002, 1902, U.S.A. 1·25 1·25
1958 $2 Pennsylvania Railroad Class H6, 1899, U.S.A. 1·25 1·25
1959 $2 John Jarvis's "De Witt Clinton", 1831, Mohawk & Hudson Railroad, U.S.A. 1·25 1·25
1960 $2 St. Clair Tunnel Company No. 598, 1891, Canada 1·25 1·25
1961 $2 Chesapeake & Ohio Railroad Class M-1 steam turbine electric locomotive No. 500, 1947, U.S.A. 1·25 1·25
1962 $2 Rutland Railroad steam locomotive No. 93, 1946, U.S.A. 1·25 1·25
1963 $2 Pennsylvania Railroad Class T1, 1942, U.S.A. 1·25 1·25
1964 $2 Chesapeake & Ohio Railroad Class H-8, 1942, U.S.A. 1·25 1·25
1965 $2 Atchison, Topeka & Santa Fe Railway Model FT diesel, 1941, U.S.A. 1·25 1·25
1966 $2 Gulf, Mobile & Ohio Railroad Models S-1 & S-2 diesels, 1940, U.S.A. 1·25 1·25
1967 $2 New York, New Haven & Hartford Railroad Class 15, 1937, U.S.A. 1·25 1·25
1968 $2 Seaboard Air Line Railroad Class R, 1936, U.S.A. 1·25 1·25
1969 $2 Newfoundland Railway Class R-2, 1930 1·25 1·25
1970 $2 Canadian National Railway diesel No. 9000, 1928 1·25 1·25

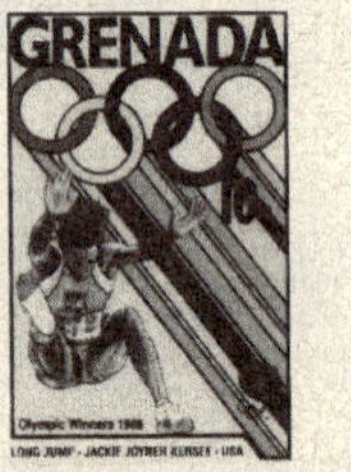

343 Women's Long Jump (Jackie Joyner-Kersee, U.S.A.)

1989. Olympic Gold Medal Winners, Seoul (1988). Multicoloured.
1971 10 c. Type **343** 20 20
1972 25 c. Women's Singles Tennis (Steffi Graf, West Germany) 50 35
1973 45 c. Men's 1500 metres (Peter Rono, Kenya) 60 40
1974 75 c. Men's 1000 metres single kayak (Greg Barton, U.S.A.) 70 60
1975 $1 Women's team foil (Italy) 85 75
1976 $2 Women's 100 metres freestyle swimming (Kristin Otto, East Germany) 1·75 2·00
1977 $3 Men's still rings gymnastics (Holger Behrendt, East Germany) 2·10 2·25
1978 $4 Synchronized swimming pair (Japan) 2·40 2·50

344 Nebulae

1989. Appearance of Halley's Comet (1986) (3rd issue).
1980 **344** 25 c. + 5 c. multicoloured 40 50
1981 – 75 c. + 5 c. black & grn 75 95
1982 – 90 c. + 5 c. multicoloured 85 1·10
1983 – $2 + 5 c. multicoloured 1·25 1·75

DESIGNS: 75 c. + 5 c. Marine astronomical experiments; 90 c. + 5 c. Moon's surface; $2 + 5c. Edmond Halley, Sir Isaac Newton and his book "Principia". (102 × 69 mm); $5 + 5 c. 17th-century warships and astrological signs.

1989. Japanese Art. Paintings by Hiroshige. As T **250** of Antigua. Multicoloured.
1985 10 c. "Shinagawa on Edo Bay" 20 20
1986 25 c. "Pine Trees on the Road to Totsuka" 30 30
1987 60 c. "Kanagawa on Edo Bay" 50 50
1988 75 c. "Crossing Banyu River to Hiratsuka" 55 55
1989 $1 "Windy Shore at Odawara" 70 70
1990 $2 "Snow-Covered Post Station of Mishima" 1·25 1·50
1991 $3 "Full Moon at Fuchu" 1·60 1·75
1992 $4 "Crossing the Stream at Okitsu" 2·25 2·50

345 Great Blue Heron

1989. Birds. Multicoloured.

1994	5 c. Type **345**	30	30
1995	10 c. Green heron	30	30
1996a	15 c. Turnstone	30	30
1997a	25 c. Blue-winged teal	30	20
1998a	35 c. Little ringed plover (vert)	35	20
1999a	45 c. Green-throated carib ("Emerald-throated hummingbird") (vert)	40	30
2000a	50 c. Rufous-breasted hermit (vert)	45	35
2001a	60 c. Lesser Antillean bullfinch (vert)	55	50
2002a	75 c. Brown pelican (vert)	60	60
2003a	$1 Black-crowned night heron (vert)	80	80
2004a	$3 American kestrel ("Sparrow hawk") (vert)	1·75	2·25
2005a	$5 Barn swallow (vert)	2·50	3·00
2006	$10 Red-billed tropic bird (vert)	6·00	7·00
2007	$20 Barn owl (vert)	12·00	13·00

1989. World Cup Football Championship, Italy (1990) (1st issue). As T **252** of Antigua. Multicoloured.

2008	10 c. Scotland player	30	20
2009	25 c. England and Brazil players	40	30
2010	60 c. Paolo Rossi (Italy)	65	55
2011	75 c. Jairzinho (Brazil)	80	70
2012	$1 Sweden striker	1·00	90
2013	$2 Pele (Brazil)	2·00	2·00
2014	$3 Mario Kempes (Argentina)	2·75	2·75
2015	$4 Pat Jennings (Northern Ireland)	3·00	3·00

See also Nos. 2174/7.

346 Xebec and Sugar Cane

1989. "Philexfrance '89" International Stamp Exhibition, Paris. Designs showing French sailing vessels and plantation crops. Mult.

2017	25 c. Type **346**	70	30
2018	75 c. Lugger and cotton	1·25	85
2019	$1 Full-rigged ship and cocoa	1·40	1·00
2020	$4 Ketch and coffee	3·50	5·00

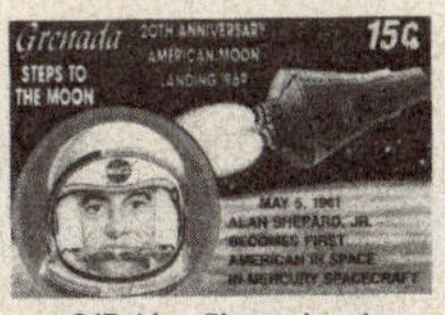

347 Alan Shepard and "Freedom 7" Spacecraft, 1961 (first American in Space)

1989. 20th Anniv of First Manned Landing on Moon. Multicoloured.

2022	15 c. Type **347**	50	40
2023	35 c. "Friendship 7" spacecraft, 1962 (first manned earth orbit)	65	55
2024	45 c. "Apollo 8" orbiting Moon, 1968 (first manned lunar orbit)	75	65
2025	70 c. "Apollo 15" lunar rover, 1972	1·00	85
2026	$1 "Apollo 11" emblem and lunar module "Eagle" on Moon, 1969	1·25	1·10
2027	$2 "Gemini 8" and "Agena" rocket, 1966 (first space docking)	2·25	2·00
2028	$3 Edward White in space, 1965 (first U.S. space walk)	3·00	2·75
2029	$4 "Apollo 7" emblem	3·50	3·25

348 "Hygrocybe occidentalis"

349 Y.W.C.A. Logo and Grenada Scenery

1989. Fungi. Multicoloured.

2031	15 c. Type **348**	50	40
2032	40 c. "Marasmius haematocephalus"	65	55
2033	50 c. "Hygrocybe hypohaemacta"	75	65
2034	70 c. "Lepiota pseudoignicolor"	1·00	90
2035	90 c. "Cookeina tricholoma"	1·25	1·25
2036	$1.10 "Leucopaxillus gracillimus"	1·50	1·50
2037	$2.25 "Hygrocybe nigrescens"	2·75	3·00
2038	$4 "Clathrus crispus"	3·75	4·00

1989. Centenary of Young Women's Christian Association. Multicoloured.

2040	50 c. Type **349**	45	45
2041	75 c. Y.W.C.A. logo and town (horiz)	80	80

350 "Historis odius"

1989. Butterflies. Multicoloured.

2042	6 c. Type **350**	30	30
2043	30 c. "Marpesia petreus"	55	55
2044	40 c. "Danaus gilippus"	60	60
2045	60 c. "Dione juno"	80	80
2046	$1.10 "Agraulis vanillae"	1·25	1·25
2047	$1.25 "Danaus plexippus"	1·50	1·50
2048	$4 "Papilio androgeus"	3·25	3·25
2049	$5 "Dryas julia"	3·25	3·25

351 Amerindian Hieroglyph

1989. 500th Anniv (1992) of Discovery of America by Columbus (2nd issue). Designs showing different hieroglyphs.

2051	**351**	45 c. brown, black & bl	70	50
2052	–	60 c. brown, black & grn	80	60
2053	–	$1 black, black & vio	1·25	1·00
2054	–	$4 dp brown, blk & brn	3·75	4·00

352 Amos leaving Home

1989. "World Stamp Expo '89" International Stamp Exhibition, Washington. Designs showing Walt Disney cartoon characters in scenes from "Ben and Me". Multicoloured.

2056	1 c. Type **352**	10	10
2057	2 c. Meeting of Benjamin Franklin and Amos	10	10
2058	3 c. The Franklin stove	10	10
2059	4 c. Ben and Amos with bi-focals	10	10
2060	5 c. Amos on page of "Pennsylvania Gazette"	10	10
2061	6 c. Ben working printing press	10	10
2062	10 c. Conducting experiment with electricity	10	10
2063	$5 Ben disembarking in England	5·00	5·50
2064	$6 Ben with Document of Agreement	5·50	6·00

1990. Christmas. Paintings by Rubens. As T **259** of Antigua. Multicoloured.

2066	20 c. "Christ in the House of Mary and Martha"	30	25
2067	35 c. "The Circumcision"	45	40
2068	60 c. "Trinity adored by Duke of Mantua and Family"	75	65
2069	$2 "Holy Family with St. Francis"	2·25	2·50
2070	$3 "The Ildefonso Altarpiece"	2·75	3·00
2071	$4 "Madonna and Child with Garland and Putti"	3·25	3·50

353 Alexander Graham Bell and Early Telephone System (150th anniv of invention)

1990. Anniversaries. Multicoloured.

2073	10 c. Type **353**	30	20
2074	25 c. George Washington and Capitol (bicentenary of presidential inauguration)	30	20
2075	35 c. Shakespeare and birthplace, Stratford (425th birth anniv)	50	30
2076	75 c. Nehru and Gandhi (birth cent of Nehru)	1·25	1·25
2077	$1 Dr. Hugo Eckener, Ferdinand von Zeppelin and airship "Graf Zeppelin" (80th anniv of first passenger Zeppelin)	1·25	1·25
2078	$2 Charlie Chaplin (birth cent)	2·25	2·25
2079	$3 Container ship in Hamburg Harbour (800th anniv)	2·50	3·00
2080	$4 Friedrich Ebert (first President) and Heidelberg gate (70th anniv of German Republic)	2·50	3·00

No. 2080 is inscribed "40th Anniversary of German Republic" in error.

354 "Odontoglossum triumphans"

1990. "EXPO '90" International Garden and Greenery Exhibition, Osaka. Caribbean Orchids. Multicoloured.

2082	1 c. Type **354**	10	10
2083	25 c. "Oncidium splendidum"	30	20
2084	60 c. "Laelia anceps"	60	60
2085	75 c. "Cattleya trianaei"	75	75
2086	$1 "Odontoglossum rossii"	1·00	1·00
2087	$2 "Brassia gireoudiana"	1·75	1·75
2088	$3 "Cattleya dowiana"	2·25	2·25
2089	$4 "Sobralia macrantha"	2·50	2·50

1990. 500th Anniv (1992) of Discovery of America by Columbus (3rd issue). New World Natural History — Butterflies. As T **260** of Antigua. Multicoloured.

2091	15 c. "Marpesia petreus"	30	20
2092	25 c. "Junonia evarete"	40	25
2093	75 c. "Siproeta stelenes"	80	70
2094	90 c. "Historis odius"	95	85
2095	$1 "Mestra cana"	1·00	90
2096	$2 "Biblis hyperia"	2·00	2·00
2097	$3 "Dryas julia"	2·50	2·75
2098	$4 "Anartia amathea"	2·50	2·75

1990. Local Fauna. As T **254** of Antigua. Mult.

2100	10 c. Caribbean monk seal	20	20
2101	15 c. Little brown bat	25	25
2102	45 c. Brown rat	50	50
2103	60 c. Common rabbit	60	60
2104	$1 Water opossum	95	95
2105	$2 White-nosed ichneumon	1·75	1·75
2106	$3 Little big-eared bat (vert)	2·25	2·25
2107	$4 Mouse opossum	2·25	2·25

1990. 50th Anniv of Second World War. As T **274** of Antigua. Multicoloured.

2109	25 c. British tanks during Operation Battleaxe, 1941	30	30
2110	35 c. Allied tank in southern France, 1944	40	40
2111	45 c. U.S. forces landing on Guadalcanal, 1942	45	45
2112	50 c. U.S. attack in New Guinea, 1943	50	50
2113	60 c. Hoisting U.S. flag on Leyte, Philippines, 1944	60	60
2114	75 c. U.S. tanks entering Cologne, 1945	75	75
2115	$1 Anzio offensive, 1944	95	95
2116	$2 Battle of the Bismarck Sea, 1943	1·75	1·75
2117	$3 U.S. battle fleet, 1944	2·25	2·25
2118	$4 Focke Wulf Fw 190A fighter attacking Salerno landing, 1943	2·50	2·50

1990. "Stamp World London '90" International Stamp Exhibition (1st issue). As T **193** of Gambia, but horiz showing Walt Disney cartoon characters and British trains.

2120	5 c. Mickey Mouse driving S.R. "King Arthur" class locomotive, 1925	20	10
2121	10 c. Mickey and Minnie Mouse with "Puffing Billy", 1813	25	10
2122	20 c. Mickey Mouse with Pluto pulling Durham colliery wagon, 1765	35	15
2123	45 c. Mickey Mouse timing L.N.E.R. locomotive No. 2509 "Silver Link", 1935	65	25
2124	$1 Mickey Mouse and Donald Duck with locomotive No. 60149 "Amadis", 1948	1·50	1·00
2125	$2 Goofy and Mickey Mouse with Liverpool & Manchester Railway locomotive, 1830	2·25	2·50
2126	$4 Goofy and Donald Duck with Great Northern locomotive No. 1, 1870	3·25	3·75
2127	$5 Mickey Mouse and Gyro the Mechanic with Advanced Passenger Train, 1972	3·25	3·75

No. 2126 is inscribed "Flying Scotsman" in error.

355 U.S. Paratroop Drop over Grenada

1990. 50th Anniv of United States Airborne Forces.

2129	**355**	75 c. multicoloured	90	90

1990. 90th Birthday of Queen Elizabeth the Queen Mother. As T **194** of Gambia showing photographs from the 1960s. Multicoloured.

2131	$2 Queen Mother in coat and hat	1·50	1·75
2132	$2 Queen Mother in evening dress	1·50	1·75
2133	$2 Queen Mother in Garter robes	1·50	1·75

1990. Olympic Games, Barcelona (1992) (1st issue). As T **268** of Antigua. Mult.

2135	10 c. Men's steeplechase	20	20
2136	15 c. Dressage	30	30
2137	45 c. Men's 200 m. butterfly swimming	45	45
2138	50 c. Men's hockey	60	60
2139	65 c. Women's beam gymnastics	60	60
2140	75 c. "Flying Dutchman" class yachting	80	80
2141	$2 Freestyle wrestling	1·75	1·75
2142	$3 Men's springboard diving	2·25	2·25
2143	$4 Women's 1000 m. sprint cycling	2·50	2·50
2144	$5 Men's basketball	3·25	3·25

See also Nos. 2414/21.

357 Yellow Goatfish

1990. Coral Reef Fishes. Multicoloured.

2147	10 c. Type **357**	20	20
2148	25 c. Black margate	35	35
2149	65 c. Blue-headed wrasse	75	75
2150	75 c. Puddingwife	85	85
2151	$1 Four-eyed butterflyfish	95	95
2152	$2 Honey damselfish	1·75	1·75
2153	$3 Queen angelfish	2·25	2·25
2154	$5 Cherub angelfish	3·00	3·00

358 Tropical Mockingbird

1990. Birds. Multicoloured.

2156	15 c. Type **358**	30	30
2157	25 c. Grey kingbird	35	35
2158	65 c. Bare-eyed thrush	75	75
2159	75 c. Antillean crested hummingbird	85	85
2160	$1 House wren	1·00	1·00
2161	$2 Purple martin	1·75	1·75
2162	$4 Hooded tanager	2·50	2·50
2163	$5 Scaly-breasted ground dove	3·00	3·00

359 Coral Crab

1990. Crustaceans. Multicoloured.

2165	5 c. Type **359**	10	10
2166	10 c. Smoothtail spiny lobster	15	15
2167	15 c. Flamestreaked box crab	15	15
2168	25 c. Spotted swimming crab	25	25
2169	75 c. Sally lightfoot rock crab	60	60
2170	$1 Spotted spiny lobster	80	80
2171	$3 Longarm spiny lobster	2·00	2·50
2172	$20 Caribbean spiny lobster	13·00	18·00

360 Cameroon Player

1990. World Cup Football Championship, Italy (2nd issue). Multicoloured.

2174	10 c. Type **360**	20	15
2175	25 c. Michel (Spain)	25	15
2176	$1 Brehme (West Germany)	85	85
2177	$5 Nevin (Scotland)	3·00	4·00

1990. Christmas. Paintings by Raphael. As T **272** of Antigua. Multicoloured.

2180	10 c. "The Ansidei Madonna" (vert)	20	10
2181	15 c. "The Sistine Madonna" (vert)	20	10
2182	$1 "The Madonna of the Baldacchino" (vert)	1·25	70
2183	$2 "The Large Holy Family" (detail) (vert)	2·00	2·25
2184	$5 "Madonna in the Meadow" (vert)	3·50	5·00

1991. 350th Death Anniv of Rubens. As T **273** of Antigua. Multicoloured.
2186 5 c. "The Brazen Serpent" (detail) 15 10
2187 10 c. "The Garden of Love" 15 10
2188 25 c. "Head of Cyrus" (detail) 30 20
2189 75 c. "Tournament in Front of a Castle" 70 60
2190 $1 "The Brazen Serpent" (different detail) 85 75
2191 $2 "Judgement of Paris" (detail) 1·75 2·00
2192 $4 "The Brazen Serpent" 2·50 3·00
2193 $5 "The Karmesse" (detail) 3·00 3·25

362 "The Sorcerer's Apprentice"

1991. 50th Anniv of "Fantasia" (cartoon film). Multicoloured.
2195 5 c. Type **362** 20 15
2196 10 c. Dancing mushrooms ("The Nutcracker Suite") 25 15
2197 20 c. Pterodactyls ("The Rite of Spring") 45 15
2198 45 c. Centaurs ("The Pastoral Symphony") 85 40
2199 $1 Bacchus and Jacchus ("The Pastoral Symphony") 1·50 1·00
2200 $2 Dancing ostrich ("Dance of the Hours") 2·50 2·75
2201 $4 Elephant ballet ("Dance of the Hours") 3·25 3·75
2202 $5 Diana ("The Pastoral Symphony") 3·25 3·75

363 "Adelpha iphicla"

1991. Butterflies. Multicoloured.
2205 5 c. Type **363** 30 15
2206 10 c. "Nymphalidae claudina" 30 20
2207 15 c. "Brassolidae polyxena" 35 20
2208 20 c. "Zebra Longwing" 40 20
2209 25 c. "Marpesia corinna" 40 25
2210 30 c. "Morpho hecuba" 40 30
2211 45 c. "Morpho rhetenor" 55 45
2212 50 c. "Dismorphia spio" 65 55
2213 60 c. "Prepona omphale" 75 65
2214 70 c. "Morpho anaxibia" 85 75
2215 75 c. "Marpesia iole" 90 80
2216 $1 "Amarynthis meneria" 1·00 90
2217 $2 "Morpho cisseis" 1·75 2·25
2218 $3 "Danaidae plexippus" 2·25 2·75
2219 $4 "Morpho achilleana" 2·75 3·50
2220 $5 "Calliona argenissa" 3·25 4·00

1991. 500th Anniv (1992) of Discovery of America by Columbus. History of Exploration. As T **277** of Antigua. Multicoloured.
2222 5 c. Vitus Bering in Bering Sea, 1728–9 20 20
2223 10 c. De Bougainville off Pacific island, 1766–69 25 25
2224 25 c. Polynesian canoe 30 25
2225 50 c. De Mendana off Solomon Islands, 1567–69 55 40
2226 $1 Darwin's H.M.S. "Beagle", 1831–35 1·00 1·00
2227 $2 Cook's H.M.S. "Endeavour", 1768–71 2·50 2·50
2228 $4 William Schouten in LeMaire Strait, 1615–17 3·00 3·00
2229 $5 Tasman off New Zealand, 1642–44 3·00 3·00

1991. "Phila Nippon '91" International Stamp Exhibition, Tokyo. Horiz designs as T **279** of Antigua showing Walt Disney cartoon characters at Japanese festivals. Multicoloured.
2231 5 c. Minnie Mouse and Daisy Duck at Dolls festival 15 10
2232 10 c. Morty and Ferdie with Boys' Day display 20 15
2233 20 c. Mickey and Minnie Mouse at Star festival 35 20
2234 45 c. Minnie and Daisy folk-dancing 60 35
2235 $1 Huey, Dewey and Louie wearing Eboshi headdresses 1·10 85
2236 $2 Mickey and Goofy pulling decorated car at Gion festival 2·50 2·75
2237 $4 Minnie and Daisy preparing rice broth, Seven Plants festival 3·25 3·50
2238 $5 Huey and Dewey with straw boat at Lanterns festival 3·25 3·50

1991. Death Centenary (1990) of Vincent van Gogh (artist). As T **278** of Antigua. Multicoloured.
2240 20 c. "Blossoming Almond Branch in Glass" 15 15
2241 25 c. "La Mousme sitting" 15 15
2242 30 c. "Still Life with Red Cabbages and Onions" (horiz) 20 20
2243 40 c. "Japonaiserie: Flowering Plum Tree" 30 30
2244 45 c. "Japonaiserie: Bridge in the Rain" 30 30
2245 60 c. "Still Life with Basket of Apples" (horiz) 50 50
2246 75 c. "Italian Woman" 60 60
2247 $1 "The Painter on his Way to Work" 80 80
2248 $2 "Portrait of Pere Tanguy" 1·50 1·50
2249 $3 "Still Life with Plaster Statuette, a Rose and Two Novels" 2·25 2·25
2250 $4 "Still Life: Bottle, Lemons and Oranges" (horiz) 2·50 2·50
2251 $5 "Orchard with Blossoming Apricot Trees" (horiz) 2·75 2·75

364 "Psilocybe cubensis"

1991. Fungi. Multicoloured.
2253 15 c. Type **364** 40 30
2254 25 c. "Leptonia caeruleocapitata" 50 30
2255 65 c. "Cystolepiota eriophora" 90 75
2256 75 c. "Chlorophyllum molybdites" 1·00 85
2257 $1 "Xerocomus hypoxanthus" 1·25 1·10
2258 $2 "Volvariella cubensis" 2·00 2·25
2259 $4 "Xerocomus coccolobae" 3·00 3·25
2260 $5 "Pluteus chrysophlebius" 3·00 3·25

365 Johannes Kepler (astronomer)

1991. Exploration of Mars. Designs showing astronomers, spacecraft and Martian landscapes. Multicoloured.
2262/97 75 c. × 9, $1.25 × 9, $2 × 9, $7 × 9 Set of 36 48·00 48·00

1991. 65th Birthday of Queen Elizabeth II. As T **280** of Antigua. Multicoloured.
2299 15 c. Royal Family on balcony after Trooping the Colour, 1985 15 15
2300 40 c. Queen and Prince Philip at Peterborough, 1988 35 35
2301 $2 Queen and Queen Mother at Windsor, 1986 1·50 1·75
2302 $4 Queen and Prince Philip on visit to United Arab Emirates 2·50 2·75

1991. 10th Wedding Anniv of the Prince and Princess of Wales. As T **280** of Antigua. Multicoloured.
2304 10 c. Prince and Princess in July 1985 20 10
2305 50 c. Separate photographs of Prince, Princess and sons 55 45
2306 $1 Prince Henry at Trooping the Colour and Prince William in Majorca 1·00 1·00
2307 $5 Separate photographs of Prince Charles and Princess Diana 3·50 4·00

366 Anglican High School Pupils

1991. 75th Anniv of Anglican High School (10, 25 c.) and 40th Anniv of University of the West Indies (45, 50 c.). Multicoloured.
2309 10 c. Type **366** 20 20
2310 25 c. Artist's impression of new Anglican High School 30 20
2311 45 c. Marryshow House, Grenada 55 55
2312 50 c. University Administrative Building, Barbados 65 75

367 George Stephenson's First Locomotive, 1814 (Great Britain)

1991. Great Railways of the World. Mult.
2313 75 c. Type **367** 60 60
2314 75 c. George Stephenson 60 60
2315 75 c. Killingworth locomotive, 1816 (Great Britain) 60 60
2316 75 c. George Stephenson's "Locomotion", 1825 (Great Britain) 60 60
2317 75 c. "Locomotion" in Darlington, 1825 (Great Britain) 60 60
2318 75 c. Opening of Stockton & Darlington Railway, 1825 60 60
2319 75 c. Timothy Hackworth's "Royal George", 1827 (Great Britain) 60 60
2320 75 c. Northumbrian T831 (Great Britain) 60 60
2321 75 c. "Planet", 1830 (Great Britain) 60 60
2322 $1 "Old Ironsides", 1832 (U.S.A.) 80 80
2323 $1 "Wilberforce", 1832 (Great Britain) 80 80
2324 $1 "Adler", 1835 (Germany) 80 80
2325 $1 "North Star", 1837 (Great Britain) 80 80
2326 $1 London & Birmingham Railway No. 1, 1838 (Great Britain) 80 80
2327 $1 Stephenson's "Austria", 1838 (Austria) 80 80
2328 $1 Baltimore & Ohio Railroad No. 378 "Muddigger", 1840 (U.S.A.) 80 80
2329 $1 Baltimore & Ohio Railroad Norris, 1840 (U.S.A.) 80 80
2330 $1 "Centaur", 1840 (Great Britain) 80 80
2331 $2 "Lion", 1841 (Great Britain) 1·50 1·50
2332 $2 "Beuth", 1843 (Germany) 1·50 1·50
2333 $2 "Derwent", 1845 (Great Britain) 1·50 1·50
2334 $2 "Bets", 1846 (Hungary) 1·50 1·50
2335 $2 Opening of Budapest to Vac railway, 1846 (Hungary) 1·50 1·50
2336 $2 Carriages, Stockton & Darlington Railway, 1846 (Great Britain) 1·50 1·50
2337 $2 "Long Boiler" type, 1847 (France) 1·50 1·50
2338 $2 Baldwin locomotive, 1850 (U.S.A.) 1·50 1·50
2339 $2 Steam locomotive, 1850 (Germany) 1·50 1·50

368 Barbu

1991. Marine Life of the Sandflats. Mult.
2341 50 c. Type **368** 55 55
2342 50 c. Beau Gregory 55 55
2343 50 c. Porcupinefish 55 55
2344 50 c. Queen or pink conch and conchfish 55 55
2345 50 c. Hermit crab 55 55
2346 50 c. Bluestripe lizardfish 55 55
2347 50 c. Spot-finned mojarra 55 55
2348 50 c. Southern stingray 55 55
2349 50 c. Long-spined sea urchin and slippery dick 55 55
2350 50 c. Peacock flounder 55 55
2351 50 c. West Indian sea star 55 55
2352 50 c. Spotted goatfish 55 55
2353 50 c. Netted olive and West Indian sea egg 55 55
2354 50 c. Pearly razorfish 55 55
2355 50 c. Spotted jawfish and yellow-headed jawfish 55 55
Nos. 2341/55 were printed together, se-tenant, forming a composite design.

1991. Christmas. Religious Paintings by Albrecht Durer. As T **287** of Antigua. Mult.
2357 10 c. "Adoration of the Magi" (detail) 25 10
2358 35 c. "Madonna with the Siskin" (detail) 50 25
2359 50 c. "Feast of the Rose Garlands" (detail) 70 45
2360 75 c. "Virgin with the Pear" (detail) 1·00 70
2361 $1 "Virgin in Half-length" (detail) 1·25 90
2362 $2 "Madonna and Child" (detail) 2·25 2·50
2363 $4 "Virgin and Child with St. Anne" (detail) 3·00 3·50
2364 $5 "Virgin and Child" (detail) 3·00 3·50

369 Goofy windsurfing

1992. Thrill Sports. Walt Disney cartoon characters. Multicoloured.
2366 5 c. Type **369** 15 10
2367 10 c. Mickey Mouse skateboarding 20 10
2368 20 c. Daisy Duck gliding 40 10
2369 45 c. Mickey's nephews stunt kite flying 70 25
2370 $1 Donald Duck mountain biking 1·25 85
2371 $2 Donald and Chipmunk parachuting 2·00 2·25
2372 $4 Mickey go-karting 3·25 3·75
2373 $5 Minnie water skiing 3·25 3·75

1992. 40th Anniv of Queen Elizabeth II's Accession. As T **288** of Antigua. Mult.
2375 10 c. Waterfall 25 15
2376 50 c. Street in St. George's 50 40
2377 $1 Colonial-style houses, St. George's 80 80
2378 $5 St. George's from the sea 3·25 3·50

1992. "Granada '92" International Stamp Exhibition, Spain. Spanish Paintings. As T **292** of Antigua. Multicoloured.
2380 10 c. "The Corpus Christi Procession in Seville" (Manuel Cabral y Aguado) (horiz) 15 15
2381 35 c. "The Mancorbo Channel" (Carlos de Haes) 25 20
2382 50 c. "Amalia de Llano y Dotres, Countess of Vilches" (Federico de Madrazo y Kuntz) 40 40
2383 75 c. "Conchita Serrano y Dominguez, Countess of Santovenia" (Eduardo Rosales Gallina) 55 55
2384 $1 "Queen Maria Isabel de Braganza" (Bernardo Lopez Piquer) 70 70
2385 $2 "The Presentation of Don John of Austria to Charles V" (detail) (Gallina) 1·40 1·75
2386 $4 "The Presentation of Don John of Austria to Charles V" (different detail) (Gallina) 2·75 3·25
2387 $5 "The Testament of Isabella the Catholic" (Gallina) (horiz) 3·00 3·25

370 Green-winged Macaw

371 Gracie Fields

1992. 500th Anniv of Discovery of America by Columbus (5th issue). World Columbian Stamp "Expo '92", Chicago. Multicoloured.
2389 10 c. Type **370** 25 15
2390 25 c. "Santa Maria" 35 20
2391 35 c. Christopher Columbus 40 30
2392 50 c. 15th-century sandglass 55 55
2393 75 c. Queen Isabella 70 80
2394 $4 Cantino map of 1502 (detail) 3·50 4·75

1992. "Genova '92" International Thematic Stamp Exhibition. Hummingbirds. As T **295** of Antigua, but vertical. Multicoloured.
2396 10 c. Ruby-throated hummingbird 20 15
2397 25 c. Vervain hummingbird 30 20
2398 35 c. Blue-headed hummingbird 35 25
2399 50 c. Cuban emerald 55 55
2400 75 c. Antillean mango 75 75
2401 $2 Purple-throated carib 1·50 1·75
2402 $4 Puerto Rican emerald 2·75 3·25
2403 $5 Green-throated carib 2·75 3·25

1992. 50th Anniv of United Service Organization (forces' entertainment programme). Multicoloured.
2405 15 c. Type **371** 15 15
2406 25 c. Jack Benny 20 20
2407 35 c. Jinx Falkenburg 25 25
2408 50 c. Francis Langford 40 40
2409 75 c. Joe E. Brown 70 70
2410 $1 Phil Silvers 80 80
2411 $2 Danny Kaye 1·50 1·75
2412 $5 Frank Sinatra 3·00 3·50

372 Badminton

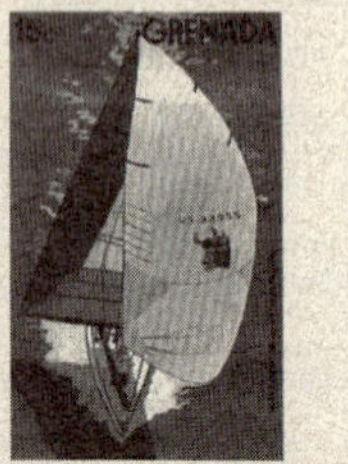

373 "Matador" (yacht), Newport News Regatta

1992. Olympic Games, Barcelona (2nd issue). Multicoloured.
2414 10 c. Type 372 . . . . 15 15
2415 25 c. Women's long jump . . 20 20
2416 35 c. Women's 100 metres . . 30 30
2417 50 c. 1000 metres cycling sprint 50 50
2418 75 c. Decathlon (horiz) . . . 70 70
2419 $2 Judo (horiz) . . . . 1·60 1·75
2420 $4 Women's gymnastics—asymmetrical bars . . . . 2·75 3·25
2421 $5 Men's javelin . . . . . 2·75 3·25

1992. 500th Anniv of Discovery of America by Columbus (6th issue). Organization of East Caribbean States. As Nos. 1670/1 of Antigua. Multicoloured.
2423 $1 Columbus meeting Amerindians 70 70
2424 $2 Ships approaching island . 1·40 1·60

1992. Toy Trains from American Manufacturers. As T 257 of Dominica. Mult.
2425 10 c. "The Blue Comet" locomotive, Boucher (1933) 15 15
2426 35 c. No. 2220 switching locomotive, Voltamp (1906) 25 25
2427 40 c. No. 221 tunnel locomotive, Knapp (1905) 30 30
2428 75 c. "Grand Canyon" locomotive, American Flyer (1931) 55 55
2429 $1 "Streamliner" tin locomotive, Hafner (1930s) 70 70
2430 $2 No. 237 switching locomotive, Elektoy (1911) 1·40 1·75
2431 $4 Parlor car, Ives (1928) . . 2·75 3·25
2432 $5 "Improved President's Special" locomotive, American Flyer (1927) . . 2·75 3·25

1992. World Regattas. Multicoloured.
2435 15 c. Type 373 . . . . 20 20
2436 25 c. "Awesome", Antigua . 25 25
2437 35 c. "Mistress Quickly", Bermuda 30 30
2438 50 c. "Emeraude", St. Tropez 50 50
2439 $1 "Diva G", German Admirals Cup 80 80
2440 $2 "Lady Be", French Admirals Cup . . . . 1·50 1·75
2441 $4 "Midnight Sun", Admirals Cup . . . . 2·75 3·25
2442 $5 "CARAT", Sardinia Cup 2·75 3·25

1992. Christmas. Religious Paintings. As T 300 of Antigua. Multicoloured.
2444 10 c. "Adoration of the Magi" (detail) (Fra Filippo Lippi) 25 15
2445 15 c. "Madonna adoring Child in a Wood" (Lippi) 30 20
2446 25 c. "Adoration of the Magi" (detail) (Botticelli) 40 20
2447 35 c. "The Epiphany—Adoration of the Magi" (detail) (Hieronymus Bosch) 45 20
2448 50 c. "Adoration of the Magi" (detail) (Giovanni de Paolo) 70 45
2449 75 c. "Adoration of the Magi" (Gentile da Fabriano) . . 90 60
2450 90 c. "Adoration of the Magi" (detail) (Juan Batista Maino) 1·10 70
2451 $1 "Adoration of the Child" (Master of Liesborn) . . . 1·25 80
2452 $2 "Adoration of the Kings" (Master of Liesborn) . . . 2·00 2·25
2453 $3 "Adoration of the Three Wise Men" (Pedro Berruguete) . . . . 2·25 3·00
2454 $4 "Adoration of the Child" (Lippi) . . . . 3·00 3·50
2455 $5 "Adoration of the Child" (Correggio) . . . . 3·00 3·50
No. 2447 is inscribed "Hieronymous" in error.

374 Cher

375 Grenada Dove

1992. Gold Record Award Winners. Mult.
2457 90 c. Type 374 . . . . 1·25 1·25
2458 90 c. Michael Jackson . . . 1·25 1·25
2459 90 c. Elvis Presley . . . . . 1·25 1·25
2460 90 c. Dolly Parton . . . . . 1·25 1·25
2461 90 c. Johnny Mathis . . . . 1·25 1·25
2462 90 c. Madonna . . . . 1·25 1·25
2463 90 c. Nat King Cole . . . . 1·25 1·25
2464 90 c. Janice Joplin . . . . 1·25 1·25
Nos. 2457/64 were printed together, se-tenant, with a composite background design.

1992. Anniversaries and Events. Mult.
2466 10 c. Type 375 . . . . 50 40
2467 25 c. Airship LZ-1 on maiden flight, 1900 (horiz) 70 30
2468 50 c. ENDOSAT (robot plane) project (horiz) 75 55
2469 75 c. Konrad Adenauer (German statesman) and industrial skyline (horiz) . 80 70
2470 $1.50 Golden lion tamarin (horiz) . . . . 2·00 2·00
2471 $2 Mountain gorilla (horiz) . 2·50 2·50
2472 $2 Outline of man and heart (horiz) . . . . 2·50 2·50
2473 $3 Wolfgang Amadeus Mozart 3·25 3·25
2474 $4 "Voyager 2" and Neptune (horiz) . . . . 3·50 3·50
2475 $4 Adenauer with flag and map of West Germany (horiz) . 3·50 3·50
2476 $5 Count von Zeppelin and "Graf Zeppelin" (horiz) . 3·50 3·50
2477 $6 Admiral Richard Byrd (polar explorer) (horiz) . . . . . 3·50 3·50
ANNIVERSARIES AND EVENTS: No. 2466, National bird; Nos. 2467, 2476, 75th death anniv of Count Ferdinand von Zeppelin; Nos. 2468, 2475, International Space Year; Nos. 2469, 2475, 25th death anniv of Konrad Adenauer; Nos. 2470/1, Earth Summit '92, Rio; No. 2472, United Nations World Health Organization Projects; No. 2473, Death bicentenary of Mozart; No. 2477, 75th anniv of International Association of Lions Clubs.

376 Care Bear on Beach

1992. Ecology.
2479 376 75 c. multicoloured . . 45 45

377 Samoyed and St. Basil's Cathedral, Moscow

378 Baha'i Shrine, Haifa

1993. Dogs of the World. Multicoloured.
2481 10 c. Type 377 . . . . . . 40 30
2482 15 c. Chow and Ling Yin Monastery, China 50 30
2483 25 c. Boxer and Tower of London 55 30
2484 90 c. Basenji and Yamma Mosque, Niger . . . . . 1·00 75
2485 $1 Golden labrador and Parliament Building, Ottawa 1·00 80
2486 $3 St. Bernard and Parsenn, Switzerland . . . . . . 2·25 2·75
2487 $4 Rhodesian ridgeback and Melrose House, South Africa 2·50 3·00
2488 $5 Afghan hound and Mazar-i-Sharif, Afghanistan . . 2·50 3·00

1993. Bicentenary of the Louvre, Paris. Paintings by Jean-Antoine Watteau. As T 305 of Antigua. Multicoloured.
2490 $1 "The Faux-pas" 65 70
2491 $1 "Portrait of a Gentleman" 65 70
2492 $1 "Young Lady with Archlute" 65 70
2493 $1 "Young Man Dancing" . 65 70
2494 $1 "Autumn, Pamona and a Cherub" 65 70
2495 $1 "Judgement of Paris" . . 65 70
2496 $1 "Pierrot" (detail) 65 70
2497 $1 "Pierrot" (different detail) 65 70

1993. Centenary of Baha'i Faith.
2499 378 75 c. multicoloured . . 60 60

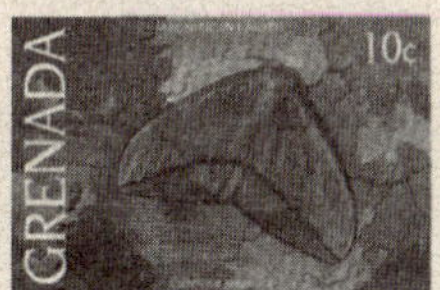

379 "Citheronia magnifica"

1993. Moths. Multicoloured.
2500 10 c. Type 379 . . . . . . 25 25
2501 35 c. "Automeris metali" . . 40 25
2502 45 c. "Thysania zenobia" . . 50 30
2503 75 c. "Agrius cingulatus" . . 70 55
2504 $1 "Composia fidelissima" . 80 65
2505 $2 "Synchlora xysteraria" . 1·50 1·75
2506 $4 "Eumorpha labruscae" . 2·50 2·75
2507 $5 "Ascalapha odorata" . . 2·50 2·75

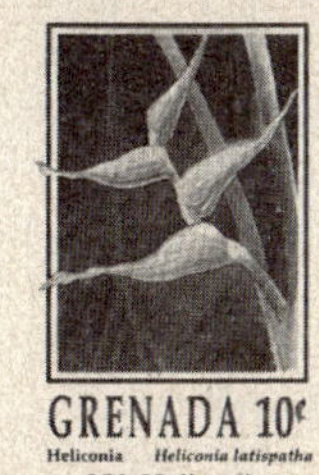

380 Heliconia

381 "Woman with Loaves" (Picasso)

1993. Flowers. Multicoloured.
2509 10 c. Type 380 . . . . . . 25 25
2510 35 c. Pansy 40 25
2511 45 c. Water lily 50 30
2512 75 c. Bougainvillea 70 55
2513 $1 Calla lily 80 65
2514 $2 California poppy . . . . 1·50 1·75
2515 $4 Red ginger . . . . 2·50 2·75
2516 $5 Anthurium . . . . 2·50 2·75

1993. 40th Anniv of Coronation. As T 307 of Antigua.
2518 35 c. multicoloured 55 65
2519 70 c. multicoloured 70 80
2520 $1 brown and black 75 85
2521 $5 multicoloured . . . . . . 2·25 2·50
DESIGNS: 35 c. Queen Elizabeth II at Coronation (photograph by Cecil Beaton); 70 c. Sceptres; $1 Queen Elizabeth receiving sceptre from Archbishop of Canterbury; $5 Queen and Prince Philip with their children, 1960s.

1993. Anniversaries and Events. Each brown, deep brown and black (Nos. 2527, 2535) or multicoloured (others).
2523 25 c. Type 381 . . . . 30 20
2524 35 c. 16th-century telescope . 35 20
2525 35 c. Public Library building . 35 20
2526 35 c. Gaetan Boucher (speed skating, 1984) 35 20
2527 50 c. Willy Brandt with Senator Edward Kennedy (horiz) . 40 30
2528 75 c. Carnival float (horiz) . . 50 40
2529 90 c. "Weeping Woman" (Picasso) 65 45
2530 $1 "Marii Prohaska" (Tyrus Czyzewski) 70 50
2531 $3 "Marysia et Burek a Geylan" (S. Wirkiewicz) . . . . . 2·25 2·25
2532 $4 "Woman seated in Airchair" (Picasso) . . . . 2·75 2·75
2533 $4 Astronaut on Moon . . . 2·75 2·75
2534 $5 Norbert Schramm (figure skating, 1984) . . . . . . 2·75 2·75
2535 $5 Willy Brandt and Kurt Waldheim (horiz) . . . . 2·75 2·75
ANNIVERSARIES AND EVENTS: Nos. 2523, 2529, 2532, 20th death anniv of Picasso (artist); Nos. 2524, 2533, 450th death anniv of Copernicus (astronomer); No. 2525, Centenary (1992) of Grenada Public Library; Nos. 2526, 2534, Winter Olympic Games '94, Lillehammer; Nos. 2527, 2535, 80th birth anniv (1992) of Willy Brandt (German politician); No. 2528, Grenada Carnival; Nos. 2530/1, "Polska '93" International Stamp Exhibition, Poznan.

382 Red-eyed Vireo

1993. Songbirds. Multicoloured.
2537 15 c. Type 382 . . . . 35 35
2538 25 c. Fork-tailed flycatcher ("Scissor-tailed flycatcher") 40 40
2539 35 c. Palm chat 45 45
2540 35 c. Chaffinch 45 45
2541 45 c. Yellow wagtail 50 50
2542 45 c. Painted bunting 50 50
2543 50 c. Short-tailed pygmy tyrant ("Short-tailed pygmy flycatcher") 50 50
2544 65 c. Orange-breasted bunting ("Rainbow Bunting") . . . 60 60
2545 75 c. Red crossbill 60 60
2546 75 c. Kauai akialoa 60 60
2547 $1 Yellow-throated longclaw ("Yellow-throated wagtail") 75 75
2548 $4 Barn swallow . . . . . . 2·25 2·25
Nos. 2537/48 were printed together, se-tenant, with the backgrounds forming a composite design.

383 Atlantic Grey Cowrie and Atlantic Yellow Cowrie

1993. Seashells. Multicoloured.
2550 15 c. Type 383 . . . . 35 35
2551 15 c. Candy-stick tellin and sunrise tellin 35 35
2552 25 c. Caribbean vase 40 40
2553 35 c. Lightning venus and royal comb venus 45 45
2554 35 c. Crown cone 45 45
2555 45 c. Reticulated cowrie-helmet 50 50
2556 50 c. Barbados mitre and variegated turret shell . . . 50 50
2557 50 c. Common egg cockle and Atlantic strawberry cockle . 50 50
2558 75 c. Measled cowrie 60 60
2559 75 c. Rooster-tail conch . . . 60 60
2560 $1 Lion's-paw scallop and Antillean scallop 75 75
2561 $4 Dog-head triton . . . . . 2·25 2·25
Nos. 2550/61 were printed together, se-tenant, with the backgrounds forming a composite design.

1993. Asian International Stamp Exhibitions. As T 268 of Dominica. Mult. (a) "Indopex '93", Surabaya, Indonesia.
2563 35 c. Megalithic carving, Sumba Island 35 25
2564 45 c. Entrance to Gao Gajah, Bali 45 30
2565 $1.50 Statue of kris holder . . 1·00 1·00
2566 $1.50 Hanuman protecting Sita 1·00 1·00
2567 $1.50 Sendi of Visu mounted on Garuda . . . . 1·00 1·00
2568 $1.50 Wahana (votif figure) . 1·00 1·00
2569 $1.50 Hanuman (different) . . 1·00 1·00
2570 $1.50 Singa (symbolic lion) . 1·00 1·00
2571 $2 Loving-mother Bridge, Taroko Gorge National Park 1·40 1·50
2572 $4 Head of Kala over temple gateway, Northern Bali . . 2·50 2·75

(b) "Taipei '93", Taiwan.
2574 35 c. Fire-breathing dragon, New Year's Fair, Chongqing 35 25
2575 45 c. Stone elephant, Ming Tomb, Nanjing 45 30
2576 $1.50 "Ornamental Cock" (Han Meilin) . . . . 1·00 1·00
2577 $1.50 "He's even afraid of Cows" (Meilin) . . . . . 1·00 1·00
2578 $1.50 "On a Moonlit Night" (Meilin) . . . . 1·00 1·00
2579 $1.50 "Eyes that see in the Dark" (Meilin) . . . . . 1·00 1·00
2580 $1.50 "He's well behaved" (Meilin) . . . . 1·00 1·00
2581 $1.50 "He doesn't Bite" (Meilin) . . . . 1·00 1·00
2582 $2 Marble peifang, Ming 13 Tombs, Beijing . . . . . 1·40 1·50
2583 $4 Stone pillar, Nanjing . . 2·50 2·75

(c) "Bangkok 1993", Thailand.
2585 35 c. Nora Nair, Prasad Phra Thepidon, Wat Phra Kaew 35 25
2586 45 c. Stucco deities at Library of Wat Phra Singh 45 30
2587 $1.50 Wooden carved horses . 1·00 1·00
2588 $1.50 Wheel of the law . . . 1·00 1·00
2589 $1.50 Lanna bronze elephant 1·00 1·00
2590 $1.50 Kendi in the form of elephant . . . . 1·00 1·00
2591 $1.50 Bronze duck . . . . . 1·00 1·00
2592 $1.50 Horseman . . . . . . 1·00 1·00
2593 $2 Naga snake, Chiang Mai's Temple . . . . 1·40 1·50
2594 $4 Stucco figures, Wat Chang Lom . . . . 2·50 2·75
No. 2590 is incorrectly inscribed "Kendi in the form of an Elphant".

1993. World Cup Football Championship, U.S.A. (1994) (1st issue). As T 310 of Antigua. Mult.
2596 10 c. Nikolai Larionov (Russia) 20 20
2597 25 c. Andrea Carnevale (Italy) 40 25
2598 35 c. Enzo Schifo (Belgium) and Soon-Ho Choi (South Korea 45 25
2599 45 c. Gary Lineker (England) 50 30
2600 $1 Diego Maradona (Argentina) . . . . 1·00 80
2601 $2 Lothar Mattaeus (Germany) 1·60 1·90
2602 $4 Jan Karas (Poland) and Julio Cesar Silva (Brazil) . . . 2·25 2·75
2603 $5 Claudio Caniggia (Argentina) . . . . 2·50 3·00
See also Nos. 2743/8.

384 James K. Spensley

1993. Centenary of Italian Football. Past and present Genoa players. Each blue, red and black.
2605 $3 Type 384 . . . . 2·00 2·00
2606 $3 Renzo de Vecchi . . . . 2·00 2·00
2607 $3 Giovanni de Pra' . . . . 2·00 2·00
2608 $3 Luigi Burlando . . . . . 2·00 2·00
2609 $3 Felice Levratto . . . . . 2·00 2·00
2610 $3 Guglielmo Stabile . . . . 2·00 2·00
2611 $3 Vittorio Sardelli . . . . 2·00 2·00
2612 $3 Juan Carlos Verdeal . . . 2·00 2·00
2613 $3 Fosco Becattini . . . . . 2·00 2·00
2614 $3 Julio Cesar Abadie . . . 2·00 2·00
2615 $3 Luigi Meroni . . . . . . 2·00 2·00
2616 $3 Roberto Pruzzo . . . . . 2·00 2·00

385 "The Band Concert", 1935

1993. 65th Anniv of Mickey Mouse. Scenes from Walt Disney cartoon films. Multicoloured.
2618 25 c. Type 385 . . . . 45 20
2619 35 c. "Mickey's Circus", 1936 50 20
2620 50 c. "Magician Mickey", 1937 60 35
2621 75 c. "Moose Hunters", 1937 80 60
2622 $1 "Mickey's Amateurs", 1937 90 80
2623 $2 "Tugboat Mickey", 1940 . 1·50 1·50
2624 $4 "Orphan's Benefit", 1941 2·50 2·75
2625 $5 "Mickey's Christmas Carol", 1983 . . . . 2·50 2·75
No. 2624 is inscribed "Oprhan's Benefit" in error.

1993. Christmas. Religious Paintings. As T 270 of Dominica. Black, yellow and red (Nos. 2627/8, 2632 and 2634) or multicoloured (others).
2627 10 c. "The Nativity" (Durer) 25 15
2628 25 c. "The Annunciation" (Durer) 35 15
2629 35 c. "The Litta Madonna" (Da Vinci) 40 20
2630 60 c. "The Virgin and Child with St. John the Baptist and St. Anne" (Da Vinci) . . . 50 40
2631 90 c. "The Madonna with the Carnation" (Da Vinci) . . 65 65

2632 $1 "Adoration of the Magi" (Durer) . . . 75 75
2633 $4 "The Benois Madonna" (Da Vinci) . . . 2·50 3·00
2634 $5 "The Virgin Mary in the Sun" (Durer) . . . 2·50 3·00
Nos. 2629/31 and 2633 are inscribed "LEONARDO DI VINCI".

386 Blanchard's Balloon over Walnut St. Prison

1993. Aviation Anniversaries. Multicoloured.
2636 35 c. Airship "Graf Zeppelin" over Vienna at night . . . 35 20
2637 45 c. Type **386** . . . 20 25
2638 50 c. Lysander . . . 50 35
2639 75 c. "Graf Zeppelin" over Pyramids . . . 75 55
2640 $2 Blanchard waving hat from balloon (vert) . . . 90 95
2641 $3 Hawker Typhoon . . . 2·00 2·50
2642 $5 "Graf Zeppelin" over Rio de Janeiro . . . 3·25 3·75
ANNIVERSARIES: Nos. 2636, 2639, 2642, 125th birth anniv of Hugo Eckener (airship commander); Nos. 2637, 2640, Bicentenary of first airmail flight; Nos. 2638, 2641, 75th anniv of Royal Air Force.

387 Mercedes Benz "370 S" Cabriolet, 1932

1993. Centenaries of Henry Ford's First Petrol Engine (Nos. 2645/6)) and Karl Benz's First Four-wheeled Car (others). Multicoloured.
2644 35 c. Type **387** . . . 15 20
2645 45 c. Ford "Mustang", 1966 . . . 40 30
2646 $3 Ford "Model A" Phaeton, 1930 . . . 1·40 1·50
2647 $4 Mercedes Benz "300 Sl" Gullwing . . . 3·50 3·75

1993. Famous Paintings by Rembrandt and Matisse. As T **316** of Antigua. Multicoloured.
2649 15 c. "Self-portrait", 1900 (Matisse) . . . 30 20
2650 35 c. "Self-portrait", 1629 (Rembrandt) . . . 35 20
2651 45 c. "Self-portrait", 1918 (Matisse) . . . 40 25
2652 50 c. "Self-portrait", 1640 (Rembrandt) . . . 50 35
2653 75 c. "Self-portrait", 1652 (Rembrandt) . . . 65 55
2654 $2 "Self-portrait", 1906 (Matisse) . . . 1·40 1·75
2655 $4 "Self-portrait", 1900 (different) (Matisse) . . . 2·50 3·25
2656 $5 "Self-portrait", 1625–31 (Rembrandt) . . . 2·75 3·25

388 Fishermen with Blue Marlin

389 National Flag and Ketch in Bay

1994. 25th Anniv of Spice Island Billfish Tournament. Multicoloured.
2658 15 c. Type **388** . . . 30 20
2659 25 c. Sailfish with angler . . . 35 20
2660 35 c. Yellow-finned tuna with angler . . . 50 25
2661 50 c. White marlin with angler . . . 60 50
2662 75 c. Catching a sailfish . . . 75 80

1994. 25th Anniv of Independence.
2663 **389** 35 c. multicoloured . . . 30 30

1994. "Hong Kong '94" International Stamp Exhibition (1st issue). As T **317** of Antigua. Multicoloured.
2665 40 c. Hong Kong 1971 Scouting 50 c. stamp and "Hong Kong Post Office, 1846" (left detail) (M. Bruce) . . . 30 40
2666 40 c. Grenada 1988 Rotary $2 and "Hong Kong Post Office, 1846" (right detail) (M. Bruce) . . . 30 40
Nos. 2665/6 were printed together, se-tenant, with the centre part of each pair forming the complete painting.
See also Nos. 2667/72.

1994. "Hong Kong '94" International Stamp Exhibition (2nd issue). Qing Dynasty Porcelain. As T **318** of Antigua, but vert. Multicoloured.
2667 45 c. Vase with dragon decoration . . . 30 35
2668 45 c. Hat stand with brown base . . . 30 35
2669 45 c. Gourd-shaped vase . . . 30 35
2670 45 c. Rotating vase with openwork . . . 30 35
2671 45 c. Candlestick with dogs . . . 30 35
2672 45 c. Hat stand with orange base . . . 30 35

390 "Hygrocybe acutoconica"

1994. Fungi. Multicoloured.
2673 35 c. Type **390** . . . 35 20
2674 45 c. "Leucopaxillus gracillimus" . . . 40 25
2675 50 c. "Leptonia caeruleocapitata" . . . 40 30
2676 75 c. "Leucocoprinus birnbaumii" . . . 60 50
2677 $1 "Marasmius atrorubens" . . . 75 75
2678 $2 "Boletellus cubensis" . . . 1·25 1·50
2679 $4 "Chlorophyllum molybdites" . . . 2·25 2·40
2680 $5 "Psilocybe cubensis" . . . 2·25 2·40

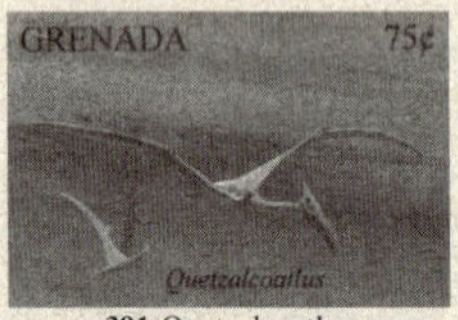
391 Quetzalcoatlus

1994. Prehistoric Animals. Multicoloured.
2682 75 c. Type **391** . . . 45 50
2683 75 c. Pteranodon ingens . . . 45 50
2684 75 c. Tropeognathus . . . 45 50
2685 75 c. Phobetor . . . 45 50
2686 75 c. Alamosaurus . . . 45 50
2687 75 c. Triceratops . . . 45 50
2688 75 c. Tyrannosaurus rex . . . 45 50
2689 75 c. Head of Tyrannosaurus rex . . . 45 50
2690 75 c. Lambeosaurus . . . 45 50
2691 75 c. Spinosaurus . . . 45 50
2692 75 c. Parasaurolophus . . . 45 50
2693 75 c. Hadrosaurus . . . 45 50
2694 75 c. Germanodactylus . . . 45 50
2695 75 c. Dimorphodon . . . 45 50
2696 75 c. Ramphorynchus . . . 45 50
2697 75 c. Apatosaurus . . . 45 50
2698 75 c. Pterodactylus . . . 45 50
2699 75 c. Stegosaurus . . . 45 50
2700 75 c. Brathiosaurus . . . 45 50
2701 75 c. Allosaurus . . . 45 50
2702 75 c. Plesiosaurus . . . 45 50
2703 75 c. Ceratosaurus . . . 45 50
2704 75 c. Compsognathus . . . 45 50
2705 75 c. Elaphosaurus . . . 45 50
Nos. 2682/93 and 2694/2705 respectively were printed together, se-tenant, forming composite designs.

1994. 25th Anniv of First Manned Moon Landing. Space Shuttle "Challenger". As T **326** of Antigua. Multicoloured.
2707 $2 Space shuttle "Challenger" . . . 1·10 1·40
2708 $2 Judith Resnick (astronaut) . . . 1·10 1·40
2709 $2 Aircraft in memorial fly past . . . 1·10 1·40
2710 $2 Dick Scobee (astronaut) . . . 1·10 1·40
2711 $2 Mission logo . . . 1·10 1·40
2712 $2 Michael Smith (astronaut) . . . 1·10 1·40

1994. Centenary of International Olympic Committee. Gold Medal Winners. As T **327** of Antigua, but vert. Multicoloured.
2714 50 c. Heike Drechsler (Germany) (long jump), 1992 . . . 40 30
2715 $1.50 Nadia Comaneci (Rumania) (gymnastics), 1976 and 1980 . . . 1·10 1·25

1994. International Year of the Family. As T **328** of Antigua. Multicoloured.
2717 $1 Grenadian family . . . 55 60

1994. 50th Anniv of D-Day. As T **331** of Antigua. Multicoloured.
2718 40 c. Sherman amphibious tank leaving landing craft . . . 40 30
2719 $2 Tank on Churchill "Ark" bridging vehicle . . . 1·40 1·50
2720 $3 Churchill "Bobbin" tank laying roadway . . . 1·75 2·00

1994. "Philakorea '94" International Stamp Exhibition, Seoul. As T **279** of Dominica. Multicoloured.
2722 40 c. Wonson Park (horiz) . . . 20 25
2723 $1 Pusan (horiz) . . . 45 50
2724 $1 "Lady in a Hooded Cloak" (left detail) (Sin Yunbok) . . . 45 50
2725 $1 "Lady in a Hooded Cloak" (right detail) . . . 45 50
2726 $1 "Kiaseng House" (left detail) (Sin Yunbok) . . . 45 50
2727 $1 "Kiaseng House" (right detail) . . . 45 50
2728 $1 "Amorous Youth on a Picnic" (left detail) (Sin Yunbok) . . . 45 50
2729 $1 "Amorous Youth on a Picnic" (right detail) . . . 45 50
2730 $1 "Chasing a Cat" (left detail) (Sin Yunbok) . . . 45 50
2731 $1 "Chasing a Cat" (right detail) . . . 45 50
2732 $4 Korean orchestra, National Theatre, Seoul (horiz) . . . 1·90 2·00
Nos. 2724/31 were printed together, se-tenant, forming composite designs of each painting.

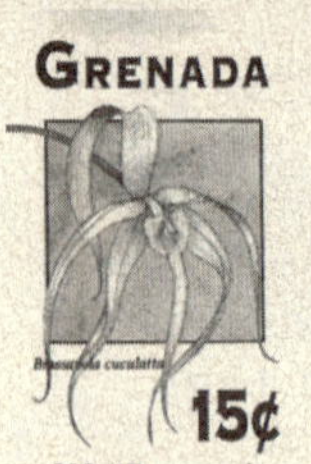
392 "Brassavola cucullatta"

393 Tony Meola (U.S.A.)

1994. Orchids. Multicoloured.
2734 15 c. Type **392** . . . 30 20
2735 25 c. "Comparettia falcata" . . . 40 20
2736 45 c. "Epidendrum ciliare" . . . 50 30
2737 75 c. "Epidendrum cochleatum" . . . 70 50
2738 $1 "Ionopsis utricularioides" . . . 80 70
2739 $2 "Onicidium cebolleta" . . . 1·25 1·40
2740 $4 "Onicidium luridium" . . . 2·25 2·50
2741 $5 "Rodriquezia secunda" . . . 2·25 2·50

1994. World Cup Football Championship, U.S.A. (2nd issue). Multicoloured.
2743 75 c. Type **393** . . . 45 50
2744 75 c. Steve Mark (Grenada) . . . 45 50
2745 75 c. Gianluigi Lentini (Italy) . . . 45 50
2746 75 c. Belloumi (Algeria) . . . 45 50
2747 75 c. Nunoz (Spain) . . . 45 50
2748 75 c. Lothar Matthaus (Germany) . . . 45 50

1994. 1st Recipients of Order of the Caribbean Community. As Nos. 2046/8 of Antigua. Multicoloured.
2750 15 c. Sir Shridath Ramphal . . . 10 10
2751 65 c. William Demas . . . 40 40
2752 $2 Derek Walcott . . . 1·40 1·60

394 Yellow-tailed Snapper

1994. Fishes. Multicoloured.
2753 15 c. Type **394** . . . 30 20
2754 20 c. Blue tang . . . 30 20
2755 25 c. Porkfish (vert) . . . 30 20
2756 75 c. Four-eyed butterflyfish . . . 65 50
2757 $1 Reid's seahorse (vert) . . . 75 70
2758 $2 Spotted moray (vert) . . . 1·25 1·50
2759 $4 Royal gramma ("Fairy basslet") . . . 2·25 2·50
2760 $5 Queen triggerfish (vert) . . . 2·25 2·50

395 Mickey Mouse bathing Pluto

1994. Chinese New Year ("Year of the Dog"). Walt Disney Cartoon Characters. Multicoloured.
2762 2 c. Type **395** . . . 10 10
2763 3 c. Dog taking mouthwash . . . 10 10
2764 4 c. Dog with curlers in tail . . . 10 10
2765 5 c. Brushing dog's eyelashes . . . 10 10
2766 10 c. Giving dog manicure . . . 15 10
2767 15 c. Mickey spraying Pluto with flea powder . . . 20 15
2768 20 c. Dogs on display . . . 25 20
2769 $4 Judge checking Pluto's teeth . . . 2·50 3·00
2770 $5 Pluto wearing "1st Prize" rosette . . . 2·50 3·00

396 "Anartia amathea"

1994. Butterflies. Multicoloured.
2772A 10 c. Type **396** . . . 10 10
2773A 15 c. "Marpesia petreus" . . . 10 10
2774A 25 c. "Hylephila phylaeus" . . . 10 10
2775A 35 c. "Junonia evarete" . . . 15 20
2776A 45 c. "Pseudolycaena marsyas" . . . 20 25
2777A 50 c. "Heliconius charitonius" . . . 20 25
2778A 75 c. "Hypolimnas misippus" . . . 35 40
2778cB 90 c. "Purgus oilcus" . . . 40 45
2779A $1 "Cepheuptychia cephus" . . . 45 50
2779cB $1.50 "Allosmaitia piplea" . . . 70 75
2780A $2 "Historis odius" . . . 85 90
2781A $3 "Phoebis philea" . . . 1·25 1·40
2782A $4 "Urbanus proteus" . . . 1·75 1·90
2783A $5 "Battus polydamas" . . . 2·10 2·25
2784A $10 "Philaethria dido" . . . 4·25 4·50
2785A $20 "Hamadryas arethusa" . . . 8·75 9·00

1994. Christmas. Religious Paintings by Francisco de Zurbaran. As T **336** of Antigua. Multicoloured.
2786 10 c. "The Virgin and Child with St. John" (1658) . . . 20 15
2787 15 c. "The Circumcision" . . . 30 20
2788 25 c. "Adoration of St. Joseph" . . . 30 20
2789 35 c. "Adoration of the Magi" . . . 30 20
2790 75 c. "The Portiuncula" . . . 60 45
2791 $1 "The Virgin and Child with St. John" (1662) . . . 75 60
2792 $2 "The Virgin and Child with St. John" (1658/64) . . . 1·25 1·25
2793 $4 "The Flight into Egypt" . . . 2·25 2·50

397 Grenada Dove on Nest

1995. Birds. Multicoloured.
2795 25 c. Type **397** . . . 40 20
2796 35 c. Pair of Grenada doves at nest . . . 45 20
2797 45 c. Cuban tody (vert) . . . 50 25
2798 75 c. Grenada dove on branch (vert) . . . 60 60
2799 75 c. Painted bunting . . . 60 60
2800 $1 Grenada dove in flight (vert) . . . 75 75
2801 $1 Red-legged honeycreeper . . . 75 75
2802 $5 Green jay . . . 2·50 2·75
Nos. 2795/6, 2798 and 2800 also show the W.W.F. Panda emblem.

1995. Centenary of First English Cricket Tour to the West Indies. As T **329** of Antigua. Multicoloured.
2804 25 c. Junior Murray (West Indies) (vert) . . . 30 20
2805 35 c. Richie Richardson (West Indies) (vert) . . . 35 25
2806 $2 Alec Stewart (England) and Wisden Trophy . . . 1·40 1·60

398 Hooded Merganser

1995. Water Birds of the World. Multicoloured.
2808 25 c. Type **398** . . . 10 10
2809 35 c. Green-winged teal . . . 15 20
2810 75 c. King eider . . . 35 40
2811 75 c. Common shoveler . . . 35 40
2812 75 c. Long-tailed duck . . . 35 40
2813 75 c. Chiloe wigeon . . . 35 40
2814 75 c. Red-breasted merganser . . . 35 40
2815 75 c. Falcated teal . . . 35 40
2816 75 c. Vericolor teal . . . 35 40
2817 75 c. Smew . . . 35 40
2818 75 c. Red-crested pochard . . . 35 40
2819 75 c. Pintail . . . 35 40
2820 75 c. Barrow's goldeneye . . . 35 40
2821 75 c. Stellar's eider . . . 35 40
2822 $1 Harlequin duck . . . 45 50
2823 $3 European wigeon . . . 1·25 1·40
Nos. 2810/21 were printed together, se-tenant, forming a composite design.
No. 2811 is inscribed "Shobeler" in error.

399 Pig Priest, China

1995. Chinese New Year ("Year of the Pig"). Ornaments. Multicoloured.
2825 50 c. Type **399** . . . 20 25
2826 75 c. Porcelain pig, Scotland . . . 35 40
2827 $1 Seated porcelain pig, Italy . . . 45 50

400 Yellow-tailed Damselfish

1995. Marine Life. Multicoloured.
2829 $1 Type **400** 45 50
2830 $1 Blue-headed wrasse 45 50
2831 $1 Balloonfish 45 50
2832 $1 Shy hamlet 45 50
2833 $1 Orange tube coral 45 50
2834 $1 Rock beauty 45 50
2835 $1 Creole wrasse 45 50
2836 $1 Queen angelfish 45 50
2837 $1 Trumpetfish 45 50
2838 $1 Barred hamlet 45 50
2839 $1 Tube sponge 45 50
2840 $1 Porcupine fish 45 50
2841 $1 Firecoral 45 50
2842 $1 Royal gramma ("Fairy basslet") 45 50
2843 $1 Sea anemone 45 50
Nos. 2829/34 and 2835/43 respectively were printed together, se-tenant, forming composite designs.

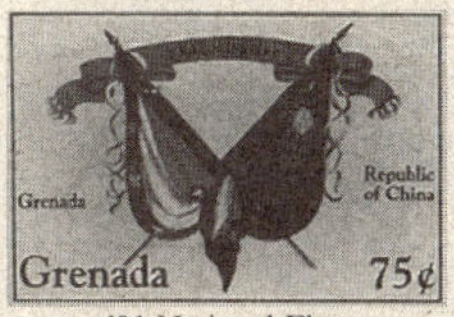

401 National Flags

1995. Grenada–Taiwan (Republic of China) Friendship. Multicoloured.
2845 75 c. Type **401** 35 40
2846 $1 Prime Minister Brathwaite and President Lee Teng-hui 45 50

402 Cocker Spaniel

404 "Swords into Ploughshares"

403 Grenadian Scout

1995. Domestic Animals. Multicoloured.
2848 10 c. Type **402** 10 10
2849 15 c. Pinto (horse) 10 10
2850 25 c. Rottweiler 10 10
2851 35 c. German shepherd 15 20
2852 45 c. Persian (cat) 20 25
2853 50 c. Snowshoe (cat) 20 25
2854 75 c. Percheron (horse) 35 40
2855 $1 Scottish fold (cat 45 50
2856 $2 Arabian (horse) 85 90
2857 $3 Andalusian (horse) 1·25 1·40
2858 $4 C.P. Shorthair (cat) 1·75 1·90
2859 $5 Chihuahua 2·10 2·25

1995. Centenary (1992) of Sierra Club (environmental protection society). Endangered Species. As T **320** of Antigua. Multicoloured.
2861 $1 Head of margay at night 45 50
2862 $1 Margay sitting 45 50
2863 $1 Head of margay in daylight 45 50
2864 $1 Head of Andean condor 45 50
2865 $1 Andean condor facing right 45 50
2866 $1 Andean condor facing left 45 50
2867 $1 White-faced saki on branch 45 50
2868 $1 White-faced saki showing mane 45 50
2869 $1 Patagonia landscape 45 50
2870 $1 Lesser rheas feeding (horiz) 45 50
2871 $1 Pair of lesser rheas (horiz) 45 50
2872 $1 Lesser rhea (horiz) 45 50
2873 $1 Sunset over snow-covered mountains, Patagonia (horiz) 45 50
2874 $1 Volcanic eruption, Patagonia (horiz) 45 50
2875 $1 White-faced Saki (horiz) 45 50
2876 $1 Common caracara on branch (horiz) 45 50
2877 $1 Pair of common caracaras at nest (horiz) 45 50
2878 $1 Common caracara facing left (horiz) 45 50

1995. 18th World Scout Jamboree, Netherlands. Multicoloured.
2879 75 c. Type **403** 35 40
2880 $1 Scout abseiling 45 50
2881 $2 Scout saluting and national flag 85 90

1995. 50th Anniv of End of Second World War in Europe. Fighter Aircraft. As T **340** of Antigua. Multicoloured.
2883 $2 Lavochkin La-7 (fighter) 85 90
2884 $2 Hawker Hurricane 85 90
2885 $2 North American P-51D Mustang 85 90
2886 $2 Messerschmitt Bf 109 85 90
2887 $2 Bristol Type 152 Beaufighter 85 90
2888 $2 Messerschmitt Me 262 85 90
2889 $2 Republic P-47 Thunderbolt 85 90
2890 $2 Hawker Tempest 85 90

1995. 50th Anniv of United Nations. Multicoloured.
2892 75 c. Type **404** 35 40
2893 $1 Globe and dove 45 50
2894 $2 U.N. Building, New York 85 90

405 Woman with Baskets

406 National Flag and Rotary Logo

1995. 50th Anniv of F.A.O. Multicoloured.
2896 75 c. Type **405** 35 40
2897 $1 Boy with basket on head 45 50
2898 $2 Men harvesting bananas 85 90

1995. 90th Anniv of Rotary International.
2900 **406** $5 multicoloured 2·10 2·25

1995. 95th Birthday of Queen Elizabeth the Queen Mother. As T **344** of Antigua.
2902 $1.50 brown, light brown and black 65 70
2903 $1.50 multicoloured 65 70
2904 $1.50 multicoloured 65 70
2905 $1.50 multicoloured 65 70
DESIGNS: No. 2902, Queen Elizabeth the Queen Mother (pastel drawing); 2903, Holding rose; 2904, At desk (oil painting); 2905, In blue hat and white coat.

1995. 50th Anniv of End of Second World War in the Pacific. As T **340** of Antigua. Multicoloured.
2907 $2 Dogfight over the Marianas 85 90
2908 $2 U.S. dive-bomber and burning aircraft carrier, Battle of Midway 85 90
2909 $2 U.S. aircraft attacking Japanese transport, Battle of the Bismarck Sea 85 90
2910 $2 "Mushashi" (Japanese battleship) on fire in Leyte Gulf 85 90
2911 $2 U.S. aircraft taking off from Henderson Field 85 90
2912 $2 Battleships at Guadalcanal 85 90

407 Tian Bingyi (China) (badminton)

408 Junior Murray (West Indies)

1995. Olympic Games, Atlanta (1996) (1st issue). Multicoloured.
2914 75 c. Type **407** 35 40
2915 75 c. Waldemar Leigien (Poland) and Frank Wieneke (West Germany) (judo) 35 40
2916 75 c. Nelli Kim (U.S.S.R.) (gymnastics) 35 40
2917 75 c. Alessandro Andri (Italy) (shot put) 35 40
2918 $2 Jackie Joyner (U.S.A.) (heptathlon) 85 90
2919 $2 Mitsuo Tsukahara (Japan) (gymnastics) 85 90
2920 $2 Flo Hyman (U.S.A.) and Zhang Rung Fang (China) (volleyball) 85 90
2921 $2 Steffi Graf (West Germany) (tennis) 85 90
See also Nos. 3102/23.

1995. Anniversaries and Events. Multicoloured.
2923 25 c. Type **408** (centenary of first English cricket tour to the West Indies) 10 10
2924 75 c. Nutmeg (opening of Grenada Spice Factory) 35 40
2925 $1 Sendall Tunnel (centenary (1994)) 45 50
2926 $1 Caribbean Development Bank building (25th anniv) 45 50

409 Ajamu

410 Elvis Presley and Signature

1995. Local Entertainers. Multicoloured.
2927 35 c. Type **409** 15 20
2928 35 c. Mighty Sparrow 15 20
2929 50 c. Mighty Sparrow in evening dress 20 25
2930 75 c. Ajamu (different) 35 40

1995. Entertainment Legends. Multicoloured.
2931 75 c. Type **410** 35 40
2932 75 c. Marilyn Monroe 35 40

411 Elvis Presley

1995. 60th Birth Anniv of Elvis Presley (singer). Multicoloured.
2933 $1 Type **411** 45 50
2934 $1 With beard 45 50
2935 $1 With long hair and microphone 45 50
2936 $1 Wearing white shirt 45 50
2937 $1 Wearing pink shirt and purple jacket 45 50
2938 $1 With short hair and microphone 45 50
2939 $1 Wearing magenta shirt 45 50
2940 $1 Wearing orange shirt 45 50
2941 $1 Wearing purple shirt 45 50

412 Film Reel and Oscar Statuette

1995. Centenary of Cinema. Multicoloured.
2942 $1 Type **412** 45 50
2943 $1 "HOLLYWOOD" sign 45 50
2944 $1 Charlie Chaplin 45 50
2945 $1 Shirley Temple 45 50
2946 $1 Spencer Tracy and Katherine Hepburn 45 50
2947 $1 Marilyn Monroe 45 50
2948 $1 John Wayne 45 50
2949 $1 Marlon Brando 45 50
2950 $1 Tom Cruise 45 50
Nos. 2942/50 were printed together, se-tenant, forming a composite design.

413 "B1 Level Vista Dome" Electric Locomotive, Japan

1995. Trains of the World (1st series). Multicoloured.
2952 $1 Type **413** 45 50
2953 $1 Rolios Rail Class 25NC steam locomotive, South Africa 45 50
2954 $1 Class 460 electric locomotive, Switzerland 45 50
2955 $1 Central Railway diesel locomotive No. 605, Peru 45 50
2956 $1 X2000 tilt body train, Sweden 45 50
2957 $1 Via Rail Toronto to Vancouver observation car, Canada 45 50
2958 $1 Intercity 125 diesel locomotive, Great Britain 45 50
2959 $1 "The Flying Scotsman" steam locomotive, Great Britain 45 50
2960 $1 "Indian Pacific" diesel locomotive, Australia 45 50
2961 $1 ETR 450 electric train, Italy 45 50
2962 $1 Isparta to Bozanonu Line steam locomotive, Turkey 45 50
2963 $1 TGV train, France 45 50
2964 $1 ICE train, Germany 45 50
2965 $1 Nishi Line electric locomotive, Japan 45 50
2966 $1 "Hikari" train, Japan 45 50
2967 $1 Central Pacific Jupiter steam locomotive, U.S.A. 45 50
2968 $1Amtrak Type 900 electric locomotive, U.S.A. 45 50
2969 $1 "Sir Nigel Gresley" steam locomotive, Great Britain 45 50
See also Nos. 3167/82.

414 Teresa Teng

1995. Teresa Teng (Chinese actress) Commem. Different portraits. Multicoloured unless otherwise indicated.
2971 35 c. Type **414** 30 30
2972 35 c. As a child (brown, ochre and yellow) 30 30
2973 35 c. Wearing feather boa (black, grey and yellow) 30 30
2974 35 c. With motor scooter 30 30
2975 35 c. Holding microphone 30 30
2976 35 c. In white sweater 30 30
2977 35 c. Playing flute 30 30
2978 35 c. With hand to hair (black, grey and yellow) 30 30
2979 35 c. Wearing gold decorated dress 30 30
2980 35 c. With fan 30 30
2981 35 c. As South-sea islander 30 30
2982 35 c. With hands clasped 30 30
2983 35 c. In kimono 30 30
2984 35 c. Holding bow tie 30 30
2985 35 c. Wearing black blouse 30 30
2986 35 c. Resting on chair arm 30 30
2987 75 c. In army uniform 45 45
2988 75 c. In navy uniform 45 45
2989 75 c. In air force uniform 45 45
2990 75 c. Singing with hand out stretched (black, grey and yellow) 45 45
2991 75 c. Singing with flowers in hair 45 45
2992 75 c. Singing in blue floral dress 45 45
2993 75 c. With pink scarf 45 45
2994 75 c. In fringed dress 45 45
2995 75 c. In pale green sweater 45 45
2996 75 c. With hands to face 45 45
Nos. 2987/96 are larger, 34×46 mm.

415 Mickey Mouse fighting Big Pete

1995. Mickey's Pirate Adventure. Walt Disney Cartoon Characters. Multicoloured.
2997 15 c. Type **415** 10 10
2998 25 c. Mickey with treasure chest 10 10
2999 35 c. Minnie Mouse trying on plunder 15 20
3000 75 c. Goofy with telescope and Mickey swimming with barrel 35 40
3001 $3 Big Pete 1·40 1·50
3002 $5 Mickey with monkey, seagull and handkerchief 2·25 2·40

416 Albert Michelson (1907 Physics)

1995. Centenary of Nobel Trust Fund. Multicoloured.

3004	$1 Type **416**	45	50
3005	$1 Ralph Bunche (1950 Peace)	45	50
3006	$1 Edwin Neher (1991 Medicine)	45	50
3007	$1 Klaus Vonklitzing (1985 Physics)	45	50
3008	$1 Johann Deisenhofer (1988 Chemistry)	45	50
3009	$1 Max Delbruck (1969 Medicine)	45	50
3010	$1 J. Georg Bednorz (1987 Physics)	45	50
3011	$1 Feodor Lynen (1964 Medicine)	45	50
3012	$1 Walther Bothe (1954 Physics)	45	50
3013	$1 James Franck (1925 Physics)	45	50
3014	$1 Gustav Hertz (1925 Physics)	45	50
3015	$1 Friedrich Bergius (1931 Chemistry)	45	50
3016	$1 Otto Loewi (1936 Medicine)	45	50
3017	$1 Fritz Lipmann (1953 Medicine)	45	50
3018	$1 Otto Meyerhof (1922 Medicine)	45	50
3019	$1 Paul Heyse (1910 Literature)	45	50
3020	$1 Jane Addams (1931 Peace)	45	50
3021	$1 Carl Braun (1909 Physics)	45	50
3022	$1 Hans Dehmelt (1989 Physics)	45	50
3023	$1 Heinrich Boll (1972 Literature)	45	50
3024	$1 Georges Kohler (1984 Medicine)	45	50
3025	$1 Wolfgang Pauli (1945 Physics)	45	50
3026	$1 Sir Bernard Katz (1970 Medicine)	45	50
3027	$1 Ernest Ruska (1986 Physics)	45	50
3028	$1 William Golding (1983 Literature)	45	50
3029	$1 Hartmut Michel (1988 Chemistry)	45	50
3030	$1 Hans Bethe (1967 Physics)	45	50

Nos. 3004/12, 3013/21 and 3022/30 respectively were printed together, se-tenant, forming composite designs.

No. 3015 is inscribed "Friedrich" in error.

1995. Christmas. Religious Paintings. As T **357** of Antigua. Multicoloured.

3032	15 c. "The Madonna" (Bartolommeo Montagna)	10	10
3033	25 c. "Sacred Conversation Piece" (Bonifacio dei Pitati)	10	10
3034	35 c. "Nativity" (Van Loo)	15	20
3035	75 c. "Madonna of the Fountain" (Van Eyck)	35	40
3036	$2 "The Apparition of the Virgin to St. Philip Neri" (Giovanni Tiepolo)	85	90
3037	$5 "The Holy Family" (Ribera)	2·10	2·25

417 Pres. Ronald Reagan at Fort George

1995. 12th Anniv of Liberation of Grenada (1st issue). Multicoloured.

3039	75 c. Type **417**	35	40
3040	75 c. Pres. Reagan with U.S. and Grenadian flags	35	40
3041	75 c. St. George's	35	40

Nos. 3039/41 were printed together, se-tenant, forming a composite design.

See also Nos. 3043/51.

418 Pres. Ronald Reagan

419 Pope John Paul II and Statue of Liberty

1995. 12th Anniv of Liberation of Grenada (2nd issue). Designs showing Pres. Ronald Reagan. Multicoloured.

3043	$1 With wife	45	50
3044	$1 Type **418**	45	50
3045	$1 With microphones	45	50
3046	$1 Wearing stetson	45	50
3047	$1 In front of U.S. flag	45	50
3048	$1 In front of Brandenburg Gate, Berlin	45	50
3049	$1 Saluting by helicopter	45	50
3050	$1 On horseback	45	50
3051	$1 Addressing troops	45	50

1995. Papal Visit to New York. Multicoloured.

3052	$1 Type **419**	45	50
3053	$1 Pope John Paul II and cathedral	45	50

420 Rat asleep

421 "Young Woman" (Durer)

1996. Chinese New Year ("Year of the Rat").

3055	**420**	75 c. buff, green and brown	35	40
3056	–	75 c. orange, red and violet	35	40
3057	–	75 c. buff, red and green	35	40

DESIGNS: No. 3056, Rat eating; 3057, Rat asleep (T **420** reversed).

1996. Famous Drawings and Paintings by Durer and Rubens. Multicoloured.

3060	15 c. Type **421**	10	10
3061	25 c. "Four Horsemen of the Apocalypse" (Durer)	10	15
3062	35 c. "Assumption and Coronation of the Virgin" (Durer)	15	20
3063	75 c. "Mulay Ahmed" (Rubens)	35	40
3064	$1 "Anthony van Dyck aged 15" (Rubens)	45	50
3065	$2 "Head of a Young Monk" (Rubens)	85	90
3066	$3 "A Scholar inspired by Nature" (Rubens)	1·25	1·40
3067	$5 "Hanns Durer" (Durer)	2·10	2·25

422 Goofy Tap-dancing

1996. Famous Dances. Walt Disney Cartoon Characters Dancing. Multicoloured.

3069	35 c. Type **422**	15	20
3070	45 c. Donald Duck doing Mexican hat dance (horiz)	20	25
3071	75 c. Daisy Duck as hula dancer	35	40
3072	90 c. Mickey and Minnie Mouse doing the tango (horiz)	40	45
3073	$1 Donald and Daisy doing the jitterbug	45	50
3074	$2 Mickey and Minnie performing Ukrainian folk dance (horiz)	90	95
3075	$3 Goofy and Pluto as ballet dancers (horiz)	1·40	1·50
3076	$4 Mickey and Minnie line-dancing	1·90	2·00

1996. 70th Birthday of Queen Elizabeth II. As T **364** of Antigua showing different photographs. Multicoloured.

3078	35 c. As Type **364** of Antigua	15	20
3079	75 c. Wearing white hat	35	40
3080	$4 With bouquet	1·75	1·90

423 Ferrari "125 F1"

1996. Ferrari Racing Cars. Multicoloured.

3082	$1.50 Type **423**	65	70
3083	$1.50 "Tipo 625"	65	70
3084	$1.50 "P4"	65	70
3085	$1.50 "312P"	65	70
3086	$1.50 "312" Formula 1	65	70
3087	$1.50 "312B"	65	70

1996. 50th Anniv of U.N.I.C.E.F. As T **366** of Antigua. Multicoloured.

3089	35 c. Child writing in book (horiz)	15	20
3090	$2 Child planting seedling (horiz)	85	90
3091	$3 Children and U.N.I.C.E.F. emblem (horiz)	1·25	1·40

424 Lions' Gate, Jerusalem

1996. 3000th Anniv of Jerusalem. Multicoloured.

3093	75 c. Type **424**	35	40
3094	$2 New Gate	85	90
3095	$3 Dung Gate	1·25	1·40

1996. Centenary of Radio. Entertainers. As T **368** of Antigua. Multicoloured.

3097	35 c. Jack Benny	15	20
3098	75 c. Gertrude Berg	35	40
3099	$1 Eddie Cantor	45	50
3100	$2 Groucho Marx	85	90

425 Olympic Stadium, Athens, 1896

1996. Olympic Games, Atlanta (2nd issue). Previous Medal Winners. Multicoloured.

3102	35 c. Gold medal of 1896 (vert)	15	20
3103	75 c. Type **425**	35	40
3104	$1 Boughera el Quafi (France) (Gold, 1928)	45	50
3105	$1 Gustav Jansson (Sweden) (Bronze, 1952)	45	50
3106	$1 Spiridon Louis (Greece) (Gold, 1896)	45	50
3107	$1 Basil Heatley (Great Britain) (Silver, 1964)	45	50
3108	$1 Emil Zatopek (Czechoslovakia) (Gold, 1952)	45	50
3109	$1 Frank Shorter (U.S.A.) (Gold, 1972)	45	50
3110	$1 Alain Minoun O'Kacha (France) (Gold, 1956)	45	50
3111	$1 Kokichi Tsu Uraya (Japan) (Bronze, 1964)	45	50
3112	$1 Delfo Cabrera (Argentina) (Gold, 1948)	45	50
3113	$1 Harald Sakata (U.S.A.) (Silver – light heavyweight, 1948)	45	50
3114	$1 Tom Kono (U.S.A.) (Gold – middleweight, 1952 and 1956)	45	50
3115	$1 Naim Suleymanoglu (Turkey) (Gold – featherweight, 1988)	45	50
3116	$1 Lee Hyung Kun (South Korea) (Gold – light heavyweight, 1988)	45	50
3117	$1 Vassily Alexeyev (U.S.S.R.) (Gold – super heavyweight, 1972 and 1976)	45	50
3118	$1 Chen Weiqiang (China) (Gold – featherweight, 1984)	45	50
3119	$1 Ye Huanming (China) (Gold – featherweight, 1988)	45	50
3120	$1 Manfred Nerlinger (Germany) (Silver – super heavyweight, 1988)	45	50
3121	$1 Joseph Depietro (U.S.A.) (Gold – bantamweight, 1948)	45	50
3122	$2 Ancient Greek runners	85	90
3123	$3 Spiridon Louis (Greece) (Gold – marathon, 1896)	1·25	1·40

Nos. 3104/12 (marathon runners) and 3113/21 (weightlifters) respectively were printed together, se-tenant, with the backgrounds forming composite designs.

426 Mercedes-Benz, 1929

1996. Classic Cars. Multicoloured.

3125	35 c. Type **426**	15	20
3126	50 c. Bugatti Type 35, 1927	25	30
3127	75 c. J. Dusenberg, 1935	35	40
3128	$1 Mercer, 1914	45	50
3129	$1 Type 57C Atalante, 1939	45	50
3130	$1 Cannstatt-Daimler, 1900	45	50
3131	$1 Delage, 1925	45	50
3132	$1 Coventry Daimler, 1899	45	50
3133	$1 Vauxhall, 1900	45	50
3134	$1 T-15 Hispano-Suza, 1912	45	50
3135	$2 Alfa Romeo, 1929	85	90
3136	$3 Rolls Royce, 1910	1·25	1·40

427 "Gorch Fock" (cadet barque), Germany, 1916

1996. Ships. Multicoloured.

3138	$1 Type **427**	45	50
3139	$1 "Henry B. Hyde", U.S.A., 1886	45	50
3140	$1 "Resolution" (galleon), Great Britain, 1652	45	50
3141	$1 Type **427**	45	50
3142	$1 "Henry B. Hyde", U.S.A., 1886	45	50
3143	$1 "Resolution" (galleon), Great Britain, 1652	45	50
3144	$1 Type **427**	45	50
3145	$1 "Henry B. Hyde", U.S.A., 1886	45	50
3146	$1 "Resolution" (galleon), Great Britain, 1652	45	50
3147	$1 H.M.S. "Bounty"	45	50
3148	$1 "Bismark" (German battleship)	45	50
3149	$1 "Chuii Apoo" and two junks	45	50
3150	$1 "Lubeck" (German frigate)	45	50
3151	$1 Dutch galleon	45	50
3152	$1 "Augsburg" (German frigate)	45	50
3153	$1 "Henri Grace a Dieu" (British galleon)	45	50
3154	$1 H.M.S. "Prince of Wales" (battleship)	45	50
3155	$1 "Santa Anna" Spanish carrack)	45	50

428 Jacqueline Kennedy

1996. Jacqueline Kennedy Onassis Commemoration. Multicoloured.

3157	$1 Type **428**	45	50
3158	$1 Wearing mauve blouse	45	50
3159	$1 In evening dress (inscr at right)	45	50
3160	$1 In evening dress (inscr at left)	45	50
3161	$1 Wearing pink dress	45	50
3162	$1 Wearing blue dress with collar embroidered	45	50
3163	$1 Wearing white jacket and brooch	45	50
3164	$1 In yellow jacket and green shirt	45	50
3165	$1 Wearing black jacket	45	50

429 Class C51 Locomotive of Imperial Train, Japan

1996. Trains of the World (2nd series). Multicoloured.

3167	35 c. Type **429**	15	20
3168	75 c. "Rheingold" express, Germany	35	40
3169	$1 Atlantic Coast Line locomotive No. 153, 1894, U.S.A.	45	50
3170	$1 Smith Compound No.1619, Great Britain	45	50
3171	$1 Trans-Siberian Soviet Railways	45	50
3172	$1 Palatinate Railway Krauss locomotive, 1898, Germany	45	50
3173	$1 Paris, Lyons and Mediterranean line, France	45	50
3174	$1 Diesel-electric 0341 locomotive, Italy	45	50
3175	$1 Class C62 locomotive, Japan	45	50
3176	$1 Shantung Railways locomotive, China	45	50
3177	$1 Class C57 locomotive, Japan	45	50
3178	$1 Diesel express train, Japan	45	50
3179	$1 Shanghai–Nanking Railway locomotive, China	45	50
3180	$1 Class D51 locomotive, Japan	45	50
3181	$2 "Pioneer", 1851, U.S.A.	85	90
3182	$3 "France", France	1·25	1·40

430 Winter Jasmine

1996. Flowers. Multicoloured.

3184	$1 Type **430**	45	50
3185	$1 Chrysanthemum	45	50
3186	$1 Lilac	45	50
3187	$1 Japanese iris	45	50
3188	$1 Hibiscus	45	50
3189	$1 Sacred lotus	45	50
3190	$1 Apple blossom	45	50
3191	$1 Gladiolus	45	50
3192	$1 Japanese quince	45	50
3193	$1 Canterbury bell (vert)	45	50
3194	$1 Rose (vert)	45	50
3195	$1 Nasturtium (vert)	45	50
3196	$1 Daffodil (vert)	45	50
3197	$1 Tulip (vert)	45	50
3198	$1 Snapdragon (vert)	45	50
3199	$1 Zinnia (vert)	45	50
3200	$1 Sweetpea (vert)	45	50
3201	$1 Pansy (vert)	45	50

Nos. 3184/92 and 3193/3201 respectively were printed together, se-tenant, with the backgrounds forming a composite design.

431 Zeppelin L-31 (Germany)

1996. Airships. Multicoloured.

3203	30 c. Type **431**	15	20
3204	30 c. Zeppelin L-35 (Germany)	15	20
3205	50 c. Zeppelin L-30 (Germany)	25	30
3206	75 c. Zeppelin L-2 10 (Germany)	35	40
3207	$1.50 Zeppelin L-21 (Germany)	65	70
3208	$1.50 Zodiac Type 13 Spiess (France)	65	70
3209	$1.50 N1 "Norge" (Roald Amundsen)	65	70
3210	$1.50 LZ-127 "Graf Zeppelin" (Germany)	65	70
3211	$1.50 LZ-129 "Hindenburg" (Germany)	65	70
3212	$1.50 Zeppelin NT (Germany)	65	70
3213	$3 Zeppelin L-3 (Germany)	1·25	1·40
3214	$3 Beardmore No. 24 (Great Britain)	1·25	1·40

432 Horned Guan

1996. West Indian Birds. Multicoloured.

3216	$1.50 Type **432**	65	70
3217	$1.50 St. Lucia parrot	65	70
3218	$1.50 Black penelopina	65	70
3219	$1.50 Grenada dove	65	70
3220	$1.50 St. Vincent parrot	65	70
3221	$1.50 White-breasted trembler	65	70

Nos. 3216/21 were printed together, se-tenant, with the backgrounds forming a composite design.

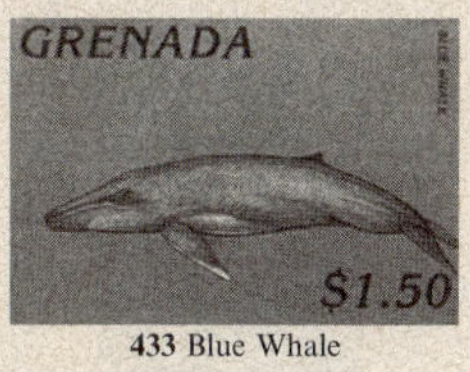

433 Blue Whale

1996. Whales and Turtles. Multicoloured.

3223	$1.50 Type **433**	65	70
3224	$1.50 Humpback whale	65	70
3225	$1.50 Right whale	65	70
3226	$1.50 Hawksbill turtle	65	70
3227	$1.50 Leatherback turtle	65	70
3228	$1.50 Green turtle	65	70

434 Killer Whale

437 Devon Rex

436 Mickey at Tram Stop

1996. Marine Life. Multicoloured.

3229	$1 Type **434**	45	50
3230	$1 Dolphin	45	50
3231	$1 Two dolphins	45	50
3232	$1 Sea lion and regal angelfish	45	50
3233	$1 Dolphins and hawksbill turtle	45	50
3234	$1 Three hawksbill turtles	45	50
3235	$1 Regal angelfish and pennant coralfish	45	50
3236	$1 Pennant coralfish	45	50
3237	$1 Sea lion and squirrelfish	45	50
3238	$1 Brown pelican	45	50
3239	$1 Killer whale (different)	45	50
3240	$1 Whale	45	50
3241	$1 Dolphins and sea lion	45	50
3242	$1 Shortfin pilot whale, blue-ringed octopus and sea lion	45	50
3243	$1 Hammerhead sharks and sea lion	45	50
3244	$1 Blue-striped grunts	45	50
3245	$1 Stingray and Van Gogh fusilier	45	50
3246	$1 Van Gogh fusilier, ribbon moray and percoid fish	45	50

Nos. 3229/37 and 3238/46 respectively were printed together, se-tenant, with the backgrounds forming a composite design.

1996. Christmas. Religious Paintings. As T **369** of Antigua. Multicoloured.

3248	25 c. "The Visitation" (Tintoretto)	10	15
3249	35 c. "Virgin with the Child" (Palma Vecchio)	15	20
3250	50 c. "The Adoration of the Magi" (Botticelli)	25	30
3251	75 c. "The Annunciation" (Titian)	35	40
3252	$1 "The Flight into Egypt" (Tintoretto)	45	50
3253	$3 "The Holy Family with the Infant Saint John" (Andrea del Sarto)	1·25	1·40

No. 3250 is inscr "Botticeli" in error.

1997. "HONG KONG '97" International Stamp Exhibition. Mickey in Hong Kong. Disney Cartoon Characters. Multicoloured.

3257	35 c. Type **436**	15	20
3258	50 c. Mickey and Donald fishing at Victoria Harbour	25	30
3259	75 c. Donald and Mickey parachuting	35	40
3260	90 c. Mickey and Minnie visiting Bank of China	40	45
3261	$1 Mickey with pet parrot	45	50
3262	$1 Mickey drinking Kung-fu Tea	45	50
3263	$1 Mickey, Minnie and Goofy shopping at Chinese Wet Market	45	50
3264	$1 Mickey, Minnie and Goofy with grasshoppers	45	50
3265	$1 Mickey and Goofy with lanterns	45	50
3266	$1 Mickey and Minnie practising Tai-chi	45	50
3267	$2 Goofy delivering bottled gas	90	95
3268	$3 Mickey, Minnie and Donald at "Jumbo" floating restaurant	1·40	1·50

1997. 50th Anniv of U.N.E.S.C.O. As T **374** of Antigua. Multicoloured.

3270	35 c. Temple, Kyoto, Japan	15	20
3271	75 c. Timbered houses, Quedlinburg, Germany	35	40
3272	90 c. View from walls, Dubrovnik, Croatia	40	45
3273	$1 Ruins at Delphi, Greece	45	50
3274	$1 Bryggen Wharf, Bergen, Norway (vert)	45	50
3275	$1 Old city, Berne, Switzerland (vert)	45	50
3276	$1 Warsaw, Poland (vert)	45	50
3277	$1 Fortress walls, Luxembourg (vert)	45	50
3278	$1 Interior of Drottningholm Palace, Sweden (vert)	45	50
3279	$1 Petajavesi Church, Finland (vert)	45	50
3280	$1 Vilnius, Lithuania (vert)	45	50
3281	$1 Jelling Church, Denmark (vert)	45	50
3282	$1 Entrance to caves, Desert of Taklamakan, China (vert)	45	50
3283	$1 House, Desert of Taklamakan, China (vert)	45	50
3284	$1 Monument, Desert of Taklamakan, China (vert)	45	50
3285	$1 Palace of Cielos Purpuras, Wudang, China (vert)	45	50
3286	$1 House, Wudang, China (vert)	45	50
3287	$1 Stone Guardian, The Great Wall, China (vert)	45	50
3288	$1 Ming Dynasty statue, Wudang, China (vert)	45	50
3289	$1 The Great Wall, China (vert)	45	50
3290	$1.50 Segovia Cathedral, Spain	65	70
3291	$1.50 Wurtzburg, Germany	65	70
3292	$1.50 Plitvice Lakes, Croatia	65	70
3293	$1.50 Batalha Monastery, Portugal	65	70
3294	$1.50 River Seine, Paris, France	65	70
3295	$2 Tomar, Portugal	85	90
3296	$3 Palace of Chaillot, Paris, France	1·25	1·40

1997. Cats and Dogs. Multicoloured.

3298	35 c. Type **437**	15	20
3299	75 c. King Charles spaniel	35	40
3300	90 c. Japanese bobtail	40	45
3301	$1 Afghan hound	45	50
3302	$1 Turkish van	45	50
3303	$1 Ragdoll	45	50
3304	$1 Siberian	45	50
3305	$1 Egyptian mau	45	50
3306	$1 American shorthair	45	50
3307	$1 Benegal	45	50
3308	$1 Asian longhair	45	50
3309	$1 Somali	45	50
3310	$1 Turkish angora	45	50
3311	$1 Lhasa apso	45	50
3312	$1 Rough collie	45	50
3313	$1 Norwich terrier	45	50
3314	$1 American cocker spaniel	45	50
3315	$1 Chinese crested dog	45	50
3316	$1 Old English sheepdog	45	50
3317	$1 Standard poodle	45	50
3318	$1 German shepherd	45	50
3319	$1 German shorthair pointer	45	50
3320	$2 Cornish rex	85	90
3321	$3 Pekingese	1·25	1·40

438 Dunkleosteus

1997. Dinosaurs. Multicoloured.

3323	35 c. Type **438**	15	20
3324	75 c. Tyrannosaurus rex	35	40
3325	$1.50 Sordes	65	70
3326	$1.50 Dimorphodon	65	70
3327	$1.50 Diplodocus	65	70
3328	$1.50 Allosaurus	65	70
3329	$1.50 Pentaceratops	65	70
3330	$1.50 Protoceratops	65	70
3331	$2 Askeptosaurus (vert)	85	90
3332	$3 Triceratops (vert)	1·25	1·40

Nos. 3325/30 were printed together, se-tenant, with the backgrounds forming a composite design.

439 Porcelain Crab

1997. Marine Life. Multicoloured.

3334	45 c. Type **439**	20	25
3335	75 c. Humpback whale	35	40
3336	90 c. Hermit crab	40	45
3337	$1 Great white shark	45	50
3338	$1.50 Octopus (vert)	65	70
3339	$1.50 Lei triggerfish (vert)	65	70
3340	$1.50 Lionfish (vert)	65	70
3341	$1.50 Harlequin wrasse (vert)	65	70
3342	$1.50 Clown fish (vert)	65	70
3343	$1.50 Moray eel (vert)	65	70
3344	$3 Green sea turtle	1·25	1·40
3345	$4 Whale shark	1·75	1·90

Nos. 3338/43 were printed together, se-tenant, with the backgrounds forming a composite design.

1997. 10th Anniv of Chernobyl Nuclear Disaster. As T **376** of Antigua. Multicoloured.

3348	$2 As Type **376** of Antigua	85	90
3349	$2 As No. 3348, but inscribed "CHABAD'S CHILDREN OF CHERNOBYL" at foot	85	90

1997. 50th Death Anniv of Paul Harris (founder of Rotary International). As T **377** of Antigua. Multicoloured.

3350	$3 Paul Harris and vocational training programme, Philippines	1·25	1·40

1997. Golden Wedding of Queen Elizabeth and Prince Philip. As T **378** of Antigua. Multicoloured.

3352	$1 Queen Elizabeth and Prince Philip waving	45	50
3353	$1 Royal coat of arms	45	50
3354	$1 Queen Elizabeth with Prince Philip in naval uniform	45	50
3355	$1 Queen Elizabeth and Prince Philip at Buckingham Palace	45	50
3356	$1 Windsor Castle	45	50
3357	$1 Prince Philip	45	50

1997. "Pacific '97" International Stamp Exhibition, San Francisco (1st issue). Death Centenary of Heinrich von Stephan (founder of the U.P.U.). As T **379** of Antigua.

3359	$2 green and black	85	90
3360	$2 brown	85	90
3361	$2 blue	85	90

DESIGNS: No. 3359, Postman on motorcycle; 3360, Von Stephan and Mercury; 3361, Postman on skis, Rocky Mountains, 1900s.

See also Nos. 3392/3408.

1997. Birth Bicentenary of Hiroshige (Japanese painter). As T **310** of Dominica. Multicoloured.

3363	$1.50 "Nihon Embankment, Yoshiwara"	65	70
3364	$1.50 "Asakusa Ricefields and Torinomachi Festival"	65	70
3365	$1.50 "Senju Great Bridge"	65	70
3366	$1.50 "Dawn inside the Yoshiwara"	65	70
3367	$1.50 "Tile Kilns and Hasiba Ferry, Sumida River"	65	70
3368	$1.50 "View from Massaki of Suijin Shrine, Uchigawa Inlet and Sekiya"	65	70

1997. 175th Anniv of Brothers Grimm's Third Collection of Fairy Tales. Snow White. As T **380** of Antigua. Multicoloured.

3370	$2 Queen looking in mirror	85	90
3371	$2 Snow White and the Seven Dwarfs	85	90
3372	$2 Snow White and Prince	85	90

440 One-man Luge

1997. Winter Olympic Games, Nagano, Japan. Multicoloured.

3374	45 c. Type **440**	20	25
3375	75 c. Men's speed skating	35	40
3376	$1 One-man luge (different)	45	50
3377	$1 Ski jumping (blue ski suit)	45	50
3378	$1 Downhill skiing	45	50
3379	$1 Speed skating	45	50
3380	$1 Two-man bobsleigh	45	50
3381	$1 Women's figure skating	45	50
3382	$1 Alpine combined	45	50
3383	$1 Ice hockey	45	50
3384	$1 Ski jumping (yellow ski suit)	45	50
3385	$2 Men's figure skating	90	95
3386	$3 Slalom	1·40	1·50

441 Bank of China

1997. Return of Hong Kong to China. Multicoloured.

3388	90 c. Type **441**	40	45
3389	$1 Skyscrapers	45	50
3390	$1.75 "Hong Kong '97" on modern buildings (63 × 32 mm)	70	75
3391	$2 Deng Xiaoping and Hong Kong (63 × 32 mm)	85	90

442 Minnie Mouse dancing the Hula

1997. "Pacific '97" International Stamp Exhibition, San Francisco (2nd issue). Centenary of the Cinema. Minnie Mouse in "Hawaiian Holiday". Multicoloured.

3392	50 c. Type **442** (Frame 1)	25	30
3393	50 c. Frame 2	25	30
3394	50 c. Frame 3	25	30
3395	50 c. Frame 4	25	30
3396	50 c. Frame 5	25	30
3397	50 c. Frame 6	25	30
3398	50 c. Frame 7	25	30
3399	50 c. Frame 8	25	30
3400	50 c. Frame 9	25	30
3401	50 c. Frame 10	25	30
3402	50 c. Frame 11	25	30
3403	50 c. Frame 12	25	30
3404	50 c. Frame 13	25	30
3405	50 c. Frame 14	25	30
3406	50 c. Frame 15	25	30
3407	50 c. Frame 16	25	30
3408	50 c. Frame 17	25	30

443 Hercules lifting Rock

1997. "Hercules" (cartoon film) (1st series). Multicoloured.

3410	$1 Type **443**	45	50
3411	$1 Pegasus	45	50
3412	$1 Megara	45	50
3413	$1 Philoktetes	45	50
3414	$1 Nessus	45	50
3415	$1 Hydra	45	50
3416	$1 Pain and Panic	45	50
3417	$1 Hades	45	50

See also Nos. 3561/84.

1997. World Cup Football Championship, France (1998). As T **383** of Antigua. Multicoloured (except Nos. 3422/3 and 3428).

3419	15 c. West German and Italian Players, 1982 (vert)	10	10
3420	75 c. Italian player holding World Cup, 1982 (vert)	35	40
3421	90 c. West German and Italian players wearing "20" shirts, 1982 (vert)	40	45
3422	$1 Uruguay team, 1950 (brown)	45	50
3423	$1 Brazilian team, 1958 (brown)	45	50
3424	$1 West German team, 1974	45	50
3425	$1 Argentine team, 1986	45	50
3426	$1 Italian team, 1982	45	50
3427	$1 West German team, 1990	45	50
3428	$1 Italian team, 1934 (brown)	45	50
3429	$1 Brazilian team, 1970	45	50
3430	$1 Seaman, England	45	50
3431	$1 Klinsmann, Germany	45	50
3432	$1 Berger, Czech Republic	45	50
3433	$1 McCoist, Scotland	45	50
3434	$1 Gascoigne, England	45	50
3435	$1 Djorkaeff, France	45	50
3436	$1 Sammer, Germany	45	50
3437	$1 Futre, Portugal	45	50
3438	$2 Italian player beating goal keeper, 1982 (vert)	85	90
3439	$3 Goal-mouth melee, 1982 (vert)	1·25	1·40
3440	$4 Two West German players tackling Italian player (vert)	1·75	1·90

444 Peacock

1997. Butterflies and Moths. Multicoloured.

3442	45 c. Type **444**	20	25
3443	75 c. Orange flambeau	35	40
3444	90 c. Eastern tailed blue	45	50
3445	$1 Brimstone	45	50
3446	$1 Mocker swallowtail	45	50
3447	$1 American painted lady	45	50
3448	$1 Tiger swallowtail	45	50
3449	$1 Long wing	45	50
3450	$1 Sunset moth	45	50
3451	$1 Australian Blue Mountain swallowtail	45	50
3452	$1 Bird wing	45	50
3453	$2 Black and red	85	90
3454	$3 Large white	1·25	1·40
3455	$4 Oriental swallowtail	1·75	1·90

445 "Paphiopedilum urbanianum"

1997. Orchids of the World. Multicoloured.

3457	20 c. Type **445**	10	10
3458	35 c. "Trichoceros parviflorus"	15	20
3459	45 c. "Euanthe sanderiana" (vert)	20	25
3460	75 c. "Oncidium macranthum" (vert)	35	40
3461	90 c. "Psychopsis kramerianum" (vert)	40	45
3462	$1 "Oncidium hastatum" (vert)	45	50
3463	$2 "Broughtonia sanguinea" (vert)	90	95
3464	$2 "Anguloa virginalis" (vert)	90	95
3465	$2 "Dendrobium bigibbum" (vert)	90	95
3466	$2 "Lucasiana" (vert)	90	95
3467	$2 "Cymbidium" (vert)	90	95
3468	$2 "Cymbidium" and vase (vert)	90	95
3469	$2 "Odontoglossum crispum" (vert)	90	95
3470	$2 "Cattleya brabantiae" (vert)	90	95
3471	$2 "Cattleya bicolor" (vert)	90	95
3472	$2 "Trichopilia suavia" (vert)	90	95
3473	$2 "Encyclia mariae" (vert)	90	95
3474	$2 "Angraecum leonis" (vert)	90	95
3475	$3 "Masdevallia saltatix" (vert)	1·40	1·50
3476	$4 "Cattleya luteola"	1·90	2·00

Nos. 3463/8 and 3469/74 respectively were printed together, se-tenant, with the backgrounds forming composite designs.

446 "Boletus erythropus"

1997. Fungi of the World. Multicoloured.

3478	35 c. Type **446**	15	20
3479	75 c. "Armillariella mellea"	35	40
3480	90 c. "Amanita flavorubens"	40	45
3481	$1 Indigo milky	45	50
3482	$1.50 "Agaricus solidipes"	65	70
3483	$1.50 Salmon waxy cap	65	70
3484	$1.50 Fused maramius	65	70
3485	$1.50 Shellfish-scented russula	65	70
3486	$1.50 Red-capped scaber stalk	65	70
3487	$1.50 "Calocybe gambosum"	65	70
3488	$1.50 "Boletus parasiticus"	65	70
3489	$1.50 "Frostis bolete"	65	70
3490	$1.50 "Amanita myscara flavilolvata"	65	70
3491	$1.50 "Volvariella volvacea"	65	70
3492	$1.50 Stuntz's blue legs	65	70
3493	$1.50 Orange-latex milky	65	70
3494	$2 "Tylopilus balloui"	85	90
3495	$4 "Boletus parasiticus"	1·75	1·90

447 Princess Diana with Landmine Victims

1997. Diana, Princess of Wales Commemoration. Multicoloured.

3497	$1.50 Type **447**	60	65
3498	$1.50 With sick child	60	65
3499	$1.50 With young boy on crutches	60	65
3500	$1.50 With leper	60	65
3501	$1.50 Holding baby	60	65
3502	$1.50 Walking through minefield	60	65

448 "Angel" (Matthias Grunewald)

1997. Christmas. Religious Paintings. Multicoloured.

3504	35 c. Type **448**	15	20
3505	50 c. "St. Demetrius" (icon)	20	25
3506	75 c. Three-panelled reliquary	35	40
3507	$1 "Angel of the Annunciation" (Jan van Eyck)	45	50
3508	$3 "The Annunciation" (Simone Martini)	1·25	1·40
3509	$4 "St. Michael" (icon)	1·75	1·90

449 Black-tailed Damselfish

1998. Fishes. Multicoloured.

3512	65 c. Type **449**	30	35
3513	90 c. Yellow sweetlips	40	45
3514	$1 Common squirrelfish	45	50
3515	$1.50 Blue tang	65	70
3516	$1.50 Porkfish	65	70
3517	$1.50 Banded butterflyfish	65	70
3518	$1.50 Thread-finned butterflyfish	65	70
3519	$1.50 Hooded butterflyfish ("Red-headed")	65	70
3520	$1.50 Emperor angelfish	65	70
3521	$1.50 Duboulay's angelfish ("Scribbled Angelfish")	65	70
3522	$1.50 Lemon-peel angelfish	65	70
3523	$1.50 Bandit angelfish	65	70
3524	$1.50 Bicoloured angelfish ("Biclor Cherub")	65	70
3525	$1.50 Palette surgeonfish ("Regal Tang")	65	70
3526	$1.50 Yellow tang	65	70
3527	$2 Powder-blue surgeonfish	85	90

Nos. 3515/20 and 3521/6 respectively were printed together, se-tenant, with the backgrounds forming composite designs.

450 "Sophronitis grandiflora"

1998. Flowers of the World. Multicoloured.

3529	$1.50 Type **450**	65	70
3530	$1.50 "Phalaenopsis amboinensis"	65	70
3531	$1.50 "Zygopetalum intermedium"	65	70
3532	$1.50 "Paphiopedilum purpuratum"	65	70
3533	$1.50 "Miltonia regnellii"	65	70
3534	$1.50 "Dendrobium parishii"	65	70
3535	$1.50 "Arachnis clarkei"	65	70
3536	$1.50 "Cymbidium eburneum"	65	70
3537	$1.50 "Dendrobium chrysotoxum"	65	70
3538	$1.50 "Paphiopedilum insigne"	65	70
3539	$1.50 "Paphiopedilum venustum"	65	70
3540	$1.50 "Renanthera imschootiana"	65	70

451 Dhow

1998. Famous Ships. Multicoloured.

3542	$1 Type **451**	45	50
3543	$1 Galleon	45	50
3544	$1 Felucca	45	50
3545	$1 Schooner	45	50
3546	$1 Aircraft carrier	45	50
3547	$1 Knau	45	50
3548	$1 Destroyer	45	50
3549	$1 Viking longship	45	50
3550	$1 "Queen Elizabeth 2" (liner)	45	50
3551	$1 Brig	45	50
3552	$1 Clipper	45	50
3553	$1 Caique	45	50
3554	$1 Mississippi riverboat	45	50
3555	$1 Luxury liner	45	50
3556	$1 "Mayflower" (Pilgrim Fathers)	45	50
3557	$1 Frigate	45	50
3558	$1 Janggolan	45	50
3559	$1 Junk	45	50

Nos. 3542/50 and 3551/9 respectively were printed together, se-tenant, forming composite background designs.

1998. "Hercules" (cartoon film) (2nd series). As T **443** showing Disney cartoon characters. Multicoloured.

3561/8	10 c. × 8 Hercules and giant statue; Hercules, Pegasus and Philoktetes; Hercules and Philoktetes with shield and arrows; Hercules swinging from blades; Nessus carrying off Megara; Hercules fighting Nessus; Hercules fighting giant lion; Hercules and Pegasus leaving prints on pavement		
3569/76	$1 × 8 Baby Hercules with Zeus and Alcmene; Baby Hercules with Hades; Hades in the Underworld; Baby Hercules and young Pegasus; Baby Hercules with Pain and Panic; Baby Hercules with mortal parents; Hercules towing hay waggon; Hercules receiving gold medallion		
3577/84	$1 × 8 Hercules and Megara; Megara and Hades; Hercules training with Philoktetes; Hercules confronting Hades; Giant destroying city; Zeus; Hercules saving Megara by lifting pillar; Hercules diving into sea		
3561/84	Set of 24	7·75	8·25

452 Arctic Skua

1998. Seabirds. Multicoloured.

3586	90 c. Type **452**	40	45
3587	$1 Northern fulmar (horiz)	45	50
3588	$1 Black-legged kittiwake (horiz)	45	50
3589	$1 Cape petrel (horiz)	45	50
3590	$1 Mediterranean gull (horiz)	45	50
3591	$1 Brandt's cormorant (horiz)	45	50
3592	$1 Greater shearwater (horiz)	45	50
3593	$1 Black-footed albatross (horiz)	45	50
3594	$1 Red-necked phalarope (horiz)	45	50
3595	$1 Black skimmer (horiz)	45	50
3596	$1.10 Humboldt penguin	50	55
3597	$2 Herring gull	85	90
3598	$3 Red knot	1·25	1·40

Nos. 3587/95 were printed together, se-tenant, with the backgrounds forming a composite design.

453 Supermarine Spitfire Mk I

1998. History of the Supermarine Spitfire (aircraft). Designs showing different versions. Multicoloured.

3600	$1.50 Type **453**	65	70
3601	$1.50 Mark VIII	65	70
3602	$1.50 Mark III	65	70
3603	$1.50 Mark XVI	65	70
3604	$1.50 Mark V	65	70
3605	$1.50 Mark XIX	65	70
3606	$1.50 Mark IX	65	70
3607	$1.50 Mark XIV	65	70
3608	$1.50 Mark XII	65	70
3609	$1.50 Mark XI	65	70
3610	$1.50 H.F. Mark VIII	65	70
3611	$1.50 Mark VB	65	70

454 Walrus

1998. International Year of the Ocean. Multicoloured.

3613	75 c. Type **454**	35	40
3614	75 c. African black-footed penguins	35	40
3615	75 c. African black-footed penguin	35	40
3616	75 c. California sealion	35	40
3617	75 c. Green turtle	35	40
3618	75 c. Redfin anthias	35	40
3619	75 c. Sperm whale	35	40
3620	75 c. French angelfish and Australian sealion	35	40
3621	75 c. Jellyfish	35	40
3622	75 c. Sawfish	35	40
3623	75 c. Cuckoo wrasse	35	40
3624	75 c. Garibaldi	35	40
3625	75 c. Spinecheek anemonefish	35	40
3626	75 c. Leafy seadragon	35	40
3627	75 c. Blue-spotted goatfish	35	40
3628	75 c. Two-spot gobies	35	40

Nos. 3613/28 were printed together, se-tenant, with the backgrounds forming a composite design.

1998. 50th Anniv of Organization of American States. As T **324** of Dominica.

3630	$1 multicoloured	45	50

1998. 25th Death Anniv of Pablo Picasso (painter). As T **325** of Dominica. Multicoloured.

3631	45 c. "The Bathers" (vert)	20	25
3632	$2 "Luncheon on the Grass"	85	90
3633	$3 "The Swimmer"	1·25	1·40

1998. Birth Centenary of Enzo Ferrari (car manufacturer). As T **326** of Dominica. Multicoloured.

3635	$2 250 GT Berlinetta Lusso	85	90
3636	$2 250 GTO	85	90
3637	$2 250 GT Boano/Ellena cabriolet	85	90

455 Scout Saluting

1998. 19th World Scout Jamboree, Chile. Multicoloured.

3639	$2 Type **455**	85	90
3640	$3 International scout flag	1·25	1·40
3641	$4 Applying first aid	1·75	1·90

1998. 50th Death Anniv of Mahatma Gandhi. As T **327** of Dominica.

3643	$1 black, grey and mauve	45	50

DESIGN: $1 Mahatma Gandhi.

1998. 80th Anniv of Royal Air Force. As T **328** of Dominica. Multicoloured.

3645	$2 Supermarine Spitfire Mk IIa	85	90
3646	$2 Supermarine Spitfire Mk IXb from above	85	90
3647	$2 Supermarine Spitfire Mk IXb from side	85	90
3648	$2 Hawker Hurricane Mk IIC of Battle of Britain Memorial Flight	85	90

3649 $2 EF-2000 Eurofighter above clouds 85 90
3650 $2 Nimrod MR2P (maritime reconnaissance) 85 90
3651 $2 EF-2000 Eurofighter at low level 85 90
3652 $2 C-47 Dakota (transport) . 85 90

456 "Knights in Combat"

1998. Birth Bicentenary of Eugene Delacroix (painter). Multicoloured.
3654 $1 Type **456** 45 50
3655 $1 "Murder of Bishop of Liege" 45 50
3656 $1 "Still Life" 45 50
3657 $1 "Battle of Nancy" 45 50
3658 $1 "Shipwreck of Don Juan" 45 50
3659 $1 "The Death of Ophelia" . 45 50
3660 $1 "Attila the Hun" 45 50
3661 $1 "Arab Entertainers" . . . 45 50

457 Flags of Grenada and CARICOM

1998. 25th Anniv of Caribbean Community.
3663 **457** $1 multicoloured 45 50

459 Dove of Peace with Stars and Streamers

460 "The Angel's parting from Tobias" (Jean Bilevelt)

1998. Grenada's Participation in U.N. Peacekeeping Operations, Beirut, 1982-4.
3672 **459** $1 multicoloured 45 50

1998. Christmas. Religious Paintings. Multicoloured.
3673 35 c. Type **460** 15 20
3674 45 c. "Allegory of Faith" (Moretto Da Brescia) . . . 20 25
3675 90 c. "Crucifixion" (Ugolino Di Tedice) 40 45
3676 $1 "The Triumphal Entry into Jerusalem" (Master of the Thuison Altarpiece) 45 50

461 Blue-hooded Euphonia

1998. Christmas. Birds. Multicoloured.
3677 45 c. Type **461** 20 25
3678 75 c. Red-billed whistling duck ("Black-bellied Whistling Duck") 35 40
3679 90 c. Purple martin 40 45
3680 $1 Imperial amazon ("Imperial Parrot") 45 50
3681 $2 Adelaide's warbler 85 90
3682 $3 Greater flamingo ("Roseate Flamingo") . . . . 1·25 1·40

462 Martin Luther King, Jr (civil rights leader)

463 Robert H. Goddard (rocket scientist)

1999. Millennium Series. Famous People of the Twentieth Century. Great Thinkers of the Past and Present. Multicoloured.
3685 $1 Type **462** 45 50
3686 $1 Socrates (Greek philosopher) (56 × 41 mm) 45 50
3687 $1 Sir Thomas More (English scholar) (56 × 41 mm) . . 45 50
3688 $1 Chaim Weizmann (first President of Israel) 45 50
3689 $1 Alexander Solzhenitsyn (Russian writer) 45 50
3690 $1 Galileo Galilei (Italian astronomer) (56 × 41 mm) 45 50
3691 $1 Michael Servetus (Spanish theologian) (56 × 41 mm) . 45 50
3692 $1 Salman Rushdie (British novelist) 45 50
No. 3691 is inscribed "MICHAEL SERVENTUS" in error.

1999. Space Exploration. Multicoloured.
3694 $1.50 Type **463** 65 70
3695 $1.50 Wernher von Braun (rocket scientist) 65 70
3696 $1.50 Yuri A. Gagarin (first cosmonaut to orbit Earth, 1961) 65 70
3697 $1.50 "Freedom 7" (first American manned Space flight, 1961) 65 70
3698 $1.50 Aleksei Leonov (first Russian to walk in Space, 1965) 65 70
3699 $1.50 Neil Armstrong and Edwin Aldrin (first astronauts on Moon, 1969) 65 70
3700 $1.50 "Mariner 9" (first spacecraft to orbit Mars, 1971) 65 70
3701 $1.50 "Voyager 1" (Jupiter probe, 1979) 65 70
3702 $1.50 Bruce McCandless (first astronaut to work in Space unattached, 1984) 65 70
3703 $1.50 "Giotto" probe (study of Halley's Comet, 1986) . . 65 70
3704 $1.50 Space Shuttle "Atlantis" (launch of "Galileo" probe, 1989) 65 70
3705 $1.50 "Magellan" (Venus probe, 1990) 65 70
Nos. 3694/99 and 3700/5 were respectively printed together, se-tenant, with the backgrounds forming composite designs.

OFFICIAL STAMPS

1992. Optd **P.R.G.** (a) Nos. 1085/97 and 1099.
O 1 5 c. West Indiaman barque, c. 1840 . . . . 15 20
O 2 6 c. R.M.S.P. "Orinoco", c. 1851 . . . . 15 20
O 3 10 c. Working schooner . . . 15 20
O 4 12 c. Trimaran at Grand Anse anchorage 15 20
O 5 15 c. Spice Island cruising yacht "Petite Amie" 20 20
O 6 20 c. Fishing pirogue 25 20
O 7 25 c. Harbour police launch . 30 30
O 8 30 c. Grand Anse speedboat 30 30
O 9 40 c. M.V. "Seimstrand" . . 35 30
O10 50 c. Three-masted schooner "Ariadne" 40 40
O11 90 c. M.V. "Geestide" . . . 70 80
O12 $1 M.V "Cunard Countess" 70 80
O13 $3 Rum-runner . . . . . . 2·00 3·75
O14 $10 Coast-guard patrol boat 6·00 12·00

(b) Nos. 1130/2 and 113/4.
O15 30 c. Prince Charles and Lady Diana Spencer . . . . . . 1·75 2·25
O16 40 c. Holyrood House . . . 2·25 2·75
O17 50 c. Prince Charles and Lady Diana Spencer . . . . . . 1·25 2·00
O18 $2 Holyrood House . . . . 2·75 3·50
O19 $4 Type **268** . . . . 6·50 8·00

POSTAGE DUE STAMPS

D 1

1892.
D 8 **D 1** 1d. black . . . . 2·50 6·50
D 9 2d. black . . . . 9·00 1·75
D10 3d. black . . . . 11·00 6·00

1892. Surch **SURCHARGE POSTAGE** and value.
D4 **13** 1d. on 6d. mauve . . . . 75·00 1·25
D5 1d. on 8d. brown . . . . £600 3·25
D6 2d. on 6d. mauve . . . . £140 2·50
D7 2d. on 8d. brown . . . . £1100 9·50

1921. As Type D 1 but inscr "POSTAGE DUE" instead of "SURCHARGE POSTAGE".
D11 **D 1** 1d. black . . . . 90 1·00
D12 1½d. black . . . . 8·50 16·00
D13 2d. black . . . . 2·00 1·75
D14 3d. black . . . . 2·00 4·25

1952. As last but currency changed.
D15 **D 1** 3 c. black . . . . 30 5·00
D16 4 c. black . . . . 30 11·00
D17 6 c. black . . . . 45 11·00
D18 8 c. black . . . . 75 11·00

GRENADINES OF GRENADA

The southern part of the group, attached to Grenada. Main islands Petit Martinique and Carriacou.

100 cents = 1 dollar

1973. Royal Wedding. Nos. 582/3 of Grenada optd **GRENADINES**.
1 **196** 25 c. multicoloured 20 10
2 $2 multicoloured 70 50

1974. Stamps of Grenada optd **GRENADINES**.
4 1 c. multicoloured (No. 306) . . 10 10
5 2 c. multicoloured (No. 307) . . 10 10
6 3 c. multicoloured (No. 308) . . 10 10
7 5 c. multicoloured (No. 309) . . 15 10
8 8 c. multicoloured (No. 311) . . 15 10
9 10 c. multicoloured (No. 312) . 15 10
10 12 c. multicoloured (No. 313) . 20 10
11 25 c. multicoloured (No. 315) . 45 10
12 $1 multicoloured (No. 318) . . 2·50 45
13 $2 multicoloured (No. 319) . . 3·00 1·00
14 $3 multicoloured (No. 320) . . 3·00 1·50
15 $5 multicoloured (No. 321) . . 3·75 1·75

1974. World Cup Football Championships. As Nos. 619/26 of Grenada, but inscr "GRENADA GRENADINES".
16 ½ c. multicoloured 10 10
17 1 c. multicoloured 10 10
18 2 c. multicoloured 10 10
19 10 c. multicoloured 15 10
20 25 c. multicoloured 20 10
21 50 c. multicoloured 25 15
22 75 c. multicoloured 25 20
23 $1 multicoloured 30 25

1974. Cent. of U.P.U. As Nos. 628/30 and 633 of Grenada, but inscr "GRENADA GRENADINES".
25 8 c. multicoloured 10 10
26 25 c. multicoloured 15 10
27 35 c. multicoloured 15 10
28 $1 multicoloured 70 40

1974. Birth Cent. of Sir Winston Churchill. As Nos. 637/8 of Grenada, but inscr "GRENADA GRENADINES".
30 35 c. multicoloured 15 10
31 $2 multicoloured 40 45

1974. Christmas. As Nos. 640/7 of Grenada but inscr "GRENADA GRENADINES" and background colours changed.
33 **204** ½ c. multicoloured 10 10
34 – 1 c. multicoloured 10 10
35 – 2 c. multicoloured 10 10
36 – 3 c. multicoloured 10 10
37 – 10 c. multicoloured 10 10
38 – 25 c. multicoloured 10 10
39 – 50 c. multicoloured 15 15
40 – $1 multicoloured 30 25

1975. Big Game Fishing. As Nos. 669/76 of Grenada inscr "GRENADA GRENADINES" and background colours changed.
42 ½ c. multicoloured 10 10
43 1 c. multicoloured 10 10
44 2 c. multicoloured 10 10
45 10 c. multicoloured 10 10
46 25 c. multicoloured 15 10
47 50 c. multicoloured 20 15
48 70 c. multicoloured 25 20
49 $1 multicoloured 35 35

1975. Flowers. As Nos. 678/85 of Grenada inscr "GRENADINES".
51 ½ c. multicoloured 10 10
52 1 c. multicoloured 10 10
53 2 c. multicoloured 10 10
54 3 c. multicoloured 10 10
55 10 c. multicoloured 10 10
56 25 c. multicoloured 10 10
57 50 c. multicoloured 20 15
58 $1 multicoloured 30 20

CANCELLED REMAINDERS*. Some of the following issues have been remaindered, cancelled-to-order, at a fraction of their face value. For all practical purposes these are indistinguishable from genuine postally used copies. Our used quotations which are indicated by an asterisk are the same for cancelled-to-order or postally used copies.

3 "Christ Crowned with Thorns" (Titian)

4 "Dawn" (detail from Medici Tomb)

1975. Easter. Paintings showing Crucifixion and Deposition by artists listed. Multicoloured.
60 ½ c. Type **3** 10 10*
61 1 c. Giotto 10 10*
62 2 c. Tintoretto 10 10*
63 3 c. Cranach 10 10*
64 35 c. Caravaggio 15 10*
65 75 c. Tiepolo 20 10*
66 $2 Velasquez 40 15*

1975. 500th Anniv of Michelangelo. Multicoloured.
68 ½ c. Type **4** 10 10*
69 1 c. "Delphic Sibyl" 10 10*
70 2 c. "Giuliano de Medici" . . . 10 10*
71 40 c. "The Creation" (detail) . . 15 10*
72 50 c. "Lorenzo de Medici" . . . 15 10*
73 75 c. "Persian Sibyl" 20 10*
74 $2 "Head of Christ" 30 15*

1975. Butterflies. As T **213** of Grenada but inscr "GRENADINES". Multicoloured.
76 ½ c. "Morpho peleides" 10 10*
77 1 c. "Danaus eresimus" ("Danaus gilippus") 10 10*
78 2 c. "Dismorphia amphione" . . 10 10*
79 35 c. "Hamadryas feronia" . . 35 10*
80 45 c. "Philaethria dido" . . . 45 10*
81 75 c. "Phoebis argante" . . . 70 15*
82 $2 "Prepona laertes" . . . . . 1·40 30*

5 Progress "Standard" Badge

1975. 14th World Scout Jamboree, Norway. Multicoloured.
84 ½ c. Type **5** 10 10*
85 1 c. Boatman's badge 10 10*
86 2 c. Coxswain's badge 10 10*
87 35 c. Interpreter's badge . . . 15 10*
88 45 c. Ambulance badge 20 10*
89 75 c. Chief Scout's award . . . 25 10*
90 $2 Queen's Scout award . . . 35 15*

6 The Surrender of Lord Cornwallis

1975. Bicentenary of America Revolution (1976) (1st issue). Multicoloured.
92 ½ c. Type **6** 10 10*
93 1 c. Minute-men 10 10*
94 2 c. Paul Revere's ride 10 10*
95 3 c. Battle of Bunker Hill . . . 10 10*
96 5 c. Fifer and drummers . . . 10 10*
97 45 c. Backwoodsman 25 10*
98 75 c. Boston Tea Party 35 10*
99 $2 Naval engagement 80 10*
100 $2 George Washington 80 35
101 $2 White House and flags . . 80 35
Nos. 100/1 are larger, 35 × 60 mm.

7 Fencing

1975. Pan-American Games, Mexico City. Multicoloured.
103 ½ c. Type **7** 10 10*
104 1 c. Hurdling 10 10*
105 2 c. Pole-vaulting 10 10*
106 35 c. Weightlifting 15 10*
107 45 c. Throwing the javelin . . 15 10*
108 75 c. Throwing the discus . . 15 10*
109 $2 Diving 35 15*

1975. Nos. 649/68 of Grenada additionally inscr "GRENADINES".
111 ½ c. Yachts, Point Saline . . . 10 30
112 1 c. Yacht Club race, St. George's 10 15
113 2 c. Carenage taxi 10 15
114 3 c. Large working boats . . 10 15
115 5 c. Deep-water dock, St. George's 10 15
116 6 c. Cocoa beans in drying trays 10 15
117 8 c. Nutmegs 10 15
118 10 c. Rum distillery, River Antoine Estate, c. 1785 . . 10 15
119 12 c. Cocoa tree 10 15
120 15 c. Fishermen at Fontenoy . 10 15
121 20 c. Parliament Building . . 10 30
122 25 c. Fort George cannons . . 10 15
123 35 c. Pearls Airport 50 15
124 50 c. General Post Office . . 20 60
125 75 c. Carib's Leap, Sauteurs Bay 40 60
126 $1 Carenage, St. George's . . 60 85
127 $2 St. George's Harbour by night 90 2·00
128 $3 Grand Anse beach . . . . 1·10 2·50
129 $5 Canoe Bay and Black Bay 1·75 5·00
130 $10 Sugar-loaf Island . . . . 3·50 5·50

8 Virgin and Child" (Durer)

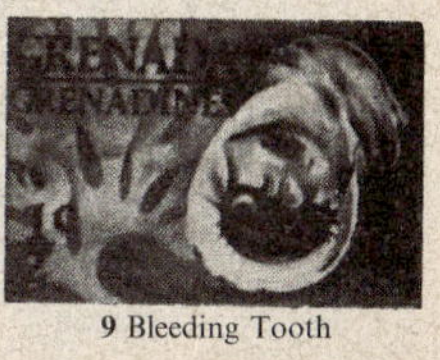

9 Bleeding Tooth

1975. Christmas. "Virgin and Child" paintings by Artists named.

131 ½ c. Type **8** 10 10*
132 1 c. Durer 10 10*
133 2 c. Correggio 10 10*
134 40 c. Botticelli 15 10*
135 50 c. Niccolo da Cremona . . 15 10*
136 75 c. Correggio 15 10*
137 $2 Correggio 30 15*

1976. Shells. Multicoloured.

139 ½ c. Type **9** 10 10*
140 1 c. Toothed donax 10 10*
141 2 c. Hawk-wing conch 10 10*
142 3 c. Atlantic distorsio 10 10*
143 25 c. Scotch bonnet 30 10*
144 50 c. King helmet 60 10*
145 75 c. Queen or pink conch . . 85 15*

10 Cocoa Thrush

1976. Flora and Fauna. Multicoloured.

147 ½ c. "Lignum vitae" 10 10*
148 1 c. Type **10** 10 10*
149 2 c. "Eurypelma sp." (spider) . 10 10*
150 35 c. Hooded tanager . . . . 1·25 10*
151 50 c. "Nyctaginaceae" . . . . 1·00 15*
152 75 c. Grenada dove . . . . . 2·50 25*
153 $1 Marine toad . . . . 2·50 25*

11 Hooked Sailfish

1976. Tourism. Multicoloured.

155 ½ c. Type **11** 10 10*
156 1 c. Careened schooner, Carriacou 10 10*
157 2 c. Carriacou Annual Regatta 10 10*
158 18 c. Boat building on Carriacou 20 10*
159 22 c. Workboat race, Carriacou Regatta 20 10*
160 75 c. Cruising off Petit Martinique 30 20*
161 $1 Water skiing 40 20*

12 Making a Camp Fire

1976. 50th Anniv of Girl Guides in Grenada. Multicoloured.

163 ½ c. Type **12** 10 10*
164 1 c. First aid 10 10*
165 2 c. Nature study 10 10*
166 50 c. Cookery 65 15*
167 $1 Sketching . . . . 1·00 25*

13 "Christ Mocked" (Bosch) **15** Piper Apache

14 "South Carolina" (frigate)

1976. Easter. Multicoloured.

169 ½ c. Type **13** 10 10*
170 1 c. "Christ Crucified" (Antonello da Messina) . . 10 10*
171 2 c. "Adoration of the Trinity" (Durer) 10 10*
172 3 c. "Lamentation of Christ" (Durer) 10 10*
173 35 c. "The Entombment" (Van der Weyden) 20 10*
174 $3 "The Entombment" (Raphael) 75 30*

1976. Bicentenary of American Revolution (2nd issue). Multicoloured.

176 ½ c. Type **14** 10 10*
177 1 c. "Lee" (schooner) 10 10*
178 2 c. H.M.S. "Roebuck" (frigate) 10 10*
179 35 c. "Andrew Doria" (brig) . 50 10*
180 50 c. "Providence" (sloop) . . 60 15*
181 $1 "Alfred" (frigate) . . . . 1·00 20*
182 $2 "Confederacy" (frigate) . 1·50 30*

1976. Aircraft. Multicoloured.

184 ½ c. Type **15** 10 10*
185 1 c. Beech 50 Twin Bonanza . 10 10*
186 2 c. De Havilland Twin Otter 10 10*
187 40 c. Britten Norman Islander 30 10*
188 50 c. De Havilland Heron 2 . 40 10*
189 $2 Hawker Siddeley H.S.748 . 1·25 25*

16 Cycling

1976. Olympic Games, Montreal. Multicoloured.

191 ½ c. Type **16** 10 10*
192 1 c. Pommel horse 10 10*
193 2 c. Hurdling 10 10*
194 35 c. Shot putting 10 10*
195 45 c. Diving 15 10*
196 75 c. Sprinting 15 10*
197 $2 Rowing 35 25*

17 "Virgin and Child" (Cima)

1976. Christmas. Multicoloured.

199 ½ c. Type **17** 10 10*
200 1 c. "The Nativity" (Romanino) 10 10*
201 2 c. "The Nativity" (Romanino) (different) 10 10*
202 35 c. "Adoration of the Kings" (Bruegel) 15 10*
203 50 c. "Madonna and Child" (Girolamo) 20 10*
204 75 c. "Adoration of the Magi" (Giorgione) (horiz) 20 15*
205 $2 "Adoration of the Kings" (School of Fra Angelico) (horiz) 40 25*

18 Alexander Graham Bell and First Telephone

1977. Centenary of First Telephone Transmission. Designs showing Alexander Graham Bell and telephone. Multicoloured.

207 ½ c. Type **18** 10 10*
208 1 c. 1895 telephone 10 10*
209 2 c. 1900 telephone 10 10*
210 35 c. 1915 telephone 15 10*
211 75 c. 1920 telephone 20 10*
212 $1 1929 telephone 25 15*
213 $2 1963 telephone 35 25*

19 Coronation Coach

1977. Silver Jubilee. Multicoloured. (a) Perf.

215 35 c. Type **19** 10 10*
216 $2 Queen entering Abbey . . 20 10*
217 $4 Queen crowned 35 25*

(b) Imperf × roul. Self-adhesive.

219 35 c. Royal visit 15 20
220 50 c. Crown of St. Edward . . 40 80
221 $2 The Queen and Prince Charles 75 1·60
222 $5 Royal Standard . . . . . 90 1·75

Nos. 219/22 come from booklets.

21 "Disrobing of Christ" (Fra Angelico) **22** "The Virgin adoring the Child" (Correggio)

1977. Easter. Paintings by artists named. Mult.

223 ½ c. Type **21** 10 10*
224 1 c. Fra Angelico 10 10*
225 2 c. El Greco 10 10*
226 18 c. El Greco 10 10*
227 35 c. Fra Angelico 15 10*
228 50 c. Giottino 20 10*
229 $2 Antonello da Messina . . . 50 25*

1977. Christmas. Multicoloured.

231 ½ c. Type **22** 10 10*
232 1 c. "Virgin and Child" (Giorgione) 10 10*
233 2 c. "Virgin and Child" (Morales) 10 10*
234 18 c. "Madonna della Tenda" (Raphael) 10 10*
235 35 c. "Rest on the Flight into Egypt" (Van Dyck) 15 10*
236 50 c. "Madonna and Child" (Lippi) 20 10*
237 $2 "Virgin and Child" (Lippi) (different) 60 25*

1977. Royal Visit. Nos. 215/17 optd **ROYAL VISIT W.I. 1977.**

239 35 c. Type **19** 10 10
240 $2 Queen entering Abbey . . 25 20
241 $4 Queen crowned 40 30

24 Life-saving

1977. Caribbean Scout Jamboree, Jamaica. Multicoloured.

243 ½ c. Type **24** 10 10*
244 1 c. Overnight hike 10 10*
245 2 c. Cubs tying knots 10 10*
246 22 c. Erecting a tent 15 10*
247 35 c. Gang show limbo dance . 25 10*
248 75 c. Campfire cooking . . . 40 15*
249 $3 Sea Scouts' yacht race . . 80 30*

25 Blast-off

1977. Space Shuttle. Multicoloured.

251 ½ c. Type **25** 10 10*
252 1 c. Booster jettison 10 10*
253 2 c. External tank jettison . . 10 10*
254 22 c. Working in orbit 15 10*
255 50 c. Shuttle re-entry 25 10*
256 $3 Shuttle landing 85 30*

26 Alfred Nobel and Physiology/Medicine Medal

1978. Nobel Prize Awards. Multicoloured.

258 ½ c. Type **26** 10 10*
259 1 c. Physics and Chemistry medal 10 10*
260 2 c. Peace medal (reverse) . . 10 10*
261 22 c. Nobel Institute, Oslo . . 25 10*
262 75 c. Peace Prize committee . 50 15*
263 $3 Literature medal . . . . 1·50 30*

27 German Zeppelin Stamp, 1930

1978. 75th Anniv of First Zeppelin Flight and 50th Anniv of Lindbergh's Transatlantic Flight. Multicoloured.

265 5 c. Type **27** 20 10*
266 15 c. French Concorde stamp, 1970 . . . . 60 10*
267 25 c. Liechtenstein Zeppelin stamp, 1931 . . . . . . 20 10*
268 35 c. Panama Lindbergh stamp, 1928 . . . . 20 10*
269 50 c. Russia Airship stamp, 1931 25 10*
270 $3 Spanish Lindbergh stamp, 1930 . . . . 75 30*

28 Coronation Ring

1978. 25th Anniv of Coronation. Multicoloured. (a) Horiz designs. Perf.

272 50 c. Type **28** 10 10
273 $2 The Orb 25 30
274 $2.50 Imperial State Crown . 30 35

(b) Vert designs. Roul × imperf. Self-adhesive.

276 18 c. Drummer, Royal Regiment of Fusiliers 15 35
277 50 c. Drummer, Royal Anglian Regiment 15 45
278 $5 Drum Major, Queen's Regiment . . . . 1·00 3·00

30 "Le Chapeau de Paille" **32** Audubon's Shearwater

31 Wright Flyer I

1978. 400th Birth Anniv of Rubens. Mult.

279 5 c. Type **30** 10 10
280 15 c. "Archilles slaying Hector" 15 10
281 18 c. "Helene Fourment and her Children" 15 10
282 22 c. "Rubens and Isabella Brandt" 20 10
283 35 c. "The Ildefonso Altarpiece" 20 10
284 $3 "Heads of Negroes" (detail) 1·10 1·00

1978. 75th Anniv of Powered Flight.

286 **31** 5 c. black, blue & brown . 10 10
287 – 15 c. black, brown & red . 10 10
288 – 18 c. black, brown & red . 10 10
289 – 25 c. black, yell. & green . 10 10
290 – 35 c. black, pink & purple 15 10
291 – 75 c. black, lilac & yellow . 25 25
292 – $3 black, violet & mve. . . 75 75

DESIGNS—HORIZ: 25 c. Wright Flyer III, 1905; 35 c. Wright glider No. 1; 75 c. Wright Flyer I (different); $3 Wright Type A. VERT: 15 c. Orville Wright; 18 c. Wilbur Wright.

1978. Birds. Multicoloured.

294 5 c. Type **32** 50 10
295 10 c. Semipalmated plover . . 70 10
296 18 c. Purple-throated carib (horiz) . . . . 1·00 15
297 22 c. Red-billed whistling duck (horiz) . . . . 1·00 20
298 40 c. Caribbean martin (horiz) 1·50 35
299 $1 Yellow-tailed tropic bird . 2·25 75
300 $2 Long-billed curlew . . . 3·25 1·25

33 Players with Ball **34** Captain Cook and Kalaniopu (King of Hawaii), 1778

1978. World Cup Football Championship, Argentina. Multicoloured.

302 15 c. Type **33** 10 10
303 35 c. Running with ball . . . 20 10
304 50 c. Player with ball 25 20
305 $3 Heading 80 80

1978. 250th Birth Anniv of Captain James Cook. Multicoloured.

307	18 c. Type **34**	45	10
308	22 c. Cook and native of Hawaii	60	15
309	50 c. Cook and death scene, 1779	1·00	30
310	$3 Cook and offering ceremony	2·25	1·75

35 "Virgin at Prayer"

36 "Strelitzia reginae"

1978. Christmas. Paintings by Durer. Multicoloured.

312	40 c. Type **35**	20	10
313	60 c. "The Dresden Altarpiece"	25	15
314	90 c. "Madonna and Child with St. Anne"	30	15
315	$2 "Madonna and Child with Pear"	60	50

1979. Flowers. Multicoloured.

317	22 c. Type **36**	15	10
318	40 c. "Euphorbia pulcherrima"	25	15
319	$1 "Heliconia humilis"	55	30
320	$3 "Thunbergia alata"	1·25	80

37 Children with Pig

1979. International Year of the Child. Multicoloured.

322	18 c. Type **37**	10	10
323	50 c. Children with donkey	20	25
324	$1 Children with goats	25	30
325	$3 Children fishing	65	80

38 "20,000 Leagues under the Sea"

1979. 150th Birth Anniv of Jules Verne (author). Multicoloured.

327	18 c. Type **38**	30	10
328	38 c. "From the Earth to the Moon"	35	20
329	75 c. "From the Earth to the Moon" (different)	45	35
330	$3 "Five Weeks in a Balloon"	85	1·00

39 Sir Rowland Hill and Mail Van

1979. Death Centenary of Sir Rowland Hill. Multicoloured.

332	15 c. Type **39**	10	10
333	$1 "Britanis" (cargo liner)	20	20
334	$2 Diesel mail train	30	30
335	$3 Concorde	90	70

40 "Virgin and Child Enthroned" (11th-century Byzantine)

42 Doctor Goofy

41 Great Hammerhead

1979. Christmas. Sculptures. Multicoloured.

337	6 c. Type **40**	10	10
338	25 c. "Presentation in the Temple" (Andre Beauneveu)	10	10
339	30 c. "Flight to Egypt" (Utrecht, c. 1510)	10	10
340	40 c. "Madonna and Child" (Jacopo della Quercia)	10	10
341	90 c. "Madonna della Mela" (Luca della Robbia)	15	15
342	$1 "Madonna and Child" (Antonio Rossellino)	20	20
343	$2 "Madonna and Child" (Antwerp, 1700)	35	35

1979. Marine Wildlife. Multicoloured.

345	40 c. Type **41**	40	30
346	45 c. Spot-finned butterflyfish	45	30
347	50 c. Permit (fish)	45	40
348	60 c. Threaded turban (shell)	65	55
349	70 c. Milk conch	75	75
350	75 c. Great blue heron	85	90
351	90 c. Colourful Atlantic moon (shell)	95	1·00
352	$1 Red-footed booby	1·50	1·75

1979. International Year of the Child. Walt Disney Cartoon Characters. Multicoloured.

354	½ c. Type **42**	10	10
355	1 c. Admiral Mickey Mouse	10	10
356	2 c. Fireman Goofy	10	10
357	3 c. Nurse Minnie Mouse	10	10
358	4 c. Drum Major Mickey Mouse	10	10
359	5 c. Policeman Donald Duck	10	10
360	10 c. Pilot Donald Duck	10	10
361	$2 Postman Goofy (horiz)	2·25	2·25
362	$2.50 Train driver Donald Duck (horiz)	2·25	2·25

See also Nos. 434/7.

1980. 1st Anniv of Revolution. Nos. 116 and 119/30 optd **PEOPLE'S REVOLUTION 13 MARCH 1979**.

364	6 c. Cocoa beans in drying trays	10	10
365	12 c. Cocoa tree	10	10
366	15 c. Fishermen at Fontenoy	10	10
367	20 c. Parliament Building, St. George's	10	10
368	25 c. Fort George cannons	15	10
369	35 c. Pearls Airport	20	10
370	50 c. General Post Office	35	15
371	75 c. Carib's Leap, Sauteurs Bay	40	20
372	$1 Carenage, St. George's	55	30
373	$2 St. George's Harbour by night	85	70
374	$3 Grand Anse Beach	1·60	1·60
375	$5 Canoe Bay and Black Bay	2·25	2·50
376	$10 Sugar-loaf Island	3·75	4·25

43 Classroom

1980. 75th Anniv of Rotary International. Multicoloured.

377	6 c. Type **43**	10	10
378	30 c. Different races encircling Rotary emblem	20	10
379	60 c. Rotary executive presenting doctor with cheque	35	20
380	$3 Nurses with young patients	1·60	75

44 Yellow-bellied Seedeater

45 Running

1980. Wild Birds. Multicoloured.

382	25 c. Type **44**	50	15
383	40 c. Blue-hooded euphonia	55	20
384	90 c. Yellow warbler	1·25	65
385	$2 Tropical mockingbird	1·75	1·25

1980. Olympic Games, Moscow. Multicoloured.

387	30 c. Type **45**	20	15
388	40 c. Football	15	20
389	90 c. Boxing	35	35
390	$2 Wrestling	70	75

1980. "London 1980" International Stamp Exhibition. Nos. 332/5 optd **LONDON 1980**.

392	15 c. Mail van	15	15
393	$1 "Britanis" (cargo liner)	75	35
394	$2 Diesel mail train	1·50	1·00
395	$3 Concorde	2·25	2·00

47 Long-jawed Squirrelfish

1980. Fishes. Multicoloured.

396	½ c. Type **47**	10	10
397	1 c. Blue chromis	10	10
398	2 c. Four-eyed butterflyfish	10	10
399	4 c. Sergeant major	10	10
400	5 c. Yellow-tailed snapper	10	10
401	6 c. Mutton snapper	10	10
402	10 c. Cocoa damselfish	10	10
403	12 c. Royal gramma	10	10
404	15 c. Cherub angelfish	10	10
405	20 c. Black-barred soldierfish	15	10
406	25 c. Mottled grouper	15	15
407	30 c. Caribbean long-nosed butterflyfish	15	20
408	40 c. Puddingwife	20	25
409	50 c. Midnight parrotfish	25	35
410	90 c. Red-spotted hawkfish	40	55
411	$1 Hogfish	45	60
412	$3 Beau Gregory	1·25	1·50
413	$5 Rock beauty	2·00	2·50
414	$10 Barred hamlet	3·50	5·00

1980. Christmas. Scenes from Walt Disney's "Bambi". As T **42**. Multicoloured.

415	½ c. Bambi with Mother	10	10
416	1 c. Bambi with quails	10	10
417	2 c. Bambi meets Thumper the rabbit	10	10
418	3 c. Bambi meets Flower the skunk	10	10
419	4 c. Bambi and Faline	10	10
420	5 c. Bambi with his father	10	10
421	10 c. Bambi on ice	10	10
422	$2.50 Faline with foals	1·75	1·25
423	$3 Bambi and Faline	1·75	1·25

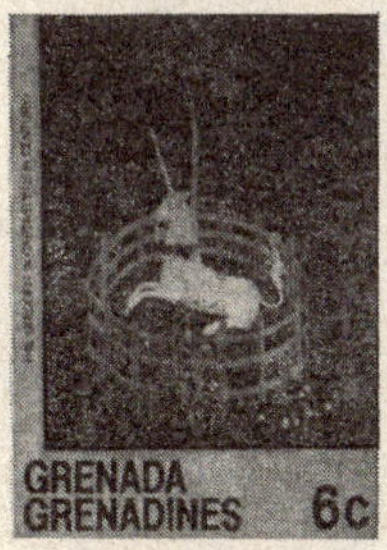

48 "The Unicorn in Captivity" (15th century unknown artist)

49 "Bust of a Woman"

1981. Art Masterpieces. Multicoloured.

425	6 c. Type **48**	10	10
426	10 c. "The Fighting 'Temeraire'" (Turner) (horiz)	10	10
427	25 c. "Sunday Afternoon on the Ile de la Grande Jatte" (Seurat) (horiz)	15	15
428	90 c. "Max Schmitt in a Single Scull" (Eakins) (horiz.)	45	45
429	$2 "The Burial of the Count of Orgaz" (El Greco)	85	85
430	$3 "Portrait of George Washington" (Stuart)	1·10	1·10

1981. 50th Anniv of Walt Disney's Pluto (cartoon character). As T **42**.

432	$2 Mickey Mouse serving birthday cake to Pluto	90	80

1981. Easter. Walt Disney Cartoon Characters. As T **42**. Multicoloured.

434	35 c. Chip	20	20
435	40 c. Dewey	20	20
436	$2 Huey	60	60
437	$2.50 Mickey Mouse	75	75

1981. Birth Centenary of Picasso. Mult.

439	6 c. Type **49**	10	10
440	40 c. Woman (study for "Les Demoiselles d'Avignon")	25	15
441	90 c. "Nude with raised Arms (The Dancer of Avignon)"	40	30
442	$4 "The Dryad"	1·25	1·25

50 Balmoral Castle

51 Lady Diana Spencer

1981. Royal Wedding (1st issue). Multicoloured.

448	30 c. Prince Charles and Lady Diana Spencer	20	20
444	40 c. As 30 c.	15	15
449	40 c. Type **50**	35	35
445	$2 Type **50**	50	50
446	$4 Prince Charles as parachutist	90	90

1981. Royal Wedding (2nd issue). Multicoloured. Self-adhesive.

450	$1 Type **51**	20	35
451	$2 Prince Charles	25	50
452	$5 Prince Charles and Lady Diana Spencer (horiz)	1·25	2·00

INDEX

Countries can be quickly located by referring to the index at the end of this volume.

52 Amy Johnson (1st solo flight, Britain to Australia by Woman, May 1930)

54 Footballer

53 Boeing 747 SCA Carrier

1981. "Decade for Women". Famous Female Aviators. Multicoloured.

453	30 c. Type **52**	45	15
454	70 c. Mme. La Baronne de Laroche (1st qualified woman pilot, March 1910)	70	30
455	$1.10 Ruth Nichols (solo Atlantic flight attempt, June 1931)	80	40
456	$3 Amelia Earhart (1st North Atlantic solo flight by woman, May 1932)	1·75	1·10

1981. Christmas. Designs as T **42** showing scenes from Walt Disney's cartoon film "Lady and the Tramp".

458	½ c. multicoloured	10	10
459	1 c. multicoloured	10	10
460	2 c. multicoloured	10	10
461	3 c. multicoloured	10	10
462	4 c. multicoloured	10	10
463	5 c. multicoloured	10	10
464	10 c. multicoloured	10	10
465	$2.50 multicoloured	2·50	1·25
466	$3 multicoloured	3·00	1·25

1981. Space Shuttle Project. Multicoloured.

468	10 c. Type **53**	30	10
469	40 c. Re-entry	65	15
470	$1.10 External tank separation	1·25	45
471	$3 Touchdown	1·75	1·00

1981. World Cup Football Championship, Spain (1982).

473	**54**	20 c. multicoloured	15	10
474	–	40 c. multicoloured	20	15
475	–	$1 multicoloured	35	30
476	–	$2 multicoloured	65	55

DESIGNS: 40 c. to $2 various designs showing footballers.

55 Mail Van and Stage-coach

1982. Cent of U.P.U. Membership. Multicoloured.

478	30 c. Type **55**	30	15
479	40 c. U.P.U. emblem	30	15
480	$2.50 "Queen Elizabeth 2" (liner) and sailing ship	1·50	70
481	$4 Concorde and De Havilland D.H.9 biplane	2·25	1·25

56 National Sports Meeting

1982. 75th Anniv of Boy Scout Movement and 125th Birth Anniv of Lord Baden-Powell. Multicoloured.

483	6 c. Type **56**	15	10
484	90 c. Sea scouts sailing	50	30
485	$1.10 Handicraft	65	60
486	$3 Animal tending	1·40	1·40

57 "Anartia jatrophae"

1982. Butterflies. Multicoloured.

488	30 c. Type **57**	75	30
489	40 c. "Chioides vintra"	80	35
490	$1.10 "Cynthia cardui"	1·75	75
491	$3 "Historis odius"	2·75	1·60

58 Prince and Princess of Wales

60 "Presentation of Christ in the Temple"

59 "New Deal" — Soil Conservation

1982. 21st Birthday of Princess of Wales. Multicoloured.

493	50 c. Blenheim Palace	50	70
494	60 c. As 50 c.	60	75
495	$1 Type **58**	70	1·40
496	$2 Type **58**	1·50	1·50
497	$3 Princess of Wales	2·00	2·25
498	$4 As $3	2·25	2·25

1982. Birth Centenary of Franklin D. Roosevelt. Multicoloured.

500	30 c. Type **59**	25	15
501	40 c. Roosevelt and George Washington Carver (scientist)	25	15
502	70 c. Civilian conservation corps (reafforestation)	45	30
503	$3 Roosevelt with Pres. Barclay of Liberia, Cassblanca Conference, 1943	1·25	90

1982. Birth of Prince William of Wales. Nos. 493/8 optd **ROYAL BABY 21.6.82**.

505	50 c. Blenheim Palace	50	50
506	60 c. As 50 c.	55	60
507	$1 Type **58**	70	75
508	$2 Type **58**	1·00	1·25
509	$3 Princess of Wales	1·25	1·75
510	$4 As $3	1·50	1·75

1982. Easter. Easter Paintings by Rembrandt. Multicoloured.

512	30 c. Type **60**	40	15
513	60 c. "Descent from the Cross"	55	20
514	$2 "Raising of the Cross"	1·25	75
515	$4 "Resurrection of Christ"	1·75	1·50

61 "Santa Fe", U.S.A.

1982. Famous Trains of the World. Mult.

517	10 c. Type **61**	50	15
518	40 c. "Mistral", France	70	20
519	70 c. "Rheingold", Germany	80	45
520	$1 "ET 403", France	1·00	50
521	$1.10 Steam locomotive "Mallard", Great Britain	1·25	60
522	$2 Tokaido Shinkansen "Hikari", Japan	1·40	90

62 Footballers

1982. World Cup Football Championship Winners.

524 **62**	60 c. multicoloured	50	35
525	$4 multicoloured	2·00	1·25

1982. Christmas. Scenes from Walt Disney's cartoon film "The Rescuers". As T **42**, but horiz.

527	½ c. multicoloured	10	10
528	1 c. multicoloured	10	10
529	2 c. multicoloured	10	10
530	3 c. multicoloured	10	10
531	4 c. multicoloured	10	10
532	5 c. multicoloured	10	10
533	10 c. multicoloured	10	10
534	$2.50 multicoloured	2·75	1·75
535	$3 multicoloured	2·75	1·75

63 Short-finned Pilot Whale

1982. Save the Whale. Multicoloured.

537	10 c. Type **63**	85	55
538	60 c. Dall's porpoise	2·00	1·75
539	$1.10 Humpback whale	3·50	2·75
540	$3 Bowhead whale	6·00	7·00

64 "David and Goliath"

1983. 500th Anniv of Raphael. Multicoloured.

542	25 c. Type **64**	15	15
543	30 c. "David sees Bathsheba"	15	15
544	90 c. "Triumph of David"	30	35
545	$4 "Anointing of Solomon"	70	90

65 Voice and Visual Communication

1983. World Communications Year. Mult.

547	30 c. Type **65**	10	10
548	60 c. Ambulance	25	20
549	$1.10 Westland Whirlwind helicopters	45	45
550	$3 Satellite	1·00	1·00

66 Chrysler "Imperial Roadster", 1931

1983. 75th Anniv of Model "T" Ford Car. Multicoloured.

552	10 c. Type **66**	15	15
553	30 c. Doble steam car, 1925	25	25
554	40 c. Ford "Mustang", 1965	25	30
555	60 c. Packard tourer, 1930	35	40
556	70 c. Mercer "Raceabout", 1913	35	40
557	90 c. Corvette "Stingray", 1963	35	40
558	$1.10 Auburn "851 Supercharger Speedster", 1935	40	45
559	$2.50 Pierce-Arrow "Silver Arrow", 1933	65	95
560	$3 Duesenberg dual cowl phaeton, 1929	75	1·25
561	$4 Mercedes-Benz "SSK", 1928	75	1·50

67 Short Solent 2 Flying Boat

1983. Bicentenary of Manned Flight. Mult.

563	40 c. Type **67**	75	20
564	70 c. Curtiss R3C-2 seaplane	90	35
565	90 c. Hawker Nimrod biplane	1·10	40
566	$4 Montgolfier balloon	3·25	2·75

68 Goofy

69 Weightlifting

1983. Christmas Disney cartoon characters in scenes from "Jingle Bells" (Christmas carol). Multicoloured.

568	½ c. Type **68**	10	10
569	1 c. Clarabelle Cow	10	10
570	2 c. Donald Duck	10	10
571	3 c. Pluto	10	10
572	4 c. Morty and Ferdie	10	10
573	5 c. Huey, Dewey and Louie	10	10
574	10 c. Daisy and Chip n'Dale	10	10
575	$2.50 Big Bad Wolf	4·75	5·00
576	$5 Mickey Mouse	5·00	5·50

1984. Olympic Games, Los Angeles. Mult.

578	30 c. Type **69**	20	15
579	60 c. Gymnastics	45	35
580	70 c. Archery	50	40
581	$4 Sailing	1·90	1·90

70 Frangipani

71 Goofy

1984. Flowers. Multicoloured.

583	15 c. Type **70**	15	10
584	40 c. Dwarf poinciana	30	25
585	70 c. Walking iris	55	45
586	$4 Lady's slipper	2·25	2·50

1984. Easter. Multicoloured.

588	½ c. Type **71**	10	10
589	1 c. Chip and Dale	10	10
590	2 c. Daisy Duck and Huey	10	10
591	3 c. Daisy Duck	10	10
592	4 c. Donald Duck	10	10
593	5 c. Merlin and Madam Mim	10	10
594	10 c. Flower	10	10
595	$2 Minnie and Mickey Mouse	1·50	2·00
596	$4 Minnie Mouse	2·25	2·75

72 Bobolink

1984. Songbirds. Multicoloured.

598	40 c. Type **72**	1·75	1·50
599	50 c. Eastern kingbird	2·00	1·60
600	60 c. Barn swallow	2·25	2·00
601	70 c. Yellow warbler	2·25	2·00
602	$1 Rose-breasted grosbeak	2·50	2·50
603	$1.10 Yellowthroat	2·75	2·75
604	$2 Catbird	3·50	4·50

1984. Universal Postal Union Congress, Hamburg. Nos. 585/6 optd **19th U.P.U. CONGRESS HAMBURG**.

606	70 c. Walking iris	1·00	1·00
607	$4 Lady's slipper	4·50	5·00

74 "Geeststar" (freighter)

1984. Ships. Multicoloured.

609	30 c. Type **74**	75	75
610	60 c. "Daphne" (liner)	1·00	1·25
611	$1.10 "Southwind" (schooner)	1·25	2·00
612	$4 "Oceanic" (liner)	2·00	5·50

1984. 450th Death Anniv of Correggio (painter). As T **296** of Grenada. Multicoloured.

614	10 c. "The Hunt — Blowing the Horn"	10	10
615	30 c. "St. John the Evangelist" (horiz)	15	15
616	90 c. "The Hunt — The Deer's Head"	50	50
617	$4 "The Virgin crowned by Christ" (horiz)	2·00	2·00

1984. 150th Birth Anniv of Edgar Degas (painter). As T **297** of Grenada. Multicoloured.

619	25 c. "The Song of the Dog"	40	15
620	70 c. "Cafe-concert"	70	50
621	$1.10 "The Orchestra of the Opera"	1·50	1·25
622	$3 "The Dance Lesson"	2·75	2·75

1984. "Ausipex" International Stamp Exhibition, Melbourne. As T **298** of Grenada. Multicoloured.

624	$1.10 Queen Victoria Gardens, Melbourne	50	50
625	$4 Ayers Rock	2·00	2·00

75 Col. Steven's Model (1825)

76 Kawasaki "750" (1972)

1984. Railway Locomotives. Multicoloured.

627	20 c. Type **75**	55	25
628	50 c. "Royal George" (1827)	70	50
629	60 c. "Stourbridge Lion" (1829)	75	65
630	70 c. "Liverpool" (1830)	80	85
631	90 c. "South Carolina" (1832)	90	1·25
632	$1.10 "Monster" (1836)	90	1·50
633	$2 "Lafayette" (1837)	1·10	2·25
634	$4 "Lion" (1838)	1·40	3·75

1984. Opening of Point Saline International Airport. Nos. 547 and 549 optd **OPENING OF POINT SALINE INT'L AIRPORT**.

636	30 c. Type **65**	30	25
637	$1.10 Westland Whirlwind helicopters	95	75

1984. Christmas. Walt Disney Cartoon Characters. As T **301** of Grenada. Multicoloured.

639	45 c. Donald Duck and nephews knitting Christmas stockings	70	40
640	60 c. Donald Duck and nephews sitting on sofa	80	65
641	90 c. Donald Duck getting out of bed	1·25	1·00
642	$2 Donald Duck putting presents in wardrobe	2·00	2·50
643	$4 Nephews singing carols outside Donald Duck's window	3·25	4·25

1985. Birth Bicentenary of John J. Audubon (ornithologist). As T **198** of Antigua. Mult.

645	50 c. Blue-winged teal	2·00	60
646	90 c. White ibis	2·50	1·25
647	$1.10 Swallow-tailed kite	3·50	2·00
648	$3 Moorhen	4·50	4·75

See also Nos. 736/9.

1985. Centenary of the Motor Cycle. Mult.

650	30 c. Type **76**	65	45
651	60 c. Honda "Goldwing GL1000" (1974) (horiz)	90	1·00
652	70 c. Kawasaki "Z650" (1976) (horiz)	1·00	1·10
653	$4 Honda "CBX" (1977)	4·00	6·50

77 Nursing Cadets folding Bandages (Health)

1985. International Youth Year. Mult.

655	50 c. Type **77**	70	45
656	70 c. Scuba diver and turtle (Environment)	1·00	80
657	$1.10 Yachting (Leisure)	1·60	1·50
658	$3 Boys playing chess (Education)	5·50	6·50

1985. 40th Anniv of International Civil Aviation Organization. As T **305** of Grenada. Multicoloured.

660	5 c. Lockheed Lodestar	40	20
661	70 c. Hawker Siddeley H.S.748	1·75	55
662	$1.10 Boeing 727-200	2·25	90
663	$4 Boeing 707	3·50	2·50

78 Lady Baden-Powell (founder) and Grenadian Guide Leaders

1985. 75th Anniv of Girl Guide Movement. Multicoloured.

665	30 c. Type **78**	40	20
666	50 c. Guide leader and guides on botany field trip	70	30
667	70 c. Guide leader and guides camping (vert)	95	45
668	$4 Guides sailing (vert)	3·25	2·25

79 "Chiomara asychis"

1985. Butterflies. Multicoloured.

670	½ c. Type **79**	10	10
671	1 c. "Anartia amathea"	10	10
672	2 c. "Pseudolycaena marsyas"	10	10
673	4 c. "Urbanus proteus"	10	10
674	5 c. "Polygonus manueli"	15	10
675	6 c. "Battus polydamas"	20	15
676	10 c. "Eurema daira"	30	15
677	12 c. "Phoebis agarithe"	45	20
678	15 c. "Aphrissa statira"	45	20
679	20 c. "Strymon simaethis"	60	20
680	25 c. "Mestra cana"	60	25
681	30 c. "Agraulis vanillae"	60	30
682	40 c. "Junonia evarete"	75	45
683	60 c. "Dryas julia"	1·00	65
684	70 c. "Philaethria dido"	1·10	75
685	$1.10 "Hamadryas feronia"	1·75	1·25
686	$2.50 "Strymon rufofusca"	3·25	3·00
687	$5 "Appias drusilla"	5·00	4·75
688	$10 "Polites dictynna"	8·00	9·00
688b	$20 "Euptychia cephus"	12·00	14·00

80 The Queen Mother before Prince William's Christening

81 Scuba Diving

1985. Life and Times of Queen Elizabeth the Queen Mother. Multicoloured.

689 $1 Type **80** 45 60
690 $1.50 In winner's enclosure at Ascot (horiz) 60 75
691 $2.50 With Prince Charles at Garter ceremony, Windsor Castle 85 1·10

Stamps as Nos. 689/91 but with face values of 70 c., $1.10 and $3 exist from additional sheetlets with changed background colours.

1985. Water Sports. Multicoloured.

693 15 c. Type **81** 30 10
694 70 c. Boys playing in waterfall 70 45
695 90 c. Water skiing 85 55
696 $4 Swimming 2·50 2·25

82 Queen or Pink Conch

1985. Marine Life. Multicoloured.

698 60 c. Type **82** 65 40
699 90 c. Porcupinefish and fire coral 85 55
700 $1.10 Ghost crab 1·00 70
701 $4 West Indies spiny lobster 2·50 2·25

1985. 300th Birth Anniv of Johann Sebastian Bach (composer). As T **206** of Antigua. Multicoloured.

703 15 c. Natural trumpet 50 10
704 60 c. Bass viol 85 40
705 $1.10 Flute 1·50 70
706 $3 Double flageolet 2·25 1·75

1985. Royal Visit. As T **207** of Antigua. Mult.

708 10 c. Arms of Great Britain and Grenada 20 20
709 $1 Queen Elizabeth II (vert) 1·25 1·75
710 $4 Royal Yacht "Britannia" 3·75 4·75

1985. 40th Anniv of United Nations Organization. Designs as T **208** of Antigua showing United Nations (New York) stamps. Multicoloured.

712 $1 Neil Armstrong (first man on Moon) and 1982 Peaceful Uses of Outer Space 20 c. 1·10 1·10
713 $2 Gandhi and 1971 Racial Equality Year 13 c. 3·25 3·75
714 $2.50 Maimonides (physician) and 1956 World Health Organization 3 c. 4·50 5·50

1985. 150th Birth Anniv of Mark Twain (author). As. T **118** of Anguilla showing Walt Disney cartoon characters illustrating scenes from "Letters from Hawaii". Multicoloured.

716 25 c. Minnie Mouse dancing the hula 60 30
717 50 c. Donald Duck surfing 90 65
718 $1.50 Donald Duck roasting marshmallow in volcano 2·25 2·25
719 $3 Mickey Mouse and Chip n'Dale canoeing 3·75 4·00

1985. Birth Bicentenaries of Grimm Brothers (folklorists). As T **119** of Anguilla, but vert, showing Walt Disney cartoon characters in scenes from "The Elves and the Shoemaker". Multicoloured.

721 30 c. Mickey Mouse as the unsuccessful Shoemaker 70 40
722 60 c. Two elves making shoes 1·10 85
723 70 c. The Shoemaker discovering the new shoes 1·40 1·00
724 $4 The Shoemaker's wife (Minnie Mouse) making clothes for the elves 4·25 5·00

83 "Madonna and Child" (Titian)

85 Two Footballers

1985. Christmas. Religious Paintings. Mult.

726 50 c. Type **83** 45 35
727 70 c. "Madonna and Child with St. Mary and John the Baptist" (Bugiardini) 55 50
728 $1.10 "Adoration of the Magi" (Di Fredi) 90 1·40
729 $3 "Madonna and Child with Young St. John the Baptist" (Bartolomeo) 1·75 3·75

1986. Centenary of Statue of Liberty (1st issue). As T **211** of Dominica. Multicoloured.

731 5 c. Croton Reservoir, New York (1875) 10 10
732 10 c. New York Public Library (1986) 10 10
733 70 c. Old Boathouse, Central Park (1894) 25 40
734 $4 Boating in Central Park (1986) 1·40 2·25

See also Nos. 892/903.

1986. Birth Bicentenary of John J. Audubon (ornithologist) (2nd issue). As T **198** of Antigua. Multicoloured.

736 50 c. Louisiana heron 2·00 1·00
737 70 c. Black-crowned night heron 2·50 1·50
738 90 c. American bittern 2·75 2·00
739 $4 Glossy ibis 5·00 6·50

1986. Visit of President Reagan of U.S.A. Nos. 684 and 687, optd **VISIT OF PRES. REAGAN 20 FEBRUARY 1986**.

741 70 c. "Philaethria dido" 1·50 1·25
742 $5 "Appias drusilla" 6·50 8·00

1986. World Cup Football Championship, Mexico. Designs showing footballers.

743 **85** 10 c. multicoloured 50 40
744 – 70 c. multicoloured 1·60 1·25
745 – $1 multicoloured 1·90 1·75
746 – $4 multicoloured 5·00 6·50

1986. Appearance of Halley's Comet (1st issue). As T **123** of Anguilla. Multicoloured.

748 5 c. Nicholas Copernicus (astronomer) and Earl of Rosse's six foot reflector telescope 40 40
749 20 c. "Sputnik I" (first satellite) orbiting Earth, 1957 60 40
750 40 c. Tycho Brahe's notes and sketch of 1577 Comet 80 60
751 $4 Edmond Halley and 1682 Comet 3·75 4·50

See also Nos. 790/3.
The captions of Nos. 750/1 are transposed.

1986. 60th Birthday of Queen Elizabeth II. As T **125** of Anguilla.

753 2 c. black and yellow 10 15
754 $1.50 multicoloured 80 1·00
755 $4 multicoloured 2·00 2·75

DESIGNS: 2 c. Princesses Elizabeth and Margaret, Windsor Park, 1933; $1.50, Queen Elizabeth; $4 In Sydney, Australia, 1970.

1986. "Ameripex '86" International stamp Exhibition, Chicago. As T **212** of Dominica. Multicoloured.

757 30 c. Donald Duck riding mule in Grand Canyon 45 45
758 60 c. Daisy Duck, Timothy Mouse and Dumbo on Golden Gate Bridge, San Francisco 70 1·00
759 $1 Mickey Mouse and Goofy in fire engine and Chicago Watertower 1·25 1·75
760 $3 Mickey Mouse as airmail pilot and White House 3·00 4·00

1986. Royal Wedding. As T **213** of Antigua. Multicoloured.

762 60 c. Prince Andrew and Miss Sarah Ferguson 55 45
763 70 c. Prince Andrew in car 65 55
764 $4 Prince Andrew with Westland Lynx naval helicopter 2·75 3·50

86 "Hygrocybe firma"

87 Giant Atlantic or Dolobrate Pyram

1986. Mushrooms of the Lesser Antilles. Mult.

766 15 c. Type **86** 80 40
767 50 c. "Xerocomus coccolobae" 1·75 1·25
768 $2 "Volvariella cubensis" 3·50 4·00
769 $3 "Lactarius putidus" 4·50 5·00

1986. Sea Shells. Multicoloured.

771 15 c. Type **87** 90 50
772 50 c. Beau's murex 2·00 1·25
773 $1.10 West Indian fighting conch 2·50 2·75
774 $4 Alphabet conch 4·75 7·00

1986. World Cup Football Championship Winners, Mexico. Nos. 743/6 optd **WINNERS Argentina 3 W.Germany 2**.

776 **85** 10 c. multicoloured 40 30
777 – 70 c. multicoloured 1·10 1·00
778 – $1 multicoloured 1·40 1·40
779 – $4 multicoloured 3·75 5·00

88 Common Opossum

89 Cycling

1986. Wildlife. Multicoloured.

781 10 c. Type **88** 20 20
782 30 c. Giant toad 40 40
783 60 c. Land tortoise 80 80
784 70 c. Murine opossum (vert) 85 85
785 90 c. Burmese mongoose (vert) 90 1·00
786 $1.10 Nine-banded armadillo 1·00 1·25
787 $2 Agouti 1·75 2·25
788 $3 Humpback whale 3·50 4·25

1986. Appearance of Halley's Comet (2nd issue). Nos. 748/51 optd with T **218** of Antigua.

790 5 c. Nicholas Copernicus (astronomer) and Earl of Rosse's six foot reflector telescope 60 60
791 20 c. "Sputnik I" orbiting Earth, 1957 80 50
792 40 c. Tycho Brahe's notes and sketch of 1577 Comet 1·00 60
793 $4 Edmond Halley and 1682 Comet 5·00 6·00

1986. Christmas. As T **220** of Antigua showing Walt Disney cartoon characters. Multicoloured.

795 25 c. Chip n'Dale with hummingbird 25 15
796 30 c. Robin delivering card to Mickey Mouse (vert) 25 20
797 50 c. Piglet, Pooh and Jose Carioca on beach 40 30
798 60 c. Grandma Duck feeding birds (vert) 50 40
799 70 c. Cinderella and birds with mistletoe (vert) 55 50
800 $1.50 Huey, Dewey and Louie windsurfing 1·25 1·75
801 $3 Mickey Mouse and Morty on beach with turtle 1·50 2·50
802 $4 Kittens playing on piano (vert) 2·00 3·25

1986. Olympic Games, Seoul, South Korea (1988). Multicoloured.

804 10 c. + 5 c. Type **89** 30 40
805 50 c + 20 c. Sailing 60 90
806 70 c. + 30 c. Gymnastics 75 1·10
807 $2 + $1 Horse trials 2·25 3·00

90 Aston-Martin "Volante" (1984)

1986. Centenary of Motoring. Multicoloured.

809 10 c. Type **90** 25 25
810 30 c. Jaguar "MK V" (1948) 45 45
811 60 c. Nash "Ambassador" (1956) 65 65
812 70 c. Toyota "Supra" (1984) 70 70
813 90 c. Ferrari "Testarosa" (1985) 80 90
814 $1 BMW "501B" (1955) 85 95
815 $2 Mercedes-Benz "280 SL" (1968) 1·40 2·00
816 $3 Austro-Daimler "ADR8" (1932) 1·90 2·50

1986. Birth Centenary of Marc Chagall (artist). As T **225** of Antigua, showing various paintings.

818/57 $1.10 × 40 multicoloured. Set of 40 28·00 28·00

1987. America's Cup Yachting Championship. As T **222** of Antigua. Multicoloured.

859 25 c. "Defender", 1895 60 40
860 45 c. "Galatea", 1886 80 60
861 70 c. "Azzurra", 1981 1·00 1·00
862 $4 "Australia II", 1983 2·00 3·50

1987. 500th Anniv (1992) of Discovery of America by Christopher Columbus (1st issue). As T **322** of Grenada. Multicoloured.

864 15 c. Christopher Columbus 25 25
865 30 c. Queen Isabella of Castile 30 30
866 50 c. "Santa Maria" 45 50
867 60 c. Claiming the New World for Spain 50 60
868 90 c. Early Spanish map of Lesser Antilles 65 75
869 $1 King Ferdinand of Aragon 70 80
870 $2 Fort La Navidad (drawing by Columbus) 1·40 2·00
871 $3 Galley and Caribs, Hispaniola (drawing by Columbus) 1·90 2·50

See also Nos. 1191/4, 1224/32, 1366/73, 1494/1500 and 1519/20.

1987. Milestones of Transportation. As T **226** of Antigua. Multicoloured.

873 10 c. Saunders Roe "SRN1" (first hovercraft), 1959 30 30
874 15 c. Bugatti "Royale" (largest car), 1931 35 35
875 30 c. Aleksei Leonov and "Voskhod II" (first spacewalk), 1965 55 55
876 50 c. C.S.S "Hunley" (first submarine to sink enemy ship), 1864 75 75
877 60 c. Rolls Royce "Flying Bedstead" (first VTOL aircraft), 1954 85 85
878 70 c. "Jenny Lind" (first mass produced locomotive class), 1847 90 1·00
879 90 c. Duryea "Buggyaut" (first U.S petrol-driven car), 1893 1·00 1·25
880 $1.50 Steam locomotive, Metropolitan Railway, London (first underground line), 1863 1·75 2·00
881 $2 S.S. "Great Britain" (first transatlantic crossing by screw-steamship), 1843 2·25 2·50
882 $3 "Budweiser Rocket" (fastest car), 1979 2·75 3·00

1987. "Capex '87" International Stamp Exhibition, Toronto. Game Fishes. As T **323** of Grenada but horiz. Multicoloured.

883 6 c. Yellow chub 15 15
884 30 c. King mackerel 40 30
885 50 c. Short-finned mako 55 55
886 60 c. Dolphin (fish) 60 60
887 90 c. Skipjack tuna ("Bonito") 75 75
888 $1.10 Cobia 1·00 1·25
889 $3 Tarpon 2·25 2·75
890 $4 Swordfish 2·50 3·25

1987. Centenary of Statue of Liberty (1986) (2nd issue). As T **227** of Antigua. Multicoloured.

892 10 c. Cleaning face of statue 20 20
893 15 c. Commemorative lapel badges 30 30
894 25 c. Band playing and statue 40 40
895 30 c. Band on parade and statue 45 45
896 45 c. Face of statue 50 50
897 50 c. Cleaning head of statue (horiz) 55 55
898 60 c. Models of statue (horiz) 65 65
899 70 c. Small boat flotilla (horiz) 75 85
900 $1 Unveiling ceremony 85 90
901 $1.10 Statue and Manhattan skyline 90 1·00
902 $2 Parade of warships 1·75 2·00
903 $3 Making commemorative flags 1·90 2·25

1987. Great Scientific Discoveries. As T **325** of Grenada. Multicoloured.

904 60 c. Newton medal 85 80
905 $1 Louis Daguerre (inventor of daguerreotype) 1·25 1·00
906 $3 Antoine Lavoisier and apparatus 2·25 2·75
907 $3 Rudolf Diesel and first oil engine 4·00 4·75

No. 907 is inscribed "JAMES WATT" in error.

1987. Bicentenary of U.S. Constitution. As T **232** of Antigua. Multicoloured.

909 10 c. Washington addressing delegates, Constitutional Convention 25 20
910 50 c. Flag and State Seal, Georgia 85 75
911 60 c. Capitol, Washington (vert) 85 80
912 $4 Thomas Jefferson (statesman) (vert) 3·75 5·50

1987. "Hafnia '87" International Stamp Exhibition, Copenhagen. Designs as T **328** of Grenada, but horiz, illustrating Hans Christian Andersen's fairy tales. Multicoloured.

914 25 c. Donald and Daisy Duck in "The Swineherd" 50 30
915 30 c. Mickey Mouse, Donald and Daisy Duck in "What the Good Man Does is Always Right" 55 35
916 50 c. Mickey and Minnie Mouse in "Little Tuk" 75 75
917 60 c. Minnie Mouse and Ferdie in "The World's Fairest Rose" 75 75
918 70 c. Mickey Mouse in "The Garden of Paradise" 80 80
919 $1.50 Goofy and Mickey Mouse in "The Naughty Boy" 2·00 2·25
920 $3 Goofy in "What the Moon Saw" 2·75 3·00
921 $4 Alice as "Thumbelina" 3·25 3·50

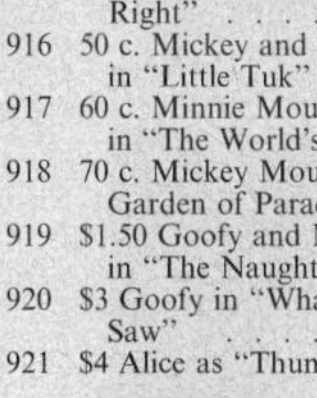

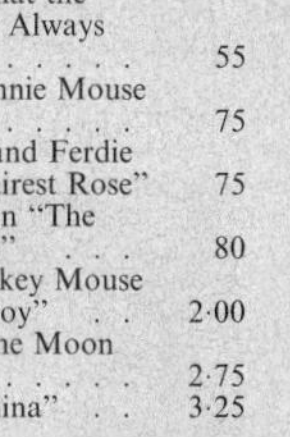

91 "The Virgin and Child with Saints Martin and Agnes"

92 Scout signalling with Semaphore Flags

1987. Christmas. Religious Paintings by El Greco. Multicoloured.

923 10 c. Type **91** 40 15
924 50 c. "St. Agnes" (detail from "The Virgin and Child with Saints Martin and Agnes") 1·25 75
925 60 c. "The Annunciation" 1·25 75
926 $4 "The Holy Family with St. Anne" 4·75 7·25

1988. Royal Ruby Wedding. As T **234** of Antigua. Multicoloured.
928 20 c. brown, black & grn 35 15
929 30 c. brown and black 40 20
930 $2 multicoloured 2·00 2·50
931 $3 multicoloured 2·50 3·25
DESIGNS: 20 c. Queen Elizabeth II with Princess Anne, c. 1957; 30 c. Wedding photograph, 1947; $2 Queen with Prince Charles and Princess Anne, c. 1955; $3 Queen Elizabeth (from photo by Tim Graham), 1980

1988. Olympic Games, Seoul. As T **331** of Grenada showing Walt Disney cartoon characters as Olympic competitors. Multicoloured.
933 1 c. Minnie Mouse as rhythmic gymnast (horiz) 10 10
934 2 c. Pete and Goofy as pankration wrestlers (horiz) 10 10
935 3 c. Huey and Dewey as synchronized swimmers (horiz) 10 10
936 4 c. Huey, Dewey and Louey in hoplite race (horiz) 10 10
937 5 c. Clarabelle and Daisy Duck playing baseball (horiz) 10 10
938 10 c. Goofy and Donald Duck in horse race (horiz) 10 10
939 $6 Donald Duck and Uncle Scrooge McDuck windsurfing (horiz) 4·50 5·50
940 $7 Mickey Mouse in chariot race (horiz) 4·75 5·50

1988. World Scout Jamboree, Australia. Mult.
942 50 c. Type **92** 50 35
943 70 c. Canoeing 60 50
944 $1 Cooking over campfire (horiz) 70 65
945 $3 Scouts around campfire (horiz) 2·00 3·00

1988. Birds. As T **334** of Grenada. Mult.
947 20 c. Yellow-crowned night heron 30 25
948 25 c. Brown pelican 30 25
949 45 c. Audubon's shearwater 40 35
950 60 c. Red-footed booby 50 45
951 70 c. Bridled tern 55 50
952 90 c. Red-billed tropic bird 70 70
953 $3 Blue-winged teal 1·75 2·25
954 $4 Sora 2·00 2·75

1988. 500th Birth Anniv of Titian (artist). As T **238** of Antigua. Multicoloured.
956 15 c. "Man with Blue Eyes" 15 15
957 30 c. "The Three Ages of Man" (detail) 20 20
958 60 c. "Don Diego Mendoza" 35 35
959 75 c. "Emperor Charles V seated" 50 50
960 $1 "A Young Man in a Fur" 60 60
961 $2 "Tobias and the Angel" 1·10 1·40
962 $3 "Pietro Bembo" 1·60 1·90
963 $4 "Pier Luigi Farnese" 1·75 2·25

1988. Airships. As T **336** of Grenada. Multicoloured.
965 10 c. "Hindenburg" over Sugarloaf Mountain, Rio de Janeiro, 1937 (horiz) 20 20
966 20 c. "Hindenburg" over New York, 1937 (horiz) 30 30
967 30 c. U.S. Navy "K" Class airships on Atlantic escort duty, 1944 (horiz) 35 35
968 40 c. "Hindenburg" approaching Lakehurst, 1937 45 45
969 60 c. "Graf Zeppelin" and "Hindenburg" over Germany, 1936 60 60
970 70 c. "Hindenburg" and "Los Angeles" moored at Lakehurst, 1936 (horiz) 65 70
971 $1 "Graf Zeppelin II" over Dover, 1939 80 85
972 $2 "Ersatz Deutschland" on scheduled passenger flight, 1912 (horiz) 1·40 1·60
973 $3 "Graf Zeppelin" over Dome of the Rock, Jerusalem, 1931 (horiz) 1·90 2·25
974 $4 "Hindenburg" over Olympic stadium, Berlin, 1936 (horiz) 2·00 2·25

93 Bambi and his Mother

1988. Disney Animal Cartoon Films.
976/1029 30 c. × 54 multicoloured Set of 54 14·00 15·00
DESIGNS: Scenes from "Bambi", "Dumbo", "Lady and the Tramp", "The Aristocats", "The Fox and the Hound" and "101 Dalmatians".

1988. "Sydpex '88" National Stamp Exhibition, Sydney and 60th Birthday of Mickey Mouse. As T **337** of Grenada. Multicoloured.
1031 1 c. Mickey Mouse conducting at Sydney Opera House 10 10
1032 2 c. Mickey Mouse and Donald Duck at Ayers Rock 10 10
1033 3 c. Goofy and Mickey Mouse on sheep station 10 10
1034 4 c. Goofy and Mickey Mouse at Lone Pine Koala Sanctuary 10 10
1035 5 c. Mickey Mouse, Donald Duck and Goofy playing Australian football 10 10
1036 10 c. Mickey Mouse and Goofy camel racing 10 10
1037 $5 Donald Duck and his nephews bowling 4·50 5·00
1038 $6 Mickey Mouse with America's Cup trophy and "Australia II" (yacht) 5·50 6·00

1988. Flowering Trees and Shrubs. As T **339** of Grenada. Multicoloured.
1040 10 c. Potato tree (vert) 15 15
1041 20 c. Wild cotton 15 15
1042 30 c. Shower of gold (vert) 20 20
1043 60 c. Napoleon's button (vert) 35 30
1044 90 c. Geiger tree 60 70
1045 $1 Fern tree 70 80
1046 $2 French cashew 1·25 2·00
1047 $4 Amherstia (vert) 2·00 3·00

1988. Cars. As T **335** of Grenada. Mult.
1049 $2 Doble "Series E", 1925 1·25 1·25
1050 $2 Alvis "12/50", 1926 1·25 1·25
1051 $2 Sunbeam 3-litre, 1927 1·25 1·25
1052 $2 Franklin "Airman", 1928 1·25 1·25
1053 $2 Delage "D8S", 1929 1·25 1·25
1054 $2 Mors, 1897 1·25 1·25
1055 $2 Peerless "Green Dragon", 1904 1·25 1·25
1056 $2 Pope-Hartford, 1909 1·25 1·25
1057 $2 Daniels "Submarine Speedstar", 1920 1·25 1·25
1058 $2 McFarlan 9.3 litre, 1922 1·25 1·25
1059 $2 Frazer Nash "Lemans" replica, 1949 1·25 1·25
1060 $2 Pegaso "Z102", 1953 1·25 1·25
1061 $2 Siata "Spyder V-8", 1953 1·25 1·25
1062 $2 Kurtis-Offenhauser, 1953 1·25 1·25
1063 $2 Kaiser-Darrin, 1954 1·25 1·25
1064 $2 Tracta, 1930 1·25 1·25
1065 $2 Maybach "Zeppelin", 1932 1·25 1·25
1066 $2 Railton "Light Sports", 1934 1·25 1·25
1067 $2 Hotchkiss, 1936 1·25 1·25
1068 $2 Mercedes-Benz "W163", 1939 1·25 1·25
1069 $2 Aston-Martin "Vantage V8", 1982 1·25 1·25
1070 $2 Porsche "956", 1982 1·25 1·25
1071 $2 Lotus "Esprit Turbo", 1983 1·25 1·25
1072 $2 McLaren "MP4/2", 1984 1·25 1·25
1073 $2 Mercedes-Benz "190E 2.3-16", 1985 1·25 1·25
1074 $2 Ferrari "250 GT Lusso", 1963 1·25 1·25
1075 $2 Porsche "904", 1964 1·25 1·25
1076 $2 Volvo "P1800", 1967 1·25 1·25
1077 $2 McLaren-Chevrolet "M8D", 1970 1·25 1·25
1078 $2 Jaguar "XJ6", 1981 1·25 1·25

1988. "Mickey's Christmas Parade". As T **246** of Antigua showing Walt Disney cartoon characters. Multicoloured.
1079 $1 Dumbo 55 65
1080 $1 Goofy as Father Christmas 55 65
1081 $1 Minnie Mouse waving from window 55 65
1082 $1 Clarabelle, Mordie and Ferdie watching parade 55 65
1083 $1 Donald Duck's nephews 55 65
1084 $1 Donald Duck as drummer 55 65
1085 $1 Toy soldiers 55 65
1086 $1 Mickey Mouse on wooden horse 55 65

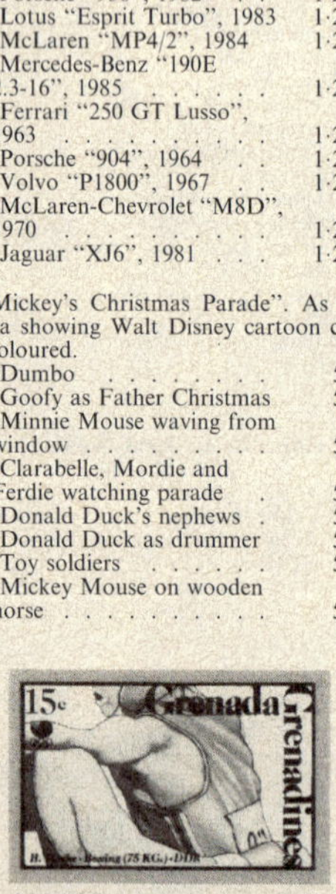

94 Middleweight Boxing (Gold, Henry Maske, East Germany)

1989. Olympic Medal Winners, Seoul (1988). Multicoloured.
1088 15 c. Type **94** 20 20
1089 50 c. Freestyle wrestling (130 kg) (Bronze, Andreas Schroeder, East Germany) 40 40
1090 60 c. Women's team gymnastics (Bronze, East Germany) 50 50
1091 75 c. Platform diving (Gold, Greg Louganis, U.S.A.) 55 55
1092 $1 Freestyle wrestling (52 kg) (Gold, Mitsuru Sato, Japan) 70 70
1093 $2 Men's freestyle 4 × 200 metres relay swimming (Bronze, West Germany) 1·25 1·50
1094 $3 Men's 5000 metres (Silver, Dieter Baumann, West Germany) 1·60 1·75
1095 $4 Women's heptathlon (Gold, Jackie Joyner-Kersee, U.S.A.) 2·00 2·50

1989. Japanese Art. Paintings by Hiroshige. As T **250** of Antigua. Multicoloured.
1097 15 c. "Crossing the Oi at Shimada by Ferry" 25 25
1098 20 c. "Daimyo and Entourage at Arai" 30 30
1099 45 c. "Cargo Portage through Goyu" 50 50
1100 75 c. "Snowfall at Fujigawa" 75 75
1101 $1 "Horses for the Emperor at Chirifu" 85 85
1102 $2 "Rainfall at Tsuchiyama" 1·60 1·60
1103 $3 "An Inn at Ishibe" 2·25 2·25
1104 $4 "On the Shore of Lake Biwa at Otsu" 2·75 2·75

1989. World Cup Football Championship, Italy (1990) (1st issue). As T **252** of Antigua. Mult.
1106 15 c. World Cup trophy 40 20
1107 20 c. Flags of Argentina (winners 1986) and International Federation of Football Associations (FIFA) (horiz) 40 20
1108 45 c. Franz Beckenbauer (West Germany) with World Cup, 1974 60 35
1109 75 c. Flags of Italy (winners 1982) and FIFA (horiz) 75 55
1110 $1 Pele (Brazil) with Jules Rimet trophy 90 70
1111 $2 Flags of West Germany (winners 1974) and FIFA (horiz) 1·40 1·75
1112 $3 Flags of Brazil (winners 1970) and FIFA (horiz) 1·75 2·50
1113 $4 Jules Rimet trophy and Brazil players 1·90 2·50
See also Nos. 1285/8.

1989. North American Railway Locomotives. As T **342** of Grenada. Multicoloured.
1115 $2 Morris & Essex Railroad "Dover", 1841, U.S.A. 1·50 1·50
1116 $2 Baltimore & Ohio Railroad No. 57 "Memnon", 1848, U.S.A. 1·50 1·50
1117 $2 Camden & Amboy Railroad "John Stevens", 1849, U.S.A. 1·50 1·50
1118 $2 Lawrence Machine Shop "Lawrence", 1853, U.S.A. 1·50 1·50
1119 $2 South Carolina Railroad "James S. Corry", 1859, U.S.A. 1·50 1·50
1120 $2 Mine Hill & Schuylkill Haven Railroad flexible beam No. 3, 1860, U.S.A. 1·50 1·50
1121 $2 Delaware, Lackawanna & Western Railroad "Montrose", 1861, U.S.A. 1·50 1·50
1122 $2 Central Pacific Railroad No. 68 "Pequop", 1868, U.S.A. 1·50 1·50
1123 $2 Boston & Providence Railroad "Daniel Nason", 1863, U.S.A. 1·50 1·50
1124 $2 Morris & Essex Railroad "Joe Scranton", 1870, U.S.A. 1·50 1·50
1125 $2 Central Railroad of New Jersey No. 124, 1871, U.S.A. 1·50 1·50
1126 $2 Baldwin tramway steam locomotive, 1876, U.S.A. 1·50 1·50
1127 $2 Lackawanna & Bloomsburg Railroad "Luzerne", 1878, U.S.A. 1·50 1·50
1128 $2 Central Mexican Railroad No. 150, 1892 1·50 1·50
1129 $2 Denver South Park & Pacific Railroad No. 15 "Breckenridge", 1879, U.S.A. 1·50 1·50
1130 $2 Miles Planting & Manufacturing Company plantation locomotive "Daisy", 1894, U.S.A. 1·50 1·50
1131 $2 Central of Georgia Railroad Baldwin 854 No. 1136, 1895, U.S.A. 1·50 1·50
1132 $2 Savannah, Florida & Western Railroad No. 111, 1900, U.S.A. 1·50 1·50
1133 $2 Douglas, Gilmore & Company contractors locomotive No. 3, 1902, U.S.A. 1·50 1·50
1134 $2 Lehigh Valley Coal Company compressed air locomotive No. 900, 1903, U.S.A. 1·50 1·50
1135 $2 Louisiana & Texas Railroad McKeen motor locomotive, 1908, U.S.A. 1·50 1·50
1136 $2 Clear Lake Lumber Company Type B Climax locomotive No. 6, 1910, U.S.A. 1·50 1·50
1137 $2 Blue Jay Lumber Company Heisler locomotive No. 10, 1912, U.S.A. 1·50 1·50
1138 $2 Stewartstown Railroad petrol locomotive No. 6, 1920s, U.S.A. 1·50 1·50
1139 $2 Bangor & Aroostock Railroad Class G No. 186, 1921, U.S.A. 1·50 1·50
1140 $2 Hammond Lumber Company Mallet locomotive, No. 6, 1923, U.S.A. 1·50 1·50
1141 $2 Central Railway of New Jersey diesel locomotive No. 1000, 1925, U.S.A. 1·50 1·50
1142 $2 Atchison Topeka & Santa Fe Railroad "Super Chief" diesel express, 1935, U.S.A. 1·50 1·50
1143 $2 Norfolk & Western Railroad Class Y-6, 1948, U.S.A. 1·50 1·50
1144 $2 Boston & Maine Railroad Budd diesel railcar, 1949, U.S.A. 1·50 1·50

1989. "Philexfrance '89" International Stamp Exn, Paris. As T **251** of Antigua showing Walt Disney cartoon characters in Paris. Multicoloured.
1145 1 c. Mickey Mouse and Donald Duck at Ecole Militaire inflating balloon 10 10
1146 2 c. Mickey and Minnie Mouse on river boat passing Conciergerie 10 10
1147 3 c. Mickey Mouse at Hotel de Ville (vert) 10 10
1148 4 c. Mickey Mouse at Genie of the Bastille monument (vert) 10 10
1149 5 c. Mickey and Minnie Mouse arriving at Opera House 10 10
1150 10 c. Mickey and Minnie Mouse on tandem in Luxembourg Gardens 10 10
1151 $5 Mickey Mouse in aeroplane over L'Arch de La Defense (vert) 5·50 6·50
1152 $6 Mickey Mouse at Place Vendome (vert) 5·50 6·50

95 Launch of "Apollo II"

97 Buddy Holly

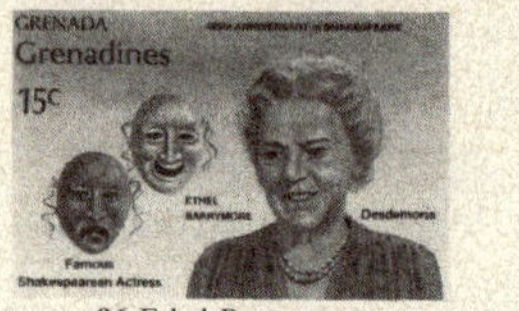

96 Ethel Barrymore

1989. 20th Anniv of First Manned Landing on Moon. Multicoloured.
1154 25 c. Type **95** 30 30
1155 50 c. Splashdown (horiz) 50 50
1156 60 c. Modules in space 60 60
1157 75 c. Aldrin setting up experiment (horiz) 70 70
1158 $1 "Apollo 11" leaving Earth orbit (horiz) 80 80
1159 $2 Moving "Apollo 11" to launch site 1·60 1·90
1160 $3 Lunar module "Eagle" leaving Moon (horiz) 2·00 2·50
1161 $4 "Eagle" landing on Moon 2·25 2·75

1989. Fungi. As T **348** of Grenada. Mult.
1163 6 c. "Agaricus purpurellus" (incorrectly inscr "Collybia aurea") 35 25
1164 10 c. "Podaxis pistillaris" 35 25
1165 20 c. "Hygrocybe firma" 55 45
1166 30 c. "Agaricus rufoaurantiacus" 65 55
1167 75 c. "Leptonia howellii" 1·40 1·40
1168 $2 "Marasmiellus purpureus" 2·50 2·75
1169 $3 "Marasmius trinitatis" 3·00 3·25
1170 $4 "Collybia aurea" (incorrectly inscr "Hygrocybe martinicensis") 3·25 3·50

1989. Butterflies. As T **350** of Grenada. Mult.
1172 25 c. "Battus polydamas" (inscr "Papilio androgeus") 40 40
1173 35 c. "Phoebis sennae" 45 45
1174 45 c. "Hamadryas feronia" 55 55
1175 50 c. "Cynthia cardui" 55 55
1176 75 c. "Ascia monuste" 80 80
1177 90 c. "Eurema lisa" 90 90
1178 $2 "Aphrissa statira" 2·00 2·00
1179 $3 "Hypolimnas misippus" 2·50 2·50

1989. 425th Birth Anniv of Shakespeare. Shakespearean Actors. Multicoloured.
1181 15 c. Type **96** 25 25
1182 $1.10 Richard Burton 1·25 1·25
1183 $2 John Barrymore 2·00 2·00
1184 $3 Paul Robeson 2·25 2·25

1989. Musicians. Multicoloured.
1186 10 c. Type **97** 35 25
1187 25 c. Jimmy Hendrix 55 40
1188 75 c. Mighty Sparrow 70 70
1189 $4 Katsutoji Kineya 3·00 4·00

1989. 500th Anniv (1992) of Discovery of America by Columbus (2nd issue). Pre-Columbian Arawak Society. As T **247** of Antigua. Multicoloured.
1191 15 c. Arawaks canoeing 25 25
1192 75 c. Family and campfire 75 75
1193 90 c. Using stone tools 95 95
1194 $3 Eating and drinking 2·50 3·00

1989. "World Stamp Expo '89" International Stamp Exhibition, Washington. Designs showing Walt Disney cartoon characters illustrating proverbs from "Poor Richard's Almanack". As T **352** of Grenada. Multicoloured.
1196 1 c. Uncle Scrooge McDuck with gold coins in sinking boat 10 10
1197 2 c. Robin Hood shooting apple off Friar Tuck 10 10
1198 3 c. Winnie the Pooh with honey 10 10
1199 4 c. Goofy, Minnie Mouse and Donald Duck exercising 10 10
1200 5 c. Pinnochio holding Jimminy Cricket 10 10
1201 6 c. Huey and Dewey putting up wallpaper 10 10
1202 8 c. Mickey Mouse asleep in storm 15 10
1203 10 c. Mickey Mouse as Benjamin Franklin selling "Pennsylvania Gazette" 15 10
1204 $5 Mickey Mouse with chicken, recipe book and egg 4·00 5·00
1205 $6 Mickey Mouse missing carriage 4·50 5·00

1990. Christmas. Paintings by Rubens. As T **259** of Antigua. Multicoloured.
1207 10 c. "The Annunciation" 35 15
1208 15 c. "The Flight of the Holy Family into Egypt" 40 15
1209 25 c. "The Presentation in the Temple" 55 15
1210 45 c. "The Holy Family under the Apple Tree" 70 25
1211 $2 "Madonna and Child with Saints" 2·00 2·50
1212 $4 "The Virgin and Child enthroned with Saints" 3·00 4·00
1213 $5 "The Holy Family" 3·00 4·00

1990. "EXPO '90" International Garden and Greenery Exhibition, Osaka. Caribbean Orchids. As T **354** of Grenada. Multicoloured.

1215 15 c. "Brassocattleya" Thalie 30 30
1216 20 c. "Odontocidium" Tigersun 35 35
1217 50 c. "Odontioda" Hambuhren 55 55
1218 75 c. "Paphiopedium" Delrosi 75 75
1219 $1 "Vuylstekeara" Yokara . 95 95
1220 $2 "Paphiopedilum" Geelong 1·75 2·00
1221 $3 "Wilsonara" Tigerwood . 2·00 2·25
1222 $4 "Cymbidium" Ormoulu . 2·50 2·75

1990. 500th Anniv (1992) of Discovery of America by Columbus (3rd issue). New World Natural History—Insects. As T **260** of Antigua. Mult.

1224 35 c. "Dynastes hercules" (beetle) 35 35
1225 40 c. "Chalcolepidius porcatus" (beetle) 35 35
1226 50 c. "Acrocinus longimanus" (beetle) 40 40
1227 60 c. "Battus polydamas" (butterfly) 75 75
1228 $1 "Orthemis ferruginea" (skimmer) 95 95
1229 $2 "Psiloptera variolosa" (beetle) . . . . 1·60 1·75
1230 $3 "Hypolimnas misippus" (butterfly) . . . . 2·50 2·75
1231 $4 Scarab beetle . . . . . . 2·50 2·75

1990. Wildlife. As T **254** of Antigua. Mult.

1233 5 c. West Indies giant rice rat 20 20
1234 25 c. Agouti 35 35
1235 30 c. Humpback whale . . . 70 65
1236 40 c. Pilot whale 70 65
1237 $1 Spotted dolphin 95 95
1238 $2 Egyptian mongoose . . . 1·75 2·00
1239 $3 Brazilian tree porcupine . 2·25 2·75
1240 $4 American manatee . . . . 2·50 3·00

1990. 50th Anniv of Second World War. As T **274** of Antigua. Multicoloured.

1242 6 c. British tanks in France, 1939 . . . . 30 30
1243 10 c. Operation "Crusader", North Africa, 1941 . . . . 30 30
1244 20 c. Retreat of the Afrika Corps, 1942 . . . . 40 40
1245 45 c. American landing on Aleutian Islands, 1943 . . 50 50
1246 50 c. U.S marines landing on Tarawa, 1943 . . . . . . 55 55
1247 60 c. U.S army entering Rome, 1944 . . . . 60 60
1248 75 c. U.S tanks crossing River Seine, 1944 . . . . 70 70
1249 $1 Battle of the Bulge, 1944 . 95 95
1250 $5 American infantry in Italy, 1945 . . . . 3·00 3·50
1251 $6 B-29 "Enola Gay" dropping atomic bomb on Hiroshima, 1945 . . . . 3·50 3·50

1990. "Stamp World London '90" International Stamp Exhibition. As T **193** of Gambia showing Walt Disney cartoon characters at Shakespeare sites. Multicoloured.

1253 15 c. Daisy Duck at Ann Hathaway's Cottage (horiz) 40 20
1254 30 c. Minnie and Bill Mouse at Shakespeare's birthplace, Stratford 55 35
1255 50 c. Minnie Mouse in front of Mary Arden's house, Wilmcote 75 70
1256 60 c. Mickey Mouse leaning on hedge in New Place gardens, Stratford (horiz) 90 90
1257 $1 Mickey Mouse walking in New Place gardens, Stratford (horiz) . . . . 1·25 1·25
1258 $2 Mickey Mouse carrying books in Scholars Lane, Stratford . . . . 2·25 2·50
1259 $4 Mickey Mouse and Royal Shakespeare Theatre, Stratford . . . . 3·25 4·00
1260 $5 Ludwig von Drake teaching Mickey Mouse at the Stratford Grammar School (horiz) . . . . 3·25 4·00

1990. 90th Birthday of Queen Elizabeth the Queen Mother. As T **194** of Gambia, showing photographs 1970–79.

1262 $2 Queen Mother wearing pink hat and coat . . . . 1·10 1·40
1263 $2 Prince Charles and Queen Mother at Garter ceremony 1·10 1·40
1264 $2 Queen Mother in blue floral outfit . . . . 1·10 1·40

1990. Birds. As T **358** of Grenada, but vert Multicoloured.

1267 25 c. Yellow-bellied seedeater 30 30
1268 45 c. Carib grackle 50 50
1269 50 c. Black-whiskered vireo . 55 55
1270 75 c. Bananaquit 70 70
1271 $1 White-collared swift . . . 95 95
1272 $2 Yellow-bellied elaenia . . 1·50 1·50
1273 $3 Blue-hooded euphonia . . 2·00 2·00
1274 $5 Eared dove . . . . 3·25 3·25

1990. Crustaceans. As T **359** of Grenada. Mult.

1276 10 c. Slipper lobster 20 20
1277 25 c. Green reef crab 30 30
1278 65 c. Caribbean lobsterette . 60 60
1279 75 c. Blind deep sea lobster . 70 70
1280 $1 Flattened crab 95 95
1281 $2 Ridged slipper lobster . . 1·75 1·75
1282 $3 Land crab . . . . 2·25 2·25
1283 $4 Mountain crab . . . . . 2·50 2·50

98 Lineker, England

1990. World Cup Football Championship, Italy (2nd issue). Multicoloured.

1285 15 c. Type **98** 25 25
1286 45 c. Burruchaga, Argentina 45 45
1287 $2 Hysen, Sweden . . . . . 1·75 2·25
1288 $4 Sang Ho, South Korea . 2·75 3·75

1990. Olympic Games, Barcelona (1992). As T **268** of Antigua. Multicoloured.

1290 10 c. Boxing 10 10
1291 25 c. Olympic flame 20 20
1292 50 c. Football 40 40
1293 75 c. Discus throwing . . . 60 60
1294 $1 Pole vaulting 85 85
1295 $2 Show jumping . . . . . 1·75 1·75
1296 $4 Women's basketball . . . 3·00 3·25
1297 $5 Men's gymnastics . . . . 3·00 3·25

1991. 350th Death Anniv of Rubens. As T **273** of Antigua. Multicoloured.

1299 5 c. "Adam and Eve" (Eve detail) (vert) 20 20
1300 15 c. "Esther before Ahasuerus" (detail) 30 20
1301 25 c. "Adam and Eve" (Adam detail) (vert) 40 25
1302 50 c. "Expulsion from Eden" 70 60
1303 $1 "Cain slaying Abel" (detail) (vert) . . . . 1·10 1·10
1304 $2 "Lot's Flight" . . . . . 1·75 2·25
1305 $4 "Samson and Delilah" (detail) . . . . 2·75 3·50
1306 $5 "Abraham and Melchizedek" . . . . . . 3·25 3·50

1991. Coral Reef Fishes. As T **357** of Grenada. Multicoloured.

1308 15 c. Barred hamlet 40 25
1309 35 c. Long-spined squirrelfish 70 50
1310 45 c. Red-spotted hawkfish . 75 60
1311 75 c. Bigeye . . . . 1·00 1·00
1312 $1 Balloonfish ("Spiny puffer") 1·25 1·25
1313 $2 Small-mouth grunt . . . 2·00 2·25
1314 $3 Harlequin bass . . . . . 2·50 2·75
1315 $4 Creole fish . . . . 3·00 3·25

99 Angel with Star and Lantern

100 "Brassia maculata"

1991. Christmas (1990). Hummel Figurines. Multicoloured.

1317 10 c. Type **99** 10 10
1318 15 c. Christ Child and Angel playing mandolin 15 15
1319 25 c. Shepherd 25 25
1320 50 c. Angel with trumpet and lantern 50 50
1321 $1 Nativity scene 95 95
1322 $2 Christ Child and Angel holding candle . . . . . . 1·75 2·25
1323 $4 Angel with baskets . . . 2·75 3·50
1324 $5 Angels singing . . . . . 3·25 3·50

1991. Orchids. Multicoloured.

1326 5 c. Type **100** 30 30
1327 10 c. "Oncidium lanceanum" 30 30
1328 15 c. "Broughtonia sanguinea" 35 20
1329 25 c. "Diacrium bicornutum" 40 20
1330 35 c. "Cattleya labiata" . . 40 20
1331 45 c. "Epidendrum fragrans" 50 25
1332 50 c. "Oncidium papilio" . . 55 30
1333 75 c. "Neocogniauxia monophylla" 70 50
1334 $1 "Epidendrum polybulbon" 80 70
1335 $2 "Spiranthes speciosa" . . 1·40 1·40
1336 $4 "Epidendrum ciliare" . . 2·25 2·75
1337 $5 "Phais tankervilliae" . . 2·50 3·00
1338 $10 "Brassia caudata" . . . 4·50 5·00
1339 $20 "Brassavola cordata" . 9·25 11·00

1991. Butterflies. As T **363** of Grenada. Mult.

1340 5 c. Crimson-patched longwing 40 30
1341 10 c. "Morpho helena" . . . 40 30
1342 15 c. "Morpho sulkowskyi" 55 35
1343 20 c. "Dynastor napoleon" . 60 40
1344 25 c. "Pieridae callinira" . . 60 45
1345 30 c. "Anartia amathea" . . 65 50
1346 35 c. "Heliconiidae dido" . . 65 50
1347 45 c. "Papilionidae columbus" 75 65
1348 50 c. "Nymphalidae praeneste" 85 70
1349 60 c. "Panacea prola" . . . 1·00 80
1350 75 c. "Dryas julia" . . . . 1·00 90
1351 $1 "Papilionidae orthosilaus" 1·25 1·10
1352 $2 "Pyrrhopyge cometes" . 1·75 2·00
1353 $3 "Papilionidae paeon" . . 2·00 2·50
1354 $4 "Morpho cypris" . . . . 2·50 3·00
1355 $5 Choringa . . . . 3·00 3·25

101 Donald and Daisy Duck with Solar-powered Car

1991. Ecology Conservation. Walt Disney cartoon characters. Multicoloured.

1357 10 c. Type **101** 30 20
1358 15 c. Goofy saving water . . 40 20
1359 25 c. Donald and Daisy on nature hike 55 35
1360 45 c. Donald Duck returning chick to nest 75 55
1361 $1 Donald Duck and balloons 1·40 1·25
1362 $2 Minnie Mouse and Daisy Duck on hot day . . . . . 2·25 2·50
1363 $4 Mickey's nephews cleaning beach . . . . 3·25 3·75
1364 $5 Donald Duck on pedal generator . . . . 3·25 3·75

1991. 500th Anniv (1992) of Discovery of America by Columbus (4th issue). History of Exploration. As T **277** of Antigua. Multicoloured.

1366 15 c. Magellan's "Vitoria" rounding Cape Horn, 1519–21 . . . . 40 30
1367 20 c. Drake's Golden Hind, 1577-80 . . . . 40 35
1368 50 c. Cook's H.M.S "Resolution", 1768-71 . . . 70 60
1369 60 c. Douglas World Cruiser seaplane , 1924 . . . . . . 70 60
1370 $1 "Sputnik I" satellite, 1957 85 90
1371 $2 Gagarin's space flight, 1961 1·50 1·75
1372 $4 Glenn's space flight, 1962 . 2·50 2·75
1373 $5 Space shuttle, 1981 . . . . 3·00 3·25

1991. "Phila Nippon '91" International Stamp Exhibition, Tokyo. As T **279** of Antigua but horiz showing Walt Disney cartoon characters in Japanese scenes. Multicoloured.

1375 15 c. Minnie Mouse with silkworms 30 20
1376 30 c. Mickey, Minnie, Morty and Ferdie at Torii Gate . 45 35
1377 50 c. Donald Duck and Mickey Mouse trying origami . . . 70 60
1378 60 c. Mickey and Minnie diving for pearls 80 70
1379 $1 Minnie Mouse in kimono . 1·25 1·10
1380 $2 Mickey making masks . . 2·25 2·50
1381 $4 Donald and Mickey making paper . . . . 3·00 3·25
1382 $5 Minnie and Pluto making pottery . . . . 3·25 3·50

1991. Fungi. As T **364** of Grenada. Multicoloured.

1384 5 c. "Pyrrhoglossum pyrrhum" 25 25
1385 45 c. "Agaricus purpurellus" . 75 50
1386 50 c. "Amanita craseoderma" 75 55
1387 90 c. "Hygrocybe acutoconica" 1·25 1·25
1388 $1 "Limacella guttata" . . . 1·25 1·25
1389 $2 "Lactarius hygrophoroides" 1·75 1·75
1390 $4 "Boletellus cubensis" . . . 3·00 3·00
1391 $5 "Psilocybe caerulescens" . 3·00 3·00

1991. 65th Birthday of Queen Elizabeth II. As T **280** of Antigua. Multicoloured.

1393 20 c. Queen, Prince Philip, Prince Charles and Prince William at Trooping the Colour, 1990 . . . . 30 20
1394 25 c. Queen and Prince Charles at polo match, 1985 . . . . 30 20
1395 $2 Queen and Prince Philip at Maundy service, 1989 . . . 2·00 2·50
1396 $4 Queen with Queen Mother on her 87th birthday, 1987 . 3·25 3·75

1991. 10th Wedding Anniv of Prince and Princess of Wales. As T **280** of Antigua. Multicoloured.

1398 5 c. Prince and Princess of Wales kissing, 1987 . . . . 15 15
1399 60 c. Portraits of Prince, Princess and sons 70 70
1400 $1 Prince Henry in 1988 and Prince William in 1987 . . 1·10 1·10
1401 $5 Princess Diana in 1990 and Prince Charles in 1988 . . . 3·75 4·75

1991. Death Centenary (1990) of Vincent van Gogh (artist). As T **278** of Antigua. Multicoloured.

1403 5 c. "Two Thistles" 20 20
1404 10 c. "Baby Marcelle Roulin" 25 20
1405 15 c. "Still Life: Basket with Six Oranges" (horiz) 30 15
1406 25 c. "Orchard in Blossom" . 35 20
1407 45 c. "Armand Roulin" . . . 50 35
1408 50 c. "Wood Gatherers in Snow" (detail) (horiz) . . . 60 40
1409 60 c. "Almond Tree in Blossom" 70 50
1410 $1 "An Old Man" . . . . . 1·00 1·00
1411 $2 "The Seine Bridge at Asnieres" (horiz) . . . . . 1·75 2·00
1412 $3 "Vase with Lilacs, Daises and Anemones" . . . . . 2·25 2·50
1413 $4 "Self Portrait" . . . . . . 2·40 2·75
1414 $5 "Patience Escalier" . . . . 2·50 2·75

102 Sargassum Triggerfish

1991. Reef Fishes. Multicoloured.

1416 50 c. Type **102** 70 70
1417 50 c. Tobaccofish 70 70
1418 50 c. Caribbean long-nosed butterflyfish 70 70
1419 50 c. Cherub angelfish . . . 70 70
1420 50 c. Black jack 70 70
1421 50 c. Masked goby and black jack 70 70
1422 50 c. Spot-finned hogfish . . 70 70
1423 50 c. Royal gramma ("Fairy basslet") 70 70
1424 50 c. Orange-backed bass . . 70 70
1425 50 c. Candy basslet 70 70
1426 50 c. Black-capped basslet . 70 70
1427 50 c. Long-jawed squirrelfish 70 70
1428 50 c. Jackknife-fish 70 70
1429 50 c. Bigeye 70 70
1430 50 c. Short bigeye 70 70

Nos. 1416/30 were printed together, se-tenant, forming a composite design.

1991. Christmas. Religious Paintings by Martin Schongauer. As T **287** of Antigua.

1432 10 c. black and brown . . . 30 15
1433 35 c. multicoloured 85 30
1434 50 c. multicoloured 75 50
1435 75 c. multicoloured . . . . . 1·00 80
1436 $1 multicoloured . . . . . . 1·40 1·25
1437 $2 multicoloured . . . . . . 2·25 2·50
1438 $4 black and brown . . . . 3·25 3·75
1439 $5 black, grey and red . . . 3·50 4·00

DESIGNS: 10 c. "Angel of the Annunciation"; 35 c. "Madonna of the Rose Hedge" (detail); 50 c. "Madonna of the Rose Hedge" (different detail); 75 c. "Nativity" (detail); $1 "Adoration of the Shepherds" (detail); $2 "The Nativity"; $4 "Nativity" (different); $5 "Symbol of St. Matthew".

1992. Great Railways of the World. As T **367** of Grenada. Multicoloured.

1441 75 c. Medoc locomotive No. J-S 58, 1857 (Switzerland) . . 80 80
1442 75 c. Stirling single locomotive No. 1, 1870 (Great Britain) 80 80
1443 75 c. Paris-Lyon-Mediterranee locomotive No. 90, 1877 (France) 80 80
1444 75 c. Standard type, 1880 (U.S.A.) 80 80
1445 75 c. Class 650 "Vittorio Emanuel II", 1884 (Italy) . 80 80
1446 75 c. Johnson single, 1887 (Great Britain) 80 80
1447 75 c. Locomotive No. 999, 1893 (U.S.A.) 80 80
1448 75 c. Class Q1, 1896 (Great Britain) 80 80
1449 75 c. "Claud Hamilton", 1900 (Great Britain) 80 80
1450 $1 Class P8, 1906 (Germany) 80 80
1451 $1 Class P, 1910 (Denmark) 80 80
1452 $1 Southern Railway Ps4, 1926 (U.S.A.) 80 80
1453 $1 "Kestrel", 1932 (Ireland) . 80 80
1454 $1 Southern Pacific Class GS2, 1937 (U.S.A.) 80 80
1455 $1 Class 12, 1938 (Belgium) 80 80
1456 $1 Norfolk and Western Railroad Class J No. 600, 1941 (U.S.A.) 80 80
1457 $1 Alco PA series diesel, 1946 (U.S.A.) 80 80
1458 $1 Class 4E electric, 1954 (South Africa) 80 80
1459 $2 Trans Europe Express train, 1957 . . . . 1·40 1·40
1460 $2 New Haven Railroad Type FL9 diesel, 1960 (U.S.A.) . 1·40 1·40
1461 $2 "Hikari" train, 1964 (Japan) 1·40 1·40
1462 $2 Class 103.1 electric, 1970 (Germany) . . . . 1·40 1·40
1463 $2 RTG diesel, 1972 (France) 1·40 1·40
1464 $2 ETR 401 Pendolino train, 1976 (Italy) . . . . 1·40 1·40
1465 $2 Advanced Passenger Train Class 370, 1981 (Great Britain) . . . . 1·40 1·40
1466 $2 Via Rail LRC diesel, 1982 (Canada) . . . . 1·40 1·40
1467 $2 MAV BZMOT 601, 1983 (Hungary) . . . . 1·40 1·40

1992. 40th Anniv of Queen Elizabeth II's Accession. As T **288** of Antigua. Multicoloured.

1469 60 c. Swimming jetty on beach 40 40
1470 75 c. View of Grenadines . . 45 45
1471 $2 Surf on beach . . . . . . 1·40 1·60
1472 $4 Secluded bay . . . . . . 2·50 3·00

1992. Olympic Games, Barcelona. As T **268** of Antigua. Multicoloured.

1474 10 c. Women's backstroke swimming 30 20
1475 15 c. Women's handball . . 35 20
1476 25 c. Men's 4 × 100 m relay . 45 30
1477 35 c. Men's hammer throw . 50 35
1478 50 c. Men's 110 m hurdles . 60 60
1479 75 c. Men's pole vault . . . 80 80
1480 $1 Men's volleyball . . . . . 1·00 1·00
1481 $2 Men's weightlifting . . . 1·75 2·00
1482 $5 Men's gymnastics . . . . 2·75 3·25
1483 $6 Football . . . . 3·00 3·50

1992. Granada '92 Int Stamp Exn, Spain. Spanish Paintings. As T **292** of Antigua. Mult.
1485 10 c. "The Surrender of Seville" (Zurbaran) 15 15
1486 35 c. "The Liberation of St. Peter by an Angel" (Antonio de Pereda) 25 25
1487 50 c. "Joseph explains the Dreams of the Pharaoh" (Antonio del Castillo Saavedra) (horiz) 55 55
1488 75 c. "The Flower Vase" (Juan de Arellano) 70 70
1489 $1 "The Duke of Pastrana" (Juan Carreno de Miranda) 80 80
1490 $2 "The Annunciation" (detail) (Francisco Rizi) 1·60 1·75
1491 $4 "The Annunciation" (different detail) (Rizi) 2·50 2·75
1492 $5 "Old Women Seated" (attr Antonio Puga) 2·50 2·75

103 Don Isaac Abarbanel, Minister of Finance

1992. 500th Anniv of Discovery of America by Columbus (5th issue). World Columbian Stamp Expo '92, Chicago. Multicoloured.
1494 10 c. Type **103** 15 15
1495 25 c. Columbus on voyage 25 25
1496 35 c. Look-out sighting land 30 30
1497 50 c. King Ferdinand and Queen Isabella of Spain 50 50
1498 60 c. Columbus showing map to Queen Isabella 55 55
1499 $5 "Santa Maria" and bird 4·00 5·50

1992. "Genova '92" International Thematic Stamp Exhibition. Hummingbirds. As T **295** of Antigua, but vert. Multicoloured.
1501 5 c. Male blue-headed hummingbird 10 10
1502 10 c. Female rufous-breasted hermit 10 10
1503 20 c. Female blue-headed hummingbird 15 15
1504 45 c. Male green-throated carib 30 30
1505 90 c. Male Antillean crested hummingbird 60 70
1506 $2 Male purple-throated carib 1·40 1·60
1507 $4 Female purple-throated carib 2·40 2·75
1508 $5 Female Antillean crested hummingbird 2·50 2·75

1992. 50th Anniv of United Service Organization (forces' entertainment programme). As T **371** of Grenada. Multicoloured.
1510 10 c. James Cagney 15 15
1511 15 c. Anne Sheridan 15 15
1512 35 c. Jerry Colonna 25 25
1513 50 c. Spike Jones 40 40
1514 75 c. Edgar Bergen 55 55
1515 $1 The Andrews Sisters 70 70
1516 $2 Dinah Shore 1·40 1·75
1517 $5 Bing Crosby 3·25 3·75
No. 1515 is incorrectly inscribed "THE ANDREW SISTERS".

1992. 500th Anniv of Discovery of America by Columbus (6th issue). Organization of East Caribbean States. As Nos. 1670/1 of Antigua.
1519 $1 Columbus meeting Amerindians 65 65
1520 $2 Ships approaching island 1·25 1·50

1992. Toy Trains from American Manufacturers. As T **257** of Dominica. Multicoloured.
1521 15 c. No. 2220 switcher locomotive, Voltamp (1910) 15 15
1522 25 c. Clockwork locomotive of Bridge Port Line, American Miniature Railroad (1907) 20 20
1523 50 c. First electric toy locomotive, Ives (1910) 40 40
1524 75 c. "J.C. Penney Special" locomotive, American Flyer (1920s) 60 60
1525 $1 Clockwork cast-metal locomotive, Hafner (1916) 80 80
1526 $2 Pull toy copper-plated locomotive, probably Hubley (1900) 1·50 1·75
1527 $4 "Mayflower" locomotive, American Flyer (1928) 2·50 3·00
1528 $5 "Olympian" locomotive, Ives (1929) 2·75 3·00

1992. Christmas. Religious Paintings. "The Annunciation" by various artists. As T **300** of Antigua. Multicoloured.
1531 5 c. Robert Campin 10 10
1532 5 c. Melchior Broederlam 15 10
1533 25 c. Fra Filippo Lippi (two-panel diptych) 20 15
1534 35 c. Simone Martini 30 20
1535 50 c. Lippi (detail from left panel) 45 45
1536 75 c. Lippi (detail from right panel) 60 60
1537 90 c. Albert Bouts 70 80
1538 $1 D. di Michelino 80 90
1539 $2 Rogier van der Weyden 1·50 1·75
1540 $3 Sandro Botticelli (detail of angel) 1·90 2·25
1541 $4 Botticelli (detail of Virgin Mary) 2·75 3·00
1542 $5 Bernardo Daddi (horiz) 2·75 3·00

1992. Gold Record Award Winners. As T **374** of Grenada. Multicoloured.
1544 90 c. Leonard Bernstein 1·00 1·00
1545 90 c. Ray Charles 1·00 1·00
1546 90 c. Bob Dylan 1·00 1·00
1547 90 c. Barbra Streisand 1·00 1·00
1548 90 c. Frank Sinatra 1·00 1·00
1549 90 c. Harry Belafonte 1·00 1·00
1550 90 c. Aretha Franklin 1·00 1·00
1551 90 c. Garth Brooks 1·00 1·00
Nos. 1544/51 were printed together, se-tenant, with a composite background design.

1992. 60th Anniv of Goofy (Disney cartoon character). Scenes from various cartoon films. As T **258** of Dominica. Multicoloured.
1553 5 c. "Father's Day Off", 1953 20 20
1554 10 c. "Cold War", 1951 25 20
1555 15 c. "Home Made Home", 1951 30 20
1556 25 c. "Get Rich Quick", 1951 35 25
1557 50 c. "Man's Best Friend", 1952 55 40
1558 75 c. "Aquamania", 1961 75 55
1559 90 c. "Tomorrow We Diet", 1951 85 65
1560 $1 "Teachers Are People", 1952 90 75
1561 $2 "The Goofy Success Story", 1955 1·60 1·60
1562 $3 "Double Dribble", 1946 2·00 2·25
1563 $4 "Hello Aloha", 1952 2·25 2·50
1564 $5 "Father's Lion", 1952 2·40 2·75

1992. Anniversaries and Events. As T **375** of Grenada. Multicoloured, except No. 1571.
1566 25 c. Zeppelin "Viktoria Luise" over Kiel Harbour (horiz) 40 30
1567 50 c. Space shuttle "Columbia" landing (horiz) 50 35
1568 75 c. German Federal Republic flag and arms (horiz) 55 50
1569 $1.50 Giant anteater (horiz) 1·00 1·00
1570 $2 Scarlet macaw 1·75 1·75
1571 $2 W.H.O. emblem (black and blue) (horiz) 1·25 1·25
1572 $3 Wolfgang Amadeus Mozart 2·50 2·50
1573 $4 The Berlin Airlift (horiz) 2·50 2·50
1574 $4 Repairing "Intelsat VI" satellite in space (horiz) 2·50 2·50
1575 $5 Zeppelin "Hindenburg" on fire (horiz) 2·75 2·75
1576 $5 Admiral Richard Byrd's Ford Trimotor aircraft (horiz) 2·75 2·75
ANNIVERSARIES AND EVENTS: Nos. 1566, 1575, 75th death anniv of Count Ferdinand von Zeppelin; Nos. 1567, 1574, International Space Year; Nos. 1568, 1573, 25th death anniv of Konrad Adenauer (German statesman); Nos. 1569/70, Earth Summit '92, Rio; No. 1571, United Nations World Health Organization Projects; No. 1572, Death bicentenary of Mozart; No. 1576, 75th anniv of International Association of Lions Clubs.

104 "Atalanta" and "Mischief" (yachts), 1881

105 "Battus polydamus"

1992. History of The Americas Cup Challenge Trophy. Multicoloured.
1578 15 c. Type **104** 20 20
1579 25 c. "Valkyrie III" and "Defender", 1895 30 30
1580 35 c. "Shamrock IV" and "Resolute", 1920 45 45
1581 75 c. "Endeavour II" and "Ranger", 1937 70 70
1582 $1 "Sceptre" and "Columbia", 1958 85 85
1583 $2 "Australia II" and "Liberty", 1983 1·50 1·75
1584 $4 "Stars & Stripes" and "Kookaburra III", 1987 2·40 3·00
1585 $5 "New Zealand" and "Stars & Stripes", 1988 2·50 3·00

1993. Dogs of the World. As T **377** of Grenada, but vert. Multicoloured.
1587 35 c. Irish setter and Glendalough, Ireland 40 30
1588 50 c. Boston terrier and Boston State House, U.S.A. 60 45
1589 75 c. Beagle and Temple to Athena, Greece 90 55
1590 $1 Weimaraner and Nesselwang, Germany 1·10 75
1591 $3 Norwegian elkhound and Urnes Stave Church, Norway 2·25 2·50
1592 $4 Mastiff and Sphinx, Egypt 2·50 2·75
1593 $5 Akita and Torii Temple, Kyoto, Japan 2·50 2·75
1594 $5 Saluki and Rub'al Khali, Saudi Arabia 2·50 2·75

1993. Bicentenary of the Louvre, Paris. As T **305** of Antigua. Multicoloured (except No. 1599).
1596 $1 "Madonna and Child with the young John the Baptist" (Botticelli) 80 80
1597 $1 "The Buffet" (Chardin) 80 80
1598 $1 "Return from Market" (Chardin) 80 80
1599 $1 "Erasmus" (Durer) (black and grey) 80 80
1600 $1 "Self-portrait with Eryngium" (Durer) 80 80
1601 $1 "Jeanne of Aragon" (Raphael) 80 80
1602 $1 "La Belle Jardiniere" (detail) (Raphael) 80 80
1603 $1 "La Belle Jardiniere" (different detail) (Raphael) 80 80

1993. Butterflies. Multicoloured.
1605 15 c. Type **105** 40 20
1606 35 c. "Astraptes talus" 55 20
1607 45 c. "Pseudolycaena marsyas" 55 25
1608 75 c. "Siproeta stelenes" 70 50
1609 $1 "Phoebis sennae" 80 60
1610 $2 "Dione juno" 1·40 1·40
1611 $4 "Chlorostrymon simaethis" 2·25 2·75
1612 $5 "Urbanus proteus" 2·50 2·75

1993. Flowers. As T **380** of Grenada. Mult.
1614 35 c. Hibiscus 50 20
1615 35 c. Columbine 50 20
1616 45 c. Red ginger 50 25
1617 75 c. Bougainvillea 70 50
1618 $1 Crown imperial 80 60
1619 $2 Fairy orchid 1·40 1·40
1620 $4 Heliconia 2·25 2·75
1621 $5 Tulip 2·50 2·75

1993. 40th Anniv of Coronation. As T **307** of Antigua.
1623 35 c. multicoloured 15 40
1624 50 c. multicoloured 25 50
1625 $2 green and black 90 1·10
1626 $4 multicoloured 1·90 2·00
DESIGNS: 35 c. Queen Elizabeth II at Coronation (photograph by Cecil Beaton); 50 c. Ampulla and spoon; $2 Queen Elizabeth II leaving for Coronation; $4 Prince Henry's christening.

1993. Anniversaries and Events. As T **381** of Grenada. Multicoloured.
1628 15 c. "Painter and Model" (Picasso) (horiz) 55 30
1629 35 c. Keith Tkachuk and Dmitri Mironov (ice hockey, 1992) (horiz) 80 40
1630 50 c. Early telescope 85 50
1631 75 c. "Gra w Gudziki" (Ludomir Slerdinski) (horiz) 90 70
1632 75 c. Willy Brandt and Lyndon Johnson, 1961 (horiz) 90 70
1633 $1 "Artist and his Model" (Picasso) (horiz) 1·00 80
1634 $2 "Pocalunek Mongolskiego Ksiecia" (S. Wirkiewicz) (horiz) 1·40 1·40
1635 $4 "The Drawing Lesson" (Picasso) (horiz) 2·25 2·25
1636 $4 Radio telescope 2·25 2·25
1637 $5 Alberto Tomba (Giant Slalom, 1984) (horiz) 2·25 2·40
1638 $5 Willy Brandt and Eleanor Hulles, 1957 (horiz) 2·25 2·40
ANNIVERSARIES AND EVENTS: Nos. 1628, 1633, 1635, 20th death anniv of Picasso (artist); Nos. 1629, 1637, Winter Olympic Games '94, Lillehammer; Nos. 1630, 1636, 450th death anniv of Copernicus (astronomer); Nos. 1631, 1634, Polska '93 International Stamp Exhibition, Poznan; Nos. 1632, 1638, 80th birth anniv of Willy Brandt (German politician).

1993. Songbirds. As T **382** of Grenada. Multicoloured.
1640 15 c. Painted bunting 35 35
1641 15 c. White-throated sparrow 35 35
1642 25 c. Common grackle 40 40
1643 25 c. Amazonian royal flycatcher 40 40
1644 35 c. Swallow tanager 45 45
1645 35 c. Vermilion flycatcher 45 45
1646 45 c. Black-headed bunting 50 50
1647 50 c. Rose-breasted grosbeak 50 50
1648 75 c. Corn bunting 60 60
1649 75 c. Rose-breasted thrush tanager 60 60
1650 $1 Buff-throated saltator 75 75
1651 $4 Plush-capped finch 2·25 2·25
Nos. 1640/51 were printed together, se-tenant, with the backgrounds forming a composite design. Nos. 1645/6 show the scientific inscriptions transposed between the designs.

1993. Shells. As T **383** of Grenada. Mult.
1653 15 c. Hawk-wing conch 25 25
1654 15 c. Music volute 25 25
1655 25 c. Globe vase and deltoid rock shell 30 30
1656 35 c. Spiny Caribbean vase 30 30
1657 35 c. American common sundial and common purple janthina 30 30
1658 45 c. Toothed donax and gaudy asaphis 35 35
1659 45 c. Mouse cone 35 35
1660 50 c. Gold-mouthed triton 40 40
1661 75 c. Tulip mussel and trigonal tivela 50 50
1662 75 c. Common dove shell and chestnut latirus 50 50
1663 $1 Wide-mouthed purpura 60 60
1664 $4 American thorny oyster and Atlantic wing oyster 1·90 2·00
Nos. 1653/64 were printed together, se-tenant, with the backgrounds forming a composite design.

1993 Asian International Stamp Exhibitions. As T **268** of Dominica. Multicoloured. (a) "Indopex '93", Surabaya, Indonesia.
1666 35 c. National Museum, Central Jakarta (horiz) 30 20
1667 45 c. Sacred wheel and deer (horiz) 35 25
1668 $1 Ramayana relief, Panataran Temple (horiz) 60 60
1669 $1.50 "Bullock Carts" (Batara Lubis) (horiz) 1·00 1·00
1670 $1.50 "Surat Irsa II" (A. D. Pirous) (horiz) 1·00 1·00
1671 $1.50 "Self-portrait with Goat" (Kartika) (horiz) 1·00 1·00
1672 $1.50 "The Cow-est Cow" (Ivan Sagito) (horiz) 1·00 1·00
1673 $1.50 "Rain Storm" (Sudjana Kerton) (horiz) 1·00 1·00
1674 $1.50 "Story of Pucuk Flower" (Effendi) (horiz) 1·00 1·00
1675 $5 Candi Tikus, Trawulan, East Java (horiz) 2·50 2·75

(b) "Taipei '93", Taiwan.
1677 35 c. Macau Palace Casino, Hong Kong (horiz) 30 20
1678 45 c. Stone lion, Ming Tomb, Nanjing (horiz) 35 25
1679 $1 Stone camels, Ming Tomb, Nanjing (horiz) 60 60
1680 $1.50 Nesting quail incense burner (horiz) 1·00 1·00
1681 $1.50 Standing quail incense burner (horiz) 1·00 1·00
1682 $1.50 Seated qilin incense burner (horiz) 1·00 1·00
1683 $1.50 Pottery horse, Han period (horiz) 1·00 1·00
1684 $1.50 Seated caparisoned elephant (horiz) 1·00 1·00
1685 $1.50 Cow in imitation of Delft faience (horiz) 1·00 1·00
1686 $5 Stone lion and elephant, Ming Tomb, Nanjing (horiz) 2·50 2·75

(c) "Bangkok 1993", Thailand.
1688 35 c. Three Naga snakes, Chiang Mai's Temple (horiz) 30 20
1689 45 c. Sri Mariamman Temple, Singapore (horiz) 35 25
1690 $1 Topiary, Hua Hin Resort (horiz) 60 60
1691 $1.50 "Buddha's Victory over Mara" (horiz) 1·00 1·00
1692 $1.50 "Mythological Elephant" (horiz) 1·00 1·00
1693 $1.50 "Battle with Mara" (Thon Buri) (horiz) 1·00 1·00
1694 $1.50 "Untitled" (Panya Wijinthanasarn) (horiz) 1·00 1·00
1695 $1.50 "Temple Mural" (horiz) 1·00 1·00
1696 $1.50 "Elephants in Pahcekha Buddha's Heaven" (horiz) 1·00 1·00
1697 $5 Pak Tai Temple, Cheung Chau Island (horiz) 2·50 2·75

1993. World Cup Football Championship, U.S.A. (1994) (1st issue). As T **310** of Antigua. Mult.
1699 15 c. McCall (Scotland) and Verri (Brazil) (horiz) 30 20
1700 25 c. Verri (Brazil) and Maradona (Argentina) (horiz) 40 20
1701 35 c. Schillaci (Italy) and Saldana (Uruguay) (horiz) 45 25
1702 45 c. Gullit (Holland) and Wright (England) (horiz) 50 35
1703 $1 Verri (Brazil) and Maradona (Argentina) (different) (horiz) 70 70
1704 $2 Zubizarreta and Fernandez (Spain) with Albert (Belgium) (horiz) 1·25 1·25
1705 $4 Hagi (Rumania) and McGrath (Ireland) (horiz) 2·25 2·40
1706 $5 Gorriz (Spain) and Scifo (Belgium) (horiz) 2·25 2·40
See also Nos. 1810/15.

1993. 65th Anniv of Mickey Mouse. Scenes from Walt Disney cartoon films. As T **385** of Grenada.
1708 15 c. "Mickey's Rival", 1936 40 25
1709 35 c. "The Worm Turns", 1937 55 25
1710 50 c. "The Pointer", 1939 70 55
1711 75 c. "Society Dog Show", 1939 90 90
1712 $1 "A Gentleman's Gentleman", 1941 1·00 1·00
1713 $2 "The Little Whirlwind", 1941 1·75 2·00
1714 $4 "Mickey Down Under", 1948 2·75 3·00
1715 $5 "R'coon Dawg", 1951 2·75 3·00

1993. Christmas. Religious Paintings. As T **270** of Dominica. Black, yellow and red (Nos. 1717 and 1721/3) or multicoloured (others).
1717 10 c. "Adoration of the Shepherds" (detail) (Durer) 30 20
1718 25 c. "Adoration of the Magi" (detail) (Raphael) 40 20
1719 35 c. "Presentation at the Temple" (detail) (Raphael) 45 20
1720 50 c. "Adoration of the Magi" (different detail) (Raphael) 55 35
1721 75 c. "Adoration of the Shepherds" (different detail) (Durer) 90 60
1722 $1 "Adoration of the Shepherds" (different detail) (Durer) 1·00 75
1723 $4 "Adoration of the Shepherds" (different detail) (Durer) 2·50 3·00
1724 $5 "Presentation at the Temple" (different detail) (Raphael) 2·50 3·00

1993. Aviation Anniversaries. As T **386** of Grenada. Multicoloured.
1726 15 c. Avro Lancaster 30 20
1727 35 c. Blanchard's balloon crossing the River Delaware 15 20
1728 50 c. Airship "Graf Zeppelin" over Rio de Janeiro 50 35
1729 75 c. Hugo Eckener 65 50
1730 $3 Pres. Washington handing passport to Blanchard 1·40 1·50
1731 $5 Short Sunderland flying boat 2·50 2·75
1732 $5 Eckener in "Graf Zeppelin" 2·50 2·75
ANNIVERSARIES: Nos. 1726, 1731, 75th anniv of Royal Air Force; Nos. 1727, 1730, Bicentenary of first airmail flight; Nos. 1728/9, 1732, 125th birth anniv of Hugo Eckener (airship commander).

1993. Centenaries of Henry Ford's First Petrol Engine (Nos. 1735/6) and Karl Benz's First Four-wheeled Car (others). As T **387** of Grenada. Multicoloured.
1734 25 c. Mercedes Benz "300 SLR", 1955 . . . . . . 30 20
1735 45 c. Ford "Thunderbird", 1957 20 25
1736 $4 Ford "150-A" station wagon, 1929 . . . . . . 1·90 2·00
1737 $5 Mercedes Benz "540 K" . 2·75 3·00

1993. Famous Paintings by Rembrandt and Matisse. As T **316** of Antigua. Multicoloured.
1739 15 c. "Hendrickje Stoffels as Flora" (Rembrandt) . . . 40 25
1740 35 c. "Lady and Gentleman in Black" (Rembrandt) . . . 50 25
1741 50 c. "Aristotle with the Bust of Homer" (Rembrandt) . . . 60 40
1742 75 c. "Interior: Flowers and Parakeets" (Matisse) . . . 85 60
1743 $1 "Goldfish" (Matisse) . . . 1·00 85
1744 $2 "The Girl with Green Eyes" (Matisse) . . . . 1·75 2·00
1745 $3 "Still Life with a Plaster Figure" (Matisse) . . . . . 2·00 2·50
1746 $5 "Christ and the Woman of Samaria" (Rembrandt) . . 2·50 2·75

1994. "Hong Kong '94" International Stamp Exhibition (1st issue). As T **317** of Antigua. Multicoloured.
1748 40 c. Hong Kong 1984 $5 aviation stamp and airliner at Kai Tak Airport 40 50
1749 40 c. Grenada Grenadines 1988 20 c. airships stamp and junk in Kowloon Bay 40 50
Nos. 1748/9 were printed together, se-tenant, forming a composite design.
See also Nos. 1750/5.

1994. "Hong Kong '94" International Stamp Exhibition (2nd issue). Jade Sculptures. As T **318** of Antigua, but horiz. Multicoloured.
1750 45 c. White jade brush washer 35 40
1751 45 c. Archaic jade brush washer 35 40
1752 45 c. Dark green jade brush washer 35 40
1753 45 c. Green jade almsbowl . . 35 40
1754 45 c. Archaic jade dog . . . 35 40
1755 45 c. Yellow jade brush washer 35 40

1994. Fungi. As T **390** of Grenada, but with white backgrounds. Multicoloured.
1756 35 c. "Hygrocybe hypohaemacta" 45 30
1757 45 c. "Cantharellus cinnabarinus" 55 35
1758 50 c. "Marasmius haematocephalus" 60 40
1759 75 c. "Mycena pura" 80 60
1760 $1 "Gymnopilus russipes" . . 90 80
1761 $2 "Calocybe cyanocephala" 1·40 1·50
1762 $4 "Pluteus chrysophlebius" . 2·50 2·75
1763 $5 "Chlorophyllum molybdites" . . . . 2·50 2·75
No. 1757 is inscribed "Cantherellus cinnabarinus" and No. 1762 "Pleuteus chrysophlebius", both in error.

1994. Prehistoric Animals. As T **391** of Grenada. Multicoloured.
1765 15 c. Spinosaurus 30 25
1766 35 c. Apatosaurus (Brontosaurus) 45 30
1767 45 c. Tyrannosaurus rex . . . 50 35
1768 55 c. Triceratops 50 40
1769 $1 Pachycephalosaurus 85 75
1770 $2 Pteranodon . . . . . . 1·40 1·50
1771 $4 Parasaurolophus . . . . . 2·50 2·75
1772 $5 Brachiosaurus . . . . . 2·50 2·75

1994. 25th Anniv of First Manned Moon Landing. Space Shuttle "Challenger". As T **326** of Antigua. Multicoloured.
1774 $1.10 "Challenger" crew in training . . . . 1·00 1·10
1775 $1.10 Christa McAuliffe (astronaut) . . . . 1·00 1·10
1776 $1.10 "Challenger" on launch pad . . . . 1·00 1·10
1777 $1.10 Gregory Jarvis (astronaut) . . . . 1·00 1·10
1778 $1.10 Ellison Onizuka (astronaut) . . . . 1·00 1·10
1779 $1.10 Ronald McNair (astronaut) . . . . 1·00 1·10

1994. Centenary of International Olympic Committee. Gold Medal Winners. As T **327** of Antigua. Multicoloured.
1781 50 c. Silke Renk (Germany) (javelin), 1992 . . . . . 35 30
1782 $1.50 Mark Spitz (U.S.A.) (swimming), 1972 . . . . 90 1·10

1994. International Year of the Family. As T **328** of Antigua. Multicoloured.
1784 $1 Grenadines family 60 60

1994. 50th Anniv of D-Day. As T **331** of Antigua. Multicoloured.
1785 40 c. Churchill bridge-laying tank 35 30
1786 $2 Sherman "Firefly" tank leaving landing craft . . . 1·00 1·25
1787 $3 Churchill "Crocodile" flame-thrower . . . . 1·60 1·75

1994. "Philakorea '94" International Stamp Exhibition, Seoul (1st issue). As T **281** of Dominica. Multicoloured.
1789 40 c. Onung Tomb (horiz) . . 30 30
1790 $1 Stone pagoda, Mt Namsam (horiz) 55 55
1791 $1 "Admiring Spring in the Country" (left detail) (Sin Yunbok) 55 55
1792 $1 "Admiring Spring in the Country" (right detail) . . 55 55
1793 $1 "Woman on Dano Day" (left detail) (Sin Yunbok) . . . 55 55
1794 $1 "Woman on Dano Day" (right detail) 55 55
1795 $1 "Enjoying Lotuses while Listening to Music" (left detail) (Sin Yunbok) . . . 55 55
1796 $1 "Enjoying Lotuses while Listening to Music" (right detail) 55 55
1797 $1 "Women by a Crystal Stream" (left detail) (Sin Yunbok) 55 55
1798 $1 "Women by a Crystal Stream" (right detail) . . 55 55
1799 $4 Pusan (horiz) . . . . . 2·25 2·25
The two details of each painting on Nos. 1791/8 were printed together, se-tenant, each pair forming a composite design.
See also Nos. 1817/30.

1994. Orchids. As T **392** of Grenada. Multicoloured.
1801 15 c. "Cattleya aurantiaca" . 35 25
1802 25 c. "Blettia patula" . . . 40 25
1803 45 c. "Sobralia macrantha" . 50 30
1804 75 c. "Encyclia belizensis" . . 70 55
1805 $1 "Sophrolaeliocattleya" . . 85 75
1806 $2 "Encyclia fragrans" . . . 1·40 1·50
1807 $4 "Schombocattleya" . . . 2·50 2·75
1808 $5 "Brassolaeliocattleya" . . 2·50 2·75

1994. World Cup Football Championship, U.S.A. (2nd issue). As T **393** of Grenada. Multicoloured.
1810 75 c. Steve Mark (Grenada) 50 50
1811 75 c. Jurgen Kohler (Germany) 50 50
1812 75 c. Almir (Brazil) 50 50
1813 75 c. Michael Windischmann (U.S.A.) 50 50
1814 75 c. Guiseppe Giannini (Italy) 50 50
1815 75 c. Rashidi Yekini (Nigeria) 50 50

106 Mickey Mouse and Unjin Miruk Window from Kwanch Ok Temple

1994. "Philakorea '94" International Stamp Exhibition, Seoul (2nd issue). Walt Disney cartoon characters. Multicoloured.
1817 3 c. Type **106** 15 15
1818 4 c. Goofy imitating statue of Admiral Yi, Chonju 15 15
1819 5 c. Cousin Gus and Donald Duck eating dinner . . . 15 15
1820 10 c. Mickey playing flute . . 20 15
1821 15 c. Goofy with Tolharubang (statue) 30 20
1822 15 c. Type **106** 30 20
1823 20 c. Mickey and Minnie at Hyang-Wonjong 30 20
1824 35 c. As 4 c. 40 25
1825 50 c. As 5 c. 50 35
1826 75 c. As 10 c. 70 55
1827 $1 As 15 c. 85 75
1828 $2 As 20 c. . . . . 1·40 1·50
1829 $4 Mickey as Somori-Kut shaman . . . . 2·50 2·75
1830 $5 Minnie holding ceremonial fan . . . . 2·50 2·75

1994. 1st Recipients of Order of the Caribbean Community. As Nos. 2046/8 of Antigua. Multicoloured.
1832 25 c. Sir Shridath Ramphal . 10 10
1833 50 c. William Demas 25 30
1834 $2 Derek Walcott . . . . . 1·40 1·60

1994. Fishes. As T **394** of Grenada. Multicoloured.
1835 75 c. Porkfish 55 55
1836 75 c. Blue chromis 55 55
1837 75 c. Caribbean reef shark (facing left) 55 55
1838 75 c. Long-spined squirrelfish 55 55
1839 75 c. Four-eyed butterflyfish 55 55
1840 75 c. Blue head 55 55
1841 75 c. Royal gramma 55 55
1842 75 c. Sharp-nosed puffer . . 55 55
1843 75 c. Reid's seahorse 55 55
1844 75 c. Black-barred soldierfish 55 55
1845 75 c. Red-lipped blenny . . . 55 55
1846 75 c. Painted wrasse 55 55
1847 75 c. Yellow-tailed snapper . . 55 55
1848 75 c. Caribbean reef shark (facing right) 55 55
1849 75 c. Great barracuda 55 55
1850 75 c. Red-tailed parrotfish . . 55 55
1851 75 c. Blue tang 55 55
1852 75 c. Queen angelfish 55 55
1853 75 c. Red hind 55 55
1854 75 c. Rock beauty 55 55
1855 75 c. Queen parrotfish 55 55
1856 75 c. Spanish hogfish 55 55
1857 75 c. Spotted moray 55 55
1858 75 c. Queen triggerfish . . . 55 55
Nos. 1835/46 and 1847/58 respectively were printed together, se-tenant, forming composite designs.

1994 Christmas. Religious Paintings by Bartolome Murillo. As T **336** of Antigua. Multicoloured.
1860 15 c. "The Annunciation" . . 20 20
1861 35 c. "The Adoration of the Shepherds" 30 20
1862 50 c. "Virgin and Child with St. Rose" 40 30
1863 50 c. "Flight into Egypt" . . 40 30
1864 75 c. "Virgin and Child" . . 60 45
1865 $1 "Virgin of the Rosary" . . 75 60
1866 $4 "The Holy Family" . . . 2·25 2·75

1995. Birds. As T **397** of Grenada. Multicoloured.
1868 25 c. Scaly-breasted ground dove (vert) 35 25
1869 50 c. White-winged dove . . . 60 45
1870 $2 Inca dove (vert) . . . . . 1·40 1·50
1871 $4 Mourning dove . . . . . 2·25 2·75

1995. Centenary of First English Cricket Tour to the West Indies. As T **329** of Antigua. Multicoloured.
1872 50 c. Mike Atherton (England) and Wisden Trophy . . . 45 35
1873 75 c. Curtly Ambrose (West Indies) (vert) 65 65
1874 $1 Brian Lara (West Indies) (vert) . . . . 85 1·00

107 Aspects of London, National Flag and Map

108 Pig

1995. Capitals of the World. Aspects of various cities, national flags and maps. Multicoloured.
1876 $1 Type **107** 45 50
1877 $1 Cairo 45 50
1878 $1 Vienna 45 50
1879 $1 Paris 45 50
1880 $1 Rome 45 50
1881 $1 Budapest 45 50
1882 $1 Moscow 45 50
1883 $1 Peking ("Beijing") 45 50
1884 $1 Tokyo 45 50
1885 $1 Washington 45 50

1995. Chinese New Year ("Year of the Pig"). Multicoloured designs showing "GRENADA GRENADINES" in colours indicated.
1886 75 c. Type **108** (violet) . . . 35 40
1887 75 c. Pig (carmine) 35 40
1888 75 c. Pig (brown) 35 40
1889 75 c. Pig (vermilion) 35 40

109 Bull Shark and Diver

1995. Marine Life of the Caribbean. Multicoloured.
1891 $1 Type **109** 45 50
1892 $1 Great white shark 45 50
1893 $1 Octopus and shoal of fish . 45 50
1894 $1 Great barracuda 45 50
1895 $1 Green moray 45 50
1896 $1 Spotted eagle ray 45 50
1897 $1 Sea snake 45 50
1898 $1 Stingray 45 50
1899 $1 Grouper 45 50
1900 $1 Dolphins 45 50
1901 $1 Lionfish 45 50
1902 $1 Sea turtle and rock beauty (fish) 45 50
1903 $1 Blue-cheeked butterflyfish and nurse shark 45 50
1904 $1 Queen angelfish 45 50
1905 $1 Grouper and coney 45 50
1906 $1 Rainbow eel and spotted moray 45 50
1907 $1 Sun flower-star and coral crab 45 50
1908 $1 Octopus on sea bed . . . 45 50

110 Suffolk Punch

1995. Domestic Animals. Multicoloured.
1910 15 c. Type **110** 10 10
1911 25 c. Shetland pony 10 10
1912 75 c. Blue persian (cat) . . . 35 40
1913 75 c. Sorrel abyssinian (cat) . 35 40
1914 75 c. White angora (cat) . . . 35 40
1915 75 c. Brown Burmese (cat) . . 35 40
1916 75 c. Red tabby exotic shorthair (cat) 35 40
1917 75 c. Seal-point birman (cat) . 35 40
1918 75 c. Korat (cat) 35 40
1919 75 c. Norwegian forest cat . . 35 40
1920 75 c. Lilac-point Balinese (cat) 35 40
1921 75 c. British shorthair (cat) . 35 40
1922 75 c. Red self longhair (cat) . 35 40
1923 75 c. Calico Manx (cat) . . . 35 40
1924 75 c. Shetland sheepdog . . . 35 40
1925 75 c. Bull terrier 35 40
1926 75 c. Afghan hound 35 40
1927 75 c. Scottish terrier 35 40
1928 75 c. Labrador retriever . . . 35 40
1929 75 c. English springer spaniel 35 40
1930 75 c. Samoyed (dog) 35 40
1931 75 c. Irish setter 35 40
1932 75 c. Border collie 35 40
1933 75 c. Pekingese 35 40
1934 75 c. Dachshund 35 40
1935 75 c. Weimaraner (dog) . . . 35 40
1936 $1 Arab 45 50
1937 $3 Shire horse . . . . . . 1·25 1·40

1995. Centenary (1992) of Sierra Club (environmental protection society). Endangered Species. As T **320** of Antigua. Multicoloured.
1939 $1 Spotted owl 45 50
1940 $1 Brown pelican on perch . 45 50
1941 $1 Head of brown pelican . 45 50
1942 $1 Head of jaguarundi . . . 45 50
1943 $1 Jaguarundi looking over shoulder 45 50
1944 $1 Maned wolf in undergrowth 45 50
1945 $1 American wood stork standing on two legs . . . 45 50
1946 $1 American wood stork standing on one leg . . . 45 50
1947 $1 Close-up of maned wolf . 45 50
1948 $1 Brown pelican (horiz) . . 45 50
1949 $1 Close-up of spotted owl (horiz) 45 50
1950 $1 Spotted owl chick (horiz) 45 50
1951 $1 Jaguarundi (horiz) 45 50
1952 $1 Central American spider monkey sitting with young (horiz) 45 50
1953 $1 Central American spider monkey carrying young (horiz) 45 50
1954 $1 Central American spider monkey swinging from branch (horiz) 45 50
1955 $1 American wood stork (horiz) 45 50
1956 $1 Pair of maned wolfs (horiz) 45 50

1995. 18th World Scout Jamboree, Netherlands. As T **403** of Grenada. Multicoloured.
1957 75 c. Grenadian scout on beach 35 40
1958 $1 Scout with staff on hill . 45 50
1959 $2 Scout saluting and national flag 85 90

1995. 50th Anniv of End of Second World War in Europe. Bombers. As T **340** of Antigua. Mult.
1961 $2 Avro Type **683** Lancaster 85 90
1962 $2 Junkers Ju 88 . . . . . 85 90
1963 $2 North American B-25 Mitchell 85 90
1964 $2 Boeing B-17 Flying Fortress 85 90
1965 $2 Petlyakov Pe-2 . . . . . 85 90
1966 $2 Martin B-26 Marauder . . 85 90
1967 $2 Heinkel He 111H 85 90
1968 $2 Consolidated B-24 Liberator 85 90

1995. 50th Anniv of United Nations. As T **404** of Grenada. Multicoloured.
1970 75 c. U.N. Headquarters, New York, and flag 35 40
1971 $1 Trygve Lie (first Secretary-General) 45 50
1972 $2 U.N. soldier 85 90
Nos. 1970/2 were printed together, se-tenant, forming a composite design.

1995. 50th Anniv of F.A.O. As T **405** of Grenada. Multicoloured.
1974 75 c. Man hoeing 35 40
1975 $1 Woman hoeing 45 50
1976 $2 Man and woman hoeing . . 90 95
Nos. 1974/6 were printed together, se-tenant, forming a composite design.

1995. 90th Anniv of Rotary International. As T **406** of Grenada. Multicoloured.
1978 $5 Paul Harris (founder) and logo (horiz) . . . . . . 2·10 2·25

1995. 95th Birthday of Queen Elizabeth the Queen Mother. As T **344** of Antigua.
1980 $1.50 brown, light brown and black 65 70
1981 $1.50 multicoloured 65 70
1982 $1.50 multicoloured 65 70
1983 $1.50 multicoloured 65 70
DESIGNS: No. 1980, Queen Elizabeth the Queen Mother (pastel drawing); 1981, At Remembrance Day service; 1982, At desk (oil painting); 1983, Wearing green hat.

1995. 50th Anniv of End of Second World War in the Pacific. As T **340** of Antigua. Multicoloured.
1985 $2 Mitsubishi G4M1 "Betty" (bomber) 85 90
1986 $2 Japanese submarine "I 14" with seaplane on catapault 85 90
1987 $2 Mitsubishi GM31 "Nell" (bomber) 85 90
1988 $2 "Akizuki" (Japanese destroyer) 85 90
1989 $2 "Kirishima" (Japanese battleship) 85 90
1990 $2 "Asigari" (Japanese cruiser) 85 90

1995. Olympic Games, Atlanta (1996). As T **407** of Grenada. Multicoloured.
1992 15 c. Rosemary Ackerman (East Germany) (high jump) (horiz) 10 10
1993 15 c. Li Ning (China) (gymnastics) (horiz) . . . 10 10
1994 15 c. Denise Parker (U.S.A.) (archery) (horiz) 10 10
1995 $3 Terry Carlisle (U.S.A.) (skeet shooting) (horiz) . . . . . 1·25 1·40
1996 $3 Kathleen Nord (East Germany) (swimming) (horiz) . . . . 1·25 1·40
1997 $3 Brigit Schmidt (East Germany) (canoeing) (horiz) 1·25 1·40

111 Brown Pelican

1995. Birds of the Caribbean. Multicoloured.
1999 10 c. Type **111** 10 10
2000 15 c. Black-necked stilt . . . 10 10
2001 25 c. Cuban trogon 10 10
2002 35 c. Greater flamingo . . . 15 20
2003 75 c. Imperial amazon . . . 35 40
2004 $1 Pintail 45 50
2005 $1 Great blue heron 45 50
2006 $1 Jamaican tody 45 50
2007 $1 Laughing gull 45 50
2008 $1 Purple-throated carib . . 45 50
2009 $1 Red-legged thrush 45 50
2010 $1 Ruddy duck 45 50
2011 $1 Common shoveler 45 50
2012 $1 West Indian red-bellied woodpecker 45 50
2013 $2 Ringed kingfisher 85 90
2014 $3 Strip-headed tanager . . . 1·25 1·40

No. 2001 is inscr "Cuban Trogan", No. 2008 "Purple-throated Carb" and No. 2013 Ringed King Fisher, all in error.

1995. Mickey's Pirate Adventure. Walt Disney Cartoon Characters. As T **415** of Grenada. Multicoloured.
2016 10 c. Goofy and Donald Duck with treasure chests (horiz) 10 10
2017 35 c. Mickey and Minnie Mouse at ship's wheel (horiz) . . . 15 20
2018 75 c. Mickey, Donald and Goofy opening chest (horiz) 35 40
2019 $1 Big Pete and rats confronting Mickey (horiz) 45 50
2020 $2 Mickey, Goofy and Donald in boat (horiz) 90 95
2021 $5 Goofy fighting rat pirate with mop (horiz) . . . . 2·25 2·40

1995. Centenary of Nobel Trust Fund. As T **416** of Grenada. Multicoloured.
2023/51 75 c. × 2, $1 × 27 Set of 29 . . . . 13·50 14·00

DESIGNS: 75 c. W. Arthur Lewis (1979 Economics); Derek Walcott (1992 Literature); $1 Jules Border (1919 Medicine); Rene Cassin (1968 Peace); Verner von Heidenstam (1916 Literature); Jose Echegaray (1904 Literature); Otto Wallach (1910 Chemistry); Corneille Heymans (1938 Medicine); Ivar Giaever (1973 Physics); Sir William Cremer (1903 Peace); John Strutt (1904 Physics); James Franck (1925 Physics); Tobias Asser (1911 Peace); Carl Spitteler (1919 Literature); Christiaan Eijkman (1929 Medicine); Ragnar Granit (1967 Medicine); Frederic Passy (1901 Peace); Louis Neel (1970 Physics); Sir William Ramsay (1904 Chemistry); Philip Noel-Baker (1959 Peace); Heike Onnes (1913 Physics); Fridtjof Nansen (1922 Peace); Sir Ronald Ross (1902 Medicine); Paul Muller (1948 Medicine); Allvar Gullstrand (1911 Medicine); Gerhart Hauptmann (1912 Literature); Hans Spemann (1935 Medicine); Cecil Powell (1950 Physics); Walther Bothe (1954 Physics).

Nos. 2025/33, 2034/42 and 2043/51 respectively were printed together, se-tenant, forming composite designs.

No. 2027 (Von Heidenstam) is inscribed "1906" and No. 2044 "Fridtjof Nanser", both in error.

112 Nita Naldi and Rudolph Valentino

114 Symbolic Rat and Candle

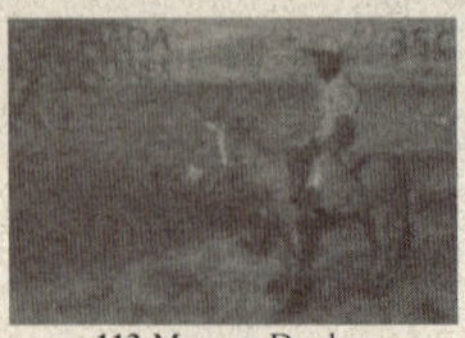
113 Man on Donkey

1995. Centenary of Cinema. Multicoloured.
2053 $1 Type **112** 45 50
2054 $1 Ramon Novaro and Alice Terry 45 50
2055 $1 Frederic March and Joan Crawford 45 50
2056 $1 Clark Gable and Vivien Leigh 45 50
2057 $1 Barbara Stanwyck and Burt Lancaster 45 50
2058 $1 Warren Beatty and Natalie Wood 45 50
2059 $1 Spencer Tracy and Katharine Hepburn 45 50
2060 $1 Humphrey Bogart and Lauren Bacall 45 50
2061 $1 Omar Sharif and Julie Christie 45 50
2062 $1 Marion Davies 45 50
2063 $1 Marlene Dietrich 45 50
2064 $1 Lillian Gish 45 50
2065 $1 Bette Davis 45 50
2066 $1 Elizabeth Taylor 45 50
2067 $1 Veronica Lake 45 50
2068 $1 Ava Gardner 45 50
2069 $1 Grace Kelly 45 50
2070 $1 Kim Novak 45 50

Nos. 2053/61 and 2062/70 respectively were printed together, se-tenant, forming composite designs.

1995. Racing Cars. As T **423** of Grenada. Multicoloured.
2072 10 c. Williams-Renault Formula 1, 1990s 10 10
2073 25 c. Porsche "956", Le Mans, 1980s 10 15
2074 35 c. Lotus "John Player Special", 1970s 15 20
2075 75 c. Ford "GT-40", 1960s . . 35 40
2076 $2 Mercedes-Benz "W196", 1950s 85 90
2077 $3 Mercedes "SSK", 1920s . 1·25 1·40

1995. Local Transport. Multicoloured.
2079 35 c. Type **113** 15 20
2080 75 c. Local bus 35 40

1995. Evolution of Sailing Ships. As T **427** of Grenada. Multicoloured.
2081 $1 "Preussen" (full-rigged ship) 45 50
2082 $1 Japanese junk 45 50
2083 $1 Caribbean pirate ship . . 45 50
2084 $1 "Mayflower" (Pilgrim Fathers) 45 50
2085 $1 Chinese junk 45 50
2086 $1 "Santa Maria" (Columbus) 45 50

1995. Christmas. Religious Paintings. As T **357** of Antigua. Multicoloured.
2088 10 c. "Immaculate Conception" (Piero di Cosimo) 10 10
2089 15 c. "St. Michael dedicating Arms to the Madonna" (Le Nain) 10 10
2090 35 c. "Annunciation" (Lorenzo di Credi) 15 20
2091 50 c. "The Holy Family" (Jacob Jordaens) 25 30
2092 $3 "Madonna and Child" (Lippi) . . . . 1·25 1·40
2093 $5 "Madonna and Child with Ten Saints" (Fiorentino) . 2·10 2·25

1996. Chinese New Year ("Year of the Rat"). Multicoloured, background colours given.
2095 **114** 75 c. blue 35 40
2096 75 c. lilac 35 40
2097 75 c. brown 35 40
2098 75 c. green 35 40

The four designs show different Chinese characters.

1996. Works of Art by Durer and Rubens. As T **421** of Grenada. Multicoloured.
2101 15 c. "The Centaur Family" (Durer) 10 10
2102 35 c. "Oriental Ruler Seated" (Durer) 15 20
2103 50 c. "The Entombment" (Durer) 25 30
2104 75 c. "Man in Armour" (Rubens) 35 40
2105 $1 "Peace embracing Plenty" (Rubens) 45 50
2106 $2 "Departure of Lot" (Rubens) 85 90
2107 $3 "The Four Evangelists" (Rubens) . . . . 1·25 1·40
2108 $5 "Knight, Death and Devil" (Durer) . . . . 2·10 2·25

115 Mickey and Minnie at New Year's Day "Hopping John" Tradition

1996. Traditional Holidays. Walt Disney Cartoon Characters. Multicoloured.
2110 25 c. Type **115** 10 15
2111 50 c. Disney characters dancing around maypole 25 30
2112 75 c. Mickey, Minnie and Pluto watching Independence Day fireworks 35 40
2113 90 c. Gyro Gearloose and Donald's nephews in Halloween costumes . . . 40 45
2114 $3 Donald Duck as Puritan and nephews as Indians on Thanksgiving Day . . . . 1·40 1·50
2115 $4 Huey and Dewey with Hanukkah dreidle . . . . 1·90 2·00

116 Gateway in Imperial Palace, Peking (½-size illustration)

1996. "CHINA '96" 9th Asian International Stamp Exhibition, Peking. Multicoloured.
2117 $1 Type **116** 45 50
2118 $1 Eastern end of Great Wall at Shanhaiguan 45 50
2119 $1 Great Wall fortress, Shanhaiguan 45 50
2120 $1 Gate of Heavenly Peace, Peking 45 50
2121 $1 Sun Yat-sen's Mausoleum, Nanjing 45 50
2122 $1 Summer Palace, Peking . . 45 50
2123 $1 Temple of Heaven, Peking 45 50
2124 $1 Hall of Supreme Harmony, Forbidden City, Peking . . 45 50

1996. 70th Birthday of Queen Elizabeth II. As T **364** of Antigua. Multicoloured.
2126 35 c. As Type **364** of Antigua 15 20
2127 $2 Queen wearing tiara and green dress 85 90
2128 $4 Windsor Castle . . . . . 1·75 1·90

1996. Flowers. As T **430** of Grenada. Multicoloured.
2130 35 c. "Camellia" "Apple Blossom" 15 20
2131 75 c. "Odontoglossum" . . . 35 40
2132 75 c. "Cattleya" 35 40
2133 75 c. "Paphiopedilum" "Venus's Slipper" 35 40
2134 75 c. "Laeliocattleya" "Marysville" 35 40
2135 75 c. Fuchsia "Citation" . . . 35 40
2136 75 c. Fuchsia "Amy Lye" . . . 35 40
2137 75 c. "Clysonimus" (butterfly) and temple 35 40
2138 75 c. Foxglove ("Digitalis purpurea") 35 40
2139 75 c. Martagon lily ("Lilium martagon") 35 40
2140 75 c. "Tulipa" "Couleur Cardinal" 35 40
2141 75 c. Snowdrop ("Galanthus nivalis") 35 40
2142 75 c. "Rosa" "Superstar" . . . 35 40
2143 75 c. Crocus "Dutch Yellow Mammoth" 35 40
2144 75 c. Japanese lily ("Lilium speciosum") 35 40
2145 75 c. "Lilium" "Joan Evans" . . 35 40
2146 75 c. "Rosa" "Rosemary Harkness" 35 40
2147 90 c. "Camellia japonica" "Extravaganza" 40 45
2148 $1 Chrysanthemum "Primrose Dorothy Else" 45 50
2149 $2 Dahlia "Brandaris" 85 90

Nos. 2135/46 were printed together, se-tenant, with the backgrounds forming a composite design.

No. 2135 is inscribed "Fuschcia" and No. 2133 "Mammouth" in error.

1996. 50th Anniv of U.N.I.C.E.F. As T **366** of Antigua. Multicoloured.
2151 75 c. Child's face (horiz) . . . 35 40
2152 $2 Child with spoon (horiz) . . 85 90
2153 $3 Girl sewing (horiz) . . . . 1·25 1·40

1996. Centenary of Radio. Entertainers. As T **368** of Antigua. Multicoloured.
2157 35 c. Ed Wynn 15 20
2158 75 c. Red Skelton 35 40
2159 $1 Joe Penner 45 50
2160 $3 Jerry Colonna . . . . . . 1·25 1·40

1996. Olympic Games, Atlanta. Previous Medal Winners. As T **425** of Grenada. Multicoloured.
2162 35 c. Los Angeles Memorial Coliseum 15 20
2163 75 c. Connie Carpenter-Phinney (U.S.A.) (Cycling) 35 40
2164 $1 Josef Neckermann (Germany) (vert) 45 50
2165 $1 Harry Boldt (Germany) (vert) 45 50
2166 $1 Elena Petouchkova (Russia) (vert) 45 50
2167 $1 Alwin Schockemoehle (Germany) (vert) 45 50
2168 $1 Hans Winkler (Germany) (vert) 45 50
2169 $1 Joe Fargis (U.S.A.) (vert) . 45 50
2170 $1 David Broome (Great Britain) (vert) 45 50
2171 $1 Reiner Klimke (Germany) (vert) 45 50
2172 $1 Richard Meade (Great Britain) (vert) 45 50
2173 $1 Julianne McNamara (U.S.A.) (vert) 45 50
2174 $1 Takuti Hayata (Japan) (vert) 45 50
2175 $1 Nikolai Adriana (Russia) (vert) 45 50
2176 $1 Mitch Gaylord (U.S.A.) (vert) 45 50
2177 $1 Ludmilla Tourischeva (Russia) (vert) 45 50
2178 $1 Karin Janz (Germany) (vert) 45 50
2179 $1 Peter Kormann (U.S.A.) (vert) 45 50
2180 $1 Sawoo Kato (Japan) (vert) . 45 50
2181 $1 Nadia Comaneci (Rumania) (vert) 45 50
2182 $2 Mohamed Bouchighe (Algeria) (Boxing) (vert) . . 85 90
2183 $3 Jackie Joyner Kersee (U.S.A.) (Javelin) . . . . 1·25 1·40

Nos. 2164/72 (equestrians) and 2173/81 (gymnasts) respectively were printed together, se-tenant, with the backgrounds forming composite designs.

1996. Classic Cars. As T **426** of Grenada. Multicoloured.
2185 35 c. Chevrolet Belair convertible 15 20
2186 50 c. V.I.P. car 25 30
2187 75 c. Rolls-Royce Torpedo . . 35 40
2188 $1 Nissan "Cepric" type . . . 45 50
2189 $1 Delaunay-Belleville HB6 . . 45 50
2190 $1 Bugatti Type-15 . . . . . 45 50
2191 $1 Mazda Type 800 . . . . . 45 50
2192 $1 Mercedes 24/100/140 Sport 45 50
2193 $1 MG K3 Rover 45 50
2194 $1 Plymouth Fury 45 50
2195 $2 Mercedes-Benz 500K . . . 85 90
2196 $3 Bugatti Type-13 . . . . . 1·25 1·40

1996. Ships. As T **427** of Grenada. Multicoloured.
2198 35 c. Grenada schooner . . . 15 20
2199 75 c. Grenada schooner (different) 35 40
2200 $1 Athenian triremes, 1000 B.C. 45 50
2201 $1 Egyptian Nile galley, 30 B.C. 45 50
2202 $1 Bangladesh dinghi, 310 B.C. 45 50
2203 $1 Warship of Queen Hatshepsut, 476 B.C. . . . 45 50
2204 $1 Chinese Junk, 200 B.C. . . 45 50
2205 $1 Polynesian ocean-going canoe, 600 B.C. 45 50
2206 $1 "Europa" (liner), 1957 . . 45 50
2207 $1 "Lusitania" (liner), 1906 . . 45 50
2208 $1 "Queen Mary" (liner), 1936 45 50
2209 $1 "Bianca C" (liner) 45 50
2210 $1 "France" (liner), 1952 . . . 45 50
2211 $1 "Orion" (liner), 1915 . . . 45 50

117 Felix Mendelssohn

120 Hong Kong

119 Springer Spaniel

1996. Composers. Multicoloured.
2213 $1 Type **117** 45 50
2214 $1 Franz Schubert 45 50
2215 $1 Franz Joseph Haydn . . . 45 50
2216 $1 Robert Schumann 45 50
2217 $1 Ludwig van Beethoven . . . 45 50
2218 $1 Gioacchino Rossini 45 50
2219 $1 George Frederick Handel . . 45 50
2220 $1 Pyotr Tchaikovsky 45 50
2221 $1 Frederic Chopin 45 50
2222 $1 Bela Bartok 45 50
2223 $1 Giacomo Puccini 45 50
2224 $1 George Gershwin 45 50
2225 $1 Leonard Bernstein 45 50
2226 $1 Kurt Weill 45 50
2227 $1 John Cage 45 50
2228 $1 Aaron Copland 45 50
2229 $1 Sergei Prokofiev 45 50
2230 $1 Igor Stravinsky 45 50

Nos. 2213/21 and 2222/30 respectively were printed together, se-tenant, with the backgrounds forming composite designs.

1996. Railway Steam Locomotives. As T **429** of Grenada. Multicoloured.
2232 $1.50 Class 38 No. 382, Germany 65 70
2233 $1.50 "Duchess of Hamilton", Great Britain 65 70
2234 $1.50 Class W.P., India . . . 65 70
2235 $1.50 Class 141R "Americaine", France 65 70
2236 $1.50 Class A4 "Mallard", Great Britain 65 70
2237 $1.50 Class 18 No. 201, Germany 65 70
2238 $1.50 Class A2 "Blue Peter", Great Britain 65 70
2239 $1.50 Class P36, Russia . . . 65 70
2240 $1.50 Class QJ, China 65 70
2241 $1.50 Class 12, Belgium . . . 65 70
2242 $1.50 Class "Challenger", U.S.A. 65 70
2243 $1.50 Class 25, South Africa . 65 70

1996. Christmas. Religious Paintings. As T **369** of Antigua. Showing different details from "Suffer Little Children to Come Unto Me" by Van Dyck.

2245 15 c. multicoloured 10 10
2246 25 c. multicoloured 10 15
2247 $1 multicoloured 45 50
2248 $1.50 multicoloured 65 70
2249 $2 multicoloured 85 90
2250 $4 multicoloured . . . . . 1·75 1·90

1997. 50th Anniv of U.N.E.S.C.O. As T **374** of Antigua. Multicoloured.

2253 15 c. Temple, Kyoto, Japan . 10 10
2254 25 c. Roman ruins, Trier, Germany 10 15
2255 $1 Gateway, Mount Taishan, China 45 50
2256 $1 Temple guardian, Kyoto, Japan (vert) 45 50
2257 $1 Temple deity, Kyoto, Japan (vert) 45 50
2258 $1 Temple lamp, Kyoto, Japan (vert) 45 50
2259 $1 Ayutthaya, Thailand (vert) 45 50
2260 $1 Statue, Borobudur Temple, Indonesia (vert) 45 50
2261 $1 Monuments at Pattadakal, India (vert) 45 50
2262 $1 Sleeping buddha, Polonnaruwa, Sri Lanka (vert) 45 50
2263 $1 Sagarmatha National Park, Nepal (vert) 45 50
2264 $1 Congonhas Sanctuary, Brazil (vert) 45 50
2265 $1 Cartagena, Colombia (vert) 45 50
2266 $1 Pueblo, Guatemala (vert) . 45 50
2267 $1 Maya statue, Honduras (vert) 45 50
2268 $1 Popocatepetl Monastery, Mexico (vert) 45 50
2269 $1 Galapagos Islands, Ecuador (vert) 45 50
2270 $1 Waterfall, Costa Rica (vert) 45 50
2271 $1 Glaciares National Park, Argentina (vert) 45 50
2272 $1.50 Notre Dame Cathedral, Paris, France 65 70
2273 $1.50 Timbered house, Maulbronn, Germany . . . 65 70
2274 $1.50 Gateway, Himeji-jo, Japan 65 70
2275 $1.50 Lion statues, Delphi, Greece 65 70
2276 $1.50 Palace of Fontainebleau, France 65 70
2277 $1.50 Scandola Nature Reserve, France 65 70
2278 $2 Citadel, Dubrovnik, Croatia 85 90
2279 $4 Angra do Heroismo, Portugal . . . . . 1·75 1·90

1997. Cats and Dogs. Multicoloured.

2281 35 c. Type **119** 15 20
2282 45 c. Abyssinian blue 20 25
2283 50 c. Burmese cream (vert) . 25 30
2284 75 c. Doberman pinscher . . 35 40
2285 90 c. Persian tortoiseshell and white 40 45
2286 $1 Italian spinone (vert) . . . 45 50
2287 $1.50 Siamese chocolate point 65 70
2288 $1.50 Oriental shorthair white 65 70
2289 $1.50 Burmese sable . . . 65 70
2290 $1.50 Abyssinian tabby . . . 65 70
2291 $1.50 Persian shaded silver . 65 70
2292 $1.50 Tonkinese natural mink 65 70
2293 $1.50 Leonberger 65 70
2294 $1.50 Newfoundland 65 70
2295 $1.50 Boxer 65 70
2296 $1.50 St. Bernard 65 70
2297 $1.50 Silky terrier 65 70
2298 $1.50 Miniature schnauzer . . 65 70
2299 $2 Cocker spaniel (vert) . . . 85 90
2300 $3 Oriental shorthair agouti (vert) . . . . . 1·25 1·40

Nos. 2287/92 (cats) and Nos. 2293/8 (dogs) respectively were printed together, se-tenant, with the backgrounds forming composite designs.

1997. Dinosaurs. As T **438** of Grenada. Mult.

2302 45 c. Stegosaurus 20 25
2303 90 c. Diplodocus 40 45
2304 $1 Pteranodon (vert) 45 50
2305 $1.50 Rhamphorhynchus and head of Brachiosaurus . . 65 70
2306 $1.50 Archaeopteryx 65 70
2307 $1.50 Anurognathus and body of Brachiosaurus 65 70
2308 $1.50 Head of Albertosaurus . 65 70
2309 $1.50 Herrerasaurus and legs of Brachiosaurus 65 70
2310 $1.50 Platyhystrix and body of Albertosaurus 65 70
2311 $2 Deinonychus and Ankylasaurus (vert) 85 90

Nos. 2305/10 were printed together, se-tenant, with the backgrounds forming a composite design.

1997. 50th Death Anniv of Paul Harris (founder of Rotary International). As T **377** of Antigua. Multicoloured.

2314 $3 Paul Harris and village women with water pump, Burkina Faso . . . . . 1·25 1·40

1997. Golden Wedding of Queen Elizabeth and Prince Philip. As T **378** of Antigua. Multicoloured (except Nos. 2318/19).

2316 $1 Engagement photograph, 1947 . . . . . 45 50
2317 $1 Royal coat of arms . . . 45 50
2318 $1 Queen Elizabeth and Duke of Edinburgh, 1953 (brown) 45 50
2319 $1 Formal portrait of Queen Elizabeth with Prince Philip in uniform (brown) 45 50
2320 $1 Sandringham House . . . 45 50
2321 $1 Queen Elizabeth and Prince Philip in carriage 45 50

1997. "Pacific '97" International Stamp Exhibition, San Francisco. Death Centenary of Heinrich von Stephan (founder of the U.P.U.). As T **379** of Antigua.

2323 $1.50 green 65 70
2324 $1.50 brown 65 70
2325 $1.50 violet 65 70

DESIGNS: No. 2323, Pony Express, 1860; 2324, Von Stephan and Mercury; 2325, American steam locomotive.

1997. Birth Bicentenary of Hiroshige (Japanese painter). "100 Famous Views of Edo". As T **310** of Dominica but horiz. Multicoloured.

2327 $1.50 "Koume Embankment" 65 70
2328 $1.50 "Azuma Shrine and the Entwined Camphor" . . . 65 70
2329 $1.50 "Yanagishima" . . . 65 70
2330 $1.50 "Inside Akiba Shrine, Ukeji" 65 70
2331 $1.50 "Distant View of Kinryuzan Temple and Azuma Bridge" 65 70
2332 $1.50 "Night View of Matsuchiyama and the San'ya Canal" 65 70

1997. 175th Anniv of Brothers Grimm's Third Collection of Fairy Tales. "The Fox and the Geese". As T **380** of Antigua. Multicoloured.

2334 $2 Fox and geese 85 90
2335 $2 Fox with knife and fork and geese 85 90
2336 $2 Fox asleep and singing geese 85 90

1997. Winter Olympic Games, Nagano, Japan. As T **440** of Grenada. Multicoloured.

2338 90 c. Slalom 40 45
2339 $1 Downhill skiing 45 50
2340 $1 Freestyle ski-jumping (blue and green ski suit) 45 50
2341 $1 Curling 45 50
2342 $1 Ski-jumping (pink ski suit) 45 50
2343 $1 Four-man bobsleigh . . . 45 50
2344 $1 Nordic combined 45 50
2345 $1 Speed skating 45 50
2346 $1 Ice hockey 45 50
2347 $1 Cross-country skiing . . 45 50
2348 $2 One-man luge 85 90
2349 $3 Men's figure-skating . . 1·25 1·40
2350 $5 Speed skating (different) . 2·10 2·25

1997. Return of Hong Kong to China. Multicoloured.

2352 **120** $1 multicoloured . . . 45 50
2353 – $1.25 multicoloured . . 50 55
2354 – $1.50 multicoloured (63 × 32 mm) 65 70
2355 – $2 multicoloured (63 × 2 mm) 85 90

DESIGNS: $1.25 to $2 Modern Hong Kong shown through inscriptions.

1997. Marine Life. As T **439** of Grenada. Mult.

2356 10 c. Wimplefish 10 10
2357 15 c. Clown triggerfish . . . 10 10
2358 25 c. Ringed emperor angelfish 10 15
2359 35 c. Hooded butterflyfish . . 15 20
2360 45 c. Semicircle angelfish . . 20 25
2361 75 c. Scribbled angelfish . . 35 40
2362 90 c. Threadfin butterflyfish 40 45
2363 $1.10 Clown surgeonfish . . 50 55
2364 $2 Bottle-nosed dolphin . . 85 90
2365 $5 Triggerfish . . . . . 2·10 2·25
2366 $10 Lionfish . . . . . 4·25 4·50
2367 $20 Jackknifefish . . . . . 8·75 9·00

121 Winnie the Pooh as Monday's Child

1997. "Monday's Child" (poem). Disney Cartoon Characters from Winnie the Pooh illustrating various verses. Multicoloured.

2368 $1 Type **121** 45 50
2369 $1 Kanga as Tuesday's child 45 50
2370 $1 Eeyore as Wednesday's child 45 50
2371 $1 Tigger as Thursday's child 45 50
2372 $1 Piglet as Friday's child . 45 50
2373 $1 Rabbit as Saturday's child 45 50

122 Snow White kissing Grumpy

1997. Disney Sweethearts. Disney Cartoon Characters kissing. Multicoloured.

2375 $1 Type **122** 45 50
2376 $1 Figaro the Cat and Cleo the Fish 45 50
2377 $1 Peter Pan and Wendy . . 45 50
2378 $1 Cinderella and the Prince . 45 50
2379 $1 Ariel and Eric 45 50
2380 $1 Beauty and the Prince . . 45 50
2381 $1 Aladdin and Jasmine . . . 45 50
2382 $1 Pocahontas and Captain John Smith 45 50
2383 $1 Phoebus and Esmeralda . . 45 50

1997. World Football Championship, France (1998). As T **383** of Antigua.

2385 10 c. blue 10 10
2386 20 c. multicoloured 10 10
2387 45 c. brown 20 25
2388 $1 black 45 50
2389 $1 brown 45 50
2390 $1 black 45 50
2391 $1 brown 45 50
2392 $1 multicoloured 45 50
2393 $1 multicoloured 45 50
2394 $1 black 45 50
2395 $1 brown 45 50
2396 $1 multicoloured 45 50
2397 $1 black 45 50
2398 $1 black 45 50
2399 $1 black 45 50
2400 $1 black 45 50
2401 $1 black 45 50
2402 $1 black 45 50
2403 $1 black 45 50
2404 $1 black 45 50
2405 $1.50 multicoloured 65 70
2406 $5 black . . . . . 2·10 2·25

DESIGNS—HORIZ: No. 2385, Italian team, 1934; 2386, Angolan team; 2387, Brazilian team, 1958; 2388, Uruguay team, 1950; 2389, Winning England team, 1966; 2390, West German team, 1954; 2391, Uruguayan officials with Jules Rimet trophy, 1930; 2392, West German players celebrating, 1990; 2393, Maradona (Argentine player), 1986; 2394, Brazilian players, 1994; 2395, Argentine players, 1978; 2396, West German player holding World Cup, 1974; 2405, West German team, 1974; 2406, Italian team, 1938. VERT: No. 2397, Ademir, Brazil; 2398, Kocsis, Hungary; 2399, Leonidas, Brazil; 2400, Nejedly, Czechoslavakia; 2401, Schiavio, Italy; 2402, Stabile, Uruguay; 2403, Pele, Brazil; 2404, Fritzwalter, West Germany.

1997. Butterflies. As T **444** of Grenada. Mult.

2408 75 c. "Polyura dehaani" . . . 35 40
2409 90 c. "Polyura dolon" . . . 40 45
2410 $1 "Charaxes candiope" . . . 45 50
2411 $1.50 "Pantaporia punctata" . 65 70
2412 $1.50 "Euthalia confucius" . . 65 70
2413 $1.50 "Euthalia kardama" . . 65 70
2414 $1.50 "Limenitis albomaculata" 65 70
2415 $1.50 "Hestina assimilis" . . 65 70
2416 $1.50 "Kallima inachus" . . . 65 70
2417 $1.50 "Euthalia teutoides" . . 65 70
2418 $1.50 "Euphaedra francina" . 65 70
2419 $1.50 "Euphaedra eleus" . . 65 70
2420 $1.50 "Euphaedra harpalyce" 65 70
2421 $1.50 "Euphaedra cyparissa" 65 70
2422 $1.50 "Euphaedra gausape" . 65 70
2423 $1.50 "Euphaedra imperialis" 65 70
2424 $2 "Charaxes etesippe" . . . 85 90
2425 $3 "Charaxes castor" . . . . 1·25 1·40

Nos. 2412/17 and 2418/23 respectively were printed together, se-tenant, with the backgrounds forming composite designs.

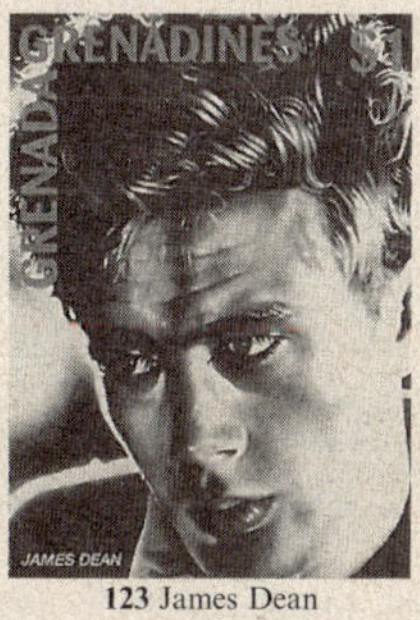

123 James Dean

124 "Symphyglossum sanguineum"

1997. James Dean (actor) Commemoration. Different portaits. Multicoloured.

2427 $1 Type **123** 45 50
2428 $1 Wearing purple jumper . . 45 50
2429 $1 Wearing stetson and smoking 45 50
2430 $1 Wearing dinner jacket and tie 45 50
2431 $1 Full-face portrait 45 50
2432 $1 Grimacing 45 50
2433 $1 Wearing stetson 45 50
2434 $1 Leaning on arms 45 50
2435 $1 Smoking 45 50

1997. Orchids of the World. Multicoloured.

2436 35 c. Type **124** 15 20
2437 45 c. "Doritaenopsis" "Mythic Beauty" 20 25
2438 75 c. "Odontoglossum cervantesii" 35 40
2439 90 c. "Cattleya" "Pumpernickel" 40 45
2440 $1 "Vanda" "Patricia Low" . 45 50
2441/9 $1 × 9 ("Lycaste" "Aquila"; "Brassolaeliocattleya" "Dorothy Bertsch"; "Phalaenopsis" "Zuma Urchin"; "Promenaea xanthina"; "Amesiella philippinensis"; "Brassocattleya" "Angel Lace"; "Brassoepidendrum" "Peggy Ann"; "Miltonia seine"; "Sophralaeliocattleya" "Precious Stones") . . . 4·25
2450/8 $1 × 9 ("Cymbidium" "Showgirl"; "Disa blackii"; "Phalaenopsis aphrodite"; "Iwanagaara" "Apple Blossom"; "Masdevallia" "Copper Angel"; "Paphiopedilum micranthum"; "Paphiopedilum" "Clare de Lune"; "Cattleya forbesii"; "Dendrobium" "Dawn Maree") . . . . 4·25
2459 $1.50 "Odontonia" "Debutante" 65 70
2460/5 $1.50 × 6 ("Miltoniopsis" "Jean Sabourin"; "Cymbidium" "Red Beauty"; "Brassocattleya" "Green Dragon"; "Phalaenopsis" hybrid; "Laeliocattleya" "Mary Ellen Carter"; "Disa" hybrid) . . . . . 4·25
2466/71 $1.50 × 6 ("Lycaste macrobulbon"; "Cochleanthes discolor"; "Cymbidium" "Nang Carpenter"; "Paphiopedilum" "Claire de Lune"; "Masdevallia caudata"; "Cymbidium" "Showgirl") . . . . . 4·25
2472 $2 "Laeliocattleya" "Mini Purple" 85 90
2473 $3 "Phragmipedium dominiarum" . . . . . 1·25 1·40
2436/73 Set of 38 20·00 21·00

Nos. 2460/5 and 2466/71 respectively were printed together, se-tenant, with the backgrounds forming composite designs.

125 "Clitocybe metachroa"

1997. Fungi. Multicoloured.

2475 75 c. Type **125** 35 40
2476 90 c. "Clavulinopsis helvola" . 40 45
2477 $1 "Lycoperdon pyriforme" . 45 50
2478 $1.50 "Auricularia auricula-judae" 65 70
2479 $1.50 "Entoloma incanum" . 65 70
2480 $1.50 "Coprinus atramentarius" 65 70
2481 $1.50 "Mycena polygramma" 65 70
2482 $1.50 "Lepista nuda" . . . 65 70
2483 $1.50 "Pleurotis cornucopiae" 65 70
2484 $1.50 "Laccaria amethystina" 65 70
2485 $2 "Clathrus archeri" . . . 85 90
2486 $3 "Lactarius trivialis" . . . 1·25 1·40

126 Ludwig van Beethoven

1997. Classical Composers. Multicoloured.

2488 $1 Type **126** 45 50
2489 $1 Pyotr Tchaikovsky . . . 45 50
2490 $1 Johann Christian Bach . . 45 50
2491 $1 Frederic Chopin 45 50
2492 $1 Igor Stravinsky 45 50
2493 $1 Franz Joseph Haydn . . . 45 50
2494 $1 Gustav Mahler 45 50
2495 $1 Gioacchino Antonio Rossini 45 50

127 Diana, Princess of Wales and Buckingham Palace

1997. Diana, Princess of Wales Commemoration. Multicoloured.

2497 $1.50 Type **127** 65 70
2498 $1.50 Princess Diana and lake at Althorp 65 70
2499 $1.50 Princess Diana and Westminster Abbey . . . 65 70
2500 $1.50 Princess Diana and gates to Althorp 65 70
2501 $1.50 Princess Diana in pink hat and gates to Kensington Palace 65 70
2502 $1.50 Princess Diana and Althorp House 65 70

1997. Christmas. Religious Paintings. As T **448** of Grenada. Multicoloured.

2504 20 c. "Choir of Angels (Simon Marmion) 10 15
2505 75 c. "The Annunciation" (Giotto) 35 40
2506 90 c. "Festival of the Rose Garlands" (Albrecht Durer) 40 45
2507 $1.50 "Madonna with Two Angels" (Hans Memling) . 65 70
2508 $2 "The Ognissanti Madonna" (Giotto) 85 90
2509 $3 "Angel with Candlestick" (Michelangelo) . . . . . . 1·25 1·40

No. 2506 is inscribed "DUER" in error.

1998. Fishes. As T **449** of Grenada. Multicoloured.

2511 Queen angelfish 45 50
2512 $1 Clown triggerfish 45 50
2513 $1 Four-spot butterflyfish . . 45 50
2514 $1 Yellow-tailed damselfish . 45 50
2515 $1 Yellow-headed wrasse . . 45 50
2516 $1 Royal gramma 45 50
2517 $1 Candy basslet 45 50
2518 $1 Smooth trunkfish 45 50
2519 $1 Coral hind 45 50

Nos. 2511/19 were printed together, se-tenant, with the backgrounds forming a composite design.

128 Tiger (hologram)

1998. Chinese New Year ("Year of the Tiger").

2521 **128** $1.50 black on silver foil 65 70

129 "Alabama" (Confederate warship)

1998. Famous Ships. Multicoloured. (a) Ships of the 1860s.

2523 75 c. Type **129** 35 40
2524 75 c. "Persia" (paddle-steamer) 35 40
2525 75 c. "Ariel" (clipper) 35 40
2526 75 c. "Florida" (Confederate cruiser) 35 40
2527 75 c. "Great Eastern" (paddle-steamer) 35 40
2528 75 c. "Jacob Bell" on fire . . 35 40
2529 75 c. "Star of India" (clipper) 35 40
2530 75 c. "Robert E. Lee" (Mississippi paddle-steamer) 35 40
2531 75 c. U.S.S. "Passaic" (monitor) 35 40
2532 75 c. "Madagascar" (clipper) 35 40
2533 75 c. H.M.S. "Devastation" (battleship) 35 40
2534 75 c. "General Grant" (clipper) 35 40

(b) Ships of the American Civil War.

2535 $1 Clark Gable as Rhett Butler in "Gone with the Wind" (vert) 45 50
2536 $1 Crew abandoning blockade runner wrecked on Sullivan's Island (vert) 45 50
2537 $1 Margaret Mitchell (author of "Gone with the Wind") (vert) 45 50
2538 $1 George Alfred Trenholm (ship owner) (vert) 45 50
2539 $1 Dock Street Theatre, Charleston (vert) 45 50
2540 $1 "Howlett" (paddle-steamer) sinking (vert) 45 50
2541 $1 U.S.S. "Tecumseh" on fire (vert) 45 50
2542 $1 City Jail, Charleston (vert) 45 50

130 Concept Strike Fighter

1998. Aircraft Designs of the Future. Multicoloured.

2544 70 c. Type **130** 30 35
2545 90 c. Concept space shuttle . 40 45
2546 $1 Velocity 173 RG Elite . . 45 50
2547 $1 Davis DA-9 . . . . 45 50
2548 $1 Concorde 45 50
2549 $1 Voyager 45 50
2550 $1 Factimobile 45 50
2551 $1 RAF 2000 . . . . 45 50
2552 $1 Boomerang 45 50
2553 $1 N1M Flying Wing 45 50
2554 $2 Concept air and space jet . 85 90
2555 $3 V Jet II . . . . 1·25 1·40

131 "Lycaste deppei"

1998. Orchids of the World. Multicoloured.

2557 $1 Type **131** 45 50
2558 $1 "Dendrobium victoriae" . 45 50
2559 $1 "Dendrobium nobile" . . 45 50
2560 $1 "Cymbidium dayanum" . 45 50
2561 $1 "Cymbidium" "Starbright" 45 50
2562 $1 "Cymbidium giganteum" 45 50
2563 $1 "Chysis aurea" 45 50
2564 $1 "Broughtonia sanguinea" 45 50
2565 $1 "Cattleya guttata" . . . 45 50
2566 $1 "Calanthe vestita" . . . 45 50
2567 $1 "Cattleya bicolor" . . . 45 50
2568 $1 "Laelia anceps" 45 50
2569 $1 "Epidendrum prismatocarpum" 45 50
2570 $1 "Coelogyne ochracea" . . 45 50
2571 $1 "Doritaenopsis eclantant" 45 50
2572 $1 "Laelia gouldiana" . . . 45 50
2573 $1 "Encyclia vitellina" . . . 45 50
2574 $1 "Maxillaria praestans" . 45 50
2575 $1 "Laelia tenebrosa" . . . 45 50
2576 $1.50 "Phragmipedium besseae" 65 70
2577 $2 "Pschopsis papilio" . . . 85 90
2578 $3 "Masdevallia coccinea" . 1·25 1·40

1998. Seabirds. As T **452** of Grenada. Multicoloured.

2580 75 c. Bonaparte's gull (horiz) 35 40
2581 90 c. Western sandpiper (horiz) 40 45
2582 $1.50 Common tern (horiz) . 65 70
2583 $1.50 Brown pelican (horiz) . 65 70
2584 $1.50 Black-legged kittiwake and white tern (horiz) . . 65 70
2585 $1.50 Herring gull (horiz) . . 65 70
2586 $1.50 Lesser noddy (horiz) . 65 70
2587 $1.50 Black-legged kittiwake (horiz) 65 70
2588 $1.50 Whimbrel (horiz) . . . 65 70
2589 $1.50 Golden white-tailed tropic bird (horiz) 65 70
2590 $1.50 Arctic tern (horiz) . . 65 70
2591 $1.50 Ruddy turnstone (horiz) 65 70
2592 $1.50 Imperial shag (horiz) . 65 70
2593 $1.50 Magellan gull (horiz) . 65 70
2594 $2 Great black-backed gull (horiz) 85 90
2595 $3 Dotterell (horiz) . . . . 1·25 1·40

1998. International Year of the Ocean. As T **454** of Grenada. Multicoloured.

2597 75 c. Great black-backed gull 35 40
2598 75 c. Common dolphin . . . 35 40
2599 75 c. Seal 35 40
2600 75 c. Amazonian catfish . . 35 40
2601 75 c. Shark 35 40
2602 75 c. Goldfish 35 40
2603 75 c. Cyathopharynx 35 40
2604 75 c. Killer whale 35 40
2605 75 c. Telmatochromis 35 40
2606 75 c. Crab 35 40
2607 75 c. Octopus 35 40
2608 75 c. Turtle 35 40
2609 90 c. Two dolphins 40 45
2610 90 c. Seal 40 45
2611 90 c. Turtle on rock 40 45
2612 90 c. Leopard shark 40 45
2613 90 c. Flame angelfish . . . 40 45
2614 90 c. Syndontis 40 45
2615 90 c. Lamprologus 40 45
2616 90 c. "Krptopterus bicirrhus" 40 45
2617 90 c. "Pterophyllum scalare" 40 45
2618 90 c. Swimming pancake . . 40 45
2619 90 c. Cowfish 40 45
2620 90 c. Seahorse 40 45

Nos. 2597/2608 and 2609/20 respectively were printed together, se-tenant, with the backgrounds forming composite designs.

132 Stylised "50"

1998. 50th Anniv of Organization of American States.

2622 **132** $1 violet, orange and black 45 50

1998. 25th Death Anniv of Pablo Picasso (painter). As T **400** of Antigua. Multicoloured.

2623 45 c. "Bust of a Woman" (vert) 20 25
2624 $2 "Three Musicians" . . . 85 90
2625 $3 "Studio at La Californie" 1·25 1·40

1998. Birth Centenary of Enzo Ferrari (car manufacturer). As T **401** of Antigua. Multicoloured.

2627 $2 275 GTB 85 90
2628 $2 340 MM 85 90
2629 $2 250 GT SWB Berlinetta "Hot Rod" 85 90

1998. 19th World Scout Jamboree, Chile. As T **402** of Antigua. Multicoloured.

2631 90 c. Scout greeting 40 45
2632 $1.50 Lord Baden-Powell . . 65 70
2633 $5 Scout salute . . . . 2·10 2·25

1998. 50th Death Anniv of Mahatma Gandhi. As T **327** of Dominica.

2635 $1 grey, brown and black . . 45 50

1998. 80th Anniv of Royal Air Force. As T **404** of Antigua. Multicoloured.

2637 $2 Tornado GR1 . . . . . . 85 90
2638 $2 BAe Hawk T1A 85 90
2639 $2 Sepecat Jaguar GR1 . . . 85 90
2640 $2 Harrier GR7 . . . . . . 85 90
2641 $2 Chinook helicopter carrying three loads 85 90
2642 $2 Silhouette of BAe Harrier GR5 . . . . 85 90
2643 $2 Panavia Tornado F3 ADV at sunset 85 90
2644 $2 Chinook HC2 carrying 105 mm light gun 85 90

1998. Birth Bicentenary of Eugene Delacroix (painter). As T **294** of Gambia. Multicoloured.

2646 $1 "The Natchez" 45 50
2647 $1 "Christ and His Disciples Crossing the Sea of Galilee" 45 50
2648 $1 "Sunset" 45 50
2649 $1 "Moroccans outside the Walls of Tangier" 45 50
2650 $1 "The Fireplace" 45 50
2651 $1 "Forest View with an Oak Tree" 45 50
2652 $1 "View of the Harbour at Dieppe" 45 50
2653 $1 "Arab Tax Collectors" . . 45 50

1998. 1st Death Anniv of Diana, Princess of Wales. As T **407** of Antigua.

2655 $1.50 multicoloured 65 70

133 Father Christmas and Hare

1998. Disney's Christmas Trains. Walt Disney cartoon characters in train carriages. Multicoloured.

2656 $1 Type **133** 45 50
2657 $1 Giraffe, elephant and tiger 45 50
2658 $1 Three Pigs and Wolf . . . 45 50
2659 $1 Pied Piper, Jiminy Cricket, penguins and children . . . 45 50
2660 $1 Swans, Little Hiawatha and tortoise 45 50
2661 $1 Mickey Mouse as train driver 45 50
2662 $1 Pluto, Chip and Dale . . . 45 50
2663 $1 Donald and Daisy Duck . 45 50
2664 $1 Goofy, Huey, Dewey and Louie 45 50
2665 $1 Minnie Mouse and presents 45 50
2666 $1 Piglet as train driver . . . 45 50
2667 $1 Winnie the Pooh and honey 45 50
2668 $1 Rabbit and Owl 45 50
2669 $1 Kanga, Roo and Christopher Robin 45 50
2670 $1 Eeyore and Tigger 45 50

134 Troodon

1999. "Australia '99" World Stamp Exhibition, Melbourne. Prehistoric Animals. Multicoloured.

2673 $1 Type **134** 45 50
2674 $1 Camptosaurus 45 50
2675 $1 Parasaurolophus 45 50
2676 $1 Dryosaurus 45 50
2677 $1 Gallimimus 45 50
2678 $1 Camarasaurus 45 50
2679 $1.50 Duckbill (horiz) 65 70
2680 $1.50 Lambeosaurus (horiz) . 65 70
2681 $1.50 Igaunodon (horiz) . . . 65 70
2682 $1.50 Euoplocephalus (horiz) 65 70
2683 $1.50 Triceratops (horiz) . . . 65 70
2684 $1.50 Brachiosaurus (horiz) . 65 70
2685 $1.50 Ponoptosaurus (horiz) . 65 70
2686 $1.50 Stegosaurus (horiz) . . 65 70

135 Eastern Railways Compound Locomotive (France)

1999. Steam Trains of the World. Multicoloured.

2688 $2 Type **135** 85 90
2689 $2 Govt Railways Class WF tank locomotive (New Zealand) 85 90
2690 $2 Burma Railways oil-burning tank locomotive, 1899 . . 85 90
2691 $2 Federated Malay States Railway Class G steam locomotive, 1899 . . . . . 85 90
2692 $2 Belfast and Northern Counties Railway narrow-gauge tank locomotive . . 85 90
2693 $2 Shunting tank locomotive (Russia) 85 90
2694 $2 G.N.R. Ivatt large-boilered "Atlantic" type 85 90
2695 $2 Palatine Railway "Atlantic" type express locomotive (Germany) 85 90

OFFICIAL STAMPS

1982. Optd **P.R.G.** (a) Nos. 400/12 and 414.

O 1 5 c. Yellow-tailed snapper . . 10 15
O 2 6 c. Mutton snapper 10 15
O 3 10 c. Cocoa damselfish . . . 10 15
O 4 12 c. Royal gramma 10 15
O 5 15 c. Cherub angelfish . . . 10 15
O 6 20 c. Black-barred soldierfish . 10 20
O 7 25 c. Mottled grouper 10 20
O 8 30 c. Long-snouted butterflyfish 15 20
O 9 40 c. Puddingwife 15 25
O10 50 c. Midnight parrotfish . . 20 30
O11 90 c. Redspotted hawkfish . 40 55
O12 $1 Hogfish 40 60
O13 $3 Beau Gregory . . . . . . 1·25 2·25
O14 $10. Barred hamlet . . . . . 4·25 6·00

(b) Nos. 444/6 and 448/9.

O15 30 c. Prince Charles and Lady Diana Spencer . . . . . . 2·00 2·00
O16 40 c. Prince Charles and Lady Diana Spencer . . . . . . 1·60 1·60
O17 40 c. Type **50** . . . . 2·00 2·75
O18 $2 Type **50** . . . . 2·50 3·50
O19 $4 Prince Charles as parachutist 6·50 8·50

(c) Nos. 473/6.

O20 **54** 20 c. multicoloured . . . 10 20
O21 – 40 c. multicoloured . . . 15 25
O22 – $1 multicoloured 35 70
O23 – $2 multicoloured . . . . 70 1·40

GRENADINES OF ST. VINCENT

Part of a group of Islands south of St. Vincent which include Bequia, Mustique, Canouan and Union.

100 cents = 1 dollar

1973. Royal Wedding. As T **47** of Anguilla. Multicoloured. Background colours given.
1 25 c. green 10 10
2 $1 brown 15 15

1974. Nos. 286/300 of St. Vincent optd **GRENADINES OF.**
3 1 c. Green heron 10 10
4 2 c. Lesser Antillean bullfinches 15 15
25 3 c. St. Vincent amazon 25 30
6 4 c. Rufous-thoated solitaire (vert) 15 10
7 5 c. Red-necked pigeon (vert) 15 10
8 6 c. Bananaquits 15 10
9 8 c. Purple-throated carib 15 10
10 10 c. Mangrove cuckoo (vert) 15 10
11 12 c. Common black hawk (vert) 20 15
12 20 c. Bare-eyed thrush 35 20
13 25 c. Hooded tanager 40 20
14 50 c. Blue hooded euphonia 70 40
15 $1 Barn owl (vert) 1·50 75
16 $2.50 Yellow-bellied elaenia (vert) 1·50 1·00
17 $5 Ruddy quail dove 1·75 1·75

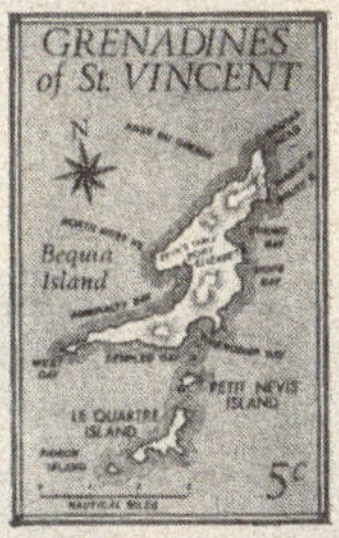

2 Map of Bequia

1974. Maps (1st series).
18 **2** 5 c. black, green & dp green 10 10
19 – 15 c. multicoloured 10 10
20 – 20 c. multicoloured 10 10
21 – 30 c. black, pink and red 10 10
22 – 40 c. black., violet & purple 10 10
23 – $1 black, ultramarine & blue 20 20
MAPS: 15 c. Prune Island; 20 c. Mayreau Island and Tobago Cays; 30 c. Mustique Island; 40 c. Union Island; $1 Canouan Island.
See also Nos. 85/8.

1974. Centenary of U.P.U. As Nos. 392/5 of St. Vincent.
26 2 c. multicoloured 10 10
27 15 c. multicoloured 10 10
28 40 c. multicoloured 10 10
29 $1 multicoloured 25 15

4 Boat-building

1974. Bequia Island (1st series). Multicoloured.
34 5 c. Type **4** 10 15
31 30 c. Careening at Port Elizabeth 10 15
32 35 c. Admiralty Bay 10 15
33 $1 Fishing-boat race 15 25
See also Nos. 185/88.

5 Music Volute

1974. Shells and Molluscs. Multicoloured.
35A 1 c. American thorny oyster 10 10
36A 2 c. Zigzag scallop 10 10
37A 3 c. Reticulated cowrie-helmet 10 10
38A 4 c. Type **5** 10 10
39A 5 c. Amber pen shell 10 10
40A 6 c. Angular triton 10 10
41A 8 c. Flame helmet 10 10
42A 10 c. Caribbean olive 10 10
43A 12 c. American or common sundial 10 10
44A 15 c. Glory of the Atlantic cone 25 20
45B 20 c. Flame auger 30 20
46A 25 c. King venus 50 20
47A 35 c. Long-spined star shell 35 25
48A 45 c. Speckled tellin 35 30
49A 50 c. Rooster-tail conch 40 25
50B $1 Green star shell 60 60
51A $2.50 Antillean or incomparable cone 80 90
52A $5 Rough file clam 1·00 1·00
52cA $10 Measled cowrie 4·50 1·50
Nos. 38/42, 45, 47 and 49/50 come with and without an imprint below the design.

1974. Birth Centenary of Sir Winston Churchill. As Nos. 403/6 of St. Vincent, but inscr "GRENADINES OF ST. VINCENT" and values (Nos. 53/5) and colours changed.
53 **75** 5 c. multicoloured 10 10
54 – 40 c. multicoloured 10 10
55 – 50 c. multicoloured 10 10
56 – $1 multicoloured 20 20

6 Cotton House, Mustique

1975. Mustique Island. Multicoloured.
57 5 c. Type **6** 10 10
58 35 c. "Blue Waters", Endeavour Bay 10 10
59 45 c. "Endeavour Bay 10 10
60 $1 "Les Jolies Eaux", Gelliceaux Bay 25 20

7 "Danaus plexippus"

1975. Butterflies. Multicoloured.
61 3 c. Type **7** 20 10
62 5 c. "Agraulis vanillae" 25 10
63 35 c. "Battus polydamas" 60 10
64 45 c. "Evenus dindymus" and "Junonia evarete" 70 10
65 $1 "Anartia jatrophae" 1·25 45

8 Resort Pavilion

1975. Petit St. Vincent. Multicoloured.
66 5 c. Type **8** 10 10
67 35 c. The Harbour 10 10
68 45 c. The Jetty 15 15
69 $1 Sailing in coral lagoon 50 80

9 Ecumenical Church, Mustique

1975. Christmas. Multicoloured.
70 5 c. Type **9** 10 10
71 25 c. Catholic Church, Union Island 10 10
72 50 c. Catholic Church, Bequia 10 10
73 $1 Anglican Church, Bequia 25 15

10 Sunset Scene

1976. Union Island (1st series). Multicoloured.
74 5 c. Type **10** 10 10
75 35 c. Customs and Post Office, Clifton 10 10
76 45 c. Anglican Church, Ashton 10 10
77 $1 Mail schooner, Clifton Harbour 25 20
See also Nos. 242/5.

11 Staghorn Coral

1976. Corals. Multicoloured.
78 5 c. Type **11** 10 10
79 35 c. Elkhorn coral 20 10
80 45 c. Pillar coral 20 10
81 $1 Brain coral 40 20

12 25 c. Bicentennial Coin

1976. Bicentenary of American Revolution.
82 **12** 25 c. silver, black and blue 10 10
83 – 50 c. silver, black and red 20 10
84 – $1 silver, black and mauve 25 20
DESIGNS: 50 c. Half-dollar coin. $1 One dollar coin.

1976. Maps (2nd series). As T **2**.
85 5 c. black, dp green & green 10 10
86 10 c. black, green and blue 10 10
87 35 c. black, brown and red 20 20
88 45 c. black, red and orange 25 25
Nos. 85/8 exist in 7 different designs to each value as follows: A, Bequia, B, Canouan, C, Mayreau, D, Mustique, E, Petit St. Vincent, F, Prune, G, Union. To indicate any particular design use the appropriate catalogue No. together with the suffix for the island concerned.

13 Station Hill School and Post Office

1977. Mayreau Island. Multicoloured.
89 5 c. Type **13** 10 10
90 35 c. Church at Old Wall 10 10
91 45 c. La Sourciere Anchorage 10 10
92 $1 Saline Bay 25 15

14 Coronation Crown Coin

1977. Silver Jubilee. Multicoloured.
93 25 c. Type **14** 15 10
94 50 c. Silver Wedding crown 20 10
95 $1 Silver Jubilee crown 20 15

15 Fiddler Crab

1977. Crustaceans. Multicoloured.
96 5 c. Type **15** 10 10
97 35 c. Ghost crab 20 10
98 50 c. Blue crab 25 10
99 $1.25 Spiny lobster 55 40

16 Snorkel Diving

1977. Prune Island. Multicoloured.
100 5 c. Type **16** 10 10
101 35 c. Palm Island Resort 10 10
102 45 c. Casuarina Beach 10 15
103 $1 Palm Island Beach Club 30 70

17 Mustique Island

1977. Royal Visit. Surch as in T **17**.
104 **17** 40 c. turquoise and green 15 10
105 $2 ochre and brown 40 25

18 The Clinic, Charlestown

1977. Canouan Island (1st series). Mult.
106 5 c. Type **18** 10 10
107 35 c. Town jetty, Charlestown 10 10
108 45 c. Mail schooner arriving at Charlestown 10 10
109 $1 Grand Bay 30 65
See also Nos. 307/10.

19 Tropical Mockingbird

1978. Birds and their Eggs. Multicoloured.
110 1 c. Type **19** 10 50
111 2 c. Mangrove cuckoo 15 50
112 3 c. Osprey 20 50
113 4 c. Smooth-billed ani 20 50
114 5 c. House wren 20 40
115 6 c. Bananaquit 20 40
116 8 c. Carib grackle 20 45
117 10 c. Yellow-bellied elaenia 20 45
118 12 c. Collared plover 30 80
119 15 c. Cattle egret 30 45
120 20 c. Red-footed booby 30 45
121 25 c. Red-billed tropic bird 30 45
122 40 c. Royal tern 45 70
123 50 c. Grenada flycatcher 45 70
124 80 c. Purple gallinule 70 90
125 $1 Broad-winged hawk 75 90
126 $2 Scaly-breasted ground dove 90 1·60
127 $3 Laughing gull 1·25 1·75
128 $5 Common noddy 2·75 2·00
129 $10 Grey kingbird 3·00 3·00

1978. 25th Anniv of Coronation. British Cathedrals. As Nos. 422/5 of Monserrat. Multicoloured.
130 5 c. Worcester Cathedral 10 10
131 40 c. Coventry Cathedral 10 10
132 $1 Winchester Cathedral 15 20
133 $3 Chester Cathedral 25 45

20 Green Turtle

1978. Turtles. Multicoloured.
135 5 c. Type **20** 10 10
136 40 c. Hawksbill turtle 15 10
137 50 c. Leatherback turtle 15 10
138 $1.25 Loggerhead turtle 40 40

21 Three Kings following Star 22 Sailing Yachts

1978. Christmas. Scenes and Verses from the Carol "We Three Kings". Multicoloured.
139 5 c. Type **21** 10 10
140 10 c. King presenting gold 10 10
141 25 c. King presenting frankincense 10 10
142 50 c. King presenting myrrh 10 10
143 $2 Kings paying homage to infant Jesus 30 20

1979. National Regatta.
145 **22** 5 c. multicoloured 10 10
146 – 40 c. multicoloured 20 10
147 – 50 c. multicoloured 25 10
148 – $2 multicoloured 75 60
DESIGNS: 40 c. to $2, Various sailing yachts.

1979. Wildlife. As T **114** of St. Vincent. Mult.
149 20 c. Green iguana 10 10
150 40 c. Common opossum ("Manicou") 15 10
151 $2 Red-legged tortoise 60 65

1979. Death Centenary of Sir Rowland Hill. As T **103** of St. Vincent. Multicoloured.
152 80 c. Sir Rowland Hill 15 15
153 $1 Great Britain 1d. and 4d. stamps of 1858 with "A10" (Kingstown, St. Vincent) postmark 15 25
154 $2 St. Vincent ½d and 1d. stamps of 1894 with Bequia postmark 25 40

1979. International Year of the Child. Designs as Nos. 570/3 of St. Vincent.
156 6 c. black, silver and blue 10 10
157 40 c. black, silver & salmon 10 10
158 $1 black, silver and buff 20 10
159 $3 black, silver and lilac 45 30

1979. Independence. As T **106** of St. Vincent. Multicoloured.
160 5 c. National flag and "Ixora salicifolia" (flower) 10 10
161 40 c. House of Assembly and "Ixora odorata" (flower) 10 10
162 $1 Prime Minister R. Milton Cato and "Ixora javanica" (flower) 20 20

23 False Killer Whale

1980. Whales and Dolphins. Multicoloured.

163	10 c. Type **23**	60	10
164	50 c. Spinner dolphin	60	35
165	90 c. Bottle-nosed dolphin	70	80
166	$2 Short-finned Pilot whale ("Blackfish")	2·00	1·50

1980. "London 1980" International Stamp Exhibition. As T **110** of St. Vincent. Multicoloured.

167	40 c. Queen Elizabeth II	10	10
168	50 c. St. Vincent 2 c. stamp of 1965	15	10
169	$3 First Grenadines stamps	40	1·00

1980. Sport. As T **112** of St. Vincent. Mult.

171	25 c. Running	10	10
172	50 c. Sailing	10	10
173	$1 Long-jumping	20	20
174	$2 Swimming	30	30

1980. Hurricane Relief. Nos. 171/4 optd **HURRICANE RELIEF 50c.**

175	**22** 25 c. + 50 c. multicoloured	10	25
176	– 50 c. + 50 c. multicoloured	15	30
177	– $1 + 50 c. multicoloured	20	40
178	– $2 + 50 c. multicoloured	30	55

24 Scene and Verse from the Carol "De Borning Day"

26 Ins. Cannaouan (from map of Windward Islands by R. Ottens, c. 1765)

25 Post Office, Port Elizabeth

1980. Christmas. Multicoloured.

179	5 c. Type **24**	10	10
180	50 c. "Mary and de Baby lonely"	10	10
181	60 c. "Mary and de Baby weary"	10	10
182	$1 "Mary and de Baby rest easy"	15	15
183	$2 "Star above shine in de sky"	25	25

1981. Bequia Island (2nd series). Mult.

185	50 c. Type **25**	15	15
186	60 c. Moonhole	15	20
187	$1.50 Fishing boats, Admiralty Bay	30	40
188	$2 "The Friendship Rose" (yacht) at jetty	40	55

1981. Details from Early Maps. Multicoloured.

189	50 c. Type **26**	30	30
190	50 c. Cannouan Is. (from chart by J. Parsons, 1861)	30	30
191	60 c. Ins. Moustiques (from map of Windward Islands by R. Ottens, c. 1765)	30	35
192	60 c. Mustique Is. (from chart by J. Parsons, 1861)	30	35
193	$2 Ins. Bequia (from map of Windward Islands by R. Ottens, c.1765)	50	75
194	$2 Bequia Is. (from map surveyed in 1763 by T. Jefferys)	50	75

1981. Royal Wedding. Royal Yachts. As T **26** of Kiribati. Multicoloured.

195	50 c. "Mary"	10	15
196	50 c. Prince Charles and Lady Diana Spencer	35	40
197	$3 "Alexandra"	20	30
198	$3 As No. 196	80	90
199	$3.50 "Britannia"	25	35
200	$3.50 As No. 196	85	90

27 Bar Jack

1981. Game Fish. Multicoloured.

204	10 c. Type **27**	15	10
205	50 c. Tarpon	30	10
206	60 c. Cobia	35	10
207	$2 Blue marlin	1·00	70

28 H.M.S. "Experiment" (frigate)

1982. Ships. Multicoloured.

208	1 c. Type **28**	10	10
209	3 c. "Lady Nelson" (cargo liner)	15	10
210	5 c. "Daisy" (brig)	20	10
211	6 c. Carib canoe	20	10
212	10 c. "Hairoun Star" (freighter)	30	10
213	15 c. "Jupiter" (liner)	40	10
214	20 c. "Christina" (steam yacht)	40	10
215	25 c. "Orinoco" (mail paddle-steamer)	55	15
216	30 c. "H.M.S. Lively" (frigate)	55	15
217	50 c. "Alabama" (Confederate warship)	70	25
218	60 c. "Denmark" (freighter)	80	30
219	75 c. "Santa Maria"	1·10	50
220	$1 "Baffin" (research vessel)	1·10	55
221	$2 "Queen Elizabeth 2" (liner)	1·50	1·25
222	$3 R.Y. "Britannia"	1·50	1·75
223	$5 "Geeststar" (freighter)	1·50	2·50
224	$10 "Grenadines Star" (ferry)	2·50	5·00

29 Prickly Pear Fruit

30 Anne Neville. Princess of Wales, 1470

1982. Prickly Pear Cactus. Multicoloured.

225	10 c. Type **29**	15	15
226	50 c. Prickly pear flower buds	35	35
227	$1 Flower of prickly pear cactus	60	60
228	$2 Prickly pear cactus	1·25	1·25

1982. 21st Birthday of Princess of Wales. Multicoloured.

229	50 c. Type **30**	10	15
230	60 c. Coat of arms of Anne Neville	10	15
231	$6 Diana, Princess of Wales	60	80

31 Old and New Uniforms

1982. 75th Anniv of Boy Scout Movement. Multicoloured.

232	$1.50 Type **31**	60	75
233	$2.50 Lord Baden-Powell	90	1·00

1982. Birth of Prince William of Wales. Nos. 224/6 optd **ROYAL BABY** and Island name.

234	50 c. Type **30**	10	15
235	60 c. Coat of arms of Anne Neville	10	15
236	$6 Diana, Princess of Wales	60	80

Nos. 229/32 exist optd with 5 different island names as follows: A, Bequia, B, Canouan, C, Mayreau, D, Mustique, E, Union Island. To indicate any particular overprint use the appropriate catalogue No. together with the suffix for the island concerned.

33 Silhouette Figures of Mary and Joseph

1982. Christmas. Silhouette of figures. Multicoloured.

237	10 c. Type **33**	10	10
238	$1.50 Animals in stable	45	45
239	$2.50 Mary and Joseph with baby Jesus	60	60

1983. No. 123 surch **45c.**

241	45 c. on 50 c. Grenada flycatcher	30	30

35 Power Station, Clifton

1983. Union Island (2nd issue). Multicoloured.

242	50 c. Type **35**	25	15
243	60 c. Sunrise, Clifton harbour	25	15
244	$1.50 Junior Secondary School, Ashton	60	40
245	$2 Frigate Rock and Conch Shell Beach	85	55

36 British Man-of-war

37 Montgolfier Balloon, 1783

1983. Bicentenary of Treaty of Versailles. Mult.

246	45 c. Type **36**	35	15
247	60 c. American man-of-war	35	15
248	$1.50 Soldiers carrying U.S flags	75	45
249	$2 British troops in battle	80	55

1983. Bicentenary of Manned Flight. Mult.

250	45 c. Type **37**	10	15
251	60 c. Ayres Turbo Thrush Commander (horiz)	15	15
252	$1.50 Lebaudy-Juillot airship No. 1 "La Jaune" (horiz)	35	45
253	$2 Space shuttle "Columbia" (horiz)	40	55

38 Coat of Arms of Henry VIII

39 Quarter Dollar and Half Dollar, 1797

1983. Leaders of the World. British Monarchs. Multicoloured.

255	60 c. Type **38**	15	25
256	60 c. Henry VIII	15	25
257	60 c. Coat of Arms of James I	15	25
258	60 c. James I	15	25
259	75 c. Henry VIII at Hampton Court	15	25
260	75 c. Hampton Court	15	25
261	75 c. James I at Edinburgh Castle	15	25
262	75 c. Edinburgh Castle	15	25
263	$2.50 The "Mary Rose"	25	35
264	$2.50 Henry VIII and Portsmouth harbour	25	35
265	$2.50 Gunpowder Plot	25	35
266	$2.50 James I and Gunpowder Plot	25	35

1983. Old Coinage. Multicoloured.

267	20 c. Type **39**	10	10
268	45 c. Nine Bitts, 1811–14	15	15
269	75 c. Twelve Bitts and Six Bitts, 1811–14	25	25
270	$3 Sixty-six Shillings, 1798	80	80

40 Class D13

1984. Leaders of the World. Railway Locomotives (1st series). The first design in each pair shows technical drawings and the second the locomotive at work.

271	5 c. multicoloured	10	10
272	5 c. multicoloured	10	10
273	10 c. multicoloured	10	10
274	10 c. multicoloured	10	10
275	15 c. multicoloured	10	15
276	15 c. multicoloured	10	15
277	35 c. multicoloured	15	20
278	35 c. multicoloured	15	20
279	45 c. multicoloured	15	20
280	45 c. multicoloured	15	20
281	60 c. multicoloured	15	20
282	60 c. multicoloured	15	20
283	$1 multicoloured	20	25
284	$1 multicoloured	20	25
285	$2.50 multicoloured	25	35
286	$2.50 multicoloured	25	35

DESIGNS: Nos. 271/2, Class D13, U.S.A., 1892 (Type **40**); 273/4, High Speed Train 125, Great Britain (1980); 275/6, Class T9, Great Britain (1899); 277/8, "Claud Hamilton", Great Britain (1900); 279/80, Class J, U.S.A. (1941); 281/2, Class D16, U.S.A (1895); 283/4, "Lode Star", Great Britain (1907); 285/6, "Blue Peter", Great Britain (1948).

See also Nos. 321/26, 351/8, 390/7, 412/9, 443/58, 504/19 and 520/35.

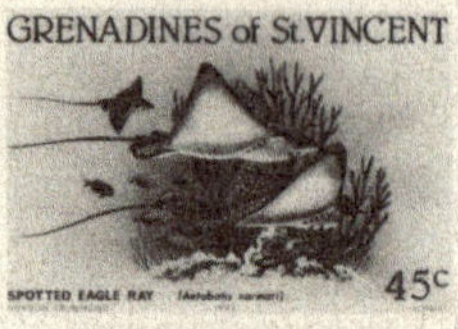

41 Spotted Eagle Ray

1984. Reef Fishes. Multicoloured.

287	45 c. Type **41**	15	20
288	60 c. Queen triggerfish	15	35
289	$1.50 White spotted filefish	25	1·00
290	$2 Schoolmaster	35	1·25

42 R. A. Woolmer

44 Lady of the Night

43 Junior Secondary School

1984. Leaders of the World. Cricketers (1st series). The first design in each pair shows a portrait and the second the cricketer in action.

291	1 c. multicoloured	10	10
292	1 c. multicoloured	10	10
293	3 c. multicoloured	10	10
294	3 c. multicoloured	10	10
295	5 c. multicoloured	10	10
296	5 c. multicoloured	10	10
297	30 c. multicoloured	20	20
298	30 c. multicoloured	20	20
299	60 c. multicoloured	30	30
300	60 c. multicoloured	30	30
301	$1 multicoloured	40	40
302	$1 multicoloured	40	40
303	$2 multicoloured	45	70
304	$2 multicoloured	45	70
305	$3 multicoloured	55	80
306	$3 multicoloured	55	80

DESIGNS: Nos. 291/2, R. A. Woolmer (Type **42**); 293/4, K. S Ranjitsinhji; 295/6, W. R Hammond; 297/8, D. L Underwood; 299/300, W. G Grace; 301/2, E. A. E. Baptiste; 303/4, A. P. E. Knott; 305/6, L. E. G. Ames.

See also Nos. 331/8 and 364/9.

1984. Canouan Island (2nd series). Multicoloured.

307	35 c. Type **43**	20	20
308	45 c. Police Station	25	25
309	$1 Post Office	50	50
310	$3 Anglican Church	1·25	1·50

1984. Leaders of the World. Railway Locomotives (2nd issue). As T **40**. The first design in each pair shows technical drawings and the second the locomotive at work.

311	1 c. multicoloured	10	10
312	1 c. multicoloured	10	10
313	5 c. multicoloured	10	10
314	5 c. multicoloured	10	10
315	20 c. multicoloured	15	15
316	20 c. multicoloured	15	15
317	35 c. multicoloured	15	15
318	35 c. multicoloured	15	15
319	60 c. multicoloured	20	20
320	60 c. multicoloured	20	20
321	$1 multicoloured	20	25
322	$1 multicoloured	20	25
323	$1.50 multicoloured	25	30
324	$1.50 multicoloured	25	30
325	$3 multicoloured	35	55
326	$3 multicoloured	35	55

DESIGNS: Nos. 311/12, Class C62, Japan (1948); 313/14, Class V, Great Britain (1903); 315/16, Richard Trevithick's "Catch-Me-Who-Can", Great Britain (1808); 317/18, Class E10, Japan (1948); 319/20, "J. B. Earle", Great Britain (1904); 321/2, No. 762 "Lyn", Great Britain (1898); 323/4, "Talyllyn", Great Britain (1865); 325/6, "Cardean", Great Britain (1906).

1984. Night-blooming Flowers. Mult.

327	35 c. Type **44**	35	30
328	45 c. Four o'clock	40	35
329	75 c. Mother-in-law's tongue	60	60
330	$3 Queen of the night	1·50	2·75

1984. Leaders of the World. Cricketers (2nd series). As T **42**. The first in each pair listed shows a head portrait and the second the cricketer in action.

331	5 c. multicoloured	10	10
332	5 c. multicoloured	10	10
333	30 c. multicoloured	25	20
334	30 c. multicoloured	25	20
335	$1 multicoloured	35	40
336	$1 multicoloured	35	40
337	$2.50 multicoloured	65	80
338	$2.50 multicoloured	65	80

DESIGNS: Nos. 331/2, S. F. Barnes; 333/4, R. Peel; 335/6, H. Larwood; 337/8, Sir John Hobbs.

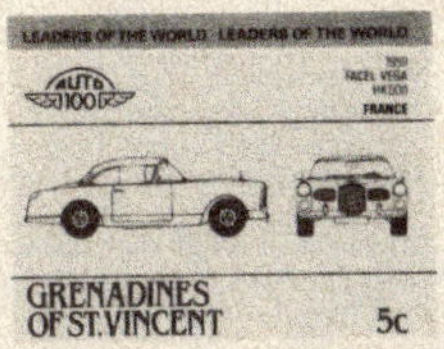

45 Facel "Vega HK500"

1984. Leaders of the World. Automobiles (1st series). The first design in each pair shows technical drawings and the second paintings.

339	5 c. black, blue and green	10	10
340	5 c. multicoloured	10	10
341	25 c. black, lilac and pink	10	10
342	25 c. multicoloured	10	10
343	50 c. black, blue and orange	15	15
344	50 c. multicoloured	15	15
345	$3 black, stone and brown	30	45
346	$3 multicoloured	30	45

DESIGNS: Nos. 339/40, Facel "Vega HK500" (Type **45**); 341/2, BMW "328"; 343/4, Frazer-Nash "TT Replica 1.5L"; 345/6, Buick "Roadmaster Riviera".

See also Nos. 378/85 and 431/42.

46 Three Wise Men and Star

1984. Christmas. Multicoloured.

347	20 c. Type **46**	10	10
348	45 c. Journeying to Bethlehem	15	25
349	$3 Presenting gifts	70	1·40

1985. Leaders of the World. Railway Locomotives (3rd series). As T **40**. The first design in each pair shows technical drawings and the second the locomotive at work.

351	1 c. multicoloured	10	10
352	1 c. multicoloured	10	10
353	15 c. multicoloured	10	10
354	15 c. multicoloured	10	10
355	75 c. multicoloured	20	25
356	75 c. multicoloured	20	25
357	$3 multicoloured	50	70
358	$3 multicoloured	50	70

DESIGNS: Nos. 351/2, P.L.M "Grosse C", France (1898); 353/4, Class C12, Japan (1932); 355/6, Class D50, Japan (1923); 357/8, "Fire Fly", Great Britain (1840).

47 Caribbean King Crab

1985. Shell Fish. Multicoloured.

360	25 c. Type **47**	20	15
361	60 c. Queen or pink conch	30	35
362	$1 White sea urchin	35	55
363	$3 West Indian top shell or wilk	75	1·75

1985. Leaders of the World. Cricketers (3rd series). As T **42** (55, 60 c.) the first in each pair showing a head portrait and the second the cricketer in action, or horiz designs showing teams ($2).

364	55 c. multicoloured	25	35
365	55 c. multicoloured	25	35
366	60 c. multicoloured	25	40
367	60 c. multicoloured	25	40
368	$2 multicoloured	60	85
369	$2 multicoloured	60	85

DESIGNS—VERT (As T **42**): Nos. 364/5, M. D Moxon; 366/7, L. Potter. HORIZ (59×42 mm): No. 368, Kent team; 369, Yorkshire team.

HAVE YOU READ THE NOTES AT THE BEGINNING OF THIS CATALOGUE?
These often provide answers to the enquiries we receive.

48 "Cypripedium calceolus"

1985. Leaders of the World. Flowers. Multicoloured.

370	5 c. Type **48**	10	10
371	5 c. "Gentiana asclepiadea"	10	10
372	55 c. "Clianthus formosus"	15	20
373	55 c. "Clemisia coriacea"	15	20
374	60 c. "Erythronium americanum"	15	20
375	60 c. "Laelia anceps"	15	20
376	$2 "Leucadendron discolor"	35	50
377	$2 "Meconopsis horridula"	35	50

1985. Leaders of the World. Automobiles (2nd series). As T **45**. The first in each pair shows technical drawings and the second paintings.

378	5 c. black, yellow and blue	10	10
379	5 c. multicoloured	10	10
380	60 c. black, yellow and orange	15	15
381	60 c. multicoloured	15	15
382	$1 black, green and blue	15	20
383	$1 multicoloured	15	20
384	$1.50 black, blue and green	15	25
385	$1.50 multicoloured	15	25

DESIGNS: Nos. 378/9, Winton (1903); 380/1, Invicta 4½ litre (1932); 382/3, Daimler "SP250 Dart" (1959); 384/5, Brabham "Repco BT19" (1966).

49 Windsurfing

1985. Tourism. Watersports. Multicoloured.

386	35 c. Type **49**	15	15
387	45 c. Water-skiing	15	15
388	75 c. Scuba-diving	15	25
389	$3 Deep-sea game fishing	35	1·40

1985. Leaders of the World. Railway Locomotives (4th series). As T **40**. The first design in each pair shows technical drawings and the second the locomotive at work.

390	10 c. multicoloured	10	10
391	10 c. multicoloured	10	10
392	40 c. multicoloured	20	20
393	40 c. multicoloured	20	20
394	50 c. multicoloured	20	20
395	50 c. multicoloured	20	20
396	$2.50 multicoloured	70	80
397	$2.50 multicoloured	70	80

DESIGNS: Nos. 390/1, Class 581 electric train, Japan (1968); 392/3, 231-132BT, Algeria (1936); 394/5, "Slieve Gullion", Ireland (1913); 396/7, Class "Beattie" well tank, Great Britain (1874).

50 Passion Fruits and Blossom

1985. Fruits and Blossoms. Multicoloured.

398	30 c. Type **50**	15	20
399	75 c. Guava	25	40
400	$1 Sapodilla	35	55
401	$2 Mango	50	1·10

51 Queen Elizabeth the Queen Mother

1985. Leaders of the World. Life and Times of Queen Elizabeth the Queen Mother. Various vertical portraits.

403	**51** 40 c. multicoloured	10	20
404	– 40 c. multicoloured	10	20
405	– 75 c. multicoloured	10	20
406	– 75 c. multicoloured	10	20
407	– $1.10 multicoloured	15	20
408	– $1.10 multicoloured	15	20
409	– $1.75 multicoloured	15	30
410	– $1.75 multicoloured	15	30

Each value, issued in pairs, shows a floral pattern across the bottom of the portraits which stops short of the left-hand edge on the first stamp and of the right-hand edge on the second.

1985. Leaders of the World. Railway Locomotives (5th series). As T **40**. The first design in each pair shows technical drawings and the second the locomotive at work.

412	35 c. multicoloured	15	20
413	35 c. multicoloured	15	20
414	70 c. multicoloured	20	30
415	70 c. multicoloured	20	30
416	$1.20 multicoloured	30	40
417	$1.20 multicoloured	30	40
418	$2 multicoloured	40	65
419	$2 multicoloured	40	65

DESIGNS: Nos. 412/13, "Coronation", Great Britain (1937); 414/15, Class E18, Germany (1935); 416/17, Hayes type, U.S.A. (1854); 418/19, Class 2120, Japan (1890).

1985. Royal Visit. Nos. 199/200, 222, 287, 398 and 407/8 optd **CARIBBEAN ROYAL VISIT 1985** or surch also.

420	**50** 30 c. multicoloured	80	1·25
421	**41** 45 c. multicoloured	1·00	1·75
422	– $1.10 multicoloured (No. 407)	1·75	3·75
423	– $1.10 multicoloured (No. 408)	1·75	3·75
424	– $1.50 on $3.50 multicoloured (No. 199)	2·00	2·25
425	– $1.50 on $3.50 multicoloured (No. 200)	15·00	17·00
426	– $3 multicoloured (No. 222)	2·25	3·25

52 Donkey Man

1985. Traditional Dances. Multicoloured.

427	45 c. Type **52**	15	30
428	75 c. Cake dance (vert)	20	40
429	$1 Bois-Bois man (vert)	25	55
430	$2 Maypole dance	45	1·10

1986. Leaders of the World. Automobiles (3rd series). As T **45**. The first in each pair shows technical drawings and the second paintings.

431	15 c. black, lilac and mauve	10	10
432	15 c. multicoloured	10	10
433	45 c. black, yellow & brown	10	20
434	45 c. multicoloured	10	20
435	60 c. black, green and blue	10	25
436	60 c. multicoloured	10	25
437	$1 black, brown and green	15	25
438	$1 multicoloured	15	25
439	$1.75 black, yellow & orange	15	35
440	$1.75 multicoloured	15	35
441	$3 multicoloured	25	45
442	$3 multicoloured	25	45

DESIGNS: Nos. 431/2, Mercedes-Benz 4.5 litre (1914); 433/4, Rolls Royce "Silver Wraith" (1954); 435/6, Lamborghini "Countach" (1974); 437/8, Marmon "V-16" (1932); 439/40, Lotus-Ford "49 B" (1968); 441/2, Delage 1.5 litre (1927).

1986. Leaders of the World. Railway Locomotives (6th series). As T **40**. The first in each pair shows technical drawings and the second the locomotive at work.

443	15 c. multicoloured	15	10
444	15 c. multicoloured	15	10
445	45 c. multicoloured	20	20
446	45 c. multicoloured	20	20
447	60 c. multicoloured	20	30
448	60 c. multicoloured	20	30
449	75 c. multicoloured	20	35
450	75 c. multicoloured	20	35
451	$1 multicoloured	25	40
452	$1 multicoloured	25	40
453	$1.50 multicoloured	25	50
454	$1.50 multicoloured	25	50
455	$2 multicoloured	30	65
456	$2 multicoloured	30	65
457	$3 multicoloured	30	80
458	$3 multicoloured	30	80

DESIGNS: Nos. 443/4, Class T15, Germany (1897); 445/6, Class 13, Great Britain (1900); 447/8, "Halesworth", Great Britain (1879); 449/50, Class "Problem", Great Britain (1859); 451/2, Class "Western" diesel, Great Britain (1961); 453/4, Drummond's "Bug", Great Britain (1899); 455/6, Class "Clan", Great Britain (1951); 457/8, Class 1800, Japan (1884).

1986. 60th Birthday of Queen Elizabeth II. As T **167** of British Virgin Islands. Multicoloured.

459	5 c. Queen Elizabeth II	15	15
460	$1 At Princess Anne's christening, 1950	30	35
461	$4 Princess Elizabeth	60	90
462	$6 In Canberra, 1982 (vert)	75	1·50

53 Handmade Dolls

1986. Handicrafts. Multicoloured.

464	10 c. Type **53**	10	10
465	60 c. Basketwork	20	35
466	$1 Scrimshaw work	30	50
467	$3 Model sailing dinghy	80	1·90

54 Uruguayan Team

1986. World Cup Football Championship, Mexico. Multicoloured.

468	1 c. Type **54**	10	10
469	10 c. Polish team	10	10
470	45 c. Bulgarian player (28×42 mm)	25	30
471	75 c. Iraqi player (28×42 mm)	35	40
472	$1.50 South Korean player (28×42 mm)	75	90
473	$2 Northern Irish player (28×42 mm)	1·00	1·40
474	$4 Portuguese team	1·50	1·75
475	$5 Canadian team	1·60	1·75

55 "Marasmius pallescens"

1986. Fungi. Multicoloured.

477	45 c. Type **55**	2·00	75
478	60 c. "Leucocoprinus fragilissimus"	2·25	1·10
479	75 c. "Hygrocybe occidentalis"	2·75	1·60
480	$3 "Xerocomus hypoxanthus"	7·50	7·00

1986. Royal Wedding (1st issue). As T **168** of British Virgin Islands. Multicoloured.

481	60 c. Miss Sarah Ferguson and Princess Diana applauding	15	25
482	60 c. Prince Andrew at shooting match	15	25
483	$2 Prince Andrew and Miss Sarah Ferguson (horiz)	50	80
484	$2 Prince Charles with Prince Andrew, Princess Anne and Princess Margaret on balcony (horiz)	50	80

1986. Royal Wedding (2nd issue). Nos. 481/4 optd **Congratulations to T.R.H. The Duke and Duchess of York.**

486	60 c. Miss Sarah Ferguson and Princess Diana applauding	30	50
487	60 c. Prince Andrew at shooting match	30	50
488	$2 Prince Andrew and Miss Sarah Ferguson (horiz)	1·00	1·25
489	$2 Prince Charles, Prince Andrew, Princess Anne and Princess Margaret on balcony (horiz)	1·00	1·25

56 "Brachymesia furcata"

1986. Dragonflies. Multicoloured.

490	45 c. Type **56**	15	20
491	60 c. "Lepthemis vesiculosa"	20	40
492	75 c. "Perithemis domitta"	20	45
493	$2.50 "Tramea abdominalis (vert)	40	1·40

57 American Kestrel

58 Santa playing Steel Band Drums

1986. Birds of Prey. Multicoloured.

495	10 c. Type **57**	65	45
496	45 c. Common black hawk	1·75	50
497	60 c. Peregrine falcon	1·90	1·25
498	$4 Osprey	4·75	6·50

1986. Christmas. Multicoloured.

499	45 c. Type **58**	30	30
500	60 c. Santa windsurfing	35	35
501	$1.25 Santa skiing	60	85
502	$2 Santa limbo dancing	1·10	1·60

1987. Railway Locomotives (7th series). As T **40**. The first in each pair shows technical drawings and the second the locomotive at work.

504 10 c. multicoloured 10 10
505 10 c. multicoloured 10 10
506 40 c. multicoloured 20 25
507 40 c. multicoloured 20 25
508 50 c. multicoloured 25 30
509 50 c. multicoloured 25 30
510 60 c. multicoloured 25 30
511 60 c. multicoloured 25 30
512 75 c. multicoloured 35 40
513 75 c. multicoloured 35 40
514 $1 multicoloured 35 50
515 $1 multicoloured 35 50
516 $1.25 multicoloured 40 60
517 $1.25 multicoloured 40 60
518 $1.50 multicoloured 55 75
519 $1.50 multicoloured 55 75

DESIGNS: Nos. 504/5, Class 1001, No. 1275, Great Britain (1874); 506/7, Class 4P Garratt, Great Britain (1927); 508/9, "Papyrus", Great Britain (1929); 510/11, Class VI, Great Britain (1930); 512/13, Class 40 diesel, No. D200, Great Britain (1958); 514/15, Class 42 "Warship" diesel, Great Britain (1958); 516/17, Class P-69, U.S.A. (1902); 518/19, Class 60-3 Shay, No. 15, U.S.A. (1913).

1987. Railway Locomotives (8th series). As T **40**. The first in each pair shows technical drawings and the second the locomotive at work.

520 10 c. multicoloured 10 15
521 10 c. multicoloured 10 15
522 40 c. multicoloured 20 30
523 40 c. multicoloured 20 30
524 50 c. multicoloured 25 35
525 50 c. multicoloured 25 35
526 60 c. multicoloured 25 40
527 60 c. multicoloured 25 40
528 75 c. multicoloured 30 45
529 75 c. multicoloured 30 45
530 $1 multicoloured 40 45
531 $1 multicoloured 40 45
532 $1.50 multicoloured 55 55
533 $1.50 multicoloured 55 55
534 $2 multicoloured 65 70
535 $2 multicoloured 65 70

DESIGNS: Nos. 520/1, Class 142, East Germany (1977); 522/3, Class 120, West Germany (1979); 524/5, Class X, Australia (1954); 526/7, Class 59, Great Britain (1986); 528/9, New York Elevated Railroad "Spuyten Duyvel", U.S.A. (1875); 530/1, Camden & Amboy Railroad "Stevens" and rebuilt "John Bull", U.S.A. (1832); 532/3, Class H1-d, No. 2850, Canada (1938); 534/5, "Pioneer Zephyr" 3-car diesel set, U.S.A. (1934).

59 Queen Elizabeth with Prince Andrew

61 "Australia IV"

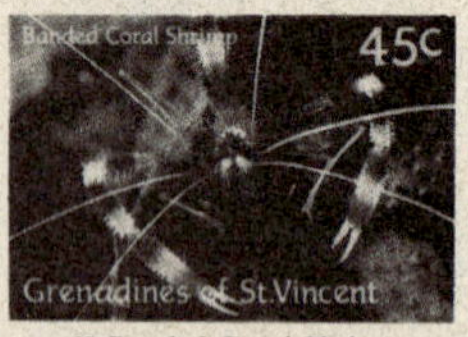

60 Banded Coral Shrimp

1987. Royal Ruby Wedding and 150th Anniv of Queen Victoria's Accession.

536 **59** 15 c. multicoloured 20 15
537 – 45 c. brown, black and yellow 25 20
538 – $1.50 multicoloured 30 50
539 – $3 multicoloured 45 80
540 – $4 multicoloured 50 1·10

DESIGNS: 45 c. Queen Victoria and Prince Albert, c. 1855; $1.50, Queen and Prince Philip after Trooping the Colour, 1977; $3 Queen and Duke of Edinburgh, 1953; $4 Queen in her study, c. 1980.

1987. Marine Life. Multicoloured.

542 45 c. Type **60** 40 35
543 50 c. Arrow crab and flamingo tongue 45 50
544 65 c. Cardinal fish 55 90
545 $5 Moray eel 2·00 3·75

1988. Ocean Racing Yachts. Multicoloured.

547 50 c. Type **61** 35 35
548 65 c. "Crusader II" 40 50
549 75 c. "New Zealand II" 45 60
550 $2 "Italia" 70 1·25
551 $4 "White Crusader" 80 2·00
552 $5 "Stars and Stripes" 85 2·25

62 Seine-fishing Boats racing

1988. Bequia Regatta. Multicoloured.

554 5 c. Type **62** 10 15
555 50 c. "Friendship Rose" (cruising yacht) 15 30
556 75 c. Fishing boats racing 20 45
557 $3.50 Yachts racing 75 2·25

63 Britten Norman Islander making Night Approach

1988. Mustique Airways. Multicoloured.

559 15 c. Type **63** 10 15
560 65 c. Beech Baron aircraft in flight 15 35
561 75 c. Britten Norman Islander over forest 15 35
562 $5 Beech Baron on airstrip 1·00 2·25

64 "Sv. Pyotr" in Arctic (Bering)

65 Asif Iqbal Razvi

1988. Explorers. Multicoloured.

564 15 c. Type **64** 35 20
565 75 c. Bering's ships in pack ice 40 30
566 $1 Livingstone's steam launch "Ma-Robert" on Zambesi 40 40
567 $2 Meeting of Livingstone and H. M Stanley at Ujiji 50 75
568 $3 Speke and Burton at Tabori 50 90
569 $3.50 Speke and Burton in canoe on Lake Victoria 50 1·10
570 $4 Sighting the New World, 1492 60 1·25
571 $4.50 Columbus trading with Indians 60 1·40

1988. Cricketers of 1988 International Season. Multicoloured.

573 20 c. Type **65** 30 30
574 45 c. R. J. Hadlee 50 50
575 75 c. M. D. Crowe 70 80
576 $1.25 C. H. Lloyd 1·00 1·25
577 $1.50 A. R. Boarder 1·25 1·50
578 $2 M. D. Marshall 1·50 2·00
579 $2.50 G. A. Hick 1·50 2·25
580 £3.50 C. G. Greenidge (horiz) 1·60 2·75

66 Pam Shriver

1988. International Tennis Players. Mult.

582 15 c. Type **66** 30 20
583 50 c. Kevin Curran (vert) 30 30
584 75 c. Wendy Turnbull (vert) 40 35
585 $1 Evonne Cawley (vert) 50 50
586 $1.50 Ilie Nastase 60 65
587 $2 Billie Jean King (vert) 65 75
588 $3 Bjorn Borg (vert) 75 1·25
589 $3.50 Virginia Wade with Wimbledon trophy (vert) 80 1·50

No. 584 is inscribed "WENDY TURNBALL" in error.

67 Mickey and Minnie Mouse visiting Fatehpur Sikri

1989. "India-'89" International Stamp Exhibition. Designs showing Walt Disney cartoon characters in India. Multicoloured.

591 1 c. Type **67** 10 10
592 2 c. Mickey and Minnie Mouse aboard "Palace on Wheels" train 10 10
593 3 c. Mickey and Minnie Mouse passing Old Fort, Delhi 10 10
594 5 c. Mickey and Minnie Mouse on camel, Pinjore Gardens, Haryana 10 10
595 10 c. Mickey and Minnie Mouse at Taj Mahal, Agra 10 10
596 25 c. Mickey and Minnie Mouse in Chandni Chowk, Old Delhi 15 10
597 $4 Goofy on elephant with Mickey and Minnie Mouse at Agra Fort, Jaipur 2·50 3·00
598 $5 Goofy, Mickey and Minnie Mouse at Gandhi Memorial Cape Comorin 2·75 3·25

1989. Japanese Art. As T **250** of Antigua. Multicoloured.

600 5 c. "The View at Yotsuya" (Hokusai) 20 20
601 30 c. "Landscape at Ochanomizu" (Hokuju) 50 50
602 45 c. "Itabashi" (Eisen) 60 60
603 65 c. "Early Summer Rain" (Kunisada) 75 75
604 75 c. "High Noon at Kasumigaseki" (Kuniyoshi) 80 80
605 $1 "The Yoshiwara Embankment by Moonlight" (Kuniyoshi) 1·00 1·00
606 $4 "The Bridge of Boats at Sano" (Hokusai) 2·75 3·00
607 $5 "Lingering Snow on Mount Hira" (Kunitora) 2·75 3·00

68 Player with Ball and Mt Vesuvius

71 "Marpesia petreus"

70 Command Module "Columbia"

1989. World Cup Football Championship, Italy (1st issue). Designs showing players and Italian landmarks. Multicoloured.

609 $1.50 Type **68** 1·25 1·25
610 $1.50 Fallen player, opponent kicking ball and Coliseum 1·25 1·25
611 $1.50 Player blocking ball and Venice 1·25 1·25
612 $1.50 Player tackling and Forum, Rome 1·25 1·25
613 $1.50 Two players competing for ball and Leaning Tower, Pisa 1·25 1·25
614 $1.50 Goalkeeper and Florence 1·25 1·25
615 $1.50 Two players competing for ball and St. Peter's, Vatican 1·25 1·25
616 $1.50 Player kicking ball and Pantheon 1·25 1·25

Nos 609/16 were printed together, se-tenant, forming a composite foreground design.
See also Nos. 680/3.

1989. 500th Anniv (1992) of Discovery of America by Columbus (1st issue). Pre-Columbian Arawak Society. As T **247** of Antigua. Multicoloured.

617 25 c. Arawak smoking tobacco 35 25
618 75 c. Arawak rolling cigar 65 65
619 $1 Applying body paint 80 80
620 $1.50 Making fire 1·10 1·40
621 $1.50 Cassava production 1·10 1·40
622 $1.50 Woman baking bread 1·10 1·40
623 $1.50 Using stone implement 1·10 1·40
624 $4 Arawak priest 2·50 2·75

Nos. 620/3 were printed together, se-tenant, forming a composite design.
See also Nos. 818/23 and 864/5.

1989. 20th Anniv of First Manned Landing on Moon. Multicoloured.

626 5 c. Type **70** 25 25
627 40 c. Astronaut Neil Armstrong saluting U.S. flag 85 85
628 55 c. "Columbia" above lunar surface 90 90
629 65 c. Lunar module "Eagle" leaving moon 90 90
630 70 c. "Eagle" on Moon 90 90
631 $1 "Columbia" re-entering Earth's atmosphere 1·25 1·25
632 $3 "Apollo II" emblem 2·50 2·50
633 $5 Armstrong and Aldrin on Moon 3·00 3·00

1989. Butterflies. Multicoloured.

635 5 c. Type **71** 30 30
636 30 c. "Papilio androgeus" 80 60
637 45 c. "Strymon maesites" 1·00 65
638 65 c. "Junonia coenia" 1·40 1·40
639 75 c. "Eurema gratiosa" 1·50 1·50
640 $1 "Hypolimnas misippus" 1·75 1·75
641 $4 "Urbanus proteus" 3·75 4·00
642 $5 "Junonia evarete" 3·75 4·00

72 "Solanum urens"

74 Exhibition Emblem

1989. Flowers from St. Vincent Botanical Gardens. Multicoloured.

644 80 c. Type **72** 1·00 1·00
645 $1.25 "Passiflora andersonii" 1·40 1·40
646 $1.65 "Miconia andersonii" 1·75 1·75
647 $1.85 "Pitcairnia sulphurea" 1·75 1·75

1989. Christmas. As T **183** of Gambia. Mult.

648 5 c. Goofy and Mickey Mouse in Rolls Royce "Silver Ghost", 1907 20 15
649 10 c. Daisy Duck driving first Stanley Steamer, 1897 20 15
650 15 c. Horace Horsecollar and Clarabelle Cow in Darracq "Genevieve", 1904 25 20
651 45 c. Donald Duck driving Detroit electric coupe, 1914 55 40
652 55 c. Mickey and Minnie Mouse in first Ford, 1896 55 40
653 $2 Mickey Mouse driving Reo "Runabout", 1904 2·00 2·00
654 $3 Goofy driving Winton mail truck, 1899 2·75 2·75
655 $5 Mickey and Minnie Mouse in Duryea car, 1893 3·50 4·00

1990. 50th Anniv of Second World War. As T **98** of Grenada Grenadines. Multicoloured.

657 10 c. Destroyer in action, First Battle of Narvik, 1940 25 25
658 15 c. Allied tank at Anzio, 1944 35 35
659 20 c. U.S. carrier under attack, Battle of Midway, 1942 40 40
660 45 c. North American B-25 Mitchell bombers over Gustav Line, 1944 70 70
661 55 c. Map showing Allied zones of Berlin, 1945 75 75
662 65 c. German U-boat pursuing convoy, Battle of the Atlantic, 1943 80 80
663 90 c. Allied tank, North Africa, 1943 1·00 1·00
664 $3 U.S. forces landing on Guam, 1944 2·50 2·50
665 $5 Crossing the Rhine, 1945 3·50 3·50
666 $6 Japanese battleships under attack, Lete Gulf, 1944 4·00 4·00

1990. "Stamp World London 90" International Stamp Exhibition (1st issue). Mickey's Shakespeare Company. As T **193** of Gambia showing Walt Disney cartoon characters. Multicoloured.

668 20 c. Goofy as Mark Anthony ("Julius Caesar") 30 20
669 30 c. Clarebelle Cow as the Nurse ("Romeo and Juliet") 35 25
670 45 c. Pete as Falstaff ("Henry IV") 50 40
671 50 c. Minnie Mouse as Portia ("The Merchant of Venice") 55 40
672 $1 Donald Duck as Hamlet ("Hamlet") 1·00 85
673 $2 Daisy Duck as Ophelia ("Hamlet") 1·75 2·00
674 $4 Donald and Daisy Duck as Benedick and Beatrice ("Much Ado About Nothing") 3·00 3·25
675 $5 Minnie Mouse and Donald Duck as Katherine and Petruchio ("The Taming of the Shrew") 3·00 3·25

1990. "Stamp World London 90" International Stamp Exhibition (2nd issue). 150th Anniv of the Penny Black.

677 **74** $1 black, pink and mauve 1·25 1·25
678 – $5 black, lilac and blue 3·50 4·00

DESIGNS: $5 Negative image of Penny Black.

1990. World Cup Football Championship, Italy (2nd issue). As T **210** of St. Vincent but horiz. Mult.

680 25 c. McCleish, Scotland 65 40
681 50 c. Rasul, Egypt 90 80
682 $2 Lindenberger, Austria 2·50 2·50
683 $4 Murray, U.S.A. 3·75 4·00

1990. "EXPO 90" International Garden and Greenery Exposition, Osaka. Orchids. As T **213** of St. Vincent. Multicoloured.

685 5 c. "Paphiopedilum" 40 40
686 25 c. "Dendrobium phalaenopsis" and "Cymbidium hybrid" 90 90
687 30 c. "Miltonia candida hybrid" 90 90
688 50 c. "Epidendrum ibaguense" and "Cymbidium" Elliot Rogers 1·25 1·25
689 $1 "Rossioglossum grande" 1·75 1·75
690 $2 "Phalaenopsis" Elisa Chang Lou and "Masdevallia coccinea" 2·00 2·00
691 $4 "Cypripedium acaule" and "Cypripedium calceolus" 3·00 3·00
692 $5 "Orchis spectabilis" 3·00 3·00

75 Scaly-breasted Ground Dove

1990. Birds of the Caribbean. Multicoloured.
694 5 c. Type **75** 20 20
695 25 c. Purple martin 40 40
696 45 c. Painted bunting 70 70
697 55 c. Blue-hooded euphonia . . . 80 80
698 75 c. Blue-grey tanager . . . . 1·00 1·00
699 $1 Red-eyed vireo . . . . . . 1·25 1·25
700 $2 Palm chat . . . . 2·00 2·00
701 $3 Northern jacana . . . . . 2·50 2·50
702 $4 Green-throated carib . . . 2·75 2·75
703 $5 St. Vincent amazon . . . . 3·00 3·00

1991. 90th Birthday of Queen Elizabeth the Queen Mother. As T **194** of Gambia.
705 $2 multicoloured . . . . . . 1·25 1·25
706 $2 multicoloured . . . . . . 1·25 1·25
707 $2 multicoloured . . . . . . 1·25 1·25
708 $2 multicoloured . . . . . . 1·25 1·25
709 $2 multicoloured . . . . . . 1·25 1·25
710 $2 multicoloured . . . . . . 1·25 1·25
711 $2 multicoloured . . . . . . 1·25 1·25
712 $2 multicoloured . . . . . . 1·25 1·25
713 $2 multicoloured . . . . . . 1·25 1·25
714 $2 multicoloured . . . . . . 1·25 1·25
715 $2 multicoloured . . . . . . 1·25 1·25
716 $2 multicoloured . . . . . . 1·25 1·25
717 $2 multicoloured . . . . . . 1·25 1·25
718 $2 multicoloured . . . . . . 1·25 1·25
719 $2 multicoloured . . . . . . 1·25 1·25
720 $2 multicoloured . . . . . . 1·25 1·25
721 $2 multicoloured . . . . . . 1·25 1·25
722 $2 multicoloured . . . . . . 1·25 1·25
723 $2 multicoloured . . . . . . 1·25 1·25
724 $2 multicoloured . . . . . . 1·25 1·25
725 $2 multicoloured . . . . . . 1·25 1·25
726 $2 multicoloured . . . . . . 1·25 1·25
727 $2 multicoloured . . . . . . 1·25 1·25
728 $2 multicoloured . . . . . . 1·25 1·25
729 $2 multicoloured . . . . . . 1·25 1·25
730 $2 multicoloured . . . . . . 1·25 1·25
731 $2 multicoloured . . . . . . 1·25 1·25
DESIGNS: No. 705, Lady Elizabeth Bowes-Lyon with sister; 706, Young Lady Elizabeth in long dress; 707, Young Lady Elizabeth wearing a hat; 708, Lady Elizabeth leaning on wall; 709, Lady Elizabeth on pony; 710, Studio portrait; 711, Lady Elizabeth in evening dress; 712, Duchess of York in fur-lined cloak; 713, Duchess of York holding rose; 714, Coronation, 1937; 715, King and Queen with Princess Elizabeth at Royal Lodge, Windsor; 716, Queen Elizabeth in blue hat; 717, King George VI and Queen Elizabeth; 718, Queen Elizabeth with Princess Elizabeth; 719, Queen Elizabeth watching sporting fixture; 720, Queen Elizabeth in white evening dress; 721, Princess Anne's christening, 1950; 722, Queen Mother with yellow bouquet; 723, Queen Mother and policewoman; 724, Queen Mother at ceremonial function; 725, Queen Mother in pink coat; 726, Queen Mother in academic robes; 727, Queen Mother in carriage with Princess Margaret; 728, Queen Mother in blue coat and hat; 729, Queen Mother with bouquet; 730, Queen Mother outside Clarence House on her birthday; 731, Queen Mother in turquoise coat and hat.

1991. Death Centenary (1990) of Vincent van Gogh (artist). As T **195** of British Virgin Islands. Multicoloured.
733 5 c. "View of Arles with Irises" 20 20
734 10 c. "Saintes-Maries" (vert) . 20 20
735 15 c. "Old Woman of Arles" (vert) 25 25
736 20 c. "Orchard in Blossom, bordered by Cypresses" . . 30 30
737 25 c. "Three White Cottages in Saintes-Maries" 30 30
738 35 c. "Boats at Saintes-Maries" 40 40
739 40 c. "Interior of a Restaurant in Arles" 45 45
740 45 c. "Peasant Women" (vert) 50 50
741 55 c. "Self-portrait" (vert) . . 60 60
742 60 c. "Pork Butcher's Shop from a Window" (vert) 70 70
743 75 c. "The Night Cafe in Arles" 80 80
744 $1 "2nd Lieut. Millet of the Zouaves" 95 95
745 $2 "The Cafe Terrace, Place du Forum, Arles at Night" (vert) 1·50 1·50
746 $3 "The Zouave" (vert) . . . 2·00 2·00
747 $4 "The Two Lovers" (detail) (vert) . . . . 2·75 2·75
748 $5 "Still Life" . . . . 3·00 3·00

1991. 65th Birthday of Queen Elizabeth II. As T **280** of Antigua. Multicoloured.
750 15 c. Inspecting the Yeomen of the Guard 30 20
751 40 c. Queen Elizabeth II with the Queen Mother at the Derby, 1988 . . . . 55 30
752 $2 The Queen and Prince Philip leaving Euston, 1986 . . . 2·00 2·00
753 $4 The Queen at the Commonwealth Institute, 1987 2·75 3·00

1991. 10th Wedding Anniv of Prince and Princess of Wales. As T **280** of Antigua. Multicoloured.
755 10 c. Prince and Princess at polo match, 1987 . . . . . . 35 20
756 50 c. Separate family portraits 70 40
757 $1 Prince William and Prince Henry at Kensington Palace, 1991 . . . . 1·00 1·00
758 $5 Portraits of Prince Charles and Princess Diana . . . . 3·50 4·00

76 Class 150 Steam Locomotive and Map

1991. "Phila Nippon '91" International Stamp Exhibition, Toyko. Japanese Railway Locomotives. Each in black, red and green.
760 10 c. Type **76** 50 50
761 25 c. Class 7100 locomotive, "Benkei", 1880 . . . . . . 80 80
762 35 c. Class 8620 steam locomotive, 1914 . . . . . 90 90
763 50 c. Class C53 steamlined steam locomotive, 1928 . . . . . 1·25 1·25
764 $1 Class DD51 diesel-hydraulic locomotive, 1962 . . . . . 1·75 1·75
765 $2 Class KTR001 electric railcar Tango Explorer (inscr "RF 22327") . . . . 2·25 2·25
766 $4 Class EF55 electric locomotive, 1936 . . . . . 3·00 3·00
767 $5 Class EF58 electric locomotive, 1946 . . . . . 3·00 3·00

77 President Gorbachev and Brandenburg Gate

1991. Anniversaries and Events. Multicoloured.
769 45 c. Type **77** 40 40
770 60 c. General de Gaulle in Djibouti, 1959 . . . . . . 75 55
771 65 c. "DIE MAUER MUSS WEG!" slogan 65 65
772 80 c. East German border guard escaping to West 80 80
773 $1 "Abduction from the Seraglio" . . . . 1·50 1·50
774 $1.50 Lilienthal and glider . . 1·75 1·75
775 $1.75 Trans-Siberian identity plate . . . . 2·00 2·00
776 $1.75 Trans-Siberian steam locomotive (vert) . . . . . 2·00 2·00
777 $2 Czechoslovakia 1918 20 h. stamp and scout delivering mail . . . . 2·25 2·25
778 $2 Zurich couple maypole dancing . . . . 2·25 2·25
779 $2 Man and woman in Vaud traditional costumes . . . . 2·25 2·25
780 $2 Georg Laves (architect) and Hoftheater . . . . 2·25 2·25
781 $3 Dresden, 1749 . . . . . . 2·50 2·50
782 $4 Scouts and cog train on Snowdon (vert) . . . . . . 2·75 2·75
ANNIVERSARIES AND EVENTS: Nos. 769, 771/2, Bicentenary of Brandenburg Gate; 770, Birth centenary of Charles de Gaulle (French statesman); 773, 781, Death bicentenary of Mozart; 774, Centenary of Otto Lilienthal's gliding experiments; 775/6, Centenary of Trans-Siberian Railway; 777, 782, 50th death anniv of Lord Baden-Powell and World Scout Jamboree, Korea; 778/9, 700th anniv of Swiss Confederation; 780, 750th anniv of Hanover.

78 Japanese Aircraft and Submarines leaving Truk

1991. 50th Anniv of Japanese Attack on Pearl Harbor. Multicoloured.
784 $1 Type **78** . . . . 1·40 1·40
785 $1 "Akagi" (Japanese aircraft carrier) . . . . 1·40 1·40
786 $1 Nakajima B5N2 "Kate" bombers . . . . 1·40 1·40
787 $1 Nakajima B5N2 "Kate" bombers attacking Battleship Row . . . . 1·40 1·40
788 $1 Burning aircraft, Ford Island airfield . . . . 1·40 1·40
789 $1 Doris Miller winning Navy Cross . . . . 1·40 1·40
790 $1 U.S.S. "West Virginia" and "Tennessee" (battleships) ablaze . . . . 1·40 1·40
791 $1 U.S.S. "Arizona" (battleship) sinking . . . . 1·40 1·40
792 $1 U.S.S. "New Orleans" (cruiser) . . . . 1·40 1·40
793 $1 President Roosevelt declaring war . . . . 1·40 1·40

1991. Christmas. Walt Disney Company Christmas Cards. As T **228** of St. Vincent. Multicoloured.
794 10 c. Pluto pulling Mickey Mouse in sledge, 1974 (horiz) 35 30
795 55 c. Mickey, Pluto and Donald Duck watching toy band, 1961 (horiz) 80 70
796 65 c. "The Same Old Wish", 1942 (horiz) 85 85
797 75 c. Mickey, Peter Pan, Donald and Nephews with Merlin the magician, 1963 (horiz) . . . 95 95
798 $1.50 Mickey and Donald with leprechauns, 1958 (horiz) . . 1·75 2·00
799 $2 Mickey and friends with book "Old Yeller", 1957 (horiz) . 2·00 2·25
800 $4 Mickey controlling Pinocchio, 1953 (horiz) . . . . 3·25 3·50
801 $5 Cinderella and Prince dancing, 1987 (horiz) . . . . 3·25 3·50

1992. 40th Anniv of Queen Elizabeth II's Accession. As T **288** of Antigua. Multicoloured.
803 15 c. View across bay 30 20
804 45 c. Schooner at anchor, Mayreau 60 25
805 $2 Hotel on hillside . . . . . 1·40 1·75
806 $4 Tourist craft at anchor . . 2·75 3·25

1992. International Stamp Exhibitions. As T **215** of Lesotho. Walt Disney cartoon characters. Multicoloured. (a) "Grenada '92", Spain. Spanish Explorers.
808 15 c. Big Pete as Hernando Cortes in Mexico (horiz) . . 20 15
809 40 c. Mickey Mouse as Hernando de Soto at Mississippi River (horiz) 40 30
810 $2 Goofy as Vasco Nunez de Balboa sights Pacific (horiz) 1·50 1·50
811 $4 Donald Duck as Francisco Coronado on Rio Grande (horiz) . . . . 2·50 2·75
(b) "World Columbian Stamp Expo '92", Chicago. Local Personalities.
813 10 c. Mickey Mouse and Pluto outside Walt Disney's birthplace (horiz) 20 20
814 50 c. Donald Duck and nephews in George Pullman's railway sleeping car (horiz) 55 55
815 $1 Daisy Duck as Jane Addams (social reformer) and Hull House (horiz) 85 85
816 $5 Mickey as Carl Sandburg (novelist, poet and historian) (horiz) . . . . 3·00 3·00

79 King Ferdinand and Queen Isabella of Spain

1992. 500th Anniv of Discovery of America by Columbus (2nd issue). Multicoloured.
818 10 c. Type **79** 25 25
819 45 c. "Santa Maria" and "Nina" in Acul Bay, Haiti 50 50
820 55 c. "Santa Maria" (vert) . . 55 55
821 $2 Ships of Columbus (vert) . 1·40 1·40
822 $4 Wreck of "Santa Maria" . . 2·50 2·50
823 $5 "Pinta" and "Nina" . . . . 2·75 2·75

1992. "Genova '92" International Thematic Stamp Exhibition (1st issue). Butterflies. As T **235** of St. Vincent. Multicoloured.
825 15 c. "Paulogramma sp" (horiz) 65 65
826 20 c. "Heliconius cydno" (horiz) 70 70
827 30 c. "Eutresis hypereia" (horiz) 75 75
828 45 c. "Eurytides columbus" . . 90 90
829 55 c. "Papilio ascolius" (horiz) 1·00 1·00
830 75 c. "Anaea pasibula" (horiz) 1·25 1·25
831 80 c. "Heliconius doris" (horiz) 1·25 1·25
832 $1 "Perisama pitheas" (horiz) 1·25 1·25
833 $2 "Batesia hypochlora" (horiz) 1·75 1·75
834 $3 "Heliconius erato" (horiz) 2·25 2·25
835 $4 "Elzunia cassandrina" (horiz) 2·50 2·50
836 $5 "Sais ivcidice" (horiz) . . . 2·50 2·50
See also Nos. 851/62.

1992. Fungi. As T **236** of St. Vincent. Multicoloured
838 10 c. "Entoloma bakeri" . . . 50 50
839 15 c. "Hydropus paraensis" . . 55 55
840 20 c. "Leucopaxillus gracillimus" 60 60
841 45 c. "Hygrotrama dennisianum" 80 80
842 50 c. "Leucoagaricus hortensis" 80 80
843 65 c. "Pyrrhoglossum pyrrhum" 1·00 1·00
844 75 c. "Amanita craeoderma" . 1·00 1·00
845 $1 "Lentinus bertieri" . . . . 1·25 1·25
846 $2 "Dennisiomyces griseus" . 2·00 2·00
847 $3 "Xerulina asprata" . . . . 2·50 2·50
848 $4 "Hygrocybe acutoconica" . 3·00 3·00
849 $5 "Lepiota spiculata" . . . . 3·00 3·00

1992. "Genova '92" International Thematic Stamp Exhibition (2nd issue). Hummingbirds. As T **237** of St. Vincent. Multicoloured.
851 5 c. Antillean crested hummingbird (female) (horiz) 30 30
852 10 c. Blue-tailed emerald (female) 30 30
853 35 c. Antillean mango (male) (horiz) 45 45
854 45 c. Antillean mango (female) (horiz) 45 45
855 55 c. Green-throated carib (horiz) 55 55
856 65 c. Green violetear (male) . . 70 70
857 75 c. Blue-tailed emerald (male) (horiz) 80 80
858 $1 Purple-throated carib . . . 1·00 1·00
859 $2 Copper-rumped hummingbird (horiz) . . . . 2·00 2·00
860 $3 Rufous-breasted hermit . . 2·75 2·75
861 $4 Antillean crested hummingbird (male) . . . . . 3·50 3·50
862 $5 Green-breasted mango (male) 3·75 3·75

1992. 500th Anniv of Discovery of America by Columbus (3rd issue). Organization of East Caribbean States. As Nos. 911/12 of Montserrat. Multicoloured.
864 $1 Columbus meeting Amerindians 60 70
865 $2 Ships approaching island . 1·50 2·00

1992. Olympic Games, Albertville and Barcelona. As T **216** of Lesotho. Multicoloured.
866 10 c. Men's volleyball 40 40
867 15 c. Men's gymnastics (horiz) 50 50
868 25 c. Men's cross-country skiing 60 60
869 30 c. Men's 110 metres hurdles (horiz) 60 60
870 45 c. Men's 120 metre ski-jumping (horiz) 70 70
871 55 c. Women's 4 × 100 metre relay 80 80
872 75 c. Men's triple jump . . . 1·00 1·00
873 80 c. Men's mogul skiing . . 1·00 1·00
874 $1 Men's 110 metre butterfly swimming (horiz) . . . . . 1·25 1·25
875 $2 "Tornado" Class yachting (horiz) . . . . 1·75 1·75
876 $3 Men's decathlon (horiz) . . 1·90 1·90
877 $5 Show jumping (horiz) . . . 2·75 2·75

1992. Christmas. Religious Paintings. As T **218** of Lesotho. Multicoloured.
879 10 c. "Our Lady with St. Roch and St. Anthony of Padua" (Giorgione) 30 30
880 40 c. "Anthony of Padua" (Master of the Embroidered Leaf) 55 55
881 45 c. "Madonna and Child" (detail) (Orazio Gentileschi) 60 60
882 50 c. "Madonna and Child with St. Anne (detail) (Da Vinci) 65 65
883 55 c. "The Holy Family" (Crespi) 70 70
884 65 c. "Madonna and Child" (Del Sarto) 80 80
885 75 c. "Madonna and Child with Sts. Lawrence and Julian" (Gentile da Fabriano) . . . 90 90
886 $1 "Virgin and Child" (detail) (School of Parma) . . . . 1·10 1·10
887 $2 "Madonna with the Iris" (detail) (style of Durer) . . 1·75 1·75
888 $3 "Virgin and Child with St. Jerome and St. Dominic" (Lippi) . . . . 2·25 2·25
889 $4 "Rapolano Madonna" (Ambrogio Lorenzetti) . . . 2·75 2·75
890 $5 "The Virgin and Child with Angels in a Garden with a Rose Hedge" (Stefano da Verona) . . . . 2·75 2·75

80 "Nina" in Baracoa Harbour

1992. Anniversaries and Events. Multicoloured.
892 10 c. Type **80** 55 55
893 75 c. Airship LZ-3 . . . . . . 1·50 1·50
894 75 c. Blind man with guide dog 1·50 1·50
895 75 c. Training guide dog . . . 1·50 1·50
896 $1 Ships of Columbus . . . . 1·50 1·50
897 $1 Adenauer, state arms and German flag . . . . 1·50 1·50
898 $1 "America III" and "Il Moro" (yachts) with trophy . . . 1·50 1·50
899 $1 Hands breaking bread and emblem (vert) . . . . . . 1·50 1·50
900 $2 "Voyager 2" and planet . . 2·50 2·50
901 $3 Adenauer and children watching Berlin Airlift . . . 2·50 2·50
902 $4 Airship LZ-37 in flames . . 2·75 2·75
903 $4 Adenauer and ruins in Cologne . . . . 2·75 2·75
904 $4 Mozart with his wife Constanze (vert) . . . . . 2·75 2·75
905 $5 Adenauer and modern office blocks . . . . 2·75 2·75
ANNIVERSARIES AND EVENTS: Nos. 892, 896, 500th anniv of discovery of America by Columbus; Nos. 893, 902, 75th death anniv of Count Ferdinand von Zeppelin (airship pioneer); Nos. 894/5, 75th anniv of International Association of Lions Clubs; Nos. 897, 901, 903, 905, 25th death anniv of Konrad Adenauer (German statesman); No. 898, Americas Cup yachting championship; No. 899, International Conference on Nutrition, Rome; No. 900, International Space Year; No. 904, Death bicentenary of Mozart.

81 Olivia and Flaversham

1992. Walt Disney Cartoon Films.
907/50 60 c. × 44 mult
Set of 44 . . . . 19·00 21·00
Nos. 907/50 were printed as five se-tenant sheetlets, each of nine different designs except for

that for "Darkwing Duck" which contains eight vertical designs (Nos. 943/50). The other four sheetlets depict scenes from "The Great Mouse Detective", "Oliver and Company", "The Legend of Sleepy Hollow" and "Ducktales the Movie".

1992. 15th Death Anniv of Elvis Presley (singer). As T **260** of Dominica. Mult.

952	$1 Elvis Presley	2·25	2·25
953	$1 Elvis with guitar	2·25	2·25
954	$1 Elvis with microphone	2·25	2·25

82 Prince Mickey searching for Bride

1992. "Tales of Uncle Scrooge" (fairy stories). Walt Disney cartoon characters.

955/1008 60 c. × 54 mult
Set of 54 . . . . . . 21·00 22·00

Nos. 955/1008 (issued as six sheetlets each of nine different designs) depict scenes from "The Princess and the Pea", "Little Red Riding Hood", "Goldilocks and the Three Bears", "The Pied Piper of Hamelin", "Hop O'-My-Thumb" and "Puss in Boots".

83 Oleander

1994. Medicinal Plants. Multicoloured.

1010	5 c. Type **83**	20	30
1011	10 c. Beach morning glory	30	20
1012	30 c. Calabash	40	30
1013	45 c. Portia tree	50	30
1014	55 c. Cashew	60	40
1015	75 c. Prickly pear	70	70
1016	$1 Shell ginger	80	80
1017	$1.50 Avocado pear	1·40	1·60
1018	$2 Mango	1·75	2·00
1019	$3 Blood flower	2·25	2·50
1020	$4 Sugar apple	2·50	2·75
1021	$5 Barbados lily	2·50	2·75

OFFICIAL STAMPS

1982. Nos. 195/200 optd **OFFICIAL**.

O1	50 c. "Mary"	10	15
O2	50 c. Prince Charles and Lady Diana Spencer	30	35
O3	$3 "Alexandra"	20	20
O4	$3 Prince Charles and Lady Diana Spencer	65	70
O5	$3.50 "Britannia"	20	20
O6	$3.50 Prince Charles and Lady Diana Spencer	65	70

APPENDIX

The following stamps have either been issued in excess of postal needs, or have not been made available to the public in reasonable quantities at face value.

BEQUIA

1984.

Leaders of the World. Railway Locomotives (1st series). Two designs for each value, the first showing technical drawings and the second the locomotive at work. 1, 5, 10, 25, 35, 45 c, $1.50, $2, each × 2.

Grenadines of St. Vincent 1982 Ships definitives (Nos. 208/24) optd **BEQUIA**. 1, 3, 5, 6, 10, 15, 20, 25, 30, 50, 60, 75c., $1, $2, $3, $5, $10.

Leaders of the World. Automobiles (1st series). Two designs for each value, the first showing technical drawings and the second the car in action. 5, 40 c., $1, $1.50, each × 2.

Leaders of the World. Olympic Games, Los Angeles. 1, 10, 60 c., $3, each × 2.

Leaders of the World. Railway Locomotives (2nd series). Two designs for each value, the first showing technical drawings and the second the locomotive at work. 1, 10, 20, 25, 75 c., $1, $2.50, $3, each × 2.

Leaders of the World. Automobiles (2nd series). Two designs for each value, the first showing technical drawings and the second the car in action. 5, 10, 20, 25, 75 c., $1.50, $3, each × 2.

1985.

Leaders of the World. Railway Locomotives (3rd series). Two designs for each value, the first showing technical drawings and the second the locomotive at work. 25, 55, 60c., $1, $2.50, each × 2.

Leaders of the World. Dogs. 25, 35, 55 c., $2, each × 2.

Leaders of the World. Warships of the Second World War. Two designs for each value, the first showing technical drawings and the second the ship at sea. 15, 50 c., $1, $1.50, each × 2.

Leaders of the World. Flowers. 10, 20, 70 c., $2.50, each × 2.

Leaders of the World. Automobiles (3rd series). Two designs for each value, the first showing technical drawings and the second the car in action. 5, 25, 50 c., $1, $1.25, $2, each × 2.

Leaders of the World. Railway Locomotives (4th series). Two designs for each value, the first showing technical drawings and the second the locomotive at work. 25, 55, 60, 75 c., $1, $2.50, each × 2.

Leaders of the World. Life and Times of Queen Elizabeth the Queen Mother. Two designs for each value showing different portraits. 20, 65 c., $1.35, $1.80, each × 2.

Leaders of the World. Automobiles (4th series). Two designs for each value, the first showing technical drawings and the second the car in action. 10, 35, 75 c., $1.15, $1.50, $2, each × 2.

1986.

Leaders of the World. Automobiles (5th series). Two designs for each value, the first showing technical drawings and the second the car in action. 25, 50, 65, 75c., $1, $3, each × 2.

60th Birthday of Queen Elizabeth II. 5, 75 c., $2, $8.

World Cup Football Championship, Mexico. 1, 2, 5, 10, 45, 60, 75 c., $1.50, $1.50, $2, $3.50, $6.

Royal Wedding (1st issue). 60 c., $2, each × 2.

Railway Engineers and Locomotives. $1, $2.50, $3, $4.

Royal Wedding (2nd issue). Previous issue optd **"Congratulations T.R.H. The Duke & Duchess of York"**. 60 c., $2, each × 2.

Automobiles (6th series). Two designs for each value, the first showing technical drawings and the second the car in action. 20, 60, 75, 90 c., $1, $3, each × 2.

1987.

Automobiles (7th series). Two designs for each value, the first showing technical drawings and the second the car in action. 5, 20, 35, 60, 75, 80 c., $1.25, $1.75, each × 2.

Royal Ruby Wedding. 15, 75 c., $1, $2.50, $5.

Railway Locomotives (5th series). Two designs for each value, the first showing technical drawings and the second the locomotive at work. 15, 25, 40, 50, 60, 75 c., $1, $2, each × 2.

1988.

Explorers. 15, 50 c., $1.75, $2, $2.50, $3, $3.50, $4.

International Lawn Tennis Players. 15, 45, 80 c., $1.25, $1.75, $2, $2.50, $3.

1989.

"Philexfrance '89" International Stamp Exhibition, Paris. Walt Disney Cartoon Characters. 1, 2, 3, 4, 5, 10 c., $5, $6.

1991.

Centenary of Otto Lilienthal's Gliding Experiments. $5.

50th Anniv of Japanese Attack on Pearl Harbor. 50 c., $1.

Death Anniv of Mozart. 10, 75 c., $4.

50th Death Anniv of Lord Baden-Powell and World Jamboree, Korea. 50 c., $1, $2, $3.

1997.

Diana, Princess of Wales Commemoration. $1.

CANOUAN

1997.

Diana, Princess of Wales Commemoration. $1.

MUSTIQUE

1997.

Diana, Princess of Wales Commemoration. $1.

UNION ISLAND

1984.

Leaders of the World. British Monarchs. Two designs for each value forming a composite picture. 1, 5, 10, 20, 60 c., $3, each × 2.

Leaders of the World. Railway Locomotives (1st series). Two designs for each value, the first showing technical drawings and the second the locomotive at work. 5, 60 c., $1, $2.

Grenadines of St. Vincent 1982 Ships definitives (Nos. 208/24) optd **UNION ISLAND**. 1, 3, 5, 6, 10, 15, 20, 25, 30, 50, 60, 75 c., $1, $2, $3, $5, $10.

Leaders of the World. Cricketers. Two designs for each value, the first showing a portrait and the second the cricketer in action. 1, 10, 15, 55, 60, 75 c., $1.50, $3, each × 2.

Leaders of the World. Railway Locomotives (2nd series). Two designs for each value, the first showing technical drawings and the second the locomotive at work. 5, 10, 20, 25, 75 c., $1, $2.50, $3, each × 2.

1985.

Leaders of the World. Automobiles (1st series). Two designs for each value, the first showing technical drawings and the second the car in action. 1, 50, 75 c., $2.50, each × 2.

Leaders of the World. Birth Bicentenary of John J. Audubon (ornithologist). Birds. 15, 50 c., $1.50, each × 2.

Leaders of the World. Railway Locomotives (3rd series). Two designs for each value, the first showing technical drawings and the second the locomotive at work. 5, 50, 60 c., $2, each × 2.

Leaders of the World. Butterflies. 15, 25, 75 c., $2, each × 2.

Leaders of the World. Automobiles (2nd series). Two designs for each value, the first showing technical drawings and the second the car in action. 5, 60 c., $1, $1.50, each × 2.

Leaders of the World. Automobiles (3rd series). Two designs for each value, the first showing technical drawings and the second the car in action. 10, 55, 60, 75, 90 c., $1, $1.50, $2, each × 2.

Leaders of the World. Life and Times of Queen Elizabeth the Queen Mother. Two designs for each value showing different portraits. 55, 70 c., $1.05, $1.70, each × 2.

1986.

Leaders of the World. Railway Locomotives (4th series). Two designs for each value, the first showing technical drawings and the second the locomotive at work. 15, 30, 45, 60, 75 c., $1.50, $2.50, $3, each × 2.

60th Birthday of Queen Elizabeth II. 10, 60 c., $2, $8.

World Cup Football Championship, Mexico. 1, 10, 30, 75 c., $1, $2.50, $3, $6.

Royal Wedding (1st issue). 60 c., $2, each × 2.

Automobiles (4th series). Two designs for each value, the first showing technical drawings and the second the car in action. 10, 60, 75 c., $1, $1.50, $3, each × 2.

Royal Wedding (2nd issue). Previous issue optd as Bequia. 60 c., $2, each × 2.

Railway Locomotive (5th series). Two designs for each value, the first showing technical drawings and the second the locomotive at work. 15, 45, 60, 75 c., $1, $2, $3, each × 2.

1987.

Railway Locomotives (6th series). Two designs for each value, the first showing technical drawings and the second the locomotives at work. 15, 25, 40, 50, 60, 75 c., $1, $2, each × 2.

Royal Ruby Wedding. 15, 45 c., $1.50, $3, $4.

Railway Locomotives (7th series). Two designs for each value, the first showing technical drawings and the second the locomotive at work. 15, 20, 30, 45, 50, 75 c., $1, $1.50, each × 2.

1989.

"Philexfrance 89" International Stamp Exhibition, Paris. Walt Disney Cartoon Characters. 1, 2, 3, 4, 5, 10 c., $5, $6.

1997.

Diana, Princess of Wales Commemoration. $1.

GRIQUALAND WEST

A British colony, later annexed to the Cape of Good Hope and now part of South Africa, whose stamps it uses.

12 pence = 1 shilling;
20 shillings = 1 pound

1874. Stamp of Cape of Good Hope ("Hope" seated) with pen-and-ink surch.

1	**4**	1d. on 4d. blue	£750	£1300

1877. Stamps of Cape of Good Hope ("Hope" seated) optd **G. W.**

2	**6**	1d. red	£425	75·00
3		4d. blue	£325	65·00

1877. Stamps of Cape of Good Hope ("Hope" seated) optd **G**.

14	**6**	½d. grey	4·50	6·00
16		1d. red	6·50	4·50
6a	**4**	4d. blue	£150	26·00
26	**6**	4d. blue	20·00	3·50
27	**4**	6d. violet	95·00	6·00
28		1s. green	80·00	3·50
29	**6**	5s. orange	£300	6·00

GUERNSEY

An island in the English Channel off N.W. coast of France. Occupied by German Forces from June, 1940, to May, 1945. "Regional" issues were introduced from 1958 (see after GREAT BRITAIN). The island's postal service was organised as a separate postal administration in 1969.

(a) War Occupation Issues.

1

1941.

1	**1**	½d. green	3·00	2·00
2		1d. red	2·50	1·25
3a		2½d. blue	4·25	4·00

(b) Independent Postal Administration.

4 Castle Cornet and Edward the Confessor

5 View of Sark

1969.

13	**4**	½d. mauve and black	10	10
14	–	1d. blue and black*	10	10
14b	–	1d. blue and black*	30	30
15	–	1½d. brown and black	10	10
16	–	2d. multicoloured	10	10
17	–	3d. multicoloured	15	15
18	–	4d. multicoloured	25	25
19	–	5d. multicoloured	25	15
20	–	6d. multicoloured	30	30
21	–	9d. multicoloured	40	30
22	–	1s. multicoloured	30	30
23	–	1s. 6d. green and black*	30	30
23b	–	1s. 6d. green and black*	2·25	1·75
24	–	1s. 9d. multicoloured	1·25	1·50
25	–	2s. 6d. violet and black	5·00	4·25
26	**5**	5s. multicoloured	3·25	3·25
27	–	10s. multicoloured	26·00	22·00
28a	–	£1 multicoloured	2·00	1·75

DESIGNS—As Type **4**: 1d. Map and William I; 1½d. Martello tower and Henry II; 2d. Arms of Sark and King John; 3d. Arms of Alderney and Edward III; 4d. Guernsey lily and Henry V; 5d. Arms of Guernsey and Elizabeth I; 6d. Arms of Alderney and Charles II; 9d. Arms of Sark and George III; 1s. Arms of Guernsey and Queen Victoria; 1s. 6d. As 1d; 1s. 9d. Guernsey lily and Elizabeth I; 2s. 6d. Martello tower and King John. As Type **5**: 10s. View of Alderney; 20s. View of Guernsey.

*On Nos. 14 and 23 the degree of latitude is inscr (incorrectly) as 40° 30′ N. On Nos. 14b and 23b it has been corrected to 49° 30.

19 Isaac Brock as Colonel

1969. Birth Bicent of Sir Isaac Brock. Mult.
29 4d. Type **19** 20 20
30 5d. Sir Isaac Brock as Major-General 20 20
31 1s. 9d. Isaac Brock as Ensign 1·40 1·25
32 2s. 6d. Arms and flags 1·40 1·25
The 2s. 6d., is horiz.

23 H.M.S. "L103" (landing craft) entering St. Peter's Harbour

1970. 25th Anniv of Liberation.
33 **23** 4d. blue 40 40
34 – 5d. brown, lake and grey 40 40
35 – 1s. 6d. brown and buff 3·25 2·50
DESIGNS—HORIZ: 5d. British ships entering St. Peter Port. VERT: 1s. 6d. Brigadier Snow reading Proclamation.

26 Guernsey "Toms"

32 St. Peter's Church, Sark

1970. Agriculture and Horticulture. Mult.
36 4d. Type **26** 80 20
37 5d. Guernsey cow 90 20
38 9d. Guernsey bull 5·00 2·75
39 1s. 6d. Freesias 6·00 3·00

1970. Christmas. Churches (1st series). Mult.
40 4d. St. Anne's Church, Alderney (horiz) 35 20
41 5d. St. Peter's Church (horiz) 45 25
42 9d. Type **32** 1·75 1·10
43 1s. 6d. St. Tugual Chapel, Herm 2·00 1·50
See also Nos. 63/6.

34 Martello Tower and King John

1971. Decimal Currency. Nos. 13, etc., but with new colours and decimal values as T **34**.
44 ½p. mauve & black (as No. 13) 10 15
45 1p. blue & black (as No. 14b) 10 10
46 1½p. brown & blk (as No. 15) 15 15
47 2p. multicoloured (as No. 18) 15 15
48 2½p. multicoloured (as No. 19) 15 10
49 3p. multicoloured (as No. 17) 20 20
50 3½p. multicoloured (as No. 24) 25 25
51 4p. multicoloured (as No. 16) 25 25
52 5p. green & black (as No. 14b) 30 25
53 6p. multicoloured (as No. 20) 30 35
54 7½p. multicoloured (as No. 22) 40 45
55 9p. multicoloured (as No. 21) 50 75
56a 10p. violet & blk (as No. 25) 1·75 1·75
57a 20p. multicoloured (as No. 26) 1·00 1·00
58 50p. multicoloured (as No. 27) 2·00 2·00

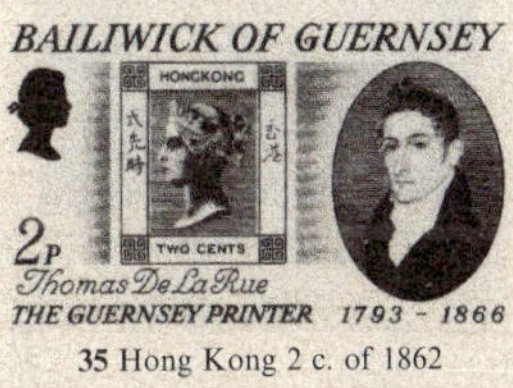

35 Hong Kong 2 c. of 1862

1971. Thomas De La Rue Commemoration.
59 **35** 2p. purple 50 30
60 – 2½p. red 50 30
61 – 4p. green 3·00 2·25
62 – 7½p. blue 3·25 2·25
DESIGNS (Each showing portraits of Queen Elizabeth and Thomas De La Rue): 2½p. Great Britain 4d. of 1855–7; 4p. Italy 5 c. of 1862; 7½p. Confederate States 5 c. of 1862.

1971. Christmas. Churches (2nd series). As T **32**. Multicoloured.
63 2p. Ebenezer Church, St. Peter Port (horiz) 25 25
64 2½p. Church of St. Pierre du Bois (horiz) 25 25
65 5p. St. Joseph's Church, St. Peter Port 2·50 2·00
66 7½p. Church of St. Philippe de Torteval 2·75 2·00

37 "Earl of Chesterfield" (1794)

1972. Mail Packet Ships (1st series). Mult.
67 2p. Type **37** 15 15
68 2½p. "Dasher" (1827) 20 20
69 7½p. "Ibex" (1891) 90 1·00
70 9p. "Alberta" (1900) 1·50 1·40
See also Nos. 80/3.

1972. World Conference of Guernsey Breeders, Guernsey. As No. 38 but size 48×29 mm, and additional inscription with face value changed.
71 5p. multicoloured 75 60

39 Bermuda Buttercup

1972. Wild Flowers. Multicoloured.
72 2p. Type **39** 15 20
73 2½p. Heath spotted orchid (vert) 15 20
74 7½p. Kaffir fig 1·00 90
75 9p. Scarlet pimpernel (vert) 1·40 1·25

40 Angels adoring Christ

42 "The Good Shepherd"

41 Supermarine Sea Eagle

1972. Royal Silver Wedding and Christmas. Stained-glass Windows from Guernsey Churches. Multicoloured.
76 2p. Type **40** 10 10
77 2½p. The Epiphany 15 15
78 7½p. The Virgin Mary 60 55
79 9p. Christ 75 60
See also Nos. 89/92.

1973. Mail Packet Boats (2nd series). As T **37**. Multicoloured.
80 2½p. "St. Julien" (1925) 20 10
81 3p. "Isle of Guernsey" (1930) 30 20
82 7½p. "St. Patrick" (1947) 1·10 60
83 9p. "Sarnia" (1961) 1·25 75

1973. 50th Anniv of Air Service. Mult.
84 2½p. Type **41** 10 10
85 3p. Westland Wessex trimotor 15 15
86 5p. De Havilland Dragon Rapide 30 25
87 7½p. Douglas DC-3 90 50
88 9p. Vickers Viscount 800 "Anne Marie" 1·00 55

1973. Christmas. Stained-glass Windows from Guernsey Churches. Multicoloured.
89 2½p. Type **42** 10 10
90 3p. Christ at the well of Samaria 10 10
91 7½p. St. Dominic 30 30
92 20p. Mary and the Child Jesus 60 60

43 Princess Anne and Capt. Mark Phillips

1973. Royal Wedding.
93 **43** 25p. multicoloured 1·00 75

44 "John Lockett", 1875

1974. 150th Anniv of Royal National Lifeboat Institution. Multicoloured.
94 2½p. Type **44** 10 10
95 3p. "Arthur Lionel", 1912 10 10
96 8p. "Euphrosyne Kendal", 1954 45 45
97 10p. "Arun", 1972 45 45

45 Private, East Regt, 1815

46 Driver, Field Battery, Royal Guernsey Artillery, 1848

1974. Guernsey Militia. Multicoloured. (a) As T **45**.
98 ½p. Type **45** 10 10
99 1p. Officer, 2nd North Regt, 1825 10 10
100 1½p. Gunner, Guernsey Artillery, 1787 10 10
101 2p. Gunner, Guernsey Artillery, 1815 10 10
102 2½p. Corporal, Royal Guernsey Artillery, 1868 10 10
103 3p. Field Officer, Royal Guernsey Artillery, 1895 10 10
104 3½p. Sergeant, 3rd Regt, 1867 10 10
105 4p. Officer, East Regt, 1822 15 15
105a 5p. Field Officer, Royal Guernsey Artillery, (1895 15 15
106 5½p. Colour-Sergeant of Grenadiers, East Regt, 1833 20 25
107 6p. Officer, North Regt, 1834 20 25
107a 7p. Officer, East Regt, 1822 25 25
108 8p. Field Officer, Rifle Company, 1868 25 30
109 9p. Private, 4th West Regt, 1785 30 30
110 10p. Field Officer, 4th West Regt, 1824 30 30

(b) As T **46**.
111 20p. Type **46** 55 40
112 50p. Officer, Field Battery, Royal Guernsey Artillery, 1868 1·50 1·25
113 £1 Cavalry Trooper, Light Dragoons, 1814 (horiz) 3·25 2·50

47 Badge of Guernsey and U.P.U. Emblem

1974. Centenary of U.P.U. Multicoloured.
114 2½p. Type **47** 10 10
115 3p. Map of Guernsey 10 10
116 8p. U.P.U. Building, Berne, and Guernsey flag 45 45
117 10p. "Salle des Etats" 45 45

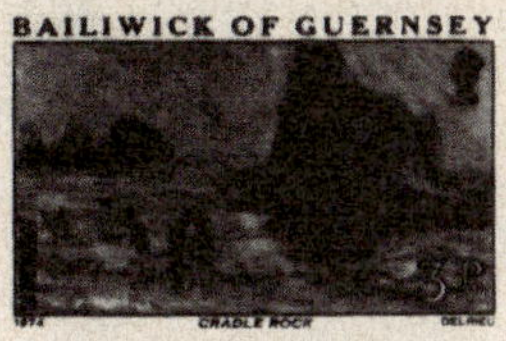

48 "Cradle Rock"

1974. Renoir Paintings. Multicoloured.
118 3p. Type **48** 10 10
119 5½p. "Moulin Huet Bay" 15 15
120 8p. "Au Bord de la Mer" (vert) 40 40
121 10p. Self-portrait (vert) 45 45

49 Guernsey Spleenwort

50 Victor Hugo House

1975. Guernsey Ferns. Multicoloured.
122 3½p. Type **49** 15 10
123 4p. Sand quillwort 15 10
124 8p. Guernsey quillwort 50 40
125 10p. Least adder's tongue 60 50

1975. Victor Hugo's Exile in Guernsey. Mult.
126 3½p. Type **50** 10 10
127 4p. Candie Gardens (vert) 20 10
128 8p. United Europe Oak, Hauteville (vert) 40 40
129 10p. Tapestry Room, Hauteville 50 50

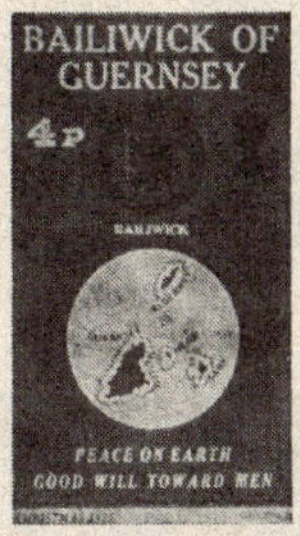

51 Globe and Seal of Bailiwick

1975. Christmas. Multicoloured.
131 4p. Type **51** 10 10
132 6p. Guernsey flag 15 15
133 10p. Guernsey flag and Alderney shield (horiz) 45 35
134 12p. Guernsey flag and Sark shield (horiz) 50 50

52 Les Hanois

1976. Bailiwick Lighthouses. Multicoloured.
135 4p. Type **52** 10 10
136 6p. Les Casquets 20 20
137 11p. Quesnard 50 45
138 13p. Point Robert 55 60

53 Milk Can

1976. Europa.
139 **53** 10p. brown and green 40 40
140 – 25p. grey and blue 85 83
DESIGN: 25p. Christening cup.

54 Pine Forest, Guernsey

1976. Bailiwick Views. Multicoloured.
141 5p. Type **54** 15 10
142 7p. Herm and Jethou 15 20
143 11p. Grand Greve Bay, Sark (vert) 55 45
144 13p. Trois Vaux Bay, Alderney (vert) 55 65

55 Royal Court House, Guernsey

1976. Christmas. Buildings. Multicoloured.
145 5p. Type **55** 15 10
146 7p. Elizabeth College, Guernsey 15 15
147 11p. La Seigneurie, Sark 55 50
148 13p. Island Hall, Alderney 55 65

56 Queen Elizabeth II

58 Statue-menhir, Castel

57 Woodland, Talbot's Valley

1977. Silver Jubilee. Multicoloured.

149	7p. Type **56**	25	25
150	35p. Queen Elizabeth (half-length portrait)	1·00	1·00

1977. Europa. Multicoloured.

151	7p. Type **57**	35	35
152	25p. Pastureland, Talbot's Valley	90	90

1977. Prehistoric Monuments. Multicoloured.

153	5p. Type **58**	10	10
154	7p. Megalithic tomb, St. Saviour (horiz)	15	15
155	11p. Cist, Tourgis (horiz)	55	55
156	13p. Statue-menhir, St. Martin	60	60

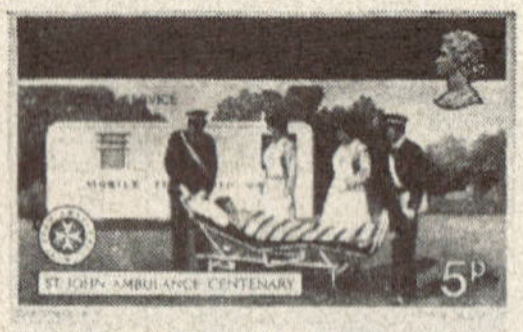

59 Mobile First Aid Unit

1977. Christmas and St. John Ambulance Centenary. Multicoloured.

157	5p. Type **59**	10	10
158	7p. Mobile radar unit	15	15
159	11p. Marine ambulance "Flying Christine II" (vert)	55	55
160	13p. Cliff rescue (vert)	60	60

60 View from Clifton, c. 1830

1978. Old Guernsey Prints (1st series).

161	**60**	5p. black and green	10	10
162	–	7p. black and stone	15	15
163	–	11p. black and pink	55	55
164	–	13p. black and blue	60	60

DESIGNS: 7p. Market Square, St. Peter Port, c. 1838; 11p. Petit-Bo Bay, c. 1839; 13p. The Quay, St. Peter Port, c. 1830.

See also Nos. 249/52.

61 "Prosperity" Memorial

62 Queen Elizabeth II

1978. Europa. Multicoloured.

165	5p. Type **61**	35	35
166	7p. Victoria Monument (vert)	40	40

1978. 25th Anniversary of Coronation.

167	**62**	20p. black, grey and blue	75	75

1978. Royal Visit. As T **62**, but inscr "VISIT OF H.M THE QUEEN AND H.R.H THE DUKE OF EDINBURGH JUNE 28-29, 1978 TO THE BAILIWICK OF GUERNSEY".

168	7p. black, grey and green	50	50

63 Northern Gannet

1978. Birds. Multicoloured.

169	5p. Type **63**	15	15
170	7p. Firecrest	25	25
171	11p. Dartford warbler	60	45
172	13p. Spotted redshank	70	55

64 Solanum

1978. Christmas. Multicoloured.

173	5p. Type **64**	10	10
174	7p. Christmas rose	20	20
175	11p. Holly (vert)	40	40
176	13p. Mistletoe (vert)	50	50

65 One Double Coin, 1830

67 Pillar-box and Post-mark, 1853, and Mail Van and Postmark, 1979

1979. Coins.

177	**65**	½p. multicoloured	10	10
178	–	1p. multicoloured	10	10
179	–	2p. multicoloured	10	10
180	–	4p. multicoloured	10	10
181	–	5p. black, silver and brown	15	10
182	–	6p. black, silver and red	15	15
183	–	7p. black, silver and green	15	20
184	–	8p. black, silver and brown	20	20
185	–	9p. multicoloured	25	20
186	–	10p. multicoloured (green background)	50	50
187	–	10p. multicoloured (orange background)	35	30
188	–	11p. multicoloured	25	30
189	–	11½p. multicoloured	25	30
190	–	12p. multicoloured	30	30
191	–	13p. multicoloured	30	30
192	–	14p. black, silver and blue	30	30
193	–	15p. black, silver and brown	35	35
194	–	20p. black, silver and brown	50	45
195	–	50p. black, silver and red	1·00	75
196	–	£1 black, silver and green	2·00	1·50
197	–	£2 black, silver and blue	4·00	2·50
198	–	£5 multicoloured	10·00	7·50

DESIGNS—VERT (As Type **65**): 1p. Two doubles, 1899; 2p. Four doubles, 1902; 4p. Eight doubles, 1959; 5p. Three pence, 1956; 6p. Five new pence, 1968; 7p. Fifty new pence, 1969; 8p. Ten new pence, 1970; 9p. Half new penny, 1971; 10p. (both) One new penny, 1971; 11p. Two new pence, 1971; 11½p. Half penny, 1979; 12p. One penny, 1977; 13p. Two pence, 1977; 14p. Five pence, 1977; 15p. Ten pence, 1977; 20p. Twenty-five pence, 1972; (26×45 mm): 50p. William I commemorative 10s., 1966; £5 Seal of the Bailiwick. HORIZ (45×26 mm): £1 Silver Jubilee crown, 1977; £2 Royal Silver Wedding crown, 1972.

1979. Europa. Communications. Multicoloured.

201	6p. Type **67**	30	30
202	8p. Telephone, 1897 and telex machine, 1979	30	30

68 Steam Train, 1879

1979. History of Public Transport. Multicoloured.

203	6p. Type **68**	15	15
204	8p. Electric tram, 1896	20	20
205	11p. Motor bus, 1911	55	55
206	13p. Motor bus, 1979	60	60

69 Bureau and Postal Headquarters

1979. 10th Anniv of Guernsey Postal Administration. Multicoloured.

207	6p. Type **69**	15	15
208	8p. "Mails and telegrams"	25	15
209	13p. "Parcels"	50	55
210	15p. "Philately"	60	60

70 Major-General Le Marchant

1980. Europa Personalities. Multicoloured.

212	10p. Type **70**	45	45
213	13½p. Admiral Lord de Saumarez	50	50

71 Policewoman with Lost Child

1980. 60th Anniv of Guernsey Police Force. Mult.

214	7p. Type **71**	20	20
215	15p. Motorcycle escort	55	55
216	17½p. Dog-handler	65	65

72 Golden Guernsey Goat

1980. Golden Guernsey Goats. Multicoloured.

217	7p. Type **72**	20	20
218	10p. Head of goat	30	35
219	15p. Goat	55	45
220	17½p. Goat and kids	65	60

73 "Sark Cottage"

1980. Peter Le Lievre Paintings. Multicoloured.

221	7p. Type **73**	25	20
222	10p. "Moulin Huet"	35	25
223	13½p. "Boats at Sea"	40	30
224	15p. "Cow Lane" (vert)	50	40
225	17½p. "Peter Le Lievre" (vert)	65	50

74 "Polyommatus icarus"

1981. Butterflies. Multicoloured.

226	8p. Type **74**	25	25
227	12p. "Vanessa atalanta"	40	40
228	22p. "Aglais urticae"	90	70
229	25p. "Lasiommata megera"	1·00	90

75 Sailors paying respect to "Le Petit Bonhomme Andriou" (rock resembling head of a man)

76 Prince Charles

1981. Europa. Folklore.

230	**75**	12p. gold, brown and light brown	45	45
231	–	18p. gold, blue and light blue	55	55

DESIGN: 18p. Fairies and Guernsey lily.

1981. Royal Wedding. Multicoloured.

232	8p. Type **76**	50	50
233	8p. Prince Charles and Lady Diana Spencer	50	50
234	8p. Lady Diana	50	50
235	12p. Type **76**	90	90
236	12p. As No. 233	90	90
237	12p. As No. 234	90	90
238	25p. Royal Family (49×32 mm)	1·50	1·50

77 Sark Launch

1981. Inter-island Transport. Multicoloured.

240	8p. Type **77**	20	20
241	12p. Britten Norman "short nose" Trislander airplane	40	40
242	18p. Hydrofoil	60	50
243	22p. Herm catamaran	75	65
244	25p. "Sea Trent" (coaster)	90	75

78 Rifle Shooting

1981. Int Year for Disabled Persons. Mult.

245	8p. Type **78**	20	20
246	12p. Riding	35	35
247	22p. Swimming	65	55
248	25p. "Work"	75	60

1982. Old Guernsey Prints (2nd series). Prints from Sketches by T. Compton. As T **60**.

249	8p. black and blue	20	20
250	12p. black and green	35	35
251	22p. black and brown	65	65
252	25p. black and lilac	75	75

DESIGNS: 8p. Jethou; 12p. Fermain Bay; 22p. The Terres; 25p. St. Peter Port.

79 Sir Edgar MacCulloch (founder-president) and Guille-Alles Library, St. Peter Port

1982. Cent of La Societe Guernesiaise. Mult.

253	8p. Type **79**	20	20
254	13p. French invasion fleet crossing English Channel, 1066 ("history")	35	35
255	20p. H.M.S "Crescent", 1793 ("history")	45	45
256	24p. Dragonfly ("entomology")	70	70
257	26p. Common snipe caught for ringing ("ornithology")	80	80
258	29p. Samian bowl, 160-200 A.D. ("archaeology")	85	85

The 13p. and 20p. designs also include the Europa C.E.P.T. emblem.

80 "Sea Scouts"

82 Flute Player and Boats

81 Midnight Mass

1982. 75th Anniv of Boy Scout Movement. Mult.

259	8p. Type **80**	20	25
260	13p. "Scouts"	50	50
261	26p. "Cub Scouts"	70	70
262	29p. "Air Scouts"	85	80

1982. Christmas. Multicoloured.

263	8p. Type **81**	20	20
264	13p. Exchanging gifts	30	30
265	24p. Christmas meal	75	75
266	26p. Exchanging cards	75	75
267	29p. Queen's Christmas message	80	80

1982. Centenary of Boys' Brigade. Multicoloured.
268 8p. Type **82** 25 25
269 13p. Cymbal player and tug o' war 40 40
270 24p. Trumpet player and bible class 85 85
271 26p. Drummer and cadets marching 90 90
272 29p. Boys' Brigade band 95 95

83 Building Albert Pier Extension, 1850s

1983. Europa. Development of St. Peter Port Harbour. Multicoloured.
273 13p. Type **83** 35 35
274 13p. St. Peter Port harbour, 1983 35 35
275 20p. St. Peter Port, 1680 75 75
276 20p. Artist's impression of future development scheme 75 75

84 "View at Guernsey" (Renoir)

1983. Cent of Renoir's Visit to Guernsey. Mult.
277 9p. Type **84** 25 25
278 13p. "Children on the Seashore" (25×39 mm) 45 45
279 26p. "Marine, Guernesey" 80 80
280 28p. "La Baie du Moulin Huet a travers les Arbres" 1·10 1·10
281 31p. "Brouillard a Guernesey" 1·25 1·25

85 Launching "Star of the West", 1869, and Capt. J. Lenfestey

1983. Guernsey Shipping (1st series). Mult.
282 9p. Type **85** 25 25
283 13p. Leaving St. Peter Port 40 40
284 26p. Off Rio Grande Bar 80 80
285 28p. Off St. Lucia 1·10 1·10
286 31p. Map of 1879–80 voyage 1·25 1·25
See also Nos. 415/19.

86 Dame of Sark as Young Woman

1984. Birth Centenary of Sibyl Hathaway, Dame of Sark. Multicoloured.
287 9p. Type **86** 25 25
288 13p. German occupation, 1940–45 40 45
289 26p. Royal visit, 1957 90 90
290 28p. Chief Pleas 95 95
291 31p. The Dame of Sark rose 1·10 1·10

87 C.E.P.T. 25th Anniversary Logo

1984. Europa.
292 **87** 13p. lt blue, blue & black 65 65
293 20½p. green, dp green & blk 85 85

88 The Royal Court and St. George's Flag

89 St. Apolline Chapel

1984. Links with the Commonwealth. Mult.
294 9p. Type **88** 40 40
295 31p. Castle Cornet and Union flag 1·10 1·10

1984. Views. Multicoloured.
296 1p. Little Chapel 20 10
297 2p. Fort Grey (horiz) 20 10
298 3p. Type **89** 20 10
299 4p. Petit Port (horiz) 20 10
300 5p. Little Russel (horiz) 20 10
301 6p. The Harbour, Herm (horiz) 20 15
302 7p. Saints (horiz) 20 20
303 8p. St. Saviour 20 20
304 9p. New Jetty (inscr "Cambridge Berth") (horiz) 20 25
305 10p. Belvoir, Herm (horiz) 25 25
306 11p. La Seigneurie, Sark (horiz) 25 25
306b 12p. Petit Bot 40 30
307 13p. St. Saviours reservoir (horiz) 30 30
308 14p. St. Peter Port 30 35
309 15p. Havelet 30 35
309c 16p. Hostel of St. John (horiz) 30 35
309d 18p. Le Variouf 35 40
310 20p. La Coupee, Sark (horiz) 50 45
310b 21p. King's Mills (horiz) 45 45
310c 26p. Town Church 70 55
311 30p. Grandes Rocques (horiz) 60 65
312 40p. Torteval Church 80 85
313 50p. Bordeaux (horiz) 1·00 1·10
314 £1 Albecq (horiz) 2·00 2·10
315 £2 L 'Ancresse (horiz) 4·25 4·25
See also Nos. 398/9a.

90 "A Partridge in a Pear Tree"

91 Sir John Doyle and Coat of Arms

1984. Christmas. "The Twelve Days of Christmas". Multicoloured.
316 5p. Type **90** 20 20
317 5p. "Two turtle doves" 20 20
318 5p. "Three French hens" 20 20
319 5p. "Four colly birds" 20 20
320 5p. "Five gold rings" 20 20
321 5p. "Six geese a-laying" 20 20
322 5p. "Seven swans a-swimming" 20 20
323 5p. "Eight maids a-milking" 20 20
324 5p. "Nine drummers drumming" 20 20
325 5p. "Ten pipers piping" 20 20
326 5p. "Eleven ladies dancing" 20 20
327 5p. "Twelve lords a-leaping" 20 20

1984. 150th Death Anniv of Lieut-General Sir John Doyle. Multicoloured.
328 13p. Type **91** 40 40
329 29p. Battle of Germantown, 1777 (horiz) 1·00 1·00
330 31p. Reclamation of Braye du Valle, 1806 (horiz) 1·25 1·25
331 34p. Mail for Alderney, 1812 (horiz) 1·25 1·25

92 Cuckoo Wrasse

1985. Fishes. Multicoloured.
332 9p. Type **92** 40 40
333 13p. Red gurnard 60 60
334 29p. Red mullet 1·50 1·10
335 31p. Mackerel 1·50 1·10
336 34p. Oceanic sunfish 1·60 1·25

93 Dove

1985. 40th Anniv of Peace in Europe.
337 **93** 22p. multicoloured 1·10 1·10

94 I.Y.Y. Emblem and Young People of Different Races

1985. International Youth Year. Multicoloured.
338 9p. Type **94** 40 40
339 31p. Girl Guides cooking over campfire 1·00 1·00

95 Stave of Music enclosing Flags

1985. Europa. European Music Year. Multicoloured.
340 14p. Type **95** 45 40
341 22p. Stave of music and musical instruments 95 1·00

96 Guide Leader, Girl Guide and Brownie

97 Santa Claus

1985. 75th Anniv of Girl Guide Movement.
342 **96** 34p. multicoloured 1·50 1·50

1985. Christmas. Gift-bearers. Multicoloured.
343 5p. Type **97** 25 25
344 5p. Lussibruden (Sweden) 25 25
345 5p. King Balthazar 25 25
346 5p. Saint Nicholas (Netherlands) 25 25
347 5p. La Befana (Italy) 25 25
348 5p. Julenisse (Denmark) 25 25
349 5p. Christkind (Germany) 25 25
350 5p. King Wenceslas (Czechoslovakia) 25 25
351 5p. Shepherd of Les Baux (France) 25 25
352 5p. King Caspar 25 25
353 5p. Baboushka (Russia) 25 25
354 5p. King Melchior 25 25

98 "Vraicing"

1985. Paintings by Paul Jacob Naftel. Multicoloured.
355 9p. Type **98** 30 30
356 14p. "Castle Cornet" 40 40
357 22p. "Rocquaine Bay" 90 90
358 31p. "Little Russel" 1·40 1·40
359 34p. "Seaweedgatherers" 1·50 1·50

99 Squadrom off Nargue Island, 1809

100 Profile of Queen Elizabeth II (after R. Maklouf)

1986. 150th Death Anniv of Admiral Lord De Saumarez. Multicoloured.
360 9p. Type **99** 40 40
361 14p. Battle of the Nile, 1798 50 50
362 29p. Battle of St. Vincent, 1797 1·25 1·25
363 31p. H.M.S "Crescent" off Cherbourg, 1793 1·40 1·40
364 34p. Battle of the Saints, 1782 1·40 1·40

1986. 60th Birthday of Queen Elizabeth II.
365 **100** 60p. multicoloured 2·50 2·50

101 Northern Gannet and Nylon Net ("Operation Gannet")

102 Prince Andrew and Miss Sarah Ferguson

1986. Europa. Nature and Environmental Protection. Multicoloured.
366 10p. Type **101** 45 45
367 14p. Loose-flowered orchid 75 75
368 22p. Guernsey elm 1·00 1·00

1986. Royal Wedding. Multicoloured.
369 14p. Type **102** 75 75
370 34p. Prince Andrew and Miss Sarah Ferguson (different) (47×30 mm) 1·50 1·50

103 Bowls

105 "While Shepherds Watched their Flocks by Night"

104 Guernsey Museum and Art Gallery, Candie Gardens

1986. Sport in Guernsey. Multicoloured.
371 10p. Type **103** 30 30
372 14p. Cricket 50 50
373 22p. Squash 75 75
374 29p. Hockey 1·25 1·25
375 31p. Swimming (horiz) 1·40 1·40
376 34p. Rifle shooting (horiz) 1·50 1·50

1986. Cent of Guernsey Museums. Mult.
377 14p. Type **104** 60 60
378 29p. Fort Grey Maritime Museum 1·10 1·10
379 31p. Castle Cornet 1·10 1·10
380 34p. National Trust of Guernsey Folk Museum 1·40 1·40

1986. Christmas. Carols. Multicoloured.
381 6p. Type **105** 40 40
382 6p. "In The Bleak Midwinter" 40 40
383 6p. "O Little Town of Bethlehem" 40 40
384 6p. "The Holly and the Ivy" 40 40
385 6p. "O Little Christmas Tree" 40 40
386 6p. "Away in a Manger" 40 40
387 6p. "Good King Wenceslas" 40 40
388 6p. "We Three Kings of Orient Are" 40 40
389 6p. "Hark the Herald Angels Sing" 40 40
390 6p. "I Saw Three Ships" 40 40
391 6p. "Little Donkey" 40 40
392 6p. "Jingle Bells" 40 40

107 Post Office Headquarters

108 Sir Edmund Andros and La Plaiderie, Guernsey

1987. Europa. Modern Architecture. Mult.
394 15p. Type **107** 55 55
395 15p. Architect's elevation of Post Office Headquarters 55 55
396 22p. Guernsey Grammar School 80 80
397 22p. Architect's elevation of Grammar School 80 80

1987. Designs as Nos. 306, 306b, 309 and 309c but smaller.
398 11p. La Seigneurie, Sark (22×18 mm) 30 40
398a 12p. Petit Bot (18×22 mm) 25 25
399 15p. Havelet (18×22 mm) 45 55
399a 16p. Hostel of St. John (22×18 mm) 35 35

1987. 350th Birth Anniv of Sir Edmund Andros (colonial administrator). Multicoloured.
400 15p. Type **108** 45 45
401 29p. Governor's Palace, Virginia 1·00 1·00
402 31p. Governor Andros in Boston 1·10 1·10
403 34p. Map of New Amsterdam (New York), 1661 1·40 1·40

109 The Jester's Warning to Young William

110 John Wesley preaching on the Quay, Alderney

1987. 900th Death Anniv of William the Conqueror. Multicoloured.

404	11p. Type **109**	45	35
405	15p. Hastings battlefield	50	50
406	15p. Norman soldier with pennant	50	50
407	22p. William the Conqueror	80	75
408	22p. Queen Matilda and Abbaye aux Dames, Caen	80	80
409	34p. William's coronation regalia and Halley's Comet	1·25	1·25

1987. Bicentenary of John Wesley's Visit to Guernsey. Multicoloured.

410	7p. Type **110**	30	30
411	15p. Wesley preaching at Mon Plaisir, St. Peter Port	45	45
412	29p. Preaching at Assembly Rooms	1·25	1·25
413	31p. Wesley and La Ville Baudu (early Methodist meeting place)	1·25	1·25
414	34p. Wesley and first Methodist Chapel, St. Peter Port	1·25	1·25

111 "Golden Spur" off St. Sampson Harbour

1988. Guernsey Shipping (2nd series). "Golden Spur". Multicoloured.

415	11p. Type **111**	35	35
416	15p. "Golden Spur" entering Hong Kong harbour	50	50
417	29p. Anchored off Macao	1·25	1·25
418	31p. In China Tea Race	1·25	1·25
419	34p. "Golden Spur" and map showing voyage of 1872–74	1·25	1·25

112 Rowing Boat and Bedford "Rascal" Mail Van

1988. Europa. Transport and Communications. Multicoloured.

420	16p. Type **112**	60	60
421	16p. Rowing boat and Vickers Viscount mail plane	60	60
422	22p. Postman on bicycle and horse-drawn carriages, Sark	95	95
423	22p. Postmen on bicycles and carriage	95	95

Nos. 420/1 and 422/3 were each printed together, se-tenant, the two stamps of each value forming a composite design.

113 Frederick Corbin Lukis and Lukis House, St. Peter Port

1988. Birth Bicentenary of Frederick Corbin Lukis (archaeologist). Multicoloured.

424	12p. Type **113**	40	40
425	16p. Natural history books and reconstructed pot	50	50
426	29p. Lukis directing excavation of Le Creux es Faies and prehistoric beaker	1·10	1·10
427	31p. Lukis House Observatory and garden	1·25	1·25
428	34p. Prehistoric artifacts	1·25	1·25

114 Powerboats and Westland Wessex Rescue Helicopter off Jethou

1988. World Off-shore Powerboat Championships. Multicoloured.

429	16p. Type **114**	60	60
430	30p. Powerboats in Gouliot Passage	1·10	1·10
431	32p. Start of race at St. Peter Port (vert)	1·25	1·25
432	35p. Admiralty chart showing course (vert)	1·50	1·50

115 Joshua Gosselin and Herbarium

116 Coutances Cathedral, France

1988. Bicentenary of Joshua Gosselin's "Flora Sarniensis". Multicoloured.

433	12p. Type **115**	40	40
434	16p. Hares-tail grass	55	55
435	16p. Dried hares-tail grass	55	55
436	23p. Variegated catchfly	80	80
437	23p. Dried variegated catchfly	80	80
438	35p. Rock sea lavender	1·40	1·40

1988. Christmas. Ecclesiastical Links. Mult.

439	8p. Type **116**	25	25
440	8p. Interior of Notre Dame du Rosaire Church, Guernsey	25	25
441	8p. Stained glass, St. Sampson's Church, Guernsey	25	25
442	8p. Dol-de-Bretagne Cathedral, France	25	25
443	8p. Bishop's throne, Town Church, Guernsey	25	25
444	8p. Winchester Cathedral	25	25
445	8p. St. John's Cathedral, Portsmouth	25	25
446	8p. High altar, St. Joseph's Church, Guernsey	25	25
447	8p. Mont Saint-Michel, France	25	25
448	8p. Chancel, Vale Church, Guernsey	25	25
449	8p. Lychgate, Forest Church, Guernsey	25	25
450	8p. Marmoutier Abbey, France	25	25

117 Le Cat (Tip Cat)

118 Outline Map of Guernsey

1989. Europa. Children's Toys and Games. Multicoloured.

451	12p. Type **117**	40	40
452	16p. Girl with Cobo Alice doll	60	60
453	23p. Le Colimachaon (hopscotch)	1·25	1·25

1989. Coil Stamp. No value expressed.

454	**118** (–) blue	40	40
455	(–) green	60	60

No. 454 is inscribed "MINIMUM BAILIWICK POSTAGE PAID" and No. 455 "MINIMUM FIRST CLASS POSTAGE TO UK PAID". They were initally sold at 14p. and 18p. but this was changed in line with postage rate rises.

119 Guernsey Airways De Havilland Dragon Express and Mail Van

1989. 50th Anniv of Guernsey Airport (Nos. 456, 458 and 460) and 201 Squadron's Affiliation with Guernsey (Nos. 457, 459 and 461). Mult.

456	12p. Type **119**	50	40
457	12p. Supermarine Southampton II flying boat at mooring	50	40
458	18p. B.E.A. De Havilland Rapide	75	75
459	18p. Short S.25 Sunderland Mk V flying boat taking off	75	75
460	35p. Air U.K. British Aerospace BAe 146	1·25	1·25
461	35p. Avro Shackleton M.R.3	1·25	1·25

MINIMUM PRICE

The minimum price quoted is 10p which represents a handling charge rather than a basis for valuing common stamps. For further notes about prices see introductory pages.

120 "Queen Elizabeth II" (June Mendoza)

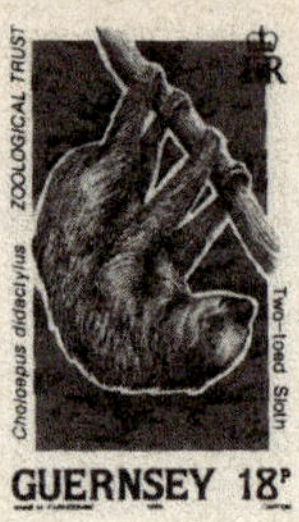

122 Two-toed Sloth

121 "Ibex" at G.W.R. Terminal, St. Peter Port

1989. Royal Visit.

462	**120** 30p. multicoloured	1·25	1·25

1989. Centenary of Great Western Railway Steamer Service to Channel Islands. Multicoloured.

463	12p. Type **121**	30	30
464	18p. "Great Western" (paddle-steamer) in Little Russel	65	65
465	29p. "St. Julien" passing Casquets Light	90	90
466	34p. "Roebuck" off Portland	1·25	1·25
467	37p. "Antelope" and boat train on Weymouth Quay	1·40	1·40

1989. 10th Anniv of Guernsey Zoological Trust. Animals of the Rainforest. Multicoloured.

469	18p. Type **122**	1·10	90
470	29p. Capuchin monkey	1·10	90
471	32p. White-lipped tamarin	1·10	90
472	34p. Common squirrel-monkey	1·10	90
473	37p. Common gibbon	1·10	90

123 Star

125 Penny Black and Mail Steamer off St. Peter Port, 1840

124 Sark Post Office, c. 1890

1989. Christmas. Christmas Tree Decorations. Multicoloured.

474	10p. Type **123**	30	30
475	10p. Fairy	30	30
476	10p. Candles	30	30
477	10p. Bird	30	30
478	10p. Present	30	30
479	10p. Carol-singer	30	30
480	10p. Christmas cracker	30	30
481	10p. Bauble	30	30
482	10p. Christmas stocking	30	30
483	10p. Bell	30	30
484	10p. Fawn	30	30
485	10p. Church	30	30

1990. Europa. Post Office Buildings.

486	**124** 20p. deep brown, sepia and light brown	60	60
487	– 20p. multicoloured	60	60
488	– 24p. deep brown, sepia and light brown	75	75
489	– 24p. multicoloured	75	75

DESIGNS: No. 487, Sark Post Office, 1990; 488, Arcade Post Office counter, St. Peter Port, c. 1840; 489, Arcade Post Office counter, St. Peter Port, 1990.

1990. 150th Anniv of the Penny Black. Mult.

490	14p. Type **125**	45	45
491	20p. Penny Red, 1841 and pillar box of 1853	60	60
492	32p. Bisected 2d., 1940 and German Army band	1·00	90
493	34p. Regional 3d., 1958 and Guernsey emblems	1·10	95
494	37p. Independent postal administration $1\frac{1}{2}$d., 1969 and queue outside Main Post Office	1·10	1·00

126 Lt. Philip Saumarez writing Log Book

1990. 250th Anniv of Anson's Circumnavigation. Multicoloured.

496	14p. Type **126**	45	45
497	20p. Anson's squadron leaving Portsmouth, 1740	60	60
498	29p. Ships at St. Catherine's Island, Brazil	1·00	90
499	34p. H.M.S "Tryal" (sloop) dismasted, Cape Horn, 1741	1·10	95
500	37p. Crew of H.M.S "Centurion" on Juan Fernandez	1·10	1·00

127 Grey Seal and Pup

1990. Marine Life. Multicoloured.

501	20p. Type **127**	60	60
502	26p. Bottle-nosed dolphin	1·00	80
503	31p. Basking shark	1·25	1·25
504	37p. Common porpoise	1·50	1·50

128 Blue Tit and Great Tit

129 Air Raid and 1941 ½d. Stamp

1990. Christmas. Winter Birds. Multicoloured.

505	10p. Type **128**	40	40
506	10p. Snow bunting	40	40
507	10p. Common kestrel	40	40
508	10p. Common starling	40	40
509	10p. Greenfinch	40	40
510	10p. European robin	40	40
511	10p. Winter wren	40	40
512	10p. Barn owl	40	40
513	10p. Mistle thrush	40	40
514	10p. Grey heron	40	40
515	10p. Chaffinch	40	40
516	10p. Common kingfisher	40	40

1991. 50th Anniv of First Guernsey Stamps. Multicoloured.

517	37p. Type **129**	1·25	1·25
518	53p. 1941 1d. stamp	1·60	1·60
519	57p. 1944 $2\frac{1}{2}$d. stamp	1·60	1·60

130 Visit of Queen Victoria to Guernsey, and Discovery of Neptune, 1846

1991. Europa. Europe in Space. Multicoloured.

520	21p. Type **130**	65	65
521	21p. Visit of Queen Elizabeth II and Prince Philip to Sark, and "Sputnik" (first artificial satellite), 1957	65	65
522	26p. Maiden voyage of "Sarnia" (ferry) and "Vostok I" (first manned space flight), 1961	90	75
523	26p. Cancelling Guernsey stamps, and first manned landing on Moon, 1969	90	75

131 Children in Guernsey Sailing Trust "GP14" Dinghy

132 Pair of Oystercatchers

1991. Centenary of Guernsey Yacht Club. Mult.

524	15p. Type **131**	50	50
525	21p. Guernsey Regatta	80	80
526	26p. Lombard Channel Islands' Challenge race	90	90
527	31p. Rolex Swan Regatta	1·00	1·00
528	37p. Old Gaffers' Association gaff-rigged yacht	1·25	1·25

1991. Nature Conservation. L'Eree Shingle Bank Reserve. Multicoloured.

530	15p. Type **132**	40	40
531	15p. Three turnstones	40	40
532	15p. Dunlins and turnstones	40	40
533	15p. Curlew and turnstones	40	40
534	15p. Ringed plover with chicks	40	40
535	21p. Gull, sea campion and sea radish	50	50
536	21p. Yellow horned poppy	50	50
537	21p. Pair of stonechats, hare's foot clover and fennel	50	50
538	21p. Hares's foot clover, fennel and slender oat	50	50
539	21p. Sea kale on shore	50	50

Nos. 530/4 and 535/9 were each printed together, se-tenant, with the backgrounds forming composite designs.

133 "Rudolph the Red-nosed Reindeer" (Melanie Sharpe)

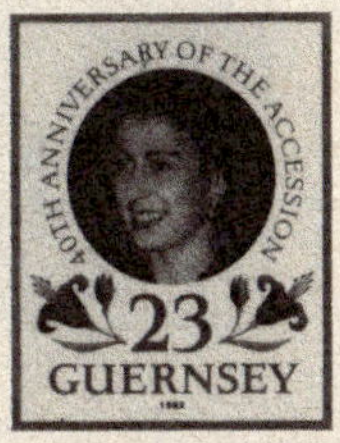

134 Queen Elizabeth II in 1952

1991. Christmas. Children's Paintings. Mult.

540	12p. Type **133**	35	35
541	12p. "Christmas Pudding" (James Quinn)	35	35
542	12p. "Snowman" (Lisa Guille)	35	35
543	12p. "Snowman in Top Hat" (Jessica Ede-Golightly)	35	35
544	12p. "Robins and Christmas Tree" (Sharon Le Page)	35	35
545	12p. "Shepherds and Angels" (Anna Coquelin)	35	35
546	12p. "Nativity" (Claudine Lihou)	35	35
547	12p. "Three Wise Men" (Jonathan Le Noury)	35	35
548	12p. "Star of Bethlehem and Angels" (Marcia Mahy)	35	35
549	12p. "Christmas Tree" (Laurel Garfield)	35	35
550	12p. "Santa Claus" (Rebecca Driscoll)	35	35
551	12p. "Snowman and Star" (Ian Lowe)	35	35

1992. 40th Anniv of Accession. Multicoloured.

552	23p. Type **134**	70	70
553	28p. Queen Elizabeth in 1977	75	75
554	33p. Queen Elizabeth in 1986	85	85
555	39p. Queen Elizabeth in 1991	1·10	1·10

135 Christopher Columbus

1992. 500th Anniv of Discovery of America by Columbus. Multicoloured.

556	23p. Type **135**	60	60
557	23p. Examples of Columbus's signature	60	60
558	28p. "Santa Maria"	1·10	1·10
559	28p. Map of first voyage	1·10	1·10

137 Stock

138 Building the Ship

1992. Horticultural Exports. Multicoloured.

562	1p. "Stephanotis floribunda"	10	10
563	2p. Potted hydrangea	10	10
564	3p. Type **137**	10	10
565	4p. Anemones	10	10
566	5p. Gladiolus	10	15
567	6p. "Asparagus plumosus" and "Gypsophila paniculata"	10	15
568	7p. Guernsey lily	15	20
569	8p. Enchantment lily	15	20
570	9p. Clematis "Freckles"	20	25
571	10p. Alstroemeria	20	25
572	16p. Standard carnation (horiz)	30	35
572b	18p. Standard rose	35	40
573	20p. Spray rose	40	45
574	23p. Mixed freesia (horiz)	45	50
575	24p. Standard rose (horiz)	50	55
576	25p. Iris "Ideal" (horiz)	50	55
576b	26p. Freesia "Pink Glow"	55	60
577	28p. Lisianthus (horiz)	55	60
578	30p. Spray chrysanthemum (horiz)	60	65
579	40p. Spray carnation	80	85
580	50p. Single freesia (horiz)	1·00	1·10
581	£1 Floral arrangement (35 × 26½ mm)	2·00	2·10
582	£2 Chelsea Flower Show exhibit (35 × 26½ mm)	4·00	4·25
582a	£3 "Floral Fantasia" (exhibit) (35 × 28 mm)	6·00	6·25

1992. "Operation Asterix" (excavation of Roman ship). Multicoloured.

583	16p. Type **138**	45	45
584	23p. Loading the cargo	60	60
585	28p. Ship at sea	80	80
586	33p. Ship under attack	95	95
587	39p. Crew swimming ashore	1·10	1·10

139 Tram No. 10 decorated for Battle of Flowers

1992. Guernsey Trams. Multicoloured.

588	16p. Type **139**	45	45
589	23p. Tram No. 10 passing Hougue a la Perre	60	60
590	28p. Tram No. 1 at St. Sampsons	80	80
591	33p. First steam tram at St. Peter Port	95	95
592	39p. Last electric tram, 1934	1·10	1·10

140 Man in Party Hat

141 Rupert Bear, Bingo and Dog

1992. Christmas. Seasonal Fayre. Multicoloured.

593	13p. Type **140**	35	35
594	13p. Girl and Christmas tree	35	35
595	13p. Woman and balloons	35	35
596	13p. Mince pies and champagne	35	35
597	13p. Roast turkey	35	35
598	13p. Christmas pudding	35	35
599	13p. Christmas cake	35	35
600	13p. Fancy cakes	35	35
601	13p. Cheese	35	35
602	13p. Nuts	35	35
603	13p. Ham	35	35
604	13p. Chocolate log	35	35

Nos. 593/604 were printed together, se-tenant, forming a composite design.

1993. Rupert Bear and Friends (cartoon characters created by Mary and Herbert Tourtel).

605	**141** 24p. multicoloured	1·00	1·00

142 Tapestry by Kelly Fletcher

1993. Europa. Contemporary Art. Multicoloured.

607	24p. Type **142**	80	80
608	24p. "Le Marchi a Paissaon" (etching and aquatint, Sally Reed) (48 × 33½ mm)	80	80
609	28p. "Red Abstract" (painting Molly Harris)	90	90
610	28p. "Dress Shop, King's Road" (painting, Damon Bell) (48 × 33½ mm)	90	90

143 Arrest of Guernsey Parliamentarians, Fermain Bay

1993. 350th Anniv of Siege of Castle Cornet. Multicoloured.

611	16p. Type **143**	40	40
612	24p. Parliamentary ships attacking Castle Cornet	65	65
613	28p. Parliamentary captives escaping	85	85
614	33p. Castle cannon firing at St. Peter Port	95	95
615	39p. Surrender of Castle Cornet, 19 December 1651	1·10	1·10

144 Playing Cards

145 "The Twelve Pearls"

1993. Birth Bicentenary of Thomas de la Rue (printer).

617	**144** 16p. multicoloured	40	40
618	– 24p. multicoloured	65	65
619	– 28p. multicoloured	80	80
620	– 33p. red	95	95
621	– 39p. green	1·10	1·10

DESIGNS: 24p. Fountain pens; 28p. Envelope-folding machine; 33p. Great Britain 1855 4d. stamp; 39p. Thomas de la Rue and Mauritius £1 banknote.

1993. Christmas. Stained Glass Windows by Mary-Eily de Putron from the Chapel of Christ the Healer. Multicoloured.

622	13p. Type **145**	45	45
623	13p. "Healing rays"	45	45
624	13p. "Hand of God over the Holy City"	45	45
625	13p. "Wing and Seabirds" (facing left)	45	45
626	13p. "Christ the Healer"	45	45
627	13p. "Wing and Seabirds" (facing right)	45	45
628	13p. "The Young Jesus in the Temple"	45	45
629	13p. "The Raising of Jairus' Daughter"	45	45
630	13p. "Suffer little Children to come unto Me"	45	45
631	13p. "Pilgrim's Progress"	45	45
632	13p. "The Light of the World"	45	45
633	13p. "Raphael, the Archangel of Healing, with Tobias"	45	45

146 Les Fouaillages (ancient burial ground)

1994. Europa. Archaeological Discoveries. Multicoloured.

634	24p. Type **146**	60	60
635	24p. Mounted Celtic warrior	60	60
636	30p. Jars, arrow heads and stone axe from Les Fouaillages	80	80
637	30p. Sword, spear head and torque from King's Road burial	80	80

148 Peugeot "Type 3", 1894

1994. Cent of First Car in Guernsey. Mult.

639	16p. Type **148**	45	45
640	24p. Mercedes "Simplex", 1903	70	70
641	35p. Humber tourer, 1906	1·00	1·00
642	41p. Bentley sports tourer, 1936	1·10	1·10
643	60p. MG TC Midget, 1948	1·75	1·75

149 "Trident" (Herm ferry)

1994. 25th Anniv of Guernsey Postal Administration. Multicoloured.

645	16p. Type **149**	35	35
646	24p. Handley Page Super Dart Herald of Channel Express	55	55
647	35p. Britten Norman Trislander of Aurigny Air Services	75	75
648	41p. "Bon Marin de Serk" (Sark ferry)	85	85
649	60p. Map of Bailiwick	1·40	1·40

MORE DETAILED LISTS
are given in the Stanley Gibbons Catalogues referred to in the country headings.
For lists of current volumes see Introduction.

150 Dolls' House

151 Seafood "Face"

1994. Christmas. Bygone Toys. Multicoloured.

651	13p. Type **150**	40	40
652	13p. Doll	40	40
653	13p. Teddy in bassinette	40	40
654	13p. Sweets in pillar box and playing cards	40	40
655	13p. Spinning top	40	40
656	13p. Building blocks	40	40
657	24p. Rocking horse	75	75
658	24p. Teddy bear	75	75
659	24p. Tricycle	75	75
660	24p. Wooden duck	75	75
661	24p. Hornby toy locomotive	75	75
662	24p. Ludo game	75	75

Nos. 651/6 and 657/62 respectively were printed together, se-tenant, forming composite designs.

1995. Greetings Stamps. "The Welcoming Face of Guernsey". Multicoloured.

663	24p. Type **151**	65	65
664	24p. Buckets and spade "face"	65	65
665	24p. Flowers "face"	65	65
666	24p. Fruit and vegetables "face"	65	65
667	24p. Sea shells and seaweed "face"	65	65
668	24p. Anchor and life belts "face"	65	65
669	24p. Glasses, cork and cutlery "face"	65	65
670	24p. Butterflies and caterpillars "face"	65	65

152 Winston Churchill and Wireless

1995. 50th Anniv of Liberation. Multicoloured.

672	16p. Type **152**	50	50
673	24p. Union Jack and Royal Navy ships off St. Peter Port	75	75
674	35p. Royal Arms and military band	1·00	1·00
675	41p. "Vega" (Red Cross supply ship)	1·00	1·00
676	60p. Rejoicing crowd	1·75	1·75

153 Silhouette of Doves on Ground (½-size illustration)

1995. Europa. Peace and Freedom. Multicoloured.

678	25p. Type **153**	65	65
679	30p. Silhouette of doves in flight	85	85

The designs of Nos. 678/9 each provide a stereogram or hidden three-dimensional image of a single dove.

154 Prince Charles, Castle Cornet and Bailiwick Arms

1995. Royal Visit.

680	**154** £1.50 multicoloured	4·00	4·00

155 Part of United Nations Emblem (face value at top left)

1995. 50th Anniv of United Nations. Designs showing different segments of the United Nations Emblem. Each blue and gold.

682	50p. Type **155**	1·25	1·25
683	50p. Face value at top right	1·25	1·25
684	50p. Face value at bottom left	1·25	1·25
685	50p. Face value at bottom right	1·25	1·25

156 "Christmas Trees for Sale in Bern" (Cornelia Huisboum-Weibel)

1995. Christmas. 50th Anniv of U.N.I.C.E.F. Multicoloured.

686	13p. Type **156** (face value at left)	40	40
687	13p. "Christmas Trees for Sale in Bern" (face value at right)	40	40
688	13p. + 1p. "Evening Snowfall" (Katerina Mertikas) (face value at left)	40	40
689	13p. + 1p. "Evening Snowfall" (face value at right)	40	40
690	24p. "It came upon a Midnight Clear" (Georgia Guback) (face value at left)	70	70
691	24p. "It came upon a Midnight Clear" (Georgia Guback) (face value at right)	70	70
692	24p. + 2p. "Children of the World" (face value at left)	70	70
693	24p. + 2p. "Children of the World" (face value at right)	70	70

Nos. 686/7, 688/9, 690/1 and 692/3 were printed together, se-tenant, each pair forming a composite design.

157 Princess Anne (President, Save the Children Fund) and Children

1996. Europa. Famous Women. Multicoloured.

694	25p. Type **157**	65	65
695	30p. Queen Elizabeth II and people of the Commonwealth	85	85

158 England v. U.S.S.R., 1968 (value at right)

1996. European Football Championship. Multicoloured.

696	16p. Type **158**	55	55
697	16p. England v. U.S.S.R., 1968 (value at left)	55	55
698	24p. Italy v. Belgium, 1972 (value at right)	75	75
699	24p. Italy v. Belgium, 1972 (value at left)	75	75
700	35p. Ireland v. Netherlands, 1988 (value at right)	80	80
701	35p. Ireland v. Netherlands, 1988 (value at left)	80	80
702	41p. Denmark v. Germany, 1992 final (value at right)	95	95
703	41p. Denmark v. Germany, 1992 final (value at left)	95	95

160 Ancient Greek Runner

162 The Annunciation

161 Humphrey Bogart as Philip Marlowe

1996. Centenary of Modern Olympic Games. Ancient Greek Athletes. Each black, yellow and orange.

705	16p. Type **160**	50	50
706	24p. Throwing the javelin	95	95
707	41p. Throwing the discus	1·10	1·10
708	55p. Wrestling (53 × 31 mm)	1·40	1·40
709	60p. Jumping	1·60	1·60

No. 708 also includes the "OLYMPHILEX '96" International Stamp Exhibition, Atlanta, logo.

1996. Centenary of Cinema. Screen Detectives. Multicoloured.

711	16p. Type **161**	30	35
712	24p. Peter Sellers as Inspector Clouseau	50	55
713	35p. Basil Rathbone as Sherlock Holmes	70	75
714	41p. Margaret Rutherford as Miss Marple	80	85
715	60p. Warner Oland as Charlie Chan	1·25	1·40

1996. Christmas. Multicoloured.

716	13p. Type **162**	25	30
717	13p. Journey to Bethlehem	25	30
718	13p. Arrival at the inn	25	30
719	13p. Angel and shepherds	25	30
720	13p. Mary, Joseph and Jesus in stable	25	30
721	13p. Shepherds worshipping Jesus	25	30
722	13p. Three Kings following star	25	30
723	13p. Three Kings with gifts	25	30
724	13p. The Presentation in the Temple	25	30
725	13p. Mary and Jesus	25	30
726	13p. Joseph warned by angel	25	30
727	13p. The Flight into Egypt	25	30
728	24p. Mary cradling Jesus (horiz)	50	55
729	25p. The Nativity (horiz)	50	55

163 Holly Blue

1997. Endangered Species. Butterflies and Moths. Multicoloured.

730	18p. Type **163**	60	60
731	25p. Hummingbird hawk-moth	75	75
732	26p. Emperor moth	90	90
733	37p. Brimstone	1·10	1·10

164 Gilliatt fighting Octopus

1997. Europa. Tales and Legends. Scenes from "Les Travailleurs de la Mer" by Victor Hugo. Multicoloured.

735	26p. Type **164**	65	65
736	31p. Gilliatt grieving on rock	75	75

165 Shell Beach, Herm

168 Teddy Bear making Cake

167 Transistor Radio, Microphone and Radio Logos

1997. Guernsey Scenes (1st series). Multicoloured. Self-adhesive.

737	18p. Type **165**	40	45
738	25p. La Seigneurie, Sark (vert)	60	60
739	26p. Castle Cornet, Guernsey	60	60

See also Nos. 770/3.

1997. Methods of Communication. Multicoloured.

741	18p. Type **167**	45	45
742	25p. Television, video camera and satellite dish	70	70
743	26p. Fax machine, telephones and mobile phone	70	70
744	37p. Printing press, newspaper and type	1·00	1·00
745	43p. Stamp, coding machine and postbox	1·10	1·10
746	63p. C.D., computer and disk	1·60	1·60

1997. Christmas. Teddy Bears. Multicoloured.

747	15p. Type **168**	45	45
748	25p. Teddy bears decorating Christmas tree	70	70
749	26p. Two teddy bears in armchair	70	70
750	37p. Teddy bear as Father Christmas	1·00	1·00
751	43p. Teddy bears unwrapping presents	1·10	1·10
752	63p. Teddy bears eating Christmas dinner	1·60	1·60

169 Visiting Guernsey, 1957

1997. Golden Wedding of Queen Elizabeth and Prince Philip. Multicoloured.

754	18p. Type **169**	45	45
755	25p. Coronation Day, 1953	70	70
756	26p. Royal family, 1957	70	70
757	37p. On royal yacht, 1972	1·00	1·00
758	43p. Queen Elizabeth and Prince Philip at Trooping the Colour, 1987	1·10	1·10
759	63p. Queen Elizabeth and Prince Philip, 1997	1·60	1·60

No. 755 is inscribed "1947" in error.

170 Tapestry of 11th-century Guernsey (St. Martin)

171 Fort Grey

1998. The Millennium Tapestries Project. Each showing a different century contributed by individual parishes. Multicoloured.

760	25p. Type **170**	50	55
761	25p. 12th-century (St. Saviour)	50	55
762	25p. 13th-century (Vale)	50	55
763	25p. 14th-century (St. Sampson)	50	55
764	25p. 15th-century (Torteval)	50	55
765	25p. 16th-century (Castel)	50	55
766	25p. 17th-century (St. Andrew)	50	55
767	25p. 18th-century (Forest)	50	55
768	25p. 19th-century (St. Pierre du Bois)	50	55
769	25p. 20th-century (St. Peter Port)	50	55

1998. Guernsey Scenes (2nd series). Multicoloured. Self-adhesive.

770	(20p.) Type **171**	40	45
771	(20p.) Grand Havre	40	45
772	(25p.) Little Chapel	50	55
773	(25p.) Guernsey cow	50	55

Nos. 770/1 are inscribed "Bailiwick Minimum Postage Paid" and were intially sold at 20p. Nos. 772/3 are inscribed "UK Minimum Postage Paid" and were initially sold at 25p.

172 Fairey IIIC, Balloon, Sopwith Camel and Avro 504

1998. 80th Anniv of the Royal Air Force. Multicoloured.

774	20p. Type **172**	40	45
775	25p. Fairey Swordfish, Tiger Moth, Supermarine Walrus and Gloster Gladiator	50	55
776	30p. Hawker Hurricane, Supermarine Spitfire, Vickers Wellington, Short Sunderland (flying boat), Westland Lysander and Bristol Blenheim	60	65
777	37p. De Havilland Mosquito, Avro Lancaster, Auster III, Gloster Meteor and Horsa glider	75	80
778	43p. Canberra, Hawker Sea Fury, Bristol Sycamore, Hawker Hunter, Handley Page Victor and BAe Lightning	85	90
779	63p. Pavania Tornado GRI, BAe Hawk, BAe Sea Harrier, Westland Lynx (helicopter) and Hawker Siddeley Nimrod	1·25	1·40

174 Girls in Traditional Costume watching Sheep Display, West Show

1998. Europa. Festivals. Multicoloured.

781	20p. Type **174**	40	45
782	25p. Marching band and "Battle of Flowers" exhibit, North Show	50	55
783	30p. Prince Charles, monument and tank, Liberation Day	60	65
784	37p. Goat, dahlias and show-jumping, South Show	75	80

The 25p. and 30p. incorporate the "EUROPA" emblem.

176 Royal Yacht "Britannia"

1998. Maritime Heritage.

809	**176** £5 multicoloured	10·00	10·50

177 Modern Tree, Teletubby and Playstation

1998. 150th Anniv of the Introduction of the Christmas Tree. Multicoloured.

810	17p. Type **177**	35	40
811	25p. 1960s tinsel tree, toy bus and doll	50	55
812	30p. 1930s gold foil tree, panda and toy tank	60	65
813	37p. 1920s tree, model of "Bluebird" and doll	75	80
814	43p. 1900 tree, teddy bear and toy train	85	90
815	63p. 1850s tree, wooden doll and spinning top	1·25	1·40

178 Elizabeth Bowes Lyon, 1907

180 Burnet Rose and Local Carriage Label

179 "Spirit of Guernsey", 1995

1999. Life and Times of Queen Elizabeth the Queen Mother. Multicoloured.

817	25p. Type **178**	50	55
818	25p. On wedding day, 1923	50	55
819	25p. Holding Princess Elizabeth, 1926	50	55
820	25p. At Coronation, 1937	50	55
821	25p. Visiting bombed areas of London, 1940 (wearing green hat)	50	55
822	25p. Fishing near Auckland, New Zealand, 1966	50	55
823	25p. At Guernsey function, 1963 (wearing tiara)	50	55
824	25p. Receiving flowers on her birthday, 1992	50	55
825	25p. Presenting trophy, Sandown Park races, 1989	50	55
826	25p. Opening Royal Norfolk Regimental Museum, Norwich, 1990 (wearing blue hat)	50	55

1999. 175th Anniv of Royal National Lifeboat Institution. Multicoloured.

827	20p. Type **179**	40	45
828	25p. "Sir William Arnold", 1973	50	55

829		30p. "Euphrosyne Kendal", 1954	60	65
830		38p. "Queen Victoria", 1929	75	80
831		44p. "Arthur Lionel", 1912	90	95
832		64p. "Vincent Kirk Ella", 1888	1·25	1·40

1999. Europa. Parks and Gardens. Herm Island. Designs each showing a different local carriage label. Multicoloured.

833		20p. Type **180**	40	45
834		25p. Puffin	50	55
835		30p. Small heath butterfly	60	65
836		38p. Shells on Shell Beach	75	80

POSTAGE DUE STAMPS

D **1** Castle Cornet

1969. Face values in black.

D1	D **1**	1d. plum	2·25	1·25
D2		2d. green	2·25	1·25
D3		3d. red	3·75	4·00
D4		4d. blue	5·00	5·00
D5		5d. ochre	5·50	5·50
D6		6d. turquoise	6·50	6·00
D7		1s. brown	17·00	17·00

1971. Decimal Currency. Face values in black.

D 8	D **1**	½p. plum	10	10
D 9		1p. green	10	10
D10		2p. red	10	10
D11		3p. blue	10	15
D12		4p. ochre	10	15
D13		5p. blue	10	15
D14		6p. violet	15	20
D15		8p. orange	25	20
D16		10p. brown	30	30
D17		15p. grey	40	40

D **2** St. Peter Port

1977. Face values in black.

D18	D **2**	½p. brown	10	10
D19		1p. purple	10	10
D20		2p. orange	10	10
D21		3p. red	10	10
D22		4p. blue	10	10
D23		5p. green	15	15
D24		6p. green	20	20
D25		8p. brown	25	25
D26		10p. blue	40	40
D27		14p. green	45	45
D28		15p. violet	45	45
D29		16p. red	55	55

D **3** Milking Cow

1982. Guernsey Scenes, c. 1900.

D30	D **3**	1p. blue and green	10	10
D31	–	2p. brown, lt brown & blue	10	10
D32	–	3p. green and lilac	10	10
D33	–	4p. green and orange	10	10
D34	–	5p. blue and green	10	10
D35	–	16p. blue and light blue	30	35
D36	–	18p. blue and green	35	40
D37	–	20p. green and blue	40	45
D38	–	25p. blue and pink	50	55
D39	–	30p. green and yellow	60	65
D40	–	50p. brown and blue	1·00	1·10
D41	–	£1 lt brown and brown	2·00	2·10

DESIGNS: 2p. Vale Mill; 3p. Sark cottage; 4p. Quay-side, St. Peter Port; 5p. Well, Water Lane, Moulin Huet; 16p. Seaweed gathering; 18p. Upper Walk, White Rock; 20p. Cobo Bay; 25p. Saint's Bay; 30p. La Coupee, Sark; 50p. Old Harbour, St. Peter Port; £1 Greenhouses, Doyle Road, St. Peter Port.

ALDERNEY

The following issues are provided by the Guernsey Post Office for use on Alderney. They are also valid for postal purposes throughout the rest of the Bailiwick of Guernsey.

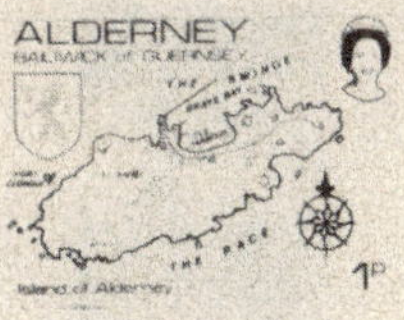

A **1** Island Map

1983. Island Scenes. Multicoloured.

A 1		1p. Type A **1**	10	10
A 2		4p. Hanging Rock	10	10
A 3		9p. States' Building, St. Anne	20	25
A 4		10p. St. Anne's Church	25	25
A 5		11p. Yachts in Braye Bay	25	25
A 6		12p. Victoria St., St. Anne	25	30
A 7		13p. Map of Channel	25	25
A 8		14p. Fort Clonque	30	35
A 9		15p. Corblets Bay and Fort	30	35
A10		16p. Old Tower, St. Anne	30	35
A11		17p. Golf course and Essex Castle	35	40
A12		18p. Old Harbour	35	40
A12a		20p. Quesnard Lighthouse	80	80
A12b		21p. Braye Harbour	80	80
A12c		23p. Island Hall	70	70
A12d		24p. "J.T. Daly" (steam locomotive)	1·75	1·75
A12e		28p. "Louis Marchesi of the Round Table" (lifeboat)	2·00	2·00

Nos. A12a/e are larger, 38×27 mm.

A **2** Oystercatcher

1984. Birds. Multicoloured.

A13		9p. Type A **2**	1·50	1·50
A14		13p. Turnstone	1·50	2·00
A15		26p. Ringed plover	5·00	4·00
A16		28p. Dunlin	5·00	4·00
A17		31p. Curlew	5·00	4·00

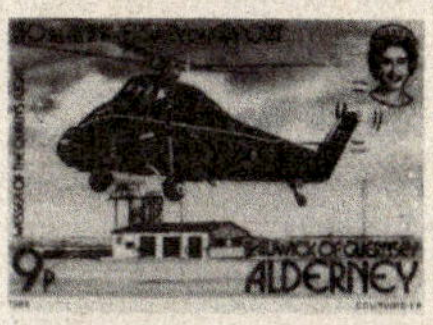

A **3** Westland Wessex HU MK 5 Helicopter of the Queen's Flight

1985. 50th Anniv of Alderney Airport. Mult.

A18		9p. Type A **3**	2·50	2·25
A19		13p. Britten Norman "Longnose" Trislander	2·50	3·00
A20		29p. De Havilland Heron 1B	6·00	5·00
A21		31p. De Havilland Dragon Rapide "Sir Henry Lawrence"	6·50	5·50
A22		34p. Saro Windhover flying boat "City of Portsmouth"	7·00	5·50

A **4** Royal Engineers, 1890 A **5** Fort Grosnez

1985. Regiments of the Alderney Garrison. Multicoloured.

A23		9p. Type A **4**	45	45
A24		14p. Duke of Albany's Own Highlanders, 1856	1·00	1·00
A25		29p. Royal Artillery, 1855	1·50	1·50
A26		31p. South Hampshire Regiment, 1810	1·75	1·75
A27		34p. Royal Irish Regiment, 1782	2·00	2·00

1986. Alderney Forts. Multicoloured.

A28		10p. Type A **5**	1·10	1·10
A29		14p. Fort Tourgis	1·75	1·75
A30		31p. Fort Clonque	4·00	4·00
A31		34p. Fort Albert	4·25	4·25

A **6** "Liverpool" (full-rigged ship), 1902

1987. Alderney Shipwrecks. Multicoloured.

A32		11p. Type A **6**	2·00	1·50
A33		15p. "Petit Raymond" (schooner), 1906	2·25	2·00
A34		29p. "Maina" (yacht), 1910	5·50	5·00
A35		31p. "Burton" (steamer), 1911	6·00	5·50
A36		34p. "Point Law" (oil tanker), 1975	6·50	6·00

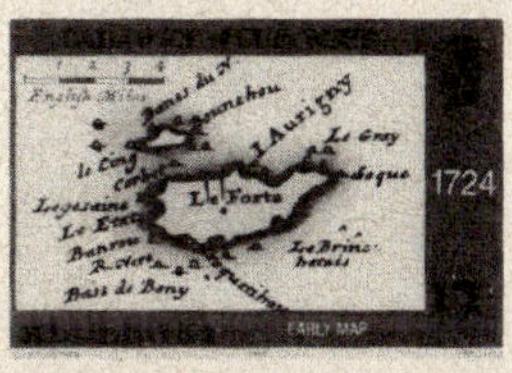

A **7** Moll's Map of 1724

1989. 250th Anniv of Bastide's Survey of Alderney.

A37	A **7**	12p. multicoloured	40	40
A38	–	18p. black, blue & brown	60	60
A39	–	27p. black, blue & green	1·10	1·10
A40	–	32p. black, blue & red	1·25	1·25
A41	–	35p. multicoloured	1·40	1·40

DESIGNS: 18p. Bastide's survey of 1739; 27p. Goodwin's map of 1831; 32p. General Staff map of 1943; 35p. Ordnance Survey map, 1988.

A **8** H.M.S. "Alderney" (bomb ketch), 1738

1990. Royal Navy Ships named after Alderney.

A42	A **8**	14p. black and bistre	45	45
A43	–	20p. black and brown	60	60
A44	–	29p. black and brown	1·10	1·10
A45	–	34p. black and blue	1·10	1·10
A46	–	37p. black and blue	1·25	1·25

DESIGNS: 20p. H.M.S. "Alderney" (sixth rate), 1742; 29p. H.M.S. "Alderney" (sloop), 1755; 34p. H.M.S. "Alderney" (submarine), 1945; 37p. H.M.S. "Alderney" (patrol vessel), 1979.

A **9** Wreck of H.M.S. "Victory", 1744

1991. Automation of The Casquets Lighthouse. Multicoloured.

A47		21p. Type A **9**	1·60	2·00
A48		26p. Lighthouse keeper's daughter rowing back to the Casquets	2·00	2·25
A49		31p. MBB-Bolkow Bo 105D helicopter leaving pad on St. Thomas Tower	2·50	2·75
A50		37p. Migrating birds over lighthouse	3·50	3·75
A51		50p. Trinity House vessel "Patricia" and arms	6·00	5·00

A **10** Two French Warships on Fire A **11** Spiny Lobster

1992. 300th Anniv of the Battle of La Hogue. Multicoloured.

A52		23p. Type A **10**	1·50	1·50
A53		28p. Crews leaving burning ships	2·25	2·25
A54		33p. French warship sinking	2·50	2·50
A55		50p. "The Battle of La Hogue" (47×32 mm)	3·75	3·75

Nos. A52/4 show details of the painting on the 50p. value.

1993. Endangered Species. Marine Life. Mult.

A56		24p. Type A **11**	90	90
A57		28p. Plumose anemone	1·00	1·00
A58		33p. Starfish	1·25	1·25
A59		39p. Sea urchin	1·60	1·60

Nos. A56/9 were printed together, se-tenant, the backgrounds forming a composite design.

A **12** Blue-tailed Damselfly, Dark Hair Water Crowfoot and Branched Bur-reed

1994. Flora and Fauna. Multicoloured.

A60		1p. Type A **12**	10	10
A61		2p. White-toothed shrew and flax-leaved St. John's wort	10	10
A62		3p. Fulmar and kaffir fig	10	10
A63		4p. Clouded yellow (butterfly) and red clover	10	10
A64		5p. Bumble bee, prostrate broom and giant broom-rape	10	10
A65		6p. Dartford warbler and lesser dodder	15	20
A66		7p. Peacock (butterfly) and stemless thistle	15	20
A67		8p. Mole and bluebell	15	20
A68		9p. Great green grasshopper and common gorse	20	25
A69		10p. Six-spot burnet (moth) and viper's bugloss	20	25
A70		16p. Common blue (butterfly) and pyramidal orchid	30	35

A70b	18p. Small tortoiseshell (butterfly) and buddleia	35	40
A71	20p. Common rabbit and creeping buttercup	40	45
A72	24p. Great black-backed gull and sand crocus	50	55
A72b	25p. Rock pipit and sea stock	50	55
A72c	26p. Sand digger wasp and sea bindweed (horiz)	50	55
A73	30p. Atlantic puffin and English stonecrop	60	65
A74	40p. Emperor (moth) and bramble	80	85
A75	50p. Pale-spined hedgehog and pink oxalis	1·00	1·10
A76	£1 Common tern and Bermuda grass (horiz)	2·00	2·10
A77	£2 Northern gannet and "Fucus vesiculosus" (seaweed) (horiz)	4·00	4·25

A **13** Royal Aircraft Factory SE5A

1995. Birth Cent of Tommy Rose (aviator). Mult.

A78	35p. Type A **13**	85	85
A79	35p. Miles Master II and other Miles aircraft	85	85
A80	35p. Miles Aerovan and Miles Monitor	85	85
A81	41p. Miles Falcon Six winning King's Cup air race, 1935	1·00	1·00
A82	41p. Miles Hawk Speed Six winning Manx Air Derby, 1947	1·00	1·00
A83	41p. Miles Falcon Six breaking U.K.–Cape record, 1936	1·00	1·00

A **15** Signallers training on Alderney

1996. 25th Anniv of Adoption of 30th Signal Regiment by Alderney. Multicoloured.

A85	24p. Type A **15**	65	65
A86	41p. Communications station, Falkland Islands	1·10	1·10
A87	60p. Dish aerial and land rover, Gulf War	1·50	1·50
A88	75p. Service with United Nations	1·75	1·75

Nos. A85/8 were printed together, se-tenant, forming a composite design.

A **16** Cat with Butterfly

A **17** Harold Larwood

1996. Cats. Multicoloured.

A89	16p. Type A **16**	45	45
A90	24p. Blue and white on table	65	65
A91	25p. Tabby kitten grooming blue and white persian kitten	65	65
A92	35p. Red persian under table	95	95
A93	41p. White cat with tortoiseshell and white in toy cart	1·10	1·10
A94	60p. Siamese playing with wool	1·75	1·75

1997. 150th Anniv of Cricket on Alderney. Multicoloured.

A96	18p. Type A **17**	50	50
A97	25p. John Arlott	65	65
A98	37p. Pelham J. Warner	1·00	1·00
A99	43p. W. G. Grace	1·25	1·25
A100	63p. John Wisden	1·60	1·60

A **18** Railway under Construction

A **19** Modern Superlite Helmet and Wreck of "Point Law" (oil tanker)

1997. Garrison Island (1st series). 150th Anniv of Harbour. Multicoloured.

A102	18p. Type A **18**	45	45
A103	18p. "Ariadne" (paddle steamer) at anchor	45	45
A104	25p. Quarrying stone	65	65
A105	25p. Quarry railway	65	65
A106	26p. Queen Victoria and Prince Albert on Alderney	70	70
A107	26p. Royal Yacht "Victoria and Albert" and guard of honour	70	70
A108	31p. Railway workers greet Queen Victoria	80	80
A109	31p. Royal party in railway wagons	80	80

See also Nos. A116/23.

1998. 21st Anniv of Alderney Diving Club. Multicoloured.

See also Nos. A116/23.

A110	20p. Type A **19**	40	45
A111	30p. Cousteau-Gagnan demand valve and wreck of "Stella" (steamer)	60	65
A112	37p. Heinke closed helmet and "Liverpool" (full-rigged ship)	75	80
A113	43p. Siebe closed helmet	85	90
A114	63p. Deane open helmet	1·25	1·40

1998. Garrison Island (2nd series). As Type A **18**. Multicoloured.

A116	20p. Alderney Post Office	40	45
A117	20p. Traders in Victoria Street	40	45
A118	25p. Court House	50	55
A119	25p. Police Station and fire engine	50	55
A120	30p. St. Anne's Church	60	65
A121	30p. Wedding party at Albert Gate	60	65
A122	37p. "Courier" (ferry) at Braye Bay	75	80
A123	37p. Fishermen at quay	75	80

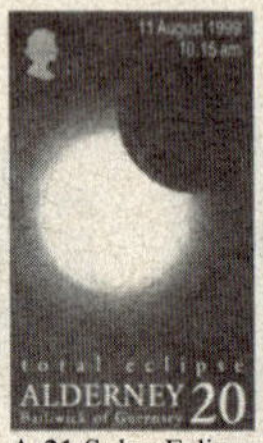

A **21** Solar Eclipse at 10.15 am

1999. Total Eclipse of the Sun (11 August). Designs showing stages of the eclipse. Multicoloured.

A125	20p. Type A **21**	40	45
A126	25p. At 10.51 am	50	55
A127	30p. At 11.14 am	60	65
A128	38p. At 11.16 am	75	80
A129	44p. At 11.17 am	90	95
A130	64p. At 11.36 am	1·25	1·40

GUYANA

Formerly British Guiana. Attained independence on 26 May, 1966, and changed its name to Guyana.

100 cents = 1 dollar

CANCELLED REMAINDERS. In 1969 remainders of some issues were put on the market cancelled-to-order in such a way as to be indistinguishable from genuine postally used copies for all practical purposes. Our quotations which are indicated by an asterisk are the same for cancelled-to-order or postally used copies.

1966. Nos. 331 etc of British Guiana optd **GUYANA INDEPENDENCE 1966.**

399	**55**	1 c. black	10	10
421	–	2 c. green	10	10
422	–	3 c. green and brown	30	10
400	–	4 c. violet	10	10
388	–	5 c. red and black	20	10
424	–	6 c. green	10	10
401	–	8 c. blue	10	10
391	–	12 c. black and brown	10	10
435	–	24 c. black and orange	2·25	10
393	–	36 c. red and black	30	30
405	–	48 c. blue and red	30	30
395	–	72 c. red and green	40	50
396	–	$1 multicoloured	1·50	35
397	–	$2 mauve	1·50	75
398	–	$5 blue and black	1·00	1·75

74 Flag and Map

1966. Independence. Multicoloured.

408		5 c. Type **74**	10	10
409		15 c. Type **74**	15	10
410		25 c. Arms of Guyana	20	10
411		$1 Arms of Guyana	65	1·00

76 Bank Building

1966. Opening of Bank of Guyana.

412	**76**	5 c. multicoloured	10	10
413		25 c. multicoloured	10	10

77 British Guiana One Cent Stamp of 1856

1967. World's Rarest Stamp Commemoration.

414	**77**	5 c. multicoloured	10	10*
415		25 c. multicoloured	10	10*

78 Chateau Margot

1967. 1st Anniv of Independence. Multicoloured.

416		6 c. Type **78**	10	10*
417		15 c. Independence Arch	10	10*
418		25 c. Fort Island	10	10*
419		$1 National Assembly	20	15

Nos. 418/9 are horiz.

MINIMUM PRICE

The minimum price quoted is 10p which represents a handling charge rather than a basis for valuing common stamps. For further notes about prices see introductory pages.

83 "Millie" (Blue and Yellow Macaw)

84 Wicket-keeping

1967. Christmas.

441	**83**	5 c. yell, bl, black & green	10	10*
443		5 c. yell, blue, black & red	10	10*
442		25 c. yell, blue, blk, & violet	15	10*
444		25 c. yell, blue, blk, & green	15	10*

1968. M.C.C.'s West Indies Tour. Multicoloured.

445		5 c. Type **84**	10	10*
446		6 c. Batting	10	10*
447		25 c. Bowling	30	10*

87 Pike Cichlid

102 "Christ of St. John of the Cross" (Salvador Dali)

1968. Multicoloured.

448		1 c. Type **87**	10	10
449		2 c. Red paranha ("Pirai")	10	10
450		3 c. Peacock cichlid ("Lukunani")	10	10
451		5 c. Armoured catfish ("Hassar")	10	10
489		6 c. Black acara ("Patua")	10	50
490		10 c. Spix's guan (vert)	30	40
491		15 c. Harpy eagle (vert)	30	10
455		20 c. Hoatzin (vert)	60	10
493		25 c. Guianan cock of the rock (vert)	30	10
457		40 c. Great kiskadee (vert)	75	40
495		50 c. Brazilian agouti ("Accouri")	35	15
459		60 c. White-lipped peccary	80	10
460		$1 Paca ("Labba")	80	10
461		$2 Nine-banded armadillo	1·25	2·00
462		$5 Ocelot	1·50	3·00

1968. Easter.

463	**102**	5 c. multicoloured	10	10*
464		25 c. multicoloured	20	10*

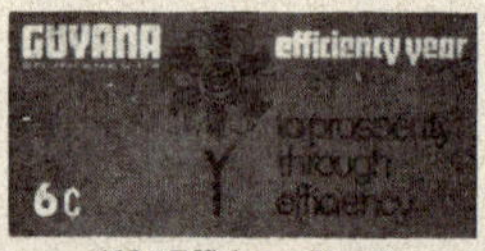

103 "Efficiency Year"

1968. "Savings Bonds and Efficiency". Multicoloured.

465		6 c. Type **103**	10	10*
466		25 c. Type **103**	10	10*
467		30 c. "Savings Bonds"	10	10*
468		40 c. "Savings Bonds"	10	10*

105 Open Book, Star and Crescent

1968. 1400th Anniv of Holy Quran.

469	**105**	6 c. black, gold & flesh	10	10*
470		25 c. black, gold & lilac	10	10*
471		30 c. black, gold & green	10	10*
472		40 c. black, gold & blue	10	10*

107 Broadcasting Greetings

1968. Christmas.

473	**107**	6 c. brown, black & green	10	10*
474		25 c. brown, violet & green	10	10*
475	–	30 c. green & turquoise	10	10*
476	–	40 c. red and turquoise	10	10*

DESIGNS: 30 c. and 40 c. Map showing radio link, Guyana—Trinidad.

109 Festival Ceremony

1969. Hindu Festival of Phagwah. Multicoloured.

477		6 c. Type **109**	10	10
478		25 c. Ladies spraying scent	10	10
479		30 c. Type **109**	10	10
480		40 c. As No. 478	10	10

111 "Sacrament of the Last Supper" (Dali)

1969. Easter.

481	**111**	6 c. multicoloured	10	10
482		25 c. multicoloured	10	10
483		30 c. multicoloured	10	10
484		40 c. multicoloured	10	10

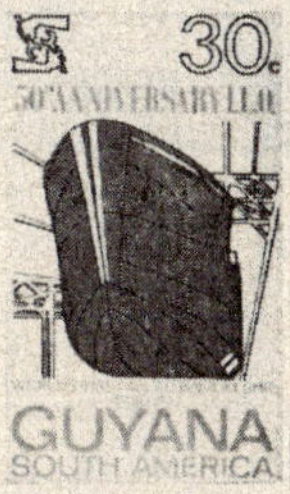

112 Map showing "CARIFTA" Countries

114 Building "Independence" (first aluminium ship)

1969. 1st Anniv of "CARIFTA".

500	**112**	6 c. red, blue & turquoise	10	10
501	–	25 c. lemon, brown & red	10	10

DESIGN—HORIZ: 25 c. "Strength in Unity".

1969. 50th Anniv of I.L.O.

502	**114**	30 c. blue, black & silver	40	20
503	–	40 c. multicoloured	50	20

DESIGN—HORIZ: 40 c. Bauxite processing plant.

116 Scouts raising Flag

1969. 3rd Caribbean Scout Jamboree and Diamond Jubilee of Scouting in Guyana. Multicoloured.

504		6 c. Type **116**	10	10
505		8 c. Camp-fire cooking	10	10
506		25 c. Type **116**	10	10
507		30 c. As 8 c.	10	10
508		50 c. Type **116**	15	15

118 Gandhi and Spinning-wheel

1969. Birth Centenary of Mahatma Gandhi.

509	**118**	6 c. black, brown & olive	20	50
510		15 c. black, brown & lilac	25	50

119 "Mother Sally" Dance Troupe

121 Forbes Burnham and Map

1969. Christmas. Unissued stamps optd as in T **119**. Multicoloured.

511		5 c. Type **119**	10	10
512		6 c. City Hall, Georgetown	10	10
513		25 c. Type **119**	10	10
514		60 c. As 6 c.	20	25

1970. Republic Day.

515	**121**	5 c. sepia, ochre and blue	10	10
516	–	6 c. multicoloured	10	10
517	–	15 c. multicoloured	15	10
518	–	25 c. multicoloured	20	15

DESIGNS—VERT: 6 c. Rural self-help. HORIZ: 15 c. University of Guyana; 25 c. Guyana House.

125 "The Descent from the Cross"

128 "Mother and Child" (Philip Moore)

127 "Peace" and U.N. Emblem

1970. Easter. Paintings by Rubens. Multicoloured.

519		5 c. Type **125**	10	10
520		6 c. "Christ on the Cross"	10	10
521		15 c. Type **125**	20	10
522		25 c. As 6 c.	20	15

1970. 25th Anniv of United Nations. Mult.

523		5 c. Type **127**	10	10
524		6 c. U.N. emblem, gold-panning and drilling	10	10
525		15 c. Type **127**	10	10
526		25 c. As 6 c.	10	15

1970. Christmas.

527	**128**	5 c. multicoloured	10	10
528		6 c. multicoloured	10	10
529		15 c. multicoloured	15	15
530		25 c. multicoloured	15	15

129 National Co-operative Bank

1971. Republic Day.

531	**129**	6 c. multicoloured	10	10
532		15 c. multicoloured	15	15
533		25 c. multicoloured	15	15

130 Racial Equality Symbol

131 Young Volunteer felling Tree (from painting by J. Criswick)

1971. Racial Equality Year.

534	**130**	5 c. multicoloured	10	10
535		6 c. multicoloured	10	10
536		15 c. multicoloured	15	15
537		25 c. multicoloured	15	15

1971. 1st Anniv of Self-help Road Project.

538	**131**	5 c. multicoloured	10	10
539		20 c. multicoloured	25	10
540		25 c. multicoloured	30	10
541		50 c. multicoloured	45	1·75

132 Yellow Allamanda

134 Obverse and Reverse of Guyana $1 Coin

133 Child praying at Bedside

1971. Flowering Plants. Multicoloured.

542		1 c. Pitcher Plant of Mt. Roraima	10	10
543		2 c. Type **132**	10	10
544		3 c. Hanging heliconia	10	10
545		5 c. Annatto tree	10	10
546		6 c. Cannon-ball tree	10	10
547		10 c. Cattleya	3·25	10
548a		15 c. Christmas orchid	65	10
549		20 c. "Paphinia cristata"	3·00	20
550		25 c. Marabunta	4·00	4·50
550ab		25 c. Marabunta	45	10
551		40 c. Tiger beard	3·50	10
552		50 c. "Guzmania lingulata"	40	85
553		60 c. Soldier's cap	30	65
554		$1 "Chelonanthus uliginoides"	30	55
555		$2 "Norantea guianensis"	35	55
556		$5 "Odontadenia grandiflora"	55	55

No. 550 shows the flowers facing upwards and has the value in the centre. No. 550ab has the flowers facing downwards with the value to the right.

1971. Christmas. Multicoloured.

557		5 c. Type **133**	10	10
558		20 c. Type **133**	10	10
559		25 c. Carnival masquerader (vert)	10	10
560		50 c. As 25 c.	20	60

1972. Republic Day.

561	**134**	5 c. silver, black and red	10	10
562	–	20 c. silver, black and red	15	10
563	**134**	25 c. silver, black & blue	15	15
564	–	50 c. silver, black & grn	25	45

DESIGN: 20 c., 50 c. Reverse and obverse of Guyana $1 coin.

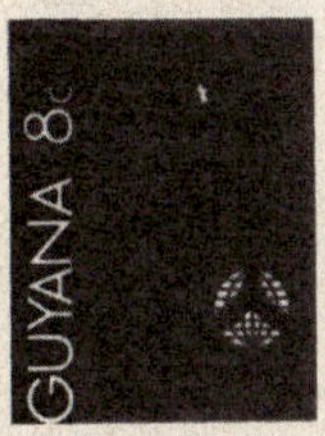

135 Hands and Irrigation Canal

136 Map and Emblem

1972. Youman Nabi (Mohammed's Birthday).

565	**135**	5 c. multicoloured	10	10
566		25 c. multicoloured	10	10
567		30 c. multicoloured	10	10
568		60 c. multicoloured	20	20

1972. Conference of Foreign Ministers of Non-aligned Countries.

569	**136**	8 c. multicoloured	10	10
570		25 c. multicoloured	10	10
571		40 c. multicoloured	15	15
572		50 c. multicoloured	20	20

137 Hand reaching for Sun

138 Joseph, Mary and the Infant Jesus

1972. 1st Caribbean Festival of Arts.

573	**137**	8 c. multicoloured	10	10
574		25 c. multicoloured	10	10
575		40 c. multicoloured	15	20
576		50 c. multicoloured	20	25

1972. Christmas.

577	**138**	8 c. multicoloured	10	10
578		25 c. multicoloured	10	10
579		40 c. multicoloured	15	25
580		50 c. multicoloured	15	25

139 Umana Yana (Meeting-house)

141 Stylized Blood Cell

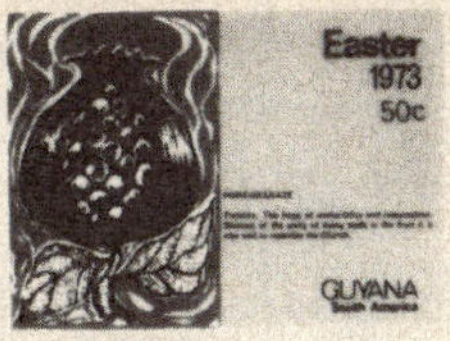

140 Pomegranate

1973. Republic Day. Multicoloured.

581		8 c. Type **139**	10	10
582		25 c. Bethel Chapel	10	10
583		40 c. As 25 c.	20	20
584		50 c. Type **139**	25	20

1973. Easter. Multicoloured.

585		8 c. Type **140**	10	10
586		25 c. Cross and map (34 × 17 mm)	10	10
587		40 c. As 25 c.	10	10
588		50 c. Type **140**	15	15

1973. 25th Anniv of Guyana Red Cross.

589	**141**	8 c. red and black	10	10
590		25 c. red and purple	25	15
591		40 c. red and blue	35	50
592		50 c. red and green	50	1·00

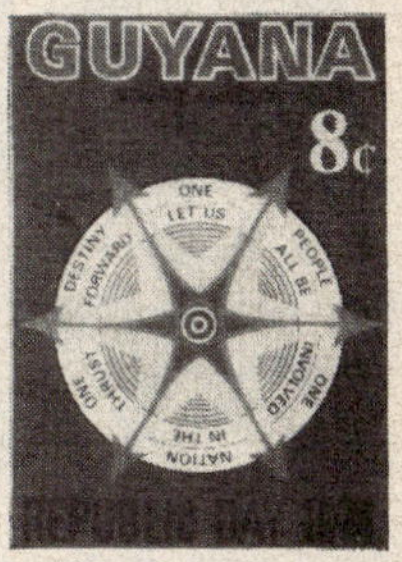

142 Steel-Band Players

143 Symbol of Progress

1973. Christmas. Multicoloured.

593		8 c. Type **142**	10	10
594		25 c. Type **142**	20	10
595		40 c. "Virgin and Child" stained-glass window (34 × 47 mm)	50	75
596		50 c. As 40 c.	55	75

1974. Republic Day. Multicoloured.

597		8 c. Type **143**	10	10
598		25 c. Wai-Wai Indian	10	10
599		40 c. Type **143**	15	30
600		50 c. As 25 c.	15	40

1974. No. 546 surch **8c**.

601		8 c. on 6 c. multicoloured	10	10

145 Kite with Crucifixion Motif

1974. Easter.

602	**145**	8 c. multicoloured	10	10
603	–	25 c. black and green	10	10
604	–	40 c. black and mauve	10	15
605	**145**	50 c. multicoloured	15	25

DESIGN: Nos. 603/4, "Crucifixion" in pre-Columbian style.

146 British Guiana 24 c. Stamp of 1874

148 Buck Toyeau

147 Guides with Banner

1974. Centenary of Universal Postal Union.

606	146	8 c. multicoloured	25	10
607	–	25 c. lt green, green & blk	35	10
608	146	40 c. multicoloured	35	20
609	–	50 c. green, brn and blk	45	45

DESIGN—VERT (42 × 25 mm): 25, 50 c. U.P.U. emblem and Guyana postman.

1974. Golden Jubilee of Girl Guides. Mult.

610	8 c. Type **147**	20	10
611	25 c. Guides in camp	30	15
612	40 c. As 25 c.	45	40
613	50 c. Type **147**	45	45

1974. Christmas. Multicoloured.

615	8 c. Type **148**	10	10
616	35 c. Five-fingers and awaras	10	10
617	50 c. Pawpaw and tangerine	15	10
618	$1 Pineapple and sapodilla	30	60

1975. No. 544 surch **8c.**

620	8 c. on 3 c. multicoloured	10	10

149 Golden Arrow of Courage

150 Old Sluice Gate

1975. Republic Day. Guyana Orders and Decorations. Multicoloured.

621	10 c. Type **149**	10	10
622	35 c. Cacique's Crown of Honour	10	15
623	50 c. Cacique's Crown of Valour	15	20
624	$1 Order of Excellence	35	60

1975. Silver Jubilee of International Commission on Irrigation and Drainage. Multicoloured.

625	10 c. Type **150**	10	10
626	35 c. Modern sluice gate (horiz)	10	15
627	50 c. Type **150**	15	30
628	$1 As 35 c.	35	60

151 I.W.Y. Emblem and Rock Drawing

1975. International Women's Year. Designs showing different rock drawings.

630	151	10 c. green and yellow	10	10
631	–	35 c. violet and blue	15	10
632	–	50 c. blue and orange	20	15
633	–	$1 brown and blue	30	45

152 Freedom Monument

153 G.N.S. Emblem

1975. Namibia Day. Multicoloured.

635	10 c. Type **152**	10	10
636	35 c. Unveiling of Monument	15	10
637	50 c. Type **152**	25	10
638	$1 As 35 c.	35	35

1975. 1st Anniv of National Service.

639	153	10 c. yellow, green & vio	10	10
640	–	35 c. orange, green & vio	10	10
641	–	50 c. blue, green & brown	15	15
642	–	$1 mauve, green & lt grn	40	40

Nos. 640/2 are as Type **153** but have different symbols within the circle.

154 Court Building, 1875, and Forester's Badge

1975. Centenary of Guyanese Ancient Order of Foresters. Multicoloured.

644	10 c. Type **154**	10	10
645	35 c. Rock drawing of hunter and quarry	10	10
646	50 c. Crossed axes and bugle-horn	15	10
647	$1 Bow and arrow	40	40

1976. No. 553 surch **35c.**

649	35 c. on 60 c. Soldier's cap	20	15

156 Shoulder Flash

157 Triumphal Arch

1976. 50th Anniv of St. John Ambulance in Guyana.

650	156	8 c. silver, black & mauve	10	10
651	–	15 c. silver, black & orge	10	10
652	–	35 c. silver, black & grn	20	20
653	–	40 c. silver, black & blue	25	25

Nos. 651/3 are as Type **156** but show different shoulder flashes.

1976. 10th Anniv of Independence. Multicoloured.

654	8 c. Type **157**	10	10
655	15 c. Stylised Victoria Regia lily	10	10
656	35 c. "Onward to Socialism"	15	15
657	40 c. Worker pointing the way	15	15

1976. West Indies Victory in World Cricket Cup. As Nos. 559/60 of Barbados.

659	15 c. Map of the Caribbean	1·50	1·75
660	15 c. Prudential Cup	1·50	1·75

158 Flame in Archway

159 Festival Emblem and "Musical Instrument"

1976. Deepavali Festival. Multicoloured.

661	8 c. Type **158**	10	10
662	15 c. Flame in hand	10	10
663	35 c. Flame in bowl	15	20
664	40 c. Goddess Latchmi	15	25

1977. Second World Black and African Festival of Arts and Culture, Nigeria.

666	159	10 c. red, black and gold	10	10
667		25 c. violet, black & gold	15	10
668		50 c. blue, black & gold	20	25
669		$1 green, black & gold	35	75

160 1 c. and 5 c. Coins

1977. New Coinage.

671	160	8 c. multicoloured	20	10
672	–	15 c. brown, grey & black	25	10
673	–	35 c. green, grey & black	45	30
674	–	40 c. red, grey and black	50	35
675	–	$1 multicoloured	1·25	1·25
676	–	$2 multicoloured	1·75	2·75

DESIGNS: 15 c. 10 and 25 c. coins; 35 c., 50 c. and $1 coins; 40 c. $5 and $10 coins; $1 $50 and $100 coins; $2 Reverse of $1 coin.

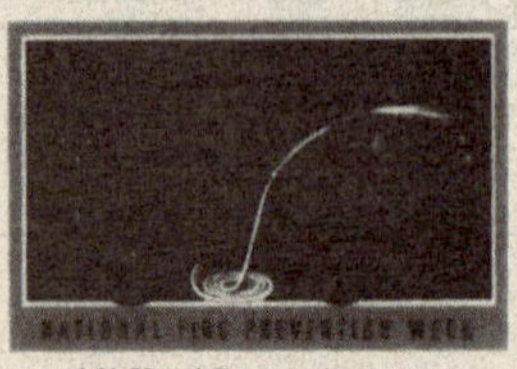

161 Hand Pump, circa 1850

1977. National Fire Prevention Week. Mult.

677	8 c. Type **161**	40	10
678	15 c. Steam engine, circa 1860	70	10
679	35 c. Fire engine, circa 1930	1·00	60
680	40 c. Fire engine, 1977	1·10	85

162 Cuffy Monument

1977. Cuffy Monument (commemorating 1763 Slave Revolt). Multicoloured.

681	8 c. Type **162**	10	10
682	15 c. Cuffy Monument (different view)	10	10
683	35 c. Type **162**	15	20
684	40 c. As 15 c.	15	30

163 American Manatee

1978. Wildlife Conservation. Multicoloured.

685	8 c. Type **163**	65	10
686	15 c. Giant sea turtle	85	20
687	35 c. Harpy eagle (vert)	3·25	1·50
688	40 c. Iguana (vert)	3·25	1·50

164 L.F.S. Burnham (Prime Minister) and Parliament Buildings, Georgetown

1978. 25th Anniv of Prime Minister's Entry into Parliament.

689	164	8 c. black, violet & grey	10	10
690	–	15 c. black, blue & grey	10	10
691	–	35 c. black, red and grey	15	20
692	–	40 c. black, orange & grey	15	20

DESIGNS: 15 c. Burnham, graduate and children ("Free Education"); 35 c. Burnham and industrial works (Nationalization of Bauxite Industry); 40 c. Burnham and village scene ("The Co-operative Village").

165 Dr. George Giglioli (scientist and physician)

166 "Prepona pheridamas"

1978. Nat Science Research Council. Mult.

694	10 c. Type **165**	15	10
695	30 c. Institute of Applied Science and Technology	20	15
696	50 c. Emblem of National Science Research Council	25	25
697	60 c. Emblem of Commonwealth Science Council (commemorating the 10th meeting) (horiz)	25	25

1978. Butterflies. Multicoloured.

698	5 c. Type **166**	1·25	10
699	10 c. "Archonias bellona"	1·25	10
700	15 c. "Eryphanis polyxena"	1·25	10
701	20 c. "Helicopis cupido"	1·25	10
702	25 c. "Nessaea batesii"	1·50	10
702a	30 c. "Nymphidium mantus"	1·25	1·75
703	35 c. "Anaea galanthis"	1·50	10
704	40 c. "Morpho rhetenor" (male)	1·50	10
705	50 c. "Hamadryas amphinome"	1·50	20
705a	60 c. "Papilio androgeus"	1·25	1·00
706	$1 "Agrias claudina"	3·25	20
707	$2 "Morpho rhetenor" (female)	5·00	35
708	$5 "Morpho deidamia"	6·50	90
708a	$10 "Elbella patrobas"	7·50	4·25

Nos. 706/8 are vertical, 25 × 39 mm.

168 Amerindian Stone-chip Grater in Preparation

169 Dish Aerial by Night

1978. National/International Heritage Year. Multicoloured.

709	10 c. Type **168**	10	10
710	30 c. Cassiri and decorated Amerindian jars	15	10
711	50 c. Fort, Kyk-over-al	20	15
712	60 c. Fort Island	20	20

1979. Satellite Earth Station. Multicoloured.

713	10 c. Type **169**	10	10
714	30 c. Dish aerial by day	20	15
715	50 c. Satellite with solar veins	30	15
716	$3 Cylinder satellite	1·50	90

170 Sir Rowland Hill and British Guiana 1850 12 c. "Cottonreel" Stamp

1979. Death Cent of Sir Rowland Hill. Mult.

717	10 c. Type **170**	15	10
718	30 c. British Guiana 1856 1 c. black on magenta stamp (vert)	25	15
719	50 c. British Guiana 1898 1 c. Mount Roraima stamp	35	25
720	$3 Printing press used for early British Guiana stamps (vert)	70	1·10

171 "Me and my Sister"

172 "An 8 Hour Day"

1979. International Year of the Child. Children's Paintings. Multicoloured.

721	10 c. Type **171**	10	10
722	30 c. "Fun with the Fowls" (horiz)	15	15
723	50 c. "Two Boys catching Ducks" (horiz)	20	20
724	$3 "Mango Season" (horiz)	65	1·25

1979. 60th Anniv of Guyana Labour Union. Multicoloured.

725	10 c. Type **172**	10	10
726	30 c. "Abolition of Night Baking" (horiz)	10	10
727	50 c. "Introduction of the Workmen's Compensation Ordinance"	15	15
728	$3 H. N. Critchlow (founder)	55	90

173 Guyana Flag

1980. 10th Anniv of Republic.

729	173	10 c. multicoloured	10	10
730	–	35 c. black and orange	30	10
731	–	60 c. multicoloured	50	20
732	–	$3 multicoloured	80	90

DESIGNS: 35 c. Demerara River Bridge; 60 c. Kaieteur Falls; $3 "Makanaima, the Great Ancestral Spirit of the Amerindians".

174 Common Snook

1980. "London 1980" International Stamp Exhibition. Fishes. Multicoloured.

733	35 c. Type **174**	35	25
734	35 c. Trahira ("Haimara")	35	25
735	35 c. Electric eel	35	25
736	35 c. Golden rivulus	35	25
737	35 c. Golden pencilfish	35	25
738	35 c. Four-eyed fish	35	25
739	35 c. Red piranha ("Pirai")	35	25
740	35 c. Smoking hassar	35	25
741	35 c. Manta	35	25
742	35 c. Festival cichlid ("Flying patwa")	35	25
743	35 c. Arapaima	35	25
744	35 c. Peacock cichlid ("Lukanani")	35	25

175 Children's Convalescent Home (Community Service)

1980. 75th Anniv of Rotary International. Multicoloured.
745 10 c. Type **175** 10 10
746 30 c. Georgetown Rotary Club and Rotary International emblems 10 10
747 50 c. District 404 emblem (vert) 20 20
748 $3 Rotary anniversary emblem (vert) 80 80

176 "C" encircling Globe, Caduceus Emblem and Sea

1980. 25th Anniv of Commonwealth Caribbean Medical Research Council. Multicoloured.
749 10 c. Type **176** 10 10
750 60 c. Researcher with microscope, Caduceus emblem, stethoscope and beach scene 40 20
751 $3 Caduceus emblem, "C" encircling researcher and island silhouettes 1·10 1·00

177 "Virola surinamensis"

1980. Christmas. Trees and Foliage. Multicoloured.
752 10 c. Type **177** 10 10
753 30 c. "Hymenaea courbaril" 20 10
754 50 c. "Mora excelsa" 30 15
755 $3 "Peltogyne venosa" 1·25 1·10

178 Brazilian Tree Porcupine **181** Map of Guyana

1981. Wildlife. Multicoloured.
756 30 c. Type **178** 60 50
757 30 c. Red howler 60 50
758 30 c. Common squirrel-monkey 60 50
759 30 c. Two-toed sloth 60 50
760 30 c. Brazilian tapir 60 50
761 30 c. Collared peccary 60 50
762a 30 c. Six-banded armadillo 60 15
763 30 c. Tamandua 60 50
764 30 c. Giant anteater 60 50
765 30 c. Murine opossum 60 50
766 30 c. Brown four-eyed opossum 60 50
767 30 c. Brazilian agouti 60 50

1981. Liberation of Southern Africa Conference. No. 635 surch **1981 CONFERENCE $1.05**.
768 $1.05 on 10 c. Type **152** 40 30

1981. Royal Wedding (1st issue). Nos. 554 and 556 surch **ROYAL WEDDING 1981** and value.
769c $3.60 on $5 "Odontadenia grandiflora" 60 65
770 $7.20 in $1 "Chelonanthus uliginoides" 80 80
See also Nos. 841/3 and 930/6.

1981. Fiscal stamps surch for postal use.
771 **181** 10 c. on 3 c. black, blue and red 40 10
940 15 c. on 2 c. black, blue and grey 50 15
941 20 c. on 2 c. black, blue and grey 3·50 30
1029 25 c. on 2 c. black, blue and grey 50 10
772 30 c. on 2 c. black, blue and grey 45 15
989 40 c. on 2 c. black, blue and grey 1·00 15
945 45 c. on 2 c. black, blue and grey 1·75 45
773 50 c. on 2 c. black, blue and grey 55 15
774 60 c. on 2 c. black, blue and grey 65 15
948 75 c. on 2 c. black, blue and grey 6·00 25
775 75 c. on 3 c. black, blue and red 65 20
949 80 c. on 2 c. black, blue and grey 5·00 20
950 85 c. on 2 c. black, blue and grey 75 25
951 **181** 100 c. on 3 c. black, blue and red 1·00 35
952 110 c. on 3 c. black, blue and red 80 30
953 120 c. on 3 c. black, blue and red 8·00 35
954 125 c. on 3 c. black, blue and red 2·25 35
955 130 c. on 3 c. black, blue and red 1·00 35
956 150 c. on 3 c. black, blue and red 8·50 40
957 160 c. on 3 c. black, blue and red 2·00 40
958 170 c. on 3 c. black, blue and red 1·40 45
959 175 c. on 3 c. black, blue and red 6·00 45
960 180 c. on 3 c. black, blue and red 2·00 60
961 200 c. on 3 c. black, blue and red 2·25 45
962 210 c. on 3 c. black, blue and red 7·00 50
963 220 c. on 3 c. black, blue and red 8·50 50
964 235 c. on 3 c. black, blue and red 8·00 50
965 240 c. on 3 c. black, blue and red 9·00 50
966 250 c. on 3 c. black, blue and red 2·25 50
967 300 c. on 3 c. black, blue and red 12·00 55
968 330 c. on 3 c. black, blue and red 2·75 65
969 375 c. on 3 c. black, blue and red 7·00 75
970 400 c. on 3 c. black, blue and red 10·00 75
971 440 c. on 3 c. black, blue and red 4·00 75
972 500 c. on 3 c. black, blue and red 3·50 1·10
973 550 c. on 3 c. black, blue and red 4·00 1·25
974 625 c. on 3 c. black, blue and red 2·75 1·75
975 1500 c. on 2 c. black, blue and grey 11·00 3·00
976 2000 c. on 2 c. black, blue and grey 11·00 3·75

1981. No. 544 surch **7.20.**
775c 720 c. on 3 c. multicoloured 70·00 15·00

1981. Various stamps optd **1981**.
791 – 15 c. mult (No. 491) 8·00 10
864 – 15 c. mult (No. 548a) 4·00 10
810 – 15 c. mult (No. 659) 6·00 20
811 – 15 c. mult (No. 660) 4·50 20
776 **105** 25 c. black, gold & lilac 10 10
777 30 c. black, gold & green 15 10
778 – 35 c. mult (No. 645) 15 10
792 – 40 c. mult (No. 457) 8·50 40
811c – 40 c. mult (No. F5) — £200
812 – 50 c. mult (No. 623) 60 20
813 **150** 50 c. multicoloured 1·00 20
814 – 50 c. blue and orange (No. 632) 23·00 2·00
815 – 50 c. mult (No. 646) 2·75 20
816 **159** 50 c. blue, blk & gold 13·00 2·00
817 – 50 c. mult (No. F6) 4·00 20
818 – 60 c. mult (No. 731) 60 20
819 – 60 c. mult (No. 750) 60 20
865 – $1 mult (No. 554) 40 20
820 – $1 mult (No. 624) 6·00 55
821 **159** $1 green, black & gold 6·00 30
866 – $2 mult (No. 555) 90 35
823 – $3 mult (No. 732) 2·50 65
824 – $5 mult (No. 556) 3·25 1·25

1981. Nos. 545 and 556 surch.
780 75 c. on 5 c. Annatto tree 50 50
781 210 c. on $5 "Odontadenia grandiflora" 80 1·00
781b 220 c. on 5 c. Annatto tree 80·00 8·50

1981. Nos. D8/11 surch **ESSEQUIBO IS OURS**.
782A D **2** 10 c. on 2 c. black 25 10
783A 15 c. on 12 c. red 25 15
784A 20 c. on 1 c. green 20 20
785A 45 c. on 2 c. black 60 20
786A 55 c. on 4 c. blue 30 20
787B 60 c. on 4 c. blue 50 15
788A 65 c. on 2 c. black 40 20
789B 70 c. on 4 c. blue 75 45
790A 80 c. on 4 c. blue 35 20

1981. Nos. 545, 554, 556, 716, 843, F7 and F9 surch.
794 50 c. on 5 c. Annatto tree (postage) 30 20
795 120 c. on $1 "Chelonanthus uliginoides" 75 40
796 140 c. on $1 "Chelonanthus uliginoides" 70 40
797 150 c. on $2 "Norantea guianensis" (F9) 75 40
800 220 c. on $3 Cylinder satellite 1·75 45
801 250 c. on $5 "Odontadenia grandiflora" 1·25 45
802 280 c. on $5 "Odontadenia grandiflora" 1·50 50
798 360 c. on $2 "Norantea guianensis" (F9) 3·00 60
803 375 c. on $5 "Odontadenia grandiflora" 1·75 55
799 720 c. on 60 c. Soldier's Cap (F7) 3·00 1·00
804 $1.10 on $2 "Norantea guianensis" (843) (air) 2·00 1·75
No. 804 has the Royal Wedding opt cancelled by three bars.

1981. No. 448 surch.
805 **87** 15 c. on 1 c. mult (postage) 70 20
806 100 c. on 1 c. mult (air) 70 40
807 110 c. on 1 c. multicoloured 70 40

1981. No. 700 optd **ESSEQUIBO IS OURS**.
808 15 c. "Eryphanis polyxena" 1·50 10

1981. Various stamps surch.
825 **116** 55 c. on 6 c mult 4·00 80
826 **111** 70 c. on 6 c. mult 1·00 20
827 100 c. on 6 c. mult 1·25 20
828 – 100 c. on 8 c. multicoloured (No. 505) 4·50 20
829 **152** 100 c. on $1.05 on 10 c. mult (No. 768) 29·00 4·00
830 **116** 110 c. on 6 c. mult 3·00 30
831 **149** 110 c. on 10 c. mult 2·50 30
832 **151** 110 c. on 10 c. green and yellow 6·00 45
834 – 125 c. on $2 multicoloured (No. 555) 12·00 80
835 **116** 180 c. on 6 c. mult 3·50 45
840 – 240 c. on $3 multicoloured (No. 728) 9·50 75
836 **116** 400 c. on 6 c. mult 3·50 80
837a 440 c. on 6 c. mult 2·00 55
838 – 550 c. on $10 multicoloured (No. O21) 5·50 1·00
839 – 625 c. on 40 c. mult (No. F5) 14·00 1·75

1981. Royal Wedding (2nd issue). Nos. 544 and 555/6 surch **Royal Wedding 1981** (No. 843 **Air Mail** also) and value.
841 60 c. on 3 c. Hanging heliconia (postage) 30 35
842 75 c. on $5 "Odontadenia grandiflora" 30 40
843 $1.10 on $2 "Norantea guianensis" (air) 30 45

1981. World Cup Football Championship, Spain (1982) (1st issue). No. 781a optd **Espana 82**.
844 220 c. on 5 c. Annatto tree 1·25 40
See also Nos. 937/9 and 1218.

1981. 150th Birth Anniv of Heinrich von Stephan (founder of U.P.U.) No. 720 surch **1831—1981 Von Stephan. 330**
845 330 c. on $3 Printing press used for early British Guiana stamps 1·50 55

1981. No. 489 surch with large figure over smaller figure.
847 12 c. on 12 c. on 6 c. Black acara ("Patua") 20 25
848 15 c. on 10 c. on 6 c. Black acara ("Patua") 15 10
849 15 c. on 30 c. on 6 c. Black acara ("Patua") 15 10
850 15 c. on 50 c. on 6 c. Black acara ("Patua") 15 10
851 15 c. on 60 c. on 6 c. Black acara ("Patua") 15 10
Nos. 847/51 are further surcharges on previously unissued stamps.

214 Coromantyn Free Negro Armed Ranger, c. 1772, and Cuffy Monument

1981. 16th Anniv of Guyana Defence Force. Multicoloured.
853 15 c. on 10 c. Type **214** 40 10
854 50 c. Private, 27th Foot Regiment, c. 1825 60 30
855 $1 on 30 c. Private, Col. Fourgeoud's Marines, c. 1775 70 45
856 $1.10 on $3 W.O. and N.C.O., Guyana Defence Force, 1966 80 70
The 15 c., $1 and $1.10 values are surcharged on previously unissued stamps.

215 Louis Braille

1981. International Year for Disabled Persons. Famous Disabled People. Multicoloured.
857 15 c. on 10 c. Type **215** 25 10
858 50 c. Helen Keller and Rajkumari Singh 50 40
859 $1 on 60 c. Beethoven and Sonny Thomas 55 50
860 $1.10 on $3 Renoir 55 55
The 15 c., $1 and $1.10 values are surcharged on previously unissued stamps.

1981. No. 489 surch (Nos. 862/3 optd **AIR** also).
861 12 c. on 6 c. Black acara ("Patua") (postage) 15 10
862b 50 c. on 6 c. Black acara ("Patua") (air) 20 15
863 $1 on 6 c. Black acara ("Patua") 50 30

1981. Nos. 601, 620, 644, O13, 717, 720, 728, 749, 751 and 755 surch (Nos. 868/9 twice).
867 110 c. on 10 c. Type **154** 3·00 30
868 110 c. on 110 c. on 8 c. on 3 c. Hanging heliconia 3·00 40
869 110 c. on 110 c. on 8 c. on 6 c. Cannon-ball tree 3·00 40
869b 110 c. on 10 c. on 25 c. Marabunta 2·25 40
870 110 c. on 10 c. Type **170** 2·00 30
871 110 c. on 10 c. Type **176** 8·00 50
872 110 c. on $3 Printing press used for early British Guiana stamps 1·75 30
873 110 c. on $3 H. N. Critchlow 6·50 45
874 110 c. on $3 Caduceus emblem, "C" encircling researcher and island silhouettes 2·00 30
875 110 c. on $3 "Peltogyne venosa" 4·00 50

1981. No. 698 surch **Nov 81 50c.**
876 50 c. on 5 c. Type **166** 5·00 20

222 Yellow Allamanda ("Allamanda cathartica") **225** Tape Measure and Guyana Metrication Board Van

1981. Flowers.
877 **222** 15 c. on 2 c. lilac, blue and green 15 15
878 – 15 c. on 8 c. lilac, blue and mauve 15 15
DESIGN: 15 c. on 8 c. Mazaruni pride ("Sipanea prolensis").
Nos. 877/8 are surcharges on previously unissued stamps.

1981. Air. Human Rights Day. No. 748 surch **Human Rights Day 1981 110 AIR**.
879 110 c. on $3 Rotary anniversary emblem 1·75 60

1981. 35th Anniv of U.N.I.C.E.F. No. 724 surch **U.N.I.C.E.F. 1946-1981 125**.
880 125 c. on $2 "Mango Season" 1·00 40

1981. "Cancun 81" International Conference. No. 698 surch **Cancun 81 50c.**
880a 50 c. on 5 c. Type **166** 4·00 55

1982. Metrication. Multicoloured.
881 15 c. Type **225** 25 25
882 15 c. "Metric man" 25 25
883 15 c. "Postal service goes metric" 25 25
884 15 c. Weighing child on metric scales 25 25
885 15 c. Canje Bridge 25 25
886 15 c. Tap filling litre bucket 25 25

1982. Various stamps optd **1982**.
887 – 20 c. multicoloured (No. 549) 2·00 20
888 **105** 25 c. black, gold and lilac 60 15
889 – 25 c. mult (No. 550ab) 2·50 20
See also Nos. 914/17, 919/21, 923/4, 977, 992/8, 1001, 1004, 1006/8, 1015, 1017, 1059, 1117 and OP3/4.

1982. No. 506 optd **POSTAGE** and Nos. 546 and 601 surch.
890 20 c. on 6 c. Cannon-ball tree 35 10
892 25 c. Type **116** 1·00 10
893 125 c. on 8 c. on 6 c. Cannon-ball tree 35 20

230 Guyana Soldier and Flag

1982. Savings Campaign.
894 **230** $1 multicoloured 30 20
No. 894 is a fiscal stamp optd for postal use.
See also Nos. 913 and 990.

1982. 125th Birth Anniv of Lord Baden-Powell and 75th Anniv of Boy Scout Movement. Nos. 543, 545 and 601 surch as given in brackets.
895 15 c. on 2 c. Type **132** (**BADEN POWELL 1857-1982**) 10 30
896 15 c. on 2 c. Type **132** (**Scout Movement 1907-1982**) 10 30
897 15 c. on 2 c. Type **132** (**1907-1982**) 15 40
898 15 c. on 2 c. Type **132** (**1857-1982**) 15 15
899 15 c. on 2 c. Type **132** (**1982**) 10 10
900 110 c. on 5 c. Annatto tree (**BADEN POWELL 1857-1982**) 1·00 20
901 110 c. on 5 c. Annatto tree (**Scout Movement 1907-1982**) 60 20
902 110 c. on 5 c. Annatto tree (**1907-1982**) 1·50 1·00
903 110 c. on 5 c. Annatto tree (**1857-1982**) 1·50 1·00
904 110 c. on 5 c. Annatto tree (**1982**) 60 20

905 125 c. on 8 c. on 6 c. Cannon-ball tree (**BADEN POWELL 1857-1982**) . . . . 1·00 20
906 125 c. on 8 c. on 6 c. Cannon-ball tree (**Scout Movement 1907-1982**) . . . . 1·00 20
907 125 c. on 8 c. on 6 c. Cannon-ball tree (**1907-1982**) . . . . . . 1·50 1·00
908 125 c. on 8 c. on 6 c. Cannon-ball tree (**1857-1982**) . . . . . . 1·50 1·00
909 125 c. on 8 c. on 6 c. Cannon-ball tree (**1982**) 75 20

1982. 250th Birth Anniv of George Washington. Nos. 718 and 720 surch **Geo Washington 1732...1982** and value and No. 708 optd **GEORGE WASHINGTON 1732-1982**.
910 100 c. on $3 Printing press used for early British Guiana stamps 45 30
911 400 c. on 30 c. British Guiana 1856 1 c. black on purple . 1·60 1·25
912 $5 "Morpho deidamia" . . . 7·50 5·50

1982. Savings Campaign. As T **230**. Mult.
913 110 c. on $5 Guyana male and female soldiers with flag . . 50 20
No. 913 is a fiscal stamp surch for postal use.
See also No. 990.

1982. Easter. Optd **1982** or surch also.
914 **111** 25 c. multicoloured . . . 20 15
915 30 c. multicoloured . . . 20 15
916 45 c. on 6 c. mult 20 25
917 75 c. on 40 c. mult 35 25

1982. No. 703 surch **20**.
918 20 c. on 35 c. "Anaea galanthis" 3·50 10

1982. No. F5 optd **1982 180**.
919 180 c. on 40 c. Tiger beard . . 3·50 40

1982. Nos. 555/6 optd **1982**.
920 $2 "Norantea guianensis" . . 80 30
921 $5 "Odontadenia grandiflora" 1·40 70

1982. No. 542 surch **220**.
922 220 c. on 1 c. Pitcher Plant of Mt. Roraima . . . . 1·25 40

1982. Nos. 472 and 684 optd **1982**.
923 **105** 40 c. black, gold & blue . 35 15
924 – 40 c. multicoloured . . . 50 25

1982. Nos. 469, 751 and 842/3 surch.
925 **105** 80 c. on 6 c. black, gold and flesh 30 20
926 85 c. on 6 c. black, gold and flesh 50 20
927 – 160 c. on $1.10 on $2 mult (No. 843) 80 30
928 – 210 c. on $3 mult (No. 751) 2·50 40
929 – 235 c. on 75 c. on 85 mult (No. 842) . . . . 2·50 60

1982. Royal Wedding (3rd issue). Nos. 841/3 surch.
930 85 c. on 60 c. on 3 c. Hanging heliconia . . . . 2·50 50
931 130 c. on 60 c. on 3 c. Hanging heliconia . . . . 1·75 45
932 160 c. on. $1.10 on $2 "Norantea guianensis" . . . . 2·25 1·00
933 170 c. on $1.10 on $2 "Norantea guianensis" . . . . 6·00 4·50
934 210 c. on 75 c. on $5 "Odontadenia grandiflora" 1·25 40
935 235 c. on 75 c. on $5 "Odontadenia grandiflora" . 2·00 1·40
936 330 c. on $1.10 on $2 "Norantea guianensis" . . . . 1·75 40

1982. World Cup Football Championship, Spain (2nd issue). Nos. 544, 546 and 554 optd **ESPANA 1982** or surch also.
937 $1 "Chelonanthus uliginoides" 75 40
938 110 c. on 3 c. Hanging heliconia 75 25
939 250 c. on 6 c. Cannon-ball tree 1·00 60
See also No. 1218.

1982. No. 548a optd **1982**.
977 15 c. Christmas orchid . . . . 7·00 10

1982. No. O26 optd **POSTAGE**.
978 110 c. on 6 c. Type **116** . . . 4·50 35

1982. Air. 21st Birthday of Princess of Wales. Nos. 542, 545 and 555 surch **AIR Princess of Wales 1961–1982**
979 110 c. on 5 c. Annatto tree . . 50 30
980 220 c. on 1 c. Pitcher Plant of Mt. Roraima 80 60
981 330 c. on $2 "Norantea guianensis" 90 90

1982. Birth of Prince William of Wales. Surch **H.R.H Prince William 21st June 1982**. (a) On stamps of British Guiana with additional opt **GUYANA**.
982 50 c. on 2 c. green (No. 332) . 40 30
983 $1.10 on 3 c. green and brown (No. 333) 80 50

(b) On stamps of Guyana previously optd **GUYANA INDEPENDENCE 1966**.
984 50 c. on 2 c. green (No. 421) . 10·00 3·25
985 $1.10 on 3 c. green and brown (No. 422) . . . . 17·00 3·25
986 $1.25 on 6 c. green (No. 424) . 60 60
987 $2.20 on 24 c. black and orange (No. 435) . . . . 1·50 1·50

1982. Savings Campaign. As No. 913 but showing inverted comma before "OURS" in opt.
990 110 c. on $5 Guyana male and female soldiers with flag . . 5·50 75

1982. Italy's Victory in World Cup Football Championship. No. F7 surch **ESPANA 1982 ITALY $2.35**.
991 $2.35 on 180 c. on 60 c. Soldier's cap . . . . 3·50 55

1982. Wildlife Protection. Nos. 687 and 733/8 optd **1982**.
992 35 c. Harpy eagle . . . . . . 2·00 40
993 35 c. Type **174** . . . . . . 2·00 40
994 35 c. Trahira ("Haimara") . . 2·00 40
995 35 c. Electric eel . . . . . 2·00 40
996 35 c. Golden rivulus . . . . 2·00 40
997 35 c. Golden pencilfish . . . 2·00 40
998 35 c. Four-eyed fish . . . . . 2·00 40

1982. Central America and Caribbean Games, Havana. Nos. 542/3 surch **C.A. & CARIB GAMES 1982**.
999 50 c. on 2 c. Type **132** . . . 1·00 25
1000 60 c. on 1 c. Pitcher plant of Mt. Roraima . . . . 1·25 15

1982. No. 730 optd **1982**.
1001 35 c. black and orange . . . 30 20

1982. Nos. 841 and 979 further surch.
1002 130 c. on 60 c. on 3 c. Hanging heliconia 40 30
1003 170 c. on 110 c. on 5 c. Annatto tree 70 45

1982. No. 841 surch **1982 440**.
1004 440 c. on 60 c. on 3 c. Hanging heliconia 75 45

1982. Commonwealth Games, Brisbane, Australia. No. 546 surch **Commonwealth GAMES AUSTRALIA 1982 1.25**
1005 $1.25 on 6 c. Cannon-ball tree 1·50 30

1982. Nos. 552, 641 and 719 optd **1982**.
1006 50 c. multicoloured (No. 552) 2·00 25
1007 50 c. blue, green and brown (No. 641) . . . . 1·50 25
1008 50 c. multicoloured (No. 719) 60 25

1982. Various Official stamps additionally optd **POSTAGE**.
1009 15 c. Christmas Orchid (No. O 23) . . . . 8·00 30
1010 50 c. "Guzmania lingulata" (No. O14) 90 15
1011 100 c. on $3 Cylinder satellite (No. O19) . . . . 1·25 35

1982. International Food Day. No. 617 optd **INT. FOOD DAY 1982**.
1012 50 c. Pawpaw and tangerine 11·00 65

1982. International Year of the Elderly. No. 747 optd **INT. YEAR OF THE ELDERLY**.
1013 50 c. District 404 emblem . 6·50 50

1982. Centenary of Robert Koch's Discovery of Tubercle Bacillus. No. 750 optd **Dr. R. KOCH CENTENARY TBC BACILLUS DISCOVERY**.
1014 60 c. Researcher with microscope, Caduceus emblem, stethoscope and beach scene . . . . 2·50 30

1982. International Decade for Women. No. 633 optd **1982**.
1015 $1 brown and blue . . . . . 2·50 60

1982. Birth Centenary of F. D. Roosevelt (American statesman). No. 706 optd **F. D. ROOSEVELT 1882-1982**.
1016 $1 "Agrias claudina" . . . . 3·25 50

1982. 1st Anniv of G.A.C. Inaugural Flight Georgetown to Boa Vista, Brazil. No. 842 optd **1982 GAC Inaug. Flight Georgetown—Boa Vista, Brasil 200**.
1017 200 c. on 75 c. on $5 "Odontadenia grandiflora" 8·00 1·40

1982. CARICOM Heads of Government Conference, Kingston, Jamaica. Nos. 881/6 surch **50 CARICOM Heads of Gov't Conference July 1982**.
1018 50 c. on 15 c. Type **225** . . 1·25 30
1019 50 c. on 15 c. "Metric man" 1·25 30
1020 50 c. on 15 c. "Postal service goes metric" . . . . . 1·25 30
1021 50 c. on 15 c. Weighing child on metric scales . . . . . 1·25 30
1022 50 c. on 15 c. Canje Bridge . 1·25 30
1023 50 c. on 15 c. Tap filling litre bucket . . . . 1·25 30

1982. Christmas. Nos. 895/9 optd **CHRISTMAS 1982**.
1024 15 c. on 2 c. Type **132** (surch **BADEN POWELL 1857–1982**) 25 15
1025 15 c. on 2 c. Type **132** (surch **Scout Movement 1907 –1982**) 25 15
1026 15 c. on 2 c. Type **132** (surch **1907–1982**) 65 50
1027 15 c. on 2 c. Type **132** (surch **1857–1982**) 65 50
1028 15 c. on 2 c. Type **132** (surch **1982**) . . . . 6·50 7·00

1982. Nos. 543 and 546 surch in figures (no "c" after face value).
1034 15 c. on 2 c. Type **132** . . . 10 10
1035 20 c. on 6 c. Cannon-ball tree 10 10
See also No. 1086.

1982. No. 489 surch.
1032 50 c. on 6 c. Black acara ("Patua") 20 15
1033 100 c. on 6 c. Black acara ("Patua") 40 30

1983. Optd **1983**.
1036 – 15 c. mult (No. 655) . . . 4·50 1·50
1037 – 15 c. brown, grey and black (No. 672) 60 10
1038 – 15 c. mult (No. 682) . . . 40 10
1039 **214** 15 c. on 10 c. mult . . . 35 10
1040 **215** 15 c. on 10 c. mult . . . 15 10
1041 – 50 c. mult (No. 646) . . . 4·00 25
1042 – 50 c. mult (No. 696) . . . 4·00 25
1043 – 50 c. mult (No. 719) . . . 1·50 25
See also Nos. 1060/1, 1069/70, 1072/9c, 1096, 1101 and 1110/16.

1983. No. O17 optd **POSTAGE**.
1044 15 c. Harpy Eagle . . . . . . 12·00 10

1983. National Heritage. Nos. 710/12 and 778 surch.
1045 90 c. on 30 c. Cassiri and decorated Amerindian jars . 1·50 50
1046 90 c. on 35 c. Rock drawing of hunter and quarry 35 20
1047 90 c. on 30 c. Fort Kyk-over-al 1·50 50
1048 90 c. on 60 c. Fort Island . . 2·25 20

258 Guyana Flag (inscr. "60TH BIRTHDAY ANNIVERSARY")

262

1983. 60th Birthday of President Burnham and 30 Years in Parliament. Multicoloured.
1049 25 c. Type **258** 15 20
1050 25 c. As T **258** but position of flag reversed and inscr. "30th ANNIVERSARY IN PARLIAMENT" 15 20
1051 $1.30 Youth display (41 × 25 mm) 40 65
1052 $6 Presidential standard (43½ × 25 mm) . . . . . . 1·00 2·75

1983. Surch in words.
1053 **170** 50 c. on 10 c. mult (No. 717) . . . . 2·00 30
1054 – 50 c. on 400 c. on 30 c. mult (No. 911) . . . . 2·50 30
1055 **152** $1 on 10 c. mult (No. 635) 7·50 45
1056 $1 on $1.05 on 10 c. mult (No. 768) . . . . . . 6·50 45
1056a – $1 on $1.10 on $2 mult (No. 843) . . . . . . 1·40 2·50
1057 – $1 on 220 c. on 5 c. mult (No. 844) . . . . . . 7·50 75
1058 – $1 on 330 c. on $2 mult (as No. 981) 60 45
1059 – $1 on $12 on $1.10 on $2 mult (No. P3) . . . . . 3·50 2·00
See also Nos. 1080/4.

1983. No. 859 optd **1983**.
1060 $1 on 60 c. Beethoven and Sonny Thomas . . . . . . 6·00 45

1983. Conference of Foreign Ministers of Non-aligned Countries, New Delhi. No. 569 surch **FIFTY CENTS** and No. 570 optd **1983**.
1061 **136** 25 c. multicoloured . . . 1·00 25
1062 50 c. on 8 c. multicoloured 2·00 25

1983. No. 771 further surch **20**.
1064 **181** 20 c. on 10 c. on 3 c. black, blue and red 55 10

1983. Commonwealth Day. Nos. 424 and 435 surch **Commonwealth Day 14 March 1983**, emblem and value.
1065 **60** 25 c. on 6 c. green . . . . 1·00 20
1066 $1.20 on 6 c. green 50 50
1067 **63** $1.30 on 24 c. black and orange . . . . 1·50 55
1068 $2.40 on 24 c. black and orange . . . . 2·00 1·25

1983. Easter. Nos. 482/3 optd **1983**.
1069 **111** 25 c. multicoloured . . . 15 10
1070 30 c. multicoloured . . . 30 15

1983. 25th Anniv of International Maritime Organization. British Guiana fiscal stamp optd.
1071 **262** $4.80 blue and green . . 2·00 4·00

1983. Optd **1983**.
1072 **152** 50 c. mult (No. 637) . . . 1·50 25
1073 **159** 50 c. blue, black and yellow (No. 668) . . . 2·75 25
1073a – 50 c. mult (No. 723) . .
1074 – 50 c. mult (No. 854) . . . 60 25
1075 – 50 c. mult (No. 858) . . . 1·00 25
1076 – $1 mult (No. 628) . . . 5·50 45
1077 – $1 mult (No. 638) . . . 4·75 45
1078 – $1 mult (No. 675) . . . 4·00 45
1079 – $1 on 30 c. mult (No. 855) 1·25 45
1079a – $3 mult (No. 720) . . . 17·00 90
1079b – $3 mult (No. 724) . . . 20·00 1·50
1079c – $3 mult (No. 748) . . . 65·00 7·00

1983. Surch **FIFTY CENTS**.
1080 **148** 50 c. on 8 c. mult (No. 615) 1·75 25
1081 **162** 50 c. on 8 c. mult (No. 681) 6·00 25
1082 **171** 50 c. on 10 c. mult (No. 721) 3·00 25
1083 – 50 c. on 10 c. on 25 c. mult (No. O13) . . . . . . 5·00 25
1084 – 50 c. on 330 c. on $3 mult (No. 845) . . . . . . 4·00 25

1983. Surch in figures with **c** after new face value.
1098 **105** 15 c. on 6 c. black, gold & pink (No. 469) 10 10
1100 – 20 c. on 6 c. multicoloured (No. 546) 15 10

1087 **111** 50 c. on 6 c. multicoloured (No. 481) 40 30
1099 – 50 c. on 6 c. multicoloured (No. 489) 30 30

1983 No. 489 surch **$1**.
1088 $1 on 6 c. Black acara ("Patua") . . . . 1·25 30

1983. No. 639 surch **110**.
1089 **153** 110 c. on 10 c. yellow, green and violet . . . . . . 1·75 50

1983. Nos. 551 and 556 surch.
1090 250 c. on 40 c. Tiger beard . 7·50 55
1091 400 c. on $5 "Odontadenia grandiflora" . . . . 5·50 70

1983. World Telecommunications and Health Day. Nos. 842 and 980 further surch.
1092 25 c. on 220 c. on 1 c. Pitcher plant of Mt. Roraima (surch **ITU 1983 25**) 30 30
1093 25 c. on 220 c. on 1 c. Pitcher plant of Mt. Roraima (surch **WHO 1983 25**) 30 30
1094 25 c. on 220 c. on 1 c. Pitcher plant of Mt. Roraima (surch **17 MAY '83 ITU/WHO 25**) 30 30
1095 $4.50 on 75 c. on $5 "Odontadenia grandiflora" (surch **ITU/WHO 17 MAY 1983**) . . . . 13·00 1·50

1983. 30th Anniv of President's Entry into Parliament. Nos. 690 and 692 surch in words, No. 1096 additionally optd **1983**.
1096 $1 on 15 c. black, blue and grey 6·00 50
1097 $1 on 40 c. black, orange and grey . . . . 9·00 50

1983. No. 611 optd **1983**.
1101 25 c. Guides in camp . . . . 48·00 4·00

1983. 15th World Scout Jamboree, Alberta. Nos. 835/6 and O25 optd **CANADA 1983**, Nos. 1103 and 1105 additionally surch.
1103 – $1.30 on 100 c. on 8 c. multicoloured . . . . 3·00 1·75
1104 **116** 180 c. on 6 c. mult . . . 3·00 3·00
1105 $3.90 on 400 c. on 6 c. multicoloured . . . . 3·50 4·50

1983. Nos. 659/60 surch.
1106 60 c. on 15 c. Map of the Caribbean . . . . 9·00 40
1107 $1.50 on 15 c. Prudential Cup 10·00 1·25

1983. As Nos. 1049/50, but without commemorative inscr above flag.
1108 25 c. As Type **258** 15 15
1109 25 c. As No. 1050 . . . . . 15 15

1983. Optd **1983**.
1110 **105** 30 c. black, gold and green (No. 471) 75 20
1111 – 30 c. multicoloured (No. 695) . . . . 9·50 30
1112 – 30 c. multicoloured (No. 718) . . . . 4·50 20
1113 – 30 c. multicoloured (No. 722) . . . . 8·00 20
1114 – 30 c. multicoloured (No. 746) . . . . 14·00 20
1115 – 60 c. multicoloured (No. 697) . . . . 4·50 20
1116 – 60 c. multicoloured (No. 731) . . . . 5·50 20

1983. No. 553 optd **1982**.
1117 60 c. Soldier's cap . . . . . 4·00 35

1983. Surch.
1118 **157** 120 c. on 8 c. mult (No. 654) 3·25 40
1119 – 120 c. on 10 c. red, black and gold (No. 666) . . . 3·50 40
1120 – 120 c. on 35 c. mult (No. 622) . . . . 3·50 40
1121 – 120 c. on 35 c. orange, grn & vio (No. 640) . . . . 3·50 40

1983. Nos. 716 and 729 surch.
1122 120 c. on 10 c. Type **173** . . 3·25 40
1123 120 c. on 375 c. on $3 Cylinder satellite . . . . 3·00 40
No. 1123 also carries an otherwise unissued surcharge in red reading **INTERNATIONAL SCIENCE YEAR 1982 375**. As issued much of this is obliterated by two heavy bars.

1983. British Guiana No. D1a and Guyana. No. D8 surch **120 GUYANA**.
1124 **D 1** 120 c. on 1 c. green . . 2·75 45
1125 **D 2** 120 c. on 1 c. olive . . . 2·75 45

1983. CARICOM Day. No. 823 additionally surch **CARICOM DAY 1983 60**.
1126 60 c. on $3 "Makanaima the Great Ancestral Spirit of the Amerindians" . . . . . . 1·75 35

271 "Kurupukari"

1983. Riverboats.
1127 **271** 30 c. black and red . . . 20 20
1128 – 60 c. black and violet . . 35 35
1129 – 120 c. black and yellow . 40 60
1130 – 130 c. black 40 65
1131 – 150 c. black and green . . 40 80
DESIGNS: 60 c. "Makouria"; 120 c. "Powis"; 130 c. "Pomeroon"; 150 c. "Lukanani".

1983. Unissued Royal Wedding surch similar to No. 843 additionally surch.
1132 $2.30 on $1.10 on $2 "Norantea guianensis" 60 40
1133 $3.20 on $1.10 on $2 "Norantea guianensis" 60 40

1983. Bicentenary of Manned Flight and 20th Anniv of Guyana Airways. Nos. 701/2a optd as indicated in brackets.
1134 20 c. multicoloured (**BW**) . . 35 35
1135 20 c. multicoloured (**LM**) . . 35 35
1136 20 c. multicoloured (**GY 1963 1983**) 35 35
1137 20 c. multicoloured (**JW**) . . 35 35
1138 20 c. multicoloured (**CU**) . . 35 35
1139 20 c. multicoloured (**Mont Golfier 1783–1983**) 35 35
1140 25 c. multicoloured (**BGI**) . . 50 25
1141 25 c. multicoloured (**GEO**) . . 15 10
1142 25 c. multicoloured (**MIA**) . . 50 25
1143 25 c. multicoloured (**BVB**) . . 50 25
1144 25 c. multicoloured (**PBM**) . . 50 25
1145 25 c. multicoloured (**Mont Golfier 1783–1983**) 20 15
1146 25 c. multicoloured (**POS**) . . 50 25
1147 25 c. multicoloured (**JFK**) . . 50 25
1148 30 c. multicoloured (**AHL**) . . 40 30
1149 30 c. multicoloured (**BCG**) . . 40 30
1150 30 c. multicoloured (**BMJ**) . . 40 30
1151 30 c. multicoloured (**EKE**) . . 40 30
1152 30 c. multicoloured (**GEO**) . . 40 30
1153 30 c. multicoloured (**GFO**) . . 40 30
1154 30 c. multicoloured (**IBM**) . . 40 30
1155 30 c. multicoloured (**Mont Golfier 1783–1983**) 25 15
1156 30 c. multicoloured (**KAI**) . . 40 30
1157 30 c. multicoloured (**KAR**) . . 40 30
1158 30 c. multicoloured (**KPG**) . . 40 30
1159 30 c. multicoloured (**KRG**) . . 40 30
1160 30 c. multicoloured (**KTO**) . . 40 30
1161 30 c. multicoloured (**LTM**) . . 40 30
1162 30 c. multicoloured (**MHA**) . . 40 30
1163 30 c. multicoloured (**MWJ**) . . 40 30
1164 30 c. multicoloured (**MYM**) . . 40 30
1165 30 c. multicoloured (**NAI**) . . 40 30
1166 30 c. multicoloured (**ORJ**) . . 40 30
1167 30 c. multicoloured (**USI**) . . 40 30
1168 30 c. multicoloured (**VEG**) . . 40 30

1983. No. 649 further surch **240**.
1169 240 c. on 35 c. on 60 c. Soldier's cap . . . . 1·25 1·00

1983. F.A.O. Fisheries Project. Nos. 448 and 450 surch **FAO 1983** and value.
1170 30 c. on 1 c. Type **87** . . . 15 15
1171 $2.60 on 3 c. Peacock cichild ("Lukunani") . . . . . . 1·50 2·25

277 G.B. 1857 1d. with Georgetown "AO3" Postmark

1983. 125th Anniv of Use of Great Britain Stamps in Guyana. (a) Inscriptions in black.
1172 **277** 25 c. brown and black . . 15 10
1173 – 30 c. red and black . . . 15 15
1174 – 60 c. violet and black . . 35 30
1175 – 120 c. green and black . . 70 55

(b) Inscriptions in blue.
1176 **277** 25 c. brown and black . . 15 10
1177 – 25 c. red and black . . . 15 10
1178 – 25 c. violet and black . . 15 10
1179 – 25 c. green and black . . 15 10
1180 **277** 30 c. brown and black . . 15 15
1181 – 30 c. red and black . . . 15 15
1182 – 30 c. violet and black . . 15 15
1183 – 30 c. green and black . . 15 15
1184 **277** 45 c. brown and black . . 30 25
1185 – 45 c. red and black . . . 30 25
1186 – 45 c. violet and black . . 30 25
1187 – 45 c. green and black . . 30 25
1188 **277** 120 c. brown and black . . 40 55
1189 – 130 c. red and black . . 40 60
1190 – 150 c. violet and black . . 40 70
1191 – 200 c. green and black . . 40 95

DESIGNS: Nos. 1173, 1177, 1181, 1185, 1189, G.B. 1857 4d. red; Nos. 1174, 1178, 1182, 1186, 1190, G.B. 1856 6d. lilac; Nos. 1175, 1179, 1183, 1187, 1191, G.B. 1856 1s. green.

Each design incorporates the "AO3" postmark except Nos. 1189/91 which show mythical postmarks of the Crowned-circle type inscribed "DEMERARA", "BERBICE" or "ESSEQUIBO".

1983. International Communications Year. No. 716 surch **INT. COMMUNICATIONS YEAR 50**.
1192 50 c. on 375 c. on $3 Cylinder satellite . . . . 4·50 30

No. 1192 also carries an otherwise unissued "375" surcharge. As issued much of this surcharge is obliterated by two groups of six horizontal lines.

1983. St. Johns Ambulance Commemoration. Nos. 650 and 653 surch.
1193 **156** 75 c. on 8 c. silver, black and mauve . . . . . . 4·50 50
1194 – $1.20 on 40 c. silver, black and blue . . . . 6·50 75

1983. International Food Day. No. 616 surch **$1.20 Int. Food Day 1983**.
1195 $1.20 on 35 c. Five-fingers and awaras . . . . 1·00 50

1983. 65th Anniv of I.L.O. and 25th Death Anniv of H. N. Critchlow (founder of Guyana Labour Union). No. 840 further optd **1918-1983 I.L.O.**
1196 240 c. on $3 H. N. Critchlow 1·50 1·50

1983. Deepavali Festival. Nos. 661 and 663/4 surch.
1197 25 c. on 8 c. Type **158** . . . 20 10
1198 $1.50 on 35 c. Flame in bowl 1·25 60
1199 $1.50 on 40 c. Goddess Latchmi 80 60

1983. No. 732 optd **1982** and No. 798 further optd **1983**.
1200 $3 "Makanaima the Great Ancestral Spirit of the Amerindians" . . . . . . 1·50 70
1201 360 c. on $2 "Norantea guianensis" . . . . 1·75 80

1983. Wildlife Protection. Nos. 686 and 688 surch and No. 852 optd **1983**.
1202 30 c. Six-banded armadillo . 50 15
1203 60 c. on 15 c. Giant sea turtle 75 30
1204 $1.20 on 40 c. Iguana . . . 1·25 50

1983. Human Rights Day. No. 1079c optd **Human Rights Day**.
1205 $3 Rotary anniversary emblem 2·00 1·25

1983. Olympic Games, Los Angeles (1984) (1st issue). Nos. 733/44 surch **LOS ANGELES 1984 125**, Nos. 1206/17 further surch **55**.
1206 55 c. on 125 c. on 35 c. Type **174** 25 25
1207 55 c. on 125 c. on 35 c. Trahira ("Haimara") 25 25
1208 55 c. on 125 c. on 35 c. Electric eel 25 25
1209 55 c. on 125 c. on 35 c. Golden rivulus 25 25
1210 55 c. on 125 c. on 35 c. Golden pencilfish 25 25
1211 55 c. on 125 c. on 35 c. Four-eyed fish 25 25
1212 55 c. on 125 c. on 35 c. Red piranha ("Pirai") 25 25
1213 55 c. on 125 c. on 35 c. Smoking hassar 25 25
1214 55 c. on 125 c. on 35 c. Manta 25 25
1215 55 c. on 125 c. on 35 c. Festive cichlid ("Flying patwa") . 25 25
1216 55 c. on 125 c. on 35 c. Arapaima 25 25
1217 55 c. on 125 c. on 35 c. Peacock cichlid ("Lukanani") . . 25 25
1217a 125 c. on 35 c. Type **174** . 5·50
1217b 125 c. on 35 c. Trahira ("Haimara") . . . . 5·50
1217c 125 c. on 35 c. Electric eel . 5·50
1217d 125 c. on 35 c. Golden rivulus 5·50
1217e 125 c. on 35 c. Golden pencilfish . . . . 5·50
1217f 125 c. on 35 c. Four-eyed fish 5·50
1217g 125 c. on 35 c. Red piranha ("Pirai") . . . . 5·50
1217h 125 c. on 35 c. Smoking hassar 5·50
1217i 125 c. on 35 c. Manta . . . 5·50
1217j 125 c. on 35 c. Festive cichlid ("Flying patwa") . . . . 5·50
1217k 125 c. on 35 c. Arapaima . . 5·50
1217l 125 c. on 35 c. Peacock cichlid ("Lukanani") . . . . . . 5·50

See also Nos. 1308/17 and 1420.

1983. No. F7 with unissued **ESPANA 1982** surch further optd **1983**.
1218 180 c. on 60 c. Soldier's cap 2·50 65

1983. Commonwealth Heads of Government Meeting, New Delhi. No. 542 surch **COMMONWEALTH HEADS OF GOV'T MEETING—INDIA 1983 150**.
1219 150 c. on 1 c. Pitcher plant of Mt. Roraima . . . . . . 2·50 60

1983. Christmas. No. 861 further surch **CHRISTMAS 1983 20c**.
1220 20 c. on 12 c. on 6 c. Black acara ("Patua") . . . . 1·50 10

1984. Nos. 838 and F9 optd **POSTAGE**.
1221 $2 "Norantea guianensis" . 3·00 70
1221b 550 c. on $10 "Elbella patrobas" . . . . 11·00 7·50

1984. Flowers. Unissued stamps as T **222** surch.
1222 17 c. on 2 c. lilac, blue and green 1·25 1·00
1223 17 c. on 8 c. lilac, blue and mauve . . . . 1·25 1·00

1984. Republic Day. No. 703 and 705a variously optd or surch..
1224 25 c. on 35 c. mult (surch **ALL OUR HERITAGE 25**) . . 35 20
1225 25 c. on 35 c. mult (surch **1984 25**) 40 20
1226 25 c. on 35 c. mult (surch **REPUBLIC DAY 25**) . . 40 20
1227 25 c. on 35 c. mult (surch **25**) 40 20
1228 25 c. on 35 c. mult (surch **BERBICE 25**) . . . . . . 1·75 1·50
1229 25 c. on 35 c. mult (surch **DEMERARA 25**) . . . . 1·75 1·50
1230 25 c. on 35 c. mult (surch **ESSEQUIBO 25**) . . . . 1·75 1·50
1232 60 c. mult (optd **ALL OUR HERITAGE**) 50 30
1233 60 c. mult (optd **REPUBLIC DAY**) 50 30
1234 60 c. mult (optd **1984**) . . . 50 30

1984. Guyana Olympic Committee Appeal. Nos. 841/3 surch **OLYMPIC GAMES 84 25c POSTAGE (+2.25 SURTAX)** and rings, the whole surch inverted.
1235 25 c. + $2.25 on 60 c. on 3 c. Hanging heliconia . . . . 2·00 4·50
1236 25 c. + $2.25 on 75 c. on $5 "Odontadenia grandiflora" 2·00 4·50
1237 25 c. + $2.25 on $1.10 on $2 "Norantea guianensis" . . 2·00 4·50

1984. Nature Protection. Various stamps optd **Protecting our Heritage**, some additionally surch.
1238 20 c. on 15 c. mult (No. 491) 8·50 10
1239 20 c. on 15 c. mult (No. 791) 8·50 10
1240a 20 c. on 15 c. mult (No. 1044) 15·00 1·25
1241 25 c. mult (No. 550ab) . . . 11·00 10
1242 30 c. on 15 c. mult (No. 548a) 20·00 30
1243 40 c. mult (No. 457) . . . . 12·00 20
1244 50 c. mult (No. 552) . . . . 1·50 25
1245 50 c. mult (No. F6) . . . . 1·50 25
1246 60 c. mult (No. 459) . . . . 9·50 30
1247 90 c. on 40 c. mult (No. 551) 16·00 50
1248 180 c. on 40 c. mult (No. 919) 16·00 90
1249 $2 multicoloured (No. 461) . 50·00 1·50
1250 225 c. on 10 c. mult (No. 490) 23·00 1·00
1251 260 c. on $1 mult (No. 460) . 11·00 1·00
1252 320 c. on 40 c. mult (No. 551) 12·00 2·25
1253 350 c. on 40 c. mult (No. 551) 20·00 2·50
1254 380 c. on 50 c. mult (No. 495) 5·00 2·50
1255 450 c. on $5 mult (No. 462) . 7·00 2·50

1984. Easter. Nos. 483 and 916/17 optd **1984** and No. 481 surch **130**.
1256 **111** 30 c. multicoloured . . . 20 20
1257 45 c. on 6 c. multicoloured 25 25
1258 75 c. on 40 c. multicoloured 35 35
1259 130 c. on 6 c. multicoloured 65 60

1984. Nos. 937/9 and 991 surch.
1260 75 c. on $1 "Chelonanthus uliginoides" . . . . 9·50 35
1261 75 c. on 110 c. on 3 c. Hanging heliconia . . . . 9·50 35
1262 225 c. on 250 c. on 6 c. Cannon-ball tree . . . . 3·00 1·25
1263 230 c. on $2.35 on 180 c. on 60 c. Soldier's cap . . . . 3·00 1·00

1984. Nos. 899/901, 904/6 and 909 surch.
1264 20 c. on 15 c. on 2 c. Type **132** (No. 899) . . . . 1·50 30
1265 75 c. on 110 c. on 5 c. Annatto tree (No. 904) . . . . . . 9·00 70
1266 90 c. on 110 c. on 5 c. Annatto tree (No. 900) . . . . . . 5·50 85
1267 90 c. on 110 c. on 5 c. Annatto tree (No. 901) . . . . . . 7·00 85
1268 120 c. on 125 c. on 8 c. on 6 c. Cannon-ball tree (No. 905) 7·00 1·00
1269 120 c. on 125 c. on 8 c. on 6 c. Cannon-ball tree (No. 906) 7·00 1·00
1270 120 c. on 125 c. on 8 c. on 6 c. Cannon-ball tree (No. 909) 2·75 1·00

1984. World Telecommunications and Health Day. Nos. 802 and 980 surch.
1271 25 c. on 220 c. on 1 c. Pitcher plant of Mt. Roraima (surch **ITU DAY 1984 25**) . . . 20 20
1272 25 c. on 220 c. on 1 c. Pitcher plant of Mt. Roraima (surch **WHO DAY 1984 25**) . . . 20 20
1273 25 c. on 220 c. on 1 c. Pitcher plant of Mt. Roraima (surch **ITU/WHO DAY 1984 25**) . 20 20
1274 $4.50 on 280 c. on $5 "Odontadenia grandiflora" (surch **ITU/WHO DAY 1984 $4.50**) . . . . 1·75 1·25

1984. No. 1005 surch **120**.
1275 120 c. on $1.25 on 6 c. Cannon-ball tree . . . . 7·00 55

1984. World Forestry Conference. No. 755 optd **1984** and Nos. 752/4 and 875 surch.
1276 55 c. on 30 c. "Hymenaea courbaril" . . . . 2·75 30
1277 75 c. on 110 c. on $3 "Peltogyne venosa" 40 35
1278 160 c. on 50 c. "Mora excelsa" 75 70
1279 260 c. on 10 c. Type **177** . . 1·25 1·25
1280 $3 "Peltogyne venosa" . . . 1·40 1·40

1984. No. 625 surch.
1281 55 c. on 110 c. on 10 c. Type **150** 75 30
1282 90 c. on 110 c. on 10 c. Type **150** 1·00 45

Nos. 1281/2 also carry an otherwise unissued 110 c. surch

1984. U.P.U. Congress, Hamburg. Nos. 1188/91 optd **UPU Congress 1984 Hamburg**.
1283 120 c. brown and black . . . 50 60
1284 130 c. red and black . . . 55 70
1285 150 c. violet and black . . . 60 75
1286 200 c. green and black . . . 80 90

1984. Nos. 982/3 and 986/7 surch.
1287 45 c. on 50 c. on 2 c. green . 60 25
1288 60 c. on $1.10 on 3 c. olive and brown . . . . 2·25 40
1289 120 c. on $1.25 on 6 c. green . 75 55
1290 200 c. on $2.20 on 24 c. black and orange . . . . 5·50 1·10

1984. Nos. 979/80 and 1003 surch and No. 981 optd **1984**.
1291 75 c. on 110 c. on 5 c. Annatto tree 60 35
1292 120 c. on 170 c. on 110 c. on 5 c. Annatto tree 80 55
1293 200 c. on 220 c. on 1 c. Pitcher plant of Mt. Roraima . . . 12·00 85
1294 330 c. on $2 "Norantea guianensis" . . . . 1·75 1·75

1984. CARICOM Day. No. 1200 additionally surch **CARICOM DAY 1984 60**.
1295 60 c. on $3 "Makanaima the Great Ancestral Spirit of the Amerindians" 40 30

1984. No. 544 surch **150**.
1296 150 c. on 3 c. Hanging heliconia 1·25 65

1984. CARICOM Heads of Government Conference. No. 544 surch **60 CARICOM HEADS OF GOV'T CONFERENCE JULY 1984**.
1297 60 c. on 3 c. Hanging heliconia 40 30

301 Children and Thatched School

1984. Cent of Guyana Teachers' Association. Mult.
1298 25 c. Type **301** 10 15
1299 25 c. Torch and graduates . . 10 15
1300 25 c. Torch and target emblem 10 15
1301 25 c. Teachers of 1884 and 1984 in front of school 10 15

1984. 60th Anniv of International Chess Federation. No. 1048 optd or surch also.
1302 25 c. on 90 c. on 60 c. Fort Island (surch **INT. CHESS FED. 1924–1984 25**) . . . 1·00 25
1303 25 c. on 90 c. on 60 c. Fort Island (surch **1984 25**) . . 1·75 45
1304 75 c. on 90 c. on 60 c. Fort Island (surch **INT. CHESS FED. 1924–1984 75**) . . . 1·10 40
1305 75 c. on 90 c. on 60 c. Fort Island (surch **1984 75**) . . 2·00 70
1306 90 c. on 60 c. Fort Island (optd **INT. CHESS FED. 1924–1984**) . . . . . . 1·25 50
1307 90 c. on 60 c. Fort Island (optd **1984**) . . . . 2·25 90

1984. Olympic Games, Los Angeles (2nd issue). No. 1051 surch.
1308 25 c. on $1.30 mult (surch **TRACK AND FIELD 25**) . 20 25
1309 25 c. on $1.30 mult (surch **BOXING 25**) 20 30
1310 25 c. on $1.30 mult (surch **OLYMPIC GAMES 1984 LOS ANGELES 25**) . . . 20 30
1311 25 c. on $1.30 mult (surch **CYCLING 25**) . . . . . . 1·00 50
1312 25 c. on $1.30 mult (surch **OLYMPIC GAMES 1984 25**) . . . . 3·00 1·25
1313 $1.20 on $1.30 mult (surch **TRACK AND FIELD $1.20**) 1·00 1·10
1314 $1.20 on $1.30 mult (surch **BOXING $1.20**) . . . . . 1·00 1·10
1315 $1.20 on $1.30 mult (surch **OLYMPIC GAMES 1984 LOS ANGELES $1.20**) . . 1·00 1·25
1316 $1.20 on $1.30 mult (surch **CYCLING $1.20**) . . . . 1·75 1·50
1317 $1.20 on $1.30 mult (surch **OLYMPIC GAMES 1984 $1.20**) . . . . 3·50 3·00

1984. 60th Anniv of Girl Guide Movement in Guyana. Nos. 900/9 surch **25 GIRL GUIDES 1924-1984**.
1318 25 c. on 110 c. on 5 c. Annatto tree (No. 900) 15 15
1319 25 c. on 110 c. on 5 c. Annatto tree (No. 901) 15 15
1320 25 c. on 110 c. on 5 c. Annatto tree (No. 902) 50 35
1321 25 c. on 110 c. on 5 c. Annatto tree (No. 903) 50 35
1322 25 c. on 110 c. on 5 c. Annatto tree (No. 904) . . . . . . 4·00 4·50
1323 25 c. on 125 c. on 8 c. on 6 c. Cannon-ball tree (No. 905) 15 15
1324 25 c. on 125 c. on 8 c. on 6 c. Cannon-ball tree (No. 906) 15 15
1325 25 c. on 125 c. on 8 c. on 6 c. Cannon-ball tree (No. 907) 50 35
1326 25 c. on 125 c. on 8 c. on 6 c. Cannon-ball tree (No. 908) 50 35
1327 25 c. on 125 c. on 8 c. on 6 c. Cannon-ball tree (No. 909) 4·00 4·50

1984. Various stamps surch.
1328 20 c. on 15 c. on 2 c. Type **132** (No. 1034) 30 10
1341 25 c. on 10 c. Cattleya (No. 547) . . . . 30·00 2·00
1343 25 c. on 15 c. Christmas orchid (No. 548a) . . . . £120 5·00
1342 25 c. on 15 c. Christmas orchid (No. 864) . . . . 14·00 15
1346 25 c. on 15 c. Christmas orchid (No. 977) . . . . 12·00 10
1347 25 c. on 15 c. Christmas orchid (No. 1009) . . . . 13·00 10
1348 25 c. on 15 c. Christmas orchid (No. O23) . . . . 13·00 10
1342a 25 c. on 35 c. on 60 c. Soldier's cap (No. 649) . . . . . . 90·00 4·50
1331 60 c. on 110 c. on 8 c. on 3 c. Hanging heliconia (As No. 868 but with only one **110**) 29·00
1332 120 c. on 125 c. on 8 c. on 6 c. Cannon-ball tree (No. 893) 5·00 50
1333 120 c. on 125 c. on $2 "Norantea guianensis" (No. 834) . . . . 38·00
1334 120 c. on 125 c. on $2 "Norantea guianensis" (No. O20) . . . . 2·00 50
1335 120 c. on 140 c. on $1 "Chelonanthus uliginoides" (No. 796) . . . . 5·50 50
1349 130 c. on 110 c. on $2 "Norantea guianensis" (No. 804) . . . . 70·00 4·00
1350 130 c. on 110 c. on $2 "Norantea guianensis" (No. O22) . . . . 2·25 1·25
1336 200 c. on 220 c. on 1 c. Pitcher plant of Mt. Roraima (No. 922) . . . . 8·00 75
1337 320 c. on $1.10 on $2 "Norantea guianensis" (No. 804) . . . . 1·75 75

1338 350 c. on 375 c. on $5 "Odontadenia grandiflora" (No. 803) . . . . 3·25 80
1339 390 c. on 400 c. on $5 "Odontadenia grandiflora" (No. 1091) . . . . 4·00 90
1340 450 c. on $5 "Odontadenia grandiflora" (No. O16) . 5·50 2·50
1351a 600 c. on $7.20 on $1 "Chelonanthus uliginoides" (No. 770) 75 75

1984. Various stamps optd **1984**.
1352 20 c. "Paphinia cristata" (No. 549) . . . . 18·00 10
1358 25 c. Marabunta (No. 550) . 85·00 4·50
1359 25 c. Marabunta (No. F4) . 4·25 50
1359a 25 c. Marabunta (No. F4a) . 2·00 30
1354 50 c. on 8 c. Type **136** (No. 1062) . . . . 10·00 25
1355 60 c. on 1 c. Pitcher plant of Mt. Roraima (No. 1000) . 65 25
1356 $2 "Norantea guianensis" (No. O33) . . . . 1·50 60
1360 $3.60 on $5 "Odontadenia grandiflora" (No. 769) . . 85 1·10

1984. No. 899 optd with fleur-de-lis.
1358a 25 c. Marabunta . . . . .

1984. 40th Anniv of I.C.A.O. Nos. 981, 1017 and 1148/68 optd **ICAO** or as indicated.
1361 30 c. multicoloured (No. 1148) 60 60
1362 30 c. multicoloured (No. 1149) 60 60
1363 30 c. multicoloured (No. 1150) 60 60
1364 30 c. multicoloured (No. 1151) 60 60
1365 30 c. multicoloured (No. 1152) 60 60
1366 30 c. multicoloured (No. 1153) 60 60
1367 30 c. multicoloured (No. 1154) (optd **IMB/ICAO**) 60 60
1368 30 c. multicoloured (No. 1155) (optd **KCV/ICAO**) 60 60
1369 30 c. multicoloured (No. 1156) (optd **KAI/ICAO**) 60 60
1370 30 c. multicoloured (No. 1157) 60 60
1371 30 c. multicoloured (No. 1158) 60 60
1372 30 c. multicoloured (No. 1155) (optd **1984**) 60 60
1373 30 c. multicoloured (No. 1155) (optd **KPM/ICA**) 60 60
1374 30 c. multicoloured (No. 1159) 60 60
1375 30 c. multicoloured (No. 1160) 60 60
1376 30 c. multicoloured (No. 1161) 60 60
1377 30 c. multicoloured (No. 1155) (optd **PMT/ICAO**) 60 60
1378 30 c. multicoloured (No. 1162) 60 60
1379 30 c. multicoloured (No. 1163) 60 60
1380 30 c. multicoloured (No. 1164) 60 60
1381 30 c. multicoloured (No. 1165) 60 60
1382 30 c. multicoloured (No. 1166) 60 60
1383 30 c. multicoloured (No. 1167) 60 60
1384 30 c. multicoloured (No. 1168) 60 60
1385 200 c. on 330 c. on $2 multicoloured (No. 981) . 65 70
1386 200 c. on 75 c. on $5 multicoloured (No. 1017) . 2·25 1·75
No. 1385 also carries an otherwise unissued surch **G.A.C. Inaug. Flight Georgetown—Toronto 200**.

1984. Wildlife Protection. Nos. 756/67 optd **1984**.
1387 30 c. Type **178** 30 25
1388 30 c. Red howler 30 25
1389 30 c. Common squirrel-monkey 30 25
1390 30 c. Two-toed sloth 30 25
1391 30 c. Brazilian tapir 30 25
1392 30 c. Collared peccary . . . 30 25
1393 30 c. Six-banded armadillo . 30 25
1394 30 c. Tamandua ("Ant Eater") 30 25
1395 30 c. Giant anteater 30 25
1396 30 c. Murine opossum . . . 30 25
1397 30 c. Brown four-eyed opossum 30 25
1398 30 c. Brazilian agouti 30 25

1984. Nos. D10/11 surch **120 GUYANA**.
1399 D **2** 120 c. on 4 c. blue . . . 3·25 45
1402 120 c. on 12 c. red . . . 3·25 45

1984. 175th Birth Anniv of Louis Braille (inventor of alphabet for the blind). No. 1040 surch **$1.50**.
1403 $1.50 on 15 c. on 10 c. Type **215** 6·50 55

1984. International Food Day. No. 1012 surch **1**.
1404 150 c. on 50 c. Pawpaw and tangerine . . . . 1·75 55
The surcharge places a "1" alongside the original face value and obliterates the "1982" date on the previous overprint.

1984. Birth Centenary of H. N. Critchlow (founder of Guyana Labour Union). No. 873 surch **240** and No. 1196, both optd **1984**.
1405 240 c. on 110 c. on $3 H. N. Critchlow (No. 873) . . . 1·00 65
1406 240 c. on $3 H. N. Critchlow (No. 1196) . . . . 6·50 70

1984. Nos. 910/12 and 1184/7 surch.
1407 **277** 25 c. on 45 c. brown and black 15 15
1408 – 25 c. on 45 c. red and black (No. 1185) 15 15
1409 – 25 c. on 45 c. violet and black (No. 1186) . . . 15 15
1410 – 25 c. on 45 c. green and black (No. 1187) . . . 15 15
1411 – 120 c. on 100 c. on $3 mult (No. 910) . . . . . 8·50 45
1412 – 120 c. on 400 c. on 30 c. mult (No. 911) 90 45
1413 – 320 c. on $5 multicoloured (No. 912) . . . . . . 16·00 1·75

1984. Deepavali Festival. Nos. 544/5 surch **MAHA SABHA 1934-1984** and new value.
1414 25 c. on 5 c. Annatto tree . . 20 10
1415 $1.50 on 3 c. Hanging heliconia 1·40 55

1984. A.S.D.A. Philatelic Exhibition, New York. Nos. 1188/91 optd **Philatelic Exhibition New York 1984**.
1416 **277** 120 c. brown and black . 40 45
1417 – 130 c. red and black . . 45 50
1418 – 150 c. violet and black . 50 55
1419 – 200 c. green and black . 70 75

1984. Olympic Games, Los Angeles (3nd issue). Design as No. 1051, but with Olympic rings and inscr "OLYMPIC GAMES 1984 LOS ANGELES".
1420 $1.20 Youth display (41 × 25 mm) . . . . 1·50 45

1984. Nos. 847, 861, 1099 and 1088 surch.
1421 20 c. on 12 c. on 12 c. on 6 c. mult (No. 847) 60 10
1422 20 c. on 12 c. on 6 c. mult (No. 861) . . . . 65·00
1423 25 c. on 50 c. on 6 c. mult (No. 1099) 30 10
1424 60 c. on $1 on 6 c. mult (No. 1088) 45 25

318 Pair of Swallow-tailed Kites on Tree

1984. Christmas. Swallow-tailed Kites. Mult.
1425 60 c. Type **318** . . . . . . 3·00 1·75
1426 60 c. Swallow-tailed kite on branch . . . . 3·00 1·75
1427 60 c. Kite in flight with wings raised . . . . 3·00 1·75
1428 60 c. Kite in flight with wings lowered . . . . 3·00 1·75
1429 60 c. Kite gliding . . . . . 3·00 1·75
Nos. 1425/9 were printed together, se-tenant, with the backgrounds forming a composite design. Each stamp is inscribed "CHRISTMAS 1982".

319 St. George's Cathedral, Georgetown

1985. Georgetown Buildings. Each black and stone.
1430 25 c. Type **319** 10 10
1431 60 c. Demerara Mutual Life Assurance Building 15 25
1432 120 c. As No. 1431 . . . . . 20 45
1433 120 c. Town Hall 20 45
1434 120 c. Victoria Law Courts . 20 45
1435 200 c. As No. 1433 . . . . 20 75
1436 300 c. As No. 1434 . . . . 20 1·10
Nos. 1432/4 were printed together, se-tenant, forming a composite design.

1985. International Youth Year. No. 1420 optd **International Youth Year 1985**.
1437 $1.20 Youth display . . . . 2·00 45
Examples of No. 1420 used for this overprint all show the second line of the original inscription as "LOS ANGELES".

1985. Republic Day. Nos. 1049/50 and 1052 optd or surch **Republic Day 1970–1985**.
1438 25 c. Type **238** 20 20
1439 25 c. Flag (inscr "30th ANNIVERSARY IN PARLIAMENT") 20 20
1440 120 c. on $6 Presidential standard 65 65
1441 130 c. on $6 Presidential standard 70 70

322 Young Ocelot on Branch

1985. Wildlife Protection. Multicoloured.
1442A 25 c. Type **322** (green background) . . . . . . 1·50 10
1443A 60 c. Young ocelot (different) (brown background) . . 30 25
1444B 120 c. As No. 1443 . . . . 15 20
1445B 120 c. Type **322** 15 20
1446B 120 c. Young ocelot (different) (brown background) 15 20
1447A 130 c. As No. 1446 . . . . 45 60
1448A 320 c. Scarlet macaw (28 × 46 mm) . . . . 3·00 1·50
1449A 330 c. Young ocelot reaching for branch (28 × 46 mm) . . 90 1·50

1985. Revenue stamp as T **181**, and Nos. 912, 940, 1016 and No. O24 surch.
1450 30 c. on 50 c. mult (No. O24) 50 10
1451 55 c. on 2 c. black, blue and grey 65 20
1452 55 c. on 15 c. on 2 c. black, blue and grey (940) 65 20
1453 90 c. on $1 mult (No. 1016) 4·50 30
1454 225 c. on $5 mult (No. 912) 7·50 90
1455 230 c. on $5 mult (No. 912) 7·50 95
1456 260 c. on $5 mult (No. 912) 7·50 1·00

1985. International Youth Year Save the Children Fund Campaign. Nos. 880, 1073a, 1079b and 1082 optd **International Youth Year 1985** or surch also.
1457 50 c. "Two Boys catching Ducks" (No. 1073a) . . . . 2·00 20
1458 50 c. on 10 c. Type **171** (No. 1082) . . . . 6·00 20
1459 120 c. on 125 c. on $3 "Mango Season" (No. 880) . . . . 2·00 45
1460 $3 "Mango Season" (No. 1079b) . . . . 2·00 1·10

1985. 125th Anniv of British Guiana Post Office (1st issue). No. 699 surch **25** and names of post offices and postal agencies open in 1860.
1461 25 c. on 10 c. mult (**Airy Hall**) 50 50
1462 25 c. on 10 c. multicoloured (**Belfield Arab Coast**) . . . 50 50
1463 25 c. on 10 c. multicoloured (**Belfield E. C. Dem.**) . . . 50 50
1464 25 c. on 10 c. mult (**Belladrum**) 50 50
1465 25 c. on 10 c. multicoloured (**Beterver-wagting**) 50 50
1466 25 c. on 10 c. multicoloured (**Blairmont Ferry**) 50 50
1467 25 c. on 10 c. mult (**Boeraserie**) 50 50
1468 25 c. on 10 c. mult (**Brahm**) . 50 50
1469 25 c. on 10 c. mult (**Bushlot**) . 50 50
1470 25 c. on 10 c. mult (**De Kinderen**) 50 50
1471 25 c. on 10 c. multicoloured (**Fort Wellington**) 50 50
1472 25 c. on 10 c. mult (**Georgetown**) 50 50
1473 25 c. on 10 c. mult (**Hague**) . 50 50
1474 25 c. on 10 c. mult (**Leguan**) . 50 50
1475 25 c. on 10 c. mult (**Mahaica**) 50 50
1476 25 c. on 10 c. mult (**Mahaicony**) 50 50
1477 25 c. on 10 c. multicoloured (**New Amsterdam**) 50 50
1478 25 c. on 10 c. mult (**Plaisance**) 50 50
1479 25 c. on 10 c. multicoloured (**No. 6 Police Station**) . . . 50 50
1480 25 c. on 10 c. mult (**Queenstown**) 50 50
1481 25 c. on 10 c. multicoloured (**Vergenoegen**) 50 50
1482 25 c. on 10 c. mult (**Vigilance**) 50 50
1483 25 c. on 10 c. multicoloured (**Vreed-en-Hoop**) 50 50
1484 25 c. on 10 c. mult (**Wakenaam**) 50 50
1485 25 c. on 10 c. multicoloured (**Windsor Castle**) 50 50
See also Nos. 1694/1717, 2140/64 and 2278/2301.

1985. I.T.U./W.H.O. Day. Nos. 1148/68 optd **1985** or with single capital letter.
1486 30 c. multicoloured (1148) . . 50 50
1487 30 c. multicoloured (1149) . . 50 50
1488 30 c. multicoloured (1150) . . 50 50
1489 30 c. multicoloured (1151) . . 50 50
1490 30 c. multicoloured (1152) . . 50 50
1491 30 c. multicoloured (1153) . . 50 50
1492 30 c. multicoloured (1154) (**I**) 50 50
1493 30 c. multicoloured (1155) (**T**) 50 50
1494 30 c. multicoloured (1156) (**U**) 50 50
1495 30 c. multicoloured (1157) . . 50 50
1496 30 c. multicoloured (1158) . . 50 50
1497 30 c. multicoloured (1155) (**W**) 50 50
1498 30 c. multicoloured (1155) (**H**) 50 50
1499 30 c. multicoloured (1155) (**O**) 50 50
1500 30 c. multicoloured (1159) . . 50 50
1501 30 c. multicoloured (1160) . . 50 50
1502 30 c. multicoloured (1161) (**D**) 50 50
1503 30 c. multicoloured (1155) (**A**) 50 50
1504 30 c. multicoloured (1162) (**Y**) 50 50
1505 30 c. multicoloured (1163) . . 50 50
1506 30 c. multicoloured (1164) . . 50 50
1507 30 c. multicoloured (1165) . . 50 50
1508 30 c. multicoloured (1166) . . 50 50
1509 30 c. multicoloured (1167) . . 50 50
1510 30 c. multicoloured (1168) . . 50 50

1985. No. 861 surch **20**.
1511 20 c. on 12 c. on 6 c. Patua . 2·50 10

1985. 10th Anniv of Caribbean Agricultural Research Development Institute. No. 544 surch **60 CARDI 1975-1985**.
1512 60 c. on 3 c. Hanging heliconia 1·25 25

1985. No. 839 surch **600**.
1513 600 c. on 625 c. on 40 c. Tiger beard . . . . 18·00 2·50

1985. 80th Anniv of Rotary International. Nos. 707 and 879 surch **ROTARY INTERNATIONAL 1905-1985**.
1514 120 c. on 110 c. on $3 Rotary anniversary emblem . . . . 9·50 45
1515 300 c. on $2 "Morpho rhetenor" . . . . 6·50 2·25

1985. CARICOM Day. No. 1200 surch **CARICOM DAY 1985 60**.
1516 60 c. on $3 "Makanaima the Great Ancestral Spirit of the Amerindians" 60 30

1985. 135th Anniv of First British Guiana Stamps. No. 870 surch **135th Anniversary Cotton Reel 1850-1985 120**.
1517 120 c. on 110 c. on 10 c. Type **170** 65 55

"REICHENBACHIA" ISSUES. Due to the proliferation of these designs the catalogue uses the book plate numbers as description for each design. The following index gives the species on each plate.

Series 1
Plate No. 1 (Series 1) "Odontoglossum crispum"
Plate No. 2 (Series 1) "Cattleya percivaliana"
Plate No. 3 (Series 1) "Cypripedium sanderianum"
Plate No. 4 (Series 1) "Odontoglossum rossi"
Plate No. 5 (Series 1) "Cattleya dowiana aurea"
Plate No. 6 (Series 1) "Coelogyne cristata maxima"
Plate No. 7 (Series 1) "Odontoglossum insleayi splendens"
Plate No. 8 (Series 1) "Laelia euspatha"
Plate No. 9 (Series 1) "Dendrobium wardianum"
Plate No. 10 (Series 1) "Laelia autumnalis xanthotropis"
Plate No. 11 (Series 1) "Phalaenopsis grandiflora aurea"
Plate No. 12 (Series 1) "Cattleya lawrenceana"
Plate No. 13 (Series 1) "Masdevallia shuttleworthii" and "M. xanthocorys"
Plate No. 14 (Series 1) "Aeranthus sesquipedalis"
Plate No. 15 (Series 1) "Cattleya mendelii Duke of Marlborough"
Plate No. 16 (Series 1) "Zygopetalum intermedium"
Plate No. 17 (Series 1) "Phaius humblotii"
Plate No. 18 (Series 1) "Chysis bractescens"
Plate No. 19 (Series 1) "Masdevallia backhousiana"
Plate No. 20 (Series 1) "Cattleya citrina"
Plate No. 21 (Series 1) "Oncidium jonesianum" and "Oncidium jonesianum phaeanthum"
Plate No. 22 (Series 1) "Saccolabium giganteum"
Plate No. 23 (Series 1) "Cypripedium io"
Plate No. 24 (Series 1) "Odontoglossum blandum"
Plate No. 25 (Series 1) "Maxillaria sanderiana"
Plate No. 26 (Series 1) "Odontoglossum Edward II"
Plate No. 27 (Series 1) "Vanda teres"
Plate No. 28 (Series 1) "Odontoglossum hallii xanthoglossum"
Plate No. 29 (Series 1) "Odontoglossum crispum hrubyanum"
Plate No. 30 (Series 1) "Oncidium concolor"
Plate No. 31 (Series 1) "Trichopilia suavis alba"
Plate No. 32 (Series 1) "Cattleya superba splendens"
Plate No. 33 (Series 1) "Odontoglossum luteo-purpureum"
Plate No. 34 (Series 1) "Cypripedium niveum"
Plate No. 35 (Series 1) "Stanhopea shuttleworthii"
Plate No. 36 (Series 1) "Laelia anceps percivaliana"
Plate No. 37 (Series 1) "Odontoglossum hebraicum"
Plate No. 38 (Series 1) "Cypripedium oenanthum superbum"
Plate No. 39 (Series 1) "Dendrobium superbiens"
Plate No. 40 (Series 1) "Laelia harpophylla"
Plate No. 41 (Series 1) "Lycaste skinneri" and "alba"
Plate No. 42 (Series 1) "Phalaenopsis stuartiana"
Plate No. 43 (Series 1) "Cattleya trianaei ernesti"
Plate No. 44 (Series 1) "Sobralia xantholeuca"
Plate No. 45 (Series 1) "Odontoglossum crispum kinlesideanum"
Plate No. 46 (Series 1) "Cattleya trianaei schroederiana"
Plate No. 47 (Series 1) "Epidendrum vitellinum"
Plate No. 48 (Series 1) "Laelia anceps stella" and "barkeriana"
Plate No. 49 (Series 1) "Odontoglossum harryanum"
Plate No. 50 (Series 1) "Dendrobium leechianum"
Plate No. 51 (Series 1) "Phalaenopsis speciosa"
Plate No. 52 (Series 1) "Laelia elegans schilleriana"
Plate No. 53 (Series 1) "Zygopetalum wendlandi"
Plate No. 54 (Series 1) "Cypripedium selligerum majus"
Plate No. 55 (Series 1) "Angraecum articulatum"
Plate No. 56 (Series 1) "Laelia anceps sanderiana"
Plate No. 57 (Series 1) "Vanda coerulea"
Plate No. 58 (Series 1) "Dendrobium nobile sanderianum"
Plate No. 59 (Series 1) "Laelia gouldiana"
Plate No. 60 (Series 1) "Odontoglossum grande"
Plate No. 61 (Series 1) "Cypripedium rothschildianum"
Plate No. 62 (Series 1) "Vanda sanderiana"
Plate No. 63 (Series 1) "Dendrobium aureum"
Plate No. 64 (Series 1) "Oncidium macranthum"
Plate No. 65 (Series 1) "Cypripedium tautzianum"
Plate No. 66 (Series 1) "Cymbidium mastersi"
Plate No. 67 (Series 1) "Angraecum caudatum"
Plate No. 68 (Series 1) "Laelia albida"
Plate No. 69 (Series 1) "Odontoglossum roezlii"
Plate No. 70 (Series 1) "Oncidium ampliatum majus"
Plate No. 71 (Series 1) "Renanthera lowii"
Plate No. 72 (Series 1) "Cattleya warscewiczii"
Plate No. 73 (Series 1) "Oncidium lanceanum"
Plate No. 74 (Series 1) "Vanda hookeriana"
Plate No. 75 (Series 1) "Cattleya labiata gaskelliana"
Plate No. 76 (Series 1) "Epidendrum prismatocarpum"
Plate No. 77 (Series 1) "Cattleya guttata leopoldi"
Plate No. 78 (Series 1) "Oncidium splendidum"
Plate No. 79 (Series 1) "Odontoglossum hebraicum aspersum"
Plate No. 80 (Series 1) "Cattleya dowiana var chrysotoxa"
Plate No. 81 (Series 1) "Cattleya trianae alba"
Plate No. 82 (Series 1) "Odontoglossum humeanum"
Plate No. 83 (Series 1) "Cypripedium argus"
Plate No. 84 (Series 1) "Odontoglossum luteo-purpureum prionopetalum"
Plate No. 85 (Series 1) "Cattleya rochellensis"
Plate No. 86 (Series 1) "Odontoglossum triumphans"
Plate No. 87 (Series 1) "Phalaenopsis casta"
Plate No. 88 (Series 1) "Oncidium tigrinum"
Plate No. 89 (Series 1) "Cypripedium lemoinierianum"
Plate No. 90 (Series 1) "Catasetum bungerothii"
Plate No. 91 (Series 1) "Cattleya ballantiniana"
Plate No. 92 (Series 1) "Dendrobium brymerianum"
Plate No. 93 (Series 1) "Cattleya eldorado crocata"
Plate No. 94 (Series 1) "Odontoglossum sanderianum"

Plate No. 95 (Series 1) "Cattleya labiata warneri"
Plate No. 96 (Series 1) "Odontoglossum schroderianum"

Series 2

Plate No. 1 (Series 2) "Cypripedium morganiae burfordiense"
Plate No. 2 (Series 2) "Cattleya bowringiana"
Plate No. 3 (Series 2) "Dendrobium formosum"
Plate No. 4 (Series 2) "Phaius tuberculosus"
Plate No. 5 (Series 2) "Odontoglossum crispum mundyanum"
Plate No. 6 (Series 2) "Laelia praestans"
Plate No. 7 (Series 2) "Dendrobium phalaenopsis var statterianum"
Plate No. 8 (Series 2) "Cypripedium boxalli atratum"
Plate No. 9 (Series 2) "Odontoglossum wattianum"
Plate No. 10 (Series 2) "Cypripedium lathamianum inversum"
Plate No. 11 (Series 2) "Paphinia rugosa" and "Zygopetalum xanthinum"
Plate No. 12 (Series 2) "Dendrobium melanodiscus"
Plate No. 13 (Series 2) "Laelia anceps schroderiana"
Plate No. 14 (Series 2) "Phaius hybridus cooksonii"
Plate No. 15 (Series 2) "Disa grandiflora"
Plate No. 16 (Series 2) "Selenipedium hybridum grande"
Plate No. 17 (Series 2) "Cattleya schroederae alba"
Plate No. 18 (Series 2) "Lycaste skinnerii armeniaca"
Plate No. 19 (Series 2) "Odontoglossum excellens"
Plate No. 20 (Series 2) "Laelio-cattleya elegans var blenheimensis"
Plate No. 21 (Series 2) "Odontoglossum coradinei"
Plate No. 22 (Series 2) "Odontoglossum wilckeanum var rothschildianum"
Plate No. 23 (Series 2) "Cypripedium lawrenceanum hyeanum"
Plate No. 24 (Series 2) "Cattleya intermedia punctatissima"
Plate No. 25 (Series 2) "Laelia purpurata"
Plate No. 26 (Series 2) "Masdevallia harryana splendens"
Plate No. 27 (Series 2) "Selenipedium hybridum nitidissimum"
Plate No. 28 (Series 2) "Cattleya mendelii var measuresiana"
Plate No. 29 (Series 20 "Odontoglossum vexillarium" ("miltonia vexillaria")
Plate No. 30 (Series 2) "Saccolabium coeleste"
Plate No. 31 (Series 2) "Cypripedium hybridum youngianum"
Plate No. 32 (Series 2) "Miltonia (hybrida) bleuana"
Plate No. 33 (Series 2) "Laelia grandis"
Plate No. 34 (Series 2) "Cattleya labiata var lueddemanniana"
Plate No. 35 (Series 2) "Odontoglossum coronarium"
Plate No. 36 (Series 2) "Cattleya granulosa var schofieldiana"
Plate No. 37 (Series 2) "Odontoglossum (hybridum) leroyanum"
Plate No. 38 (Series 2) "Cypripedium (hybridum) laucheanum" and "eyermanianum"
Plate No. 39 (Series 2) "Cychnoches chlorochilon"
Plate No. 40 (Series 2) "Cattleya O'Brieniana"
Plate No. 41 (Series 2) "Odontoglossum ramosissimum"
Plate No. 42 (Series 2) "Dendrobium phalaenopsis var"
Plate No. 43 (Series 2) "Cypripedium (hybridum) pollettianum" and "maynardii"
Plate No. 44 (Series 2) "Odontoglossum naevium"
Plate No. 45 (Series 2) "Cypripedium (hybridum) castleanum"
Plate No. 47 (Series 2) "Cattleya amethystoglossa"
Plate No. 48 (Series 2) "Cattleya (hybrida) arnoldiana"
Plate No. 49 (Series 2) "Cattleya labiata"
Plate No. 50 (Series 2) "Dendrobium (hybridum) venus" and "cassiope"
Plate No. 51 (Series 2) "Selenipedium (hybridum) weidlichianum"
Plate No. 52 (Series 2) "Cattleya mossiae var reineckiana"
Plate No. 53 (Series 2) "Cymbidium lowianum"
Plate No. 54 (Series 2) "Oncidium loxense"
Plate No. 56 (Series 2) "Coelogyne sanderae"
Plate No. 58 (Series 2) "Coelogyne pandurata"
Plate No. 59 (Series 2) "Schomburgkia sanderiana"
Plate No. 60 (Series 2) "Oncidium superbiens"
Plate No. 61 (Series 2) "Dendrobium johnsoniae"
Plate No. 62 (Series 2) "Laelia hybrida behrensiana"
Plate No. 63 (Series 2) Hybrid "Calanthes Victoria Regina", "Bella" and "Burfordiense"
Plate No. 64 (Series 2) "Cattleya mendelii Quorndon House var"
Plate No. 65 (Series 2) "Arachnanthe clarkei"
Plate No. 66 (Series 2) "Zygopetalum burtii"
Plate No. 67 (Series 2) "Cattleya (hybrida) parthenia"
Plate No. 68 (Series 2) "Phalaenopsis sanderiana" and "intermedia portei"
Plate No. 69 (Series 2) "Phaius blumei var assamicus"
Plate No. 70 (Series 2) "Angraecum humblotii"
Plate No. 71 (Series 2) "Odontoglossum pescatorei"
Plate No. 72 (Series 2) "Cattleya rex"
Plate No. 73 (Series 2) "Zygopetalum crinitum"
Plate No. 74 (Series 2) "Cattleya lueddemanniana alba"
Plate No. 75 (Series 2) "Cymbidium (hybridum) winnianum"
Plate No. 76 (Series 2) Hybrid "Masdevallias courtauldiana", "geleniana" and "measuresiana"
Plate No. 77 (Series 2) "Cypripedium (hybridum) calypso"
Plate No. 78 (Series 2) "Masdevallia chimaera var mooreana"
Plate No. 79 (Series 2) "Miltonia phalaenopsis"
Plate No. 80 (Series 2) "Lissochilus giganteus"
Plate No. 82 (Series 2) "Thunia brymeriana"
Plate No. 83 (Series 2) "Miltonia moreliana"
Plate No. 84 (Series 2) "Oncidium kramerianum"
Plate No. 85 (Series 2) "Cattleya Victoria Regina"
Plate No. 86 (Series 2) "Zygopetalum klabochorum"
Plate No. 87 (Series 2) "Laelia autumnalis alba"
Plate No. 88 (Series 2) "Spathoglottis kimballiana"
Plate No. 89 (Series 2) "Laelio-cattleya" ("The Hon. Mrs. Astor")
Plate No. 90 (Series 2) "Phaius hybridus amabilis" and "marthiae"
Plate No. 91 (Series 2) "Zygopetalum rostratum"
Plate No. 92 (Series 2) "Coelogyne swaniana"
Plate No. 93 (Series 2) "Laelio-cattleya (hybrida) phoebe"
Plate No. 94 (Series 2) "Epidendrum atropurpureum var randianum"
Plate No. 95 (Series 2) "Dendrobium imperatrix"
Plate No. 96 (Series 2) "Vanda parishii var marriottiana"

331 "Cattleya lawrenceana" (Plate No. 12 (Series 1))

1985. Centenary of Publication of Sanders' "Reichenbachia" (1st issue). Orchids. Mult.
1518 25 c. Type **331** . . . 40 30
1519 60 c. Plate No. 2 (Series 1) . 50 35
1520 60 c. Plate No. 7 (Series 1) . 50 35
1521 60 c. Plate No. 10 (Series 1) 50 35
1522 60 c. Plate No. 19 (Series 1) 50 35
1523 60 c. Plate No. 31 (Series 1) 50 35
1524 120 c. Plate No. 27 (Series 1) 75 55
1525 130 c. Plate No. 3 (Series 1) 75 55
1759 130 c. Plate No. 6 (Series 1) 55 20
1760 130 c. Plate No. 13 (Series 1) 55 20
1528 130 c. Plate No. 18 (Series 1) 2·00 55
1761 130 c. Plate No. 20 (Series 1) 55 20
1762 130 c. Plate No. 25 (Series 1) 55 20
1531 130 c. Plate No. 29 (Series 1) 1·50 55
1532 130 c. Plate No. 30 (Series 1) 1·50 55
1533 200 c. Plate No. 4 (Series 1) 1·50 85
See also Nos. 1551/66, 1571/1806, 1597, 1620/1863, 1663/73, 1679/83, 1731/8, 1747/54, 1809/19, 1822, 1868/9, 1872/81, 1884/7, 1907, 1912/15, 1916/24, 1925/9, 2066/73, 2171/8, 2180/2, 2190/3, 2216/18, 2219/20, 2225/7, 2235/42, 2314/18, 2322/5, 2328, 2314/18, 2322/5, 2329/31, 2468/71, 2498/2511 and 2605/8.

332 Arms of Guyana

337 Leaders of the 1763 Rebellion

1985.
1535b **332** 25 c. multicoloured . . 15 20
For Type **332** within frame, see No. 2183.

1985. 85th Birthday of Queen Elizabeth the Queen Mother (1st issue). Nos. 1528 and 1531/2 optd **QUEEN MOTHER 1900-1985.**
1536 130 c. Plate No. 18 (Series 1) 60 70
1537 130 c. Plate No. 29 (Series 1) 60 70
1538 130 c. Plate No. 30 (Series 1) 60 70

1985. International Youth Year. Nos. 900/4 surch **25 International Youth Year 1985.**
1540 25 c. on 110 c. on 5 c. multicoloured (900) . . . 10 10
1541 25 c. on 110 c. on 5 c. multicoloured (901) . . . 15 15
1542 25 c. on 110 c. on 5 c. multicoloured (902) . . . 35 25
1543 25 c. on 110 c. on 5 c. multicoloured (903) . . . 35 25
1544 25 c. on 100 c. on 5 c. multicoloured (904) . . . 2·50 2·25

1985. 75th Anniv of Girl Guide Movement. No. 612 surch **225 1910-1985.**
1545 225 c. on 350 c. on 225 c. on 40 c. Guides in camp . . . 27·00 1·75
No. 1545 also carries two otherwise unissued surcharges at top right.

1985. Birth Bicentenary of John J. Audubon (ornithologist). No. 992 surch **J. J. Audubon 1785-1985 240.**
1546 240 c. on 35 c. Harpy eagle . 19·00 2·00

1985. 150th Anniv (1984) of Abolition of Slavery (1st issue).
1547 **337** 25 c. black and grey . . 25 10
1548 – 60 c. black and mauve . 20 25
1549 – 130 c. black and blue . . 25 50
1550 – 150 c. black and lilac . . 60 55
DESIGNS: 60 c. Damon and Parliament Buildings, Georgetown; 130 c. Quamina and Demerara, 1823; 150 c. "Den Arendt" (slave ship), 1627.
For these designs in changed colours see Nos. 2552/5.

1985. Centenary of Publication of Sanders' "Reichenbachia" (2nd issue). As T **331** showing orchids. Multicoloured.
1551 25 c. Plate No. 52 (Series 1) . 60 25
1763 55 c. Plate No. 9 (Series 1) . . 55 10
1764 55 c. Plate No. 22 (Series 1) . 55 10
1765 55 c. Plate No. 49 (Series 1) . 55 10
1766 55 c. Plate No. 64 (Series 1) . 55 10
1556 60 c. Plate No. 44 (Series 1) . 70 35
1557 60 c. Plate No. 47 (Series 1) . 70 35
1558 120 c. Plate No. 36 (Series 1) 1·00 55
1559 130 c. Plate No. 16 (Series 1) 1·00 55
1560 130 c. Plate No. 38 (Series 1) 1·00 55
1561 150 c. Plate No. 32 (Series 1) 1·00 55
1562 150 c. Plate No. 34 (Series 1) 1·00 55
1563 150 c. Plate No. 35 (Series 1) 1·00 55
1564 150 c. Plate No. 41 (Series 1) 1·00 55
1565 150 c. Plate No. 48 (Series 1) 1·00 55
1566 150 c. Plate No. 62 (Series 1) 1·00 55

1985. Signing of Guyana—Libya Friendship Treaty. No. 621 surch **Guyana/Libya Friendship 1985 150.**
1567 **149** 150 c. on 10 c. multi . . 9·00 2·75

1985. Namibia Day. No. 636 surch **150.**
1568 150 c. on 35 c. Unveiling of monument . . . . 2·75 55

1985. World Cup Football Championship, Mexico (1986) (1st issue). No. F2 surch **Mexico 1986 275.**
1569 275 c. on 3 c. Hanging heliconia 5·50 1·10
See also No. 1727.

1985. Centenary of Publication of Sanders' "Reichenbachia" (3rd issue). As T **331** showing orchids. Multicoloured.
1571 25 c. Plate No. 8 (Series 1) . . 70 20
1572 25 c. Plate No. 23 (Series 1) . 70 20
1573 25 c. Plate No. 51 (Series 1) . 70 20
1574 25 c. Plate No. 61 (Series 1) . 70 20
1575 25 c. Plate No. 63 (Series 1) . 70 20
1576 25 c. Plate No. 70 (Series 1) . 70 20
1577 25 c. Plate No. 72 (Series 1) . 70 20
1578 120 c. Plate No. 1 (Series 1) (horiz) . . . . 1·00 55
1579 120 c. Plate No. 11 (Series 1) (horiz) . . . . 1·00 55
1580 120 c. Plate No. 28 (Series 1) (horiz) . . . . 1·00 55
1767 150 c. Plate No. 40 (Series 1) (horiz) 45 20
1768 150 c. Plate No. 42 (Series 1) (horiz) 45 20
1769 150 c. Plate No. 45 (Series 1) (horiz) 45 20
1584 200 c. Plate No. 14 (Series 1) 1·50 80
1585 200 c. Plate No. 21 (Series 1) (horiz) . . . . 1·50 80
1770 200 c. Plate No. 43 (Series 1) (horiz) 55 30

1985. 30th Anniv of Commonwealth Caribbean Medical Research Council. Nos. 819, 871, 874, 928 and 1014 optd **1955–1985** or surch also.
1587 – 60 c. mult (No. 819) . . 20 25
1588 – 60 c. mult (No. 1014) . . 20 25
1589 **176** 120 c. on 110 c. on 10 c. multicoloured (No. 871) 40 45
1590 – 120 c. on 110 c. on $3 mult (No. 874) 40 45
1592 – 120 c. on 210 c. on $3 mult (No. 928) 40 45

1985. 20th Anniv of Guyana Defence Force. No. 856 surch **1965–1985.**
1593 25 c. on $1.10 on $3 W.O. and N.C.O; Guyana Defence Force, 1966 . . . . 1·00 10
1594 225 c. on $1.10 on $3 W.O. and N.C.O; Guyana Defence Force, 1966 . . . . 2·50 1·25

1985. Fire Prevention. Nos. 678 and 680 optd **1985** and surch.
1595 25 c. on 40 c. Fire engine, 1977 8·00 20
1596 320 c. on 15 c. Steam engine, circa 1860 . . . . 14·00 3·75

1985. Centenary of Publication of Sanders' "Reichenbachia" (4th issue). As T **331**. Mult.
1597 60 c. Plate No. 55 (Series 1) . 75 30

1985. Columbus Day. Unissued value as T **331** surch **350 CRISTOBAL COLON 1492–1992.** Mult.
1598 350 c. on 120 c. Plate No. 65 (Series 1) . . . . 4·50 2·50

1985. 20th Death Anniv of Sir Winston Churchill. No. 707 optd **SIR WINSTON CHURCHILL 1965–1985.**
1599 $2 "Morpho rhetenor" (female) 7·00 1·60

1985. 35th Anniv of International Commission of Irrigation and Drainage. No. 625 with unissued surcharge further surch **1950–1985.**
1600 **150** 25 c. on 110 c. on 10 c. multicoloured 15 10
1601 200 c. on 110 c. on 10 c. multicoloured 85 85

1985. 40th Anniv of U.N.O. Nos. 714/16, 800 and O19 optd **United Nations 1945–1985.**
1602 30 c. mult (No. 714) . . . . 1·50 10
1603 50 c. mult (No. 715) . . . . 1·50 20
1604 100 c. on $3 mult (No. O19) . 1·50 40
1605 225 c. on 220 c. on $3 mult (No. 800) . . . . 7·00 75
1606 $3 mult (No. 716) . . . . . 3·00 1·40

1985. Nos. 551/3, O14/15, O18, O21, OP1/2 and F7 optd **POSTAGE.**
1607 30 c. on $2 "Norantea guianensis" (No. O18) . . 40 10
1608 40 c. Tiger beard (No. 551) . 32·00 40
1609 50 c. "Guzmania lingulata" (No. 552) 40 20
1610 50 c. "Guzmania lingulata" (No. O14) 40 20
1611 60 c. Soldier's cap (No. 553) 3·00 25
1612 60 c. Soldier's cap (No. O15) 2·75 25
1613 60 c. Soldier's cap (No. F7) . 1·50 25
1614 $10 "Elbella patrobas" (No. O21) . . . . 16·00 5·50
1615 $15 on $1 "Chelonanthus uliginoides" (No. OP1) . . 8·00 9·00
1616 $20 on $1 "Chelonanthus uliginoides" (No. OP2) . . 9·00 11·00

1985. Deepavali Festival. Nos. 542/3 surch **Deepavali 1985.**
1617 25 c. on 2 c. Type **132** . . . 20 10
1618 150 c. on 1 c. Pitcher plant of Mt. Roraima . . . . . . 1·40 55

1985. Centenary of Publication of Sanders' "Reichenbachia" (5th issue). As T **331** showing orchids. Multicoloured.
1620 25 c. Plate No. 59 (Series 1) . 65 20
1771 30 c. Plate No. 53 (Series 1) . 30 10
1622 60 c. Plate No. 57 (Series 1) (horiz) 80 35
1623 60 c. Plate No. 73 (Series 1) (horiz) 80 35
1624 60 c. Plate No. 75 (Series 1) (horiz) 80 35
1772 75 c. Plate No. 55 (Series 1) . 35 15
1773 100 c. Plate No. 65 (Series 1) 35 15
1627 120 c. Plate No. 37 (Series 1) 1·25 55
1628 120 c. Plate No. 46 (Series 1) 1·25 55
1629 120 c. Plate No. 56 (Series 1) 1·25 55
1630 120 c. Plate No. 58 (Series 1) 1·25 55
1631 120 c. Plate No. 67 (Series 1) 1·25 55
1632 130 c. Plate No. 66 (Series 1) 1·40 65
1633 150 c. Plate No. 26 (Series 1) 1·50 75
1634 200 c. Plate No. 33 (Series 1) (horiz) . . . . 1·75 85
1774 225 c. Plate No. 24 (Series 1) 45 35
The 30, 75, 100 and 225 c. values have "GUYANA" in blue.

351 Clive Lloyd (cricketer)

1985. Clive Lloyd's Testimonial Year. Multicoloured.
1636 25 c. Type **351** 50 60
1637 25 c. Clive Lloyd, bat and wicket 50 60
1638 25 c. Cricket equipment . . . 50 60
1639 60 c. As No. 1638 (25 × 33 mm) 60 40
1640 $1.30 As No. 1637 (25 × 33 mm) 70 85
1641 $2.25 Type **351** (25 × 33 mm) 80 1·25
1642 $3.50 Clive Lloyd with the Prudential Cup (36 × 56 mm) 90 1·75

1985. Wildlife Protection. Nos. 756/67 optd **1985.**
1643 30 c. Type **178** 75 75
1644 30 c. Red howler 75 75
1645 30 c. Common squirrel-monkey 75 75
1646 30 c. Two-toed sloth 75 75
1647 30 c. Brazilian tapir 75 75
1648 30 c. Collared peccary . . . 75 75
1649 30 c. Six-banded armadillo . . 75 75
1650 30 c. Tamandua 75 75
1651 30 c. Giant anteater 75 75
1652 30 c. Murine opossum . . . 75 75
1653 30 c. Brown four-eyed opossum 75 75
1654 30 c. Brazilian agouti 75 75

1985. No. 847 surch **20.**
1655 20 c. on 12 c. on 12 c. on 6 c. Black acara ("Patua") . . 1·50 15

1986. Centenary of the Appearance of "Reichenbachia" Volume 1. Nos. 1768 and 1770 optd **REICHENBACHIA 1886–1986.**
1657 150 c. Plate No. 42 (Series 1) 2·25 60
1658 200 c. Plate No. 43 (Series 1) 2·25 75

1986. Republic Day. Nos. 1108/9 and 1052 optd **Republic Day 1986** or surch also.
1659 25 c. As Type **258** 10 10
1660 25 c. As No. 1050 . . . . . 10 10
1661 120 c. on $6 Presidential standard 40 45
1662 225 c. on $6 Presidential standard 70 75

1986. Centenary of Publication of Sanders' "Reichenbachia" (6th issue). As T **331**. Mult.
1663 40 c. Plate No. 77 (Series 1) . 55 20
1664 45 c. Plate No. 54 (Series 1) . 55 25
1665 50 c. Plate No. 92 (Series 1) . 55 25
1666 60 c. Plate No. 95 (Series 1) . 60 30
1667 75 c. Plate No. 5 (Series 1) . 65 35
1668 90 c. Plate No. 84 (Series 1) . 75 40
1669 150 c. Plate No. 78 (Series 1) 95 60
1670 200 c. Plate No. 79 (Series 1) 1·25 80
1671 300 c. Plate No. 83 (Series 1) 1·75 1·25
1672 320 c. Plate No. 50 (Series 1) 1·75 1·40
1673 360 c. Plate No. 85 (Series 1) 1·90 1·50

1986. Easter. No. 481 optd **1986** and surch also.
1674 **111** 25 c. on 6 c. mult . . . 25 10
1675 50 c. on 6 c. mult . . . 40 20
1676 100 c. on 6 c. mult . . . 65 40
1677 200 c. on 6 c. mult . . . 1·25 70

1986. 60th Anniv of St. John's Ambulance in Guyana. No. 652 surch **1926 1986 150.**
1678 150 c. on 35 c. silver, black and green . . . . 3·00 55

1986. Centenary of Publication of Sanders' "Reichenbachia" (7th issue). As T **331**. Mult.
1679 25 c. Plate No. 71 (Series 1) (horiz) 60 20
1680 120 c. Plate No. 69 (Series 1) (horiz) . . . . 1·50 55
1681 150 c. Plate No. 87 (Series 1) (horiz) . . . . 1·75 65
1682 225 c. Plate No. 60 (Series 1) 1·75 90
1683 350 c. Plate No. 94 (Series 1) (horiz) . . . . 2·25 1·50

1986. 60th Birthday of Queen Elizabeth II. No. 1760 optd **1926 1986 QUEEN ELIZABETH**.
1684 130 c. Plate No. 13 (Series 1) 1·25 50

1986. Wildlife Protection. Nos. 685, 739/44 and 993/8 surch **Protect the** and value.
1686 60 c. on 35 c. Type **174** . . . 35 35
1687 60 c. on 35 c. Trahira ("Haimara") 35 35
1688 60 c. on 35 c. Electric eel . . 35 35
1689 60 c. on 35 c. Golden rivulus 35 35
1690 60 c. on 35 c. Golden pencilfish 35 35
1691 60 c. on 35 c. Four-eyed fish 35 35
1691a 60 c. on 35 c. Red piranha ("Pirai") . . . . 4·75 2·00
1691b 60 c. on 35 c. Smoking hassar 4·75 2·00
1691c 60 c. on 35 c. Manta . . . . 4·75 2·00
1691d 60 c. on 35 c. Festive cichlid ("Flying patwa") . . . . 4·75 2·00
1691e 60 c. on 35 c. Arapaima . . 4·75 2·00
1691f 60 c. on 35 c. Peacock cichlid ("Lukanani") . . . . . 4·75 2·00
1692 $6 on 8 c. Type **163** . . . . 3·00 2·50

1986. No. 799 surch **600**.
1693 600 c. on 720 c. on 60 c. Soldier's cap . . . . 9·00 75

1986. 125th Anniv of British Guiana Post Office (2nd issue). No. 702a surch **25** and names of postal agencies opened between 1860 and 1880.
1694 25 c. on 30 c. mult (surch **Abary**) 50 50
1695 25 c. on 30 c. multicoloured (surch **Anna Regina**) . . . 50 50
1696 25 c. on 30 c. multicoloured (surch **Aurora**) 50 50
1697 25 c. on 30 c. multicoloured (surch **Bartica Grove**) . . . 50 50
1698 25 c. on 30 c. multicoloured (surch **Bel Air**) 50 50
1699 25 c. on 30 c. multicoloured (surch **Belle Plaine**) 50 50
1700 25 c. on 30 c. multicoloured (surch **Clonbrook**) 50 50
1701 25 c. on 30 c. multicoloured (surch **T.P.O. Dem. Railway**) 50 50
1702 25 c. on 30 c. multicoloured (surch **Enmore**) 50 50
1703 25 c. on 30 c. multicoloured (surch **Fredericksburg**) . . 50 50
1704 25 c. on 30 c. multicoloured (surch **Good Success**) . . . 50 50
1705 25 c. on 30 c. mult (surch **1986**) 50 50
1706 25 c. on 30 c. multicoloured (surch **Mariabba**) 50 50
1707 25 c. on 30 c. multicoloured (surch **Massaruni**) 50 50
1708 25 c. on 30 c. mult (surch **Nigg**) 50 50
1709 25 c. on 30 c. multicoloured (surch **No. 50**) 50 50
1710 25 c. on 30 c. multicoloured (surch **No. 63 Benab**) . . . 50 50
1711 25 c. on 30 c. multicoloured (surch **Philadelphia**) . . . 50 50
1712 25 c. on 30 c. multicoloured (surch **Sisters**) 50 50
1713 25 c. on 30 c. multicoloured (surch **Skeldon**) 50 50
1714 25 c. on 30 c. multicoloured (surch **Suddie**) 50 50
1715 25 c. on 30 c. multicoloured (surch **Taymouth Manor**) . 50 50
1716 25 c. on 30 c. mult (surch **Wales**) 50 50
1717 25 c. on 30 c. mult (surch **Whim**) 50 50

1986. 20th Anniv of Independence. (a) No. 332 of British Guiana surch **GUYANA INDEPENDENCE 1966–1986**, Nos. 424 and 435 of Guyana surch **1986** and No. 656 surch **25**.
1718 25 c. on 2 c. green (No. 332) 15 10
1719 25 c. on 35 c. mult (No. 656) 15 10
1720 60 c. on 2 c. green (No. 332) 25 10
1721 120 c. on 6 c. green (No. 424) 40 20
1722 130 c. on 24 c. black and orange (No. 435) . . . . 4·25 30

(b) Nos. 1188/91 surch **INDEPENDENCE 1966–1986**.
1723 **277** 25 c. on 120 c. brown, black and blue (No. 1188) . 25 20
1724 – 25 c. on 130 c. red, black and blue (No. 1189) . 25 20
1725 – 25 c. on 150 c. violet and blue (No. 1190) 25 20
1726 – 225 c. on 200 c. green, black and blue (No. 1191) . 65 60

1986. World Cup Football Championship, Mexico (2nd issue). No. 544 surch **MEXICO 1986 225**.
1727 225 c. on 3 c. Hanging heliconia 7·50 70

1986. CARICOM Day. No. 705a optd **CARICOM DAY 1986**.
1728 60 c. "Papilio androgeus" . . 5·50 30

1986. CARICOM Heads of Government Conference, Georgetown. Nos. 544 and 601 surch **CARICOM HEADS OF GOV'T CONFERENCE JULY 1986** and value.
1729 25 c. on 8 c. on 6 c. Cannon-ball tree . . . . 1·00 10
1730 60 c. on 3 c. Hanging heliconia 1·50 25

1986. Centenary of Publication of Sanders' "Reichenbachia" (8th issue). As T **331**. Mult.
1731 30 c. Plate No. 86 (Series 1) . 50 15
1732 55 c. Plate No. 17 (Series 1) . 50 20
1733 60 c. Plate No. 93 (Series 1) . 50 20
1734 100 c. Plate No. 68 (Series 1) 85 20
1735 130 c. Plate No. 91 (Series 1) 90 30
1736 250 c. Plate No. 74 (Series 1) 1·00 60
1737 260 c. Plate No. 39 (Series 1) 1·00 60
1738 375 c. Plate No. 90 (Series 1) 1·50 85

1986. International Peace Year. Nos. 542 and 546 surch **INT. YEAR OF PEACE** and value.
1739 25 c. on 1 c. Pitcher plant of Mt. Roraima 20 20
1740 60 c. on 6 c. Cannon-ball tree 40 40
1741 120 c. on 6 c. Cannon-ball tree 40 40
1742 130 c. on 6 c. Cannon-ball tree 40 40
1743 150 c. on 6 c. Cannon-ball tree 40 40

363 Halley's Comet and British Guiana 1907 2 c. Stamp

1986. Appearance of Halley's Comet.
1744 **363** 320 c. red, black and lilac 30 50
1745 – 320 c. multicoloured . . 30 50
DESIGN: No. 1745, Guyana 1985 320 c. scarlet macaw stamp.

1986. Centenary of Publication of Sanders' "Reichenbachia" (9th issue). As T **331**. Mult.
1747 40 c. Plate No. 96 (Series 1) 60 15
1748 45 c. Plate No. 81 (Series 1) 60 15
1749 90 c. Plate No. 89 (Series 1) 80 20
1750 100 c. Plate No. 88 (Series 1) 80 20
1751 150 c. Plate No. 76 (Series 1) 90 35
1752 180 c. Plate No. 15 (Series 1) 90 40
1753 320 c. Plate No. 82 (Series 1) 1·10 70
1754 330 c. Plate No. 80 (Series 1) 1·25 90

1986. No. 489 surch **20**.
1755 20 c. on 6 c. Patua . . . . . 3·00 15

1986. 50th Anniv of Guyana United Sadr Islamic Association. Nos. 469/70 optd **GUSIA 1936–1986**, No. 1757 surch also.
1756 **105** 25 c. black, gold and lilac 1·25 10
1757 $1.50 on 6 c. black, gold and flesh . . . . . . 2·50 80

1986. Regional Pharmacy Conference. No. 545 surch **REGIONAL PHARMACY CONFERENCE 1986 130**.
1758 130 c. on 5 c. Annatto tree . 4·00 30

1986. Centenary of Publication of Sanders' "Reichenbachia" (10th issue). As T **331**. Mult.
1809 30 c. Plate No. 30 (Series 2) 35 15
1810 45 c. Plate No. 21 (Series 2) (horiz) 40 15
1811 75 c. Plate No. 8 (Series 2) . 65 15
1812 80 c. Plate No. 42 (Series 2) (horiz) 65 15
1813 90 c. Plate No. 4 (Series 2) . 75 25
1814 130 c. Plate No. 38 (Series 2) 80 35
1815 160 c. Plate No. 5 (Series 2) (horiz) 95 40
1816 200 c. Plate No. 9 (Series 2) 1·25 50
1817 320 c. Plate No. 12 (Series 2) 2·00 70
1818 350 c. Plate No. 29 (Series 2) (horiz) . . . . 2·25 70
1819 360 c. Plate No. 34 (Series 2) 2·25 70

1986. 20th Anniv of Independence (2nd issue). As T **332** but additionally inscr "1966–1986" at foot.
1820 25 c. multicoloured 20 25

1986. Centenary of Publication of Sanders' "Reichenbachia" (11th issue). Design as No. 1735, but with different face value. Mult.
1822 40 c. Plate No. 91 (Series 1) 75 15

1986. Nos. 1361/84 surch **120**.
1823 120 c. on 30 c. mult (No. 1361) 70 70
1824 120 c. on 30 c. mult (No. 1362) 70 70
1825 120 c. on 30 c. mult (No. 1363) 70 70
1826 120 c. on 30 c. mult (No. 1364) 70 70
1827 120 c. on 30 c. mult (No. 1365) 70 70
1828 120 c. on 30 c. mult (No. 1366) 70 70
1829 120 c. on 30 c. mult (No. 1367) 70 70
1830 120 c. on 30 c. mult (No. 1368) 70 70
1831 120 c. on 30 c. mult (No. 1369) 70 70
1832 120 c. on 30 c. mult (No. 1370) 70 70
1833 120 c. on 30 c. mult (No. 1371) 70 70
1834 120 c. on 30 c. mult (No. 1372) 70 70
1835 120 c. on 30 c. mult (No. 1373) 70 70
1836 120 c. on 30 c. mult (No. 1374) 70 70
1837 120 c. on 30 c. mult (No. 1375) 70 70
1838 120 c. on 30 c. mult (No. 1376) 70 70
1839 120 c. on 30 c. mult (No. 1377) 70 70
1840 120 c. on 30 c. mult (No. 1378) 70 70
1841 120 c. on 30 c. mult (No. 1379) 70 70
1842 120 c. on 30 c. mult (No. 1380) 70 70
1843 120 c. on 30 c. mult (No. 1381) 70 70
1844 120 c. on 30 c. mult (No. 1382) 70 70
1845 120 c. on 30 c. mult (No. 1383) 70 70
1846 120 c. on 30 c. mult (No. 1384) 70 70

1986. 12th World Orchid Conference, Tokyo (1st issue). Unissued design as No. 1731, but with different face value, surch **12th World Orchid Conference TOKYO JAPAN MARCH 1987 650**.
1847 650 c. on 40 c. Plate No. 86 (Series 1) . . . . 7·50 3·50
No. 1847 is inscribed "ONTOGLOSSUM TRIUMPHANS" in error.
See also No. 2138.

1986. Columbus Day. Unissued design as No. 1774, but with different face value, surch **1492-1992 CHRISTOPHER COLUMBUS 320**.
1864 320 c. on 150 c. Plate No. 24 (Series 1) . . . . 2·50 80

1986. International Food Day. Nos. 1170/1 further surch **1986** and value.
1866 50 c. on 30 c. on 1 c. Type **87** 1·25 15
1867 225 c. on $2.60 on 3 c. Peacock cichlid ("Lukunani") . . . 4·00 60

1986. Centenary of Publication of Sanders' "Reichenbachia" (12th issue). As T **331**, one as No. 1731 with different face value. Mult.
1868 40 c. Plate No. 86 (Series 1) . 50 15
1869 90 c. Plate No. 10 (Series 2) . 75 30

1986. Air. 40th Annivs of U.N.I.C.E.F. and U.N.E.S.C.O. No. 706 surch.
1870 120 c. on $1 "Agrias claudina" (surch **UNICEF 1946–1986 AIR 120**) . . . . 3·00 3·00
1871 120 c. on $1 "Agrias claudina" (surch **UNESCO 1946–1986 AIR 120**) . . . . 6·00 6·00

1986. Centenary of Publication of Sanders' "Reichenbachia" (13th issue). As T **331**. Mult.
1872 45 c. Plate No. 17 (Series 2) . 30 15
1873 50 c. Plate No. 33 (Series 2) . 30 15
1874 60 c. Plate No. 27 (Series 2) . 45 15
1875 75 c. Plate No. 56 (Series 2) . 55 20
1876 85 c. Plate No. 45 (Series 2) . 55 20
1877 90 c. Plate No. 13 (Series 2) . 70 20
1878 200 c. Plate No. 44 (Series 2) 1·00 45
1879 300 c. Plate No. 50 (Series 2) 1·60 60
1880 320 c. Plate No. 10 (Series 2) 1·75 70
1881 390 c. Plate No. 6 (Series 2) . 2·00 95

1986. Deepavali Festival. Nos. 543 and 601 surch **Deepavali 1986** and value.
1882 25 c. on 2 c. Type **132** . . . 50 10
1883 200 c. on 8 c. on 6 c. Cannon-ball tree . . . . 1·50 40

1986. Centenary of Publication of Sanders' "Reichenbachia" (14th issue). As T **331**, two as Nos. 1732 and 1734 with different face values. Multicoloured.
1884 40 c. Plate No. 68 (Series 1) . 90 15
1885 80 c. Plate No. 17 (Series 1) . 1·50 25
1886 200 c. Plate No. 2 (Series 2) . 1·75 60
1887 225 c. Plate No. 24 (Series 2) 2·00 70

1986. Christmas. No. 489 surch **CHRISTMAS 1986 20**.
1888 20 c. on 6 c. Black acara ("Patua") 75 10

1986. Wildlife Protection. Nos. 756/67 optd **1986**.
1894 30 c. Type **178** 80 80
1895 30 c. Red howler 80 80
1896 30 c. Common squirrel-monkey 80 80
1897 30 c. Two-toed sloth 80 80
1898 30 c. Brazilian tapir 80 80
1899 30 c. Collared peccary 80 80
1900 30 c. Six-banded armadillo . . 80 80
1901 30 c. Tamandua 80 80
1902 30 c. Giant anteater 80 80
1903 30 c. Murine opossum 80 80
1904 30 c. Brown four-eyed opossum 80 80
1905 30 c. Brazilian agouti 80 80

1986. No. 1642 surch **$15**.
1906 $15 on $3.50 Clive Lloyd with Prudential Cup . . . . . . 18·00 12·00

1986. Centenary of Publication of Sanders' "Reichenbachia" (15th issue). Design as No. 1877, but with different face value. Mult.
1907 50 c. Plate No. 13 (Series 2) . 65 15

375 Memorial

1986. President Burnham Commemoration. Multicoloured.
1908 25 c. Type **375** 10 10
1909 120 c. Map of Guyana and flags 20 20
1910 130 c. Parliament Buildings and mace 20 20
1911 $6 L. F. Burnham and George-town mayoral chain (vert) . 60 1·25

1986. Centenary of Publication of Sanders' "Reichenbachia" (16th issue). As Nos. 1765/6, 1874 and 1887 but with different face values. Multicoloured.
1912 50 c. Plate No. 49 (Series 1) . 1·00 20
1913 50 c. Plate No. 64 (Series 1) . 1·00 20
1914 85 c. Plate No. 24 (Series 2) . 1·50 35
1915 90 c. Plate No. 27 (Series 2) . 1·50 35

1986. Centenary of Publication of Sanders' "Reichenbachia" (17th issue). As T **331**. Mult.
1916 25 c. Plate No. 20 (Series 2) . 35 15
1917 40 c. Plate No. 7 (Series 2) . . 35 15
1918 85 c. Plate No. 15 (Series 2) . 50 20
1919 90 c. Plate No. 3 (Series 2) . . 50 20
1920 120 c. Plate No. 14 (Series 2) 65 30
1921 130 c. Plate No. 32 (Series 2) 65 30
1922 150 c. Plate No. 22 (Series 2) 80 35
1923 320 c. Plate No. 18 (Series 2) 1·25 55
1924 330 c. Plate No. 28 (Series 2) 1·25 70

1987. Centenary of Publication of Sanders' "Reichenbachia" (18th issue). As Nos. 1772, 1876, 1886, 1918 and 1923 but with different face values. Multicoloured.
1925 35 c. Plate No. 45 (Series 2) . 40 15
1926 50 c. Plate No. 15 (Series 2) . 40 15
1927 50 c. Plate No. 55 (Series 1) . 40 15
1928 85 c. Plate No. 18 (Series 2) . 65 25
1929 90 c. Plate No. 2 (Series 2) . 65 25

1987. 10th Anniv of Guyana Post Office Corporation (1st issue). Unissued designs as Nos. 1771 and 1774, but with different face values, surch or optd **G P O C 1977 – 1987**.
1930 $2.25 Plate No. 53 (Series 1) 1·25 35
1931 $10 on 150 c. Plate No. 24 (Series 1) . . . . 3·50 4·00
See also Nos. 2074/80.

1987. Various "Reichenbachia" issues surch.
2375 120 c. on 40 c. Plate No. 91 (Series 1) (No. 1822) . . . 60 40
2380 120 c. on 40 c. Plate No. 90 (Series 1) 60 40
2387 120 c. on 50 c. Plate No. 9 (Series 1) 60 40
1994 120 c. on 50 c. Plate No. 49 (Series 1) (No. 1912) . . 50 40
1995 120 c. on 50 c. Plate No. 64 (Series 1) (No. 1913) . . 50 40
2388 120 c. on 50 c. Plate No. 22 (Series 1) 60 40
2389 120 c. on 50 c. Plate No. 3 (Series 2) 60 40
2390 120 c. on 50 c. Plate No. 6 (Series 2) 60 40
2391 120 c. on 50 c. Plate No. 20 (Series 2) 60 40
2392 120 c. on 50 c. Plate No. 32 (Series 2) 60 40
2019 120 c. on 50 c. Plate No. 24 (Series 1) 50 40
2020 120 c. on 50 c. Plate No. 53 (Series 1) 50 40
2021 120 c. on 50 c. Plate No. 65 (Series 1) 50 40
1980 120 c. on 55 c. Plate No. 9 (Series 1) (No. 1763) . . 50 40
2003 120 c. on 55 c. Plate No. 49 (Series 1) (No. 1765) . . 50 40
1981 120 c. on 55 c. Plate No. 64 (Series 1) (No. 1766) . . 50 30
2006 120 c. on 55 c. Plate No. 22 (Series 1) (No. 1764) . . 50 40
2009 120 c. on 55 c. Plate No. 15 (Series 1) 50 40
2010 120 c. on 55 c. Plate No. 81 (Series 1) 50 40
2011 120 c. on 55 c. Plate No. 82 (Series 1) 50 40
2012 120 c. on 55 c. Plate No. 89 (Series 1) 50 40
2394 120 c. on 60 c. Plate No. 2 (Series 1) (No. 1519) . . 60 30
2027 120 c. on 60 c. Plate No. 10 (Series 1) (No. 1521) . . 50 40
2028 120 c. on 60 c. Plate No. 19 (Series 1) (No. 1522) . . 50 40
2029 120 c. on 60 c. Plate No. 31 (Series 1) (No. 1523) . . 50 40
2030 120 c. on 60 c. Plate No. 5 (Series 1) 50 40
2403 120 c. on 60 c. Plate No. 50 (Series 1) 60 40
2404 120 c. on 60 c. Plate No. 54 (Series 1) 60 40
2405 120 c. on 60 c. Plate No. 69 (Series 1) 60 40
2034 120 c. on 60 c. Plate No. 71 (Series 1) 50 40
2406 120 c. on 60 c. Plate No. 79 (Series 1) 60 40
2036 120 c. on 60 c. Plate No. 87 (Series 1) 50 40
2407 120 c. on 60 c. Plate No. 94 (Series 1) 60 40
2038 120 c. on 75 c. Plate No. 60 (Series 1) 50 40
2039 120 c. on 75 c. Plate No. 83 (Series 1) 50 40
2040 120 c. on 75 c. Plate No. 92 (Series 1) 50 40
2041 120 c. on 75 c. Plate No. 95 (Series 1) 50 40
1933 200 c. on 25 c. Plate No. 8 (Series 1) (No. 1571) . . 60 50
1934 200 c. on 25 c. Plate No. 51 (Series 1) (No. 1573) . . 60 50
1949 200 c. on 25 c. Plate No. 52 (Series 1) (No. 1551) . . 60 50
1951 200 c. on 25 c. Plate No. 72 (Series 1) (No. 1577) . . 60 50
1952 200 c. on 25 c. Plate No. 71 (Series 1) (No. 1679) . . 60 50
1953 200 c. on 30 c. Plate No. 86 (Series 1) (No. 1731) . . 60 50
1954 200 c. on 30 c. Plate No. 53 (Series 1) (No. 1771) . . 60 50
1932 200 c. on 40 c. Plate No. 90 (Series 1) 60 50
1937 200 c. on 40 c. Plate No. 68 (Series 1) (No. 1884) . . 60 50
1955 200 c. on 40 c. Plate No. 77 (Series 1) (No. 1663) . . 60 50
1956 200 c. on 40 c. Plate No. 86 (Series 1) (No. 1868) . . 60 50
1957 200 c. on 45 c. Plate No. 81 (Series 1) (No. 1748) . . 60 50
1958 200 c. on 45 c. Plate No. 77 (Series 1) 60 50
1959 200 c. on 45 c. Plate No. 78 (Series 1) 60 50
1960 200 c. on 45 c. Plate No. 85 (Series 1) 60 50
2044 200 c. on 45 c. Plate No. 84 (Series 1) 50 40
1939 200 c. on 50 c. Plate No. 92 (Series 1) (No. 1665) . . 60 50
1940 200 c. on 50 c. Plate No. 22 (Series 1) 60 50
1961 200 c. on 50 c. Plate No. 24 (Series 1) 60 50
1962 200 c. on 50 c. Plate No. 53 (Series 1) 60 50
1963 200 c. on 50 c. Plate No. 65 (Series 1) 60 50

2046 200 c. on 50 c. Plate No. 55 (Series 1) (No. 1927) . . . 90 50
1941 200 c. on 55 c. Plate No. 22 (Series 1) (No. 1764) . . . 60 50
1964 200 c. on 55 c. Plate No. 49 (Series 1) (No. 1765) . . . 60 50
1965 200 c. on 55 c. Plate No. 17 (Series 1) (No. 1732) . . . 60 50
2050 200 c. on 55 c. Plate No. 15 (Series 1) . . . . 2·00 50
2051 200 c. on 55 c. Plate No. 81 (Series 1) . . . . 2·00 50
2052 200 c. on 55 c. Plate No. 82 (Series 1) . . . . 5·00 50
2053 200 c. on 55 c. Plate No. 89 (Series 1) . . . . 2·00 50
1942 200 c. on 60 c. Plate No. 5 (Series 1) 60 50
1967 200 c. on 60 c. Plate No. 7 (Series 1) (No. 1520) . . . 60 50
1968 200 c. on 60 c. Plate No. 10 (Series 1) (No. 1521) . . . 60 50
1969 200 c. on 60 c. Plate No. 19 (Series 1) (No. 1522) . . . 60 50
1970 200 c. on 60 c. Plate No. 31 (Series 1) (No. 1523) . . . 60 50
1971 200 c. on 60 c. Plate No. 44 (Series 1) (No. 1556) . . . 60 50
1972 200 c. on 60 c. Plate No. 47 (Series 1) (No. 1557) . . . 60 50
1973 200 c. on 60 c. Plate No. 57 (Series 1) (No. 1622) . . . 60 50
1974 200 c. on 60 c. Plate No. 73 (Series 1) (No. 1623) . . . 60 50
1975 200 c. on 60 c. Plate No. 75 (Series 1) (No. 1624) . . . 60 50
1976 200 c. on 60 c. Plate No. 71 (Series 1) 60 50
1977 200 c. on 60 c. Plate No. 87 (Series 1) 60 50
1943 200 c. on 75 c. Plate No. 5 (Series 1) (No. 1667) . . . 60 50
1944 200 c. on 75 c. Plate No. 60 (Series 1) 60 50
1945 200 c. on 75 c. Plate No. 92 (Series 1) 60 50
1946 200 c. on 85 c. Plate No. 18 (Series 2) (No. 1928) . . . 60 50
1947 200 c. on 375 c. Plate No. 90 (Series 1) (No. 1738) . . . 60 50
1987 225 c. on 40 c. Plate No. 91 (Series 1) (No. 1822) . . . 70 60
1988 225 c. on 40 c. Plate No. 90 (Series 1) 70 60
2055 225 c. on 40 c. Plate No. 86 (Series 1) (No. 1868) . . . 1·25 60
2056 225 c. on 40 c. Plate No. 68 (Series 1) (No. 1884) . . . 90 60
1988a 225 c. on 50 c. Plate No. 92 (Series 1) (No. 1665) . . . 10·00 3·00
1989 225 c. on 50 c. Plate No. 22 (Series 1) 70 60
1990 225 c. on 60 c. Plate No. 55 (Series 1) (No. 1597) . . . 70 60
1990a 225 c. on 60 c. Plate No. 95 (Series 1) (No. 1666) . . . 10·00 3·00
1991 225 c. on 60 c. Plate No. 93 (Series 1) (No. 1733) . . . 70 60
2058 225 c. on 65 c. Plate No. 76 (Series 1) 90 60
2059 225 c. on 65 c. Plate No. 80 (Series 1) 90 60
2060 225 c. on 65 c. Plate No. 88 (Series 1) 90 60
2061 225 c. on 65 c. Plate No. 96 (Series 1) 90 60
1992 225 c. on 80 c. Plate No. 93 (Series 1) 70 60
1978 225 c. on 90 c. Plate No. 89 (Series 1) (No. 1749) . . . 65 55
1993 225 c. on 150 c. Plate No. 42 (Series 1) (No. 1657) . . . 70 60
2062 600 c. on 80 c. Plate No. 17 (Series 1) (No. 1885) . . . 1·50 1·50
2063 600 c. on 80 c. Plate No. 39 (Series 1) . . . . 1·50 1·50
2064 600 c. on 80 c. Plate No. 74 (Series 1) . . . . 1·50 1·50
2065 600 c. on 80 c. Plate No. 93 (Series 1) . . . . 1·50 1·50

1987. Nos. 1518 and 1572 surch **TWO DOLLARS**.
1935 $2 on 25 c. Plate No. 12 (Series 1) (No. 1518) . . . 60 50
1936 $2 on 25 c. Plate No. 23 (Series 1) (No. 1572) . . . 60 50

1987. Various "Reichenbachia" issues surch. **1987**.
1983 $10 on 25 c. Plate No. 53 (Series 1) . . . . 2·00 2·25
1984 $12 on 80 c. Plate No. 74 (Series 1) . . . . 2·25 2·50
1985 $15 on 80 c. Plate No. 39 (Series 1) . . . . 2·75 3·00
1986 $25 on 25 c. Plate No. 53 (Series 1) . . . . 4·50 5·00

1987. Centenary of Publication of Sanders' "Reichenbachia" (19th issue). Multicoloured.
2066 180 c. Plate 41 (Series 2) . . 1·25 40
2067 230 c. Plate 25 (Series 2) . . 1·40 50
2068 300 c. Plate 85 (Series 2) . . 2·00 65
2069 330 c. Plate 82 (Series 2) . . 2·25 70
2070 425 c. Plate 87 (Series 2) . . 2·50 85
2071 440 c. Plate 88 (Series 2) . . 2·50 85
2072 590 c. Plate 52 (Series 2) . . 2·50 1·25
2073 650 c. Plate 65 (Series 2) . . 3·25 1·50

1987. 10th Anniv of Guyana Post Office Corporation (2nd issue). Nos. 543, 545, 548a and 601 surch **Post Office Corp. 1977-1987**.
2074 25 c. on 2 c. Type **132** . . . 15 10
2075 25 c. on 5 c. Annatto tree . . 15 10
2076 25 c. on 8 c. on 6 c. Cannon-ball tree 15 10
2077 25 c. on 15 c. Christmas orchid 1·25 10
2078 60 c. on 15 c. Christmas orchid 2·50 15
2079 $1.20 on 2 c. Type **132** . . . 75 65
2080 $1.30 on 15 c. Christmas orchid 3·00 85

1987. No. 1535b surch **1987 200**.
2081 **332** 200 c. on 25 c. mult . . 85 85

1987. Various "Reichenbachia" issues optd **1987**.
2112 120 c. Plate No. 1 (Series 1) (No. 1578) . . . . 2·00 60
2113 120 c. Plate No. 11 (Series 1) (No. 1579) . . . . 1·50 60
2114 120 c. Plate No. 28 (Series 1) (No. 1580) . . . . 2·00 60
2115 120 c. Plate No. 37 (Series 1) (No. 1627) . . . . 1·00 60
2116 120 c. Plate No. 46 (Series 1) (No. 1628) . . . . 4·50 60
2117 120 c. Plate No. 56 (Series 1) (No. 1629) . . . . 1·50 60
2118 120 c. Plate No. 58 (Series 1) (No. 1630) . . . . 1·50 60
2132 120 c. Plate No. 67 (Series 1) (No. 1631) 50 40
2084 130 c. Plate No. 3 (Series 1) (No. 1525) 50 40
2093 130 c. Plate No. 6 (Series 1) (No. 1759) 50 40
2094 130 c. Plate No. 20 (Series 1) (No. 1761) 50 40
2087 130 c. Plate No. 18 (Series 1) (No. 1536) 50 40
2088 130 c. Plate No. 29 (Series 1) (No. 1537) 50 40
2089 130 c. Plate No. 30 (Series 1) (No. 1538) 50 40
2090 130 c. Plate No. 16 (Series 1) (No. 1559) 50 40
2091 130 c. Plate No. 66 (Series 1) (No. 1632) 50 40
2092 130 c. Plate No. 13 (Series 1) (No. 1684) 50 40
2109 130 c. Plate No. 91 (Series 1) (No. 1735) 50 40
2111 130 c. Plate No. 25 (Series 1) (No. 1762) 50 40
2123 150 c. Plate No. 40 (Series 1) (No. 1767) . . . . 1·25 70
2124 150 c. Plate No. 45 (Series 1) (No. 1769) . . . . 1·00 70
2125 150 c. Plate No. 42 (Series 1) (No. 1657) . . . . 3·00 70
2137 150 c. Plate No. 26 (Series 1) (No. 1633) 50 50
2095 200 c. Plate No. 4 (Series 1) (No. 1533) 60 50
2096 200 c. Plate No. 14 (Series 1) (No. 1584) 60 50
2097 200 c. Plate No. 21 (Series 1) (No. 1585) 60 50
2098 200 c. Plate No. 33 (Series 1) (No. 1634) 60 50
2099 200 c. Plate No. 43 (Series 1) (No. 1658) 60 50
2100 200 c. Plate No. 79 (Series 1) (No. 1670) 60 50
2101 200 c. Plate No. 9 (Series 2) (No. 1816) 60 50
2102 200 c. Plate No. 2 (Series 2) (No. 1886) 60 50
2103 250 c. Plate No. 74 (Series 1) (No. 1736) 70 60
2104 260 c. Plate No. 39 (Series 1) (No. 1737) 70 60

1987. 12th World Orchid Conference, Tokyo (2nd issue). Nos. 1763 surch **12th World Orchid Conference 650**.
2138 650 c. on 55 c. Plate No. 9 (Series 1) . . . . 3·50 2·50

1987. 125th Anniv of British Guiana Post Office (3rd issue). No. 699 surch **25** and names of postal agencies opened by 1885.
2140 25 c. on 10 c. multicoloured (surch **AGRICOLA**) . . . 50 30
2141 25 c. on 10 c. multicoloured (surch **BAGOTVILLE**) . . 50 30
2142 25 c. on 10 c. multicoloured (surch **BOURDA**) 50 30
2143 25 c. on 10 c. multicoloured (surch **BUXTON**) 50 30
2144 25 c. on 10 c. multicoloured (surch **CABACABURI**) . . 50 30
2145 25 c. on 10 c. mult (surch **CARMICHAEL STREET**) . . 50 30
2146 25 c. on 10 c. mult (surch **COTTON TREE**) 50 30
2147 25 c. on 10 c. multicoloured (surch **DUNOON**) 50 30
2148 25 c. on 10 c. multicoloured (surch **FELLOWSHIP**) . . 50 30
2149 25 c. on 10 c. multicoloured (surch **GROVE**) 50 30
2150 25 c. on 10 c. multicoloured (surch **HACKNEY**) . . . 50 30
2151 25 c. on 10 c. multicoloured (surch **LEONORA**) . . . 50 30
2152 25 c. on 10 c. mult (surch **1987**) 50 30
2153 25 c. on 10 c. multicoloured (surch **MALLALI**) . . . 50 30
2154 25 c. on 10 c. multicoloured (surch **PROVIDENCE**) . . 50 30
2155 25 c. on 10 c. multicoloured (surch **RELIANCE**) . . . 50 30
2156 25 c. on 10 c. multicoloured (surch **SPARTA**) 50 30
2157 25 c. on 10 c. multicoloured (surch **STEWARTVILLE**) 50 30
2158 25 c. on 10 c. multicoloured (surch **TARLOGY**) . . . 50 30
2159 25 c. on 10 c. mult (surch **T.P.O. BERBICE RIV.**) . . . 50 30
2160 25 c. on 10 c. multicoloured (surch **T.P.O. DEM. RIV.**) 50 30
2161 25 c. on 10 c. multicoloured (surch **T.P.O. ESSEO. RIV.**) 50 30
2162 25 c. on 10 c. mult (surch **T.P.O. MASSARUNI RIV.**) . . . 50 30
2163 25 c. on 10 c. multicoloured (surch **TUSCHEN (De VRIENDEN)**) 50 30
2164 25 c. on 10 c. multicoloured (surch **ZORG**) 50 30

1987. 50th Anniv of First Georgetown to Port-of-Spain Flight by P.A.A. No. 708a optd **28 MARCH 1927 PAA GEO-POS**.
2165 $10 "Elbella patrobas" . . . 8·50 4·50

1987. No. 704 surch **25**.
2166 25 c. on 40 c. "Morpho rhetenor" (male) . . . . . 4·00 10

1987. Easter. Nos. 481/2 and 484 optd **1987** or surch also.
2167 **111** 25 c. multicoloured . . . 30 10
2168 120 c. on 6 c. mult . . . 40 20
2169 320 c. on 6 c. mult . . . 75 55
2170 500 c. on 40 c. mult . . . 1·25 90

1987. Centenary of Publication of Sanders' "Reichenbachia" (20th issue). As T **331**. Mult.
2171 240 c. Plate No. 47 (Series 2) 80 45
2172 260 c. Plate No. 39 (Series 2) 90 55
2173 275 c. Plate No. 58 (Series 2) (horiz) 90 55
2174 390 c. Plate No. 37 (Series 2) (horiz) . . . . 1·10 70
2175 450 c. Plate No. 19 (Series 2) (horiz) . . . . 1·50 90
2176 460 c. Plate No. 54 (Series 2) (horiz) . . . . 1·50 90
2177 500 c. Plate No. 51 (Series 2) 1·75 1·10
2178 560 c. Plate No. 1 (Series 2) . 2·00 1·50

1987. No. 706 optd **1987**.
2179 **167** $1 multicoloured . . . . 3·00 15

1987. Centenary of Publication of Sanders' "Reichenbachia" (21st issue). As T **331**. Mult.
2180 500 c. Plate No. 86 (Series 2) 1·75 1·10
2181 520 c. Plate No. 89 (Series 2) 1·90 1·25
2182 $20 Plate No. 83 (Series 2) . . 6·00 7·00

1987. As T **332** but within frame.
2183 25 c. multicoloured 30 30
2184 25 c. multicoloured 30 30
No. 2183 has a bird with a short tail (as in Type **332**) in the lower part of the arms; No. 2184 has a bird with crest and long tail.

1987. "Capex '87" International Stamp Exhibition, Toronto. Nos. 1744/5 optd **CAPEX '87**.
2185 **363** 320 c. red, black & lilac . 75 1·00
2186 – 320 c. multicoloured . . . 75 1·00

1987. Commonwealth Heads of Government Meeting, Vancouver. Nos. 1066/8 further optd **1987**.
2187 $1.20 on 6 c. green 45 20
2188 $1.30 on 24 c. black & orange 3·00 30
2189 $2.40 on 24 c. black & orange 3·75 90

1987. Centenary of Publication of Sanders' "Reichenbachia" (22nd issue). As T **331**. Mult.
2190 400 c. Plate No. 80 (Series 2) 1·25 80
2191 480 c. Plate No. 77 (Series 2) 1·50 1·00
2192 600 c. Plate No. 94 (Series 2) 2·00 1·50
2193 $25 Plate No. 72 (Series 2) . . 6·50 8·00

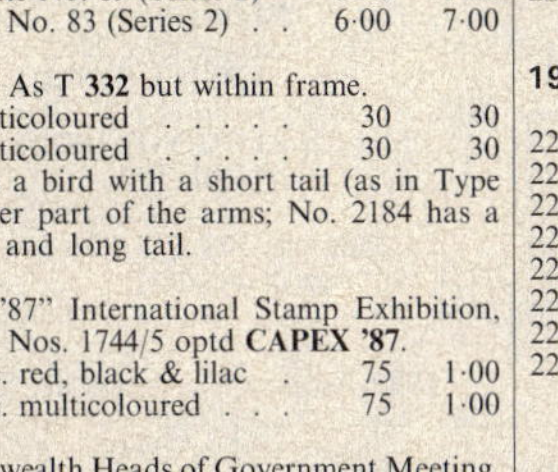

396 Steam Locomotive No. 4 "Alexandra"

1987. Guyana Railways.
2194 **396** $1.20 green 25 30
2195 – $1.20 green 25 30
2196 – $1.20 green 25 30
2197 – $1.20 green 25 30
2198 **396** $1.20 purple 25 30
2199 – $1.20 purple 25 30
2200 – $1.20 purple 25 30
2201 – $1.20 purple 25 30
2202 **396** $3.20 blue 80 90
2203 – $3.20 blue 80 90
2204 – $3.20 blue 80 90
2205 – $3.20 blue 80 90
2206 – $3.20 blue 80 90
2207 – $3.30 black 80 90
2208 **396** $3.30 black 80 90
2209 – $3.30 black 80 90
2210 – $3.30 black 80 90
2211 – $3.30 black 80 90
2212 – $10 multicoloured . . . . 1·00 1·50
2213 – $12 multicoloured . . . . 1·25 1·75
DESIGNS:—As T **396**: Nos. 2195, 2199, 2203, 2207, Front view of diesel locomotive; Nos. 2196, 2200, 2204, 2210, Steam locomotive with searchlight; Nos. 2197, 2201, 2205, 2209, Side view of diesel locomotive No. 21. (82 × 55 mm): No. 2206, Molasses warehouses and early locomotive; No. 2211, Diesel locomotive and passenger train. (88 × 39 mm): No. 2212, Cattle train and Parika–Rosignol Railway route map; No. 2213, Molasses train and Parika–Rosignol Railway route map.

1987. 50th Anniv of First Flights from Georgetown to Massaruni and Mabaruma. No. 706 optd.
2214 $1 multicoloured (optd **FAIREY NICHOLL 8 AUG 1927 GEO-MAZ**) . . . . . 4·00 4·00
2215 $1 multicoloured (optd **FAIREY NICHOLL 15 AUG 1927 GEO-MAB**) . . . . . 4·00 4·00

1987. Centenary of Publication of Sanders' "Reichenbachia" (23rd issue). As T **331**. Mult.
2216 200 c. Plate No. 43 (Series 2) 2·00 65
2217 200 c. Plate No. 48 (Series 2) 2·00 65
2218 200 c. Plate No. 92 (Series 2) 2·00 65

1987. Centenary of Publication of Sanders' "Reichenbachia" (24th issue). No. 2219 surch **600**. Multicoloured.
2219 600 c. on 900 c. Plate No. 74 (Series 2) . . . . 2·25 2·50
2220 900 c. Plate No. 74 (Series 2) 2·25 2·50

1987. Columbus Day.
2221 225 c. on 350 c on 120 c. Plate No. 65 (Series 1) (No. 1598 further surch **225**) 75 40
2222 950 c. on 900 c. Plate No. 74 (Series 2) (No. 2220 surch **950 CRISTOVAO COLOMBO 1492 – 1992**) . . . . 1·75 2·25
2223 950 c. on 900 c. Plate No. 74 (Series 2) (No. 2220 surch **950 CHRISTOPHE COLOMB 1492 – 1992**) . . . . 1·75 2·25

1987. Centenary of Publication of Sanders' "Reichenbachia" (25th issue). As T **331**. Mult.
2225 325 c. Plate No. 68 (Series 2) (horiz) . . . . 2·25 90
2226 420 c. Plate No. 95 (Series 2) (horiz) . . . . 2·50 1·25
2227 575 c. Plate No. 60 (Series 2) 3·00 2·25

1987. Deepavali Festival. Nos. 544/5 surch **DEEPAVALI 1987** and new value.
2228 25 c. on 3 c. Hanging heliconia 30 10
2229 $3 on 5 c. Annatto tree . . . 1·25 60

1987. Christmas. No. 489 surch **CHRISTMAS 1987 20**.
2230 20 c. on 6 c. Black acara ("Patua") 60 10

1987. Royal Ruby Wedding. No. 1684 optd **1987**.
2233 130 c. Plate No. 13 (Series 1) 1·25 30

1987. Centenary of Publication of Sanders' "Reichenbachia" (26th issue). As T **331**. Mult.
2235 255 c. Plate No. 61 (Series 2) 2·00 1·25
2236 290 c. Plate No. 53 (Series 2) 2·25 1·50
2237 375 c. Plate No. 96 (Series 2) 2·75 1·60
2238 680 c. Plate No. 64 (Series 2) 4·00 2·50
2239 720 c. Plate No. 49 (Series 2) 4·50 4·00
2240 750 c. Plate No. 66 (Series 2) 4·50 4·00
2241 800 c. Plate No. 79 (Series 2) 5·00 4·50
2242 850 c. Plate No. 76 (Series 2) 5·00 4·50

1987. Air. No. 1620 surch **AIR 75**.
2243 75 c. on 25 c. Plate No. 59 (Series 1) . . . . 3·00 40

1987. Wildlife Protection. Nos. 756/67 optd **1987**, Nos. 1432/4 surch **Protect our Heritage '87 320** and Nos. 1631/3, 1752/3 and 1847 optd **PROTECT OUR HERITAGE '87**.
2244 30 c. Type **178** 20 15
2245 30 c. Red howler 20 15
2246 30 c. Common squirrel-monkey 20 15
2247 30 c. Two-toed sloth 20 15
2248 30 c. Brazilian tapir 20 15
2249 30 c. Collared peccary . . . 20 15
2250 30 c. Six-banded armadillo . 20 15
2251 30 c. Tamandua 20 15
2252 30 c. Giant anteater 20 15
2253 30 c. Murine opossum . . . 20 15
2254 30 c. Brown four-eyed opossum 20 15
2255 30 c. Brazilian agouti 20 15
2256 120 c. Plate No. 67 (Series 1) 50 30
2257 130 c. Plate No. 66 (Series 1) 50 30
2258 150 c. Plate No. 26 (Series 1) 55 35
2259 180 c. Plate No. 15 (Series 1) 60 40
2260 320 c. Plate No. 82 (Series 1) 80 60
2261 320 c. on 120 c. Demerara Mutual Life Assurance Building 80 80
2262 320 c. on 120 c. Town Hall . . 80 80
2263 320 c. on 120 c. Victoria Law Courts 80 80
2264 650 c. on 40 c. Plate No. 86 (Series 1) . . . . 2·00 2·00

1987. Air. Various "Reichenbachia" issues optd **AIR**.
2265 60 c. Plate No. 55 (Series 1) (No. 1597) . . . . 3·50 4·00
2463 75 c. Plate No. 55 (Series 1) (No. 1772) 90 55
2464 75 c. Plate No. 5 (Series 1) (No. 1667) 90 55
2466 75 c. Plate No. 83 (Series 1) . 90 55
2467 75 c. Plate No. 95 (Series 1) . 90 55

1988. World Scout Jamboree, Australia. No. 837a optd **AUSTRALIA 1987 JAMBOREE 1988** and Nos. 830, 837a and 1104 surch **$10 AUSTRALIA 1987 JAMBOREE 1988**.
2266 **116** 440 c. on 6 c. mult (No. 837a) . . . . 3·75 30
2267 $10 on 110 c. on 6 c. mult (No. 830) 75 70
2268 $10 on 180 c. on 6 c. mult (No. 1104) 75 70
2269a $10 on 440 c. on 6 c. mult (No. 837a) 75 70

1988. 10th Anniv of International Fund for Agricultural Development. Nos. 448 and 450 surch **IFAD For a World Without Hunger**.
2270 25 c. on 1 c. Type **87** 30 10
2271 $5 on 3 c. Lukunani . . . . 1·25 70

1988 Republic Day. Nos. 545, 548a and 555 surch **Republic Day 1988**.
2272 25 c. on 5 c. Annatto tree . . 10 10
2273 120 c. on 15 c. Christmas orchid 1·75 50
2274 $10 on $2 "Noranthea guianensis" . . . . 2·00 1·75

1988. Centenary of Publication of Sanders' "Reichenbachia" (28th series). As T **331**. Multicoloured.
2276 $10 Plate No. 40 (Series 2) . 1·75 2·00
2277 $12 Plate No. 91 (Series 2) . 1·75 2·00

1988. 125th Anniv of British Guiana Post Office (4th issue). No. 702a surch **25** and names of postal agencies opened between 1886 and 1900.
2278 25 c. on 30 c. multicoloured (surch **Albouystown**) 50 40
2279 25 c. on 30 c. multicoloured (surch **Anns Grove**) 50 40
2280 25 c. on 30 c. multicoloured (surch **Amacura**) 50 40
2281 25 c. on 30 c. multicoloured (surch **Arakaka**) 50 40
2282 25 c. on 30 c. multicoloured (surch **Baramanni**) 50 40
2283 25 c. on 30 c. multicoloured (surch **Cuyuni**) 50 40
2284 25 c. on 30 c. multicoloured (surch **Hope Placer**) 50 40
2285 25 c. on 30 c. multicoloured (surch **H M P S**) 50 40
2286 25 c. on 30 c. mult (surch **Kitty**) 50 40
2287 25 c. on 30 c. multicoloured (surch **M'M'Zorg**) 50 40
2288 25 c. on 30 c. multicoloured (surch **Maccaseema**) 50 40
2289 25 c. on 30 c. mult (surch **1988**) 50 40
2290 25 c. on 30 c. multicoloured (surch **Morawhanna**) 50 40
2291 25 c. on 30 c. multicoloured (surch **Naamryck**) 50 40
2292 25 c. on 30 c. mult (surch **Purini**) 50 40
2293 25 c. on 30 c. multicoloured (surch **Potaro Landing**) 50 40
2294 25 c. on 30 c. multicoloured (surch **Rockstone**) 50 40
2295 25 c. on 30 c. multicoloured (surch **Rosignol**) 50 40
2296 25 c. on 30 c. multicoloured (surch **Stanleytown**) 50 40
2297 25 c. on 30 c. multicoloured (surch **Santa Rosa**) 50 40
2298 25 c. on 30 c. multicoloured (surch **Tumatumari**) 50 40
2299 25 c. on 30 c. multicoloured (surch **Weldaad**) 50 40
2300 25 c. on 30 c. multicoloured (surch **Wismar**) 50 40
2301 25 c. on 30 c. mult (surch **TPO Berbice Railway**) 50 40

1988. Olympic Games, Seoul (1st issue). Nos. 1206/17 further surch **120 Olympic Games 1988**.
2302 120 c. on 55 c. on 125 c. on 35 c. Type **174** 70 70
2303 120 c. on 35 c. on 125 c. on 35 c. Trahira ("Haimara") 70 70
2304 120 c. on 55 c. on 125 c. on 35 c. Electric eel 70 70
2305 120 c. on 55 c. on 125 c. on 35 c. Golden rivulus 70 70
2306 120 c. on 55 c. on 125 c. on 35 c. Golden pencilfish 70 70
2307 120 c. on 55 c. on 125 c. on 35 c. Four-eyed fish 70 70
2308 120 c. on 55 c. on 125 c. on 35 c. Red piranha ("Pirai") 70 70
2309 120 c. on 55 c. on 125 c. on 35 c. Smoking hassar 70 70
2310 120 c. on 55 c. on 125 c. on 35 c. Manta 70 70
2311 120 c. on 55 c. on 125 c. on 35 c. Festive cichlid ("Flying patwa") 70 70
2312 120 c. on 55 c. on 125 c. on 35 c. Arapaima 70 70
2313 120 c. on 55 c. on 125 c. on 35 c. Peacock cichlid ("Lukanani") 70 70
See also Nos. 2476/95.

1988. Centenary of Publication of Sanders' "Reichenbachia" (29th issue). As T **331**. Mult.
2314 320 c. Plate No. 62 (Series 2) 80 40
2315 475 c. Plate No. 73 (Series 2) 1·00 70
2316 525 c. Plate No. 36 (Series 2) 1·50 90
2317 530 c. Plate No. 69 (Series 2) 1·50 90
2318 $15 Plate No. 67 (Series 2) . 3·00 4·00

1988. CARICOM Day. Nos. 545/6 and 555 surch **Caricom Day 1988** and new value.
2319 25 c. on 5 c. Annatto tree 15 10
2320 $1.20 on 6 c. Cannon-ball tree 30 10
2321 $10 on $2 "Norantea guianensis" 2·00 2·00

1988. Centenary of Publication of Sanders' "Reichenbachia" (30th issue). As T **331**. Mult.
2322 700 c. Plate No. 62 (Series 2) 1·50 1·25
2323 775 c. Plate No. 59 (Series 2) 1·75 1·40
2324 875 c. Plate No. 31 (Series 2) 2·00 1·50
2325 950 c. Plate No. 78 (Series 2) 2·25 1·75

1988. 40th Anniv of World Health Day. No. 705a optd.
2326 60 c. "Papilio androgeus" (optd **WHO 1948–1988**) 7·50 8·50
2327 60 c. "Papilio androgeus" (optd **1988**) 15 10

1988. Centenary of Publication of Sanders' "Reichenbachia" (31st issue). As T **331**. Mult.
2328 350 c. Plate No. 74 (Series 2) 90 40

1988. Centenary of Publication of Sanders' "Reichenbachia" (32nd issue). As T **331**, but additionally inscr "1985–1988". Multicoloured.
2329 130 c. Plate No. 73 (Series 2) 85 25
2330 200 c. Plate No. 96 (Series 2) 1·00 30
2331 260 c. Plate No. 16 (Series 2) 1·50 45

1988. Conservation of Resources. (a) Nos. 1444/6 optd.
2333 120 c. Young Ocelot (No. 1444) (optd **CONSERVE TREES**) 50 40
2334 120 c. Young Ocelot (No. 1444) (optd **CONSERVE ELECTRICITY**) 50 40
2335 120 c. Young Ocelot (No. 1444) (optd **CONSERVE WATER**) 50 40
2336 120 c. Type **322** (optd **CONSERVE ELECTRICITY**) 50 40
2337 120 c. Type **322** (optd **CONSERVE WATER**) 50 40
2338 120 c. Type **322** (optd **CONSERVE TREES**) 50 40
2339 120 c. Young Ocelot (No. 1446) (optd **CONSERVE WATER**) 50 40
2340 120 c. Young Ocelot (No. 1446) (optd **CONSERVE TREES**) 50 40
2341 120 c. Young Ocelot (No. 1446) (optd **CONSERVE ELECTRICITY**) 50 40

(b) Nos. 1634, 1670, 1683 and 1774 optd **CONSERVE WATER**.
2342 200 c. Plate No. 33 (Series 1) 50 40
2343 200 c. Plate No. 79 (Series 1) 50 40
2344 225 c. Plate No. 24 (Series 1) 50 40
2345 350 c. Plate No. 94 (Series 1) 50 40

1988. Road Safety Campaign. Nos. 2194/2201 optd.
2346 **396** $1.20 green (optd **BEWARE OF ANIMALS**) 1·00 1·00
2347 – $1.20 green (No. 2195) (optd **BEWARE OF CHILDREN**) 1·00 1·00
2348 – $1.20 green (No. 2196) (optd **DRIVE SAFELY**) 1·00 1·00
2349 – $1.20 green (No. 2197) (optd **DO NOT DRINK AND DRIVE**) 1·00 1·00
2350 **396** $1.20 purple (optd **BEWARE OF ANIMALS**) 1·00 1·00
2351 – $1.20 purple (No. 2199) (optd **BEWARE OF CHILDREN**) 1·00 1·00
2352 – $1.20 purple (No. 2200) (optd **DRIVE SAFELY**) 1·00 1·00
2353 – $1.20 purple (No. 2201) (optd **DO NOT DRINK AND DRIVE**) 1·00 1·00

1988. No. 706 optd **1988** or surch **120**.
2354 $1 "Agrias claudina" 2·50 50
2355 120 c. on $1 "Agrias claudina" 2·50 50

1988. Various "Reichenbachia" issues surch.
2356 120 c. on 25 c. Plate No. 61 (Series 1) (No. 1574) 60 40
2357 120 c. on 25 c. Plate No. 63 (Series 1) (No. 1575) 60 40
2358 120 c. on 25 c. Plate No. 70 (Series 1) (No. 1576) 60 40
2359 120 c. on 25 c. Plate No. 59 (Series 1) (No. 1620) 60 40
2360 120 c. on 25 c. Plate No. 71 (Series 1) (No. 1679) 60 40
2429 120 c. on 25 c. Plate No. 72 (Series 1) (No. 1577) 60 40
2361 120 c. on 30 c. Plate No. 53 (Series 1) (No. 1771) 60 40
2362 120 c. on 30 c. Plate No. 86 (Series 1) (No. 1731) 60 40
2363 120 c. on 30 c. Plate No. 30 (Series 2) (No. 1809) 60 40
2365 120 c. on 30 c. Plate No. 7 (Series 2) 60 40
2366 120 c. on 30 c. Plate No. 14 (Series 2) 60 40
2368 120 c. on 30 c. Plate No. 22 (Series 2) 60 40
2369 120 c. on 30 c. Plate No. 28 (Series 2) 60 40
2371 120 c. on 35 c. Plate No. 45 (Series 2) (No. 1925) 60 40
2372 120 c. on 40 c. Plate No. 77 (Series 1) (No. 1663) 60 40
2374 120 c. on 40 c. Plate No. 96 (Series 1) (No. 1747) 60 40
2377 120 c. on 40 c. Plate No. 86 (Series 1) (No. 1868) 60 40
2378 120 c. on 40 c. Plate No. 68 (Series 1) (No. 1884) 60 40
2381 120 c. on 45 c. Plate No. 54 (Series 1) (No. 1664) 60 40
2382 120 c. on 45 c. Plate No. 81 (Series 1) (No. 1748) 60 40
2383 120 c. on 45 c. Plate No. 21 (Series 2) (No. 1810) 60 40
2384 120 c. on 50 c. Plate No. 92 (Series 1) (No. 1665) 60 40
2385 120 c. on 50 c. Plate No. 13 (Series 2) (No. 1907) 60 40
2386 120 c. on 50 c. Plate No. 15 (Series 2) (No. 1926) 60 40
2393 120 c. on 55 c. Plate No. 17 (Series 1) (No. 1732) 60 40
2395 120 c. on 60 c. Plate No. 57 (Series 1) (No. 1622) 60 40
2397 120 c. on 60 c. Plate No. 73 (Series 1) (No. 1623) 60 40
2398 120 c. on 60 c. Plate No. 75 (Series 1) (No. 1624) 60 40
2400 120 c. on 60 c. Plate No. 95 (Series 1) (No. 1666) 60 40
2401 120 c. on 60 c. Plate No. 93 (Series 1) (No. 1733) 60 40
2402 120 c. on 60 c. Plate No. 27 (Series 2) (No. 1874) 60 40
2408 120 c. on 70 c. Plate No. 8 (Series 2) 60 40
2409 120 c. on 70 c. Plate No. 9 (Series 2) 60 40
2411 120 c. on 70 c. Plate No. 12 (Series 2) 60 40
2413 120 c. on 70 c. Plate No. 17 (Series 2) 60 40
2414 120 c. on 80 c. Plate No. 39 (Series 1) 60 40
2415 120 c. on 80 c. Plate No. 74 (Series 1) 60 40
2416 120 c. on 80 c. Plate No. 93 (Series 1) 60 40
2417 120 c. on 85 c. Plate No. 45 (Series 2) (No. 1876) 60 40
2418 120 c. on 85 c. Plate No. 24 (Series 2) (No. 1914) 60 40
2419 120 c. on 85 c. Plate No. 15 (Series 2) (No. 1918) 60 40
2420 120 c. on 85 c. Plate No. 18 (Series 2) (No. 1928) 60 40
2421 120 c. on 90 c. Plate No. 84 (Series 1) (No. 1668) 60 40
2422 120 c. on 90 c. Plate No. 89 (Series 1) (No. 1749) 60 40
2423 120 c. on 90 c. Plate No. 10 (Series 2) (No. 1869) 60 40
2424 120 c. on 90 c. Plate No. 13 (Series 2) (No. 1877) 60 40
2425 120 c. on 90 c. Plate No. 27 (Series 2) (No. 1915) 60 40
2426 120 c. on 90 c. Plate No. 2 (Series 2) (No. 1929) 60 40
2427 200 c. on 80 c. Plate No. 42 (Series 2) (No. 1812) 60 40
2428 200 c. on 90 c. Plate No. 4 (Series 2) (No. 1813) 60 40
2430 240 c. on 140 c. Plate No. 30 (Series 2) 60 40
2431 240 c. on 140 c. Plate No. 34 (Series 2) 60 40
2432 240 c. on 425 c. Plate No. 87 (Series 2) (No. 2070) 60 40
2433 260 c. on 375 c. Plate No. 90 (Series 1) (No. 1378) 60 40

1988. Conservation of Resources. Various "Reichenbachia" issues optd **CONSERVE OUR RESOURCES**.
2434 100 c. Plate No. 65 (Series 1) (No. 1773) 60 40
2435 100 c. Plate No. 68 (Series 1) (No. 1734) 60 40
2436 100 c. Plate No. 88 (Series 1) (No. 1750) 60 40
2438 120 c. Plate No. 27 (Series 1) (No. 1524) 60 40
2439 120 c. Plate No. 36 (Series 1) (No. 1558) 60 40
2440 120 c. Plate No. 37 (Series 1) (No. 1627) 60 40
2441 120 c. Plate No. 56 (Series 1) (No. 1629) 60 40
2442 120 c. Plate No. 58 (Series 1) (No. 1630) 60 40
2443 120 c. Plate No. 67 (Series 1) (No. 1631) 60 40
2444 120 c. Plate No. 69 (Series 1) (No. 1680) 60 40
2445 130 c. Plate No. 38 (Series 1) (No. 1560) 60 40
2446 130 c. Plate No. 66 (Series 1) (No. 1632) 60 40
2447 130 c. Plate No. 91 (Series 1) (No. 1735) 60 40
2448 130 c. Plate No. 13 (Series 1) (No. 1760) 60 40
2249 130 c. Plate No. 20 (Series 1) (No. 1761) 60 40
2450 150 c. Plate No. 26 (Series 1) (No. 1633) 60 40
2451 150 c. Plate No. 78 (Series 1) (No. 1669) 60 40
2452 150 c. Plate No. 87 (Series 1) (No. 1681) 60 40
2453 150 c. Plate No. 76 (Series 1) (No. 1751) 60 40
2454 250 c. Plate No. 74 (Series 1) (No. 1736) 60 40

1988. 125th Anniv of International Red Cross. Nos. 2202/5 and 2207/10 optd with cross.
2455 **396** $3.20 blue 80 80
2456 – $3.20 blue (No. 2203) 80 80
2457 – $3.20 blue (No. 2204) 80 80
2458 – $3.20 blue (No. 2205) 80 80
2459 – $3.30 black (No. 2207) 80 80
2460 **396** $3.30 black 80 80
2461 – $3.30 black (No. 2209) 80 80
2462 – $3.30 black (No. 2210) 80 80

1988. Centenary of Publication of Sanders' "Reichenbachia" (33rd issue). As T **331**. Mult.
2468 270 c. Plate No. 90 (Series 2) 85 60
2469 360 c. Plate No. 84 (Series 2) 1·25 75
2470 550 c. Plate No. 70 (Series 2) (horiz) 2·00 1·00
2471 670 c. Plate No. 71 (Series 2) (horiz) 2·50 1·75

1988. 60th Anniv of Cricket in Guyana. Nos. 1584, 1670, 1681 and 1815 optd **1928-1988 CRICKET JUBILEE** or surch also.
2472 200 c. Plate No. 14 (Series 1) 9·00 11·00
2473 200 c. Plate No. 79 (Series 1) 1·00 40
2474 800 c. on 150 c. Plate No. 87 (Series 1) 6·00 8·00
2475 800 c. on 160 c. Plate No. 5 (Series 2) 3·25 3·25

1988. Olympic Games, Seoul. (a) Nos. 1628, 1634, 1671, 1681, 1683, 1814, 1818/19, 1880 and 2069 optd **OLYMPIC GAMES 1988** or surch also.
2476 120 c. Plate No. 46 (Series 1) 20 20
2477 130 c. Plate No. 38 (Series 2) 20 20
2478 150 c. Plate No. 87 (Series 1) 20 20
2479 200 c. Plate No. 33 (Series 1) 20 20
2480 300 c. Plate No. 83 (Series 1) 20 20
2481 300 c. on 360 c. Plate No. 34 (Series 2) 30 30
2482 320 c. Plate No. 10 (Series 2) 30 30
2483 330 c. Plate No. 82 (Series 2) 30 30
2484 350 c. Plate No. 94 (Series 1) 30 30
2485 350 c. Plate No. 29 (Series 2) 30 30

(b) Design as No. 1420 but incorrectly inscr "LOS ANGELLES" optd or surch **OLYMPICS 1988** (A) or **KOREA 1988** (B).
2486 $1.20 multicoloured (A) 20 20
2487 $1.20 multicoloured (B) 20 20
2488 130 c. on $1.20 mult (A) 20 20
2489 130 c. on $1.20 mult (B) 20 20
2490 150 c. on $1.20 mult (A) 20 20
2491 150 c. on $1.20 mult (B) 20 20
2492 200 c. on $1.20 mult (A) 25 25
2493 200 c. on $1.20 mult (B) 25 25
2594 350 c. on $1.20 mult (A) 35 35
2495 350 c. on $1.20 mult (B) 35 35

1988. Columbus Day. Nos. 1672/3 optd or surch **V CENTENARY OF THE LANDING OF CHRISTOPHER COLUMBUS IN THE AMERICAS**.
2496 320 c. Plate No. 50 (Series 1) 1·00 30
2497 $15 on 360 c. Plate No. 85 (Series 1) 2·50 3·00

1988. Centenary of Publication of Sanders' "Reichenbachia" (34th issue). As T **331**. Mult.
2498 100 c. Plate No. 44 (Series 2) 1·00 55
2499 130 c. Plate No. 42 (Series 2) (horiz) 1·00 55
2500 140 c. Plate No. 4 (Series 2) . 1·25 65
2501 160 c. Plate No. 50 (Series 2) 1·25 65
2502 175 c. Plate No. 51 (Series 2) 1·50 75
2503 200 c. Plate No. 11 (Series 2) 1·50 75
2504 200 c. Plate No. 23 (Series 2) 1·50 75
2505 200 c. Plate No. 26 (Series 2) 1·50 75
2506 200 c. Plate No. 75 (Series 2) 1·50 75
2507 200 c. Plate No. 93 (Series 2) 1·50 75
2508 250 c. Plate No. 79 (Series 2) 1·75 90
2509 280 c. Plate No. 62 (Series 2) 1·75 1·00
2510 285 c. Plate No. 63 (Series 2) 2·00 1·00
2511 380 c. Plate No. 35 (Series 2) 2·25 1·25

1988. Christmas (1st issue). Various "Reichenbachia" issues optd or surch. (a) Optd or surch **SEASON'S GREETINGS**.
2519 120 c. on 100 c. Plate No. 6 (Series 1) 50 50
2520 120 c. on 100 c. Plate No. 13 (Series 1) 50 50
2521 120 c. on 100 c. Plate No. 20 (Series 1) 50 50
2522 120 c. on 100 c. Plate No. 25 (Series 1) 50 50
2523 120 c. on 100 c. Plate No. 40 (Series 1) (horiz) 20 20
2524 120 c. on 100 c. Plate No. 42 (Series 1) (horiz) 20 20
2525 120 c. on 100 c. Plate No. 43 (Series 1) (horiz) 20 20
2526 120 c. on 100 c. Plate No. 45 (Series 1) (horiz) 20 20
2512 150 c. Plate No. 32 (Series 1) (No. 1561) 50 50
2513 150 c. Plate No. 62 (Series 1) (No. 1566) 50 50
2514 225 c. Plate No. 60 (Series 1) (No. 1682) 50 50
2532 240 c. on 180 c. Plate No. 15 (Series 1) (No. 1752) 50 50
2515 260 c. Plate No. 39 (Series 1) (No. 1737) 50 50
2516 320 c. Plate No. 82 (Series 1) (No. 1753) 50 50
2517 330 c. Plate No. 80 (Series 1) (No. 1754) 50 50
2518 360 c. Plate No. 85 (Series 1) (No. 1673) 50 50

(b) Optd **SEASON'S GREETINGS 1988**.
2527 225 c. Plate No. 24 (Series 1) (No. 1774) 75 75
2528 225 c. Plate No. 60 (Series 1) (No. 1682) 75 75
2530 225 c. on 350 c. on 120 c. Plate No. 65 (Series 1) (No. 2221) 75 75

1988. Christmas (2nd issue). Nos. 489, 1188/91 and 1449 surch or optd **CHRISTMAS 1988**.
2533 – 20 c. on 6 c. mult (No. 489) 10 10
2534 **277** 120 c. brown, blk & bl . 20 25
2535 – 120 c. on 130 c. red, black and blue (No. 1189) . 20 25
2536 – 120 c. on 150 c. violet, black and blue (No. 1190) . 20 25
2537 – 120 c. on 200 c. green, black and blue (No. 1191) . 20 25
2538 – 500 c. on 330 c. mult (No. 1449) 1·00 1·10

1988. AIDS Information Campaign. Nos. 707/8a optd or surch with various slogans.
2539 120 c. on $5 "Morpho deidamia" (A) 1·75 1·75
2540 120 c. on $5 "Morpho deidamia" (B) 1·75 1·75
2541 120 c. on $5 "Morpho deidamia" (C) 1·75 1·75
2542 120 c. on $5 "Morpho deidamia" (D) 1·75 1·75
2543 120 c. on $5 "Morpho deidamia" (E) 1·75 1·75
2544 120 c. on $10 "Elbella patrobas" (A) 1·75 1·75
2545 120 c. on $10 "Elbella patrobas" (B) 1·75 1·75
2546 120 c. on $10 "Elbella patrobas" (C) 1·75 1·75
2547 120 c. on $10 "Elbella patrobas" (D) 1·75 1·75
2548 120 c. on $10 "Elbella patrobas" (E) 1·75 1·75
2549 $2 "Morpho rhetenor" (female) (E) 4·50 1·75
2550 $5 "Morpho deidamia" (E) . 7·00 4·25
2551 $10 "Elbella patrobas" (E) . 8·50 6·00
OVERPRINTS: (A) **Be compassionate towards AIDS victims**; (B) **Get information on AIDS. it may save your life.**; (C) **Get the facts. Education helps to prevent AIDS.**; (D) **Say no to Drugs and limit the spread of AIDS.**; (E) **Protect yourself from AIDS. Better safe than sorry.**

1988. 150th Anniv of Abolition of Slavery (1984) (2nd issue). Designs as Nos. 1547/50, but colours changed.
2552 **337** 25 c. black and brown . 15 10
2553 – 60 c. black and lilac . . . 20 15
2254 – 130 c. black and green . 25 40
2555 – 150 c. black and blue . . 30 45

1989. Olympic Medal Winners, Seoul. Nos. 1672, 1923 and 2178 surch **SALUTING WINNERS OLYMPIC GAMES 1988**.
2556 550 c. on 560 c. Plate No. 1 (Series 2) . . . . 1·00 1·00
2557 900 c. on 320 c. Plate No. 18 (Series 2) . . . . 1·50 1·75
2558 1050 c. on 320 c. Plate No. 50 (Series 1) . . . . 2·00 2·25

1989. Republic Day. Nos. 2194/2201 and 2212 optd **REPUBLIC DAY 1989**.
2559 **396** $1.20 green 20 30
2560 – $1.20 green (No. 2195) . 20 30
2561 – $1.20 green (No. 2196) . 20 30
2562 – $1.20 green (No. 2197) . 20 30
2563 **396** $1.20 purple 20 30
2564 – $1.20 purple (No. 2199) . 20 30
2565 – $1.20 purple (No. 2200) . 20 30
2566 – $1.20 purple (No. 2201) . 20 30
2567 – $10 multicoloured . . . 1·75 2·00

1989. Nos. 2202/5 and 2207/10 surch **$5.00**.
2568 **396** $5 on $3.20 blue . . . . 1·00 1·25
2569 – $5 on $3.20 blue (No. 2203) 1·00 1·25
2570 – $5 on $3.20 blue (No. 2204) 1·00 1·25
2571 – $5 on $3.20 blue (No. 2205) 1·00 1·25
2572 – $5 on $3.30 black (No. 2207) . . . . 1·00 1·25
2573 **396** $5 on $3.30 black . . . . 1·00 1·25
2574 – $5 on $3.30 black (No. 2209) . . . . 1·00 1·25
2575 – $5 on $3.30 black (No. 2210) . . . . 1·00 1·25

1989. Various "Reichenbachia" issues surch.
2576 120 c. on 140 c. Plate No. 25 (Series 2) 80 80
2577 120 c. on 140 c. Plate No. 52 (Series 2) 80 80
2578 120 c. on 140 c. Plate No. 65 (Series 2) 80 80
2580 120 c. on 140 c. Plate No. 38 (Series 2) 80 80
2581 120 c. on 140 c. Plate No. 41 (Series 2) 80 80
2579 120 c. on 175 c. Plate No. 54 (Series 2) 80 80
2582 170 c. on 175 c. Plate No. 58 (Series 2) 90 90
2583 250 c. on 280 c. Plate No. 66 (Series 2) . . . . 1·25 1·25
2584 250 c. on 280 c. Plate No. 67 (Series 2) . . . . 1·25 1·25
2585 300 c. on 290 c. Plate No. 53 (Series 2) (No. 2236) . . 1·40 1·40

1989. Nos. 1744/5 and 2185/6 surch **TEN DOLLARS $10.00** (Nos. 2586, 2588) or **TEN DOLLARS** (Nos. 2587, 2589).
2586 **363** $10 on 320 c. red, black and lilac (No. 1744) . . . . 1·50 2·00
2587 – $10 on 320 c. mult (No. 1745) . . . . 1·50 2·00
2588 **363** $10 on 320 c. red, black and lilac (No. 2185) . . . . 1·50 2·00
2589 – $10 on 320 c. mult (No. 2186) . . . . 1·50 2·00

1989. Nos. O54/7, O59/63 and O65/9 optd **POSTAGE** or surch also.
2591 125 c. on 130 c. Plate No. 92 (Series 2) 60 60
2592 125 c. on 140 c. Plate No. 36 (Series 2) 60 60
2593 150 c. Plate No. 43 (Series 2) 60 60
2594 150 c. on 175 c. Plate No. 31 (Series 2) 60 60
2595 250 c. Plate No. 59 (Series 2) 75 75
2596 250 c. on 225 c. Plate No. 26 (Series 2) 75 75
2597 250 c. on 230 c. Plate No. 68 (Series 2) 75 75
2598 250 c. on 275 c. Plate No. 69 (Series 2) 75 75
2599 300 c. on 275 c. Plate No. 90 (Series 2) 75 75
2750 350 c. Plate No. 95 (Series 2) 75 75
2601 350 c. on 330 c. Plate No. 23 (Series 2) 60 60
2602 600 c. Plate No. 70 (Series 2) 1·00 1·00
2603 $12 Plate No. 71 (Series 2) . 1·75 2·00
2604 $15 Plate No. 84 (Series 2) . 2·00 2·25

1989. Centenary of Publication of Sanders' "Reichenbachia" (35th issue). As T **331**. Mult.
2605 200 c. Plate No. 49 (Series 2) 50 50
2606 200 c. Plate No. 53 (Series 2) 50 50
2607 200 c. Plate No. 60 (Series 2) 50 50
2608 200 c. Plate No. 64 (Series 2) 50 50

1989. No. 1442 surch **250**.
2609 **322** 250 c. on 25 c. mult . . . 1·00 15

1989. 40th Anniv of Guyana Red Cross. No. 1872 surch **RED CROSS 1948 1988** and new value.
2610 375 c. on 45 c. Plate No. 17 (Series 2) . . . . 1·25 65
2611 425 c. on 45 c. Plate No. 17 (Series 2) . . . . 1·25 65

1989. World Health Day. Nos. 1875 and 2239 surch with new value and inscr as indicated.
2612 250 c. on 75 c. Plate No. 56 (Series 2) surch **HEALTH FOR ALL** 65 65
2613 250 c. on 75 c. Plate No. 56 (Series 2) surch **ALL FOR HEALTH** 65 65
2614 675 c. on 720 c. Plate No. 49 (Series 2) surch **ALL FOR HEALTH** . . . . 1·25 1·25
2615 675 c. on 720 c. Plate No. 49 (Series 2) surch **HEALTH FOR ALL** . . . . 1·25 1·25

1989. Scouting Anniversaries. Nos. 1873, 1879, 2322, 2509 and unissued value as No. 1873 optd or surch also.
2616 250 c. on 50 c. Plate No. 33 (Series 2) (surch **BOY SCOUTS 1909 1989**) . . . 60 60
2617 250 c. on 50 c. Plate No. 33 (Series 2) (surch **GIRL GUIDES 1924 1989**) . . . 60 60
2618 250 c. on 100 c. Plate No. 33 (Series 2) (surch **BOY SCOUTS 1909 1989**) . . . 60 60
2619 250 c. on 100 c. Plate No. 33 (Series 2) (surch **GIRL GUIDES 1924 1989**) . . . 60 60
2620 300 c. Plate No. 50 (Series 2) (optd **BOY SCOUTS 1909 1989**) 75 75
2621 300 c. Plate No. 50 (Series 2) (optd **GIRL GUIDES 1924 1989**) 75 75
2622 $25 on 280 c. Plate No. 62 (Series 2) (surch **LADY BADEN POWELL 1889 - 1989**) . . . . 3·50 4·00
2623 $25 on 700 c. Plate No. 62 (Series 2) (surch **LADY BADEN POWELL 1889 - 1989**) . . . . 3·50 4·00

The events commemorated are the 80th anniv of Boy Scout Movement in Guyana, 65th anniv of Girl Guide Movement in Guyana and birth centenary of Lady Baden-Powell.

1989. 150 Years of Photography. No. 1881 surch **PHOTOGRAPHY 1839-1989** and new value.
2624 550 c. on 390 c. Plate No. 6 (Series 2) 70 70
2625 650 c. on 390 c. Plate No. 6 (Series 2) 70 70

1989. 70th Anniv of International Labour Organization. No. 1875 surch **I.L.O. 1919-1989 300**.
2627 300 c. on 75 c. Plate No. 56 (Series 2) . . . . 3·00 40

1989. Various stamps surch.
2628 80 c. on 6 c. Patua (No. 489) 40 20
2629 $1 on 2 c. Type **132** 40 20
2630 $2.05 on 3 c. Hanging heliconia (No. 544) 40 25
2641 $2.55 on 5 c. Annatto tree (No. 545) 40 25
2642 $3.25 on 6 c. Cannon-ball tree (No. 546) 40 25
2633 $5 on 6 c. Type **111** 40 30
2634 $6.40 on 10 c. "Archonias bellona" (No. 699) . . . 2·75 75
2648 $6.40 on $3.30 black (No. 2207) . . . . 2·50 1·50
2649 $6.40 on $3.30 black (No. 2208) . . . . 2·50 1·50
2650 $6.40 on $3.30 black (No. 2209) . . . . 2·50 1·50
2651 $6.40 on $3.30 black (No. 2210) . . . . 2·50 1·50
2646 640 c. on 675 c. on 720 c. Plate No. 49 (Series 2) (No. 2614) 1·25 1·25
2647 640 c. on 675 c. on 720 c. Plate No. 49 (Series 2) (No. 2615) 1·25 1·25
2637a $7.65 on 35 c. "Anaea galanthus" (No. 703) . 3·25 80
2638 $7.65 on 40 c. "Morpho retenor" (male) (No. 704) 3·25 80
2652 $7.65 on $3.20 blue (No. 2202) 2·50 1·50
2653 $7.65 on $3.20 blue (No. 2203) 2·50 1·50
2654 $7.65 on $3.20 blue (No. 2204) 2·50 1·50
2655 $7.65 on $3.20 blue (No. 2205) 2·50 1·50
2635 $8.90 on 60 c. "Papilio androgeus" (No. 705a) . 3·75 85
2643 $50 on $2 "Morpho rhetenor" (female) (No. 707) . 10·00 3·50
2644 $100 on $2 "Morpho rhetenor" (female) (No. 707) 15·00 8·50

1989. CARICOM Day. No. 1878 surch **CARICOM DAY 125**.
2656 125 c. on 200 c. Plate No. 44 (Series 2) . . . . 1·50 30

454 "Stalachtis calliope"

455 Kathryn Sullivan (first U.S. woman to walk in space)

1989. Butterflies (1st series). Multicoloured.
2657 80 c. Type **454** 40 10
2658 $2.25 "Morpho rhetenor" . 50 10
2659 $5 "Agrias claudia" . . . 55 10
2660 $6.40 "Marpesia marcella" . 60 15
2661 $7.65 "Papilio zagreus" . . 65 20
2662 $8.90 "Chorinea faunus" . . 80 25
2663 $25 "Euptychia cephus" . . 2·25 2·25
2664 $100 "Nessaea regina" . . . 6·00 7·00
See also Nos. 2789/2860.

1989. 25 Years of Women in Space. Mult.
2665 $6.40 Type **455** 40 15
2666 $12.80 Svetlana Savitskaya (first Soviet woman to walk in space) 65 35
2667 $15.30 Judy Resnik and Christa McAuliffe with "Challenger" logo 65 35
2668 $100 Sally Ride (first U.S. woman astronaut) . . . 4·00 5·00

1989. Centenary of Ahmadiyya (Moslem organization). Nos. 543/5 surch **AHMADIYYA CENTENARY 1899-1989**.
2669 80 c. on 2 c. Type **132** . . . . 1·25 40
2670 $6.40 on 3 c. Hanging heliconia 5·00 2·75
2671 $8.90 on 5 c. Annatto tree . . 6·00 3·50

457 Head of Harpy Eagle

458 Channel-billed Toucan

1990. Endangered Species. Harpy Eagle. Multicoloured.
2672 $2.25 Type **457** 50 25
2673 $5 Harpy eagle with monkey prey 75 30
2674 $8.90 Eagle on branch (facing right) . . . . 1·10 50
2675 $30 Eagle on branch (facing left) 3·00 3·50

1990. Birds of Guyana. Multicoloured.
2676 $15 Type **458** 90 70
2677 $25 Blue and yellow macaw . 1·40 50
2678 $50 Wattled jacana (horiz) . . 2·75 2·25
2679 $60 Hoatzin . . . . 3·00 2·50

1990. 85th Anniv of Rotary International. Optd **Rotary International 1905–1990** and emblem. (a) On Nos. 2657/64.
2681 80 c. Type **454** 60 20
2682 $2.25 "Morpho rhetenor" . . 90 30
2683 $5 "Agrias claudia" . . . . 1·25 30
2684 $6.40 "Marpesia marcella" . . 1·40 35
2685 $7.65 "Papilio zagreus" . . . 1·50 50
2686 $8.90 "Chorinea faunus" . . 1·60 55
2687 $25 "Euptychia cephus" . . 2·75 3·25
2688 $100 "Nessaea regina" . . . 8·00 9·00

(b) On Nos. 2665/8.
2689 $6.40 Type **455** 85 40
2690 $12.80 Svetlana Savitskaya (first Soviet woman to walk in space) . . . . 1·50 80
2691 $15.30 Judy Resnik and Christa McAuliffe with "Challenger" logo . . . . 1·60 90
2692 $100 Sally Ride (first U.S. woman astronaut) . . . 6·00 7·00

460 Indian Post Runner, 1837

1990. 150th Anniv of the Penny Black and 500th Anniv of Thurn and Taxis Postal Service. Multicoloured.
2693/2746 $15.30 × 27, $17.80 × 9, $20 × 18
Set of 54 . . . . . . 23·00 26·00
Nos. 2693/2746 depict various forms of mail transport.

1990. 9th Conference of Rotary District 405, Georgetown. Nos. 1759, 1762/3 and 1765/6 surch **ROTARY DISTRICT 405 9th CONFERENCE MAY 1990 GEORGETOWN** and new value.
2748 80 c. on 55 c. Plate No. 9 (Series 1)
2749 80 c. on 55 c. Plate No. 49 (Series 1)
2750 80 c. on 55 c. Plate No. 64 (Series 1)
2751 $6.40 on 130 c. Plate No. 6 (Series 1)
2752 $6.40 on 130 c. Plate No. 25 (Series 1)
2753 $7.65 on 130 c. Plate No. 25 (Series 1)

1990. 90th Birthday of Queen Elizabeth the Queen Mother. Nos. 2657/64 surch **90th Birthday H.M. The Queen Mother**.
2754 80 c. Type **454** 40 20
2755 $2.25 "Morpho rhetenor" . . 65 30
2756 $5 "Agrias claudia" 80 30
2757 $6.40 "Marpesia marcella" . . 90 35
2758 $7.65 "Papilio zagreus" . . . 1·00 40
2759 $8.90 "Chorinea faunus" . . 1·25 45
2760 $25 "Euptychia cephus" . . 2·50 2·75
2761 $100 "Nessaea regina" . . . 7·50 8·50

463 Collared Trogon

464 "Melinaea idae"

1990. Birds. Multicoloured.
2762 80 c. Guiana partridge (horiz) 10 10
2763 $2.55 Type **463** 10 10
2764 $3.25 Derby aracari 10 10
2765 $5 Black-necked aracari . . 20 20
2766 $5.10 Green aracari 20 20
2767 $5.80 Ivory-billed aracari . . 20 20
2768 $6.40 Guiana toucanet . . . 20 20
2769 $6.50 Sulphur-breasted toucan 20 20
2770 $7.55 Red-billed toucan . . . 25 25
2771 $7.65 Toco toucan 25 25
2772 $8.25 Natterers toucanet . . 25 25
2773 $8.90 Welcome trogon . . . 25 25
2774 $9.75 Doubtful trogon . . . 25 25
2775 $11.40 Banded aracari . . . 30 30
2776 $12.65 Golden-headed train bearer 30 30
2777 $12.80 Rufous-breasted hermit 30 30
2778 $13.90 Band tail barbthroat . 30 30
2779 $15.30 White-tipped sickle bill 35 35
2780 $17.80 Black jacobin 40 40
2781 $19.20 Fiery topaz 40 40
2782 $22.95 Tufted coquette . . . 45 45
2783 $26.70 Ecuadorian pied-tail . 45 45
2784 $30 Quetzal 50 50
2785 $50 Green-crowned brilliant . 80 80
2786 $100 Emerald-chinned hummingbird . . . . . . 1·50 1·50
2787 $190 Lazuline sabre-wing . . 2·50 2·50
2788 $225 Beryline hummingbird . 2·75 2·75

1990. Butterfiles (2nd series). Multicoloured.
2789/2860 80 c., $2.55, $5, $6.40, $7.65, $8.90, $10 × 64, $50 and $100
Set of 72 . . . . . . 9·50 10·00

DESIGNS—VERT: $2.55, "Rhetus dysonii"; $5 "Actinote anteas"; $6.40, "Heliconius tales"; $7.65, "Thecla telemus"; $8.90, "Theope eudocia"; $10 (2795), "Heleconius vetustus"; 2796, "Mesosemia eumene"; 2797, "Parides phosphorus"; 2798, "Polystichtis emylius"; 2799, "Xanthocleis aedesia"; 2800, "Doxocopa agathina"; 2801, "Adelpha plesaure"; 2802, "Heliconius wallacei"; 2803, "Notheme eumeus"; 2804, "Melinaea mediatrix"; 2805, "Theritas coronata"; 2806, "Dismorphia orise"; 2807, "Phyciodes ianthe"; 2808, "Morpho aega"; 2809, "Zaretis isidora"; 2810, "Pierella lena"; 2811, "Heliconius silvana"; 2812, "Eunica alcmena"; 2813, "Mechanitis polymnia"; 2814, "Mesosemia ephyne"; 2815, "Thecla erema"; 2816, "Callizona acesta"; 2817, "Stalachtis phaedusa"; 2818, "Battus belus"; 2819, "Nymula phliasus"; 2820, "Parides childrenae"; 2821, "Stalachtis euterpe"; 2822, "Dysmathia portia"; 2823, "Tithorea hermias"; 2824, "Prepona pheridamas"; 2825, "Dismorphia fortunata"; 2826, "Hamadryas amphinome"; $50 "Heliconius vicini"; $100 "Amarynthis meneria". HORIZ: $10 (2827), "Thecla falerina"; 2828, "Pheles heliconides"; 2829, "Echenias leucocyana"; 2830, "Heliconius xanthocles"; 2831, "Mesopthalma idotea"; 2832, "Parides aeneas"; 2833, "Heliconius numata"; 2834, "Thecla critola"; 2835, "Themone pais"; 2836, "Nymula agle"; 2837, "Adelpha cocala"; 2838, "Anaea eribotes"; 2839, "Prepona demophon"; 2840, "Selenophanes cassiope"; 2841, "Consul hippona"; 2842, "Antirrhaea avernus"; 2843, "Thecla telemus"; 2844, "Thyridia confusa"; 2845, "Heliconius burneyi"; 2846, "Parides lysander"; 2847, "Eunica orphise"; 2848, "Adelpha melona"; 2849, "Morpho menelaus"; 2850, "Nymula phylleus"; 2851, "Stalachtis phlegia"; 2852, "Theope barea"; 2853, "Morpho perseus"; 2854, "Lycorea ceres"; 2855, "Archonias bellona"; 2856; "Caeronis chorinaeus"; 2857, "Vila azeca"; 2858, "Nessaea batesii".

Nos. 2795/2810, 2811/26, 2827/42 and 2843/58 respectively were printed together, se-tenant, forming composite designs.

465 "Vanilla inodora"

466 Ivory-billed Woodpecker

1990. Flowers. Multicoloured.
2862/2965 $7.65, $8.90, $10 × 32, $12.80 × 65, $15.30, $17.80, $20, $25 and $100
Set of 104 . . . . 12·00 13·00

DESIGNS—VERT: $8.90, "Epidendrum ibaguense"; $10 (2864), "Dichea muricata"; 2865, "Octomeria erosilabia"; 2866, "Spiranthes orchioides"; 2867, "Brassavola nodosa"; 2868, "Epidendrum rigidum"; 2869, "Brassia caudata"; 2870, "Pleurothallis diffusa"; 2871, "Aspasia variegata"; 2872, "Stenia pallida"; 2873, "Cyrtopodium punctatum"; 2874, "Cattleya deckeri"; 2875, "Cryptarrhena lunata"; 2876, "Cattleya violacea"; 2877, "Caularthron bicornutum"; 2878, "Oncidium carthagenense"; 2879, "Galeandra devoniana"; 2880, "Bifrenaria aurantiaca"; 2881, "Epidendrum ciliare"; 2882, "Dichaea picta"; 2883, "Scaphyglottis violacea"; 2884, "Cattleya percivaliana"; 2885, Map and national flag; 2886, "Epidendrum difforme"; 2887, "Eulophia maculata"; 2888, "Spiranthes tenuis"; 2889, "Peristoria guttata"; 2890, "Pleurothallis pruinosa"; 2891, "Cleistes rosea"; 2892, "Maxillaria variabilis"; 2893, "Brassavola cucullata"; 2894,"Epidendrum moyobambae"; 2895, "Oncidium orthostate"; $12.80, "Maxillaria parkeri"; $12.80 (2897), "Brassavola martiana"; 2898, "Paphinia cristata"; 2899, "Aganisia pulchella"; 2900, "Oncidium lanceanum"; 2901, "Lockhartia imbricata"; 2902, "Caularthron bilamellatum"; 2903, "Oncidium nanum"; 2904, "Pleurothallis ovalifolia";

2905, "Galeandra dives"; 2906, "Cycnoches loddigesii"; 2907, "Ada aurantiaca"; 2908, "Catasetum barbatum"; 2909, "Palmorchis pubescens"; 2910, "Epidendrum anceps"; 2911, "Huntleya meleagris"; 2912, "Sobralia sessilis"; $15.30, "Epidendrum nocturnum"; $17.80, "Catasetum discolor"; $20 "Scuticaria hadwenii"; $25 "Epidendrum fragrans"; $100 "Epistephium parviflorum". HORIZ: $12.80 (2913), "Cochlospermum vitifolium"; 2914, "Eugenia malaccensis"; 2915, "Plumiera rubra"; 2916, "Erythrina glauca"; 2917, "Spathodea campanulata"; 2918, "Jacaranda filicifolia"; 2919, "Samanea saman"; 2920, "Cassia fistula"; 2921, "Abutilon integerrimum"; 2922, "Lagerstroemia speciosa"; 2923, "Tabebuia serratifolia"; 2924, "Guaiacum officinale"; 2925, "Solanum macranthum"; 2926, "Peltophorum roxburghii"; 2927, "Bauhinia variegata"; 2928, "Plumiera alba"; 2929, "Maxillaria camaridii"; 2930, "Vanilla pompona"; 2931, "Stanhopea grandiflora"; 2932, "Oncidium pusillum"; 2933, "Polycycnis vittata"; 2934, "Cattleya lawrenceana"; 2935, "Menadenium labiosum"; 2936, "Rodriguezia secunda"; 2937, "Mormodes buccinator"; 2938, "Otostylis brachystalix"; 2939, "Maxillaria discolor"; 2940, "Liparis elata"; 2941, "Gongora maculata"; 2942, "Koellensteinia graminea"; 2943, "Rudolfiella aurantiaca"; 2944, "Scuticaria steelei"; 2945, "Gloriosa rothschildiana"; 2946, "Pseudocalymma alliaceum"; 2947, "Callichlamys latifolia"; 2948, "Distictis riversii"; 2949, "Maurandya barclaiana"; 2950, "Beaumontia fragrans"; 2951, "Phaseolus caracalla"; 2952, "Mandevilla splendens"; 2953, "Solandra longiflora"; 2954, "Passiflora coccinea"; 2955, "Allamanda cathartica"; 2956, "Bauhinia galpini"; 2957, "Verbena maritima"; 2958, "Mandevilla sauveolens"; 2959, "Phryganocydia corymbosa"; 2960, "Jasminum sambac".

Nos. 2864/79, 2880/95, 2897/2912, 2913/28, 2929/44 and 2945/60 respectively were printed together, se-tenant, forming composite designs.

1990. Fauna. Multicoloured.

2967/86 $12.80 × 20 (vert designs showing endangered birds)
2987/3006 $12.80 × 20 (vert designs showing tropical birds)
3007/26 $12.80 × 20 (vert designs showing prehistoric animals)
3027/46 $12.80 × 20 (horiz designs showing endangered wildlife)
Set of 80 . . . . . . 30·00 30·00

DESIGNS—VERT: No. 2968, Cauca guan; 2969, Sun conure; 2970, Quetzal; 2971, Long-wattled umbrellabird; 2972, Banded cotinga; 2973, Blue-chested parakeet; 2974, Rufous-bellied chachalaca; 2975, Yellow-faced amazon; 2976, Toucan barbet; 2977, Red siskin; 2978, Cock-of-the-rock; 2979, Hyacinth macaw; 2980, Yellow cardinal; 2981, Bare-necked umbrellabird; 2982, Saffron toucanet; 2983, Red-billed curassow; 2984, Spectacled parrotlet; 2985, Lovely cotinga; 2986, Black-breasted gnateater; 2987, Swallow-tailed kite; 2988, Hoatzin; 2989, Ruby-topaz hummingbird; 2990, American black vulture; 2991, Rufous-tailed jacamar; 2992, Scarlet macaw; 2993, Rose-breasted thrush tanager; 2994, Toco toucan; 2995, Bearded bellbird; 2996, Blue-crowned motmot; 2997, Green oropendola; 2998, Pompadour cotinga; 2999; Vermilion flycatcher; 3000, Blue and yellow macaw; 3001, White-barred piculet; 3002, Great razor-billed curassow; 3003, Ruddy quail dove; 3004, Paradise tanager; 3005, American darter ("Anhinga"); 3006, Greater flamingo; 3007, Palaelodus; 3008, Archaeotrogon; 3009, Vulture; 3010, Bradypus tridactylus; 3011, Natalus stramineus bat; 3012, Cebidae; 3013, Cuvieronius; 3014, Phororhacos; 3015, Smilodectes; 3016, Megatherium; 3017, Titanotylopus; 3018, Teleoceras; 3019, Macrauchenia; 3020, Mylodon; 3021, Smilodon; 3022, Glyptodon; 3023, Protohydrocherus; 3024, Archaeohyrax; 3025, Pyrotherium; 3026, Platypittamys. HORIZ: $12.80 (3027), Harpy eagle and hyacinth macaw; 3028, Andean condor; 3029, Amazonian umbrellabird; 3030, Spider monkeys; 3031, Hyacinth macaws; 3032, Red siskin; 3033, Toucan barbet; 3034, Three-toed sloth; 3035, Guanacos; 3036, Spectacled bear; 3037, White-lipped peccary; 3038, Maned wolf; 3039, Jaguar; 3040, Spectacled cayman; 3041, Giant armadillo; 3042, Giant anteater; 3043, South American river otter; 3044, Yapok; 3045, Central American river turtle; 3046, Cauca guan.

Nos. 2967/86, 2987/3006, 3007/26 and 3027/46 respectively were printed together, se-tenant, forming composite designs.

No. 2982 is inscribed "Toucanette" and No. 2995 "Belllbird", both in error.

468 Ramon Folist (Cuba) (fencing, 1900)

1991. Winter Olympic Games, Albertville (1st issue), and Olympic Games, Barcelona. Previous Gold Medal Winners. Multicoloured.

3048/3119 $15.30 × 9, $17.80 × 9, $20 × 18, $25 × 18 and $30 × 18
Set of 72 . . . . . . 30·00 32·00

DESIGNS: $15.30 (3049), Lucien Gaudin (France) (fencing, 1924); 3050, Ole Lilloe-Olsen (Norway) (shooting, 1924); 3051, Morris Fisher (U.S.A.) (rifle shooting, 1924); 3052, Ray Ewry (U.S.A.) (long jump, 1900); 3053, Hubert van Innes (Belgium) (archery, 1900); 3054, Alvin Kraenzlein (U.S.A.) (hurdles, 1900); 3055, Johnny Weissmuller (U.S.A.) (swimming, 1924); 3056, Hans Winkler (West Germany) (show jumping, 1956); $17.80 (3057), Viktor Chukarin (Russia) (gymnastics, 1952); 3058, Agnes Keleti (Hungary) (gymnastics, 1952); 3059, Barbel Wochel (East Germany) (200 metres, 1980); 3060, Eric Heiden (U.S.A.) (speed skating, 1980); 3061, Alvodar Gerevich (Hungary) (fencing, 1932); 3062, Giuseppe Delfino (Italy) (fencing, 1952); 3063, Alexander Tikhonov (Russia) (skiing, 1980); 3064, Pahud de Mortanges (Netherlands) (equestrian, 1932); 3065, Patricia McCormick (U.S.A.) (diving, 1952); $20 (3066), Olga Korbut (Russia) (gymnastics, 1972); 3067, Lyudmila Turischeva (Russia) (gymnastics, 1972); 3068, Lasse Viren (Finland) (10,000 metres, 1972); 3069, George Miez (Switzerland) (gymnastics, 1936); 3070, Roland Matthes (East Germany) (swimming, 1972); 3071, Pal Kovaks (Hungary) (fencing, 1936); 3072, Jesse Owens (U.S.A.) (200 metres, 1936); 3073, Mark Spitz (U.S.A.) (swimming, 1972); 3074, Eduardo Mangiarotti (Italy) (fencing, 1936); 3075, Nelli Kim (Russia) (gymnastics, 1976); 3076, Viktor Krovopuskov (Russia) (fencing, 1976); 3077, Viktor Sidiak (Russia) (fencing, 1976); 3078, Nikolai Andrianov (Russia) (gymnastics, 1976); 3079, Nadia Comaneci (Rumania) (gymnastics, 1976); 3080, Mitsuo Tsukahara (Japan) (gymnastics, 1976); 3081, Yelena Novikova-Belova (Russia) (fencing, 1976); 3082, John Naber (U.S.A.) (swimming, 1976); 3083, Kornella Ender (Rumania) (swimming, 1976); $25 (3084), Lydia Skoblikova (Russia) (speed skating, 1964); 3085, Ivar Ballangrud (Norway) (speed skating, 1936); 3086, Clas Thunberg (Finland) (speed skating, 1928); 3087, Anton Heida (U.S.A.) (gymnastics, 1904); 3088, Akinori Nakayama (Japan) (gymnastics, 1968); 3089, Sixten Jernberg (Sweden) (skiing, 1964); 3090, Yevgeniy Grischin (Russia) (speed skating, 1956); 3091, Paul Radmilovic (East Germany) (waterpolo, 1920); 3092, Charles Daniels (U.S.A.) (swimming, 1904); 3093, Sawao Kato (Japan) (gymnastics, 1968); 3094, Rudolf Karpati (Hungary) (fencing, 1948); 3095, Jeno Fuchs (Hungary) (fencing, 1908); 3096, Emil Zatopek (Czechoslovakia) (10,000 metres, 1948); 3097, Fanny Blankers-Koen (Netherlands) (hurdles, 1948); 3098, Melvin Sheppard (U.S.A.) (4 x 400 metres relay, 1908); 3099, Gert Fredriksson (Sweden) (kayak, 1948); 3100, Paul Elvstrom (Denmark) (yachting, 1948); 3101, Harrison Dillard (U.S.A.) (100 metres, 1948); $30 (3102), Al Oerter (U.S.A.) (discus, 1956); 3103, Polina Atsakhova (Russia) (gymnastics, 1956); 3104, Takashi Ono (Japan) (gymnastics, 1956); 3105, Valentin Muratov (Russia) (gymnastics, 1956); 3106, Henri St. Cyr (Sweden) (equestrian, 1956); 3107, Iain Murray Rose (Australia) (swimming, 1956); 3108, Larisa Latynina (Russia) (gymnastics, 1956); 3109, Carlo Pavesi (Italy) (fencing, 1956); 3110, Dawn Fraser (Australia) (swimming, 1956); 3111, Betty Cuthbert (Australia) (400 metres, 1964); 3112, Vera Caslavska (Czechoslovakia) (gymnastics, 1964); 3113, Galin Kulakova (Russia) (skiing, 1972); 3114, Yukio Endo (Japan) (gymnastics, 1972); 3115, Vladimir Morozov (Russia) (kayak, 1972); 3116, Boris Shaklin (Russia) (gymnastics, 1964); 3117, Don Schollander (U.S.A.) (swimming, 1964); 3118, Gyozo Kulscar (Hungary) (fencing, 1964); 3119, Christian D'Oriloa (France) (fencing, 1956).

Nos. 3048/56, 3057/65, 3066/74, 3075/83, 3084/92, 3093/3101, 3102/10 and 3111/19 respectively were printed together, se-tenant, forming composite designs.

Sheetlets containing Nos. 3057/65, 3084/92 and 3111/19 were subsequently re-issued with Nos. 3063, 3086 and 3113 overprinted "ALBERTVILLE '92".

See also Nos. 3186/94 and 3246/53.

1991. 85th Anniv of Rotary International (1990). (a) Nos. 2789/94 and 2859/60 optd or surch **Paul Percy Harris Founder 1868–1947** and emblem (A) or with Rotary emblem and **1905–1990** (B).

3121 80 c. Type **464** (B) 10 10
3122 $2.55 "Rhetus dysonii" (A) . 10 10
3123 $5 "Actinote anteas" (A) . . 10 10
3124 $6.40 "Heliconius tales" (A) 10 10
3125 $7.65 "Thecla telemus" (A) . 10 10
3126 $100 on $8.90 "Theope eudocia" (A) . . . . . . 1·25 1·40
3127 $190 on $50 "Heliconius vicini" (B) . . . . 2·25 2·50
3128 $225 on $100 "Amarynthis meneria" (B) . . . . . . 2·50 2·75

(b) Nos. 2795/2810 optd or surch as Nos. 3121/8 or with emblems and inscriptions of other international organizations.

3129 $10 "Heliconius vetustus" (B) 15 15
3130 $10 "Mesosemia eumene" (optd Boy Scout emblem and **1907–1992**) 15 15
3131 $10 "Parides phosphorus" (optd Lions Club emblem and **1917–1992**) 15 15
3132 $10 "Polystichtis emylius" (A) 15 15
3133 $10 "Xanthocleis aedesia" (optd **125 Years Red Cross** and cross) 15 15
3134 $10 "Doxocopa agathina" (optd with part Rotary emblem) 15 15
3135 $10 "Adelpha plesaure" (optd with part Rotary emblem) 15 15
3136 $10 "Heliconius wallacei" (optd **125 Years Red Cross** and cross) 15 15
3137 $10 "Notheme eumeus" (optd Lions Club emblem and **1917–1992**) 15 15
3138 $10 "Melinaea mediatrix" (optd with part Rotary emblem) 15 15
3139 $10 "Theritas coronata" (optd with part Rotary emblem) 15 15
3140 $10 "Dismorphia orise" (optd Boy Scout emblem and **1907–1992**) 15 15
3141 $50 on $10 "Phyciodes ianthe" (A) 65 65
3142 $75 on $10 "Morpho aega" (surch Boy Scout emblem and **1907–1992**) . . . . 1·00 1·10
3143 $100 on $10 "Zaretis isidora" (surch Lions Club emblem and **1917–1992**) . . . . . . 1·25 1·40
3144 $190 on $10 "Pierella lena" (B) 2·25 2·50

1991. 65th Birthday of Queen Elizabeth II and 70th Birthday of Prince Philip. As T **280** of Antigua. Multicoloured.

3146 $12.80 Queen and Prince Philip in evening dress 15 20
3147 $15.30 Queen Elizabeth II . . 15 20
3148 $100 Queen and Prince Philip 1·00 1·10
3149 $130 Prince Philip . . . . . 1·25 1·40
3150 $150 Prince Philip in R.A.F. uniform . . . . 1·50 1·60
3151 $200 The Queen with Queen Elizabeth the Queen Mother 2·25 2·40

1991. 10th Wedding Anniv of Prince and Princess of Wales. As T **280** of Antigua. Multicoloured.

3153 $8.90 Prince and Princess of Wales 20 20
3154 $50 Separate portraits of Princess and sons 80 80
3155 $75 Prince Charles with Prince William . . . . 1·25 1·25
3156 $190 Princess Diana with Prince Henry . . . . 2·75 3·00

1991. 75th Anniv of Lions International (1992). (a) Nos. 2789/94 and 2859/60 optd or surch **Melvin Jones Founder 1880–1961** (A) or with Lions Club emblem and **Lions International 1917–1992** (B).

3158 80 c. Type **464** (B) 15 10
3159 $2.55 "Rhetus dysonii" (B) . 20 15
3160 $5 "Actinote anteas" (A) . . 30 20
3161 $6.40 "Heliconius tales" (A) . 30 25
3162 $7.65 "Thecla telemus" (A) . 30 25
3163 $100 on $8.90 "Theope eudocia" (A) . . . . 1·50 1·50
3164 $190 on $50 "Heliconius vicini" (B) . . . . 2·50 2·75
3165 $225 on $100 "Amarynthis meneria" (B) . . . . 2·50 2·75

(b) Nos. 2843/58 optd or surch as Nos. 3158/65 or with emblems and inscriptions of other international organizations.

3166 $10 "Thecla telemus" (optd Lions Club emblem and **1917–1992**) 15 15
3167 $10 "Thyridia confusa" (optd Rotary emblem and **1905–1990**) 15 15
3168 $10 "Heliconius burneyi" (optd Boy Scout emblem and **1907–1992**) 15 15
3169 $10 "Parides lysander" (A) . 15 15
3170 $10 "Eunica orphise" (optd **125 Years Red Cross** and cross) 15 15
3171 $10 "Adelpha melona" (optd with part Lions Club emblem) 15 15
3172 $10 "Morpho menelaus" (optd with part Lions Club emblem) 15 15
3173 $10 "Nymula phylleus" (optd **125 Years Red Cross** and cross) 15 15
3174 $10 "Stalachtis phlegia" (optd Rotary emblem and **1905–1990**) 15 15
3175 $10 "Theope barea" (optd with part Lions Club emblem) . 15 15
3176 $10 "Morpho perseus" (optd with part Lions Club emblem) 15 15
3177 $10 "Lycorea ceres" (optd Boy Scout emblem and **1907–1992**) 15 15
3178 $50 on $10 "Archonias bellona" (A) 65 65
3179 $75 on $10 "Caerois chorinaeus" (surch Boy Scout emblem and **1907–1992**) . . 1·00 1·10
3180 $100 on $10 "Vila azeca" (surch Rotary emblem and **1905–1990**) . . . . 1·25 1·40
3181 $190 on $10 "Nessaea batesii" (surch Lions Club emblem and **1917–1992**) . . . . . . 2·25 2·50

1991. Winter Olympic Games, Albertville (1992) (2nd issue). Nos. 2738/46 optd or surch **ALBERTVILLE 92** or **XVIth Olympic Winter Games in Albertville** (No. 3190).

3186/94 $20 x 6, $70 on $20, $100 on $20, $190 on $20
Set of 9 . . . . 7·50 8·00

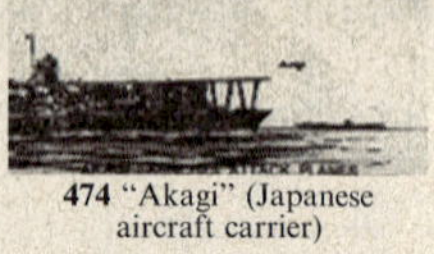

474 "Akagi" (Japanese aircraft carrier)

1991. 50th Anniv of Japanese Attack on Pearl Harbor. Each blue, red and black.

3197 $50 Type **474** 85 85
3198 $50 Beached Japanese midget submarine 85 85
3199 $50 Mitsubishi A6M Zero-Sen fighter 85 85
3200 $50 U.S.S. "Arizona" (battleship) under attack . . 85 85
3201 $50 Aichi D3A1 "Val" dive bomber 85 85
3202 $50 U.S.S. "California" (battleship) sinking 85 85
3203 $50 Curtiss P-40 fighters taking off 85 85
3204 $50 U.S.S. "Cassin" and U.S.S. "Downes" damaged in dry dock 85 85
3205 $50 Boeing B-17 Flying Fortress crash landing at Bellows Field 85 85
3206 $50 U.S.S. "Nevada" (battleship) on fire 85 85

475 Brandenburg Gate and Location Plan

1991. Anniversaries and Events. Multicoloured.

3207 $10 Type **475** 20 20
3208 $25 President Bush, President Lech Walesa of Poland and Brandenburg Gate 50 50
3209 $25 Scout handshake 50 50
3210 $30 Scouts hiking at Philmont Scout Ranch 60 60
3211 $40 Jamboree and Scout Movement emblems . . . 70 70
3212 $60 General de Gaulle at Venice, 1944 . . . . 90 90
3213 $75 De Gaulle with Khrushchev, 1960 . . . . 1·25 1·25
3214 $75 Mozart and Castle of Laxenburg . . . . 1·25 1·25
3215 $75 Caroline Herschel (astronomer) and Old Town Hall, Hanover . . . . . . 1·25 1·25
3216 $75 Map of Switzerland and woman in Valais costume . 1·25 1·25
3217 $80 De Gaulle at Algiers, 1958 1·40 1·40
3218 $80 Mozart and death of Leopold II . . . . 1·40 1·40
3219 $80 Otto Lilienthal and "Flugzeug Nr. 3" . . . . 1·40 1·40
3220 $100 Chancellor Kohl, Foreign Minister Genscher and Brandenburg Gate . . . . 1·50 1·50
3221 $100 Lord Baden-Powell (vert) 1·50 1·50
3222 $100 De Gaulle with Pope Paul VI, 1967 . . . . 1·50 1·50
3223 $100 Mozart and birthplace, Salzburg . . . . 1·50 1·50
3224 $100 Class P36 steam locomotive . . . . 1·50 1·50

ANNIVERSARIES and EVENTS: Nos. 3207/8, 3220, Bicentenary of Brandenburg Gate, Berlin; 3209/11, 3221, 17th World Scout Jamboree, Korea; 3212/13, 3217, 3222, Birth centenary (1990) of Charles de Gaulle (French statesman); 3214, 3218, 3223, Death bicentenary of Mozart; 3215, 750th anniv of Hanover; 3216, 700th anniv of Swiss Confederation; 3219, Centenary of Otto Lilienthal's first gliding experiments; 3224, Centenary of Trans-Siberian Railway.

No. 3222 is inscribed "Pope John VI" in error.

476 Disney Characters Carol Singing, 1989

1991. Christmas. Walt Disney Christmas Cards. Multicoloured.

3226 80 c. Type **476** 10 10
3227 $2.55 Disney characters and carol singers in tram, 1962 10 10
3228 $5 Donald Duck and Pluto with parcel, 1971 . . . . 10 10
3229 $6.40 "SEASON'S GREETINGS" and Mickey Mouse with candle, 1948 . 10 10
3230 $7.65 Mickey Mouse as Father Christmas, 1947 . . . . . 10 10
3231 $8.90 Shadow of Pinocchio with candle, 1939 . . . . 10 10
3232 $50 Three Little Pigs dancing on wolf rug, 1933 . . . . . . 65 65
3233 $50 Conductor and Donald Duck, 1940 (vert) 65 65
3234 $50 Elephant and ostrich carol singing, 1940 (vert) 65 65
3235 $50 Hippo, centaurs, Pinocchio and Goofy, 1940 (vert) . . 65 65
3236 $50 Snow White, Dopey, Mickey and Minnie, 1940 (vert) 65 65
3237 $50 Dino, Pluto and Walt Disney, 1940 (vert) 65 65
3238 $50 Mickey Mouse in sleigh, 1974 (vert) 65 65
3239 $50 Three Little Pigs, Winnie the Pooh, Bambi and Thumper, 1974 (vert) . . . 65 65
3240 $50 Baloo, King Louis, Lady and the Tramp, 1974 (vert) 65 65
3241 $50 Alice, Robin Hood, the Cheshire Cat and Goofy, 1974 (vert) 65 65
3242 $50 Dumbo, Pinocchio, Peter Pan, Tinkerbelle, Seven Dwarfs and Donald Duck, 1974 (vert) 65 65

3243 $50 Pluto pulling sleigh, 1974 (vert) 65 65
3244 $200 Mickey and mice carol singing, 1949 2·75 2·75

477 Gus Gander playing Ice Hockey

1991. Winter Olympic Games, Albertville (1992) (3rd issue). Walt Disney Cartoon Characters. Multicoloured.

3246 $6.40 Type **477** 20 10
3247 $7.65 Mickey and Minnie Mouse in bobsleigh 20 10
3248 $8.90 Donald's Nephews on luge and skis 25 10
3249 $12.80 Goofy freestyle skiing 40 20
3250 $50 Goofy ski jumping 1·00 1·00
3251 $100 Donald and Daisy Duck speed skating 1·50 1·50
3252 $130 Pluto cross-country skiing 1·75 2·00
3253 $190 Mickey and Minnie Mouse ice dancing 2·50 3·00

478 Columbus landing on Trinidad

1992. 500th Anniv of Discovery of America by Columbus. Multicoloured.

3255 $6.40 Type **478** 40 40
3256 $7.65 Columbus the map-maker 45 45
3257 $8.90 Fleet blown off course 45 45
3258 $12.80 Map of third voyage and Columbus in chains 55 55
3259 $15.30 Sighting land 55 55
3260 $50 "Nina" and "Pinta" 90 90
3261 $75 "Santa Maria" 1·25 1·25
3262 $100 Columbus trading with Amerindians 1·75 1·75
3263 $125 Crew and sea monster 2·00 2·00
3264 $130 Columbus landing on San Salvador and map of first voyage 2·00 2·00
3265 $140 Priest and Amerindians 2·00 2·00
3266 $150 Columbus before King Ferdinand and Queen Isabella of Spain 2·00 2·00

479 Tom Mix in "The Great K&A Train Robbery", 1926

1992. Classic Movie Posters. Multicoloured.

3268 $8.90 Type **479** 30 30
3269 $12.80 Richard Dix and Irene Dunne in "Cimarron", 1931 40 40
3270 $15.30 Fatty Arbuckle in "Buzzin' Around", 1934 40 40
3271 $25 Tom Tyler in "The Adventures of Captain Marvel", 1941 55 55
3272 $30 Boris Karloff in "The Mummy", 1932 70 70
3273 $50 Rudolph Valentino in "A Sainted Devil", 1924 90 90
3274 $75 Seven posters for "A Tale of Two Cities", 1935 1·25 1·25
3275 $100 Chester Conklin in "A Tugboat Romeo", 1916 1·75 1·75
3276 $130 Douglas Fairbanks in "The Thief of Bagdad", 1924 2·00 2·00
3277 $150 Laurel and Hardy in "Bacon Grabbers", 1929 2·50 2·50
3278 $190 Marx Brothers in "A Night at the Opera", 1935 3·00 3·00
3279 $200 Orson Welles in "Citizen Kane", 1941 3·00 3·00

1992. Easter. Paintings by Durer. As T **291** of Antigua, but vert. Multicoloured.

3281 $6.40 "The Martyrdom of Ten Thousand" (detail) 25 10
3282 $7.65 "Adoration of the Trinity" (detail of Virgin Mary) 25 10
3283 $12.80 "The Martyrdom of Ten Thousand" (execution detail) 40 20
3284 $15.30 "Adoration of the Trinity" (different detail) 45 25
3285 $50 "The Martyrdom of Ten Thousand" (detail of bishop) 1·00 75
3286 $100 "Adoration of the Trinity" (different detail) 1·50 1·50
3287 $130 "The Martyrdom of Ten Thousand" (different detail) 1·75 2·00
3288 $190 "Adoration of the Trinity" (different detail) 3·25 3·50

1992. Baha'i Holy Year. Surch **BAHA'I HOLY YEAR 1992** and value.

3290 $6.40 on 60 c. Plate No. 10 (Series 1) (No. 1521)
3291 $7.65 on 60 c. Plate No. 31 (Series 1) (No. 1523)
3292 $8.90 on 60 c. Plate No. 19 (Series 1) (No. 1522)
3293 $50 on 60 c. Plate No. 2 (Series 1) (No. 1519)

481 Queen Elizabeth II and Duke of Edinburgh

1992. 40th Anniv of Queen Elizabeth II's Accession. Multicoloured.

3294 $8.90 Type **481** 25 25
3295 $12.80 Queen at Trooping the Colour 30 30
3296 $100 Queen at Coronation 2·00 2·25
3297 $130 Queen in Garter robes 2·25 2·50

482 Holy Cross Church, Annai Rupununi

1992. 150th Anniv of Diocese of Guyana. Multicoloured.

3299 $6.40 Type **482** 15 10
3300 $50 St. Peter's Church 80 65
3301 $100 Interior of St. George's Cathedral (vert) 1·50 1·60
3302 $190 Map of Guyana (vert) 2·75 3·25

483 Burmese

1992. Cats. Multicoloured.

3304 $5 Type **483** 10 10
3305 $6.40 Turkish van 10 10
3306 $12.80 American shorthair 15 20
3307 $15.30 Sphynx 15 20
3308 $50 Egyptian mau 50 55
3309 $50 Russian blue 50 55
3310 $50 Havana brown 50 55
3311 $50 Himalayan 50 55
3312 $50 Manx 50 55
3313 $50 Cornish rex 50 55
3314 $50 Black Persian 50 55
3315 $50 Scottish fold 50 55
3316 $50 Siamese 50 55
3317 $100 Japanese bobtail 1·00 1·10
3318 $130 Abyssinian 1·25 1·40
3319 $225 Oriental shorthair 2·25 2·40

484 Red Howler

1992. Animals of Guyana. Multicoloured.

3321 $8.90 Type **484** 20 10
3322 $12.80 Ring-tailed coati 25 20
3323 $15.30 Jaguar 30 20
3324 $25 Two-toed sloth 50 30
3325 $50 Giant armadillo 1·00 80
3326 $75 Giant anteater 1·50 1·75
3327 $100 Capybara 1·75 1·90
3328 $130 Ocelot 2·00 2·25

485 Oligocene Mammoth

1992. Elephants. Multicoloured.

3330 $50 Type **485** 1·25 1·25
3331 $50 Mid-Miocene stegodon 1·25 1·25
3332 $50 Pliocene mammoth 1·25 1·25
3333 $50 Carthaginian elephant crossing Alps, 219 B.C. 1·25 1·25
3334 $50 Ceremonial elephant of Maharaja of Mysore, India 1·25 1·25
3335 $50 Elephant pulling teak trunks, Burma 1·25 1·25
3336 $50 Tiger-hunting by elephant, India 1·25 1·25
3337 $50 Elephant towing raft on River Kwai, Thailand 1·25 1·25

486 Palomino

1992. Horses. Multicoloured.

3339 $190 Type **486** 3·00 3·00
3340 $190 Appaloosa 3·00 3·00
3341 $190 Clydesdale 3·00 3·00
3342 $190 Arab 3·00 3·00
3343 $190 Morgan 3·00 3·00
3344 $190 Friesian 3·00 3·00
3345 $190 Pinto 3·00 3·00
3346 $190 Thoroughbred 3·00 3·00

No. 3340 is inscribed "APALOOSA" in error.

1992. International Conference on Nutrition, Rome. Surch **INT. CONFERENCE ON NUTRITION 1992** and value.

3348 $6.40 on 150 c. Plate No. 45 (Series 1) (No. 1769)
3349 $7.65 on 150 c. Plate No. 42 (Series 1) (No. 1768)
3350 $8.90 on 150 c. Plate No. 40 (Series 1) (No. 1767)
3351 $10 on 200 c. Plate No. 43 (Series 1) (No. 1658)
3352 $50 on 200 c. Plate No. 43 (Series 1) (No. 1658)

488 Marklin Swiss "Crocodile" Locomotive, 1933

1992. "Genova '92" International Thematic Stamp Exhibition. Toy Trains from German Manufacturers. Multicoloured.

3353/61 $45 × 9 (Made by Marklin: Type **488**; French tramcar, 1902; British "Flatiron" tank engine, 1913; German switching engine, 1970; Third class carriage, 1909; American style locomotive, 1904; Zurich tramcar, 1928; Central London Railway locomotive in Paris–Orleans livery, 1904; British GWR "Great Bear" locomotive, 1909

3362/70 $45 × 9 (Made by Marklin: LMS "Precursor" tank engine, 1923; American "Congressional Limited" passenger carriage, 1908; Swiss Type "Ae 3/6" locomotive, 1934; German Class 80, 1975; British Southern Railways third class carriage, 1926; LNWR Bowen-Cooke tank engine, 1913; London Underground "Two Penny Tube", 1901; French Paris–Orsay steeplecab, 1920; Passenger locomotive, 1895

3371/9 $45 × 9 (Made by Marklin: American style locomotive, 1907; German passenger carriage, 1908; British Great Eastern Railway locomotive, 1908; London Underground steeplecab, 1904; Santa Fe Railroad diesel locomotive, 1962; British GNR locomotive, 1903; Caledonian Railway "Cardean", 1906; British LNWR passenger carriage, 1903; Swiss St. Gotthard Railway locomotive, 1920

3380/8 $45 × 9 (Made by Marklin: British LB & SCR tank engine No. 22, 1920; Central London Railway steeplecab locomotive, 1904; German "Borsig" streamlined, 1935; French Paris–Lyon–Mediterranee first class carriage, 1929; American style locomotive No. 1021, 1904; French Paris–Orsay long-nose steeplecab, 1920; British LNER "Cock o' the North", 1936; Prussian State Railways Class P8, 1975; German diesel railcar set, 1937

3389/97 $45 × 9 (Marklin North British Railway "Atlantic", 1913; Bing British LNWR "Precursor", 1916; Marklin British GWR "King George V", 1937; Marklin "Kaiser Train" passenger carriage, 1901; Bing side tank locomotive No. 88, 1904; Marklin steeplecab, 1912; Marklin "Adler", 1935; Bing British GWR "County of Northampton", 1909; Bing British Midland Railway "Black Prince", 1908

3398/3406 $45 × 9 (Made by Bing: Midland Railway "Deeley Type" No. 483, 1909; British Midland Railway No. 2631, 1903; German Pacific, 1927; British GWR third class coach, 1926; British LSWR "M7" No. 109, 1909; Side tank engine "Pilot", 1901; British LNWR Webb "Cauliflower", 1912; Side tank locomotive No. 112, 1910; British GNR "Stirling Single", 1904

3407/15 $45 × 9 (Carette tin "Penny Bazaar" train, 1904; Winteringham locomotive, 1917; Carette British Northeastern Railway Smith Compound, 1905; Carette S.E. & C.R. steam railcar, 1908; Carette British Great Northern Railway Stirling Single No. 776, 1903; Carette British Midland Railways locomotive No. 1132M, 1911; Carette London Metropolitan Railway Co. "Westinghouse" locomotive No. 5, 1908; Carette Clestory carriage, 1907; Carette steam railcar No. 1, 1906

3416/24 $45 × 9 (Made by Bing: Engine and tender, 1895; British Midland Railway "Single" No. 650, 1913; No. 524/510 reversible locomotive, 1916; "Kaiser Train" passenger carriage, 1902; British rural station, 1915; British LSWR M7 tank locomotive, 1909; "Windcutter", 1912; British Great Central Railway "Sir Sam Fay", 1914; Scottish Caledonian Railway "Dunalastair" locomotive, 1910)

3353/3424 Set of 72 35·00 40·00

489 Aquarius

1992. Signs of the Zodiac. Multicoloured.

3427 $30 Type **489** 60 60
3428 $30 Pisces 60 60
3429 $30 Aries 60 60
3430 $30 Taurus 60 60
3431 $30 Gemini 60 60
3432 $30 Cancer 60 60
3433 $30 Leo 60 60
3434 $30 Virgo 60 60
3435 $30 Libra 60 60
3436 $30 Scorpio 60 60
3437 $30 Sagittarius 60 60
3438 $30 Capricorn 60 60

490 City Walls and Two Birds

1992. Bible Stories (1st series). David and Goliath. Multicoloured.

3439 $25 Type **490** 50 50
3440 $25 City walls and one bird at right 50 50
3441 $25 Sun over city gateway 50 50
3442 $25 City walls and one bird at left 50 50
3443 $25 City walls and no birds 50 50
3444 $25 Philistine army and edge of shield 50 50
3445 $25 Goliath's head and torso 50 50
3446 $25 Goliath's arm and spear 50 50
3447 $25 Philistine army and spearhead 50 50
3448 $25 Philistine infantry 50 50
3449 $25 Philistine cavalry and infantry 50 50
3450 $25 Goliath's shield 50 50
3451 $25 Goliath's waist and thigh 50 50
3452 $25 David with sling 50 50
3453 $25 Israelite soldier with spear 50 50
3454 $25 Two Israelite soldiers with spears and shields 50 50
3455 $25 Goliath's right leg 50 50
3456 $25 Goliath's left leg (face value at foot) 50 50
3457 $25 David's legs and Israelite standard 50 50
3458 $25 Three Israelite soldiers 50 50
3459 $25 Israelite soldier and parts of two shields 50 50
3460 $25 Israelite soldier with sword 50 50
3461 $25 Back of Israelite soldier 50 50
3462 $25 Israelite soldier leaning on rock 50 50
3463 $25 Israelite soldier looking left 50 50

Nos. 3439/63 were printed together, se-tenant, forming a composite design.

See also Nos. 4020/4116.

491 Count Ferdinand von Zeppelin and Airship over Lake Constance, 1909

1992. Anniversaries and Events. Multicoloured.

3464 $12.80 Type **491** 50 35
3465 $50 "Voyager I" and Jupiter 1·50 1·00
3466 $50 Chancellor Adenauer with President Kennedy, 1961 1·00 1·00
3467 $100 Aeromedical airlift 2·00 2·00
3468 $100 Boutu ("Amazon Dolphin") 2·00 2·00

3469 $130 Baby gorilla . . . . . . 2·50 2·50
3470 $130 Mobile eye screening unit and doctor with child . . . 2·50 2·50
3471 $130 "Stars and Stripes" (winning yacht, 1987) . . . 2·50 2·50
3472 $130 Lift-off of "Voyager I", 1977 . . . . . . 2·50 2·50
3473 $190 Adenauer with President De Gaulle of France, 1962 3·25 3·25
3474 $225 Von Zeppelin and airship preparing for take-off, 1905 3·50 3·50

ANNIVERSARIES and EVENTS: Nos. 3464, 3474, 75th death anniv of Count Ferdinand von Zeppelin; 3465, 3472, International Space Year; 3466, 3473, 75th death anniv of Konrad Adenauer (German statesman); 3467, United Nations World Health Organization projects; 3468/9, Earth Summit '92, Rio; 3470, 75th anniv of International Association of Lions Clubs; 3471, Americas Cup Yachting Championship.

492 Hyacinth Macaw

1993. South American Parrots. Multicoloured.

3476 80 c. Type **492** 30 15
3477 $6.40 Scarlet macaw (preening) 50 25
3478 $7.65 Buffon's macaw ("Green Macaw") (vert) 50 25
3479 $15.30 Orange-chinned parakeet ("Tovi Parakeet") 70 50
3480 $50 Blue and yellow macaw . 1·00 80
3481 $100 Military macaw (vert) . 1·50 1·25
3482 $130 Green-winged macaw ("Red and Green Macaw") (vert) . . . . 1·75 1·75
3483 $190 Chestnut-fronted macaw ("Severa Macaw") . . . . 2·50 3·00

493 Crimson Topaz

1993. Birds of Guyana. Multicoloured.

3485 $50 Type **493** 75 75
3486 $50 Bearded bellbird 75 75
3487 $50 Amazonian umbrellabird 75 75
3488 $50 Paradise jacamar 75 75
3489 $50 Paradise tanager 75 75
3490 $50 White-tailed trogon . . . 75 75
3491 $50 Scarlet macaw 75 75
3492 $50 Hawk-headed parrot ("Red-fan Parrot") 75 75
3493 $50 Cuvier's toucan ("Red-billed Toucan") 75 75
3494 $50 White-faced antcatcher ("White-plumed Antbird") 75 75
3495 $50 Crimson-hooded manakin 75 75
3496 $50 Guianan cock of the rock 75 75

Nos. 3485/96 were printed together, se-tenant, with the backgrounds forming a composite design.

494 Manatee surfacing

495 Tamandua

1993. Endangered Species. American Manatee ("Caribbean Manatee"). Multicoloured.

3498 $6.40 Type **494** 40 40
3499 $7.60 Cow and calf feeding . 40 40
3500 $8.90 Manatee underwater . 40 40
3501 $50 Two manatees . . . . . 2·00 1·50

1993. Animals of Guyana. Multicoloured.

3502 $50 Type **495** 75 75
3503 $50 Pale-throated sloth ("Three-toed Sloth") 75 75
3504 $50 Red howler 75 75
3505 $50 Four-eyed opossum . . . 75 75
3506 $50 Black spider monkey . . . 75 75
3507 $50 Giant otter 75 75
3508 $50 Red brocket 75 75
3509 $50 Brazilian tree porcupine . 75 75
3510 $50 Tayra 75 75
3511 $50 Brazilian tapir 75 75
3512 $50 Ocelot 75 75
3513 $50 Giant armadillo 75 75

Nos. 3502/13 were printed together, se-tenant, the backgrounds forming a composite design.

496 Pteranodon

1993. Prehistoric Animals. Multicoloured.

3515/26 $30 × 12 (Type **496**; Cearadactylus; Eudimorphodon; Pterodactylus; Staurikosaurus; Euoplocephalus; Tuojiangosaurus; Oviraptor; Protoceratops; Panaoplosaurus; Psittacosaurus; Corythosaurus)
3527/38 $30 × 12 (Sordes; Quetzalcoatlus; Archaeopteryx in flight; Rhamphorynchus; Spinosaurus; Anchisaurus; Stegosaurus; Leaellynosaurus; Minmi; Heterdontosaurus; esothosaurus; Deninonychus)
3539/50 $30 × 12 (Archaeopteryx on branch; Pteranodon (different); Quetzalcoatlus (three); Protoavis; Dicraeosaurus; Moschops; Lystrosaurus; Dimetrondon; Staurikosaurus; Cacops; Diarthrognathus; Estemmenosuchus)
3515/50 Set of 36 . . . . . . 13·50 15·00

Nos. 3515/26, 3527/38 and 3539/50 respectively were printed together, se-tenant, with the backgrounds forming composite designs.

1993. 40th Anniv of Coronation. As T **307** of Antigua. Multicoloured.

3551 $25 Queen Elizabeth II in Coronation robes (photograph by Cecil Beaton) 75 75
3552 $50 Royal gems . . . . . . 1·00 1·00
3553 $75 Queen Elizabeth and Prince Philip . . . . 1·25 1·40
3554 $130 Queen opening Parliament . . . . 1·50 1·75

497 Gabriel Marquez (author)

1993. Famous People of the Twentieth Century. Multicoloured. (a) Arts and Literature.

3556 $50 Type **497** 50 55
3557 $50 Pablo Picasso (artist) . . 50 55
3558 $50 Cecil De Mille (film director) 50 55
3559 $50 Martha Graham (dancer) 50 55
3560 $50 Peace dove (inscr "20th Century Arts and Literature") 50 55
3561 $50 Charlie Chaplin (actor) . 50 55
3562 $50 Paul Robeson (actor) . . 50 55
3563 $50 Rudolph Dunbar (musician) 50 55
3564 $50 Louis Armstrong (musician) 50 55

(b) Science and Medicine.

3566 $50 Louis Leakey (archaeologist and anthropologist) . . . 50 55
3567 $50 Jonas Salk (discoverer of polio vaccine) 50 55
3568 $50 Hideyo Noguchi (bacteriologist) 50 55
3569 $50 Karl Landsteiner (pathologist) 50 55
3570 $50 As No. 3550, but inscr "20th Century Science and Medicine" 50 55
3571 $50 Sigmund Freud (founder of psychoanalysis) 50 55
3572 $50 Louis Pasteur (chemist) . 50 55
3573 $50 Madame Curie (physicist) 50 55
3574 $50 Jean Baptiste Perrin (physicist) 50 55

(c) Sports Personalities.

3576 $50 O. J. Simpson (American football) 50 55
3577 $50 Rohan Kanhai (cricket) 50 55
3578 $50 Gabriela Sabatini (tennis) 50 55
3579 $50 Severiano Ballesteros (golf) 50 55
3580 $50 As No. 3550, but inscr "20th Century Sports" . . 50 55
3581 $50 Franz Beckenbauer (football) 50 55
3582 $50 Pele (football) 50 55
3583 $50 Wilt Chamberlain (basketball) 50 55
3584 $50 Nadia Comaneci (gymnastics) 50 55

(d) Peace and Humanity.

3586 $100 Mahatma Gandhi (India) 1·00 1·10
3587 $100 Dalai Lama (Tibet) . . 1·00 1·10
3588 $100 Michael Manley (Jamaica) . . . . 1·00 1·10
3589 $100 Perez de Cuellar (U.N. Secretary-General) . . . 1·00 1·10
3590 $100 Peace dove and globe . 1·00 1·10
3591 $100 Mother Teresa (India) . 1·00 1·10
3592 $100 Martin Luther King (U.S.A.) . . . . 1·00 1·10
3593 $100 Pres. Nelson Mandela (South Africa) . . . . . . 1·00 1·10
3594 $100 Raoul Wallenberg (Sweden) . . . . 1·00 1·10

(e) Politics.

3596 $100 Nehru (India) . . . . . 1·00 1·10
3597 $100 Dr. Eric Williams (Trinidad and Tobago) . . 1·00 1·10
3598 $100 Pres. John F. Kennedy (U.S.A.) . . . . 1·00 1·10
3599 $100 Pres. Hugh Desmond Hoyte (Guyana) . . . . . 1·00 1·10
3600 $100 Peace dove and map of the Americas . . . . 1·00 1·10
3601 $100 Friedrich Ebert (Germany) . . . . 1·00 1·10
3602 $100 Pres. F. D. Roosevelt (U.S.A.) . . . . 1·00 1·10
3603 $100 Mikhail Gorbachev (Russia) . . . . 1·00 1·10
3604 $100 Sir Winston Churchill (Great Britain) . . . . . . 1·00 1·10

(f) Transportation and Technology.

3606 $100 Douglas DC-3 cargo plane . . . . 1·00 1·10
3607 $100 Space shuttle . . . . . 1·00 1·10
3608 $100 Concord . . . . 1·00 1·10
3609 $100 Count Ferdinand von Zeppelin and "Graf Zeppelin" . . . . 1·00 1·10
3610 $100 Peace dove and rocket trails . . . . 1·00 1·10
3611 $100 Marconi and aerial tower 1·00 1·10
3612 $100 Adrian Thompson (mountaineer) and Mt. Roraima . . . . 1·00 1·10
3613 $100 "Hikari" express train, Japan . . . . 1·00 1·10
3614 $100 Johann von Neumann and computer . . . . 1·00 1·10

Nos. 3556/64, 3566/74, 3576/84, 3586/94, 3596/3604 and 3606/14 respectively were printed together, se-tenant, with composite background designs on Nos. 3586/94, 3596/3604 and 3606/14.

No. 3562 is inscribed "Paul Roebeson" in error.

498 "Bather, Paris" (Picasso)

1993. Anniversaries and Events. Multicoloured.

3616 $15.30 Type **498** 15 20
3617 $25 Willy Brandt with Prime Minister of Israel Golda Meir, 1969 (horiz) . . . 40 40
3618 $50 "Pantaloons" (left half) (Tadeusz Brzozowski) . . . 50 55
3619 $50 Georg Hackl (men's single luge, 1992) 70 70
3620 $50 Astrolabe 70 70
3621 $75 Miedzyrecz Castle 75 80
3622 $100 "Two Nudes" (Picasso) . 1·00 1·10
3623 $130 "Pantaloons" (right half) (Tadeusz Brzozowski) . . . 1·25 1·40
3624 $130 Karen Magnussen (women's figure skating, 1972) . . . . 1·50 1·50
3625 $190 "Nude seated on a Rock" (Picasso) . . . . 1·90 2·00
3626 $190 Willy Brandt at Georgsmarienhutten Steel Mill, 1969 (horiz) . . . . . 2·25 2·25
3627 $190 Dish aerial . . . . . . 2·25 2·25

ANNIVERSARIES and EVENTS: Nos. 3616, 3622, 3625, 20th death anniv of Picasso (artist); 3617, 3626, 80th birth anniv (1992) of Willy Brandt (German politician); 3618, 3621, 3623, "Polska '93" International Stamp Exhibition, Poznan; 3619, 3624, Winter Olympic Games '94, Lillehammer; 3620, 3627, 450th death anniv of Copernicus (astronomer).

Nos. 3618 and 3623 were printed together, se-tenant, forming a composite design showing the complete painting.

499 Audie Murphy (most decorated U.S. serviceman)

1993. 50th Anniv of Second World War (1st issue). Multicoloured.

3629 $6.40 Type **499** 30 20
3630 $7.65 Allied troops in Normandy (8 June 1944) . 30 25
3631 $8.90 American howitzer crew, Battle of Montecassino (18 May 1944) 35 30
3632 $12.80 American aircraft attacking "Yamato" (Japanese battleship), Battle of East China Sea (7 April 1945) 50 40
3633 $15.30 St. Basil's Cathedral, Moscow (Foreign Ministers' Conference, 19 October 1943) 50 40
3634 $50 American troops crossing Rhine at Remagen (7 March 1945) 80 65
3635 $100 Boeing B-29 Super-fortresses raiding Japan from China (15 June 1944) . . . 1·50 1·50
3636 $130 General Patton and map of Sicily (17 August 1943) . 1·60 1·60
3637 $190 Destruction of "Tirpitz" (German battleship) (12 November 1944) . . . . . 2·40 2·50
3638 $200 American forces in Brittany (1 August 1944) . 2·50 2·75
3639 $225 American half-track (ceasefire in Italy, 2 May 1945) . . . . 2·75 3·00

No. 3631 is inscribed "Monte Casino" in error. See also Nos. 3641/60 and 3942/61.

500 R.A.A.F. Bristol Type 156 Beaufighter, Battle of the Bismarck Sea (2–4 March 1943)

1993. 50th Anniv of Second World War (2nd issue). Multicoloured.

3641 $50 Type **500** 80 80
3642 $50 Lockheed P-38 Lightning attacking Admiral Yamamoto's plane, Bougainville (7 April 1943) 80 80
3643 $50 Consolidated B-24 Liberator bombers, Tarawa (17–19 September 1943) . . 80 80
3644 $50 North American B-25 Mitchell bomber, Rabaul (12 October 1943) 80 80
3645 $50 U.S. Navy aircraft attacking Makin (19 November 1943) 80 80
3646 $50 U.S.A.A.F. bombers on first daylight raid over Germany (27 January 1943) 80 80
3647 $50 R.A.F. De Havilland D.H.98 Mosquito bombers on first daylight raid over Berlin (30 January 1943) . 80 80
3648 $50 Allied aircraft over Hamburg (24–30 July 1943) 80 80
3649 $50 Consolidated B-24 Liberators bombing Ploesti oil refineries, Rumania (1 August 1943) 80 80
3650 $50 German nightfighter attacking Allied bombers over Berlin (18 November 1943) 80 80
3651 $50 Japanese aircraft carriers during Operation 1 (7 April 1943) 80 80
3652 $50 Lt. John F. Kennedy's motor torpedo boat U.S.S. "PT109" in Blackett Strait (1 August 1943) 80 80
3653 $50 U.S.S. "Enterprise" (aircraft carrier) 80 80
3654 $50 American battleships bombarding Rabaul (12 October 1943) 80 80
3655 $50 American landing craft at Cape Gloucester (26 December 1943) 80 80
3656 $50 Commissioning of U.S.S. "Bogue" (first anti-submarine escort carrier) (February 1943) 80 80
3657 $50 Grumman FM-2 Wildcat fighters from U.S.S. "Bogue" sinking "U-118" 80 80
3658 $50 U-boat launching torpedo during peak of Battle of the Atlantic (March 1943) . . 80 80
3659 $50 Surrender of Italian fleet at Malta (10 September 1943) 80 80
3660 $50 H.M.S. "Duke of York" (battleship) sinking "Scharnhorst" (26 December 1943) 80 80

501 Stuart Pearce (England)

502 Sir Shridath Ramphal

1993. World Cup Football Championship, U.S.A. (1994) (1st issue). Multicoloured.

3661 $5 Type **501** 15 10
3662 $6.40 Ronald Koeman (Netherlands) 15 10
3663 $7.65 Gianluca Vialli (Italy) . 20 10
3664 $12.80 McStay (Scotland) and Alemao (Brazil) 30 20
3665 $15.30 Ceulemans (Belgium) and Butcher (England) . . 30 20
3666 $50 Dragan Stojkovic (Yugoslavia) 75 65
3667 $100 Ruud Gullit (Netherlands) . . . . 1·25 1·25
3668 $130 Miloslav Kadlec (Czechoslovakia) . . . . . 1·40 1·50
3669 $150 Ramos (Uruguay) and Berthold (Germany) . . . 1·75 2·00
3670 $190 Baggio (Italy) and Wright (England) . . . . 2·25 2·50
3671 $200 Yaremtchuck (Russia) and Renquin (Belgium) . . . . 2·40 2·75

3672 $225 Timofte (Rumania) and Aleinikov (Russia) . . . . 2·50 3·00
See also Nos. 4142/58.

1993. 1st Recipients of Order of the Caribbean Community. Multicoloured.
3674 $7.65 Type **502** 50 30
3675 $7.65 William Demas 50 30
3676 $7.65 Derek Walcott 50 30

1993. Christmas. Paintings by Rubens and Durer. As T **270** of Dominica. Each black, yellow and red (Nos. 3678, 3680/1, 3684) or multicoloured (others).
3677 $6.40 "The Holy Family under the Apple Tree" (detail) (Rubens) 10 10
3678 $7.65 "The Virgin in Glory" (detail) (Durer) 10 10
3679 $12.80 "The Holy Family under the Apple Tree" (different detail) (Rubens) 10 15
3680 $15.30 "The Virgin in Glory" (different detail) (Durer) . 15 20
3681 $50 "The Virgin in Glory" (different detail) (Durer) . 50 55
3682 $130 "The Holy Family under the Apple Tree" (different detail) (Rubens) . . . . . 1·25 1·40
3683 $190 "The Holy Family under the Apple Tree" (different detail) (Rubens) . . . . . 1·90 2·00
3684 $250 "The Virgin in Glory" (different detail) (Durer) . 2·50 2·75

1993. Bicentenary of the Louvre, Paris. As T **305** of Antigua. Multicoloured.
3686 $50 "Mona Lisa" (Leonardo da Vinci)
3687/94 $50 × 8 "Self-portrait with Spectacles" (Chardin), "Infanta Maria Theresa" (Velazquez); "Spring" (Arcimboldo); "The Virgin of Sorrows" (Bouts); "The Student" (Fragonard); "Francois I" (Clouet); "Le Condottiere" (Antonello da Messina); "La Bohemienne" (Hals)
3695/3702 $50 × 8 "The Village Bride" (left detail) (Greuze); "The Village Bride" (centre detail); "The Village Bride" (right detail); "Self-portrait" (Melendez); "The Knight, the Girl and the Mountain" (Baldung-Grien); "The Young Beggar" (Murillo); "The Pilgrims of Emmaus" (left detail) (Le Nain); "The Pilgrims of Emmaus" (right detail)
3703/10 $50 × 8 "Woman with a Flea" (detail) (Crespi); "The Woman with Dropsy" (detail) (Dou); "Portrait of a Couple" (Ittenbach); "Cleopatra" (Moreau); "Riches" (Vouet); "Old Man and Young Boy" (Ghirlandaio); "Louis XIV" (Rigaud); "The Drinker" (Pieter de Hooch)
3711/18 $50 × 8 "Woman with a Flea" (Crespi); "Self-portrait at Easel" (Rembrandt); "Algerian Women" (detail) (Delacroix); "Head of a Young Man" (Raphael); "Venus and The Graces" (detail) (Botticelli); "Still Life with Chessboard" (detail) (Lubin Baugin); "Lady Macbeth" (Fussli); "The Smoke-filled Room" (detail) (Chardin)
3719/26 $50 × 8 "The Virgin with the Rabbit" (Titian); "The Virgin with the Rabbit" (detail of head) (Titian); "The Beautiful Gardener" (detail) (Raphael); "The Lace-maker" (Vermeer); "Jeanne d'Aragon" (detail) (Raphael); "The Astronomer" (Vermeer); "The Rialto Bridge" (detail) (Canaletto); "Sigismond Malatesta" (Piero della Francesca)
3686/3726 Set of 41 . . . . . . 18·00 19·00

503 "Donald's Better Self", 1938

505 President Dr. Cheddi Jagan

504 Aladdin

1993. Donald Duck Film Posters. Multicoloured.
3728/35 $60 × 8 Type **503**; "Donald's Golf Game", 1938; "Sea Scouts", 1939; "Donald's Penguin", 1939; "A Good Time for a Dime", 1941; "Truant Officer Donald"; "Orphan's Benefit", 1941; "Chef Donald", 1941
3736/43 $60 × 8 "The Village Smithy"; "Donald's Snow Fight"; "Donald's Garden"; "Donald's Gold Mine"; "The Vanishing Private"; "Sky Trooper"; "Bellboy Donald"; "The New Spirit", all 1942
3744/51 $60 × 8 "Saludos Amigos", 1943; "The Eyes Have It", 1945; "Donald's Crime", 1945; "Straight Shooters", 1947; "Donald's Dilemma", 1947; "Bootle Beetle", 1947; "Daddy Duck", 1948; "Soup's On", 1948
3752/9 $80 × 8 "Donald's Happy Birthday", 1949; "Sea Salts", 1949; "Honey Harvester", 1949; "All in a Nutshell", 1949; "The Greener Yard", 1949; "Slide, Donald, Slide", 1949; "Lion Around", 1950; "Trailer Horn", 1950
3760/7 $80 × 8 "Bee at the Beach", 1950; "Out on a Limb", 1950; "Corn Chips", 1951; "Test Pilot Donald", 1951; "Lucky Number", 1951; "Out of Scale", 1951; "Bee on Guard", 1951; "Let's Stick Together", 1952
3768/75 $80 × 8 "Trick or Treat", 1952; "Don's Fountain of Youth", 1953; "Rugged Bear", 1953; "Canvas Back Duck", 1953; "Dragon Around", 1954; "Grin and Bear It", 1954; "The Flying Squirrel", 1954; "Up a Tree", 1955
3776/81 $80 × 8 Scenes from "Pirate Gold": In the crow's nest; Aracuan Bird carrying treasure chest; Donald with treasure map; Donald at souvenir stall; Aracuan Bird with Donald; Donald on jetty (all horiz)
3728/81 Set of 56 . . . . 38·00 40·00

1993. "Aladdin" (film). Disney Cartoon Characters. Multicoloured.
3783/90 $7.65 × 8 Type **504**; Abu the monkey; Jasmine; Rajah the tiger; Jafar; Iago the parrot; The Sultan; The Genie
3791/9 $50 × 9 Jafar and magic scarab; Tiger Head entrance, Cave of Wonders; Jafar; Aladdin and Abu at breakfast; Aladdin rescuing Jasmine; Aladdin, Jasmine and Abu; Rajah comforts Jasmine; Jafar disguised as an old man; Aladdin and Abu in treasure chamber (all horiz)
3800/8 $65 × 9 Aladdin with lamp and magic carpet; The Genie measuring Aladdin; Abu turned into an elephant; Aladdin in disguise at palace; Aladdin and Jasmine on magic carpet; Aladdin in disguise, Jasmine and Sultan; Aladdin fighting Jafar; Aladdin and Jasmine; The Genie with suitcase and golf clubs (all horiz)
3783/3808 Set of 26 . . . . . . 10·50 11·00

1993. 1st Anniv of Election of President Jagan.
3810 **505** $6.40 multicoloured . . 30 30

1994. "Hong Kong '94" International Stamp Exhibition (1st issue). As T **317** of Antigua. Multicoloured.
3812 $50 Hong Kong 1984 Royal Hong Kong Jockey Club $1.30 stamp and Happy Valley Racecourse 70 80
3813 $50 Guyana 1992 Movie Posters $190 stamp and Happy Valley Racecourse 70 80
Nos. 3812/13 were printed together, se-tenant, with the centre part of each pair forming a composite design.

1994. "Hong Kong '94" International Stamp Exhibition (2nd issue). Ch'ing Dynasty Snuff Boxes (Nos. 3814/19) or Porcelain (Nos. 3820/5). As T **318** of Antigua but vert. Multicoloured.
3814 $20 Painted enamel in shape of bamboo 30 30
3815 $20 Painted enamel showing woman 30 30
3816 $20 Amber with lions playing ball 30 30
3817 $20 Agate in shape of two gourds 30 30
3818 $20 Glass overlay with dog design 30 30
3819 $20 Glass with foliage design 30 30
3820 $20 Covered jar with dragon design 30 30
3821 $20 Rotating brush-holder . 30 30
3822 $20 Covered jar with horses design 30 30
3823 $20 Amphora vase with bats and peaches 30 30
3824 $20 Tea caddy with Fo dogs 30 30
3825 $20 Vase with camellias and peaches design 30 30

1994. Centenary of the Sign for the Mahdi. Nos. 1622/4 and 1634 surch **CENTENARY Sign For The MAHDI 1894-1994** and new value.
3826 $6 on 60 c. Plate No. 73 (Series 1) (horiz) . . . . .
3827 $20 on 200 c. Plate No. 33 (Series 1) (horiz) . . . . .
3828 $30 on 60 c. Plate No. 57 (Series 1) (horiz) . . . . .
3829 $35 on 60 c. Plate No. 75 (Series 1) (horiz) . . . . .
The surcharges on Nos. 3826 and 3828 show the third line as "MADHI".

1994. Hummel Figurines. As T **302** of Antigua. Multicoloured.
3830 $20 Girl holding inscribed heart 20 25
3831 $25 Boy with heart under arm 25 30
3832 $35 Baker 35 40
3833 $50 Girl with pot of flowers . 50 55
3834 $60 Girl with trumpet, pot plant and bird 60 65
3835 $130 Four girls . . . . . . 1·25 1·40
3836 $190 Boy and two girls with dog . . . . 1·90 2·00
3837 $250 Boy with cake and dog . 2·50 2·75

1994. 75th Anniv of I.L.O. Nos. 1760 and 1629/30 surch **I L O 75th Anniversary 1919-1994** and new value.
3839 $6 on 130 c. Plate No. 13 (Series 1) . . . .
3840 $30 on 120 c. Plate No. 58 (Series 1) . . . .
3841 $35 on 120 c. Plate No. 56 (Series 1) . . . .

1994. Centenary (1992) of Sierra Club (environmental protection society). Endangered Species. As T **320** of Antigua. Multicoloured.
3842 $70 Red Kangaroo with young 90 90
3843 $70 Head of American alligator 90 90
3844 $70 Head of bald eagle . . . 90 90
3845 $70 Giant panda eating bamboo 90 90
3846 $70 Head of red kangaroo . . 90 90
3847 $70 Alaskan brown bear sitting 90 90
3848 $70 Bald eagle 90 90
3849 $70 Head of giant panda . . 90 90
3850 $70 Red kangaroo (horiz) . . 90 90
3851 $70 Whooping crane facing left (horiz) 90 90
3852 $70 Male whooping crane in courtship display (horiz) . . 90 90
3853 $70 Whooping crane looking right (horiz) 90 90
3854 $70 Alaskan brown bear and cub (horiz) 90 90
3855 $70 Alaskan brown bear fishing (horiz) 90 90
3856 $70 Bald eagle on branch (horiz) 90 90
3857 $70 Giant panda (horiz) . . . 90 90
3858 $70 American alligator (logo at left) (horiz) 90 90
3859 $70 American alligator (logo at right) (horiz) 90 90
3860 $70 Italian Alps at sunrise (horiz) 90 90
3861 $70 Italian Alps and meadow (horiz) 90 90
3862 $70 Mono Lake at sunset (horiz) 90 90
3863 $70 Rock pinnacles, Mono Lake (horiz) 90 90
3864 $70 Sea lion 90 90
3865 $70 Head of sea lion 90 90
3866 $70 Sea lions on rocks . . . 90 90
3867 $70 Rock pinnacles, Mono Lake 90 90
3868 $70 Sierra Club Centennial emblem (black, brown and green) 90 90
3869 $70 Lake, Italian Alps 90 90
3870 $70 Summit of Matterhorn . . 90 90
3871 $70 Matterhorn and village . . 90 90
3872 $70 Clouds over Matterhorn . 90 90

1994. Royal Visit. Nos. 3551/4 optd **ROYAL VISIT FEB 19-22, 1994.**
3873 $25 Queen Elizabeth II in Coronation robes (photograph by Cecil Beaton) 40 50
3874 $50 Royal gems 75 85
3875 $75 Queen Elizabeth and Prince Philip . . . . 90 1·00
3876 $130 Queen opening Parliament . . . . 1·25 1·40

509 "Cestrum parqui"

1994. Flowers. Multicoloured.
3878 $6.40 Type **509** 10 10
3879 $7.65 "Brunfelsia calycina" . 10 10
3880 $12.80 "Datura rosei" 10 15
3881 $15.30 "Ruellia macrantha" . 15 20
3882 $50 "Portlandia albiflora" . . 50 55
3883 $50 "Clusia grandiflora" . . 50 55
3884 $50 "Begonia haageana" . . 50 55
3885 $50 "Fuchsia simplicicaulis" . 50 55
3886 $50 "Guaiacum officinale" . . 50 55
3887 $50 "Pithecoctenium cynanchoides" 50 55
3888 $50 "Sphaeralcea umbellata" . 50 55
3889 $50 "Erythrina poeppigiana" . 50 55
3890 $50 "Steriphoma paradoxa" . 50 55
3891 $50 "Allemanda violacea" . . 50 55
3892 $50 "Centropogon cornutus" 50 55
3893 $50 "Passiflora quadrangularis" 50 55
3894 $50 "Victoria amazonica" . . 50 55
3895 $50 "Cobaea scandens" . . . 50 55
3896 $50 "Pyrostegia venusta" . . 50 55
3897 $50 "Petrea kohautiana" . . 50 55
3898 $50 "Hippobroma longiflora" 50 55
3899 $50 "Cleome hassleriana" . . 50 55
3900 $50 "Verbena peruviana" . . 50 55
3901 $50 "Tropaeolum peregrinum" 50 55
3902 $50 "Plumeria rubra" 50 55
3903 $50 "Selenicereus grandiflorus" 50 55
3904 $50 "Mandevilla splendens" . 50 55
3905 $50 "Pereskia aculeata" . . . 50 55
3906 $50 "Ipomoea learii" 50 55
3907 $130 "Pachystachys coccinea" 1·25 1·40
3908 $190 "Beloperone guttata" . . 1·90 2·00
3909 $250 "Ferdinandusa speciosa" 2·50 2·75
Nos. 3883/94 and 3895/3906 respectively were printed together, se-tenant, forming composite background designs.

1994. 25th Anniv of First Moon Landing (1st issue). As T **326** of Antigua. Multicoloured.
3911 $60 Walter Dornberger and launch of first A-4 rocket . 90 90
3912 $60 Rudolph Nebel and "Surveyor 1" 90 90
3913 $60 Robert H. Goddard and "Apollo 7" 90 90
3914 $60 Kurt Debus and view of Earth from Moon ("Apollo 8") 90 90
3915 $60 James T. Webb and "Apollo 9" 90 90
3916 $60 George E. Mueller and "Apollo 10" lunar module 90 90
3917 $60 Wernher von Braun and launch of "Apollo 11" . . 90 90
3918 $60 Rocco A. Petrone and "Apollo 11" astronaut on Moon 90 90
3919 $60 Eberhard Rees and "Apollo 12" astronaut on Moon . 90 90
3920 $60 Charles A. Berry and damaged "Apollo 13" . . 90 90
3921 $60 Thomas O. Paine and "Apollo 14" before splashdown 90 90
3922 $60 A. F. Staats and "Apollo 15" on Moon 90 90
3923 $60 Robert R. Gilruth and "Apollo 16" astronaut on Moon 90 90
3924 $60 Ernst Stuhlinger and "Apollo 17" crew on Moon 90 90
3925 $60 Christopher C. Kraft and X-30 National Aero-Space Plane 90 90
3926 $60 Rudolf Opitz and Messerschmitt Me 163B Komet (rocket engine), 1943 90 90
3927 $60 Clyde W. Tombaugh and "face" on Mars 90 90
3928 $60 Hermann Oberth and scene from "The Girl in the Moon" 90 90
See also Nos. 4169/86.

1994. Centenary of International Olympic Committee. Medal Winners. As T **327** of Antigua but vert. Multicoloured.
3930 $20 Nancy Kerrigan (U.S.A.) (1994 figure skating silver) 30 30
3931 $35 Sawao Kato (Japan) (1976 gymnastics gold) 50 50
3932 $130 Florence Griffith Joyner (U.S.A.) (1988 100 and 200 metres gold) . . . . 1·75 2·00

1994. Centenary of First English Cricket Tour to the West Indies (1995). As T **329** of Antigua. Multicoloured.
3934 $20 Clive Lloyd (Guyana and West Indies) (vert) 40 30
3935 $35 Carl Hooper (Guyana and West Indies) and Wisden Trophy 55 50
3936 $60 Graham Hick (England) and Wisden Trophy . . . 90 1·00

1994. 50th Anniv of D-Day. Aircraft. As T **331** of Antigua. Multicoloured.
3938 $6 Supermarine Spitfire Mk XI fighter on photo reconnaissance 20 15
3939 $35 North American B-25 Mitchell bomber 60 50
3940 $190 Republic P-47 Thunderbolt fighters . . . 2·50 3·00

1994. 50th Anniv of Second World War (3rd issue). As T **500**. Multicoloured.
3942 $60 Paratroops drop, D-Day 80 80
3943 $60 Glider assault, D-Day . 80 80
3944 $60 U.S.S. "Arkansas" (battleship) bombarding Omaha Beach, D-Day . . 80 80
3945 $60 U.S. fighters attacking train 80 80
3946 $60 Allied landing craft approaching beaches . . . 80 80
3947 $60 Troops in beach obstacles 80 80
3948 $60 Commandos leaving landing craft 80 80
3949 $60 U.S. flail tank destroying mines 80 80
3950 $60 U.S. tank breaking through sea wall 80 80
3951 $60 Tanks and infantry advancing 80 80
3952 $60 Landings at Anzio (22 January 1944) 80 80
3953 $60 R.A.F. attacking Amiens Prison (18 February 1944) 80 80
3954 $60 Soviet Army tank in Sevastopol (9 May 1944) . 80 80
3955 $60 British bren-gun carriers at the Gustav Line (19 May 1944) 80 80
3956 $60 D-Day landings (6 June 1944) 80 80
3957 $60 "V-1" over London (13 June 1944) 80 80
3958 $60 Allies entering Paris (19 August 1944) 80 80
3959 $60 German "V-2" rocket ready for launch (8 September 1944) 80 80
3960 $60 Sinking of "Tirpitz" (German battleship) (12 November 1944) 80 80
3961 $60 U.S. tanks at Bastogne (29 December 1944) 80 80

1994. "Philakorea '94" International Stamp Exhibition, Seoul (1st issue). As T **330** of Antigua. Multicoloured.
3962 $6 Socialist ideals statue, Pyongyang (vert) 10 10
3963 $25 Statue of Admiral Yi Sun-sin (vert) 25 30
3964 $60 Fruits and mountain peaks 60 65

3965 $60 Manchurian crane, bamboo and peaks 60 65
3966 $60 Rising sun and two cranes on pine 60 65
3967 $60 Five cranes on pine and peak 60 65
3968 $60 Three cranes in flight . . . 60 65
3969 $60 Sea, rocky shore and fungi 60 65
3970 $60 Sea, rocky shore and fruit 60 65
3971 $60 Hind at seashore and fruit 60 65
3972 $60 Stag in pine forest . . . 60 65
3973 $60 Deer and fungi by waterfall 60 65
3974 $60 Tops of pines and mountain peaks 60 65
3975 $60 Manchurian crane in flight 60 65
3976 $60 Three cranes on pine tree 60 65
3977 $60 Crane on pine tree . . . 60 65
3978 $60 Top of fruit tree 60 65
3979 $60 Stag and two hinds on mountainside 60 65
3980 $60 Deer and fungi 60 65
3981 $60 Stag by waterfall and hind drinking 60 65
3982 $60 Pine tree, fruit and fungi 60 65
3983 $60 Fungi on mountainside . 60 65
3984 $120 Sokkat'ap Pagoda, Pulguksa . . . . 1·25 1·40
3985 $130 Village Guardian (statue), Chejudo Island . . . . . 1·25 1·40

Nos. 3964/73 and 3974/83, all 23×49 mm, were printed together, se-tenant, in sheetlets of 10, each sheetlet forming a composite design showing panels from a screen painting of longevity symbols from the late Chosun dynasty.

See also Nos. 4117/40.

510 Miki Maya

1994. 80th Anniv of Takarazuka Revue of Japan. Multicoloured.

3987 $20 Type **510** 40 45
3988 $20 Fubuki Takane 40 45
3989 $20 Seika Kuze 40 45
3990 $20 Saki Asaji 40 45
3991 $60 Mira Anju (34×47 mm) 70 75
3992 $60 Yuki Amami (34×47 mm) 70 75
3993 $60 Maki Ichiro (34×47 mm) 70 75
3994 $60 Yu Shion (34×47 mm) . 70 75

511 "Heliconius melpomene"

1994. Butterflies. Multicoloured.

3995 $6 Type **511** 10 10
3996 $20 "Helicopis cupido" . . . 10 25
3997 $25 "Agrias claudina" . . . 25 30
3998 $30 "Parides coelus" 30 35
3999 $50 "Heliconius hecale" . . . 50 55
4000 $50 "Anaea marthesia" . . . 50 55
4001 $50 "Brassolis astyra" . . . 50 55
4002 $50 "Heliconius melpomene" 50 55
4003 $50 "Haetera piera" 50 55
4004 $50 "Morpho diana" 50 55
4005 $50 "Parides coelus" 50 55
4006 $50 "Catagramma pitheas" . 50 55
4007 $50 "Nessaea obrinus" . . . 50 55
4008 $50 "Automeris janus" . . . 50 55
4009 $50 "Papilio torquatus" . . 50 55
4010 $50 "Eunica sophonisba" . . 50 55
4011 $50 "Ceratinia nise" 50 55
4012 $50 "Panacea procilla" . . . 50 55
4013 $50 "Pyrrhogyra neaerea" . . 50 55
4014 $50 "Morpho deidamia" . . . 50 55
4015 $50 "Dismorphia orise" . . . 50 55
4016 $60 "Morpho diana" 60 65
4017 $190 "Dismorphia orise" . . 1·90 2·00
4018 $250 "Morpho deidamia" . . 2·50 2·75

512 Jacob

513 Peregrine Falcon

1994. Bible Stories (2nd series). Multicoloured. (a) Joseph.

4020/43 $20×24 arranged as blocks of 4 depicting Jacob giving Joseph a coat of many colours (Type **512** at top left); Joseph thrown into a pit; Joseph sold as a slave; Joseph accused by Potiphar's wife; Joseph interprets Pharoah's dreams; Joseph reunited with his brothers

(b) The Parting of the Red Sea.

4044/67 $20×24 Palm trees on shore; Pyramids; Palm trees on shore and black cloud; Three palm trees; Blue and white dove; Red and white bird; Egyptian army engulfed by sea; Yellow and white dove; Red and green fishes; Egyptian chariot with wall of water at left; Chariots between walls of water; Dolphins; Two doves; Israelites and water to left; Israelites and water to right; Turquoise and purple fishes; Israelites with tree at left; Israelites with goats; Moses; Israelites with tree at right; Israelites with woman on horse; Israelites with old man and woman carrying pack; Israelites with woman carrying young child; Israelites with cart

(c) Ruth.

4068/91 $20×24 arranged as blocks of 6 depicting Ruth and Naomi; Ruth gleaning in cornfield; Boaz establishing kinsman's rights; Naomi with Ruth, Boaz and Obed

(d) Daniel in the Lions' Den.

4092/4116 $20×25 Palm fronds and hibiscus flower; Frigate bird and palm fronds; Frigate birds and tops of stone pillars; Frigate bird, pillars and sail at bottom right; Hibiscus, sails of ship and top of pillar; Yellow arum lilies and palm trees; Heads of adult and immature frigate birds and palm trees; Palm trees, butterfly and stone pillars; Two butterflies and stone pillars; Stone pillar and sailing ship; Standing heron; Purple irises and palm trees; Daniel; Angel; Donkey foal; Orchids; Lioness and two cubs; Daniel's legs and lions; Lion; Three crowns; Goat and kid; Kid; Cub and head of lion; Lioness; Heron in flight

4020/4116 Set of 97 . . . . . . 22·00 24·00

Nos. 4020/43, 4044/67, 4068/91 and 4092/4116 respectively were printed together, se-tenant, forming composite designs.

1994. "Philakorea '94" International Stamp Exhibition, Seoul (2nd issue). Birds of the World. Multicoloured.

4117 $35 Type **513** 45 50
4118 $35 Great spotted woodpecker 45 50
4119 $35 White-throated kingfisher 45 50
4120 $35 Peruvian cock of the rock 45 50
4121 $35 Yellow-headed amazon . 45 50
4122 $35 Victoria crowned pigeon 45 50
4123 $35 Little owl 45 50
4124 $35 Ring-necked pheasant . 45 50
4125 $35 Goldfinch 45 50
4126 $35 Jay 45 50
4127 $35 Sulphur-breasted toucan 45 50
4128 $35 Japanese blue flycatcher 45 50
4129 $35 Northern goshawk . . . 45 50
4130 $35 Lapwing 45 50
4131 $35 Ornate umbrellabird . . 45 50
4132 $35 Slaty-headed parakeet . 45 50
4133 $35 Regent bowerbird . . . 45 50
4134 $35 Egyptian goose 45 50
4135 $35 White-winged crossbill . 45 50
4136 $35 Waxwing 45 50
4137 $35 Ruff 45 50
4138 $35 Hoopoe 45 50
4139 $35 Superb starling 45 50
4140 $35 Great jacamar 45 50

514 Paulo Futre (Portugal)

1994. World Cup Football Championship, U.S.A. (2nd issue). Multicoloured.

4142 $6 Type **514** 10 10
4143 $35 Lyndon Hooper (Canada) 35 40
4144 $60 Enzo Francescoli (Uruguay) 60 65
4145 $60 Paolo Maldini (Italy) . . 60 65
4146 $60 Guyana player 60 65
4147 $60 Bwalya Kalusha (Zambia) 60 65
4148 $60 Diego Maradona (Argentina) 60 65
4149 $60 Andreas Brehme (Germany) 60 65
4150 $60 Eric Wynalda (U.S.A.) (pursuing ball) 60 65
4151 $60 John Doyle (U.S.A.) . . 60 65
4152 $60 Eric Wynalda (U.S.A.) (kicking ball) 60 65
4153 $60 Thomas Dooley (U.S.A.) 60 65
4154 $60 Ernie Stewart (U.S.A.) . 60 65
4155 $60 Marcelo Balboa (U.S.A.) 60 65
4156 $60 Bora Milutinovic (U.S.A. coach) 60 65
4157 $190 Freddy Rincon (Colombia) . . . . 1·90 2·00

Nos. 4145/50 and 4151/6 respectively were printed together, se-tenant, forming composite background designs.

515 Anja Fichtel (individual foil, 1988)

1994. Olympic Games, Atlanta (1996) (1st issue). Previous German Gold Medal Winners. Mult.

4159 $6 Type **515** 10 10
4160 $25 Annegret Richter (100 metres, 1976) (vert) . . . 25 30
4161 $30 Heike Henkel (high jump, 1992) (vert) 30 35
4162 $35 Armin Hary (100 metres, 1960) (vert) 35 40
4163 $50 Heide Rosendahl (long jump, 1972) (vert) 50 55
4164 $60 Josef Neckermann (dressage, 1968) (vert) . . . 60 65
4165 $130 Heike Drechsler (long jump, 1988) (vert) . . . . 1·25 1·40
4166 $190 Ulrike Mayfarth (high jump, 1984) (vert) . . . . 1·90 2·00
4167 $250 Michael Gross (200 metres freestyle and 100 metres butterfly, 1984) . . . . . 2·50 2·75

See also Nos. 4492/4507 and 4739/87.

516 Dog Laika and Rocket, 1957

1994. 25th Anniv of First Moon Landing (2nd issue). Multicoloured.

4169 $60 Type **516** 80 80
4170 $60 Yury Gagarin (first man in space), 1961 . . . . 80 80
4171 $60 John Glenn (first American to orbit Earth), 1962 . . . 80 80
4172 $60 Edward White walking in space, 1965 . . . . 80 80
4173 $60 Neil Armstrong, walking on Moon and "Apollo 11" logo 80 80
4174 $60 "Luna 16" leaving Moon, 1970 . . . . 80 80
4175 $60 Lunar Module 1 on Moon, 1970 . . . . 80 80
4176 $60 Skylab 1, 1973 . . . . . 80 80
4177 $60 Astronauts and Apollo–Soyuz link-up, 1975 . . . . 80 80
4178 $60 "Mars 3" 80 80
4179 $60 "Mariner 10" 80 80
4180 $60 "Voyager" 80 80
4181 $60 "Pioneer" 80 80
4182 $60 "Giotto" 80 80
4183 $60 "Magellan" 80 80
4184 $60 "Galileo" 80 80
4185 $60 "Ulysses" 80 80
4186 $60 "Cassini" 80 80

Nos. 4178/86 were printed together, se-tenant, with the backgrounds forming a composite design of Space.

517 South Caroline Railroad "Best Friend of Charleston", 1830, U.S.A.

1994. History of Trains. Steam Locomotives. Multicoloured.

4188 $25 Type **517** 40 40
4189 $25 South Eastern Railway No. 285, 1882 . . . . 40 40
4190 $30 Camden & Amboy Railway No. 1 "John Bull", 1831, U.S.A. 45 45
4191 $30 Stephenson "Patentee" type locomotive, 1837 . . . . 45 45
4192 $30 "Atlantic", 1832 . . . . 45 45
4193 $30 "Stourbridge Lion", 1829, U.S.A. 45 45
4194 $30 Polonceau locomotive, 1854 . . . . 45 45
4195 $30 "Thomas Rogers", 1855, U.S.A. 45 45
4196 $30 "Vulcan", 1858 . . . . 45 45
4197 $30 "Namur", 1846 . . . . 45 45
4198 $30 John Jarvis's "De Witt Clinton", 1831, U.S.A. . . 45 45
4199 $30 Seguin locomotive, 1829 . 45 45
4200 $30 Stephenson's "Planet", 1830 . . . . 45 45
4201 $30 Norris locomotive, 1840 . 45 45
4202 $30 "Sampson", 1867, U.S.A. 45 45
4203 $30 "Andrew Jackson", 1832 . 45 45
4204 $30 "Herald", 1831 . . . . . 45 45
4205 $30 "Cumberland", 1845, U.S.A. 45 45
4206 $30 Pennsylvania Railroad Class K, 1880 . . . . . . 45 45
4207 $30 Cooke locomotive No. 11, 1885 . . . . 45 45
4208 $30 "John B. Turner", 1867, U.S.A. 45 45
4209 $30 Baldwin locomotive, 1871 45 45
4210 $30 Richard Trevithick's locomotive, 1803 . . . . . 45 45
4211 $30 John Stephens's locomotive, 1825 . . . . 45 45
4212 $30 John Blenkinsop's locomotive, 1814 . . . . . 45 45
4213 $30 "Pennsylvania," 1803 . . 45 45
4214 $300 Mount Washington Cog Railway locomotive No. 6, 1886 . . . . 3·00 3·00
4215 $300 Stroudley locomotive "Brighton", 1872 . . . . 3·00 3·00

No. 4198 is inscribed "West Point Foundry 1832 Locomotive" and No. 4202 "Union Iron Works os San Francisco", both error.

1994. Christmas. Religious Paintings. As T **336** of Antigua. Multicoloured.

4217 $6 "Joseph with the Christ Child" (Guido Reni) . . . 15 10
4218 $20 "Adoration of the Christ Child" (Girolamo Romanino) 25 25
4219 $25 "Adoration of the Christ Child with St. Barbara and St. Martin" (Raffaello Botticini) 30 30
4220 $30 "Holy Family" (Pompeo Batoni) 35 35
4221 $35 "Flight into Egypt" (Bartolommeo Carducci) . 40 40
4222 $60 "Holy Family and the Baptist" (Andrea del Sarto) 70 70
4223 $120 "Sacred Conversation" (Cesare de Sesto) . . . . 1·50 1·75
4224 $190 "Madonna and Child with Saints Joseph and John the Baptist" (Pontormo) . . . 2·40 2·75

518 Riker and Dr. Crusher

1994. "Star Trek Generations" (film). Designs showing "Enterprise" crew in 19th-century naval uniforms (Nos. 4226/34) or in 23rd-century (Nos. 4235/43). Multicoloured.

4226 $100 Type **518** . . . . . . 1·25 1·25
4227 $100 Geordi, Dr. Crusher with Lt. Worf in chains . . . . 1·25 1·25
4228 $100 Captain Picard . . . . 1·25 1·25
4229 $100 Data and Geordi . . . 1·25 1·25
4230 $100 "U.S.S. Enterprise" (sailing ship) . . . . . . 1·25 1·25
4231 $100 Captain Picard and Riker on quarterdeck . . . . . 1·25 1·25
4232 $100 Data . . . . 1·25 1·25
4233 $100 Lt. Worf . . . . 1·25 1·25
4234 $100 Dr. Crusher . . . . . . 1·25 1·25
4235 $100 Captain Picard . . . . 1·25 1·25
4236 $100 Riker . . . . 1·25 1·25
4237 $100 Captain Kirk . . . . . 1·25 1·25
4238 $100 Soron with phaser . . 1·25 1·25
4239 $100 Captains Kirk and Picard on horseback . . . . . 1·25 1·25
4240 $100 Klingon women . . . . 1·25 1·25
4241 $100 Captains Kirk and Picard . . . . 1·25 1·25
4242 $100 Troi . . . . 1·25 1·25
4243 $100 Captain Picard and Data 1·25 1·25
4244 $100 "BOLDLY GO" film poster . . . . 1·25 1·25

519 Cross and Map of Guyana

1994. Centenary of Sisters of Mercy in Guyana.

4246 **519** $60 multicoloured . . . 80 80

1994. 1st Recipients of Order of the Caribbean Community. As Nos. 2046/8 of Antigua. Multicoloured.

4247 $60 Sir Shridath Ramphal . . 60 65
4248 $60 William Demas 60 65
4249 $60 Derek Walcott 60 65

520 Garfield Sobers congratulating Brian Lara

1995. Brian Lara's Achievements in Cricket. Multicoloured.

4250	$20 Type **520**	20	25
4251	$30 Brian Lara setting world record for highest Test Match score (vert)	30	35
4252	$375 Lara and Chanderpaul	3·75	4·00

521 Babe Ruth

1995. Birth Centenary of Babe Ruth (baseball player). Each brown and black.

4254	$65 Type **521**	65	70
4255	$65 Preparing to bat (full-length photo)	65	70
4256	$65 Head and shoulders portrait (cap with limp brim)	65	70
4257	$65 In retirement (bare-headed)	65	70
4258	$65 Running (in plain shirt)	65	70
4259	$65 Head and shoulders portrait (cap with emblem and stiff brim)	65	70
4260	$65 Wearing "NEW YORK" shirt	65	70
4261	$65 Preparing to hit (in "NEW YORK" shirt)	65	70
4262	$65 Wearing "YANKEES" shirt	65	70
4263	$65 At base with bat on shoulder (in striped shirt)	65	70
4264	$65 Watching the ball (in striped shirt)	65	70
4265	$65 In cap and coat at Old Timer's Day, Yankee Stadium, 1948	65	70

522 Mickey Mouse as Family Doctor

1995. Disney Characters at Work. Multicoloured.

4267/75	$30×9 Type **522**; Goofy and optometrist; Daisy Duck as nurse; Scrooge McDuck as psychiatrist; Daisy Duck as physiotherapist; Horace Horsecollar and dentist; Goofy and radiologist; Goofy as pharmacist; Big Pete as chiropractor		
4276/84	$30×9 Mickey Mouse as vet; Donald Duck training seals; Ludwig von Duck as animal psychiatrist; Goofy as ornithologist; Daisy Duck grooming Old English sheepdog; Minnie Mouse as herpetologist; Mickey Mouse as pet shop keeper with Pluto; J. Audubon Woodlore as park ranger; Donald Duck as aquarist		
4285/93	$30×9 Mickey Mouse as animator with Pluto; Goofy the tailor with Mickey Mouse; Pete the glassblower with Morty; Minnie Mouse painting Clarabelle; Daisy Duck sculpting Donald; Donald Duck as potter; Chip and Dale the watchmakers; Donald Duck the locksmith; Grandma Duck making quilt		
4294/4301	$35×8 Mickey Mouse as policeman; Donald Duck as fireman; Uncle Scrooge as ambulance driver; Grandma Duck as crossing patrol; Daisy Duck as museum attendant and Donald as visitor; Goofy as census taker and family of rabbits; Horace Horsecollar and Big Pete as street maintenance workers; Donald Duck as sanitation worker at recycling bin (all vert)		
4302/9	$35×8 Mickey Mouse with Pluto driving lorry; Mickey Mouse as carpenter sawing; Goofy riding road drill; Minnie Mouse with electric drill; Donald Duck driving forklift; Minnie Mouse and Goofy as construction contractors; Mickey Mouse with Pluto as carpenter making table; Pluto driving bulldozer (all vert)		
4310/17	$35×8 Mickey Mouse as plumber; Mickey Mouse the paperboy; Huey, Dewey and Louie moving furniture; Big Pete as handyman; Donald Duck and nephews house painting; Goofy as washing machine repairman; Minnie Mouse as babysitter; Daisy Duck as carer (all vert)		
4267/4317	Set of 51	18·00	20·00

No. 4271 is inscribed "PHYSICAL THEREPIST" in error.

1995. Centenary of Salvation Army. Nos. 1519 and 1521/3 surch **SALVATION ARMY 1895 — 1995** and new value.

4319	$6 on 60 c. Plate No. 10 (Series 1)		
4320	$20 on 60 c. Plate No. 19 (Series 1)		
4321	$30 on 60 c. Plate No. 2 (Series 1)		
4322	$35 on 60 c. Plate No. 31 (Series 1)		

524 Pig

525 Goshawk

1995. Chinese New Year ("Year of the Pig"). Symbolic pigs. Multicoloured.

4323	$20 Type **524**	20	25
4324	$30 Pig facing left	30	35
4325	$50 Pig facing front (face value bottom right)	50	55
4326	$100 Pig facing front (face value bottom left)	1·00	1·10

1995. Birds. Multicoloured.

4329	$5 Type **525**	10	10
4330	$6 Lapwing	10	10
4331	$8 Ornate umbrellabird	10	10
4332	$15 Slaty-headed parakeet	10	10
4333	$19 Regent bowerbird	20	25
4334	$20 Egyptian goose	20	25
4335	$25 White-winged crossbill	25	30
4336	$30 Waxwing	30	35
4337	$35 Ruff	35	40
4338	$60 Hoopoe	60	65
4339	$100 Superb starling	1·00	1·10
4340	$500 Great jacamar	5·00	5·25

526 Norwegian Forest Cat

1995. "Singapore '95" International Stamp Exhibition. Multicoloured.

4341/52	$35 × 12 Cats (Type **526**; Scottish fold; Red Burmese; British blue-hair; Abyssinian; Siamese; Exotic shorthair; Turkish van cat; Black Persian; Black-tipped burmilla; Singapura; Calico shorthair)		
4353/64	$35 × 12 Dogs (Gordon setter; Long-haired chihuahua; Dalmatian; Afghan hound; Old English bulldog; Miniature schnauzer; Clumber spaniel; Pekingese; St. Bernard; English cocker spaniel; Alaskan malamute; Rottweiler)		
4365/76	$35 × 12 Horses (chestnut thoroughbred colt; liver chestnut quarter horse; black Friesian; chestnut Belgian; Appaloosa; Lippizaner; chestnut hunter; British shire; Palomino; pinto ("Seal Brown Point"); Arab; Afghanistan kabardin)		
4341/76	Set of 36	13·00	15·00

No. 4355 is inscribed "Dalmation", No. 4367 "Freisian" and No. 4370 "Lipizzanas", all in error.

527 Captain John Smith leaving for New World, 1607

1995. "Pocahontas". Characters and scenes from Disney cartoon film. Multicoloured. (a) Vert designs showing characters.

4378/85	$50×8 Pocahontas and Meeko; John Smith; Chief Powhatan; Kocoum; Ratcliffe; Wiggins; Nakoma; Thomas		

(b) Horiz designs showing film scenes.

4386/94	$8×9 Type **527**; Ratcliffe; Chief Powhatan greeted by his people; Pocahontas standing on cliff; Pocahontas, Nakoma and Meeko in canoe; Powhatan asking Pocahontas to marry Kocoum; Pocahontas receiving her mother's necklace; Pocahontas seeking guidance from Grandmother Willow; Pocahontas watching arrival of "Susan Constant"		
4395/4403	$30×9 Ratcliffe claiming land for English Crown; Kekata having vision; Meeting of John Smith and Pocahontas; Namantack watching settlers; Powhatan and wounded Namantack; Pocahontas showing John Smith the colours of the wind; Nakoma finds Pocahontas with John Smith; Pocahontas offering John "Indian gold" (corn); Pocahontas, John Smith and Grandmother Willow		
4404/12	$35×9 Kocoum telling Pocahontas about the war council; Nakoma telling Kocoum to find Pocahontas; John Smith and Kocoum wrestling over knife; Powhatan sentencing John to death; Pocahontas and Grandmother Willow; Pocahontas saving John Smith; Ratcliffe under arrest; Powhatan draping his cloak over wounded John Smith; Pocahontas and John Smith saying goodbye		
4378/4412	Set of 35	20·00	21·00

1995. 95th Birthday of Queen Elizabeth the Queen Mother. As T **344** of Antigua.

4414	$100 brown, light brown and black	1·00	1·10
4415	$100 multicoloured	1·00	1·10
4416	$100 multicoloured	1·00	1·10
4417	$100 multicoloured	1·00	1·10

DESIGNS: No. 4414, Queen Elizabeth the Queen Mother (pastel drawing); 4415, Wearing purple hat; 4416, Wearing turquoise hat; 4417, At desk (oil painting).

528 Paul Harris (founder) and Rotary Emblem

1995. 90th Anniv of Rotary International. Multicoloured.

4419	**528** $200 multicoloured	2·00	2·10

529 Girl carrying Sack on Head

1995. 50th Anniv of F.A.O. Multicoloured.

4421	$35 Type **529**	35	40
4422	$60 Man and woman carrying sacks of food aid	60	65
4423	$200 Woman holding sack	2·00	2·10

Nos. 4421/3 were printed together, se-tenant, forming a composite design.

530 Scouts around Campfire

1995. 18th World Scout Jamboree, Netherlands. Multicoloured.

4425	$20 Type **530**	20	25
4426	$25 Scout on beach	25	30
4427	$30 Scouts hiking	30	35
4428	$35 Scout snorkelling	35	40
4429	$60 Scout saluting and flag of Guyana	60	65
4430	$200 Scout fishing from boat	2·00	2·10

1995. 50th Anniv of End of World War II in Europe. As T **340** of Antigua. Multicoloured.

4432	$60 American tank during Battle of the Bulge	60	65
4433	$60 Allied tanks crossing Siegfried Line	60	65
4434	$60 Liberated concentration camp prisoners	60	65
4435	$60 Allied plane dropping food to Dutch	60	65
4436	$60 U.S. infantry patrol, North Italy	60	65
4437	$60 "Daily Mail" headline announcing Hitler's death	60	65
4438	$60 Soviet tanks entering Berlin	60	65
4439	$60 Surrender of "U858" in U.S. waters	60	65

No. 4433 was incorrectly inscribed "SIGFRIED LINE".

1995. 50th Anniv of End of Second World War in the Pacific. As T **340** 0f Antigua. Multicoloured.

4441	$60 P61 Black Widow	60	65
4442	$60 PT boat	60	65
4443	$60 Martin B-26 Marauder bomber	60	65
4444	$60 U.S.S. "San Juan" (cruiser)	60	65
4445	$60 Gato class submarine	60	65
4446	$60 Destroyer	60	65

531 Thanksgiving (U.S.A.)

1995. Holidays of the World. Multicoloured.

4448	$60 Type **531**	60	65
4449	$60 Christmas (Germany)	60	65
4450	$60 Hanukkah (Israel)	60	65
4451	$60 Easter (Spain)	60	65
4452	$60 Carnivale (Brazil)	60	65
4453	$60 Bastille Day (France)	60	65
4454	$60 Independence Day (India)	60	65
4455	$60 St. Patrick's Day (Ireland)	60	65

532 Map of the Americas and U.N. Soldier

1995. 50th Anniv of United Nations. Multicoloured.

4457	$35 Type **532**	35	40
4458	$60 Map of Africa and Western Asia	60	65
4459	$200 Map of Eastern Asia and Australasia with refugees	2·00	2·10

Nos. 4457/9 were printed together, se-tenant, forming a composite design.

533 Four-eyed Butterflyfish

1995. Marine Life. Multicoloured.

4461	$30 Type **533**	30	35
4462	$30 Lemon shark	30	35
4463	$35 Blue-headed wrasse	35	40
4464	$35 Green turtle	35	40
4465	$60 Three-spotted damselfish	60	65
4466	$60 Sawfish	60	65
4467	$60 Sei whales	60	65
4468	$60 Great barracuda	60	65
4469	$60 Mutton snapper	60	65
4470	$60 Hawksbill turtle	60	65
4471	$60 Spanish hogfish	60	65
4472	$60 Queen angelfish	60	65
4473	$60 Porkfish	60	65
4474	$60 Trumpetfish	60	65
4475	$60 Lesser electric ray	60	65
4476	$60 Tiger shark	60	65
4477	$60 Needlefish	60	65
4478	$60 Horse-eyed jack	60	65
4479	$60 Princess parrotfish	60	65
4480	$60 Yellow-tailed snapper	60	65
4481	$60 Spotted snake eel	60	65
4482	$60 Buffalo trunkfish	60	65
4483	$60 Cherubfish angelfish	60	65
4484	$60 French angelfish	60	65
4485	$80 Cocoa damselfish (vert)	80	85
4486	$80 Sergeant major (vert)	80	85
4487	$80 Beaugregory (vert)	80	85
4488	$80 Yellow-tailed damselfish (vert)	80	85
4489	$200 Fin-spot wrasse	2·00	2·10
4490	$200 Stingray	2·00	2·10

Nos. 4461, 4463, 4465 and 4489; Nos. 4462, 4464, 4466 and 4490; Nos. 4467/75; Nos. 4476/84 and Nos. 4485/8 respectively were printed together, se-tenant, the backgrounds forming composite designs.

534 Pole Vaulting

535 Sand Martin

1995. Olympic Games, Atlanta (1996) (2nd issue). Multicoloured.

4492	$60 Type **534**	60	65
4493	$60 Long jumping	60	65
4494	$60 Woman with relay baton	60	65
4495	$60 Wrestling	60	65

4496 $60 Discus (side view) . . . 60 65
4497 $60 Basketball 60 65
4498 $60 Boxing 60 65
4499 $60 Weightlifting 60 65
4500 $60 Shot put 60 65
4501 $60 Man in relay race 60 65
4502 $60 Female gymnast on beam 60 65
4503 $60 Cycling 60 65
4504 $60 Synchronized swimming . 60 65
4505 $60 Hurdling 60 65
4506 $60 Male gymnast on pommel horse 60 65
4507 $60 Discus (front view) . . . 60 65
Nos. 4492/9 and 4500/7 respectively were printed together, se-tenant, the backgrounds forming composite designs.

1995. Wildlife. Multicoloured.
4509 $20 Type **535** 20 25
4510 $35 House martin 35 40
4511 $60 Hobby 60 65
4512 $60 Olive colobus 60 65
4513 $60 Violet-backed starling . . 60 65
4514 $60 Diana monkey 60 65
4515 $60 African palm civet . . . 60 65
4516 $60 Giraffe and zebras . . . 60 65
4517 $60 African linsang 60 65
4518 $60 Royal antelope 00 00
4519 $60 Duikers 60 65
4520 $60 Palm squirrel 60 65
4521 $200 Long-tailed skua . . . 60 65
Nos. 4509/11 and 4521; and 4512/20 respectively were printed together, se-tenant, forming composite background designs.

536 Queenstown Jama Masjid

1995. Centenary of Queenstown Jama Masjid (mosque), Georgetown.
4523 **536** $60 multicoloured . . . 60 65

537 Woman Soldier with Sub-machine Gun

1995. 30th Anniv of Guyana Defence Force. Multicoloured.
4524 $6 Type **537** 10 10
4525 $60 Soldier with rifle 60 65

538 Bank Logo and Headquarters

1995. 25th Anniv of Caribbean Development Bank.
4526 **538** $60 multicoloured . . . 60 65

1995. Christmas. Religious Paintings. As T **357** of Antigua. Multicoloured.
4527 $25 "Angel of the Annunciation" (Carracci) . 25 30
4528 $30 "Virgin of the Annunciation" (Carracci) . 30 35
4529 $35 "Assumption of the Madonna" (Carracci) . . . 35 40
4530 $60 "Baptism of Christ" (Carracci) 60 65
4531 $100 "Madonna and Child with Saints" (detail) (Carracci) . 1·00 1·10
4532 $300 "Birth of the Virgin" (Carracci) . . . . . . 3·00 3·25

539 John Lennon

540 Albrecht Kossel (1910 Medicine)

1995. 15th Death Anniv of John Lennon (musician).
4534 **539** $35 multicoloured . . . 35 40

1995. Centenary of Nobel Trust Fund. Multicoloured.
4535/43 $35 × 9 Type **540**; Arthur H. Compton (1927 Physics); N. M. Butler (1931 Peace); Charles Laveran (1907 Medicine); George R. Minot (1934 Medicine); Henry H. Dale (1936 Medicine); Jacques Monod (1965 Medicine); Alfred Hershey (1969 Medicine); Par Lagerkvist (1951 Literature)
4544/52 $35 × 9 Norman F. Ramsey (1989 Physics); Chen Ning Yang (1957 Physics); Earl W. Sutherland Jr. (1971 Medicine); Paul Karrer (1937 Chemistry); Harmut Michel (1988 Chemistry); Richard Kuhn (1938 Chemistry); P. A. M. Dirac (1933 Physics); Victor Grignard (1912 Chemistry); Richard Willstatter (1915 Chemistry)
4553/61 $35 × 9 Adolf von Baeyer (1905 Chemistry); Hideki Yukawa (1949 Physics); George W. Beadle (1958 Medicine); Edwin M. McMillan (1951 Chemistry); Samuel C. C. Ting (1976 Physics); Saint-John Perse (1960 Literature); John F. Enders (1954 Medicine); Felix Bloch (1952 Physics); P. B. Medawar (1960 Medicine)
4562/70 $35 × 9 Nikolai Basov (1964 Physics); Klas Arnoldson (1908 Peace); Rene Sully-Prudhomme (1901 Literature); Robert W. Wilson (1978 Physics); Hugo Theorell (1955 Medicine); Nelly Sachs (1966 Literature); Hans von Euler-Chelpin (1929 Chemistry); Mairead Corrigan (1976 Peace); Willis E. Lamb Jr. (1955 Physics)
4571/9 $35 × 9 Francis Crick (1962 Medicine); Manne Siegbahn (1924 Physics); Eisaku Sato (1974 Peace); Robert Koch (1905 Medicine); Edgar D. Adrian (1932 Medicine); Erwin Neher (1991 Medicine); Henry Taube (1983 Chemistry); Norman Angell (1933 Peace); Robert Robinson (1947 Chemistry)
4580/8 $35 × 9 Henri Becquerel (1903 Physics); Igor Tamm (1958 Physics); Georges Kohler (1984 Medicine); Gerhard Domagk (1939 Medicine); Yasunari Kawabata (1968 Literature); Maurice Allais (1988 Economic Sciences); Aristide Briand (1926 Peace); Pavel Cherenkov (1958 Physics); Feodor Lynen (1964 Medicine)
4535/88 Set of 54 . . . . . . 20·00 21·00
Nos. 4535/43, 4544/52, 4553/61, 4562/70, 4571/9 and 4580/8 respectively were printed together, se-tenant, with the backgrounds forming composite designs.

541 David Copperfield

1995. David Copperfield (magician). Multicoloured.
4590 $60 Type **541** 60 65
4591 $60 David Copperfield in cloak and top hat 60 65
4592 $60 With flaming torch . . 60 65
4593 $60 David Copperfield in close up 60 65
4594 $60 Head of Statue of Liberty 60 65
4595 $60 David Copperfield climbing rope 60 65
4596 $60 With handcuffs 60 65
4597 $60 With woman dancer . . 60 65
4598 $60 David Copperfield wearing white shirt 60 65
Nos. 4590/8 were printed together, se-tenant, forming a composite background design.

542 Marilyn Monroe

1995. 70th Birth Anniv of Marilyn Monroe (entertainer). Multicoloured.
4600 $60 Type **542** 60 65
4601 $60 Marilyn Monroe with circular earrings 60 65
4602 $60 Marilyn Monroe (red top right corner) 60 65
4603 $60 Marilyn Monroe (signature at bottom right) 60 65
4604 $60 With hair over left eye . 60 65
4605 $60 With pink satin at left . . 60 65
4606 $60 With arm raised 60 65
4607 $60 With pink satin at bottom right 60 65
4608 $60 With square earring . . . 60 65
Nos. 4600/8 were printed together, se-tenant, with the background forming a composite design.

543 Rat

1995. Chinese New Year ("Year of the Rat").
4610 **543** $20 multicoloured 20 25
4611 – $30 multicoloured (face value bottom left) . . . 30 35
4612 – $50 multicoloured (face value top right) 50 55
4613 – $100 multicoloured (face value top left) . . . . 1·00 1·10
DESIGNS: $30 to $100 Symbolic rats.

1996. Paintings by Rubens. As T **421** of Grenada. Multicoloured.
4617 $6 "The Garden of Love" (detail) 10 10
4618 $10 "Two Sleeping Children" 10 10
4619 $20 "All Saints Day" 20 25
4620 $25 "Sacrifice of Abraham" . 25 30
4621 $30 "The Last Supper" . . . 30 35
4622 $35 "The Birth of Henry of Navarre" 35 40
4623 $40 "Study of standing female saint 40 45
4624 $50 "The Garden of Love" (different detail) 50 55
4625 $60 "The Garden of Love" (different detail) 60 65
4626 $200 "The Martyrdom of St. Livinus" . . . . 2·00 2·10
4627 $200 "St. Francis of Paola" . 2·00 2·10
4628 $300 "The Union of Maria de Medici and Henry IV" . . 3·00 3·25

545 Apatosaurus

1996. Prehistoric Animals. Multicoloured.
4630/41 $35 × 12 Type **545**; Archaeopteryx; Dimorphodon; Deinonychus; Coelophysis; Tyrannosaurus; Triceratops; Anatosaurus; Saltasaurus; Allosaurus; Oviraptor; Stegosaurus
4642/53 $35 × 12 Ornithomimus; Pteranodon; Rhamphorynchus; Ornitholestes; Brachiosaurus; Parasaurolophus; Ceratosaurus; Camarasaurus; Euoplocephalus; Scutellosaurus; Compsognathus; Stegoceras
4654/65 $35 × 12 Eudimorphodon; Criorhynchus; Elasmosaurus; Rhomaleosaurus; Ceresiosaurus; Mesosaurus; Grendelius; Nothosaurus; Mixosaurus; Placodus; Coelacanth; Mosasaurus
4666/77 $35 × 12 Tarbosaurus; Hadrosaurus; Polacanthus; Psittacosaurus; Ornitholestes; Yangchuanosaurus; Scelidosaurus; Kentrosaurus; Coelophysis; Lesothosaurus; Plateosaurus; Staurikosaurus (all vert)
4630/77 Set of 48 . . . . . . 16·00 17·00
Nos. 4630/41, 4642/53, 4654/65 and 4666/77 respectively were printed together, se-tenant, with the backgrounds forming composite designs.

547 "Morchella esculenta" and "Doryphorella princeps" (leaf beetle)

549 Hulda Gates

1996. Fungi of Guyana. Multicoloured.
4682 $20 Type **547** 20 25
4683 $25 Green-spored mushroom . 25 30
4684 $30 Common mushroom and leaf beetle 30 35
4685 $35 Pine cone mushroom and "Danaus plexippus" caterpillar 35 40
4686 $60 "Armillaria mellea" . . . 60 65
4687 $60 "Gomphus floccosus" . . 60 65
4688 $60 "Pholiota astragalina" . . 60 65
4689 $60 "Helvellaa crispa" 60 65
4690 $60 "Hygrophorus miniatus" . 60 65
4691 $60 "Omphalotus olearius" . 60 65
4692 $60 "Hygrocybe acutoconica" . 60 65
4693 $60 "Mycena viscosa" . . . 60 65
4694 $60 Cockle-shell lentinus . . 60 65
4695 $60 "Volvariella surrecta" . . 60 65
4696 $60 "Lepiota josserandii" . . 60 65
4697 $60 "Boletellus betula" . . . 60 65
4698 $60 "Amanita muscaria" . . 60 65
4699 $60 "Russula claroflava" and "Semiotus angulatus" (click beetle) 60 65
4700 $60 "Dictyophora duplicata" and "Musca domestica" (house fly) 60 65
4701 $60 "Stropharia" and "Editha magnifica" (butterfly hunter) 60 65
4702 $60 "Leotia viscosa" 60 65
4703 $60 "Calostoma cinnabarina" . 60 65
4704 $60 Stalkless paxillus 60 65
4705 $60 "Amanita spissa" 60 65
Nos. 4686 and 4692 are inscribed "Armillauella mellea" and "Hygzocybe acutoconica", both in error.

1996. 70th Birthday of Queen Elizabeth II. As T **364** of Antigua. Multicoloured.
4707 $100 As Type **364** of Antigua 1·00 1·10
4708 $100 Queen wearing green and blue jacket and hat . . . . 1·00 1·10
4709 $100 Queen at State Opening of Parliament . . . . 1·00 1·10

1996. Commonwealth Pharmacy Week. Unissued values in designs of Nos. 1810 and 1873 surch **COMMONWEALTH PHARMACY WEEK JUNE 16th 22nd 1996.**
4711 $6 on 130 c. Plate No. 21 (Series 2) . . . .
4712 $60 on 100 c. Plate No. 33 (Series 2) . . . .

1996. Centenary of Radio Entertainers. As T **368** of Antigua. Multicoloured.
4713 $20 Frank Sinatra 20 25
4714 $35 Gene Autry 50 55
4715 $60 Groucho Marx 60 65
4716 $200 Red Skelton . . . . . 2·00 2·10

1996. 3000th Anniv of Jerusalem. Multicoloured.
4718 $30 Type **549** 30 35
4719 $35 Church of St. Mary Magdalene 35 40
4720 $200 Absalom's Tomb, Kidron Valley . . . . 2·00 2·10

550 Long-billed Starthroat

1996. Birds of the World. Multicoloured.
4722 $60 Type **550** 60 65
4723 $60 Velvet-purple coronet . . 60 65
4724 $60 Racquet-tailed coquette . 60 65
4725 $60 Violet-tailed sylph . . . 60 65
4726 $60 Broad-tailed hummingbird 60 65
4727 $60 Blue-tufted starthroat . . 60 65
4728 $60 White-necked jacobin . . 60 65
4729 $60 Ruby-throated hummingbird 60 65
4730 $60 Blue and yellow macaw . 60 65
4731 $60 Andean condor 60 65
4732 $60 Guiana crested eagle . . 60 65
4733 $60 White-tailed trogon . . . 60 65
4734 $60 Toco toucan 60 65
4735 $60 Great horned owl 60 65
4736 $60 Andean cock-of-the-rock 60 65
4737 $60 Great curassow 60 65
Nos. 4722/9 and 4730/7 respectively were printed together, se-tenant, the backgrounds forming composite designs.

551 Pancratium (ancient Olympic event)

1996. Olympic Games, Atlanta (3rd issue). Multicoloured.
4739 $20 Type **551** 20 25
4740 $30 Olympic Stadium, Melbourne, 1956 . . . . 30 35
4741/9 $50 × 9 Volleyball; Basketball; Tennis; Table tennis; Baseball; Handball; Hockey; Water polo; Football
4750/8 $50 × 9 Cycling; Hurdling; High jumping; Diving; Weight- lifting; Canoeing; Wrestling; Gymnastics; Running (all vert)

4759/67	$50 × 9 Florence Griffith-Joyner (track and field) (U.S.A.); Ines Geissler (swimming) (Germany); Nadia Comaneci (gymnastics) (Rumania); Tatiana Gutsu (gymnastics) (Unified team); Ogla Korbut (gymnastics) (Russia); Barbara Krause (swimming) (Germany); Olga Bryzgina (track and field) (Russia); Fanny Blankers-Koen (track and field) (Holland); Irena Szewinska (track and field) (Poland) (all vert)		
4768/76	$50 × 9 Gerd Wessig (Germany); Jim Thorpe (U.S.A.); Norman Read (New Zealand); Lasse Viren (Finland); Milt Campbell (U.S.A.); Abebe Bikila (Ethiopia); Jesse Owens (U.S.A.); Viktor Saneev (Russia); Waldemer Cierpinski (Germany) (all track and field) (all vert)		
4777/85	$50 × 9 Ditmar Schmidt (handball) (Germany); Pam Shriver (tennis doubles) (U.S.A.); Zina Garrison (tennis doubles) (U.S.A); Hyun Jung-Hua (table tennis doubles) (Korea); Steffi Graf (tennis) (Germany); Michael Jordan (basketball) (U.S.A.); Karch Kiraly (volleyball) (U.S.A.); "Magic" Johnson (basketball) (U.S.A.); Ingolf Weigert (handball) (Germany) (all vert)		
4786	$60 Leonid Spirin winning 20 kilometre walk, 1956 (vert)	60	65
4787	$200 Lars Hall, Gold medal winner, Modern Pentathalon, 1952 and 1956 (Sweden) (vert)	2·00	2·10
4739/87	Set of 49	26·00	27·00

Nos. 4741/9, 4750/8, 4759/67, 4768/76 and 4777/85 (the last three showing Gold medal winners) respectively were printed together, se-tenant, forming composite background designs.

552 Mickey's Bait Shop

1996. Mickey Mouse and Friends Outdoors. Multicoloured.

4789	$60 Type **552**	60	65
4790	$60 Mickey and Pluto as lumberjacks	60	65
4791	$60 Mickey fishing	60	65
4792	$80 Donald Duck in BMX bike championships (vert)	80	85
4793	$80 Goofy as ice hockey superstar (vert)	80	85
4794	$80 Donald Duck at Malibu Surf City (vert)	80	85
4795	$100 Mickey as naval captain (vert)	1·00	1·10
4796	$100 Captain Mickey's Seamanship School (vert)	1·00	1·10
4797	$100 Mickey as sailor with ship's wheel and full-rigged sailing ship (vert)	1·00	1·10

553 Two Gun Mickey

1996. Disney Antique Toys. Multicoloured.

4799	$6 Type **553**	10	10
4800	$6 Wood-jointed Mickey figure	10	10
4801	$6 Donald jack-in-the-box	10	10
4802	$6 Rocking Minnie	10	10
4803	$6 Fireman Donald Duck	10	10
4804	$6 Long-billed Donald Duck	10	10
4805	$6 Painted-wood Mickey figure	10	10
4806	$6 Wind-up Jiminy Cricket	10	10

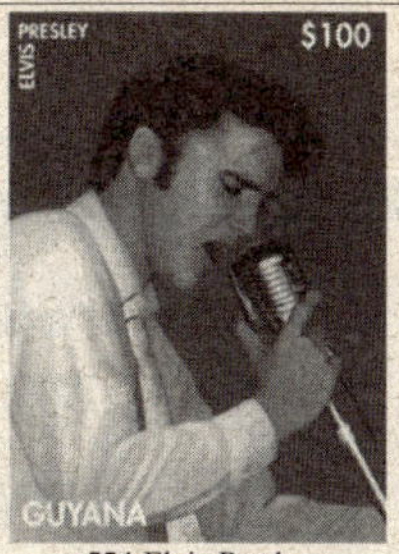

554 Elvis Presley

1996. 60th Birth Anniv (1995) of Elvis Presley. Multicoloured, background colours given.

4808	**554**	$100 red	1·00	1·10
4809	–	$100 mauve	1·00	1·10
4810	–	$100 brown	1·00	1·10
4811	–	$100 blue	1·00	1·10
4812	–	$100 purple	1·00	1·10
4813	–	$100 blue	1·00	1·10

DESIGNS: Nos. 4809/13, Various portraits.

556 Birman

1996. Cats of the World. Multicoloured.

4815	$60 Type **556**	60	65
4816	$60 American curl	60	65
4817	$60 Turkish angora	60	65
4818	$60 European shorthair (Italy)	60	65
4819	$60 Persian (Great Britain)	60	65
4820	$60 Scottish fold	60	65
4821	$60 Sphynx (Canada)	60	65
4822	$60 Malayan (Thailand)	60	65
4823	$60 Cornish rex (Great Britain)	60	65
4824	$60 Norwegian forest (vert)	60	65
4825	$60 Russian shorthair (vert)	60	65
4826	$60 European shorthair (Italy) (vert)	60	65
4827	$60 Birman (vert)	60	65
4828	$60 Ragdoll (U.S.A.) (vert)	60	65
4829	$60 Egyptian mau (vert)	60	65
4830	$60 Persian (Great Britain) (vert)	60	65
4831	$60 Turkish angora (vert)	60	65
4832	$60 Siamese (vert)	60	65

Nos. 4815/23 and 4824/32 respectively were printed together, se-tenant, with the backgrounds forming composite designs.

557 Hyed Snapper

1996. Marine Life. Multicoloured.

4834	$6 Type **557**	10	10
4835	$6 Angelfish	10	10
4836	$20 Boxfish	20	25
4837	$25 Golden damselfish	25	30
4838	$30 Goblin shark and coelacanth	30	35
4839	$30 "Jason" remote-controlled submersible	30	35
4840	$30 Deep-water invertebrates	30	35
4841	$30 Submarine NR-1	30	35
4842	$30 Giant squid	30	35
4843	$30 Sperm whale	30	35
4844	$30 Volcanic vents and "Alvin" submersible	30	35
4845	$30 Air-recycling pressure suits and shipwreck	30	35
4846	$30 "Shinkai" 6500 submersible	30	35
4847	$30 Giant tube worms	30	35
4848	$30 Anglerfish	30	35
4849	$30 Six-gill shark	30	35
4850	$30 Autonomous underwater vehicle ABE	30	35
4851	$30 Octopus and viperfish	30	35
4852	$30 Swallower and hatchetfish	30	35
4853	$35 Clown triggerfish	35	40
4854	$60 Red gorgonians	60	65
4855	$60 Soft coral and butterflyfish	60	65
4856	$60 Soft coral and slender snapper	60	65
4857	$60 Common clownfish, anemone and mushroom coral	60	65
4858	$60 Anemone and horse-eyed jack	60	65
4859	$60 Splendid coral trout	60	65
4860	$60 Anemones	60	65
4861	$60 Brain coral	60	65
4862	$60 Cup coral	60	65
4863	$200 Harlequin tuskfish	2·00	2·10

Nos. 4838/52 and 4854/62 respectively were printed together, se-tenant, with the backgrounds forming composite designs.

No. 4853 is inscribed "CLOWN TUGGERFISH" in error.

558 Snow White and Reindeer

1996. Christmas. Disney's "Snow White and the Seven Dwarfs". Multicoloured.

4865	$6 Type **558**	10	10
4866	$20 Doc with presents	20	25
4867	$25 Dopey and Sneezy	25	30
4868	$30 Sleepy, Happy and Bashful	30	35
4869	$35 Dopey and Santa Claus	35	40
4870	$60 Dopey with socks at fireplace	60	65
4871	$100 Dopey and Grumpy	1·00	1·10
4872	$200 Dopey dressed as Santa Claus	2·00	2·10

559 Hotel Tower

1996. 50th Anniv of Hotel Tower, Georgetown.

4874	**559**	$30 multicoloured	30	35

EXPRESS LETTER STAMPS

1986. Various stamps surch **EXPRESS** and new values.

E1	$12 on 350 c. on 120 c. multicoloured (No. 1598)	6·00	6·00
E2	$15 on 40 c. multicoloured (No. 1868)	8·00	8·00
E3	$20 on $6.40 multicoloured	6·00	6·00
E4	$25 on 25 c. multicoloured (as No. 1771, but value changed)	11·00	11·00

No. E3 was previously a miniature sheet for Halley's Comet containing two 320 c. stamps. As surch the original values on both designs have been cancelled and replaced by a single $20 face value.

1987. No. E3 additionally optd with small Maltese cross above surch.

E5	$20 on $6.40 multicoloured	6·50	6·50

1987. Centenary of Publication of Sanders' "Reichenbachia". As T **331** additionally inscr "EXPRESS". Multicoloured.

E6	$15 Plate No. 11 (Series 2)	4·00	4·00
E7	$20 Plate No. 93 (Series 2)	3·50	4·00
E8	$25 Plate No. 63 (Series 2)	3·75	4·25
E9	$45 Plate No. 35 (Series 2)	7·00	8·00

1987.

Nos. 1744/5 imperf between surch **EXPRESS FORTY DOLLARS** and star.

E10	$40 on $6.40 multicoloured	11·00	11·00

1987. No. E2 additionally optd **1987**.

E11	$15 on 40 c. multicoloured	9·00	5·00

1988. Nos. 2206 and 2211 surch **SPECIAL DELIVERY** and new value.

E12	$40 on $3.20 blue	8·50	9·00
E13	$45 on $3.30 black	9·00	10·00

1989. Imperf between pairs of Nos. 1744/5 and 2185/6 surch **EXPRESS FORTY DOLLARS** (without stars).

E14	$40 on $6.40 multicoloured (Nos. 1744/5)	4·50	5·00
E15	$40 on $6.40 multicoloured (Nos. 2185/6)	4·50	5·00

1989. Nos. 2206 and 2211 surch **SPECIAL DELIVERY** and new value.

E16	$190 on $3.30 black	13·00	15·00
E17	$225 on $3.20 blue	14·00	16·00

OFFICIAL STAMPS

1981. Nos. 556, F4a and F6/7 optd **OPS** or surch also.

O13	10 c. on 25 c. Marabunta	1·50	2·00
O14	50 c. "Guzmania lingulata"	1·60	30
O15	60 c. Soldier's cap	1·25	20
O16	$5 "Odontadenia grandiflora"	3·00	1·75

1981. Nos. 491, 708a, 716, 804, 834 and F9 optd **OPS** or surch also.

O17	15 c. Harpy eagle (postage)	8·50	65
O18	30 c. on $2 "Norantea guianensis" (F9)	45	30
O19	100 c. on $3 Cylinder satellite	3·00	40
O20	125 c. on $2 "Norantea guianensis"	1·75	60
O21	$10 "Elbella patrobas"	7·00	8·00
O22	$1.10 on $2 "Norantea guianensis" (804) (air)	1·50	2·50

1981. Nos. 548a, 719, 828 and 830 optd **OPS** or surch also.

O23	15 c. Christmas orchid	8·00	1·50
O24	50 c. British Guiana 1898 1 c. stamp	1·25	35
O25	100 c. on 8 c. Camp-fire cooking	2·00	50
O26	110 c. on 6 c. Type **116**	3·50	1·25

1982. Various stamps optd **OPS**.

O27	–	20 c. multicoloured (No. 701)	3·25	60
O28	**136**	40 c. multicoloured	75	15
O29	–	40 c. red, grey and black (No. 674)	1·00	15
O30	–	$2 multicoloured (No. 676)	7·00	75

1982. Nos. 911 and 980 optd or surch **OPS**.

O31	250 c. on 400 c. on 30 c. multicoloured (postage)	80	60
O32	220 c. on 1 c. multicoloured (air)	1·50	60

1982. No. F9 optd **OPS**.

O33	$2 "Norantea guianensis"	10·00	2·00

1982. Air. No. 979 optd **OPS**.

O34	110 c. on 5 c. Annatto tree	1·75	60

1984. No. 912 surch **OPS**.

O35	150 c. on $5 multicoloured	5·00	2·75
O36	200 c. on $5 multicoloured	5·50	3·00
O37	225 c. on $5 multicoloured	5·50	3·25
O38	230 c. on $5 multicoloured	5·50	3·25
O39	260 c. on $5 multicoloured	5·50	3·50
O40	320 c. on $5 multicoloured	6·50	4·00
O41	350 c. on $5 multicoloured	7·00	4·50
O42	600 c. on $5 multicoloured	8·50	5·50

1984. Nos. O32 and O34 surch and No. 981 optd **OPS**.

O43	25 c. on 110 c. on 5 c. Annatto tree	70	30
O44	30 c. on 110 c. on 5 c. Annatto tree	80	35
O45	45 c. on 220 c. on 1 c. Pitcher plant of Mt. Roraima	90	40
O46	55 c. on 110 c. on 5 c. Annatto tree	1·10	50
O47	60 c. on 220 c. on 1 c. Pitcher plant of Mt. Roraima	1·10	50

O48 75 c. on 220 c. on 1 c. Pitcher plant of Mt. Roraima . . . 1·25 60
O49 90 c. on 220 c. on 1 c. Pitcher plant of Mt. Roraima . . . 1·25 70
O50 120 c. on 220 c. on 1 c. Pitcher plant of Mt. Roraima . . . 1·40 85
O51 130 c. on 220 c. on 1 c. Pitcher plant of Mt. Roraima . . . 1·50 90
O52 330 c. on $2 "Norantea guianensis" . . . . 3·00 2·25

1987. Centenary of Publication of Sanders' "Reichenbachia". As T **331** additionally inscr "OFFICIAL". Multicoloured.

O53 120 c. Plate No. 48 (Series 2) 60 25
O54 130 c. Plate No. 92 (Series 2) 60 25
O55 140 c. Plate No. 36 (Series 2) 60 25
O56 150 c. Plate No. 43 (Series 2) 60 25
O57 175 c. Plate No. 31 (Series 2) 70 30
O58 200 c. Plate No. 61 (Series 2) 75 35
O59 225 c. Plate No. 26 (Series 2) 75 35
O60 230 c. Plate No. 68 (Series 2) (horiz) 75 35
O61 250 c. Plate No. 59 (Series 2) 75 40
O62 260 c. Plate No. 69 (Series 2) 75 40
O63 275 c. Plate No. 90 (Series 2) 75 40
O64 320 c. Plate No. 75 (Series 2) 75 50
O65 330 c. Plate No. 23 (Series 2) 85 60
O66 350 c. Plate No. 95 (Series 2) (horiz) 85 60
O67 600 c. Plate No. 70 (Series 2) (horiz) . . . . 1·25 1·25
O68 $12 Plate No. 71 (Series 2) (horiz) . . . . 2·00 2·00
O69 $15 Plate No. 84 (Series 2) . . 2·25 2·25

OFFICIAL PARCEL POST STAMPS

1981. Nos. P1/2 optd **OPS**.

OP1 $15 on $1 "Chelonanthus uliginoides" . . . . 7·50 2·25
OP2 $20 on $1 "Chelonanthus uliginoides" . . . . 10·00 2·75

1983. No. 843 surch **OPS Parcel Post $12.00** and additionally optd **1982**.

OP3 $12 on $1.10 on $2 "Norantea guianensis" . . . . 65·00 17·00

1983. No. OP3 with additional **OPS** opt.

OP4 $12 on $1.10 on $2 "Norantea guianensis" . . . . 29·00 5·00

1983. No. P4 optd **OPS**.

OP5 $12 on $1.10 on $2 "Norantea guianensis" . . . . 7·50 5·00

PARCEL POST STAMPS

1981. No. 554 surch **PARCEL POST** and new value.

P1 $15 on $1 "Chelonanthus uliginoides" . . . . 10·00 3·00
P2 $20 on $1 "Chelonanthus uliginoides" . . . . 10·00 6·00

1983. No. 843 surch **PARCEL POST $12.00**.

P3 $12 on $1.10 on $2 "Norantea guianensis" . . . . 4·50 2·50

1983. Unissued Royal Wedding surch, similar to No. 843, further surch **Parcel Post $12.00**.

P4 $12 on $1.10 on $2 "Norantea guianensis" . . . . 1·00 1·75

1985. No. 673 surch **TWENTY FIVE DOLLARS PARCEL POST 25.00**.

P5 $25 on 35 c. green, grey and black 20·00 18·00

POSTAGE DUE STAMPS

D 2

1987.

D 8 D **2** 1 c. green . . . . 20 3·00
D 9 2 c. black . . . . 20 3·00
D10 4 c. blue . . . . 20 3·00
D11 12 c. red . . . . 30 3·00

POSTAL FISCAL STAMPS

1975. Nos. 543/5 and 550ab/6 optd **REVENUE ONLY**.

F 1 2 c. Type **132** 40 40
F 2 3 c. Hanging heliconia . . . 40 40
F 3 5 c. Annatto tree 65 30
F 4 25 c. Marabunta . . . . 2·50 30
F 4a 25 c. Marabunta (No. 550) . 15·00 13·00
F 5 40 c. Tiger beard . . . . 5·00 30
F 6 50 c. "Guzmania lingulata" . 60 40
F 7 60 c. Soldier's cap 75 50
F 8 $1 "Chelonanthus uliginoides" 75 1·25
F 9 $2 "Norantea guianensis" . . 1·00 2·75
F10 $5 "Odontadenis grandiflora" 1·75 9·00

Although intended for fiscal use Nos. F1/F10 were allowed by the postal authorities as an "act of grace" to do duty as postage stamps until 30 June 1976.

GWALIOR

A "convention" state of Central India.

12 pies = 1 anna; 16 annas = 1 rupee

1885. Queen Victoria stamps of India optd **GWALIOR** at foot and native opt at top.

1	**23**	½ a. turquoise	85·00	16·00
2	–	1 a. purple	60·00	22·00
6	–	1½ a. brown	50·00	
3	–	2 a. blue	50·00	11·00
8	–	4 a. green (No. 69)	60·00	
9	–	6 a. brown (No. 80)	60·00	
10	–	8 a. mauve	55·00	
11	–	1 r. grey (No. 101)	55·00	

Stamps of India overprinted **GWALIOR** above native overprint unless otherwise stated.

1885. Queen Victoria.

16c	**23**	½ a. turquoise	20	10
17	–	9 p. red	27·00	50·00
18	–	1 a. purple	35	15
20c	–	1 a. 6 p. brown	65	40
21c	–	2 a. blue	50	10
23	–	2 a. 6 p. green	4·50	13·00
25c	–	3 a. orange	50	15
14	–	4 a. green (No. 69)	16·00	9·00
27c	–	4 a. green (No. 96)	1·50	45
29	–	6 a. brown (No. 80)	1·00	4·50
30c	–	8 a. mauve	1·75	60
32c	–	12 a. purple on red	2·50	65
33c	–	1 r. grey (No. 101)	1·40	85
34	**37**	1 r. green and red	2·25	2·75
35	**38**	2 r. red and orange	5·00	3·00
36		3 r. brown and green	7·00	3·50
37		5 r. blue and violet	12·00	6·50

1899. Queen Victoria.

38	**40**	3 p. red	10	20
39		3 p. grey	6·00	60·00
40	**23**	½ a. green	20	1·00
41	–	1 a. red	40	35
42	–	2 a. lilac	60	3·25
43	–	2½ a. blue	85	3·75

1903. King Edward VII.

46A	**41**	3 p. grey	45	20
48A	–	½ a. green (No. 122)	10	10
49A	–	1 a. red (No. 123)	10	10
50Af	–	2 a. lilac	1·00	20
52B	–	2 a. 6 p. blue	60	5·50
53A	–	3 a. orange	1·00	30
54A	–	4 a. olive	1·10	40
56B	–	6 a. bistre	3·25	80
57A	–	8 a. mauve	2·75	1·25
59B	–	12 a. purple on red	3·00	3·25
60A	–	1 r. green and red	1·50	1·75
61B	**52**	2 r. red and orange	7·50	11·00
62B		3 r. brown and green	24·00	40·00
63B		5 r. blue and violet	17·00	25·00

1907. King Edward VII inscr "INDIA POSTAGE AND REVENUE".

65	½ a. green (No. 149)	40	15
66	1 a. red (No. 150)	75	10

1912. King George V.

67	**55**	3 p. grey	10	10
68	**58**	½ a. green	20	10
102	**79**	½ a. green	20	10
88	**80**	9 p. green	1·25	20
69	**57**	1 a. red	25	10
80		1 a. brown	20	10
103	**81**	1 a. brown	10	10
90	**82**	1 a. 3 p. mauve	30	10
81	**58**	1½ a. brown (No. 165)	70	50
82		1½ a. red	15	20
70	**59**	2 a. lilac	40	10
91	**70**	2 a. lilac	45	20
104	**59**	2 a. red	35	1·40
83	**61**	2½ a. blue	1·00	1·75
84		2½ a. orange	20	50
71	**62**	3 a. orange	40	15
92		3 a. blue	60	40
72	**63**	4 a. olive	50	60
93	**71**	4 a. green	80	90
73	**64**	6 a. bistre	70	75
74	**65**	8 a. mauve	80	30
75	**66**	12 a. red	95	2·00
76	**67**	1 r. brown and green	2·50	40
77		2 r. red and orange	4·50	4·25
78		5 r. blue and violet	18·00	6·50

1922. No. 192 (King George V) optd **GWALIOR** only.

79	**57**	9 p. on 1a. red	10	40

1928. King George V. Optd in larger type (19 mm long).

96	**67**	1 r. brown and green	1·40	2·50
97		2 r. red and orange	3·00	3·00
98		5 r. blue and violet	13·00	20·00
99		10 r. green and red	40·00	30·00
100		15 r. blue and olive	65·00	48·00
101		25 r. orange and blue	£130	£100

1938. King George V.

105	**91**	3 p. slate	3·25	10
106		½ a. brown	3·75	10
107		9 p. green	32·00	2·50
108		1 a. red	3·25	15
109		3 a. green (No. 253)	9·00	2·50
110		4 a. brown (No. 255)	38·00	1·50
111		6 a. green (No. 256)	2·50	5·50
112	**93**	1 r. slate and brown	5·00	1·50
113		2 r. purple and brown	26·00	6·00
114		5 r. green and blue	38·00	30·00
115		10 r. purple and red	38·00	38·00
116		15 r. brown and green	£120	£150
117		25 r. slate and purple	£110	£120

1942. King George VI.

118	**100a**	3 p. slate	45	10
119		½ a. mauve	45	10
120		9 p. green	45	10
121		1 a. red	40	10
122	**101**	1½ a. violet	3·25	20
123		2 a. red	55	20
124		3 a. violet	5·50	30
125	**102**	4 a. brown	1·25	20
126		6 a. green	20·00	17·00
127		8 a. violet	2·75	2·75
128		12 a. purple	4·50	15·00

OFFICIAL STAMPS

Stamps of India overprinted with native inscription at top and bottom, unless otherwise stated.

1895. Queen Victoria.

O 1	**23**	½ a. turquoise	10	10
O 3	–	1 a. purple	65	10
O 4	–	2 a. blue	1·00	35
O 7	–	4 a. green (No. 96)	1·10	85
O 9	–	8 a. mauve	1·10	70
O10	**37**	1 r. green and red	3·50	3·00

1901. Queen Victoria.

O23	**40**	3 p. red	30	30
O24		3 p. grey	90	1·60
O26	**23**	½ a. green	20	10
O27	–	1 a. red	3·00	10
O28	–	2 a. lilac	55	1·50

1903. King Edward VII.

O29	**41**	3 p. grey	30	10
O41	–	½ a. green (No. 122)	1·50	15
O32	–	1 a. red (No. 123)	40	10
O33a	–	2 a. lilac	90	20
O44	–	4 a. olive	2·50	75
O36	–	8 a. mauve	3·00	70
O38	–	1 r. green and red	2·75	1·40

1907. King Edward VII inscr "POSTAGE & REVENUE".

O49	–	½ a. green (No. 149)	65	15
O48	–	1 a. red (No. 150)	3·50	15

1913. King George V.

O51	**55**	3 p. grey	20	10
O62	**56**	½ a. green	10	15
O73	**79**	½ a. green	15	15
O63	**80**	9 p. green	10	15
O53a	**57**	1 a. red	20	10
O64		1 a. brown	10	10
O74	**81**	1 a. brown	15	15
O65	**82**	1 a. 3 p. mauve	50	15
O55	**59**	2 a. lilac	45	20
O66	**70**	2 a. lilac	20	15
O75	**59**	2 a. red	20	35
O77	**63**	4 a. olive	50	60
O67	**71**	4 a. green	50	30
O68	**65**	8 a. mauve	50	70
O58	**67**	1 r. brown and green	14·00	13·00

1922. No. O97 (King George V Official) optd **GWALIOR** only.

O59	**57**	9 p. on 1a. red	10	30

1927. King George V. Optd in large type (21 mm long).

O69	**67**	1 r. brown and green	80	1·75
O70		2 r. red and orange	6·00	8·00
O71		5 r. blue and violet	11·00	£120
O72		10 r. green and red	85·00	£250

1938. King George VI.

O78	**91**	½ a. brown	6·50	30
O79		1 a. red	1·10	20
O91	**93**	1 r. slate and brown	8·00	12·00
O92		2 r. purple and brown	20·00	60·00
O93		5 r. green and blue	38·00	£325
O94		10 r. purple and red	£110	£650

1940. King George VI. Optd at bottom only.

O80	**O 20**	3 p. slate	50	10
O81		½ a. brown	3·00	25
O82		½ a. purple	50	10
O83		9 p. green	70	50
O84		1 a. red	2·25	10
O85		1 a. 3 p. brown.	28·00	1·60
O86		1 a. 6 p. violet	1·00	30
O87		2 a. orange	1·00	30
O88		4 a. brown	1·25	1·50
O89		8 a. violet	2·50	5·50

1942. No. O65 surch **1A 1A** and bar.

O90	**82**	1 a. on 1¼a. mauve	16·00	2·50

HELIGOLAND

An island off the N. coast of Germany, ceded to that country by Great Britain in 1890.

1867. 16 schillings = 1 mark.
1875. 100 pfennig = 1 mark.

Many of the Heligoland stamps found in old collections and the majority of those offered at a small fraction of catalogue prices today, are reprints which have very little value.

1

1867. Perf (½, 1, 2 and 6 sch. also roul).

5	**1**	¼ sch. green and red	26·00	£1500
6b		½ sch. green and red	95·00	£150
7		¾ sch. red and green	29·00	£1100
8a		1 sch. red and green	£120	£180
9		1½ sch. green and red	65·00	£250
3		2 sch. red and green	10·00	55·00
4		6 sch. green and red	12·00	£250

2

3

4

5

1875.

10	**2**	1 pf. (¼d.) green and red	10·00	£500
11		2 pf. (½d.) red and green	10·00	£600
12a	**3**	3 pf. (⅝d.) green, red & yell	£160	£850
13	**2**	5 pf. (¾d.) green and red	10·00	18·00
14a		10 pf. (1½d.) red and green	10·00	20·00
15b	**3**	20 pf. (2½d.) green, red and yellow	12·00	28·00
16	**2**	25 pf. (3d.) green and red	12·00	26·00
17		50 pf. (6d.) red and green	18·00	32·00
18	**4**	1 m. (1s.) green, red & black	£140	£200
19	**5**	5 m. (5s.) green, red & black	£150	£950

HONG KONG

Former British colony at the mouth of the Canton R., consisting of the island of Hong Kong and peninsula of Kowloon. Under Japanese Occupation from 25 December, 1941, until liberated by British forces on 16 September, 1945.

Hong Kong became a Special Administrative Region of the People's Republic of China on 1 July 1997.

100 cents = 1 Hong Kong dollar

1

1862.

8a	**1**	2 c. brown	£110	7·00
34		4 c. grey	9·00	85
10		6 c. lilac	£300	9·50
11b		8 c. yellow	£350	11·00
12a		12 c. blue	25·00	5·50
22		16 c. yellow	£1200	65·00
4		18 c. lilac	£500	45·00
14		24 c. green	£450	8·50
15a		30 c. red	£650	15·00
16		30 c. mauve	£180	5·50
17a		48 c. red	£800	23·00
18		96 c. olive	£25000	£550
19		96 c. grey	£1000	42·00

1877. Surch in figures and words, thus **5 cents.**

23	**1**	5 c. on 8 c. yellow	£600	85·00
24		5 c. on 18 c. lilac	£600	55·00
25		10 c. on 12 c. blue	£700	55·00
26		10 c. on 16 c. yellow	£3500	£140
27		10 c. on 24 c. green	£1200	80·00
20		16 c. on 18 c. lilac	£1900	£150
21		28 c. on 30 c. mauve	£1000	48·00

1880.

33	**1**	2 c. red	25·00	85
56		2 c. green	25·00	85
57		4 c. red	14·00	85
35		5 c. blue	20·00	85
58		5 c. yellow	17·00	6·50
30		10 c. mauve	£425	13·00
37a		10 c. green	£110	1·00
38		10 c. purple on red	18·00	85
59		10 c. blue	45·00	1·75
39a		30 c. green	60·00	16·00
61		30 c. brown	30·00	20·00
31		48 c. brown	£950	85·00

1885. Surch in figures and words, thus **20 CENTS**.

54	**1**	10 c. on 30 c. green	£450	£750
40		20 c. on 30 c. red	85·00	5·00
45a		20 c. on 30 c. green	95·00	£130
41		50 c. on 48 c. brown	£300	26·00
46		50 c. on 48 c. purple	£225	£250
42		$1 on 96 c. olive	£550	48·00
47		$1 on 96 c. purple on red	£600	£325
53a		$1 on 96 c. black	£2750	£3500

1891. Surch in figures and words, thus **7 cents.**

43	**1**	7 c. on 10 c. green	60·00	7·50
44		14 c. on 30 c. mauve	£120	50·00

弍 **13** (20 c.)   五十 **14** (50 c.)   壹圓 **15** ($1)

1891. T **1** surch with figures and words and with Chinese surch also.

55	–	10 c. on 30 c. green	38·00	70·00
48a	**13**	20 c. on 30 c. green	25·00	4·50
49	**14**	50 c. on 48 c. purple	65·00	5·50
50	**15**	$1 on 96 c. purple on red	£375	22·00
52		$1 on 96 c. black	£130	27·00

The Chinese surch on No. 55 is larger than Type **13**.

1891. 50th Anniv of Colony. Optd **1841 Hong Kong JUBILEE 1891**.

51	**1**	2 c. red	£375	95·00

20

24

1903.

62	**20**	1 c. purple and brown	2·00	50
91		1 c. brown	3·00	90
77		2 c. green	4·00	1·25
78a		4 c. purple on red	4·75	40
93		4 c. red	4·25	40
79a		5 c. green and orange	9·00	5·00
94		6 c. brown and purple	15·00	3·00
66		8 c. grey and violet	7·00	1·25
81		10 c. purple & blue on blue	12·00	75
95		10 c. blue	15·00	40
68		12 c. green & purple on yell	7·00	4·25
83a		20 c. grey and brown	20·00	2·25
96		20 c. purple and green	32·00	35·00
84		30 c. green and black	24·00	12·00
97		30 c. purple and yellow	45·00	18·00
85		50 c. green and purple	45·00	6·50
98		50 c. black on green	35·00	13·00
86a		$1 purple and olive	85·00	17·00
87a		$2 grey and red	£140	75·00
99		$2 red and black	£250	£225
88		$3 grey and blue	£150	£180
89		$5 purple and green	£325	£300
76		$10 grey & orange on blue	£800	£375

1912.

117	**24**	1 c. brown	1·00	40
118		2 c. green	2·25	30
118c		2 c. grey	13·00	5·00
119		3 c. grey	4·00	1·00
120a		4 c. red	2·25	30
121		5 c. violet	4·50	30
103		6 c. orange	3·75	85
104		8 c. grey	22·00	4·50
123		8 c. orange	3·00	90
124		10 c. blue	2·25	30
106		12 c. purple on yellow	3·50	5·50
125		20 c. purple and olive	3·50	30
126		25 c. purple	2·50	40
127		30 c. purple and orange	10·00	1·50
128		50 c. black on green	8·50	30
129		$1 purple & blue on blue	22·00	50
130		$2 red and black	80·00	5·50
131		$3 green and purple	£140	45·00
132		$5 green and red on green	£375	60·00
116		$10 purple & black on red	£475	75·00

1935. Silver Jubilee. As T **13** of Antigua.

133	3 c. blue and black	4·00	3·00
134	5 c. green and blue	8·00	3·00
135	10 c. brown and blue	20·00	1·50
136	20 c. grey and purple	38·00	7·00

1937. Coronation. As T **2** of Aden.

137	4 c. green	6·00	2·50
138	15 c. red	12·00	3·25
139	25 c. blue	15·00	2·50

29 King George VI

30 Street Scene

1938.

140	**29**	1 c. brown	1·75	80
141		2 c. grey	2·00	30
142		4 c. orange	2·75	1·25
143		5 c. green	1·25	20
144		8 c. brown	1·75	2·25
145b		10 c. violet	5·50	70
146		15 c. red	1·50	30
147		20 c. black	1·25	30
148		20 c. red	7·00	40
149		25 c. blue	24·00	80
150		25 c. olive	4·75	1·25
151a		30 c. olive	20·00	8·00
152		30 c. blue	7·00	20
153b		50 c. lilac	9·00	20
154		80 c. red	5·00	95
155		$1 purple and blue	8·00	2·50
156		$1 orange and green	16·00	30
157		$2 orange and green	70·00	14·00
158		$2 violet and red	26·00	1·50
159		$5 purple and red	55·00	48·00
160		$5 green and violet	80·00	5·00
161		$10 green and violet	£375	80·00
162		$10 violet and blue	£140	23·00

1941. Centenary of British Occupation. Dated "1841 1941".

163	**30**	2 c. orange and brown	4·00	1·75
164	–	4 c. purple and mauve	4·50	1·75
165	–	5 c. black and green	2·50	50
166	–	15 c. black and red	5·50	1·00
167	–	25 c. brown and blue	12·00	3·25
168	–	$1 blue and orange	45·00	7·00

DESIGNS—HORIZ: 4 c. "Empress of Japan" (liner) and junk; 5 c. University; 15 c. Harbour; $1 "Falcon" (clipper) and Short S.23 Empire "C" Class flying boat. VERT: 25 c. Hong Kong Bank.

For Japanese issues see "Japanese Occupation of Hong Kong".

36

1946. Victory.

169 **36** 30 c. blue and red . . . . 1·75 1·25
170 $1 brown and red . . . . . 3·50 75

1948. Silver Wedding. As T **10/11** of Aden.

171 10 c. violet . . . . 2·50 80
172 $10 red . . . . £250 70·00

1949. U.P.U. As T **20/23** of Antigua.

173 10 c. violet . . . . 3·75 50
174 20 c. red . . . . 15·00 3·00
175 30 c. blue . . . . 12·00 1·75
176 80 c. mauve . . . . 35·00 9·50

1953. Coronation. As T **13** of Aden.

177 10 c. black and purple . . . . 5·00 30

1954. As T **29** but portrait of Queen Elizabeth, facing left.

178 5 c. orange . . . . 1·50 20
179 10 c. lilac . . . . 2·50 10
180a 15 c. green . . . . 4·00 45
181 20 c. brown . . . . 5·00 30
182a 25 c. red . . . . 3·00 70
183 30 c. grey . . . . 4·50 20
184 40 c. blue . . . . 4·00 40
185 50 c. purple . . . . 4·75 20
186 65 c. grey . . . . 19·00 7·50
187 $1 orange and green . . . . 7·50 20
188 $1.30 blue and red . . . . . 23·00 1·00
189 $2 violet and red . . . . . . 12·00 40
190 $5 green and purple . . . . 75·00 1·50
191 $10 violet and blue . . . . . 60·00 8·50

38 University Arms

1961. Golden Jubilee of Hong Kong University.

192 **38** $1 multicoloured . . . . . 7·00 2·00

39 Statue of Queen Victoria

40 Queen Elizabeth II (after Annigoni)

1962. Stamp Centenary.

193 **39** 10 c. black and mauve . . 60 10
194 20 c. black and blue . . . 1·75 1·75
195 50 c. black and bistre . . . 4·00 40

1962.

196 **40** 5 c. orange 50 50
223 10 c. violet 70 30
198 15 c. green . . . . 2·50 75
199 20 c. brown . . . . 1·75 75
200 25 c. mauve . . . . 2·50 1·50
201 30 c. blue . . . . 2·50 10
202 40 c. turquoise . . . . . . 2·00 30
203 50 c. red . . . . 1·75 20
230a 65 c. blue . . . . 6·00 6·50
231 $1 sepia . . . . 12·00 1·50
206 – $1.30 multicoloured . . . 5·00 20
207 – $2 multicoloured . . . . 7·00 40
208 – $5 multicoloured . . . . 17·00 1·25
209 – $10 multicoloured . . . . 30·00 2·25
210 – $20 multicoloured . . . . £140 22·00

Nos. 206/10 are as T **40** but larger $26 \times 40\frac{1}{2}$ mm.

1963. Freedom from Hunger. As T **28** of Aden.

211 $1.30 green . . . . 55·00 8·00

1963. Cent of Red Cross. As T **33** of Antigua.

212 10 c. red and black . . . . . 5·00 30
213 $1.30 red and blue . . . . . . 35·00 8·00

1965. Cent of I.T.U. As T **36** of Antigua.

214 10 c. purple and yellow . . . 4·00 25
215 $1.30 olive and green . . . . 25·00 5·50

1965. I.C.Y. As T **37** of Antigua.

216 10 c. purple and turquoise . . 3·00 25
217 $1.30 green and lavender . . . 20·00 5·50

1966. Churchill Commen. As T **38** of Antigua.

218 10 c. blue . . . . 3·00 15
219 50 c. green . . . . 3·50 30
220 $1.30 brown . . . . 24·00 3·00
221 $2 violet . . . . 38·00 10·00

1966. Inauguration of W.H.O. Headquarters, Geneva. As T **41** of Antigua.

237 10 c. black, green and blue . . 3·00 30
238 50 c. black, purple & ochre . . 10·00 1·75

1966. 20th Anniv of U.N.E.S.C.O. As T **54/6** of Antigua.

239 10 c. multicoloured . . . . . 3·50 20
240 50 c. yellow, violet and olive . 13·00 90
241 $2 black, purple & orange . . 55·00 17·00

42 Rams' Heads on Chinese Lanterns

1967. Chinese New Year ("Year of the Ram").

242 **42** 10 c. red, olive and yellow . 4·00 50
243 – $1.30 green, red & yellow . 32·00 11·00

DESIGN: $1.30, Three rams.

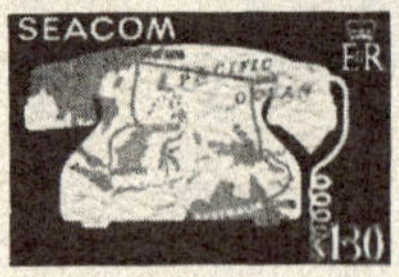

44 Cable Route Map

1967. Completion of Malaysia–Hong Kong Link of SEACOM Telephone Cable.

244 **44** $1.30 blue and red . . . . 17·00 4·50

45 Rhesus Macaques in Tree

1968. Chinese New Year ("Year of the Monkey").

245 **45** 10 c. gold, black and red . 4·50 50
246 – $1.30 gold, black and red . 30·00 9·50

DESIGN: $1.30, Family of rhesus macaques.

47 "Iberia" (liner) at Ocean Terminal

53 "Bauhinia blakeana"

1968. Sea Craft.

247 **47** 10 c. multicoloured . . . . 2·00 15
248 – 20 c. blue, black and brown 3·25 1·00
249 – 40 c. orange, black & mve 11·00 9·00
250 – 50 c. red, black and green 7·50 75
251 – $1 yellow, black & red . . 16·00 4·50
252 – $1.30 blue, black and pink 45·00 4·25

DESIGNS: 20 c. Pleasure launch; 40 c. Car ferry; 50 c. Passenger ferry; $1 Sampan; $1.30, Junk.

1968. Multicoloured.

253 65 c. Type **53** . . . . . . 9·00 50
254 $1 Arms of Hong Kong . . . 9·00 40

55 "Aladdin's Lamp" and Human Rights Emblem

1968. Human Rights Year.

255 **55** 10 c. orange, black & grn . 1·50 75
256 50 c. yellow, black & pur . 4·50 2·25

56 Cockerel

1969. Chinese New Year ("Year of the Cock"). Multicoloured.

257 10 c. Type **56** . . . . 5·00 1·00
258 $1.30 Cockerel (vert) . . . . 65·00 14·00

58 Arms of Chinese University

1969. Establishment of Chinese University of Hong Kong.

259 **58** 40 c. violet, gold and blue 7·00 3·00

59 Earth Station and Satellite

1969. Opening of Communications Satellite Tracking Station.

260 **59** $1 multicoloured . . . . . 24·00 4·50

60 Chow's Head

62 "Expo '70" Emblem

1970. Chinese New Year ("Year of the Dog"). Multicoloured.

261 10 c. Type **60** . . . . . . 5·50 1·25
262 $1.30 Chow standing (horiz) . . 65·00 14·00

1970. World Fair, Osaka. Multicoloured.

263 15 c. Type **62** 65 85
264 25 c. "Expo '70" emblem and junks (horiz) . . . . 1·40 1·50

64 Plaque in Tung Wah Hospital

1970. Centenary of Tung Wah Hospital.

265 **64** 10 c. multicoloured 75 25
266 50 c. multicoloured . . . . 3·25 1·50

65 Symbol

1970. Asian Productivity Year.

267 **65** 10 c. multicoloured . . . . 1·00 60

66 Pig

1971. Chinese New Year ("Year of the Pig").

268 **66** 10 c. multicoloured . . . . 5·00 90
269 $1.30 multicoloured . . . . 30·00 11·00

67 "60" and Scout Badge

68 Festival Emblem

1971. Diamond Jubilee of Scouting in Hong Kong.

270 **67** 10 c. black, red & yellow . . 65 10
271 50 c. black, green and blue . 3·25 1·00
272 $2 black, mauve & violet . 18·00 9·50

1971. Hong Kong Festival.

273 **68** 10 c. orange and purple . . 1·25 20
274 – 50 c. multicoloured . . . 2·50 90
275 – $1 multicoloured . . . . 7·50 6·00

DESIGNS—39×23 mm: 50 c. Coloured streamers. 23×39 mm: $1 "Orchid".

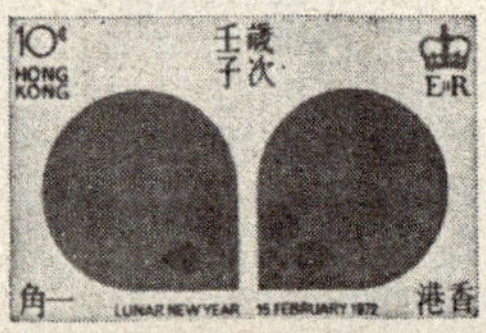

69 Stylised Rats

1972. Chinese New Year. ("Year of the Rat").

276 **69** 10 c. red, black and gold . 3·50 50
277 $1.30 red, black and gold . 32·00 11·00

70 Tunnel Entrance

1972. Opening of Cross-Harbour Tunnel.

278 **70** $1 multicoloured . . . . . 5·00 2·25

1972. Royal Silver Wedding. As T **52** of Ascension, but with Phoenix and Dragon in background.

279 10 c. multicoloured 30 15
280 50 c. multicoloured . . . . . 1·10 1·40

72 Ox

73 Queen Elizabeth II

1973 Chinese New Year ("Year of the Ox").

281 **72** 10 c. orange, brown & blk 2·00 40
282 – $1.30 yellow, orange & blk 6·50 6·50

DESIGN—HORIZ: $1.30, Ox.

1973.

311 **73** 10 c. orange 55 30
284 15 c. green . . . . 7·00 6·00
313 20 c. violet 50 10
286 25 c. brown . . . . 10·00 6·50
315 30 c. blue 70 30
316 40 c. blue . . . . 1·25 1·25
289 50 c. red . . . . 1·25 50
318 60 c. lavender . . . . . . 1·75 1·75
290 65 c. brown . . . . 12·00 11·00
320 70 c. yellow . . . . 1·75 30
321 80 c. red . . . . 2·25 2·50
321c 90 c. brown . . . . 7·50 1·40
291 $1 green . . . . 2·25 70
323 – $1.30 yellow and violet . 2·50 30
324 – $2 green and brown . . . 3·00 1·25
324c – $5 pink and blue . . . . 4·75 1·75
324d – $10 pink and green . . . 8·00 5·50
324e – $20 pink and black . . . 13·00 11·00

Values of $1.30 and above are size 27×32 mm.

1973. Royal Wedding. As T **47** of Anguilla. Multicoloured. Background colours given.

297 50 c. brown 50 15
298 $2 mauve . . . . 2·25 1·50

75 Festival Symbols forming Chinese Character

1973. Hong Kong Festival.

299 **75** 10 c. red and green 40 10
300 – 50 c. mauve and orange . . 2·00 90
301 – $1 green and mauve . . . 4·75 4·25

DESIGNS—Festival symbols arranged to form a Chinese character: 10 c. "Hong"; 50 c. "Kong"; $1 "Festival".

76 Tiger

1974. Chinese New Year ("Year of the Tiger").

302 **76** 10 c. multicoloured . . . . 3·50 50
303 – $1.30 multicoloured . . . . 11·00 12·00

DESIGN—VERT: $1.30, similar to Type **76**.

77 Chinese Mask

1974. Arts Festival.
304 **77** 10 c. multicoloured 75 10
305 – $1 multicoloured . . . . 6·00 4·25
306 – $2 multicoloured . . . . 9·00 8·50
DESIGNS: $1, $2, Chinese masks similar to T **77**.

78 Pigeons with Letters

1974. Centenary of U.P.U.
308 **78** 10 c. blue, green & black . . 40 10
309 – 50 c. mauve, orange & blk . 1·00 40
310 – $2 multicoloured . . . . 5·25 4·25
DESIGNS: 50 c. Globe within letters; $2 Hands holding letters.

79 Stylized Hare

1975. Chinese New Year ("Year of the Hare").
327 **79** 10 c. silver and red . . . . 1·00 60
328 – $1.30 gold and green . . . 8·00 8·00
DESIGN: $1.30, Pair of hares.

80 Queen Elizabeth II, the Duke of Edinburgh and Hong Kong Arms

1975. Royal Visit.
329 **80** $1.30 multicoloured . . . . 2·75 2·00
330 $2 multicoloured . . . . 3·75 4·00

81 Mid-Autumn Festival **82** Hwamei

1975. Hong Kong Festivals of 1975. Mult.
331 50 c. Type **81** . . . . . . 2·00 50
332 $1 Dragon-boat Festival . . . 8·00 2·50
333 $2 Tin Hau Festival . . . . 28·00 7·50

1975. Birds. Multicoloured.
335 50 c. Type **82** . . . . . . 2·00 50
336 $1.30 Chinese bulbul . . . . 8·00 5·00
337 $2 Black-capped kingfisher . . 14·00 12·00

83 Dragon

1976. Chinese New Year ("Year of the Dragon").
338 **83** 20 c. mauve, purple & gold . 75 10
339 – $1.30 green, red and gold . 6·50 3·25
DESIGN: $1.30, As Type **83** but dragon reversed.

84 "60" and Girl Guides Badge

1976. Diamond Jubilee of Girl Guides. Multicoloured.
354 20 c. Type **84** 50 10
355 $1.30 Badge, stylised diamond and "60" . . . . 5·00 3·50

85 "Postal Services" in Chinese Characters

1976. Opening of New G.P.O.
356 **85** 20 c. green, grey and black . 75 10
357 – $1.30 orange, grey and blk . 3·75 2·00
358 – $2 yellow, grey and black . 6·50 4·50
DESIGNS: $1.30, Old G.P.O.; $2 New G.P.O.

86 Tree Snake on Branch

1977. Chinese New Year ("Year of the Snake"). Multicoloured.
359 20 c. Type **86** 50 15
360 $1.30 Snake facing left . . . 4·00 4·75

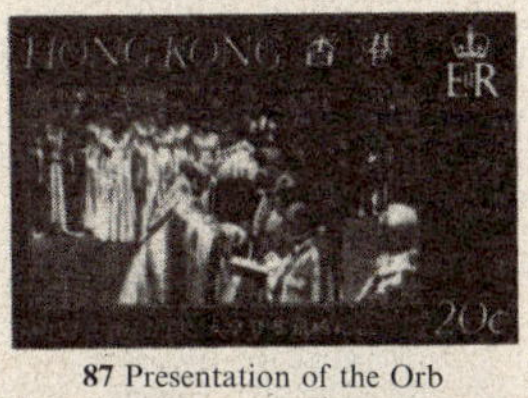

87 Presentation of the Orb

1977. Silver Jubilee. Multicoloured.
361 20 c. Type **87** 40 10
362 $1.30 The Queen's visit, 1975 . 1·25 1·25
363 $2 The Orb (vert) . . . . . 1·50 1·50

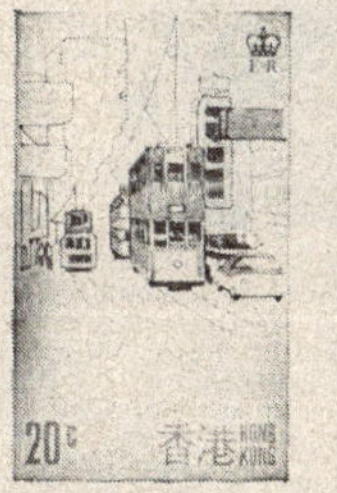

88 Tram Cars **89** Buttercup Orchid

1977. Tourism. Multicoloured.
364 20 c. Type **88** 55 10
365 60 c. Star ferryboat . . . . 1·50 2·25
366 $1.30 The Peak Railway . . . 2·50 2·25
367 $2 Junk and sampan . . . . 3·25 3·75

1977. Orchids. Multicoloured.
368 20 c. Type **89** . . . . . . 1·25 15
369 $1.30 Lady's slipper orchid . 4·00 2·25
370 $2 Susan orchid . . . . . . 6·00 4·25

90 Horse

1978. Chinese New Year ("Year of the Horse").
371 **90** 20 c. mauve, olive and bistre 50 10
372 $1.30 orange, brn & lt brn 3·50 4·00

91 Queen Elizabeth II

1978. 25th Anniv of Coronation.
373 **91** 20 c. mauve and blue . . . 40 10
374 $1.30 blue and mauve . . 1·50 2·25

92 Girl and Boy holding Hands

1978. Centenary of Po Leung Kuk (children's charity). Multicoloured.
375 20 c. Type **92** 30 15
376 $1.30 Ring of children . . . . 1·75 2·00

93 Electronics Industry

1979. Hong Kong Industries.
377 **93** 20 c. yellow, olive & orge . 30 10
378 – $1.30 multicoloured . . . . 1·10 1·75
379 – $2 multicoloured . . . . 1·10 2·25
DESIGNS: $1.30, Toy industry; $2 Garment industry.

94 "Precis orithya" **96** Tsui Shing Lau Pagoda

95 Diagrammatic View of Railway Station

1979. Butterflies. Multicoloured.
380 20 c. Type **94** . . . . . . 1·00 10
381 $1 "Graphium sarpedon" . . . 1·75 80
382 $1.30 "Heliophorus epicles" . . 2·50 1·60
383 $2 "Danaus genutia" . . . . 2·75 3·50

1979. Mass Transit Railway. Multicoloured.
384 20 c. Type **95** 80 10
385 $1.30 Diagrammatic view of car 2·25 80
386 $2 Plan showing route of railway 2·50 1·75

1980. Rural Architecture.
387 **96** 20 c. black, mauve & yellow 40 20
388 – $1.30 multicoloured . . . 1·10 1·25
389 – $2 multicoloured . . . . 1·60 2·50
DESIGNS—HORIZ: $1.30, Village house, Sai O; $2 Ching Chung Koon Temple.

97 Queen Elizabeth the Queen Mother

1980. 80th Birthday of The Queen Mother.
390 **97** $1.30 multicoloured . . . . 1·00 1·25

98 Botanical Gardens

1980. Parks. Multicoloured.
391 20 c. Type **98** 40 15
392 $1 Ocean Park 75 60
393 $1.30 Kowloon Park 80 85
394 $2 Country parks . . . . . 1·75 2·50

99 Red-spotted Grouper

1981. Fishes. Multicoloured.
395 20 c. Type **99** 30 15
396 $1 Golden thread-finned bream 1·00 70
397 $1.30 Scar-breasted tuskfish . 1·10 95
398 $2 Blue-barred orange parrotfish . . . . 2·00 3·25

100 Wedding Bouquet from Hong Kong **101** Suburban Development

1981. Royal Wedding. Multicoloured.
399 20 c. Type **100** 30 10
400 $1.30 Prince Charles in Hong Kong 70 50
401 $5 Prince Charles and Lady Diana Spencer . . . . . . 2·25 2·75

1981. Public Housing.
402 **101** 20 c. multicoloured . . . 20 10
403 – $1 multicoloured 80 60
404 – $1.30 multicoloured . . . 1·00 1·00
405 – $2 multicoloured . . . . 1·25 2·00
DESIGNS: $1 to $2, Various suburban developments.

102 "Victoria from the Harbour, c. 1855"

1982. Hong Kong Port, Past and Present. Multicoloured.
407 20 c. Type **102** 60 15
408 $1 "West Point, Hong Kong, 1847" . . . . 1·75 90
409 $1.30 Fleet of junks . . . . 2·25 1·10
410 $2 Liner "Queen Elizabeth 2" at Hong Kong . . . . 3·00 2·75

103 Large Indian Civet

1982. Wild Animals.
411 **103** 20 c. black, pink & brown 60 15
412 – $1 multicoloured . . . . 1·25 90
413 – $1.30 black, green & orge 1·50 1·10
414 – $5 black, brown & yellow 3·00 4·50
DESIGNS: $1 Chinese pangolin; $1.30, Chinese porcupine; $5 Indian muntjac.

104 Queen Elizabeth II **107** Dancing

106 Table Tennis

1982.

415 **104** 10 c. lt red, red & yellow . . 70 60
416 20 c. blue, violet & lavender 90 70
417 30 c. lt violet, vio & pink . 1·25 30
418 40 c. red and blue . . . . 1·25 30
475 50 c. chestnut, brn & grn 90 40
476 60 c. purple and grey . . 1·50 1·10
477 70 c. green, myrtle & yell 1·75 40
478 80 c. bistre, brown & green 2·00 1·75
479 90 c. dp green, grn & turq 2·00 50
480 $1 dp orange, orge & red . 1·75 40
481 $1.30 blue and mauve . . 2·25 45
482 $1.70 dp blue, bl & grn . 3·50 1·50
483 $2 blue and pink . . . . 3·75 1·50
484 – $5 red, purple & yellow . 6·50 3·25
485 – $10 brown & lt brown . . 7·50 4·00
486 – $20 red and blue . . . . 10·00 7·50
487 – $50 red and grey . . . . 30·00 25·00
Nos. 484/7 are as Type **104** but larger, 26×30 mm.

1982. Sport for the Disabled. Multicoloured.

431 30 c. Type **106** 50 10
432 $1 Racing 75 80
433 $1.30 Basketball . . . . . . 2·75 1·50
434 $5 Archery . . . . 5·00 6·50

1983. Performing Arts.

435 **107** 30 c. light blue and blue . . 50 10
436 – $1.30 red and purple . . . 2·00 1·25
437 – $5 green and deep green . . 6·50 5·50
DESIGNS: $1.30, "Theatre"; $5 "Music".

108 Aerial View of Hong Kong

1983. Commonwealth Day. Multicoloured.

438 30 c. Type **108** 70 10
439 $1 "Liverpool Bay" (container ship) . . . . 1·75 1·25
440 $1.30 Hong Kong flag . . . 1·75 1·25
441 $5 Queen Elizabeth II and Hong Kong . . . . 3·50 5·00

109 Victoria Harbour

1983. Hong Kong by Night. Multicoloured.

442 30 c. Type **109** . . . . . . 1·25 15
443 $1 Space Museum, Tsim Sha Tsui Cultural Centre . . . . 3·75 1·50
444 $1.30 Fireworks display . . . 4·75 2·00
445 $5 "Jumbo", floating restaurant 15·00 8·50

110 Old and new Observatory Buildings

1983. Centenary of Hong Kong Observatory.

446 **110** 40 c. orange, brown & black 75 10
447 – $1 mauve, dp mve & blk . 2·00 1·75
448 – $1.30 blue, dp blue & blk . 2·75 1·75
449 – $5 yellow, green & black . 8·00 9·00
DESIGNS: $1 Wind measuring equipment; $1.30, Thermometer; $5 Ancient and modern seismometers.

111 De Havilland D.H.86 Dragon Express "Dorado" (Hong Kong–Penang Service, 1936)

1984. Aviation in Hong Kong. Multicoloured.

450 40 c. Type **111** . . . . . . 1·00 15
451 $1 Sikorsky S-42B flying boat (San Francisco–Hong Kong Service, 1937) . . . . . . 2·25 1·75
452 $1.30 Cathay-Pacific Boeing 747 jet leaving Kai Tak Airport 3·25 1·75
453 $5 Baldwin brothers' balloon, 1891 (vert) . . . . 9·00 10·00

112 Map by Capt. E. Belcher, 1836

1984. Maps of Hong Kong.

454 40 c. Type **112** . . . . . . 1·00 20
455 $1 Bartholomew map of 1929 1·75 1·25
456 $1.30 Early map of Hong Kong waters . . . . 3·00 1·75
457 $5 Chinese-style map of 1819 11·00 10·00

113 Cockerel

1984. Chinese Lanterns. Multicoloured.

458 40 c. Type **113** 80 15
459 $1 Dog . . . . 1·75 1·25
460 $1.30 Butterfly . . . . . . 3·00 1·75
461 $5 Fish . . . . 9·00 8·50

114 Jockey on Horse and Nurse with Baby ("Health Care")

1984. Centenary of Royal Hong Kong Jockey Club. Designs showing aspects of Club's charity work. Multicoloured.

462 40 c. Type **114** . . . . . . 1·25 20
463 $1 Disabled man playing handball ("Support for Disabled") . . . . 2·00 1·75
464 $1.30 Ballerina ("The Arts") . 3·00 2·00
465 $5 Humboldt penguins ("Ocean Park") . . . . 9·00 11·00

115 Hung Sing Temple

1985. Historic Buildings. Multicoloured.

467 40 c. Type **115** 60 20
468 $1 St. John's Cathedral . . . 1·75 1·60
469 $1.30 The Old Supreme Court Building . . . . 2·25 1·75
470 $5 Wan Chai Post Office . . 9·50 8·50

116 Prow of Dragon Boat

1985. 10th International Dragon Boat Festival. Designs showing different parts of dragon boat. Multicoloured.

488 40 c. Type **116** 50 15
489 $1 Drummer and rowers . . 1·75 1·25
490 $1.30 Rowers . . . . 3·00 1·60
491 $5 Stern of boat . . . . . . 9·25 8·00

117 The Queen Mother with Prince Charles and Prince William, 1984

1985. Life and Times of Queen Elizabeth the Queen Mother. Multicoloured.

493 40 c. At Glamis Castle, aged 7 60 10
494 $1 Type **117** . . . . 1·75 1·25
495 $1.30 The Queen Mother, 1970 (from photo by Cecil Beaton) 2·00 1·40
496 $5 With Prince Henry at his christening (from photo by Lord Snowdon) . . . . . . 3·25 4·00

118 Melastoma

1985. Native Flowers. Multicoloured.

497 40 c. Type **118** . . . . . . 1·50 20
498 50 c. Chinese lily . . . . . . 1·75 40
499 60 c. Grantham's camellia . . 2·00 90
500 $1.30 Narcissus . . . . . . 3·25 1·25
501 $1.70 Bauhinia . . . . 3·75 1·50
502 $5 Chinese New Year flower 7·00 9·00

119 Hong Kong Academy for Performing Arts

1985. New Buildings. Multicoloured.

503 50 c. Type **119** 80 15
504 $1.30 Exchange Square (vert) 1·75 1·50
505 $1.70 Hong Kong Bank Headquarters (vert) . . . . 2·50 1·75
506 $5 Hong Kong Coliseum . . . 8·00 11·00

120 Halley's Comet in the Solar System

1986. Appearance of Halley's Comet. Mult.

507 50 c. Type **120** . . . . . . 1·25 20
508 $1.30 Edmond Halley and Comet 2·00 1·40
509 $1.70 Comet over Hong Kong 2·75 1·50
510 $5 Comet passing the Earth . . 11·00 8·00

1986. 60th Birthday of Queen Elizabeth II. As T **110** of Ascension. Multicoloured.

512 50 c. At wedding of Miss Celia Bowes-Lyon, 1931 . . . . . 40 10
513 $1 Queen in Garter procession, Windsor Castle 1977 . . . . 75 60
514 $1.30 In Hong Kong, 1975 . . 1·00 70
515 $1.70 At Royal Lodge, Windsor, 1980 (from photo by Norman Parkinson) . . . . 1·10 75
516 $5 At Crown Agents Head Office, London, 1983 . . . . 3·25 4·00

121 Mass Transit Train, Boeing 747 Airliner and Map of World

1986. "Expo '86" World Fair, Vancouver. Multicoloured.

517 50 c. Type **121** 80 30
518 $1.30 Hong Kong Bank Headquarters and map of world . . . . 1·50 1·00
519 $1.70 Container ship and map of world . . . . 2·25 1·40
520 $5 Dish aerial and map of world 6·50 7·00

122 Hand-liner Sampan

1986. Fishing Vessels. Designs showing fishing boat and outline of fish. Multicoloured.

521 50 c. Type **122** 80 15
522 $1.30 Stern trawler . . . . . 1·50 1·10
523 $1.70 Long liner junk . . . . 2·25 1·40
524 $5 Junk trawler . . . . . . 7·00 7·50

123 "The Second Puan Khequa" (attr Spoilum)

1986. 19th-century Hong Kong Portraits. Multicoloured.

525 50 c. Type **123** 55 15
526 $1.30 "Chinese Lady" (19th-century copy) . . . . 1·50 1·10
527 $1.70 "Lamqua" (self-portrait) 1·75 1·40
528 $5 "Wife of Wo Hing Qua" (attr G. Chinnery) . . . . 5·50 5·50

124 Rabbit

1987. Chinese New Year ("Year of the Rabbit"). Designs showing stylized rabbits.

529 **124** 50 c. multicoloured . . . 65 15
530 – $1.30 multicoloured . . . 1·50 1·25
531 – $1.70 multicoloured . . . 1·75 1·40
532 – $5 multicoloured . . . . 6·50 6·00
Nos. 530/1 have the "0" omitted from their face values.

125 "Village Square, Hong Kong Island, 1838" (Auguste Borget)

1987. 19th-century Hong Kong Scenes. Mult.

534 50 c. Type **125** 60 15
535 $1.30 "Boat Dwellers, Kowloon Bay, 1838 (Auguste Borget) 1·75 1·10
536 $1.70 "Flagstaff House, 1846" (Murdoch Bruce) . . . . 2·25 1·40
537 $5 "Wellington Street, late 19th-century" (C. Andrasi) . . . 7·00 6·50

126 Queen Elizabeth II and Central Victoria

127 Hong Kong Flag

1987.

600 **126** 10 c. multicoloured . . . 50 60
601 40 c. multicoloured . . . 1·25 1·50
602 50 c. multicoloured . . . 70 30
603 60 c. multicoloured . . . 70 30
604 70 c. multicoloured . . . 70 50
605 80 c. multicoloured . . . 70 40
606 90 c. multicoloured . . . 80 40
607 $1 multicoloured 80 30
607a $1.20 multicoloured . . 2·75 2·25
608 $1.30 multicoloured . . 1·50 50
609 $1.40 multicoloured . . 1·50 70
547A $1.70 multicoloured . . 3·00 80
610 $1.80 multicoloured . . 1·00 60
611 $2 multicoloured . . . 1·25 50
611a $2.30 multicoloured . . 2·75 2·25
612 – $5 multicoloured . . . 3·50 1·25
613 – $10 multicoloured . . . 5·00 3·00
614 – $20 multicoloured . . . 7·50 7·00
615 – $50 multicoloured . . . 18·00 15·00
DESIGNS—25×31 mm: Queen Elizabeth II and $5 Kowloon; $10 Victoria Harbour; $20 Legislative Council Building; $50 Government House.
With the exception of Nos. 607a and 611a which are dated, all the above exist with or without a date in the design.

1987.

554a **127** 10 c. multicoloured . . . 50 50
554b – 50 c. brown, red & black 1·25 1·50
554c – 80 c. mauve, green & blk 70 1·00
554d – 90 c. blue, brown & black 70 90
554e – $1.30 green, blue & black 1·40 1·75
554f – $2.30 brown, violet & blk 1·60 2·25
DESIGN: 50 c. to $2.30, Map of Hong Kong.

128 Alice Ho Miu Ling Nethersole Hospital, 1887

1987. Hong Kong Medical Centenaries. Mult.

555 50 c. Type **128** . . . . . . 1·00 20
556 $1.30 Matron and nurses, Nethersole Hospital, 1891 . 2·25 1·40
557 $1.70 Scanning equipment, Faculty of Medicine . . . . 2·75 1·40
558 $5 Nurse and patient, Faculty of Medicine . . . . 8·50 8·00

129 Casual Dress with Fringed Hem, 220–589

1987. Historical Chinese Costumes. Multicoloured.

559	50 c. Type **129**	55	10
560	$1.30 Two-piece dress and wrap, 581–960	1·40	1·25
561	$1.70 Formal dress, Song Dynasty, 960–1279	1·75	1·50
562	$5 Manchu empress costume, 1644–1911	5·75	6·50

130 Dragon

1988. Chinese New Year ("Year of the Dragon"). Designs showing dragons.

563	**130**	50 c. multicoloured	75	15
564	–	$1.30 multicoloured	1·75	1·25
565	–	$1.70 multicoloured	2·00	1·40
566	–	$5 multicoloured	4·00	5·00

131 White-breasted Kingfisher
132 Chinese Banyan

1988. Hong Kong Birds. Multicoloured.

568	50 c. Type **131**	1·10	30
569	$1.30 Fukien niltava	2·25	1·40
570	$1.70 Black kite	2·75	1·50
571	$5 Lesser pied kingfisher	5·00	6·00

1988. Trees of Hong Kong. Multicoloured.

572	50 c. Type **132**	35	10
573	$1.30 Hong Kong orchid tree	75	65
574	$1.70 Cotton tree	1·10	85
575	$5 Schima	3·50	4·00

133 Lower Terminal, Peak Tramway
134 Hong Kong Catholic Cathedral

1988. Centenary of The Peak Tramway. Mult.

577	50 c. Type **133**	60	10
578	$1.30 Tram on incline	1·00	90
579	$1.70 Peak Tower Upper Terminal	1·10	90
580	$5 Tram	3·50	4·00

1988. Centenary of Hong Kong Catholic Cathedral.

582	**134**	60 c. multicoloured	1·25	75

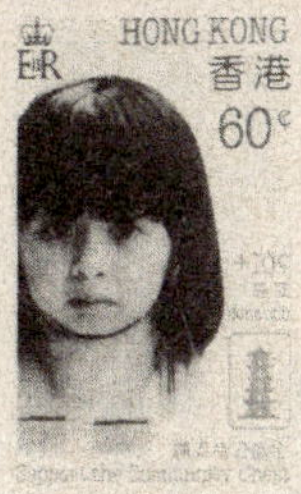

135 Deaf Girl
137 Girl and Doll

136 Snake

1988. Community Chest Charity.

583	**135**	60 c. + 10 c. blk, red & blue	60	75
584	–	$1.40 + 20 c. black, red and green	80	1·00
585	–	$1.80 + 30 c. black, red and orange	1·50	1·60
586	–	$5 + $1 black, red & brn	4·25	5·50

DESIGNS: $1.40, Elderly woman; $1.80, Blind boy using braille typewriter; $5 Mother and baby.

1989. Chinese New Year ("Year of the Snake"). Multicoloured.

587	60 c. Type **136**	30	15
588	$1.40 Snake and fish	1·25	60
589	$1.80 Snake on branch	1·75	75
590	$5 Coiled snake	5·00	5·00

1989. Cheung Chau Bun Festival. Multicoloured.

592	60 c. Type **137**	45	15
593	$1.40 Girl in festival costume	1·10	60
594	$1.80 Paper effigy of god Taai Si Wong	1·25	70
595	$5 Floral gateway	3·00	3·75

138 "Twins" (wood carving, Cheung Yee)
139 Lunar New Year Festivities

1989. Modern Art. Multicoloured.

596	60 c. Type **138**	40	15
597	$1.40 "Figures" (acrylic on paper, Chan Luis)	1·00	60
598	$1.80 "Lotus" (copper sculpture, Van Lau)	1·25	70
599	$5 "Zen Painting" (ink and colour on paper, Lui Shou-kwan)	3·00	3·75

1989. Hong Kong People. Multicoloured.

616	60 c. Type **139**	50	10
617	$1.40 Shadow boxing and horse racing	1·25	70
618	$1.80 Foreign-exchange dealer and traditional builder	1·60	80
619	$5 Multi-racial society	4·00	5·00

140 University of Science and Technology
141 Prince and Princess of Wales and Hong Kong Skyline

1989. Building for the Future.

620	**140**	60 c. black, yellow & brn	35	15
621	–	70 c. blk, pale pink & pink	40	20
622	–	$1.30 black, lt green & grn	80	55
623	–	$1.40 black, lt blue & bl	80	55
624	–	$1.80 black, turquoise & bl	95	80
625	–	$5 brown, orange & red	3·25	3·50

DESIGNS: 70 c. Cultural Centre; $1.30, Eastern Harbour motorway interchange; $1.40, New Bank of China Building; $1.80, Convention and Exhibition Centre; $5 Mass Transit electric train.

1989. Royal Visit. Multicoloured.

626	60 c. Type **141**	60	15
627	$1.40 Princess of Wales	1·00	60
628	$1.80 Prince of Wales	1·25	95
629	$5 Prince and Princess of Wales in evening dress	5·00	5·50

143 Horse

1990. Chinese New Year ("Year of the Horse").

631	**143**	60 c. multicoloured	60	20
632	–	$1.40 multicoloured	1·25	1·00
633	–	$1.80 multicoloured	1·50	1·25
634	–	$5 multicoloured	4·25	4·75

DESIGNS: $1.40 to $5, Different horse designs.

144 Chinese Lobster Dish
145 Air Pollution and Clean Air

1990. International Cuisine. Designs showing various dishes. Multicoloured.

636	60 c. Type **144**	50	15
637	70 c. Indian	50	20
638	$1.30 Chinese vegetables	80	50
639	$1.40 Thai	80	50
640	$1.80 Japanese	1·25	70
641	$5 French	4·00	5·00

1990. U.N. World Environment Day. Mult.

642	60 c. Type **145**	40	15
643	$1.40 Noise pollution and music	75	50
644	$1.80 Polluted and clean water	90	60
645	$5 Litter on ground and in bin	2·40	2·75

146 Street Lamp and Des Voeux Road, 1890

1990. Centenary of Electricity Supply.

647	**146**	60 c. black, bistre & brn	40	10
648	–	$1.40 multicoloured	1·00	80
649	–	$1.80 black, bistre & blue	1·10	90
650	–	$5 multicoloured	2·50	3·75

DESIGNS: $1.40, Street Lamp and "Jumbo" (floating restaurant), 1940; $1.80, Street lamp and pylon, 1960; $5 Street lamp and Hong Kong from harbour, 1980.

147 Christmas Tree and Skyscrapers

1990. Christmas. Multicoloured.

652	50 c. Type **147**	20	10
653	60 c. Dove with holly	20	15
654	$1.40 Firework display	70	40
655	$1.80 Father Christmas hat on skyscraper	90	50
656	$2 Children with Father Christmas	1·25	1·25
657	$5 Candy stick with bow and Hong Kong skyline	2·75	4·00

148 Ram

1991. Chinese New Year ("Year of the Ram").

658	**148**	60 c. multicoloured	25	15
659	–	$1.40 multicoloured	65	45
660	–	$1.80 multicoloured	80	60
661	–	$5 multicoloured	2·50	3·50

DESIGNS: $1.40 to $5, Different ram designs.

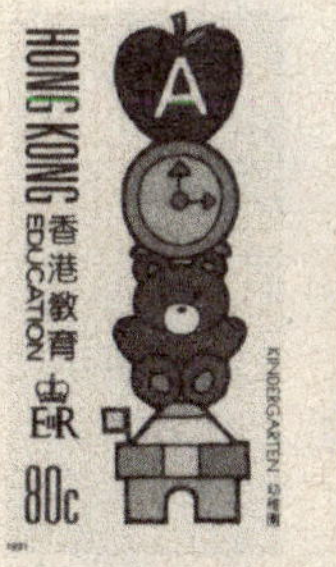

149 Letter "A", Clock, Teddy Bear and Building Bricks (Kindergarten)
150 Rickshaw

1991. Education. Multicoloured.

663	80 c. Type **149**	40	20
664	$1.80 Globe, laboratory flask and mathematical symbols (Primary and Secondary)	1·00	70
665	$2.30 Machinery (Vocational)	1·25	1·25
666	$5 Mortar board, computer and books (Tertiary)	2·75	4·00

1991. 100 Years of Public Transport. Mult.

667	80 c. Type **150**	30	15
668	90 c. Double-decker bus	55	30
669	$1.70 Harbour ferry	90	60
670	$1.80 Double-deck tram	1·25	60
671	$2.30 Mass Transit electric train	1·75	1·75
672	$5 Jetfoil	3·50	4·50

151 Victorian Pillar Box and Cover of 1888
152 Bronze Buddha, Lantau Island

1991. 150th Anniv of Hong Kong Post Office. Multicoloured.

673	80 c. Type **151**	40	15
674	$1.70 Edwardian pillar box and cover	90	65
675	$1.80 King George V pillar box and cover of 1935	1·00	65
676	$2.30 King George VI pillar box and cover of 1938	1·40	1·75
677	$5 Queen Elizabeth II pillar box and cover of 1989	3·75	4·75

1991. Landmarks.

679	**152**	80 c. red and black	40	15
680	–	$1.70 green and black	90	70
681	–	$1.80 violet and black	1·00	70
682	–	$2.30 blue and black	1·25	1·75
683	–	$5 orange and black	3·50	4·50

DESIGNS: $1.70, Peak Pavilion; $1.80, Clocktower of Kowloon–Canton Railway Station; $2.30, Catholic Cathedral; $5 Wong Tai Sin Temple.

153 Monkey

1992. Chinese New Year ("Year of the Monkey").

686	**153**	80 c. multicoloured	40	15
687	–	$1.80 multicoloured	70	55
688	–	$2.30 multicoloured	1·25	1·40
689	–	$5 multicoloured	2·75	4·00

DESIGNS: $1.80 to $5, Different monkey designs.

1992. 40th Anniv of Queen Elizabeth II's Accession. As T **143** of Ascension. Multicoloured.

691	80 c. Royal barge in Hong Kong harbour	30	15
692	$1.70 Queen watching dancing display	60	35
693	$1.80 Fireworks display	60	35
694	$2.30 Three portraits of Queen Elizabeth	90	85
695	$5 Queen Elizabeth II	2·00	2·50

154 Running

1992. Olympic Games, Barcelona. Multicoloured.

696	80 c. Type **154**	40	20
697	$1.80 Swimming and javelin	80	80
698	$2.30 Cycling	1·60	1·75
699	$5 High jump	2·25	3·25

155 Queen Elizabeth II
157 Principal Male Character

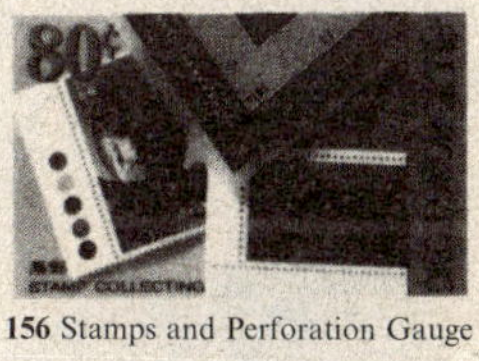

156 Stamps and Perforation Gauge

1992.

702	**155**	10 c. mauve, blk & cerise	30	40
702bp		20 c. black, indigo & bl	50	60
703		50 c. red, black & yellow	30	30
704		60 c. blue, black and light blue	50	45
705		70 c. mauve, black and lilac	50	50

706	155	80 c. mauve, black and pink	30	20
707		90 c. green, black & grey	30	20
708		$1 brown, black and yellow	35	20
708b		$1.10 red, black & orge	35	35
709		$1.20 violet, blk & lilac	35	25
757c		$1.30 blue, black & orge	45	60
709c		$1.40 green, black and yellow	35	30
709d		$1.50 brown, black and blue	60	45
709e		$1.60 green, black and lilac	45	50
710		$1.70 ultram, blk & bl	55	45
711		$1.80 mauve, blk & grey	85	45
711a		$1.90 green, blk & stone	55	50
764		$2 blue, black & green	60	75
712b		$2.10 red, black & green	85	60
713		$2.30 brown, blk & pink	80	60
759		$2.40 blue, black & grey	85	1·25
713b		$2.50 green, black and yellow	55	70
713c		$2.60 choc, blk & brn	75	80
713d		$3.10 brown, black and blue	65	80
759e		$5 green, black & lt grn	1·00	1·50
715	–	$10 brown, black and cinnamon	2·75	2·75
716	–	$20 red, black & orange	4·00	4·50
717	–	$50 dp grey, blk & grey	8·50	11·00

Nos. 715/17 are as Type **155**, but larger, 26 × 30 mm.

1992. Stamp Collecting. Multicoloured.

718	80 c. Type **156**	30	20
719	$1.80 Handstamp of 1841, 1891 Jubilee overprint and tweezers	60	55
720	$2.30 Stamps of 1946 and 1949 under magnifying glass	85	90
721	$5 2 c. of 1862 and watermark detector	2·00	3·00

1992. Chinese Opera. Multicoloured.

724	80 c. Type **157**	50	25
725	$1.80 Martial character	1·00	85
726	$2.30 Principal female character	1·40	1·50
727	$5 Comic character	2·50	4·00

158 Hearts

1992. Greetings Stamps. Multicoloured.

728	80 c. Type **158**	30	20
729	$1.80 Stars	55	60
730	$2.30 Presents	75	95
731	$5 Balloons	1·60	2·50

159 Cockerel

1993. Chinese New Year ("Year of the Cock").

732	159	80 c. multicoloured	30	20
733	–	$1.80 multicoloured	70	70
734	–	$2.30 multicoloured	95	1·10
735	–	$5 multicoloured	2·25	3·00

DESIGNS: $1.80 to $5, Different cock designs.

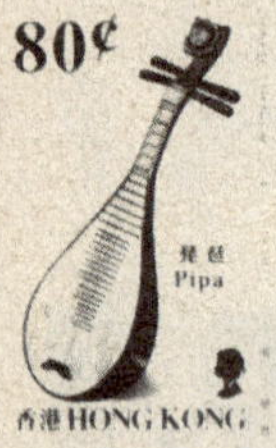

160 Pipa

161 Central Waterfront, Hong Kong in 1954

1993. Chinese String Musical Instruments. Multicoloured.

737	80 c. Type **160**	40	20
738	$1.80 Erhu	70	60
739	$2.30 Ruan	95	1·00
740	$5 Gehu	2·00	3·00

1993. 40th Anniv of Coronation. Multicoloured.

741	80 c. Type **161**	40	20
742	$1.80 Hong Kong in 1963	70	50
743	$2.30 Hong Kong in 1975	90	1·00
744	$5 Hong Kong in 1992	2·25	2·75

162 University of Science and Technology Building and Student

1993. Hong Kong's Contribution to Science and Technology. Multicoloured.

747	80 c. Type **162**	30	20
748	$1.80 Science Museum building and energy machine exhibit	50	40
749	$2.30 Governor's Award and circuit board	70	90
750	$5 Dish aerials and world map	1·75	3·00

163 Red Calico Egg-fish

1993. Goldfish. Multicoloured.

752	$1 Type **163**	35	20
753	$1.90 Red cap oranda	60	50
754	$2.40 Red and white fringetail	90	1·00
755	$5 Black and gold dragon-eye	2·25	3·25

164 Dog

1994. Chinese New Year ("Year of the Dog").

766	164	$1 multicoloured	30	20
767	–	$1.90 multicoloured	50	45
768	–	$2.40 multicoloured	70	90
769	–	$5 multicoloured	1·75	3·75

DESIGNS: $1.90 to $5, Different dog designs.

165 Modern Police Constables on Traffic Duty

1994. 150th Anniv of Royal Hong Kong Police Force. Multicoloured.

772	$1 Type **165**	30	20
773	$1.20 Marine policeman with binoculars	40	25
774	$1.90 Police uniforms of 1950	55	35
775	$2 Tactical firearms unit officer with sub-machine gun	75	55
776	$2.40 Early 20th-century police uniforms	90	90
777	$5 Sikh and Chinese constables of 1900	2·75	3·50

166 Dragon Boat Festival

1994. Traditional Chinese Festivals. Multicoloured.

778	$1 Type **166**	35	20
779	$1.90 Lunar New Year	60	50
780	$2.40 Seven Sisters Festival	85	1·10
781	$5 Mid-Autumn Festival	1·75	2·75

167 Swimming

1994. 15th Commonwealth Games, Victoria, Canada. Multicoloured.

783	$1 Type **167**	25	20
784	$1.90 Bowls	50	50
785	$2.40 Gymnastics	70	85
786	$5 Weightlifting	1·60	2·50

168 Dr. James Legge and Students

1994. Dr. James Legge (Chinese scholar) Commemoration.

787	168	$1 multicoloured	55	50

169 Alcyonium Coral

1994. Corals. Multicoloured.

788	$1 Type **169**	35	20
789	$1.90 Zoanthus	60	55
790	$2.40 Tubastrea	75	1·00
791	$5 Platygyra	1·75	2·50

170 Pig

1995. Chinese New Year ("Year of the Pig").

793	170	$1 multicoloured	30	30
794	–	$1.90 multicoloured	60	70
795	–	$2.40 multicoloured	70	95
796	–	$5 multicoloured	1·25	2·00

DESIGNS: $1.90 to $5, Different pig designs.

171 Hong Kong Rugby Sevens

1995. International Sporting Events in Hong Kong. Multicoloured.

798	$1 Type **171**	45	20
799	$1.90 The China Sea Yacht Race	60	55
800	$2.40 International Dragon Boat Races	85	1·00
801	$5 Hong Kong International Horse Races	1·75	2·50

172 Tsui Shing Lau Pagoda

1995. Hong Kong Traditional Rural Buildings. Multicoloured.

802	$1 Type **172**	30	20
803	$1.90 Sam Tung Uk village	55	55
804	$2.40 Lo Wai village	75	1·00
805	$5 Man Shek Tong house	1·50	2·50

173 Regimental Badge

1995. Disbandment of the Royal Hong Kong Regiment. Multicoloured.

806	$1.20 Type **173**	40	25
807	$2.10 Regimental guidon (horiz)	60	55
808	$2.60 Colour of Hong Kong Volunteer Defence Corps, 1928 (horiz)	75	85
809	$5 Cap badge of Royal Hong Kong Defence Force, 1951	1·25	2·00

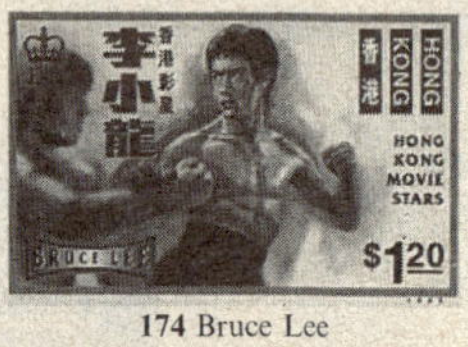

174 Bruce Lee

1995. Hong Kong Film Stars. Multicoloured.

812	$1.20 Type **174**	1·50	45
813	$2.10 Leung Sing-por	1·75	1·25
814	$2.60 Yam Kim-fai	2·75	1·40
815	$5 Lin Dai	2·75	3·00

175 Rat

1996. Chinese New Year ("Year of the Rat").

816	175	$1.20 multicoloured	25	30
817	–	$2.10 multicoloured	45	55
818	–	$2.60 multicoloured	50	65
819	–	$5 multicoloured	1·25	1·75

DESIGNS: $2.10 to $5, Rats (different).

176 Rhythmic Gymnastics

1996. Olympic Games, Atlanta. Multicoloured with Royal cypher and face values in black and Olympic rings multicoloured.

822	$1.20 Type **176**	25	25
823	$2.10 Diving	45	50
824	$2.60 Athletics	55	75
825	$5 Basketball	1·25	2·00

See also Nos. 832/5.

177 Painted Pottery Basin, c. 4500–3700 B.C.

1996. Archaeological Discoveries. Multicoloured.

828	$1.20 Type **177**	40	25
829	$2.10 Stone "yue" (ceremonial axe), c. 2900–2200 B.C.	50	65
830	$2.60 Stone "ge" (halberd), c. 2200–1500 B.C.	60	1·00
831	$5 Pottery tripod, c. 25–220 A.D.	1·25	2·50

1996. Opening of Centennial Olympic Games, Atlanta. Designs as Nos. 822/5, but with Royal Cypher and Olympic Rings in gold and face values in colours quoted.

832	$1.20 Type **176** (mauve)	35	25
833	$2.10 As No. 823 (blue)	50	60
834	$2.60 As No. 824 (green)	60	90
835	$5 As No. 825 (red)	1·25	2·25

178 Pat Sin Leng Mountain

1996. Mountains. Multicoloured.

837	$1.30 Type **178**	50	35
838	$2.50 Ma On Shan (40 × 35 mm)	70	1·00
839	$3.10 Lion Rock (35 × 40 mm)	90	1·00
840	$5 Lantau Peak (25 × 46½ mm)	1·25	2·25

179 Main Building, University of Hong Kong, 1912

1996. Urban Heritage. Multicoloured.

843	$1.30 Type **179**	40	70
844	$2.50 Western Market, 1906	60	85
845	$3.10 Old Pathological Institute, 1905	65	1·00
846	$5 Flagstaff House, 1846	80	1·75

180 Part of Hong Kong Skyline

1997.

848	**180**	10 c. purple and pink	10	10
849	–	20 c. brown and red	10	10
850	–	50 c. green and orange	10	10
851	–	$1 blue and yellow	15	20
852	–	$1.20 green and yellow	20	25
853	–	$1.30 violet and green	20	25
854	–	$1.40 purple and green	20	25
855	–	$1.60 purple and green	25	30
856	–	$2 green and blue	30	35
857	–	$2.10 turquoise and blue	30	35
858	–	$2.50 violet and mauve	40	45
859	–	$3.10 purple and mauve	50	55
860	–	$5 mauve and orange	80	85
861	–	$10 multicoloured (28 × 32 mm)	1·60	1·75
862	–	$20 multicoloured (28 × 32 mm)	3·25	3·50
863	–	$50 multicoloured (28 × 32 mm)	8·00	8·25

DESIGNS: 20 c. to $50 Different sections of Hong Kong skyline.

181 Ox

1997. Chinese New Year ("Year of the Ox").

874	**181**	$1.30 multicoloured	25	25
875		$2.50 multicoloured	50	55
876		$3.10 multicoloured	75	90
877		$5 multicoloured	1·25	2·00

182 Yellow-breasted Bunting

1997. Migratory Birds. Multicoloured.

884	$1.30 Type **182**	30	35
885	$2.50 Great knot	50	55
886	$3.10 Falcated teal	75	90
887	$5 Black-faced spoonbill	1·25	2·00

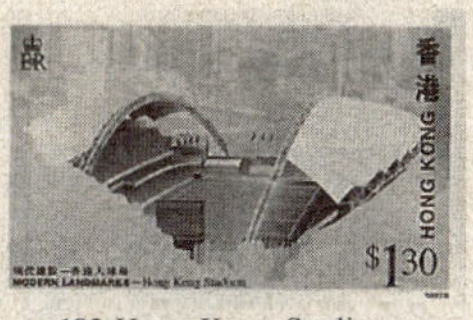

183 Hong Kong Stadium

1997. Modern Landmarks. Multicoloured.

888	$1.30 Type **183**	25	25
889	$2.50 Peak Tower	50	55
890	$3.10 Hong Kong Convention and Exhibition Centre	75	1·00
891	$5 Lantau bridge	1·10	2·00

For later issues see Volume 1.

POSTAGE DUE STAMPS

D 1 Post-office Scales

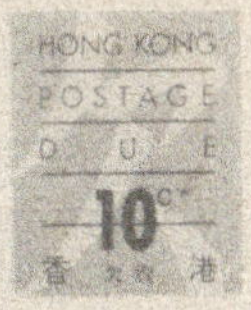

D 2

1923.

D 1ab	**D 1**	1 c. brown	30	1·00
D 2a		2 c. green	10·00	5·00
D 6a		2 c. grey	1·10	10·00
D 3a		4 c. red	27·00	7·00
D 7a		4 c. orange	2·50	9·00
D18		5 c. red (21 × 18 mm)	2·00	4·50
D 4		6 c. yellow	26·00	13·00
D 8		6 c. red	9·50	5·50
D 9		8 c. brown	5·50	32·00
D 5		10 c. blue	23·00	8·00
D15		10 c. violet	3·50	4·00
D16		20 c. black	5·00	4·00
D22		50 c. blue	4·50	9·50

1976. As Type D 1 but smaller design 21 × 17 mm with redrawn value.

D25a	**D 1**	10 c. violet	70	1·75
D26a		20 c. grey	70	2·00
D27a		50 c. blue	70	2·50
D28a		$1 yellow	1·10	3·25

1987.

D31	**D 2**	10 c. green	10	10
D32		20 c. brown	10	10
D33		50 c. violet	10	10
D34		$1 orange	15	20
D35		$5 blue	80	85
D36		$10 red	1·60	1·75

JAPANESE OCCUPATION OF HONG KONG

100 sen = 1 yen

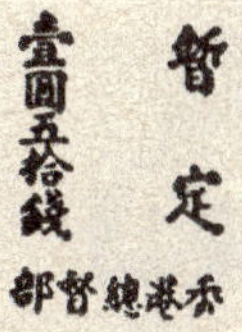
(1)

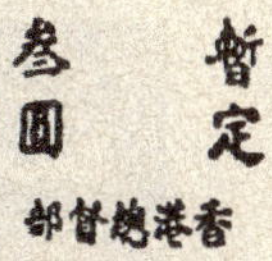
(2)

1945. Stamps of Japan surch as T **1** (No. J1) or T **2**.

J1	**126**	1.50 yen on 1 s. brown	25·00	21·00
J2	**84**	3 yen on 2 s. red	12·00	17·00
J3		5 yen on 5 s. red (No. 396)	£850	£130

HYDERABAD

A state in India. Now uses Indian stamps.

12 pies = 1 anna; 16 annas = 1 rupee

1

1869.

1	**1**	1 a. green	12·00	6·00

2

3

1870.

2	**2**	½ a. brown	4·00	4·00
3		2 a. green	40·00	35·00

1871.

13	**3**	½ a. brown	1·25	10
13d		½ a. red	1·00	10
14		1 a. purple	3·75	3·75
14b		1 a. brown	50	15
14c		1 a. black	1·00	10
15		2 a. green	2·00	15
16b		3 a. brown	85	85
17b		4 a. grey	3·00	1·75
17c		4 a. green	3·00	85
18		8 a. brown	1·25	1·90
19		12 a. blue	3·00	4·25
19a		12 a. green	2·50	2·75

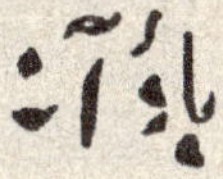
(4)

1898. Surch with T **4**.

20	**3**	¼ a. on ½ a. brown	50	85

5

6

1900.

21	**5**	¼ a. blue	3·75	2·50

1905.

22	**6**	¼ a. blue	1·25	45
32d		¼ a. grey	30	10
33		¼ a. purple	50	10
23b		½ a. red	1·60	25
34		½ a. green	40	10
26		1 a. red	1·00	10
27cb		2 a. lilac	1·10	10
28b		3 a. orange	90	60
29c		4 a. green	90	30
30c		8 a. purple	1·10	35
31c		12 a. green	3·00	1·40

8 Symbol

9

1915.

35	**8**	½ a. green	60	10
58		½ a. red	1·00	50
36		1 a. red	80	10
37	**9**	1 r. yellow	9·00	11·00

(10)

1930. Surch as T **10**.

38	**6**	4 p. on ¼ a. grey	48·00	15·00
39		4 p. on ¼ a. purple	25	10
40	**8**	8 p. on ½ a. green	25	10

12 Symbols

13 The Char Minar

1931.

60	**12**	2 p. brown	1·00	1·60
41		4 p. black	30	10
59		6 p. red	5·50	4·50
42		8 p. green	30	10
43	**13**	1 a. brown	30	10
44	–	2 a. violet	1·75	10
45	–	4 a. blue	1·25	30
46	–	8 a. orange	3·50	2·25
47	–	12 a. red	3·75	8·00
48	–	1 r. yellow	3·25	2·75

In No. 59 "POSTAGE" is at foot.

DESIGNS—HORIZ (32½ × 21 mm): 2 a. High Court of Justice; 4 a. Osman Sagar Reservoir; 12 a. Bidar College. VERT: 8 a. Entrance to Ajanta Caves; 1 r. Victory Tower, Daulatabad.

15 Unani General Hospital

1937. Inscr "H.E.H. THE NIZAM'S SILVER JUBILEE".

49	**15**	4 p. slate and violet	35	75
50	–	8 p. slate and brown	65	80
51	–	1 a. slate and yellow	65	55
52	–	2 a. slate and green	85	2·75

DESIGNS: 8 p. Osmania General Hospital; 1 a. Osmania University; 2 a. Osmania Jubilee Hall.

16 Family Reunion

17 Town Hall

1945. Victory Commemoration.

53	**16**	1 a. blue	10	10

1947. Reformed Legislature.

54	**17**	1 a. black	60	90

18 Power House, Hyderabad

1947. Inscr as in T **18**.

55	**18**	1 a. 4 p. green	65	1·40
56	–	3 a. blue	75	2·00
57	–	6 a. brown	3·00	9·50

DESIGNS—HORIZ: 3 a. Kaktayi Arch, Warangal Fort; 6 a. Golkunda Fort.

OFFICIAL STAMPS

(O 1)

1873. Optd with Type O **1**.

O2	**2**	½ a. brown	—	£375
O1	**1**	1 a. green	55·00	19·00
O3a	**2**	2 a. olive	—	£120

1873. Optd with Type O **1**.

O 9a	**3**	½ a. brown	5·50	2·25
O11		1 a. brown	65·00	45·00
O12a		1 a. drab	1·40	1·50
O19		1 a. black	55·00	10
O13a		2 a. green	2·75	3·75
O20d		3 a. brown	3·00	1·00
O15a		4 a. grey	10·00	10·00
O20e		4 a. green	£275	3·25
O16b		8 a. brown	28·00	22·00
O17a		12 a. blue	32·00	48·00
O20g		12 a. green	—	55·00

1909. Optd as Type O **1**, or similar smaller opt.

O37e	**6**	¼ a. grey	70	30
O38		¼ a. lilac	1·40	10
O21a		½ a. red	95·00	15
O39d		½ a. green	1·25	10
O40	**8**	½ a. green	1·40	10
O54		½ a. red	9·00	5·00
O31d	**6**	1 a. red	75	15
O41e	**8**	1 a. red	75	10
O32b	**6**	2 a. lilac	85	20
O33b		3 a. orange	8·50	1·50
O34d		4 a. green	2·25	10
O35		8 a. purple	2·75	20
O36		12 a. green	9·50	40

1930. Official stamps surch as T **10**.

O42	**6**	4 p. on ¼ a. grey	£190	17·00
O43		4 p. on ¼ a. lilac	65	10
O45		8 p. on ½ a. green	35·00	45·00
O44	**8**	8 p. on ½ a. green	60	10

1934. Optd as Type O **1** but smaller.

O55	**12**	2 p. brown	7·00	5·50
O46		4 p. black	85	10
O56		6 p. red	8·50	16·00
O47		8 p. green	35	10
O48	**13**	1 a. brown	50	10
O49	–	2 a. violet (No. 44)	3·50	10
O50	–	4 a. blue (No. 45)	1·60	20
O51	–	8 a. orange (No. 46)	7·50	50
O52	–	12 a. red (No. 47)	5·50	1·25
O53	–	1 r. yellow (No. 48)	12·00	2·00

IDAR

A state in Western India. Now uses Indian stamps.

12 pies = 1 anna; 16 annas = 1 rupee

1 Maharaja Singh Himat 2

1939.

1b	**1**	½ a. green	9·50	16·00

1944.

3b	**2**	½ a. green	1·40	48·00
4		1 a. violet	1·75	42·00
5		2 a. blue	2·25	70·00
6		4 a. red	2·50	75·00

INDIA

A peninsula in the S. of Asia. Formerly consisted of British India and numerous Native States, some of which issued stamps of their own. Divided in 1947 into the Dominion of India and the Dominion of Pakistan. Now a republic within the British Commonwealth.

1852. 12 pies = 1 anna; 16 annas = 1 rupee.
1957. 100 naye paise = 1 rupee.
1964. 100 paisa = 1 rupee.

1

3

9

10

1852. "Scinde Dawk". Imperf.

S1	**1**	½ a. white	£4500	£800
S2		½ a. blue	£12000	£3500
S3		½ a. red	£65000	£8000

1854. Imperf.

1	**3**	½ a. red	£800	
2		½ a. blue	55·00	14·00
14		1 a. red	42·00	35·00
31	**10**	2 a. green	85·00	23·00
23	**9**	4 a. blue and red	£2500	£225

11

12

1855. Perf.

75	**11**	½ a. blue	3·25	50
59		1 a. brown	3·00	40
41		2 a. pink	£375	22·00
63		2 a. orange	21·00	2·00
46		4 a. black	£160	4·75
64		4 a. green	£325	18·00
73		8 a. red	24·00	4·75

1860. Inscr "EAST INDIA POSTAGE". Various frames.

57	**12**	8 p. mauve	9·00	8·00
77	–	9 p. lilac	11·00	11·00
71	–	4 a. green	16·00	1·40
81	–	6 a. brown	5·00	1·50
72	–	6 a. 8 p. grey	30·00	18·00
82	–	12 a. brown	7·00	18·00
79	–	1 r. grey	32·00	20·00

14

23

1866. Optd **POSTAGE.**

66	**14**	6 a. purple	£600	£110

1882. Inscr "INDIA POSTAGE". Various frames.

84	**23**	½ a. turquoise	3·25	10
86	–	9 p. red	60	1·50
88	–	1 a. purple	3·25	30
90	–	1 a. 6 p. brown	60	80
91	–	2 a. blue	3·25	30
94	–	3 a. orange	5·50	50
96	–	4 a. green	12·00	50
97	–	4 a. 6 p. green	14·00	4·00
98	–	8 a. mauve	19·00	2·00
100	–	12 a. purple on red	6·50	2·50
101	–	1 r. grey	12·00	5·00

1891. No. 97 surch **2½ As.**

102	2½ a. on 4½ a. green	2·00	60

40

37

38

1892. As 1882 and some new designs.

111	**40**	3 p. red	10	10
112		3 p. grey	50	70
113	**23**	½ a. green	1·25	45
115	–	1 a. red	1·00	15
116	–	2 a. lilac	3·25	1·00
103	–	2 a. 6 p. green	1·25	40
118	–	2 a. 6 p. blue	3·25	3·75
106	**37**	1 r. green and red	7·50	2·00
107	**38**	2 r. red and orange	35·00	11·00
108		3 r. brown and green	25·00	10·00
109		5 r. blue and violet	35·00	23·00

1898. Surch ¼.

110	**23**	¼ a. on ½ a. turquoise	10	50

41

52

1902. As 1882 and 1892, but portrait of King Edward VII (inscribed "INDIA POSTAGE").

119	**41**	3 p. grey	90	10
121	–	½ a. green	75	20
123	–	1 a. red	90	10
124	–	2 a. violet	3·25	40
125	–	2 a. mauve	2·50	10
126	–	2 a. 6 p. blue	4·00	30
127	–	3 a. orange	3·75	35
128	–	4 a. green	3·00	35
132	–	6 a. bistre	10·00	4·50
133	–	8 a. purple	8·00	1·00
135	–	12 a. purple on red	7·50	2·00
136	–	1 r. green and red	6·50	70
139	**52**	2 r. red and brown	35·00	4·00
140		3 r. brown and green	24·00	19·00
142		5 r. blue and violet	50·00	35·00
144		10 r. green and red	£100	25·00
146		15 r. blue and brown	£130	42·00
147		25 r. orange and blue	£750	£800

1905. No. 121 surch ¼.

148	¼ a. on ½ a. green	55	10

1906. As Nos. 121 and 123, but inscr "INDIA POSTAGE & REVENUE".

149	½ a. green	2·25	10
150	1 a. red	1·25	10

55

56

57

58

59

70

60

61

62

63

71

64

65

66

67

1911.

*Two types of 1½ a. brown. Type A as illustrated. Type B inscr "1½ As. ONE AND A HALF ANNAS".

201	**55**	3 p. grey	30	10
202	**56**	½ a. green	60	10
161	**57**	1 a. red	1·90	15
203		1 a. brown	50	10
163	**58**	1½ a. brown (A)*	2·25	30
165		1½ a. brown (B)*	2·50	3·25
204		1½ a. red (B)*	1·25	10
166	**59**	2 a. mauve	2·75	30
168		2 a. violet	4·50	40
206	**70**	2 a. purple	1·00	10
170	**60**	2 a. 6 p. blue	1·90	3·00
171	**61**	2 a. 6 p. blue	1·75	20
207		2 a. 6 p. orange	1·25	10
173	**62**	3 a. orange	3·00	20
209		3 a. blue	5·50	10
210	**63**	4 a. olive	1·50	10
211	**71**	4 a. green	6·00	10
176	**64**	6 a. bistre	3·75	90
212	**65**	8 a. mauve	4·00	10
213	**66**	12 a. red	5·00	30
214	**67**	1 r. brown and green	5·00	45
215		2 r. red and orange	9·00	70
216		5 r. blue and violet	22·00	1·25
217		10 r. green and red	40·00	2·75
218w		15 r. blue and olive	24·00	26·00
219		25 r. orange and blue	90·00	29·00

See also Nos. 232, etc.

1921. Surch **NINE PIES** and bar.

192	**57**	9 p. on 1 a. red	60	30

1922. Surch ¼.

195	**56**	¼ a. on ½ a. green	30	35

72 De Havilland Hercules

1929. Air.

220w	**72**	2 a. green	1·50	60
221		3 a. blue	1·00	1·40
222		4 a. olive	2·25	85
223		6 a. bistre	2·25	90
224		8 a. purple	2·50	1·00
225		12 a. red	9·00	4·50

73 Purana Qila

1931. Inauguration of New Delhi.

226	**73**	¼ a. green and orange	1·25	2·25
227	–	½ a. violet and green	1·25	40
228	–	1 a. mauve and brown	1·25	20
229	–	2 a. green and blue	1·50	1·50
230	–	3 a. brown and red	2·50	2·50
231	–	1 r. violet and green	7·50	20·00

DESIGNS: ½ a. War Memorial Arch; 1 a. Council House; 2 a. Viceroy's House; 3 a. Secretariat; 1 r. Dominion Columns and Secretariat.

79

80

81

82

83

84 Gateway of India, Bombay

1932.

232	**79**	½ a. green	1·00	10
233	**80**	9 p. green	30	10
234	**81**	1 a. brown	3·00	10
235	**82**	1¼ a. mauve	30	10
236	**70**	2 a. red	9·00	3·75
236b	**59**	2 a. red	3·75	50
237	**62**	3 a. red	3·00	10
238	**83**	3½ a. blue	2·50	10

1935. Silver Jubilee.

240	**84**	½ a. black and green	60	15
241	–	9 p. black and green	45	20
242w	–	1 a. black and brown	45	10
243	–	1¼ a. black and violet	45	10
244w	–	2½ a. black and orange	1·50	95
245	–	3½ a. black and blue	3·25	2·75
246	–	8 a. black and purple	3·25	3·00

DESIGNS: 9 p. Victoria Memorial, Calcutta; 1 a. Rameswaram Temple, Madras; 1¼ a. Jain Temple, Calcutta; 2½ a. Taj Mahal, Agra; 3½ a. Golden Temple, Amritsar; 8 a. Pagoda in Mandalay.

91 King George VI

93 King George VI

92 Dak Runner

1937.

247	**91**	3 p. slate	50	10
248		½ a. brown	1·50	10
249		9 p. green	4·00	20
250		1 a. red	50	10
251	**92**	2 a. red	2·75	30
252	–	2 a. 6 p. violet	75	20
253	–	3 a. green	4·50	30
254	–	3 a. 6 p. blue	3·25	50
255	–	4 a. brown	13·00	20
256	–	6 a. blue	14·00	80
257	–	8 a. violet	7·50	50
258	–	12 a. red	18·00	1·10
259	**93**	1 r. slate and brown	1·00	15
260		2 r. purple and brown	3·75	30
261		5 r. green and blue	15·00	50
262		10 r. purple and red	15·00	70
263		15 r. brown and green	70·00	55·00
264		25 r. slate and purple	90·00	17·00

DESIGNS—As Type **92**: 2 a. 6 p. Dak bullock cart; 3 a. Dak tonga; 3 a. 6 p. Dak camel; 4 a. Mail train; 6 a. "Strathnaver" (liner); 8 a. Mail lorry; 12 a. Armstrong Whitworth Ensign 1 mail plane (small head).

100a King George VI

101

102 King George VI

1940.

265	**100a**	3 p. slate	25	10
266		½ a. mauve	40	10
267		9 p. green	40	10
268		1 a. red	40	10
269	**101**	1 a. 3 p. brown	90	10
269a		1½ a. violet	60	10
270		2 a. red	1·25	10
271		3 a. violet	2·25	10
272		3½ a. blue	70	10
273	**102**	4 a. brown	45	10
274		6 a. green	3·00	10
275		8 a. violet	1·50	30
276		12 a. purple	2·50	50
277	–	14 a. purple	18·00	1·25

No. 277 is as No. 258, but with large head.

105 "Victory" and King George VI

1946. Victory Commemoration.

278	**105**	9 p. green	30	30
279		1½ a. purple	30	30
280		3½ a. blue	75	60
281		12 a. red	1·50	55

1946. Surch **3 PIES** and bars.

282	**101**	3 p. on 1 a. 3 p. brown	10	15

DOMINION OF INDIA

303 Douglas DC-4

1947. Independence. Inscr "15TH AUG 1947".

301	–	1½ a. green	15	10
302	–	3½ a. red, blue and green	30	85
303	**303**	12 a. blue	1·50	1·75

DESIGNS—VERT: 1½ a. Asokan capital. HORIZ: 3½ a. Indian national flag.

1948. Air. Inauguration of India–U.K. Service. As T **303**, but showing Lockheed Constellation flying in opposite direction and inscr "AIR INDIA INTERNATIONAL FIRST FLIGHT 8TH JUNE 1948".

304	12 a. black and blue	1·00	2·00

305 Mahatma Gandhi

1948. 1st Anniv of Independence.

305	305	1½ a. brown	1·75	30
306		3½ a. violet	4·25	1·50
307		12 a. green	6·00	60
308	–	10 r. brown and red	55·00	40·00

DESIGN—22½×37 mm: 10 r. Profile portrait of Mahatma Gandhi.

307 Ajanta Panel

308 Konarak Horse

314 Bhuvanesvara

315 Gol Gumbad, Bijapur

319 Red Fort, Delhi

322 Satrunjaya Temple, Palitana

1949.

309	307	3 p. violet	15	10
310	308	6 p. brown	25	10
311	–	9 p. green	40	10
312	–	1 a. blue (A)	60	10
313	–	1 a. blue (B)	2·50	10
313	–	2 a. red	80	10
333b	–	2½ a. lake	2·50	2·50
314	–	3 a. salmon	1·50	10
315	–	3½ a. blue	1·50	2·75
316	314	4 a. lake	4·00	10
333c		4 a. blue	6·00	10
317	315	6 a. violet	1·50	10
318	–	8 a. green	1·50	10
319	–	12 a. blue	1·50	20
320	–	1 r. violet and green	9·00	10
321	319	2 r. red and violet	10·00	20
322	–	5 r. green and brown	28·00	90
323	–	10 r. brown and blue	45·00	4·75
324	322	15 r. brown and red	14·00	17·00

1 anna: (A) Left arm of statue outstretched. (B) Reversed—right arm outstretched.
DESIGNS—As Type **307**: 9 p. Trimurti; 1 a. Bodhisattva; 2 a. Nataraja. As Type **314**: 2½ a., 3½ a. Bodh Gaya Temple; 3 a. Sanchi Stupa, East Gate. As Type **315**: 8 a. Kandarya Mahadeva Temple; 12 a. Golden Temple, Amritsar. As Type **319**—VERT: 1 r. Victory Tower, Chittorgarh; 10 r. Qutb Minar, Delhi. HORIZ: 5 r. Taj Mahal, Agra.

323 Globe and Asokan Capital

1949. 75th Anniv of U.P.U.

325	323	9 p. green	1·00	2·00
326		2 a. red	1·00	2·00
327		3½ a. blue	1·75	2·25
328		12 a. red	3·00	2·50

REPUBLIC OF INDIA

324 Rejoicing Crowds

1950. Inauguration of Republic.

329	324	2 a. red	1·00	40
330	–	3½ a. blue	1·50	2·75
331	–	4 a. violet	1·50	65
332	–	12 a. purple	3·25	2·25

DESIGNS—VERT: 3½ a. Quill, ink-well and verse. HORIZ: 4 a. Ear of corn and plough; 12 a. Spinning-wheel and cloth.

329 "Stegodon ganesa"

1951. Centenary of Geological Survey.

334	329	2 a. black and red	2·00	40

330 Torch

331 Kabir

1951. 1st Asian Games, New Delhi.

335	330	2 a. purple and orange	1·00	30
336		12 a. brown and blue	4·00	90

1952. Indian Saints and Poets.

337	331	9 p. green	30	40
338	–	1 a. red (Tulsidas)	30	15
339	–	2 a. orange (Meera)	1·00	20
340	–	4 a. blue (Surdas)	1·25	40
341	–	4½ a. mauve (Ghalib)	30	80
342	–	12 a. brown (Tagore)	2·00	80

332 Locomotives of 1853 and 1953

1953. Centenary of Indian Railways.

343	332	2 a. black	75	10

333 Mount Everest

1953. Conquest of Mount Everest.

344	333	2 a. violet	50	10
345		14 a. brown	3·00	25

334 Telegraph Poles of 1851 and 1951

1953. Centenary of Indian Telegraphs.

346	334	2 a. green	30	10
347		12 a. blue	2·50	40

335 Postal Transport, 1854

1954. Indian Stamp Centenary.

348	335	1 a. purple	30	20
349	–	2 a. mauve	30	10
350	–	4 a. brown	2·75	50
351	–	14 a. blue	1·50	40

DESIGNS: 2, 14 a. "Airmail"; 4 a. Postal transport, 1954.

338 U.N. Emblem and Lotus

1954. U.N. Day.

352	338	2 a. turquoise	40	30

339 Forest Research Institute

1954. 4th World Forestry Congress, Dehra Dun.

353	339	2 a. blue	20	10

340 Tractor

344 Woman Spinning

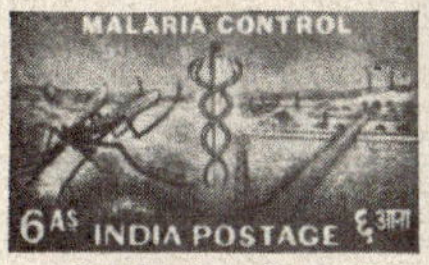

347 "Malaria Control" (Mosquito and Staff of Aesculapius)

358 Bodhi Tree

1955. Five Year Plan.

354	340	3 p. mauve	30	10
355	–	6 p. violet	30	10
356	–	9 p. brown	40	10
357	–	1 a. green	45	10
358	344	2 a. blue	30	10
359	–	3 a. green	50	10
360	–	4 a. red	50	10
361	347	6 a. brown	1·50	10
362	–	8 a. blue	6·00	10
363	–	10 a. turquoise	2·25	1·50
364	–	12 a. blue	1·75	10
365	–	14 a. green	3·25	20
413	–	1 r. myrtle	3·75	10
367	–	1 r. 2 a. grey	2·00	2·75
368	–	1 r. 8 a. purple	7·00	4·00
369	–	2 r. mauve	4·25	10
415	–	5 r. brown	9·00	30
371	–	10 r. orange	14·00	4·00

DESIGNS—As Type **340**: 6 p. Power loom; 9 p. Bullock-driven well; 1 a. Damodar Valley Dam; 4 a. Bullocks; 8 a. Chittaranjan Locomotive Works; 12 a. Hindustan Aircraft Factory, Bangalore; 1 r. Telephone engineer; 2 r. Rare Earth Factory, Alwaye; 5 r. Sindri Fertiliser Factory; 10 r. Steel plant. As Type **344**: 3 a. Woman hand-weaving. As Type **347**: 10 a. Marine Drive, Bombay; 14 a. Kashmir landscape; 1 r. 2 a. Cape Comorin; 1 r. 8 a. Mt. Kangchenjunga.

1956. Buddha Jayanti.

372	358	2 a. sepia	75	10
373	–	14 a. red	4·00	3·50

DESIGN—HORIZ: 14 a. Round parasol and Bodhi tree.

360 Lokmanya Bal Gangadhar Tilak

361 Map of India

1956. Birth Centenary of Tilak (journalist).

374	360	2 a. brown	10	10

1957. Value in naye paise.

375	361	1 n.p. green	10	10
376		2 n.p. brown	10	10
377		3 n.p. brown	10	10
402		5 n.p. green	10	10
379		6 n.p. grey	10	10
404		8 n.p. turquoise	90	10
405		10 n.p. myrtle	15	10
381		13 n.p. red	30	10
407		15 n.p. violet	60	10
408		20 n.p. blue	30	10
409		25 n.p. blue	30	10
410		50 n.p. orange	30	10
411		75 n.p. purple	40	10
385a		90 n.p. purple	3·00	1·50

MORE DETAILED LISTS
are given in the Stanley Gibbons Catalogues referred to in the country headings.
For lists of current volumes see Introduction.

362 The Rani of Jhansi

363 Shrine

1957. Centenary of Indian Mutiny.

386	362	15 n.p. brown	15	10
387	363	90 n.p. purple	1·50	60

364 Henri Dunant and Conference Emblem

1957. 19th Int Red Cross Conf, New Delhi.

388	364	15 n.p. grey and red	10	10

365 "Nutrition"

369 Calcutta University

1957. Children's Day.

389	365	8 n.p. purple	10	15
390	–	15 n.p. turquoise	10	10
391	–	90 n.p. brown	25	15

DESIGNS—HORIZ: 15 n.p. "Education". VERT: 90 n.p. "Recreation".

1957. Centenary of Indian Universities.

392	–	10 n.p. violet	15	20
393	369	10 n.p. grey	15	20
394	–	10 n.p. brown	30	20

DESIGNS—21½×38 mm: No. 392, Bombay University. As Type **369**: No. 394, Madras University.

371 J. N. Tata (founder) and Steel Plant

372 Dr. D. K. Karve

1958. 50th Anniv of Steel Industry.

395	371	15 n.p. red	10	10

1958. Birth Centenary of Karve (educationist).

396	372	15 n.p. brown	10	10

373 Westland Wapiti Biplane and Hawker Hunter

375 Bipin Chandra Pal

1958. Silver Jubilee of Indian Air Force.

397	373	15 n.p. blue	1·00	10
398		90 n.p. blue	1·25	1·25

1958. Birth Centenary of Pal (patriot).

418	375	15 n.p. green	10	10

376 Nurse with Child Patient

377 Jagadish Chandra Bose

1958. Children's Day.

419	376	15 n.p. violet	10	10

1958. Birth Centenary of Bose (botanist).

420	377	15 n.p. turquoise	20	10

378 Exhibition Gate

1958. India 1958 Exhibition, New Delhi.
421 **378** 15 n.p. purple 10 10

379 Sir Jamsetjee Jejeebhoy

381 Boys awaiting admission to Children's Home

380 "The Triumph of Labour" (after Chowdhury)

1959. Death Centenary of Sir Jamsetjee Jejeebhoy (philanthropist).
422 **379** 15 n.p. brown 10 10

1959. 40th Anniv of I.L.O.
423 **380** 5 n.p. green 10 10

1959. Children's Day.
424 **381** 15 n.p. green 10 10

382 "Agriculture" 383 Thiruvalluvar (philosopher)

1959. 1st World Agriculture Fair, New Delhi.
425 **382** 15 n.p. grey 20 10

1960. Thiruvalluvar Commemoration.
426 **383** 15 n.p. purple 10 10

384 Yaksha pleading with the Cloud (from the "Meghaduta") 385 Shakuntala writing a letter to Dushyanta (from the "Shakuntala")

1960. Kalidasa (poet) Commemoration.
427 **384** 15 n.p. grey 30 10
428 **385** 1 r. 3 n.p. yellow & brown 1·40 75

386 S. Bharati (poet) 387 Dr. M. Visvesvaraya

1960. Subramania Bharati Commemoration.
429 **386** 15 n.p. blue 10 10

1960. Birth Centenary of Dr. M. Visvesvaraya (engineer).
430 **387** 15 n.p. brown and red . . 10 10

388 "Children's Health"

1960. Children's Day.
431 **388** 15 n.p. green 10 10

389 Children greeting U.N. Emblem

1960. U.N.I.C.E.F. Day.
432 **389** 15 n.p. brown and drab . 10 10

390 Tyagaraja 391 "First Aerial Post" Cancellation

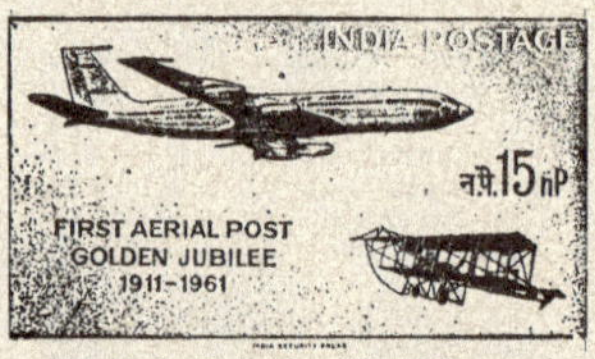

392 Air India Boeing 707 Airliner and Humber Sommer Biplane

1961. 114th Death Anniv of Tyagaraja (musician).
433 **390** 15 n.p. blue 10 10

1961. 50th Anniv of 1st Official Airmail Flight, Allahabad-Naini.
434 **391** 5 n.p. olive . . . . 1·10 30
435 **392** 15 n.p. green and grey . . 1·10 30
436 – 1 r. purple and grey . . . 3·75 1·60
DESIGN—As Type **392**: 1 r. H. Pecquet flying Humber Sommer plane, and "Aerial Post" cancellation.

394 Shivaji on Horseback 395 Motilal Nehru (politician)

1961. Chatrapati Shivaji (Maratha ruler) Commemoration.
437 **394** 15 n.p. brown and green . 70 30

1961. Birth Centenary of Pandit Motilal Nehru.
438 **395** 15 n.p. brown & orange . 10 10

396 Tagore (poet) 397 All India Radio Emblem and Transmitting Aerials

1961. Birth Centenary of Rabindranath Tagore.
439 **396** 15 n.p. orange & turq . . 70 30

1961. Silver Jubilee of All India Radio.
440 **397** 15 n.p. blue 10 10

398 Ray 399 Bhatkande

1961. Birth Centenary of Prafulla Chandra Ray (social reformer).
441 **398** 15 n.p. grey 10 20

1961. Birth Centenary (1960) of V. N Bhatkande (composer).
442 **399** 15 n.p. drab 10 10

400 Child at Lathe 401 Fair Emblem and Main Gate

1961. Children's Day.
443 **400** 15 n.p. brown 10 20

1961. Indian Industries Fair, New Delhi.
444 **401** 15 n.p. blue and red . . . 10 10

402 Indian Forest 403 Pitalkhora: Yaksha

1961. Centenary of Scientific Forestry.
445 **402** 15 n.p. green and brown . 30 20

1961. Cent of Indian Archaeological Survey.
446 **403** 15 n.p. brown 20 10
447 – 90 n.p. olive and brown . 40 20
DESIGN—HORIZ: 90 n.p. Kalibangan seal.

405 M. M. Malaviya 406 Gauhati Refinery

1961. Birth Centenary of Malaviya (educationist).
448 **405** 15 n.p. slate 10 20

1962. Inauguration of Gauhati Oil Refinery.
449 **406** 15 n.p. blue 30 20

407 Bhikaiji Cama 408 Village Panchayati and Parliament Building

1962. Birth Centenary of Bhikaiji Cama (patriot).
450 **407** 15 n.p. purple 10 10

1962. Inauguration of Panchayati System of Local Government.
451 **408** 15 n.p. mauve 10 10

409 D. Saraswati (religious reformer) 410 G. S. Vidhyarthi (journalist)

1962. Dayanand Saraswati Commem.
452 **409** 15 n.p. brown 10 10

1962. Ganesh Shankar Vidhyarthi Commem.
453 **410** 15 n.p. brown 10 10

411 Malaria Eradication Emblem 412 Dr. R. Prasad

1962. Malaria Eradication.
454 **411** 15 n.p. yellow and lake . 10 10

1962. Retirement of President Dr. Rajendra Prasad.
455 **412** 15 n.p. purple 20 10

413 Calcutta High Court 416 Ramabai Ranade

1962. Centenary of Indian High Courts.
456 **413** 15 n.p. green 50 20
457 – 15 n.p. brown (Madras) . 50 20
458 – 15 n.p. slate (Bombay) . . 50 20

1962. Birth Centenary of Ramabai Ranade (social reformer).
459 **416** 15 n.p. orange 10 20

417 Indian Rhinoceros

1962. Wild Life Week.
460 **417** 15 n.p. brown & turquoise 40 15

418 "Passing the Flag to Youth"

1962. Children's Day.
461 **418** 15 n.p. red and green . . 15 20

419 Human Eye within Lotus Blossom 420 S. Ramanujan

1962. 19th Int Ophthalmology Congress, New Delhi.
462 **419** 15 n.p. brown 20 10

1962. 75th Birth Anniv of Srinivasa Ramanujan (mathematician).
463 **420** 15 n.p. brown 60 40

421 S. Vivekananda

423 Hands reaching for F.A.O. Emblem

1963. Birth Cent of Vivekananda (philosopher).
464 **421** 15 n.p. brown and olive . 15 20

1963. Surch.
465 **385** 1 r. on 1 r. 3 n.p. yellow and brown 30 10

1963. Freedom from Hunger.
466 **423** 15 n.p. blue . . . . 1·00 30

424 Henri Dunant (founder) and Centenary Emblem

427 D. Naoroji (parliamentarian)

425 Artillery and Mil Mi-4 Helicopter

1963. Centenary of Red Cross.
467 **424** 15 n.p. red and grey . . . 2·50 30

1963. Defence Campaign.
468 **425** 15 n.p. green 40 10
469 – 1 r. brown 70 65
DESIGN: 1 r. Sentry and parachutists.

1963. Dadabhai Naoroji Commemoration.
470 **427** 15 n.p. grey 10 10

428 Annie Besant (patriot and theosophist)

434 "School Meals"

1963. Annie Besant Commemoration.
471 **428** 15 n.p. green 15 10
No. 471 is incorrectly dated "1837". Mrs. Besant was born in 1847.

1963. Wild Life Preservation. Animal designs as T **417**.
472 10 n.p. black and orange . . . 75 1·50
473 15 n.p. brown and green . . . 1·50 60
474 30 n.p. slate and ochre . . . . 3·75 1·50
475 50 n.p. orange and green . . . 3·50 80
476 1 r. brown and blue . . . . . 2·50 50
ANIMALS—As Type **417**: 10 n.p. Gaur. $25\frac{1}{2} \times 35\frac{1}{2}$ mm: 15 n.p. Lesser panda; 30 n.p. Indian elephant. $35\frac{1}{2} \times 25\frac{1}{2}$ mm: 50 n.p. Tiger; 1 r. Lion.

1963. Children's Day.
477 **434** 15 n.p. bistre 10 10

435 Eleanor Roosevelt at Spinning-wheel

1963. 15th Anniv of Declaration of Human Rights.
478 **435** 15 n.p. purple 10 15

436 Dipalakshmi (bronze)

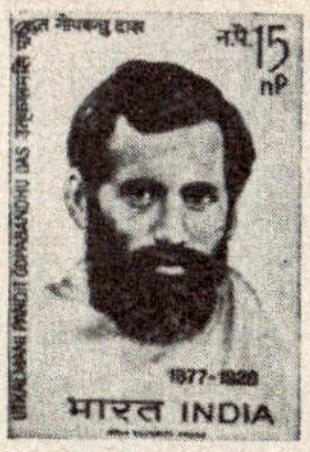
437 Gopabandhu Das (social reformer)

1964. 26th Int Orientalists Congress, New Delhi.
479 **436** 15 n.p. blue 20 15

1964. Gopabandhu Das Commemoration.
480 **437** 15 n.p. purple 10 10

438 Purandaradasa

439 S. C. Bose and I.N.A. Badge

1964. 400th Death Anniv of Purandaradasa (composer).
481 **438** 15 n.p. brown 15 10

1964. 67th Birth Anniv of Subhas Chandra Bose (nationalist).
482 **439** 15 n.p. olive 40 20
483 – 55 n.p. black, orge & red 40 45
DESIGN: 35 n.p. Bose and Indian National Army.

441 Sarojini Naidu

442 Kasturba Gandhi

1964. 85th Birth Anniv of Sarojini Naidu (poetess).
484 **441** 15 n.p. green and purple . 10 10

1964. 20th Death Anniv of Kasturba Gandhi.
485 **442** 15 n.p. brown 10 10

443 Dr. W. M. Haffkine (immunologist)

444 Jawaharlal Nehru (statesman)

1964. Haffkine Commemoration.
486 **443** 15 n.p. brown on buff . . 10 10

1964. Nehru Mourning Issue.
487 **444** 15 p. slate 10 10

445 Sir Asutosh Mookerjee

446 Sri Aurobindo

1964. Birth Centenary of Sir Asutosh Mookerjee (education reformer).
488 **445** 15 p. brown and olive . . 10 10

1964. 92nd Birth Anniv of Sri Aurobindo (religious teacher).
489 **446** 15 p. purple 15 10

447 Raja R. Roy (social reformer)

448 I.S.O. Emblem and Globe

1964. Raja Rammohun Roy Commemoration.
490 **447** 15 n.p. brown 10 10

1964. 6th Int Organization for Standardisation General Assembly, Bombay.
491 **448** 15 p. red 15 20

449 Jawaharlal Nehru (from 1 r. commemorative coin)

450 St. Thomas (after statue, Ortona Cathedral, Italy)

1964. Children's Day.
492 **449** 15 p. slate 10 10

1964. St. Thomas Commemoration.
493 **450** 15 p. purple 10 30
No. 493 was issued on the occasion of Pope Paul's visit to India.

451 Globe

452 J. Tata (industrialist)

1964. 22nd International Geological Congress.
494 **451** 15 p. green 30 30

1965. Jamsetji Tata Commemoration.
495 **452** 15 p. dull purple & orange 30 20

453 Lala Lajpat Rai

454 Globe and Congress Emblem

1965. Birth Centenary of Lala Lajpat Rai (social reformer).
496 **453** 15 p. brown 20 10

1965. 20th International Chamber of Commerce Congress, New Delhi.
497 **454** 15 p. green and red . . . 15 15

455 Freighter "Jalausha" and Visakhapatnam

456 Abraham Lincoln

1965. National Maritime Day.
498 **455** 15 p. blue 30 30

1965. Death Centenary of Lincoln.
499 **456** 15 p. brown and ochre . . 15 10

457 I.T.U. Emblem and Symbols

1965. Centenary of I.T.U.
500 **457** 15 p. purple 90 30

458 "Everlasting Flame"

459 I.C.Y. Emblem

1965. 1st Death Anniv of Nehru.
501 **458** 15 p. red and blue 15 10

1965. International Co-operation Year.
502 **459** 15 p. green and brown . . 90 60

460 Climbers on Summit

466 Electric Locomotive

475 Dal Lake, Kashmir

1965. Indian Mount Everest Expedition.
503 **460** 15 p. purple 20 10

1965.

504	–	2 p. brown	10	50
505	–	3 p. olive	10	2·00
505a	–	4 p. brown	10	2·00
506	–	5 p. red	10	10
507	–	6 p. black	10	2·25
508	–	8 p. brown	30	3·50
509	**466**	10 p. blue	40	10
510	–	15 p. green	1·50	10
511	–	20 p. purple	5·00	10
512	–	30 p. sepia	15	10
513	–	40 p. purple	15	10
514	–	50 p. green	20	10
515	–	60 p. grey	35	10
516	–	70 p. blue	60	10
517	–	1 r. brown and plum	60	10
518	**475**	2 r. blue and violet	2·00	10
519	–	5 r. violet and brown	2·50	70
520	–	10 r. black and green	13·00	80

DESIGNS—VERT (as Type **466**): 2 p. Bidri vase; 3 p. Brass lamp; 5 p. "Family Planning"; 6 p. Konarak elephant; 8 p. Spotted deer ("Chital"); 30 p. Indian dolls; 50 p. Mangoes; 60 p. Somnath Temple. (as Type **475**): 1 r. Medieval sculpture. HORIZ (as Type **466**): 4 p. Coffee berries; 15 p. Plucking tea; 20 p. Hindustan Aircraft Industries Ajeet jet fighter; 40 p. Calcutta G.P.O.; 70 p. Hampi Chariot (sculpture). (As Type **475**): 5 r. Bhakra Dam, Punjab; 10 r. Atomic reactor, Trombay.
See also Nos. 721/38c.

479 G. B. Pant (statesman)

480 V. Patel

1965. Govind Ballabh Pant Commemoration.
522 **479** 15 p. brown and green . . 10 20

1965. 90th Birth Anniv of Vallabhbhai Patel (statesman).
523 **480** 15 p. brown 10 30

481 C. Das

482 Vidyapati (poet)

1965. 95th Birth Anniv of Chittaranjan Das (lawyer and patriot).
524 **481** 15 p. brown 10 10

1965. Vidyapati Commemoration.
525 **482** 15 p. brown 10 10

483 Sikandra, Agra

484 Soldier, Hindustan Aircraft Industries Ajeet Jet Fighters and Cruiser "Mysore"

1966. Pacific Area Travel Assn Conf, New Delhi.
526 **483** 15 p. slate 10 10

1966. Indian Armed Forces.
527 **484** 15 p. violet 70 30

485 Lal Bahadur Shastri (statesman)

486 Kambar (poet)

1966. Shastri Mourning Issue.
528 **485** 15 p. black 40 10

1966. Kambar Commemoration.
529 **486** 15 p. green 10 10

487 B. R. Ambedkar

488 Kunwar Singh (patriot)

1966. 75th Birth Anniv of Dr. Bhim Rao Ambedkar (lawyer).
530 **487** 15 p. purple 10 10

1966. Kunwar Singh Commemoration.
531 **488** 15 p. brown 10 10

489 G. K. Gokhale

1966. Birth Centenary of Gopal Krishna Gokhale (patriot).
532 **489** 15 p. purple and yellow . 10 10

490 Acharya Dvivedi (poet)

491 Maharaja Ranjit Singh (warrior)

1966. Dvivedi Commemoration.
533 **490** 15 p. drab 10 10

1966. Maharaja Ranjit Singh Commemoration.
534 **491** 15 p. purple 30 15

492 Homi Bhabha (scientist) and Nuclear Reactor

1966. Dr. Homi Bhabha Commemoration.
535 **492** 15 p. purple 15 30

493 A. K. Azad (scholar)

1966. Abul Kalam Azad Commemoration.
536 **493** 15 p. blue 15 15

494 Swami Tirtha

1966. 60th Death Anniv of Swami Rama Tirtha (social reformer).
537 **494** 15 p. blue 20 30

495 Infant and Dove Emblem

496 Allahabad High Court

1966. Children's Day.
538 **495** 15 p. purple 30 20

1966. Centenary of Allahabad High Court.
539 **496** 15 p. purple 30 30

497 Indian Family

1966. Family Planning.
540 **497** 15 p. brown 15 15

498 Hockey Game

1966. India's Hockey Victory in 5th Asian Games.
541 **498** 15 p. blue . . . . 1·00 50

499 "Jai Kisan"

500 Voter and Polling Booth

1967. 1st Death Anniv of Shastri.
542 **499** 15 p. green 15 30

1967. Indian General Election.
543 **500** 15 p. brown 15 15

501 Gurudwara Shrine, Patna

502 Taj Mahal, Agra

1967. 300th Birth Anniv (1966) of Guru Gobind Singh (Sikh religious leader).
544 **501** 15 p. violet 15 15

1967. International Tourist Year.
545 **502** 15 p. brown and orange . 15 15

503 Nandalal Bose and "Garuda"

504 Survey Emblem and Activities

1967. 1st Death Anniv of Nandalal Bose (painter).
546 **503** 15 p. brown 15 15

1967. Bicentenary of Survey of India.
547 **504** 15 p. lilac 30 30

505 Basaveswara

1967. 800th Anniv of Basaveswara (reformer and statesman).
548 **505** 15 p. red 15 15

506 Narsinha Mehta (poet)

507 Maharana Pratap

1967. Narsinha Mehta Commemoration.
549 **506** 15 p. sepia 15 15

1967. Maharana Pratap (Rajput leader) Commem.
550 **507** 15 p. brown 15 15

508 Narayana Guru

509 Pres. Radhakrishnan

1967. Narayana Guru (philosopher) Commem.
551 **508** 15 p. brown 15 20

1967. 75th Birth Anniv of Sarvepalli Radhakrishnan (former President).
552 **509** 15 p. red 40 15

510 Martyrs' Memorial, Patna

1967. 25th Anniv of "Quit India" Movement.
553 **510** 15 p. lake 15 15

511 Route Map

512 Wrestling

1967. Centenary of Indo-European Telegraph Service.
554 **511** 15 p. black and blue . . . 20 20

1967. World Wrestling Championships, New Delhi.
555 **512** 15 p. purple and brown . . 30 20

513 Nehru leading Naga Tribesmen

514 Rashbehari Basu (nationalist)

1967. 4th Anniv of Nagaland as a State of India.
556 **513** 15 p. blue 15 15

1967. Rashbehari Basu Commemoration.
557 **514** 15 p. purple 15 20

515 Bugle, Badge and Scout Salute

1967. 60th Anniv of Scout Movement in India.
558 **515** 15 p. brown 60 30

516 Men embracing Universe

517 Globe and Book of Tamil

1968. Human Rights Year.
559 **516** 15 p. green 30 30

1968. Int Conf and Seminar of Tamil Studies, Madras.
560 **517** 15 p. lilac 30 15

518 U.N. Emblem and Transport

1968. United Nations Conference on Trade and Development, New Delhi.
561 **518** 15 p. blue 40 15

519 Quill and Bow Symbol

520 Maxim Gorky

1968. Centenary of "Amrita Bazar Patrika" (newspaper).
562 **519** 15 p. sepia and yellow . . 15 15

1968. Birth Centenary of Maxim Gorky.
563 **520** 15 p. plum 15 20

521 Emblem and Medal

522 Letter-box and "100,000"

1968. 1st Triennale Art Exhibition, New Delhi.
564 **521** 15 p. orange, blue & lt bl 30 20

1968. Opening of 100,000th Indian Post Office.
565 **522** 20 p. red, blue and black . 30 15

523 Stalks of Wheat, Agricultural Institute and Production Graph

1968. Wheat Revolution.
566 **523** 20 p. green and brown . . 30 15

524 "Self-portrait"

525 Lakshminath Bezbaruah

1968. 30th Death Anniv of Gaganendranath Tagore (painter).
567 524 20 p. purple and ochre . . 30 15

1968. Birth Cent of Lakshminath Bezbaruah (writer).
568 525 20 p. brown 15 15

526 Athlete's Legs and Olympic Rings

1968. Olympic Games, Mexico.
569 526 20 p. brown and grey . . 15 15
570 1 r. sepia and olive . . . 40 15

527 Bhagat Singh and Followers

1968. 61st Birth Anniv of Bhagat Singh (patriot).
571 527 20 p. brown 20 20

528 Azad Hind Flag, Swords and Chandra Bose (founder)

529 Sister Nivedita

1968. 25th Anniv of Azad Hind Government.
572 528 20 p. blue 20 15

1968. Birth Cent of Sister Nivedita (social reformer).
573 529 20 p. green 30 30

530 Marie Curie and Radium Treatment

1968. Birth Centenary of Marie Curie.
574 530 20 p. lilac . . . . 1·40 50

531 Map of the World

532 Cochin Synagogue

1968. 21st Int Geographical Congress, New Delhi.
575 531 20 p. blue 15 15

1968. 400th Anniv of Cochin Synagogue.
576 532 20 p. blue and red 55 40

533 I.N.S. "Nilgiri"

1968. Navy Day.
577 533 20 p. blue . . . . 1·50 40

534 Red-billed Blue Magpie

1968. Birds.
578 534 20 p. multicoloured . . . 55 40
579 – 50 p. red, black & green . 1·10 1·50
580 – 1 r. blue and brown . . . 1·75 1·00
581 – 2 r. multicoloured . . . . 1·75 1·50

DESIGNS—HORIZ: 50 p. Brown-fronted pied woodpecker; 2 r. Yellow-backed sunbird. VERT: 1 r. Slaty-headed scimitar babbler.

538 Bankim Chandra Chatterjee

539 Dr. Bhagavan Das

1969. 130th Birth Anniv of Chatterjee (writer).
582 538 20 p. blue 15 20

1969. Birth Centenary of Das (philosopher).
583 539 20 p. brown 15 15

540 Dr. Martin Luther King

1969. Martin Luther King Commemoration.
584 540 20 p. brown 40 20

541 Mirza Ghalib and Letter Seal

1969. Death Centenary of Mirza Ghalib (poet).
585 541 20 p. sepia, red and flesh 15 15

542 Osmania University

1969. 50th Anniv of Osmania University.
586 542 20 p. green 15 20

543 Rafi Ahmed Kidwai and Lockheed Constellation Mail Plane

1969. 20th Anniv of "All-up" Airmail Scheme.
587 543 20 p. blue 60 30

544 I.L.O. Badge and Emblem

1969. 50th Anniv of Int Labour Organization.
588 544 20 p. brown 15 20

545 Memorial, and Hands dropping Flowers

546 K. Nageswara Rao Pantulu (journalist)

1969. 50th Anniv of Jallianwala Bagh Massacre, Amritsar.
589 545 20 p. red 15 20

1969. Kasinadhuni Nageswara Rao Pantulu Commemoration.
590 546 20 p. brown 15 20

547 Ardaseer Cursetjee Wadia, and Ships

1969. Ardaseer Cursetjee Wadia (ship-builder) Commemoration.
591 547 20 p. turquoise 40 30

548 Serampore College

549 Dr. Zakir Husain

1969. 150th Anniv of Serampore College.
592 548 20 p. plum 15 20

1969. President Dr. Zakir Husain Commemoration.
593 549 20 p. sepia 15 20

550 Laxmanrao Kirloskar

1969. Birth Centenary of Laxmanrao Kirloskar (agriculturist).
594 550 20 p. black 15 15

551 Gandhi and his Wife

1969. Birth Centenary of Mahatma Gandhi.
595 551 20 p. brown 60 30
596 – 75 p. flesh and drab . . . 1·25 90
597 – 1 r. blue . . . . 1·25 63
598 – 5 r. brown and orange . . 4·50 6·50

DESIGNS AND SIZES—VERT: 75 p. Gandhi's head and shoulders (28×38 mm); 1 r. Gandhi walking (woodcut) (20×38 mm). HORIZ: 5 r. Gandhi with charkha (36×26 mm).

555 "Ajanta" (bulk carrier) and I.M.C.O. Emblem

1969. 10th Anniv of Inter-Governmental Maritime Consulative Organization.
599 555 20 p. blue . . . . 1·50 40

556 Outline of Parliament Building and Globe

1969. 57th Inter-Parliamentary Conf, New Delhi.
600 556 20 p. blue 15 20

557 Astronaut walking beside Space Module on Moon

558 Gurudwara Nankana Sahib (birthplace)

1969. 1st Man on the Moon.
601 557 20 p. brown 40 30

1969. 500th Birth Anniv of Guru Nanak Dev (Sikh religious leader).
602 558 20 p. violet 15 20

559 Tiger's Head and Hands holding Globe

1969. Int Union for the Conservation of Nature and Natural Resources Conf, New Delhi.
603 559 20 p. brown and green . . 30 30

560 Sadhu Vaswani

561 Thakkar Bapa

1969. 90th Birth Anniv of Sadhu Vaswani (educationist).
604 560 20 p. grey 15 15

1969. Birth Centenary of Thakkar Bapa (humanitarian).
605 561 20 p. brown 15 20

562 Satellite, Television, Telephone and Globe

1970. 12th Plenary Assembly of Int Radio Consultative Committee.
606 562 20 p. blue 40 20

563 C. N. Annadurai

564 M. N. Kishore and Printing Press

1970. 1st Death Anniv of Conjeevaram Natrajan Annadurai (statesman).
607 563 20 p. purple and blue . . 15 15

1970. 75th Death Anniv of Munshi Newal Kishore (publisher).
608 564 20 p. lake 15 20

565 Nalanda College

1970. Centenary of Nalanda College.
609 565 20 p. brown 60 40

566 Swami Shraddhanand (social reformer)

567 Lenin

1970. Swami Shraddhanand Commemoration.
610 566 20 p. brown 60 40

1970. Birth Centenary of Lenin.
611 567 20 p. brown and sepia . . 30 20

568 New U.P.U. H.Q. Building

569 Sher Shah Suri (15th century ruler)

1970. New U.P.U. Headquarters Building, Berne.
612 **568** 20 p. green, grey & black . . . 15 20

1970. Sher Shah Suri Commemoration.
613 **569** 20 p. green 15 20

570 V. D. Savarkar (patriot) and Cellular Jail, Andaman Islands

571 "U N" and Globe

1970. Vinayak Damodar Savarkar Commem.
614 **570** 20 p. brown 15 20

1970. 25th Anniv of United Nations.
615 **571** 20 p. blue 30 20

572 Symbol and Workers

1970. Asian Productivity Year.
616 **572** 20 p. violet 20 20

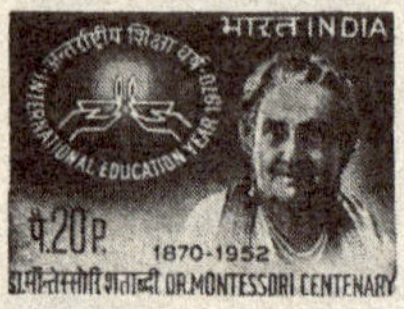

573 Dr. Montessori and I.E.Y. Emblem

1970. Birth Centenary of Dr. Maria Montessori (educationist).
617 **573** 20 p. purple 30 30

574 J. N. Mukherjee (revolutionary) and Horse

1970. Jatindra Nath Mukherjee Commem.
618 **574** 20 p. brown 75 30

575 V. S. Srinivasa Sastri

576 I. C. Vidyasagar

1970. Srinivasa Sastri (educationist) Commemoration.
619 **575** 20 p. yellow and purple . . 30 30

1970. 150th Birth Anniv of Iswar Chandra Vidyasagar (educationist).
620 **576** 20 p. brown and purple . 30 30

577 Maharishi Valmiki

1970. Maharishi Valmiki (ancient author) Commem.
621 **577** 20 p. purple 30 30

578 Calcutta Port

1970. Centenary of Calcutta Port Trust.
622 **578** 20 p. blue 90 50

579 University Building

1970. 50th Anniv of Jamia Millia Islamia University.
623 **579** 20 p. green 40 40

580 Jamnalal Bajaj

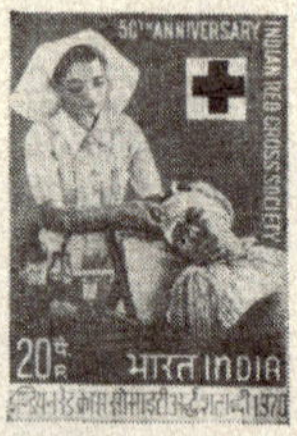

581 Nurse and Patient

1970. Jamnalal Bajaj (industrialist) Commemoration.
624 **580** 20 p. grey 15 30

1970. 50th Anniv of Indian Red Cross.
625 **581** 20 p. red and blue . . . 50 40

582 Sant Namdeo

583 Beethoven

1970. 700th Birth Anniv of Sant Namdeo (mystic).
626 **582** 20 p. orange 15 30

1970. Birth Bicentenary of Beethoven.
627 **583** 20 p. orange and black . . 1·50 60

584 Children examining Stamps

1970. Indian National Philatelic Exhibition, New Delhi.
628 **584** 20 p. orange and green . 30 10
629 – 1 r. brown and ochre . . 2·25 80
DESIGN: 1 r. Gandhi commemorative through magnifier.

585 Girl Guide

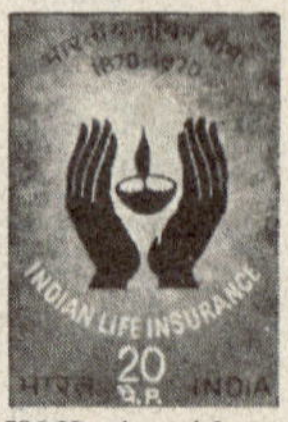

586 Hands and Lamp (emblem)

1970. Diamond Jubilee of Girl Guide Movement in India.
630 **585** 20 p. purple 60 30

1971. Centenary of Indian Life Insurance.
631 **586** 20 p. brown and red . . 20 30

587 Vidyapith Building

1971. 50th Anniv of Kashi Vidyapith University.
632 **587** 20 p. brown 20 30

588 Sant Ravidas

1971. Sant Ravidas (15th-century mystic) Commemoration.
633 **588** 20 p. red 30 30

589 C. F. Andrews

590 Acharya Narendra Deo (scholar)

1971. Birth Centenary of Charles Freer Andrews (missionary).
634 **589** 20 p. brown 35 30

1971. 15th Death Anniv of Acharya Narendra Deo.
635 **590** 20 p. green 15 30

591 Crowd and "100"

1971. Centenary of Decennial Census.
636 **591** 20 p. brown and blue . . . 30 30

592 Sri Ramana Maharishi (mystic)

593 Raja Ravi Varma and "Damayanti and the Swan"

1971. 21st Death Anniv of Ramana Maharishi.
637 **592** 20 p. orange and brown . 20 30

1971. 65th Death Anniv of Ravi Varma (artist).
638 **593** 20 p. green 40 40

594 Dadasaheb Phalke and Camera

1971. Birth Centenary of Dadasaheb Phalke (cinematographer).
639 **594** 20 p. purple 70 40

595 "Abhisarika" (Tagore)

596 Swami Virjanand (Vedic scholar)

1971. Birth Centenary of Abanindranath Tagore (painter).
640 **595** 20 p. grey, yellow & brn . 30 30

1971. Swami Virjanand Commemoration.
641 **596** 20 p. brown 30 40

597 Cyrus the Great and Procession

1971. 2500th Anniv of Charter of Cyrus the Great.
642 **597** 20 p. brown 75 55

598 Globe and Money Box

1971. World Thrift Day.
643 **598** 20 p. grey 20 30

599 Ajanta Caves Painting

600 "Women at Work" (Geeta Gupta)

1971. 25th Anniv of U.N.E.S.C.O.
644 **599** 20 p. brown . . . . . . 1·25 50

1971. Children's Day.
645 **600** 20 p. red 20 40

607 Refugees

608 C. V. Raman (scientist) and Light Graph

1971. Obligatory Tax. Refugee Relief. (a) Optd **REFUGEE RELIEF** in Hindi and English.
646 – 5 p. red (No. 506) 50 10

(b) Optd **Refugee Relief**.
647 – 5 p. red (No. 506) . . . . . 2·50 1·00

(c) Optd **REFUGEE RELIEF**.
649 – 5 p. red (No. 506) . . . . . 3·25 1·50

(d) Optd **Refugee relief**.
650c – 5 p. red (No. 506) . . . . 14·00 3·75

(e) Optd **Refugee Relief** in Hindi and English.
650d – 5 p. red (No. 506) . . . .

(f) Type **607**.
651 **607** 5 p. red 30 10

From 15 November 1971 until 31 March 1973 the Indian Government levied a 5 p. surcharge on all mail, except postcards and newspapers, for the relief of refugees from the former East Pakistan.

1971. 1st Death Anniv of Chandrasekhara Venkata Raman.
652 **608** 20 p. orange and brown . 50 30

609 Visva Bharati Building and Rabindranath Tagore (founder)

1971. 50th Anniv of Visva Bharati University.
653 **609** 20 p. sepia and brown . . 20 30

610 Cricketers

1971. Indian Cricket Victories.
654 **610** 20 p. green, myrtle & sage 2·00 65

INDEX

Countries can be quickly located by referring to the index at the end of this volume.

611 Map and Satellite

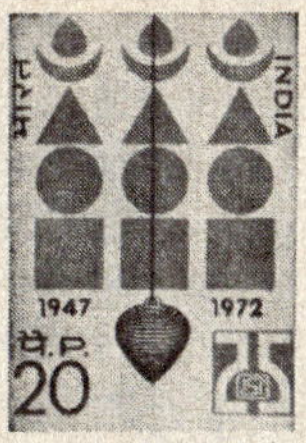

612 Elemental Symbols and Plumb-line

1972. 1st Anniv of Arvi Satellite Earth Station.
655 **611** 20 p. purple 15 30

1972. 25th Anniv of Indian Standards Institution.
656 **612** 20 p. grey and black . . . 15 40

613 Signal Box Panel

614 Hockey-player

1972. 50th Anniv of Int Railways Union.
657 **613** 20 p. multicoloured . . . 50 40

1972. Olympic Games, Munich.
658 **614** 20 p. violet . . . . 1·50 25
659 – 1 r. 45 green and lake . . 2·00 2·00
DESIGN: 1 r. 45, Various sports.

615 Symbol of Sri Aurobindo

617 Inter-Services Crest

616 Celebrating Independence Day in front of Parliament

1972. Birth Centenary of Sri Aurobindo (religious teacher).
660 **615** 20 p. yellow and blue . . 20 30

1972. 25th Anniv of Independence. (1st issue).
661 **616** 20 p. multicoloured . . . 15 30
See also Nos. 673/4.

1972. Defence Services Commemoration.
662 **617** 20 p. multicoloured . . . 30 40

618 V. O. Chidambaran Pillai (trade union leader) and Ship

1972. Birth Cent of V. O. Chidambaran Pillai.
663 **618** 20 p. blue and brown . . 75 40

619 Bhai Vir Singh

620 T. Prakasam

1972. Birth Centenary of Bhai Vir Singh (poet).
664 **619** 20 p. purple 30 40

1972. Birth Centenary of Tanguturi Prakasam (lawyer).
665 **620** 20 p. brown 20 40

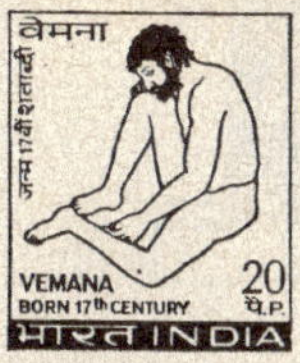

621 Vemana

622 Bertrand Russell

1972. 300th Birth Anniv of Vemana (poet).
666 **621** 20 p. black 20 40

1972. Birth Centenary of Bertrand Russell (philosopher).
667 **622** 1 r. 45 black . . . . . . 3·25 2·75

623 Symbol of "Asia '72"

1972. "Asia '72" (Third Asian International Trade Fair), New Delhi.
668 **623** 20 p. black and orange . . 10 20
669 – 1 r. 45 orange and black . . 60 1·75
DESIGN: 1 r. 45, Hand of Buddha.

624 V. A. Sarabhai and Rocket

1972. 1st Death Anniv of Dr. Vikram A. Sarabhai (scientist).
670 **624** 20 p. brown and green . . 20 40

625 Flag of U.S.S.R. and Kremlin Tower

1972. 50th Anniv of U.S.S.R.
671 **625** 20 p. red and yellow . . 20 40

626 Exhibition Symbol

627 "Democracy"

1973. "Indipex '73" Stamp Exhibition (1st issue).
672 **626** 1 r. 45 mauve, gold & blk 45 1·25
See also No. 701.3.

1973. 25th Anniv of Independence (2nd issue). Multicoloured.
673 20 p. Type **627** 15 15
674 1 r. 45 Hindustan Aircraft Industries Ajeet jet fighters over India Gate (38 × 20 mm) 1·10 1·60

628 Sri Ramakrishna Paramahamsa (religious leader)

629 Postal Corps Emblem

1973. Sri Ramakrishna Paramahamsa Commem.
675 **628** 20 p. brown 20 40

1973. 1st Anniv of Army Postal Service Corps.
676 **629** 20 p. blue and red . . . 40 50

630 Flag and Map of Bangladesh

631 Kumaran Asan

1973. "Jai Bangla" (Inauguration of 1st Bangladesh Parliament).
677 **630** 20 p. multicoloured . . . 15 40

1973. Birth Centenary of Kumaran Asan (writer and poet).
678 **631** 20 p. brown 20 45

632 Flag and Flames

634 "Radha-Kishangarh" (Nihal Chand)

633 Dr. Bhim Rao Ambedkar (lawyer)

1973. Homage to Martyrs for Independence.
679 **632** 20 p. multicoloured . . . 15 40

1973. Ambedkar Commemoration.
680 **633** 20 p. green and purple . . 20 75

1973. Indian Miniature Paintings. Multicoloured.
681 20 p. Type **634** 30 35
682 50 p. "Dance Duet" (Aurangzeb's period) . . . . 60 1·50
683 1 r. "Lovers on a Camel" (Nasir-ud-din) . . . . 1·50 2·75
684 2 r. "Chained Elephant" (Zain-al-Abidin) . . . . 2·00 3·25

635 Mount Everest

1973. 15th Anniv of Indian Mountaineering Foundation.
685 **635** 20 p. blue 40 50

636 Tail of Boeing 747

1973. 25th Anniv of Air-India's International Services.
686 **636** 1 r. 45 blue and red . . . 4·00 4·00

637 Cross, Church of St. Thomas' Mount, Madras

638 Michael Madhusudan Dutt (poet—Death Centenary)

1973. 19th Death Centenary of St. Thomas.
687 **637** 20 p. grey and brown . . 20 50

1973. Centenaries.
688 **638** 20 p. green and brown . . 1·00 65
689 – 30 p. brown . . . . . . 1·25 2·50
690 – 50 p. brown . . . . . . 1·50 2·50
691 – 1 r. violet and red . . . 1·50 1·50
DESIGNS—HORIZ: 30 p. Vishnu Digambar Paluskar (musician, birth cent); 50 p. Dr. G. A. Hansen (cent of discovery of leprosy bacillus); 1 r. Nicolaus Copernicus (astronomer, 5th birth cent).

639 A. O. Hume

641 R. C. Dutt

640 Gandhi and Nehru

1973. Allan Octavian Hume (founder of Indian National Congress) Commemoration.
692 **639** 20 p. grey 20 40

1973. Gandhi and Nehru Commemoration.
693 **640** 20 p. multicoloured . . . 20 40

1973. Romesh Chandra Dutt (writer) Commem.
694 **641** 20 p. brown 20 40

642 K. S. Ranjitsinhji

643 Vithalbhai Patel

1973. K. S. Ranjitsinhji (cricketer) Commemoration.
695 **642** 30 p. green . . . . 3·50 3·25

1973. Vithalbhai Patel (lawyer) Commemoration.
696 **643** 50 p. brown 20 65

644 Sowar of President's Bodyguard

645 Interpol Emblem

1973. Bicentenary of President's Bodyguard.
697 **644** 20 p. multicoloured . . . 35 40

1973. 50th Anniv of Interpol.
698 **645** 20 p. brown 30 40

646 Syed Ahmad Khan (social reformer)

1973. Syed Ahmad Khan Commemoration.
699 **646** 20 p. brown 20 60

647 "Children at Play" (Bela Raval)

1973. Children's Day.
700 **647** 20 p. multicoloured . . . 20 30

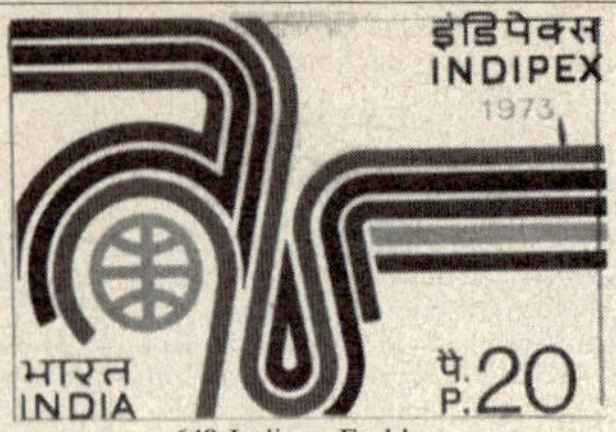

648 Indipex Emblem

1973. "Indipex '73" Philatelic Exhibition, New Delhi (2nd issue). Multicoloured.

701 20 p. Type **648** 20 30
702 1 r. Ceremonial elephant and 1½ a. stamp of 1947 (vert) . 1·25 2·00
703 2 r. Common peafowl (vert) . 1·50 2·75

649 Emblem of National Cadet Corps

650 C. Rajagopalachari (statesman)

1973. 25th Anniv of National Cadet Corps.
705 **649** 20 p. multicoloured . . . 20 30

1973. Chakravarti Rajagopalachari Commemoration.
706 **650** 20 p. brown 20 50

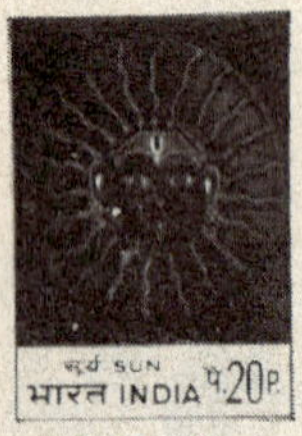

651 "Sun" Mask

652 Chhatrapati

1974. Indian Masks. Multicoloured.
707 20 p. Type **651** 15 15
708 50 p. "Moon" mask 30 55
709 1 r. "Narasimha" . . . . . . 70 1·25
710 2 r. "Ravana" (horiz) . . . . 1·00 2·00

1974. 300th Anniv of Coronation of Chhatrapati Shri Shivaji Maharaj (patriot and ruler).
712 **652** 25 p. multicoloured . . . 30 30

653 Maithili Sharan Gupta (poet)

654 Kandukuri Veeresalingam (social reformer)

1974. Indian Personalities (1st series).
713 **653** 25 p. brown 15 45
714 – 25 p. brown 15 45
715 – 25 p. brown 15 45
PORTRAITS: No. 714, Jainarain Vyas (politician and journalist); No. 715, Utkal Gourab Madhusudan Das (social reformer).

1974. Indian Personalities (2nd series).
716 **654** 25 p. brown 25 50
717 – 50 p. purple . . . . 55 1·75
718 – 1 r. brown . . . . 70 1·75
PORTRAITS: 50 p. Tipu Sultan; 1 r. Max Mueller (Sanskrit scholar).

655 Kamala Nehru

1974. Kamala Nehru Commemoration.
719 **655** 25 p. multicoloured . . . 50 50

656 W.P.Y. Emblem

657 Spotted Deer

657a Sitar

1974. World Population Year.
720 **656** 25 p. purple and brown . 20 30

1974. (a) Values expressed with "p" or "Re".
721 – 15 p. brown . . . . . . 3·25 70
722 **657** 25 p. brown . . . . . . 75 1·00
723 **657a** 1 r. brown and black . . 2·50 30

(b) Values expressed as numerals only.
724 – 2 p. brown . . . . . . 70 2·00
725 – 5 p. red 30 10
729 – 10 p. blue 30 15
730 – 15 p. brown . . . . . 1·50 10
731 – 20 p. green 15 10
732 – 25 p. brown . . . . . 5·00 1·75
732b – 30 p. brown . . . . . 2·75 55
733 – 50 p. violet . . . . . 4·00 10
734 – 60 p. grey 75 80
735 **657a** 1 r. brown and black . . 3·25 10
736a – 2 r. violet and brown . 11·00 40
737 – 5 r. violet and brown . 1·25 1·00
738d – 10 r. grey and green . . 1·10 1·10
DESIGNS—VERT (as Type **657**): 2 p. Bidri vase; 5 p. "Family Planning"; 15 p. Tiger; 25 p. Gandhi; 30 p. Indian dolls; 60 p. Somnath Temple. HORIZ (as Type **657a**): 10 p. Electric locomotive; 20 p. Handicrafts toy; 50 p. Great egret in flight. (As Type **657a**): 2 r. Himalayas; 5 r. Bhakra Dam, Punjab; 10 r. Atomic reactor, Trombay.
For 30, 35, 50, 60 p. and 1 r. values as No. 732 see Nos. 968, 979, 1073, 1320 and 1436.

658 President V. Giri

660 Woman Flute-player (sculpture)

659 U.P.U. Emblem

1974. Retirement of President Giri.
739 **658** 25 p. multicoloured . . . 15 30

1974. Centenary of U.P.U.
740 **659** 25 p. violet, blue & black . 40 10
741 – 1 r. multicoloured . . . . 1·00 1·50
742 – 2 r. multicoloured . . . . 1·25 2·00
DESIGNS:—1 r. Birds and nest, "Madhubani" style. VERT: 2 r. Arrows around globe.

1974. Centenary of Mathura Museum.
744 **660** 25 p. chestnut and brown 50 45
745 – 25 p. chestnut and brown 50 45
DESIGN: No. 745, Vidyadhara with garland.

661 Nicholas Roerich (medallion by H. Dropsy)

1974. Birth Centenary of Professor Roerich (humanitarian).
746 **661** 1 r. green and yellow . . 50 55

662 Pavapuri Temple

1974. 2,500th Anniv of Bhagwan Mahavira's Attainment of Nirvana.
747 **662** 25 p. black 40 20

663 "Cat" (Rajesh Bhatia)

664 "Indian Dancers" (Amita Shah)

1974. Children's Day.
748 **663** 25 p. multicoloured . . . 60 40

1974. 25th Anniv of U.N.I.C.E.F. in India.
749 **664** 25 p. multicoloured . . . 55 45

665 Territorial Army Badge

666 Krishna as Gopal Bal with Cows (Rajasthan painting on cloth)

1974. 25th Anniv of Indian Territorial Army.
750 **665** 25 p. black, yellow & grn . 60 40

1974. 19th International Dairy Congress, New Delhi.
751 **666** 25 p. purple and brown . . 40 30

667 Symbols and Child's Face

668 Marconi

1974. Help for Retarded Children.
752 **667** 25 p. red and black . . . 40 50

1974. Birth Centenary of Guglielmo Marconi (radio pioneer).
753 **668** 2 r. blue . . . . 2·00 1·25

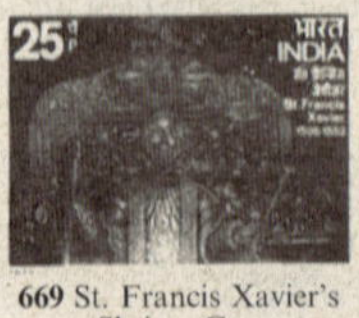

669 St. Francis Xavier's Shrine, Goa

670 Saraswati (Deity of Language and Learning)

1974. St. Francis Xavier Celebration.
754 **669** 25 p. multicoloured . . . 15 30

1975. World Hindi Convention, Nagpur.
755 **670** 25 p. grey and red 30 30

671 Parliament House, New Delhi

1975. 25th Anniv of Republic.
756 **671** 25 p. black, silver and blue 30 30

672 Table-tennis Bat

1975. World Table-tennis Championships, Calcutta.
757 **672** 25 p. black, red & green . 55 30

673 "Equality, Development and Peace"

1975. International Women's Year.
758 **673** 25 p. multicoloured . . . 85 45

674 Stylised Cannon

676 Saraswati

675 Arya Samaj Emblem

1975. Bicent of Indian Army Ordnance Corps.
759 **674** 25 p. multicoloured . . . 55 45

1975. Centenary of Arya Samaj Movement.
760 **675** 25 p. red and brown . . . 30 30

1975. World Telugu Language Conf, Hyderabad.
761 **676** 25 p. black and green . . 45 30

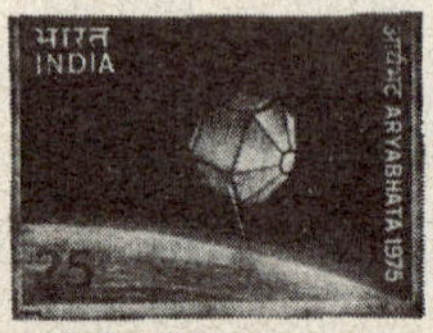

677 Satellite "Aryabhata"

1975. Launch of First Indian Satellite.
762 **677** 25 p. lt blue, blue & pur . 50 40

678 Blue-winged Pitta

1975. Indian Birds. Multicoloured.
763 25 p. Type **678** 55 25
764 50 p. Asian black-headed oriole 1·25 1·75
765 1 r. Western tragopan (vert) . 2·25 2·75
766 2 r. Himalayan monal pheasant (vert) . . . . 2·75 4·50

679 Page from "Ramcharitmanas" (manuscript)

1975. 4th Centenary of "Ramcharitmanas" (epic poem by Goswami Tulsidas).
767 **679** 25 p. black, yellow & red 40 20

680 Young Women within Y.W.C.A. Badge

681 "The Creation"

1975. Centenary of Indian Y.W.C.A.
768 **680** 25 p. multicoloured . . . 30 30

1975. 500th Birth Anniv of Michelangelo. "Creation" Frescoes from Sistine Chapel.
769 **681** 50 p. multicoloured . . . 80 80
770 – 50 p. multicoloured . . . 80 80
771 – 50 p. multicoloured . . . 80 80
772 – 50 p. multicoloured . . . 80 80
Nos. 770 and 772 are size 49 × 34 mm. The four stamps form a composite design.

682 Commission Emblem

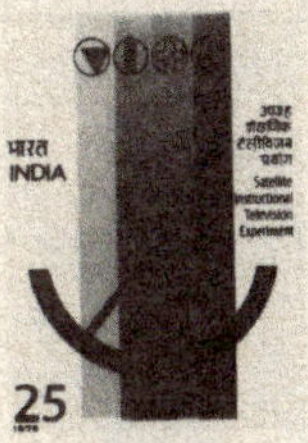

683 Stylised Ground Antenna

1975. 25th Anniv of Int Commission on Irrigation and Drainage.
773 **682** 25 p. multicoloured . . . 40 20

1975. Inauguration of Satellite Instructional Television Experiment.
774 **683** 25 p. multicoloured . . . 40 20

684 St. Arunagirinathar

685 Commemorative Text

1975. 600th Birth Anniv of St. Arunagirinathar.
775 **684** 50 p. purple and black . . 1·00 1·00

1975. Namibia Day.
776 **685** 25 p. black and red . . . 40 40

686 Mir Anees (poet)

687 Memorial Temple to Ahilyabai Holkar (ruler)

1975. Indian Celebrities.
777 **686** 25 p. green 25 65
778 **687** 25 p. brown 25 65

688 Bharata Natyam

689 Ameer Khusrau

1975. Indian Dances. Multicoloured.
779 25 p. Type **688** 65 20
780 50 p. Orissi . . . . 1·00 1·25
781 75 p. Kathak . . . . 1·25 1·50
782 1 r. Kathakali . . . . 1·50 1·25
783 1 r. 50 Kuchipudi . . . . . . 2·25 3·00
784 2 r. Manipuri . . . . 2·25 3·75

1975. 650th Death Anniv of Ameer Khusrau (poet).
785 **689** 50 p. brown and bistre . . 80 1·50

690 V. K. Krishna Menon

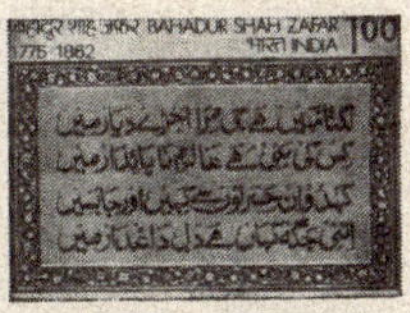

691 Text of Poem

1975. 1st Death Anniv of V. K. Krishna Menon (statesman).
786 **690** 25 p. green 50 60

1975. Birth Bicentenary of Emperor Bahadur Shah Zafar.
787 **691** 1 r. black, buff & brown . 65 90

692 Sansadiya Soudha, New Delhi

1975. 21st Commonwealth Parliamentary Conference, New Delhi.
788 **692** 2 r. green . . . . 2·00 2·50

693 V. Patel

694 N. C. Bardoloi

1975. Birth Centenary of Vallabhbhai Patel (statesman).
789 **693** 25 p. green 15 40

1975. Birth Centenary of Nabin Chandra Bardoloi (politician).
790 **694** 25 p. brown 30 50

695 "Cow" (Sanjay Nathubhai Patel)

1975. Children's Day.
791 **695** 25 p. multicoloured . . . 60 60

696 Original Printing Works, Nasik Road

697 Gurdwara Sisganj (site of martyrdom)

1975. 50th Anniv of India Security Press.
792 **696** 25 p. multicoloured . . . 40 40

1975. Tercentenary of the Martyrdom of Guru Tegh Bahadur (Sikh leader).
793 **697** 25 p. multicoloured . . . 40 40

698 Theosophical Society Emblem

699 Weather Cock

1975. Centenary of Theosophical Society.
794 **698** 25 p. multicoloured . . . 40 40

1975. Cent of Indian Meteorological Department.
795 **699** 25 p. multicoloured . . . 50 50

700 Early Mail Cart

1975. "Inpex '75" Nat Philatelic Exn, Calcutta.
796 **700** 25 p. black and brown . . 50 30
797 – 2 r. brown, purple & blk . 2·25 3·25
DESIGN: 2 r. Indian bishop mark, 1775.

701 L. N. Mishra

702 Tiger

1976. 1st Death Anniv of Lalit Narayan Mishra (politician).
798 **701** 25 p. brown 40 40

1976. Birth Cent of Jim Corbett (naturalist).
799 **702** 25 p. multicoloured . . . 1·00 70

703 Painted Storks

1976. Keoladeo Ghana Bird Sanctuary, Bharatpur.
800 **703** 25 p. multicoloured . . . 80 50

704 Vijayanta Tank

1976. Bicent of 16th Light Cavalry Regiment.
801 **704** 25 p. green and brown . . 1·40 30

705 Alexander Graham Bell

706 Muthuswami Dikshitar

1976. Alexander Graham Bell Commem.
802 **705** 25 p. brown and black . . 70 40

1976. Birth Bicentenary of Muthuswami Dikshitar (composer).
803 **706** 25 p. violet 70 40

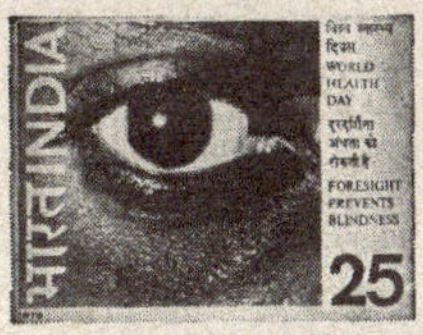

707 Eye and Red Cross

1976. World Health Day. Prevention of Blindness.
804 **707** 25 p. brown and red . . . 80 50

708 "Industries"

710 Nehru

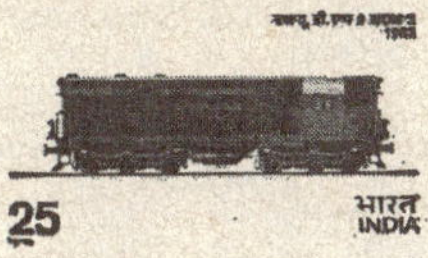

709 Type WDM Diesel Locomotive, 1963

1976. Industrial Development.
805 **708** 25 p. multicoloured . . . 30 30

1976. Locomotives. Multicoloured.
806 25 p. Type **709** 55 10
807 50 p. Radjustan Malvan Railway Class F/1 steam locomotive, 1895 . . . . 1·50 55
808 1 r. Southern Railway Class WP/1 steam locomotive, 1963 2·75 1·25
809 2 r. Great Peninsular Railway Class GIP steam locomotive, 1853 . . . . 3·50 2·50

1976.
810b **710** 25 p. violet . . . . . . 4·00 80
811 – 25 p. brown . . . . . . 1·00 30
DESIGN: No. 811, Gandhi.
For these designs in a smaller format see Nos. 732, 968/9, 979/80, 1073/4 and 1320.

713 "Spirit of '76" (Willard)

714 K. Kamaraj (politician)

1976. Bicentenary of American Revolution.
812 **713** 2 r. 80 multicoloured . . 1·25 1·25

1976. Kumaraswamy Kamaraj Commemoration.
813 **714** 25 p. brown 15 15

715 "Shooting"

716 Subhadra Kumari Chauhan (poetess)

1976. Olympic Games, Montreal.
814 **715** 25 p. violet and red . . . 30 10
815 – 1 r. multicoloured . . . . 1·00 90
816 – 1 r. 50 mauve and black . 1·75 2·50
817 – 2 r. 80 multicoloured . . 1·75 3·75
DESIGNS: 1 r. Shot-put; 1 r. 50, Hockey; 2 r. 80, Sprinting.

1976. S. K. Chauhan Commemoration.
818 **716** 25 p. blue 15 40

717 Param Vir Chakra Medal

718 University Building, Bombay

1976. Param Vir Chakra Commemoration.
819 **717** 25 p. multicoloured . . . 15 50

1976. 60th Anniv of Shreemati Nathibai Damodar Thackersey Women's University.
820 **718** 25 p. violet 30 30

719 Bharatendu Harischandra (writer)

720 S. C. Chatterji

1976. Harischandra Commemoration.
821 **719** 25 p. brown 15 30

1976. Birth Centenary of Sarat Chandra Chatterji (writer).
822 **720** 25 p. black 15 30

721 Planned Family

722 Maharaja Agrasen and Coins

1976. Family Planning.
823 **721** 25 p. multicoloured . . . 15 30

1976. Maharaja Agrasen Commemoration.
824 **722** 25 p. brown 10 30

723 Swamp Deer

724 Hands holding Hearts

1976. Indian Wildlife. Multicoloured.

825 25 p. Type **723** 45 40
826 50 p. Lion . . . . 1·25 2·25
827 1 r. Leopard (horiz) . . . . . 1·75 2·25
828 2 r. Caracal (horiz) . . . . . 2·00 3·50

1976. Voluntary Blood Donation.
829 **724** 25 p. yellow, red & black . 50 40

725 Suryakant Tripathi ("Nirala")

726 "Loyal Mongoose" (H. D. Bhatia)

1976. 80th Birth Anniv of "Nirala" (poet and novelist).
830 **725** 25 p. violet 15 30

1976. Children's Day.
831 **726** 25 p. multicoloured . . . 40 40

727 Hiralal Shastri (social reformer)

728 Dr. Hari Singh Gour (lawyer)

1976. Shastri Commemoration.
832 **727** 25 p. brown 20 30

1976. Dr. Hari Singh Gour Commemoration.
833 **728** 25 p. purple 20 30

729 Airbus Industrie A300B4

1976. Inauguration of Indian Airlines' Airbus Service.
834 **729** 2 r. multicoloured . . . . 2·25 2·25

730 Hybrid Coconut Palm

731 First Stanza of "Vande Mataram"

1976. Diamond Jubilee of Coconut Research.
835 **730** 25 p. multicoloured . . . 20 30

1976. Centenary of "Vande Mataram" (patriotic song by B. C. Chatterjee).
836 **731** 25 p. multicoloured . . . 20 30

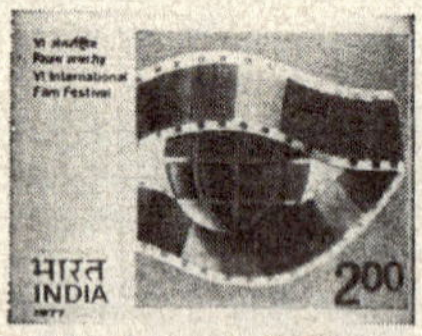

732 Globe and Film Strip

1977. 6th International Film Festival of India, New Delhi.
837 **732** 2 r. multicoloured . . . . 1·10 2·00

733 Seismograph and Crack in Earth's Crust

734 Tarun Ram Phookun

1977. 6th World Conference on Earthquake Engineering, New Delhi.
838 **733** 2 r. lilac . . . . 1·00 2·00

1977. Birth Cent of Tarun Ram Phookun (politician).
839 **734** 25 p. grey 15 30

735 Paramahansa Yogananda

736 Asian Regional Red Cross Emblem

1977. Paramahansa Yogananda (religious leader) Commem.
840 **735** 25 p. orange 40 30

1977. 1st Asian Regional Red Cross Conference, New Delhi.
841 **736** 2 r. red, pink and blue . . 2·00 2·50

737 Fakhruddin Ali Ahmed

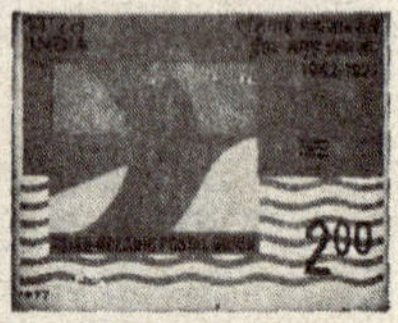

738 Emblem of Asian–Oceanic Postal Union

1977. Death of President Ahmed.
842 **737** 25 p. multicoloured . . . 35 35

1977. 15th Anniv of Asian–Oceanic Postal Union.
843 **738** 2 r. multicoloured . . . . 1·10 1·75

739 Narottam Morarjee and "Loyalty" (liner)

740 Makhanlal Chaturvedi (writer and poet)

1977. Birth Cent of Morarjee (ship owner).
844 **739** 25 p. blue 75 70

1977. Chaturvedi Commemoration.
845 **740** 25 p. brown 15 30

741 Mahaprabhu Vallabhacharya (philosopher)

742 Federation Emblem

1977. Vallabhacharya Commemoration.
846 **741** 1 r. brown 30 40

1977. 50th Anniv of Federation of Indian Chambers of Commerce and Industry.
847 **742** 25 p. purple, brown and yellow 15 40

744 "Environment Protection"

1977. World Environment Day.
848 **744** 2 r. multicoloured . . . . 60 1·25

745 Rajya Sabha Chamber

1977. 25th Anniv of Rajya Sabha (Upper House of Parliament).
849 **745** 25 p. multicoloured . . . 15 30

746 Lotus

1977. Indian Flowers. Multicoloured.

850 25 p. Type **746** 25 15
851 50 p. Rhododendron (vert) . . 45 90
852 1 r. Kadamba (vert) . . . . . 60 1·00
853 2 r. Gloriosa lily . . . . . . 90 2·25

747 Berliner Gramophone

1977. Centenary of Sound Recording.
854 **747** 2 r. brown and black . . . 1·00 2·00

748 Coomaraswamy and Siva

750 Dr. Samuel Hahnemann (founder of homeopathy)

749 Ganga Ram and Hospital

1977. Birth Centenary of Ananda Kentish Coomaraswamy (art historian).
855 **748** 25 p. multicoloured . . . 40 40

1977. 50th Death Anniv of Sir Ganga Ram (social reformer).
856 **749** 25 p. purple 30 30

1977. 32nd Int Homeopathic Congress, New Delhi.
857 **750** 2 r. black and green . . . 3·50 2·75

751 Ram Manohar Lohia (politician)

752 Early Punjabi Postman

1977. Ram Manohar Lohia Commemoration.
858 **751** 25 p. brown 35 30

1977. "Inpex '77" Philatelic Exn, Bangalore.
859 **752** 25 p. multicoloured . . . 50 30
860 – 2 r. grey and red . . . . 2·00 2·75
DESIGN: 2 r. "Lion and Palm" essay, 1853.

753 Scarlet "Scinde Dawks" of 1852

1977. "Asiana '77" Philatelic Exn, Bangalore.
861 **753** 1 r. multicoloured . . . . 1·50 1·00
862 – 3 r. blue, orange and black 2·50 3·00
DESIGN: 3 r. Foreign mail arriving at Ballard Pier, Bombay, 1927.

754 "Mother and Child" (Khajuraho sculpture)

756 Symbolic Sun

755 Statue of Kittur Rani Channamma, Belgaum

1977. 15th Int Congress of Pediatrics, New Delhi.
863 **754** 2 r. blue and brown . . . 2·25 2·75

1977. Kittur Rani Channama, (ruler) Commem.
864 **755** 25 p. green 80 40

1977. Union Public Service Commission.
865 **756** 25 p. multicoloured . . . 35 30

757 Ear of Corn

759 Jotirao Phooley (social reformer)

758 "Cats" (Nikur Dilipbhai Mody)

1977. "Agriexpo '77" Agricultural Exhibition, New Delhi.
866 **757** 25 p. green 40 40

1977. Children's Day. Multicoloured.
867 25 p. Type **758** 50 30
868 1 r. "Friends" (Bhavsar Ashish Ramanlal) . . . . 2·25 3·00

1977. Indian Personalities.
869 **759** 25 p. olive 30 45
870 – 25 p. brown 30 45
DESIGN: No. 870, Senapti Bapat (patriot).

760 Diagram of Population Growth
761 Kamta Prasad Guru and Vyakarna (Hindi Grammar)

1977. 41st Session of International Statistical Institute, New Delhi.
871 **760** 2 r. turquoise and red . . 60 1·00

1977. Kamta Prasad Guru (writer) Commem.
872 **761** 25 p. brown 20 30

762 Kremlin Tower and Soviet Flag
763 Climber crossing a Crevice

1977. 60th Anniv of October Revolution.
873 **762** 1 r. multicoloured 45 75

1978 Conquest of Kanchenjunga (1977). Multicoloured.
874 25 p. Type **763** 10 10
875 1 r. Indian flag near summit (horiz) 45 80

764 "Shikara" on Lake Dal, Kashmir

1978. 27th Pacific Area Travel Association Conference, New Delhi.
876 **764** 1 r. multicoloured . . . . . 2·00 1·50

765 Children in Library

1978. 3rd World Book Fair, New Delhi.
877 **765** 1 r. brown and slate . . . 45 80

766 Mother-Pondicherry

767 Wheat and Globe

1978. Birth Centenary of Mother-Pondicherry (philosopher).
878 **766** 25 p. brown and grey . . 20 30

1978. 5th International Wheat Genetics Symposium, New Delhi.
879 **767** 25 p. yellow & turquoise . 20 30

768 Nanalal Dalpatram Kavi (poet)
769 Surjya Sen (revolutionary)

1978. Nanalal Dalpatram Kavi Commemoration.
880 **768** 25 p. brown 20 30

1978. Surjya Sen Commemoration.
881 **769** 25 p. bistre and red . . . 20 30

770 "Two Vaishnavas" (Jamini Roy)

1978. Modern Indian Paintings. Multicoloured.
882 25 p. Type **770** 20 30
883 50 p. "The Mosque" (Sailoz Mookherjea) . . . . 40 1·25
884 1 r. "Head" (Rabindranath Tagore) . . . . 70 1·50
885 2 r. "Hill Women" (Amrita Sher Gil) . . . . 90 2·00

771 "Self-portrait" (Rubens)
772 Charlie Chaplin

1978. 400th Birth Anniv of Peter Paul Rubens.
886 **771** 2 r. multicoloured . . . . 2·00 3·00

1978. Charlie Chaplin Commemoration.
887 **772** 25 p. blue and gold . . . 90 45

773 Deendayal Upadhyaya (politician)
774 Syama Prasad Mookerjee

1978. Deendayal Upadhyaya Commemoration.
888 **773** 25 p. brown and orange . 20 40

1978. Syama Prasad Mookerjee (politician) Commemoration.
889 **774** 25 p. brown 30 50

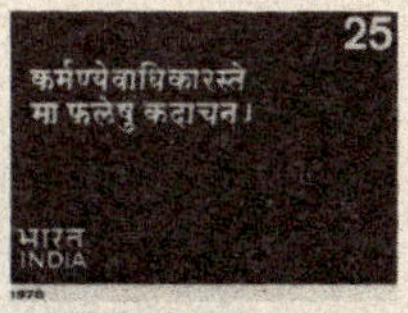

775 Airavat (mythological elephant). Jain Temple, Gujerat (Kachchh Museum)
776 Krishna and Arjuna in Battle Chariot

1978. Treasures from Indian Museums. Mult.
890 25 p. Type **775** 30 30
891 50 p. Kalpadruma (magical tree), Besnagar (Indian Museum) . 50 1·25
892 1 r. Obverse and reverse of Kushan gold coin (National Museum) . . . . 70 1·50
893 2 r. Dagger and knife of Emperor Jehangir, Mughal (Salar Jung Museum) . . . . 1·00 2·00

1978. Bhagawadgeeta (Divine Song of India) Commemoration.
894 **776** 25 p. gold and red 20 30

777 Bethune College
778 E. V. Ramasami

1978. Centenary of Bethune College, Calcutta.
895 **777** 25 p. brown and green . . 20 30

1978. E. V. Ramasami (social reformer) Commemoration.
896 **778** 25 p. black 20 20

779 Uday Shankar
780 Leo Tolstoy

1978. Uday Shankar (dancer) Commem.
897 **779** 25 p. brown 20 30

1978. 150th Birth Anniv of Leo Tolstoy (writer).
898 **780** 1 r. multicoloured 30 30

781 Vallathol Narayana Menon
783 Machine Operator

782 "Two Friends" (Dinesh Sharma)

1978. Birth Centenary of Vallathol Narayana Menon (poet).
899 **781** 25 p. purple and brown . . 15 40

1978. Children's Day.
900 **782** 25 p. multicoloured . . . 20 40

1978. National Small Industries Fair, New Delhi.
901 **783** 25 p. green 20 30

784 Sowars of Skinner's Horse
785 Mohammad Ali Jauhar

1978. 175th Anniv of Skinner's Horse (cavalry regiment).
902 **784** 25 p. multicoloured . . . 60 60

1978. Birth Centenary of Mohammad Ali Jauhar (patriot).
903 **785** 25 p. olive 20 30

786 Chakravarti Rajagopalachari
787 Wright Brothers and Flyer I

1978. Birth Centenary of Chakravarti Rajagopalachari (first post-independence Governor-General).
904 **786** 25 p. brown 20 30

1978. 75th Anniv of Powered Flight.
905 **787** 1 r. violet and yellow . . 65 30

788 Ravenshaw College
789 Schubert

1978. Centenary of Ravenshaw College, Cuttack.
906 **788** 25 p. red and green . . . 20 30

1978. 150th Death Anniv of Franz Schubert (composer).
907 **789** 1 r. multicoloured 70 55

790 Uniforms of 1799, 1901 and 1979 with Badge

1979. 4th Reunion of Punjab Regiment.
908 **790** 25 p. multicoloured . . . 90 70

791 Bhai Parmanand
792 Gandhi with Young Boy

1979. Bhai Parmanand (scholar) Commemoration.
909 **791** 25 p. violet 20 30

1979. International Year of the Child.
910 **792** 25 p. brown and red . . . 40 30
911 – 1 r. brown and orange . . 60 1·50
DESIGN: 1 r. India I.Y.C. emblem.

793 Albert Einstein
794 Rajarshi Shahu Chhatrapati

1979. Birth Centenary of Albert Einstein (physicist).
912 **793** 1 r. blue 30 50

1979. Rajarshi Shahu Chhatrapati (ruler of Kolhapur State, and precursor of social reform in India) Commemoration.
913 **794** 25 p. purple 20 30

795 Exhibition Logo

1979. "India '80" International Stamp Exhibition (1st issue).
914 **795** 30 p. green and orange . . 20 30
See also Nos. 942/5 and 955/8.

796 Postcards under Magnifying Glass · 797 Raja Mahendra Pratap

1979. Centenary of Indian Postcards.
915 **796** 50 p. multicoloured . . . 20 40

1979. Raja Mahendra Pratap (patriot) Commemoration.
916 **797** 30 p. green 20 40

798 Hilsa, Pomfret and Prawn · 800 Jatindra Nath Das

1979.

920	–	2 p. violet	10	10
921	**798**	5 p. blue	10	10
922a	–	10 p. green	10	10
923a	–	15 p. green	10	10
924a	–	20 p. red	10	10
925a	–	25 p. brown	30	10
925bb	–	25 p. green	10	10
926ab	–	30 p. green	10	10
927	–	35 p. purple	40	10
928c	–	50 p. violet	10	10
929b	–	1 r. brown	10	10
932b	–	2 r. lilac	10	10
933c	–	2 r. 25 red and green	10	10
934	–	2 r. 80 red and green	50	30
934ca	–	3 r. 25 orange & green	10	10
935c	–	5 r. red and green	60	40
936b	–	10 r. purple and green	30	35

DESIGNS—HORIZ: 2 p. Adult education class; 10 p. Irrigation canal; 25 p. (925a) Chick hatching from egg; 25 p. (925ba) Village, wheat and tractor; 30 p. Harvesting maize; 50 p. Woman dairy farmer, cows and milk bottles. (36 × 19 mm): 10 r. Forest on hillside. VERT (17 × 20 mm): 15 p. Farmer and agricultural symbols; 20 p. Mother feeding child; 35 p. "Family". (17 × 28 mm): 1 r. Cotton plant; 2 r. Weaving. (20 × 38 mm): 2 r. 25, Cashew; 2 r. 80, Apples; 3 r. 25, Oranges; 5 r. Rubber tapping.
For 75 p. in same design as No. 927 see No. 1214.

1979. 50th Death Anniv of Jatindra Nath Das (revolutionary).
941 **800** 30 p. brown 20 30

801 De Havilland Puss Moth · 802 Early and Modern Lightbulbs

1979. "Air India 80" International Stamp Exhibition (2nd issue). Mail-carrying Aircraft. Multicoloured.
942 30 p. Type **801** 30 25
943 50 p. Indian Air Force Hindustan Aircraft Industries Chetak helicopter 50 45
944 1 r. Indian Airlines Boeing 737 airliner 65 75
945 2 r. Air India Boeing 747 airliner 75 95

1979. Centenary of Electric Lightbulb.
946 **802** 1 r. purple 20 30

803 Gilgit Record

1979. International Archives Week.
947 **803** 30 p. yellow and brown . 20 50

804 Hirakud Dam, Orissa

1979. 50th Anniv and 13th Congress of International Commission on Large Dams.
948 **804** 30 p. brown & turquoise . 20 30

805 Fair Emblem · 806 Child learning to Read

1979. India International Trade Fair, New Delhi.
949 **805** 1 r. black and red 20 30

1979. International Children's Book Fair, New Delhi.
950 **806** 30 p. multicoloured . . . 20 30

807 Dove with Olive Branch and I.A.E.A. Emblem

1979. 23rd International Atomic Energy Agency Conference, New Delhi.
951 **807** 1 r. multicoloured 20 45

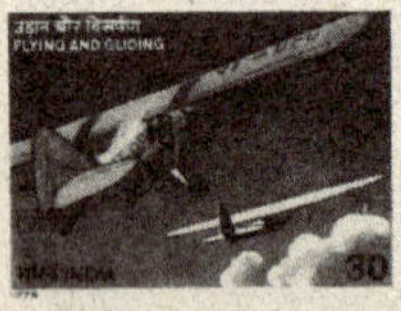

808 Hindustan Aircraft Industries HAL-26 Pushpak Light Plane and Rohini-1 Glider

1979. Flying and Gliding.
952 **808** 30 p. black, brown & bl . 1·00 80

809 Gurdwara Baoli Sahib Temple, Goindwal, Amritsar District · 810 Ring of People encircling U.N. Emblem and Cogwheel

1979. 500th Birth Anniv of Guru Amar Das (Sikh leader).
953 **809** 30 p. multicoloured . . . 20 30

1980. 3rd United Nations Industrial Development Organization General Conference, New Delhi.
954 **810** 1 r. multicoloured 20 30

811 Army Post Office and Postmarks · 812 Energy Symbols

1980. "India '80" International Stamp Exhibition (3rd issue).
955 **811** 30 p. green 40 30
956 – 50 p. brown & dp brown . 70 1·00
957 – 1 r. red . . . . 80 1·00
958 – 2 r. brown . . . . 80 2·00
DESIGNS: 50 p. Money order transfer document, 1879; 1 r. Copper prepayment ticket, 1774; 2 r. Sir Rowland Hill and birthplace at Kidderminster.

1980. Institution of Engineers (India) Commem.
959 **812** 30 p. gold and blue . . . 20 30

813 Uniforms of 1780 and 1980, Crest and Ribbon · 814 Books

1980. Bicentenary of Madras Sappers.
960 **813** 30 p. multicoloured . . . 60 50

1980. 4th World Book Fair, New Delhi.
961 **814** 30 p. blue 30 30

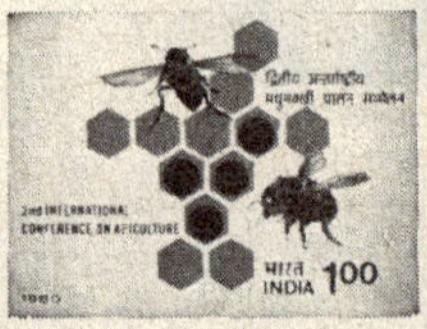

815 Bees and Honey-Comb · 816 Welthy Fisher and Saksharta Nicketan (Literacy House), Lucknow

1980. 2nd International Conference on Agriculture.
962 **815** 1 r. bistre and brown . . . 40 45

1980. Welthy Fisher (teacher) Commemoration.
963 **816** 30 p. blue 30 30

817 Darul-Uloom, Deoband · 818 Keshub Chunder Sen

1980. Darul-Uloom College Commemoration.
964 **817** 30 p. green 20 30

1980. Keshub Chunder Sen (religious and social reformer) Commemoration.
965 **818** 30 p. brown 20 30

819 Chhatrapati Shivaji Maharaj · 820 Table Tennis

1980. 300th Death Anniv of Chhatrapati Shivaji Maharaj (warrior).
966 **819** 30 p. multicoloured . . . 20 30

1980. 5th Asian Table Tennis Championships, Calcutta.
967 **820** 30 p. purple 30 30

1980. As Nos. 732 and 810, but 17 × 20 mm in size.
968 30 p. brown (Gandhi) . . . . 3·75 80
969 30 p. violet (Nehru) . . . . 1·00 40

821 N. M. Joshi · 822 Ulloor S. Parameswara Iyer

1980. Narayan Malhar Joshi (trade unionist) Commemoration.
970 **821** 30 p. mauve 60 40

1980. Ulloor S. Parameswara Iyer (poet) Commemoration.
971 **822** 30 p. purple 60 40

823 S. M. Zamin Ali · 824 Helen Keller

1980. Syed Mohammed Zamin Ali (educationist and poet) Commemoration.
972 **823** 30 p. green 20 40

1980. Birth Centenary of Helen Keller (campaigner for the handicapped).
973 **824** 30 p. black and orange . 50 40

825 High-jumping · 826 Prem Chand

1980. Olympic Games, Moscow. Multicoloured.
974 1 r. Type **825** 40 40
975 2 r. 80 Horse-riding . . . . . 1·10 2·25

1980. Birth Cent of Prem Chand (novelist).
976 **826** 30 p. brown 20 40

827 Mother Teresa and Nobel Peace Prize Medallion · 828 Lord Mountbatten

1980. Award of 1979 Nobel Peace Prize to Mother Teresa.
977 **827** 30 p. violet 40 30

1980. Lord Mountbatten Commemoration.
978 **828** 2 r. 80 multicoloured . . 1·75 2·50

1980. As Nos. 968/9, but new face value.
979 35 p. brown 85 30
980 35 p. violet 30 20
DESIGNS: No. 979, Gandhi; No. 980, Nehru.

829 Scottish Church College, Calcutta · 830 Rajah Annamalai Chettiar

1980. 150th Anniv of Scottish Church College, Calcutta.
981 **829** 35 p. lilac 20 30

1980. Rajah Annamalai Chettiar (banker and educationist) Commemoration.
982 **830** 35 p. lilac 20 30

831 Gandhi marching to Dandi
832 Jayaprakash Narayan

1980. 50th Anniv of "Dandi March" (Gandhi's defiance of Salt Tax Law).
983 **831** 35 p. black, blue & gold . 20 65
984 – 35 p. black, mauve & gold 20 65
DESIGN: No. 984, Gandhi picking up handful of salt at Dandi.

1980. Jayaprakash Narayan (socialist) Commemoration.
985 **832** 35 p. brown 40 40

833 Great Indian Bustard
834 Arabic Commemorative Inscription

1980. International Symposium on Bustards, Juipur.
986 **833** 2 r. 30 multicoloured . . . 1·00 2·00

1980. Moslem Year 1400 A.H. Commemoration.
987 **834** 35 p. multicoloured . . . 15 30

835 "Girls Dancing" (Pampa Paul)
836 Dhyan Chand

1980. Children's Day.
988 **835** 35 p. multicoloured . . . 40 40

1980. Dhyan Chand (hockey player). Commemoration.
989 **836** 35 p. brown 80 75

837 Gold Mining
838 M. A. Ansari

1980. Cent of Kolar Gold Fields, Karnataka.
990 **837** 1 r. multicoloured . . . . 1·10 30

1980. Mukhtayar Ahmad Ansari (medical practitioner and politician) Commemoration.
991 **838** 35 p. green 40 40

839 India Government Mint, Bombay

1980. 150th Anniv of India Government Mint, Bombay.
992 **839** 35 p. black, blue & silver . 20 30

840 Bride from Tamil Nadu
841 Mazharul Haque

1980. Brides in Traditional Costume. Multicoloured.
993 1 r. Type **840** 40 75
994 1 r. Rajasthan 40 75
995 1 r. Kashmir 40 75
996 1 r. Bengal 40 75

1981. Mazharul Haque (journalist) Commem.
997 **841** 35 p. blue 20 40

842 St. Stephen's College

1981. Centenary of St. Stephen's College, Delhi.
998 **842** 35 p. red 20 40

843 Gommateshwara
844 G. V. Mavalankar

1981. Millenium of Gommateshwara (statue at Shravanabelgola).
999 **843** 1 r. multicoloured 20 30

1981. 25th Death Anniv of Ganesh Vasudeo Mavalankar (parliamentarian).
1000 **844** 35 p. red 20 40

845 Flame of Martyrdom
846 Heinrich von Stephan and U.P.U. Emblem

1981. "Homage to Martyrs".
1001 **845** 35 p. multicoloured . . 20 30

1981. 150th Birth Anniv of Heinrich von Stephan (founder of U.P.U.).
1002 **846** 1 r. brown 20 50

847 Disabled Child being helped by Able-bodied Child

1981. International Year for Disabled Persons.
1003 **847** 1 r. black and blue . . . 20 30

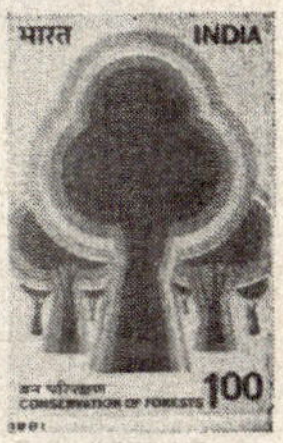

848 Bhil
849 Stylised Trees

1981. Tribes of India. Muticoloured.
1004 1 r. Type **848** 40 35
1005 1 r. Dandami Maria 40 35
1006 1 r. Toda 40 35
1007 1 r. Khlamngam Naga . . . 40 35

1981. Forests Conservation.
1008 **849** 1 r. multicoloured . . . 20 30

850 Nilmoni Phukan
851 Sanjay Gandhi

1981. Nilmoni Phukan (poet) Commemoration.
1009 **850** 35 p. brown 20 40

1981. 1st Death Anniv of Sanjay Gandhi (politician).
1010 **851** 35 p. multicoloured . . . 40 55

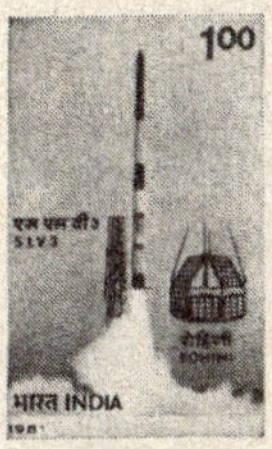

852 Launch of "SLV 3" and Diagram of "Rohini"
853 Games Logo

1981. Launch of "SLV 3" Rocket with "Rohini" Satellite.
1011 **852** 1 r. black, pink and blue . 30 30

1981. Asian Games, New Delhi (1st issue). Multicoloured.
1012 1 r. Type **853** . . . . 1·25 65
1013 1 r. Games emblem and stylised hockey players . . . . . . 1·25 65
See also Nos. 1026, 1033, 1057, 1059 and 1061/6.

854 Flame of the Forest
855 W. F. D. Emblem and Wheat

1981. Flowering Trees. Multicoloured.
1014 35 p. Type **854** 40 15
1015 50 p. Crateva 75 75
1016 1 r. Golden shower . . . . 1·00 50
1017 2 r. Bauhinia . . . . 1·40 2·25

1981. World Food Day.
1018 **855** 1 r. yellow and blue . . . 20 20

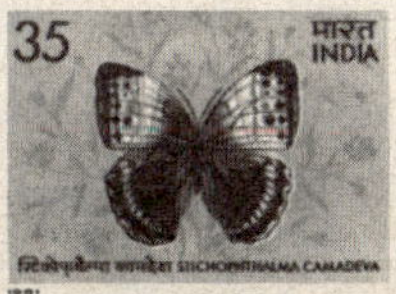

856 "Stichophthalma camadeva"

1981. Butterflies. Multicoloured.
1019 35 p. Type **856** 90 15
1020 50 p. "Cethosia biblis" . . . 1·75 1·40
1021 1 r. "Cyrestis achates" (vert) . 2·25 70
1022 2 r. "Teinopalpus imperialis" (vert) . . . . 2·75 5·00

857 Bellary Raghava

1981. Bellary Raghava (actor) Commemoration.
1023 **857** 35 p. green 70 30

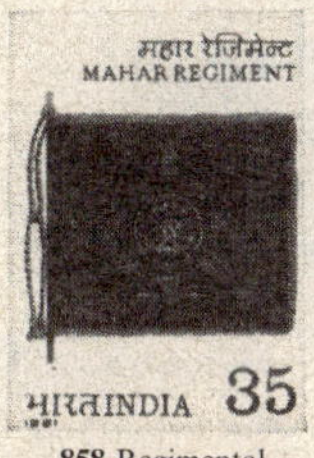

858 Regimental Colour
859 "Toyseller" (Kumari Ruchita Sharma)

1981. 40th Anniv of Mahar Regiment.
1024 **858** 35 p. multicoloured . . . 90 30

1981. Children's Day.
1025 **859** 35 p. multicoloured . . . 75 30

860 Rajghat Stadium
861 Kashi Prasad Jayasawal and Yaudheya Coin

1981. Asian Games, New Delhi (2nd issue).
1026 **860** 1 r. multicoloured . . . 1·50 30

1981. Birth Centenary of Kashi Prasad Jayasawal (lawyer and historian).
1027 **861** 35 p. blue 50 30

862 Indian and P.L.O. Flags, and People

1981. Palestinian Solidarity.
1028 **862** 1 r. multicoloured . . . 2·00 40

863 I.N.S. "Taragiri" (frigate)

1981. Indian Navy Day.
1029 **863** 35 p. multicoloured . . . 2·25 1·25

864 Henry Heras and Indus Valley Seal

1981. Henry Heras (historian) Commemoration.
1030 **864** 35 p. lilac 45 30

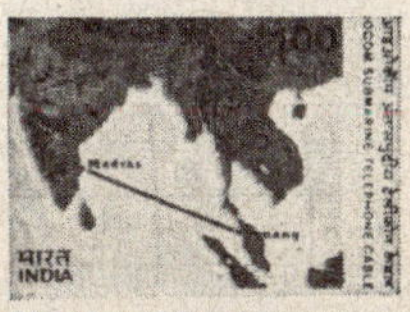

865 Map of South-East Asia showing Cable Route

1981. Inauguration of I.O.C.O.M. (Indian Ocean Commonwealth Cable) Submarine Telephone Cable.
1031 **865** 1 r. multicoloured . . . 2·00 35

866 Stylised Hockey-players and Championship Emblem

1981. World Cup Hockey Championship, Bombay.
1032 **866** 1 r. multicoloured . . . 95 30

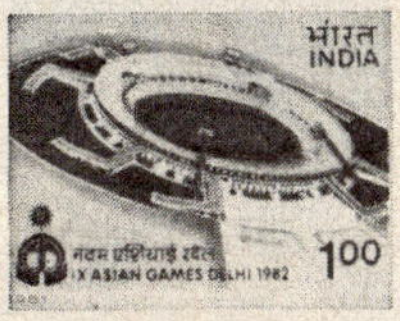

867 Jawaharlal Nehru Stadium
868 Early and Modern Telephones

1981. Asian Games, New Delhi (3rd issue).
1033 **867** 1 r. multicoloured . . . 30 20

1982. Centenary of Telephone Services.
1034 **868** 2 r. black, blue and grey 30 30

869 Map of World

870 Sir J. J. School of Art

1982. International Soil Science Congress, New Delhi.
1035 **869** 1 r. multicoloured . . . 30 20

1982. 125th Anniv of Sir J. J. School of Art, Bombay.
1036 **870** 35 p. multicoloured . . . 20 20

871 "Three Musicians"

872 Deer (stone carving), 5th-century A.D.

1982. Birth Centenary (1981) of Picasso.
1037 **871** 2 r. 85 multicoloured . . 1·00 50

1982. Festival of India. Ancient Sculpture. Multicoloured.
1038 2 r. Type **872** 20 40
1039 3 r. 05 Kaliya Mardana (bronze statue), 9th-century A.D. . . 35 60

873 Radio Telescope, Ooty

1982. Festival of India. Science and Technology.
1040 **873** 3 r. 05 multicoloured . . 35 40

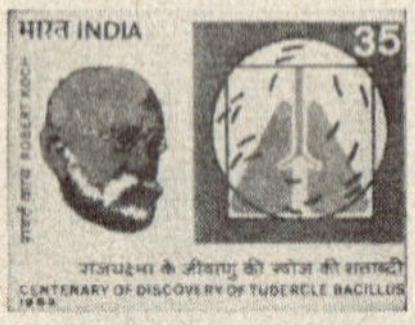

874 Robert Koch and Symbol of Disease

1982. Centenary of Robert Koch's Discovery of Tubercle Bacillus.
1041 **874** 35 p. lilac . . . . 1·40 75

875 Durgabai Deshmukh

1982. 1st Death Anniv of Durgabai Deshmukh (social reformer).
1042 **875** 35 p. blue 60 70

876 Blue Poppy

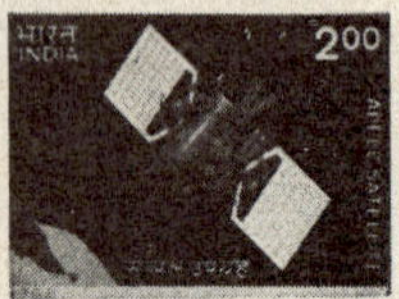

877 "Apple" Satellite

1982. Himalayan Flowers. Multicoloured.
1043 35 p. Type **876** 65 20
1044 1 r. Showy inula . . . . . . 1·50 30
1045 2 r. Cobra lily . . . . 2·00 2·50
1046 2 r. 85 Brahma kamal . . . . 2·50 3·25

1982. 1st Anniv of "Apple" Satellite Launch.
1047 **877** 2 r. multicoloured . . . 50 80

878 Bidhan Chandra Roy

1982. Birth Centenary of Bidhan Chandra Roy (doctor and politician).
1048 **878** 50 p. brown . . . . . . 80 1·10

879 "Sagar Samrat" Oil Rig

1982. 25th Anniv of Oil and Natural Gas Commission.
1049 **879** 1 r. multicoloured . . . 1·00 60

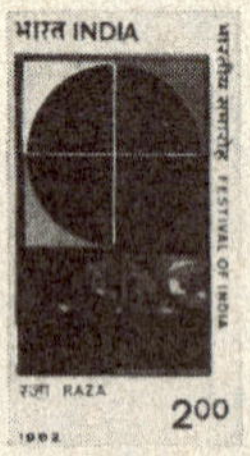

880 "Bindu" (S. H. Raza)

881 Red Deer Stag, Kashmir

1982. Festival of India. Contemporary Paintings. Multicoloured.
1050 2 r. Type **880** 40 50
1051 3 r. 05 "Between the Spider and the Lamp" (M. F. Hussain) 60 1·25

1982. Wildlife Conservation.
1052 **881** 2 r. 85 multicoloured . . 1·50 1·25

882 Westland Wapiti Biplane and Mikoyan Gurevich MiG-25 Aircraft

1982. 50th Anniv of Indian Air Force.
1053 **882** 1 r. multicoloured . . . 3·75 1·25

883 J. Tata with De Havilland Puss Moth

1982. 50th Anniv of Civil Aviation in India.
1054 **883** 3 r. 25 multicoloured . . 3·50 1·60

884 Police Patrol

1982. Police Commemoration Day.
1055 **884** 50 p. green 50 30

885 Coins and Economic Symbols

1982. Centenary of Post Office Savings Bank.
1056 **885** 50 p. brown and light brown 20 20

886 Wrestling Bout

888 Arjuna shooting Arrow at Fish

887 Troposcatter Communication Link

1982. Asian Games, New Delhi (4th issue).
1057 **886** 1 r. multicoloured 30 30

1982. 1st Anniv of Troposcatter Communication Link between India and U.S.S.R.
1058 **887** 3 r. 05 multicoloured . . 30 40

1982. Asian Games, New Delhi (5th issue).
1059 **888** 1 r. multicoloured . . . . 1·75 30

889 "Mother and Child" (Deepak Sharma)

890 Stylised Cyclists

1982. Children's Day.
1060 **889** 50 p. multicoloured . . . 30 30

1982. Asian Games, New Delhi (6th issue). Multicoloured.
1061 50 p. Type **890** 10 10
1062 2 r. Javelin-throwing 25 30
1063 2 r. 85 Discus-throwing . . . 30 45
1064 3 r. 25 Football 40 55

891 Yachting

1982. Asian Games, New Delhi (7th issue). Multicoloured.
1065 2 r. Type **891** 90 30
1066 2 r. 85 Rowing . . . . 1·10 55

892 Chetwode Building

1982. 50th Anniv of Indian Military Academy Dehradun.
1067 **892** 50 p. multicoloured . . . 30 50

893 Purushottamdas Tandon

1982. Birth Cent of Purushottamdas Tandon (politician).
1068 **893** 50 p. brown 30 70

894 Darjeeling Himalayan Railway

1982. Cent of Darjeeling Himalayan Railway.
1069 **894** 2 r. 85 multicoloured . . 4·00 4·00

895 Vintage Rail Coach and Silhouette of Steam Locomotive

1982. "Inpex 82" Stamp Exhibition. Multicoloured.
1070 50 p. Type **895** 65 85
1071 2 r. 1854 ½ anna blue stamp and 1947 3½ anna Independence commem (33 × 44 mm) . . 1·90 2·25

896 Antarctic Camp

1983. 1st Indian Antarctic Expedition.
1072 **896** 1 r. multicoloured . . . 3·50 2·25

1983. As Nos. 968/9, but with new face value.
1073a 50 p. brown (Gandhi) . . . 3·00 1·50
1074a 50 p. blue (Nehru) . . . . 1·50 55

897 Roosevelt with Stamp Collection

1983. Birth Centenary of Franklin D. Roosevelt (American statesman).
1075 **897** 3 r. 25 brown . . . . . 55 1·25

898 "Siberian Cranes at Bharatpur" (Diane Pierce)

899 Jat Regiment Uniforms Past and Present

1983. International Crane Workshop, Bharatpur.
1076 **898** 2 r. 85 multicoloured . . 2·00 2·50

1983. Presentation of Colours to Battalions of the Jat Regiment.
1077 **899** 50 p. multicoloured . . . 1·50 1·00

900 Non-aligned Summit Logo

1983. 7th Non-aligned Summit Conference, New Delhi.
1078 **900** 1 r. lt brown, brn & blk . 20 30
1079 – 2 r. multicoloured . . . 30 95
DESIGN: 2 r. Nehru.

901 Shore Temple, Mahabalipuram

1983. Commonwealth Day. Multicoloured.
1080 1 r. Type **901** 15 30
1081 2 r. Gomukh, Gangotri Glacier 30 1·25

902 Acropolis and Olympic Emblems

1983. Int Olympic Committee Session, New Delhi.
1082 **902** 1 r. multicoloured . . . 30 50

903 "St. Francis and Brother Falcon" (statue by Giovanni Collina)

904 Karl Marx and "Das Kapital"

1983. 800th Birth Anniv of St. Francis of Assisi.
1083 **903** 1 r. brown 30 30

1983. Death Centenary of Karl Marx.
1084 **904** 1 r. brown 20 30

905 Darwin and Map of Voyage

1983. Death Centenary (1982) of Charles Darwin (naturalist).
1085 **905** 2 r. multicoloured . . . 2·25 2·75

906 Swamp Deer

907 Globe and Satellite

1983. 50th Anniv of Kanha National Park.
1086 **906** 1 r. multicoloured . . . 1·50 75

1983. World Communications Year.
1087 **907** 1 r. multicoloured . . . 40 40

908. Simon Bolivar.

908 Simon Bolivar

909 Meera Behn

1983. Birth Bicentenary of Simon Bolivar (South American statesman).
1088 **908** 2 r. multicoloured . . . 1·75 2·00

1983. India's Struggle for Freedom (1st series).
1089 50 p. red and green . . . . . 90 2·00
1090 50 p. brown, green and red . 90 2·00
1091 50 p. multicoloured . . . . . 90 1·50
1092 50 p. brown, green and red . 15 30
1093 50 p. brown, green & orange 15 30
1094 50 p. green, yellow & orange 15 30
DESIGNS—VERT: No. 1089, Type **909**; 1090, Mahadev Desai; 1092, Hemu Kalani (revolutionary); 1093, Acharya Vinoba Bhave (social reformer); 1094, Surendranath Banerjee (political reformer). HORIZ (43 × 31 mm): No. 1091, Quit India Resolution.
See also Nos. 1119/24, 1144/9, 1191/4, 1230/5, 1287/96 and 1345/9.

910 Ram Nath Chopra

1983. Ram Nath Chopra (pharmacologist) Commemoration.
1095 **910** 50 p. red 40 80

911 Nanda Devi Mountain

1983. 25th Anniv of Indian Mountaineering Federation.
1096 **911** 2 r. multicoloured . . . 1·10 90

912 Great Indian Hornbill

913 View of Garden

1983. Centenary of Natural History Society, Bombay.
1097 **912** 1 r. multicoloured . . . 2·50 90

1983. Rock Garden, Chandigarh.
1098 **913** 1 r. multicoloured . . . 1·25 85

914 Golden Langur

1983. Indian Wildlife. Monkeys. Multicoloured.
1099 1 r. Type **914** . . . . 1·10 50
1100 2 r. Lion-tailed macaque . . 2·25 3·00

915 Ghats of Varanasi

1983. 5th General Assembly of World Tourism Organization.
1101 **915** 2 r. multicoloured . . . 40 40

916 Krishna Kanta Handique

918 Woman and Child (from "Festival" by Kashyap Premsawala)

1983. Krishna Kanta Handique (scholar).
1102 **916** 50 p. blue 30 70

1983. Children's Day.
1103 **918** 50 p. multicoloured . . 30 50

920 "Udan Khatola", First Indian Hot Air Balloon

921 Tiger

1983. Bicentenary of Manned Flight.
1104 1 r. Type **920** 75 20
1105 2 r. Montgolfier balloon . . 1·00 80

1983. Ten Years of "Project Tiger".
1106 **921** 2 r. multicoloured . . . 2·50 3·00

922 Commonwealth Logo

923 "Pratiksha"

1983. Commonwealth Heads of Government Meeting, New Delhi. Multicoloured.
1107 1 r. Type **922** 10 15
1108 2 r. Goanese couple, early 19th century 25 30

1983. Birth Centenary of Nanda Lal Bose (artist).
1109 **923** 1 r. multicoloured 30 30

925 Lancer in Ceremonial Uniform

926 Troopers in Ceremonial Uniform and Tank

1984. Bicentenary of 7th Light Cavalry.
1110 **925** 1 r. multicoloured . . . . 3·25 1·40

1984. Presentation of Regimental Guidon to the Deccan Horse.
1111 **926** 1 r. multicoloured . . . . 3·25 1·40

927 Society Building and Sir William Jones (founder)

928 Insurance Logo

1984. Bicentenary of Asiatic Society.
1112 **927** 1 r. green and purple . . 30 50

1984. Centenary of Postal Life Insurance.
1113 **928** 1 r. multicoloured 30 30

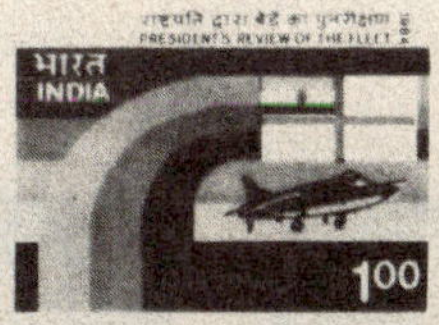

929 Hawker Siddeley Sea Harrier

1984. President's Review of the Fleet. Multicoloured.
1114 1 r. Type **929** . . . . 1·40 1·60
1115 1 r. "Vikrant" (aircraft carrier) 1·40 1·60
1116 1 r. "Vela" (submarine) . . . 1·40 1·60
1117 1 r. "Kashin" (destroyer) . . 1·40 1·60
Nos. 1114/17 were printed together, se-tenant, forming a composite design.

930 I.L.A. Logo and Hemispheres

1984. 12th International Leprosy Congress.
1118 **930** 1 r. multicoloured 30 30

1984. India's Struggle for Freedom (2nd series). As T **909**.
1119 50 p. green, lt green & orge . 30 40
1120 50 p. brown, green & orge . . 30 40
1121 50 p. multicoloured 50 60
1122 50 p. multicoloured 50 60
1123 50 p. multicoloured 50 60
1124 50 p. multicoloured 50 60
DESIGNS: No. 1119, Vasudeo Balvant Phadke (revolutionary); 1120, Baba Kanshi Ram (revolutionary); 1121, Tatya Tope; 1122, Nana Sahib; 1123, Begum Hazrat Mahal; 1124, Mangal Pandey.

932 "Salyut 7"

1984. Indo-Soviet Manned Space Flight.
1125 **932** 3 r. multicoloured . . . 55 55

935 G. D. Birla

1984. 90th Birth Anniv of G. D. Birla (industrialist).
1126 **935** 50 p. brown 30 70

936 Basketball

937 Gwalior

1984. Olympic Games, Los Angeles. Multicoloured.
1127 50 p. Type **936** 90 65
1128 1 r. High jumping 75 30
1129 2 r. Gymnastics (horiz) . . . 1·00 1·50
1130 2 r. 50 Weightlifting (horiz) . 1·25 2·50

1984. Forts. Multicoloured.
1131 50 p. Type **937** 70 55
1132 1 r. Vellore (vert) 95 30
1133 1 r. 50 Simhagad (vert) . . . 1·75 2·75
1134 2 r. Jodhpur . . . . 2·00 3·00

938 B. V. Paradkar and Newspaper

939 Dr. D. N. Wadia and Institute of Himalayan Geology, Dehradun

1984. B. V. Paradkar (journalist) Commemoration.
1135 **938** 50 p. brown 30 60

1984. Birth Centenary (1983) of Dr. D. N. Wadia (geologist).
1136 **939** 1 r. multicoloured . . . 1·25 30

940 "Herdsman and Cattle in Forest" (H. Kassam)

942 Congress Emblem

941 Indira Gandhi

1984. Children's Day.
1137 **940** 50 p. multicoloured . . . 75 95

1984. Prime Minister Indira Gandhi Commemoration (1st issue).
1138 **941** 50 p. black, violet & orange 2·25 2·25
See also Nos. 1151, 1167 and 1170.

1984. 12th World Mining Congress, New Delhi.
1139 **942** 1 r. black and yellow . . 1·25 30

943 Dr. Rajendra Prasad at Desk **944** Mrinalini (rose)

1984. Birth Centenary of Dr. Rajendra Prasad (former President).
1140 **943** 50 p. multicoloured . . . 1·00 85

1984. Roses. Multicoloured.
1141 1 r. 50 Type **944** . . . . 2·00 2·00
1142 2 r. Sugandha . . . . 2·25 2·25

945 "Fergusson College" (Gopal Deuskar)

1985. Centenary of Fergusson College, Pune.
1143 **945** 1 r. multicoloured . . . 55 55

1985. India's Struggle for Freedom (3rd series). As T **909**.
1144 50 p. brown, green & orge . . 50 60
1145 50 p. brown, green & orge . . 50 60
1146 50 p. brown, green & orge . . 50 60
1147 50 p. brown, green & orge . . 50 60
1148 50 p. blue, green & orge . . 50 60
1149 50 p. black, green & orge . . 50 60
DESIGNS—VERT: No. 1144, Narhar Vishnu Gadgil (politician); 1145, Jairamdas Doulatram (journalist); 1147, Kakasaheb Kalelkar (author); 1148, Master Tara Singh (politician); 1149, Ravishankar Maharaj (politician). HORIZ: No. 1146, Jatindra and Nellie Sengupta (politicians).

947 Gunner and Howitzer from Mountain Battery

1985. 50th Anniv of Regiment of Artillery.
1150 **947** 1 r. multicoloured . . . 3·50 1·50

948 Indira Gandhi making Speech

1985. Indira Gandhi Commemoration (2nd issue).
1151 **948** 2 r. multicoloured . . . 2·50 3·00

949 Minicoy Lighthouse **950** Medical College Hospital

1985. Centenary of Minicoy Lighthouse.
1152 **949** 1 r. multicoloured . . . 3·75 85

1985. 150th Anniv of Medical College, Calcutta.
1153 **950** 1 r. yellow, brown & purple 2·50 70

951 Medical College, Madras

1985. 150th Anniv of Medical College, Madras.
1154 **951** 1 r. light brown and brown 2·50 70

952 Riflemen of 1835 and 1985 and Map of North-East India **953** Potato Plant

1985. 150th Anniv of Assam Rifles.
1155 **952** 1 r. multicoloured . . . 3·25 1·25

1985. 50th Anniv of Potato Research in India.
1156 **953** 50 p. deep brown and brown . . . . 1·50 1·60

954 Baba Jassa Singh Ahluwalia **956** White-winged Wood Duck

955 St. Xavier's College

1985. Death Bicentenary (1983) of Baba Jassa Singh Ahluwalia (Sikh leader).
1157 **954** 50 p. purple . . . . . . 1·50 1·60

1985. 125th Anniv of St. Xavier's College, Calcutta.
1158 **955** 1 r. multicoloured . . . 1·00 50

1985. Wildlife Conservation. White-winged Wood Duck.
1159 **956** 2 r. multicoloured . . . 4·50 4·50

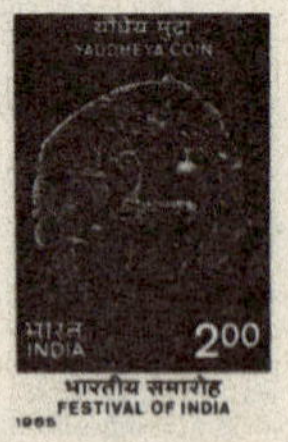
957 "Mahara" **958** Yaudheya Copper Coin, c. 200 B.C.

1985. Bougainvillea. Multicoloured.
1160 50 p. Type **957** . . . . . 1·25 1·75
1161 1 r. "H. B. Singh" . . . . . 1·50 1·50

1985. Festival of India (1st issue).
1162 **958** 2 r. multicoloured . . . 2·00 2·00

959 Statue of Didarganj Yakshi (deity) **962** Swami Haridas

1985. Festival of India (2nd issue).
1163 **959** 1 r. multicoloured . . . 1·00 40

1985. Swami Haridas (philosopher) Commemoration.
1164 **962** 1 r. multicoloured . . . . 1·75 1·50

963 Stylised Mountain Road

1985. 25th Anniv of Border Roads Organization.
1165 **963** 2 r. red, violet and black . 2·00 2·25

964 Nehru addressing General Assembly

1985. 40th Anniv of United Nations Organization.
1166 **964** 2 r. multicoloured 90 90

965 Indira Gandhi with Crowd

1985. Indira Gandhi Commemoration (3rd issue).
1167 **965** 2 r. brown and black . . 2·50 2·75

966 Girl using Home Computer

1985. Children's Day.
1168 **966** 50 p. multicoloured . . . 90 90

967 Halley's Comet **968** Indira Gandhi

1985. 19th General Assembly of International Astronomical Union, New Delhi.
1169 **967** 1 r. multicoloured . . . . 1·75 1·25

1985. Indira Gandhi Commemoration (4th issue).
1170 **968** 3 r. multicoloured . . . . 2·50 3·00

969 St. Stephen's Hospital

1985. Centenary of St. Stephen's Hospital, Delhi.
1171 **969** 1 r. black and brown . . 80 40

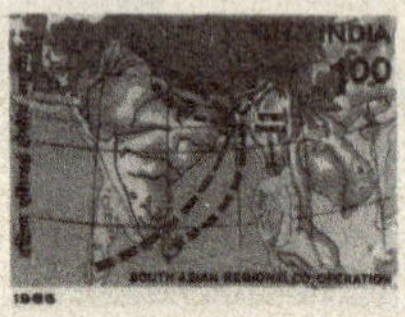
971 Map showing Member States

1985. 1st Summit Meeting of South Asian Association for Regional Co-operation, Dhaka, Bangladesh. Multicoloured.
1172 1 r. Type **971** . . . . 1·50 35
1173 3 r. Flags of member nations (44 × 32 mm) . . . . 2·50 3·25

972 Shyama Shastri **975** Young Runners and Emblem

1985. Shyama Shastri (composer) Commemoration.
1174 **972** 1 r. multicoloured . . . 2·25 1·50

1985. International Youth Year.
1175 **975** 2 r. multicoloured . . . 1·25 75

976 Handel and Bach

1985. 300th Birth Annivs of George Frederick Handel and Johann Sebastian Bach (composers).
1176 **976** 5 r. multicoloured . . . 3·25 3·75

977 A. O. Hume (founder) and Early Congress Presidents

1985. Centenary of Indian National Congress. Designs showing miniature portraits of Congress Presidents.
1177 **977** 1 r. black, orange, green and grey . . . . 1·50 1·75
1178 – 1 r. black, orange and green 1·50 1·75
1179 – 1 r. black, orange and green 1·50 1·75
1180 – 1 r. black, orange, green and grey . . . . . . 1·50 1·75
Nos. 1178/80 each show sixteen miniature portraits. The individual stamps can be distinguished by the position of the face value and inscription which are at the top on Nos. 1177/8 and at the foot on Nos. 1179/80. No. 1180 shows a portrait of Prime Minister Rajiv Gandhi in a grey frame at bottom right.

978 Bombay and Duncan Dry Docks, Bombay.

1181 **978** 2 r. 50 multicoloured . . 3·25 3·50

979 Hawa Mahal and Jaipur 1904 2 a. Stamp

1986. "INPEX '86" Philatelic Exhibition, Jaipur. Multicoloured.
1182 50 p. Type **979** . . . . . . 1·00 1·00
1183 2 r. Mobile camel post office, Thar Desert . . . . 2·25 2·75

MORE DETAILED LISTS
are given in the Stanley Gibbons Catalogues referred to in the country headings. For lists of current volumes see Introduction.

980 I.N.S. "Vikrant" (aircraft carrier)

981 Humber Sommer Biplane and Later Mail Planes

1986. Completion of 25 Years Service by I.N.S. "Vikrant".
1184 **980** 2 r. multicoloured . . . 4·25 4·25

1986. 75th Anniv of First Official Airmail Flight, Allahabad–Naini. Multicoloured.
1185 50 p. Type **981** . . . . 2·25 1·75
1186 3 r. Modern Air India Airbus Industries A300 mail plane and Humber Sommer biplane (37 × 24 mm) . . . . 4·75 6·00

982 Triennale Emblem

983 Chaitanya Mahaprabhu

1986. 6th Triennale Art Exhibition, New Delhi.
1187 **982** 1 r. purple, yellow & black 1·50 95

1986. 500th Birth Anniv of Chaitanya Mahaprabhu (religious leader).
1188 **983** 2 r. multicoloured . . . 2·75 3·50

984 Main Building, Mayo College

1986. Mayo College (public school), Ajmer, Commemoration.
1189 **984** 1 r. multicoloured . . . 1·50 1·00

985 Two Footballers

1986. World Cup Football Championship, Mexico.
1190 **985** 5 r. multicoloured . . . 4·00 4·00

1986. India's Struggle for Freedom (4th series). As T **909**.
1191 50 p. brown, green and red . 1·25 1·50
1192 50 p. brown, green and red . 1·25 1·50
1193 50 p. black, green & orange . 1·25 1·50
1194 50 p. brown, green and red . 1·25 1·50
DESIGNS: No. 1191, Bhim Sen Sachar; 1192, Alluri Seeta Rama Raju; 1193, Sagarmal Gopa; 1194, Veer Surendra Sai.

987 Swami Sivananda

988 Volleyball

1986. Birth Centenary of Swami Sivananda (spiritual leader).
1195 **987** 2 r. multicoloured . . . 3·00 3·50

1986. Asian Games, Seoul, South Korea. Multicoloured.
1196 1 r. 50 Type **988** . . . . . 2·50 2·75
1197 3 r. Hurdling . . . . 3·00 3·75

989 Madras G.P.O.

1986. Bicentenary of Madras G.P.O.
1198 **989** 5 r. black and red . . . 4·50 5·00

990 Parachutist

991 Early and Modern Policemen

1986. 225th Anniv of 8th Battalion of Coast Sepoys (now 1st Battalion Parachute Regiment).
1199 **990** 3 r. multicoloured . . . 5·00 5·00

1986. 125th Anniv of Indian Police. Designs showing early and modern police.
1200 **991** 1 r. 50 multicoloured . . 3·50 3·75
1201 – 2 r. multicoloured . . . 3·50 3·75
Nos. 1200/1 were printed together, se-tenant, forming a composite design.

992 Hand holding Flower and World Map

1986. International Peace Year.
1202 **992** 5 r. multicoloured . . . 2·25 1·25

993 "Girl Rock Climber" (Sujasha Dasgupta)

994 Windmill

1986. Children's Day.
1203 **993** 50 p. multicoloured . . 2·25 2·25

1986. Science and Technology.
1211 – 35 p. red 10 10
1212 – 40 p. red 10 10
1213 – 60 p. green and red . . 10 10
1214a – 75 p. red 30 20
1215 – 1 r. black and red . . 15 10
1217 – 5 r. brown and orange 15 20
1218 – 20 r. brown and blue . 55 60
1219 **994** 50 r. black, blue and mauve . . . . . . 1·40 1·50
DESIGNS—20 × 17 mm: 35 p. Family planning. 37 × 20 mm: 60 p. Indian family; 20 r. Bio gas. 17 × 20 mm: 40 p. Television set, dish aerial and transmitter; 75 p. "Family" (as No. 927). 20 × 37 mm: 1 r. Petrol pump nozzle (Oil conservation); 5 r. Solar energy.

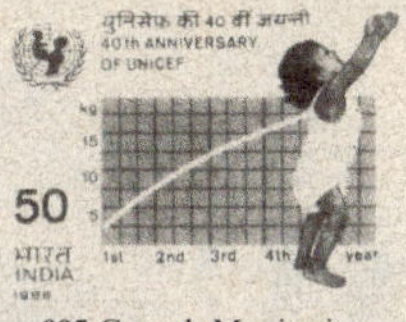

995 Growth Monitoring

1986. 40th Anniv of U.N.I.C.E.F. Multicoloured.
1221 50 p. Type **995** . . . . . . 2·00 2·00
1222 5 r. Immunization . . . . . 4·25 6·00

996 Tansen

997 Indian Elephant

1986. Tansen (musician and composer) Commem.
1223 **996** 1 r. multicoloured . . . 2·00 60

1986. 50th Anniv of Corbett National Park. Multicoloured.
1224 1 r. Type **997** . . . . 3·50 1·00
1225 2 r. Gharial . . . . 4·00 6·00

998 St. Martha's Hospital

1986. Centenary of St. Martha's Hospital, Bangalore.
1226 **998** 1 r. blue, orange & black 2·00 1·40

999 Yacht "Trishna" and Route Map

1987. Indian Army Round the World Yacht Voyage, 1985–7.
1227 **999** 6 r. 50 multicoloured . . 4·50 4·00

1000 Map of Southern Africa and Logo

1001 Emblem

1987. Inauguration of AFRICA Fund.
1228 **1000** 6 r. 50 black . . . . . . 4·50 4·75

1987. 29th Congress of International Chamber of Commerce, New Delhi.
1229 **1001** 5 r. violet, blue and red . 3·00 1·75

1987. India's Struggle for Freedom (5th series). As T **909**.
1230 60 p. brown, green and orge . 2·00 30
1231 60 p. violet, green and red . . 30 30
1232 60 p. brown, green and red . . 30 30
1233 60 p. blue, green & orange . . 30 30
1234 60 p. brown, green and red . . 30 30
1235 60 p. brown, green and red . . 30 30
1236 60 p. red, green & orange . . 30 30
DESIGNS: No. 1230, Hakim Ajmal Khan; No. 1231, Lala Har Dayal; No. 1232, M. N Roy; No. 1233, Tripuraneni Ramaswamy Chowdary; No. 1234, Dr. Kailas Nath Katju; No. 1235, S. Satyamurti; No. 1236, Pandit Hriday Nath Kunzru.

1002 Blast Furnace and Railway Emblem

1003 Kalia Bhomora Bridge, Tezpur, Assam

1987. Cent of South Eastern Railway. Mult.
1237 1 r. Type **1002** 40 15
1238 1 r. 50 Tank locomotive No. 691, 1887 (horiz) 45 35
1239 2 r. Electric train on viaduct, 1987 . . . . 55 60
1240 4 r. Steam locomotive, c. 1900 (horiz) . . . . 80 1·25

1987. Inauguration of Brahmaputra Bridge.
1241 **1003** 2 r. multicoloured . . . 30 30

1004 Madras Christian College

1987. 150th Anniv of Madras Christian College.
1242 **1004** 1 r. 50 black and red . . 20 20

MINIMUM PRICE

The minimum price quoted is 10p which represents a handling charge rather than a basis for valuing common stamps. For further notes about prices see introductory pages.

1005 Shree Shree Ma Anandamayee

1006 "Rabindranath Tagore" (self-portrait)

1987. Shree Shree Ma Anandamayee (Hindu spiritual leader) Commemoration.
1243 **1005** 1 r. brown 30 20

1987. Rabindranath Tagore (poet) Commem.
1244 **1006** 2 r. multicoloured . . . 40 30

1007 Garhwal Rifles Uniforms of 1887

1008 J. Krishnamurti

1987. Centenary of Garhwal Rifles Regiment.
1245 **1007** 1 r. multicoloured . . . 50 20

1987. J. Krishnamurti (philosopher) Commem.
1246 **1008** 60 p. brown 60 90

1009 Regimental Uniforms of 1887

1987. Centenary of 37th Dogra Regt (now 7th Battalion) (1 Dogra), Mechanised Infantry Regt.
1247 **1009** 1 r. multicoloured . . . 40 20

1010 Hall of Nations, Pragati Maidan, New Delhi

1011 "Sadyah-Snata" Sculpture, Sanghol

1987. "India '89" International Stamp Exhibition, New Delhi (1st issue). Multicoloured.
1248 50 p. Exhibition logo 10 15
1249 5 r. Type **1010** 45 50
See also Nos. 1264/7, 1333/4, 1341/2 and 1358/61.

1987. Festival of India, U.S.S.R.
1251 **1011** 6 r. 50 multicoloured . . 1·00 75

1012 Flag and Stylized Birds with "40" in English and Hindi

1987. 40th Anniv of Independence.
1252 **1012** 60 p. orange, green & bl 20 20

1013 Sant Harchand Singh Longowal

1014 Guru Ghasidas

1987. Sant Harchand Singh Longowal (Sikh leader) Commemoration.
1253 **1013** 1 r. multicoloured . . . 40 20

1987. Guru Ghasidas (Hindu leader) Commemoration.
1254 **1014** 60 p. red 20 20

1015 Thakur Anukul Chandra — **1016** University of Allahabad

1987. Thakur Anukul Chandra (spiritual leader) Commemoration.
1255 **1015** 1 r. multicoloured . . . 40 20

1987. Centenary of Allahabad University.
1256 **1016** 2 r. multicoloured . . . 30 40

1017 Pankha Offering — **1018** Chhatrasal on Horseback

1987. Phoolwalon Ki Sair Festival, Delhi.
1257 **1017** 2 r. multicoloured . . . 30 40

1987. Chhatrasal (Bundela ruler) Commemoration.
1258 **1018** 60 p. brown 30 20

1019 Family and Stylized Houses

1987. International Year of Shelter for the Homeless.
1259 **1019** 5 r. multicoloured . . . 45 60

1020 Map of Asia and Logo

1987. Asia Regional Conference of Rotary International.
1260 **1020** 60 p. brown and green . 15 15
1261 – 6 r. 50 multicoloured . . 60 80
DESIGN: 6 r. 50, Oral polio vaccination.

1021 Blind Boy, Braille Books and Computer

1987. Centenary of Service to Blind.
1262 **1021** 1 r. multicoloured . . . 15 15
1263 – 2 r. deep blue & blue . . 35 30
DESIGN: 2 r. Eye donation.

1022 Iron Pillar, Delhi

1987. "India '89" International Stamp Exhibition, New Delhi (2nd issue). Delhi Landmarks. Mult.
1264 60 p. Type **1022** 10 15
1265 1 r. 50 India Gate 15 20
1266 5 r. Dewan-e-Khas, Red Fort 45 50
1267 6 r. 50 Old Fort 60 65

1023 Tyagmurti Goswami Ganeshdutt — **1024** "My Home" (Siddharth Deshprabha)

1987. Tyagmurti Goswami Ganeshdutt (spiritual leader and social reformer) Commemoration.
1269 **1023** 60 p. red 20 20

1987. Children's Day.
1270 **1024** 60 p. multicoloured . . 30 20

1025 Chinar — **1026** Logo (from sculpture "Worker and Woman Peasant" by V. Mukhina)

1987. Indian Trees. Multicoloured.
1271 **1025** 60 p. multicoloured . . 15 15
1272 – 1 r. 50 multicoloured . 20 20
1273 – 5 r. black, green & brown 55 65
1274 – 6 r. 50 brown, red & green 80 80
DESIGNS—HORIZ: 1 r. 50, Pipal; 6 r. 50, Banyan. VERT: 5 r. Sal.

1987. Festival of U.S.S.R., India.
1275 **1026** 5 r. multicoloured . . . 50 50

1027 White Tiger — **1028** Execution of Veer Narayan Singh

1987. Wildlife. Multicoloured.
1276 1 r. Type **1027** 50 15
1277 5 r. Snow leopard (horiz) . . 1·25 85

1987. Veer Narayan Singh (patriot) Commemoration.
1278 **1028** 60 p. brown 20 20

1029 Rameshwari Nehru — **1030** Father Kuriakose Elias Chavara

1987. Rameshwari Nehru (women's rights campaigner) Commemoration.
1279 **1029** 60 p. brown 20 20

1987. Father Kuriakose Elias Chavara (founder of Carmelites of Mary Immaculate) Commemoration.
1280 **1030** 60 p. brown 20 20

1031 Dr. Rajah Sir Muthiah Chettiar

1987. Dr. Rajah Sir Muthiah Chettiar (politician) Commemoration.
1281 **1031** 60 p. grey 20 20

1032 Golden Temple, Amritsar — **1033** Rukmini Devi and Dancer

1987. 400th Anniv of Golden Temple, Amritsar.
1282 **1032** 60 p. multicoloured . . 30 20

1987. Rukmini Devi (Bharatanatyam dance pioneer). Commemoration.
1283 **1033** 60 p. red 30 20

1034 Dr. Hiralal — **1035** Light Frequency Experiment and Bodhi Tree

1987. Dr. Hiralal (historian) Commemoration.
1284 **1034** 60 p. blue 20 20

1988. 75th Session of Indian Science Congress Association.
1285 **1035** 4 r. multicoloured . . . 50 60

1036 Rural Patient — **1037** U Tirot Singh

1988. 13th Asian Pacific Dental Congress.
1286 **1036** 4 r. multicoloured . . . 50 50

1988. India's Struggle for Freedom (6th series). As T **909**.
1287 60 p. black, green and orange 20 40
1288 60 p. brown, green & orange . 20 40
1289 60 p. red, green and orange . 20 40
1290 60 p. purple, green & orange . 20 40
1291 60 p. purple, green and red . 20 40
1292 60 p. black, green and orange 20 40
1293 60 p. lilac, green and red . . 20 40
1294 60 p. deep green, green & red 20 30
1295 60 p. brown, green and green 20 30
1296 60 p. mauve, green & orange . 20 30
DESIGNS: No. 1287, Mohan Lal Sukhadia; 1288, Dr. S. K. Sinha; 1289, Chandra Shekhar Azad; 1290, G. B. Pant; 1291, Dr. Anugrah Narain Singh; 1292, Kuladhor Chaliha; 1293, Shivprasad Gupta; 1294, Sarat Chandra Bose; 1295, Baba Kharak Singh; 1296, Sheikh Mohammad Abdullah.

1988. U Tirot Singh (Khasis leader) Commem.
1297 **1037** 60 p. brown 20 20

1038 Early and Modern Regimental Uniforms — **1039** Balgandharva

1988. Bicentenary of 4th Battalion of the Kumaon Regiment.
1298 **1038** 1 r. multicoloured . . . 30 20

1988. Birth Centenary of Balgandharva (actor).
1299 **1039** 60 p. brown 20 20

1040 Soldiers and Infantry Combat Vehicle — **1041** B. N. Rau

1988. Presentation of Colours to Mechanised Infantry Regiment.
1300 **1040** 1 r. multicoloured . . . 35 20

1988. B. N. Rau (constitutional lawyer) Commemoration.
1301 **1041** 60 p. black 20 20

1042 Mohindra Government College — **1043** Dr. D. V. Gundappa

1988. Mohindra Government College, Patiala.
1302 **1042** 1 r. mauve 20 20

1988. Dr. D. V. Gundappa (scholar) Commem.
1303 **1043** 60 p. grey 20 20

1044 Rani Avantibai — **1045** "Malayala Manorama" Office, Kottayam

1988. Rani Avantibai of Ramgarh Commem.
1304 **1044** 60 p. mauve 20 20

1988. Centenary of "Malayala Manorama" (newspaper).
1305 **1045** 1 r. black and blue . . 20 20

1046 Maharshi Dadhichi — **1047** Mohammad Iqbal

1988. Maharshi Dadhichi (Hindu saint) Commemoration.
1306 **1046** 60 p. red 20 20

1988. 50th Death Anniv of Mohammad Iqbal (poet).
1307 **1047** 60 p. gold and red . . . 20 20

1048 Samarth Ramdas — **1049** Swati Tirunal Rama Varma

1988. Samarth Ramdas (Hindu spiritual leader) Commemoration.
1308 **1048** 60 p. green 20 20

1988. 175th Birth Anniv of Swati Tirunal Rama Varma (composer).
1309 **1049** 60 p. mauve 20 20

1050 Bhaurao Patil and Class

1988. Bhaurao Patil (educationist) Commem.
1310 **1050** 60 p. brown 20 20

1051 "Rani Lakshmi Bai" (M. F. Husain)

1988. Martyrs from 1st War of Independence.
1311 **1051** 60 p. multicoloured . . 20 20

1052 Broad Peak

1988. Himalayan Peaks.
1312 **1052** 1 r. 50 lilac, violet and blue 35 30
1313 – 4 r. multicoloured . . . 70 60
1314 – 5 r. multicoloured . . . 80 70
1315 – 6 r. 50 multicoloured . . 95 85
DESIGNS: 4 r. K 2 (Godwin Austen); 5 r. Kanchenjunga; 6 r. 50, Nanda Devi.

1053 Child with Grandparents

1988. "Love and Care for Elders".
1316 **1053** 60 p. multicoloured . . 20 20

1054 Victoria Terminus, Bombay

1988. Centenary of Victoria Terminus Station, Bombay.
1317 **1054** 1 r. multicoloured . . . 40 20

1055 Lawrence School, Lovedale

1988. 130th Anniv of Lawrence School, Lovedale.
1318 **1055** 1 r. brown and green . . 30 20

1056 Khejri Tree

1988. World Environment Day.
1319 **1056** 60 p. multicoloured . . 20 15

1988. As No. 732, but new face value.
1320 60 p. black (Gandhi) . . . 55 15

1057 Rani Durgawati

1058 Acharya Shanti Dev

1988. Rani Durgawati (Gondwana ruler) Commemoration.
1322 **1057** 60 p. red 20 20

1988. Acharya Shanti Dev (Buddhist scholar) Commemoration.
1323 **1058** 60 p. brown 20 20

1059 Y. S. Parmar

1061 Durgadas Rathore

1060 Arm pointing at Proclamation in Marathi

1988. Dr. Yashwant Singh Parmar (former Chief Minister of Himachal Pradesh) Commemoration.
1324 **1059** 60 p. violet 20 20

1988. 40th Anniv of Independence. Bal Gangadhar Tilak (patriot) Commemoration. Multicoloured.
1325 60 p. Type **1060** 20 20
1326 60 p. Battle scene 20 20
Nos. 1325/6 were printed together, se-tenant, forming a composite design showing a painting by M. F. Husain.

1988. 150th Birth Anniv of Durgadas Rathore (Regent of Marwar).
1327 **1061** 60 p. brown 20 20

1062 Gopinath Kaviraj

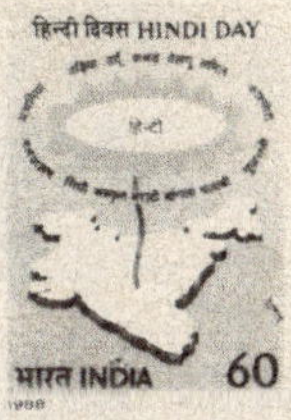

1063 Lotus and Outline Map of India

1988. Gopinath Kaviraj (scholar) Commem.
1328 **1062** 60 p. brown 20 20

1988. Hindi Day.
1329 **1063** 60 p. red, green & brown 20 20

1064 Indian Olympic Association Logo

1065 Jerdon's Courser

1988. "Sports–1988" and Olympic Games, Seoul.
1330 **1064** 60 p. purple 35 15
1331 – 5 r. multicoloured . . . 1·90 60
DESIGN—HORIZ: 5 r. Various sports.

1988. Wildlife Conservation. Jerdon's Courser.
1332 **1065** 1 r. multicoloured . . . 1·00 30

1988. "India '89" International Stamp Exhibition, New Delhi (3rd issue). General Post Offices. As T **1022**. Multicoloured.
1333 4 r. Bangalore G.P.O. . . . 40 35
1334 5 r. Bombay G.P.O. 50 45

1066 "Times of India" Front Page

1988. 150th Anniv of "The Times of India".
1335 **1066** 1 r. 50 black, gold & yell 20 20

1067 "Maulana Abul Kalam Azad" (K. Hebbar)

1988. Birth Centenary of Maulana Abul Kalam Azad (politician).
1336 **1067** 60 p. multicoloured . . 20 20

1068 Nehru

1988. Birth Centenary (1989) of Jawaharlal Nehru (1st issue).
1337 **1068** 60 p. black, orange and green 30 15
1338 – 1 r. multicoloured . . . 35 15
DESIGN—VERT: 1 r. "Jawaharlal Nehru" (Svetoslav Roerich).
See also No. 1393.

1069 Birsa Munda

1988. Birsa Munda (Munda leader) Commem.
1339 **1069** 60 p. brown 20 20

1070 Bhakra Dam

1988. 25th Anniv of Dedication of Bhakra Dam.
1340 **1070** 60 p. red 35 60

1071 Dead Letter Office Cancellations of 1886

1988. "India '89" International Stamp Exhibition, New Delhi (4th series). Postal Cancellations.
1341 **1071** 60 p. brown, blk & red . 25 15
1342 – 6 r. 50 brown and black 1·00 1·00
DESIGN: 6 r. 50, Allahabad–Cawnpore travelling post office handstamp of 1864.

1072 K. M. Munshi

1988. Birth Centenary (1987) of K. M. Munshi (author and politician).
1343 **1072** 60 p. green 20 20

1073 Mannathu Padmanabhan

1074 Lok Sabha Secretariat

1989. Mannathu Padmanabhan (social reformer) Commemoration.
1344 **1073** 60 p. brown 20 20

1989. India's Struggle for Freedom (7th series). As T **909**.
1345 60 p. black, green & orange . 20 30
1346 60 p. orange, green & lilac . 20 50
1347 60 p. black, green & orange . 20 50
1348 60 p. brown, green & orange . 20 50
1349 60 p. brown, green & orange . 20 30
DESIGNS: No. 1345, Hare Krishna Mahtab; 1346, Balasaheb Gangadhar Kher; 1347, Raj Kumari Amrit Kaur; 1348, Saifuddin Kitchlew; 1349, Asaf Ali.

1989. 60th Anniv of Lok Sabha Secretariat (formerly Legislative Assembly Department).
1355 **1074** 60 p. green 20 20

1075 Goddess Durga seated on Lion (5th-cent terracotta plaque)

1076 Baldev Ramji Mirdha

1989. 125th Anniv of Lucknow Museum.
1356 **1075** 60 p. deep blue and blue 20 20

1989. Birth Centenary of Baldev Ramji Mirdha (nationalist).
1357 **1076** 60 p. green 20 20

1077 Girl with Stamp Collection

1989. "India'89" International Stamp Exhibition, New Delhi (5th issue). Philately.
1358 **1077** 60 p. yellow, red & blue 15 10
1359 – 1 r. 50 grey, yellow and black 20 15
1360 – 5 r. red and blue . . . 60 50
1361 – 6 r. 50 black, brown & bl 70 60
DESIGNS: 1 r. 50, Dawk gharry, c. 1842; 5 r. Travancore 1888 2 ch. conch shell stamp; 6 r. 50, Early Indian philatelic magazines.

1078 St. John Bosco and Boy

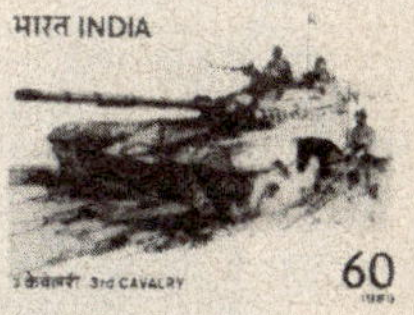

1079 Modern Tank and 19th-century Sowar

1989. St. John Bosco (founder of Salesian Brothers) Commemoration.
1362 **1078** 60 p. red 20 20

1989. 3rd Cavalry Regiment.
1363 **1079** 60 p. multicoloured . . 30 20

1080 Dargah Sharif, Ajmer

1989. Dargah Sharif (Sufi shrine), Ajmer.
1364 **1080** 1 r. multicoloured . . . 20 20

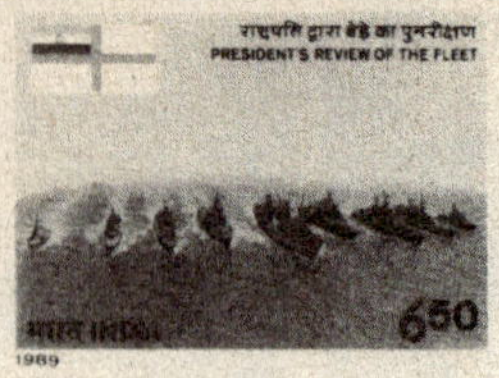

1081 Task Force and Indian Naval Ensign

1989. President's Review of the Fleet.
1365 **1081** 6 r. 50 multicoloured . . 1·25 1·00

1082 Shaheed Laxman Nayak and Barbed Wire Fence

1989. Shaheed Laxman Nayak Commemoration.
1366 **1082** 60 p. brown, grn & orge 20 20

1083 Rao Gopal Singh

1085 Bishnu Ram Medhi

1084 Sydenham College

1989. Rao Gopal Singh Commemoration.
1367 **1083** 60 p. brown 20 20

1989. 75th Anniv (1988) of Sydenham College, Bombay.
1368 **1084** 60 p. black 30 20

1989. Birth Centenary (1988) of Bishnu Ram Medhi (politician).
1369 **1085** 60 p. grn, dp grn & red 30 20

1086 Dr. N. S. Hardikar

1087 "Advaita" in Devanagari Script

1989. Birth Centenary of Dr. Narayana Subbarao Hardikar (nationalist).
1370 **1086** 60 p. brown 20 20

1989. Sankaracharya (philosopher) Commem.
1371 **1087** 60 p. multicoloured . . 20 20

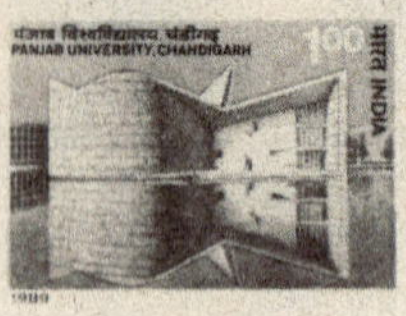

1088 Gandhi Bhavan, Punjab University

1988. Punjab University, Chandigarh.
1372 **1088** 1 r. brown and blue . . 20 20

1089 Scene from Film "Raja Harischandra"

1090 Cactus and Cogwheels

1989. 75 Years of Indian Cinema.
1373 **1089** 60 p. black and yellow 20 20

1989. Centenary of Kirloskar Brothers Ltd (engineering group).
1374 **1090** 1 r. multicoloured . . . 20 20

1091 Early Class and Modern University Students

1989. Centenary of First D.A.V. College.
1375 **1091** 1 r. multicoloured . . . 20 20

1092 Post Office, Dakshin Gangotri Base, Antarctica

1989. Opening of Post Office, Dakshin Gangotri Research Station, Antarctica.
1376 **1092** 1 r. multicoloured . . . 80 20

1093 First Allahabad Bank Building

1989. 125th Anniv (1990) of Allahabad Bank.
1377 **1093** 60 p. purple and blue . 20 20

1094 Nehru inspecting Central Reserve Police, Neemuch, 1954

1989. 50th Anniv of Central Reserve Police Force (formerly Crown Representative's Police).
1378 **1094** 60 p. brown 60 20

1095 Dairy Cow

1989. Centenary of Military Farms.
1379 **1095** 1 r. multicoloured . . . 50 20

1096 Mustafa Kemal Ataturk

1989. 50th Death Anniv (1988) of Mustafa Kemal Ataturk (Turkish statesman).
1380 **1096** 5 r. multicoloured . . . 1·25 45

1097 Dr. S. Radhakrishnan

1989. Birth Centenary (1988) of Dr. Sarvepalli Radhakrishnan (former President).
1381 **1097** 60 p. black 20 20

1098 Football Match

1989. Cent of Mohun Bagan Athletic Club.
1382 **1098** 1 r. multicoloured . . . 40 20

1099 Dr. P. Subbarayan

1100 Shyamji Krishna Varma

1989. Birth Centenary of Dr. P. Subbarayan (politician).
1383 **1099** 60 p. brown 20 20

1989. Shyamji Krishna Varma (nationalist) Commemoration.
1384 **1100** 60 p. brown, grn & red . 20 20

1101 Sayajirao Gaekwad III

1103 Namakkal Kavignar

1102 Symbolic Bird with Letter

1989. 50th Death Anniv of Maharaja Sayajirao Gaekwad III of Baroda.
1385 **1101** 60 p. grey 20 20

1989. "Use Pincode" Campaign.
1386 **1102** 60 p. multicoloured . . 20 20

1989. Namakkal Kavignar (writer) Commem.
1387 **1103** 60 p. black 20 20

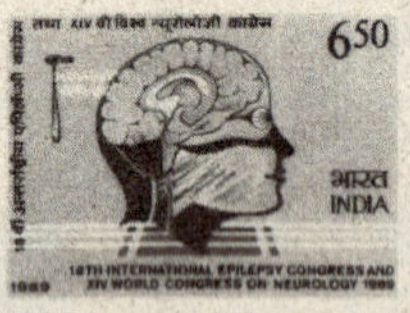

1104 Diagram of Human Brain

1989. 18th International Epilepsy Congress and 14th World Congress on Neurology, New Delhi.
1388 **1104** 6 r. 50 multicoloured . . 2·25 75

1105 Pandita Ramabai and Original Sharada Sadan Building

1989. Pandita Ramabai (women's education pioneer) Commemoration.
1389 **1105** 60 p. brown 30 20

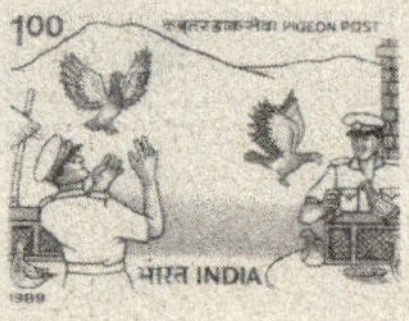

1106 Releasing Homing Pigeons

1989. Orissa Police Pigeon Post.
1390 **1106** 1 r. red 50 20

1107 Acharya Narendra Deo

1108 Acharya Kripalani

1989. Birth Centenary of Acharya Narendra Deo (scholar).
1391 **1107** 60 p. brown, grn & orge 20 20

1989. Acharya Kripalani (politician) Commemoration.
1392 **1108** 60 p. black, green & red 20 20

1109 Nehru

1989. Birth Cent of Jawaharlal Nehru (2nd issue).
1393 **1109** 1 r. brown, deep brown and buff 65 20

1110 Meeting Logo

1111 Sir Gurunath Bewoor

1989. 8th Asian Track and Field Meeting, New Delhi.
1394 **1110** 1 r. black, orange & grn 30 20

1989. Sir Gurunath Bewoor (former Director-General, Posts and Telegraphs) Commemoration.
1395 **1111** 60 p. brown 20 20

1112 Balkrishna Sharma Navin

1113 Abstract Painting of Houses

1989. Balkrishna Sharma Navin (politician and poet) Commemoration.
1396 **1112** 60 p. black 20 20

1989. Cent of Bombay Art Society (1988).
1397 **1113** 1 r. multicoloured . . . 20 20

1114 Lesser Florican

1115 Centenary Logo

1989. Wildlife Conservation. Lesser Florican.
1398 **1114** 2 r. multicoloured . . . 1·50 55

1989. Centenary of Indian Oil Production.
1399 **1115** 60 p. brown 30 20

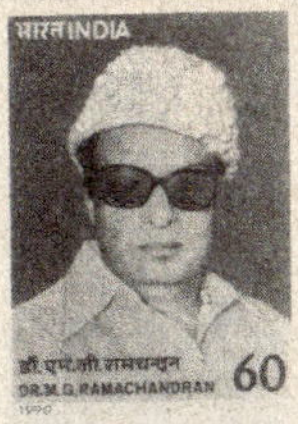

1116 Dr. M. G. Ramachandran

1117 Volunteers working at Sukhna Lake, Chandigarh

1990. Dr. M. G. Ramachandran (former Chief Minister of Tamil Nadu) Commemoration.

1400 **1116** 60 p. brown 40 20

1990. Save Sukhna Lake Campaign.

1401 **1117** 1 r. multicoloured . . . 20 20

1118 Gallantry Medals

1990. Presentation of New Colours to Bombay Sappers.

1402 **1118** 60 p. multicoloured . . 80 80

1119 Indian Chank Shell and Logo

1990. 23rd Annual General Meeting of Asian Development Bank, New Delhi.

1403 **1119** 2 r. black, orange & yell 75 30

1120 Penny Black and Envelope

1990. 150th Anniv of the Penny Black.

1404 **1120** 6 r. multicoloured . . . 1·25 40

1121 Ho Chi-Minh and Vietnamese House

1122 Chaudhary Charan Singh

1990. Birth Centenary of Ho Chi-Minh (Vietnamese leader).

1405 **1121** 2 r. brown and green . . 30 30

1990. 3rd Death Anniv of Chaudhary Charan Singh (former Prime Minister).

1406 **1122** 1 r. brown 20 20

1123 Armed Forces' Badge and Map of Sri Lanka

1124 Wheat

1990. Indian Peace-keeping Operations in Sri Lanka.

1407 **1123** 2 r. multicoloured . . . 30 30

1990. 60th Anniv of Indian Council of Agricultural Research (1989).

1408 **1124** 2 r. black, grn & dp grn 30 30

1125 Khudiram Bose

1127 K. Kelappan

1126 "Life in India" (Tanya Vorontsova)

1990. Khudiram Bose (patriot) Commemoration.

1409 **1125** 1 r. orange, green & red 20 20

1990 Indo-Soviet Friendship. Children's Paintings. Multicoloured.

1410 1 r. Type **1126** . . . . . . 1·50 2·00

1411 6 r. 50 "St. Basil's Cathedral and Kremlin, Moscow" (Sanjay Adhikari) . . . . 1·50 2·00

Stamps in similar designs were also issued by U.S.S.R.

1990. K. Kelappan (social reformer) Commem.

1412 **1127** 1 r. brown 20 20

1128 Girl in Garden

1129 Hand guiding Child's Writing

1990. Year of the Girl Child.

1413 **1128** 1 r. multicoloured . . . 50 30

1990. International Literacy Year.

1414 **1129** 1 r. multicoloured . . . 50 30

1130 Woman using Water Pump

1131 Sunder Lal Sharma

1990. Safe Drinking Water Campaign.

1415 **1130** 4 r. black, red & green 1·25 1·75

1990. 50th Death Anniv of Sunder Lal Sharma (patriot).

1416 **1131** 60 p. red 50 50

1132 Kabbadi

1133 A. K. Gopalan

1990. 11th Asian Games, Peking. Mult.

1417 1 r. Type **1132** 40 20

1418 4 r. Athletics . . . . 1·50 2·00

1419 4 r. Cycling . . . . 1·50 2·00

1420 6 r. 50 Archery . . . . . . 1·75 2·50

1990. Ayillyath Kuttiari Gopalan (social reformer) Commemoration.

1421 **1133** 1 r. brown 50 30

1134 Gurkha Soldier

1135 Suryamall Mishran

1990. 50th Anniv of 3rd and 5th Battalions, 5th Gurkha Rifles.

1422 **1134** 2 r. black and brown . . 1·40 1·60

1990. 75th Birth Anniv of Suryamall Mishran (poet).

1423 **1135** 2 r. brown and orange . 50 65

1136 "Doll and Cat" (Subhash Kumar Nagarajan)

1990. Children's Day.

1424 **1136** 1 r. multicoloured . . . 60 30

1137 Security Post and Border Guard on Camel

1138 Hearts and Flowers

1990. 25th Anniv of Border Security Force.

1425 **1137** 5 r. blue, brown & black 1·50 1·75

1990. Greetings Stamps. Multicoloured.

1426 1 r. Type **1138** 20 15

1427 4 r. Ceremonial elephants (horiz) 50 65

1139 Bikaner

1990. Cities of India. Multicoloured.

1428 4 r. Type **1139** 55 60

1429 5 r. Hyderabad 65 75

1430 6 r. 50 Cuttack . . . . . . 90 1·25

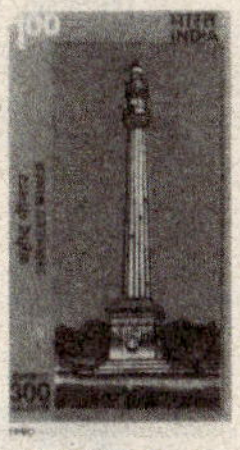

1140 Bhakta Kanakadas and Udipi Temple

1141 Shaheed Minar Monument

1990. Bhakta Kanakadas (mystic and poet) Commemoration.

1431 **1140** 1 r. red 55 30

1990. 300th Anniv of Calcutta.

1432 **1141** 1 r. multicoloured . . . 30 20

1433 – 6 r. black, brown & red 1·25 1·50

DESIGN—HORIZ (44 × 36 mm): 6 r. 18th-century shipping on the Ganges.

1142 Dnyaneshwari (poet) and Manuscript

1143 Madan Mohan Malaviya (founder) and University

1990. 700th Anniv of Dnyaneshwari (spiritual epic).

1434 **1142** 2 r. multicoloured . . . 30 50

1991. 75th Anniv of Banaras Hindu University.

1435 **1143** 1 r. red 30 20

1991. As No. 732 but new face value.

1436 1 r. brown (Gandhi) 10 10

1144 Road Users

1145 Exhibition Emblem

1991. International Traffic Safety Conference, New Delhi.

1437 **1144** 6 r. 50 black, blue & red 75 1·00

1991. 7th Triennale Art Exhibition, New Delhi.

1438 **1145** 6 r. 50 multicoloured . 60 75

1146 Jagannath Sunkersett and Central Railways Headquarters

1147 Tata Memorial Centre

1991. 125th Death Anniv (1990) of Jagannath Sunkersett (educationist and railway pioneer).

1439 **1146** 2 r. blue and red . . . 50 60

1991. 50th Anniv of Tata Memorial Medical Centre.

1440 **1147** 2 r. brown and stone . 30 40

1148 River Dolphin

1991. Endangered Marine Mammals.

1441 **1148** 4 r. brown, blue & green 1·50 1·50

1442 – 6 r. 50 multicoloured . 2·00 2·00

DESIGN: 6 r. 50, Sea cow.

1149 Drugs

1150 Hand, Bomb Explosion and Dove

1991. International Conference on Drug Abuse, Calcutta.

1443 **1149** 5 r. violet and red . . . 1·60 1·60

1991. World Peace.

1444 **1150** 6 r. 50 blk, lt brn & brn 75 1·00

1151 Remote Sensing Satellite "IA"

1152 Babu Jagjivan Ram

1991. Launch of Indian Remote Sensing Satellite "IA".

1445 **1151** 6 r. 50 brown and blue 60 85

1991. Babu Jagjivan Ram (politician) Commemoration.

1446 **1152** 1 r. brown 20 20

1153 Dr. B. R. Ambedkar and Demonstration

1991. Birth Centenary of Dr. Bhimrao Ramji Ambedkar (social reformer).
1447 **1153** 1 r. brown and blue . . 30 20

1154 Valar Dance

1991. Tribal Dances. Multicoloured.
1448 2 r. 50 Type **1154** 50 40
1449 4 r. Kayang 70 80
1450 5 r. Hozagiri 80 90
1451 6 r. 50 Velakali . . . . 1·00 1·40

1155 Ariyakudi Ramanuja Iyengar and Temples

1156 Karpoori Thakur

1991. Ariyakudi Ramanuja Iyengar (singer and composer) Commemoration.
1452 **1155** 2 r. brown and green . . 50 65

1991. Jan Nayak Karpoori Thakur (politician and social reformer) Commemoration.
1453 **1156** 1 r. brown 20 20

1157 Emperor Penguins

1991. 30th Anniv of Antarctic Treaty. Mult.
1454 5 r. Type **1157** . . . . 1·75 2·00
1455 6 r. 50 Antarctic map and pair of Adelie penguins . . . . 1·75 2·00
Nos. 1454/5 were printed together, se-tenant, forming a composite design.

1158 Rashtrapati Bhavan Building, New Delhi

1991. 60th Anniv of New Delhi. Multicoloured.
1456 5 r. Type **1158** . . . . 1·00 1·40
1457 6 r. 50 New Delhi monuments 1·00 1·40
Nos. 1456/7 were printed together, se-tenant, forming a composite design.

1159 Sri Ram Sharma Acharya

1991. Sri Ram Sharma Acharya (social reformer) Commemoration.
1458 **1159** 1 r. green and red . . . 20 20

1160 "Shankar awarded Padma Vibhushan" (cartoon)

1991. Keshav Shankar Pillai (cartoonist) Commemoration.
1459 **1160** 4 r. brown . . . . . . 1·00 1·40
1460 – 6 r. 50 lilac . . . . . . 1·40 1·75
DESIGN—VERT: 6 r. 50, "The Big Show".

1161 Sriprakash and Kashi Vidyapith University

1162 Gopinath Bardoloi

1991. 20th Death Anniv of Sriprakash (politician).
1461 **1161** 2 r. brown & light brown 30 30

1991. Birth Centenary (1990) of Gopinath Bardoloi (Assamese politician).
1462 **1162** 1 r. lilac 20 20

1163 Rajiv Gandhi

1991. Rajiv Gandhi (Congress Party leader) Commemoration.
1463 **1163** 1 r. multicoloured . . . 40 40

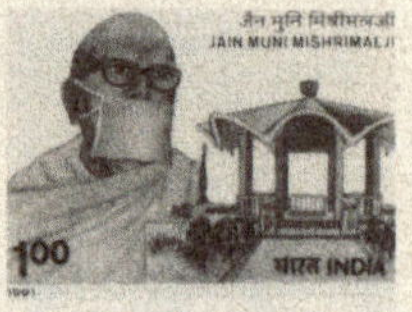

1164 Muni Mishrimalji and Memorial

1991. Birth Centenary of Muni Mishrimalji (Jain religious leader).
1464 **1164** 1 r. brown 30 20

1165 Mahadevi Verma (poetess) and "Varsha"

1991. Hindu Writers.
1465 **1165** 2 r. black and blue 15 25
1466 – 2 r. black and blue 15 25
DESIGN: No. 1466, Jayshankar Prasad (poet and dramatist) and scene from "Kamayani".

1166 Parliament House and C.P.A. Emblem

1991. 37th Commonwealth Parliamentary Association Conference, New Delhi.
1467 **1166** 6 r. 50 blue and brown 40 60

1167 Frog

1168 "Cymbidium aloifolium"

1991. Greetings Stamps.
1468 **1167** 1 r. green and red . . . 20 40
1469 – 6 r. 50 red and green . . 35 55
DESIGN: 6 r. 50, Symbolic bird carrying flower.

1991. Orchids. Multicoloured.
1470 1 r. Type **1168** 30 15
1471 2 r. 50 "Paphiopedilum venustum" 35 35
1472 3 r. "Aerides crispum" . . . 40 50
1473 4 r. "Cymbidium bicolour" . . 50 65
1474 5 r. "Vanda spathulata" . . . 55 70
1475 6 r. 50 "Cymbidium devonianum" . . . . 70 1·00

1169 Gurkha Soldier in Battle Dress

1170 Couple on Horse (embroidery)

1991. 90th Anniv of 2nd Battalion, Third Gurkha Rifles.
1476 **1169** 4 r. multicoloured . . . 1·50 1·50

1991. 3rd Death Anniv of Kamaladevi Chattopadhyaya (founder of All India Handicrafts Board).
1477 **1170** 1 r. lake, red & yellow . 40 20
1478 – 6 r. 50 multicoloured . . 1·50 1·75
DESIGN: 6 r. 50, Traditional puppet.

1171 Chithira Tirunal and Temple Sculpture

1172 "Children in Traditional Costume" (Arpi Snehalbhai Shah)

1991. Chithira Tirunal Bala Rama Varma (former Maharaja of Travancore) Commemoration.
1479 **1171** 2 r. violet 65 75

1991. Children's Day.
1480 **1172** 1 r. multicoloured . . . 70 30

1173 Mounted Sowar and Tanks

1991. 70th Anniv (1992) of the 18th Cavalry Regiment.
1481 **1173** 6 r. 50 multicoloured . . 2·00 2·50

1174 Kites

1175 Sports on Bricks

1991. India Tourism Year.
1482 **1174** 6 r. 50 multicoloured . . . 60 1·00

1991. International Conference on Youth Tourism, New Delhi.
1483 **1175** 6 r. 50 multicoloured . . 1·10 1·50

1176 "Mozart at Piano" (unfinished painting, J. Lange)

1177 Homeless Family

1991. Death Bicentenary of Mozart.
1484 **1176** 6 r. 50 multicoloured . . 1·50 2·00

1991. South Asian Association for Regional Co-operation Year of Shelter.
1485 **1177** 4 r. brown and ochre . 55 70

1178 People running on Heart

1179 "Sidhartha with an Injured Bird" (Asit Kumar Haldar)

1991. "Run for Your Heart" Marathon, New Delhi.
1486 **1178** 1 r. black, grey and red 20 20

1991. Birth Centenary (1990) of Asit Kumar Haldar (artist).
1487 **1179** 2 r. yellow, red and black 30 50

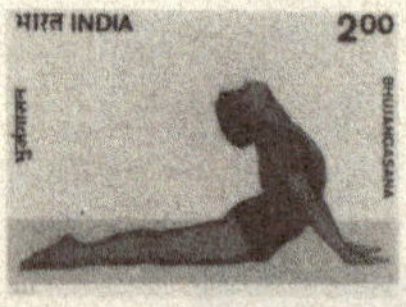

1180 Bhujangasana

1181 Y.M.C.A. Logo

1991. Yoga Exercises. Multicoloured.
1488 2 r. Type **1180** 20 25
1489 5 r. Dhanurasana 40 55
1490 6 r. 50 Ustrasana 50 70
1491 10 r. Utthita trikonasana . . 85 1·25

1992. Centenary (1991) of National Council of Young Men's Christian Association.
1492 **1181** 1 r. red and blue . . . 20 20

1182 Madurai Temple Tower and Hooghly River Bridge

1183 Goat Seal from Harappa Culture, 2500 to 1500 B.C.

1992. 14th Congress of International Association for Bridge and Structural Engineering, New Delhi.
1493 **1182** 2 r. brown, red and blue 45 65
1494 – 2 r. brown, red and blue 45 65
DESIGN: No. 1494, Gate, Sanchi Stupa and Hall of Nations, New Delhi.

1992. 5th International Goat Conference, New Delhi.
1495 **1183** 6 r. blue and brown . . 1·50 2·00

1184 Early 19th-century Letter with Mail Pouch and National Archives Building, New Delhi

1185 Krushna Chandra Gajapathi

1992. Centenary (1991) of National Archives.
1496 **1184** 6 r. multicoloured . . . 50 65

1992. Krushna Chandra Gajapathi (former Chief Minister of Orissa) Commemoration.
1497 **1185** 1 r. lilac 15 15

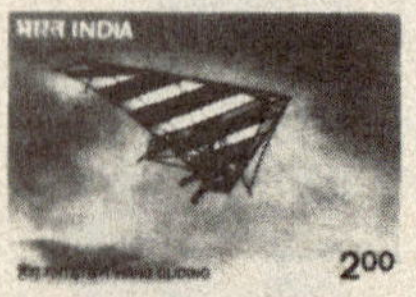

1186 Vijay Singh Pathik

1187 Hang-gliding

1992. Vijay Singh Pathik (writer) Commem.
1498 **1186** 1 r. brown 15 15

1992. Adventure Sports. Multicoloured.
1499 2 r. Type **1187** 25 20
1500 4 r. Windsurfing 50 60
1501 5 r. River rafting 60 70
1502 11 r. Skiing 1·25 2·00

1188 Henry Gidney and Anglo-Indians

1992. 50th Death Anniv of Sir Henry Gidney (ophthalmologist).
1503 **1188** 1 r. black and blue 30 15

1189 Telecommunications Training Centre, Jabalpur **1190** Sardar Udham Singh

1992. 50th Anniv of Telecommunications Training Centre, Jabalpur.
1504 **1189** 1 r. bistre 20 15

1992. Sardar Udham Singh (patriot) Commemoration.
1505 **1190** 1 r. black and brown 20 15

1191 Men's Discus **1192** Spinning Wheel Emblem

1992. Olympic Games, Barcelona. Mult.
1506 1 r. Type **1191** 30 10
1507 6 r. Women's gymnastics 80 90
1508 8 r. Men's hockey 1·75 2·00
1509 11 r. Boxing 1·75 2·25

1992. 50th Anniv of "Quit India" Movement.
1510 **1192** 1 r. black and pink 60 30
1511 – 2 r. black, brown & grey 1·40 1·60
DESIGN: 2 r. Mahatma Gandhi and mantra.

1193 Treating Casualty

1992. 50th Anniv of 60th Parachute Field Ambulance.
1512 **1193** 1 r. multicoloured 1·00 40

1194 Dr. S. R. Ranganathan and Madras University

1992. Birth Centenary of Shiyali Ramamrita Ranganathan (librarian).
1513 **1194** 1 r. blue 55 30

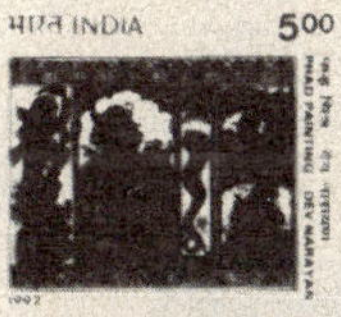

1195 "Dev Narayan" **1196** Hanuman Prasad Poddar

1992. Phad Scroll Paintings from Rajasthan.
1514 **1195** 5 r. multicoloured 55 70

1992. Hanuman Prasad Poddar (editor) Commemoration.
1515 **1196** 1 r. green 15 15

1197 Mikoyan Guerevich MiG-29 Fighter and Ilyushin Il-76 Transport **1198** Lighting Candle

1992. 60th Anniv of Indian Air Force. Mult.
1516 1 r. Type **1197** 40 60
1517 10 r. MiG-27 fighter and Westland Wapiti biplane 1·00 1·25

1992. 150th Anniv of Sisters of Jesus and Mary's Arrival in India.
1518 **1198** 1 r. blue and grey 15 15

1199 "Sun" (Harshit Prashant Patel) **1200** Yogiji Maharaj

1992. Children's Day.
1519 **1199** 1 r. multicoloured 20 15

1992. Birth Centenary of Yogiji Maharaj (Hindu reformer).
1520 **1200** 1 r. blue 30 15

1201 Army Service Corps Transport

1992. Army Service Corps Commemoration.
1521 **1201** 1 r. multicoloured 1·00 40

1202 Stephen Smith and Early Rocket Post Covers

1992. Birth Centenary (1991) of Stephen Smith (rocket mail pioneer).
1522 **1202** 11 r. multicoloured 90 1·25

1203 Electricity Pylons, Farmers and Crops

1992. 25th Anniv of Haryana State.
1523 **1203** 2 r. red, dp green & grn 15 15

1204 Madanlal Dhingra **1205** Osprey

1992. Madanlal Dhingra (revolutionary) Commemoration.
1524 **1204** 1 r. brown, red & grn 30 15

1992. Birds of Prey. Multicoloured.
1525 2 r. Type **1205** 75 50
1526 6 r. Peregrine falcon 1·00 1·00
1527 8 r. Lammergeier 1·25 1·60
1528 11 r. Golden eagle 1·50 1·90

1206 Pandit Ravishankar Shukla **1208** Fakirmohan Senapati

1207 William Carey

1992. Pandit Ravishankar Shukla (social reformer) Commemoration.
1529 **1206** 1 r. purple 15 15

1993. Bicent of William Carey's Appointment as Baptist Missionary to India.
1530 **1207** 6 r. multicoloured 90 1·00

1993. Fakirmohan Senapati Commemoration.
1531 **1208** 1 r. red 30 15

1209 Workers and C.S.I.R emblem

1993. 50th Anniv of Council of Scientific and Industrial Research.
1532 **1209** 1 r. purple 30 15

1210 Parachute Drop and Field Gun

1993. 50th Anniv of 9th Parachute Field Artillery Regiment.
1533 **1210** 1 r. multicoloured 1·00 30

1211 Westland Wapiti Biplane

1993. 60th Anniv of No. 1 Squadron, Indian Air Force.
1534 **1211** 1 r. multicoloured 1·00 30

1212 Rahul Sankrityayan

1993. Birth Centenary of Rahul Sankrityayan (politician).
1535 **1212** 1 r. black, cinnamon and brown 15 15

1213 Parliament Building and Emblem

1993. 89th Inter-Parliamentary Union Conference, New Delhi.
1536 **1213** 1 r. black 15 15

1214 Neral Matheran Railway Tank Locomotive, 1905

1993. Mountain Locomotives. Multicoloured.
1537 1 r. Type **1214** 60 20
1538 6 r. Darjeeling and Himalayan Railway, 1889 1·25 1·25
1539 8 r. Nilgiri Mountain Railway, 1914 1·40 1·60
1540 11 r. Kalka–Simla Railway, 1934 1·90 2·25

1215 Students and College Building

1993. Centenary of Meerut College.
1541 **1215** 1 r. black and brown 15 15

1216 Mahalanobis and Office Block

1993. Prasanta Chandra Mahalanobis Commemoration.
1542 **1216** 1 r. brown 15 15

1217 Bombay Town Hall

1993. Centenary of Bombay Municipal Corporation.
1543 **1217** 2 r. multicoloured 20 30

1218 Abdul Ghaffar Khan and Mountainside

1993. Abdul Ghaffar Khan Commemoration.
1544 **1218** 1 r. multicoloured 15 15

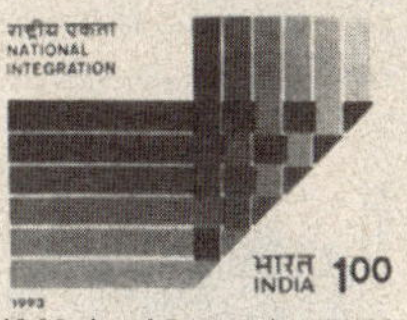

1219 National Integration Emblem

1993. National Integration Campaign.
1545 **1219** 1 r. orange and green 15 15

1220 Dadabhai Naoroji and Houses of Parliament, London **1221** Swami Vivekananda and Art Institute, Chicago

1993. Centenary of Dadabhai Naoroji's Election to the House of Commons.
1546 **1220** 6 r. multicoloured 45 60

1993. Centenary of Swami Vivekananda's Chicago Address.
1547 **1221** 2 r. orange and grey 40 40

1222 "Lagerstroemia speciosa" **1223** College Building and Emblem

1993. Flowering Trees.

1548 **1222** 1 r. red, green & brn . . 20 15
1549 – 6 r. multicoloured . . . 40 55
1550 – 8 r. multicoloured . . . 55 70
1551 – 11 r. multicoloured . . 75 1·00

DESIGNS: 6 r. "Cochlospermum religiosum"; 8 r. "Erythrina variegata"; 11 r. "Thespesia populnea".

1993. 50th Anniv of College of Military Engineering, Pune.

1552 **1223** 2 r. multicoloured . . . 20 30

1224 Dr. Dwaram Venkataswamy Naidu playing Violin **1225** Children on Elephant

1993. Birth Centenary of Dwaram Venkataswamy Naidu (violinist).

1553 **1224** 1 r. red 20 20

1993. Children's Day.

1554 **1225** 1 r. multicoloured . . . 20 20

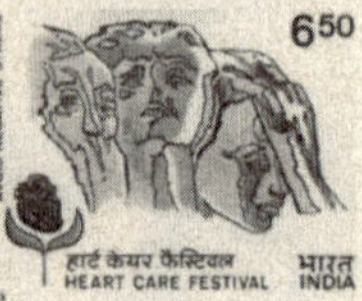

1226 People with Stress

1993. Heart Care Festival.

1555 **1226** 6 r. 50 multicoloured . . 60 70

1227 Dr. Kotnis performing Operation

1993. Dr. Dwarkanath Kotnis (surgeon) Commemoration.

1556 **1227** 1 r. black 20 20

1228 Tea Symbol

1993. Indian Tea Production.

1557 **1228** 6 r. green and red . . . 50 65

1229 Papal Seminary Arms and Building

1993. Centenary of Papal Seminary, Pune.

1558 **1229** 6 r. multicoloured . . . 50 65

1230 Meghnad Saha and Eclipse of the Sun

1993. Meghnad Saha (astronomer) Commem.

1559 **1230** 1 r. blue 30 20

1231 Speedpost Letter and Arrows circling Globe

1993. Inpex '93 National Stamp Exn, Calcutta. Multicoloured.

1560 1 r. Type **1231** 15 15
1561 2 r. "Custom-house Wharf, Calcutta" (Sir Charles D'Oyly) 25 35

1232 Dinanath Mangeshkar **1233** Nargis Dutt

1993. Dinanath Mangeshkar Commem.

1562 **1232** 1 r. red 15 15

1993. Nargis Dutt Commemoration.

1563 **1233** 1 r. red 15 15

1234 S. C. Bose inspecting Troops

1993. 50th Anniv of Indian National Army.

1564 **1234** 1 r. grn, dp grn & red . 30 20

1235 Satyendra Nath Bose and Equation

1994. Birth Centenary of Satyendra Nath Bose (scientist).

1565 **1235** 1 r. brown 30 15

1236 Dr. Sampurnanand

1994. Dr. Sampurnanand (politician) Commemoration.

1566 **1236** 1 r. brown, green and red 15 10

1237 Scene from "Pather Panchali" (½-size illustration)

1994. Satyajit Ray (film director) Commemoration. Multicoloured.

1567 6 r. Type **1237** . . . . 1·00 1·25
1568 11 r. Satyajit Ray and Oscar (35 × 35 mm) . . . . . . 1·25 1·50

1238 Dr. Bhatnagar and University Building

1994. Dr. Shanti Swarup Bhatnagar (scientist) Commemoration.

1569 **1238** 1 r. blue 15 10

1239 Prajapita Brahma and Memorial

1994. 25th Death Anniv of Prajapita Brahma (social reformer).

1570 **1239** 1 r. lilac and blue . . . 15 10

1240 "Window" (K. Subramanyan) **1241** Agricultural Products and Tea Garden

1994. 8th Triennale Art Exhibition, New Delhi.

1571 **1240** 6 r. orange, red and blue 40 60

1994. Centenary of United Planters' Association of Southern India.

1572 **1241** 2 r. multicoloured . . . 20 20

1242 Indian Family **1242a** Sanchi Stupa

1994.

1573 **1242** 75 p. brown and red . 10 10
1574 – 1 r. mauve and green . 10 10
1575 – 3 r. purple 15 20
1576 **1242a** 5 r. brown and green . 15 20

DESIGNS (as T **1242**)—HORIZ: 1 r. Family outside home. VERT: 3 r. Baby and drop of polio vaccine.

1243 Rani Rashmoni on River Bank

1994. Birth Bicentenary of Rani Rashmoni.

1589 **1243** 1 r. brown 15 10

1244 Indians releasing Peace Doves

1994. 75th Anniv of Jallianwala Bagh Massacre, Amritsar.

1590 **1244** 1 r. black and red . . . 15 10

1245 Chandra Singh Garhwali

1994. 15th Death Anniv of Chandra Singh Garhwali (nationalist).

1591 **1245** 1 r. green and orange . . 15 10

1246 Emblems and National Flag **1247** Silhouette of Drummer and Logo

1994. 75th Anniv of I.L.O.

1592 **1246** 6 r. multicoloured . . . 40 60

1994. 50th Anniv of Indian People's Theatre Association.

1593 **1247** 2 r. black, green and gold 15 15

1248 Statue of Sepoy **1249** Institute Building and Emblem

1994. Bicentenary of 4th Battalion, The Madras Regiment.

1594 **1248** 6 r. 50 multicoloured . . 55 65

1994. Bicentenary of Institute of Mental Health, Madras.

1595 **1249** 2 r. red and blue . . . 15 15

1250 Mahatma Gandhi and Indian Flag **1251** Symbols of Cancer

1994. 125th Birth Anniv of Mahatma Gandhi. Multicoloured.

1596 6 r. Type **1250** . . . . . . 1·00 1·25
1597 11 r. Aspects of Gandhi's life on flag (69 × 34 mm) . . . . 1·25 1·50

Nos. 1596/7 were printed together, se-tenant, forming a composite design.

1994. 16th International Cancer Congress, New Delhi.

1598 **1251** 6 r. multicoloured . . . 55 65

1252 Human Resources Emblem

1994. Human Resource Development World Conference, New Delhi.

1599 **1252** 6 r. blue, red and azure 55 65

1253 "Me and My Pals" (Namarata Amit Shah) **1254** Family and Emblem

1994. Children's Day.

1600 **1253** 1 r. multicoloured . . . 10 10

1994. International Year of the Family.

1601 **1254** 2 r. multicoloured . . . 20 15

1255 "Taj Mahal" (illustration from Badsha Nama)

1994. Khuda Bakhsh Oriental Public Library, Patna, Commemoration.

1602 **1255** 6 r. multicoloured . . . 4·00 1·00

1256 Andaman Teal

1994. Endangered Water Birds. Multicoloured.
1603 1 r. Type 1256 . . . . 5·00 2·00
1604 6 r. Eastern white stork . . . 8·00 4·00
1605 8 r. Black-necked crane . . . 9·00 4·50
1606 11 r. Pink-headed duck . . . 11·00 6·00
It is reported that Nos. 1603/6 were withdrawn shortly after issue.

1257 J. R. D. Tata and Aspects of Industrial Symbols

1994. J. R. D. Tata (industrialist) Commemoration.
1607 1257 2 r. multicoloured . . . 30 30

1258 School Building and Computer Class

1994. Centenary of Calcutta Blind School.
1608 1258 2 r. red, brown and cinnamon 20 15

1259 Begum Akhtar

1261 Cavalryman, Infantryman and Dog Handler

1260 College Building

1994. 80th Birth Anniv of Begum Akhtar (singer).
1609 1259 2 r. multicoloured . . . 4·00 4·00

1994. 125th Anniv of St. Xavier's College, Bombay.
1610 1260 2 r. brown and blue . . 15 15

1994. 215th Anniv of Remount Veterinary Corps.
1611 1261 6 r. multicoloured . . . 75 60

1262 College Building

1994. Bicentenary of College of Engineering, Guindy, Madras.
1612 1262 2 r. red, brown and black 15 10

1263 Righthand Ornament of Bronze Stand

1265 Statue of King Rajaraja Chola

1264 "200" and Aspects of Postal Service (½-size illustration)

1994. Centenary of Baroda Museum.
1613 1263 6 r. yellow and brown 3·00 75
1614 – 11 r. yellow and brown 3·00 75
DESIGN: 11 r. Bronze Rishabhanatha statue of Buddha on stand.

1994. Bicentenary of Bombay General Post Office.
1615 1264 6 r. multicoloured . . 6·00 1·50

1995. 8th International Conference-Seminar of Tamil Studies, Thanjavur.
1616 1265 2 r. blue, ultramarine and black . . . . 3·50 75

1266 Globe and Emblem

1267 Chhotu Ram

1995. 60th Anniv of National Science Academy.
1617 1266 6 r. multicoloured . . 50 60

1995. Chhotu Ram (social reformer) Commem.
1618 1267 1 r. brown . . . . . 1·00 25

1268 Film Reel and Globe

1995. Centenary of Cinema. Multicoloured.
1619 6 r. Type 1268 . . . . 60 70
1620 11 r. Film reel and early equipment 80 90

1269 Symbolic Hands and Children

1270 Prithviraj Kapoor and Mask

1995. South Asian Association for Regional Cooperation Youth Year.
1621 1269 2 r. multicoloured . . 20 20

1995. 50th Anniv of Prithvi Theatre.
1622 1270 2 r. multicoloured . . 3·75 75

1271 Field-Marshal Cariappa

1272 Textile Pattern

1995. Field-Marshal K. Cariappa Commemoration.
1623 1271 2 r. multicoloured . . 30 20

1995. "TEX-STYLES INDIA '95" Fair, Bombay.
1624 1272 2 r. brown, buff and red 20 20

1273 Rafi Ahmed Kidwai

1274 K. L. Saigal, Film Reel and Gramophone

1995. Birth Centenary (1994) of Rafi Ahmed Kidwai (politician).
1625 1273 1 r. brown 15 10

1995. 90th Birth Anniv of K. L. Saigal (singer).
1626 1274 5 r. brown, grey and black 75 80

1275 R. S. Ruikar

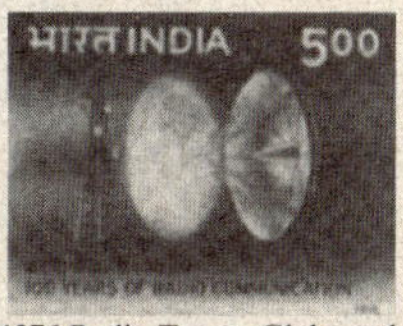

1276 Radio Tower, Globe and Dish Aerial

1995. Birth Centenary of R. S. Ruikar (trade unionist).
1627 1275 1 r. brown 15 10

1995. Centenary of Telecommunications.
1628 1276 5 r. multicoloured . . . 60 70

1277 Leaves and Symbolic Houses

1995. Delhi Development Authority.
1629 1277 2 r. multicoloured . . . 20 20

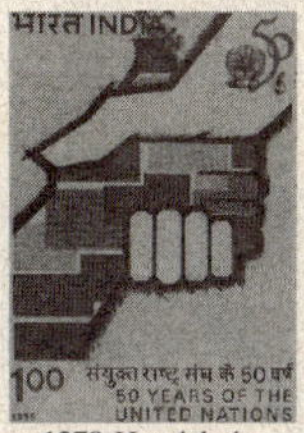

1278 Handshake

1279 Colonnade on Book Cover

1995. 50th Anniv of United Nations. Multicoloured.
1630 1 r. Type 1278 . . . . 10 10
1631 6 r. Work of U.N. Agencies . 45 55

1995. Centenary of Bharti Bhawan Library, Allahabad.
1632 1279 6 r. black, brown and red 55 65

1280 Globe showing South-east Asia

1281 "75" and Taurus Formation Sign

1995. 25th Anniv of Asian-Pacific Postal Training Centre, Bangkok.
1633 1280 10 r. multicoloured . . 80 90

1995. 75th Anniv of Area Army Headquarters, Delhi.
1634 1281 2 r. multicoloured . . . 30 20

1282 Louis Pasteur in Laboratory (from painting by Edelfelt)

1995. Death Centenary of Louis Pasteur (chemist).
1635 1282 5 r. black and stone . . 60 70

1283 La Martiniere College, Lucknow

1284 Gandhi in South Africa

1995. 150th Anniv of La Martiniere College, Lucknow.
1636 1283 2 r. multicoloured . . 20 20

1995. India–South Africa Co-operation. 125th Birth Anniv (1994) of Mahatma Gandhi.
1637 1284 1 r. red 25 25
1638 – 2 r. red 30 30
DESIGN: 2 r. Gandhi wearing dhoti.

1285 Ears of Grain, "50" and Emblem on Globe

1286 P. M. Thevar

1995. 50th Anniv of F.A.O.
1640 1285 5 r. multicoloured . . 60 70

1995. Pasumpon Muthuramalingam Thevar (social reformer) Commemoration.
1641 1286 1 r. red 15 10

1287 W. C. Rontgen

1288 Children in Circle

1995. 150th Birth Anniv of W. C. Rontgen (discoverer of X-rays).
1642 1287 6 r. multicoloured . . 65 75

1995. Children's Day.
1643 1288 1 r. multicoloured . . 20 10

1289 Sitar

1290 Jat War Memorial, Bareilly

1995. Communal Harmony Campaign.
1644 1289 2 r. multicoloured . . 40 20

1995. Bicentenary of Jat Regiments.
1645 1290 5 r. multicoloured . . 65 75

1291 Men of Rajputana Rifles

1995. 175th Anniv of 5th (Napier's) Battalion, Rajputana Rifles.
1646 1291 5 r. multicoloured . . 70 70

1292 Sant Tukdoji Maharaj and Rural Meeting

1293 Dr. Yellapragada Subbarow

1995. Sant Tukdoji Maharaj Commemoration.
1647 1292 1 r. brown 15 10
Although dated "1993", No. 1647 was not issued until the date quoted above.

1995. Dr. Yellapragada Subbarow (pharmaceutical scientist) Commemoration.
1648 1293 1 r. brown 30 10

1294 Pres. Giani Zail Singh

1295 Dargah of Ala Hazrat Barelvi

1995. 1st Death Anniv of Pres. Giani Zail Singhn.
1649 **1294** 1 r. multicoloured . . 15 10

1995. 75th Death Anniv of Ala Hazrat Barelvi (Moslem scholar).
1650 **1295** 1 r. multicoloured . . 15 10

1296 Tata Institute Building

1996. 50th Anniv (1995) of Tata Institute of Fundamental Research.
1651 **1296** 2 r. multicoloured . . 20 20

1297 Kasturba Gandhi

1298 Sectioned Heart

1996. 50th Anniv of the Kasturba Trust.
1652 **1297** 1 r. grey, green and red 15 10

1996. 100 Years of Cardiac Surgery.
1653 **1298** 5 r. multicoloured . . 60 70

1299 C. K. Nayudu

1300 "Vasant" (Spring) (Ragini Basanti)

1996. Cricketers. Multicoloured.
1654 2 r. Type **1299** 20 20
1655 2 r. Vinoo Mankad 20 20
1656 2 r. Deodhar 20 20
1657 2 r. Vijay Merchant 20 20

1996. Miniature Paintings of the Seasons. Multicoloured.
1658 5 r. Type **1300** 50 60
1659 5 r. "Greeshma" (Summer) (Jyestha) 50 60
1660 5 r. "Varsha" (Monsoon) (Rag Megh Malbar) 50 60
1661 5 r. "Hemant" (Winter) (Pausha) 50 60

1301 Kunjilal Dubey

1302 Morarji Desai

1996. Kunjilal Dubey Commemoration.
1662 **1301** 1 r. brown & chocolate 15 10

1996. Birth Centenary of Morarji Desai (former Prime Minister) (1st issue).
1663 **1302** 1 r. red 20 10
See also No. 1702.

1303 Blood Pheasant

1996. Himalayan Ecology. Multicoloured.
1664 5 r. Type **1303** 50 60
1665 5 r. Markhor (goat) 50 60
1666 5 r. "Meconopsis horridula" (Tsher Gnoin) (plant) . . 50 60
1667 5 r. "Saussurea simpsoniana" (Sunflower) 50 60

1304 S.K.C.G. College Building

1305 Muhammad Ismail Sahib

1996. Centenary of S.K.C.G. College, Gajapati.
1669 **1304** 1 r. brown and cream 15 10

1996. Birth Centenary of Muhammad Ismail Sahib (Moslem politician).
1670 **1305** 1 r. purple 15 10

1306 Modern Stadium and Ancient Athens

1307 Sister Alphonsa

1996. Olympic Games, Atlanta. Multicoloured.
1671 5 r. Type **1306** 35 40
1672 5 r. Hand holding Olympic torch 35 40

1996. 50th Death Anniv of Sister Alphonsa.
1673 **1307** 1 r. black and blue . . 15 10

1308 "Communications"

1309 Sir Pherozeshah Mehta

1996. 125th Anniv of Videsh Sanchar Nigam Limited (telecommunications company).
1674 **1308** 5 r. multicoloured . . 35 40

1996. 150th Birth Anniv of Sir Pherozeshah Mehta (politician).
1675 **1309** 1 r. blue 15 10

1310 Ahilyabai

1311 Chembai Vaidyanatha Bhagavathar

1996. Death Bicentenary (1995) of Ahilyabai (ruler of Holkar).
1676 **1310** 2 r. brown and deep brown 20 20

1996. Birth Centenary of Chembai Vaidanatha Bhagavathar (musician).
1677 **1311** 1 r. brown and green . 15 10

1312 Red Junglefowl Cockerel

1996. 20th World Poultry Congress, New Delhi.
1678 **1312** 5 r. multicoloured . . . 50 55

1313 Rani Gaidinliu

1314 Nath Pai

1996. Rani Gaidinliu (Naga leader) Commemoration.
1679 **1313** 1 r. blue 15 10

1996. 25th Death Anniv of Nath Pai (politician).
1680 **1314** 1 r. blue 15 10

1315 Exhibition Logo

1317 Jananayak Debeswar Sarmah

1316 Historic Steam Locomotives

1996. INDEPEX '97 International Stamp Exhibition, New Delhi (1st issue).
1681 **1315** 2 r. gold and purple . . 20 20
See also Nos. 1713/16, 1722/5, 1741/4 and 1758/61.

1996. 25th Anniv of National Rail Museum.
1682 **1316** 5 r. multicoloured . . . 50 55

1996. Birth Centenary of Jananayak Debeswar Sarmah (politician).
1683 **1317** 2 r. brown and deep brown 20 20

1318 Monument and Sikh Sentry

1996. 150th Anniv of Sikh Regiment.
1684 **1318** 5 r. multicoloured . . . 50 55

1319 Dr. Salim Ali

1996. Birth Centenary of Salim Ali (ornithologist). Multicoloured.
1685 8 r. Type **1319** 70 80
1686 11 r. Storks at nest . . . . . 90 1·10
Nos. 1685/6 were printed together, se-tenant, with the backgrounds forming a composite design.

1320 "Indian Village" (child's painting)

1996. Children's Day.
1687 **1320** 8 r. multicoloured . . . 50 55

1321 Seeds in a Test-tube

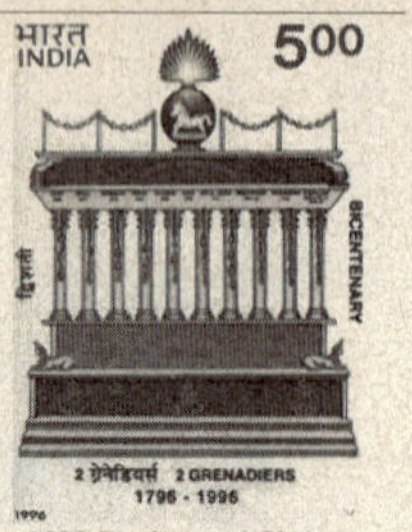
1322 Regimental Shrine

1996. 2nd International Crop Science Congress.
1688 **1321** 2 r. multicoloured . . 20 20

1996. Bicentenary of 2nd Battalion, Grenadiers.
1689 **1322** 5 r. multicoloured . . 50 55

1323 Woman writing

1324 Abai Konunbaev

1996. 10th Anniv of South Asian Association for Regional Co-operation (S.A.A.R.C.).
1690 **1323** 11 r. multicoloured . . 65 70

1996. 150th Birth Anniv (1995) of Abai Konunbaev (Kazakh poet).
1691 **1324** 5 r. chestnut, brown and lilac 35 40

1325 Buglers in front of Memorial

1327 Victorian Doctors performing Operation

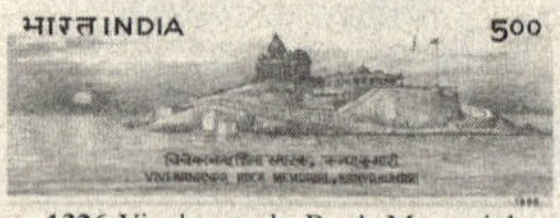
1326 Vivekananda Rock Memorial (½-size illustration)

1996. 25th Anniv of the Liberation of Bangladesh.
1692 **1325** 2 r. multicoloured . . 20 20

1996. 25th Anniv of Vivekananda Rock Memorial, Kanyakumari.
1693 **1326** 5 r. multicoloured . . 50 55

1996. 150th Anniv of Anaesthetics.
1694 **1327** 5 r. multicoloured . . 50 55

1328 Roorkee University Buildings

1329 Dr. Vrindavanlal Verma

1997. 150th Anniv of Roorkee University.
1695 **1328** 8 r. multicoloured . . 60 70

1997. Dr. Vrindavanlal Verma (writer) Commemoration.
1696 **1329** 2 r. red 20 20

1330 Field Post Office

1331 Subhas Chandra Bose

1997. 25th Anniv of Army Postal Service Corps.
1697 **1330** 5 r. multicoloured . . 35 40

1997. Birth Centenary of Subhas Chandra Bose (nationalist).
1698 **1331** 1 r. brown 20 10

1332 Jose Marti

1333 Conference Logo

1997. Jose Marti (Cuban writer) Commemoration.
1699 **1332** 11 r. black and pink . 65 70

1996. "Towards Partnership between Men and Women in Politics" Inter-Parliamentary Conference, New Delhi.
1700 **1333** 5 r. multicoloured . . 35 40

1334 St. Andrew's Church

1335 Morarji Desai

1997. St. Andrew's Church, Egmore, Madras Commemoration.
1701 **1334** 8 r. multicoloured . . 50 55

1997. Birth Centenary of Morarji Desai (former Prime Minister) (2nd issue).
1702 **1335** 1 r. brown and deep brown 10 10

1336 Shyam Lal Gupt

1337 Saint Dnyaneshwar

1997. Birth Centenary (1996) of Shyam Lal Gupt (social reformer).
1703 **1336** 1 r. cinnamon and brown 10 10

1997. 700th Death Anniv (1996) of Saint Dnyaneshwar.
1704 **1337** 5 r. multicoloured . . 30 35

1338 Parijati Tree

1339 Monument, Rashtriya Military College

1997. Parijati Tree. Multicoloured.
1705 5 r. Type **1338** 30 40
1706 6 r. Parijati flower 30 40

1997. 75th Anniv of Rashtriya Military College, Dehra Dun.
1707 **1339** 2 r. multicoloured . . 20 20

1340 Ram Manohar Lohia

1341 Society Centenary Emblem

1997. Ram Manohar Lohia Commemoration.
1708 **1340** 1 r. multicoloured . . 10 10

1997. Centenary of the Philatelic Society of India. Multicoloured.
1709 2 r. Type **1341** 20 25
1710 2 r. Cover of 1st "Philatelic Journal of India", 1897 . 20 25

1342 Gyandith Award Winners

1343 Madhu Limaye

1997. Gyandith Award Scheme.
1711 **1342** 2 r. multicoloured . . 15 15

1997. Madhu Limaye Commemoration.
1712 **1343** 2 r. green 15 15

1344 Nalanda Monastic University

1997. "INDEPEX '97" International Stamp Exhibition, New Delhi (2nd issue). Buddhist Cultural Sites. Multicoloured.
1713 2 r. Type **1344** 10 10
1714 6 r. The Bodhi Tree, Bodhgaya 25 30
1715 10 r. Stupa and Pillar, Vaishali 40 45
1716 11 r. Stupa, Kushinagar . . 40 45

1345 Pandit Omkarnath Thakur

1346 Ram Sewak Yadav

1997. Birth Centenary of Pandit Omkarnath Thakur (musician).
1717 **1345** 2 r. black and blue . . 15 15

1997. Ram Sewak Yadav (politician) Commemoration.
1718 **1346** 2 r. brown 15 15

1347 Sibnath Banerjee

1348 Rukmini Lakshmipathi

1997. Birth Centenary of Sibnath Banerjee (trade unionist).
1719 **1347** 2 r. red and purple . . 15 15

1997. Rukmini Lakshmipathi (social reformer) Commemoration.
1720 **1348** 2 r. brown 15 15

1349 Sri Basaveswara

1350 Gopalpur-on-Sea Beach

1997. Sri Basaveswara (reformer and statesman) Commemoration.
1721 **1349** 2 r. purple 15 15

1997. "INDEPEX '97" International Stamp Exhibition, New Delhi (3rd issue). Beaches. Multicoloured.
1722 2 r. Type **1350** 10 10
1723 6 r. Kovalam 20 30
1724 10 r. Anjuna 40 45
1725 11 r. Bogmalo 40 45

1351 Newspaper Masthead

1997. 50th Anniv of "Swatantra Bharat" (Hindi daily newspaper).
1726 **1351** 2 r. multicoloured . . . 15 15

1352 Shah Nawaz Khan, P.K. Sahgal and G.S. Dhillon

1997. I.N.A. Trials Commemoration.
1727 **1352** 2 r. multicoloured . . . 15 15

1353 Sir Ronald Ross (bacteriologist)

1354 Firaq Gorakhpuri

1997. Centenary of the Discovery of the Malaria Parasite by Sir Ronald Ross.
1728 **1353** 2 r. grey 15 15

1997. Birth Centenary (1996) of Firaq Gorakhpuri (poet).
1729 **1354** 2 r. brown 15 15

1355 Bhaktivedanta Swami

1997. Birth Centenary (1996) of Bhaktivedanta Swami (philosopher).
1730 **1355** 5 r. brown 30 35

1356 Parachute Regiment Emblem

1997. Bicentenary of 2nd (Maratha) Battalion, Parachute Regiment.
1731 **1356** 2 r. multicoloured . . . 15 15

1357 Fossil of "Birbalsahnia divyadarshanii"

1358 Swami Brahmanand

1997. 50th Anniv of Birbal Sahni Institute of Palaeobotany, Lucknow. Plant Fossils. Multicoloured.
1732 2 r. Type **1357** 15 15
1733 2 r. "Glossopteris" 15 15
1734 6 r. "Pentoxylon" (reconstruction) 35 40
1735 10 r. "Williamsonia sewardiana" (model) . . . 55 65

1997. Swami Brahmanand (social reformer) Commemoration.
1736 **1358** 2 r. grey and stone . . 15 15

1359 "Sir William Jones"

1361 V. K. Krishna Menon

1360 Lawrence School Building and Crest

1997. 250th Birth Anniv (1996) of Sir William Jones (Sanskrit scholar).
1737 **1359** 4 r. multicoloured . . 30 30

1997. 150th Anniv of Lawrence School, Sanawar.
1738 **1360** 2 r. multicoloured . . 15 15

1997. Birth Centenary (1996) of V. K. Krishna Menon (politician).
1739 **1361** 2 r. red 15 15

1362 Policemen and Globe

1997. 66th General Assembly Session of ICPO Interpol.
1740 **1362** 4 r. multicoloured . . 30 30

1363 Woman from Arunachal Pradesh

1364 Students in Meditation, Astachai

1997. "INDEPEX '97" International Stamp Exhibition, New Delhi (4th issue). Women's Costumes. Multicoloured.
1741 2 r. Type **1363** 10 10
1742 6 r. Gujarat costume 25 30
1743 10 r. Ladakh costume . . . 40 45

1997. Centenary of Scindia School, Gwalior. Multicoloured.
1745 5 r. Type **1364** 30 35
1746 5 r. Gwalior Fort 30 35

1365 "Ocimum sanctum"

1997. Medicinal Plants. Multicoloured.

1747		2 r. Type 1365	10	10
1748		5 r. "Curcuma longa"	20	25
1749		10 r. "Rauvolfia serpentina"	40	45
1750		11 r. "Aloe barbadensis"	45	50

1366 Sant Kavi Sunderdas

1367 K. Rama Rao

1997. 400th Birth Anniv (1996) of Sant Kavi Sunderdas (Hindu theologian).
1751 **1366** 2 r. brown 15 15

1997. Birth Centenary of K. Rama Rao (parliamentarian and journalist).
1752 **1367** 2 r. bistre and brown . 15 15

1368 Jawaharlal Nehru and Child

1997. Children's Day.
1753 **1368** 2 r. multicoloured . . 15 15

1369 Animals on Globe

1370 Hazari Prasad Dwivedi

1997. World Convention on Reverence for All Life, Pune.
1754 **1369** 4 r. multicoloured . . 20 25

1997. 90th Birth Anniv of Hazari Prasad Dwivedi (scholar).
1755 **1370** 2 r. grey 15 15

1372 Vallabhbhai Patel and Marchers

1997. 47th Death Anniv of Vallabhbhai Patel (politician).
1757 **1372** 2 r. brown 15 15

1373 Head Post Office, Pune

1997. "INDEPEX '97" International Stamp Exhibition, New Delhi (5th issue). Post Office Heritage. Multicoloured.

1758	2 r. Type 1373	20	20
1759	6 r. River mail barge	40	45
1760	10 r. Jal Cooper (philatelist) and cancellations	70	75
1761	11 r. "Hindoostan" (paddle-steamer)	70	75

1374 50th Anniversary Emblem

1997. 50th Anniv of Indian Armed Forces.
1762 **1374** 2 r. multicoloured . . 15 15

1375 Dr. Pattabhi Sitaramayya

1377 Ram Prasad Bismil and Ashfaqullah Khan

1376 Father Jerome d'Souza and Cathedral

1997. Dr. Pattabhi Sitaramayya (politician) Commemoration.
1763 **1375** 2 r. brown 15 15

1997. Birth Centenary of Father Jerome d'Souza (academic).
1764 **1376** 2 r. brown 15 15

1997. 70th Death Anniv of Ram Prasad Bismil and Ashfaqullah Khan (revolutionaries).
1765 **1377** 2 r. brown 15 15

1378 Jail Buildings

1379 Sword and Kukri

1997. Cellular Jail, Port Blair.
1766 **1378** 2 r. multicoloured . . 15 15

1998. 50th Anniv of 11th Gorkha Rifles.
1767 **1379** 4 r. multicoloured . . 30 35

1380 Nahar Singh

1381 Nanak Singh

1998. 140th Death Anniv of Nahar Singh (Sikh leader).
1768 **1380** 2 r. purple 15 15

1998. Birth Centernary (1997) of Nanak Singh (writer).
1769 **1381** 2 r. red 15 15

1382 Rotary International Emblem

1998. Meeting of Rotary International Council on Legislation, Delhi.
1770 **1382** 8 r. yellow and blue . 50 55

1383 Maharana Pratap

1384 V. S. Khandekar

1998. 400th Death Anniv of Maharana Pratap (Rajput leader).
1771 **1383** 2 r. purple 15 15

1998. Birth Centenary of V. S. Khandekar (writer).
1772 **1384** 2 r. red 15 15

1385 Elephant and Dancers

1998. India Tourism Day.
1773 **1385** 10 r. multicoloured . . 60 65

1386 Jagdish Chandra Jain

1998. Jagdish Chandra Jain (educationist) Commemoration.
1774 **1386** 2 r. brown 15 15

1387 Gandhi as a Young Man and Peasants in Fields

1388 A. Vedaratnam

1998. 50th Death Anniv of Mahatma Gandhi. Multicoloured.

1775	2 r. Type 1387	10	10
1776	6 r. Woman weaving and Gandhi distributing food	25	30
1777	10 r. Gandhi collecting salt	40	45
1778	11 r. Gandhi carrying flag	45	50

Nos. 1775/8 were printed together, se-tenant, with the backgrounds forming a composite design.

1998. Birth Centenary (1997) of A. Vedaratnam (social reformer).
1779 **1388** 2 r. purple 15 15

1389 Anniversary Emblem

1391 Sir Syed Ahmad Khan

1390 Savitribai Phule

1998. 50th Anniv of Universal Declaration of Human Rights.
1780 **1389** 6 r. multicoloured . . . 30 35

1998. Death Centenary (1997) of Savitribai Phule (educational reformer).
1781 **1390** 2 r. brown 15 15

1998. Death Centenary of Sir Syed Ahmed Khan (social reformer).
1782 **1391** 2 r. brown 15 15

1392 Barren Landscape and Living Forest

1998. 1st Assembly Meeting of Global Environment Facility, Delhi.
1783 **1392** 11 r. multicoloured . . 45 50

1393 Ramana Maharshi

1998. Ramana Maharshi (religious leader) Commemoration.
1784 **1393** 2 r. lilac 15 15

1394 College Arms

1998. 50th Anniv of Defence Services Staff College, Wellington.
1785 **1394** 6 r. red 30 35

1395 Diesel Train on Viaduct (⅔-size illustration)

1998. Konkan Railway.
1786 **1395** 8 r. multicoloured . . 40 45

1396 Narayan Ganesh Goray

1397 Dr. Zakir Husain

1998. Narayan Ganesh Goray (social reformer) Commemoration.
1787 **1396** 2 r. brown 15 15

1998. Birth Centenary (1997) of Dr. Zakir Husain (former President of India).
1788 **1397** 2 r. brown 10 15

1398 Mohammed Abdurahiman Shahib

1399 Lokanayak Omeo Kumar Das

1998. Mohammed Abdurahiman Shahib (nationalist) Commemoration.
1789 **1398** 2 r. brown 10 15

1998. Lokanayak Omeo Kumar Das (writer) Commemoration.
1790 **1399** 2 r. brown 10 15

1400 Vakkom Abdul Khader, Satyendra Chandra Bardhan and Fouja Singh

1998. Nationalist Martyrs Commemoration.
1791 **1400** 2 r. brown and cinnamon 10 15

1401 Bishnu Dey, Tarashankar Bandopadhyay and Ashapurna Devi

1402 Big Ben, London

1998. Bangla Jnanpith Literary Award Winners Commemoration.
1792 **1401** 2 r. brown 10 15

1998. 50th Anniv of First Air India International Flight.
1793 5 r. Type **1402** 15 20
1794 6 r. Lockheed Super Constellation airliner, globe and Gateway of India, Bombay (55×35 mm) . . . 20 25

Nos. 1793/4 were printed together, se-tenant, forming a composite design.

1403 Dr. C. Vijiaraghavachariar

1405 Bhagawan Gopinathji

1404 Anniversary Logo and Savings Stream

1998. Dr. C. Vijiaraghavachariar (lawyer and social reformer) Commemoration.
1795 **1403** 2 r. brown 10 15

1998. 50th Anniv of National Savings Organization. Multicoloured.
1796 5 r. Type **1404** 15 20
1797 6 r. Hand dropping coin into jar 20 25

Nos. 1796/7 were printed together, se-tenant, forming a composite design.

1998. Birth Centenary of Bhagawan Gopinathji (spiritual leader).
1798 **1405** 3 r. brown 15 20

1406 Ardeshir and Pirojsha Godrej

1998. Centenary of Godrej (industrial conglomerate).
1799 **1406** 3 r. green 15 20

1407 Aruna Asaf Ali

1998. Aruna Asaf Ali (nationalist) Commemoration.
1800 **1407** 3 r. brown 15 20

1408 Iswar Chandra Vidyasagar (educationist) and College

1998. 125th Anniv of Vidyasagar College, Calcutta.
1801 **1408** 2 r. black 10 15

1409 Shivpujan Sahai

1998. Shivpujan Sahai (writer) Commemoration.
1802 **1409** 2 r. brown 10 15

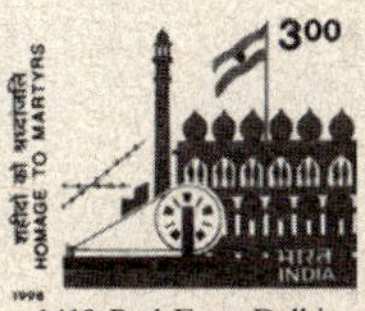

1410 Red Fort, Delhi, and Spinning Wheel

1411 Gostha Behari Paul

1998. Homage to Martyrs for Independence. Multicoloured.
1803 3 r. Type **1410** 15 20
1804 8 r. Industrial and scientific development in modern India 25 30

1998. Gostha Paul (footballer) Commemoration.
1805 **1411** 3 r. purple 15 20

1412 Youth Hostel and Logo

1998. 50th Anniv of Youth Hostels Association of India.
1806 **1412** 5 r. multicoloured . . 20 25

1413 Uniforms, Badge and Tank

1998. Bicentenary of 4th Battalion, Guards' Brigade (1 Rajput).
1807 **1413** 6 r. multicoloured . . 25 30

1414 Bhai Kanhaiyaji

1998. Bhai Kanhaiyaji (Sikh social reformer) Commemoration.
1808 **1414** 2 r. red 10 15

1415 Emblem and Diagram of Head

1998. 20th International Congress of Radiology.
1809 **1415** 8 r. multicoloured . . 30 35

1416 Dove of Peace and Boy reading Book

1417 Dr. Tristao Braganza Cunha

1998. 26th International Books for Young People Congress.
1810 **1416** 11 r. multicoloured . . 30 35

1998. Dr. Tristao Braganza Cunha (nationalist) Commemoration.
1811 **1417** 3 r. brown 15 20

1418 Jananeta Hijam Irawat Singh

1419 Women Aviators and Bi-plane

1998. Jananeta Hijam Irawat Singh (social reformer) Commemoration.
1812 **1418** 3 r. brown 15 20

1998. Indian Women's Participation in Aviation.
1813 **1419** 8 r. blue 25 30

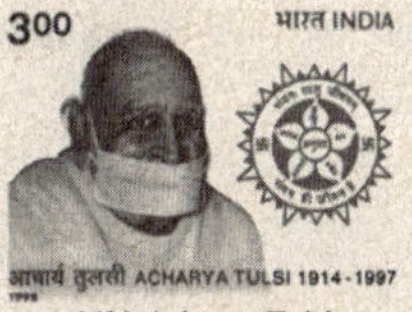

1420 Acharya Tulsi

1998. 1st Death Anniv of Acharya Tulsi (Jain religious leader).
1814 **1420** 3 r. brown and orange 15 20

1421 Girl and Bird reading Book

1998. Children's Day.
1815 **1421** 3 r. multicoloured . . . 15 20

1422 I.N.S. "Delhi" (destroyer)

1998. Navy Day.
1816 **1422** 3 r. multicoloured . . . 15 20

1423 Mounted Trumpeter

1424 Sir David Sassoon and Library, Bombay

1998. 225th Anniv of President's Bodyguard.
1817 **1423** 3 r. multicoloured . . . 15 20

1998. David Sassoon Library and Reading Room Commemoration.
1818 **1424** 3 r. ultramarine and blue 15 20

1425 Regimental Arms and Soldier

1998. Bicentenary of 2nd Battalion, Rajput Regiment.
1819 **1425** 3 r. multicoloured . . 15 20

1426 Army Postal Service Centre, Kamptee

1998. 50th Anniv of Army Postal Service Training Centre.
1820 **1426** 3 r. multicoloured . . 15 20

1427 Connemara Public Library, Madras

1998. Centenary (1996) of Connemara Public Library.
1821 **1427** 3 r. brown and ochre . 15 20

1428 Neem Tree and Leaves

1429 Baba Raghav Das

1998. 50th Anniv of The Indian Pharmaceutical Congress Association.
1822 **1428** 3 r. multicoloured . . 15 20

1998. 40th Death Anniv of Baba Raghav Das (social reformer).
1823 **1429** 2 r. violet 10 15

1430 Lt. Indra Lal Roy D.F.C.

1998. Birth Centenary of Indra Lal Roy (First World War pilot).
1824 **1430** 3 r. multicoloured . . 15 20

1431 Sant Gadge Baba

1998. Sant Gadge Baba (social reformer) Commemoration.
1825 **1431** 3 r. lilac, blue and black 15 20

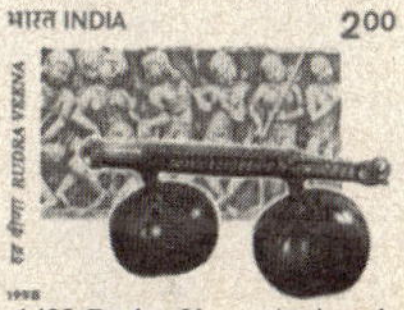

1432 Rudra Veena (stringed instrument)

1998. Musical Instruments. Multicoloured.
1826 2 r. Type **1432** 10 15
1827 6 r. Flute 20 25
1828 8 r. Pakhawaj (wooden barrel drum) 25 30
1829 10 r. Sarod (stringed instrument) 30 35

1433 "Chicoreus brunneus" (Murex shell)

1998. Shells. Multicoloured.

1830		3 r. Type **1433**	15	20
1831		3 r. "Cassis cornuta" (horned helmet)	15	20
1832		3 r. "Cypraea staphylaea" (cowrie)	15	20
1833		11 r. "Lambis lambis" (common spider conch)	30	35

1434 Stylised Police Officers

1999. 50th Anniv of Indian Police Service.

1834	**1434**	3 r. multicoloured	15	20

1435 Modern Weapon Systems

1999. 40th Anniv of Defence Research and Development Organization.

1835	**1435**	10 r. multicoloured	30	35

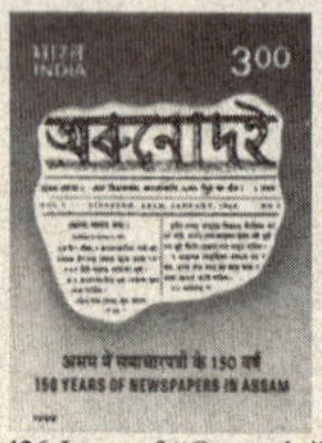

1436 Issue of "Orunodoi" (Assamese newspaper) for January, 1846

1999. 150th Anniv of Newspapers in Assam.

1836	**1436**	3 r. black, yellow and orange	15	20

OFFICIAL STAMPS

1866. Optd **Service.**

O20	**11**	½ a. blue	24·00	40
O 8	**12**	8 p. mauve	18·00	42·00
O23	**11**	1 a. brown	30·00	45
O27		2 a. orange	4·75	2·25
O13		4 a. green	£160	70·00
O29	–	4 a. green (No. 69)	3·00	1·50
O30	**11**	8 a. red	3·25	1·50

1866. Fiscal stamp with head of Queen Victoria surch **SERVICE TWO ANNAS.**

O15		2 a. purple	£275	£225

1866. Fiscal stamps optd **SERVICE POSTAGE.**

O19		½ a. mauve on lilac	£375	85·00
O16		2 a. purple	£800	£400
O17		4 a. purple	£3000	£1100
O18		8 a. purple	£3750	£3250

1874. Optd **On H. M. S.** (Queen Victoria).

O31	**11**	½ a. blue	6·50	20
O32		1 a. brown	10·00	20
O33a		2 a. orange	32·00	11·00
O34	–	4 a. green (No. 69)	11·00	3·00
O35	**11**	8 a. red	4·75	3·50

1883. Queen Victoria stamps of 1882 and 1892 optd **On H. M. S.**

O37a	**40**	3 p. red	20	10
O39	**23**	½ a. turquoise	60	10
O49		½ a. green	1·75	70
O41	–	1 a. purple	30	10
O50	–	1 a. red	2·50	10
O42	–	2 a. blue	3·75	60
O51	–	2 a. lilac	27·00	90
O44a	–	4 a. green	11·00	35
O46	–	8 a. mauve	7·50	50
O48	**37**	1 r. green and red	8·50	40

1902. King Edward VII stamps optd **On H. M. S.**

O54	**41**	3 p. grey	1·75	30
O56	–	½ a. green (No. 122)	1·25	30
O57	–	1 a. red (No. 123)	1·00	10
O59	–	2 a. lilac	3·00	10
O61	–	4 a. olive	6·50	30
O62	–	6 a. bistre	1·50	15
O63	–	8 a. mauve	6·00	85
O65	–	1 r. green and red	4·00	70
O68	**52**	2 r. red and orange	8·00	95
O69		5 r. blue and violet	14·00	1·50
O70		10 r. green and red	25·00	10·00
O71		15 r. blue and olive	60·00	32·00
O72		25 r. orange and blue	£140	60·00

1906. Nos. 149/50 optd **On H. M. S.**

O66		½ a. green	75	10
O67		1 a. red	1·50	10

1912. King George V stamps optd **SERVICE.**

O109	**55**	3 p. grey	15	10
O 76	**56**	½ a. green	30	10
O 81	**57**	1 a. red	1·25	10
O111		1 a. brown	15	10
O 83	**59**	2 a. lilac	55	10
O112	**70**	2 a. lilac	20	10
O129		2 a. red	1·00	2·00
O132	**63**	4 a. olive	1·00	10
O113	**71**	4 a. green	40	20
O 87	**64**	6 a. bistre	1·50	2·00
O115	**65**	8 a. mauve	60	10
O116	**66**	12 a. red	60	1·40
O117	**67**	1 r. brown and green	1·90	1·00
O 92		2 r. red and orange	3·25	3·75
O 93		5 r. blue and violet	12·00	16·00
O 94		10 r. green and red	40·00	40·00
O 95		15 r. blue and olive	90·00	£100
O 96		25 r. orange and blue	£200	£160

1921. No. O81 surch **NINE PIES.**

O97	**57**	9 p. on 1 a. red	75	65

1925. Nos. O70/2 surch in words.

O 99	**52**	1 r. on 15 r. blue & olive	4·25	3·25
O100		1 r. on 25 r. orange & blue	20·00	60·00
O101		2 r. on 10 r. green & red	3·75	3·50

1925. Nos. O94/6 surch in words.

O102	**67**	1 r. on 15 r. blue & olive	19·00	70·00
O103		1 r. on 25 r. orange & bl	5·00	9·00
O104		2 r. on 10 r. green & red	£750	

1926. No. O62 surch **ONE ANNA.**

O105		1 a. on 6 a. bistre	30	30

1926. Surch **SERVICE ONE ANNA** and two bars.

O106	**58**	1 a. on 1½ a. brown (A)	20	10
O107		1 a. on 1½ a. brown (B)	1·25	3·50
O108	**61**	1 a. on 2 a. 6 p. blue	60	80

1932. Optd **SERVICE.**

O126	**79**	½ a. green	60	10
O127	**80**	9 p. green	30	10
O127a	**81**	1 a. brown	2·25	10
O128	**82**	1 a. 3 p. mauve	30	10
O130a	**59**	2 a. red	1·00	10
O131	**61**	2 a. 6 p. orange	30	10

1937. King George VI stamps optd **SERVICE.**

O135	**91**	½ a. brown	16·00	15
O136		9 p. green	16·00	20
O137		1 a. red	2·50	10
O138	**93**	1 r. slate and brown	50	50
O139		2 r. purple and brown	1·50	2·50
O140		5 r. green and blue	2·50	5·50
O141		10 r. purple and red	14·00	4·75

1939. King George V stamp surch **SERVICE 1A.**

O142	**82**	1 a. on 1¼ a. mauve	10·00	20

O 20 King George VI

O 21 Asokan Capital

1939.

O143	**O 20**	3 p. slate	40	10
O144		½ a. brown	3·50	10
O144a		½ a. purple	30	10
O145		9 p. green	30	10
O146		1 a. red	30	10
O146a		1 a. 3p. brown	3·00	70
O146b		1½ a. violet	65	10
O147		2 a. orange	60	10
O148		2½ a. violet	60	40
O149		4 a. brown	60	10
O150		8 a. violet	90	30

1948. 1st Anniv of Independence. Optd **SERVICE.**

O150a	**305**	1½ a. brown	42·00	30·00
O150b		3½ a. violet	£750	£450
O150c		12 a. green	£2000	£1600
O150d	–	10 r. brown and red (No. 308)	£10000	

1950.

O151	**O 21**	3 p. violet	10	10
O152		6 p. brown	10	10
O153		9 p. green	30	10
O154		1 a. blue	70	10
O155		2 a. red	1·00	10
O156		3 a. red	3·00	1·75
O157		4 a. purple	5·00	20
O158		4 a. blue	50	10
O159		6 a. violet	3·00	40
O160		8 a. brown	1·50	10
O186	–	1 r. violet	15	10
O187	–	2 r. red	25	10
O188	–	5 r. green	50	60
O189	–	10 r. brown	1·25	80

The rupee values are larger and with a different frame.

1957. Value in naye paise.

O175	**O 21**	1 n.p. slate	10	10
O166		2 n.p. violet	10	10
O167		3 n.p. brown	10	10
O168		5 n.p. green	10	10
O169		6 n.p. turquoise	10	10
O180		10 n.p. green	1·50	1·25
O170		13 n.p. red	10	10
O182		15 n.p. violet	10	10
O183		20 n.p. red	30	10
O184		25 n.p. blue	10	10
O185		50 n.p. brown	15	10

O 23

O 25

O 26

1967.

O200	**O 23**	2 p. violet	10	80
O201		3 p. brown	10	90
O202		5 p. green	10	10
O203		6 p. blue	65	85
O204		10 p. green	10	30
O205		15 p. plum	10	30
O206		20 p. red	10	30
O207		25 p. red	7·50	3·75
O208		30 p. blue	10	50
O209		50 p. brown	10	50
O197		1 r. purple	40	10

1971. Obligatory Tax. Refugee Relief. Optd **REFUGEE RELIEF** in English and Devanagari (No. O210) or in English only (No. O211).

O210	**O 23**	5 p. green	30	30
O211		5 p. green	1·25	40
O213	**O 25**	5 p. green	15	15

See note below Nos. 646/51.

1977. Designs redrawn showing face-value in figures only and smaller Capital with Hindi motto beneath as Type **O 26.**

O214	**O 26**	2 p. blue	20	85
O254		5 p. green	10	10
O255		10 p. green	10	10
O256		15 p. purple	10	10
O257		20 p. red	15	10
O258		25 p. red	15	10
O259		30 p. blue	20	10
O260		35 p. violet	10	10
O268		40 p. violet	10	10
O269		50 p. brown	10	10
O263		60 p. brown	20	10
O270		1 r. purple	10	10
O225b	–	2 r. red	40	1·50
O226b	–	5 r. green	60	2·25
O227	–	10 r. red	1·25	3·50

The 2, 5 and 10 r. values are larger.

O 27

O 28

1981. Redrawn with face value figures in bottom corners.

O271	**O 27**	2 r. red	10	15
O272		5 r. green	15	20
O273		10 r. brown	30	35

1982. As 1977 and 1981 issue but with simulated perforations. Imperf.

O231	**O 28**	5 p. green	50	60
O232		10 p. green	55	65
O233		15 p. purple	55	65
O234		20 p. red	60	70
O235		25 p. red	1·25	1·50
O236		35 p. violet	70	45
O237		50 p. brown	1·25	1·00
O238		1 r. brown	1·50	1·00
O239		2 r. red	1·75	3·50
O240		5 r. green	2·00	4·25
O241		10 r. brown	2·50	6·00

INDIAN CUSTODIAN FORCES IN KOREA

Stamps used by the Indian Forces on custodian duties in Korea in 1953.

12 pies = 1 anna; 16 annas = 1 rupee

(I)

1953. Stamps of India (archaeological series) optd with T **1**.

K 1	**307**	3 p. violet	1·50	4·50
K 2	**308**	6 p. brown	1·50	4·50
K 3	–	9 p. green	1·75	4·50
K 4	–	1 a. blue (B)	1·50	4·50
K 5	–	2 a. red	1·50	4·50
K 6	–	2½ a. lake	1·50	4·75
K 7	–	3 a. salmon	1·50	4·75
K 8	**314**	4 a. blue	2·00	4·75
K 9	**315**	6 a. violet	8·50	9·00
K10	–	8 a. green	3·25	9·00
K11	–	12 a. blue	4·50	17·00
K12	–	1 r. violet and green	6·00	17·00

INDIAN EXPEDITIONARY FORCES

Stamps used by Indian Forces during, and after, the War of 1914-18.

12 pies = 1 anna; 16 annas = 1 rupee

1914. Stamps of India (King George V) optd **I. E. F.**

E 1	**55**	3 p. grey	15	25
E 2	**56**	½ a. green	20	20
E 3	**57**	1 a. red	50	20
E 5	**59**	2 a. lilac	70	30
E 6	**61**	2 a. 6 p. blue	1·25	2·75
E 7	**62**	3 a. orange	80	70
E 8	**63**	4 a. olive	70	70
E 9	**65**	8 a. mauve	1·00	1·75
E12	**66**	12 a. red	2·25	5·50
E13	**67**	1 r. brown and green	2·50	4·00

INDIAN FORCES IN INDO-CHINA

Stamps used by Indian Forces engaged in the International Commission in Indo-China.

1954. 12 pies = 1 anna; 16 annas = 1 rupee.
1957. 100 naye paise = 1 rupee.
1964. 100 paisa = 1 rupee.

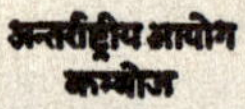

(N 1)

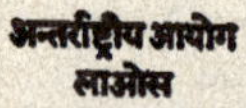

(N 2)

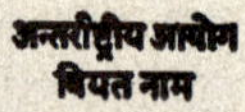

(N 3)

1954. Stamps of India (archaeological series) overprinted. (a) Optd with Type N **1** for use in Cambodia.

N1	**307**	3 p. violet	90	7·50
N2	–	1 a. blue (B)	90	75
N3	–	2 a. red	90	80
N4	–	8 a. green	2·00	3·50
N5	–	12 a. blue	2·00	4·00

(b) Optd with Type N **2** for use in Laos.

N 6	**307**	3 p. violet	90	7·50
N 7	–	1 a. blue (B)	90	75
N 8	–	2 a. red	90	80
N 9	–	8 a. green	2·00	3·50
N10	–	12 a. blue	2·00	4·00

(c) Optd with Type N **3** for use in Vietnam.

N11	**307**	3 p. violet	90	7·50
N12	–	1 a. blue (B)	90	75
N13	–	2 a. red	90	80
N14	–	8 a. green	2·00	3·50
N15	–	12 a. blue	2·00	4·00

1957. Map type of India overprinted. (a) Optd with Type N **1** for use in Cambodia.

N16	**361**	2 n.p. brown	75	30
N17		6 n.p. grey	50	30
N18		13 n.p. red	70	40
N19		50 n.p. orange	2·25	1·25
N20		75 n.p. purple	2·25	1·25

(b) Optd with Type N **2** for use in Laos.

N21	**361**	2 n.p. brown	75	30
N39		3 n.p. brown	10	20
N40		5 n.p. green	10	15
N22		6 n.p. grey	50	30
N23		13 n.p. red	70	40
N24		50 n.p. orange	2·25	1·25
N25		75 n.p. purple	2·25	1·25

(c) Optd with Type N **3** for use in Vietnam.

N43	**361**	1 n.p. turquoise	10	20
N26		2 n.p. brown	75	30
N45		3 n.p. brown	10	20
N46		5 n.p. green	10	15
N27		6 n.p. grey	50	30
N28		13 n.p. red	70	40
N29		50 n.p. orange	2·25	1·25
N30		75 n.p. purple	2·25	1·25

1965. Children's Day stamp of India optd **ICC** for use in Laos and Vietnam.

N49	**469**	15 p. slate	60	3·25

1968. Nos. 504/6, 509/10, 515 and 517/18, of India optd ICC in English and Devanagari, for use in Laos and Vietnam.

N50	–	2 p. brown	10	2·25
N51	–	3 p. olive	10	2·25
N52	–	5 p. red	10	75
N53	–	10 p. blue	1·75	1·75
N54	**467**	15 p. green	60	1·75
N55	–	60 p. grey	35	1·25
N56	–	1 r. brown and plum	50	1·75
N57	–	2 r. blue and violet	1·25	7·50

INDIAN U.N. FORCE IN CONGO

Stamps used by Indian Forces attached to the United Nations Force in Congo.

100 naye paise = 1 rupee

1962. Map type of India optd **U.N. FORCE (INDIA) CONGO**.

U1	**361**	1 n.p. turquoise	80	2·00
U2		2 n.p. brown	80	80
U3		5 n.p. green	80	55
U4		8 n.p. turquoise	80	30
U5		13 n.p. red	80	40
U6		50 n.p. orange	80	70

INDIAN U.N. FORCE IN GAZA (PALESTINE)

Stamps used by Indian Forces attached to the United Nations Force in Gaza.

100 paise = 1 rupee

1965. Children's Day stamp of India optd **UNEF**.

G1	**449**	15 p. slate	1·25	5·50

INDORE (HOLKAR STATE)

A state in C. India. Now uses Indian stamps.

12 pies = 1 anna; 16 annas = 1 rupee

1 Maharaja Tukoji Rao Holkar II

2

1886.

2	**1**	½ a. mauve	1·50	1·10

1889. No gum. Imperf.

4	**2**	½ a. black on pink	1·90	2·50

3 Maharaja Shivaji Rao Holkar

5 Maharaja Tukoji Holkar III

1889.

5	**3**	¼ a. orange	60	40
6a		½ a. purple	70	15
7		1 a. green	80	50
8		2 a. red	2·75	1·00

1904.

9	**5**	¼ a. orange	30	10
10		½ a. red	8·50	10
11		1 a. green	1·60	10
12		2 a. brown	7·50	45
13		3 a. violet	12·00	4·50
14a		4 a. blue	5·00	1·10

The ¼ a. is inscr "HOLKAR".

पाव आना.

(6)

1905. No. 6a. surch as T **6**.

15	**3**	¼ a. on ½ a. purple	3·00	16·00

7 Maharaja Yeshwant Rao Holkar II 9

1928.

16	**7**	¼ a. orange	30	10
17		½ a. purple	30	10
18		1 a. green	80	10
19		1¼ a. green	1·25	15
20		2 a. brown	3·50	90
21		2 a. green	9·00	60
22		3 a. violet	1·50	8·50
23		3 a. blue	15·00	
24		3½ a. violet	4·50	9·00
25		4 a. blue	3·25	3·00
26		4 a. yellow	21·00	1·50
27		8 a. grey	5·50	4·50
28		8 a. orange	15·00	18·00
29		12 a. red	5·00	10·00
30	–	1 r. black and blue	8·00	14·00
31	–	2 r. black and red	35·00	35·00
32	–	5 r. black and brown	55·00	60·00

The rupee values are larger 23×28 mm.

1940. Surch diagonally in words.

33	–	¼ a. on 5 r. (No. 32)	6·50	75
34	–	½ a. on 2 r. (No. 31)	10·00	1·60
35	**7**	1 a. on 1¼ a. green (No. 19)	10·00	40

1941.

36	**9**	¼ a. orange	2·00	10
37		½ a. red	1·40	10
38		1 a. green	8·00	10
39		1¼ a. green	14·00	40
40		2 a. blue	11·00	1·00
41		4 a. yellow	12·00	9·00
42	–	2 r. black and red	9·00	95·00
43	–	5 r. black and orange	9·00	£130

The rupee values are larger 23×28 mm.

OFFICIAL STAMPS

1904. Optd **SERVICE**.

S1	**5**	¼ a. orange	10	45
S2		½ a. red	10	10
S3		1 a. green	10	20
S4		2 a. brown	30	25
S5		3 a. violet	1·75	1·50
S6		4 a. blue	2·75	1·40

IONIAN ISLANDS

A group of islands off the W. coast of Greece, placed under the protection of Gt. Britain in 1815 and ceded to Greece in 1864.

12 pence = 1 shilling
20 shillings = 1 pound

1

1859. Imperf.

1	**1**	(½d.) orange	75·00	£500
2		(1d.) blue	20·00	£180
3		(2d.) red	15·00	£180

IRELAND

Ireland (Eire) consisting of Ireland less the six counties of Ulster, became the Irish Free State in 1922 and left the British Empire in 1949 when it became an independent republic.

12 pence = 1 shilling
20 shillings = 1 pound

Rialtap Sealatac na hÉipeann 1922 | **Rialtap Sealadac na hÉipeann 1922.**

(1) "Provisional Government (2) of Ireland, 1922"

1922. Optd with T **1** (date in thin figures and no full point).

1	**105**	½d. green	85	40
2	**104**	1d. red	1·25	35
4a		2½d. blue	85	3·25
5	**106**	3d. violet	4·00	3·75
6		4d. green	3·25	9·50
7	**107**	5d. brown	3·75	8·50
8	**108**	9d. brown	10·00	20·00
9		10d. blue	8·00	35·00
17	**109**	2s. 6d. brown	35·00	65·00
19		5s. red	60·00	£120
21		10s. blue	£120	£250

On Nos. 17, 19 and 21 the overprint is in four lines instead of five.

1922. Optd with T **2** (date in thick figures followed by full point).

30	**105**	½d. green	1·75	80
31	**104**	1d. red	1·00	50
10	**105**	1½d. brown	1·25	85
12	**1[illegible]**	2d. orange	2·25	50
35	**104**	2½d. blue	6·00	18·00
36	**106**	3d. violet	2·25	2·00
37		4d. green	3·00	4·50
38	**107**	5d. brown	4·00	8·50
39	**107**	6d. purple	7·50	3·00
40	**108**	9d. black	12·00	15·00
41		9d. green	4·75	30·00
42		10d. blue	25·00	48·00
43		1s. brown	8·50	11·00

Saorstát Éireann 1922

(5 "Irish Free State, 1922")

1922. Optd with T **5**.

52	**105**	½d. green	1·00	30
53	**104**	1d. red	75	40
54	**105**	1½d. brown	3·25	8·50
55	**106**	2d. orange	1·00	1·50
56	**104**	2½d. blue	6·00	7·00
57	**106**	3d. violet	3·50	11·00
58		4d. green	2·75	5·50
59	**107**	5d. brown	3·25	4·75
60		6d. purple	2·00	2·00
61	**108**	9d. green	3·00	5·50
62		10d. blue	16·00	48·00
63		1s. brown	7·00	10·00
86	**109**	2s. 6d. brown	40·00	42·00
87		5s. red	60·00	80·00
88		10s. blue	£150	£170

6 "Sword of Light"

7 Map of Ireland

8 Arms of Ireland

9 Celtic Cross

1922.

71	**6**	½d. green	85	75
112	**7**	1d. red	30	10
73		1½d. purple	1·40	1·75
114		2d. green	30	10
75	**8**	2½d. brown	3·75	3·50
116	**9**	3d. blue (18¾×22½ mm)	60	10
227		3d. blue (17×21 mm)	40	15
117	**8**	4d. blue	55	10
118	**6**	5d. violet (18¾×22½ mm)	65	10
228		5d. violet (17×21 mm)	30	15
119b		6d. purple	1·25	20
119c		8d. red	80	70
120	**8**	9d. violet	1·50	70
121	**9**	10d. brown	60	70
121b		11d. red	1·50	2·25
82	**6**	1s. blue	17·00	5·50

12 Daniel O'Connell

13 Shannon Barrage

1929. Centenary of Catholic Emancipation.

89	**12**	2d. green	50	45
90		3d. blue	4·00	8·50
91		9d. violet	4·00	4·00

1930. Completion of Shannon Hydro-Electric Scheme.

92	**13**	2d. deep brown	80	55

14 Reaper

15 The Cross of Cong

1931. Bicentenary of Royal Dublin Society.

93	**14**	2d. blue	65	30

1932. International Eucharistic Congress.

94	**15**	2d. green	90	30
95		3d. blue	2·25	5·00

16 Adoration of the Cross

17 Hurler

1933. "Holy Year".

96	**16**	2d. green	1·00	15
97		3d. blue	2·50	2·00

1934. 50th Anniv of Gaelic Athletic Assn.

98	**17**	2d. green	75	45

18 St. Patrick

19 Ireland and New Constitution

1937.

123a	**18**	2s. 6d. green	1·50	2·25
124ca		5s. purple	6·00	7·50
125ba		10s. blue	9·00	16·00

1937. Constitution Day.

105	**19**	2d. red	1·00	20
106		3d. blue	4·00	3·50

For similar stamps see No. 176/7 in Volume 1.

20 Father Mathew

1938. Centenary of Temperance Crusade.

107	**20**	2d. black	1·50	30
108		3d. blue	8·50	6·00

21 George Washington, American Eagle and Irish Harp

1939. 150th Anniv of U.S. Constitution and Installation of First U.S. President.

109	**21**	2d. red	1·75	60
110		3d. blue	3·25	4·00

24 Volunteer and G.P.O., Dublin

1941. 25th Anniv of Easter Rising (1916). (a) Provisional issue. Optd with two lines of Irish characters between the dates "1941" and "1916".

126	**7**	2d. orange	1·50	50
127	**9**	3d. blue	27·00	9·50

(b) Definitive Issue.

128	**24**	2½d. blue	70	60

25 Dr. Douglas Hyde

26 Sir William Rowan Hamilton

1943. 50th Anniv of Gaelic League.

129	**25**	½d. green	40	30
130		2½d. purple	1·25	10

1943. Centenary of Announcement of Discovery of Quaternions.

131	**26**	½d. green	40	40
132		2½d. brown	1·75	10

27 Bro. Michael O'Clery

28 Edmund Ignatius Rice

1944. Death Tercentenary of Michael O'Clery (Franciscan historian) (commemorating the "Annals of the Four Masters").

133	**27**	½d. green	10	10
134		1s. brown	70	10

1944. Death Centenary of Edmund Rice (founder of Irish Christian Brothers).

135	**28**	2½d. slate	60	45

29 "Youth sowing Seeds of Freedom"

30 "Country and Homestead"

1945. Death Centenary of Thomas Davis (founder of Young Ireland Movement).

136 29 2½d. blue . . . . 1·00 25
137 6d. purple . . . . 7·00 3·75

1946. Birth Centenaries of Michael Davitt and Charles Parnell (land reformers).

138 30 2½d. red . . . . 1·50 15
139 3d. blue . . . . 3·50 3·50

31 Angel Victor over Rock of Cashel

1948. Air. Inscr "VOX HIBERNIAE".

140 31 1d. brown . . . . 2·00 3·50
141 – 3d. blue . . . . 4·00 2·25
142 – 6d. purple . . . . 1·00 1·50
142a – 8d. lake . . . . 7·00 7·00
143 – 1s. green . . . . 1·25 1·50
143a 31 1s. 3d. orange . . . . . . 7·50 1·25
143b 1s. 5d. blue . . . . 3·50 1·00

DESIGNS: 3d., 8d. Angel Victor over Lough Derg; 6d. Over Croagh Patrick; 1s. Over Glendalough.

35 Theobald Wolfe Tone

1948. 150th Anniv of Insurrection.

144 35 2½d. purple . . . . 1·00 10
145 3d. violet . . . . 3·25 3·25

For later issues see Volume 1.

POSTAGE DUE STAMPS

D 1

1925.

D 1 D 1 ½d. green . . . . 12·00 16·00
D 6 1d. red . . . . 1·50 70
D 7 1½d. red . . . . 1·75 6·50
D 8 2d. green . . . . 2·75 70
D 9 3d. blue . . . . 2·25 2·75
D10 5d. violet . . . . 4·50 3·00
D11a 6d. plum 70 85
D12 8d. orange . . . . 8·50 8·00
D13 10d. purple . . . . 8·50 7·50
D14 1s. green . . . . 6·00 9·00

ISLE OF MAN

An island in the Irish Sea to the north-west of England. Man became a possession of the English Crown during the Middle Ages, but retains its own Assembly.

Regional issues from 1958–71 are listed at end of "GREAT BRITAIN".

Isle of Man had an independent postal administration from 1973.

100 pence = 1 pound

4 Castletown 5 Manx Cat

1973. Multicoloured.

12 ½p. Type 4 . . . . 10 10
13 1p. Port Erin 10 10
14 1½p. Snaefell 10 10
15 2p. Laxey 10 10
16 2½p. Tynwald Hill 10 10
17 3p. Douglas Promenade 10 10
18 3½p. Port St. Mary 15 15
19 4p. Fairy Bridge 15 15
20 4½p. As 2½p. 20 20
21 5p. Peel 20 20
22 5½p. As 3p. 25 25
23 6p. Cregneish 25 25
24 7p. As 2p. 30 30
25 7½p. Ramsey Bay 25 25
26 8p. As 7½p. 35 35
27 9p. Douglas Bay 30 35
28 10p. Type 5 . . . . 40 35
29 11p. Monk's Bridge, Ballasalla . . . 30 30
30 13p. Derbyhaven 40 40
31 20p. Manx loaghtyn ram 50 50
32 50p. Manx shearwater . . . . . 1·50 1·25
33 £1 Viking longship . . . . . . 3·00 2·50

SIZES: Nos. 13/27 and 29/30 as Type 4; Nos. 31/3 as Type 5.

6 Viking Landing on Man, A.D. 938

1973. Inauguration of Postal Independence.

34 6 15p. multicoloured 60 60

7 No. 1 "Sutherland", 1873

1973. Cent of Steam Railway. Multicoloured.

35 2½p. Type 7 . . . . 20 20
36 3p. No. 4 "Caledonia", 1885 . . . 20 20
37 7½p. No. 13 "Kissack", 1910 . . . 80 90
38 9p. No. 3 "Pender", 1873 . . . 1·00 90

8 Leonard Randles, First Winner, 1923

1973. Golden Jubilee of Manx Grand Prix. Multicoloured.

39 3p. Type 8 . . . . 30 20
40 3½p. Alan Holmes, Double Winner, 1957 . . . . 30 20

9 Princess Anne and Capt. Mark Phillips

1973. Royal Wedding.

41 9 25p. multicoloured . . . . . 1·00 1·00

10 Badge, Citation and Sir William Hillary (founder)

1974. 150th Anniv of Royal National Lifeboat Institution. Multicoloured.

42 3p. Type 10 . . . . 10 10
43 3½p. Wreck of "St. George", 1830 . 15 15
44 8p. R.N.L.B. "Manchester and Salford", 1868–87 . . . . . 40 40
45 10p. R.N.L.B. "Osman Gabriel" . . 45 45

11 Stanley Woods, 1935

1974. Tourist Trophy Motor-cycle Races (1st issue). Multicoloured.

46 3p. Type 11 . . . . 10 10
47 3½p. Freddy Frith, 1937 . . . . 10 10
48 8p. Max Deubel and Emil Horner, 1961 . . . . 45 45
49 10p. Mike Hailwood, 1961 . . . 60 45

See also Nos. 63/6.

12 Rushen Abbey and Arms

1974. Historical Anniversaries. Multicoloured.

50 3½p. Type 12 . . . . 10 10
51 4½p. Magnus Haraldson rows King Edgar on the Dee . . . 10 10
52 8p. King Magnus and Norse fleet 40 40
53 10p. Bridge at Avignon and bishop's mitre 50 50

COMMEMORATIONS: Nos. 50 and 53, William Russell, Bishop of Sodor and Man, 600th death anniv; Nos. 51/2, 1000th anniv of rule of King Magnus Haraldson.

13 Churchill and Bugler Dunne at Colenso, 1899

1974. Birth Centenary of Sir Winston Churchill. Multicoloured.

54 3½p. Type 13 . . . . 10 10
55 4½p. Churchill and Government Buildings, Douglas 10 10
56 8p. Churchill and Manx ack-ack crew 25 35
57 20p. Churchill as Freeman of Douglas 75 55

14 Cabin School and Names of Pioneers

1975. Manx Pioneers in Cleveland, Ohio. Multicoloured.

59 4½p. Type 14 . . . . 10 10
60 5½p. Terminal Tower Building, J. Gill and R. Carran 15 10
61 8p. Clague House Museum, and Robert and Margaret Clague . 35 40
62 10p. S.S. "William T. Graves" and Thomas Quayle 50 50

15 Tom Sheard, 1923

1975. Tourist Trophy Motor-cycle Races (2nd issue). Multicoloured.

63 5½p. Type 15 . . . . 20 15
64 7p. Walter Handley, 1925 . . . 30 20
65 10p. Geoff Duke, 1955 . . . . 50 30
66 12p. Peter Williams, 1973 . . . 50 45

16 Sir George Goldie and Birthplace

1975. 50th Death Anniv of Sir George Goldie. Multicoloured.

67 5½p. Type 16 . . . . 10 15
68 7p. Goldie and map of Africa (vert) 20 20
69 10p. Goldie as President of Geographical Society (vert) . . 40 30
70 12p. River scene on the Niger . . 40 45

17 Title Page of Manx Bible 18 William Christian listening to Patrick Henry

1975. Christmas and Bicentenary of Manx Bible. Multicoloured.

71 5½p. Type 17 . . . . 15 15
72 7p. Rev. Philip Moore and Ballaugh Old Church 20 20
73 11p. Bishop Hildesley and Bishops Court 35 35
74 13p. John Kelly saving Bible manuscript 40 40

1976. Bicent of American Independence. Mult.

75 5½p. Type 18 . . . . 15 15
76 7p. Conveying the Fincastle Resolutions 20 20
77 13p. Patrick Henry and William Christian 35 35
78 20p. Christian as an Indian fighter 50 50

19 First Horse Tram, 1876

1976. Cent of Douglas Horse-Trams. Mult.

80 5½p. Type 19 . . . . 10 15
81 7p. "Toast-rack" tram, 1890 . . 15 15
82 11p. Horse-bus, 1895 . . . . . 45 35
83 13p. Royal tram, 1972 . . . . 50 45

20 Barrose Beaker 21 Diocesan Banner

1976. Europa. Ceramic Art. Multicoloured.

84 5p. Type 20 . . . . 25 20
85 5p. Souvenir teapot 25 20
86 5p. Laxey jug 25 20
87 10p. Cronk Aust food vessel (horiz) 40 35
88 10p. Sansbury bowl (horiz) . . 40 35
89 10p. Knox urn (horiz) 40 35

1976. Christmas and Centenary of Mothers' Union. Multicoloured.

90 6p. Type 21 . . . . 15 15
91 7p. Onchan banner 15 15
92 11p. Castletown banner 40 35
93 13p. Ramsey banner 40 45

22 Queen Elizabeth II

1977. Silver Jubilee. Multicoloured.

94 6p. Type 22 . . . . 20 20
95 7p. Queen Elizabeth and Prince Philip (vert) 20 20
96 25p. Queen Elizabeth (different) 80 70

23 Carrick Bay from "Tom-the-Dipper"

1977. Europa. Landscapes. Multicoloured.

97 6p. Type 23 . . . . 20 20
98 10p. View from Ramsey . . . 30 30

24 F. A. Applebee, 1912

1977. Linked Anniversaries. Multicoloured.

99 6p. Type 24 . . . . 20 15
100 7p. St. John's Ambulance Brigade at Governor's Bridge, 1938 . . . . 20 20
101 11p. Scouts operating the scoreboard 50 40
102 13p. John Williams, 1976 . . . 50 40

The events commemorated are: 70th anniv of Manx TT races; 70th anniv of Boy Scouts; Centenary of St. John's Ambulance Brigade.

25 Old Summer House, Mount Morrison, Peel 27 Watch Tower, Langness

26 Short Type 184 Seaplane and H.M.S. "Ben-My-Chree", 1915

1977. Bicent of First Visit of John Wesley. Multicoloured.

103	6p. Type **25**	20	15
104	7p. Wesley preaching in Castletown Square	30	20
105	11p. Wesley preaching outside Braddan Church	45	35
106	13p. New Methodist Church, Douglas	50	40

Nos. 104/5 are larger, 38×26 mm.

1978. 60th Anniv of Royal Air Force. Mult.

107	6p. Type **26**	20	15
108	7p. Bristol Scout C and H.M.S. "Vindex", 1915	30	20
109	11p. Boulton Paul Defiant over Douglas Bay, 1941	45	35
110	13p. Sepecat Jaguar over Ramsey, 1977	50	40

1978. Multicoloured.

111	½p. Type **27**	10	10
112	1p. Jurby Church (horiz)	10	10
113	6p. Government Buildings	30	30
114	7p. Tynwald Hill (horiz)	35	35
115	8p. Milner's Tower	25	25
116	9p. Laxey Wheel	35	35
117a	10p. Castle Rushen (horiz)	35	35
118	11p. St. Ninian's Church	40	40
119a	12p. Tower of Refuge (horiz)	50	40
120a	13p. St. German's Cathedral (horiz)	40	40
121a	14p. Point of Ayre Lighthouse (horiz)	50	50
122a	15p. Corrin's Tower (horiz)	40	40
123	16p. Douglas Head Lighthouse (horiz)	90	90
124	20p. Fuchsia	40	40
125	25p. Manx cat	50	50
126	50p. Chough	1·00	1·00
127	£1 Viking warrior	2·00	2·00
128	£2 Queen Elizabeth II	4·25	4·25

Nos. 124/7 are larger, 25×31 mm and No. 128, 38×48 mm.

28 Queen Elizabeth in Coronation Regalia

29 Wheel-headed Cross-slab

1978. 25th Anniv of Coronation.

132	**28**	25p. multicoloured	75	75

1978. Europa. Celtic and Norse Crosses. Multicoloured.

133	6p. Type **29**	20	15
134	6p. Celtic wheel-cross	20	15
135	6p. Keeil Chiggyrt Stone	20	15
136	11p. Olaf Liotulfson Cross	35	30
137	11p. Odd's and Thorleif's Crosses	35	30
138	11p. Thor Cross	35	30

30 J. K. Ward and Ward Library, Peel

1978. Anniversaries and Events. Multicoloured.

139	6p. Type **30**	15	15
140	7p. Swimmer, cyclist and walker (42×26 mm)	20	20
141	11p. American bald eagle, Manx arms and maple leaf (42×26 mm)	35	35
142	13p. Lumber camp, Three Rivers, Quebec	40	40

ANNIVERSARIES AND EVENTS: 6, 13p. James Kewley Ward (Manx pioneer in Canada) commemoration; 7p. Commonwealth Games, Edmonton; 11p. 50th anniv of North American Manx Association.

MINIMUM PRICE

The minimum price quoted is 10p which represents a handling charge rather than a basis for valuing common stamps. For further notes about prices see introductory pages.

31 Hunt the Wren

33 Postman, 1859

32 P. M. C. Kermode and "Nassa kermodei"

1978. Christmas.

143	**31**	5p. multicoloured	50	50

1979. Centenary of Natural History and Antiquarian Society. Multicoloured.

144	6p. Type **32**	15	15
145	7p. Peregrine falcon	20	20
146	11p. Fulmar	35	35
147	13p. "Epitriptus cowini" (fly)	40	40

1979. Europa. Communications. Multicoloured.

148	6p. Type **33**	25	25
149	11p. Postman, 1979	50	50

34 Viking Longship Emblem

35 Viking Raid at Garwick

1979. Millennium of Tynwald. Multicoloured.

150b	3p. Type **34**	10	10
151	4p. "Three Legs of Man" emblem	15	15
152	6p. Type **35**	15	15
153	7p. 10th-century meeting of Tynwald	20	20
154	11p. Tynwald Hill and St. John's Church	30	30
155	13p. Procession to Tynwald Hill	45	35

The 4p. value is as Type **34** and the remainder as Type **35**.

36 Queen and Court on Tynwald Hill

1979. Royal Visit. Multicoloured.

156	7p. Type **36**	35	35
157	13p. Queen and procession from St. John's Church to Tynwald Hill	50	50

37 "Odin's Raven"

1979. Voyage of "Odin's Raven".

158	**37**	15p. multicoloured	70	70

38 John Quilliam seized by the Press Gang

1979. 150th Death Anniv of Captain John Quilliam. Multicoloured.

159	6p. Type **38**	15	15
160	8p. Steering H.M.S. "Victory", Battle of Trafalgar	20	20
161	13p. Captain John Quilliam and H.M.S. "Spencer"	35	35
162	15p. Captain John Quilliam (member of the House of Keys)	40	40

39 Young Girl with Teddybear and Cat

1979. Christmas. Int Year of the Child. Mult.

163	5p. Type **39**	25	25
164	7p. Father Christmas with young children	35	35

40 Conglomerate Arch, Langness

1980. 150th Anniv of Royal Geographical Society. Multicoloured.

165	7p. Type **40**	20	20
166	8p. Braaid Circle	20	20
167	12p. Cashtal-yn-Ard	25	25
168	13p. Volcanic rocks at Scarlett	35	35
169	15p. Sugar-loaf Rock	40	40

41 "Mona's Isle I"

1980. 150th Anniv of Isle of Man Steam Packet Company. Multicoloured.

170	7p. Type **41**	20	20
171	8p. "Douglas I"	20	20
172	11½p. H.M.S. "Mona's Queen II" sinking U-boat	30	30
173	12p. H.M.S. "King Orry III" at surrender of German fleet, 1918	30	30
174	13p. "Ben-My-Chree IV"	40	35
175	15p. "Lady of Mann II"	50	40

42 Stained Glass Window, T. E. Brown Room, Manx Museum

1980. Europa. Personalities. Thomas Edward Brown (poet and scholar) Commemoration. Multicoloured.

177	7p. Type **42**	20	20
178	13½p. Clifton College, Bristol	40	40

43 King Olav V and "Norge" (Norwegian royal yacht)

1980. Visit of King Olav of Norway, August 1979.

179	**43**	12p. multicoloured	50	50

44 Winter Wren and View of Calf of Man

1980. Christmas and Wildlife Conservation Year. Multicoloured.

181	6p. Type **44**	20	20
182	8p. European robin and view of Port Erin Marine Biological Station	30	30

45 William Kermode and Brig "Robert Quayle", 1819

46 Peregrine Falcon

1980. Kermode Family in Tasmania Commemoration. Multicoloured.

183	7p. Type **45**	20	20
184	9p. "Mona Vale", Van Diemen's Land, 1834	25	25
185	13½p. Ross Bridge, Tasmania	40	35
186	15p. "Mona Vale", Tasmania (completed 1868)	45	40
187	17½p. Robert Quayle Kermode and Parliament Buildings, Tasmania	50	45

1980. Multicoloured.

188	1p. Type **46**	40	40
189	5p. Loaghtyn ram	40	40

47 Luggers passing Red Pier, Douglas

1981. Centenary of Royal National Mission to Deep Sea Fishermen. Multicoloured.

190	8p. Type **47**	25	25
191	9p. Peel Lugger "Wanderer" rescuing survivors from "Lusitania"	30	30
192	18p. Nickeys leaving Port St. Mary	45	45
193	20p. Nobby entering Ramsey Harbour	50	50
194	22p. Nickeys "Sunbeam" and "Zebra" at Port Erin	50	50

48 "Crosh Cuirn" Superstition

1981. Europa. Folklore. Multicoloured.

195	8p. Type **48**	25	25
196	18p. "Bollan Cross" superstition	75	75

49 Lt. Mark Wilks (Royal Manx Fencibles) and Peel Castle

1981. 150th Death Anniv of Colonel Mark Wilks. Multicoloured.

197	8p. Type **49**	25	25
198	20p. Ensign Mark Wilks and Fort St. George, Madras	50	50
199	22p. Governor Mark Wilks and Napoleon, St. Helena	70	55
200	25p. Col. Mark Wilks (Speaker of the House of Keys) and estate, Kirby	80	80

50 Miss Emmeline Goulden (Mrs. Pankhurst) and Mrs. Sophia Jane Goulden

1981. Centenary of Manx Women's Suffrage.

201	**50**	9p. black, grey and stone	50	50

51 Prince Charles and Lady Diana Spencer

1981. Royal Wedding.

202	**51**	9p. black, blue and lt blue	50	50
203		25p. black, blue and pink	1·50	1·50

52 Douglas War Memorial, Poppies and Commemorative Inscription

1981. 60th Anniv of The Royal British Legion. Multicoloured.

205 8p. Type **52** 25 25
206 10p. Major Robert Cain (war hero) 30 35
207 18p. Festival of Remembrance, Royal Albert Hall 65 65
208 20p. T.S.S. "Tynwald" at Dunkirk, May 1940 . . . . 75 75

53 Nativity Scene (stained glass window, St. George's Church)

1981. Christmas. Multicoloured.

209 7p. Type **53** 25 25
210 9p. Children from Special School performing nativity play (48 × 30 mm) 35 35

54 Joseph and William Cunningham (founders of Isle of Man Boy Scout Movement) and Cunningham House Headquarters

1982. 75th Anniv of Boy Scout Movement and 125th Birth Anniv of Lord Baden-Powell. Multicoloured.

211 9p. Type **54** 30 30
212 10p. Baden-Powell visiting Isle of Man, 1911 . . . . 30 30
213 19½p. Baden-Powell and Scout emblem (40 × 31 mm) . . . 60 60
214 24p. Scouts and Baden-Powell's last message 70 70
215 29p. Scout salute, handshake, emblem and globe 90 90

55 "The Principals and Duties of Christianity" (Bishop T. Wilson) (first book printed in Manx, 1707)

1982. Europa. Historic Events. Multicoloured.

216 9p. Type **55** 25 25
217 19½p. Landing at Derbyhaven (visit of Thomas, 2nd Earl of Derby, 1507) 50 50

56 Charlie Collier (first TT race (single cylinder) winner) and Tourist Trophy Race, 1907

1982. 75th Anniv of Tourist Trophy Motorcycle Racing. Multicoloured.

218 9p. Type **56** 20 20
219 10p. Freddie Dixon (Sidecar and Junior TT winner) and Junior TT Race, 1927 . . . . . . 25 25
220 24p. Jimmie Simpson (TT winner and first to lap at 60, 70 and 80 mph) and Senior TT, 1932 . 80 70
221 26p. Mike Hailwood (winner of fourteen TT's) and Senior TT, 1961 . . . . 85 75
222 29p. Jock Taylor (Sidecar TT winner, 1978, 1980 and 1981) and Sidecar TT (with Benga Johansson), 1980 . . . . . 1·00 90

57 "Mona I"

1982. 150th Anniv of Isle of Man Steam Packet Company Mail Contract. Multicoloured.

223 12p. Type **57** 50 50
224 19½p. "Manx Maid II" . . . 75 75

58 Three Wise Men bearing Gifts

1982. Christmas. Multicoloured.

225 8p. Type **58** 50 50
226 11p. Christmas snow scene (vert) 50 50

60 Opening of Salvation Army Citadel, and T. H. Cannell, J.P.

1983. Centenary of Salvation Army in Isle of Man. Multicoloured.

228 10p. Type **60** 30 30
229 12p. Early meeting place and Gen. William Booth . . . 40 40
230 19½p. Salvation Army band . . 60 60
231 26p. Treating lepers and Lt.-Col. Thomas Bridson 90 90

61 Atlantic Puffins

61a "Queen Elizabeth II" (Ricardo Macarron)

1983. Sea Birds. Multicoloured.

232 1p. Type **61** 30 30
233 2p. Northern gannets 30 30
234 5p. Lesser black-backed gulls 60 40
235 8p. Common cormorants . . 60 40
236 10p. Kittiwakes 60 35
237 11p. Shags 60 35
238 12p. Grey herons 70 40
239 13p. Herring gulls 70 40
240 14p. Razorbills 70 40
241 15p. Great black-backed gulls 80 50
242 16p. Common shelducks . . . 80 50
243 18p. Oystercatchers 80 60
244 20p. Arctic terns . . . . . . 90 1·00
245 25p. Common guillemots . . 1·00 1·00
246 50p. Redshanks . . . . 1·75 1·75
247 £1 Mute swans . . . . 3·25 3·00
248 £5 Type **61a** . . . . 10·00 10·00
Nos. 244/7 are larger, 39 × 26 mm.

62 Design Drawings by Roger Casement for the Great Laxey Wheel (½-size illustration)

1983. Europa. The Great Laxey Wheel.

249 **62** 10p. black, blue and buff . 40 35
250 – 20½p. multicoloured . . . 60 70
DESIGN: 20½p. Roger Casement and the Great Laxey Wheel.

63 Nick Keig (international yachtsman) and Trimaran "Three Legs of Man III"

1983. 150th Anniv of King William's College. Multicoloured.

251 10p. Type **63** 20 20
252 12p. King William's College, Castletown 30 30
253 28p. Sir William Bragg (winner of Nobel Prize for Physics) and spectrometer 80 80
254 31p. General Sir George White, V.C. and action at Charasiah 1·00 1·00

64 New Post Office Headquarters, Douglas

1983. World Communications Year and 10th Anniv of Isle of Man Post Office Authority. Multicoloured.

255 10p. Type **64** 40 40
256 15p. As Type **64** but inscr "POST OFFICE DECENNIUM 1983" 60 60

65 Shepherds

1983. Christmas. Multicoloured.

257 9p. Type **65** 50 50
258 12p. Three Kings 50 50

66 "Manx King" (full-rigged ship)

1984. The Karran Fleet. Multicoloured.

259 10p. Type **66** 40 40
260 13p. "Hope" (barque) 55 55
261 20½p. "Rio Grande" (brig) . . 85 85
262 28p. "Lady Elizabeth" (barque) 1·00 1·00
263 31p. "Sumatra" (barque) . . . 1·10 1·10

67 C.E.P.T. 25th Anniversary Logo

69 Window from Glencrutchery House, Douglas

68 Railway Air Services De Havilland D.H.84 Dragon Mk 2

1984. Europa.

265 **67** 10p. orange, brown and light orange 35 35
266 20½p. blue, deep blue and light blue 70 70

1984. 50th Anniv of First Official Airmail to the Isle of Man and 40th Anniv of International Civil Aviation Organization. Multicoloured.

267 11p. Type **68** 45 45
268 13p. West Coast Air Services De Havilland D.H. 86A Dragon Express "Ronaldsway" . . 55 55
269 26p. B.E.A. Douglas DC-3 . . 95 95
270 28p. B.E.A. Vickers Viscount 800 1·00 1·00
271 31p. Telair Britten Norman Islander . . . . 1·25 1·25

1984. Christmas. Stained-glass Windows. Multicoloured.

272 10p. Type **69** 50 50
273 13p. Window from Lonan Old Church 50 50

70 William Cain's Birthplace, Ballasalla

1984. William Cain (civic leader, Victoria) Commemoration. Multicoloured.

274 11p. Type **70** 35 35
275 22p. The "Anna" leaving Liverpool, 1852 . . . . . . 75 75
276 28p. Early Australian railway . 1·00 1·00
277 30p. William Cain as Mayor of Melbourne, and Town Hall 1·10 1·10
278 33p. Royal Exhibition Building, Melbourne . . . . 1·25 1·25

71 Queen Elizabeth II and Commonwealth Parliamentary Association Badge

1984. Links with the Commonwealth. 30th Commonwealth Parliamentary Association Conference. Multicoloured.

279 14p. Type **71** 50 50
280 33p. Queen Elizabeth II and Manx emblem . . . . . . 1·10 1·10

72 Cunningham House Headquarters and Mrs. Willie Cunningham and Mrs. Joseph Cunningham (former Commissioners)

1985. 75th Anniv of Girl Guide Movement. Multicoloured.

281 11p. Type **72** 45 45
282 14p. Princess Margaret, Isle of Man standard and guides . . 75 75
283 29p. Lady Olave Baden-Powell opening Guide Headquarters, 1955 . . . . 1·10 1·10
284 31p. Guide uniforms from 1910 to 1985 . . . . 1·40 1·40
285 34p. Guide handclasp, salute and early badge . . . . . . 1·60 1·60

73 Score of Manx National Anthem

1985. Europa. European Music Year.

286 **73** 12p. black, light brown and brown 50 45
287 – 12p. black, light brown and brown 50 45
288 – 22p. black, lt blue and blue . 1·00 95
289 – 22p. black, lt blue and blue . 1·00 95
DESIGNS: No. 287, William H. Gill (lyricist); 288, Score of hymn "Crofton"; 289, Dr. John Clague (composer).

74 Charles Rolls in 20 h.p. Rolls-Royce (1906 Tourist Trophy Race)

1985. Century of Motoring. Multicoloured.

290 12p. Type **74** 40 40
291 12p. W. Bentley in 3 litre Bentley (1922 Tourist Trophy Race) 40 40
292 14p. F. Gerrard in E.R.A. (1950 British Empire Trophy Race) 55 55
293 14p. Brian Lewis in Alfa Romeo (1934 Mannin Moar Race) 55 55
294 31p. Jaguar "XJ-SC" ("Roads Open" car, 1984 Motor Cycle TT Races) . . . . 1·40 1·25
295 31p. Tony Pond and Mike Nicholson in Vauxhall "Chevette" (1981 Rothmans International Rally) . . . . 1·40 1·25

75 Queen Alexandra and Victorian Sergeant with Wife

1985. Centenary of Soldiers', Sailors' and Airmen's Families Association. Association Presidents. Multicoloured.

296 12p. Type **75** 40 40
297 15p. Queen Mary and Royal Air Force family 55 55
298 29p. Earl Mountbatten and Royal Navy family . . . . 1·10 1·10
299 34p. Prince Michael of Kent and Royal Marine with parents, 1982 . . . . 1·25 1·25

76 Kirk Maughold (birthplace)

1985. Birth Bicentenary of Lieutenant-General Sir Mark Cubbon (Indian administrator). Mult.

300 12p. Type **76** 45 45
301 22p. Lieutenant-General Sir Mark Cubbon (vert) . . . . 1·10 1·10
302 45p. Memorial statue, Bangalore, India (vert) . . . . 1·90 1·90

77 St. Peter's Church, Onchan

1985. Christmas. Manx Churches. Multicoloured.

303 11p. Type **77** 45 45
304 14p. Royal Chapel of St. John, Tynwald 55 55
305 31p. Bride Parish Church . . . 1·25 1·25

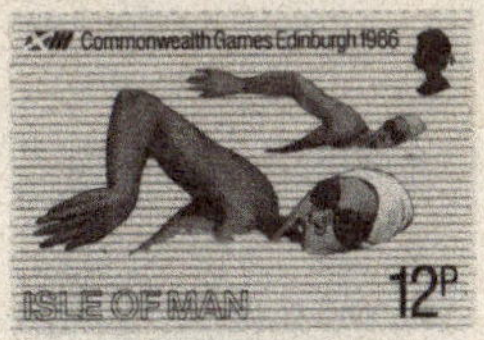

78 Swimming

1986. Commonwealth Games, Edinburgh. Multicoloured.

306 12p. Type **78** 40 40
307 15p. Race walking 50 50
308 31p. Rifle-shooting . . . . . 1·50 1·50
309 34p. Cycling . . . . 1·50 1·50

No. 309 also commemorates the 50th anniversary of Manx International Cycling Week.

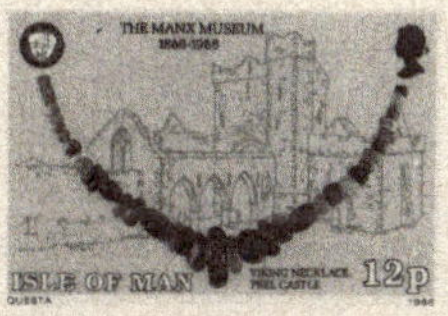

79 Viking Necklace and Peel Castle

1986. Centenary of Manx Museum. Multicoloured.

310 12p. Type **79** 35 35
311 15p. Meayll Circle, Rushen . . 45 45
312 22p. Skeleton of Great Deer and Manx Museum (vert) . . . 85 85
313 26p. Viking longship model (vert) 1·00 1·00
314 29p. Open Air Museum, Cregneash . . . . 1·25 1·25

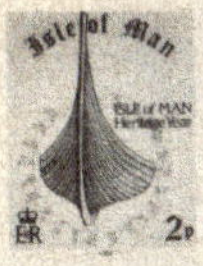

80 Viking Longship

81 "Usnea articulata" (lichen) and "Neotinea intacta" (orchid), The Ayres

1986. Manx Heritage Year.

315 **80** 2p. multicoloured 20 20
316 – 10p. black, green and grey 55 55

DESIGN: 10p. Celtic cross logo.

1986. Europa. Protection of Nature and the Environment. Multicoloured.

317 12p. Type **81** 60 60
318 12p. Hen harrier, Calf of Man 60 60
319 22p. Manx stoat, Eary Cushlin 95 95
320 22p. "Stenobothus stigmaticus" (grasshopper), St. Michael's Isle 95 95

82 Ellanbane (home of Myles Standish)

1986. "Ameripex '86" International Stamp Exhibition, Chicago. Captain Myles Standish of the "Mayflower". Multicoloured.

321 12p. Type **82** 35 35
322 15p. "Mayflower" crossing the Atlantic, 1620 . . . . 55 55
323 31p. Pilgrim Fathers landing at Plymouth, 1620 . . . . . . 1·40 1·40
324 34p. Captain Myles Standish 1·60 1·60

83 Prince Andrew in Naval Uniform and Miss Sarah Ferguson

1986. Royal Wedding. Multicoloured.

326 15p. Type **83** 75 75
327 40p. Engagement photograph 1·75 1·50

84 Prince Philip (from photo by Karsh)

85 European Robins on Globe and "Peace and Goodwill" in Braille

1986. Royal Birthdays. Multicoloured.

328 15p. Type **84** 80 80
329 15p. Queen Elizabeth II (from photo by Karsh) 80 80
330 34p. Queen Elizabeth and Prince Philip (from photo by Karsh) (48 × 35 mm) . . . . 1·75 1·75

Nos. 328/30 also commemorate "Stockholmia '86" International Stamp Exhibition, Sweden and the 350th anniversary of the Swedish Post Office.

1986. Christmas and International Peace Year. Multicoloured.

331 11p. Type **85** 50 50
332 14p. Hands releasing peace dove 55 55
333 31p. Clasped hands and "Peace" in sign language . . . . . 1·25 1·25

86 North Quay

1987. Victorian Douglas. Multicoloured.

334 2p. Type **86** 10 10
335 3p. Old Fishmarket 10 10
336 10p. The Breakwater 35 35
337 15p. Jubilee Clock 50 50
338 31p. Loch Promenade . . . . 1·50 1·50
339 34p. Beach . . . . 1·75 1·75

87 "The Old Fishmarket and Harbour, Douglas"

1987. Paintings by John Miller Nicholson. Multicoloured.

340 12p. Type **87** 35 35
341 26p. "Red Sails at Douglas" . 90 90
342 29p. "The Double Corner, Peel" 1·40 1·40
343 34p. "Peel Harbour" . . . . . 1·60 1·60

88 Sea Terminal, Douglas

1987. Europa. Architecture. Multicoloured.

344 12p. Type **88** 60 60
345 12p. Tower of Refuge, Douglas 60 60
346 22p. Gaiety Theatre, Douglas 1·10 1·10
347 22p. Villa Marina, Douglas . . 1·10 1·10

89 Supercharged "BMW" 500cc Motor Cycle, 1939

1987. 80th Anniv of Tourist Trophy Motor Cycle Races. Multicoloured.

348 12p. Type **89** 40 40
349 15p. Manx "Kneeler" Norton 350cc, 1953 . . . . 60 60
350 29p. MV Agusta 500cc 4, 1956 1·00 1·00
351 31p. Guzzi 500cc V8, 1957 . . 1·10 1·10
352 34p. Honda 250cc 6, 1967 . . 1·40 1·40

Nos. 348/52 also commemorate the Centenary of the St. John Ambulance Brigade.

90 Fuchsia and Wild Roses

91 Stirring the Christmas Pudding

1987. Wild Flowers. Multicoloured.

354 16p. Type **90** 60 60
355 29p. Field scabious and ragwort 1·10 1·10
356 31p. Wood anemone and celandine . . . . 1·25 1·25
357 34p. Violets and primroses . . 1·50 1·50

1987. Christmas. Victorian Scenes. Multicoloured.

358 12p. Type **91** 50 50
359 15p. Bringing home the Christmas tree 75 75
360 31p. Decorating the Christmas tree . . . . 1·25 1·25

92 Russell Brookes in Vauxhall "Opel" (Manx Rally winner, 1985)

1988. Motor Sport. Multicoloured.

361 13p. Type **92** 75 70
362 26p. Ari Vatanen in Ford "Escort" (Manx Rally winner, 1976) . . . . 1·25 1·10
363 31p. Terry Smith in Repco "March 761" (Hill Climb winner, 1980) . . . . 1·40 1·25
364 34p. Nigel Mansell in Williams/ Honda (British Grand Prix winner, 1986 and 1987) . . . 1·60 1·40

93 Horse Tram Terminus, Douglas Bay Tramway

93a Queen Elizabeth II taking Salute at Trooping the Colour

1988. Manx Railways and Tramways. Mult.

365 1p. Type **93** 10 10
366 2p. Snaefell Mountain Railway 10 10
367 3p. Marine Drive Tramway . 10 10
367c 4p. Douglas Cable Tramway 10 10
368 5p. Douglas Head Incline Railway 20 20
369 10p. Douglas & Laxey Coast Electric Tramway car at Maughold Head 30 30
370 13p. As 4p. 50 50
371 14p. Manx Northern Railway No. 4, "Caledonia", at Gob-y-Deigan 50 50
372 15p. Laxey Mine Railway Lewin locomotive "Ant" . . 50 50
373 16p. Port Erin Breakwater Tramway locomotive "Henry B. Loch" 50 50
374 17p. Ramsey Harbour Tramway 50 50
375 18p. Locomotive No. 7, "Tynwald", on Foxdale line 55 55
375a 18p. T.P.O. Special leaving Douglas, 3 July 1991 . . . 55 55
376 19p. Baldwin Reservoir Tramway steam locomotive No. 1, "Injebreck" 60 60
377 20p. I.M.R. No. 13, "Kissack", near St. Johns 60 60
377a 21p. As 14p. 60 60
377b 23p. Double-deck horse tram, Douglas 60 60
378 25p. I.M.R. No. 12, "Hutchinson", leaving Douglas 70 70
379 50p. Groudle Glen Railway locomotive "Polar Bear" . 1·50 1·50
380 £1 I.M.R. No. 11, "Maitland", pulling Royal Train, 1963 . 3·00 3·00
380a £2 Type **93a** . . . . 6·00 6·00

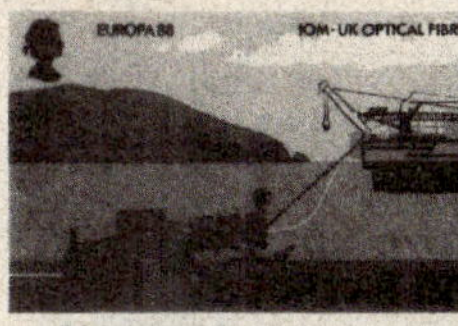

94 Laying Isle of Man–U.K. Submarine Cable

1988. Europa. Transport and Communications. Multicoloured.

381 13p. Type **94** 50 50
382 13p. "Flex Services" (cable ship) 50 50
383 22p. Earth station, Braddan . . 90 90
384 22p. "INTELSAT 5" satellite 90 90

Nos. 381/2 and 383/4 were each printed together, se-tenant Nos. 381/2 forming a composite design.

95 "Euterpe" (full-rigged ship) off Ramsey, 1863

1988. Manx Sailing Ships. Multicoloured.

385 16p. Type **95** 50 50
386 29p. "Vixen" (topsail schooner) leaving Peel for Australia, 1853 1·00 1·00
387 31p. "Ramsey" (full-rigged ship) off Brisbane, 1870 . . . . . 1·25 1·25
388 34p. "Star of India" (formerly "Euterpe") (barque) off San Diego, 1976 . . . . 1·40 1·40

Nos. 386/7 also commemorate the Bicent of Australian Settlement.

96 "Magellanica"

1988. 50th Anniv of British Fuchsia Society. Multicoloured.

390 13p. Type **96** 50 50
391 16p. "Pink Cloud" 60 60
392 22p. "Leonora" 80 80
393 29p. "Satellite" . . . . 1·10 1·00

394	31p. "Preston Guild"	1·25	1·25
395	34p. "Thalia"	1·40	1·40

97 Long-eared Owl

1988. Christmas. Manx Birds. Multicoloured.

396	12p. Type **97**	55	55
397	15p. European robin	85	85
398	31p. Grey partridge	1·40	1·40

98 Ginger Cat

1989. Manx Cats. Multicoloured.

399	16p. Type **98**	50	50
400	27p. Black and white cat	1·00	1·00
401	30p. Tortoiseshell and white cat	1·40	1·40
402	40p. Tortoiseshell cat	1·60	1·60

99 Tudric Pewter Clock, c. 1903

1989. 125th Birth Anniv of Archibald Knox (artist and designer). Multicoloured.

403	13p. Type **99**	35	35
404	16p. "Celtic Cross" watercolour	45	45
405	23p. Silver cup and cover 1902–03	75	75
406	32p. Gold and silver brooches from Liberty's Cymric range (horiz)	1·40	1·40
407	35p. Silver jewel box, 1900 (horiz)	1·50	1·50

100 William Bligh and Old Church, Onchan

1989. Bicentenary of the Mutiny on the "Bounty". Multicoloured.

408	13p. Type **100**	25	30
409	16p. Bligh and loyal crew cast adrift	30	35
410	23p. Pitcairn Islands 1989 Settlement Bicentenary 90 c., No. 345	1·10	1·10
411	27p. Norfolk Island 1989 Bicentenary 39 c., No. 461	1·10	1·10
412	30p. Midshipman Peter Heywood and Tahiti	70	70
413	32p. H.M.S. "Bounty" anchored off Pitcairn Island	75	75
414	35p. Fletcher Christian and Pitcairn Island	80	80

101 Skipping and Hopscotch

1989. Europa. Children's Games. Multicoloured.

416	13p. Type **101**	60	60
417	13p. Wheelbarrow, leapfrog and piggyback	60	60
418	23p. Completing model house and blowing bubbles	95	95
419	23p. Girl with doll and doll's house	95	95

Nos. 416/17 and 418/19 were printed together, se-tenant, forming composite designs.

INDEX

Countries can be quickly located by referring to the index at the end of this volume.

102 Atlantic Puffin

104 Mother with Baby, Jane Crookall Maternity Home

103 Red Cross Cadets learning Resuscitation

1989. Sea Birds. Multicoloured.

420	13p. Type **102**	80	80
421	13p. Black guillemot	80	80
422	13p. Common cormorant	80	80
423	13p. Kittiwake	80	80

1989. 125th Anniv of International Red Cross and Centenary of Noble's Hospital, Isle of Man.

424	**103**	14p. multicoloured	40	40
425	–	17p. grey and red	65	65
426	–	23p. multicoloured	90	90
427	–	30p. multicoloured	1·25	1·25
428	–	35p. multicoloured	1·50	1·50

DESIGNS: 17p. Anniversary logo; 23p. Signing Geneva Convention, 1864; 30p. Red Cross ambulance; 35p. Henri Dunant (founder).

1989. Christmas. 50th Anniv of Jane Crookall Maternity Home and 75th Anniv of St. Ninian's Church, Douglas. Multicoloured.

429	13p. Type **104**	45	45
430	16p. Mother with child	55	55
431	34p. Madonna and Child	1·10	1·10
432	37p. Baptism, St. Ninian's Church	1·25	1·25

105 "The Isle of Man Express going up a Gradient"

1990. Isle of Man Edwardian Postcards. Mult.

433	15p. Type **105**	30	30
434	19p. "A way we have in the Isle of Man"	55	55
435	32p. "Douglas—waiting for the male boat"	1·00	1·00
436	34p. "The last toast rack home, Douglas Parade"	1·40	1·40
437	37p. "The last Isle of Man boat"	1·50	1·50

106 Modern Postman

107 Penny Black

1990. Europa. Post Office Buildings. Mult.

438	15p. Type **106**	55	55
439	15p. Ramsey Post Office, 1990 (40 × 26 mm)	55	55
440	24p. Postman, 1890	95	95
441	24p. Douglas Post Office, 1890 (40 × 26 mm)	95	95

1990. 150th Anniv of the Penny Black.

442	**107**	1p. black, buff and gold	10	10
443	–	1p. gold, black & buff	65	65
444	–	32p. multicoloured	1·25	1·25
445	–	34p. multicoloured	1·25	1·25
446	–	37p. multicoloured	1·40	1·40

DESIGNS: 19p. Wyon Medal, 1837; 32p. Wyon's stamp essay; 34p. Perkins Bacon engine-turned essay, 1839; 37p. Twopence Blue, 1840.

108 Queen Elizabeth the Queen Mother

110 Churchill with Freedom of Douglas Casket

109 Hawker Hurricane Mk 1, Bristol Type 142 Blenheim Mk 1 and Home Defence

1990. 90th Birthday of Queen Elizabeth the Queen Mother.

448	**108**	90p. multicoloured	3·00	3·00

1990. 50th Anniv of Battle of Britain. Mult.

449	15p. Type **109**	40	40
450	15p. Supermarine Spitfire with Westland Lysander Mk I rescue aircraft and launch	40	40
451	24p. Rearming Hawker Hurricanes Mk I fighters	90	90
452	24p. Ops room and scramble	90	90
453	29p. Civil Defence personnel	95	95
454	29p. Anti-aircraft battery	95	95

1990. 25th Death Anniv of Sir Winston Churchill. Multicoloured.

455	19p. Type **110**	60	60
456	32p. Churchill and London blitz	1·10	1·10
457	34p. Churchill and searchlights over Westminster	1·40	1·40
458	37p. Churchill with R.A.F. Hawker Hurricane Mk I fighters	1·40	1·40

111 Boy on Toboggan and Girl posting Letter

112 Henry Bloom Noble and Orphans (Marshall Wane)

1990. Christmas. Multicoloured.

459	14p. Type **111**	40	40
460	18p. Girl on toboggan and skaters	60	60
461	34p. Boy with snowman	1·25	1·25
462	37p. Children throwing snowballs	1·40	1·40

1991. Manx Photography.

464	**112**	17p. brown, grey & black	45	45
465	–	21p. brown and ochre	60	60
466	–	26p. brown, stone & blk	90	90
467	–	31p. brown, lt brn & blk	1·25	1·25
468	–	40p. multicoloured	1·50	1·50

DESIGNS: 21p. Douglas (Frederick Frith); 26p. Studio portrait of three children (Hilda Newby); 31p. Cashtal yn Ard (Christopher Killip); 40p. Peel Castle (Colleen Corlett).

113 Lifeboat "Sir William Hillary", Douglas

1991. Manx Lifeboats. Multicoloured.

469	17p. Type **113**	45	45
470	21p. "Osman Gabriel", Port Erin	60	60
471	26p. "Ann and James Ritchie", Ramsey	90	90
472	31p. "The Gough Ritchie", Port St. Mary	1·25	1·25
473	37p. "John Batstone", Peel	1·50	1·50

No. 469 is inscribed "HILARY" and No. 471 "JAMES & ANN RITCHIE", both in error.

114 "Intelsat" Communications Satellite

116 Laxey Hand-cart, 1920

115 Oliver Godfrey with Indian 500cc at Start, 1911

1991. Europa. Europe in Space. Multicoloured.

474	17p. Type **114**	70	70
475	17p. "Ariane" rocket launch and fishing boats in Douglas harbour	70	70
476	26p. Weather satellite and space station	1·00	1·00
477	26p. Ronaldsway Airport, Manx Radio transmitter and Space shuttle launch	1·00	1·00

Nos. 474/5 and 476/7 were each printed together, se-tenant, each pair forming a composite design.

1991. 80th Anniv of Tourist Trophy Mountain Course. Multicoloured.

478	17p. Type **115**	40	40
479	21p. Freddie Dixon on Douglas "banking" sidecar, 1923	60	60
480	26p. Bill Ivy on Yamaha 125cc, 1968	85	85
481	31p. Giacomo Agostini on MV Agusta 500cc, 1972	1·25	1·25
482	37p. Joey Dunlop on RVF Honda 750cc, 1985	1·40	1·40

1991. Fire Engines. Multicoloured.

485	17p. Type **116**	40	40
486	21p. Horse-drawn steamer, Douglas, 1909	60	60
487	30p. Merryweather "Hatfield" pump, 1936	85	85
488	33p. Dennis "F8" pumping appliance, Peel, 1953	1·25	1·25
489	37p. Volvo turntable ladder, Douglas, 1989	1·40	1·40

117 Mute Swans, Douglas Harbour

1991. Swans. Multicoloured.

490	17p. Type **117**	55	55
491	17p. Black swans, Curraghs Wildlife Park	55	55
492	26p. Whooper swans, Bishop's Dub, Ballaugh	1·10	1·10
493	26p. Whistling ("Bewick's") swans, Eairy Dam, Foxdale	1·10	1·10
494	37p. Coscoroba swans, Curraghs Wildlife Park	1·40	1·40
495	37p. Whooper ("Trumpeter") swans, Curraghs Wildlife Park	1·40	1·40

The two designs of each value were printed together, se-tenant, forming a composite design.

118 The Three Kings

120 Queen Elizabeth II at Coronation, 1953

119 North African and Italian Campaigns, 1942–43

1991. Christmas. Paper Sculptures. Multicoloured.

496	16p. Type **118**	50	40
497	20p. Mary with manger	65	70
498	26p. Shepherds with sheep	80	85
499	37p. Choir of angels	1·10	1·10

1992. 50th Anniv of Parachute Regiment. Mult.

502	23p. Type **119**	75	75
503	23p. D-Day, 1944	75	75
504	28p. Arnhem, 1944	80	80
505	28p. Rhine crossing, 1945	80	80
506	39p. Operations in Near, Middle and Far East, 1945–68	1·25	1·25
507	39p. Liberation of Falkland Islands, 1982	1·25	1·25

1992. 40th Anniv of Accession. Multicoloured.

508	18p. Type **120**	50	50
509	23p. Queen visiting Isle of Man, 1979	60	60
510	28p. Queen in evening dress	70	70
511	33p. Queen visiting Isle of Man, 1989	1·25	1·25
512	39p. Queen arriving for film premiere, 1990	1·40	1·40

121 Brittle-stars

1992. Centenary of Port Erin Marine Laboratory. Multicoloured.

513 18p. Type **121** 50 50
514 23p. Phytoplankton 60 60
515 28p. Atlantic herring 70 70
516 33p. Great scallop 1·25 1·25
517 39p. Dahlia anemone and delesseria 1·40 1·40

122 The Pilgrim Fathers embarking at Delfshaven

1992. Europa. 500th Anniv of Discovery of America by Columbus. Multicoloured.

518 18p. Type **122** 60 60
519 18p. "Speedwell" leaving Delfshaven 60 60
520 28p. "Mayflower" setting sail for America 1·00 1·00
521 28p. "Speedwell" anchored at Dartmouth 1·00 1·00

The two designs for each value were printed together, se-tenant, in horizontal pairs forming composite designs.

123 Central Pacific Locomotive "Jupiter", 1869

1992. Construction of the Union Pacific Railroad, 1866–69. Multicoloured.

522 33p. Type **123** 95 95
523 33p. Union Pacific locomotive No. 119, 1869 95 95
524 39p. Union Pacific locomotive No. 844, 1992 1·25 1·25
525 39p. Union Pacific locomotive No. 3985, 1992 1·25 1·25

124 "King Orry V" in Douglas Harbour

1992. Manx Harbours. Multicoloured.

527 18p. Type **124** 50 50
528 23p. Castletown 60 60
529 37p. Port St. Mary 1·25 1·25
530 40p. Ramsey 1·25 1·25

126 Stained Glass Window, St. German's Cathedral, Peel

127 Mansell on Lap of Honour, British Grand Prix, 1992

1992. Christmas. Manx Churches. Mult.

532 17p. Type **126** 50 50
533 22p. Reredos, St. Matthew the Apostle Church, Douglas 70 70
534 28p. Stained glass window, St. George's Church, Douglas 85 85
535 37p. Reredos, St. Mary of the Isle Catholic Church, Douglas 1·00 1·00
536 40p. Stained glass window, Trinity Methodist Church, Douglas 1·10 1·10

1992. Nigel Mansell's Victory in Formula 1 World Motor Racing Championship. Multicoloured.

537 20p. Type **127** 70 70
538 24p. Mansell in French Grand Prix, 1992 80 80

128 H.M.S. "Amazon" (frigate)

128a Manx Red Ensign **128b** Queen Elizabeth II (hologram)

1993. Ships. Multicoloured.

539 1p. Type **128** 10 10
540 2p. "Fingal" (lighthouse tender) 10 10
541 4p. "Sir Winston Churchill" (cadet schooner) 10 10
542 5p. "Dar Mlodziezy" (full-rigged cadet ship) 10 10
543 20p. "Tynwald I" (paddle-steamer) 40 45
544 21p. "Ben Veg" (freighter) 40 45
545 22p. "Waverley" (paddle-steamer) 45 50
546 23p. Royal Yacht "Britannia" 45 50
547 24p. "Francis Drake" (ketch) 50 55
548 25p. "Royal Viking Sky" (liner) 50 55
549 26p. "Lord Nelson" (cadet barque) 55 60
550 27p. "Europa" (liner) 55 60
551 30p. "Snaefell V" (ferry) leaving Ardrossan 60 65
552 35p. "Seacat" (catamaran ferry) 70 75
553 40p. "Lady of Mann I" (ferry) off Ramsey 80 85
554 50p. "Mona's Queen II" (paddle ferry) leaving Fleetwood 1·00 1·10
555 £1 "Queen Elizabeth 2" (liner) and "Mona's Queen V" (ferry) off Liverpool 2·00 2·10
556 £2 Type **128a** 4·00 4·25
557 £5 Type **128b** 10·00 10·50

For 4, 20 and 24p. in smaller size, 21 × 18 mm, see Nos. 687/93.

129 No. 1 Motor Car and No. 13 Trailer at Groudle Glen Hotel

1993. Cent of Manx Electric Railway. Mult.

559 20p. Type **129** 50 50
560 24p. No. 9 Tunnel Car and No. 19 Trailer at Douglas Bay Hotel 75 75
561 28p. No. 19 Motor Car and No. 59 Royal Trailer Special at Douglas Bay 85 85
562 39p. No. 33 Motor Car, No. 45 Trailer and No. 13 Van at Derby Castle 1·25 1·25

130 "Sir Hall Caine" (statue) (Bryan Kneale)

1993. Europa. Contemporary Art. Works by Bryan Kneale. Multicoloured.

563 20p. Type **130** 55 55
564 20p. "The Brass Bedstead" (painting) 55 55
565 28p. Abstract bronze sculpture 90 90
566 28p. "Polar Bear Skeleton" (drawing) 90 90

131 Graham Oates and Bill Marshall (1933 International Six Day Trial) on Ariel Square Four

1993. Manx Motor Cycling Events. Mult.

567 20p. Type **131** 50 50
568 24p. Sergeant Geoff Duke (1947 Royal Signals Display Team) on Triumph 3T Twin 70 70
569 28p. Denis Parkinson (1953 Senior Manx Grand Prix) on Manx Norton 90 90
570 33p. Richard Swallow (1991 Junior Classic MGP) on Aermacchi 1·25 1·25
571 39p. Steve Colley (1992 Scottish Six Day Trial) on Beta Zero 1·40 1·40

132 "Inachis io" (Peacock)

133 Children decorating Christmas Tree

1993. Butterflies. Multicoloured.

573 24p. Type **132** 80 80
574 24p. "Argynnis aglaja" (Dark green fritillary) 80 80
575 24p. "Cynthia cardui" (Painted lady) 80 80
576 24p. "Celastrina argiolus" (Holly blue) 80 80
577 24p. "Vanessa atalanta" (Red admiral) 80 80

1993. Christmas. Multicoloured.

578 19p. Type **133** 55 55
579 23p. Girl with snowman 65 65
580 28p. Boy opening presents 80 80
581 39p. Girl with teddy bear 1·10 1·10
582 40p. Children with toboggan 1·10 1·10

134 White-throated Robin

1994. Calf of Man Bird Observatory. Mult.

583 20p. Type **134** 60 60
584 20p. Black-eared wheatear 60 60
585 24p. Goldcrest 90 90
586 24p. Northern oriole 90 90
587 30p. Common kingfisher 1·00 1·00
588 30p. Hoopoe 1·00 1·00

135 Gaiety Theatre, Douglas

1994. Manx Tourism Centenary. Multicoloured.

590 24p. Type **135** 60 60
591 24p. Sports 60 60
592 24p. Artist at work and yachts racing 60 60
593 24p. TT Races and British Aerospace Hawk T.1s of Red Arrows display team 60 60
594 24p. Musical instruments 60 60
595 24p. Laxey Wheel and Manx cat 60 60
596 24p. Tower of Refuge, Douglas, with bucket and spade 60 60
597 24p. Cyclist 60 60
598 24p. Tynwald Day and classic car 60 60
599 24p. Santa Mince Pie train, Groudle Glen 60 60

136 "Eubranchus tricolor" (sea slug)

1994. Europa. Discoveries of Edward Forbes (marine biologist). Multicoloured.

600 20p. Type **136** 50 50
601 20p. "Loligo forbesii" (common squid) 50 50
602 20p. Edward Forbes and signature 50 50
603 30p. "Solaster moretonis" (fossil starfish) 90 90
604 30p. "Adamsia carciniopados" (anenome) on hermit crab 90 90
605 30p. "Solaster endeca" (starfish) 90 90

137 Maj-Gen. Bedell Smith and Naval Landing Force including "Ben-my-Chree IV" (ferry)

1994. 50th Anniv of D-Day. Multicoloured.

606 4p. Type **137** 15 15
607 4p. Admiral Ramsay and naval ships including "Victoria" and "Lady of Mann" (ferries) 15 15
608 20p. Gen. Montgomery and British landings 70 70
609 20p. Lt-Gen. Dempsey and 2nd Army landings 70 70
610 30p. Air Chief Marshal Leigh-Mallory and U.S. paratroops and aircraft 1·00 1·00
611 30p. Air Chief Marshal Tedder and British paratroops and aircraft 1·00 1·00
612 41p. Lt-Gen. Bradley and U.S. 1st Army landings 1·25 1·25
613 41p. Gen. Eisenhower and American landings 1·25 1·25

138 Postman Pat, Jess and Ffinlo at Sea Terminal, Douglas

1994. Postman Pat visits the Isle of Man. Multicoloured.

614 1p. Type **138** 10 10
615 20p. Laxey Wheel 60 60
616 24p. Cregneash 80 80
617 30p. Manx Electric Railway trains 90 90
618 36p. Peel Harbour 1·10 1·10
619 41p. Douglas Promenade 1·25 1·25

139 Cycling

1994. Centenary of International Olympic Committee. Multicoloured.

621 10p. Type **139** 30 30
622 20p. Downhill skiing 55 55
623 24p. Swimming 70 70
624 35p. Hurdling 95 95
625 48p. Centenary logo 1·40 1·40

140 Santa Train to Santon

1994. Christmas. Father Christmas in the Isle of Man. Multicoloured.

626 19p. Type **140** 50 50
627 23p. Father Christmas and Postman Pat on mini tractor, Douglas (vert) 70 70
628 60p. Father Christmas and majorettes in sleigh, Port St. Mary 1·60 1·60

141 Foden Steam Wagon, Highway Board Depot, Douglas

1995. Steam Traction Engines. Multicoloured.

629 20p. Type **141** 60 60
630 24p. Clayton & Shuttleworth and Fowler engines pulling dead whale 70 70
631 30p. Wallis and Steevens engine at Ramsey Harbour 85 85
632 35p. Marshall engine with threshing machine, Ballarhenny 1·10 1·10
633 41p. Marshall convertible steam roller 1·25 1·25

142 Car No. 2 and First Train, 1895

1995. Centenary of Snaefell Mountain Railway. Multicoloured.

634 20p. Type **142** 60 60
635 24p. Car No. 4 in green livery and Car No. 3 in Laxey Valley 70 70
636 35p. Car No. 6 and Car No. 5 in 1971 . . . . 95 95
637 42p. Goods Car No. 7 and "Caledonia" steam locomotive pulling construction train . 1·10 1·10

143 Peace Doves forming Wave and Tower of Refuge, Douglas Bay

1995. Europa. Peace and Freedom. Multicoloured.

639 20p. Type **143** 50 50
640 30p. Peace dove breaking barbed wire 75 75

144 Spitfire, Tank and Medals

1995. 50th Anniv of End of Second World War. Multicoloured.

641 10p. Type **144** 30 30
642 10p. Typhoon, anti-aircraft gun and medals 30 30
643 20p. Lancaster, escort carrier and medals 55 55
644 20p. U.S. Navy aircraft, jungle patrol and medals 55 55
645 24p. Celebrations in Parliament Square 70 70
646 24p. V.E. Day bonfire 70 70
647 40p. Street party . . . . . . 1·10 1·10
648 40p. King George VI and Queen Elizabeth on Isle of Man in July 1945 . . . . 1·10 1·10

145 Reg Parnell in Maserati "4 CLT", 1951

1995. 90th Anniv of Motor Racing on Isle of Man. Multicoloured.

649 20p. Type **145** 60 60
650 24p. Stirling Moss in Frazer Nash, 1951 . . . . 75 75
651 30p. Richard Seaman in Delage, 1936 . . . . 85 85
652 36p. Prince Bira in ERA R2B "Romulus", 1937 . . . . . 1·00 1·00
653 41p. Kenelm Guinness in Sunbeam 1, 1914 . . . . . 1·10 1·10
654 42p. Freddie Dixon in Riley, 1934 . . . . 1·10 1·10

146 Thomas the Tank Engine and Bertie Bus being Unloaded

1995. 50th Anniv of Thomas the Tank Engine Stories by Revd. Awdry. "Thomas the Tank Engine's Dream". Multicoloured.

656 20p. Type **146** 60 60
657 24p. Mail train 75 75
658 30p. Bertie and engines at Ballasalla 85 85
659 36p. "Viking" the diesel engine, Port Erin . . . . 1·00 1·00
660 41p. Thomas and railcar at Snaefell summit . . . . . . 1·10 1·10
661 45p. Engines racing past Laxey Wheel . . . . 1·25 1·25

147 "Amanita muscaria"

148 St. Catherine's Church, Port Erin

1995. Fungi. Multicoloured.

662 20p. Type **147** 50 50
663 24p. "Boletus edulis" 65 65
664 30p. "Coprinus disseminatus" 85 85
665 35p. "Pleurotus ostreatus" . . 95 95
666 45p. "Geastrum triplex" . . . 1·50 1·50

1995. Christmas. Multicoloured.

668 19p. Type **148** 50 50
669 23p. European robin on holly branch 60 60
670 42p. St. Peter's Church and wild flowers . . . . 1·10 1·10
671 50p. Hedgehog hibernating under farm machinery . . . 1·40 1·40

149 Langness Lighthouse

151 Douglas Borough Arms

150 White Manx Cat and Celtic Interlaced Ribbons

1996. Lighthouses. Multicoloured.

672 20p. Type **149** 55 55
673 24p. Point of Ayre lighthouse (horiz) 65 65
674 30p. Chicken Rock lighthouse 85 85
675 36p. Calf of Man lighthouse (horiz) . . . . 1·00 1·00
676 41p. Douglas Head lighthouse 1·10 1·10
677 42p. Maughold Head lighthouse (horiz) . . . . 1·10 1·10

1996. Manx Cats. Multicoloured.

678 20p. Type **150** 60 60
679 24p. Cat and Union Jack ribbons 75 75
680 36p. Cat on rug in German colours, mouse and Brandenburg Gate . . . . 1·00 1·00
681 42p. Cat, U.S.A. flag and Statue of Liberty . . . . 1·10 1·10
682 48p. Cat, map of Australia and kangaroo . . . . 1·25 1·25

1996. Centenary of Douglas Borough. Self-adhesive.

684 **151** (20p.) multicoloured . . 50 50

1996. Ships. As Nos. 541, 543 and 547, but smaller, 21 × 18 mm. Multicoloured.

687 4p. "Sir Winston Churchill" (cadet schooner) 10 10
689 20p. "Tynwald I" (paddle-steamer), 1846 . . . . . . 60 60
693 24p. "Francis Drake" (ketch) 75 75

The 20p. and 24p. show the positions of the face value and Queen's head reversed.

152 Princess Anne (President, Save the Children Fund) and Children

1996. Europa. Famous Women. Multicoloured.

701 24p. Type **152** 60 60
702 30p. Queen Elizabeth II and people of the Commonwealth 90 90

153 Alec Bennett

1996. Tourist Trophy Motorcycle Races. Irish Winners. Multicoloured.

703 20p. Type **153** 65 65
704 24p. Stanley Woods 70 70
705 45p. Artie Bell . . . . 1·25 1·25
706 60p. Joey and Robert Dunlop . 1·50 1·50

154 National Poppy Appeal Trophy

1996. 75th Anniv of Royal British Legion. Mult.

708 20p. Type **154** 60 60
709 24p. Manx War Memoial, Braddan 65 65
710 42p. Poppy appeal collection box 1·10 1·10
711 75p. Royal British Legion badge 2·10 2·10

155 U.N.I.C.E.F. Projects in Mexico

1996. 50th Anniv of U.N.I.C.E.F. Multicoloured.

713 24p. Type **155** 50 55
714 24p. Projects in Sri Lanka . . 50 55
715 30p. Projects in Colombia . . 60 65
716 30p. Projects in Zambia . . . 60 65
717 42p. Projects in Afghanistan . 85 90
718 42p. Projects in Vietnam . . . 85 90

156 Labrador

1996. Dogs. Multicoloured.

719 20p. Type **156** 55 55
720 24p. Border collie 65 65
721 31p. Dalmatian 75 75
722 38p. Mongrel 90 90
723 43p. English setter . . . . . 1·10 1·10
724 63p. Alsatian . . . . 1·60 1·60

157 "Snowman and Pine Trees" (David Bennett)

158 Primroses and Cashtyl ny Ard

1996. Christmas. Children's Paintings. Multicoloured.

726 19p. Type **157** 50 50
727 23p. "Three-legged Father Christmas" (Louis White) 65 65
728 50p. "Family around Christmas Tree" (Robyn Whelan) . . . 1·25 1·25
729 75p. "Father Christmas in Sleigh" (Claire Bradley) . . 1·75 1·75

1997. Spring in Man. Multicoloured.

730 20p. Type **158** 40 45
731 24p. Lochtan sheep and lambs 50 55
732 43p. Daffodils, duck and ducklings 85 90
733 63p. Dabchick with young and frog on lily pad . . . . . 1·25 1·40

159 Barn Owl

160 Moddey Dhoo, Peel Castle

1997. Owls. Multicoloured.

734 20p. Type **159** 60 60
735 24p. Short-eared owl 75 75
736 31p. Long-eared owl 90 90
737 36p. Little owl . . . . 1·10 1·10
738 43p. Snowy owl . . . . 1·25 1·25
739 56p. Tawny owl . . . . 1·50 1·50

1997. Europa. Tales and Legends. Multicoloured.

741 21p. Type **160** 50 50
742 25p. Fairies in tree and cottage 60 60
743 31p. Fairies at Fairy bridge . 70 70
744 36p. Giant Finn MacCooil and Calf of Man 80 80
745 37p. The Buggane of St. Trinian's 85 85
746 43p. Fynoderee and farm . . 1·00 1·00

Nos. 742/3 include the "EUROPA" emblem.

161 Sopwith Tabloid

1997. Manx Aircraft. Multicoloured.

747 21p. Type **161** 50 50
748 21p. Grumman Tiger (winner of 1996 Schneider Trophy) . . 50 50
749 25p. BAe ATP (15th anniv of Manx Airlines) 60 60
750 25p. BAe 146-200 (15th anniv of Manx Airlines) 60 60
751 31p. Boeing 757-200 (largest aircraft to land on Isle of Man) 75 75
752 31p. Farman biplane (1st Manx flight, 1911) 75 75
753 36p. Spitfire 90 90
754 36p. Hawker Hurricane . . . 90 90

Nos. 747/8, 749/50, 751/2 and 753/4 respectively were each printed together, se-tenant, the backgrounds forming composite of Isle of Man.

No. 752 is inscribed "EARMAN BIPLANE" in error.

162 14th Hole, Ramsey Golf Club

1997. Golf. Multicoloured.

755 21p. Type **162** 50 50
756 25p. 15th Hole, King Edward Bay Golf and Country Club 60 60
757 43p. 17th Hole, Rowany Golf Club . . . . 1·10 1·10
758 50p. 8th Hole, Castletown Golf Links . . . . 1·50 1·50

163 Steve Colley

1997. F.I.M. "Trial de Nations" Motorcycle Team Trials. Multicoloured.

761 21p. Type **163** 50 50
762 25p. Steve Saunders (vert) . . 60 60
763 37p. Sammy Miller (vert) . . 1·00 1·00
764 44p. Don Smith . . . . 1·25 1·25

164 Angel and Shepherd

165 Engagement of Princess Elizabeth and Lieut. Philip Mountbatten, 1947

1997. Christmas. Multicoloured.

765 20p. Type **164** 55 55
766 24p. Angel and King 70 70
767 63p. The Nativity (54 × 39 mm) 1·50 1·50

1997. Golden Wedding of Queen Elizabeth and Prince Philip. Multicoloured (except No. 768).

768 50p. Type **165** (brown and gold) 1·25 1·25
769 50p. Wedding photograph, 1947 1·25 1·25
770 50p. At Ascot, 1952 . . . . . 1·25 1·25
771 50p. Golden Wedding photograph, 1997 . . . . . 1·25 1·25

166 Shamrock

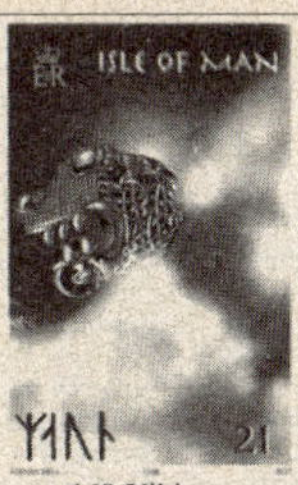
168 Viking Figurehead

167 Queen Elizabeth II and Queen Elizabeth the Queen Mother

1998. Flowers. Multicoloured
773 1p. Bearded iris 10 10
774 2p. Daisy 10 10
775 4p. Type **166** 10 10
776 5p. Silver Jubilee rose 10 15
777 10p. Oriental poppy 20 25
778 20p. Heath spotted orchid . . 40 45
779 21p. Cushag 40 45
780 22p. Gorse 45 50
781 25p. Princess of Wales rose . . 50 55
782 26p. Dog rose 50 55
783 30p. Fuchsia "Lady Thumb" . 60 65
784 50p. Daffodil . . . . 1·00 1·10
785 £1 Spear thistle . . . . . . 2·00 2·10
790 £2.50 Type **167** . . . . . . 5·00 5·25

1998. Viking Longships. Multicoloured.
793 21p. Type **168** 40 45
794 25p. Viking longship at sea . . 50 55
795 31p. Viking longship on beach 60 65
796 75p. Stern of ship . . . . . . 1·50 1·60

169 Bottle-nosed Dolphins

1998. U.N.E.S.C.O. International Year of the Ocean. Multicoloured.
798 10p. Type **169** 20 25
799 21p. Basking shark 40 45
800 25p. Front view of basking shark 50 55
801 31p. Minke whale 60 65
802 63p. Killer whale and calf . . 1·25 1·40

170 Locomotive No. 12 "Hutchinson"

1998. 125th Anniv of Isle of Man Steam Railway. Multicoloured.
803 21p. Type **170** 40 45
804 25p. Locomotive No. 10 "G. H. Wood" 50 55
805 31p. Locomotive No. 11 "Maitland" 60 65
806 63p. Locomotive No. 4 "Loch" 1·25 1·40

171 Purple Helmets Display Team

1998. Isle of Man T.T. Races and 50th Anniv of Honda (manufacturer). Multicoloured.
808 21p. Type **171** 40 45
809 25p. Joey Dunlop 50 55
810 31p. Dave Molyneux 60 65
811 43p. Naomi Taniguchi 85 90
812 63p. Mike Hailwood . . . . . 1·25 1·40

172 Princess Diana wearing Protective Clothing, Angola

1998. Diana, Princess of Wales Commemoration. Multicoloured.
813 25p. Type **172** 50 55
814 25p. Receiving award from United Cerebral Palsy Charity, New York, 1995 . . . . . 50 55
815 25p. With children, South Korea, 1992 . . . . 50 55
816 25p. Wearing blue jacket, July 1993 . . . . 50 55

173 Tynwald Day Ceremony

1998. Europa. Festivals. Multicoloured.
817 25p. Type **173** 50 60
818 30p. Traditional dancers, Tynwald Fair 60 65

174 Father Christmas at North Pole

1998. Christmas. "A Very Special Delivery". Multicoloured.
819 20p. Type **174** 40 45
820 24p. Father Christmas checking list 50 55
821 30p. Flying over Spring Valley sorting office 60 65
822 43p. Passing through Baldrine village 85 90
823 63p. Father Christmas delivering presents . . . . 1·25 1·40

175 Large Oval Pillar Box, Kirk Onchan

176 Cottage, Ballaglass Glen

1999. Local Post Boxes. Multicoloured.
824 10p. Type **175** 20 25
825 20p. Wall box, Ballaterson . . 40 45
826 21p. King Edward VII pillar box, Laxey Station 45 50
827 25p. Wall box, Spaldrick . . . 50 55
828 44p. Small oval pillar box, Derby Road, Douglas 90 95
829 63p. Wall box, Baldrine Station 1·25 1·40

1999. Europa. Parks and Gardens. Multicoloured.
830 25p. Type **176** 50 55
831 30p. Glen Maye Waterfall . . 60 65

177 "Ann and James Ritchie", Ramsey

1999. 175th Anniv of Royal National Lifeboat Institution. Multicoloured.
832 21p. Type **177** 45 50
833 25p. "Sir William Hillary", Douglas 50 55
834 37p. "Ruby Clery, Peel" . . . 75 80
835 43p. Inshore lifeboat, Port Erin 85 90
836 43p. 1974 150th Anniv 8p. stamp 85 90
837 56p. "Gough Ritchie II", Port St. Mary . . . . 1·10 1·25
838 56p. 1991 Manx Lifeboats 21p. stamp . . . . 1·10 1·25

178 Winter

1999. Jewels of the Manx Language. The Seasons. Multicoloured.
840 22p. Type **178** 45 50
841 26p. Spring 55 60
842 50p. Summer . . . . 1·00 1·10
843 63p. Autumn . . . . 1·25 1·40
Nos. 840/3 are inscribed "Ellan Vannin", the Manx name for the Isle of Man.

180 Tilling-Stevens Double-deck Bus, 1922

1999. Manx Buses. Multicoloured.
845 22p. Type **180** 45 50
846 26p. Thornycroft BC single-deck, 1928 . . . . 55 60
847 28p. Cumberland ADC 416 single-deck, 1927 . . . . . 55 60
848 37p. Straker-Squire single-deck, 1914 . . . . 75 80
849 38p. Thornycroft A2 single-deck, 1927 . . . . 75 80
850 40p. Leyland Lion LT9 single-deck, 1938 . . . . 80 85

POSTAGE DUE STAMPS

D 1

D 2

1973.
D1 **D 1** ½p. red, black and yellow . 1·75 1·50
D2 1p. red, black and brown . 65 65
D3 2p. red, black and green . 15 20
D4 3p. red, black and grey . . 25 25
D5 4p. red, black and pink . . 35 35
D6 5p. red, black and blue . . 40 40
D7 10p. red, black and violet . 50 50
D8 20p. red, black and green . 90 90

1975.
D 9 **D 2** ½p. yellow, black & red . 10 10
D10 1p. brown, black & red . 10 10
D11 4p. lilac, black and red . 10 10
D12 7p. blue, black and red . 20 20
D13 9p. grey, black and red . 25 25
D14 10p. mauve, black and red 30 30
D15 50p. orange, black and red 1·25 1·25
D16 £1 green, black & red . . 1·50 1·50

D 3

D 4

1982.
D17 **D 3** 1p. multicoloured 10 10
D18 2p. multicoloured 10 10
D19 5p. multicoloured 10 10
D20 10p. multicoloured . . . 20 25
D21 20p. multicoloured . . . 40 45
D22 50p. multicoloured . . . 1·00 1·10
D23 £1 multicoloured . . . . 2·00 2·10
D24 £2 multicoloured . . . . 4·00 4·25

1992.
D25 **D 4** £5 multicoloured . . . . 10·00 10·50

JAIPUR

A state of Rajasthan, India. Now uses Indian stamps.

12 pies = 1 anna; 16 annas = 1 rupee

2 Chariot of the Sun God, Surya **3**

1904.
3 **2** ½ a. blue . . . . 2·75 4·25
4 1 a. red . . . . 4·00 11·00
5 2 a. green . . . . 3·00 10·00

1904.
9 **3** ¼ a. olive 55 40
10a ½ a. blue 50 40
28 1 a. red . . . . 1·40 1·40
12 2 a. green . . . . 1·00 75
13 4 a. brown . . . . 4·75 2·00
14 8 a. violet . . . . 3·00 2·75
15a 1 r. yellow . . . . 14·00 16·00
This set was issued engraved in 1904 and surface-printed in 1913.

4 Chariot of the Sun God, Surya

३ आना
(**5**)

1911. No gum.
17 **4** ¼ a. olive 30 55
18 ½ a. blue 30 55
20 1 a. red 40 60
21 2 a. green . . . . 2·00 5·50

1926. Surch with T **5**.
32 **3** 3 a. on 8 a. violet . . . . . 1·00 1·90
33 3 a. on 1 r. yellow . . . . . 1·75 3·50

6 Chariot of the Sun God, Surya

7 Maharaja Sawai Man Singh II

1931. Investiture of Maharaja. Centres in black.
40 **6** ¼ a. purple . . . . 80 1·10
58 **7** ¼ a. red 30 15
41 ½ a. violet 30 10
59 ¾ a. red . . . . 4·25 2·50
42 – 1 a. blue . . . . 4·75 5·00
60 **7** 1 a. blue . . . . 5·00 1·90
43 – 2 a. orange . . . . 3·25 5·00
61 **7** 2 a. orange . . . . 5·00 2·50
44 – 2½ a. red . . . . 28·00 42·00
62 **7** 2½ a. red . . . . 2·00 1·40
45 – 3 a. green . . . . 10·00 35·00
63 **7** 3 a. green . . . . 1·25 40
46 – 4 a. green . . . . 12·00 38·00
64 **7** 4 a. green . . . . 16·00 75·00
47 – 6 a. blue . . . . 6·00 35·00
65 **7** 6 a. blue . . . . 1·90 17·00
48 – 8 a. brown . . . . 10·00 50·00
66 **7** 8 a. brown . . . . 13·00 70·00
49 – 1 r. olive . . . . 23·00 £150
67 **7** 1 r. bistre . . . . 20·00 95·00
50 – 2 r. green . . . . 20·00 £160
51 – 5 r. purple . . . . 30·00 £170
DESIGNS—VERT: 1 a. (No. 42), Elephant and banner; 2 a. (No. 43), Sowar in armour; 2½ a. (No. 44), Common peafowl; 8 a. (No. 48), Sireh-Deorhi Gate. HORIZ: 3 a. (No. 45), Bullock carriage; 4 a. (No. 46), Elephant carriage; 6 a. (No. 47), Albert Museum; 1 r. (No. 49), Chandra Mahal; 2 r. Amber Palace; 5 r. Maharajas Sawai Jai Singh and Man Singh.

1932. As T **7**, but inscr "POSTAGE & REVENUE". Portrait in black.
52 1 a. blue 45 50
53 2 a. brown . . . . 1·50 1·00
54 4 a. green . . . . 3·00 5·00
55 8 a. brown . . . . 4·50 8·00
56 1 r. bistre . . . . 15·00 70·00
57 2 r. green . . . . 70·00 £275

1936. Nos. 57 and 51 surch **One Rupee**.
68 1 r. on 2 r. green . . . . . . 5·50 60·00
69 1 r. on 5 r. purple . . . . . . 5·50 48·00

1938. No. 41 surch in native characters.
70 **7** ¼ a. on ½ a. violet . . . . . 8·50 12·00

13 Maharaja and Amber Palace

1947. Silver Jubilee of Maharaja's Accession to the Throne. Inscr as in T **13**.
71 – ¼ a. brown and green . . . . 65 2·50
72 **13** ½ a. green and violet . . . . 20 2·25
73 – ¾ a. black and red . . . . 65 3·00
74 – 1 a. brown and blue . . . . 35 2·25
75 – 2 a. violet and red . . . . 30 2·50
76 – 3 a. green and black . . . . 80 3·30
77 – 4 a. blue and brown . . . . 50 2·25
78 – 8 a. red and brown . . . . 60 3·25
79 – 1 r. purple and green . . . . 1·25 17·00
DESIGNS: ¼ a. Palace Gate; ¾ a. Map of Jaipur; 1 a. Observatory; 2 a. Wind Palace; 3 a. Coat of Arms; 4 a. Amber Fort Gate; 8 a. Chariot of the Sun; 1 r. Maharaja's portrait between State flags.

1947. No. 41 surch **3 PIES** and bars.
80 **7** 3 p. on ½ a. violet . . . . . . 14·00 22·00

OFFICIAL STAMPS

1929. Optd **SERVICE**. No gum (except for No. O6a).
O1a **3** ¼ a. bistre . . . . 1·25 1·25
O2 ½ a. blue 65 20
O3c 1 a. red 70 20
O5 2 a. green 65 40
O6a 4 a. brown (with gum) . . . 2·00 1·75
O7 8 a. violet . . . . 16·00 48·00
O8 1 r. orange . . . . 32·00 £180

1931. Stamps of 1931–32 optd **SERVICE**.
O23 **7** ¼ a. red 40 10
O13 ½ a. violet 30 10
O24 ¾ a. red . . . . 1·50 40
O25 1 a. blue . . . . 7·50 30
O14 – 1 a. blue (No. 42) . . . . £200 1·60
O18 – 1 a. blue (No. 52) . . . . 1·25 10
O15 – 2 a. orange (No. 43) . . . . 2·00 4·00
O19 – 2 a. brown (No. 53) . . . . 1·75 10
O26 **7** 2 a. orange . . . . 6·50 1·50
O27 2¾ a. red . . . . 9·00 65·00
O16 – 4 a. green (No. 46) . . . . 24·00 22·00
O20 – 4 a. green (No. 54) . . . . £225 5·00
O28 **7** 4 a. green . . . . 5·00 2·75
O21 – 8 a. brown (No. 55) . . . . 4·75 1·10
O29 **7** 8 a. brown . . . . 5·00 4·00
O22 – 1 r. bistre (No. 56) . . . . 13·00 14·00
O30 **7** 1 r. bistre £100

1932. No. O5 surch in native characters.
O17 **3** ½ a. on 2 a. green £120 85

1947. Official stamps surch.
O33 **7** 3 p. on ½ a. violet . . . . . 3·50 9·50
O32 9 p. on 1 a. blue . . . . . 2·25 2·50

1949. No. O13 surch in native characters.
O34 **7** ¼ a. on ½ a. violet . . . . . . 12·00 12·00

For later issues see **RAJASTHAN**.

JAMAICA

An island in the W. Indies. Part of the Br. Caribbean Federation from 3 Jan. 1958, until 6 Aug. 1962 when Jamaica became an independent state within the Commonwealth.

1860. 12 pence = 1 shilling;
20 shillings = 1 pound.
1969. 100 cents = 1 dollar.

8

11

1860. Portrait as T **8**. Various frames.
7 **8** ½d. red . . . . 12·00 3·50
16a ½d. green 80 10
8 1d. blue . . . . 55·00 75
18a 1d. red . . . . 24·00 60
9 2d. red . . . . 55·00 70
20a 2d. grey . . . . 50·00 50
21a 3d. green . . . . 2·50 1·00
22a 4d. orange . . . . 2·00 35
52a 6d. lilac . . . . 9·00 15·00
23a 6d. yellow . . . . 4·00 3·50
24 1s. brown . . . . 5·00 5·50
25 2s. red . . . . 27·00 18·00
26 5s. lilac . . . . 48·00 60·00
See also Nos. 47a etc.

1889.
27 **11** 1d. purple and mauve . . . 2·25 10
28a 2d. green . . . . 4·50 6·00
29 2½d. purple and blue . . . 4·75 40

1890. No. 22a surch **TWO PENCE HALF-PENNY**.
30 **8** 2½d. on 4d. orange . . . . . 27·00 8·50

13 Llandovery Falls, Jamaica

1900.
31 **13** 1d. red . . . . 1·25 20
32 1d. black and red . . . . . 2·00 20

14 Arms of Jamaica 16

1903.
33 **14** ½d. grey and green . . . . 1·50 20
34 1d. grey and red . . . . 1·50 10
35 2½d. grey and blue . . . . 2·25 30
42 2½d. blue . . . . 2·50 1·25
36 5d. grey and yellow . . . . 15·00 23·00
44 6d. purple . . . . 12·00 12·00
45 5s. grey and violet . . . . 40·00 30·00

1906.
38a **16** ½d. green . . . . 3·75 20
40 1d. red . . . . 1·25 10

1908. Queen Victoria portraits as 1860.
47a 3d. purple on yellow . . . . 2·00 1·50
48 4d. brown . . . . 70·00 55·00
49 4d. black on yellow . . . . 7·00 35·00
50 4d. red on yellow . . . . . 1·50 7·50
54 1s. black on green . . . . 3·75 8·50
56 2s. purple on blue . . . . 6·00 3·50

17

1911.
57 **17** 2d. grey . . . . 2·00 13·00

1912. As T **17**, but King George V.
89a ½d. green . . . . 1·25 10
58a 1d. red . . . . 1·25 50
59 1½d. orange . . . . 1·00 60
60 2d. grey . . . . 1·75 1·75
61 2½d. blue . . . . 1·00 15
62 3d. purple on yellow 40 45
63 4d. black and red on yellow . . 50 3·25
64a 6d. purple and mauve . . . . 70 1·00
65a 1s. black on green . . . . 70 4·50
66 2s. purple and blue on blue . . 11·00 24·00
67 5s. green and red on yellow . . 45·00 75·00

1916. Optd **WAR STAMP.** in one line (with full point).
68 **16** ½d. green 10 35
69a – 3d. purple on yellow (62) . . 1·00 16·00
See also Nos. 76/77a.

1916. Optd **WAR STAMP.** in two lines.
73 **16** ½d. green 10 20
74 – 1½d. orange (No. 59) . . . 10 10
75 – 3d. purple on yellow (No. 62) . 15 90

1919. Optd **WAR STAMP** in one line (no full point).
76 **15** ½d. green 10 15
77a – 3d. purple on yell (No. 62) . 2·00 1·25

23 Jamaica Exhibition, 1891

24 Arawak Woman preparing Cassava

27 Return of War Contingent, 1919

34

1919.
91a **23** ½d. green and olive . . . 25 40
79 **24** 1d. red and orange (A)* . . 1·75 1·75
92 1d. red and orange (B)* . . 1·50 10
93 – 1½d. green 30 45
81 – 2d. blue and green . . . 1·00 3·75
82a **27** 2½d. blue . . . . 1·25 1·50
96a **27** 3d. green and blue 60 15
97a – 4d. brown and green . . . 65 30
98a – 6d. black and blue . . . . 11·00 1·25
99a – 1s. orange . . . . 1·40 50
100 – 2s. blue and brown . . . . 2·50 50
101 – 3s. violet and orange . . . 9·00 8·50
102c – 5s. blue and bistre . . . . 24·00 22·00
103 **34** 10s. green . . . . 48·00 65·00
*Two types of the 1d. (A) Without and (B) with "POSTAGE & REVENUE" at foot.
DESIGNS—HORIZ (41½ × 26 mm): 1½d. War Contingent embarking, 1915; 6d. Port Royal, 1853. (27 × 22 mm): 3d. Landing of Columbus, 1494. VERT (22 × 29 mm): 2d. King's House, Spanish Town; 4d. Cathedral, Spanish Town. (25 × 30 mm): 1s. Statue of Queen Victoria, Kingston; 2s. Admiral Rodney Memorial, Spanish Town; 3s. Sir Charles Metcalfe Monument; 5s. Jamaican scenery.

37

41

1923. Child Welfare. Designs as T **37**.
104 **37** ½d. + ½d. black and green . . 60 5·00
105 – 1d. + ½d. black and red . . 1·50 10·00
106 – 2½d. + ½d. black and blue . 8·00 18·00

1929. Various frames.
108 **41** 1d. red . . . . 1·50 10
109 1½d. brown . . . . 1·50 15
110 9d. red . . . . 3·00 1·00

43 Coco Palms at Don Christopher's Cove

45 Priestman's River, Portland

1932.
111 **43** 2d. black and green . . . . 7·00 2·25
112 – 2½d. turquoise and blue . . 1·50 1·50
113 **45** 6d. black and purple . . . 7·00 1·25
DESIGN—As T **43**: 2½d. Wag Water River, St. Andrew.

1935. Silver Jubilee. As T **13** of Antigua.
114 1d. blue and red 20 15
115 1½d. blue and black 50 85
116 6d. green and blue . . . . . 5·00 10·00
117 1s. grey and purple . . . . . 4·00 6·50

1937. Coronation. As T **2** of Aden.
118 1d. red 30 15
119 1½d. grey 50 30
120 2½d. blue 85 70

48 King George VI

49 Coco Palms at Don Christopher's Cove

50 Bananas

54 Bamboo Walk

1938.
121 **48** ½d. green . . . . 1·00 10
121b ½d. orange 20 30
122 1d. red 80 10
122a 1d. green 30 10
123 1½d. brown 80 10
124b **49** 2d. black and green 75 10
125 – 2½d. green and blue . . . 3·00 1·50
126 **50** 3d. blue and green . . . . 70 1·25
126b **50** 3d. green and blue . . . . 1·75 1·40
126c 3d. green and red . . . . 1·50 30
127 – 4d. brown and green . . . 40 10
128a – 6d. black and purple . . . 1·75 10
129 – 9d. red 40 40
130 – 1s. green and brown . . . 5·50 20
131 **54** 2s. blue and brown . . . . 20·00 90
132ba – 5s. blue and brown . . . . 6·50 3·00
133aa – 10s. green . . . . 9·00 5·00
133a – £1 brown and violet . . . 27·00 26·00
DESIGNS—As Type **49**: 2½d. Wag Water River, St. Andrew. As Type **50**: 4d. Citrus grove; 9d. Kingston Harbour; 1s. Sugar industry; £1 Tobacco growing and cigar making. As previous issues, but with portrait of King George VI: 6d. As Type **45**; 5 s. As No. 102c; 10s. As Type **34**.

57 Courthouse, Falmouth

59 Institute of Jamaica

1945. New Constitution.
134 **57** 1½d. brown 20 30
135a – 2d. green 20 50
136 **59** 3d. blue 20 50
137 – 4½d. black 30 30
138 – 2s. brown 30 50
139 – 5s. blue . . . . 1·00 1·00
140 **59** 10s. green . . . . 85 2·25
DESIGNS—VERT (as Type **57**): 2s. "Labour and Learning". HORIZ (as Type **57**): 2d. Kings Charles II and George VI. (As Type **59**): 4½d. House of Assembly; 5s. Scroll, flag and King George VI.

1946. Victory. As T **9** of Aden.
141a 1½d. brown 30 55
142 3d. blue . . . . 2·25 2·25

1948. Silver Wedding. As T **10/11** of Aden.
143 1½d. brown 30 10
144 £1 red . . . . 24·00 45·00

1949. U.P.U. As T **20/23** of Antigua.
145 1½d. brown 30 15
146 2d. green . . . . 1·00 1·75
147 3d. blue . . . . 55 1·25
148 6d. purple . . . . 65 2·50

1951. Inauguration of B.W.I. University College. As T **24/25** of Antigua.
149 2d. black and brown 30 30
150 6d. black and purple 35 30

69 Scout Badge and Map of Caribbean

70 Scout Badge and Map of Jamaica

1952. 1st Caribbean Scout Jamboree.
151 **69** 2d. blue, green and black . 15 10
152 **70** 6d. green, red and black . 15 40

1953. Coronation. As T **13** of Aden.
153 2d. black and green 40 10

1953 Royal Visit. As T **49** but with portrait of Queen Elizabeth II and inscr "ROYAL VISIT 1953".
154 2d. black and green 30 10

73 Man-o'-War at Port Royal

1955. Tercentenary Issue.
155 **73** 2d. black and green . . . 35 10
156 – 2½d. black and blue . . . 15 35
157 – 3d. black and claret . . . 15 30
158 – 6d. black and red . . . 20 20
DESIGNS: 2½d. Old Montego Bay; 3d. Old Kingston; 6d. Proclamation of Abolition of Slavery, 1838.

74 Coconut Palms

76 Blue Mountain Peak

75 Mahoe

77 Arms of Jamaica

1956.

159	**74**	½d. black and red	10	10
160	–	1d. black and green	10	10
161	–	2d. black and red	10	10
162	–	2½d. black and blue	30	40
163	**75**	3d. green and brown	20	10
164	–	4d. green and blue	20	10
165	–	5d. red and green	20	1·00
166	–	6d. black and red	1·25	10
167	**76**	8d. blue and orange	15	10
168	–	1s. green and blue	50	10
169	–	1s. 6d. blue and purple	50	10
170	–	2s. blue and green	6·00	1·50
171	**77**	3s. black and blue	1·25	1·50
172	–	5s. black and red	3·25	3·00
173	–	10s. black and green	23·00	12·00
174	–	£1 black and purple	23·00	12·00

DESIGNS—As Type **74**: 1d. Sugar cane; 2d. Pineapples; 2½d. Bananas. As Type **75**: 4d. Breadfruit; 5d. Ackee; 6d. Streamertail. As Type **76**: 1s. Royal Botanic Gardens, Hope; 1s. 6d. Rafting on the Rio Grande; 2s. Fort Charles. As Type **77** but vert: 10s., £1 Arms without portrait.

1958. British Caribbean Federation. As T **28** of Antigua.

175	2d. green	50	10
176	5d. blue	95	3·25
177	6d. red	95	40

81 Bristol Britannia 312 flying over "City of Berlin", 1860

83 1s. Stamps of 1860 and 1956

1960. Centenary of Jamaica Postage Stamps.

178	**81**	2d. blue and purple	45	10
179	–	6d. red and olive	45	20
180	**83**	1s. brown, green and blue	45	25

DESIGN—As Type **81**: 6d. Postal mule-cart and motor-van.

1962. Independence. (a) Nos. 159/74 optd **INDEPENDENCE** and **1962** (3d. to 2s.) or **1962 1962** (others).

205	**74**	½d. black and red	10	15
182	–	1d. black and green	10	10
183	–	2½d. black and blue	10	85
184	**75**	3d. green and brown	10	10
185	–	5d. red and olive	15	60
186	–	6d. black and red	2·00	10
187	**76**	8d. blue and orange	15	10
188	–	1s. green and blue	15	10
189	–	2s. blue and olive	80	1·50
190	**77**	3s. black and blue	90	1·50
191	–	10s. black and green	2·75	4·25
192	–	£1 black and purple	2·75	5·50

86 Military Bugler and Map

(b) As T **86** inscr "INDEPENDENCE".

193	**86**	2d. multicoloured	60	10
194		4d. multicoloured	60	10
195	–	1s. 6d. black and red	2·00	85
196	–	5s. multicoloured	2·75	3·50

DESIGNS: 1s. 6d. Gordon House and banner; 5s. Map, factories and fruit.

89 Kingston Seal, Weightlifting, Boxing, Football and Cycling

1962. 9th Central American and Caribbean Games, Kingston.

197	**89**	1d. sepia and red	20	10
198	–	6d. sepia and blue	20	10
199	–	8d. sepia and bistre	20	10
200	–	2s. multicoloured	30	70

DESIGNS: 6d. Diver, sailing, swimming and water polo; 8d. Javelin, discus, pole-vault, hurdles and relay-racing; 2s. Kingston coat of arms and athlete.

93 Farmer and Crops

1963. Freedom from Hunger.

201	**93**	1d. multicoloured	20	10
202		8d. multicoloured	60	60

1963. Cent of Red Cross. As T **33** of Antigua.

203	2d. red and black	20	10
204	1s. 6d. red and blue	70	1·25

95 Carole Joan Crawford ("Miss World 1963")

1964. "Miss World 1963" Commem.

214	**95**	3d. multicoloured	10	10
215		1s. multicoloured	15	10
216		1s. 6d. multicoloured	20	30

96 Lignum Vitae

103 Gypsum Industry

1964.

217	**96**	1d. blue, green & brown	10	10
218	–	1½d. multicoloured	15	10
219	–	2d. red, yellow and green	15	10
220	–	2½d. multicoloured	90	60
221	–	3d. yellow, black & grn	15	10
222	–	4d. ochre and violet	45	10
223	–	6d. multicoloured	2·25	10
224	–	8d. multicoloured	1·50	1·25
225	**103**	9d. blue and bistre	1·50	10
226	–	1s. black and brown	20	10
227	–	1s. 6d. black, blue & buff	2·75	15
228	–	2s. brown, black & blue	2·75	15
229b	–	3s. blue and green	35	65
230	–	5s. black, ochre & blue	1·25	1·00
231	–	10s. multicoloured	1·25	1·00
232	–	£1 multicoloured	1·50	1·00

DESIGNS—HORIZ (As T **96**): 1½d. Ackee (fruit); 2½d. Land shells; 3d. National flag over Jamaica; 4d. Antillean murex (sea shell); 6d. "Papilio homerus" (butterfly); 8d. Streamertail. VERT (As T **96**): 2d. Blue Mahoe (tree). HORIZ (As T **103**): 1s. National Stadium; 1s. 6d. Palisadoes International Airport; 2s. Bauxite mining; 3s. Blue marlin (sport fishing); 5s. Exploration of sunken city, Port Royal; £1 Queen Elizabeth II and national flag. VERT (As T **96**): 10s. Arms of Jamaica.

114 Scout Badge and Alligator

1964. 6th Inter-American Scout Conf, Kingston.

233	–	3d. red, black and pink	10	10
234	–	8d. blue, olive and black	15	25
235	**114**	1s. gold, blue & light blue	20	35

DESIGNS—VERT (25½×30 mm): 3d. Scout belt; 8d. Globe, scout hat and scarf.

115 Gordon House, Kingston

118 Eleanor Roosevelt

1964. 10th Commonwealth Parliamentary Conf, Kingston.

236	**115**	3d. black and green	10	10
237	–	6d. black and red	30	10
238	–	1s. 6d. black and blue	50	30

DESIGNS: 6d. Headquarters House, Kingston; 1s. 6d. House of Assembly, Spanish Town.

1964. 16th Anniv of Declaration of Human Rights.

239	**118**	1s. black, red & green	10	10

119 Guides' Emblem on Map

121 Uniform Cap

1965. Golden Jubilee of Jamaica Girl Guides' Assn. Inscr "1915–1965".

240	**119**	3d. yellow, green & black	10	10
241	–	1s. yellow, black & green	20	30

DESIGN—TRIANGULAR (61½×30½ mm): 1s. Guide emblems.

1965. Centenary of Salvation Army. Mult.

242	3d. Type **121**	25	10
243	1s. 6d. Flag-bearer and drummer (vert)	50	35

123 Paul Bogle, William Gordon and Morant Bay Court House

1965. Centenary of Morant Bay Rebellion.

244	**123**	3d. brown, blue & black	10	10
245		1s. 6d. brown, green & blk	15	10
246		3s. brown, red & black	25	65

124 Abeng-blower, "Telstar", Morse Key and I.T.U. Emblem

1965. Centenary of I.T.U.

247	**124**	1s. black, slate & red	40	15

1966. Royal Visit. Nos. 221, 223, 226/7 optd **ROYAL VISIT MARCH 1966**.

248	3d. yellow, black and green	15	10
249	6d. multicoloured	1·75	20
250	1s. black and brown	55	10
251	1s. 6d. black, blue and buff	1·75	1·75

126 Sir Winston Churchill

1966. Churchill Commemoration.

252	**126**	6d. black and green	35	20
253		1s. brown and blue	65	70

127 Statue of Athlete and Flags

1966. 8th British Empire and Commonwealth Games.

254	**127**	3d. multicoloured	10	10
255	–	6d. multicoloured	30	10
256	–	1s. multicoloured	10	10
257	–	3s. gold and blue	35	35

DESIGNS: 6d. Racing cyclists; 1s. National Stadium, Kingston; 3s. Games emblem.

131 Bolivar's Statue and Flags of Jamaica and Venezuela

133 Sir Donald Sangster (Prime Minister)

132 Jamaican Pavilion

1966. 150th Anniv of "Jamaica Letter".

259	**131**	8d. multicoloured	10	10

1967. World Fair, Montreal.

260	**132**	6d. multicoloured	10	10
261		1s. multicoloured	10	10

1967. Sangster Memorial Issue.

262	**133**	3d. multicoloured	10	10
263		1s. 6d. multicoloured	20	20

134 Traffic Duty

1967. Centenary of Constabulary Force. Mult

264	3d. Type **134**	40	10
265	1s. Personnel of the Force (56½×20½ mm)	40	10
266	1s. 6d. Badge and Constables of 1867 and 1967	50	60

1968. M.C.C.'s West Indies Tour. As Nos. 445/7 of Guyana.

267	6d. multicoloured	50	50
268	6d. multicoloured	50	50
269	6d. multicoloured	50	50

137 Sir Alexander and Lady Bustamante

1968. Labour Day.

270	**137**	3d. red and black	10	10
271		1s. olive and black	10	10

138 Human Rights Emblem over Map of Jamaica

1968. Human Rights Year. Multicoloured.

272	3d. Type **138**	10	10
273	1s. Hands cupping Human Rights emblem	10	10
274	3s. Jamaican holding "Human Rights"	30	80

141 I.L.O. Emblem

1969. 50th Anniv of I.L.O.

275	**141**	6d. yellow and brown	10	10
276		3s. green and brown	30	30

142 Nurse and Children being Weighed and Measured

146 "The Adoration of the Kings" (detail, Foppa)

1969. 20th Anniv of W.H.O. Multicoloured.
277 6d. Type **142** 10 10
278 1s. Malaria eradication (horiz) 10 10
279 3s. Trainee nurse 20 45

1969. Decimal Currency. Nos. 217, 219, 221/3 and 225/32 surch **C-DAY 8th September 1969** and value.
280 **95** 1 c. on 1d. bl, grn & brn . 10 10
281 – 2 c. on 2d. red, yellow & grn 10 10
282 – 3 c. on 3d. yellow, blk & grn 10 10
283 – 4 c. on 4d. ochre & violet 1·25 10
284 – 5 c. on 6d. multicoloured . 1·25 10
285 **103** 8 c. on 9d. blue & bistre . 10 10
286 – 10 c. on 1s. black & brn . 10 10
287 – 15 c. on 1s. 6d. black, blue and buff 30 90
288 – 20 c. on 2s. brn, blk & bl 1·50 1·00
289 – 30 c. on 3s. blue & green 1·50 2·75
290 – 50 c. on 5s. black, ochre and blue . . . . 1·25 3·00
291 – $1 on 10s. multicoloured 1·25 6·00
292 – $2 on £1 multicoloured . 1·50 6·50

1969. Christmas. Paintings. Multicoloured.
293 2 c. Type **146** 20 40
294 5 c. "Madonna, Child and St. John" (Raphael) . . . 25 40
295 8 c. "The Adoration of the Kings" (detail, Dosso Dossi) 25 40

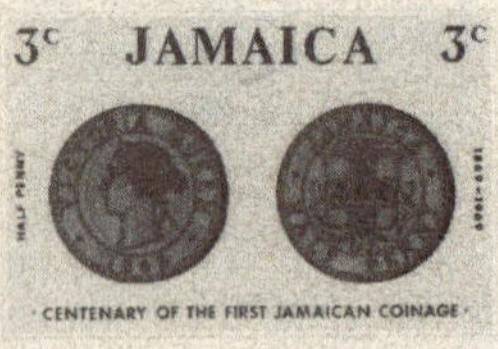

149 Half Penny, 1869

1969. Centenary of 1st Jamaican Coins.
296 **149** 3 c. silver, black and mauve 15 25
297 – 15 c. silver, black & grn . 10 10
DESIGN: 15 c. One penny, 1869.

151 George William Gordon

156 "Christ appearing to St. Peter" (Carracci)

1970. National Heroes. Multicoloured; background colours given.
298 **151** 1 c. mauve 10 10
299 – 3 c. blue 10 10
300 – 5 c. grey 10 10
301 – 10 c. red 15 10
302 – 15 c. green 20 15
PORTRAITS: 3 c. Sir Alexander Bustamante; 5 c. Norman Manley; 10 c. Marcus Garvey; 15 c. Paul Bogle.

1970. Easter. Centres multicoloured; frame colours given.
303 **156** 3 c. red 10 10
304 – 10 c. green 10 10
305 – 20 c. grey 20 50
DESIGNS: 10 c. "Christ Crucified" (Antonello); 20 c. Easter lily.

1970. No. 219 surch **2c.**
306 2 c. on 2d. red, yellow & grn . 20 20

160 Lignum Vitae

164 Bananas, Citrus, Sugar-Cane and Tobacco

161 Cable Ship "Dacia"

1970. Decimal Currency. Designs as Nos. 217, 219, 221/23, 225/32, but with values inscr as T **160** in new currency.
307 **160** 1 c. blue, green & brown 60 1·25
308 – 2 c. red, yellow and green (as 2d.) 30 10
309 – 3 c. yellow, black and green (as 3d.) 30 60
310 – 4 c. ochre and violet (as 4d.) 2·00 10
311 – 5 c. multicoloured (as 6d.) 3·00 30
312 **103** 8 c. blue and yellow . . 1·50 10
313 – 10 c. black & brn (as 1s.) 30 10
314 – 15 c. black, blue and buff (as 1s. 6d.) . . . . 1·75 2·25
315 – 20 c. brown, black and blue (as 2s.) . . . . 1·25 2·00
316 – 30 c. blue & green (as 3s.) 2·75 3·50
317 – 50 c. black, ochre and blue (as 5s.) . . . . 1·25 3·75
318 – $1 multicoloured (as 10s.) 1·25 3·75
319 – $2 multicoloured (as £1) . 1·50 4·00

1970. Centenary of Telegraph Service.
320 **161** 3 c. yellow, black and red 15 10
321 – 10 c. black and green . 20 10
322 – 50 c. multicoloured . . 50 1·00
DESIGNS: 10 c. Bright's cable gear aboard "Dacia"; 50 c. Morse key and chart.

1970. 75th Anniv of Jamaican Agricultural Society.
323 **164** 2 c. multicoloured . . . 25 60
324 10 c. multicoloured . . . 45 10

165 Locomotive "Projector" (1845)

168 Church of St. Jago de la Vega

1970. 125th Anniv of Jamaican Railways.
325 3 c. Type **165** 30 10
326 15 c. Steam locomotive No. 54 (1944) 80 30
327 50 c. Steam locomotive No. 102 (1967) . . . . 2·00 2·00

1971. Centenary of Disestablishment of Church of England in Jamaica.
328 **168** 3 c. multicoloured . . . 10 10
329 10 c. multicoloured . . . 10 10
330 20 c. multicoloured . . . 30 30
331 – 30 c. multicoloured . . . 30 65
DESIGN: 30 c. Emblem of Church of England in Jamaica.

169 Henry Morgan and Ships

1971. Pirates and Buccaneers. Multicoloured.
332 3 c. Type **169** 60 10
333 15 c. Mary Read, Anne Bonny and trial pamphlet . . . 1·00 15
334 30 c. Pirate schooner attacking merchantman . . . . 1·75 1·25

170 1s. Stamp of 1919 with Frame Inverted

1971. Tercentenary of Post Office.
335 – 3 c. black and brown . . 20 20
336 – 5 c. black and green . . 20 20
337 – 8 c. black and violet . . 20 10
338 – 10 c. brown, black and blue 20 10
339 – 20 c. multicoloured . . . 50 45
340 **170** 50 c. brown, blk & grey . 75 1·25
DESIGNS—HORIZ: 3 c. Dummer packet letter, 1705; 5 c. Pre-stamp inland letter, 1793; 8 c. Harbour St. P.O., Kingston, 1820; 10 c. Modern stamp and cancellation; 20 c. British stamps used in Jamaica, 1859.

171 Satellite and Dish Aerial

172 Causeway, Kingston Harbour

1972. Opening of Jamaican Earth Satellite Station.
341 **171** 3 c. multicoloured . . . 15 10
342 15 c. multicoloured . . . 20 15
343 50 c. multicoloured . . . 65 1·25

1972. Multicoloured.
344 1 c. Pimento (vert) 10 10
345 2 c. Red ginger (vert) . . . 10 10
346 3 c. Bauxite Industry . . . 10 10
347 4 c. Type **172** 10 10
348 5 c. Oil refinery 10 10
349 6 c. Senate Building, University of the West Indies . . . 10 10
350 8 c. National Stadium . . . 10 10
351 9 c. Devon House 10 10
352 10 c. Air Jamaica Hostess and Vickers VC-10 . . . . 20 10
353 15 c. Old Iron Bridge, Spanish Town (vert) . . . . 1·75 10
354 20 c. College of Arts, Science and Technology 30 15
355 30 c. Dunn's River Falls (vert) 35 15
356 50 c. River rafting . . . . 1·50 40
357 $1 Jamaica House . . . . 75 1·25
358 $2 Kings House . . . . 1·00 1·50
Designs for 8 c. to $2 are larger, 35 × 27 or 27 × 35 mm..

1972. 10th Anniv of Independence Nos. 346, 352 and 356 optd **TENTH ANNIVERSARY INDEPENDENCE 1962-1972.**
359 3 c. multicoloured 30 20
360 10 c. multicoloured 30 10
361 50 c. multicoloured . . . . 75 1·90

175 Arms of Kingston

1972. Centenary of Kingston as Capital.
362 **175** 5 c. multicoloured . . . 10 10
363 30 c. multicoloured . . . 20 35
364 – 50 c. multicoloured . . . 40 1·50
DESIGN—HORIZ: 50 c. design similar to Type **175**.

176 Mongoose on Map

1973. Centenary of Introduction of the Small Indian Mongoose.
365 **176** 8 c. green, yellow & black . 15 10
366 – 40 c. dp blue, blue & blk . 35 50
367 – 60 c. pink, salmon & blk . 60 1·00
DESIGNS: 40 c. Mongoose and rat; 60 c. Mongoose and chicken.

177 "Euphorbia punicea"

1973. Flora. Multicoloured.
369 1 c. Type **177** 10 10
370 6 c. "Hylocereus triangularis" . 15 10
371 9 c. "Columnea argentea" . . 15 10
372 15 c. "Portlandia grandiflora" . 25 15
373 30 c. "Samyda pubescens" . . 50 60
374 50 c. "Cordia sebestena" . . 80 1·25

178 "Broughtonia sanguinea"

1973. Orchids. Multicoloured.
375 5 c. Type **178** 40 10
376 10 c. "Arpophyllum jamaicense" (vert) 50 10
377 20 c. "Oncidium pulchellum" (vert) . . . . 1·25 25
378 $1 "Brassia maculata" . . . 2·75 2·75

179 "Mary", 1808–15

1974. Mail Packet Boats. Multicoloured.
380 5 c. Type **179** 55 10
381 10 c. "Queensbury", 1814–27 . 55 10
382 15 c. "Sheldrake", 1829–34 . 90 40
383 50 c. "Thames I", 1842 . . 2·00 2·50

180 "Journeys"

1974. National Dance Theatre Company. Mult.
385 5 c. Type **180** 10 10
386 10 c. "Jamaican Promenade" . 10 10
387 30 c. "Jamaican Promenade" (different) 30 30
388 50 c. "Misa Criolla" 50 80

181 U.P.U. Emblem and Globe

1974. Centenary of U.P.U.
390 **181** 5 c. multicoloured . . . 10 10
391 9 c. multicoloured . . . 10 10
392 50 c. multicoloured . . . 35 80

182 Senate Building and Sir Hugh Wooding

1975. 25th Anniv of University of West Indies. Mult.
393 5 c. Type **182** 10 10
394 10 c. University Chapel and Princess Alice 10 10
395 30 c. Type **182** 20 25
396 50 c. As 10 c. 35 60

183 Commonwealth Symbol

1975. Heads of Commonwealth Conf. Mult.
397 5 c. Type **183** 10 10
398 10 c. Jamaican coat of arms . 10 10
399 30 c. Dove of Peace . . . 15 30
400 50 c. Jamaican flag . . . 30 1·10

184 Jamaican Kite Swallowtail

185 Koo Koo or Actor Boy

1975. Butterflies (1st series), showing the family "Papilionidae". Multicoloured.

401	10 c. Type **184**	55	20
402	20 c. Orange swallowtail ("Papilo thoas")	1·10	1·10
403	25 c. False androyeus swallowtail ("Papilo thersites")	1·25	2·00
404	30 c. Homerus swallowtail ("Papilo homerus")	1·40	2·75

See also Nos. 429/32 and 443/6.

1975. Christmas. Belisario prints of "John Canoe" Festival (1st series). Multicoloured.

406	8 c. Type **185**	15	10
407	10 c. Red Set-girls	15	10
408	20 c. French Set-girls	35	20
409	50 c. Jaw-bone or House John Canoe	70	1·90

See also Nos. 421/3.

186 Bordone Map, 1528

1976. 16th Century Maps of Jamaica.

411	**186** 10 c. brown, lt brn & red	20	10
412	– 20 c. multicoloured	35	25
413	– 30 c. multicoloured	60	85
414	– 50 c. multicoloured	85	2·25

DESIGNS: 20 c. Porcacchi map, 1576; 30 c. De Bry map, 1594; 50 c. Langenes map, 1598.
See also Nos. 425/8.

187 Olympic Rings

1976. Olympic Games, Montreal.

415	**187** 10 c. multicoloured	15	10
416	20 c. multicoloured	25	20
417	25 c. multicoloured	25	25
418	50 c. multicoloured	40	1·75

1976. West Indian Victory in World Cricket Cup. As Nos. 559/60 of Barbados.

419	10 c. Map of the Caribbean	40	50
420	25 c. Prudential Cup	85	1·75

1976. Christmas. Belisario Prints (2nd series). As T **185**. Multicoloured.

421	10 c. Queen of the set-girls	10	10
422	20 c. Band of the Jaw-bone John Canoe	25	10
423	50 c. Koo Koo (actor-boy)	45	1·75

1977. 17th Cent Maps of Jamaica. As T **186**.

425	9 c. multicoloured	30	30
426	10 c. red, brown and buff	30	10
427	25 c. black, blue and lt blue	70	60
428	40 c. black, blue and green	80	1·75

DESIGNS: 9 c. Hickeringill map, 1661; 10 c. Ogilby map, 1671; 25 c. Visscher map, 1680; 40 c. Thornton map, 1689.

1977. Butterflies (2nd series). As T **184**. Mult.

429	10 c. False barred sulphur ("Eurema elathea")	35	10
430	20 c. Bronze wing ("Dynamine egaea")	75	55
431	25 c. Jamaican harlequin ("Chlosyne pantoni")	1·00	1·50
432	40 c. Mimic ("Hypolimnas misippus")	1·50	3·00

188 Map, Scout Emblem and Streamertail

190 Half-figure with Canopy

189 Trumpeter

1977. Sixth Caribbean Scout Jamboree, Jamaica.

434	**188** 10 c. multicoloured	30	10
435	20 c. multicoloured	60	25
436	25 c. multicoloured	65	35
437	50 c. multicoloured	90	1·75

1977. 50th Anniv of Jamaica Military Band. Mult.

438	9 c. Type **189**	15	10
439	10 c. Clarinet players	15	10
440	20 c. Two kettle drummers (vert)	40	35
441	25 c. Double-bass player and trumpeter (vert)	55	65

1978. Butterflies (3rd series). As T **184**. Multicoloured.

443	10 c. Jamaican hairstreak ("Callophrys crethona")	50	10
444	20 c. Malachite ("Siproeta stelenes")	85	20
445	25 c. Common long-tailed skipper ("Urbanus proteus")	95	50
446	50 c. Troglodyte ("Anaea troglodyta")	2·00	2·50

1978. Arawak Artefacts (1st series).

448	**190** 10 c. brown, yellow & black	10	10
449	– 20 c. brown, mauve, & black	15	10
450	– 50 c. brown, green & blk	35	35

DESIGNS: 20 c. Standing figure; 50 c. Birdman.
See also Nos. 479/83.

191 Norman Manley (statue)

193 "Negro Aroused" (sculpture by Edna Manley)

192 Band and Banner

1978. 24th Commonwealth Parliamentary Conference. Multicoloured.

452	10 c. Type **191**	10	10
453	20 c. Sir Alexander Bustamante (statue)	20	15
454	25 c. City of Kingston Crest	20	20
455	40 c. Gordon House Chamber, House of Representatives	30	55

1978. Christmas. Centenary of Salvation Army. Multicoloured.

456	10 c. Type **192**	40	10
457	20 c. Trumpeter	45	20
458	25 c. Banner	45	30
459	50 c. William Booth (founder)	80	2·50

1978. International Anti-Apartheid Year.

460	**193** 10 c. multicoloured	30	20

194 Tennis, Montego Bay

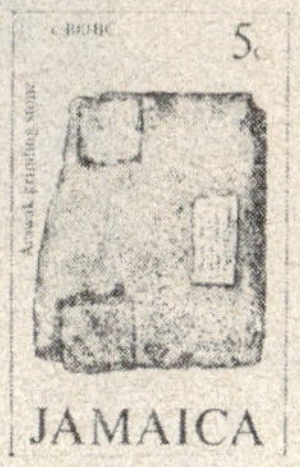

197 Grinding Stone, circa 400 B.C.

1979. Multicoloured.

461	1 c. Type **194**	70	55
462	2 c. Golf, Tryall, Hanover	1·75	1·75
463	4 c. Horse riding, Negril Beach	40	80
464	5 c. Old waterwheel, Tryall, Hanover	55	20
465	6 c. Fern Gully, Ocho Rios	70	1·25
466	7 c. Dunn's River Falls, Ocho Rios	40	30
467	8 c. Jamaican tody	80	65
468	10 c. Jamaican mango	80	20
469	12 c. Yellow-billed amazon	80	1·00
470	15 c. Streamertail	80	30
471	35 c. White-chinned thrush	80	30
472	50 c. Jamaican woodpecker	1·00	30
473	65 c. Rafting, Martha Brae Trelawny	70	1·25
474	75 c. Blue Marlin fleet, Port Antonio	1·00	30
475	$1 Scuba diving, Ocho Rios	1·25	1·25
476	$2 Sailing boats, Montego Bay	75	50
477	$5 Arms and map of Jamaica (37×27 mm)	1·00	1·60

1979. 10th Anniv of Air Jamaica. No. 352 optd **TENTH ANNIVERSARY AIR JAMAICA 1st APRIL 1979**.

478	10 c. multicoloured	50	50

1979. Arawak Artefacts (2nd series). Multicoloured.

479	5 c. Type **197**	10	10
480	10 c. Stone implements, c. 500 B.C. (horiz)	10	10
481	20 c. Cooking pot, c. 300 A.D. (horiz)	10	15
482	25 c. Serving boat, c. 300 A.D. (horiz)	10	20
483	50 c. Storage jar fragment, c. 300 A.D.	25	35

198 1962 1s. 6d. Independence Commemorative Stamp

1979. Death Centenary of Sir Rowland Hill.

484	**198** 10 c. black, brown and red	15	10
485	– 20 c. yellow and brown	20	15
486	– 25 c. mauve and blue	25	20
487	– 50 c. multicoloured	35	70

DESIGNS: 20 c. 1920 1s. with frame inverted; 25 c. 1860 6d. stamp; 50 c. 1968 3d. Human Rights Year commemorative.

199 Group of Children

1979. Christmas. International Year of the Child. Multicoloured.

489	10 c. Type **199**	10	10
490	20 c. Doll (vert)	10	10
491	25 c. "The Family" (painting by child)	15	15
492	50 c. "House on the Hill" (painting by child)	25	40

200 Date Tree Hall, 1886 (original home of Institute)

1980. Centenary of Institute of Jamaica. Mult.

493	5 c. Type **200**	10	10
494	15 c. Institute building, 1980	15	10
495	35 c. Microfilm reader (vert)	25	20
496	50 c. Hawksbill turtle and green turtle	45	70
497	75 c. Jamaican owl (vert)	1·50	2·75

201 Don Quarrie (200 Metres, 1976)

1980. Olympic Games, Moscow. Jamaican Olympic Gold Medal Winners. Multicoloured.

498	15 c. Type **201**	40	15
499	35 c. Arthur Wint (4×400 Metres Relay, 1952)	45	70
500	35 c. Leslie Laing (4×400 Metres Relay, 1952)	45	70
501	35 c. Herbert McKenley (4×400 Metres Relay, 1952)	45	70
502	35 c. George Rhoden (4×400 Metres Relay, 1952)	45	70

202 Parish Church

1980. Christmas. Churches (1st series). Multicoloured.

503	15 c. Type **202**	10	10
504	20 c. Coke Memorial Church	10	10
505	25 c. Church of the Redeemer	15	10
506	$5 Holy Trinity Cathedral	1·00	2·00

See also No. 537/9 and 570/2.

203 Blood Cup Sponge

205 White Orchid

204 Brown's Hutia (or Indian Coney)

1981. Marine Life (1st series). Multicoloured.

508	20 c. Type **203**	15	10
509	45 c. Tube sponge (horiz)	25	35
510	60 c. Black coral	35	45
511	75 c. Tyre reef (horiz)	40	75

See also Nos. 541/5.

1981. Brown's Hutia (or Indian Coney).

512	20 c. Hutia facing right	15	20
513	20 c. Type **204**	15	20
514	20 c. Hutia facing left and eating	15	20
515	20 c. Hutia family	15	20

1981. Royal Wedding. Multicoloured.

516	20 c. Type **205**	10	10
517	45 c. Royal Coach	15	10
518	60 c. Prince Charles and Lady Diana Spencer	20	20
519	$5 St. James' Palace	60	85

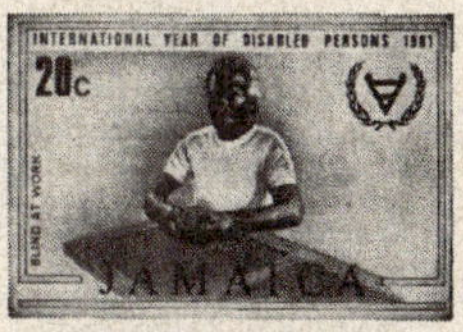

206 Blind Man at Work

1981. International Year for Disabled Persons. Multicoloured.

521	20 c. Type **206**	15	15
522	45 c. Painting with the mouth	40	40
523	60 c. Deaf student communicating with sign language	50	75
524	$1.50 Basketball players	1·25	2·00

207 W.F.D. Emblem on 1964 1½d. Definitive

208 "Survival" (song title)

1981. World Food Day. Stamps on Stamps.

525	**207** 20 c. multicoloured	35	15
526	– 45 c. black, red and orge	70	40
527	– $2 black, blue and green	2·00	1·40
528	– $4 black, green and brown	3·25	2·50

DESIGNS—VERT (As T **207**): 45 c. 1922 1d. value. HORIZ (40×26 mm): $2 As 1938 3d. but with W.F.D. emblem replacing King's head; $4 As 1938 1s. but with W.F.D. emblem replacing King's head.

1981. Bob Marley (musician) Commemoration. Song Titles. Multicoloured.

529	1 c. Type **208**	30	40
530	2 c. "Exodus"	30	40
531	3 c. "Is this Love"	30	40
532	15 c. "Coming in from the Cold"	1·75	30
533	20 c. "Positive Vibration"	1·75	30
534	60 c. "War"	2·50	2·75
535	$3 "Could you be Loved"	7·50	10·00

No. 533 is incorrectly inscribed "OSITIVE VIBRATION".

209 Webb Memorial Baptist Church

1981. Christmas. Churches (2nd series). Multicoloured.

537	10 c. Type **209**	10	10
538	45 c. Church of God in Jamaica	30	15
539	$5 Bryce United Church	2·25	2·50

210 Gorgonian Coral

211 Cub Scout

1982. Marine Life (2nd series). Multicoloured.

541	20 c. Type **210**	45	10
542	45 c. Hard sponge and diver (horiz)	65	25
543	60 c. American manatee (horiz)	90	55
544	75 c. Plume worm (horiz)	1·00	65
545	$3 Coral banded shrimp (horiz)	2·50	1·75

1982. 75th Anniv of Boy Scout Movement. Mult.

546	20 c. Type **211**	50	15
547	45 c. Scout camp	85	40
548	60 c. "Out of Many, One People"	1·10	90
549	$2 Lord Baden-Powell	1·75	2·50

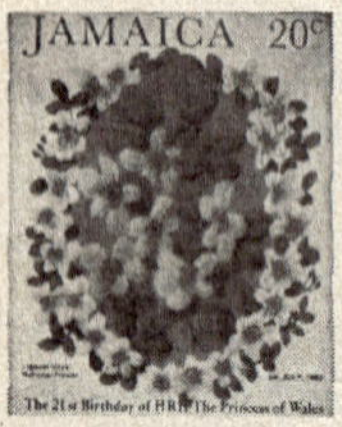

212 "Lignum vitae" (national flower)

213 Prey Captured

1982. 21st Birthday of Princess of Wales.

551	20 c. Type **212**	20	20
552	45 c. Carriage ride	35	35
553	60 c. Wedding	50	60
554	75 c. "Saxifraga longifolia"	1·00	1·75
555	$2 Princess of Wales	1·40	2·00
556	$3 "Viola gracilis major"	1·40	2·75

1982. Birth of Prince William of Wales. Nos. 551/6 optd **ROYAL BABY 21.6.82.**

558	20 c. Type **212**	20	20
559	45 c. Carriage ride	30	35
560	60 c. Wedding	40	60
561	75 c. "Saxifraga longifolia"	70	1·00
562	$2 Princess of Wales	75	1·50
563	$3 "Viola gracilis major"	1·00	2·50

1982. Jamaican Birds (1st series). Jamaican Lizard Cuckoo. Multicoloured.

565	$1 Type **213**	1·10	1·25
566	$1 Searching for prey	1·10	1·25
567	$1 Calling prior to prey search	1·10	1·25
568	$1 Adult landing	1·10	1·25
569	$1 Adult flying in	1·10	1·25

See also Nos. 642/5 and 707/10.

1982. Christmas. Churches (3rd series). As T **209**. Multicoloured.

570	20 c. United Pentecostal Church	40	10
571	45 c. Disciples of Christ Church	75	25
572	75 c. Open Bible Church	1·40	2·75

214 Queen Elizabeth II

1983. Royal Visit. Multicoloured.

573	$2 Type **214**	3·00	3·50
574	$3 Coat of arms	4·00	5·00

215 Folk Dancing

1983. Commonwealth Day. Multicoloured.

575	20 c. Type **215**	15	15
576	45 c. Bauxite mining	35	35
577	75 c. World map showing position of Jamaica	45	45
578	$2 Coat of arms and family	60	1·40

216 General Cargo Ship at Wharf

1983. 25th Anniv of International Maritime Organization. Multicoloured.

579	15 c. Type **216**	75	30
580	20 c. "Veendam" (cruise liner) at Kingston	1·00	40
581	45 c. Container ship entering port	1·75	85
582	$1 Tanker passing International Seabed Headquarters Building	2·75	3·75

217 Norman Manley and Sir Alexander Bustamante

218 Ship-to-Shore Radio

1983. 21st Anniv of Independence.

583	**217** 15 c. multicoloured	15	20
584	20 c. multicoloured	15	25
585	45 c. multicoloured	30	50

1983. World Communications Year. Multicoloured.

586	20 c. Type **218**	40	15
587	45 c. Postal services	75	40
588	75 c. Telephone communications	1·00	2·00
589	$1 T.V. via satellite	1·25	2·50

219 "Racing at Caymanas" (Sidney McLaren)

1983. Christmas. Paintings. Multicoloured.

590	15 c. Type **219**	15	10
591	20 c. "Seated Figures" (Karl Parboosingh)	15	10
592	75 c. "The Petitioner" (Henry Daley) (vert)	50	50
593	$2 "Banana Plantation" (John Dunkley) (vert)	1·25	2·25

220 Sir Alexander Bustamante

1984. Birth Centenary of Sir Alexander Bustamante. Multicoloured.

594	20 c. Type **220**	65	1·00
595	20 c. Birthplace, Blenheim	65	1·00

221 De Havilland Gipsy Moth Seaplane

1984. Seaplanes and Flying Boats. Multicoloured.

596	25 c. Type **221**	1·25	15
597	55 c. Consolidated Commodore flying boat	1·75	85
598	$1.50 Sikorsky S-38A flying boat	3·00	4·00
599	$3 Sikorsky S-40 flying boat "American Clipper"	4·00	5·50

222 Cycling

1984. Olympic Games, Los Angeles. Multicoloured.

600	25 c. Type **222**	75	30
601	55 c. Relay running	60	30
602	$1.50 Start of race	1·00	2·00
603	$3 Finish of race	1·40	3·00

1984. Nos. 465 and 469 surch.

605	5 c. on 6 c. Fern Gully, Ocho Rios	15	40
606	10 c. on 12 c. Yellow-billed amazon	85	60

224 Head of Jamaican Boa Snake

1984. Jamaican Boa Snake. Multicoloured.

607	25 c. Type **224**	2·75	40
608	55 c. Boa snake on branch over tree	4·00	80
609	70 c. Snake with young	4·75	2·50
610	$1 Snake on log	5·50	3·25

225 Locomotive "Enterprise" (1845)

1984. Railway Locomotives (1st series). Mult.

612	25 c. Type **225**	1·25	30
613	55 c. Tank locomotive (1880)	1·50	70
614	$1.50 Kitson-Meyer tank locomotive (1904)	2·50	3·00
615	$3 Super-heated locomotive No. 40 (1916)	3·50	4·75

See also Nos. 634/7.

226 "Accompong Madonna" (Namba Roy)

227 Brown Pelicans flying

1984. Christmas. Sculptures. Multicoloured.

616	20 c. Type **226**	25	10
617	25 c. "Head" (Alvin Marriott)	30	10
618	55 c. "Moon" (Edna Manley)	70	65
619	$1.50 "All Women are Five Women" (Mallica Reynolds (Kapo))	1·75	3·25

1985. Birth Bicentenary of John J. Audubon (ornithologist). Brown Pelican. Multicoloured.

620	20 c. Type **227**	90	20
621	55 c. Diving for fish	1·25	40
622	$2 Young pelican taking food from adult	2·25	2·75
623	$5 "Brown Pelican" (John J. Audubon)	3·75	6·00

228 The Queen Mother at Belfast University

1985. Life and Times of Queen Elizabeth the Queen Mother. Multicoloured.

625	25 c. With photograph album, 1963	15	10
626	55 c. With Prince Charles at Garter Ceremony, Windsor Castle, 1983	20	15
627	$1.50 Type **228**	40	65
628	$3 With Prince Henry at his christening (from photo by Lord Snowdon)	75	1·50

229 Maps and Emblems

1985. International Youth Year and 5th Pan-American Scout Jamboree.

630	**229** 25 c. multicoloured	30	10
631	55 c. multicoloured	45	25
632	70 c. multicoloured	55	70
633	$4 multicoloured	2·25	4·00

1985. Railway Locomotives (2nd series). As T **225**. Multicoloured.

634	25 c. Baldwin steam locomotive No. 16	1·00	30
635	55 c. Rogers locomotive	1·50	35
636	$1.50 Locomotive "Projector", 1845	2·00	2·25
637	$4 Diesel locomotive No. 102	3·50	4·50

230 "The Old Settlement" (Ralph Campbell)

1985. Christmas. Jamaican Paintings. Mult.

638	20 c. Type **230**	10	10
639	55 c. "The Vendor" (Albert Huie) (vert)	15	15
640	75 c. "Road Menders" (Gaston Tabois)	20	35
641	$4 "Woman, must I not be about my Father's business?" (Carl Abrahams) (vert)	1·10	2·25

1986. Jamaican Birds (2nd series). As T **213**. Multicoloured.

642	25 c. Chestnut-bellied cuckoo	50	10
643	55 c. Jamaican becard	65	30
644	$1.50 White-eyed thrush	85	1·75
645	$5 Rufous-tailed flycatcher	1·75	4·00

1986. 60th Birthday of Queen Elizabeth II. As T **110** of Ascension. Multicoloured.

646	20 c. Princess Elizabeth and Princess Margaret, 1939	15	10
647	25 c. With Prince Charles and Prince Andrew, 1962	15	10
648	70 c. Queen visiting War Memorial, Montego Bay, 1983	25	25
649	$3 On state visit to Luxembourg, 1976	50	90
650	$5 At Crown Agents Head Office, London, 1983	75	1·75

231 Bustamante Children's Hospital

232 Richard "Shrimpy" Clarke

1986. "Ameripex '86" International Stamp Exhibition, Chicago. Multicoloured.

651	25 c. Type **231**	40	15
652	55 c. Air Jamaica Boeing 737 airliner and map of holiday resorts	1·00	40
653	$3 Norman Manley Law School	1·25	2·50
654	$5 Bauxite and agricultural exports	5·50	7·00

1986. Royal Wedding. As T **112** of Ascension. Multicoloured.

656	20 c. Prince Andrew and Miss Sarah Ferguson, Ascot, 1985	15	10
657	$5 Prince Andrew making speech, Fredericton, Canada, 1985	1·00	1·90

1986. Jamaican Boxing Champions. Multicoloured.

658	45 c. Type **232**	20	15
659	70 c. Michael McCallum	30	30
660	$2 Trevor Berbick	70	1·25
661	$4 Richard "Shrimpy" Clarke, Michael McCallum and Trevor Berbick	1·25	2·25

1986. Nos. 472/3 surch.

662	5 c. on 50 c. Jamaican woodpecker	1·25	1·75
663	10 c. on 65 c. Rafting, Martha Brae Trelawny	1·00	1·40

234 "Heliconia wagneriana"

235 Crown Cone

1986. Christmas. Flowers (1st series). Mult.

664 20 c. Type **234** 10 10
665 25 c. "Heliconia psittacorum" (horiz) 10 10
666 55 c. "Heliconia rostrata" . . 20 30
667 $5 "Strelitzia reginae" (horiz) . 1·60 3·50
See also Nos. 703/6 and 739/42.

1987. Sea Shells. Multicoloured.

668 35 c. Type **235** 45 15
669 75 c. Measled cowrie 65 60
670 $1 Atlantic trumpet triton . . 75 90
671 $5 Rooster-tail conch . . . . 1·50 3·25

236 Norman Manley

237 Arms of Jamaica

1987. Portraits.

672A **236** 1 c. red and pink . . 10 20
673A 2 c. red and pink . . 10 20
674A 3 c. green and stone . 10 20
675A 4 c. green & light green 10 20
676B 5 c. blue and grey . . 10 10
677A 6 c. blue and grey . . 20 20
678A 7 c. violet and mauve . 20 20
679A 8 c. mauve and pink . 20 10
680A 9 c. sepia and brown . 20 10
681B – 10 c. red and pink . . 10 10
682B – 20 c. orange and flesh 20 10
683A – 30 c. green & light green 40 10
684B – 40 c. dp green & green 30 20
685B – 50 c. green and grey . 30 20
685cB – 55 c. bistre and cream 30 10
686A – 60 c. blue & light blue 30 20
687A – 70 c. violet & light violet 30 20
688A – 80 c. violet and lilac . 30 30
689B – 90 c. brown & lt brown 40 30
690A **237** $1 brown and cream . 50 30
690cB $1.10 brown and cream 40 30
691aB $2 orange and cream . 40 40
692A $5 green and stone . . 60 70
693A $10 blue and azure . . 70 1·00
693cB $25 violet and lilac . . 90 1·10
693dB $50 mauve and lilac . 1·75 2·25
DESIGN: 10 c. to 90 c. Sir Alexander Bustamante.
The 5, 20, 40, 50, 90 c. and $1 exist with or without imprint date at foot.

238 Jamaican Flag and Coast at Sunset

239 Marcus Garvey

1987. 25th Anniv of Independence. Multicoloured.

694 55 c. Type **238** 75 60
695 70 c. Jamaican flag and inscription (horiz) . . . . . 1·00 2·00

1987. Birth Centenary of Marcus Garvey (founder of Universal Negro Improvement Association). Each black, green and yellow.

696 25 c. Type **239** . . . . 80 1·40
697 25 c. Statue of Marcus Garvey 80 1·40

240 Salvation Army School for the Blind

1987. Cent of Salvation Army in Jamaica. Mult.

698 25 c. Type **240** . . . . 1·25 30
699 55 c. Col. Mary Booth and Bramwell Booth Memorial Hall . . . . 1·25 30
700 $3 Welfare Service lorry, 1929 3·00 4·00
701 $5 Col. Abram Davey and S.S. "Alene", 1887 . . . . 4·00 5·50

1987. Christmas. Flowers (2nd series). As T **234**. Multicoloured.

703 20 c. Hibiscus hybrid 15 10
704 25 c. "Hibiscus elatus" 15 10
705 $4 "Hibiscus cannabinus" . . 2·00 2·75
706 $5 "Hibiscus rosasinensis" . . 2·25 2·75

1988. Jamaican Birds (3rd series). As T **213**. Multicoloured.

707 45 c. Chestnut-bellied cuckoo, black-billed amazon and Jamaican euphonia . . . . 1·50 2·00
708 45 c. Black-billed amazon, jamaican white-eyed vireo, rufous-throated solitaire and yellow elaenia . . . . 1·50 2·00
709 $5 Snowy plover, little blue heron and great blue heron (white phase) . . . . 4·00 4·50
710 $5 Black-necked stilt, snowy egret, snowy plover and black-crowned night heron . . . 4·00 4·50
The two designs of each value were printed together, se-tenant, each pair forming a composite design.

243 Blue Whales

1988. Marine Mammals. Multicoloured.

711 20 c. Type **243** . . . . 1·75 60
712 25 c. Gervais's whales . . . . 1·75 60
713 55 c. Killer whales . . . . . 2·75 70
714 $5 Common dolphins . . . . 4·50 7·00

1988. West Indian Cricket. As T **186** of Barbados, each showing portrait, cricket equipment and early belt buckle. Multicoloured.

715 25 c. Jackie Hendriks . . . . 1·25 40
716 55 c. George Headley . . . . 1·40 40
717 $2 Michael Holding . . . . . 3·00 2·50
718 $3 R. K. Nunes . . . . . . 3·25 3·75
719 $4 Allan Rae . . . . 3·50 4·00

244 Jamaican Red Cross Workers with Ambulance

1988. 125th Anniv of Int Red Cross. Mult.

720 55 c. Type **244** 50 30
721 $5 Henri Dunant (founder) in field hospital . . . . 2·00 3·25

245 Boxing

1988. Olympic Games, Seoul. Multicoloured.

722 25 c. Type **245** 15 10
723 45 c. Cycling 55 30
724 $4 Athletics . . . . 1·25 2·00
725 $5 Hurdling . . . . 1·25 2·00

246 Bobsled Team Members and Logo

1988. Jamaican Olympic Bobsled Team. Mult.

727 25 c. Type **246** 40 65
728 25 c. Two-man bobsled . . . 40 65
729 $5 Bobsled team members (different) and logo . . . . 1·25 2·00
730 $5 Four-man bobsled . . . . 1·25 2·00

1988. Hurricane Gilbert Relief Fund. Nos. 722/5 surch + **25c HURRICANE GILBERT RELIEF FUND.**

731 25 c. + 25 c. Type **245** . . . 10 15
732 45 c. + 45 c. Cycling 20 25
733 $4 + $4 Athletics . . . . . 1·10 1·90
734 $5 + $5 Hurdling . . . . . 1·10 2·25

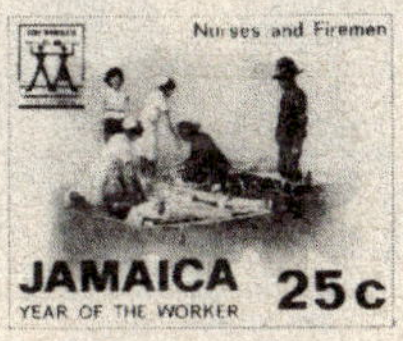

248 Nurses and Firemen

1988. Year of the Worker. Multicoloured.

735 25 c. Type **248** 45 20
736 55 c. Woodcarver 45 30
737 $3 Textile workers . . . . . 1·00 2·50
738 $5 Workers on fish farm . . . 1·25 3·00

1988. Christmas. Flowers (3rd series). As T **234**. Multicoloured.

739 25 c. "Euphorbia pulcherrima" 40 10
740 55 c. "Spathodea campanulata" (horiz) 50 15
741 $3 "Hylocereus triangularis" . 1·10 1·40
742 $4 "Broughtonia sanguinea" (horiz) . . . . 1·10 1·50

249 Old York Castle School

1989. Bicent of Methodist Church in Jamaica.

743 **249** 25 c. black and blue . . . 15 10
744 – 45 c. black and red . . . 20 10
745 – $5 black and green . . . 2·50 3·00
DESIGNS: 45 c. Revd. Thomas Coke and Parade Chapel, Kingston; $5 Father Hugh Sherlock and St. John's Church.

250 "Syntomidopsis variegata"

251 Arawak Fisherman with Catch

1989. Jamaican Moths (1st series). Multicoloured.

746 25 c. Type **250** 50 10
747 55 c. "Himantoides perkinsae" 80 30
748 $3 "Arctia nigriplaga" . . . . 1·50 2·50
749 $5 "Sthenognatha toddi" . . . 1·90 3·00
See also Nos. 758/61 and 790/3.

1989. 500th Anniv (1992) of Discovery of America by Columbus (1st issue). Multicoloured.

750 25 c. Type **251** 20 10
751 70 c. Arawak man smoking . . 45 30
752 $5 King Ferdinand and Queen Isabella inspecting caravels . . 2·00 2·75
753 $10 Columbus with chart . . . 3·75 5·50
See also Nos. 774/7 and 802/7.

252 Girl Guide

1990. 75th Anniv of Girl Guide Movement in Jamaica. Multicoloured.

755 45 c. Type **252** 65 20
756 55 c. Guide leader 75 20
757 $5 Brownie, guide and ranger . 3·50 5·50

1990. Jamaican Moths (2nd series). As T **250**. Multicoloured.

758 25 c. "Eunomia rubripunctata" 75 35
759 55 c. "Perigonia jamaicensis" . 1·00 35
760 $4 "Uraga haemorrhoa" . . . 2·25 3·50
761 $5 "Empyreuma pugione" . . 2·25 3·50

1990. "EXPO '90" International Garden and Greenery Exhibition, Osaka. Nos. 758/61 optd **EXPO '90** and logo.

762 25 c. "Eunomia rubripunctata" 75 35
763 55 c. "Perigonia jamaicensis" . 1·00 35
764 $4 "Uraga haemorrhoa" . . . 2·25 3·50
765 $5 "Empyreuma pugione" . . 2·25 3·50

254 Teaching English

1990. International Literacy Year. Mult.

766 55 c. Type **254** 40 25
767 $5 Teaching maths . . . . . . 3·00 4·00

255 "To the Market"

1990. Christmas. Children's Paintings. Mult.

768 20 c. Type **255** 35 10
769 25 c. "House and Garden" . . 35 10
770 55 c. "Jack and Jill" 50 15
771 70 c. "Market" 65 40
772 $1.50 "Lonely" . . . . 1·50 2·25
773 $5 "Market Woman" (vert) . 3·00 4·50

256 Map of First Voyage, 1492

1990. 500th Anniv (1992) of Discovery of America by Columbus (2nd issue). Multicoloured.

774 25 c. Type **256** 60 20
775 45 c. Map of second voyage, 1493 75 20
776 $5 Map of third voyage, 1498 2·75 3·50
777 $10 Map of fourth voyage, 1502 3·75 5·00

257 Weather Balloon, Dish Aerial and Map of Jamaica

1991. 11th World Meteorological Congress, Kingston.

780 **257** 50 c. multicoloured 50 20
781 $10 multicoloured . . . . 5·50 6·50

258 Bust of Mary Seacole

1991. International Council of Nurses Meeting of National Representatives. Multicoloured.

782 50 c. Type **258** 50 30
783 $1.10 Mary Seacole House . . 1·25 1·75

259 Jamaican Iguana

1991. 50th Anniv of Natural History Society of Jamaica. Jamaican Iguana. Multicoloured.

785 $1.10 Type **259** 55 70
786 $1.10 Head of iguana looking right 55 70
787 $1.10 Iguana climbing 55 70
788 $1.10 Iguana on rock looking left 55 70
789 $1.10 Close-up of iguana's head 55 70

1991. Jamaican Moths (3rd series). As T **250**. Multicoloured.

790 50 c. "Urania sloanus" . . . 65 20
791 $1.10 "Phoenicoprocta jamaicensis" 90 60
792 $1.40 "Horama grotei" . . . 1·10 90
793 $8 "Amplypterus gannascus" . 3·25 5·50

1991. "Phila Nippon '91" International Stamp Exhibition, Tokyo. Nos. 790/3 optd **PHILA NIPPON 91** and emblem.

794 50 c. "Urania sloanus" . . . 65 20
795 $1.10 "Phoenicoprocta jamaicensis" 90 60
796 $1.40 "Horama grotei" . . . 1·10 90
797 $8 "Amplypterus gannascus" . 3·25 5·50

261 "Doctor Bird"

1991. Christmas. Children's Paintings. Mult.

798 50 c. Type **261** 40 10
799 $1.10 "Road scene" 80 25
800 $5 "Children and house" . . 2·00 2·50
801 $10 "Cows grazing" . . . . . 3·25 4·50

262 Indians threatening Ships

263 Compasses and Square Symbol

1991. 500th Anniv (1992) of Discovery of America by Columbus (3rd issue). Multicoloured.

802	50 c. Type **262**	45	15
803	$1.10 Spaniards setting dog on Indians	55	30
804	$1.40 Indian with gift of pineapple	55	30
805	$25 Columbus describes Jamaica with crumpled paper	5·50	7·00

1992. 250th Anniv of First Provisional Grand Master of English Freemasonry in Jamaica. Multicoloured.

808	50 c. Type **263**	55	20
809	$1.10 Symbol in stained glass window	70	35
810	$1.40 Compasses and square on book	70	35
811	$25 Eye in triangle symbol	5·50	7·00

264 Ship in Flooded Street

1992. 300th Anniv of Destruction of Port Royal. Multicoloured.

813	50 c. Type **264**	45	20
814	$1.10 Church tower falling	60	35
815	$1.40 Houses collapsing	60	35
816	$25 Inhabitants falling into fissure	3·75	5·00

265 Credit Union Symbol

1992. 50th Anniv of Credit Union Movement.

818 **265**	50 c. blue, emerald, & grn	75	40
819 –	$1.40 multicoloured	1·40	1·75

DESIGN: $1.40, O'Hare Hall.

266 Jamaican Flag and Beach Scene

1992. 30th Anniv of Independence.

820 **266**	50 c. multicoloured	10	10
821	$1.10 multicoloured	20	20
822	$25 multicoloured	2·75	4·50

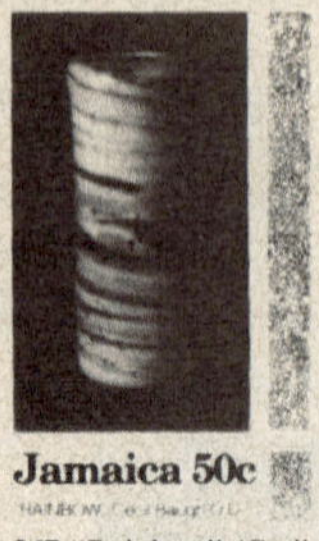

267 "Rainbow" (Cecil Baugh)

269 Cadet, Armoured Car and Emblem

268 Girls' Brigade Parade

1993. Art Ceramics and Pottery. Multicoloured.

823	50 c. Type **267**	10	10
824	$1.10 "Yabba Pot" (Louisa Jones)	20	20
825	$1.40 "Sculptured Vase" (Gene Pearson)	20	20
826	$25 "Lidded Form" (Norma Harrack)	3·50	4·50

1993. Centenary of Girls' Brigade. Mult.

827	50 c. Type **268**	40	30
828	$1.10 Brigade members	50	55

1993. 50th Anniv of Jamaica Combined Cadet Force. Multicoloured.

829	50 c. Type **269**	25	20
830	$1.10 Cadet and Britten Norman Islander aircraft (horiz)	40	30
831	$1.40 Cadet and patrol boats	40	30
832	$3 Cadet and emblem (horiz)	60	1·40

270 Constant Spring Golf Course

1993. Golf Courses. Multicoloured.

833	50 c. Type **270**	20	10
834	$1.10 Type **270**	20	10
835	$1.40 Half Moon	25	15
836	$2 As $1.40	30	35
837	$3 Jamaica Jamaica	35	45
838	$10 As $3	90	1·75

271 Norman Manley

273 Flags of Great Britain and Jamaica

1994. Birth Centenary of Norman Manley.

840 **271**	$25 multicoloured	2·00	2·75
841	$50 multicoloured	2·50	3·25

1994. Royal Visit. Multicoloured.

843	$1.10 Type **273**	20	10
844	$1.40 Royal Yacht "Britannia"	50	20
845	$25 Queen Elizabeth II	1·50	2·50
846	$50 Queen Elizabeth and Prince Philip	2·50	3·50

274 Douglas DC-9

1994. 25th Anniv of Air Jamaica. Mult.

847	50 c. Type **274**	25	20
848	$1.10 Douglas DC-8	25	20
849	$5 Boeing 727	50	65
850	$50 Airbus A300	3·25	5·00

275 Giant Swallowtail

1994. Giant Swallowtail Butterfly Conservation. Multicoloured.

851	50 c. Type **275**	25	20
852	$1.10 With wings closed	35	20
853	$10 On flower	1·25	2·00
854	$25 With wings spread	2·50	3·75

276 "Royal Botanical Gardens" (Sidney McLaren)

1994. Tourism. Multicoloured.

856	50 c. Type **276**	30	20
857	$1.10 Blue Mountains	45	25
858	$5 Tourist in hammock and water sports	1·25	1·75

277 Jamaican Red Poll Calf

1994. Jamaican Red Poll Cattle. Multicoloured.

860	50 c. Type **277**	10	10
861	$1.10 Red Poll heifer	10	10
862	$25 Red Poll cow	1·25	2·25
863	$50 Red Poll bull	2·50	3·75

278 Refuse Collectors

1994. Christmas. Children's Paintings. Multicoloured.

864	50 c. Type **278**	10	10
865	90 c. Hospital ward	10	10
866	$1.10 House	10	10
867	$50 Landscape	2·75	4·00

279 Jamaican Band-tailed Pigeon ("Ring-tailed Pigeon")

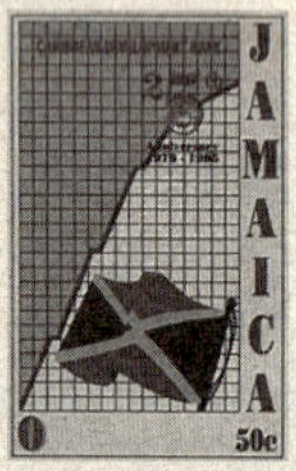

280 Graph, National Flag and Logo

1995. Jamaican Wild Birds. Multicoloured.

868	50 c. Type **279**	30	15
869	90 c. Yellow-billed amazon ("Yellow-billed parrot")	40	30
870	$1.10 Black-billed amazon ("Black-billed parrot")	40	30
871	$50 Jamaican owl ("Brown owl")	3·75	4·50

1995. 25th Anniv of Caribbean Development Bank.

873 **280**	50 c. green, black and yellow	10	10
874	$1 green, black and yellow	10	10
875 –	$1.10 multicoloured	10	10
876 –	$50 multicoloured	2·75	4·00

DESIGNS—HORIZ: $1.10, Industry, agriculture and commerce; $50 Jamaican currency.

281 "Song of Freedom"

1995. 50th Birth Anniv of Bob Marley (reggae singer). Record covers. Multicoloured.

877	50 c. Type **281**	10	10
878	$1.10 "Fire"	15	15
879	$1.40 "Time will Tell"	15	15
880	$3 "Natural Mystic"	30	40
881	$10 "Live at Lyceum"	1·00	1·75

283 Michael Manley

1995. Recipients of the Order of the Caribbean Community. Multicoloured.

884	50 c. Type **283**	10	10
885	$1.10 Sir Alister McIntyre	10	10
886	$1.40 Justice P. Telford Georges	10	10
887	$50 Dame Nita Barrow	2·75	4·00

284 Dish Aerial and Landrover, Balkans

1995. 50th Anniv of United Nations. Multicoloured.

889	50 c. Type **284**	10	10
890	$1.10 Antonov An-32 aircraft, Balkans	15	15
891	$3 Bedford articulated road tanker, Balkans	25	40
892	$5 Fairchild C-119 Flying Boxcar, Korea	35	55

285 Landing of Indian Immigrants

1996. 150th Anniv of Indian Immigration to Jamaica. Multicoloured.

894	$2.50 Type **285**	20	10
895	$10 Indian musicians and traditional dancers	60	80

286 Jamaican Flag and U.N.I.C.E.F. Emblem

1996. 50th Anniv of U.N.I.C.E.F.

896 **286**	$2.50 multicoloured	15	10
897	$8 multicoloured	45	70
898	$10 multicoloured	50	75

287 Brown's Hutia

1996. Endangered Species. Brown's Hutia ("Jamaican Hutia"). Multicoloured.

899	$2.50 Type **287**	15	10
900	$10 Hutia on rock	50	65
901	$12.50 Female with young	60	80
902	$25 Head of hutia	1·25	1·75

288 High Altar, Church of St. Thomas the Apostle

1997. 300th Anniv of Kingston Parish Church. Multicoloured.

903	$2 Type **288**	10	10
904	$8 Church of St. Thomas the Apostle	50	50
905	$12.50 "The Angel" (wood carving by Edna Manley) (vert)	80	90

No. 903 is inscribed "ALTER" in error.

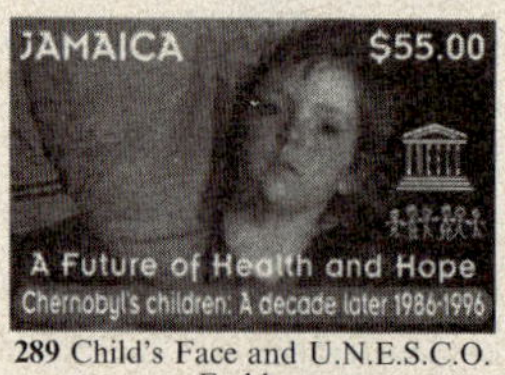

289 Child's Face and U.N.E.S.C.O. Emblem

1998. 10th Anniv of Chernobyl Nuclear Disaster.

907 **289**	$55 multicoloured	1·75	1·90

290 "Coelia triptera" **291** Diana, Princess of Wales

1997. Orchids. Multicoloured.

908A	$1 Type **290**	10	10
909A	$2 "Oncidium pulchellum" (horiz)	10	10
910A	$2.50 "Oncidium triquetium"	10	10
911A	$3 "Broughtonia negrilensis"	10	15
912A	$4.50 "Oncidium gauntlettii" (horiz)	20	25
913A	$5 "Encyclia fragans" (horiz)	20	25
914A	$8 "Broughtonia sanguinea" (horiz)	30	35
915A	$12 "Phaius tankervilleae"	45	50
916A	$25 "Cochleanthes flabelliformis" (horiz)	90	95
917A	$50 "Broughtonia sanguinea" (three varieties) (horiz)	1·75	1·90

1998. Diana, Princess of Wales Commemoration.

918	**291**	$20 multicoloured	85	90

292 University Chapel, Mona

1998. 50th Anniv of University of West Indies. Multicoloured.

920	$8 Type **292**	40	40
921	$10 Philip Sherlock Centre for Creative Arts, Mona	40	40
922	$50 University arms (vert)	2·25	2·50

293 Flags of Jamaica and CARICOM

1998. 25th Anniv of Caribbean Community.

923	**293**	$30 multicoloured	1·10	1·10

294 Jamaican Footballer **295** Coral Reef

1998. World Cup Football Championship, France. Multicoloured.

924	$10 Type **294**	45	40
925	$25 Jamaican team (horiz)	1·10	1·10
926	$100 As $25	4·00	4·50

1998. Christmas. International Year of the Ocean. Multicoloured.

927	$10 Type **295**	35	40
928	$30 Fishing boats, Negril	1·10	1·25
929	$50 Black spiny sea urchin	1·75	1·90
930	$100 Composite design as Nos. 927/9 (22×41 mm)	3·50	3·75

OFFICIAL STAMPS

1890. Optd **OFFICIAL**.

O3	**8**	½d. green	6·00	40
O4	**11**	1d. red	4·00	65
O5		2d. grey	7·00	1·00

JAMMU AND KASHMIR

A state in the extreme N. of India.

12 pies = 1 anna; 16 annas = 1 rupee

1

Gum. The stamps of Jammu and Kashmir were issued without gum.

1866. Imperf.

29	**1**	½ a. black	23·00	42·00
26		½ a. red	24·00	42·00
44		½ a. blue	30·00	£200
20		½ a. green	65·00	£180
48		½ a. yellow	£100	
15		1 a. black	£200	
27		1 a. red	27·00	£150
5		1 a. blue	£275	70·00
21		1 a. green	75·00	£180
24		1 a. yellow	£550	
16		4 a. black	£200	
10		4 a. red	50·00	90·00
19		4 a. blue	£130	
22		4 a. green	£160	£300
25		4 a. yellow	£350	

Prices for the circular stamps (Nos. 5/48) are for cut-square examples. Cut-to-shape examples are worth from 10% to 20% of these prices, according to condition.

½ a. ½ a

1 a. **4** ½ a

1867.

69a	**4**	½ a. black	95·00	£130
58		½ a. blue	£130	70·00
60		½ a. red	4·50	2·50
64		½ a. orange	85·00	90·00
68		½ a. green	£1300	£800
69b		1 a. black	£1100	£950
55		1 a. blue	£500	£275
61		1 a. red	10·00	8·00
65		1 a. orange	£1400	£900
69		1 a. green	£2250	£1400

The characters denoting the value are in the upper part of the inner circle.

8 (¼ a.) **12** (¼ a.)

1867. Imperf.

90	**8**	¼ a. black	1·75	2·00
91		½ a. blue	1·75	90
93		1 a. blue	£2750	£1200
94		1 a. orange	7·00	7·50
97		2 a. yellow	9·00	11·00
99		4 a. green	24·00	24·00
101		8 a. red	26·00	24·00

1878. Imperf or perf.

139	**12**	⅛ a. yellow	60	90
125		¼ a. red	2·25	2·50
131		¼ a. orange	8·00	9·00
130a		¼ a. blue	£750	£450
142		¼ a. brown	50	40
105		½ a. violet	13·00	12·00
147		½ a. red	80	35
132		½ a. orange	18·00	12·00
143		½ a. blue	4·00	
127		1 a. red	1·75	2·25
106		1 a. mauve	19·00	20·00
133		1 a. orange	16·00	8·50
148		1 a. grey	60	50
150		1 a. green	60	50
108		2 a. violet	20·00	20·00
110		2 a. blue	35·00	35·00
128		2 a. red	2·50	3·25
134		2 a. orange	14·00	8·50
152		2 a. red on yellow	1·00	80
153		2 a. red on green	1·75	2·25
129		4 a. red	6·00	6·00
135		4 a. orange	24·00	38·00
155		4 a. green	2·25	3·25
130		8 a. red	6·00	7·00
136		8 a. orange	48·00	55·00
159		8 a. blue	4·75	6·50
161a		8 a. lilac	10·00	15·00

OFFICIAL STAMPS

1878. Imperf or perf.

O 6	**12**	½ a. black	60	65
O 7		½ a. black	15	30
O 8		1 a. black	20	40
O 9		2 a. black	30	40
O10		4 a. black	35	65
O11		8 a. black	90	1·00

JASDAN

A state of India. Now uses Indian Stamps.

12 pie = 1 anna; 16 annas = 1 rupee

1 Sun

1942.

4	**1**	1 a. green	11·00	90·00

JERSEY

Island in the English Channel off N.W. coast of France. Occupied by German forces from June 1940 to May 1945 with separate stamp issues.

The general issue of 1948 for Channel Islands and the regional issues of 1958 are listed at end of GREAT BRITAIN.

Jersey had its own postal administration from 1969.

1941. 12 pence = 1 shilling;
20 shillings = 1 pound.
1971. 100 (new) pence = 1 pound sterling.

(a) War Occupation Issues.

1 **2** Old Jersey Farm

1941.

1	**1**	½d. green	4·00	3·25
2		1d. red	4·25	3·25

1943.

3	**2**	½d. green	7·00	5·50
4	–	1d. red	1·50	75
5	–	1½d. brown	3·00	3·00
6	–	2d. yellow	4·00	3·00
7a	–	2½d. blue	1·00	1·50
8	–	3d. violet	1·00	2·75

DESIGNS: 1d. Portelet Bay; 1½d. Corbiere Lighthouse; 2d. Elizabeth Castle; 2½d. Mont Orgueil Castle; 3d. Gathering vraic (seaweed).

(b) Independent Postal Administration.

10 Elizabeth Castle

1969. Multicoloured.

15	½d. Type **10**	10	70
16	1d. La Hougue Bie (prehistoric tomb)	15	20
17	2d. Portelet Bay	10	15
18	3d. La Corbiere Lighthouse	20	15
19	4d. Mont Orgueil Castle by night	15	10
20	5d. Arms and Royal Mace	15	10
21	6d. Jersey cow	25	30
22	9d. Chart of the English Channel	40	75
23	1s. Mont Orgueil Castle by day	75	75
24	1s. 6d. Chart of the English Channel	1·25	1·25
25	1s. 9d. Queen Elizabeth II (after Cecil Beaton) (vert)	1·25	1·25
26	2s. 6d. Jersey Airport	2·00	1·75
27	5s. Legislative Chamber	11·00	7·00
28	10s. The Royal Court	26·00	17·00
29	£1 Queen Elizabeth II (after Cecil Beaton) (vert)	2·00	1·50

24 First Day Cover

1969. Inauguration of Post Office.

30	**24**	4d. multicoloured	25	20
31		5d. multicoloured	30	30
32		1s. 6d. multicoloured	1·25	1·60
33		1s. 9d. multicoloured	1·25	1·60

25 Lord Coutanche, former Bailiff of Jersey

1970. 25th Anniv of Liberation. Multicoloured.

34	4d. Type **25**	25	25
35	5d. Sir Winston Churchill	25	25
36	1s. 6d. "Liberation" (Edmund Blampied)	1·75	1·75
37	1s. 9d. S.S. "Vega"	1·75	1·75

Nos. 36/7 are horiz.

29 "A Tribute to Enid Blyton"

1970. "Battle of Flowers" Parade. Multicoloured.

38	4d. Type **29**	25	25
39	5d. "Rags to Riches" (Cinderella and pumpkin)	40	40
40	1s. 6d. "Gourmet's Delight" (lobster and cornucopia)	7·00	2·50
41	1s. 9d. "We're the Greatest" (ostriches)	7·25	2·50

33 Jersey Airport

1970. Decimal Currency. Nos. 15, etc, but with new colours, new design (6p.) and decimal values, as T **33**.

42	½p. mult (as No. 15)	10	10
43	1p. mult (as No. 18)	10	10
44	1½p. mult (as No. 21)	10	10
45	2p. mult (as No. 19)	10	10
46	2½p. mult (as No. 20)	10	10
47	3p. mult (as No. 16)	10	10
48	3½p. mult (as No. 17)	15	15
49	4p. mult (as No. 22)	15	15
49a	4½p. mult (as No. 20)	20	20
50	5p. mult (as No. 23)	10	15
50a	5½p. mult (as No. 21)	40	25
51	6p. multicoloured (Martello Tower, Archirondel, 23×22 mm)	25	30
52	7½p. mult (as No. 24)	30	40
52a	8p. mult (as No. 19)	25	25
53	9p. mult (as No. 25)	50	30
54	10p. mult (as No. 26)	50	55
55	20p. mult (as No. 27)	75	75
56	50p. mult (as No. 28)	1·75	1·75

34 White Eared-Pheasant

1971. Wildlife Preservation Trust (1st series). Multicoloured.

57	2p. Type **34**	75	25
58	2½p. Thick-billed parrot (vert)	75	25
59	7½p. Western black-and-white colobus monkey (vert)	7·75	3·75
60	9p. Ring-tailed lemur	8·00	3·75

See also Nos. 73/6, 217/21, 324/9, 447/51 and 824/9.

35 Poppy Emblem and Field

1971. 50th Anniv of Royal British Legion. Mult.

61	2p. Royal British Legion Badge	50	50
62	2½p. Type **35**	50	50
63	7½p. Jack Counter and Victoria Cross	2·40	2·40
64	9p. Crossed Tricolour and Union Jack	2·40	2·40

36 "Tante Elizabeth" (E. Blampied)   37 Jersey Fern

1971. Paintings (1st series). Multicoloured.

65	2p. Type **36**	15	15
66	2½p. "English Fleet in the Channel" (P. Monamy) (horiz)	25	20
67	7½p. "The Boyhood of Raleigh" (Millais) (horiz)	3·00	2·50
68	9p. "The Blind Beggar" (W. W. Ouless)	3·25	2·75

See also Nos. 115/118.

1972. Wild Flowers of Jersey. Multicoloured.

69	3p. Type **37**	25	15
70	5p. Jersey thrift	60	45
71	7½p. Jersey orchid	2·25	2·25
72	9p. Jersey viper's bugloss	2·50	2·25

1972. Wildlife Preservation Trust (2nd series). As T **34**. Multicoloured.

73	2½p. Cheetah	65	20
74	3p. Rothschild's mynah (vert)	40	35
75	7½p. Spectacled bear	1·40	1·50
76	9p. Tuatara	2·00	1·75

38 Artillery Shako   39 Princess Anne

1972. Royal Jersey Militia. Multicoloured.

77	2½p. Type **38**	15	15
78	3p. Shako (2nd North Regt.)	20	20
79	7½p. Shako (5th South-West Regt.)	85	50
80	9p. Helmet (3rd Jersey Light Infantry)	1·00	60

1972. Royal Silver Wedding. Multicoloured.

81	2½p. Type **39**	10	10
82	3p. Queen Elizabeth and Prince Philip (horiz)	10	10
83	7½p. Prince Charles	40	40
84	20p. The Royal Family (horiz)	60	50

40 Armorican Bronze Coins

1973. Centenary of La Societe Jersiaise. Mult.

85	2½p. Silver cups	10	10
86	3p. Gold torque (vert)	10	10
87	7½p. Royal Seal of Charles II (vert)	40	40
88	9p. Type **40**	50	50

41 Balloon "L'Armee de la Loire" and Letter, Paris, 1870

1973. Jersey Aviation History. Multicoloured.

89	3p. Type **41**	10	10
90	5p. Astra seaplane, 1912	15	15
91	7½p. Supermarine Sea Eagle	50	40
92	9p. De Havilland Dragon Express "Giffard Bay"	65	50

42 "North Western", 1870

1973. Centenary of Jersey Eastern Railway. Early Locomotives. Multicoloured.

93	2½p. Type **42**	10	10
94	3p. "Calvados", 1873	10	10
95	7½p. "Carteret" at Grouville station, 1893	60	40
96	9p. "Caesarea", 1873, and route map	80	50

43 Princess Anne and Capt. Mark Phillips

1973. Royal Wedding.

97	**43**	3p. multicoloured	10	10
98		20p. multicoloured	90	90

44 Spider Crab

1973. Marine Life. Multicoloured.

99	2½p. Type **44**	10	10
100	3p. Conger eel	10	10
101	7½p. Lobster	45	35
102	20p. Tuberculate ormer	70	55

45 Freesias   47 John Wesley

46 First Letter Box and Contemporary Cover

1974. Spring Flowers. Multicoloured.

103	3p. Type **45**	10	10
104	5½p. Anemones	20	10
105	8p. Carnations and Gladioli	60	40
106	10p. Daffodils and Iris	80	50

1974. Centenary of U.P.U. Multicoloured.

107	2½p. Type **46**	10	10
108	3p. Postmen, 1862 and 1969	10	10
109	5½p. Letter-box and letter, 1974	35	30
110	20p. R.M.S. "Aquila" (1874) and B.A.C. One Eleven 200 (1974)	85	60

1974. Anniversaries.

111	**47**	3p. black and brown	10	10
112	–	3½p. violet and blue	10	10
113	–	8p. black and lilac	30	35
114	–	20p. black and stone	70	65

PORTRAITS AND EVENTS: 3p. (Bicentenary of Methodism in Jersey). 3½p. Sir William Hillary, founder (150th anniv of R.N.L.I.). 8p. Canon Wace (poet and historian) (800th death anniv. 20p. Sir Winston Churchill (Birth cent)

48 "Catherine" and "Mary" (Royal yachts)

1974. Marine Paintings by Peter Monamy. Mult.

115	3½p. Type **48**	10	10
116	5½p. French two-decker	20	15
117	8p. Dutch vessel (horiz)	30	30
118	25p. Battle of Cap La Hague, 1692 (55×27 mm)	80	60

49 Potato Digger

1975. 19th-Century Farming. Multicoloured.

119	3p. Type **49**	10	10
120	3½p. Cider crusher	10	15
121	8p. Six-horse plough	35	35
122	10p. Hay cart	55	50

50 H.M. Queen Elizabeth, the Queen Mother (photograph by Cecil Beaton)   51 Nautilus Shell

1975. Royal Visit.

123	**50**	20p. multicoloured	1·00	1·00

1975. Jersey Tourism. Multicoloured.

124	5p. Type **51**	10	10
125	8p. Parasol	15	15
126	10p. Deckchair	35	35
127	12p. Sandcastle with flags of Jersey and the U.K.	50	50

52 Common Tern   53 Armstrong Whitworth Siskin IIIA

1975. Sea Birds. Multicoloured.

129	4p. Type **52**	15	15
130	5p. British storm petrel	15	15
131	8p. Brent geese	50	35
132	25p. Shag	85	45

1975. 50th Anniv of Royal Air Force Association, Jersey Branch. Multicoloured.

133	4p. Type **53**	10	10
134	5p. Supermarine Southampton I flying boat	15	15
135	10p. Supermarine Spitfire Mk I	50	30
136	25p. Folland Gnat T.1	95	60

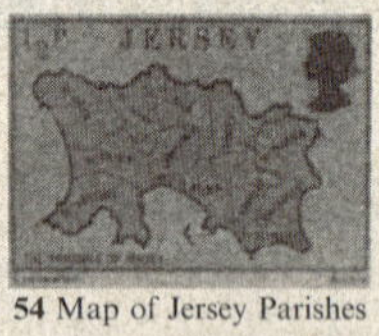

54 Map of Jersey Parishes

55 Parish Arms and Island Scene

1976. Multicoloured. (a) Parish Arms and Views.

137	½p. Type **54**	10	10
138	1p. Zoological Park	10	10
139	5p. St. Mary's Church	15	15
140	6p. Seymour Tower	15	15
141	7p. La Corbiere Lighthouse	20	20
142	8p. St. Saviour's Church	20	20
143	9p. Elizabeth Castle	25	25
144	10p. Gorey Harbour	25	25
145	11p. Jersey Airport	30	25
146	12p. Grosnez Castle	30	30
147	13p. Bonne Nuit Harbour	35	35
148	14p. Le Hocq Tower	35	40
149	15p. Morel Farm	40	45

(b) Emblems.

150	20p. Type **55**	50	50
151	30p. Flag and map	75	75
152	40p. Postal H.Q. and badge	1·00	1·00
153	50p. Parliament, Royal Court and arms	1·25	1·00
154	£1 Lieutenant-Governor's flag and Government House	2·50	2·25
155	£2 Queen Elizabeth II (vert)	4·50	4·25

56 Sir Walter Raleigh and Map of Virginia

1976. Bicentenary of American Independence. Multicoloured.

160	5p. Type **56**	10	10
161	7p. Sir George Carteret and map of New Jersey	15	15
162	11p. Philippe Dauvergne and Long Island landing	40	35
163	13p. John Copley and sketch	45	50

57 Dr. Grandin and Map of China

1976. Birth Centenary of Dr. Lilian Grandin (medical missionary).

164	**57**	5p. multicoloured	10	10
165	–	7p. yellow, brown & black	15	15
166	–	11p. multicoloured	50	35
167	–	13p. multicoloured	50	50

DESIGNS: 7p. Sampan on the Yangtze; 11p. Overland trek; 13p. Dr. Grandin at work.

58 Coronation, 1953 (photographed by Cecil Beaton)

1977. Silver Jubilee. Multicoloured.

168	5p. Type **58**	25	15
169	7p. Visit to Jersey, 1957	30	20
170	25p. Queen Elizabeth II (photo by Peter Grugeon)	90	80

59 Coins of 1871 and 1877

1977. Centenary of Currency Reform. Mult.

171	5p. Type **59**	10	10
172	7p. One-twelfth shilling, 1949	15	15
173	11p. Silver crown, 1966	40	35
174	13p. £2 piece, 1972	45	50

60 Sir William Weston and "Santa Anna", 1530

1977. Centenary of St. John Ambulance. Mult.

175	5p. Type **60**	10	10
176	7p. Sir William Drogo and ambulance, 1877	15	15
177	11p. Duke of Connaught and ambulance, 1917	40	35
178	13p. Duke of Gloucester and stretcher-team, 1977	45	50

61 Arrival of Queen Victoria, 1846

1977. 125th Anniv of Victoria College. Mult.

179	7p. Type **61**	20	20
180	10½p. Victoria College, 1852	25	20
181	11p. Sir Galahad Statue, 1924 (vert)	30	35
182	13p. College Hall (vert)	35	35

62 Harry Vardon Statuette and Map of Royal Jersey Golf Course

1978. Cent of Royal Jersey Golf Club. Mult.

183	6p. Type **62**	15	15
184	8p. Harry Vardon's grip and swing	20	20
185	11p. Harry Vardon's putt	65	35
186	13p. Golf trophies and book by Harry Vardon	65	40

63 Mont Orgueil Castle

1978. Europa. Castles from Paintings by Thomas Phillips. Multicoloured.

187	6p. Type **63**	20	20
188	8p. St. Aubin's Fort	40	40
189	10½p. Elizabeth Castle	50	50

64 "Gaspe Basin" (P. J. Ouless)

1978. Links with Canada. Multicoloured.

190	6p. Type **64**	15	15
191	8p. Map of Gaspe Peninsula	20	20
192	10½p. "Century" (brigantine)	25	25
193	11p. Early map of Jersey	40	30
194	13p. St. Aubin's Bay, town and harbour	45	35

65 Queen Elizabeth and Prince Philip

66 Mail Cutter, 1778–1827

1978. 25th Anniv of Coronation.

195	**65**	8p. silver, black and red	30	30
196	–	25p. silver, black and blue	70	70

DESIGN: 25p. Hallmarks of 1953 and 1977.

1978. Bicentenary of England–Jersey Government Mail Packet Service.

197	**66**	6p. black, brown & yellow	15	15
198	–	8p. black, green & yellow	20	20
199	–	10½p. black, ultram & bl	40	30
200	–	11p. black, purple and lilac	45	35
201	–	13p. black, red and pink	50	45

DESGNS—SHIPS: 8p. "Flamer", 1831–7; 10½p. "Diana", 1877–90; 11p. "Ibex", 1891–1925; 13p. "Caesarea", 1960–75.

67 Jersey Calf

68 Jersey Pillar Box, c. 1860

1979. 9th Conference of World Jersey Cattle Bureau. Multicoloured.

202	6p. Type **67**	20	20
203	25p. "Ansom Designette" (calf presented to the Queen, 1978) (46 × 29 mm)	80	80

1979. Europa. Multicoloured.

204	8p. Type **68**	25	25
205	8p. Clearing modern post box	25	25
206	10½p. Telephone switchboard, c. 1900	30	30
207	10½p. Modern SPC telephone system	30	30

69 Percival Mew Gull "Golden City"

70 "My First Sermon"

1979. 25th International Air Rally. Mult.

208	6p. Type **69**	15	15
209	8p. De Havilland Chipmunk	20	20
210	10½p. Druine Turbulent	40	20
211	11p. De Havilland Tiger Moth	45	25
212	13p. North American Harvard	50	30

1979. International Year of the Child and 150th Birth Anniversary of Sir John Millais (painter). Paintings. Multicoloured.

213	8p. Type **70**	25	15
214	10½p. "Orphans"	30	25
215	11p. "The Princes in the Tower"	30	25
216	25p. "Christ in the House of his Parents" (50 × 32 mm)	55	45

1979. Wildlife Preservation Trust (3rd series). As T **34**. Multicoloured.

217	6p. Pink pigeon (vert)	15	15
218	8p. Orang-utan (vert)	20	20
219	11½p. Waldrapp	50	25
220	13p. Lowland gorilla (vert)	65	25
221	15p. Rodriguez flying fox (vert)	75	30

71 Plan of Mont Orgueil

73 Planting

72 Sir Walter Raleigh and Paul Ivy (engineer) discussing Elizabeth Castle

1980. Jersey Fortresses. Drawings by Thomas Phillips. Multicoloured.

222	8p. Type **71**	30	25
223	11½p. Plan of La Tour de St. Aubin	35	30
224	13p. Plan of Elizabeth Castle	55	45
225	25p. Map of Jersey (38 × 27 mm)	80	70

1980. Europa. Links with Britain. Multicoloured.

226	9p. Type **72**	20	20
227	9p. Type **72**	20	20
228	13½p. Charles II presenting deeds of Smith's Island, Virginia to Sir George Carteret	40	35
229	13½p. Lady Carteret, maid and Jean Chevalier	40	35

Nos. 226/7 and Nos. 228/9 were issued together, se-tenant, forming composite designs.

1980. Cent of Jersey Royal Potato. Mult.

230	7p. Type **73**	15	15
231	15p. Digging	35	35
232	17½p. Weighbridge	60	60

74 Three Lap Event

75 "Eye of the Wind"

1980. 60th Anniv of Jersey Motor Cycle and Light Car Club. Multicoloured.

233	7p. Type **74**	25	25
234	9p. Jersey International Road Race	25	25
235	13½p. Scrambling	45	45
236	15p. Sand racing (saloon cars)	50	50
237	17½p. National Hill Climb	55	55

1980. "Operation Drake" and 150th Anniv of Royal Geographical Society (14p). Multicoloured.

238	7p. Type **75**	20	20
239	9p. Inflatable raft	25	25
240	13½p. Shooting rapids	35	35
241	14p. "Discovery"	45	35
242	15p. Aerial walkway	45	35
243	17½p. Goodyear Aerospace airship "Europa"	55	45

76 Detail of "The Death of Major Peirson"

1981. Bicentenary of Battle of Jersey. Details of J. S. Copley's painting.

244	**76**	7p. multicoloured	25	25
245	–	10p. multicoloured	30	30
246	–	15p. multicoloured	60	60
247	–	17½p. multicoloured	80	80

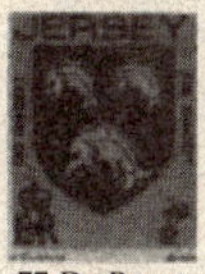

77 De Bagot

78a "Queen Elizabeth II" (Norman Hepple)

1981. Crests of Jersey Families.

249	**77**	½p. black, silver & grn	20	20
250	–	1p. multicoloured	10	10
251	–	2p. multicoloured	10	10
252	–	3p. multicoloured	10	10
253	–	4p. silver, black & mve	25	15
254	–	5p. multicoloured	15	15
255	–	6p. multicoloured	20	20
256	–	7p. multicoloured	20	20
257	–	8p. multicoloured	25	25
258	–	9p. multicoloured	30	30
259b	–	10p. multicoloured	35	35
260	–	11p. multicoloured	35	35
261a	–	12p. multicoloured	40	25
262	–	13p. multicoloured	40	40
263	–	14p. multicoloured	45	45
264	–	15p. multicoloured	45	45
265	–	16p. multicoloured	45	45
266	–	17p. multicoloured	50	50
266a	–	18p. multicoloured	75	75
266b	–	19p. multicoloured	80	80
267	–	20p. black, silver & yellow	60	60
268	–	25p. black and blue	60	60
268a	**77**	26p. black, silver & red	60	60
269	–	30p. multicoloured	90	90
270a	–	40p. multicoloured	1·25	1·25
271	–	50p. multicoloured	1·50	1·60
272	–	75p. multicoloured	2·25	1·75
273	–	£1 multicoloured	3·25	3·00
274	**78a**	£5 multicoloured	15·00	10·50

DESIGNS—As T **77**: 1p. De Carteret; 2p. La Cloche; 3p. Dumaresq; 4p. Payn; 5p. Janvrin; 6p. Poingdestre; 7p. Pipon; 8p. Marett; 9p. Le Breton; 10p. Le Maistre; 11p. Bisson; 12p. Robin; 13p. Herault; 14p. Messervy; 15p. Fiott; 16p. Malet; 17p. Mabon; 18p. De St. Martin; 19p. Hamptonne; 20p. Badier; 25p. L'Arbalestier; 30p. Journeaux; 40p. Lempriere; 50p. Auvergne; 75p. Remon. 38 × 22 mm: £1 Jersey crest and map of Channel.

79 Knight of Hambye slaying Dragon

1981. Europa. Folklore. Multicoloured.

275	10p. Type **79**	25	25
276	10p. Servant slaying Knight of Hambye and awaiting execution	25	25
277	18p. St. Brelade celebrating Easter on island	50	50
278	18p. Island revealing itself as a huge fish	50	50

LEGENDS: 10p. (both) Slaying of the Dragon of Lawrence by the Knight of Hambye; 18p. (both) Voyages of St. Brelade.

80 The Harbour by Gaslight

1981. 150th Anniv of Gas in Jersey. Multicoloured.

279	7p. Type **80**	25	25
280	10p. The Quay	30	30
281	18p. Royal Square	45	45
282	22p. Halkett Place	55	55
283	25p. Central Market	65	65

81 Prince Charles and Lady Diana Spencer

1981. Royal Wedding.

284	**81**	10p. multicoloured	75	75
285		25p. multicoloured	1·75	1·75

82 Christmas Tree in Royal Square

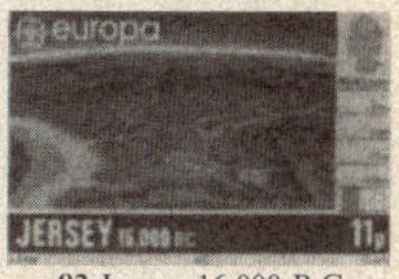

83 Jersey, 16,000 B.C.

1981. Christmas. Multicoloured.

286	7p. Type **82**	25	25
287	10p. East window, Parish Church, St. Helier	40	40
288	18p. Boxing Day meet of Jersey Drag Hunt	50	50

1982. Europa. Formation of Jersey. Mult.

289	11p. Type **83**	30	30
290	11p. In 10,000 B.C. (vert)	30	30
291	19½p. In 7,000 B.C. (vert)	70	60
292	19½p. In 4,000 B.C.	70	60

84 Duke Rollo of Normandy, William the Conqueror and "Clameur de Haro" (traditional procedure for obtaining justice)

1982. Links with France. Multicoloured.

293	8p. Type **84**	25	25
294	8p. John of England, Philippe Auguste of France, and Siege of Rouen	25	25
295	11p. Jean Martell (brandy merchant), early still and view of Cognac	35	35
296	11p. Victor Hugo, "Le Rocher des Proscrits" (rock where he used to meditate) and Marine Terrace	35	35
297	19½p. Pierre Teilhard de Chardin (philosopher) and "Maison Saint Louis" (science institute)	60	60
298	19½p. Pere Charles Rey (scientist), anemotachymeter and The Observatory, St. Louis	60	60

85 Sir William Smith, Founder of Boys' Brigade

1982. Youth Organizations. Multicoloured.

299	8p. Type **85**	25	25
300	11p. Boys' Brigade "Old Boys" band, Liberation Parade, 1945 (vert)	30	30
301	24p. William Smith and Lord Baden-Powell at Royal Albert Hall, 1903	60	60
302	26p. Lord and Lady Baden-Powell, St. Helier, 1924 (vert)	75	75
303	29p. Scouts at "Westward Ho" campsite, St. Ouen's Bay	90	90

Nos. 299/301 commemorate the centenary of the Boys' Brigade and Nos. 302/3 the 75th anniversary of the Boy Scout Movement.

86 H.M.S. "Tamar" and H.M.S. "Dolphin" at Port Egmont

1983. Jersey Adventurers (1st series). Mult.

304	8p. Type **86**	25	25
305	11p. H.M.S. "Dolphin" and H.M.S. "Swallow" off Magellan Strait	30	30
306	19½p. Discovering Pitcairn Island	50	50
307	24p. Carteret taking possession of English Cove, New Ireland	70	70
308	26p. H.M.S. "Swallow" sinking a pirate, Macassar Strait	85	75
309	29p. H.M.S. "Endymion" leading convoy from West Indies	1·00	85

See also Nos. 417/21 and 573/8.

HAVE YOU READ THE NOTES AT THE BEGINNING OF THIS CATALOGUE?

These often provide answers to the enquiries we receive.

87 1969 5s. Legislative Chamber Definitive

1983. Europa. Multicoloured.

310 11p. Type **87** 50 50
311 11p. Royal Mace (23 × 32 mm) 50 50
312 19½p. 1969 10s. Royal Court definitive showing green border error 75 75
313 19½p. Bailiff's Seal (23 × 32 mm) 75 75

88 Charles Le Geyt and Battle of Minden (1759)

1983. World Communications Year and 250th Birth Anniv of Charles Le Geyt (1st Jersey postmaster). Multicoloured.

314 8p. Type **88** 25 25
315 11p. London to Weymouth mail coach 35 35
316 24p. P.O. Mail Packet "Chesterfield" attacked by French privateer 75 75
317 26p. Mary Godfray and the Hue Street Post Office 90 90
318 29p. Mail steamer leaving St. Helier harbour . . . . . . 1·10 1·10

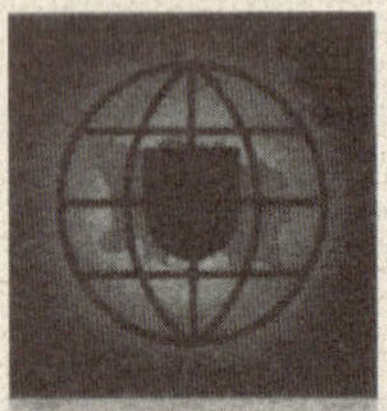

89 Assembly Emblem

1983. 13th General Assembly of the A.I.P.L.F. (Association Internationale des Parlementaires de Langue Francaise) Jersey.

319 **89** 19½p. multicoloured 75 75

90 "Cardinal Newman" 91 Golden Lion Tamarin

1983. 50th Death Anniv of Walter Ouless (artist). Multicoloured.

320 8p. Type **90** 25 25
321 11p. "Incident in the French Revolution" 45 45
322 20½p. "Thomas Hardy" . . . 85 85
323 31p. "David with the head of Goliath" (38 × 32 mm) . . . 1·25 1·25

1984. Wildlife Preservation Trust (4th series). Multicoloured.

324 9p. Type **91** 30 30
325 12p. Snow leopard 40 40
326 20½p. Jamaican boa 60 60
327 26p. Round island gecko . . . 95 75
328 28p. Coscoroba swan . . . 1·10 90
329 31p. St. Lucia amazon . . . . 1·10 90

92 C.E.P.T. 25th Anniversary Logo

1984. Europa.

330 **92** 9p. lt blue, blue & black . . 30 30
331 12p. lt green, grn & blk . . 40 40
332 20½p. lilac, purple & blk . . 70 70

94 "Sarah Bloomshoft" at Demie de Pas Light, 1906

1984. Centenary of Jersey R.N.L.I. Lifeboat Station. Multicoloured.

334 9p. Type **94** 40 40
335 9p. "Hearts of Oak" and "Maurice Georges", 1949 . 40 40
336 12p. "Elizabeth Rippon" and "Hanna", 1949 . . . . . 50 50
337 12p. "Elizabeth Rippon" and "Santa Maria", 1951 . . 50 50
338 20½p. "Elizabeth Rippon" and "Bacchus", 1973 . . . . 90 75
339 20½p. "Thomas James King" and "Cythara", 1983 . . . . . 90 75

95 Bristol Type 170 Freighter Mk 32

1984. 40th Anniv of I.C.A.O. Multicoloured.

340 9p. Type **95** 30 30
341 12p. Airspeed A.S.57 Ambassador 2 . . . . . . 40 40
342 26p. De Havilland D.H.114 Heron 1B . . . . 1·10 90
343 31p. De Havilland D.H.89A Dragon Rapide . . . . . . 1·40 1·10

96 "Robinson Crusoe leaves the Wreck"

1984. Links with Australia. Paintings by John Alexander Gilfillan. Multicoloured.

344 9p. Type **96** 30 30
345 12p. "Edinburgh Castle" . . 40 40
346 20½p. "Maori Village" 75 75
347 26p. "Australian Landscape" 95 95
348 28p. "Waterhouse's Corner, Adelaide" . . . . 1·00 1·00
349 31p. "Captain Cook at Botany Bay" . . . . 1·10 1·10

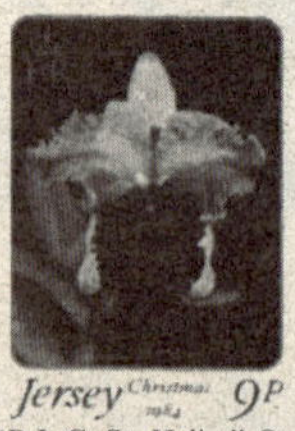

97 "B.L.C. St. Helier" Orchid

1984. Christmas. Jersey Orchids (1st series). Multicoloured.

350 9p. Type **97** 50 45
351 12p. "Oda Mt. Bingham" . . 75 65

See also Nos. 433/7, 613/17 and 892/7.

98 "'Hebe' off Corbiere, 1874"

1984. Death Centenary of Philip John Ouless (artist). Multicoloured.

352 9p. Type **98** 30 30
353 12p. "The 'Gaspe' engaging the 'Diomede'" 40 40
354 22p. "The Paddle-steamer 'London' entering Naples, 1856" 80 80
355 31p. "'The Rambler' entering Cape Town, 1840" . . . . 1·40 1·10
356 34p. "St. Aubin's Bay from Mount Bingham, 1871" . . 1·50 1·25

99 John Ireland (composer) and Faldouet Dolmen

1985. Europa. European Music Year. Mult.

357 10p. Type **99** 40 40
358 13p. Ivy St. Helier (actress) and His Majesty's Theatre, London 55 55
359 22p. Claude Debussy (composer) and Elizabeth Castle . . . . 1·00 90

100 Girls' Brigade 101 "Duke of Normandy" at Cheapside

1985. International Youth Year. Mult.

360 10p. Type **100** 30 30
361 13p. Girl Guides (75th anniversary) 50 50
362 29p. Prince Charles and Jersey Youth Service Activities Base 1·00 1·00
363 31p. Sea Cadet Corps . . . . 1·10 1·00
364 34p. Air Training Corps . . . 1·25 1·10

1985. The Jersey Western Railway. Mult.

365 10p. Type **101** 55 55
366 13p. Saddletank at First Tower 70 70
367 22p. "La Moye" at Millbrook 1·10 1·10
368 29p. "St. Heliers" at St. Aubin 1·25 1·25
369 34p. "St. Aubyns" at Corbiere 1·40 1·40

102 Memorial Window to Revd. James Hemery (former Dean) and St. Helier Parish Church

1985. 300th Anniv of Huguenot Immigration. Multicoloured.

370 10p. Type **102** 30 30
371 10p. Judge Francis Jeune, Baron St. Helier, and Houses of Parliament 30 30
372 13p. Silverware by Pierre Amiraux 45 45
373 13p. Francis Voisin (merchant) and Russian port 45 45
374 22p. Robert Brohier, Schweppes carbonation plant and bottles 75 75
375 22p. George Ingouville, V.C. R.N. and attack on Viborg . 75 75

103 Howard Davis Hall, Victoria College

1985. Thomas Benjamin Davis (philanthropist) Commemoration. Multicoloured.

376 10p. Type **103** 40 40
377 13p. Racing schooner "Westward" 60 60
378 31p. Howard Davis Park, St. Helier . . . . 1·10 1·10
379 34p. Howard Davis Experimental Farm, Trinity 1·25 1·25

104 "Amaryllis belladonna" (Pandora Sellars)

1986. Jersey Lilies. Multicoloured.

380 13p. Type **104** 75 75
381 34p. "A Jersey Lily" (Lily Langtry) (Sir John Millais) (30 × 48 mm) . . . . 1·75 1·75

105 King Harold, William of Normandy and Halley's Comet, 1066 (from Bayeux Tapestry)

1986. Appearance of Halley's Comet. Multicoloured.

383 10p. Type **105** 40 40
384 22p. Lady Carteret, Edmond Halley, map and Comet . . 1·00 1·00
385 31p. Aspects of communications in 1910 and 1986 on TV screen 1·40 1·40

106 Dwarf Pansy 107 Queen Elizabeth II (from photo by Karsh)

1986. Europa. Environmental Conservation. Multicoloured.

386 10p. Type **106** 40 40
387 14p. Sea stock 75 75
388 22p. Sand crocus . . . . . . 1·10 1·10

1986. 60th Birthday of Queen Elizabeth II.

389 **107** £1 multicoloured . . . . 3·25 3·25

See also No. 491b.

108 Le Rat Cottage

1986. 50th Anniv of National Trust for Jersey. Multicoloured.

390 10p. Type **108** 30 30
391 14p. The Elms (Trust headquarters) 45 45
392 22p. Morel Farm 80 80
393 29p. Quetivel Mill 90 90
394 31p. La Vallette 95 95

109 Prince Andrew and Miss Sarah Ferguson 110 "Gathering Vraic"

1986. Royal Wedding.

395 **109** 14p. multicoloured . . . 50 50
396 40p. multicoloured . . . 1·50 1·50

1986. Birth Centenary of Edmund Blampied (artist).

397 **110** 10p. multicoloured . . . 40 40
398 – 14p. black, blue & grey . . 70 70
399 – 29p. multicoloured . . . 1·00 1·00
400 – 31p. black, orge & grey . 1·25 1·25
401 – 34p. multicoloured . . . 1·40 1·40

DESIGNS: 14p. "Driving Home in the Rain"; 29p. "The Miller"; 31p. "The Joy Ride"; 34p. "Tante Elizabeth".

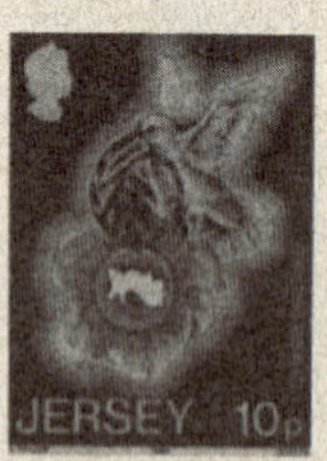

111 Island Map on Jersey Lily, and Dove holding Olive Branch

1986. Christmas. Int Peace Year. Mult.

402 10p. Type **111** 40 40
403 14p. Mistletoe wreath encircling European robin and dove . 60 60
404 34p. Christmas cracker releasing dove . . . . 1·25 1·25

112 "Westward" under Full Sail

1987. Racing Schooner "Westward". Mult.

405 10p. Type **112** 40 40
406 14p. T. B. Davis at the helm . 60 60
407 31p. "Westward" overhauling "Britannia" . . . . 1·25 1·10
408 34p. "Westward" fitting-out at St. Helier . . . . 1·40 1·25

113 De Havilland Dragon Express "Belcroute Bay"

1987. 50th Anniv of Jersey Airport. Multicoloured.
409 10p. Type **113** 30 30
410 14p. Boeing 757 and Douglas DC-9-15 . . . . 50 50
411 22p. Britten Norman "long nose" Trislander and Islander aircraft 70 70
412 29p. Short 330 and Vickers Viscount 800 . . . . 1·00 1·10
413 31p. B.A.C. One Eleven 500 and Handley Page Dart Herald . 1·25 1·25

114 St. Mary and St. Peter's Roman Catholic Church

1987. Europa. Modern Architecture. Mult.
414 11p. Type **114** 45 45
415 15p. Villa Devereux, St. Brelade 65 65
416 22p. Fort Regent Leisure Centre, St. Helier (57 × 29 mm) . . 90 90

115 H.M.S. "Racehorse" and H.M.S. "Carcass" (bomb ketches) trapped in Arctic

1987. Jersey Adventurers (2nd series). Philippe D'Auvergne. Multicoloured.
417 11p. Type **115** 40 40
418 15p. H.M.S. "Alarm" on fire, Rhode Island 50 50
419 29p. H.M.S. "Arethusa" wrecked off Ushant 90 80
420 31p. H.M.S. "Rattlesnake" stranded on Isle de Trinidad 1·00 90
421 34p. Mont Orgueil Castle and fishing boats . . . . 1·10 1·00
See also Nos. 501/6 and 539/44.

116 Grant of Lands to Normandy, 911 and 933

1987. 900th Death Anniv of William the Conqueror. Multicoloured.
422 11p. Type **116** 40 40
423 15p. Edward the Confessor and Duke Robert I of Normandy landing on Jersey, 1030 . . 45 45
424 22p. King William's coronation, 1066 and fatal fall, 1087 . . 80 80
425 29p. Death of William Rufus, 1100 and Battle of Tinchebrai, 1106 . . . . 95 95
426 31p. Civil war between Matilda and Stephen, 1135–41 . . . 1·10 1·10
427 34p. Henry inherits Normandy, 1151; John asserts ducal rights in Jersey, 1213 . . . . . . 1·25 1·25

117 "Grosnez Castle"

1987. Christmas. Paintings by John Le Capelain. Multicoloured.
428 11p. Type **117** 40 40
429 15p. "St. Aubin's Bay" 60 60
430 22p. "Mont Orgueil Castle" . . 80 80
431 31p. "Town Fort and Harbour, St. Helier" . . . . 1·10 1·10
432 34p. "The Hermitage" . . . . 1·25 1·25

HAVE YOU READ THE NOTES AT THE BEGINNING OF THIS CATALOGUE?
These often provide answers to the enquiries we receive.

118 "Cymbidium pontac"

1988. Jersey Orchids (2nd series). Multicoloured.
433 11p. Type **118** 50 50
434 15p. "Odontioda" "Eric Young" (vert) 60 60
435 29p. "Lycaste auburn" "Seaford" and "Ditchling" 1·00 1·00
436 31p. "Odontoglossum" "St. Brelade" (vert) . . . . . . 1·10 1·10
437 34p. "Cymbidium mavourneen" "Jester" . . . . 1·25 1·25

119 Labrador Retriever

1988. Centenary of Jersey Dog Club. Mult.
438 11p. Type **119** 50 50
439 15p. Wire-haired dachshund . 75 75
440 22p. Pekingese . . . . 1·10 1·10
441 31p. Cavalier King Charles spaniel . . . . 1·10 1·10
442 34p. Dalmatian . . . . 1·25 1·25

120 De Havilland D.H.C.7 Dash Seven, London Landmarks and Jersey Control Tower

1988. Europa. Transport and Communications. Multicoloured.
443 16p. Type **120** 50 50
444 16p. Weather radar and Jersey airport landing system (vert) 50 50
445 22p. Hydrofoil, St. Malo and Elizabeth Castle, St. Helier 90 90
446 22p. Port control tower and Jersey Radio maritime communication centre, La Moye (vert) 90 90

121 Rodriguez Fody

122 Rain Forest Leaf Frog, Costa Rica

1988. Wildlife Preservation Trust (5th series). Multicoloured.
447 12p. Type **121** 55 55
448 16p. Volcano rabbit (horiz) . 70 70
449 29p. White-faced marmoset . 1·10 1·10
450 31p. Ploughshare tortoise (horiz) 1·25 1·25
451 34p. Mauritius kestrel . . . . 1·40 1·40

1988. Operation Raleigh. Multicoloured.
452 12p. Type **122** 45 45
453 16p. Archaeological survey, Peru 55 55
454 22p. Climbing glacier, Chile . 80 80
455 29p. Red Cross Centre, Solomon Islands . . . . 1·00 1·00
456 31p. Underwater exploration, Australia . . . . 1·10 1·10
457 34p. "Zebu" (brigantine) returning to St. Helier . . . 1·25 1·25

123 St. Clement Parish Church

1988. Christmas. Jersey Parish Churches (1st series). Multicoloured.
458 12p. Type **123** 35 35
459 16p. St. Ouen 60 60
460 31p. St. Brelade 90 90
461 34p. St. Lawrence 95 95
See also Nos. 535/8 and 597/600.

124 Talbot "Type 4 CT Tourer", 1912

1989. Vintage Cars (1st series). Multicoloured.
462 12p. Type **124** 40 40
463 16p. De Dion "Bouton Type 1-D", 1920 . . . . 60 60
464 23p. Austin 7 "Chummy", 1926 75 75
465 30p. Ford "Model T", 1926 . . 90 90
466 32p. Bentley 8 litre, 1930 . . . 1·10 1·10
467 35p. Cadillac "452A–V16 Fleetwood Sports Phaeton", 1931 . . . . 1·25 1·25
See also Nos. 591/6.

125 Belcroute Bay

125a Arms of King George VI

1989. Jersey Scenes. Multicoloured.
468 1p. Type **125** 10 10
469 2p. High Street, St. Aubin . . 10 10
470 4p. Royal Jersey Golf Course 10 10
471 5p. Portelet Bay 10 10
472 10p. Les Charrieres D'Anneport 20 25
473 13p. St. Helier Marina . . . 25 30
474 14p. Sand yacht racing, St. Ouen's Bay 30 35
475 15p. Rozel Harbour 30 35
476 16p. St. Aubin's Harbour . . 30 35
477 17p. Jersey Airport 35 40
478 18p. Corbiere Lighthouse . . . 35 40
479 19p. Val de la Mare 40 45
480 20p. Elizabeth Castle 40 45
481 21p. Greve de Lecq 40 45
482 22p. Samares Manor 45 50
483 23p. Bonne Nuit Harbour . . 45 50
484 24p. Grosnez Castle 50 55
485 25p. Augres Manor 50 55
486 26p. Central Market 50 55
487 27p. St. Brelade's Bay 55 60
488 30p. St. Ouen's Manor . . . 60 65
489 40p. La Hougue Bie 80 85
490 50p. Mont Orgueil Castle . . 1·00 1·10
491 75p. Royal Square, St. Helier 1·50 1·60
491b £2 Type **107** . . . . 4·50 4·25
491c £4 Type **125a** . . . . . . 8·00 8·25
Nos. 469/91 are as Type **125**.

126 Agile Frog

1989. Endangered Jersey Fauna. Multicoloured.
492 13p. Type **126** . . . . . . 1·00 1·00
493 13p. "Heteropterus morpheus" (butterfly) (vert) . . . . . 1·00 1·00
494 17p. Barn owl (vert) . . . . . 1·10 1·10
495 17p. Green lizard . . . . . . 1·10 1·10

127 Toddlers' Toys

1989. Europa. Children's Toys and Games. Designs showing clay plaques. Multicoloured.
496 17p. Type **127** 50 50
497 17p. Playground games 50 50
498 23p. Party games 90 90
499 23p. Teenage sports 90 90

128 Queen Elizabeth II and Royal Yacht "Britannia" in Elizabeth Harbour

1989. Royal Visit.
500 **128** £1 multicoloured . . . . 3·00 3·00

129 Philippe D'Auvergne presented to Louis XVI, 1786

1989. Bicentenary of the French Revolution. Philippe D'Auvergne. Multicoloured.
501 13p. Type **129** 45 45
502 17p. Storming the Bastille, 1789 60 60
503 23p. Marie de Bouillon and revolutionaries, 1790 . . . 80 80
504 30p. Auvergne's headquarters at Mont Orgueil, 1795 . . . . 1·10 1·10
505 32p. Landing arms for Chouan rebels, 1796 . . . . 1·25 1·25
506 35p. The last Chouan revolt, 1799 . . . . 1·40 1·40
See also Nos. 539/44.

130 "St. Helier" off Elizabeth Castle

1989. Centenary of Great Western Railway Steamer Service to Channel Islands. Multicoloured.
507 13p. Type **130** 40 40
508 17p. "Caesarea II" off Corbiere Lighthouse 50 50
509 27p. "Reindeer" in St. Helier harbour . . . . 1·00 1·00
510 32p. "Ibex" racing "Frederica" off Portelet . . . . 1·25 1·25
511 35p. "Lynx" off Noirmont . . 1·40 1·40

131 "Gorey Harbour"

1989. 150th Birth Anniv of Sarah Louisa Kilpack (artist). Multicoloured.
512 13p. Type **131** 40 40
513 17p. "La Corbiere" 50 50
514 23p. "Greve de Lecq" . . . . 1·00 1·00
515 32p. "Bouley Bay" . . . . . 1·25 1·25
516 35p. "Mont Orgueil" . . . . 1·40 1·40

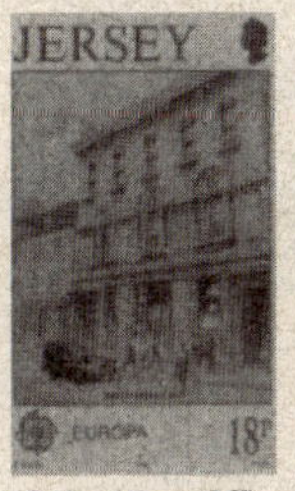

132 Head Post Office, Broad Street, 1969

133 "Battle of Flowers" Parade

1990. Europa. Post Office Buildings. Mult.
517 18p. Type **132** 50 50
518 18p. Postal Headquarters, Mont Millais, 1990 . . . . 50 50
519 24p. Hue Street Post Office, 1815 (horiz) 90 90
520 24p. Head Post Office, Halkett Place, 1890 (horiz) 90 90

1990. Festival of Tourism. Multicoloured.
521 18p. Type **133** 60 60
522 24p. Sports 75 75
523 29p. Mont Orgueil Castle and German Underground Hospital Museum 95 95
524 32p. Salon Culinaire . . . . . 1·00 1·00

134 Early Printing Press and Jersey Newspaper Mastheads

1990. International Literacy Year. Jersey News Media. Multicoloured.
526 14p. Type **134** 55 55
527 18p. Modern press, and offices of "Jersey Evening Post" in 1890 and 1990 . . . . 60 60
528 34p. Radio Jersey broadcaster 1·10 1·10
529 37p. Channel Television studio cameraman . . . . 1·10 1·10

135 British Aerospace Hawk T.1

1990. 50th Anniv of Battle of Britain. Multicoloured.
530 14p. Type **135** 45 45
531 18p. Supermarine Spitfire . . . 60 60
532 24p. Hawker Hurricane Mk I . 85 85
533 34p. Vickers-Armstrong Wellington . . . . . . 1·50 1·50
534 37p. Avro Lancaster . . . . . 1·60 1·60

1990. Christmas. Jersey Parish Churches (2nd series). As T **123**. Multicoloured.
535 14p. St. Helier 40 40
536 18p. Grouville 60 60
537 34p. St. Saviour . . . . 1·10 1·10
538 37p. St. John . . . . 1·25 1·25

1991. 175th Death Anniv of Philippe d'Auvergne. As T **129**. Multicoloured.
539 15p. Prince's Tower, La Hougue Bie 50 50
540 20p. Auvergne's arrest in Paris 60 60
541 26p. Auvergne plotting against Napoleon 80 80
542 31p. Execution of George Cadoudal . . . . 1·00 1·00
543 37p. H.M.S. "Surly" (cutter) attacking French convoy . . 1·25 1·25
544 44p. Auvergne's last days in London . . . . 1·40 1·40

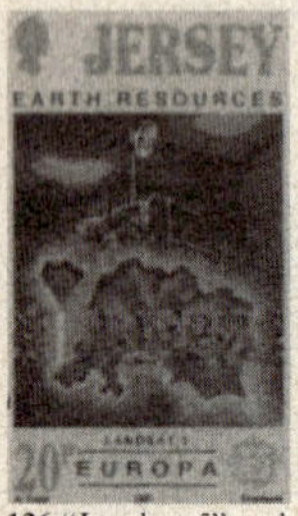

136 "Landsat 5" and Thematic Mapper Image over Jersey

137 1941 1d. Stamp (50th anniv of first Jersey postage stamp)

1991. Europa. Europe in Space. Multicoloured.
545 20p. Type **136** 55 55
546 20p. "ERS-1" earth resources remote sensing satellite . . . 55 55
547 26p. "Meteosat" weather satellite 85 85
548 26p. "Olympus" direct broadcasting satellite 85 85

1991. Anniversaries. Multicoloured.
549 15p. Type **137** 40 40
550 20p. Steam train (centenary of Jersey Eastern Railway extension to Gorey Pier) . 60 60
551 26p. Jersey cow and Herd Book (125th anniv of Jersey Herd Book) 80 80
552 31p. Stone-laying ceremony (from painting by P. J. Ouless) (150th anniv of Victoria Harbour) 90 90
553 53p. Marie Bartlett and hospital (250th anniv of Marie Bartlett's hospital bequest) . 1·75 1·75

138 "Melitaea cinxia"

1991. Butterflies and Moths. Multicoloured.
554 15p. Type **138** 40 40
555 20p. "Euplagia quadripunctaria" 50 50
556 37p. "Deilephila porcellus" . 1·60 1·60
557 57p. "Inachis io" . . . . . . 2·00 2·00

139 Drilling for Water, Ethiopia

1991. Overseas Aid. Multicoloured.
558 15p. Type **139** 50 40
559 20p. Building construction, Rwanda 60 65
560 26p. Village polytechnic, Kenya 80 80
561 31p. Treating leprosy, Tanzania 1·00 1·00
562 37p. Ploughing, Zambia . . . 1·25 1·25
563 44p. Immunisation clinic, Lesotho . . . . 1·40 1·40

140 "This is the Place for Me"

141 Pied Wagtail

1991. Christmas. Illustrations by Edmund Blampied for J. M. Barrie's "Peter Pan". Multicoloured.
564 15p. Type **140** 40 40
565 20p. "The Island Come True" 65 65
566 37p. "The Never Bird" . . . 1·25 1·25
567 53p. "The Great White Father" 1·60 1·60

1992. Winter Birds. Multicoloured.
568 16p. Type **141** 55 45
569 22p. Firecrest 80 60
570 28p. Common snipe 90 70
571 39p. Lapwing . . . . 1·40 1·00
572 57p. Fieldfare . . . . 1·90 1·50
See also Nos. 635/9.

142 Shipping at Shanghai, 1860

1992. Jersey Adventurers (3rd series). 150th Birth Anniv of William Mesny. Multicoloured.
573 16p. Type **142** 50 50
574 16p. Mesny's junk running Taiping blockade, 1862 . . 50 50
575 22p. General Mesny outside river gate, 1874 . . . . . . 75 75
576 22p. Mesny in Burma, 1877 . 75 75
577 33p. Mesny and Governor Chang, 1882 . . . . . . 1·00 1·00
578 33p. Mesny in mandarin's sedan chair, 1886 . . . . 1·00 1·00

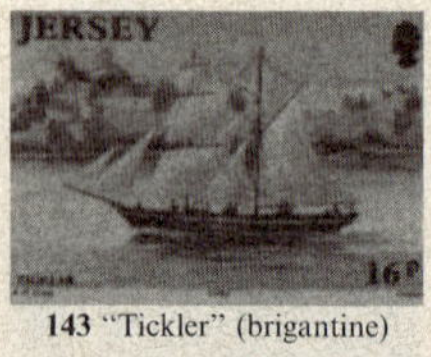

143 "Tickler" (brigantine)

1992. Jersey Shipbuilding. Multicoloured.
579 16p. Type **143** 50 50
580 22p. "Hebe" (brig) 80 70
581 50p. "Gemini" (barque) . . . 1·60 1·50
582 57p. "Percy Douglas" (full-rigged ship) . . . . 1·90 1·75

144 John Bertram (ship owner) and Columbus

1992. Europa. 500th Anniv of Discovery of America by Columbus. Multicoloured.
584 22p. Type **144** 70 70
585 28p. Sir George Carteret (founder of New Jersey) . . 85 85
586 39p. Sir Walter Raleigh (founder of Virginia) . . . . 1·25 1·25

145 "Snow Leopards" (Allison Griffiths)

146 Farmhouse

1992. Batik Designs. Multicoloured.
587 16p. Type **145** 50 50
588 22p. "Three Elements" (Nataly Miorin) 70 70
589 39p. "Three Men in a Tub" (Amanda Crocker) . . . . 1·25 1·25
590 57p. "Cockatoos" (Michelle Millard) . . . . 1·75 1·75

1992. Vintage Cars (2nd series). As T **124**. Multicoloured.
591 16p. Morris Cowley "Bullnose", 1925 . . . . 35 35
592 22p. Rolls Royce "20/25", 1932 50 50
593 28p. Chenard and Walcker "T5", 1924 . . . . 80 80
594 33p. Packard 900 series "Light Eight", 1932 . . . . . . 90 90
595 39p. Lanchester "21", 1927 . . 1·10 1·10
596 50p. Buick "30 Roadster", 1913 1·50 1·50

1992. Christmas. Jersey Parish Churches (3rd series). As T **123**. Multicoloured.
597 16p. Trinity 40 35
598 22p. St. Mary 55 60
599 39p. St. Martin . . . . . . 1·00 1·00
600 57p. St. Peter . . . . 1·40 1·40

1993. Multicoloured.
601 (–) Type **146** 40 45
602 (–) Trinity Church 40 45
603 (–) Daffodils and cows 40 45
604 (–) Jersey cows 40 45
605 (–) Sunbathing 50 55
606 (–) Windsurfing 50 55
607 (–) Crab (Queen's head at left) 50 55
608 (–) Crab (Queen's head at right) 50 55
609 (–) "Singin' in the Rain" float 60 65
610 (–) "Dragon Dance" float . . 60 65
611 (–) "Bali, Morning of the World" float 60 65
612 (–) "Zulu Fantasy" float . . . 60 65

The above do not show face values, but are inscribed "BAILIWICK POSTAGE PAID" (Nos. 601/4), "U.K. MINIMUM POSTAGE PAID" (Nos. 605/8) or "EUROPE POSTAGE PAID" (Nos. 609/12). They were initially sold at 17p., 23p. or 28p., but it is intended that these face values will be increased to reflect postage rate changes in the future.

147 "Phragmipedium" Eric Young "Jersey"

149 "Jersey's Opera House" (Ian Rolls)

148 Douglas DC-3 Dakota

1993. Jersey Orchids (3rd series). Multicoloured.
613 17p. Type **147** 50 35
614 23p. "Odontoglossum" Augres "Trinity" 75 45
615 28p. "Miltonia" St. Helier "Colomberie" 90 65
616 39p. "Phragmipedium pearcei" 1·25 1·25
617 57p. "Calanthe" Grouville "Grey" . . . . 1·75 1·75

1993. 75th Anniv of Royal Air Force. Mult.
618 17p. Type **148** 50 50
619 23p. Wight seaplane 70 70
620 28p. Avro Shackleton A.E.W.2 80 80
621 33p. Gloster Meteor Mk III and De Havilland Vampire FB.5 90 90
622 39p. Hawker Siddeley Harrier GR.1A . . . . 1·10 1·10
623 57p. Panavia Tornado F Mk 3 1·60 1·60
Nos. 618/23 also commemorate the 50th anniv of the Royal Air Force Association and the 40th anniv of the first air display on Jersey.

1993. Europa. Contemporary Art. Multicoloured.
625 23p. Type **149** 70 70
626 28p. "The Ham and Tomato Bap" (Jonathan Hubbard) . 85 85
627 39p. "Vase of Flowers" (Neil MacKenzie) . . . . 1·25 1·25

150 1943 ½d. Occupation Stamp

1993. 50th Anniv of Edmund Blampied's Occupation Stamps. Designs showing stamps from the 1943 issue.
628 **150** 17p. green, lt grn & blk . 40 45
629 – 23p. red, pink & black . . 55 55
630 – 28p. brown, cinnamon and black 75 75
631 – 33p. orange, salmon & blk 90 90
632 – 39p. blue, cobalt & black 1·25 1·25
633 – 50p. mauve, lt mve & blk 1·40 1·40
DESIGNS: 23p. 1d. value; 28p. 1½d. value; 33p. 2d. value; 39p. 2½d. value; 50p. 3d. value.

151 Queen Elizabeth II (from painting by Marca McGregor)

1993. 40th Anniv of Coronation.
634 **151** £1 multicoloured . . . . 2·50 2·50

152 Short-toed Treecreeper

153 Two Angels holding "Hark the Herald Angels Sing" Banner

1993. Summer Birds. Multicoloured.
635 17p. Type **152** 50 50
636 23p. Dartford warbler 75 75
637 28p. Common wheatear . . . 85 85
638 39p. Cirl bunting . . . . . . 1·25 1·25
639 57p. Jay . . . . 1·75 1·75

1993. Christmas. Stained Glass Windows by Henry Bosdet from St. Aubin on the Hill Church. Multicoloured.
640 17p. Type **153** 45 45
641 23p. Two angels playing harps 65 65
642 39p. Two angels playing violins 1·25 1·25
643 57p. Two angels holding "Once in Royal David's City" banner 1·90 1·90

154 "Coprinus comatus"

156 Maine Coon

1994. Fungi. Multicoloured.
644 18p. Type **154** 45 45
645 23p. "Amanita muscaria" . . 70 70
646 30p. "Cantharellus cibarius" . 90 90
647 41p. "Macrolepiota procera" . 1·25 1·25
648 60p. "Clathrus ruber" . . . . 1·75 1·75

1994. 21st Anniv of Jersey Cat Club. Mult.
650 18p. Type **156** 45 45
651 23p. British shorthair (horiz) . 70 60
652 35p. Persian 90 80
653 41p. Siamese (horiz) . . . . 1·25 1·10
654 60p. Non-pedigree . . . . . 1·75 1·75

157 Mammoth Hunt, La Cotte de St. Brelade

1994. Europa. Archaeological Discoveries. Multicoloured.
655 23p. Type **157** 50 50
656 23p. Stone Age hunters pulling mammoth into cave . . . 50 50
657 30p. Chambered passage, La Hougue Bie 75 75
658 30p. Transporting stones . . . 75 75

158 Gliders and Towing Aircraft approaching France

1994. 50th Anniv of D-Day. Multicoloured.
659 18p. Type **158** 60 50
660 18p. Landing craft approaching beaches 60 50
661 23p. Disembarking from landing craft on Gold Beach 80 60
662 23p. British troops on Sword Beach 80 70
663 30p. Spitfires over beaches . . 90 80
664 30p. Invasion map 90 80

159 Sailing

1994. Centenary of International Olympic Committee. Multicoloured.
665 18p. Type **159** 45 45
666 23p. Rifle shooting 60 60
667 30p. Hurdling 85 85
668 41p. Swimming . . . . 1·25 1·25
669 60p. Hockey . . . . 1·60 1·60

160 Strawberry Anemone

1994. Marine Life. Multicoloured.
670 18p. Type **160** 50 50
671 23p. Hermit crab and parasitic anemone 75 75
672 41p. Velvet swimming crab . . 1·40 1·40
673 60p. Common jellyfish . . . . 1·75 1·75

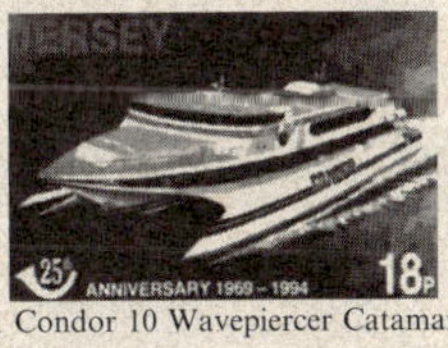

161 Condor 10 Wavepiercer Catamaran

1994. 25th Anniv of Jersey Postal Administration. Multicoloured.
674 18p. Type **161** 45 45
675 23p. Map of Jersey and pillar box 60 60
676 35p. Vickers Type 953 Vanguard of B.E.A. 85 75
677 41p. Shorts 360 of Aurigny Air Services . . . . 1·10 1·00
678 60p. "Caesarea" (Sealink ferry) 1·50 1·40

162 "Away in a Manger"

1994. Christmas. Carols. Multicoloured.
680 18p. Type **162** 45 45
681 23p. "Hark! the Herald Angels Sing" 60 60
682 41p. "While Shepherds watched" 1·25 1·25
683 60p. "We Three Kings of Orient Are" . . . . 1·60 1·60

163 Dog and "GOOD LUCK"

164 Camellia "Captain Rawes"

1995. Greetings Stamps. Multicoloured.
684 18p. Type **163** 45 45
685 18p. Rose and "WITH LOVE" 45 45
686 18p. Chick and "CONGRATULATIONS" . 45 45
687 18p. Bouquet of flowers and "THANK YOU" 45 45
688 23p. Dove with letter and "WITH LOVE" 55 55
689 23p. Cat and "GOOD LUCK" 55 55
690 23p. Carnations and "THANK YOU" 55 55
691 23p. Parrot and "CONGRATULATIONS" 55 55
692 60p. Pig and "HAPPY NEW YEAR" (25×63 mm) . . . 1·40 1·40
No. 692 commemorates the Chinese New Year of the Pig.

1994. Camellias. Multicoloured.
693 18p. Type **164** 60 60
694 23p. "Brigadoon" 80 80
695 30p. "Elsie Jury" 95 95
696 35p. "Augusto L'Gouveia Pinto" 1·00 1·00
697 41p. "Bella Romana" . . . . 1·10 1·10

165 "Liberation" (sculpture, Philip Jackson)

1995. Europa. Peace and Freedom
698 **165** 23p. black and blue . . . 55 55
699 30p. black and pink . . . 70 75

166 Bailiff and Crown Officers in Launch

1995. 50th Anniv of Liberation. Multicoloured.
700 18p. Type **166** 40 40
701 18p. "Vega" (Red Cross supply ship) 40 40
702 23p. H.M.S. "Beagle" (destroyer) 60 60
703 23p. British troops in Ordnance Yard, St. Helier 60 60
704 60p. King George VI and Queen Elizabeth in Jersey . . . . 1·50 1·50
705 60p. Unloading supplies from landing craft, St. Aubin's . 1·50 1·50

167 Bell Heather

1995. European Nature Conservation Year. Wild Flowers. Multicoloured.
707 19p. Type **167** 45 45
708 19p. Sea campion 45 45
709 19p. Spotted rock-rose . . . 45 45
710 19p. Thrift 45 45
711 19p. Sheep's-bit scabious . . . 45 45
712 23p. Field bind-weed 50 50
713 23p. Common bird's-foot-trefoil 50 50
714 23p. Sea-holly 50 50
715 23p. Common centaury . . . 50 50
716 23p. Dwarf pansy 50 50
Nos. 707/11 and 712/16 respectively were printed together, se-tenant, forming composite designs.

168 "Precis almana"

1995. Butterflies. Multicoloured.
717 19p. Type **168** 55 55
718 23p. "Papilio palinurus" . . . 70 70
719 30p. "Catopsilia scylla" . . . 90 90
720 41p. "Papilio rumanzovia" . . 1·10 1·10
721 60p. "Troides helena" . . . . 1·75 1·75

INDEX

Countries can be quickly located by referring to the index at the end of this volume.

169 Peace Doves and United Nations Anniversary Emblem

1995. 50th Anniv of United Nations.
723 **169** 19p. cobalt and blue . . . 45 45
724 – 23p. turquoise and green . 50 50
725 – 41p. green and turquoise . 85 85
726 **169** 60p. blue and cobalt . . . 1·40 1·40
DESIGN: 23p., 41p. Symbolic wheat and anniversary emblem.

170 "Puss in Boots"

1995. Christmas. Pantomimes. Multicoloured.
727 19p. Type **170** 45 45
728 23p. "Cinderella" 50 50
729 41p. "Sleeping Beauty" 85 85
730 60p. "Aladdin" . . . . 1·40 1·40

172 African Child and Map

1996. 50th Anniv of U.N.I.C.E.F. Multicoloured.
732 19p. Type **172** 50 50
733 23p. Children and globe . . . 60 60
734 30p. European child and map . 80 80
735 35p. South American child and map 95 95
736 41p. Asian child and map . . 1·10 1·10
737 60p. South Pacific child and map 1·60 1·60

173 Queen Elizabeth II (from photo by T. O'Neill)

1996. 70th Birthday of Queen Elizabeth II.
738 **173** £5 multicoloured . . . . . 10·00 10·50

174 Elizabeth Garrett (first British woman doctor)

1996. Europa. Famous Women. Multicoloured.
739 23p. Type **174** 60 60
740 30p. Emmeline Pankhurst (suffragette) 80 80

175 Player shooting at Goal

1996. European Football Championship, England. Multicoloured.
741 19p. Type **175** 50 50
742 23p. Two players chasing ball . 70 70
743 35p. Player avoiding tackle . . 95 95
744 41p. Two players competing for ball . . . . 1·10 1·10
745 60p. Players heading ball . . . 1·75 1·75

176 Rowing

1996. Sporting Anniversaries. Multicoloured.
746 19p. Type **176** 50 50
747 23p. Judo 70 70
748 35p. Fencing 95 95
749 41p. Boxing . . . . 1·10 1·10
750 60p. Basketball . . . . 1·75 1·75
ANNIVERSARIES: Nos. 746/8, 750/1, Centenary of modern Olympic Games; 749, 50th anniv of International Amateur Boxing Association.

177 Bay on North Coast

1996. Tourism. Beaches. Multicoloured.
752 19p. Type **177** 50 50
753 23p. Portelet Bay 60 60
754 30p. Greve de Lecq Bay . . . 80 80
755 35p. Beauport Beach 95 95
756 41p. Plemont Bay . . . . . . 1·10 1·10
757 60p. St. Brelade's Bay . . . . 1·60 1·60

178 Drag Hunt

1996. Horses. Multicoloured.
758 19p. Type **178** 50 50
759 23p. Pony and trap 60 60
760 30p. Training racehorses on beach 80 80
761 35p. Show jumping 95 95
762 41p. Pony Club event . . . . 1·10 1·10
763 60p. Shire mare and foal . . . 1·60 1·60

179 The Journey to Bethlehem

1996. Christmas. Multicoloured.
764 19p. Type **179** 40 45
765 23p. The Shepherds 45 50
766 30p. The Nativity 60 65
767 60p. The Three Kings . . . . 1·25 1·40

181 Lillie the Cow on the Beach

182 Red-breasted Merganser

1997. Tourism. "Lillie the Cow". Multicoloured. Self-adhesive.
770 (23p.) Type **181** 45 50
771 (23p.) Lillie taking photograph 45 50
772 (23p.) Carrying bucket and spade 45 50
773 (23p.) Eating meal at Mont Orgueil 45 50

1997. Seabirds and Waders. Multicoloured.
774 1p. Type **182** 10 10
775 2p. Sanderling 10 10
776 4p. Northern gannet 10 10
777 5p. Great crested grebe . . . 10 15
778 10p. Common tern 20 25
779 15p. Black-headed gull . . . 30 35
780 20p. Dunlin 40 45
781 21p. Sandwich tern 40 45
782 22p. Ringed plover 40 50
783 24p. Puffin 45 50
784 25p. Brent goose 50 55
785 26p. Grey plover 50 55
786 30p. Fulmar 60 65
787 31p. Golden plover 60 65
788 32p. Greenshank 65 70
789 35p. Curlew 70 75
790 37p. Oystercatcher 75 80
791 40p. Turnstone 80 65
792 44p. Herring gull 90 95
793 50p. Great black-backed gull . 1·00 1·10
794 60p. Avocet . . . . 1·25 1·40
795 75p. Redshank . . . . 1·50 1·60
796 £1 Razorbill . . . . 2·00 2·10
797 £2 Shag . . . . 4·00 4·25

183 De Havilland D.H.95 Flamingo

1997. 60th Anniv of Jersey Airport. Multicoloured.
807 20p. Type **183** 55 55
808 24p. Handley Page H.P.R. Marathon 65 65
809 31p. De Havilland D.H.114 Heron 80 80
810 37p. Boeing 737-236 . . . . . 1·00 1·00
811 43p. Britten Norman Trislander 1·10 1·10
812 63p. BAe 146-200 . . . . . . 1·75 1·75

184 The Bull of St. Clement

1997. Europa. Tales and Legends. Multicoloured.
813 20p. Type **184** 50 50
814 24p. The Black Horse of St. Ouen 60 60
815 31p. The Black Dog of Bouley Bay 70 70
816 63p. Les Fontaines des Mittes 1·40 1·40
Nos. 814/15 include the "EUROPA" emblem.

185 Cycling

1997. 7th Island Games, Jersey. Multicoloured.
818 20p. Type **185** 55 55
819 24p. Archery 65 65
820 31p. Windsurfing 80 80
821 37p. Gymnastics . . . . 1·00 1·00
822 43p. Volleyball . . . . 1·10 1·10
823 63p. Running . . . . 1·75 1·75

186 Mallorcan Midwife Toad

1997. Wildlife Preservation Trust (6th series). Multicoloured.
824 20p. Type **186** 55 50
825 24p. Aye-aye 65 65
826 31p. Echo parakeet 80 80
827 37p. Pigmy hog . . . . 1·00 1·00
828 43p. St. Lucia whip-tail . . . 1·10 1·10
829 63p. Madagascar teal . . . . 1·75 1·75

187 Ash

1997. Trees. Multicoloured.
830 20p. Type **187** 55 55
831 24p. Elder 65 65
832 31p. Beech 80 80
833 37p. Sweet chestnut . . . . . 1·00 1·00
834 43p. Hawthorn . . . . 1·10 1·10
835 63p. Common oak . . . . . . 1·75 1·75

188 Father Christmas and Reindeer outside Jersey Airport

1997. Christmas. Multicoloured.
836 20p. Type **188** 55 55
837 24p. Father Christmas with presents, St. Aubin's Harbour 65 65
838 31p. Father Christmas in sleigh, Mont Orgueil Castle . . . 80 80
839 63p. Father Christmas with children, Royal Square, St. Helier . . . . 1·60 1·60

189 Wedding Photograph, 1947

1997. Golden Wedding of Queen Elizabeth and Prince Philip. Multicoloured.
840 50p. Type **189** . . . . 1·50 1·50
841 50p. Queen Elizabeth and Prince Philip, 1997 . . . . 1·50 1·50

191 J.M.T. Bristol 4 Tonner, 1923

1998. 75th Anniv of Jersey Motor Transport Company. Buses. Multicoloured.
844 20p. Type **191** 40 45
845 24p. Safety Coach Service Regent double decker, 1934 . . . . 50 55
846 31p. Slade's Dennis Lancet, circa 1936 . . . . 60 65
847 37p. Tantivy Leyland PLSC Lion, 1947 . . . . 75 80
848 43p. J.B.S. Morris, circa 1958 85 90
849 63p. J.M.T. Titan TD4 double decker, circa 1961 . . . . 1·25 1·40

192 Creative Arts Festival

193 Hobie Cat and "Duke of Normandy" (launch)

1998. Europa. National Festivals. Multicoloured.
850 20p. Type **192** 40 45
851 24p. Jazz Festival 50 55
852 31p. Good Food Festival . . 60 65
853 63p. Floral Festival . . . . . 1·25 1·40
Nos. 851/2 include the "EUROPA" emblem.

1998. Opening of Elizabeth Marina, St. Helier. Multicoloured.
854 20p. Type **193** 40 45
855 20p. Hobie Cat with white, yellow, red and green sails . 40 45
856 20p. Hobie Cats with pink, purple and orange sails . . 40 45
857 20p. Bow of Hobie Cat with yellow, blue and purple sail 40 45
858 20p. Hobie Cat heeling 40 45
859 24p. Yacht with red, white and blue spinnaker 40 45
860 24p. Yacht with pink spinnaker 40 45
861 24p. Yacht with two white sails 40 45
862 24p. Trimaran 40 45
863 24p. Yacht with blue, white and yellow spinnaker in foreground 40 45
Nos. 854/8 and 859/63 respectively were printed together, se-tenant, forming composite designs of yacht races.

194 Bass

1998. International Year of the Ocean. Fishes. Multicoloured.
864 20p. Type **194** 40 45
865 24p. Red gurnard 50 55
866 31p. Skate 60 65
867 37p. Mackerel 75 80
868 43p. Tope 85 90
869 63p. Cuckoo wrasse . . . . . 1·25 1·40

195 Cider-making

196 Irises

1998. Days Gone By. Multicoloured. Self-adhesive.
870 (20p.) Type **195** 40 45
871 (20p.) Potato barrels on cart . 40 45
872 (20p.) Collecting seaweed for fertiliser 40 45
873 (20p.) Milking Jersey cows . . 40 45

1998. Flowers. Multicoloured.
874 20p. Type **196** 40 45
875 24p. Carnations 50 55
876 31p. Chrysanthemums 60 65
877 37p. Pinks 75 80
878 43p. Roses 85 90
879 63p. Lilies . . . . 1·25 1·40

197 Central Market Crib

1998. Christmas. Cribs. Multicoloured.
881 20p. Type **197** 40 45
882 24p. St. Thomas's Church crib 50 55
883 31p. Trinity Parish Church crib 60 65
884 63p. Royal Square crib . . . . 1·25 1·40

199 Jersey Eastern Railway Mail Train

1999. 125th Anniv of U.P.U. Multicoloured.
886 20p. Type **199** 40 45
887 24p. "Brighton" (paddle-steamer) 50 55
888 43p. De Havilland D.H.86 Dragon Express at Jersey Airport 85 90
889 63p. Jersey Postal Service Morris Minor van . . . . 1·25 1·40

200 "Jessie Eliza", St. Catherine

1999. 175th Anniv of Royal National Lifeboat Institute. Multicoloured.
890 75p. Type **200** . . . . 1·50 1·60
891 £1 "Alexander Coutanche", St. Helier . . . . 2·00 2·10

201 "Cymbidium" Maufant "Jersey"

1999. Jersey Orchids (4th series). Multicoloured.
892 21p. Type **201** 45 50
893 25p. "Miltonia" Millbrook "Jersey" 50 55
894 31p. "Paphiopedilum" "Transvaal" 65 70
895 37p. "Paphiopedilum" "Elizabeth Castle" 75 80
896 43p. "Calanthe" "Five Oaks" . 85 90
897 63p. "Cymbidium" Icho Tower "Trinity" . . . . 1·25 1·40

202 Howard Davis Park

1999. Europa. Parks and Gardens. Multicoloured.
899 21p. Type **202** 45 50
900 25p. Sir Winston Churchill Memorial Park 50 55
901 31p. Coronation Park 65 70
902 63p. La Collette Gardens . . 1·25 1·40
Nos. 900/1 include the "EUROPA" logo at top left and all four values show the "iBRA '99" International Stamp Exhibition, Nuremberg, emblem at top right.

POSTAGE DUE STAMPS

D 1

D 3 Arms of St. Clement and Dovecote at Samares

1969.
D1 D 1 1d. violet . . . . 1·50 1·50
D2 2d. sepia . . . . 2·25 2·00
D3 3d. mauve . . . . 3·00 2·75
D4 – 1s. green . . . . 9·00 7·50
D5 – 2s. 6d. grey . . . . . . 21·00 16·00
D6 – 5s. red . . . . 30·00 27·00
DESIGNS: 1s., 2s. 6d. and 5s. Map.

1971. Decimal Currency. Design as Nos. D4/6, but values in new currency.
D 7 ½p. black 10 10
D 8 1p. blue 10 10
D 9 2p. brown 10 10
D10 3p. purple 10 10
D11 4p. red 10 10
D12 5p. green 15 15
D13 6p. orange 20 15
D14 7p. yellow 20 15
D15 8p. blue 30 25
D16 10p. green 40 35
D17 11p. brown 40 40
D18 14p. violet 45 45
D19 25p. green 90 90
D20 50p. purple . . . . 1·50 1·50

1978. Parish Arms and Views.
D21 D 3 1p. black and green . . 10 10
D22 – 2p. black and yellow . . 10 10
D23 – 3p. black and brown . . 10 10
D24 – 4p. black and red . . . 10 10
D25 – 5p. black and blue . . . 10 10
D26 – 10p. black and olive . . 30 20
D27 – 12p. black and blue . . 35 25
D28 – 14p. black and orange . 35 30
D29 – 15p. black and mauve . 35 30
D30 – 20p. black and green . . 50 40
D31 – 50p. black and brown . 1·10 1·10
D32 – £1 black and blue . . . 2·25 2·25
DESIGNS: 2p. Arms of St. Lawrence and Handois Reservoir; 3p. Arms of St. John and Sorel Point; 4p. Arms of St. Ouen and Pinnacle Rock; 5p. Arms of St. Peter and Quetivel Mill; 10p. Arms of St. Martin and St. Catherine's Breakwater; 12p. Arms of St. Helier and Harbour; 14p. Arms of St. Saviour and Highlands College; 15p. Arms of St. Brelade and Beauport Bay; 20p. Arms of Grouville and La Hougue Bie; 50p. Arms of St. Mary and Perry Farm; £1 Arms of Trinity and Bouley Bay.

D 4 St. Brelade

1982. Jersey Harbours.
D33 D 4 1p. green 10 10
D34 – 2p. yellow 10 10
D35 – 3p. brown 10 10
D36 – 4p. red 10 10
D37 – 5p. blue 10 10
D38 – 6p. green 10 15
D39 – 7p. mauve 15 20
D40 – 8p. red 15 20
D41 – 9p. green 20 45
D42 – 10p. blue 20 25
D43 – 20p. green 40 45
D44 – 30p. purple 60 65
D45 – 40p. orange 80 85
D46 – £1 violet . . . . 2·00 2·10
DESIGNS: 2p. St. Aubin; 3p. Rozel; 4p. Greve de Lecq; 5p. Bouley Bay; 6p. St. Catherine; 7p. Gorey; 8p. Bonne Nuit; 9p. La Roque; 10p. St. Helier; 20p. Ronez; 30p. La Collette; 40p. Elizabeth Castle; £1 Upper Harbour Marina.

JHALAWAR

A state of Rajasthan, India. Now uses Indian stamps.

4 paisa = 1 anna

1 Apsara (dancing nymph of Hindu Paradise)

1886. Imperf.

1	**1**	1 p. green	3·00	8·00
2	–	¼ a. green	70	1·50

The ¼ a. is larger and has a different frame.

JIND

A "convention" state of the Punjab, India, which now uses Indian stamps.

12 pies = 1 anna; 16 annas = 1 rupee

J **1** (½ a.)

J **6** (¼ a.)

1874. Imperf.

J 8	J **1**	½ a. blue	50	3·00
J 9		1 a. purple	1·40	7·00
J 3		2 a. bistre	1·00	3·00
J11		4 a. green	1·25	9·50
J12		8 a. purple	7·00	10·00

1882. Various designs and sizes. Imperf or perf.

J16A	J **6**	¼ a. brown	30	1·25
J19A		½ a. bistre	70	60
J20A		1 a. brown	1·60	3·25
J22A		2 a. blue	2·00	1·00
J23A		4 a. green	90	90
J25A		8 a. red	4·75	4·25

Stamps of India (Queen Victoria) overprinted.

1885. Optd **JHIND STATE** vert (curved).

1	**23**	½ a. turquoise	1·25	2·25
2	–	1 a. purple	20·00	28·00
3	–	2 a. blue	6·50	11·00
4	–	4 a. green (No. 71)	40·00	55·00
5	–	8 a. mauve	£375	
6	–	1 r. grey (No. 101)	£400	

1885. Optd **JEEND STATE**.

7	**23**	½ a. turquoise	75·00	
8	–	1 a. purple	80·00	
9	–	2 a. blue	80·00	
10	–	4 a. green (No. 71)	£110	
11	–	8 a. mauve	£110	
12	–	1 r. grey (No. 101)	£120	

1886. Optd **JHIND STATE** horiz.

17	**23**	½ a. turquoise	15	10
18	–	1 a. purple	55	20
20	–	1 a. 6 p. brown	90	2·25
21	–	2 a. blue	1·00	40
23	–	3 a. orange	1·00	50
15	–	4 a. green (No. 71)	35·00	
24	–	4 a. green (No. 96)	2·25	1·50
27	–	6 a. brown	90	6·50
28	–	8 a. mauve	3·50	10·00
30	–	12 a. purple on red	3·50	15·00
31	–	1 r. grey (No. 101)	6·00	30·00
32	**37**	1 r. green and red	6·50	35·00
33	**38**	2 r. red and orange	£200	£600
34		3 r. brown and green	£350	£600
35		5 r. blue and violet	£400	£600

1900. Optd **JHIND STATE** horiz.

36	**40**	3 p. red	70	1·00
37		3 p. grey	15	2·25
38	**23**	½ a. green	2·25	3·75
40	–	1 a. red	20	3·75

Stamps of India optd **JHIND STATE**.

1903. King Edward VII.

41	**41**	3 p. grey	10	10
43	–	½ a. green (No. 122)	40	1·25
44	–	1 a. red (No. 123)	1·75	1·00
46	–	2 a. lilac	1·25	55
47	–	2½ a. blue	30	4·50
48	–	3 a. orange	35	35
50	–	4 a. olive	4·50	6·50
51	–	6 a. bistre	4·50	13·00
52	–	8 a. mauve	2·00	16·00
54	–	12 a. purple on red	1·75	10·00
55	–	1 r. green and red	2·25	11·00

1907. King Edward VII (inscr "INDIA POSTAGE and REVENUE").

56	½ a. green (No. 149)	10	20
57	1 a. red (No. 150)	15	55

1913. King George V.

58	**55**	3 p. grey	10	1·60
59	**56**	½ a. green	10	60
60	**57**	1 a. red	10	35
61	**59**	2 a. lilac	15	3·50
62	**62**	3 a. orange	1·50	8·00
63	**64**	6 a. bistre	4·00	20·00

1914. Stamps of India (King George V) optd **JIND STATE** in two lines.

64	**55**	3 p. grey	40	20
65	**56**	½ a. green	1·25	15
66	**57**	1 a. red	50	15
80		1 a. brown	2·75	1·00
67	**58**	1½ a. brown (A. No. 163)	60	3·00
68		1½ a. brown (B. No. 165)	35	1·50
81		1½ a. red (B.)	20	1·50
69	**59**	2 a. lilac	1·00	45
70	**61**	2 a. 6 p. blue	35	3·75
82		2 a. 6 p. orange	30	4·75
71	**62**	3 a. orange	50	2·00
83		3 a. blue	1·00	3·25
72	**63**	4 a. olive	95	4·50
73	**64**	6 a. brown	1·10	9·00
74	**65**	8 a. mauve	3·00	5·00
75	**66**	12 a. red	1·25	9·00
76	**67**	1 r. brown and green	5·50	11·00
77		2 r. red and orange	4·00	80·00
78		5 r. blue and violet	27·00	£160

1922. No. 192 of India optd **JIND**.

79	**57**	9 p. on 1 a. red	1·25	13·00

Stamps of India optd **JIND STATE** in one line.

1927. King George V.

84	**55**	3 p. grey	10	10
85	**56**	½ a. green	10	35
86	**80**	9 p. green	40	40
87	**57**	1 a. brown	15	10
88	**82**	1 a. 3 p. mauve	20	30
89	**58**	1½ a. red	35	1·40
90	**70**	2 a. lilac	90	30
91w	**61**	2 a. 6 p. orange	70	6·50
92	**62**	3 a. blue	1·75	7·00
93w	**83**	3 a. 6 p. blue	50	11·00
94w	**71**	4 a. green	90	1·40
95	**64**	6 a. bistre	55	12·00
96	**65**	8 a. mauve	1·75	1·90
97w	**66**	12 a. red	2·75	13·00
98	**67**	1 r. brown and green	2·75	3·00
99		2 r. red and orange	22·00	90·00
100		5 r. blue and violet	8·00	26·00
101		10 r. green and red	10·00	18·00
102		15 r. blue and olive	60·00	£375
103		25 r. orange and blue	90·00	£450

1934. King George V.

104	**79**	½ a. green	30	15
105	**81**	1 a. brown	70	20
106	**59**	2 a. orange	70	50
107	**62**	3 a. red	1·10	40
108	**63**	4 a. olive	1·40	75

1937. King George VI.

109	**91**	3 p. slate	5·50	1·00
110		½ a. brown	60	2·25
111		9 p. green	60	2·00
112		1 a. red	60	35
113	**92**	2 a. red	1·50	10·00
114	–	2 a. 6 p. violet	1·00	11·00
115	–	3 a. green	4·50	9·50
116	–	3 a. 6 p. blue	1·50	11·00
117	–	4 a. brown	5·50	10·00
118	–	6 a. green	3·00	14·00
119	–	8 a. violet	2·00	14·00
120	–	12 a. red	1·75	16·00
121	**93**	1 r. slate and brown	14·00	26·00
122		2 r. purple and brown	16·00	75·00
123		5 r. green and blue	30·00	55·00
124		10 r. purple and red	55·00	60·00
125		15 r. brown and green	£150	£550
126		25 r. slate and purple	£325	£550

1941. Stamps of India (King George VI) optd **JIND**.

(a) On issue of 1937.

127	**91**	3 p. slate	9·50	13·00
128		½ a. brown	1·00	40
129		9 p. green	8·50	10·00
130		1 a. red	1·00	3·00
131	**93**	1 r. slate and brown	8·00	19·00
132		2 r. purple and brown	16·00	24·00
133		5 r. green and blue	38·00	65·00
134		10 r. purple and red	55·00	65·00
135		15 r. brown and green	£120	£130
136		25 r. slate and purple	£100	£325

(b) On issue of 1940.

137	**100a**	3 p. slate	50	50
138		½ a. mauve	50	85
139		9 p. green	60	2·25
140		1 a. red	65	85
141	**101**	1 a. 3 p. yellow-brown	1·00	2·75
142		1½ a. violet	5·00	3·50
143		2 a. red	1·75	2·50
144		3 a. violet	11·00	2·75
145		3½ a. blue	5·00	5·50
146	**102**	4 a. brown	3·00	2·50
147		6 a. green	3·50	8·50
148		8 a. violet	2·50	8·50
149		12 a. purple	9·50	8·50

OFFICIAL STAMPS

Postage stamps of Jind optd **SERVICE**.

1885. Nos. 1/3 (Queen Victoria).

O1	**23**	½ a. green	30	30
O2	–	1 a. purple	30	10
O3	–	2 a. blue	26·00	35·00

1886. Nos. 17/32 and No. 38 (Q.V.).

O12	**23**	½ a. turquoise	50	10
O22	–	½ a. green (No. 38)	1·00	20
O14	–	1 a. purple	7·00	20
O16	–	2 a. blue	50	30
O17	–	4 a. green (No. 24)	85	45
O19	–	8 a. mauve	2·75	2·00
O21	**37**	1 r. green and red	6·00	27·00

1903. Nos. 42/55 (King Edward VII).

O24	**41**	3 p. grey	10	10
O25	–	½ a. green (No. 43)	1·90	10
O26	–	1 a. red (No. 44)	80	10
O28	–	2 a. lilac	30	10
O29	–	4 a. olive	40	45
O31	–	8 a. mauve	2·75	1·50
O32	–	1 r. green and red	2·50	2·25

1907. Nos. 56/7 (King Edward VII).

O33	½ a. green	15	10
O34	1 a. red	30	10

1914. Official stamps of India. Nos. O75/96 (King George V) optd **JIND STATE**.

O35	**55**	3 p. grey	10	10
O36	**56**	½ a. green	10	10
O37	**57**	1 a. red	20	10
O46		1 a. brown	40	10
O39	**59**	2 a. lilac	15	15
O40	**63**	4 a. olive	40	15
O41	**64**	6 a. bistre	45	2·25
O42	**65**	8 a. mauve	30	1·00
O43	**67**	1 r. brown and green	1·00	1·60
O44		2 r. red and orange	10·00	50·00
O45		5 r. blue and violet	17·00	£140

Stamps of India optd **JIND STATE SERVICE**.

1927. King George V.

O47	**55**	3 p. grey	10	20
O48	**56**	½ a. green	10	90
O49	**80**	9 p. green	40	15
O50	**57**	1 a. brown	10	10
O51	**82**	1 a. 3 p. mauve	40	15
O52	**70**	2 a. lilac	25	15
O64	**59**	2 a. orange	30	15
O53	**61**	2 a. 6 p. orange	45	14·00
O54	**71**	4 a. green	35	25
O55w	**64**	6 a. bistre	1·75	12·00
O56w	**65**	8 a. mauve	40	1·25
O57	**66**	12 a. red	90	9·50
O58	**67**	1 r. brown and green	1·75	2·50
O59		2 r. red and orange	27·00	22·00
O60		5 r. blue and purple	12·00	£150
O61		10 r. green and red	24·00	85·00

1934. King George V.

O62	**79**	½ a. green	20	15
O63	**81**	1 a. brown	20	15
O65	**63**	4 a. olive	3·50	30

1937. King George VI.

O66	**91**	½ a. brown	48·00	30
O67		9 p. green	85	6·50
O68		1 a. red	55	30
O69	**93**	1 r. slate and brown	24·00	42·00
O70		2 r. purple and brown	42·00	£170
O71		5 r. green and blue	85·00	£300
O72		10 r. purple and red	£170	£700

1939. Official stamps of India optd **JIND**.

O73	O **20**	3 p. slate	50	60
O74		½ a. brown	1·50	50
O75		½ a. purple	60	30
O76		9 p. green	1·50	7·00
O77		1 a. red	1·50	15
O78		1½ a. violet	5·00	1·00
O79		2 a. orange	2·50	30
O80		2½ a. violet	1·50	5·50
O81		4 a. brown	3·25	1·10
O82		8 a. violet	3·00	2·75

1943. Stamps of India (King George VI) optd **JIND SERVICE**.

O83	**93**	1 r. slate and brown	18·00	40·00
O84		2 r. purple and brown	42·00	£120
O85		5 r. green and blue	90·00	£275
O86		10 r. purple and red	£160	£350

JOHORE

A state of the Federation of Malaya incorporated in Malaysia in 1963.

100 cents = 1 dollar (Straits or Malayan)

Queen Victoria stamps of Straits Settlements overprinted.

1876. Optd with Crescent and Star.

1	**1**	2 c. brown	£8500	£3500

1882. Optd **JOHORE**.

8	**1**	2 c. pink (no full point)	60·00	75·00
6		2 c. pink (with full point)	£120	£130

1884. Optd **JOHOR**.

10	**1**	2 c. pink (no full point)	5·50	4·50
14		2 c. pink (with full point)	85·00	42·00

1891. Surch **JOHOR Two CENTS**.

17	**1**	2 c. on 24 c. green	23·00	35·00

21 Sultan Aboubakar

24 Sultan Ibrahim

1891.

21	**21**	1 c. purple	30	50
22		2 c. purple and yellow	50	1·50
23		3 c. purple and red	55	50
24		4 c. purple and black	2·75	11·00
25		5 c. purple and green	7·00	20·00
26		6 c. purple and blue	8·00	20·00
27		$1 green and red	55·00	£120

1892. Surch **3 cents.**

28	**21**	3 c. on 4 c. purple and black	1·75	50
29		3 c. on 5 c. purple and green	80	2·00
30		3 c. on 6 c. purple and blue	1·75	2·00
31		3 c. on $1 green and red	10·00	45·00

1896. Sultan's Coronation. Optd **KEMAHKOTAAN**.

32	**21**	1 c. purple	45	85
33		2 c. purple and yellow	45	1·00
34		3 c. purple and red	55	1·00
35		4 c. purple and black	80	2·25
36		5 c. purple and green	5·50	7·50
37		6 c. purple and blue	3·50	6·00
38		$1 green and red	40·00	90·00

1896.

39	**24**	1 c. green	70	45
40		2 c. green and blue	40	30
41		3 c. green and purple	2·50	1·50
42		4 c. green and red	50	50
43		4 c. yellow and red	75	65
44		5 c. green and brown	75	1·40
45	**24**	6 c. green and yellow	80	2·25
46		10 c. green and black	7·00	45·00
47		25 c. green and mauve	9·00	38·00
48		50 c. green and red	13·00	40·00
49		$1 purple and green	26·00	65·00
50		$2 purple and red	27·00	65·00
51		$3 purple and blue	28·00	90·00
52		$4 purple and brown	28·00	75·00
53		$5 purple and yellow	60·00	£110

1903. Surch in figures and words.

54	**24**	3 c. on 4 c. yellow and red	50	1·10
55		10 c. on 4 c. grn & red (A)	2·50	6·50
59		10 c. on 4 c. grn & red (B)	9·00	35·00
58		10 c. on 4 c. yell & red (B)	20·00	35·00
56		50 c. on $3 purple & blue	26·00	80·00
60		50 c. on $5 purple & yellow	65·00	£130
57		$1 on $2 purple and red	60·00	£110

10 c. on 4 c. Type A, "cents" in small letters. Type B, "CENTS" in capitals.

33 Sultan Sir Ibrahim

1904.

78	**33**	1 c. purple and green	30	15
90		2 c. purple and orange	50	2·50
63		3 c. purple and black	2·50	40
91		4 c. purple and red	75	60
109		5 c. purple and green	30	30
83		8 c. purple and blue	4·00	5·00
84		10 c. purple and black	35·00	2·75
116		25 c. purple and green	2·00	1·00
119		50 c. purple and red	3·00	1·60
120		$1 green and mauve	2·50	85
121		$2 green and red	5·50	3·50
72		$3 green and blue	23·00	70·00
73		$4 green and brown	24·00	90·00
124		$5 green and orange	50·00	50·00
75		$10 green and black	48·00	£130
76		$50 green and blue	£140	£200
77		$100 green and red	£275	£425
128		$500 blue and red	£16000	

1912. Surch **3 CENTS.** and bars.

88	**33**	3 c. on 8 c. purple and blue	2·50	4·50

1918.

103	**33**	1 c. purple and black	30	20
89		2 c. purple and green	40	80
104		2 c. purple and sepia	85	2·75
105		2 c. green	40	40
106		3 c. green	1·50	4·00
107		3 c. purple and sepia	1·10	1·50
110		6 c. purple and red	40	45
93		10 c. purple and blue	1·50	1·40
112		10 c. purple and yellow	30	25
113		12 c. purple and blue	1·00	1·25
114		12 c. blue	32·00	5·00
115		21 c. purple and orange	2·00	3·00
117		30 c. purple and orange	4·50	4·00
118		40 c. purple and brown	4·50	4·50

37 Sultan Sir Ibrahim and Sultana

38 Sultan Sir Ibrahim

1935.

129	**37**	8 c. violet and grey	2·75	50

1940.

130	**38**	8 c. black and blue	14·00	30

1948. Silver Wedding. As T **10/11** of Aden.

131	10 c. violet	20	30
132	$5 green	24·00	35·00

39 Sultan Sir Ibrahim

40 Sultan Sir Ibrahim

1949.

133	**39**	1 c. black	10	10
134		2 c. orange	10	10
135		3 c. green	35	50
136		4 c. brown	10	10
136a		5 c. purple	30	30
137		6 c. grey	20	10
138		8 c. red	2·00	90
138a		8 c. green	2·75	1·50
139		10 c. mauve	30	10
139a		12 c. red	2·25	3·00
140		15 c. blue	1·50	10
141		20 c. black and green	45	1·00
141a		20 c. blue	80	10
142		25 c. purple and orange	60	10
142a		30 c. red and purple	1·75	2·25
142b		35 c. red and purple	3·25	1·00
143		40 c. red and purple	3·00	7·50
144		50 c. black and blue	70	10
145		$1 blue and purple	3·50	1·50
146		$2 green and red	14·00	3·50
147		$5 green and brown	40·00	9·00

1949. U.P.U. As T **20/23** of Antigua.

148	10 c. purple	30	15
149	15 c. blue	1·25	1·00
150	25 c. orange	65	2·00
151	50 c. black	1·25	2·00

1953. Coronation. As T **13** of Aden.

152		10 c. black and purple	50	10

1955. Diamond Jubilee of Sultan.

153	**40**	10 c. red	10	10

41 Sultan Sir Ismail and Johore Coat of Arms

1960. Coronation of Sultan.

154	**41**	10 c. multicoloured	20	20

1960. As Nos. 92/102 of Kedah but with inset portrait of Sultan Sir Ismail.

155	1 c. black	10	30
156	2 c. red	10	40
157	4 c. sepia	10	10
158	5 c. lake	10	10
159	8 c. green	1·50	2·25
160	10 c. purple	30	10
161	20 c. blue	80	20
162	50 c. black and blue	20	10
163	$1 blue and purple	1·25	1·75
164	$2 green and red	7·00	9·50
165	$5 brown and green	23·00	24·00

42 "Vanda hookeriana"

1965. Inset portrait of Sultan Ismail. Multicoloured.

166	1 c. Type **42**	10	30
167	2 c. "Arundina graminifolia"	10	40
168	5 c. "Paphiopedilum niveum"	10	10
169	6 c. "Spathoglottis plicata"	40	30
170	10 c. "Arachnis flos-aeris"	40	10
171	15 c. "Rhyncostylis retusa"	1·50	10
172	20 c. "Phalaenopsis violacea"	1·50	50

The higher values used in Johore were Nos. 20/7 of Malaysia (National Issues).

44 "Delias ninus"

1971. Butterflies. Inset portrait of Sultan Ismail. Multicoloured.

175	1 c. Type **44**	30	90
176	2 c. "Danaus melanippus"	75	90
177	5 c. "Parthenos sylvia"	95	20
178	6 c. "Papilio demoleus"	95	1·40
179	10 c. "Hebomoia glaucippe"	95	20
180	15 c. "Precis orithya"	95	10
181	20 c. "Valeria valeria"	95	30

The higher values in use with this issue were Nos. 64/71 of Malaysia (National Issues).

45 "Rafflesia hasseltii" (inset portrait of Sultan Ismail)

46 Coconuts. (Inset portrait of Sultan Mahmood)

1979. Flowers. Multicoloured.

188	1 c. Type **45**	10	40
189	2 c. "Pterocarpus indicus"	10	40
190	5 c. "Lagerstroemia speciosa"	10	10
191	10 c. "Durio zibethinus"	15	10
192	15 c. "Hibiscus rosa-sinensis"	15	10
193	20 c. "Rhododendron scortechinii"	20	10
194	25 c. "Etlingera elatior" (inscr "Phaeomeria speciosa")	40	10

1986. Agricultural Products of Malaysia. Mult.

202	1 c. Coffee	10	10
203	2 c. Type **46**	10	10
204	5 c. Cocoa	10	10
205	10 c. Black pepper	10	10
206	15 c. Rubber	10	10
207	20 c. Oil palm	10	10
208	30 c. Rice	15	20

POSTAGE DUE STAMPS

D 1

1938.

D1	D **1**	1 c. red	12·00	32·00
D2		4 c. green	40·00	40·00
D3		8 c. orange	48·00	£140
D4		10 c. brown	48·00	48·00
D5		12 c. purple	55·00	£110

KEDAH

A state of the Federation of Malaya, incorporated in Malaysia in 1963.

100 cents = 1 dollar (Straits or Malayan)

1 Sheaf of Rice

2 Malay ploughing

1912.

1	**1**	1 c. black and green	30	25
26		1 c. brown	40	20
52		1 c. black	30	10
27		2 c. green	85	20
2		3 c. black and red	2·50	30
19		3 c. purple	65	70
53		3 c. green	1·50	90
3		4 c. red and grey	9·50	25
20		4 c. red	1·50	20
54		4 c. violet	90	10
4		5 c. green and brown	2·25	3·00
55		5 c. yellow	1·50	10
56		6 c. red	70	65
5		8 c. black and blue	2·25	3·50
57		8 c. black	9·00	10
6	**2**	10 c. blue and brown	1·75	90
58		12 c. black and blue	2·25	4·00
31		20 c. black and green	3·25	2·00
32		21 c. mauve and purple	2·00	13·00
33		25 c. blue and purple	2·25	5·50
34		30 c. black and pink	3·00	6·50
59		35 c. purple	5·00	25·00
9		40 c. black and purple	3·50	14·00
36		50 c. brown and blue	2·25	10·00
37w	–	$1 black and red on yellow	6·50	7·50
38	–	$2 green and brown	13·00	75·00
39w	–	$3 black and blue on blue	45·00	55·00
40w	–	$5 black and red	50·00	£100

DESIGN:—As Type **2**: $1 to $5, Council Chamber.

1919. Surch in words.

24	50 c. on $2 green and brown	50·00	65·00
25	$1 on $3 black and blue on blue	20·00	85·00

1922. Optd **MALAYA- BORNEO EXHIBITION.**

45	**1**	1 c. brown	2·25	13·00
41		2 c. green	3·50	19·00
46		3 c. purple	3·00	35·00
47		4 c. red	3·00	25·00
48	**2**	10 c. blue and sepia	4·50	32·00
42		21 c. purple	24·00	70·00
43		25 c. blue and purple	24·00	70·00
44		50 c. brown and blue	24·00	85·00

6 Sultan Abdul Hamid Halimshah

1937.

60	**6**	10 c. blue and brown	3·50	70
61		12 c. black and violet	27·00	12·00
62		25 c. blue and purple	7·50	4·50
63		30 c. green and red	8·50	10·00
64		40 c. black and purple	3·50	16·00
65		50 c. brown and blue	5·50	4·50
66		$1 black and green	3·50	10·00
67		$2 green and brown	£120	85·00
68		$5 black and red	32·00	£130

1948. Silver Wedding. As T **10/11** of Aden.

70	10 c. violet	20	20
71	$5 red	25·00	32·00

1949. U.P.U. As T **20/23** of Antigua.

72	10 c. purple	25	20
73	15 c. blue	1·50	1·25
74	25 c. orange	65	1·25
75	50 c. black	1·00	2·25

7 Sheaf of Rice

8 Sultan Badlishah

1950.

76	**7**	1 c. black	20	30
77		2 c. orange	20	15
78		3 c. green	90	1·00
79		4 c. brown	50	10
79ab		5 c. purple	45	45
80		6 c. grey	40	15
81		8 c. red	85	2·00
81a		8 c. green	75	1·75
82		10 c. mauve	40	10
82a		12 c. red	85	2·50
83		15 c. blue	65	35
84		20 c. black and green	70	2·50
84a		20 c. blue	85	10
85	**8**	25 c. purple and orange	65	30
85a		30 c. red and purple	1·25	1·25
85b		35 c. red and purple	85	1·50
86		40 c. red and purple	1·50	6·00
87	**8**	50 c. black and blue	1·50	20
88		$1 blue and purple	2·75	2·25
89		$2 green and red	20·00	22·00
90		$5 green and brown	42·00	32·00

1953. Coronation. As T **13** of Aden.

91	10 c. black and purple	65	20

15 Fishing Craft

20 Sultan Abdul Halim Mu' Adzam Shah

1957. Inset portrait of Sultan Badlishah.

92	–	1 c. black	10	35
93	–	2 c. red	10	50
94	–	4 c. sepia	10	20
95	–	5 c. lake	10	30
96	–	8 c. green	2·00	5·50
97	–	10 c. sepia	30	10
98	**15**	20 c. blue	1·75	1·25
99	–	50 c. black and blue	1·50	2·00
100	–	$1 blue and purple	3·25	7·50
101	–	$2 green and red	19·00	19·00
102	–	$5 brown and green	35·00	32·00

DESIGNS—HORIZ: 1 c. Copra; 2 c. Pineapples; 4 c. Ricefield; 5 c. Masjid Alwi Mosque, Kangar; 8 c. East Coast Railway "Golden Blowpipe" Express; $1 Govt Offices; $2 Bersilat (form of wrestling); $5 Weaving. VERT: 10 c. Tiger; 50 c. Aborigines with blowpipe.

1959. Installation of Sultan.

103	**20**	10 c. yellow, brown and blue	10	10

21 Sultan Abdul Halim Shah

1959. As Nos. 92/102 but with inset portrait of Sultan Abdul Halim Shah as in T **21**.

104	1 c. black	10	40
105	2 c. red	10	50
106	4 c. sepia	10	20
107	5 c. lake	10	10
108	8 c. green	3·50	2·25
109	10 c. sepia	75	10
109a	10 c. purple	3·50	30
110	20 c. blue	60	20
111a	50 c. black and blue	30	10
112	$1 blue and purple	1·75	2·25
113	$2 green and red	13·00	13·00
114a	$5 brown and green	20·00	11·00

22 "Vanda hookeriana"

1965. Flowers. Multicoloured.

115	1 c. Type **22**	10	40
116	2 c. "Arundina graminifolia"	10	70
117	5 c. "Paphiopedilum niveum"	10	10
118	6 c. "Spathoglottis plicata"	15	30
119	10 c. "Arachnis flos-aeris"	30	10
120	15 c. "Rhyncostylis retusa"	1·50	10
121	20 c. "Phalaenopsis violacea"	1·75	50

The higher values used in Kedah were Nos. 20/7 of Malaysia.

23 "Danaus melanippus"

1971. Butterflies. Multicoloured.

124	1 c. "Delias ninus"	30	75
125	2 c. Type **23**	40	75
126	5 c. "Parthenos sylvia"	90	10
127	6 c. "Papilio demoleus"	90	90
128	10 c. "Hebomoia glaucippe"	65	10
129	15 c. "Precis orithya"	80	10
130	20 c. "Valeria valeria"	1·10	45

The higher values in use with this issue were Nos. 64/71 of Malaysia.

24 "Pterocarpus indicus"

1979. Flowers. Multicoloured.

135	1 c. "Rafflesia hasseltii"	10	40
136	2 c. Type **24**	10	40
137	5 c. "Lagerstroemia speciosa"	10	10
138	10 c. "Durio zibethinus"	15	10
139	15 c. "Hibiscus rosa-sinensis"	15	10
140	20 c. "Rhododendron scortechinii"	20	10
141	25 c. "Etlingera elatior" (inscr "Phaeomeria speciosa")	40	10

25 Sultan Abdul Halim Shah

26 Cocoa

1983. Silver Jubilee of Sultan's Installation. Multicoloured.

142	20 c. Type **25**	70	30
143	40 c. Paddy fields (horiz)	1·50	1·00
144	60 c. Paddy fields and Mount Jerai (horiz)	2·25	3·75

1986. Agricultural Products of Malaysia. Mult.

152	1 c. Coffee	10	10
153	2 c. Coconuts	10	10
154	5 c. Type **26**	10	10
155	10 c. Black pepper	10	10
156	15 c. Rubber	10	10
157	20 c. Oil palm	10	10
158	30 c. Rice	15	20

KELANTAN

A state in the Federation of Malaya, incorporated in Malaysia in 1963.

100 cents = 1 dollar (Straits or Malayan)

1

3 Sultan Ismail

1911.

1a **1** 1 c. green . . . . 2·25 30
15 1 c. black 50 50
16 2 c. brown . . . . 4·50 3·75
16a 2 c. green . . . . 1·25 40
2 3 c. red . . . . 3·50 15
16b 3 c. brown . . . . 2·75 1·00
17 4 c. black and red 85 10
18 5 c. green & red on yellow . 70 10
19 6 c. purple . . . . 2·50 1·50
19a 6 c. red . . . . 4·00 5·50
5 8 c. blue . . . . 5·50 1·00
20 10 c. black and mauve . . . 2·00 10
21 30 c. purple and red . . . 4·00 5·50
8 50 c. black and orange . . . 6·50 2·50
9 $1 green . . . . 45·00 48·00
9a $1 green and brown . . . 32·00 2·00
10 $2 green and red . . . 1·00 4·00
11 $5 green and blue . . . 4·00 7·50
12 $25 green and orange . . . 38·00 75·00

1922. Optd **MALAYA BORNEO EXHIBITION**.

37 **1** 1 c. green . . . . 2·50 38·00
30 4 c. black and red . . . 2·75 38·00
31 5 c. green and red on yellow . 4·50 38·00
38 10 c. black and mauve . . . 4·75 48·00
32 30 c. purple and red . . . 4·50 55·00
33 50 c. black and orange . . . 7·50 60·00
34 $1 green and brown . . . 21·00 80·00
35 $2 green and red . . . 45·00 £150
36 $5 green and blue . . . £130 £300

1928.

40 **3** 1 c. olive and yellow . . . 30 55
41 2 c. green . . . . 2·50 10
42 4 c. red . . . . 4·75 70
43 5 c. brown . . . . 4·75 10
44 6 c. red . . . . 11·00 4·75
45 8 c. olive . . . . 4·75 10
46 10 c. purple . . . . 22·00 2·75
47 12 c. blue . . . . 3·25 4·00
48 25 c. red and purple . . . 4·75 3·50
49 30 c. violet and red . . . 40·00 16·00
50 40 c. orange and green . . . 8·00 23·00
51 50 c. olive and orange . . . 55·00 6·50
39 $1 blue . . . . 9·50 75·00
52 $1 violet and green . . . 48·00 12·00
53 $2 red £170 £180
54 $5 red £300 £450

All except No. 39 are larger than T **3**.

1948. Silver Wedding. As T **10/11** of Aden.

55 10 c. violet . . . . 60 1·50
56 $5 red . . . . 24·00 48·00

1949. U.P.U. As T **20/23** of Antigua.

57 10 c. purple 25 30
58 15 c. blue . . . . 1·50 90
59 25 c. orange . . . . 60 2·25
60 50 c. black . . . . 1·00 2·25

5 Sultan Ibrahim

6 Sultan Yahya Petra and Crest of Kelantan

1951.

61 **5** 1 c. black 20 30
62 2 c. orange 70 35
63 3 c. green . . . . 3·25 1·25
64 4 c. brown 20 15
65 5 c. purple 45 50
66 6 c. grey 30 20
67 8 c. red . . . . 1·25 3·25
68 8 c. green . . . . 75 1·75
69 10 c. mauve 20 10
70 12 c. red . . . . 75 2·25
71 15 c. blue . . . . 3·00 60
72 20 c. black and green . . . 45 5·50
73 20 c. blue 80 25
74 25 c. purple and orange . . . 75 55
75 30 c. red and purple . . . 1·25 1·75
76 35 c. red and purple . . . 90 1·50
77 40 c. red and purple . . . 4·75 12·00
78 50 c. black and blue . . . 1·50 40
79 $1 blue and purple . . . 6·00 4·00
80 $2 green and red . . . 22·00 20·00
81 $5 green and brown . . . 48·00 40·00

1953. Coronation. As T **13** of Aden.

82 10 c. black and purple . . . 60 80

1957. As Nos. 92/102 of Kedah but inset portrait of Sultan Ibrahim.

83 1 c. black 10 30
84 2 c. red 50 50
85 4 c. sepia 10 10
86 5 c. lake 10 10
87 8 c. green . . . . 80 2·25
88 10 c. sepia . . . . 1·25 10
89 10 c. purple . . . . 5·00 5·00
90 20 c. blue . . . . 1·00 30
91 50 c. black and blue . . . 50 50
92 $1 blue and purple . . . 4·50 1·50
93 $2 green and red . . . 11·00 6·00
94 $5 brown and green . . . 15·00 12·00

1961. Coronation of the Sultan.

95 **6** 10 c. multicoloured . . . 40 30

7 Sultan Yahya Petra

8 "Vanda hookeriana"

1961. As Nos. 83, etc, but with inset portrait of Sultan Yahya Petra as in T **7**.

96 1 c. black 10 75
97 2 c. red 10 75
98 4 c. sepia 15 10
99 5 c. lake 15 10
100 8 c. green . . . . 5·50 6·50
101 10 c. purple 70 10
102 20 c. blue . . . . 3·00 40

1965. As Nos. 115/21 of Kedah but with inset portrait of Sultan Yahya Petra as in T **8**.

103 **8** 1 c. multicoloured . . . 10 50
104 – 2 c. multicoloured . . . 10 60
105 – 5 c. multicoloured . . . 15 10
106 – 6 c. multicoloured . . . 70 1·00
107 – 10 c. multicoloured . . . 30 10
108 – 15 c. multicoloured . . . 1·50 20
109 – 20 c. multicoloured . . . 1·50 1·25

The higher values used in Kelantan were Nos. 20/7 of Malaysia (National Issues).

9 "Parthenos sylvia"

1971. Butterflies. As Nos. 124/30 of Kedah but with portrait of Sultan Yahya Petra as in T **9**.

112 – 1 c. multicoloured . . . 30 1·25
113 – 2 c. multicoloured . . . 40 1·25
114 **9** 5 c. multicoloured . . . 1·25 30
115 – 6 c. multicoloured . . . 1·25 1·50
116 – 10 c. multicoloured . . . 1·25 20
117 – 15 c. multicoloured . . . 1·25 10
118 – 20 c. multicoloured . . . 1·75 1·00

The higher values in use with this series were Nos. 64/71 of Malaysia (National Issues).

10 "Lagerstroemia speciosa"

1979. Flowers. As Nos. 135/41 of Kedah but with portrait of Sultan Yahya Petra as in T **10**.

123 1 c. "Rafflesia hasseltii" . . 10 50
124 2 c. "Pterocarpus indicus" . . 10 50
125 5 c. Type **10** 10 40
126 10 c. "Durio zibethinus" . . 15 10
127 15 c. "Hibiscus rosa-sinensis" . 15 10
128 20 c. "Rhododendron scortechinii" 20 10
129 25 c. "Etlingera elatior" (inscr "Phaeomeria speciosa") . . 40 50

11 Sultan Tengku Ismail Petra

12 Black Pepper

1980. Coronation of Sultan Tengku Ismail Petra.

130 **11** 10 c. multicoloured . . . 40 75
131 15 c. multicoloured . . . 40 15
132 50 c. multicoloured . . . 90 2·50

1986. Agricultural Products of Malaysia. Mult.

140 1 c. Coffee 10 10
141 2 c. Coconuts 10 10
142 5 c. Cocoa 10 10
143 10 c. Type **12** 10 10
144 15 c. Rubber 10 10
145 20 c. Oil palm 10 10
146 30 c. Rice 15 20

KENYA

Formerly part of Kenya, Uganda and Tanganyika (q.v.). Became Independent in 1963 and a Republic in 1964.

100 cents = 1 shilling

1 Cattle Ranching

4 Cockerel

3 National Assembly

1963. Independence.

1 **1** 5 c. multicoloured . . . 10 55
2 – 10 c. brown 10 10
3 – 15 c. mauve 85 10
4 – 20 c. black and green . . . 15 10
5 – 30 c. black and yellow . . . 15 10
6 – 40 c. brown and blue . . . 15 30
7 – 50 c. red, black and green . . 15 10
8 – 65 c. turquoise and yellow . . 55 65
9 **3** 1 s. multicoloured . . . 20 10
10 – 1 s. 30 brown, black & grn . 4·25 20
11 – 2 s. multicoloured . . . 1·25 40
12 – 5 s. brown, blue and green . . 1·25 40
13 – 10 s. brown and blue . . . 8·50 2·50
14 – 20 s. black and red . . . 5·50 7·50

DESIGNS—As Type **1**: 10 c. Wood-carving; 15 c. Heavy industry; 20 c. Timber industry; 30 c. Jomo Kenyatta facing Mt. Kenya; 40 c. Fishing industry; 50 c. Kenya flag; 65 c. Pyrethrum industry. As Type **3**: 1 s. 30, Tourism (Treetops hotel); 2 s. Coffee industry; 5 s. Tea industry; 10 s. Mombasa Port; 20 s. Royal College, Nairobi.

1964. Inauguration of Republic. Multicoloured.

15 15 c. Type **4** 20 15
16 30 c. Pres. Kenyatta . . . 25 10
17 50 c. African lion 35 10
18 1 s. 30 Hartlaub's turaco . . 3·75 50
19 2 s. 50 Nandi flame . . . 75 3·75

5 Thomson's Gazelle

7 Greater Kudu

1966.

20 **5** 5 c. orange, black and sepia . 20 20
21 – 10 c. black and green . . . 10 10
22 – 15 c. black and orange . . . 10 10
23 – 20 c. ochre, black and blue . . 10 15
24 – 30 c. indigo, blue and black . . 20 10
25 – 40 c. black and brown . . . 60 30
26 – 50 c. black and orange . . . 60 10
27 – 65 c. black and green . . . 1·25 2·00
28 – 70 c. black and red . . . 6·00 1·25
29 **7** 1 s. brown, black and blue . . 30 10
30 – 1 s. 30 blue, green and black . 4·00 20
31 – 1 s. 50 black, brown and green 4·25 2·00
32 – 2 s. 50 yellow, black & brown 3·25 1·25
33 – 5 s. yellow, black and green . 1·00 70
34 – 10 s. ochre, black and brown . 2·50 3·00
35 – 20 s. multicoloured . . . 8·00 13·00

DESIGNS—As Type **5**: 10 c. Sable antelope; 15 c. Aardvark ("Ant Bear"); 20 c. Lesser bushbaby; 30 c. Warthog; 40 c. Common zebra; 50 c. African buffalo; 65 c. Black rhinoceros; 70 c. Ostrich. As Type **7**: 1 s. 30, African elephant; 1 s. 50, Bat-eared fox; 2 s. 50, Cheetah; 5 s. Savanna monkey ("Vervet Monkey"); 10 s. Giant ground pangolin; 20 s. Lion.

8 Perna Tellin

9 Ramose Murex

1971. Sea Shells. Multicoloured.

36 5 c. Type **8** 10 30
37 10 c. Episcopal mitre . . . 15 10
38 15 c. Purplish clanculus . . . 15 20
39 20 c. Humpback cowrie . . . 15 20
40 30 c. Variable abalone . . . 20 10
41 40 c. Flame top shell . . . 20 10
42 50 c. Common purple janthina . 30 20
43 50 c. Common purple janthina . 9·50 2·25
44 60 c. Bullmouth helmet . . . 30 1·25
45 70 c. Chambered or pearly nautilus . . . . 45 1·50
46 70 c. Chambered or pearly nautilus . . . . 9·00 4·50
47a 1 s. Type **9** 20 10
48 1 s. 50 Trumpet triton . . . 1·25 10
49 2 s. 50 Trapezium horse conch . 1·25 10
50a 5 s. Great green turban . . . 1·00 10
51 10 s. Textile or cloth of gold cone . . . . 4·25 15
52a 20 s. Scorpion conch . . . 3·75 25

INSCRIPTIONS: No. 42, "Janthina globosa"; 43, "Janthina janthina"; 45, "Nautilus pompileus"; 46, "Nautilus pompilius".

Nos. 47/52 are larger, as Type **9**.

1975. Nos. 48/9 and 52a surch.

53 2 s. on 1 s. 50 Trumpet triton . 6·00 4·50
54 3 s. on 2 s. 50 Trapezium horse conch . . . . 9·50 18·00
55 40 s. on 20 s. Scorpion conch . 6·00 13·00

11 Microwave Tower

1976. Telecommunications Development. Mult.

56 50 c. Type **11** 10 10
57 1 s. Cordless switchboard (horiz) 10 10
58 2 s. Telephones 20 30
59 3 s. Message switching centre (horiz) 25 45

12 Akii Bua, Ugandan Hurdler

1976. Olympic Games, Montreal. Multicoloured.

61 50 c. Type **12** 10 10
62 1 s. Filbert Bayi, Tanzanian runner 15 10
63 2 s. Steve Muchoki, Kenyan boxer 45 35
64 3 s. Olympic flame and East African flags 60 50

13 Diesel-hydraulic Train, Tanzania–Zambia Railway

1976. Railway Transport. Multicoloured.

66 50 c. Type **13** 35 10
67 1 s. Nile Bridge, Uganda . . . 60 15
68 2 s. Nakuru Station, Kenya . . 2·25 1·25
69 3 s. Uganda Railway Class A steam locomotive, 1896 . . . 2·50 1·75

14 Nile Perch

1977. Game Fish of East Africa. Multicoloured.

71 50 c. Type **14** 25 10
72 1 s. Nile mouthbrooder ("Tilapia") 35 10
73 3 s. Sailfish . . . . 1·00 90
74 5 s. Black marlin . . . . 1·50 1·25

15 Maasai Manyatta (village), Kenya

1977. Second World Black and African Festival of Arts and Culture, Nigeria. Multicoloured.

76	50 c. Type **15**	15	10
77	1 s. "Heartbeat of Africa" (Ugandan dancers)	20	10
78	2 s. Makonde sculpture, Tanzania	75	1·25
79	3 s. "Early man and technology" (skinning hippopotamus)	1·00	1·75

16 Rally Car and Villagers

1977. 25th Anniv of Safari Rally. Multicoloured.

81	50 c. Type **16**	20	10
82	1 s. Pres. Kenyatta starting rally	30	10
83	2 s. Car fording river	80	1·00
84	5 s. Car and elephants	1·50	1·75

17 Canon Kivebulaya

1977. Centenary of Ugandan Church. Multicoloured.

86	50 c. Type **17**	10	10
87	1 s. Modern Namirembe Cathedral	10	10
88	2 s. The first Cathedral	30	55
89	5 s. Early congregation, Kigezi	50	1·00

18 Sagana Royal Lodge, Nyeri, 1952

1977. Silver Jubilee. Multicoloured.

91	2 s. Type **18**	15	15
92	5 s. Treetops Hotel (vert)	20	35
93	10 s. Queen Elizabeth and Pres. Kenyatta	30	60
94	15 s. Royal visit, 1972	45	1·00

19 Pancake Tortoise

1977. Endangered Species. Multicoloured.

96	50 c. Type **19**	30	10
97	1 s. Nile crocodile	40	10
98	2 s. Hunter's hartebeest	1·60	75
99	3 s. Red colobus monkey	1·75	1·00
100	5 s. Dugong	2·00	1·50

20 Kenya-Ethiopia Border Point

1977. Nairobi–Addis Ababa Highway. Mult.

102	50 c. Type **20**	15	10
103	1 s. Archer's Post	20	10
104	2 s. Thika Flyover	55	60
105	5 s. Marsabit Game Lodge	1·25	1·50

21 Gypsum

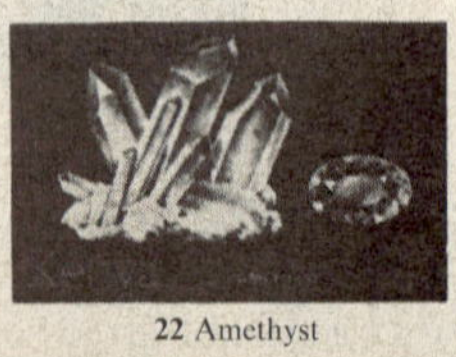

22 Amethyst

1977. Minerals. Multicoloured.

107	10 c. Type **21**	1·25	20
108	20 c. Trona	1·25	20
109	30 c. Kyanite	1·40	20
110	40 c. Amazonite	1·40	10
111	50 c. Galena	1·40	10
112	70 c. Silicified wood	4·50	40
113	80 c. Fluorite	4·50	60
114	1 s. Type **22**	2·00	10
115	1 s. 50 Agate	2·00	30
116	2 s. Tourmaline	2·00	20
117	3 s. Aquamarine	2·25	55
118	5 s. Rhodolite garnet	2·25	1·40
119	10 s. Sapphire	2·25	2·50
120	20 s. Ruby	6·00	3·50
121	40 s. Green grossular garnet	16·00	16·00

23 Joe Kadenge (Kenya) and Forwards

1978. World Cup Football Championship, Argentina. Multicoloured.

122	50 c. Type **23**	10	10
123	1 s. Mohamed Chuma (Tanzania) and cup presentation	10	10
124	2 s. Omari Kidevu (Zanzibar) and goalmouth scene	30	70
125	3 s. Polly Ouma (Uganda) and three forwards	40	95

24 Boxing

1978. Commonwealth Games, Edmonton. Mult.

127	50 c. Type **24**	15	10
128	1 s. Welcoming the Olympic Games Team, 1968	20	10
129	3 c. Javelin throwing	60	1·00
130	5 s. Pres. Kenyatta admiring boxer's trophy	75	1·60

25 "Overloading is Dangerous"

1978. Road Safety. Multicoloured.

131	50 c. Type **25**	50	10
132	1 s. "Speed does not pay"	70	20
133	1 s. 50 "Ignoring Traffic Signs may cause death"	85	55
134	2 s. "Slow down at School Crossing"	1·25	1·00
135	3 s. "Never cross a continuous line"	1·40	2·50
136	5 s. "Approach Railway Level Crossing with extreme caution"	2·00	3·50

26 Pres. Kenyatta at Mass Rally, 1963

1978. Kenyatta Day. Multicoloured.

137	50 c. "Harambee Water Project"	20	10
138	1 s. Handing over of Independence Instruments, 1963	30	10
139	2 s. Type **26**	65	50
140	3 s. "Harambee, 15 Great Years"	90	1·25
141	5 s. "Struggle for Independence, 1952"	1·10	2·00

27 Freedom Fighters, Namibia

1978. International Anti-Apartheid Year.

142	**27** 50 c. multicoloured	20	10
143	– 1 s. black and blue	25	10
144	– 2 s. multicoloured	60	30
145	– 3 s. multicoloured	80	65
146	– 5 s. multicoloured	90	1·00

DESIGNS: 1 s. International seminar on apartheid; 2 s. Steve Biko's tombstone; 3 s. Nelson Mandela; 5 s. Bishop Lamont.

28 Children Playing

1979. International Year of the Child. Multicoloured.

147	50 c. Type **28**	20	10
148	2 s. Boy fishing	60	60
149	3 s. Children singing and dancing	80	90
150	5 s. Children with camels	1·00	1·40

29 "The Lion and the Jewel"

1979. Kenya National Theatre. Multicoloured.

151	50 c. Type **29**	15	10
152	1 s. "Utisi"	20	10
153	2 s. Theatre programmes	40	30
154	3 s. Kenya National Theatre	60	45
155	5 s. "Genesis"	1·00	75

30 Blind Telephone Operator

31 "Father of the Nation" (Kenyatta's funeral procession)

1979. 50th Anniv of Salvation Army Social Services.

156	50 c. Type **30**	45	10
157	1 s. Care for the aged	45	10
158	3 s. Village polytechnic (horiz)	1·25	1·50
159	5 s. Vocational training (horiz)	1·50	2·50

1979. 1st Death Anniv of President Kenyatta. Multicoloured.

160	50 c. Type **31**	10	10
162	1 s. "First President of Kenya" (Kenyatta receiving independence)	15	10
163	3 s. "Kenyatta the politician" (speaking at rally)	35	50
164	5 s. "A true son of Kenya" (Kenyatta as a boy carpenter)	60	95

32 British East Africa Company 1890 1 a. Stamp

1979. Death Centenary of Sir Rowland Hill.

164	**32** 50 c. multicoloured	15	10
165	– 1 s. multicoloured	15	10
166	– 2 s. black, red and brown	30	40
167	– 5 s. multicoloured	60	1·00

DESIGNS: 1 s. Kenya, Uganda and Tanganyika 1935 1 s. stamp; 2 s. Penny Black; 5 s. 1964 2 s. 50, Inauguration of Republic commemorative.

33 Roads, Globe and Conference Emblem

1980. International Road Federation. African Highway Conference, Nairobi. Multicoloured.

168	50 c. Type **33**	15	10
169	1 s. New weighbridge, Athi River	20	10
170	3 s. New Nyali Bridge, Mombasa	55	85
171	5 s. Highway to Jomo Kenyatta International Airport	60	2·00

34 Mobile Unit in action in Masailand

1980. Flying Doctor Service. Multicoloured.

172	50 c. Type **34**	10	10
173	1 s. Donkey transport to Turkana airstrip (vert)	20	10
174	3 s. Surgical team in action at outstation (vert)	65	1·00
175	5 s. Emergency airlift from North Eastern Province	90	1·60

35 Statue of Sir Rowland Hill

37 Blue-spotted Stingray

36 Pope John Paul II

1980. "London 1980" International Stamp Exhibition.

177	**35** 25 s. multicoloured	1·00	2·50

1980. Papal Visit. Multicoloured.

179	50 c. Type **36**	40	10
180	1 s. Pope, arms and cathedral (vert)	50	10
181	5 s. Pope, flags and dove (vert)	1·10	70
182	10 s. Pope, President Moi and map of Africa	1·60	1·40

1980. Marine Life. Multicoloured.

183	50 c. Type **37**	30	10
184	2 s. Allard's anemonefish	1·00	80
185	3 s. Four-coloured nudibranch	1·25	1·75
186	5 s. "Eretmochelys imbricata"	1·75	2·75

38 National Archives

1980. Historic Buildings. Multicoloured.

187	50 c. Type **38**	10	10
188	1 s. Provincial Commissioner's Office, Nairobi	15	10
189	1 s. 50 Nairobi House	20	20
190	2 s. Norfolk Hotel	25	50
191	3 s. McMillan Library	35	75
192	5 s. Kipande House	55	1·25

39 "Disabled enjoys Affection"

1981. Int Year for Disabled Persons. Mult.

193	50 c. Type **39**	15	10
194	1 s. President Moi presenting flag to Disabled Olympic Games team captain	20	10
195	3 s. Blind people climbing Mount Kenya, 1975	65	55
196	5 s. Disabled artist at work	95	1·00

HAVE YOU READ THE NOTES AT THE BEGINNING OF THIS CATALOGUE?

These often provide answers to the enquiries we receive.

40 Longonot Complex

1981. Satellite Communications. Multicoloured.

197	50 c. Type **40**	15	10
198	2 s. "Intelsat V"	50	35
199	3 s. "Longonot I"	60	55
200	5 s. "Longonot II"	85	85

41 Kenyatta Conference Centre

1981. O.A.U. (Organization of African Unity) Summit Conference, Nairobi.

201	**41** 50 c. multicoloured	15	10
202	– 1 s. black, yellow & blue	20	10
203	– 3 s. multicoloured	50	40
204	– 5 s. multicoloured	90	65
205	– 10 s. multicoloured	1·00	1·00

DESIGNS: 1 s. "Panaftel" earth stations; 3 s. Parliament Building; 5 s. Jomo Kenyatta International Airport; 10 s. O.A.U. flag.

42 St. Paul's Cathedral 43 Giraffe

1981. Royal Wedding. Multicoloured.

207	50 c. Prince Charles and President Daniel Arap Moi	10	10
208	3 s. Type **42**	15	20
209	5 s. Royal Yacht "Britannia"	25	30
210	10 s. Prince Charles on safari in Kenya	40	55

1981. Rare Animals. Multicoloured.

212	50 c. Type **43**	15	10
213	2 s. Bongo	35	25
214	5 s. Roan antelope	70	1·25
215	10 s. Agile mangabey	1·25	2·75

44 "Technical Development" 45 Kamba

1981. World Food Day. Multicoloured.

216	50 c. Type **44**	10	10
217	1 s. "Mwea rice projects"	15	10
218	2 s. "Irrigation schemes"	30	55
219	5 s. "Breeding livestock"	60	1·75

1981. Ceremonial Costumes (1st series). Mult.

220	50 c. Type **45**	40	10
221	1 s. Turkana	45	10
222	2 s. Giriama	1·25	85
223	3 s. Masai	1·60	1·75
224	5 s. Luo	1·75	2·50

See also Nos. 329/33, 413/17 and 515/19.

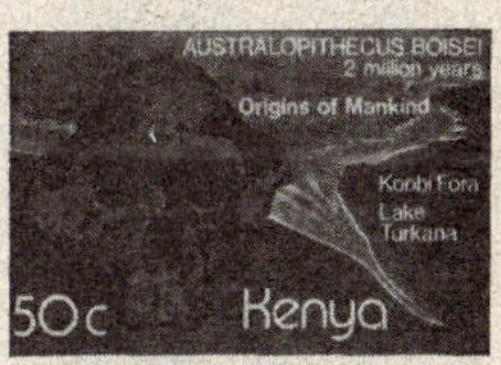

46 "Australopithecus boisei"

1982. "Origins of Mankind". Skulls. Multicoloured.

225	50 c. Type **46**	1·10	20
226	2 s. "Homo erectus"	2·50	1·50
227	3 s. "Homo habilis"	3·00	3·75
228	5 s. "Proconsul africanus"	3·50	5·00

47 Tree-planting

1982. 75th Anniv of Boy Scout Movement (Nos. 229, 231, 233 and 235) and 60th Anniv of Girl Guide Movement (Nos. 230, 232, 234 and 236). Multicoloured.

229	70 c. Type **47**	50	65
230	70 c. Paying homage	50	65
231	3 s. 50 "Be Prepared"	1·25	1·75
232	3 s. 50 "International Friendship"	1·25	1·75
233	5 s. Helping disabled	1·75	2·50
234	5 s. Community service	1·75	2·50
235	6 s. 50 Paxtu Cottage (Lord Baden-Powell's home)	2·00	2·75
236	6 s. 50 Lady Baden-Powell	2·00	2·75

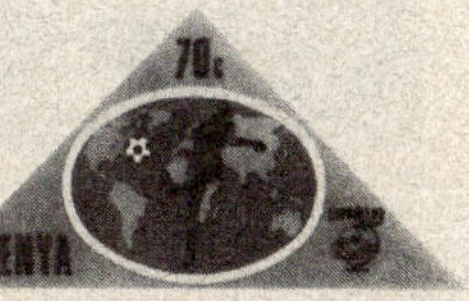

48 Footballer displaying Shooting Skill

1982. World Cup Football Championship, Spain. Footballers silhouetted against Map of World. Multicoloured.

238	70 c. Type **48**	1·50	65
239	3 s. 50 Heading	2·75	2·75
240	5 s. Goalkeeping	3·25	4·25
241	10 s. Dribbling	5·50	8·00

49 Cattle Judging 50 Micro-wave Radio System

1982. 80th Anniv of Agricultural Society of Kenya. Multicoloured.

243	70 c. Type **49**	70	10
244	2 s. 50 Farm machinery	1·75	1·75
245	3 s. 50 Musical ride	2·00	3·00
246	6 s. 50 Agricultural Society emblem	2·50	4·75

1982. I.T.U. Plenipotentiary Conference, Nairobi. Multicoloured.

247	70 c. Type **50**	60	10
248	3 s. 50 Sea-to-shore service link	2·00	2·25
249	5 s. Rural telecommunications system	2·50	3·75
250	6 s. 50 I.T.U. emblem	3·00	4·50

1982. No. 113 surch **70c.**

251	70 c. on 80 c. Fluorite	1·00	1·00

52 Container Cranes

1983. 5th Anniv of Kenya Ports Authority. Mult.

252	70 c. Type **52**	85	10
253	2 s. Port by night	1·75	1·90
254	3 s. 50 Container cranes (different)	2·50	3·50
255	5 s. Map of Mombasa Port	3·25	4·50

53 Shada Zambarau 54 Waridi Kikuba

1983. Flowers. Multicoloured.

257	10 c. Type **53**	40	40
258	20 c. Kilua Kingulima	55	40
259	30 c. Mwalika Mwiya	55	40
260	40 c. Ziyungi Buluu	55	40
261	50 c. Kilua Habashia	55	30
262	70 c. Chanuo Kato	60	20
262a	80 c. As 40 c.	4·00	2·25
262b	1 s. Waridi Kikuba	4·00	80
263	1 s. Type **54**	65	20
264	1 s. 50 Mshomoro Mtambazi	1·75	60
265	2 s. Papatuo Boti	1·75	60
266	2 s. 50 Tumba Mboni	2·25	60
266a	3 s. Mkuku Mrembo	7·00	7·00
267	3 s. 50 Mtongo Mbeja	2·00	1·50
267b	4 s. Mnukia Muuma	4·75	6·50
268	5 s. Nyungu Chepuo	2·00	1·50
268a	7 s. Mlua Miba	6·50	8·00
269	10 s. Muafunili	2·00	2·50
270	20 s. Mbake Nyanza	2·50	3·75
271	40 s. Njuga Pagwa	4·25	8·00

The 1 s. 50 to 40 s. are in the same format as T **54**.

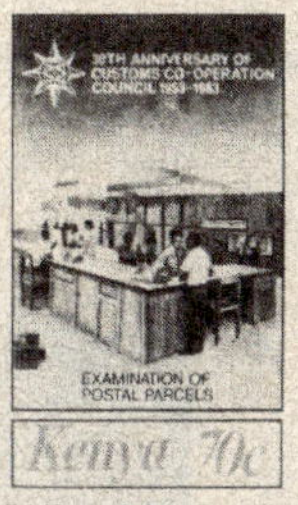

55 Coffee Plucking 56 Examining Parcels

1983. Commonwealth Day. Multicoloured.

272	70 c. Type **55**	10	10
273	2 s. President Daniel Arap Moi	15	20
274	5 s. Satellite view of Earth (horiz)	35	45
275	10 s. Masai dance (horiz)	65	1·00

1983. 30th Anniv of Customs Co-operation Council. Multicoloured.

276	70 c. Type **56**	25	10
277	2 s. 50 Customs Headquarters, Mombasa	65	30
278	3 s. 50 Customs Council Headquarters, Brussels	75	40
279	10 s. Customs patrol boat	2·40	2·50

57 Communications via Satellite

1983. World Communications Year. Multicoloured.

280	70 c. Type **57**	60	10
281	2 s. 50 "Telephone and Postal Services"	1·50	1·75
282	3 s. 50 Communications by sea and air (horiz)	2·00	3·00
283	5 s. Road and rail communications (horiz)	2·50	4·00

58 Ships in Kilindini Harbour

1983. 25th Anniv of Intergovernmental Maritime Organization. Multicoloured.

284	70 c. Type **58**	95	10
285	2 s. 50 Life-saving devices	2·00	1·75
286	3 s. 50 Mombasa container terminal	2·50	3·00
287	10 s. Marine park	3·50	6·50

59 President Moi signing Visitors' Book

1983. 29th Commonwealth Parliamentary Conference. Multicoloured.

288	70 c. Type **59**	25	10
289	2 s. 50 Parliament building, Nairobi (vert)	90	1·10
290	5 s. State opening of Parliament (vert)	1·60	2·75

60 Kenyan and British Flags

1983. Royal Visit. Multicoloured.

292	70 c. Type **60**	50	10
293	3 s. 50 Sagana State Lodge	2·00	1·50
294	5 s. Treetops Hotel	2·25	2·50
295	10 s. Queen Elizabeth II and President Moi	3·50	6·50

61 President Moi

1983. 20th Anniv of Independence. Mult.

297	70 c. Type **61**	10	10
298	2 s. President Moi planting tree	20	20
299	3 s. 50 Kenyan flag and emblem	35	35
300	5 s. School milk scheme	50	50
301	10 s. People of Kenya	1·00	1·10

62 White-backed Night Heron 63 Radar Tower

1984. Rare Birds of Kenya. Multicoloured.

303	70 c. Type **62**	1·50	30
304	2 s. 50 Quail plover	2·75	2·50
305	3 s. 50 Taita olive thrush	3·50	3·75
306	5 s. Mufumbiri shrike	4·00	4·25
307	10 s. White-winged apalis	5·50	7·00

1984. 40th Anniv of International Civil Aviation Organization. Multicoloured.

308	70 c. Type **63**	15	10
309	2 s. 50 Kenya School of Aviation (horiz)	45	45
310	3 s. 50 Boeing 707 taking off from Moi airport (horiz)	65	70
311	5 s. Air traffic control centre	95	1·00

64 Running

1984. Olympic Games, Los Angeles.

312	**64** 70 c. black, green & dp green	30	10
313	– 2 s. 50 black, purple & vio	60	70
314	– 5 s. black, blue & dp blue	1·50	2·50
315	– 10 s. black, yellow & brn	3·50	5·50

DESIGNS: 2 s. 50, Hurdling; 5 s. Boxing; 10 s. Hockey.

65 Conference and Kenya Library Association Logos

1984. 50th Conference of the International Federation of Library Associations. Multicoloured.

317	70 c. Type **65**	10	10
318	3 s. 50 Mobile library	50	60
319	5 s. Adult library	65	1·25
320	10 s. Children's library	1·00	2·50

66 Doves and Cross

67 Export Year Logo

1984. 4th World Conference on Religion and Peace. As T **66**, each design showing a different central symbol. Multicoloured.

321 70 c. Type **66** 30 10
322 2 s. 50 Arabic inscription . . . 1·25 1·50
323 3 s. 50 Peace emblem . . . . 1·60 2·00
324 6 s. 50 Star and Crescent . . . 2·00 3·00

1984. Kenya Export Year. Multicoloured.

325 70 c. Type **67** 30 10
326 3 s. 50 Forklift truck with air cargo (horiz) . . . . . . 1·75 2·00
327 5 s. Loading ship's cargo . . . 2·50 2·75
328 10 s. Kenyan products (horiz) . . 3·75 5·25

1984. Ceremonial Costumes (2nd series). As T **45**. Multicoloured.

329 70 c. Luhya 70 15
330 2 s. Kikuyu . . . . 1·75 1·75
331 3 s. 50 Pokomo . . . . 2·25 2·25
332 5 s. Nandi . . . . 2·50 2·50
333 10 s. Rendile . . . . 3·50 5·00

68 Staunton Knight and Nyayo National Stadium

1984. 60th Anniv of International Chess Federation. Multicoloured.

334 70 c. Type **68** . . . . 1·50 30
335 2 s. 50 Staunton rook and Fort Jesus . . . . 2·50 1·75
336 3 s. 50 Staunton bishop and National Monument . . . . 3·00 2·50
337 5 s. Staunton queen and Parliament Building . . . . 3·25 3·50
338 10 s. Staunton king and Nyayo Fountain . . . . 5·00 7·00

69 Cooking with Wood-burning Stove and Charcoal Fire

1985. Energy Conservation. Multicoloured.

339 70 c. Type **69** 20 10
340 2 s. Solar energy panel on roof 75 75
341 3 s. 50 Production of gas from cow dung . . . . 1·00 1·25
342 10 s. Ploughing with oxen . . 2·75 4·50

70 Crippled Girl Guide making Table-mat

1985. 75th Anniv of Girl Guide Movement. Multicoloured.

344 1 s. Type **70** 75 15
345 3 s. Girl Guides doing community service . . . . . 1·75 1·50
346 5 s. Lady Olave Baden-Powell (founder) . . . . 2·50 3·00
347 7 s. Girl Guides gardening . . 4·00 6·00

71 Stylised Figures and Globe

1985. World Red Cross Day.

348 **71** 1 s. black and red 80 15
349 – 4 s. multicoloured . . . . 3·00 3·00
350 – 5 s. multicoloured . . . . 3·25 3·50
351 – 7 s. multicoloured . . . . 4·50 6·00

DESIGNS: 4 s. First Aid team; 5 s. Hearts containing crosses ("Blood Donation"); 7 s. Cornucopia ("Famine Relief").

72 Man with Malaria

73 Repairing Water Pipes

1985. 7th International Congress of Protozoology, Nairobi. Multicoloured.

352 1 s. Type **72** 90 15
353 3 s. Child with Leishmaniasis . 2·75 2·75
354 5 s. Cow with Trypanosomiasis 3·25 3·50
355 7 s. Dog with Babesiosis . . 4·75 6·50

1985. United Nations Women's Decade Conference. Multicoloured.

356 1 s. Type **73** 20 10
357 3 s. Traditional food preparation 60 85
358 5 s. Basket-weaving . . . . . 1·00 1·50
359 7 s. Dressmaking . . . . . . 1·40 2·50

74 The Last Supper

1985. 43rd International Eucharistic Congress, Nairobi. Multicoloured.

360 1 s. Type **74** 50 10
361 3 s. Village family ("The Eucharist and the Christian Family") . . . . 2·25 2·00
362 5 s. Congress altar, Uhuru Park 2·50 2·75
363 7 s. St. Peter Claver's Church, Nairobi . . . . 3·00 4·50

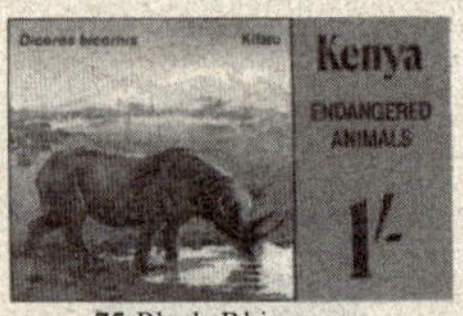

75 Black Rhinoceros

1985. Endangered Animals. Multicoloured.

365 1 s. Type **75** . . . . 1·75 40
366 3 s. Cheetah . . . . 3·00 2·75
367 5 s. De Brazza's monkey . . 3·25 3·75
368 10 s. Grevy's zebra . . . . . 5·50 7·50

76 "Borassus aethiopum"

1986. Indigenous Trees. Multicoloured.

370 1 s. Type **76** 65 15
371 3 s. "Acacia xanthophloea" . . 2·50 2·50
372 5 s. "Ficus natalensis" . . . . 3·50 3·75
373 7 s. "Spathodea nilotica" . . 4·50 6·00

77 Dove and U.N. Logo (from poster)

78 Dribbling the Ball

1986. International Peace Year. Multicoloured.

375 1 s. Type **77** 30 10
376 3 s. U.N. General Assembly (horiz) . . . . 1·00 65
377 7 s. Nuclear explosion . . . 2·25 2·75
378 10 s. Quotation from Wall of Isaiah, U.N. Building, New York (horiz) . . . . . . 2·50 2·75

1986. World Cup Football Championship, Mexico. Multicoloured.

379 1 s. Type **78** 80 15
380 3 s. Scoring from a penalty . 2·25 1·25
381 5 s. Tackling . . . . 3·00 2·00
382 7 s. Cup winners . . . . . . 3·75 3·50
383 10 s. Heading the ball . . . . 4·75 4·25

79 Rural Post Office and Telephone

1986. "Expo '86" World Fair, Vancouver. Mult.

385 1 s. Type **79** 50 15
386 3 s. Container depot, Embakasi 2·50 1·75
387 5 s. Piper Twin Commanche airplane landing at game park airstrip . . . . 3·50 2·50
388 7 s. Container ship . . . . . 4·00 4·25
389 10 s. Transporting produce to market . . . . 4·25 4·75

80 Telephone, Computer and Dish Aerial

1986. African Telecommunications. Multicoloured.

390 1 s. Type **80** 35 10
391 3 s. Telephones of 1876, 1936 and 1986 . . . . 1·00 85
392 5 s. Dish aerial, satellite, telephones and map of Africa 1·25 1·25
393 7 s. Kenyan manufacture of telecommunications equipment 1·75 2·25

81 Mashua

1986. Dhows of Kenya. Multicoloured.

394 1 s. Type **81** 65 20
395 3 s. Mtepe . . . . 1·75 1·50
396 5 s. Dau La Mwao . . . . . 2·25 2·50
397 10 s. Jahazi . . . . 3·75 4·75

82 Nativity

83 Immunization

1986. Christmas. Multicoloured.

399 1 s. Type **82** 30 10
400 3 s. Shepherd and sheep . . . 1·00 55
401 5 s. Angel and slogan "LOVE PEACE UNITY" (horiz) . . 1·60 1·40
402 7 s. The Magi riding camels (horiz) . . . . 1·90 2·75

1987. 40th Anniv of U.N.I.C.E.F. Multicoloured.

403 1 s. Type **83** 45 10
404 3 s. Food and nutrition . . . 1·00 60
405 4 s. Oral rehydration therapy . 1·75 1·25
406 5 s. Family planning . . . . 1·75 1·25
407 10 s. Female literacy . . . . 2·50 3·00

84 Akamba Woodcarvers

1987. Tourism. Multicoloured.

408 1 s. Type **84** 30 10
409 3 s. Tourism on beach . . . . 2·25 1·75
410 5 s. Tourist and guide at view point . . . . 2·50 3·25
411 7 s. Pride of lions . . . . . . 3·50 5·00

1987. Ceremonial Costumes (3rd series). As T **45**. Multicoloured.

413 1 s. Embu 45 10
414 3 s. Kisii . . . . 1·25 70
415 5 s. Samburu . . . . 1·60 1·40
416 7 s. Taita . . . . 2·25 2·50
417 10 s. Boran . . . . 2·75 3·00

85 Telecommunications by Satellite

1987. 10th Anniv of Kenya Posts and Telecommunications Corporation. Multicoloured.

418 1 s. Type **85** 35 30
419 3 s. Rural post office, Kajiado 80 80
420 4 s. Awarding trophy, Welfare Sports . . . . 1·10 1·25
421 5 s. Village and telephone box 1·25 1·40
422 7 s. Speedpost labels and outline map of Kenya . . . . . . 1·75 2·25

86 Volleyball

87 "Aloe volkensii"

1987. 4th All-Africa Games, Nairobi. Mult.

424 1 s. Type **86** 20 10
425 3 s. Cycling 25 30
426 4 s. Boxing 35 55
427 5 s. Swimming 40 60
428 7 s. Steeplechasing . . . . . 50 1·10

1987. Medicinal Herbs. Multicoloured.

430 1 s. Type **87** 40 10
431 3 s. "Cassia didymobotrya" . . 1·10 1·00
432 5 s. "Erythrina abyssinica" . . 1·75 1·75
433 7 s. "Adenium obesum" . . . 2·25 2·50
434 10 s. Herbalist's clinic . . . 2·50 2·75

88 "Epamera sidus"

89 "Papilio rex"

1988. Butterflies. Multicoloured.

434a 10 c. "Cyrestis camillus" . . 60 1·25
435 20 c. Type **88** 30 70
436 40 c. "Cynthia cardui" . . . 40 70
437 50 c. "Colotis evippe" . . . 40 70
438 70 c. "Precis westermanni" . . 40 70
439 80 c. "Colias electo" 40 70
440 1 s. "Eronia leda" 40 30
440a 1 s. 50 "Papilio dardanus" . . 1·25 30
441 2 s. Type **89** 70 40
442 2 s. 50 "Colotis phisadia" . . 75 90
443 3 s. "Papilio desmondi" . . . 80 90
444 3 s. 50 "Papilio demodocus" . 80 60
445 4 s. "Papilio phorcas" . . . 85 60
446 5 s. "Charaxes druceanus" . . 90 70
447 7 s. "Cymothoe teita" . . . 1·00 1·50
448 10 s. "Charaxes zoolina" . . 1·25 1·50
449 20 s. "Papilio dardanus" . . 1·60 3·00
450 40 s. "Charaxes cithaeron" . . 3·00 5·00

The 10 c. to 1 s. 50 are in the same format as T **88**.

90 Samburu Lodge and Crocodiles

1988. Kenyan Game Lodges. Multicoloured.

451 1 s. Type **90** 30 10
452 3 s. Naro Moru River Lodge and rock climbing 75 60
453 4 s. Mara Serena Lodge and zebra with foal . . . . . 85 1·00
454 5 s. Voi Safari Lodge and buffalo 95 1·10
455 7 s. Kilimanjaro Buffalo Lodge and giraffes . . . . 1·25 1·75
456 10 s. Meru Mulika Lodge and rhinoceroses . . . . . . 1·75 2·00

91 Athletes and Stadium, Commonwealth Games, Brisbane, 1982

1988. "Expo '88" World Fair, Brisbane, and Bicent of Australian Settlement. Multicoloured.

457 1 s. Type **91** 20 10
458 3 s. Flying Doctor Service De Havilland Drover 3 and Piper Twin Commanche aircraft 1·25 90
459 4 s. H.M.S. "Sirius" (frigate), 1788 1·40 1·40
460 5 s. Ostrich and emu 1·75 1·75
461 7 s. Queen Elizabeth II, Pres. Arap Moi of Kenya and Prime Minister Hawke of Australia 2·00 2·50

92 W.H.O. Logo and Slogan

1988. 40th Anniv of W.H.O.

463 **92** 1 s. blue, gold & dp blue 25 10
464 – 3 s. multicoloured 85 70
465 – 5 s. multicoloured 1·25 1·25
466 – 7 s. multicoloured 1·75 2·25
DESIGNS: 3 s. Mother with young son and nutritious food; 5 s. Giving oral vaccine to baby; 7 s. Village women drawing clean water from pump.

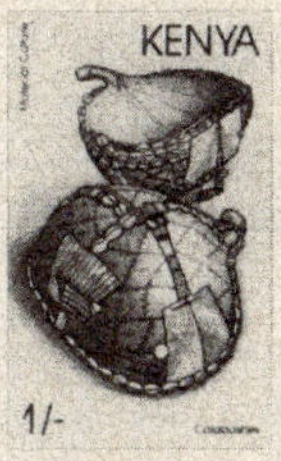

93 Handball **94** Calabashes

1988. Olympic Games, Seoul. Multicoloured.

467 1 s. Type **93** 15 10
468 3 s. Judo 30 35
469 5 s. Weightlifting 40 50
470 7 s. Javelin 55 80
471 10 s. Relay racing 65 1·00

1988. Kenyan Material Culture (1st issue). Mult.

473 1 s. Type **94** 20 10
474 3 s. Milk gourds 60 55
475 5 s. Cooking pots (horiz) 70 65
476 7 s. Winnowing trays (horiz) 95 1·10
477 10 s. Reed baskets (horiz) 1·40 1·60
See also Nos. 646/50.

95 Pres. Arap Moi taking Oath, 1978

1988. 10th Anniv of "Nyayo" Era. Mult.

479 1 s. Type **95** 25 10
480 3 s. Building soil conservation barrier 85 70
481 3 s. 50 Passengers boarding bus 1·25 80
482 4 s. Metalwork shop 1·25 1·25
483 5 s. Moi University, Eldoret 1·25 1·25
484 7 s. Aerial view of hospital 2·50 2·75
485 10 s. Pres. Arap Moi and Mrs. Thatcher at Kapsabet Telephone Exchange 4·25 3·75

96 Kenya Flag

1988. 25th Anniv of Independence. Mult.

486 1 s. Type **96** 30 10
487 3 s. Coffee picking 50 50
488 5 s. Proposed Kenya Posts and Telecommunications Headquarters building 95 95
489 7 s. Kenya Airways Airbus Industrie A310-300 "Harambee Star" 2·50 2·00
490 10 s. New diesel locomotive No. 9401 3·75 3·50

97 Gedi Ruins, Malindi

1989. Historic Monuments. Multicoloured.

491 1 s. 20 Type **97** 25 10
492 3 s. 40 Vasco Da Gama Pillar, Malindi (vert) 70 70
493 4 s. 40 Ishiakani Monument, Kiunga 80 80
494 5 s. 50 Fort Jesus, Mombasa 1·00 1·25
495 7 s. 50 She Burnan Omwe, Lamu (vert) 1·50 2·00

98 125th Anniversary and Kenya Red Cross Logos

1989 125th Anniv of International Red Cross. Multicoloured.

496 1 s. 20 Type **98** 30 10
497 3 s. 40 Red Cross workers with car crash victim 85 85
498 4 s. 40 Disaster relief team distributing blankets 95 1·25
499 5 s. 50 Henri Dunant (founder) 1·10 1·50
500 7 s. 70 Blood donor 1·50 2·50

99 Female Giraffe and Calf **100** "Lentinus sajor-caju"

1989. Reticulated Giraffe. Multicoloured.

501 1 s. 20 Type **99** 1·75 30
502 3 s. 40 Giraffe drinking 3·25 2·75
503 4 s. 40 Two giraffes 3·75 3·50
504 5 s. 50 Giraffe feeding 4·50 4·50

1989. Mushrooms. Multicoloured.

506 1 s. 20 Type **100** 1·25 30
507 3 s. 40 "Agaricus bisporus" 2·00 1·75
508 4 s. 40 "Agaricus bisporus" (different) 2·25 2·25
509 5 s. 50 "Termitomyces schimperi" 3·00 3·25
510 7 s. 70 "Lentinus edodes" 3·75 4·75

101 Independence Monuments

1989. Birth Centenary of Jawaharlal Nehru (Indian statesman). Multicoloured.

511 1 s. 20 Type **101** 80 30
512 3 s. 40 Nehru with graduates and open book 2·00 1·75
513 5 s. 50 Jawaharlal Nehru 2·75 3·25
514 7 s. 70 Industrial complex and cogwheels 3·75 4·50

1989. Ceremonial Costumes (4th series). As T **45**. Multicoloured.

515 1 s. 20 Kipsigis 65 20
516 3 s. 40 Rabai 1·50 1·50
517 5 s. 50 Duruma 2·00 2·25
518 7 s. 70 Kuria 2·75 3·25
519 10 s. Bajuni 3·00 3·50

102 EMS Speedpost Letters and Parcel

1990. 10th Anniv of Pan African Postal Union. Multicoloured.

520 1 s. 20 Type **102** 15 10
521 3 s. 40 Mail runner 35 35
522 5 s. 50 Mandera Post Office 55 70
523 7 s. 70 EMS Speedpost letters and globe (vert) 80 1·60
524 10 s. P.A.P.U. logo (vert) 90 1·60

103 "Stamp King" with Tweezers and Magnifying Glass **104** Moi Golden Cup

1990. "Stamp World London '90" International Stamp Exhibition.

525 **103** 1 s. 50 multicoloured 35 10
526 – 4 s. 50 multicoloured 1·25 1·25
527 – 6 s. 50 black, red and blue 1·40 1·40
528 – 9 s. multicoloured 1·75 2·50
DESIGNS: 4 s. 50, Penny Black and Kenya Stamp Bureau postmark; 6 s. 50, Early British cancellations; 9 s. Ronald Ngala Street Post Office, Nairobi.

1990. World Cup Football Championship, Italy. Trophies. Multicoloured.

530 1 s. 50 Type **104** 50 10
531 4 s. 50 East and Central Africa Challenge Cup 1·60 1·60
532 6 s. 50 East and Central Africa Club Championship Cup 2·50 2·75
533 9 s. World Cup 2·75 3·50

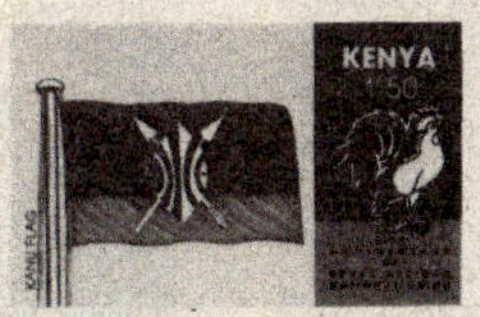

105 K.A.N.U. Flag

1990. 30th Anniv of Kenya African National Union. Multicoloured.

534 1 s. 50 Type **105** 15 10
535 2 s. 50 Nyayo Monument 15 15
536 4 s. 50 Party Headquarters 35 35
537 5 s. Jomo Kenyatta (Party founder) 40 40
538 6 s. 50 President Arap Moi 50 75
539 9 s. President Moi addressing rally 70 1·40
540 10 s. Queue of voters 80 1·40

106 Desktop Computer

1990. 125th Anniv of I.T.U. Multicoloured.

541 1 s. 50 Type **106** 15 10
542 4 s. 50 Telephone switchboard assembly, Gilgil 35 50
543 6 s. 50 "125 YEARS" 45 80
544 9 s. Urban and rural telecommunications 70 2·00

1990. 90th Birthday of Queen Elizabeth the Queen Mother. As T **134** of Ascension.

545 10 s. multicoloured 1·50 1·75
546 40 s. black and green 3·25 4·75
DESIGNS—21 × 36 mm: 10 s. Queen Mother at British Museum, 1988. 29 × 37 mm: 40 s. Queen Elizabeth at hospital garden party, 1947.

109 Kenya 1988 2 s. Definitive **110** Adult Literacy Class

1990. Cent. of Postage Stamps in Kenya. Mult.

547 1 s. 50 Type **109** 65 10
548 4 s. 50 East Africa and Uganda 1903 1 a 1·25 90
549 6 s. 50 British East Africa Co 1890 ½ a. optd on G.B. 1d. 1·75 1·75
550 9 s. Kenya and Uganda 1922 20 c. 2·25 2·75
551 20 s. Kenya, Uganda, Tanzania 1971 2 s. 50 railway commemorative 3·75 5·00

1990. International Literacy Year. Multicoloured.

552 1 s. 50 Type **110** 30 10
553 4 s. 50 Teaching by radio 1·00 90
554 6 s. 50 Technical training 1·25 1·40
555 9 s. International Literacy Year logo 2·00 3·00

111 National Flag

1991. Olympic Games, Barcelona (1992) (1st issue). Multicoloured.

556 2 s. Type **111** 30 10
557 6 s. Basketball 1·75 1·25
558 7 s. Hockey 2·00 1·75
559 8 s. 50 Table tennis 2·00 2·50
560 11 s. Boxing 2·00 2·75
See also Nos. 580/4.

112 Symbolic Man and Pointing Finger **114** Leopard

1992. AIDS Day. Multicoloured.

561 2 s. Type **112** 50 15
562 6 s. Victim and drugs 1·25 90
563 8 s. 50 Male and female symbols 1·75 2·00
564 11 s. Symbolic figure and hypodermic syringe 2·50 3·25

1992. 40th Anniv of Queen Elizabeth II's Accession. As T **143** of Ascension. Multicoloured.

565 3 s. Queen and Prince Philip with Pres. Moi 35 10
566 8 s. Marabou storks in tree 80 70
567 11 s. Treetops Hotel 90 90
568 14 s. Three portraits of Queen Elizabeth 1·10 1·25
569 40 s. Queen Elizabeth II 2·50 4·00

1992. Kenya Wildlife. Multicoloured.

570 3 s. Type **114** 75 30
571 8 s. Lion 1·50 1·50
572 10 s. Elephant 2·25 2·25
573 11 s. Buffalo 1·75 2·25
574 14 s. Black rhinoceros 3·00 3·25

115 International Harvester Safari Truck, 1926

1992. Vintage Cars. Multicoloured.

575 3 s. Type **115** 60 20
576 8 s. Fiat "509", 1924 1·50 1·10
577 10 s. Hupmobile, 1923 1·75 1·75
578 11 s. Chevrolet "Box Body", 1928 1·75 1·75
579 14 s. Bentley/Parkward, 1934 2·00 2·50

116 Kenyan Athlete winning Race

1992. Olympic Games, Barcelona (2nd issue). Mult.

580 3 s. Type **116** 55 10
581 8 s. Men's judo 1·10 1·10
582 10 s. Kenyan women's volleyball players 1·75 1·75
583 11 s. Kenyan men's 4 × 100 metres relay runners 1·75 1·75
584 14 s. Men's 10,000 metres 2·00 2·50

117 Holy Child, Joseph and Animals **118** Asembo Bay Lighthouse, Lake Victoria

1992. Christmas. Multicoloured.

585	3 s. Type **117**	20	10
586	8 s. Mary with Holy Child	55	50
587	11 s. Christmas tree	70	80
588	14 s. Adoration of the Magi	1·00	1·75

1993. Lighthouses. Multicoloured.

589	3 s. Type **118**	75	30
590	8 s. Old Ras Serani lighthouse, Mombasa	1·50	1·25
591	11 s. New Ras Serani lighthouse, Mombasa	1·75	1·60
592	14 s. Gingira, Lake Victoria	2·25	2·75

119 Superb Starling

120 Yellow-billed Hornbill

1993. Birds. Multicoloured. (a) As T **119**.

593	50 c. Type **119**	10	10
594	1 s. Red and yellow barbet	10	10
594a	1 s. 50 Lady Ross's turaco	10	10
595	3 s. Black-throated honeyguide ("Greater honeyguide")	10	10
595a	5 s. African fish eagle	10	10
596	7 s. Malachite kingfisher	15	20
597	8 s. Speckled pigeon	15	20
598	10 s. Cinnamon-chested bee eater	20	25
599	11 s. Scarlet-chested sunbird	20	25
600	14 s. Bagalafecht weaver ("Reichenow's weaver")	25	30

(b) As T **120**.

601	50 s. Type **120**	1·00	1·10
602	80 s. Lesser flamingo	1·60	1·75
603	100 s. Hadada ibis	2·00	2·10

121 Nurse bandaging Boy's Legs

123 "Ansellia africana"

122 Maendeleo House, Nairobi

1993. 17th World Congress of Rehabilitation International.

611 **121**	3 s. multicoloured	45	10
612 –	8 s. multicoloured	65	65
613 –	10 s. multicoloured	75	80
614 –	11 s. multicoloured	75	80
615 –	14 s. black, blue & orge	1·10	1·40

DESIGNS—HORIZ: 8 s. Singing group on crutches; 10 s. Vocational training; 11 s. Wheelchair race. VERT: 14 s. Congress emblem.

1994. 40th Anniv of Maendeleo Ya Wanawake Organization. Multicoloured.

616	3 s. 50 Type **122**	30	10
617	9 s. Planting saplings	50	50
618	11 s. Rural family planning clinic (vert)	60	60
619	12 s. 50 Women carrying water	75	1·00
620	15 s. 50 Improved wood-burning cooking stove (vert)	1·00	1·40

1994. Orchids. Multicoloured.

621	3 s. 50 Type **123**	60	15
622	9 s. "Aerangis luteoalba var rhodosticta"	90	75
623	12 s. 50 "Polystachya bella"	1·10	1·25
624	15 s. 50 "Brachycorythis kalbreyeri"	1·40	1·50
625	20 s. "Eulophia guineensis"	1·50	1·75

124 Emblem and K.I.C.C. Building, Nairobi

1994. 30th Anniv of African Development Bank. Multicoloured.

626	6 s. Type **124**	50	25
627	25 s. Isinya-Kajiado project	1·75	2·50

125 Kenyan Family

126 Paul Harris (founder of Rotary)

1994. International Year of the Family. Mult.

628	6 s. Type **125**	40	10
629	14 s. 50 Nurse with mother and baby	1·50	1·25
630	20 s. Schoolchildren and teacher (horiz)	1·75	1·75
631	25 s. Emblem (horiz)	2·00	2·50

1994. 50th Anniv of Rotary Club of Mombasa. Multicoloured.

632	6 s. Type **126**	25	10
633	14 s. 50 Anniversary logo	70	70
634	17 s. 50 Administering polio vaccine	1·00	1·25
635	20 s. Women at stand pipe	1·00	1·40
636	25 s. Rotary emblem	1·10	1·60

127 Donkey

128 Male Golfer in Bunker

1995. Kenya Society for Prevention of Cruelty to Animals. Multicoloured.

637	6 s. Type **127**	30	10
638	14 s. 50 Cow	45	45
639	17 s. 50 Sheep	55	75
640	20 s. Dog	1·10	1·40
641	25 s. Cat	1·25	1·60

1995. Golf. Multicoloured.

642	6 s. Type **128**	40	15
643	17 s. 50 Female golfer on fairway	1·10	1·10
644	20 s. Male golfer teeing-off	1·25	1·60
645	25 s. Head of golf club	1·40	1·75

129 Perfume Containers

1995. Kenyan Material Culture (2nd issue). Mult.

646	6 s. Type **129**	30	10
647	14 s. 50 Basketry	75	75
648	17 s. 50 Preserving pots	85	1·00
649	20 s. Gourds	1·10	1·50
650	25 s. Wooden containers	1·25	1·75

130 Tsetse Fly

131 Maize

1995. 25th Anniv of I.C.I.P.E. Insect Pests. Multicoloured.

651	14 s. Type **130**	50	30
652	26 s. Tick	80	80
653	32 s. Wild silkmoth	95	95
654	33 s. Maize borer	1·00	1·50
655	40 s. Locust	1·60	2·00

1995. 50th Anniv of F.A.O. Multicoloured.

656	14 s. Type **131**	50	30
657	28 s. Cattle	80	80
658	32 s. Chickens	95	95
659	33 s. Fisherman with catch	1·00	1·50
660	40 s. Fruit	1·60	2·00

132 Kenyan and United Nations Flags over Headquarters, Nairobi

1995. 50th Anniv of United Nations.

661 **132**	23 s. multicoloured	70	70
662 –	26 s. multicoloured	80	90
663 –	32 s. multicoloured	95	1·10
664 –	40 s. blue, red and black	1·40	2·00

DESIGNS: 26 s. Multi-racial group with emblem; 32 s. United Nations helmet; 40 s. 50th anniversary emblem.

133 Swimming

1996. Olympic Games, Atlanta (1st issue). Events and Gold Medal Winners. Multicoloured.

665	14 s. Type **133**	60	65
666	20 s. Archery	60	65
667	20 s. Weightlifting	60	65
668	20 s. Pole vault (vert)	60	65
669	20 s. Equestrian (vert)	60	65
670	20 s. Diving (vert)	60	65
671	20 s. Sprinting (vert)	60	65
672	20 s. Athlete carrying Olympic Torch (vert)	60	65
673	20 s. Hurdling (vert)	60	65
674	20 s. Kayak (vert)	60	65
675	20 s. Boxing (vert)	60	65
676	20 s. Gymnastics (vert)	60	65
677	25 s. Greg Louganis (U.S.A.) (diving, 1984 and 1988) (vert)	60	65
678	25 s. Cassius Clay (U.S.A.) (boxing, 1960) (vert)	60	65
679	25 s. Nadia Comaneci (Rumania) (gymnastics, 1980) (vert)	60	65
680	25 s. Daley Thompson (Great Britain) (decathlon, 1980 and 1984) (vert)	60	65
681	25 s. Kipchoge Keino (Kenya) (running, 1968) (vert)	60	65
682	25 s. Kornelia Enders (Germany) (swimming, 1976) (vert)	60	65
683	25 s. Jackie Joyner-Kersee (U.S.A.) (long jump, 1988) (vert)	60	65
684	25 s. Michael Jordan (U.S.A.) (basketball, 1984) (vert)	60	65
685	25 s. Shun Fujimoto (Japan) (gymnastics, 1972) (vert)	60	65
686	32 s. Javelin	65	70
687	40 s. Fencing	80	85
688	50 s. Discus	1·00	1·10

Nos. 665/7 with 686/8, 668/76 and 677/85 respectively were printed together, se-tenant, forming composite designs.

See also Nos. 702/6.

134 Lions

135 Water Buck

1996. Tourism. Multicoloured. (a) Designs as T **134**.

690	6 s. Type **134**	30	10
691	14 s. Mt. Kenya	35	30
692	20 s. Sail boards	55	70
693	25 s. Hippopotami	1·00	1·25
694	40 s. Couple in traditional dress	1·25	1·75

(b) Horiz designs as T **135**.

696	20 s. Type **135**	70	90
697	20 s. Pair of rhinoceroses	70	90
698	20 s. Cheetah	70	90
699	20 s. Group of oryx	70	90
700	20 s. Pair of giraffes	70	90
701	20 s. Monkey and bongo	70	90

136 Women's 10,000 Metres

137 Red Cross Emblem

1996. Olympic Games, Atlanta (2nd issue). Multicoloured.

702	6 s. Type **136**	20	10
703	14 s. Steeple-chasing	35	30
704	20 s. Victorious athletes with flag	60	70
705	25 s. Boxing	70	90
706	40 s. Men's 1500 metres	1·25	2·00

1996. Kenya Red Cross Society.

707 **137**	6 s. red and black	25	10
708 –	14 s. multicoloured	45	35
709 –	20 s. multicoloured	70	80
710 –	25 s. multicoloured	80	95
711 –	40 s. multicoloured	1·40	2·00

DESIGNS: 14 s. Giving blood; 20 s. Immunization; 25 s. Refugee child with food; 40 s. Cleaning the environment.

138 Impala

139 Kenya Lions Club Logo

1996. East African Wildlife Society. Multicoloured.

712	6 s. Type **138**	20	10
713	20 s. Colobus monkey	60	60
714	25 s. African elephant	1·10	1·25
715	40 s. Black rhinoceros	1·75	2·25

1996. Work of Lions Club International in Kenya. Multicoloured.

716	6 s. Type **139**	15	10
717	14 s. Eye operation	45	45
718	20 s. Two disabled children in wheelchair	70	80
719	25 s. Modern ambulance	80	1·00

140 C.O.M.E.S.A. Logo

1997. Inauguration of Common Market for Eastern and Southern Africa. Multicoloured.

720	6 s. Type **140**	15	15
721	20 s. Kenyan flag and logo	70	95

141 "Haplochromis cinctus"

1997. Endangered Species. Lake Victoria Cichlid Fishes. Multicoloured.

722	25 s. Type **141**	75	90
723	25 s. "Haplochromis" "Orange Rock Hunter"	75	90
724	25 s. "Haplochromis chilotes"	75	90
725	25 s. "Haplochromis nigricans"	75	90

142 Class 94 Diesel-electric Locomotive No. 9401, 1981

1997. Kenya Railway Locomotives. Multicoloured.

726	6 s. Type **142**	20	15
727	14 s. Class 87 diesel-electric No. 8721, 1964	40	40
728	20 s. Class 59 Garratt steam No. 5905, 1955	60	60
729	25 s. Class 57 Garratt steam No. 5701, 1939	65	70
730	30 s. Class 23 steam No. 2305, 1923	70	80
731	40 s. Class 10 steam No. 1001, 1914	90	1·25

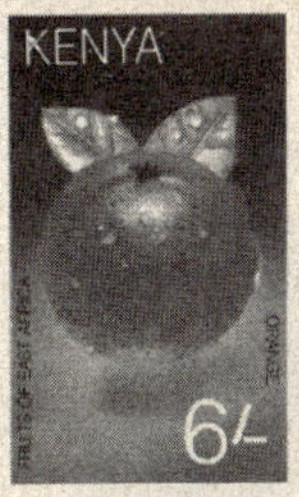

143 Orange

145 Girl Guides Anniversary Logo

144 Crocodile

1997. Fruits of East Africa. Multicoloured.

732	6 s. Type **143**	25	15
733	14 s. Pineapple	45	45
734	20 s. Mango	65	70
735	25 s. Pawpaw	70	85

1997. Local Tourist Attractions. Multicoloured.

736	10 s. Type **144**	45	25
737	27 s. Lake Bogoria hot springs	85	80
738	30 s. Warthogs	95	90
739	33 s. Windsurfing	1·00	1·10
740	42 s. Traditional huts	1·40	1·75

1997. 75th Anniv of Kenyan Girl Guides Anniversary. Multicoloured.

741	10 s. Type **145**	30	35
742	10 s. Lord Baden Powell	30	35
743	27 s. Girl guides hiking	70	75
744	27 s. Rangers in camp	70	75
745	33 s. Girl guides planting seedlings	80	90
746	33 s. Boy scouts giving first aid	80	90
747	42 s. Boy scouts in camp	90	1·00
748	42 s. Brownies entertaining the elderly	90	1·00

146 Portuguese Ships arriving at Malinda

1998. 500th Anniv of Vasco da Gama's Arrival at Malinda. Multicoloured.

749	10 s. Type **146**	30	25
750	24 s. Portuguese ships	70	70
751	33 s. Map of Africa	90	95
752	42 s. Vasco da Gama Pillar and harbour	1·00	1·25

147 Lion

1998. 18th Anniv of Pan African Postal Union. Wildlife. Multicoloured.

753	10 s. Type **147**	30	25
754	24 s. Buffalo	70	70
755	33 s. Grant's gazelle	90	95
756	42 s. Cheetah	1·40	1·50

148 Pres. Arap Moi taking Oath, 1998

1998. Daniel Arap Moi's 5th Presidential Term.

758	**148**	14 s. multicoloured	25	30

OFFICIAL STAMPS

Intended for use on official correspondence of the Kenya Government only, but there is no evidence that they were so used.

1964. Stamps of 1963 optd **OFFICIAL**.

O21	**46**	5 c. multicoloured	10
O22	–	10 c. brown	10
O23	–	15 c. mauve	1·25
O24	–	20 c. black and green	20
O25	–	30 c. black and yellow	30
O26	–	50 c. red, black and green	2·75

POSTAGE DUE STAMPS

D 3

1967.

D13	D **3**	5 c. red	15	2·50
D41		10 c. green	30	60
D42		20 c. blue	30	60
D44		30 c. brown	15	40
D45		40 c. purple	15	40
D49		50 c. green	10	10
D46		80 c. red	20	55
D50		1 s. orange	10	10
D51		2 s. violet	10	10
D52		3 s. blue	10	10
D53		5 s. red	10	10

KENYA, UGANDA AND TANGANYIKA (TANZANIA)

From 1903 joint issues were made for British East Africa (later Kenya) and Uganda. In 1933 the postal administrations of Kenya, Uganda and Tanganyika were combined.

On independence of the constituent territories in the 1960s the postal administration became the East African Posts and Telecommunications Corporation. As well as separate issues for each state (q.v.), joint commemorative issues (which however were not valid in Zanzibar) were made until the dissolution of the Corporation in 1977.

1903. 16 annas = 100 cents = 1 rupee.
1922. 100 cents = 1 shilling.

1

2

1903.

17a	**1**	½ a. green	4·25	2·75
2		1 a. grey and red	1·75	40
19a		2 a. purple	2·50	2·00
21		2½ a. blue	7·50	17·00
22a		3 a. purple and green	3·75	25·00
23		4 a. green and black	7·50	17·00
24		5 a. grey and brown	8·00	15·00
25		8 a. grey and blue	7·00	8·50
9	**2**	1 r. green	15·00	50·00
27		2 r. purple	35·00	55·00
28		3 r. green and black	50·00	90·00
29		4 r. grey and green	55·00	£120
30		5 r. grey and red	65·00	95·00
31		10 r. grey and blue	£130	£150
15		20 r. grey and stone	£425	£850
16		50 r. grey and brown	£1100	£1900

1907.

34	**1**	1 c. brown	1·40	15
35		3 c. green	7·00	40
36		6 c. red	2·75	10
37		10 c. lilac and olive	9·00	8·50
38		12 c. purple	8·00	2·75
39		15 c. blue	11·00	8·50
40		25 c. green and black	5·00	7·00
41		50 c. green and brown	11·00	12·00
42		75 c. grey and blue	4·50	32·00

1912. As T **1/2** but portraits of King George V.

44	1 c. black	30	1·60
45	3 c. green	2·00	50
46	6 c. red	70	50
47	10 c. orange	2·00	40
48	12 c. grey	2·75	50
49	15 c. blue	2·75	70
50	25 c. black & red on yellow	45	1·00
51	50 c. black and lilac	1·50	1·00
52b	75 c. black and green	6·00	6·50
53	1 r. black and green	1·75	4·00
54	2 r. red and black on blue	20·00	32·00
55	3 r. violet and green	20·00	65·00
56	4 r. red and green on yellow	45·00	£100
57	5 r. blue and purple	48·00	£120
58	10 r. red and green on green	80·00	£140
59	20 r. black & purple on red	£275	£300
60	20 r. purple & blue on blue	£275	£300
61	50 r. red and green	£500	£600
62	100 r. purple & black on red	£3250	£2250
63	500 r. green & red on green	£14000	

1919. No. 46 surch **4 cents**.

64	4 c. on 6 c. red	85	15

6

7

1922.

76	**6**	1 c. brown	80	2·25
77		5 c. violet	3·25	60
78		5 c. green	2·00	20
79		10 c. green	1·50	20
80		10 c. black	3·50	10
81a		12 c. black	2·75	25·00
82		15 c. red	1·25	10
83		20 c. orange	3·25	10
84		30 c. blue	2·00	40
85		50 c. grey	2·50	10
86		75 c. olive	3·00	8·50
87	**7**	1 s. green	3·25	2·25
88		2 s. purple	8·00	8·50
89		2 s. 50 brown	18·00	65·00
90		3 s. grey	17·00	6·00
91		4 s. grey	20·00	75·00
92		5 s. red	22·00	19·00
93		7 s. 50 orange	60·00	£140
94		10 s. blue	48·00	48·00
95		£1 black and orange	£140	£200
96		£2 green and purple	£600	
97		£3 purple and yellow	£750	
98		£4 black and mauve	£1300	
99		£5 black and blue	£1600	
100		£10 black and green	£7500	
101		£20 red and green	£14000	
102		£25 black and red	£17000	
103		£50 black and brown	£24000	
104		£75 purple and grey	£50000	
105		£100 red and black	£50000	

8 South African Crowned Cranes

9 Dhow on Lake Victoria

1935. King George V.

110	**8**	1 c. black and brown	30	1·50
111	**9**	5 c. black and green	1·50	50
112	–	10 c. black and yellow	2·50	50
113	–	15 c. black and red	85	10
114	**8**	20 c. black and orange	1·50	20
115	–	30 c. black and blue	1·50	1·25
116	**9**	50 c. purple and black	1·25	10
117	–	65 c. black and brown	2·25	2·00
118	–	1 s. black and green	75	55
119	–	2 s. red and purple	4·25	3·75
120	–	3 s. blue and black	6·00	14·00
121	–	5 s. black and red	17·00	26·00
122	**8**	10 s. purple and blue	48·00	70·00
123	–	£1 black and red	£110	£130

DESIGNS—VERT: 10 c., £1 Lion; 30 c., 5 s. Nile Railway Bridge, Ripon Falls. HORIZ: 15 c., 2 s. Kilimanjaro; 65 c. Mt. Kenya; 1 s., 3 s. Lake Naivasha.

1935. Silver Jubilee. As T **13** of Antigua.

124	20 c. blue and olive	50	10
125	30 c. brown and blue	2·50	3·00
126	65 c. green and blue	1·75	2·75
127	1 s. grey and purple	2·00	2·25

1937. Coronation. As T **2** of Aden.

128	5 c. green	20	10
129	20 c. orange	40	30
130	30 c. blue	60	1·25

15 Dhow on Lake Victoria

1938. As 1935 (except 10 c.) but with portrait of King George VI as in T **15**.

131a	**8**	1 c. black and brown	30	40
132	**15**	5 c. black and green	2·25	40
133		5 c. brown and orange	40	2·75
134	–	10 c. brown and orange	1·75	10
135	–	10 c. black and green	30	85
136	–	10 c. brown and grey	75	55
137a	–	15 c. black and red	3·50	3·50
138	–	15 c. black and green	1·40	2·75
139b	**8**	20 c. black and orange	6·00	10
140	**15**	25 c. black and red	1·25	2·00
141b	–	30 c. black and blue	2·75	10
142	–	30 c. purple and brown	1·25	40
143	**8**	40 c. black and blue	1·75	3·00
144e	**15**	50 c. purple and black	7·00	55
145a	–	1 s. black and brown	8·50	30
146b	–	2 s. red and purple	14·00	30
147b	–	3 s. blue and black	22·00	2·00
148b	–	5 s. black and red	22·00	1·00
149b	**8**	10 s. purple and blue	30·00	3·00
150ab	–	£1 black and red	16·00	15·00

DESIGN—HORIZ: 10 c. Lake Naivasha.

1941. Stamps of South Africa surch **KENYA TANGANYIKA UGANDA** and value. Alternate stamps inscr in English or Afrikaans.

151	**7**	5 c. on 1d. black and red	60	15
152	**22a**	10 c. on 3d. blue	1·00	30
153	**8**	20 c. on 6d. green & red	85	20
154	–	70 c. on 1s. brown and blue (No. 120)	9·00	40

Prices for Nos. 151/4 are for unused pairs and used singles.

1946. Victory. As T **9** of Aden.

155	20 c. orange	20	10
156	30 c. blue	20	50

1948. Silver Wedding. As T **10/11** of Aden.

157	20 c. orange	15	10
158	£1 red	35·00	48·00

1949. U.P.U. As T **20/23** of Antigua.

159	20 c. orange	20	10
160	30 c. blue	1·25	1·00
161	50 c. grey	60	20
162	1 s. brown	75	40

1952. Visit of Queen Elizabeth II (as Princess) and Duke of Edinburgh. As Nos. 135 and 145ba but inscr "ROYAL VISIT 1952".

163	10 c. black and green	10	1·25
164	1 s. black and brown	20	1·75

1953. Coronation. As T **13** of Aden.

165	20 c. black and orange	15	10

1954. Royal Visit. As No. 171 but inscr "ROYAL VISIT 1954".

166	**18**	30 c. black and blue	20	15

18 Owen Falls Dam

21 Queen Elizabeth II

20 Royal Lodge, Sagana

1954.

167	18	5 c. black and brown	20	40
168	–	10 c. red	75	10
169a	–	15 c. black and blue	55	80
170	–	20 c. black and orange	70	10
171	18	30 c. black and blue	80	10
172	–	40 c. brown	3·00	75
173	–	50 c. purple	1·25	10
174	–	65 c. green and purple	2·75	1·25
175	–	1 s. black and purple	1·00	10
176	–	1 s. 30 lilac and orange	8·00	10
177	–	2 s. black and green	4·00	70
178	–	5 s. black and orange	12·00	1·25
179	20	10 s. black and blue	18·00	2·00
180	21	£1 red and black	16·00	11·00

DESIGNS—VERT (Size as Type **18**): 10 c., 50 c. Giraffe; 20 c., 40 c., 1 s. Lion. HORIZ: 1 c., 1 s. 30, 5 s. Elephants; 65 c., 2 s. Mount Kilimanjaro.

25 Map of E. Africa showing Lakes

1958. Cent of Discovery of Lakes Tanganyika and Victoria by Burton and Speke.

181	25	40 c. blue and green	30	30
182		1 s. 30 green and purple	30	1·25

26 Sisal

29 Queen Elizabeth II

28 Mt. Kenya and Giant Plants

1960.

183	26	5 c. blue	10	15
184	–	10 c. green	10	10
185	–	15 c. purple	30	10
186	–	20 c. mauve	20	10
187	–	25 c. green	3·25	1·00
188	–	30 c. red	15	10
189	–	40 c. blue	15	10
190	–	50 c. violet	15	10
191	–	65 c. olive	30	75
192	28	1 s. violet and purple	80	10
193	–	1 s. 30 brown and red	2·00	15
194	–	2 s. indigo and blue	2·00	30
195	–	2 s. 50 olive & turquoise	3·50	2·75
196	–	5 s. red and purple	3·75	60
197	–	10 s. myrtle and green	7·50	6·00
198	29	20 s. blue and lake	16·00	16·00

DESIGNS—As Type **26**: 10 c. Cotton; 15 c. Coffee; 20 c. Blue wildebeest; 25 c. Ostrich; 30 c. Thomson's gazelle; 40 c. Manta; 50 c. Common zebra; 65 c. Cheetah. As Type **28**: 1 s. 30, Murchison Falls and hippopotamus; 2 s. Mt. Kilimanjaro and giraffe; 2 s. 50, Candelabra tree and black rhinoceros; 5 s. Crater Lake and Mountains of the Moon; 10 s. Ngorongoro Crater and African buffalo.

30 Land Tillage

1963. Freedom from Hunger.

199	30	15 c. blue and olive	10	10
200	–	30 c. brown and yellow	20	10
201	30	50 c. blue and orange	30	10
202	–	1 s. 30 brown and blue	55	1·75

DESIGN: 30 c., 1 s. 30, African with corncob.

31 Scholars and Open Book

1963. Founding of East African University.

203	31	30 c. multicoloured	10	10
204		1 s. 30 multicoloured	20	20

32 Red Cross Emblem

1963. Centenary of Red Cross.

205	32	30 c. red and blue	1·00	10
206		50 c. red and brown	1·25	45

35 East African "Flags"

1964. Olympic Games, Tokyo.

207	–	30 c. yellow and purple	10	10
208	–	50 c. purple and yellow	15	10
209	35	1 s. 30 yellow, green & blue	30	10
210		2 s. 50 mauve, violet & bl	40	1·40

DESIGN—VERT: 30 c., 50 c. Chrysanthemum emblem.

36 Rally Badge

1965. 13th East African Safari Rally.

211	36	30 c. black, yellow & turq	10	10
212		50 c. black, yellow & brn	10	10
213	–	1 s. 30 green, ochre & blue	25	10
214	–	2 s. 50 green, red and blue	40	1·50

DESIGN: 1 s. 30, 2 s. 50, Cars en route.

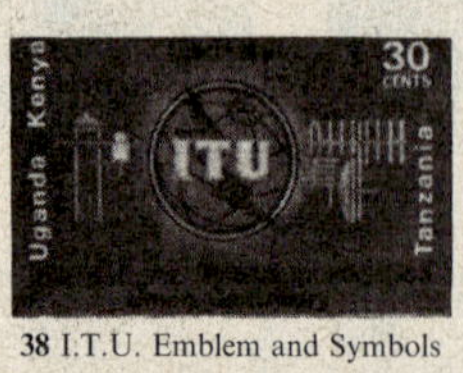

38 I.T.U. Emblem and Symbols

1965. Centenary of I.T.U. "I.T.U." and symbols in gold.

215	38	30 c. brown and mauve	20	10
216		50 c. brown and grey	20	10
217		1 s. 30 brown and blue	45	10
218		2 s. 50 brown and turquoise	90	2·25

39 I.C.Y. Emblem

1965. International Co-operation Year.

219	39	30 c. green and gold	10	10
220		50 c. black and gold	15	10
221		1 s. 30 blue and gold	30	10
222		2 s. 50 red and gold	75	2·50

40 Game Park Lodge, Tanzania

1966. Tourism. Multicoloured.

223	30 c. Type **40**	15	10
224	50 c. Murchison Falls, Uganda	50	10
225	1 s. 30 Lesser flamingoes, Lake Nakuru, Kenya	2·25	30
226	2 s. 50 Deep sea fishing, Tanzania	2·00	3·00

41 Games Emblem

1966. 8th British Empire and Commonwealth Games, Jamaica.

227	41	30 c. multicoloured	10	10
228		50 c. multicoloured	15	10
229		1 s. 30 multicoloured	20	10
230		2 s. 50 multicoloured	35	1·25

42 U.N.E.S.C.O. Emblem

1966. 20th Anniv of U.N.E.S.C.O.

231	42	30 c. black, green & red	25	10
232		50 c. black, green & brn	35	10
233		1 s. 30 black, green & grey	85	15
234		2 s. 50 black, green & yell	1·50	2·75

43 De Havilland Dragon Rapide

1967. 21st Anniv of East African Airways.

235	43	30 c. violet, blue and green	30	10
236	–	50 c. multicoloured	40	10
237	–	1 s. 30 multicoloured	85	30
238	–	2 s. 50 multicoloured	1·25	3·00

DESIGNS: 50 c. Vickers Super VC-10; 1 s. 30, Hawker Siddeley Comet 4B; 2 s. 50, Fokker Friendship.

44 Pillar Tomb

1967. Archaeological Relics.

239	44	30 c. ochre, black & purple	15	10
240	–	50 c. red, black & brown	65	10
241	–	1 s. 30 black, yellow & grn	85	15
242	–	2 s. 50 black, ochre & red	1·40	3·00

DESIGNS: 50 c. Rock painting; 1 s. 30, Clay head; 2 s. 50, Proconsul skull.

48 Unified Symbols of Kenya, Tanzania, and Uganda.

1967. Foundation of East African Community.

243	48	5 s. gold, black and grey	40	1·25

49 Mountaineering

1968. Mountains of East Africa. Multicoloured.

244	30 c. Type **49**	15	10
245	50 c. Mount Kenya	30	10
246	1 s. 30 Mount Kilimanjaro	60	10
247	2 s. 50 Ruwenzori Mountains	90	2·25

50 Family and Rural Hospital

1968. World Health Organization.

248	50	30 c. green, lilac & brown	10	10
249	–	50 c. slate, lilac and black	15	10
250	–	1 s. 30 brown, lilac & lt brown	20	15
251	–	2 s. 50 grey, black & lilac	30	1·90

DESIGNS: 50 c. Family and nurse; 1 s. 30, Family and microscope; 2 s. 50, Family and hypodermic syringe.

51 Olympic Stadium, Mexico City

1968. Olympic Games, Mexico.

252	51	30 c. green and black	10	10
253	–	50 c. green and black	15	10
254	–	1 s. 30 red, black & grey	25	15
255	–	2 s. 50 sepia and brown	35	1·25

DESIGNS—HORIZ: 50 c. High-diving boards; 1 s. 30, Running tracks. VERT: 2 s. 50, Boxing ring.

52 "Umoja" (railway ferry)

1969. Water Transport.

256	52	30 c. blue and grey	40	10
257	–	50 c. multicoloured	45	10
258	–	1 s. 30 green and blue	85	20
259	–	2 s. 50 orange and blue	1·40	3·00

DESIGNS: 50 c. S.S. "Harambee"; 1 s. 30, M.V. "Victoria"; 2 s. 50, "St. Michael".

53 I.L.O. Emblem and Agriculture

1969. 50th Anniv of Int Labour Organization.

260	53	30 c. black, green & yellow	10	10
261	–	50 c. multicoloured	10	10
262	–	1 s. 30 black, brown and orange	10	10
263	–	2 s. 50 black, blue & turq	20	90

DESIGNS—I.L.O. emblem and: 50 c. Building-work; 1 s. 30, Factory-workers; 2 s. 50, Shipping.

54 Pope Paul VI and Ruwenzori Mountains

55 Euphorbia Tree shaped as Africa, and Emblem

1969. Visit of Pope Paul VI to Uganda.

264	54	30 c. black, gold and blue	20	10
265		70 c. black, gold and red	25	10
266		1 s. 50 black, gold & blue	35	20
267		2 s. 50 black, gold & violet	50	1·40

1969. 5th Anniv of African Development Bank.

268	55	30 c. green and gold	10	10
269		70 c. green, gold & violet	15	10
270		1 s. 50 green, gold & blue	30	10
271		2 s. 50 green, gold & brown	35	1·00

56 Marimba

1970. Musical Instruments.
272 **56** 30 c. buff and brown . . . 15 10
273 – 70 c. green, brown & yell . . 25 10
274 – 1 s. 50 brown & yellow . . 50 10
275 – 2 s. 50 orange, yellow & brn 75 2·00
DESIGNS: 70 c. Amadinda; 1 s. 50, Nzomari; 2 s. 50, Adeudeu.

57 Satellite Earth Station

1970. Inauguration of Satellite Earth Station.
276 **57** 30 c. multicoloured 10 10
277 – 70 c. multicoloured 15 10
278 – 1 s. 50 black, violet & orge 25 10
279 – 2 s. 50 multicoloured . . . 55 2·25
DESIGNS: 70 c. Transmitter—daytime; 1 s. 50, Transmitter—night; 2 s 50, Earth and satellite.

58 Athlete

1970. 9th Commonwealth Games.
280 **58** 30 c. brown and black . . 10 10
281 70 c. green, brown and black 10 10
282 1 s. 50 lilac, brown and black 15 10
283 2 s. 50 blue, brown and black 20 1·25

59 "25" and U.N. Emblem

1970. 25th Anniversary of United Nations.
284 **59** 30 c. multicoloured 10 10
285 70 c. multicoloured 10 10
286 1 s. 50 multicoloured . . . 20 10
287 2 s. 50 multicoloured . . . 45 2·00

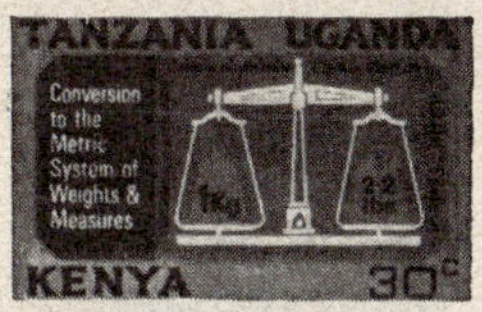

60 Balance and Weight Equivalents

1970. Conversion to Metric System. Multicoloured.
288 30 c. Type **60** 10 10
289 70 c. Fahrenheit and Centigrade thermometers 10 10
290 1 s. 50 Petrol pump and liquid capacities 15 10
291 2 s. 50 Surveyors and land measures . . . . 35 2·00

61 Class 11 Tank Locomotive

1971. Railway Transport. Multicoloured.
292 30 c. Type **61** 35 10
293 70 c. Class 90 diesel-electric locomotive 55 10
294 1 s. 50 Class 59 steam locomotive 1·25 50
295 2 s. 50 Class 30 steam locomotive 2·25 3·25

62 Syringe and Cow

1971. O.A.U. Rinderpest Campaign.
297 **62** 30 c. black, brown & grn . 10 10
298 – 70 c. black, blue & brown . 10 10
299 **62** 1 s. 50 black, purple & brn 15 10
300 – 2 s. 50 black, red & brown 25 70
DESIGN: 70 c., 2 s 50, As Type **62** but with bull facing right.

63 Livingstone meets Stanley

1971. Centenary of Livingstone and Stanley meeting at Ujiji.
301 **63** 5 s. multicoloured 30 75

64 Pres. Nyerere and Supporters

1971. 10th Anniv of Tanzanian Independence. Multicoloured.
302 30 c. Type **64** 10 10
303 70 c. Ujamaa village 15 10
304 1 s. 50 Dar-es-Salaam University 30 25
305 2 s. 50 Kilimanjaro International Airport . . . . 1·00 3·25

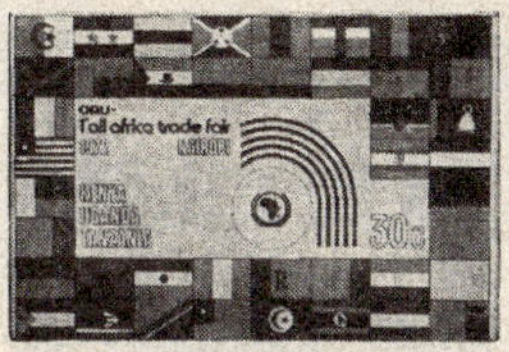

65 Flags and Trade Fair Emblem

1972. All-Africa Trade Fair.
306 **65** 30 c. multicoloured . . . 10 10
307 70 c. multicoloured . . . 10 10
308 1 s. 50 multicoloured . . . 10 10
309 2 s. 50 multicoloured . . . 25 80

66 Child with Cup

1972. 25th Anniv of U.N.I.C.E.F. Multicoloured.
310 30 c. Type **66** 10 10
311 70 c. Children with ball . . . 10 10
312 1 s. 50 Child at blackboard . . 10 10
313 2 s. 50 Child and tractor . . 25 80

67 Hurdling

1972. Olympic Games, Munich. Multicoloured.
314 40 c. Type **67** 10 10
315 70 c. Running 10 10
316 1 s. 50 Boxing 20 15
317 2 s. 50 Hockey . . . . 30 1·75

68 Ugandan Kobs

1972. 10th Anniv of Ugandan Independence. Multicoloured.
319 40 c. Type **68** 30 10
320 70 c. Conference Centre . . . 30 10
321 1 s. 50 Makerere University . . 65 30
322 2 s. 50 Coat of arms . . . . 1·00 3·25

69 Community Flag

1972. 5th Anniv of East African Community.
324 **69** 5 s. multicoloured . . . . 55 1·40

70 Run-of-the-wind Anemometer

1972. Centenary of IMO/WMO. Multicoloured.
325 40 c. Type **70** 10 10
326 70 c. Weather balloon (vert) . 15 10
327 1 s. 50 Meteorological rocket . 25 15
328 2 s. 50 Satellite receiving aerial 55 2·25

71 "Learning by Serving"

73 Police Dog-handler

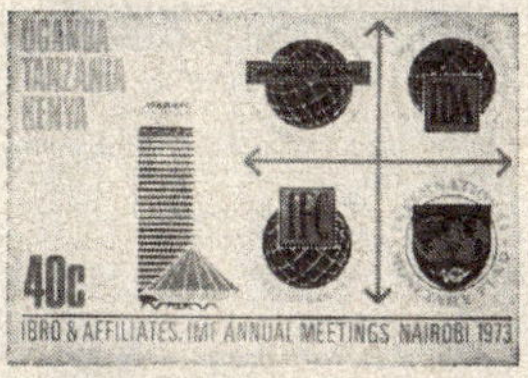

72 Kenyatta Conference Centre

1973. 24th World Scouting Conference, Nairobi.
329 **71** 40 c. multicoloured 15 10
330 – 70 c. red, violet & black . . 20 10
331 – 1 s. 50 blue, violet & black . 45 30
332 – 2 s. 50 multicoloured . . . 1·00 2·25
DESIGN: 70 c. Baden-Powell's grave, Nyeri; 1 s. 50, World Scout emblem; 2 s. 50, Lord Baden-Powell.

1973. I.M.F./World Bank Conference.
333 **72** 40 c. green, grey & black . 10 10
334 – 70 c. brown, grey & black . 10 10
335 – 1 s. 50 multicoloured . . . 25 35
336 – 2 s. 50 orange, grey & black 35 1·75
DESIGNS: Nos. 334/6 show different arrangements of Bank emblems and the Conference Centre, the 1 s. 50 being vertical.

1973. 50th Anniv of Interpol.
338 **73** 40 c. yellow, blue & black . 55 15
339 – 70 c. green, yellow & blk . 90 15
340 – 1 s. 50 violet, yellow & blk 1·50 90
341 – 2 s. 50 green, orange & blk 3·75 6·00
342 – 2 s. 50 green, orange & blk 3·75 6·00
DESIGNS: 70 c. East African policemen; 1 s. 50, Interpol emblem; 2 s. 50 (2), Interpol H.Q. No. 341 is inscribed "St. Clans" and No. 342 "St. Cloud".

74 Tea Factory

1973. 10th Anniv of Kenya's Independence. Mult.
343 40 c. Type **74** 10 10
344 70 c. Kenyatta Hospital . . . 15 10
345 1 s. 50 Nairobi Airport . . . 50 20
346 2 s. 50 Kindaruma hydro-electric scheme . . . . 65 1·75

75 Party H.Q.

1973. 10th Anniv of Zanzibar's Revolution. Mult.
347 40 c. Type **75** 10 10
348 70 c. Housing scheme 15 10
349 1 s. 50 Colour T.V. 35 30
350 2 s. 50 Amaan Stadium . . . . 70 2·50

76 "Symbol of Union"

1974. 10th Anniv of Tanganyika–Zanzibar Union. Multicoloured.
351 40 c. Type **76** 10 10
352 70 c. Handclasp and map . . 20 10
353 1 s. 50 "Communications" . . 40 30
354 2 s. 50 Flags of Tanu, Tanzania and Afro-Shirazi Party . . 80 2·50

77 East African Family ("Stability of the Home")

1974. 17th Social Welfare Conference, Nairobi.
355 **77** 40 c. yellow, brown & blk . 10 10
356 – 70 c. multicoloured 15 10
357 – 1 s. 50 yellow, green & blk 30 30
358 – 2 s. 50 red, violet & black . 1·25 2·00
DESIGNS: 70 c. Dawn and drummer (U.N. Second Development Plan); 1 s. 50, Agricultural scene (Rural Development Plan); 2 s. 50, Transport and telephone ("Communications").

78 New Postal H.Q., Kampala

1974. Centenary of U.P.U. Multicoloured.
359 40 c. Type **78** 10 10
360 70 c. Mail-train and post-van 20 10
361 1 s. 50 U.P.U. Building, Berne 15 20
362 2 s. 50 Loading mail into Vickers Super VC-10 . . . . 55 1·50

79 Family-planning Clinic

1974. World Population Year.
363 **79** 40 c. multicoloured 10 10
364 – 70 c. mauve and red . . . 10 10
365 – 1 s. 50 multicoloured . . . 15 20
366 – 2 s. 50 blue, emerald and green . . . . 30 1·90
DESIGNS: 70 c. "Tug of War"; 1 s. 50, "Population scales"; 2 s. 50, W.P.Y. emblem.

80 Seronera Wildlife Lodge, Tanzania

1975. East African Game Lodges. Multicoloured.
367 40 c. Type **80** 15 10
368 70 c. Mweya Safari Lodge, Uganda 20 10
369 1 s. 50 "Ark"—Aberdare Forest Lodge, Kenya 35 30
370 2 s. 50 Paraa Safari Lodge, Uganda . . . . 80 2·25

81 Kitana (wooden comb), Bajun of Kenya

83 Ahmed ("Presidential" Elephant)

82 International Airport, Entebbe

1975. African Arts. Multicoloured.

371	50 c. Type **81**	10	10
372	1 s. Earring, Chaga of Tanzania	15	10
373	2 s. Okoco (armlet), Acholi of Uganda	35	70
374	3 s. Kitete, Kamba gourd, Kenya	65	1·40

1975. O.A.U. Summit Conf, Kampala. Mult.

375	50 c. Type **82**	30	10
376	1 s. Map of Africa and flag (vert)	30	10
377	2 s. Nile Hotel, Kampala	40	85
378	3 s. Martyrs' Shrine, Namugongo (vert)	50	1·60

1975. Rare Animals. Multicoloured.

379	50 c. Type **83**	50	10
380	1 s. Albino buffalo	50	10
381	2 s. Ahmed in grounds of National Museum	1·60	1·50
382	3 s. Abbott's duiker	1·60	3·00

84 Maasai Manyatta (village), Kenya

1975. 2nd World Black and African Festival of Arts and Culture, Nigeria (1977). Multicoloured.

383	50 c. Type **84**	15	10
384	1 s. "Heartbeat of Africa" (Ugandan Dancers)	20	10
385	2 s. Makonde sculpture, Tanzania	65	85
386	3 s. "Early Man and Technology" (Skinning animal)	95	1·40

85 Fokker Friendship at Nairobi Airport

1975. 30th Anniv of East African Airways. Multicoloured.

387	50 c. Type **85**	1·00	30
388	1 s. Douglas DC-9 at Kilimanjaro Airport	1·10	30
389	2 s. Vickers Super VC-10 at Entebbe Airport	3·50	3·00
390	3 s. East African Airways crest	3·75	3·75

Further commemorative sets were released during 1976–78 using common designs, but each inscribed for one republic only. See Kenya, Tanzania and Uganda.

Co-operation between the postal services of the three member countries virtually ceased after 30 June 1977. The postal services of Kenya, Tanzania and Uganda then operated independently.

OFFICIAL STAMPS

For use on official correspondence of the Tanganyika Government only.

1959. Stamps of 1954 optd **OFFICIAL**.

O 1	18	5 c. black and brown	10	40
O 2	–	10 c. red	15	40
O 3	–	15 c. black and blue	30	50
O 4	–	20 c. black and orange	20	20
O 5	18	30 c. black and blue	15	30
O 6	–	50 c. purple	20	20
O 7	–	1 s. black and red	20	30
O 8	–	1 s. 30 orange and lilac	1·90	1·00
O 9	–	2 s. black and green	1·25	1·00
O10	–	5 s. black and orange	3·00	2·25
O11	20	10 s. black and blue	2·00	2·75
O12	21	£1 red and black	6·50	12·00

1960. Stamps of 1960 optd **OFFICIAL**.

O13	26	5 c. blue	10	65
O14	–	10 c. green	10	55
O15	–	15 c. purple	10	65
O16	–	20 c. mauve	10	10
O17	–	30 c. red	10	10
O18	–	50 c. violet	30	30
O19	28	1 s. violet and purple	30	10
O20	–	5 s. red and purple	8·50	65

POSTAGE DUE STAMPS

D 1

D 2

1923.

D1	D 1	5 c. violet	2·50	40
D2		10 c. red	2·00	15
D3		20 c. green	2·00	2·75
D4		30 c. brown	15·00	14·00
D5		40 c. blue	6·00	13·00
D6		1 s. green	45·00	90·00

1935.

D 7	D 2	5 c. violet	2·75	1·50
D 8		10 c. red	30	40
D 9	D 2	20 c. green	30	40
D10		30 c. brown	70	50
D11		40 c. blue	1·50	3·00
D12		1 s. grey	18·00	19·00

KING EDWARD VII LAND

Stamp issued in connection with the Shackleton Antarctic Expedition in 1908. The expedition landed at Cape Royds in Victoria Land, instead of King Edward VII Land the intended destination.

1908. Stamp of New Zealand optd **KING EDWARD VII LAND**.

A1	42	1d. red	£400	35·00

KIRIBATI

This group of islands in the Pacific, formerly known as the Gilbert Islands, achieved independence on 12 July 1979 and was renamed Kiribati.

100 cents = 1 dollar

15 National Flag

1979. Independence. Multicoloured.

84	10 c. Type **15**	10	25
85	45 c. Houses of Parliament and Maneaba ni Maungatabu (House of Assembly)	20	65

16 "Teraaka" (training ship)

1979. Multicoloured.

86	1 c. Type **16**	10	75
122	3 c. "Tautunu" (inter-island freighter)	15	30
88	5 c. Hibiscus	10	20
89	7 c. Catholic Cathedral, Tarawa	10	20
90	10 c. Maneaba, Bikenibeu	10	20
91	12 c. Betio Harbour	15	20
92	15 c. Eastern reef heron	35	25
93	20 c. Flamboyant tree	20	25
129	25 c. Moorish idol (fish)	30	30
95	30 c. Frangipani	25	30
96	35 c. G.I.P.C. Chapel, Tangintebu	25	30
97	50 c. "Hypolimnas bolina" (butterfly)	75	55
98	$1 "Tabakea" (Tarawa Lagoon ferry)	70	75
99	$2 Evening scene	70	80
135	$5 National flag	1·40	4·50

17 Gilbert and Ellice Islands 1911 ½d. Stamp

18 Boy with Giant Clam Shell

1979. Death Cent of Sir Rowland Hill. Mult.

100	10 c. Type **17**	10	10
101	20 c. Gilbert & Ellice Islands 1956 2s. 6d. definitive	15	20
102	25 c. G.B. Edward VII 2s. 6d.	15	20
103	45 c. Gilbert and Ellice Islands 1924 10s.	25	35

1979. International Year of the Child. Mult.

105	10 c. Type **18**	10	10
106	20 c. Child climbing coconut palm (horiz)	10	10
107	45 c. Girl reading	15	20
108	$1 Child in traditional costume	30	50

19 Downrange Station, Christmas Island

1980. Satellite Tracking. Multicoloured.

109	25 c. Type **19**	10	10
110	45 c. Map showing satellite trajectory	15	15
111	$1 Rocket launch, Tanegashima, Japan (vert)	30	35

20 T.S. "Teraaka"

1980. "London 1980" Int Stamp Exhibition. Mult.

112	12 c. Type **20**	15	10
113	25 c. Loading Air Tungaru Britten Norman Islander, Bonriki Airport	15	10
114	30 c. Radio operator	15	10
115	$1 Bairiki Post Office	20	35

21 "Achaea janata"

1980. Moths. Multicoloured.

117	12 c. Type **21**	10	10
118	25 c. "Ethmia nigroapicella"	15	15
119	30 c. "Utetheisa pulchelloides"	15	15
120	50 c. "Anua coronata"	25	25

22 Captain Cook Hotel

1980. Development. Multicoloured.

136	10 c. Type **22**	10	10
137	20 c. Sports stadium	10	10
138	25 c. International Airport, Bonriki	15	10
139	35 c. National Library and Archives, Bairiki	15	10
140	$1 Otintai Hotel, Bikenibeu	20	40

23 "Acalypha godseffiana"

1981. Flowers. Multicoloured.

141	12 c. Type **23**	10	10
142	30 c. "Hibiscus schizopetalus"	15	15
143	35 c. "Calotropis gigantea"	15	15
144	50 c. "Euphorbia pulcherrima"	20	20

25 Maps of Abaiang and Marakei, and String Figures

1981. Islands (1st series). Multicoloured.

145	12 c. Type **25**	15	10
146	30 c. Maps of Little Makin and Butaritari, and village house	20	10
147	35 c. Map of Maiana and coral road	25	15
148	$1 Map of Christmas Island, and Captain Cook's H.M.S. "Resolution"	70	75

See also Nos. 201/4, 215/18, 237/40, 256/60 and 270/3.

26 "Katherine"

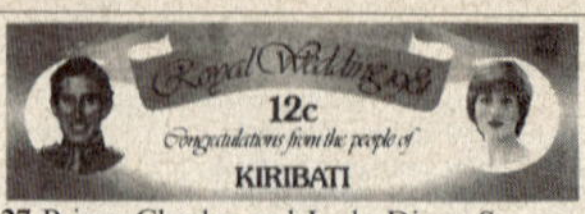

27 Prince Charles and Lady Diana Spencer (½-size illustration)

1981. Royal Wedding. Royal Yachts. Multicoloured.

149	12 c. Type **26**	10	15
150	12 c. Type **27**	20	30
151	50 c. "Osborne"	25	40
152	50 c. Type **27**	50	75
153	$2 "Britannia"	35	80
154	$2 Type **27**	1·50	2·50

28 Tuna Bait Breeding Centre, Bonriki Fish Farm

1981. Tuna Fishing Industry. Multicoloured.

158	12 c. Type **28**	15	10
159	30 c. Tuna fishing	25	20
160	35 c. Cold storage, Betio	25	25
161	50 c. Government Tuna Fishing Vessel "Nei Manganibuka"	50	50

29 Pomarine Skua

1982. Birds. Multicoloured.

163	1 c. Type **29**	15	15
164	2 c. Mallard	15	15
165	4 c. Collared petrel	20	20
166	5 c. Blue-faced booby	20	20
167	7 c. Friendly quail dove	20	20
168	8 c. Common shoveler	20	20
169	12 c. Polynesian reed warbler	20	20
170	15 c. American golden plover	25	25
171	20 c. Eastern reef heron	30	30
171a	25 c. Common noddy	3·00	1·50
172	30 c. Brown booby	30	30
173	35 c. Audubon's shearwater	30	35
174	40 c. White-throated storm petrel (vert)	35	40
175	50 c. Bristle-thighed curlew (vert)	40	45
175a	55 c. White tern (vert)	11·00	15·00
176	$1 Kuhl's lory (vert)	70	55
177	$2 Long-tailed koel (vert)	90	75
178	$5 Great frigate bird (vert)	1·75	1·75

30 Riley Turbo Skyliner

1982. Air. Inaug of Tungaru Airline. Mult.

179	12 c. Type **30**	15	10
180	30 c. Britten Norman "short nose" Trislander	20	20
181	35 c. Casa-212 Aviocar	20	25
182	50 c. Boeing 727-200	30	35

No. 179 is inscr "De Havilland DH114 Heron" in error.

31 Mary of Teck, Princess of Wales, 1893

1982. 21st Birthday of Princess of Wales. Mult.

183	12 c. Type **31**	10	10
184	50 c. Coat of arms of Mary of Teck	20	20
185	$1 Diana, Princess of Wales	30	35

1982. Birth of Prince William of Wales. Nos. 183/5 optd **ROYAL BABY**.

186	12 c. Type **31**	10	10
187	50 c. Coat of arms of Mary of Teck	25	25
188	$1 Diana, Princess of Wales	40	45

32 First Aid Practice

1982. 75th Anniv of Boy Scout Movement. Mult.

189	12 c. Type **32**	20	15
190	25 c. Boat repairs	20	30
191	30 c. On parade	25	35
192	40 c. Gilbert Islands 1977 8 c. Scouting stamp and "75"	25	60

33 Queen and Duke of Edinburgh with Local Dancer

1982. Royal Visit. Multicoloured.

193	12 c. Type **33**	15	15
194	25 c. Queen, Duke of Edinburgh and outrigger canoe	20	20
195	35 c. New Philatelic Bureau building	30	30

34 "Obaia, The Feathered" (Kiribati legend)

1983. Commonwealth Day. Multicoloured.

197	12 c. Type **34**	10	10
198	30 c. Robert Louis Stevenson Hotel, Abemama	15	20
199	50 c. Container ship off Betio	15	25
200	$1 Map of Kiribati	20	50

1983. Island Maps (2nd series). As T **25**. Mult.

201	12 c. Beru, Nikunau and canoe	20	15
202	25 c. Abemama, Aranuka, Kuria and fish	20	20
203	35 c. Nonouti and reef fishing (vert)	25	35
204	50 c. Tarawa and House of Assembly (vert)	30	50

35 Collecting Coconuts

1983. Copra Industry. Multicoloured.

205	12 c. Type **35**	25	20
206	25 c. Selecting coconuts for copra	45	35
207	30 c. Removing husks	45	40
208	35 c. Drying copra	45	45
209	50 c. Loading copra at Betio	50	55

36 War Memorials

1983. 40th Anniv of Battle of Tarawa. Multicoloured.

210	12 c. Type **36**	15	15
211	30 c. Maps of Tarawa and Pacific Ocean	25	30
212	35 c. Gun emplacement	25	35
213	50 c. Modern and war-time landscapes	35	55
214	$1 Aircraft carrier U.S.S. "Tarawa"	55	75

1983. Island Maps (3rd series). As T **25**. Mult.

215	12 c. Teraina and Captain Fanning's ship "Betsey", 1798	25	15
216	30 c. Nikumaroro and hawksbill turtle	30	35
217	35 c. Kanton and local postmark	35	40
218	50 c. Banaba and flying fish	40	55

37 Tug "Riki"

1984. Kiribati Shipping Corporation. Mult.

219	12 c. Type **37**	50	15
220	35 c. Ferry "Nei Nimanoa"	75	35
221	50 c. Ferry "Nei Tebaa"	1·10	60
222	$1 Cargo ship "Nei Momi"	1·50	1·10

38 Water and Sewage Schemes

1984. "Ausipex" International Stamp Exhibition, Melbourne. Multicoloured.

224	12 c. Type **38**	20	15
225	30 c. "Nouamake" (game fishing boat)	25	30
226	35 c. Overseas training schemes	25	40
227	50 c. International communications link	35	55

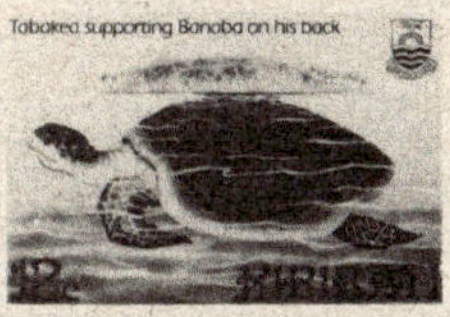

39 "Tabakea supporting Banaba"

1984. Kiribati Legends (1st series). Multicoloured.

228	12 c. Type **39**	15	20
229	30 c. "Nakaa, Judge of the Dead"	20	35
230	35 c. "Naareau and Dragonfly"	20	45
231	50 c. "Whistling Ghosts"	30	55

See also Nos. 245/8.

40 Sail-finned Tang

1985. Reef Fishes. Multicoloured.

232	12 c. Type **40**	60	25
233	25 c. Picasso triggerfish	1·00	65
234	35 c. Clown surgeonfish	1·25	85
235	80 c. Red squirrelfish	2·00	2·50

1985. Island Maps (4th series). As T **25**. Mult.

237	12 c. Tabuaeran and great frigate bird	75	15
238	35 c. Rawaki and germinating coconuts	1·40	40
239	50 c. Arorae and xanthid crab	1·60	65
240	$1 Tamana and fish hook	2·25	1·25

41 Youths playing Football on Beach

1985. International Youth Year. Multicoloured.

241	15 c. Type **41**	75	55
242	35 c. Logos of I.Y.Y. and Kiribati Youth Year	1·10	1·25
243	40 c. Girl preparing food (vert)	1·25	1·60
244	55 c. Map illustrating Kiribati's youth exchange links	1·40	2·25

1985. Kiribati Legends (2nd series). As T **39**. Mult.

245	15 c. "Nang Kineia and the Tickling Ghosts"	50	30
246	35 c. "Auriaria and Tituabine"	85	85
247	40 c. "The first coming of Babai at Arorae"	1·00	1·25
248	55 c. "Riiki and the Milky Way"	1·25	1·75

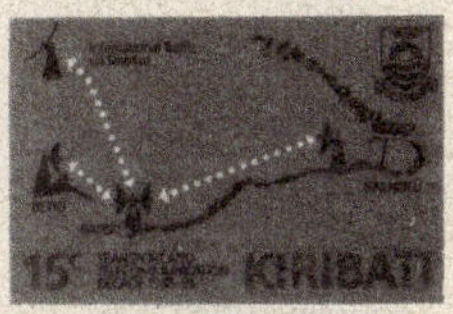

42 Map showing Telecommunications Satellite Link

1985. Transport and Telecommunications Decade (1st issue). Multicoloured.

249	15 c. Type **42**	1·50	1·00
250	40 c. M. V. "Moanaraoi" (Tarawa–Suva service)	2·75	3·00

See also Nos. 268/9, 293/4 and 314/15.

1986. 60th Birthday of Queen Elizabeth II. As T **110** of Ascension. Multicoloured.

251	15 c. Princess Elizabeth in Girl Guide uniform, Windsor Castle, 1938	15	15
252	35 c. At Trooping the Colour, 1980	20	30
253	40 c. With Duke of Edinburgh in Kiribati, 1982	20	35
254	55 c. At banquet, Austrian Embassy, London, 1966	25	50
255	$1 At Crown Agents Head Office, London, 1983	45	1·25

1986. Island Maps (5th series). As T **25**. Mult.

256	15 c. Manra and coconut crab	1·75	65
257	30 c. Birnie and McKean Islands and cowrie shells	2·50	1·60
258	35 c. Orona and red-footed booby	3·00	1·90
259	40 c. Malden Island and whaling ship, 1844	3·00	2·50
260	55 c. Vostok, Flint and Caroline Islands and Bellingshausen's "Vostok", 1820	3·00	3·25

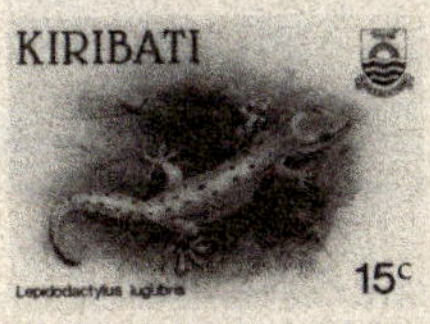

43 "Lepidodactylus lugubris"

1986. Geckos. Multicoloured.

261	15 c. Type **43**	1·00	70
262	35 c. "Gehyra mutilata"	1·75	1·50
263	40 c. "Hemidactylus frenatus"	1·90	1·75
264	55 c. "Gehyra oceanica"	2·25	2·50

See also Nos. 274/7.

44 Maps of Australia and Kiribati

46 Henri Dunant (founder)

45 Freighter "Moamoa"

1986. America's Cup Yachting Championship. Multicoloured.

265	15 c. Type **44**	20	65
266	55 c. America's Cup and map of course	50	1·25
267	$1.50 "Australia II" (1983 winner)	1·25	1·50

1987. Transport and Telecommunications Decade (2nd issue). Multicoloured.

268	30 c. Type **45**	2·25	2·25
269	55 c. Telephone switchboard and automatic exchange	3·25	3·50

1987. Island Maps (6th series). As T **25**. Multicoloured.

270	15 c. Starbuck and red-tailed tropic bird	55	50
271	30 c. Enderbury and white tern	65	55
272	55 c. Tabiteuea and pandanus tree	65	80
273	$1 Onotoa and okai (house)	70	1·75

1987. Skinks. As T **43**. Multicoloured.

274	15 c. "Emoia nigra"	15	20
275	35 c. "Cryptoblepharus sp."	20	35
276	40 c. "Emoia cyanura"	25	45
277	$1 "Lipinia noctua"	40	1·00

1987. Royal Ruby Wedding. Nos. 251/5 optd **40TH WEDDING ANNIVERSARY**.

279	15 c. Princess Elizabeth in Girl Guide uniform, Windsor Castle, 1938	15	25
280	35 c. At Trooping the Colour, 1980	20	30
281	40 c. With Duke of Edinburgh in Kiribati, 1982	25	35
282	55 c. At banquet, Austrian Embassy, London, 1966	30	45
283	$1 At Crown Agents Head Office, London, 1983	50	1·25

1988. 125th Anniv of Int Red Cross. Mult.

284	15 c. Type **46**	70	55
285	35 c. Red Cross workers in Independence parade, 1979	1·10	1·25
286	40 c. Red Cross workers with patient	1·25	1·40
287	55 c. Gilbert & Ellice Islands 1970 British Red Cross Centenary 10 c. stamp	1·60	1·75

47 Causeway built by Australia

1988. Bicent of Australian Settlement and "Sydpex '88" National Stamp Exn, Sydney. Mult.

288	15 c. Type **47**	25	20
289	35 c. Capt. Cook and Pacific map	60	60
290	$1 Obverse of Australian $10 Bicentenary banknote	1·25	1·75
291	$1 Reverse of $10 Bicentenary banknote	1·25	1·75

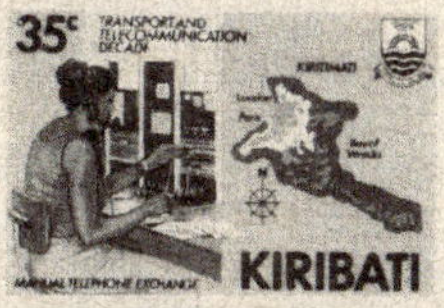

48 Manual Telephone Exchange and Map of Kiritimati

1988. Transport and Telecommunications Decade (3rd issue). Multicoloured.

293	35 c. Type **48**	75	75
294	45 c. Betio–Bairiki Causeway	1·00	1·00

49 "Hound" (brigantine), 1835

1989. Nautical History (1st series). Multicoloured.

295	15 c. Type **49**	90	55
296	30 c. "Phantom" (brig), 1854	1·50	1·10
297	40 c. H.M.S. "Alacrity" (schooner), 1873	1·60	1·60
298	$1 "Charles W. Morgan" (whaling ship), 1851	3·00	3·75

See also Nos. 343/7 and 523/6.

50 Eastern Reef Heron

51 House of Assembly

1989. Birds with Young. Multicoloured.

299	15 c. Type **50**	1·00	1·25
300	15 c. Eastern reef heron chicks in nest	1·00	1·25
301	$1 White-tailed tropic bird	2·25	3·00
302	$1 Young white-tailed tropic bird	2·25	3·00

Nos. 299/300 and 301/2 were each printed together, se-tenant, each pair forming a composite design.

1989. 10th Anniv of Independence. Mult.

303	15 c. Type **51**	25	25
304	$1 Constitution	1·25	1·75

1989. 20th Anniv of First Manned Landing on Moon. As T **126** of Ascension. Multicoloured.

305	20 c. "Apollo 10" on launch gantry	30	30
306	50 c. Crew of "Apollo 10" (30 × 30 mm)	70	90
307	60 c. "Apollo 10" emblem (30 × 30 mm)	80	1·00
308	75 c. "Apollo 10" splashdown, Hawaii	95	1·25

1989. "Philexfrance 89" International Stamp Exhibition, Paris and "World Stamp Expo '89", Washington. As T **127** of Ascension showing Statue of Liberty. Multicoloured.

311	35 c. Examining fragment of Statue	1·10	1·40
312	35 c. Workman drilling Statue	1·10	1·40
313	35 c. Surveyor with drawing	1·10	1·40

52 Telecommunications Centre

1989. Transport and Telecommunications Decade (4th issue). Multicoloured.

314	30 c. Type **52**	1·50	1·25
315	75 c. "Mataburo" (inter-island freighter)	3·00	3·75

1989. "Melbourne Stampshow '89". Nos. 301/2 optd with Exhibition emblem showing tram.
316 $1 White-tailed tropic bird . . 2·75 3·25
317 $1 Young white-tailed tropic bird 5·50 6·50

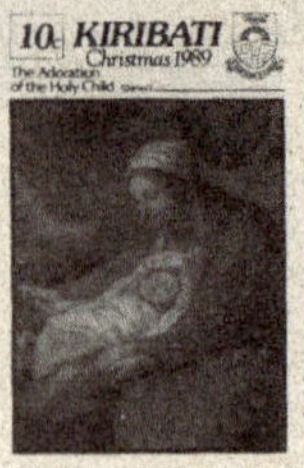

54 Virgin and Child (detail, "The Adoration of the Holy Child" (Denys Calvert)

1989. Christmas. Paintings. Multicoloured.
318 10 c. Type **54** 65 30
319 15 c. "The Adoration of the Holy Child" (Denys Calvert) . . . 85 40
320 55 c. "The Holy Family and St. Elizabeth" (Rubens) . . . . 2·50 1·25
321 $1 "Madonna with Child and Maria Magdalena" (School of Correggio) . . . . 3·75 6·00

55 Gilbert and Ellice Islands 1912 1d. and G.B. Twopence Blue Stamps

1990. 150th Anniv of the Penny Black and "Stamp World London 90" International Stamp Exhibition. Multicoloured.
322 15 c. Type **55** 90 55
323 50 c. Gilbert and Ellice Islands 1911 ½d. and G.B. Penny Black 2·25 2·25
324 60 c. Kiribati 1982 1 c. bird and G.B. 1870 ½d. . . . . . . 2·25 2·25
325 $1 Gilbert Islands 1976 1 c. ship and G.B. 1841 1d. brown . 2·75 3·25

56 Blue-barred Orange Parrotfish

1990. Fishes. Multicoloured.
326 1 c. Type **56** 30 60
327 5 c. Honeycomb grouper . . . 45 60
328 10 c. Blue-finned trevally . . . 55 70
329 15 c. Hump-backed snapper . . 70 40
330 20 c. Variegated emperor . . . 75 60
356 23 c. Bennett's pufferfish . . . 70 70
331 25 c. Rainbow runner 80 65
332 30 c. Black-saddled coral grouper 90 65
333 35 c. Great barracuda . . . . 1·00 75
334 40 c. Convict tang . . . . . . 1·00 80
335 50 c. Violet squirrelfish . . . 1·25 90
336 60 c. Stocky hawkfish . . . . 1·75 1·40
337 75 c. Pennant coralfish . . . . 1·90 1·60
338 $1 Common blue-striped snapper ("Yellow and blue sea perch") 2·25 1·90
339 $2 Sailfish . . . . 3·25 4·50
340 $5 White-tipped reef shark . . 6·50 9·50

1990. 90th Birthday of Queen Elizabeth the Queen Mother. As T **134** of Ascension.
341 75 c. multicoloured . . . . . 1·25 1·50
342 $2 black and green . . . . . 2·75 3·50
DESIGNS—21 × 36 mm: 75 c. Queen Elizabeth the Queen Mother. 29 × 37 mm: $2 King George VI and Queen Elizabeth with air raid victim, London, 1940.

1990. Nautical History (2nd series). As T **49**. Multicoloured.
343 15 c. "Herald" (whaling ship), 1851 . . . . 75 55
344 50 c. "Belle" (barque), 1849 . 1·50 1·50
345 60 c. "Supply" (schooner), 1851 1·75 2·25
346 75 c. "Triton" (whaling ship), 1848 . . . . 1·75 2·25

57 Manta

1991. Endangered Species. Fishes. Multicoloured.
348 15 c. Type **57** . . . . 1·10 55
349 20 c. Manta (different) . . . . 1·25 90
350 30 c. Whale shark . . . . . . 1·75 2·00
351 35 c. Whale shark (different) . 2·00 2·25

1991. 65th Birthday of Queen Elizabeth II and 70th Birthday of Prince Philip. As T **139** of Ascension. Multicoloured.
366 65 c. Queen Elizabeth II . . . 1·00 1·25
367 70 c. Prince Philip in R.A.F. uniform . . . . 1·00 1·25

59 Aerial View of Hospital

1991. "Phila Nippon '91" International Stamp Exhibition, Tokyo, and Opening of Tungaru Central Hospital. Multicoloured.
368 23 c. Type **59** 40 30
369 50 c. Traditional dancers . . 75 85
370 60 c. Hospital entrance . . . 85 1·10
371 75 c. Foundation stone and plaques . . . . 1·25 1·60

60 Mother and Child

1991. Christmas. Multicoloured.
373 23 c. Type **60** 60 40
374 50 c. The Holy Family in Pacific setting . . . . 1·10 90
375 60 c. The Holy Family in traditional setting . . . . . 1·25 1·50
376 75 c. Adoration of the Shepherds 1·50 2·00

1992. 40th Anniv of Queen Elizabeth II's Accession. As T **143** of Ascension. Multicoloured.
377 23 c. Kiribati village 30 30
378 30 c. Lagoon at sunset . . . 40 45
379 50 c. Tarawa waterfront . . . 60 70
380 60 c. Three portraits of Queen Elizabeth 70 90
381 75 c. Queen Elizabeth II . . . 90 1·10

1992. "EXPO '92" Worlds Fair, Seville. Nos. 356, 336/7 and 339 optd **EXPO'92 SEVILLA**.
382 23 c. Bennett's pufferfish . . . 55 40
383 60 c. Stocky hawkfish . . . . 1·25 1·50
384 75 c. Pennant coralfish . . . 1·40 1·60
385 $2 Sailfish . . . . 3·00 4·00

62 Marine Training Centre Sign

1992. 25th Anniv of Marine Training Centre. Multicoloured.
386 23 c. Type **62** 45 40
387 50 c. Cadets on parade . . . 80 90
388 60 c. Fire school 80 90
389 75 c. Lifeboat training . . . 1·10 1·40

63 Healthy Children

1992. United Nations World Health and Food and Agriculture Organizations. Multicoloured.
390 23 c. Type **63** 55 50
391 50 c. Fishing at night . . . . 1·00 1·00
392 60 c. Fruit . . . . 1·25 1·50
393 75 c. "Papuan Chief" (container ship) . . . . 1·75 2·25

64 Phoenix Petrel

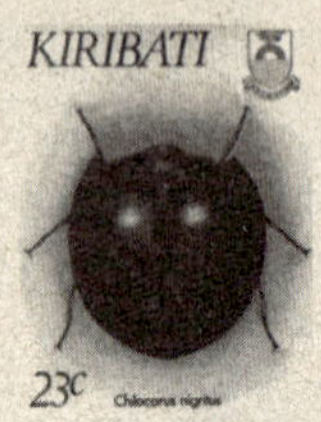

65 "Chilocorus nigritus"

1993. Birds. Multicoloured.
394 23 c. Type **64** 40 50
395 23 c. Cook's petrel 40 50
396 60 c. European pintail . . . . 90 1·10
397 60 c. Eurasian wigeon . . . . 90 1·10
398 75 c. Spectacled tern . . . . 1·00 1·25
399 75 c. Black-naped tern . . . . 1·00 1·25
400 $1 Australian stilt . . . . . 1·25 1·40
401 $1 Wandering tattler . . . . 1·25 1·40

1993. Insects. Multicoloured.
402 23 c. Type **65** 75 45
403 60 c. "Rodolia pumila" (ladybird) . . . . 1·50 1·75
404 75 c. "Rodolia cardinalis" (ladybird) . . . . 1·75 2·00
405 $1 "Cryptolaemus montrouzieri" 2·00 2·50

66 U.S. Air Reconnaissance Consolidated B-24 Liberator

1993. 50th Anniv of Battle of Tarawa. Multicoloured.
406 23 c. Type **66** 60 65
407 23 c. U.S.S. "Nautilus" (submarine) 60 65
408 23 c. U.S.S. "Indianapolis" (cruiser) 60 65
409 23 c. U.S.S. "Pursuit" (destroyer) 60 65
410 23 c. Vought Sikorsky Kingfisher spotter seaplane 60 65
411 23 c. U.S.S. "Ringgold" and "Dashiell" (destroyers) . . . 60 65
412 23 c. Sherman tank on seabed . 60 65
413 23 c. Grumman Hellcat fighter aircraft in lagoon 60 65
414 23 c. Naval wreck on seabed . . 60 65
415 23 c. First U.S. aircraft to land on Betio 60 65
416 75 c. Landing craft leaving transports . . . . 1·00 1·10
417 75 c. Marines landing on Betio . 1·00 1·10
418 75 c. Landing craft approaching beach . . . . 1·00 1·10
419 75 c. Marines pinned down in surf . . . . 1·00 1·10
420 75 c. U.S.S. "Maryland" (battleship) . . . . 1·00 1·10
421 75 c. Aerial view of Betio Island 1·00 1·10
422 75 c. U.S. Navy memorial . . 1·00 1·10
423 75 c. Memorial to expatriates . 1·00 1·10
424 75 c. Japanese memorial . . . 1·00 1·10
425 75 c. Plan of Betio Island . . . 1·00 1·10

67 Shepherds and Angels

1993. Christmas. Pacific Nativity Scenes. Mult.
426 23 c. Type **67** 30 25
427 40 c. Three Kings 55 60
428 60 c. Holy Family . . . . . . 85 1·00
429 75 c. Virgin and Child . . . . 1·10 1·40

69 Bryde's Whale and Calf

1994. Whales. Multicoloured.
432 23 c. Type **69** 75 80
433 23 c. Bryde's whale with two calves 75 80
434 40 c. Blue whale and calf (face value at left) . . . . 90 1·00
435 40 c. Blue whales and calf (face value at right) . . . . . . 90 1·00
436 60 c. Humpback whale and calf (face value at left) . . . . 1·50 2·00
437 60 c. Humpback whale and calf (face value at right) . . . . 1·50 2·00
438 75 c. Killer whale and calf . . 1·50 2·00
439 75 c. Killer whale and two calves 1·50 2·00

70 Family silhouetted on Beach

1994. 15th Anniv of Independence. Protecting the Environment. Multicoloured.
440 40 c. Type **70** 60 60
441 60 c. Fish and coral . . . . . 1·00 1·25
442 75 c. Great frigate birds in flight 1·25 1·50

71 "Diaphania indica"

72 "Nerium oleander"

1994. Butterflies and Moths. Multicoloured.
443 1 c. Type **71** 10 10
444 5 c. "Herpetogramma licarsisalis" 10 10
445 10 c. "Parotis suralis" 10 10
446 12 c. "Sufetula sunidesalis" . . 10 10
447 20 c. "Aedia sericea" 15 20
448 23 c. "Anomis vitiensis" . . . 20 25
449 30 c. "Anticarsia irrorata" . . 25 30
450 35 c. "Spodoptera litura" . . 25 30
451 40 c. "Mocis frugalis" 30 35
452 45 c. "Agrius convolvuli" . . 35 40
453 50 c. "Cephonodes picus" . . 40 45
454 55 c. "Gnathothlibus erotus" . 40 45
455 60 c. "Macroglossum hirundo" 45 50
456 75 c. "Badamia exclamationis" 55 60
457 $1 "Precis villida" 75 80
458 $2 "Danaus plexippus" . . . 1·50 1·60
459 $3 "Hypolimnas bolina" (male) 2·25 2·40
460 $5 "Hypolimnas bolina" (female) 3·75 4·00

1994. Seasonal Flowers. Multicoloured.
461 23 c. Type **72** 30 30
462 60 c. "Catharanthus roseus" . 80 1·00
463 75 c. "Ipomea pes-caprae" . . 1·00 1·25
464 $1 "Calophyllum inophyllum" 1·40 2·00

73 Gemini (The Twins)

74 Church and Traditional Meeting Hut

1995. Night Sky over Kiribati. Multicoloured.
465 50 c. Type **73** 75 70
466 60 c. Cancer (The Crab) . . . 85 90
467 75 c. Cassiopeia (The Queen of Ethiopia) . . . . 1·00 1·25
468 $1 Southern Cross . . . . . 1·25 1·75

1995. Tourism. Multicoloured.
469 30 c. Type **74** 50 60
470 30 c. Fishermen and outrigger canoes 50 60
471 30 c. Gun emplacement and map 50 60
472 30 c. Children with marine creatures 50 60
473 30 c. Sports 50 60
474 40 c. Local girls in traditional costume 55 65
475 40 c. Windsurfing 55 65
476 40 c. Fishermen and wood carver 55 65
477 40 c. Under water sport . . . 55 65
478 40 c. Women weaving 55 65

1995. 50th Anniv of End of Second World War. American Aircraft. As T **161** of Ascension. Multicoloured.
489 23 c. Grumman TBF Avenger 50 40
490 40 c. Curtiss SOC.3-1 Seagull seaplane 70 70
491 50 c. Consolidated B-24 Liberator bomber 80 80
492 60 c. Grumman G-21 Goose amphibian 95 95
493 75 c. Martin B-26 Marauder bomber . . . . 1·25 1·25
494 $1 Northrop P-61 Black Widow bomber . . . . 1·50 1·60

76 Eclectus Parrots, Great Frigate Bird and Coconut Crabs

1995. Protecting the Environment. Multicoloured.
496 60 c. Type **76** 85 95
497 60 c. Red-tailed tropic birds, common dolphin and pantropical spotted dolphin 85 95
498 60 c. Blue-striped snapper ("Yellow and blue sea perch"), blue-barred orange parrotfish and green turtle 85 95
499 60 c. Red-breasted wrasse, pennant coralfish and violet squirrelfish 85 95

1995. "Jakarta '95" Stamp Exhibition, Indonesia. Nos. 496/9 optd **JAKARTA 95** within emblem.
500 60 c. Type **76** . . . . 1·10 1·25
501 60 c. Red-tailed tropic birds, common dolphin and pantropical spotted dolphin 1·10 1·25
502 60 c. Blue-striped snapper, blue-barred orange parrotfish and green turtle . . . . 1·10 1·25
503 60 c. Red-breasted wrasse, pennant coralfish and violet squirrelfish . . . . 1·10 1·25

79 "Teanoai" (police patrol boat)

1995. Police Maritime Unit. Multicoloured.
506 75 c. Type **79** . . . . 1·40 1·50
507 75 c. "Teanoai" at sea . . . . 1·40 1·50

80 Pantropical Spotted Dolphins

1996. Dolphins. Multicoloured.
508 23 c. Type **80** 65 45
509 60 c. Spinner dolphins . . . . 1·25 1·00
510 75 c. Fraser's dolphins . . . . 1·40 1·40
511 $1 Rough-toothed dolphins . . 1·75 2·00

81 Tap and Top Left Segment of U.N.I.C.E.F. Emblem

1996. 50th Anniv of U.N.I.C.E.F. Multicoloured.
512 30 c. Type **81** 50 60
513 30 c. Documents and top right segment 50 60
514 30 c. Syringe and bottom left segment 50 60
515 30 c. Open book and bottom right segment 50 60
Nos. 512/15 were printed together, se-tenant, with each block of 4 showing the complete emblem.

84 Rathbun Red Crab

1996. Sea Crabs. Multicoloured.
518 23 c. Type **84** 40 40
519 60 c. Red and white painted crab 80 80
520 75 c. Red-spotted crab . . . . 95 1·10
521 $1 Red-spotted white crab . . 1·40 2·00

1996. Nautical History (3rd series). As T **49**. Multicoloured.
523 23 c. "Potomac" (whaling ship), 1843 . . . . 40 40
524 50 c. "Southern Cross IV" (missionary barquentine), 1891 . . . . 70 70
525 60 c. "John Williams III" (missionary barque), 1890 . . 85 90
526 $1 H.M.S. "Dolphin" (frigate), 1765 . . . . 1·25 1·60

1997. "Pacific '97" International Stamp Exhibition, San Francisco. Nos. 489/94 optd **PACIFIC 97 World Philatelic Exhibition San Francisco, California 29 May - 8 June.**
528 23 c. Type **75** 40 35
529 40 c. Curtiss SOC.3-1 Seagull seaplane 60 55
530 50 c. Consolidated B-24 Liberator bomber 70 70
531 60 c. Grumman G-21 Goose amphibian 80 80
532 75 c. Martin B-26 Marauder bomber . . . . 90 1·00
533 $1 Northrop P-61 Black Widow bomber . . . . 1·10 1·25

87 Queen Elizabeth II in 1996 **88** Young Rock Dove

1997. Golden Wedding of Queen Elizabeth and Prince Philip. Multicoloured.
535 50 c. Type **87** 80 90
536 50 c. Prince Philip carriage-driving at Windsor Horse Show 80 90
537 60 c. Queen in phaeton at Trooping the Colour . . . 90 1·00
538 60 c. Prince Philip on Montserrat, 1993 . . . . . 90 1·00
539 75 c. Queen Elizabeth and Prince Philip, 1989 . . . . . . 1·00 1·25
540 75 c. Prince Edward on horseback . . . . 1·00 1·25
Nos. 535/6, 537/8 and 539/40 respectively were printed together, se-tenant, with the backgrounds forming composite designs.

1997. Birds. Multicoloured.
542 50 c. Type **88** 75 80
543 50 c. Adult rock dove 75 80
544 60 c. Adult Pacific pigeon . . 80 90
545 60 c. Young Pacific pigeon . . 80 90
546 75 c. Adult Micronesian pigeon 90 1·00
547 75 c. Young Micronesian pigeon 90 1·00

1997. "ASIA '97" Stamp Exhibition, Bangkok. Nos. 542/3 and 546/7 optd **ASIA '97 KIRIBATI 5 - 14 OCTOBER** and elephant.
548 50 c. Type **88** 75 80
549 50 c. Adult rock dove 75 80
550 75 c. Adult Micronesian pigeon 90 1·00
551 75 c. Young Micronesian pigeon 90 1·00

90 Spiny Lobster

1998. Endangered Species. Spiny Lobster. Multicoloured.
552 25 c. Type **90** 30 40
553 25 c. Facing right 30 40
554 25 c. With coral in foreground 30 40
555 25 c. On sponge 30 40

91 Diana, Princess of Wales, 1992

1998. Diana, Princess of Wales Commemoration.
557 **91** 25 c. multicoloured . . . 30 40

93 Indo-Pacific Humpbacked Dolphin

1998. Whales and Dolphins. Multicoloured.
560 25 c. Type **93** 35 40
561 25 c. Bottlenose dolphin . . . 35 40
562 60 c. Short-snouted spinner dolphin 70 75
563 60 c. Risso's dolphin 70 75
564 75 c. Striped dolphin 80 90
565 75 c. Sei whale 80 90
566 $1 Fin whale . . . . 90 1·00
567 $1 Minke whale . . . . 90 1·00

95 Pollutants and Harmful Emissions

1998. The Greenhouse Effect. Multicoloured.
569 25 c. Type **95** 20 25
570 50 c. Diagram of greenhouse effect 40 45
571 60 c. Diagram of rising sea levels on Tarawa 45 50
572 75 c. Diagram of rising sea levels on Kiritimati 55 60

97 Common Shoveler ("Northern Shoveler") (male)

1999. "iBRA '99" International Stamp Exhibition, Nuremberg. Ducks. Multicoloured.
575 25 c. Type **97** 20 25
576 50 c. Common Shoveler ("Northern Shoveler") (female) and ducklings . . . 40 45
577 60 c. Green-winged teal (male) 45 50
578 75 c. Green-winged teal (female) and ducklings 55 60

OFFICIAL STAMPS

1981. Nos. 86/135 optd **O.K.G.S.**
O11 1 c. Type **16** 10 30
O12 3 c. M.V. "Tautunu" (inter-island freighter) 10 20
O13 5 c. Hibiscus 10 15
O14 7 c. Catholic Cathedral, Tarawa 10 15
O15 10 c. Maneaba, Bikenibeu . . 10 15
O16 12 c. Betio Harbour 30 30
O17 15 c. Eastern reef heron . . . 1·50 30
O18 20 c. Flamboyant tree 20 30
O19 25 c. Moorish idol (fish) . . . 30 30
O20 30 c. Frangipani 30 35
O21 35 c. G.I.P.C. Chapel, Tangintebu 35 40
O22 50 c. "Hypolimnas bolina" (butterfly) 50 55
O23 $1 "Tabakea" (Tarawa Lagoon ferry) . . . . 1·00 75
O24 $2 Evening scene . . . . . . 1·50 1·25
O25 $5 National flag . . . . . . 3·00 3·25

1983. Nos. 169, 172/3, 175 and 177 optd **O.K.G.S.**
O36 12 c. Polynesian reed warbler . . 40 30
O37 30 c. Brown booby 70 50
O38 35 c. Audubon's shearwater . . 80 60
O39 50 c. Bristle-thighed curlew . . 1·00 80
O40 $2 Long-tailed koel . . . . . 3·00 2·75

POSTAGE DUE STAMPS

D 1 Kiribati Coat of Arms

1981.
D1 **D 1** 1 c. black and mauve . . 10 10
D2 2 c. black and blue . . . 10 10
D3 5 c. black and green . . . 10 10
D4 10 c. black and brown . . 10 15
D5 20 c. black and blue . . . 15 25
D6 30 c. black and brown . . 20 35
D7 40 c. black and purple . . 25 45
D8 50 c. black and green . . 25 50
D9 $1 black and red 40 75

KISHANGARH

A state of Rajasthan, India. Now uses Indian stamps.

12 pies = 1 anna; 16 annas = 1 rupee

1

1899. Imperf or perf.
1 **1** 1 a. green . . . . 20·00 50·00
3 1 a. blue £400

2 (¼ a.) **5** (2 a.) Maharaja Sardul Singh

1899. Various arms designs. Perf or imperf.
21 **2** ¼ a. green £200 £350
22a ¼ a. red 25 40
25 ½ a. green . . . . 13·00 16·00
8 ½ a. red £1700 £1100
26a ½ a. blue 55 45
7 ½ a. lilac . . . . 95·00 £170
27 **2** 1 a. grey . . . . 4·25 2·75
29 1 a. mauve 75 90
12b 1 a. pink . . . . 50·00 £140
15 **5** 2 a. orange . . . . 4·00 4·50
31 **2** 4 a. brown . . . . 2·00 5·00
32 1 r. green . . . . 10·00 15·00
17 1 r. lilac . . . . 20·00 25·00
33 1 r. yellow £650
34 2 r. red . . . . 38·00 45·00
35 5 r. mauve . . . . 32·00 45·00

11 (½ a.) **12** Maharaja Sardul Singh

1903. Imperf or perf.
39 **11** ½ a. pink . . . . 8·00 3·00
40 **12** 2 a. orange . . . . 3·00 5·00
41 **2** 8 a. grey . . . . 5·00 7·50

13 Maharaja Madan Singh **14** Maharaja Madan Singh

1904.
42a **13** ¼ a. red 45 45
43a ½ a. brown 45 30
44a 1 a. blue . . . . 1·25 1·25
45 2 a. orange . . . . 12·00 7·00
46a 4 a. brown . . . . 10·00 13·00
47 8 a. violet . . . . 6·00 16·00
48 1 r. green . . . . 21·00 27·00
49 2 r. yellow . . . . 20·00 95·00
50 5 r. brown . . . . 21·00 £120

1912.
63 **14** ¼ a. blue 20 45
64 ½ a. green 20 80
65 1 a. red . . . . 1·00 2·50
54 2 a. purple . . . . 2·50 5·00
67 4 a. blue . . . . 6·00 8·00
68 8 a. brown . . . . 7·00 38·00
69 1 r. mauve . . . . 15·00 95·00
70 2 r. green . . . . 70·00 £180
71 5 r. brown . . . . 85·00 £350

15 **16** Maharaja Yagyanarayan Singh

1913.
59 **15** ¼ a. blue 20 80
60 2 a. purple . . . . 7·00 18·00

1928.

72	16	½ a. blue	60	2·00
73		½ a. green	2·00	1·10
74	–	1 a. red	60	1·50
75	–	2 a. purple	3·00	7·50
76	16	4 a. brown	1·25	1·75
77		8 a. violet	3·50	22·00
78		1 r. green	11·00	42·00
79		2 r. yellow	26·00	£130
80		5 r. red	30·00	£150

Nos. 74/5 are larger.

OFFICIAL STAMPS

1918. Optd **ON K S D.**

O 5	2	¼ a. green	—	£120
O 6		¼ a. pink	2·25	60
O 7		½ a. blue	£120	35·00
O 9		1 a. mauve	28·00	1·50
O10	5	2 a. orange	—	£120
O11	2	4 a. brown	40·00	16·00
O16		8 a. grey	55·00	22·00
O12		1 r. green	£120	90·00
O13		2 r. brown	—	£750
O14		5 r. mauve	—	£1400

1918. Optd **ON K S D.**

O15	12	2 a. orange	55·00	5·00

1918. Optd **ON K S D.**

O17	13	¼ a. red	—	£200
O18		½ a. brown	75	35
O19		1 a. blue	7·00	4·00
O20		2 a. orange	—	£750
O21		4 a. brown	42·00	18·00
O22		8 a. violet	£250	£150
O23		1 r. green	£475	£425
O24		5 r. brown		

1918. Optd **ON K S D.**

O28	14	¼ a. blue	50	50
O29		½ a. green	75	75
O30a		1 a. red	1·00	1·00
O31		2 a. purple	6·00	4·00
O32		4 a. blue	20·00	15·00
O33		8 a. brown	90·00	40·00
O34		1 r. mauve	£275	£275
O35		2 r. green		
O36		5 r. brown	£1200	

1918. Optd **ON K S D.**

O25	15	¼ a. blue	6·00	
O27		2 a. purple	£350	£375

For later issues see **RAJASTHAN.**

KUWAIT

An independent Arab Shaikhdom on the N.W. coast of the Persian Gulf with Indian and later British postal administration. On 1 February, 1959, the Kuwait Government assumed responsibility for running its own postal service. In special treaty relations with Great Britain until 19 June 1961 when Kuwait became completely independent.

1923. 12 pies = 1 anna; 16 annas = 1 rupee.
1957. 100 naye paise = 1 rupee.

Stamps of India optd **KUWAIT.**

1923. King George V.

16	56	½ a. green	2·25	1·40
16b	79	½ a. green	4·50	95
2	57	1 a. brown	2·25	2·25
17b	81	1 a. brown	4·50	75
3	58	1½ a. brown (No. 163)	1·50	4·25
4	59	2 a. lilac	3·25	2·25
19c		2 a. red	4·50	1·75
18	70	2 a. lilac	3·00	80
19		2 a. red	20·00	80·00
5	61	2 a. 6 p. blue	2·00	8·00
6	62	3 a. orange	4·25	18·00
20		3 a. blue	2·75	1·60
21		3 a. red	5·50	4·25
22a	63	4 a. green	5·50	12·00
22	71	4 a. green	25·00	75·00
9	64	6 a. bistre	8·50	13·00
23	65	8 a. mauve	16·00	13·00
11	66	12 a. red	14·00	38·00
12	67	1 r. brown and green	16·00	22·00
26		2 r. red and orange	10·00	60·00
27		5 r. blue and violet	75·00	£190
28		10 r. green and red	£170	£375
29		15 r. blue and olive	£475	£750

1933. Air.

31	72	2 a. green	13·00	25·00
32		3 a. blue	2·50	2·50
33		4 a. olive	85·00	£170
34		6 a. bistre	2·50	4·50

1939. King George VI.

36	91	½ a. brown	7·00	1·75
38		1 a. red	7·00	1·50
39	92	2 a. red	7·00	2·50
41	–	3 a. green	7·00	2·00
43	–	4 a. brown	35·00	14·00
44	–	6 a. green	25·00	7·50
45	–	8 a. violet	28·00	32·00
46	–	12 a. red	20·00	45·00
47	93	1 r. slate and brown	6·00	2·75
48		2 r. purple and brown	3·75	13·00
49		5 r. green and blue	12·00	18·00
50		10 r. purple and red	60·00	75·00
51		15 r. brown and green	£120	£190

1942. King George VI stamps of 1940.

52	100a	3 p. slate	1·00	2·25
53		½ a. purple	1·00	2·25
54		9 p. green	2·50	7·00
55		1 a. red	1·50	1·75
56	101	1½ a. violet	3·00	7·00
57		2 a. red	3·25	2·50
58	101	3 a. violet	3·50	3·25
59		3½ a. blue	4·00	7·00
60	102	4 a. brown	3·25	2·25
60a		6 a. green	14·00	8·50
61		8 a. violet	7·00	2·50
62		12 a. purple	7·00	3·00
63	–	14 a. purple (No. 277)	13·00	15·00

From 1948 onwards, for stamps with similar surcharges, but without name of country, see British Postal Agencies in Eastern Arabia.

Stamps of Great Britain surch **KUWAIT** and new values in Indian currency.

1948. King George VI.

64	128	½ a. on ½d. green	1·00	1·00
84		½ a. on ½d. orange	1·50	1·50
65		1 a. on 1d. red	1·00	1·00
85		1 a. on 1d. blue	1·50	85
66		1½ a. on 1½d. brown	1·50	75
86		1½ a. on 1½d. green	1·50	2·25
67		2 a. on 2d. orange	1·00	90
87		2 a. on 2d. brown	1·50	85
68		2½ a. on 2½d. blue	1·50	1·00
88		2½ a. on 2½d. red	1·50	2·25
69		3 a. on 3d. violet	1·00	30
89	129	4 a. on 4d. blue	1·25	80
70		6 a. on 6d. purple	1·00	60
71	130	1 r. on 1s. brown	2·50	1·00
72	131	2 r. on 2s. 6d. green	3·00	4·00
73		5 r. on 5s. red	5·00	4·50
73a	–	10 r. on 10s. blue (No. 478a)	38·00	6·00

1948. Silver Wedding.

74	137	2½ a. on 2½d. blue	1·25	50
75	138	15 r. on £1 blue	30·00	30·00

1948. Olympic Games.

76	139	2½ a. on 2½d. blue	1·00	1·50
77	140	3 a. on 3d. violet	1·00	1·50
78	–	6 a. on 6d. purple	1·25	1·50
79	–	1 r. on 1s. brown	1·25	1·50

1949. U.P.U.

80	143	2½ a. on 2½d. blue	90	1·75
81	144	3 a. on 3d. violet	1·25	2·25
82	–	6 a. on 6d. purple	1·40	2·25
83	–	1 r. on 1s. brown	1·60	1·25

1951. Pictorial high values.

90	147	2 r. on 2s. 6d. green	15·00	4·50
91	–	5 r. on 5s. red (No. 510)	21·00	5·00
92	–	10 r. on 10s. blue (No. 511)	29·00	6·50

1952. Queen Elizabeth II.

93	154	½ a. on ½d. orange	20	60
94		1 a. on 1d. blue	20	10
95		1½ a. on 1½d. green	15	30
96		2 a. on 2d. brown	35	10
97	155	2½ a. on 2½d. red	15	30
98		3 a. on 3d. lilac	40	10
99		4 a. on 4d. blue	1·25	75
100	157	6 a. on 6d. purple	1·25	10
101	160	12 a. on 1s. 3d. green	5·00	2·50
102		1 r. on 1s. 6d. blue	4·50	10

1953. Coronation.

103	161	2½ a. on 2½d. red	3·00	2·25
104	–	4 a. on 4d. blue	3·00	2·25
105	163	12 a. on 1s. 3d. green	4·50	3·50
106	–	1 r. on 1s. 6d. blue	4·00	80

1955. Pictorials.

107	166	2 r. on 2 s. 6d. brown	7·00	2·00
108	–	5 r. on 5s. red	7·50	4·50
109	–	10 r. on 10s. blue	8·00	4·50

1957. Queen Elizabeth II.

120	157	1 n.p. on 5d. brown	10	70
121	154	3 n.p. on ½d. orange	60	2·25
122		6 n.p. on 1d. blue	60	1·25
123		9 n.p. on 1½d. green	60	1·75
124		12 n.p. on 2d. brown	60	1·75
125	155	15 n.p. on 2½d. red	60	1·50
126		20 n.p. on 3d. lilac	60	30
127		25 n.p. on 4d. blue	2·25	3·25
128	157	40 n.p. on 6d. purple	1·00	30
129	158	50 n.p. on 9d. olive	5·50	4·00
130	160	75 n.p. on 1s. 3d. green	5·50	4·25

For stamps issued by Kuwait government see volume 2.

OFFICIAL STAMPS

1923. Stamps of India (King George V) optd **KUWAIT SERVICE.**

O 1	56	½ a. green	1·00	19·00
O 2	57	1 a. brown	2·00	10·00
O 3	58	1½ a. brown (No. 163)	2·75	26·00
O 4	59	2 a. lilac	4·00	22·00
O17	70	2 a. lilac	55·00	£150
O 5	61	2 a. 6 p. blue	3·75	48·00
O 6	62	3 a. orange	3·25	55·00
O19		3 a. blue	3·75	38·00
O 8	63	4 a. green	3·25	50·00
O20	71	4 a. green	4·25	65·00
O 9	65	8 a. mauve	5·00	60·00
O22	66	12 a. red	24·00	£140
O10	67	1 r. brown and green	13·00	£120
O11		2 r. red and orange	18·00	£170
O12		5 r. blue and violet	60·00	£350
O13		10 r. green and red	£110	£350
O14		15 r. blue	£180	£475

LABUAN

An Island off the N. coast of Borneo, ceded to Great Britain in 1846, and a Crown Colony from 1902. Incorporated with Straits Settlements in 1906, it used Straits stamps till it became part of N. Borneo in 1946.

100 cents = 1 dollar

1

18

1879.

17	1	2 c. green	12·00	21·00
39		2 c. red	3·00	3·50
6		6 c. orange	80·00	85·00
40		6 c. green	6·00	4·50
7		8 c. red	80·00	80·00
41		8 c. violet	2·50	6·50
43		10 c. brown	7·00	8·00
9		12 c. red	£190	£250
45		12 c. blue	3·50	6·50
4		16 c. blue	48·00	£100
46		16 c. grey	4·00	8·00
47		40 c. orange	18·00	32·00

1880. (a) Surch **8.**

11	1	8 on 12 c. red	£900	£650

(b) Surch **6 6** or **8 8.**

12	1	6 on 16 c. blue	£1600	£650
13		8 on 12 c. red	£1000	£750

1881. Surch **EIGHT CENTS.**

14	1	8 c. on 12 c. red	£200	£250

1881. Surch **Eight Cents.**

15	1	8 c. on 12 c. red	£100	£110

1883. Manuscript surch **one Dollar A.S.H.**

22	1	$1 on 16 c. blue	£2500	

1885. Surch **2 CENTS** horiz.

23	1	2 c. on 8 c. red	£150	£325
24		2 c. on 16 c. blue	£800	£750

1885. Surch **2 Cents** horiz.

25	1	2 c. on 16 c. blue	£110	£160

1885. Surch with large **2 Cents** diag.

26	1	2 c. on 8 c. red	60·00	95·00

1891. Surch **6 Cents.**

35	1	6 c. on 8 c. violet	6·50	6·50
37		6 c. on 16 c. blue	£1600	£1500
38		6 c. on 40 c. orange	£7000	£3750

1892. Surch as **Two CENTS** or **Six CENTS.**

49	1	2 c. on 40 c. orange	£140	90·00
50		6 c. on 16 c. grey	£275	£140

Most issues from 1894 exist cancelled-to-order with black bars. Our prices are for stamps postally used, cancelled-to-order examples being worth considerably less.

1894. Types of North Borneo (different colours) optd **LABUAN.**

62	24	1 c. black and mauve	1·50	6·00
63	25	2 c. black and blue	2·50	6·00
64a	26	3 c. black and yellow	5·50	9·00
65a	27	5 c. black and green	25·00	10·00
67	28	6 c. black and red	2·50	9·50
69	29	8 c. black and pink	7·00	23·00
70	30	12 c. black and orange	23·00	40·00
71	31	18 c. black and brown	22·00	45·00
74a	32	24 c. blue and mauve	13·00	38·00
80	10	25 c. green	20·00	24·00
81	–	50 c. purple (as No. 82)	20·00	24·00
82	–	$1 blue (as No. 83)	48·00	40·00

1895. No. 83 of North Borneo surch **LABUAN** and value in cents.

75		4 c. on $1 red	1·00	1·75
76		10 c. on $1 red	1·90	1·40
77		20 c. on $1 red	21·00	8·00
78		30 c. on $1 red	23·00	28·00
79		40 c. on $1 red	20·00	22·00

1896. Jubilee of Cession of Labuan to Gt. Britain. Nos. 62/8 optd **1846 JUBILEE 1896.**

83	24	1 c. black and mauve	17·00	21·00
84d	25	2 c. black and blue	28·00	14·00
85	26	3 c. black and yellow	28·00	22·00
86	27	5 c. black and green	48·00	16·00
87	28	6 c. black and red	23·00	20·00
88b	29	8 c. black and pink	32·00	11·00

1897. Stamps of North Borneo, Nos. 92 to 106 (different colours), optd **LABUAN.** Opt at top of stamp.

89		1 c. black and purple	4·00	4·75
90		2 c. black and blue	9·50	4·25
91b		3 c. black and yellow	8·50	6·50
92a		5 c. black and green	32·00	38·00
93b		6 c. black and red	4·50	19·00
94a		8 c. black and pink	15·00	12·00
95a		12 c. black and orange	24·00	42·00

Overprint at foot of stamp.

98a	–	12 c. black and orange (as No. 106)	35·00	42·00

Opt at foot. Inscr "POSTAL REVENUE".

96b	–	18 c. black and bistre (as No. 108)	15·00	38·00

Opt at foot. Inscr "POSTAGE AND REVENUE".

99a	–	18 c. black and bistre (as No. 110)	75·00	60·00

Opt at top. Inscr "POSTAGE AND REVENUE".

101b	–	18 c. black and bistre (as No. 110)	27·00	45·00

Opt at top. "POSTAGE AND REVENUE" omitted.

97a	–	24 c. blue and lilac (as No. 109)	10·00	40·00

Opt at top. Inscr "POSTAGE AND REVENUE".

100	–	24 c. blue and mauve (No. 111)	22·00	48·00

1899. Stamps of Labuan surch **4 CENTS.**

102		4 c. on 5 c. blk & grn (92a)	29·00	26·00
103		4 c. on 6 c. blk & red (93b)	18·00	19·00
104a		4 c. on 8 c. black and pink (94a)	21·00	32·00
105		4 c. on 12 c. black and orange (98a)	32·00	35·00
106		4 c. on 18 c. black and olive (101b)	20·00	17·00
107		4 c. on 24 c. blue and mauve (100)	19·00	26·00
108		4 c. on 25 c. green (80)	5·50	7·50
109		4 c. on 50 c. purple (81)	5·50	7·50
110		4 c. on $1 blue (82)	5·50	7·50

1900. Stamps of North Borneo, as Nos. 95 to 107, optd **LABUAN.**

111		2 c. black and green	3·75	2·50
112		4 c. black and brown	6·00	30·00
113a		4 c. black and red	6·50	7·00
114		5 c. black and blue	24·00	18·00
115		10 c. brown and grey	45·00	65·00
116		16 c. green and brown	55·00	85·00

1902.

117	18	1 c. black and purple	3·50	6·50
118		2 c. black and green	3·00	4·00
119		3 c. black and brown	3·00	7·50
120		4 c. black and red	3·00	3·25
121		8 c. black and orange	7·00	8·00
122		10 c. brown and blue	3·00	8·00
123		12 c. black and yellow	3·50	10·00
124		16 c. green and brown	4·75	13·00
125		18 c. black and brown	3·25	13·00
126		25 c. green and blue	6·00	15·00
127		50 c. purple and lilac	10·00	38·00
128		$1 red and orange	8·00	42·00

1904. Surch **4 cents.**

129	–	4 c. on 5 c. black and green (92a)	27·00	32·00
130	–	4 c. on 6 c. black and red (93b)	12·00	30·00
131	–	4 c. on 8 c. black and pink (94a)	22·00	32·00
132	–	4 c. on 12 c. black and orange (98a)	19·00	32·00
133	–	4 c. on 18 c. black and olive (101b)	18·00	35·00
134	–	4 c. on 24 c. blue and mauve (100)	16·00	35·00
135	10	4 c. on 25 c. green (80)	8·50	20·00
136		4 c. on 50 c. purple (81)	8·50	20·00
137		4 c. on $1 blue (82)	8·50	20·00

POSTAGE DUE STAMPS

1901. Optd **POSTAGE DUE.**

D1	2 c. black and green (111)	11·00	20·00
D2	3 c. black and yellow (91)	16·00	70·00
D3b	4 c. black and red (113)	23·00	70·00
D4	5 c. black and blue (114)	35·00	85·00
D5	6 c. black and red (93b)	17·00	75·00
D6	8 c. black and pink (94a)	42·00	75·00
D7	12 c. black and orange (98a)	65·00	85·00
D8	18 c. black and olive (101b)	16·00	80·00
D9	24 c. blue and mauve (100)	29·00	70·00

LAGOS

A British colony on the southern coast of Nigeria. United with Southern Nigeria in 1906 to form the Colony and Protectorate of Southern Nigeria.

12 pence = 1 shilling;
20 shillings = 1 pound

1

3

1874.

21	1	½d. green	1·75	70
17		1d. mauve	17·00	10·00
22		1d. red	1·75	70
11		2d. blue	35·00	12·00
23		2d. grey	50·00	5·00
19		3d. brown	13·00	5·00
5		4d. red	60·00	40·00
24		4d. lilac	90·00	8·50
25		6d. green	7·00	30·00
26		1s. orange	6·00	18·00
27		2s. 6d. black	£275	£250
28		5s. blue	£475	£400
29		10s. brown	£1200	£800

1887.

30	1	2d. mauve and blue	2·25	1·75
31		2½d. blue	3·00	1·75
32		3d. mauve and brown	2·50	3·25
33		4d. mauve and black	2·25	1·75
34		5d. mauve and green	2·00	11·00
35		6d. mauve	4·50	3·00
35a		6d. mauve and red	4·50	12·00
36		7½d. mauve and red	2·00	26·00
37		10d. mauve and yellow	3·25	13·00
38		1s. green and black	4·50	22·00
39		2s. 6d. green and red	22·00	75·00
40		5s. green and blue	38·00	£130
41		10s. green and brown	65·00	£170

1893. Surch **HALF PENNY** and bars.

42	**1**	$\frac{1}{2}$d. on 4d. mauve and black	3·75	2·50

1904.

44	**3**	$\frac{1}{2}$d. green	1·50	5·50
45		1d. purple and black on red	1·00	15
56		2d. purple and blue	2·00	1·40
47		$2\frac{1}{2}$d. purple and blue on blue	1·00	1·50
48		3d. purple and brown	1·75	1·75
59a		6d. purple and mauve	4·25	1·25
60a		1s. green and black	18·00	2·25
61		2s. 6d. green and red	12·00	38·00
62		5s. green and blue	22·00	90·00
63		10s. green and brown	50·00	£170

LAS BELA

A state of Baluchistan. Now part of Pakistan.

12 pies = 1 anna; 16 annas = 1 rupee

1

1897.

1	**1**	$\frac{1}{2}$ a. black on white	19·00	12·00
11		$\frac{1}{2}$ a. black on blue	9·50	6·50
3		$\frac{1}{2}$ a. black on grey	10·00	6·50
12		$\frac{1}{2}$ a. black on green	9·50	6·50
8	–	1 a. black on orange	14·00	16·00

The 1 a. has the English inscriptions in a circle with the native inscription across the centre.

LEEWARD ISLANDS

A group of islands in the Br. W. Indies, including Antigua, Barbuda, British Virgin Islands, Dominica (till end of 1939), Montserrat, Nevis and St. Christopher (St. Kitts). Stamps of Leeward Islands were used concurrent with the issues for the respective islands until they were withdrawn on the 1 July, 1956.

1890. 12 pence = 1 shilling;
20 shillings = 1 pound.
1951. 100 cents = 1 West Indian dollar.

1

(3)

1890.

1	**1**	$\frac{1}{2}$d. mauve and green	3·00	1·00
2		1d. mauve and red	3·00	20
3		$2\frac{1}{2}$d. mauve and blue	3·50	20
4		4d. mauve and orange	3·75	7·00
5		6d. mauve and brown	9·00	10·00
6		7d. mauve and grey	3·00	10·00
7		1s. green and red	15·00	38·00
8		5s. green and blue	£120	£225

1897. Diamond Jubilee. Optd with T **3**.

9	**1**	$\frac{1}{2}$d. mauve and green	3·00	9·50
10		1d. mauve and red	3·50	9·50
11		$2\frac{1}{2}$d. mauve and blue	3·75	9·50
12		4d. mauve and orange	27·00	65·00
13		6d. mauve and brown	48·00	85·00
14		7d. mauve and grey	48·00	85·00
15		1s. green and red	£120	£190
16		5s. green and blue	£450	£750

1902. Surch **One Penny**.

17	**1**	1d. on 4d. mauve and orange	1·40	4·50
18		1d. on 6d. mauve and brown	2·25	9·00
19		1d. on 7d. mauve and grey	2·00	4·00

1902. As T **1**, but portrait of King Edward VII.

20	$\frac{1}{2}$d. purple and green	4·00	70
21	1d. purple and red	5·00	20
22	2d. purple and brown	2·50	4·25
23	$2\frac{1}{2}$d. purple and blue	4·00	2·00
24	3d. purple and black	3·25	7·00
25	6d. purple and brown	2·00	7·50
26	1s. green and red	2·25	17·00
27	2s. 6d. green and black	26·00	60·00
28	5s. green and blue	48·00	70·00

1907. As last, colours changed.

36	$\frac{1}{4}$d. brown	1·75	1·25
37	$\frac{1}{2}$d. green	2·00	75
38	1d. red	6·00	70
39	2d. grey	2·50	7·50
40	$2\frac{1}{2}$d. blue	4·00	3·50
41	3d. purple and yellow	3·00	7·00
42	6d. purple	6·00	7·00
43	1s. black on green	3·00	20·00
44	2s. 6d. black and red on blue	38·00	48·00
45	5s. green and red on yellow	40·00	65·00

10 King George V

14 King George VI

1912.

46	**10**	$\frac{1}{4}$d. brown	1·00	65
59		$\frac{1}{2}$d. green	60	60
60		1d. red	1·50	40
61		1d. violet	2·00	1·00
63		$1\frac{1}{2}$d. red	2·50	1·75
64		$1\frac{1}{2}$d. brown	75	10
65		2d. grey	1·50	70
67		$2\frac{1}{2}$d. blue	2·25	75
66		$2\frac{1}{2}$d. yellow	5·50	42·00
69		3d. purple on yellow	75	6·50
68		3d. blue	3·50	20·00
70		4d. black & red on yellow	2·25	18·00
71		5d. purple and green	2·00	4·25
53		6d. purple	1·75	7·50
54		1s. black on green	1·75	7·50
55		2s. purple & blue on blue	6·00	42·00
75		2s. 6d. black & red on blue	6·50	23·00
76		3s. green and violet	11·00	24·00
77		4s. black and red	11·00	40·00
57b		5s. green & red on yellow	15·00	50·00

Larger type, as T **15** of Malta.

79	10s. green and red on green	48·00	75·00
80	£1 purple and black on red	£225	£250

1935. Silver Jubilee. As T **13** of Antigua.

88	1d. blue and red	1·40	1·00
89	$1\frac{1}{2}$d. blue and grey	2·00	70
90	$2\frac{1}{2}$d. brown and blue	2·00	3·25
91	1s. grey and purple	5·50	13·00

1937. Coronation. As T **2** of Aden.

92	1d. red	30	15
93	$1\frac{1}{2}$d. brown	40	35
94	$2\frac{1}{2}$d. blue	40	45

1938.

95a	**14**	$\frac{1}{4}$d. brown	10	90
96		$\frac{1}{2}$d. green	60	60
97		$\frac{1}{2}$d. grey	30	1·00
99		1d. red	1·50	1·50
100		1d. green	55	15
101		$1\frac{1}{2}$d. brown	80	50
102		$1\frac{1}{2}$d. orange and black	50	30
103		2d. grey	2·50	1·00
104		2d. red	1·40	80
105a		$2\frac{1}{2}$d. blue	60	1·25
106		$2\frac{1}{2}$d. black and purple	55	15
107a		3d. orange	40	85
108		3d. blue	65	15
109a		6d. purple	4·50	2·25
110b		1s. black on green	4·25	90
111a		2s. purple & blue on blue	10·00	1·50
112a		5s. green & red on yellow	32·00	14·00
113c	–	10s. green & red on green	£120	70·00
114b	–	£1 purple and black on red	35·00	24·00

Nos. 113b/4b are as Type **15** of Bermuda but with portrait of King George VI.

1946. Victory. As T **9** of Aden.

115	$1\frac{1}{2}$d. brown	15	30
116	3d. orange	15	30

1949. Silver Wedding. As T **10/11** of Aden.

117	$2\frac{1}{2}$d. blue	10	10
118	5s. green	3·75	2·75

1949. U.P.U. As T **20/23** of Antigua.

119	$2\frac{1}{2}$d. black	15	60
120	3d. blue	1·00	80
121	6d. mauve	40	80
122	1s. turquoise	45	80

1951. Inauguration of B.W.I. University College. As T **24/25** of Antigua.

123	3 c. orange and black	30	60
124	12 c. red and violet	60	60

1953. Coronation. As T **13** of Aden.

125	3 c. black and green	30	1·50

1954. As T **14** but portrait of Queen Elizabeth II facing left.

126	$\frac{1}{2}$ c. brown	10	40
127	1 c. grey	40	75
128	2 c. green	40	10
129	3 c. yellow and black	80	75
130	4 c. red	80	10
131	5 c. black and purple	1·50	75
132	6 c. yellow	1·25	30
133	8 c. blue	2·00	10
134	12 c. purple	1·50	10
135	24 c. black and green	1·75	20
136	48 c. purple and blue	6·00	2·75
137	60 c. brown and green	6·00	2·25
138	\$1.20 green and red	5·00	2·75

Larger type as T **15** of Malta.

139	\$2.40 green and red	6·50	5·00
140	\$4.80 purple and black	6·50	6·50

LESOTHO

Formerly Basutoland, attained independence on 4 October, 1966 and changed its name to Lesotho.

1966. 100 cents = 1 rand.
1979. 100 lisente = 1 (ma)loti.

33 Moshoeshoe I and Moshoeshoe II

1966. Independence.

106	**33**	$2\frac{1}{2}$ c. brown, black & red	10	10
107		5 c. brown, black & blue	10	10
108		10 c. brown, black & green	15	10
109		20 c. brown, black & purple	20	15

1966. Nos. 69 etc. of Basutoland optd **LESOTHO**.

110A	**8**	$\frac{1}{2}$ c. black and sepia	10	10
111A	–	1 c. black and green	10	10
112A	–	2 c. blue and orange	60	10
113B	**26**	$2\frac{1}{2}$ c. sage and red	50	10
114A	–	$3\frac{1}{2}$ c. indigo and blue	30	10
115A	–	5 c. brown and green	10	10
116A	–	10 c. bronze and purple	10	10
117B	–	$12\frac{1}{2}$ c. brown & turquoise	30	20
118A		25 c. blue and red	30	20
119B	–	50 c. black and red	60	50
120B	**9**	1 r. black and purple	65	75

35 "Education, Culture and Science"

36 Maize

1966. 20th Anniv of U.N.E.S.C.O.

121	**35**	$2\frac{1}{2}$ c. yellow and green	10	10
122		5 c. green and olive	15	10
123		$12\frac{1}{2}$ c. blue and red	35	10
124		25 c. orange and blue	60	25

1967.

125	**36**	$\frac{1}{2}$ c. green and violet	10	10
126	–	1 c. sepia and red	10	10
149	–	2 c. yellow and green	10	10
128	–	$2\frac{1}{2}$ c. black and ochre	10	10
151	–	3 c. chocolate, green & brn	15	15
152	–	$3\frac{1}{2}$ c. blue and yellow	15	10
130	–	5 c. bistre and blue	10	10
131	–	10 c. brown and grey	10	10
132	–	$12\frac{1}{2}$ c. black and orange	20	10
133	–	25 c. black and blue	55	20
134	–	50 c. black, blue & turquoise	4·50	45
135	–	1 r. multicoloured	65	75
136	–	2 r. black, gold and purple	1·00	1·75

DESIGNS—HORIZ: 1 c. Cattle; 2 c. Aloes; $2\frac{1}{2}$ c. Basotho hat; 3 c. Sorghum; $3\frac{1}{2}$ c. Merino sheep ("Wool"); 5 c. Basotho pony; 10 c. Wheat; $12\frac{1}{2}$ c. Angora goat ("Mohair"); 25 c. Maletsunyane Falls; 50 c. Diamonds; 1 r. Arms of Lesotho. VERT: 2 r. Moshoeshoe II.

See also Nos. 191/203.

46 Students and University

1967. 1st Conferment of University Degrees.

137	**46**	1 c. sepia, blue and orange	10	10
138		$2\frac{1}{2}$ c. sepia, ultramarine & bl	10	10
139		$12\frac{1}{2}$ c. sepia, blue and red	10	10
140		25 c. sepia, blue and violet	15	15

47 Statue of Moshoeshoe I

1967. 1st Anniv of Independence.

141	**47**	$2\frac{1}{2}$ c. black and green	10	10
142	–	$12\frac{1}{2}$ c. multicoloured	25	15
143	–	25 c. black, green & ochre	35	25

DESIGNS: $12\frac{1}{2}$ c. National flag; 25 c. Crocodile (national emblem).

50 Lord Baden-Powell and Scout Saluting

1967. 60th Anniv of Scout Movement.

144	**50**	15 c. multicoloured	20	10

51 W.H.O. Emblem and World Map

1968. 20th Anniv of World Health Organization.

145	**51**	$2\frac{1}{2}$ c. blue, gold and red	15	10
146	–	25 c. multicoloured	45	20

DESIGN: 25 c. Nurse and child.

55 Running Hunters

1968. Rock Paintings.

160	**55**	3 c. brown, turq & grn	25	10
161	–	$3\frac{1}{2}$ c. yellow, olive & sepia	30	10
162	–	5 c. red, ochre & brown	35	10
163	–	10 c. yellow, red & purple	45	10
164	–	15 c. buff, yellow and brown	75	30
165	–	20 c. green, yell & brown	90	55
166	–	25 c. yellow, brown & black	1·00	75

DESIGNS—HORIZ: $3\frac{1}{2}$ c. Baboons; 10 c. Archers; 20 c. Eland; 25 c. Hunting scene. VERT: 5 c. Javelin thrower; 15 c. Blue cranes.

62 Queen Elizabeth II Hospital

1969. Centenary of Maseru (capital). Mult.

167	$2\frac{1}{2}$ c. Type **62**	10	10
168	10 c. Lesotho Radio Station	10	10
169	$12\frac{1}{2}$ c. Leabua Jonathan Airport	35	10
170	25 c. Royal Palace	25	15

66 Rally Car passing Basuto Tribesman

1969. "Roof of Africa" Car Rally.

171	**66**	$2\frac{1}{2}$ c. yellow, mve & plum	15	10
172	–	$12\frac{1}{2}$ c. blue, yellow & grey	20	10
173	–	15 c. blue, black & mauve	20	10
174	–	20 c. black, red and yellow	20	10

DESIGNS: $12\frac{1}{2}$ c. Rally car on mountain road; 15 c. Chequered flags and "Roof of Africa" Plateau; 20 c. Map of rally route and Independence Trophy.

71 Gryponyx and Footprints

1970. Prehistoric Footprints (1st series).

175	–	3 c. brown and sepia	70	50
176	**71**	5 c. purple, pink & sepia	85	30
177	–	10 c. yellow, black & sepia	1·00	35
178	–	15 c. yellow, black & sepia	1·60	2·00
179	–	25 c. blue and black	2·50	2·00

DESIGNS: 3 c. Dinosaur footprints at Moyeni; 10 c. Plateosauravus and footprints; 15 c. Tritylodon and footprints; 25 c. Massospondylus and footprints.

No. 175 is larger, 60×23 mm.

See also Nos. 596/8.

75 Moshoeshoe I as a Young Man

1970. Death Centenary of Chief Moshoeshoe I.
180 **75** 2½ c. green and mauve . . . 10 10
181 – 25 c. blue and brown . . . 20 20
DESIGN: 25 c. Moshoeshoe I as an old man.

77 U.N. Emblem and "25"

1970. 25th Anniv of United Nations.
182 **77** 2½ c. pink, blue & purple . 10 10
183 – 10 c. multicoloured 10 10
184 – 12½ c. red, blue and drab . 10 10
185 – 25 c. multicoloured 15 15
DESIGNS: 10 c. U.N. Building; 12½ c. "People of the World"; 25 c. Symbolic dove.

78 Gift Shop, Maseru

1970. Tourism. Multicoloured.
186 2½ c. Type **78** 10 10
187 5 c. Trout fishing 20 10
188 10 c. Pony trekking 25 10
189 12½ c. Skiing, Maluti Mountains 50 10
190 20 c. Holiday Inn, Maseru . . 40 50

79 Maize 80 Lammergeier

1971. As Nos. 147/58 but in new format omitting portrait, as in T **79**. New designs for 4 c., 2 r.
191 **79** ½ c. green and violet . . . 10 10
192 – 1 c. brown and red . . . 10 10
193 – 2 c. yellow and green . . 10 10
194 – 2½ c. black, green & yell . 10 10
195 – 3 c. brown, green & yell . 10 10
196 – 3½ c. blue and yellow . . . 10 10
196a – 4 c. multicoloured 20 10
197 – 5 c. brown and blue . . . 15 10
198 – 10 c. brown and grey . . 15 10
199 – 12½ c. brown and orange . 25 30
200 – 25 c. slate and blue . . . 60 40
201 – 50 c. black, blue & green . 6·00 4·25
202 – 1 r. multicoloured . . . . 2·25 2·25
401 – 2 r. brown and blue . . . 1·10 3·00
DESIGNS—HORIZ: 4 c. National flag. VERT: 2 r. Statue of Moshoeshoe I.

1971. Birds. Multicoloured.
204 2½ c. Type **80** . . . . 1·75 20
205 5 c. Bald ibis . . . . 2·50 2·00
206 10 c. Rufous rockjumper . . . 3·00 2·00
207 12½ c. Blue bustard . . . . . 3·50 3·25
208 15 c. Painted snipe . . . . . 4·25 4·25
209 20 c. Golden-breasted bunting 4·25 4·25
210 25 c. Ground woodpecker . . . 4·75 4·25

81 Lionel Collett Dam

1971. Soil Conservation. Multicoloured.
211 4 c. Type **81** 10 10
212 10 c. Contour ridges 10 10
213 15 c. Earth dams 25 10
214 25 c. Beaver dams 35 35

82 Diamond Mining

1971. Development. Multicoloured.
215 4 c. Type **82** 75 40
216 10 c. Pottery 30 10
217 15 c. Weaving 45 60
218 20 c. Construction . . . . . 55 1·25

83 Mail Cart

1972. Centenary of Post Office.
219 **83** 5 c. brown and pink 15 10
220 – 10 c. multicoloured . . . 15 10
221 – 15 c. blue, black and brown 30 15
222 – 20 c. multicoloured . . . 45 70
DESIGNS—HORIZ: 10 c. Postal bus; 20 c. Maseru Post Office. VERT: 15 c. 4d. Cape of Good Hope stamp of 1876.

84 Sprinting

1972. Olympic Games, Munich. Multicoloured.
223 4 c. Type **84** 15 10
224 10 c. Shot putting 20 10
225 15 c. Hurdling 30 10
226 25 c. Long-jumping 35 40

85 "Adoration of the Shepherds" (Matthias Stomer)

1972. Christmas.
227 **85** 4 c. multicoloured 10 10
228 10 c. multicoloured 10 10
229 25 c. multicoloured 15 20

86 W.H.O. Emblem

1973. 25th Anniv of W.H.O.
230 **86** 20 c. yellow and blue 30 30

1973. O.A.U. 10th Anniv Nos. 194 and 196a/8 optd **O.A.U. 10th Anniversary Freedom in Unity**.
231 2½ c. black, green and brown . 10 10
232 4 c. multicoloured 10 10
233 5 c. brown and blue 10 10
234 10 c. brown and blue 15 15

88 Basotho Hat and W.F.P. Emblem

1973. 10th Anniv of World Food Programme. Multicoloured.
235 4 c. Type **88** 10 10
236 15 c. School feeding 20 15
237 20 c. Infant feeding 20 20
238 25 c. "Food for work" 25 25

89 "Aeropetes tulbaghia"

1973. Butterflies. Multicoloured.
239 4 c. Type **89** 65 10
240 5 c. "Papilio demodocus" . . . 75 50
241 10 c. "Cynthia cardui" . . . . 1·25 50
242 15 c. "Precis hierta" . . . . . 2·00 1·75
243 20 c. "Precis oenone" . . . . 2·00 1·75
244 25 c. "Danaus chrysippus" . . 2·25 2·50
245 30 c. "Colotis evenina" . . . . 2·25 3·00

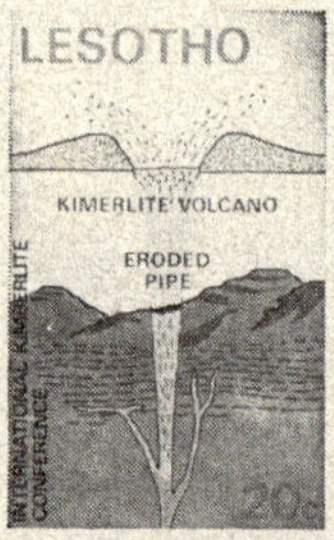

90 Kimberlite Volcano **92** Open Book and Wreath

91 "Health"

1973. International Kimberlite Conference. Mult.
246 10 c. Map of diamond mines (horiz) . . . . 2·00 50
247 15 c. Kimberlite-diamond rock (horiz) . . . . 2·25 2·25
248 20 c. Type **90** . . . . 2·25 2·50
249 30 c. Diamond prospecting . . 3·75 6·00

1974. Youth and Development. Multicoloured.
250 4 c. Type **91** 10 10
251 10 c. "Education" 15 10
252 20 c. "Agriculture" 20 10
253 25 c. "Industry" 30 20
254 30 c. "Service" 30 25

1974. 10th Anniv of U.B.L.S. Multicoloured.
255 10 c. Type **92** 15 10
256 15 c. Flags, mortar-board and scroll 20 20
257 20 c. Map of Africa 25 20
258 25 c. King Moshoeshoe II capping a graduate 25 30

93 Senqunyane River Bridge, Marakabei

1974. Rivers and Bridges. Multicoloured.
259 4 c. Type **93** 10 10
260 5 c. Tsoelike River and bridge 10 10
261 10 c. Makhaleng River Bridge . 20 10
262 15 c. Seaka Bridge, Orange/Senqu River 35 35
263 20 c. Masianokeng Bridge Phuthiatsana River 40 40
264 25 c. Mahobong Bridge, Hlotse River 45 45

94 U.P.U. Emblem

1974. Centenary of U.P.U.
265 **94** 4 c. green and black 10 10
266 – 10 c. orange, yellow & blk . 15 10
267 – 15 c. multicoloured . . . 20 50
268 – 20 c. multicoloured . . . 45 65
DESIGNS: 10 c. Map of air-mail routes; 15 c. Post Office H.Q., Maseru; 20 c. Horseman taking rural mail.

95 Siege of Thaba-Bosiu

1974. 150th Anniv of Siege of Thaba-Bosiu. Multicoloured.
269 4 c. Type **95** 10 10
270 5 c. The wreath-laying 10 10
271 10 c. Moshoeshoe I (vert) . . . 25 10
272 20 c. Makoanyane, the warrior (vert) 90 55

96 Mamokhorong

1974. Basotho Musical Instruments. Multicoloured.
273 4 c. Type **96** 10 10
274 10 c. Lesiba 10 10
275 15 c. Setolotolo 15 20
276 20 c. Meropa 15 20

97 Horseman in Rock Archway

1975. Sehlabathebe National Park. Mult.
278 4 c. Type **97** 30 10
279 5 c. Mountain view through arch 30 10
280 15 c. Antelope by stream . . 50 45
281 20 c. Mountains and lake . . 50 50
282 25 c. Tourists by frozen waterfall 65 75

98 Morena Moshoeshoe I **99** Mokhibo Dance

1975. Leaders of Lesotho.
283 **98** 3 c. black and blue 10 10
284 – 4 c. black and mauve . . . 10 10
285 – 5 c. black and pink 10 10
286 – 6 c. black and brown . . . 10 10
287 – 10 c. black and red 10 10
288 – 15 c. black and red 20 20
289 – 20 c. black and green . . . 25 30
290 – 25 c. black and blue . . . 25 40
DESIGNS: 4 c. King Moshoeshoe II; 5 c. Morena Letsie I; 6 c. Morena Lerotholi; 10 c. Morena Letsie II; 15 c. Morena Griffith; 20 c. Morena Seeiso Griffith Lerotholi; 25 c. Mofumahali Mantsebo Seeiso, O.B.E.
The 25 c. also commemorates International Women's Year.

1975. Traditional Dances. Multicoloured.
291 4 c. Type **99** 10 10
292 10 c. Ndlamo 15 10
293 15 c. Baleseli 30 55
294 20 c. Mohobelo 35 65

100 Enrolment

1976. 25th Anniv of Lesotho Red Cross. Mult.
296 4 c. Type **100** 50 10
297 10 c. Medical aid 70 10
298 15 c. Rural service . . . . . 1·00 1·25
299 25 c. Relief supplies . . . . . 1·40 1·75

101 Tapestry

1976. Multicoloured.

300	2 c. Type **101**	10	30
301	3 c. Mosotho horseman	20	30
302	4 c. Map of Lesotho	65	10
303	5 c. Lesotho Brown diamond	55	60
304	10 c. Lesotho Bank	30	10
305	15 c. Lesotho and O.A.U. flags	90	50
306	25 c. Sehlabathebe National Park	80	35
307	40 c. Pottery	80	1·00
308	50 c. Prehistoric rock art	2·00	2·00
309	1 r. King Moshoeshoe II (vert)	1·10	1·75

102 Football

103 "Rising Sun"

1976. Olympic Games, Montreal. Mult.

310	4 c. Type **102**	15	10
311	10 c. Weightlifting	15	10
312	15 c. Boxing	25	10
313	25 c. Throwing the discus	40	35

1976. 10th Anniv of Independence. Multicoloured.

314	4 c. Type **103**	10	10
315	10 c. Open gates	10	10
316	15 c. Broken chains	40	20
317	25 c. Britten Norman Islander aircraft over hotel	50	35

104 Telephones, 1876 and 1976

1976. Centenary of Telephone. Multicoloured.

318	4 c. Type **104**	10	10
319	10 c. Early handset and telephone-user, 1976	15	10
320	15 c. Wall telephone and telephone exchange	25	15
321	25 c. Stick telephone and Alexander Graham Bell	45	40

105 "Aloe striatula"

106 Large-toothed Rock Hyrax

1977. Aloes and Succulents. Multicoloured.

322	3 c. Type **105**	25	10
323	4 c. "Aloe aristata"	30	10
324	5 c. "Kniphofia caulescens"	35	10
325	10 c. "Euphorbia pulvinata"	50	10
326	15 c. "Aloe saponaria"	1·50	40
327	20 c. "Caralluma lutea"	1·50	65
328	25 c. "Aloe polyphylla"	1·75	90

See also Nos. 347/54.

1977. Animals. Multicoloured.

329	4 c. Type **106**	2·00	20
330	5 c. Cape porcupine	2·00	30
331	10 c. Zorilla (polecat)	2·50	20
332	15 c. Klipspringer	9·00	2·25
333	25 c. Chacma baboon	11·00	3·00

107 "Rheumatic Man"

110 Black and White Heads

108 Small-mouthed Yellowfish

1977. World Rheumatism Year.

334	**107** 4 c. yellow and red	10	10
335	– 10 c. blue and deep blue	15	10
336	– 15 c. yellow and blue	30	10
337	– 25 c. red and black	40	45

DESIGNS—Each show the "Rheumatic Man" as Type **107**: 10 c. Surrounded by "pain"; 15 c. Surrounded by "chain"; 25 c. Supporting globe.

1977. Fish. Multicoloured.

338	4 c. Type **108**	30	10
339	10 c. Mudfish	45	10
340	15 c. Rainbow trout	1·00	35
341	25 c. Barnard's mudfish	1·10	60

1977. No. 198 surch **3**.

342	3 c. on 10 c. brown and blue	90	90

1977. Decade for Action to Combat Racism.

343	**110** 4 c. black and mauve	10	10
344	– 10 c. black and blue	10	10
345	– 15 c. black and orange	15	15
346	– 25 c. black and green	25	25

DESIGNS: 10 c. Jigsaw pieces; 15 c. Cogwheels; 25 c. Handshake.

1978. Flowers. As T **105**. Multicoloured.

347	2 c. "Papaver aculeatum"	10	20
348	3 c. "Diascia integerrima"	10	20
349	4 c. "Helichrysum trilineatum"	10	10
350	5 c. "Zaluzianskya maritima"	10	10
351	10 c. "Gladiolus natalensis"	20	20
352	15 c. "Chironia krebsii"	30	40
353	25 c. "Wahlenbergia undulata"	50	1·00
354	40 c. "Brunsvigia radulosa"	85	2·00

111 Edward Jenner vaccinating Child

112 Tsoloane Falls

1978. Global Eradication of Smallpox. Mult.

355	5 c. Type **111**	20	10
356	25 c. Head of child and W.H.O. emblem	60	65

1978. Waterfalls. Multicoloured.

357	4 c. Type **112**	15	10
358	10 c. Qiloane Falls	25	10
359	15 c. Tsoelikana Falls	45	60
360	25 c. Maletsunyane Falls	75	1·50

113 Wright Flyer III, 1903

1978. 75th Anniv of First Powered Flight. Mult.

361	5 c. Type **113**	15	10
362	25 c. Wilbur and Orville Wright	40	55

114 "Orthetrum farinosum"

115 Oudehout Branch in Flower

1978. Insects. Multicoloured.

363	4 c. Type **114**	10	10
364	10 c. "Phymateus viridipes"	20	10
365	15 c. "Belonogaster lateritis"	30	40
366	25 c. "Sphodromantis gastrica"	50	80

1979. Trees. Multicoloured.

367	4 c. Type **115**	15	10
368	10 c. Wild olive	20	10
369	15 c. Blinkblaar	35	80
370	25 c. Cape holly	70	1·50

116 Mampharoane

1979. Reptiles. Multicoloured.

371A	4 s. Type **116**	10	10
372A	10 s. Qoaane	20	10
373A	15 s. Leupa	30	60
374A	25 s. Masumu	60	1·25

117 Basutoland 1933 1d. Stamp

118 Detail of painting "Children's Games" by Brueghel

1979. Death Centenary of Sir Rowland Hill.

375	**117** 4 s. multicoloured	10	10
376	– 15 s. multicoloured	30	20
377	– 25 s. black, orange & bistre	40	30

DESIGNS: 15 s. Basutoland 1962 ½ c. new currency definitive; 25 s. Penny Black.

1979. International Year of the Child.

379	**118** 4 s. multicoloured	10	10
380	– 10 s. multicoloured	10	10
381	– 15 s. multicoloured	15	15

DESIGNS: 10, 15 s. Different details taken from Brueghel's "Children's Games".

119 Beer Strainer, Broom and Mat

1980. Grasswork. Multicoloured.

383	4 s. Type **119**	10	10
384	10 s. Winnowing basket	10	10
385	15 s. Basotho hat	20	25
386	25 s. Grain storage	35	40

120 Praise Poet

1980. Centenary of Gun War. Multicoloured.

387	4 s. Type **120**	15	10
388	5 s. Lerotholi, Commander of Basotho Army	15	10
389	10 s. Ambush at Qalabane	20	10
390	15 s. Snider and Martini-Henry rifles	60	45
391	25 s. Map showing main areas of action	70	55

121 Olympic Flame, Flags and Kremlin

1980. Olympic Games, Moscow. Multicoloured.

392	25 s. Type **121**	25	25
393	25 s. Doves, flame and flags	25	25
394	25 s. Football	25	25
395	25 s. Running	25	25
396	25 s. Opening ceremony	25	25

1980. Nos. 203 and 300/9 surch **s** or new value.

402A	2 s. on 2 c. Type **101**	10	10
403A	3 s. on 3 c. Mosotho horseman	20	10
410A	5 s. on 5 c. Lesotho Brown diamond	60	10
404A	6 s. on 4 c. Map of Lesotho	30	10
411B	10 s. on 10 c. Lesotho Bank	10	10
412A	25 s. on 25 c. Sehlabathebe National Park	25	30
406A	40 s. on 40 c. Pottery	45	50
407B	50 s. on 50 c. Prehistoric rock art	1·25	55
408A	75 s. on 15 c. Lesotho and O.A.U. flags	70	75
409A	1 m. on 1 r. King Moshoeshoe II	80	1·00
417A	2 m. on 2 r. Statue of King Moshoeshoe I	80	1·40

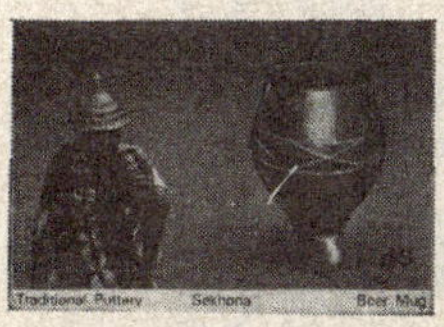

123 Beer Mug

124 Queen Elizabeth the Queen Mother with Prince Charles

1980. Pottery. Multicoloured.

418	4 s. Type **123**	10	10
419	10 s. Beer brewing pot	10	10
420	15 s. Water pot	15	15
421	25 s. Pot shapes	25	30

1980. 80th Birthday of The Queen Mother. Mult.

423	5 s. Type **124**	25	25
424	10 s. The Queen Mother	25	25
425	1 m. 1947 Basutoland Royal Visit 2d. stamp (54 × 43 mm)	90	90

125 Lesotho Evangelical Church, Morija

1980. Christmas. Multicoloured.

426	4 s. Type **125**	10	10
427	15 s. St. Agnes' Anglican Church, Teyateyaneng	10	10
428	25 s. Cathedral of Our Lady of Victories, Maseru	15	10
429	75 s. University Chapel, Roma	45	50

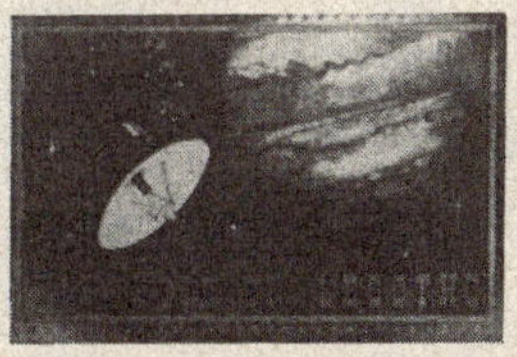

126 "Voyager" Satellite and Jupiter

1981. Space Exploration. Multicoloured.

431	25 c. Type **126**	30	25
432	25 c. "Voyager" and Saturn	30	25
433	25 c. "Voyager" passing Saturn	30	25
434	25 c. "Space Shuttle" releasing satellite	30	25
435	25 c. "Space Shuttle" launching into space	30	25

127 Greater Kestrel

128 Wedding Bouquet from Lesotho

1981. Birds. Multicoloured.

437	1 s. Type **127**	15	20
438	2 s. Speckled pigeon (horiz)	15	20
439	3 s. South African crowned crane	20	20
440	5 s. Bokmakierie shrike	20	20
504	6 s. Cape robin chat	30	10
505	7 s. Yellow canary	30	10
506	10 s. Red-billed pintail (horiz)	30	10
507	25 s. Malachite kingfisher	80	30
508	40 s. Yellow-tufted malachite sunbird (horiz)	1·00	45
509	60 s. Cape longclaw (horiz)	1·25	90
510	75 s. Hoopoe (horiz)	1·75	90
448	1 m. Red bishop (horiz)	2·50	1·00
449	2 m. Egyptian goose (horiz)	3·50	3·00
450	5 m. Lilac-breasted roller (horiz)	6·00	7·00

1981. Royal Wedding. Multicoloured.

451	25 s. Type **128**	10	10
452	50 s. Prince Charles riding	20	25
453	75 s. Prince Charles and Lady Diana Spencer	30	50

130 "Santa planning his Annual Visit"

1981. Christmas. Paintings by Norman Rockwell. Multicoloured.

455 6 s. Type **130** 15 10
456 10 s. "Santa reading his Mail" 25 10
457 15 s. "The Little Spooners" 30 20
458 20 s. "Raleigh Rockwell Travels" 30 25
459 25 s. "Ride 'em Cowboy" . . 30 30
460 60 s. "The Discovery" . . . . 50 1·00

131 Duke of Edinburgh, Award Scheme Emblem and Flags

1981. 25th Anniv of Duke of Edinburgh Award Scheme. Multicoloured.

462 6 s. Type **131** 10 10
463 7 s. Tree planting 10 10
464 25 s. Gardening 25 20
465 40 s. Mountain climbing . . . 40 40
466 75 s. Award Scheme emblem . 70 75

132 Wild Cat

1981. Wildlife. Multicoloured.

468 6 s. Type **132** . . . . 1·25 30
469 20 s. Chacma baboon (44 × 31 mm) . . . . 1·75 70
470 25 s. Cape eland . . . . 2·25 75
471 40 s. Porcupine . . . . 3·00 1·75
472 50 s. Oribi (44 × 31 mm) . . . 3·00 1·75

133 Scout Bugler

1982. 75th Anniv of Boy Scout Movement. Multicoloured.

474 6 s. Type **133** 50 25
475 30 s. Scouts hiking 70 50
476 40 s. Scout sketching 75 60
477 50 s. Scout with flag 75 65
478 75 s. Scouts saluting 80 80

134 Jules Rimet Trophy with Footballers and Flags of 1930 Finalists (Argentina and Uruguay)

1982. World Cup Football Championship, Spain. Each showing Trophy with Players and Flags from Past Finals. Multicoloured.

480 15 s. Type **134** 25 25
481 15 s. Czechoslovakia and Italy, 1934 . . . . 25 25
482 15 s. Hungary and Italy, 1938 25 25
483 15 s. Brazil and Uruguay, 1950 25 25
484 15 s. Hungary and W. Germany, 1954 . . . . 25 25
485 15 s. Sweden and Brazil, 1958 25 25
486 15 s. Czechoslovakia and Brazil, 1962 . . . . 25 25
487 15 s. W. Germany and England, 1966 . . . . 25 25
488 15 s. Italy and Brazil, 1970 . . 25 25
489 15 s. Holland and W. Germany, 1974 . . . . 25 25
490 15 s. Holland and Argentina, 1978 . . . . 25 25
491 15 s. Map of World on footballs 25 25

Nos. 480/8 show the Jules Rimet Trophy and Nos. 489/91 the World Cup Trophy.

135 Portrait of George Washington

1982. 250th Birth Anniv of George Washington. Mult.

493 6 s. Type **135** 10 10
494 7 s. Washington with step-children and dog 10 10
495 10 s. Washington with Indian chief 15 10
496 25 s. Washington with troops 30 30
497 40 s. Washington arriving in New York 40 40
498 1 m. Washington on parade . 1·00 1·10

136 Lady Diana Spencer in Tetbury, May 1981

137 Mosotho reading Sesotho Bible

1982. 21st Birthday of Princess of Wales. Mult.

514a 30 s. Lesotho coat of arms . 40 40
515 50 s. Type **136** 60 60
516 75 s. Wedding picture at Buckingham Palace . . . 80 1·00
517 1 m. Formal portrait . . . . 1·25 1·40

1982. Centenary of Sesotho Bible. Multicoloured.

518 6 s. Type **137** 15 20
519 15 s. Sesotho bible and Virgin Mary holding infant Jesus . 20 25
520 1 m. Sesotho bible and Cathedral (62 × 42 mm) 50 75

138 Birthday Greetings

1982. Birth of Prince William of Wales. Mult.

521 6 s. Type **138** . . . . 1·50 2·00
522 60 s. Princess Diana and Prince William . . . . 1·00 1·00

139 "A Partridge in a Pear Tree"

1982. Christmas. "The Twelve Days of Christmas". Walt Disney cartoon characters. Multicoloured.

523 2 s. Type **139** 10 10
524 2 s. "Two turtle doves" . . 10 10
525 3 s. "Three French hens" . . 10 10
526 3 s. "Four calling birds" . . 10 10
527 4 s. "Five golden rings" . . . 10 10
528 4 s. "Six geese a-laying" . . . 10 10
529 75 s. "Seven swans a-swimming" 1·40 1·75
530 75 s. "Eight maids a-milking" 1·40 1·75

140 "Lepista caffrorum"

1983. Fungi. Multicoloured.

532 10 s. Type **140** 15 10
533 30 s. "Broomeia congregata" . 30 40
534 50 s. "Afroboletus luteolus" . 60 90
535 75 s. "Lentinus tuber-regium" . 90 1·40

141 Ba-Leseli Dance

1983. Commonwealth Day. Multicoloured.

536 5 s. Type **141** 10 10
537 30 s. Tapestry weaving 20 30
538 60 s. Queen Elizabeth II (vert) 35 65
539 75 s. King Moshoeshoe II (vert) 40 80

142 "Dancers in a Trance" (rock painting from Ntloana Tsoana)

1983. Rock Paintings. Multicoloured.

540 6 s. Type **142** 20 10
541 25 s. "Baboons", Sehonghong . 55 35
542 60 s. "Hunters attacking Mountain Reedbuck", Makhetha . . . . 75 1·10
543 75 s. "Eland", Lehaha la Likhomo . . . . 80 1·60

143 Montgolfier Balloon, 1783

1983. Bicentenary of Manned Flight. Mult.

545 7 s. Type **143** 15 10
546 30 s. Wright brothers and Flyer I 40 40
547 60 s. First airmail flight . . . 75 1·00
548 1 m. Concorde . . . . 2·00 2·00

144 Rev. Eugene Casalis

1983. 150th Anniv of Arrival of the French Missionaries. Multicoloured.

550 6 s. Type **144** 10 10
551 25 s. The founding of Morija . 10 10
552 40 s. Baptism of Libe 10 15
553 75 s. Map of Lesotho 20 25

145 Mickey Mouse and Pluto greeted by Friends

1983. Christmas. Walt Disney Characters in scenes from "Old Christmas" (Washington Irving's sketchbook). Multicoloured.

554 1 s. Type **145** 10 10
555 2 s. Donald Duck and Pluto . 10 10
556 3 s. Donald Duck with Huey, Dewey and Louie 10 10
557 4 s. Goofy, Donald Duck and Mickey Mouse 10 10
558 5 s. Goofy holding turkey, Donald Duck and Mickey Mouse 10 10
559 6 s. Goofy and Mickey Mouse 10 10
560 7 s. Donald and Daisy Duck . 2·00 2·40
561 1 m. Goofy and Clarabell . . 2·50 2·75

146 "Danaus chrysippus"

1984. Butterflies. Multicoloured.

563 1 s. Type **146** 30 40
564 2 s. "Aeropetes tulbaghia" . . 30 40
565 3 s. "Colotis evenina" 35 40
566 4 s. "Precis oenone" 35 40
567 5 s. "Precis hierta" 35 40
568 6 s. "Catopsilia florella" . . . 35 10
569 7 s. "Phalanta phalantha" . . 35 10
570 10 s. "Acraea stenobea" . . . 40 10
571 15 s. "Cynthia cardui" 90 10
572 20 s. "Colotis subfasciatus" . . 1·00 10
573 30 s. "Charaxes jasius" . . . 1·25 30
574 50 s. "Terias brigitta" . . . . 1·50 40
575 60 s. "Pontia helice" . . . . 1·60 50
576 75 s. "Colotis regina" . . . . 1·75 50
577 1 m. "Hypolimnas misippus" 2·00 1·50
578 5 m. "Papilio demodocus" . . 4·50 7·50

147 "Thou shalt not have Strange Gods before Me"

1984. Easter. The Ten Commandments. Mult.

579 20 s. Type **147** 30 30
580 20 s. "Thou shalt not take the name of the Lord thy God in vain" 30 30
581 20 s. "Remember thou keep holy the Lord's Day" 30 30
582 20 s. "Honour thy father and mother" 30 30
583 20 s. "Thou shalt not kill" . . 30 30
584 20 s. "Thou shalt not commit adultery" 30 30
585 20 s. "Thou shalt not steal" . . 30 30
586 20 s. "Thou shalt not bear false witness against thy neighbour" 30 30
587 20 s. "Thou shalt not covet thy neighbour's wife" 30 30
588 20 s. "Thou shalt not covet thy neighbour's goods" 30 30

148 Torch Bearer

1984. Olympic Games, Los Angeles. Multicoloured.

590 10 s. Type **148** 10 10
591 30 s. Horse-riding 10 10
592 50 s. Swimming 15 20
593 75 s. Basketball 20 25
594 1 m. Running 25 30

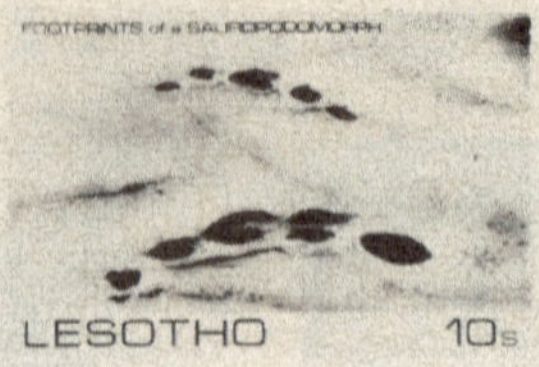

149 Sauropodomorph Footprints

1984. Prehistoric Footprints (2nd series). Mult.

596 10 s. Type **149** 55 30
597 30 s. Lesothosaurus footprints 1·00 1·25
598 50 s. Footprint of carnivorous dinosaur . . . . 1·25 2·00

150 Wells Fargo Coach, 1852

1984. "Ausipex" Int Stamp Exhibition, Melbourne. Bicent of First Mail Coach Run. Mult.
599 6 s. Type **150** . . . 10 10
600 7 s. Basotho mail cart, circa 1900 . . 10 10
601 10 s. Bath mail coach, 1784 . . 10 10
602 30 s. Cobb coach, 1853 . . 30 35
603 50 s. Exhibition logo and Royal Exhibition Buildings, Melbourne (82 × 25 mm) . . 50 55

151 "The Orient Express" (1900)

1984. Railways of the World. Multicoloured.
605 6 s. Type **151** . . . 40 15
606 15 s. Class 05 streamlined steam locomotive No. 001, Germany (1935) . . . 40 30
607 30 s. Caledonian Railway steam locomotive "Cardean" (1906) 60 60
608 60 s. Atchison, Topeka & Santa Fe "Super Chief" express (1940) . . . 80 1·75
609 1 m. L.N.E.R. "Flying Scotsman" (1934) . . . 85 2·00

152 Eland Calf

1984. Baby Animals. Multicoloured.
611 15 s. Type **152** . . . 35 20
612 20 s. Young chacma baboons . 40 25
613 30 s. Oribi calf . . . 55 40
614 75 s. Young Natal red hares . 1·25 1·60
615 1 m. Black-backed jackal pups (46 × 27 mm) . . . 1·50 2·00

153 Crown of Lesotho

154 Christ condemned to Death

1985. Silver Jubilee of King Moshoeshoe II. Mult.
616 6 s. Type **153** . . . 10 10
617 30 s. King Moshoeshoe in 1960 20 30
618 75 s. King Moshoeshoe in traditional dress, 1985 . . . 50 75
619 1 m. King Moshoeshoe in uniform, 1985 . . . 70 1·10

1985. Easter. The Stations of the Cross. Mult.
620 20 s. Type **154** . . . 20 25
621 20 s. Christ carrying the Cross 20 25
622 20 s. Falling for the first time 20 25
623 20 s. Christ meets Mary . . 20 25
624 20 s. Simon of Cyrene helping to carry the Cross . . . 20 25
625 20 s. Veronica wiping the face of Christ . . . 20 25
626 20 s. Christ falling a second time 20 25
627 20 s. Consoling the women of Jerusalem . . . 20 25
628 20 s. Falling for the third time 20 25
629 20 s. Christ being stripped . . 20 25
630 20 s. Christ nailed to the Cross 20 25
631 20 s. Dying on the Cross . . 20 25
632 20 s. Christ taken down from the Cross . . . 20 25
633 20 s. Christ being laid in the sepulchre . . . 20 25

155 Duchess of York with Princess Elizabeth, 1931

1985. Life and Times of Queen Elizabeth the Queen Mother. Multicoloured.
635 10 s. Type **155** . . . 15 10
636 30 s. The Queen Mother in 1975 50 50
637 60 s. Queen Mother with Queen Elizabeth and Princess Margaret, 1980 . . . 60 90
638 2 m. Four generations of Royal Family at Prince Henry's christening, 1984 . . . 1·25 2·50

156 B.M.W. "732i"

1985. Century of Motoring. Multicoloured.
640 6 s. Type **156** . . . 25 15
641 10 s. Ford "Crown Victoria" 35 15
642 30 s. Mercedes-Benz "500SE" 75 50
643 90 s. Cadillac "Eldorado Biarritz" . . . 2·00 2·50
644 2 m. Rolls-Royce "Silver Spirit" 3·00 4·00

157 American Cliff Swallow

158 Two Youths Rock-climbing

1985. Birth Bicentenary of John J. Audubon (ornithologist). Designs showing original paintings. Multicoloured.
646 5 s. Type **157** . . . 40 20
647 6 s. Great crested grebe (horiz) 40 20
648 10 s. Vesper sparrow (horiz) . 55 20
649 30 s. Greenshank (horiz) . . 1·25 75
650 60 s. Stilt sandpiper (horiz) . 2·00 2·50
651 2 m. Glossy ibis (horiz) . . 3·50 5·00

1985. International Youth Year and 75th Anniv of Girl Guide Movement. Multicoloured.
652 10 s. Type **158** . . . 20 10
653 30 s. Young technician in hospital laboratory . . . 50 40
654 75 s. Three guides on parade . 1·00 1·25
655 2 m. Guide saluting . . . 2·40 3·00

159 U.N. (New York) 1951 1 c. Definitive and U.N. Flag

160 Cosmos

1985. 40th Anniversary of U.N.O.
657 **159** 10 s. multicoloured . . 25 10
658 – 30 s. multicoloured . . 60 35
659 – 50 s. multicoloured . . 95 85
660 – 2 m. black and green . 5·00 6·50
DESIGNS—VERT: 30 s. Ha Sofonia Earth Satellite Station; 2 m. Maimonides (physician, philosopher and scholar). HORIZ: 50 s. Lesotho Airways Fokker F.27 Friendship at Maseru Airport.

1985. Wild Flowers. Multicoloured.
661 6 s. Type **160** . . . 40 15
662 10 s. Small agapanthus . . 55 15
663 30 s. Pink witchweed . . 1·10 70
664 60 s. Small iris . . . 1·75 2·00
665 90 s. Wild geranium or cranesbill 2·40 3·00
666 1 m. Large spotted orchid . 3·75 5·00

1985. 150th Birth Anniv of Mark Twain. Walt Disney cartoon characters illustrating various Mark Twain quotations. As T **118** of Anguilla. Multicoloured.
667 6 s. Mrs Jumbo and baby Dumbo 40 15
668 50 s. Uncle Scrooge and Goofy reading newspaper . . . 1·25 1·00
669 90 s. Winnie the Pooh, Tigger, Piglet and Owl . . . 1·75 2·00
670 1 m. 50 Goofy at ship's wheel 2·75 3·00

1985. Birth Bicentenaries of Grimm Brothers (folklorists). Walt Disney cartoon characters in scenes from "The Wishing Table". As T **119** of Anguilla. Multicoloured.
672 10 s. The tailor (Donald Duck) 35 15
673 60 s. The second son (Dewey) with magic donkey and gold coins . . . 1·25 1·25
674 75 s. The eldest son (Huey) with wishing table laden with food 1·50 1·50
675 1 m. The innkeeper stealing the third son's (Louie) magic cudgel . . . 2·00 2·50

161 Male Lammergeier on Watch

162 Two Players chasing Ball

1986. Flora and Fauna of Lesotho. Multicoloured.
677 7 s. Type **161** . . . 90 30
678 9 s. Prickly pear . . . 70 20
679 12 s. Stapelia . . . 70 20
680 15 s. Pair of lammergeiers . . 1·75 50
681 35 s. Pig's ears . . . 1·10 60
682 50 s. Male lammergeier in flight 3·00 2·50
683 1 m. Adult and juvenile lammergeiers . . . 3·75 4·50
684 2 m. Columnar cereus . . 3·75 6·00

1986. World Cup Football Championship, Mexico. Multicoloured.
686 35 s. Type **162** . . . 1·25 50
687 50 s. Goalkeeper saving goal . 1·75 1·25
688 1 m. Three players chasing ball 3·00 2·75
689 2 m. Two players competing for ball . . . 5·00 5·00

1986. Appearance of Halley's Comet. As T **123** of Anguilla. Multicoloured.
691 9 s. Galileo and 200 inch Hale telescope, Mount Palomar Observatory, California . . 50 15
692 15 s. Halley's Comet and "Pioneer Venus 2" spacecraft 75 20
693 70 s. Halley's Comet of 684 A.D. (from "Nuremberg Chronicle", 1493) . . . 1·60 1·40
694 3 m. Comet and landing of William the Conqueror, 1066 4·00 5·50

163 International Year of the Child Gold Coin

1986. First Anniv of New Currency (1980). Multicoloured.
696 30 s. Type **163** . . . 5·00 6·50
697 30 s. Five maloti banknote . 5·00 6·50
698 30 s. Fifty lisente coin . . 5·00 6·50
699 30 s. Ten maloti banknote . . 5·00 6·50
700 30 s. One sente coin . . . 5·00 6·50
These stamps were prepared in 1980, but were not issued at that time.

1986. 60th Birthday of Queen Elizabeth II. As T **125** of Anguilla.
701 90 s. black and yellow . . 50 60
702 1 m. multicoloured . . . 55 65
703 2 m. multicoloured . . . 90 1·40
DESIGNS: 90 s. Princess Elizabeth in pantomime; 1 m. Queen at Windsor Horse Show, 1971; 2 m. At Royal Festival Hall, 1971.

1986. Centenary of Statue of Liberty. Immigrants to the U.S.A. As T **211** of Dominica. Multicoloured.
705 15 s. Bela Bartok (composer) . 85 30
706 35 s. Felix Adler (philosopher) 85 30
707 1 m. Victor Herbert (composer) 3·00 2·00
708 3 m. David Niven (actor) . . 4·25 4·00

1986. "Ameripex" International Stamp Exhibition, Chicago. Walt Disney cartoon characters delivering mail. As T **212** of Dominica. Multicoloured.
710 15 s. Mickey Mouse and Goofy as Japanese mail runners . . 55 20
711 35 s. Mickey Mouse and Pluto with mail sledge . . . 90 30
712 1 m. Goofy as postman riding Harley-Davidson motorcycle 1·75 1·75
713 2 m. Donald Duck operating railway mailbag apparatus . 2·25 2·75

1986. Various stamps surch. (a) On Nos. 437 etc (Birds)
729 9 s. on 5 s. Bokmakierie shrike 15 20
715 9 s. on 10 s. Red-billed pintail (horiz) . . . 2·50 1·25
716 15 s. on 1 s. Type **127** . . 6·00 3·00
717 15 s. on 2 s. Speckled pigeon (horiz) . . . 4·00 4·50
718 15 s. on 5 s. Bokmakierie shrike 1·00 35
719 15 s. on 60 s. Cape longclaw (horiz) . . . 20 10
730 16 s. on 25 s. Malachite kingfisher . . . 2·25 1·00
731 35 s. on 25 s. Malachite kingfisher . . . 60 60
721 35 s. on 75 s. Hoopoe . . 22·00 18·00

(b) On Nos. 563, etc (Butterflies).
722 9 s. on 30 s. "Charaxes jasius" 15 10
723 9 s. on 60 s. "Pontia helice" . 4·00 4·00
724 15 s. on 1 s. Type **146** . . 2·75 2·75
725 15 s. on 2 s. "Aeropetes tulbaghia" . . . 20 20
726 15 s. on 3 s. "Colotis evenina" 20 20
727 15 s. on 5 s. "Precis hierta" . 20 20
732 20 s. on 4 s. "Precis oenone" 10 10
728 35 s. on 75 s. "Colotis regina" 35 35
733 40 s. on 7 s. "Phalanta phalantha" . . . 15 20

(c) No. 722 further surch.
734 3 s. on 9 s. on 30 s. "Charaxes jasius" . . . 15 15
735 7 s. on 9 s. on 30 s. "Charaxes jasius" . . . 25 25

1986. Royal Wedding. As T **213** of Antigua. Multicoloured.
736 50 s. Prince Andrew and Miss Sarah Ferguson . . . 40 40
737 1 m. Prince Andrew . . . 70 70
738 3 m. Prince Andrew piloting helicopter . . . 2·25 2·25

171 Basotho Pony and Rider

1986. 20th Anniv of Independence. Multicoloured.
740 9 s. Type **171** . . . 30 10
741 15 s. Basotho woman spinning mohair . . . 30 15
742 35 s. Crossing river by rowing boat . . . 40 30
743 3 m. Thaba Tseka Post Office 1·50 3·00

1986. Christmas. Walt Disney cartoon characters. As T **220** of Antigua. Multicoloured.
745 15 s. Chip'n' Dale pulling Christmas cracker . . . 35 20
746 35 s. Mickey and Minnie Mouse 60 30
747 1 m. Pluto pulling Christmas taffy . . . 1·50 2·00
748 2 m. Aunt Matilda baking . . 2·00 3·00

172 Rally Car

173 Lawn Tennis

1987. Roof of Africa Motor Rally. Multicoloured.
750 9 s. Type **172** . . . 30 10
751 15 s. Motorcyclist . . . 35 15
752 35 s. Motorcyclist (different) . 55 35
753 4 m. Rally car (different) . . 3·00 4·50

1987. Olympic Games, Seoul (1988) (1st issue). Multicoloured.
754 9 s. Type **173** . . . 40 10
755 15 s. Judo . . . 40 15
756 20 s. Athletics . . . 45 20
757 35 s. Boxing . . . 60 30
758 1 m. Diving . . . 1·25 1·60
759 3 m. Ten-pin bowling . . 2·75 4·50
See also Nos. 838/41.

174 Isaac Newton and Reflecting Telescope

1987. Great Scientific Discoveries. Multicoloured.
761 5 s. Type **174** . . . 30 10
762 9 s. Alexander Graham Bell and first telephone . . . 30 15
763 75 s. Robert Goddard and liquid fuel rocket . . . 80 65
764 4 m. Chuck Yeager and Bell XS-1 rocket plane . . . 2·75 4·00

175 Grey Rhebuck

1987. Flora and Fauna. Multicoloured.
766 5 s. Type **175** . . . 40 15
767 9 s. Cape clawless otter . . 40 15
768 15 s. Cape grey mongoose . . 55 20
769 20 s. Free State daisy (vert) . 60 20

770	35 s. River bells (vert)	75	30
771	1 m. Turkey flower (vert)	1·75	2·25
772	2 m. Sweet briar (vert)	2·25	3·50
773	3 m. Mountain reedbuck	2·75	4·50

176 Scouts hiking

178 "Madonna and Child" (detail)

177 Spotted Trunkfish and Columbus's Fleet

1987. World Scout Jamboree, Australia. Mult.

775	9 s. Type **176**	50	20
776	15 s. Scouts playing football	55	20
777	35 s. Kangaroos	70	50
778	75 s. Scout saluting	1·50	1·25
779	4 m. Australian scout windsurfing	3·75	6·00

1987. 500th Anniv (1992) of Discovery of America by Columbus. Multicoloured.

781	9 s. Type **177**	45	20
782	15 s. Green turtle and ships	60	20
783	35 s. Columbus watching common dolphins from ship	80	40
784	5 m. White-tailed tropic bird and fleet at sea	4·25	6·50

No. 782 is inscribed "Carribbean" in error.

1987. Christmas. Paintings by Raphael. Mult.

786	9 s. Type **178**	30	10
787	15 s. "Marriage of the Virgin"	45	15
788	35 s. "Coronation of the Virgin" (detail)	90	40
789	90 s. "Madonna of the Chair"	2·00	3·50

179 Lesser Pied Kingfisher

1988. Birds. Multicoloured.

791	2 s. Type **179**	20	30
792	3 s. Three-banded plover	20	30
793	5 s. Spur-winged goose	20	30
794	10 s. Clapper lark	20	20
795	12 s. Red-eyed bulbul	30	10
796	16 s. Cape weaver	30	10
797	20 s. Paradise sparrow ("Red-headed Finch")	30	10
798	30 s. Mountain chat	35	20
799	40 s. Stonechat	40	20
800	55 s. Pied barbet	50	25
801	60 s. Red-shouldered glossy starling	55	50
802	75 s. Cape sparrow	65	60
803	1 m. Cattle egret	75	80
804	3 m. Giant kingfisher	1·50	2·50
805	10 m. Helmet guineafowl	4·00	7·00

1988. Royal Ruby Wedding. Nos. 701/3 optd **40TH WEDDING ANNIVERSARY H.M. QUEEN ELIZABETH II H.R.H. THE DUKE OF EDINBURGH.**

806	90 s. black and yellow	50	65
807	1 m. multicoloured	60	80
808	2 m. multicoloured	1·00	1·40

181 Mickey Mouse and Goofy outside Presidential Palace, Helsinki

1988. "Finlandia '88" International Stamp Exhibition, Helsinki. Designs showing Walt Disney cartoon characters in Finland. Mult.

810	1 s. Type **181**	10	10
811	2 s. Goofy and Mickey Mouse in sauna	10	10
812	3 s. Goofy and Mickey Mouse fishing in lake	10	10
813	4 s. Mickey and Minnie Mouse and Finlandia Hall, Helsinki	10	10
814	5 s. Mickey Mouse photographing Goofy at Sibelius Monument, Helsinki	10	10
815	10 s. Mickey Mouse and Goofy pony trekking	10	10
816	3 m. Goofy, Mickey and Minnie Mouse at Helsinki Olympic Stadium	2·75	3·00
817	5 m. Mickey Mouse and Goofy meeting Santa at Arctic Circle	3·50	4·00

182 Pope John Paul II giving Communion

183 Large-toothed Rock Hyrax

1988. Visit of Pope John Paul II. Mult.

819	55 s. Type **182**	40	25
820	2 m. Pope leading procession	1·25	1·50
821	3 m. Pope at airport	1·75	2·00
822	4 m. Pope John Paul II	2·25	2·75

1988. Small Mammals of Lesotho. Mult.

824	16 s. Type **183**	30	15
825	40 s. Ratel and black-throated honey guide (bird)	70	40
826	75 s. Small-spotted genet	90	75
827	3 m. Yellow mongoose	2·75	3·75

184 "Birth of Venus" (detail) (Botticelli)

1988. Famous Paintings. Multicoloured.

829	15 s. Type **184**	30	15
830	25 s. "View of Toledo" (El Greco)	35	20
831	40 s. "Maids of Honour" (detail) (Velasquez)	45	25
832	50 s. "The Fifer" (Manet)	55	30
833	55 s. "Starry Night" (detail) (Van Gogh)	55	30
834	75 s. "Prima Ballerina" (Degas)	70	70
835	2 m. "Bridge over Water Lilies" (Monet)	1·75	2·00
836	3 m. "Guernica" (detail) (Picasso)	1·75	2·50

185 Wrestling

1988. Olympic Games, Seoul (2nd series). Mult.

838	12 s. Type **185**	10	10
839	16 s. Show jumping (vert)	10	10
840	55 s. Shooting	20	30
841	3 m. 50 As 16 s. (vert)	1·40	2·00

186 Yannick Noah and Eiffel Tower, Paris

1988. 75th Anniv of Int Tennis Federation. Mult.

843	12 s. Type **186**	20	15
844	20 s. Rod Laver and Sydney Harbour Bridge and Opera House	25	20
845	30 s. Ivan Lendl and Prague	30	25
846	65 s. Jimmy Connors and Tokyo (vert)	45	40
847	1 m. Arthur Ashe and Barcelona (vert)	70	60
848	1 m. 55 Althea Gibson and New York (vert)	90	90
849	2 m. Chris Evert and Vienna (vert)	1·25	1·25
850	2 m. 40 Boris Becker and Houses of Parliament, London (vert)	1·60	1·75
851	3 m. Martina Navratilova and Golden Gate Bridge, San Francisco	1·75	2·00

No. 844 is inscribed "SIDNEY" in error.

1988. Christmas. 500th Birth Anniv of Titian (artist). As T **238** of Antigua but inscr "CHRISTMAS 1988". Multicoloured.

853	12 s. "The Averoldi Polyptych" (detail)	20	10
854	20 s. "Christ and the Adulteress" (detail)	20	10
855	35 s. "Christ and the Adulteress" (different detail)	30	20
856	45 s. "Angel of the Annunciation"	40	30
857	65 s. "Saint Dominic"	55	50
858	1 m. "The Vendramin Family" (detail)	75	80
859	2 m. "Mary Magdalen"	1·25	1·75
860	3 m. "The Tribute Money"	1·75	2·50

187 Pilatus PC-6 Turbo Porter

1989. 125th Anniv of International Red Cross. Aircraft. Multicoloured.

862	12 s. Type **187**	15	10
863	20 s. Unloading medical supplies from Cessna Caravan I	20	15
864	55 s. De Havilland D.H.C.6 Twin Otter 200/300	40	40
865	3 m. Douglas DC-3	2·00	3·00

1989. Japanese Art. Paintings by Hiroshige. As T **250** of Antigua. Multicoloured.

867	12 s. "Dawn Mist at Mishima"	30	10
868	16 s. "Night Snow at Kambara"	35	10
869	20 s. "Wayside Inn at Mariko Station"	35	10
870	35 s. "Shower at Shono"	55	10
871	55 s. "Snowfall on the Kisokaido near Oi"	65	40
872	1 m. "Autumn Moon at Seba"	85	85
873	3 m. 20 "Evening Moon at Ryogoku Bridge"	2·25	3·00
874	5 m. "Cherry Blossoms at Arashiyama"	2·75	3·75

188 Mickey Mouse as General

189 "Paxillus involutus"

1989. "Philexfrance 89" International Stamp Exhibition, Paris. Designs showing Walt Disney cartoon characters in French military uniforms of the Revolutionary period. Multicoloured.

876	1 s. Type **188**	10	10
877	2 s. Ludwig von Drake as infantryman	10	10
878	3 s. Goofy as grenadier	10	10
879	4 s. Horace Horsecollar as cavalryman	10	10
880	5 s. Pete as hussar	10	10
881	10 s. Donald Duck as marine	10	10
882	3 m. Gyro Gearloose as National Guard	3·00	3·25
883	5 m. Scrooge McDuck as admiral	3·75	4·25

1989. Fungi. Multicoloured.

900	12 s. Type **189**	20	10
901	16 s. "Ganoderma applanatum"	20	15
902	55 s. "Suillus granulatus"	45	35
903	5 m. "Stereum hirsutum"	3·25	4·50

190 Sesotho Huts

192 Launch of "Apollo 11"

191 Marsh Sandpiper

1989. Maloti Mountains. Multicoloured.

905	1 m. Type **190**	70	90
906	1 m. American aloe and mountains	70	90
907	1 m. River valley with waterfall	70	90
908	1 m. Sesotho tribesman on ledge	70	90

Nos. 905/8 were printed together, se-tenant, forming a composite design.

1989. Migrant Birds. Multicoloured.

910	12 s. Type **191**	70	30
911	65 s. Little stint	1·25	70
912	1 m. Ringed plover	1·75	1·50
913	4 m. Curlew sandpiper	3·50	5·50

1989. 20th Anniv of First Manned Landing on Moon. Multicoloured.

915	12 s. Type **192**	25	10
916	16 s. Lunar module "Eagle" landing on Moon (horiz)	25	15
917	40 s. Neil Armstrong leaving "Eagle"	45	25
918	55 s. Edwin Aldrin on Moon (horiz)	50	30
919	1 m. Aldrin performing scientific experiment (horiz)	85	85
920	2 m. "Eagle" leaving Moon (horiz)	1·50	1·75
921	3 m. Command module "Columbia" in Moon orbit (horiz)	2·00	2·25
922	4 m. Command module on parachutes	2·50	2·75

193 English Penny Post Paid Mark, 1680

1989. "World Stamp Expo '89" International Stamp Exhibition, Washington. Stamps and Postmarks.

924	**193**	75 s. red, black and stone	60	65
925	–	75 s. black, grey and red	60	65
926	–	75 s. violet, black & brn	60	65
927	–	75 s. brown, black & lt brn	60	65
928	–	75 s. black and yellow	60	65
929	–	75 s. multicoloured	60	65
930	–	75 s. black and lilac	60	65
931	–	75 s. black, red & brown	60	65
932	–	75 s. red, black & yellow	60	65

DESIGNS: No. 925, German postal seal and feather, 1807; 926, British Post Office in Crete 1898 20 pa. stamp; 927, Bermuda 1848 Perot 1d. provisional; 928, U.S.A. Pony Express cancellation, 1860; 929, Finland 1856 5 k. stamp; 930, Fiji 1870 "Fiji Times" 1d. stamp, 1870; 931, Sweden newspaper wrapper handstamp, 1823; 932, Bhor 1879 ½ a. stamp.

1989. Christmas. Paintings by Velazquez. As T **259** of Antigua. Multicoloured.

934	12 s. "The Immaculate Conception"	10	10
935	20 s. "St. Anthony Abbot and St. Paul the Hermit"	15	10
936	35 s. "St. Thomas the Apostle"	25	25
937	55 s. "Christ in the House of Martha and Mary"	35	35
938	1 m. "St. John writing The Apocalypse on Patmos"	60	75
939	3 m. "The Virgin presenting the Chasuble to St. Ildephonsus"	1·60	2·25
940	4 m. "The Adoration of the Magi"	2·00	2·75

194 Scene from 1966 World Cup Final, England

1989. World Cup Football Championship, Italy. Scenes from past finals. Multicoloured.

942	12 s. Type **194**	30	10
943	16 s. 1970 final, Mexico	30	15
944	55 s. 1974 final, West Germany	75	40
945	5 m. 1982 final, Spain	3·50	5·00

1990. No. 889 and 798/9 surch **16 s.**

948	16 s. on 12 s. Red-eyed bulbul	50	15
948*e*	16 s. on 30 s. Mountain chat	50	15
948*f*	16 s. on 40 s. Stonechat	50	15

197 "Byblia anvatara"

1990. Butterflies. Multicoloured.

949	12 s. Type **197**	50	15
950	16 s. "Cynthia cardui"	65	15
951	55 s. "Precis oenone"	90	40
952	65 s. "Pseudacraea boisduvali"	1·00	65
953	1 m. "Precis orithya"	1·50	1·25
954	2 m. "Precis sophia"	2·50	2·50
955	3 m. "Danaus chrysippus"	3·25	3·75
956	4 m. "Druryia antimachus"	4·25	6·00

198 "Satyrium princeps"

1990. "EXPO 90" International Garden and Greenery Exhibition, Osaka. Local Orchids. Multicoloured.

958	12 s. Type **198**	45	15
959	16 s. "Huttonaea pulchra"	50	15
960	55 s. "Herschelia graminifolia"	1·00	30
961	1 m. "Ansellia gigantea"	1·50	75
962	1 m. 55 "Polystachya pubescens"	1·75	1·75
963	2 m. 40 "Penthea filicornis"	1·75	2·25
964	3 m. "Disperis capensis"	2·25	3·25
965	4 m. "Disa uniflora"	3·00	4·00

1990. 90th Birthday of Queen Elizabeth the Queen Mother. As T **99** of Grenada Grenadines.

967	1 m. 50 black and mauve	95	1·00
968	1 m. 50 black and mauve	95	1·00
969	1 m. 50 black and mauve	95	1·00

DESIGNS: No. 967, Lady Elizabeth Bowes-Lyon and brother in fancy dress; 968, Lady Elizabeth Bowes-Lyon in evening dress; 969, Lady Elizabeth Bowes-Lyon wearing hat.

199 King Moshoeshoe II and Prince Mohato wearing Seana-Marena Blankets

200 Filling Truck at No. 1 Quarry

1990. Traditional Blankets. Multicoloured.

971	12 s. Type **199**	10	10
972	16 s. Prince Mohato wearing Seana-Marena blanket	10	10
973	1 m. Pope John Paul II wearing Seana-Marena blanket	1·50	1·10
974	3 m. Basotho horsemen wearing Matlama blankets	2·00	2·75

1990. Lesotho Highlands Water Project. Mult.

976	16 s. Type **200**	35	10
977	20 s. Tanker lorry on Pitseng–Malibamatso road	35	10
978	55 s. Piers for Malibamatso Bridge	55	30
979	2 m. Excavating Mphosong section of Pitseng–Malibamatso road	2·00	3·00

201 Mother breastfeeding Baby

203 "Virgin and Child" (detail, Rubens)

1990. U.N.I.C.E.F. Child Survival Campaign. Multicoloured.

981	12 s. Type **201**	40	10
982	55 s. Baby receiving oral rehydration therapy	70	45
983	1 m. Weight monitoring	1·00	2·00

1990. Olympic Games, Barcelona (1992). As T **268** of Antigua. Multicoloured.

984	16 s. Men's triple jump	30	10
985	55 s. Men's 200 metres race	50	25
986	1 m. Men's 5000 metres race	80	90
987	4 m. Show jumping	2·75	4·00

1990. Christmas. Paintings by Rubens. Mult.

989	12 s. Type **203**	20	10
990	16 s. "Adoration of the Magi" (detail)	20	10
991	55 s. "Head of One of the Three Kings"	45	25
992	80 s. "Adoration of the Magi" (different detail)	60	60
993	1 m. "Virgin and Child" (different detail)	70	70
994	2 m. "Adoration of the Magi" (different detail)	1·25	1·50
995	3 m. "Virgin and Child" (different detail)	2·00	2·25
996	4 m. "Adoration of the Magi" (different detail)	2·25	2·75

204 Mickey Mouse at Nagasaki Peace Park

1991. "Phila Nippon '91" International Stamp Exhibition, Tokyo. Walt Disney cartoon characters in Japan. Multicoloured.

998	20 s. Type **204**	45	15
999	30 s. Mickey Mouse on Kamakura Beach	50	20
1000	40 s. Mickey and Donald Duck with Bunraku puppet	55	25
1001	50 s. Mickey and Donald eating soba	60	35
1002	75 s. Mickey and Minnie Mouse at tea house	85	70
1003	1 m. Mickey running after "Hikari" express train	1·00	1·00
1004	3 m. Mickey Mouse with deer at Todaiji Temple, Nara	2·50	3·25
1005	4 m. Mickey and Minnie outside Imperial Palace	2·75	3·50

205 Stewart Granger ("King Solomon's Mines")

207 Victim of Drug Abuse

206 "Satyrus aello"

1991. Famous Films with African Themes. Mult.

1007	12 s. Type **205**	35	20
1008	16 s. Johnny Weissmuller ("Tarzan the Ape Man")	35	20
1009	30 s. Clark Gable and Grace Kelly ("Mogambo")	50	35
1010	55 s. Sigourney Weaver and gorilla ("Gorillas in the Mist")	75	55
1011	70 s. Humphrey Bogart and Katharine Hepburn ("The African Queen")	90	80
1012	1 m. John Wayne and capture of rhinoceros ("Hatari!")	1·25	1·00
1013	2 m. Meryl Streep and De Havilland Gipsy Moth light aircraft ("Out of Africa")	2·00	2·25
1014	4 m. Arsenio Hall and Eddie Murphy ("Coming to America")	2·75	3·50

1991. Butterflies. Multicoloured.

1016B	2 s. Type **206**	10	10
1017B	3 s. "Erebia medusa"	10	10
1018A	5 s. "Melanargia galathea"	30	30
1019B	10 s. "Erebia aethiops"	10	10
1020A	20 s. "Coenonympha pamphilus"	35	30
1021B	25 s. "Pyrameis atalanta"	10	10
1022B	30 s. "Charaxes jasius"	10	10
1023B	40 s. "Colias palaeno"	10	10
1024B	50 s. "Colias cliopatra"	15	20
1025B	60 s. "Colias philodice"	15	20
1026B	70 s. "Rhumni gonepterix"	25	25
1027B	1 m. "Colias caesonia"	25	30
1028B	2 m. "Pyrameis cardui"	50	55
1029B	3 m. "Danaus chrysippus"	80	85
1030B	10 m. "Apatura iris"	2·50	3·75

1991. "Say No To Drugs" Campaign.

1031	**207** 16 s. multicoloured	70	60

208 Wattled Cranes

1991. Southern Africa Development Co-ordination Conference Tourism Promotion. Multicoloured.

1032	12 s. Type **208**	70	70
1033	16 s. Butterfly on flowers	70	70
1034	25 s. Zebra and tourist bus at Mukurub (rock formation), Namibia	85	30

209 De Gaulle in 1939

211 "St. Anne with Mary and the Child Jesus"

1991. Birth Centenary of Charles de Gaulle (French statesman).

1036	**209**	20 s. black and brown	40	15
1037	–	40 s. black and purple	60	25
1038	–	50 s. black and green	60	40
1039	–	60 s. black and blue	70	65
1040	–	4 m. black and red	2·25	3·75

DESIGNS: 40 s. General De Gaulle as Free French leader; 50 s. De Gaulle as provisional President of France, 1944–46; 60 s. Charles de Gaulle in 1958; 4 m. Pres. De Gaulle.

1991. 10th Wedding Anniv of Prince and Princess of Wales. As T **280** of Antigua. Multicoloured.

1041	50 s. Prince and Princess of Wales	65	25
1042	70 s. Prince Charles at polo and Princess Diana holding Prince Henry	65	45
1043	1 m. Prince Charles with Prince Henry and Princess Diana in evening dress	85	65
1044	3 m. Prince William and Prince Henry in school uniform	1·75	2·75

1991. Christmas. Drawings by Albrecht Durer.

1046	**211**	20 s. black and mauve	25	10
1047	–	30 s. black and blue	35	20
1048	–	50 s. black and green	50	25
1049	–	60 s. black and red	55	30
1050	–	70 s. black and yellow	60	45
1051	–	1 m. black and orange	75	75
1052	–	2 m. black and purple	1·50	2·00
1053	–	4 m. black and blue	2·25	3·50

DESIGNS: 30 s. "Mary on Grass Bench"; 50 s. "Mary with Crown of Stars"; 60 s. "Mary with Child beside Tree"; 70 s. "Mary with Child beside Wall"; 1 m. "Mary in Halo on Crescent Moon"; 2 m. "Mary breastfeeding Child"; 4 m. "Mary with Infant in Swaddling Clothes".

212 Mickey Mouse and Pluto pinning the Tail on the Donkey

1991. Children's Games. Walt Disney cartoon characters. Multicoloured.

1055	20 s. Type **212**	40	15
1056	30 s. Mickey playing mancala	45	20
1057	40 s. Mickey rolling hoop	50	20
1058	50 s. Minnie Mouse hula-hooping	55	25
1059	70 s. Mickey and Pluto throwing a frisbee	75	60
1060	1 m. Donald Duck with a diabolo	1·00	1·00
1061	2 m. Donald's nephews playing marbles	2·00	2·50
1062	3 m. Donald with Rubik's cube	2·50	3·25

213 Lanner Falcon

1992. Birds. Multicoloured.

1064	30 s. Type **213**	45	45
1065	30 s. Bateleur	45	45
1066	30 s. Paradise sparrow (inscr "Red-headed Finch")	45	45
1067	30 s. Lesser striped swallow	45	45
1068	30 s. Alpine swift	45	45
1069	30 s. Didric cuckoo	45	45
1070	30 s. Yellow-tufted malachite sunbird	45	45
1071	30 s. Burchell's gonolek ("Crimson-breasted Shrike")	45	45
1072	30 s. Pin-tailed whydah	45	45
1073	30 s. Lilac-breasted roller	45	45
1074	30 s. Little black bustard ("Korhaan")	45	45
1075	30 s. Black-collared barbet	45	45
1076	30 s. Secretary bird	45	45
1077	30 s. Red-billed quelea	45	45
1078	30 s. Red bishop	45	45
1079	30 s. Ring-necked dove	45	45
1080	30 s. Yellow canary	45	45
1081	30 s. Cape longclaw	45	45
1082	30 s. Cordon-bleu (inscr "Blue Waxbill")	45	45
1083	30 s. Golden bishop	45	45

Nos. 1064/83 were printed together, se-tenant, forming a composite design.

1992. 40th Anniv of Queen Elizabeth II's Accession. As T **288** of Antigua. Multicoloured.

1084	20 s. Huts on mountain	20	15
1085	30 s. View from mountains	25	20
1086	1 m. Cacti and mountain	65	65
1087	4 m. Thaba-Bosiu	2·25	3·00

215 Minnie Mouse as Spanish Lady, 1540–1660

1992. International Stamp Exhibitions. Walt Disney cartoon characters. Multicoloured. (a) "Granada '92", Spain. Traditional Spanish Costumes.

1089	20 s. Type **215**	40	15
1090	50 s. Mickey Mouse as Don Juan at Lepanto, 1571	55	30
1091	70 s. Donald in Galician costume, 1880	70	50
1092	2 m. Daisy Duck in Aragonese costume, 1880	1·75	2·50

(b) "World Columbian Stamp Expo '92". Red Indian Life.

1094	30 s. Donald Duck making arrowheads	30	30
1095	40 s. Goofy playing lacrosse	40	40
1096	1 m. Mickey Mouse and Donald Duck planting corn	70	80
1097	3 m. Minnie Mouse doing bead work	1·60	2·50

216 Stegosaurus

1992. Prehistoric Animals. Multicoloured.

1099	20 s. Type **216**	30	30
1100	30 s. Ceratosaurus	35	35
1101	40 s. Procompsognathus	45	45
1102	50 s. Lesothosaurus	55	55
1103	70 s. Plateosaurus	70	70
1104	1 m. Gasosaurus	1·00	1·00
1105	2 m. Massospondylus	1·50	1·50
1106	3 m. Archaeopteryx	2·00	2·00

217 Men's Discus

218 "Virgin and Child" (Sassetta)

1992. Olympic Games, Albertville and Barcelona. Multicoloured.

1108	20 s. Type **217**	20	15
1109	30 s. Men's long jump	25	15
1110	40 s. Women's 4 × 100 metres relay	30	25
1111	70 s. Women's 100 metres	50	50
1112	1 m. Men's parallel bars	70	70
1113	2 m. Men's double luge (horiz)	1·40	1·60
1114	3 m. Women's 30k cross-country skiing (horiz)	1·75	2·25
1115	4 m. Men's biathlon	2·00	2·50

1992. Christmas. Religious Paintings. Mult.

1117	20 s. Type **218**	25	15
1118	30 s. "Coronation of the Virgin" (Master of Bonastre)	30	20
1119	40 s. "Virgin and Child" (Master of SS. Cosmas and Damian)	40	25
1120	70 s. "The Virgin of Great Panagia" (detail) (12th-century Russian school)	70	55
1121	1 m. "Madonna and Child" (Vincenzo Foppa)	95	95
1122	2 m. "Madonna and Child" (School of Lippo Memmi)	1·75	2·00
1123	3 m. "Virgin and Child" (Barnaba da Modena)	2·25	2·75
1124	4 m. "Virgin and Child with Saints" (triptych) (Simone dei Crocifissi)	2·50	3·00

220 Baby Harp Seal (Earth Summit '92, Rio)

1993. Anniversaries and Events. Multicoloured.

1127	20 s. Type **220**	40	30
1128	30 s. Giant panda (Earth Summit '92, Rio)	55	30
1129	40 s. Airship "Graf Zeppelin" over globe (75th death anniv of Count Ferdinand von Zeppelin)	55	30
1130	70 s. Woman grinding maize (International Conference on Nutrition, Rome)	55	45
1131	4 m. Lt. Robinson's Royal Aircraft Factory B.E.2C shooting down Schutte Lanz SL-11 airship (75th death anniv of Count Ferdinand von Zeppelin)	2·50	2·75
1132	5 m. Valentina Tereshkova and "Vostok 6" (30th anniv of first woman in space)	2·50	2·75

221 "Orpheus and Eurydice" (detail)

1993. Bicentenary of the Louvre, Paris. Paintings by Poussin. Multicoloured.

1134	70 s. Type **221**	70	70
1135	70 s. "Rape of the Sabine Women" (left detail)	70	70
1136	70 s. "Rape of the Sabine Women" (right detail)	70	70
1137	70 s. "The Death of Sapphira" (left detail)	70	70
1138	70 s. "The Death of Sapphira" (right detail)	70	70
1139	70 s. "Echo and Narcissus" (left detail)	70	70
1140	70 s. "Echo and Narcissus" (right detail)	70	70
1141	70 s. "Self-portrait"	70	70

222 Aloe

1993. Flowers. Multicoloured.

1143	20 s. Type **222**	25	10
1144	30 s. Calla lily	30	15
1145	40 s. Bird of paradise plant	35	15
1146	70 s. Amaryllis	55	40
1147	1 m. Agapanthus	75	60
1148	2 m. Crinum	1·50	1·25
1149	4 m. Watsonia	1·60	2·00
1150	5 m. Gazania	1·75	2·25

223 "Precis westermanni"

1993. Butterflies. Multicoloured.

1152	20 s. Type **223**	40	15
1153	40 s. "Precis sophia"	50	20
1154	70 s. "Precis terea"	65	45
1155	1 m. "Byblia acheloia"	75	75
1156	2 m. "Papilio antimachus"	1·25	1·50
1157	5 m. "Pseudacraea boisduvali"	1·75	2·50

No. 1157 is inscribed "Pesudacraea boisduvali" in error.

1993. 40th Anniv of Coronation. As T **307** of Antigua.

1159	20 s. multicoloured	30	45
1160	40 s. multicoloured	45	60
1161	1 m. black and green	70	90
1162	5 m. multicoloured	3·00	3·25

DESIGNS: 20 s. Queen Elizabeth II at Coronation (photograph by Cecil Beaton); 40 s. St. Edward's Crown and Sceptre; 1 m. Queen Elizabeth the Queen Mother; 5 m. Queen Elizabeth II and family.

225 East African Railways Vulcan Steam Locomotive, 1929

1993. African Railways. Multicoloured.

1164	20 s. Type **225**	30	15
1165	30 s. Beyer-Garratt Class 15A steam locomotive, Zimbabwe Railways, 1952	40	20
1166	40 s. Class 25 steam locomotive, South African Railways, 1953	50	20
1167	70 s. Class A 58 steam locomotive, East African Railways	65	40
1168	1 m. Class 9E electric locomotives, South African Railways	80	70
1169	2 m. Class 87 diesel-electric locomotive, East African Railways, 1971	1·25	1·25
1170	3 m. Class 92 diesel locomotive, East African Railways, 1971	1·60	1·75
1171	5 m. Class 26 steam locomotive No. 3450, South African Railways, 1982	2·00	2·50

226 Court-house

1993. Traditional Houses. Multicoloured.

1173	20 s. Type **226**	25	10
1174	30 s. House with reed fence	30	15
1175	70 s. Unmarried girls' house	55	35
1176	4 m. Hut made from branches	2·75	3·25

227 Black and White Shorthair

1993. Domestic Cats. Multicoloured.

1178	20 s. Type **227**	10	10
1179	30 s. shorthair tabby lying down	10	10
1180	70 s. Head of Shorthair tabby	15	20
1181	5 m. Black and white shorthair with shorthair tabby	1·00	1·10

228 Pluto in Chung Cheng Park, Keelung

1993. "Taipei '93" Asian International Stamp Exhibition, Taiwan. Walt Disney cartoon characters in Taiwan. Multicoloured.

1183	20 s. Type **228**	30	10
1184	30 s. Donald Duck at Chiao-Tienkung Temple Festival	35	15
1185	40 s. Goofy with lantern figures	40	20
1186	70 s. Minnie Mouse shopping at temple festival	65	40
1187	1 m. Daisy Duck at Queen's Head Rock, Yehliu (vert)	80	70
1188	1 m. 20 Mickey and Minnie at National Concert Hall (vert)	1·00	1·00
1189	2 m. Donald at Chiang Kai-shek Memorial Hall (vert)	1·40	1·50
1190	2 m. 50 Donald and Daisy at the Grand Hotel, Taipei	1·75	2·00

229 Tseliso "Frisco" Khomari (Lesotho)

230 King Letsie III signing Oath of Office

1994. World Cup Football Championship '94, U.S.A. Multicoloured.

1192	20 s. Type **229**	30	10
1193	30 s. Thato "American Spoon" Mohale (Lesotho)	35	15
1194	40 s. Jozic Davor (Yugoslavia) and Freddy Rincorn (Colombia)	40	20
1195	50 s. Lefika "Mzee" Lekhotla (Lesotho)	45	25
1196	70 s. Litsiso "House-on-fire" Khali (Lesotho)	60	45
1197	1 m. Roger Milla (Cameroun)	75	70
1198	1 m. 20 David Platt (England)	1·00	1·25
1199	2 m. Karl Heinz Rummenigge (Germany) and Soren Lerby (Denmark)	1·60	1·75

1994. 1st Anniv of Restoration of Democracy. Multicoloured.

1201	20 s. Type **230**	10	10
1202	30 s. Parliament building (horiz)	10	10
1203	50 s. Swearing-in of Dr. Ntsu Mokhehle as Prime Minister (horiz)	10	10
1204	70 s. Maj-Gen P. Ramaema handing Instruments of Government to Dr. Ntsu Mokhehle (horiz)	15	10

231 Aquatic River Frog

1994. "Philakorea '94" International Stamp Exhibition, Seoul. Frogs and Toads. Mult.

1205	35 s. Type **231**	10	10
1206	50 s. Bubbling kassina	10	10
1207	1 m. Guttural toad	20	10
1208	1 m. 50 Common river frog	30	40

232 De Havilland D.H.C.6 Twin Otter and Emblem

1994. 50th Anniv of I.C.A.O. Multicoloured.

1210	35 s. Type **232**	10	10
1211	50 s. Fokker F.27 Friendship on runway	10	10
1212	1 m. Fokker F.27 Friendship over Moshoeshoe I International Airport	20	15
1213	1 m. 50 Cessna light aircraft over mountains	30	35

1995. No. 1022 surch **20s.**

1214a	20 s. on 30 s. "Charaxes jasius"	40	20

234 "Tagetes minuta"

235 Pius XII College, 1962

1995. Medicinal Plants. Multicoloured.

1215	35 s. Type **234**	10	10
1216	50 s. "Plantago lanceolata"	10	10
1217	1 m. "Amaranthus spinosus"	20	25
1218	1 m. 50 "Taraxacum officinale"	30	35

1995. 50th Anniv of University Studies in Lesotho. Multicoloured.

1220	35 s. Type **235**	10	10
1221	50 s. Campus, University of Basutoland, Bechuanaland and Swaziland, 1966	10	10
1222	70 s. Campus, University of Botswana, Lesotho and Swaziland, 1970	15	20
1223	1 m. Administration Block, University of Botswana, Lesotho and Swaziland, 1975	20	25
1224	1 m. 50 Administration Block, National University of Lesotho, 1988	30	35
1225	2 m. Procession of Vice-Chancellors, National University of Lesotho, 1995	45	50

236 Qiloane Pinnacle, Thaba-Bosiu

237 "Peace"

1995. 20th Anniv of World Tourism Organization. Multicoloured.

1226	35 s. Type **236**	10	10
1227	50 s. Ha Mohalenyane rock formation	10	10
1228	1 m. Botsoela Falls (vert)	20	25
1229	1 m. 50 Backpackers in Makhaleng River Gorge	30	35

1995. 50th Anniv of United Nations. Multicoloured.

1231	35 s. Type **237**	10	10
1232	50 s. "Justice" (scales)	10	10
1233	1 m. 50 "Reconciliation" (clasped hands) (horiz)	30	35

238 "Sutter's Gold Rose"

240 Adding Iodised Salt to Cooking Pot

239 Part of 1911 Map showing Lephaqhoa

1995. Christmas. Roses. Multicoloured.

1234	5 s. Type **238**	10	10
1235	50 s. "Michele Meilland"	10	10
1236	1 m. "J. Otto Thilow"	20	25
1237	2 m. "Papa Meilland"	40	45

1996. Completion of New Standard Map of Lesotho (1994). Map Sections of Malibamatso Valley. Multicoloured. (a) 1911 Map.

1238	35 s. Type **239**	10	10
1239	35 s. Boritsa Tsuene	10	10
1240	35 s. Molapo	10	10
1241	35 s. Nkeu	10	10
1242	35 s. Three rivers flowing east	10	10
1243	35 s. Tibedi and Rafanyane	10	10
1244	35 s. Two rivers flowing east	10	10
1245	35 s. Madibatmatso River	10	10
1246	35 s. Bokung River	10	10
1247	35 s. Semena River	10	10

(b) 1978 Map.

1248	35 s. Mountains and river valley	10	10
1249	35 s. Pelaneng and Lepaqoa	10	10
1250	35 s. Mamohau	10	10
1251	35 s. Ha Lejone	10	10

1252 35 s. Ha Thoora 10 10
1253 35 s. Ha Mikia 10 10
1254 35 s. Ha Kosetabole 10 10
1255 35 s. Ha Seshote 10 10
1256 35 s. Ha Rapooane 10 10
1257 35 s. Bokong Ha Kennan 10 10

(c) 1994 Map.

1258 35 s. Mafika-Lisiu Pass 10 10
1259 35 s. Ha Lesaoana 10 10
1260 35 s. Ha Masaballa 10 10
1261 35 s. Ha Nkisi 10 10
1262 35 s. Ha Rafanyane 10 10
1263 35 s. Laitsoka Pass 10 10
1264 35 s. "Katse Reservoir" 10 10
1265 35 s. Seshote 10 10
1266 35 s. Sephareng 10 10
1267 35 s. Katse Dam 10 10

Nos. 1238/47, 1248/57 and 1258/67 respectively were printed together, se-tenant, forming composite designs.

1996. 50th Anniv of U.N.I.C.E.F. Multicoloured.

1268 35 s. Type **240** 10 10
1269 50 s. Herdboys with livestock (horiz) 10 10
1270 70 s. Children in class (horiz) 15 20
1271 1 m. 50 Boys performing traditional dance (horiz) 30 35

241 U.S.A. Basketball Team, 1936

1996. Olympic Games, Atlanta. Previous Gold Medal Winners. Multicoloured.

1272 1 m. Type **241** 20 25
1273 1 m. 50 Brandenburg Gate and stadium, Berlin, 1936 30 35
1274 1 m. 50 Glen Morris (U.S.A.) (decathlon, 1936) (vert) 30 35
1275 1 m. 50 Saidi Aouita (Morocco) (5000m running, 1984) (vert) 30 35
1276 1 m. 50 Arnie Robinson (U.S.A.) (long jump, 1976) (vert) 30 35
1277 1 m. 50 Hans Woellke (Germany) (shot put, 1936) (vert) 30 35
1278 1 m. 50 Renate Stecher (Germany) (100m running, 1972) (vert) 30 35
1279 1 m. 50 Evelyn Ashford (U.S.A.) (100m running, 1984) (vert) 30 35
1280 1 m. 50 Willie Davenport (U.S.A.) (110m hurdles, 1968) (vert) 30 35
1281 1 m. 50 Bob Beamon (U.S.A.) (long jump, 1968) (vert) 30 35
1282 1 m. 50 Heidi Rosendhal (Germany) (long jump, 1972) (vert) 30 35
1283 2 m. Jesse Owens (U.S.A.) (track and field, 1936) (vert) 40 45
1284 3 m. Speed boat racing 60 65

No. 1273 is inscribed "BRANDEBOURG GATE" in error. No. 1274 incorrectly identifies Glen Morris as the gold medal winner in the 1936 long jump.

Nos. 1274/82 were printed together, se-tenant, with the backgrounds forming a composite design.

242 Class WP Steam Locomotive (India)

1996. Trains of the World. Multicoloured.

1286 1 m. 50 Type **242** 30 35
1287 1 m. 50 Canadian Pacific steam locomotive No. 2471 (Canada) 30 35
1288 1 m. 50 The "Caledonian" (Great Britain) 30 35
1289 1 m. 50 Steam locomotive "William Mason" (U.S.A.) 30 35
1290 1 m. 50 "Trans-Siberian Express" (Russia) 30 35
1291 1 m. 50 Steam train (Switzerland) 30 35
1292 1 m. 50 ETR 450 high speed train (Italy) 30 35
1293 1 m. 50 TGV express train (France) 30 35
1294 1 m. 50 XPT high speed train (Australia) 30 35
1295 1 m. 50 "Blue Train" (South Africa) 30 35
1296 1 m. 50 Intercity 225 express train (Great Britain) 30 35
1297 1 m. 50 "Hikari" express train (Japan) 30 35

243 Mother's Union Member, Methodist Church

1996. Christmas. Mothers' Unions. Multicoloured.

1299 35 s. Type **243** 10 10
1300 50 s. Roman Catholic Church 10 10
1301 1 m. Lesotho Evangelical Church 20 25
1302 1 m. 50 Anglican Church 30 35

No. 1302 is inscribed "Anglian" in error.

244 Hand Clasp (Co-operation for Development)

1997. 10th Anniv of Lesotho Highland Water Project (1996). Multicoloured.

1303 35 s. Type **244** 10 10
1304 50 s. Bearded vulture and rock painting (Nature and Heritage) 10 10
1305 1 m. Malibamatso Bridge (Engineering) 20 25
1306 1 m. 50 Katse Valley in 1986 and 1996 (75×28 mm) 30 35

No. 1305 is inscribed "Developement" in error.

245 Land Reclamation

246 Schmeichel, Denmark

1997. Environment Protection. Multicoloured.

1307 35 s. Type **245** 10 10
1308 50 s. Throwing rubbish into bin 15 20
1309 1 m. Hands holding globe and tree 25 30
1310 1 m. 20 Recycling symbol and rubbish 30 35
1311 1 m. 50 Collecting rain water 40 45

1997. World Cup Football Championship, France (1998). Multicoloured.

1312 1 m. Type **246** 20 25
1313 1 m. 50 Bergkamp, Netherlands 30 35
1314 1 m. 50 Argentine players celebrating 30 35
1315 1 m. 50 Argentine and Dutch players competing for ball 30 35
1316 1 m. 50 Players heading ball 30 35
1317 1 m. 50 Goalkeeper deflecting ball 30 35
1318 1 m. 50 Goal-mouth melee 30 35
1319 1 m. 50 Argentine player kicking ball 30 35
1320 2 m. Southgate, England 40 45
1321 2 m. 50 Asprilla, Colombia 50 55
1322 3 m. Gascoigne, England 60 65
1323 4 m. Giggs, Wales 80 85

247 "Spialia spio"

1997. Butterflies. Multicoloured.

1325 1 m. 50 Type **247** 30 35
1326 1 m. 50 "Leptotes pirithous" 30 35
1327 1 m. 50 "Acratea satis" 30 35
1328 1 m. 50 "Belenois aurota aurota" 30 35
1329 1 m. 50 "Spindasis natalensis" 30 35
1330 1 m. 50 "Torynesis orangica" 30 35
1331 1 m. 50 "Lepidochysops variabilis" 30 35
1332 1 m. 50 "Pinacopteryx eriphia" 30 35
1333 1 m. 50 "Anthene butleri livida" 30 35

Nos. 1325/33 were printed together, se-tenant, with the backgrounds forming a composite design.

No. 1326 is inscribed "Cyclyrius pirithous", No. 1332 "Pinacopteryx eriphea", both in error.

248 Rock Paintings and Boy

249 Diana, Princess of Wales

1998. 40th Anniv of Morija Museum and Archives. Multicoloured.

1335 35 s. Type **248** 10 10
1336 45 s. Hippopotamus and lower jaw bone (horiz) 10 15
1337 50 s. Woman and cowhide skirt 15 20
1338 1 m. Drum and "thomo" (musical bow) 25 30
1339 1 m. 50 Warrior with "khau" (gorget awarded for valour) 40 45
1340 2 m. Herders with ox (horiz) 50 55

1998. Diana, Princess of Wales Commemoration. Multicoloured.

1341 3 m. Type **249** 60 65
1342 3 m. Wearing grey jacket 60 65
1343 3 m. Wearing white polo-necked jumper 60 65
1344 3 m. Wearing pearl necklace 60 65
1345 3 m. Wearing white evening dress 60 65
1346 3 m. Wearing pale blue jacket 60 65

250 Atitlan Grebe

1998. Fauna of the World. Multicoloured. (a) Vert designs as T **250**.

1348 1 m. Type **250** 20 25
1349 1 m. Cabot's tragopan 20 25
1350 1 m. Spider monkey 20 25
1351 1 m. Dibatag 20 25
1352 1 m. Right whale 20 25
1353 1 m. Imperial parrot 20 25
1354 1 m. Cheetah 20 25
1355 1 m. Brown-eared pheasant 20 25
1356 1 m. Leatherback turtle 20 25
1357 1 m. Imperial woodpecker 20 25
1358 1 m. Andean condor 20 25
1359 1 m. Barbary deer 20 25
1360 1 m. Grey gentle lemur 20 25
1361 1 m. Cuban parrot 20 25
1362 1 m. Numbat 20 25
1363 1 m. Short-tailed albatross 20 25
1364 1 m. Green turtle 20 25
1365 1 m. White rhinoceros 20 25
1366 1 m. Diademed sifaka 20 25
1367 1 m. Galapagos penguin 20 25

(b) Horiz designs, each 48×31 mm.

1368 1 m. 50 Impala 30 35
1369 1 m. 50 Black bear 30 35
1370 1 m. 50 American buffalo 30 35
1371 1 m. 50 African elephant 30 35
1372 1 m. 50 Kangaroo 30 35
1373 1 m. 50 Lion 30 35
1374 1 m. 50 Giant panda 30 35
1375 1 m. 50 Tiger 30 35
1376 1 m. 50 Zebra 30 35

251 Cape Vulture

1998. Endangered Species. Cape Vulture. Mult.

1378 1 m. Type **251** 20 25
1379 1 m. Looking towards ground 20 25
1380 1 m. Looking over shoulder 20 25
1381 1 m. Facing right 20 25

252 Siamese

1998. Cats of the World. Multicoloured.

1382 70 s. Type **252** 15 20
1383 1 m. Chartreux 20 25
1384 2 m. Korat 40 45
1385 2 m. Japanese bobtail 40 45
1386 2 m. British white 40 45
1387 2 m. Bengal 40 45
1388 2 m. Abyssinian 40 45
1389 2 m. Snowshoe 40 45
1390 2 m. Scottish fold 40 45
1391 2 m. Maine coon 40 45
1392 2 m. Balinese 40 45
1393 2 m. Persian 40 45
1394 2 m. Javanese 40 45
1395 2 m. Turkish angora 40 45
1396 2 m. Tiffany 40 45
1397 3 m. Egyptian mau 60 65
1398 4 m. Bombay 80 85
1399 5 m. Burmese 1·00 1·10

Nos. 1385/90 and 1391/6 respectively were printed together, se-tenant, with the backgrounds forming composite designs.

253 "Laccaria laccata"

1998. Fungi of the World. Multicoloured.

1401 70 s. Type **253** 15 20
1402 1 m. "Mutinus caninus" 20 25
1403 1 m. "Hygrophorus psittacinus" 20 25
1404 1 m. "Cortinarius obtusus" 20 25
1405 1 m. "Volvariella bombycina" 20 25
1406 1 m. "Cortinarius caerylescens" 20 25
1407 1 m. "Laccaria amethystina" 20 25
1408 1 m. "Tricholoma aurantium" 20 25
1409 1 m. "Amanita excelsa (spissa)" 20 25
1410 1 m. "Clavaria helvola" 20 25
1411 1 m. Unidentified species (inscr "Cortinarius caerylescens") 20 25
1412 1 m. "Russula queletii" 20 25
1413 1 m. "Amanita phalloides" 20 25
1414 1 m. "Lactarius deliciosus" 20 25
1415 1 m. 50 "Tricholoma lascivum" 30 35
1416 2 m. "Clitocybe geotropa" 40 45
1417 3 m. "Amanita excelsa" 60 65
1418 4 m. Red-capped bolete 80 85

Nos. 1406, 1407, 1414 and 1416 are inscribed "Continarius caerylescens", "Laccaria amethystea", "Lactarius delicious", and "Clitocybe geotrapa", all in error.

254 "Simba"

1998. World Cinema. Multicoloured. (a) Films about Africa.

1420 2 m. Type **254** 40 45
1421 2 m. "Call to Freedom" 40 45
1422 2 m. "Cry the Beloved Country" 40 45
1423 2 m. "King Solomon's Mines" 40 45
1424 2 m. "Flame and the Fire" 40 45
1425 2 m. "Cry Freedom" 40 45
1426 2 m. "Bopha!" 40 45
1427 2 m. "Zulu" 40 45

(b) Japanese Film Stars.

1428 2 m. Takamine Hideko 40 45
1429 2 m. James Shigeta 40 45
1430 2 m. Miyoshi Umeki 40 45
1431 2 m. May Ishimara 40 45
1432 2 m. Sessue Hayakawa 40 45
1433 2 m. Miiko Taka 40 45
1434 2 m. Mori Masayuki 40 45
1435 2 m. Hara Setsuko 40 45
1436 2 m. Kyo Machiko 40 45

Nos. 1420/7 and 1428/36 respectively were printed together, se-tenant, with the backgrounds forming composite designs.

No. 1423 is inscribed "KING SOLOMAN'S MINES" in error.

255 Ceresiosaurus

1998. Prehistoric Animals. Multicoloured.

1438 2 m. Type **255** 40 45
1439 2 m. Rhomaleosaurus 40 45
1440 2 m. Anomalocaris 40 45
1441 2 m. Mixosaurus 40 45
1442 2 m. Stethacanthus 40 45
1443 2 m. Dunklosteus 40 45
1444 2 m. Tommotia 40 45
1445 2 m. Sanctacaris 40 45
1446 2 m. Ammonites 40 45
1447 2 m. Rhamphorhynchus 40 45
1448 2 m. Brachiosaurus 40 45
1449 2 m. Mamenchisaurus hochuanensis 40 45
1450 2 m. Ceratosaurus nasicornis 40 45
1451 2 m. Archaeopteryx 40 45
1452 2 m. Leaellynasaura amicagraphica 40 45

1453	2 m. Chasmosaurus belli	40	45
1454	2 m. Deinonychus and Pachyrhinosaurus	40	45
1455	2 m. Deinonychus	40	45
1456	2 m. Nyctosaurus	40	45
1457	2 m. Volcanoes	40	45
1458	2 m. Eudimorphodon	40	45
1459	2 m. Apatosaurus	40	45
1460	2 m. Peteinosaurus	40	45
1461	2 m. Tropeognathus	40	45
1462	2 m. Pteranodon ingens	40	45
1463	2 m. Ornithodesmus	40	45
1464	2 m. Wuerhosaurus	40	45

Nos. 1438/46, 1447/55 and 1456/64 respectively were printed together, se-tenant, with the backgrounds forming composite designs.

256 Crowning of King Letsie III

1998. 1st Anniv of Coronation of King Letsie III. Multicoloured.

1466	1 m. Type **256**	20	25
1467	1 m. King saluting Basotho nation	20	25
1468	1 m. King Letsie in profile	20	25

257 "Pelargonium sidoides"

1998. Flowers. Multicoloured.

1469	10 s. Type **257**	10	10
1470	15 s. "Aponogeton ranunculiflorus"	10	10
1471	20 s. "Sebaea leiostyla"	10	10
1472	40 s. "Sebaea grandis"	10	10
1473	50 s. "Satyrium neglectum"	10	10
1474	60 s. "Massonia jasminiflora"	10	10
1475	70 s. "Ajuga ophrydis"	15	20
1476	80 s. "Nemesia fruticans"	20	25
1477	1 m. "Aloe broomii"	20	25
1478	2 m. "Wahlenbergia androsacea"	40	45
1479	2 m. 50 "Phygelius capensis"	50	55
1480	3 m. "Dianthus basuticus"	60	65
1481	4 m. 50 "Rhodohypoxis baurii"	90	95
1482	5 m. "Turbina oblongata"	1·00	1·10
1483	6 m. "Hibiscus microcarpus"	1·10	1·40
1484	10 m. "Lobelia erinus ("Moraea stricta")	2·00	2·10

POSTAGE DUE STAMPS

1966. Nos. D9/10 of Basutoland optd **LESOTHO**.

D11	**D 2**	1 c. red	30	75
D12		5 c. violet	30	90

D 1

D 2

1967.

D13	**D 1**	1 c. blue	15	3·00
D14		2 c. red	15	3·25
D15		5 c. green	20	3·25

1986.

D19	**D 2**	2 s. green	15	70
D20		5 s. blue	15	70
D21		35 s. violet	50	1·25

APPENDIX

The following stamps have either been issued in excess of postal needs, or have not been available to the public in reasonable quantities at face value.

1981-83.

15th Anniv of Independence. Classic Stamps of the World. 10 m. × 40, each embossed on gold foil.

MAFEKING

A town in the Cape of Good Hope. Special stamps issued by British garrison during Boer War.

12 pence = 1 shilling;
20 shillings = 1 pound

1900. Surch **MAFEKING, BESIEGED.** and value.

(a) On Cape of Good Hope stamps.

1	**6**	1d. on ½d. green	£170	50·00
2	**17**	1d. on ½d. green	£225	60·00
3		3d. on 1d. red	£170	50·00
4	**6**	6d. on 3d. mauve	£25000	£250
5		1s. on 4d. olive	£5500	£325

(b) On stamps of Bechuanaland Protectorate (opts on Great Britain).

6	**71**	1d. on ½d. red (No. 59)	£170	50·00
7	**57**	3d. on 1d. lilac (No. 61)	£850	80·00
13	**73**	6d. on 2d. green and red (No. 62)	£1100	60·00
9	**75**	6d. on 3d. purple on yell (No. 63)	£4000	£250
14	**79**	1s. on 6d. purple on red (No. 65)	£3750	85·00

(c) On stamps of British Bechuanaland (opts on Great Britain).

10	**3**	6d. on 3d. lilac and black (No. 12)	£350	60·00
11	**76**	1s. on 4d. green and brown (No. 35)	£1200	65·00
15	**79**	1s. on 6d. purple on red (No. 36)	£13000	£600
16	**82**	2s. on 1s. green (No. 37)	£7000	£325

3 Cadet Sgt.-Major Goodyear

4 General Baden-Powell

1900.

17	**3**	1d. blue on blue	£800	£275
19	**4**	3d. blue on blue	£1200	£400

MALACCA

A British Settlement on the Malay Peninsula which became a state of the Federation of Malaya, incorporated in Malaysia in 1963.

100 cents = 1 dollar (Malayan)

1948. Silver Wedding. As T **10/11** of Aden.

1	10 c. violet	30	60
2	$5 brown	26·00	35·00

1949. As T **58** of Straits Settlements.

3	1 c. black	20	70
4	2 c. orange	70	45
5	3 c. green	30	1·75
6	4 c. brown	15	10
6a	5 c. purple	45	1·50
7	6 c. grey	60	85
8	8 c. red	30	5·50
8a	8 c. green	85	4·50
9	10 c. mauve	15	10
9a	12 c. red	95	4·00
10	15 c. blue	50	60
11	20 c. black and green	30	6·00
11a	20 c. blue	1·50	2·50
12	25 c. purple and orange	30	70
12a	35 c. red and purple	1·00	3·00
13	40 c. red and purple	1·25	11·00
14	50 c. black and blue	75	1·25
15	$1 blue and purple	6·00	17·00
16	$2 green and red	20·00	19·00
17	$5 green and brown	42·00	35·00

1949. U.P.U. As T **20/23** of Antigua.

18	10 c. purple	20	45
19	15 c. blue	1·10	1·75
20	25 c. orange	45	3·75
21	50 c. black	1·00	4·00

1953. Coronation. As T **13** of Aden.

22	10 c. black and purple	55	65

1 Queen Elizabeth II

1954.

23	**1**	1 c. black	10	60
24		2 c. orange	30	1·00
25		4 c. brown	40	10
26		5 c. mauve	30	1·75
27		6 c. grey	10	30
28		8 c. green	30	1·75
29		10 c. purple	40	10
30		12 c. red	20	2·00
31		20 c. blue	20	80
32		25 c. purple and orange	20	90
33		30 c. red and purple	20	30
34		35 c. red and purple	20	60
35	**1**	50 c. black and blue	30	1·50
36		$1 blue and purple	4·00	5·50
37		$2 green and red	22·00	29·00
38		$5 green and brown	22·00	35·00

1957. As Nos. 92/102 of Kedah but inset portrait of Queen Elizabeth II.

39	1 c. black	10	40
40	2 c. red	10	40
41	4 c. sepia	10	10
42	5 c. lake	10	10
43	8 c. green	1·25	2·50
44	10 c. sepia	30	10
45	20 c. blue	30	40
46	50 c. black and blue	30	50
47	$1 blue and purple	2·25	2·50
48	$2 green and red	11·00	16·00
49	$5 brown and green	14·00	26·00

2 Copra

1960. As Nos. 39/49 but with inset picture of Melaka tree and Pelandok (mouse-deer) as in T **2**.

50	1 c. black	10	30
51	2 c. red	10	30
52	4 c. sepia	10	10
53	5 c. lake	10	10
54	8 c. green	2·50	2·25
55	10 c. purple	30	10
56	20 c. blue	40	50
57	50 c. black and blue	30	50
58	$1 blue and purple	1·75	2·50
59	$2 green and red	4·50	6·00
60	$5 brown and green	9·00	11·00

3 "Vanda hookeriana"

1965. As Nos. 115/21 of Kedah but with Arms of Malacca inset and inscr "MELAKA" as in T **3**.

61	**3**	1 c. multicoloured	10	70
62	–	2 c. multicoloured	10	70
63	–	5 c. multicoloured	10	10
64	–	6 c. multicoloured	30	55
65	–	10 c. multicoloured	20	10
66	–	15 c. multicoloured	1·75	40
67	–	20 c. multicoloured	2·25	90

The higher values used in Malacca were Nos. 20/7 of Malaysia.

4 "Papilio demoleus"

1971. Butterflies. As Nos. 124/30 of Kedah but with Arms of Malacca as in T **4**. Inscr "melaka".

70	–	1 c. multicoloured	40	1·25
71	–	2 c. multicoloured	60	1·25
72	–	5 c. multicoloured	1·00	50
73	**4**	6 c. multicoloured	1·00	2·00
74	–	10 c. multicoloured	1·00	40
75	–	15 c. multicoloured	1·75	20
76	–	20 c. multicoloured	1·75	1·75

The higher values in use with this issue were Malaysia Nos. 64/71.

5 "Durio zibethinus"

6 Rubber

1979. Flowers. As Nos. 135/41 of Kedah but with Arms of Malacca and inscr "melaka" as in T **5**.

82	1 c. "Rafflesia hasseltii"	10	70
83	2 c. "Pterocarpus indicus"	10	70
84	5 c. "Lagerstroemia speciosa"	15	60
85	10 c. Type **5**	20	20
86	15 c. "Hibiscus rosa-sinesis"	20	10
87	20 c. "Rhododendron scortechinii"	25	10
88	25 c. "Etlingera elatior" (inscr "Phaeomeria speciosa")	45	60

1986. As Nos. 152/8 of Kedah but with Arms of Malacca and inscr "MELAKA" as in T **6**.

96	1 c. Coffee	10	10
97	2 c. Coconuts	10	10
98	5 c. Cocoa	10	10
99	10 c. Black pepper	10	10
100	15 c. Type **6**	10	10
101	20 c. Oil palm	10	10
102	30 c. Rice	15	20

MALAWI

Formerly Nyasaland, became an independent Republic within the Commonwealth on 6 July 1966.

1964. 12 pence = 1 shilling;
20 shillings = 1 pound.
1970. 100 tambalas = 1 kwacha.

44 Dr. H. Banda (Prime Minister) and Independence Monument

1964. Independence.

211	**44**	3d. olive and sepia	10	10
212	–	6d. multicoloured	10	10
213	–	1s. 3d. multicoloured	35	10
214	–	2s. 6d. multicoloured	45	1·00

DESIGNS—each with Dr. Hastings Banda: 6d. Rising sun; 1s. 3d. National flag; 2s. 6d. Coat of arms.

48 Tung Tree

1964. As Nos. 199/210 of Nyasaland but inscr "MALAWI" as in T **48**. The 9d., 1s. 6d. and £2 are new values and designs.

252	½d. violet	10	10
216	1d. black and green	10	10
217	2d. brown	10	10
218	3d. brown, green & bistre	15	10
219	4d. blue and yellow	60	15
220	6d. purple, green and blue	75	10
221	9d. brown, green & yellow	30	15
258	1s. brown, blue and yellow	25	10
223	1s. 3d. green and brown	50	60
259	1s. 6d. brown and green	30	10
224	2s. 6d. brown and blue	1·10	1·00
225	5s. multicoloured (I)	65	2·25
225a	5s. multicoloured (II)	5·00	90
226	10s. green, salmon & black	1·50	2·00
227	£1 brown and yellow	7·00	5·50
262	£2 multicoloured	25·00	24·00

DESIGNS (New): 1s. 6d. Burley tobacco; £2 "Cyrestis camillus" (butterfly).

Two types of 5s. I, inscr "LAKE NYASA". II, inscr "LAKE MALAWI".

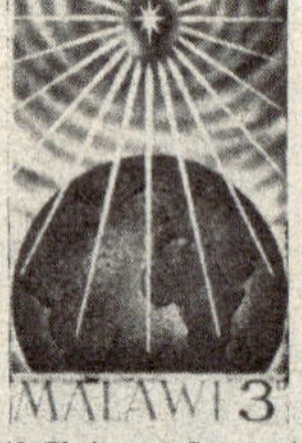

49 Christmas Star and Globe

1964. Christmas.

228	**49**	3d. green and gold	10	10
229		6d. mauve and gold	10	10
230		1s. 3d. violet and gold	10	10
231		2s. 6d. blue and gold	20	25

50 Coins

1964. Malawi's First Coinage. Coins in black and silver.

232	**50**	3d. green	10	10
233		9d. mauve	20	10
234		1s. 6d. purple	25	10
235		3s. blue	35	50

1965. Nos. 223/4 surch.

236	1s. 6d. on 1s. 3d. green & brown	10	10
237	3s. on 2s. 6d. brown & blue	20	20

52 Chilembwe leading Rebels

1965. 50th Anniv of 1915 Rising.

238	52	3d. violet and green	10	10
239		9d. olive and orange	10	10
240		1s. 6d. brown and blue	15	10
241		3s. turquoise and blue	20	25

53 "Learning and Scholarship"

1965. Opening of Malawi University.

242	53	3d. black and green	10	10
243		9d. black and mauve	10	10
244		1s. 6d. black and violet	10	10
245		3s. black and blue	15	40

54 "Papilio ophidicephalus"

1966. Malawi Butterflies. Multicoloured.

247		4d. Type **54**	80	10
248		9d. "Papilio desmondi" (magdae)	1·25	10
249		1s. 6d. "Epamera handmani"	1·75	30
250		3s. "Amauris crawshayi"	2·75	6·00

58 British Central Africa 6d. Stamp of 1891

59 President Banda

1966. 75th Anniv of Postal Services.

263	58	4d. blue and green	10	10
264		9d. blue and red	15	10
265		1s. 6d. blue and lilac	20	10
266		3s. grey and blue	30	50

1966. Republic Day.

268	59	4d. brown, silver & green	10	10
269		9d. brown, silver & mauve	10	10
270		1s. 6d. brown, silver & vio	15	10
271		3s. brown, silver and blue	25	15

60 Bethlehem

1966. Christmas.

273	60	4d. green and gold	10	10
274		9d. purple and gold	10	10
275		1s. 6d. red and gold	15	10
276		3s. blue and gold	40	50

61 "Ilala I"

1967. Lake Malawi Steamers.

277	61	4d. black, yellow & green	40	10
278	–	9d. black, yellow & mauve	45	10
279	–	1s. 6d. black, red & violet	65	15
280	–	3s. black, red and blue	1·25	1·50

DESIGNS: 9d. "Dove"; 1s. 9d. "Chauncy Maples I" (wrongly inscr "Chauncey"); 3s. "Gwendolen".

62 Golden Mbuna (female)

1967. Lake Malawi Cichlids. Multicoloured.

281		4d. Type **62**	20	10
282		9d. Scraped-mouthed mbuna	30	10
283		1s. 6d. Zebra mbuna	40	15
284		3s. Orange mbuna	1·25	1·50

63 Rising Sun and Gearwheel

1967. Industrial Development.

285	63	4d. black and green	10	10
286		9d. black and red	10	10
287		1s. 6d. black and violet	10	10
288		3s. black and blue	15	15

64 Mary and Joseph beside Crib

1967. Christmas.

290	64	4d. blue and green	10	10
291		9d. blue and red	10	10
292		1s. 6d. blue and yellow	10	10
293		3s. deep blue and blue	15	15

65 "Calotropis procera"

1968. Wild Flowers. Multicoloured.

295		4d. Type **65**	15	10
296		9d. "Borreria dibrachiata"	15	10
297		1s. 6d. "Hibiscus rhodanthus"	15	10
298		3s. "Bidens pinnatipartita"	20	75

66 Bagnall Steam Locomotive, No. 1 "Thistle"

1968. Malawi Locomotives.

300	66	4d. green, blue and red	40	10
301	–	9d. red, blue and green	50	10
302	–	1s. 6d. multicoloured	75	25
303	–	3s. multicoloured	1·40	2·75

DESIGNS: 9d. Class G steam locomotive No. 49; 1s. 6d. Class "Zambesi" diesel locomotive No. 202; 3s. Diesel railcar No. DR1.

67 "The Nativity" (Piero della Francesca)

1968. Christmas. Multicoloured.

305		4d. Type **67**	10	10
306		9d. "The Adoration of the Shepherds" (Murillo)	10	10
307		1s. 6d. "The Adoration of the Shepherds" (Reni)	10	15
308		3s. "Nativity, with God the Father and Holy Ghost" (Pittoni)	15	15

69 Nyassa Lovebird

70 Carmine Bee Eater

1968. Birds (1st series). Multicoloured.

310		1d. Scarlet-chested sunbird (horiz)	15	10
311		2d. Violet starling (horiz)	15	10
312		3d. White-browed robin chat (horiz)	20	10
313		4d. Red-billed fire finch (horiz)	35	40
314		6d. Type **69**	45	15
315		9d. Yellow-rumped bishop	50	60
316		1s. Type **70**	60	15
317		1s. 6d. Grey-headed bush shrike	5·00	8·00
318		2s. Paradise whydah	5·00	8·00
319		3s. African paradise flycatcher (vert)	4·50	4·25
320		5s. Bateleur (vert)	7·00	4·25
321		10s. Saddle-bill stork (vert)	5·50	7·50
322		£1 Purple heron (vert)	10·00	18·00
323		£2 Knysna turaco ("Livingstone's Loerie")	40·00	48·00

SIZES: 1d. to 9d. as Type **69**; 1s. 6d. to £2 as Type **70**.

See also Nos. 473/85.

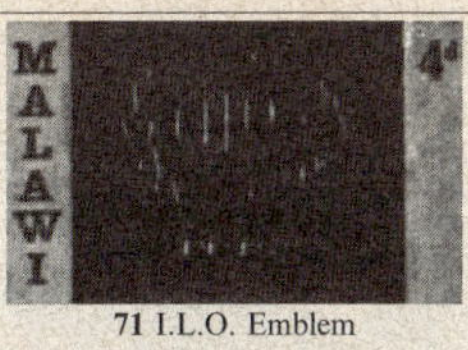

71 I.L.O. Emblem

1969. 50th Anniv of Int Labour Organization.

324	71	4d. gold and green	10	10
325		9d. gold and brown	10	10
326		1s. 6d. gold and brown	10	10
327		3s. gold and blue	15	15

72 White-fringed Ground Orchid

1969. Orchids of Malawi. Multicoloured.

329		4d. Type **72**	15	10
330		9d. Red ground orchid	20	10
331		1s. 6d. Leopard tree orchid	30	10
332		3s. Blue ground orchid	60	1·75

73 African Development Bank Emblem

74 Dove over Bethlehem

1969. 5th Anniv of African Development Bank.

334	73	4d. yellow, brown & ochre	10	10
335		9d. yellow, ochre & green	10	10
336		1s. 6d. yellow, ochre & brn	10	10
337		3s. yellow, ochre and blue	15	15

1969. Christmas.

339	74	2d. black and yellow	10	10
340		4d. black and turquoise	10	10
341		9d. black and red	10	10
342		1s. 6d. black and violet	10	10
343		3s. black and blue	15	15

75 "Zonocerus elegans" (grasshopper)

77 Runner

1970. Insects of Malawi. Multicoloured.

345		4d. Type **75**	15	10
346		9d. "Mylabris dicincta" (beetle)	15	10
347		1s. 6d. "Henosepilachna elaterii" (ladybird)	20	10
348		3s. "Sphodromantis speculabunda" (mantid)	35	45

1970. Rand Easter Show. No. 317 optd **Rand Easter Show 1970**.

350		1s. 6d. multicoloured	50	1·75

1970. 9th Commonwealth Games, Edinburgh.

351	77	4d. blue and green	10	10
352		9d. blue and red	10	10
353		1s. 6d. blue and yellow	10	10
354		3s. deep blue and blue	15	15

1970. Decimal Currency. Nos. 316 and 318 surch.

356		10 t. on 1s. multicoloured	1·75	25
357		20 t. on 2s. multicoloured	2·25	2·50

79 "Aegocera trimeni"

1970. Moths. Multicoloured.

358		4d. Type **79**	20	10
359		9d. "Faidherbia bauhiniae"	30	10
360		1s. 6d. "Parasa karschi"	50	20
361		3s. "Teracotona euprepia"	1·25	3·25

80 Mother and Child

1970. Christmas.

363	80	2d. black and yellow	10	10
364		4d. black and green	10	10
365		9d. black and red	10	10
366		1s. 6d. black and purple	10	10
367		3s. black and blue	15	15

1971. No. 319 surch **30t Special United Kingdom Delivery Service**.

369		30 t. on 3s. multicoloured	50	2·00

No. 369 was issued for use on letters carried by an emergency airmail service from Malawi to Great Britain during the British postal strike. The fee of 30 t. was to cover the charge for delivery by a private service, and ordinary stamps to pay the normal airmail postage had to be affixed as well. These stamps were in use from 8 February to 8 March.

82 Decimal Coinage and Cockerel

83 Greater Kudu

1971. Decimal Coinage.

370	82	3 t. multicoloured	15	10
371		8 t. multicoloured	20	10
372		15 t. multicoloured	25	15
373		30 t. multicoloured	35	1·25

1971. Decimal Currency. Antelopes. Mult.

375		1 t. Type **83**	10	10
376		2 t. Nyala	15	10
377		3 t. Mountain reedbuck	20	50
378		5 t. Puku	40	75
379		8 t. Impala	45	60
380		10 t. Eland	60	10
381		15 t. Klipspringer	1·00	20
382		20 t. Suni	1·50	90
383		30 t. Roan antelope	8·00	90
384		50 t. Waterbuck	90	65
385		1 k. Bushbuck	1·50	85
386		2 k. Red forest duiker	2·75	1·50
387		4 k. Common duiker	20·00	17·00

Nos. 380/7 are larger, size 25×42 mm.

No. 387 is incorrectly inscr "Gray Duiker".

85 Christ on the Cross

87 "Holarrhena febrifuga"

1971. Easter. Multicoloured.

388	85	3 t. black and green	10	20
389	–	3 t. black and green	10	20
390	85	8 t. black and red	10	20
391	–	8 t. black and red	10	20
392	85	15 t. black and violet	20	30
393	–	15 t. black and violet	20	30
394	85	30 t. black and blue	25	45
395	–	30 t. black and blue	25	45

DESIGN: Nos. 389, 391, 393, 395, The Resurrection.

Both designs from "The Small Passion" (Durer).

1971. Flowering Shrubs and Trees. Mult.

397		3 t. Type **87**	10	10
398		8 t. "Brachystegia spiciformis"	15	10
399		15 t. "Securidaca longepedunculata"	25	10
400		30 t. "Pterocarpus rotundifolius"	40	50

88 Drum Major

89 "Madonna and Child" (William Dyce)

1971. 50th Anniv of Malawi Police Force.

402	88	30 t. multicoloured	65	1·25

1971. Christmas. Multicoloured.

403	3 t. Type **89**	10	10
404	8 t. "The Holy Family" (M. Schongauer)	15	10
405	15 t. "The Holy Family with St. John" (Raphael)	20	20
406	30 t. "The Holy Family" (Bronzino)	50	1·00

90 Vickers Viscount 700

1972. Air. Malawi Aircraft. Multicoloured.

408	3 t. Type **90**	30	10
409	8 t. Hawker Siddeley H.S.748	50	10
410	15 t. Britten Norman Islander	75	30
411	30 t. B.A.C. One Eleven	1·25	2·00

91 Figures (Chencherere Hill)

1972. Rock Paintings.

413	**91** 3 t. green and black	35	10
414	– 8 t. red, grey and black	45	10
415	– 15 t. multicoloured	70	30
416	– 30 t. multicoloured	1·00	1·00

DESIGNS: 8 t. Lizard and cat (Chencherere Hill); 15 t. Schematics (Diwa Hill); 30 t. Sun through rain (Mikolongwe Hill).

92 Boxing

1972. Olympic Games, Munich.

418	**92** 3 t. multicoloured	10	10
419	8 t. multicoloured	10	10
420	15 t. multicoloured	15	10
421	30 t. multicoloured	35	45

93 Arms of Malawi **94** "Adoration of the Kings" (Orcagna)

1972. Commonwealth Parliamentary Conf.

423	**93** 15 t. multicoloured	30	35

1972. Christmas. Multicoloured.

424	3 t. Type **94**	10	10
425	8 t. "Madonna and Child Enthroned" (Florentine School)	10	10
426	15 t. "Virgin and Child" (Crivelli)	20	10
427	30 t. "Virgin and Child with St. Anne" (Flemish School)	45	70

95 "Charaxes bohemani"

1973. Butterflies. Multicoloured.

429	3 t. Type **95**	20	10
430	8 t. "Uranothauma crawshayi"	45	10
431	15 t. "Charaxes acuminatus"	65	30
432	30 t. "Amauris ansorgei" (inscr in error "EUPHAEDRA ZADDACHI")	3·00	7·50
433	30 t. "Amauris ansorgei" (inscr corrected)	3·00	7·50

96 Livingstone and Map

1973. Death Cent of David Livingstone (1st issue).

435	**96** 3 t. multicoloured	10	10
436	8 t. multicoloured	15	10
437	15 t. multicoloured	20	10
438	30 t. multicoloured	35	60

See also No. 450.

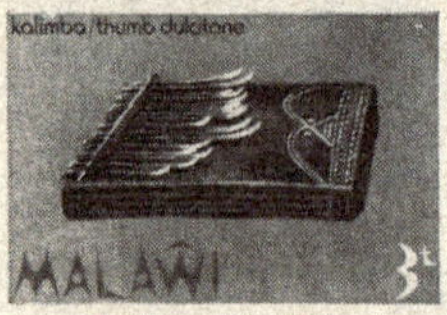

97 Thumb Dulcitone

1973. Musical Instruments. Multicoloured.

440	3 t. Type **97**	10	10
441	8 t. Hand zither (vert)	15	10
442	15 t. Hand drum (vert)	25	10
443	30 t. One-stringed fiddle	45	60

98 The Magi

1973. Christmas.

445	**98** 3 t. blue, lilac & ultramarine	10	10
446	8 t. red, lilac and brown	10	10
447	15 t. mauve, blue & dp mve	15	10
448	30 t. yellow, lilac & brown	30	55

99 Stained-glass Window, Livingstonia Mission

1973. Death Cent of David Livingstone (2nd issue).

450	**99** 50 t. multicoloured	45	1·00

100 Large-mouthed Black Bass

1973. 35th Anniv of Malawi Angling Society. Multicoloured.

452	3 t. Type **100**	25	10
453	8 t. Rainbow trout	30	10
454	15 t. Silver alestes ("Lake salmon")	55	20
455	30 t. Tigerfish	85	75

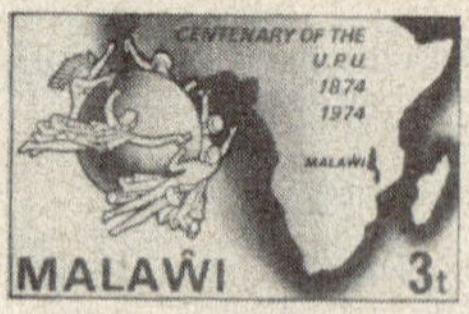

101 U.P.U. Monument and Map of Africa

1974. Centenary of U.P.U.

457	**101** 3 t. green and brown	10	10
458	8 t. red and brown	10	10
459	15 t. violet and brown	15	10
460	30 t. blue and brown	30	70

102 Capital Hill, Lilongwe

1974. 10th Anniv of Independence.

462	**102** 3 t. multicoloured	10	10
463	8 t. multicoloured	10	10
464	15 t. multicoloured	10	10
465	30 t. multicoloured	25	35

103 "Madonna of the Meadow" (Bellini)

1974. Christmas. Multicoloured.

467	3 t. Type **103**	10	10
468	8 t. "The Holy Family with Sts. John and Elizabeth" (Jordaens)	10	10
469	15 t. "The Nativity" (Pieter de Grebber)	15	10
470	30 t. "Adoration of the Shepherds" (Lorenzo di Credi)	30	50

104 Arms of Malawi **105** African Snipe

106 Spur-winged Goose

1975.

472	**104** 1 t. blue	20	40
472a	5 t. red	50	1·10

1975. Birds (2nd series). Mult. (a) As T **105**.

473	1 t. Type **105**	30	1·50
474	2 t. Double-banded sandgrouse (horiz)	50	1·50
475	3 t. Blue quail (horiz)	1·50	1·50
476	5 t. Bare-throated francolin	3·50	1·25
477	8 t. Harlequin quail (horiz)	4·75	1·00

(b) As T **106**.

502	10 t. Type **106**	2·00	1·25
503	15 t. Barrow's bustard	2·00	1·75
480	20 t. Comb duck	1·00	2·25
481	30 t. Helmet guineafowl	1·25	70
482	50 t. African pygmy goose (horiz)	2·00	1·60
483	1 k. Garganey	3·00	7·50
504	2 k. White-faced whistling duck	6·50	9·50
485	4 k. African green pigeon	13·00	16·00

107 M.V. "Mpasa"

1975. Ships of Lake Malawi. Multicoloured.

486	3 t. Type **107**	30	10
487	8 t. M.V. "Ilala II"	40	10
488	15 t. M.V. "Chauncy Maples II"	75	30
489	30 t. M.V. "Nkwazi"	1·00	2·50

108 "Habenaria splendens" **109** Thick-tailed Bushbaby

1975. Malawi Orchids. Multicoloured.

491	3 t. Type **108**	40	10
492	10 t. "Eulophia cucullata"	50	10
493	20 t. "Disa welwitschii"	80	25
494	40 t. "Angraecum conchiferum"	1·10	1·50

1976. Malawi Animals. Multicoloured.

496	3 t. Type **109**	10	10
497	10 t. Leopard	35	10
498	20 t. Roan antelope	55	35
499	40 t. Common zebra	1·00	2·75

1975. 10th Africa, Caribbean and Pacific Ministerial Conference. No. 482 optd **10th ACP Ministerial Conference 1975**.

514	50 t. African pygmy goose	85	1·75

111 "A Castle with the Adoration of the Magi"

1975. Christmas. Religious Medallions. Mult.

515	3 t. Type **111**	10	10
516	10 t. "The Nativity"	15	10
517	20 t. "Adoration of the Magi" (different)	20	10
518	40 t. "Angel appearing to Shepherds"	50	1·90

112 Alexander Graham Bell **113** President Banda

1976. Centenary of Telephone.

520	**112** 3 t. green and black	10	10
521	10 t. purple and black	10	10
522	20 t. violet and black	20	10
523	40 t. blue and black	50	70

1976. 10th Anniv of Republic. Multicoloured.

525	**113** 3 t. green	10	10
526	10 t. purple	10	10
527	20 t. blue	20	10
528	40 t. blue	50	70

114 Bagnall Diesel Shunter No. 100

1976. Malawi Locomotives. Multicoloured.

530	3 t. Type **114**	40	10
531	10 t. Class "Shire" diesel locomotive No. 503	70	10
532	20 t. Nippon Sharyo diesel-hydraulic locomotive No. 301	1·40	45
533	40 t. Hunslet diesel-hydraulic locomotive No. 110	2·10	4·75

1976. Centenary of Blantyre Mission. Nos. 479 and 481 optd **Blantyre Mission Centenary 1876–1976**.

535	15 t. Barrow's bustard	1·25	1·00
536	30 t. Helmet guineafowl	1·50	2·50

116 Child on Bed of Straw **117** Man and Woman

1976. Christmas.

537	**116** 3 t. multicoloured	10	10
538	10 t. multicoloured	10	10
539	20 t. multicoloured	20	10
540	40 t. multicoloured	40	60

1977. Handicrafts. Wood-carvings. Mult.

542	4 t. Type **117**	10	10
543	10 t. Elephant (horiz)	15	10
544	20 t. Rhinoceros (horiz)	20	10
545	40 t. Antelope	50	70

118 Chileka Airport

1977. Transport. Multicoloured.

547	4 t. Type **118**	40	10
548	10 t. Blantyre–Lilongwe Road	40	10
549	20 t. M.V. "Ilala II"	1·25	35
550	40 t. Blantyre–Nacala rail line	2·00	3·75

119 Blue-grey Mbuna

1977. Fish of Lake Malawi. Multicoloured.

552B	4 t. Type **119**	30	10
553B	10 t. Livingston mbuna	40	20
554A	20 t. Zebra mbuna	1·40	30
555B	40 t. Malawi scale-eater	1·25	95

120 "Madonna and Child with St. Catherine and the Blessed Stefano Maconi" (Borgognone)

121 "Entry of Christ into Jerusalem" (Giotto)

1977. Christmas.

557	**120** 4 t. multicoloured	10	10
558	– 10 t. multicoloured	10	10
559	– 20 t. multicoloured	20	10
560	– 40 t. multicoloured	50	70

DESIGNS: 10 t. "Madonna and Child with the Eternal Father and Angels" (Borgognone); 20 t. Bottigella altarpiece (detail, Foppa); 40 t. "Madonna of the Fountain" (van Eyck).

1978. Easter. Paintingss by Giotto. Multicoloured.

562	4 t. Type **121**	10	10
563	10 t. "The Crucifixion"	15	10
564	20 t. "Descent from the Cross"	30	10
565	40 t. "Jesus appears before Mary"	50	55

122 Nyala

124 "Vanilla polylepis"

123 Malamulo Seventh Day Adventist Church

1978. Wildlife. Multicoloured.

567	4 t. Type **122**	1·00	10
568	10 t. Lion (horiz)	3·00	30
569	20 t. Common zebra (horiz)	5·50	80
570	40 t. Mountain reedbuck	7·50	4·75

1978. Christmas. Multicoloured.

572	4 t. Type **123**	10	10
573	10 t. Likoma Cathedral	10	10
574	20 t. St. Michael's and All Angels', Blantyre	20	10
575	40 t. Zomba Catholic Cathedral	40	60

1979. Orchids. Multicoloured.

577	1 t. Type **124**	50	30
578	2 t. "Cirrhopetalum umbellatum"	50	30
579	5 t. "Calanthe natalensis"	50	10
580	7 t. "Ansellia gigantea"	50	50
581	8 t. "Tridactyle bicaudata"	50	30
582	10 t. "Acampe pachyglossa"	50	10
583	15 t. "Eulophia quartiniana"	50	15
584	20 t. "Cyrtorchis arcuata"	50	50
585	30 t. "Eulophia tricristata"	1·25	30
586	50 t. "Disa hamatopetala"	85	50
587	75 t. "Cynorchis glandulosa"	2·00	4·00
588	1 k. "Aerangis kotschyana"	1·60	1·25
589	1 k. 50 "Polystachya dendrobiiflora"	1·75	2·25
590	2 k. "Disa ornithantha"	1·75	2·00
591	4 k. "Cyrtorchis praetermissa"	3·00	3·50

125 Tsamba

1979. National Tree Planting Day. Mult.

592	5 t. Type **125**	20	10
593	10 t. Mulanje cedar	25	10
594	20 t. Mlombwa	40	20
595	40 t. Mbawa	70	2·25

126 Train crossing Viaduct

1979. Opening of Salima–Lilongwe Railway Line. Multicoloured.

597	5 t. Type **126**	25	10
598	10 t. Diesel railcar at station	40	10
599	20 t. Diesel train rounding bend	60	30
600	40 t. Diesel train passing through cutting	85	1·25

127 Young Child

1979. International Year of the Child. Designs showing young children. Multicoloured; background colours given.

602	**127** 5 t. green	10	10
603	– 10 t. red	10	10
604	– 20 t. mauve	25	10
605	– 40 t. blue	45	60

128 1964 3d. Independence Commemorative Stamp

1979. Death Centenary of Sir Rowland Hill. Designs showing 1964 Independence Commemorative Stamps. Multicoloured.

606	5 t. Type **128**	10	10
607	10 t. 6d. value	10	10
608	20 t. 1s. 3d. value	20	10
609	40 t. 2s. 6d. value	35	60

129 River Landscape

1979. Christmas. Multicoloured.

611	5 t. Type **129**	10	10
612	10 t. Sunset	10	10
613	20 t. Forest and hill	25	15
614	40 t. Plain and mountains	50	1·75

130 Limbe Rotary Club Emblem

132 Agate Nodule

131 Mangochi District Post Office

1980. 75th Anniv of Rotary International.

615	**130** 5 t. multicoloured	10	10
616	– 10 t. multicoloured	10	10
617	– 20 t. blue, gold and red	30	15
618	– 40 t. gold and blue	75	1·60

DESIGNS: 10 t. Blantyre Rotary Club pennant; 20 t. Lilongwe Rotary Club pennant; 40 t. Rotary International emblem.

1980. "London 1980" International Stamp Exhibition.

620	**131** 5 t. black and green	10	10
621	– 10 t. black and red	10	10
622	– 20 t. black and violet	15	10
623	– 1 k. black and blue	65	1·10

DESIGNS: 10 t. New Blantyre Sorting Office; 20 t. Mail transfer hut, Walala; 1 k. First Nyasaland Post Office, Chiromo.

1980. Gemstones. Multicoloured.

625	5 t. Type **132**	60	10
626	10 t. Sunstone	80	10
627	20 t. Smoky quartz	1·40	30
628	1 k. Kyanite crystal	3·50	6·00

133 Elephants

1980. Christmas. Children's Paintings. Multicoloured.

629	5 t. Type **133**	40	10
630	10 t. Flowers	30	10
631	20 t. Class "Shire" diesel train	75	20
632	1 k. Malachite kingfisher	1·60	2·00

134 Suni

1981. Wildlife. Multicoloured.

633	7 t. Type **134**	15	10
634	10 t. Blue duiker	20	10
635	20 t. African buffalo	30	15
636	1 k. Lichtenstein's hartebeest	1·25	1·60

135 "Kanjedza II" Standard "A" Earth Station

1981. International Communications. Mult.

637	7 t. Type **135**	10	10
638	10 t. Blantyre International Gateway Exchange	15	10
639	20 t. "Kanjedza I" standard "B" earth station	25	15
640	1 k. "Satellite communications"	1·50	1·90

136 Maize

1981. World Food Day. Agricultural Produce. Multicoloured.

642	7 t. Type **136**	15	10
643	10 t. Rice	20	10
644	20 t. Finger-millet	30	20
645	1 k. Wheat	1·00	1·40

137 "The Adoration of the Shepherds" (Murillo)

138 Impala Herd

1981. Christmas. Paintings. Multicoloured.

646	7 t. Type **137**	20	10
647	10 t. "The Holy Family" (Lippi) (horiz)	25	10
648	20 t. "The Adoration of the Shepherds" (Louis le Nain) (horiz)	45	15
649	1 k. "The Virgin and Child, St. John the Baptist and an Angel" (Paolo Morando)	1·10	1·75

1982. National Parks. Wildlife. Multicoloured.

650	7 t. Type **138**	20	10
651	10 t. Lions	35	10
652	20 t. Greater kudu	50	20
653	1 k. Greater flamingoes	2·25	4·25

139 Kamuzu Academy

1982. Kamuzu Academy.

654	**139** 7 t. multicoloured	15	10
655	– 20 t. multicoloured	20	10
656	– 30 t. multicoloured	30	45
657	– 1 k. multicoloured	1·00	2·75

DESIGNS: 20 t. to 1 k. Various views of the Academy.

140 Attacker challenging Goalkeeper

1982. World Cup Football Championship, Spain. Multicoloured.

658	7 t. Type **140**	65	10
659	20 t. FIFA World Cup trophy	1·40	1·10
660	30 t. Football stadium	1·75	3·00

141 Blantyre War Memorial, St. Paul's Church

1982. Remembrance Day. Multicoloured.

662	7 t. Type **141**	10	10
663	20 t. Zomba war memorial	15	10
664	30 t. Chichiri war memorial	20	30
665	1 k. Lilongwe war memorial	65	3·25

142 Kwacha International Conference Centre

1983. Commonwealth Day. Multicoloured.

666	7 t. Type **142**	10	10
667	20 t. Tea-picking, Mulanje	20	10
668	30 t. World map showing position of Malawi	25	30
669	1 k. Pres. Dr. H. Kamuzu Banda	60	1·50

143 "Christ and St. Peter"

144 Pair by Lake

1983. 500th Birth Anniv of Raphael. Details from the cartoon for "The Miraculous Draught of Fishes" Tapestry. Multicoloured.

670	7 t. Type **143**	35	10
671	20 t. "Hauling in the Catch"	75	80
672	30 t. "Fishing Village" (horiz)	90	2·50

1983. African Fish Eagle. Multicoloured.

674	30 t. Type **144**	1·40	1·75
675	30 t. Making gull-like call	1·40	1·75
676	30 t. Diving on prey	1·40	1·75
677	30 t. Carrying fish	1·40	1·75
678	30 t. Feeding on catch	1·40	1·75

145 Kamuzu International Airport

1983. Bicentenary of Manned Flight. Mult.

679	7 t. Type **145**	10	10
680	20 t. Kamuzu International Airport (different)	25	15
681	30 t. B.A.C. One Eleven	40	45
682	1 k. Short Empire "C" Class flying boat at Cape Maclear	1·10	2·25

146 "Clerodendrum myricoides"

147 Golden Mbuna

1983. Christmas. Flowers. Multicoloured.

684	7 t. Type **146**	40	10
685	20 t. "Gloriosa superba"	90	15
686	30 t. "Gladiolus laxiflorus"	1·25	60
687	1 k. "Aframomum angustifolium"	3·00	6·50

1984. Fishes. Multicoloured.

688	1 t. Type **147**	30	60
689	2 t. Malawi eyebiter	30	60
690	5 t. Blue mbuna	30	50
691	7 t. Lombardo's mbuna	30	10
692	8 t. Golden zebra mbuna	30	10
693	10 t. Fairy cichlid	30	10
694	15 t. Crabro mbuna	30	10
695	20 t. Marbled zebra mbuna	30	10
696	30 t. Sky-blue mbuna	40	10
697	40 t. Venustus cichlid	60	30
698	50 t. Thumbi emperor cichlid	1·75	2·00
699	75 t. Purple mbuna	2·25	3·00
700	1 k. Zebra mbuna	2·50	3·25
701	2 k. Fairy cichlid (different)	3·50	4·50
702	4 k. Mbenje emperor cichlid	4·75	7·50

Nos. 688 and 691/7 exist with different imprint dates at foot.

148 Smith's Red Hare

1984. Small Mammals. Multicoloured.

703	7 t. Type **148**	40	10
704	20 t. Gambian sun squirrel	75	50
705	30 t. South African hedgehog	1·10	1·10
706	1 k. Large-spotted genet	1·40	5·50

149 Running

150 "Euphaedra neophron"

1984. Olympic Games, Los Angeles. Mult.

707	7 t. Type **149**	15	10
708	20 t. Boxing	35	20
709	30 t. Cycling	75	70
710	1 k. Long jumping	1·40	3·50

1984. Butterflies.

712	**150**	7 t. multicoloured	95	30
713	–	20 t. yellow, brown and red	2·25	45
714	–	30 t. multicoloured	2·50	1·10
715	–	1 k. multicoloured	4·25	9·00

DESIGNS: 20 t. "Papilio dardanus"; 30 t. "Antanartia schaeneia"; 1 k. "Spindasis nyassae".

151 "Virgin and Child" (Duccio)

152 "Leucopaxillus gracillimus"

1984. Christmas. Religious Paintings. Multicoloured.

716	7 t. Type **151**	45	10
717	20 t. "Madonna and Child" (Raphael)	1·25	20
718	30 t. "Virgin and Child" (ascr to Lippi)	1·75	70
719	1 k. "The Wilton Diptych"	3·25	7·00

1985. Fungi. Multicoloured.

720	7 t. Type **152**	1·25	30
721	20 t. "Limacella guttata"	2·50	45
722	30 t. "Termitomyces eurrhizus"	3·00	1·25
723	1 k. "Xerulina asprata"	5·50	8·50

153 Map showing Member States and Lumberjack (Forestry)

1985. 5th Anniv of Southern African Development Co-ordination Conference. Designs showing map and aspects of development.

724	**153**	7 t. black, green and light green	75	10
725	–	15 t. black, red and pink	1·25	20
726	–	20 t. black, violet and mauve	4·00	1·75
727	–	1 k. black, blue and light blue	4·50	8·00

DESIGNS: 15 t. Radio mast (Communications); 20 t. Diesel locomotive (Transport); 1 k. Trawler and net (Fishing).

154 M.V. "Ufulu"

1985 Ships of Lake Malawi (2nd series). Mult.

728	7 t. Type **154**	90	10
729	15 t. M.V. "Chauncy Maples II"	1·75	20
730	20 t. M.V. "Mtendere"	2·25	65
731	1 k. M.V. "Ilala II"	4·50	6·00

155 Stierling's Woodpecker

156 "The Virgin of Humility" (Jaime Serra)

1985. Birth Bicentenary of John J. Audubon (ornithologist). Multicoloured.

733	7 t. Type **155**	1·25	20
734	15 t. Lesser seedcracker	2·25	20
735	20 t. East coast akelat	2·25	55
736	1 k. Boehm's bee eater	4·25	5·50

1985. Christmas. Nativity Paintings. Mult.

738	7 t. Type **156**	30	10
739	15 t. "The Adoration of the Magi" (Stefano da Zevio)	75	15
740	20 t. "Madonna and Child" (Gerard van Honthorst)	85	25
741	1 k. "Virgin of Zbraslav" (Master of Vissy Brod)	2·25	3·00

157 Halley's Comet and Path of "Giotto" Spacecraft

1986. Appearance of Halley's Comet. Mult.

742	8 t. Type **157**	60	10
743	15 t. Halley's Comet above Earth	65	15
744	20 t. Comet and dish aerial, Malawi	1·00	30
745	1 k. "Giotto" spacecraft	2·00	3·50

158 Two Players competing for Ball

1986. World Cup Football Championship, Mexico. Multicoloured.

746	8 t. Type **158**	70	10
747	15 t. Goalkeeper saving goal	95	20
748	20 t. Two players competing for ball (different)	1·10	35
749	1 k. Player kicking ball	4·00	3·50

159 President Banda

160 "Virgin and Child" (Botticelli)

1986. 20th Anniv of Republic. Multicoloured.

751	8 t. Type **159**	1·50	2·00
752	15 t. National flag	80	15
753	20 t. Malawi coat of arms	85	25
754	1 k. Kamuzu International Airport and emblem of national airline	3·50	4·00

1986. Christmas. Multicoloured.

755	8 t. Type **160**	45	10
756	15 t. "Adoration of the Shepherds" (Guido Reni)	80	15
757	20 t. "Madonna of the Veil" (Carlo Dolci)	1·25	35
758	1 k. "Adoration of the Magi" (Jean Bourdichon)	3·75	7·00

161 Wattled Crane

1987. Wattled Crane. Multicoloured.

763	8 t. Type **161**	1·25	30
764	15 t. Two cranes	2·00	40
765	20 t. Cranes at nest	2·25	70
766	75 t. Crane in lake	4·50	8·00

162 Bagnall Steam Locomotive No. 2 "Shamrock"

1987. Steam Locomotives. Multicoloured.

767	10 t. Type **162**	1·75	30
768	25 t. Class D steam locomotive No. 8, 1914	2·25	40
769	30 t. Bagnall steam locomotive No. 1 "Thistle"	2·50	75
770	1 k. Kitson steam locomotive No. 6, 1903	4·50	8·00

163 Hippopotamus grazing

164 "Stathmostelma spectabile"

1987. Hippopotamus. Multicoloured.

771	10 t. Type **163**	1·25	30
772	25 t. Hippopotami in water	2·00	40
773	30 t. Female and calf in water	2·00	70
774	1 k. Hippopotami and cattle egret	5·50	8·00

1987. Christmas. Wild Flowers. Multicoloured.

776	10 t. Type **164**	65	10
777	25 t. "Pentanisia schweinfurthii"	1·50	25
778	30 t. "Chironia krebsii"	1·75	55
779	1 k. "Ochna macrocalyx"	3·00	7·00

165 African and Staunton Knights

166 High Jumping

1988. Chess. Local and Staunton chess pieces. Multicoloured.

780	15 t. Type **165**	70	20
781	35 t. Bishops	1·25	70
782	50 t. Rooks	1·50	1·50
783	2 k. Queens	4·75	7·00

1988. Olympic Games, Seoul. Multicoloured.

784	15 t. Type **166**	30	10
785	35 t. Javelin throwing	50	20
786	50 t. Tennis	75	50
787	2 k. Shot-putting	1·60	2·50

167 Scrub Warbler

168 "Madonna in the Church" (Jan van Eyck)

1988. Birds. Multicoloured.

789	1 t. Type **167**	10	10
790	2 t. Yellow-throated woodland warbler	10	10
791	5 t. Moustached green tinkerbird	10	10
792	7 t. Waller's red-winged starling	10	10
793	8 t. Oriole-finch	10	10
794	10 t. Starred robin	1·75	30
795	15 t. Bar-tailed trogon	10	10
796	20 t. Green-backed twin-spot	10	10
797	30 t. African grey cuckoo shrike	10	10
798	40 t. Black-fronted bush shrike	10	10
799	50 t. White-tailed crested flycatcher	2·25	60
800	75 t. Green barbet	10	10
801	1 k. Lemon dove ("Cinnamon Dove")	10	10
802	2 k. Silvery-cheeked hornbill	10	15
803	4 k. Crowned eagle	10	15
804	10 k. Anchieta's sunbird	4·00	4·50
804a	10 k. As 10 t.	30	35

1988. 300th Anniv of Lloyd's of London. As T **123** of Ascension. Multicoloured.

805	15 t. Rebuilt Royal Exchange, 1844	30	10
806	35 t. Opening ceremony, Nkula Falls Hydro-electric Power Station	60	20
807	50 t. Air Malawi B.A.C. One Eleven airliner (horiz)	1·50	50
808	2 k. "Seawise University" (formerly "Queen Elizabeth") on fire, Hong Kong, 1972	3·25	3·00

1988. Christmas. Multicoloured.

809	15 t. Type **168**	50	10
810	35 t. "Virgin, Infant Jesus and St. Anna" (da Vinci)	80	25
811	50 t. "Virgin and Angels" (Cimabue)	1·10	70
812	2 k. "Virgin and Child" (Baldovinetti Apenio)	2·75	4·50

169 Robust Cichlid

1989. 50th Anniv of Malawi Angling Society. Multicoloured.
813 15 t. Type 169 . . . . 50 10
814 35 t. Small-scaled minnow ("Mpasa") 95 30
815 50 t. Long-scaled yellowfish . 1·40 1·40
816 2 k. Tigerfish . . . . 3·75 7·00

170 Independence Arch, Blantyre

1989. 25th Anniv of Independence. Multicoloured.
817 15 t. Type 170 . . . . 60 10
818 35 t. Grain silos . . . . 1·00 30
819 50 t. Capital Hill, Lilongwe . 1·60 1·50
820 2 k. Reserve Bank Headquarters 4·00 7·00

171 Blantyre Digital Telex Exchange

1989. 25th Anniv of African Development Bank. Multicoloured.
821 15 t. Type 171 . . . . 60 10
822 40 t. Dzalanyama steer . . . . 1·00 30
823 50 t. Mikolongwe heifer . . . 1·60 1·50
824 2 k. Zebu bull . . . . 4·00 7·00

172 Rural House with Verandah

1989. 25th Anniv of Malawi–United Nations Co-operation. Multicoloured.
825 15 t. Type 172 . . . . 60 10
826 40 t. Rural house . . . . . . 1·00 30
827 50 t. Traditional hut and modern houses . . . . 1·60 1·50
828 2 k. Tea plantation . . . . . 4·00 7·00

173 St. Michael and All Angels Church

1989. Christmas. Churches of Malawi. Mult.
829 15 t. Type 173 . . . . . . 60 10
830 40 t. Catholic Cathedral, Limbe 1·00 30
831 50 t. C.C.A.P. Church, Nkhoma 1·60 1·50
832 2 k. Cathedral, Likoma Island 4·00 7·00

174 Ford "Sedan", 1915

175 Player heading Ball into Net

1990. Vintage Vehicles. Multicoloured.
833 15 t. Type 174 . . . . 70 10
834 40 t. Two-seater Ford, 1915 . 1·00 30
835 50 t. Ford pick-up, 1915 . . . 1·60 1·50
836 1 k. Chevrolet bus, 1930 . . . 4·00 7·00

1990. World Cup Football Championship, Italy. Multicoloured.
838 15 t. Type 175 . . . . 85 10
839 40 t. Player tackling . . . . . 1·25 30
840 50 t. Player scoring goal . . . 1·75 1·50
841 2 k. World Cup . . . . 4·00 7·00

176 Anniversary Emblem on Map

1990. 10th Anniv of Southern Africa Development Co-ordination Conference. Multicoloured.
843 15 t. Type 176 . . . . 75 10
844 40 t. Tilapia . . . . 1·25 40
845 50 t. Cedar plantation . . . . 1·60 1·50
846 2 k. Male nyala (antelope) . . 3·75 7·00

177 "Aerangis kotschyana"

178 "The Virgin and the Child Jesus" (Raphael)

1990. Orchids. Multicoloured.
848 15 t. Type 177 . . . . 1·25 15
849 40 t. "Angraecum eburneum" . 2·00 70
850 50 t. "Aerangis luteo-alba rhodostica" . . . . 2·00 1·60
851 2 k. "Cyrtorchis arcuata whytei" 4·75 7·00

1990. Christmas. Paintings by Raphael. Mult.
853 15 t. Type 178 . . . . 70 10
854 40 t. "Transfiguration" (detail) 1·25 30
855 50 t. "St. Catherine of Alexandrie" (detail) . . . . 1·50 90
856 2 k. "Transfiguration" . . . . 4·00 7·00

179 Buffalo

1991. Wildlife. Multicoloured.
858 20 t. Type 179 . . . . 70 15
859 60 t. Cheetah . . . . 1·75 1·00
860 75 t. Greater kudu . . . . . . 1·75 1·00
861 2 k. Black rhinoceros . . . . 6·00 8·00

180 Chiromo Post Office, 1891

1991. Centenary of Postal Services. Mult.
863 20 t. Type 180 . . . . 70 10
864 60 t. Re-constructed mail exchange hut at Walala . . 1·40 85
865 75 t. Mangochi post office . . 1·50 95
866 2 k. Satellite Earth station . . 4·25 7·00

181 Red Locust

182 Child in a Manger

1991. Insects. Multicoloured.
868 20 t. Type 181 . . . . 75 20
869 60 t. Weevil . . . . 1·75 1·00
870 75 t. Cotton stainer bug . . . 1·75 1·25
871 2 k. Pollen beetle . . . . . . 4·75 7·50

1991. Christmas. Multicoloured.
872 20 t. Type 182 . . . . 55 10
873 60 t. Adoration of the Kings and Shepherds . . . . 1·40 45
874 75 t. Nativity . . . . 1·50 75
875 2 k. Virgin and Child . . . . 3·75 6·50

183 Red Bishop

1992. Birds. Multicoloured.
876 75 t. Type 183 . . . . 90 1·00
877 75 t. Lesser striped swallow . . 90 1·00
878 75 t. Long-crested eagle . . . 90 1·00
879 75 t. Lilac-breasted roller . . . 90 1·00
880 75 t. African paradise flycatcher 90 1·00
881 75 t. White-fronted bee eater . 90 1·00
882 75 t. White-winged black tern . 90 1·00
883 75 t. African fire finch . . . . 90 1·00
884 75 t. White-browed robin chat 90 1·00
885 75 t. African fish eagle . . . . 90 1·00
886 75 t. Malachite kingfisher . . . 90 1·00
887 75 t. Lesser masked weaver . . 90 1·00
888 75 t. Barn owl . . . . 90 1·00
889 75 t. Variable sunbird . . . . 90 1·00
890 75 t. Lesser flamingo . . . . . 90 1·00
891 75 t. South African crowned crane . . . . 90 1·00
892 75 t. African pitta . . . . . . 90 1·00
893 75 t. African darter . . . . . . 90 1·00
894 75 t. White-faced whistling duck 90 1·00
895 75 t. African pied wagtail . . . 90 1·00

184 Long Jumping

1992. Olympic Games, Barcelona. Multicoloured.
896 20 t. Type 184 . . . . 60 10
897 60 t. High jumping 95 60
898 75 t. Javelin . . . . 1·25 90
899 2 k. Running . . . . 2·50 4·00

185 "The Angel Gabriel" (detail, "The Annunciation") (Philippe de Champaigne)

186 "Voyager 2" passing Saturn

1992. Christmas. Religious Paintings. Mult.
901 20 t. Type 185 . . . . 50 10
902 75 t. "Virgin and Child" (Bernandino Luini) . . . . . 1·10 50
903 95 t. "Virgin and Child" (Sassoferrato) . . . . 1·40 90
904 2 k. "Virgin Mary" (detail, "The Annunciation") (De Champaigne) . . . . 3·50 4·75

1992. International Space Year. Multicoloured.
905 20 t. Type 186 . . . . 75 30
906 75 t. Centre of galaxy . . . . 1·50 90
907 95 t. Kanjedza II Standard A Earth Station . . . . . . 1·60 1·00
908 2 k. Communications satellite . 3·50 4·50

187 "Strychnos spinosa"

188 "Apaturopsis cleocharis"

1993. World Forestry Day. Indigenous Fruit Trees. Multicoloured.
909 20 t. Type 187 . . . . 45 10
910 75 t. "Adansonia digitata" . . 1·00 60
911 95 t. "Ximenia caffra" . . . . 1·25 90
912 2 k. "Uapaca kirkiana" . . . 2·25 3·50

1993. Butterflies. Multicoloured.
913 20 t. Type 188 . . . . 70 30
914 75 t. "Euryphura achlys" . . . 1·25 70
915 95 t. "Cooksonia aliciae" . . . 1·50 1·00
916 2 k. "Charaxes protoclea azota" 2·25 3·50

189 The Holy Family

190 Kentrosaurus

1993. Christmas. Multicoloured.
917 20 t. Type 189 . . . . 10 10
918 75 t. Shepherds and star . . . 20 20
919 95 t. Three Kings 25 30
920 2 k. Adoration of the Kings . 65 1·50

1993. Prehistoric Animals. Multicoloured.
921 20 t. Type 190 . . . . 35 25
922 75 t. Stegosaurus 70 80
923 95 t. Sauropod 75 90

191 Socolof's mbuna

1994. Fishes. Multicoloured.
925 20 t. Type 191 . . . . 15 10
926 75 t. Golden mbuna 40 30
927 95 t. Lombardo's mbuna . . . 45 35
928 1 k. Scraper-mouthed mbuna . 50 55
929 2 k. Zebra mbuna . . . . . . 1·00 1·40
930 4 k. Elongate mbuna . . . . . 1·75 2·75

192 "Ilala II" (lake vessel)

1994. Ships of Lake Malawi. Multicoloured.
931 20 t. Type 192 . . . . 15 10
932 75 t. "Ufulu" (tanker) 20 20
933 95 t. "Pioneer" (steam launch) 25 25
934 2 k. "Dove" (paddle-steamer) 35 80

193 "Virgin and Child" (detail) (Durer)

194 Pres. Bakili Muluzi (C.O.M.E.S.A. chairman, 1994–95)

1994. Christmas. Religious Paintings. Multicoloured.
936 20 t. Type 193 . . . . 15 10
937 75 t. "Wise Men present Gifts" (Franco-Flemish Book of Hours) 20 15
938 95 t. "The Nativity" (detail) (Fra Filippo Lippi) (horiz) . . . 25 15
939 2 k. "Nativity Scene with Wise Men" (Rogier van der Weyden) (horiz) 60 90

1995. Establishment of C.O.M.E.S.A. (Common Market for Eastern and Southern African States).
940 194 40 t. multicoloured . . . 10 10
941 1 k. 40 multicoloured . . . 20 20
942 1 k. 80 multicoloured . . . 25 30
943 2 k. multicoloured . . . 30 50

195 Telecommunications Training

1995. 50th Anniv of the United Nations. Mult.
944 40 t. Type 195 . . . . 10 10
945 1 k. 40 Village women collecting water 20 20
946 1 k. 80 Mt. Mulanje 25 30
947 2 k. Villagers in field 30 40

196 Teacher and Class

1995. Christmas. Multicoloured.
949 40 t. Type 196 . . . . 10 10
950 1 k. 40 Dispensing medicine . 25 20
951 1 k. 80 Crowd at water pump 30 35
952 2 k. Refugees on ferries . . . 30 45

197 "Precis tugela"

1996. Butterflies. Multicoloured.

953		60 t. Type **197**	15	10
954		3 k. "Papilio pelodorus"	35	30
955		4 k. "Acrea acrita"	40	35
956		10 k. "Melanitis leda"	90	1·50

198 Children's Party

1996. Christmas. Multicoloured.

957		10 t. Type **198**	10	10
958		20 t. Nativity play	15	10
959		30 t. Children wearing party hats	20	10
960		60 t. Mother and child	35	50

199 Mother and Child 200 The Nativity

1997. 50th Anniv of U.N.I.C.E.F. Multicoloured.

961		60 t. Type **199**	15	10
962		3 k. Children in class	25	25
963		4 k. 40 Boy with fish	30	40
964		5 k. Nurse inoculating child	40	50

1997. Christmas. Multicoloured.

965		60 t. Type **200**	15	10
966		3 k. The Nativity (different)	25	20
967		4 k. 40 Adoration of the Magi	30	40
968		5 k. The Holy Family	40	50

1998. Diana, Princess of Wales Commemoration. As T **91** of Kiribati. Multicoloured.

969		60 t. Wearing red dress	15	10
970		6 k. Wearing lilac jacket	20	15
971		7 k. With head scarf	25	25
972		8 k. Wearing blue evening dress	35	35

201 Tattooed Rock, Mwalawamphini, Cape Maclear

1998. Monuments. Multicoloured.

974		60 t. Type **201**	10	10
975		6 k. War Memorial Tower, Zomba	10	15
976		7 k. Mtengatenga Postal Hut, Walala (horiz)	15	20
977		8 k. P.I.M. Church, Chiradzulu (horiz)	20	25

No. 974 is inscribed "tatooed" and No. 975 "Memoral", both in error.

202 Woman voting

1998. 50th Anniv of Declaration of Human Rights. Multicoloured.

978		60 t. Type **202**	10	10
979		6 k. Books, pens and pencils ("Education")	10	15
980		7 k. Man and woman on scales ("Justice")	15	20
981		8 k. Person hugging house and land ("Property")	20	25

POSTAGE DUE STAMPS

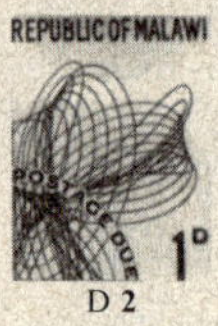

D 2

1967.

D 6	**D 2**	1d. red	15	3·00
D 7		2d. brown	20	3·00
D 8		4d. violet	25	3·25
D 9		6d. blue	25	3·50
D10		8d. green	35	3·75
D11		1s. black	45	4·00

1971. Values in tambalas. No accent over "W" of "MALAWI".

D12	**D 2**	2 t. brown	30	2·75
D13		4 t. mauve	70	2·75
D14		6 t. blue	65	3·00
D15		8 t. green	75	3·00
D16		10 t. brown	85	3·00

1975. With circumflex over "W" of "MALAWI".

D27	**D 2**	2 t. brown	40	70
D28		4 t. purple	40	70
D29		6 t. blue	40	70
D21		8 t. green	1·00	2·00
D31		10 t. black	50	70

MALAYA (BRITISH MILITARY ADMINISTRATION)

The following stamps were for use throughout the Malayan States and in Singapore during the period of the British Military Administration and were gradually replaced by individual issues for each state.

100 cents = 1 dollar

1945. Straits Settlements stamps optd **B M A MALAYA.**

1a	**58**	1 c. black	10	20
2a		2 c. orange	20	10
4		3 c. green	30	50
5		5 c. brown	70	80
6a		6 c. grey	30	20
7		8 c. red	30	10
8a		10 c. purple	40	10
10		12 c. blue	1·75	4·25
12a		15 c. blue	75	20
13a		25 c. purple and red	1·40	30
14a		50 c. black on green	60	10
15		$1 black and red	2·00	10
16		$2 green and red	2·75	75
17		$5 green and red on green	80·00	75·00
18		$5 purple and orange	3·75	3·00

For stamps inscribed "MALAYA" at top and with Arabic characters at foot see under Kelantan, Negri Sembilan, Pahang, Perak, Selangor or Trengganu.

MALAYA (JAPANESE OCCUPATION OF)

Japanese forces invaded Malaya on 8 December 1941 and the conquest of the Malay peninsula was completed by the capture of Singapore on 15 February.

The following stamps were used in Malaya until the defeat of Japan in 1945.

100 cents = 1 dollar

(a) **JOHORE**

POSTAGE DUE STAMPS

(1)

(2)

1942. Nos. D1/5 of Johore optd with T **1**.

JD1	**D 1**	1 c. red	28·00	70·00
JD2		4 c. green	60·00	80·00
JD3		8 c. orange	75·00	90·00
JD4		10 c. brown	16·00	50·00
JD5		12 c. purple	28·00	50·00

1943. Postage Due stamps of Johore optd with T **2**.

JD 6	**D 1**	1 c. red	4·00	18·00
JD 7		4 c. green	4·25	19·00
JD 8		8 c. orange	4·50	20·00
JD 9		10 c. brown	4·00	24·00
JD10		12 c. purple	5·00	35·00

(b) **KEDAH**

1942. Stamps of Kedah optd **DAI NIPPON 2602**.

J 1	**1**	1 c. black	3·25	4·75
J 2		2 c. green	24·00	30·00
J 3		4 c. violet	3·50	4·00
J 4		5 c. yellow	2·75	3·25
J 5		6 c. red	1·90	7·50
J 6		8 c. black	2·75	1·75
J 7	**6**	10 c. blue and brown	7·50	7·50
J 8		12 c. black and violet	20·00	26·00
J 9		25 c. blue and purple	6·00	9·00
J10		30 c. green and red	65·00	75·00
J11		40 c. black and purple	26·00	38·00
J12		50 c. brown and blue	28·00	40·00
J13		$1 black and green	£130	£150
J14		$2 green and brown	£160	£170
J15		$5 black and red	65·00	75·00

(c) **KELANTAN**

(**5**) Sunagawa Seal

(**6**) Handa Seal

1942. Stamps of Kelantan surch. (a) With T **5**. (i) New value in **CENTS**.

J16	**4**	1 c. on 50 c. green & orge	£225	£180
J17		2 c. on 40 c. orange & grn	£425	£275
J18		4 c. on 30 c. violet & red	£1700	£1200
J19		5 c. on 12 c. blue	£200	£180
J20		6 c. on 25 c. red & violet	£250	£190
J21		8 c. on 5 c. brown	£300	£140
J22		10 c. on 6 c. red	75·00	£120
J23		12 c. on 8 c. green	48·00	£110
J24		25 c. on 10 c. purple	£1100	£1200
J25		30 c. on 4 c. red	£1800	£2000
J26		40 c. on 2 c. green	55·00	85·00
J27		50 c. on 1 c. green & yell	£1200	£1100
J28		$1 on 4 c. black and red	50·00	75·00
J29		$2 on 5 c. green & red on yell	50·00	75·00
J30		$5 on 6 c. red	50·00	75·00

(ii) New Value in **Cents**.

J32	**4**	1 c. on 50 c. green & orge	£120	85·00
J33		2 c. on 40 c. orange & grn	£110	90·00
J34		5 c. on 12 c. blue	£100	£100
J35	**4**	8 c. on 5 c. brown	95·00	70·00
J36		10 c. on 6 c. red	£225	£250
J37		12 c. on 8 c. green	£375	£400
J38		30 c. on 4 c. red	£1800	£2000
J39		40 c. on 2 c. green	£400	£425
J40		50 c. on 1 c. green & yell	£1000	£1100

(b) With T **6** and new value.

J41	**4**	1 c. on 50 c. green & orge	90·00	£130
J42		2 c. on 40 c. orange & grn	95·00	£140
J43		8 c. on 5 c. brown	65·00	£120
J44		10 c. on 6 c. red	85·00	£140
J31		12 c. on 8 c. green	£130	£190

(d) **PENANG**

(**11**) Okugawa Seal

(**12**) Ochiburi Seal

1942. Straits Settlements stamps optd. (a) As T **11**.

J56	**58**	1 c. black	9·50	11·00
J57		2 c. orange	24·00	22·00
J58		3 c. green	20·00	22·00
J59		5 c. brown	24·00	24·00
J60		8 c. grey	26·00	26·00
J61		10 c. purple	50·00	50·00
J62		12 c. blue	27·00	35·00
J63		15 c. blue	35·00	42·00
J64		40 c. red and purple	90·00	£100
J65		50 c. black/green	£190	£200
J66		$1 black and red on blue	£200	£225
J67		$2 green and red	£475	£500
J68		$5 green and red on green	£1400	£1400

(b) With T **12**.

J69	**58**	1 c. black	£100	£100
J70		2 c. orange	95·00	85·00
J71		3 c. green	80·00	85·00
J72		5 c. brown	£1200	£1200
J73		8 c. grey	55·00	70·00
J74		10 c. purple	85·00	95·00
J75		12 c. blue	80·00	90·00
J76		15 c. blue	80·00	90·00

1942. Stamps of Straits Settlements optd **DAI NIPPON 2602 PENANG**.

J77	**58**	1 c. black	2·00	1·75
J78		2 c. orange	4·25	2·75
J79		3 c. green	3·50	2·00
J80		5 c. brown	2·00	3·50
J81		8 c. grey	2·25	1·40
J82		10 c. purple	1·50	2·00
J83		12 c. blue	2·75	9·00
J84		15 c. blue	1·75	2·00
J85		40 c. red and purple	3·75	9·00
J86		50 c. black and green	3·75	17·00
J87		$1 black and red on blue	6·00	24·00
J88		$2 green and red	38·00	75·00
J89		$5 green and red on green	£450	£550

(e) **SELANGOR**.

1942. Agri-horticultural Exhibition. Stamps of Straits Settlements optd **SELANGOR EXHIBITION DAI NIPPON 2602 MALAYA**.

J90	**58**	2 c. orange	12·00	24·00
J91		8 c. grey	13·00	24·00

(f) **SINGAPORE**

(**15**) "Malay Military Government Division Postal Services Bureau Seal"

1942. Stamps of Straits Settlements optd with T **15**.

J92	**58**	1 c. black	12·00	16·00
J93		2 c. orange	12·00	13·00
J94		3 c. green	50·00	70·00
J95		8 c. grey	22·00	18·00
J96		15 c. blue	15·00	15·00

(g) **TRENGGANU**

1942. Stamps of Trengganu optd with T **1**.

J 97	**4**	1 c. black	95·00	85·00
J 98		2 c. green	£140	£140
J 99a		2 c. on 5 c. purple on yellow (No. 59)	45·00	70·00
J100		3 c. brown	80·00	80·00
J101		4 c. red	£140	£140
J102		5 c. purple on yellow	10·00	18·00
J103		6 c. orange	8·50	24·00
J104		8 c. grey	9·00	13·00
J105		8 c. on 10 c. blue (No. 60)	13·00	35·00
J106		10 c. blue	15·00	26·00
J107		12 c. blue	8·00	27·00
J108		20 c. purple and orange	8·50	25·00
J109		25 c. green and purple	7·50	30·00
J110		30 c. purple and black	8·00	25·00
J111		35 c. red on yellow	21·00	35·00
J112		50 c. green and red	60·00	70·00
J113		$1 purple and blue on blue	£2000	£2000
J114		$3 green and red on green	48·00	80·00
J115	–	$5 green and red on yellow (No. 31)	£130	£180
J116	–	$25 purple and blue (No. 40)	£950	
J117	–	$50 green and yellow (No. 41)	£7000	
J118	–	$100 green and red (No. 42)	£1000	

1942. Stamps of Trengganu optd **DAI NIPPON 2602 MALAYA**.

J119	4	1 c. black	12·00	10·00
J120		2 c. green	£160	£180
J121		2 c. on 5 c. purple on yellow (No. 59)	6·00	8·00
J122		3 c. brown	9·00	16·00
J123		4 c. red	9·00	11·00
J124		5 c. purple on yellow	5·50	11·00
J125		6 c. orange	5·00	11·00
J126		8 c. grey	70·00	24·00
J127		8 c. on 10 c. blue (No. 60)	5·50	10·00
J128		12 c. blue	5·00	18·00
J129		20 c. purple and orange	9·50	13·00
J130		25 c. green and purple	7·00	26·00
J131		30 c. purple and black	7·50	23·00
J132		$3 green and red on green	60·00	£110

1942. Stamps of Trengganu optd with T **2**.

J133	4	1 c. black	8·50	16·00
J134		2 c. green	7·50	22·00
J135		2 c. on 5 c. purple on yellow (No. 59)	6·00	18·00
J136		5 c. purple on yellow	6·50	23·00
J137		6 c. orange	8·00	26·00
J138		8 c. grey	55·00	75·00
J139		8 c. on 10 c. blue (No. 60)	18·00	38·00
J140		10 c. blue	75·00	£170
J141		12 c. blue	12·00	32·00
J142		20 c. purple and orange	14·00	32·00
J143		25 c. green and purple	12·00	35·00
J144		30 c. purple and black	15·00	38·00
J145		35 c. red on yellow	15·00	40·00

1942. Postage Due stamps of Trengganu optd with T **2**.

JD17	D 1	1 c. red	50·00	80·00
JD18a		4 c. green	50·00	85·00
JD19		8 c. yellow	14·00	50·00
JD20		10 c. brown	14·00	50·00

(h) GENERAL ISSUES

1942. Stamps of various states optd with T **1**. (a) Straits Settlements.

J146	58	1 c. black	3·25	3·25
J147		2 c. green	£1600	£1600
J148		2 c. orange	3·00	2·25
J149		3 c. green	2·75	2·25
J150		5 c. brown	22·00	28·00
J151		8 c. grey	3·75	2·25
J152		10 c. purple	40·00	40·00
J153		12 c. blue	75·00	95·00
J154		15 c. blue	3·50	3·50
J155		30 c. purple and orange	£1400	£1500
J156		40 c. red and purple	80·00	90·00
J157		50 c. black and green	45·00	48·00
J158		$1 black & red on blue	75·00	75·00
J159		$2 green and red	£130	£140
J160		$5 green & red on green	£170	£180

There also exists a similar overprint with double-lined frame.

(b) Negri Sembilan

J161b	6	1 c. black	15·00	16·00
J162		2 c. orange	20·00	16·00
J163		3 c. green	26·00	20·00
J164c		5 c. brown	15·00	11·00
J165		6 c. grey	£140	£120
J166		8 c. red	80·00	70·00
J167		10 c. purple	£130	£130
J168		12 c. blue	£1100	£1100
J169		15 c. blue	18·00	8·00
J170		25 c. purple and red	28·00	38·00
J171		30 c. purple and orange	£170	£150
J172		40 c. red and purple	£800	£800
J173		50 c. black on green	£500	£500
J174a		$1 black and red on blue	£160	£170
J175		$5 green and red on green	£425	£450

(c) Pahang

J176	15	1 c. black	40·00	38·00
J177		3 c. green	£200	£200
J178		5 c. brown	12·00	9·00
J179		8 c. grey	£400	£400
J180		8 c. red	22·00	10·00
J181		10 c. purple	£150	£100
J182a		12 c. blue	£1200	£1200
J183		15 c. blue	95·00	95·00
J184		25 c. purple and red	19·00	29·00
J185		30 c. purple and orange	12·00	28·00
J186		40 c. red and purple	17·00	32·00
J187		50 c. black on green	£500	£500
J188		$1 black and red on blue	£110	£130
J189		$5 green & red on green	£600	£700

(d) Perak

J190	51	1 c. black	48·00	32·00
J191		2 c. orange	27·00	20·00
J192		3 c. green	26·00	28·00
J193		5 c. brown	7·00	6·00
J194		8 c. grey	48·00	40·00
J195		8 c. red	26·00	35·00
J196		10 c. purple	24·00	24·00
J197		12 c. blue	£225	£225
J198		15 c. blue	23·00	30·00
J199		25 c. purple and red	14·00	24·00
J200		30 c. purple and orange	17·00	32·00
J201		40 c. red and purple	£300	£325
J202		50 c. black on green	38·00	50·00
J203		$1 black & red on blue	£400	£400
J204		$2 green and red	£1900	£1900
J205		$5 green & red on green	£475	

(e) Selangor

J206	46	1 c. black	12·00	21·00
J207		2 c. green	£850	£850
J208		2 c. orange	65·00	48·00
J210a		3 c. green	18·00	17·00
J211		5 c. brown	6·00	5·50
J212a		6 c. red	£200	£200
J213		8 c. grey	17·00	17·00
J214		10 c. purple	13·00	21·00
J215		12 c. blue	55·00	55·00
J216		15 c. blue	16·00	21·00
J217a		25 c. purple and red	60·00	80·00
J218		30 c. purple and orange	11·00	24·00
J219		40 c. red and purple	£120	£120
J220a		50 c. black on green	80·00	85·00
J221	48	$1 black & red on blue	30·00	42·00
J222		$2 green and red	35·00	60·00
J223		$5 green and red on green	65·00	85·00

1942. Various stamps optd **DAI NIPPON 2602 MALAYA**. (a) Stamps of Straits Settlements.

J224	58	2 c. orange	85	50
J225		3 c. green	50·00	65·00
J226		8 c. grey	3·25	1·75
J227		15 c. blue	9·00	6·00

(b) Stamps of Negri Sembilan

J228	6	1 c. black	1·50	60
J229		2 c. orange	3·75	50
J230		3 c. green	2·50	45
J231		5 c. brown	50	75
J232		6 c. grey	2·25	1·00
J233		8 c. red	2·75	1·25
J234		10 c. purple	3·00	2·50
J235		15 c. blue	9·00	2·50
J236		25 c. purple and red	2·50	8·50
J237		30 c. purple and orange	4·50	3·00
J238		$1 black and red on blue	£100	£110

(c) Stamps of Pahang

J239	15	1 c. black	1·25	1·25
J240		5 c. brown	1·00	70
J241		8 c. red	25·00	2·50
J242		10 c. purple	8·50	6·00
J243		12 c. blue	1·00	7·00
J244		25 c. purple and red	3·75	13·00
J245		30 c. purple and orange	1·60	6·50

(d) Stamps of Perak

J246	51	2 c. orange	1·40	80
J247		3 c. green	60	60
J248		8 c. red	60	40
J249		10 c. purple	8·00	5·00
J250		15 c. blue	3·75	2·00
J251		50 c. black on green	1·75	2·75
J252		$1 black and red on blue	£350	£400
J253		$5 green and red on green	32·00	65·00

(e) Stamps of Selangor

J254	46	3 c. green	50	1·50
J255		12 c. blue	1·10	8·50
J256		15 c. blue	3·25	1·50
J257		40 c. red and purple	2·00	2·50
J258	48	$2 green and red	10·00	28·00

1942. No. 108 of Perak surch **DAI NIPPON 2602 MALAYA 2 Cents.**

J259	88	2 c. on 5 c. brown	1·25	1·60

1942. Stamps of Perak optd **DAI NIPPON YUBIN** ("Japanese Postal Service") or surch also in figures and words.

J260	51	1 c. black	2·50	6·00
J261		2 c. on 5 c. brown	2·00	6·50
J262		8 c. red	3·25	2·00

1943. Various stamps optd vert or horiz with T **2** or surch in figures and words. (a) Stamps of Straits Settlements.

J263	58	8 c. grey	1·40	50
J264		12 c. blue	55	6·00
J265		40 c. red and purple	65	2·75

(b) Stamps of Negri Sembilan.

J266	6	1 c. black	30	60
J267		2 c. on 5 c. brown	40	45
J268		6 c. on 5 c. brown	40	85
J269		25 c. purple and red	1·10	9·00

(c) Stamp of Pahang

J270	7	6 c. on 5 c. brown	50	75

(d) Stamps of Perak

J272	51	1 c. black	80	60
J274		2 c. on 5 c. brown	45	45
J275		5 c. brown	45	40
J276		8 c. red	55	60
J277		10 c. purple	60	50
J278		30 c. purple and orange	1·50	2·50
J279		50 c. black on green	3·00	12·00
J280		$5 green & red on green	50·00	80·00

(e) Stamps of Selangor

J288	46	1 c. black	35	50
J289		2 c. on 5 c. brown	30	50
J282		3 c. green	40	45
J290		3 c. on 5 c. brown	30	2·75
J291		5 c. brown	40	2·75
J293		6 c. on 5 c. brown	20	70
J283		12 c. blue	45	1·60
J284		15 c. blue	2·75	3·00
J285	48	$1 black and red on blue	3·00	15·00
J295	46	$1 on 10 c. purple	30	1·00
J296		$1.50 on 30 c. purple and orange	30	1·00
J286	48	$2 green and red	10·00	35·00
J287		$5 green & red on green	22·00	70·00

25 Tapping Rubber

27 Japanese Shrine, Singapore

1943.

J297	25	1 c. green	15	55
J298	–	2 c. green	15	15
J299	25	3 c. grey	15	15
J300	–	4 c. red	45	15
J301	–	8 c. blue	15	15
J302	–	10 c. purple	15	15
J303	27	15 c. violet	35	2·00
J304	–	30 c. olive	35	35
J305	–	50 c. blue	1·25	2·00
J306	–	70 c. blue	16·00	10·00

DESIGNS—VERT: 2 c. Fruit; 4 c. Tin dredger; 8 c. War Memorial, Bukit Batok, Singapore; 10 c. Fishing village; 30 c. Sago palms; 50 c. Straits of Johore. HORIZ: 70 c. Malay Mosque, Kuala Lumpur.

28 Ploughman

29 Rice-planting

1943. Savings Campaign.

J307	28	8 c. violet	7·50	2·75
J308		15 c. red	6·00	2·75

1944. "Re-birth of Malaya".

J309	29	8 c. red	9·50	2·75
J310		15 c. mauve	4·00	3·00

大日本

マライ郵便

50 セント

(30)

1944. Stamps intended for use on Red Cross letters. Surch with T **30**. (a) On Straits Settlements.

J311	58	50 c. on 50 c. black on grn	10·00	24·00
J312		$1 on $1 black and red on bl	18·00	35·00
J313		$1.50 on $2 grn on red	30·00	70·00

(b) On Johore

J314	24	50 c. on 50 c. pur & red	8·00	20·00
J315		$1.50 on $2 green & red	5·50	14·00

(c) On Selangor

J316	48	$1 on $2 black & red on bl	4·00	14·00
J317		$1.50 on $2 green & red	6·50	20·00

POSTAGE DUE STAMPS

1942. Postage Due stamps of Malayan Postal Union optd with T **1**.

JD21	D 1	1 c. violet	12·00	19·00
JD22		3 c. green	45·00	48·00
JD23		4 c. green	27·00	25·00
JD24		8 c. red	55·00	50·00
JD25		10 c. orange	20·00	28·00
JD26		12 c. blue	20·00	35·00
JD27		50 c. black	50·00	65·00

1942. Postage Due stamps of Malayan Postal Union optd **DAI NIPPON 2602 MALAYA**.

JD28	D 1	1 c. violet	1·40	7·50
JD29		3 c. green	9·00	14·00
JD30		4 c. green	7·50	10·00
JD31		8 c. red	10·00	13·00
JD32		10 c. orange	1·60	9·50
JD33		12 c. blue	1·60	22·00

1943. Postage Due stamps of Malayan Postal Union optd with T **2**.

JD34	D 1	1 c. violet	60	2·50
JD35		3 c. green	60	2·50
JD36		4 c. green	35·00	38·00
JD37		5 c. red	50	3·00
JD38		9 c. orange	60	4·50
JD39		10 c. orange	60	4·25
JD40		12 c. blue	70	8·50
JD41		15 c. blue	70	4·50

MALAYA (THAI OCCUPATION OF)

Stamps issued for use in the four Malay states of Kedah, Kelantan, Perlis and Trengganu ceded by Japan to Thailand on 19 October 1943 and restored to British rule on the defeat of the Japanese.

100 cents = 1 dollar

TM 1 War Memorial

1943.

TM1	TM 1	1 c. yellow	30·00	32·00
TM2		2 c. brown	12·00	20·00
TM3		3 c. green	20·00	38·00
TM4		4 c. purple	14·00	28·00
TM5		8 c. red	14·00	20·00
TM6		15 c. blue	38·00	60·00

MALAYAN FEDERATION

An independent country within the British Commonwealth, comprising all the Malay States (except Singapore) and the Settlements of Malacca and Penang. The component units retained their individual stamps. In 1963 the Federation became part of Malaysia (q.v.).

100 cents (sen) = 1 Malayan dollar

1 Tapping Rubber

1957.

1	1	6 c. blue, red and yellow	50	10
2	–	12 c. multicoloured	85	30
3	–	25 c. multicoloured	2·00	10
4	–	30 c. red and lake	80	20

DESIGNS—HORIZ: 12 c. Federation coat of arms; 25 c. Tin dredge. VERT: 30 c. Map of the Federation.

5 Prime Minister Tunku Abdul Rahman and Populace greeting Independence

1957. Independence Day.

5	5	10 c. brown	10	10

6 United Nations Emblem

8 Merdeka Stadium, Kuala Lumpur

1958. U.N. Economic Commission for Asia and Far East Conference, Kuala Lumpur.

6	6	12 c. red	30	50
7	–	30 c. purple	40	50

DESIGN: 30 c. As Type **6** but vert.

1958. 1st Anniv of Independence.

8	8	10 c. multicoloured	15	10
9	–	30 c. multicoloured	40	50

DESIGN—VERT: 30 c. Portrait of the Yang di-Pertuan Agong (Tuanku Abdul Rahman).

11 Malayan with "Torch of Freedom"

12 Mace and Malayan Peoples

1958. 10th Anniv of Declaration of Human Rights.

10	–	10 c. multicoloured	10	10
11	11	30 c. green	30	40

DESIGN—VERT: 10 c. "Human Rights".

1959. Inauguration of Parliament.

12	12	4 c. red	10	10
13		10 c. violet	10	10
14		25 c. green	35	20

14

15 Seedling Rubber Tree and Map

1960. World Refugee Year.

15	–	12 c. purple	10	40
16	14	30 c. green	10	10

DESIGN: 12 c. As Type **14** but horiz.

1960. Natural Rubber Research Conf and 15th Int Rubber Study Group Meeting, Kuala Lumpur.

17	15	6 c. multicoloured	20	85
18		30 c. multicoloured	50	50

No. 18 is inscr "INTERNATIONAL RUBBER STUDY GROUP 15th MEETING KUALA LUMPUR" at foot.

16 The Yang di-Pertuan Agong (Tuanku Syed Putra)

1961. Installation of Yang di-Pertuan Agong, Tuanku Syed Putra.

19	16	10 c. black and blue	10	10

17 Colombo Plan Emblem

18 Malaria Eradication Emblem

1961. Colombo Plan Conf, Kuala Lumpur.

20	17	12 c. black and mauve	35	2·00
21		25 c. black and green	80	2·00
22		30 c. black and blue	70	30

1962. Malaria Eradication.

23	18	25 c. brown	20	35
24		30 c. lilac	20	15
25		50 c. blue	40	30

19 Palmyra Palm Leaf

1962. National Language Month.

26	19	10 c. brown and violet	15	10
27		20 c. brown and green	25	35
28		50 c. brown and mauve	60	90

20 "Shadows of the Future"

1962. Introduction of Free Primary Education.

29	20	10 c. purple	10	10
30		25 c. ochre	30	40
31		30 c. green	1·50	10

21 Harvester and Fisherman

1963. Freedom from Hunger.

32	21	25 c. pink and green	85	2·25
33		30 c. pink and lake	1·50	85
34		50 c. pink and blue	1·50	2·25

22 Dam and Pylon

1963. Cameron Highlands Hydro-Electric Scheme.

35	22	20 c. green and violet	35	10
36		30 c. turquoise and blue	45	70

MALAYAN POSTAL UNION

In 1936 postage due stamps were issued in Type D 1 for use in Negri Sembilan, Pahang, Perak, Selangor and Straits Settlements but later their use was extended to the whole of the Federation and Singapore, and from 1963 throughout Malaysia.

POSTAGE DUE STAMPS

D 1

1936.

D 7	D 1	1 c. purple	2·75	1·75
D14		1 c. violet	30	1·25
D15		2 c. slate	80	2·00
D 8		3 c. green	6·00	10·00
D 2		4 c. green	12·00	1·00
D17		4 c. sepia	45	4·25
D 9		5 c. red	6·00	7·50
D 3		8 c. red	6·00	3·50
D19		8 c. orange	2·00	4·00
D11		9 c. orange	50·00	48·00
D 4		10 c. orange	8·00	30
D 5		12 c. blue	9·00	14·00
D20		12 c. mauve	1·00	5·50
D12		15 c. blue	£140	35·00
D21		20 c. blue	4·00	6·50
D 6		50 c. black	28·00	6·00

1965. Surch **10 cents**.

D29	D 1	10 c. on 8 c. orange	30	2·00

MALAYSIA

Issues for use by the new Federation comprising the old Malayan Federation (Johore ("JOHOR"), Kedah, Kelantan, Malacca ("MELAKA"), Negri Sembilan ("NEGERI SEMBILAN"), Pahang, Penang ("PULAU PINANG"), Perak, Perlis, Selangor and Trengganu), Sabah (North Borneo), Sarawak and Singapore, until the latter became an independent state on 9 August, 1965.

Stamps inscr "MALAYSIA" and state name are listed under the various states, as above.

100 cents (sen) = 1 Malaysian dollar

A. NATIONAL SERIES

General issues for use throughout the Federation.

1 Federation Map

2 Bouquet of Orchids

1963. Inauguration of Federation.

1	1	10 c. yellow and violet	40	10
2		12 c. yellow and green	80	60
3		50 c. yellow and brown	1·25	10

1963. 4th World Orchid Congress, Singapore.

4	2	6 c. multicoloured	1·25	1·25
5		25 c. multicoloured	1·25	25

4 Parliament House, Kuala Lumpur

1963. 9th Commonwealth Parliamentary Conference, Kuala Lumpur.

7	4	20 c. mauve and gold	50	40
8		30 c. green and gold	50	15

5 "Flame of Freedom" and Emblems of Goodwill, Health and Charity

1964. Eleanor Roosevelt Commemoration.

9	5	25 c. black, red & turquoise	15	10
10		30 c. black, red and lilac	15	15
11		50 c. black, red & yellow	15	10

6 Microwave Tower and I.T.U. Emblem

1965. Centenary of I.T.U.

12	6	2 c. multicoloured	15	80
13		25 c. multicoloured	1·00	50
14		50 c. multicoloured	1·75	10

7 National Mosque

1965. Opening of National Mosque, Kuala Lumpur.

15	7	6 c. red	10	10
16		15 c. brown	20	10
17		20 c. green	20	15

8 Air Terminal

1965. Opening of Int Airport, Kuala Lumpur.

18	8	15 c. black, green and blue	15	10
19		30 c. black, green & mauve	30	20

9 Crested Wood Partridge

17 Sepak Raga (ball game) and Football

1965. Birds. Multicoloured.

20		25 c. Type **9**	50	10
21		30 c. Blue-backed fairy bluebird	60	10
22		50 c. Black-naped oriole	80	10
23		75 c. Rhinoceros hornbill	90	10
24		$1 Zebra dove	1·50	10
25		$2 Great argus pheasant	3·50	30
26		$5 Asiatic paradise flycatcher	18·00	2·50
27		$10 Blue-tailed pitta	48·00	11·00

For the lower values see the individual sets listed under each of the states which form Malaysia.

1965. 3rd South East Asian Peninsular Games.

28	17	25 c. black and green	40	90
29	–	30 c. black and purple	40	20
30	–	50 c. black and blue	70	30

DESIGNS: 30 c. Running; 50 c. Diving.

20 National Monument

21 The Yang di-Pertuan Agong (Tuanku Ismail Nasiruddin Shah)

1966. National Monument, Kuala Lumpur.

31	20	10 c. multicoloured	15	10
32		20 c. multicoloured	25	40

1966. Installation of Yang di-Pertuan Agong, Tuanku Ismail Nasiruddin Shah.

33	21	15 c. black and yellow	10	10
34		50 c. black and blue	20	20

22 School Building

1966. 150th Anniv of Penang Free School.

35	22	20 c. multicoloured	40	10
36		50 c. multicoloured	60	10

23 "Agriculture"

1966. 1st Malaysia Plan. Multicoloured.

37		15 c. Type **23**	20	10
38		15 c. "Rural Health"	20	10
39		15 c. "Communications"	1·00	15
40		15 c. "Education"	20	10
41		15 c. "Irrigation"	20	10

28 Cable Route Maps (½-size illustration)

1967. Completion of Malaysia–Hong Kong Link of SEACOM Telephone Cable.

42	28	30 c. multicoloured	80	30
43		75 c. multicoloured	2·50	3·00

29 Hibiscus and Paramount Rulers

1967. 10th Anniv of Independence.

44	29	15 c. multicoloured	20	10
45		50 c. multicoloured	65	65

30 Mace and Shield

1967. Centenary of Sarawak Council.

46	30	15 c. multicoloured	10	10
47		50 c. multicoloured	30	50

31 Straits Settlements 1867 8 c. Stamp and Malaysian 1965 25 c. Stamp

1967. Stamp Centenary.

48	31	25 c. multicoloured	1·40	2·25
49	–	30 c. multicoloured	1·40	1·75
50	–	50 c. multicoloured	2·25	2·50

DESIGNS: 30 c. Straits Settlements 1867 24 c. stamp and Malaysian 1965 30 c. stamp; 50 c. Straits Settlements 1867 32 c. stamp and Malaysian 1965 50 c. stamp.

34 Tapping Rubber, and Molecular Unit

1968. Natural Rubber Conf, Kuala Lumpur. Multicoloured.

51		25 c. Type **34**	25	10
52		30 c. Tapping rubber and export consignment	40	20
53		50 c. Tapping rubber and aircraft tyres	40	10

37 Mexican Sombrero and Blanket with Olympic Rings

39 Tunku Abdul Rahman against background of Pandanus Weave

1968. Olympic Games, Mexico. Multicoloured.

54		30 c. Type **37**	20	10
55		75 c. Olympic Rings and Mexican Embroidery	40	20

1969. Solidarity Week.

56	39	15 c. multicoloured	15	10
57	–	20 c. multicoloured	30	80
58	–	50 c. multicoloured	30	20

DESIGNS—VERT: 20 c. As Type **39** (different). HORIZ: 50 c. Tunku Abdul Rahman with pandanus pattern.

42 Peasant Girl with Sheaves of Paddy

1969. National Rice Year.

59	42	15 c. multicoloured	15	10
60		75 c. multicoloured	55	85

43 Satellite-tracking Aerial

1970. Satellite Earth Station.

61	43	15 c. drab, black and blue	95	15
62	–	30 c. multicoloured	95	1·60
63	–	30 c. multicoloured	95	1·60

DESIGN—40 × 27 mm: Nos. 62/3, "Intelsat III" in Orbit.

No. 62 has inscriptions and value in white and No. 63 has them in gold.

45 "Euploea leucostictus"

46 Emblem

1970. Butterflies. Multicoloured.

64	25 c. Type **45**	1·00	10
65	30 c. "Zeuxidia amethystus"	1·50	10
66	50 c. "Polyura athamas"	1·75	10
67	75 c. "Papilio memnon"	2·00	10
68	$1 "Appias nero"	2·50	10
69	$2 "Trogonoptera brookiana"	3·50	10
70	$5 "Narathura centaurus"	5·00	2·75
71	$10 "Terinos terpander"	16·00	5·00

Lower values were issued for use in the individual States.

1970. 50th Anniv of Int Labour Organization.

72 **46**	30 c. grey and blue	10	20
73	75 c. pink and blue	20	30

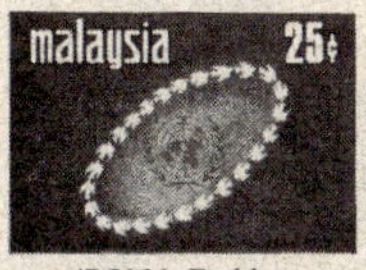

47 U.N. Emblem encircled by Doves

50 The Yang di-Pertuan Agong (Tuanku Abdul Halim Shah)

1970. 25th Anniv of United Nations.

74 **47**	25 c. gold, black and brown	30	40
75 –	30 c. multicoloured	30	35
76 –	50 c. black and green	40	75

DESIGNS: 30 c. Line of doves and U.N. emblem; 50 c. Doves looping U.N. emblem.

1971. Installation of Yang di-Pertuan Agong (Paramount Ruler of Malaysia).

77 **50**	10 c. black, gold & yellow	20	30
78	15 c. black, gold & mauve	20	30
79	50 c. black, gold and blue	60	1·60

51 Bank Negara Complex

1971. Opening of Bank Negara Building.

80 **51**	25 c. black and silver	80	90
81	50 c. black and gold	80	1·10

52 Aerial View of Parliament Buildings

1971. 17th Commonwealth Parliamentary Association Conference, Kuala Lumpur. Multicoloured.

82	25 c. Type **52**	1·25	50
83	75 c. Ground view of Parliament Buildings (horiz 73 × 23½ mm)	2·75	1·75

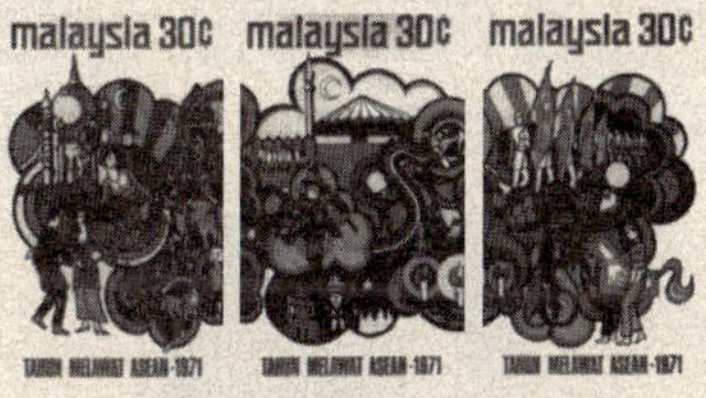

53 54 55
Malaysian Carnival

1971. Visit ASEAN Year.

84 **53**	30 c. multicoloured	1·50	55
85 **54**	30 c. multicoloured	1·50	55
86 **55**	30 c. multicoloured	1·50	55

ASEAN = Association of South East Asian Nations.

Nos. 84/6 form a composite design of a Malaysian Carnival, as Types **53/5**.

56 Trees, Elephant and Tiger

1971. 25th Anniv of U.N.I.C.E.F. Multicoloured.

87	15 c. Type **56**	1·75	45
88	15 c. Cat and kittens	1·75	45
89	15 c. Sun, flower and bird (22 × 29 mm)	1·75	45
90	15 c. Monkey, elephant and lion in jungle	1·75	45
91	15 c. Spider and butterflies	1·75	45

57 Athletics

1971. 6th S.E.A.P. Games, Kuala Lumpur. Mult.

92	25 c. Type **57**	45	40
93	30 c. Sepak Raga players	60	50
94	50 c. Hockey	1·50	95

S.E.A.P. = South East Asian Peninsula.

58 59 60
Map and Tourist Attractions

1971. Pacific Area Tourist Association Conference.

95 **58**	30 c. multicoloured	2·25	70
96 **59**	30 c. multicoloured	2·25	70
97 **60**	30 c. multicoloured	2·25	70

Nos. 95/7 form a composite design of a map showing tourist attractions, as Types **58/60**.

61 Kuala Lumpur City Hall

1972. City Status for Kuala Lumpur. Multicoloured.

98	25 c. Type **61**	1·25	1·25
99	50 c. City Hall in floodlights	2·00	1·25

62 SOCSO Emblem

64 Fireworks, National Flag and Flower

63 W.H.O. Emblem

1973. Social Security Organization.

100 **62**	10 c. multicoloured	15	15
101	15 c. multicoloured	25	10
102	50 c. multicoloured	60	1·40

1973. 25th Anniv of W.H.O.

103 **63**	30 c. multicoloured	65	25
104 –	75 c. multicoloured	1·60	1·75

The 75 c. is similar to Type **63**, but vertical.

1973. 10th Anniv of Malaysia.

105 **64**	10 c. multicoloured	40	25
106	15 c. multicoloured	55	15
107	50 c. multicoloured	1·90	1·60

65 Emblems of Interpol and Royal Malaysian Police

1973. 50th Anniv of Interpol. Multicoloured.

108	25 c. Type **65**	1·00	50
109	75 c. Emblems within "50"	2·25	2·00

66 Boeing 737 and M.A.S. Emblem

1973. Foundation of Malaysian Airline System.

110 **66**	15 c. multicoloured	35	10
111	30 c. multicoloured	65	60
112	50 c. multicoloured	95	1·60

67 Kuala Lumpur

1974. Establishment of Kuala Lumpur as Federal Territory.

113 **67**	25 c. multicoloured	50	85
114	50 c. multicoloured	1·00	1·75

68 Development Projects

1974. 7th Annual Meeting of Asian Development Bank's Board of Governors, Kuala Lumpur.

115 **68**	30 c. multicoloured	25	50
116	75 c. multicoloured	80	1·75

69 Scout Badge and Map

1974. Malaysian Scout Jamboree. Multicoloured.

117	10 c. Type **69**	45	30
118	15 c. Scouts saluting and flags (46 × 24 mm)	55	30
119	50 c. Scout badge	1·50	2·25

70 Coat of Arms and Power Installations

1974. 25th Anniv of National Electricity Board. Multicoloured.

120	30 c. Type **70**	30	50
121	75 c. National Electricity Board Building (37 × 27 mm)	1·00	2·00

71 U.P.U. and Post Office Emblems within "100"

1974. Centenary of U.P.U.

122 **71**	25 c. green, yellow & red	20	35
123	30 c. blue, yellow and red	25	35
124	75 c. orange, yellow & red	65	1·75

72 Gravel Pump in Tin Mine

1974. 4th World Tin Conf, Kuala Lumpur. Mult.

125	15 c. Type **72**	1·75	20
126	20 c. Open-cast mine	2·00	1·25
127	50 c. Dredger within "ingot"	3·75	4·50

73 Hockey-players, World Cup and Federation Emblem

74 Congress Emblem

1975. 3rd World Cup Hockey Championships.

128 **73**	30 c. multicoloured	90	60
129	75 c. multicoloured	2·10	2·25

1975. 25th Anniv of Malaysian Trade Union Congress.

130 **74**	20 c. multicoloured	20	25
131	25 c. multicoloured	30	30
132	30 c. multicoloured	45	60

75 Emblem of M.K.P.W. (Malayan Women's Organization)

76 Ubudiah Mosque, Kuala Kangsar

1975. International Women's Year.

133 **75**	10 c. multicoloured	15	25
134	15 c. multicoloured	30	25
135	50 c. multicoloured	1·25	2·25

1975. Koran Reading Competition. Multicoloured.

136	15 c. Type **76**	1·50	40
137	15 c. Zahir Mosque, Alor Star	1·50	40
138	15 c. National Mosque, Kuala Lumpur	1·50	40
139	15 c. Sultan Abu Bakar Mosque, Johore Bahru	1·50	40
140	15 c. Kuching State Mosque, Sarawak	1·50	40

77 Plantation and Emblem

1975. 50th Anniv of Malaysian Rubber Research Institute. Multicoloured.

141	10 c. Type **77**	40	15
142	30 c. Latex cup and emblem	1·10	70
143	75 c. Natural rubber in test-tubes	2·25	2·25

77a "Hebomoia glaucippe"

1976. Multicoloured.

144	10 c. Type **77a**	2·00	5·50
145	15 c. "Precis orithya"	2·00	5·50

78 Scrub Typhus

79 The Yang di-Pertuan Agong (Tuanku Yahya Petra)

1976. 75th Anniv of Institute of Medical Research. Multicoloured.

146	20 c. Type **78**	25	15
147	25 c. Malaria diagnosis	40	20
148	$1 Beri-beri	1·60	2·50

1976. Installation of Yang di-Pertuan Agong.

149 **79**	10 c. black, brown & yell	25	10
150	15 c. black, brown & mve	40	10
151	50 c. black, brown & blue	2·25	2·50

80 State Council Complex

1976. Opening of State Council Complex and Administrative Building, Sarawak.

152 **80**	15 c. green and yellow	35	10
153	20 c. green and mauve	45	40
154	50 c. green and blue	1·00	1·40

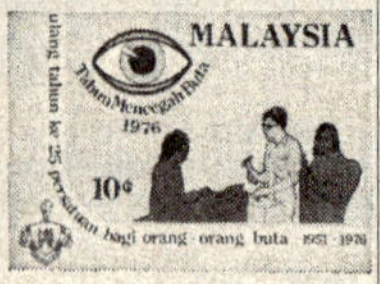

81 E.P.F. Building **82** Blind People at Work

1976. 25th Anniv of Employees' Provident Fund. Multicoloured.

155	10 c. Type **81**	15	10
156	25 c. E.P.F. emblems (27 × 27 mm)	25	35
157	50 c. E.P.F. Building at night	60	1·00

1976. 25th Anniv of Malayan Assn for the Blind. Multicoloured.

158	10 c. Type **82**	15	15
159	75 c. Blind man and shadow	1·25	2·40

83 Independence Celebrations, 1957 **84** F.E.L.D.A. Village Scheme

1977. 1st Death Anniv of Tun Abdul Razak (Prime Minister).

160	15 c. Type **83**	1·50	40
161	15 c. "Education"	1·50	40
162	15 c. Tun Razak and map ("Development")	1·50	40
163	15 c. "Rukunegara" (National Philosophy)	1·50	40
164	15 c. ASEAN meeting	1·50	40

1977. 21st Anniv of Federal Land Development Authority (F.E.L.D.A.). Multicoloured.

165	15 c. Type **84**	30	10
166	30 c. Oil palm settlement	80	1·50

85 Figure "10" **86** Games Logos

1977. 10th Anniv of Association of South East Asian Nations (A.S.E.A.N.). Multicoloured.

167	10 c. Type **85**	10	10
168	75 c. Flags of members	1·25	65

1977. Ninth South East Asia Games, Kuala Lumpur. Multicoloured.

169	10 c. Type **86**	15	15
170	20 c. "Ball"	20	15
171	75 c. Symbolic athletes	75	1·50

87 Islamic Development Bank Emblem

1978. Islamic Development Bank Board of Governors' Meeting, Kuala Lumpur.

172 **87**	30 c. multicoloured	25	15
173	75 c. multicoloured	65	55

88 Mobile Post Office

1978. Fourth Commonwealth Postal Administrations Conference, Kuala Lumpur. Multicoloured.

174	10 c. Type **88**	30	10
175	25 c. G.P.O., Kuala Lumpur	75	1·00
176	50 c. Rural delivery by motorcycle	2·00	2·50

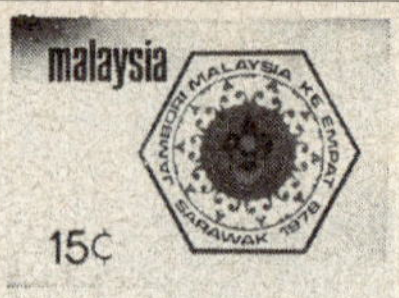

89 Boy Scout Emblem

1978. Fourth Malaysian Scout Jamboree, Sarawak. Multicoloured.

177	15 c. Type **89**	50	10
178	$1 Bees and honeycomb	2·50	2·25

90 Dome of the Rock, Jerusalem

1978. Palestinian Welfare.

179 **90**	15 c. multicoloured	60	10
180	30 c. multicoloured	90	1·25

91 Globe and Emblems

1978. Global Eradication of Smallpox.

181 **91**	15 c. black, red and blue	20	20
182	30 c. black, red and green	35	10
183	50 c. black, red and pink	55	45

92 "Seratus Tahun Getah Asli" and Tapping Knives Symbol

1978. Centenary of Rubber Industry.

184 **92**	10 c. gold and green	10	10
185 –	20 c. blue, brown & green	10	10
186 –	75 c. gold and green	45	65

DESIGNS: 20 c. Rubber tree seedling and part of "maxi stump"; 75 c. Graphic design of rubber tree, latex cup and globe arranged to form "100".

93 Sultan of Selangor's New Palace

1978. Inaug of Shah Alam New Town as State Capital of Selangor. Multicoloured.

187	10 c. Type **93**	10	10
188	30 c. Aerial view of Shah Alam	20	15
189	75 c. Shah Alam	55	1·25

94 Tiger

1979. Animals. Multicoloured.

190	30 c. Type **94**	1·75	10
191	40 c. Malayan flying lemur	80	10
192	50 c. Lesser Malay chevrotain	1·50	10
193	75 c. Leathery pangolin	1·00	10
194	$1 Malayan turtle	1·50	10
195	$2 Malayan tapir	1·50	10
196	$5 Gaur	4·50	1·75
197	$10 Orang-utang (vert)	7·00	3·25

96 View of Central Bank of Malaysia **97** I.Y.C. Emblem

1979. 20th Anniv of Central Bank of Malaysia. Multicoloured.

198	10 c. Type **96**	10	10
199	75 c. Central Bank (vert)	40	60

1979. International Year of the Child.

200 **97**	10 c. gold, blue and salmon	30	10
201 –	15 c. multicoloured	40	10
202 –	$1 multicoloured	2·10	3·00

DESIGNS: 15 c. Children holding hands in front of globe; $1 Children playing.

98 Dam and Power Station

1979. Opening of Hydro-Electric Power Station, Temengor.

203 **98**	15 c. multicoloured	20	15
204 –	25 c. multicoloured	35	60
205 –	50 c. multicoloured	55	1·25

DESIGNS: 25 c., 50 c. Different views of Dam.

99 Exhibition Emblem **100** Tuanku Haji Ahmad Shah

1979. 3rd World Telecommunications Exhibition, Geneva.

206 **99**	10 c. orange, blue & silver	10	30
207 –	15 c. multicoloured	15	10
208 –	50 c. multicoloured	40	1·75

DESIGNS—34 × 24 mm: 15 c. Telephone receiver joining the one half of World to the other. 39 × 28 mm: 50 c. Communications equipment.

1980. Installation of Tuanku Haji Ahmad Shah as Yang di-Pertuan Agong.

209 **100**	10 c. black, gold & yellow	10	20
210	15 c. black, gold & purple	15	10
211	50 c. black, gold and blue	40	1·50

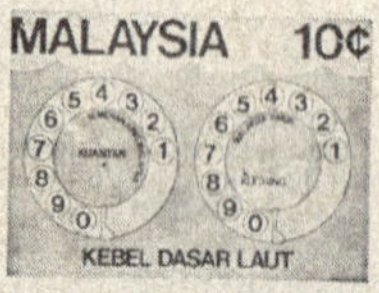

101 Pahang and Sarawak Maps within Telephone Dials

1980. Kuantan–Kuching Submarine Cable Project. Multicoloured.

212	10 c. Type **101**	10	30
213	15 c. Kuantan and Kuching views within telephone dials	15	10
214	50 c. Pahang and Sarawak maps within telephone receiver	35	1·40

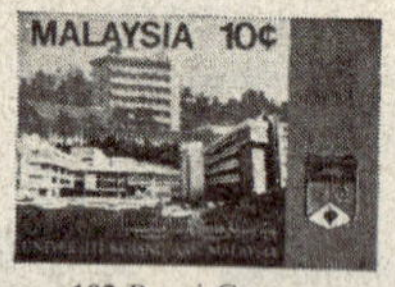

102 Bangi Campus

1980. 10th Anniv of National University of Malaysia. Multicoloured.

215	10 c. Type **102**	15	20
216	15 c. Jalan Pantai Baru campus	20	10
217	75 c. Great Hall	65	2·50

103 Mecca

1980. Moslem Year 1400 A.H. Commemoration.

218 **103**	15 c. multicoloured	10	10
219	50 c. multicoloured	30	1·25

No. 219 is inscribed in Roman lettering.

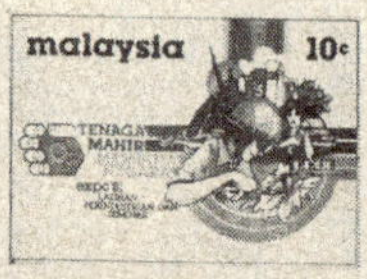

104 Disabled Child learning to Walk **105** Industrial Scene

1981. International Year for Disabled Persons. Multicoloured.

220	10 c. Type **104**	30	30
221	15 c. Girl sewing	55	10
222	75 c. Disabled athlete	1·50	3·25

1981. Expo "81" Industrial Training Exposition, Kuala Lumpur and Seminar, Genting Highlands. Multicoloured.

223	10 c. Type **105**	10	10
224	15 c. Worker and bulldozer	15	10
225	30 c. Workers at shipbuilding plant	25	35
226	75 c. Agriculture and fishing produce, workers and machinery	65	2·00

106 "25"

1981. 25th Anniv of Malaysian National Committee for World Energy Conferences. Multicoloured.

227	10 c. Type **106**	15	20
228	15 c. Drawings showing importance of energy sources in industry	30	10
229	75 c. Symbols of various energy sources	1·50	2·75

107 Drawing showing development of Sabah from Village to Urbanised Area

1981. Centenary of Sabah. Multicoloured.

230	15 c. Type **107**	50	15
231	80 c. Drawing showing traditional and modern methods of agriculture	2·00	4·00

108 "Samanea saman"

1981. Trees. Multicoloured.

232	15 c. Type **108**	55	10
233	50 c. "Dyera costulata" (vert)	1·75	1·40
234	80 c. "Dryobalanops aromatica" (vert)	2·00	4·00

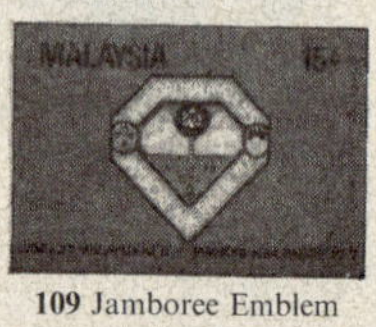

109 Jamboree Emblem

1982. 5th Malaysian/7th Asia-Pacific Boy Scout Jamboree. Multicoloured.

235	15 c. Type **109**	35	10
236	50 c. Malaysian flag and scout emblem	80	85
237	80 c. Malaysian and Asia-Pacific scout emblem	1·25	4·00

110 A.S.E.A.N. Building and Emblem

1982. 15th Anniv of Ministerial Meeting of A.S.E.A.N. (Association of South East Asian Nations). Multicoloured.

238	15 c. Type **110**	15	10
239	$1 Flags of members	60	2·50

111 Dome of the Rock, Jerusalem

1982. "Freedom for Palestine".

240 **111**	15 c. gold, green and blk	75	15
241	$1 silver, green and black	3·00	3·75

112 Views of Kuala Lumpur in 1957 and 1982

1982. 25th Anniv of Independence. Multicoloured.

242	10 c. Type **112**	10	10
243	15 c. Malaysian industries	15	15
244	50 c. Soldiers on parade	40	55
245	80 c. Independence ceremony	70	2·25

113 Shadow Play

1982. Traditional Games. Multicoloured.

247	10 c. Type **113**	50	30
248	15 c. Cross Top	50	15
249	75 c. Kite flying	2·00	3·75

114 Sabah Hats

1982. Malaysian Handicrafts. Multicoloured.

250	10 c. Type **114**	25	30
251	15 c. Gold-threaded cloth	25	20
252	75 c. Sarawak pottery	1·25	3·00

115 Gas Exploitation Logo

1983. Export of Liquefied Natural Gas from Bintulu Field, Sarawak. Multicoloured.

253	15 c. Type **115**	75	15
254	20 c. "Tenaga Satu" (liquid gas tanker)	1·50	70
255	$1 Gas drilling equipment	3·50	5·50

116 Flag of Malaysia

1983. Commonwealth Day. Multicoloured.

256	15 c. Type **116**	10	10
257	20 c. The King of Malaysia	15	20
258	40 c. Oil palm tree and refinery	25	45
259	$1 Satellite view of earth	60	2·00

117 Nile Mouthbrooder

1983. Freshwater Fishes. Multicoloured.

260	20 c. Type **117**	1·25	1·50
261	20 c. Common carp	1·25	1·50
262	40 c. Lampan barb	2·00	2·50
263	40 c. Grass carp	2·00	2·50

118 Lower Pergau River Bridge

1983. Opening of East-West Highway. Mult.

264	15 c. Type **118**	80	15
265	20 c. Perak river reservoir bridge	1·00	60
266	$1 Map showing East–West highway	3·25	5·00

119 Northrop Tiger II Fighter

1983. 50th Anniv of Malaysian Armed Forces. Multicoloured.

267	15 c. Type **119**	1·25	15
268	20 c. Missile boat	1·75	45
269	40 c. Battle of Pasir Panjang	2·25	2·25
270	80 c. Trooping the Colour	3·25	4·50

120 Helmeted Hornbill

122 Sky-scraper and Mosque, Kuala Lumpur

121 Bank Building, Ipoh

1983. Hornbills of Malaysia. Multicoloured.

280	15 c. Type **120**	85	15
281	20 c. Wrinkled hornbill	1·10	50
282	50 c. Long-crested hornbill	1·75	1·75
283	$1 Rhinoceros hornbill	2·75	4·50

1984. 25th Anniv of Bank Negara. Multicoloured.

284	20 c. Type **121**	40	30
285	$1 Bank building, Alor Setar	2·00	3·50

1984. 10th Anniv of Federal Territory of Kuala Lumpur. Multicoloured.

286	20 c. Type **122**	70	20
287	40 c. Aerial view	1·40	1·40
288	80 c. Gardens and clock-tower (horiz)	2·25	4·00

123 Map showing Industries

124 Semenanjung Keris

1984. Formation of Labuan Federal Territory. Multicoloured.

289	20 c. Type **123**	75	25
290	$1 Flag and map of Labuan	3·50	4·25

1984. Traditional Malay Weapons. Multicoloured.

291	40 c. Type **124**	1·25	1·75
292	40 c. Pekakak keris	1·25	1·75
293	40 c. Jawa keris	1·25	1·75
294	40 c. Lada tumbuk	1·25	1·75

125 Map of World and Transmitter

1984. 20th Anniv of Asia–Pacific Broadcasting Union. Multicoloured.

295	20 c. Type **125**	40	25
296	$1 Clasped hands within "20"	2·00	3·75

126 Facsimile Service

127 Yang di-Pertuan Agong (Tuanku Mahmood)

1984. Opening of New General Post Office, Kuala Lumpur. Multicoloured.

297	15 c. Type **126**	35	20
298	20 c. New G.P.O. building	45	45
299	$1 Mailbag conveyor	2·00	3·75

1984. Installation of Yang di-Pertuan Agong (Tuanku Mahmood).

300	**127** 15 c. multicoloured	40	20
301	20 c. multicoloured	45	20
302	– 40 c. multicoloured	85	1·00
303	– 80 c. multicoloured	2·00	3·50

DESIGN—HORIZ: 40 c., 80 c. Yang di-Pertuan Agong and federal crest.

128 White Hibiscus

129 Parliament Building

1984. Hibiscus. Multicoloured.

304	10 c. Type **128**	50	30
305	20 c. Red hibiscus	1·00	20
306	40 c. Pink hibiscus	1·75	2·00
307	$1 Orange hibiscus	2·75	4·75

1985. 25th Anniv of Federal Parliament. Mult.

308	20 c. Type **129**	30	15
309	$1 Parliament Building (different) (horiz)	1·75	2·00

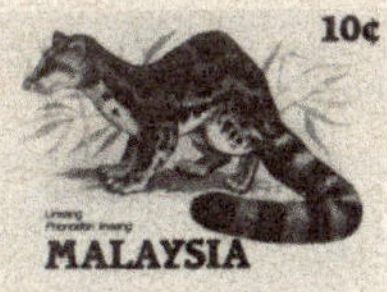

130 Banded Linsang

1985. Protected Animals of Malaysia (1st series). Multicoloured.

310	10 c. Type **130**	60	10
311	40 c. Slow loris (vert)	1·75	1·40
312	$1 Spotted giant flying squirrel (vert)	3·50	4·50

See also Nos. 383/6.

131 Stylised Figures

1985. International Youth Year. Multicoloured.

313	20 c. Type **131**	30	15
314	$1 Young workers	3·00	4·00

132 Steam Locomotive No. 1, 1885

1985. Centenary of Malayan Railways.

315	**132** 15 c. black, red and orange	1·25	30
316	– 20 c. multicoloured	1·40	40
317	– $1 multicoloured	3·50	4·50

DESIGNS: 20 c. Class 20 diesel-electric locomotive, 1957; $1 Hitachi Class 23 diesel-electric locomotive, 1983.

133 Blue Proton "Saga 1.3s" Car

1985. Production of Proton "Saga" (Malaysian national car). Multicoloured.

319	20 c. Type **133**	70	15
320	40 c. White Proton "Saga 1.3s"	1·25	1·00
321	$1 Red Proton "Saga 1.5s"	2·25	3·50

134 Penang Bridge

135 Offshore Oil Rig

1985. Opening of Penang Bridge. Multicoloured.

322	20 c. Type **134**	80	15
323	40 c. Penang Bridge and location map	1·60	90
324	$1 Symbolic bridge linking Penang to mainland (40 × 24 mm)	3·00	3·75

1985. Malaysian Petroleum Production. Mult.

325	15 c. Type **135**	1·00	20
326	20 c. Malaysia's first oil refinery (horiz)	1·10	50
327	$1 Map of Malaysian offshore oil and gas fields (horiz)	3·00	4·00

136 Sultan Azlan Shah and Perak Royal Crest

137 Crested Fireback Pheasant

1985. Installation of the Sultan of Perak.

328	**136** 15 c. multicoloured	30	10
329	20 c. multicoloured	40	25
330	$1 multicoloured	2·25	3·75

1986. Protected Birds of Malaysia (1st series). Multicoloured.

331	20 c. Type **137**	2·00	2·50
332	20 c. Malay peacock-pheasant	2·00	2·50
333	40 c. Bulwer's pheasant (horiz)	2·50	3·00
334	40 c. Great argus pheasant (horiz)	2·50	3·00

See also Nos. 394/7.

139 Two Kadazan Dancers, Sabah

140 Stylised Competitors

1986. Pacific Area Travel Association Conference, Malaysia. Multicoloured.

335	20 c. Type **139**	75	95
336	20 c. Dyak dancer and longhouse, Sarawak	75	95
337	20 c. Dancers and fortress, Malacca	75	95
338	40 c. Malay dancer and Kuala Lumpur	1·10	1·40
339	40 c. Chinese opera dancer and Penang Bridge	1·10	1·40
340	40 c. Indian dancer and Batu Caves	1·10	1·40

1986. Malaysia Games. Multicoloured.

341	20 c. Type **140**	1·25	20
342	40 c. Games emblems (vert)	2·25	2·00
343	$1 National and state flags (vert)	5·50	6·50

141 Rambutan

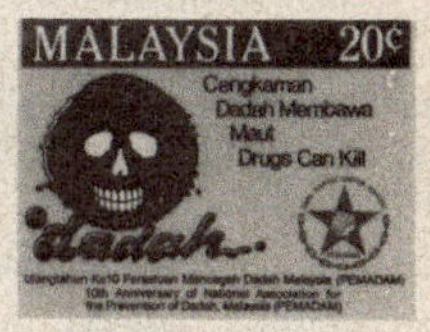

142 Skull and Slogan "Drugs Can Kill"

1986. Fruits of Malaysia. Multicoloured.

344	40 c. Type **141**	15	20
345	50 c. Pineapple	15	20
346	80 c. Durian	25	30
347	$1 Mangosteen	30	35
348	$2 Star fruit	60	65
349	$5 Banana	1·60	1·75
350	$10 Mango	3·25	3·50
351	$20 Papaya	6·25	6·50

1986. 10th Anniv of National Association for Prevention of Drug Addiction. Multicoloured.

352	20 c. Type **142**	1·00	30
353	40 c. Bird and slogan "Stay Free From Drugs"	1·40	1·10
354	$1 Addict and slogan "Drugs Can Destroy" (vert)	2·25	3·50

143 MAS Logo and Map showing Routes

144 Building Construction

1986. Inaugural Flight of Malaysian Airlines Kuala Lumpur–Los Angeles Service. Multicoloured.

355	20 c. Type **143**	95	15
356	40 c. Logo, stylized aircraft and route diagram	1·60	60
357	$1 Logo and stylized aircraft	2·75	2·25

1986. 20th Anniv of National Productivity Council and 25th Anniv of Asian Productivity Organization (40 c., $1). Multicoloured.

358	20 c. Type **144**	85	25
359	40 c. Planning and design (horiz)	1·40	1·00
360	$1 Computer-controlled car assembly line (horiz)	3·75	5·00

145 Old Seri Menanti Palace, Negri Sembilan

1986. Historic Buildings of Malaysia (1st series). Multicoloured.

361	15 c. Type **145**	40	20
362	20 c. Old Kenangan Palace, Perak	45	20
363	40 c. Old Town Hall, Malacca	90	60
364	$1 Astana, Kuching, Sarawak	2·00	3·00

See also Nos. 465/8.

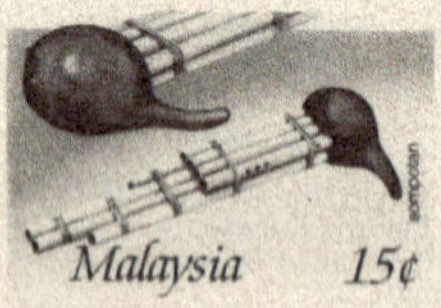

146 Sompotan (bamboo pipes)

1987. Malaysian Musical Instruments. Multicoloured.

365	15 c. Type **146**	45	10
366	20 c. Sapih (four-stringed chordophone)	55	15
367	50 c. Serunai (pipes) (vert)	1·25	40
368	80 c. Rebab (three-stringed fiddle) (vert)	1·75	90

147 Modern Housing Estate

1987. International Year of Shelter for the Homeless. Multicoloured.

369	20 c. Type **147**	30	15
370	$1 Stylised families and houses	1·25	75

148 Drug Addict and Family

1987. International Conference on Drug Abuse, Vienna. Multicoloured.

371	20 c. Type **148**	1·00	65
372	20 c. Hands holding drugs and damaged internal organs	1·00	65
373	40 c. Healthy boy and broken drug capsule	1·50	90
374	40 c. Drugs and healthy internal organs	1·50	90

Nos. 371/2 and 373/4 were printed together, se-tenant, forming composite designs.

149 Spillway and Power Station

1987. Opening of Sultan Mahmud Hydro-electric Scheme, Kenyir, Trengganu. Multicoloured.

375	20 c. Type **149**	50	10
376	$1 Dam, spillway and reservoir	2·50	1·50

150 Crossed Maces and Parliament Building, Kuala Lumpur

1987. 33rd Commonwealth Parliamentary Conference. Multicoloured.

377	20 c. Type **150**	25	10
378	$1 Parliament building and crossed mace emblem	1·00	1·00

151 Dish Aerial, Satellite and Globe

1987. Asia/Pacific Transport and Communications Decade. Multicoloured.

379	15 c. Type **151**	40	10
380	20 c. Diesel train and car	1·00	55
381	40 c. Container ships and lorry	1·25	1·25
382	$1 Malaysian Airlines Boeing 747, Kuala Lumpur Airport	2·50	3·50

152 Temminck's Golden Cat

1987. Protected Animals of Malaysia (2nd series). Multicoloured.

383	15 c. Type **152**	1·25	30
384	20 c. Flatheaded cat	1·25	30
385	40 c. Marbled cat	2·25	1·75
386	$1 Clouded leopard	4·25	4·75

153 Flags of Member Nations and "20"

1987. 20th Anniv of Association of South East Asian Nations. Multicoloured.

387	20 c. Type **153**	20	10
388	$1 Flags of member nations and globe	80	1·00

154 Mosque and Portico

1988. Opening of Sultan Salahuddin Abdul Aziz Shah Mosque. Multicoloured.

389	15 c. Type **154**	20	10
390	20 c. Dome, minarets and Sultan of Selangor	20	15
391	$1 Interior and dome (vert)	70	1·00

155 Aerial View

1988. Sultan Ismail Hydro-electric Power Station, Paka, Trengganu. Multicoloured.

392	20 c. Type **155**	20	10
393	$1 Power-station and pylons	80	90

156 Black-naped Blue Monarch

157 Outline Map and Products of Sabah

1988. Protected Birds of Malaysia (2nd series). Multicoloured.

394	20 c. Type **156**	1·50	1·50
395	20 c. Scarlet-backed flowerpecker	1·50	1·50
396	50 c. Yellow-backed sunbird	2·25	2·25
397	50 c. Black and red broadbill	2·25	2·25

1988. 25th Anniv of Sabah and Sarawak as States of Malaysia. Multicoloured.

398	20 c. Type **157**	30	40
399	20 c. Outline map and products of Sarawak	30	40
400	$1 Flags of Malaysia, Sabah and Sarawak (30 × 40 mm)	80	1·25

158 "Glossodoris atromarginata"

159 Sultan's Palace, Malacca

1988. Marine Life (1st series). Multicoloured.

401	20 c. Type **158**	60	70
402	20 c. Ocellate nudibranch	60	70
403	20 c. "Chromodoris annae"	60	70
404	20 c. "Flabellina macassarana"	60	70
405	20 c. Ruppell's nudibranch	60	70

Nos. 401/5 were printed together, se-tenant, forming a composite background design.

See also Nos. 410/13, 450/3, 492/6 and 559/62.

1989. Declaration of Malacca as Historic City. Multicoloured.

407	20 c. Type **159**	20	15
408	20 c. Independence Memorial Building	20	15
409	$1 Porta De Santiago Fortress (vert)	1·00	1·40

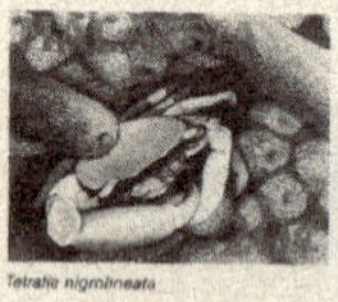

160 "Tetralia nigrolineata"

161 Map of Malaysia and Scout Badge

1989. Marine Life (2nd series). Crustaceans. Multicoloured.

410	20 c. Type **160**	45	65
411	20 c. "Neopetrolisthes maculatus" (crab)	45	65
412	40 c. "Periclimenes holthuisi" (shrimp)	55	90
413	40 c. "Synalpheus neomeris" (shrimp)	55	90

1989. 7th National Scout Jamboree. Multicoloured.

414	10 c. Type **161**	25	10
415	20 c. Saluting national flag	40	25
416	80 c. Scouts around camp fire (horiz)	1·25	2·00

162 Cycling

163 Sultan Azlan Shah

1989. 15th South East Asian Games, Kuala Lumpur. Multicoloured.

417	10 c. Type **162**	15	15
418	20 c. Athletics	25	20
419	50 c. Swimming (vert)	50	75
420	$1 Torch bearer (vert)	85	1·90

1989. Installation of Sultan Azlan Shah as Yang di-Pertuan Agong.

421	**163** 20 c. multicoloured	20	15
422	40 c. multicoloured	30	35
423	$1 multicoloured	70	1·75

164 Putra World Trade Centre and Pan-Pacific Hotel

1989. Commonwealth Heads of Government Meeting, Kuala Lumpur. Multicoloured.

424	20 c. Type **164**	20	10
425	50 c. Traditional dancers (vert)	65	75
426	$1 National flag and map showing Commonwealth countries	1·25	2·25

165 Clock Tower, Kuala Lumpur City Hall and Big Ben

166 Sloth and Map of Park

1989. Inaugural Malaysia Airlines "747" Non-stop Flight to London. Each showing Malaysia Airlines Boeing "747-400". Multicoloured.

427	20 c. Type **165**	75	1·00
428	20 c. Parliament Buildings, Kuala Lumpur, and Palace of Westminster	75	1·00
429	$1 World map showing route	2·00	2·25

1989. 50th Anniv of National Park. Multicoloured.

430	20 c. Type **166**	30	15
431	$1 Pair of Malay ocellated pheasants	1·50	2·50

167 Outline Map of South-east Asia and Logo

168 "Dillenia suffruticosa"

1990. "Visit Malaysia Year". Multicoloured.

432	20 c. Type **167**	30	15
433	50 c. Traditional drums	65	80
434	$1 Scuba diving, windsurfing and yachting	1·00	2·00

1990. Wildflowers (1st series). Multicoloured.

435	15 c. Type **168**	25	15
436	20 c. "Mimosa pudica"	30	20
437	50 c. "Ipmoea carnea"	60	70
438	$1 "Nymphaea pubescens"	80	1·75

See also Nos. 505/8.

169 Monument and Rainbow

171 Alor Setar

170 Seri Negara Building

1990. Kuala Lumpur, Garden City of Lights. Multicoloured.

439	20 c. Type **169**	15	20
440	40 c. Mosque and skyscrapers at night (horiz)	30	45
441	$1 Kuala Lumpur skyline (horiz)	75	1·75

1990. 1st Summit Meeting of South–South Consultation and Co-operation Group, Kuala Lumpur. Multicoloured.

442	20 c. Type **170**	20	15
443	80 c. Summit logo	80	1·75

1990. 250th Anniv of Alor Setar. Multicoloured.

444	20 c. Type **171**	20	20
445	40 c. Musicians and monument (vert)	30	35
446	$1 Zahir Mosque (vert)	85	1·75

172 Sign Language Letters

1990. International Literacy Year. Multicoloured.

447	20 c. Type **172**	10	10
448	40 c. People reading	25	35
449	$1 Symbolic person reading (vert)	65	1·75

173 Leatherback Turtle

1990. Marine Life (3rd series). Sea Turtles. Mult.

450	15 c. Type **173**	50	10
451	20 c. Common green turtle	50	15
452	40 c. Olive Ridley turtle	1·00	80
453	$1 Hawksbill turtle	2·25	2·75

174 Safety Helmet, Dividers and Industrial Skyline

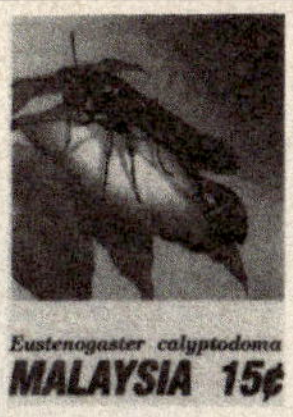

175 "Eustenogaster calyptodoma"

1991. 25th Anniv of MARA (Council of the Indigenous People). Multicoloured.

454	20 c. Type **174**	15	10
455	40 c. Documents and graph	30	35
456	$1 25th Anniversary logo	75	1·75

1991. Insects. Wasps. Multicoloured.

457	15 c. Type **175**	25	30
458	20 c. "Vespa affinis indonensis"	25	20
459	50 c. "Sceliphorn javanum"	60	70
460	$1 "Ampulex compressa"	1·00	1·50

176 Tunku Abdul Rahman Putra and Independence Rally

1991. Former Prime Ministers of Malaysia. Multicoloured.

462	$1 Type **176**	70	1·00
463	$1 Tun Abdul Razak Hussein and jungle village	70	1·00
464	$1 Tun Hussein Onn and standard-bearers	70	1·00

177 Maziah Palace, Trengganu

1991. Historic Buildings of Malaysia (2nd series). Multicoloured.

465	15 c. Type **177**	20	10
466	20 c. Grand Palace, Johore	20	15
467	40 c. Town Palace, Kuala Langat, Selangor	45	50
468	$1 Jahar Palace, Kelantan	90	1·75

178 Museum Building in 1891, Brass Lamp and Fabric

179 Rural Postman on Cycle

1991. Centenary of Sarawak Museum. Mult.

469	30 c. Type **178**	20	15
470	$1 Museum building in 1991, vase and fabric	80	1·25

1992. Inauguration of Post Office Corporation. Multicoloured.

471	30 c. Type **179**	50	65
472	30 c. Urban postman on motorcycle	50	65
473	30 c. Inner city post van	50	65
474	30 c. Industrial post van	50	65
475	30 c. Malaysian Airlines Boeing 747 and globe	50	65

180 Hill Forest and Jelutong Tree

1992. Tropical Forests. Multicoloured.

476	20 c. Type **180**	15	10
477	50 c. Mangrove swamp and Bakau Minyak tree	35	50
478	$1 Lowland forest and Chengal tree	75	1·50

181 Tuanku Ja'afar and Coat of Arms

182 Badminton Players

1992. 25th Anniv of Installation of Tuanku Ja'afar as Yang di-Pertuan Besar of Negri Sembilan. Multicoloured.

479	30 c. Type **181**	20	20
480	$1 Palace, Negri Sembilan	80	1·60

1992. Malaysian Victory in Thomas Cup Badminton Championship. Multicoloured.

481	$1 Type **182**	55	75
482	$1 Thomas Cup and Malaysian flag	55	75

183 Women in National Costumes

1992. 25th Anniv of A.S.E.A.N. (Association of South East Asian Nations). Multicoloured.

484	30 c. Type **183**	40	30
485	50 c. Regional flowers	65	75
486	$1 Traditional architecture	1·25	2·25

184 Straits Settlements 1867 1½ c. and Malaysian Federation 1957 10 c. Stamps

1992. 125th Anniv of Postage Stamps and "Kuala Lumpur '92" Int Stamp Exn. Multicoloured.

487	30 c. Type **184**	35	50
488	30 c. Straits Settlements 1867 2 c. and Malaysia 1963 Federation Inauguration 12 c.	35	50
489	50 c. Straits Settlements 1868 4 c. and Malaysia 1990 Kuala Lumpur 40 c.	65	80
490	50 c. Straits Settlements 1867 12 c. and Malaysia "Kuala Lumpur '92" $2	65	80

185 "Acropora"

186 Girls smiling

1992. Marine Life (4th series). Corals. Multicoloured.

492	30 c. Type **185**	65	80
493	30 c. "Dendronephthya"	65	80
494	30 c. "Dendrophyllia"	65	80
495	30 c. "Sinularia"	65	80
496	30 c. "Melithaea"	65	80

1993. 16th Asian–Pacific Dental Congress. Multicoloured.

498	30 c. Type **186**	50	65
499	30 c. Girls smiling with koala bear	50	65
500	50 c. Dentists with Japanese, Malaysian and South Korean flags	80	1·00
501	$1 Dentists with New Zealand, Thai, Chinese and Indonesian flags	1·00	1·25

187 View of Golf Course

188 "Alpinia rafflesiana"

1993. Cent of Royal Selangor Golf Club. Mult.

502	30 c. Type **187**	60	20
503	50 c. Old and new club houses	90	80
504	$1 Bunker on course (horiz)	1·75	2·00

1993. Wildflowers (2nd series). Gingers. Mult.

505	20 c. Type **188**	35	10
506	30 c. "Achasma megalocheilos"	45	20
507	50 c. "Zingiber spectabile"	80	80
508	$1 "Costus speciosus"	1·60	2·00

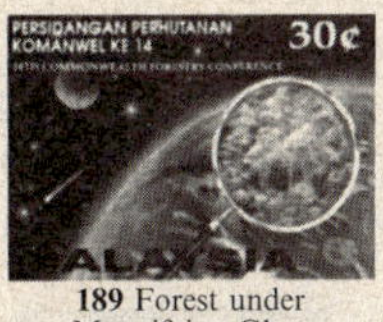

189 Forest under Magnifying Glass

190 White-breasted Kingfisher

1993. 14th Commonwealth Forestry Conference, Kuala Lumpur. Multicoloured.

509	30 c. Type **189**	40	20
510	50 c. Hand holding forest	65	70
511	$1 Forest in glass dome (vert)	1·40	2·25

1993. Kingfishers. Multicoloured

512	30 c. Type **190**	60	80
513	30 c. Pair of blue-eared kingfishers	60	80
514	50 c. Chestnut-collared kingfisher	80	1·00
515	50 c. Pair of three-toed kingfishers	80	1·00

191 SME MD3-160m Light Aircraft

1993. Langkawi International Maritime and Aerospace Exhibition '93. Multicoloured.

516	30 c. Type **191**	35	20
517	50 c. Eagle X-TS light aircraft	65	75
518	$1 "Kasturi" (frigate)	1·25	2·00

192 Jeriau Waterfalls

1994. Visit Malaysia. Multicoloured.

520	20 c. Type **192**	25	10
521	30 c. Flowers	30	25
522	50 c. Turtle and fishes	45	55
523	$1 Orang-utan and other wildlife	90	1·50

193 Planetarium and Planets

1994. National Planetarium, Kuala Lumpur. Mult.

524	30 c. Type **193**	50	20
525	50 c. Static displays	65	75
526	$1 Planetarium auditorium	1·50	2·00

194 "Spathoglottis aurea"

195 Decorative Bowl

1994. Orchids. Multicoloured.

527	20 c. Type **194**	35	10
528	30 c. "Paphiopedilum barbatum"	45	25
529	50 c. "Bulbophyllum lobbii"	75	85
530	$1 "Aerides odorata"	1·25	1·75

1994. World Islamic Civilisation Festival '94, Kuala Lumpur. Multicoloured.

532	20 c. Type **195**	15	10
533	30 c. Celestial globe	25	20
534	50 c. Dinar coins	40	55
535	$1 Decorative tile	75	1·25

196 Flock of Chickens and Vet examining Cat

197 Workers laying Electric Cable

1994. Centenary of Veterinary Services. Mult.

536	30 c. Type **196**	25	20
537	50 c. Vet in abattoir	50	50
538	$1 Herd of cows and veterinary equipment	90	1·25

1994. Centenary of Electricity Supply. Multicoloured.

539	30 c. Type **197**	25	45
540	30 c. Illuminated city	25	45
541	$1 City of the future	70	1·10

198 Expressway from the Air

199 Sultan Tuanku Ja'afar

1994. Opening of North–South Expressway. Mult.

542	30 c. Type **198**	20	20
543	50 c. Expressway junction	35	50
544	$1 Expressway bridge	80	1·25

1994. Installation of Sultan Tuanku Ja'afar as Yang di-Pertuan Agong.

545	**199** 30 c. multicoloured	20	20
546	50 c. multicoloured	40	50
547	$1 multicoloured	80	1·25

200 Map of Malaysia and Logo

201 Tunku Abdul Rahman Putra and National Flag

1994. 16th Commonwealth Games, Kuala Lumpur (1998) (1st issue). Multicoloured.

548	$1 Type **200**	80	1·00
549	$1 Wira (games mascot) holding national flag	80	1·00

See also Nos. 575/6, 627/30, 668/71 and 693/708.

1994. 5th Death Anniv of Tunku Abdul Rahman Putra (former Prime Minister). Multicoloured.

550	30 c. Type **201**	25	20
551	$1 The Residency, Kuala Lumpur	75	1·00

202 Library Building

1994. Opening of New National Library Building. Multicoloured.

552	30 c. Type **202**	20	25
553	50 c. Computer plan on screen	45	50
554	$1 Ancient Koran	1·00	1·40

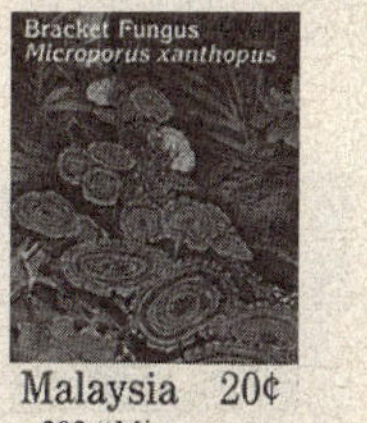

203 "Microporus xanthopus"

1995. Fungi. Multicoloured.

555	20 c. Type **203**	15	10
556	30 c. "Cookeina tricholoma"	25	20
557	50 c. "Phallus indusiatus" ("Dictyophora phalloidea")	45	55
558	$1 "Ramaria sp."	90	1·50

204 Seafans

1995. Marine Life (5th series). Corals. Multicoloured.

559	20 c. Type **204**	40	55
560	20 c. Feather stars	40	55
561	30 c. Cup coral	45	55
562	30 c. Soft coral	45	55

205 Clouded Leopard on Branch

1995. Endangered Species. Clouded Leopard. Mult.

563	20 c. Type **205**	25	25
564	30 c. With cubs	30	30
565	50 c. Crouched on branch	45	50
566	$1 Climbing tree	70	1·00

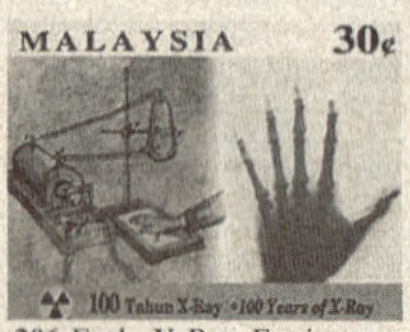

206 Early X-Ray Equipment and X-Ray of Hand

1995. Centenary of Discovery of X-Rays by Wilhelm Conrad Rontgen. Multicoloured.

567	30 c. Type **206**	30	50
568	30 c. Body scanner and brain scan	30	50
569	$1 Chest X-rays	95	1·00

207 Jembiah (curved dagger)

1995. "Singapore '95" International Stamp Exhibition. Traditional Malay Weapons. Mult.

570	20 c. Type **207**	15	10
571	30 c. Keris panjang (sword)	25	20
572	50 c. Kerambit (curved dagger)	40	50
573	$1 Keris sundang (sword)	80	1·50

208 Badminton, Cricket, Shooting, Tennis, Hurdling, Hockey and Weightlifting

1995. 16th Commonwealth Games, Kuala Lumpur (1998) (2nd issue). Multicoloured.

575	$1 Type **208**	1·00	1·25
576	$1 Cycling, bowls, boxing, basketball, rugby, gymnastics and swimming	1·00	1·25

209 Leatherback Turtle ("Dermochelys coriacea")

1995. Turtles. Multicoloured.

577	30 c. Type **209**	40	50
578	30 c. Green turtle ("Chelonia mydas")	40	50

210 Anniversary Emblem and Symbolic People around Globe

1995. 50th Anniv of United Nations. Multicoloured.

579	30 c. Type **210**	15	20
580	$1 United Nations emblem	60	80

211 Boeing 747, Globe, Emblem and Malaysian Scenes

212 Proton "Saga 1.5" Saloon, 1985

1995. 50th Anniv of International Air Transport Association. Designs each showing Boeing 747 and Globe. Multicoloured.

581	30 c. Type **211**	30	40
582	30 c. Asian and Australasian scenes	30	40
583	50 c. European and African scenes	45	65
584	50 c. North and South American scenes	45	65

1995. 10th Anniv of Proton Cars. Multicoloured.

585	30 c. Type **212**	20	25
586	30 c. "Iswara 1.5" aeroback, 1992	20	25
587	30 c. "Iswara 1.5" saloon, 1992	20	25
588	30 c. "Wira 1.6" saloon, 1993	20	25
589	30 c. "Wira 1.6" aeroback, 1993	20	25
590	30 c. Proton rally car, 1994	20	25
591	30 c. "Satria 1.6" hatchback, 1994	20	25
592	30 c. "Perdana 2.0" saloon, 1995	20	25
593	30 c. "Wira 1.6" aeroback, 1995	20	25
594	30 c. "Wira 1.8" saloon, 1995	20	25

213 "Ariane 4" Launch Rocket

214 "Nepenthes sanguinea"

1996. Launch of MEASAT I (Malaysia East Asia Satellite). Multicoloured.

595	30 c. Type **213**	25	20
596	50 c. Satellite over Eastern Asia	40	45
597	$1 Satellite Earth station, Langkawi	90	1·40

1996. Pitcher Plants. Multicoloured.

599	30 c. Type **214**	25	35
600	30 c. "Nepenthes macfarlanei"	25	35
601	50 c. "Nepenthes rajah"	35	50
602	50 c. "Nepenthes lowii"	35	50

215 Brahminy Kite

1996. Birds of Prey. Multicoloured.

603	20 c. Type **215**	20	15
604	30 c. Crested serpent eagle	30	25
605	50 c. White-bellied sea eagle	45	55
606	$1 Crested hawk eagle	90	1·50

216 Family, Globe and Burning Drugs

1996. International Day against Drug Abuse and Illicit Trafficking. Multicoloured.

608	30 c. Type **216**	25	35
609	30 c. Sporting activities	25	35
610	$1 Family and rainbow	60	80

217 "Graphium sarpedon"

218 Kuala Lumpur Tower

1996. "ISTANBUL '96" International Stamp Exhibition. Butterflies. Multicoloured.

611	30 c. Type **217**	30	40
612	30 c. "Terinos terpander"	30	40
613	30 c. "Melanocyma faunula"	30	40
614	30 c. "Trogonoptera brookiana"	30	40
615	30 c. "Delias hyparete"	30	40

1996. Opening of Kuala Lumpur Telecommunications Tower. Multicoloured.

616	30 c. Type **218**	20	20
617	50 c. Diagram of top of tower	30	35
618	$1 Kuala Lumpur Tower at night	80	1·00

219 C.A.P.A. Logo on Kite

1996. 14th Conference of the Confederation of Asian and Pacific Accountants. Multicoloured.

620	30 c. Type **219**	20	20
621	$1 Globe and C.A.P.A. logo	60	70

220 Model of D.N.A. Molecule

1996. Opening of National Science Centre, Kuala Lumpur. Multicoloured.

623	30 c. Type **220**	20	20
624	50 c. Planetary model and Science Centre	30	35
625	$1 National Science Centre	70	1·00

222 Running

1996. 16th Commonwealth Games, Kuala Lumpur (1998) (3rd issue). Multicoloured.

627	30 c. Type **222**	20	30
628	30 c. Hurdling	20	30
629	50 c. High jumping	30	50
630	50 c. Javelin	30	50

223 Pygmy Blue Flycatcher

224 Transit Train leaving Station

1997. Highland Birds. Multicoloured.

631	20 c. Type **223**	25	10
632	30 c. Silver-eared mesia	30	20
633	50 c. Black-sided flower-pecker	40	45
634	$1 Scarlet sunbird	70	90

1997. Opening of Kuala Lumpur Light Rail Transit System. Multicoloured.

636	30 c. Type **224**	30	40
637	30 c. Trains in central Kuala Lumpur	30	40

225 Bowler

1997. International Cricket Council Trophy, Kuala Lumpur. Multicoloured.

638	30 c. Type **225**	30	15
639	50 c. Batsman	45	40
640	$1 Wicket-keeper	80	1·00

226 Boeing 747-400 over World Map

1997. 50th Anniv of Aviation in Malaysia. Mult.

641	30 c. Type **226**	30	15
642	50 c. Boeing 747-400 over Kuala Lumpur	40	40
643	$1 Tail fins of four airliners	70	90

227 "Schima wallichii"

228 World Youth Football Championship Mascot

1997. Highland Flowers. Multicoloured.

644	30 c. Type **227**	25	30
645	30 c. "Aeschynanthus longicalyx"	25	30
646	30 c. "Aeschynanthus speciosa"	25	30
647	30 c. "Phyllagathis tuberculata"	25	30
648	30 c. "Didymocarpus quinquevulnerus"	25	30

1997. 9th World Youth Football Championship, Malaysia. Multicoloured.

649	30 c. Type **228**	15	10
650	50 c. Football and players	25	30
651	$1 Map of Malaysia and football	50	70

229 Members of First Conference, 1897

1997. Centenary of Rulers' Conference. Mult.

652	30 c. Type **229**	15	10
653	50 c. State emblem	25	25
654	$1 Seal and press	50	55

230 A.S.E.A.N. Logo and Ribbons

1997. 30th Anniv of Association of South-east Asian Nations. Multicoloured.

655	30 c. Type **230**	15	10
656	50 c. "30" enclosing logo	25	30
657	$1 Chevrons and logo	50	70

231 "Tubastrea sp."

232 Women Athletes, Scientist and Politician

1997. International Year of the Coral Reefs. Multicoloured.

658	20 c. Type **231**	10	10
659	30 c. "Melithaea sp."	10	10
660	50 c. "Aulostomus chinensis"	20	25
661	$1 "Symphillia sp."	30	50

1997. 20th International Pan-Pacific and South-east Asia Women's Association Conference, Kuala Lumpur. Multicoloured.

663	30 c. Type **232**	10	10
664	30 c. Family and house	10	10

234 Group of 15 Emblem

237 Kundang

235 Hockey

1997. 7th Summit Conference of the Group of 15, Kuala Lumpur. Multicoloured.

666	30 c. Type **234**	10	10
667	$1 Flags of member countries	70	85

1997. 16th Commonwealth Games, Kuala Lumpur (1998) (4th issue). Multicoloured.

668	30 c. Type **235**	20	20
669	30 c. Netball	20	20
670	50 c. Cricket	30	30
671	50 c. Rugby	30	30

1998. Fruit. Multicoloured.

674	20 c. Type **237**	10	10
675	30 c. Sentul	10	10
676	50 c. Pulasan	15	20
677	$1 Asam gelugur	60	65

239 Mas (coin) from Trengganu, 1793–1808

1998. Gold coins. Multicoloured.

679	20 c. Type **239**	10	10
680	30 c. Kupang from Kedah, 1661–1687	15	10
681	50 c. Kupang from Johore, 1597–1615	30	25
682	$1 Kupang from Kelantan, 1400–1780	40	50

240 Red Crescent Boat and Emblem

1998. 50th Anniv of Malaysian Red Crescent Society. Multicoloured.

683	30 c. Type **240**	10	10
684	$1 Ambulance and casualty	40	45

241 Transit Train at Airport

1998. Opening of Kuala Lumpur International Airport. Designs showing control tower. Mult.

685	30 c. Type **241**	15	10
686	50 c. Airport Terminals	30	25
687	$1 Airliner in flight	50	60

242 "Solanum torvum"

243 Weightlifting

1998. Medicinal Plants. Multicoloured.

689	20 c. Type **242**	10	10
690	30 c. "Tinospora crispa"	15	10
691	50 c. "Jatropha podagrica"	25	25
692	$1 "Hibiscus rosa-sinensis"	40	50

1998. 16th Commonwealth Games, Kuala Lumpur, Malaysia (5th issue). (Sports). Multicoloured.

693	20 c. Type **243**	10	10
694	20 c. Badminton	10	10
695	20 c. Netball	10	10
696	20 c. Shooting	10	10
697	30 c. Men's hockey	10	10
698	30 c. Women's hockey	10	10
699	30 c. Cycling	10	10
700	30 c. Bowls	10	10
701	50 c. Gymnastics	15	20
702	50 c. Cricket	15	20
703	50 c. Rugby	15	20
704	50 c. Running	15	20
705	$1 Swimming	30	35
706	$1 Squash	30	35
707	$1 Boxing	30	35
708	$1 Ten-pin bowling	30	35

244 L.R.T. "Putra" Type Train

1998. Modern Kuala Lumpur Rail Transport. Multicoloured.

709b	30 c. Type **244**	10	10
710	50 c. L.R.T. "Star" type train	15	20
711	$1 K.T.M commuter train	30	35

245 Globe and A.P.E.C. Logo

1998. Asia–Pacific Economic Co-operation Conference. Multicoloured.

712	30 c. Type **245**	10	10
713	$1 Business meeting and computer office	30	35

B. FEDERAL TERRITORY ISSUES

For use in the Federal Territories of Kuala Lumpur and (from 1984) Labuan.

K 1 "Rafflesia hasseltii"

K 2 Coffee

1979. Flowers. Multicoloured.

K1	1 c. Type K **1**	10	30
K2	2 c. "Pterocarpus indicus"	10	30
K3	5 c. "Lagerstroemia speciosa"	10	30
K4	10 c. "Durio zibethinus"	10	10
K5	15 c. "Hibiscus rosa-sinensis"	20	10
K6	20 c. "Rhododendron scortechinii"	20	10
K7	25 c. "Etlingera elatior" (inscr "Phaeomeria speciosa")	40	10

1986. Agricultural Products of Malaysia. Mult.

K15	1 c. Type K **2**	10	10
K16	2 c. Coconuts	10	10
K17	5 c. Cocoa	10	10
K18	10 c. Black pepper	10	10
K19	15 c. Rubber	10	10
K20	20 c. Oil palm	10	10
K21	30 c. Rice	15	20

POSTAGE DUE STAMPS

Until 15 August, 1966, the postage due stamps of Malaysian Postal Union were in use throughout Malaysia.

D 1

D 2

1966.

D 1	D **1**	1 c. red	20	2·50
D 2		2 c. blue	25	2·50
D 3		4 c. green	85	4·00
D18		8 c. green	45	2·75
D19		10 c. blue	45	2·25
D 6		12 c. violet	60	4·00
D20		20 c. brown	55	2·75
D21		50 c. bistre	90	3·50

1986.

D22	D **2**	5 c. mauve and lilac	10	10
D23		10 c. black and grey	10	10
D24		20 c. red and brown	10	10
D25		50 c. green and blue	25	30
D26		$1 blue and cobalt	50	55

MALDIVE ISLANDS

A group of islands W. of Ceylon. A republic from 1 Jan., 1953, but reverted to a sultanate in 1954. Became independent on 26 July, 1965 and left the British Commonwealth, but was re-admitted as an Associate Member on 9 July, 1982.

1906. 100 cents = 1 rupee.
1951. 100 larees = 1 rupee.

1906. Nos. 268, 277/9 and 283/4 of Ceylon optd **MALDIVES**.

1	**44**	2 c. brown	13·00	28·00
2	**48**	3 c. green	17·00	28·00
3		4 c. orange and blue	32·00	65·00
4	–	5 c. purple	4·50	6·50
5	**48**	15 c. blue	55·00	£110
6		25 c. brown	65·00	£120

2 Minaret, Juma Mosque, Male

5 Palm Tree and Dhow

1909.

7a	**2**	2 c. brown	2·50	90
11A		2 c. grey	2·75	2·00
8		3 c. green	40	70
12A		3 c. brown	70	2·00
9		5 c. purple	40	35
15A		6 c. red	1·50	4·50
10		10 c. red	7·00	80
16A		10 c. green	85	55
17A		15 c. black	6·50	11·00
18A		25 c. brown	6·50	11·00
19A		50 c. purple	6·50	11·00
20B		1 r. blue	11·00	2·75

1950.

21	**5**	2 l. olive	1·25	40
22		3 l. blue	7·50	40
23		5 l. green	7·50	50
24		6 l. brown	70	30
25		10 l. red	70	30
26		15 l. orange	70	30
27		25 l. purple	70	30
28		50 l. violet	70	30
29		1 r. brown	8·00	25·00

8 Native Products

1952.

30	–	3 l. blue (Fish)	85	30
31	**8**	5 l. green	50	1·25

9 Male Harbour

10 Fort and Building

1956.

32	**9**	2 l. purple	10	10
33		3 l. slate	10	10
34		5 l. brown	10	10
35		6 l. violet	10	10
36		10 l. green	10	10
37		15 l. brown	10	40
38		25 l. red	10	10
39		50 l. orange	10	10
40	**10**	1 r. green	15	10
41		5 r. blue	60	30
42		10 r. mauve	1·10	85

11 Cycling

1960. Olympic Games.

43	**11**	2 l. purple and green	15	10
44		3 l. slate and purple	15	10
45		5 l. brown and blue	15	10
46		10 l. green and brown	15	10
47		15 l. sepia and blue	15	25
48	–	25 l. red and olive	15	25
49	–	50 l. orange and violet	20	40
50	–	1 r. green and purple	40	1·25

DESIGN—VERT: 25 l. to 1 r. Basketball.

13 Tomb of Sultan

1960.

51	**13**	2 l. purple	10	10
52	–	3 l. green	10	10
53	–	5 l. brown	2·75	2·75
54	–	6 l. blue	10	10
55	–	10 l. red	10	10
56	–	15 l. sepia	10	10
57	–	25 l. violet	10	10
58	–	50 l. grey	10	10
59	–	1 r. orange	15	10
60	–	5 r. blue	2·50	60
61	–	10 r. green	7·00	1·25

DESIGNS: 3 l. Custom House; 5 l. Cowrie shells; 6 l. Old Royal Palace; 10 l. Road to Juma Mosque, Male; 15 l. Council House; 25 l. New Government Secretariat; 50 l. Prime Minister's Office; 1 r. Old Ruler's Tomb; 5 r. Old Ruler's Tomb (distant view); 10 r. Maldivian port.

Higher values were also issued, intended mainly for fiscal use.

24 "Care of Refugees"

1960. World Refugee Year.

62	**24**	2 l. violet, orange & green	10	10
63		3 l. brown, green and red	10	10
64		5 l. green, sepia and red	10	10
65		10 l. green, violet and red	10	10
66		15 l. violet, green and red	10	10
67		25 l. blue, brown and green	10	10
68		50 l. olive, red and blue	10	10
69		1 r. red, slate and violet	15	35

25 Coconuts

26 Map of Male

1961.

70	**25**	2 l. brown and green	10	10
71		3 l. brown and blue	10	10
72		5 l. brown and mauve	10	10
73		10 l. brown and orange	10	10
74		15 l. brown and black	10	10
75	**26**	25 l. multicoloured	15	15
76		50 l. multicoloured	15	25
77		1 r. multicoloured	20	40

27 5 c. Stamp of 1906

1961. 55th Anniv of First Maldivian Stamp.

78	**27**	2 l. purple, blue and green	10	10
79		3 l. purple, blue and green	10	10
80		5 l. purple, blue and green	10	10
81		6 l. purple, blue and green	10	10
82	–	10 l. green, red and purple	10	10
83	–	15 l. green, red and purple	15	15
84	–	20 l. green, red and purple	15	20
85	–	25 l. red, green and black	15	20
86	–	50 l. red, green and black	25	80
87	–	1 r. red. green and black	40	1·50

DESIGNS: 10 l. to 20 l. Posthorn and 3 c. stamp of 1906; 25 l. to 1 r. Olive sprig and 2 c. stamp of 1906.

30 Malaria Eradication Emblem

31 Children of Europe and America

1962. Malaria Eradication.

88	**30**	2 l. brown	10	10
89		3 l. green	10	10
90		5 l. turquoise	10	10
91		10 l. red	10	10
92	–	15 l. sepia	15	10
93	–	25 l. blue	20	15
94	–	50 l. myrtle	25	30
95	–	1 r. purple	55	45

Nos. 92/5 are as Type **30**, but have English inscriptions at the side.

1962. 15th Anniv of U.N.I.C.E.F.

96	**31**	2 l. multicoloured	10	10
97		6 l. multicoloured	10	10
98		10 l. multicoloured	10	10
99		15 l. multicoloured	10	10
100	–	25 l. multicoloured	10	10
101	–	50 l. multicoloured	10	10
102	–	1 r. multicoloured	10	20
103	–	5 r. multicoloured	65	2·75

DESIGN: Nos. 100/3, Children of Middle East and Far East.

33 Sultan Mohamed Farid Didi

39 Fishes in Net

34 Royal Angelfish

1962. 9th Anniv of Enthronement of Sultan.

104	**33**	3 l. brown and green	10	10
105		5 l. brown and blue	10	10
106		10 l. brown and blue	10	10
107		20 l. brown and olive	15	20
108		50 l. brown and mauve	20	30
109		1 r. brown and violet	30	45

1963. Tropical Fish. Multicoloured.

110	2 l. Type **34**	10	15
111	3 l. Type **34**	10	15
112	5 l. Type **34**	15	15
113	10 l. Moorish idol (fish)	20	15
114	25 l. As 10 l.	55	20
115	50 l. Diadem soldierfish	80	40
116	1 r. Powder-blue surgeonfish	1·10	55
117	5 r. Racoon butterflyfish	6·00	8·50

1963. Freedom from Hunger.

118	**39**	2 l. brown and green	30	80
119	–	5 l. brown and red	50	70
120	**39**	7 l. brown and turquoise	70	70
121	–	10 l. brown and blue	85	70
122	**39**	25 l. brown and red	3·00	3·25
123	–	50 l. brown and violet	4·75	7·00
124	**39**	1 r. brown and mauve	7·50	11·00

DESIGN—VERT: 5 l., 10 l., 50 l. Handful of grain.

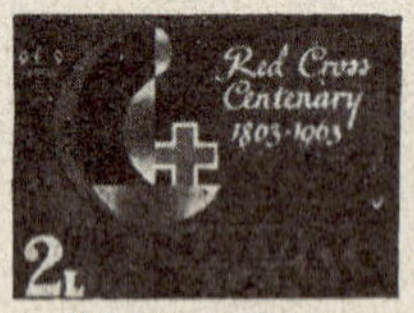

41 Centenary Emblem

42 Maldivian Scout Badge

1963. Centenary of Red Cross.

125	**41**	2 l. red and purple	30	1·25
126		15 l. red and green	65	80
127		50 l. red and brown	1·50	1·75
128		1 r. red and blue	2·25	2·00
129		4 r. red and olive	7·00	20·00

1964. World Scout Jamboree, Marathon (1963).

130	**42**	2 l. green and violet	10	10
131		3 l. green and brown	10	10
132		25 l. green and blue	15	15
133		1 r. green and red	55	1·50

43 Mosque, Male

1964. "Maldives Embrace Islam".

134	**43**	2 l. purple	10	10
135		3 l. green	10	10
136		10 l. red	10	10
137		40 l. purple	30	15
138		60 l. blue	50	15
139		85 l. brown	60	20

44 Putting the Shot

1964. Olympic Games, Tokyo.

140	**44**	2 l. purple and blue	10	10
141		3 l. red and brown	10	10
142		5 l. bronze and green	15	10
143		10 l. violet and purple	20	10
144	–	15 l. sepia and brown	30	10
145	–	25 l. indigo and blue	50	10
146	–	50 l. bronze and olive	75	25
147	–	1 r. purple and grey	1·25	50

DESIGN: 15 l. to 1 r. Running.

46 Telecommunications Satellite

1965. International Quiet Sun Years.

148	**46**	5 l. blue	15	15
149		10 l. brown	20	15
150		25 l. green	40	15
151		1 r. mauve	90	55

47 Isis (wall carving, Abu Simbel)

49 "XX" and U.N. Flag

48 Pres. Kennedy and Doves

1965. Nubian Monuments Preservation.

152	**47**	2 l. green and purple	10	10
153	–	3 l. lake and green	10	10
154	**47**	5 l. green and purple	15	10
155	–	10 l. blue and orange	20	10
156	**47**	15 l. brown and violet	30	15
157	–	25 l. purple and blue	50	15
158	**47**	50 l. green and sepia	65	35
159	–	1 r. ochre and green	1·00	55

DESIGN: 3, 10, 25 l., 1 r. Rameses II on throne (wall carving, Abu Simbel).

1965. 2nd Death Anniv of Pres. Kennedy.

160	**48**	2 l. black and mauve	10	10
161		5 l. brown and mauve	10	10
162		25 l. blue and mauve	10	10
163	–	1 r. purple, yellow & green	25	25
164	–	2 r. bronze, yellow & green	40	40

DESIGN: 1 r., 2 r. Pres. Kennedy and hands holding olive-branch.

1965. 20th Anniv of U.N.

165	**49**	3 l. blue and brown	10	10
166		10 l. blue and violet	15	10
167		1 r. blue and green	50	35

50 I.C.Y. Emblem

1965. International Co-operation Year.

168	**50**	5 l. brown and bistre	15	10
169		15 l. brown and lilac	20	10
170		50 l. brown and olive	45	30
171		1 r. brown and red	1·25	1·50
172		2 r. brown and blue	1·75	3·00

INDEX

Countries can be quickly located by referring to the index at the end of this volume.

51 Princely Cone Shells

1966. Multicoloured.

174		2 l. Type **51**	20	40
175		3 l. Yellow flowers	20	40
176		5 l. Reticulate distorsio and leopard shells	30	15
177		7 l. Camellias	30	15
178		10 l. Type **51**	60	15
179		15 l. Crab plover and seagull	2·50	30
180		20 l. As 3 l.	80	30
181		30 l. Type **51**	2·00	35
182		50 l. As 15 l.	4·50	55
183		1 r. Type **51**	3·00	55
184		1 r. As 7 l.	3·00	55
185		1 r. 50 As 3 l.	3·50	2·00
186		2 r. As 7 l.	4·75	2·50
187		5 r. As 15 l.	17·00	10·00
188		10 r. As 5 l.	17·00	14·00

The 3 l., 7 l., 20 l., 1 r. (No. 184), 1 r. 50 and 2 r. are DIAMOND (43½ × 43½ mm).

52 Maldivian Flag

1966. 1st Anniv of Independence.

189	**52**	10 l. green, red & turquoise	35	10
190		1 r. multicoloured	1·40	40

53 "Luna 9" on Moon

1966. Space Rendezvous and Moon Landing.

191	**53**	10 l. brown, indigo & blue	20	10
192	–	25 l. green and red	30	10
193	**53**	50 l. brown and green	40	15
194	–	1 r. turquoise and brown	70	35
195	–	2 r. green and violet	1·50	65
196	–	5 r. pink and turquoise	2·25	1·60

DESIGNS: 25 l., 1 r., 5 r. "Gemini 6" and "7" rendezvous in space; 2 r. "Gemini" spaceship as seen from the other spaceship.

54 U.N.E.S.C.O. Emblem and Owl on Book

1966. 20th Anniv of U.N.E.S.C.O. Multicoloured.

198		2 l. Type **54**	10	40
199		3 l. U.N.E.S.C.O. emblem and globe and microscope	10	40
200		5 l. U.N.E.S.C.O. emblem and mask, violin and palette	30	15
201		50 l. Type **54**	1·50	45
202		1 r. Design as 3 l.	2·25	75
203		5 r. Design as 5 l.	7·50	12·00

55 Sir Winston Churchill and Cortege

1966. Churchill Commem. Flag in red and blue.

204	**55**	2 l. brown	15	40
205	–	10 l. turquoise	60	10
206	**55**	15 l. green	85	10
207	–	25 l. violet	1·40	15
208	–	1 r. brown	3·75	75
209	**55**	2 r. 50 red	9·00	9·50

DESIGN: 10 l., 25 l., 1 r. Churchill and catafalque.

56 Footballers and Jules Rimet Cup

1967. England's Victory in World Cup Football Championship. Multicoloured.

210		2 l. Type **56**	10	40
211		3 l. Player in red shirt kicking ball	10	40
212		5 l. Scoring goal	10	10
213		25 l. As 3 l.	60	10
214		50 l. Making a tackle	1·00	20
215		1 r. Type **56**	2·00	55
216		2 r. Emblem on Union Jack	3·25	3·00

57 Ornate Butterflyfish

1967. Tropical Fishes. Multicoloured.

218		2 l. Type **57**	10	30
219		3 l. Black-saddled pufferfish	15	30
220		5 l. Blue boxfish	20	10
221		6 l. Picasso triggerfish	20	20
222		50 l. Semicircle angelfish	3·25	30
223		1 r. As 3 l.	4·50	75
224		As 50 l.	8·50	8·00

58 Hawker Siddeley H.S.748 over Hulule Airport Building

1967. Inauguration of Hulule Airport.

225	**58**	2 l. violet and olive	15	40
226	–	5 l green and lavender	20	10
227	**58**	10 l. violet and green	25	10
228	–	15 l. green and ochre	40	10
229	**58**	30 l. ultramarine & blue	90	10
230	–	50 l. brown and mauve	1·50	20
231	**58**	5 r. blue and orange	4·50	5·50
232	–	10 r. brown and blue	6·50	9·00

DESIGN: 5, 15, 50 l., 10 r. Airport building and Hawker Siddeley H.S.748.

59 "Man and Music" Pavilion

1967. World Fair, Montreal. Multicoloured.

233		2 l. Type **59**	10	10
234		5 l. "Man and His Community" Pavilion	10	10
235		10 l. Type **59**	10	10
236		50 l. As 5 l.	30	20
237		1 r. Type **59**	65	40
238		2 r. As 5 l.	1·25	90

1968. Int Tourist Year (1967). Nos. 225/32 optd **International Tourist Year 1967**.

240	**58**	2 l. violet and olive	10	30
241	–	5 l. green and lavender	15	15
242	**58**	10 l. violet and green	20	15
243	–	15 l. green and ochre	20	15
244	**58**	30 l. ultramarine & blue	30	20
245	–	50 l. brown and mauve	45	30
246	**58**	5 r. blue and orange	3·50	3·75
247	–	10 r. brown and blue	5·00	6·00

61 Cub signalling and Lord Baden-Powell

63 Putting the Shot

62 French Satellite "A 1"

1968. Maldivian Scouts and Cubs.

248	**61**	2 l. brown, green & yellow	10	30
249	–	3 l. red, blue and lt blue	10	30
250	**61**	25 l. violet, lake and red	1·50	30
251	–	1 r. green, brown and light green	3·50	1·60

DESIGN: 3 l. and 1 r. Scouts and Lord Baden-Powell.

1968. Space Martyrs.

252	**62**	2 l. mauve and blue	10	30
253	–	3 l. violet and brown	10	30
254	–	7 l. brown and lake	15	30
255	–	10 l. blue, drab and black	15	15
256	–	25 l. green and violet	40	15
257	**62**	50 l. blue and brown	75	30
258	–	1 r. purple and green	1·10	50
259	–	2 r. brown, blue and black	1·75	1·75
260	–	5 r. mauve, drab & black	2·75	3·00

DESIGNS: 3 l., 25 l. "Luna 10"; 7 l., 1 r. "Orbiter" and "Mariner"; 10 l., 2 r. Astronauts White, Grissom and Chaffee; 5 r. Cosmonaut V. M. Komarov.

1968. Olympic Games, Mexico (1st Issue). Multicoloured.

262		2 l. Type **63**	10	15
263		6 l. Throwing the discus	10	15
264		10 l. Type **63**	10	10
265		25 l. As 6 l.	15	10
266		1 r. Type **63**	50	35
267		2 r. 50 As 6 l.	1·25	1·50

See also Nos. 294/7.

64 "Adriatic Seascape" (Bonington)

1968. Paintings. Multicoloured.

268		50 l. Type **64**	60	30
269		1 r. "Ulysses deriding Polyphemus" (Turner)	1·00	45
270		2 r. "Sailing Boat at Argenteuil" (Monet)	1·75	1·60
271		5 r. "Fishing Boat at Les Saintes-Maries" (Van Gogh)	4·00	4·00

65 LZ-130 "Graf Zeppelin II" and Montgolfier's Balloon

1968. Development of Civil Aviation.

272	**65**	2 l. brown, green and blue	15	40
273	–	3 l. blue, violet and brown	15	40
274	–	5 l. green, red and blue	15	15
275	–	7 l. blue, purple & orange	90	55
276	**65**	10 l. brown, blue & purple	35	15
277	–	50 l. red, green and olive	1·50	20
278	–	1 r. green, blue and red	2·25	50
279	–	2 r. purple, bistre and blue	14·00	10·00

DESIGNS: 3 l., 1 r. Boeing 707-420 and Douglas DC-3; 5 l., 50 l. Wright Type A and Lilienthal's glider; 7 l., 2 r. Projected Boeing 733 and Concorde.

66 W.H.O. Building, Geneva

1968. 20th Anniv of World Health Organization.

280	**66**	10 l. violet, turquoise & blue	60	10
281		25 l. green, brown & yellow	1·00	15
282		1 r. brown, emerald & grn	3·25	90
283		2 r. violet, purple & mauve	5·25	5·50

1968. 1st Anniv of Scout Jamboree, Idaho. Nos. 248/51 optd **International Boy Scout Jamboree, Farragut Park, Idaho, U.S.A. August 1–9, 1967.**

284	**61**	2 l. brown, green & yellow	10	40
285	–	3 l. red, blue and lt blue	10	40
286	**61**	25 l. violet, lake and red	1·50	40
287	–	1 r. green, brown and light green	4·50	2·10

68 Curlew and Redshank

1968. Multicoloured.

288		2 l. Type **68**	50	60
289		10 l. Pacific grinning tun and Papal mitre shells	1·25	20
290		25 l. Oriental angel wing and tapestry turban shells	1·75	25
291		50 l. Type **68**	6·00	90
292		1 r. As 10 l.	4·50	95
293		2 r. As 25 l.	4·75	4·50

69 Throwing the Discus

71 "The Thinker" (Rodin)

70 Fishing Dhow

1968. Olympic Games, Mexico (2nd issue). Multicoloured.

294		10 l. Type **69**	10	10
295		50 l. Running	20	10
296		1 r. Cycling	2·00	35
297		2 r. Basketball	2·75	1·25

1968. Republic Day.

298	**70**	10 l. brown, blue & green	75	20
299	–	1 r. green, red and blue	2·75	80

DESIGN: 1 r. National flag, crest and map.

1969. U.N.E.S.C.O. "Human Rights". Designs showing sculptures by Rodin. Multicoloured.

300		6 l. Type **71**	30	15
301		10 l. "Hands"	30	15
302		1 r. 50 "Eve"	2·00	2·25
303		2 r. 50 "Adam"	2·50	3·00

72 Module nearing Moon's Surface

1969. First Man on the Moon. Multicoloured.

305		6 l. Type **72**	15	15
306		10 l. Astronaut with hatchet	15	15
307		1 r. 50 Astronaut and module	2·00	1·40
308		2 r. 50 Astronaut using camera	2·25	2·00

1969. Gold Medal Winner, Olympic Games, Mexico (1968). Nos. 295/6 optd **Gold Medal Winner Mohamed Gammoudi 5000 m. run Tunisia REPUBLIC OF MALDIVES** or similar opt.

310		50 l. multicoloured	60	60
311		1 r. multicoloured	90	90

The inscription on No. 310 honours P. Trentin (cycling, France).

74 Racoon Butterflyfish

1970. Tropical Fishes. Multicoloured.

312		2 l. Type **74**	40	70
313		5 l. Clown triggerfish	65	40
314		25 l. Broad-barred lionfish	1·75	40
315		50 l. Long-nosed butterflyfish	2·50	1·00
316		1 r. Emperor angelfish	3·75	1·00
317		2 r. Royal angelfish	5·50	6·50

75 Columbia Dauman Victoria, 1899

1970. "75 Years of the Automobile". Multicoloured.

318	2 l. Type **75**	20	30
319	5 l. Duryea phaeton, 1902	25	30
320	7 l. Packard S-24, 1906	30	30
321	10 l. Autocar Runabout, 1907	35	30
322	25 l. Type **75**	1·00	30
323	50 l. As 5 l.	2·25	55
324	1 r. As 7 l.	3·50	90
325	2 r. As 10 l.	4·50	5·50

76 U.N. Headquarters, New York

1970. 25th Anniv of United Nations. Mult.

327	2 l. Type **76**	10	50
328	10 l. Surgical operation (W.H.O.)	75	15
329	25 l. Student, actress and musician (U.N.E.S.C.O.)	1·75	30
330	50 l. Children at work and play (U.N.I.C.E.F.)	1·75	60
331	1 r. Fish, corn and farm animals (F.A.O.)	1·75	90
332	2 r. Miner hewing coal (I.L.O.)	4·50	5·00

77 Ship and Light Buoy

78 "Guitar-player and Masqueraders" (A. Watteau)

1970. 10th Anniv of I.M.C.O. Multicoloured.

333	50 l. Type **77**	50	40
334	1 r. Ship and lighthouse	3·25	85

1970. Famous Paintings showing the Guitar. Multicoloured.

335	3 l. Type **78**	10	30
336	7 l. "Spanish Guitarist" (Manet)	10	30
337	50 l. "Costumed Player" (Watteau)	50	35
338	1 r. "Mandoline-player" (Roberti)	85	55
339	2 r. 50 "Guitar-player and Lady" (Watteau)	2·25	2·75
340	5 r. "Mandoline-player" (Frans Hals)	4·00	4·50

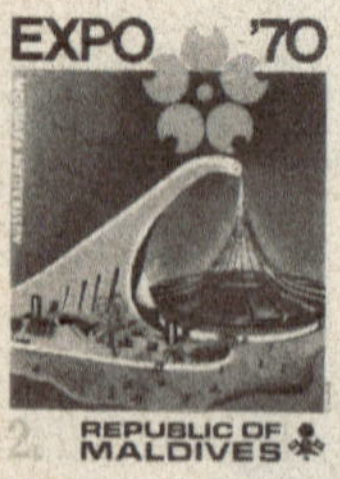

79 Australian Pavilion

82 Footballers

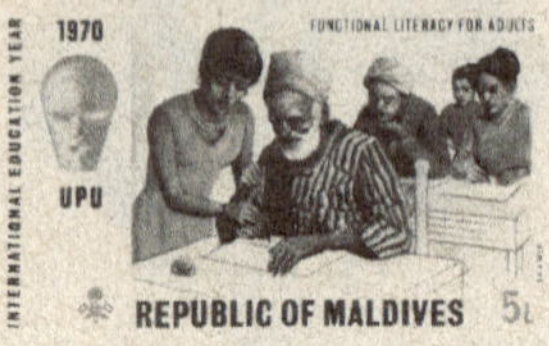

80 Learning the Alphabet

1970. "EXPO 70" World Fair, Osaka, Japan. Multicoloured.

342	2 l. Type **79**	10	40
343	3 l. West German Pavilion	10	40
344	10 l. U.S. Pavilion	30	10
345	25 l. British Pavilion	70	15
346	50 l. Soviet Pavilion	1·25	35
347	1 r. Japanese Pavilion	1·75	65

1970. Int Education Year. Multicoloured.

348	5 l. Type **80**	15	15
349	10 l. Training teachers	20	10
350	25 l. Geography lesson	50	15
351	50 l. School inspector	70	45
352	1 r. Education by television	1·00	75

1970. "Philympia 1970" Stamp Exn, London. Nos. 306/8 optd **Philympia London 1970**.

353	10 l. multicoloured	10	10
354	1 r. 50 multicoloured	65	75
355	2 r. 50 multicoloured	1·00	1·50

1970. World Cup Football Championships, Mexico.

357	**82** 3 l. multicoloured	15	40
358	– 6 l. multicoloured	20	40
359	– 7 l. multicoloured	20	30
360	– 25 l. multicoloured	90	20
361	– 1 r. multicoloured	2·50	90

DESIGNS: 6 l. to 1 r. Different designs showing footballers in action.

83 Little Boy and U.N.I.C.E.F. Flag

84 Astronauts Lovell, Haise and Swigert

1970. 25th Anniv of U.N.I.C.E.F. Multicoloured.

362	5 l. Type **83**	10	15
363	10 l. Little girl with U.N.I.C.E.F. "balloon"	10	15
364	1 r. Type **83**	1·75	85
365	2 r. As 10 l.	2·75	3·00

1971. Safe Return of "Apollo 13". Multicoloured.

366	5 l. Type **84**	20	15
367	20 l. Explosion in Space	40	15
368	1 r. Splashdown	1·10	50

85 "Multiracial Flower"

86 "Mme. Charpentier and her Children" (Renoir)

1971. Racial Equality Year.

369	**85** 10 l. multicoloured	10	15
370	25 l. multicoloured	20	15

1971. Famous Paintings showing "Mother and Child". Multicoloured.

371	5 l. Type **86**	20	20
372	7 l. "Susanna van Collen and her Daughter" (Rembrandt)	25	20
373	10 l. "Madonna nursing the Child" (Titian)	35	20
374	20 l. "Baroness Belleli and her Children" (Degas)	85	20
375	25 l. "The Cradle" (Morisot)	90	20
376	1 r. "Helena Fourment and her Children" (Reubens)	2·50	85
377	3 r. "On the Terrace" (Renoir)	5·00	6·00

87 Alan Shepard

1971. Moon Flight of "Apollo 14". Multicoloured.

378	6 l. Type **87**	30	20
379	10 l. Stuart Roosa	35	20
380	1 r. 50 Edgar Mitchell	4·50	3·00
381	5 r. Mission insignia	9·50	9·50

88 "Ballerina" (Degas)

1971. Famous Paintings showing "Dancers". Multicoloured.

382	5 l. Type **88**	20	20
383	10 l. "Dancing Couple" (Renoir)	25	20
384	2 r. "Spanish Dancer" (Manet)	2·75	2·50
385	5 r. "Ballerinas" (Degas)	5·00	5·00
386	10 r. "La Goulue at the Moulin Rouge" (Toulouse-Lautrec)	7·50	8·00

1972. Visit of Queen Elizabeth II and Prince Philip. Nos. 382/6 optd **ROYAL VISIT 1972**.

387	**88** 5 l. multicoloured	15	10
388	– 10 l. multicoloured	20	10
389	– 2 r. multicoloured	4·50	4·00
390	– 5 r. multicoloured	8·00	8·00
391	– 10 r. multicoloured	9·50	10·00

90 Book Year Emblem

1972. International Book Year.

392	**90** 25 l. multicoloured	15	10
393	5 r. multicoloured	1·60	2·00

91 Scottish Costume

1972. National Costumes of the World. Mult.

394	10 l. Type **91**	50	10
395	15 l. Netherlands	55	15
396	25 l. Norway	90	15
397	50 l. Hungary	1·75	55
398	1 r. Austria	2·25	80
399	2 r. Spain	4·00	3·25

92 Stegosaurus

1972. Prehistoric Animals. Multicoloured.

400	2 l. Type **92**	50	50
401	7 l. Dimetrodon (inscr "Edaphosaurus")	90	40
402	25 l. Diplodocus	1·75	40
403	50 l. Triceratops	2·00	75
404	2 r. Pteranodon	5·00	5·00
405	5 r. Tyrannosaurus	9·00	9·50

93 Cross-country Skiing

1972. Winter Olympic Games, Sapporo, Japan. Multicoloured.

406	3 l. Type **93**	10	30
407	6 l. Bobsleighing	10	30
408	15 l. Speed skating	20	20
409	50 l. Ski jumping	1·00	45
410	1 r. Figure skating (pair)	1·75	70
411	2 r. 50 Ice hockey	5·50	3·25

94 Scout Saluting

95 Cycling

1972. 13th Boy Scout Jamboree, Asagiri, Japan (1971). Multicoloured.

412	10 l. Type **94**	65	20
413	15 l. Scout signalling	85	20
414	50 l. Scout blowing bugle	3·00	1·25
415	1 r. Scout playing drum	4·50	2·25

1972. Olympic Games, Munich. Multicoloured.

416	5 l. Type **95**	30	20
417	10 l. Running	20	20
418	25 l. Wrestling	30	20
419	50 l. Hurdling	50	35
420	2 r. Boxing	1·10	1·75
421	5 r. Volleyball	2·50	3·25

96 Globe and Conference Emblem

97 "Flowers" (Van Gogh)

1972. U.N. Environmental Conservation Conf, Stockholm.

423	**96** 2 l. multicoloured	10	30
424	3 l. multicoloured	10	30
425	15 l. multicoloured	30	15
426	50 l. multicoloured	75	45
427	2 r. 50 multicoloured	3·25	4·00

1973. Floral Paintings. Multicoloured.

428	1 l. Type **97**	10	30
429	2 l. "Flowers in Jug" (Renoir)	10	30
430	3 l. "Chrysanthemums" (Renoir)	10	30
431	50 l. "Mixed Bouquet" (Bosschaert)	1·00	20
432	1 r. As 3 l.	1·50	40
433	5 r. As 2 l.	3·50	5·00

1973. Gold-medal Winners, Munich Olympic Games. Nos. 420/1 optd as listed below.

435	2 r. multicoloured	3·00	2·25
436	5 r. multicoloured	4·00	2·50

OVERPRINTS: 2 r. **LEMECHEV MIDDLE-WEIGHT GOLD MEDALLIST**; 5 r. **JAPAN GOLD MEDAL WINNERS**.

99 Animal Care

1973. International Scouting Congress, Nairobi and Addis Ababa. Multicoloured.

438	1 l. Type **99**	10	20
439	2 l. Lifesaving	10	20
440	3 l. Agricultural training	10	20
441	4 l. Carpentry	10	20
442	5 l. Playing leapfrog	10	20
443	1 r. As 2 l.	2·75	75
444	2 r. As 4 l.	5·00	4·75
445	3 r. Type **99**	6·50	7·00

100 Blue Marlin

1973. Fishes. Multicoloured.
447 1 l. Type **100** . . . 10 30
448 2 l. Skipjack tuna . . . 10 30
449 3 l. Blue-finned tuna . . . 10 30
450 5 l. Dolphin (fish) . . . 10 30
451 60 l. Humpbacked snapper . . 80 40
452 75 l. As 60 l. . . . 1·00 40
453 1 r. 50 Yellow-edged lyretail . 1·75 1·75
454 2 r. 50 As 5 l. . . . 2·25 2·75
455 3 r. Spotted coral grouper . . 2·25 3·00
456 10 r. Spanish mackerel . . 4·75 8·00
Nos. 451/2 are smaller, size 29 × 22 mm.

101 Golden-fronted Leafbird

1973. Fauna. Multicoloured.
458 1 l. Type **101** . . . 10 30
459 2 l. Indian flying fox . . . 10 30
460 3 l. Land tortoise . . . 10 30
461 4 l. Butterfly ("Kallima inachus") 30 30
462 50 l. As 3 l. . . . 60 35
463 2 r. Type **101** . . . 4·00 4·00
464 3 r. As 2 l. . . . 3·50 4·00

102 "Lantana camara"

1973. Flowers of the Maldive Islands. Mult.
466 1 l. Type **102** . . . 10 20
467 2 l. "Nerium oleander" . . . 10 20
468 3 l. "Rosa polyantha" . . . 10 20
469 4 l. "Hibiscus manihot" . . . 10 20
470 5 l. "Bougainvillea glabra" . . 10 20
471 10 l. "Plumera alba" . . . 10 20
472 50 l. "Poinsettia pulcherrima" . 55 30
473 5 r. "Ononis natrix" . . . 3·75 5·00

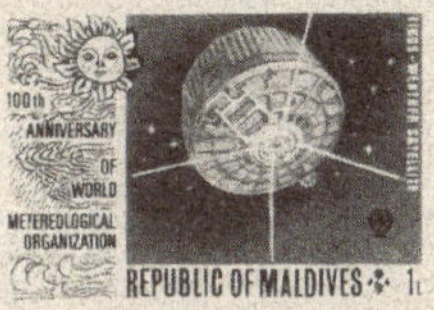
103 "Tiros" Weather Satellite

1974. Centenary of World Meteorological Organization. Multicoloured.
475 1 l. Type **103** . . . 10 10
476 2 l. "Nimbus" satellite . . . 10 10
477 3 l. "Nomad" (weather ship) . . 10 10
478 4 l. Scanner, A.P.T. Instant Weather Picture equipment . 10 10
479 5 l. Richard's wind-speed recorder . . . 10 10
480 2 r. Type **103** . . . 3·00 3·50
481 3 r. As 3 l. . . . 3·25 3·75

104 "Apollo" Spacecraft and Pres. Kennedy

1974. American and Russian Space Exploration Projects. Multicoloured.
483 1 l. Type **104** . . . 10 15
484 2 l. "Mercury" capsule and John Glenn . . . 10 15
485 3 l. "Vostok 1" and Yuri Gagarin 10 20
486 4 l. "Vostok 6" and Valentina Tereshkova . . . 10 20
487 5 l. "Soyuz 11" and "Salyut" space-station . . . 10 20
488 2 r. "Skylab" space laboratory 3·50 3·50
489 3 r. As 2 l. . . . 4·00 4·00

MINIMUM PRICE

The minimum price quoted is 10p which represents a handling charge rather than a basis for valuing common stamps. For further notes about prices see introductory pages.

105 Copernicus and "Skylab" Space Laboratory
106 "Maternity" (Picasso)

1974. 500th Birth Anniv of Nicholas Copernicus (astronomer). Multicoloured.
491 1 l. Type **105** . . . 10 15
492 2 l. Orbital space-station of the future . . . 10 15
493 3 l. Proposed "Space-shuttle" craft . . . 10 15
494 4 l. "Mariner 2" Venus probe . 10 20
495 5 l. "Mariner 4" Mars probe . 10 20
496 25 l. Type **105** . . . 90 20
497 1 r. 50 As 2 l. . . . 3·25 3·25
498 5 r. As 3 l. . . . 8·00 10·00

1974. Paintings by Picasso. Multicoloured.
500 1 l. Type **106** . . . 10 10
501 2 l. "Harlequin and Friend" . 10 10
502 3 l. "Pierrot Sitting" . . . 10 10
503 20 l. "Three Musicians" . . 25 15
504 75 l. "L'Aficionado" . . . 55 40
505 5 r. "Still Life" . . . 3·50 4·75

107 U.P.U. Emblem, Steam and Diesel Locomotives

1974. Cent of Universal Postal Union. Mult.
507 1 l. Type **107** . . . 10 10
508 2 l. Paddle-steamer and modern mailboat . . . 10 10
509 3 l. Airship "Graf Zeppelin" and Boeing 747 airliner . . 10 10
510 1 r. 50 Mailcoach and motor van 85 85
511 2 r. 50 As 2 l. . . . 1·40 1·60
512 5 r. Type **107** . . . 2·75 3·50

108 Footballers
109 "Capricorn"

1974. World Cup Football Championships, West Germany.
514 **108** 1 l. multicoloured . . . 15 10
515 – 2 l. multicoloured . . . 15 10
516 – 3 l. multicoloured . . . 15 10
517 – 4 l. multicoloured . . . 15 10
518 – 75 l. multicoloured . . . 1·25 75
519 – 4 r. multicoloured . . . 3·50 4·00
520 – 5 r. multicoloured . . . 3·75 4·00
DESIGNS: Nos. 515/20 show football scenes similar to Type **108**.

1974. Signs of the Zodiac. Multicoloured.
522 1 l. Type **109** . . . 20 30
523 2 l. "Aquarius" . . . 20 30
524 3 l. "Pisces" . . . 20 30
525 4 l. "Aries" . . . 20 30
526 5 l. "Taurus" . . . 20 30
527 6 l. "Gemini" . . . 20 30
528 7 l. "Cancer" . . . 20 30
529 10 l. "Leo" . . . 30 30
530 15 l. "Virgo" . . . 30 30
531 20 l. "Libra" . . . 30 30
532 25 l. "Scorpio" . . . 30 30
533 5 r. "Sagittarius" . . . 11·00 12·00

110 Churchill and Avro Type 683 Lancaster
111 Bullmouth Helmet

1974. Birth Cent of Sir Winston Churchill. Mult.
535 1 l. Type **110** . . . 15 30
536 2 l. Churchill as pilot . . . 15 30
537 3 l. Churchill as First Lord of the Admiralty . . . 20 30
538 4 l. Churchill and H.M.S. "Indomitable" (aircraft carrier) . . . 20 30
539 5 l. Churchill and De Havilland Mosquito bombers . . . 20 30
540 60 l. Churchill and anti-aircraft battery . . . 2·75 1·50
541 75 l. Churchill and tank in desert 3·00 1·50
542 5 r. Churchill and Short S.25 Sunderland flying boat . . 11·00 12·00

1975. Sea Shells and Cowries. Multicoloured.
544 1 l. Type **111** . . . 10 30
545 2 l. Venus comb murex . . . 10 30
546 3 l. Common or major harp . . 10 30
547 4 l. Chiragra spider conch . . 10 30
548 5 l. Geography cone . . . 10 30
549 60 l. Dawn cowrie (22 × 30 mm) 3·00 2·00
550 75 l. Purplish clanculus (22 × 30 mm) . . . 3·50 2·00
551 5 r. Ramose murex . . . 8·50 11·00

112 Royal Throne
113 Guavas

1975. Historical Relics and Monuments. Multicoloured.
553 1 l. Type **112** . . . 10 10
554 10 l. Candlesticks . . . 10 10
555 25 l. Lamp-tree . . . 15 10
556 60 l. Royal umbrellas . . . 30 30
557 75 l. Eid-Miskith Mosque (horiz) 35 35
558 3 r. Tomb of Al-Hafiz Abu-al Barakath-al Barubari (horiz) 1·60 2·75

1975. Exotic Fruits. Multicoloured.
559 2 l. Type **113** . . . 10 30
560 4 l. Maldive mulberry . . . 15 30
561 5 l. Mountain apples . . . 15 30
562 10 l. Bananas . . . 20 15
563 20 l. Mangoes . . . 40 25
564 50 l. Papaya . . . 1·00 60
565 1 r. Pomegranates . . . 1·75 70
566 5 r. Coconut . . . 8·50 11·00

114 "Phyllangia"

1975. Marine Life. Corals, Urchins and Sea Stars. Multicoloured.
568 1 l. Type **114** . . . 10 10
569 2 l. "Madrepora oculata" . . 10 10
570 3 l. "Acropora gravida" . . 10 10
571 4 l. "Stylotella" . . . 10 10
572 5 l. "Acrophora cervicornis" . 10 10
573 60 l. "Strongylocentrotus purpuratus" . . . 75 65
574 75 l. "Pisaster ochraceus" . . 85 75
575 5 r. "Marthasterias glacialis" . 5·00 6·50

115 Clock Tower and Customs Building within "10"

1975. 10th Anniv of Independence. Multicoloured.
577 4 l. Type **115** . . . 10 10
578 5 l. Government offices . . . 10 10
579 7 l. Waterfront . . . 10 10
580 15 l. Mosque and minaret . . 10 10
581 10 r. Sultan Park and museum . 2·75 6·00

1975. "Nordjamb 75" World Scout Jamboree, Norway. Nos. 443/5 optd **14th Boy Scout Jamboree July 29–August 7, 1975.**
582 – 1 r. multicoloured . . . 40 40
583 – 2 r. multicoloured . . . 60 60
584 **99** 3 r. multicoloured . . . 1·25 1·25

117 Madura Prau

1975. Ships. Multicoloured.
586 1 l. Type **117** . . . 10 10
587 2 l. Ganges patela . . . 10 10
588 3 l. Indian palla (vert) . . . 10 10
589 4 l. Odhi (dhow) (vert) . . . 10 10
590 5 l. Maldivian schooner . . . 10 10
591 25 l. "Cutty Sark" (British tea clipper) . . . 90 40
592 1 r. Maldivian baggala (vert) . 1·50 70
593 5 r. "Maldive Courage" (freighter) . . . 4·00 6·00

118 "Brahmophthalma wallichi" (moth)

1975. Butterflies and Moth. Multicoloured.
595 1 l. Type **118** . . . 15 30
596 2 l. "Teinopalpus imperialis" . 15 30
597 3 l. "Cethosia biblis" . . . 15 30
598 4 l. "Idea jasonia" . . . 15 30
599 5 l. "Apatura ilia" . . . 15 30
600 25 l. "Kallima horsfieldi" . . 1·25 35
601 1 r. 50 "Hebomoia leucippe" . 3·50 3·75
602 5 r. "Papilio memnon" . . . 8·00 10·00

119 "The Dying Captive"
120 Beaker and Vase

1975. 500th Birth Anniv of Michelangelo. Multicoloured.
604 1 l. Type **119** . . . 10 10
605 2 l. Detail of "The Last Judgement" . . . 10 10
606 3 l. "Apollo" . . . 10 10
607 4 l. Detail of Sistine Chapel ceiling . . . 10 10
608 5 l. "Bacchus" . . . 10 10
609 1 r. Detail of "The Last Judgement" (different) . . 1·50 40
610 2 r. "David" . . . 2·50 2·50
611 5 r. "Cumaean Sibyl" . . . 4·25 5·50

1975. Maldivian Lacquerware. Multicoloured.
613 2 l. Type **120** . . . 10 30
614 4 l. Boxes . . . 10 30
615 50 l. Jar with lid . . . 40 20
616 75 l. Bowls with covers . . . 50 30
617 1 r. Craftsman at work . . . 65 40

121 Map of Maldives

1975. Tourism. Multicoloured.
618 4 l. Type **121** . . . 20 20
619 5 l. Motor launch and small craft 20 20
620 7 l. Sailing-boats . . . 20 20
621 15 l. Underwater fishing . . 20 20
622 3 r. Hulule Airport . . . 2·00 2·00
623 10 r. Motor cruisers . . . 4·50 6·50

122 Cross-country Skiing
123 "General Burgoyne" (Reynolds)

1976. Winter Olympic Games, Innsbruck. Multicoloured.
624 1 l. Type **122** . . . 10 10
625 2 l. Speed-skating (pairs) . . 10 10
626 3 l. Figure-skating (pairs) . . 10 10
627 4 l. Four-man bobsleighing . . 10 10
628 5 l. Ski-jumping . . . 10 10
629 25 l. Figure-skating (women's) . 35 10
630 1 r. 15 Skiing (slalom) . . . 1·00 1·25
631 4 r. Ice-hockey . . . 3·25 4·00

1976. Bicent of American Revolution. Mult.
633 1 l. Type **123** . . . 10 10
634 2 l. "John Hancock" (Copley) . 10 10
635 3 l. "Death of Gen. Montgomery" (Trumbull) (horiz) . . . 10 10

636 4 l. "Paul Revere" (Copley) . 10 10
637 5 l. "Battle of Bunker Hill" (Trumbull) (horiz) 10 10
638 2 r. "The Crossing of the Delaware" (Sully) (horiz) . . 2·00 2·50
639 3 r. "Samuel Adams" (Copley) 2·50 3·00
640 5 r. "Surrender of Cornwallis" (Trumbull) (horiz) . . . . . 3·00 3·25

124 Thomas Edison

1976. Centenary of Telephone. Multicoloured.
642 1 l. Type **124** 10 20
643 2 l. Alexander Graham Bell . 10 20
644 3 l. Telephone of 1919, 1937 and 1972 . . . . 10 20
645 10 l. Cable entrance into station 20 20
646 20 l. Equaliser circuit assembly 30 20
647 1 r. "Salernum" (cable ship) . 1·75 55
648 10 r. "Intelsat IV-A" and Earth Station . . . . 4·75 7·50

1976. "Interphil 76" International Stamp Exhibition, Philadelphia. Nos. 638/40 optd **MAY 29TH-JUNE 6TH "INTERPHIL" 1976.**
650 2 r. multicoloured . . . . . . 1·50 1·75
651 3 r. multicoloured . . . . . . 2·00 2·25
652 5 r. multicoloured . . . . . . 2·50 2·75

126 Wrestling

127 "Dolichos lablab"

1976. Olympic Games, Montreal. Multicoloured.
654 1 l. Type **126** 10 10
655 2 l. Putting the shot 10 10
656 3 l. Hurdling 10 10
657 4 l. Hockey 10 10
658 5 l. Running 10 10
659 6 l. Javelin-throwing 10 10
660 1 r. 50 Discus-throwing . . . 1·25 1·75
661 5 r. Volleyball . . . . 4·25 5·25

1976. Vegetables. Multicoloured.
663 2 l. Type **127** 10 20
664 4 l. "Moringa pterygosperma" . 10 20
665 10 l. "Solanum melongena" . . 10 10
666 20 l. "Moringa pterygosperma" 1·25 1·50
667 50 l. "Cucumis sativus" . . . 80 65
668 75 l. "Trichosanthes anguina" . 85 75
669 1 r. "Momordica charantia" . 95 85
670 2 r. "Trichosanthes anguina" . 3·75 6·00

128 "Viking" approaching Mars

1977. "Viking" Space Mission.
671 **128** 5 r. multicoloured . . . . 2·25 2·75

129 Coronation Ceremony

1977. Silver Jubilee of Queen Elizabeth II. Multicoloured.
673 1 l. Type **129** 10 10
674 2 l. Queen and Prince Philip . 10 10
675 3 l. Royal couple with Princes Andrew and Edward 10 10
676 1 r. 15 Queen with Archbishops 35 35
677 3 r. State coach in procession . 60 55
678 4 r. Royal couple with Prince Charles and Princess Anne . 60 90

130 Beethoven and Organ

1977. 150th Death Anniv of Ludwig van Beethoven. Multicoloured.
680 1 l. Type **130** 15 20
681 2 l. Portrait and manuscript of "Moonlight Sonata" . . . 15 20
682 3 l. With Goethe at Teplitz . 15 20
683 4 l. Beethoven and string instruments 15 20
684 5 l. Beethoven's home, Heiligenstadt 15 20
685 25 l. Hands and gold medals . 85 20
686 2 r. Portrait and "Missa solemnis" . . . . 2·75 3·00
687 5 r. Composer's hearing-aids . 4·75 5·00

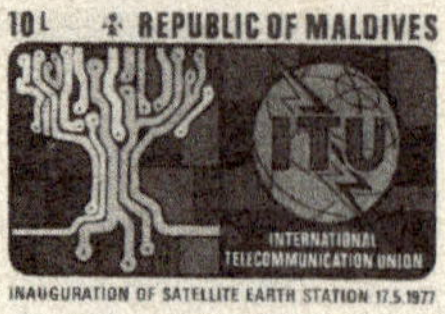

131 Printed Circuit and I.T.U. Emblem

1977. Inauguration of Satellite Earth Station. Multicoloured.
689 10 l. Type **131** 10 10
690 90 l. Central Telegraph Office 45 45
691 10 r. Satellite Earth Station . 5·00 7·00

132 "Miss Anne Ford" (Gainsborough)

133 Lesser Frigate Birds

1977. Artists' Birth Anniversaries. Multicoloured.
693 1 l. Type **132** (250th anniv) . 10 10
694 2 l. Group painting by Rubens (400th anniv) 10 10
695 3 l. "Girl with Dog" (Titian) (500th Anniv) 10 10
696 4 l. "Mrs. Thomas Graham" (Gainsborough) 10 10
697 5 l. "Artist with Isabella Brant" (Rubens) 10 10
698 95 l. Portrait by Titian . . . 75 40
699 1 r. Portrait by Gainsborough 75 40
700 10 r. "Isabella Brant" (Rubens) 4·75 7·00

1977. Birds. Multicoloured.
702 1 l. Type **133** 20 30
703 2 l. Crab plover 20 30
704 3 l. White-tailed tropic bird . 20 30
705 4 l. Wedge-tailed shearwater . 20 30
706 5 l. Grey heron 20 30
707 20 l. White tern 90 30
708 95 l. Cattle egret . . . . . 2·25 1·60
709 1 r. 25 Black-naped tern . . 2·50 2·50
710 5 r. Pheasant coucal . . . . 6·50 8·00

134 Charles Lindbergh

136 Rheumatic Heart

135 Boat Building

1977. 50th Anniv of Lindbergh's Transatlantic Flight and 75th Anniv of First Navigable Airships. Multicoloured.
712 1 l. Type **134** 10 10
713 2 l. Lindbergh and "Spirit of St. Louis" 10 10
714 3 l. Lindbergh's Miles Mohawk aircraft (horiz) 10 10
715 4 l. Lebaudy-Juillot airship "Morning Post" (horiz) . . 10 10
716 5 l. Airship "Graf Zeppelin" and portrait of Zeppelin . . . 10 10
717 1 r. Airship "Los Angeles" (horiz) 60 30
718 3 r. Lindbergh and Henry Ford 1·40 1·75
719 10 r. Vickers airship R-23 rigid airship . . . . 3·50 5·50
No. 715 is inscr "Lebaudy 1 built by H. Juillot 1902".

1977. Occupations. Multicoloured.
721 6 l. Type **135** 35 20
722 15 l. Fishing 55 20
723 20 l. Cadjan weaving 65 20
724 90 l. Mat-weaving . . . . . . 1·75 1·40
725 2 r. Lace-making (vert) . . . . 3·00 4·00

1977. World Rheumatism Year. Multicoloured.
726 1 l. Type **136** 10 30
727 50 l. Rheumatic shoulder . . . 60 30
728 2 r. Rheumatic hands . . . . 1·50 1·50
729 3 r. Rheumatic knees . . . . 1·75 1·75

137 Lilienthal's Biplane Glider

1978. 75th Anniv of First Powered Aircraft. Multicoloured.
730 1 l. Type **137** 20 30
731 2 l. Chanute's glider 20 30
732 3 l. Wright glider No. II, 1901 20 30
733 4 l. A. V. Roe's Triplane I . . 20 30
734 5 l. Wilbur Wright demonstrating Wright Type A for King Alfonso of Spain 20 30
735 10 l. A. V. Roe's Avro Type D biplane 50 30
736 20 l. Wright Brothers and A. G. Bell at Washington 90 30
737 95 l. Hadley's triplane . . . . 2·75 2·25
738 5 r. Royal Aircraft Factory B.E.2A biplanes at Upavon, 1914 . . . . 8·00 10·00
No. 732 is wrongly dated "1900".

138 Newgate Prison

139 Television Set

1978. World Eradication of Smallpox. Mult.
740 15 l. Foundling Hospital, London (horiz) 75 30
741 50 l. Type **138** . . . . 1·50 60
742 2 r. Edward Jenner (discoverer of smallpox vaccine) . . . . . 3·75 4·00

1978. Inaug of Television in Maldive Islands. Mult.
743 15 l. Type **139** 40 30
744 25 l. Television aerials 55 30
745 1 r. 50 Control desk (horiz) . . 2·25 2·75

140 Mas Odi

1978. Ships. Multicoloured.
746 1 l. Type **140** 10 15
747 2 l. Battela 10 15
748 3 l. Bandu odi (vert) 10 15
749 5 l. "Maldive Trader" (freighter) 20 20
750 1 r. "Fath-hul Baaree" (brigantine) 65 30
751 1 r. 25 Mas dhoni . . . . . . 1·00 1·00
752 3 r. Baggala (vert) . . . . . . 1·40 2·00
753 4 r. As 1 r. 25 . . . . 1·40 2·00

141 Ampulla

142 Capt. Cook

1978. 25th Anniv of Coronation. Multicoloured.
755 1 l. Type **141** 10 10
756 2 l. Sceptre with Dove 10 10
757 3 l. Golden Orb 10 10
758 1 r. 15 St. Edward's Crown . . 15 15
759 2 r. Sceptre with Cross 20 25
760 5 r. Queen Elizabeth II 55 70

1978. 250th Birth Anniv of Capt. James Cook and Bicent of Discovery of Hawaiian Islands. Mult.
762 1 l. Type **142** 10 15
763 2 l. Statue of Kamehameha I of Hawaii 10 15
764 3 l. H.M.S. "Endeavour" . . 10 15
765 25 l. Route of third voyage . 45 45
766 75 l. H.M.S. "Discovery" H.M.S. "Resolution" and map of Hawaiian Islands (horiz) . . 1·25 1·25
767 1 r. 50 Cook meeting Hawaiian islanders (horiz) . . . . . 2·00 2·25
768 10 r. Death of Capt. Cook (horiz) 7·50 10·00

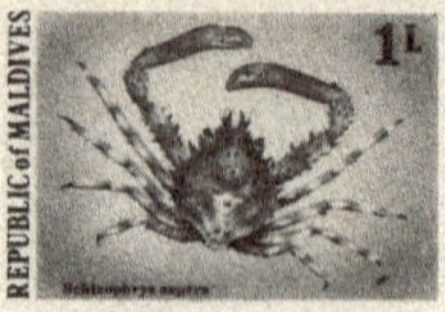

143 "Schizophrys aspera"

1978. Crustaceans. Multicoloured.
770 1 l. Type **143** 10 10
771 2 l. "Atergatis floridus" . . . 10 10
772 3 l. "Perenon planissimum" . . 10 10
773 90 l. "Portunus granulatus" . . 50 40
774 1 r. "Carpilius maculatus" . . 50 40
775 2 r. "Huenia proteus" . . . . 1·00 1·40
776 25 r. "Etisus laevimanus" . . 9·00 13·00

144 "Four Apostles"

145 T.V. Tower and Building

1978. 450th Death Anniv of Albrecht Durer (artist).
778 **144** 10 l. multicoloured . . . 10 10
779 – 20 l. multicoloured . . . 15 10
780 – 55 l. multicoloured . . . 20 20
781 – 1 r. black, brown and buff 30 30
782 – 1 r. 80 multicoloured . . 45 60
783 – 3 r. multicoloured . . . . 70 1·25
DESIGNS—VERT: 20 l. "Self-portrait at 27"; 55 l. "Madonna and Child with a Pear"; 1 r. 80, "Hare"; 3 r. "Great Piece of Turf". HORIZ: 1 r. "Rhinoceros".

1978. 10th Anniv of Republic. Multicoloured.
785 1 l. Fishing boat 10 10
786 5 l. Montessori School 10 10
787 10 l. Type **145** 10 10
788 25 l. Islet 15 15
789 50 l. Boeing 737 aircraft . . . 40 15
790 95 l. Beach scene 40 30
791 1 r. 25 Dhow at night 65 55
792 3 r. President's residence . . 85 1·25
793 5 r. Masjidh Afeefuddin Mosque 1·25 2·50
The 1, 5, 25 to 95 l., 1 r. 25 and 3, 5 r. are horiz designs.

146 Human Rights Emblem

1978. 30th Anniv of Declaration of Human Rights.
795 **146** 30 l. pink, lilac and green 15 15
796 90 l. yellow, brown and green 40 60
797 1 r. 80 blue, deep blue and green . . . . 70 1·00

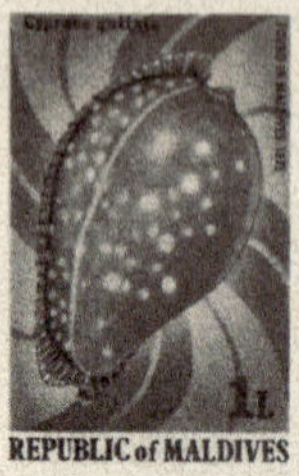

147 Great Spotted or Rare Spotted Cowrie

148 Delivery by Bellman

1979. Shells. Multicoloured.
798 1 l. Type **147** 10 10
799 2 l. Imperial cone 10 10
800 3 l. Great green turban 10 10
801 10 l. Giant spider conch . . . 45 10
802 1 r. White-toothed cowrie . . 1·75 40
803 1 r. 80 Fig cone . . . . . . 2·75 2·50
804 3 r. Glory of the sea cone . . 3·75 3·75

1979. Death Cent of Sir Rowland Hill. Mult.

806	1 l. Type **148**	10	10
807	2 l. Mail coach, 1840 (horiz)	10	10
808	3 l. First London letter box, 1855	10	10
809	1 r. 55 Penny Black	35	50
810	5 r. First Maldive Islands stamp	90	1·25

149 Girl with Teddy Bear

151 Sari with Overdress

150 "White Feathers"

1979. Int Year of the Child (1st issue). Mult.

812	5 l. Type **149**	10	10
813	1 r. 25 Boy with sailing boat	40	50
814	2 r. Boy with toy rocket	45	55
815	3 r. Boy with toy airship	60	75

See also Nos. 838/46.

1979. 25th Death Anniv of Henri Matisse (artist). Multicoloured.

817	20 l. Type **150**	15	15
818	25 l. "Joy of Life"	15	15
819	30 l. "Eggplants"	15	15
820	1 r. 50 "Harmony in Red"	55	65
821	5 r. "Still-life"	1·00	2·25

1979. National Costumes. Multicoloured.

823	50 l. Type **151**	15	15
824	75 l. Sashed apron dress	20	20
825	90 l. Serape	25	25
826	95 l. Ankle-length printed dress	30	30

152 "Gloriosa superba"

1979. Flowers. Multicoloured.

827	1 l. Type **152**	10	10
828	3 l. "Hibiscus tiliaceus"	10	10
829	50 l. "Barringtonia asiatica"	20	20
830	1 r. "Abutilon indicum"	40	40
831	5 r. "Guettarda speciosa"	1·75	2·25

153 Weaving

1979. Handicraft Exhibition. Multicoloured.

833	5 l. Type **153**	10	10
834	10 l. Lacquerwork	10	10
835	1 r. 30 Tortoiseshell jewellery	45	55
836	2 r. Carved woodwork	70	1·00

154 Mickey Mouse attacked by Bird

1979. International Year of the Child (2nd issue). Disney Characters. Multicoloured.

838	1 l. Goofy delivering parcel on motor-scooter (vert)	10	10
839	2 l. Type **154**	10	10
840	3 l. Goofy half-covered with letters	10	10
841	4 l. Pluto licking Minnie Mouse's envelopes	10	10
842	5 l. Mickey Mouse delivering letters on roller skates (vert)	10	10
843	10 l. Donald Duck placing letter in mail-box	10	10
844	15 l. Chip and Dale carrying letter	10	10
845	1 r. 50 Donald Duck on monocycle (vert)	75	95
846	5 r. Donald Duck with ostrich in crate (vert)	2·25	3·25

155 Post-Ramadan Dancing

1980. National Day. Multicoloured.

848	5 l. Type **155**	10	10
849	15 l. Musicians and dancer, Eeduu Festival	10	10
850	95 l. Sultan's ceremonial band	30	30
851	2 r. Dancer and drummers Circumcision Festival	55	85

156 Leatherback Turtle

1980. Turtle Conservation Campaign. Mult.

853	1 l. Type **156**	10	20
854	2 l. Flatback turtle	10	20
855	5 l. Hawksbill turtle	15	20
856	10 l. Loggerhead turtle	30	20
857	75 l. Olive ridley turtle	80	45
858	10 r. Atlantic ridley turtle	3·50	4·25

157 Paul Harris (founder)

1980. 75th Anniv of Rotary Int. Mult.

860	75 l. Type **157**	35	10
861	90 l. Humanity	40	20
862	1 r. Hunger	40	25
863	10 r. Health	3·00	4·50

1980. "London 1980" International Stamp Exhibition. Nos. 809/10 optd **LONDON 1980**.

865	1 r. 55 Penny Black	1·75	1·00
866	5 r. First Maldives stamp	3·25	2·75

159 Swimming

1980. Olympic Games, Moscow. Multicoloured.

868	10 l. Type **159**	10	10
869	50 l. Running	20	20
870	3 r. Putting the shot	70	1·10
871	4 r. High jumping	80	1·40

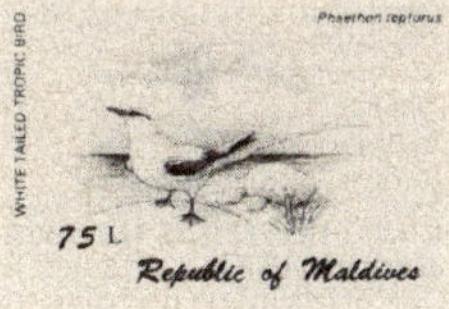

160 White-tailed Tropic Bird

1980. Birds. Multicoloured.

873	75 l. Type **160**	25	15
874	95 l. Sooty tern	35	30
875	1 r. Common noddy	35	30
876	1 r. 55 Curlew	50	70
877	2 r. Wilson's petrel	60	85
878	4 r. Caspian tern	1·10	1·60

161 Seal of Ibrahim II

1980. Seals of the Sultans.

880	**161** 1 l. brown and black	10	10
881	– 2 l. brown and black	10	10
882	– 5 l. brown and black	10	10
883	– 1 r. brown and black	30	30
884	– 2 r. brown and black	50	70

DESIGNS: 2 l. Mohammed Imadudeen II; 5 l. Bin Haji Ali; 1 r. Kuda Mohammed Rasgefaanu; 2 r. Ibrahim Iskander I.

162 Queen Elizabeth the Queen Mother

1980. 80th Birthday of the Queen Mother.

886	**162** 4 r. multicoloured	1·00	1·25

163 Munnaru

1980. 1400th Anniv of Hegira. Multicoloured.

888	5 l. Type **163**	15	10
889	10 l. Hukuru Miskiiy mosque	15	10
890	30 l. Medhuziyaaraiy (shrine of saint	30	30
891	55 l. Writing tablets with verses of Koran	35	35
892	90 l. Mother teaching child Koran	60	70

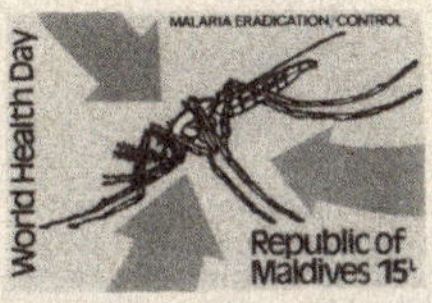

164 Malaria Eradication

1980. World Health Day. Multicoloured.

894	15 l. Type **164**	10	10
895	25 l. Nutrition	10	10
896	1 r. 50 Dental health	1·25	1·00
897	5 r. Clinics	2·50	2·75

165 White Rabbit

1980. Walt Disney's "Alice in Wonderland". Multicoloured.

899	1 l. Type **165**	10	10
900	2 l. Alice falling into Wonderland	10	10
901	3 l. Alice too big to go through door	10	10
902	4 l. Alice with Tweedledum and Tweedledee	10	10
903	5 l. Alice and caterpillar	10	10
904	10 l. The Cheshire cat	10	10
905	15 l. Alice painting the roses	10	10
906	2 r. 50 Alice and the Queen of Hearts	2·50	2·25
907	4 r. Alice on trial	2·75	2·50

166 Indian Ocean Ridley Turtle

1980. Marine Animals. Multicoloured.

909	90 l. Type **166**	2·00	60
910	1 r. 25 Pennant coralfish	2·50	1·25
911	2 r. Spiny lobster	3·25	1·75

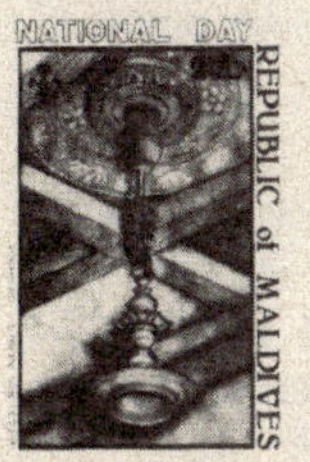

167 Pendant Lamp

168 Prince Charles and Lady Diana Spencer

1981. National Day. Multicoloured.

913	10 l. Tomb of Ghaazee Muhammad Thakurufaan (horiz)	10	10
914	20 l. Type **167**	15	10
915	30 l. Chair used by Muhammad Thakurufaan	20	10
916	95 l. Muhammad Thakurufaan's palace (horiz)	45	45
917	10 r. Cushioned divan	3·00	4·50

1981. British Royal Wedding. Multicoloured.

918	1 r. Type **168**	15	15
919	2 r. Buckingham Palace	25	25
920	5 r. Prince Charle, polo player	40	50

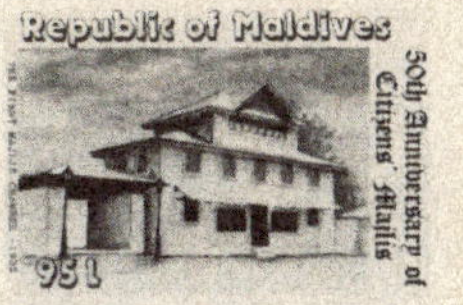

169 First Majlis Chamber

1981. 50th Anniv of Citizens' Majlis (grievance rights). Multicoloured.

922	95 l. Type **169**	30	30
923	1 r. Sultan Muhammed Shamsuddin III	35	35

170 "Self-portrait with a Palette"

171 Airmail Envelope

1981. Birth Centenary of Pablo Picasso. Mult.

925	5 l. Type **170**	15	10
926	10 l. "Woman in Blue"	20	10
927	25 l. "Boy with Pipe"	35	10
928	30 l. "Card Player"	35	10
929	90 l. "Sailor"	65	40
930	3 r. "Self-portrait"	1·25	1·25
931	5 r. "Harlequin"	1·75	1·75

1981. 75th Anniv of Postal Service.

933	**171** 25 l. multicoloured	10	10
934	75 l. multicoloured	20	25
935	5 r. multicoloured	70	1·25

172 Boeing 737 taking off

1981. Male International Airport. Multicoloured.

936	5 l. Type **172**	20	20
937	20 l. Passengers leaving Boeing 737	55	20
938	1 r. 80 Refuelling	1·25	1·50
939	4 r. Plan of airport	1·50	2·50

173 Homer

174 Preparation of Maldive Fish

1981. International Year of Disabled People. Multicoloured.

941	2 l. Type **173**	10	10
942	5 l. Miguel Cervantes	10	10
943	1 r. Beethoven	2·00	85
944	5 r. Van Gogh	3·00	5·00

1981. Decade for Women. Multicoloured.

946	20 l. Type **174**	10	10
947	90 l. 16th-century Maldive women	25	25
948	1 r. Farming	30	30
949	2 r. Coir rope-making	55	1·10

MINIMUM PRICE

The minimum price quoted is 10p which represents a handling charge rather than a basis for valuing common stamps. For further notes about prices see introductory pages.

175 Collecting Bait

1982. Fishermen's Day. Multicoloured.

950	5 l. Type **175**	35	15
951	15 l. Fishing boats	65	25
952	90 l. Fisherman with catch	1·25	60
953	1 r. 30 Sorting fish	1·50	1·10

176 Bread Fruit

1981. World Food Day. Multicoloured.

955	10 l. Type **176**	25	10
956	25 l. Hen with chicks	60	15
957	30 l. Maize	60	20
958	75 l. Skipjack tuna	1·75	65
959	1 r. Pumpkin	2·00	70
960	2 r. Coconuts	2·25	2·75

177 Pluto and Cat

1982. 50th Anniv of Pluto (Walt Disney Cartoon Character).

962	**177**	4 r. multicoloured	3·00	2·75

178 Balmoral

1982. 21st Birthday of Princess of Wales. Mult.

964	95 l. Type **178**	20	20
965	3 r. Prince and Princess of Wales	60	65
966	5 r. Princess on aircraft steps	1·00	95

179 Scout saluting and Camp-site

1983. 75th Anniv of Boy Scout Movement. Multicoloured.

968	1 r. 30 Type **179**	40	45
969	1 r. 80 Lighting a fire	50	60
970	4 r. Life-saving	1·10	1·40
971	5 r. Map-reading	1·40	1·75

180 Footballer

1982. World Cup Football Championship, Spain.

973	**180**	90 l. multicoloured	1·25	60
974	–	1 r. 50 multicoloured	1·75	1·10
975	–	3 r. multicoloured	2·50	1·75
976	–	5 r. multicoloured	3·25	2·50

DESIGNS: 1 r. 50 to 5 r. Various footballers.

1982. Birth of Prince William of Wales. Nos. 964/6 optd **ROYAL BABY 21.6.82.**

978	95 l. Type **178**	15	20
979	3 r. Prince and Princess of Wales	45	65
980	5 r. Princess on aircraft steps	70	95

181 Basic Education Scheme

1983. National Education. Multicoloured.

982	90 l. Type **181**	15	25
983	95 l. Primary education	15	25
984	1 r. 30 Teacher training	20	30
985	2 r. 50 Printing educational material	40	60

182 Koch isolates the Bacillus

183 Blohm and Voss Seaplane "Nordsee"

1983. Centenary of Robert Koch's Discovery of Tubercle Bacillus. Multicoloured.

987	5 l. Type **182**	10	15
988	15 l. Micro-organism and microscope	15	15
989	95 l. Dr. Robert Koch in 1905	35	45
990	3 r. Dr. Koch and plates from publication	85	1·50

1983. Bicentenary of Manned Flight. Mult.

992	90 l. Type **183**	2·25	70
993	1 r. 45 Macchi Castoldi MC.72 seaplane	2·75	1·75
994	4 r. Boeing F4B-3 biplane fighter	4·50	3·25
995	5 r. Renard and Krebs airship "La France"	4·50	3·50

184 "Curved Dash" Oldsmobile, 1902

1983. Classic Motor Cars. Multicoloured.

997	5 l. Type **184**	20	40
998	30 l. Aston Martin "Tourer", 1932	60	40
999	40 l. Lamborghini "Muira", 1966	60	45
1000	1 r. Mercedes-Benz "300SL", 1945	1·00	70
1001	1 r. 40 Stutz "Bearcat", 1913	1·25	2·00
1002	5 r. Lotus "Elite", 1958	2·75	4·25

185 Rough-toothed Dolphin

1983. Marine Mammals. Multicoloured.

1004	30 l. Type **185**	1·60	60
1005	40 l. Indo-Pacific hump-backed dolphin	1·60	65
1006	4 r. Finless porpoise	5·00	4·00
1007	6 r. Pygmy sperm whale	10·00	7·00

186 Dish Aerial

1983. World Communications Year. Multicoloured.

1009	50 l. Type **186**	40	20
1010	1 r. Land, sea and air communications	1·00	60
1011	2 r. Ship-to-shore communications	1·40	1·50
1012	10 r. Air traffic controller	3·75	6·50

187 "La Donna Gravida"

1983. 500th Birth Anniv of Raphael. Mult.

1014	90 l. Type **187**	25	25
1015	3 r. "Giovanna d'Aragona" (detail)	75	1·25
1016	4 r. "Woman with Unicorn"	1·00	1·75
1017	6 r. "La Muta"	1·25	2·25

188 Refugee Camp

1983. Solidarity with the Palestinian People. Multicoloured.

1019	4 r. Type **188**	1·50	2·00
1020	5 r. Refugee holding dead child	1·60	2·00
1021	6 r. Child carrying food	1·90	2·50

189 Education Facilities

1983. National Development Programme. Multicoloured.

1022	7 l. Type **189**	20	10
1023	10 l. Health service and education	30	10
1024	5 r. Growing more food	1·50	1·25
1025	6 r. Fisheries development	2·00	1·50

190 Baseball

194 Island Resort and Common Terns

193 Hands breaking Manacles

1984. Olympic Games, Los Angeles. Multicoloured.

1027	50 l. Type **190**	25	15
1028	1 r. 55 Backstroke swimming	55	40
1029	3 r. Judo	1·00	90
1030	4 r. Shot-putting	1·40	1·40

1984. U.P.U. Congress, Hamburg. Nos. 994/5 optd **19th UPU CONGRESS HAMBURG.**

1032	4 r. Boeing "F4B-3"	1·40	1·40
1033	5 r. "La France" airship	1·60	1·60

1984. Surch **Rf1.45.** (a) Nos. 964/6.

1035	1 r. 45 on 95 l. Type **178**	2·50	1·75
1036	1 r. 45 on 3 r. Prince and Princess of Wales	2·50	1·75
1037	1 r. 45 on 5 r. Princess on aircraft steps	2·50	1·75

(b) Nos. 978/80.

1039	1 r. 45 on 95 l. Type **178**	2·50	1·75
1040	1 r. 45 on 3 r. Prince and Princess of Wales	2·50	1·75
1041	1 r. 45 on 5 r. Princess on aircraft steps	2·50	1·75

1984. Namibia Day. Multicoloured.

1043	6 r. Type **193**	1·50	1·60
1044	8 r. Namibian family	2·00	2·10

1984. Tourism. Multicoloured.

1046	7 l. Type **194**	30	10
1047	15 l. Dhow	30	10
1048	20 l. Snorkelling	30	10
1049	2 r. Wind-surfing	75	40
1050	4 r. Aqualung diving	1·25	75
1051	6 r. Night fishing	2·00	1·25
1052	8 r. Game fishing	2·25	1·50
1053	10 r. Turtle on beach	2·50	1·75

195 Frangipani

1984. "Ausipex" International Stamp Exhibition, Melbourne. Multicoloured.

1054	5 r. Type **195**	2·25	1·75
1055	10 r. Cooktown orchid	4·75	3·75

196 Facade of Male Mosque

1984. Opening of Islamic Centre. Multicoloured.

1057	2 r. Type **196**	45	50
1058	5 r. Male Mosque and minaret (vert)	1·10	1·25

197 Air Maldives Boeing 737

1984. 40th Anniv of I.C.A.O. Multicoloured.

1059	7 l. Type **197**	40	15
1060	4 r. Air Lanka Lockheed L-1011 Tristar	2·25	1·25
1061	6 r. Alitalia Douglas DC-10-30	2·75	1·60
1062	8 r. L.T.U. Lockheed L-1011 Tristar	3·00	2·25

198 Daisy Duck

1984. 50th Birthday of Donald Duck. Walt Disney Cartoon Characters. Multicoloured.

1064	3 l. Type **198**	10	10
1065	4 l. Huey, Dewey and Louie	10	10
1066	5 l. Ludwig von Drake	10	10
1067	10 l. Gyro Gearloose	10	10
1068	15 l. Uncle Scrooge painting self-portrait	15	10
1069	25 l. Donald Duck with camera	15	10
1070	5 r. Donald Duck and Gus Goose	2·25	1·25
1071	8 r. Gladstone Gander	2·50	2·00
1072	10 r. Grandma Duck	3·00	2·50

199 "The Day" (detail)

200 "Edmond Iduranty" (Degas)

1984. 450th Death Anniv of Correggio (artist). Mult.

1075	5 r. Type **199**	1·25	1·25
1076	10 r. "The Night" (detail)	1·75	2·00

1984. 150th Birth Anniv of Edgar Degas (artist). Multicoloured.

1078	75 l. Type **200**	20	20
1079	2 r. "James Tissot"	50	50
1080	5 r. "Achille de Gas in Uniform"	1·25	1·25
1081	10 r. "Lady with Chrysanthemums"	2·50	2·75

201 Pale-footed Shearwater

204 Queen Elizabeth the Queen Mother, 1981

202 Squad Drilling

1985. Birth Bicentenary of John J. Audubon (ornithologist) (1st issue). Designs showing original paintings. Multicoloured.

1083	3 r. Type **201**	1·75	80
1084	3 r. 50 Little grebe (horiz)	2·00	90
1085	4 r. Common cormorant	2·00	1·00
1086	4 r. 50 White-faced storm petrel (horiz)	2·00	1·10

See also Nos. 1192/9.

1985. National Security Service. Multicoloured.

1088	15 l. Type **202**	40	10
1089	20 l. Combat patrol	40	10
1090	1 r. Fire fighting	1·75	40
1091	2 r. Coastguard cutter	2·25	1·00
1092	10 r. Independence Day Parade (vert)	3·00	3·50

1985. Olympic Games Gold Medal Winners, Los Angeles. Nos. 1027/30 optd.

1094	50 l. Type **190** (optd **JAPAN**)	15	10
1095	1 r. 55 Backstroke swimming (optd **GOLD MEDALIST THERESA ANDREWS USA**)	35	40
1096	3 r. Judo (optd **GOLD MEDALIST FRANK WIENEKE USA**)	65	75
1097	4 r. Shot-putting (optd **GOLD MEDALIST CLAUDIA LOCH WEST GERMANY**)	90	95

1985. Life and Times of Queen Elizabeth the Queen Mother. Multicoloured.

1099	3 r. Type **204**	45	60
1100	5 r. Visiting the Middlesex Hospital (horiz)	65	1·00
1101	7 r. The Queen Mother	85	1·25

Stamps as Nos. 1099/1101 but with face values of 1 r., 4 r. and 10 r. exist from additional sheetlets with changed background colours.

1985. 300th Birth Anniversary of Johann Sebastian Bach (composer). As T **206** of Antigua. Mult.

1103	15 l. Lira da braccio	10	10
1104	2 r. Tenor oboe	50	45
1105	4 r. Serpent	90	85
1106	10 r. Table organ	1·90	2·25

205 Mas Odi (fishing boat)

1985. Maldives Ships and Boats. Multicoloured.

1108	5 l. Type **205**	10	10
1109	5 l. Battela (dhow)	10	10
1110	10 l. Addu odi (dhow)	10	10
1111	2 r. 60 Modern dhoni (fishing boat)	1·25	1·50
1112	2 r. 70 Mas dhoni (fishing boat)	1·25	1·50
1113	3 r. Baththeli dhoni	1·40	1·60
1114	5 r. "Inter I" (inter-island vessel)	2·25	2·75
1115	10 r. Dhoni-style yacht	4·00	6·00

206 Windsurfing

207 United Nations Building, New York

1985. 10th Anniv of World Tourism Organization. Multicoloured.

1116	6 r. Type **206**	1·75	1·75
1117	8 r. Scuba diving	2·00	2·00

1985. 40th Anniv of U.N.O. and International Peace Year. Multicoloured.

1119	15 l. Type **207**	10	10
1120	2 r. Hands releasing peace dove	40	45
1121	4 r. U.N. Security Council meeting (horiz)	80	1·00
1122	10 r. Lion and lamb	1·90	2·50

208 Maldivian Delegate voting in U.N. General Assembly

1985. 20th Anniv of United Nations Membership. Multicoloured.

1124	20 l. Type **208**	10	10
1125	15 r. U.N. and Maldivian flags, and U.N. Building, New York	2·75	3·50

209 Youths playing Drums

1985. International Youth Year. Multicoloured.

1126	90 l. Type **209**	15	20
1127	6 r. Tug-of-war	1·00	1·40
1128	10 r. Community service (vert)	1·60	2·25

210 Quotation and Flags of Member Nations

1985. 1st Summit Meeting of South Asian Association for Regional Co-operation, Dhaka, Bangladesh.

1130	**210** 3 r. multicoloured	1·50	1·25

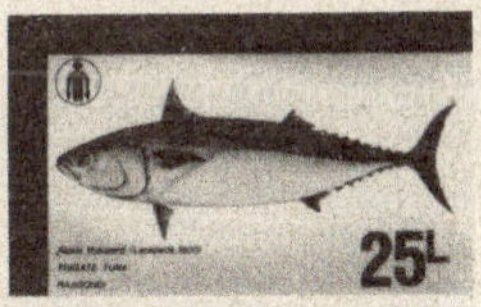

211 Mackerel Frigate

1985. Fishermen's Day. Species of Tuna. Multicoloured.

1131	25 l. Type **211**	35	10
1132	75 l. Kawakawa ("Little tuna")	65	15
1133	3 r. Dog-toothed tuna	2·00	75
1134	5 r. Yellow-finned tuna	2·50	1·25

1985. 150th Birth Anniv of Mark Twain. Designs as T **118** of Anguilla, showing Walt Disney cartoon characters illustrating various Mark Twain quotations. Multicoloured.

1136	2 l. Winnie the Pooh	10	10
1137	3 l. Gepetto and Figaro the cat	10	10
1138	4 l. Goofy and basket of broken eggs	10	10
1139	20 l. Goofy as doctor scolding Donald Duck	25	10
1140	4 r. Mowgli and King Louis	1·40	1·75
1141	13 r. The wicked Queen and mirror	5·00	7·00

1985. Birth Bicentenaries of Grimm Brothers (folklorists). Designs as T **119** of Anguilla, showing Walt Disney cartoon characters in scenes from "Dr. Knowall". Multicoloured.

1143	1 l. Donald Duck as Crabb driving oxcart	10	10
1144	5 l. Donald Duck as Dr. Knowall	10	10
1145	10 l. Dr. Knowall in surgery	10	10
1146	15 l. Dr. Knowall with Uncle Scrooge as a lord	10	10
1147	3 r. Dr. and Mrs. Knowall in pony and trap	1·10	1·50
1148	15 r. Dr. Knowall and thief	5·50	7·00

1986. Appearance of Halley's Comet (1st issue). As T **123** of Anguilla. Multicoloured.

1150	20 l. N.A.S.A. space telescope and Comet	50	25
1151	1 r. 50 E.S.A. "Giotto" spacecraft and Comet	1·25	1·50
1152	2 r. Japanese "Planet A" spacecraft and Comet	1·50	1·75
1153	4 r. Edmond Halley and Stonehenge	2·75	3·25
1154	5 r. Russian "Vega" spacecraft and Comet	3·00	3·50

See also Nos. 1206/10.

1986. Centenary of Statue of Liberty. Multicoloured. As T **211** of Dominica, showing the Statue of Liberty and immigrants to the U.S.A.

1156	50 l. Walter Gropius (architect)	40	30
1157	70 l. John Lennon (musician)	1·50	1·00
1158	1 r. George Balanchine (choreographer)	1·50	1·00
1159	10 r. Franz Werfel (writer)	3·75	6·50

1986. "Ameripex" International Stamp Exhibition, Chicago. As T **212** of Dominica, showing Walt Disney cartoon characters and U.S.A. stamps. Multicoloured.

1161	3 l. Johnny Appleseed and 1966 Johnny Appleseed stamp	10	10
1162	4 l. Paul Bunyan and 1958 Forest Conservation stamp	10	10
1163	5 l. Casey and 1969 Professional Baseball Centenary stamp	10	10
1164	10 l. Ichabod Crane and 1974 "Legend of Sleepy Hollow" stamp	10	10
1165	15 l. John Henry and 1944 75th Anniv of completion of First Transcontinental Railroad stamp	15	15
1166	20 l. Windwagon Smith and 1954 Kansas Territory Centenary stamp	15	15
1167	13 r. Mike Fink and 1970 Great Northwest stamp	6·50	6·50
1168	14 r. Casey Jones and 1950 Railroad Engineers stamp	7·50	7·50

1986. 60th Birthday of Queen Elizabeth II. As T **125** of Anguilla.

1170	1 r. black and yellow	30	25
1171	2 r. multicoloured	40	55
1172	12 r. multicoloured	1·50	2·50

DESIGNS: 1 r. Royal Family at Girl Guides Rally, 1938; 2 r. Queen in Canada; 12 r. At Sandringham, 1970.

212 Player running with Ball

1986. World Cup Football Championship, Mexico. Multicoloured.

1174	15 l. Type **212**	75	30
1175	2 r. Player gaining control of ball	2·50	1·75
1176	4 r. Two players competing for ball	4·00	3·50
1177	10 r. Player bouncing ball on knee	7·50	8·00

1986. Royal Wedding. As T **213** of Antigua. Multicoloured.

1179	10 l. Prince Andrew and Miss Sarah Ferguson	15	10
1180	2 r. Prince Andrew	70	70
1181	12 r. Prince Andrew in naval uniform	3·00	3·75

213 Moorish Idol and Sea Fan

1986. Marine Wildlife. Multicoloured.

1183	50 l. Type **213**	1·25	40
1184	90 l. Regal angelfish	1·75	55
1185	1 r. Maldive anemonefish	1·75	55
1186	2 r. Tiger cowrie and stinging coral	2·25	1·60
1187	3 r. Emperor angelfish and staghorn coral	2·75	2·00
1188	4 r. Black-naped tern	3·50	2·75
1189	5 r. Fiddler crab and staghorn coral	3·50	2·75
1190	10 r. Hawksbill turtle	4·00	5·00

1986. Birth Bicentenary (1985) of John J. Audubon (ornithologist) (2nd issue). As T **201** showing original paintings. Multicoloured.

1192	3 l. Little blue heron (horiz)	30	40
1193	4 l. White-tailed kite	30	40
1194	5 l. Greater shearwater (horiz)	30	40
1195	10 l. Magnificent frigate bird	40	40
1196	15 l. Black-necked grebe	70	40
1197	20 l. Goosander	75	40
1198	13 r. Peregrine falcon (horiz)	5·50	6·50
1199	14 r. Prairie chicken (horiz)	5·50	6·50

1986. World Cup Football Championship Winners, Mexico. Nos. 1174/7 optd **WINNERS Argentina 3 W. Germany 2**.

1201	15 l. Type **212**	30	30
1202	2 r. Player gaining control of ball	1·10	1·10
1203	4 r. Two players competing for ball	1·75	2·00
1204	10 r. Player bouncing ball on knee	3·25	4·25

1986. Appearance of Halley's Comet (2nd issue). Nos. 1150/4 optd as **218** of Antigua.

1206	20 l. N.A.S.A. space telescope and Comet	65	40
1207	1 r. 50 E.S.A. "Giotto" spacecraft and Comet	1·25	1·00
1208	2 r. Japanese "Planet A" spacecraft and Comet	1·50	1·50
1209	4 r. Edmond Halley and Stonehenge	2·00	2·25
1210	5 r. Russia "Vega" spacecraft and Comet	2·00	2·25

214 Servicing Aircraft

216 Ixora

215 "Hypholoma fasciculare"

1986. 40th Anniv of U.N.E.S.C.O. Multicoloured.

1212	1 r. Type **214**	70	30
1213	2 r. Boat building	90	90
1214	3 r. Children in classroom	1·00	1·25
1215	5 r. Student in laboratory	1·40	2·00

1986. Fungi of the Maldives. Multicoloured.

1217	15 l. Type **215**	80	25
1218	50 l. "Kuehneromyces mutabilis" (vert)	1·50	45
1219	1 r. "Amanita muscaria" (vert)	1·75	60
1220	2 r. "Agaricus campestris"	2·50	1·50
1221	3 r. "Amanita pantherina" (vert)	2·50	1·75
1222	4 r. "Coprinus comatus" (vert)	2·50	2·25
1223	5 r. "Gymnopilus junonius" ("Pholiota spectabilis")	2·50	2·75
1224	10 r. "Pluteus cervinus"	3·75	4·50

1987. Flowers. Multicoloured.

1226	10 l. Type **216**	10	10
1227	20 l. Frangipani	15	10
1228	50 l. Crinum	1·25	50
1229	2 r. Pink rose	75	80
1230	4 r. Flamboyant flower	1·00	1·50
1231	10 r. Ground orchid	5·00	6·00

217 Guides studying Wild Flowers

1987. 75th Anniv (1985) of Girl Guide Movement. Multicoloured.

1233	15 l. Type **217**	30	20
1234	2 r. Guides with pet rabbits	70	80
1235	4 r. Guide observing white spoonbill	2·00	2·00
1236	12 r. Lady Baden-Powell and Guide flag	3·00	4·50

218 "Thespesia populnea"

219 "Precis octavia"

1987. Trees and Plants. Multicoloured.

1238	50 l. Type **218**	10	10
1239	1 r. "Cocos nucifera"	15	20
1240	2 r. "Calophyllum mophyllum"	30	40
1241	3 r. "Xanthosoma indica" (horiz)	45	60
1242	5 r. "Ipomoea batatas" (horiz)	80	1·10
1243	7 r. "Artocarpus altilis"	1·10	1·75

No. 1241 is inscr "Xyanthosomaindica" in error.

1987. America's Cup Yachting Championship. As T **222** of Antigua. Multicoloured.

1245	15 l. "Intrepid", 1970	10	10
1246	1 r. "France II", 1974	20	20
1247	2 r. "Gretel", 1962	40	60
1248	12 r. "Volunteer", 1887	2·00	3·00

1987. Butterflies. Multicoloured.

1250	15 l. Type **219**	45	30
1251	20 l. "Atrophaneura hector"	45	30
1252	50 l. "Teinopalpus imperialis"	75	40
1253	1 r. "Kallima horsfieldi"	1·00	45

1254	2 r. "Cethosia biblis"	1·60	1·25
1255	4 r. "Idea jasonia"	2·50	2·25
1256	7 r. "Papilio memnon"	3·50	4·00
1257	10 r. "Aeropetes tulbaghia"	4·00	5·00

220 Isaac Newton experimenting with Spectrum

1988. Great Scientific Discoveries. Multicoloured.

1259	1 r. 50 Type **220**	1·25	1·00
1260	3 r. Euclid composing "Principles of Geometry" (vert)	1·60	1·75
1261	4 r. Mendel formulating theory of Genetic Evolution (vert)	1·75	2·00
1262	5 r. Galileo and moons of Jupiter	3·00	3·00

221 Donald Duck and Weather Satellite

1988. Space Exploration. Walt Disney cartoon characters. Multicoloured.

1264	3 l. Type **221**	10	10
1265	4 l. Minnie Mouse and navigation satellite	10	10
1266	5 l. Mickey Mouse's nephews talking via communication satellite	10	10
1267	10 l. Goofy in lunar rover (vert)	10	10
1268	20 l. Minnie Mouse delivering pizza to flying saucer (vert)	10	10
1269	13 r. Mickey Mouse directing spacecraft docking (vert)	5·00	5·00
1270	14 r. Mickey Mouse and "Voyager 2"	5·00	5·00

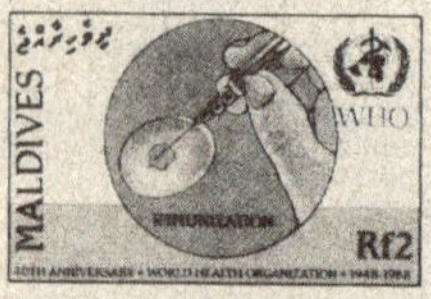

222 Syringe and Bacterium ("Immunization")

1988. 40th Anniv of W.H.O. Multicoloured.

1272	2 r. Type **222**	35	40
1273	4 r. Tap ("Clean Water")	60	85

223 Water Droplet and Atoll

1988. World Environment Day (1987). Mult.

1274	15 l. Type **223**	10	10
1275	75 l. Coral reef	20	30
1276	2 r. Audubon's shearwaters in flight	75	1·25

224 Globe, Carrier Pigeon and Letter

226 Discus-throwing

1988. Transport and Telecommunications Decade. Each showing central globe. Multicoloured.

1278	2 r. Type **224**	60	65
1279	3 r. Dish aerial and girl using telephone	1·00	1·10
1280	5 r. Satellite, television, telephone and antenna tower	1·75	2·00
1281	10 r. Car, ship and Lockheed Tristar airliner	5·00	5·50

1988. Royal Ruby Wedding. Nos. 1170/2 optd **40TH WEDDING ANNIVERSARY H.M. QUEEN ELIZABETH II H.R.H. THE DUKE OF EDINBURGH.**

1282	1 r. black and yellow	35	25
1283	2 r. multicoloured	50	60
1284	12 r. multicoloured	2·50	3·50

1988. Olympic Games, Seoul. Multicoloured.

1286	15 l. Type **226**	10	10
1287	2 r. 100 metres race	40	40
1288	4 r. Gymnastics (horiz)	70	80
1289	12 r. Three-day equestrian event (horiz)	2·25	3·25

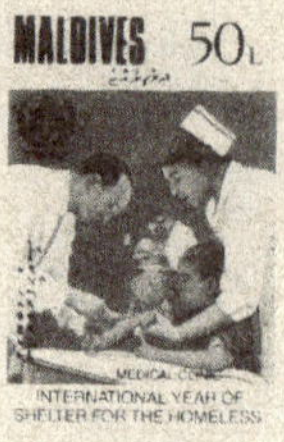

227 Immunization at Clinic

230 Pres. Kennedy and Launch of "Apollo" Spacecraft

228 Breadfruit

1988. Int Year of Shelter for the Homeless. Mult.

1291	50 l. Type **227**	30	30
1292	3 r. Prefab housing estate	1·10	1·40

1988. 10th Anniv of International Fund for Agricultural Development. Multicoloured.

1294	7 r. Type **228**	1·00	1·40
1295	10 r. Mangoes (vert)	1·50	1·90

1988. World Aids Day. Nos. 1272/3 optd **WORLD AIDS DAY** and emblem.

1297	2 r. Type **222**	35	45
1298	4 r. "Tap" ("Clean Water")	65	80

1989. 25th Death Anniv (1988) of John F. Kennedy (American statesman). U.S. Space Achievements. Multicoloured.

1299	5 r. Type **230**	1·60	1·90
1300	5 r. Lunar module and astronaut on Moon	1·60	1·90
1301	5 r. Astronaut and buggy on Moon	1·60	1·90
1302	5 r. President Kennedy and spacecraft	1·60	1·90

1989. Olympic Medal Winners, Seoul. Nos. 1286/9 optd.

1304	15 l. Type **226** (optd **J. SCHULT DDR**)	20	20
1305	2 r. 100 metres race (optd **C. LEWIS USA**)	65	65
1306	4 r. Gymnastics (horiz) (optd **MEN'S ALL AROUND V. ARTEMOV USSR**)	1·25	1·25
1307	12 r. Three-day equestrian event (horiz) (optd **TEAM SHOW JUMPING W. GERMANY**)	2·75	3·50

1989. 500th Birth Anniv of Titian (artist). As T **238** of Antigua showing paintings. Multicoloured.

1309	15 l. "Benedetto Varchi"	10	10
1310	1 r. "Portrait of a Young Man"	20	15
1311	2 r. "King Francis I of France"	40	40
1312	5 r. "Pietro Aretino"	1·10	1·25
1313	15 r. "The Bravo"	5·00	6·00
1314	20 r. "The Concert" (detail)	5·50	6·50

1989. 10th Anniversary of Asia–Pacific Telecommunity. Nos. 1279/80 optd **ASIA-PACIFIC TELECOMMUNITY 10 YEARS** and emblem. Multicoloured.

1316	3 r. Dish aerial and girl using telephone	1·25	1·50
1317	5 r. Satellite, television, telephone and antenna tower	1·75	2·00

1989. Japanese Art. Paintings by Hokusai. As T **250** of Antigua. Multicoloured.

1318	15 l. "Fuji from Hodogaya"	10	10
1319	50 l. "Fuji from Lake Kawaguchi"	15	15
1320	1 r. "Fuji from Owari"	25	25
1321	2 r. "Fuji from Tsukudajima in Edo"	50	50
1322	4 r. "Fuji from a Teahouse at Yoshida"	90	90
1323	6 r. "Fuji from Tagonoura"	1·25	1·25
1324	10 r. "Fuji from Mishima-goe"	3·00	3·25
1325	12 r. "Fuji from the Sumida River in Edo"	3·00	3·25

233 Clown Triggerfish

1989. Tropical Fishes. Multicoloured.

1327	20 l. Type **233**	25	20
1328	50 l. Blue-striped snapper	35	25
1329	1 r. Powder-blue surgeonfish	45	30
1330	2 r. Oriental sweetlips	75	65
1331	3 r. Six-barred wrasse	1·00	85
1332	8 r. Thread-finned butterflyfish	2·00	2·50
1333	10 r. Bicoloured parrotfish	2·40	2·75
1334	12 r. Scarlet-finned squirrelfish	2·40	2·75

234 Goofy, Mickey and Minnie Mouse with Takuri "Type 3", 1907

1989. "World Stamp Expo '89" International Stamp Exhibition, Washington (1st issue). Designs showing Walt Disney cartoon characters with Japanese cars. Multicoloured.

1336	15 l. Type **234**	20	15
1337	50 l. Donald and Daisy Duck in Mitsubishi "Model A", 1917	40	30
1338	1 r. Goofy in Datsun "Roadstar", 1935	70	50
1339	2 r. Donald and Daisy Duck with Mazda, 1940	1·00	75
1340	4 r. Donald Duck with Nissan "Bluebird 310", 1959	1·50	1·25
1341	6 r. Donald and Daisy Duck with Subaru "360", 1958	1·75	1·75
1342	10 r. Mickey Mouse and Pluto in Honda "5800", 1966	3·25	3·75
1343	12 r. Mickey Mouse and Goofy in Daihatsu "Fellow", 1966	3·75	4·25

235 Lunar Module "Eagle"

1989. 20th Anniv of First Manned Landing on Moon. Multicoloured.

1346	1 r. Type **235**	30	20
1347	2 r. Astronaut Aldrin collecting dust samples	50	60
1348	6 r. Aldrin setting up seismometer	1·25	1·75
1349	10 r. Pres. Nixon congratulating "Apollo 11" astronauts	1·90	2·50

236 Jawaharlal Nehru with Mahatma Gandhi

1989. Anniversaries and Events. Multicoloured.

1351	20 l. Type **236** (birth cent)	90	45
1352	50 l. Opium poppies and logo (anti-drugs campaign) (vert)	90	45
1353	1 r. William Shakespeare (425th birth anniv)	90	45
1354	2 r. Storming the Bastille (bicent of French Revolution) (vert)	90	90
1355	3 r. Concorde (20th anniv of first flight)	2·50	1·75
1356	8 r. George Washington (bicent of inauguration)	2·00	2·50
1357	10 r. William Bligh (bicent of mutiny on the "Bounty")	4·00	4·00
1358	12 r. Hamburg harbour (800th anniv) (vert)	3·50	4·00

237 Sir William van Horne (Chairman of Canadian Pacific), Locomotive and Map, 1894

239 "Louis XVI in Coronation Robes" (Duplesis)

238 Bodu Thakurufaanu Memorial Centre, Utheemu

1989. Railway Pioneers. Multicoloured.

1360	10 l. Type **237**	15	15
1361	25 l. Matthew Murray (engineer) with Blenkinsop and Murray's rack locomotive, 1810	20	20
1362	50 l. Louis Favre (railway engineer) and steam locomotive entering tunnel	25	25
1363	2 r. George Stephenson (engineer) and "Locomotion", 1825	55	55
1364	6 r. Richard Trevithick and "Catch-Me-Who-Can", 1808	1·50	1·50
1365	8 r. George Nagelmackers and "Orient Express" dining car	1·75	1·75
1366	10 r. William Jessop and horse-drawn wagon, Surrey Iron Railway, 1770	2·50	2·50
1367	12 r. Isambard Brunel (engineer) and GWR steam locomotive, 1833	3·00	3·00

1990. 25th Anniv of Independence. Multicoloured.

1369	20 l. Type **238**	10	10
1370	25 l. Islamic Centre, Male	10	10
1371	50 l. National flag and logos of international organizations	10	10
1372	2 r. Presidential Palace, Male	30	40
1373	5 r. National Security Service	85	1·25

1990. Bicentenary of French Revolution and "Philexfrance '89" International Stamp Exhibition, Paris. French Paintings. Multicoloured.

1375	15 l. Type **239**	15	15
1376	50 l. "Monsieur Lavoisier and his Wife" (David)	25	25
1377	1 r. "Madame Pastoret" (David)	35	35
1378	2 r. "Oath of Lafayette, 14 July 1790" (anon)	55	70
1379	4 r. "Madame Trudaine" (David)	1·00	1·50
1380	6 r. "Chenard celebrating the Liberation of Savoy" (Boilly)	1·40	1·90
1381	10 r. "An Officer swears Allegiance to the Constitution" (anon)	2·75	3·50
1382	12 r. "Self Portrait" (David)	3·00	3·50

1990. "Stamp World London '90" International Stamp Exhibition. As T **193** of Gambia, showing Walt Disney cartoon characters playing British sports. Multicoloured.

1384	15 l. Donald Duck, Mickey Mouse and Goofy playing rugby	30	15
1385	50 l. Donald Duck and Chip-n-Dale curling	35	25
1386	1 r. Goofy playing polo	55	40
1387	2 r. Mickey Mouse and nephews playing soccer	80	70
1388	4 r. Mickey Mouse playing cricket	1·50	1·50
1389	6 r. Minnie and Mickey Mouse at Ascot races	1·90	1·90
1390	10 r. Mickey Mouse and Goofy playing tennis	3·25	3·50
1391	12 r. Donald Duck and Mickey Mouse playing bowls	3·25	3·50

240 Silhouettes of Queen Elizabeth II and Queen Victoria

1990. 150th Anniv of the Penny Black.

1393	**240**	8 r. black and green	2·25	2·50
1394	–	12 r. black and blue	2·75	3·00

DESIGN: 12 r. As Type **240**, but with position of silhouettes reversed.

1990. 90th Birthday of Queen Elizabeth the Queen Mother. As T **103** of Grenada Grenadines.

1396	6 r. black, mauve and blue	80	1·10
1397	6 r. black, mauve and blue	80	1·10
1398	6 r. black, mauve and blue	80	1·10

DESIGNS: No. 1396, Lady Elizabeth Bowes-Lyon; 1397, Lady Elizabeth Bowes-Lyon wearing headband; 1398, Lady Elizabeth Bowes-Lyon leaving for her wedding.

241 Sultan's Tomb

1990. Islamic Heritage Year. Each black and blue.

1400	1 r. Type **241**	25	35
1401	1 r. Thakurufaan's Palace	25	35
1402	1 r. Male Mosque	25	35
1403	2 r. Veranda of Friday Mosque	25	35
1404	2 r. Interior of Friday Mosque	25	35
1405	2 r. Friday Mosque and Monument	25	35

1990. 50th Anniv of Second World War. As T **101** of Grenada Grenadines. Multicoloured.

1406	15 l. Defence of Wake Island, 1941	15	15
1407	25 l. Stilwell's army in Burma, 1944	20	20
1408	50 l. Normandy offensive, 1944	25	25
1409	1 r. Capture of Saipan, 1944	40	40
1410	2 r. 50 D-Day landings, 1944	70	70
1411	3 r. 50 Allied landings in Norway, 1940	90	90
1412	4 r. Lord Mountbatten, Head of Combined Operations, 1943	1·10	1·10
1413	6 r. Japanese surrender, Tokyo Bay, 1945	1·50	1·50
1414	10 r. Potsdam Conference, 1945	2·50	2·50
1415	12 r. Allied invasion of Sicily, 1943	2·75	2·75

243 Crested Tern

1990. Birds. Multicoloured.

1417	25 l. Type **243**	15	15
1418	50 l. Koel	25	25
1419	1 r. White tern	35	35
1420	3 r. 50 Cinnamon bittern	90	1·00
1421	6 r. Sooty tern	1·40	1·60
1422	8 r. Audubon's shearwater	1·60	2·00
1423	12 r. Common noddy	2·50	3·00
1424	15 r. Lesser frigate bird	2·75	3·25

244 Emblem, Dish Aerial and Sailboards

245 "Spathoglottis plicata"

1990. 5th South Asian Association for Regional Co-operation Summit.

1426	**244** 75 l. black and orange	20	25
1427	– 3 r. 50 multicoloured	90	1·25

DESIGN: 3 r. 50, Flags of member nations.

1990. "EXPO '90" International Garden and Greenery Exhibition, Osaka. Flowers. Multicoloured.

1429	20 l. Type **245**	50	30
1430	75 l. "Hippeastrum puniceum"	70	40
1431	2 r. "Tecoma stans" (horiz)	1·00	90
1432	3 r. 50 "Catharanthus roseus" (horiz)	1·25	1·50
1433	10 r. "Ixora coccinea" (horiz)	2·50	2·75
1434	12 r. "Clitorea ternatea" (horiz)	2·75	3·00
1435	15 r. "Caesalpinia pulcherrima"	2·75	3·00

1990. International Literacy Year. As T **269** of Antigua showing Walt Disney cartoon characters illustrating fables by Aesop. Multicoloured.

1437	15 l. "The Hare and the Tortoise" (horiz)	30	15
1438	50 l. "The Town Mouse and the Country Mouse" (horiz)	50	25
1439	1 r. "The Fox and the Crow"	70	35
1440	3 r. 50 "The Travellers and the Bear" (horiz)	1·40	1·40
1441	4 r. "The Fox and the Lion" (horiz)	1·50	1·50
1442	6 r. "The Mice Meeting" (horiz)	2·00	2·00
1443	10 r. "The Fox and the Goat" (horiz)	2·50	2·75
1444	12 r. "The Dog in the Manger" (horiz)	2·50	3·00

247 East African Railways Class 31 Steam Locomotive

248 Ruud Gullit of Holland

1990. Railway Steam Locomotives. Multicoloured.

1446	20 l. Type **247**	55	30
1447	50 l. Steam locomotive, Sudan	75	45
1448	1 r. Class GM Garratt, South Africa	1·00	60
1449	3 r. 7th Class, Rhodesia	2·00	2·00
1450	5 r. Central Pacific Class No. 229, U.S.A.	2·25	2·25
1451	8 r. Reading Railroad No. 415, U.S.A.	2·50	2·75
1452	10 r. Porter narrow gauge, Canada	2·50	2·75
1453	12 r. Great Northern Railway No. 515, U.S.A.	2·50	3·00

1990. World Cup Football Championship, Italy. Multicoloured.

1455	1 r. Type **248**	75	50
1456	2 r. 50 Paul Gascoigne of England	1·25	1·25
1457	3 r. 50 Brazilian challenging Argentine player	1·60	1·60
1458	5 r. Brazilian taking control of ball	2·00	2·00
1459	7 r. Italian and Austrian jumping for header	2·50	2·50
1460	10 r. Russian being chased by Turkish player	2·75	3·00
1461	15 r. Andres Brehme of West Germany	3·00	3·25

249 Winged Euonymus

251 Greek Messenger from Marathon, 490 BC (2480th Anniv)

250 "Summer" (Rubens)

1991. Bonsai Trees and Shrubs. Multicoloured.

1463	20 l. Type **249**	30	20
1464	50 l. Japanese black pine	45	35
1465	1 r. Japanese five needle pine	70	55
1466	3 r. 50 Flowering quince	1·60	1·60
1467	5 r. Chinese elm	2·00	2·00
1468	8 r. Japanese persimmon	2·25	2·50
1469	10 r. Japanese wisteria	2·25	2·50
1470	12 r. Satsuki azalea	2·50	2·75

1991. 350th Death Anniv of Rubens. Mult.

1472	20 l. Type **250**	20	15
1473	50 l. "Landscape with Rainbow" (detail)	35	25
1474	1 r. "Wreck of Aeneas"	55	40
1475	2 r. 50 "Chateau de Steen" (detail)	1·00	1·00
1476	3 r. 50 "Landscape with Herd of Cows"	1·25	1·25
1477	7 r. "Ruins on the Palantine"	2·00	2·50
1478	10 r. "Landscape with Peasants and Cows"	2·25	2·50
1479	12 r. "Wagon fording Stream"	2·50	2·75

1991. Anniversaries and Events (1990). Mult.

1481	50 l. Type **251**	45	25
1482	1 r. Anthony Fokker in Haarlem Spin monoplane (birth centenary)	80	45
1483	3 r. 50 "Early Bird" satellite (25th anniv)	1·50	1·50
1484	7 r. Signing Reunification of Germany agreement (horiz)	1·75	2·50
1485	8 r. King John signing Magna Carta (775th anniv)	2·25	2·50
1486	10 r. Dwight D. Eisenhower (birth centenary)	2·25	2·50
1487	12 r. Sir Winston Churchill (25th death anniv)	3·25	3·50
1488	15 r. Pres. Reagan at Berlin Wall (German reunification) (horiz)	2·75	3·50

252 Arctic Iceberg and Maldives Dhoni

1991. Global Warming. Multicoloured.

1490	3 r. 50 Type **252**	1·25	1·25
1491	7 r. Antarctic iceberg and "Maldive Trader" (freighter)	2·75	2·75

253 S.A.A.R.C. Emblem and Medal

1991. Year of the Girl Child.

1492	**253** 7 r. multicoloured	1·75	1·75

254 Children on Beach

1991. Year of the Maldivian Child. Children's Paintings. Multicoloured.

1493	3 r. 50 Type **254**	1·50	1·25
1494	5 r. Children in a park	2·00	1·75
1495	10 r. Hungry child dreaming of food	3·00	3·25
1496	25 r. Scuba diver	5·50	7·00

1991. Death Centenary (1990) of Vincent van Gogh (artist). As T **278** of Antigua. Multicoloured.

1497	15 l. "Still Life: Japanese Vase with Roses and Anemones"	30	20
1498	20 l. "Still Life: Red Poppies and Daisies"	30	20
1499	2 r. "Vincent's Bedroom in Arles" (horiz)	90	80
1500	3 r. 50 "The Mulberry Tree" (horiz)	1·25	1·00
1501	7 r. "Blossoming Chestnut Branches" (horiz)	2·00	2·25
1502	10 r. "Peasant Couple going to Work" (horiz)	2·50	2·75
1503	12 r. "Still Life: Pink Roses" (horiz)	2·75	3·00
1504	15 r. "Child with Orange"	3·00	3·25

1991. 65th Birthday of Queen Elizabeth II. As T **280** of Antigua. Multicoloured.

1506	2 r. Queen at Trooping the Colour, 1990	75	60
1507	5 r. Queen with Queen Mother and Princess Margaret, 1973	1·50	1·50
1508	8 r. Queen and Prince Philip in open carriage, 1986	2·25	2·50
1509	12 r. Queen at Royal Estates Ball	2·75	3·25

1991. 10th Wedding Anniv of Prince and Princess of Wales. As T **280** of Antigua. Multicoloured.

1511	1 r. Prince and Princess skiing, 1986	30	20
1512	3 r. 50 Separate photographs of Prince, Princess and sons	1·00	90
1513	7 r. Prince Henry in Christmas play and Prince William watching polo	1·50	1·75
1514	15 r. Princess Diana at Ipswich, 1990, and Prince Charles playing polo	2·75	3·00

256 Boy painting

257 Class C57 Steam Locomotive

1991. Hummel Figurines. Multicoloured.

1516	10 l. Type **256**	10	10
1517	25 l. Boy reading at table	15	15
1518	50 l. Boy with school satchel	30	30
1519	2 r. Girl with basket	60	60
1520	3 r. 50 Boy reading	90	1·00
1521	8 r. Girl and young child reading	1·75	2·00
1522	10 r. School girls	2·00	2·25
1523	25 r. School boys	4·00	5·00

1991. "Phila Nippon '91" Int Stamp Exn, Tokyo. Japanese Steam Locomotives. Mult.

1525	15 l. Type **257**	15	15
1526	25 l. Class 6250 locomotive, 1915 (horiz)	25	25
1527	1 r. Class D51 locomotive, 1936	40	40
1528	3 r. 50 Class 8620 locomotive, 1914 (horiz)	95	1·10
1529	5 r. Class 10 locomotive, 1889 (horiz)	1·25	1·50
1530	7 r. Class C61 locomotive, 1947	1·60	1·90
1531	10 r. Class 9600 locomotive, 1913 (horiz)	2·00	2·25
1532	12 r. Class D52 locomotive, 1943 (horiz)	2·40	2·50

258 "Salamis temora" and "Vanda caerulea"

1991. Butterflies and Flowers. Multicoloured.

1534	10 l. Type **258**	40	40
1535	25 l. "Meneris tulbaghia" and "Incarvillea younghusbandii"	55	30
1536	50 l. "Polyommatus icarus" and "Campsis grandiflora"	75	40
1537	2 r. "Danaus plexippus" and "Thunbergia grandiflora"	1·25	90
1538	3 r. 50 "Colias interior" and "Medinilla magnifica"	1·75	1·75
1539	5 r. "Ascalapha ordorata" and "Meconopsis horridula"	2·00	2·00
1540	8 r. "Papilio memnon" and "Dillenia obovata"	2·50	3·00
1541	10 r. "Precis octavia" and "Thespesia populnea"	2·50	3·00

259 "H-II" Rocket

1991. Japanese Space Programme. Multicoloured.

1543	15 l. Type **259**	40	20
1544	20 l. Projected "H-II" orbiting plane	40	20
1545	2 r. Satellite "GMS-5"	1·00	75
1546	3 r. 50 Satellite "MOMO-1"	1·40	1·40
1547	7 r. Satellite "CS-3"	2·25	2·50
1548	10 r. Satellite "BS-2a, 2b"	2·50	2·75
1549	12 r. "H-I" Rocket (vert)	2·75	3·00
1550	15 r. Space Flier unit and U.S. Space shuttle	2·75	3·00

260 Williams "FW-07"

1991. Formula 1 Racing Cars. Multicoloured.

1552	20 l. Type **260**	30	20
1553	50 l. Brabham/BMW "BT50" turbo	40	30
1554	1 r. Williams/Honda "FW-11"	60	45
1555	3 r. 50 Ferrari "312 T3"	1·25	1·25
1556	5 r. Lotus/Honda "99T"	1·75	1·75
1557	7 r. Benetton/Ford "B188"	2·00	2·25
1558	10 r. Tyrrell "P34" six-wheeler	2·25	2·50
1559	21 r. Renault "RE-30B" turbo	4·00	5·00

261 "Testa Rossa", 1957

1991. Ferrari Cars. Multicoloured.

1561	5 r. Type **261**	1·50	1·75
1562	5 r. "275GTB", 1966	1·50	1·75
1563	5 r. "Aspirarta", 1951	1·50	1·75
1564	5 r. "Testarossa"	1·50	1·75
1565	5 r. Enzo Ferrari	1·50	1·75
1566	5 r. "Dino 246", 1958	1·50	1·75
1567	5 r. "Type 375", 1952	1·50	1·75
1568	5 r. Nigel Mansell's Formula 1 racing car	1·50	1·75
1569	5 r. "312T", 1975	1·50	1·75

262 Franklin D. Roosevelt

1991. 50th Anniv of Japanese Attack on Pearl Harbor. American War Leaders. Multicoloured.

1570	3 r. 50 Type **262**	1·10	1·25
1571	3 r. 50 Douglas MacArthur and map of Philippines	1·10	1·25
1572	3 r. 50 Chester Nimitz and Pacific island	1·10	1·25
1573	3 r. 50 Jonathan Wainwright and barbed wire	1·10	1·25
1574	3 r. 50 Ernest King and aircraft carrier	1·10	1·25
1575	3 r. 50 Claire Chennault and Curtiss Tomahawk II fighters	1·10	1·25
1576	3 r. 50 William Halsey and aircraft carrier	1·10	1·25
1577	3 r. 50 Marc Mitscher and aircraft carrier	1·10	1·25

1578 3 r. 50 James Doolittle and North American B-25 Mitchell bomber 1·10 1·25
1579 3 r. 50 Raymond Spruance and Douglas Dauntless dive bomber 1·10 1·25

1992. Anniversaries and Events. As T **285** of Antigua. Multicoloured.

1580 20 l. Brandenburg Gate and postcard commemorating Berlin Wall 10 10
1581 50 l. Schwarzenburg Palace 10 10
1582 1 r. Spa at Baden 15 15
1583 1 r. 75 Berlin Wall and man holding child 30 30
1584 2 r. Royal Palace, Berlin 35 35
1585 4 r. Demonstrator and border guards 75 75
1586 5 r. Viennese masonic seal 1·75 1·50
1587 6 r. De Gaulle and Normandy landings, 1944 (vert) 1·75 1·75
1588 6 r. Lilienthal's signature and "Flugzeug Nr. 16" 1·75 1·75
1589 7 r. St. Marx 1·75 1·75
1590 7 r. Trans-Siberian Railway Class VL80T electric locomotive No. 1406 (vert) 1·75 1·75
1591 8 r. Kurt Schwitters (artist) and Landesmuseum 1·75 1·75
1592 9 r. Map of Switzerland and man in Uri traditional costume 1·75 1·75
1593 10 r. De Gaulle in Madagascar, 1958 1·75 1·75
1594 10 r. Scouts exploring coral reef 2·00 2·00
1595 11 r. Scout salute and badge (vert) 2·00 2·00
1596 12 r. Trans-Siberian Railway steam locomotive 2·25 2·25
1597 15 r. Imperial German badges 2·00 2·00
1598 20 r. Josepsplatz, Vienna 2·75 2·75

ANNIVERSARIES AND EVENTS: Nos. 1580, 1583, 1585, 1597, Bicentenary of Brandenburg Gate, Berlin; Nos. 1581/2, 1584, 1586, 1589, 1598, Death bicentenary of Mozart (1991); Nos. 1587, 1593, Birth centenary of Charles de Gaulle (French statesman) (1990); No. 1588, Centenary of Otto Lilienthal's first gliding experiments; Nos. 1590, 1596, Centenary of Trans-Siberian Railway; No. 1591, 750th anniv of Hannover; No. 1592, 700th anniv of Swiss Confederation; Nos. 1594/5, 17th World Scout Jamboree, Korea.

264 Mickey Mouse on Flying Carpet, Arabia

1992. Mickey's World Tour. Designs showing Walt Disney cartoon characters in different countries. Multicoloured.

1600 25 l. Type **264** 30 20
1601 50 l. Goofy and Big Ben, Great Britain 40 25
1602 1 r. Mickey wearing clogs, Netherlands 50 35
1603 2 r. Pluto eating pasta, Italy 85 65
1604 3 r. Mickey and Donald doing Mexican hat dance 1·10 1·10
1605 3 r. 50 Mickey, Goofy and Donald as tiki, New Zealand 1·25 1·25
1606 5 r. Goofy skiing in Austrian Alps 1·50 1·50
1607 7 r. Mickey and city gate, Germany 1·75 2·00
1608 10 r. Donald as samurai, Japan 2·00 2·25
1609 12 r. Mickey as heroic statue, Russia 2·25 2·50
1610 15 r. Mickey, Donald, Goofy and Pluto as German band 2·50 2·75

265 Whimbrel **266** Powder-blue Surgeonfish

1992. Birds. Multicoloured.

1612 10 l. Type **265** 10 10
1613 25 l. Great egret 10 10
1614 50 l. Grey heron 10 10
1615 2 r. Shag 20 25
1616 3 r. 50 Roseate tern 35 40
1617 5 r. Greenshank 50 55
1617a 6 r. 50 + 50 l. Egyptian vulture 70 75
1618 8 r. Hoopoe 80 85
1619 10 r. Black-shouldered kite 1·00 1·10
1620 25 r. Scarlet ibis 2·50 2·75
1620a 30 r. Peregrine falcon 3·00 3·25
1620b 40 r. Black kite 4·00 4·25
1621 50 r. Grey plover 5·00 5·50
1621a 100 r. Common shoveler 10·00 10·50

Nos. 1617a, 1620a/b and 1621a are larger, 23×32 mm.

1992. 40th Anniv of Queen Elizabeth II's Accession. As T **288** of Antigua. Multicoloured.

1622 1 r. Palm trees on beach 40 25
1623 3 r. 50 Path leading to jetty 1·25 1·00
1624 7 r. Tropical plant 2·00 2·50
1625 10 r. Palm trees on beach (different) 2·40 3·00

1992. Fishes. Multicoloured.

1627 7 l. Type **266** 30 20
1628 20 l. Catalufa 40 25
1629 50 l. Yellow-finned tuna 55 30
1630 1 r. Twin-spotted red snapper 75 35
1631 3 r. 50 Hawaiian squirrelfish 1·50 1·25
1632 5 r. Picasso triggerfish 2·00 2·00
1633 8 r. Bennet's butterflyfish 2·25 2·50
1634 10 r. Parrotfish 2·50 2·75
1635 12 r. Coral hind 2·75 3·00
1636 15 r. Skipjack tuna 2·75 3·00

1992. International Stamp Exhibitions. As T **215** of Lesotho showing Walt Disney cartoon characters. Multicoloured. (a) "Granada '92", Spain. The Alhambra.

1638 2 r. Minnie Mouse in Court of the Lions 90 60
1639 5 r. Goofy in Lions Fountain 1·75 1·50
1640 8 r. Mickey Mouse at the Gate of Justice 2·25 2·50
1641 12 r. Donald Duck serenading Daisy at the Vermilion Towers 2·75 3·00

(b) "World Columbian Stamp Expo '92". Chicago Landmarks

1643 1 r. Mickey meeting Jean Baptiste du Sable (founder) 60 35
1644 3 r. 50 Donald Duck at Old Chicago Post Office 1·50 1·00
1645 7 r. Donald at Old Fort Dearborn 2·25 2·50
1646 15 r. Goofy in Museum of Science and Industry 3·00 3·50

On No. 1646 the design is wrongly captioned as the Science and Industry Museum.

267 Coastguard Patrol Boats

1992. Cent of National Security Service. Mult.

1648 3 r. 50 Type **267** 1·50 1·25
1649 5 r. Infantry in training 2·00 1·75
1650 10 r. Aakoatey fort 2·25 2·50
1651 15 r. Fire Service 4·50 4·75

268 Flowers of the United States of America **269** "Laetiporus sulphureus"

1992. National Flowers. Multicoloured.

1653 25 l. Type **268** 40 20
1654 50 l. Australia 60 30
1655 2 r. England 1·10 75
1656 3 r. 50 Brazil 1·50 1·25
1657 5 r. Holland 2·00 2·00
1658 8 r. France 2·25 2·50
1659 10 r. Japan 2·50 2·75
1660 15 r. Africa 2·75 3·00

1992. Fungi. Multicoloured.

1662 10 l. Type **269** 30 30
1663 25 l. "Coprinus atramentarius" 40 30
1664 50 l. "Ganoderma lucidum" 60 40
1665 3 r. 50 "Russula aurata" 1·25 1·00
1666 5 r. "Grifola umbellata" ("Polyporus umbellatus") 1·75 1·75
1667 8 r. "Suillus grevillei" 2·25 2·50
1668 10 r. "Clavaria zollingeri" 2·50 2·50
1669 25 r. "Boletus edulis" 5·00 6·00

1992. Olympic Games, Albertville and Barcelona (1st issue). As T **216** of Lesotho. Multicoloured.

1671 10 l. Pole vault 20 10
1672 25 l. Men's pommel horse (horiz) 25 15
1673 50 l. Men's shot put 30 25
1674 1 r. Men's horizontal bar (horiz) 35 30
1675 2 r. Men's triple jump (horiz) 80 65
1676 3 r. 50 Table tennis 1·10 1·10
1677 5 r. Two-man bobsled 1·40 1·40
1678 7 r. Freestyle wrestling (horiz) 1·75 2·00
1679 8 r. Freestyle ski-jump 1·75 2·00
1680 9 r. Baseball 2·00 2·25
1681 10 r. Women's cross-country Nordic skiing 2·00 2·25
1682 12 r. Men's 200 metres backstroke (horiz) 2·00 2·25

See also Nos. 1684/91.

270 Hurdling **271** Deinonychus

1992. Olympic Games, Barcelona (2nd issue). Multicoloured.

1684 10 l. Type **270** 10 10
1685 1 r. Boxing 30 30
1686 3 r. 50 Women's sprinting 80 70
1687 5 r. Discus 1·25 1·25
1688 7 r. Basketball 2·50 2·25
1689 10 r. Long-distance running 2·00 2·25
1690 12 r. Aerobic gymnastics 2·25 2·50
1691 20 r. Fencing 3·00 3·75

1992. "Genova '92" International Thematic Stamp Exhibition. Prehistoric Animals. Multicoloured.

1693 5 l. Type **271** 20 20
1694 10 l. Styracosaurus 20 20
1695 25 l. Mamenchisaurus 30 30
1696 50 l. Stenonychosaurus 30 30
1697 1 r. Parasaurolophus 40 40
1698 1 r. 25 Scelidosaurus 50 50
1699 1 r. 75 Tyrannosaurus 55 55
1700 2 r. Stegosaurus 60 60
1701 3 r. 50 Iguanodon 80 80
1702 4 r. Anatosaurus 90 90
1703 5 r. Monoclonius 1·00 1·00
1704 7 r. Tenontosaurus 1·25 1·50
1705 8 r. Brachiosaurus 1·25 1·50
1706 10 r. Euoplocephalus 1·25 1·50
1707 25 r. Triceratops 2·75 3·50
1708 50 r. Apatosaurus 5·50 6·50

1992. 60th Anniv of Goofy (Disney cartoon character). Goofy in various cartoon films. As T **258** of Dominica. Multicoloured.

1714 10 l. "Father's Weekend", 1953 10 10
1715 50 l. "Symphony Hour", 1942 35 20
1716 75 l. "Frank Duck Brings 'Em Back Alive", 1946 45 20
1717 1 r. "Crazy with the Heat", 1947 45 20
1718 2 r. "The Big Wash", 1948 70 60
1719 3 r. 50 "How to Ride a Horse", 1950 1·25 1·25
1720 5 r. "Two Gun Goofy", 1952 1·50 1·50
1721 8 r. "Saludos Amigos", 1943 (vert) 2·00 2·25
1722 10 r. "How to be a Detective", 1952 2·00 2·25
1723 12 r. "For Whom the Bulls Toil", 1953 2·25 2·50
1724 15 r. "Double Dribble", 1946 (vert) 2·25 2·50

276 Minnie Mouse in "Le Missioner" (Toulouse-Lautrec)

1992. Opening of Euro-Disney Resort, France. Disney cartoon characters superimposed on Impressionist paintings. Multicoloured.

1726 5 r. Type **276** 1·40 1·50
1727 5 r. Goofy in "The Card Players" (Cezanne) 1·40 1·50
1728 5 r. Mickey and Minnie Mouse in "The Cafe Terrace, Place du Forum" (Van Gogh) 1·40 1·50
1729 5 r. Mickey in "The Bridge at Langlois" (Van Gogh) 1·40 1·50
1730 5 r. Goofy in "Chocolate Dancing" (Toulouse-Lautrec) 1·40 1·50
1731 5 r. Mickey and Minnie in "The Seine at Asnieres" (Renoir) 1·40 1·50
1732 5 r. Minnie in "Ball at the Moulin Rouge" (Toulouse-Lautrec) 1·40 1·50
1733 5 r. Mickey in "Wheatfield with Cypresses" (Van Gogh) 1·40 1·50
1734 5 r. Minnie in "When will you Marry?" (Gauguin) 1·40 1·50

277 Rivers

1992. South Asian Association for Regional Co-operation Year of the Environment. Natural and Polluted Environments. Multicoloured.

1736 25 l. Type **277** 15 10
1737 50 l. Beaches 25 10
1738 5 r. Oceans 80 1·00
1739 10 r. Weather 1·50 2·00

278 Jurgen Klinsmann (Germany)

1993. World Cup Football Championship, U.S.A. (1994) (1st issue). German Players and Officials. Multicoloured.

1740 10 l. Type **278** 15 20
1741 25 l. Pierre Littbarski 20 20
1742 50 l. Lothar Matthaus 30 20
1743 1 r. Rudi Voller 35 25
1744 2 r. Thomas Hassler 60 60
1745 3 r. 50 Thomas Berthold 1·00 1·00
1746 4 r. Jurgen Kohler 1·25 1·25
1747 5 r. Berti Vogts 1·40 1·40
1748 6 r. Bodo Illgner 1·60 1·90
1749 7 r. Klaus Augenthaler 1·75 2·00
1750 8 r. Franz Beckenbauer 1·75 2·00
1751 10 r. Andreas Brehme 2·00 2·25
1752 12 r. Guido Buchwald 2·00 2·50

See also Nos. 1990/7 and 2089/2100.

279 German Navy Airship L-13 bombing London, 1914–18

1993. Anniversaries and Events. Mult.

1754 1 r. Type **279** 45 30
1755 3 r. 50 Radio telescope 70 70
1756 3 r. 50 Chancellor Adenauer and Pres. de Gaulle 70 70
1757 6 r. Indian rhinoceros 1·50 1·50
1758 6 r. Columbus and globe 1·25 1·25
1759 7 r. Conference emblems 1·00 1·00
1760 8 r. Green seaturtle 1·40 1·40
1761 10 r. "America" (yacht), 1851 1·75 1·75
1762 10 r. Melvin Jones (founder) and emblem 1·75 1·75
1763 12 r. Columbus landing on San Salvador 1·75 1·75
1764 15 r. "Voyager I" approaching Saturn 3·00 3·00
1765 15 r. Adenauer, N.A.T.O. flag and Lockheed Starfighter aircraft 3·00 3·00
1766 20 r. "Graf Zeppelin" over New York, 1929 3·25 3·25

ANNIVERSARIES AND EVENTS: Nos. 1754, 1766, 75th death anniv of Count Ferdinand von Zeppelin; Nos. 1755, 1764, International Space Year; Nos. 1756, 1765, 25th death anniv of Konrad Adenauer; Nos. 1757, 1760, Earth Summit '92, Rio; Nos. 1758, 1763, 500th anniv of discovery of America by Columbus; No. 1759, International Conference on Nutrition, Rome; No. 1761, Americas Cup Yachting Championship; No. 1762, 75th anniv of International Association of Lions Clubs.

1993. 15th Death Anniv of Elvis Presley (singer). As T **260** of Dominica. Mult.

1768 3 r. 50 Elvis Presley 60 60
1769 3 r. 50 Elvis with guitar 60 60
1770 3 r. 50 Elvis with microphone 60 60

1993. Bicentenary of the Louvre, Paris. As T **305** of Antigua. Multicoloured.

1771 8 r. "The Study" (Fragonard) 90 95
1772 8 r. "Denis Diderot" (Fragonard) 90 95
1773 8 r. "Marie-Madelaine Guimard" (Fragonard) 90 95
1774 8 r. "Inspiration" (Fragonard) 90 95
1775 8 r. "Waterfalls, Tivoli" (Fragonard) 90 95
1776 8 r. "The Music Lesson" (Fragonard) 90 95
1777 8 r. "The Bolt" (Fragonard) 90 95
1778 8 r. "Blind-man's Buff" (Fragonard) 90 95
1779 8 r. "Self-portrait" (Corot) 90 95
1780 8 r. "Woman in Blue" (Corot) 90 95
1781 8 r. "Woman with a Pearl" (Corot) 90 95
1782 8 r. "Young Girl at her Toilet" (Corot) 90 95
1783 8 r. "Haydee" (Corot) 90 95
1784 8 r. "Chartres Cathedral" (Corot) 90 95
1785 8 r. "The Belfry of Douai" (Corot) 90 95
1786 8 r. "The Bridge of Mantes" (Corot) 90 95
1787 8 r. "Madame Seriziat" (David) 90 95
1788 8 r. "Pierre Seriziat" (David) 90 95
1789 8 r. "Madame De Verninac" (David) 90 95
1790 8 r. "Madame Recamier" (David) 90 95
1791 8 r. "Self-portrait" (David) 90 95
1792 8 r. "General Bonaparte" (David) 90 95

1793	8 r. "The Lictors bringing Brutus his Son's Body" (David) (left detail)	90	95
1794	8 r. "The Lictors bringing Brutus his Son's Body" (David) (right detail)	90	95

281 James Stewart and Marlene Dietrich ("Destry Rides Again")

1993. Famous Western Films. Multicoloured.

1796	5 r. Type **281**	80	80
1797	5 r. Gary Cooper ("The Westerner")	80	80
1798	5 r. Henry Fonda ("My Darling Clementine")	80	80
1799	5 r. Alan Ladd ("Shane")	80	80
1800	5 r. Kirk Douglas and Burt Lancaster ("Gunfight at the O.K. Corral")	80	80
1801	5 r. Steve McQueen ("The Magnificent Seven")	80	80
1802	5 r. Robert Redford and Paul Newman ("Butch Cassidy and The Sundance Kid")	80	80
1803	5 r. Jack Nicholson and Randy Quaid ("The Missouri Breaks")	80	80

1993. 40th Anniv of Coronation. As T **307** of Antigua.

1805	3 r. 50 multicoloured	80	85
1806	5 r. multicoloured	1·00	1·10
1807	10 r. blue and black	1·40	1·50
1808	10 r. blue and black	1·40	1·50

DESIGNS: No. 1805, Queen Elizabeth II at Coronation (photograph by Cecil Beaton); No. 1806, St. Edward's Crown; No. 1807, Guests in the Abbey; No. 1808, Queen Elizabeth II and Prince Philip.

282 Blue Goatfish

1993. Fishes. Multicoloured.

1809	3 r. 50 Type **282**	60	70
1810	3 r. 50 Emperor angelfish	60	70
1811	3 r. 50 Madagascar butterflyfish	60	70
1812	3 r. 50 Regal angelfish	60	70
1813	3 r. 50 Forceps fish ("Longnose butterflyfish")	60	70
1814	3 r. 50 Racoon butterflyfish	60	70
1815	3 r. 50 Harlequin filefish	60	70
1816	3 r. 50 Rectangle triggerfish	60	70
1817	3 r. 50 Yellow-tailed anemonefish	60	70
1818	3 r. 50 Clown triggerfish	60	70
1819	3 r. 50 Zebra lionfish	60	70
1820	3 r. 50 Maldive anemonefish ("Clownfish")	60	70
1821	3 r. 50 Black-faced butterflyfish	60	70
1822	3 r. 50 Bird wrasse	60	70
1823	3 r. 50 Checkerboard wrasse	60	70
1824	3 r. 50 Yellow-faced angelfish	60	70
1825	3 r. 50 Masked bannerfish	60	70
1826	3 r. 50 Thread-finned butterflyfish	60	70
1827	3 r. 50 Painted triggerfish	60	70
1828	3 r. 50 Coral hind	60	70
1829	3 r. 50 Pennant coralfish	60	70
1830	3 r. 50 Black-backed butterflyfish	60	70
1831	3 r. 50 Red-toothed triggerfish	60	70
1832	3 r. 50 Melon butterflyfish	60	70

Nos. 1809/20 and 1821/32 were printed together, se-tenant, with the backgrounds forming composite designs.

283 Gull-billed Tern

1993. Birds. Multicoloured.

1834	3 r. 50 Type **283**	60	70
1835	3 r. 50 White-tailed tropic bird	60	70
1836	3 r. 50 Great frigate bird	60	70
1837	3 r. 50 Wilson's petrel	60	70
1838	3 r. 50 White tern	60	70
1839	3 r. 50 Brown booby	60	70
1840	3 r. 50 Marsh harrier	60	70
1841	3 r. 50 Common noddy	60	70
1842	3 r. 50 Green heron ("Little Heron")	60	70
1843	3 r. 50 Turnstone	60	70
1844	3 r. 50 Curlew	60	70
1845	3 r. 50 Crab plover	60	70
1846	3 r. 50 Pallid harrier (vert)	60	70
1847	3 r. 50 Cattle egret (vert)	60	70
1848	3 r. 50 Koel (vert)	60	70
1849	3 r. 50 Tree pipit (vert)	60	70
1850	3 r. 50 Short-eared owl (vert)	60	70
1851	3 r. 50 Common kestrel ("European Kestrel") (vert)	60	70
1852	3 r. 50 Yellow wagtail (vert)	60	70
1853	3 r. 50 Grey heron ("Common Heron") (vert)	60	70
1854	3 r. 50 Black bittern (vert)	60	70
1855	3 r. 50 Common snipe (vert)	60	70
1856	3 r. 50 Little egret (vert)	60	70
1857	3 r. 50 Little stint (vert)	60	70

Nos. 1834/45 and 1846/57 were printed together, se-tenant, with the backgrounds forming composite designs.

284 Precious Wentletrap

285 Sifaka Lemur

1993. Shells. Multicoloured.

1859	7 l. Type **284**	15	20
1860	15 l. Common purple janthina	20	20
1861	50 l. Asiatic arabian cowrie	30	20
1862	3 r. 50 Common or major harp	1·00	1·00
1863	4 r. Amplustre or royal paper bubble	1·25	1·25
1864	5 r. Sieve cowrie	1·40	1·40
1865	6 r. Episcopal mitre	1·60	1·75
1866	7 r. Camp pitar venus	1·75	2·00
1867	8 r. Spotted or eyed auger	1·75	2·00
1868	10 r. Exposed cowrie	2·00	2·25
1869	12 r. Geographic map cowrie	2·00	2·50
1870	20 r. Bramble murex	2·50	3·00

1993. Endangered Species. Multicoloured.

1872	7 l. Type **285**	30	20
1873	10 l. Snow leopard	30	20
1874	15 l. Numbat	30	20
1875	25 l. Gorilla	50	30
1876	2 r. Koala	70	55
1877	3 r. 50 Cheetah	90	90
1878	5 r. Yellow-footed rock wallaby	1·25	1·25
1879	7 r. Orang-utan	1·75	2·00
1880	8 r. Black lemur	1·75	2·00
1881	10 r. Black rhinoceros	2·00	2·25
1882	15 r. Humpback whale	2·25	2·50
1883	20 r. Mauritius parakeet	2·75	3·00

286 Symbolic Heads and Arrows

287 Early Astronomical Equipment

1993. Productivity Year. Multicoloured.

1885	7 r. Type **286**	1·25	1·40
1886	10 r. Abstract	1·60	1·75

1993. Anniversaries and Events. Mult.

1887	3 r. 50 Type **287**	60	60
1888	3 r. 50 "Still Life with Pitcher and Apples" (Picasso)	60	60
1889	3 r. 50 "Zolte Roze" (Menasze Seidenbeurel)	60	60
1890	3 r. 50 Prince Naruhito and engagement photographs (horiz)	60	60
1891	5 r. "Bowls and Jug" (Picasso)	70	70
1892	5 r. Krysztofory Palace, Cracow	70	70
1893	8 r. "Jabtka i Kotara" (Waclaw Borowski)	1·25	1·25
1894	8 r. Marina Kiehl (Germany) (women's downhill skiing)	1·25	1·25
1895	10 r. "Bowls of Fruit and Loaves on a Table" (Picasso)	1·40	1·40
1896	10 r. Masako Owada and engagement photographs (horiz)	1·40	1·40
1897	15 r. American astronaut in space	1·90	1·90
1898	15 r. Vegard Ulvang (Norway) (30km cross-country skiing)	1·90	1·90

ANNIVERSARIES AND EVENTS: Nos. 1887, 1897, 450th death anniv of Copernicus (astronomer); Nos. 1888, 1891, 1895, 20th death anniv of Picasso (artist); Nos. 1889, 1892/3, "Polska '93" International Stamp Exhibition, Poznan; Nos. 1890, 1896, Marriage of Crown Prince Naruhito of Japan; Nos. 1894, 1898, Winter Olympic Games '94, Lillehammer.

288 "Limenitis procris" and "Mussaenda"

1993. Butterflies and Flowers. Multicoloured.

1900	7 l. Type **288**	20	20
1901	20 l. "Danaus limniace" and "Thevetia neriifolia"	30	20
1902	25 l. "Amblypodia centaurus" and "Clitoria ternatea"	30	20
1903	50 l. "Papilio crino" and "Crossandra infundibuliformis"	35	20
1904	5 r. "Mycalesis patnia" and "Thespesia populnia"	1·40	1·40
1905	6 r. 50 + 50 l. "Idea jasonia" and "Cassia glauca"	1·75	2·00
1906	7 r. "Catopsilia pomona" and "Calotropis"	1·75	2·00
1907	10 r. "Precis orithyia" and "Thunbergia grandiflora"	2·00	2·25
1908	12 r. "Vanessa cardui" and "Caesalpinia pulcherrima"	2·25	2·75
1909	15 r. "Papilio polymnestor" and "Nerium oleander"	2·50	3·00
1910	18 r. "Cirrochroa thais" and "Vinca rosea"	2·75	3·00
1911	20 r. "Pachliopta hector" and "Ixora coccinea"	2·75	3·00

289 Airship "Graf Zeppelin" in Searchlights

1993. Aviation Anniversaries. Multicoloured.

1913	3 r. 50 Type **289**	70	55
1914	5 r. Homing pigeon and message from Santa Catalina mail service, 1894	90	90
1915	10 r. Eckener and airship "Graf Zeppelin"	1·50	1·60
1916	15 r. Pilot's badge and loading Philadelphia–Washington mail, 1918	2·25	2·40
1917	20 r. U.S.S. "Macon" (airship) and mooring mast, 1933	2·50	2·75

ANNIVERSARIES: Nos. 1913, 1915, 1917, 125th birth anniv of Hugo Eckener (airship pioneer); Nos. 1914, 1916, Bicent of first airmail flight.

290 Ford Model "T"

1993. Centenaries of Henry Ford's First Petrol Engine (Nos. 1919/30) and Karl Benz's First Four-wheeled Car (others).

1919	**290** 3 r. 50 multicoloured	60	60
1920	– 3 r. 50 multicoloured	60	60
1921	– 3 r. 50 black and violet	60	60
1922	– 3 r. 50 multicoloured	60	60
1923	– 3 r. 50 multicoloured	60	60
1924	– 3 r. 50 multicoloured	60	60
1925	– 3 r. 50 multicoloured	60	60
1926	– 3 r. 50 multicoloured	60	60
1927	– 3 r. 50 multicoloured	60	60
1928	– 3 r. 50 multicoloured	60	60
1929	– 3 r. 50 multicoloured	60	60
1930	– 3 r. 50 black, brown and violet	60	60
1931	– 3 r. 50 multicoloured	60	60
1932	– 3 r. 50 multicoloured	60	60
1933	– 3 r. 50 green, black and violet	60	60
1934	– 3 r. 50 multicoloured	60	60
1935	– 3 r. 50 multicoloured	60	60
1936	– 3 r. 50 multicoloured	60	60
1937	– 3 r. 50 multicoloured	60	60
1938	– 3 r. 50 multicoloured	60	60
1939	– 3 r. 50 multicoloured	60	60
1940	– 3 r. 50 multicoloured	60	60
1941	– 3 r. 50 multicoloured	60	60
1942	– 3 r. 50 black, brown and violet	60	60

DESIGNS: No. 1920, Henry Ford; No. 1921, Plans of first petrol engine; No. 1922, Ford "Probe GT", 1993; No. 1923, Front of Ford "Sportsman", 1947; No. 1924, Back of Ford "Sportsman"; No. 1925, Advertisement of 1915; No. 1926, Ford "Thunderbird", 1955; No. 1927, Ford logo; No. 1928, Ford "Edsel Citation", 1958; No. 1929, Ford half-ton pickup, 1941; No. 1930, Silhouette of early Ford car; No. 1931, Daimler-Benz "Straight 8", 1937; No. 1932, Karl Benz; No. 1933, Mercedes-Benz poster; No. 1934, Mercedes "38-250SS", 1929; No. 1935, Benz "Viktoria", 1893; No. 1936, Benz logo; No. 1937, Plan of Mercedes engine; No. 1938, Mercedes-Benz "300SL Gullwing", 1952; No. 1939, Mercedes-Benz "SL", 1993; No. 1940, Front of Benz 4-cylinder car, 1906; No. 1941, Back of Benz 4-cylinder car and advertisement; No. 1942, Silhouette of early Benz car.

Nos. 1919/30 and 1931/42 were printed together, se-tenant, forming a composite design.

INDEX
Countries can be quickly located by referring to the index at the end of this volume.

291 Ivan, Sonia, Sasha and Peter in the Snow

1993. "Peter and the Wolf". Scenes from Walt Disney's cartoon film. Multicoloured.

1944	7 l. Type **291**	15	15
1945	15 l. Grandpa and Peter	20	20
1946	20 l. Peter on bridge	20	20
1947	25 l. Yascha, Vladimir and Mischa	20	20
1948	50 l. Sasha on lookout	30	20
1949	1 r. The Wolf	35	25
1950	3 r. 50 Peter dreaming	60	60
1951	3 r. 50 Peter taking gun	60	60
1952	3 r. 50 Peter with gun in snow	60	60
1953	3 r. 50 Sasha and Peter	60	60
1954	3 r. 50 Sonia and Peter	60	60
1955	3 r. 50 Peter with Ivan and Sasha	60	60
1956	3 r. 50 Ivan warning Peter of the wolf	60	60
1957	3 r. 50 Ivan, Peter and Sasha in tree	60	60
1958	3 r. 50 Wolf below tree	60	60
1959	3 r. 50 Wolf and Sonia	60	60
1960	3 r. 50 Sasha attacking the wolf	60	60
1961	3 r. 50 Sasha walking into wolf's mouth	60	60
1962	3 r. 50 Peter firing pop gun at wolf	60	60
1963	3 r. 50 Wolf chasing Sonia	60	60
1964	3 r. 50 Ivan tying rope to wolf's tail	60	60
1965	3 r. 50 Peter and Ivan hoisting wolf	60	60
1966	3 r. 50 Sasha and the hunters	60	60
1967	3 r. 50 Ivan and Peter on wolf hanging from tree	60	60

1994. Famous Paintings by Rembrandt and Matisse. As T **316** of Antigua. Multicoloured.

1969	50 l. "Girl with a Broom" (Rembrandt)	20	15
1970	2 r. "Girl with Tulips" (Matisse)	45	45
1971	3 r. 50 "Young Girl at half-open Door" (Rembrandt)	70	70
1972	3 r. 50 "Portrait of Greta Moll" (Matisse)	70	70
1973	5 r. "The Prophetess Hannah" (Rembrandt)	90	90
1974	6 r. 50 "The Idol" (Matisse)	1·25	1·50
1975	7 r. "Woman with a Pink Flower" (Rembrandt)	1·25	1·50
1976	9 r. "Mme Matisse in a Japanese Robe" (Matisse)	1·50	1·75
1977	10 r. "Portrait of Mme Matisse" (Matisse)	1·50	1·75
1978	12 r. "Lucretia" (Rembrandt)	1·75	2·00
1979	15 r. "Lady with a Ostrich Feather Fan" (Rembrandt)	2·00	2·25
1980	15 r. "The Woman with the Hat" (Matisse)	2·00	2·25

No. 1979 is inscribed "The Lady with an Ostich Feather Fan" in error.

1994. "Hong Kong '94" International Stamp Exn (1st issue). As T **317** of Antigua. Mult.

1982	4 r. Hong Kong 1983 $1 Space Museum stamp and Moon-lantern festival	50	70
1983	4 r. Maldive Islands 1976 5 r. "Viking" space mission stamp and Moon-lantern festival	50	70

Nos. 1982/3 were printed together, se-tenant, forming a composite design.

1994. "Hong Kong '94" International Stamp Exhibition (2nd issue). Ching Dynasty Cloisonne Enamelware. As T **318** of Antigua but vert. Multicoloured.

1984	2 r. Vase	35	35
1985	2 r. Flower holder	35	35
1986	2 r. Elephant with vase on back	35	35
1987	2 r. Tibetan style lama's teapot	35	35
1988	2 r. Fo-Dog	35	35
1989	2 r. Teapot with swing handle	35	35

295 Windischmann (U.S.A.) and Giannini (Italy)

297 Dome of the Rock, Jerusalem

1994. World Cup Football Championship, U.S.A. (2nd issue). Multicoloured.

1990	7 l. Type **295**	15	15
1991	20 l. Carnevale (Italy) and Gascoigne (England)	20	20
1992	25 l. England players congratulating Platt	20	20
1993	3 r. 50 Koeman (Holland) and Klinsmann (Germany)	60	60

1994 5 r. Quinn (Ireland) and Maldini (Italy) 80 80
1995 7 r. Lineker (England) 1·10 1·25
1996 15 r. Hassam (Egypt) and Moran (Ireland) 2·00 2·50
1997 18 r. Canniggia (Argentina) 2·25 2·50

1994. Centenary (1992) of Sierra Club (environmental protection society). Endangered Species. As T **320** of Antigua. Multicoloured.
1999 6 r. 50 Humpback whale 1·00 1·00
2000 6 r. 50 Ocelot crouched in grass 1·00 1·00
2001 6 r. 50 Ocelot sitting 1·00 1·00
2002 6 r. 50 Snow monkey 1·00 1·00
2003 6 r. 50 Prairie dog 1·00 1·00
2004 6 r. 50 Golden lion tamarin 1·00 1·00
2005 6 r. 50 Prairie dog eating (horiz) 1·00 1·00
2006 6 r. 50 Prairie dog outside burrow (horiz) 1·00 1·00
2007 6 r. 50 Herd of woodland caribou (horiz) 1·00 1·00
2008 6 r. 50 Woodland caribou facing left (horiz) 1·00 1·00
2009 6 r. 50 Woodland caribou facing right (horiz) 1·00 1·00
2010 6 r. 50 Pair of Galapagos penguins (horiz) 1·00 1·00
2011 6 r. 50 Galapagos penguin facing right 1·00 1·00
2012 6 r. 50 Galapagos penguin looking straight ahead 1·00 1·00
2013 6 r. 50 Bengal tiger looking straight ahead 1·00 1·00
2014 6 r. 50 Bengal tiger looking right 1·00 1·00
2015 6 r. 50 Philippine tarsier with tree trunk at left 1·00 1·00
2016 6 r. 50 Philippine tarsier with tree trunk at right 1·00 1·00
2017 6 r. 50 Head of Phillippine tarsier 1·00 1·00
2018 6 r. 50 Sierra Club centennial emblem (black, buff and green) 1·00 1·00
2019 6 r. 50 Golden lion tamarin between two branches (horiz) 1·00 1·00
2020 6 r. 50 Golden lion tamarin on tree trunk (horiz) 1·00 1·00
2021 6 r. 50 Tail fin of humpback whale and coastline (horiz) 1·00 1·00
2022 6 r. 50 Tail fin of humpback whale at night (horiz) 1·00 1·00
2023 6 r. 50 Bengal tiger (horiz) 1·00 1·00
2024 5 r. 50 Ocelot (horiz) 1·00 1·00
2025 6 r. 50 Snow monkey in water climbing out of pool (horiz) 1·00 1·00
2026 6 r. 50 Snow monkey swimming (horiz) 1·00 1·00

1994. Solidarity with the Palestinians.
2027 **297** 8 r. multicoloured 1·40 1·50

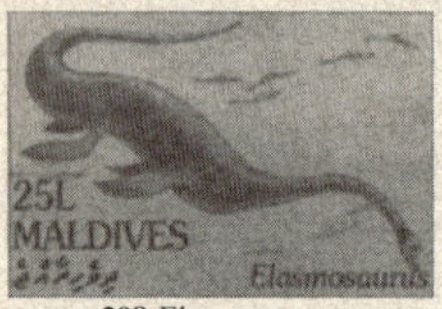

298 Elasmosaurus

1994. Prehistoric Animals. Multicoloured.
2028/59 25 l., 50 l., 1 r., 3 r. × 24, 5 r., 8 r., 10 r., 15 r., 20 r.
Set of 32 22·00 23·00

Nos. 2031/42 and 2043/54 respectively were printed together, se-tenant, forming composite designs. The species depicted are, in addition to Type **298**, Dilophosaurus, Avimimus, Dimorphodon, Megalosaurus, Kuehneosaurus, Dryosaurus, Kentrosaurus, Baraposaurus, Tenontosaurus, Elaphrosaurus, Maiasaura, Huayangosaurus, Rutiodon, Pianitzkysaurus, Quetzalcoatlus, Daspletosaurus, Pleurocoelus, Baryonyx, Pentaceratops, Kritosaurus, Microvenator, Nodosaurus, Montanaceratops, Dromiceiomimus, Dryptosaurus, Parkosaurus, Chasmosaurus, Edmontonia, Anatosaurus, Velociraptor and Spinosaurus.

299 Mallet Steam Locomotive, Indonesia

1994. Railway Locomotives of Asia. Multicoloured.
2061 25 l. Type **299** 20 20
2062 50 l. Class C62 steam locomotive, Japan, 1948 25 20
2063 1 r. Class D51 steam locomotive, Japan, 1936 (horiz) 30 20
2064 5 r. Steam locomotive, India (horiz) 90 90
2065 6 r. 50 + 50 l. Class W steam locomotive, India (horiz) 1·25 1·50
2066 6 r. 50 + 50 l. Class C53 steam locomotive, Indonesia (horiz) 1·25 1·50
2067 6 r. 50 + 50 l. Class C10 steam locomotive, Japan (horiz) 1·25 1·50
2068 6 r. 50 + 50 l. Hanomag steam locomotive, India (horiz) 1·25 1·50
2069 6 r. 50 + 50 l. "Hikari" express train, Japan (horiz) 1·25 1·50
2070 6 r. 50 + 50 l. Class C55 steam locomotive, Japan, 1935 (horiz) 1·25 1·50
2071 8 r. Class 485 electric locomotive, Japan (horiz) 1·50 1·75
2072 10 r. Class WP steam locomotive, India (horiz) 1·75 2·00
2073 15 r. Class RM steam locomotive, China (horiz) 2·00 2·25
2074 20 r. Class C57 steam locomotive, Japan, 1937 2·25 2·50

No. 2069 is inscribed "Hakari" in error.

300 Japanese Bobtail

1994. Cats. Multicoloured.
2076 7 l. Type **300** 15 20
2077 20 l. Siamese (vert) 25 20
2078 25 l. Persian longhair 25 20
2079 50 l. Somali (vert) 30 20
2080 3 r. 50 Oriental shorthair 80 80
2081 5 r. Burmese 1·00 1·00
2082 7 r. Bombay carrying kitten 1·25 1·50
2083 10 r. Turkish van (vert) 1·50 1·75
2084 12 r. Javanese (vert) 1·75 2·00
2085 15 r. Singapura 2·00 2·25
2086 18 r. Turkish angora (vert) 2·25 2·50
2087 20 r. Egyptian mau (vert) 2·25 2·50

301 Franco Baresi (Italy) and Stuart McCall (Scotland)

1994. World Cup Football Championship, U.S.A. (3rd issue). Multicoloured. (a) Horiz designs.
2089 10 l. Type **301** 30 30
2090 25 l. Mick McCarthy (Ireland) and Gary Lineker (England) 30 30
2091 50 l. J. Helt (Denmark) and R. Gordillo (Spain) 30 30
2092 5 r. Martin Vasquez (Spain) and Enzo Scifo (Belgium) 80 85
2093 10 r. Championship emblem 1·25 1·40
2094 12 r. Tomas Brolin (Sweden) and Gordon Durie (Scotland) 1·40 1·60

(b) Vert designs.
2095 6 r. 50 Bebeto (Brazil) 1·00 1·10
2096 6 r. 50 Lothar Matthaus (Germany) 1·00 1·10
2097 6 r. 50 Diego Maradona (Argentina) 1·00 1·10
2098 6 r. 50 Stephane Chapuasti (Switzerland) 1·00 1·10
2099 6 r. 50 George Hagi (Rumania) 1·00 1·10
2100 6 r. 50 Carlos Valderama (Colombia) 1·00 1·10

1994. 25th Anniv of First Manned Moon Landing. As T **238** of Antigua. Multicoloured.
2102 5 r. Crew of "Apollo 11" 90 90
2103 5 r. "Apollo 11" mission logo 90 90
2104 5 r. Edwin Aldrin (astronaut) and "Eagle" 90 90
2105 5 r. Crew of "Apollo 12" 90 90
2106 5 r. "Apollo 12" mission logo 90 90
2107 5 r. Alan Bean (astronaut) and equipment 90 90
2108 5 r. Crew of "Apollo 16" 90 90
2109 5 r. "Apollo 16" mission logo 90 90
2110 5 r. Astronauts with U.S. flag 90 90
2111 5 r. Crew of "Apollo 17" 90 90
2112 5 r. "Apollo 17" mission logo 90 90
2113 5 r. Launch of "Apollo 17" 90 90

1994. Centenary of International Olympic Committee. Gold Medal Winners. As T **327** of Antigua. Multicoloured.
2115 7 r. Linford Christie (Great Britain) (100 metres), 1992 (vert) 1·25 1·25
2116 12 r. Koji Gushiken (Japan) (gymnastics), 1984 (vert) 1·50 1·75

1994. 50th Anniv of D-Day. As T **331** of Antigua. Multicoloured.
2118 2 r. U.S. amphibious DUKW 35 30
2119 4 r. Landing Craft Tank unloading at Sword Beach 60 60
2120 18 r. Landing Craft Infantry at Omaha Beach 2·50 3·00

1994. "Philakorea '94" International Stamp Exn, Seoul. As T **330** of Antigua. Mult.
2122 50 l. Duckpond, Suwan Folk Village 15 15
2123 3 r. Pear-shaped bottle 45 45
2124 3 r. Vase with dragon decoration 45 45
2125 3 r. Vase with repaired lip 45 45
2126 3 r. Stoneware vase with floral decoration 45 45
2127 3 r. Celadon-glazed vase 45 45
2128 3 r. Unglazed stone vase 45 45
2129 3 r. Ritual water sprinkler 45 45
2130 3 r. Long-necked celadon-glazed vase 45 45
2131 3 r. 50 Yongduson Park 50 50
2132 20 r. Ploughing with ox, Hahoe 2·50 3·00

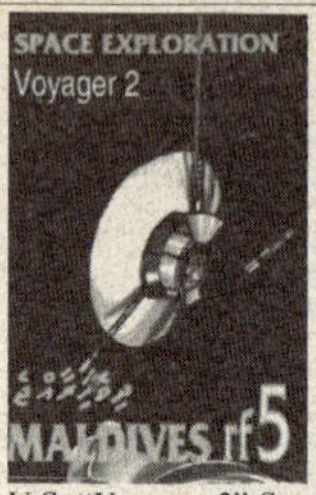

306 U.S. "Voyager 2" Satellite

1994. Space Exploration. Multicoloured.
2134 5 r. Type **306** 80 80
2135 5 r. Russian "Sputnik" satellite 80 80
2136 5 r. "Apollo-Soyuz" mission 80 80
2137 5 r. "Apollo 10" on parachutes 80 80
2138 5 r. "Apollo 11" mission flag 80 80
2139 5 r. Hubble space telescope 80 80
2140 5 r. Edwin "Buzz" Aldrin (astronaut) 80 80
2141 5 r. RCA lunar camera 80 80
2142 5 r. Lunar Rover (space buggy) 80 80
2143 5 r. Jim Irwin (astronaut) 80 80
2144 5 r. "Apollo 12" lunar module 80 80
2145 5 r. Astronaut holding equipment 80 80

307 Mother, Child, Old Man and Town Skyline

1994. United Nations Development Programme. Multicoloured.
2147 1 r. Type **307** 15 10
2148 8 r. Fisherman with son and island 1·40 1·50

308 School Band

1994. 50th Anniv of Aminiya School. Children's Paintings. Multicoloured.
2149 15 l. Type **308** 10 10
2150 50 l. Classroom 20 15
2151 1 r. School emblem and hand holding book (vert) 30 15
2152 8 r. School girls holding books (vert) 1·40 1·50
2153 10 r. Sporting activities 1·50 1·60
2154 11 r. School girls holding crown (vert) 1·60 1·90
2155 13 r. Science lesson 1·75 2·00

309 Boeing 747

1994. 50th Anniv of I.C.A.O. Multicoloured.
2156 50 l. Type **309** 30 15
2157 1 r. Hawker Siddeley ("de Havilland") Comet 4 35 20
2158 2 r. Male International Airport 60 50
2159 3 r. Lockheed L.1649 Super Star 75 75
2160 8 r. European Airbus 1·40 1·50
2161 10 r. Dornier Do-228 1·50 1·60

310 Pintail ("Northern Pintail")

1995. Ducks. Multicoloured.
2163 5 r. Type **310** 50 55
2164 5 r. Comb duck 50 55
2165 5 r. Ruddy shelduck 50 55
2166 5 r. Garganey 50 55
2167 5 r. Indian whistling duck ("Lesser whistling duck") 50 55
2168 5 r. Green-winged teal 50 55
2169 5 r. Fulvous whistling duck 50 55
2170 5 r. Common shoveler ("Northern shoveler") 50 55
2171 5 r. Cotton pygmy goose 50 55
2172 6 r. 50 + 50 l. European pochard (vert) 70 75
2173 6 r. 50 + 50 l. Mallard (vert) 70 75
2174 6 r. 50 + 50 l. European wigeon (vert) 70 75
2175 6 r. 50 + 50 l. Common shoveler ("Northern shoveler") (vert) 70 75
2176 6 r. 50 + 50 l. Pintail (vert) 70 75
2177 6 r. 50 + 50 l. Garganey (vert) 70 75
2178 6 r. 50 + 50 l. Tufted duck (vert) 70 75
2179 6 r. 50 + 50 l. Red-crested pochard ("Ferruginous duck") (vert) 70 75
2180 6 r. 50 + 50 l. Ferruginous duck ("Red-crested pochard") (vert) 70 75

Nos. 2163/71 and 2172/80 were printed together, se-tenant, forming composite designs.

311 Taj Mahal, India

1995. Famous Monuments of the World. Multicoloured.
2182 7 l. Type **311** 10 10
2183 10 l. Washington Monument, U.S.A. 10 10
2184 15 l. Mount Rushmore, U.S.A. 10 10
2185 25 l. Arc de Triomphe, Paris (vert) 10 10
2186 50 l. Sphinx, Egypt (vert) 10 10
2187 5 r. El Castillo, Toltec pyramid, Yucatan 50 55
2188 8 r. Toltec statue, Tula, Mexico (vert) 80 85
2189 12 r. Victory Column, Berlin (vert) 1·25 1·40

312 Donald Duck driving Chariot

1995. History of Wheeled Transport. Scenes from Disney cartoon film "Donald and the Wheel". Multicoloured.
2191 3 l. Type **312** 10 10
2192 4 l. Donald with log 10 10
2193 5 l. Donald driving Stephenson's "Rocket" 10 10
2194 10 l. Donald pondering over circle (vert) 10 10
2195 20 l. Donald in crashed car (vert) 10 10
2196 25 l. Donald listening to early grammaphone 10 10
2197 5 r. Donald on mammoth 75 75
2198 20 r. Donald pushing early car 2·75 3·25

313 Donald Duck playing Saxophone

1995. 60th Birthday of Donald Duck. Walt Disney Cartoon Characters. Multicoloured.
2199 5 r. Type **313** 80 80
2200 5 r. Moby Duck playing fiddle 80 80
2201 5 r. Feathry Duck with banjo and drum 80 80
2202 5 r. Daisy Duck playing harp 80 80
2203 5 r. Gladstone Gander with clarinet 80 80
2204 5 r. Huey, Dewey and Louie with bassoon 80 80
2205 5 r. Gus Goose playing flute 80 80
2206 5 r. Prof. Ludwig von Drake playing trombone 80 80
2207 5 r. Daisy picking flowers 80 80
2208 5 r. Donald with backpack 80 80
2209 5 r. Grandma Duck with kitten 80 80
2210 5 r. Gus Goose and pie 80 80
2211 5 r. Gyro Gearloose in space 80 80
2212 5 r. Huey, Dewey and Louie photographing porcupine 80 80
2213 5 r. Prof. Ludwig von Drake 80 80
2214 5 r. Scrooge McDuck with money 80 80

314 Islamic Centre, Male

1995. Eid Greetings. Multicoloured.
2216 1 r. Type **314** 10 10
2217 1 r. Rose 10 10
2218 8 r. Orchid 80 85
2219 10 r. Orchid (different) 1·00 1·10

315 Killer Whale

1995. "Singapore '95" International Stamp Exhibition (1st issue). Whales, Dolphins and Porpoises. Multicoloured.
2220 1 r. Type **315** 10 10
2221 2 r. Bottlenose dolphins 20 25
2222 3 r. Right whale 30 35
2223 3 r. Pair of killer whales 30 35
2224 3 r. Humpback whale 30 35
2225 3 r. Pair of belugas 30 35
2226 3 r. Narwhal 30 35
2227 3 r. Head of blue whale 30 35
2228 3 r. Bowhead whale 30 35
2229 3 r. Head of fin whale 30 35
2230 3 r. Pair of pilot whales 30 35
2231 3 r. Grey whale 30 35
2232 3 r. Sperm whale 30 35
2233 3 r. Pair of goosebeaked whales 30 35
2234 3 r. Hourglass dolphin 30 35
2235 3 r. Bottlenose dolphin (different) 30 35
2236 3 r. Dusky dolphin 30 35
2237 3 r. Spectacled porpoise 30 35
2238 3 r. Fraser's dolphin 30 35
2239 3 r. Cameron's dolphin 30 35
2240 3 r. Pair of spinner dolphins 30 35
2241 3 r. Pair of Dalls dolphins 30 35
2242 3 r. Spotted dolphin 30 35
2243 3 r. Indus River dolphin 30 35
2244 3 r. Hector's dolphin 30 35
2245 3 r. Amazon River dolphin 30 35
2246 8 r. Humpback whale and calf 80 85
2247 10 r. Common dolphin 1·00 1·10
See also Nos. 2302/10.

316 Scout Camp and National Flag

1995. 18th World Scout Jamboree, Netherlands. Multicoloured.
2249 10 r. Type **316** 1·00 1·10
2250 12 r. Campfire cooking 1·25 1·40
2251 15 r. Scouts erecting tent 1·50 1·60
Nos. 2249/51 were printed together, se-tenant, forming a composite design.

1995. 50th Anniv of End of Second World War in Europe. As T **340** of Antigua. Multicoloured.
2253 5 r. Soviet heavy howitzer battery 50 55
2254 5 r. Ruins of Berchtesgaden 50 55
2255 5 r. U.S. Boeing B-17 Flying Fortress dropping food over the Netherlands 50 55
2256 5 r. Soviet Ilyushin Il-1 bomber 50 55
2257 5 r. Liberation of Belsen 50 55
2258 5 r. Supermarine Spitfire and V-1 flying bomb 50 55
2259 5 r. U.S. tanks advancing through Cologne 50 55
2260 5 r. Reichstag in ruins 50 55

318 Asian Child and Dove

320 Asian Child eating Rice

319 United Nations Emblem

1995. 50th Anniv of United Nations (1st issue). Multicoloured.
2262 6 r. 50 + 50 l. Type **318** 70 75
2263 8 r. Globe and dove 80 85
2264 10 r. African child and dove 1·00 1·10
Nos. 2262/4 were printed together, se-tenant, forming a composite design.

1995. 50th Anniv of United Nations (2nd issue).
2266 **319** 30 l. black, blue and green 10 10
2267 – 8 r. multicoloured 80 85
2268 – 11 r. multicoloured 1·10 1·25
2269 – 13 r. black, grey and red 1·40 1·50
DESIGNS: 8 r. Symbolic women, flag and map; 11 r. U.N. soldier and symbolic dove; 13 r. Gun barrels, atomic explosion and bomb sight.

1995. 50th Anniv of F.A.O. (1st issue). Multicoloured.
2270 6 r. 50 + 50 l. Type **320** 70 75
2271 8 r. F.A.O. emblem 80 85
2272 10 r. African mother and child 1·00 1·10
See also Nos. 2311/12.

1995. 95th Birthday of Queen Elizabeth the Queen Mother. As T **344** of Antigua.
2274 5 r. brown, light brown and black 50 55
2275 5 r. multicoloured 50 55
2276 5 r. multicoloured 50 55
2277 5 r. multicoloured 50 55
DESIGNS: No. 2274, Queen Elizabeth the Queen Mother (pastel drawing); 2275, Without hat; 2276, At desk (oil painting); 2277, Queen Elizabeth the Queen Mother.

1995. 50th Anniv of End of Second World War in the Pacific. As T **340** of Antigua.
2279 6 r. 50 + 50 l. Grumman F6F-3 Hellcat aircraft 70 75
2280 6 r. 50 + 50 l. F4-U1 fighter aircraft attacking beach 70 75
2281 6 r. 50 + 50 l. Douglas SBD Dauntless aircraft 70 75
2282 6 r. 50 + 50 l. American troops in landing craft, Guadalcanal 70 75
2283 6 r. 50 + 50 l. U.S. marines in Alligator tanks 70 75
2284 6 r. 50 + 50 l. U.S. landing ship 70 75

322 Students using Library

1995. 50th Anniv of National Library. Multicoloured.
2286 2 r. Type **322** 20 25
2287 8 r. Students using library (different) 80 85

323 Spur-thighed Tortoise

1995. Turtles and Tortoises. Multicoloured.
2289 3 r. Type **323** 30 35
2290 3 r. Aldabra turtle 30 35
2291 3 r. Loggerhead turtle 30 35
2292 3 r. Olive Ridley turtle 30 35
2293 3 r. Leatherback turtle 30 35
2294 3 r. Green turtle 30 35
2295 3 r. Atlantic ridley turtle 30 35
2296 3 r. Hawksbill turtle 30 35
2297 10 r. Hawksbill turtle on beach 1·00 1·10
2298 10 r. Pair of hawksbill turtles 1·00 1·10
2299 10 r. Hawksbill turtle climbing out of water 1·00 1·10
2300 10 r. Hawksbill turtle swimming 1·00 1·10
Nos. 2289/96 were printed together, se-tenant, forming a composite design.
Nos. 2297/2300 include the W.W.F. Panda emblem.

324 "Russula aurata" (fungi) and "Papilio demodocus" (butterfly)

1995. "Singapore '95" International Stamp Exhibition. Butterflies and Fungi. Multicoloured.
2302 2 r. Type **324** 20 25
2303 2 r. "Lepista saeva" and "Kallimoides rumia" 20 25
2304 2 r. "Lepista nuda" and "Hypolimnas salmacis" 20 25
2305 2 r. "Xerocomus subtomentosus" ("Boletus subtomentosus" and "Precis octavia") 20 25
2306 5 r. "Gyroporus castaneus" and "Hypolimnas salmacis" 50 55
2307 8 r. "Gomphidius glutinosus" and "Papilio dardanus" 80 85
2308 10 r. "Russula olivacea" and "Precis octavia" 1·00 1·10
2309 12 r. "Boletus edulis" and "Prepona praeneste" 1·25 1·40
Nos. 2302/5 and 2306/9 respectively were printed together, se-tenant, forming composite designs.
No. 2304 is inscribed "Lapista" in error.

325 Planting Kaashi

1995. 50th Anniv of F.A.O. (2nd issue). Mult.
2311 7 r. Type **325** 70 75
2312 8 r. Fishing boat 85 85

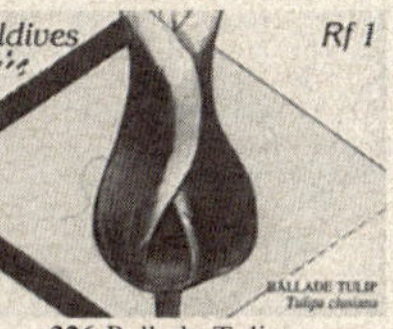

326 Ballade Tulip

1995. Flowers. Multicoloured.
2313 1 r. Type **326** 10 10
2314 3 r. White mallow 30 35
2315 5 r. Regale trumpet lily 50 55
2316 5 r. "Dendrobium Waipahu Beauty" 50 55
2317 5 r. "Brassocattleya Jean Murray" 50 55
2318 5 r. "Cymbidium Fort George" 50 55
2319 5 r. "Paphiopedilum malipoense" 50 55
2320 5 r. "Cycnoches chlorochilon" 50 55
2321 5 r. "Rhyncholaelia digbgana" 50 55
2322 5 r. "Lycaste deppei" 50 55
2323 5 r. "Masdevallia constricta" 50 55
2324 5 r. "Paphiopedilum Clair de Lune" 50 55
2325 7 r. "Lilactime dahlia" 70 75
2326 8 r. Blue ideal iris 80 85
2327 10 r. Red crown imperial 1·00 1·10

327 John Lennon with Microphone

328 Elvis Presley with Microphone

1995. 15th Death Anniv of John Lennon (musician). Multicoloured.
2329 5 r. Type **327** 1·00 1·00
2330 5 r. With glasses and moustache 1·00 1·00
2331 5 r. With guitar 1·00 1·00
2332 5 r. With guitar and wearing glasses 1·00 1·00
2333 5 r. Wearing sun glasses and red jacket 1·00 1·00
2334 5 r. Wearing headphones 1·00 1·00

1995. 60th Birth Anniv of Elvis Presley (entertainer). Multicoloured.
2337 5 r. Type **328** 50 55
2338 5 r. Wearing red jacket 50 55
2339 5 r. Wearing blue jacket 50 55
2340 5 r. With microphone and wearing blue jacket 50 55
2341 5 r. In army uniform 50 55
2342 5 r. Wearing yellow bow tie 50 55
2343 5 r. In yellow shirt 50 55
2344 5 r. In light blue shirt 50 55
2345 5 r. Wearing red and white high-collared jacket 50 55

329 Johannes van der Waals (1919 Physics)

1995. Cent of Nobel Prize Trust Fund. Mult.
2347/55 5 r. × 9 (Type **329**; Charles Guillaume (1920 Physics); Sir James Chadwick (1935 Physics); Willem Einthoven (1924 Medicine); Henrik Dam (1943 Medicine); Sir Alexander Fleming (1945 Medicine); Hermann Muller (1946 Medicine); Rodney Porter (1972 Medicine); Werner Arber (1978 Medicine))
2356/64 5 r. × 9 (Niels Bohr (1922 Physics); Ben Mottelson (1975 Physics); Patrick White (1973 Literature); Elias Canetti (1981 Literature); Theodor Kocher (1909 Medicine); August Krogh (1920 Medicine); William Murphy (1934 Medicine); John Northrop (1946 Chemistry); Luis Leloir (1970 Chemistry))
2365/73 5 r. × 9 (Dag Hammarskjold (1961 Peace); Alva Myrdal (1982 Peace); Archbishop Desmond Tutu (1984 Peace); Rudolf Eucken (1908 Literature); Aleksandr Solzhenitsyn (1970 Literature); Gabriel Marquez (1982 Literature); Chen Yang (1957 Physics); Karl Muller (1987 Physics); Melvin Schwartz (1988 Physics))
2374/82 5 r. × 9 (Robert Millikan (1923 Physics); Louis de Broglie (1929 Physics); Ernest Walton (1951 Physics); Richard Willstatter (1915 Chemistry); Lars Onsager (1968 Chemistry); Gerhard Herzberg (1971 Chemistry); William B. Yeats (1923 Literature); George Bernard Shaw (1925 Literature); Eugene O'Neill (1936 Literature))
2383/91 5 r. × 9 (Bernardo Houssay (1947 Medicine); Paul Muller (1948 Medicine); Walter Hess (1949 Medicine); Sir MacFarlane Burnet (1960 Medicine); Baruch Blumberg (1976 Medicine); Daniel Nathans (1978 Medicine); Glenn Seaborg (1951 Chemistry); Ilya Prigogine (1977 Chemistry); Kenichi Fukui (1981 Chemistry))
2392/2400 5 r. × 9 (Carl Spitteler (1919 Literature); Henri Bergson (1927 Literature); Johannes Jensen (1944 Literature); Antoine-Henri Becquerel (1903 Physics); Sir William H. Bragg (1915 Physics); Sir William L. Bragg (1915 Physics); Frederik Bajer (1908 Peace); Leon Bourgeois (1920 Peace); Karl Benning (1921 Peace))
Set of 54 27·00 29·00

330 Rythmic Gymnast and Japanese Fan

1996. Olympic Games, Atlanta (1st issue). Mult.
2402 1 r. Type **330** 10 10
2403 3 r. Archer and Moscow Olympics logo 30 35
2404 5 r. Diver and Swedish flag 50 55
2405 5 r. Canadian Maple Leaf 50 55

2406 5 r. Shot putting (decathlon) . . 50 55
2407 5 r. Moscow Olympic medal and ribbon 50 55
2408 5 r. Fencer 50 55
2409 5 r. Gold medal 50 55
2410 5 r. Equestrian competitor . . 50 55
2411 5 r. Sydney Opera House . . 50 55
2412 5 r. Athlete on starting blocks 50 55
2413 5 r. South Korean flag . . . 50 55
2414 7 r. High jumper and Tower Bridge, London 70 75
2415 10 r. Athlete on starting blocks and Brandenburg Gate, Germany . . . . 1·00 1·10
2416 12 r. Hurdler and Amsterdam Olympic logo . . . . . . 1·25 1·40

See also Nos. 2469/87.

331 "Self Portrait" (Degas)

1996. 125th Anniv of Metropolitan Museum of Art, New York. Multicoloured.

2418/25 4 r. × 8 (Type **331**; "Andromache and Astyanax" (Prud'hon); "Rene Grenier" (Toulouse-Lautrec); "The Banks of the Bievre near Bicetre" (Rousseau); "The Repast of the Lion" (Rousseau); "Portrait of Yves Gobillard-Morisot" (Degas); "Sunflowers" (Van Gogh); "The Singer in Green" (Degas))
2426/33 4 r. × 8 ("Still Life" (Fantin-Latour); "Portrait of a Lady in Grey" (Degas); "Apples and Grapes" (Monet); "The Englishman" (Toulouse-Lautrec); "Cypresses" (Van Gogh); "Flowers in a Chinese Vase" (Redon); "The Gardener" (Seurat); "Large Sunflowers I" (Nolde))
2434/41 4 r. × 8 (All by Manet: "The Spanish Singer"; "Young Man in Costume of Majo"; "Mademoiselle Victorine"; "Boating"; "Peonies"; "Woman with a Parrot"; "George Moore"; "The Monet Family in their Garden")
2442/9 4 r. × 8 ("Goldfish" (Matisse); "Spanish Woman: Harmony in Blue" (Matisse); "Nasturtiums and the "Dance" II" (Matisse); "The House behind Trees" (Braque); "Mada Primavesi" (Klimt); "Head of a Woman" (Picasso); "Woman in White" (Picasso); "Harlequin" (Picasso))
2418/49 Set of 32 . . . . 12·00 13·00

332 Mickey Mouse on Great Wall of China

1996. "CHINA '96" 9th Asian International Stamp Exhibition, Peking. Walt Disney Cartoon Characters in China. Multicoloured.

2451 2 r. Type **332** 35 35
2452 2 r. Pluto with temple guardian 35 35
2453 2 r. Minnie Mouse with pandas 35 35
2454 2 r. Mickey windsurfing near junks 35 35
2455 2 r. Goofy cleaning grotto statue 35 35
2456 2 r. Donald and Daisy Duck at Marble Boat 35 35
2457 2 r. Mickey with terracotta warriors 35 35
2458 2 r. Goofy with geese and masks 35 35
2459 2 r. Donald and Goofy on traditional fishing boat . . 35 35
2460 2 r. Mickey and Minnie in dragon boat 35 35
2461 2 r. Donald at Peking opera . 35 35
2462 2 r. Mickey and Minnie in Chinese garden 35 35
2463 3 r. Mickey and Minnie at the Ice Pagoda (vert) 50 50
2464 3 r. Donald and Mickey flying Chinese kites (vert) . . . 50 50
2465 3 r. Goofy playing anyiwu (vert) 50 50
2466 3 r. Paper cutouts of Mickey and Goofy (vert) 50 50
2467 3 r. Donald and Mickey in dragon dance (vert) 50 50

INDEX

Countries can be quickly located by referring to the index at the end of this volume.

333 Stella Walsh (Poland) (10m sprint, 1932) on Medal

1996. Olympic Games, Atlanta (2nd issue). Previous Gold Medal Winners. Multicoloured.

2469 1 r. Type **333** 10 10
2470 3 r. Emile Zatopek (Czechoslovakia) (10,000m running, 1952) and Olympic torch (vert) 30 35
2471 5 r. Yanko Rousseu (Bulgaria) (lightweight, 1980) (vert) . 50 55
2472 5 r. Peter Baczako (Hungary) (middle heavyweight, 1980) (vert) 50 55
2473 5 r. Leonid Taranenko (Russia) (heavyweight, 1980) (vert) 50 55
2474 5 r. Aleksandr Kurlovich (Russia) (heavyweight, 1988) (vert) 50 55
2475 5 r. Assen Zlateu (Bulgaria) (middleweight, 1980) (vert) 50 55
2476 5 r. Zeng Guoqiang (China) (flyweight, 1984) (vert) . . 50 55
2477 5 r. Yurik Vardanyan (Russia) (heavyweight, 1980) (vert) 50 55
2478 5 r. Sultan Rakhmanov (Russia) (super heavyweight, 1980) (vert) 50 55
2479 5 r. Vassily Alexeev (Russia) (super heavyweight, 1972) (vert) 50 55
2480 5 r. Ethel Catherwood (Canada) (high jump, 1928) . . . 50 55
2481 5 r. Mildred Didrikson (U.S.A.) (javelin, 1932) 50 55
2482 5 r. Francina Blankers-Koen (Netherlands) (80m hurdles, 1948) 50 55
2483 5 r. Tamara Press (Russia) (shot put, 1960) 50 55
2484 5 r. Lia Manoliu (Rumania) (discus, 1968) 50 55
2485 5 r. Rosa Mota (Portugal) (marathon, 1988) 50 55
2486 10 r. Olga Fikotova (Czechoslovakia) (discus, 1956) on medal . . . . . 1·00 1·10
2487 12 r. Joan Benoit (U.S.A.) (marathon, 1984) on medal 1·25 1·40

1996. 70th Birthday of Queen Elizabeth II. As T **363** of Antigua. Multicoloured.

2489 8 r. As Type **363** of Antigua 80 85
2490 8 r. Wearing hat 80 85
2491 8 r. At desk 80 85

335 African Child

1996. 50th Anniv of U.N.I.C.E.F. Multicoloured.

2493 5 r. Type **335** 50 55
2494 7 r. European girl 70 75
2495 7 r. Maldivian boy 70 75
2496 10 r. Asian girl . . . . 1·00 1·10

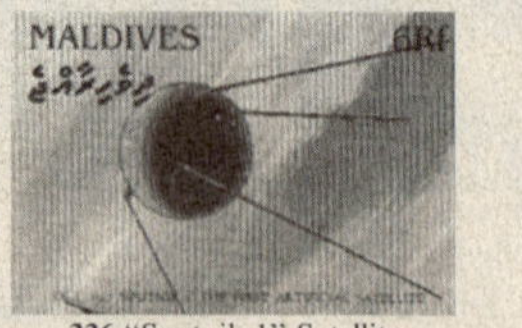

336 "Sputnik 1" Satellite

1996. Space Exploration. Multicoloured.

2498 6 r. Type **336** 60 65
2499 6 r. "Apollo 11" command module 60 65
2500 6 r. "Skylab" 60 65
2501 6 r. Astronaut Edward White walking in space 60 65
2502 6 r. "Mariner 9" 60 65
2503 6 r. "Apollo" and "Soyuz" docking 60 65

337 "Epiphora albida"

1996. Butterflies. Multicoloured.

2505 7 r. Type **337** 70 75
2506 7 r. "Satyrus dryas" 70 75
2507 7 r. "Satyrus lena" 70 75
2508 7 r. "Papilio tynderaeus" . . 70 75
2509 7 r. "Urota suraka" 70 75
2510 7 r. "Satyrus nercis" 70 75
2511 7 r. "Papilio troilus" (vert) . . 70 75
2512 7 r. "Papilio cresphontes" (vert) 70 75
2513 7 r. Lime swallowtail caterpillar (vert) 70 75
2514 7 r. "Cynthia virginiensis" (vert) 70 75
2515 7 r. Monarch caterpillar (vert) 70 75
2516 7 r. "Danaus plexippus" (vert) 70 75
2517 7 r. Monarch caterpillar and pupa (vert) 70 75
2518 7 r. "Chlosyne harrisii" (vert) 70 75
2519 7 r. "Cymothoe coccinata" (vert) 70 75
2520 7 r. "Morpho rhetenor" (vert) 70 75
2521 7 r. "Callicore lidwina" (vert) 70 75
2522 7 r. "Heliconius erato reductimacula" (vert) . . . 70 75

338 Amtrak F40H Diesel-electric Locomotive, U.S.A.

1996. Trains of the World. Multicoloured.

2524 3 r. Type **338** 30 35
2525 3 r. Stephenson's "Experiment" 30 35
2526 3 r. Indian-Pacific Intercontinental, Australia . 30 35
2527 3 r. Stephenson's Killingworth type steam locomotive, 1815 30 35
2528 3 r. George Stephenson . . . 30 35
2529 3 r. Stephenson's "Rocket", 1829 . . . . 30 35
2530 3 r. High Speed Train 125, Great Britain 30 35
2531 3 r. First rail passenger coach "Experiment", 1825 . . . 30 35
2532 3 r. Union Pacific Class U25B diesel locomotive (inscr "Tofac"), U.S.A. 30 35
2533 3 r. Southern Pacific's "Daylight" express, 1952, U.S.A. 30 35
2534 3 r. Timothy Hackworth's "Sans Pareil", 1829 . . . . 30 35
2535 3 r. Chicago and North Western diesel locomotive, U.S.A. . 30 35
2536 3 r. Richard Trevithick's "Pen-y-Darren" locomotive, 1804 30 35
2537 3 r. Isambard Kingdom Brunel 30 35
2538 3 r. Great Western locomotive, 1838 . . . . 30 35
2539 3 r. Vistadome observation car, Canada 30 35
2540 3 r. Mohawk and Hudson Railroad "Experiment", 1832 30 35
2541 3 r. ICE high speed train, Germany 30 35
2542 3 r. Electric container locomotive, Germany . . . 30 35
2543 3 r. John Blenkinsop's rack locomotive, 1811 . . . . . 30 35
2544 3 r. Diesel-electric locomotive, Western Australia 30 35
2545 3 r. Timothy Hackworth's "Royal George", 1827 . . . 30 35
2546 3 r. Robert Stephenson . . . 30 35
2547 3 r. Trevithick's "Newcastle" 30 35
2548 3 r. Deltic diesel-electric locomotive, Great Britain . . 30 35
2549 3 r. Stockton and Darlington Railway locomotive No. 5 "Stockton", 1826 . . . . . 30 35
2550 3 r. Channel Tunnel "Le Shuttle" train 30 35

339 Bongo

1996. Wildlife of the World. Multicoloured.

2552 5 r. Type **339** 50 55
2553 5 r. Bushbuck 50 55
2554 5 r. Namaqua dove 50 55
2555 5 r. Hoopoe 50 55
2556 5 r. African fish eagle . . . 50 55
2557 5 r. Egyptian goose 50 55
2558 5 r. Saddle-bill stork 50 55
2559 5 r. Blue-breasted kingfisher . 50 55
2560 5 r. Yellow baboon 50 55
2561 5 r. Banded duiker ("Zebra Duiker") 50 55
2562 5 r. Yellow-backed duiker . . . 50 55
2563 5 r. Pygmy hippopotamus . . 50 55
2564 5 r. Large-spotted genet . . . 50 55
2565 5 r. African spoonbill 50 55
2566 5 r. White-faced whistling duck 50 55
2567 5 r. Helmet guineafowl . . . 50 55
2568 7 r. Cotton-headed tamarin (horiz) 70 75
2569 7 r. European bison (horiz) . 70 75
2570 7 r. Tiger (horiz) 70 75
2571 7 r. Capercaillie (horiz) . . . 70 75
2572 7 r. Giant panda (horiz) . . . 70 75
2573 7 r. "Trogonoptera brookiana" (butterfly) (horiz) 70 75
2574 7 r. American beaver (horiz) 70 75
2575 7 r. "Leiopelma hamiltoni" (frog) (horiz) 70 75
2576 7 r. Manatee (horiz) 70 75

Nos. 2552/9, 2560/7 and 2568/76 respectively were printed together, se-tenant, with the backgrounds forming composite designs.

No. 2553 is inscribed "BUSHBACK" in error.

340 Giant Panda

1996. Endangered Species. Multicoloured.

2578 5 r. Type **340** 50 55
2579 5 r. Indian elephant 50 55
2580 5 r. Arrow-poison frog . . . 50 55
2581 5 r. Mandrill 50 55
2582 5 r. Snow leopard 50 55
2583 5 r. California condor . . . 50 55
2584 5 r. Whale-headed stork ("Shoebill Stork") 50 55
2585 5 r. Red-billed hornbill . . . 50 55
2586 5 r. Hippopotamus 50 55
2587 5 r. Gorilla 50 55
2588 5 r. Lion 50 55
2589 5 r. South African crowned crane 50 55

341 Mickey Mouse climbing out of Puddle

1996. Centenary of the Cinema. Cartoon Frames from "The Little Whirlwind" (Nos. 2591/2607) or "Pluto and the Flypaper" (Nos. 2608/24). Mult.

2591 4 r. Type **341** 60 60
2592 4 r. Frame 2 . . . . 60 60
2593 4 r. Frame 3 . . . . 60 60
2594 4 r. Frame 4 . . . . 60 60
2595 4 r. Frame 5 . . . . 60 60
2596 4 r. Frame 6 . . . . 60 60
2597 4 r. Frame 7 . . . . 60 60
2598 4 r. Frame 8 . . . . 60 60
2599 4 r. Frame 9 . . . . 60 60
2600 4 r. Frame 10 . . . . 60 60
2601 4 r. Frame 11 . . . . 60 60
2602 4 r. Frame 12 . . . . 60 60
2603 4 r. Frame 13 . . . . 60 60
2604 4 r. Frame 14 . . . . 60 60
2605 4 r. Frame 15 . . . . 60 60
2606 4 r. Frame 16 (Mickey holding fish above head) 60 60
2607 4 r. Frame 17 (Mickey throwing fish into pool) 60 60
2608 4 r. Frame 1 (Pluto) 60 60
2609 4 r. Frame 2 . . . . 60 60
2610 4 r. Frame 3 . . . . 60 60
2611 4 r. Frame 4 . . . . 60 60
2612 4 r. Frame 5 . . . . 60 60
2613 4 r. Frame 6 . . . . 60 60
2614 4 r. Frame 7 . . . . 60 60
2615 4 r. Frame 8 . . . . 60 60
2616 4 r. Frame 9 . . . . 60 60
2617 4 r. Frame 10 . . . . 60 60
2618 4 r. Frame 11 . . . . 60 60
2619 4 r. Frame 12 . . . . 60 60
2620 4 r. Frame 13 . . . . 60 60
2621 4 r. Frame 14 . . . . 60 60
2622 4 r. Frame 15 . . . . 60 60
2623 4 r. Frame 16 . . . . 60 60
2624 4 r. Frame 17 . . . . 60 60

342 Letter "O" with Chinese Character

1997. "HONG KONG '97" International Stamp Exhibition. Multicoloured.

2626 5 r. Letter "H" and Chinese couple 50 55
2627 5 r. Type **342** 50 55
2628 5 r. Letter "N" and Chinese dragon 50 55
2629 5 r. Letter "G" and carnival dragon 50 55
2630 5 r. Letter "K" and modern office block 50 55
2631 5 r. Letter "O" and Chinese character (different) . . . 50 55

2632 5 r. Letter "N" and Chinese fan cases 50 55
2633 5 r. Letter "G" and Chinese junk 50 55

343 California Condor

344 Ye Qiabo (China) (women's 500/1000m speed skating, 1992)

1997. Birds of the World. Multicoloured.
2635 5 r. Type **343** 50 55
2636 5 r. Audouin's gull 50 55
2637 5 r. Atlantic puffin 50 55
2638 5 r. Resplendent quetzal . . . 50 55
2639 5 r. Puerto Rican amazon . . 50 55
2640 5 r. Lesser bird of paradise . . 50 55
2641 5 r. Japanese crested ibis . . 50 55
2642 5 r. Mauritius kestrel . . . 50 55
2643 5 r. Kakapo 50 55
Nos. 2635/43 were printed together, se-tenant, with the backgrounds forming a composite design.

1997. Winter Olympic Games, Nagano, Japan (1998). Multicoloured.
2645 2 r. Type **344** 20 25
2646 3 r. Leonhard Stock (Austria) (downhill skiing, 1980) . . 30 35
2647 5 r. Herma von Szabo-Planck (Austria) (figure skating, 1924) 50 55
2648 5 r. Katarina Witt (Germany) (figure skating, 1988) . . . 50 55
2649 5 r. Natalia Bestemianova and Andrei Bukin (Russia) (pairs ice dancing, 1988) 50 55
2650 5 r. Jayne Torvill and Christopher Dean (Great Britain) (pairs ice dancing, 1984) 50 55
2651 8 r. Bjorn Daehlie (Norway) (cross-country skiing, 1992) 80 85
2652 12 r. Wolfgang Hoppe (Germany) (bobsleigh, 1984) 1·25 1·40

345 Crowned Solitary Eagle

1997. Eagles. Multicoloured.
2654 1 r. Type **345** 10 15
2655 2 r. African hawk eagle (horiz) 20 25
2656 3 r. Lesser spotted eagle . . 30 35
2657 5 r. Stellar's sea eagle . . . 50 55
2658 5 r. Bald eagle attacking . . 50 55
2659 5 r. Bald eagle on branch . . 50 55
2660 5 r. Bald eagle looking left . . 50 55
2661 5 r. Bald eagle looking right . 50 55
2662 5 r. Bald eagle sitting on branch with leaves 50 55
2663 5 r. Bald eagle soaring . . . 50 55
2664 8 r. Spanish imperial eagle (horiz) 80 85
2665 10 r. Harpy eagle . . . . . 1·00 1·10
2666 12 r. Crested serpent eagle (horiz) . . . . 1·25 1·40

346 Blitzer Benz, 1911

1997. Classic Cars. Multicoloured.
2668 5 r. Type **346** 50 55
2669 5 r. Datsun, 1917 . . . . . 50 55
2670 5 r. Auburn 8-120, 1929 . . . 50 55
2671 5 r. Mercedes-Benz C280, 1996 50 55
2672 5 r. Suzuki UR-1 . . . . . 50 55
2673 5 r. Chrysler Atlantic . . . 50 55
2674 5 r. Mercedes-Benz 190SL, 1961 50 55
2675 5 r. Kwaishinha D.A.T., 1916 50 55
2676 5 r. Rolls-Royce Roadster 20/25 50 55
2677 5 r. Mercedes-Benz SLK, 1997 50 55
2678 5 r. Toyota Camry, 1996 . . 50 55
2679 5 r. Jaguar MK 2, 1959 . . 50 55

347 "Patris II", Greece (1926)

1997. Passenger Ships. Multicoloured.
2681 1 r. Type **347** 10 15
2682 2 r. "Infanta Beatriz", Spain (1928) 20 25
2683 3 r. "Vasilefs Constantinos", Greece (1914) 30 35
2684 3 r. "Cunene", Portugal (1911) 30 35
2685 3 r. "Selandia", Denmark (1912) 30 35
2686 3 r. "President Harding", U.S.A. (1921) 30 35
2687 3 r. "Ulster Monarch", Great Britain (1929) 30 35
2688 3 r. "Matsonia", U.S.A. (1913) 30 35
2689 3 r. "France", France (1911) 30 35
2690 3 r. "Campania", Great Britain (1893) 30 35
2691 3 r. "Klipfontein", Holland (1922) 30 35
2692 3 r. "Eridan", France (1929) 30 35
2693 3 r. "Mount Clinton", U.S.A. (1921) 30 35
2694 3 r. "Infanta Isabel", Spain (1912) 30 35
2695 3 r. "Suwa Maru", Japan (1914) 30 35
2696 3 r. "Yorkshire", Great Britain (1920) 30 35
2697 3 r. "Highland Chieftain", Great Britain (1929) . . . 30 35
2698 3 r. "Sardinia", Norway (1920) 30 35
2699 3 r. "San Guglielmo", Italy (1911) 30 35
2700 3 r. "Avila", Great Britain (1927) 30 35
2701 8 r. "Stavangerfjord", Norway (1918 . . . . 80 85
2702 12 r. "Baloeran", Netherlands (1929) . . . . 1·25 1·40

348 Prayer Wheels, Lhasa

1997. 50th Anniv of U.N.E.S.C.O. Multicoloured.
2704 1 r. Type **348** 10 15
2705 2 r. Ruins of Roman Temple of Diana, Portugal (horiz) . . 20 25
2706 3 r. Santa Maria Cathedral, Hildesheim, Germany (horiz) 30 35
2707 5 r. Vivunga National Park, Zaire 50 55
2708 5 r. Valley of Mai Nature Reserve, Seychelles . . . 50 55
2709 5 r. Kandy, Sri Lanka . . . 50 55
2710 5 r. Taj Mahal, India . . . 50 55
2711 5 r. Istanbul, Turkey 50 55
2712 5 r. Sana'a, Yemen 50 55
2713 5 r. Bleinheim Palace, England 50 55
2714 5 r. Grand Canyon National Park, U.S.A. 50 55
2715 5 r. Tombs, Gondar, Ethiopia 50 55
2716 5 r. Bwindi National Park, Uganda 50 55
2717 5 r. Bemaraha National Reserve, Madagascar . . . 50 55
2718 5 r. Buddhist ruins at Takht-I-Bahi, Pakistan 50 55
2719 5 r. Anuradhapura, Sri Lanka 50 55
2720 5 r. Cairo, Egypt 50 55
2721 5 r. Ruins, Petra, Jordan . . 50 55
2722 5 r. Volcano, Ujung Kulon National Park, Indonesia . . 50 55
2723 5 r. Terrace, Mount Taishan, China 50 55
2724 5 r. Temple, Mount Taishan, China 50 55
2725 5 r. Temple turret, Mount Taishan, China 50 55
2726 5 r. Standing stones, Mount Taishan, China 50 55
2727 5 r. Courtyard, Mount Taishan, China 50 55
2728 5 r. Staircase, Mount Taishan, China 50 55
2729 5 r. Terracotta Warriors, China 50 55
2730 5 r. Head of Terracota Warrior, China 50 55
2731 7 r. Doorway, Abu Simbel, Egypt 70 75
2732 8 r. Mandraki, Rhodes, Greece (horiz) 80 85
2733 8 r. Agios Stefanos Monastery, Meteora, Greece (horiz) . . 80 85
2734 8 r. Taj Mahal, India (horiz) 80 85
2735 8 r. Cistercian Abbey of Fontenay, France (horiz) . 80 85
2736 8 r. Yarushima, Japan (horiz) 80 85
2737 8 r. Cloisters, San Gonzalo Convent, Portugal (horiz) . 80 85
2738 8 r. Olympic National Park, U.S.A. (horiz) 80 85
2739 8 r. Waterfall, Nahanni National Park, Canada (horiz) 80 85
2740 8 r. Mountains, National Park, Argentina (horiz) . . . 80 85
2741 8 r. Bonfin Salvador Church, Brazil (horiz) 80 85
2742 8 r. Convent of the Companions of Jesus, Morelia, Mexico (horiz) 80 85
2743 8 r. Two-storey temple, Horyu Temple, Japan (horiz) . . 80 85
2744 8 r. Summer house, Horyu Temple, Japan (horiz) . . 80 85
2745 8 r. Temple and cloister, Horyu Temple, Japan (horiz) . . 80 85
2746 8 r. Single storey temple, Horyu Temple, Japan (horiz) . . 80 85
2747 8 r. Well, Horyu Temple, Japan (horiz) 80 85
2748 10 r. Scandola Nature Reserve, France (horiz) . . . . 1·00 1·10
2749 12 r. Temple on the Lake, China (horiz) . . . . . . 1·25 1·40
No. 2717 is inscribed "MADAGASGAR" and 2737 "COVENT", both in error.

349 White Doves and S.A.A.R.C. Logo

1997. 9th South Asian Association for Regional Cooperation Summit, Male. Multicoloured.
2751 3 r. Type **349** 30 35
2752 5 r. Flags of member countries 50 55

350 Queen Elizabeth II

1997. Golden Wedding of Queen Elizabeth and Prince Philip. Multicoloured.
2753 5 r. Type **350** 50 55
2754 5 r. Royal coat of arms . . . 50 55
2755 5 r. Queen Elizabeth and Prince Philip at opening of Parliament 50 55
2756 5 r. Queen Elizabeth and Prince Philip with Prince Charles, 1948 . . . . 50 55
2757 5 r. Buckingham Palace from the garden 50 55
2758 5 r. Prince Philip 50 55

351 Early Indian Mail Messenger

1997. "Pacific '97" International Stamp Exhibition, San Francisco. Death Centenary of Heinrich von Stephan (founder of the U.P.U.).
2760 **351** 2 r. green and black . . . 20 25
2761 – 2 r. brown and black . . . 20 25
2762 – 2 r. violet 20 25
DESIGNS: No. 2761, Von Stephan and Mercury; 2762, Autogyro, Washington.

352 "Dawn at Kanda Myojin Shrine"

1997. Birth Bicentenary of Hiroshige (Japanese painter). "One Hundred Famous Views of Edo". Multicoloured.
2763 8 r. Type **352** 80 85
2764 8 r. "Kiyomizu Hall and Shinobazu Pond at Ueno" . . 80 85
2765 8 r. "Ueno Yamashita" . . . 80 85
2766 8 r. "Moon Pine, Ueno" . . . 80 85
2767 8 r. "Flower Pavilion, Dango Slope, Sendagi" 80 85
2768 8 r. "Shitaya Hirokoji" . . . 80 85

353 Common Noddy

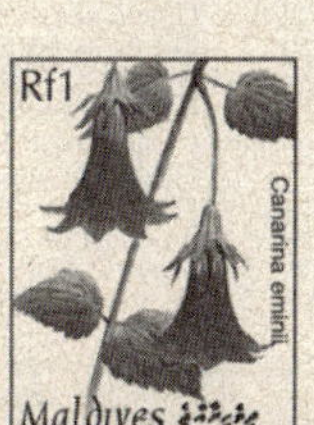

354 "Canarina eminii"

1997. Birds. Multicoloured.
2770 30 l. Type **353** 10 10
2771 1 r. Spectacled owl 10 10
2772 2 r. Malay fish owl 20 25
2773 3 r. Peregrine falcon 30 35
2774 5 r. Golden eagle 50 55
2775 7 r. Ruppell's parrot 70 75
2776 7 r. Blue-headed parrot . . . 70 75
2777 7 r. St. Vincent amazon . . . 70 75
2778 7 r. Grey parrot 70 75
2779 7 r. Masked lovebird 70 75
2780 7 r. Sun conure 70 75
2781 8 r. Bateleur 80 85
2782 10 r. Whiskered tern with chicks 1·00 1·10
2783 10 r. Common caracara . . . 1·00 1·10
2784 15 r. Red-footed booby . . . 1·50 1·60

1997. Flowers. Multicoloured.
2786 1 r. Type **354** 10 10
2787 2 r. "Delphinium macrocentron" 20 25
2788 3 r. "Leucadendron discolor" 30 35
2789 5 r. "Nymphaea caerulea" . 50 55
2790 7 r. "Rosa multiflora polyantha" (20 × 23 mm) . 70 75
2791 8 r. "Bulbophyllum barbigerum" 80 85
2792 8 r. "Acacia seyal" (horiz) . . 80 85
2793 8 r. "Gloriosa superba" (horiz) 80 85
2794 8 r. "Gnidia subcordata" (horiz) 80 85
2795 8 r. "Platycelyphium voense" (horiz) 80 85
2796 8 r. "Aspilia mossambicensis" (horiz) 80 85
2797 8 r. "Adenium obesum" (horiz) 80 85
2798 12 r. "Hibiscus vitifolius" . . 1·25 1·40
Nos. 2792/7 were printed together, se-tenant, with the backgrounds forming a composite design.

355 Archaeopteryx

1997. Prehistoric Animals. Multicoloured. (a) Horiz designs.
2800 5 r. Type **355** 50 55
2801 7 r. Diplodocus 70 75
2802 7 r. Tyrannosaurus rex . . . 70 75
2803 7 r. Pteranodon 70 75
2804 7 r. Montanceratops 70 75
2805 7 r. Dromaeosaurus 70 75
2806 7 r. Oviraptor 70 75
2807 8 r. Mosasaurus 80 85
2808 12 r. Deinonychus . . . . . 1·25 1·40
2809 15 r. Triceratops . . . . . 1·50 1·60

(b) Square designs, 31 × 31 mm.
2810 7 r. Troodon 70 75
2811 7 r. Brachiosaurus 70 75
2812 7 r. Saltasaurus 70 75
2813 7 r. Oviraptor 70 75
2814 7 r. Parasaurolophus 70 75
2815 7 r. Psittacosaurus 70 75
2816 7 r. Triceratops 70 75
2817 7 r. Pachycephalosaurus . . . 70 75
2818 7 r. Iguanodon 70 75
2819 7 r. Tyrannosaurus rex . . . 70 75
2820 7 r. Corythosaurus 70 75
2821 7 r. Stegosaurus 70 75
2822 7 r. Euophlocephalus 70 75
2823 7 r. Compsognathus 70 75
2824 7 r. Herrerasaurus 70 75
2825 7 r. Styracosaurus 70 75
2826 7 r. Baryonyx 70 75
2827 7 r. Lesothosaurus 70 75
Nos. 2801/6, 2810/15, 2816/21 and 2822/7 respectively were printed together, se-tenant, with the backgrounds of Nos. 2801/6 and 2810/15 forming composite designs.

1997. World Cup Football Championship, France. As T **246** of Lesotho but horizontal.
2829 1 r. black 10 10
2830 2 r. black 25 25
2831 3 r. multicoloured 30 35
2832/39 3 r. × 8 (black; black; multicoloured; multi-coloured; black; multi-coloured; black; multi-coloured) . . . . 2·40 2·50
2840/47 3 r. × 8 (multicoloured; multicoloured; black; black; black; multi-coloured; multicoloured; black) . 2·40 2·50
2848/55 3 r. × 8 (multicoloured; multicoloured; multi-coloured; black; black; multicoloured; multi-coloured; multicoloured) 2·40 2·50
2856 7 r. black 70 75
2857 8 r. black 80 85
2858 10 r. multicoloured . . . . 1·00 1·10
DESIGNS: No. 2829, Brazilian team, 1994; 2830, German player, 1954; 2831, Maradona holding World Cup, 1986; 2832, Brazilian team, 1958; 2833, Luis Bellini, Brazil, 1958; 2834, Brazilian team, 1962; 2835, Carlos Alberto, Brazil, 1970; 2836, Mauro, Brazil, 1962; 2837, Brazilian team, 1970; 2838, Dunga, Brazil, 1994; 2839, Brazilian team, 1994; 2840, Paulo Rossi, Italy, 1982; 2841, Zoff and Gentile, Italy, 1982; 2842, Angelo Schavio, Italy; 2843, Italian team, 1934; 2844, Italian team with flag, 1934; 2845, Italian team, 1982; 2846, San Paolo Stadium, Italy; 2847, Italian team, 1938; 2848, English player with ball, 1966; 2849, Wembley Stadium, London; 2850, English player heading ball, 1966; 2851, English players celebrating, 1966; 2852, English and German players chasing ball, 1966; 2853, English player wearing No. 21 shirt, 1966; 2854, English team

with Jules Rimet trophy, 1966; 2855, German player wearing No. 5 shirt, 1966; 2856, Argentine player holding trophy, 1978; 2857, English players with Jules Rimet trophy, 1966; 2858, Brazilian player with trophy, 1970.

1998. Diana, Princess of Wales Commemoration. As T **249** of Lesotho. Multicoloured (except Nos. 2864, 2870, 2872 and 2877).

2860 7 r. Laughing 70 75
2861 7 r. With Prince William and Prince Harry 70 75
2862 7 r. Carrying bouquets . . . 70 75
2863 7 r. In white evening dress . . 70 75
2864 7 r. Wearing bow tie (brown and black) 70 75
2865 7 r. Wearing black jacket . . 70 75
2866 7 r. With Indian child on lap 70 75
2867 7 r. Wearing blue evening dress 70 75
2868 7 r. Wearing blue jacket and poppy 70 75
2869 7 r. Wearing cream jacket . . 70 75
2870 7 r. Wearing blouse and jacket (brown and black) . . . 70 75
2871 7 r. Wearing red jacket . . . 70 75
2872 7 r. Wearing hat (blue and black) 70 75
2873 7 r. Wearing red evening dress 70 75
2874 7 r. With Sir Richard Attenborough 70 75
2875 7 r. Wearing jeans and white shirt 70 75
2876 7 r. Wearing white jacket . . 70 75
2877 7 r. Carrying bouquet (brown and black) 70 75

356 Pres. Nelson Mandela

357 Pres. John F. Kennedy

1998. 80th Birthday of Nelson Mandela (President of South Africa).

2879 **356** 7 r. multicoloured . . . 70 75

1998. Pres. John F. Kennedy Commemoration. Multicoloured, background colours given.

2880 **357** 5 r. green 50 55
2881 – 5 r. green 50 55
2882 – 5 r. brown (inscr at right) 50 55
2883 – 5 r. yellow 50 55
2884 – 5 r. violet 50 55
2885 – 5 r. blue 50 55
2886 – 5 r. grey 50 55
2887 – 5 r. brown (inscr at left) . 50 55
2888 – 5 r. blue (value at bottom right) 50 55

DESIGNS: Nos. 2881/8, Various portraits.

358 Yakovlev Yak-18 (from 1947)

1998. Aircraft in Longest Continuous Production. Multicoloured.

2889 5 r. Type **358** 50 55
2890 5 r. Beechcraft Bonanza (from 1947) 50 55
2891 5 r. Piper Cub (1937–82) . . 50 55
2892 5 r. Tupolev Tu-95 (1954–90) 50 55
2893 5 r. Lockheed C-130 Hercules (from 1954) 50 55
2894 5 r. Piper PA-28 Cherokee (from 1961) 50 55
2895 5 r. Mikoyan Gurevich MiG-21 (from 1959) 50 55
2896 5 r. Pilatus PC-6 Turbo Porter (from 1960) 50 55
2897 5 r. Antonov An-2 (from 1949) 50 55

359 White American Shorthair

1998. Cats. Multicoloured.

2899 5 r. Type **359** 50 55
2900 7 r. American curl and Maine coon (horiz) 70 75
2901 7 r. Maine coon (horiz) . . . 70 75
2902 7 r. Siberian (horiz) 70 75
2903 7 r. Somali (horiz) 70 75
2904 7 r. European Burmese (horiz) 70 75
2905 7 r. Nebelung (horiz) 70 75
2906 7 r. Bicolor British shorthair (horiz) 70 75
2907 7 r. Manx (horiz) 70 75
2908 7 r. Tabby American shorthair (horiz) 70 75
2909 7 r. Silver tabby Persian (horiz) 70 75
2910 7 r. Oriental white (horiz) . . 70 75
2911 7 r. Norwegian forest cat (horiz) 70 75
2912 8 r. Sphynx cat 80 85
2913 10 r. Tabby American shorthair 1·00 1·10
2914 12 r. Scottish fold . . . . . 1·25 1·25

Nos. 2900/5 and 2906/11 respectively were printed together, se-tenant, forming composite designs.

360 Boeing 737 HS

1998. Aircraft. Multicoloured.

2916 2 r. Type **360** 20 25
2917 5 r. CL-215 (flying boat) . . 50 55
2918 5 r. Orion 50 55
2919 5 r. Yakolev Yak-54 . . . . 50 55
2920 5 r. Cessna sea plane 50 55
2921 5 r. CL-215 (amphibian) . . 50 55
2922 5 r. CL-215 SAR (amphibian) 50 55
2923 5 r. Twin Otter 50 55
2924 5 r. Rockwell Quail 50 55
2925 5 r. F.S.W. fighter 50 55
2926 5 r. V-Jet II 50 55
2927 5 r. Pilatus PC-12 . . . . . 50 55
2928 5 r. Citation Exel 50 55
2929 5 r. Stutz Bearcat 50 55
2930 5 r. Cessna T-37 (B) 50 55
2931 5 r. Peregrine Business Jet . 50 55
2932 5 r. Beech 58 Baron 50 55
2933 7 r. Boeing 727 . . . . . . 70 75
2934 8 r. Boeing 747-400 . . . . 80 85
2935 10 r. Boeing 737 . . . . . . 1·00 1·10

361 Captain Edward Smith's Cap

1998. "Titanic" Commemoration. Multicoloured.

2937 7 r. Type **361** 70 75
2938 7 r. Deck chair 70 75
2939 7 r. Fifth Officer Harold Lowe's coat button 70 75
2940 7 r. Lifeboat 70 75
2941 7 r. "Titanic's" wheel . . . 70 75
2942 7 r. Passenger's lifejacket . . 70 75

362 Guava Tree

1998. 20th Anniv of International Fund of Agriculture. Multicoloured.

2944 1 r. Type **362** 10 15
2945 5 r. Selection of fruit . . . 50 55
2946 7 r. Fishing boat 70 75
2947 8 r. Papaya tree 80 85
2948 10 r. Vegetable produce . . 1·00 1·10

363 Thread-finned Butterflyfish

1998. Fish. Multicoloured.

2949 50 l. Type **363** 10 10
2950 50 l. Queen angelfish . . . 10 10
2951 1 r. Oriental sweetlips . . . 10 15
2952 3 r. Mandarin fish 30 35
2953 3 r. Copper-banded butterflyfish 30 35
2954 3 r. Harlequin tuskfish . . . 30 35
2955 3 r. Yellow-tailed demoiselle 30 35
2956 3 r. Wimplefish 30 35
2957 3 r. Red emperor snapper . 30 35
2958 3 r. Clown triggerfish . . . 30 35
2959 3 r. Common clown 30 35
2960 3 r. Palette surgeonfish ("Regal Tang") 30 35
2961 5 r. Emperor angelfish . . . 50 55
2962 5 r. Common squirrelfish ("Diadem Squirrelfish") . . 50 55
2963 5 r. Lemon-peel angelfish . . 50 55
2964 5 r. Powder-blue surgeonfish 50 55
2965 5 r. Moorish idol 50 55
2966 5 r. Bicolor angelfish ("Bicolor Cherub") 50 55
2967 5 r. Duboulay's angelfish ("Scribbled Angelfish") . 50 55
2968 5 r. Two-banded anemonefish 50 55
2969 5 r. Yellow tang 50 55
2970 7 r. Red-tailed surgeonfish ("Achilles Tang") 70 75
2971 7 r. Bandit angelfish 70 75
2972 8 r. Hooded butterflyfish ("Red-headed Butterflyfish") . . . 80 85
2973 50 r. Blue-striped butterflyfish 5·00 5·25

364 Baden-Powell inspecting Scouts, Amesbury, 1909

1998. 19th World Scout Jamboree, Chile. Multicoloured.

2975 12 r. Type **364** . . . . . . 1·25 1·40
2976 12 r. Sir Robert and Lady Baden-Powell with children, 1927 . . . . 1·25 1·40
2977 12 r. Sir Robert Baden-Powell awarding merit badges, Chicago, 1926 . . . . . . 1·25 1·40

365 Diana, Princess of Wales

1998. 1st Death Anniv of Diana, Princess of Wales.

2978 **365** 10 r. multicoloured . . . 1·00 1·10

MALTA

An island in the Mediterranean Sea, south of Italy. After a period of self-government under various Constitutions, independence was attained on 21 September 1964. The island became a republic on 13 December 1974.

1860. 12 pence = 1 shilling;
20 shillings = 1 pound.
1972. 10 mils = 1 cent;
100 cents = M£1.

1

5

1860. Various frames.

18 **1** ½d. yellow . . . . 26·00 35·00
20 ½d. green . . . . 1·60 50
22 – 1d. red . . . . 2·00 35
23 – 2d. grey . . . . 4·50 1·25
26 – 2½d. blue . . . . 32·00 90
27 – 4d. brown . . . . 10·00 3·00
28 – 1s. violet . . . . 32·00 9·00
30 **5** 5s. red . . . . £110 80·00

6 Harbour of Valletta

7 Gozo Fishing Boat

8 Ancient Maltese Galley

9 Emblematic Figure of Malta

10 Shipwreck of St. Paul

12

1899.

45 **6** ¼d. brown . . . . 1·40 10
79 4d. black . . . . 11·00 2·75
32 **7** 4½d. brown . . . . 12·00 9·50
58 4½d. orange . . . . 4·00 3·25
59 **8** 5d. red . . . . 24·00 4·50
60 5d. green . . . . 3·75 3·25
34 **9** 2s. 6d. olive . . . . . . 40·00 12·00
35 **10** 10s. black . . . . 80·00 60·00

1902. No. 26 surch **One Penny**.

36 1d. on 2½d. blue 70 90

1903.

47b **12** ½d. green . . . . 2·50 10
48 1d. black and red . . . . 9·00 10
49 1d. red . . . . 1·50 10
50 2d. purple and grey . . . . 6·00 1·40
51 2d. grey . . . . 2·50 4·50
52 2½d. purple and blue . . . 13·00 40
53 2½d. blue . . . . 5·00 2·25
42 3d. grey and purple . . . . 1·50 50
54 4d. black and brown . . . 9·00 5·00
55 4d. black & red on yellow . 3·75 3·25
44 1s. grey and violet . . . . 13·00 7·00
62 1s. black on green . . . . 6·50 2·25
63 5s. green & red on yellow . 60·00 65·00

13

15

17

18

1914.

69	**13**	¼d. brown	50	10
71		½d. green	1·60	20
73		1d. red	80	10
75		2d. grey	5·50	2·75
77		2½d. blue	1·50	40
78		3d. purple on yellow	2·50	7·50
80		6d. purple	9·00	15·00
81a		1s. black on green	10·00	13·00
86	**15**	2s. purple & blue on blue	50·00	28·00
88		5s. green & red on yellow	75·00	90·00
104	**17**	10s. black	£300	£550

1918. Optd **WAR TAX.**

92	**13**	½d. green	50	15
93	**12**	3d. grey and purple	1·25	7·00

1921.

100	**18**	2d. grey	2·50	1·50

1922. Optd **SELF-GOVERNMENT.**

114	**13**	¼d. brown	10	40
106		½d. green	50	1·25
116		1d. red	50	15
117	**18**	2d. grey	1·40	45
118	**13**	2½d. blue	65	55
108		3d. purple on yellow	1·75	13·00
109		6d. purple	1·75	13·00
110		1s. black on green	2·75	12·00
120	**15**	2s. purple & blue on blue	38·00	75·00
112	**9**	2s. 6d. olive	20·00	38·00
113	**15**	5s. green & red on yellow	50·00	75·00
105	**10**	10s. black	£170	£275
121	**17**	10s. black	£100	£150

1922. Surch **One Farthing.**

122	**18**	¼d. on 2d. grey	40	30

22

23

1922.

123a	**22**	¼d. brown	1·40	30
124		½d. green	1·25	10
125		1d. orange and purple	1·90	15
126		1d. violet	1·90	65
127		1½d. red	1·75	10
128		2d. brown and blue	2·00	80
129		2½d. blue	1·50	60
130		3d. blue	2·25	70
131		3d. black on yellow	1·75	8·50
132		4d. yellow and blue	1·25	1·75
133		6d. green and violet	2·25	1·50
134	**23**	1s. blue and brown	4·25	2·50
135		2s. brown and blue	7·00	8·50
136		2s. 6d. purple and black	8·50	13·00
137		5s. orange and blue	19·00	30·00
138		10s. grey and brown	50·00	£120
140	**22**	£1 black and red	90·00	£250

1925. Surch **Two pence halfpenny.**

141	**22**	2½d. on 3d. blue	1·00	2·00

1926. Optd **POSTAGE.**

143	**22**	¼d. brown	30	2·25
144		½d. green	40	15
145		1d. violet	50	25
146		1½d. red	50	40
147		2d. brown and blue	50	30
148		2½d. blue	80	50
149		3d. black on yellow	40	50
150		4d. yellow and blue	3·75	12·00
151		6d. green and violet	2·25	2·00
152	**23**	1s. blue and brown	4·50	8·50
153		2s. brown and blue	45·00	£130
154		2s. 6d. purple and black	9·00	24·00
155		5s. orange and blue	8·00	26·00
156		10s. grey and brown	6·50	14·00

26

27 Valletta Harbour

28 St. Publius

1926. Inscr "POSTAGE".

157	**26**	¼d. brown	70	15
158		½d. green	50	15
159		1d. red	2·00	80
160		1½d. brown	1·50	10
161		2d. grey	3·75	8·00
162		2½d. blue	3·25	30
162a		3d. violet	3·50	2·00
163		4d. black and red	2·75	7·50
164		4½d. violet and yellow	3·00	2·50
165		6d. violet and red	3·50	2·25
166	**27**	1s. black	5·50	3·00
167	**28**	1s. 6d. black and green	5·50	12·00
168	–	2s. black and purple	5·50	14·00
169	–	2s. 6d. black and red	13·00	40·00
170	–	3s. black and blue	15·00	27·00
171	–	5s. black and green	21·00	55·00
172	–	10s. black and red	55·00	£100

DESIGNS—As Type **27**: 2s. Mdina (Notabile); 5s. Neolithic temple, Mnajdra. As Type **28**: 2s. 6d. Gozo boat; 3s. Neptune; 10s. St. Paul.

1928. Air. Optd **AIR MAIL.**

173	**26**	6d. violet and red	1·25	90

1928. Optd **POSTAGE AND REVENUE.**

174	**26**	¼d. brown	1·25	10
175		½d. green	1·00	10
176		1d. red	1·50	2·50
177		1d. brown	3·50	10
178		1½d. brown	1·75	30
179		1½d. red	3·75	10
180		2d. grey	3·25	8·00
181		2½d. blue	1·50	10
182		3d. violet	1·25	30
183		4d. black and red	1·25	1·00
184		4½d. violet and yellow	2·25	1·00
185		6d. violet and red	2·25	1·00
186	**27**	1s. black	4·25	2·25
187	**28**	1s. 6d. black and green	5·00	9·00
188	–	2s. black and purple	20·00	48·00
189	–	2s. 6d. black and red	15·00	23·00
190	–	3s. black and blue	18·00	30·00
191	–	5s. black and green	26·00	65·00
192	–	10s. black and red	55·00	90·00

1930. As Nos. 157/72, but inscr "POSTAGE & REVENUE".

193	¼d. brown	50	10
194	½d. green	50	10
195	1d. brown	60	10
196	1½d. red	70	10
197	2d. grey	1.00	20
198	2½d. blue	2·00	10
199	3d. violet	1·50	20
200	4d. black and red	1·25	3·25
201	4½d. violet and yellow	2·50	1·00
202	6d. violet and red	2·00	85
203	1s. black	8·50	10·00
204	1s. 6d. black and green	6·50	17·00
205	2s. black and purple	8·50	17·00
206	2s. 6d. black and red	16·00	48·00
207	3s. black and blue	23·00	55·00
208	5s. black and green	28·00	65·00
209	10s. black and red	65·00	£120

1935. Silver Jubilee. As T **13** of Antigua.

210	½d. black and green	40	50
211	2½d. brown and blue	2·50	3·75
212	6d. blue and olive	6·00	3·75
213	1s. grey and purple	10·00	15·00

1937. Coronation. As T **2** of Aden.

214	½d. green	10	10
215	1½d. red	50	15
216	2½d. blue	50	35

37 Grand Harbour, Valletta

38 H.M.S. "St. Angelo"

39 Verdala Palace

1938. Various designs with medallion King George VI.

217	**37**	¼d. brown	10	10
218	**38**	½d. green	1·75	10
218a		½d. brown	55	30
219	**39**	1d. brown	4·25	30
219a		1d. green	60	10
220	–	1½d. red	1·00	15
220b	–	1½d. black	30	15
221	–	2d. black	40	1·50
221a	–	2d. red	40	10
222	–	2½d. blue	75	30
222a	–	2½d. violet	60	10
223	–	3d. violet	45	70
223a	–	3d. blue	30	10
224	–	4½d. olive and brown	50	10
225	–	6d. olive and red	75	15
226	–	1s. black	75	30
227	–	1s. 6d. black and olive	7·00	3·50
228	–	2s. green and blue	3·25	3·75
229	–	2s. 6d. black and red	7·00	4·50
230	–	5s. black and green	5·50	5·50
231	–	10s. black and red	14·00	14·00

DESIGNS—As Types **38/9**. VERT: 1½d. Hypogeum, Hal Saflieni; 3d. St. John's Co-Cathedral; 6d. Statue of Manoel de Vilhena; 1s. Maltese girl wearing faldetta; 5s. Palace Square, Valletta; 10s. St. Paul. HORIZ: 2d. Victoria and Citadel, Gozo; 2½d. De I'Isle Adam entering Mdina; 4½d. Ruins at Mnajdra; 1s. 6d. St. Publius; 2s. Mdina Cathedral; 2s. 6d. Statue of Neptune.

1946. Victory. As T **9** of Aden.

232	1d. green	10	10
233	3d. blue	10	30

1948. Self-Government. As 1938 issue optd **SELF-GOVERNMENT 1947.**

234	¼d. brown	20	20
235	½d. brown	20	10
236	1d. green	20	10
236a	1d. grey	20	10
237	1½d. black	75	10
237b	1½d. green	30	10
238	2d. red	75	10
238a	2d. yellow	30	10
239	2½d. violet	80	10
239a	2½d. red	30	85
240	3d. blue	30	15
240a	3d. violet	35	15
241	4½d. olive and brown	2·00	1·50
241a	4½d. olive and blue	50	90
242	6d. olive and red	1·25	15
243	1s. black	2·25	40
244	1s. 6d. black and olive	2·50	45
245	2s. green and blue	5·00	1·50
246	2s. 6d. black and red	12·00	2·50
247	5s. black and green	17·00	4·50
248	10s. black and red	17·00	20·00

1949. Silver Wedding. As T **10/11** of Aden.

249	1d. green	50	10
250	£1 blue	38·00	35·00

1949. U.P.U. As T **20/23** of Antigua.

251	2½d. violet	30	10
252	3d. blue	2·50	50
253	6d. red	1·25	50
254	1s. black	1·25	1·75

53 Queen Elizabeth II when Princess

54 "Our Lady of Mount Carmel" (attrib Palladino)

1950. Visit of Princess Elizabeth.

255	**53**	1d. green	10	10
256		3d. blue	20	10
257		1s. black	55	45

1951. 7th Centenary of the Scapular.

258	**54**	1d. green	10	10
259		3d. violet	20	10
260		1s. black	60	40

1953. Coronation. As T **13** of Aden.

261	1½d. black and green	30	10

55 St. John's Co-Cathedral

56 "Immaculate Conception" (Caruana) (altar-piece, Cospicua)

1954. Royal Visit.

262	**55**	3d. violet	30	10

1954. Centenary of Dogma of the Immaculate Conception.

263	**56**	1½d. green	10	10
264		3d. blue	10	10
265		1s. grey	35	20

57 Monument of the Great Siege, 1565

74 "Defence of Malta"

1956.

266	**57**	¼d. violet	20	10
267	–	½d. orange	50	10
314	–	1d. black	50	30
269	–	1½d. green	30	10
270	–	2d. sepia	1·25	10
271	–	2½d. brown	45	30
272	–	3d. red	75	10
273	–	4½d. blue	1·00	20
274	–	6d. blue	50	10
275	–	8d. ochre	1·50	1·00
276	–	1s. violet	50	10
277	–	1s. 6d. turquoise	8·50	20
278	–	2s. olive	10·00	80
279	–	2s. 6d. brown	6·50	2·25
280	–	5s. green	12·00	2·75
281	–	10s. red	35·00	9·00
282	–	£1 brown	35·00	20·00

DESIGNS—VERT: ½d. Wignacourt aqueduct horsetrough; 1d. Victory church; 1½d. War memorial; 2d. Mosta dome; 3d. The King's scroll; 4½d. Roosevelt's scroll; 8d. Vedette; 1s. Mdina Gate; 1s. 6d. "Les Gavroches" (statue); 2s. Monument of Christ the King; 2s. 6d. Monument of Grand Master Cottoner; 5s. Grand Master Perellos's monument; 10s. St. Paul (statue); £1 Baptism of Christ (statue). HORIZ: 2½d. Auberge de Castile; 6d. Neolithic Temples at Tarxien.

1957. George Cross Commem. Cross in Silver.

283	**74**	1½d. green	15	10
284	–	3d. red	15	10
285	–	1s. brown	15	10

DESIGNS—HORIZ: 3d. Searchlights over Malta. VERT: 1s. Bombed buildings.

77 Design

81 Sea Raid on Grand Harbour, Valletta

1958. Technical Education in Malta. Inscr "TECHNICAL EDUCATION".

286	**77**	1½d. black and green	10	10
287	–	3d. black, red and grey	10	10
288	–	1s. grey, purple and black	15	10

DESIGNS—VERT: 3d. "Construction". HORIZ: 1s. Technical School, Paola.

1958. George Cross Commem. Cross in first colour outlined in silver.

289	–	1½d. green and black	15	10
290	**81**	3d. red and black	15	10
291	–	1s. mauve and black	15	10

DESIGNS—HORIZ: 1½d. Bombed-out family; 1s. Searchlight crew.

83 Air Raid Casualties

86 Shipwreck of St. Paul (after Palombi)

87 Statue of St. Paul, Rabat, Malta

1959. George Cross Commemoration.

292	**83**	1½d. green, black & gold	20	10
293	–	3d. mauve, black & gold	20	10
294	–	1s. grey, black and gold	70	65

DESIGNS—HORIZ: 3d. "For Gallantry". VERT: 1s. Maltese under bombardment.

1960. 19th Centenary of the Shipwreck of St. Paul. Inscr as in T **86/7**.

295	**86**	1½d. blue, gold & brown	15	10
296	–	3d. purple, gold and blue	15	10
297	–	6d. red, gold and grey	25	10
298	**87**	8d. black and gold	30	50
299	–	1s. purple and gold	25	10
300	–	2s. 6d. blue, green & gold	1·00	2·00

DESIGNS—As Type **88**: 3d. Consecration of St. Publius, First Bishop of Malta; 6d. Departure of St. Paul (after Palombi). As Type **87**: 1s. Angel with the "Acts of the Apostles"; 2s. 6d. St. Paul with the "Second Epistle to the Corinthians".

92 Stamp of 1860

1960. Centenary of Malta Stamps. Stamp in buff and blue.

301	92	1½d. green	25	10
302		3d. red	30	10
303		6d. blue	40	80

93 George Cross

1961. George Cross Commemoration.

304	93	1½d. black, cream & bistre	15	10
305	–	3d. brown and blue	30	10
306	–	1s. green, lilac and violet	60	1·40

DESIGNS: 3d. and 1s. show George Cross as Type **93** over backgrounds with different patterns.

96 "Madonna Damascena" 100 Bruce, Zammit and Microscope

1962. Great Siege Commemoration.

307	96	2d. blue	10	10
308	–	3d. red	10	10
309	–	6d. bronze	25	10
310	–	1s. purple	25	30

DESIGNS: 3d. Great Siege Monument; 6d. Grand Master La Valette; 1s. Assault on Fort St. Elmo.

1963. Freedom from Hunger. As T **28** of Aden.

311	1s. 6d. sepia	2·00	2·50

1963. Cent of Red Cross. As T **33** of Antigua.

312	2d. red on black	25	15
313	1s. 6d. red and blue	3·00	3·75

1964. Anti-Brucellosis Congress.

316	100	2d. brown, black & green	10	10
317	–	1s. 6d. black and purple	75	20

DESIGN: 1s. 6d. Goat and laboratory equipment.

102 "Nicola Cotoner tending Sick Man" (M. Preti)

1964. 1st European Catholic Doctors' Congress, Valletta. Multicoloured.

318	2d. Type **102**	20	10
319	6d. St. Luke and hospital	50	15
320	1s. 6d. Sacra Infermeria, Valletta	1·10	1·60

106 Dove and British Crown 110 Neolithic Era

109 "The Nativity"

1964. Independence.

321	106	2d. olive, red and gold	30	10
322	–	3d. brown, red and gold	30	10
323	–	6d. slate, red and gold	70	15
324	106	1s. blue, red and gold	70	15
325	–	1s. 6d. blue, red & gold	2·00	1·00
326	–	2s. 6d. blue, red & gold	2·00	2·25

DESIGNS: 3d., 1s. 6d. Dove and Pope's Tiara; 6d., 2s. 6d. Dove and U.N. emblem.

1964. Christmas.

327	109	2d. purple and gold	10	10
328		4d. blue and gold	20	15
329		8d. green and gold	45	45

1965. Multicoloured.

330	½d. Type **110**	10	10
331	1d. Punic era	10	10
332	1½d. Roman era	30	10
333	2d. Proto Christian era	10	10
334	2½d. Saracenic era	40	10
335	3d. Siculo Norman era	10	10
336	4d. Knights of Malta	30	10
337	4½d. Maltese Navy	85	40
337b	5d. Fortifications	30	20
338	6d. French occupation	20	10
339	8d. British rule	40	10
339c	10d. Naval Arsenal	45	1·60
340	1s. Maltese Corps of the British Army	30	10
341	1s. 3d. International Eucharistic Congress, 1913	2·00	1·40
342	1s. 6d. Self-Government, 1921	60	10
343	2s. Gozo Civic Council	70	10
344	2s. 6d. State of Malta	70	50
345	3s. Independence, 1964	1·25	75
346	5s. HAFMED (Allied Forces, Mediterranean)	5·50	1·00
347	10s. The Maltese Islands (map)	3·50	3·00
348	£1 Patron Saints	3·75	5·00

Nos. 339/48 are larger, 41 × 29 mm from perf to perf and include portrait of Queen Elizabeth II.

129 "Dante" (Raphael) 131 Turkish Fleet

1965. 700th Birth Anniv of Dante.

349	129	2d. blue	10	10
350		6d. green	25	10
351		2s. brown	1·10	1·25

1965. 400th Anniv of Great Siege. Multicoloured.

352	2d. Turkish camp	30	10
353	3d. Battle scene	30	10
354	6d. Type **131**	50	10
355	8d. Arrival of relief force	90	90
356	1s. Grand Master J. de La Valette's arms	50	10
357	1s. 6d. "Allegory of Victory" (from mural by M. Preti)	1·25	30
358	2s. 6d. Victory medal	1·50	3·00

SIZES—As Type **131**: 1s. SQUARE (32½ × 32½ mm): others.

137 "The Three Kings"

1965. Christmas.

359	137	1d. purple and red	10	10
360		4d. purple and blue	30	25
361		1s. 3d. slate and purple	30	30

138 Sir Winston Churchill

1966. Churchill Commemoration.

362	138	2d. black, red and gold	20	10
363	–	3d. green, olive and gold	20	10
364	138	1s. purple, red and gold	25	10
365	–	1s. 6d. blue, ultram & gold	35	40

DESIGN: 3d., 1s. 6d. Sir Winston Churchill and George Cross.

140 Grand Master La Valette 145 Pres. Kennedy and Memorial

1966. 400th Anniv of Valletta. Multicoloured.

366	2d. Type **140**	10	10
367	3d. Pope Pius V	10	10
368	6d. Map of Valletta	15	10
369	1s. F. Laparelli (architect)	15	10
370	2s. 6d. G. Cassar (architect)	35	50

1966. Pres. Kennedy Commemoration.

371	145	3d. olive, gold and black	10	10
372		1s. 6d. blue, gold & black	10	10

146 "Trade" 147 "The Child in the Manger"

1966. 10th Malta Trade Fair.

373	146	2d. multicoloured	10	10
374		8d. multicoloured	30	25
375		2s. 6d. multicoloured	30	25

1966. Christmas.

376	147	1d. multicoloured	10	10
377		4d. multicoloured	10	10
378		1s. 3d. multicoloured	10	10

148 George Cross 149 Crucifixion of St. Peter

1967. 25th Anniv of George Cross Award to Malta.

379	148	2d. multicoloured	10	10
380		4d. multicoloured	10	10
381		3s. multicoloured	15	15

1967. 1,900th Anniv of Martyrdom of Saints Peter and Paul.

382	149	2d. brown, orange and blk	10	10
383	–	8d. olive, gold and black	15	10
384	–	3s. blue and black	20	15

DESIGNS—As Type **149**: 3s. Beheading of St. Paul. HORIZ (47 × 25 mm): 8d. Open Bible and episcopal emblems.

152 "St. Catherine of Siena" 156 Temple Ruins, Tarxien

1967. 300th Death Anniv of Melchior Gafa (sculptor). Multicoloured.

385	2d. Type **152**	10	10
386	4d. "St. Thomas of Villanova"	10	10
387	1s. 6d. "Baptism of Christ" (detail)	15	10
388	2s. 6d. "St. John the Baptist" (from "Baptism of Christ")	15	10

1967. 15th Int Historical Architecture Congress, Valletta. Multicoloured.

389	2d. Type **156**	10	10
390	6d. Facade of Palazzo Falzon, Notabile	10	10
391	1s. Parish Church, Birkirkara	10	10
392	3s. Portal, Auberge de Castille	25	25

160 "Angels" 166 Human Rights Emblem and People

163 Queen Elizabeth II and Arms of Malta

1967. Christmas. Multicoloured.

393	1d. Type **160**	10	10
394	8d. "Crib"	15	10
395	1s. 4d. "Angels"	15	10

1967. Royal Visit.

396	163	2d. multicoloured	10	10
397	–	4d. black, purple and gold	10	10
398	–	3s. multicoloured	20	25

DESIGNS—VERT: 4d. Queen in Robes of Order of St. Michael and St. George. HORIZ: 3s. Queen and outline of Malta.

1968. Human Rights Year. Multicoloured.

399	2d. Type **166**	10	10
400	6d. Human Rights emblem and people (different)	10	10
401	2s. Type **166** (reversed)	10	10

169 Fair "Products" 170 Arms of the Order of St. John and La Valette

1968. Malta International Trade Fair.

402	169	4d. multicoloured	10	10
403		8d. multicoloured	10	10
404		3s. multicoloured	15	10

1968. 4th Death Cent of Grand Master La Valette. Multicoloured.

405	1d. Type **170**	10	10
406	8d. "La Valette" (A. de Favray)	15	10
407	1s. 6d. La Valette's tomb (28 × 23 mm)	15	10
408	2s. 6d. Angels and scroll bearing date of death	20	20

The 8d., 2s. 6d. are vert.

174 Star of Bethlehem and Angel waking Shepherds 177 "Agriculture"

1968. Christmas. Multicoloured.

409	1d. Type **174**	10	10
410	8d. Mary and Joseph with shepherd watching over Cradle	15	10
411	1s. 4d. Three Wise Men and Star of Bethlehem	15	20

1968. 6th Food and Agricultural Organization Regional Conference for Europe. Mult.

412	4d. Type **177**	10	10
413	1s. F.A.O. emblem and coin	10	10
414	2s. 6d. "Agriculture" sowing Seeds	10	15

180 Mahatma Gandhi 181 ILO Emblem

1969. Birth Centenary of Mahatma Gandhi.

415	180	1s. 6d. brown, blk & gold	15	10

1969. 50th Anniv of Int Labour Organization.

416	181	2d. blue, gold and turq	10	10
417		6d. sepia, gold & brown	10	10

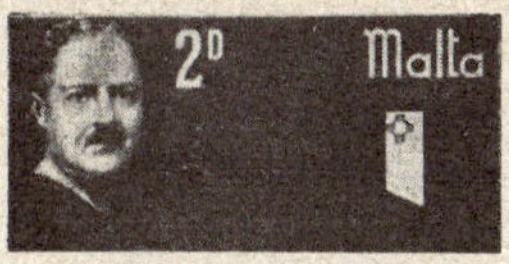

182 Robert Samut

1969. Birth Centenary of Robert Samut (composer of Maltese National Anthem).

418	**182**	2d. multicoloured	10	10

183 Dove of Peace, U.N. Emblem and Sea-Bed

1969. United Nations Resolution on Oceanic Resources.

419	**183**	5d. multicoloured	10	10

184 "Swallows" returning to Malta

1969. Maltese Migrants' Convention.

420	**184**	10d. black, gold and olive	10	10

185 University Arms and Grand Master de Fonseca (founder)

1969. Bicentenary of University of Malta.

421	**185**	2s. multicoloured	10	20

187 Flag of Malta and Birds

1969. 5th Anniv of Independence.

422	–	2d. multicoloured	10	10
423	**187**	5d. black, red and gold . .	10	10
424	–	10d. black, blue & gold . .	10	10
425	–	1s. 6d. multicoloured . . .	15	30
426	–	2s. 6d. black, brn & gold .	20	35

DESIGNS—SQUARE (31 × 31 mm): 2d. 1919 War Monument. VERT: 10d. "Tourism"; 1s. 6d. U.N. and Council of Europe emblems; 2s. 6d. "Trade and Industry".

191 Peasants playing Tambourine and Bagpipes

1969. Christmas. Children's Welfare Fund. Multicoloured.

427		1d. + 1d. Type **191**	10	20
428		5d. + 1d. Angels playing trumpet and harp	15	20
429		1s. 6d. + 3d. Choir boys singing	15	45

194 "The Beheading of St. John" (Caravaggio)

1970. 13th Council of Europe Art Exn. Mult.

430		1d. Type **194**	10	10
431		2d. "St. John the Baptist" (M. Preti)	10	10
432		5d. Interior of St. John's Co-Cathedral, Valletta	10	10
433		6d. "Allegory of the Order" (Neapolitan school)	10	10
434		8d. "St. Jerome" (Caravaggio)	15	20
435		10d. Articles from the Order of St. John in Malta	15	10
436		1s. 6d. "The Blessed Gerard receiving Godfrey de Bouillon" (A. de Favray)	20	25
437		2s. Cape and Stolone (16th cent)	25	35

SIZES—HORIZ: 1d., 8d. 56 × 30 mm; 2d., 6d. 45 × 32 mm; 10d. 2s. 63 × 21 mm; 1s. 6d. 45 × 34 mm. SQUARE: 5d. 39 × 39 mm.

202 Artist's Impression of Fujiyama

1970. World Fair, Osaka.

438	**202**	2d. multicoloured	10	10
439		5d. multicoloured	10	10
440		3s. multicoloured	15	15

203 "Peace and Justice" **204** Carol-singers, Church and Star

1970. 25th Anniv of United Nations.

441	**203**	2d. multicoloured	10	10
442		5d. multicoloured	10	10
443		2s. 6d. multicoloured . . .	15	15

1970. Christmas. Multicoloured.

444		1d. + ½d. Type **204**	10	10
445		10d. + 2d. Church, star and angels with Infant	10	20
446		1s. 6d. + 3d. Church, star and nativity scene	15	35

207 Books and Quill

1971. Literary Anniversaries. Multicoloured.

447		1s. 6d. Type **207** (De Soldanis (historian) death bicent) . .	10	10
448		2s. Dun Karm (poet), books, pens and lamp (birth cent) .	10	15

209 Europa "Chain" **211** "Centaurea spathulata"

210 "St. Joseph, Patron of the Universal Church" (G. Cali)

1971. Europa.

449	**209**	2d. orange, black & olive	10	10
450		5d. orange, black and red	10	10
451		1s. 6d. orange, blk & slate	45	90

1971. Cent of Proclamation of St. Joseph as Patron Saint of Catholic Church, and 50th Anniv of Coronation of the Statue of "Our Lady of Victories". Multicoloured.

452		2d. Type **210**	10	10
453		5d. Statue of "Our Lady of Victories" and galley . . .	10	10
454		10d. Type **210**	15	10
455		1s. 6d. As 5d.	30	40

1971. National Plant and Bird of Malta. Multicoloured.

456		2s. Type **211**	10	10
457		5d. Blue rock thrush (horiz) .	20	10
458		10d. As 5d.	30	15
459		1s. 6d. Type **211**	30	1·25

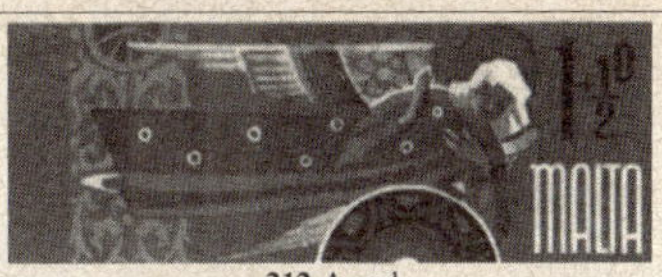

212 Angel

1971. Christmas. Multicoloured.

460		1d. + ½d. Type **212**	10	10
461		10d. + 2d. Mary and the Child Jesus	15	20
462		1s. 6d. + 3d. Joseph lying awake	20	30

213 Heart and W.H.O. Emblem

1972. World Health Day.

464	**213**	2d. multicoloured	10	10
465		10d. multicoloured	15	10
466		2s. 6d. multicoloured . . .	40	80

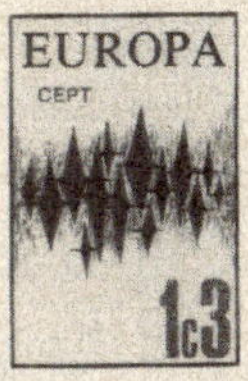

214 Maltese Cross **216** "Communications"

1972. Decimal Currency. Coins. Multicoloured.

467		2 m. Type **214**	10	10
468		3 m. Bee on honeycomb . . .	10	10
469		5 m. Earthen lampstand . . .	10	10
470		1 c. George Cross	10	10
471		2 c. Classical head	10	10
472		5 c. Ritual altar	10	10
473		10 c. Grandmaster's galley . .	20	10
474		50 c. Great Siege Monument .	1·25	1·25

SIZES: 3 m., 2 c. As Type **214**: 5 m., 1 c., 5 c. 25 × 30 mm; 10 c., 50 c. 31 × 38 mm.

1972. Nos. 337a, 339 and 341 surch.

475		1 c. 3 on 5d. multicoloured . .	10	10
476		3 c. on 8d. multicoloured . . .	15	10
477		5 c. on 1s. 3d. multicoloured .	15	20

1972. Europa.

478	**216**	1 c. 3 multicoloured . . .	10	10
479		3 c. multicoloured	10	10
480		5 c. multicoloured	15	35
481		7 c. 5 multicoloured . . .	20	75

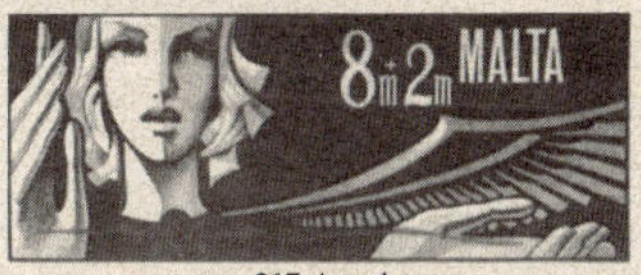

217 Angel

1972. Christmas.

482	**217**	8 m. + 2 m. brown, grey and gold	10	10
483	–	3 c. + 1 c. purple, violet and gold	15	40
484	–	7 c. 5 + 1 c. 5 indigo, blue and gold	20	50

DESIGNS: No. 483, Angel with tambourine; No. 484, Singing angel.

See also Nos. 507/9.

218 Archaeology **219** Europa "Posthorn"

1973. Multicoloured.

486		2 m. Type **218**	10	10
487		4 m. History	10	10
488		5 m. Folklore	10	10
489		8 m. Industry	10	10
490		1 c. Fishing industry	10	10
491		1 c. 3 Pottery	10	10
492		2 c. Agriculture	10	10
493		3 c. Sport	10	10
494		4 c. Yacht marina	15	10
495		5 c. Fiesta	15	10
496		7 c. 5 Regatta	25	10
497		10 c. Voluntary service	25	10
498		50 c. Education	75	1·00
499		£1 Religion	2·00	2·75
500		£2 Coat of arms (32 × 27 mm)	12·00	17·00
500b		£2 National Emblem (32 × 27 mm)	7·00	13·00

1973. Europa.

501	**219**	3 c. multicoloured	15	10
502		5 c. multicoloured	15	35
503		7 c. 5 multicoloured . . .	25	60

220 Emblem, and Woman holding Corn **221** Girolamo Cassar (architect)

1973. Anniversaries.

504	**220**	1 c. 3 multicoloured . . .	10	10
505	–	7 c. 5 multicoloured . . .	25	40
506	–	10 c. multicoloured . . .	30	50

ANNIVERSARIES: 1 c. 3, 10th anniv of World Food Programme; 7 c. 5, 25th anniv of W.H.O.; 10 c. 25th anniv of Universal Declaration of Human Rights.

1973. Christmas. As T **217**. Multicoloured.

507		8 m. + 2 m. Angels and organ pipes	15	10
508		3 c. + 1 c. Madonna and Child	25	55
509		7 c. 5 + 1 c. 5 Buildings and Star	45	1·00

1973. Prominent Maltese.

511	**221**	1 c. 3 deep green, green and gold	10	10
512	–	3 c. green, blue & gold . .	15	10
513	–	5 c. brown, grn & gold .	20	15
514	–	7 c. 5 blue, lt bl & gold .	20	30
515	–	10 c. deep purple, purple and gold	20	40

DESIGNS: 3 c. Giuseppe Barth (ophthalmologist); 5 c. Nicolo' Isouard (composer); 7 c. 5, John Borg (botanist); 10 c. Antonio Sciortino (sculptor).

222 "Air Malta" Emblem

1974. Air. Multicoloured.

516		3 c. Type **222**	15	10
517		4 c. Boeing 720B	15	10
518		5 c. Type **222**	20	10
519		7 c. 5 As 4 c.	25	10
520		20 c. Type **222**	80	60
521		25 c. As 4 c.	80	60
522		35 c. Type **222**	1·10	1·40

223 Prehistoric Sculpture

1974. Europa.

523	**223**	1 c. 3 blue, black & gold .	15	10
524	–	3 c. brown, black & gold .	20	15
525	–	5 c. purple, black & gold .	25	50
526	–	7 c. 5 green, black & gold .	35	1·00

DESIGNS—VERT: 3 c. Old Cathedral Door, Mdina; 7 c. 5, "Vetlina" (sculpture by A. Sciortino). HORIZ: 5 c. Silver monstrance.

224 Heinrich von Stephan (founder) and Land Transport **225** Decorative Star and Nativity Scene

1974. Centenary of U.P.U.

527	**224**	1 c. 3 green, blue & orge .	30	10
528	–	5 c. brown, red & green .	30	10
529	–	7 c. 5 blue, violet & grn .	35	20
530	–	50 c. purple, red & orge .	1·00	1·25

DESIGNS (each containing portrait as Type **224**): 5 c. "Washington" (paddle-steamer) and "Royal Viking Star" (liner); 7 c. 5, Balloon and Boeing 747-100; 50 c. U.P.U. Buildings, 1874 and 1974.

1974. Christmas. Multicoloured.

532		8 m. + 2 m. Type **225**	10	10
533		3 c. + 1 c. "Shepherds" . . .	15	20
534		5 c. + 1 c. "Shepherds with gifts"	20	35
535		7 c. 5 + 1 c. 5 "The Magi" .	30	40

226 Swearing-in of Prime Minister

1975. Inauguration of Republic.

536	**226**	1 c. 3 multicoloured . . .	10	10
537	–	5 c. red and black	20	10
538	–	25 c. multicoloured . . .	60	1·00

DESIGNS: 5 c. National flag; 25 c. Minister of Justice, President and Prime Minister.

227 Mother and Child ("Family Life")

1975. International Women's Year.

539	227	1 c. 3 violet and gold	15	10
540	–	3 c. blue and gold	20	10
541	227	5 c. brown and gold	30	20
542	–	20 c. brown and gold	1·10	2·75

DESIGN: 3 c., 20 c. Office secretary ("Public Life").

228 "Allegory of Malta" (Francesco de Mura)

1975. Europa. Multicoloured.

543	5 c. Type 228	30	10
544	15 c. "Judith and Holofernes" (Valentin de Boulogne)	50	75

The 15 c. is similar: 47 × 23 mm.

229 Plan of Ggantija Temple

1975. European Architectural Heritage Year.

545	229	1 c. 3 black and red	10	10
546	–	3 c. purple, red & brown	20	10
547	–	5 c. brown and red	40	35
548	–	25 c. green, red & black	1·40	3·25

DESIGNS: 3 c. Mdina skyline; 5 c. View of Victoria, Gozo; 25 c. Silhouette of Fort St. Angelo.

230 Farm Animals

231 "The Right to Work"

1975. Christmas. Multicoloured.

549	8 m. + 2 m. Type 230	30	25
550	3 c. + 1 c. Nativity scene (50 × 23 mm)	50	75
551	7 c. 5 + 1 c. 5 Approach of the Magi	60	1·40

1975. 1st Anniv of Republic.

552	231	1 c. 3 multicoloured	10	10
553	–	5 c. multicoloured	20	10
554	–	25 c. red, blue and black	70	1·10

DESIGNS: 5 c. "Safeguarding the Environment"; 25 c. National flag.

232 "Festa Tar-Rahal"

233 Water Polo

1976. Maltese Folklore. Multicoloured.

555	1 c. 3 Type 232	10	10
556	5 c. "L-Imnarja" (horiz)	15	10
557	7 c. 5 "Il-Karnival" (horiz)	35	70
558	10 c. "Il-Gimgha L-Kbira"	55	1·40

1976. Olympic Games, Montreal. Multicoloured.

559	1 c. 7 Type 233	10	10
560	5 c. Sailing	25	10
561	30 c. Athletics	85	1·50

234 Lace-making

1976. Europa. Multicoloured.

562	7 c. Type 234	20	35
563	15 c. Stone carving	25	60

235 Nicola Cotoner

1976. 300th Anniv of School of Anatomy and Surgery. Multicoloured.

564	2 c. Type 235	10	10
565	5 c. Arm	15	10
566	7 c. Giuseppe Zammit	20	10
567	11 c. Sacra Infermeria	35	65

236 St. John the Baptist and St. Michael

237 Jean de la Valette's Armour

1976. Christmas. Multicoloured.

568	1 c. + 5 m. Type 236	15	20
569	5 c. + 1 c. Madonna and Child	20	60
570	7 c. + 1 c. 5 St. Christopher and St. Nicholas	30	80
571	10 c. + 2 c. Complete painting (32 × 27 mm)	40	1·25

Nos. 568/71 show portions of "Madonna and Saints" by Domenico di Michelino.

1977. Suits of Armour. Multicoloured.

572	2 c. Type 237	10	10
573	7 c. Aloph de Wignacourt's armour	20	10
574	11 c. Jean Jacques de Verdelin's armour	25	50

1977. No. 336 surch **1c7**.

575	1 c. 7 on 4d. multicoloured	25	25

239 "Annunciation"

1977. 400th Birth Anniv of Rubens. Flemish Tapestries. Multicoloured.

576	2 c. Type 239	10	10
577	7 c. "Four Evangelists"	25	10
578	11 c. "Nativity"	45	45
579	20 c. "Adoration of the Magi"	80	1·00

See also Nos. 592/5, 615/18 and 638/9.

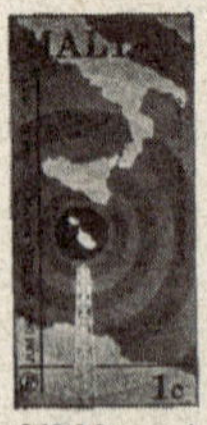

240 Map and Radio Aerial

242 "Aid to Handicapped Workers" (detail from Workers' Monument)

241 Ta' L-Isperanza

1977. World Telecommunications Day.

580	240	1 c. black, green and red	10	10
581		6 c. black, blue and red	20	10
582	–	8 c. black, brn and red	30	10
583	–	17 c. black, mauve & red	60	40

DESIGN—HORIZ: 8, 17 c. Map, aerial and airplane tail-fin.

1977. Europa. Multicoloured.

584	7 c. Type 241	30	15
585	20 c. Is-Salini	35	1·00

1977. Maltese Worker Commemoration.

586	242	2 c. orange and brown	10	10
587	–	7 c. light brown & brown	15	10
588	–	20 c. multicoloured	40	60

DESIGNS—VERT: 7 c. "Stoneworker, modern industry and ship-building" (monument detail). HORIZ: 20 c. "Mother with Dead Son" and Service Medal.

243 The Shepherds

1977. Christmas. Multicoloured.

589	1 c. + 5 m. Type 243	10	20
590	7 c. + 1 c. The Nativity	15	30
591	11 c. + 1 c. 5 The Flight into Egypt	20	45

1978. Flemish Tapestries. (2nd series). As T **239**. Multicoloured.

592	2 c. "The Entry into Jerusalem"	10	10
593	7 c. "The Last Supper" (after Poussin)	25	10
594	11 c. "The Raising of the Cross" (after Rubens)	30	25
595	25 c. "The Resurrection" (after Rubens)	70	80

244 "Young Lady on Horseback and Trooper"

1978. 450th Death Anniv of Albrecht Durer.

596	244	1 c. 7 black, red and blue	10	10
597	–	8 c. black, red and grey	15	10
598	–	17 c. black, red and grey	40	45

DESIGNS: 8 c. "The Bagpiper"; 17 c. "The Virgin and Child with a Monkey".

245 Monument to Grand Master Nicola Cotoner (Foggini)

246 Goalkeeper

1978. Europa. Monuments. Multicoloured.

599	7 c. Type 245	15	10
600	25 c. Monument to Grand Master Ramon Perellos (Mazzuoli)	35	90

1978. World Cup Football Championship, Argentina. Multicoloured.

601	2 c. Type 246	10	10
602	11 c. Players heading ball	15	10
603	15 c. Tackling	25	35

247 Boeing 707 over Megalithic Temple

1978. Air. Multicoloured.

605	5 c. Type 247	20	10
606	7 c. Air Malta Boeing 720B	20	10
607	11 c. Boeing 747 taking off from Luqa Airport	35	10
608	17 c. Type 247	45	30
609	20 c. As 7 c.	60	40
610	75 c. As 11 c.	1·75	2·75

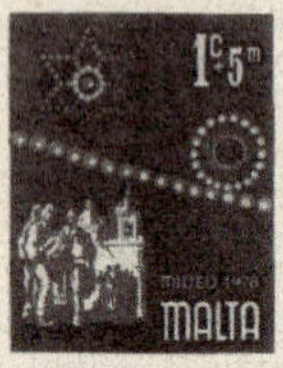

248 Folk Musicians and Village Church

249 Fishing Boat and Aircraft Carrier

1978. Christmas. Multicoloured.

611	1 c. + 5 m. Type 248	10	10
612	5 c. + 1 c. Choir of Angels	15	20
613	7 c. + 1 c. 5 Carol singers	20	35
614	11 c. + 3 c. Folk musicians, church, angels and carol singers (58 × 22 mm)	25	45

1979. Flemish Tapestries (3rd series) showing paintings by Rubens. As T **239**. Multicoloured.

615	2 c. "The Triumph of the Catholic Church"	10	10
616	7 c. "The Triumph of Charity"	20	10
617	11 c. "The Triumph of Faith"	30	25
618	25 c. "The Triumph of Truth"	95	80

1979. End of Military Facilities Agreement. Multicoloured.

619	2 c. Type 249	10	10
620	5 c. Raising the flag ceremony	10	10
621	7 c. Departing soldier and olive sprig	15	10
622	8 c. Type 249	40	40
623	17 c. As 5 c.	55	60
624	20 c. As 7 c.	55	60

250 Speronara (fishing boat) and Tail of Air Malta Airliner

251 Children on Globe

1979. Europa. Communications. Multicoloured.

625	7 c. Type 250	20	10
626	25 c. Coastal watch tower and radio link towers	40	65

1979. International Year of the Child. Multicoloured.

627	2 c. Type 251	10	10
628	7 c. Children flying kites (27 × 33 mm)	15	10
629	11 c. Children in circle (27 × 33 mm)	20	35

252 Shells

1979. Marine Life. Multicoloured.

630	2 c. Type 252	10	10
631	5 c. Loggerhead turtle	20	10
632	7 c. Dolphin (fish)	25	10
633	25 c. Noble pen shell	90	1·25

253 "The Nativity" (detail)

1979. Christmas. Paintings by Giuseppe Cali. Multicoloured.

634	1 c. + 5 m. Type 253	10	10
635	5 c. + 1 c. "The Flight into Egypt" (detail)	10	15
636	7 c. + 1 c. 5 "The Nativity"	15	20
637	11 c. + 3 c. "The Flight into Egypt"	25	50

1980. Flemish Tapestries (4th series). As T **239**. Multicoloured.

638	2 c. "The Institution of Corpus Domini" (Rubens)	10	10
639	8 c. "The Destruction of Idolatry" (Rubens)	20	20

254 Hal Saflieni Hypogeum, Paola

255 Dun Gorg Preca

1980 Int Restoration of Monuments Campaign. Multicoloured.

641	2 c. 5 Type 254	10	15
642	6 c. Vilhena Palace, Mdina	25	20
643	8 c. Citadel of Victoria, Gozo (horiz)	30	40
644	12 c. Fort St. Elmo, Valletta (horiz)	40	60

1980. Birth Centenary of Dun Gorg Preca (founder of Society of Christian Doctrine).
645 **255** 2 c. 5 grey and black . . . 10 10

256 Ruzar Briffa (poet)

1980. Europa.
646 **256** 8 c. yellow, brown & grn . 20 10
647 – 30 c. green, brown & lake 55 1·10
DESIGN: 30 c. Nikiol Anton Vassalli (scholar and patriot).

257 "Annunciation" **258** Rook and Pawn

1980. Christmas. Paintings by A. Inglott. Multicoloured.
648 2 c. + 5 m. Type **257** 10 10
649 6 c. + 1 c. "Conception" . . 20 20
650 8 c. + 1 c. 5 "Nativity" . . . 25 35
651 12 c. + 3 c. "Annunciation", "Conception" and "Nativity" (47 × 38 mm) 30 50

1980. 24th Chess Olympiad and International Chess Federation Congress. Multicoloured.
652 2 c. 5 Type **258** 25 10
653 8 c. Bishop and pawn 65 20
654 30 c. King, queen and pawn (vert) . . . . 1·00 1·25

259 Barn Owl **260** Traditional Horse Race

1981. Birds. Multicoloured.
655 3 c. Type **259** 30 25
656 8 c. Sardinian warbler 50 25
657 12 c. Woodchat shrike 60 80
658 23 c. British storm petrel . . . 1·10 1·75

1981. Europa. Folklore. Multicoloured.
659 8 c. Type **260** 20 10
660 30 c. Attempting to retrieve flag from end of "gostra" (greasy pole) 40 65

261 Stylised "25" **262** Disabled Artist at Work

1981. 25th Maltese International Trade Fair.
661 **261** 4 c. multicoloured 15 15
662 25 c. multicoloured 50 60

1981. International Year for Disabled Persons. Multicoloured.
663 3 c. Type **262** 20 10
664 35 c. Disabled child playing football 75 75

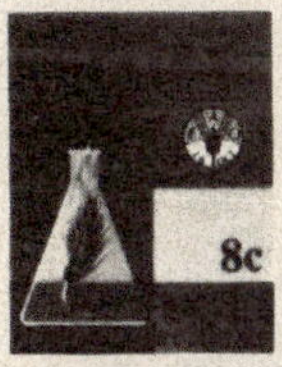

263 Wheat Ear in Conical Flask **264** Megalithic Building

1981. World Food Day.
665 **263** 8 c. multicoloured 15 15
666 23 c. multicoloured . . . 60 50

1981. History of Maltese Industry. Multicoloured.
667 5 m. Type **264** 10 20
668 1 c. Cotton production 10 10
669 2 c. Early ship-building . . . 60 10
670 3 c. Currency minting 30 10
671 5 c. "Art" 30 25
672 6 c. Fishing 80 25
673 7 c. Agriculture 30 70
674 8 c. Stone quarrying 45 35
675 10 c. Grape pressing 35 50
676 12 c. Modern ship-building . 1·25 1·25
677 15 c. Energy . . . . 70 1·25
678 20 c. Telecommunications . . . 70 75
679 25 c. "Industry" . . . . . . 90 1·60
680 50 c. Drilling for Water . . . 1·75 2·50
681 £1 Sea transport . . . . . . 6·00 7·00
682 £3 Air transport . . . . . . 11·00 17·00

265 Children and Nativity Scene **266** Shipbuilding

1981. Christmas. Multicoloured.
683 2 c. + 1 c. Type **265** 15 10
684 8 c. + 2 c. Christmas Eve procession (horiz) 25 20
685 20 c. + 3 c. Preaching midnight sermon 50 60

1982. Shipbuilding Industry.
686 **266** 3 c. multicoloured 15 10
687 – 8 c. multicoloured 30 30
688 – 13 c. multicoloured 55 55
689 – 27 c. multicoloured . . . 1·25 1·25
DESIGNS: 8 c. to 27 c. Differing shipyard scenes.

267 Elderly Man and Has-Serh (home for elderly)

1982. Care of Elderly. Multicoloured.
690 8 c. Type **267** 40 20
691 30 c. Elderly woman and Has-Zmien (hospital for elderly) 1·40 1·40

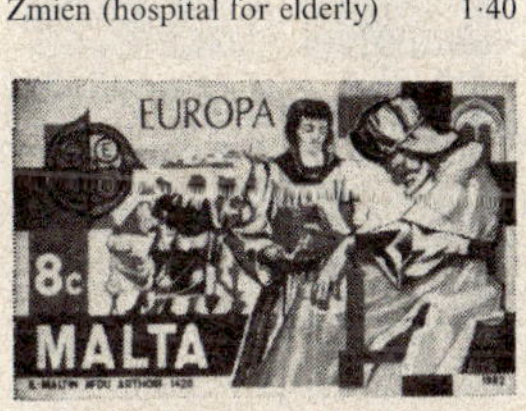

268 Redemption of Islands by Maltese, 1428

1982. Europa. Historical Events. Multicoloured.
692 8 c. Type **268** 40 20
693 30 c. Declaration of rights by Maltese, 1802 . . . . . . 1·00 1·40

269 Stylised Footballer

1982. World Cup Football Championship, Spain.
694 **269** 3 c. multicoloured 20 10
695 – 12 c. multicoloured 60 55
696 – 15 c. multicoloured 70 65
DESIGNS: 12 c., 15 c. Various stylised footballers.

270 Angel appearing to Shepherds

1982. Christmas. Multicoloured.
698 2 c. + 1 c. Type **270** 15 15
699 8 c. + 2 c. Nativity and Three Wise Men bearing gifts . . 50 50
700 20 c. + 3 c. Nativity scene (45 × 37 mm) . . . . 1·00 1·00

MINIMUM PRICE

The minimum price quoted is 10p which represents a handling charge rather than a basis for valuing common stamps. For further notes about prices see introductory pages.

271 "Ta Salvo Serafino" (oared brigantine), 1531

1982. Maltese Ships (1st series). Multicoloured.
701 3 c. Type **271** 40 10
702 8 c. "La Madonna del Rosaria" (tartane), 1740 . . . . . . 80 30
703 12 c. "San Paulo" (xebec), 1743 1·25 55
704 20 c. "Ta' Pietro Saliba" (xprunara), 1798 . . . . . . 1·60 90
See also Nos. 725/8, 772/5, 792/5 and 809/12.

272 Locomotive "Manning Wardle", 1883

1983. Centenary of Malta Railway. Multicoloured.
705 3 c. Type **272** 45 15
706 13 c. Locomotive "Black Hawthorn", 1884 . . . . . 1·00 1·00
707 27 c. Beyer Peacock locomotive, 1895 . . . . 2·00 3·25

273 Peace Doves leaving Malta

1983. Commonwealth Day. Multicoloured.
708 8 c. Type **273** 25 30
709 12 c. Tourist landmarks . . . 40 60
710 15 c. Holiday beach (vert) . . . 45 75
711 23 c. Ship-building (vert) . . . 70 1·00

274 Ggantija Megalithic Temples, Gozo

1983. Europa. Multicoloured.
712 8 c. Type **274** 50 40
713 30 c. Fort St. Angelo . . . . . 1·25 2·40

275 Dish Aerials (World Communications Year)

1983. Anniversaries and Events. Multicoloured.
714 3 c. Type **275** 45 15
715 7 c. Ships' prows and badge (25th anniv of I.M.O. Convention) 70 55
716 13 c. Container lorries and badge (30th anniv of Customs Co-operation Council) 90 90
717 20 c. Stadium and emblem (9th Mediterranean Games) . . . 1·00 2·25

276 Monsignor Giuseppe de Piro **277** Annunciation

1983. 50th Death Anniv of Monsignor Giuseppe de Piro.
718 **276** 3 c. multicoloured 15 15

1983. Christmas. Multicoloured.
719 2 c. + 1 c. Type **277** 30 15
720 8 c. + 2 c. The Nativity . . . 75 60
721 20 c. + 3 c. Adoration of the Magi . . . . 1·40 2·25

278 Workers at Meeting

1983. 40th Anniv of General Workers' Union. Multicoloured.
722 3 c. Type **278** 25 10
723 8 c. Worker with family . . . 50 40
724 27 c. Union H.Q. Building . . 1·50 1·75

1983. Maltese Ships (2nd series). As T **271**. Multicoloured.
725 2 c. "Strangier" (full-rigged ship), 1813 . . . . 30 25
726 12 c. "Tigre" (topsail schooner), 1839 . . . . 1·25 1·25
727 13 c. "La Speranza" (brig), 1844 1·25 1·25
728 20 c. "Wignacourt" (barque), 1844 . . . . 1·75 2·75

279 Boeing 737

1984. Air. Multicoloured.
729 7 c. Type **279** 50 30
730 8 c. Boeing 720B 60 35
731 16 c. Vickers Vanguard . . . 1·25 70
732 23 c. Vickers Viscount . . . . 1·50 70
733 27 c. Douglas DC-3 . . . . . 1·75 80
734 38 c. Armstrong Whitworth Atalanta "Artemis" . . . . 2·25 2·75
735 75 c. "Marina" Fiat MF.5 flying boat . . . . 3·25 5·00

280 Bridge

1984. Europa. 25th Anniv of C.E.P.T.
736 **280** 8 c. green, black & yell . 35 35
737 30 c. red, black & yellow . 1·25 1·25

281 Early Policeman **282** Running

1984. 170th Anniv of Malta Police Force. Multicoloured.
738 3 c. Type **281** 65 15
739 8 c. Mounted police . . . . . 1·50 65
740 11 c. Motorcycle policeman . . 1·75 2·00
741 25 c. Policeman and firemen . 2·75 3·75

1984. Olympic Games, Los Angeles. Multicoloured.
742 7 c. Type **282** 25 30
743 12 c. Gymnastics 50 70
744 23 c. Swimming . . . . 85 1·25

283 "The Visitation" (Pietru Caruana) **284** Dove on Map

1984. Christmas. Paintings from Church of Our Lady of Porto Salvo, Valletta. Multicoloured.
745 2 c. + 1 c. Type **283** 55 55
746 8 c. + 2 c. "The Epiphany" (Rafel Caruana) (horiz) . . 1·00 1·25
747 20 c. + 3 c. "Jesus among the Doctors" (Rafel Caruana) (horiz) . . . . 2·00 3·75

1984. 10th Anniv of Republic. Multicoloured.

748	3 c. Type **284**	40	20
749	8 c. Fort St. Angelo	75	65
750	30 c. Hands	2·50	4·75

285 1885 ½d. Green Stamp

287 Nicolo Baldacchino (tenor)

286 Boy, and Hands planting Vine

1985. Centenary of Malta Post Office. Mult.

751	3 c. Type **285**	45	15
752	8 c. 1885 1d. rose	65	45
753	12 c. 1885 2½d. blue	90	1·40
754	20 c. 1885 4d. brown	1·40	3·00

1985. International Youth Year. Multicoloured.

756	2 c. Type **286**	15	15
757	13 c. Young people and flowers (vert)	85	60
758	27 c. Girl holding flame in hand	1·75	1·40

1985. Europa. European Music Year. Mult.

759	8 c. Type **287**	2·00	50
760	30 c. Francesco Azopardi (composer)	3·00	5·00

288 Guzeppi Bajada and Manwel Attard (victims)

1985. 66th Anniv of 7 June 1919 Demonstrations. Multicoloured.

761	3 c. Type **288**	35	15
762	7 c. Karmnu Abela and Wenzu Dyer (victims)	75	35
763	35 c. Model of projected Demonstration monument by Anton Agius (vert)	2·50	2·00

289 Stylized Birds

1985. 40th Anniv of United Nations Organization. Multicoloured.

764	4 c. Type **289**	25	15
765	11 c. Arrow-headed ribbons	85	1·25
766	31 c. Stylized figures	2·00	3·25

290 Giorgio Mitrovich (nationalist) (death centenary)

291 The Three Wise Men

1985. Celebrities' Anniversaries. Multicoloured.

767	8 c. Type **290**	80	35
768	12 c. Pietru Caxaru (poet and administrator) (400th death anniversary)	1·60	2·50

1985. Christmas. Designs showing details of terracotta relief by Ganni Bonnici. Multicoloured.

769	2 c. + 1 c. Type **291**	55	75
770	8 c. + 2 c. Virgin and Child	1·25	1·75
771	20 c. + 3 c. Angels	2·50	4·00

1985. Maltese Ships (3rd series). Steamships. As T **271**. Multicoloured.

772	3 c. "Scotia" (paddle-steamer), 1844	75	20
773	7 c. "Tagliaferro" (screw-steamer), 1822	1·40	1·00
774	15 c. "Gleneagles" (screw-steamer), 1885	2·00	3·25
775	23 c. "L'Isle Adam" (screw-steamer), 1886	2·75	4·00

292 John XXIII Peace Laboratory and Statue of St. Francis of Assisi

1986. International Peace Year. Multicoloured.

776	8 c. Type **292**	1·00	50
777	11 c. Dove and hands holding olive branch (40 × 19 mm)	1·50	2·50
778	27 c. Map of Africa, dove and two heads	3·00	4·75

293 Symbolic Plant and "Cynthia cardui", "Vanessa atalanta" and "Polyommatus icarus"

294 Heading the Ball

1986. Europa. Environmental Conservation. Multicoloured.

779	8 c. Type **293**	1·75	50
780	35 c. Island, Neolithic frieze, sea and sun	3·25	6·00

1986. World Cup Football Championship, Mexico. Multicoloured.

781	3 c. Type **294**	60	20
782	7 c. Saving a goal	1·25	1·00
783	23 c. Controlling the ball	4·00	6·50

295 Father Diegu

1986. Maltese Philanthropists. Multicoloured.

785	2 c. Type **295**	40	30
786	3 c. Adelaide Cini	50	30
787	8 c. Alfonso Maria Galea	1·25	60
788	27 c. Vincenzo Bugeja	3·25	6·00

296 "Nativity"

1986. Christmas. Paintings by Giuseppe D'Arena. Multicoloured.

789	2 c. + 1 c. Type **296**	80	90
790	8 c. + 2 c. "Nativity" (detail) (vert)	2·25	2·75
791	20 c. + 3 c. "Epiphany"	3·50	5·00

1986. Maltese Ships (4th series). As T **271**. Multicoloured.

792	7 c. "San Paul" (freighter), 1921	1·25	50
793	10 c. "Knight of Malta" (mail steamer), 1930	1·50	1·75
794	12 c. "Valetta City" (freighter), 1948	1·75	2·75
795	20 c. "Saver" (freighter), 1959	3·00	4·50

297 European Robin

1987. 25th Anniv of Malta Ornithological Society. Multicoloured.

796	3 c. Type **297**	85	50
797	8 c. Peregrine falcon (vert)	2·00	1·00
798	13 c. Hoopoe (vert)	2·75	3·50
799	23 c. Coy's shearwater	3·25	5·50

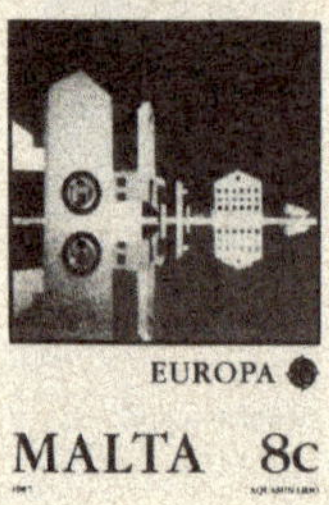

298 Aquasun Lido

299 16th-century Pikeman

1987. Europa. Modern Architecture. Multicoloured.

800	8 c. Type **298**	1·25	75
801	35 c. Church of St. Joseph, Manikata	3·50	6·25

1987. Maltese Uniforms (1st series). Multicoloured.

802	3 c. Type **299**	65	40
803	7 c. 16th-century officer	1·25	90
804	10 c. 18th-century standard bearer	1·50	2·25
805	27 c. 18th-century General of the Galleys	3·25	4·75

See also Nos. 832/5, 851/4, 880/3 and 893/6.

300 Maltese Scenes, Wheat Ears and Sun

1987. Anniversaries and Events. Multicoloured.

806	5 c. Type **300** (European Environment Year)	1·00	50
807	8 c. Esperanto star as comet (Centenary of Esperanto)	1·25	60
808	23 c. Family at house door (International Year of Shelter for the Homeless)	3·00	3·00

1987. Maltese Ships (5th series). As T **271**. Multicoloured.

809	2 c. "Medina" (freighter), 1969	60	60
810	11 c. "Rabat" (container ship), 1974	2·25	2·50
811	13 c. "Ghawdex" (passenger ferry), 1979	2·50	2·75
812	20 c. "Pinto" (car ferry), 1987	3·50	4·00

301 "The Visitation"

1987. Christmas. Illuminated illustrations, score and text from 16th-century choral manuscript. Multicoloured.

813	2 c. + 1 c. Type **301**	50	50
814	8 c. + 2 c. "The Nativity"	2·00	2·75
815	20 c. + 3 c. "The Adoration of the Magi"	3·25	4·50

302 Dr. Arvid Pardo (U.N. representative)

1987. 20th Anniv of United Nations Resolution on Peaceful Use of the Seabed. Multicoloured.

816	8 c. Type **302**	1·00	75
817	12 c. U.N. emblem and sea	1·75	3·00

303 Ven. Nazju Falzon (Catholic catechist)

304 "St. John Bosco with Youth" (statue)

1988. Maltese Personalities. Multicoloured.

819	2 c. Type **303**	25	30
820	3 c. Mgr. Sidor Formosa (philanthropist)	25	30
821	4 c. Sir Luigi Preziosi (ophthalmologist)	30	30
822	10 c. Fr. Anastasju Cuschieri (poet)	70	85
823	25 c. Mgr. Pietru Pawl Saydon (Bible translator)	2·00	3·25

1988. Religious Anniversaries. Multicoloured.

824	10 c. Type **304** (death centenary)	1·00	1·00
825	12 c. "Assumption of Our Lady" (altarpiece by Perugino, Ta' Pinu, Gozo) (Marian Year)	1·25	1·50
826	14 c. "Christ the King" (statue by Sciortino) (75th anniv of International Eucharistic Congress, Valletta)	1·75	2·50

305 Bus, Ferry and Aircraft

306 Globe and Red Cross Emblems

1988. Europa. Transport and Communications. Multicoloured.

827	10 c. Type **305**	1·25	75
828	35 c. Control panel, dish aerial and pylons	2·75	4·50

1988. Anniversaries and Events. Multicoloured.

829	4 c. Type **306** (125th anniv of Int Red Cross)	40	50
830	18 c. Divided globe (Campaign for North–South Inter-dependence and Solidarity)	1·75	2·50
831	19 c. Globe and symbol (40th anniv of W.H.O.)	1·75	2·50

1988. Maltese Uniforms (2nd series). As T **299**. Multicoloured.

832	3 c. Private, Maltese Light Infantry, 1800	30	30
833	4 c. Gunner, Malta Coast Artillery, 1802	35	35
834	10 c. Field Officer, 1st Maltese Provincial Battalion, 1805	85	1·25
835	25 c. Subaltern, Royal Malta Regiment, 1809	2·25	4·25

307 Athletics

308 Shepherd with Flock

1988. Olympic Games, Seoul. Multicoloured.

836	4 c. Type **307**	30	30
837	10 c. Diving	70	80
838	35 c. Basketball	2·00	3·00

1988. Christmas. Multicoloured.

839	3 c. + 1 c. Type **308**	30	30
840	10 c. + 2 c. The Nativity	70	1·25
841	25 c. + 3 c. Three Wise Men	1·75	2·75

309 Commonwealth Emblem

311 Two Boys flying Kite

310 New State Arms

1989. 25th Anniv of Independence. Multicoloured.
842 2 c. Type **309** 25 35
843 3 c. Council of Europe flag . . 25 35
844 4 c. U.N. flag 30 35
845 10 c. Workers, hands gripping ring and national flag . . . 75 95
846 12 c. Scales and allegorical figure of Justice . . . . 90 1·40
847 25 c. Prime Minister Borg Olivier with Independence constitution (42 × 28 mm) . 1·90 3·25

1989.
848 **310** £1 multicoloured . . . . 4·00 4·50

1989. Europa. Children's Games. Multicoloured.
849 10 c. Type **311** . . . . 1·25 75
850 35 c. Two girls with dolls . . 3·25 4·50

1989. Maltese Uniforms (3rd series). As T **299**. Multicoloured.
851 3 c. Officer, Maltese Veterans, 1815 . . . . 45 45
852 4 c. Subaltern, Royal Malta Fencibles, 1839 . . . . . . 50 50
853 10 c. Private, Malta Militia, 1856 1·50 1·50
854 25 c. Colonel, Royal Malta Fencible Artillery, 1875 . . 2·75 3·75

312 Human Figures and Buildings

1989. Anniversaries and Commemorations. Designs showing logo and stylized human figures. Multicoloured.
855 3 c. Type **312** (20th anniv of U.N. Declaration on Social Progress and Development) 30 30
856 4 c. Workers and figure in wheelchair (Malta's Ratification of European Social Charter) 35 35
857 10 c. Family (40th anniv of Council of Europe) . . . . 80 1·25
858 14 c. Teacher and children (70th anniv of Malta Union of Teachers) . . . . 1·00 1·75
859 25 c. Symbolic knights (Knights of the Sovereign Military Order of Malta Assembly) . 2·25 3·50

313 Angel and Cherub

315 General Post Office, Auberge d'Italie, Valletta

314 Presidents Bush and Gorbachev

1989. Christmas. Vault paintings by Mattia Preti from St. John's Co-Cathedral, Valletta.
860 3 c. + 1 c. Type **313** 50 50
861 10 c. + 2 c. Two angels . . . 1·25 1·75
862 20 c. + 3 c. Angel blowing trumpet . . . . 1·75 3·00

1989. U.S.A.–U.S.S.R. Summit Meeting, Malta.
863 **314** 10 c. multicoloured . . . . 1·00 1·25

1990. Europa. Post Office Buildings. Multicoloured.
864 10 c. Type **315** 75 50
865 35 c. Branch Post Office, Zebbug (horiz) . . . . 2·25 3·50

316 Open Book and Letters from Different Alphabets (International Literacy Year)

318 St. Paul

317 Samuel Taylor Coleridge (poet) and Government House

1990. Anniversaries and Events. Multicoloured.
866 3 c. Type **316** 25 25
867 4 c. Count Roger of Sicily and Norman soldiers (900th anniv of Sicilian rule) (horiz) . . 45 30
868 19 c. Communications satellite (25th anniv of I.T.U.) (horiz) 1·75 2·50
869 20 c. Football and map of Malta (Union of European Football Association 20th Ordinary Congress, Malta) . . . . . 1·75 2·50

1990. British Authors. Multicoloured.
870 4 c. Type **317** 30 30
871 10 c. Lord Byron (poet) and map of Valletta 60 70
872 12 c. Sir Walter Scott (novelist) and Great Siege 70 95
873 25 c. William Makepeace Thackeray (novelist) and Naval Arsenal . . . . . . 1·40 2·25

1990. Visit of Pope John Paul II. Bronze Bas-reliefs.
874 **318** 4 c. black, flesh and red . . 50 1·50
875 – 25 c. black, flesh & red . . 1·50 1·75
DESIGN: 25 c. Pope John Paul II.

319 Flags and Football

320 Innkeeper

1990. World Cup Football Championship, Italy. Multicoloured.
876 5 c. Type **319** 35 30
877 10 c. Football in net . . . . 65 1·00
878 14 c. Scoreboard and football 1·00 1·75

1990. Maltese Uniforms (4th series). As T **299**. Multicoloured.
880 3 c. Captain, Royal Malta Militia, 1889 . . . . 55 55
881 4 c. Field officer, Royal Malta Artillery, 1905 . . . . . . 60 60
882 10 c. Labourer, Malta Labour Corps, 1915 . . . . 1·50 1·50
883 25 c. Lieutenant, King's Own Malta Regiment of Militia, 1918 . . . . 2·50 3·00

1990. Christmas. Figures from Crib by Austin Galea, Marco Bartolo and Rosario Zammit. Multicoloured.
884 3 c. + 1 c. Type **320** 30 40
885 10 c. + 2 c. Nativity (41 × 28 mm) 70 1·25
886 25 c. + 3 c. Shepherd with sheep 1·60 2·25

321 1919 10s. Stamp under Magnifying Glass

1991. 25th Anniv of Philatelic Society of Malta.
887 **321** 10 c. multicoloured . . . 60 70

322 "Eurostar" Satellite and V.D.U. Screen

324 Interlocking Arrows

323 St. Ignatius Loyola (founder of Jesuits) (500th birth anniv)

1991. Europa. Europe in Space. Multicoloured.
888 10 c. Type **322** . . . . 1·25 70
889 35 c. "Ariane 4" rocket and projected HOTOL aerospace-plane . . . . 2·25 2·75

1991. Religious Commemorations. Multicoloured.
890 3 c. Type **323** 30 20
891 4 c. Abbess Venerable Maria Adeodata Pisani (185th birth anniversary) (vert) 35 25
892 30 c. St. John of the Cross (400th death anniversary) . . . . . 2·00 2·25

1991. Maltese Uniforms (5th series). As T **299**. Multicoloured.
893 3 c. Officer with colour, Royal Malta Fencibles, 1860 . . . 30 25
894 10 c. Officer with colour, Royal Malta Regiment of Militia, 1903 . . . . 70 60
895 19 c. Officer with Queen's colour, King's Own Malta Regiment, 1968 . . . . 1·40 1·75
896 25 c. Officer with colour, Malta Armed Forces, 1991 . . . . 1·75 2·00

1991. 25th Anniv of Union Haddiema Maghqudin (public services union).
897 **324** 4 c. multicoloured 30 30

325 Honey Buzzard

326 Three Wise Men

1991. Endangered Species. Birds. Multicoloured.
898 4 c. Type **325** . . . . 1·50 1·75
899 4 c. Marsh harrier . . . . 1·50 1·75
900 10 c. Eleonora's falcon . . . . 1·50 1·75
901 10 c. Lesser kestrel . . . . . . 1·50 1·75

1991. Christmas. Multicoloured.
902 3 c. + 1 c. Type **326** 25 25
903 10 c. + 2 c. Holy Family . . . 65 85
904 25 c. + 3 c. Two shepherds . . 1·25 2·25

327 Ta' Hagrat Neolithic Temple

1991. National Heritage of the Maltese Islands. Multicoloured.
905 1 c. Type **327** 10 10
906 2 c. Cottoner Gate 10 10
907 3 c. St. Michael's Bastion, Valletta 10 10
908 4 c. Spinola Palace, St. Julian's 15 20
909 5 c. Birkirkara Church 15 20
910 10 c. Mellieha Bay 30 35
911 12 c. Wied iz-Zurrieq 40 45
912 14 c. Mgarr harbour, Gozo . . . 45 50
913 20 c. Yacht marina 60 65
914 50 c. Gozo Channel . . . . . 1·50 1·60
915 £1 "Arab Horses" (sculpture by Antonio Sciortino) . . . . . 3·25 3·50
916 £2 Independence Monument (Ganni Bonnici) (vert) . . . 6·25 6·50

328 Aircraft Tailfins and Terminal

1992. Opening of Int Air Terminal. Mult.
917 4 c. Type **328** 45 30
918 10 c. National flags and terminal 65 65

329 Ships of Columbus

1992. Europa. 500th Anniv of Discovery of America by Columbus. Multicoloured.
919 10 c. Type **329** 55 55
920 35 c. Columbus and map of Americas . . . . 2·00 2·25

330 George Cross and Anti-aircraft Gun Crew

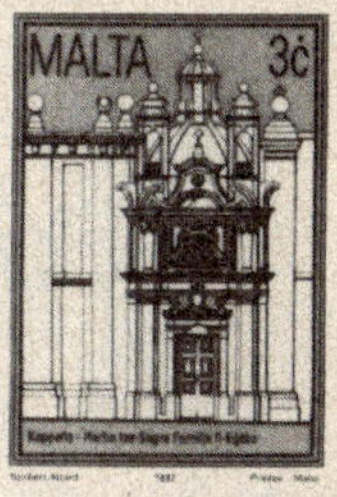

332 Church of the Flight into Egypt

331 Running

1992. 50th Anniv of Award of George Cross to Malta. Multicoloured.
921 4 c. Type **330** 40 25
922 10 c. George Cross and memorial bell . . . . 1·00 80
923 50 c. Tanker "Ohio" entering Grand Harbour . . . . . . 4·00 5·50

1992. Olympic Games, Barcelona. Multicoloured.
924 3 c. Type **331** 45 20
925 10 c. High jumping 95 70
926 30 c. Swimming . . . . 2·25 3·50

1992. Rehabilitation of Historical Buildings.
927 **332** 3 c. black, stone & grey . 25 20
928 – 4 c. black, stone & pink . 30 20
929 – 19 c. black, stone & lilac . 1·50 2·00
930 – 25 c. black, stone & green . 1·75 2·00
DESIGNS—HORIZ: 4 c. St. John's Co-Cathedral; 25 c. Auberge de Provence. VERT: 19 c. Church of Madonna del Pillar.

333 "The Nativity" (Giuseppe Cali)

1992. Christmas. Religious Paintings by Giuseppe Cali from Mosta Church. Multicoloured.
931 3 c. + 1 c. Type **333** 50 50
932 10 c. + 2 c. "Adoration of the Magi" . . . . 1·25 1·50
933 25 c. + 3 c. "Christ with the Elders in the Temple" . . . 2·50 3·25

334 Malta College Building, Valletta

335 Lions Club Emblem

1992. 400th Anniv of University of Malta. Multicoloured.
934 4 c. Type **334** 40 25
935 30 c. Modern University complex, Tal-Qroqq (horiz) 2·00 3·00

1993. 75th Anniv of International Association of Lions Club. Multicoloured.
936 4 c. Type **335** 50 25
937 50 c. Eye (Sight First Campaign) 2·75 3·25

336 Untitled Painting by Paul Carbonaro

1993. Europa. Contemporary Art. Mult.

938 10 c. Type **336** 75 50
939 35 c. Untitled painting by Alfred Chircop (horiz) 2·25 3·50

337 Mascot holding Flame

1993. 5th Small States of Europe Games. Multicoloured.

940 3 c. Type **337** 20 20
941 4 c. Cycling 20 90
942 10 c. Tennis 1·00 3·00
943 35 c. Yachting 2·25 4·00

338 Learning First Aid **339** "Papilio machaon"

1993. 50th Anniv of Award of Bronze Cross to Maltese Scouts and Guides. Multicoloured.

945 3 c. Type **338** 30 15
946 4 c. Bronze Cross 30 20
947 10 c. Scout building camp fire 80 75
948 35 c. Governor Lord Gort presenting Bronze Cross, 1943 2·25 3·00

1993. European Year of the Elderly. Butterflies. Multicoloured.

949 5 c. Type **339** 35 20
950 35 c. "Vanessa atalanta" 1·75 2·25

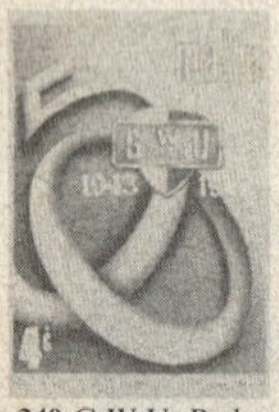

340 G.W.U. Badge and Interlocking "50" **341** Child Jesus and Star

1993. 50th Anniv of General Workers Union.

951 **340** 4 c. multicoloured 35 40

1993. Christmas. Multicoloured.

952 3 c. + 1 c. Type **341** 30 30
953 10 c. + 2 c. Christmas tree 85 95
954 25 c. + 3 c. Star in traditional window 1·60 2·25

343 Symbolic Tooth and Probe **344** Sir Themistocles Zammit (discoverer of Brucella microbe)

1994. 50th Anniv of Maltese Dental Association. Multicoloured.

956 5 c. Type **343** 35 30
957 44 c. Symbolic mouth and dental mirror 3·00 3·00

1994. Europa. Discoveries. Multicoloured.

958 14 c. Type **344** 50 30
959 30 c. Bi-lingually inscribed candelabrum of 2nd century B.C. (deciphering of ancient Phoenician language) 1·90 3·00

345 Family in Silhouette (International Year of the Family) **346** Football and Map

1994. Anniversaries and Events. Multicoloured.

960 5 c. Type **345** 25 20
961 9 c. Stylised Red Cross (International recognition of Malta Red Cross Society) 50 40
962 14 c. Animals and crops (150th anniv of Agrarian Society) 85 80
963 20 c. Worker in silhouette (75th anniv of I.L.O.) 1·25 1·40
964 25 c. St. Paul's Anglican Cathedral (155th anniv) (vert) 1·40 1·60

1994. World Cup Football Championship, U.S.A. Multicoloured.

965 5 c. Type **346** 30 20
966 14 c. Ball and goal 85 80
967 30 c. Ball and pitch superimposed on map 2·25 2·50

347 Falcon Trophy, Twin Comanche and Auster (25th anniv of Malta International Rally)

1994. Aviation Anniversaries and Events. Multicoloured.

969 5 c. Type **347** 50 20
970 14 c. Alouette helicopter, display teams and logo (Malta International Airshow) 1·40 85
971 20 c. De Havilland Dove "City of Valetta" and Avro York aircraft with logo (50th anniv of I.C.A.O.) 1·60 1·40
972 25 c. Airbus 320 "Nicolas Cottoner" and De Havilland Comet aircraft with logo (50th anniv of I.C.A.O.) 1·75 1·75

348 National Flags and Astronaut on Moon **350** Helmet-shaped Ewer

349 Virgin Mary and Child with Angels

1994. 25th Anniv of First Manned Moon Landing.

973 **348** 14 c. multicoloured 1·10 95

1994. Christmas. Multicoloured.

974 5 c. Type **349** 25 10
975 9 c. + 2 c. Angel in pink (vert) 65 60
976 14 c. + 3 c. Virgin Mary and Child (vert) 90 1·25
977 20 c. + 3 c. Angel in green (vert) 1·60 2·25

Nos. 975/7 are larger, 28 × 41 mm, and depict details from Type **349**.

1994. Maltese Antique Silver Exhibition. Multicoloured.

978 5 c. Type **350** 25 20
979 14 c. Balsamina 70 80
980 20 c. Coffee pot 1·25 1·40
981 25 c. Sugar box 1·50 1·75

351 "60 plus" and Hands touching **352** Hand holding Leaf and Rainbow

1995. Anniversaries and Events. Multicoloured.

982 2 c. Type **351** (25th anniv of National Association of Pensioners) 15 15
983 5 c. Child's drawing (10th anniv of National Youth Council) 25 20
984 14 c. Conference emblem (4th World Conference on Women, Peking, China) 70 80
985 20 c. Nurse and thermometer (50th anniv of Malta Memorial District Nursing Association) 1·25 1·40
986 25 c. Louis Pasteur (biologist) (death centenary) 1·50 1·75

1995. Europa. Peace and Freedom. Multicoloured.

987 14 c. Type **352** 75 55
988 30 c. Peace doves (horiz) 1·50 2·00

353 Junkers Ju 87B "Stuka" Dive Bombers over Valletta and Anti-aircraft Gun

1995. Anniversaries. Multicoloured.

989 5 c. Type **353** (50th anniv of end of Second World War) 25 25
990 14 c. Silhouetted people holding hands (50th anniv of United Nations) 70 80
991 35 c. Hands holding bowl of wheat (50th anniv of F.A.O.) (vert) 2·00 2·25

354 Light Bulb **356** Pinto's Turret Clock

355 Rock Wall and Girna

1995. Maltese Electricity and Telecommunications. Multicoloured.

992 2 c. Type **354** 15 15
993 5 c. Symbolic owl and binary codes 25 25
994 9 c. Dish aerial 45 50
995 14 c. Sun and rainbow over trees 70 80
996 20 c. Early telephone, satellite and Moon's surface 1·25 1·50

1995. European Nature Conservation Year. Multicoloured.

997 5 c. Type **355** 25 25
998 14 c. Maltese wall lizards 70 80
999 44 c. Aleppo pine 2·75 3·00

1995. Treasures of Malta. Antique Maltese Clocks. Multicoloured.

1000 1 c. Type **356** 10 10
1001 5 c. Michelangelo Sapiano (horologist) and clocks 30 25
1002 14 c. Arlogg tal-lira clock 90 80
1003 25 c. Sundials 1·75 2·00

357 Children's Christmas Eve Procession

1995. Christmas. Multicoloured.

1004 5 c. Type **357** 25 10
1005 5 c. + 2 c. Children with crib (vert) 30 40
1006 14 c. + 3 c. Children with lanterns (vert) 85 90
1007 25 c. + 3 c. Boy with lantern and balustrade (vert) 1·60 1·75

Nos. 1005/7 are 27 × 32 mm and depict details from Type **357**.

358 Silhouetted Children and President's Palace, San Anton

1996. Anniversaries. Multicoloured.

1008 5 c. Type **358** (35th anniv of the President's Award) 25 25
1009 14 c. Nazzareno Camilleri (priest) and St. Patrick's Church, Salesjani (90th birth anniv) 65 65
1010 20 c. St. Mary Euphrasia and convent (birth bicentenary) 1·00 1·10
1011 25 c. Silhouetted children and fountain (50th anniv of U.N.I.C.E.F.) 1·25 1·40

359 Carved Figures from Skorba

1996. Maltese Prehistoric Art Exhibition. Multicoloured.

1012 5 c. Type **359** 30 20
1013 14 c. Temple carving, Gozo 80 85
1014 20 c. Carved figure of a woman, Skorba (vert) 1·10 1·25
1015 35 c. Ghar Dalam pot (vert) 1·90 2·25

360 Mabel Strickland (politician and journalist) **361** Face and Emblem (United Nations Decade against Drug Abuse)

1996. Europa. Famous Women. Multicoloured.

1016 14 c. Type **360** 70 55
1017 30 c. Inez Soler (artist, musician and writer) 1·75 2·00

1996. Anniversaries and Events. Multicoloured.

1018 5 c. Type **361** 25 25
1019 5 c. "Fi" and emblem (50th anniv of Malta Federation of Industry) 25 25
1020 14 c. Commemorative plaque and national flag (75th anniv of self-government) 80 80
1021 44 c. Guglielmo Marconi and early radio equipment (centenary of radio) 2·25 2·50

362 Judo

1996. Olympic Games, Atlanta. Multicoloured.

1022 2 c. Type **362** 10 10
1023 5 c. Athletics 30 25
1024 14 c. Diving 80 80
1025 25 c. Rifle-shooting 1·40 1·60

363 "Harvest Time" (Cali)

1996. 150th Birth Anniv of Guiseppe Cali (painter). Multicoloured.

1026 5 c. Type **363** 30 25
1027 14 c. "Dog" (Cali) 80 70
1028 20 c. "Countrywoman in a Field" (Cali) (vert) 1·10 1·10
1029 25 c. "Cali at his Easel" (Edward Dingli) (vert) 1·25 1·25

364 Bus No. 1990 "Diamond Star", 1920s

1996. Buses. Multicoloured.

1030 2 c. Type **364** 15 10
1031 5 c. No. 434 "Tom Mix", 1930s 30 25
1032 14 c. No. 1764 "Verdala", 1940s 80 80
1033 30 c. No. 3495, 1960s 1·60 1·75

365 Stained Glass Window

1996. Christmas. Multicoloured.

1034 5 c. Type **365** 35 10
1035 5 c. + 2 c. Madonna and Child (29 × 35 mm) 40 45
1036 14 c. + 3 c. Angel facing right (29 × 35 mm) 80 85
1037 25 c. + 3 c. Angel facing left (29 × 35 mm) 1·25 1·40

Nos. 1035/7 show details from Type **365**.

366 Hompesch Arch and Arms, Zabbar

368 Gahan carrying Door

367 Captain-General of the Galleys' Sedan Chair

1997. Bicentenary of Maltese Cities. Multicoloured.

1038 6 c. Type **366** 30 25
1039 16 c. Statue, church and arms, Siggiewi 70 70
1040 26 c. Seated statue and arms, Zejtun 1·10 1·10

1997. Treasures of Malta. Sedan Chairs. Multicoloured.

1042 2 c. Type **367** 15 15
1043 6 c. Cotoner Grandmasters' chair 30 30
1044 16 c. Chair from Cathedral Museum, Mdina (vert) 70 70
1045 27 c. Chevalier D'Arezzo's chair (vert) 1·10 1·10

1997. Europa. Tales and Legends. Multicoloured.

1046 16 c. Type **368** 75 75
1047 35 c. St. Dimitrius appearing from painting 1·25 1·50

369 Modern Sculpture (Antonio Sciortino)

370 Dr. Albert Laferla

1997. Anniversaries. Multicoloured.

1048 1 c. Type **369** 10 10
1049 6 c. Joseph Calleia and film reel (horiz) 30 30
1050 6 c. Gozo Cathedral (horiz) 30 30
1051 11 c. City of Gozo (horiz) 50 50
1052 16 c. Sculpture of head (Sciortino) 70 70
1053 22 c. Joseph Calleia and film camera (horiz) 1·00 1·00

ANNIVERSARIES: 1, 16 c. 50th death anniv of Antonio Sciortino (sculptor); 6 (No. 1049), 22 c. Birth centenary of Joseph Calleia (actor); 6 (No. 1050), 11 c. 300th anniv of construction of Gozo Cathedral.

1997. Pioneers of Education. Multicoloured.

1054 6 c. Type **370** 30 25
1055 16 c. Sister Emilie de Vialar 70 70
1056 19 c. Mgr. Paolo Pullicino 80 80
1057 26 c. Mgr. Tommaso Gargallo 1·00 1·10

371 The Nativity

1997. Christmas. Multicoloured.

1058 6 c. Type **371** 25 10
1059 6 c. + 2 c. Mary and baby Jesus (vert) 30 35
1060 16 c. + 3 c. Joseph with donkey (vert) 70 75
1061 26 c. + 3 c. Shepherd with lamb (vert) 1·00 1·40

Nos. 1059/61 show details from Type **371**.

372 Plan of Fort and Soldiers in Victoria Lines

1997. Anniversaries. Multicoloured (except 6 c.).

1062 2 c. Type **372** 15 10
1063 6 c. Sir Paul Boffa making speech (black and red) 25 25
1064 16 c. Plan of fort and gun crew 70 65
1065 37 c. Queue of voters 1·40 1·60

ANNIVERSARIES: 2, 16 c. Centenary of Victoria Lines; 6, 37 c. 50th anniv of 1947 Self-Government Constitution.

373 "Maria Amelia Grognet" (Antonine de Favray)

1998. Treasures of Malta. Costumes and Paintings.

1066 6 c. Type **373** 30 30
1067 6 c. Gentleman's waistcoat, c. 1790–1810 30 30
1068 16 c. Lady's dinner dress, c. 1880 60 70
1069 16 c. "Veneranda, Baroness Abela, and her Grandson" (De Favray) 60 70

374 Grand Master Ferdinand von Hompesch

1998. Bicentenary of Napoleon's Capture of Malta. Multicoloured.

1071 6 c. Type **374** 25 30
1072 6 c. French fleet 25 30
1073 16 c. French landing 65 75
1074 16 c. General Napoleon Bonaparte 65 75

375 Racing Two-man Luzzus

376 Dolphin and Diver

1998. Europa. Sailing Regatta, Grand Harbour. Multicoloured.

1075 16 c. Type **375** 65 55
1076 35 c. Racing four-man luzzus 1·25 1·50

1998. International Year of the Ocean. Multicoloured.

1077 2 c. Type **376** 15 15
1078 6 c. Diver and sea-urchin 30 25
1079 16 c. Jacques Cousteau and diver (horiz) 70 70
1080 27 c. Two divers (horiz) 95 1·10

377 Goalkeeper saving Goal

378 Ships' Wheels (50th anniv of Int Maritime Organization)

1998. World Cup Football Championship, France. Players and flags. Multicoloured.

1081 6 c. Type **377** 30 25
1082 16 c. Two players and referee 70 70
1083 22 c. Two footballers 90 1·00

1998. Anniversaries. Multicoloured.

1085 1 c. Type **378** 10 10
1086 6 c. Symbolic family (50th anniv of Universal Declaration of Human Rights) 20 25
1087 11 c. "GRTU" and cogwheels (50th anniv of General Retailers and Traders Union) 35 40
1088 19 c. Mercury (50th anniv of Chamber of Commerce) 60 65
1089 26 c. Aircraft tailfins (25th anniv of Air Malta) 85 90

379 "Rest on the Flight to Egypt"

1998. Christmas. Paintings by Mattia Preti. Mult.

1090 6 c. Type **379** 20 25
1091 6 c. + 2 c. "Virgin and Child with Sts. Anthony and John the Baptist" 25 30
1092 16 c. + 3 c. "Virgin and Child with Sts. Raphael, Nicholas and Gregory" 60 65
1093 26 c. + 3 c. "Virgin and Child with Sts. John the Baptist and Nicholas" 90 95

380 Fort St. Angelo

1999. 900th Anniv of the Sovereign Military Order of Malta. Multicoloured.

1094 2 c. Type **380** 10 10
1095 6 c. Grand Master De l'Isle Adam (vert) 20 25
1096 16 c. Grand Master La Valette (vert) 50 55
1097 27 c. Auberge de Castille 85 90

381 Little Ringed Plover, Ghadira Nature Reserve

1999. Europa. Parks and Gardens. Multicoloured.

1098 16 c. Type **381** 50 55
1099 35 c. Common kingfisher, Simar Nature Reserve 1·10 1·25

382 Council of Europe Assembly

1999. 50th Anniv of Council of Europe. Mult.

1100 6 c. Type **382** 20 25
1101 16 c. Council of Europe Headquarters, Strasbourg 50 55

POSTAGE DUE STAMPS

D 1 D 2

1925. Imperf.

D 1 D 1 ½d. black 1·25 4·50
D 2 1d. black 3·00 2·50
D 3 1½d. black 3·00 3·50
D 4 2d. black 5·50 9·50
D 5 2½d. black 2·75 2·75
D 6 3d. black on grey 9·00 11·00
D 7 4d. black on yellow 5·00 9·00
D 8 6d. black on yellow 5·00 13·00
D 9 1s. black on yellow 7·50 17·00
D10 1s. 6d. black on yellow 13·00 50·00

1925. Perf.

D32 D 2 ½d. green 35 1·50
D33 1d. violet 30 1·00
D13 1½d. brown 1·50 80
D14 2d. grey 11·00 1·00
D35 2d. brown 85 70
D36 2½d. orange 60 70
D37 3d. blue 60 60
D38 4d. green 1·00 80
D39 6d. purple 75 1·00
D40 1s. black 90 1·50
D41 1s. 6d. red 2·25 5·50

D 3 Maltese Lace D 4

1973.

D42 D 3 2 m. brown and red 10 10
D43 3 m. orange and red 10 15
D44 5m. pink and red 15 20
D45 1 c. blue and green 30 35
D46 2 c. grey and black 30 35
D47 3 c. lt brown and brn 30 35
D48 5 c. dull blue and blue 55 70
D49 10 c. lilac and plum 75 1·00

1993.

D50 D 4 1 c. magenta & mauve 10 10
D51 2 c. blue and light blue 15 15
D52 5 c. green & turquoise 20 20
D53 10 c. orange & yellow 35 35

MAURITIUS

An island in the Indian Ocean, east of Madagascar. Attained self-government on 1 September 1967, and became independent on 12 March 1968.

1847. 12 pence = 1 shilling;
20 shillings = 1 pound.
1878. 100 cents = 1 rupee.

1 ("POST OFFICE") 2 ("POST PAID")

1847. Imperf.

1	1	1d. red	–	£450000
2		2d. blue	–	£550000

1848. Imperf.

23	2	1d. red	£1400	£375
25		2d. blue	£1900	£500

3 5

1854. Surch FOUR-PENCE. Imperf.

26	3	4d. green	£750	£375

1858. No value on stamps. Imperf.

27	3	(4d.) green	£425	£200
28		(6d.) red	25·00	40·00
29		(9d.) purple	£550	£200

1859. Imperf.

32	5	6d. blue	£550	30·00
33		6d. black	19·00	28·00
34		1s. red	£2000	45·00
35		1s. green	£400	90·00

6 8

1859. Imperf.

39	6	2d. blue	£1100	£400

1859. Imperf.

42	8	1d. red	£3000	£750
44		2d. blue	£1500	£350

9 10

1860.

56	9	1d. purple	48·00	8·50
57		1d. brown	65·00	5·50
60		2d. blue	65·00	7·00
61a		3d. red	40·00	8·50
62		4d. red	80·00	2·75
65		6d. green	95·00	3·75
50		6d. grey	£180	75·00
63		6d. violet	£150	24·00
51		9d. purple	85·00	35·00
66		9d. green	£100	£170
67	10	10d. red	£170	29·00
70	9	1s. yellow	£140	12·00
53		1s. green	£550	£150
69		1s. blue	£130	18·00
71		5s. mauve	£150	45·00

1862. Perf.

54	5	6d. black	16·00	40·00
55		1s. green	£1800	£325

HALF
PENNY
(11)

HALF PENNY
(13)

1876. Surcharged with T **11**.

76	9	½d. on 9d. purple	6·00	9·00
77	10	½d. on 10d. red	1·50	13·00

1877. Surch with T **13**.

79	10	½d. on 10d. red	2·75	25·00

1877. Surch in words.

80	9	1d. on 4d. red	7·50	12·00
82		1s. on 5s. mauve	£200	£100

1878. Surch.

83	10	2 c. red	5·50	4·50
84	9	4 c. on 1d. brown	7·50	4·25
85		8 c. on 2d. blue	65·00	1·25
86		13 c. on 3d. red	7·50	23·00
87		17 c. on 4d. red	£140	1·75
88		25 c. on 6d. blue	£170	4·75
89		38 c. on 9d. purple	18·00	48·00
90		50 c. on 1s. green	85·00	2·50
91		2 r. 50 on 5s. mauve	12·00	13·00

18 19

1879. Various frames.

101	18	1 c. violet	1·50	45
102		2 c. red	29·00	4·75
103		2 c. green	2·00	55
104	19	4 c. orange	65·00	2·50
105		4 c. red	2·50	60
106	–	8 c. blue	1·75	90
95	–	13 c. grey	£120	£160
107	–	15 c. brown	3·50	1·00
108	–	15 c. blue	5·50	75
109	–	16 c. brown	3·50	90
96	–	17 c. red	48·00	4·75
110	–	25 c. olive	4·25	1·75
98	–	38 c. purple	£150	£190
99	–	50 c. green	3·50	2·50
111	–	50 c. orange	28·00	8·00
100	–	2 r. 50 purple	29·00	50·00

1883. No. 96 surch **16 CENTS**.

112		16 c. on 17 c. red	£130	50·00

1883. No. 96 surch **SIXTEEN CENTS**.

115		16 c. on 17 c. red	55·00	90

1885. No. 98 surch **2 CENTS** with bar.

116		2 c. on 38 c. purple	85·00	32·00

1887. No. 95 surch **2 CENTS** without bar.

117		2 c. on 13 c. grey	35·00	65·00

1891. Surch in words with or without bar.

123	18	1 c. on 2 c. violet	90	50
124	–	1 c. on 16 c. brown (No. 109)	90	2·50
118	19	2 c. on 4 c. red	1·25	50
119	–	2 c. on 17 c. red (No. 96)	90·00	90·00
120	9	2 c. on 38 c. on 9d. purple (No. 89)	1·60	3·50
121	–	2 c. on 38 c. purple (No. 98)	2·25	3·50

36 37

1895.

127	36	1 c. purple and blue	75	1·00
128		2 c. purple and orange	2·00	50
129		3 c. purple	60	50
130		4 c. purple and green	3·75	60
131		6 c. green and red	3·75	3·75
132		18 c. green and blue	6·50	5·00

1898. Diamond Jubilee.

133	37	36 c. orange and blue	9·50	14·00

1899. Surch in figures and words.

137	–	4 c. on 16 c. brown (No. 109)	2·25	7·00
134	36	6 c. on 18 c. (No. 132)	90	90
156		12 c. on 18 c. (No. 132)	1·50	5·00
163	37	12 c. on 36 c. (No. 133)	1·25	1·25
135		15 c. on 36 c. (No. 133)	1·25	1·75

40 Admiral Mahe de Labourdonnais, Governor of Mauritius 1735–46

42

1899. Birth Bicentenary of Labourdonnais.

136	40	15 c. blue	10·00	3·00

1900.

138	36	1 c. grey and black	50	10
139		2 c. purple	75	20
140		3 c. green & red on yellow	3·25	1·00
141		4 c. purple & red on yellow	1·50	40
142		4 c. green and violet	60	1·75
167a		4 c. black & red on blue	1·50	10
144		5 c. purple on buff	5·00	50·00
145		5 c. purple & blk on buff	2·25	2·50
168a		6 c. purple & red on red	1·75	10
147		8 c. green & blk on buff	1·75	5·50
148		12 c. black and red	1·75	1·90
149		15 c. green and orange	8·50	6·00
171		15 c. black & blue on blue	4·00	35
151a	36	25 c. green & red on grn	2·75	11·00
174		50 c. green on yellow	1·50	2·25
175	42	1 r. grey and red	20·00	45·00
154		2 r. 50 green & blk on bl	15·00	75·00
155		5 r. purple & red on red	55·00	75·00

1902. Optd **Postage & Revenue.**

157	36	4 c. purple and red on yellow	50	20
158		6 c. green and red	55	2·50
159		15 c. green and orange	1·50	30
160	–	25 c. olive (No. 110)	1·75	2·25
161	–	50 c. green (No. 99)	3·75	2·25
162	–	2 r. 50 purple (No. 100)	70·00	90·00

46 47

1910.

205	46	1 c. black	90	90
206		2 c. brown	90	10
207		2 c. purple on yellow	60	20
183		3 c. green	2·50	10
184		4 c. green and red	3·00	10
210		4 c. green	1·00	10
211		4 c. brown	2·50	1·25
186		6 c. red	1·75	10
213		6 c. mauve	1·25	10
187		8 c. orange	2·50	1·25
215		10 c. grey	2·00	3·25
216		10 c. red	3·25	1·25
217		12 c. red	1·50	40
218		12 c. grey	1·50	2·75
219b		15 c. blue	75	25
220		20 c. blue	2·00	80
221		20 c. purple	8·00	10·00

1910.

185	47	5 c. grey and red	2·25	2·50
188		12 c. grey	1·50	2·25
190		25 c. black & red on yell	1·75	10·00
191		50 c. purple and black	1·75	16·00
192		1 r. black on green	5·50	10·00
193		2 r. 50 black & red on blue	9·50	60·00
194		5 r. green & red on yellow	25·00	85·00
195		10 r. green & red on green	85·00	£170

48 51

1913.

223	48	1 c. black	70	90
224		2 c. brown	55	10
225		3 c. green	60	30
226		4 c. green and red	45	30
226c		4 c. green	4·00	45
227		5 c. grey and red	80	10
228		6 c. brown	70	60
229		8 c. orange	60	8·50
230		10 c. red	1·00	20
232b		12 c. grey	3·75	20
232		12 c. red	30	3·00
233		15 c. blue	70	20
234		20 c. purple	45	40
235		20 c. blue	9·50	80
236		25 c. black & red on yell	30	15
237		50 c. purple and black	7·50	3·50
238		1 r. black on green	2·75	40
239		2 r. 50 black & red on bl	17·00	6·00
240		5 r. green & red on yell	26·00	60·00
204d		10 r. green & red on grn	26·00	85·00

1924. As T **42** but Arms similar to T **46**.

222		50 r. purple and green	£700	£1300

1925. Surch with figures, words and bar.

242	46	3 c. on 4 c. green	2·50	3·75
243		10 c. on 12 c. red	30	30
244		15 c. on 20 c. blue	55	20

1935. Silver Jubilee. As T **13** of Antigua.

245		5 c. blue and grey	50	10
246		12 c. green and blue	4·50	10
247		20 c. brown and blue	4·50	20
248		1 r. grey and purple	29·00	40·00

1937. Coronation. As T **2** of Aden.

249		5 c. violet	40	10
250		12 c. red	40	1·50
251		20 c. blue	40	10

1938.

252	51	2 c. grey	30	10
253		3 c. purple and red	2·00	1·50
254b		4 c. green	1·00	1·50
255a		5 c. violet	2·25	20
256b		10 c. red	2·25	10
257		12 c. orange	1·00	20
258		20 c. blue	1·00	10
259b		25 c. purple	4·50	10
260b		1 r. brown	15·00	80
261a		2 r. 50 violet	25·00	9·00
262a		5 r. olive	27·00	22·00
263a		10 r. purple	10·00	20·00

1946. Victory. As T **9** of Aden.

264		5 c. violet	10	10
265		20 c. blue	10	10

52 1d. "Post Office" Mauritius and King George VI

1948. Cent of First British Colonial Stamp.

266	52	5 c. orange and mauve	10	30
267		12 c. orange and green	10	10
268	–	20 c. blue	10	10
269	–	1 r. blue and brown	15	30

DESIGN: 20 c., 1 r. As Type **52**, but showing 2d. "Post Office" Mauritius.

1948. Silver Wedding. As T **10/11** of Aden.

270		5 c. violet	10	10
271		10 r. mauve	9·50	20·00

1949. U.P.U. As T **20/3** of Antigua.

272		12 c. red	60	65
273		20 c. blue	1·25	1·25
274		35 c. purple	60	65
275		1 r. brown	60	20

55 Aloe Plant 60 Legend of Paul and Virginie

67 Arms of Mauritius 69 Historical Museum, Mahebourg

1950.

276	–	1 c. purple	10	50
277	–	2 c. red	15	10
278	55	3 c. green	60	2·25
279	–	4 c. green	20	95
280	–	5 c. blue	15	10
281	–	10 c. red	30	75
282	–	12 c. green	1·25	1·75
283	60	20 c. blue	60	15
284	–	25 c. red	1·25	40
285	–	35 c. violet	30	10
286	–	50 c. green	2·00	50
287	–	1 r. brown	4·25	10
288	–	2 r. 50 orange	12·00	6·00
289	–	5 r. brown	13·00	13·00
290	67	10 r. blue	14·00	17·00

DESIGNS—HORIZ: 1 c. Labourdonnais sugar factory; 2 c. Grand Port; 5 c. Rempart Mountain; 10 c. Transporting cane; 12 c. Mauritius dodo and map; 35 c. Government House, Reduit; 1 r. Timor deer; 2 r. 50, Port Louis; 5 r. Beach scene. VERT: 4 c. Tamarind Falls; 25 c. Labourdonnais statue; 50 c. Pieter Both Mountain.

1953. Coronation. As T **13** of Aden.

291		10 c. black and green	70	15

1953. As 1950 but portrait of Queen Elizabeth II. Designs as for corresponding values except where stated.

293	–	2 c. red	10	10
294	–	3 c. green	30	40
295	–	4 c. purple (as 1 c.)	10	60
296	–	5 c. blue	10	10
314	–	10 c. green (as 4 c.)	15	10
298	69	15 c. red	10	10
299	–	20 c. red (as 25 c.)	15	20
300	–	25 c. blue (as 20 c.)	1·50	10
301	–	35 c. violet	20	10
302	–	50 c. green	55	75
315	–	60 c. green (as 12 c.)	1·75	10
303	–	1 r. sepia	30	10
316	–	2 r. 50 orange	4·75	8·00
305	–	5 r. brown	14·00	8·00
306	–	10 r. blue	13·00	65

70 Queen Elizabeth II and King George III (after Lawrence)

1961. 150th Anniv of British Post Office in Mauritius.

307	70	10 c. black and red	10	10
308		20 c. ultramarine and blue	30	25
309		35 c. black and yellow	40	25
310		1 r. purple and green	60	25

1963. Freedom from Hunger. As T **28** of Aden.

311		60 c. violet	40	10

1963. Cent of Red Cross. As T **33** of Antigua.

312		10 c. red and black	15	10
313		60 c. red and blue	60	20

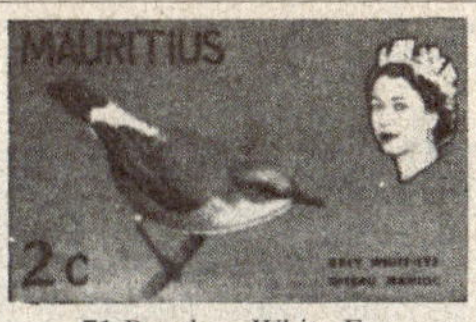

71 Bourbon White Eye

1965. Birds. Multicoloured.
317 2 c. Type **71** (yellow background) 40 15
318 3 c. Rodriguez fody (brown background) 1·00 15
319 4 c. Mauritius olive white eye 30 15
340 5 c. Mascarene paradise flycatcher 40 15
321 10 c. Mauritius fody 30 10
322 15 c. Mauritius parakeet (grey background) 2·00 40
323 20 c. Mauritius greybird (yellow background) 2·00 10
324 25 c. Mauritius kestrel 2·00 30
341 35 c. Pink pigeon 30 15
326 50 c. Reunion bulbul 50 40
327 60 c. Mauritius blue pigeon (extinct) (yellow background) 60 10
328 1 r. Mauritius dodo (extinct) (olive background) 5·50 10
329 2 r. 50 Rodriguez solitaire (extinct) 5·00 6·00
330 5 r. Mauritius red rail (extinct) 14·00 9·00
331 10 r. Broad-billed parrot (extinct) 26·00 17·00
For some values with background colours changed see Nos. 370/5.

1965. Centenary of I.T.U. As T **36** of Antigua.
332 10 c. orange and green 15 10
333 60 c. yellow and violet 40 20

1965. I.C.Y. As T **37** of Antigua.
334 10 c. purple and turquoise 15 10
335 60 c. green and violet 30 20

1966. Churchill Commem. As T **38** of Antigua.
336 2 c. blue 10 2·00
337 10 c. green 25 10
338 60 c. brown 1·10 20
339 1 r. violet 1·25 20

1966. 20th Anniv of U.N.E.S.C.O. As T **54/6** of Antigua.
342 5 c. multicoloured 15 20
343 10 c. yellow, violet & green 25 10
344 60 c. black, purple & orange 70 15

86 Red-tailed Tropic Bird

1967. Self-Government. Multicoloured.
345 2 c. Type **86** 20 80
346 10 c. Rodriguez brush warbler 50 10
347 60 c. Rose-ringed parakeet (extinct) 60 10
348 1 r. Grey-rumped swiftlet 60 10

1967. Self-Government. Nos. 317/31 optd **SELF GOVERNMENT 1967**.
349 **71** 2 c. multicoloured 10 50
350 – 3 c. multicoloured 10 50
351 – 4 c. multicoloured 10 50
352 – 5 c. multicoloured 10 10
353 – 10 c. multicoloured 10 10
354 – 15 c. multicoloured 10 30
355 – 20 c. multicoloured 15 10
356 – 25 c. multicoloured 15 10
357 – 35 c. multicoloured 20 10
358 – 50 c. multicoloured 30 15
359 – 60 c. multicoloured 30 10
360 – 1 r. multicoloured 35 10
361 – 2 r. 50 multicoloured 1·00 2·25
362 – 5 r. multicoloured 6·00 3·25
363 – 10 r. multicoloured 8·00 14·00

91 Flag of Mauritius

1968. Independence. Multicoloured.
364 2 c. Type **91** 10 1·25
365 3 c. Arms and Mauritius dodo emblem 15 1·25
366 15 c. Type **91** 20 10
367 20 c. As 3 c. 40 10
368 60 c. Type **91** 60 10
369 1 r. As 3 c. 75 10

1968. As Nos. 317/8, 322/3 and 327/8 but background colours changed as below.
370 **71** 2 c. olive 20 1·60
371 – 3 c. blue 1·75 3·50
372 – 15 c. brown 55 20
373 – 20 c. buff 3·50 2·75
374 – 60 c. red 1·50 15
375 – 1 r. purple 2·50 1·00

93 Dominique rescues Paul and Virginie

1968. Bicentenary of Bernardin de St. Pierre's Visit to Mauritius. Multicoloured.
376 2 c. Type **93** 10 65
377 15 c. Paul and Virginie crossing the river 25 10
378 50 c. Visit of Labourdonnais to Madame de la Tour 40 10
379 60 c. Meeting of Paul and Virginie in Confidence 40 10
380 1 r. Departure of Virginie for Europe 50 20
381 2 r. 50 Bernardin de St. Pierre 1·25 3·25
Nos. 377, 379 and 381 are vert.

99 Black-spotted Emperor

1969. Multicoloured (except 10, 15, 25, 60 c.).
382 2 c. Type **99** 10 1·50
383 3 c. Red reef crab 10 2·25
384 4 c. Episcopal mitre 1·40 2·50
385 5 c. Black-saddled pufferfish ("Bourse") 30 10
386 10 c. Starfish (red, black and flesh) 1·00 10
387 15 c. Sea urchin (brown, black and blue) 30 10
480 20 c. Fiddler crab 70 30
389 25 c. Spiny shrimp (red, black and green) 30 1·75
390 30 c. Single harp shells and double harp shell 1·50 1·50
483 35 c. Common paper nautilus 1·00 15
484 40 c. Spanish dancer 1·00 60
448 50 c. Orange spider conch and violet spider conch 45 10
449b 60 c. Blue marlin (black, pink and blue) 65 10
487 75 c. "Conus clytospira" 1·25 1·50
396 1 r. Dolphin (fish) 60 10
452 2 r. 50 Spiny lobster 2·00 4·00
453 5 r. Ruby snapper ("Sacre chien rouge") 3·00 2·00
399w 10 r. Yellow-edged lyretail ("Croissant queue jaune") 2·50 4·00

117 Gandhi as Law Student

1969. Birth Cent of Mahatma Gandhi. Mult.
400 2 c. Type **117** 10 10
401 15 c. Gandhi as stretcher-bearer during Zulu Revolt 25 10
402 50 c. Gandhi as Satyagrahi in South Africa 30 30
403 60 c. Gandhi at No. 10 Downing Street, London 30 10
404 1 r. Gandhi in Mauritius, 1901 40 10
405 2 r. 50 Gandhi, the "Apostle of Truth and Non-Violence" 90 1·50

124 Frangourinier Cane-crusher (18th cent)

1969. 150th Anniv of Telfair's Improvements to the Sugar Industry. Multicoloured.
407 2 c. Three-roller Vertical Mill 10 20
408 15 c. Type **124** 10 10
409 60 c. Beau Rivage Factory, 1867 10 10
410 1 r. Mon Desert-Alma Factory, 1969 10 10
411 2 r. 50 Dr. Charles Telfair (vert) 25 80

1970. Expo '70. Nos. 394 and 396 optd **EXPO '70' OSAKA**.
413 60 c. black, red and blue 10 10
414 1 r. multicoloured 10 10

129 Morne Plage, Mountain and Boeing 707

1970. Inauguration of Lufthansa Flight, Mauritius–Frankfurt. Multicoloured.
415 25 c. Type **129** 10 10
416 50 c. Boeing 707 and map (vert) 10 10

131 Lenin as a Student

1970. Birth Centenary of Lenin.
417 **131** 15 c. green and silver 10 10
418 – 75 c. brown 20 20
DESIGN: 75 c. Lenin as founder of U.S.S.R.

133 2d. "Post Office" Mauritius and original Post Office

1970. Port Louis, Old and New. Multicoloured.
419 5 c. Type **133** 10 10
420 15 c. G.P.O. Building (built 1870) 10 10
421 50 c. Mail coach (c. 1870) 40 10
422 75 c. Port Louis Harbour (1970) 55 10
423 2 r. 50 Arrival of Pierre A. de Suffren (1783) 70 70

138 U.N. Emblem and Symbols

1970. 25th Anniv of U.N.
425 **138** 10 c. multicoloured 10 10
426 60 c. multicoloured 40 10

139 Rainbow over Waterfall

1971. Tourism. Multicoloured.
427 10 c. Type **139** 35 10
428 15 c. Trois Mamelles Mountains 35 10
429 60 c. Beach scene 55 10
430 2 r. 50 Marine life 1·50 1·50
Nos. 427/30 have inscriptions on the reverse.

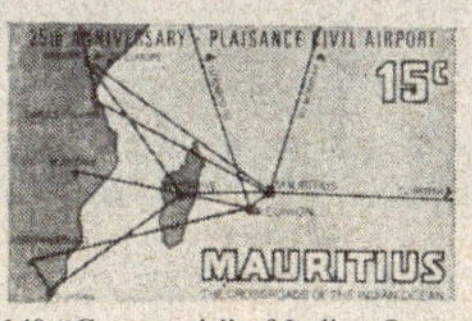

140 "Crossroads" of Indian Ocean

1971. 25th Anniv of Plaisance Airport. Multicoloured.
431 15 c. Type **140** 20 10
432 60 c. Boeing 707 and Terminal buildings 40 10
433 1 r. Air hostesses on gangway 45 10
434 2 r. 50 Farman F.190, "Roland Garros" airplane, Choisy Airfield, 1937 1·75 3·75

141 Princess Margaret Orthopaedic Centre

1971. 3rd Commonwealth Medical Conference. Multicoloured.
435 10 c. Type **141** 10 10
436 75 c. Operating theatre in National Hospital 20 20

142 Queen Elizabeth II and Prince Philip

1972. Royal Visit. Multicoloured.
455 15 c. Type **142** 15 10
456 2 r. 50 Queen Elizabeth II (vert) 2·50 2·50

143 Theatre Facade

1972. 150th Anniv of Port Louis Theatre. Multicoloured.
457 10 c. Type **143** 10 10
458 1 r. Theatre auditorium 40 20

144 Pirate Dhow

1972. Pirates and Privateers. Multicoloured.
459 15 c. Type **144** 65 15
460 60 c. Treasure chest (vert) 1·00 20
461 1 r. Lemene and "L'Hirondelle" (vert) 1·25 20
462 2 r. 50 Robert Surcouf 4·50 7·50

145 Mauritius University

1973. 5th Anniv of Independence. Multicoloured.
463 15 c. Type **145** 10 10
464 60 c. Tea development 15 15
465 1 r. Bank of Mauritius 15 15

146 Map and Hands

1973. O.C.A.M. Conference. Multicoloured.
466 10 c. O.C.A.M. emblem (horiz) 10 10
467 2 r. 50 Type **146** 40 45
O.C.A.M. = Organisation Commune Africaine Malgache et Mauricienne.

147 W.H.O. Emblem

1973. 25th Anniv of W.H.O.
468 **147** 1 r. multicoloured 10 10

148 Meteorological Station, Vacoas

1973. Centenary of I.M.O./W.M.O.
469 **148** 75 c. multicoloured . . . 30 60

149 Capture of the "Kent" 1800

1973. Birth Bicentenary of Robert Surcouf (privateer).
470 **149** 60 c. multicoloured . . . 50 85

150 P. Commerson

1974. Death Bicentenary (1973) of Philibert Commerson (naturalist).
471 **150** 2 r. 50 multicoloured . . . 30 40

151 Cow being Milked

1974. Eighth F.A.O. Regional Conf for Africa, Mauritius.
472 **151** 60 c. multicoloured . . . 20 20

152 Mail Train

1974. Centenary of U.P.U. Multicoloured.
473 15 c. Type **152** 40 15
474 1 r. New G.P.O., Port Louis . 40 20

153 "Cottage Life" (F. Leroy)

1975. Aspects of Mauritian Life. Paintings. Multicoloured.
493 15 c. Type **153** 10 10
494 60 c. "Milk Seller" (A. Richard) (vert) 35 10
495 1 r. "Entrance of Port Louis Market" (Thuillier) 35 10
496 2 r. 50 "Washerwoman" (Max Boullee) (vert) 95 80

154 Mace across Map

1975. French-speaking Parliamentary Assemblies Conference, Port Louis.
497 **154** 75 c. multicoloured . . . 30 90

155 Woman with Lamp ("The Light of the World")

1976. International Women's Year.
498 **155** 2 r. 50 multicoloured . . 35 1·00

156 Parched Landscape

1976. Drought in Africa. Multicoloured.
499 50 c. Type **156** 15 15
500 60 c. Map of Africa and carcass (vert) 15 15

157 "Pierre Loti", 1953–70

1976. Mail Carriers to Mauritius. Multicoloured.
501 10 c. Type **157** 55 10
502 15 c. "Secunder", 1907 . . . 80 10
503 50 c. "Hindoostan", 1842 . . 1·25 15
504 60 c. "St. Geran", 1740 . . . 1·40 15
505 2 r. 50 "Maen", 1638 . . . . 3·25 6·50

158 "The Flame of Hindi carried across the Seas"

1976. 2nd World Hindi Convention. Multicoloured.
507 10 c. Type **158** 10 10
508 75 c. Type **158** 10 15
509 1 r. 20 Hindi script 20 50

159 Conference Logo and Map of Mauritius

160 King Priest and Breastplate

1976. 22nd Commonwealth Parliamentary Association Conf. Multicoloured.
510 1 r. Type **159** 35 10
511 2 r. 50 Conference logo . . . 65 1·00

1976. Moenjodaro Excavations, Pakistan. Multicoloured.
512 60 c. Type **160** 30 10
513 1 r. House with well and goblet 50 10
514 2 r. 50 Terracotta figurine and necklace . . . . 1·25 65

161 Sega Scene

1977. 2nd World Black and African Festival of Arts and Culture, Nigeria.
515 **161** 1 r. multicoloured 30 15

162 The Queen with Sceptre and Rod

1977. Silver Jubilee. Multicoloured.
516 50 c. The Queen at Mauritius Legislative Assembly, 1972 . 15 10
517 75 c. Type **162** 20 10
518 5 r. Presentation of Sceptre and Rod 55 75

163 "Hugonia tomentosa"

1977. Indigenous Flowers. Multicoloured.
519 20 c. Type **163** 20 10
520 1 r. "Ochna mauritiana" (vert) 40 10
521 1 r. 50 "Dombeya acutangula" 50 20
522 5 r. "Trochetia blackburniana" (vert) . . . . 1·10 1·25

164 De Havilland Twin Otter 200/300

1977. Inaugural Int Flight of Air Mauritius. Multicoloured.
524 25 c. Type **164** 60 10
525 50 c. De Havilland Twin Otter 200/300 and Air Mauritius emblem 80 10
526 75 c. Piper Navajo and Boeing 747-100 . . . . 95 10
527 5 r. Boeing 707 . . . . 3·00 2·50

165 Portuguese Map of Mauritius, 1519

166 Mauritius Dodo

1978.
529B **165** 10 c. multicoloured . . 75 90
530A – 15 c. multicoloured . . 1·25 2·00
740 – 20 c. multicoloured . . 1·75 90
532A – 25 c. multicoloured . . 60 60
533B – 35 c. multicoloured . . 1·00 20
534A – 50 c. multicoloured . . 50 60
535A – 60 c. multicoloured . . 60 1·50
536A – 70 c. multicoloured . . 2·25 2·75
537B – 75 c. multicoloured . . 1·50 2·00
538A – 90 c. multicoloured . . 2·25 2·75
539A – 1 r. multicoloured . . . 60 40
540A – 1 r. 20 multicoloured . . 1·75 2·50
541B – 1 r. 25 multicoloured . . 1·25 20
542A – 1 r. 50 multicoloured . . 1·00 1·00
543A – 2 r. multicoloured . . . 60 40
544A – 3 r. multicoloured . . . 60 40
545A – 5 r. multicoloured . . . 60 1·00
546A – 10 r. multicoloured . . . 1·00 1·00
547A – 15 r. multicoloured . . . 1·50 2·25
548A – 25 r. green, black & brn 2·00 3·00

DESIGNS—HORIZ: 15 c. Dutch Occupation, 1638-1710; 20 c. Map by Van Keulen, c. 1700; 50 c. Construction of Port Louis, c. 1736; 70 c. Map by Bellin, 1763; 90 c. Battle of Grand Port, 1810; 1 r. Landing of the British, 1810; 1 r. 20, Government House, c. 1840; 1 r. 50, Indian immigration, 1835; 2 r. Race Course, c. 1870; 3 r. Place d'Armes, c. 1880; 5 r. Royal Visit postcard, 1901; 10 r. Royal College, 1914; 25 r. First Mauritian Governor-General and Prime Minister. VERT: 25 c. Settlement on Rodriguez, 1691; 35 c. French settlers Charter, 1715; 60 c. Pierre Poivre, c. 1767; 75 c. First coinage, 1794; 1 r. 25 Lady Gomm's Ball, 1847; 15 r. Unfurling of Mauritian flag.

1978. 25th Anniv of Coronation.
549 – 3 r. grey, black and blue . 25 45
550 – 3 r. multicoloured 25 45
551 **166** 3 r. grey, black and blue . 25 45
DESIGNS: No. 549, Antelope of Bohun; No. 550, Queen Elizabeth II.

167 Problem of Infection, World War I

1978. 50th Anniv of Discovery of Penicillin.
552 **167** 20 c. multicoloured 50 10
553 – 1 r. multicoloured . . . . 1·10 10
554 – 1 r. 50 black, brn & grn . 1·50 1·25
555 – 5 r. multicoloured . . . . 2·25 5·00
DESIGNS: 1 r. First mould growth, 1928; 1 r. 50, "Penicillium chrysogenum" ("notatum"); 5 r. Sir Alexander Fleming.

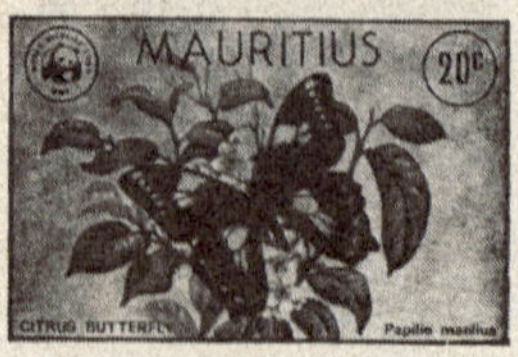
168 "Papilio manlius" (butterfly)

1978. World Wildlife. Multicoloured.
557 20 c. Type **168** . . . . 1·50 10
558 1 r. Geckos 90 10
559 1 r. 50 Greater Mascarene flying fox . . . . 1·25 55
560 5 r. Mauritius kestrel . . . . 11·00 6·00

169 Ornate Table

171 Father Laval and Crucifix

170 Whitcomb Diesel Locomotive 65H.P., 1949

1978. Bicentenary of Reconstruction of Chateau Le Reduit. Multicoloured.
562 15 c. Type **169** 10 10
563 75 c. Chateau Le Reduit . . . 10 10
564 3 r. Le Reduit gardens 30 45

1979. Railway Locomotives. Multicoloured.
565 20 c. Type **170** 20 10
566 1 r. "Sir William", 1922 . . . 40 10
567 1 r. 50 Kitson type 1930 . . . 60 45
568 2 r. Garratt type, 1927 . . . . 75 85

1979. Beatification of Father Laval (missionary). Mult.
570 20 c. Type **171** 10 10
571 1 r. 50 Father Laval 10 10
572 5 r. Father Laval's tomb (horiz) 35 50

172 Astronaut descending from Lunar Module

173 Great Britain 1855 4d. Stamp and Sir Rowland Hill

1979. 10th Anniv of Moon Landing. Multicoloured. Self-adhesive.
574 20 c. Type **172** 25 30
575 3 r. Astronaut performing experiment on Moon . . . 70 90
576 5 r. Astronaut on Moon . . . 2·50 4·50

1979. Death Cent of Sir Rowland Hill. Mult.
577 25 c. Type **173** 10 10
578 2 r. 1954 60 c. definitive . . . 55 50
579 5 r. 1847 1d. "POST OFFICE" 1·00 1·25

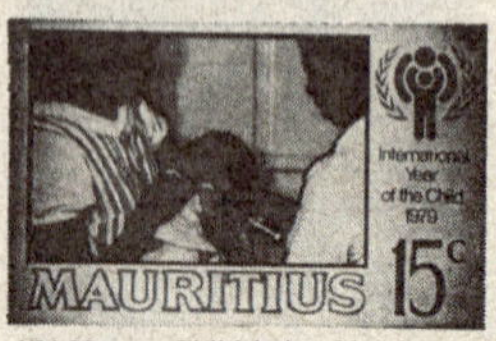
174 Young Child being Vaccinated

1979. International Year of the Child.
581 **174** 15 c. multicoloured . . . 10 10
582 – 25 c. multicoloured . . . 10 10
583 – 1 r. black, blue and light blue 15 10
584 – 1 r. 50 multicoloured . . . 30 20
585 – 3 r. multicoloured 50 50
DESIGNS—HORIZ: 25 c. Children playing; 1 r. 50, Girls in Chemistry laboratory; 3 r. Boy operating lathe. VERT: 1 r. I.Y.C. emblem.

175 The Lienard Obelisk

1980. Pamplemousses Botanical Gardens. Multicoloured.

586	20 c. Type **175**	10	10
587	25 c. Poivre Avenue	10	10
588	1 r. Varieties of Vacoas	20	10
589	2 r. Giant water lilies	45	55
590	5 r. Mon Plaisir (mansion)	80	2·25

176 "Emirne" (French steam packet)

1980. "London 1980" International Stamp Exhibition. Mail-carrying Ships. Multicoloured.

592	25 c. Type **176**	30	10
593	1 r. "Boissevain" (cargo liner)	50	10
594	2 r. "La Boudeuse" (Bougainville's ship)	70	60
595	5 r. "Sea Breeze" (English clipper)	95	2·00

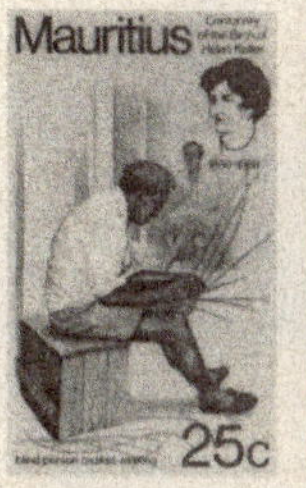

177 Blind Person Basket-making

178 Prime Minister Sir Seewoosagur Ramgoolam

1980. Birth Centenary of Helen Keller (campaigner for the handicapped). Multicoloured.

596	25 c. Type **177**	20	10
597	1 r. Deaf child under instruction	45	10
598	2 r. 50 Helen reading braille	70	35
599	5 r. Helen at graduation, 1904	1·25	1·25

1980. 80th Birthday and 40th Year in Parliament of Prime Minister Sir Seewoosagur Ramgoolam.

600	**178**	15 r. multicoloured	1·00	1·40

179 Headquarters, Mauritius Institute

1980. Centenary of Mauritius Institute. Mult.

601	25 c. Type **179**	15	10
602	2 r. Rare copy of Veda	40	15
603	2 r. Glory of India cone shell	55	20
604	5 r. "Le Torrent" (painting by Harpignies)	65	60

180 "Hibiscus liliiflorus"

181 Beau-Bassin/ Rose Hill

1981. Flowers. Multicoloured.

605	25 c. Type **180**	20	10
606	2 r. "Erythrospermum monticolum"	70	65
607	2 r. 50 "Chasalia boryana"	80	1·25
608	5 r. "Hibiscus columnaris"	1·40	2·50

1981. Coats of Arms of Mauritius Towns. Multicoloured.

609	25 c. Type **181**	10	10
610	1 r. 50 Curepipe	30	20
611	2 r. Quatre-Bornes	35	25
612	2 r. 50 Vacoas/Phoenix	40	30
613	5 r. Port Louis	75	75

182 Prince Charles as Colonel-in-Chief, Royal Regiment of Wales

184 Drummer and Piper

183 Emmanuel Anquetil and Guy Rozemont

1981. Royal Wedding. Multicoloured.

615	25 c. Wedding bouquet from Mauritius	10	10
616	2 r. 50 Type **182**	40	15
617	10 r. Prince Charles and Lady Diana Spencer	80	90

1981. Famous Politicians and Physician.

618	**183**	20 c. black and red	10	10
619	–	25 c. black and yellow	10	10
620	–	1 r. 25 black and green	30	25
621	–	1 r. 50 black and red	35	15
622	–	2 r. black and blue	45	20
623	–	2 r. 50 black and brown	50	30
624	–	5 r. black and blue	1·25	90

DESIGNS: 25 c. Remy Ollier and Sookdeo Bissoondoyal; 1 r. 25, Maurice Cure and Barthelemy Ohsan; 1 r. 50, Sir Guy Forget and Renganaden Seeneevassen; 2 r. Sir Abdul Razak Mohamed and Jules Koenig; 2 r. 50, Abdoollatiff Mahomed Osman and Dazzi Rama (Pandit Sahadeo); 5 r. Sir Thomas Lewis (physician) and electrocardiogram.

1981. Religion and Culture. Multicoloured.

625	20 c. Type **184**	10	10
626	2 r. Swami Sivananda (vert)	1·00	1·00
627	5 r. Chinese Pagoda	1·25	3·00

The 20 c. value commemorates the World Tamil Culture Conference (1980).

185 "Skills"

186 Ka'aba (sacred shrine, Great Mosque of Mecca)

1981. 25th Anniv of Duke of Edinburgh Award Scheme. Multicoloured.

628	25 c. Type **185**	10	10
629	1 r. 25 "Service"	10	10
630	5 r. "Expeditions"	20	30
631	10 r. Duke of Edinburgh	40	70

1981. Moslem Year 1400 A.H Commemoration. Multicoloured.

632	25 c. Type **186**	30	10
633	2 r. Mecca	80	80
634	5 r. Mecca and Ka'aba	1·40	2·75

187 Scout Emblem

189 Bride and Groom at Buckingham Palace

188 Charles Darwin

1982. 75th Anniv of Boy Scout Movement and 70th Anniv of Scouting in Mauritius.

635	**187**	25 c. lilac and green	10	10
636	–	2 r. brown and ochre	40	30
637	–	5 r. green and olive	85	1·00
638	–	10 r. green and blue	1·25	2·00

DESIGNS: 2 r. Lord Baden-Powell and Baden-Powell House; 5 r. Grand Howl; 10 r. Ascent of Pieter Both.

1982. 150th Anniv of Charles Darwin's Voyage. Multicoloured.

639	25 c. Type **188**	10	10
640	2 r. Darwin's telescope	30	45
641	2 r. 50 Darwin's elephant ride	35	55
642	10 r. H.M.S. "Beagle" beached for repairs	1·40	2·75

1982. 21st Birthday of Princess of Wales. Mult.

643	25 c. Mauritius coat of arms	10	10
644	2 r. 50 Princess Diana in Chesterfield, November, 1981	60	35
645	5 r. Type **189**	75	90
646	10 r. Formal portrait	2·50	2·25

190 Prince and Princess of Wales with Prince William

1982. Birth of Prince William of Wales.

647	**190**	2 r. 50 multicoloured	75	30

191 Bois Fandamane Plant

193 Early Wall-mounted Telephone

192 Arms and Flag of Mauritius

1982. Centenary of Robert Koch's Discovery of Tubercle Bacillus. Multicoloured.

648	25 c. Type **191**	10	10
649	1 r. 25 Central market, Port Louis	40	40
650	2 r. Bois Banane plant	65	75
651	5 r. Platte de Lezard plant	1·00	2·25
652	10 r. Dr. Robert Koch	1·75	3·75

1983. Commonwealth Day. Multicoloured.

653	25 c. Type **192**	10	10
654	2 r. 50 Satellite view of Mauritius	15	30
655	5 r. Harvesting sugar cane	30	75
656	10 r. Port Louis harbour	70	1·50

1983. World Communications Year. Mult.

657	25 c. Type **193**	10	10
658	1 r. 25 Early telegraph apparatus (horiz)	40	20
659	2 r. Earth satellite station	60	50
660	10 r. First hot-air balloon in Mauritius, 1784 (horiz)	1·25	2·75

194 Map of Nambia

195 Fish Trap

1983. Namibia Day. Multicoloured.

661	25 c. Type **194**	45	10
662	2 r. 50 Hand breaking chains	1·50	75
663	5 r. Family and settlement	2·00	2·25
664	10 r. Diamond mining	4·25	3·75

1983. Fishery Resources. Multicoloured.

665	25 c. Type **195**	15	10
666	1 r. Fishing boat (horiz)	55	15
667	5 r. Game fishing	1·00	2·25
668	10 r. Octopus drying (horiz)	1·40	4·00

196 Swami Dayananda

197 Adolf von Plevitz

1983. Death Centenary of Swami Dayananda. Multicoloured.

669	25 c. Type **196**	10	10
670	35 c. Last meeting with father	10	10
671	2 r. Receiving religious instruction	50	65
672	5 r. Swami demonstrating strength	90	2·50
673	10 r. At a religious gathering	1·40	3·75

1983. 125th Anniv of Arrival in Mauritius of Adolf von Plevitz (social reformer). Multicoloured.

674	25 c. Type **197**	10	10
675	1 r. 25 La Laura, Government school	30	30
676	5 r. Von Plevitz addressing Commission of Enquiry, 1872	1·00	2·50
677	10 r. Von Plevitz with Indian farm workers	1·75	3·75

198 Courtship Chase

1984. The Mauritius Kestrel. Multicoloured.

678	25 c. Type **198**	75	30
679	2 r. Kestrel in tree (vert)	1·75	1·25
680	2 r. 50 Young kestrel	2·00	2·25
681	10 r. Head (vert)	3·25	7·00

199 Wreck of S.S "Tayeb"

200 Blue Latan Palm

1984. 250th Anniv of "Lloyd's List" (newspaper). Multicoloured.

682	25 c. Type **199**	30	10
683	1 r. S.S. "Taher"	95	15
684	5 r. East Indiaman "Triton"	2·75	3·25
685	10 r. M.S. "Astor"	3·25	6·00

1984. Palm Trees. Multicoloured.

686	25 c. Type **200**	10	10
687	50 c. "Hyophorbe vaughanii"	20	20
688	2 r. 50 "Tectiphiala ferox"	1·25	1·50
689	5 r. Round Island bottle-palm	2·00	3·00
690	10 r. "Hyophorbe amaricaulis"	3·25	5·25

201 Slave Girl

203 The Queen Mother on Clarence House Balcony, 1980

202 75th Anniversary Production of "Faust" and Leoville L'Homme

1984. 150th Anniv of Abolition of Slavery and Introduction of Indian Immigrants.

691	**201**	25 c. purple, lilac and brown	15	10
692	–	1 r. purple, lilac and brown	70	10
693	–	2 r. purple and lilac	1·50	1·00
694	–	10 r. purple and lilac	5·00	7·25

DESIGNS—VERT: 1 r. Slave market. HORIZ: 2 r. Indian immigrant family; 10 r. Arrival of Indian immigrants.

1984. Centenary of Alliance Francaise (cultural organization). Multicoloured.
695 25 c. Type **202** 20 10
696 1 r. 25 Prize-giving ceremony and Aunauth Beejadbur 70 50
697 5 r. First headquarters and Hector Clarenc 2·00 3·00
698 10 r. Lion Mountain and Labourdonnais 2·50 5·00

1985. Life and Times of Queen Elizabeth the Queen Mother. Multicoloured.
699 25 c. The Queen Mother in 1926 15 10
700 2 r. With Princess Margaret at Trooping the Colour 40 30
701 5 r. Type **203** 75 1·40
702 10 r. With Prince Henry at his christening (from photo by Lord Snowdon) 1·25 2·50

204 High Jumping

205 Adult and Fledgling Pink Pigeons

1985. 2nd Indian Ocean Islands Games. Multicoloured.
704 25 c. Type **204** 20 10
705 50 c. Javelin-throwing 45 30
706 1 r. 25 Cycling 2·25 1·50
707 10 r. Wind surfing 5·50 7·50

1985. Pink Pigeon. Multicoloured.
708 25 c. Type **205** 1·75 30
709 2 r. Pink pigeon displaying at nest 4·00 1·75
710 2 r. 50 On nest 4·50 3·50
711 5 r. Pair preening 8·50 8·50

206 Caverne Patates, Rodrigues

1985. 10th Anniv of World Tourism Organization. Multicoloured.
712 25 c. Type **206** 50 10
713 35 c. Coloured soils, Chamarel 50 30
714 5 r. Serpent Island 4·00 4·50
715 10 r. Coin de Mire Island 6·00 7·50

207 Old Town Hall, Port Louis

1985. 250th Anniv of Port Louis. Multicoloured.
716 25 c. Type **207** 10 10
717 1 r. Al-Aqsa Mosque (180th anniv) 90 10
718 2 r. 50 Vase and trees (250th anniv of settlement of Tamil-speaking Indians) 1·25 1·50
719 10 r. Port Louis Harbour 5·50 7·50

208 Edmond Halley and Diagram

1986. Appearance of Halley's Comet. Mult.
720 25 c. Type **208** 40 10
721 1 r. 25 Halley's Comet (1682) and Newton's Reflector 1·10 50
722 3 r. Halley's Comet passing Earth 1·60 2·00
723 10 r. "Giotto" spacecraft 3·50 5·50

1986. 60th Birthday of Queen Elizabeth II. As T **110** of Ascension. Multicoloured.
724 25 c. Princess Elizabeth wearing badge of Grenadier Guards, 1942 10 10
725 75 c. Investiture of Prince of Wales, 1969 10 10
726 2 r. With Prime Minister of Mauritius, 1972 20 25
727 3 r. In Germany, 1978 30 40
728 15 r. At Crown Agents Head Office, London, 1983 1·25 2·00

209 Maize (World Food Day)

210 "Cryptopus elatus"

1986. International Events. Multicoloured.
729 25 c. Type **209** 10 10
730 1 r. African Regional Industrial Property Organization emblem (10th anniv) 30 10
731 1 r. 25 International Peace Year emblem 65 50
732 10 r. Footballer and Mauritius Football Association emblem (World Cup Football Championship, Mexico) 5·50 6·50

1986. Orchids. Multicoloured.
733 25 c. Type **210** 40 10
734 2 r. "Jumellea recta" 1·10 45
735 2 r. 50 "Angraecum mauritianum" 1·25 60
736 10 r. "Bulbophyllum longiflorum" 2·25 3·00

211 Hesketh Bell Bridge

1987. Mauritius Bridges. Multicoloured.
758 25 c. Type **211** 25 10
759 50 c. Sir Colville Deverell Bridge 35 20
760 2 r. 50 Cavendish Bridge 1·10 75
761 5 r. Tamarin Bridge 1·75 2·00
762 10 r. Grand River North West Bridge 2·50 2·50

212 Supreme Court, Port Louis

213 Mauritius Dodo Mascot

1987. Bicentenary of the Mauritius Bar. Mult.
763 25 c. Type **212** 10 10
764 1 r. District Court, Flacq 40 10
765 1 r. 25 Statue of Justice 50 20
766 10 r. Barristers of 1787 and 1987 2·00 2·00

1987. International Festival of the Sea. Mult.
767 25 c. Type **213** 20 10
768 1 r. 50 Yacht regatta (horiz) 1·00 90
769 3 r. Water skiing (horiz) 2·00 2·50
770 5 r. "Svanen" (barquentine) 2·75 4·00

214 Toys

1987. Industrialisation. Multicoloured.
771 20 c. Type **214** 10 10
772 35 c. Spinning factory 10 10
773 50 c. Rattan furniture 10 10
774 2 r. 50 Spectacle factory 85 80
775 10 r. Stone carving 2·50 2·75

215 Maison Ouvriere (Int Year of Shelter for the Homeless)

1987. Art and Architecture.
776 **215** 25 c. multicoloured 10 10
777 – 1 r. black and grey 25 10
778 – 1 r. 25 multicoloured 30 30
779 – 2 r. multicoloured 55 55
780 – 5 r. multicoloured 1·00 1·25
DESIGNS: 1 r. "Paul et Virginie" (lithograph); 1 r. 25, Chateau de Rosnay; 2 r. "Vielle Ferme" (Boulle); 5 r. "Trois Mamelles".

216 University of Mauritius

1988. 20th Anniv of Independence. Mult.
781 25 c. Type **216** 10 10
782 75 c. Anniversary gymnastic display 20 10
783 2 r. 50 Hurdlers and aerial view of Sir Maurice Rault Stadium 70 55
784 5 r. Air Mauritius aircraft at Sir Seewoosagur Ramgoolam International Airport 1·40 1·60
785 10 r. Governor-General Sir Veerasamy Ringadoo and Prime Minister Aneerood Jugnauth 2·25 2·75

217 Breast Feeding

218 Modern Bank Building

1988. 40th Anniv of W.H.O. Multicoloured.
786 20 c. Type **217** 15 10
787 2 r. Baby under vaccination umbrella and germ droplets 1·25 70
788 3 r. Nutritious food 1·40 1·25
789 10 r. W.H.O logo 2·75 3·25

1988. 150th Anniv of Mauritius Commercial Bank Ltd.
790 **218** 25 c. black, green & blue 10 10
791 – 1 r. black and red 15 10
792 – 1 r. 25 multicoloured 30 30
793 – 25 r. multicoloured 6·00 7·00
DESIGNS—HORIZ: 1 r. Mauritius Commercial Bank, 1897; 25 r. Fifteen dollar bank note of 1838. VERT: 1 r. 25, Bank arms.

219 Olympic Rings and Athlete

1988. Olympic Games, Seoul. Multicoloured.
794 25 c. Type **219** 10 10
795 35 c. Wrestling 15 15
796 1 r. 50 Long distance running 75 60
797 10 r. Swimming 2·50 3·75

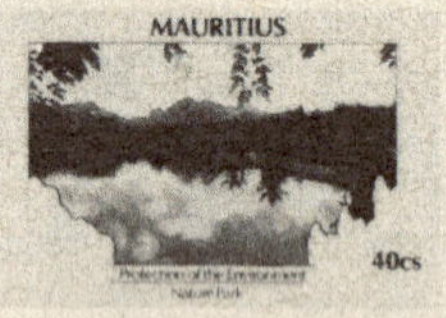

220 Nature Park

1989. Protection of the Environment. Mult.
798A 15 c. Underwater view 10 10
799B 20 c. As 15 c. 10 10
800B 30 c. Greenshank 10 10
801B 40 c. Type **220** 10 10
810A 50 c. Round Island (vert) 10 10
801cB 60 c. As 50 c. 10 10
811A 75 c. Bassin Blanc 10 10
812A 1 r. Mangrove (vert) 10 10
802A 1 r. 50 Whimbrel 10 10
813A 2 r. Le Morne 10 15
803A 3 r. Marine life 15 20
804B 4 r. Fern tree (vert) 20 25
814A 5 r. Riviere du Poste estuary 30 35
805A 6 r. Ecological scenery (vert) 35 40
806B 10 r. "Phelsuma ornata" (gecko) on plant (vert) 55 60
816A 15 r. Benares waves 80 85
817B 25 r. Migratory birds and map (vert) 1·40 1·50

221 La Tour Sumeire, Port Louis

222 Cardinal Jean Margeot

1989. Bicentenary of the French Revolution.
818 **221** 30 c. black, green & yell 10 10
819 – 1 r. black, brown and light brown 20 10
820 – 8 r. multicoloured 1·50 1·50
821 – 15 r. multicoloured 2·00 2·25
DESIGNS: 1 r. Salle de Spectacle du Jardin; 8 r. Portrait of Comte de Malartic; 15 r. Bicentenary logo.

1989. Visit of Pope John Paul II. Multicoloured.
822 30 c. Type **222** 30 10
823 40 c. Pope John Paul II and Prime Minister Jugnauth, Vatican, 1988 60 25
824 3 r. Mere Marie Magdeleine de la Croix and Chapelle des Filles de Marie, Port Louis, 1864 1·25 1·25
825 6 r. St. Francois d'Assise Church, Pamplemousses, 1756 2·00 3·00
826 10 r. Pope John Paul II 3·75 4·25

223 Nehru

1989. Birth Centenary of Jawaharlal Nehru (Indian statesman). Multicoloured.
827 40 c. Type **223** 60 20
828 1 r. 50 Nehru with daughter, Indira, and grandsons 1·25 70
829 3 r. Nehru and Gandhi 2·25 2·25
830 4 r. Nehru with Presidents Nasser and Tito 2·25 2·50
831 10 r. Nehru with children 4·25 5·50

224 Cane Cutting

1990. 350th Anniv of Introduction of Sugar Cane to Mauritius. Multicoloured.
832 30 c. Type **224** 10 10
833 40 c. Sugar factory, 1867 15 10
834 1 r. Mechanical loading of cane 30 10
835 25 r. Modern sugar factory 7·00 8·00

225 Industrial Estate

226 Desjardins (naturalist) (150th death anniv)

1990. 60th Birthday of Prime Minister Sir Anerood Jugnauth. Multicoloured.
836 35 c. Type **225** 10 10
837 40 c. Sir Aneerood Jugnauth at desk 10 10
838 1 r. 50 Mauritius Stock Exchange symbol 30 30
839 4 r. Jugnauth with Governor-General Sir Seewoosagur Ramgoolam 1·50 2·00
840 10 r. Jugnauth greeting Pope John Paul II 4·25 6·00

1990. Anniversaries. Multicoloured.
841 30 c. Type **226** 20 10
842 35 c. Logo on TV screen (25th anniv of Mauritius Broadcasting Corporation) (horiz) 20 10
843 6 r. Line Barracks (now Police Headquarters) (250th anniv) 3·25 3·50
844 8 r. Town Hall, Curepipe (centenary of municipality) (horiz) 3·25 3·75

227 Letters from Alphabets

1990. International Literacy Year. Multicoloured.
845 30 c. Type **227** 15 10
846 1 r. Blind child reading Braille 70 15
847 3 r. Open book and globe 1·60 1·60
848 10 r. Book showing world map with quill pen 4·00 6·00

1991. 65th Birthday of Queen Elizabeth II and 70th Birthday of Prince Philip. As T **139** of Ascension. Multicoloured.

849 8 r. Queen Elizabeth II . . . . 1·40 2·00
850 8 r. Prince Philip in Grenadier Guards ceremonial uniform . . 1·40 2·00

228 City Hall, Port Louis (25th anniv of City status)

1991. Anniversaries and Events. Multicoloured.

851 40 c. Type **228** 10 10
852 4 r. Colonel Draper (race course founder) (150th death anniv) (vert) . . . . 1·75 1·75
853 6 r. Joseph Barnard (engraver) and "POST PAID" 2d. stamp (175th birth anniv) (vert) . . 2·00 2·25
854 10 r. Supermarine Spitfire "Mauritius II" (50th anniv of Second World War) . . . . 4·50 5·50

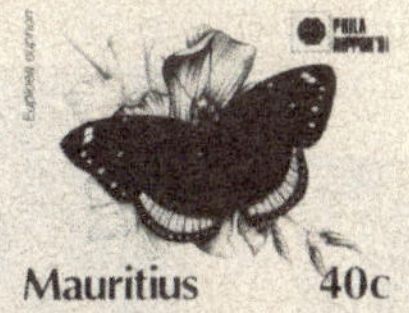

229 "Euploea euphon"

1991. "Phila Nippon '91" International Stamp Exn, Tokyo. Butterflies. Multicoloured.

855 40 c. Type **229** 50 20
856 3 r. "Hypolimnas misippus" (female) . . . . 1·60 90
857 8 r. "Papilio manlius" . . . . 2·75 3·50
858 10 r. "Hypolimnas misippus" (male) . . . . 2·75 3·75

230 Green Turtle, Tromelin

1991. Indian Ocean Islands. Multicoloured.

859 40 c. Type **230** 40 20
860 1 r. Glossy ibis, Agalega . . . 1·25 40
861 2 r. Takamaka flowers, Chagos Archipelago . . . . 1·40 1·10
862 15 r. Violet spider conch sea shell, St. Brandon . . . . . 6·00 7·50

231 Pres. Veerasamy Ringadoo and President's Residence

1992. Proclamation of Republic. Multicoloured.

863 40 c. Type **231** 10 10
864 4 r. Prime Minister Anerood Jugnauth and Government House . . . . 80 1·25
865 8 r. Children and rainbow . . 1·75 2·75
866 10 r. Presidential flag . . . . 2·00 3·00

232 Ticolo (mascot)

233 Bouquet (25th anniv of Fleurir Maurice)

1992. 8th African Athletics Championships, Port Louis. Multicoloured.

867 40 c. Type **232** 10 10
868 4 r. Sir Anerood Jugnauth Stadium (horiz) 65 95
869 5 r. High jumping (horiz) . . . 75 1·10
870 6 r. Championships emblem . . 90 1·60

1992. Local Events and Anniversaries. Mult.

871 40 c. Type **233** 10 10
872 1 r. Swami Krishnanandji Maharaj (25th anniv of arrival) 40 10
873 2 r. Boy with dog (humane education) (horiz) 85 60
874 3 r. Commission Headquarters (10th anniv of Indian Ocean Commission) (horiz) . . . 85 1·00
875 15 r. Radio telescope antenna, Bras d'Eau (project inauguration) (horiz) . . . 4·00 5·50

234 Bank of Mauritius Headquarters

235 Housing Development

1992. 25th Anniv of Bank of Mauritius. Mult.

876 40 c. Type **234** 10 10
877 4 r. Dodo gold coin (horiz) . 1·00 80
878 8 r. First bank note issue (horiz) 2·00 2·50
879 15 r. Graph of foreign exchange reserves, 1967–92 (horiz) . . 3·50 4·50

1993. 25th Anniv of National Day. Multicoloured.

880 30 c. Type **235** 10 10
881 40 c. Gross domestic product graph on computer screen . 10 10
882 3 r. National colours on map of Mauritius 40 50
883 4 r. Ballot box 45 60
884 15 r. Grand Commander's insignia for Order of Star and Key of the Indian Ocean . . 1·75 3·00

236 Bell 206 B JetRanger Helicopter

1993. 25th Anniv of Air Mauritius Ltd. Mult.

885 40 c. Type **236** 60 30
886 3 r. Boeing 747SP . . . . . . 1·00 1·00
887 4 r. Aerospatiale/Aeritalia ATR 42 . . . . 1·25 1·25
888 10 r. Boeing 767-200ER . . . 2·50 3·50

1993. No. 811 surch **40cs.**

890 40 c. on 75 c. Bassin Blanc . 30 30

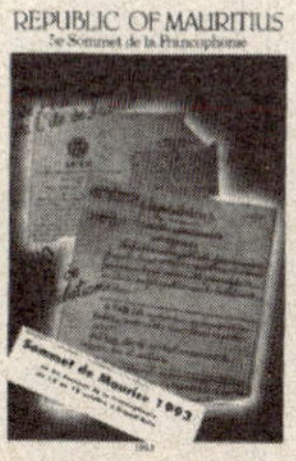

238 French Royal Charter, 1715, and Act of Capitulation, 1810

239 "Scotia" (cable ship) and Map of Cable Route

1993. 5th Summit of French-speaking Nations. Multicoloured.

891 1 r. Type **238** 30 10
892 5 r. Road signs . . . . 1·50 1·25
893 6 r. Code Napoleon . . . . . 1·50 1·75
894 7 r. Early Mauritius newspapers 1·75 2·00

1993. Cent of Telecommunications. Mult.

895 40 c. Type **239** 20 10
896 3 r. Morse key and code . . . 60 70
897 4 r. Signal Mountain Earth station . . . . 75 1·00
898 8 r. Communications satellite 1·40 2·00

240 Indian Mongoose

1994. Mammals. Multicoloured.

899 40 c. Type **240** 20 10
900 2 r. Indian black-naped hare . 45 35
901 8 r. Pair of crab-eating macaque 1·50 2·25
902 10 r. Adult and infant common tenrec . . . . 1·75 2·50

241 Dr Edouard Brown-Sequard (physiologist) (death cent)

1994. Anniversaries and Events. Multicoloured.

903 40 c. Type **241** 10 10
904 4 r. Family in silhouette (International Year of the Family) 45 55
905 8 r. World Cup and map of U.S.A. (World Cup Football Championship, U.S.A.) . . . 1·00 1·50
906 10 r. Control tower, SSR International Airport (50th anniv of Civil Aviation Organization) . . . . 1·25 1·75

242 "St. Geran" leaving L'Orient for Isle de France, 1744

1994. 250th Anniv of Wreck of "St. Geran" (sailing packet). Multicoloured.

907 40 c. Type **242** 20 10
908 5 r. In rough seas off Isle de France 65 70
909 6 r. Bell and main mast . . . 75 1·00
910 10 r. Artifacts from wreck . . 1·25 2·00

243 Ring-a-ring-a-roses

1994. Children's Games and Pastimes. Children's paintings. Multicoloured.

912 30 c. Type **243** 10 10
913 40 c. Skipping and ball games . 10 10
914 8 r. Water sports . . . . . . 1·25 1·75
915 10 r. Blind man's buff . . . . 1·25 1·75

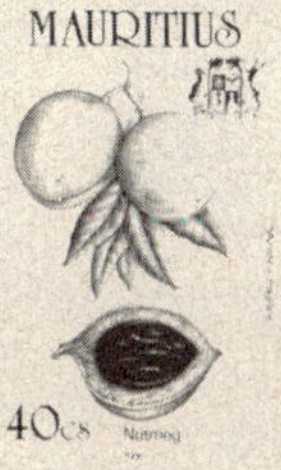

244 Nutmeg

245 Mare Longue Reservoir

1995. Spices. Multicoloured.

916 40 c. Type **244** 10 10
917 4 r. Coriander 55 65
918 5 r. Cloves 65 75
919 10 r. Cardamom . . . . 1·25 2·00

1995. 50th Anniv of End of Second World War. As T **161** of Ascension, but 35 × 28 mm. Mult.

920 5 r. H.M.S. "Mauritius" (cruiser) 90 1·25
921 5 r. Mauritian soldiers and map of North Africa . . . . . . 90 1·25
922 5 r. Consolidated PBY-5 Catalina flying boat, Tombeau Bay . . . . 90 1·25

1995. Anniversaries. Multicoloured.

923 40 c. Type **245** (50th anniv of construction) 10 10
924 4 r. Mahebourg to Curepipe road (bicentenary of construction) 60 70
925 10 r. Buildings on fire (centenary of Great Fire of Port Louis) 1·25 2·00

MORE DETAILED LISTS
are given in the Stanley Gibbons Catalogues referred to in the country headings.
For lists of current volumes see Introduction.

246 Ile Plate Lighthouse

247 Symbolic Children under U.N.I.C.E.F. Umbrella

1995. Lighthouses. Multicoloured.

926 30 c. Type **246** 30 15
927 40 c. Pointe aux Caves . . . 30 15
928 8 r. Ile aux Fouquets . . . . 1·50 2·00
929 10 r. Pointe aux Canonniers . 1·75 2·00

1995. 50th Anniv of United Nations. Multicoloured.

931 40 c. Type **247** 10 10
932 4 r. Hard hat and building construction (I.L.O.) 35 45
933 8 r. Satellite picture of cyclone (W.M.O.) . . . . 70 1·10
934 10 r. Bread and grain (F.A.O.) 90 1·40

248 C.O.M.E.S.A. Emblem

1995. Inauguration of Common Market for Eastern and Southern Africa.

935 **248** 60 c. black and pink . . 10 10
936 4 r. black and blue . . . 35 45
937 8 r. black and yellow . . 70 1·10
938 10 r. black and green . . 90 1·40

249 "Pachystyla bicolor"

1996. Snails. Multicoloured.

939 60 c. Type **249** 15 10
940 4 r. "Gonidomus pagodus" . . 45 50
941 5 r. "Harmogenanina implicata" 45 60
942 10 r. "Tropidophora eugeniae" 85 1·60

250 Boxing

1996. Centenary of Modern Olympic Games. Multicoloured.

943 60 c. Type **250** 10 10
944 4 r. Badminton 45 50
945 5 r. Basketball 60 65
946 10 r. Table tennis . . . . . . 1·00 1·50

251 "Zambezia" (freighter)

1996. Ships. Multicoloured.

947 60 c. Type **251** 15 10
948 4 r. "Sir Jules" (coastal freighter) 45 50
949 5 r. "Mauritius" (cargo liner) 50 60
950 10 r. "Mauritius Pride" (container ship) . . . . . . 1·00 1·50

252 Posting a Letter

1996. 150th Anniv of the Post Office Ordinance. Multicoloured.

952		60 c. Type **252**	10	10
953		4 r. "B53" duplex postmark	45	50
954		5 r. Modern mobile post office	55	60
955		10 r. Carriole (19th-century horse-drawn postal carriage)	1·00	1·50

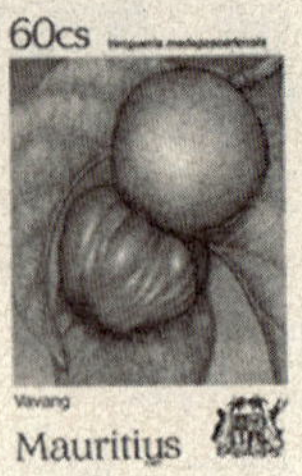

253 Vavang

1997. Fruits. Multicoloured.

956		60 c. Type **253**	10	10
957		4 r. Pom zako	45	50
958		5 r. Zambos	55	60
959		10 r. Sapot negro	1·00	1·50

254 Governor Mahe de la Bourdonnais and Map

1997. Aspects of Mauritius History. Multicoloured.

960		60 c. Type **254**	10	10
961		1 r. La Perouse and map of Pacific	15	10
962		4 r. Governor Sir William Gomm and Lady Gomm's Ball, 1847	40	40
963		6 r. George Clark discovering skeleton of dodo, 1865	60	60
964		10 r. Professor Brian Abel-Smith and Social Policies report of 1960	90	1·25

255 1d. "POST OFFICE" Mauritius

1997. 150th Anniv of "POST OFFICE" Stamps. Multicoloured.

965		60 c. Type **255**	15	10
966		4 r. 2d. "POST OFFICE" Mauritius	30	30
967		5 r. "POST OFFICE" 1d. and 2d. on gold background	40	40
968		10 r. "POST OFFICE" 2d. and 1d. on silver background	80	1·00

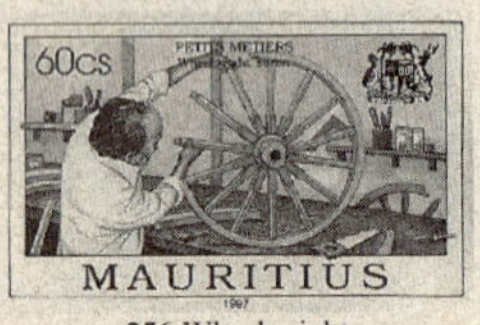

256 Wheelwright

1997. Small Businesses. Multicoloured.

970		60 c. Type **256**	10	10
971		4 r. Laundryman	30	30
972		5 r. Shipwright	40	40
973		15 r. Quarryman	1·25	1·50

257 "Phelsuma guentheri" (gecko)

1998. Geckos. Multicoloured.

974		1 r. Type **257**	15	10
975		6 r. "Nactus serpensinsula durrelli"	45	45
976		7 r. "Nactus coindemirensis"	55	55
977		8 r. "Phelsuma edwardnewtonii"	65	70

258 Steam Train on Viaduct

1998. Inland Transport. Multicoloured.

978		40 c. Type **258**	15	10
979		5 r. Early lorry	45	45
980		6 r. Bus in town street	50	50
981		10 r. Sailing barge at wharf	1·50	1·75

259 President Nelson Mandela

1998. State Visit of President Nelson Mandela of South Africa.

982	**259**	25 r. multicoloured	1·40	1·50

260 Count Maurice of Nassau and Dutch Landing

1998. 400th Anniv of Dutch Landing on Mauritius. Multicoloured.

983		50 c. Type **260**	10	10
984		1 r. Fort Frederik Hendrik and sugar cane	10	10
985		7 r. Dutch map of Mauritius (1670)	40	45
986		8 r. Diagram of landing	45	50

261 Cascade Balfour

1998. Waterfalls. Multicoloured.

988		1 r. Type **261**	10	10
989		5 r. Rochester Falls	30	35
990		6 r. Cascade G.R.S.E. (vert)	35	40
991		10 r. 500 ft. Cascade (vert)	55	60

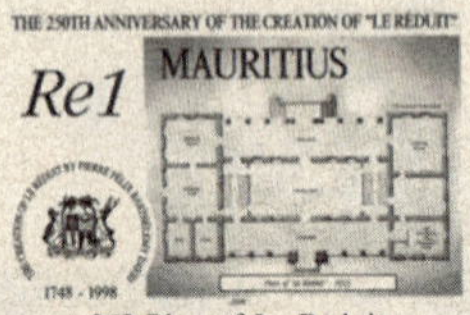

262 Plan of Le Reduit

1998. 250th Anniv of Chateau Le Reduit. Multicoloured.

992		1 r. Type **262**	10	10
993		4 r. "Le Chateau du Reduit, 1814" (P. Thuillier)	20	25
994		5 r. "Le Reduit, 1998" (Hassen Edun)	30	35
995		15 r. Commemorative monument	80	85

263 Governor Mahe de la Bourdonnais on 15 c. Stamp of 1899

1999. 300th Birth Anniv of Governor Mahe de la Bourdonnais.

996	**263**	7 r. blue, black and red	40	45

264 "Clerodendron laciniatum"

1999. Local Plants. Multicoloured.

997		1 r. Type **264**	10	10
998		2 r. "Senecio lamarckianus"	10	15
999		5 r. "Cylindrocline commersonii"	30	35
1000		9 r. "Psiadia pollicina"	50	55

265 "The Washerwomen" (Herve Masson)

1999. Mauritius through Local Artists' Eyes. Multicoloured.

1001		1 r. Type **265**	10	10
1002		3 r. "The Casino" (Gaetan de Rosnay)	15	20
1003		4 r. "The Four Elements" (Andree Poilly)	20	25
1004		6 r. "Going to Mass" (Xavier Le Juge de Segrais)	35	40

EXPRESS DELIVERY STAMPS

1903. No. 136 surch **EXPRESS DELIVERY 15 c.**

E1	**40**	15 c. on 15 c. blue	5·50	17·00

1903. No. 136 surch **EXPRESS DELIVERY (INLAND) 15 c.**

E3	**40**	15 c. on 15 c. blue	6·00	2·25

1904. T **42** without value in label (a) Surch **(FOREIGN) EXPRESS DELIVERY 18 CENTS**.

E5	**42**	18 c. green	1·50	18·00

(b) Surch **EXPRESS DELIVERY (INLAND) 15 c.**

E6	**42**	15 c. green	3·00	3·00

POSTAGE DUE STAMPS

D 1

1933.

D 1	**D 1**	2 c. black	75	50
D 2		4 c. violet	40	65
D 3		6 c. red	40	80
D 4		10 c. green	40	70
D 5		20 c. blue	50	90
D13		50 c. purple	75	10·00
D 7		1 r. orange	70	14·00

1982. Nos. 530/1, 535, 540, 542 and 547 surch **POSTAGE DUE** and value.

D14		10 c. on 15 c. Dutch Occupation, 1638–1710	20	30
D15		20 c. on 20 c. Van Keulen's map, c. 1700	30	30
D16		50 c. on 60 c. Pierre Poivre, c. 1767 (vert)	30	30
D17		1 r. on 1 r. 20 Government House, c. 1840	40	30
D18		1 r. 50 on 1 r. 50 Indian immigration, 1835	50	75
D19		5 r. on 15 r. Unfurling Mauritian flag, 1968	1·00	2·00

MONTSERRAT

One of the Leeward Is., Br. W. Indies. Used general issues for Leeward Is. concurrently with Montserrat stamps until 1 July 1956, when Leeward Is. stamps were withdrawn.

1876. 12 pence = 1 shilling;
20 shillings = 1 pound.
1951. 100 cents = 1 West Indian dollar.

1876. Stamps of Antigua as T **1** optd **MONTSERRAT**.

8c		1d. red	15·00	14·00
2		6d. green	55·00	40·00

3

1880.

7	**3**	½d. green	1·00	7·00
9		2½d. brown	£225	65·00
10		2½d. blue	18·00	17·00
5		4d. blue	£140	40·00
12		4d. mauve	4·25	3·00

4 Device of the Colony

5

1903.

24a	**4**	½d. green	40	75
15		1d. grey and red	75	40
26a		2d. grey and brown	1·75	1·00
17		2½d. grey and blue	1·50	1·75
28a		3d. orange and purple	6·00	2·50
29a		6d. purple and olive	6·00	5·50
30		1s. green and purple	8·50	7·00
21		2s. green and brown	23·00	16·00
22		2s. 6d. green and black	17·00	30·00
33	**5**	5s. black and red	80·00	£110

1908.

36	**4**	1d. red	1·40	30
38		2d. grey	1·75	13·00
39		2½d. blue	2·25	3·50
40		3d. purple on yellow	1·00	17·00
43		6d. purple	6·50	45·00
44		1s. black on green	8·00	42·00
45		2s. purple and blue on blue	25·00	50·00
46		2s. 6d. black & red on blue	30·00	65·00
47	**5**	5s. red and green on yellow	50·00	65·00

1914. As T **5**, but portrait of King George V.

48		5s. red and green on yellow	55·00	85·00

8

10 Plymouth

1916.

63	**8**	¼d. brown	15	4·75
64		½d. green	20	30
50		1d. red	35	75
65		1d. violet	30	50
67		1½d. yellow	1·75	9·50
68		1½d. red	30	2·75
69		1½d. brown	70	50
70		2d. grey	45	1·50
71a		2½d. blue	60	90
72		2½d. yellow	1·25	18·00
74		3d. purple on yellow	1·10	4·75
73		3d. blue	50	14·00
75		4d. black & red on yellow	60	10·00
76		5d. purple and olive	2·50	10·00
77		6d. purple	2·00	6·00
78		1s. black on green	3·00	7·00
79		2s. purple and blue on blue	6·00	13·00
80		2s. 6d. black & red on blue	11·00	48·00
81		3s. green and violet	12·00	18·00
82		4s. black and red	15·00	29·00
83		5s. green and red on yellow	23·00	35·00

1917. Optd **WAR STAMP**.

60	**8**	½d. green	10	1·00
62		1½d. black and orange	10	30

1932. 300th Anniv of Settlement of Montserrat.

84	**10**	½d. green	75	5·50
85		1d. red	75	5·00
86		1½d. brown	1·25	2·50
87		2d. grey	1·25	14·00
88		2½d. blue	1·25	12·00
89		3d. orange	1·50	13·00
90		6d. violet	2·25	25·00
91		1s. olive	12·00	32·00
92		2s. 6d. purple	48·00	65·00
93		5s. brown	£100	£160

1935. Silver Jubilee. As T **13** of Antigua.

94 1d. blue and red . . . . 85 3·00
95 1½d. blue and grey . . . . . . 1·00 2·75
96 2½d. brown and blue . . . . . 2·25 3·00
97 1s. grey and purple . . . . . . 3·00 13·00

1937. Coronation. As T **2** of Aden.

98 1d. red 30 50
99 1½d. brown 40 30
100 2½d. blue 40 75

11 Carr's Bay

1938. King George VI.

101a **11** ½d. green 15 20
102a – 1d. red 30 30
103a – 1½d. purple 30 50
104a – 2d. orange 85 70
105a – 2½d. blue 40 30
106 **11** 3d. brown . . . . 1·50 40
107a – 6d. violet . . . . 2·50 60
108a **11** 1s. red . . . . 2·00 30
109 – 2s. 6d. blue . . . . . . 18·00 80
110a **11** 5s. red . . . . 21·00 3·00
111 – 10s. blue . . . . 13·00 17·00
112 **11** £1 black . . . . 13·00 27·00
DESIGNS: 1d., 1½d., 2½d. Sea Island cotton; 2d., 6d., 2s. 6d., 10s. Botanic station.

1946. Victory. As T **9** of Aden.

113 1½d. purple 10 10
114 3d. brown 10 10

1949. Silver Wedding. As T **10/11** of Aden.

115 2½d. blue 10 10
116 5s. red . . . . 4·50 6·00

1949. U.P.U. As T **20/23** of Antigua.

117 2½d. blue 20 30
118 3d. brown . . . . 1·50 30
119 6d. purple 40 30
120 1s. purple 40 30

1951. Inauguration of B.W.I. University College. As T **24/25** of Antigua.

121 3 c. black and purple 20 60
122 12 c. black and violet 20 60

14 Government House

21 Pineapple

1951.

123 **14** 1 c. black . . . . 10 1·25
124 – 2 c. green 15 70
125 – 3 c. brown 30 70
126 – 4 c. red 30 40
127 – 5 c. violet 30 70
128 – 6 c. brown 30 30
129 – 8 c. blue 35 20
130 – 12 c. blue and brown . . . 35 30
131 – 24 c. red and green 35 30
132 – 60 c. black and red . . . . 5·50 2·50
133 – $1.20 green and blue . . . 5·50 4·00
134 – $2.40 black and green . . . 4·50 12·00
135 – $4.80 black and purple . . 16·00 16·00
DESIGNS: 2 c., $1.20, Sea Island cotton: cultivation; 3 c. Map; 4 c., 24 c. Picking tomatoes; 5 c., 12 c. St. Anthony's Church; 6 c., $4.80, Badge; 8 c., 60 c. Sea Island cotton: ginning; $2.40, Government House (portrait on right).

1953. Coronation. As T **13** of Aden.

136 2 c. black and green 40 15

1953. As 1951 but portrait of Queen Elizabeth II.

136a ½ c. violet (As 3 c.) (I) 50 10
136b ½ c. violet (II) 70 10
137 1 c. black 10 10
138 2 c. green 15 10
139 3 c. brown (I) 50 10
139a 3 c. brown (II) 70 90
140 4 c. red 30 20
141 5 c. violet 30 30
142 6 c. brown (I) 30 10
142a 6 c. brown (II) 40 15
143 8 c. blue . . . . 1·00 10
144 12 c. blue and brown . . . . . 1·50 10
145 24 c. red and green . . . . . 1·50 20
145a 48 c. olive & pur (As 2 c.) . . 12·00 2·25
146 60 c. black and red . . . . . 7·00 2·00
147 $1.20 green and blue . . . . 14·00 4·25
148 $2.40 black and green . . . . 12·00 10·00
149 $4.80 black and purple (I) . . 6·00 10·00
149a $4.80 black and purple (II) . . 11·00 7·50
I. Inscr "Presidency". II. Inscr "Colony".

1958. British Caribbean Federation. As T **28** of Antigua.

150 3 c. green 55 20
151 6 c. blue 75 45
152 12 c. red 90 15

1963. Freedom from Hunger. As T **28** of Aden.

153 12 c. violet 30 15

1963. Cent of Red Cross. As T **33** of Antigua.

154 4 c. red and black 10 20
155 12 c. red and blue 25 50

1964. 400th Birth Anniv of Shakespeare. As T **34** of Antigua.

156 12 c. blue 10 10

1965. Cent of I.T.U. As T **36** of Antigua.

158 4 c. red and violet 15 10
159 48 c. green and red 30 20

1965. Multicoloured.

160 1 c. Type **21** 10 10
161 2 c. Avocado 10 10
162 3 c. Soursop 10 10
163 4 c. Pepper 10 10
164 5 c. Mango 10 10
165 6 c. Tomatoe 10 10
166 8 c. Guava 10 10
167 10 c. Ochro 10 10
168 12 c. Lime 15 10
169 20 c. Orange 20 10
170 24 c. Banana 20 10
171 42 c. Onion 75 60
172 48 c. Cabbage . . . . 1·50 75
173 60 c. Pawpaw . . . . 2·25 90
174 $1.20 Pumpkin . . . . 2·00 2·25
175 $2.40 Sweet potato . . . . . 6·00 4·75
176 $4.80 Egg plant . . . . 6·00 8·00

1965. I.C.Y. As T **37** of Antigua.

177 2 c. purple and turquoise . . . 10 20
178 12 c. green and lavender . . . 25 10

1966. Churchill Commem. As T **38** of Antigua.

179 1 c. blue 10 10
180 2 c. green 10 10
181 24 c. brown 15 10
182 42 c. violet 20 15

1966. Royal Visit. As T **39** of Antigua.

183 14 c. black and blue 40 15
184 24 c. black and mauve 60 15

1966. Inauguration of W.H.O. Headquarters, Geneva. As T **41** of Antigua.

185 12 c. black, green and blue . . 10 10
186 60 c. black, purple and ochre . . 25 40

1966. 20th Anniv of U.N.E.S.C.O. As T **54/6** of Antigua.

187 4 c. multicoloured 10 10
188 60 c. yellow, violet and olive . . 30 10
189 $1.80 black, purple & orange . . 1·25 70

25 Yachting

1967. International Tourist Year. Multicoloured.

190 5 c. Type **25** 15 10
191 15 c. Waterfall near Chance Mountain 20 10
192 16 c. Fishing, skin diving and swimming 20 30
193 24 c. Playing golf . . . . . . 1·40 35
No. 191 is vert.

1968. Nos. 168, 170, 172, 174/6 surch.

194 15 c. on 12 c. Lime 20 15
195 25 c. on 24 c. Banana 25 15
196 50 c. on 48 c. Cabbage 45 15
197 $1 on $1.20 Pumpkin 80 40
198 $2.50 on $2.40 Sweet potato . 1·25 3·25
199 $5 on $4.80 Egg plant . . . . 1·40 3·75

27 Sprinting

1968. Olympic Games, Mexico.

200 **27** 15 c. mauve, green & gold . . 10 10
201 – 25 c. blue, orange & gold . . 15 10
202 – 50 c. green, red and gold . . 25 10
203 – $1 multicoloured 35 20
DESIGNS—HORIZ: 25 c. Weightlifting; 50 c. Gymnastics. VERT: $1 Sprinting and Aztec pillars.

31 Alexander Hamilton

1968. Human Rights Year. Multicoloured.

204 5 c. Type **31** 10 10
205 15 c. Albert T. Marryshow . . . 10 10
206 25 c. William Wilberforce . . . 10 10
207 50 c. Dag Hammarskjold . . . 10 10
208 $1 Dr. Martin Luther King . . . 25 30

32 "The Two Trinities" (Murillo)

34 Map showing CARIFTA Countries

1968. Christmas.

209 **32** 5 c. multicoloured 10 10
210 – 15 c. multicoloured 10 10
211 **32** 25 c. multicoloured 10 10
212 – 50 c. multicoloured 25 20
DESIGN: 15, 50 c. "The Adoration of the Kings" (detail, Botticelli).

1969. 1st Anniv of CARIFTA (Caribbean Free Trade Area). Multicoloured.

223 15 c. Type **34** 10 10
224 20 c. Type **34** 10 10
225 35 c. "Strength in Unity" . . . 10 10
226 50 c. As 35 c. 15 15
Nos. 225/6 are horiz.

36 Telephone Receiver and Map of Montserrat

41 King Caspar before the Virgin and Child (detail) (Norman 16th-cent stained glass window)

40 Dolphin (fish)

1969. Development Projects. Multicoloured.

227 15 c. Type **36** 10 10
228 25 c. School symbols and map . . 10 10
229 50 c. Hawker Siddeley H.S.748 aircraft and map 15 10
230 $1 Electricity pylon and map . . 25 20

1969. Game Fish. Multicoloured.

231 5 c. Type **40** 35 10
232 15 c. Atlantic sailfish 50 10
233 25 c. Blackfin tuna 60 10
234 40 c. Spanish mackerel 80 55

1969. Christmas Paintings multicoloured; frame colours given.

235 **41** 15 c. black, gold & violet . . 10 10
236 25 c. black and red 10 10
237 – 50 c. black, blue & orge . . 15 15
DESIGN—HORIZ: 50 c. "Nativity" (Leonard Limosin).

43 "Red Cross Sale"

1970. Centenary of British Red Cross. Mult.

238 3 c. Type **43** 10 10
239 4 c. School for deaf children . . 10 10
240 15 c. Transport services for disabled 10 20
241 20 c. Workshop 10 60

44 Red-footed Booby

1970. Birds. Multicoloured.

242 1 c. Type **44** 10 10
243 2 c. American kestrel 15 15
244 3 c. Magnificent frigate bird . . 15 15
245 4 c. Great egret . . . . 1·00 15
299a 5 c. Brown pelican 60 55
247 10 c. Bananaquit 40 10
248 15 c. Smooth-billed ani . . . 30 15
249 20 c. Red-billed tropic bird . . 35 15
250 25 c. Montserrat oriole 50 50
251 50 c. Green-throated carib . . 5·00 1·00
252 $1 Antillean crested hummingbird . . . . . . 6·50 1·00
253 $2.20 Little blue heron . . . 5·00 9·00
254 $5 Purple-throated carib . . 7·50 11·00
254c $10 Forest thrush . . . . . 15·00 15·00
The 2, 3, 4, 5, 10, 50 c. and $2.50 are vert.

45 "Madonna and Child with Animals" (Brueghel the Elder, after Durer)

1970. Christmas. Multicoloured.

255 5 c. Type **45** 10 10
256 15 c. "The Adoration of the Shepherds" (Domenichino) . . 10 10
257 20 c. Type **45** 10 10
258 $1 As 15 c. 35 90

46 War Memorial

1970. Tourism. Multicoloured.

259 5 c. Type **46** 10 10
260 15 c. Plymouth from Fort St. George 10 10
261 25 c. Carr's Bay 15 15
262 50 c. Golf Fairway . . . . . 1·00 1·00

47 Girl Guide and Badge

48 "Descent from the Cross" (Van Hemessen)

1970. Diamond Jubilee of Montserrat Girl Guides. Multicoloured.

264 10 c. Type **47** 10 10
265 15 c. Brownie and badge . . . 10 10
266 25 c. As 15 c. 15 10
267 40 c. Type **47** 20 40

1971. Easter. Multicoloured.

268 5 c. Type **48** 10 10
269 15 c. "Noli me tangere" (Orcagna) 10 10
270 20 c. Type **48** 10 10
271 40 c. As 15 c. 15 15

49 D.F.C. and D.F.M. in Searchlights

50 "The Nativity with Saints" (Romanino)

1971. Golden Jubilee of Commonwealth Ex-Services League. Multicoloured.

272 10 c. Type **49** 10 10
273 20 c. M.C., M.M. and jungle patrol 15 10
274 40 c. D.S.C., D.S.M. and submarine action 20 15
275 $1 V.C. and soldier attacking bunker 50 70

1971. Christmas. Multicoloured.

276 5 c. Type **50** 10 10
277 15 c. "Choir of Angels" (Simon Marmion) 10 10
278 20 c. Type **50** 10 10
279 $1 As 15 c. 35 40

51 Piper Apache

1971. 14th Anniv of Inauguration of L.I.A.T. (Leeward Islands Air Transport). Multicoloured.

280	5 c. Type **51**	10	10
281	10 c. Beech 50 Twin Bonanza	15	15
282	15 c. De Havilland Heron	30	15
283	20 c. Britten Norman Islander	35	15
284	40 c. De Havilland Twin Otter 100	65	45
285	75 c. Hawker Siddeley H.S.748	2·00	2·25

52 "Chapel of Christ in Gethsemane", Coventry Cathedral

1972. Easter. Multicoloured.

287	5 c. Type **52**	10	10
288	10 c. "The Agony in the Garden" (Bellini)	10	10
289	20 c. Type **52**	10	10
290	75 c. As 10 c.	35	50

53 Lizard

54 "Madonna of the Chair" (Raphael)

1972. Reptiles. Multicoloured.

291	15 c. Type **53**	15	10
292	20 c. Mountain chicken (frog)	20	10
293	40 c. Iguana (horiz)	35	20
294	$1 Tortoise (horiz)	1·50	1·50

1972. Christmas. Multicoloured.

303	10 c. Type **54**	10	10
304	35 c. "Virgin and Child with Cherub" (Fungai)	20	10
305	50 c. "Madonna of the Magnificat" (Botticelli)	30	30
306	$1 "Virgin and Child with St. John and an Angel" (Botticelli)	40	65

1972. Royal Silver Wedding. As T **52** of Ascension, but with lime, tomatoes and pawpaw in background.

307	35 c. pink	10	10
308	$1 blue	20	20

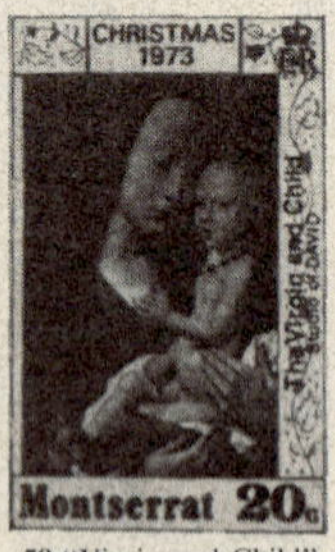

56 "Passiflora herbertiana"

58 "Virgin and Child" (School of Gerard David)

57 Montserrat Monastery, Spain

1973. Easter. Passion-flowers. Multicoloured.

309	20 c. Type **56**	25	10
310	35 c. "P. vitifolia"	30	10
311	75 c. "P. amabilis"	75	75
312	$1 "P. alata-caerulea"	80	80

1973. 480th Anniv of Columbus's Discovery of Montserrat. Multicoloured.

313	10 c. Type **57**	15	10
314	35 c. Columbus sighting Montserrat	30	15
315	60 c. Columbus's ship off Montserrat	1·10	1·10
316	$1 Island badge and map of voyage	1·25	1·10

1973. Christmas. Multicoloured.

318	20 c. Type **58**	25	10
319	35 c. "The Holy Family with St. John" (Jordaens)	30	10
320	50 c. "Virgin and Child" (Bellini)	45	50
321	90 c. "Virgin and Child with Flowers" (Dolci)	65	1·00

1973. Royal Wedding. As T **47** of Anguilla. Multicoloured, background colours given.

322	35 c. green	10	10
323	$1 blue	20	20

59 Steel Band

1974. 25th Anniv of University of West Indies. Multicoloured.

324	20 c. Type **59**	15	10
325	35 c. Masqueraders (vert)	15	10
326	60 c. Student weaving (vert)	25	45
327	$1 University Centre, Montserrat	30	55

60 Hands with Letters

1974. Centenary of U.P.U.

329	**60**	1 c. multicoloured	10	10
330	–	2 c. red, orange and black	10	10
331	**60**	3 c. multicoloured	10	10
332	–	5 c. orange, red and black	10	10
333	**60**	50 c. multicoloured	20	20
334	–	$1 blue, green and black	40	65

DESIGN: 2 c., 5 c., $1 Figures from U.P.U. Monument.

1974. Various stamps surch.

335	2 c. on $1 mult (No. 252)	30	1·25
336	5 c. on 50 c. mult (No. 333)	30	60
337	10 c. on 60 c. mult (No. 326)	65	1·75
338	20 c. on $1 mult (No. 252)	30	1·00
339	35 c. on $1 blue, green and black (No. 334)	40	1·25

62 Churchill and Houses of Parliament

1974. Birth Cent of Sir Winston Churchill. Mult.

340	35 c. Type **62**	15	10
341	70 c. Churchill and Blenheim Palace	20	20

63 Carib "Carbet"

1975. Carib Artefacts.

343	**63**	5 c. brown, yellow & black	10	10
344	–	20 c. black, brown & yell	10	10
345	–	35 c. black, yellow & brn	15	10
346	–	70 c. yellow, brown & blk	45	40

DESIGNS: 20 c. "Caracoli"; 35 c. Club or mace; 70 c. Canoe.

Nos. 343/46 also come self-adhesive from booklet panes.

64 One-Bitt Coin

1975. Local Coinage, 1785–1801.

351	**64**	5 c. black, blue and silver	10	10
352	–	10 c. black, pink and silver	15	10
353	–	35 c. black, green & silver	20	15
354	–	$2 black, red and silver	90	1·50

DESIGNS: 10 c. Eighth dollar; 35 c. Quarter dollar; $2 One dollar.

65 1d. and 6d. Stamps of 1876

1976. Centenary of First Montserrat Postage Stamp.

356	**65**	5 c. red, green and black	15	10
357	–	10 c. yellow, red and black	20	10
358	–	40 c. multicoloured	50	40
359	–	55 c. mauve, green & blk	60	50
360	–	70 c. multicoloured	70	70
361	–	$1.10 green, blue and black	1·00	1·00

DESIGNS: 10 c. G.P.O. and bisected 1d. stamp; 40 c. Bisects on cover; 55 c. G.B. 6d. used in Montserrat and local 6d. of 1876; 70 c. Stamps for 2½d. rate, 1876; $1.10, Packet boat "Antelope" and 6d. stamp.

66 "The Trinity"

69 Mary and Joseph

68 White Frangipani

1976. Easter. Paintings by Orcagna. Multicoloured.

363	15 c. Type **66**	10	10
364	40 c. "The Resurrection"	15	15
365	55 c. "The Ascension"	15	15
366	$1.10 "Pentecost"	30	40

1976. Nos. 244, 246 and 247 surch.

368	2 c. on 5 c. multicoloured	10	15
369	30 c. on 10 c. multicoloured	30	20
370	45 c. on 3 c. multicoloured	40	25

1976. Flowering Trees. Multicoloured.

371	1 c. Type **68**	10	10
372	2 c. Cannon-ball tree	10	10
373	3 c. Lignum vitae	10	10
374	5 c. Malay apple	15	10
375	10 c. Jacaranda	30	10
376	15 c. Orchid tree	30	10
377	20 c. Manjak	30	10
378	25 c. Tamarind	40	30
379	40 c. Flame of the forest	40	30
380	55 c. Pink cassia	50	30
381	70 c. Long john	50	30
382	$1 Saman	65	60
383	$2.50 Immortelle	1·25	1·50
384	$5 Yellow poui	1·75	2·25
385	$10 Flamboyant	2·75	4·25

1976. Christmas. Multicoloured.

386	5 c. Type **69**	10	10
387	20 c. The Shepherds	10	10
388	55 c. Mary and Jesus	15	15
389	$1.10 The Magi	30	50

MINIMUM PRICE

The minimum price quoted is 10p which represents a handling charge rather than a basis for valuing common stamps. For further notes about prices see introductory pages.

70 Hudson River Review, 1976

1976. Bicent of American Revolution. Mult.

391	15 c. Type **70**	40	20
392	40 c. "Raleigh" (American frigate), 1777*	70	40
393	75 c. H.M.S. "Druid" (frigate), 1777*	70	40
394	$1.25 Hudson River Review (different detail)	1·25	60

*The date is wrongly given on the stamps as "1776".

Nos. 391 and 394 and 392/3 respectively were issued in se-tenant pairs, each pair forming a composite design.

71 The Crowning

1977. Silver Jubilee. Multicoloured.

396	30 c. Royal Visit, 1966	10	10
397	45 c. Cannons firing salute	15	10
398	$1 Type **71**	25	50

72 "Ipomoea alba"

75 The Stable at Bethlehem

73 Princess Anne laying Foundation Stone of Glendon Hospital

1977. Flowers of the Night. Multicoloured.

399	15 c. Type **72**	20	10
400	40 c. "Epiphyllum hookeri" (horiz)	45	30
401	55 c. "Cereus hexagonus" (horiz)	45	45
402	$1.50 "Cestrum nocturnum"	1·25	1·25

1977. Development. Multicoloured.

404	20 c. Type **73**	15	10
405	40 c. "Statesman" (freighter) in Plymouth Port	35	15
406	55 c. Glendon Hospital	35	20
407	$1.50 Jetty at Plymouth Port	90	1·00

1977. Royal Visit. Nos. 380/1 and 383 surch **$1.00 SILVER JUBILEE 1977 ROYAL VISIT TO THE CARIBBEAN.**

409	$1 on 55 c. Pink cassia	30	45
410	$1 on 70 c. Long john	30	45
411	$1 on $2.50 Immortelle	30	45

1977. Christmas. Multicoloured.

412	5 c. Type **75**	10	10
413	40 c. The Three Kings	15	10
414	55 c. Three Ships	20	10
415	$2 Three Angels	65	1·00

76 Four-eyed Butterflyfish

1978. Fish. Multicoloured.

417	30 c. Type **76**	45	10
418	40 c. French angelfish	50	15
419	55 c. Blue tang	65	15
420	$1.50 Queen triggerfish	1·10	1·25

77 St. Paul's Cathedral

1978. 25th Anniv of Coronation. Multicoloured.

422	40 c. Type **77**	10	10
423	55 c. Chichester Cathedral	10	10
424	$1 Lincoln Cathedral	20	25
425	$2.50 Llandaff Cathedral	40	50

78 "Alpinia speciosa" **79** Private, 21st (Royal North British Fusiliers), 1786

1978. Flowers. Multicoloured.

427	40 c. Type **78**	20	10
428	55 c. "Allamanda cathartica"	25	15
429	$1 "Petrea volubilis"	45	45
430	$2 "Hippeastrum puniceum"	70	80

1978. Military Uniforms (1st series). British Infantry Regiments. Multicoloured.

431	30 c. Type **79**	15	15
432	40 c. Corporal, 86th (Royal County Down), 1831	20	15
433	55 c. Sergeant, 14th (Buckinghamshire), 1837	30	20
434	$1.50 Officer, 55th (Westmorland), 1784	75	80

See also Nos. 441/4.

80 Cub Scouts

1979. 50th Anniv of Boy Scout Movement on Montserrat. Multicoloured.

436	40 c. Type **80**	20	10
437	55 c. Scouts with signalling equipment	30	20
438	$1.25 Camp fire (vert)	50	55
439	$2 Oath ceremony (vert)	65	1·00

1979. Military Uniforms (2nd series). As T **79**. Multicoloured.

441	30 c. Private, 60th (Royal American), 1783	15	15
442	40 c. Private, 1st West India, 1819	20	15
443	55 c. Officer, 5th (Northumberland), 1819	30	25
444	$2.50 Officer, 93rd (Sutherland Highlanders), 1830	1·00	1·10

81 Child reaching out to Adult

1979. International Year of the Child.

446	**81**	$2 black, brown and flesh	50	55

82 Sir Rowland Hill with Penny Black and Montserrat 1876 1d. Stamp

1979. Death Cent of Sir Rowland Hill and Cent of U.P.U. Membership. Multicoloured.

448	40 c. Type **82**	20	10
449	55 c. U.P.U. emblem and notice announcing Leeward Islands entry into Union	20	15
450	$1 1883 letter following U.P.U. membership	30	50
451	$2 Great Britain Post Office Regulations Notice and Sir Rowland Hill	40	80

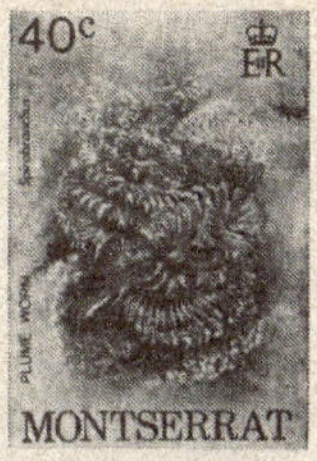

83 Plume Worm

1979. Marine Life. Multicoloured.

453	40 c. Type **83**	30	15
454	55 c. Sea fans	40	20
455	$2 Sponge and coral	1·00	2·10

84 Tree Frog

1980. Reptiles and Amphibians. Mult.

456	40 c. Type **84**	20	15
457	55 c. Tree lizard	25	25
458	$1 Crapaud	45	50
459	$2 Wood slave	80	90

85 "Marquess of Salisbury" and 1838 Handstamps

1980. "London 1980" Int Stamp Exhibition. Mult.

460	40 c. Type **85**	20	15
461	55 c. Hawker Siddeley H.S.748 aircraft and 1976 55 c. definitive	25	25
462	$1.20 "La Plata" (liner) and 1903 5s. Stamp	30	45
463	$1.20 "Lady Hawkins" (packet steamer) and 1932 Tercentenary 5s. commem	30	45
464	$1.20 "Avon" (paddle-steamer) and Penny Red stamp with "A 08" postmark	30	45
465	$1.20 Aeronca Champion 17 airplane and 1953 $1.20 definitive	30	45

1980. 75th Anniv of Rotary International. No. 383 optd **75th Anniversary of Rotary International**.

467	$2.50 Immortelle	55	85

87 Greek, French and U.S.A. Flags

1980. Olympic Games, Moscow. Multicoloured.

468	40 c. Type **87**	20	15
469	55 c. Union, Swedish and Belgian flags	20	15
470	70 c. French, Dutch and U.S.A. flags	30	20
471	$1 German, Union and Finnish flags	35	25
472	$1.50 Australian, Italian and Japanese flags	45	55
473	$2 Mexican, West German and Canadian flags	50	70
474	$2.50 "The Discus Thrower" (sculpture, Miron)	55	1·00

1980. Nos. 371, 373, 376 and 379 surch.

476	5 c. on 3 c. Lignum vitae	10	10
477	35 c. on 1 c. Type **68**	15	15
478	35 c. on 3 c. Lignum vitae	15	15
479	35 c. on 15 c. Orchid tree	15	15
480	55 c. on 40 c. Flame of the forest	15	15
481	$5 on 40 c. Flame of the forest	85	2·00

89 "Lady Nelson", 1928

1980. Mail Packet Boats (1st series). Mult.

482	40 c. Type **89**	30	15
483	55 c. "Chignecto", 1913	40	25
484	$1 "Solent II", 1878	80	60
485	$2 "Dee", 1841	1·10	1·25

See also Nos. 615/19.

90 "Heliconius charithonia" **91** Atlantic Spadefish

1981. Butterflies. Multicoloured.

486	50 c. Type **90**	60	40
487	65 c. "Pyrgus oileus"	70	45
488	$1.50 "Phoebis agarithe"	90	85
489	$2.50 "Danaus plexippus"	1·25	1·10

1981. Fishes. Multicoloured.

555	5 c. Type **91**	20	10
556	10 c. Hogfish and neon goby	25	10
492	15 c. Creole wrasse	80	30
493	20 c. Three-spotted damselfish	70	10
559	25 c. Sergeant major	35	20
560	35 c. Fin-spot wrasse	45	30
496	45 c. Schoolmaster	80	40
497	55 c. Striped parrotfish	1·10	45
498	65 c. Bigeye	80	60
564	75 c. French grunt	75	55
565	$1 Rock beauty	85	65
501	$2 Blue chromis	1·75	1·10
502	$3 Royal gramma ("Fairy basslet") and blueheads	1·90	1·75
503	$5 Cherub angelfish	2·75	2·75
504	$7.50 Long-jawed squirrelfish	4·00	4·75
570	$10 Caribbean long-nosed butterflyfish	5·50	6·00

92 Fort St. George

1981. Montserrat National Trust. Multicoloured.

506	50 c. Type **92**	25	20
507	65 c. Bird sanctuary, Fox's Bay	45	35
508	$1.50 Museum	50	65
509	$2.50 Bransby Point Battery, c. 1780	60	1·10

1981. Royal Wedding. Royal Yachts. As T **26/27** of Kiribati. Multicoloured.

510	90 c. "Charlotte"	25	25
511	90 c. Prince Charles and Lady Diana Spencer	85	85
512	$3 "Portsmouth"	60	60
513	$3 As No. 511	1·50	1·50
514	$4 "Britannia"	75	75
515	$4 As No. 511	1·75	1·75

93 H.M.S. "Dorsetshire" and Fairey Firefly Seaplane

1981. 50th Anniv of Montserrat Airmail Service. Multicoloured.

519	50 c. Type **93**	50	30
520	65 c. Beech 50 Twin Bonanza	65	30
521	$1.50 De Havilland Dragon Rapide "Lord Shaftesbury"	1·10	1·75
522	$2.50 Hawker Siddeley H.S.748 and maps of Montserrat and Antigua	1·40	2·75

94 Methodist Church, Bethel **95** Rubiaceae ("Rondeletia buxifolia")

1981. Christmas. Churches. Multicoloured.

523	50 c. Type **94**	20	15
524	65 c. St. George's Anglican Church, Harris	25	15
525	$1.50 St. Peter's Anglican Church, St. Peter's	60	60
526	$2.50 St. Patrick's R.C. Church, Plymouth	75	1·00

1982. Plant Life. Multicoloured.

528	50 c. Type **95**	25	30
529	65 c. Boraginaceae ("Heliotropium ternatum") (horiz)	30	40
530	$1.50 Simarubaceae ("Picramnia pentandra")	65	85
531	$2.50 Ebenaceae ("Diospyrus revoluta") (horiz)	1·00	1·25

96 Plymouth

1982. 350th Anniv of Settlement of Montserrat by Sir Thomas Warner.

532	**96**	40 c. green	30	30
533		55 c. red	35	35
534		65 c. brown	40	50
535		75 c. grey	45	60
536		85 c. blue	45	75
537		95 c. orange	45	80
538		$1 violet	45	80
539		$1.50 olive	50	1·25
540		$2 claret	65	1·50
541		$2.50 brown	80	1·50

The design of Nos. 532/41 is based on the 1932 Tercentenary set.

97 Catherine of Aragon, Princess of Wales, 1501 **98** Local Scout

1982. 21st Birthday of Princess of Wales. Mult.

542	75 c. Type **97**	15	15
543	$1 Coat of Arms of Catherine of Aragon	15	15
544	$5 Diana, Princess of Wales	80	1·25

1982. 75th Anniv of Boy Scout Movement. Multicoloured.

545	$1.50 Type **98**	75	70
546	$2.20 Lord Baden-Powell	1·00	1·10

99 Annunciation

1982. Christmas. Multicoloured.

547	35 c. Type **99**	15	15
548	75 c. Shepherds' Vision	30	35
549	$1.50 The Stable	55	85
550	$2.50 Flight into Egypt	80	1·10

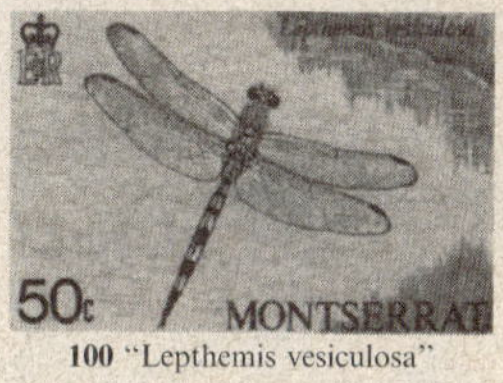

100 "Lepthemis vesiculosa"

1983. Dragonflies. Multicoloured.

551	50 c. Type **100**	40	20
552	65 c. "Orthemis ferruginea"	50	25
553	$1.50 "Triacanthagyna trifida"	1·00	1·25
554	$2.50 "Erythrodiplax umbrata"	1·40	2·00

101 Blue-headed Hummingbird **102** Montserrat Emblem

1983. Hummingbirds. Multicoloured.
571 35 c. Type **101** . . . . 1·50 35
572 75 c. Green-throated carib . . 1·75 85
573 $2 Antilean crested hummingbird 2·75 2·75
574 $3 Purple-throated carib . . . 3·00 3·75

1983.
575 **102** $12 blue and red . . . . 4·25 5·00
576 $30 red and blue . . . . 9·00 12·00

1983. Various stamps surch. (a) Nos. 491, 494, 498/9, 501.
577 40 c. on 25 c. Sergeant major (No. 494) 30 30
578 70 c. on 10 c. Hogfish and neon goby (No. 491) 45 45
579 90 c. on 65 c. Bigeye (No. 498) 55 60
580 $1.15 on 75 c. French grunt (No. 499) 65 70
581 $1.50 on $2 Blue chromis (No. 501) 85 90
(b) Nos. 512/15.
582 70 c. on $3 "Portsmouth" . . 65 85
583 70 c. on $3 Prince Charles and Lady Diana Spencer . . . 1·50 2·25
584 $1.15 on $4 "Britannia" . . . 1·10 1·25
585 $1.15 on $4, As No. 583 . . . 1·75 2·50

104 Montgolfier Balloon, 1783

106 Statue of Discus Thrower

105 Boys dressed as Clowns

1983. Bicentenary of Manned Flight. Mult.
586 35 c. Type **104** 15 15
587 75 c. De Havilland Twin Otter 200/300 (horiz) 30 30
588 $1.50 Lockheed Vega V (horiz) 60 75
589 $2 Beardmore airship R.34 (horiz) . . . . 85 1·25

1983. Christmas. Carnival. Multicoloured.
591 55 c. Type **105** 10 10
592 90 c. Girls dressed as silver star bursts 15 20
593 $1.15 Flower girls 20 35
594 $2 Masqueraders 35 80

1984. Olympic Games, Los Angeles. Mult.
595 90 c. Type **106** 30 35
596 $1 Olympic torch 35 45
597 $1.25 Los Angeles Olympic stadium 40 50
598 $2.50 Olympic and American flags . . . . 65 1·00

107 Cattle Egret

1984. Birds of Montserrat. Multicoloured.
600 5 c. Type **107** 30 30
601 10 c. Carib grackle 30 30
602 15 c. Moorhen 30 30
603 20 c. Brown booby 40 30
604 25 c. Black-whiskered vireo . . 40 40
605 40 c. Scaly-breasted thrasher . . 60 50
606 55 c. Laughing gull 75 30
607 70 c. Glossy ibis 90 45
608 90 c. Green heron . . . . . . 1·00 60
609 $1 Belted kingfisher (vert) . . . 1·25 70
610 $1.15 Bananaquit (vert) . . . 1·50 1·40
611 $3 American kestrel (vert) . . 3·25 5·00
612 $5 Forest thrush (vert) . . . . 4·50 7·00
613 $7.50 Black-crowned night heron (vert) . . . . 6·00 12·00
614 $10 Bridled quail dove (vert) . 7·00 13·00

1984. Mail Packet Boats (2nd series). As T **89**. Multicoloured.
615 55 c. "Tagus II", 1907 . . . . 20 40
616 90 c. "Cobequid", 1913 . . . 30 50
617 $1.15 "Lady Drake", 1942 . . . 40 70
618 $2 "Factor", 1948 . . . . . . 60 1·25

108 Hermit Crab and West Indian Top Shell

1984. Marine Life. Multicoloured.
620 90 c. Type **108** . . . . . . 1·50 1·00
621 $1.15 Rough file shell . . . . 1·75 1·40
622 $1.50 True tulip . . . . . . 2·50 3·00
623 $2.50 Queen or pink conch . . 3·25 4·75

109 "Bull Man"

1984. Christmas. Carnival Costumes. Mult.
624 55 c. Type **109** 50 25
625 $1.15 Masquerader Captain . . 1·50 1·25
626 $1.50 "Fantasy" Carnival Queen 1·75 2·25
627 $2.30 "Ebony and Ivory" Carnival Queen . . . . . . 2·50 4·00

110 Mango

111 "Oncidium urophyllum"

1985. National Emblems. Multicoloured.
628 $1.15 Type **110** 30 60
629 $1.50 Lobster claw . . . . . 40 1·00
630 $3 Montserrat oriole . . . . 60 2·00

1985. Orchids of Montserrat. Multicoloured.
631 90 c. Type **111** 45 55
632 $1.15 "Epidendrum difforme" . . 55 80
633 $1.50 "Epidendrum ciliare" . . 60 1·10
634 $2.50 "Brassavola cucullata" . 1·00 2·50

112 Queen Elizabeth the Queen Mother

115 Black-throated Blue Warbler

113 Cotton Plants

1985. Life and Times of Queen Elizabeth the Queen Mother. Various vertical portraits.
636 **112** 55 c. multicoloured . . . 25 40
637 – 55 c. multicoloured . . . 25 40
638 – 90 c. multicoloured . . . 25 60
639 – 90 c. multicoloured . . . 25 60
640 – $1.15 multicoloured . . . 25 60
641 – $1.15 multicoloured . . . 25 60
642 – $1.50 multicoloured . . . 30 60
643 – $1.50 multicoloured . . . 30 60

Each value was issued in pairs showing a floral pattern across the bottom of the portraits which stops short of the left-hand edge on the first stamp and of the right-hand edge on the second.

1985. Montserrat Sea Island Cotton Industry. Multicoloured.
645 90 c. Type **113** 25 45
646 $1 Operator at carding machine 25 50
647 $1.15 Threading loom 25 65
648 $2.50 Weaving with hand loom 50 2·25

1985. Royal Visit. Nos. 514/15, 543, 587/8 and 640/1 optd **CARIBBEAN ROYAL VISIT 1985** or surch also.
650 75 c. multicoloured (No. 587) 2·75 2·50
651 $1 multicoloured (No. 543) . 4·25 3·50
652 $1.15 multicoloured (No. 640) 4·25 5·00
653 $1.15 multicoloured (No. 641) 4·25 5·00
654 $1.50 multicoloured (No. 588) 6·00 6·00
655 $1.60 on $4 mult" (No. 514) . 3·00 3·75
656 $1.60 on $4 mult (No. 515) . . 12·00 16·00

No. 656 shows a new face value only, "CARIBBEAN ROYAL VISIT 1985" being omitted from the surcharge.

1985. Leaders of the World. Birth Bicentenary of John J. Audubon (ornithologist). Designs showing original paintings. Multicoloured.
657 15 c. Type **115** 15 20
658 15 c. Palm warbler 15 20
659 30 c. Bobolink 15 30
660 30 c. Lark sparrow 15 30
661 55 c. Chipping sparrow 20 40
662 55 c. Northern oriole 20 40
663 $2.50 American goldfinch . . . 40 1·25
664 $2.50 Blue grosbeak . . . . . 40 1·25

116 Herald Angel appearing to Goatherds

1985. Christmas. Designs showing Caribbean Nativity. Multicoloured.
665 70 c. Type **116** 15 15
666 $1.15 Three Wise Men following Star 25 40
667 $1.50 Carol singing around War Memorial, Plymouth 30 70
668 $2.30 Praying to "Our Lady of Montserrat", Church of Our Lady, St. Patrick's Village 45 1·60

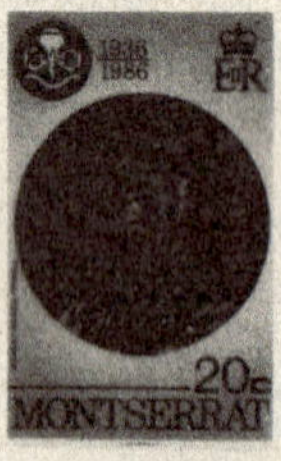

117 Lord Baden-Powell

1986. 50th Anniv of Montserrat Girl Guide Movement. Multicoloured.
669 20 c. Type **117** 15 40
670 20 c. Girl Guide saluting . . . 15 40
671 75 c. Lady Baden-Powell . . . 25 75
672 75 c. Guide assisting in old people's home 25 75
673 90 c. Lord and Lady Baden-Powell 30 75
674 90 c. Guides serving meal in old people's home 30 75
675 $1.15 Girl Guides of 1936 . . 40 80
676 $1.15 Two guides saluting . . 40 80

1986. 60th Birthday of Queen Elizabeth II. As T **167** of British Virgin Islands. Multicoloured.
677 10 c. Queen Elizabeth II . . . 10 10
678 $1.50 Princess Elizabeth in 1928 25 50
679 $3 In Antigua, 1977 . . . . . 40 85
680 $6 In Canberra, 1982 (vert) . . 65 1·75

118 King Harold and Halley's Comet, 1066 (from Bayeux Tapestry)

1986. Appearance of Halley's Comet. Multicoloured.
682 35 c. Type **118** 25 25
683 50 c. Comet of 1301 (from Giotto's "Adoration of the Magi") 30 30
684 70 c. Edmond Halley and Comet of 1531 . . . . 40 40
685 $1 Comets of 1066 and 1910 . 40 40
686 $1.15 Comet of 1910 . . . . . 50 50
687 $1.50 E.S.A. "Giotto" spacecraft and Comet 50 80
688 $2.30 U.S. space telescope and Comet . . . . 60 1·75
689 $4 Computer reconstruction of 1910 Comet . . . . 80 2·75

1986. Royal Wedding (1st isssue). As T **168** of British Virgin Islands. Multicoloured.
691 70 c. Prince Andrew 25 35
692 70 c. Miss Sarah Ferguson . . 25 35
693 $2 Prince Andrew wearing stetson (horiz) 40 80
694 $2 Miss Sarah Ferguson on skiing holiday (horiz) 40 80

See also Nos. 705/8.

119 "Antelope" being attacked by "L'Atalante"

1986. Mail Packet Sailing Ships. Mult.
696 90 c. Type **119** . . . . 2·00 1·50
697 $1.15 "Montagu" (1810) . . . 2·25 2·00
698 $1.50 "Little Catherine" being pursued by "L'Etoile" (1813) 2·75 2·75
699 $2.30 "Hinchingbrook I" (1813) 3·50 5·00

120 Radio Montserrat Building, Dagenham

123 Christmas Rose

122 Sailing and Windsurfing

1986. Communications. Multicoloured.
701 70 c. Type **120** . . . . 1·00 70
702 $1.15 Radio Gem dish aerial, Plymouth . . . . 1·00 1·50
703 $1.50 Radio Antilles studio, O'Garro's . . . . 1·75 2·25
704 $2.30 Cable and Wireless building, Plymouth . . . . 2·25 4·25

1986. Royal Wedding (2nd issue). Nos. 691/4 optd **Congratulations to T.R.H. The Duke & Duchess of York.**
705 70 c. Prince Andrew . . . . . 70 1·25
706 70 c. Miss Sarah Ferguson . . 70 1·25
707 $2 Prince Andrew wearing stetson (horiz) . . . . . . 1·25 1·75
708 $2 Miss Sarah Ferguson on skiing holiday (horiz) . . . 1·25 1·75

1986. Tourism. Multicoloured.
710 70 c. Type **122** 40 70
711 $1.15 Golf . . . . 80 1·50
712 $1.50 Plymouth market . . . 80 2·00
713 $2.30 Air Recording Studios . 1·25 3·00

1986. Christmas. Flowering Shrubs. Mult.
714 70 c. Type **123** 70 40
715 $1.15 Candle flower 95 85
716 $1.50 Christmas tree kalanchoe 1·50 1·50
717 $2.30 Snow on the mountain . 2·00 4·50

124 Tiger Shark

1987. Sharks. Multicoloured.
719 40 c. Type **124** . . . . 1·50 55
720 90 c. Lemon shark . . . . . 2·50 1·50
721 $1.15 Great white shark . . . 2·75 2·00
722 $3.50 Whale shark . . . . . 5·50 8·00

1987. Nos. 601, 603, 607/8 and 611 surch.
724 5 c. on 70 c. Glossy ibis . . . 50 75
725 $1 on 20 c. Brown booby . . 1·75 90
726 $1.15 on 10 c. Carib grackle . 2·00 1·40
727 $1.50 on 90 c. Green heron . 2·25 2·50
728 $2.30 on $3 American kestrel (vert) . . . . 3·25 5·00

127 "Phoebis trite"

128 "Oncidium variegatum"

1987. Butterflies. Multicoloured.
730 90 c. Type **127** . . . . 2·00 1·10
731 $1.15 "Biblis hyperia" . . . . 2·50 1·60
732 $1.50 "Polygonus leo" . . . . 3·00 2·50
733 $2.50 "Hypolimnas misippus" 4·50 6·50

1987. Christmas. Orchids. Multicoloured.
734 90 c. Type **128** 60 45
735 $1.15 "Vanilla planifolia" (horiz) 85 55
736 $1.50 "Gongora quinquenervis" 1·10 1·00
737 $3.50 "Brassavola nodosa" (horiz) . . . . 2·00 4·00

1987. Royal Ruby Wedding. Nos. 601, 604/5 and 608 surch **40th Wedding Anniversary HM Queen Elizabeth II HRH Duke of Edinburgh. November 1987.** and value.
739B 5 c. on 90 c. Green heron . . 30 40
740B $1.15 on 10 c. Carib grackle 1·00 1·00
741B $2.30 on 25 c. Black-whiskered vireo . . . . 1·75 2·25
742B $5 on 40 c. Scaly-breasted thrasher . . . . 3·50 4·50

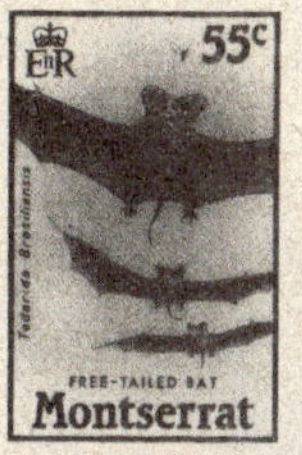

130 Free-tailed Bat

131 Magnificent Frigate Bird

1988. Bats. Multicoloured.
743 55 c. Type **130** 80 40
744 90 c. "Chiroderma improvisum" (fruit bat) . . . . 1·25 90
745 $1.15 Fisherman bat . . . . . 1·60 1·50
746 $2.30 "Brachyphylla cavernarum" (fruit bat) . . 3·00 5·00

1988. Easter. Birds. Multicoloured.
748 90 c. Type **131** 60 45
749 $1.15 Caribbean elaenia . . . 80 75
750 $1.50 Glossy ibis . . . . . . 1·00 1·50
751 $3.50 Purple-throated carib . . 2·00 3·50

132 Discus throwing

1988. Olympic Games, Seoul. Multicoloured.
753 90 c. Type **132** 50 50
754 $1.15 High jumping 60 55
755 $3.50 Athletics . . . . 2·00 3·00

133 Golden Tulip

1988. Sea Shells. Multicoloured.
757 5 c. Type **133** 30 30
758 10 c. Little knobbed scallop . 40 40
759 15 c. Sozoni's cone 40 40
760 20 c. Globular coral shell . . 50 40
761 25 c. American or common sundial 50 40
762 40 c. King helmet 60 40
763 55 c. Channelled turban . . . 80 40
764 70 c. True tulip . . . . . . 1·00 75
765 90 c. Music volute . . . . . 1·25 75
766 $1 Flame auger . . . . 1·40 80
767 $1.15 Rooster-tail conch . . . 1·50 90
768 $1.50 Queen or pink conch . . 1·60 1·40
769 $3 Teramachi's slit shell . . 2·75 4·00
770 $5 Common or Florida crown conch . . . . 4·50 6·50
771 $7.50 Beau's murex . . . . . 6·50 10·00
772 $10 Atlantic trumpet triton . . 7·50 10·00

134 University Crest

1988. 40th Anniv of University of West Indies.
773 **134** $5 multicoloured . . . . 2·40 3·25

1988. Princess Alexandra's Visit. Nos. 763, 766 and 769/70 surch **HRH PRINCESS ALEXANDRA'S VISIT NOVEMBER 1988** and new value.
774 40 c. on 55 c. Channelled turban 45 45
775 90 c. on $1 Flame auger . . . 70 80
776 $1.15 on $3 Teramachi's slit shell 85 95
777 $1.50 on $5 Common or Florida crown conch . . . . 1·10 1·50

136 Spotted Sandpiper

1988. Christmas. Sea Birds. Multicoloured.
778 90 c. Type **136** 70 55
779 $1.15 Turnstone 85 70
780 $3.50 Red-footed booby . . . 2·00 3·50

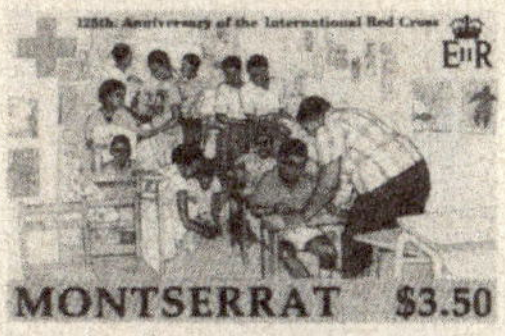

137 Handicapped Children in Classroom

1988. 125th Anniv of International Red Cross.
782 **137** $3.50 multicoloured . . . 1·50 2·25

138 Drum Major in Ceremonial Uniform

1989. 75th Anniv (1986) of Montserrat Defence Force. Uniforms. Multicoloured.
783 90 c. Type **138** 70 50
784 $1.15 Field training uniform . 85 75
785 $1.50 Cadet in ceremonial uniform . . . . 1·25 1·75
786 $3.50 Gazetted Police Officer in ceremonial uniform . . . . 2·50 3·50

139 Amazon Lily

1989. Easter. Lilies. Multicoloured.
788 90 c. Type **139** 50 50
789 $1.15 Salmon blood lily (vert) 70 70
790 $1.50 Amaryllis (vert) . . . . 85 1·25
791 $3.50 Amaryllis (vert) . . . . 1·90 2·75

140 "Morning Prince" (schooner), 1942

1989. Shipbuilding in Montserrat. Mult.
793 90 c. Type **140** 90 60
794 $1.15 "Western Sun" (inter-island freighter) . . . . . 1·40 1·10
795 $1.50 "Kim G" (inter-island freighter) under construction 1·75 2·00
796 $3.50 "Romaris" (inter-island ferry), c. 1942 . . . . . 2·75 4·00

141 The Scarecrow

1989. 50th Anniv of "The Wizard of Oz" (film). Multicoloured.
797 90 c. Type **141** 40 45
798 $1.15 The Lion 55 60
799 $1.50 The Tin Man 70 85
800 $3.50 Dorothy . . . . 1·60 2·25

1989. Hurricane Hugo Relief Fund. Nos. 795/6 surch **Hurricane Hugo Relief Surcharge $2.50**.
802 $1.50 + $2.50 "Kim G" (inter-island freighter under construction) . . . . 2·25 3·00
803 $3.50 + $2.50 "Romaris" (inter-island ferry), c. 1942 . . . . 2·50 4·00

143 "Apollo 11" above Lunar Surface

1989. 20th Anniv of First Manned Landing on Moon. Multicoloured.
804 90 c. Type **143** 35 40
805 $1.15 Astronaut alighting from lunar module "Eagle" . . . 45 50
806 $1.50 "Eagle" and astronaut conducting experiment . . . 60 80
807 $3.50 Opening "Apollo 11" hatch after splashdown . . . 1·40 2·25

144 "Yamato" (Japanese battleship)

145 The Empty Tomb

1990. World War II Capital Ships. Multicoloured.
809 70 c. Type **144** . . . . 1·50 70
810 $1.15 U.S.S. "Arizona" at Pearl Harbor . . . . 2·00 95
811 $1.50 "Bismarck" (German battleship) in action . . . 2·50 2·25
812 $3.50 H.M.S. "Hood" (battle cruiser) . . . . 4·00 6·00

1990. Easter. Stained glass windows from St. Michael's Parish Church, Bray, Berkshire. Multicoloured.
814 $1.15 Type **145** . . . . 1·00 1·25
815 $1.50 The Ascension . . . . . 1·25 1·60
816 $3.50 The Risen Christ with Disciples . . . . 1·75 2·25

1990. "Stamp World London '90" International Stamp Exhibition. Nos. 460/4 surch **Stamp World London 90**, emblem and value.
818 70 c. on 40 c. Type **85** 50 50
819 90 c. on 55 c. Hawker Siddeley H.S.748 aircraft and 1976 55 c. definitive 70 70
820 $1 on $1.20 "La Plata" (liner) and 1903 5s. stamp 80 90
821 $1.15 on $1.20 "Lady Hawkins" (packet steamer) and 1932 Tercentenary 5s. commem . 90 1·10
822 $1.50 on $1.20 "Avon" (paddle-steamer) and Penny Red stamp with "A 08" postmark . . . 1·25 1·75

147 General Office, Montserrat and 1884 ½d. Stamp

1990. 150th Anniv of the Penny Black. Mult.
823 90 c. Type **147** 65 65
824 $1.15 Sorting letters and Montserrat 1d. stamp of 1876 (vert) 85 90
825 $1.50 Posting letters and Penny Black (vert) . . . . 1·25 1·75
826 $3.50 Postman delivering letters and 1840 Twopence Blue . . 3·00 4·00

148 Montserrat v. Antigua Match

1990. World Cup Football Championship, Italy. Multicoloured.
828 90 c. Type **148** 65 55
829 $1.15 U.S.A. v. Trinidad match 85 75
830 $1.50 Montserrat team . . . 1·25 1·50
831 $3.50 West Germany v. Wales match . . . . 2·25 3·25

149 Spinner Dolphin

1990. Dolphins. Multicoloured.
833 90 c. Type **149** . . . . 1·50 85
834 $1.15 Common dolphin . . . 1·75 1·25
835 $1.50 Striped dolphin . . . . 2·50 2·50
836 $3.50 Atlantic spotted dolphin 3·75 5·00

150 Spotted Goatfish

1991. Tropical Fishes. Multicoloured.
838 90 c. Type **150** . . . . 1·50 85
839 $1.15 Cushion star . . . . . 1·75 1·25
840 $1.50 Rock beauty . . . . . 2·50 2·50
841 $3.50 French grunt . . . . . 3·75 5·00

1991. Nos. 760/1, 768 and 771 surch.
843 5 c. on 20 c. Globular coral shell 65 1·00
844 5 c. on 25 c. American or common sundial . . . . . . 65 1·00
845 $1.15 on $1.50 Queen or pink conch . . . . 2·75 3·25
846 $1.15 on $7.50 Beau's murex . 2·75 3·25

152 Duck

1991. Domestic Birds. Multicoloured.
847 90 c. Type **152** 60 60
848 $1.15 Hen and chicks 80 90
849 $1.50 Red junglefowl . . . . 1·10 1·50
850 $3.50 Helmet guineafowl . . . 2·40 3·50

153 "Panaeolus antillarum"

1991. Fungi
851 **153** 90 c. grey . . . . 1·25 1·00
852 – $1.15 red . . . . 1·50 1·25
853 – $1.50 brown . . . . 2·25 2·25
854 – $2 purple . . . . 2·50 3·25
855 – $3.50 blue . . . . 3·75 5·00
DESIGNS: $1.15, "Cantharellus cinnabarinus"; $1.50, "Gymnopilus chrysopellus"; $2 "Psilocybe cubensis"; $3.50, "Leptonia caeruleocapitata".

154 Red Water Lily

155 Tree Frog

1991. Lilies. Multicoloured.
856 90 c. Type **154** 65 65
857 $1.15 Shell ginger 75 85
858 $1.50 Early day lily . . . . . 1·00 1·60
859 $3.50 Anthurium . . . . . . 2·50 3·50

1991. Frogs and Toad. Multicoloured.
860 $1.15 Type **155** . . . . 2·25 1·25
861 $2 Crapaud toad . . . . . . 3·25 3·75
862 $3.50 Mountain chicken (frog) 5·50 6·50

156 Black British Shorthair Cat

1991. Cats. Multicoloured.

864	90 c. Type **156**	1·50	90
865	$1.15 Seal point Siamese	1·75	1·10
866	$1.50 Silver tabby Persian	2·25	2·25
867	$2.50 Birman temple cat	3·00	3·75
868	$3.50 Egyptain mau	4·00	5·00

157 Navigational Instruments

1992. 500th Anniv of Discovery of America by Columbus. Multicoloured.

869	$1.50 Type **157**	1·25	1·50
870	$1.50 Columbus and coat of arms	1·25	1·50
871	$1.50 Landfall on the Bahamas	1·25	1·50
872	$1.50 Petitioning Queen Isabella	1·25	1·50
873	$1.50 Tropical birds	1·25	1·50
874	$1.50 Tropical fruits	1·25	1·50
875	$3 Ships of Columbus (81 × 26 mm)	1·75	2·00

158 Runner with Olympic Flame

1992. Olympic Games, Barcelona. Multicoloured.

876	$1 Type **158**	90	60
877	$1.15 Montserrat, Olympic and Spanish flags	1·25	90
878	$2.30 Olympic flame on map of Montserrat	2·25	2·50
879	$3.60 Olympic events	2·75	3·75

159 Tyrannosaurus

1992. Death Centenary of Sir Richard Owen (zoologist). Multicoloured.

880	$1 Type **159**	1·75	1·10
881	$1.15 Diplodocus	2·00	1·40
882	$1.50 Apatosaurus	2·50	2·50
883	$3.45 Dimetrodon	5·00	7·00

160 Male Montserrat Oriole

1992. Montserrat Oriole. Multicoloured.

885	$1 Type **160**	1·10	1·10
886	$1.15 Male and female orioles	1·40	1·40
887	$1.50 Female oriole with chicks	1·75	2·00
888	$3.60 Map of Montserrat and male oriole	3·50	5·00

161 "Psophus stridulus" (grasshopper)

1992. Insects. Multicoloured.

889	5 c. Type **161**	30	40
890	10 c. "Gryllus campestris" (field cricket)	35	40
891	15 c. "Lepthemis vesiculosa" (dragonfly)	40	40
892	20 c. "Orthemis ferruginea" (red skimmer)	45	45
893	25 c. "Gerris lacustris" (pond skater)	45	45
894	40 c. "Byctiscus betulae" (leaf weevil)	60	50
895	55 c. "Atta texana" (leaf-cutter ants)	60	40
896	70 c. "Polistes fuscatus" (paper wasp)	70	60
897	90 c. "Sparmopolius fulvus" (bee fly)	80	60
898	$1 "Chrysopa carnea" (lace wing)	1·25	65
899	$1.15 "Phoebis philea" (butterfly)	2·00	90
900	$1.50 "Cynthia cardui" (butterfly)	2·25	1·75
901	$3 "Utetheisa bella" (moth)	3·00	4·00
902	$5 "Alucita pentadactyla" (moth)	4·25	5·50
903	$7.50 "Anartia jatropha" (butterfly)	5·50	7·50
904	$10 "Heliconius melpomene" (butterfly)	5·50	7·50

162 Adoration of the Magi

1992. Christmas. Multicoloured.

905	$1.15 Type **162**	1·50	75
906	$4.60 Appearance of angel to shepherds	4·00	6·00

163 $1 Coin and $20 Banknote

164 Columbus meeting Amerindians

1993. East Caribbean Currency. Multicoloured.

907	$1 Type **163**	90	70
908	$1.15 10 c. and 25 c. coins with $10 banknote	1·25	85
909	$1.50 5 c. coin and $5 banknote	1·75	2·00
910	$3.60 1 c. and 2 c. coins with $1 banknote	4·00	6·00

1993. Organization of East Caribbean States. 500th Anniv of Discovery of America by Columbus. Multicoloured.

911	$1 Type **164**	1·10	90
912	$2 Ships approaching island	2·00	2·75

165 Queen Elizabeth II on Montserrat with Chief Minister W. H. Bramble, 1966

1993. 40th Anniv of Coronation. Multicoloured.

913	$1.15 Type **165**	1·50	75
914	$4.60 Queen Elizabeth II in State Coach, 1953	4·50	5·50

1993. 500th Anniv of Discovery of Montserrat. As Nos. 869/75, some with new values, each showing "500th ANNIVERSARY DISCOVERY OF MONTSERRAT" at foot and with additional historical inscr across the centre.

915	$1.15 mult (As Type **157**)	1·25	1·50
916	$1.15 multicoloured (As No. 870)	1·25	1·50
917	$1.15 multicoloured (As No. 871)	1·25	1·50
918	$1.50 multicoloured (As No. 872)	1·60	1·90
919	$1.50 multicoloured (As No. 873)	1·60	1·90
920	$1.50 multicoloured (As No. 874)	1·60	1·90
921	$3.45 multicoloured (As No. 875)	2·50	3·25

Additional inscriptions: No. 915, "PRE-COLUMBUS CARIB NAME OF ISLAND ALLIOUGANA"; No. 916, "COLUMBUS NAMED ISLAND SANTA MARIA DE MONTSERRATE"; No. 917, "COLUMBUS SAILED ALONG COASTLINE 11th NOV. 1493"; No. 918, "ISLAND OCCUPIED BY FRENCH BRIEFLY IN 1667"; No. 919, "ISLAND DECLARED ENGLISH BY TREATY OF BREDA 1667"; No. 920, "AFRICAN SLAVES BROUGHT IN DURING 1600's"; No. 921, "IRISH CATHOLICS FROM ST. KITTS AND VIRGINIA SETTLED ON ISLAND BETWEEN 1628–1634".

166 Boeing Sentry, 1993

1993. 75th Anniv of Royal Air Force. Mult.

922	15 c. Type **166**	45	20
923	55 c. Vickers Valiant B Mk1, 1962	65	40
924	$1.15 Handley Page Hastings C Mk 2, 1958	1·25	75
925	$3 Lockheed Ventura, 1943	2·50	4·00

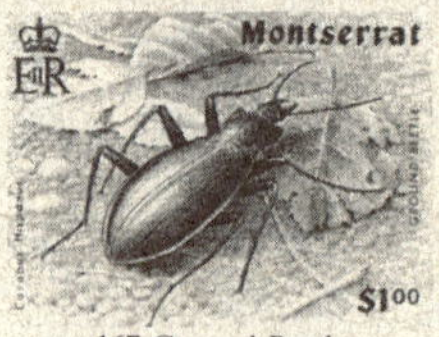

167 Ground Beetle

1994. Beetles. Multicoloured.

927	$1 Type **167**	65	65
928	$1.15 Click beetle	80	80
929	$1.50 Harlequin beetle	1·25	1·50
930	$3.45 Leaf beetle	3·00	4·25

168 "Gossypium barbadense"

1994. Flowers. Multicoloured.

932	90 c. Type **168**	1·00	80
933	$1.15 "Hibiscus sabdariffa"	1·25	1·00
934	$1.50 "Hibiscus esculentus"	1·60	1·75
935	$3.50 "Hibiscus rosa-sinensis"	3·50	5·00

169 Coaching Young Players and Logo

1994. World Cup Football Championship, U.S.A. Multicoloured.

936	90 c. Type **169**	1·25	1·75
937	$1 United States scoring against England, 1950	1·25	1·75
938	$1.15 Rose Bowl stadium, Los Angeles, and trophy	1·25	1·75
939	$3.45 German players celebrating with trophy, 1990	2·75	3·25

170 Elasmosaurus

1994. Aquatic Dinosaurs. Multicoloured.

941	$1 Type **170**	1·75	2·00
942	$1.15 Plesiosaurus	1·75	2·00
943	$1.50 Nothosaurus	2·25	2·50
944	$3.45 Mosasaurus	3·00	3·75

1994. Space Anniversaries. Nos. 804/7 variously surch or optd, each including **Space Anniversaries**.

945	40 c. on 90 c. Type **143**	1·00	60
946	$1.15 Astronaut alighting from lunar module "Eagle"	1·75	1·25
947	$1.50 "Eagle" and astronaut conducting experiment	2·25	2·25
948	$2.30 on $3.50 Opening "Apollo 11" hatch after splashdown	3·25	5·00

Surcharges and overprints: No. 945, **Juri Gagarin First man in space April 12, 1961**; No. 946, **First Joint US Soviet Mission July 15, 1975**; No. 947 **25th Anniversary First Moon Landing Apollo XI – July 20, 1994**; No. 948, **Columbia First Space Shuttle April 12, 1981**.

172 1969 Festival Logo

1994. 25th Anniv of Woodstock Music Festival. Multicoloured.

949	$1.15 Type **172**	1·00	1·00
950	$1.50 1994 anniversary festival logo	1·25	1·25

173 Sea Fan

1995. Marine Life. Multicoloured.

951	$1 Type **173**	60	50
952	$1.15 Sea lily	70	60
953	$1.50 Sea pen	90	1·00
954	$3.45 Sea fern	2·00	2·75

174 Marilyn Monroe

1995. Centenary of Cinema. Portraits of Marilyn Monroe (film star). Multicoloured.

956	$1.15 Type **174**	90	1·00
957	$1.15 Puckering lips	90	1·00
958	$1.15 Laughing in brown evening dress and earrings	90	1·00
959	$1.15 Wearing red earrings	90	1·00
960	$1.15 In brown dress without earrings	90	1·00
961	$1.15 With white boa	90	1·00
962	$1.15 In red dress	90	1·00
963	$1.15 Wearing white jumper	90	1·00
964	$1.15 Looking over left shoulder	90	1·00

176 Atmospheric Sounding Experiments using V2 Rockets

1995. 50th Anniv of End of Second World War. Scientific Achievements. Multicoloured.

967	$1.15 Type **176**	80	90
968	$1.15 American space shuttle "Challenger"	80	90
969	$1.15 Nuclear experiment, Chicago, 1942	80	90
970	$1.15 Calder Hall Atomic Power Station, 1956	80	90
971	$1.50 Radar-equipped Ju 88G 7a nightfighter	1·00	1·25
972	$1.50 Boeing E6 A.W.A.C.S. aircraft	1·00	1·25
973	$1.50 Gloster G.41 Meteor Mk III jet fighter	1·00	1·25
974	$1.50 Concorde (airliner)	1·00	1·25

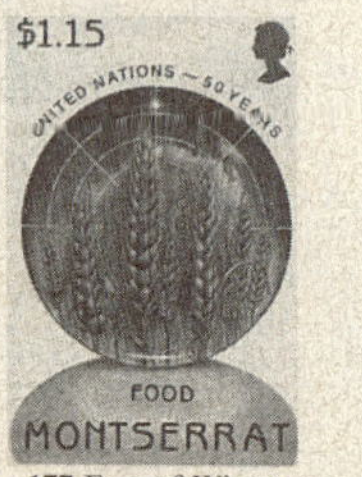

177 Ears of Wheat ("Food")

1995. 50th Anniv of United Nations. Multicoloured.

975	$1.15 Type **177**	90	75
976	$1.50 Open book ("Education")	1·25	1·00
977	$2.30 P.T. class ("Health")	1·75	2·25
978	$3 Dove ("Peace")	2·25	3·00

178 Headquarters Building

1995. 25th Anniv of Montserrat National Trust. Multicoloured.

980	$1.15 Type **178**	80	75
981	$1.50 17th-century cannons, Bransby Point	1·25	1·00
982	$2.30 Impression of Galways Sugar Mill (vert)	2·25	2·50
983	$3 Great Alps Falls (vert)	3·50	4·50

1995. 25th Anniv of Air Recording Studios. No. 713 surch **air 25TH ANNIVERSARY 1970 - 1995.**

984	$2.30 + $5 Air Recording Studios	4·25	4·75

The $5 premium on No. 984 was for relief following a volcanic eruption.

180 Bull Shark

1996. Scavengers of the Sea. Multicoloured.

985	$1 Type **180**	80	70
986	$1.15 Sea mouse	90	80
987	$1.50 Bristleworm	1·25	1·25
988	$3.45 Prawn "Xiphocaris"	2·50	3·00

181 Marconi and Radio Equipment, 1901

1996. Centenary of Radio. Multicoloured.

990	$1.15 Type **181**	90	80
991	$1.50 Marconi's steam yacht "Elettra"	1·25	1·00
992	$2.30 Receiving first Trans-atlantic radio message, Newfoundland, 1901	1·75	2·00
993	$3 Imperial Airways airplane at Croydon Airport, 1920	2·25	2·75

182 Paul Masson (France) (Cycling)

1996. Olympic Games, Atlanta. Gold Medal Winners of 1896. Multicoloured.

995	$1.15 Type **182**	80	80
996	$1.50 Robert Garrett (U.S.A.) (Discus)	1·00	1·00
997	$2.30 Spyridon Louis (Greece) (Marathon)	1·50	1·75
998	$3 John Boland (Great Britain) (Tennis)	2·00	2·50

183 James Dean

1996. James Dean (film star) Commemoration. Multicoloured.

999	$1.15 Type **183**	80	80
1000	$1.15 Wearing stetson facing right	80	80
1001	$1.15 Wearing blue sweater	80	80
1002	$1.15 Wearing black sweater	80	80
1003	$1.15 Full face portrait wearing stetson	80	80
1004	$1.15 Wearing fawn jacket	80	80
1005	$1.15 Wearing red wind-cheater	80	80
1006	$1.15 Smoking a cigarette	80	80
1007	$1.15 In open-necked shirt and green jumper	80	80

184 Leprechaun

185 Blue and Green Teddybears

1996. Mythical Creatures. Multicoloured.

1009	5 c. Type **184**	10	10
1010	10 c. Pegasus	10	10
1011	15 c. Griffin	10	10
1012	20 c. Unicorn	10	10
1013	25 c. Gnomes	10	15
1014	40 c. Mermaid	15	20
1015	55 c. Cockatrice	25	30
1016	70 c. Fairy	30	35
1017	90 c. Goblin	40	45
1018	$1 Faun	45	50
1019	$1.15 Dragon	50	55
1020	$1.50 Giant	65	70
1021	$3 Elves	1·25	1·40
1022	$5 Centaur	2·10	2·25
1023	$7.50 Phoenix	3·25	3·50
1024	$10 Erin	4·75	4·50

1996. Jerry Garcia and the Grateful Dead (rock group) Commemoration. Multicoloured.

1025	$1.15 Type **185**	1·00	1·00
1026	$1.15 Green and yellow teddybears	1·00	1·00
1027	$1.15 Brown and pink teddybears	1·00	1·00
1028	$6 Jerry Garcia (37 × 50 mm)	5·50	5·50

Nos. 1025/7 were printed together, se-tenant, forming a composite design.

186 Turkey Vulture

1997. Scavengers of the Sky. Multicoloured.

1029	$1 Type **186**	75	60
1030	$1.15 American crow	90	70
1031	$1.50 Great skua	1·25	1·25
1032	$3.45 Kittiwake	2·25	2·50

1997. "HONG KONG '97" International Stamp Exhibition. Nos. 1025/7 optd **HONG KONG '97**.

1034	$1.15 Type **185**	70	80
1035	$1.15 Green and yellow teddybears	70	80
1036	$1.15 Brown and pink teddybears	70	80

1997. "PACIFIC '97" International Stamp Exhibition, San Francisco. Nos. 999/1007 optd **PACIFIC 97 World Philatelic Exhibition San Francisco, California 29 May - 8 June**.

1037	$1.15 Type **183**	80	90
1038	$1.15 Wearing stetson facing right	80	90
1039	$1.15 Wearing blue sweater	80	90
1040	$1.15 Wearing black sweater	80	90
1041	$1.15 Full-face portrait wearing stetson	80	90
1042	$1.15 Wearing fawn jacket	80	90
1043	$1.15 Wearing red wind-cheater	80	90
1044	$1.15 Smoking a cigarette	80	90
1045	$1.15 In open-necked shirt and green jumper	80	90

189 Heavy Ash Eruption over Plymouth, 1995

1997. Eruption of Soufriere Volcano. Multicoloured.

1046	$1.50 Type **189**	1·10	1·10
1047	$1.50 Burning rock flow entering sea	1·10	1·10
1048	$1.50 Double venting at Castle Peak	1·10	1·10
1049	$1.50 Mangrove cuckoo	1·10	1·10
1050	$1.50 Lava flow at night, 1996	1·10	1·10
1051	$1.50 Antillean crested hummingbird	1·10	1·10
1052	$1.50 Ash cloud over Plymouth	1·10	1·10
1053	$1.50 Lava spine, 1996	1·10	1·10
1054	$1.50 Burning rock flows forming new land	1·10	1·10

190 Elvis Presley

1997. Rock Legends. Multicoloured.

1055	$1.15 Type **190**	1·00	1·10
1056	$1.15 Jimi Hendrix	1·00	1·10
1057	$1.15 Jerry Garcia	1·00	1·10
1058	$1.15 Janis Joplin	1·00	1·10

191 Untitled Painting by Frama

1997. Frama Exhibition at Guggenheim Museum, New York.

1059	**191** $1.50 multicoloured	85	95

1997. No. 1028 surch **$1.50**.

1060	$1.50 on $6 Jerry Garcia (37 × 50 mm)	65	70

193 Prickly Pear

194 Eva and Juan Peron (Argentine politicians)

1998. Medicinal Plants. Multicoloured.

1061	$1 Type **193**	45	50
1062	$1.15 Pomme coolie	50	55
1063	$1.50 Aloe	65	70
1064	$3.45 Bird pepper	1·40	1·50

1998. Famous People of the 20th Century. Multicoloured.

1065	$1.15 Type **194**	50	55
1066	$1.15 Pablo Picasso (painter)	50	55
1067	$1.15 Wernher von Braun (space scientist)	50	55
1068	$1.15 David Ben Gurion (Israeli statesman)	50	55
1069	$1.15 Jean Henri Dunant (founder of Red Cross)	50	55
1070	$1.15 Dwight Eisenhower (President of U.S.A.)	50	55
1071	$1.15 Mahatma Gandhi (leader of Indian Independence movement)	50	55
1072	$1.15 King Leopold III and Queen Astrid of Belgium	50	55
1073	$1.15 Grand Duchess Charlotte and Prince Felix of Luxembourg	50	55
1074	$1.50 Charles Augustus Lindbergh (pioneer aviator)	65	70
1075	$1.50 Mao Tse-tung (Chinese communist leader)	65	70
1076	$1.50 Earl Mountbatten (last Viceroy of India)	65	70
1077	$1.50 Konrad Adenauer (German statesman)	65	70
1078	$1.50 Anne Frank (Holocaust victim)	65	70
1079	$1.50 Queen Wilhelmina of the Netherlands	65	70
1080	$1.50 King George VI of Great Britain	65	70
1081	$1.50 King Christian X of Denmark	65	70
1082	$1.50 King Haakon VII and Crown Prince Olav of Norway	65	70
1083	$1.50 King Alfonso XIII of Spain	65	70
1084	$1.50 King Gustavus V of Sweden	65	70

195 Jerry Garcia

1998. Rock Music Legends. Multicoloured. (a) Jerry Garcia.

1086	$1.15 In long-sleeved blue shirt	50	55
1087	$1.15 With drum kit in background	50	55
1088	$1.15 Type **195**	50	55
1089	$1.15 Wearing long-sleeved black t-shirt	50	55
1090	$1.15 Close-up with left hand in foreground	50	55
1091	$1.15 With purple and black background	50	55
1092	$1.15 Holding microphone	50	55
1093	$1.15 In short-sleeved blue t-shirt	50	55
1094	$1.15 In sunglasses with cymbal in background	50	55

(b) Bob Marley. Predominant colour for each design given.

1095	$1.15 Pointing (green)	50	55
1096	$1.15 Wearing neck chain (green)	50	55
1097	$1.15 Singing into microphone (green)	50	55
1098	$1.15 Singing with eyes closed (yellow)	50	55
1099	$1.15 Facing audience (yellow)	50	55
1100	$1.15 In striped t-shirt with fingers on chin (red)	50	55
1101	$1.15 In Rastafarian hat (red)	50	55
1102	$1.15 In striped t-shirt with hand closed (red)	50	55

196 Ash Eruption from Soufriere Hills Volcano

1998. Total Eclipse of the Sun on 26 February. Multicoloured.

1104	$1.15 Type **196**	50	55
1105	$1.15 Volcano emitting black cloud	50	55
1106	$1.15 Village below volcano	50	55
1107	$1.15 Lava flow and wrecked house	50	55

197 Princess Diana on Wedding Day, 1981

1998. Diana, Princess of Wales Commemoration. Multicoloured.

1109	$1.15 Type **197**	50	55
1110	$1.50 Accepting bouquet from children	65	70
1111	$3 At Royal Ascot	1·25	1·40

1998. 19th World Scout Jamboree, Chile. Nos. 669/72 optd **19 th WORLD JAMBOREE MONDIAL CHILE 1999** and emblem.

1113	20 c. Type **117**	10	10
1114	20 c. Girl Guide saluting	10	10
1115	75 c. Lady Baden-Powell	35	40
1116	75 c. Guide assisting in old people's home	35	40

1999. "iBRA '99" International Stamp Exhibition, Nuremberg. Nos. 975/6 optd **iBRA INTERNATIONALE BRIEFMARKEN WELTAUSSTELLUNG NURNBERG 27.-4.5.99.**

1117	$1.15 Type **177**	50	55
1118	$1.50 Open book ("Education")	65	70

OFFICIAL STAMPS

1976. Various stamps, some already surch, optd **O.H.M.S.**

O1	5 c. multicoloured (No. 246)	†	65
O2	10 c. multicoloured (No. 247)	†	75
O3	30 c. on 10 c. mult (No. 369)	†	1·50
O4	45 c. on 3 c. mult (No. 370)	†	2·00
O5	$5 multicoloured (No. 254)	†	£100
O6	$10 multicoloured (No. 254a)	†	£550

These stamps were issued for use on mail from the Montserrat Philatelic Bureau. They were not sold to the public, either unused or used.

1976. Nos. 372, 374/82, 384/5 and 476 optd **O.H.M.S.** or surch also.

O17	5 c. Malay apple	†	10
O28	5 c. on 3 c. Lignum vitae	†	20
O18	10 c. Jacaranda	†	10
O19	15 c. Orchid tree	†	10
O20	20 c. Manjak	†	10
O21	25 c. Tamarind	†	15
O33	30 c. on 15 c. Orchid tree	†	30
O34	35 c. on 2 c. Cannon-ball tree	†	30
O35	40 c. Flame of the forest	†	40
O22	55 c. Pink cassia	†	35
O23	70 c. Long john	†	45
O24	$1 Saman	†	60
O39	$2.50 on 40 c. Flame of the forest	†	2·00
O25	$5 Yellow poui	†	2·00
O16	$10 Flamboyant	†	3·75

1981. Nos. 490/4, 496, 498, 500, 502/3 and 505 optd **O.H.M.S.**

O42	5 c. Type **91**	10	10
O43	10 c. Hogfish and neon goby	10	10
O44	15 c. Creole wrasse	10	10
O45	20 c. Three-spotted damselfish	15	15
O46	25 c. Sergeant major	15	15
O47	45 c. Schoolmaster	25	20
O48	65 c. Bigeye	35	30
O49	$1 Rock beauty	65	65
O50	$3 Royal gramma ("Fairy basslet") and blueheads	1·75	1·75
O51	$5 Cherub angelfish	2·50	2·25
O52	$10 Caribbean long-nosed butterflyfish	4·00	2·25

1983. Nos. 510/15 surch **O.H.M.S.** and value.

O53	45 c. on 90 c. "Charlotte"	15	30
O54	45 c. on 90 c. Prince Charles and Lady Diana Spencer	50	60
O55	75 c. on $3 "Portsmouth"	25	35
O56	75 c. on $3 Prince Charles and Lady Diana Spencer	65	80
O57	$1 on $4 "Britannia"	35	50
O58	$1 on $4 Prince Charles and Lady Diana Spencer	75	90

1983. Nos. 542/4 surch on **O.H.M.S.**

O59	70 c. on 75 c. Type **97**	60	40
O60	$1 Coat of Arms of Catherine of Aragon	70	50
O61	$1.50 on $5 Diana, Princess of Wales	1·00	80

1985. Nos. 600/12 and 614 optd **O H M S**.

O62	5 c. Type **107**	60	70
O63	10 c. Carib grackle	60	70
O64	15 c. Moorhen	70	70
O65	20 c. Brown booby	75	60
O66	25 c. Black-whiskered vireo	75	60
O67	40 c. Scaly-breasted thrasher	1·00	60
O68	55 c. Laughing gull	1·25	65
O69	70 c. Glossy ibis	1·40	80
O70	90 c. Green heron	1·75	80
O71	$1 Belted kingfisher	1·75	60
O72	$1.15 Bananaquit	2·50	90
O73	$3 American kestrel	3·75	3·50
O74	$5 Forest thrush	4·50	3·50
O75	$10 Bridled quail dove	6·50	3·50

1989. Nos. 757/70 and 772 optd **O H M S**.

O76	5 c. Type **133**	20	20
O77	10 c. Little knobbed scallop	20	20
O78	15 c. Sozoni's cone	20	20
O79	20 c. Globular coral shell	20	20
O80	25 c. American or common sundial	25	25
O81	40 c. King helmet	30	30
O82	55 c. Channelled turban	40	40
O83	70 c. True tulip shell	50	50
O84	90 c. Music volute	65	65
O85	$1 Flame auger	70	70
O86	$1.15 Rooster-tail conch	80	80
O87	$1.50 Queen or pink conch	95	95
O88	$3 Teramachi's slit shell	1·75	1·75
O89	$5 Common or Florida crown conch	3·00	3·00
O90	$10 Atlantic trumpet triton	5·50	5·50

1989. Nos. 578 and 580/1 surch **OHMS**.

O91	70 c. on 10 c. Hogfish and neon goby	1·50	1·50
O92	$1.15 on 75 c. French grunt	2·00	1·50
O93	$1.50 on $2 Blue chromis	2·25	2·75

1992. Nos. 838/41, 847/50, 856/9 surch or optd **OHMS**.

O 94	70 c. on 90 c. Type **150**	1·25	1·25
O 95	70 c. on 90 c. Type **152**	1·25	1·25
O 96	70 c. on 90 c. Type **154**	1·25	1·25
O 97	70 c. on $3.50 French grunt	1·25	1·25
O 98	$1 on $3.50 Helmeted guineafowl	1·40	1·50
O 99	$1 on $3.50 Anthurium	1·40	1·40
O100	$1.15 Cushion star	1·40	1·40
O101	$1.15 Hen and chicks	1·40	1·40
O102	$1.15 Shell ginger	1·40	1·40
O103	$1.50 Rock beauty	1·50	1·50
O104	$1.50 Red junglefowl	1·50	1·50
O105	$1.50 Early day lily	1·50	1·50

1993. Nos. 889/902 and 904 optd **OHMS**.

O106	5 c. Type **161**	40	60
O107	10 c. "Gryllus campestris" (field cricket)	40	60
O108	15 c. "Lepthemis vesiculosa" (dragonfly)	50	60
O109	20 c. "Orthemis ferruginea" (red skimmer)	50	50
O110	25 c. "Gerris lacustris" (pond skater)	50	50
O111	40 c. "Byctiscus betulae" (leaf weevil)	60	40
O112	55 c. "Atta texana" (leaf-cutter ants)	65	40
O113	70 c. "Polistes fuscatus" (paper wasp)	70	70
O114	90 c. "Sparmopolius fulvus" (bee fly)	80	70
O115	$1 "Chrysopa carnea" (lace wing)	1·00	70
O116	$1.15 "Phoebis philea" (butterfly)	1·75	1·50
O117	$1.50 "Cynthia cardui" (butterfly)	2·00	2·25
O118	$3 "Utetheisa bella" (moth)	2·50	3·00
O119	$5 "Alucita pentadactyla" (moth)	3·50	3·75
O120	$10 "Heliconius melpomene" (butterfly)	5·50	6·00

1997. Nos. 1009/22 and 1024 optd **O.H.M.S.**

O121	5 c. Type **184**	10	10
O122	10 c. Pegasus	10	10
O123	15 c. Griffin	10	10
O124	20 c. Unicorn	10	10
O125	25 c. Gnomes	10	10
O126	40 c. Mermaid	15	20
O127	55 c. Cockatrice	25	30
O128	70 c. Fairy	30	35
O129	90 c. Goblin	40	45
O130	$1 Faun	45	50
O131	$1.15 Dragon	50	55
O132	$1.50 Giant	65	70
O133	$3 Elves	1·25	1·40
O134	$5 Centaur	2·10	2·25
O135	$10 Erin	4·25	4·50

MOROCCO AGENCIES

Stamps used at British postal agencies in Morocco, N. Africa, the last of which closed on 30 April, 1957.

I. GIBRALTAR ISSUES OVERPRINTED.

For use at all British Post Offices in Morocco.

All British P.O.'s in Morocco were under the control of the Gibraltar P.O. until 1907 when control was assumed by H.M. Postmaster-General.

1898. Stamps of Gibraltar (Queen Victoria) optd **Morocco Agencies**.

9	**7**	5 c. green	30	30
10		10 c. red	45	20
11		20 c. olive	3·50	70
3		20 c. olive and brown	3·50	1·25
4		25 c. blue	2·25	60
5		40 c. brown	3·50	3·25
14		50 c. lilac	6·00	3·50
7		1 p. brown and blue	10·00	23·00
8		2 p. black and red	11·00	24·00

1903. Stamps of Gibraltar (King Edward VII) optd **Morocco Agencies**.

24	**8**	5 c. light green and green	4·25	2·75
18		10 c. purple on red	5·00	30
26		20 c. green and red	2·75	25·00
20		25 c. purple & black on blue	4·25	15
28		50 c. purple and violet	6·00	32·00
29		1 p. black and red	23·00	75·00
30		2 p. black and blue	15·00	35·00

II. BRITISH CURRENCY.

On sale at British P.O.s throughout Morocco, including Tangier, until 1937.

PRICES. Our prices for used stamps with these overprints are for examples used in Morocco. These stamps could also be used in the United Kingdom, with official sanction, from the summer of 1950 onwards, and with U.K. postmarks are worth about 50 percent less.

Stamps of Great Britain optd **MOROCCO AGENCIES**.

1907. King Edward VII.

31	**83**	½d. green	1·25	7·00
32		1d. red	6·50	4·00
33	–	2d. green and red	5·50	4·50
34	–	4d. green and brown	3·75	3·25
35a	–	4d. orange	7·50	7·50
36	–	6d. purple	11·00	13·00
37	–	1s. green and red	24·00	17·00
38	–	2s. 6d. purple	60·00	£100

1914. King George V.

55	**105**	½d. green	60	30
43	**104**	1d. red	60	10
44	**105**	1½d. brown	2·00	11·00
45	**106**	2d. orange	2·00	35
58	**104**	2½d. blue	2·00	5·00
46	**106**	3d. violet	1·00	35
47		4d. green	2·00	70
60a	**107**	6d. purple	55	60
49	**108**	1s. brown	5·00	75
53	**109**	2s. 6d. brown	32·00	25·00
74		5s. red	23·00	80·00

1935. Silver Jubilee.

62	**123**	½d. green	1·25	5·50
63		1d. red	1·25	5·50
64		1½d. brown	2·00	9·00
65		2½d. blue	2·00	2·50

1935. King George V.

66	**119**	1d. red	3·25	7·00
67	**118**	1½d. brown	2·50	11·00
68	**120**	2d. orange	40	3·75
69	**119**	2½d. blue	1·75	4·25
70	**120**	3d. violet	40	20
71		4d. green	40	20
72	**122**	1s. brown	80	1·50

1936. King Edward VIII.

75	**124**	1d. red	10	30
76		2½d. blue	10	15

In 1937 unoverprinted Great Britain stamps replaced overprinted **MOROCCO AGENCIES** issues as stocks became exhausted. In 1949 overprinted issues reappeared and were in use at Tetuan (Spanish Zone), the only remaining British P.O. apart from that at Tangier.

1949. King George VI.

77	**128**	½d. green	1·75	6·00
94		½d. orange	1·75	50
78		1d. red	2·75	8·00
95		1d. blue	1·75	65
79		1½d. brown	2·75	7·50
96		1½d. green	1·75	1·50
80		2d. orange	3·00	8·00
97		2d. brown	1·75	3·00
81		2½d. blue	3·25	9·00
98		2½d. red	1·75	2·75
82		3d. violet	1·50	1·40
83	**129**	4d. green	45	80
84		5d. brown	3·00	14·00
85		6d. purple	1·50	1·00
86	**130**	7d. green	40	15·00
87		8d. red	3·00	5·50
88		9d. olive	40	10·00
89		10d. blue	40	5·00
90		11d. plum	70	5·00
91		1s. brown	2·75	5·00
92	**131**	2s. 6d. green	10·00	28·00
93		5s. red	28·00	48·00

1951. Pictorials.

99	**147**	2s. 6d. green	11·00	17·00
100	–	5s. red (No. 510)	11·00	18·00

1952. Queen Elizabeth II.

101	**154**	½d. orange	10	10
102		1d. blue	15	90
103		1½d. green	15	20
104		2d. brown	20	1·00
105	**155**	2½d. red	15	50
106		4d. blue	85	3·25
107	**156**	5d. brown	65	60
108		6d. purple	85	3·25
109	**158**	8d. mauve	70	1·00
110	**159**	1s. bistre	70	60

III. SPANISH CURRENCY.

Stamps surcharged in Spanish currency were sold at British P.O's throughout Morocco until the establishment of the French Zone and the Tangier International Zone, when their use was confined to the Spanish Zone.

Stamps of Great Britain surch **MOROCCO AGENCIES** and value in Spanish currency.

1907. King Edward VII.

112	**83**	5 c. on ½d. green	2·75	15
113		10 c. on 1d. red	5·50	10
114a	–	15 c. on 1½d. purple and green	1·50	15
115	–	20 c. on 2d. green & red	1·00	15
116a	**83**	25 c. on 2½d. blue	1·25	15
117	–	40 c. on 4d. grn & brn	1·00	1·75
118a	–	40 c. on 4d. orange	75	60
119a	–	50 c. on 5d. pur & blue	1·25	1·00
120a	–	1 p. on 10d. pur & red	17·00	7·50
121	–	3 p. on 2s. 6d. purple	19·00	24·00
122	–	6 p. on 5s. red	35·00	45·00
123	–	12 p. on 10s. blue	75·00	75·00

1912. King George V.

126	**101**	5 c. on ½d. green	2·00	10
127	**102**	10 c. on 1d. red	70	10

1914. King George V.

128	**105**	3 c. on ½d. green	30	3·25
129	**105**	5 c. on ½d. green	30	10
130	**104**	10 c. on 1d. red	50	10
131	**105**	15 c. on 1½d. brown	50	10
132	**106**	20 c. on 2d. orange	50	25
133	**104**	25 c. on 2½d. blue	1·25	25
148	**106**	40 c. on 4d. green	1·25	1·25
135	**108**	1 p. on 10d. blue	1·50	3·75
142	**109**	3 p. on 2s. 6d. brown	23·00	70·00
136		6 p. on 5s. red	28·00	48·00
138		12 p. on 10s. blue	£110	£160

1935. Silver Jubilee.

149	**123**	5 c. on ½d. green	1·00	55
150		10 c. on 1d. red	2·75	2·25
151		15 c. on 1½d. brown	4·00	14·00
152		25 c. on 2½d. blue	5·00	2·25

1935. King George V.

153	**118**	5 c. on ½d. green	75	13·00
154	**119**	10 c. on 1d. red	2·50	4·50
155	**118**	15 c. on 1½d. brown	3·25	3·25
156	**120**	20 c. on 2d. orange	40	25
157	**119**	25 c. on 2½d. blue	1·25	3·75
158	**120**	40 c. on 4d. green	45	3·00
159	**122**	1 p. on 10d. blue	3·50	30

1936. King Edward VIII.

160	**124**	5 c. on ½d. green	10	10
161		10 c. on 1d. red	50	1·50
162		15 c. on 1½d. brown	10	10
163		25 c. on 2½d. blue	10	10

1937. Coronation.

164	**126**	15 c. on 1½d. brown	50	30

1937. King George VI.

165	**128**	5 c. on ½d. green	55	15
182		5 c. on ½d. orange	2·00	2·25
166		10 c. on 1d. red	50	10
183		10 c. on 1d. blue	3·25	4·00
167		15 c. on 1½d. brown	55	25
184		15 c. on 1½d. green	1·75	12·00
168		25 c. on 2½d. blue	60	50
185		25 c. on 2½d. red	1·75	4·00
169	**129**	40 c. on 4d. green	24·00	9·50
186		40 c. on 4d. blue	60	9·00
170	**130**	70 c. on 7d. green	50	8·50
171		1 p. on 10d. blue	85	3·50

1940. Stamp Centenary.

172	**134**	5 c. on ½d. green	30	1·50
173		10 c. on 1d. red	2·40	1·75
174		15 c. on 1½d. brown	30	1·75
175		25 c. on 2½d. blue	30	50

1948. Silver Wedding.

176	**137**	25 c. on 2½d. blue	40	15
177	**138**	45 p. on £1 blue	17·00	22·00

1948. Olympic Games.

178	**139**	25 c. on 2½d. blue	40	60
179	**140**	30 c. on 3d. violet	40	60
180	–	60 c. on 6d. purple	40	60
181	–	1 p. 20 on 1s. brown	55	60

1954. Queen Elizabeth II.

189	**154**	5 c. on ½d. orange	15	75
188		10 c. on 1d. blue	50	75
190	**155**	40 c. on 4d. blue	70	1·75

IV. FRENCH CURRENCY.

Stamps surch in French currency were sold at British P.O.'s in the French Zone.

Stamps of Great Britain surch **MOROCCO AGENCIES** and value in French currency.

1917. King George V.

191	**105**	3 c. on ½d. green	50	2·50
192		5 c. on ½d. green	30	10
203	**104**	10 c. on 1d. red	30	70
194	**105**	15 c. on 1½d. brown	2·00	15
205	**104**	25 c. on 2½d. blue	30	40
206	**106**	40 c. on 4d. green	50	80
207	**107**	50 c. on 5d. brown	50	10

198	**108**	75 c. on 9d. green	50	75
209		90 c. on 9d. green	9·50	4·25
210		1 f. on 10d. blue	70	10
211		1 f. 50 on 1s. brown	5·50	2·25
200	**109**	3 f. on 2s. 6d. brown	7·50	1·50
226		6 f. on 5s. red	6·00	20·00

1935. Silver Jubilee.

212	**123**	5 c. on ½d. green	15	15
213		10 c. on 1d. red	1·90	50
214		15 c. on 1½d. brown	20	50
215		25 c. on 2½d. blue	30	15

1935. King George V.

216	**118**	5 c. on ½d. green	45	3·50
217	**119**	10 c. on 1d. red	35	30
218	**118**	15 c. on 1½d. brown	2·50	3·00
219	**119**	25 c. on 2½d. blue	30	15
220	**120**	40 c. on 4d. green	30	15
221	**121**	50 c. on 5d. brown	30	15
222	**122**	90 c. on 9d. olive	35	1·00
223		1 f. on 10d. blue	30	30
224		1 f. 50 on 1s. brown	40	2·00

1936. King Edward VIII.

227	**124**	5 c. on ½d. green	10	15
228		15 c. on 1½d. brown	10	15

1937. Coronation.

229	**126**	15 c. on 1½d. brown	30	20

1937. King George VI.

230	**128**	5 c. on ½d. green	90	1·40

V. TANGIER INTERNATIONAL ZONE.

This Zone was established in 1924 and the first specially overprinted stamps issued in 1927.

PRICES. Our note re U.K. usage (at beginning of Section II) also applies to **TANGIER** optd stamps.

Stamps of Great Britain optd **TANGIER**.

1927. King George V.

231	**105**	½d. green	1·00	10
232	**104**	1d. red	1·25	10
233	**105**	1½d. brown	3·50	2·00
234	**106**	2d. orange	3·25	10

1934. King George V.

235	**118**	½d. green	1·00	1·40
236	**119**	1d. red	1·60	70
237	**118**	1½d. brown	15	10

1935. Silver Jubilee optd **TANGIER TANGIER**.

238	**123**	½d. green	1·00	2·25
239		1d. red	12·00	8·00
240		1½d. brown	1·25	30

1936. King Edward VIII.

241	**124**	½d. green	10	15
242		1d. red	10	10
243		1½d. brown	15	10

1937. Coronation optd **TANGIER TANGIER**.

244	**126**	1½d. brown	40	30

1937. King George VI.

245	**128**	½d. green	90	30
280		½d. orange	45	1·00
246		1d. red	3·00	30
281		1d. blue	70	2·50
247		1½d. brown	60	10
282		1½d. green	70	13·00
261		2d. orange	3·50	3·50
283		2d. brown	70	2·00
262		2½d. blue	50	2·50
284		2½d. red	70	2·75
263		3d. violet	35	50
264	**129**	4d. green	6·50	9·00
285		4d. blue	1·25	2·50
265		5d. brown	2·75	9·00
266		6d. purple	35	30
267	**130**	7d. green	80	9·00
268		8d. red	3·00	8·00
269		9d. olive	60	10·00
270		10d. blue	60	10·00
271		11d. plum	60	8·00
272		1s. brown	60	1·50
273	**131**	2s. 6d. green	4·00	10·00
274		5s. red	12·00	35·00
275	–	10s. blue (No. 478a)	35·00	90·00

1940. Stamp Centenary.

248	**134**	½d. green	30	3·25
249		1d. red	45	50
250		1½d. brown	2·00	2·25

1946. Victory.

253	**135**	2½d. blue	30	20
254	–	3d. violet	30	40

1948. Silver Wedding.

255	**137**	2½d. blue	30	15
256	**138**	£1 blue	25·00	25·00

1948. Olympic Games.

257	**139**	2½d. blue	65	1·00
258	**140**	3d. violet	65	1·00
259	–	6d. purple	65	1·00
260	–	1s. brown	65	50

1949. U.P.U.

276	**143**	2½d. blue	50	1·00
277	**144**	3d. violet	50	85
278	–	6d. purple	50	85
279	–	1s. brown	50	1·75

1951. Pictorial stamps.

286	**147**	2s. 6d. green	7·50	4·50
287	–	5s. red (No. 510)	13·00	15·00
288	–	10s. blue (No. 511)	17·00	15·00

1952. Queen Elizabeth II.

313	**154**	½d. orange	10	20
290		1d. blue	15	30
291		1½d. green	10	30
292		2d. brown	20	30
293	**155**	2½d. red	10	30
294		3d. lilac	20	30
320		4d. blue	65	2·00
296	**157**	5d. brown	60	90
297		6d. purple	45	15
298		7d. green	80	2·00
299	**158**	8d. mauve	60	1·50
300		9d. olive	1·40	75
301		10d. blue	1·40	2·75
302		11d. purple	1·40	3·25
303	**159**	1s. brown	50	30
304		1s. 3d. green	65	2·00
305		1s. 6d. blue	1·00	1·75

1953. Coronation.

306	**161**	2½d. red	50	30
307	–	4d. blue	1·00	30
308	**163**	1s. 3d. green	1·25	1·25
309	–	1s. 6d. blue	1·25	60

1955. Pictorials.

310	**166**	2s. 6d. brown	3·50	6·00
311	–	5s. red	5·50	11·00
312	–	10s. blue	19·00	21·00

1957. Cent of British Post Office in Tangier. Queen Elizabeth II stamps optd **1857–1957 TANGIER**.

323	**154**	½d. orange	10	10
324		1d. blue	10	10
325		1½d. green	10	10
326		2d. brown	10	10
327	**155**	2½d. red	15	50
328		3d. lilac	15	10
329		4d. blue	30	20
330	**157**	5d. brown	30	35
331		6d. purple	30	15
332		7d. green	30	30
333	**158**	8d. mauve	30	70
334		9d. olive	30	30
335		10d. blue	30	30
336		11d. plum	30	30
337	**159**	1s. bistre	30	30
338		1s. 3d. green	45	2·00
339		1s. 6d. blue	50	1·00
340	**166**	2s. 6d. brown	2·00	3·00
341	–	5s. red	2·75	3·75
342	–	10s. blue	5·00	5·00

MORVI

A state of India, Bombay district. Now uses Indian stamps.

12 pies = 1 anna

1 Maharaja Lakhdirji 3

1931.

8	**1**	3 p. red	2·00	7·00
9b		6 p. green	2·75	7·00
5a		½ a. blue	1·90	9·00
6		1 a. brown	3·25	18·00
10		1 a. blue	2·00	7·50
7		2 a. brown	4·00	25·00
11		2 a. violet	10·00	27·00

1934.

16	**3**	3 p. red	70	2·25
17		6 p. green	75	2·00
14		1 a. brown	1·10	8·00
15		2 a. violet	2·50	15·00

MOZAMBIQUE

The Republic of Mozambique joined the Commonwealth on 12 November 1995. For previous issues see Volume 2.

100 centavos = 1 metical

267 Child wearing Blue Cloak

1995. 20th Anniv of U.N.I.C.E.F. in Mozambique.

1417	**267**	5000 m. multicoloured	60	65

268 Player scoring Goal

1996. Football. Multicoloured.

1418	1000 m. Type **268**	10	15
1419	2000 m. Goalkeeper holding ball	20	25
1420	4000 m. Referee admonishing players	40	45
1421	6000 m. Two players tackling for ball	60	65

269 Mask

270 "Mae Africa" (De Malangatana)

1996. Local Masks.

1422	**269**	1000 m. multicoloured	10	15
1423	–	2000 m. multicoloured	20	25
1424	–	4000 m. multicoloured	40	45
1425	–	6000 m. multicoloured	60	65

DESIGNS: 2000 to 6000 m. Different masks.

1996. 15th Anniv of Mozambique Red Cross.

1426	**270**	5000 m. multicoloured	50	55

271 African Elephant

272 Mine Field

1996. Wild Animals. Multicoloured.

1427	1000 m. Type **271**	25	20
1428	2000 m. White rhinoceros	40	35
1429	4000 m. Leopard	60	65
1430	6000 m. Pel's fishing owl	90	1·00

1996. Land Mine Clearance Campaign. Mult.

1431	2000 m. Type **272**	20	25
1432	6000 m. Warning sign	60	65
1433	8000 m. Soldier with mine detector	80	85
1434	10000 m. Soldier lifting mine	1·00	1·10

273 City Street

274 5 r. Stamp of 1876 and Magnifying Glass

1996. "Keeping the City Clean".

1435	**273**	2000 m. multicoloured	20	25

1996. 120th Anniv of Mozambique Stamps.

1436	**274**	2000 m. multicoloured	20	25

275 Mitumbui

1997. Local Boats. Multicoloured.

1437	2000 m. Type **275**	20	25
1438	6000 m. Muterere	60	65
1439	8000 m. Lancha	80	85
1440	10000 m. Dhow	1·00	1·10

276 Village Scene

1997. International Children's Day.

1441	**276**	2000 m. multicoloured	20	25

277 Enaretta Conitera

1997. Beetles. Multicoloured.

1442	2000 m. Type **277**	20	25
1443	6000 m. "Zographus hieroglyphicus	60	65
1444	8000 m. "Tragiscoschema bertolonii"	80	85
1445	10000 m. "Tragocephala ducalis"	1·00	1·10

278 Yellow-billed Stork

280 Sun and Globe

279 Abstract Patterns

1997. Aquatic Birds. Multicoloured.

1447	2000 m. Type **278**	20	25
1448	4000 m. Black-winged stilt	40	45
1449	8000 m. Long-toed stint (horiz)	80	85
1450	10000 m. Eastern white pelican	1·00	1·10

1997. Centenary of Joao Ferreira dos Santos Group.

1451	**279**	2000 m. multicoloured	20	25

1997. Protection of Ozone Layer.

1452	**280**	2000 m. multicoloured	20	25

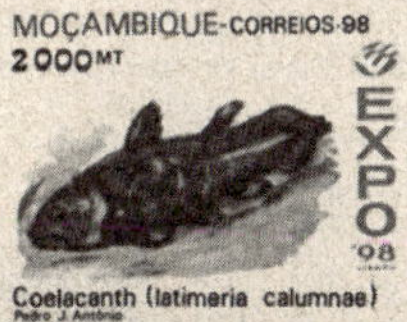

282 Coelacanth

1998. "EXPO '98" International Stamp Exhibition, Lisbon.

1454	**282**	2000 m. multicoloured	20	25

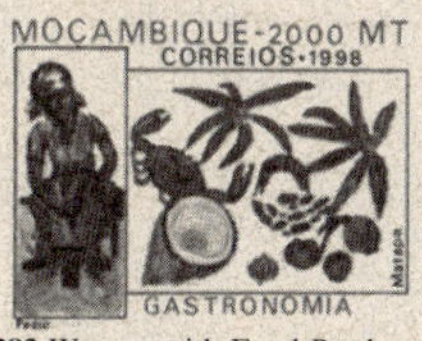

283 Woman with Food Products

1998. Food Production.

1455	**283**	2000 m. multicoloured	20	25

MUSCAT

Independent Sultanate in Eastern Arabia with Indian and, subsequently, British postal administration.

12 pies = 1 anna. 16 annas = 1 rupee

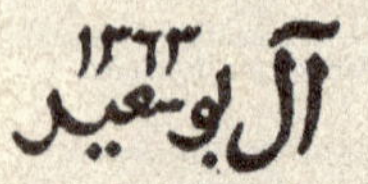

(2)

1944. Bicentenary of Al-Busaid Dynasty. Stamps of India (King George VI) optd as T **2**.

1	**100a**	3 p. slate	30	4·50
2		½ a. mauve	30	4·50
3		9 p. green	30	4·50
4		1 a. red	30	4·50
5	**101**	1½ a. plum	30	4·50
6		2 a. red	30	4·50
7		3 a. violet	50	4·50
8		3½ a. blue	50	4·50
9	**102**	4 a. brown	50	4·50
10		6 a. green	65	4·50
11		8 a. violet	65	4·50
12		12 a. red	80	5·00
13	–	14 a. purple (No. 277)	1·75	7·00
14	**93**	1 r. slate and brown	50	9·00
15		2 r. purple and brown	1·10	15·00

OFFICIAL STAMPS

1944. Bicentenary of Al-Busaid Dynasty. Official stamps of India optd as T **2**.

O 1	**O 20**	3 p. slate	50	9·00
O 2		½ a. purple	50	9·00
O 3		9 p. green	50	9·00
O 4		1 a. red	50	9·00
O 5		1½ a. violet	50	9·00
O 6		2 a. orange	50	9·00
O 7		2½ a. violet	1·25	9·00
O 8		4 a. brown	1·00	9·00
O 9		8 a. violet	1·40	9·50
O10	**93**	1 r. slate and brown (No. O138)	2·25	18·00

For later issues see **BRITISH POSTAL AGENCIES IN EASTERN ARABIA**.

NABHA

A "Convention" state in the Punjab, India.

12 pies = 1 anna; 16 annas = 1 rupee

Stamps of India optd **NABHA STATE**.

1885. Queen Victoria. Vert opt.

1	**23**	½ a. turquoise	1·40	3·00
2	–	1 a. purple	28·00	£100
3	–	2 a. blue	9·50	32·00
4	–	4 a. green (No. 96)	55·00	£140
5	–	8 a. mauve	£300	
6	–	1 r. grey (No. 79)	£275	

1885. Queen Victoria. Horiz opt.

36	**40**	3 p. red	10	15
14	**23**	½ a. turquoise	10	10
15	–	9 p. red	50	2·25
17	–	1 a. purple	80	40
18	–	1 a. 6 p. brown	60	1·75
20	–	2 a. blue	1·00	70
22	–	3 a. orange	1·75	1·10
12	–	4 a. green (No. 69)	24·00	£120
24	–	4 a. green (No. 96)	3·25	1·40
26	–	6 a. brown (No. 80)	1·25	2·00
27	–	8 a. mauve	1·25	1·60
28	–	12 a. purple on red	2·25	3·00
29	–	1 r. grey (No. 101)	6·50	32·00
30	**37**	1 r. green and red	6·00	3·75
31	**38**	2 r. red and orange	85·00	£170
32		3 r. brown and green	85·00	£200
33		5 r. blue and violet	85·00	£300

1903. King Edward VII.

37	3 p. grey	25	15
38	½ a. green (No. 122)	35	30
39	1 a. red (No. 123)	60	60
40a	2 a. lilac	1·50	30
40b	2½ a. blue	17·00	75·00
41	3 a. orange	45	30
42	4 a. olive	1·10	1·75
43	6 a. bistre	90	9·00
44	8 a. mauve	5·50	14·00
45	12 a. purple on red	2·50	16·00
46	1 r. green and red	5·50	8·50

1907. As last, but inscr "INDIA POSTAGE & REVENUE".

47	½ a. green (No. 149)	45	1·10
48	1 a. red (No. 150)	35	70

1913. King George V. Optd in two lines.

49	**55**	3 p. grey	20	15
50	**56**	½ a. green	20	10
51	**57**	1 a. red	45	10
59		1 a. brown	2·25	1·25
52	**59**	2 a. lilac	45	35
53	**62**	3 a. orange	50	35
54	**63**	4 a. olive	55	90
55	**64**	6 a. bistre	55	4·00
56	**65**	8 a. mauve	1·25	3·00
57	**66**	12 a. red	1·10	16·00
58	**67**	1 r. brown and green	6·00	2·75

1928. King George V. Optd in one line.

60	**55**	3 p. grey	60	15
61	**56**	½ a. green	30	20
73	**79**	½ a. green	30	30
61a	**80**	9 p. green	1·25	1·10
62	**57**	1 a. brown	50	15
74	**81**	1 a. brown	30	30
63	**82**	1¼ a. mauve	60	3·50
64	**70**	2 a. lilac	1·40	35
65	**61**	2½ a. orange	45	5·50
66	**62**	3 a. blue	1·10	1·00
75	**57**	3 a. red	3·25	8·00
76	**63**	4 a. olive	2·25	2·25
67	**71**	4 a. green	1·50	1·40
71	**67**	2 r. red and orange	21·00	70·00
72		5 r. blue and purple	70·00	£190

1938. King George VI. Nos. 247/63.

77	**91**	3 p. slate	4·75	30
78		½ a. brown	2·75	50
79		9 p. green	16·00	3·00
80		1 a. red	1·25	30
81	**92**	2 a. red	1·00	4·00
82	–	2 a. 6 p. violet	1·00	6·50
83	–	3 a. green	1·10	3·50
84	–	3 a. 6 p. blue	1·10	13·00
85	–	4 a. brown	4·50	4·75
86	–	6 a. green	2·00	13·00
87	–	8 a. violet	1·90	13·00
88	–	12 a. red	2·25	15·00
89	**93**	1 r. slate and brown	10·00	20·00
90		2 r. purple and brown	19·00	70·00
91		5 r. green and blue	45·00	£140
92		10 r. purple and red	70·00	£275
93		15 r. brown and green	£180	£500
94		25 r. slate and purple	£180	£500

1942. King George VI. Optd **NABHA** only.

95	**91**	3 p. slate	27·00	2·50
105	**100a**	3 p. slate	80	45
96	**91**	½ a. brown	65·00	3·50
106	**100a**	½ a. mauve	3·75	45
97	**91**	9 p. green	10·00	9·50
107	**100a**	9 p. green	3·00	45
98	**91**	1 a. red	10·00	2·00
108	**100a**	1 a. red	80	2·00
109	**101**	1 a. 3 p. brown	80	1·50
110		1½ a. violet	1·00	1·00
111		2 a. red	80	2·75
112		3 a. violet	2·00	2·50
113		3½ a. blue	9·50	35·00
114	**102**	4 a. brown	1·60	75
115		6 a. green	7·00	35·00
116		8 a. violet	5·00	25·00
117		12 a. purple	4·25	35·00

OFFICIAL STAMPS

Stamps of Nabha optd **SERVICE**.

1885. Nos. 1/3 (Queen Victoria).

O1	½ a. turquoise	1·50	55
O2	1 a. purple	30	15
O3	2 a. blue	48·00	95

1885. Nos. 14/30 (Queen Victoria).

O 6	½ a. turquoise	10	10
O 8	1 a. purple	75	25
O 9	2 a. blue	1·40	55
O12	3 a. orange	15·00	48·00
O13	4 a. green (No. 4)	1·60	50
O15	6 a. brown	11·00	18·00
O17	8 a. mauve	1·00	70
O18	12 a. purple on red	4·00	13·00
O19	1 r. grey	26·00	£170
O20	1 r. green and red	22·00	50·00

1903. Nos. 37/46 (King Edward VII).

O25	3 p. grey	65	9·00
O26	½ a. green	35	10
O27	1 a. red	15	10
O29	2 a. lilac	1·00	40
O30	4 a. olive	1·25	50
O32	8 a. mauve	1·10	1·00
O34	1 r. green and red	1·50	2·25

1907. Nos. 47/8 (King Edward VII inscr "INDIA POSTAGE & REVENUE").

O35	½ a. green	20	35
O36	1 a. red	25	25

1913. Nos. 54 and 58, (King George V).

O37	**63**	4 a. olive	10·00	42·00
O38	**67**	1 r. brown and green	55·00	£275

1913. Official stamps of India (King George V) optd **NABHA STATE**.

O39	**55**	3 p. grey	30	5·50
O40	**56**	½ a. green	15	10
O41	**57**	1 a. red	15	10
O42	**59**	2 a. lilac	30	15
O43	**63**	4 a. olive	40	40
O44	**65**	8 a. mauve	65	80
O46	**67**	1 r. brown and green	2·75	2·00

1932. Stamps of India (King George V) optd **NABHA STATE SERVICE**.

O47	**55**	3 p. grey	10	15
O48	**81**	1 a. brown	15	15
O49	**63**	4 a. olive	18·00	2·25
O50	**65**	8 a. mauve	1·00	1·90

1938. Stamps of India (King George VI) optd **NABHA STATE SERVICE**.

O53	**91**	9 p. green	1·50	2·25
O54		1 a. red	8·50	45

1943. Stamps of India (King George VI) optd **NABHA**.

O55	**O 20**	3 p. slate	55	60
O56		½ a. brown	70	30
O57		½ a. purple	2·50	45
O58		9 p. green	1·25	20
O59		1 a. red	50	20
O61		1½ a. violet	60	40
O62		2 a. orange	1·25	60
O64		4 a. brown	3·50	1·75
O65		8 a. violet	5·50	12·00

1943. Stamps of India (King George VI) optd **NABHA SERVICE**.

O66	**93**	1 r. slate and brown	8·50	27·00
O67		2 r. purple and brown	23·00	£140
O68		5 r. green and blue	£200	£450

NAMIBIA

Formerly South West Africa which became independent on 21 March 1990.

1990. 100 cents = 1 rand.
1993. 100 cents = 1 Namibia dollar.

141 Pres. Sam Nujoma, Map of Namibia and National Flag

1990. Independence. Multicoloured.

538	18 c. Type **141**	30	15
539	45 c. Hands releasing dove and map of Namibia (vert)	70	1·00
540	60 c. National flag and map of Africa	1·25	1·75

142 Fish River Canyon

1990. Namibia Landscapes. Multicoloured.

541	18 c. Type **142**	35	20
542	35 c. Quiver-tree forest, Keetmanshoop	65	35
543	45 c. Tsaris Mountains	75	55
544	60 c. Dolerite boulders, Keetmanshoop	85	65

143 Stores on Kaiser Street, c. 1899

1990. Centenary of Windhoek. Multicoloured.

545	18 c. Type **143**	25	20
546	35 c. Kaiser Street, 1990	45	35
547	45 c. City Hall, 1914	55	65
548	60 c. City Hall, 1990	70	1·00

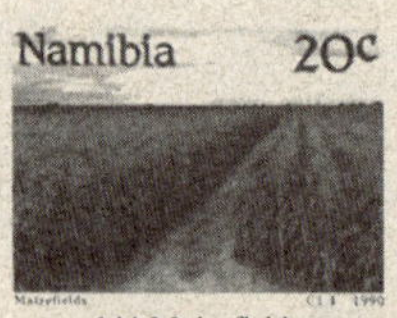

144 Maizefields **145** Gypsum

1990. Farming. Multicoloured.

549	20 c. Type **144**	25	20
550	35 c. Sanga bull	45	35
551	50 c. Damara ram	60	45
552	65 c. Irrigation in Okavango	75	60

1991. Minerals. As Nos. 519/21 and 523/33 of South West Africa, some with values changed and new design (5 r.), inscr "Namibia" as T **145**. Multicoloured.

553	1 c. Type **145**	10	10
554	2 c. Fluorite	15	10
555	5 c. Mimetite	20	10
556	10 c. Azurite	30	10
557	20 c. Dioptase	35	10
558	25 c. Type **139**	35	15
559	30 c. Tsumeb lead and copper complex	50	20
560	35 c. Rosh Pinah zinc mine	50	20
561	40 c. Diamonds	65	25
562	50 c. Uis tin mine	65	25
563	65 c. Boltwoodite	65	35
564	1 r. Rossing uranium mine	70	50
565	1 r. 50 Wulfenite	1·10	70
566	2 r. Gold	1·50	1·10
567	5 r. Willemite (vert as T **145**)	3·00	2·75

146 Radiosonde Weather Balloon

1991. Centenary of Weather Service. Mult.

568	20 c. Type **146**	30	20
569	35 c. Sunshine recorder	45	30
570	50 c. Measuring equipment	60	50
571	65 c. Meteorological station, Gobabeb	70	60

147 Herd of Zebras

1991. Endangered Species. Mountain Zebra. Multicoloured.

572	20 c. Type **147**	1·00	60
573	25 c. Mare and foal	1·10	70
574	45 c. Zebras and foal	1·75	1·75
575	60 c. Two zebras	2·25	2·50

148 Karas Mountains

1991. Mountains of Namibia. Multicoloured.

576	20 c. Type **148**	35	20
577	25 c. Gamsberg Mountains	40	30
578	45 c. Mount Brukkaros	70	70
579	60 c. Erongo Mountains	80	1·00

149 Bernabe de la Bat Camp

1991. Tourist Camps. Multicoloured.

580	20 c. Type **149**	40	30
581	25 c. Von Bach Dam Recreation Resort	50	45
582	45 c. Gross Barmen Hot Springs	75	65
583	60 c. Namutoni Rest Camp	90	1·00

150 Artist's Pallet

1992. 21st Anniv of Windhoek Conservatoire. Multicoloured.

584	20 c. Type **150**	20	15
585	25 c. French horn and cello	25	20
586	45 c. Theatrical masks	50	50
587	60 c. Ballet dancers	65	90

151 Mozambique Mouthbrooder

1992. Freshwater Angling. Multicoloured.

588	20 c. Type **151**	40	20
589	25 c. Large-mouthed yellowfish	45	20
590	45 c. Common carp	85	50
591	60 c. Sharp-toothed catfish	95	65

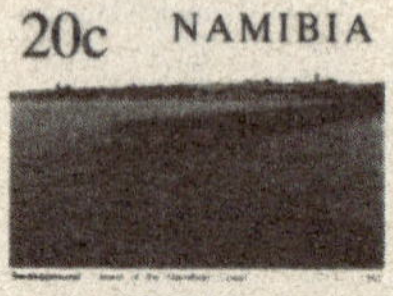

152 Old Jetty

1992. Centenary of Swakopmund. Mult.

592	20 c. Type **152**	25	25
593	25 c. Recreation centre	25	25
594	45 c. State House and lighthouse	80	60
595	60 c. Sea front	85	75

153 Running

154 Wrapping English Cucumbers

1992. Olympic Games, Barcelona. Mult.

597	20 c. Type **153**	25	20
598	25 c. Map of Namibia, Namibian flag and Olympic rings	30	20
599	45 c. Swimming	50	40
600	60 c. Olympic Stadium, Barcelona	65	55

1992. Integration of the Disabled. Mult.

602	20 c. Type **154**	20	15
603	25 c. Weaving mats	20	15
604	45 c. Spinning thread	40	30
605	60 c. Preparing pot plants	55	50

155 Elephants in Desert

1993. Namibia Nature Foundation. Rare and Endangered Species. Multicoloured.

606	20 c. Type **155**	40	20
607	25 c. Sitatunga in swamp	30	20
608	45 c. Black rhinoceros	65	50
609	60 c. Hunting dogs	65	60

156 Herd of Simmentaler Cattle

1993. Centenary of Simmentalar Cattle in Namibia. Multicoloured.

611	20 c. Type **156**	30	10
612	25 c. Cow and calf	30	15
613	45 c. Bull	60	40
614	60 c. Cattle on barge	85	75

157 Sand Dunes, Sossusvlei

1993. Namib Desert Scenery. Multicoloured.

615	30 c. Type **157**	25	20
616	40 c. Blutkuppe	25	20
617	65 c. River Kuiseb, Homeb	40	45
618	85 c. Desert landscape	60	65

158 Smiling Child

1993. S.O.S. Child Care in Namibia. Mult.

619	30 c. Type **158**	30	20
620	40 c. Family	35	20
621	65 c. Modern house	60	55
622	85 c. Young artist with mural	80	80

159 "Charaxes jasius"

160 White Seabream

1993. Butterflies. Multicoloured.

707	5 c. Type **159**	10	10
624	10 c. "Acraea anemosa"	20	20
625	20 c. "Papilio nireus"	30	10
626	30 c. "Junonia octavia"	30	10
627	40 c. "Hypolimnus misippus"	30	10
708	50 c. "Physcaeneura panda"	30	30
629	65 c. "Charaxes candiope"	40	30
630	85 c. "Junonia hierta"	50	40
631	90 c. "Colotis cellmene"	50	40
632	$1 "Cacyreus dicksoni"	55	35
633	$2 "Charaxes bohemani"	80	80
634	$2.50 "Stugeta bowkeri"	1·00	1·10
635	$5 "Byblia anvatara"	1·50	1·75

See also No. 648.

1994. Coastal Angling. Multicoloured.

636	30 c. Type **160**	25	25
637	40 c. Kob	25	25
638	65 c. West coast steenbras	40	40
639	85 c. Galjoen	60	60

161 Container Ship at Wharf

1994. Incorporation of Walvis Bay Territory into Namibia. Multicoloured.

641	30 c. Type **161**	30	30
642	65 c. Aerial view of Walvis Bay	50	70
643	85 c. Map of Namibia	75	1·00

162 "Adenolobus pechuelii"

163 Yellow-billed Stork

1994. Flowers. Multicoloured.

644	35 c. Type **162**	30	25
645	40 c. "Hibiscus elliottiae"	30	25
646	65 c. "Pelargonium cortusifolium"	55	40
647	85 c. "Hoodia macrantha"	75	60

1994. Butterflies. As T **159**, but inscr "STANDARDISED MAIL". Multicoloured.

648	(–) "Graphium antheus"	15	20

No. 648 was initially sold at 35 c., but this was subsequently increased to reflect changes in postal rates.

1994. Storks. Multicoloured.

649	35 c. Type **163**	30	30
650	40 c. Abdim's stork	30	30
651	80 c. African open-bill stork	50	50
652	$1.10 White stork	65	65

164 Steam Railcar, 1908

1994. Steam Locomotives. Multicoloured.

653	35 c. Type **164**	40	30
654	70 c. Krauss side-tank locomotive No. 106, 1904	70	50
655	80 c. Class 24 locomotive, 1948	75	55
656	$1.10 Class 7C locomotive, 1914	1·10	80

165 Cape Cross Locomotive No. 84 "Prince Edward", 1895

1995. Cent of Railways in Namibia. Mult.

657	35 c. Type **165**	45	25
658	70 c. Steam locomotive, German South West Africa	70	35
659	80 c. South African Railways Class 8 steam locomotive	75	40
660	$1.10 Trans-Namib Class 33-400 diesel-electric locomotive	1·10	55

166 National Arms

167 Living Tortoise and "Geochelone stromeri" (fossil)

1995. 5th Anniv of Independence.

662	**166**	(–) multicoloured	30	30

No. 662 is inscribed "STANDARDISED MAIL" and was initially sold for 35 c., but this was subsequently increased to reflect changes in postal rates.

1995. Fossils. Multicoloured.

663	40 c. Type **167**	40	25
664	80 c. Ward's diamond bird and "Diamantornis wardi" (fossil eggs)	70	60
665	90 c. Hyraxes and "Prohyrax hendeyi" skull	80	70
666	$1.20 Crocodiles and "Crocodylus lloydi" skull	1·10	90

168 Martii Rautanen and Church

169 Ivory Buttons

1995. 125th Anniv of Finnish Missionaries in Namibia. Multicoloured.

667	40 c. Type **168**	25	20
668	80 c. Albin Savola and hand printing press	50	50
669	90 c. Karl Weikkolin and wagon	60	65
670	$1.20 Dr. Selma Rainio and Onandjokwe Hospital	85	95

1995. Personal Ornaments. Multicoloured.

671	40 c. Type **169**	20	20
672	80 c. Conus shell pendant	45	45
673	90 c. Cowrie shell headdress	55	55
674	$1.20 Shell button pendant	85	95

170 U.N. Flag

1995. 50th Anniv of the United Nations.

676	**170**	40 c. blue and black	20	20

171 Bogenfels Arch

1996. Tourism. Multicoloured.

677	(–) Type **171**	15	15
678	90 c. Ruacana Falls	30	30
679	$1 Epupa Falls	30	30
680	$1.30 Herd of wild horses	35	50

No. 677 is inscribed "Standardised Mail" and was initially sold at 45 c.

172 Sister Leoni Kreitmeier and Dobra Education and Training Centre

1996. Centenary of Catholic Missions in Namibia. Multicoloured.

681	50 c. Type **172**	20	20
682	95 c. Father Johann Malinowski and Heirachabis Mission	30	35
683	$1 St. Mary's Cathedral, Windhoek	30	35
684	$1.30 Archbishop Joseph Gotthardt and early church, Ovamboland	35	65

173 Children and U.N.I.C.E.F. Volunteer

1996. 50th Anniv of U.N.I.C.E.F. Multicoloured.

686	(–) Type **173**	15	15
687	$1.30 Girls in school	60	60

No. 686 is inscribed "STANDARD POSTAGE" and was initially sold at 50 c.

174 Boxing

1996. Centennial Olympic Games, Atlanta. Multicoloured.

688	(–) Type **174**	15	15
689	90 c. Cycling	30	40
690	$1 Swimming	30	40
691	$1.30 Running	35	55

No. 688 is inscribed "Standard Postage" and was initially sold at 50 c.

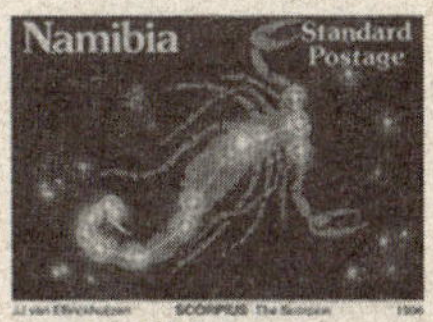
175 Scorpius

1996. Stars in the Namibian Sky. Multicoloured.

692	(–) Type **175**	15	15
693	90 c. Sagittarius	25	30
694	$1 Southern Cross	30	30
695	$1.30 Orion	35	50

No. 692 is inscribed "Standard Postage" and was initially sold at 50 c.

176 Urn-shaped Pot

179 Heinrich von Stephan

177 Khauxa!nas Ruins

1996. Early Pottery. Multicoloured.

697	(–) Type **176**	15	15
698	90 c. Decorated storage pot	25	35
699	$1 Reconstructed cooking pot	30	35
700	$1.30 Storage pot	35	50

No. 697 is inscribed "Standard Postage" and was initially sold at 50 c.

1997. Khaux!nas Ruins.

701	**177**	(–) multicoloured	25	20
702	–	$1 multicoloured	45	50
703	–	$1.10 multicoloured	50	55
704	–	$1.50 multicoloured	70	80

DESIGNS: $1 to $1.50, Different views.

No. 701 is inscribed "Standard postage" and was initially sold at 50 c.

1997. Death Centenary of Heinrich von Stephan (founder of U.P.U.).

709	**179**	$2 multicoloured	75	75

180 Cinderella Waxbill

182 Jackass Penguins calling

181 Helmet Guineafowl

1997. Waxbills. Multicoloured.

710	50 c. Type **180**	15	20
711	60 c. Black-cheeked waxbill	15	20

1997. Greetings Stamp.

712 **181**	$1.20 multicoloured	30	35

For similar designs see Nos. 743/6.

1997. Endangered Species. Jackass Penguin. Multicoloured.

713	(–) Type **182**	25	30
714	$1 Incubating egg	40	40
715	$1.10 Adult with chick	50	50
716	$1.50 Penguins swimming	55	60

No. 713 is inscribed "STANDARD POSTAGE" and was initially sold at 50 c.

183 Caracal

1997. Wildcats. Multicoloured.

718	(–) Type **183**	20	20
719	$1 "Felis lybic"	30	30
720	$1.10 Serval	35	40
721	$1.50 Black-footed cat	50	55

No. 718 is inscribed "STANDARD POSTAGE" and was initially sold at 50 c.

184 "Catophractes alexandri"

1997. Greeting Stamps. Flowers and Helmet Guineafowl. Multicoloured.

723	(–) Type **184**	15	20
724	(–) "Crinum paludosum"	15	20
725	(–) "Gloriosa superba"	15	20
726	(–) "Tribulus zeyheri"	15	20
727	(–) "Aptosimum pubescens"	15	20
728	50 c. Helmet guineafowl raising hat	15	20
729	50 c. Holding bouquet	15	20
730	50 c. Ill in bed	15	20
731	$1 With heart round neck	25	20
732	$1 With suitcase and backpack	25	20

Nos. 723/7 are inscribed "Standard Postage" and were initially sold at 50 c. each.

185 Collecting Bag

1997. Basket Work. Multicoloured.

733	50 c. Type **185**	20	20
734	90 c. Powder basket	30	30
735	$1.20 Fruit basket	35	35
736	$2 Grain basket	70	75

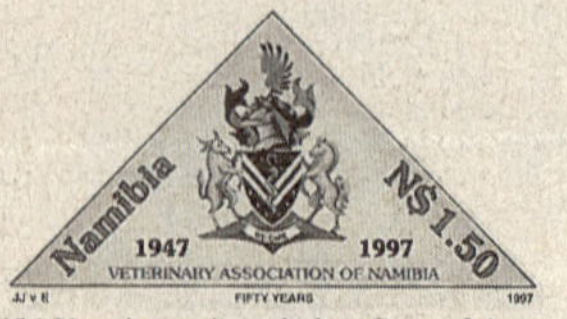

186 Veterinary Association Coat of Arms

1997. 50th Anniv of Namibian Veterinary Association.

737 **186**	$1.50 multicoloured	50	50

MINIMUM PRICE

The minimum price quoted is 10p which represents a handling charge rather than a basis for valuing common stamps. For further notes about prices see introductory pages.

188 German South West Africa Postman

189 False Mopane

1997. World Post Day.

739 **188**	(–) multicoloured	15	20

No. 739 is inscribed "STANDARD POSTAGE" and was initially sold at 50 c.

1997. Trees. Multicoloured.

740	(–) Type **189**	15	20
741	$1 Ana tree	30	40
742	$1.10 Shepherd's tree	35	45
743	$1.50 Kiaat	50	55

No. 740 is inscribed "STANDARD POSTAGE" and was initially sold at 50 c.

1997. Christmas. As T **181**, showing Helmet Guineafowl, each with festive frame. Multicoloured.

744	(–) Guineafowl facing right	15	20
745	$1 Guineafowl in grass	30	30
746	$1.10 Guineafowl on rock	35	40
747	$1.50 Guineafowl in desert	50	55

No. 744 is inscribed "standard postage" and was initially sold at 50 c.

190 Flame Lily

191 John Muafangejo

1997. Flora and Fauna. Multicoloured.

749	5 c. Type **190**	10	10
750	10 c. Bushman poison	10	10
751	20 c. Camel's foot	10	10
752	30 c. Western rhigozum	10	10
753	40 c. Blue-checked bee-eater	10	10
754	50 c. Laughing dove	10	10
755	(–) Peach-faced lovebird	10	10
756	60 c. Lappet-faced vulture	10	10
757	90 c. Yellow-billed hornbill	20	25
758	$1 Lilac-breasted roller	20	25
759	$1.10 Hippopotamus	20	25
760	$1.20 Giraffe	30	35
761	(–) Leopard	30	35
762	$1.50 Elephant	30	35
763	$2 Lion	40	45
764	$4 Buffalo	80	85
765	$5 Black rhinoceros	1·00	1·10
766	$10 Cheetah	2·00	2·10

No. 755 is inscribed "standard postage" and was initially sold at 50 c.; No. 761 is inscribed "postcard rate" and was initially sold at $1.20.

Nos. 755, 758 and 761 exist with ordinary or self-adhesive gum.

1997. 10th Death Anniv of John Muafangejo (artist).

770 **191**	(50 c.) multicoloured	15	20

No. 770 is inscribed "STANDARD POSTAGE" and was initially sold at 50 c.

192 Gabriel B. Taapopi

1998. Gabriel B. Taapopi (writer) Commemoration.

771 **192**	(–) silver and brown	10	10

No. 771 is inscribed "STANDARD POSTAGE" and was initially sold at 50 c.

194 Leopard

1998. Large Wild Cats. Multicoloured.

782	$1.20 Type **194**	20	25
783	$1.90 Lioness and cub	40	45
784	$2 Lion	40	45
785	$2.50 Cheetah	50	55

195 Narra Plant

196 Collecting Rain Water

1998. Narra Cultivation.

787 **195**	$2.40 multicoloured	35	40

1998. World Water Day.

788 **196**	(–) multicoloured	10	10

No. 788 is inscribed "STANDARD POSTAGE" and was initially sold at 50 c. On 1 April 1998 the standard postage rate was increased to 55 c.

197 White-faced Scops Owl

1998. Owls of Namibia. Multicoloured.

790	55 c. Black-tailed tree rat (20 × 24 mm)	10	10
791	$1.50 Type **197**	30	35
792	$1.50 Barred owl	30	35
793	$1.90 Spotted eagle owl	40	45
794	$1.90 Barn owl (61 × 24 mm)	40	45

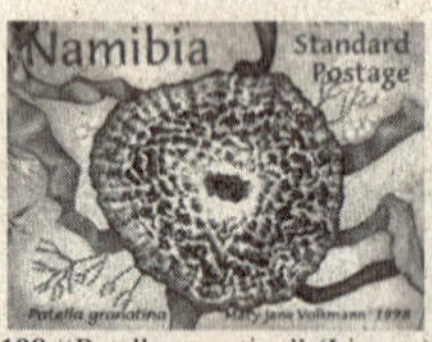

198 "Patella ganatina" (Limpet)

1998. Shells. Multicoloured.

795	(–) Type **198**	10	10
796	$1.10 "Cymatium cutaceum africanum" (Triton)	20	25
797	$1.50 "Conus mozambicus" (Cone)	30	35
798	$6 "Venus verrucosa" (Venus clam)	1·25	1·40

No. 795 is inscribed "Standard Postage" and was initially sold at 55 c.

201 Namibian Beach

1998. World Environment Day. Multicoloured.

802	(–) Type **201**	10	10
803	$1.10 Okavango sunset	20	25
804	$1.50 Sossusvlei	30	35
805	$1.90 African Moringo tree	40	45

No. 802 is inscribed "STANDARD POSTAGE" and was initially sold at 55 c.

204 Carmine Bee-eater

1998. Wildlife of the Caprivi Strip. Multicoloured.

808	60 c. Type **204**	10	15
809	60 c. Sable antelope (40 × 40 mm)	10	15
810	60 c. Lechwe (40 × 40 mm)	10	15
811	60 c. Woodland waterberry	10	15
812	60 c. Nile monitor (40 × 40 mm)	10	15
813	60 c. African jacana	10	15
814	60 c. African fish eagle	10	15
815	60 c. Woodland kingfisher	10	15
816	60 c. Nile crocodile (55 × 30 mm)	10	15
817	60 c. Black mamba (32 × 30 mm)	10	15

Nos. 808/17 were printed together, se-tenant, with the backgrounds forming a composite design.

NANDGAON

A state of central India. Now uses Indian stamps.

12 pies = 1 anna; 16 annas = 1 rupee

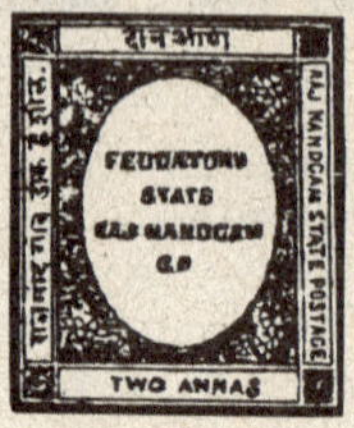

1

2 (2 a.)

1891. Imperf.

1 **1**	$\frac{1}{2}$ a. blue	3·75	£110
2	2 a. pink	17·00	£300

1893. Imperf.

5 **2**	$\frac{1}{2}$ a. green	19·00	42·00
6	1 a. red	35·00	85·00
4b	2 a. red	7·00	55·00

OFFICIAL STAMPS

1893. Optd **M.B.D.** in oval.

O1 **1**	$\frac{1}{2}$ a. blue	£350	
O4 **2**	$\frac{1}{2}$ a. green	4·50	7·50
O5	1 a. red	7·00	26·00
O6	2 a. red	6·00	16·00

NATAL

On the east coast of S. Africa. Formerly a British Colony, later a province of the Union of S. Africa.

12 pence = 1 shilling;
20 shillings = 1 pound

1

1857. Embossed stamps. Various designs.

1 **1**	1d. red	—	£1700
2	1d. buff	—	£1000
3	1d. blue	—	£1100
4	3d. red	—	£400
5 –	6d. green	—	£1100
6 –	9d. blue	—	£7000
7 –	1s. buff	—	£5500

The 3d., 6d., 9d. and 1s. are larger. Beware of reprints.

6

7

1859.

19 **6**	1d. red	85·00	25·00
12	3d. blue	£100	32·00
13	6d. grey	£160	50·00
24	6d. violet	40·00	26·00

1867.

25 **7**	1s. green	£130	27·00

1869. Variously optd **POSTAGE** or **Postage.**

50 **6**	1d. red	85·00	30·00
82	1d. yellow	70·00	65·00
53	3d. blue	£140	40·00
83	6d. violet	50·00	5·50
84 **7**	1s. green	80·00	4·75

1870. Optd **POSTAGE** in a curve.

59 **7**	1s. green	65·00	10·00
108	1s. orange	3·50	85

1870. Optd **POSTAGE** twice, reading up and down.

60 **6**	1d. red	70·00	13·00
61	3d. blue	75·00	13·00
62	6d. violet	£150	25·00

1873. Optd **POSTAGE** once, reading up.

63 **7**	1s. brown	£140	18·00

23

28

16

1874. Queen Victoria. Various frames.

97a	23	½d. green	1·00	30
99	–	1d. red	1·75	10
107	–	2d. olive	2·25	1·40
113	28	2½d. blue	3·50	50
68	–	3d. blue	85·00	14·00
101	–	3d. grey	2·50	95
102	–	4d. brown	3·00	75
103	–	6d. lilac	3·25	80
73	16	5s. red	60·00	26·00

1877. No. 99 surch ½ HALF.

85		½d. on 1d. red	22·00	65·00

POSTAGE
Half-penny
(21)

POSTAGE.
Half-Penny
(29)

1877. Surch as T 21.

91	6	½d. on 1d. yellow	8·00	12·00
92		1d. on 6d. violet	50·00	8·50
93		1d. on 6d. red	95·00	35·00

1885. Surch in words.

104		½d. on 1d. red (No. 99)	16·00	11·00
105		2d. on 3d. grey (No. 101)	18·00	5·50
109		2½d. on 4d. brown (No. 102)	11·00	8·50

1895. No. 23 surch with T 29.

114	6	½d. on 6d. violet	1·25	2·75

1895. No. 99 surch HALF.

125		HALF on 1d. red	1·00	75

31

32

1902.

127	31	½d. green	90	15
128		1d. red	3·25	15
129		1½d. green and black	1·75	1·75
130		2d. red and olive	1·25	25
131		2½d. blue	1·25	3·00
132		3d. purple and grey	1·00	90
152		4d. red and brown	2·75	1·00
134		5d. black and orange	1·50	2·75
135		6d. green and purple	1·50	1·75
136		1s. red and blue	2·75	1·75
137		2s. green and violet	48·00	9·00
138		2s. 6d. purple	35·00	12·00
139		4s. red and yellow	60·00	70·00
140	32	5s. blue and red	20·00	9·00
141		10s. red and purple	60·00	26·00
142		£1 black and blue	£140	48·00
143		£1.10s. green and violet	£275	80·00
162		£1.10s. orange & purple	£1000	£1800
144		£5 mauve and black	£1800	£475
145		£10 green and orange	£6000	£2500
145a		£20 red and green	£12000	£5500

1908. As T 31/2 but inscr "POSTAGE POSTAGE".

165	31	6d. purple	4·50	2·25
166		1s. black on green	6·00	2·00
167		2s. purple & blue on blue	15·00	3·00
168		2s. 6d. black & red on blue	25·00	3·00
169	32	5s. green & red on yellow	18·00	20·00
170		10s. green & red on green	50·00	55·00
171		£1 purple & black on red	£225	£190

OFFICIAL STAMPS

1904. Optd OFFICIAL.

O1	31	½d. green	3·00	35
O2		1d. red	2·00	60
O3		2d. red and olive	17·00	9·50
O4		3d. purple and grey	9·00	4·00
O5		6d. green and purple	30·00	38·00
O6		1s. red and blue	90·00	£150

NAURU

An island in the W. Pacific Ocean, formerly a German possession and then administered by Australia under trusteeship. Became a Republic on 31 January 1968.

1916. 12 pence = 1 shilling;
20 shillings = 1 pound.
1966. 100 cents = 1 Australian dollar.

1916. Stamps of Gt. Britain (King George V) optd NAURU.

1	105	½d. green	1·50	6·00
2	104	1d. red	1·50	4·00
15	105	1½d. brown	23·00	40·00
4	106	2d. orange	2·00	9·50
6	104	2½d. blue	2·75	7·00
7	106	3d. violet	2·00	3·50
8		4d. green	2·00	8·50
9	107	5d. brown	2·25	8·50
10		6d. purple	3·25	10·00
11	108	9d. black	8·50	19·00
12		1s. brown	7·00	19·00
25	109	2s. 6d. brown	65·00	95·00
22		5s. red	£100	£140
23		10s. blue	£250	£325

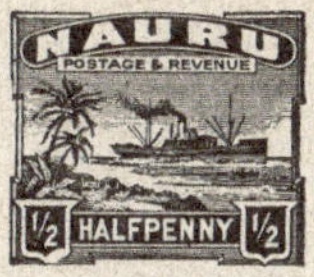

4

6

1924.

26A	4	½d. brown	1·50	2·75
27B		1d. green	2·50	3·00
28B		1½d. red	90	1·50
29B		2d. orange	1·75	8·00
30dB		2½d. blue	1·75	3·75
31cB		3d. blue	2·50	9·50
32B		4d. green	4·25	11·00
33B		5d. brown	3·50	4·00
34B		6d. violet	3·25	4·50
35A		9d. brown	8·50	19·00
36B		1s. red	5·50	2·75
37B		2s. 6d. green	25·00	35·00
38B		5s. purple	35·00	50·00
39B		10s. yellow	£100	£130

1935. Silver Jubilee. Optd HIS MAJESTY'S JUBILEE. 1910-1935.

40	4	1½d. red	75	80
41		2d. orange	1·25	4·00
42		2½d. blue	1·50	1·50
43		1s. red	5·00	3·50

1937. Coronation.

44	6	1½d. red	45	1·25
45		2d. orange	45	1·75
46		2½d. blue	45	60
47		1s. purple	65	90

8 Anibare Bay

18 "Iyo" ("calophyllum")

21 White Tern

1954.

48	–	½d. violet	20	40
49a	8	1d. green	20	40
50	–	3½d. red	1·50	60
51	–	4d. blue	1·50	1·75
52	–	6d. orange	70	20
53	–	9d. red	60	20
54	–	1s. purple	30	20
55	–	2s. 6d. green	2·75	1·00
56	–	5s. mauve	9·00	2·75

DESIGNS—HORIZ: ½d. Nauruan netting fish; 3½d. Loading phosphate from cantilever; 4d. Great frigate bird; 6d. Canoe; 9d. Domaneab (meeting house); 2s. 6d. Buada Lagoon. VERT: 1s. Palm trees; 5s. Map of Nauru.

1963.

57	–	2d. multicoloured	75	2·25
58	–	3d. multicoloured	55	35
59	18	5d. multicoloured	55	75
60	–	8d. black and green	2·50	80
61	–	10d. black	50	30
62	21	1s. 3d. blue, black & green	3·75	4·00
63	–	2s. 3d. blue	3·50	55
64	–	3s. 3d. multicoloured	3·75	2·75

DESIGNS—VERT (As Type 21): 2d. Micronesian pigeon. (26 × 29 mm): 10d. Capparis (flower). HORIZ (As Type 18): 3d. Poison nut (flower); 8d. Black lizard; 2s. 3d. Coral pinnacles. 3s. 3d. Finsch's reed warbler.

1965. 50th Anniv of Gallipoli Landing. As T 184 of Australia, but slightly larger 22 × 34½ mm.

65		5d. sepia, black and green	15	10

24 Anibare Bay

27 "Towards the Sunrise"

1966. Decimal Currency. As earlier issues but with values in cents and dollars as in T 24. Some colours changed.

66	24	1 c. blue	15	10
67	–	2 c. purple (as No. 48)	15	40
68	–	3 c. green (as No. 50)	30	1·25
69	–	4 c. multicoloured (as T 18)	25	10
70	–	5 c. blue (as No. 54)	25	60
71	–	7 c. black and brown (as No. 60)	30	10
72	–	8 c. green (as No. 61)	30	10
73	–	10 c. red (as No. 51)	40	10
74	–	15 c. blue, black and green (as T 21)	80	1·50
75	–	25 c. brown (as No. 63)	45	60
76	–	30 c. mult (as No. 58)	70	30
77	–	35 c. mult (as No. 64)	1·25	35
78	–	50 c. mult (as No. 57)	2·50	80
79	–	$1 mauve (as No. 56)	2·00	1·00

The 25 c. is as No. 63 but larger, 27½ × 25 mm.

1968. Nos. 66/79 optd REPUBLIC OF NAURU.

80	24	1 c. blue	10	30
81	–	2 c. purple	10	10
82	–	3 c. green	15	10
83	–	4 c. multicoloured	15	10
84	–	5 c. blue	15	10
85	–	7 c. black and brown	25	10
86	–	8 c. green	25	10
87	–	10 c. red	30	15
88	–	15 c. blue, black and green	2·25	2·50
89	–	25 c. brown	30	15
90	–	30 c. multicoloured	55	15
91	–	35 c. multicoloured	2·00	30
92	–	50 c. multicoloured	2·00	50
93	–	$1 purple	1·25	75

1968. Independence.

94	27	5 c. multicoloured	10	10
95	–	10 c. black, green & blue	10	10

DESIGN: 10 c. Planting seedling, and Map.

29 Flag of Independent Nauru

1969.

96	29	15 c. yellow, orange & blue	40	15

30 Island, "C" and Stars

1972. 25th Anniv of South Pacific Commission.

97	30	25 c. multicoloured	30	30

1973. 5th Anniv of Independence. No. 96 optd Independence 1968–1973.

98	29	15 c. yellow, orange & blue	20	30

32 Denea

33 Artefacts and Map

1973. Multicoloured.

99	1 c. Ekwenababae	50	20
100	2 c. Kauwe iud	65	20
101	3 c. Rimone	65	20
102	4 c. Type 32	65	40
103	5 c. Erekogo	65	40
104	7 c. Racoon butterflyfish ("Ikimago")	30	40
105	8 c. Catching flying fish	30	20
106	10 c. Itsibweb (ball game)	30	20
107	15 c. Nauruan wrestling	35	20
108	20 c. Snaring great frigate birds	50	30
109	25 c. Nauruan girl	50	30
110	30 c. Catching common noddy birds	85	40
111	50 c. Great frigate birds	1·25	75
112	$1 Type 33	1·25	75

Nos. 104/106 and 110/111 are horiz designs.

34 Co-op Store

1973. 50th Anniv of Nauru Co-operative Society. Multicoloured.

113		5 c. Type 34	20	30
114		25 c. Timothy Detudamo (founder)	20	15
115		50 c. N.C.S. trademark (vert)	45	55

35 Phosphate Mining

1974. 175th Anniv of First Contact with the Outside World. Multicoloured.

116	7 c. M.V. "Eigamoiya" (bulk carrier)	1·00	90
117	10 c. Type 35	75	25
118	15 c. Fokker Fellowship "Nauru Chief"	1·00	30
119	25 c. Nauruan chief in early times	85	35
120	35 c. Capt. Fearn and H.M.S. "Hunter" (70 × 22 mm)	4·00	2·50
121	50 c. H.M.S. "Hunter" off Nauru (70 × 22 mm)	2·00	1·40

36 Map of Nauru

37 Rev. P. A. Delaporte

1974. Centenary of U.P.U. Multicoloured.

122	5 c. Type 36	20	20
123	8 c. Nauru Post Office	20	20
124	20 c. Nauruan postman	20	10
125	$1 U.P.U. Building and Nauruan flag	50	60

1974. Christmas and 75th Anniv of Rev. Delaporte's Arrival.

127	37	15 c. multicoloured	20	20
128		20 c. multicoloured	30	30

38 Map of Nauru, Lump of Phosphate Rock and Albert Ellis

1975. Phosphate Mining Anniversaries. Mult.

129	5 c. Type 38	30	40
130	7 c. Coolies and mine	40	40
131	15 c. Electric phosphate train, barges and ship	1·25	1·40
132	25 c. Modern ore extraction	1·50	1·50

ANNIVERSARIES: 5 c. 75th anniv of discovery; 7 c. 70th anniv of Mining Agreement; 15 c. 55th anniv of British Phosphate Commissioners; 25 c. 5th anniv of Nauru Phosphate Corporation.

39 Micronesian Outrigger

41 "Our Lady" (Yaren Church)

40 New Civic Centre

1975. South Pacific Commission Conf, Nauru (1st issue). Multicoloured.

133	20 c. Type 39	75	40
134	20 c. Polynesian double-hull	75	40
135	20 c. Melanesian outrigger	75	40
136	20 c. Polynesian outrigger	75	40

1975. South Pacific Commission Conf, Nauru (2nd issue). Multicoloured.

137	30 c. Type 40	15	15
138	50 c. Domaneab (meeting-house)	30	30

1975. Christmas. Stained-glass Windows. Multicoloured.

139	5 c. Type 41	15	15
140	7 c. "Suffer little children" (Orro Church)	15	15
141	15 c. As 7 c.	30	55
142	25 c. Type 41	45	70

42 Flowers floating towards Nauru

1976. 30th Anniv of Islanders' Return from Truk. Multicoloured.

143 10 c. Type **42** 10 10
144 14 c. Nauru encircled by garland 15 10
145 25 c. Finsch's reed warbler and maps 35 25
146 40 c. Return of the islanders . 45 35

43 3d. and 9d. Stamps of 1916

1976. 60th Anniv of Nauruan Stamps. Mult.

147 10 c. Type **43** 15 15
148 15 c. 6d. and 1s. stamps . . . 20 15
149 25 c. 2s. 6d. stamp 30 25
150 50 c. 5s. "Specimen" stamp . . 40 35

44 "Pandanus mei" and "Enna G" (cargo liner)

1976. South Pacific Forum, Nauru. Mult.

151 10 c. Type **44** 15 10
152 20 c. "Tournefortia argentea" with Boeing 737 and Fokker Fellowship aircraft 20 15
153 30 c. "Thespesia populnea" and Nauru Tracking Station . . 25 15
154 40 c. "Cordia subcordata" and produce 35 25

45 Nauruan Choir

46 Nauru House and Coral Pinnacles

1976. Christmas. Multicoloured.

155 15 c. Type **45** 10 10
156 15 c. Nauruan choir 10 10
157 20 c. Angel in white dress . . 15 15
158 20 c. Angel in red dress . . . 15 15

1977. Opening of Nauru House, Melbourne. Multicoloured.

159 15 c. Type **46** 15 15
160 30 c. Nauru House and Melbourne skyline 25 25

47 Cable Ship "Anglia"

48 Father Kayser and First Catholic Church

1977. 75th Anniv of First Trans-Pacific Cable and 20th Anniv of First Artificial Earth Satellite.

161 **47** 7 c. multicoloured 30 10
162 – 15 c. blue, grey and black . . 40 15
163 – 20 c. blue, grey and black . . 40 20
164 – 25 c. multicoloured 45 20

DESIGNS: 15 c. Tracking station, Nauru; 20 c. Stern of "Anglia"; 25 c. Dish aerial.

1977. Christmas. Multicoloured.

165 15 c. Type **48** 10 10
166 25 c. Congregational Church, Orro 15 15
167 30 c. Catholic Church, Arubo . . 15 15

49 Arms of Nauru

1978. 10th Anniv of Independence.

168 **49** 15 c. multicoloured . . . 20 15
169 60 c. multicoloured . . . 35 30

1978. Nos. 159/60 surch.

170 **46** 4 c. on 15 c. multicoloured 70 1·75
171 5 c. on 15 c. multicoloured 70 1·75
172 – 8 c. on 30 c. multicoloured 70 1·75
173 – 10 c. on 30 c. multicoloured 70 1·75

51 Collecting Shellfish

1978.

174 **51** 1 c. multicoloured 50 30
175 – 2 c. multicoloured 50 30
176 – 3 c. multicoloured 90 40
177 – 4 c. brown, blue and black 50 30
178 – 5 c. multicoloured . . . . 1·50 40
179 – 7 c. multicoloured 30 55
180 – 10 c. multicoloured . . . 30 20
181 – 15 c. multicoloured . . . 40 30
182 – 20 c. grey, black and blue . 30 30
183 – 25 c. multicoloured . . . 30 30
184 – 30 c. multicoloured . . . 1·50 45
185 – 32 c. multicoloured . . . 2·00 65
186 – 40 c. multicoloured . . . 1·50 1·50
187 – 50 c. multicoloured . . . 85 75
188 – $1 multicoloured 70 55
189 – $2 multicoloured . . . . 95 1·00
190 – $5 grey, black and blue . . 1·50 2·25

DESIGNS: 2 c. Coral outcrop; 3 c. Reef scene; 4 c. Girl with fish; 5 c. Eastern reef heron; 7 c. Catching fish, Buada Lagoon; 10 c. Ijuw Lagoon; 15 c. Girl framed by coral; 20 c. Pinnacles, Anibare Bay reef; 25 c. Pinnacle at Meneng; 30 c. Head of great frigate bird; 32 c. White-capped noddy birds in coconut palm; 40 c. Wandering tattler; 50 c. Great frigate birds on perch; $1 Old coral pinnacles at Topside; $2 New pinnacles at Topside; $5 Blackened pinnacles at Topside.

52 A.P.U. Emblem

53 Virgin and Child

1978. 14th General Assembly of Asian Parliamentarians' Union, Nauru.

191 **52** 15 c. multicoloured . . . 20 25
192 – 20 c. black, blue and gold 20 25

DESIGN: 20 c. As Type **52**, but with different background.

1978. Christmas. Multicoloured.

193 7 c. Type **53** 10 10
194 15 c. Angel in sun-rise scene (horiz) 10 10
195 20 c. As 15 c. 15 15
196 30 c. Type **53** 20 20

54 Baden-Powell and Cub Scout

1978. 70th Anniv of Boy Scout Movement. Multicoloured.

197 20 c. Type **54** 20 15
198 30 c. Scout 25 20
199 50 c. Rover Scout 35 30

55 Wright Flyer I over Nauru

1979. Flight Anniversaries. Multicoloured.

200 10 c. Type **55** 20 15
201 15 c. Fokker F.VIIa/3m "Southern Cross" superimposed on nose of Boeing 737 . . . . 30 20
202 15 c. "Southern Cross" and Boeing 737 (front view) . . . 30 20
203 30 c. Wright Flyer I over Nauru airfield 55 30

ANNIVERSARIES: Nos. 200, 203, 75th anniv of powered flight; Nos. 201/2, 50th anniv of Kingsford-Smith's Pacific flight.

56 Sir Rowland Hill and Marshall Islands 10 pf. stamp of 1901

1979. Death Cent of Sir Rowland Hill. Mult.

204 5 c. Type **56** 15 10
205 15 c. Sir Rowland Hill and "Nauru" opt on G.B. 10s. "Seahorse" stamp of 1916–23 25 20
206 60 c. Sir Rowland Hill and Nauru 60 c. 10th anniv of Independence stamp, 1978 . 55 40

57 Dish Antenna, Transmitting Station and Radio Mast

1979. 50th Anniv of International Consultative Radio Committee. Multicoloured.

208 7 c. Type **57** 15 10
209 32 c. Telex operator 35 25
210 40 c. Radio operator 40 25

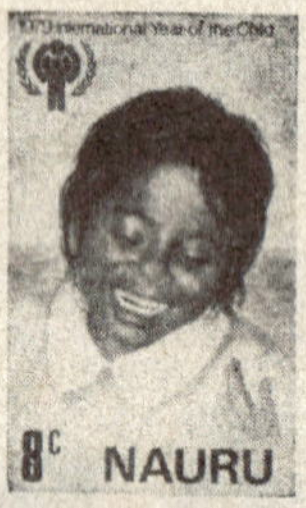

58 Smiling Child

1979. International Year of the Child.

211 **58** 8 c. multicoloured 10 10
212 – 15 c. multicoloured . . . 15 15
213 – 25 c. multicoloured . . . 20 20
214 – 32 c. multicoloured . . . 20 20
215 – 50 c. multicoloured . . . 25 25

DESIGNS: 15 c. to 50 c. Smiling children.

59 Ekwenababae (flower), Scroll inscribed "Peace on Earth" and Star

1979. Christmas. Multicoloured.

216 7 c. Type **59** 10 10
217 15 c. "Thespia populnea" (flower), scroll inscribed "Goodwill towards Men" and star 10 10
218 20 c. Denea (flower), scroll inscribed "Peace on Earth" and star 10 10
219 30 c. Erekogo (flower), scroll inscribed "Goodwill toward Men" and star 20 20

60 Dassault Bregeut Mystere Falcon 50 over Melbourne

1980. 10th Anniv of Air Nauru. Mult.

220 15 c. Type **60** 35 15
221 20 c. Fokker F.28 Fellowship over Tarawa 40 15
222 25 c. Boeing 727-100 over Hong Kong 40 15
223 30 c. Boeing 737 over Auckland 40 15

61 Steam Locomotive

1980. 10th Anniv of Nauru Phosphate Corporation. Multicoloured.

224 8 c. Type **61** 10 10
225 32 c. Electric locomotive . . . 20 20
226 60 c. Diesel-hydraulic locomotive 35 35

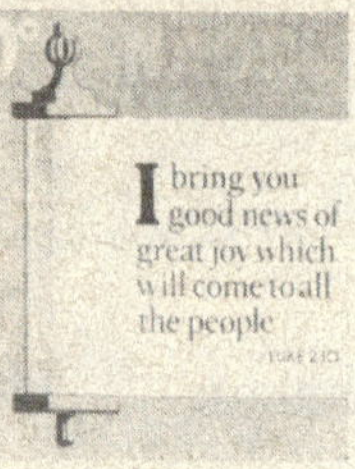

62 Verse 10 from Luke, Chapter 2 in English

1980. Christmas. Verses from Luke, Chapter 2. Multicoloured.

228 20 c. Type **62** 10 10
229 20 c. Verse 10 in Nauruan . . 10 10
230 30 c. Verse 14 in English . . . 15 15
231 30 c. Verse 14 in Nauruan . . 15 15

See also Nos. 248/51.

63 Nauruan, Australia, Union and New Zealand Flags on Aerial View of Nauru

1980. 20th Anniv of U.N. Declaration on the Granting of Independence to Colonial Countries and Peoples. Multicoloured.

232 25 c. Type **63** 15 15
233 50 c. U.N. Trusteeship Council (72 × 23 mm) 15 15
234 50 c. Nauru independence ceremony, 1968 (72 × 23 mm) 25 25

64 Timothy Detudamo

1981. 30th Anniv of Nauru Local Government Council. Head Chiefs. Multicoloured.

235 20 c. Type **64** 15 15
236 30 c. Raymond Gadabu . . . 15 15
237 50 c. Hammer DeRoburt . . 25 25

65 Casting Net by Hand

1981. Fishing. Multicoloured.

238 8 c. Type **65** 10 10
239 20 c. Outrigger canoe 20 15
240 32 c. Outboard motor boat . . 25 20
241 40 c. Trawler 30 25

66 Bank of Nauru Emblem and Building

1981. 5th Anniv of Bank of Nauru.

243 **66** $1 multicoloured 60 60

67 Inaugural Speech

1981. U.N. Day. E.S.C.A.P. (United Nations Economic and Social Commission for Asia and the Pacific) Events. Multicoloured.

244 15 c. Type **67** 15 15
245 20 c. Presenting credentials . . 15 15
246 25 c. Unveiling plaque 20 20
247 30 c. Raising U.N. flag . . . 25 25

1981. Christmas. Bible Verses. Designs as T **62**. Multicoloured.

248 20 c. Matthew 1, 23 in English 15 15
249 20 c. Matthew 1, 23 in Nauruan 15 15
250 30 c. Luke 2, 11 in English . . 20 20
251 30 c. Luke 2, 11 in Nauruan . 20 20

68 Earth Satellite Station

1981. 10th Anniv of South Pacific Forum. Multicoloured.

252 10 c. Type **68** 30 20
253 20 c. "Enna G" (cargo liner) . 35 25
254 30 c. Boeing 737 airliner . . . 35 30
255 40 c. Local produce 45 40

69 Nauru Scouts leaving for 1935 Frankston Scout Jamboree

1982. 75th Anniv of Boy Scout Movement. Multicoloured.

256 7 c. Type **69** 15 15
257 8 c. Two Nauru scouts on "Nauru Chief", 1935 (vert) . 15 15
258 15 c. Nauru scouts making pottery, 1935 (vert) 15 20
259 20 c. Lord Huntingfield addressing Nauru scouts, Frankston Jamboree, 1935 . 20 25
260 25 c. Nauru cub and scout, 1982 20 30
261 40 c. Nauru cubs, scouts and scouters, 1982 . . . . 30 45

70 100 kw Electricity Generating Plant under Construction (left side)

1982. Ocean Thermal Energy Conversion. Multicoloured.

263 25 c. Type **70** 50 30
264 25 c. 100 kw Electricity Generating Plant under construction (right side) . . 50 30
265 40 c. Completed plant (left) . 70 40
266 40 c. Completed plant (right) . 70 40

Nos. 263/4 and 265/6 were each issued as horizontal se-tenant pairs, forming composite designs.

71 S.S. "Fido"

1982. 75th Anniv of Phosphate Shipments. Multicoloured.

267 5 c. Type **71** 55 10
268 10 c. Steam locomotive "Nellie" 80 20
269 30 c. Class "Clyde" diesel locomotive 90 50
270 60 c. M.V. "Eigamoiya" (bulk carrier) 95 80

72 Queen Elizabeth II on Horseback

1982. Royal Visit. Multicoloured.

272 20 c. Type **72** 40 30
273 50 c. Prince Philip, Duke of Edinburgh 50 60
274 $1 Queen Elizabeth II and Prince Philip (horiz) . . . . . . 80 1·25

73 Father Bernard Lahn

1982. Christmas. Multicoloured.

275 10 c. Type **73** 30 30
276 30 c. Reverend Itubwa Amram 35 45
277 40 c. Pastor James Aingimen 40 70
278 50 c. Bishop Paul Mea . . . 40 1·00

74 Speaker of the Nauruan Parliament

75 Nauru Satellite Earth Station

1983. 15th Anniv of Independence. Mult.

279 15 c. Type **74** 15 15
280 20 c. Family Court in session 20 20
281 30 c. Law Courts building (horiz) 25 25
282 50 c. Parliamentary chamber (horiz) 40 40

1983. World Communications Year. Mult.

283 5 c. Type **75** 20 10
284 10 c. Omni-directional range installation 20 15
285 20 c. Emergency short-wave radio 25 25
286 25 c. Radio Nauru control room 40 30
287 40 c. Unloading air mail . . . 90 45

76 Return of Exiles from Truk on M.V. "Trienza", 1946

1983. Angam Day. Multicoloured.

288 15 c. Type **76** 20 25
289 20 c. Mrs. Elsie Agio (exile community leader) 20 25
290 30 c. Child on scales 35 40
291 40 c. Nauruan children . . . 45 50

Nos. 289/91 are vert, each 25 × 41 mm.

77 "The Holy Virgin, Holy Child and St. John" (School of Raphael)

78 S.S. "Ocean Queen"

1983. Christmas. Multicoloured.

292 5 c. Type **77** 10 10
293 15 c. "Madonna on the Throne, surrounded by Angels" (School of Sevilla) 20 15
294 50 c. "The Mystical Betrothal of St. Catherine with Jesus" (School of Veronese) (horiz) 60 40

1984. 250th Anniv of "Lloyd's List" (newspaper). Multicoloured.

295 20 c. Type **78** 50 30
296 25 c. M.V "Enna G" 55 35
297 30 c. M.V "Baron Minto" . . 60 40
298 40 c. Sinking of M.V. "Triadic", 1940 . . . . 85 55

79 1974 U.P.U. $1 Stamp

1984. Universal Postal Union Congress, Hamburg.

299 **79** $1 multicoloured . . . . . 1·25 1·25

80 "Hypolimnas bolina" (female)

1984. Butterflies. Multicoloured.

300 25 c. Type **80** 50 40
301 30 c. "Hypolimnas bolina" (male) 55 55
302 50 c. "Danaus plexippus" . . . 70 85

81 Coastal Scene

1984. Life in Nauru. Multicoloured.

303 1 c. Type **81** 10 40
304 3 c. Nauruan woman (vert) . . 15 40
305 5 c. Modern trawler 40 50
306 10 c. Golfer on the links . . . 90 50
307 15 c. Excavating phosphate (vert) 90 65
308 20 c. Surveyor (vert) 65 55
309 25 c. Air Nauru Boeing 727 airliner 80 55
310 30 c. Elderly Nauruan (vert) . . 50 50
311 40 c. Loading hospital patient on to Boeing 727 aircraft . . . 90 55
312 50 c. Skin-diver with fish (vert) 1·00 80
313 $1 Tennis player (vert) . . . . 2·50 3·25
314 $2 Anabar Lagoon . . . . . . 2·50 3·75

82 Buada Chapel

1984. Christmas. Multicoloured.

315 30 c. Type **82** 60 50
316 40 c. Detudamo Memorial Church 80 65
317 50 c. Candle-light service, Kayser College (horiz) 90 70

83 Air Nauru Boeing 737 Jet on Tarmac

1985. 15th Anniv of Air Nauru. Mult.

318 20 c. Type **83** 65 35
319 30 c. Stewardesses on Boeing 737 aircraft steps (vert) 85 60
320 40 c. Fokker F.28 Fellowship over Nauru . . . . 1·10 75
321 50 c. Freight being loaded onto Boeing 727 (vert) . . . . . 1·25 85

84 Open Cut Mining

1985. 15th Anniv of Nauru Phosphate Corporation. Multicoloured.

322 20 c. Type **84** 80 60
323 25 c. Diesel locomotive hauling crushed ore . . . . 1·50 1·00
324 30 c. Phosphate drying plant . 1·50 1·00
325 50 c. Early steam locomotive . 2·25 1·75

85 Mother and Baby on Beach

86 Adult Common Noddy with Juvenile

1985. Christmas. Multicoloured.

326 50 c. Beach scene . . . . . . 1·40 2·00
327 50 c. Type **85** . . . . 1·40 2·00

Nos. 326/7 were printed se-tenant forming a composite design.

1985. Birth Bicentenary of John J. Audubon (ornithologist). Common ("Brown") Noddy. Multicoloured.

328 10 c. Type **86** 35 35
329 20 c. Adult and immature birds in flight 50 70
330 30 c. Adults in flight 65 85
331 50 c. "Brown Noddy" (John J. Audubon) . . . . 80 1·10

87 Douglas Motor Cycle

1986. Early Transport on Nauru. Mult.

332 15 c. Type **87** 80 70
333 20 c. Primitive lorry 95 95
334 30 c. German-built steam locomotive, 1910 . . . . . 1·50 1·50
335 40 c. "Baby" Austin car . . . 1·75 1·75

88 Island and Bank of Nauru

1986. 10th Anniv of Bank of Nauru. Children's Paintings. Multicoloured.

336 20 c. Type **88** 30 30
337 25 c. Borrower with notes and coins 35 35
338 30 c. Savers 40 40
339 40 c. Customers at bank counter 55 55

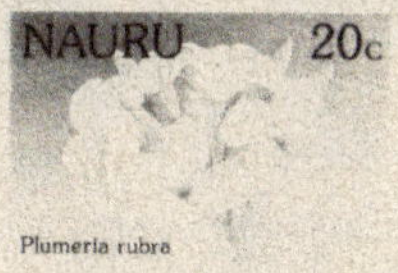

89 "Plumeria rubra"

1986. Flowers. Multicoloured.

340 20 c. Type **89** 55 70
341 25 c. "Tristellateia australis" . 65 85
342 30 c. "Bougainvillea cultivar" 75 1·00
343 40 c. "Delonix regia" . . . . 1·00 1·25

90 Carol Singers

1986. Christmas. Multicoloured.

344 20 c. Type **90** 45 30
345 $1 Carol singers and hospital patient . . . . 2·00 3·00

91 Young Girls Dancing

1987. Nauruan Dancers. Multicoloured.

346 20 c. Type **91** 80 80
347 30 c. Stick dance . . . . . . 1·00 1·25
348 50 c. Boy doing war dance (vert) 1·75 2·50

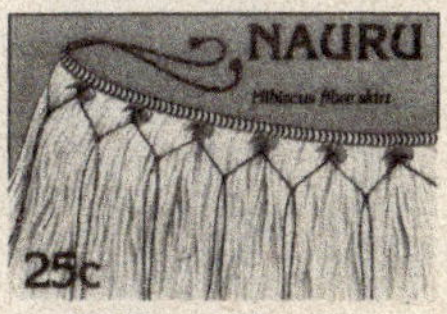

92 Hibiscus Fibre Skirt

1987. Personal Artefacts. Multicoloured.

349 25 c. Type **92** 75 75
350 30 c. Headband and necklets . . 85 85
351 45 c. Decorative necklets . . . 1·10 1·10
352 60 c. Pandanus leaf fan . . . 1·60 1·60

93 U.P.U. Emblem and Air Mail Label

94 Open Bible

1987. World Post Day.
353 93 40 c. multicoloured 90 75

1987. Centenary of Nauru Congregational Church.
355 94 40 c. multicoloured . . . . 75 1·00

95 Nauruan Children's Party

1987. Christmas. Multicoloured.
356 20 c. Type **95** 75 50
357 $1 Nauruan Christmas dinner . 2·75 3·25

96 Loading Phosphate on Ship

1988. 20th Anniv of Independence. Mult.
358 25 c. Type **96** . . . . 1·00 1·00
359 40 c. Tomano flower (vert) . . 1·50 1·50
360 55 c. Great frigate bird (vert) . 2·25 2·25
361 $1 Arms of Republic (35 × 35 mm) . . . . . . 2·50 3·50

97 Map of German Marshall Is. and 1901 5 m. Yacht Definitive

1988. 80th Anniv of Nauru Post Office. Mult.
362 30 c. Type **97** 75 75
363 50 c. Letter and post office of 1908 . . . . 1·00 1·25
364 70 c. Nauru Post Office and airmail letter . . . . 1·25 1·50

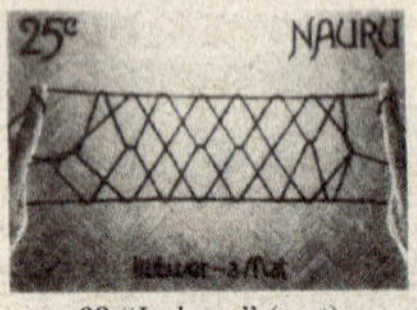

98 "Itubwer" (mat)

1988. String Figures. Multicoloured.
365 25 c. Type **98** 35 35
366 40 c. "Etegerer – the Pursuer" . 50 60
367 55 c. "Holding up the Sky" . 65 70
368 80 c. "Manujie's Sword . . . 1·00 1·25

99 U.P.U. Emblem and National Flag

1988. Cent of Nauru's Membership of U.P.U.
369 99 $1 multicoloured . . . . . 1·25 1·25

100 "Hark the Herald Angels"

1988. Christmas. Designs showing words and music from "Hark the Herald Angels Sing".
370 100 20 c. black, red & yellow . 40 30
371 – 60 c. black, red & mauve . 1·00 85
372 – $1 black, red and green . 1·60 1·40

101 Logo (15th anniv of Nauru Insurance Corporation)

102 Mother and Baby

1989. Anniversaries and Events. Mult.
373 15 c. Type **101** 30 30
374 50 c. Logos (World Telecommunications Day and 10th anniv of Asian-Pacific Telecommunity) 75 85
375 $1 Photograph of island scene (150 years of photography) 1·75 2·00
376 $2 Capitol and U.P.U. emblem (20th U.P.U. Congress, Washington) . . . . 2·75 3·75

1989. Christmas. Multicoloured.
377 20 c. Type **102** 50 30
378 $1 Children opening presents . 2·25 3·00

103 Eigigu working while Sisters play

104 Early Mining by Hand

1989. 20th Anniv of First Manned Landing on Moon. Legend of "Eigigu, the Girl in the Moon". Multicoloured.
379 25 c. Type **103** . . . . . . 2·50 2·50
380 30 c. Eigigu climbing tree . . 2·75 2·75
381 50 c. Eigigu stealing toddy from blind woman . . . . 4·75 4·75
382 $1 Eigigu on Moon . . . . . 7·00 7·00

1990. 20th Anniv of Nauru Phosphate Corporation. Multicoloured.
383 50 c. Type **104** 75 75
384 $1 Modern mining by excavator 1·25 1·25

105 Sunday School Class

106 Eoiyepiang laying Baby on Mat

1990. Christmas. Multicoloured.
385 25 c. Type **105** 90 90
386 25 c. Teacher telling Christmas story 90 90

Nos. 385/6 were printed together, se-tenant, forming a composite design.

1990. Legend of "Eoiyepiang, the Daughter of Thunder and Lightning". Multicoloured.
387 25 c. Type **106** . . . . 1·00 60
388 30 c. Eoiyepiang making floral decoration . . . . 1·25 70
389 50 c. Eoiyepiang left on snow-covered mountain . . . . 1·75 2·00
390 $1 Eoiyepiang and warrior . 2·75 3·50

107 Oleander

1991. Flowers. Multicoloured.
391 15 c. Type **107** 15 20
392 20 c. Lily 15 20
393 25 c. Passion flower 25 30
394 30 c. Lily (different) 25 30
395 35 c. Caesalpinia 30 35
396 40 c. Clerodendron 35 40
397 45 c. "Baubina pinnata" . . 40 45
398 50 c. Hibiscus (vert) 45 50
399 75 c. Apocymaceae 65 70
400 $1 Bindweed (vert) 90 95
401 $2 Tristellateia (vert) . . . . 1·75 1·90
402 $3 Impala lily (vert) . . . . . 2·50 2·75

109 Star and Symbol of Asian Development Bank

1992. 25th Annual Meeting of Asian Development Bank.
404 109 $1.50 multicoloured . . . 2·00 2·50

110 Gifts under Christmas Tree

1992. Christmas. Children's Paintings. Mult.
405 45 c. Type **110** 75 75
406 60 c. Father Christmas in sleigh 1·00 1·25

111 Hammer DeRoburt

112 Running, Constitution Day Sports

1993. 25th Anniv of Independence and Hammer DeRoburt (former President) Commemoration.
407 111 $1 multicoloured . . . . . 2·00 2·50

1993. 15th Anniv of Constitution Day. Mult.
408 70 c. Type **112** 75 75
409 80 c. Part of Independence Proclamation . . . . 1·00 1·25

113 Great Frigate Birds, Flying Fish and Island

1993. 24th South Pacific Forum Meeting, Nauru. Multicoloured.
410 60 c. Type **113** . . . . 1·40 1·50
411 60 c. Red-tailed tropic bird, great frigate bird, dolphin and island 1·40 1·50
412 60 c. Racoon butterflyfish ("Ikimago"), coral and sea urchins . . . . 1·40 1·50
413 60 c. Three different types of fish with corals . . . . 1·40 1·50

Nos. 410/13 were printed together, se-tenant, forming a composite design.

114 "Peace on Earth, Goodwill to Men" and Star

1993. Christmas. Multicoloured.
415 55 c. Type **114** 85 85
416 65 c. "Hark the Herald Angels Sing" and star 90 90

115 Girls with Dogs

1994. "Hong Kong '94" International Stamp Exhibition. Chinese New Year ("Year of the Dog"). Multicoloured.
417 $1 Type **115** . . . . 1·50 1·75
418 $1 Boys with dogs . . . . . 1·50 1·75

116 Weightlifting

117 Peace Dove and Star over Island

1994. 15th Commonwealth Games, Victoria, Canada.
421 116 $1.50 multicoloured . . . 1·40 1·50

1994. Christmas. Multicoloured.
422 65 c. Type **117** 60 65
423 75 c. Star over Bethlehem . . 70 75

118 Air Nauru Airliner and Emblems

1994. 50th Anniv of I.C.A.O. Multicoloured.
424 55 c. Type **118** 50 55
425 65 c. Control tower, Nauru International Airport . . . 60 65
426 80 c. D.V.O.R. equipment . . 70 75
427 $1 Crash tenders 90 95

119 Emblem and Olympic Rings

1994. Nauru's Entry into International Olympic Committee.
429 119 50 c. multicoloured . . . 45 50

120 Nauruan Flag

1995. 50th Anniv of United Nations (1st issue). Multicoloured.
430 75 c. Type **120** 80 90
431 75 c. Arms of Nauru 80 90
432 75 c. Outrigger canoe on coastline 80 90
433 75 c. Airliner over phosphate freighter 80 90

Nos. 430/3 were printed together, se-tenant, forming a composite design.

See also Nos. 444/5.

121 Signing Phosphate Agreement, 1967

1995. 25th Anniv of Nauru Phosphate Corporation. Multicoloured.
435 60 c. Type **121** 80 90
436 60 c. Pres. Bernard Dowiyogo and Prime Minister Keating of Australia shaking hands . . 80 90

1995. International Stamp Exhibitions. No. 309 surch.
438 50 c. on 25 c. multicoloured (surch "at Beijing") . . . . 1·00 1·10
439 $1 on 25 c. multicoloured (surch "at Jakarta") . . . . 1·25 1·40
440 $1 on 25 c. multicoloured (surch "at Singapore") . . . . . . 1·25 1·40

124 Children playing on Gun

1995. 50th Anniv of Peace. Multicoloured

442		75 c. Type **124**	1·25	1·50
443		$1.50 Children making floral garlands	1·75	2·00

125 Nauru Crest, Coastline and U.N. Anniversary Emblem
126 Young Girl praying

1995. 50th Anniv of United Nations (2nd issue). Multicoloured.

444		75 c. Type **125**	90	1·00
445		$1.50 Aerial view of Nauru and U.N. Headquarters, New York	1·60	2·00

1995. Christmas. Multicoloured.

446		60 c. Type **126**	90	1·00
447		70 c. Man praying	90	1·00

127 Returning Refugees and Head Chief Timothy Detudamo

1996. 50th Anniv of Nauruans' Return from Truk.

448	**127**	75 c. multicoloured	90	1·00
449		$1.25 multicoloured	1·60	2·00

129 Symbolic Athlete

1996. Centenary of Modern Olympic Games. Multicoloured.

452		40 c. Type **129**	60	60
453		50 c. Symbolic weightlifter	70	80
454		60 c. Weightlifter (horiz)	80	90
455		$1 Athlete (horiz)	1·25	1·75

130 The Nativity and Angel

1996. Christmas. Multicoloured.

456		50 c. Type **130**	60	60
457		70 c. Angel, world map and wild animals	80	80

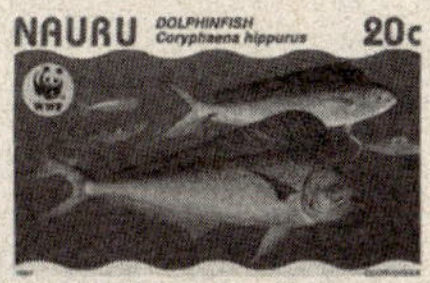

131 Dolphin (fish)

1997. Endangered Species. Fishes. Multicoloured.

458		20 c. Type **131**	45	45
459		30 c. Wahoo	55	55
460		40 c. Sailfish	60	60
461		50 c. Yellow-finned tuna	70	70

132 Statue of Worshipper with Offering
133 Princess Elizabeth and Lieut. Philip Mountbatten, 1947

1997. "HONG KONG '97" International Stamp Exhibition. Statues of different worshippers (1 c. to 15 c.) or Giant Buddha of Hong Kong (25 c.).

462	**132**	1 c. multicoloured	10	10
463	–	2 c. multicoloured	15	15
464	–	5 c. multicoloured	25	25
465	–	10 c. multicoloured	30	30
466	–	12 c. multicoloured	30	30
467	–	15 c. multicoloured	30	30
468	–	25 c. multicoloured	40	40

1997. Golden Wedding of Queen Elizabeth and Prince Philip.

469	**133**	80 c. black and gold	80	85
470	–	$1.20 multicoloured	1·25	1·40

DESIGN: $1.20, Queen Elizabeth and Prince Philip, 1997.

135 Commemorative Pillar

1997. Christmas. 110th Anniv of Nauru Congregational Church. Multicoloured.

473		60 c. Type **135**	50	55
474		80 c. Congregational Church	70	75

137 Juan Antonio Samaranch and Aerial View

1998. Visit of International Olympic Committee President.

476	**137**	$2 multicoloured	1·50	1·60

138 Diana, Princess of Wales
139 Gymnastics

1998. Diana, Princess of Wales Commemoration. Multicoloured.

477		70 c. Type **138**	55	60
478		70 c. Wearing white shirt	55	60
479		70 c. With tiara	55	60
480		70 c. In white jacket	55	60
481		70 c. Wearing pink hat	55	60
482		70 c. In white suit	55	60

1998. 16th Commonwealth Games, Kuala Lumpur, Malaysia. Multicoloured.

483		40 c. Type **139**	30	35
484		60 c. Athletics	45	50
485		70 c. Sprinting	55	60
486		80 c. Weightlifting	60	65

140 Sqn. Ldr. Hicks (Composer of Nauru's National Anthem) conducting

1998. 30th Anniv of Independence. Multicoloured.

488		$1 Type **140**	75	80
489		$2 Sqn. Ldr. Hicks and score	1·50	1·60

141 Palm Trees, Fish, Festive Candle and Flower

1998. Christmas. Multicoloured.

491		85 c. Type **141**	65	70
492		95 c. Flower, present, fruit and island scene	75	80

142 "Hunter" (snow)

1998. Bicentenary of First Contact with the Outside World. Multicoloured.

493		$1.50 Type **142**	1·10	1·25
494		$1.50 Capt. John Fearn	1·10	1·25

NAWANAGAR

A state of India, Bombay District. Now uses Indian stamps.

6 docra = 1 anna

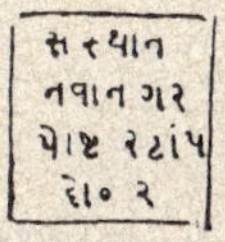
1 (1 docra)
2 (2 docra)

1877. Imperf or perf.

1	**1**	1 doc. blue	50	22·00

1880. Imperf.

6	**2**	1 doc. lilac	2·00	6·50
8c		2 doc. green	2·75	7·00
9b		3 doc. yellow	4·00	8·00

4 (1 docra)

1893. Imperf or perf.

13	**4**	1 doc. black	70	3·50
14		2 doc. green	75	4·00
15b		3 doc. yellow	75	6·50

NEGRI SEMBILAN

A state of the Federation of Malaya, incorporated in Malaysia in 1963.

100 cents = 1 dollar (Straits or Malayan)

1891. Stamp of Straits Settlements optd **Negri Sembilan.**

1	**5**	2 c. red	2·50	4·25

2 Tiger
3

1891.

2	**2**	1 c. green	2·75	1·00
3		2 c. red	3·25	5·50
4		5 c. blue	28·00	38·00

1896.

5	**3**	1 c. purple and green	6·50	3·00
6		2 c. purple and brown	30·00	£100
7		3 c. purple and red	8·00	75
8		5 c. purple and yellow	7·00	5·50
9		8 c. purple and blue	28·00	15·00
10		10 c. purple and orange	27·00	14·00
11		15 c. green and violet	38·00	75·00
12		20 c. green and olive	45·00	38·00
13		25 c. green and red	70·00	90·00
14		50 c. green and black	50·00	60·00

1898. Surch in words and bar.

15	**3**	1 c. on 15 c. green & violet	80·00	£170
16	**2**	4 c. on 1 c. green	1·25	15·00
17	**3**	4 c. on 3 c. purple and red	3·00	15·00
18	**2**	4 c. on 5 c. blue	1·25	15·00

1898. Surch in words only.

19	**3**	4 c. on 8 c. purple and blue	2·50	3·75

6 Arms of Negri Sembilan 7

1935.

21	**6**	1 c. black	75	10
22		2 c. green	80	20
23		2 c. orange	3·25	55·00
24		3 c. green	5·50	8·00
25		4 c. orange	50	10
26		5 c. brown	1·25	10
27		6 c. red	9·00	2·50
28		6 c. grey	4·00	70·00
29		8 c. grey	2·00	10
30		10 c. purple	70	10
31		12 c. blue	1·40	40
32		15 c. blue	8·00	48·00
33		25 c. purple and red	90	70
34		30 c. purple and orange	3·50	2·00
35		40 c. red and purple	85	2·00
36		50 c. black on green	3·75	2·00
37		$1 black and red on blue	2·25	3·00
38		$2 green and red	25·00	16·00
39		$5 green and red on green	14·00	45·00

1948. Silver Wedding. As T **10/11** of Aden.

40		10 c. violet	15	50
41		$5 green	18·00	28·00

1949.

42	**7**	1 c. black	10	10
43		2 c. orange	10	10
44		3 c. green	10	30
45		4 c. brown	10	10
46a		5 c. purple	30	45
47		6 c. grey	30	10
48		8 c. red	20	75
49		8 c. green	1·50	1·60
50		10 c. mauve	15	10
51		12 c. red	1·50	2·25
52		15 c. blue	2·00	10
53		20 c. black and green	25	75
54		20 c. blue	80	10
55		25 c. purple and orange	25	10
56		30 c. red and purple	1·25	2·50
57		35 c. red and purple	70	1·00
58		40 c. red and purple	80	4·50
59		50 c. black and blue	70	20
60		$1 blue and purple	3·00	1·75
61		$2 green and red	12·00	14·00
62		$5 green and brown	50·00	35·00

1949. U.P.U. As T **20/23** of Antigua.

63	10 c. purple	20	10
64	15 c. blue	1·10	2·00
65	25 c. orange	50	2·00
66	50 c. black	1·00	2·50

1853. Coronation. As T **13** of Aden.

67	10 c. black and purple	60	30

1957. As Nos. 92/102 of Kedah but inset Arms of Negri Sembilan.

68	1 c. black	10	10
69	2 c. red	10	10
70	4 c. sepia	10	10
71	5 c. lake	10	10
72	8 c. green	85	1·40
73	10 c. sepia	1·00	10
74	10 c. purple	2·75	10
75	20 c. blue	60	10
76a	50 c. black and blue	30	10
77	$1 blue and purple	1·50	1·75
78	$2 green and red	5·00	11·00
79	$5 brown and green	11·00	15·00

8 Tuanku Munawir

1961. Installation of Tuanku Munawir as Yang di-Pertuan Besar of Negri Sembilan.

80	**8**	10 c. multicoloured	20	30

9 "Vanda hookeriana"

1965. As Nos. 115/21 of Kedah but with Arms of Negri Sembilan inset and inscr "NEGERI SEMBILAN" as in T **6**.

81	**9**	1 c. multicoloured	10	60
82	–	2 c. multicoloured	10	75
83	–	5 c. multicoloured	40	10
84	–	6 c. multicoloured	40	40
85	–	10 c. multicoloured	40	10
86	–	15 c. multicoloured	80	10
87	–	20 c. multicoloured	1·25	75

The higher values used in Negri Sembilan were Nos. 20/7 of Malaysia (National Issues).

10 Negri Sembilan Crest and Tuanku Ja'afar

1968. Installation of Tuanku Ja'afar as Yang di-Pertuan Besar of Negri Sembilan.

88	**10**	15 c. multicoloured	15	40
89		50 c. multicoloured	30	1·10

11 "Hebomoia glaucippe"

1971. Butterflies. As Nos. 124/30 of Kedah but with Arms of Negri Sembilan inset as T **11** and inscr "negeri sembilan".

91	–	1 c. multicoloured	40	1·00
92	–	2 c. multicoloured	60	1·00
93	–	5 c. multicoloured	90	10
94	–	6 c. multicoloured	90	1·25
95	**11**	10 c. multicoloured	90	10
96	–	15 c. multicoloured	1·25	10
97	–	20 c. multicoloured	1·25	40

The higher values in use with this issue were Nos. 64/71 of Malaysia (National Issues).

12 "Hibiscus rosa-sinensis"

13 Oil Palm

1979. Flowers. As Nos. 135/41 of Kedah but with Arms of Negri Sembilan and inscr "negeri sembilan" as in T **12**.

103	1 c. "Rafflesia hasseltii"	10	60
104	2 c. "Pterocarpus indicus"	10	60
105	5 c. "Lagerstroemia speciosa"	15	20
106	10 c. "Durio zibethinus"	20	10
107	15 c. Type **12**	20	10
108	20 c. "Rhododendron scortechinii"	25	10
109	25 c. "Etlingera elatior" (inscr "Phaeomeria speciosa")	45	20

1986. As Nos. 152/8 of Kedah but with Arms of Negri Sembilan and inscr "NEGERI SEMBILAN" as T **13**.

117	1 c. Coffee	10	10
118	2 c. Coconuts	10	10
119	5 c. Cocoa	10	10
120	10 c. Black pepper	10	10
121	15 c. Rubber	10	10
122	20 c. Type **13**	10	10
123	30 c. Rice	15	20

NEVIS

One of the Leeward Islands, Br. W. Indies. Used stamps of St. Kitts–Nevis from 1903 until June 1980 when Nevis, although remaining part of St. Kitts–Nevis, had a separate postal administration.

1861. 12 pence = 1 shilling;
20 shillings = 1 pound.
1980. 100 cents = 1 dollar.

1

2

5

(The design on the stamps refers to a medicinal spring on the Island).

1861. Various frames.

15	**1**	1d. red	16·00	13·00
6	**2**	4d. red	80·00	55·00
12		4d. orange	95·00	19·00
7	–	6d. lilac	80·00	40·00
20	–	1s. green	65·00	85·00

1879.

25	**5**	½d. green	3·00	8·50
23		1d. mauve	50·00	27·00
27a		1d. red	4·50	5·00
28		2½d. brown	£100	45·00
29		2½d. blue	13·00	9·50
30		4d. blue	£275	45·00
31		4d. grey	6·00	2·75
32		6d. green	£350	£350
33		6d. brown	17·00	48·00
34		1s. violet	85·00	£160

1883. Half of No. 23 surch **NEVIS. ½d.**

35	**5**	½d. on half 1d. mauve	£700	30·00

1980. Nos. 394/406 of St. Christopher, Nevis and Anguilla with "St. Christopher" and "Anguilla" obliterated.

37	5 c. Radio and T.V station	10	10
38	10 c. Technical college	10	10
39	12 c. T.V. assembly plant	10	30
40	15 c. Sugar cane harvesting	10	10
41	25 c. Crafthouse (craft centre)	10	10
42	30 c. "Europa" (liner)	20	15
43	40 c. Lobster and sea crab	20	40
44	45 c. Royal St. Kitts Hotel and golf course	80	70
45	50 c. Pinney's Beach, Nevis	20	30
46	55 c. New runway at Golden Rock	40	15
47	$1 Picking cotton	15	30
48	$5 Brewery	30	75
49	$10 Pineapples and peanuts	40	1·00

1980. 80th Birthday of Queen Elizabeth the Queen Mother. As T **10** of St. Kitts.

50	$2 multicoloured	20	30

8 Nevis Lighter

9 Virgin and Child

1980. Boats. Multicoloured.

51	5 c. Type **8**	10	10
52	30 c. Local fishing boat	10	10
53	55 c. "Caona" (catamaran)	15	10
54	$3 "Polynesia" (cruise schooner) (39 × 53 mm)	30	40

1980. Christmas. Multicoloured.

55	5 c. Type **9**	10	10
56	30 c. Angel	10	10
57	$2.50 The Wise Men	20	30

10 Charlestown Pier

11 New River Mill

1981. Multicoloured.

58A	5 c. Type **10**	10	10
59A	10 c. Court House and Library	10	10
60A	15 c. Type **11**	10	10
61A	20 c. Nelson Museum	10	10
62A	25 c. St. James' Parish Church	15	15
63A	30 c. Nevis Lane	15	15
64A	40 c. Zetland Plantation	20	20
65A	45 c. Nisbet Plantation	20	25
66A	50 c. Pinney's Beach	25	25
67A	55 c. Eva Wilkin's Studio	25	30
68A	$1 Nevis at dawn	40	45
69A	$2.50 Ruins of Fort Charles	45	80
70A	$5 Old Bath House	55	1·00
71A	$10 Beach at Nisbet's	65	2·00

1981. Royal Wedding. Royal Yachts. As T **26/27** of Kiribati. Multicoloured.

72	55 c. "Royal Caroline"	15	15
73	55 c. Prince Charles and Lady Diana Spencer	40	40
74	$2 "Royal Sovereign"	30	30
75	$2 As No. 73	80	1·25
76	$5 "Britannia"	45	80
77	$5 As No. 73	1·00	2·00

12 "Heliconius charithonia"

1982. Butterflies (1st series). Multicoloured.

81	5 c. Type **12**	10	10
82	30 c. "Siproeta stelenes"	15	10
83	55 c. "Marpesia petreus"	20	15
84	$2 "Phoebis agarithe"	60	70

See also Nos. 105/8.

13 Caroline of Brunswick, Princess of Wales, 1793

1982. 21st Birthday of Princess of Wales. Mult.

85	30 c. Type **13**	10	10
86	55 c. Coat of arms of Caroline of Brunswick	15	15
87	$5 Diana, Princess of Wales	60	1·00

1982. Birth of Prince William of Wales. Nos. 85/7 optd **ROYAL BABY**.

88	30 c. As Type **13**	10	10
89	55 c. Coat of arms of Caroline of Brunswick	15	15
90	$5 Diana, Princess of Wales	60	1·00

14 Cyclist

1982. 75th Anniv of Boy Scout Movement. Multicoloured.

91	5 c. Type **14**	20	10
92	30 c. Athlete	25	10
93	$2.50 Camp cook	50	65

15 Santa Claus

1982. Christmas. Children's Paintings. Mult.

94	15 c. Type **15**	10	10
95	30 c. Carollers	10	10
96	$1.50 Decorated house and local band (horiz)	15	25
97	$2.50 Adoration of the Shepherds (horiz)	25	40

16 Tube Sponge

19 Montgolfier Balloon, 1783

17 H.M.S. "Boreas" off Nevis

1983. Corals (1st series). Multicoloured.
98 15 c. Type **16** 10 10
99 30 c. Stinging coral 15 10
100 55 c. Flower coral 15 10
101 $3 Sea rod and red fire sponge 50 80
See also Nos. 423/6.

1983. Commonwealth Day. Multicoloured.
103 55 c. Type **17** 15 10
104 $2 Capt. Horatio Nelson and H.M.S. "Boreas" at anchor 45 60

1983. Butterflies (2nd series). As T **12**. Mult.
105 30 c. "Pyrgus oileus" 15 10
106 55 c. "Junonia evarete" (vert) . 20 10
107 $1.10 "Urbanus proteus" (vert) 30 40
108 $2 "Hypolimnas misippus" . . 40 75

1983. Nos. 58 and 60/71 optd **INDEPENDENCE 1983**.
109B 5 c. Type **10** 10 10
110B 15 c. Type **11** 10 10
111B 20 c. Nelson Museum . . . 10 10
112B 25 c. St. James' Parish Church 10 15
113B 30 c. Nevis Lane 15 15
114B 40 c. Zetland Plantation . . . 15 20
115B 45 c. Nisbet Plantation . . . 20 25
116B 50 c. Pinney's Beach . . . 20 25
117B 55 c. Eva Wilkin's Studio . . 25 30
118B $1 Nevis at dawn 40 45
119B $2.50 Ruins of Fort Charles 45 60
120B $5 Old Bath House 50 70
121B $10 Beach at Nisbet's . . . 65 90

1983. Bicentenary of Manned Flight. Mult.
122 10 c. Type **19** 10 10
123 45 c. Sikorsky S-38 flying boat (horiz) 15 10
124 50 c. Beech 50 Twin Bonanza (horiz) 15 10
125 $2.50 Hawker Siddeley Sea Harrier (horiz) 30 60

20 Mary praying over Holy Child

1983. Christmas. Multicoloured.
127 5 c. Type **20** 10 10
128 30 c. Shepherds with flock . . 10 10
129 55 c. Three Angels 10 10
130 $3 Boy with two girls 30 60

21 "County of Oxford" (1945)

1983. Leaders of the World. Railway Locomotives (1st series). The first in each pair shows technical drawings and the second the locomotive at work.
132 **21** 55 c. multicoloured 10 20
133 – 55 c. multicoloured 10 20
134 – $1 red, blue and black . . 15 20
135 – $1 multicoloured 15 20
136 – $1 purple, blue and black . 15 20
137 – $1 multicoloured 15 20
138 – $1 red, black and yellow . 15 20
139 – $1 multicoloured 15 20
140 – $1 multicoloured 15 20
141 – $1 multicoloured 15 20
142 – $1 yellow, black and blue . 15 20
143 – $1 multicoloured 15 20
144 – $1 yellow, black and purple 15 20
145 – $1 multicoloured 15 20
146 – $1 multicoloured 15 20
147 – $1 multicoloured 15 20
DESIGNS: Nos. 132/3, "County of Oxford", Great Britain (1945); 134/5, "Evening Star", Great Britain (1960); 136/7, Stanier Class 5 No. 44806, Great Britain (1934); 138/9, "Pendennis Castle", Great Britain (1924); 140/1, "Winston Churchill", Great Britain (1946); 142/3, "Mallard", Great Britain (1938) (inscr "1935" in error); 144/5, "Britannia", Great Britain (1951); 146/7, "King George V", Great Britain.
See also Nos. 219/26, 277/84, 297/308, 352/9 and 427/42.

22 Boer War

1984. Leaders of the World. British Monarchs (1st series). Multicoloured.
148 5 c. Type **22** 10 10
149 5 c. Queen Victoria 10 10
150 50 c. Queen Victoria at Osborne House 10 30
151 50 c. Osborne House 10 30
152 60 c. Battle of Dettingen . . 10 30
153 60 c. George II 10 30
154 75 c. George II at the Bank of England 15 30
155 75 c. Bank of England 15 30
156 $1 Coat of Arms of George II 15 30
157 $1 George II (different) . . . 15 30
158 $3 Coat of Arms of Queen Victoria 30 50
159 $3 Queen Victoria (different) . 30 50
See also Nos. 231/6.

23 Golden Rock Inn

1984. Tourism (1st series). Multicoloured.
160 55 c. Type **23** 25 20
161 55 c. Rest Haven Inn 25 20
162 55 c. Cliffdwellers Hotel . . . 25 20
163 55 c. Pinney's Beach Hotel . . 25 20
See also Nos. 245/8.

24 Early Seal of Colony

1984.
164 **24** $15 red . . . . 2·25 4·00

25 Cadillac

1984. Leaders of the World Automobiles (1st series). As T **25**. The first design in each pair shows technical drawings and the second paintings.
165 1 c. yellow, black and mauve 10 10
166 1 c. multicoloured 10 10
167 5 c. blue, mauve and black . 10 10
168 5 c. multicoloured 10 10
169 15 c. multicoloured 10 15
170 15 c. multicoloured 10 15
171 35 c. mauve, yellow and black 10 25
172 35 c. multicoloured 10 25
173 45 c. blue, mauve and black . 10 25
174 45 c. multicoloured 10 25
175 55 c. multicoloured 10 25
176 55 c. multicoloured 10 25
177 $2.50 mauve, black and yellow 25 60
178 $2.50 multicoloured 25 60
179 $3 blue, yellow and black . . 25 70
180 $3 multicoloured 25 70
DESIGNS: No. 165/6, Cadillac "V16 Fleetwood Convertible" (1932); 167/8, Packard "Twin Six Touring Car" (1916); 169/70, Daimler "2 Cylinder" (1886); 171/2, Porsche "911 S Targa" (1970); 173/4, Benz "Three Wheeler" (1885); 175/6, M.G. "TC" (1947); 177/8, Cobra "Roadster 289" (1966); 179/80, Aston Martin "DB6 Hardtop" (1966).
See also Nos. 203/10, 249/64, 326/37, 360/371 and 411/22.

26 Carpentry

1984. 10th Anniv of Culturama Celebrations. Multicoloured.
181 30 c. Type **26** 10 10
182 55 c. Grass mat and basket making 10 10
183 $1 Pottery firing 15 25
184 $3 Culturama Queen and dancers 40 55

27 Yellow Bell

29 C. P. Mead

28 Cotton-picking and Map

1984. Flowers. Multicoloured.
185A 5 c. Type **27** 10 10
186A 10 c. Plumbago 10 10
187A 15 c. Flamboyant 10 10
188B 20 c. Eyelash orchid 40 30
189A 30 c. Bougainvillea 10 15
190B 40 c. Hibiscus 30 30
191A 50 c. Night-blooming cereus . 15 20
192A 55 c. Yellow mahoe 20 25
193A 60 c. Spider-lily 20 25
194A 75 c. Scarlet cordia 25 30
195A $1 Shell-ginger 35 40
196A $3 Blue petrea . . . . . . 60 1·10
197A $5 Coral hibiscus . . . . . 75 2·00
198A $10 Passion flower . . . . 1·10 3·50

1984. 1st Anniv of Independence of St. Kitts–Nevis. Multicoloured.
199 15 c. Type **28** 10 10
200 55 c. Alexander Hamilton's birthplace 10 10
201 $1.10 Local agricultural produce 20 40
202 $3 Nevis Peak and Pinney's Beach . . . . 50 1·00

1984. Leaders of the World. Automobiles (2nd series). As T **25**. The first in each pair shows technical drawings and the second paintings.
203 5 c. black, blue and brown . . 10 10
204 5 c. multicoloured 10 10
205 30 c. black, turquoise and brown 15 15
206 30 c. multicoloured 15 15
207 50 c. black, drab and brown . 15 15
208 50 c. multicoloured 15 15
209 $3 black, brown and green . . 30 45
210 $3 multicoloured 30 45
DESIGNS: Nos. 203/4, Lagonda "Speed Model" touring car (1929); 205/6, Jaguar "E-Type" 4.2 litre (1967); 207/8, Volkswagen "Beetle" (1947); 209/10, Pierce Arrow "V12" (1932).

1984. Leaders of the World. Cricketers (1st series). As T **29**. The first in each pair shows a head portrait and the second the cricketer in action. Multicoloured.
211 5 c. Type **29** 10 10
212 5 c. C. P. Mead 10 10
213 25 c. J. B. Statham 30 30
214 25 c. J. B. Statham 30 30
215 55 c. Sir Learie Constantine . . 40 40
216 55 c. Sir Learie Constantine . . 40 40
217 $2.50 Sir Leonard Hutton . . 1·00 1·25
218 $2.50 Sir Leonard Hutton . . 1·00 1·25
See also Nos. 237/4.

1984. Leaders of the World. Railway Locomotives (2nd series). As T **21**. The first in each pair shows technical drawings and the second the locomotive at work.
219 5 c. multicoloured 10 10
220 5 c. multicoloured 10 10
221 10 c. multicoloured 10 10
222 10 c. multicoloured 10 10
223 60 c. multicoloured 25 25
224 60 c. multicoloured 25 25
225 $2 multicoloured 70 70
226 $2 multicoloured 70 70
DESIGNS: Nos. 219/20, Class EF81 electric locomotive, Japan (1968); 221/22, Class 5500 electric locomotive, France (1927); 223/4, Class 240P, France (1940); 225/6, "Hikari" express train, Japan (1964).

30 Fifer and Drummer from Honeybees Band

1984. Christmas. Local Music. Multicoloured.
227 15 c. Type **30** 15 10
228 40 c. Guitar and "barhow" players from Canary Birds Band 25 10
229 60 c. Shell All Stars steel band 30 10
230 $3 Organ and choir, St. John's Church, Fig Tree . . . . 1·25 1·00

1984. Leaders of the World. British Monarchs (2nd series). As T **22**. Multicoloured.
231 5 c. King John and Magna Carta 10 10
232 5 c. Barons and King John . . 10 10
233 55 c. King John 10 15
234 55 c. Newark Castle 10 15
235 $2 Coat of arms 25 40
236 $2 King John (different) . . . 25 40

1984. Leaders of the World. Cricketers (2nd series). As T **29**. The first in each pair listed shows a head portrait and the second the cricketer in action. Multicoloured.
237 5 c. J. D. Love 10 10
238 5 c. J. D. Love 10 10
239 15 c. S. J. Dennis 15 15
240 15 c. S. J. Dennis 15 15
241 55 c. B. W. Luckhurst 20 20
242 55 c. B. W. Luckhurst 20 20
243 $2.50 B. L. D'Oliveira 50 60
244 $2.50 B. L. D'Oliveira 50 60

1984. Tourism (2nd series). As T **23**. Multicoloured.
245 $1.20 Croney's Old Manor Hotel 15 25
246 $1.20 Montpelier Plantation Inn 15 25
247 $1.20 Nisbet's Plantation Inn . 15 25
248 $1.20 Zetland Plantation Inn . 15 25

1985. Leaders of the World. Automobiles (3rd series). As T **25**. The first in each pair shows technical drawings and the second paintings.
249 1 c. black, green and light green 10 10
250 1 c. multicoloured 10 10
251 5 c. black, blue and light blue 10 10
252 5 c. multicoloured 10 10
253 10 c. black, green and light green 10 10
254 10 c. multicoloured 10 10
255 50 c. black, green and brown . 10 10
256 50 c. multicoloured 10 10
257 60 c. black, green and blue . . 10 10
258 60 c. multicoloured 10 10
259 75 c. black, red and orange . 10 10
260 75 c. multicoloured 10 10
261 $2.50 black, green and blue . 20 30
262 $2.50 multicoloured 20 30
263 $3 black, green and light green 20 30
264 $3 multicoloured 20 30
DESIGNS: Nos. 249/50, Delahaye "Type 35 Cabriolet" (1935); 251/2, Ferrari "Testa Rossa" (1958); 253/4, Voisin "Aerodyne" (1934); 255/6, Buick "Riviera" (1963); 257/8, Cooper "Climax" (1960); 259/60, Ford "999" (1904); 261/2, MG "M-Type Midget" (1930); 263/4, Rolls-Royce "Corniche" (1971).

31 Broad-winged Hawk

1985. Local Hawks and Herons. Multicoloured.
265 20 c. Type **31** . . . . 1·00 20
266 40 c. Red-tailed hawk . . . . 1·25 30
267 60 c. Little blue heron . . . . 1·25 40
268 $3 Great blue heron (white phase) . . . . 2·50 1·90

32 Eastern Bluebird

1985. Leaders of the World. Birth Bicentenary of John J. Audubon (ornithologist) (1st issue). Multicoloured.
269 5 c. Type **32** 10 10
270 5 c. Common cardinal 10 10
271 55 c. Belted kingfisher 20 55
272 55 c. Mangrove cuckoo . . . 20 55
273 60 c. Yellow warbler 20 55
274 60 c. Cerulean warbler 20 55
275 $2 Burrowing owl . . . . . . 60 1·25
276 $2 Long-eared owl . . . . . 60 1·25
See also Nos. 285/92.

1985. Leaders of the World. Railway Locomotives (3rd series). As T **21**, the first in each pair showing technical drawings and the second the locomotive at work.
277 1 c. multicoloured 10 10
278 1 c. multicoloured 10 10
279 60 c. multicoloured 20 20
280 60 c. multicoloured 20 20
281 90 c. multicoloured 25 25
282 90 c. multicoloured 25 25
283 $2 multicoloured 40 60
284 $2 multicoloured 40 60
DESIGNS: Nos. 277/8, Class "Wee Bogie", Great Britain (1882); 279/80, "Comet", Great Britain (1851); 281/2, Class 8H No. 6173, Great Britain (1908); 283/4, Class A No. 23, Great Britain (1866).

1985. Leaders of the World. Birth Bicentenary of John J. Audubon (ornithologist) (2nd issue). As T **32**. Multicoloured.
285 1 c. Painted bunting 10 10
286 1 c. Golden-crowned kinglet . 10 10
287 40 c. Common flicker 25 40
288 40 c. Western tanager 25 40
289 60 c. Varied thrush 25 45
290 60 c. Evening grosbeak 25 45
291 $2.50 Blackburnian warbler . . 50 80
292 $2.50 Northern oriole 50 80

33 Guides and Guide Headquarters

1985. 75th Anniv of Girl Guide Movement. Multicoloured.
293 15 c. Type **33** 10 10
294 60 c. Girl Guide uniforms of 1910 and 1985 (vert) 15 25
295 $1 Lord and Lady Baden-Powell (vert) 20 40
296 $3 Princess Margaret in Guide uniform (vert) . . . . . . 50 1·25

1985. Leaders of the World. Railway Locomotives (4th series). As T **21**. The first in each pair shows technical drawings and the second the locomotive at work.
297 5 c. multicoloured 10 10
298 5 c. multicoloured 10 10
299 30 c. multicoloured 10 15
300 30 c. multicoloured 10 15
301 60 c. multicoloured 15 20
302 60 c. multicoloured 15 20
303 75 c. multicoloured 15 25
304 75 c. multicoloured 15 25
305 $1 multicoloured 15 25
306 $1 multicoloured 15 25
307 $2.50 multicoloured 25 60
308 $2.50 multicoloured 25 60
DESIGNS: Nos. 297/8, "Snowdon Ranger" (1878); 299/300, Large Belpaire locomotive, Great Britain (1904); 301/2, Class "County" No. 3821, Great Britain (1904); 303/4, "L'Outrance", France (1877); 305/6, Class PB-15, Australia (1899); 307/8, Class 64, Germany (1928).

34 The Queen Mother at Garter Ceremony **35** Isambard Kingdom Brunel

1985. Leaders of the World. Life and Times of Queen Elizabeth the Queen Mother. Various vertical portraits.
309 **34** 45 c. multicoloured 10 15
310 – 45 c. multicoloured 10 15
311 – 75 c. multicoloured 10 20
312 – 75 c. multicoloured 10 20
313 – $1.20 multicoloured 15 35
314 – $1.20 multicoloured 15 35
315 – $1.50 multicoloured 15 40
316 – $1.50 multicoloured 15 40
Each value was issued in pairs showing a floral pattern across the bottom of the portraits which stops short of the left-hand edge on the first stamp and of the right-hand edge on the second.

1985. 150th Anniv of Great Western Railway. Designs showing railway engineers and their achievements. Multicoloured.
318 25 c. Type **35** 15 35
319 25 c. Royal Albert Bridge, 1859 15 35
320 50 c. William Dean 20 45
321 50 c. Locomotive "Lord of the Isles", 1895 . . . . 20 45
322 $1 Locomotive "Lode Star", 1907 . . . . 25 65
323 $1 G. J. Churchward 25 65
324 $2.50 Locomotive "Pendennis Castle", 1924 . . . . 35 80
325 $2.50 C. B. Collett 35 80
Nos. 318/19, 320/1, 322/3 and 324/5 were printed together se-tenant, each pair forming a composite design.

1985. Leaders of the World. Automobiles (4th series). As T **25**. The first in each pair shows technical drawings and the second paintings.
326 10 c. black, blue and red . . . 10 10
327 10 c. multicoloured 10 10
328 35 c. black, turquoise and blue 10 25
329 35 c. multicoloured 10 25
330 75 c. black, green and brown . 10 40
331 75 c. multicoloured 10 40
332 $1.15 black, brown and green . 15 45
333 $1.15 multicoloured 15 45
334 $1.50 black, blue and red . . . 20 50
335 $1.50 multicoloured 20 50
336 $2 black, lilac and violet . . . 25 60
337 $2 multicoloured 25 60
DESIGNS: Nos. 326/7, Sunbeam "Coupe de l'Auto" (1912); 328/9, Cisitalia "Pininfarina Coupe" (1948); 330/1, Porsche "928S" (1980); 332/3, MG "K3 Magnette" (1933); 334/5, Lincoln "Zephyr" (1937); 336/7, Pontiac 2 Door (1926).

INDEX

Countries can be quickly located by referring to the index at the end of this volume.

1985. Royal Visit. Nos. 76/7, 83, 86, 92/3, 98/9 and 309/10 optd **CARIBBEAN ROYAL VISIT 1985** or surch also.
338 **16** 15 c. multicoloured . . . 75 1·25
339 – 30 c. multicoloured (No. 92) 1·75 1·75
340 – 30 c. multicoloured (No. 99) 75 1·25
341 – 40 c. on 55 c. mult (No. 86) 1·75 2·00
342 **34** 45 c. multicoloured . . . 1·50 2·75
343 – 45 c. multicoloured (No. 310) 1·50 2·75
344 – 55 c. multicoloured (No. 83) 1·25 1·25
345 – $1.50 on $5 multicoloured (No. 76) . . . . 2·00 2·50
346 – $1.50 on $5 multicoloured (No. 77) . . . . 10·00 13·00
347 – $2.50 mult (No. 93) . . . 2·25 3·00

36 St. Paul's Anglican Church, Charlestown

1985. Christmas. Churches of Nevis (1st series). Multicoloured.
348 10 c. Type **36** 15 10
349 40 c. St. Theresa Catholic Church, Charlestown . . . 35 30
350 60 c. Methodist Church, Gingerland 50 50
351 $3 St. Thomas Anglican Church, Lowland . . . . 1·25 2·75
See also Nos. 462/5.

1986. Leaders of the World. Railway Locomotives (5th series). As T **21**. The first in each pair shows technical drawings and the second the locomotive at work.
352 30 c. multicoloured 15 25
353 30 c. multicoloured 15 25
354 75 c. multicoloured 25 50
355 75 c. multicoloured 25 50
356 $1.50 multicoloured 40 70
357 $1.50 multicoloured 40 70
358 $2 multicoloured 50 80
359 $2 multicoloured 50 80
DESIGNS: Nos. 352/3, "Stourbridge Lion", U.S.A. (1829); 354/5, EP-2 Bi-Polar electric locomotive, U.S.A. (1919); 356/7, Gas turbine No. 59, U.S.A. (1953); 358/9 Class FL9 diesel locomotive No. 2039, U.S.A. (1955).

1986. Leaders of the World. Automobiles (5th series). As T **25**, the first in each pair showing technical drawings and the second paintings.
360 10 c. black, brown and green 10 10
361 10 c. multicoloured 10 10
362 60 c. black, orange and red . 15 25
363 60 c. multicoloured 15 25
364 75 c. black, light brown and brown 15 25
365 75 c. multicoloured 15 25
366 $1 black, light grey and grey . 15 30
367 $1 multicoloured 15 30
368 $1.50 black, yellow and green 20 35
369 $1.50 multicoloured 20 35
370 $3 black, light blue and blue . 30 65
371 $3 multicoloured 30 65
DESIGNS: Nos. 360/1, Adler "Trumpf" (1936); 362/3, Maserati "Tipo 250F" (1957); 364/5, Oldsmobile "Limited" (1910); 366/7, Jaguar "C-Type" (1951); 368/9, ERA "1.5L B Type" (1937); 370/1, Chevrolet "Corvette" (1953).

37 Supermarine Spitfire Prototype, 1936

1986. 50th Anniv of Spitfire (fighter aircraft). Multicoloured.
372 $1 Type **37** 20 50
373 $2.50 Supermarine Spitfire Mk 1A in Battle of Britain, 1940 30 1·00
374 $3 Supermarine Spitfire Mk XII over convoy, 1944 . . . . 40 1·25
375 $4 Supermarine Spitfire Mk XXIV, 1948 . . . . 50 1·40

38 Head of Amerindian **39** Brazilian Player

1986. 500th Anniv (1992) of Discovery of America by Columbus (1st issue). Multicoloured.
377 75 c. Type **38** 55 55
378 75 c. Exchanging gifts for food from Amerindians 55 55
379 $1.75 Columbus's coat of arms 1·40 1·75
380 $1.75 Breadfruit plant . . . . 1·40 1·75
381 $2.50 Columbus's fleet . . . . 1·75 2·00
382 $2.50 Christopher Columbus . . 1·75 2·00
The two designs of each value were printed together, se-tenant, each pair forming a composite design showing charts of Columbus's route in the background.
See also Nos. 546/53, 592/99, 678/83 and 685/6.

1986. 60th Birthday of Queen Elizabeth II. As T **167** of British Virgin Islands. Multicoloured.
384 5 c. Queen Elizabeth in 1976 . 10 10
385 75 c. Queen Elizabeth in 1953 . 15 25
386 $2 In Australia 20 60
387 $8 In Canberra, 1982 (vert) . . 75 2·00

1986. World Cup Football Championship, Mexico. Multicoloured.
389 1 c. Official World Cup mascot (horiz) 10 10
390 2 c. Type **39** 10 10
391 5 c. Danish player 10 10
392 10 c. Brazilian player (different) 10 10
393 20 c. Denmark v Spain 20 20
394 30 c. Paraguay v Chile 30 30
395 60 c. Italy v West Germany . . 45 55
396 75 c. Danish team (56 × 36 mm) 50 65
397 $1 Paraguayan team (56 × 36 mm) 55 70
398 $1.75 Brazilian team (56 × 36 mm) . . . . . . 75 1·25
399 $3 Italy v England . . . . . 1·10 1·90
400 $6 Italian team (56 × 36 mm) 1·75 3·00

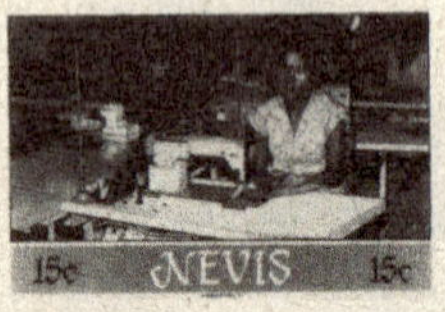

40 Clothing Machinist

1986. Local Industries. Multicoloured.
402 15 c. Type **40** 20 15
403 40 c. Carpentry/joinery workshop 45 30
404 $1.20 Agricultural produce market . . . . 1·25 1·50
405 $3 Fishing boats landing catch 2·50 3·25

1986. Royal Wedding. As T **168** of British Virgin Islands. Multicoloured.
406 60 c. Prince Andrew in midshipman's uniform . . . 15 25
407 60 c. Miss Sarah Ferguson . . 15 25
408 $2 Prince Andrew on safari in Africa (horiz) 40 60
409 $2 Prince Andrew at the races (horiz) 40 60

1986. Automobiles (6th series). As T **25**, the first in each pair showing technical drawings and the second paintings.
411 15 c. multicoloured 10 10
412 15 c. multicoloured 10 10
413 45 c. black, light blue and blue 20 25
414 45 c. multicoloured 20 25
415 60 c. multicoloured 20 30
416 60 c. multicoloured 20 30
417 $1 black, light green and green 25 40
418 $1 multicoloured 25 40
419 $1.75 black, lilac and deep lilac 30 50
420 $1.75 multicoloured 30 50
421 $3 multicoloured 50 90
422 $3 multicoloured 50 90
DESIGNS: Nos. 411/12, Riley "Brooklands Nine" (1930); 413/14, Alfa Romeo "GTA" (1966); 415/16, Pierce Arrow "Type 66" (1913); 417/18, Willys-Knight "66A" (1928); 419/20, Studebaker "Starliner" (1953); 421/2, Cunningham "V-8" (1919).

41 Gorgonia **41a** Statue of Liberty and World Trade Centre, Manhattan

1986. Corals (2nd series). Multicoloured.
423 15 c. Type **41** 25 15
424 60 c. Fire coral 55 55
425 $2 Elkhorn coral . . . . . . 90 2·00
426 $3 Vase sponge and feather star 1·10 2·50

1986. Railway Locomotives (6th series). As T **21**, the first in each pair showing technical drawings and the second the locomotive at work.
427 15 c. multicoloured 10 10
428 15 c. multicoloured 10 10
429 45 c. multicoloured 15 25
430 45 c. multicoloured 15 25
431 60 c. multicoloured 20 30
432 60 c. multicoloured 20 30
433 75 c. multicoloured 20 40
434 75 c. multicoloured 20 40
435 $1 multicoloured 25 50
436 $1 multicoloured 25 50
437 $1.50 multicoloured 30 60
438 $1.50 multicoloured 30 60
439 $2 multicoloured 40 65
440 $2 multicoloured 40 65
441 $3 multicoloured 55 80
442 $3 multicoloured 55 80
DESIGNS: Nos. 427/8, Connor Single Class, Great Britain (1859); 429/30, Class P2 "Cock o' the North", Great Britain (1934); 431/2, Class 7000 electric locomotive, Japan (1926); 433/4, Class P3, Germany (1897); 435/6, "Dorchester", Canada (1836); 436/7, Class "Centennial" diesel locomotive, U.S.A. (1969); 439/40, "Lafayette", U.S.A. (1837); 441/2, Class C-16 No. 222, U.S.A. (1882).

1986. Centenary of Statue of Liberty. Multicoloured.
443 15 c. Type **41a** 20 15
444 25 c. Sailing ship passing statue 30 20
445 40 c. Statue in scaffolding . . 30 25
446 60 c. Statue (side view) and scaffolding 30 30
447 75 c. Statue and regatta . . . 40 40
448 $1 Tall Ships parade passing statue (horiz) 40 45
449 $1.50 Head and arm of statue above scaffolding 40 60
450 $2 Ships with souvenir flags (horiz) 55 80
451 $2.50 Statue and New York waterfront 60 90
452 $3 Restoring statue . . . . . 80 1·25

1986. Royal Wedding (2nd issue). Nos. 406/9 optd **Congratulations to T.R.H. The Duke & Duchess of York**.
454 60 c. Prince Andrew in midshipman's uniform . . . 15 40
455 60 c. Miss Sarah Ferguson . . 15 40
456 $2 Prince Andrew on safari in Africa (horiz) . . . . . . 40 1·00
457 $2 Prince Andrew at the races (horiz) . . . . 40 1·00

42 Dinghy sailing

1986. Sports. Multicoloured.
458 10 c. Type **42** 10 10
459 25 c. Netball 30 15
460 $2 Cricket . . . . 2·25 2·50
461 $3 Basketball . . . . 2·75 3·00

43 St. George's Anglican Church, Gingerland **44** Constitution Document, Quill and Inkwell

1986. Christmas. Churches of Nevis (2nd series). Multicoloured.
462 10 c. Type **43** 15 10
463 40 c. Trinity Methodist Church, Fountain 30 25
464 $1 Charlestown Methodist Church 60 65
465 $5 Wesleyan Holiness Church, Brown Hill . . . . 2·75 3·75

1987. Bicentenary of U.S. Constitution and 230th Birth Anniv of Alexander Hamilton (U.S. statesman). Multicoloured.
466 15 c. Type **44** 10 10
467 40 c. Alexander Hamilton and Hamilton House 20 25
468 60 c. Alexander Hamilton . . 25 35
469 $2 Washington and his Cabinet 90 1·25

1987. Victory of "Stars and Stripes" in America's Cup Yachting Championship. No. 54 optd **America's Cup 1987 Winners 'Stars & Stripes'**.
471 $3 Windjammer S.V "Polynesia" 1·10 1·60

46 Fig Tree Church

1987. Bicentenary of Marriage of Horatio Nelson and Frances Nisbet. Multicoloured.
472 15 c. Type **46** 15 10
473 60 c. Frances Nisbet 40 30
474 $1 H.M.S. "Boreas" (frigate) . 1·25 1·00
475 $3 Captain Horatio Nelson . . 2·50 3·25

47 Queen Angelfish

1987. Coral Reef Fishes. Multicoloured.

477 60 c. Type **47** 35 60
478 60 c. Blue angelfish 35 60
479 $1 Stoplight parrotfish (male) 40 80
480 $1 Stoplight parrotfish (female) 40 80
481 $1.50 Red hind 45 90
482 $1.50 Rock hind 45 90
483 $2.50 Coney (bicoloured phase) 50 1·50
484 $2.50 Coney (red-brown phase) 50 1·50
Nos. 478, 480, 482 and 484 are inverted triangles.

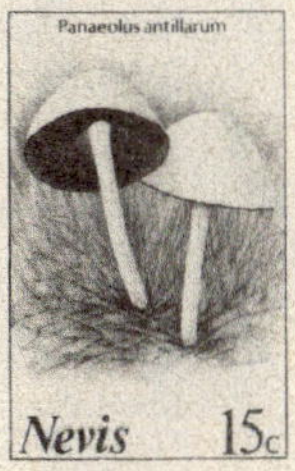

48 "Panaeolus antillarum" **50** Hawk-wing Conch

49 Rag Doll

1987. Fungi (1st series). Multicoloured.

485 15 c. Type **48** 80 30
486 50 c. "Pycnoporus sanguineus" 1·50 80
487 $2 "Gymnopilus chrysopellus" 2·75 3·25
488 $3 "Cantharellus cinnabarinus" 3·25 4·25
See also Nos. 646/53.

1987. Christmas. Toys. Multicoloured.

489 10 c. Type **49** 10 10
490 40 c. Coconut boat 20 25
491 $1.20 Sandbox cart 55 60
492 $5 Two-wheeled cart 2·25 3·75

1988. Sea Shells and Pearls. Multicoloured.

493 15 c. Type **50** 20 15
494 40 c. Rooster-tail conch 30 20
495 60 c. Emperor helmet 50 40
496 $2 Queen or pink conch 1·60 2·00
497 $3 King helmet 1·75 2·25

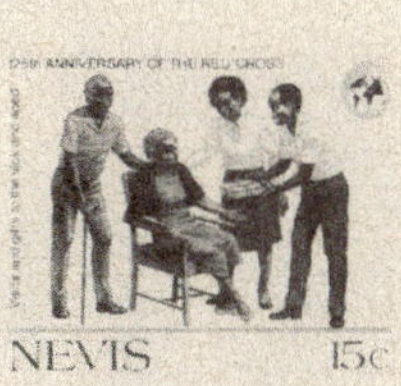

51 Visiting Pensioners at Christmas **52** Athlete on Starting Blocks

1988. 125th Anniv of International Red Cross. Multicoloured.

498 15 c. Type **51** 10 10
499 40 c. Teaching children first aid 15 20
500 60 c. Providing wheelchairs for the disabled 25 35
501 $5 Helping cyclone victim 2·10 3·25

1988. Olympic Games, Seoul. Multicoloured.

502 10 c. Type **52** 10 35
503 $1.20 At start 50 85
504 $2 During race 85 1·25
505 $3 At finish 1·25 1·50
Nos. 502/5 were printed together, se-tenant, each strip forming a composite design showing an athlete from start to finish of race.

53 Outline Map and Arms of St. Kitts-Nevis **54** Poinsettia

1988. 5th Anniv of Independence.

507 **53** $5 multicoloured 2·10 2·75

1988. 300th Anniv of Lloyd's of London. As T **123** of Ascension. Multicoloured.

508 15 c. House of Commons passing Lloyd's Bill, 1871 20 10
509 60 c. "Cunard Countess" (liner) (horiz) 1·10 65
510 $2.50 Space shuttle deploying satellite (horiz) 2·25 3·00
511 $3 "Viking Princess" (cargo liner) on fire, 1966 2·25 3·00

1988. Christmas. Flowers. Multicoloured.

512 15 c. Type **54** 10 10
513 40 c. Tiger claws 15 20
514 60 c. Sorrel flower 25 30
515 $1 Christmas candle 40 60
516 $5 Snow bush 2·10 3·50

55 British Fleet off St. Kitts **56** Cicada

1989. "Philexfrance 89" International Stamp Exhibition, Paris. Battle of Frigate Bay, 1782. Multicoloured.

517 50 c. Type **55** 75 1·00
518 $1.20 Battle off Nevis 1·00 1·40
519 $2 British and French fleets exchanging broadsides 1·25 1·60
520 $3 French map of Nevis, 1764 1·60 2·00
Nos. 517/19 were printed together, se-tenant, forming a composite design.

1989. "Sounds of the Night". Multicoloured.

521 10 c. Type **56** 20 15
522 40 c. Grasshopper 40 35
523 60 c. Cricket 55 50
524 $5 Tree frog 3·75 5·50

1989. 20th Anniv of First Manned Landing on Moon. As T **126** of Ascension. Multicoloured.

526 15 c. Vehicle Assembly Building, Kennedy Space Centre 15 10
527 40 c. Crew of "Apollo 12" (30 × 30 mm) 20 20
528 $2 "Apollo 12" emblem (30 × 30 mm) 1·00 1·60
529 $3 "Apollo 12" astronaut on Moon 1·40 1·90

57 Queen or Pink Conch feeding

1990. Queen or Pink Conch. Multicoloured.

531 10 c. Type **57** 50 30
532 40 c. Queen or pink conch from front 80 40
533 60 c. Side view of shell 1·10 80
534 $1 Black and flare 1·40 1·75

58 Wyon Medal Portrait **59**

1990. 150th Anniv of the Penny Black.

536 **58** 15 c. black and brown 15 10
537 – 40 c. black and green 30 25
538 – 60 c. black 45 55
539 – $4 black and blue 2·50 3·25
DESIGNS: 40 c. Engine-turned background; 60 c. Heath's engraving of portrait; $4 Essay with inscriptions.

1990. 500th Anniv of Regular European Postal Services.

541 **59** 15 c. brown 20 15
542 – 40 c. green 35 25
543 – 60 c. violet 55 65
544 – $4 blue 2·75 3·50
Nos. 541/4 commemorate the Thurn and Taxis postal service and the designs are loosely based on those of the initial 1852–58 series.

1990. 500th Anniv (1992) of Discovery of America by Columbus (2nd issue). New World Natural History—Crabs. As T **260** of Antigua. Mult.

546 5 c. Sand fiddler 10 10
547 15 c. Great land crab 15 15
548 20 c. Blue crab 15 15
549 40 c. Stone crab 30 30
550 60 c. Mountain crab 45 45
551 $2 Sargassum crab 1·40 1·60
552 $3 Yellow box crab 1·75 2·00
553 $4 Spiny spider crab 2·25 2·50

1990. 90th Birthday of Queen Elizabeth the Queen Mother. As T **103** of Grenada Grenadines.

555 $2 black, mauve and buff 1·40 1·60
556 $2 black, mauve and buff 1·40 1·60
557 $2 black, mauve and buff 1·40 1·60
DESIGNS: No. 555, Duchess of York with corgi; 556, Queen Elizabeth in Coronation robes, 1937; 557, Duchess of York in garden.

61 MaKanaky, Cameroons **62** "Cattleya deckeri"

1990. World Cup Football Championship, Italy. Star Players. Multicoloured.

559 10 c. Type **61** 30 10
560 25 c. Chovanec, Czechoslovakia 35 15
561 $2.50 Robson, England 2·50 3·00
562 $5 Voller, West Germany 3·50 4·50

1990. Christmas. Native Orchids. Mult.

564 10 c. Type **62** 40 20
565 15 c. "Epidendrum ciliare" 40 20
566 20 c. "Epidendrum fragrans" 50 20
567 40 c. "Epidendrum ibaguense" 75 25
568 60 c. "Epidendrum latifolium" 1·00 50
569 $1.20 "Maxillaria conferta" 1·40 1·60
570 $2 "Epidendrum strobiliferum" 1·75 2·50
571 $3 "Brassavola cucullata" 2·00 3·00

1991. 350th Death Anniv of Rubens. As T **273** of Antigua, showing details from "The Feast of Acheloüs". Multicoloured.

573 10 c. Two jugs (vert) 20 15
574 40 c. Woman at table (vert) 40 30
575 60 c. Two servants with fruit (vert) 55 45
576 $4 Acheloüs (vert) 2·50 3·25

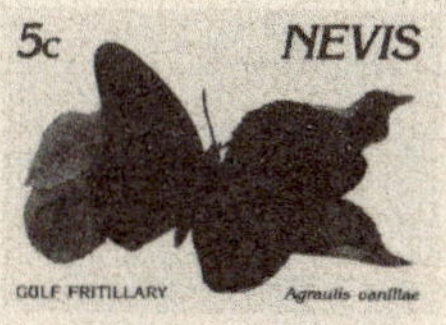

63 "Agraulis vanillae"

1991. Butterflies. Multicoloured.

578B 5 c. Type **63** 20 30
579A 10 c. "Historis odius" 25 15
580B 15 c. "Marpesia corinna" 20 20
581A 20 c. "Anartia amathea" 40 20
582A 25 c. "Junonia evarete" 40 20
583B 40 c. "Heliconius charithonia" 40 30
584B 50 c. "Marpesia petreus" 45 35
585A 60 c. "Dione juno" 40 45
586B 75 c. "Heliconius doris" 60 60
586B 80 c. As 60 c. 60 60
587A $1 "Hypolimnas misippus" 70 70
588A $3 "Danaus plexippus" 1·75 2·25
589A $5 "Heliconius sara" 2·50 3·50
590A $10 "Tithorea harmonia" 4·75 7·00
591A $20 "Dryas julia" 9·50 12·00

64 "Viking Mars Lander", 1976

1991. 500th Anniv of Discovery of America by Columbus (1992) (3rd issue). History of Exploration. Multicoloured.

592 15 c. Type **64** 20 15
593 40 c. "Apollo 11", 1969 30 25
594 60 c. "Skylab", 1973 45 45
595 75 c. "Salyut 6", 1977 55 55
596 $1 "Voyager 1", 1977 65 65
597 $2 "Venera 7", 1970 1·25 1·40
598 $4 "Gemini 4", 1965 2·50 2·75
599 $5 "Luna 3", 1959 2·75 3·00

65 Magnificent Frigate Bird

1991. Island Birds. Multicoloured.

601 40 c. Type **65** 50 50
602 40 c. Roseate tern 50 50
603 40 c. Red-tailed hawk 50 50
604 40 c. Zenaida dove 50 50
605 40 c. Bananaquit 50 50
606 40 c. American kestrel 50 50
607 40 c. Grey kingbird 50 50
608 40 c. Prothonotary warbler 50 50
609 40 c. Blue-hooded euphonia 50 50
610 40 c. Antillean crested hummingbird 50 50
611 40 c. White-tailed tropic bird 50 50
612 40 c. Yellow-bellied sapsucker 50 50
613 40 c. Green-throated carib 50 50
614 40 c. Purple-throated carib 50 50
615 40 c. Red-billed whistling duck ("Black-bellied tree-duck") 50 50
616 40 c. Ringed kingfisher 50 50
617 40 c. Burrowing owl 50 50
618 40 c. Turnstone 50 50
619 40 c. Great blue heron 50 50
620 40 c. Yellow-crowned night-heron 50 50
Nos. 601/20 were printed together, se-tenant, forming a composite design.

1991. 65th Birthday of Queen Elizabeth II. As T **280** of Antigua. Multicoloured.

622 15 c. Queen Elizabeth at polo match with Prince Charles 30 20
623 40 c. Queen and Prince Philip on Buckingham Palace balcony 45 35
624 $2 In carriage at Ascot, 1986 1·40 1·75
625 $4 Queen Elizabeth II at Windsor polo match, 1989 2·75 3·75

1991. 10th Wedding Anniv of Prince and Princess of Wales. As T **280** of Antigua. Multicoloured.

627 10 c. Prince Charles and Princess Diana 20 20
628 50 c. Prince of Wales and family 50 30
629 $1 Prince William and Prince Harry 85 90
630 $5 Prince and Princess of Wales 3·00 3·50

1991. "Phila Nippon '91" International Stamp Exhibition, Tokyo. Japanese Railway Locomotives. As T **257** of Maldives. Mult.

632 10 c. Class C62 steam locomotive 35 30
633 15 c. Class C56 steam locomotive (horiz) 40 30
634 40 c. Class C55 streamlined steam locomotive (horiz) 60 50
635 60 c. Class 1400 steam locomotive (horiz) 80 80
636 $1 Class 485 diesel rail car 1·00 1·00
637 $2 Class C61 steam locomotive 2·00 2·00
638 $3 Class 485 diesel train (horiz) 2·25 2·25
639 $4 Class 7000 electric train (horiz) 2·75 2·75

1991. Christmas. Drawings by Albrecht Dürer. As T **211** of Lesotho.

641 10 c. black and green 10 10
642 40 c. black and orange 20 25
643 60 c. black and blue 25 30
644 $3 black and mauve 1·40 2·40
DESIGNS: 10 c. "Mary being Crowned by an Angel"; 40 c. "Mary with the Pear"; 60 c. "Mary in a Halo"; $3 "Mary with Crown of Stars and Sceptre".

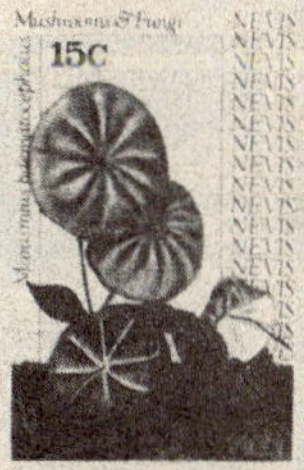

66 "Marasmius haematocephalus" **67** Monique Knol (cycling), Netherlands

1991. Fungi (2nd series). Multicoloured.

646 15 c. Type **66** 30 20
647 40 c. "Psilocybe cubensis" 40 30
648 60 c. "Hygrocybe acutoconica" 50 40
649 75 c. "Hygrocybe occidentalis" 60 60
650 $1 "Boletellus cubensis" 70 70
651 $2 "Gymnopilus chrysopellus" 1·25 1·50
652 $4 "Cantharellus cinnabarinus" 2·25 2·50
653 $5 "Chlorophyllum molybdites" 2·25 2·50

1992. 40th Anniv of Queen Elizabeth II's Accession. As T **292** of Antigua. Multicoloured.

655 10 c. Charlestown from the sea 20 10
656 40 c. Charlestown square 30 25
657 $1 Mountain scenery 60 50
658 $5 Early cottage 2·50 3·00

1992. Olympic Games, Barcelona. Gold Medal Winners of 1988. Multicoloured.

660 20 c. Type **67** 30 30
661 25 c. Roger Kingdom (hurdles), U.S.A. 30 30
662 50 c. Yugoslavia (men's waterpolo) 50 50
663 80 c. Anja Fichtel (foil), West Germany 70 70
664 $1 Said Aouita (mid-distance running), Morocco 80 80
665 $1.50 Yuri Sedykh (hammer throw), U.S.S.R. 1·10 1·10
666 $3 Shushunova (women's gymnastics), U.S.S.R. 2·00 2·50
667 $5 Valimir Artemov (men's gymnastics), U.S.S.R. 2·50 3·00

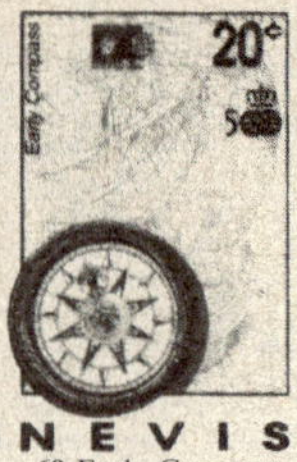

68 "Landscape" (Mariano Fortuny i Marsal)
69 Early Compass and Ship

1992. "Granada '92" International Stamp Exhibition, Spain. Spanish Paintings. Multicoloured.

669	20 c. Type **68**	30	30
670	25 c. "Dona Juana la Loca" (Francisco Pradilla Ortiz) (horiz)	30	30
671	50 c. "Idyll" (Fortuny i Marsal)	50	50
672	80 c. "Old Man Naked in the Sun" (Fortuny i Marsal)	70	70
673	$1 "The Painter's Children in the Japanese Salon" (detail) (Fortuny i Marsal)	80	80
674	$2 "The Painter's Children in the Japanese Salon" (different detail) (Fortuny i Marsal)	1·25	1·25
675	$3 "Still Life: Sea Bream and Oranges" (Luis Eugenio Melendez) (horiz)	2·00	2·50
676	$5 "Still Life: Box of Sweets, Pastry and Other Objects" (Melendez)	2·50	3·00

1992. 500th Anniv of Discovery of America by Columbus (4th issue) and "World Columbian Stamp Expo '92", Chicago. Multicoloured.

678	20 c. Type **69**	25	25
679	50 c. Manatee and fleet	50	50
680	80 c. Green turtle and "Santa Maria"	70	80
681	$1.50 "Santa Maria" and arms	1·25	1·75
682	$3 Queen Isabella of Spain and commission	2·25	2·75
683	$5 Pineapple and colonists	3·00	3·50

1992. 500th Anniv of Discovery of America by Columbus (5th issue). Organization of East Caribbean States. As Nos. 911/12 of Montserrat. Multicoloured.

685	$1 Columbus meeting Amerindians	50	50
686	$2 Ships approaching island	1·25	1·40

70 Minnie Mouse
71 Care Bear and Butterfly

1992. Mickey's Portrait Gallery. Mult.

688	10 c. Type **70**	30	20
689	15 c. Mickey Mouse	30	20
690	40 c. Donald Duck	45	30
691	80 c. Mickey Mouse, 1930	70	70
692	$1 Daisy Duck	80	80
693	$2 Pluto	1·50	1·50
694	$4 Goofy	2·50	2·75
695	$5 Goofy, 1932	2·50	2·75

1992. Christmas. Religious Paintings. As T **218** of Lesotho. Multicoloured.

697	20 c. "The Virgin and Child between Two Saints" (Giovanni Bellini)	30	15
698	40 c. "The Virgin and Child surrounded by Four Angels" (Master of the Castello Nativity)	45	25
699	50 c. "Virgin and Child surrounded by Angels with St. Frediano and St. Augustine" (detail) (Filippo Lippi)	50	30
700	80 c. "The Virgin and Child between St. Peter and St. Sebastian" (Bellini)	70	70
701	$1 "The Virgin and Child with St. Julian and St. Nicholas of Myra" (Lorenzo di Credi)	80	80
702	$2 "St. Bernadino and a Female Saint presenting a Donor to Virgin and Child" (Francesco Bissolo)	1·50	1·50
703	$4 "Madonna and Child with Four Cherubs" (ascr Barthel Bruyn)	2·50	3·00
704	$5 "The Virgin and Child" (Quentin Metsys)	2·75	3·25

No. 699 is inscribed "Fillipo Lippi" in error.

1993. Ecology.

706	**71** 80 c. multicoloured	60	60

1993. Bicentenary of the Louvre, Paris. As T **305** of Antigua. Multicoloured.

708	$1 "The Card Cheat" (left detail) (La Tour)	75	75
709	$1 "The Card Cheat" (centre detail) (La Tour)	75	75
710	$1 "The Card Cheat" (right detail) (La Tour)	75	75
711	$1 "St. Joseph, the Carpenter" (La Tour)	75	75
712	$1 "St. Thomas" (La Tour)	75	75
713	$1 "Adoration of the Shepherds" (left detail) (La Tour)	75	75
714	$1 "Adoration of the Shepherds" (right detail) (La Tour)	75	75
715	$1 "Mary Magdalene with a Candle" (La Tour)	75	75

1993. 15th Death Anniv of Elvis Presley (singer). As T **260** of Dominica. Mult.

717	$1 Elvis Presley	75	75
718	$1 Elvis with guitar	75	75
719	$1 Elvis with microphone	75	75

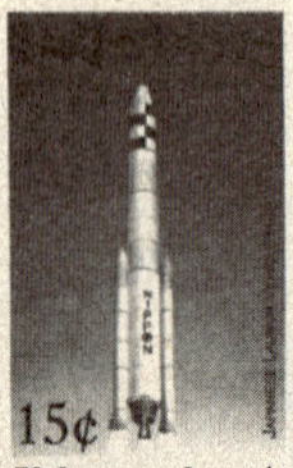

72 Japanese Launch Vehicle H-11
73 "Plumeria rubra"

1993. Anniversaries and Events. Mult.

720	15 c. Type **72**	40	20
721	50 c. Airship "Hindenburg" on fire, 1937 (horiz)	65	65
722	75 c. Konrad Adenauer and Charles de Gaulle (horiz)	65	65
723	80 c. Red Cross emblem and map of Nevis (horiz)	70	70
724	80 c. "Resolute", 1920	70	70
725	80 c. Nelson Museum and map of Nevis (horiz)	70	70
726	80 c. St. Thomas's Church (horiz)	70	70
727	$1 Blue whale (horiz)	1·25	80
728	$3 Mozart	1·75	1·75
729	$3 Graph and U.N. emblems (horiz)	1·60	1·60
730	$3 Lions Club emblem	1·60	1·60
731	$5 Soviet "Energia" launch vehicle SL-17	3·00	3·50
732	$5 Lebaudy-Juillot airship No. 1 "La Jaune" (horiz)	3·00	3·50
733	$5 Adenauer and Pres. Kennedy (horiz)	3·00	3·50

ANNIVERSARIES AND EVENTS: Nos. 720, 731, International Space Year; Nos. 721, 732, 75th death anniv of Count Ferdinand von Zeppelin (airship pioneer); Nos. 722, 733, 25th death anniv of Konrad Adenauer (German statesman); No. 723, 50th anniv of St. Kitts-Nevis Red Cross; No. 724, Americas Cup Yachting Championship; No. 725, Opening of Nelson Museum; No. 726, 150th anniv of Anglican Diocese of North-eastern Caribbean and Aruba; No. 727, Earth Summit '92, Rio; No. 728, Death bicentenary of Mozart; No. 729, International Conference on Nutrition, Rome; No. 730, 75th anniv of International Association of Lions Clubs.

1993. West Indian Flowers. Multicoloured.

735	10 c. Type **73**	40	30
736	25 c. "Bougainvillea"	50	30
737	50 c. "Allamanda cathartica"	65	50
738	80 c. "Anthurium andraeanum"	85	70
739	$1 "Ixora coccinea"	95	75
740	$2 "Hibiscus rosa-sinensis"	1·75	1·75
741	$4 "Justicia brandegeeana"	3·00	3·50
742	$5 "Antigonon leptopus"	3·00	3·50

74 Antillean Blue (male)

1993. Butterflies. Multicoloured.

744	10 c. Type **74**	50	40
745	25 c. Cuban crescentspot (female)	65	40
746	50 c. Ruddy daggerwing	80	50
747	80 c. Little yellow (male)	1·00	75
748	$1 Atala	1·25	90
749	$1.50 Orange-barred giant sulphur	1·75	1·75
750	$4 Tropic queen (male)	3·00	3·75
751	$5 Malachite	3·00	3·75

1993. 40th Anniv of Coronation. As T **307** of Antigua.

753	10 c. multicoloured	10	10
754	80 c. brown and black	35	40
755	$2 multicoloured	90	95
756	$4 multicoloured	1·90	2·00

DESIGNS—38 × 47 mm: 10 c. Queen Elizabeth II at Coronation (photograph by Cecil Beaton); 80 c. Queen wearing Imperial State Crown; $2 Crowning of Queen Elizabeth II; $4 Queen and Prince Charles at polo match.

75 Flag and National Anthem
76 "Annunciation of Mary"

1993. 10th Anniv of Independence of St. Kitts-Nevis. Multicoloured.

758	25 c. Type **75**	30	20
759	80 c. Brown pelican and map of St. Kitts-Nevis	95	75

1993. World Cup Football Championship 1994, U.S.A. As T **278** of Maldive Islands. Mult.

760	10 c. Imre Garaba (Hungary) and Michel Platini (France) (horiz)	30	20
761	25 c. Diego Maradona (Argentina) and Giuseppe Bergomi (Italy) (horiz)	40	20
762	50 c. Luis Fernandez (France) and Vasily Rats (Russia) (horiz)	60	45
763	80 c. Victor Munez (Spain) (horiz)	80	55
764	$1 Preben Elkjaer (Denmark) and Andoni Goicoechea (Spain) (horiz)	90	70
765	$2 Elzo Coelho (Brazil) and Jean Tigana (France) (horiz)	1·75	1·75
766	$3 Pedro Troglio (Argentina) and Sergei Alejnikov (Russia) (horiz)	2·00	2·25
767	$5 Jan Karas (Poland) and Antonio Luiz Costa (Brazil) (horiz)	2·75	3·50

1993. Christmas. Religious Paintings by Durer. Black, yellow and red (Nos. 769/73 and 776) or multicoloured (others).

769	20 c. Type **76**	30	10
770	40 c. "The Nativity" (drawing)	50	25
771	50 c. "Holy Family on a Grassy Bank"	60	30
772	80 c. "The Presentation of Christ in the Temple"	80	50
773	$1 "Virgin in Glory on the Crescent"	90	60
774	$1.60 "The Nativity" (painting)	1·50	1·75
775	$3 "Madonna and Child"	2·25	2·50
776	$5 "The Presentation of Christ in the Temple" (detail)	2·75	3·50

77 Mickey Mouse playing Basketball

1994. Sports and Pastimes. Walt Disney cartoon characters. Multicoloured.

778	10 c. Type **77**	30	30
779	25 c. Minnie Mouse sunbathing (vert)	35	20
780	50 c. Mickey playing volleyball	55	35
781	80 c. Minnie dancing (vert)	70	50
782	$1 Mickey playing football	85	60
783	$1.50 Minnie hula hooping (vert)	1·50	1·50
784	$4 Minnie skipping (vert)	2·75	3·00
785	$5 Mickey wrestling Big Pete	2·75	3·00

1994. Hummel Figurines. As T **302** of Antigua. Multicoloured.

788	5 c. Girl with umbrella	10	30
789	25 c. Boy holding beer mug and parsnips	35	10
790	50 c. Girl sitting in tree	55	35
791	80 c. Boy in hat and scarf	75	50
792	$1 Boy with umbrella	85	60
793	$1.60 Girl with bird	1·50	1·50
794	$2 Boy on sledge	1·75	1·75
795	$5 Boy sitting in apple tree	2·75	3·50

79 Beekeeper collecting Wild Nest

1994. Beekeeping. Multicoloured.

797	50 c. Type **79**	45	30
798	80 c. Beekeeping club	70	40
799	$1.60 Extracting honey from frames	1·40	1·50
800	$3 Keepers placing queen in hive	2·25	2·75

80 Blue Point Himalayan

1994. Persian Cats. Multicoloured.

802	80 c. Type **80**	55	55
803	80 c. Black and white Persian	55	55
804	80 c. Cream Persian	55	55
805	80 c. Red Persian	55	55
806	80 c. Persian	55	55
807	80 c. Persian black smoke	55	55
808	80 c. Chocolate smoke Persian	55	55
809	80 c. Black Persian	55	55

81 Black Coral
83 Symbol 1. Turtles and Cloud

82 Striped Burrfish

1994. Endangered Species. Black Coral.

811	**81** 25 c. multicoloured	40	50
812	– 40 c. multicoloured	50	60
813	– 50 c. multicoloured	50	60
814	– 80 c. multicoloured	60	70

DESIGNS: 40 c. to 80 c. Different forms of coral.

1994. Fishes. Multicoloured.

815	10 c. Type **82**	20	20
816	50 c. Flame-backed angelfish	35	35
817	50 c. Reef bass	35	35
818	50 c. Long-finned damselfish ("Honey Gregory")	35	35
819	50 c. Saddle squirrelfish	35	35
820	50 c. Cobalt chromis	35	35
821	50 c. Genie's neon goby	35	35
822	50 c. Slender-tailed cardinalfish	35	35
823	50 c. Royal gramma	35	35
824	$1 Blue-striped grunt	60	60
825	$1.60 Blue angelfish	1·00	1·25
826	$3 Cocoa damselfish	1·50	1·75

Nos. 816/23 were printed together, se-tenant, forming a composite design.

No. 824 is inscribed "BLUESRIPED GRUNT" in error.

1994. "Philakorea '94" International Stamp Exhibition, Seoul. Longevity symbols. Multicoloured.

828	50 c. Type **83**	25	30
829	50 c. Symbol 2. Cranes and bamboo	25	30
830	50 c. Symbol 3. Deer and bamboo	25	30
831	50 c. Symbol 4. Turtles and Sun	25	30
832	50 c. Symbol 5. Cranes under tree	25	30
833	50 c. Symbol 6. Deer and tree	25	30
834	50 c. Symbol 7. Turtles and rock	25	30
835	50 c. Symbol 8. Cranes above tree	25	30

84 Twin-roofed House with Veranda

1994. Island Architecture. Multicoloured.

836	25 c. Type **84**	30	10
837	50 c. Two-storey house with outside staircase	50	30
838	$1 Government Treasury	80	70
839	$5 Two-storey house with red roof	3·00	3·75

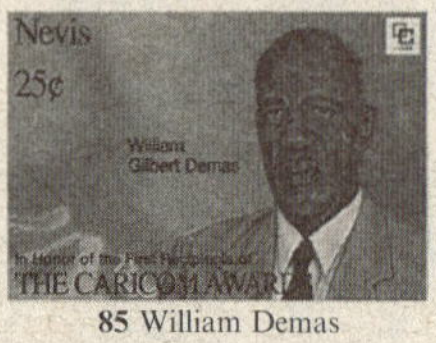

85 William Demas

1994. First Recipients of Order of Caribbean Community. Multicoloured.

841	25 c. Type **85**	30	10
842	50 c. Sir Shridath Ramphal	50	45
843	$1 Derek Walcott	1·00	80

86 "The Virgin Mary as Queen of Heaven" (detail) (Jan Provost)

88 Rufous-breasted Hermit

87 Mickey and Minnie Mouse

1994. Christmas. Religious Paintings. Multicoloured.
844 20 c. Type **86** 20 10
845 40 c. "The Virgin Mary as Queen of Heaven" (different detail) (Provost) 35 25
846 50 c. "The Virgin Mary as Queen of Heaven" (different detail) (Provost) 40 30
847 80 c. "Adoration of the Magi" (detail) (Circle of Van der Goes) 60 40
848 $1 "Adoration of the Magi" (different detail) (Circle of Van der Goes) 70 50
849 $1.60 "Adoration of the Magi" (different detail) (Circle of Van der Goes) 1·25 1·25
850 $3 "Adoration of the Magi" (different detail) (Circle of Van der Goes) 2·00 2·25
851 $5 "The Virgin Mary as Queen of Heaven" (different detail) (Provost) 3·00 3·50

1995. Disney Sweethearts (1st series). Walt Disney Cartoon Characters. Multicoloured.
853 10 c. Type **87** 20 20
854 25 c. Donald and Daisy Duck 35 20
855 50 c. Pluto and Fifi 50 35
856 80 c. Clarabelle Cow and Horace Horsecollar 70 50
857 $1 Pluto and Figaro 85 65
858 $1.50 Polly and Peter Penguin 1·25 1·50
859 $4 Prunella Pullet and Hick Rooster 2·50 3·00
860 $5 Jenny Wren and Cock Robin 2·50 3·00
See also Nos. 998/1006.

1995. Birds. Multicoloured.
862 50 c. Type **88** 20 25
863 50 c. Purple-throated carib 20 25
864 50 c. Green mango 20 25
865 50 c. Bahama woodstar 20 25
866 50 c. Hispaniolan emerald 20 25
867 50 c. Antillean crested hummingbird 20 25
868 50 c. Green-throated carib 20 25
869 50 c. Antillean mango 20 25
870 50 c. Vervain hummingbird 20 25
871 50 c. Jamaican mango 20 25
872 50 c. Cuban emerald 20 25
873 50 c. Blue-headed hummingbird 20 25
874 50 c. Hooded merganser 20 25
875 80 c. Green-backed heron 35 40
876 $2 Double-crested cormorant 85 90
877 $3 Ruddy duck 1·25 1·40
No. 870 is inscribed "VERVIAN" in error.

89 Pointer

1995. Dogs. Multicoloured.
879 25 c. Type **89** 10 10
880 50 c. Old Danish pointer 20 25
881 80 c. Irish setter 35 40
882 80 c. Weimaraner 35 40
883 80 c. Gordon setter 35 40
884 80 c. Brittany spaniel 35 40
885 80 c. American cocker spaniel 35 40
886 80 c. English cocker spaniel 35 40
887 80 c. Labrador retriever 35 40
888 80 c. Golden retriever 35 40
889 80 c. Flat-coated retriever 35 40
890 $1 German short-haired pointer 45 50
891 $2 English setter 85 90
"POINTER" is omitted from the inscription on No. 890.

INDEX
Countries can be quickly located by referring to the index at the end of this volume.

90 "Schulumbergera truncata"

92 Oriental and African People

91 Scouts backpacking

1995. Cacti. Multicoloured.
893 40 c. Type **90** 15 20
894 50 c. "Echinocereus pectinatus" 20 25
895 80 c. "Mammillaria zeilmanniana alba" 35 40
896 $1.60 "Lobivia hertriehiana" 70 75
897 $2 "Hammatocactus setispinus" 85 90
898 $3 "Astrophytum myriostigma" 1·25 1·90

1995. 18th World Scout Jamboree, Netherlands. Multicoloured.
900 $1 Type **91** 45 50
901 $2 Scouts building aerial rope way 85 90
902 $4 Scout map reading 1·75 1·90
Nos. 900/2 were printed together, se-tenant, forming a composite design.

1995. 50th Anniv of End of Second World War in Europe. As T **340** of Antigua. Multicoloured.
904 $1.25 Clark Gable and aircraft 55 60
905 $1.25 Audie Murphy and machine-gunner 55 60
906 $1.25 Glenn Miller playing trombone 55 60
907 $1.25 Joe Louis and infantry 55 60
908 $1.25 Jimmy Doolittle and U.S.S. "Hornet" (aircraft carrier) 55 60
909 $1.25 John Hersey and jungle patrol 55 60
910 $1.25 John F. Kennedy in patrol boat 55 60
911 $1.25 James Stewart and bombers 55 60

1995. 50th Anniv of United Nations. Each lilac and black.
913 $1.25 Type **92** 55 60
914 $1.60 Asian people 75 80
915 $3 American and European people 1·40 1·50
Nos. 913/15 were printed together, se-tenant, forming a composite design.

1995. 50th Anniv of F.A.O. As T **92**. Multicoloured.
917 40 c. Woman wearing yellow headdress 15 20
918 $2 Babies and emblem 85 90
919 $3 Woman wearing blue headdress 1·25 1·40
Nos. 917/19 were printed together, se-tenant, forming a composite design.

93 Rotary Emblem on Nevis Flag

1995. 90th Anniv of Rotary International.
921 **93** $5 multicoloured 2·10 2·25

1995. 95th Birthday of Queen Elizabeth the Queen Mother. As T **344** of Antigua.
923 $1.50 brown, light brown and black 65 70
924 $1.50 multicoloured 65 70
925 $1.50 multicoloured 65 70
926 $1.50 multicoloured 65 70
DESIGNS: No. 923, Queen Elizabeth the Queen Mother (pastel drawing); 924, Wearing pink hat; 925, At desk (oil painting); 926, Wearing blue hat.

1995. 50th Anniv of End of Second World War in the Pacific. United States Aircraft. As T **344** of Antigua. Multicoloured.
928 $2 Grumman F4F Wildcat 85 90
929 $2 Chance Vought F4U-1A Corsair 85 90
930 $2 Vought SB2U Vindicator 85 90
931 $2 Grumman F6F Hellcat 85 90
932 $2 Douglas SDB Dauntless 85 90
933 $2 Grumman TBF-1 Avenger 85 90

94 Emil von Behring (1901 Medicine)

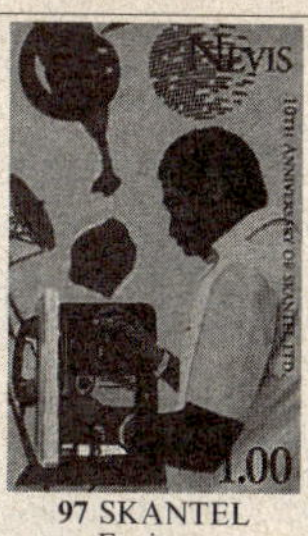

97 SKANTEL Engineer

96 Great Egrets

1995. Centenary of Nobel Trust Fund. Past Prize Winners. Multicoloured.
935 $1.25 Type **94** 55 60
936 $1.25 Wilhelm Rontgen (1901 Physics) 55 60
937 $1.25 Paul Heyse (1910 Literature) 55 60
938 $1.25 Le Duc Tho (1973 Peace) 55 60
939 $1.25 Yasunari Kawabata (1968 Literature) 55 60
940 $1.25 Tsung-dao Lee (1957 Physics) 55 60
941 $1.25 Werner Heisenberg (1932 Physics) 55 60
942 $1.25 Johannes Stark (1919 Physics) 55 60
943 $1.25 Wilhelm Wien (1911 Physics) 55 60

1995. Marine Life. Multicoloured.
946 50 c. Type **96** 20 25
947 50 c. 17th-century galleon 20 25
948 50 c. Galleon and marlin 20 25
949 50 c. Herring gulls 20 25
950 50 c. Nassau groupers 20 25
951 50 c. Spotted eagleray 20 25
952 50 c. Leopard shark and hammerhead 20 25
953 50 c. Hourglass dolphins 20 25
954 50 c. Spanish hogfish 20 25
955 50 c. Jellyfish and seahorses 20 25
956 50 c. Angelfish and buried treasure 20 25
957 50 c. Hawksbill turtle 20 25
958 50 c. Common octopus 20 25
959 50 c. Moray eel 20 25
960 50 c. Queen angelfish and butterflyfish 20 25
961 50 c. Ghost crab and sea star 20 25
Nos. 946/61 were printed together, se-tenant, forming a composite design.

1995. 10th Anniv of SKANTEL (telecommunications company). Multicoloured.
963 $1 Type **97** 45 50
964 $1.50 SKANTEL sign outside Nevis office 65 70

98 "Rucellai Madonna and Child" (detail) (Duccio)

1995. Christmas. Religious Paintings by Duccio di Buoninsegna. Multicoloured.
966 20 c. Type **98** 10 10
967 50 c. "Angel form the Rucellai Madonna" (detail) 20 25
968 80 c. "Madonna and Child" (different) 35 40
969 $1 "Angel from the Annunciation" (detail) 45 50
970 $1.60 "Madonna and Child" (different) 70 75
971 $3 "Angel from the Rucellai Madonna" (different) 1·25 1·40

99 View of Nevis Four Seasons Resort

1996. 5th Anniv of Four Seasons Resort, Nevis. Multicoloured.
973 25 c. Type **99** 10 15
974 50 c. Catamarans, Pinney's Beach 20 25
975 80 c. Robert Trent Jones II Golf Course 35 40
976 $2 Prime Minister Simeon Daniel laying foundation stone 85 90

100 Rat, Plant and Butterfly

1996. Chinese New Year ("Year of the Rat"). Multicoloured.
978 $1 Type **100** 45 50
979 $1 Rat with prickly plant 45 50
980 $1 Rat and bee 45 50
981 $1 Rat and dragonfly 45 50

101 Ancient Greek Boxers

1996. Olympic Games, Atlanta. Previous Medal Winners. Multicoloured.
984 25 c. Type **101** 10 10
985 50 c. Mark Spitz (U.S.A.) (Gold – swimming, 1972) 20 25
986 80 c. Siegbert Horn (East Germany) (Gold – single kayak slalom, 1972) 35 40
987 $1 Jim Thorpe on medal (U.S.A.), 1912 (vert) 45 50
988 $1 Glenn Morris on medal (U.S.A.), 1936 (vert) 45 50
989 $1 Bob Mathias on medal (U.S.A.), 1948 and 1952 (vert) 45 50
990 $1 Rafer Johnson on medal (U.S.A.), 1960 (vert) 45 50
991 $1 Bill Toomey (U.S.A.), 1968 (vert) 45 50
992 $1 Nikolay Avilov (Russia), 1972 (vert) 45 50
993 $1 Bruce Jenner (U.S.A.), 1976 (vert) 45 50
994 $1 Daley Thompson (Great Britain), 1980 and 1984 (vert) 45 50
995 $1 Christian Schenk (East Germany), 1988 (vert) 45 50
996 $3 Olympic Stadium and Siegestor Arch, Munich (vert) 1·25 1·40

1996. Disney Sweethearts (2nd series). As T **87**. Walt Disney Cartoon Characters. Multicoloured.
998 $2 Pocahontas and John Smith 1·25 1·25
999 $2 Mowgli and the Girl 1·25 1·25
1000 $2 Belle and the Beast 1·25 1·25
1001 $2 Cinderella and Prince Charming 1·25 1·25
1002 $2 Pinocchio and the Dutch Girl 1·25 1·25
1003 $2 Grace Martin and Henry Coy 1·25 1·25
1004 $2 Snow White and the Prince 1·25 1·25
1005 $2 Aladdin and Jasmine 1·25 1·25
1006 $2 Pecos Bill and Slue Foot Sue 1·25 1·25

102 Qian Qing Gong, Peking

1996. "CHINA '96" 9th Asian International Stamp Exhibition, Peking. Peking Pagodas. Multicoloured.
1008 $1 Type **102** 45 50
1009 $1 Temple of Heaven 45 50
1010 $1 Zhongnanhai 45 50
1011 $1 Da Zing Hall, Shehyang Palace 45 50
1012 $1 Temple of the Sleeping Buddha 45 50
1013 $1 Huang Qiong Yu, Altar of Heaven 45 50
1014 $1 The Grand Bell Temple 45 50
1015 $1 Imperial Palace 45 50
1016 $1 Pu Tuo Temple 45 50

1996. 70th Birthday of Queen Elizabeth II. As T **363** of Antigua. Multicoloured.
1018 $2 As Type **363** of Antigua 85 90
1019 $2 Wearing evening dress 85 90
1020 $2 In purple hat and coat 85 90

103 Children reading Book

1996. 50th Anniv of U.N.I.C.E.F. Multicoloured.

1022	25 c. Type **103**	10	10
1023	50 c. Doctor and child	20	30
1024	$4 Children	1·75	1·90

104 Cave Paintings, Tassili n'Ajjer, Algeria

1996. 50th Anniv of U.N.E.S.C.O. Multicoloured.

1026	25 c. Type **104**	10	10
1027	$2 Temple, Tikai National Park, Guatemala (vert)	85	90
1028	$3 Temple of Hera, Samos, Greece	1·25	1·40

105 American Academy of Ophthalmology Logo

1996. Centenary of American Academy of Ophthalmology.

1030	**105**	$5 multicoloured	2·10	2·25

106 "Rothmannia longiflora" **107** Western Meadowlark on Decoration

1996. Flowers. Multicoloured.

1031	25 c. Type **106**	10	10
1032	50 c. "Gloriosa simplex"	20	25
1033	$1 "Monodora myristica"	45	50
1034	$1 Giraffe	45	50
1035	$1 "Adansonia digitata"	45	50
1036	$1 "Ansellia gigantea"	45	50
1037	$1 "Geissorhiza rochensis"	45	50
1038	$1 "Arctotis venusta"	45	50
1039	$1 "Gladiotus cardinalis"	45	50
1040	$1 "Eucomis bicolor"	45	50
1041	$1"Protea obtusifolia"	45	50
1042	$2 "Catharanthus roseus"	85	90
1043	$3 "Plumbago auriculata"	1·25	1·40

1996. Christmas. Birds. Multicoloured.

1045	25 c. Type **107**	10	10
1046	50 c. Bird (incorrectly inscr as "American goldfinch") with decorations (horiz)	20	25
1047	80 c. Santa Claus, sleigh and reindeer (horiz	35	40
1048	$1 American goldfinch on stocking	45	50
1049	$1.60 Mockingbird with snowman decoration	70	75
1050	$5 Yellow-rumped cacique and bauble	2·10	2·25

No. 1048 is inscribed "WESTERN MEADOWLARK" and No. 1050 "YELLOW-RUMPED CAIEQUE", both in error.

109 Giant Panda eating Bamboo Shoots **110** Elquemedo Willett

1997. "HONG KONG '97" International Stamp Exhibition. Giant Pandas. Multicoloured.

1053	$1.60 Type **109**	70	75
1054	$1.60 Head of panda	70	75
1055	$1.60 Panda with new-born cub	70	75
1056	$1.60 Panda hanging from branch	70	75
1057	$1.60 Panda asleep on tree	70	75
1058	$1.60 Panda climbing trunk	70	75

1997. Nevis Cricketers. Multicoloured.

1060	25 c. Type **110**	10	15
1061	80 c. Stuart Williams	35	40
1062	$2 Keith Arthurton	85	90

111 Crimson-speckled Moth

1997. Butterflies and Moths. Multicoloured.

1064	10 c. Type **111**	10	10
1065	25 c. Purple emperor	10	15
1066	50 c. Regent skipper	20	25
1067	80 c. Provence burnet moth	35	40
1068	$1 Common wall butterfly	45	50
1069	$1 Red-lined geometrid	45	50
1070	$1 Boisduval's autumnal moth	45	50
1071	$1 Blue pansy	45	50
1072	$1 Common clubtail	45	50
1073	$1 Tufted jungle king	45	50
1074	$1 Lesser marbled fritillary	45	50
1075	$1 Peacock royal	45	50
1076	$1 Emperor gum moth	45	50
1077	$1 Orange swallow-tailed moth	45	50
1078	$4 Cruiser butterfly	1·75	1·90

No. 1073 is inscribed "TUFTED JUNGLE QUEEN" in error.

113 Paul Harris and Literacy Class

1997. 50th Death Anniv of Paul Harris (founder of Rotary International).

1081	**113**	$2 multicoloured	85	90

1997. Golden Wedding of Queen Elizabeth and Prince Philip. As T **350** of Maldive Islands. Multicoloured.

1083	$1 Queen Elizabeth II	45	50
1084	$1 Royal Coat of Arms	45	50
1085	$1 Queen Elizabeth wearing red hat and coat with Prince Philip	45	50
1086	$1 Queen Elizabeth in blue coat and Prince Philip	45	50
1087	$1 Caernarvon Castle	45	50
1088	$1 Prince Philip in R.A.F. uniform	45	50

1997. "Pacific '97" International Stamp Exhibition, San Francisco. Death Centenary of Heinrich von Stephan. As T **351** of Maldive Islands.

1090	$1.60 green	70	75
1091	$1.60 brown	70	75
1092	$1.60 blue	70	75

DESIGNS: No. 1090, Russian reindeer post, 1859; 1091, Von Stephan and Mercury; 1092, "City of Cairo" (paddle-steamer), Mississippi, 1800s.

1997. Birth Bicentenary of Hiroshige (Japanese painter). "One Hundred Famous Views of Edo". As T **352** of Maldive Islands. Multicoloured.

1094	$1.60 "Scattered Pines, Tone River"	70	75
1095	$1.60 "Mouth of Nakagawa River"	70	75
1096	$1.60 "Niijuku Ferry"	70	75
1097	$1.60 "Horie and Nekozane"	70	75
1098	$1.60 "Konodai and the Tone River"	70	75
1099	$1.60 "Maple Trees, Tekona Shrine and Bridge, Mama"	70	75

114 Augusta National Course, U.S.A.

1997. Golf Courses of the World. Multicoloured.

1101	$1 Type **114**	45	50
1102	$1 Cabo del Sol, Mexico	45	50
1103	$1 Cypress Point, U.S.A.	45	50
1104	$1 Lost City, South Africa	45	50
1105	$1 Moscow Country Club, Russia	45	50
1106	$1 New South Wales, Australia	45	50
1107	$1 Royal Montreal, Canada	45	50
1108	$1 St. Andrews, Scotland	45	50
1109	$1 Four Seasons Resort, Nevis	45	50

115 "Cantharellus cibarius" **116** Diana, Princess of Wales

1997. Fungi. Multicoloured.

1110	25 c. Type **115**	10	10
1111	50 c. "Stropharia aeruginosa"	20	25
1112	80 c. "Suillus hiteus"	35	40
1113	80 c. "Amanita muscaria"	35	40
1114	80 c. "Lactarius rufus"	35	40
1115	80 c. "Amanita rubescens"	35	40
1116	80 c. "Armillaria mellea"	35	40
1117	80 c. "Russula sardonia"	35	40
1118	$1 "Boletus edulis"	45	50
1119	$1 "Pholiota lenta"	45	50
1120	$1 "Cortinarius bolaris"	45	50
1121	$1 "Coprinus picaceus"	45	50
1122	$1 "Amanita phalloides"	45	50
1123	$1 "Cystolepiota aspera"	45	50
1124	$3 "Lactarius turpis"	1·25	1·40
1125	$4 "Entoloma clypeatum"	1·75	1·90

Nos. 1112/17 and 1118/23 respectively were printed together, se-tenant, with the backgrounds forming composite designs.

1997. Diana, Princess of Wales Commemoration. Multicoloured.

1127	$1 Type **116**	45	50
1128	$1 Wearing white blouse	45	50
1129	$1 In wedding dress, 1981	45	50
1130	$1 Wearing turquoise blouse	45	50
1131	$1 Wearing tiara	45	50
1132	$1 Wearing blue blouse	45	50
1133	$1 Wearing pearl necklace	45	50
1134	$1 Wearing diamond drop earrings	45	50
1135	$1 Wearing sapphire necklace and earrings	45	50

117 Victoria Govt Class S Pacific Locomotive, Australia

1997. Trains of the World. Multicoloured.

1136	10 c. Type **117**	10	10
1137	50 c. Express steam-locomotive, Japan	20	30
1138	80 c. L.M.S. steam-turbine locomotive, Great Britain	35	40
1139	$1 Electric locomotive, Switzerland	45	50
1140	$1.50 "Mikado" steam locomotive, Sudan	65	70
1141	$1.50 "Mohammed Ali el Kebir" steam locomotive, Egypt	65	70
1142	$1.50 Southern Region steam locomotive "Leatherhead"	65	70
1143	$1.50 Great Southern Railway Drumm battery-powered railcar, Ireland	65	70
1144	$1.50 Pacific locomotive, Germany	65	70
1145	$1.50 Canton–Hankow Railway Pacific locomotive, China	65	70
1146	$2 L.M.S. high-pressure locomotive, Great Britain	85	90
1147	$3 Great Northern Railway "Kestrel", Ireland	1·25	1·40

118 "Selection of Angels" (detail) (Durer)

1997. Christmas. Paintings. Multicoloured.

1149	20 c. Type **118**	10	10
1150	25 c. "Selection of Angels" (different detail) (Durer)	10	15
1151	50 c. "Andromeda and Perseus" (Rubens)	20	25
1152	80 c. "Harmony" (detail) (Raphael)	35	40
1153	$1.60 "Harmony" (different detail) (Raphael)	70	75
1154	$5 "Holy Trinity" (Raphael)	2·10	2·25

119 Tiger (semi-circular character at top left)

1998. Chinese New Year ("Year of the Tiger"). Multicoloured.

1156	80 c. Type **119**	35	40
1157	80 c. Oblong character at bottom right	35	40
1158	80 c. Circular character at top left	35	40
1159	80 c. Square character at bottom right	35	40

120 Social Security Board Emblem **121** Soursop

1998. 20th Anniv of Social Security Board. Multicoloured.

1161	30 c. Type **120**	15	20
1162	$1.20 Opening of Social Security building, Charlestown (horiz)	50	55

1998. Fruits. Multicoloured.

1164	5 c. Type **121**	10	10
1165	10 c. Carambola	10	10
1166	25 c. Guava	10	15
1167	30 c. Papaya	15	20
1168	50 c. Mango	20	25
1169	60 c. Golden apple	25	30
1170	80 c. Pineapple	35	40
1171	90 c. Watermelon	40	45
1172	$1 Bananas	45	50
1173	$1.80 Orange	80	85
1174	$3 Honeydew	1·25	1·40
1175	$5 Cantelope	2·10	2·25
1176	$10 Pomegranate	4·25	4·50
1177	$20 Cashew	8·75	9·00

122 African Fish Eagle

1998. Endangered Species. Multicoloured.

1178	30 c. Type **122**	15	20
1179	80 c. Summer tanager at nest	35	40
1180	90 c. Orang Utan and young	40	45
1181	$1 Young chimpanzee	45	50
1182	$1 Keel-billed toucan	45	50
1183	$1 Chaco peccary	45	50
1184	$1 Spadefoot toad and insect	45	50
1185	$1 Howler monkey	45	50
1186	$1 Alaskan brown bear	45	50
1187	$1 Koala bears	45	50
1188	$1 Brown pelican	45	50
1189	$1 Iguana	45	50
1190	$1.20 Tiger cub	50	55
1191	$2 Cape pangolin	85	90
1192	$3 Hoatzin	1·25	1·40

No. 1185 is inscribed "MOWLER MONKEY" and No. 1192 "MOATZIN", both in error.

123 Chaim Topol (Israeli actor)

1998. "Israel 98" International Stamp Exhibition, Tel-Aviv.

1194	**123**	$1.60 multicoloured	70	75

124 Boeing 747 200B (U.S.A.)

1998. Aircraft. Multicoloured.
1195 10 c. Type **124** 10 10
1196 90 c. Cessna 185 Skywagon (U.S.A.) 40 45
1197 $1 Northrop B-2 A (U.S.A.) . 45 50
1198 $1 Lockheed SR-71A (U.S.A.) . 45 50
1199 $1 Beechcraft T-44A (U.S.A.) . 45 50
1200 $1 Sukhoi Su-27UB (U.S.S.R.) . 45 50
1201 $1 Hawker Siddeley Harrier GR. Mk1 (Great Britain) . 45 50
1202 $1 Boeing E-3A Sentry (U.S.A.) . 45 50
1203 $1 Convair B-36H (U.S.A.) . 45 50
1204 $1 IAI KFIR C2 (Israel) . . 45 50
1205 $1.80 McDonnell Douglas DC-9 SO (U.S.A.) 75 80
1206 $5 Airbus A-300 B4 (U.S.A.) . 2·10 2·25

125 Anniversary Logo

127 Prime Minister Kennedy Simmonds receiving Constitutional Instruments from Princess Margaret, 1983

126 Butterflyfish

1998. 10th Anniv of "Voice of Nevis" Radio.
1208 **125** 20 c. violet, light violet and black 10 10
1209 – 30 c. multicoloured . . . 15 20
1210 – $1.20 multicoloured . . . 50 55
DESIGNS: 30 c. Evered Herbert (Station Manager); $1.20, V.O.N. studio.

1998. International Year of the Ocean. Multicoloured.
1212 30 c. Type **126** 15 20
1213 80 c. Bicolor cherub 35 40
1214 90 c. Copperbanded butterfly-fish (vert) 40 45
1215 90 c. Forcepsfish (vert) . . . 40 45
1216 90 c. Double-saddled butterfly-fish (vert) 40 45
1217 90 c. Blue surgeonfish (vert) . 40 45
1218 90 c. Orbiculate batfish (vert) 40 45
1219 90 c. Undulated triggerfish (vert) 40 45
1220 90 c. Rock beauty (vert) . . 40 45
1221 90 c. Flamefish (vert) 40 45
1222 90 c. Queen angelfish (vert) . 40 45
1223 $1 Pyjama cardinal fish . . . 45 50
1224 $1 Wimplefish 45 50
1225 $1 Long-nosed filefish . . . 45 50
1226 $1 Oriental sweetlips 45 50
1227 $1 Blue-spotted boxfish . . . 45 50
1228 $1 Blue-stripe angelfish . . . 45 50
1229 $1 Goldrim tang 45 50
1230 $1 Blue chromis 45 50
1231 $1 Common clownfish 45 50
1232 $1.20 Silver badgerfish . . . 50 55
1233 $2 Asfur angelfish 85 90
Nos. 1214/22 and 1223/31 respectively were printed together, se-tenant, with the backgrounds forming composite designs.
No. 1223 is inscribed "Pygama" in error.

1998. 15th Anniv of Independence.
1235 **127** $1 multicoloured 45 50

128 Stylised "50"

1998. 50th Anniv of Organization of American States.
1236 **128** $1 blue, light blue and black 45 50

129 365 "California"

1998. Birth Centenary of Enzo Ferrari (car manufacturer). Multicoloured.
1237 $2 Type **129** 85 90
1238 $2 Pininfarina's P6 . . . . . 85 90
1239 $2 250 LM 85 90

130 Scouts of Different Nationalities

1998. 19th World Scout Jamboree, Chile. Multicoloured.
1241 $3 Type **130** . . . . 1·25 1·40
1242 $3 Scout and Gettysburg veterans, 1913 . . . . . . 1·25 1·40
1243 $3 First black scout troop, Virginia, 1928 . . . . . 1·25 1·40

131 Gandhi in South Africa, 1914

133 Princess Diana

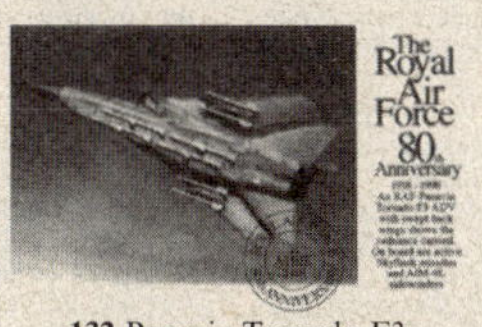
132 Panavia Tornado F3

1998. 50th Death Anniv of Mahatma Gandhi. Multicoloured.
1244 $1 Type **131** 45 50
1245 $1 Gandhi in Downing Street, London 45 50

1998. 80th Anniv of Royal Air Force. Multicoloured.
1246 $2 Type **132** 85 90
1247 $2 Panavia Tornado F3 firing Skyflash missile 85 90
1248 $2 Tristar Mk1 Tanker refuelling Tornado GR1 . 85 90
1249 $2 Panavia Tornado GR1 firing AIM-9L missile 85 90

1998. 1st Death Anniv of Diana, Princess of Wales.
1251 **133** $1 multicoloured . . . 45 50

134 Kitten and Santa Claus Decoration

1998. Christmas. Multicoloured.
1252 25 c. Type **134** 10 15
1253 60 c. Kitten playing with bauble 25 30
1254 80 c. Kitten in Christmas stocking (vert) 35 40
1255 90 c. Fox Terrier puppy and presents 40 45
1256 $1 Angel with swallows . . 45 50
1257 $3 Boy wearing Santa hat (vert) 1·25 1·40

135 Mickey Mouse

1998. 70th Birthday of Mickey Mouse. Walt Disney cartoon characters playing basketball. Mult.
1259 $1 Type **135** 45 50
1260 $1 Donald Duck bouncing ball 45 50
1261 $1 Minnie Mouse in green kit 45 50
1262 $1 Goofy wearing purple . . 45 50
1263 $1 Huey in green baseball cap 45 50
1264 $1 Goofy and Mickey 45 50
1265 $1 Mickey bouncing ball . . 45 50
1266 $1 Huey, Dewey and Louie . 45 50
1267 $1 Mickey, in purple, shooting ball 45 50
1268 $1 Goofy in yellow shorts and vest 45 50
1269 $1 Minnie in purple 45 50
1270 $1 Mickey in yellow vest and blue shorts 45 50
1271 $1 Minnie in yellow 45 50
1272 $1 Donald spinning ball on finger 45 50
1273 $1 Donald and Mickey . . . 45 50
1274 $1 Dewey shooting for goal . 45 50

136 Black Silver Fox Rabbits

1999. Chinese New Year ("Year of the Rabbit"). Multicoloured.
1276 $1.60 Type **136** 70 75
1277 $1.60 Dutch rabbits (brown with white "collar") 70 75
1278 $1.60 Dwarf rabbits (brown) . 70 75
1279 $1.60 Netherlands Dwarf rabbits (white with brown markings) 70 75

137 Laurent Blanc (France)

1999. Leading Players of 1998 World Cup Football Championship, France. Multicoloured.
1281 $1 Type **137** 45 50
1282 $1 Dennis Bergkamp (Holland) 45 50
1283 $1 Davor Sukor (Croatia) . . 45 50
1284 $1 Ronaldo (Brazil) 45 50
1285 $1 Didier Deschamps (France) 45 50
1286 $1 Patrick Kluivert (Holland) 45 50
1287 $1 Rivaldo (Brazil) 45 50
1288 $1 Zinedine Zidane (France) . 45 50
Nos. 1281/8 were printed together, se-tenant, with the backgrounds forming a composite design.

138 Kritosaurus

1999. "Australia '99" World Stamp Exhibition, Melbourne. Prehistoric Animals. Multicoloured.
1290 30 c. Type **138** 15 20
1291 60 c. Oviraptor 25 30
1292 80 c. Eustreptospondylus . . 35 40
1293 $1.20 Tenontosaurus 50 55
1294 $1.20 Edmontosaurus 50 55
1295 $1.20 Avimimus 50 55
1296 $1.20 Minmi 50 55
1297 $1.20 Segnosaurus 50 55
1298 $1.20 Kentrosaurus 50 55
1299 $1.20 Deinonychus 50 55
1300 $1.20 Saltasaurus 50 55
1301 $1.20 Compsoganthus 50 55
1302 $1.20 Hadrosaurus 50 55
1303 $1.20 Tuojiangosaurus . . . 50 55
1304 $1.20 Euoplocephalus 50 55
1305 $1.20 Anchisaurus 50 55
1306 $2 Ouranosaurus 85 90
1307 $3 Muttaburrasaurus . . . . 1·25 1·40
Nos. 1294/9 and 1300/5 respectively were printed together, se-tenant, with the backgrounds forming composite designs.

139 Emperor Haile Selassie of Ethiopia

1999. Millennium Series. Famous People of the Twentieth Century. World Leaders. Multicoloured.
1309 90 c. Type **139** 40 45
1310 90 c. Haile Selassie and Ethiopian warriors (56×41 mm) 40 45
1311 90 c. David Ben-Gurion, woman soldier and ancient Jewish prophet (56×41 mm) 40 45
1312 90 c. David Ben-Gurion (Prime Minister of Israel) 40 45
1313 90 c. President Franklin D. Roosevelt of U.S.A. and Mrs. Roosevelt 40 45
1314 90 c. Franklin and Eleanor Roosevelt campaigning (56×41 mm) 40 45
1315 90 c. Mao Tse-tung and the Long March, 1934 (56×41 mm) 40 45
1316 90 c. Poster of Mao Tse-tung (founder of People's Republic of China) 40 45

OFFICIAL STAMPS

1980. Nos. 40/49 optd **OFFICIAL**.
O 1 15 c. Sugar cane being harvested 10 10
O 2 25 c. Crafthouse (craft centre) 10 10
O 3 30 c. "Europa" (liner) . . . 10 10
O 4 40 c. Lobster and sea crab . 15 15
O 5 45 c. Royal St. Kitts Hotel and golf course 20 20
O 6 50 c. Pinney's Beach, Nevis . 15 20
O 7 55 c. New runway at Golden Rock 15 20
O 8 $1 Picking cotton 15 25
O 9 $5 Brewery 45 55
O10 $10 Pineapples and peanuts . 70 90

1981. Nos. 60/71 optd **OFFICIAL**.
O11 15 c. New River Mill 10 10
O12 20 c. Nelson Museum 10 10
O13 25 c. St. James' Parish Church 10 15
O14 30 c. Nevis Lane 15 15
O15 40 c. Zetland Plantation . . 15 20
O16 45 c. Nisbet Plantation . . . 20 25
O17 50 c. Pinney's Beach 20 25
O18 55 c. Eva Wilkin's Studio . . 25 30
O19 $1 Nevis at dawn 30 35
O20 $2.50 Ruins of Fort Charles . 50 65
O21 $5 Old Bath House 70 80
O22 $10 Beach at Nisbet's . . . . 1·25 1·40

1983. Nos. 72/7 optd or surch **OFFICIAL**.
O23 45 c. on $2 "Royal Sovereign" 10 15
O24 45 c. on $2 Prince Charles and Lady Diana Spencer . . . 20 25
O25 55 c. "Royal Caroline" . . . 10 15
O26 55 c. Prince Charles and Lady Diana Spencer 25 25
O27 $1.10 on $5 "Britannia" . . 20 25
O28 $1.10 on $5 Prince Charles and Lady Diana Spencer . . . 55 60

1985. Nos. 187/98 optd **OFFICIAL**.
O29 15 c. Flamboyant 15 15
O30 20 c. Eyelash orchid 30 20
O31 30 c. Bougainvillea 30 30
O32 40 c. Hibiscus sp. 30 30
O33 50 c. Night-blooming cereus . 35 35
O34 55 c. Yellow mahoe 35 35
O35 60 c. Spider-lily 40 40
O36 75 c. Scarlet cordia 45 45
O37 $1 Shell-ginger 60 60
O38 $3 Blue petrea . . . . 1·25 1·75
O39 $5 Coral hibiscus . . . . . . 2·00 2·25
O40 $10 Passion flower . . . . . 3·00 3·00

1993. Nos. 578/91 optd **OFFICIAL**.
O41 5 c. Type **63** 10 10
O42 10 c. "Historis odius" 10 10
O43 15 c. "Marpesia corinna" . . 10 10
O44 20 c. "Anartia amathea" . . 10 10
O45 25 c. "Junonia evarete" . . . 10 10
O46 40 c. "Heliconius charithonia" 20 25
O47 50 c. "Marpesia petreus" . . 25 30
O48 75 c. "Heliconius doris" . . 35 40
O49 80 c. "Dione juno" 35 40
O50 $1 "Hypolimnas misippus" . . 45 50
O51 $3 "Danaus plexippus" . . . 1·40 1·50
O52 $5 "Heliconius sara" . . . . 2·25 2·40
O53 $10 "Tithorea harmonia" . . 4·50 4·75
O54 $20 "Dryas julia" . . . . . 9·25 9·50

NEW BRUNSWICK

An eastern province of the Dominion of Canada, whose stamps are now used.

1851. 12 pence = 1 shilling;
20 shilling = 1 pound.
1860. 100 cents = 1 dollar.

1 Royal Crown and Heraldic Flowers of the United Kingdom

1851.

1	**1**	3d. red	£1600	£325
4		6d. yellow	£4500	£700
5		1s. mauve	£13000	£4000

2 Locomotive

3 Queen Victoria

1860.

9	**2**	1 c. purple	30·00	30·00
10	**3**	2 c. orange	14·00	14·00
13	–	5 c. brown	£3500	
14	–	5 c. green	12·00	12·00
17	–	10 c. red	35·00	35·00
18	–	12½ c. blue	50·00	40·00
19	–	17 c. black	32·00	40·00

DESIGNS—VERT: 5 c. brown, Charles Connell; 5 c. green; 10 c. Queen Victoria; 17 c. King Edward VII when Prince of Wales. HORIZ: 12½ c. Steamship.

NEWFOUNDLAND

An island off the east coast of Canada. A British Dominion merged since 1949 with Canada, whose stamps it now uses.

1857. 12 pence = 1 shilling;
20 shillings = 1 pound.
1866. 100 cents = 1 dollar.

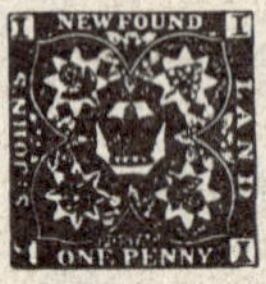

1

2

3 Royal Crown and Heraldic Flowers of the United Kingdom

1857. Imperf.

1	**1**	1d. purple	85·00	£140
10	**2**	2d. red	£300	£375
11	**3**	3d. green	65·00	£150
12	**2**	4d. red	£2250	£800
13	**1**	5d. brown	90·00	£275
14	**2**	6d. red	£2750	£600
7		6½d. red	£2250	£2500
8		8d. red	£225	£300
9		1s. red	£13000	£4750

The frame design of Type **2** differs for each value.

1861. Imperf.

21	**1**	1d. brown	£150	£225
22	**2**	2d. lake	£150	£375
23		4d. lake	26·00	90·00
24a	**1**	5d. brown	45·00	£190
24b	**2**	6d. lake	20·00	£100
24c		6½d. lake	65·00	£425
24d		8d. lake	70·00	£475
24e		1s. lake	35·00	£300

6 Codfish

7 Common Seal on Ice-floe

8 Prince Consort

9 Queen Victoria

10 Schooner

11 Queen Victoria

1866. Perf (2 c. also roul).

31	**6**	2 c. green	65·00	28·00
26	**7**	5 c. brown	£450	£170
32	**8**	10 c. black	£160	35·00
33	**9**	12 c. brown	40·00	40·00
29	**10**	13 c. orange	85·00	60·00
30	**11**	24 c. blue	32·00	32·00

12 King Edward VII, when Prince of Wales

14 Queen Victoria

1868. Perf or roul.

34	**12**	1 c. purple	48·00	45·00
36		3 c. orange	£250	£100
42		3 c. blue	£250	3·50
38	**7**	5 c. black	£225	£100
43		5 c. blue	£170	2·75
39	**14**	6 c. red	6·50	16·00

19 Newfoundland Dog

15 King Edward VII, when Prince of Wales

16 Codfish

17

18 Common Seal on Ice-floe

20 Atlantic Brigantine

21 Queen Victoria

1880.

49	**19**	½ c. red	8·00	6·50
59		½ c. black	8·00	4·00
44a	**15**	1 c. brown	22·00	7·50
50a		1 c. green	5·50	2·50
46	**16**	2 c. green	42·00	20·00
51		2 c. orange	12·00	4·00
47a	**17**	3 c. blue	65·00	2·50
52		3 c. brown	55·00	1·00
59a	**18**	5 c. blue	55·00	2·50
54	**20**	10 c. black	45·00	48·00

1890.

55	**21**	3 c. grey	24·00	1·00

This stamp on pink paper was stained by sea-water.

22 Queen Victoria

23 John Cabot

24 Cape Bonavista

25 Caribou-hunting

1897. 400th Anniv of Discovery of Newfoundland and 60th Year of Queen Victoria's Reign. Dated "1497 1897".

66	**22**	1 c. green	2·00	4·00
67	**23**	2 c. red	1·25	2·25
68	**24**	3 c. blue	3·00	50
69	**25**	4 c. olive	9·00	2·75
70	–	5 c. violet	11·00	2·75
71	–	6 c. brown	8·00	2·75
72	–	8 c. orange	16·00	7·50
73	–	10 c. brown	35·00	5·00
74	–	12 c. blue	32·00	5·00
75	–	15 c. red	18·00	15·00
76	–	24 c. violet	22·00	18·00
77	–	30 c. blue	42·00	55·00
78	–	35 c. red	60·00	55·00
79	–	60 c. black	16·00	11·00

DESIGNS—As Type **24**: 5 c. Mining; 6 c. Logging; 8 c. Fishing; 10 c. Cabot's ship, the "Matthew"; 15 c. Seals; 24 c. Salmon-fishing; 35 c. Iceberg. As Type **23**: 12 c. Willow/red grouse; 30 c. Seal of the Colony; 60 c. Henry VII.

1897. Surch **ONE CENT** and bar.

80	**21**	1 c. on 3 c. grey	40·00	17·00

39 Prince Edward later Duke of Windsor

40 Queen Victoria

1897. Royal portraits.

83	**39**	½ c. olive	2·00	1·25
84	**40**	1 c. red	2·75	2·75
85a	–	1 c. green	6·00	10
86	–	2 c. orange	2·75	1·75
87	–	2 c. red	12·00	30
88	–	3 c. orange	12·00	20
89	–	4 c. violet	22·00	3·75
90	–	5 c. blue	35·00	2·75

DESIGNS: 2 c. King Edward VII when Prince of Wales; 3 c. Queen Alexandra when Princess of Wales; 4 c. Queen Mary when Duchess of York; 5 c. King George V when Duke of York.

45 Map of Newfoundland

46 King James I

47 Arms of Colonisation Co

49 "Endeavour' (immigrant ship), 1610

1908.

94	**45**	2 c. lake	25·00	60

1910. Dated "1610 1910".

109	**46**	1 c. green	1·25	20
107	**47**	2 c. red	3·50	35
97	–	3 c. olive	5·00	14·00
98	**49**	4 c. violet	12·00	12·00
108	–	5 c. blue	8·00	2·50
111	–	6 c. purple	17·00	42·00
112	–	8 c. bistre	48·00	60·00
102	–	9 c. green	40·00	75·00
103	–	10 c. grey	55·00	95·00
115	–	12 c. brown	60·00	60·00
105	–	15 c. black	65·00	95·00

DESIGNS—HORIZ: 5 c. Cupids; 8 c. Mosquito; 9 c. Logging camp, Red Indian Lake; 10 c. Paper mills, Grand Falls. VERT: 3 c John Guy; 6 c. Sir Francis Bacon; 12 c. King Edward VII; 15 c. King George V. (Cupids and Mosquito are places).

57 Queen Mary

58 King George V

67 Seal of Newfoundland

1911. Coronation.

117	**57**	1 c. green	5·50	20
118	**58**	2 c. red	3·00	20
119	–	3 c. brown	17·00	26·00
120	–	4 c. purple	16·00	25·00
121	–	5 c. blue	4·75	1·25
122	–	6 c. grey	10·00	24·00
123	–	8 c. blue	48·00	75·00
124	–	9 c. blue	14·00	40·00
125	–	10 c. green	26·00	38·00
126	–	12 c. plum	20·00	38·00
127	**67**	15 c. lake	16·00	45·00

PORTRAITS—VERT (As Type **57/8**): 3 c. Duke of Windsor when Prince of Wales; 4 c. King George VI when Prince Albert; 5 c. Princess Mary, the Princess Royal; 6 c. Duke of Gloucester when Prince Henry; 8 c. Duke of Kent when Prince George; 9 c. Prince John; 10 c. Queen Alexandra; 12 c. Duke of Connaught.

68 Caribou

1919. Newfoundland Contingent. 1914–18.

130	**68**	1 c. green	3·00	20
131		2 c. red	2·75	85
132		3 c. brown	4·00	20
133		4 c. mauve	4·25	60
134		5 c. blue	4·50	1·10
135		6 c. grey	4·50	30·00
136		8 c. purple	8·00	38·00
137		10 c. green	4·50	3·25
138		12 c. orange	18·00	45·00
139		15 c. blue	15·00	55·00
140		24 c. brown	22·00	25·00
141		36 c. olive	12·00	24·00

DESIGNS—Each inscr with the name of a different action: 1 c. Suvla Bay; 3 c. Gueudecourt; 4 c. Beaumont Hamel; 6 c. Monchy; 10 c. Steenbeck; 15 c. Langemarck; 24 c. Cambrai; 36 c. Combles. The 2, 5, 8 and 12 c. are inscribed "Royal Naval Reserve. Ubique".

1919. Air. Hawker Flight. No. 132a optd **FIRST TRANS- ATLANTIC AIR POST April, 1919.**

142	**68**	3 c. brown	£15000	£8000

1919. Air. Alcock and Brown Flight. Surch **Trans-Atlantic AIR POST, 1919. ONE DOLLAR.**

143	$1 on 15 c. red (No. 75)	£110	£110

1920. Surch in words between bars.

144	2 c. on 30 c. blue (No. 77)	3·50	15·00
146	3 c. on 15 c. red (No. 75)	12·00	11·00
147	3 c. on 35 c. red (No. 78)	5·00	9·00

1921. Air. Optd **AIR MAIL to Halifax, N.S. 1921.**

148a	35 c. red (No. 78)	80·00	80·00

73 Twin Hills, Tor's Cove

75 Statue of Fighting Newfoundlander, St. John's

1923.

149	**73**	1 c. green	60	10
150	–	2 c. red	60	10
151	**75**	3 c. brown	60	10
152	–	4 c. purple	90	30
153	–	5 c. blue	1·50	1·50
154	–	6 c. grey	2·50	7·00
155	–	8 c. purple	3·00	3·25
156	–	9 c. green	17·00	28·00
157	–	10 c. violet	4·25	2·50
158	–	11 c. olive	2·25	15·00
159	–	12 c. lake	2·50	8·00
160	–	15 c. blue	2·50	12·00
161	–	20 c. brown	4·75	10·00
162	–	24 c. brown	45·00	75·00

DESIGNS—HORIZ: 2 c. South-west Arm, Trinity; 6 c. Upper Steadies, Humber River; 8 c. Quidi Vidi, near St. John's; 9 c. Caribou crossing lake; 11 c. Shell Bird Island; 12 c. Mount Moriah, Bay of Islands; 20 c. Placentia. VERT: 4 c. Humber River; 5 c. Coast at Trinity; 10 c. Humber River Canon; 15 c. Humber River, near Little Rapids; 24 c. Topsail Falls.

1927. Air. Optd **Air Mail DE PINEDO 1927**.

163	60 c. black (No. 79)	£23000	£7000

88 Newfoundland and Labrador

89 S.S. "Caribou"

90 King George V and Queen Mary

91 Duke of Windsor when Prince of Wales

1928. Publicity issue.

164	**88**	1 c. green	2·00	1·00
180	**89**	2 c. red	1·50	20
181	**90**	3 c. brown	1·00	10
201	**91**	4 c. mauve	1·75	70
183	–	5 c. grey	5·50	2·00
184a	–	6 c. blue	2·25	11·00
170	–	8 c. brown	2·00	23·00
171	–	9 c. green	2·00	10·00
185	–	10 c. violet	3·50	3·00
173	–	12 c. lake	2·00	18·00
174a	–	14 c. purple	5·00	7·50
175	–	15 c. blue	2·75	26·00
176a	–	20 c. black	2·50	6·50
177	–	28 c. green	27·00	48·00
178	–	30 c. brown	6·00	15·00

DESIGNS—HORIZ: 5 c. Express train; 6 c. Newfoundland Hotel, St. John's; 8 c. Heart's Content; 10 c. War Memorial, St. John's; 15 c. Vickers Vimy aircraft; 20 c. Parliament House, St. John's. VERT: 9, 14 c. Cabot Tower, St. John's; 12, 28 c. G.P.O., St. John's; 30 c. Grand Falls, Labrador.

1929. Surch **THREE CENTS.**

188		3 c. on 6 c. (No. 154)	85	4·00

1930. Air. No. 141 surch **Trans-Atlantic AIR MAIL By B. M. "Columbia" September 1930** Fifty Cents.

191	**68**	50 c. on 36 c. olive	£4500	£4250

103 Westland Limousine III and Dog-team

104 Vickers-Vimy Biplane and early Sailing Packet

105 Routes of historic Trans-Atlantic Flights

1931. Air.

192	**103**	15 c. brown	4·00	10·00
193	**104**	50 c. green	26·00	42·00
194	**105**	$1 blue	45·00	85·00

107 Codfish

108 King George V

110 Duke of Windsor when Prince of Wales

111 Reindeer

112 Queen Elizabeth II when Princess

121 Corner Brook Paper Mills

1932.

209	**107**	1 c. green	2·00	20
276		1 c. grey	20	30
210	**108**	2 c. red	1·50	10
223		2 c. green	40	10
211	–	3 c. brown	1·50	10
212	**110**	4 c. lilac	5·00	1·75
224		4 c. red	1·60	40
213	**111**	5 c. purple	2·25	1·00
225c		5 c. violet	70	30
214	**112**	6 c. blue	4·00	13·00
226	–	7 c. lake	2·25	3·00
282	**121**	8 c. red	1·00	1·75
215	–	10 c. brown	70	40
216	–	14 c. black	3·25	4·00
217	–	15 c. purple	1·25	1·75
218	–	20 c. green	1·00	80
228	–	24 c. blue	60	2·75
219	–	25 c. grey	2·00	2·00
220	–	30 c. blue	26·00	26·00
289	–	48 c. brown	3·00	5·50

DESIGNS—VERT: 3 c. Queen Mary; 7 c. Queen Mother when Duchess of York. HORIZ: 10 c. Salmon; 14 c. Newfoundland dog; 15 c. Harp seal; 20 c. Cape Race; 24 c. Loading iron ore, Bell Island; 25 c. Sealing fleet; 30, 48 c. Fishing fleet.

1932. Air. Surch **TRANS-ATLANTIC WEST TO EAST Per Dornier DO-X May, 1932. One Dollar and Fifty Cents.**

221	**105**	$1.50 c. on $1 blue	£180	£225

1933. Optd **L. & S. Post.** ("Land and Sea") between bars.

229	**103**	15 c. brown	2·75	8·50

124 Put to Flight

1933. Air.

230	**124**	5 c. brown	13·00	15·00
231	–	10 c. yellow	9·00	24·00
232	–	30 c. blue	27·00	38·00
233	–	60 c. green	45·00	75·00
234	–	75 c. brown	45·00	70·00

DESIGNS: 10 c. Land of Heart's Delight; 30 c. Spotting the herd; 60 c. News from home; 75 c. Labrador.

1933. Air. Balbo Trans-Atlantic Mass Formation Flight. No. 234 surch **1933 GEN. BALBO FLIGHT. $4.50.**

235		$4.50 on 75 c. brown	£250	£300

130 Sir Humphrey Gilbert

131 Compton Castle, Devon

1933. 350th Anniv of Annexation. Dated "1583 1933".

236	**130**	1 c. black	70	90
237	**131**	2 c. green	1·00	50
238	–	3 c. brown	1·75	1·00
239	–	4 c. red	80	40
240	–	5 c. violet	2·00	70
241	–	7 c. blue	10·00	15·00
242	–	8 c. orange	7·00	11·00
243	–	9 c. blue	7·00	9·00
244	–	10 c. brown	4·00	7·00
245	–	14 c. black	12·00	30·00
246	–	15 c. red	10·00	18·00
247	–	20 c. green	13·00	15·00
248	–	24 c. purple	11·00	22·00
249	–	32 c. black	7·00	45·00

DESIGNS—VERT: 3 c. Gilbert coat of arms; 5 c. Anchor token; 14 c. Royal Arms; 15 c. Gilbert in the "Squirrel"; 24 c. Queen Elizabeth I; 32 c. Gilbert's statue at Truro. HORIZ: 4 c. Eton College; 7 c. Gilbert commissioned by Elizabeth; 8 c. Fleet leaving Plymouth, 1583; 9 c. Arrival at St. John's; 10 c. Annexation, 5 August, 1583; 20 c. Map of Newfoundland.

1935. Silver Jubilee. As T **13** of Antigua.

250		4 c. red	1·00	1·75
251		5 c. violet	1·25	1·75
252		7 c. blue	1·50	6·00
253		24 c. olive	5·00	6·00

1937. Coronation. As T **2** of Aden.

254		2 c. green	1·00	2·25
255		4 c. red	1·60	2·75
256		5 c. purple	3·00	2·75

144 Atlantic Cod

155 King George VI

1937. Coronation.

257	**144**	1 c. grey	2·00	20
258a	–	3 c. brown	3·25	2·25
259	–	7 c. blue	2·00	75
260	–	8 c. red	1·75	2·50
261	–	10 c. black	3·25	6·00
262	–	14 c. black	1·40	2·00
263	–	15 c. red	8·50	4·00
264	–	20 c. green	2·25	5·00
265	–	24 c. blue	2·25	2·50
266	–	25 c. black	2·75	1·75
267	–	48 c. purple	8·50	4·50

DESIGNS: 3 c. Map of Newfoundland; 7 c. Reindeer; 8 c. Corner Brook Paper Mills; 10 c. Atlantic salmon; 14 c. Newfoundland dog; 15 c. Harp seal; 20 c. Cape Race; 24 c. Bell Island; 25 c. Sealing fleet; 48 c. The Banks fishing fleet.

1938.

277	**155**	2 c. green	30	20
278	–	3 c. red	30	10
270	–	4 c. blue	1·75	20
271	–	7 c. blue	75	3·50

DESIGNS: 3 c. Queen Mother; 4 c. Queen Elizabeth II, aged 12; 7 c. Queen Mary.

159 King George VI and Queen Elizabeth

1938. Royal Visit.

272	**159**	5 c. blue	1·50	30

1939. Surch in figures and triangles.

273	**159**	2 c. on 5 c. blue	1·75	30
274		4 c. on 5 c. blue	90	50

161 Grenfell on the "Strathcona" (after painting by Gribble)

1941. 50th Anniv of Sir Wilfred Grenfell's Labrador Mission.

275	**161**	5 c. blue	30	55

162 Memorial University College

1942.

290	**162**	30 c. red	1·00	1·40

163 St. John's

165 Queen Elizabeth II when Princess

1943. Air.

291	**163**	7 c. blue	40	65

1946. Surch **TWO CENTS.**

292	**162**	2 c. on 30 c. red	30	65

1947. 21st Birthday of Princess Elizabeth.

293	**165**	4 c. blue	30	65

166 Cabot off Cape Bonavista

1947. 450th Anniv of Cabot's Discovery of Newfoundland.

294	**166**	5 c. violet	20	80

POSTAGE DUE STAMPS

D 1

1939.

D1	**D 1**	1 c. green	2·00	8·00
D2		2 c. red	11·00	7·00
D3		3 c. blue	4·50	18·00
D4		4 c. orange	9·00	16·00
D5		5 c. brown	5·50	23·00
D6		10 c. purple	6·00	16·00

NEW GUINEA

Formerly a German Colony, part of the island of New Guinea. Occupied by Australian forces during the 1914–18 war and subsequently joined with Papua and administered by the Australian Commonwealth under trusteeship. After the Japanese defeat in 1945 Australian stamps were used until 1952 when the combined issue appeared for Papua and New Guinea (q.v.). The stamps overprinted "N.W. PACIFIC ISLANDS" were also used in Nauru and other ex-German islands.

12 pence = 1 shilling;
20 shillings = 1 pound

1914. "Yacht" key-types of German New Guinea surch **G.R.I.** and value in English currency.

16	N	1d on 3 pf. brown	42·00	50·00
17		1d. on 5 pf. green	17·00	27·00
18		2d. on 10 pf. red	22·00	35·00
19		2d. on 20 pf. blue	27·00	40·00
5		2½d. on 10 pf. red	65·00	£140
6		2½d. on 20 pf. blue	70·00	£140
22		3d. on 25 pf. black and red on yellow	95·00	£130
23		3d. on 30 pf. black and orange on buff	80·00	£110
24		4d. on 40 pf. black & red	95·00	£130
25		5d. on 50 pf. black and purple on buff	£130	£170
26		8d. on 80 pf. black and red on rose	£325	£400
12	O	1s on 1 m. red	£1500	£2000
13		2s. on 2 m. blue	£1700	£2500
14		3s. on 3 m. black	£3250	£4250
15		5s. on 5 m. red and black	£6500	£8000

Nos. 3/4 surch **1**.

31	N	"1" on 2d. on 10 pf. red	£13000	£13000
32		"1" on 2d. on 20 pf. blue	£12000	£7500

4

1914. Registration labels with names of various town surch **G.R.I. 3d.**

33	**4**	3d. black and red	£150	£200

1914. "Yacht" key-types of German Marshall Islands surch **G.R.I.** and value in English currency.

50	N	1d on 3 pf. brown	45·00	75·00
51		1d. on 5 pf. green	48·00	55·00
52		2d. on 10 pf. red	16·00	25·00
53		2d. on 20 pf. blue	17·00	28·00
64g		2½d. on 10 pf. red	£6500	
64h		2½d. on 20 pf. blue	£9500	
54		3d. on 25 pf. black and red on yellow	£275	£375
55		3d. on 30 pf. black and orange on buff	£300	£400
56		4d. on 40 pf. black & red	95·00	£130
57		5d. on 50 pf. black and purple on buff	£140	£180
58		8d. on 80 pf. black and red on rose	£400	£500
59	O	1s on 1 m. red	£1800	£3000
60		2s. on 2 m. blue	£1200	£2000
61		3s. on 3 m. black	£3250	£4500
62		5s. on 5 m. red & black	£6500	£8000

1915. Nos. 52 and 53 surch **1**.

63	N	"1" on 2d. on 10 pf. red	£140	£170
64		"1"on 2d. on 20 pf. blue	£3000	£2250

1915. Stamps of Australia optd **N. W. PACIFIC ISLANDS.**

102	**3**	½d. green	1·00	3·50
103		1d. red	2·50	1·60
120		1d. violet	1·25	6·50
94	**1**	2d. grey	5·00	12·00
121	**3**	2d. orange	4·50	3·25
122		2d. red	8·00	4·50
74	**1**	2½d. blue	2·75	16·00
96		3d. olive	5·00	11·00
70	**3**	4d. orange	4·00	13·00
123		4d. violet	29·00	48·00
124		4d. blue	11·00	50·00
105		5d. brown	1·75	12·00
110	**1**	6d. blue	4·50	14·00
89		9d. violet	15·00	19·00
90		1s. green	11·00	24·00
115		2s. brown	21·00	38·00
116		5s. grey and yellow	60·00	65·00
84		10s. grey and pink	£110	£160
99		£1 brown and blue	£250	£400

1918. Nos. 105 and 90 surch **One Penny**.

100	**3**	1d. on 5d. brown	90·00	80·00
101	**1**	1d. on 1s. green	90·00	75·00

12 Native Village

14 Raggiana Bird of Paradise (Dates either side of value)

1925.

125	12	½d. orange	2·50	5·50
126		1d. green	2·50	5·50
126a		1½d. red	3·25	2·50
127		2d. red	2·50	4·50
128		3d. blue	4·50	4·00
129		4d. olive	13·00	17·00
130b		6d. brown	4·50	48·00
131		9d. purple	13·00	42·00
132		1s. green	15·00	23·00
133		2s. lake	30·00	45·00
134		5s. brown	48·00	65·00
135		10s. red	£100	£160
136		£1 grey	£180	£250

1931. Air. Optd with biplane and **AIR MAIL**.

137	12	½d. orange	1·00	4·50
138		1d. green	1·60	4·50
139		1½d. red	1·00	5·00
140		2d. red	1·00	7·00
141		3d. blue	1·75	13·00
142		4d. olive	1·25	8·50
143		6d. brown	1·75	13·00
144		9d. purple	3·00	17·00
145		1s. green	3·00	17·00
146		2s. lake	7·00	38·00
147		5s. brown	20·00	65·00
148		10s. red	70·00	£100
149		£1 grey	£120	£190

1931. 10th Anniv of Australian Administration. Dated "1921–1931".

150	14	1d. green	3·00	60
151		1½d. red	4·25	10·00
152		2d. red	4·50	4·25
153		3d. blue	4·50	4·50
154		4d. olive	6·50	15·00
155		5d. green	4·50	16·00
156		6d. brown	4·50	16·00
157		9d. violet	8·00	16·00
158		1s. grey	5·50	15·00
159		2s. lake	10·00	27·00
160		5s. brown	38·00	50·00
161		10s. red	75·00	£120
162		£1 grey	£170	£225

1931. Air. Optd with biplane and **AIR MAIL**.

163	14	½d. orange	2·50	3·00
164		1d. green	3·25	4·00
165		1½d. red	3·00	9·00
166		2d. red	1·75	2·75
167		3d. blue	5·00	5·00
168		4d. olive	5·00	6·00
169		5d. green	5·00	9·00
170		6d. brown	7·00	25·00
171		9d. violet	8·00	15·00
172		1s. grey	7·00	15·00
173		2s. lake	15·00	48·00
174		5s. brown	40·00	65·00
175		10s. red	60·00	£110
176		£1 grey	£100	£190

1932. As T **14**, but without dates.

177	1d. green	70	20
178	1½d. red	80	10·00
179	2d. red	90	20
179a	2½d. green	5·00	15·00
180	3d. blue	1·50	80
180a	3½d. red	11·00	9·00
181	4d. olive	75	4·50
182	5d. green	85	70
183	6d. brown	2·25	3·00
184	9d. violet	9·00	20·00
185	1s. grey	4·00	10·00
186	2s. lake	4·00	17·00
187	5s. brown	27·00	45·00
188	10s. red	48·00	70·00
189	£1 grey	95·00	£100

1932. Air. T **14**, but without dates, optd with biplane and **AIR MAIL**.

190	½d. orange	50	1·50
191	1d. green	70	1·50
192	1½d. mauve	90	5·50
193	2d. red	80	30
193a	2½d. green	4·25	2·25
194	3d. blue	2·25	2·25
194a	3½d. red	3·75	3·25
195	4d. olive	4·00	8·50
196	5d. green	7·00	7·50
197	6d. brown	4·00	13·00
198	9d. violet	6·00	9·00
199	1s. grey	6·00	8·00
200	2s. lake	8·50	42·00
201	5s. brown	45·00	55·00
202	10s. red	75·00	75·00
203	£1 grey	75·00	55·00

16 Bulolo Goldfields

18 King George VI

1935. Air.

204	16	£2 violet	£200	£120
205		£5 green	£500	£375

1935. Silver Jubilee. Nos. 177 and 179 optd **HIS MAJESTY'S JUBILEE. 1910–1935**.

206	1d. green	50	35
207	2d. red	1·50	35

1937. Coronation.

208	18	2d. red	50	30
209		3d. blue	50	55
210		5d. green	50	45
211		1s. purple	50	35

1939. Air. As T **16** but inscr "AIR MAIL POSTAGE".

212	½d. orange	2·50	5·50
213	1d. green	3·25	3·75
214	1½d. red	2·75	7·00
215	2d. red	7·50	3·25
216	3d. blue	9·50	16·00
217	4d. olive	9·00	7·50
218	5d. green	7·50	2·50
219	6d. brown	17·00	14·00
220	9d. violet	17·00	19·00
221	1s. green	18·00	17·00
222	2s. red	48·00	45·00
223	5s. brown	£110	90·00
224	10s. pink	£300	£200
225	£1 olive	£100	£110

OFFICIAL STAMPS

1915. Nos. 16 and 17 optd **O. S.**

O1	N	1d on 3 pf. brown	25·00	70·00
O2		1d. on 3 pf. green	80·00	£140

1925. Optd **O S**.

O 3	12	1d. green	1·00	4·50
O 4		1½d. red	5·50	17·00
O 5		2d. red	1·75	3·75
O 6		3d. blue	3·50	6·00
O 7		4d. olive	4·50	8·50
O 8a		6d. brown	7·00	35·00
O 9		9d. purple	4·00	35·00
O10		1s. green	5·50	35·00
O11		2s. lake	28·00	60·00

1931. Optd **O S**.

O12	14	1d. green	3·75	13·00
O13		1½d. red	4·00	12·00
O14		2d. red	7·50	7·00
O15		3d. blue	5·00	6·00
O16		4d. olive	3·75	8·50
O17		5d. green	9·00	12·00
O18		6d. brown	12·00	17·00
O19		9d. violet	15·00	28·00
O20		1s. grey	15·00	28·00
O21		2s. lake	38·00	65·00
O22		5s. brown	90·00	£150

1932. T **14**, but without dates, optd **O S**.

O23	1d. green	4·00	4·00
O24	1½d. red	4·50	12·00
O25	2d. red	4·75	3·00
O26	2½d. green	3·00	6·00
O27	3d. blue	6·50	20·00
O28	3½d. red	3·00	9·00
O29	4d. olive	5·00	15·00
O30	5d. green	5·00	15·00
O31	6d. brown	7·50	32·00
O32	9d. violet	10·00	40·00
O33	1s. grey	15·00	28·00
O34	2s. lake	35·00	75·00
O35	5s. brown	£120	£160

For later issues see **PAPUA AND NEW GUINEA**.

NEW HEBRIDES

A group of islands in the Pacific Ocean, E. of Australia, under joint administration of Gt. Britain and France. The Condominium ended in 1980, when the New Hebrides became independent as the Republic of Vanuatu.

1908. 12 pence = 1 shilling;
20 shillings = 1 pound.
1938. 100 gold centimes = 1 gold franc.
1977. 100 centimes = 1 New Hebrides franc.

BRITISH ADMINISTRATION

1908. Stamps of Fiji optd (a) **NEW HEBRIDES. CONDOMINIUM.** (with full points).

1a	23	½d. green	40	7·00
2		1d. red	45	40
5		2d. purple and orange	60	70
6		2½d. purple & blue on blue	60	70
7		5d. purple and green	80	2·00
8		6d. purple and red	70	1·25
3		1s. green and red	17·00	4·50

(b) **NEW HEBRIDES CONDOMINIUM** (without full points).

10	23	½d. green	3·50	24·00
11		1d. red	10·00	8·50
12		2d. grey	60	3·00
13		2½d. blue	65	3·75
14		5d. purple and green	65	5·50
15		6d. purple and deep purple	85	5·00
16		1s. black and green	85	7·50

3 Weapons and Idols

1911.

18	3	½d. green	85	1·60
19		1d. red	3·25	2·00
20		2d. grey	6·50	4·00
21		2½d. blue	2·50	5·00
24		5d. green	4·00	6·00
25		6d. purple	3·00	5·00
26		1s. black on green	2·00	13·00
27		2s. purple on blue	17·00	22·00
28		5s. green on yellow	32·00	48·00

1920. Surch (a) On T **3**.

40	3	1d. on ½d. green	3·75	20·00
30		1d. on 5d. green	7·00	60·00
31		1d. on 1s. black on green	1·25	12·00
32		1d. on 2s. purple on blue	1·00	10·00
33	3	1d. on 5s. green on yellow	1·00	10·00
41		3d. on 1d. red	3·75	11·00
42		5d. on 2½d. blue	7·00	20·00

(b) On No. F16 of French New Hebrides.

34	3	2d. on 40 c. red on yellow	1·00	15·00

5

1925.

43	5	½d. (5 c.) black	1·25	8·00
44		1d. (10 c.) green	1·00	8·00
45		2d. (20 c.) grey	1·75	2·50
46		2½d. (25 c.) brown	1·00	11·00
47		5d. (50 c.) blue	2·75	2·50
48		6d. (60 c.) purple	3·50	10·00
49		1s. (1 f. 25) black on green	3·25	19·00
50		2s. (2 f. 50) purple on blue	6·00	21·00
51		5s. (6 f. 25) green on yellow	6·00	24·00

6 Lopevi Islands and Outrigger Canoe

1938.

52	6	5 c. green	2·50	2·75
53		10 c. orange	1·25	1·00
54		15 c. violet	3·00	3·00
55		20 c. red	1·60	1·75
56		25 c. brown	1·60	1·75
57		30 c. blue	1·90	1·25
58		40 c. olive	4·50	3·75
59		50 c. purple	1·60	1·00
60		1 f. red on green	4·00	7·50
61		2 f. blue on green	30·00	16·00
62		5 f. red on yellow	70·00	48·00
63		10 f. violet on blue	£200	75·00

1949. U.P.U. As T **20/23** of Antigua.

64	10 c. orange	30	30
65	15 c. violet	30	30
66	30 c. blue	30	30
67	50 c. purple	40	30

7 Outrigger Sailing Canoes

1953.

68	7	5 c. green	60	10
69		10 c. red	60	10
70		15 c. yellow	60	10
71		20 c. blue	60	10
72	–	25 c. olive	60	10
73	–	30 c. brown	60	10
74	–	40 c. sepia	60	10
75	–	50 c. violet	1·00	10
76	–	1 f. orange	7·50	70
77	–	2 f. purple	7·50	9·00
78	–	5 f. red	12·00	32·00

DESIGNS: 25 c. to 50 c. Native carving; 1 f. to 5 f. Two natives outside hut.

1953. Coronation. As T **13** of Aden.

79	10 c. black and red	60	50

10 Quiros Galleon and Map

1956. 50th Anniv of Condominium. Inscr "1906 1956".

80	10	5 c, green	15	10
81		10 c. red	15	10
82	–	20 c. blue	10	10
83	–	50 c. lilac	15	15

DESIGN: 20, 50 c. "Marianne", "Talking Drum" and "Britannia".

12 Port Villa; Iririki Islet

1957.

84	12	5 c. green	40	50
85		10 c. red	30	10
86		15 c. yellow	50	50
87		20 c. blue	40	10
88	–	25 c. olive	45	10
89	–	30 c. brown	45	10
90	–	40 c. sepia	45	10
91	–	50 c. violet	45	10
92	–	1 f. orange	1·00	80
93	–	2 f. mauve	6·00	4·00
94	–	5 f. black	15·00	6·00

DESIGNS: 25 c. to 50 c. River scene and spear fisherman; 1 f. to 5 f. Woman drinking from coconut.

1963. Freedom from Hunger. As T **28** of Aden.

95	60 c. green	50	15

1963. Cent of Red Cross. As T **33** of Antigua, but with British and French cyphers in place of Queen's portrait.

96	15 c. red and black	35	10
97	45 c. red and blue	45	20

17 Cocoa Beans

1963.

98	–	5 c. red, brown and blue	1·00	40
99	17	10 c. brown, buff & green	15	10
100	–	15 c. bistre, brown & violet	15	10
101	–	20 c. black, green and blue	55	10
102	–	25 c. violet, brown & red	50	70
103	–	30 c. brown, bistre & violet	75	10
104	–	40 c. red and blue	80	1·40
105	–	50 c. green, yellow & blue	60	10
129	–	60 c. red and blue	40	15
106	–	1 f. red, black and green	2·50	3·25
107	–	2 f. black, purple & green	2·50	1·75
108	–	3 f. multicoloured	13·00	8·00
109	–	5 f. blue, deep blue & black	18·00	21·00

DESIGNS: 5 c Exporting manganese, Forari; 15 c. Copra; 20 c. Fishing from Palikulo Point; 25 c. Picasso triggerfish; 30 c. New Caledonian nautilus shell; 40, 60 c. Lionfish; 50 c. Clown surgeonfish; 1 f. Cardinal honeyeater (bird); 2 f. Buff-bellied flycatcher; 3 f. Thicket warbler; 5 f. White-collared kingfisher.

1965. Centenary of I.T.U. As T **36** of Antigua, but with British and French cyphers in place of the Queen's portrait.

110	15 c. red and drab	20	10
111	60 c. blue and red	35	20

1965. I.C.Y. As T **37** of Antigua, but with British and French cyphers in place of the Queen's portrait.

112	5 c. purple and turquoise	15	10
113	55 c. green and lavender	20	20

1966. Churchill Commemoration. As T **38** of Antigua, but with British and French cyphers in place of Queen's portrait.

114	5 c. blue	20	10
115	15 c. green	40	10
116	25 c. brown	50	10
117	30 c. violet	50	10

1966. World Cup Championship. As T **40** of Antigua, but with British and French cyphers in place of the Queen's portrait.

118	20 c. multicoloured	20	15
119	40 c. multicoloured	30	15

1966. Inauguration of W.H.O. Headquarters, Geneva. As T **41** of Antigua, but with British and French cyphers in place of the Queen's portrait.

120	25 c. black, green and blue	20	10
121	60 c. black, purple and ochre	55	20

1966. 20th Anniv of U.N.E.S.C.O. As T **54/6** of Antigua, but with British and French cyphers in place of the Queen's portrait.

122	15 c. multicoloured	20	10
123	30 c. yellow, violet and olive	50	10
124	45 c. black, purple & orange	60	15

36 The Coast Watchers

1967. 25th Anniv of Pacific War. Mult.

125	15 c. Type **36**	15	10
126	25 c. Map of war zone, U.S. marine and Australian soldier	40	15
127	60 c. H.M.A.S. "Canberra" (cruiser)	50	20
128	1 f. Boeing B-17 "Flying Fortress"	55	30

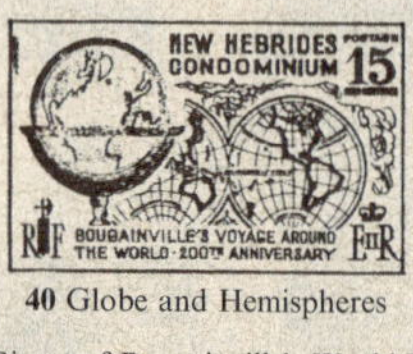

40 Globe and Hemispheres

1968. Bicent of Bougainville's World Voyage.

130	40	15 c. green, violet and red	15	10
131	–	25 c. olive, purple and blue	30	10
132	–	60 c. brown, purple & green	35	10

DESIGNS: 25 c. Ships "La Boudeuse" and "L'Etoile", and map; 60 c. Bougainville, ship's figure-head and bougainvillea flowers.

43 Concorde and Vapour Trails

1968. Anglo-French Concorde Project.
133 43 25 c. blue, red and blue 50 20
134 – 60 c. red, black and blue 60 25
DESIGN: 60 c. Concorde in flight.

45 Kauri Pine

1969. Timber Industry.
135 45 20 c. multicoloured 10 10

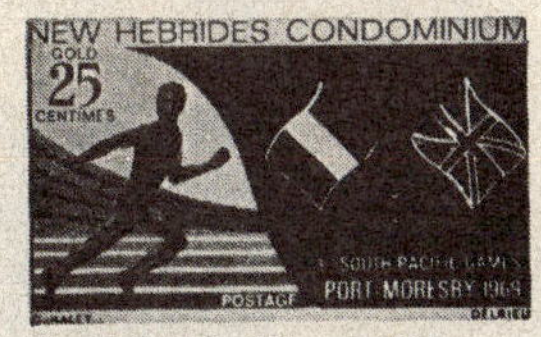
46 Cyphers, Flags and Relay Runner receiving Baton

1969. 3rd South Pacific Games, Port Moresby. Multicoloured.
136 25 c. Type 46 10 10
137 1 f. Runner passing baton 20 20

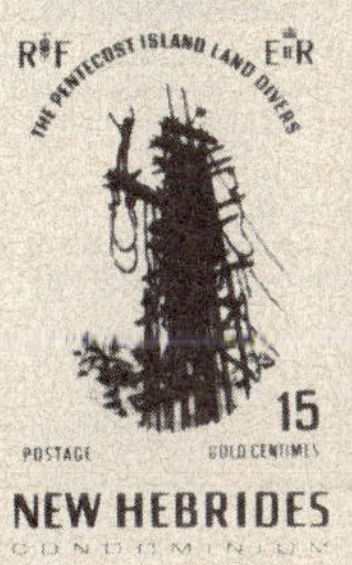
48 Diver on Platform

52 General Charles de Gaulle

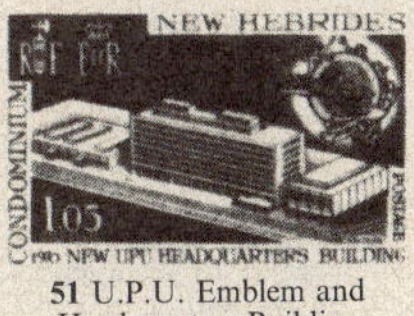
51 U.P.U. Emblem and Headquarters Building

1969. Pentecost Island Land Divers. Mult.
138 15 c. Type 48 10 10
139 25 c. Diver jumping 10 10
140 1 f. Diver at end of fall 20 20

1970. New U.P.U. Headquarters Building.
141 51 1 f. 05 slate, orange & purple 15 15

1970. 30th Anniv of New Hebrides' Declaration for the Free French Government.
142 52 65 c. multicoloured 35 50
143 1 f. 10 multicoloured 45 50

1970. No. 101 surch 35.
144 35 c. on 20 c. black, green and blue 30 30

54 "The Virgin and Child" (Bellini)

57 Kauri Pine, Cone and Arms of Royal Society

56 Football

1970. Christmas. Multicoloured.
145 15 c. Type 54 10 10
146 50 c. "The Virgin and Child" (Cima) 20 20

1971. Death of General Charles de Gaulle. Nos. 142/3 optd **1890-1970 IN MEMORIAM 9-11-70.**
147 52 65 c. multicoloured 15 10
148 1 f. 10 multicoloured 15 20

1971. 4th South Pacific Games, Papeete, French Polynesia.
149 20 c. Type 56 10 10
150 65 c. Basketball (vert) 30 20

1971. Royal Society's Expedition to New Hebrides.
151 57 65 c. multicoloured 20 15

58 "The Adoration of the Shepherds" (detail, Louis le Nain)

60 Ceremonial Headdress, South Malekula

59 De Havilland Drover 3

1971. Christmas. Multicoloured.
152 25 c. Type 58 10 10
153 50 c. "The Adoration of the Shepherds" (detail, Tintoretto) 30 40

1972. Aircraft. Multicoloured.
154 20 c. Type 59 40 15
155 25 c. Short S.25 Sandringham 4 flying boat 40 15
156 30 c. De Havilland Dragon Rapide 40 15
157 65 c. Sud Aviation SE 210 Caravelle 1·00 1·25

1972. Multicoloured.
158 5 c. Type 60 10 10
159 10 c. Baker's pigeon 25 10
160 15 c. Gong and carving, North Ambrym 15 15
161 20 c. Red-headed parrot finch 40 25
162 25 c. Graskoin's cowrie (shell) 40 25
163 30 c. Red-lip olive (shell) 50 30
164 35 c. Chestnut-bellied kingfisher 65 40
165 65 c. Pretty conch (shell) 75 60
166 1 f. Gong (North Malekula) and carving (North Ambrym) 90 1·00
167 2 f. Palm lorikeet 4·00 4·50
168 3 f. Ceremonial headdress, South Malekula (different) 3·75 6·00
169 5 f. Great green turban (shell) 6·50 14·00

61 "Adoration of the Kings" (Spranger)

63 "Dendrobium teretifolium"

1972. Christmas. Multicoloured.
170 25 c. Type 61 10 10
171 70 c. "The Virgin and Child in a Landscape" (Provoost) 20 20

1972. Royal Silver Wedding. As T 52 of Ascension, but with Royal and French cyphers in background.
172 35 c. violet 15 10
173 65 c. green 20 10

1973. Orchids. Multicoloured.
174 25 c. Type 63 30 10
175 30 c. "Ephemerantha comata" 35 10
176 35 c. "Spathoglottis petri" 40 10
177 65 c. "Dendrobium mohlianum" 75 55

64 New Wharf at Vila

65 Wild Horses

1973. Opening of New Wharf at Villa. Multicoloured.
178 25 c. Type 64 20 10
179 70 c. As T 64 but horiz format 40 30

1973. Tanna Island. Multicoloured.
180 35 c. Type 65 30 15
181 70 c. Yasur Volcano 55 20

66 Mother and Child

1973. Christmas. Multicoloured.
182 35 c. Type 66 10 10
183 70 c. Lagoon scene 20 20

67 Pacific Pigeon

1974. Wild Life. Multicoloured.
184 25 c. Type 67 80 25
185 35 c. "Lyssa curvata" (moth) 80 60
186 70 c. Green sea turtle 80 70
187 1 f. 15 Grey-headed flying fox 1·00 1·50

1974. Royal Visit. Nos. 164 and 167 optd **ROYAL VISIT 1974.**
188 35 c. multicoloured 25 10
189 2 f. multicoloured 40 40

69 Old Post Office

1974. Inaug of New Post Office, Vila. Mult.
190 35 c. Type 69 15 50
191 70 c. New Post Office 15 60

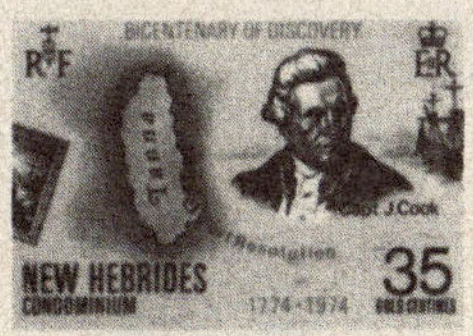
70 Capt. Cook and Map

1974. Bicent of Discovery. Multicoloured.
192 35 c. Type 70 1·50 2·00
193 35 c. William Wales and beach landing 1·50 2·00
194 35 c. William Hodges and island scene 1·50 2·00
195 1 f. 15 Capt. Cook map and H.M.S. "Resolution" (59 × 34 mm) 2·75 3·50

71 U.P.U. Emblem and Letters

1974. Centenary of U.P.U.
196 71 70 c. multicoloured 30 70

72 "Adoration of the Magi" (Velazquez)

74 Canoeing

73 Charolais Bull

1974. Christmas. Multicoloured.
197 35 c. Type 72 10 10
198 70 c. "The Nativity" (Gerard van Honthorst) 20 20

1975.
199 73 10 f. brown, green & blue 9·50 20·00

1975. World Scout Jamboree, Norway. Mult.
200 25 c. Type 74 20 10
201 35 c. Preparing meal 20 10
202 1 f. Map-reading 50 15
203 5 f. Fishing 1·75 2·50

75 "Pitti Madonna" (Michelangelo)

77 Telephones of 1876 and 1976

76 Concorde in British Airways Livery

1975. Christmas. Michelangelo's Sculptures. Multicoloured.
204 35 c. Type 75 10 10
205 70 c. "Bruges Madonna" 15 10
206 2 f. 50 "Taddei Madonna" 70 50

1976. 1st Commercial Flight of Concorde.
207 76 5 f. multicoloured 6·00 5·00

1976. Centenary of Telephone. Multicoloured.
208 25 c. Type 77 15 10
209 70 c. Alexander Graham Bell 30 10
210 1 f. 15 Satellite and Noumea Earth Station 50 50

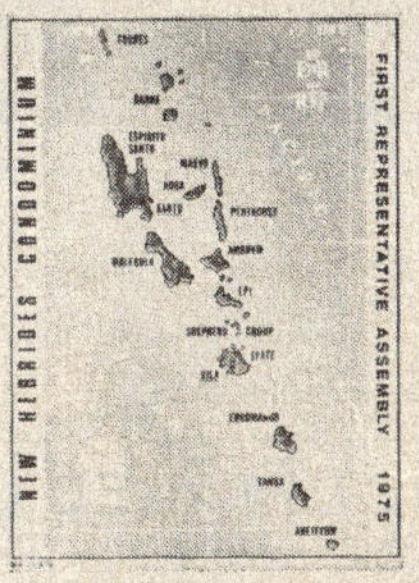
78 Map of the Islands

1976. Constitutional Changes. Multicoloured.
211 25 c. Type 78 35 15
212 1 f. View of Santo (horiz) 65 60
213 2 f. View of Vila (horiz) 95 1·50
Nos. 212/13 are smaller, 36 × 26 mm.

79 "The Flight into Egypt" (Lusitano)

80 Royal Visit, 1974

1976. Christmas. Multicoloured.
214 35 c. Type **79** 10 10
215 70 c. "Adoration of the Shepherds" . . . 15 10
216 2 f. 50 "Adoration of the Magi" 45 50
Nos. 215/16 show retables by the Master of Santos-o-Novo.

1977. Silver Jubilee. Multicoloured.
217 35 c. Type **80** 10 10
218 70 c. Imperial State Crown . . 15 10
219 2 f. The Blessing 30 65

1977. Currency change. Nos. 158/69 and 199 surch.
233 5 f. on 5 c. Type **60** 50 15
234 10 f. on 10 c. Baker's pigeon . 50 15
222 15 f. on 15 c. Gong and carving 60 80
223 20 f. on 20 c. Red-headed parrot finch . . . . 1·25 55
224 25 f. on 25 c. Gaskoin's cowrie (shell) . . . . 1·00 1·00
225 30 f. on 30 c. Red-lip olive (shell) 1·25 50
238 35 f. on 35 c. Chestnut-bellied kingfisher . . . . 2·25 55
239 40 f. on 65 c. Pretty conch (shell) 1·50 55
228 50 f. on 1 f. Gong and carving 1·50 1·50
229 70 f. on 2 f. Palm lorikeet . . 3·00 1·00
230 100 f. on 3 f. Ceremonial headdress . . . . 1·75 4·25
231 200 f. on 5 f. Great green turban (shell) . . . . 7·00 14·00
241 500 f. on 10 f. Type **73** . . . . 17·00 13·00

89 Island of Erromango and Kauri Pine

90 "Tempi Madonna" (Raphael)

1977. Islands. Multicoloured.
242 5 f. Type **89** 30 10
243 10 f. Territory map and copra-making 40 30
244 15 f. Espiritu Santo and cattle 30 30
245 20 f. Efate and Vila P.O. . . . 30 25
246 25 f. Malekula and headdresses 40 40
247 30 f. Aobe, Maewo and pigs' tusks 45 50
248 35 f. Pentecost and land diver 50 65
249 40 f. Tanna and John Frum Cross 70 60
250 50 f. Shepherd Is. and canoe . 1·00 40
251 70 f. Banks Is. and dancers . . 1·75 2·50
252 100 f. Ambrym and idols . . . 1·75 90
253 200 f. Aneityum and baskets . 1·75 2·50
254 500 f. Torres Is. and archer fisherman . . . . 4·00 7·50

1977. Christmas. Multicoloured.
255 10 f. Type **90** 20 15
256 15 f. "The Flight into Egypt" (Gerard David) 30 20
257 30 f. "Virgin and Child" (Batoni) 40 70

91 Concorde over New York

1978. Concorde Commemoration.
258 10 f. Type **91** . . . . 1·00 75
259 20 f. Concorde over London . 1·25 1·00
260 30 f. Concorde over Washington 1·60 1·40
261 40 f. Concorde over Paris . . 1·90 1·60

92 White Horse of Hanover

93 "Madonna and Child"

1978. 25th Anniv of Coronation.
262 **92** 40 f. brown, blue & silver . 15 30
263 – 40 f. multicoloured 15 30
264 – 40 f. brown, blue & silver . 15 30
DESIGNS: No. 263, Queen Elizabeth II; No. 264, Gallic Cock.

1978. Christmas. Paintings by Durer. Multicoloured.
265 10 f. Type **93** 10 10
266 15 f. "The Virgin and Child with St. Anne" 10 10
267 30 f. "Madonna of the Siskin" 15 10
268 40 f. "Madonna of the Pear" 20 15

1979. 1st Anniv of Internal Self-Government. Surch **166°E 11.1.79 FIRST ANNIVERSARY INTERNAL SELF-GOVERNMENT** and new value.
269 **78** 10 f. on 25 f. mult (blue background) 10 10
270 40 f. on 25 f. mult (green background) 20 20

95 1938 5 c. Stamp and Sir Rowland Hill

96 Chubwan Mask

1979. Death Centenary of Sir Rowland Hill. Multicoloured.
271 10 f. Type **95** 10 10
272 20 f. 1969 25 c. Pentecost Island Land Divers commemorative 20 10
273 40 f. 1925 2d. (20 c.) 25 20

1979. Arts Festival. Multicoloured.
275 5 f. Type **96** 10 10
276 10 f. Nal-Nal clubs and spears 10 10
277 20 f. Ritual puppet 15 10
278 40 f. Neqatmalow headdress . 25 15

97 "Native Church" (Metas Masongo)

1979. Christmas and International Year of the Child. Children's Drawings. Multicoloured.
279 5 f. Type **97** 10 10
280 10 f. "Priest and Candles" (Herve Rutu) 10 10
281 20 f. "Cross and Bible" (Mark Deards) (vert) 10 10
282 40 f. "Green Candle and Santa Claus" (Dev Raj) (vert) . . 15 15

98 White-bellied Honeyeater

1980. Birds. Multicoloured.
283 10 f. Type **98** 50 10
284 20 f. Scarlet robin 70 10
285 30 f. Yellow-fronted white eye 90 45
286 40 f. Fan-tailed cuckoo . . . 1·00 70

POSTAGE DUE STAMPS

1925. Optd **POSTAGE DUE**.
D1 **5** 1d. (10 c.) green . . . . . 40·00 1·00
D2 2d. (20 c.) grey . . . . . 48·00 1·00
D3 3d. (30 c.) red . . . . . 50·00 2·50
D4 5d. (50 c.) blue . . . . . 55·00 4·50
D5 10d. (1 c.) red on blue . . . 60·00 5·50

1938. Optd **POSTAGE DUE**.
D 6 **6** 5 c. green . . . . 20·00 28·00
D 7 10 c. orange . . . . 20·00 28·00
D 8 20 c. red . . . . 26·00 42·00
D 9 40 c. olive . . . . 35·00 55·00
D10 1 f. red on green . . . . . 45·00 65·00

1953. Nos. 68/9, 71, 74 and 76 optd **POSTAGE DUE**.
D11 **7** 5 c. green . . . . 5·00 10·00
D12 10 c. red . . . . 1·75 7·50
D13 20 c. blue . . . . 6·00 16·00
D14 – 40 c. sepia (No. 74) . . . 8·50 26·00
D15 – 1 f. orange (No. 76) . . . 6·00 26·00

1957. Optd **POSTAGE DUE**.
D16 **12** 5 c. green . . . . 30 1·50
D17 10 c. red . . . . 30 1·50
D18 20 c. blue . . . . 1·25 2·00
D19 – 40 c. sepia (No. 90) . . . 2·00 3·75
D20 – 1 f. orange (No. 92) . . . 3·00 7·00

FRENCH ADMINISTRATION

1908. Stamps of New Caledonia optd **NOUVELLES HEBRIDES**.
F1 **15** 5 c. green . . . . 2·75 2·75
F2 10 c. red . . . . 3·25 3·50
F3 **16** 25 c. blue on green . . . . 4·00 3·75
F4 50 c. red on green . . . . 5·50 5·25
F5 **17** 1 f. blue on green . . . . . 11·50 11·50

1910. Nos. F1/5 further optd **CONDOMINIUM**.
F 6 **15** 5 c. green . . . . 2·00 1·75
F 7 10 c. red . . . . 2·00 70
F 8 **16** 25 c. blue on green . . . . 2·25 3·50
F 9 50 c. red on orange . . . . 6·50 6·50
F10 **17** 1 f. blue on green . . . . . 13·00 16·00

The following issues are as stamps of British Administration but are inscr "NOUVELLES HEBRIDES" except where otherwise stated.

1911.
F11 **3** 5 c. green . . . . 1·00 2·50
F12 10 c. red 45 90
F13 20 c. grey . . . . 1·10 2·00
F25 25 c. blue . . . . 85 3·75
F26 30 c. brown on yellow . . . 2·25 7·00
F16 40 c. red on yellow . . . . 1·40 3·25
F17 50 c. olive . . . . 2·00 3·00
F18 75 c. orange . . . . 6·75 16·00
F19 1 f. red on blue . . . . . 2·25 2·50
F20 2 f. violet . . . . 8·50 18·00
F21 5 f. red on green . . . . . 12·00 24·00

1920. Surch in figures.
F34 5 c. on 40 c. red on yellow (No. F16) . . . . 26·00 75·00
F32a 5 c. on 50 c. red on orange (No. F4) £425 £425
F33 5 c. on 50 c. red on orange (No. F9) . . . . 2·50 6·50
F38 10 c. on 5 c. green (No. F11) 1·60 3·50
F33a 10 c. on 25 c. blue on green (No. F8) . . . . 50 1·25
F35 20 c. on 30 c. brown on yellow (No. F26) . . . . 10·00 48·00
F39 30 c. on 10 c. red (No. F12) 1·75 2·00
F41 50 c. on 25 c. blue (No. F25) 3·25 22·00

1921. Stamp of New Hebrides (British) surch **10c.**
F37 10 c. on 5d. green (No. 24) . . 15·00 30·00

1925.
F42 **5** 5 c. (½d.) black . . . . . . 1·50 9·00
F43 10 c. (1d.) green . . . . . 1·50 8·50
F44 20 c. (2d.) grey . . . . . 1·50 2·50
F45 25 c. (2½d.) brown . . . . 2·00 10·00
F46 30 c. (3d.) red . . . . . . 1·50 4·50
F47 40 c. (4d.) red on yellow . . 1·50 4·50
F48 50 c. (5d.) blue . . . . . 1·50 3·25
F49 75 c. (7½d.) brown . . . . 2·00 9·50
F50 1 f. (10d.) red on blue . . . 2·00 3·00
F51 2 f. (1s. 8d.) violet . . . . 4·25 20·00
F52 5 f. (4d.) red on green . . . 5·50 21·00

1938.
F53 **6** 5 c. green . . . . 1·60 2·75
F54 10 c. orange . . . . 1·60 2·50
F55 15 c. violet . . . . 1·25 2·75
F56 20 c. red . . . . 1·60 2·50
F57 25 c. brown . . . . 4·00 2·75
F58 30 c. blue . . . . 4·00 2·25
F59 40 c. olive . . . . 1·25 6·00
F60 50 c. purple . . . . . . 1·25 1·75
F61 1 f. red on green . . . . . 1·60 3·50
F62 2 f. blue on green . . . . . 25·00 27·00
F63 5 f. red on yellow . . . . . 50·00 40·00
F64 10 f. violet and blue . . . . £120 85·00

1941. Free French Issue. As last optd **France Libre**.
F65 **6** 5 c. green . . . . 2·50 21·00
F66 10 c. orange . . . . 4·00 20·00
F67 15 c. violet . . . . 6·00 28·00
F68 20 c. red . . . . 14·00 26·00
F69 25 c. brown . . . . 14·00 30·00
F70 30 c. blue . . . . 14·00 27·00
F71 40 c. olive . . . . 14·00 30·00
F72 50 c. purple . . . . . . 14·00 26·00
F73 1 f. red on green . . . . . 14·00 26·00
F74 2 f. blue on green . . . . . 14·00 30·00
F75 5 f. red on yellow . . . . . 14·00 30·00
F76 10 f. violet on blue . . . . . 14·00 30·00

1949. 75th Anniv of U.P.U.
F77 10 c. orange . . . . 2·25 4·00
F78 15 c. violet . . . . 3·50 6·50
F79 30 c. blue . . . . 5·00 9·50
F80 50 c. purple . . . . . . 6·00 10·00

1953.
F81 **7** 5 c. green . . . . 40 1·25
F82 10 c. red 70 90
F83 15 c. yellow . . . . 70 1·25
F84 20 c. blue 70 90
F85 – 25 c. olive 70 90
F86 – 30 c. brown 70 90
F87 – 40 c. sepia . . . . 70 1·25
F88 – 50 c. violet 70 90
F89 – 1 f. orange . . . . 19·00 6·00
F90 – 2 f. purple . . . . 21·00 45·00
F91 – 5 f. red . . . . 28·00 75·00

1956. 50th Anniv of Condominium.
F92 **10** 5 c. green . . . . 1·50 1·25
F93 10 c. red . . . . 1·50 1·25
F94 – 20 c. blue . . . . 1·50 1·50
F95 – 50 c. violet . . . . 1·50 2·00

1957.
F 96 **12** 5 c. green 80 60
F 97 10 c. red 80 40
F 98 15 c. yellow . . . . 1·25 60
F 99 20 c. blue . . . . 1·25 50
F100 – 25 c. olive . . . . 1·25 50
F101 – 30 c. brown . . . . 1·25 60
F102 – 40 c. sepia . . . . 1·25 60
F103 – 50 c. violet . . . . 1·25 50
F104 – 1 f. orange . . . . 8·00 2·75
F105 – 2 f. mauve . . . . 22·00 27·00
F106 – 5 f. black . . . . 32·00 35·00

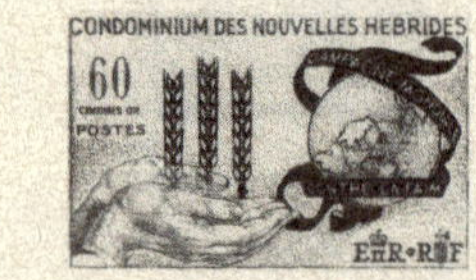

F 7 Emblem and Globe

1963. Freedom from Hunger.
F107 **F 7** 60 c. green and brown . 17·00 11·00

F 8 Centenary Emblem

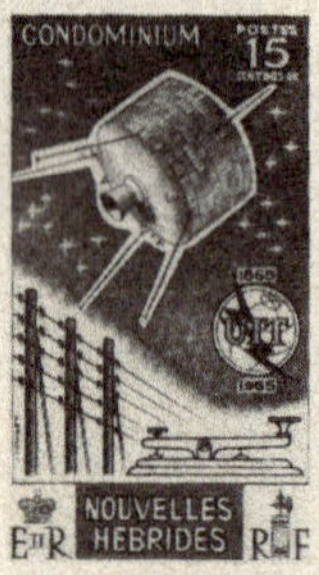

F 9 "Syncom" Communications Satellite, Telegraph Poles and Morse Key

1963. Centenary of Red Cross.
F108 **F 8** 15 c. red, grey & orange 10·00 6·00
F109 45 c. red, grey and bistre 18·00 18·00

1963.
F110 – 5 c. lake, brown and blue 60 30
F111 – 10 c. brown, buff & green* 80 80
F112 – 10 c. brown, buff & green 65 15
F113 **18** 15 c. bistre, brown and violet . . . . 10·00 40
F114 – 20 c. black, green & blue* 2·25 3·00
F115 – 20 c. black, green and blue 2·00 25
F116 – 25 c. violet, brown and red 60 60
F117 – 30 c. brown, bistre & violet 11·00 60
F118 – 40 c. red and blue . . . 3·50 6·00
F119 – 50 c. green, yellow and turquoise . . . . . . 11·00 60
F120 – 60 c. red and blue . . . 1·50 80
F121 – 1 f. red, black & green . 2·00 3·25
F122 – 2 f. black, brown & olive 24·00 9·00
F123 – 3 f. multicoloured* . . . 12·00 20·00
F124 – 3 f. multicoloured . . . 10·00 11·00
F125 – 5 f. blue, indigo & black . 22·00 28·00
The stamps indicated by an asterisk have "RF" wrongly placed on the left.

1965. Centenary of I.T.U.
F126 **F 9** 15 c. blue, green and brown . . . . 10·00 6·00
F127 60 c. red, grey & green . 22·00 22·00

1965. I.C.Y. As Nos. 112/13.
F128 5 c. purple and turquoise . . 4·00 3·00
F129 55 c. green and lavender . . 10·00 9·00

1966. Churchill Commem. As Nos. 114/17.
F130 5 c. multicoloured . . . . 1·00 75
F131 15 c. multicoloured . . . . 2·75 1·00
F132 25 c. multicoloured . . . . 3·00 3·50
F133 30 c. multicoloured . . . . 3·75 4·50

1966. World Cup Football Championships. As Nos. 118/19.
F134 20 c. multicoloured . . . . 3·50 2·75
F135 40 c. multicoloured . . . . 5·00 4·25

1966. Inauguration of W.H.O. Headquarters, Geneva. As Nos. 120/1.
F136 25 c. black, green and blue . 3·00 2·00
F137 60 c. black, mauve and ochre 5·00 5·00

1966. 20th Anniv of U.N.E.S.C.O. As Nos. 122/4.
F138 15 c. multicoloured . . . . 1·75 1·25
F139 30 c. yellow, violet & olive . 2·75 2·50
F140 45 c. black, purple & orange 3·00 3·00

1967. 25th Anniv of Pacific War. As Nos. 125/8.
F141 15 c. multicoloured 75 40
F142 25 c. multicoloured . . . . 1·25 50
F143 60 c. multicoloured . . . . 1·75 1·25
F144 1 f. multicoloured . . . . 2·25 2·00

1968. Bicentenary of Bougainville's World Voyage. As Nos. 130/2.

F145	15 c. green, violet and red	20	20
F146	25 c. olive, purple and blue	40	40
F147	60 c. brown, purple & green	90	90

1968. Anglo-French Concorde Project. As Nos. 133/4.

F148	25 c. blue, red and violet	2·25	1·50
F149	60 c. red, black and blue	3·75	3·00

1969. Timber Industry. As No. 135.

F150	20 c. multicoloured	20	30

1969. 3rd South Pacific Games, Port Moresby, Papua New Guinea. As Nos. 136/7.

F151	25 c. multicoloured	50	30
F152	1 f. multicoloured	1·75	2·00

1969. Land Divers of Pentecost Island. As Nos. 138/40.

F153	15 c. multicoloured	30	30
F154	25 c. multicoloured	40	40
F155	1 f. multicoloured	1·40	1·40

1970. Inauguration of New U.P.U. Headquarters Building, Berne. As No. 141.

F156	1 f. 05 slate, orange & purple	50	70

1970. New Hebrides' Declaration for the Free French Government. As Nos. 142/3.

F157	65 c. multicoloured	65	65
F158	1 f. 10 multicoloured	1·25	1·25

1970. No. F115 surch **35**.

F159	35 c. on 20 c. black, green and blue	60	50

1970. Christmas. As Nos. 145/6.

F160	15 c. multicoloured	15	15
F161	50 c. multicoloured	25	40

1971. Death of General Charles de Gaulle. Nos. F157/8 optd **1890–1970 IN MEMORIAM 9-11-70**.

F162	65 c. multicoloured	75	55
F163	1 f. 10 multicoloured	1·50	1·50

1971. 4th South Pacific Games, Papeete, French Polynesia. As Nos. 149/50.

F164	20 c. multicoloured	35	20
F165	65 c. multicoloured	95	80

1971. Royal Society Expedition to New Hebrides. As No. 151.

F166	65 c. multicoloured	50	50

1971. Christmas. As Nos. 152/3.

F167	25 c. multicoloured	15	20
F168	50 c. multicoloured	30	35

1972. Aircraft. As Nos. 154/7.

F169	20 c. multicoloured	1·00	60
F170	25 c. multicoloured	1·00	70
F171	30 c. multicoloured	1·10	80
F172	65 c. multicoloured	3·00	4·50

1972. As Nos. 158/69.

F173	5 c. multicoloured	40	10
F174	10 c. multicoloured	1·75	50
F175	15 c. multicoloured	50	15
F176	20 c. multicoloured	2·25	30
F177	25 c. multicoloured	1·75	30
F178	30 c. multicoloured	1·75	30
F179	35 c. multicoloured	3·00	40
F180	65 c. multicoloured	2·50	60
F181	1 f. multicoloured	2·50	1·75
F182	2 f. multicoloured	15·00	10·00
F183	3 f. multicoloured	9·50	13·00
F184	5 f. multicoloured	17·00	22·00

1972. Christmas. As Nos. 170/1.

F185	25 c. multicoloured	25	20
F186	70 c. multicoloured	50	45

1972. Royal Silver Wedding. As Nos. 172/3.

F187	35 c. multicoloured	40	40
F188	65 c. multicoloured	50	1·00

1973. Orchids. As Nos. 174/7.

F189	25 c. multicoloured	2·25	60
F190	30 c. multicoloured	2·25	80
F191	35 c. multicoloured	2·25	95
F192	65 c. multicoloured	3·75	4·75

1973. Opening of New Wharf at Vila. As Nos. 178/9.

F193	25 c. multicoloured	60	50
F194	70 c. multicoloured	90	1·50

1973. Tanna Island. As Nos. 180/1.

F195	35 c. multicoloured	2·25	1·25
F196	70 c. multicoloured	3·25	3·25

1973. Christmas. As Nos. 182/3.

F197	35 c. multicoloured	40	35
F198	70 c. multicoloured	70	75

1974. Wild Life. As Nos. 184/7.

F199	25 c. multicoloured	3·75	1·50
F200	35 c. multicoloured	5·50	1·75
F201	70 c. multicoloured	5·50	4·00
F202	1 f. 15 multicoloured	6·00	10·00

1974. Royal Visit of Queen Elizabeth II. Nos. F179 and F182 optd **VISITE ROYALE 1974**.

F203	35 c. Chestnut-bellied kingfisher	2·50	50
F204	2 f. Green palm lorikeet	5·50	6·50

1974. Inauguration of New Post Office, Vila. As Nos. 190/1.

F205	35 c. multicoloured	50	65
F206	70 c. multicoloured	60	85

1974. Bicent of Discovery. As Nos. 192/5.

F207	35 c. multicoloured	4·50	4·00
F208	35 c. multicoloured	4·50	4·00
F209	35 c. multicoloured	4·50	4·00
F210	1 f. 15 multicoloured	10·00	8·50

1974. Centenary of U.P.U. As No. 196.

F210a	70 c. blue, red and black	1·50	1·75

1974. Christmas. As Nos. 197/8.

F211	35 c. multicoloured	25	20
F212	70 f. multicoloured	55	45

1975. Charolais Bull. As No. 199.

F213	10 f. brown, green and blue	28·00	35·00

1975. World Scout Jamboree, Norway. As Nos. 200/3.

F214	25 c. multicoloured	55	20
F215	35 c. multicoloured	65	30
F216	1 f. multicoloured	1·25	1·10
F217	5 f. multicoloured	5·50	9·00

1975. Christmas. As Nos. 204/6.

F218	35 c. multicoloured	25	15
F219	70 c. multicoloured	40	25
F220	2 f. 50 multicoloured	1·75	2·75

1976. 1st Commercial Flight of Concorde. As No. 207, but Concorde in Air France livery.

F221	5 f. multicoloured	15·00	14·00

1976. Centenary of Telephone. As Nos. 208/10.

F222	25 c. multicoloured	55	40
F223	70 c. multicoloured	1·40	1·50
F224	1 f. 15 multicoloured	1·75	2·50

1976. Constitutional Changes. As Nos. 211/13.

F225	25 c. multicoloured	50	30
F226	1 f. multicoloured	1·50	1·25
F227	2 f. multicoloured	2·50	2·25

1976. Christmas. Paintings. As Nos. 214/16.

F228	35 c. multicoloured	25	15
F229	70 c. multicoloured	40	25
F230	2 f. 50 multicoloured	1·75	2·75

1977. Silver Jubilee. As Nos. F217/9.

F231	35 c. multicoloured	30	15
F232	70 c. multicoloured	50	25
F233	2 f. multicoloured	60	60

1977. Currency change. Nos. F173/84 and F213, surch.

F234	5 f. on 5 c. multicoloured	40	40
F235	10 f. on 10 c. multicoloured	85	40
F236	15 f. on 15 c. multicoloured	70	60
F237	20 f. on 20 c. multicoloured	1·50	85
F238	25 f. on 25 c. multicoloured	1·50	1·00
F239	30 f. on 30 c. multicoloured	1·75	1·50
F240	35 f. on 35 c. multicoloured	2·50	1·50
F241	40 f. on 65 c. multicoloured	2·50	2·00
F242	50 f. on 1 f. multicoloured	2·50	2·00
F243	70 f. on 2 f. multicoloured	4·25	2·75
F244	100 f. on 3 f. multicoloured	4·50	4·50
F245	200 f. on 5 f. multicoloured	14·00	19·00
F246	500 f. on 10 f. multicoloured	26·00	35·00

1977. Islands. As Nos. 242/54.

F256	5 f. multicoloured	65	20
F257	10 f. multicoloured	75	20
F258	15 f. multicoloured	75	20
F259	20 f. multicoloured	1·00	30
F260	25 f. multicoloured	80	40
F261	30 f. multicoloured	80	45
F262	35 f. multicoloured	2·25	60
F263	40 f. multicoloured	1·25	75
F264	50 f. multicoloured	2·00	75
F265	70 f. multicoloured	4·50	3·25
F266	100 f. multicoloured	3·00	2·50
F267	200 f. multicoloured	4·75	9·00
F268	500 f. multicoloured	11·00	15·00

1977. Christmas. As Nos. 255/7.

F269	10 f. multicoloured	20	20
F270	15 f. multicoloured	35	35
F271	30 f. multicoloured	85	85

1978. Concorde. As Nos. 258/61.

F272	10 f. multicoloured	2·50	1·00
F273	20 f. multicoloured	2·75	1·50
F274	30 f. multicoloured	3·25	2·00
F275	40 f. multicoloured	3·75	3·25

1978. Coronation. As Nos. 262/4.

F276	40 f. brown, blue & silver	25	60
F277	40 f. multicoloured	25	60
F278	40 f. brown, blue & silver	25	60

1978. Christmas. As Nos. 265/8.

F279	10 f. multicoloured	20	20
F280	15 f. multicoloured	25	30
F281	30 f. multicoloured	40	60
F282	40 f. multicoloured	50	70

1979. Internal Self-Government. As T **37** surch **166°E. PREMIER GOUVERNEMENT AUTONOME 11.1.78. 11.1.79** and new value.

F283	10 f. on 25 f. mult (blue background)	55	30
F284	40 f. on 25 f. mult (green background)	1·25	1·50

1979. Death Centenary of Sir Rowland Hill. As Nos. 271/3.

F285	10 f. multicoloured	25	35
F286	20 f. multicoloured	30	55
F287	40 f. multicoloured	40	75

1979. Arts Festival. As Nos. 275/8.

F288	5 f. multicoloured	20	10
F289	10 f. multicoloured	25	15
F290	20 f. multicoloured	35	40
F291	40 f. multicoloured	60	1·00

1979. Christmas and International Year of the Child. As Nos. 279/82.

F292	5 f. multicoloured	65	35
F293	10 f. multicoloured	85	35
F294	20 f. multicoloured	1·25	1·00
F295	40 f. multicoloured	2·00	2·00

1980. Birds. As Nos. 283/6.

F296	10 f. multicoloured	1·50	45
F297	20 f. multicoloured	1·75	1·00
F298	30 f. multicoloured	2·25	1·75
F299	40 f. multicoloured	2·25	2·25

POSTAGE DUE STAMPS

1925. Nos. F32 etc, optd **CHIFFRE TAXE**

FD53	5	10 c. (1d.) green	48·00	3·25
FD54		20 c. (2d.) grey	48·00	3·25
FD55		30 c. (3d.) red	48·00	3·25
FD56		50 c. (5d.) blue	48·00	3·25
FD57		1 f. (10d.) red on blue	48·00	3·25

1938. Optd **CHIFFRE TAXE**.

FD65	6	5 c. green	14·00	35·00
FD66		10 c. orange	17·00	35·00
FD67		20 c. red	23·00	45·00
FD68		40 c. olive	45·00	90·00
FD69		1 f. red on green	48·00	£100

1941. Free French Issue. As last optd **France Libre**.

FD77	6	5 c. green	8·75	35·00
FD78		10 c. orange	8·75	35·00
FD79		20 c. red	8·75	35·00
FD80		40 c. olive	8·75	35·00
FD81		1 f. red on green	17·00	35·00

1953. Optd **TIMBRE-TAXE**.

FD92	7	5 c. green	4·00	16·00
FD93		10 c. red	4·00	14·00
FD94		20 c. blue	12·00	22·00
FD95	–	40 c. sepia (No. F87)	15·00	45·00
FD96	–	1 f. orange (No. F89)	25·00	48·00

1957. Optd **TIMBRE-TAXE**.

FD107	12	5 c. green	2·25	7·00
FD108		10 c. red	2·25	7·00
FD109		20 c. blue	5·50	9·50
FD110	–	40 c. sepia (No. F102)	11·00	17·00
FD111	–	1 f. orange (No. F104)	13·00	20·00

For later issues see **VANUATU**.

NEW REPUBLIC

A Boer republic originally part of Zululand. It was incorporated with the South African Republic in 1888 and annexed to Natal in 1903.

12 pence = 1 shilling;
20 shillings = 1 pound

1

1886. On yellow or blue paper.

1	1	1d. black	—	£2750
2		1d. violet	10·00	12·00
73		2d. violet	8·50	8·50
74		3d. violet	13·00	13·00
75		4d. violet	13·00	13·00
81		6d. violet	8·00	8·00
82		9d. violet	8·50	8·50
83		1s. violet	8·50	8·50
77		1s. 6d. violet	14·00	14·00
85		2s. violet	18·00	16·00
86		2s. 6d. violet	23·00	23·00
87		3s. violet	42·00	42·00
88		4s. violet	11·00	11·00
89		5s. violet	13·00	13·00
90		5s. 6d. violet	12·00	12·00
91		7s. 6d. violet	14·00	17·00
92		10s. violet	12·00	12·00
93		10s. 6d. violet	16·00	16·00
44		12s. violet	£300	
23		13s. violet	£400	
94		£1 violet	45·00	45·00
25		30s. violet	95·00	

Some stamps are found with Arms embossed in the paper, and others with the Arms and without a date above "ZUID-AFRIKA".

NEW SOUTH WALES

A S.E. state of the Australian Commonwealth, whose stamps it now uses.

12 pence = 1 shilling;
20 shillings = 1 pound

1 Seal of the Colony

8

1850. Imperf.

11	1	1d. red	£2250	£275
25		2d. blue	£1800	£130
42		3d. green	£2500	£225

1851. Imperf.

47	8	1d. red	£900	£100
83		1d. orange	£170	17·00
86		2d. blue	£110	8·00
87		3d. green	£200	27·00
76		6d. brown	£1600	£250
79		8d. yellow	£3500	£600

14

15

1854. Imperf.

104	14	1d. red	£150	22·00
107		2d. blue	£130	8·00
111		3d. green	£800	80·00
114	15	5d. green	£1000	£550
116		6d. grey	£400	32·00
122		6d. brown	£450	32·00
126		8d. orange	£3500	£800
128		1s. red	£750	65·00

For these stamps perforated, see No. 134 etc.

24

1860. Perf.

173	14	1d. red	40·00	14·00
134		2d. blue	90·00	10·00
226		3d. green	6·00	80
243	15	5d. green	6·00	90
143		6d. brown	£275	45·00
165		6d. violet	55·00	4·50
218		8d. orange	£100	17·00
168		1s. red	70·00	7·50
297c	24	5s. purple	32·00	12·00

26

28

1862. Queen Victoria. Various frames.

207	26	1d. red	5·00	20
210	28	2d. blue	7·00	20
230c	–	4d. brown	28·00	1·00
234	–	6d. lilac	40·00	1·00
310	–	10d. lilac	12·00	3·50
237	–	1s. black	65·00	2·00

1871. As No. 310 surch **NINEPENCE**.

236d	9d. on 10d. brown	8·00	4·25

43

1885.

244b	43	5s. green and lilac	£325	80·00
251b		10s. red and violet	£150	45·00
246a		£1 red and lilac	£2250	

45 View of Sydney

46 Emu

52 Capt. Arthur Phillip, 1st Governor, and Lord Carrington, Governor in 1888

55 Allegorical Figure of Australia

1888. Cent of New South Wales.

253	**45**	1d. mauve	3·75	10
254	**46**	2d. blue	4·25	10
335	–	4d. brown	9·50	3·25
256	–	6d. red	20·00	3·50
297fa	–	6d. green	22·00	8·00
339	–	6d. yellow	11·00	1·25
257	–	8d. purple	15·00	2·00
343	–	1s. brown	16·00	1·25
263	–	5s. violet	£120	27·00
346b	**52**	20s. blue	£140	60·00

DESIGNS—As Type **45**: 4d. Capt. Cook; 6d. Queen Victoria and Arms; 8d. Superb lyrebird; 1s. Kangaroo. As Type **52**: 5s. Map of Australia.

1890.

281	**55**	2½d. blue	2·50	40

1891. Types as 1862, but new value and colours, surch in words.

282	**26**	½d. on 1d. grey	3·00	3·00
283a	–	7½d. on 6d. brown	5·00	2·75
284d	–	12½d. on 1s. red	10·00	7·00

58

59

60

61

62 Superb Lyrebird

63

1892.

286	**58**	½d. grey	2·00	10
298		½d. green	1·00	10
300	**59**	1d. red	1·00	10
333	**60**	2d. blue	1·75	10
296	**61**	2½d. violet	4·25	80
303		2½d. blue	2·75	70
348	**63**	9d. brown and blue	6·50	90
345a	**62**	2s. 6d. green	27·00	16·00

58a

1897. Diamond Jubilee and Hospital Charity.

287c	**58a**	1d. (1s.) green & brown	40·00	40·00
287d	–	2½d. (2s. 6d.) gold & blue	£150	£150

DESIGN—VERT: 2½d. Two female figures.

OFFICIAL STAMPS

1879-92. Various issues optd **O S**

A. Issues of 1854 to 1871.

O20b	**26**	1d. red	5·50	1·40
O21c	**28**	2d. blue	6·00	1·00
O25c	**14**	3d. green	5·00	3·50
O27a	–	4d. brown (No. 230c)	12·00	3·00
O28	**15**	5d. green	12·00	10·00
O31	–	6d. lilac (No. 234)	18·00	5·00
O32b	**15**	8d. orange	20·00	9·00
O11	–	9d. on 10d. (No. 236d)	£350	
O18a	–	10d. lilac (No. 310)	£130	80·00
O33	–	1s. black (No. 237)	25·00	6·00
O18	**24**	5s. purple	£170	80·00

B. Fiscal stamps of 1885.

O37	**24**	10s. red and violet	£1200	£600
O38		£1 red and violet	£4000	£3000

C. Issue of 1888 (Nos. 253/346b).

O39	1d. mauve	2·00	15
O40	2d. blue	3·75	15
O41	4d. brown	9·00	2·50
O42	6d. red	8·50	3·50
O43	8d. purple	16·00	8·50
O44	1s. brown	15·00	3·00
O49a	5s. violet	£160	70·00
O48	20s. blue	£1600	£800

D. Issues of 1890 and 1892.

O58a	**58**	½d. grey	6·00	8·00
O55	**26**	½d. on 1d. grey	50·00	45·00
O54	**55**	2½d. blue	7·00	3·00
O56	–	7½d. on 6d. (No. 283)	35·00	30·00
O57	–	12½d. on 1s. (No. 284c)	60·00	55·00

POSTAGE DUE STAMPS

D 1

1891.

D 1	**D 1**	½d. green	3·00	2·25
D 2		1d. green	4·50	90
D 3		2d. green	6·50	1·00
D 4		3d. green	11·00	2·75
D 5		4d. green	8·50	80
D 6		6d. green	17·00	2·00
D 7		8d. green	60·00	9·00
D 8		5s. green	£120	30·00
D 9a		10s. green	£180	80·00
D10b		20s. green	£225	£100

REGISTRATION STAMPS

13

1856.

88	**13**	(6d.) red and blue (Imp)	£700	£150
92		(6d.) orange and blue (Imp)	£800	£150
101		(6d.) red and blue (Perf)	75·00	15·00
94		(6d.) orange and blue (Perf)	£325	50·00

NEW ZEALAND

A group of islands in the south Pacific Ocean. A Commonwealth Dominion.

1855. 12 pence = 1 shilling;
20 shillings = 1 pound.
1967. 100 cents = 1 dollar.

1

3

1855. Imperf.

35	**1**	1d. red	£375	£225
34		1d. orange	£425	£190
39		2d. blue	£250	70·00
40		3d. lilac	£325	£120
43		6d. brown	£650	90·00
45		1s. green	£850	£225

1862. Perf.

110	**1**	1d. orange	£100	24·00
132		1d. brown	£100	27·00
114		2d. blue	£100	17·00
133		2d. orange	85·00	23·00
117		3d. lilac	85·00	27·00
119		4d. red	£2250	£250
120		4d. yellow	£120	85·00
122		6d. brown	£140	23·00
136		6d. blue	£100	45·00
125		1s. green	£130	75·00

1873.

151	**3**	½d. pink	7·50	60

5

6

7

8

9

10

11

1874. Inscr "POSTAGE".

180	**5**	1d. lilac	35·00	3·00
181	**6**	2d. red	35·00	1·40
154	**7**	3d. brown	£100	55·00
182	**8**	4d. purple	£140	40·00
183	**9**	6d. blue	80·00	10·00
184	**10**	1s. green	£110	35·00
185	**11**	2s. red	£325	£275
186		5s. grey	£350	£275

13

16

19

F 4

1882. Inscr "POSTAGE & REVENUE".

236	**13**	½d. black	3·00	15
237	**10**	1d. red	3·75	10
238	**9**	2d. mauve	7·50	30
239	**16**	2½d. blue	40·00	3·75
198	**10**	3d. yellow	40·00	6·50
222	**6**	4d. green	45·00	2·50
200	**19**	5d. black	42·00	9·00
224b	**8**	6d. brown	45·00	5·50
202	**9**	8d. blue	65·00	45·00
226	**7**	1s. brown	75·00	5·50

1882.

F 90	**F 4**	2s. blue	25·00	4·00
F 99		2s. 6d. brown	27·00	4·50
F100		3s. mauve	70·00	5·50
F102		5s. green	70·00	7·50
F 87		10s. brown	£130	13·00
F 77		£1 red	£170	45·00

The above are revenue stamps authorised for use as postage stamps as there were no other postage stamps available in these denominations. Other values in this and similar types were mainly used for revenue purposes.

23 Mount Cook or Aorangi

24 Lake Taupo and Mount Ruapehu

26 Lake Wakatipu and Mount Earnslaw

25 Pembroke Peak, Milford Sound

28 Sacred Huia Birds

29 White Terrace, Rotomahana

30 Otira Gorge and Mount Ruapehu

31 Brown Kiwi

32 Maori War Canoe

33 Pink Terrace, Rotomahana

34 Kea and Kaka

35 Milford Sound

1898.

246	**23**	½d. purple	4·25	60
302		½d. green	5·00	30
247	**24**	1d. blue and brown	3·25	20
248	**25**	2d. red	26·00	20
249	**26**	2½d. blue (A)*	6·50	23·00
320		2½d. blue (B)*	9·00	2·50
309	**28**	3d. brown	23·00	1·00
252	**29**	4d. red	12·00	15·00
311a	**30**	5d. brown	20·00	4·50
254	**31**	6d. green	50·00	26·00
265		6d. red	35·00	3·75
325	**32**	8d. blue	26·00	7·50
326	**33**	9d. purple	26·00	6·00
268a	**34**	1s. orange	48·00	3·00
328	**35**	2s. green	65·00	22·00
329	–	5s. red	£170	£190

DESIGN—As Type **30**: 5 s. Mount Cook.
* Type A of 2½d. is inscr "WAKITIPU", Type B "WAKATIPU".

40 Commemorative of the New Zealand Contingent in the South African War

1900.

274	**29**	1d. red	13·00	10
275b	**40**	1½d. brown	9·00	4·00
319	**25**	2d. purple	5·50	1·25
322d	**24**	4d. blue and brown	4·00	1·50

The 1d., 2d. and 4d. are smaller than the illustrations of their respective types.

42

44 Maori Canoe "Te Arawa"

1901.

303	**42**	1d. red	3·00	10

1906. New Zealand Exhibition, Christchurch. Inscr "COMMEMORATIVE SERIES OF 1906".

370	**44**	½d. green	17·00	28·00
371	–	1d. red	15·00	16·00
372	–	3d. brown and blue	45·00	75·00
373	–	6d. red and green	£160	£250

DESIGNS: 1d. Maori art; 3d. Landing of Cook; 6d. Annexation of New Zealand.

50

51 King Edward VII

53 Dominion

1907.

386	**50**	1d. red	22·00	60
383	**28**	3d. brown	35·00	10·00
376	**31**	6d. red	45·00	6·50
385	**34**	1s. orange	£120	24·00

These are smaller in size than the 1898 and 1901 issues. Type **50** also differs from Type **42** in the corner ornaments.

1909.

387	**51**	½d. green	3·50	10
405	**53**	1d. red	1·25	10
388	**51**	2d. mauve	14·00	6·50
389		3d. brown	22·00	70
390a		4d. orange	7·00	5·00
391a		5d. brown	15·00	1·50
392		6d. red	40·00	80
393		8d. blue	10·00	65
394		1s. red	48·00	1·75

1913. Auckland Industrial Exhibition. Optd **AUCKLAND EXHIBITION, 1913.**

412	**51**	½d. green	13·00	38·00
413	**53**	1d. red	19·00	38·00
414	**51**	3d. brown	£130	£250
415		6d. red	£140	£275

62 King George V

1915.

446	**62**	½d. green	50	10
416		1½d. grey	2·00	1·50
438		1½d. brown	2·25	10
417		2d. violet	7·00	26·00
439		2d. yellow	1·75	10
419		2½d. blue	3·25	3·50
449		3d. brown	7·00	30
421		4d. yellow	4·25	45·00
422e		4d. violet	7·00	30
423		4½d. green	12·00	13·00
424		5d. blue	6·50	1·00
425		6d. red	7·00	40
426		7½d. brown	13·00	23·00
427		8d. blue	14·00	45·00
428		8d. brown	18·00	1·50
429		9d. green	17·00	2·25
430c		1s. orange	14·00	50

1915. No. 446 optd **WAR STAMP** and stars.

452	**62**	½d. green	1·60	30

64 "Peace" and Lion

65 "Peace" and Lion

1920. Victory. Inscr "VICTORY" or dated "1914 1919" (6d.).

453	**64**	½d. green	2·25	2·25
454	**65**	1d. red	4·00	40
455	–	1½d. orange	3·50	30
456	–	3d. brown	13·00	11·00
457	–	6d. violet	14·00	15·00
458	–	1s. orange	24·00	48·00

DESIGNS—HORIZ (As Type **65**): 1½d. Maori chief. (As Type **64**): 3d. Lion; 1s. King George V. VERT (As Type **64**): 6d. "Peace" and "Progress".

1922. No. 453 surch **2d. 2d. TWOPENCE.**

459	**64**	2d. on ½d. green	3·25	1·25

69 New Zealand

70 Exhibition Buildings

1923. Restoration of Penny Postage.

460	**69**	1d. red	2·50	40

1925. Dunedin Exhibition.

463	**70**	½d. green on green	3·00	11·00
464		1d. red on rose	3·25	5·50
465		4d. mauve on mauve	40·00	70·00

71

73 Nurse

1926.

468	**71**	1d. red	40	10
469	–	2s. blue	48·00	19·00
470	–	3s. mauve	80·00	£120

The 2s. and 3s. are larger, 21 × 25 mm.

1929. Anti-T.B Fund.

544	**73**	1d. + 1d. red	11·00	18·00

1930. Inscr "HELP PROMOTE HEALTH".

545	**73**	1d. + 1d. red	21·00	30·00

74 Smiling Boy

F **6** "Arms" Type

75 New Zealand Lake Scenery

1931. Health Stamps.

546	**74**	1d. + 1d. red	75·00	75·00
547		2d. + 1d. blue	75·00	65·00

1931. Air.

548	**75**	3d. brown	23·00	13·00
549		4d. purple	23·00	16·00
550		7d. orange	26·00	7·50

1931. Air. Surch **FIVE PENCE.**

551	**75**	5d. on 3d. green	11·00	7·50

1931. Various frames.

F191	F **6**	1s. 3d. yellow	7·00	1·50
F192		1s. 3d. yellow & black	1·00	70
F193		2s. 6d. brown	6·50	40
F194		4s. red	11·00	70
F195		5s. green	17·00	80
F196w		6s. red	30·00	2·50
F197		7s. blue	30·00	4·25
F198		7s. 6d. grey	60·00	50·00
F153		8s. violet	28·00	28·00
F154		9s. orange	30·00	28·00
F201		10s. red	28·00	2·25
F156		12s. 6d. purple	£140	£140
F202		15s. green	42·00	18·00
F203		£1 pink	26·00	3·50
F159		25s. blue	£250	£375
F205w		30s. brown	£200	£100
F161		35s. yellow	£2500	£2750
F206		£2 violet	80·00	18·00
F207		£2 10s. red	£250	£250
F208w		£3 green	£100	45·00
F165		£3 10s. red	£1300	£1000
F210		£4 blue	£130	95·00
F167		£4 10s. grey	£1000	£1100
F211w		£5 blue	£160	45·00

77 Hygeia Goddess of Health

78 The Path to Health

1932. Health Stamp.

552	**77**	1d. + 1d. red	23·00	26·00

1933. Health Stamp.

553	**78**	1d. + 1d. red	12·00	17·00

1934. Air. Optd **TRANS-TASMAN AIR MAIL "FAITH IN AUSTRALIA".**

554	**75**	7d. blue	35·00	40·00

80 Crusader

1934. Health Stamp.

555	**80**	1d. + 1d. red	9·50	15·00

81 Collared Grey Fantail

83 Maori Woman

86 Maori Girl

85 Mt. Cook

87 Mitre Peak

89 Harvesting

91 Maori Panel

93 Capt. Cook at Poverty Bay

1935.

556	**81**	½d. green	1·50	40
557	–	1d. red	1·50	30
558a	**83**	1½d. brown	4·75	5·00
580	–	2d. orange	30	10
581c	**85**	2½d. brown and grey	50	3·75
561	**86**	3d. brown	12·00	1·50
583d	**87**	4d. black and brown	90	10
584c	–	5d. blue	3·00	65
585c	**89**	6d. red	75	10
586d	–	8d. brown	3·50	60
631	**91**	9d. red and black	3·25	2·25
588	–	1s. green	2·50	60
589e	**93**	2s. olive	10·00	1·50
590c	–	3s. chocolate and brown	5·00	2·00

DESIGNS—As Type **81**: 1d. Brown kiwi; 2d. Maori carved house; 1s. Tui. As Type **87**: 8d. Tuatara lizard. As Type **85**: 5d. Swordfish; 3s. Mt. Egmont.

95 Bell Block Aerodrome

1935. Air.

570	**95**	1d. red	85	50
571		3d. violet	4·50	3·00
572		6d. blue	8·50	2·00

96 King George V and Queen Mary

1935. Silver Jubilee.

573	**96**	½d. green	75	70
574		1d. red	1·25	60
575		6d. orange	20·00	22·00

97 "The Key to Health"

99 N.Z. Soldier at Anzac Cove

1935. Health Stamp.

576	**97**	1d. + 1d. red	2·25	2·50

1936. Charity. 21st Anniv of "Anzac" Landing at Gallipoli.

591	**99**	½d. + ½d. green	50	1·60
592		1d. + 1d. red	50	1·25

100 Wool

1936. Congress of British Empire Chambers of Commerce, Wellington. Inscr as in T **100**.

593	**100**	½d. green	30	30
594	–	1d. red (Butter)	30	20
595	–	2½d. blue (Sheep)	1·00	7·50
596	–	4d. violet (Apples)	80	4·75
597	–	6d. brown (Exports)	1·75	4·00

105 Health Camp

1936. Health Stamp.

598	**105**	1d. + 1d. red	1·25	3·50

106 King George VI and Queen Elizabeth

1937. Coronation.

599	**106**	1d. red	30	10
600		2½d. blue	1·25	2·25
601		6d. orange	1·75	1·75

107 Rock climbing

108 King George VI

1937. Health Stamp.

602	**107**	1d. + 1d. red	2·00	3·00

1938.

603	**108**	½d. green	6·50	10
604		½d. orange	20	20
605		1d. red	5·00	10
606		1d. green	20	10
607		1½d. brown	26·00	1·75
608		1½d. red	20	30
680		2d. orange	15	10
609		3d. blue	20	10
681		4d. purple	60	30
682		5d. grey	50	60
683		6d. red	40	10
684		8d. violet	65	30
685		9d. brown	1·50	30
686b	–	1s. brown and red	50	60
687	–	1s. 3d. brown and blue	1·00	80
688	–	2s. orange and green	2·75	1·75
689	–	3s. brown and grey	3·25	3·00

The shilling values are larger, 22 × 25½ mm, and "NEW ZEALAND" appears at the top.

109 Children playing

110 Beach Ball

1938. Health Stamp.

610	**109**	1d. + 1d. red	3·50	2·25

1939. Health Stamps. Surch.

611	**110**	1d. on ½d. + ½d. green	3·50	3·50
612		2d. on 1d. + 1d. red	3·50	3·50

1939. Surch in bold figures.

F212	F **6**	3/6 on 3s. 6d. green	20·00	6·50
F214		5/6 on 5s. 6d. lilac	40·00	17·00
F215		11/- on 11s. yellow	75·00	48·00
F216		22/- on 22s. red	£250	£130
F186		35/- on 35s. orange	£400	£225

112 "Endeavour", Chart of N.Z. and Captain Cook

1940. Centenary of Proclamation of British Sovereignty. Inscr "CENTENNIAL OF NEW ZEALAND 1840–1940".

613	–	½d. green	30	10
614	**112**	1d. brown and red	2·75	10
615	–	1½d. blue and mauve	30	20
616	–	2d. green and brown	1·50	10
617	–	2½d. green and blue	1·75	65
618	–	3d. purple and red	3·50	65
619	–	4d. brown and red	16·00	1·00
620	–	5d. blue and brown	6·00	3·00
621	–	6d. green and violet	13·00	80
622	–	7d. black and red	1·50	3·75
623	–	8d. black and red	13·00	2·50
624	–	9d. green and orange	7·50	1·50
625	–	1s. green and deep green	17·00	3·25

DESIGNS—HORIZ (as T **112**): ½d. Arrival of the Maoris, 1350; 1½d. British Monarchs; 2d. Abel Tasman with "Heemskerk" and chart; 3d. Landing of immigrants, 1840; 4d. Road, rail, ocean and air transport; 6d. "Dunedin" and "frozen mutton" sea route to London; 7, 8d. Maori council; 9d. Gold mining methods, 1861 and 1940. (25 × 21 mm): 5d. H.M.S. "Britomart" at Akaroa, 1840. VERT (21 × 25 mm): 2½d. Treaty of Waitangi. (As T **112**): 1s. Giant kauri tree.

1940. Health Stamps.

626	**110**	1d. + ½d. green	12·00	13·00
627		2d. + 1d. orange	12·00	13·00

1941. Surch.

628	**108**	1d. on ½d. green	80	10
629		2d. on 1½d. brown	80	10

1941. Health Stamps. Optd **1941**.

632	**110**	1d. + ½d. green	25	1·75
633		2d. + 1d. orange	25	1·75

125 Boy and Girl on Swing

1942. Health Stamps.

634	**125**	1d. + ½d. green	20	75
635		2d. + 1d. orange	20	75

126 Princess Margaret

1943. Health Stamps.

636	**126**	1d. + ½d. green	15	80
637	–	2d. + 1d. brown	15	15

DESIGN: 2d. Queen Elizabeth II as Princess.

1944. Surch **TENPENCE** between crosses.

662	–	10d. on 1½d. blue and mauve (No. 615)	10	10

129 Queen Elizabeth II as Princess and Princess Margaret

130 Peter Pan Statue, Kensington Gardens

1944. Health Stamps.

663	**129**	1d. + ½d. green	20	25
664		2d. + 1d. blue	20	25

1945. Health Stamps.

665	**130**	1d. + ½d. green and buff	10	20
666		2d. + 1d. red and buff	10	20

131 Lake Matheson

132 King George VI and Parliament House, Wellington

133 St. Paul's Cathedral

139 "St. George" (Wellington College War Memorial window)

1946. Peace Issue.

667	**131**	½d. green and brown	15	30
668	**132**	1d. green	10	10
669	**133**	1½d. red	10	15
670	–	2d. purple	15	10
671	–	3d. blue and grey	30	15
672	–	4d. green and orange	20	20
673	–	5d. green and blue	30	50
674	–	6d. brown and red	15	20
675	**139**	8d. black and red	15	15
676	–	9d. blue and black	15	15
677	–	1s. grey	15	15

DESIGNS—As Type **132**: 2d. The Royal Family. As Type **131**: 3d. R.N.Z.A.F. badge and airplanes; 4d. Army badge, tank and plough; 5d. Navy badge, H.M.N.Z.S. "Achilles" (cruiser) and "Dominion Monarch" (liner); 6d. N.Z. coat of arms, foundry and farm; 9d. Southern Alps and Franz Josef Glacier. As T **139**: 1s. National Memorial campanile.

142 Soldier helping Child over Stile

145 Statue of Eros

1946. Health Stamps.

678	**142**	1d. + ½d. green & orange	10	10
679		2d. + 1d. brown & orange	10	10

1947. Health Stamps.

690	**145**	1d. + ½d. green	10	10
691		2d. + 1d. red	10	10

146 Port Chalmers, 1848

1948. Centenary of Otago. Various designs inscr "CENTENNIAL OF OTAGO".

692	**146**	1d. blue and green	15	20
693	–	2d. green and brown	15	20
694	–	3d. purple	15	30
695	–	6d. black and red	15	30

DESIGNS—HORIZ: 2d. Cromwell, Otago; 6d. Otago University. VERT: 3d. First Church, Dunedin.

150 Boy sunbathing and Children playing

151 Nurse and Child

1948. Health Stamps.

696	**150**	1d. + ½d. blue and green	10	10
697		2d. + 1d. purple and red	10	10

1949. Health Stamps.

698	**151**	1d. + ½d. green	15	15
699		2d. + 1d. blue	15	15

1950. As Type F **6**, but without value, surch **1½d. POSTAGE**.

700		1½d. red	20	20

Type F **6** is illustrated next to Type **74**.

153 Queen Elizabeth II and Prince Charles

155 Cairn on Lyttleton Hills

1950. Health Stamps.

701	**153**	1d. + ½d. green	15	10
702		2d. + 1d. purple	15	10

1950. Centenary of Canterbury, N.Z.

703	–	1d. green and blue	15	35
704	**155**	2d. red and orange	15	35
705	–	3d. deep blue and blue	20	50
706	–	6d. brown and blue	20	50
707	–	1s. purple and blue	20	70

DESIGNS—VERT: 1d. Christchurch Cathedral; 3d. John Robert Godley. HORIZ: 6d. Canterbury University College; 1s. Aerial view of Timaru.

159 "Takapuna" class Yachts

1951. Health Stamps.

708	**159**	1½d. + ½d. red & yellow	15	70
709		2d. + 1d. green & yellow	15	10

160 Princess Anne

161 Prince Charles

1952. Health Stamps.

710	**160**	1½d. + ½d. red	15	20
711	**161**	2d. + 1d. brown	15	20

1952. Surch in figures.

712	**108**	1d. on ½d. orange	20	75
713		3d. on 1d. green	10	10

164 Queen Elizabeth II

166 Westminster Abbey

165 Coronation State Coach

1953. Coronation.

714	–	2d. blue	30	30
715	**164**	3d. brown	30	10
716	**165**	4d. red	1·25	2·50
717	**166**	8d. grey	80	1·25
718	–	1s. 6d. purple and blue	2·00	2·50

DESIGNS—As Type **165**: 2d. Queen Elizabeth II and Buckingham Palace; 1s. 6d. St. Edward's Crown and Royal Sceptre.

168 Girl Guides

169 Boy Scouts

1953. Health Stamps.

719	**168**	1½d. + ½d. blue	15	10
720	**169**	2d. + 1d. green	15	30

170 Queen Elizabeth II

171 Queen Elizabeth II and Duke of Edinburgh

1953. Royal Visit.

721	**170**	3d. purple	10	10
722	**171**	4d. blue	10	50

172

173

174 Queen Elizabeth II

1953. Small figures of value.

723	**172**	½d. black	15	30
724		1d. orange	15	10
725		1½d. red	20	10
726		2d. green	20	10
727		3d. red	20	10
728		4d. blue	40	40
729		6d. purple	70	1·40
730		8d. red	60	60
731	**173**	9d. brown and green	60	30
732		1s. black and red	65	10
733		1s. 6d. black and blue	1·25	50
733c		1s. 9d. black & orange	7·00	1·00
733d	**174**	2s. 6d. brown	27·00	7·50
734		3s. green	12·00	30
735		5s. red	20·00	3·25
736		10s. blue	45·00	16·00

175 Young Climber and Mts. Aspiring and Everest

176 Maori Mail-carrier

177 Queen Elizabeth II

179 Children's Health Camps Federation Emblem

1954. Health Stamps.

737	**175**	1½d. + ½d. brown and violet	15	25
738		2d. + 1d. brown and blue	15	25

1955. Centenary of First New Zealand Stamps. Inscr "1855–1955".

739	**176**	2d. brown and green	10	10
740	**177**	3d. red	10	10
741	–	4d. black and blue	25	70

DESIGN—HORIZ (As Type **176**): 4d. Douglas DC-3 airliner.

1955. Health Stamps.

742	**179**	1½d. + ½d. brown and chestnut	10	40
743		2d. + 1d. red and green	10	20
744		3d. + 1d. brown and red	15	10

180

183 Takahe

181 "The Whalers of Foveaux Strait"

1955. As 1953 but larger figures of value and stars omitted from lower right corner.

745	**180**	1d. orange	50	10
746		1½d. red	60	60
747		2d. green	40	10
748b		3d. red	75	10
749		4d. blue	1·50	55
750		6d. purple	9·50	10
751		8d. brown	6·50	7·50

1956. Southland Centennial.

752	**181**	2d. green	30	15
753	–	3d. brown	10	10
754	**183**	8d. violet and red	1·25	1·50

DESIGN—As Type **181**: 3d. Allegory of farming.

184 Children picking Apples

185 New Zealand Lamb and Map

1956. Health Stamps.
755 184 1½d. + ½d. brown 15 50
756 2d. + 1d. green 15 40
757 3d. + 1d. red 15 15

1957. 75th Anniv of First Export of N.Z. Lamb.
758 185 4d. blue 40 90
759 – 8d. red . . . . 60 1·00
DESIGN—HORIZ: 8d. Lamb, sailing ship "Dunedin" and "Port Brisbane" (refrigerated freighter).

187 Sir Truby King

188 Life-savers in Action

1957. 50th Anniv of Plunket Society.
760 187 3d. red 10 10

1957. Health Stamps.
761 188 2d. + 1d. black and green 15 50
762 – 3d. + 1d. blue and red . . 15 10
DESIGN: 3d. Children on seashore.

1958. Surch.
763 180 2d. on 1½d. brown 70 10
808 2½d. on 3d. red 15 15

192 Boys' Brigade Bugler

194 Seal of Nelson

1958. Health Stamps.
764 – 2d. + 1d. green 20 30
765 192 3d. + 1d. blue 20 30
DESIGN: 2d. Girls' Life Brigade cadet.

1958. 30th Anniv of 1st Air Crossing of Tasman Sea. As T 120 of Australia.
766 6d. blue 40 50

1958. Centenary of City of Nelson.
767 194 3d. red 10 10

195 "Pania" Statue, Napier

196 Australian Gannets on Cape Kidnappers

1958. Centenary of Hawke's Bay Province.
768 195 2d. green 10 10
769 196 3d. blue 20 10
770 – 8d. brown . . . . 55 1·25
DESIGN—As Type 195: 8d. Maori sheep-shearer.

197 "Kiwi", Jamboree Badge

198 Careening H.M.S. "Endeavour" at Ship Cove

1959. Pan-Pacific Scout Jamboree, Auckland.
771 197 3d. brown and red 30 10

1959. Centenary of Marlborough Province. Inscr as in T 198.
772 198 2d. green 30 10
773 – 3d. blue 30 10
774 – 8d. brown . . . . 1·00 2·00
DESIGNS: 3d. Shipping wool, Wairau Bar, 1857; 8d. Salt industry, Grassmere.

201 Red Cross Flag

1959. Red Cross Commemoration.
775 201 3d. + 1d. red and blue . 20 10

202 Grey Teal

204 "The Explorer"

1959. Health Stamps.
776 202 2d. + 1d. yellow, olive and red 40 50
777 – 3d. + 1d. black, pink and blue 40 50
DESIGN: 3d. New Zealand stilt.

1960. Centenary of Westland Province.
778 204 2d. green 20 10
779 – 3d. salmon 20 10
780 – 8d. black . . . . 70 2·75
DESIGNS: 3d. "The Gold Digger"; 8d. "The Pioneer Woman".

207 Manuka (Tea Tree)

215 Timber Industry

219 Taniwha (Maori Rock Drawing)

225 Sacred Kingfisher

1960.
781 207 ½d. green and red . . . 10 10
782 – 1d. multicoloured . . . 10 10
783 – 2d. multicoloured . . . 10 10
784 – 2½d. multicoloured . . . 80 10
785 – 3d. multicoloured . . . 30 10
786 – 4d. multicoloured . . . 40 10
787 – 5d. multicoloured . . . 1·00 10
788 – 6d. lilac, green & turquoise 60 10
788d – 7d. red, green and yellow 35 1·00
789 – 8d. multicoloured . . . 40 10
790 – 9d. red and blue 40 10
791 215 1s. brown and green . . . 30 10
792b – 1s. 3d. red, sepia and blue 1·50 10
793 – 1s. 6d. olive and brown . 80 10
794 – 1s. 9d. brown . . . . . 16·00 15
795 – 1s. 9d. multicoloured . . 8·50 90
796 219 2s. black and buff . . . 3·50 10
797 – 2s. 6d. yellow and brown 1·75 85
798 – 3s. sepia . . . . 32·00 65
799 – 3s. bistre, blue & green . 6·50 1·75
800 – 5s. myrtle . . . . 5·50 80
801 – 10s. blue . . . . 9·00 3·00
802 – £1 mauve . . . . 13·00 6·00
DESIGNS—VERT (as Type 207): 1d. Karaka; 2d. Kowhai Ngutu-kaka (Kaka Beak); 2½d. Titoki (plant); 3d. Kowhai; 4d. Puarangi (Hibiscus); 5d. Matua tikumu (Mountain daisy); 6d. Pikiarero (Clematis); 7d. Koromiko; 8d. Rata. (As T 215): 1s. 3d. Rainbow trout; 1s. 6d. Tiki. (As T 219): 5s. Sutherland Falls; £1 Potutu Geyser. HORIZ (as T 215): 9d. National flag; 1s. 9d. Aerial top-dressing. (As Type 219): 2s. 6d. Butter-making; 3s. Tongariro National Park and Chateau; 10s. Tasman Glacier.

1960. Health Stamps.
803 225 2d. + 1d. sepia and blue 90 50
804 – 3d. + 1d. purple & orange 90 50
DESIGN: 3d. New Zealand pigeon.

227 "The Adoration of the Shepherds" (Rembrandt)

228 Great Egret

1960. Christmas.
805 227 2d. red & brown on cream 15 10

1961. Health Stamps.
806 228 2d. + 1d. black & purple . 50 50
807 – 3d. + 1d. sepia and green 50 50
DESIGN: 3d. New Zealand falcon.

232 "Adoration of the Magi" (Durer)

236 Tieke Saddleback

233 Morse Key and Port Hills, Lyttleton

1961. Christmas.
809 232 2½d. multicoloured 10 10

1962. Telegraph Centenary.
810 233 3d. sepia and green 10 10
811 – 8d. black and red 65 55
DESIGN: 8d. Modern teleprinter.

1962. Health Stamps.
812 – 2½d. + 1d. multicoloured . 40 50
813 236 3d. + 1d. multicoloured . 40 50
DESIGN: 2½d. Red-fronted parakeet.

237 "Madonna in Prayer" (Sassoferrato)

238 Prince Andrew

1962. Christmas.
814 237 2½d. multicoloured 10 10

1963. Health Stamps.
815 238 2½d. + 1d. blue 30 60
816 – 3d. + 1d. red 30 10
DESIGN: 3d. Prince Andrew (different).

240 "The Holy Family" (Titian)

1963. Christmas.
817 240 2½d. multicoloured 10 10

241 Steam Locomotive "Pilgrim" (1863) and Class DG Diesel Electric Locomotive

1963. Centenary of New Zealand Railway. Inscr as in T 241. Multicoloured.
818 3d. Type 241 . . . . 40 10
819 1s. 9d. Diesel express and Mt. Ruapehu . . . . 2·25 1·50

1963. Opening of COMPAC (Trans-Pacific Telephone Cable). As T 174 of Australia.
820 8d. multicoloured . . . . . . 50 1·25

244 Road Map and Car Steering-wheel

1964. Road Safety Campaign.
821 244 3d. black, yellow & blue . 20 10

245 Silver Gulls

1964. Health Stamps. Multicoloured.
822 2½d. + 1d. Type 245 . . . . 30 30
823 3d. + 1d. Little penguin . . . 30 30

246 Rev. S. Marsden taking first Christian Service at Rangihoua Bay, 1814

1964. Christmas.
824 246 2½d. multicoloured 10 10

1964. Surch **7D POSTAGE**.
825 F 6 7d. on (–) red . . . . . . 60 1·00

248 Anzac Cove

1965. 50th Anniv of Gallipoli Landing.
826 248 4d. brown 10 10
827 – 5d. green and red 10 45
DESIGN: 5d. Anzac Cove and poppy.

249 I.T.U. Emblem and Symbols

1965. Centenary of I.T.U.
828 249 9d. blue and brown . . . 40 35

1965. Churchill Commem. As T 186 of Australia.
829 7d. black, grey and blue . . . 15 50

251 Wellington Provincial Council Building

252 Kaka

1965. Centenary of Government in Wellington.
830 251 4d. multicoloured 10 10

1965 Health Stamps. Multicoloured.
831 3d. + 1d. Type 252 . . . . . 30 30
832 4d. + 1d. Collared grey fantail 30 30

254 I.C.Y. Emblem

255 "The Two Trinities" (Murillo)

1965. International Co-operation Year.
833 254 4d. red and olive 15 10

1965. Christmas.
834 255 3d. multicoloured 10 10

256 Arms of New Zealand

1965. 11th Commonwealth Parliamentary Conf. Multicoloured.
835 4d. Type **256** 25 20
836 9d. Parliament House, Wellington, and Badge . . . 55 1·25
837 2s. Wellington from Mt. Victoria 4·00 5·50

259 "Progress" Arrowhead

260 New Zealand Bell Bird

1966. 4th National Scout Jamboree, Trentham.
838 **259** 4d. gold and green 10 10

1966. Health Stamps. Multicoloured.
839 3d. + 1d. Type **260** 30 45
840 4d. + 1d. Weka rail 30 45

262 "The Virgin with Child" (Maratta)

263 Queen Victoria and Queen Elizabeth II

1966. Christmas.
842 **262** 3d. multicoloured 10 10

1967. Centenary of New Zealand Post Office Savings Bank.
843 **263** 4d. black, gold & purple . 10 10
844 – 9d. multicoloured 10 20
DESIGN: 9d. Half-sovereign of 1867 and commemorative dollar coin.

265 Manuka (Tea Tree)

268 Running with Ball

1967. Decimal Currency. Designs as earlier issues, but with values inscr in decimal currency as T **265**.
845 **265** ½ c. blue, green and red 10 10
846 – 1 c. mult (No. 782) . 10 10
847 – 2 c. mult (No. 783) . 10 10
848 – 2½ c. mult (No. 785) . 10 10
849 – 3 c. mult (No. 786) . 10 10
850 – 4 c. mult (No. 787) . 30 10
851 – 5 c. lilac, olive and green (No. 788) . . . 65 10
852 – 6 c. mult (No. 788d) . 70 20
853 – 7 c. mult (No. 789) . 85 20
854 – 8 c. red and blue (No. 790) 85 10
855 **215** 10 c. brown and green 90 10
856 – 15 c. green and brown (No. 793) . . . . 1·00 70
857 **219** 20 c. black and buff . 2·50 10
858 – 25 c. yellow and brown (No. 797) . . . . 3·25 1·75
859 – 30 c. yellow, green and blue (No. 799) . . . 3·25 25
860 – 50 c. green (No. 800) . 3·50 75
861 – $1 blue (No. 801) . . 12·00 1·25
862 – $2 mauve (No. 802) . 7·00 10·00
F219w **F 6** $4 violet . . . . . 3·00 1·50
F220w $6 green . . . . . 4·50 2·50
F221w $8 blue . . . . . 6·00 4·50
F222w $10 blue . . . . . 7·50 4·50
For 15 c. in different colours, see No. 874.

1967. Health Stamps. Rugby Football.
867 **268** 2½ c. + 1 c. multicoloured 15 10
868 – 3 c. + 1 c. multicoloured 15 10
DESIGN—HORIZ: 3 c. Positioning for place-kick.

271 Brown Trout

273 Forest and Timber

1967.
870 – 7 c. multicoloured . . . . 1·50 90
871 **271** 7½ c. multicoloured . . . 30 70
872 – 8 c. multicoloured . . . 75 70
873 **273** 10 c. multicoloured . . . 50 10
874 – 15 c. green, deep green & red (as No. 793) . . . . . 1·00 80
875 – 18 c. multicoloured . . . 1·00 55
876 – 20 c. multicoloured . . . 1·00 20
877 – 25 c. multicoloured . . . 3·00 2·00
878 – 28 c. multicoloured . . . 60 10
879 – $2 black, ochre & blue (as No. 802) . . . . . . 22·00 15·00
DESIGNS: 7 c. "Kaitia" (trawler) and catch; 8 c. Apples and orchard; 18 c. Sheep and the "Woolmark"; 20 c. Consignments of beef and herd of cattle; 25 c. Dairy farm, Mt. Egmont and butter consignment. VERT: 28 c. Fox Glacier, Westland National Park.
No. 871 was originally issued to commemorate the introduction of the brown trout into New Zealand.
No. 874 is slightly larger than No. 793, measuring 21 × 25 mm. and the inscr and numerals differ in size.

278 "The Adoration of the Shepherds" (Poussin)

279 Mount Aspiring, Aurora Australis and Southern Cross

1967. Christmas.
880 **278** 2½ c. multicoloured . . . 10 10

1967. Cent of Royal Society of New Zealand.
881 **279** 4 c. multicoloured 25 20
882 – 8 c. multicoloured 25 70
DESIGN: 8 c. Sir James Hector (founder).

281 Open Bible

282 Soldiers and Tank

1968. Centenary of Maori Bible.
883 **281** 3 c. multicoloured 10 10

1968. New Zealand Armed Forces. Mult.
884 4 c. Type **282** 30 15
885 10 c. Airmen, Fairey Firefly and English Electric Canberra aircraft 50 60
886 28 c. Sailors and H.M.N.Z.S. "Achilles", 1939, and H.M.N.Z.S. "Waikato", 1968 70 2·25

285 Boy breasting Tape and Olympic Rings

1968. Health Stamps. Multicoloured.
887 2½ c. + 1 c. Type **285** 20 15
888 3 c. + 1 c. Girl swimming and Olympic rings 20 15

287 Placing Votes in Ballot Box

288 Human Rights Emblem

1968. 75th Anniv of Universal Suffrage in New Zealand.
890 **287** 3 c. ochre, green & blue . 10 10

1968. Human Rights Year.
891 **288** 10 c. red, yellow & green . 10 30

289 "Adoration of the Holy Child" (G. van Honthorst)

1968. Christmas.
892 **289** 2½ c. multicoloured . . . 10 10

290 I.L.O. Emblem

1969. 50th Anniv of Int Labour Organization.
893 **290** 7 c. black and red 15 30

291 Supreme Court Building, Auckland

1969. Centenary of New Zealand Law Society.
894 **291** 3 c. multicoloured 10 10
895 – 10 c. multicoloured 35 55
896 – 18 c. multicoloured . . . . 45 1·00
DESIGNS—VERT: 10 c. Law Society's coat of arms; 18 c. "Justice" (from Memorial Window in University of Canterbury, Christchurch).

295 Student being conferred with Degree

1969. Centenary of Otago University. Mult.
897 3 c. Otago University (vert) . . 10 10
898 10 c. Type **295** 20 25

296 Boys playing Cricket

1969. Health Stamps.
899 **296** 2½ c. + 1 c. multicoloured 40 50
900 – 3 c. + 1 c. multicoloured . 40 50
901 – 4 c. + 1 c. brown and ultramarine . . . . 40 1·75
DESIGNS—HORIZ: 3 c. Girls playing cricket. VERT: 4 c. Dr. Elizabeth Gunn (founder of first Children's Health Camp).

299 Oldest existing House in New Zealand, and Old Stone Mission Store, Kerikeri

1969. Early European Settlement in New Zealand, and 150th Anniv of Kerikeri. Multicoloured.
903 4 c. Type **299** 20 25
904 6 c. View of Bay of Islands . . 30 1·75

301 "The Nativity" (Federico Fiori (Barocci))

306 Girl, Wheat Field and C.O.R.S.O. Emblem

302 Captain Cook, Transit of Venus and "Octant"

1969. Christmas.
905 **301** 2½ c. multicoloured 10 10

1969. Bicentenary of Captain Cook's Landing in New Zealand.
906 **302** 4 c. black, red and blue . . 1·00 35
907 – 6 c. green, brown & black 1·25 2·75
908 – 18 c. brown, green & black 2·25 2·75
909 – 28 c. red, black and blue . 3·25 4·75
DESIGNS: 6 c. Sir Joseph Banks (naturalist) and outline of H.M.S. "Endeavour"; 18 c. Dr. Daniel Solander (botanist) and his plant; 28 c. Queen Elizabeth II and Cook's chart, 1769.

1969. 25th Anniv of C.O.R.S.O. (Council of Organizations for Relief Services Overseas). Multicoloured.
911 7 c. Type **306** . . . . 55 1·25
912 8 c. Mother feeding her child, dairy herd and C.O.R.S.O. emblem (horiz) . . . . . . 55 1·25

308 "Cardigan Bay" (champion trotter)

1970. Return of "Cardigan Bay" to New Zealand.
913 **308** 10 c. multicoloured . . . 30 30

309 "Vanessa gonerilla" (butterfly)

310 Queen Elizabeth II and New Zealand Coat of Arms

1970.
914 – ½ c. multicoloured . . . 10 20
915 **309** 1 c. multicoloured . . . 10 10
916 – 2 c. multicoloured . . . 10 10
917 – 2½ c. multicoloured . . 40 10
918 – 3 c. multicoloured . . . 15 10
919 – 4 c. multicoloured . . . 15 10
920 – 5 c. multicoloured . . . 45 10
921 – 6 c. black, green and red 45 20
922 – 7 c. multicoloured . . . 55 45
923 – 7½ c. multicoloured . . 1·00 1·50
924 – 8 c. multicoloured . . 65 70
925 **310** 10 c. multicoloured . . 40 15
926 – 15 c. black, flesh & brown 1·00 50
927 – 18 c. green, brown & black 1·00 40
928 – 20 c. black and brown . 1·00 15
929 – 23 c. multicoloured . . 80 30
930b – 25 c. multicoloured . . 70 40
931 – 30 c. multicoloured . . 1·00 15
932 – 50 c. multicoloured . . 60 20
933 – $1 multicoloured . . . 1·75 85
934 – $2 multicoloured . . . 2·75 1·25
DESIGNS—VERT (as T **309**): ½ c. "Lycaena salustius" (butterfly); 2 c. "Argyrophenga antipodum" (butterfly); 2½ c. "Nyctemera annulata" (moth); 3 c. "Detunda egregia" (moth); 4 c. "Charagia virescens" (moth); 5 c. Scarlet wrasse ("Scarlet parrot fish"); 6 c. Big-bellied sea horses; 7 c. Leather jacket (fish); 7½ c. Intermediate halfbeak ("Garfish"); 8 c. John Dory (fish). (As T **310**): 18 c. Maori club; 25 c. Hauraki Gulf Maritime Park; 30 c. Mt. Cook National Park. HORIZ (as T **310**): 15 c. Maori fish hook; 20 c. Maori tattoo pattern; 23 c. Egmont National Park; 50 c. Abel Tasman National Park; $1 Geothermal power; $2 Agricultural technology.

311 Geyser Restaurant

312 U.N. H.Q. Building

1970. World Fair, Osaka. Multicoloured.
935 7 c. Type **311** . . . . 40 1·00
936 8 c. New Zealand Pavilion . . 40 1·00
937 18 c. Bush Walk . . . . . . 60 1·00

1970. 25th Anniv of United Nations.
938 **312** 3 c. multicoloured 10 10
939 – 10 c. red and yellow . . . 20 20
DESIGN: 10 c. Tractor on horizon.

313 Soccer

314 "The Virgin adoring the Child" (Correggio)

1970. Health Stamps. Multicoloured.
940 2½ c. + 1 c. Netball (vert) . . 25 50
941 3 c. + 1 c. Type **313** 25 50

1970. Christmas.
943 **314** 2½ c. multicoloured . . . 10 10
944 – 3 c. multicoloured . . . 10 10
945 – 10 c. black, orange & silver 30 75
DESIGNS—VERT: 3 c. Stained Glass Window, Invercargill Presbyterian Church "The Holy Family". HORIZ: 10 c. Tower of Roman Catholic Church, Sockburn.

316 Chatham Islands Lily

1970. Chatham Islands. Multicoloured.

946 1 c. Type **316** 10 25
947 2 c. Shy albatross 30 35

317 Country Women's Institute Emblem

1971. 50th Annivs of Country Women's Institutes and Rotary International in New Zealand. Multicoloured.

948 4 c. Type **317** 10 10
949 10 c. Rotary emblem and map of New Zealand 10 30

318 "Rainbow II" (yacht)

1971. One Ton Cup Racing Trophy. Mult.

950 5 c. Type **318** 20 25
951 8 c. One Ton Cup . . . . . . 30 1·00

319 Civic Arms of Palmerston North

1971. City Centenaries. Multicoloured.

952 3 c. Type **319** 10 10
953 4 c. Arms of Auckland 10 10
954 5 c. Arms of Invercargill . . . 15 70

320 Antarctica on Globe

1971. 10th Anniv of Antarctic Treaty.

955 **320** 6 c. multicoloured . . . . 1·00 1·00

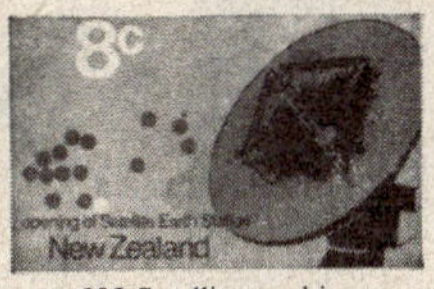

321 Child on Swing — 323 Satellite-tracking Aerial

1971. 25th Anniv of U.N.I.C.E.F.

956 **321** 7 c. multicoloured 50 70

1971. No. 917 surch **4c**.

957 4 c. on $2\frac{1}{2}$ c. multicoloured . . 15 10

1971. Opening of Satellite Earth Station.

958 **323** 8 c. black, grey and red . . 60 1·25
959 – 10 c. black, green and violet 65 1·00
DESIGN: 10 c. Satellite.

324 Girls playing Hockey

1971. Health Stamps. Multicoloured.

960 3 c. + 1 c. Type **324** 45 50
961 4 c. + 1 c. Boys playing hockey 45 50
962 5 c. + 1 c. Dental health . . . 1·10 2·00

325 "Madonna bending over the Crib" (Maratta)

1971. Christmas. Multicoloured.

964 3 c. Type **325** 10 10
965 4 c. "The Annunciation" (stained-glass window) . . 10 10
966 10 c. "The Three Kings" . . 70 1·25
Nos. 965/6 are smaller, size $21\frac{1}{2}\times38$ mm.

326 "Tiffany" Rose — 327 Lord Rutherford and Alpha Particles

1971. 1st World Rose Convention, Hamilton. Multicoloured.

967 2 c. Type **326** 15 30
968 5 c. "Peace" 35 35
969 8 c. "Chrysler Imperial" . . . 60 1·10

1971. Birth Centenary of Lord Rutherford (scientist). Multicoloured.

970 1 c. Type **327** 25 40
971 7 c. Lord Rutherford and formula . . . . 85 1·40

328 Benz (1895) — 329 Coat of Arms of Wanganui

1972. International Vintage Car Rally. Mult.

972 3 c. Type **328** 20 10
973 4 c. Oldsmobile (1904) . . . 25 10
974 5 c. Ford "Model T" (1914) . 25 10
975 6 c. Cadillac Service car (1915) 40 45
976 8 c. Chrysler (1924) . . . . . 1·00 1·90
977 10 c. Austin "7" (1923) . . . 1·00 1·40

1972. Anniversaries.

978 **329** 3 c. multicoloured 15 10
979 – 4 c. orange, brown & black 15 10
980 – 5 c. multicoloured 25 10
981 – 8 c. multicoloured . . . . 90 1·40
982 – 10 c. multicoloured . . . . 90 1·40
DESIGNS AND EVENTS—VERT: 3 c. Type **329** (centenary of Wanganui Council); 5 c. De Havilland D.H.89 Dragon Rapide and Boeing 737 (25th anniv of National Airways Corp); 8 c. French frigate and Maori palisade (bicentenary of landing by Marion du Fresne). HORIZ: 4 c. Postal Union symbol (10th anniv of Asian–Oceanic Postal Union); 10 c. Stone cairn (150th anniv of New Zealand Methodist Church).

330 Black Scree Cotula — 331 Boy playing Tennis

1972. Alpine Plants. Multicoloured.

983 4 c. Type **330** 30 10
984 6 c. North Island edelweiss . 50 50
985 8 c. Haast's buttercup . . . . 70 1·00
986 10 c. Brown Mountain daisy . 90 1·40

1972. Health Stamps.

987 **331** 3 c. + 1 c. grey & brown 30 45
988 – 4 c. + 1 c. brown, grey and yellow 30 45
DESIGN: No. 988, Girl playing tennis.

332 "Madonna with Child" (Murillo) — 333 Lake Waikaremoana

1972. Christmas. Multicoloured.

990 3 c. Type **332** 10 10
991 5 c. "The Last Supper" (stained-glass window, St. John's Church, Levin) 15 10
992 10 c. Pohutukawa flower . . . 55 1·00

1972. Lake Scenes. Multicoloured.

993 6 c. Type **333** . . . . 1·00 1·25
994 8 c. Lake Hayes . . . . 1·10 1·25
995 18 c. Lake Wakatipu . . . . . 1·50 2·25
996 23 c. Lake Rotomahana . . . 1·75 2·75

334 Old Pollen Street

1973. Commemorations.

997 **334** 3 c. multicoloured 10 10
998 – 4 c. multicoloured 15 10
999 – 5 c. multicoloured 15 15
1000 – 6 c. multicoloured 60 65
1001 – 8 c. grey, blue and gold . 50 65
1002 – 10 c. multicoloured . . . 70 1·00
DESIGNS AND EVENTS. 3 c. (centenary of Thames Borough); 4 c. Coalmining and pasture (centenary of Westport Borough); 5 c. Cloister (centenary of Canterbury University); 6 c. Forest, birds and lake (50th anniv of Royal Forest and Bird Protection Society); 8 c. Rowers (Success of N.Z. rowers in 1972 Olympics); 10 c. Graph and people (25th anniv of E.C.A.F.E.).

335 Class W Locomotive

1973. New Zealand Steam Locomotives. Multicoloured.

1003 3 c. Type **335** 40 10
1004 4 c. Class X 40 10
1005 5 c. Class Ab 40 10
1006 10 c. Class Ja No. 1274 . . . 2·25 1·75

336 "Maori Woman and Child" — 337 Prince Edward

1973. Paintings by Frances Hodgkins. Multicoloured.

1027 5 c. Type **336** 40 15
1028 8 c. "Hilltop" 60 75
1029 10 c. "Barn in Picardy" . . . 80 1·25
1030 18 c. "Self-portrait Still Life" . 1·25 2·50

1973. Health Stamps.

1031 **337** 3 c. + 1 c. green & brown 30 30
1032 4 c. + 1 c. red & brown . . 30 30

338 "Tempi Madonna" (Raphael) — 339 Mitre Peak

1973. Christmas. Multicoloured.

1034 3 c. Type **338** 10 10
1035 5 c. "Three Kings" (stained-glass window, St. Theresa's Church, Auckland) 10 10
1036 10 c. Family entering church . 25 50

1973. Mountain Scenery. Multicoloured.

1037 6 c. Type **339** 70 80
1038 8 c. Mt. Ngauruhoe . . . . 80 1·25
1039 18 c. Mt. Sefton (horiz) . . . 1·40 2·50
1040 23 c. Burnett Range (horiz) . 1·50 2·75

340 Hurdling — 342 "Spirit of Napier" Fountain

1974. 10th British Commonwealth Games, Christchurch.

1041 **340** 4 c. multicoloured . . . 10 10
1042 – 5 c. black and violet . . 15 10
1043 – 10 c. multicoloured . . . 20 15
1044 – 18 c. multicoloured . . . 25 50
1045 – 23 c. multicoloured . . . 35 70
DESIGNS: 5 c. Ball-player (4th Paraplegic Games, Dunedin); 10 c. Cycling; 18 c. Rifle-shooting; 23 c. Bowls.

1974. Centenaries of Napier and U.P.U. Mult.

1047 4 c. Type **342** 10 10
1048 5 c. Clock Tower, Berne . . 15 25
1049 8 c. U.P.U. Monument, Berne 65 1·40

343 Boeing Seaplane, 1919 — 344 Children, Cat and Dog

1974. History of New Zealand Airmail Transport. Multicoloured.

1050 3 c. Type **343** 30 10
1051 4 c. Lockheed 10 Electra "Kauha", 1937 . . . . . 35 10
1052 5 c. Bristol Type 170 Freighter Mk 31, 1958 . . . . . . 40 30
1053 23 c. Short S.30 modified "G" Class flying boat "Aotearoa", 1940 . . . . 1·75 2·50

1974. Health Stamps.

1054 **344** 3 c. + 1 c. multicoloured 20 35
1055 – 4 c. + 1 c. multicoloured 25 35
1056 – 5 c. + 1 c. multicoloured 1·00 1·50
Nos. 1055/6 are similar to Type **344** showing children with pets.

345 "The Adoration of the Magi" (Konrad Witz) — 346 Great Barrier Island

1974. Christmas. Multicoloured.

1058 3 c. Type **345** 10 10
1059 5 c. "The Angel Window" (stained glass window, Old St. Pauls Church, Wellington) 10 10
1060 10 c. Madonna lily 30 70

1974. Offshore Islands. Multicoloured.

1061 6 c. Type **346** 30 40
1062 8 c. Stewart Island . . . . . 50 1·25
1063 18 c. White Island . . . . . 70 1·25
1064 23 c. The Brothers . . . . . 75 1·50

347 Crippled Child

1975. Anniversaries and Events. Multicoloured.

1065 3 c. Type **347** 10 10
1066 5 c. Farming family 15 10
1067 10 c. I.W.Y. symbols 20 65
1068 18 c. Medical School Building, Otago University . . . . . 55 1·50
COMMEMORATIONS: 3 c. 40th anniv of New Zealand Crippled Children Society; 5 c. 50th anniv of Women's Division, Federated Farmers of New Zealand; 10 c. International Women's Year; 18 c. Centenary of Otago Medical School.

348 Scow "Lake Erie"

1975. Historic Sailing Ships.

1069 **348** 4 c. black and red . . . 30 10
1070 – 5 c. black and blue . . . 30 10
1071 – 8 c. black and yellow . . 55 60
1072 – 10 c. black and yellow . . 60 60
1073 – 18 c. black and brown . . 1·00 1·75
1074 – 23 c. black and lilac . . . 1·10 1·75

SHIPS: 5 c. Schooner "Herald"; 8 c. Brigantine "New Zealander"; 10 c. Topsail schooner "Jessie Kelly"; 18 c. Barque "Tory"; 23 c. Full-rigged clipper "Rangitiki".

349 Lake Sumner Forest Park

1975. Forest Park Scenes. Multicoloured.

1075 6 c. Type **349** 50 70
1076 8 c. North-west Nelson . . . 60 1·00
1077 18 c. Kaweka . . . . . . 1·00 1·75
1078 23 c. Coromandel . . . . . 1·25 2·00

350 Girl feeding Lamb

351 "Virgin and Child" (Zanobi Machiavelli)

1975. Health Stamps. Multicoloured.

1079 3 c. + 1 c. Type **350** 20 30
1080 4 c. + 1 c. Boy with hen and chicks 20 30
1081 5 c. + 1 c. Boy with duck and duckling . . . . 60 1·25

1975. Christmas. Multicoloured.

1083 3 c. Type **351** 10 10
1084 5 c. "Cross in Landscape" (stained-glass window, Greendale Church) 10 10
1085 10 c. "I saw three ships" (carol) 35 65

The 5 c. and 10 c. are horizontal.

352 "Sterling Silver"

353 Queen Elizabeth II (photograph by W. Harrison)

353a Maripi (knife)

353b Rainbow Abalone or Paua

1975. (a) Garden Roses. Multicoloured.

1086 1 c. Type **352** 10 10
1087 2 c. "Lilli Marlene" 10 10
1088 3 c. "Queen Elizabeth" . . . 60 10
1089 4 c. "Super Star" 10 20
1090 5 c. "Diamond Jubilee" . . . 10 10
1091a 6 c. "Cresset" 40 70
1092a 7 c. "Michele Meilland" . . . 40 10
1093a 8 c. "Josephine Bruce" . . . 45 10
1094 9 c. "Iceberg" 30 40

(b) Type **353**.

1094ab 10 c. multicoloured 30 10

(c) Maori Artefacts.

1095 **353a** 11 c. brown, yell & blk . . 30 50
1096 – 12 c. brown, yell & blk . . 30 15
1097 – 13 c. brown, mve & blk . . 40 65
1098 – 14 c. brown, yell & blk . . 30 20

DESIGNS: 12 c. Putorino (flute); 13 c. Wahaika (club); 14 c. Kotiate (club).

(d) Sea Shells. Multicoloured.

1099 20 c. Type **353b** 15 20
1100 30 c. Toheroa clam 25 30
1101 40 c. Old woman or coarse dosinia 30 35
1102 50 c. New Zealand or spiny murex 40 45
1103 $1 New Zealand scallop . . . 70 85
1104 $2 Circular saw . . . . . . 1·00 1·75

(e) Building. Multicoloured.

1105 $5 "Beehive" (section of Parliamentary Buildings, Wellington) (22 × 26 mm) . 2·50 1·50

354 Family and League of Mothers Badge

1976. Anniversaries and Metrication. Mult.

1110 6 c. Type **354** 10 10
1111 7 c. Weight, temperature, linear measure and capacity . . 10 10
1112 8 c. "William Bryon" (immigrant ship), mountain and New Plymouth . . . 15 10
1113 10 c. Two women shaking hands and Y.W.C.A. badge . . . 15 50
1114 25 c. Map of the world showing cable links . . . . . . 30 1·25

ANNIVERSARIES: 6 c. 50th anniv of League of Mothers; 7 c. Metrication; 8 c. Centenary of New Plymouth; 10 c. 50th anniv of New Zealand Y.W.C.A.; 25 c. Link with International Telecommunications Network.

355 Gig

1976. Vintage Farm Transport. Multicoloured.

1115 6 c. Type **355** 15 40
1116 7 c. Thornycroft lorry . . . 20 10
1117 8 c. Scandi wagon 40 20
1118 9 c. Traction engine 30 50
1119 10 c. Wool wagon 30 50
1120 25 c. Cart . . . . 85 2·25

356 Purakaunui Falls

357 Boy and Pony

1976. Waterfalls. Multicoloured.

1121 10 c. Type **356** 35 10
1122 14 c. Marakopa Falls . . . 60 85
1123 15 c. Bridal Veil Falls . . . 65 95
1124 16 c. Papakorito Falls . . . 70 1·10

1976. Health Stamps. Multicoloured.

1125 7 c. + 1 c. Type **357** 20 30
1126 8 c. + 1 c. Girl and calf . . 20 30
1127 10 c. + 1 c. Girls and bird . . 40 90

358 "Nativity" (Spanish carving)

359 Arms of Hamilton

1976. Christmas. Multicoloured.

1129 7 c. Type **358** 15 10
1130 11 c. "Resurrection" (stained-glass window, St. Joseph's Catholic Church, Grey Lynn) (horiz) 25 30
1131 18 c. Angels (horiz) 40 90

1977. Anniversaries. Multicoloured.

1132 8 c. Type **359** 15 10
1133 8 c. Arms of Gisborne . . . 15 10
1134 8 c. Arms of Masterton . . . 15 10
1135 10 c. A.A. emblem 15 40
1136 10 c. Arms of the Royal Australasian College of Surgeons 15 40

ANNIVERSARIES: No. 1132, Cent of Hamilton; No. 1133, Cent of Gisborne; No. 1134, Cent of Masterton; No. 1135, 75th anniv of Automobile Association in New Zealand; No. 1136, 50th anniv of R.A.C.S.

361 Physical Education and Maori Culture

363 Karitane Beach

1977. Education. Multicoloured.

1138 8 c. Type **361** 40 70
1139 8 c. Geography, science and woodwork 40 70
1140 8 c. Teaching the deaf, kindergarten and woodwork 40 70
1141 8 c. Tertiary and language classes 40 70
1142 8 c. Home science, correspondence school and teacher training 40 70

1977. Nos. 918/19 surch.

1143 7 c. on 3 c. "Detunda egregia" (moth) 40 70
1144 8 c. on 4 c. "Charagia virescens" (moth) 40 70

1977. Seascapes. Multicoloured.

1145 10 c. Type **363** 15 10
1146 16 c. Ocean Beach, Mount Maunganui 30 30
1147 18 c. Piha Beach 30 30
1148 30 c. Kaikoura Coast 35 40

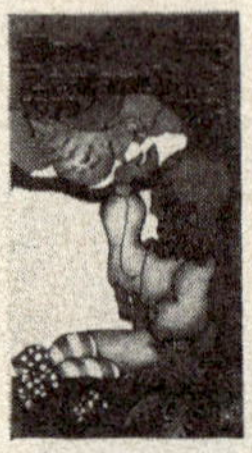

364 Girl with Pigeon

365 "The Holy Family" (Correggio)

1977. Health Stamps. Multicoloured.

1149 7 c. + 2 c. Type **364** 20 35
1150 8 c. + 2 c. Boy with frog . . 25 40
1151 10 c. + 2 c. Girl with butterfly 45 80

1977. Christmas. Multicoloured.

1153 7 c. Type **365** 15 10
1154 16 c. "Madonna and Child" (stained-glass window, St. Michael's and All Angels, Dunedin) 25 25
1155 23 c. "Partridge in a Pear Tree" 40 1·00

The 16 c. and 23 c. are vertical.

366 Merryweather Manual Pump, 1860

1977. Fire Fighting Appliances. Mult.

1156 10 c. Type **366** 15 10
1157 11 c. 2-wheel hose, reel and ladder, 1880 . . . . . . 15 25
1158 12 c. Shand Mason steam fire engine, 1873 . . . . . 20 30
1159 23 c. Chemical fire engine, 1888 30 50

367 Town Clock and Coat of Arms, Ashburton

368 Students and Ivey Hall, Lincoln College

1978. Centenaries.

1160 **367** 10 c. multicoloured . . . 15 10
1161 – 10 c. multicoloured . . . 15 10
1162 – 12 c. red, yellow & black . 15 15
1163 – 20 c. multicoloured . . . 20 30

DESIGNS—VERT: No. 1161, Mount Egmont (cent of Stratford); No. 1162, Early telephone (cent of telephone in New Zealand). HORIZ: No. 1163, Aerial view of the Bay of Islands (cent of the Bay of Islands County).

1978. Land Resources and Centenary of Lincoln College of Agriculture. Multicoloured.

1164 10 c. Type **368** 15 10
1165 12 c. Sheep grazing 15 25
1166 15 c. Fertiliser ground spreading 15 30
1167 16 c. Agricultural Field Days 15 30
1168 20 c. Harvesting grain . . . 20 40
1169 30 c. Dairy farming 20 70

369

370 Maui Gas Drilling Platform

1978. Coil Stamps.

1170 **369** 1 c. purple 10 30
1171 2 c. orange 10 30
1172 5 c. brown 10 35
1173 10 c. blue 30 70

1978. Resources of the Sea. Multicoloured.

1174 12 c. Type **370** 20 15
1175 15 c. Trawler 25 30
1176 20 c. Map of 200 mile fishing limit 30 40
1177 23 c. Humpback whale and bottle-nosed dolphins . . . 40 50
1178 35 c. Kingfish, snapper, grouper and squid 60 75

371 First Health Charity Stamp

372 "The Holy Family" (El Greco)

1978. Health Stamps.

1179 **371** 10 c. + 2 c. black, red and gold 30 35
1180 – 12 c. + 2 c. multicoloured 30 40

DESIGNS: 10 c. Type **371** (50th anniv of Health Stamps); 12 c. Heart Operation (National Heart Foundation).

1978. Christmas. Multicoloured.

1182 7 c. Type **372** 10 10
1183 16 c. All Saint's Church, Howick (horiz) 25 35
1184 23 c. Beach scene (horiz) . . 30 50

373 Sir Julius Vogel

374 Riverlands Cottage, Blenheim

1979. Statesmen. Designs each brown and drab.

1185 10 c. Type **373** 30 65
1186 10 c. Sir George Grey . . . 30 65
1187 10 c. Richard John Seddon . . 30 65

1979. Architecture (1st series).

1188 **374** 10 c. black, light blue and blue 10 10
1189 – 12 c. black, light green and green 15 25
1190 – 15 c. black and grey . . 20 30
1191 – 20 c. black, brown and sepia 25 30

DESIGNS: 12 c. The Mission House, Waimate North; 15 c. "The Elms", Tauranga; 20 c. Provincial Council Buildings, Christchurch.

See also Nos. 1217/20 and 1262/5.

375 Whangaroa Harbour

1979. Small Harbours. Multicoloured.

1192 15 c. Type **375** 20 10
1193 20 c. Kawau Island 25 40
1194 23 c. Akaroa Harbour (vert) . 30 50
1195 35 c. Picton Harbour (vert) . 45 70

376 Children with Building Bricks

1979. International Year of the Child.
1196 **376** 10 c. multicoloured . . . 15 10

377 Two-spotted Chromis

1979. Health Stamps. Marine Life. Multicoloured.
1197 10 c. + 2 c. Type **377** 40 60
1198 10 c. + 2 c. Sea urchin 40 60
1199 12 c. + 2 c. Red goatfish and underwater cameraman (vert) 40 60

1979. Nos. 1091a/3a and 1094ab surch.
1201 4 c. on 8 c. "Josephine Bruce" 10 20
1202 14 c. on 10 c. Type **353** . . 30 20
1203 17 c. on 6 c. "Cresset" . . . 30 70
1203a 20 c. on 7 c. "Michele Meilland" 30 10

379 "Madonna and Child" (sculpture, Ghiberti)
380 Chamber, House of Representatives

1979. Christmas. Multicoloured.
1204 10 c. Type **379** 15 10
1205 25 c. Christ Church, Russell . 30 40
1206 35 c. Pohutukawa (tree) . . . 40 55

1979. 25th Commonwealth Parliamentary Conference, Wellington. Multicoloured.
1207 14 c. Type **380** 15 10
1208 20 c. Mace and Black Rod . 20 30
1209 30 c. "Beehive" wall hanging 30 70

381 1855 1d. Stamp

1980. Anniversaries and Events.
1210 **381** 14 c. black, red & yellow 20 30
1211 – 14 c. black, blue & yellow 20 30
1212 – 14 c. black, green & yell . 20 30
1213 – 17 c. multicoloured . . . 20 30
1214 – 25 c. multicoloured . . . 25 35
1215 – 30 c. multicoloured . . . 25 40
DESIGNS: No. 1211, 1855 2d. stamp; No. 1212, 1855 1s. stamp (125th anniv of New Zealand stamps); No. 1213, Geyser, wood-carving and building (Centenary of Rotorua (town)); No. 1214, "Earina autumnalis" and "Thelymitra venosa" (International Orchid Conference, Auckland); No. 1215, Ploughing and Golden Plough Trophy (World Ploughing Championships, Christchurch).

382 Ewelme Cottage, Parnell

1980. Architecture (2nd series). Multicoloured.
1217 14 c. Type **382** 15 10
1218 17 c. Broadgreen, Nelson . . 25 35
1219 25 c. Courthouse, Oamaru . . 30 45
1220 30 c. Government Buildings, Wellington 35 45

383 Auckland Harbour

1980. Large Harbours. Multicoloured.
1221 25 c. Type **383** 25 20
1222 30 c. Wellington Harbour . . 30 30
1223 35 c. Lyttelton Harbour . . . 30 35
1224 50 c. Port Chalmers 50 65

384 Surf-fishing
385 "Madonna and Child with Cherubim" (sculpture, Andrea della Robbia)

1980. Health Stamps. Fishing. Multicoloured.
1225 14 c. + 2 c. Type **384** . . . 45 70
1226 14 c. + 2 c. Wharf-fishing . 45 70
1227 17 c. + 2 c. Spear-fishing . 45 55

1980. Christmas. Multicoloured.
1229 10 c. Type **385** 15 10
1230 25 c. St. Mary's Church, New Plymouth 25 25
1231 35 c. Picnic scene 40 65

386 Te Heu Heu (chief)
387 Lt. Col. the Hon. W. H. A. Feilding and Borough of Feilding Crest (cent)

1980. Maori Personalities. Multicoloured.
1232 15 c. Type **386** 10 10
1233 25 c. Te Hau (chief) 15 20
1234 35 c. Te Puea (princess) . . 20 10
1235 45 c. Ngata (politician) . . . 30 20
1236 60 c. Te Ata-O-Tu (warrior) 35 25

1981. Commemorations.
1237 **387** 20 c. multicoloured . . 20 20
1238 – 25 c. orange and black . 25 25
DESIGN AND COMMEMORATION: 25 c. I.Y.D. emblem and cupped hands (International Year of the Disabled).

388 The Family at Play
389 Kaiauai River

1981. "Family Life". Multicoloured.
1239 20 c. Type **388** 20 10
1240 25 c. The family young and old 25 30
1241 30 c. The family at home . . 30 40
1242 35 c. The family at church . 35 55

1981. River Scenes. Multicoloured.
1243 30 c. Type **389** 25 25
1244 35 c. Mangahao 30 30
1245 40 c. Shotover (horiz) . . . 35 40
1246 60 c. Cleddau (horiz) 55 65

390 St. Paul's Cathedral

1981. Royal Wedding. Multicoloured.
1247 20 c. Type **390** 20 30
1248 20 c. Prince Charles and Lady Diana Spencer 20 30

391 Girl with Starfish
392 "Madonna suckling the Child" (painting, d'Oggiono)

1981. Health Stamps. Children playing by the Sea. Multicoloured.
1249 20 c. + 2 c. Type **391** 25 50
1250 20 c. + 2 c. Boy fishing . . . 25 50
1251 25 c. + 2 c. Children exploring rock pool 25 35
Nos. 1249/50 were printed together, se-tenant, forming a composite design.

1981. Christmas. Multicoloured.
1253 14 c. Type **392** 15 10
1254 30 c. St. John's Church, Wakefield 35 25
1255 40 c. Golden tainui (flower) . 45 35

393 Tauranga Mission House
394 Map of New Zealand

1981. Commemorations. Multicoloured.
1256 20 c. Type **393** 25 10
1257 20 c. Water tower, Hawera . 25 10
1258 25 c. Cat 35 35
1259 30 c. "Dunedin" (refrigerated sailing ship) 35 40
1260 35 c. Scientific research equipment 40 45
COMMEMORATIONS: No. 1256, Centenary of Tauranga (town); No. 1257, Centenary of Hawera (town); No. 1258, Centenary of S.P.C.A. (Society for the Prevention of Cruelty to Animals in New Zealand); No. 1259, Centenary of frozen meat exports; No. 1260, International Year of Science.

1982.
1261 **394** 24 c. green and blue . . . 30 10

395 Alberton, Auckland

1982. Architecture (3rd series). Multicoloured.
1262 20 c. Type **395** 20 15
1263 25 c. Caccia Birch, Palmerston North 25 25
1264 30 c. Railway station, Dunedin 50 30
1265 35 c. Post Office, Ophir . . . 40 40

396 Kaiteriteri Beach, Nelson (Summer)

1982. New Zealand Scenes. Multicoloured.
1266 35 c. Type **396** 30 30
1267 40 c. St. Omer Park, Queenstown (Autumn) . . 35 35
1268 45 c. Mt. Ngauruhoe, Tongariro National Park (Winter) . . 40 40
1269 70 c. Wairarapa farm (Spring) 60 60

397 Labrador
398 "Madonna with Child and Two Angels" (painting by Piero di Cosimo)

1982. Health Stamps. Dogs. Multicoloured.
1270 24 c. + 2 c. Type **397** . . . 80 1·00
1271 24 c. + 2 c. Border collie . . 80 1·00
1272 30 c. + 2 c. Cocker spaniel . 80 1·00

1982. Christmas. Multicoloured.
1274 18 c. Type **398** 20 10
1275 35 c. Rangiatea Maori Church, Otaki 35 30
1276 45 c. Surf life-saving 50 40

399 Nephrite
399a Grapes

399b Kokako
400 Old Arts Building, Auckland University

1982. (a) Minerals. Multicoloured.
1277 1 c. Type **399** 10 10
1278 2 c. Agate 10 10
1279 3 c. Iron pyrites 10 10
1280 4 c. Amethyst 10 10
1281 5 c. Carnelian 10 10
1282 9 c. Native sulphur 20 10

(b) Fruits. Multicoloured.
1283 10 c. Type **399a** 50 10
1284 20 c. Citrus fruit 35 10
1285 30 c. Nectarines 30 10
1286 40 c. Apples 35 10
1287 50 c. Kiwifruit 40 10

(c) Native Birds. Multicoloured.
1288 30 c. Kakapo 50 25
1289 40 c. Mountain ("Blue") duck 60 35
1290 45 c. New Zealand falcon . . 1·00 35
1291 60 c. New Zealand teal . . . 1·00 40
1292 $1 Type **399b** . . . . 1·00 30
1293 $2 Chatham Island robin . . 1·75 50
1294 $3 Stitchbird . . . . 2·00 1·40
1295 $4 Saddleback . . . . 2·25 2·50
1296 $5 Takahe . . . . 3·00 3·00
1297 $10 Little spotted kiwi . . . 6·00 6·75

1983. Commemorations. Multicoloured.
1303 24 c. Salvation Army Centenary logo 20 10
1304 30 c. Type **400** 30 35
1305 35 c. Stylised kangaroo and Kiwi 35 35
1306 40 c. Rainbow trout 40 45
1307 45 c. Satellite over Earth . . 45 50
COMMEMORATIONS: 24 c. Salvation Army Centenary; 30 c. Auckland University Centenary; 35 c. Closer Economic Relationship agreement with Australia; 40 c. Centenary of Introduction of Rainbow Trout into New Zealand; 45 c. World Communications Year.

401 Queen Elizabeth II
402 "Boats, Island Bay" (Rita Angus)

1983. Commonwealth Day. Multicoloured.
1308 24 c. Type **401** 30 10
1309 35 c. Maori rock drawing . . 35 50
1310 40 c. Woolmark and woolscouring symbols . . 35 80
1311 45 c. Coat of arms 35 80

1983. Paintings by Rita Angus. Mult.
1312 24 c. Type **402** 35 10
1313 30 c. "Central Otago Landscape" 40 45
1314 35 c. "Wanaka Landscape" . 50 50
1315 45 c. "Tree" 70 70

403 Mt. Egmont
404 Tabby

1983. Beautiful New Zealand. Mult.
1316 35 c. Type **403** 30 35
1317 40 c. Cooks Bay 35 40
1318 45 c. Lake Matheson (horiz) 40 45
1319 70 c. Lake Alexandrina (horiz) 65 70

1983. Health Stamps. Cats. Multicoloured.
1320 24 c. + 2 c. Type **404** . . . 40 50
1321 24 c. + 2 c. Siamese 40 50
1322 30 c. + 2 c. Persian 75 90

405 "The Family of the Holy Oak Tree" (Raphael)

406 Geology

1983. Christmas. Multicoloured.

1324	18 c. Type **405**	15	10
1325	35 c. St. Patrick's Church, Greymouth	40	40
1326	45 c. "The Glory of Christmas"	55	55

1984. Antarctic Research. Multicoloured.

1327	24 c. Type **406**	35	10
1328	40 c. Biology	45	40
1329	58 c. Glaciology	60	55
1330	70 c. Meteorology	70	70

407 "Mountaineer", Lake Wakatipu

1984. New Zealand Ferry Boats. Mult.

1332	24 c. Type **407**	25	10
1333	40 c. "Waikana", Otago	30	45
1334	58 c. "Britannia", Waitemata	40	1·10
1335	70 c. "Wakatere", Firth of Thames	55	85

408 Mount Hutt

1984. Ski-slope Scenery. Multicoloured.

1336	35 c. Type **408**	40	40
1337	40 c. Coronet Park	45	45
1338	45 c. Turoa	50	50
1339	70 c. Whakapapa	75	75

409 Hamilton's Frog

1984. Amphibians and Reptiles. Multicoloured.

1340	24 c. Type **409**	30	30
1341	24 c. Great Barrier skink	30	30
1342	30 c. Harlequin gecko	35	35
1343	58 c. Otago skink	70	70
1344	70 c. Gold-striped gecko	75	75

410 Clydesdales ploughing

1984. Health Stamps. Horses. Multicoloured.

1345	24 c. + 2 c. Type **410**	30	50
1346	24 c. + 2 c. Shetland ponies	30	50
1347	30 c. + 2 c. Thoroughbreds	45	50

411 "Adoration of the Shepherds" (Lorenzo di Credi)

1984. Christmas. Multicoloured.

1349	18 c. Type **411**	20	10
1350	35 c. Old St. Paul's, Wellington (vert)	40	40
1351	45 c. "The Joy of Christmas" (vert)	50	65

412 Mounted Riflemen, South Africa, 1901

1984. New Zealand Military History. Multicoloured.

1352	24 c. Type **412**	25	10
1353	40 c. Engineers, France, 1917	35	45
1354	58 c. Tanks of 2nd N.Z. Divisional Cavalry, North Africa, 1942	50	90
1355	70 c. Infantryman in jungle kit, and 25-pounder gun, Korea and South-East Asia, 1950–72	60	80

413 St. John Ambulance Badge

1985. Centenary of St. John Ambulance in New Zealand.

1357	**413** 24 c. black, gold and red	25	15
1358	30 c. black, silver & blue	35	45
1359	40 c. black and grey	40	1·10

The colours of the badge depicted are those for Bailiffs and Dames Grand Cross (24 c.), Knights and Dames of Grace (30 c.) and Officer Brothers and Sisters (40 c.).

414 Nelson Horse Tram, 1862

1985. Vintage Trams. Multicoloured.

1360	24 c. Type **414**	40	10
1361	30 c. Graham's Town steam tram, 1871	50	60
1362	35 c. Dunedin cable car, 1881	50	70
1363	40 c. Auckland electric tram, 1902	50	70
1364	45 c. Wellington electric tram, 1904	60	90
1365	58 c. Christchurch electric tram, 1905	70	1·75

415 Shotover Bridge

416 Queen Elizabeth II (from photo by Camera Press)

1985. Bridges of New Zealand. Multicoloured.

1366	35 c. Type **415**	60	60
1367	40 c. Alexandra Bridge	65	60
1368	45 c. South Rangitikei Railway Bridge (vert)	70	1·25
1369	70 c. Twin Bridges (vert)	90	1·25

1985. Mult, background colours given.

1370	**416** 25 c. red	50	10
1371	35 c. blue	90	10

417 Princess of Wales and Prince William

418 The Holy Family in the Stable

1985. Health Stamps. Designs showing photographs by Lord Snowdon. Multicoloured.

1372	25 c. + 2 c. Type **417**	75	1·00
1373	25 c. + 2 c. Princess of Wales and Prince Henry	75	1·00
1374	35 c. + 2 c. Prince and Princess of Wales with Princes William and Henry	75	1·00

1985. Christmas. Multicoloured.

1376	18 c. Type **418**	20	10
1377	40 c. The shepherds	40	85
1378	50 c. The angels	45	1·00

419 H.M.N.Z.S. "Philomel" (1914–47)

1985. New Zealand Naval History. Multicoloured.

1379	25 c. Type **419**	70	15
1380	45 c. H.M.N.Z.S. "Achilles" (1936–46)	1·10	1·40
1381	60 c. H.M.N.Z.S. "Rotoiti" (1949–65)	1·40	2·00
1382	75 c. H.M.N.Z.S. "Canterbury" (from 1971)	1·75	2·25

420 Police Computer Operator

1986. Centenary of New Zealand Police. Designs showing historical aspects above modern police activities. Multicoloured.

1384	25 c. Type **420**	35	50
1385	25 c. Detective and mobile control room	35	50
1386	25 c. Policewoman and badge	35	50
1387	25 c. Forensic scientist, patrol car and policeman with child	35	50
1388	25 c. Police College, Porirua, "Lady Elizabeth II" (patrol boat) and dog handler	35	50

421 Indian "Power Plus" 1000cc Motor Cycle (1920)

1986. Vintage Motor Cycles. Multicoloured.

1389	35 c. Type **421**	50	45
1390	45 c. Norton "CS1" 500cc (1927)	60	65
1391	60 c. B.S.A. "Sloper". 500cc (1930)	75	1·25
1392	75 c. Triumph "Model H" 550cc (1915)	85	1·25

422 Tree of Life

1986. International Peace Year. Mult.

1393	25 c. Type **422**	30	30
1394	25 c. Peace dove	30	30

423 Knights Point

424 "Football" (Kylie Epapara)

1986. Coastal Scenery. Multicoloured.

1395	55 c. Type **423**	55	65
1396	60 c. Becks Bay	55	80
1397	65 c. Doubtless Bay	60	80
1398	80 c. Wainui Bay	75	1·10

1986. Health Stamps. Children's Paintings (1st series). Multicoloured.

1400	30 c. + 3 c. Type **424**	40	40
1401	30 c. + 3 c. "Children at Play" (Philip Kata)	40	40
1402	45 c. + 3 c. "Children Skipping" (Mia Flannery) (horiz)	50	50

See also Nos. 1433/5.

425 "A Partridge in a Pear Tree"

426 Conductor and Orchestra

1986. Christmas. "The Twelve Days of Christmas" (carol). Multicoloured.

1404	25 c. Type **425**	20	10
1405	55 c. "Two turtle doves"	45	45
1406	65 c. "Three French hens"	50	50

1986. Music in New Zealand.

1407	**426** 30 c. multicoloured	25	10
1408	– 60 c. black, blue & orange	45	70
1409	– 80 c. multicoloured	70	1·40
1410	– $1 multicoloured	80	1·10

DESIGNS: 60 c. Cornet and brass band; 80 c. Piper and Highland pipe band; $1 Guitar and country music group.

427 Jetboating

428 Southern Cross Cup

1987. Tourism. Multicoloured.

1411	60 c. Type **427**	50	50
1412	70 c. Sightseeing flights	60	60
1413	80 c. Camping	70	75
1414	85 c. Windsurfing	70	75
1415	$1.05 Mountaineering	90	1·00
1416	$1.30 River rafting	1·10	1·25

1987. Yachting Events. Designs showing yachts. Multicoloured.

1417	40 c. Type **428**	35	15
1418	80 c. Admiral's Cup	70	80
1419	$1.05 Kenwood Cup	85	1·25
1420	$1.30 America's Cup	1·10	1·40

429 Hand writing Letter and Postal Transport

1987. New Zealand Post Ltd Vesting Day. Multicoloured.

1421	40 c. Type **429**	1·00	1·40
1422	40 c. Posting letter, train and mailbox	1·00	1·40

430 Avro Type 626 and Wigram Airfield, 1937

1987. 50th Anniv of Royal New Zealand Air Force. Multicoloured.

1423	40 c. Type **430**	65	15
1424	70 c. Curtiss Kittyhawk I over World War II Pacific airstrip	90	1·50
1425	80 c. Short S.25 Sunderland flying boat and Pacific lagoon	1·00	1·50
1426	85 c. Douglas A-4F Skyhawk and Mt. Ruapehu	1·10	1·25

431 Urewera National Park and Fern Leaf

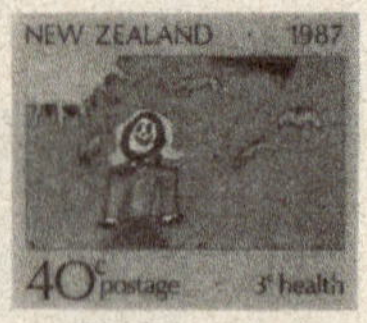

432 "Kite Flying" (Lauren Baldwin)

1987. Centenary of National Parks Movement. Multicoloured.

1428	70 c. Type **431**	70	55
1429	80 c. Mt. Cook and buttercup	75	60
1430	85 c. Fiordland and pineapple shrub	80	65
1431	$1.30 Tongariro and tussock	1·40	95

1987. Health Stamps. Children's Paintings (2nd series). Multicoloured.

1433	40 c. + 3 c. Type **432**	80	1·25
1434	40 c. + 3 c. "Swimming" (Ineke Schoneveld)	80	1·25
1435	60 c. + 3 c. "Horse Riding" (Aaron Tylee) (vert)	1·25	1·50

433 "Hark the Herald Angels Sing"

434 Knot ("Pona")

1987. Christmas. Multicoloured.

1437	35 c. Type **433**	45	10
1438	70 c. "Away in a Manger"	90	55
1439	85 c. "We Three Kings of Orient Are"	1·10	65

1987. Maori Fibre-work. Multicoloured.

1440	40 c. Type **434**	35	10
1441	60 c. Binding ("Herehere")	45	55
1442	80 c. Plait ("Whiri")	60	80
1443	85 c. Cloak weaving ("Korowai") with flax fibre ("Whitau")	65	85

435 "Geothermal"

1988. Centenary of Electricity. Each shows radiating concentric circles representing energy generation.

1444	**435** 40 c. multicoloured	30	35
1445	– 60 c. black, red and brown	40	45
1446	– 70 c. multicoloured	50	55
1447	– 80 c. multicoloured	55	60

DESIGNS: 60 c. "Thermal"; 70 c. "Gas"; 80 c. "Hydro".

436 Queen Elizabeth II and 1882 Queen Victoria 1d. Stamp

1988. Centenary of Royal Philatelic Society of New Zealand. Multicoloured.

1448	40 c. Type **436**	35	50
1449	40 c. As Type **436**, but 1882 Queen Victoria 2d.	35	50

437 "Mangopare"

438 "Good Luck"

1988. Maori Rafter Paintings. Multicoloured.

1451	40 c. Type **437**	40	40
1452	40 c. "Koru"	40	40
1453	40 c. "Raupunga"	40	40
1454	60 c. "Koiri"	55	65

1988. Greetings Stamps. Multicoloured.

1455	40 c. Type **438**	60	70
1456	40 c. "Keeping in touch"	60	70
1457	40 c. "Happy birthday"	60	70
1458	40 c. "Congratulations" (41 × 27 mm)	60	70
1459	40 c. "Get well soon" (41 × 27 mm)	60	70

439 Paradise Shelduck

440 Milford Track

1988. Native Birds. Multicoloured.

1459a	5 c. Sooty crake	10	10
1460	10 c. Double-banded plover	10	10
1461	20 c. Yellowhead	15	20
1462	30 c. Grey-backed white eye ("Silvereye")	30	30
1463	40 c. Brown kiwi	35	40
1589a	45 c. Rock wren	30	45
1464	50 c. Sacred kingfisher	50	50
1465	60 c. Spotted cormorant ("Spotted shag")	50	55
1466	70 c. Type **439**	55	70
1467	80 c. Fiordland crested penguin	80	70
1467a	80 c. New Zealand falcon	70	70
1468	90 c. New Zealand robin	85	80

The 40 and 45 c. also exist self-adhesive.

1988. Scenic Walking Trails. Multicoloured.

1469	70 c. Type **440**	50	60
1470	80 c. Heaphy Track	55	75
1471	85 c. Copland Track	60	80
1472	$1.30 Routeburn Track	90	1·25

441 Kiwi and Koala at Campfire

1988. Bicent of Australian Settlement.

1474	**441** 40 c. multicoloured	60	35

A stamp in a similar design was also issued by Australia.

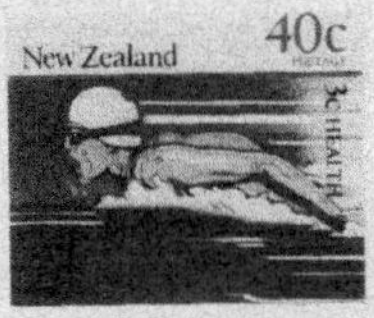

442 Swimming

443 "O Come All Ye Faithful"

1988. Health Stamps. Olympic Games, Seoul. Multicoloured.

1475	40 c. + 3 c. Type **442**	40	65
1476	60 c. + 3 c. Athletics	60	1·00
1477	70 c. + 3 c. Canoeing	70	1·00
1478	80 c. + 3 c. Show-jumping	90	1·25

1988. Christmas. Carols. Designs showing illuminated verses. Multicoloured.

1480	35 c. Type **443**	35	30
1481	70 c. "Hark the Herald Angels Sing"	65	65
1482	80 c. "Ding Dong Merrily on High"	70	70
1483	85 c. "The First Nowell"	80	80

444 "Lake Pukaki" (John Gully)

1988. New Zealand Heritage (1st issue). "The Land". Designs showing 19th-century paintings. Multicoloured.

1484	40 c. Type **444**	35	35
1485	60 c. "On the Grass Plain below Lake Arthur" (William Fox)	45	45
1486	70 c. "View of Auckland" (John Hoyte)	55	55
1487	80 c. "Mt. Egmont from the Southward" (Charles Heaphy)	60	60
1488	$1.05 "Anakiwa, Queen Charlotte Sound" (John Kinder)	80	80
1489	$1.30 "White Terraces, Lake Rotomahana", (Charles Barraud)	95	95

See also Nos. 1505/10, 1524/9, 1541/6, 1548/53 and 1562/7.

445 Brown Kiwi

1988.

1490	**445** $1 green	2·00	2·75
1490b	$1 red	1·25	1·40
1490c	$1 blue	90	1·25
2090	$1 violet	75	80

446 Humpback Whale and Calf

1988. Whales. Multicoloured.

1491	60 c. Type **446**	80	85
1492	70 c. Killer whales	1·00	1·10
1493	80 c. Southern right whale	1·10	1·25
1494	85 c. Blue whale	1·25	1·50
1495	$1.05 Southern bottlenose whale and calf	1·50	2·00
1496	$1.30 Sperm whale	1·60	2·00

Although inscribed "ROSS DEPENDENCY" Nos. 1491/6 were available from post offices throughout New Zealand.

447 Clover

448 Katherine Mansfield

1989. Wild Flowers. Multicoloured.

1497	40 c. Type **447**	40	35
1498	60 c. Lotus	50	60
1499	70 c. Montbretia	60	80
1500	80 c. Wild ginger	70	90

1989. New Zealand Authors. Multicoloured.

1501	40 c. Type **448**	30	35
1502	60 c. James K. Baxter	40	50
1503	70 c. Bruce Mason	50	60
1504	80 c. Ngaio Marsh	55	70

449 Moriori Man and Map of Chatham Islands

1989. New Zealand Heritage (2nd issue). The People.

1505	**449** 40 c. multicoloured	45	35
1506	– 60 c. brown, grey and deep brown	60	70
1507	– 70 c. green, grey and deep green	65	75
1508	– 80 c. blue, grey and deep blue	75	85
1509	– $1.05 grey, light grey and black	1·00	1·10
1510	– $1.30 red, grey & brown	1·25	1·40

DESIGNS: 60 c. Gold prospector; 70 c. Settler ploughing; 80 c. Whaling; $1.05, Missionary preaching to Maoris; $1.30, Maori village.

450 White Pine (Kahikatea)

451 Duke and Duchess of York with Princess Beatrice

1989. Native Trees. Multicoloured.

1511	80 c. Type **450**	75	80
1512	85 c. Red pine (Rimu)	80	85
1513	$1.05 Totara	1·00	1·10
1514	$1.30 Kauri	1·25	1·40

1989. Health Stamps. Multicoloured.

1516	40 c. + 3 c. Type **451**	80	1·00
1517	40 c. + 3 c. Duchess of York with Princess Beatrice	80	1·00
1518	80 c. + 3 c. Princess Beatrice	1·40	1·75

452 One Tree Hill, Auckland through Bedroom Window

453 Windsurfing

1989. Christmas. Designs showing Star of Bethlehem. Multicoloured.

1520	35 c. Type **452**	40	30
1521	65 c. Shepherd and dog in mountain valley	75	70
1522	80 c. Star over harbour	95	90
1523	$1 Star over globe	1·25	1·40

1989. New Zealand Heritage (3rd issue). The Sea. Multicoloured.

1524	40 c. Type **453**	40	35
1525	60 c. Fishes of many species	70	70
1526	65 c. Striped marlin and game fishing launch	75	75
1527	80 c. Rowing boat and yachts in harbour	85	85
1528	$1 Coastal scene	1·10	1·10
1529	$1.50 "Rotoiti" (container ship) and tug	1·50	1·60

454 Games Logo

1989. 14th Commonwealth Games, Auckland. Multicoloured.

1530	40 c. Type **454**	40	35
1531	40 c. Goldie (games kiwi mascot)	40	35
1532	40 c. Gymnastics	40	35
1533	50 c. Weightlifting	50	55
1534	65 c. Swimming	65	70
1535	80 c. Cycling	80	90
1536	$1 Lawn bowling	1·00	1·25
1537	$1.80 Hurdling	1·75	1·90

455 Short S.30 modified "G" Class Flying Boat "Aotearoa" and Boeing 747-200

1990. 50th Anniv of Air New Zealand.

1539	**455** 80 c. multicoloured	1·40	80

457 Maori Voyaging Canoe

1990. New Zealand Heritage (4th issue). The Ships. Multicoloured.

1541	40 c. Type **457**	60	35
1542	50 c. H.M.S. "Endeavour" (Cook), 1769	85	75
1543	60 c. "Tory" (barque), 1839	95	85
1544	80 c. "Crusader" (full-rigged immigrant ship), 1871	1·40	1·25
1545	$1 "Edwin Fox" (full-rigged immigrant ship), 1873	1·60	1·40
1546	$1.50 "Arawa" (steamer), 1884	2·00	2·25

459 Grace Neill (social reformer) and Maternity Hospital, Wellington

1990. New Zealand Heritage (5th issue). Famous New Zealanders. Multicoloured.

1548	40 c. Type **459**	55	30
1549	50 c. Jean Batten (pilot) and Percival P.3 Gull Six aircraft	65	75
1550	60 c. Katherine Sheppard (suffragette) and 19th-century women	85	1·25
1551	80 c. Richard Pearse (inventor) and early flying machine	1·10	1·25
1552	$1 Lt.-Gen. Sir Bernard Freyberg and tank	1·25	1·25
1553	$1.50 Peter Buck (politician) and Maori pattern	1·50	2·00

460 Akaroa

461 Jack Lovelock (athlete) and Race

1990. 150th Anniv of European Settlements. Multicoloured.

1554	80 c. Type **460**	75	75
1555	$1 Wanganui	95	95
1556	$1.50 Wellington	1·40	2·25
1557	$1.80 Takapuna Beach, Auckland	1·60	2·25

1990. Health Stamps. Sportsmen (1st series). Multicoloured.

1559	40 c. + 5 c. Type **461**	50	65
1560	80 c. + 5 c. George Nepia (rugby player) and match	75	1·10

See also Nos. 1687/8.

462 Creation Legend of Rangi and Papa

464 Angel

1990. New Zealand Heritage (6th issue). The Maori. Multicoloured.

1562	40 c. Type **462**	40	30
1563	50 c. Pattern from Maori feather cloak	55	70
1564	60 c. Maori women's choir	60	80
1565	80 c. Maori facial tattoos	75	90
1566	$1 War canoe prow (detail)	90	1·10
1567	$1.50 Maori haka	1·40	2·50

1990. Christmas.

1569	**464** 40 c. purple, blue & brn	40	30
1570	– $1 purple, green & brown	80	80
1571	– $1.50 purple, red & brown	1·40	1·75
1572	– $1.80 purple, red & brown	1·60	1·75

DESIGNS: $1 to $1.80, Different angels.

465 Antarctic Petrel

466 Coopworth Ewe and Lambs

1990. Antarctic Birds. Multicoloured.

1573	40 c. Type **465**	70	30
1574	50 c. Wilson's petrel	80	50
1575	60 c. Snow petrel	95	75
1576	80 c. Southern fulmar	1·00	75
1577	$1 Chinstrap penguin	1·25	85
1578	$1.50 Emperor penguin	1·60	2·00

Although inscribed "Ross Dependency" Nos. 1573/8 were available from post offices throughout New Zealand.

1991. New Zealand Farming and Agriculture. Sheep Breeds. Multicoloured.

1579	40 c. Type **466**	40	40
1580	60 c. Perendale	55	75
1581	80 c. Corriedale	70	85
1582	$1 Drysdale	85	90
1583	$1.50 South Suffolk	1·25	2·00
1584	$1.80 Romney	1·50	2·00

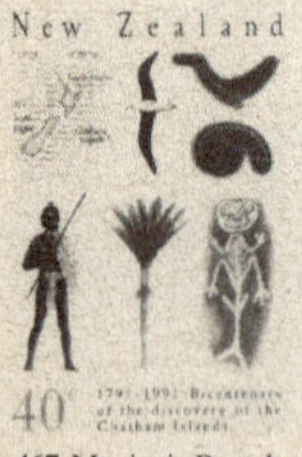

467 Moriori, Royal Albatross, Nikau Palm and Artefacts

469 Tuatara on Rocks

468 Goal and Footballers

1991. Bicentenary of Discovery of Chatham Islands. Multicoloured.

1585	40 c. Type **467**	50	50
1586	80 c. Carvings, H.M.S. "Chatham", Moriori house of 1870, and Tommy Solomon	1·25	1·60

1991. Centenary of New Zealand Football Association. Multicoloured.

1587	80 c. Type **468**	1·00	1·40
1588	80 c. Five footballers and referee	1·00	1·40

Nos. 1587/8 were printed together, se-tenant, forming a composite design.

1991. Endangered Species. The Tuatara. Multicoloured.

1590	40 c. Type **469**	40	55
1591	40 c. Tuatara in crevice	40	55
1592	40 c. Tuatara with foliage	40	55
1593	40 c. Tuatara in dead leaves	40	55

470 Clown

471 Cat at Window

1991. "Happy Birthday". Multicoloured.

1594	40 c. Type **470**	45	60
1595	40 c. Balloons	45	60
1596	40 c. Party hat	45	60
1597	40 c. Birthday present (41 × 27 mm)	45	60
1598	40 c. Birthday cake (41 × 27 mm)	45	60
1599	45 c. Type **470**	45	60
1600	45 c. As No. 1595	45	60
1601	45 c. As No. 1596	45	60
1602	45 c. As No. 1597	45	60
1603	45 c. As No. 1598	45	60

1991. "Thinking of You". Multicoloured.

1604	40 c. Type **471**	45	60
1605	40 c. Cat playing with slippers	45	60
1606	40 c. Cat with alarm clock	45	60
1607	40 c. Cat in window (41 × 27 mm)	45	60
1608	40 c. Cat at door (41 × 27 mm)	45	60
1609	45 c. Type **471**	45	60
1610	45 c. As No. 1605	45	60
1611	45 c. As No. 1606	45	60
1612	45 c. As No. 1607	45	60
1613	45 c. As No. 1608	45	60

472 Punakaiki Rocks

473 Dolphins Underwater

1991. Scenic Landmarks. Multicoloured.

1614	40 c. Type **472**	40	30
1615	50 c. Moeraki Boulders	55	55
1616	80 c. Organ Pipes	85	85
1617	$1 Castle Hill	95	95
1618	$1.50 Te Kaukau Point	1·50	1·60
1619	$1.80 Ahuriri River Clay Cliffs	1·75	1·90

1991. Health Stamps. Hector's Dolphin. Multicoloured.

1620	45 c. + 5 c. Type **473**	90	1·00
1621	80 c. + 5 c. Dolphins leaping	1·25	1·60

474 Children's Rugby

475 "Three Shepherds"

1991. World Cup Rugby Championship. Multicoloured.

1623	80 c. Type **474**	1·00	1·25
1624	$1 Women's rugby	1·10	95
1625	$1.50 Senior rugby	1·75	2·50
1626	$1.80 "All Blacks" (national team)	2·00	2·50

1991. Christmas. Multicoloured.

1628	45 c. Type **475**	55	75
1629	45 c. Two Kings on camels	55	75
1630	45 c. Mary and Baby Jesus	55	75
1631	45 c. King with gift	55	75
1632	65 c. Star of Bethlehem	70	80
1633	$1 Crown	85	95
1634	$1.50 Angel	1·40	2·00

476 "Dodonidia helmsii"

1991. Butterflies. Multicoloured.

1640	$1 Type **476**	65	70
1641	$2 "Zizina otis oxleyi"	1·25	1·40
1642	$3 "Vanessa itea"	1·90	2·00
1643	$4 "Lycaena salustius"	2·50	2·75
1644	$5 "Bassaris gonerilla"	3·25	3·50

479 Yacht "Kiwi Magic", 1987

1992. New Zealand Challenge for America's Cup. Multicoloured.

1655	45 c. Type **479**	45	35
1656	80 c. Yacht "New Zealand", 1988	80	70
1657	$1 Yacht "America", 1851	95	85
1658	$1.50 "America's Cup" Class yacht, 1992	1·60	1·40

480 "Heemskerk"

1992. Great Voyages of Discovery. Mult.

1659	45 c. Type **480**	55	35
1660	80 c. "Zeehan"	90	85
1661	$1 "Santa Maria"	1·25	85
1662	$1.50 "Pinta" and "Nina"	1·50	1·60

Nos. 1659/60 commemorate the 350th anniv of Tasman's discovery of New Zealand and Nos. 1661/2 the 500th anniv of discovery of America by Columbus.

481 Sprinters

1992. Olympic Games, Barcelona (1st issue).

1663	**481** 45 c. multicoloured	50	40

See also Nos. 1670/3.

482 Weddell Seal and Pup

1992. Antarctic Seals. Multicoloured.

1664	45 c. Type **482**	70	40
1665	50 c. Crabeater seals swimming	80	40
1666	65 c. Leopard seal and Adelie penguins	1·00	85
1667	80 c. Ross seal	1·25	90
1668	$1 Southern elephant seal and harem	1·40	95
1669	$1.80 Hooker's sea lion and pup	2·25	2·25

Although inscribed "ROSS DEPENDENCY" Nos. 1664/9 were available from post offices throughout New Zealand.

483 Cycling

1992. Olympic Games, Barcelona (2nd issue). Multicoloured.

1670	45 c. Type **483**	65	35
1671	80 c. Archery	90	70
1672	$1 Equestrian three-day eventing	1·00	85
1673	$1.50 Sailboarding	1·50	1·40

484 Ice Pinnacles, Franz Josef Glacier

1992. Glaciers. Multicoloured.

1675	45 c. Type **484**	40	35
1676	50 c. Tasman Glacier	50	45
1677	80 c. Snowball glacier, Marion Plateau	70	70
1678	$1 Brewster Glacier	85	85
1679	$1.50 Fox Glacier	1·40	1·40
1680	$1.80 Franz Josef Glacier	1·50	1·60

485 "Grand Finale" Camellia

486 Tree and Hills

1992. Camellias. Multicoloured.

1681	45 c. Type **485**	40	35
1682	50 c. "Showa-No-Sakae"	50	45
1683	80 c. "Sugar Dream"	70	70
1684	$1 "Night Rider"	85	85
1685	$1.50 "E.G. Waterhouse"	1·40	1·40
1686	$1.80 "Dr. Clifford Parks"	1·50	1·50

1992. Health Stamps. Sportsmen (2nd series). As T **461**. Multicoloured.

1687	45 c. + 5 c. Anthony Wilding (tennis player) and match	80	85
1688	80 c. + 5 c. Stewie Dempster (cricketer) and batsman	95	1·10

1992. Landscapes. Multicoloured.

1690	45 c. Type **486**	40	50
1691	45 c. River and hills	40	50
1692	45 c. Hills and mountain	40	50
1693	45 c. Glacier	40	50
1694	45 c. Hills and waterfall	40	50
1695	45 c. Tree and beach	40	50
1696	45 c. Estuary and cliffs	40	50
1697	45 c. Fjord	40	50
1698	45 c. River delta	40	50
1699	45 c. Ferns and beach	40	50

487 Reindeer over Houses

488 1920s Fashions

1992. Christmas. Multicoloured.

1700	45 c. Type **487**	70	75
1701	45 c. Santa Claus on sleigh over houses	70	75
1702	45 c. Christmas tree in window	70	75
1703	45 c. Christmas wreath and children at window	70	75
1704	65 c. Candles and fireplace	80	80
1705	$1 Family going to church	1·00	1·00
1706	$1.50 Picnic under Pohutukawa tree	1·75	1·90

1992. New Zealand in the 1920s. Mult.

1707	45 c. Type **488**	50	35
1708	50 c. Dr. Robert Jack and early radio announcer	55	55
1709	80 c. "All Blacks" rugby player, 1924	85	85
1710	$1 Swaggie and dog	95	95
1711	$1.50 Ford "Model A" car and young couple	1·75	1·75
1712	$1.80 Amateur aviators and biplane	2·00	2·50

489 "Old Charley" Toby Jug

490 Women's Fashions of the 1930s

1993. Royal Doulton Ceramics Exhibition, New Zealand. Multicoloured.

1713	45 c. Type **489**	45	35
1714	50 c. "Bunnykins" nursery plate	50	50
1715	80 c. "Maori Art" tea set	75	75
1716	$1 "Ophelia" handpainted plate	90	90
1717	$1.50 "St. George" figurine	1·50	2·00
1718	$1.80 "Lambeth" salt-glazed stoneware vase	1·75	2·25

1993. New Zealand in the 1930s. Mult.

1720	45 c. Type **490**	50	45
1721	50 c. Unemployed protest march	55	75
1722	80 c. "Phar Lap" (racehorse)	85	95
1723	$1 State housing project	1·00	1·00
1724	$1.50 Boys drinking free school milk	1·75	2·25
1725	$1.80 Cinema queue	1·90	2·00

491 Women signing Petition

492 Champagne Pool

1993. Centenary of Women's Suffrage. Mult.
1726 45 c. Type **491** . . . 50 35
1727 80 c. Aircraft propeller and woman on tractor . . . 1·00 85
1728 $1 Housewife with children . 1·00 95
1729 $1.50 Modern women . . . 1·60 1·60

1993. Thermal Wonders, Rotorua. Mult.
1730 45 c. Type **492** . . . 60 40
1731 50 c. Boiling mud . . . 60 40
1732 80 c. Emerald pool . . . 85 70
1733 $1 Hakereteke Falls . . . 95 80
1734 $1.50 Warbrick Terrace . . . 1·50 1·50
1735 $1.80 Pohutu Geyser . . . 1·60 1·75

493 Yellow-eyed Penguin, Hector's Dolphin and New Zealand Fur Seal

1993. Endangered Species Conservation. Mult.
1736 45 c. Type **493** . . . 55 60
1737 45 c. Chatham Island taiko (bird), Mount Cook lily and mountain duck . . . 55 60
1738 45 c. Giant snail, rock wren and Hamilton's frog . . . 55 60
1739 45 c. Kaka (bird), New Zealand pigeon and giant weta . . 55 60
1740 45 c. Tusked weta (23 × 28 mm) 55 60

494 Boy with Puppy

495 Christmas Decorations (value at left)

1993. Health Stamps. Children's Pets. Mult.
1741 45 c. + 5 c. Type **494** . . . 60 70
1742 80 c. + 5 c. Girl with kitten . 90 1·25

1993. Christmas. Multicoloured.
1746 45 c. Type **495** . . . 60 70
1747 45 c. Christmas decorations (value at right) . . . 60 70
1748 45 c. Sailboards, gifts and Christmas pudding (value at left) . . . 60 70
1749 45 c. Sailboards, gifts and Christmas pudding (value at right) . . . 60 70
1750 $1 Sailboards, baubles and Christmas cracker . . . 1·50 1·25
1751 $1.50 Sailboards, present and wreath . . . 2·00 2·50

496 Rainbow Abalone or Paua

497 Sauropod

1993. Marine Life. Multicoloured.
1752 45 c. Type **496** . . . 60 70
1753 45 c. Green mussels . . . 60 70
1754 45 c. Tarakihi . . . 60 70
1755 45 c. Salmon . . . 60 70
1756 45 c. Southern blue-finned tuna, yellow-finned tuna and kahawai . . . 60 70
1757 45 c. Rock lobster . . . 60 70
1758 45 c. Snapper . . . 60 70
1759 45 c. Grouper . . . 60 70
1760 45 c. Orange roughy . . . 60 70
1761 45 c. Squid, hoki and black oreo 60 70

1993. Prehistoric Animals. Multicoloured.
1762 45 c. Type **497** . . . 45 45
1763 45 c. Carnosaur and sauropod (30 × 25 mm) . . . 45 45
1764 80 c. Pterosaur . . . 85 85
1765 $1 Ankylosaur . . . 95 95
1766 $1.20 Mauisaurus . . . 1·40 1·40
1767 $1.50 Carnosaur . . . 1·50 1·50

498 Soldiers, National Flag and Pyramids

499 Bungy Jumping

1993. New Zealand in the 1940s. Multicoloured.
1771 45 c. Type **498** . . . 45 40
1772 50 c. Aerial crop spraying . 50 50
1773 80 c. Hydro-electric scheme . 80 80
1774 $1 Marching majorettes . . 90 90
1775 $1.50 American troops . . . 1·50 1·50
1776 $1.80 Crowd celebrating victory 1·60 1·60

1994. Tourism. Multicoloured.
1777 45 c. Type **499** . . . 50 40
1778 45 c. White water rafting (25 × 25 mm) . . . 50 55
1779 80 c. Trout fishing . . . 70 70
1780 $1 Jet boating (horiz) . . . 80 80
1781 $1.50 Tramping . . . 1·40 1·40
1782 $1.80 Heli-skiing . . . 1·90 2·00

500 "New Zealand Endeavour" (yacht)

503 Rock and Roll Dancers

501 Mt. Cook and New Zealand Symbols

1994. Round the World Yacht Race.
1783 **500** $1 multicoloured . . . 1·40 1·40

1994.
1784 **501** $20 blue and gold . . . 12·50 13·50

1994. New Zealand in the 1950s. Mult.
1787 45 c. Type **503** . . . 45 40
1788 80 c. Sir Edmund Hillary on Mt. Everest . . . 75 75
1789 $1 Aunt Daisy (radio personality) . . . 85 85
1790 $1.20 Queen Elizabeth II during 1953 royal visit . . . 1·25 1·25
1791 $1.50 Children playing with Opo the dolphin . . . 1·60 1·60
1792 $1.80 Auckland Harbour Bridge 1·90 2·00

504 Mt. Cook and Mt. Cook Lily ("Winter")

1994. The Four Seasons. Mult.
1793 45 c. Type **504** . . . 45 40
1794 70 c. Lake Hawea and Kowhai ("Spring") . . . 65 65
1795 $1.50 Opononi Beach and Pohutukawa ("Summer") . 1·40 1·40
1796 $1.80 Lake Pukaki and Puriri ("Autumn") . . . 1·75 1·75

505 Rainbow Abalone or Paua Shell

506 Maui pulls up Te Ika

1994. New Zealand Life. Multicoloured.
1797 45 c. Type **505** (25 × 20 mm) . 35 40
1798 45 c. Pavlova dessert (35 × 20 mm) . . . 35 40
1799 45 c. Hokey pokey ice cream (25 × 20 mm) . . . 35 40
1800 45 c. Fish and chips (35 × 20 mm) . . . 35 40
1801 45 c. Jandals (30 × 20 mm) . . 35 40
1802 45 c. Bush shirt (25 × 30½ mm) 35 40
1803 45 c. Buzzy Bee (toy) (35 × 30½ mm) . . . 35 40
1804 45 c. Gumboots and black singlet (25 × 30½ mm) . . 35 40
1805 45 c. Rugby boots and ball (35 × 30½ mm) . . . 35 40
1806 45 c. Kiwifruit (30 × 30½ mm) 35 40

1994. Maori Myths. Multicoloured.
1807 45 c. Type **506** . . . 50 40
1808 80 c. Rona snatched up by Marama . . . 85 85
1809 $1 Maui attacking Tuna . . . 1·00 1·00
1810 $1.20 Tane separating Rangi and Papa . . . 1·40 1·75
1811 $1.50 Matakauri slaying the Giant of Wakatipu . . . 1·50 2·00
1812 $1.80 Panenehu showing crayfish to Tangaroa . . . 1·75 2·00

507 1939 2d. on 1d. + 1d. Health Stamp and Children playing with Ball

508 Astronaut on Moon (hologram)

1994. Health Stamps. 75th Anniv of Children's Health Camps. Multicoloured.
1813 45 c. + 5 c. Type **507** . . . 50 70
1814 45 c. + 5 c. 1949 1d. + ½d. stamp and nurse holding child 50 70
1815 45 c. + 5 c. 1969 4 c. + 1 c. stamp and children reading 50 70
1816 80 c. + 5 c. 1931 2d. + 1d. stamp and child in cap . . 75 90

1994. 25th Anniv of First Manned Moon Landing.
1818 **508** $1.50 multicoloured . . . 1·25 1·50

509 "people reaching people"

1994. Self-adhesive.
1818ab **509** 40 c. multicoloured . . 45 40
1819 45 c. multicoloured . . 50 45

510 African Elephants

1994. Stamp Month. Wild Animals. Multicoloured.
1820 45 c. Type **510** . . . 45 45
1821 45 c. White rhinoceros . . . 45 45
1822 45 c. Lions . . . 45 45
1823 45 c. Common zebras . . . 45 45
1824 45 c. Giraffe and calf . . . 45 45
1825 45 c. Siberian tiger . . . 45 45
1826 45 c. Hippopotami . . . 45 45
1827 45 c. Spider monkey . . . 45 45
1828 45 c. Giant panda . . . 45 45
1829 45 c. Polar bear and cub . . . 45 45

511 Children with Crib

512 Batsman

1994. Christmas. Multicoloured.
1832 45 c. Father Christmas and children (30 × 25 mm) . . . 45 40
1833 45 c. Type **511** . . . 45 40
1834 70 c. Man and toddler with crib 65 80
1835 80 c. Three carol singers . . . 70 85
1836 $1 Five carol singers . . . 90 90
1837 $1.50 Children and candles . 1·25 1·75
1838 $1.80 Parents with child . . . 1·60 2·00

1994. Centenary of New Zealand Cricket Council. (a) Horiz designs, each 30 × 25 mm. Multicoloured.
1840 45 c. Bathers catching balls . 40 60
1841 45 c. Child on surf board at top 40 60
1842 45 c. Young child with rubber ring at top . . . 40 60
1843 45 c. Man with beach ball at top 40 60
1844 45 c. Woman with cricket bat at right . . . 40 60
1845 45 c. Boy in green cap with bat 40 60
1846 45 c. Man in spotted shirt running . . . 40 60
1847 45 c. Woman in striped shorts with bat . . . 40 60
1848 45 c. Boy in wet suit with surf board at right . . . 40 60
1849 45 c. Sunbather with newspaper at right . . . 40 60

(b) T **512** and similar vert designs. Multicoloured.
1850 45 c. Type **512** . . . 45 40
1851 80 c. Bowler . . . 80 80
1852 $1 Wicket keeper . . . 1·00 1·00
1853 $1.80 Fielder . . . 1·75 1·75

513 Auckland

1995. New Zealand by Night. Multicoloured.
1855 45 c. Type **513** . . . 35 40
1856 80 c. Wellington . . . 60 65
1857 $1 Christchurch . . . 80 85
1858 $1.20 Dunedin . . . 95 1·00
1859 $1.50 Rotorua . . . 1·10 1·25
1860 $1.80 Queenstown . . . 1·40 1·50

514 The 15th Hole, Waitangi

515 New Zealand Pigeon and Nest

1995. New Zealand Golf Courses. Multicoloured.
1861 45 c. Type **514** . . . 65 40
1862 80 c. The 6th hole, New Plymouth . . . 1·00 90
1863 $1.20 The 9th hole, Rotorua . 1·50 1·50
1864 $1.80 The 5th hole, Queenstown 2·40 2·50

1995. Environment. Multicoloured.
1865 45 c. Type **515** . . . 60 60
1866 45 c. Planting sapling . . . 60 60
1867 45 c. Dolphins and whales . . 60 60
1868 45 c. Thunder storm . . . 60 60
1869 45 c. Backpackers . . . 60 60
1870 45 c. Animal pests . . . 60 60
1871 45 c. Noxious plants . . . 60 60
1872 45 c. Undersized fish and shellfish . . . 60 60
1873 45 c. Pollution from factories 60 60
1874 45 c. Family at picnic site . . 60 60

516 Teacher with Guitar and Children

517 Map of Australasia and Asia

1995. Maori Language Year. Multicoloured.
1875 45 c. Type **516** . . . 50 45
1876 70 c. Singing group . . . 75 75
1877 80 c. Mother and baby . . . 85 85
1878 $1 Women performing traditional welcome . . . 1·10 1·10
1879 $1.50 Grandfather reciting family genealogy . . . 1·75 1·75
1880 $1.80 Tribal orator . . . 2·00 2·00

1995. Meetings of Asian Development Bank Board of Governors and International Pacific Basin Economic Council, Auckland. Multicoloured.
1881 $1 Type **517** . . . 1·25 1·00
1882 $1.50 Map of Australasia and Pacific . . . 1·75 2·25

MORE DETAILED LISTS
are given in the Stanley Gibbons Catalogues referred to in the country headings.
For lists of current volumes see Introduction.

518 "Black Magic" (yacht)

1995. New Zealand's Victory in 1995 America's Cup.

1883	**518**	45 c. multicoloured	55	55

519 Boy on Skateboard

1995. Health Stamps. Children's Sports. Mult.

1884	45 c. + 5 c. Type **519**	65	70
1885	80 c. + 5 c. Girl on bicyle	1·25	1·40

520 Lion Red Cup and Players

1995. Centenary of Rugby League. Multicoloured.

1888	45 c. Trans Tasman test match (30 × 25 mm)	50	45
1889	45 c. Type **520**	50	45
1890	$1 Children's rugby and mascot	1·25	1·10
1891	$1.50 George Smith, Albert Baskerville and early match	2·00	2·00
1892	$1.80 Courtney Goodwill Trophy and match against Great Britain	2·25	2·25

521 Sheep and Lamb

522 Archangel Gabriel

1995. Farmyard Animals. Multicoloured.

1894	40 c. Type **521**	50	55
1895	40 c. Deer	50	55
1896	40 c. Mare and foal	50	55
1897	40 c. Cow with calf	50	55
1898	40 c. Goats and kid	50	55
1899	40 c. Common turkey	50	55
1900	40 c. Ducks	50	55
1901	40 c. Red junglefowl	50	55
1902	40 c. Sow with piglets	50	55
1903	40 c. Border collie	50	55
1904	45 c. As Type **521**	60	65
1905	45 c. As No. 1895	60	65
1906	45 c. As No. 1896	60	65
1907	45 c. As No. 1897	60	65
1908	45 c. As No. 1898	60	65
1909	45 c. As No. 1899	60	65
1910	45 c. As No. 1900	60	65
1911	45 c. As No. 1901	60	65
1912	45 c. As No. 1902	60	65
1913	45 c. As No. 1903	60	65

1995. Christmas. Stained Glass Windows from St. Mary's Anglican Church, Merivale (Nos. 1916/18), The Lady Chapel of St. Luke's Anglican Church, Christchurch (Nos. 1919/22) or St. John the Evangelist Church, Cheviot (No. 1923). Multicoloured. (a) As T **522**.

1916	40 c. Type **522**	50	40
1917	45 c. Type **522**	60	45
1918	70 c. Virgin Mary	90	90
1919	80 c. Shepherds	1·00	1·00
1920	$1 Virgin and Child	1·25	1·10
1921	$1.50 Two Wise Men	2·00	2·50
1922	$1.80 Wise Man kneeling	2·25	2·50

(b) Smaller design, 25 × 30 mm.

1923	40 c. Angel with trumpet	50	50

523 Face and Nuclear Disarmament Symbol

524 Mt. Cook

1995. Nuclear Disarmament.

1924	**523**	$1 multicoloured	1·00	1·00

1995. New Zealand Scenery. Multicoloured.

1925	5 c. Type **524**	10	10
1926	10 c. Champagne Pool	10	10
1927	20 c. Cape Reinga	15	20
1928	30 c. Mackenzie Country	20	25
1929	40 c. Mitre Peak (vert)	25	30
1930	50 c. Mt. Ngauruhoe	30	35
1931	60 c. Lake Wanaka (vert)	40	45
1932	70 c. Giant kauri tree (vert)	45	50
1933	80 c. Doubtful Sound (vert)	50	55
1934	90 c. Waitomo Limestone Cave (vert)	55	60
1935	$10 Mt. Ruapela (40 × 34 mm)	6·25	6·50

For similar self-adhesive designs see Nos. 1984/91.

525 Dame Kiri te Kanawa (opera singer)

526 National Flags, Peace Dove and "50"

1995. Famous New Zealanders. Multicoloured.

1936	40 c. Type **525**	65	40
1937	80 c. Charles Upham, V.C. (war hero)	90	85
1938	$1 Barry Crump (author)	1·25	1·00
1939	$1.20 Sir Brian Barratt-Boyes (surgeon)	1·50	1·25
1940	$1.50 Dame Whina Cooper (Maori leader)	1·75	1·75
1941	$1.80 Sir Richard Hadlee (cricketer)	2·50	2·25

1995. 50th Anniv of United Nations.

1942	**526**	$1.80 multicoloured	2·25	1·90

527 Fern and Globe

1995. Commonwealth Heads of Government Meeting, Auckland. Multicoloured.

1943	40 c. Type **527**	60	40
1944	$1.80 Fern and New Zealand flag	2·50	2·00

528 "Kiwi"

1996. Famous Racehorses. Multicoloured.

1945	40 c. Type **528**	55	40
1946	80 c. "Rough Habit"	95	95
1947	$1 "Blossom Lady"	1·25	1·25
1948	$1.20 "Il Vicolo"	1·60	1·60
1949	$1.50 "Horlicks"	1·75	1·75
1950	$1.80 "Bonecrusher"	2·50	2·50

529 Kete (basket)

530 Black-backed Gulls

1996. Maori Crafts. Multicoloured.

1952	40 c. Type **529**	50	40
1953	80 c. Head of Taiaha (spear)	90	90
1954	$1 Taniko (embroidery)	1·25	1·25
1955	$1.20 Pounamu (greenstone)	1·50	1·50
1956	$1.50 Hue (gourd)	1·75	1·75
1957	$1.80 Korowai (feather cloak)	2·00	2·25

1996. Marine Life. Multicoloured. Self-adhesive or ordinary gum.

1958	40 c. Type **530**	45	50
1959	40 c. Children, sea cucumber and spiny starfish	45	50
1960	40 c. Yacht, gull and common shrimps	45	50
1961	40 c. Gaudy nudibranch	45	50
1962	40 c. Large rock crab and clingfish	45	50
1963	40 c. Snake skin chiton and red rock crab	45	50
1964	40 c. Estuarine triplefin and cat's-eye shell	45	50
1965	40 c. Cushion star and sea horses	45	50
1966	40 c. Blue-eyed triplefin and Yaldwyn's triplefin	45	50
1967	40 c. Common octopus	45	50

531 Fire and Ambulance Services

532 Mt. Egmont, Taranaki

1996. Rescue Services. Multicoloured.

1979	40 c. Type **531**	50	40
1980	80 c. Civil Defence	90	90
1981	$1 Air-sea rescue	1·10	1·10
1982	$1.50 Air ambulance and rescue helicopter	1·60	1·60
1983	$1.80 Mountain rescue and Red Cross	2·25	2·40

1996. New Zealand Scenery. Self-adhesive. Multicoloured.

1984b	40 c. Type **532**	25	30
1985	40 c. Piercy Island, Bay of Islands	25	30
1986	40 c. Tory Channel, Malborough Sounds	25	30
1987	40 c. "Earnslaw" (ferry), Lake Wakatipu	25	30
1988	40 c. Lake Matheson	25	30
1989	40 c. Fox Glacier	25	30
1990	80 c. Doubtful Sound (as No. 1933)	50	55
1991	$1 Pohutukawa tree (33 × 22 mm)	65	70

533 Yellow-eyed Penguin

534 Baby in Car Seat

1996. Marine Wildlife. Multicoloured.

1992	40 c. Type **533**	50	50
1993	80 c. Royal albatross (horiz)	90	90
1994	$1 White herons (horiz)	1·10	1·10
1995	$1.20 Flukes of sperm whale (horiz)	1·40	1·40
1996	$1.50 Fur seals	1·60	1·60
1997	$1.80 Bottlenose dolphin	2·00	2·00

1996. Health Stamps. Child Safety. Multicoloured. Self-adhesive (1991) or ordinary (others) gum.

2000	40 c. + 5 c. Type **534**	50	50
2003	40 c. + 5 c. Type **534** (21½ × 38 mm)	50	50
2001	80 c. + 5 c. Child and adult on zebra crossing	90	90

535 Violin

1996. 50th Anniv of New Zealand Symphony Orchestra. Multicoloured.

2006	40 c. Type **535**	40	40
2007	80 c. French horn	1·00	1·25

536 Swimming

537 "Hinemoa"

1996. Centennial Olympic Games, Atlanta. Multicoloured.

2008	40 c. Type **536**	50	40
2009	80 c. Cycling	1·25	90
2010	$1 Running	1·25	1·00
2011	$1.50 Rowing	1·75	2·00
2012	$1.80 Yachting	2·00	2·25

1996. Centenary of New Zealand Cinema. Multicoloured.

2014	40 c. Type **537**	50	40
2015	80 c. "Broken Barrier"	1·00	80
2016	$1.50 "Goodbye Pork Pie"	1·75	2·00
2017	$1.80 "Once Were Warriors"	1·75	2·00

538 Danyon Loader (swimmer) and Blyth Tait (horseman)

539 Beehive Ballot Box

1996. New Zealand Olympic Gold Medal Winners, Atlanta.

2018	**538**	40 c. multicoloured	45	45

1996. New Zealand's First Mixed Member Proportional Representation Election.

2019	**539**	40 c. black, red and yellow	45	45

540 King following Star

1996. Christmas. Multicoloured. (a) Size 35 × 35 mm.

2020	40 c. Type **540**	50	40
2021	70 c. Shepherd and Baby Jesus	80	80
2022	80 c. Angel and shepherd	90	90
2023	$1 Mary, Joseph and Baby Jesus	1·25	1·00
2024	$1.50 Mary and Joseph with donkey	2·00	2·25
2025	$1.80 The Annunciation	2·00	2·25

(b) Size 30 × 24 mm. Self-adhesive.

2026	40 c. Angels with trumpets	45	50
2027	40 c. King with gift	45	50

541 Adzebill

1996. Extinct Birds. Multicoloured. (a) Size 40 × 28 mm.

2028	40 c. Type **541**	60	40
2029	80 c. South Island whekau ("Laughing Owl")	1·25	1·25
2030	$1 Piopio	1·25	1·10
2031	$1.20 Huia	1·50	1·60
2032	$1.50 Giant eagle	1·75	2·00
2033	$1.80 Giant moa	2·00	2·00

(b) Size 30 × 24 mm. Self-adhesive.

2035	40 c. Stout-legged wren	45	50

542 Seymour Square, Blenheim

543 Holstein Friesian Cattle

1996. Scenic Gardens. Multicoloured.

2038	40 c. Type **542**	50	40
2039	80 c. Pukekura Park, New Plymouth	1·00	1·00
2040	$1 Wintergarden, Auckland	1·25	1·10
2041	$1.50 Botanic Garden, Christchurch	1·75	2·00
2042	$1.80 Marine Parade Gardens, Napier	1·90	2·00

1997. Cattle Breeds. Multicoloured.

2043	40 c. Type **543**	50	40
2044	80 c. Jersey	1·00	1·00
2045	$1 Simmental	1·25	1·00
2046	$1.20 Ayrshire	1·50	1·60
2047	$1.50 Angus	1·60	2·00
2048	$1.80 Hereford	1·90	2·00

544 James Cook and Sextant

1997. Millennium Series (1st issue). Discoverers of New Zealand. Multicoloured.

2051	40 c. Type **544**	70	45
2052	80 c. Kupe and ocean-going canoe	1·00	90
2053	$1 Carved panel depicting Maui (vert)	1·25	1·00
2054	$1.20 Anchor and Jean de Surville's ship (vert)	1·50	1·60
2055	$1.50 Dumont d'Urville, crab and ship	1·75	2·00
2056	$1.80 Abel Tasman and illustration from journal	1·90	2·00

See also Nos. 2140/5, 2216/21 and 2239/44.

545 Rippon Vineyard, Central Otago

1997. New Zealand Vineyards. Multicoloured.

2057	40 c. Type **545**	60	40
2058	80 c. Te Mata Estate, Hawke's Bay	1·00	90
2059	$1 Cloudy Bay Vineyard, Marlborough	1·25	1·00
2060	$1.20 Pegasus Bay Vineyard, Waipara	1·50	1·60
2061	$1.50 Milton Vineyard, Gisborne	1·75	2·00
2062	$1.80 Goldwater Estate, Waiheke Island	1·90	2·00

546 Cottage Letterbox

1997. Curious Letterboxes. Multicoloured. Self-adhesive.

2064	40 c. Type **546**	45	50
2065	40 c. Owl letterbox	45	50
2066	40 c. Blue whale letterbox	45	50
2067	40 c. "Kilroy is Back" letterbox	45	50
2068	40 c. Nesting box letterbox	45	50
2069	40 c. Piper letterbox	45	50
2070	40 c. Diver's helmet letterbox	45	50
2071	40 c. Aircraft letterbox	45	50
2072	40 c. Water tap letterbox	45	50
2073	40 c. Indian palace letterbox	45	50

547 "The Promised Land", 1948 (Colin McCahon)

1997. Contemporary Paintings by Colin McCahon. Multicoloured.

2074	40 c. Type **547**	50	35
2075	$1 "Six Days in Nelson and Canterbury", 1950	1·10	90
2076	$1.50 "Northland Panels" (detail), 1958	1·75	2·25
2077	$1.80 "Moby Dick is sighted off Muriwai Beach", 1972	2·25	2·25

548 Carrier Pigeon (based on 1899 "Pigeon-gram" local stamp)

1997. Centenary of Great Barrier Island Pigeon Post.

2078	**548**	40 c. red	50	60
2079		80 c. blue	90	1·00

549 Rainbow Trout and Red Setter Fly

1997. Fly Fishing. Multicoloured.

2082	40 c. Type **549**	40	35
2083	$1 Sea-run brown trout and grey ghost fly	90	90
2084	$1.50 Brook charr and twilight beauty fly	1·40	1·50
2085	$1.80 Brown trout and Hare and Cooper fly	1·60	1·75

550 "Beach Scene" (Fern Petrie)

1997. Children's Health. Children's paintings. Multicoloured. (a) Ordinary gum.

2086	40 c. + 5 c. Type **550**	45	45
2087	80 c. + 5 c. "Horse-riding on the Waterfront" (Georgia Dumergue)	80	85
	(b) Self-adhesive.		
2089	40 c. + 5 c. "Picking Fruit" (Anita Pitcher)	45	45

551 The "Overlander" at Paremata, Wellington

1997. Scenic Railway Services. Multicoloured.

2091	40 c. Type **551**	50	35
2092	80 c. The "Tranz Alpine" in the Southern Alps	90	80
2093	$1 The "Southener" at Canterbury	1·00	90
2094	$1.20 The "Coastal Pacific" on the Kaikoura Coast	1·40	1·75
2095	$1.50 The "Bay Express" at Central Hawke's Bay	1·60	2·00
2096	$1.80 The "Kaimai Express" at Tauranga Harbour	1·75	2·00

552 Samuel Marsden's "Active", Bay of Islands

553 Huhu Beetle

1997. Christmas. Multicoloured. (a) Ordinary gum.

2097	40 c. Type **552**	45	40
2098	70 c. Revd. Marsden preaching	75	65
2099	80 c. Marsden and Maori chiefs	85	75
2100	$1 Maori family	1·00	90
2101	$1.50 Handshake and cross	1·60	1·75
2102	$1.80 Pohutukawa (flower) and Rangihoua Bay	1·75	2·00
	(b) Smaller design, 29 × 24 mm. Self-adhesive.		
2103	40 c. Memorial cross, Pohutukawa and Bay of Islands	40	40

1997. Insects. Multicoloured. Self-adhesive.

2104	40 c. Type **553**	30	35
2105	40 c. Giant land snail	30	35
2106	40 c. Giant weta	30	35
2107	40 c. Giant dragonfly	30	35
2108	40 c. Peripatus	30	35
2109	40 c. Cicada	30	35
2110	40 c. Puriri moth	30	35
2111	40 c. Veined slug	30	35
2112	40 c. Katipo	30	35
2113	40 c. Flax weevil	30	35

MORE DETAILED LISTS
are given in the Stanley Gibbons Catalogues referred to in the country headings.
For lists of current volumes see Introduction.

554 "Rosa rugosa"

555 Queen Elizabeth II and Prince Philip

1997. New Zealand–China Joint Issue. Roses. Multicoloured.

2114	40 c. Type **554**	40	40
2115	40 c. "Aotearoa"	40	40

1997. Golden Wedding of Queen Elizabeth and Prince Philip.

2117	**555**	40 c. multicoloured	40	35

556 Cartoon Kiwi on Busy-bee

1997. New Zealand Cartoons. "Kiwis Taking on the World". Multicoloured.

2118	40 c. Type **556**	45	35
2119	$1 "Let's have 'em for Breakfast"	85	80
2120	$1.50 Kiwi dinghy winning race	1·25	1·50
2121	$1.80 "CND" emblem cut in forest	1·60	1·75

557 Modern Dancer

1998. Performing Arts. Multicoloured.

2124	40 c. Type **557**	40	35
2125	80 c. Trombone player	75	75
2126	$1 Opera singer	90	85
2127	$1.20 Actor	1·25	1·25
2128	$1.50 Singer	1·40	1·50
2129	$1.80 Ballet dancer	1·60	1·75

558 Museum of New Zealand

1998. Opening of Museum of New Zealand, Wellington. Multicoloured.

2131	40 c. Type **558**	30	35
2132	$1.80 Museum and seabirds	1·40	1·40

559 Domestic Cat

560 Maoris and Canoe

1998. Cats. Multicoloured.

2133	40 c. Type **559**	40	35
2134	80 c. Burmese	75	80
2135	$1 Birman	85	80
2136	$1.20 British blue	1·00	1·10
2137	$1.50 Persian	1·25	1·50
2138	$1.80 Siamese	1·75	2·00

1998. Millennium Series (2nd issue). Immigrants. Multicoloured.

2140	40 c. Type **560**	30	35
2141	80 c. 19th-century European settlers and immigrant ship	60	65
2142	$1 Gold miners and mine	75	80
2143	$1.20 Post 1945 European migrants and liner	90	95
2144	$1.50 Pacific islanders and hurch	1·10	1·25
2145	$1.80 Asian migrant and jumbo jet	1·25	1·40

561 "With Great Respect to the Mehmetcik" Statue, Gallipoli

562 Mother and Son Hugging

1998. Joint Issue New Zealand–Turkey. Memorial Statues. Multicoloured.

2146	40 c. Type **561**	30	35
2147	$1.80 "Mother with Children", National War Memorial, Wellington	1·25	1·40

1998. "Stay in Touch" Greetings Stamps. Multicoloured. Self-adhesive.

2148	40 c. Type **562**	25	30
2149	40 c. Couple on beach	25	30
2150	40 c. Boys striking hands	25	30
2151	40 c. Grandmother and grandson	25	30
2152	40 c. Young boys in pool (horiz)	25	30
2153	40 c. "I'LL MISS YOU... PLEASE WRITE" (horiz)	25	30
2154	40 c. Symbolic couple and clouds (horiz)	25	30
2155	40 c. Young couple kissing (horiz)	25	30
2156	40 c. Couple sat on sofa (horiz)	25	30
2157	40 c. Maoris rubbing noses (horiz)	25	30

563 Mount Cook or Aorangi

565 Girl wearing Lifejacket

564 "Wounded at Cassino"

1998. Centenary of 1898 Pictorial Stamps. Designs as T **23/26** and **28/35** with modern face values as T **563**.

2158	**563**	40 c. brown	25	30
2159	**24**	40 c. blue and brown	25	30
2160	**25**	40 c. brown	25	30
2161	**28**	40 c. brown	25	30
2162	**29**	40 c. red	25	30
2163	**31**	40 c. green	25	30
2164	**32**	40 c. blue	25	30
2165	**34**	40 c. orange	25	30
2166	**26**	80 c. blue (inscr "LAKE WAKITIPU") (35 × 23 mm)	50	55
2167		80 c. blue (inscr "LAKE WAKATIPU") (35 × 23 mm)	50	55
2168	**30**	$1 brown (23 × 35 mm)	65	70
2169	**33**	$1.20 brown (35 × 23 mm)	75	80
2170	**35**	$1.50 green (35 × 23 mm)	95	1·00
2171	–	$1.80 red (as No. 329) (23 × 35 mm)	1·10	1·25

1998. Paintings by Peter McIntyre. Multicoloured.

2174	40 c. Type **564**	35	30
2175	$1 "The Cliffs of Rangitikei"	85	75
2176	$1.50 "Maori Children, King Country"	1·25	1·40
2177	$1.80 "The Anglican Church, Kakahi"	1·40	1·50

1998. Children's Health. Water Safety. Multicoloured. (a) Ordinary gum.

2178	40 c. + 5 c. Type **565**	40	40
2179	80 c. + 5 c. Boy learning to swim	60	60
	(b) Smaller design, 25 × 37 mm. Self-adhesive.		
2181	40 c. + 5 c. Type **565**	30	35

566 Sunrise near Cambridge

1998. Scenic Skies. Multicoloured.

2182	40 c. Type **566**	35	30
2183	80 c. Clouds over Lake Wanaka	65	65
2184	$1 Sunset over Mount Maunganui	75	75
2185	$1.20 Rain clouds over South Bay, Kaikoura	90	90
2186	$1.50 Sunset near Statue of Wairaka, Whakatane Harbour	1·25	1·25
2187	$1.80 Cloud formation above Lindis Pass	1·60	1·75

567 Virgin Mary and Christ Child

568 Lemon and Mineral Water Bottle, Paeroa

1998. Christmas. Multicoloured. (a) Ordinary gum.

2189	40 c. Type **567**	35	30
2190	70 c. Shepherds approaching the stable	55	55
2191	80 c. Virgin Mary, Joseph and Christ Child	65	65
2192	$1 Magi with gift of gold	80	80
2193	$1.50 Three magi	1·25	1·25
2194	$1.80 Angel and shepherds	1·40	1·50

(b) Smaller design, 24 × 29 mm. Self-adhesive.

2195	40 c. Type **567**	30	30

1998. Town Icons. Self-adhesive. Multicoloured.

2196	40 c. Type **568**	25	30
2197	40 c. Carrot, Ohakune	25	30
2198	40 c. Brown Trout, Gore (25 × 36 mm)	25	30
2199	40 c. Crayfish, Kaikoura (25 × 36 mm)	25	30
2200	40 c. Sheep-shearer, Te Kuiti (25 × 36 mm)	25	30
2201	40 c. "Pania of the Reef" (Maori legend), Napier (25 × 36 mm)	25	30
2202	40 c. Paua Shell, Riverton (24 × 29 mm)	25	30
2203	40 c. Kiwifruit, Te Puke (24 × 29 mm)	25	30
2204	40 c. Border Collie, Lake Tekapo (24 × 29 mm)	25	30
2205	40 c. "Big Cow", Hawera (24 × 29 mm)	25	30

569 Moonfish

571 "Fuchsia excorticata"

570 Wellington in 1841 and 1998

1998. International Year of the Ocean. Multicoloured.

2206	40 c. Type **569**	25	30
2207	40 c. Mako shark	25	30
2208	40 c. Yellowfin tuna	25	30
2209	40 c. Giant squid	25	30
2210	80 c. Striped marlin	50	55
2211	80 c. Porcupine fish	50	55
2212	80 c. Eagle ray	50	55
2213	80 c. Sandager's wrasse	50	55

Nos. 2206/9 and 2210/13 respectively were printed together, se-tenant, forming composite designs.

1998. Millennium Series (3rd issue). Urban Transformations. Multicoloured.

2216	40 c. Type **570**	25	30
2217	80 c. Auckland in 1852 and 1998	50	55
2218	$1 Christchurch in 1851 and 1998	65	70
2219	$1.20 Westport in 1919 and 1998	75	80
2220	$1.50 Tauranga in 1880 and 1998	95	1·00
2221	$1.80 Dunedin in 1862 and 1998	1·10	1·25

1999. Flowering Trees of New Zealand. Mult.

2222	40 c. Type **571**	25	30
2223	80 c. "Solanum laciniatum"	50	55
2224	$1 "Sophora tetraptera"	65	70
2225	$1.20 "Carmichaelia stevensonii"	75	80
2226	$1.50 "Olearia angustfolia"	95	1·00
2227	$1.80 "Metrosideros umbellata"	1·10	1·25

572 Civic Theatre, Auckland

573 Labrador Puppy and Netherland Dwarf Rabbit

1999. Art Deco Architecture. Multicoloured.

2228	40 c. Type **572**	25	30
2229	$1 Masonic Hotel, Napier	65	70
2230	$1.50 Medical and Dental Chambers, Hastings	95	1·00
2231	$1.80 Buller County Chambers, Westport	1·10	1·25

1999. Popular Pets. Multicoloured.

2232	40 c. Type **573**	25	30
2233	80 c. Netherland dwarf rabbit	50	55
2234	$1 Tabby kitten and Netherland dwarf rabbit	65	70
2235	$1.20 Lamb	75	80
2236	$1.50 Welsh pony	95	1·00
2237	$1.80 Two budgerigars	1·10	1·25

574 Toy Fire Engine and Marbles

1999. Millennium Series (4th issue). Nostalgia. Multicoloured.

2239	40 c. Type **574**	25	30
2240	80 c. Commemorative tin of biscuits and cereal packet	50	55
2241	$1 Tram, tickets and railway crockery	65	70
2242	$1.20 Radio and "Woman's Weekly" magazine	75	80
2243	$1.50 Coins, postcards and stamps	95	1·00
2244	$1.80 Lawn mower and seed packets	1·10	1·25

575 Hunter Building, Victoria University

576 Auckland Blues Player kicking Ball

1999. Centenary of Victoria University, Wellington.

2247	**575** 40 c. multicoloured	25	30

1999. New Zealand U-Bix Rugby Super 12 Championship. Multicoloured. Ordinary or self-adhesive gum.

2248	40 c. Type **576**	25	30
2249	40 c. Auckland Blues player being tackled	25	30
2250	40 c. Chiefs player being tackled	25	30
2251	40 c. Chiefs lineout jump	25	30
2252	40 c. Wellington Hurricanes player being tackled	25	30
2253	40 c. Wellington Hurricanes player passing ball	25	30
2254	40 c. Canterbury Crusaders lineout jump	25	30
2255	40 c. Canterbury Crusaders player kicking ball	25	30
2256	40 c. Otago Highlanders diving for try	25	30
2257	40 c. Otago Highlanders player running with ball	25	30

577 "The Lake, Tuai"

1999. Paintings by Doris Lusk. Multicoloured.

2268	40 c. Type **577**	25	30
2269	$1 "The Pumping Station"	65	70
2270	$1.50 "Arcade Awning, St. Mark's Square, Venice (2)"	95	1·00
2271	$1.80 "Tuam St. II"	1·10	1·25

578 "A Lion in the Meadow" (Margaret Mahy)

1999. Children's Health. Children's Books. Multicoloured. Ordinary gum.

2272	40 c. + 5 c. Type **578**	30	35
2273	80 c. + 5 c. "Greedy Cat" (Joy Cowley)	55	60

(b) Smaller design 37 × 25 mm. Self-adhesive.

2275	40 c. + 5 c. "Hairy Maclary's Bone" (Lynley Dodd) (37 × 25 mm)	30	35

EXPRESS DELIVERY STAMPS

E 1

1903.

E1	**E 1** 6d. red and violet	35·00	22·00

E 2 Express Mail Delivery Van

1939.

E6	**E 2** 6d. violet	1·50	1·75

LIFE INSURANCE DEPARTMENT

L 1

L 3 Castlepoint Lighthouse

1891.

L13	**L 1** ½d. purple	55·00	2·75
L14	1d. blue	55·00	75
L15	2d. brown	70·00	3·50
L 4	3d. brown	£160	20·00
L 5	6d. green	£275	60·00
L 6	1s. pink	£500	£120

1905. Similar type but "V.R." omitted.

L24	½d. green	10·00	90
L22	1d. blue	£160	30·00
L38	1d. red	2·50	2·00
L26	1½d. black	40·00	6·50
L27	1½d. brown	1·50	2·25
L21	2d. brown	£1000	80·00
L28	2d. purple	48·00	26·00
L29	2d. yellow	4·00	2·00
L30	3d. brown	45·00	24·00
L35	3d. red	18·00	22·00
L41	6d. pink	11·00	32·00

1947. Lighthouses.

L42	**L 3** ½d. green and orange	1·00	60
L43	– 1d. olive and blue	1·00	65
L44	– 2d. blue and black	70	40
L45	– 2½d. black and blue	9·50	13·00
L46	– 3d. mauve and blue	2·50	35
L47	– 4d. brown and orange	3·25	1·25
L48	– 6d. brown and blue	3·50	1·50
L49	– 1s. brown and blue	3·50	2·50

LIGHTHOUSES—HORIZ: 1d. Taiaroa; 2d. Cape Palliser; 6d. The Brothers. VERT: 2½d. Cape Campbell; 3d. Eddystone; 4d. Stephens Island; 1s. Cape Brett.

1967. Decimal currency. Stamps of 1947–65 surch.

L50a	1 c. on 1d. (No. L43)	1·75	4·25
L51	2 c. on 2½d. (No. L45)	11·00	13·00
L52	2½ c. on 3d. (No. L46)	2·00	4·50
L53	3 c. on 4d. (No. L47)	4·50	5·50
L54	5 c. on 6d. (No. L48)	1·00	6·00
L55a	10 c. on 1s. (No. L49)	1·00	4·00

L 13 Moeraki Point Lighthouse

1969.

L56	**L 13** ½ c. yellow, red & violet	1·50	2·25
L57	– 2½ c. blue, green & buff	75	1·25
L58	– 3 c. stone, yellow & brn	75	75
L59	– 4 c. green, ochre & blue	1·00	1·00
L60	– 8 c. multicoloured	45	2·50
L61	– 10 c. multicoloured	45	2·50
L62	– 15 c. multicoloured	60	2·00

DESIGNS—HORIZ: 2½ c. Puysegur Point Lighthouse; 4 c. Cape Egmont Lighthouse. VERT: 3 c. Baring Head Lighthouse; 8 c. East Cape; 10 c. Farewell Spit; 15 c. Dog Island Lighthouse.

1978. No. L57 surch **25c**.

L63	25 c. on 2½ c. blue, green and buff	75	1·75

L 17

1981.

L64	L **17**	5 c. multicoloured	10	10
L65		10 c. multicoloured	10	10
L66		20 c. multicoloured	15	15
L67		30 c. multicoloured	25	25
L68		40 c. multicoloured	35	30
L69		50 c. multicoloured	45	35

OFFICIAL STAMPS

1891. Optd **O.P.S.O.**

O 1	**3**	½d. pink	—	£450
O 2	**13**	½d. black	—	£180
O13	**23**	½d. green	—	£180
O 4	**10**	1d. pink	—	£180
O19	**42**	1d. red	—	£180
O 6	**9**	2d. mauve	—	£325
O 8	**16**	2½d. blue	—	£225
O14	**26**	2½d. blue (A)	—	£400
O21		2½d. blue (B)	—	£275
O22		3d. brown . **28**.	—	£400
O16	**24**	4d. blue and brown	—	£375
O11	**19**	5d. black	—	£375
O17a	**30**	5d. brown	—	£375
O12	**8**	6d. brown (No. 224b)	—	£500
O18	**32**	8d. blue	—	£475
O23	**34**	1s. red	—	£800
O24	**35**	2s. green	—	£1200

Optd **OFFICIAL.**

1907. Pictorials.

O59	**23**	½d. green	8·00	50
O61a	**25**	2d. purple	8·50	1·25
O63	**28**	3d. brown	42·00	1·75
O64	**31**	6d. red	£130	18·00
O65	**34**	1s. orange	85·00	15·00
O66	**35**	2s. green	70·00	48·00
O67	–	5s. red (No. 329)	£150	£170

1907. "Universal" type.

O60b	**42**	1d. red	8·00	30

1908.

O70	**50**	1d. red	65·00	2·25
O72	**31**	6d. red (No. 254)	£110	35·00

1910. King Edward VII etc.

O73	**51**	½d. green	4·25	30
O78	**53**	1d. red	3·25	10
O74	**51**	3d. brown	14·00	80
O75		6d. red	19·00	4·50
O76		8d. blue	14·00	18·00
O77		1s. orange	50·00	15·00

1913. Queen Victoria.

O82	F **4**	2s. blue	48·00	35·00
O83		5s. green	75·00	90·00
O84		£1 red	£550	£450

1915. King George V.

O 96	**62**	½d. green	80	10
O 90		1½d. grey	4·25	65
O 91		1½d. brown	4·25	30
O 98		2d. yellow	2·00	40
O 99		3d. brown	4·00	40
O101		4d. violet	14·00	3·25
O102		6d. red	5·00	75
O103		8d. brown	70·00	90·00
O104		9d. green	38·00	32·00
O105b		1s. orange	7·00	2·00

1927. King George V.

O111c	**71**	1d. red	1·50	10
O112		2s. blue	70·00	£100

1933. "Arms".

O113	F **6**	5s. green	£250	£300

Optd **OFFICIAL.**

1936. "Arms".

O133	F **6**	5s. green	38·00	5·00

1936. As 1935.

O120	**81**	½d. green	6·00	4·00
O115	–	1d. red (No. 557)	2·25	70
O122	**83**	1½d. brown	14·00	4·00
O123	–	2d. orange (No. 580)	2·00	10
O124a	**85**	2½d. brown and grey	14·00	20·00
O125	**86**	3d. brown	48·00	3·00
O126c	**87**	4d. black and brown	3·50	75
O127c	**89**	6d. red	8·00	30
O128a	–	8d. brown (No. 586b)	8·00	15·00
O130	**91**	9d. red and black	20·00	22·00
O131b	–	1s. green (No. 588)	22·00	85
O132d	**93**	2s. olive	42·00	7·00

1938. King George VI.

O134	**108**	½d. green	15·00	2·25
O135		½d. orange	1·60	2·75
O136		1d. red	15·00	15
O137		1d. green	2·25	10
O138		1½d. brown	75·00	18·00
O139		1½d. red	9·00	5·00
O152		2d. orange	1·75	10
O140		3d. blue	2·25	10
O153		4d. purple	4·25	1·50
O154		6d. red	11·00	40
O155		8d. violet	8·00	6·50
O156		9d. brown	9·00	6·50
O157a	–	1s. brn & red (No. 686b)	8·50	8·50
O158	–	2s. orange and green (No. 688)	23·00	16·00

1940. Centenary stamps.

O141	½d. green	1·75	35
O142	1d. brown and red	4·00	10
O143	1½d. blue and mauve	2·75	2·00
O144	2d. green and brown	4·00	10
O145	2½d. green and blue	4·00	2·75
O146	3d. purple and red	8·00	90
O147	4d. brown and red	40·00	2·00
O148	6d. green and violet	25·00	2·00
O149	8d. black and red	30·00	17·00
O150	9d. olive and red	11·00	7·00
O151	1s. green	48·00	4·00

O **6** Queen Elizabeth II

1954.

O159	O **6**	1d. orange	60	30
O160		1½d. brown	3·25	4·00
O161		2d. green	40	15
O162		2½d. olive	4·25	1·50
O163		3d. red	60	10
O164		4d. blue	1·25	20
O165		9d. red	6·50	75
O166		1s. purple	1·00	10
O167		3s. slate	35·00	48·00

1959. Surch.

O169	O **6**	2½d. on 2d. green	85	1·50
O168		6d. on 1½d. brown	40	1·10

POSTAGE DUE STAMPS

D 1

D 2

1899.

D 9	D **1**	½d. red and green	2·50	16·00
D10		1d. red and green	9·50	1·25
D15		2d. red and green	45·00	4·75
D12		3d. red and green	13·00	3·50
D16		4d. red and green	32·00	9·00
D 6		5d. red and green	21·00	21·00
D 7		6d. red and green	28·00	23·00
D 2		8d. red and green	60·00	75·00
D 8		10d. red and green	70·00	85·00
D 3		1s. red and green	65·00	80·00
D 4		2s. red and green	£120	£140

1902.

D18	D **2**	½d. red and green	1·50	1·50
D30		1d. red and green	3·75	80
D22a		2d. red and green	5·00	1·50
D36		3d. red and green	15·00	42·00

D 3

1939.

D41	D **3**	½d. green	5·00	5·00
D42		1d. red	2·75	30
D46		2d. blue	7·50	1·40
D47aw		3d. brown	9·00	8·00

NIGER COAST PROTECTORATE

A district on the west coast of Africa. In 1900 became part of Southern Nigeria.

12 pence = 1 shilling;
20 pence = 1 pound

1892. Stamps of Gt. Britain (Queen Victoria) optd **BRITISH PROTECTORATE OIL RIVERS.**

1	**71**	½d. red	8·50	4·50
2	**57**	1d. lilac	5·50	6·00
3	**73**	2d. green and red	17·00	8·00
4	**74**	2½d. purple and blue	6·50	2·25
5	**78**	5d. purple and blue	7·50	7·50
6	**82**	1s. green	50·00	70·00

1893. Half of No. 2 surch **½d.**

7	**57**	½d. on half of 1d. lilac	£150	£140

1893. Nos. 1 to 6 surch in words (½d., 1s.) or figures (others).

20	**73**	½d. on 2d. green and red	£275	£225
21	**74**	½d. on 2½d. purple on blue	£250	£180
37	**73**	1s. on 2d. green and red	£400	£350
40		5s. on 2d. green and red	£8000	£9000
41	**78**	10s. on 5d. purple & blue	£6000	£8000
42	**82**	20s. on 1s. green	£70000	

13

14

1893. Various frames with "OIL RIVERS" barred out and "NIGER COAST" above.

45	**13**	½d. red	4·00	3·75
46		1d. blue	5·00	3·25
47d		2d. green	17·00	13·00
48		2½d. red	7·00	3·50
49		3d. lilac	14·00	12·00
50		1s. black	14·00	12·00

1894. Various frames.

66	**14**	½d. green	3·00	1·50
67		1d. red	3·50	1·50
68		2d. red	1·75	1·25
69a		2½d. blue	6·50	1·50
55		5d. purple	6·00	5·50
71		6d. brown	7·00	6·50
56a		1s. black	27·00	7·00
73b		2s. 6d. brown	22·00	75·00
74b		10s. violet	80·00	£160

1894. Surch with large figures.

58	½ on half 1d. (No. 46)	£650	£275
59	1 on half 2d. (No. 2)	£1400	£275

1894. No. 67 bisected and surch.

64	**14**	½d. on half of 1d. red	£1600	£350

1894. Surch **ONE HALF PENNY** and bars.

65	**14**	½d. on 2½d. blue	£350	£225

NIGERIA

A former British colony on the west coast of Africa, comprising the territories of Northern and Southern Nigeria and Lagos. Attained full independence within the British Commonwealth in 1960 and became a Federal Republic in 1963.

The Eastern Region (known as Biafra (q.v)) seceded in 1967, remaining independent until overrun by Federal Nigerian troops during January 1970.

1914. 12 pence = 1 shilling;
20 shillings = 1 pound.
1973. 100 kobo = 1 naira.

1

1914.

15	**1**	½d. green	1·00	40
16		1d. red	3·00	30
17		1½d. orange	3·25	15
18		2d. grey	1·50	3·50
20		2d. brown	1·25	15
21		2½d. blue	1·00	4·50
5a		3d. purple on yellow	1·50	2·50
22		3d. violet	5·00	3·25
23		3d. blue	5·00	1·50
24		4d. black & red on yellow	65	55
25a		6d. purple	7·00	8·00
26		1s. black on green	1·25	1·75
9		2s. 6d. black & red on blue	12·00	5·50
10		5s. green & red on yellow	11·00	38·00
11d		10s. green & red on green	38·00	90·00
12a		£1 purple & black on red	£160	£190

1935. Silver Jubilee. As T **13** of Antigua.

30	1½d. blue and grey	80	50
31	2d. green and blue	1·50	50
32	3d. brown and blue	3·00	8·50
33	1s. grey and purple	3·00	22·00

3 Apapa Wharf

5 Victoria–Buea Road

1936.

34	**3**	½d. green	1·25	1·40
35	–	1d. red	40	40
36	–	1½d. brown	1·25	40
37	–	2d. black	40	80
38	–	3d. blue	1·25	1·25
39	–	4d. brown	1·50	2·00
40	–	6d. violet	40	60
41	–	1s. green	1·50	4·50
42	**5**	2s. 6d. black and blue	3·50	19·00
43	–	5s. black and green	6·00	24·00
44	–	10s. black and grey	45·00	65·00
45	–	£1 black and orange	70·00	£140

DESIGNS—VERT: 1d. Cocoa; 1½d. Tin dredger; 2d. Timber industry; 3d. Fishing village; 4d. Cotton ginnery; 6d. Habe minaret; 1s. Fulani cattle. HORIZ: 5s. Oil palms; 10s. River Niger at Jebba; £1 Canoe pulling.

1937. Coronation. As T **2** of Aden.

46	1d. red	30	1·50
47	1½d. brown	1·25	2·25
48	3d. blue	1·40	2·25

15 King George VI

1938.

49	**15**	½d. green	10	10
50a		1d. red	75	30
50b		1d. lilac	10	20
51a		1½d. brown	10	10
52		2d. black	10	1·00
52ab		2d. red	10	40
52b		2½d. orange	10	70
53		3d. blue	10	10
53b		3d. black	15	40
54		4d. orange	48·00	2·75
54a		4d. blue	15	1·75
55		6d. violet	40	10
56a		1s. olive	15	10
57		1s. 3d. blue	90	30
58b	–	2s. 6d. black and blue	2·00	2·75
59b	–	5s. black and orange	6·00	3·00

DESIGNS: 2s. 6d., 5s. As Nos. 42 and 44 but with portrait of King George VI.

1946. Victory. As T **9** of Aden.

60	1½d. brown	25	10
61	4d. blue	25	90

1948. Royal Silver Wedding. As T **10/11** of Aden.

62	1d. mauve	35	30
63	5s. orange	5·00	8·00

1949. U.P.U. As T **20/23** of Antigua.

64	1d. purple	20	10
65	3d. blue	1·25	2·25
66	6d. purple	70	2·00
67	1s. olive	80	1·75

1953. Coronation. As T **13** of Aden.

68	1½d. black and green	40	10

18 Old Manilla Currency

26 Victoria Harbour

29 New and Old Lagos

1953.
69 **18** ½d. black and orange . . . 15 30
70 – 1d. black and bronze . . . 20 10
71 – 1½d. turquoise 50 40
72 – 2d. black and ochre . . . 4·00 30
72cb – 2d. slate . . . . 3·50 40
73 – 3d. black and purple . . . 55 10
74 – 4d. black and blue . . . . 2·50 20
75 – 6d. brown and black . . . 30 10
76 – 1s. black and purple . . . 40 10
77 **26** 2s. 6d. black and green . . 5·50 50
78 – 5s. black and red . . . . 3·50 1·00
79 – 10s. black and brown . . . 12·00 2·50
80 **29** £1 black and violet . . . 21·00 6·50
DESIGNS—HORIZ (As Type **18**): 1d. Bornu horsemen; 1½d. "Groundnuts"; 2d. "Tin"; 3d. Jebba Bridge and R. Niger; 4d. "Cocoa"; 1s. "Timber". (As Type **26**): 5s. "Palm oil"; 10s. "Hides and skins". VERT (As Type **18**): 6d. Ife bronze.

1956. Royal Visit. No. 72 optd **ROYAL VISIT 1956**.
81 2d. black and ochre 40 20

31 Victoria Harbour

1958. Centenary of Victoria, S. Cameroons.
82 **31** 3d. black and purple 20 30

32 Lugard Hall

1959. Attainment of Self-Government. Northern Region of Nigeria.
83 **32** 3d. black and purple 15 10
84 – 1s. black and green 55 75
DESIGN: 1s. Kano Mosque.

35 Legislative Building

1960. Independence Commemoration.
85 **35** 1d. black and red 10 10
86 – 3d. black and blue 15 10
87 – 6d. green and brown 20 20
88 – 1s. 3d. blue and yellow . . . 40 20
DESIGNS—As Type **35**: 3d. African paddling canoe; 6d. Federal Supreme Court. LARGER (40 × 24 mm): 1s. 3d. Dove, torch and map.

39 Groundnuts

48 Central Bank

1961.
89 **39** ½d. green 10 50
90 – 1d. violet 80 10
91 – 1½d. red . . . . 70 2·00
92 – 2d. blue 30 10
93 – 3d. green 40 10
94 – 4d. blue 40 55
95 – 6d. yellow and black 80 10
96 – 1s. green . . . . 4·50 10
97 – 1s. 3d. orange . . . . . . 1·25 10
98 **48** 2s. 6d. black and yellow . . 2·50 15
99 – 5s. black and green 65 70
100 – 10s. black and blue . . . . 1·75 2·00
101 – £1 black and red . . . . . 8·50 9·50
DESIGNS—VERT (as Type **39**): 1d. Coal mining; 1½d. Adult education; 2d. Pottery; 3d. Oyo carver; 4d. Weaving; 6d. Benin mask; 1s. Yellow casqued hornbill; 1s. 3d. Camel train. HORIZ (as Type **48**: 5s. Nigeria Museum; 10s. Kano airport; £1 Lagos railway station.

52 Globe and Diesel-electric Locomotive

1961. Admission into U.P.U. Inscr as in T **52**.
102 **52** 1d. orange and blue 20 10
103 – 3d. olive and black 20 10
104 – 1s. 3d. blue and red . . . 70 20
105 – 2s. 6d. green and blue . . . 85 1·75
DESIGNS: 3d. Globe and mail van; 1s. 3d. Globe and Bristol 175 Britannia aircraft; 2s. 6d. Globe and liner.

56 Coat of Arms

61 "Health"

1961. 1st Anniv of Independence.
106 **56** 3d. multicoloured 10 10
107 – 4d. green and orange . . . 20 10
108 – 6d. green 30 10
109 – 1s. 3d. grey and blue . . . 35 10
110 – 2s. 6d. green and blue . . 40 1·50
DESIGNS—HORIZ: 4d. Natural resources map; 6d. Nigerian eagle; 1s 3d. Eagles in flight; 2s. 6d. Nigerians and flag.

1962. Lagos Conf of African and Malagasy States.
111 **61** 1d. bistre 10 10
112 – 3d. purple 10 10
113 – 6d. green 15 10
114 – 1s. brown 20 10
115 – 1s. 3d. blue 25 20
DESIGNS: Map and emblems symbolising Culture (3d.); Commerce (6d.); Communications (1s.); Co-operation (1s. 3d.).

66 Malaria Eradication Emblem and Parasites

1962. Malaria Eradication.
116 **66** 3d. green and red 15 10
117 – 6d. blue and purple 20 10
118 – 1s. 3d. mauve and blue . . 20 10
119 – 2s. 6d. blue and brown . . 30 60
DESIGNS (embodying emblem): 6d. Insecticide-spraying; 1s. 3d. Aerial spraying; 2s. 6d. Mother, child and microscope.

70 National Monument

1962. 2nd Anniv of Independence.
120 **70** 3d. green and blue 10 10
121 – 5s. red, green and violet . 1·00 70
DESIGN—VERT: 5s. Benin bronze.

72 Fair Emblem

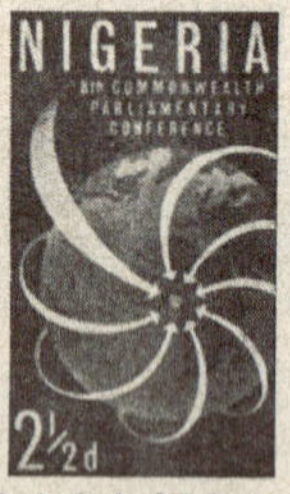

76 "Arrival of Delegates"

1962. International Trade Fair, Lagos.
122 **72** 1d. red and olive 10 10
123 – 6d. black and red 15 10
124 – 1s. black and brown . . . 15 10
125 – 2s. 6d. yellow and blue . . 60 20
DESIGNS—HORIZ: 6d. "Cogwheels of Industry"; 1s. "Cornucopia of Industry"; 2s. 6d. Oilwells and tanker.

1962. 8th Commonwealth Parliamentary Conference, Lagos.
126 **76** 2½d. blue 15 20
127 – 4d. blue and rose 15 15
128 – 1s. 3d. sepia and yellow . . 20 20
DESIGNS—HORIZ: 4d. National Hall. VERT: 1s. 3d. Mace as Palm Tree.

80 Tractor and Maize

81 Mercury Capsule and Kano Tracking Station

1963. Freedom from Hunger.
129 – 3d. olive . . . . 1·00 20
130 **80** 6d. mauve . . . . 1·50 20
DESIGN—VERT: 3d. Herdsman.

1963. "Peaceful Use of Outer Space".
131 **81** 6d. blue and green 25 10
132 – 1s. 3d. black & turquoise . 35 20
DESIGN: 1s. 3d. Satellite and Lagos Harbour.

83 Scouts shaking Hands

1963. 11th World Scout Jamboree. Marathon.
133 **83** 3d. red and bronze 30 15
134 – 1s. black and red 95 65
DESIGN: 1s. Campfire.

85 Emblem and First Aid Team

88 President Azikiwe and State House

1963. Centenary of Red Cross.
135 **85** 3d. red and blue 75 10
136 – 6d. red and green . . . . 1·25 10
137 – 1s. 3d. red and sepia . . . 1·75 70
DESIGNS: 6d. Emblem and "Hospital Services"; 1s. 3d. Patient and emblem.

1963. Republic Day.
138 **88** 3d. olive and green 10 10
139 – 1s. 3d. brown and sepia . . 10 10
140 – 2s. 6d. turquoise and blue . 15 15
The buildings on the 1s. 3d. and the 2s. 6d. are the Federal Supreme Court and the Parliament Building respectively.

90 "Freedom of Worship"

93 Queen Nefertari

1963. 15th Anniv of Declaration of Human Rights.
141 – 3d. red 10 10
142 **90** 6d. green 15 10
143 – 1s. 3d. blue 30 10
144 – 2s. 6d. purple 45 30
DESIGNS—HORIZ: 3d. (Inscr "1948–1963"), Charter and broken whip. VERT: 1s. 3d. "Freedom from Want"; 2s. 6d. "Freedom of Speech".

1964. Nubian Monuments Preservation.
145 **93** 6d. olive and green 50 10
146 – 2s. 6d. brown, olive & green 2·00 1·75
DESIGN: 2s. 6d. Rameses II.

95 President Kennedy

98 President Azikiwe

1964. Pres. Kennedy Memorial Issue.
147 **95** 1s. 3d. lilac and black . . . 50 15
148 – 2s. 6d. multicoloured . . . 70 55
149 – 5s. multicoloured . . . . . 1·25 1·60
DESIGNS: 2s. 6d. Kennedy and flags; 5s. Kennedy (U.S. coin head) and flags.

1964. 1st Anniv of Republic.
150 **98** 3d. brown 10 10
151 – 1s. 3d. green 35 10
152 – 2s. 6d. green 70 50
DESIGNS—25 × 42 mm: 1s. 3d. Herbert Macaulay; 2s. 6d. King Jaja of Opobo.

101 Boxing Gloves

1964. Olympic Games, Tokyo.
153 **101** 3d. sepia and green . . . 45 10
154 – 6d. green and blue 60 10
155 – 1s. 3d. sepia and olive . . 1·25 15
156 – 2s. 6d. sepia and brown . 2·25 3·50
DESIGNS—HORIZ: 6d. High-jumping. VERT: 1s. 3d. Running. TRIANGULAR (60 × 30 mm): 2s. 6d. Hurdling.

105 Scouts on Hill-top

109 "Telstar"

1965. 50th Anniv of Nigerian Scout Movement.
157 **105** 1d. brown 10 10
158 – 3d. red, black and green . 15 10
159 – 6d. red, sepia and green . 25 20
160 – 1s. 3d. brown, yellow and deep green 40 85
DESIGNS: 3d. Scout badge on shield; 6d. Scout badges; 1s. 3d. Chief Scout and Nigerian scout.

1965. International Quiet Sun Years.
161 **109** 6d. violet and turquoise . 15 15
162 – 1s. 3d. green and lilac . . 15 15
DESIGN: 1s. 3d. Solar satellite.

111 Native Tom-tom and Modern Telephone

1965. Centenary of I.T.U.
163 **111** 3d. black, red and brown . 20 10
164 – 1s. 3d. black, green & blue 1·75 1·00
165 – 5s. multicoloured . . . . 4·75 6·50
DESIGNS—VERT: 1s. 3d. Microwave aerial. HORIZ: 5s. Telecommunications satellite and part of globe.

114 I.C.Y. Emblem and Diesel-hydraulic Locomotive

1965. International Co-operation Year.
166 **114** 3d. green, red & orange . 3·00 20
167 – 1s. black, blue & lemon . 3·00 40
168 – 2s. 6d. green, blue & yell . 9·00 6·50
DESIGNS: 1s. Students and Lagos Teaching Hospital; 2s. 6d. Kainji (Niger) Dam.

117 Carved Frieze

1965. 2nd Anniv of Republic.
169 **117** 3d. black, red & yellow . 10 10
170 – 1s. 3d. brown, green & blue 50 10
171 – 5s. brown, sepia and green 1·00 1·25
DESIGNS—VERT: 1s. 3d. Stone Images at Ikom; 5s. Tada bronze.

121 African Elephants

1965.
172 – ½d. multicoloured . . . 80 1·75
173 **121** 1d. multicoloured . . . 40 15
174 – 1½d. multicoloured . . . 5·50 7·00
222 – 2d. multicoloured . . . 1·50 90
176 – 3d. multicoloured . . . 1·25 30
177a – 4d. multicoloured . . . 30 10
225 – 6d. multicoloured . . . 1·75 30
179 – 9d. blue and red . . . . 3·00 60
227 – 1s. multicoloured . . . 2·00 35
181 – 1s. 3d. multicoloured . . 8·50 90

182 **227** 2s. 6d. light brown, buff and brown . . . . . . 75 1·00
183 – 5s. chestnut, yellow and brown . . . . 1·75 2·50
184 – 10s. multicoloured . . . 6·50 3·00
185 – £1 multicoloured . . . . 15·00 9·00

DESIGNS—VERT (as T **121**): ½d. Lion and cubs; 6d. Saddle-bill stork. (26½ × 46mm): 10s. Hippopotamus. HORIZ (as T **121**): 1½d. Splendid sunbird; 2d. Village weaver and red-headed malimbe; 3d. Cheetah; 4d. Leopards; 9d. Grey parrots. (46 × 26½ mm): 1s. Blue-breasted kingfishers; 1s. 3d. Crowned cranes; 2s. 6d. Kobs; 5s. Giraffes; £1 African buffalo.

The 1d., 3d., 4d., 1s., 1s. 3d., 2s. 6d., 5s. and £1 exist optd **F.G.N.** (Federal Government of Nigeria) twice in black. They were prepared in November 1968 as official stamps, but the scheme was abandoned. Some stamps held at a Head Post Office were sold in error and passed through the post. The Director of Posts then decided to put limited supplies on sale, but they had no postal validity.

1966. Commonwealth Prime Ministers' Meeting, Lagos. Optd **COMMONWEALTH P. M. MEETING 11. JAN. 1966.**
186 **48** 2s. 6d. black and yellow . . 30 30

135 Y.W.C.A. Emblem and H.Q., Lagos

1966. Diamond Jubilee of Nigerian Y.W.C.A.
187 **135** 4d. multicoloured 15 10
188 9d. multicoloured 15 60

137 Telephone Handset and Linesman

1966. 3rd Anniv of Republic.
189 – 4d. green 10 10
190 **137** 1s. 6d. black, brown & violet 45 50
191 – 2s. 6d. multicoloured . . . 1·25 2·25

DESIGNS—VERT: 4d. Dove and flag. HORIZ: 2s. 6d. North Channel Bridge over River Niger, Jebba.

139 "Education, Science and Culture"

1966. 20th Anniv of U.N.E.S.C.O.
192 **139** 4d. black, lake & orange . 40 10
193 1s. 6d. black, lake & turq . 1·75 2·50
194 2s. 6d. black, lake & pink 2·75 5·00

140 Children drinking

1966. Nigerian Red Cross.
195 **140** 4d. + 1d. black, vio & red 40 30
196 – 1s. 6d. + 3d. multicoloured 1·00 3·75
197 – 2s. 6d. + 3d. multicoloured 1·10 4·25

DESIGNS—VERT: 1s. 6d. Tending patient. HORIZ: 2s. 6d. Tending casualties and badge.

143 Surveying

1967. Int Hydrological Decade. Mult.
198 4d. Type **143** 10 10
199 2s. 6d. Water gauge on dam (vert) . . . . 25 1·00

145 Globe and Weather Satellite

1967. World Meteorological Day.
200 **145** 4d. mauve and blue . . . 15 10
201 – 1s. 6d. black, yellow & bl 65 65

DESIGN: 1s. 6d. Passing storm and sun.

147 Eyo Masqueraders

1967. 4th Anniv of Republic. Multicoloured.
202 4d. Type **147** 15 10
203 1s. 6d. Crowds watching acrobat 50 1·50
204 2s. 6d. Stilt dancer (vert) . . 75 3·00

150 Tending Sick Animal

1967. Rinderpest Eradication Campaign.
205 **150** 4d. multicoloured 15 10
206 1s. 6d. multicoloured . . 55 1·25

151 Smallpox Vaccination

1968. 20th Anniv of W.H.O.
207 **151** 4d. mauve and black . . 15 10
208 – 1s. 6d. orge, lemon & blk 55 40

DESIGN: 1s. 6d. African and mosquito.

153 Chained Hands and Outline of Nigeria

155 Hand grasping at Doves of Freedom

1968. Human Rights Year.
209 **153** 4d. blue, black & yellow . 10 10
210 – 1s. 6d. green, red & black 20 30

DESIGN—VERT: 1s. 6d. Nigerian flag and Human Rights emblem.

1968. 5th Anniv of Federal Republic.
211 **155** 4d. multicoloured 10 10
212 1s. 6d. multicoloured . . 20 20

156 Map of Nigeria and Olympic Rings

1968. Olympic Games, Mexico.
213 **156** 4d. black, green and red . 10 10
214 – 1s. 6d. multicoloured . . 20 20

DESIGN: 1s. 6d. Nigerian athletes, flag and Olympic rings.

158 G.P.O., Lagos

1969. Inauguration of Philatelic Service.
215 **158** 4d. black and green . . . 10 10
216 1s. 6d. black and blue . . 20 20

159 Yakubu Gowon and Victoria Zakari

160 Bank Emblem and "5th Anniversary"

1969. Wedding of General Gowon.
217 **159** 4d. brown and green . . 10 10
218 1s. 6d. black and green . 50 20

1969. 5th Anniv of African Development Bank.
233 **160** 4d. orange, black & blue . 10 10
234 – 1s. 6d. yellow, black and purple 20 30

DESIGN: 1s. 6d. Bank emblem and rays.

162 I.L.O. Emblem

1969. 50th Anniv of I.L.O.
235 **162** 4d. black and violet . . . 10 10
236 – 1s. 6d. green and black . . 75 85

DESIGN: 1s. 6d. World map and I.L.O. emblem.

164 Olumo Rock

1969. International Year of African Tourism.
237 **164** 4d. multicoloured 15 10
238 – 1s. black and green 20 10
239 – 1s. 6d. multicoloured . . . 1·10 35

DESIGNS—VERT: 1s. Traditional musicians; 1s. 6d. Assob Falls.

167 Symbolic Tree

169 Scroll

168 U.P.U. Headquarters Building

1970. "Stamp of Destiny". End of Civil War.
240 **167** 4d. gold, blue and black . 10 10
241 – 1s. multicoloured 10 10
242 – 1s. 6d. green and black . . 15 10
243 – 2s. multicoloured 20 20

DESIGNS—VERT: 1s. Symbolic Wheel; 1s. 6d. United Nigerians supporting Map. HORIZ: 2s. Symbolic Torch.

1970. New U.P.U. Headquarters Building.
244 **168** 4d. violet and yellow . . . 10 10
245 1s. 6d. blue and indigo . . 40 20

1970. 25th Anniv of United Nations.
246 **169** 4d. brown, buff and black 10 10
247 – 1s. 6d. blue, brown & gold 30 20

DESIGN: 1s. 6d. U.N. Building.

170 Oil Rig

172 Ibibio Face Mask

171 Children and Globe

1970. 10th Anniv of Independence.
248 2d. Type **170** 25 10
249 4d. University graduate . . . 15 10
250 6d. Durbar horsemen 30 10
251 9d. Servicemen raising flag . . 40 10
252 1s. Footballer 40 10
253 1s. 6d. Parliament building . . 40 40
254 2s. Kainji Dam 70 90
255 2s. 6d. Agricultural produce . . 70 1·00

1971. Racial Equality Year. Multicoloured.
256 4d. Type **171** 10 10
257 1s. Black and white men uprooting "Racism" (vert) . . 10 10
258 1s. 6d. "The World in Black and White" (vert) 15 60
259 2s. Black and white men united 15 85

1971. Antiquities of Nigeria.
260 **172** 4d. black and blue 10 10
261 – 1s. 3d. brown and ochre . 15 30
262 – 1s. 9d. green, brown & yell 20 80

DESIGNS: 1s. 3d. Benin bronze; 1s. 9d. Ife bronze.

173 Children and Symbol

174 Mast and Dish Aerial

1971. 25th Anniv of U.N.I.C.E.F.
263 **173** 4d. multicoloured 10 10
264 – 1s. 3d. orange, red & brn 15 40
265 – 1s. 9d. turquoise and deep turquoise 15 85

DESIGNS: Each with U.N.I.C.E.F. symbol: 1s. 3d. Mother and child; 1s. 9d. Mother carrying child.

1971. Opening of Nigerian Earth Satellite Station.
266 **174** 4d. multicoloured 15 10
267 – 1s. 3d. green, blue & black 30 50
268 – 1s. 9d. brown, orge & blk 40 1·00
269 – 3s. mauve, black & purple 85 2·00

DESIGNS: Nos. 267/9 as Type **174**, but showing different views of the Satellite Station.

175 Trade Fair Emblem

177 Nok Style Terracotta Head

176 Traffic

1972. All-Africa Trade Fair.
270 **175** 4d. multicoloured 10 10
271 – 1s. 3d. lilac, yellow & gold 15 35
272 – 1s. 9d. yellow, orge & blk 15 90

DESIGNS—HORIZ: 1s. 3d. Map of Africa with pointers to Nairobi. VERT: 1s. 9d. Africa on globe.

1972. Change to Driving on the Right.
273 **176** 4d. orange, brown & black 50 10
274 – 1s. 3d. multicoloured . . 1·25 70
275 – 1s. 9d. multicoloured . . 1·40 1·25
276 – 3s. multicoloured . . . . 2·25 3·00

DESIGNS: 1s. 3d. Roundabout; 1s. 9d. Highway; 3s. Road junction.

1972. All-Nigeria Arts Festival. Multicoloured.
277 4d. Type **177** 10 10
278 1s. 3d. Bronze pot from Igbo-Ukwu 25 60
279 1s. 9d. Bone harpoon (horiz) . 30 1·50

178 Hides and Skins

1973.
290 **178** 1 k. multicoloured . . . 10 20
281 – 2 k. multicoloured . . . 35 10
292 – 3 k. multicoloured . . . 15 10
282a – 5 k. multicoloured . . . 50 10
294 – 7 k. multicoloured . . . 30 1·25
295 – 8 k. multicoloured . . . 40 10
344 – 10 k. multicoloured . . . 1·00 20
297 – 12 k. black, green & blue 30 2·25
298 – 15 k. multicoloured . . . 30 60
299 – 18 k. multicoloured . . . 50 30
300 – 20 k. multicoloured . . . 65 30
301 – 25 k. multicoloured . . . 85 45
302 – 30 k. black, yellow & blue 40 1·50
303 – 35 k. multicoloured . . . 6·00 4·25
288a – 50 k. multicoloured . . . 1·00 90
305 – 1 n. multicoloured . . . 75 75
306 – 2 n. multicoloured . . . 1·75 3·00

DESIGNS—HORIZ: 2 k. Natural gas tanks; 3 k. Cement works; 5 k. Cattle-ranching; 7 k. Timber mill; 8 k. Oil refinery; 10 k. Cheetahs, Yankari Game Reserve; 12 k. New Civic Building; 15 k. Sugar-cane harvesting; 20 k. Vaccine production; 25 k. Modern wharf; 35 k. Textile machinery; 1 n. Eko Bridge; 2 n. Teaching Hospital, Lagos. VERT: 18 k. Palm oil production; 30 k. Argungu Fishing Festival; 50 k. Pottery.

179 Athlete

1973. Second All-African Games, Lagos.
307 **179** 5 k. lilac, blue and black . 15 10
308 – 12 k. multicoloured . . . 25 50
309 – 18 k. multicoloured . . . 60 1·00
310 – 25 k. multicoloured . . . 70 1·50
DESIGNS—HORIZ: 12 k. Football; 18 k. Table tennis. VERT: 25 k. National stadium.

180 All-Africa House, Addis Ababa

1973. 10th Anniv of O.A.U. Multicoloured.
311 5 k. Type **180** 10 10
312 18 k. O.A.U. flag (vert) . . . 30 40
313 30 k. O.A.U. emblem and symbolic flight of ten stairs (vert) 50 80

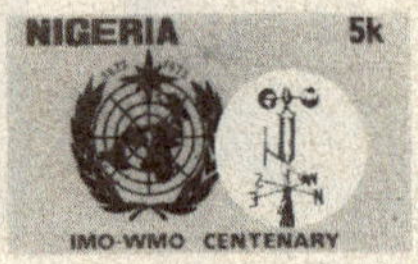

181 Dr. Hansen **182** W.M.O. Emblem and Weather-vane

1973. Cent of Discovery of Leprosy Bacillus.
314 **181** 5 k. + 2 k. brown, pink and black 30 70

1973. Centenary of I.M.O./W.M.O.
315 **182** 5 k. multicoloured 30 10
316 30 k. multicoloured . . . 1·50 2·25

183 University Complex

1973. 25th Anniv of Ibadan University. Multicoloured.
317 5 k. Type **183** 10 10
318 12 k. Students' population growth (vert) 25 30
319 18 k. Tower and students . . . 35 55
320 30 k. Teaching Hospital . . . 50 85

184 Lagos 1d. Stamp of 1874

1974. Stamp Centenary.
321 – 5 k. green, orange & black . 20 10
322 – 12 k. multicoloured . . . 60 60
323 **184** 18 k. green, mauve & blk . 80 1·00
324 – 30 k. multicoloured . . . 2·25 2·50
DESIGNS: 5 k. Graph of mail traffic growth; 12 k. Northern Nigeria £25 stamp of 1904; 30 k. Forms of mail transport.

185 U.P.U. Emblem on Globe

1974. Centenary of U.P.U.
325 **185** 5 k. blue, orange & black . . 15 10
326 – 18 k. multicoloured . . . 2·00 60
327 – 30 k. brown, green & black 1·75 1·75
DESIGNS: 18 k. World transport map; 30 k. U.P.U. emblem and letters.

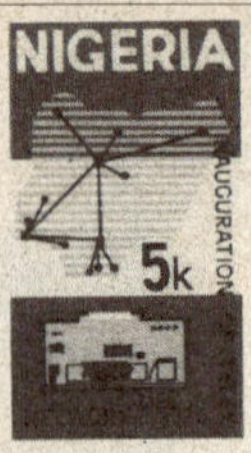

186 Starving and Well-fed Children **187** Telex Network and Teleprinter

1974. Freedom from Hunger Campaign.
328 **186** 5 k. green, buff and black 10 10
329 – 12 k. multicoloured . . . 40 50
330 – 30 k. multicoloured . . . 1·10 1·75
DESIGNS—HORIZ: 12 k. Poultry battery. VERT: 30 k. Water-hoist.

1975. Inauguration of Telex Network.
331 **187** 5 k. black, orange & green 10 10
332 – 12 k. black, yellow & brn 20 20
333 – 18 k. multicoloured . . . 30 30
334 – 30 k. multicoloured . . . 50 50
DESIGNS: 12, 18, 30 k. are as Type **187** but with the motifs arranged differently.

188 Queen Amina of Zaria **190** Alexander Graham Bell

1975. International Women's Year.
335 **188** 5 k. green, yellow and blue 20 10
336 18 k. purple, blue & mauve 80 80
337 30 k. multicoloured . . . 95 1·60

1976. Centenary of Telephone.
355 **190** 5 k. multicoloured . . . 10 10
356 – 18 k. multicoloured . . . 40 55
357 – 25 k. blue, light blue and brown . . . . 70 1·00
DESIGNS—HORIZ: 18 k. Gong and modern telephone system. VERT: 25 k. Telephones, 1876 and 1976.

191 Child writing

1976. Launching of Universal Primary Education.
358 **191** 5 k. yellow, violet & mauve 10 10
359 – 18 k. multicoloured . . . 45 60
360 – 25 k. multicoloured . . . 70 85
DESIGNS—VERT: 18 k. Children entering school; 25 k. Children in class.

192 Festival Emblem

1976. 2nd World Black and African Festival of Arts and Culture, Nigeria.
361 **192** 5 k. gold and brown . . . 25 10
362 – 10 k. brown, yellow & blk 35 40
363 – 12 k. multicoloured . . . 60 55
364 – 18 k. yellow, brown & blk 80 80
365 – 30 k. red and black . . . 1·00 1·50
DESIGNS: 10 k. National Arts Theatre; 12 k. African hair-styles; 18 k. Musical instruments; 30 k. "Nigerian arts and crafts".

193 General Murtala Muhammed and Map of Nigeria **194** Scouts saluting

1977. 1st Death Anniv of General Muhammed (Head of State). Multicoloured.
366 5 k. Type **193** 10 10
367 18 k. General in dress uniform (vert) 20 35
368 30 k. General in battle dress (vert) 30 70

1977. 1st All-African Scout Jamboree, Jos, Nigeria. Multicoloured.
369 5 k. Type **194** 15 10
370 18 k. Scouts cleaning street (horiz) 70 70
371 25 k. Scouts working on farm (horiz) . . . . 85 1·25
372 30 k. Jamboree emblem and map of Africa (horiz) . . . . . . 1·10 2·00

195 Trade Fair Complex

1977. 1st Lagos Int Trade Fair.
373 **195** 5 k. black, blue & green . 10 10
374 – 18 k. black, blue & purple 20 25
375 – 30 k. multicoloured . . . 30 45
DESIGNS: 18 k. Globe and Trade Fair emblem; 30 k. Weaving and basketry.

196 Map showing Nigerian Universities

1978. Global Conference on Technical Co-operation between Developing Countries, Buenos Aires.
376 **196** 5 k. multicoloured 10 10
377 – 12 k. multicoloured . . . 15 15
378 – 18 k. multicoloured . . . 25 25
379 – 30 k. yellow, violet & black 45 60
DESIGNS: 12 k. Map of West African highways and telecommunications; 18 k. Technologists undergoing training; 30 k. World map.

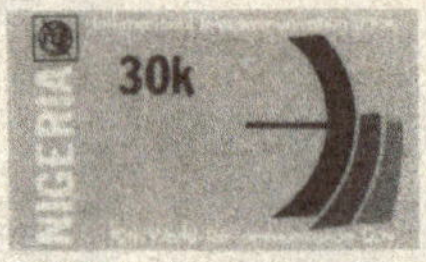

197 Microwave Antenna

1978. 10th World Telecommunications Day.
380 **197** 30 k. multicoloured . . . 50 60

198 Students on "Operation Feed the Nation"

1978. "Operation Feed the Nation" Campaign. Multicoloured.
381 5 k. Type **198** 10 10
382 18 k. Family backyard farm . 20 20
383 30 k. Plantain farm (vert) . . . 35 60

199 Mother with Infected Child

1978. Global Eradication of Smallpox.
384 **199** 5 k. black, brown & lilac . 20 10
385 – 12 k. multicoloured . . . 30 20
386 – 18 k. black, brown & yell 55 40
387 – 30 k. black, silver & pink . 70 70
DESIGNS—HORIZ: 12 k. Doctor and infected child; 18 k. Group of children being vaccinated. VERT: 30 k. Syringe.

200 Nok Terracotta Human Figure Bwari, (900 B.C.–100 A.D.) **201** Anti-Apartheid Emblem

1978. Antiquities.
388 **200** 5 k. black, blue and red . 10 10
389 – 12 k. multicoloured . . . 15 10
390 – 18 k. black, blue and red . 20 15
391 – 30 k. multicoloured . . . 25 20
DESIGNS—HORIZ: 12 k. Igbo-Ukwu bronze snail shell, Igbo Isaiah (9th-century A.D.). VERT: 18 k. Ife bronze statue of a king (12th–15th century A.D.); 30 k. Benin bronze equestrian figure (about 1700 A.D.).

1978. International Anti-Apartheid Year.
392 **201** 18 k. black, yellow and red 15 15

202 Wright Brothers and Wright Type A

1978. 75th Anniv of Powered Flight.
393 **202** 5 k. multicoloured 25 10
394 – 18 k. black, blue and light blue . . . . 1·00 20
DESIGN: 18 k. Nigerian Air Force formation.

203 Murtala Muhammed Airport

1979. Opening of Murtala Muhammed Airport.
395 **203** 5 k. black, grey and blue . 40 30

204 Child with Stamp Album

1979. 10th Anniv of National Philatelic Service.
396 **204** 5 k. multicoloured 10 10

205 Mother and Child

1979. International Year of the Child. Multicoloured.
397 5 k. Type **205** 15 10
398 18 k. Children studying . . . 50 30
399 25 k. Children playing (vert) . 60 50

206 Trainee Teacher making Audio Visual Aid Materials **207** Necom House

1979. 50th Anniv of International Bureau of Education. Multicoloured.
400 10 k. Type **206** 10 10
401 30 k. Adult education class . 25 30

1979. 50th Anniv of Consultative Committee of International Radio.
402 **207** 10 k. multicoloured . . . 15 20

208 Trainees of the Regional Air Survey School, Ile-Ife

1979. 21st Anniv of Economic Commission for Africa.
403 **208** 10 k. multicoloured . . . 20 20

209 Football Cup and Map of Nigeria

1980. African Cup of Nations Football Competition, Nigeria. Multicoloured.
404 10 k. Type **209** 20 10
405 30 k. Footballer (vert) 60 50

210 Wrestling

1980. Olympic Games, Moscow.

406	210	10 k. multicoloured	10	10
407	–	20 k. black and green	10	10
408	–	30 k. black, orange & blue	15	15
409	–	45 k. multicoloured	20	20

DESIGNS—VERT: 20 k. Long jump; 45 k. Netball. HORIZ: 30 k. Swimming.

211 Figures supporting O.P.E.C. Emblem

1980. 20th Anniv of O.P.E.C. (Organization of Petroleum Exporting Countries).

410	211	10 k. black, blue & yellow	25	10
411	–	45 k. black, blue & mauve	1·00	60

DESIGN—VERT: 45 k. O.P.E.C. emblem and globe.

212 Tank Locomotive No. 2, Wushishi Tramway

1980. 25th Anniv of Nigerian Railway Corporation. Multicoloured.

412	10 k. Type 212	75	10
413	20 k. Loading goods train	1·50	85
414	30 k. Freight train	2·00	1·25

213 Metric Scales

215 Disabled Woman sweeping

214 "Communication" Symbols and Map of West Africa

1980. World Standards Day.

415	213	10 k. red and black	10	10
416	–	30 k. multicoloured	35	40

DESIGN—HORIZ: 30 k. Quality control.

1980. 5th Anniv of Economic Community of West African States.

417	214	10 k. black, orange & olive	10	10
418	–	25 k. black, green & red	30	10
419	–	30 k. black, yellow & brn	20	15
420	–	45 k. black, turq & blue	25	25

DESIGNS: 25 k. "Transport"; 30 k. "Agriculture"; 45 k. "Industry".

1981. International Year for Disabled Persons.

421	215	10 k. multicoloured	20	10
422	–	30 k. black, brown & blue	65	65

DESIGN: 30 k. Disabled man filming.

216 President launching "Green Revolution" (food production campaign)

1981. World Food Day.

423	216	10 k. multicoloured	10	10
424	–	25 k. black, yellow & green	20	50
425	–	30 k. multicoloured	25	55
426	–	45 k. black, brown & yell	45	85

DESIGNS—VERT: 25 k. Food crops; 30 k. Harvesting tomatoes. HORIZ: 45 k. Pig farming.

217 Rioting in Soweto

1981. Anti-Apartheid Movement.

427	217	30 k. multicoloured	35	45
428	–	45 k. black, red and green	50	80

DESIGN—VERT: 45 k. "Police brutality".

218 "Preservation of Wildlife"

1982. 75th Anniv of Boy Scout Movement. Multicoloured.

429	30 k. Type 218	50	55
430	45 k. Lord Baden-Powell taking salute	75	95

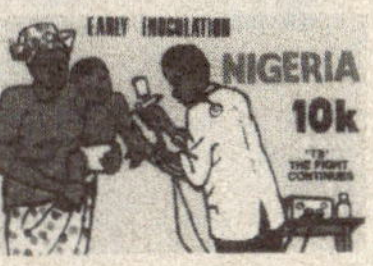

219 Early Inoculation

1982. Centenary of Robert Koch's Discovery of Tubercle Bacillus.

431	219	10 k. multicoloured	20	15
432	–	30 k. black, brown and green	50	65
433	–	45 k. black, brown and green	80	1·40

DESIGNS—HORIZ: 30 k. Technician and microscope. VERT: 45 k. Patient being X-rayed.

220 "Keep Your Environment Clean"

1982. 10th Anniv of U.N. Conference on Human Environment.

434	220	10 k. multicoloured	15	10
435	–	20 k. orange, grey and black	30	40
436	–	30 k. multicoloured	45	60
437	–	45 k. multicoloured	65	85

DESIGNS: 20 k. "Check air pollution"; 30 k. "Preserve natural environment"; 45 k. "Reafforestation concerns all".

221 "Salamis parhassus"

222 Carving of "Male and Female Twins"

1982. Nigerian Butterflies. Multicoloured.

438	10 k. Type 221	15	10
439	20 k. "Iterus zalmoxis"	30	30
440	30 k. "Cymothoe beckeri"	40	40
441	45 k. "Papilio hesperus"	70	70

1982. 25th Anniv of National Museum. Multicoloured.

442	10 k. Type 222	20	10
443	20 k. Royal bronze leopard (horiz)	30	35
444	30 k. Soapstone seated figure	50	90
445	45 k. Wooden helmet mask	70	1·50

223 Three Generations

1983. Family Day. Multicoloured.

446	10 k. Type 223	15	10
447	30 k. Parents with three children (vert)	50	65

224 Satellite View of Globe

1983. Commonwealth Day.

448	224	10 k. brown and black	10	10
449	–	25 k. multicoloured	20	30
450	–	30 k. black, purple & grey	55	35
451	–	45 k. multicoloured	35	45

DESIGNS—HORIZ: 25 k. National Assembly Buildings. VERT: 30 k. Drilling for oil; 45 k. Athletics.

225 Corps Members on Building Project

226 Postman on Bicycle

1983. 10th Anniv of National Youth Service Corps. Multicoloured.

452	10 k. Type 225	15	10
453	25 k. On the assault-course (vert)	30	30
454	30 k. Corps members on parade	40	40

1983. World Communications Year. Multicoloured.

455	10 k. Type 226	15	10
456	25 k. Newspaper kiosk (horiz)	30	40
457	30 k. Town crier blowing elephant tusk (horiz)	35	45
458	45 k. T.V. newsreader (horiz)	45	55

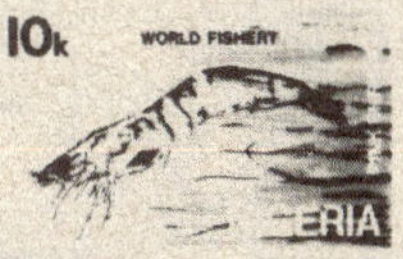

227 Pink Shrimp

1983. World Fishery Resources.

459	227	10 k. red, blue and black	15	10
460	–	25 k. multicoloured	30	40
461	–	30 k. multicoloured	30	45
462	–	45 k. multicoloured	40	70

DESIGNS: 25 k. Long-necked croaker; 30 k. Barracuda; 45 k. Fishing techniques.

228 On Parade

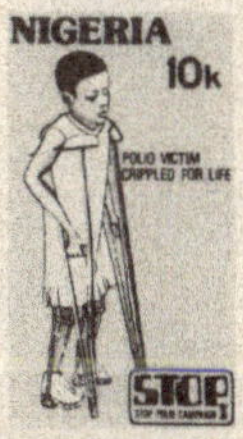

229 Crippled Child

1983. Centenary of Boys' Brigade and 75th Anniv of Founding in Nigeria. Multicoloured.

463	10 k. Type 228	40	10
464	30 k. Members working on cassava plantation (horiz)	1·50	1·50
465	45 k. Skill training (horiz)	2·25	2·75

1984. Stop Polio Campaign.

466	229	10 k. blue, black & brown	20	15
467	–	25 k. orange, black & yell	40	75
468	–	30 k. red, black & brown	60	1·10

DESIGNS—HORIZ: 25 k. Child receiving vaccine. VERT: 30 k. Healthy child.

230 Waterbuck

232 Boxing

231 Obverse and Reverse of 1969 £1 Note

1984. Nigerian Wildlife.

469	230	10 k. green, brown & black	20	10
470	–	25 k. multicoloured	40	50
471	–	30 k. brown, black & green	50	90
472	–	45 k. blue, orange & black	60	1·25

DESIGNS—HORIZ: 25 k. Hartebeest; 30 k. African buffalo. VERT: 45 k. Diademed monkey.

1984. 25th Anniv of Nigerian Central Bank.

473	231	10 k. multicoloured	20	10
474	–	25 k. brown, black & green	45	50
475	–	30 k. red, black and green	55	60

DESIGNS: 25 k. Central Bank; 30 k. Obverse and reverse of 1959 £5 note.

1984. Olympic Games, Los Angeles. Mult.

476	10 k. Type 232	15	10
477	25 k. Discus-throwing	35	50
478	30 k. Weightlifting	40	60
479	45 k. Cycling	60	90

233 Irrigation Project, Lesotho

234 Pin-tailed Whydah

1984. 20th Anniv of African Development Bank.

480	233	10 k. multicoloured	15	10
481	–	25 k. multicoloured	30	50
482	–	30 k. black, yellow & blue	35	60
483	–	45 k. black, brown & blue	1·75	90

DESIGNS—HORIZ: 25 k. Bomi Hills Road, Liberia; 30 k. School building project, Seychelles; 45 k. Coal mining Niger.

1984. Rare Birds. Multicoloured.

484	10 k. Type 234	75	20
485	25 k. Spur-winged plover	1·50	70
486	30 k. Red bishop	1·50	1·75
487	45 k. Double-spurred francolin	1·75	2·50

235 Boeing 747 Airliner taking-off

1984. 40th Anniv of International Civil Aviation Organization. Multicoloured.

488	10 k. Type 235	40	10
489	45 k. Boeing 707 airliner circling globe	1·50	2·25

236 Office Workers and Clocks ("Punctuality")

1985. "War against Indiscipline". Mult.

490	20 k. Type 236	30	35
491	50 k. Cross over hands passing banknotes ("Discourage Bribery")	55	75

237 Footballers receiving Flag from Major-General Buhari

239 Globe and O.P.E.C. Emblem

238 Rolling Mill

1985. International Youth Year. Mult.

492	20 k. Type 237	30	20
493	50 k. Girls of different tribes with flag (vert)	55	70
494	55 k. Members of youth organizations with flags (vert)	55	80

1985. 25th Anniv of Independence. Mult.

495	20 k. Type 238	25	10
496	50 k. Map of Nigeria	40	35
497	55 k. Remembrance Arcade	40	40
498	60 k. Eleme, first Nigerian oil refinery	1·00	50

1985. 25th Anniv of Organization of Petroleum Exporting Countries.

500	239	20 k. blue and red	75	35
501	–	50 k. black and blue	1·50	75

DESIGN—HORIZ: 50 k. World map and O.P.E.C. emblem.

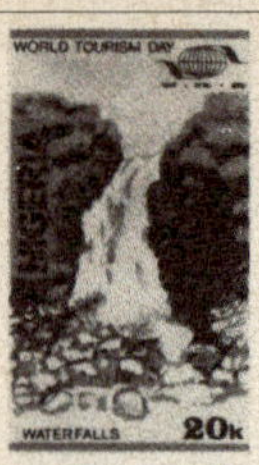

240 Waterfall

241 Map of Nigeria and National Flag

1985. World Tourism Day. Multicoloured.
502 20 k. Type **240** 35 10
503 50 k. Pottery, carved heads and map of Nigeria (horiz) 45 50
504 55 k. Calabash carvings and Nigerian flag 45 50
505 60 k. Leather work 45 55

1985. 40th Anniv of United Nations Organization and 25th Anniv of Nigerian Membership.
506 **241** 20 k. black, green & blue 20 10
507 – 50 k. black, blue & red 35 50
508 – 55 k. black, blue & red 35 60
DESIGNS—HORIZ: 50 k. United Nations Building, New York; 55 k. United Nations logo.

242 Rock Python

243 Social Worker with Children

1986. African Reptiles.
509 **242** 10 k. multicoloured 30 10
510 – 20 k. black, brown & blue 50 70
511 – 25 k. multicoloured 50 80
512 – 30 k. multicoloured 50 80
DESIGNS: 20 k. Long snouted crocodile; 25 k. Gopher tortoise; 30 k. Chameleon.

1986. Nigerian Life. Multicoloured.
513 1 k. Type **243** 10 20
514 2 k. Volkswagen motor assembly line (horiz) 10 20
515 5 k. Modern housing estate (horiz) 10 20
516 10 k. Harvesting oil palm fruit 10 10
517 15 k. Unloading freighter (horiz) 10 10
518 20 k. "Tecoma stans" (flower) 10 10
519 25 k. Hospital ward (horiz) 10 10
519a 30 k. Birom dancers (horiz) 10 10
520 35 k. Telephonists operating switchboard (horiz) 10 10
521 40 k. Nkpokiti dancers 10 10
522 45 k. Hibiscus (horiz) 10 10
523a 50 k. Post Office counter (horiz) 10 10
524 1 n. Stone quarry (horiz) 10 10
525a 2 n. Students in laboratory (horiz) 10 10
525ba 10 n. Lekki Beach (horiz) 55 60
525c 20 n. Ancient wall, Kano (horiz) 4·00 1·50
525d 50 n. Rock bridge (horiz) 2·75 3·00
525e 100 n. Ekpe masquerader 5·50 5·75
525f 500 n. National Theatre (horiz) 27·00 28·00

244 Emblem and Globe

1986. International Peace Year. Mult.
526 10 k. Type **244** 20 10
527 20 k. Hands of five races holding globe 60 1·00

245 "Goliathus goliathus" (beetle)

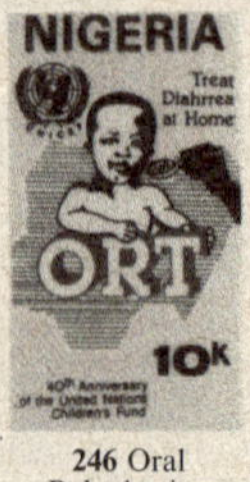

246 Oral Rehydration Therapy

1986. Nigerian Insects. Multicoloured.
528 10 k. Type **245** 30 10
529 20 k. "Vespa vulgaris" (wasp) 40 40
530 25 k. "Acheta domestica" (cricket) 45 70
531 30 k. "Anthrenus verbasci" (beetle) 55 1·00

1986. 40th Anniv of U.N.I.C.E.F.
533 **246** 10 k. multicoloured 30 10
534 – 20 k. black, brown & yell 40 40
535 – 25 k. multicoloured 45 70
536 – 30 k. multicoloured 55 1·00
DESIGNS: 20 k. Immunisation; 25 k. Breast feeding; 30 k. Mother and child.

247 Stylized Figures on Wall ("International Understanding")

1986. 25th Anniv of Nigerian Institute of International Affairs.
537 **247** 20 k. black, blue & green 50 50
538 – 30 k. multicoloured 75 1·25
DESIGN—VERT: 30 k. "Knowledge" (bronze sculpture).

248 Freshwater Clam

1987. Shells.
539 **248** 10 k. multicoloured 65 10
540 – 20 k. black, brown & pink 1·25 1·75
541 – 25 k. multicoloured 1·50 2·00
542 – 30 k. multicoloured 1·75 2·50
DESIGNS: 20 k. Periwinkle; 25 k. Bloody cockle (inscr "BLODDY COCKLE"); 30 k. Mangrove oyster.

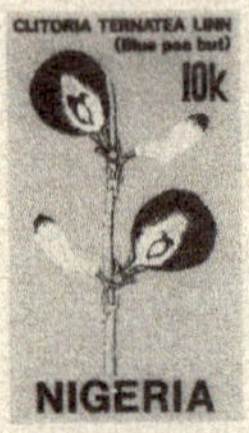

249 "Clitoria ternatea"

250 Doka Hairstyle

1987. Nigerian Flowers.
543 **249** 10 k. multicoloured 10 10
544 – 20 k. brown, yellow and green 15 10
545 – 25 k. multicoloured 15 15
546 – 30 k. multicoloured 20 30
DESIGNS: 20 k. "Hibiscus tiliaceus"; 25 k. "Acanthus montanus"; 30 k. "Combretum racemosum".

1987. Women's Hairstyles.
547 **250** 10 k. black, brown and grey 10 10
548 – 20 k. multicoloured 15 20
549 – 25 k. black, brown and red 20 30
550 – 30 k. multicoloured 20 30
DESIGNS: 20 k. Eting; 25 k. Agogo; 30 k. Goto.

251 Family sheltering under Tree

252 Red Cross Worker distributing Food

1987. International Year of Shelter for the Homeless. Multicoloured.
551 20 k. Type **251** 15 10
552 30 k. Family and modern house 15 20

1988. 125th Anniv of International Red Cross. Multicoloured.
553 20 k. Type **252** 65 30
554 30 k. Carrying patient to ambulance 65 95

253 Doctor vaccinating Baby

254 O.A.U. Logo

1988. 40th Anniv of W.H.O. Multicoloured.
555 10 k. Type **253** 25 10
556 20 k. W.H.O. logo and outline map of Nigeria 60 60
557 30 k. Doctor and patients at mobile clinic 60 60

1988. 25th Anniv of Organization of African Unity.
558 **254** 10 k. brown, green & orge 15 15
559 – 20 k. multicoloured 15 15
DESIGN: 20 k. Four Africans supporting map of Africa.

255 Pink Shrimp

1988. Shrimps.
560 **255** 10 k. multicoloured 25 10
561 – 20 k. black and green 40 15
562 – 25 k. black, red & brown 45 25
563 – 30 k. orange, brown & blk 55 50
DESIGNS: 20 k. Tiger shrimp; 25 k. Deepwater roseshrimp; 30 k. Estuarine prawn.

256 Weightlifting

1988. Olympic Games, Seoul. Multicoloured.
565 10 k. Type **256** 25 10
566 20 k. Boxing 35 35
567 30 k. Athletics (vert) 45 55

257 Banknote Production Line (½-size illustration)

1988. 25th Anniv of Nigerian Security Printing and Minting Co. Ltd.
568 **257** 10 k. multicoloured 10 10
569 – 20 k. black, silver & green 20 20
570 – 25 k. multicoloured 30 30
571 – 30 k. multicoloured 45 45
DESIGNS—HORIZ (As T **257**): 20 k. Coin production line. VERT (37 × 44 mm): 25 k. Montage of products; 30 k. Anniversary logos.

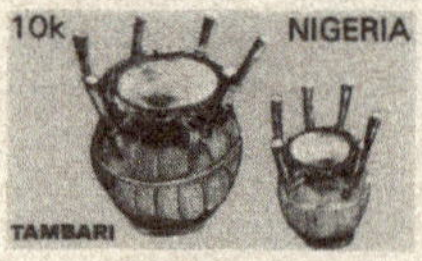

258 Tambari

1989. Nigerian Musical Instruments.
572 **258** 10 k. multicoloured 10 10
573 – 20 k. multicoloured 20 20
574 – 25 k. brown, green & black 30 30
575 – 30 k. brown and black 45 45
DESIGNS: 20 k. Kundung; 25 k. Ibid; 30 k. Dundun.

259 Construction of Water Towers, Mali

1989. 25th Anniv of African Development Bank. Multicoloured.
576 10 k. Type **259** 10 10
577 20 k. Paddy field, Gambia 15 15
578 25 k. Bank Headquarters, Abidjan, Ivory Coast 25 25
579 30 k. Anniversary logo (vert) 35 35

260 Lighting Campfire

1989. 70th Anniv of Nigerian Girl Guides Association. Multicoloured.
580 10 k. Type **260** 30 10
581 20 k. Guide on rope bridge (vert) 60 60

261 Etubom Costume

262 Dove with Letter and Map of Africa

1989. Traditional Costumes. Multicoloured.
582 10 k. Type **261** 15 10
583 20 k. Fulfulde 25 25
584 25 k. Aso-Ofi 35 40
585 30 k. Fuska Kura 45 60

1990. 10th Anniv of Pan African Postal Union. Multicoloured.
586 10 k. Type **262** 25 10
587 20 k. Parcel and map of Africa 50 50

263 Oil Lamps

1990. Nigerian Pottery.
588 **263** 10 k. black, brown & violet 10 10
589 – 20 k. black, brown & violet 20 20
590 – 25 k. brown and violet 25 25
591 – 30 k. multicoloured 35 35
DESIGNS: 20 k. Water pots; 25 k. Musical pots; 50 k. Water jugs.

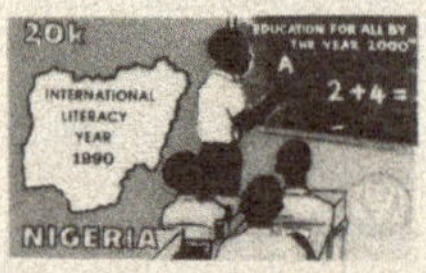

264 Teacher and Class

1990. International Literacy Year.
593 **264** 20 k. multicoloured 20 10
594 – 30 k. brown, blue & yellow 30 30
DESIGN: 30 k. Globe and book.

265 Globe and OPEC Logo

1990. 30th Anniv of the Organization of Petroleum Exporting Countries. Multicoloured.
595 10 k. Type **265** 10 10
596 20 k. Logo and flags of member countries (vert) 20 20
597 25 k. World map and logo 25 25
598 30 k. Logo within inscription "Co-operation for Global Energy Security" (vert) 35 35

266 Grey Parrot

267 Eradication Treatment

1990. Wildlife. Multicoloured.
599 20 k. Type **266** 20 10
600 30 k. Roan antelope 20 10
601 1 n. 50 Grey-necked bald crow ("Rockfowl") 60 80
602 2 n. 50 Mountain gorilla 85 1·25

1991. National Guineaworm Eradication Day. Multicoloured.
604 10 k. Type **267** 15 10
605 20 k. Women collecting water from river (horiz) 25 25
606 30 k. Boiling pot of water 25 25

268 Hand holding Torch (Progress)

269 National Flags

1991. Organization of African Unity Heads of State and Governments Meeting, Abuja. Each showing outline map of Africa. Multicoloured.
607 20 k. Type **268** 15 10
608 30 k. Cogwheel (Unity) 20 25
609 50 k. O.A.U. flag (Freedom) 20 45

1991. Economic Community of West African States Summit Meeting, Abuja. Multicoloured.
610 20 k. Type **269** 15 10
611 50 k. Map showing member states 30 45

270 Electric Catfish

1991. Nigerian Fishes. Multicoloured.

612	10 k. Type **270**	15	10
613	20 k. Nile perch	25	25
614	30 k. Nile mouthbrooder ("Talapia")	35	35
615	50 k. Sharp-toothed catfish	50	55

271 Telecom '91 Emblem

1991. "Telecom '91" 6th World Telecommunication Exhibition, Geneva.

617	**271**	20 k. black, green & violet	30	10
618	–	50 k. multicoloured	40	30

DESIGN—VERT: 50 k. Emblem and patchwork.

272 Boxing

1992. Olympic Games, Barcelona (1st issue). Multicoloured.

619	50 k. Type **272**	15	15
620	1 n. Nigerian athlete winning race	25	25
621	1 n. 50 Table tennis	35	35
622	2 n. Taekwondo	45	45

See also No. 624.

273 Football — 274 Blood Pressure Gauge

1992. Olympic Games, Barcelona (2nd issue).

624	**273**	1 n. 50 multicoloured	50	50

1992. World Health Day. Multicoloured.

625	50 k. Type **274**	15	15
626	1 n. World Health Day '92 emblem	20	20
627	1 n. 50 Heart and lungs	30	30
628	2 n. Interior of heart	40	40

275 Map of World and Stamp on Globe

1992. "Olymphilex '92" Olympic Stamp Exhibition, Barcelona. Multicoloured.

630	50 k. Type **275**	20	10
631	1 n. 50 Examining stamps	40	40

276 Gathering Plantain Fruit — 277 Centre Emblem

1992. 25th Anniv of International Institute of Tropical Agriculture.

633	**276**	50 k. multicoloured	10	10
634	–	1 n. multicoloured	15	15
635	–	1 n. 50 black, brown & grn	20	20
636	–	2 n. multicoloured	25	25

DESIGNS—VERT: 1 n. 50, Harvesting cassava tubers; 2 n. Stacking yams. HORIZ: 1 n. Tropical foods.

1992. Commissioning of Maryam Babangida National Centre for Women's Development.

638	**277**	50 k. gold, emerald and green	10	10
639	–	1 n. multicoloured	15	15
640	–	1 n. 50 multicoloured	20	20
641	–	2 n. multicoloured	30	30

DESIGNS—VERT: 1 n. Women working in fields; 2 n. Woman at loom. HORIZ: 1 n. 50, Maryam Babangida National Centre.

All examples of No. 641 are without a "NIGERIA" inscription.

278 Healthy Food and Emblem — 279 Sabada Dance

1992. International Conference on Nutrition, Rome. Multicoloured.

642	50 k. Type **278**	10	10
643	1 n. Child eating	15	15
644	1 n. 50 Fruit (vert)	20	20
645	2 n. Vegetables	25	25

1992. Traditional Dances. Multicoloured.

647	50 k. Type **279**	10	10
648	1 n. Sato	15	15
649	1 n. 50 Asian Ubo Ikpa	20	20
650	2 n. Dundun	25	25

280 African Elephant

1993. Wildlife. Multicoloured.

652	1 n. 50 Type **280**	20	10
653	5 n. Stanley crane (vert)	60	25
654	20 n. Roan antelope	2·50	1·40
655	30 n. Lion	4·00	2·00

281 Suburban Garden

1993. World Environment Day. Multicoloured.

656	1 n. Type **281**	10	10
657	1 n. 50 Water pollution	15	10
658	5 n. Forest road	50	50
659	10 n. Rural house	90	90

282 Oni Figure — 283 "Bulbophyllum distans"

1993. 50th Anniv of National Museums and Monuments Commission. Multicoloured.

660	1 n Type **282**	10	10
661	1 n. 50 Bronze head of Queen Mother	10	10
662	5 n. Bronze pendant (horiz)	30	35
663	10 n. Nok head	70	75

1993. Orchids. Multicoloured.

664	1 n. Type **283**	10	10
665	1 n. 50 "Eulophia cristata"	15	10
666	5 n. "Eulophia horsfalli"	45	45
667	10 n. "Eulophia quartiniana"	1·00	1·10

284 Children in Classroom and Adults carrying Food

1994. International Year of the Family. Mult.

669	1 n. 50 Type **284**	10	10
670	10 n. Market	1·00	1·00

285 Hand with Tweezers holding 1969 4d. Philatelic Service Stamp

1994. 25th Anniv of Nat Philatelic Service. Mult.

671	1 n. Type **285**	10	10
672	1 n. 50 Philatelic Bureau	15	10
673	5 n. Stamps forming map of Nigeria	45	45
674	10 n. Philatelic counter	1·00	1·10

286 "I Love Stamps"

1994. 120th Anniv of First Postage Stamps in Nigeria. Multicoloured.

675	1 n. Type **286**	10	10
676	1 n. 50 "I Collect Stamps"	15	15
677	5 n. 19th-century means of communication	45	45
678	10 n. Lagos stamp of 1874	1·00	1·10

287 Magnifying Glass over Globe

1994. "Philakorea '94" International Stamp Exhibition, Seoul.

679	**287**	30 n. multicoloured	1·75	2·40

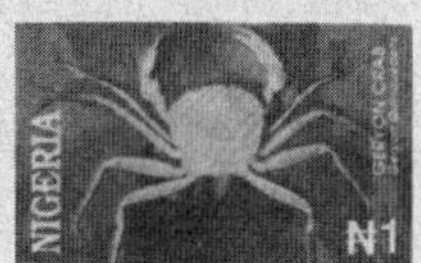

288 Geryon Crab

1994. Crabs. Multicoloured.

681	1 n. Type **288**	10	10
682	1 n. 50 Spider crab	10	10
683	5 n. Red spider crab	45	45
684	10 n. Geryon maritae crab	90	90

289 Sewage Works — 290 Letterbox

1994. 30th Anniv of African Development Bank. Multicoloured.

685	1 n. 50 Type **289**	15	10
686	30 n. Development Bank emblem and flowers	1·75	2·40

1995. 10th Anniv of Nigerian Post and Telecommunication Corporations. Multicoloured.

687	1 n. Type **290**	10	10
688	1 n. 50 Letter showing "1 JAN 1985" postmark (horiz)	10	10
689	5 n. Nipost and Nitel emblems (horiz)	30	35
690	10 n. Mobile telephones	60	65

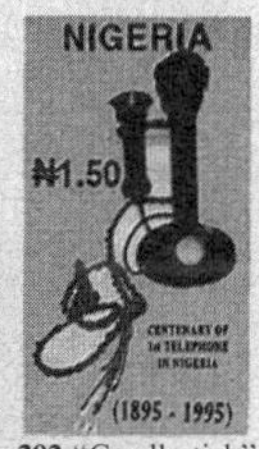

291 Woman preparing Food — 292 "Candlestick" Telephone

1995. Family Support Programme. Multicoloured.

691	1 n. Type **291**	10	10
692	1 n. 50 Mother teaching children	10	10
693	5 n. Family meal	30	35
694	10 n. Agricultural workers and tractor	60	65

1995. Cent of First Telephone in Nigeria. Mult.

695	1 n. 50 Type **292**	10	10
696	10 n. Early equipment	60	65

293 F.A.O. Emblem — 294 "Justice" and 50th Anniversary Emblem

1995. 50th Anniv of F.A.O. Multicoloured.

697	1 n. 50 Type **293**	10	10
698	30 n. Fishing canoes	1·90	2·00

1995. 50th Anniv of United Nations. Multicoloured.

699	1 n. Type **294**	10	10
700	1 n. 50 Toxic waste (horiz)	10	10
701	5 n. Tourist hut (horiz)	30	35
702	10 n. Nigerian armoured car on U.N. duty (horiz)	90	95

295 Container Ship in Dock

1996. 10th Anniv of Niger Dock. Multicoloured.

703	5 n. Type **295**	35	30
704	10 n. "Badagri" (tourist launch) on crane	65	60
705	20 n. Shipping at dock	1·25	1·50
706	30 n. "Odoragushin" (ferry)	2·00	2·50

296 Scientist and Crops

1996. 21st Anniv of E.C.O.W.A.S. (Economic Community of West African States). Multicoloured.

707	5 n. Type **296**	30	30
708	30 n. Queue at border crossing	1·50	2·00

297 Judo — 298 Nigerian Flag and Exhibition Emblem

1996. Olympic Games, Atlanta. Multicoloured.

709	5 n. Type **297**	35	30
710	10 n. Tennis	80	60
711	20 n. Relay race	1·25	1·50
712	30 n. Football	1·75	2·25

1996. "ISTANBUL '96" International Stamp Exhibition.

713	**298**	30 n. mauve, green and black	1·50	2·00

299 "Volvariella esculenta" — 300 Boy with Toys

1996. Fungi. Multicoloured.

714	5 n. Type **299**	45	30
715	10 n. "Lentinus subnudus"	90	60
716	20 n. "Tricholoma lobayensis"	1·50	1·50
717	30 n. "Pleurotus tuber-regium"	2·00	2·25

1996. 50th Anniv of U.N.I.C.E.F. Multicoloured.

718	5 n. Type **300**	30	30
719	30 n. Girl reading book (horiz)	1·50	2·00

301 Literacy Logo

1996. 5th Anniv of Mass Literacy Commission.
720 **301** 5 n. emerald, green and black 30 30
721 – 30 n. emerald, green and black . . . . 1·50 2·00
DESIGN: 30 n. Hands holding book and literacy logo.

302 University Tower and Complex

1998. 50th Anniv of Ibadan University. Mult.
722 5 n. Type **302** 25 30
723 30 n. Anniversary logo and University crest . . . . . . 1·60 1·75

303 Ship and Logo

1998. 8th Anniv of Economic Community of West African States Military Arm (ECOMOG). Multicoloured.
724 5 n. Type **303** 25 30
725 30 n. Logo and original member states . . . . 1·60 1·75
726 50 n. Current member states . 2·75 3·00

304 Football and Globe

1999. 11th World Youth Football Championship, Nigeria. Multicoloured.
727 5 n. + 5 n. Type **304** 15 20
728 10 n. + 5 n. Player throwing ball 20 25
729 20 n. + 5 n. Player scoring goal 35 40
730 30 n. + 5 n. Map of Nigeria showing venues 50 55
731 40 n. + 5 n. World Youth Football Championship logo 60 65
732 50 n. + 5 n. Player being tackled 75 80

POSTAGE DUE STAMPS

D 1

1959.
D1 D 1 1d. orange 10 65
D2 2d. orange 15 80
D3 3d. orange . . . . 20 1·25
D4 6d. orange . . . . 20 4·50
D5 1s. black . . . . 45 6·00

1961.
D 6 D 1 1d. red 10 30
D 7 2d. blue 10 35
D 8 3d. green 15 50
D 9 6d. yellow . . . . 30 1·00
D10 1s. blue . . . . 45 2·00

1973. As Type D **1**.
D11 2 k. red 10 10
D12 3 k. blue 10 10
D13 5 k. yellow 10 10
D14 10 k. green 10 10

NIUAFO'OU

A remote island, part of the Kingdom of Tonga, with local autonomy.

100 seniti = 1 pa'anga

1 Map of Niuafo'ou

4 Eruption of Niuafo'ou

1983.
1 **1** 1 s. stone, black and red . . 20 50
2 2 s. stone, black and green . 20 50
3 3 s. stone, black and blue . . 20 60
4 3 s. stone, black and brown . 20 60
5 5 s. stone, black and purple . 30 60
6 6 s. stone, black and blue . . 30 60
7 9 s. stone, black and green . 30 60
8 10 s. stone, black and blue . 30 60
9 13 s. stone, black and green . 55 65
10 15 s. stone, black and brown 60 90
11 20 s. stone, black and blue . 65 90
12 29 s. stone, black and purple 90 80
13 32 s. stone, black and green . 1·00 90
14 47 s. stone, black and red . . 1·40 1·40

1983. No. 820 of Tonga optd **NIUAFO'OU KINGDOM OF TONGA** or surch also.
15 1 p. on 2 p. green and black . 2·50 3·00
16 2 p. green . . . . 3·50 4·50

1983. Inauguration of Niuafo'ou Airport. As T **153** of Tonga.
17 29 s. multicoloured . . . . . 80 1·00
18 1 p. multicoloured . . . . . . 2·50 3·25

1983. As T **1**, but without value, surch.
19 3 s. stone, black and blue . . . 20 20
20 5 s. stone, black and blue . . . 20 20
21 32 s. stone, black and blue . . 1·50 1·25
22 2 p. stone, black and blue . . 8·00 9·00

1983. 25th Anniv of Re-settlement. Mult.
23 5 s. Type **4** 40 30
24 29 s. Lava flow . . . . 1·00 1·00
25 32 s. Islanders fleeing to safety 1·10 1·00
26 1 p. 50 Evacuation by canoe . 3·50 5·00

5 Purple Swamphen

6 Green Turtle

1983. Birds of Niuafo'ou.
27 **5** 1 s. black and mauve 70 80
28 – 2 s. black and blue 70 80
29 – 3 s. black and green 70 80
30 – 5 s. black and yellow 90 80
31 – 6 s. black and orange . . . 1·00 95
32 – 9 s. multicoloured . . . . . 1·40 95
33 – 10 s. multicoloured . . . . . 1·40 1·40
34 – 13 s. multicoloured . . . . . 1·75 1·40
35 – 15 s. multicoloured . . . . . 1·75 1·75
36 – 20 s. multicoloured . . . . . 2·00 2·00
37 – 29 s. multicoloured . . . . . 2·25 1·50
38 – 32 s. multicoloured . . . . . 2·25 1·60
39 – 47 s. multicoloured . . . . . 3·00 2·25
40 – 1 p. multicoloured . . . . . 5·00 7·00
41 – 2 p. multicoloured . . . . . 7·00 9·50
DESIGNS—VERT (22×29 mm): 2 s. White collared kingfisher; 3 s. Red-headed parrot finch; 5 s. Banded rail; 6 s. Polynesian scrub hen ("Niuafo'ou megapode"); 9 s. Green honeyeater; 10 s. Purple swamphen (different). (22×36 mm): 29 s. Red-headed parrot finch (different); 32 s. White-collared kingfisher (different). (29×42 mm): 1 p. As 10 s. HORIZ (29×22 mm): 13 s. Banded rail (different): 15 s. Polynesian scrub hen (different). (36×22 mm): 20 s. As 13 s.; 47 s. As 15 s. (42×29 mm): 2 p. As 15 s.

1984. Wildlife and Nature Reserve. Mult.
42 29 s. Type **6** 70 70
43 32 s. Insular flying fox (vert) . 70 70
44 47 s. Humpback whale . . . . 2·50 1·75
45 1 p. 50 Polynesian scrub hen ("Niuafo'ou megapode") (vert) 4·50 6·00

7 Diagram of Time Zones

1984. Cent of International Dateline. Mult.
46 47 s. Type **7** 60 50
47 2 p. Location map showing Niuafo'ou . . . . 1·90 2·75

8 Australia 1913 £2 Kangaroo Definitive

9 Dutch Brass Band entertaining Tongans

1984. "Ausipex" International Stamp Exhibition, Melbourne. Multicoloured.
48 32 s. Type **8** 75 60
49 1 p. 50 Niuafo'ou 1983 10 s. map definitive . . . . 2·25 3·00

1985. 400th Birth Anniv of Jacob Le Maire (discoverer of Niuafo'ou).
51 **9** 13 s. brown, yellow & orange 25 40
52 – 32 s. brown, yellow and blue 55 60
53 – 47 s. brown, yellow and green 75 80
54 – 1 p. 50 brown, cinnamon and yellow . . . . 2·25 3·00
DESIGNS: 32 s. Tongans preparing kava; 47 s. Tongan canoes and outriggers; 1 p. 50, "Eendracht" at anchor off Tafahi Island.

10 "Ysabel", 1902

1985. Mail Ships. Multicoloured.
56B 9 s. Type **10** 35 55
57A 13 s. "Tofua I", 1908 . . . . 60 55
58B 47 s. "Mariposa", 1934 . . . 1·10 1·60
59A 1 p. 50 "Matua", 1936 . . . 3·00 3·50

11 Preparing to fire Rocket

1985. Niuafo'ou Rocket Mails. Multicoloured.
60B 32 s. Type **11** 80 80
61A 42 s. Rocket in flight . . . . 1·00 1·00
62B 57 s. Ship's crew watching rocket's descent . . . . . . 1·40 1·40
63A 1 p. 50 Islanders reading mail 3·25 4·00

12 Halley's Comet, 684 A.D.

1986. Appearance of Halley's Comet. Multicoloured.
64 42 s. Type **12** . . . . 4·75 3·00
65 42 s. Halley's Comet, 1066, from Bayeux Tapestry . . . . . . 4·75 3·00
66 42 s. Edmond Halley . . . . . 4·75 3·00
67 42 s. Halley's Comet, 1910 . . . 4·75 3·00
68 42 s. Halley's Comet, 1986 . . . 4·75 3·00
69 57 s. Type **12** . . . . 4·75 3·50
70 57 s. As No. 65 . . . . 4·75 3·50
71 57 s. As No. 66 . . . . 4·75 3·50
72 57 s. As No. 67 . . . . 4·75 3·50
73 57 s. As No. 68 . . . . 4·75 3·50
Nos. 64/8 and 69/73 were printed together, se-tenant, forming composite designs.

1986. Nos. 32/9 surch.
74 4 s. on 9 s. Green honeyeater . 75 1·00
75 4 s. on 10 s. Purple swamphen . 75 1·00
76 42 s. on 13 s. Banded rail . . . 1·75 1·25
77 42 s. on 15 s. Polynesian scrub hen 1·75 1·25
78 57 s. on 29 s. Red-headed parrot finch . . . . 2·25 1·75
79 57 s. on 32 s. White-collared kingfisher . . . . 2·25 1·75
80 2 p. 50 on 20 s. Banded rail . . 6·00 7·00
81 2 p. 50 on 47 s. Polynesian scrub hen . . . . 6·00 7·00

1986. "Ameripex '86" International Stamp Exhibition, Chicago. 25th Anniv of United States Peace Corps. As T **173** of Tonga. Multicoloured.
82 57 s. Peace Corps surveyor and pipeline . . . . 1·25 1·25
83 1 p. 50 Inspecting crops . . . . 2·25 2·75

14 Swimmers with Mail

1986. Centenary of First Tonga Stamps. Designs showing Niuafo'ou mail transport. Multicoloured.
85 42 s. Type **14** 90 90
86 57 s. Collecting tin can mail . . 1·10 1·10
87 1 p. Ship firing mail rocket . . 2·00 2·50
88 2 p. 50 "Collecting the Mails" (detail) (C. Mayger) . . . . 3·50 4·50

15 Woman with Nourishing Foods ("Eat a balanced diet")

1987. Red Cross. Preventive Medicine. Mult.
90 15 s. Type **15** 60 60
91 42 s. Nurse with baby ("Give them post-natal care") . . . . . . 1·00 1·60
92 1 p. Man with insecticide ("Insects spread disease") . . . . . . 2·50 3·00
93 2 p. 50 Boxer ("Say no to alcohol, drugs, tobacco") . . . . . . 4·00 4·75

16 Hammerhead

1987. Sharks. Multicoloured.
94 29 s. Type **16** . . . . 2·00 1·75
95 32 s. Tiger shark . . . . 2·00 1·75
96 47 s. Grey nurse shark . . . . 2·50 2·25
97 1 p. Great white shark . . . . 4·00 5·50

17 Capt. E. C. Musick and Sikorsky S.42A Flying Boat "Samoan Clipper"

1987. Air Pioneers of the South Pacific. Multicoloured.
99 42 s. Type **17** . . . . 1·40 1·40
100 57 s. Capt. J. W. Burgess and Short S.30 modified "G" Class flying boat "Aotearoa" . . 1·75 1·75
101 1 p. 50 Sir Charles Kingsford Smith and Fokker F.VIIa/3m "Southern Cross" . . . . . 2·50 3·00
102 2 p. Amelia Earhart and Lockheed 10E Electra . . . 3·00 3·50

18 Polynesian Scrub Hen and 1983 1 s. Map Definitive

1988. 5th Annivs of First Niuafo'ou Postage Stamp (42, 57 s.) and Niuafo'ou Airport Inauguration (1, 2 p.). Multicoloured.
103 42 s. Type **18** 80 75
104 57 s. As Type **18**, but with stamp at left . . . . 1·00 95
105 1 p. Concorde and 1983 Airport Inauguration 29 s. stamp . 3·00 3·00
106 2 p. As 1 p. but with stamp at left 3·50 3·75

20 Audubon's Shearwaters and Blowholes, Houma, Tonga

23 Formation of Earth's Surface

22 Spiny Hatchetfish

1988. Islands of Polynesia. Multicoloured.

108	42 s. Type **20**	95	95
109	57 s. Brown kiwi at Akaroa Harbour, New Zealand	1·40	1·40
110	90 s. Red-tailed tropic birds at Rainmaker Mountain, Samoa	2·00	2·25
111	2 p. 50 Laysan albatross at Kapoho Volcano, Hawaii	4·50	5·50

1989. Fishes of the Deep. Multicoloured.

113	32 s. Type **22**	85	1·00
114	42 s. Snipe eel	1·00	1·00
115	57 s. Viperfish	1·25	1·50
116	1 p. 50 Football anglerfish	3·00	3·75

1989. The Evolution of the Earth. Mult. (a) Size $27 \times 35\frac{1}{2}$ mm.

117	1 s. Type **23**	10	10
118	2 s. Cross-section of Earth's crust	10	10
119	5 s. Volcano	10	10
120	10 s. Cross-section of Earth during cooling	10	10
120a	13 s. Gem stones	15	20
121	15 s. Sea	15	20
122	20 s. Mountains	15	20
123	32 s. River gorge	25	30
124	42 s. Early plant life, Silurian era	30	35
124a	45 s. Early marine life	35	40
125	50 s. Fossils and Cambrian lifeforms	40	45
126	57 s. Carboniferous forest and coal seams	45	50
126a	60 s. Dinosaurs feeding	45	50
126b	80 s. Tyrannosaurus and triceratops fighting	60	65

(b) Size $25\frac{1}{2} \times 40$ mm

127	1 p. Dragonfly and amphibians, Carboniferous era	75	80
128	1 p. 50 Dinosaurs, Jurassic era	1·10	1·25
129	2 p. Archaeopteryx and mammals, Jurassic era	1·50	1·60
130	5 p. Human family and domesticated dog, Pleistocene era	3·75	4·00
130a	10 p. Mammoth and sabre-tooth tiger	7·50	7·75

24 Astronaut on Moon and Newspaper Headline

1989. "World Stamp Expo '89" International Stamp Exhibition, Washington.

131	**24**	57 s. multicoloured	1·00	1·00

25 Lake Vai Lahi

1990. Niuafo'ou Crater Lake. Multicoloured.

133	42 s. Type **25**	70	90
134	42 s. Islands in centre of lake	70	90
135	42 s. South-west end of lake and islet	70	90
136	1 p. Type **25**	1·40	1·50
137	1 p. As No. 134	1·40	1·50
138	1 p. As No. 135	1·40	1·50

Nos. 133/8 were printed together in se-tenant strips of each value, forming a composite design.

26 Penny Black and Tin Can Mail Service

1990. 150th Anniv of the Penny Black. Mult.

139	42 s. Type **26**	80	80
140	57 s. U.S.A. 1847 10 c. stamp	1·10	1·25
141	75 s. Western Australia 1854 1d. stamp	1·25	1·50
142	2 p. 50 Mafeking Siege 1900 1d. stamp	4·00	4·75

27 Humpback Whale surfacing

1990. Polynesian Whaling. Multicoloured.

143	15 s. Type **27**	1·50	1·40
144	42 s. Whale diving under canoe	2·00	1·75
145	57 s. Tail of Blue whale	2·25	1·90
146	2 p. Old man and pair of whales	5·50	6·00

1990. 40th Anniv of U.N. Development Programme. As T **203** of Tonga. Multicoloured.

148	57 s. Agriculture and Fisheries	90	1·25
149	57 s. Education	90	1·25
150	2 p. 50 Healthcare	3·25	3·75
151	2 p. 50 Communications	3·25	3·75

28 H.M.S. "Bounty"

30 Longhorned Beetle Grub

1991. Bicentenary of Charting of Niuafo'ou. Multicoloured.

152	32 s. Type **28**	1·00	1·25
153	42 s. Chart of "Pandora's" course	1·10	1·40
154	57 s. H.M.S. "Pandora" (frigate)	1·25	1·50

1991. Longhorned Beetle. Multicoloured.

157	42 s. Type **30**	80	80
158	57 s. Adult beetle	90	90
159	1 p. 50 Grub burrowing	2·75	3·00
160	2 p. 50 Adult on tree trunk	4·00	4·25

31 Heina meeting the Eel

1991. Christmas. The Legend of the Coconut Tree. Multicoloured.

161	15 s. Type **31**	35	40
162	42 s. Heina crying over the eel's grave	90	1·00

1992. 50th Anniv of War in the Pacific. As T **215** of Tonga each showing contemporary newspaper headline. Multicoloured.

165	42 s. American battleship ablaze, Pearl Harbor	1·10	1·25
166	42 s. Destroyed American Douglas B-18 Bolo aircraft, Hawaii	1·10	1·25
167	42 s. Newspaper and Japanese Mitsubishi A6M Zero-Sen fighter	1·10	1·25
168	42 s. Pres. Roosevelt signing Declaration of War	1·10	1·25
169	42 s. Japanese T 95 light tank and Gen. MacArthur	1·10	1·25
170	42 s. Douglas SBD Dauntless dive bomber and Admiral Nimitz	1·10	1·25
171	42 s. Bren gun and Gen. Sir Thomas Blamey	1·10	1·25
172	42 s. Australian mortar crew, Kokoda	1·10	1·25
173	42 s. U.S.S. "Mississippi" in action and Maj. Gen. Julian C. Smith	1·10	1·25
174	42 s. U.S.S. "Enterprise" (aircraft carrier)	1·10	1·25
175	42 s. American marine and Maj. Gen. Curtis Lemay	1·10	1·25
176	42 s. Boeing B-29 Superfortress bomber and Japanese surrender, Tokyo Bay	1·10	1·25

Nos. 165/76 were printed together, se-tenant, forming a composite design.

1992. 25th Anniv of the Coronation of King Tupou IV. As T **217** of Tonga.

177	45 s. multicoloured	75	75
178	80 s. multicoloured	1·50	1·75
179	80 s. black and brown	1·50	1·75
180	80 s. multicoloured	1·50	1·75
181	2 p. multicoloured	2·50	3·00

DESIGNS—(34×23 mm): No. 177, King Taufa'-ahau Tupou IV and Queen Halaevalu during Coronation. (48×35 mm): No. 178, King Tupou IV and Tongan national anthem; 179, Extract from Investiture ceremony; 180, Tongan choir; 181, As 45 s.

32 Male and Female Scrub Hens searching for Food

1992. Endangered Species. Polynesian Scrub Hen. Multicoloured.

182	45 s. Type **32**	1·00	1·25
183	60 s. Female guarding egg	1·25	1·40
184	80 s. Chick	1·60	1·75
185	1 p. 50 Head of male	2·75	3·50

33 1983 2 s. Map Definitive and 1993 60 s. Dinosaur Definitive

1993. 10th Anniv of First Niuafo'ou Stamp. Multicoloured.

186	60 s. Type **33**	1·00	1·10
187	80 s. 1983 5 s. definitive and 1993 80 s. dinosaurs definitive	1·25	1·40

34 De Havilland Twin Otter 200/300 of South Pacific Island Airways

35 Blue-crowned Lorikeets

1993. 10th Anniv of First Flight to Niuafo'ou. Multicoloured.

188	1 p. Type **34**	1·50	2·00
189	2 p. 50 De Havilland Twin Otter 200/300 of Friendly Islands Airways	3·50	4·25

1993. 75th Birthday of King Taufa'ahau Tupou IV. As T **229** of Tonga. Multicoloured.

190	45 s. King Tupou IV and "Pangai" (patrol boat)	55	55
191	80 s. King Tupou IV and musical instruments ($38\frac{1}{2} \times 51$ mm)	1·25	1·75
192	80 s. King Tupou IV and sporting events ($38\frac{1}{2} \times 51$ mm)	1·25	1·75
193	80 s. King Tupou IV with De Havilland Twin Otter 200/300 airplane and telecommunications	1·25	1·75
194	2 p. As 45 s. but larger ($38\frac{1}{2} \times 51$ mm)	2·75	3·00

1993. Natural History of Lake Vai Lahi. Multicoloured.

195	60 s. Type **35**	1·00	1·25
196	60 s. White-tailed tropic bird and eastern reef heron	1·00	1·25
197	60 s. Black admiral (butterfly) and Niuafo'ou coconut beetle	1·00	1·25
198	60 s. Niuafo'ou dragonfly, spotbill ducks and Niuafo'ou moths	1·00	1·25
199	60 s. Niuafo'ou megapode	1·00	1·25

Nos. 195/9 were printed together, se-tenant, forming a composite design.

1993. Children's Painting Competition Winners. As T **231** of Tonga.

200	10 s. multicoloured	40	55
201	10 s. black and grey	40	55
202	1 p. multicoloured	2·75	3·00
203	1 p. multicoloured	2·75	3·00

DESIGNS: Nos. 200 and 202, "Crater Lake Megapode and Volcano" (Paea Puletau); Nos. 201 and 203, "Ofato Beetle Grubs of Niuafo'ou" (Peni Finau).

36 "Scarabaeidea"

1994. Beetles. Multicoloured.

204	60 s. Type **36**	85	1·00
205	80 s. "Coccinellidea"	1·10	1·40
206	1 p. 50 "Cerambycidea"	2·00	2·50
207	2 p. 50 "Pentatomidae"	3·75	4·25

37 Stern of H.M.S. "Bounty"

38 Blue-crowned Lory and Lava Flows

1994. Sailing Ships. Multicoloured.

208	80 s. Type **37**	1·75	2·00
209	80 s. Bow of H.M.S. "Bounty"	1·75	2·00
210	80 s. H.M.S. "Pandora" (frigate)	1·75	2·00
211	80 s. Whaling ship	1·75	2·00
212	80 s. Trading schooner	1·75	2·00

1994. Volcanic Eruptions on Niuafo'ou. Multicoloured.

213	80 s. Type **38**	1·25	1·50
214	80 s. Spotbill ducks over lava flows	1·25	1·50
215	80 s. Megapodes and palm trees	1·25	1·50
216	80 s. White-tailed tropic birds and inhabitants	1·25	1·50
217	80 s. Eastern heron and evacuation, 1946	1·25	1·50

Nos. 213/17 were printed together, se-tenant, forming a composite design.

1995. Visit South Pacific Year '95. Save the Whales. Nos. 143/6 surch **SAVE THE WHALES VISIT SOUTH PACIFIC YEAR '95**, emblem and value.

218	60 s. on 42 s. Whale diving under canoe	1·00	1·00
219	80 s. on 15 s. Type **27**	1·25	1·25
220	80 s. on 57 s. Tail of blue whale	1·25	1·25
221	2 p. on 2 p. Old man and pair of whales	3·00	3·50

1995. 50th Anniv of End of World War II in the Pacific. As T **242** of Tonga.

223	60 s. yellow, black and blue	1·10	1·10
224	60 s. yellow, black and blue	1·10	1·10
225	60 s. yellow, black and blue	1·10	1·10
226	60 s. yellow, black and blue	1·10	1·10
227	60 s. yellow, black and blue	1·10	1·10
228	80 s. yellow, black and red	1·10	1·10
229	80 s. yellow, black and red	1·10	1·10
230	80 s. yellow, black and red	1·10	1·10
231	80 s. yellow, black and red	1·10	1·10
232	80 s. yellow, black and red	1·10	1·10

DESIGNS: Nos. 223 and 228, American marine; 224 and 229, Marine firing and side of tank; 225 and 230, Tank; 226 and 231, Marines leaving landing craft; 227 and 232, Beach assault and palm trees.

Nos. 223/32 were printed together, se-tenant, forming two composite designs.

1995. "Singapore '95" International Stamp Exhibitions. As T **243** of Tonga, each with exhibition emblem. Multicoloured.

233	45 s. Dinosaurs feeding (as No. 126a) (vert)	1·00	1·25
234	60 s. Tyrannosaurus fighting Triceratops (as No. 126b) (vert)	1·00	1·25

1995. 50th Anniv of United Nations and End of Second World War. As T **245** of Tonga.

237	60 s. multicoloured	1·00	1·00
238	60 s. black and blue	1·00	1·00
239	60 s. multicoloured	1·00	1·00
240	80 s. multicoloured	1·25	1·25
241	80 s. blue and black	1·25	1·25
242	80 s. multicoloured	1·25	1·25

DESIGNS—As T **245** of Tonga: No. 237, St. Paul's Cathedral and searchlights; 239, Concorde; 240, Allied prisoners of war and Burma Railway; 242, Mt. Fuji and express train. 25×35 mm: Nos. 238 and 241, U.N. anniversary emblem.

40 Charles Ramsay and Swimmers with Poles

1996. Tin Can Mail Pioneers. Multicoloured.

243	45 s. Type **40**	90	90
244	60 s. Charles Ramsay and encounter with shark	1·25	1·25
245	1 p. Walter Quensell and transferring mail from canoes to ship	2·00	2·00
246	3 p. Walter Quensell and Tin Can Mail cancellations	6·00	6·00

1996. 13th Congress of International Union of Prehistoric and Protohistoric Sciences, Forli, Italy. As T **250** of Tonga. Multicoloured.

247	1 p. Cave painting, lake village and hunter	2·25	2·25
248	1 p. Egyptians with Pyramid, Greek temple, and Romans with Colosseum	2·25	2·25

1996. 50th Anniv of U.N.I.C.E.F. Children's Toys. As T **252** of Tonga. Multicoloured.

249	80 s. Dolls, model truck and counting balls	1·25	1·25
250	80 s. Teddy bear, tricycle and model car	1·25	1·25
251	80 s. Book, model helicopter, pedal car and roller skates	1·25	1·25

Nos. 249/51 were printed together, se-tenant, forming a composite design.

41 Island and Two Canoes

1996. 50th Anniv of Evacuation of Niuafo'ou. Multicoloured.

252	45 s. Type **41**	70	75
253	45 s. Erupting volcano and canoes	70	75
254	45 s. End of island, volcanic cloud and canoe	70	75
255	45 s. Family and livestock in outrigger canoe	70	75
256	45 s. Islanders reaching Matua	70	75
257	60 s. Type **41**	95	1·00
258	60 s. As No. 253	95	1·00
259	60 s. As No. 254	95	1·00
260	60 s. As No. 255	95	1·00
261	60 s. As No. 256	95	1·00

Nos. 252/6 and 257/61 respectively were printed together, se-tenant, forming the same composite design.

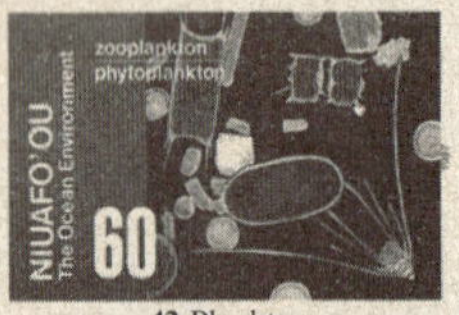

42 Plankton

1997. The Ocean Environment.

262	**42**	60 s. multicoloured	85	85
263	–	80 s. multicoloured	1·10	1·10
264	–	1 p. 50 multicoloured	2·00	2·25
265	–	2 p. 50 multicoloured	2·75	3·00

DESIGNS: 80 s. to 2 p. 50, Different plankton.

1997. King and Queen of Tonga's Golden Wedding and 30th Anniv of Coronation. As T **261** of Tonga, but 50 × 37 mm. Multicoloured.

267	80 s. King and Queen on wedding day	1·25	1·25
268	80 s. King Tupou in Coronation robes	1·25	1·25

43 Blue-crowned Lory Nestlings

1998. Endangered Species. Blue-crowned Lory. Multicoloured.

270	10 s. Type **43**	30	30
271	55 s. Feeding on flowers	75	75
272	80 s. Perched on branch	1·00	1·00
273	3 p. Pair on branch	3·50	3·50

1998. 80th Birthday of King Taufa'ahau Tupou IV. Portrait as T **263** of Tonga.

276	$2.70 multicoloured	2·50	2·75

1998. International Year of the Ocean. As T **265** of Tonga. Multicoloured.

278	10 s. "Amphiprion melanopus"	10	15
279	55 s. "Amphiprion perideraion"	40	45
280	80 s. "Amphiprion chrysopterus"	60	65

1998. Christmas. As T **266** of Tonga. Multicoloured.

281	20 s. Angel playing lute (inscr in Tongan)	15	20
282	55 s. Angel playing violin (inscr in English)	40	45
283	1 p. Children and bells (inscr in Tongan)	75	80
284	1 p. 60 Children and candles (inscr in English)	1·10	1·25

44 "Eendracht" (Le Maire)

1999. Early Explorers. Multicoloured.

286	80 s. Type **44**	60	65
287	2 p. 70 Tongiaki (outrigger canoe)	2·00	2·10

NIUE

One of the Cook Is. group in the S. Pacific. A dependency of New Zealand, the island achieved local self-government in 1974.

1902. 12 pence = 1 shilling;
20 shillings = 1 pound.
1967 100 cents = 1 dollar.

1902. T **42** of New Zealand optd **NIUE** only.

1	**42**	1d. red	£300	£300

Stamps of New Zealand surch **NIUE.** and value in native language.

1902. Pictorials of 1898 etc.

8	**23**	½d. green	75	80
9	**42**	1d. red	50	70
2	**26**	2½d. blue (B)	1·25	4·00
13	**28**	3d. brown	9·50	5·00
14	**31**	6d. red	12·00	11·00
16	**34**	1s. orange	35·00	35·00

1911. King Edward VII stamps.

17	**51**	½d. green	45	40
18		6d. red	2·00	7·00
19		1s. orange	6·50	45·00

1917. Dominion and King George V stamps.

21	**53**	1d. red	8·00	5·50
22	**62**	3d. brown	48·00	80·00

1917. Stamps of New Zealand (King George V, etc) optd **NIUE.** only.

23	**62**	½d. green	70	2·00
24	**53**	1d. red	7·00	7·00
25	**62**	1½d. grey	80	2·00
26		1½d. brown	70	3·50
28a		2½d. blue	1·25	3·75
29a		3d. brown	1·25	1·50
30a		6d. red	4·75	20·00
31a		1s. orange	5·50	20·00

1918. Stamps of New Zealand optd **NIUE.**

33	F **4**	2s. blue	15·00	32·00
34		2s. 6d. brown	20·00	48·00
35		5s. green	24·00	50·00
36		10s. red	85·00	95·00
37		£1 red	£130	£150

1920. Pictorial types as Cook Islands (1920), but inscr "NIUE".

38	**9**	½d. black and green	3·75	3·75
45	–	1d. black and red	1·75	75
40	–	1½d. black and red	2·50	6·00
46	–	2½d. black and blue	4·00	10·00
41	–	3d. black and blue	60	11·00
47	**7**	4d. black and violet	7·00	16·00
42	–	6d. brown and green	1·75	17·00
43	–	1s. black and brown	1·75	17·00

1927. Admiral type of New Zealand optd **NIUE.**

49	**71**	2s. blue	18·00	32·00

1931. No. 40 surch **TWO PENCE.**

50	2d. on 1½d. black and red	2·25	1·00

1931. Stamps of New Zealand (Arms types) optd **NIUE.**

83	F **6**	2s. 6d. brown	3·50	8·90
84		5s. green	7·50	11·00
53		10s. red	35·00	85·00
86		£1 pink	42·00	55·00

1932. Pictorial stamps as Cook Islands (1932) but inscr additionally "NIUE".

89	**20**	½d. black and green	50	1·75
90	–	1d. black and red	50	80
64	**22**	2d. black and brown	40	1·00
92	–	2½d. black and blue	60	95
66	–	4d. black and blue	1·75	2·25
67	–	6d. black and orange	70	75
61	–	1s. black and violet	2·25	5·00

1935. Silver Jubilee. As Nos. 63, 92 and 67, with colours changed, optd **SILVER JUBILEE OF KING GEORGE V. 1910–1935.**

69	1d. red	60	2·50
70	2½d. blue	3·25	5·50
71	6d. green and orange	3·25	5·50

1937. Coronation. New Zealand stamps optd **NIUE.**

72	**106**	1d. red	30	10
73		2½d. blue	40	50
74		6d. orange	40	20

1938. As 1938 issue of Cook Islands, but inscr "NIUE COOK ISLANDS".

95	**29**	1s. black and violet	1·25	85
96	**30**	2s. black and brown	8·50	2·75
97	–	3s. blue and green	15·00	7·00

1940. As T **32** of Cook Islands but inscr "NIUE COOK ISLANDS".

78	**32**	3d. on 1½d. black and purple	40	10

1946. Peace. New Zealand stamps optd **NIUE** (twice on 2d.).

98	**132**	1d. green	20	10
99	–	2d. purple (No. 670)	20	10
100	–	6d. brown & red (No. 674)	20	40
101	**139**	8d. black and red	30	40

18 Map of Niue

19 H.M.S. "Resolution"

1950.

113	**18**	½d. orange and blue	10	40
114	**19**	1d. brown and green	2·25	1·50
115	–	2d. black and red	20	40
116	–	3d. blue and violet	10	15
117	–	4d. olive and purple	10	15
118	–	6d. green and orange	60	50
119	–	9d. orange and brown	10	50
120	–	1s. purple and black	10	15
121	–	2s. brown and green	1·00	3·50
122	–	3s. blue and black	4·50	4·00

DESIGNS—HORIZ: 2d. Alofi landing; 3d. Native hut; 4d. Arch at Hikutavake; 6d. Alofi bay; 1s. Cave, Makefu. VERT: 9d. Spearing fish; 2s. Bananas; 3s. Matapa Chasm.

1953. Coronation. As Types of New Zealand but inscr "NIUE".

123	**164**	3d. brown	65	40
124	**168**	6d. grey	95	40

26

27 "Pua"

1967. Decimal Currency. (a) Nos. 113/22 surch.

125	**17**	½ c. on ½d.	10	10
126	**18**	1 c. on 1d.	1·10	15
127	–	2 c. on 2d.	10	10
128	–	2½ c. on 3d.	10	10
129	–	3 c. on 4d.	10	10
130	–	5 c. on 6d.	10	10
131	–	8 c. on 9d.	10	10
132	–	10 c. on 1s.	10	10
133	–	20 c. on 2s.	50	1·00
134	–	30 c. on 3s.	1·00	1·50

(b) Arms type of New Zealand without value, surch as in T **26**.

135	**26**	25 c. brown	55	55
136		50 c. green	80	80
137		$1 mauve	60	1·25
138		$2 pink	90	2·00

1967. Christmas. As T **278** of New Zealand but inscr "NIUE".

139	2½ c. multicoloured	10	10

1969. Christmas. As No. 905 of New Zealand but inscr "NIUE".

140	2½ c. multicoloured	10	10

1969. Flowers. Multicoloured; frame colours given.

141	**27**	½ c. green	10	10
142	–	1 c. red	10	10
143	–	2 c. olive	10	10
144	–	2½ c. brown	10	10
145	–	3 c. blue	10	10
146	–	5 c. red	10	10
147	–	8 c. violet	10	10
148	–	10 c. yellow	10	10
149	–	20 c. blue	1·00	1·25
150	–	30 c. green	1·75	1·75

DESIGNS: 1 c. "Golden Shower"; 2 c. Flamboyant; 2½ c. Frangipani; 3 c. Niue crocus; 5 c. Hibiscus; 8 c. "Passion Fruit"; 10 c. "Kampui"; 20 c. Queen Elizabeth II (after Anthony Buckley); 30 c. Tapeu orchid .

For 20 c. design as 5 c. see No. 801.

37 Kalahimu

1970. Indigenous Edible Crabs. Mult.

151	3 c. Type **37**	10	10
152	5 c. Kalavi	10	10
153	30 c. Unga	30	25

1970. Christmas. As T **314** of New Zealand, but inscr "NIUE".

154	2½ c. multicoloured	10	10

38 Outrigger Canoe, and Fokker F.27 Friendship over Jungle

1970. Opening of Niue Airport. Multicoloured.

155	3 c. Type **38**	10	15
156	5 c. "Tofua II" (cargo liner) and Fokker F.27 Friendship over harbour	15	15
157	8 c. Fokker F.27 Friendship over airport	15	20

39 Spotted Triller

1971. Birds. Multicoloured.

158 5 c. Type **39** 15 20
159 10 c. Purple-capped fruit dove 70 20
160 20 c. Blue-crowned lory . . . 80 20

1971. Christmas. As T **325** of New Zealand, but inscr "Niue".

161 3 c. multicoloured 10 10

40 Niuean Boy

41 Octopus Lure

1971. Niuean Portraits. Multicoloured.

162 4 c. Type **40** 10 10
163 6 c. Girl with garland 10 15
164 9 c. Man 10 25
165 14 c. Woman with garland . . 15 40

1972. South Pacific Arts Festival, Fiji. Multicoloured.

166 3 c. Type **41** 10 10
167 5 c. War weapons 15 15
168 10 c. Sika throwing (horiz) . . 20 15
169 25 c. Vivi dance (horiz) . . . 30 25

42 Alofi Wharf

1972. 25th Anniversary of South Pacific Commission. Multicoloured.

170 4 c. Type **42** 10 10
171 5 c. Medical services 15 10
172 6 c. Schoolchildren 15 10
173 18 c. Dairy cattle 25 20

1972. Christmas. As T **332** of New Zealand, but inscr "NIUE".

174 3 c. multicoloured 10 10

43 Silver Sweeper

1973. Fishes. Multicoloured.

175 8 c. Type **43** 25 25
176 10 c. Peacock hind ("Loi") . . 30 30
177 15 c. Yellow-edged lyretail ("Malau") 40 40
178 20 c. Ruby snapper ("Palu") . 45 45

44 "Large Flower Piece" (Jan Brueghel)

46 King Fataaiki

45 Capt. Cook and Bowsprit

1973. Christmas. Flower studies by the artists listed. Multicoloured.

179 4 c. Type **44** 10 10
180 5 c. Bollongier 10 10
181 10 c. Ruysch 20 20

1974. Bicent of Capt. Cook's Visit. Mult.

182 2 c. Type **45** 20 20
183 3 c. Niue landing place 20 20
184 8 c. Map of Niue 35 30
185 20 c. Ensign of 1774 and Administration Building . . 55 65

1974. Self-Government. Multicoloured.

186 4 c. Type **46** 10 10
187 8 c. Annexation Ceremony, 1900 10 10
188 10 c. Legislative Assembly Chambers (horiz) 10 10
189 20 c. Village meeting (horiz) . 15 15

47 Decorated Bicycles

48 Children going to Church

1974. Christmas. Multicoloured.

190 3 c. Type **47** 10 10
191 10 c. Decorated motorcycle . 10 10
192 20 c. Motor transport to church 20 30

1975. Christmas. Multicoloured.

193 4 c. Type **48** 10 10
194 5 c. Child with balloons on bicycle 10 10
195 10 c. Balloons and gifts on tree 20 20

49 Hotel Buildings

1975. Opening of Tourist Hotel. Mult.

196 8 c. Type **49** 10 10
197 20 c. Ground-plan and buildings 20 20

50 Preparing Ground for Taro

1976. Food Gathering. Multicoloured.

198 1 c. Type **50** 10 10
199 2 c. Planting taro 10 10
200 3 c. Banana gathering 10 10
201 4 c. Harvesting taro 10 10
202 5 c. Gathering shell fish . . . 30 10
203 10 c. Reef fishing 20 10
204 20 c. Luku gathering 20 15
205 50 c. Canoe fishing 30 60
206 $1 Coconut husking 35 80
207 $2 Uga gathering . . . . . . 60 1·40

See also Nos. 249/58 and 264/73.

51 Water

1976. Utilities. Multicoloured.

208 10 c. Type **51** 10 10
209 15 c. Telecommunications . . 15 15
210 20 c. Power 15 15

52 Christmas Tree, Alofi

1976. Christmas. Multicoloured.

211 9 c. Type **52** 15 15
212 15 c. Church service, Avatele 15 15

53 Queen Elizabeth II and Westminster Abbey

1977. Silver Jubilee. Multicoloured.

213 $1 Type **53** 60 50
214 $2 Coronation regalia 80 75

54 Child Care

1977. Personal Services. Multicoloured.

216 10 c. Type **54** 15 10
217 15 c. School dental clinic . . . 20 20
218 20 c. Care of the aged 20 20

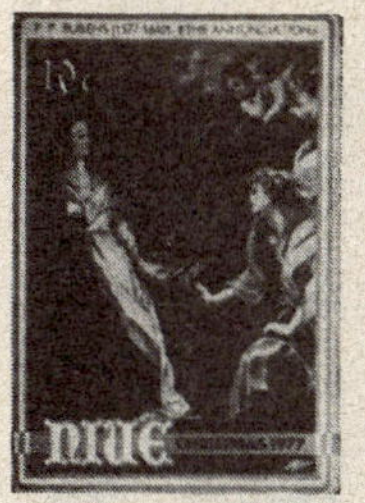

55 "The Annunciation"

58 "The Deposition of Christ" (Caravaggio)

57 "An Island View in Atooi"

1977. Christmas. Paintings by Rubens. Multicoloured.

219 10 c. Type **55** 20 10
220 12 c. "Adoration of the Magi" 20 15
221 20 c. "Virgin in a Garland" . . 35 40
222 35 c. "The Holy Family" . . . 55 90

1977. Nos. 198/207, 214, 216 and 218 surch.

224 12 c. on 1 c. Type **50** 25 25
225 16 c. on 2 c. Planting taro . . 30 30
226 20 c. on 3 c. Banana gathering 40 40
227 35 c. on 4 c. Harvesting taro . 45 45
228 40 c. on 5 c. Gathering shell fish 45 50
229 60 c. on 20 c. Luku gathering . 45 55
230 70 c. on $1 Coconut husking . 45 55
231 85 c. on $2 Uga gathering . . 45 60
232 $1.10 on 10 c. Type **22** 45 60
233 $2.60 on 20 c. Care of the aged 50 70
234 $3.20 on $2 Coronation regalia 60 80

1978. Bicent of Discovery of Hawaii. Paintings by John Webber. Multicoloured.

235 12 c. Type **57** 85 40
236 16 c. "A View of Karakaooa, in Owhyhee" 95 50
237 20 c. "An Offering before Capt. Cook in the Sandwich Islands" 1·00 60
238 30 c. "Tereoboo, King of Owhyhee bringing presents to Capt. Cook" . . . . 1·10 70
239 35 c. "A Canoe in the Sandwich Islands, the rowers masked" 1·25 80

1978. Easter. Paintings from the Vatican Galleries. Multicoloured.

241 10 c. Type **58** 30 10
242 20 c. "The Burial of Christ" (Bellini) 60 25

59 Flags of Niue and U.K.

1978. 25th Anniv of Coronation. Mult.

245 $1.10 Type **59** 60 90
246 $1.10 Coronation portrait by Cecil Beaton 60 90
247 $1.10 Queen's personal flag for New Zealand 60 90

1978. Designs as Nos. 198/207 but margin colours changed and silver frame.

249 12 c. Type **50** 20 20
250 16 c. Planting taro 20 20
251 30 c. Banana gathering 30 25
252 35 c. Harvesting taro 30 30
253 40 c. Gathering shell fish . . . 40 40
254 60 c. Reef fishing 40 35
255 75 c. Luku gathering 40 40
256 $1.10 Canoe fishing 50 80
257 $3.20 Coconut husking 60 90
258 $4.20 Uga gathering 65 95

60 "Festival of the Rosary"

1978. Christmas. 450th Death Anniv of Durer. Multicoloured.

259 20 c. Type **60** 40 20
260 30 c. "The Nativity" 50 30
261 35 c. "Adoration of the Magi" 60 35

1979. Air. Designs as Nos. 249/58 but gold frames and additionally inscr "AIRMAIL".

264 15 c. Planting taro 20 15
265 20 c. Banana gathering . . . 25 15
266 23 c. Harvesting taro 30 15
267 50 c. Canoe fishing 70 20
268 90 c. Reef fishing 80 35
269 $1.35 Type **50** . . . . 80 1·50
270 $2.10 Gathering shell fish . . 80 1·75
271 $2.60 Luku gathering . . . . 80 1·75
272 $5.10 Coconut husking . . . 80 1·75
273 $6.35 Uga gathering . . . . . 80 1·75

61 "Pieta" (Gregorio Fernandez)

1979. Easter. Paintings. Multicoloured.

274 30 c. Type **61** 30 25
275 35 c. "Burial of Christ" (Pedro Roldan) 35 25

62 "The Nurse and Child" (Franz Hals)

63 Penny Black Stamp

1979. International Year of the Child. Details of Paintings. Multicoloured.

278 16 c. Type **62** 30 15
279 20 c. "Child of the Duke of Osuna" (Goya) 35 20
280 30 c. "Daughter of Robert Strozzi" (Titian) 55 35
281 35 c. "Children eating Fruit" (Murillo) 60 40

1979. Death Cent of Sir Rowland Hill. Mult.

284 20 c. Type **63** 20 15
285 20 c. Sir Rowland Hill and original Bath mail coach . . 20 15
286 30 c. Basel 1845 $2\frac{1}{2}$ r. stamp . 30 20
287 30 c. Sir Rowland Hill and Alpine village coach 30 20
288 35 c. U.S.A. 1847 5 c. stamp . 35 25
289 35 c. Sir Rowland Hill and "Washington" (first transatlantic U.S.A. mail vessel) 35 25
290 50 c. France 1849 20 c. stamp 40 35
291 50 c. Sir Rowland Hill and French Post Office railway van, 1849 . . . . 40 35
292 60 c. Bavaria 1849 1 k. stamp 40 40
293 60 c. Sir Rowland Hill and Bavarian coach with mail . 40 40

The two versions of each value were issued se-tenant within the sheet, forming composite designs.

64 Cook's Landing at Botany Bay

1979. Death Bicentenary of Captain Cook. Multicoloured.

295 20 c. Type **64** 55 30
296 30 c. Cook's men during a landing on Erromanga . . . 75 40
297 35 c. H.M.S. "Resolution" and H.M.S. "Discovery" in Queen Charlotte's Sound 85 45
298 75 c. Death of Captain Cook, Hawaii . . . . 1·50 70

65 Launch of "Apollo 11"

66 "Virgin of Tortosa" (P. Serra)

1979. 10th Anniv of First Manned Moon Landing. Multicoloured.

300 30 c. Type **65** 35 20
301 35 c. Lunar module on Moon 45 25
302 60 c. Sikorsky Sea King helicopter, recovery ship and command module after splashdown 60 40

1979. Christmas. Paintings. Multicoloured.

304 20 c. Type **66** 10 10
305 25 c. "Virgin with Milk" (R. di Mur) 15 15
306 30 c. "Virgin and Child" (S. di G. Sassetta) 20 20
307 50 c. "Virgin and Child" (J. Huguet) 25 25

1980. Hurricane Relief. Surch **HURRICANE RELIEF Plus 2c.** (a) On Nos. 284/93 **HURRICANE RELIEF** spread over each se-tenant pair.

310 **63** 20 c. + 2 c. multicoloured . 30 30
311 – 20 c. + 2 c. multicoloured (No. 285) 30 30
312 – 30 c. + 2 c. multicoloured (No. 286) 35 35
313 – 30 c. + 2 c. multicoloured (No. 287) 35 35
314 – 35 c. + 2 c. multicoloured (No. 288) 40 40
315 – 35 c. + 2 c. multicoloured (No. 289) 40 40
316 – 50 c. + 2 c. multicoloured (No. 290) 55 55
317 – 50 c. + 2 c. multicoloured (No. 291) 55 55
318 – 60 c. + 2 c. multicoloured (No. 292) 65 65
319 – 60 c. + 2 c. multicoloured (No. 293) 65 65

(b) On Nos. 295/8.

320 **64** 20 c. + 2 c. multicoloured . 40 40
321 – 30 c. + 2 c. multicoloured . 50 50
322 – 35 c. + 2 c. multicoloured . 55 55
323 – 75 c. + 2 c. multicoloured . 1·00 1·00

(c) On Nos. 300/2.

324 **65** 30 c. + 2 c. multicoloured . 35 35
325 – 35 c. + 2 c. multicoloured . 40 40
326 – 60 c. + 2 c. multicoloured . 65 65

(d) On Nos. 304/7.

327 **66** 20 c. + 2 c. multicoloured . 25 25
328 – 25 c. + 2 c. multicoloured . 30 30
329 – 30 c. + 2 c. multicoloured . 35 35
330 – 50 c. + 2 c. multicoloured . 55 55

68 "Pieta" (Bellini)

1980. Easter. "Pieta". Paintings. Mult.

331 25 c. Type **68** 30 15
332 30 c. Botticelli 35 20
333 35 c. A. van Dyck 35 20

69 Ceremonial Stool, New Guinea

72 Queen Elizabeth the Queen Mother

1980. South Pacific Festival of Arts, New Guinea. Multicoloured.

336 20 c. Type **69** 10 10
337 20 c. Ku-Tagwa plaque, New Guinea 10 10
338 20 c. Suspension hook, New Guinea 10 10
339 20 c. Ancestral board, New Guinea 10 10
340 25 c. Platform post, New Hebrides 15 15
341 25 c. Canoe ornament, New Ireland 15 15
342 25 c. Carved figure, Admiralty Islands 15 15
343 25 c. Female with child, Admiralty Islands 15 15
344 30 c. The God A'a, Rurutu (Austral Islands) 15 15
345 30 c. Statue of Tangaroa, Cook Islands 15 15
346 30 c. Ivory pendant, Tonga . . 15 15
347 30 c. Tapa (Hiapo) cloth, Niue 15 15
348 35 c. Feather box (Waka), New Zealand 15 15
349 35 c. Hei-Tiki amulet, New Zealand 15 15
350 35 c. House post, New Zealand 15 15
351 35 c. Feather image of god Ku, Hawaii 15 15

1980. "Zeapex '80" International Stamp Exhibition, Auckland. Nos. 284/93 optd (A) **ZEAPEX'80 AUCKLAND** or (B) **NEW ZEALAND STAMP EXHIBITION** and emblem.

353 **63** 20 c. multicoloured (A) . . 30 20
354 – 20 c. multicoloured (B) . . 30 20
355 – 30 c. multicoloured (A) . . 30 25
356 – 30 c. multicoloured (B) . . 30 25
357 – 35 c. multicoloured (A) . . 30 25
358 – 35 c. multicoloured (B) . . 30 25
359 – 50 c. multicoloured (A) . . 40 30
360 – 50 c. multicoloured (B) . . 40 30
361 – 60 c. multicoloured (A) . . 40 35
362 – 60 c. multicoloured (B) . . 40 35

1980. 80th Birthday of The Queen Mother.

364 **72** $1.10 multicoloured . . . . 80 1·50

73 100 Metre Dash

74 "The Virgin and Child"

1980. Olympic Games, Moscow.

366 **73** 20 c. multicoloured . . . 20 15
367 – 20 c. multicoloured . . . 20 15
368 – 25 c. multicoloured . . . 20 20
369 – 25 c. multicoloured . . . 20 20
370 – 30 c. multicoloured . . . 25 20
371 – 30 c. multicoloured . . . 25 20
372 – 35 c. multicoloured . . . 25 25
373 – 35 c. multicoloured . . . 25 25

DESIGNS: No. 367, Allen Wells, Great Britain (winner 100 metre dash); 368, 400 metre freestyle 369, Ines Diers (winner, D.D.R.); 370, Soling Class; 371, Winner, Denmark; 372, Football; 373, Winner, Czechoslovakia.

Nos. 366/7, 368/9, 370/1 and 372/3 were printed se-tenant in pairs each pair forming a composite design. On the 25 c. and 35 c. stamps the face value is at right on the first design and at left on the second in each pair. For the 30 c. No. 370 has a yacht with a green sail at left and No. 371 a yacht with a red sail.

1980. Christmas. Various Virgin and Child paintings by Andrea del Sarto.

375 **74** 20 c. multicoloured . . . 15 15
376 – 25 c. multicoloured . . . 15 15
377 – 30 c. multicoloured . . . 20 20
378 – 35 c. multicoloured . . . 20 20

75 "Phalaenopsis sp."

77 Prince Charles

76 "Jesus Defiled" (El Greco)

1981. Flowers (1st series). Multicoloured.

381 2 c. Type **75** 10 10
382 2 c. Moth orchid 10 10
383 5 c. "Euphorbia pulcherrima" 10 10
384 5 c. Poinsettia 10 10
385 10 c. "Thunbergia alata" . . 10 10
386 10 c. Black-eyed Susan . . . 10 10
387 15 c. "Cochlospermum hibiscoides" 15 15
388 15 c. Buttercup tree 15 15
389 20 c. "Begonia sp." 20 20
390 20 c. Begonia 20 20
391 25 c. "Plumeria sp." 25 25
392 25 c. Frangipani 25 25
393 30 c. "Strelitzia reginae" . . 30 30
394 30 c. Bird of Paradise 30 30
395 35 c. "Hibiscus syriacus" . . 30 30
396 35 c. Rose of Sharon 30 30
397 40 c. "Nymphaea sp." 35 35
398 40 c. Water lily 35 35
399 50 c. "Tibouchina sp." 45 45
400 50 c. Princess flower 45 45
401 60 c. "Nelumbo sp." 55 55
402 60 c. Lotus 55 55
403 80 c. "Hybrid hibiscus" . . . 75 75
404 80 c. Yellow Hibiscus 75 75
405 $1 Golden shower tree ("cassia fistula") . . . . 1·25 1·00
406 $2 "Orchid var" . . . . . . 3·50 2·50
407 $3 "Orchid sp." . . . . . . 4·50 3·50
408 $4 Euphorbia pulcherrima poinsettia" . . . . 3·50 4·00
409 $6 "Hybrid hibiscus" . . . . 5·50 6·00
410 $10 Scarlet hibiscus ("hibiscus rosa-sinensis") . . . . . . 8·50 9·00

Nos. 405/10 are larger, 47 × 35 mm.
See also Nos. 527/36.

1981. Easter. Details of Paintings. Mult.

425 35 c. Type **76** 40 30
426 50 c. "Pieta" (Fernando Gallego) 60 50
427 60 c. "The Supper of Emmaus" (Jacopo de Pontormo) . . . 65 55

1981. Royal Wedding. Multicoloured.

430 75 c. Type **77** 25 60
431 95 c. Lady Diana Spencer . . 50 70
432 $1.20 Prince Charles and Lady Diana Spencer 50 80

78 Footballer Silhouettes

1981. World Cup Football Championship, Spain (1982).

434 **78** 30 c. green, gold and blue . 20 20
435 – 30 c. green, gold and blue . 20 20
436 – 30 c. green, gold and blue . 20 20
437 – 35 c. blue, gold & orange . 20 20
438 – 35 c. blue, gold & orange . 20 20
439 – 35 c. blue, gold & orange . 20 20
440 – 40 c. orange, gold & green . 20 20
441 – 40 c. orange, gold & green . 20 20
442 – 40 c. orange, gold & green . 20 20

DESIGNS—Various footballer silhouettes: 435, gold figure 3rd from left; 436, gold figure 4th from left; 437, gold figure 3rd from left; 438, gold figure 4th from left; 439, gold figure 2nd from left; 440, gold figure 3rd from left displaying close control; 441, gold figure 2nd from left; 442, gold figure 3rd from left, heading.

1982. International Year for Disabled Persons. Nos. 430/2 surch **+5c.**

444 75 c. + 5 c. Type **77** . . . . 60 1·00
445 95 c. + 5 c. Lady Diana Spencer 70 1·25
446 $1.20 + 5 c. Prince Charles and Lady Diana . . . . 75 1·50

80 "The Holy Family with Angels" (detail)

81 Prince of Wales

1981. Christmas. 375th Birth Anniv of Rembrandt. Multicoloured.

448 20 c. Type **80** 65 45
449 35 c. "Presentation in the Temple" 85 55
450 50 c. "Virgin and Child in Temple" . . . . 95 1·10
451 60 c. "The Holy Family" . . . . 1·25 1·50

1982. 21st Birthday of Princess of Wales. Multicoloured.

454 50 c. Type **81** 40 55
455 $1.25 Prince and Princess of Wales 60 90
456 $2.50 Princess of Wales . . . . 1·50 1·40

1982. Birth of Prince William of Wales (1st issue). Nos. 430/2 optd.

458 75 c. Type **77** . . . . 1·50 2·00
459 75 c. Type **77** . . . . 1·50 2·00
460 95 c. Lady Diana Spencer . . 2·50 2·50
461 95 c. Lady Diana Spencer . . 2·50 2·50
462 $1.20 Prince Charles and Lady Diana Spencer . . . . . . 2·50 2·75
463 $1.20 Prince Charles and Lady Diana Spencer . . . . . . 2·50 2·75

OVERPRINTS: Nos. 458, 460 and 462 **COMMEMORATING THE ROYAL BIRTH 21 JUNE 1982**; 459, 461 and 463 **BIRTH OF PRINCE WILLIAM OF WALES 21 JUNE 1982.**

1982. Birth of Prince William of Wales (2nd issue). As Nos. 454/6, but with changed inscriptions. Multicoloured.

465 50 c. Type **81** 45 55
466 $1.25 Prince and Princess of Wales . . . . 85 1·25
467 $2.50 Princess of Wales . . . . 2·75 2·25

83 Infant

1982. Christmas. Paintings of Infants by Bronzion, Murillo and Boucher.

469 **83** 40 c. multicoloured . . . . 1·10 50
470 – 52 c. multicoloured . . . . 1·25 60
471 – 83 c. multicoloured . . . . 2·00 1·50
472 – $1.05 multicoloured . . . . 2·25 1·75

85 Prime Minister Rober Rex

1983. Commonwealth Day. Multicoloured.

475 70 c. Type **85** 50 55
476 70 c. H.M.S. "Resolution" and H.M.S. "Adventure" off Niue, 1774 . . . . 50 55
477 70 c. Passion flower 50 55
478 70 c. Limes 50 55

86 Scouts signalling

1983. 75th Anniv of Boy Scout Movement and 125th Birth Anniv of Lord Baden-Powell. Multicoloured.

479 40 c. Type **86** 35 40
480 50 c. Planting sapling 45 50
481 83 c. Map-reading 85 90

1983. 15th World Scout Jamboree, Alberta, Canada. Nos. 479/81 optd **XV WORLD JAMBOREE CANADA.**

483 40 c. Type **86** 35 40
484 50 c. Planting sapling 45 50
485 83 c. Map-reading 85 90

88 Black Right Whale

1983. Protect the Whales. Multicoloured.

487 12 c. Type **88** 75 65
488 25 c. Fin whale 95 80
489 35 c. Sei whale . . . . 1·50 1·25
490 40 c. Blue whale . . . . 1·75 1·50
491 58 c. Bowhead whale . . . . 1·90 1·60
492 70 c. Sperm whale . . . . . . 2·25 1·75
493 83 c. Humpback whale . . . 2·50 2·25
494 $1.05 Minke whale . . . . . 3·00 2·50
495 $2.50 Grey whale . . . . . . 4·25 4·00

89 Montgolfier Balloon, 1783

1983. Bicentenary of Manned Flight. Mult.

496 25 c. Type **89** 35 25
497 40 c. Wright Brothers Flyer I, 1903 . . . . 75 45
498 58 c. Airship "Graf Zeppelin", 1928 . . . . 90 60
499 70 c. Boeing 247, 1933 . . . . 1·25 85
500 83 c. "Apollo 8", 1968 . . . 1·25 1·00
501 $1.05 Space shuttle "Columbia", 1982 . . . . 1·40 1·40

90 "The Garvagh Madonna"

91 Morse Key Transmitter

1983. Christmas. 500th Birth Anniv of Raphael. Multicoloured.
503 30 c. Type **90** 40 30
504 40 c. "Madonna of the Granduca" 45 35
505 58 c. "Madonna of the Goldfish" 65 50
506 70 c. "The Holy Family of Francis I" 80 60
507 83 c. "The Holy Family with Saints" . . . . 1·00 70

1983. Various stamps surch. (a) Nos. 393/4, 399/404 and 407.
509 52 c. on 30 c. "Strelitzia reginae" 60 45
510 52 c. on 30 c. Bird of paradise 60 45
511 58 c. on 50 c. "Tibouchina sp." 70 55
512 58 c. on 50 c. Princess flower . 70 55
513 70 c. on 60 c. "Nelumbo sp." . 75 60
514 70 c. on 60 c. Lotus 75 60
515 83 c. on 80 c. "Hybrid hibiscus" 90 75
516 83 c. on 80 c. Yellow hibiscus 90 75
517 $3.70 on $3 "Orchid sp." . . . 5·00 3·25

(b) Nos. 431/2 and 455/6.
518 $1.10 on 95 c. Lady Diana Spencer . . . . 2·50 2·25
519 $1.10 on $1.25 Prince and Princess of Wales . . . . 2·00 2·00
520 $2.60 on $1.20 Prince Charles and Lady Diana . . . . . 4·00 3·50
521 $2.60 on $2.50 Princess of Wales 2·75 3·25

1984. World Communications Year. Multicoloured.
523 40 c. Type **91** 30 35
524 52 c. Wall-mounted phone . . 40 45
525 83 c. Communications satellite 60 65

92 "Phalaenopsis sp."

93 Discus throwing

1984. Flowers (2nd series). Multicoloured.
527 12 c. Type **92** 25 15
528 25 c. "Euphorbia pulcherrima" 35 20
529 30 c. "Cochlospermum hibiscoides" 40 25
530 35 c. "Begonia sp." 40 25
531 40 c. "Plumeria sp." 50 30
532 52 c. "Strelitzia reginae" . . . 65 40
533 58 c. "Hibiscus syriacus" . . . 70 45
534 70 c. "Tibouchina sp." . . . . 1·00 60
535 83 c. "Nelumbo sp." . . . . . 1·10 70
536 $1.05 "Hybrid hibiscus" . . . 1·25 85
537 $1.75 "Cassia fistula" . . . . 2·00 1·50
538 $2.30 "Orchid var" . . . . . 3·50 2·00
539 $3.90 "Orchid sp." . . . . . 5·00 4·00
540 $5 "Euphorbia pulcherrima poinsettia" . . . . 6·50 4·50
541 $6.60 "Hybrid hibiscus" . . . 7·00 6·00
542 $8.30 "Hibiscus rosa-sinensis" 8·00 7·00
Nos. 537/42 are larger, 39 × 31 mm.

1984. Olympic Games, Los Angeles. Multicoloured.
547 30 c. Type **93** 25 30
548 35 c. Sprinting (horiz) 30 35
549 40 c. Horse racing (horiz) . . . 35 40
550 58 c. Boxing (horiz) 50 55
551 70 c. Javelin-throwing 60 65

94 Koala

98 "The Nativity" (A. Vaccaro)

96 Niue National Flag and Premier Sir Robert Rex

1984. "Ausipex" International Stamp Exhibition, Melbourne. (a) Designs showing Koala Bears.
552 **94** 25 c. mult (postage) 60 30
553 – 35 c. multicoloured 65 35
554 – 40 c. multicoloured 70 40
555 – 58 c. multicoloured 90 65
556 – 70 c. multicoloured . . . . 1·10 75

(b) Vert designs showing Kangaroos.
557 – 83 c. multicoloured (air) . . . 1·25 85
558 – $1.05 multicoloured . . . . 1·50 1·25
559 – $2.50 multicoloured . . . . 3·00 3·50

1984. Olympic Gold Medal Winners, Los Angeles. Nos. 547/51 optd.
561 30 c. Type **93** 25 30
562 35 c. Sprinting 30 35
563 40 c. Horse racing 30 35
564 58 c. Boxing 45 50
565 70 c. Javelin-throwing 55 60
OPTS: 30 c. **Discus Throw Rolf Danneberg Germany**; 35 c. **1,500 Metres Sebastian Coe Great Britain**; 40 c. **Equestrian Mark Todd New Zealand**; 58 c. **Boxing Tyrell Biggs United States**; 70 c. **Javelin Throw Arto Haerkoenen Finland**.

1984. 10th Anniv of Self-Government. Mult.
568 40 c. Type **96** 55 35
569 58 c. Map of Niue and Premier Rex 70 50
570 70 c. Premier Rex receiving proclamation of self-government 70 60

1984. Birth of Prince Henry. Nos. 430 and 454 surch **$2 Prince Henry 15. 9. 84.**
573 $2 on 50 c. Type **81** . . . . . 2·50 1·75
574 $2 on 75 c. Type **77** . . . . . 2·50 1·75

1984. Christmas. Multicoloured.
575 40 c. Type **98** 40 35
576 58 c. "Virgin with Fly" (anon, 16th-century) 55 50
577 70 c. "The Adoration of the Shepherds" (B. Murillo) . . 65 60
578 80 c. "Flight into Egypt" (B. Murillo) 65 70

99 House Wren

1985. Birth Bicentenary of John J. Audubon (ornithologist). Multicoloured.
581 40 c. Type **99** . . . . 2·75 1·00
582 70 c. Veery . . . . 3·00 1·60
583 83 c. Grasshopper sparrow . . 3·25 2·00
584 $1.50 Henslow's sparrow . . . 3·50 2·00
585 $2.50 Vesper sparrow . . . . 5·00 3·75

100 The Queen Mother in Garter Robes

1985. Life and Times of Queen Elizabeth the Queen Mother. Multicoloured.
587 70 c. Type **100** 55 60
588 $1.15 In open carriage with the Queen 80 95
589 $1.50 With Prince Charles during 80th birthday celebrations . 90 1·25

1985. South Pacific Mini Games, Rarotonga. Nos. 547/8 and 550/1 surch **MINI SOUTH PACIFIC GAMES, RAROTONGA** and emblem.
591 52 c. on 70 c. Javelin throwing 40 45
592 83 c. on 58 c. Boxing 65 70
593 95 c. on 35 c. Sprinting . . . 75 80
594 $2 on 30 c. Type **93** . . . . . 1·50 1·60

1985. Pacific Islands Conference, Rarotonga. Nos. 475/8 optd **PACIFIC ISLANDS CONFERENCE, RAROTONGA** and emblem.
595 70 c. Type **85** 55 60
596 70 c. "Resolution" and "Adventure" off Niue, 1774 55 60
597 70 c. Passion flower 55 60
598 70 c. Limes 55 60
Nos. 595 also shows an overprinted amendment to the caption which now reads **Premier Sir Robert Rex K.B.E.**

103 "R. Strozzi's Daughter" (Titian)

104 "Virgin and Child"

1985. International Youth Year. Mult.
599 58 c. Type **103** . . . . 1·00 90
600 70 c. "The Fifer" (E. Manet) 1·25 1·00
601 $1.15 "Portrait of a Young Girl" (Renoir) . . . . 1·90 1·90
602 $1.50 "Portrait of M. Berard" (Renoir) . . . . 2·25 2·50

1985. Christmas. Details of Paintings by Correggio. Multicoloured.
604 58 c. Type **104** . . . . 1·25 85
605 85 c. "Adoration of the Magi" 1·60 1·25
606 $1.05 "Virgin with Child and St. John" . . . . 2·00 2·25
607 $1.45 "Virgin and Child with St. Catherine" . . . . 2·50 3·00

105 "The Constellations" (detail)

1986. Appearance of Halley's Comet. Designs showing details from ceiling painting "The Constellations" by Giovanni de Vecchi. Nos. 611/13 show different spacecraft at top left. Multicoloured.
610 60 c. Type **105** 50 50
611 75 c. "Vega" spacecraft . . . 65 65
612 $1.10 "Planet A" spacecraft . . 90 90
613 $1.50 "Giotto" spacecraft . . . 1·25 1·25

106 Queen Elizabeth II and Prince Philip

107 U.S.A. 1847 Franklin 5 c. Stamp and Washington Sculpture, Mt. Rushmore, U.S.A.

1986. 60th Birthday of Queen Elizabeth II. Multicoloured.
615 $1.10 Type **106** . . . . . . 70 1·00
616 $1.50 Queen and Prince Philip at Balmoral . . . . 90 1·25
617 $2 Queen at Buckingham Palace 1·25 1·75

1986. "Ameripex '86" International Stamp Exhibition, Chicago. Multicoloured.
620 $1 Type **107** . . . . 2·75 2·75
621 $1 Flags of Niue and U.S.A. and Mt. Rushmore sculptures . . 2·75 2·75
Nos. 620/1 were printed together, se-tenant, forming a composite design.

108 "Statue under Construction, Paris, 1883" (Victor Dargaud)

1986. Centenary of Statue of Liberty. Multicoloured.
622 $1 Type **108** . . . . 2·00 2·00
623 $2.50 "Unveiling of Statue of Liberty" (Edmund Morand) 2·75 2·75

109 Prince Andrew, Miss Sarah Ferguson and Westminster Abbey

1986. Royal Wedding.
625 **109** $2.50 multicoloured . . . 2·75 3·00

110 Great Egret

111 "Virgin and Child" (Perugino)

1986. "Stampex '86" Stamp Exhibition, Adelaide. Australian Birds. Multicoloured.
628 40 c. Type **110** . . . . 2·50 1·75
629 60 c. Painted finch (horiz) . . 2·75 2·00
630 75 c. Australian king parrot . 3·00 2·25
631 80 c. Variegated wren (horiz) . 3·25 2·50
632 $1 Peregrine falcon . . . . . 3·75 2·75
633 $1.65 Azure kingfisher (horiz) 5·00 4·00
634 $2.20 Budgerigars . . . . . . 6·00 6·00
635 $4.25 Emu (horiz) . . . . . . 7·50 7·50

1986. Christmas from Vatican Museum. Multicoloured.
636 80 c. Type **111** . . . . 2·00 1·75
637 $1.15 "Virgin of St. N. dei Frari" (Titian) . . . . 2·25 2·00
638 $1.80 "Virgin with Milk" (Lorenzo di Credi) . . . . 3·25 3·50
639 $2.60 "Madonna of Foligno" (Raphael) . . . . 4·00 4·50

1986. Visit of Pope John Paul II to South Pacific. Nos. 636/9 surch **CHRISTMAS VISIT TO SOUTH PACIFIC OF POPE JOHN II NOVEMBER 21-24 1986.**
642 80 c. + 10 c. Type **111** . . . . 2·50 2·50
643 $1.15 + 10 c. "Virgin of St. N. dei Frari" (Titian) . . . . 3·00 3·00
644 $1.80 + 10 c. "Virgin with Milk" (Lorenzo di Credi) . . . . 4·00 4·00
645 $2.60 + 10 c. "Madonna of Foligno" (Raphael) . . . . 5·00 5·00

113 Boris Becker, Olympic Rings and Commemorative Coin

1987. Olympic Games, Seoul (1988). Tennis (1st issue). Designs showing Boris Becker in play.
649 **113** 80 c. multicoloured . . . 2·00 2·00
650 – $1.15 multicoloured . . . 2·25 2·25
651 – $1.40 multicoloured . . . 2·50 2·50
652 – $1.80 multicoloured . . . 3·25 3·25

1987. Olympic Games, Seoul (1988). Tennis (2nd issue). As T **113** but showing Steffi Graf.
653 85 c. multicoloured . . . . . 1·25 1·25
654 $1.05 multicoloured . . . . . 1·50 1·50
655 $1.30 multicoloured . . . . . 1·75 1·75
656 $1.75 multicoloured . . . . . 2·00 2·00

1987. Royal Ruby Wedding. Nos. 616/17 surch **40TH WEDDING ANNIV. 4.85.**
657 $4.85 on $1.50 Queen and Prince Philip at Balmoral . . . . 3·50 4·50
658 $4.85 on $2 Queen at Buckingham Palace . . . . 3·50 4·50

115 "The Nativity"

1987. Christmas. Religious Paintings by Durer. Multicoloured.
659 80 c. Type **115** . . . . 1·50 1·25
660 $1.05 "Adoration of the Magi" 1·75 1·75
661 $2.80 "Celebration of the Rosary" . . . . 3·25 3·50
Nos. 659/61 each include detail of an angel with lute as in T **115**.

116 Franz Beckenbauer in Action

1988. West German Football Victories. Multicoloured.
664 20 c. Type **116** 70 70
665 40 c. German "All Star" team in action 90 90
666 60 c. Bayern Munich team with European Cup, 1974 . . . 1·10 1·10
667 80 c. World Cup match, England, 1966 . . . . 1·40 1·40
668 $1.05 World Cup match, Mexico, 1970 . . . . 1·60 1·60
669 $1.30 Beckenbauer with pennant, 1974 . . . . 2·00 2·00
670 $1.80 Beckenbauer and European Cup, 1974 . . . 2·25 2·25

1988. Steffi Graf's Tennis Victories. Nos. 653/6 optd.
671 85 c. mult (optd **Australia 24 Jan 88 French Open 4 June 88**) . 1·50 1·50
672 $1.05 multicoloured (optd **Wimbledon 2 July 88 U S Open 10 Sept. 88**) . . . . 1·75 1·75
673 $1.30 multicoloured (optd **Women's Tennis Grand Slam: 10 September 88**) . . . . . 1·90 1·90
674 $1.75 mult (optd **Seoul Olympic Games Gold Medal Winner**) 2·10 2·10

118 Angels

1988. Christmas. Details from "The Adoration of the Shepherds" by Rubens. Multicoloured.
675 60 c. Type **118** . . . . 1·50 1·50
676 80 c. Shepherds . . . . 1·75 1·75
677 $1.05 Virgin Mary . . . . . . 2·50 2·50
678 $1.30 Holy Child . . . . . . 3·00 3·00

119 Astronaut and "Apollo 11" Emblem

1989. 20th Anniv of First Manned Landing on Moon. Multicoloured.
680 $1.50 Type **119** . . . . 3·50 3·50
681 $1.50 Earth and Moon . . . . 3·50 3·50
682 $1.50 Astronaut and "Apollo 11" emblem . . . . 3·50 3·50

120 Priests

1989. Christmas. Details from "Presentation in the Temple" by Rembrandt. Multicoloured.
684 70 c. Type **120** . . . . 2·00 2·00
685 80 c. Virgin and Christ Child in Simeon's arms . . . . 2·00 2·00
686 $1.05 Joseph . . . . 2·50 2·50
687 $1.30 Simeon and Christ Child 3·00 3·00

121 Fritz Walter

1990. World Cup Football Championship, Italy. German Footballers. Multicoloured.
689 80 c. Type **121** . . . . 2·50 2·50
690 $1.15 Franz Beckenbauer . . . 2·75 2·75
691 $1.40 Uwe Seeler . . . . . . 3·00 3·00
692 $1.80 German team emblem and signatures of former captains 4·00 4·00

122 "Merchant Maarten Looten" (Rembrandt)

123 Queen Elizabeth the Queen Mother

1990. 150th Anniv of the Penny Black. Rembrandt Paintings. Multicoloured.
693 80 c. Type **122** . . . . 2·25 2·25
694 $1.05 "Rembrandt's Son Titus with Pen in Hand" . . . . 2·50 2·50
695 $1.30 "The Shipbuilder and his Wife" . . . . 2·75 2·75
696 $1.80 "Bathsheba with King David's Letter" . . . . . . 3·00 3·00

1990. 90th Birthday of Queen Elizabeth the Queen Mother.
698 **123** $1.25 multicoloured . . . 3·75 3·75

124 "Adoration of the Magi" (Dirk Bouts)

129 "The Virgin and Child with Sts. Jerome and Dominic" (Lippi)

1990. Christmas. Religious Paintings. Mult.
700 70 c. Type **124** . . . . 2·00 2·00
701 80 c. "Holy Family" (Fra Bartolommeo) . . . . 2·25 2·25
702 $1.05 "Nativity" (Memling) . . 2·50 2·50
703 $1.30 "Adoration of the Kings" (Bruegel the Elder) . . . . 3·25 3·25

1990. "Birdpex '90" Stamp Exhibition, Christchurch, New Zealand. No. 410 optd **Birdpex '90** and logo.
705 $10 Scarlet hibiscus . . . . . 11·00 12·00

1991. 65th Birthday of Queen Elizabeth II. No. 409 optd **SIXTY FIFTH BIRTHDAY QUEEN ELIZABETH II**.
706 $6 "Hybrid hibiscus" . . . . 8·50 10·00

1991. 10th Wedding Anniv of Prince and Princess of Wales. Nos. 430/2 optd **TENTH ANNIVERSARY**.
707A 75 c. Type **77** . . . . 1·75 1·75
708A 95 c. Lady Diana Spencer . . 2·75 2·75
709A $1.20 Prince Charles and Lady Diana . . . . 2·75 2·75

1991. Christmas. Religious Paintings. Mult.
710 20 c. Type **129** 50 50
711 50 c. "The Isenheim Altarpiece" (M. Grunewald) . . . . . . 1·00 1·00
712 $1 "The Nativity" (G. Pittoni) 1·75 2·00
713 $2 "Adoration of the Kings" (J. Brueghel the Elder) . . 2·50 2·75

130 Banded Rail

1992. Birds. Multicoloured.
718 20 c. Type **130** 15 20
719 50 c. Red-tailed tropic bird . . 30 30
720 70 c. Purple swamphen . . . 45 45
721 $1 Pacific pigeon 65 65
722 $1.50 White-collared kingfisher 95 95
723 $2 Blue-crowned lory . . . . 1·25 1·25
724 $3 Purple-capped fruit dove . . 1·90 1·90
726 $5 Barn owl . . . . 3·25 3·25
727 $7 Longtailed koel ("Cuckoo") ($48\frac{1}{2} \times 35$ mm) . . . . . . 4·50 4·75
728 $10 Eastern reef heron ($48\frac{1}{2} \times 35$ mm) . . . . . . 6·25 6·50
729 $15 Spotted triller ("Polynesian Triller") ($48\frac{1}{2} \times 35$ mm) . . . 9·50 9·75

131 Columbus before King Ferdinand and Queen Isabella

1992. 500th Anniv of Discovery of America by Columbus. Multicoloured.
731 $2 Type **131** . . . . 2·75 2·75
732 $3 Fleet of Columbus . . . . 4·50 4·50
733 $5 Claiming the New World for Spain . . . . 6·00 6·00

132 Tennis and $10 Commemorative Coin

1992. Olympic Games, Barcelona. Mult.
734 $2.50 Type **132** . . . . . . 4·00 4·00
735 $2.50 Olympic flame and national flags . . . . . . 4·00 4·00
736 $2.50 Gymnastics and different $10 coin . . . . 4·00 4·00

1992. 6th Festival of Pacific Arts, Rarotonga. Nos. 336/51 surch **$1**.
738 $1 on 20 c. Type **69** . . . . . 1·00 1·00
739 $1 on 20 c. Ku-Tagwa plaque, New Guinea . . . . 1·00 1·00
740 $1 on 20 c. Suspension hook, New Guinea . . . . 1·00 1·00
741 $1 on 20 c. Ancestral board, New Guinea . . . . 1·00 1·00
742 $1 on 25 c. Platform post, New Hebrides . . . . 1·00 1·00
743 $1 on 25 c. Canoe ornament, New Ireland . . . . 1·00 1·00
744 $1 on 25 c. Carved figure, Admiralty Islands . . . . . 1·00 1·00
745 $1 on 25 c. Female with child, Admiralty Islands . . . . . 1·00 1·00
746 $1 on 30 c. The God A'a, Rurutu, Austral Islands . . 1·00 1·00
747 $1 on 30 c. Statue of Tangaroa, Cook Islands . . . . . . 1·00 1·00
748 $1 on 30 c. Ivory pendant, Tonga 1·00 1·00
749 $1 on 30 c. Tapa (Hiapo) cloth, Niue . . . . 1·00 1·00
750 $1 on 35 c. Feather box (Waka), New Zealand . . . . . . 1·00 1·00
751 $1 on 35 c. Hei-Tiki amulet, New Zealand . . . . 1·00 1·00
752 $1 on 35 c. House post, New Zealand . . . . 1·00 1·00
753 $1 on 35 c. Feather image of god Ku, Hawaii . . . . 1·00 1·00

134 "St. Catherine's Mystic Marriage" (detail) (Memling)

135 Queen on Official Visit

1992. Christmas.
754 **134** 20 c. multicoloured 50 40
755 – 50 c. multicoloured 85 85
756 – $1 multicoloured . . . . . 1·50 1·50
757 – $2 multicoloured . . . . . 2·50 3·25
DESIGNS: 50 c., $1, $2 Different details from "St. Catherine's Mystic Marriage" by Hans Memling.

1992. 40th Anniv of Queen Elizabeth II's Accession. Multicoloured.
759 70 c. Type **135** . . . . 1·50 1·50
760 $1 Queen in green evening dress 2·00 2·00
761 $1.50 Queen in white embroidered evening dress . 2·50 2·50
762 $2 Queen with bouquet . . . 2·75 2·75

136 Rough-toothed Dolphin

1993. Endangered Species. South Pacific Dolphins. Multicoloured.
763 20 c. Type **136** . . . . 1·00 80
764 50 c. Fraser's dolphin . . . . 1·75 1·50
765 75 c. Pantropical spotted dolphin 2·25 2·25
766 $1 Risso's dolphin . . . . . 2·75 3·25

1993. Premier Sir Robert Rex Commemoration. Nos. 568/70 optd **1909 IN MEMORIAM 1992 SIR ROBERT R REX K.B.E.** or surch also.
767 40 c. Type **96** . . . . 1·00 1·00
768 58 c. Map of Niue and Premier Rex . . . . 1·25 1·25
769 70 c. Premier Rex receiving proclamation of self-government . . . . 1·50 1·50
770 $1 on 40 c. Type **96** . . . . . 1·75 1·75
771 $1 on 58 c. Map of Niue and Premier Rex . . . . 1·75 1·75
772 $1 on 70 c. Premier Rex receiving proclamation of self-government . . . . 1·75 1·75

138 Queen Elizabeth II in Coronation Robes and St. Edward's Crown

1993. 40th Anniv. of Coronation.
773 **138** $5 multicoloured . . . . 7·00 7·50

139 "Virgin of the Rosary" (detail) (Guido Reni)

1993. Christmas.
774 **139** 20 c. multicoloured . . . 55 45
775 – 70 c. multicoloured . . . 1·25 1·00
776 – $1 multicoloured . . . . 1·40 1·25
777 – $1. 50 multicoloured . . . 2·25 2·50
778 – $3 multicoloured ($32 \times 47$ mm) . . . . . 3·75 4·50
DESIGNS: 70 c. to $3 Different details of "Virgin of the Rosary" (Reni).

140 World Cup and Globe with Flags of U.S.A. and Previous Winners

1994. World Cup Football Championship, U.S.A.
779 **140** $4 multicoloured . . . . 5·50 6·00

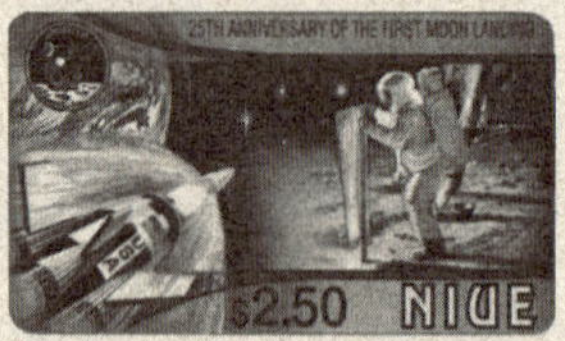

141 "Apollo 11" and Astronaut on Moon

1994. 25th Anniv of First Manned Moon Landing. Multicoloured.
780 $2.50 Type **141** . . . . . . 5·50 5·50
781 $2.50 Astronaut and flag . . 5·50 5·50
782 $2.50 Astronaut and equipment 5·50 5·50

142 "The Adoration of the Kings" (Jan Gossaert)

1994. Christmas. Religious Paintings. Multicoloured.
783 70 c. Type **142** . . . . 1·00 1·25
784 70 c. "Madonna and Child with Sts. John and Catherine" (Titian) . . . . 1·00 1·25
785 70 c. "The Holy Family and Shepherd" (Titian) . . . . 1·00 1·25
786 70 c. "The Virgin and Child with Saints" (Gerard David) . . 1·00 1·25
787 $1 "The Adoration of the Shepherds" (cherubs detail) (Poussin) . . . . 1·25 1·50
788 $1 "The Adoration of the Shepherds" (Holy Family detail) (Poussin) . . . . . 1·25 1·50
789 $1 "Madonna and Child with Sts. Joseph and John" (Sebastiano) . . . . 1·25 1·50
790 $1 "The Adoration of the Kings" (Veronese) . . . . 1·25 1·50

143 Long John Silver and Jim Hawkins ("Treasure Island")

145 Tapeu Orchid

1994. Death Centenary of Robert Louis Stevenson (author). Multicoloured.

791	$1.75 Type **143**	2·50	2·50
792	$1.75 Transformation of Dr. Jekyll ("Dr. Jekyll and Mr. Hyde")	2·50	2·50
793	$1.75 Attack on David Balfour ("Kidnapped")	2·50	2·50
794	$1.75 Robert Louis Stevenson, tomb and inscription	2·50	2·50

1996. Nos. 720 and 722 surch.

795	50 c. on 70 c. Purple swamphen	2·00	1·50
796	$1 on $1.50 White-collared kingfisher	3·00	2·50

1996. Flowers. Multicoloured.

797	70 c. Type **145**	80	80
798	$1 Frangipani	1·00	1·00
799	$1.20 "Golden Shower"	1·40	1·60
800	$1.50 "Pua"	1·90	2·25

1996. Redrawn design as No. 146.

801	20 c. red and green	15	20

146 "Jackfish" (yacht)

1996. Sailing Ships. Multicoloured.

802	70 c. Type **146**	90	90
803	$1 "Jennifer" (yacht)	1·40	1·40
804	$1.20 "Mikeva" (yacht)	1·75	2·00
805	$2 "Eye of the Wind" (cadet brig)	2·25	2·50

148 "Acropora gemmifera"

1996. Corals. Multicoloured.

807	20 c. Type **148**	15	20
808	50 c. "Acropora nobilis"	35	40
809	70 c. "Goniopora lobata"	50	55
810	$1 "Sylaster sp."	75	80
811	$1.20 "Alveopora catalai"	90	95
812	$1.50 "Fungia scutaria"	1·10	1·25
813	$2 "Porites solida"	1·50	1·60
814	$3 "Millepora sp."	2·25	2·40
815	$4 "Pocillopora eydouxi"	3·00	3·25
816	$5 "Platygyra pini"	3·75	4·00

150 Steps to Lagoon

1997. Island Scenes. Multicoloured.

818	$1 Type **150**	1·00	1·10
819	$1 Islands in lagoon	1·00	1·10
820	$1 Beach with rocks in foreground	1·00	1·10
821	$1 Over-hanging rock on beach	1·00	1·10

Nos. 818/21 were printed together, se-tenant, forming a composite design.

151 Humpback Whale

1997. Whales (1st series). Multicoloured.

822	20 c. Type **151**	30	25
823	$1 Humpback whale and calf (vert)	1·10	1·10
824	$1.50 Humpback whale surfacing (vert)	1·60	1·75

See also Nos. 827/9.

1997. Whales (2nd series). As T **151**. Multicoloured.

827	50 c. Killer whale (vert)	60	60
828	70 c. Minke whale (vert)	80	80
829	$1.20 Sperm whale (vert)	1·10	1·10

154 Floral Display in Woven Basket

1997. Christmas. Floral Displays. Multicoloured.

831	20 c. Type **154**	25	20
832	50 c. Display in white pot	50	50
833	70 c. Display in white basket	70	70
834	$1 Display in purple vase	80	85

155 Divers and Turtle

1998. Diving. Multicoloured.

836	20 c. Type **155**	30	30
837	70 c. Diver exploring coral reef	65	65
838	$1 Exploring underwater chasm (vert)	80	80
839	$1.20 Divers and coral fronds	90	90
840	$1.50 Divers in cave	1·25	1·25

157 Pacific Black Duck

1998. Coastal Birds. Multicoloured.

841	20 c. Type **157**	30	30
842	70 c. Fairy tern	65	65
843	$1 Great frigate bird (vert)	85	85
844	$1.20 Lesser golden plover	95	95
845	$2 Brown noddy	1·50	1·50

158 Golden Cowrie

1998. Shells. Multicoloured.

846	20 c. Type **158**	30	30
847	70 c. Cowrie shell	65	65
848	$1 Spider conch	85	85
849	$5 Helmet shell	4·25	4·25

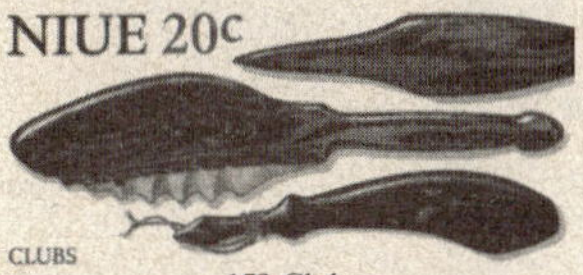

159 Clubs

1998. Ancient Weapons. Multicoloured.

850	20 c. Type **159**	15	20
851	$1.20 Three spears (59 × 24 mm)	75	80
852	$1.50 Five spears (59 × 24 mm)	95	1·00
853	$2 Throwing stones	1·25	1·40

160 Outrigger Canoe (first migration of Niue Fekai)

1999. "Australia '99" World Stamp Exhibition, Melbourne. Maritime History. Each blue.

854	70 c. Type **160**	45	50
855	$1 H.M.S. "Resolution" (Cook)	65	70
856	$1.20 "John Williams" (missionary sailing ship)	75	80
857	$1.50 Captain James Cook	95	1·00

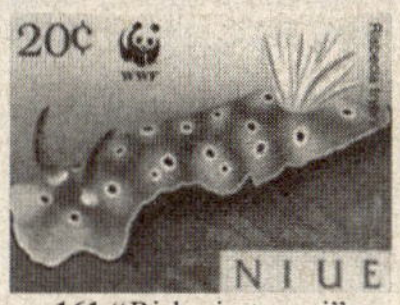

161 "Risbecia tryoni"

1999. Endangered Species. Nudibranchs. Mult.

858	20 c. Type **161**	15	20
859	$1 "Chromodoris lochi"	65	70
860	$1.20 "Chromodoris elizabethina"	75	80
861	$1.50 "Chromodoris bullocki"	95	1·00

OFFICIAL STAMPS

1985. Nos. 409/10 and 527/42 optd **O.H.M.S.**

O 1	12 c. Type **92**	35	30
O 2	25 c. "Euphorbia pulcherrima"	40	35
O 3	30 c. "Cochlospermum hibiscoides"	45	35
O 4	35 c. "Begonia sp."	50	40
O 5	40 c. "Plumeria sp."	50	45
O 6	52 c. "Strelitzia reginae"	60	50
O 7	58 c. "Hibiscus syriacus"	60	55
O 8	70 c. "Tibouchina sp."	75	70
O 9	83 c. "Nelumbo sp."	90	80
O10	$1.05 "Hybrid hibiscus"	1·25	1·00
O11	$1.75 "Cassia fistula"	1·75	1·75
O12	$2.30 Orchid var.	5·00	2·50
O13	$3.90 Orchid sp.	5·50	3·75
O14	$4 "Euphorbia pulcherrima poinsettia"	4·00	4·00
O15	$5 "Euphorbia pulcherrima poinsettia"	4·25	5·00
O16	$6 "Hybrid hibiscus"	5·50	6·50
O17	$6.60 "Hybrid hibiscus"	6·00	7·00
O18	$8.30 "Hibiscus rosa-sinensis"	7·00	8·00
O19	$10 Scarlet hibiscus	8·00	9·00

1993. Nos. 718/29 optd **O.H.M.S.**

O20	20 c. Type **130**	15	20
O21	50 c. Red-tailed tropic bird	30	35
O22	70 c. Purple swamphen	45	50
O23	$1 Pacific pigeon	65	70
O24	$1.50 White-collared kingfisher	95	1·00
O25	$2 Blue-crowned lory	1·25	1·40
O26	$3 Crimson-crowned fruit dove	1·90	2·00
O27	$5 Barn owl	3·25	3·50
O28	$7 Longtailed cuckoo ($48\frac{1}{2} \times 35$ mm)	4·50	4·75
O29	$10 Eastern reef heron ($48\frac{1}{2} \times 35$ mm)	6·25	6·50
O30	$15 Spotted triller ("Polynesian Triller") ($48\frac{1}{2} \times 35$ mm)	9·50	9·75

NORFOLK ISLAND

A small island East of New South Wales, administered by Australia until 1960 when local government was established.

1947. 12 pence = 1 shilling;
20 shillings = 1 pound.
1966. 100 cents = $1 Australian.

1 Ball Bay

1947.

1	1	$\frac{1}{2}$d. orange	35	60
2		1d. violet	50	60
3		$1\frac{1}{2}$d. green	50	70
4		2d. violet	55	40
5		$2\frac{1}{2}$d. red	80	30
6		3d. brown	70	70
6a		3d. green	16·00	6·50
7		4d. red	1·00	40
8		$5\frac{1}{2}$d. blue	70	30
9		6d. brown	70	30
10		9d. pink	1·25	40
11		1s. green	70	40
12		2s. brown	1·50	1·00
12a		2s. blue	24·00	7·00

12 "Hibiscus insularis"

2 Warder's Tower

4 Old Stores (Crankmill)

17 Queen Elizabeth II (after Annigoni and Cereus)

22 Red-tailed Tropic Bird

1953.

24	**12**	1d. green	15	10
25	–	2d. red and green	20	10
26	–	3d. green	70	15
13	**2**	$3\frac{1}{2}$d. red	1·50	90
27	–	5d. purple	55	20
14	–	$6\frac{1}{2}$d. green	2·50	2·75
15	**4**	$7\frac{1}{2}$d. blue	2·00	3·00
28	–	8d. red	80	50
16	–	$8\frac{1}{2}$d. brown	2·25	4·25
29	**17**	9d. blue	80	45
17	–	10d. violet	1·50	75
30	–	10d. brown and violet	2·75	1·25
31	–	1s. 1d. red	80	35
32	–	2s. brown	6·00	90
33	–	2s. 5d. violet	1·00	40
34	–	2s. 8d. brown and green	2·75	55
18	–	5s. brown	45·00	10·00
35	–	5s. brown and green	6·00	75
36	**22**	10s. green	50·00	26·00

DESIGNS—VERT: 2d. "Lagunaria patersonii"; 5d. Lantana; 8d. Red hibiscus; $8\frac{1}{2}$d. Barracks entrance; 10d. Salt house; 1s. 1d. Fringed hibiscus; 2s. Solander's petrel; 2s. 5d. Passion-flower; 2s. 8d. Rose apple. HORIZ: 3d. White tern; $6\frac{1}{2}$d. Airfield; 5s. Bloody Bridge.

For Nos. 25 and 28 with face values in decimal currency see Nos. 600/1.

8 Norfolk Is. Seal and Pitcairners Landing

1956. Cent of Landing of Pitcairners on Norfolk Is.

19	**8**	3d. green	1·50	40
20		2s. violet	2·00	75

1958. Surch.

21	**4**	7d. on $7\frac{1}{2}$d. blue	1·00	1·00
22	–	8d. on $8\frac{1}{2}$d. brown (No. 16)	1·00	1·00

1959. 150th Anniv of Australian P.O. No. 331 of Australia surch **NORFOLK ISLAND 5D.**

23	**143**	5d. on 4d. slate	35	30

1960. As Nos. 13 and 14/15 but colours changed and surch.

37	**2**	1s. 1d. on $3\frac{1}{2}$d. blue	3·50	2·50
38		2s. 5d. on $6\frac{1}{2}$d. turquoise	4·00	1·50
39	**4**	2s. 8d. on $7\frac{1}{2}$d. sepia	10·00	4·75

26 Queen Elizabeth II and Map

29 Stripey

1960. Introduction of Local Government.

40	**26**	2s. 8d. purple	16·00	9·50

1960. Christmas. As No. 338 of Australia.

41	**150**	5d. mauve	80	50

1961. Christmas. As No. 341 of Australia.

42	**153**	5d. blue	30	40

1962. Fishes.

43	**29**	6d. sepia, yellow & green	75	25
44	–	11d. orange, brown & blue	2·00	80
45	–	1s. blue, pink and olive	75	25
46	–	1s. 3d. blue, brown & green	2·00	1·75
47	–	1s. 6d. sepia, violet & blue	2·75	80
48	–	2s. 3d. multicoloured	5·00	80

DESIGNS: 11d. Gold-mouthed emperor; 1s. Surge wrasse ("Po'ov"); 1s. 3d. Seachub ("Dreamfish"); 1s. 6d. Giant grouper; 2s. 3d. White trevally.

1962. Christmas. As No. 345 of Australia.

49	**157**	5d. blue	45	70

1963. Christmas. As No. 361 of Australia.

50	**173**	5d. red	40	60

32 Overlooking Kingston

33 Norfolk Pine

1964. Multicoloured.

51	5d. Type **32**	75	40
52	8d. Kingston	1·00	1·00
53	9d. The Arches (Bumboras)	2·25	30
54	10d. Slaughter Bay	2·25	30

1964. 50th Anniv of Norfolk Island as Australian Territory.

55	**33**	5d. black, red and orange	40	15
56		8d. black, red and green	40	80

1964. Christmas. As No. 372 of Australia.

57	**183**	5d. multicoloured	30	40

1965. 50th Anniv of Gallipoli Landing. As T **184** of Australia, but slightly larger (22×34½ mm).

58	5d. brown, black and green	15	10

1965. Christmas. As No. 381 of Australia.

59	**190**	5d. multicoloured	15	10

38 "Hibiscus insularis"

39 Headstone Bridge

1966. Decimal Currency. As earlier issue but with values in cents and dollars. Surch in black on silver tablets obliterating old value as in T **38**.

60	**38**	1 c. on 1d.	20	10
61	–	2 c. on 2d. (No. 25)	20	10
62	–	3 c. on 3d. (No. 26)	50	30
63	–	4 c. on 5d. (No. 27)	25	10
64	–	5 c. on 8d. (No. 28)	30	10
65	–	10 c. on 10d. (No. 30)	60	15
66	–	15 c. on 1s. 1d. (No. 31)	45	30
67	–	20 c. on 2s. (No. 32)	3·50	2·75
68	–	25 c. on 2s. 5d. (No. 33)	1·50	40
69	–	30 c. on 2s. 8d. (No. 34)	1·00	50
70	–	50 c. on 5s. (No. 35)	3·50	75
71	**22**	$1 on 10s.	2·75	2·00

1966. Multicoloured.

72	7 c. Type **39**	40	15
73	9 c. Cemetery Road	40	15

41 St. Barnabas' Chapel (interior)

43 Star over Philip Island

1966. Centenary of Melanesian Mission. Mult.

74	4 c. Type **41**	10	10
75	25 c. St. Barnabas' Chapel (exterior)	20	20

1966. Christmas.

76	**43**	4 c. multicoloured	10	10

44 H.M.S. "Resolution", 1774

1967. Multicoloured.

77	1 c. Type **44**	10	10
78	2 c. "La Boussole" and "L'Astrolabe", 1788	15	10
79	3 c. H.M.S. "Supply" (brig), 1788	15	10
80	4 c. H.M.S. "Sirius" (frigate), 1790	30	10
81	5 c. "Norfolk" (cutter), 1798	20	10
82	7 c. H.M.S. "Mermaid" (survey cutter), 1825	20	10
83	9 c. "Lady Franklin" (full-rigged ship), 1853	20	10
84	10 c. "Morayshire" (full-rigged transport), 1856	20	30
85	15 c. "Southern Cross" (missionary ship), 1866	45	30
86	20 c. "Pitcairn" (missionary schooner), 1891	60	40
87	25 c. "Black Billy" (Norfolk Island whaleboat), 1895	1·50	75
88	30 c. "Iris" (cable ship), 1907	1·50	2·00
89	50 c. "Resolution" (schooner), 1926	4·00	3·25
90	$1 "Morinda" (freighter), 1931	5·50	3·25

1967. 50th Anniv of Lions Int. As T **205** of Australia.

91	4 c. black, green and yellow	10	10

46 Prayer of John Adams and Candle

1967. Christmas.

92	**46**	5 c. black, olive and red	10	10

1968. As T **191** of Australia, but inscr "NORFOLK ISLAND".

93	3 c. black, brown and red	10	10
94	4 c. black, brown and green	10	10
95	5 c. black, brown and violet	10	10
95a	6 c. black, brown and lake	30	45

59 Avro Type 691 Lancastrian and Douglas DC-4 Aircraft

1968. 21st Anniv of QANTAS Air Service, Sydney–Norfolk Island.

96	**59**	5 c. black, red and blue	15	10
97		7 c. brown, red & turq	15	10

60 Bethlehem Star and Flowers

61 Captain Cook, Quadrant and Chart of Pacific Ocean

1968. Christmas.

98	**60**	5 c. multicoloured	10	10

1969. Captain Cook Bicentenary (1st issue). Observation of the transit of Venus across the Sun from Tahiti.

99	**61**	10 c. multicoloured	10	10

See also Nos. 118/19, 129, 152/5, 200/2 and 213/14.

62 Van Diemen's Land, Norfolk Island and Sailing Cutter

63 "The Nativity" (carved mother-of-pearl plaque)

1969. 125th Anniv of Annexation of Norfolk Island to Van Diemen's Land.

100	**62**	5 c. multicoloured	10	10
101		30 c. multicoloured	50	70

1969. Christmas.

102	**63**	5 c. multicoloured	10	10

64 New Zealand Grey Flyeater

1970. Birds. Multicoloured.

103	1 c. Scarlet robin	30	10
104	2 c. Golden whistler	30	20
105	3 c. Type **64**	30	10
106	4 c. Long-tailed koels	60	10
107	5 c. Red-fronted parakeet	1·50	45
108	7 c. Long-tailed triller	45	10
109	9 c. Island thrush	70	10
110	10 c. Boobook owl	1·75	1·25
111	15 c. Norfolk Island pigeon	1·50	65
112	20 c. White-chested white-eye	7·00	3·25
113	25 c. Norfolk Island parrots	2·50	40
114	30 c. Collared grey fantail	7·00	1·75
115	45 c. Norfolk Island starlings	3·00	80
116	50 c. Crimson rosella	3·50	1·75
117	$1 Sacred kingfisher	10·00	10·00

Nos. 105/6, 109, 112, 114/15 and 117 are horiz; the remainder being vert.

65 Cook and Map of Australia

1970. Captain Cook Bicentenary (2nd issue). Discovery of Australia's East Coast. Mult.

118	5 c. Type **65**	15	10
119	20 c. H.M.S. "Endeavour" and aborigine	40	10

66 First Christmas Service, 1788

67 Bishop Patteson, and Martyrdom of St. Stephen

1970. Christmas.

120	**66**	5 c. multicoloured	10	10

1971. Death Cent of Bishop Patteson. Multicoloured.

121	6 c. Type **67**	10	20
122	6 c. Bible, Martyrdom of St. Stephen and knotted palm-frond	10	20
123	10 c. Bishop Patteson and stained glass	10	20
124	10 c. Cross and Bishop's Arms	10	20

68 Rose Window, St. Barnabas Chapel, Kingston

69 Map and Flag

1971. Christmas.

125	**68**	6 c. multicoloured	10	10

1972. 25th Anniv of South Pacific Commission.

126	**69**	7 c. multicoloured	15	20

70 "St. Mark" (stained glass window) (All Saints, Norfolk Is.)

71 Cross and Pines (stained glass-window All Saints Church)

1972. Christmas.

127	**70**	7 c. multicoloured	10	10

1972. Cent of First Pitcairner-built Church.

128	**71**	12 c. multicoloured	10	10

72 H.M.S. "Resolution" in the Antarctic

1973. Capt. Cook Bicentenary (3rd issue). Crossing of the Antarctic Circle.

129	**72**	35 c. multicoloured	3·00	2·25

73 Child and Christmas Tree

1973. Christmas. Multicoloured.

130	7 c. Type **73**	20	10
131	12 c. Type **73**	25	10
132	35 c. Fir trees and star	70	80

74 Protestant Clergyman's Quarters

1973. Historic Buildings. Multicoloured.

133	1 c. Type **74**	10	10
134	2 c. Royal Engineers' Office	10	10
135	3 c. Double Quarters for Free Overseers	25	30
136	4 c. Guard House	20	20
137	5 c. Entrance to Pentagonal Gaol	25	15
138	7 c. Pentagonal Gaol	35	35
139	8 c. Prisoners' Barracks	1·25	1·50
140	10 c. Officer's Quarters, New Military Barracks	50	55
141	12 c. New Military Barracks	50	30
142	14 c. Beach Stores	60	70
143	15 c. The Magazine	1·25	50
144	20 c. Entrance, Old Military Barracks	70	90
145	25 c. Old Military Barracks	1·25	1·00
146	30 c. Old Stores (Crankmill)	70	60
147	50 c. Commissariat Stores	70	2·00
148	$1 Government House	1·50	4·00

75 Royal Couple and Map

1974. Royal Visit.

149	**75**	7 c. multicoloured	40	15
150		25 c. multicoloured	1·25	75

76 Chichester's De Havilland Gipsy Moth Seaplane "Madame Elijah"

1974. 1st Aircraft Landing on Norfolk Island.

151	**76**	14 c. multicoloured	1·00	70

77 "Captain Cook" (engraving by J. Basire)

78 Nativity Scene (pearl-shell pew carving)

1974. Capt. Cook Bicentenary (4th issue). Discovery of Norfolk Is. Multicoloured.

152		7 c. Type **77**	1·00	75
153		10 c. H.M.S. "Resolution" (H. Roberts)	2·00	1·75
154		14 c. Norfolk Island pine	1·75	2·25
155		25 c. "Norfolk Island flax" (G. Raper)	2·00	3·00

1974. Christmas.

156	**78**	7 c. multicoloured	15	10
157		30 c. multicoloured	60	75

79 Norfolk Pine

1974. Centenary of Universal Postal Union. Multicoloured. Imperf. Self-adhesive.

158		10 c. Type **79**	25	40
159		15 c. Offshore islands	35	45
160		35 c. Crimson rosella and sacred kingfisher	60	75
161		40 c. Pacific map	60	90

80 H.M.S. "Mermaid" (survey cutter)

1975. 150th Anniv of Second Settlement. Multicoloured.

163		10 c. Type **80**	40	75
164		35 c. Kingston, 1835 (from painting by T. Seller)	60	1·00

81 Star on Norfolk Island Pine

82 Memorial Cross

1975. Christmas.

165	**81**	10 c. multicoloured	15	10
166		15 c. multicoloured	20	10
167		35 c. multicoloured	30	35

1975. Cent of St. Barnabas Chapel. Mult.

168		30 c. Type **82**	20	15
169		60 c. Laying foundation stone, and Chapel in 1975	40	40

83 Launching of "Resolution"

1975. 50th Anniv of Launching of "Resolution" (schooner). Multicoloured.

170		25 c. Type **83**	25	40
171		45 c. "Resolution" at sea	40	70

84 Whaleship "Charles W. Morgan"

1976. Bicent of American Revolution. Mult.

172		18 c. Type **84**	30	30
173		25 c. Thanksgiving Service	40	30
174		40 c. Boeing B-17 Flying Fortress over Norfolk Island	75	65
175		45 c. California quail	1·00	85

85 Swallow-tailed Tern and Sun

86 "Vanessa ita"

1976. Christmas.

176	**85**	18 c. multicoloured	30	15
177		25 c. multicoloured	55	20
178		45 c. multicoloured	90	50

1977. Butterflies and Moths. Multicoloured.

179		1 c. Type **86**	10	40
180		2 c. "Utetheisa pulchelloides"	10	40
181		3 c. "Agathia asterias"	10	20
182		4 c. "Cynthia kershawi"	10	25
183		5 c. "Leucania loreyimima"	15	30
184		10 c. "Hypolimnas bolina"	30	35
185		15 c. "Pyrrhorachis pyrrhogona"	30	30
186		16 c. "Austrocarea iocephala"	30	30
187		17 c. "Pseudocoremia christiani"	35	30
188		18 c. "Cleora idiocrossa"	35	30
189		19 c. "Simplicia caeneusalis"	35	30
190		20 c. "Austrocidaria ralstonae"	40	30
191		30 c. "Hippotion scrofa"	50	40
192		40 c. "Papilio amynthor (ilioneus)"	55	40
193		50 c. "Tiracola plagiata"	70	60
194		$1 "Precis villida"	75	75
195		$2 "Cepora perimale"	1·25	1·40

87 Queen's View, Kingston

1977. Silver Jubilee.

196	**87**	25 c. multicoloured	35	30

88 Hibiscus Flowers and Oil Lamp

89 Captain Cook (from a portrait by Nathaniel Dance)

1977. Christmas.

197	**88**	18 c. multicoloured	15	10
198		25 c. multicoloured	15	10
199		45 c. multicoloured	30	35

1978. Capt. Cook Bicentenary (5th issue). Discovery of Hawaii. Multicoloured.

200		18 c. Type **89**	30	20
201		25 c. Discovery of northern Hawaiian islands	40	30
202		80 c. British flag against island background	90	70

90 Guide Flag and Globe

1978. 50th Anniv of Girl Guides. Multicoloured. Imperf. Self-adhesive.

203		18 c. Type **90**	25	30
204		25 c. Trefoil and scarf badge	30	40
205		35 c. Trefoil and Queen Elizabeth	45	60
206		45 c. Trefoil and Lady Baden-Powell	55	70

91 St. Edward's Crown

1978. 25th Anniv of Coronation. Mult.

207		25 c. Type **91**	15	15
208		70 c. Coronation regalia	40	45

92 View of Duncombe Bay with Scout at Camp Fire

1978. 50th Anniv of Boy Scout Movement. Multicoloured. Imperf. Self-adhesive.

209		20 c. Type **92**	30	45
210		25 c. View from Kingston and emblem	35	55
211		35 c. View of Anson Bay and Link Badge	50	90
212		45 c. Sunset scene and Lord Baden-Powell	55	95

93 Chart showing Route of Arctic Voyage

1978. Captain Cook Bicentenary (6th issue). Northern-most Voyages. Multicoloured.

213		25 c. Type **93**	30	30
214		90 c. "H.M.S. "Resolution" and H.M.S. "Discovery" in Pack Ice" (Webber)	80	80

94 Poinsettia and Bible

95 Cook and Village of Staithes near Marton

1978. Christmas. Multicoloured.

215		20 c. Type **94**	15	10
216		30 c. Native oak and bible	20	15
217		55 c. Hibiscus and bible	30	30

1978. 250th Birth Anniv of Captain Cook. Multicoloured.

218		20 c. Type **95**	30	25
219		80 c. Cook and Whitby Harbour	70	1·25

96 H.M.S. "Resolution"

1979. Death Bicent of Captain Cook. Mult.

220		20 c. Type **96**	30	30
221		20 c. Cook (statue)	30	30
222		40 c. Cook's death	40	50
223		40 c. Cook's death (different)	40	50

Nos. 220/1 were issued se-tenant, in horizontal pairs throughout the sheet, forming a composite design. A chart of Cook's last voyage is shown in the background. Nos. 222/3 were also issued se-tenant, the horizontal pair forming a composite design taken from an aquatint by John Clevely.

97 Assembly Building

1979. First Norfolk Island Legislative Assembly.

224	**97**	$1 multicoloured	50	50

98 Tasmania 1853 1d. Stamp and Sir Rowland Hill

1979. Death Centenary of Sir Rowland Hill.

225	**98**	20 c. blue and brown	20	10
226	–	30 c. red and grey	25	15
227	–	55 c. violet and indigo	40	30

DESIGNS: 30 c. Great Britain 1841 1d. red; 55 c. 1947 "Ball Bay" 1d. stamp.

99 I.Y.C. Emblem and Map of Pacific showing Norfolk Island as Pine Tree

1979. International Year of the Child.

229	**99**	80 c. multicoloured	40	45

100 Emily Bay

101 Lions International Emblem

1979. Christmas.

230	**100**	15 c. multicoloured	15	15
231	–	20 c. multicoloured	15	15
232	–	30 c. multicoloured	15	15

DESIGNS: 20, 30 c. Different scenes.

Nos. 230/2 were printed together, se-tenant, forming a composite design.

1980. Lions Convention.

234	**101**	50 c. multicoloured	35	30

102 Rotary International Emblem

1980. 75th Anniv of Rotary International.

235	**102**	50 c. multicoloured	35	30

103 De Havilland Gipsy Moth Seaplane "Madame Elijah"

1980. Airplanes. Multicoloured.

236		1 c. Hawker Siddeley H.S.748	15	20
237		2 c. Type **103**	15	20
238		3 c. Curtis P-40E Kittyhawk I	15	20
239		4 c. Chance Vought F4U-1 Corsair	15	30
240		5 c. Grumman TBF Avenger	30	30
241		15 c. Douglas SBD-5 Dauntless	30	30
242		20 c. Cessna 172D Skyhawk	25	30
243		25 c. Lockheed 414 Hudson	30	35
244		30 c. Lockheed PV-1 Ventura	40	90
245		40 c. Avro Type 685 York	50	55
246		50 c. Douglas DC-3	65	65
247		60 c. Avro Type 691 Lancastrian	75	75
248		80 c. Douglas DC-4	95	95
249		$1 Beech 200 Super King Air	1·25	90
250		$2 Fokker F.27 Friendship	2·50	2·25
251		$5 Lockheed C-130 Hercules	6·00	2·00

104 Queen Elizabeth the Queen Mother

1980. 80th Birthday of The Queen Mother.

252	**104**	22 c. multicoloured	20	20
253		60 c. multicoloured	35	40

105 Red-tailed Tropic Birds

1980. Christmas. Birds. Multicoloured.

254	15 c. Type **105**	30	25
255	22 c. White terns	30	25
256	35 c. White-capped noddys	30	25
257	60 c. White terns (different)	40	45

106 "Morayshire" and View of Norfolk Island

1981. 125th Anniv of Pitcairn Islanders' Migration to Norfolk Island. Multicoloured.

258	5 c. Type **106**	15	15
259	35 c. Islanders arriving ashore	40	30
260	60 c. View of new settlement	60	45

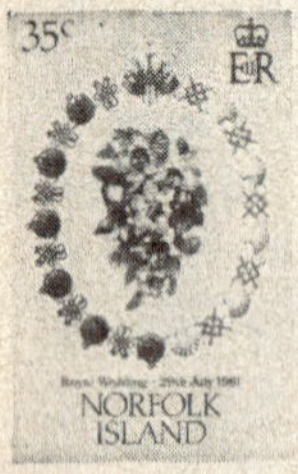

107 Wedding Bouquet from Norfolk Island

109 Pair of White-chested White Eyes

108 Uniting Church in Australia

1981. Royal Wedding. Multicoloured.

262	35 c. Type **107**	15	15
263	55 c. Prince Charles at horse trials	25	25
264	60 c. Prince Charles and Lady Diana Spencer	25	35

1981. Christmas. Churches. Multicoloured.

265	18 c. Type **108**	15	10
266	24 c. Seventh Day Adventist Church	15	15
267	30 c. Church of the Sacred Heart	20	20
268	$1 St. Barnabas Chapel	50	70

1981. White-chested White Eye. ("Silver-eye") Mult.

269	35 c. Type **109**	35	40
270	35 c. Bird on nest	35	40
271	35 c. Bird with egg	35	40
272	35 c. Parents with chicks	35	40
273	35 c. Fledgelings	35	40

110 Aerial view of Philip Island

1982. Philip and Nepean Islands. Mult.

274	24 c. Type **110**	25	25
275	24 c. Close-up view of Philip Island landscape	25	25
276	24 c. Gecko ("Phyllodactylus guentheri"), Philip Island	25	25
277	24 c. Sooty tern, Philip Island	25	25
278	24 c. Philip Island hibiscus ("hibiscus insularis")	25	25
279	35 c. Aerial view of Nepean Island	30	30
280	35 c. Close-up view of Nepean Island landscape	30	30
281	35 c. Gecko ("phyllodactylus guentheri"), Nepean Island	30	30
282	35 c. Blue-faced boobies, Nepean Island	30	30
283	35 c. "Carpobrotus glaucescens" (flower), Nepean Island	30	30

111 Sperm Whale

1982. Whales.

248	**111**	24 c. multicoloured	45	35
285	–	55 c. multicoloured	85	95
286	–	80 c. black, mauve & stone	1·10	2·00

DESIGNS: 55 c. Black right whale; 80 c. Humpback whale.

112 "Diocet", Wrecked 20 April 1873

1982. Shipwrecks. Multicoloured.

287	24 c. H.M.S. "Sirius", wrecked 19 March 1790	50	50
288	27 c. Type **112**	50	50
289	35 c. "Friendship", wrecked 17 May 1835	90	80
290	40 c. "Mary Hamilton", wrecked 6 May 1873	90	1·25
291	55 c. "Fairlie", wrecked 14 February 1840	1·25	1·25
292	65 c. "Warrigal", wrecked 18 March 1918	1·25	1·75

113 R.N.Z.A.F. Lockheed 414 Hudson dropping Christmas Supplies, 1942

1982. Christmas. 40th Anniv of First Supply-plane Landings on Norfolk Island (Christmas Day 1942). Multicoloured.

293	27 c. Type **113**	55	35
294	40 c. R.N.Z.A.F. Lockheed 414 Hudson landing Christmas supplies 1942	75	65
295	75 c. Christmas, 1942	90	1·40

114 50th (Queen's Own) Regiment

115 "Panaeolus papilionaceus"

1982. Military Uniforms. Multicoloured.

296	27 c. Type **114**	30	35
297	40 c. 58th (Rutlandshire) Regiment	40	75
298	55 c. 80th (Staffordshire Volunteers) Battalion Company	50	95
299	65 c. 11th (North Devonshire) Regiment	60	1·25

1983. Fungi. Multicoloured.

300	27 c. Type **115**	45	35
301	40 c. "Coprinus domesticus"	70	50
302	55 c. "Marasmius niveus"	95	70
303	65 c. "Cymatoderma elegans var lamellatum"	1·25	85

116 Beechcraft 18

1983. Bicentenary of Manned Flight. Mult.

304	10 c. Type **116**	15	15
305	27 c. Fokker F.28 Fellowship	25	35
306	45 c. French military Douglas C-54	40	60
307	75 c. Sikorsky S-61N helicopter	60	95

117 St. Matthew

118 Cable Ship "Chantik"

1983. Christmas. 150th Birth Anniv of Sir Edward Burne-Jones.

309	5 c. Type **117**	10	10
310	24 c. St. Mark	20	30
311	30 c. Jesus Christ	25	40
312	45 c. St. Luke	35	55
313	85 c. St. John	55	1·10

DESIGNS: showing stained glass windows from St. Barnabas Chapel, Norfolk Island.

1983. World Communications Year. ANZCAN Cable. Multicoloured.

314	30 c. Type **118**	30	40
315	45 c. "Chantik" during in-shore operations	40	55
316	75 c. Cable ship "Mercury"	55	95
317	85 c. Diagram of cable route	55	1·10

119 Popwood

120 Morwong

1984. Flowers. Multicoloured.

318	1 c. Type **119**	30	70
319	2 c. Strand morning glory	40	70
320	3 c. Native phreatia	45	70
321	4 c. Philip Island wisteria	45	70
322	5 c. Norfolk Island palm	45	70
323	10 c. Evergreen	50	70
324	15 c. Bastard oak	60	70
325	20 c. Devil's guts	60	70
326	25 c. White oak	70	80
327	30 c. Ti	70	90
328	35 c. Philip Island hibiscus	70	90
329	40 c. Native wisteria	80	1·25
330	50 c. Native jasmine	1·25	1·25
331	$1 Norfolk Island hibiscus	1·25	1·75
332	$3 Native oberonia	2·75	4·00
333	$5 Norfolk Island pine	3·75	4·50

1984. Reef Fishes. Multicoloured.

334	30 c. Type **120**	40	45
335	45 c. Black-spotted goatfish	60	65
336	75 c. Surgeonfish	1·00	1·10
337	85 c. Three-striped butterflyfish	1·25	1·40

121 Owl with Eggs

123 Font, Kingston Methodist Church

122 1953 7½d. and 1974 Cook Bicent 10 c. Stamps

1984. Boobook Owl. Multicoloured.

338	30 c. Type **121**	65	60
339	30 c. Fledgeling	65	60
340	30 c. Young owl on stump	65	60
341	30 c. Adult on branch	65	60
342	30 c. Owl in flight	65	60

1984. "Ausipex" International Stamp Exhibition, Melbourne. Multicoloured.

343	30 c. Type **122**	30	35
344	45 c. John Buffett commemorative postal stationery envelope	50	75
345	75 c. Design from Presentation Pack for 1982 Military Uniforms issue	90	1·75

1984. Christmas. Centenary of Methodist Church on Norfolk Island. Multicoloured.

347	5 c. Type **123**	10	10
348	24 c. Church service in Old Barracks, Kingston, late 1800s	25	40
349	30 c. The Revd. & Mrs. A. H. Phelps and sailing ship	35	45
350	45 c. The Revd. A. H. Phelps and First Congregational Church, Chester, U.S.A.	40	65
351	85 c. Interior of Kingston Methodist Church	80	1·40

124 The Revd. Nobbs teaching Pitcairn Islanders

125 "Fanny Fisher"

1984. Death Centenary of Revd. George Hunn Nobbs (leader of Pitcairn community). Multicoloured.

352	30 c. Type **124**	30	45
353	45 c. The Revd. Nobbs with sick islander	45	65
354	75 c. Baptising baby	75	1·10
355	85 c. Presented to Queen Victoria, 1852	80	1·40

1985. 19th-Century Whaling Ships (1st series). Multicoloured.

356	5 c. Type **125**	40	25
357	33 c. "Costa Rica Packet"	1·00	55
358	50 c. "Splendid"	1·50	1·25
359	90 c. "Onward"	1·90	2·00

See also Nos. 360/3.

1985. 19th-Century Whaling Ships (2nd series). As T **125**. Multicoloured.

360	15 c. "Waterwitch"	70	70
361	20 c. "Canton"	80	80
362	60 c. "Aladdin"	1·50	2·00
363	80 c. "California"	1·75	2·50

126 The Queen Mother (from photo by Norman Parkinson)

127 "Swimming"

1985. Life and Times of Queen Elizabeth the Queen Mother. Multicoloured.

364	5 c. The Queen Mother (from photo by Dorothy Wilding)	10	10
365	33 c. With Princess Anne at Trooping the Colour	25	25
366	50 c. Type **126**	40	55
367	90 c. With Prince Henry at his christening (from photo by Lord Snowdon)	60	1·00

1985. International Youth Year. Children's Paintings. Multicoloured.

369	33 c. Type **127**	40	40
370	50 c. "A Walk in the Country"	70	85

128 Prize-winning Cow and Owner

129 Shepherds with Flock

1985. 125th Anniv of Royal Norfolk Island Agricultural and Horticultural Show. Mult.

371	80 c. Type **128**	75	80
372	90 c. Show exhibits	85	90

1985. Christmas. Multicoloured.

374	27 c. Type **129**	50	30
375	33 c. Mary and Joseph with donkey	60	40
376	50 c. The Three Wise Men	1·10	65
377	90 c. The Nativity	1·50	1·25

130 Long-spined Sea Urchin

131 "Giotto" Spacecraft

1986. Marine Life. Multicoloured.
378 5 c. Type **130** 10 10
379 33 c. Blue starfish 30 35
380 55 c. Southern eagle ray . . . 50 85
381 75 c. Snowflake moray . . . . 70 1·25

1986. Appearance of Halley's Comet. Mult.
383 $1 Type **131** . . . . 75 1·50
384 $1 Halley's Comet . . . . . . 75 1·50
Nos. 383/4 were printed together, se-tenant, forming a composite design.

132 Isaac Robinson (U.S. Consul 1887–1908)

133 Princess Elizabeth and Dog

1986. "Ameripex '86" International Stamp Exhibition, Chicago. Multicoloured.
385 33 c. Type **132** 40 35
386 50 c. Ford "Model T" (first vehicle on island) (horiz) . . 60 50
387 80 c. Statue of Liberty 65 80
No. 387 also commemorates the Centenary of the Statue of Liberty.

1986. 60th Birthday of Queen Elizabeth II. Multicoloured.
389 5 c. Type **133** 10 10
390 33 c. Queen Elizabeth II . . . 40 35
391 80 c. Opening Norfolk Island Golf Club . . . . 1·25 1·40
392 90 c. With Duke of Edinburgh in carriage . . . . 1·25 1·60

134 Stylized Dove and Norfolk Island

135 British Convicts, 1787

1986. Christmas.
393 **134** 30 c. multicoloured . . . 25 30
394 40 c. multicoloured . . . 35 45
395 $1 multicoloured . . . . 1·00 1·50

1986. Bicentenary (1988) of Norfolk Island Settlement (1st issue). Governor Phillip's Commission. Multicoloured.
396 36 c. Type **135** 80 35
397 55 c. Judge passing sentence of transportation . . . . 1·50 85
398 90 c. Governor Phillip meeting Home Secretary (inscr "Home Society") . . . . 2·50 3·50
399 90 c. As No. 398, but correctly inscr "Home Secretary" . . 2·25 3·25
400 $1 Captain Arthur Phillip . . 2·50 2·50
See also Nos. 401/4, 421/4, 433/5, 436/7 and 438/43.

136 Stone Tools

1986. Bicentenary (1988) of Norfolk Island Settlement (2nd issue). Pre-European Occupation. Multicoloured.
401 36 c. Type **136** 65 75
402 36 c. Bananas and taro . . . 65 75
403 36 c. Polynesian outrigger canoe 65 75
404 36 c. Maori chief 65 75

137 Philip Island from Point Ross

138 Male Red-fronted Parakeet

1987. Norfolk Island Scenes. Multicoloured.
405 1 c. Cockpit Creek Bridge . . 50 70
406 2 c. Cemetery Bay Beach . . 50 70
407 3 c. Island guesthouse 50 70
408 5 c. Type **137** 30 50
409 15 c. Cattle in pasture . . . . 80 1·25
410 30 c. Rock fishing . . . . . . 30 1·00
411 37 c. Old Pitcairner-style house 1·40 1·50
412 40 c. Shopping centre . . . . 35 1·25
413 50 c. Emily Bay . . . . . . 45 1·25
414 60 c. Bloody Bridge . . . . . 2·00 2·25
415 80 c. Pitcairner-style shop . . 1·75 2·50
416 90 c. Government House . . 1·25 2·00
417 $1 Melanesian Memorial Chapel 1·00 1·75
418 $2 Convict Settlement, Kingston 1·75 3·50
419 $3 Ball Bay . . . . 5·00 6·00
420 $5 Northern cliffs . . . . . . 7·00 8·50

1987. Bicentenary of Norfolk Island Settlement (1988) (3rd issue). The First Fleet. As T **135**. Multicoloured.
421 5 c. Loading supplies, Deptford 50 75
422 55 c. Fleet leaving Spithead . 1·75 2·25
423 55 c. H.M.S. "Sirius" leaving Spithead . . . . 1·75 2·25
424 $1 Female convicts below decks 2·25 3·00
Nos. 422/3 were printed together, se-tenant, forming a composite design.

1987. Red-fronted Parakeet ("Green Parrot"). Multicoloured.
425 5 c. Type **138** . . . . 2·00 1·75
426 15 c. Adult with fledgeling and egg . . . . 2·50 2·25
427 36 c. Young parakeets . . . 3·50 3·25
428 55 c. Female parakeet . . . . 4·50 3·75

139 Christmas Tree and Restored Garrison Barracks

140 Airliner, Container Ship and Sydney Harbour Bridge

1987. Christmas. Multicoloured.
429 30 c. Type **139** 30 30
430 42 c. Children opening presents 45 55
431 58 c. Father Christmas with children . . . . 60 1·00
432 63 c. Children's party . . . . 70 1·25

1987. Bicentenary of Norfolk Island Settlement (1988) (4th issue). Visit of La Perouse (navigator). As T **135**. Multicoloured.
433 37 c. La Perouse with King Louis XVI 95 55
434 90 c. "L'Astrolabe" and "La Boussole" off Norfolk Island 2·75 3·00
435 $1 "L'Astrolabe" wrecked in Solomon Islands . . . . . 2·75 3·00

1988. Bicentenary of Norfolk Island Settlement (5th issue). Arrival of First Fleet at Sydney. As T **135**. Multicoloured.
436 37 c. Ship's cutter approaching Port Jackson . . . . 1·25 75
437 $1 Landing at Sydney Cove . 2·75 3·25

1988. Bicentenary of Norfolk Island Settlement (6th issue). Foundation of First Settlement. As T **135**. Multicoloured.
438 5 c. Lt. Philip Gidley King . 20 50
439 37 c. Raising the flag, March 1788 . . . . 85 75
440 55 c. King exploring . . . . 1·75 1·50
441 70 c. Landing at Sydney Bay, Norfolk Island . . . . . . 2·00 2·50
442 90 c. H.M.S. "Supply" (brig) 2·25 2·75
443 $1 Sydney Bay settlement, 1788 2·25 2·75

1988. "Sydpex '88" National Stamp Exhibition, Sydney. Multicoloured.
444 37 c. Type **140** . . . . 95 1·10
445 37 c. Exhibition label under magnifying glass (horiz) . . 95 1·10
446 37 c. Telephone and dish aerial 95 1·10

141 Flowers and Decorations

142 Pier Store and Boat Shed

1988. Christmas. Multicoloured.
448 30 c. Type **141** 50 40
449 42 c. Flowers 70 70
450 58 c. Fishes and beach . . . 85 95
451 63 c. Norfolk Island . . . . . 95 1·25

1988. Restored Buildings from the Convict Era. Multicoloured.
452 39 c. Type **142** 45 40
453 55 c. Royal Engineers Building 60 60
454 90 c. Old Military Barracks . . 1·00 1·50
455 $1 Commissariat Store and New Military Barracks . . . . . 1·10 1·50

143 "Lamprima aenea"

1989. Endemic Insects. Multicoloured.
456 39 c. Type **143** 65 40
457 55 c. "Insulascirtus nythos" . . 90 75
458 90 c. "Caedicia araucariae" . . 1·40 2·00
459 $1 "Thrincophora aridela" . . 1·60 2·00

144 H.M.S. "Bounty" off Tasmania

1989. Bicentenary of the Mutiny on the "Bounty". Multicoloured.
460 5 c. Type **144** 60 60
461 39 c. Mutineers and Polynesian women, Pitcairn Island . . . 1·75 1·25
462 55 c. Lake Windermere, Cumbria (Christian's home county) . 2·25 2·25
463 $1.10 "Mutineers casting Bligh adrift" (Robert Dodd) . . . 3·50 4·50

145 Norfolk Island Flag

146 Red Cross

1989. 10th Anniv of Internal Self-Government. Multicoloured.
465 41 c. Type **145** 90 55
466 55 c. Old ballot box 95 65
467 $1 Norfolk Island Act, 1979 . 1·75 2·00
468 $1.10 Island crest . . . . . . 1·75 2·75

1989. 75th Anniv of Red Cross on Norfolk Island.
469 **146** $1 red and blue . . . . 3·00 3·00

147 "Gethsemane"

1989. Christmas. Designs showing opening lines of hymns and local scenes. Multicoloured.
470 36 c. Type **147** 90 40
471 60 c. "In the Sweet Bye and Bye" 1·75 2·00
472 75 c. "Let the Lower Lights be Burning" . . . . 2·25 2·75
473 80 c. "The Beautiful Stream" . 2·25 3·00

148 John Royle (first announcer)

149 H.M.S. "Bounty" on fire, Pitcairn Island, 1790

1989. 50th Anniv of Radio Australia. Designs each showing Kingston buildings. Mult.
474 41 c. Type **148** 95 55
475 65 c. Radio waves linking Australia and Norfolk Island 1·75 2·25
476 $1.10 Anniversary kookaburra logo . . . . 2·75 3·75

1990. History of the Norfolk Islanders (1st series). Settlement on Pitcairn Island. Mult.
477 70 c. Type **149** . . . . . . 2·50 2·50
478 $1.10 Arms of Norfolk Island 2·75 3·00
See also Nos. 503/4 and 516/17.

150 H.M.S. "Sirius" striking Reef

1990. Bicentenary of Wreck of H.M.S. "Sirius". Multicoloured.
479 41 c. Type **150** . . . . 1·75 2·00
480 41 c. H.M.S. "Sirius" failing to clear bay . . . . 1·75 2·00
481 65 c. Divers at work on wreck 2·50 3·00
482 $1 Recovered artifacts and chart of site . . . . 2·75 3·25
Nos. 479/80 were printed together, se-tenant, forming a composite design.

151 Unloading Lighter, Kingston

152 "Ile de Lumiere" (freighter)

1990. Ships.
483 **151** 5 c. brown 20 30
484 10 c. brown 20 30
485 – 45 c. multicoloured . . . 80 60
486 – 50 c. multicoloured . . . 90 1·00
487 – 65 c. multicoloured . . . 1·00 1·25
488 **152** 70 c. multicoloured . . . 90 1·00
489 – 75 c. multicoloured . . . 1·50 1·75
490 – 80 c. multicoloured . . . 1·50 2·00
491 – 90 c. multicoloured . . . 1·50 2·00
492 – $1 multicoloured . . . . 1·50 1·75
493 – $2 multicoloured . . . . 2·25 3·00
494 – $5 multicoloured . . . . 5·00 7·00
DESIGNS—As T **152**: 45 c. "La Dunkerquoise" (French patrol vessel); 50 c. "Dmitri Mendeleev" (Russian research vessel); 65 c. "Pacific Rover" (tanker); 75 c. "Norfolk Trader" (freighter); 80 c. "Roseville" (transport); 90 c. "Kalia" (container ship); $1 "Bounty" (replica); $2 H.M.A.S. "Success" (supply ship); $5 H.M.A.S. "Whyalla" (patrol vessel).

153 Santa on House Roof

154 William Charles Wentworth

1990. Christmas. Multicoloured.
499 38 c. Type **153** 75 45
500 43 c. Santa at Kingston Post Office 80 50
501 65 c. Santa over Sydney Bay, Kingston (horiz) . . . . . 1·75 2·25
502 85 c. Santa on Officers' Quarters (horiz) . . . . 2·00 2·75

1990. History of the Norfolk Islanders (2nd series). The First Generation.
503 **154** 70 c. brown & cinnamon . 1·25 1·50
504 – $1.20 brown & cinnamon . 2·00 2·50
DESIGN: $1.20, Thursday October Christian.

155 Adult Robin and Chicks in Nest

156 Map of Norfolk Island

1990. "Birdpex '90" Stamp Exhibition, Christchurch, New Zealand. Scarlet Robin. Multicoloured.
505 65 c. Type **155** . . . . 1·00 1·25
506 $1 Hen on branch . . . . . . 1·50 1·75
507 $1.20 Cock on branch . . . . 1·60 2·00

1991. Ham Radio Network. Multicoloured.
509 43 c. Type **156** . . . . 1·25 70
510 $1 Globe showing Norfolk Island 2·75 3·00
511 $1.20 Map of south-west Pacific 2·75 4·00

157 Display in "Sirius" Museum — **158** H.M.S. "Pandora" wrecked on Great Barrier Reef (1791)

1991. Norfolk Island Museums. Mult.

512 43 c. Type **157** 90 50
513 70 c. 19th-century sitting room, House Museum (horiz) 1·75 2·00
514 $1 Carronade, "Sirius" Museum (horiz) 2·50 2·75
515 $1.20 Reconstructed jug and beaker, Archaeological Museum 2·50 3·25

1991. History of the Norfolk Islanders (3rd series). Search for the "Bounty". Multicoloured.

516 $1 Type **158** 2·75 2·50
517 $1.20 H.M.S. "Pandora" leaving bay 2·75 3·00

159 Hibiscus and Island Scene

1991. Christmas.

518 **159** 38 c. multicoloured 90 45
519 43 c. multicoloured 1·00 55
520 65 c. multicoloured 1·50 2·00
521 85 c. multicoloured 1·75 2·50

160 Tank and Soldier in Jungle — **161** Coat of Arms

1991. 50th Anniv of Outbreak of Pacific War. Multicoloured.

522 43 c. Type **160** 1·00 55
523 70 c. Boeing B-17 Flying Fortress on jungle airstrip 2·00 2·50
524 $1 Warships 2·50 3·25

1992. 500th Anniv of Discovery of America by Columbus. Multicoloured.

525 45 c. Type **161** 85 55
526 $1.05 "Santa Maria" 2·00 2·75
527 $1.20 Columbus and globe 2·50 3·25

162 Deployment Map — **163** Norfolk Pines above Ball Bay

1992. 50th Anniv of Battle of the Coral Sea. Multicoloured.

528 45 c. Type **162** 1·00 50
529 70 c. H.M.A.S. "Australia" (cruiser) 1·75 2·25
530 $1.05 U.S.S. "Yorktown" (aircraft carrier) 2·50 3·25

1992. 50th Anniv of Battle of Midway. As T **162**. Multicoloured.

531 45 c. Battle area 1·00 50
532 70 c. Consolidated PBY-5 Catalina flying boat over task force 1·75 2·25
533 $1.05 Douglas SBD Dauntless dive bomber and burning Japanese aircraft carrier 2·50 3·25

1992. 50th Anniv of Battle of Guadalcanal. As T **162**. Multicoloured.

534 45 c. American troops landing (horiz) 1·00 50
535 70 c. Machine-gun crew (horiz) 1·75 2·25
536 $1.05 Map of Pacific with Japanese and American flags (horiz) 2·50 3·25

1992. Christmas. Multicoloured.

537 40 c. Type **163** 70 40
538 45 c. Headstone Creek 75 45
539 75 c. South side of Ball Bay 1·50 2·25
540 $1.20 Rocky Point Reserve 2·00 3·00

164 Boat Shed and Flaghouses, Kingston

1993. Tourism. Historic Kingston. Mult.

541 45 c. Type **164** 80 1·00
542 45 c. Old Military Barracks 80 1·00
543 45 c. All Saints Church 80 1·00
544 45 c. Officers' Quarters 80 1·00
545 45 c. Quality Row 80 1·00

Nos. 541/5 were printed together, se-tenant, forming a composite design.

165 Fire Engine

1993. Emergency Services. Multicoloured.

546 45 c. Type **165** 1·00 60
547 70 c. Cliff rescue squad 1·10 1·75
548 75 c. Ambulance 1·40 1·90
549 $1.20 Police car 2·50 3·00

166 Blue-sea Lizard ("Glaucus atlanticus")

1993. Nudibranchs. Multicoloured.

550 45 c. Type **166** 80 55
551 45 c. Ocellate nudibranch ("Phyllidia ocellata") 80 55
552 75 c. "Bornella sp." 1·50 1·75
553 85 c. "Glossodoris rubroannolata" 1·75 2·25
554 95 c. "Halgerda willeyi" 2·00 2·50
555 $1.05 "Ceratosoma amoena" 2·00 3·00

167 Christmas Wreath — **168** Maori Stone Clubs

1993. Christmas.

556 **167** 40 c. multicoloured 60 45
557 45 c. multicoloured 60 45
558 75 c. multicoloured 1·00 1·50
559 $1.20 multicoloured 1·90 2·50

1993. Bicentenary of Contact with New Zealand. Multicoloured.

560 70 c. Type **168** 1·25 1·50
561 $1.20 First Maori map of New Zealand, 1793 2·00 2·50

169 Alvaro de Saavedra, Route Map and "Florida"

1994. Pacific Explorers. Multicoloured.

562 5 c. Vasco Nunez de Balboa, map and "Barbara" 40 40
563 10 c. Ferdinand Magellan, map and "Vitoria" 40 40
564 20 c. Juan Sebastian del Cano, map and "Vitoria" 50 50
565 50 c. Type **169** 75 75
566 70 c. Ruy Lopez de Villalobos, map and "San Juan" 1·00 1·00
567 75 c. Miguel Lopez de Legaspi, map and "San Lesmes" 1·00 1·00
568 80 c. Sir Francis Drake, map and "Golden Hind" 1·25 1·25
569 85 c. Alvaro de Mendana, map and "Santiago" 1·25 1·25
570 90 c. Pedro Fernandes de Quiros, map and "San Pedro y Pablo" 1·25 1·25
571 $1 Luis Baez de Torres, map and "San Pedrico" 1·40 1·40
572 $2 Abel Tasman, map and "Heemskerk" 2·00 2·25
573 $5 William Dampier, map and "Cygnet" 4·25 5·00

170 Sooty Tern — **171** House and Star

1994. Sea Birds. Multicoloured.

575 45 c. Type **170** 95 1·00
576 45 c. Red-tailed tropic bird 95 1·00
577 45 c. Australian gannet 95 1·00
578 45 c. Wedge-tailed shearwater 95 1·00
579 45 c. Masked booby 95 1·00

Nos. 575/9 were printed together, se-tenant, forming a composite design.

1994. Christmas. Multicoloured. Self-adhesive.

580 45 c. Type **171** 80 55
581 75 c. Figures from stained-glass windows 1·50 2·00
582 $1.20 Rainbow and full-rigged sailing ship 2·50 3·00

172 Chevrolet, 1926

1995. Vintage Motor Vehicles. Multicoloured.

583 45 c. Type **172** 75 55
584 75 c. Ford Model "A", 1928 1·25 1·75
585 $1.05 Ford Model "A A/C", 1929 1·60 2·00
586 $1.20 Ford Model "A", 1930 1·75 2·25

173 Tail Flukes of Humpback Whale

1995. Humpback Whale Conservation. Multicoloured.

587 45 c. Type **173** 1·00 55
588 75 c. Mother and calf 1·50 2·00
589 $1.05 Whale breaching (vert) 1·75 2·50

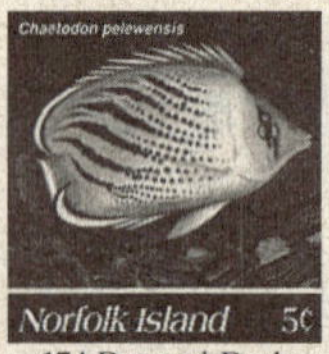

174 Dot-and-Dash Butterflyfish

1995. Butterflyfishes. Multicoloured.

591 5 c. Type **174** 30 50
592 45 c. Blue-spotted butterflyfish 85 50
593 $1.20 Three-belted butterflyfish 2·25 2·75
594 $1.50 Three-finned butterflyfish 2·50 3·00

175 International 4 × 4 Refueller, 1942

1995. Second World War Vehicles. Multicoloured.

596 5 c. Type **175** 30 40
597 45 c. Ford Sedan, 1942 75 45
598 $1.20 Ford 3 ton tipper, 1942 2·00 2·50
599 $2 D8 caterpillar with scraper 3·00 3·50

1995. Flower designs as 1960 issues, but with face values in decimal currency.

600 5 c. pink and green (as No. 25) 10 10
601 5 c. red (as No. 28) 10 10

176 Servicing Fighter — **177** Peace Dove and Anniversary Emblem

1995. 50th Anniv of End of Second World War in the Pacific. Multicoloured.

602 5 c. Type **176** 40 50
603 45 c. Sgt. Tom Derrick, VC (vert) 70 45
604 75 c. Gen. Douglas MacArthur (vert) 1·25 1·50
605 $1.05 Girls celebrating victory 1·75 2·00
606 $10 Pacific War medals (50 × 30 mm) 16·00 18·00

The $10 also includes the "Singapore '95" International stamp exhibition logo.

1995. Christmas. 50th Anniv of United Nations. Each including U.N. anniversary emblem.

607 **177** 45 c. gold and blue 60 45
608 – 75 c. gold and violet 1·00 1·25
609 – $1.05 gold and red 1·40 2·00
610 – $1.20 gold and green 1·60 2·25

DESIGNS: 75 c. Star of Bethlehem; $1.05, Symbolic candles on cake; $1.20, Olive branch.

178 Skink on Bank — **179** Sopwith Pup Biplane and Emblem

1996. Endangered Species. Skinks and Geckos. Multicoloured.

611 5 c. Type **178** 40 45
612 5 c. Gecko on branch 40 45
613 45 c. Skink facing right 70 75
614 45 c. Gecko on flower 70 75

1996. 75th Anniv of Royal Australian Air Force. Aircraft. Multicoloured.

615 45 c. Type **179** 60 60
616 45 c. Wirraway fighter 60 60
617 75 c. F-111C jet fighter 1·00 1·40
618 85 c. F/A-18 Hornet jet fighter 1·10 1·50

181 "Naticarlus oncus"

1996. Shells. Multicoloured.

620 45 c. Type **181** 70 85
621 45 c. "Janthina janthina" 70 85
622 45 c. "Cypraea caputserpentis" 70 85
623 45 c. "Argonauta nodosa" 70 85

182 Shopping — **183** The Nativity

1996. Tourism. Multicoloured.

624 45 c. Type **182** 50 50
625 75 c. Celebrating Bounty Day 1·00 1·00
626 $2.50 Horse riding 3·75 4·25
627 $3.70 Unloading lighter 4·50 5·25

1996. Christmas. Multicoloured.

628 45 c. Type **183** 50 50
629 45 c. Star and boat sheds 50 50
630 75 c. Star, bungalow and ox 90 1·50
631 85 c. Star, fruit, flowers and ox 1·10 1·75

184 Coat of Arms — **186** "Cepora perimale"

1997.

632 **184** 5 c. blue and yellow 20 30
633 – 5 c. brown 20 30

DESIGN: No. 633, Great Seal of Norfolk Island.

1997. Butterflies. Multicoloured.

636 75 c. Type **186** 1·00 85
637 90 c. "Danaus chrysippus" 1·25 1·50
638 $1 "Danaus hamata" 1·40 1·50
639 $1.20 "Danaus plexippus" 1·50 2·00

187 Dusky Dolphins

1997. Dolphins. Multicoloured.

640 45 c. Type **187** 60 50
641 75 c. Common dolphin and calf 80 1·00

188 Ball Bay, Norfolk Island

1997. 50th Anniv of Norfolk Island Stamps. Multicoloured.

644 $1 Type **188** . . . . 1·50 2·00
645 $1.50 1947 2d. stamp . . . . 2·00 2·25
646 $8 Ball Bay and 1947 2s. bistre stamp (90 × 45 mm) . . . . 10·00 12·00

1997. Golden Wedding of Queen Elizabeth and Prince Philip. As T **173** of Ascension. Multicoloured.

647 20 c. Queen Elizabeth 30 40
648 25 c. Prince Philip in carriage-driving trials 30 40
649 25 c. Prince Philip 30 40
650 50 c. Queen in phaeton at Trooping the Colour 60 60

190 Christmas Tree 193 "Pepper"

1997. Annual Festivals. Multicoloured.

653 45 c. Type **190** 50 45
654 75 c. Fireworks (New Year's Eve) 80 1·00
655 $1.20 Rose (Valentine's Day) . 1·25 1·50

1998. Cats. Multicoloured.

658 45 c. Type **193** 55 50
659 45 c. "Tabitha" at window . . 55 50
660 75 c. "Midnight" 75 90
661 $1.20 "Rainbow" with flower pot 1·10 1·40

194 Entrance to Pentagonal Goal

1998.

662 **194** 5 c. black and blue . . . 10 15
663 – 5 c. black and green . . . 10 15
DESIGN: No. 663, Ruined First Settlement cottage.

1998. Diana, Princess of Wales Commemoration. As T **91** of Kiribati.

664 45 c. Princess Diana with bouquet, 1991 . . . . 40 40

195 Tweed Trousers 196 Hammer Throwing

1998. Reef Fishes. Multicoloured.

666 10 c. Type **195** 10 15
667 20 c. Conspicuous angelfish . 15 20
668 30 c. Moon wrasse 25 30
669 45 c. Wide-striped clownfish . 35 40
670 50 c. Racoon butterflyfish . . 40 45
671 70 c. Artooti (juvenile) 55 60
672 75 c. Splendid hawkfish . . . 55 60
673 85 c. Scorpion fish 65 70
674 90 c. Orange fairy basslet . . 70 75
675 $1 Sweetlips 75 80
676 $3 Moorish idol . . . . 2·25 2·40
677 $4 Gold-ribbon soapfish . . . 2·25 2·40
Nos. 672 and 675 are incorrectly inscribed "Splendid Hawkefish" and "Sweetlip".

1998. 16th Commonwealth Games, Kuala Lumpur.

679 **196** 75 c. red and black . . . 75 80
680 – 95 c. violet and black . . 90 1·00
681 – $1.05 mauve and black . 95 1·10
DESIGNS—HORIZ: 95 c. Trap shooting. VERT: $1.05, Lawn bowls.

197 "Norfolk" (sloop)

1998. Bicentenary of the Circumnavigation of Tasmania by George Bass and Matthew Flinders.

683 **197** 45 c. multicoloured . . . 40 40

199 "Peace on Earth"

1998. Christmas. Multicoloured.

686 45 c. Type **199** 35 40
687 75 c. "Joy to the World" . . 55 60
688 $1.05 "A Season of Love" . . 80 85
689 $1.20 "Light of the World" . 90 95

200 Short S.23 Sandringham (flying boat) 204 Solander's Petrel in Flight

202 Hull of "Resolution" under Construction

1999. Aircraft. Each red and green.

690 5 c. Type **200** 10 10
691 5 c. DC-4 "Norfolk Trader" . 10 10

1999. "Australia '99" International Stamp Exhibition, Melbourne. Schooner "Resolution". Multicoloured.

693 45 c. Type **202** 35 40
694 45 c. After being launched . . 35 40
695 45 c. In Emily Bay 35 40
696 45 c. Off Cascade 35 40
697 45 c. Alongside at Auckland . 35 40

1999. Endangered Species. Solander's Petrel ("Providence Petrel"). Multicoloured.

699 75 c. Type **204** 55 60
700 $1.05 Head of Solander's petrel (horiz) 80 85
701 $1.20 Adult and fledgling (horiz) 90 95

NORTH BORNEO

A territory in the north of the Island of Borneo in the China Sea, formerly under the administration of the British North Borneo Company. A Crown Colony since 1946. Joined Malaysia in 1963 and renamed Sabah in 1964.

100 cents = 1 dollar (Malayan)

1

1883. "POSTAGE NORTH BORNEO" at top.

8 **1** ½ c. mauve . . . . 75·00 £160
9 1 c. orange £160 £275
10 2 c. brown . . . . 20·00 20·00
11 4 c. pink . . . . 17·00 48·00
12 8 c. green . . . . 19·00 48·00
13 10 c. blue . . . . 24·00 42·00

1883. Surch **8 Cents.** vert.

2 **1** 8 c. on 2 c. brown £900 £600

1883. Surch **EIGHT CENTS.**

3 **1** 8 c. on 2 c. brown £400 £170

Where there are three price columns, prices in the second column are for postally used stamps and those in the third column are for stamps cancelled with black bars.

4 5

1883. Inscr "NORTH BORNEO".

4 **4** 50 c. violet . . . . . . 90·00 — 19·00
5 **5** $1 red . . . . 85·00 — 9·50
For these designs with "BRITISH" in place of value in words at top, see Nos. 46/7.

1886. Optd **and Revenue**.

14 **1** ½ c. mauve . . . . 85·00 £170
15 10 c. blue £120 £170

1886. Surch in words and figures.

18 **1** 3 c. on 4 c. pink . . . . . . 70·00 £100
19 5 c. on 8 c. green . . . . . . 75·00 £100

9 10

13 19

1886. Inscr "BRITISH NORTH BORNEO".

22 **9** ½ c. red . . . . 2·50 13·00
24 1 c. orange . . . . 2·00 8·00
25 2 c. brown . . . . 2·00 8·50
26 4 c. pink . . . . 2·25 9·00
27 8 c. green . . . . 7·00 16·00
28 10 c. blue . . . . 7·00 25·00
45 **10** 25 c. blue . . . . 38·00 80·00 75
46 – 50 c. violet . . . . . . 65·00 £120 75
47 – $1 red . . . . 27·00 £110 75
48 **13** $2 green . . . . £100 £160 1·50
49 **19** $5 purple . . . . £130 £140 8·50
50 – $10 brown . . . . £180 £250 12·00
DESIGNS: 50 c. As Type **4**; $1, As Type **5**. $10 As Type **19** but with different frame.

14

1888. Inscr "POSTAGE & REVENUE".

36b **14** ½ c. red . . . . 90 4·00 60
37 1 c. orange . . . . . 1·40 3·25 50
38b 2 c. brown . . . . . 2·50 9·50 50
39 3 c. violet . . . . . 2·50 11·00 50
40 4 c. pink . . . . . . 4·00 23·00 50
41 5 c. grey . . . . . . 2·75 16·00 50
42 6 c. red . . . . 7·00 17·00 50
43a 8 c. green . . . . . 14·00 20·00 50
44b 10 c. blue . . . . . . 6·50 17·00 50

1890. Surch in words.

51 **10** 2 c. on 25 c. blue . . . . . 50·00 70·00
52 8 c. on 25 c. blue . . . . . 80·00 95·00

1891. Surch in figures and words.

63 **14** 1 c. on 4 c. pink . . . . . 19·00 14·00
64 1 c. on 5 c. grey . . . . . . 6·50 6·00
54 **9** 6 c. on 8 c. green £6500 £3500
55 **14** 6 c. on 8 c. green . . . . . 15·00 9·00
56 **9** 6 c. on 10 c. blue . . . . . 50·00 18·00
57 **14** 6 c. on 10 c. blue . . . . . £110 26·00
65 **10** 8 c. on 25 c. blue £120 £140

24 Dyak Chief 25 Sambar Stag ("Cervus unicolor")

26 Sago Palm 27 Great Argus Pheasant

28 Arms of the Company 29 Malay Prau

30 Estuarine Crocodile 31 Mt. Kinabalu

32 Arms of the Company with Supporters

1894.

66 **24** 1 c. black & bistre . . 1·25 8·00 50
69 **25** 2 c. black & red . . . 4·75 4·75 50
70 **26** 3 c. green & mauve . . 2·25 7·50 50
72 **27** 5 c. black & red . . . 11·00 11·00 60
73a **28** 6 c. black & brown . . 3·75 15·00 60
74 **29** 8 c. black & lilac . . . 4·50 9·50 60
75 **30** 12 c. black & blue . . 26·00 75·00 2·50
78 **31** 18 c. black & green . . 22·00 48·00 2·00
79 **32** 24 c. blue & red . . . 20·00 65·00 2·00

1894. As Nos. 47, etc, but inscr "THE STATE OF NORTH BORNEO".

81 25 c. blue . . . . 8·50 26·00 90
82 50 c. violet . . . . 14·00 48·00 90
83 $1 red . . . . 12·00 24·00 1·00
84 $2 green . . . . 15·00 70·00 1·25
85b $5 purple . . . . £150 £190 5·50
86 $10 brown . . . . £180 £250 10·00

1895. No. 83 surch in figures and words.

87 4 cents on $1 red . . . . . 4·25 1·50 40
88 10 cents on $1 red . . . . 11·00 1·75 40
89 20 cents on $1 red . . . . 28·00 13·00 40
90 30 cents on $1 red . . . . 22·00 20·00 40
91 40 cents on $1 red . . . . 22·00 42·00 40

37 Orang-utan 41 Sun Bear

43 Borneo Steam Train

1897. As 1894 issue with insertion of native inscriptions.

92a	**24**	1 c. black & bistre .	7·00	2·50	40
94a	**25**	2 c. black & red . .	15·00	3·00	40
95		2 c. black & green .	38·00	1·50	40
97	**26**	3 c. green & mauve	8·50	3·00	50
98	**37**	4 c. black & green .	8·00	—	1·50
99		4 c. black & red . .	27·00	6·00	50
100a	**27**	5 c. black & orange	70·00	3·00	50
101a	**28**	6 c. black & brown	13·00	3·25	50
102b	**29**	8 c. black & lilac .	27·00	2·75	60
104	**41**	10 c. brown & grey	65·00	35·00	1·75
106b	**30**	12 c. black & blue .	75·00	30·00	1·50
107	**43**	16 c. green & brown	£120	85·00	3·00
108	**31**	18 c. black & green	16·00	55·00	1·00
110b		18 c. black & green*	55·00	12·00	1·50
109	**32**	24 c. blue & red* .	14·00	70·00	1·60
111		24 c. blue & red* .	50·00	35·00	2·00

*No. 110 is inscribed "POSTAGE & REVENUE" at the sides instead of "POSTAL REVENUE" as in No. 108. No. 111 has the words "POSTAGE & REVENUE" at the sides below the Arms; these words were omitted in No. 109.

1899. Stamps of 1897 and Nos. 81/6 surch **4 CENTS**.

112a	4 c. on 5 c. black & orange .	16·00	10·00
113	4 c. on 6 c. black & brown .	17·00	22·00
114	4 c. on 8 c. black and lilac .	14·00	10·00
115	4 c. on 12 c. black & blue . .	15·00	13·00
116	4 c. on 18 c. black and green (110)	9·50	13·00
117	4 c. on 24 c. bl & red (111) .	14·00	14·00
118	4 c. on 25 c. blue	5·00	8·50
119	4 c. on 50 c. violet	6·00	13·00
121	4 c. on $1 red	5·00	9·50
122	4 c. on $2 green	5·00	12·00
125	4 c. on $5 purple	5·50	12·00
126	4 c. on $10 brown	5·50	12·00

1901. Stamps of 1897 and Nos. 81/6 optd **BRITISH PROTECTORATE.**

127a	1 c. black & bistre . .	2·25	1·75	30
128	2 c. black & green . .	2·75	1·75	30
129	3 c. green & mauve . .	1·60	3·75	30
130	4 c. black and red . .	7·00	1·50	30
131a	5 c. black & orange . .	8·50	2·50	30
132b	6 c. black & brown . .	3·25	9·00	70
133	8 c. black and lilac . .	3·00	3·25	50
134	10 c. brown & grey . .	32·00	5·00	60
135	12 c. black and blue .	38·00	12·00	1·50
136	16 c. green & brown .	85·00	20·00	2·25
137	18 c. black & green (110)	10·00	25·00	1·25
138	24 c. blue & red (111) .	15·00	38·00	1·50
139	25 c. blue	2·00	10·00	50
140	50 c. violet	2·75	11·00	55
142	$1 red	6·50	35·00	2·50
143	$2 green	30·00	95·00	3·50
144	$5 purple (with full point)	£170	£425	7·00
184	$5 purple (without full point)	£800	£900	7·50
145	$10 brown (with full point)	£300	£550	8·00
185	$10 brown (without full point)	£1000	—	7·50

1904. Stamps of 1897 and Nos. 81/6 surch **4 cents**.

146	4 c. on 5 c. blk & orge	27·00	40·00	7·00
147	4 c. on 6 c. blk & brn	7·00	19·00	6·00
148	4 c. on 8 c. blk & lilac	12·00	26·00	6·50
149	4 c. on 12 c. blk & bl .	22·00	40·00	7·00
150	4 c. on 18 c. black and green (110)	14·00	38·00	7·00
151a	4 c. on 24 c. bl & red (111)	16·00	48·00	7·00
152	4 c. on 25 c. blue . . .	3·50	25·00	7·00
153	4 c. on 50 c. violet . .	3·75	38·00	7·00
154	4 c. on $1 red	4·25	48·00	7·00
155	4 c. on $2 green . . .	5·50	48·00	7·50
156	4 c. on $5 purple . . .	11·00	48·00	7·50
157	4 c. on $10 brown . .	11·00	48·00	7·50

51 Malayan Tapir

52 Traveller's Tree

64

(68)

1909. No. 177 is surch **20 CENTS**.

277	**51**	1 c. black & brown .	1·00	70	—
160	**52**	2 c. black & green .	1·00	70	30
278		2 c. black & red . .	40	60	—
162	–	3 c. black & red . .	2·50	1·50	40
279	–	3 c. black & green .	2·75	1·10	—
280	–	4 c. black & red . .	45	10	—
281	–	5 c. black & brown .	4·50	2·75	—
282	–	6 c. black & green .	5·00	90	—
283	–	8 c. black & red . .	3·25	50	—
284	–	10 c. black & blue .	3·00	90	—
285	–	12 c. black & blue .	17·00	80	—
174	–	16 c. black & brown .	22·00	7·00	70
175	–	18 c. black & green .	85·00	30·00	1·00
177	–	20 c. on 18 c. blk & grn	6·00	95	20
176	–	24 c. black & green .	26·00	3·50	80
178	**64**	25 c. black & green .	6·00	3·75	1·50
179	–	50 c. black & blue . .	6·50	3·75	1·75
180	–	$1 black & brown . .	15·00	4·00	1·75
181	–	$2 black & lilac . . .	42·00	14·00	4·25
182	–	$5 black & red . . .	90·00	£100	23·00
183	–	$10 black & orge . .	£225	£275	45·00

DESIGNS—As T **51**: 3 c. Jesselton railway station; 4 c. Sultan of Sulu, his staff and W. C. Cowie, first Chairman of the Company; 5 c. Asiatic elephant; 8 c. Ploughing with buffalo; 24 c. Dwarf Cassowary. As T **52**: 6 c. Sumatran rhinoceros; 10 c. Wild boar; 12 c. Palm Cockatoo; 16 c Rhinoceros hornbill; 18 c Banteng. As T **64** but Arms with supporters: $5, $10.

1916. Stamps of 1909 surch.

186	2 c. on 3 c. black and red . .	18·00	12·00
187	4 c. on 6 c. black and olive .	15·00	15·00
188	10 c. on 12 c. black & blue .	45·00	50·00

1916. Nos. 277 etc, optd with T **68**.

189	1 c. black and brown	7·50	32·00
203	2 c. black and green	27·00	48·00
191	3 c. black and red	27·00	48·00
192	4 c. black and red	5·50	30·00
193	5 c. black and brown	30·00	55·00
206	6 c. black and green	40·00	65·00
207	8 c. black and red	24·00	55·00
208	10 c. black and blue	45·00	65·00
197	12 c. black and blue	85·00	90·00
210	16 c. black and brown . . .	75·00	95·00
199	20 c. on 18 c. black & green .	32·00	85·00
200	24 c. black and mauve . . .	80·00	85·00
201	25 c. black and green	£275	£350

1918. Nos. 159, etc, surch **RED CROSS TWO CENTS**.

214	1 c. + 2 c. black and brown .	3·50	9·00
215	2 c. + 2 c. black and green .	1·00	8·50
216	3 c. + 2 c. black and red . .	10·00	15·00
218	4 c. + 2 c. black and red . .	70	4·00
219	5 c. + 2 c. black and brown .	8·00	22·00
221	6 c. + 2 c. black and olive .	5·00	18·00
222	8 c. + 2 c. black and red . .	5·50	9·00
223	10 c. + 2 c. black and blue .	7·50	23·00
224	12 c. + 2 c. black and blue .	18·00	40·00
225	16 c. + 2 c. black and brown	20·00	40·00
226	24 c. + 2 c. black and mauve	20·00	40·00
229	25 c. + 2 c. black and green .	10·00	38·00
230	50 c. + 2 c. black and blue .	12·00	38·00
231	$1 + 2 c. black and brown .	45·00	50·00
232	$2 + 2 c. black and lilac . .	70·00	95·00
233	$5 + 2 c. black and red . . .	£300	£425
234	$10 + 2 c. black and orange	£300	£425

The premium of 2 c. on each value was for Red Cross Funds.

1918. Nos. 159, etc, surch **FOUR CENTS** and a red cross.

235	1 c. + 4 c. black and brown .	60	5·00
236	2 c. + 4 c. black and green .	65	8·00
237	3 c. + 4 c. black and red . .	90	3·75
238	4 c. + 4 c. black and red . .	40	4·75
239	5 c. + 4 c. black and brown .	2·00	18·00
240	6 c. + 4 c. black and olive .	1·90	12·00
241	8 c. + 4 c. black and red . .	1·25	9·50
242	10 c. + 4 c. black and blue .	3·75	12·00
243	12 c. + 4 c. black and blue .	10·00	14·00
244	16 c. + 4 c. black and brown	7·00	16·00
245	24 c. + 4 c. black and mauve	8·00	20·00
246	25 c. + 4 c. black and green .	5·00	48·00
248	50 c. + 4 c. black and blue .	15·00	42·00
249	$1 + 4 c. black and brown .	15·00	55·00
250	$2 + 4 c. black and lilac . .	48·00	80·00
251	$5 + 4 c. black and red . . .	£250	£375
252	$10 + 4 c. black and orange	£250	£375

The premium of 4 c. on each value was for Red Cross Funds.

1922. Nos. 159, etc, optd **MALAYA-BORNEO EXHIBITION 1922.**

253	1 c. black and brown	8·00	48·00
255	2 c. black and green	1·75	17·00
256	3 c. black and red	12·00	40·00
257	4 c. black and red	1·75	27·00
258	5 c. black and brown	9·00	48·00
260	6 c. black and green	4·50	48·00
262	8 c. black and red	5·00	42·00
263	10 c. black and blue	6·50	45·00
265	12 c. black and blue	4·75	21·00
267	16 c. black and brown . . .	13·00	50·00
268	20 c. on 18 c. black & green .	13·00	55·00
270	24 c. black and mauve . . .	26·00	55·00
274	25 c. black and green	4·00	50·00
275	50 c. black and blue	7·50	40·00

1923. No. 280 surch **THREE CENTS** and bars.

276	–	3 c. on 4 c. black & red . .	1·00	4·75

73 Head of a Murut

76 Mount Kinabalu

1931. 50th Anniv of North Borneo Company.

295	**73**	3 c. black and green . . .	80	80
296	–	6 c. black and orange . .	16·00	3·25
297	–	10 c. black and red	3·50	11·00
298	**76**	12 c. black and blue . . .	4·00	8·00
299	–	25 c. black and violet . .	38·00	35·00
300	–	$1 black and green	26·00	85·00
301	–	$2 black and brown . . .	48·00	£110
302	–	$5 black and purple . . .	£140	£300

DESIGNS—VERT: 6 c. Orang-utan; 10 c. Dyak warrior; $1, $2, $5 Arms. HORIZ: 25 c. Clouded leopard.

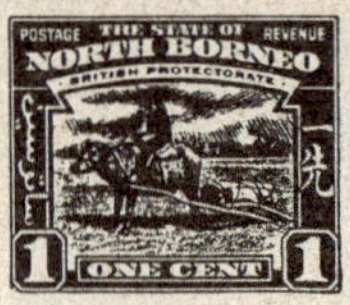

81 Buffalo Transport

82 Palm Cockatoo

1939.

303	**81**	1 c. green and brown . . .	90	1·00
304	**82**	2 c. purple and blue	5·00	1·00
305	–	3 c. blue and green	1·75	2·00
306	–	4 c. green and violet	3·25	50
307	–	6 c. blue and red	2·50	5·00
308	–	8 c. red	6·50	1·50
309	–	10 c. violet and green . . .	38·00	6·00
310	–	12 c. green and blue	16·00	5·00
311	–	15 c. green and brown . . .	16·00	7·00
312	–	20 c. violet and blue	10·00	3·25
313	–	25 c. green and brown . . .	12·00	8·00
314	–	50 c. brown and violet . . .	15·00	7·00
315	–	$1 brown and red	65·00	19·00
316	–	$2 violet and olive	£100	85·00
317	–	$5 blue	£300	£225

DESIGNS—VERT: 3 c. Native; 4 c. Proboscis monkey; 6 c. Mounted Bajaus; 10 c. Orang-utan; 15 c. Dyak; $1, $2 Arms. HORIZ: 8 c. Map of Eastern Archipelago; 12 c. Murut with blow-pipe; 20 c. River scene; 25 c. Native boat; 50 c. Mt. Kinabalu; $5 Arms with supporters.

1941. Optd **WAR TAX**.

318	**81**	1 c. green and brown . . .	75	2·00
319	**82**	2 c. purple and blue	4·50	3·50

1945. British Military Administration. Stamps of 1939 optd **BMA**.

320	**81**	1 c. green and brown . . .	4·25	1·50
321	**82**	2 c. purple and blue	12·00	1·50
322	–	3 c. blue and green	1·25	1·25
323	–	4 c. green and violet	16·00	13·00
324	–	6 c. blue and red	1·25	50
325	–	8 c. red	3·00	55
326	–	10 c. violet and green . . .	3·00	30
327	–	12 c. green and blue	4·75	2·00
328	–	15 c. green and brown . . .	1·50	1·00
329	–	20 c. violet and blue	3·00	1·25
330	–	25 c. green and brown . . .	4·50	1·25
331	–	50 c. brown and violet . . .	3·00	1·00
332	–	$1 brown and red	40·00	28·00
333	–	$2 violet and olive	38·00	20·00
334	–	$5 blue	15·00	10·00

1947. Stamps of 1939 optd with Crown over GR monogram and bars obliterating "THE STATE OF" and "BRITISH PROTECTORATE".

335	**81**	1 c. green and brown . . .	15	1·00
336	**82**	2 c. purple and blue	1·75	90
337	–	3 c. blue and green	15	90
338	–	4 c. green and violet	50	40
339	–	6 c. blue and red	15	20
340	–	8 c. red	20	20
341	–	10 c. violet and green . . .	60	40
342	–	12 c. green and blue	2·00	2·25
343	–	15 c. green and brown . . .	2·25	30
344	–	20 c. violet and blue	1·00	85
345	–	25 c. green and brown . . .	2·00	45
346	–	50 c. brown and violet . . .	1·50	85
347	–	$1 brown and red	2·00	1·25
348	–	$2 violet and olive	6·00	11·00
349	–	$5 blue	15·00	11·00

1948. Silver Wedding. As T **10/11** of Antigua.

350	8 c. red	30	80
351	$10 mauve	20·00	35·00

1949. U.P.U. As T **20/23** of Antigua.

352	8 c. red	40	30
353	10 c. brown	2·50	1·00
354	30 c. brown	90	1·75
355	55 c. blue	90	2·25

100 Mt. Kinabalu

102 Coconut Grove

1950.

356	**100**	1 c. brown	15	70
357	–	2 c. blue	15	50
358	**102**	3 c. green	15	15
359	–	4 c. purple	15	10
360	–	5 c. violet	15	10
361	–	8 c. red	75	85
362	–	10 c. purple	60	15
363	–	15 c. blue	1·50	65
364	–	20 c. brown	1·00	10
365	–	30 c. buff	2·00	20
366	–	50 c. red ("JESSLETON")	85	3·00
366a	–	50 c. red ("JESSELTON")	6·50	2·00
367	–	$1 orange	2·00	1·00
368	–	$2 green	2·00	8·00
369	–	$5 green	11·00	15·00
370	–	$10 blue	32·00	42·00

DESIGNS—VERT: 4 c. Hemp drying; 5 c. Cattle at Kota Belud; 30 c. Suluk river canoe; 50 c. Clock tower, Jesselton; $1 Bajau horsemen. HORIZ: 2 c. Musician; 8 c. Map; 10 c. Log pond; 15 c. Malay prau, Sandakan; 20 c. Bajau chief; $2 Murut with blowpipe; $5 Net fishing; $10, King George VI and arms.

1953. Coronation. As T **13** of Aden.

371	10 c. black and red	1·25	60

1954. As 1950 but with portrait of Queen Elizabeth II.

372	1 c. brown	10	30
373	2 c. blue	50	15
374	3 c. green	40	2·00
375	4 c. purple	60	20
376	5 c. violet	75	10
377	8 c. red	50	30
378	10 c. purple	30	10
379	15 c. blue	75	10
380	20 c. brown	30	15
381	30 c. buff	2·00	20
382	50 c. red (No. 366a)	5·00	20
383	$1 orange	6·00	20
384	$2 green	12·00	1·25
385	$5 green	10·00	23·00
386	$10 blue	23·00	35·00

117 Malay Prau

1956. 75th Anniv of Foundation of British North Borneo Co. Inscr "CHARTER 1ST NOVEMBER 1881".

387	–	10 c. black and red . . .	1·00	40
388	**117**	15 c. black and brown . .	30	30
389	–	35 c. black and green . .	30	1·50
390	–	$1 black and slate	65	2·50

DESIGNS—HORIZ: 10 c. Borneo Railway, 1902; 35 c. Mt. Kinabalu. VERT: $1 Arms of Chartered Company.

120 Sambar Stag

1961.

391	**120**	1 c. green and red	20	10
392	–	4 c. olive and orange . .	20	90
393	–	5 c. sepia and violet . . .	30	10
394	–	6 c. black and turquoise .	50	40
395	–	10 c. green and red . . .	30	10
396	–	12 c. brown and myrtle .	30	10
397	–	20 c. turquoise and blue .	3·50	10
398	–	25 c. black and red . . .	70	90
399	–	30 c. sepia and olive . . .	70	20
400	–	35 c. slate and brown . .	1·75	90
401	–	50 c. green and bistre . .	1·75	20
402	–	75 c. blue and purple . .	7·00	90
403	–	$1 brown and green . . .	11·00	80
404	–	$2 brown and slate . . .	23·00	3·00
405	–	$5 green and purple . . .	35·00	14·00
406	–	$10 red and blue	24·00	25·00

DESIGNS—HORIZ: 4 c. Sun bear; 5 c. Clouded leopard; 6 c. Dusun woman with gong; 10 c. Map of Borneo; 12 c. Banteng; 20 c. Butterfly orchid; 25 c. Sumatran rhinoceros; 30 c. Murut with blow-pipe; 35 c. Mt. Kinabalu; 50 c. Dusun and buffalo transport; 75 c. Bajau horseman. VERT: $1 Orang-utan; $2 Rhinoceros hornbill; $5 Crested wood partridge; $10 Arms of N. Borneo.

1963. Freedom from Hunger. As T **28** of Aden.

407	12 c. blue	1·50	65

POSTAGE DUE STAMPS

Overprinted **POSTAGE DUE**

1895. Issue of 1894.

D 2	**25**	2 c. black & red	13·00	20·00	1·25
D 3	**26**	3 c. green & mve	4·75	13·00	1·00
D 4	**27**	5 c. black & red .	38·00	25·00	2·50
D 5a	**28**	6 c. black & brn .	10·00	35·00	2·50
D 7	**29**	8 c. blk & lilac . .	32·00	42·00	2·50
D 8b	**30**	12 c. blk & blue .	50·00	42·00	2·50
D10	**31**	18 c. blk & grn . .	50·00	55·00	4·00
D11b	**32**	24 c. blue & red .	22·00	48·00	4·00

1897. Issue of 1897.

D12	**25**	2 c. black & red .	7·00	8·00	1·00
D15		2 c. black & green	30·00	42·00	70
D16b	**26**	3 c. green & mve .	9·50	19·00	50
D18		4 c. black & red .	25·00	25·00	50
D19	**27**	5 c. black & orge .	19·00	30·00	1·40
D20a	**28**	6 c. black & brn .	3·50	22·00	70
D21a	**29**	8 c. blk and lilac .	3·75	22·00	50
D22	**30**	12 c. black & bl	70·00	£160	4·00
D23a	**31**	18 c. black and green (No. 108)	†	†	£425
D24		18 c. black and green (No. 110) . . .	35·00	£160	4·00
D25	**32**	24 c. blue and red (No. 109)	—	—	£150
D26a		24 c. blue and red (No. 111) .	17·00	£130	2·25

1902. Issue of 1901.

D47	1 c. black & bistre . .	4·25	55·00	—
D36	2 c. black and green .	7·50	2·75	30
D37	3 c. green & mauve .	2·50	2·75	30
D38	4 c. black and red . .	5·50	5·50	30
D39	5 c. black & orange .	13·00	4·00	30
D40	6 c. black & brown .	8·50	8·50	40
D41	8 c. black and lilac .	16·00	4·25	40
D42b	10 c. brown & grey .	60·00	13·00	1·40
D43	12 c. black and blue .	15·00	12·00	1·50
D44	16 c. green & brown .	25·00	17·00	1·50
D45	18 c. black & green .	5·50	17·00	1·50
D46	24 c. blue and red . .	9·00	21·00	1·50

1919. Issue of 1909.

D49	2 c. black and green . . .	10·00	75·00
D57	2 c. black and red	50	1·75
D58	3 c. black and green . . .	4·00	17·00

D51		4 c. black and red	80	1·00
D52		5 c. black and brown	7·50	16·00
D61		6 c. black and olive	4·00	2·50
D54		8 c. black and red	1·25	1·25
D55		10 c. black and blue	11·00	17·00
D56		12 c. black and blue	38·00	38·00
D56ba		16 c. black and brown	6·50	50·00

D 2 Crest of the Company

1939.

D66	D 2	2 c. brown	6·50	70·00
D67		4 c. red	6·50	90·00
D68		6 c. violet	20·00	£110
D69		8 c. green	20·00	£190
D70		10 c. blue	42·00	£325

For later issues see SABAH.

JAPANESE OCCUPATION

1942. Stamps of North Borneo optd as T **1** of Japanese Occupation of Brunei. (a) Issue of 1939.

J 1	81	1 c. green and brown	£130	£180
J 2	82	2 c. purple and blue	£130	£180
J 3	–	3 c. blue and green	£110	£180
J 4a	–	4 c. green and violet	50·00	£100
J 5	–	6 c. blue and red	£120	£180
J 6	–	8 c. red	£120	£160
J 7	–	10 c. violet and green	£130	£180
J 8	–	12 c. green and blue	£150	£300
J 9	–	15 c. green and brown	£150	£300
J10	–	20 c. violet and blue	£180	£350
J11	–	25 c. green and brown	£180	£350
J12	–	50 c. brown and violet	£250	£400
J13	–	$1 brown and red	£250	£475
J14	–	$2 violet and olive	£350	£650
J15	–	$5 blue	£425	£750

(b) War Tax Issue of 1941.

J16	81	1 c. green and brown	£400	£250
J17	82	2 c. purple and blue	£1100	£350

2 Mt. Kinabalu

3 Borneo Scene

1943.

J18	2	4 c. red	14·00	32·00
J19	3	8 c. blue	14·00	32·00

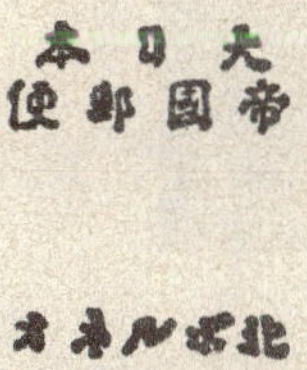
(4)

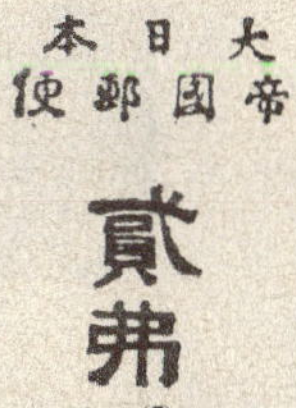
(5)

("Imperial Japanese Postal Service, North Borneo")

1944. Optd with T 4. (a) On stamps of North Borneo.

J20	81	1 c. green and brown	4·25	8·50
J21	82	2 c. purple and blue	7·50	8·50
J22	–	3 c. blue and green	3·75	6·50
J23	–	4 c. green and violet	4·00	9·50
J24	–	6 c. blue and red	3·50	6·00
J25	–	8 c. red	5·50	17·00
J26	–	10 c. violet and green	8·00	13·00
J27	–	12 c. green and blue	6·00	13·00
J28	–	15 c. green and brown	6·00	14·00
J29	–	20 c. violet and blue	16·00	38·00
J30	–	25 c. green and brown	16·00	38·00
J31	–	50 c. brown and violet	50·00	£100
J32	–	$1 brown and red	80·00	£140

(b) On stamps of Japanese Occupation of North Borneo.

J21a		2 c. purple and blue (J2)	£425	
J22a		3 c. blue and green (J3)	£425	
J25a		8 c. red (J6)	£425	
J26b		10 c. violet and green (J7a)	£180	£350
J27a		12 c. green and blue (J8)	£425	
J28a		15 c. green and brown (J9)	£425	

1944. No. J1 surch with T 5.

J33	81	$2 on 1 c. green & brown	£4500	£3750

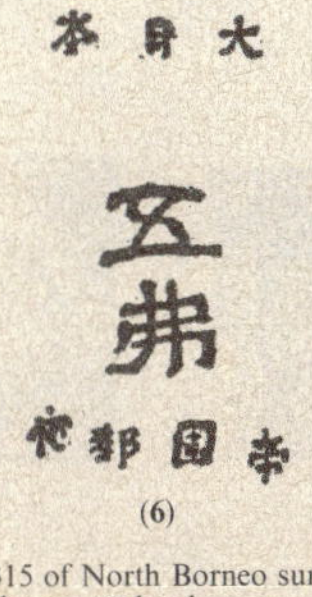
(6)

1944. No. 315 of North Borneo surch with T 6.

J34		$5 on $1 brown and red	£4000	£2750

1944. Stamps of Japan optd as bottom line in T 4.

J35	126	1 s. brown	5·50	14·00
J36	84	2 s. red	5·50	13·00
J37	–	3 s. green (No. 319)	4·50	14·00
J38	129	4 s. green	5·50	12·00
J39	–	5 s. red (No. 396)	6·50	15·00
J40	–	6 s. orange (No. 322)	7·50	16·00
J41	–	8 s. violet (No. 324)	4·75	16·00
J42	–	10 s. red (No. 399)	5·00	16·00
J43	–	15 s. blue (No. 401)	7·00	16·00
J44	–	20 s. blue (No. 328)	85·00	85·00
J45	–	25 s. brown (No. 329)	55·00	70·00
J46	–	30 s. blue (No. 330)	£160	95·00
J47	–	50 s. olive and brown (No. 331)	60·00	60·00
J48	–	1 y. brown (No. 332)	60·00	80·00

NORTHERN NIGERIA

A British protectorate on the west coast of Africa. In 1914 incorporated into Nigeria.

12 pence = 1 shilling;
20 shillings = 1 pound

1

5

1900.

1	1	½d. mauve and green	2·00	9·00
2		1d. mauve and red	2·25	3·25
3		2d. mauve and yellow	7·50	30·00
4		2½d. mauve and blue	6·50	30·00
5		5d. mauve and brown	15·00	32·00
6		6d. mauve and violet	13·00	24·00
7		1s. green and black	17·00	55·00
8		2s. 6d. green and blue	75·00	£350
9		10s. green and brown	£190	£450

1902. As T **1**, but portrait of King Edward VII.

10		½d. purple and green	1·75	80
11		1d. purple and red	1·75	40
12		2d. purple and yellow	1·75	2·50
13		2½d. purple and blue	1·50	6·00
14		5d. purple and brown	1·75	4·75
15		6d. purple and violet	4·50	4·50
16		1s. green and black	2·75	4·75
17		2s. 6d. green and blue	8·00	32·00
18		10s. green and brown	45·00	50·00

1910. As last. New colours etc.

28		½d. green	1·40	90
29		1d. red	1·50	85
30		2d. grey	3·00	2·25
31		2½d. blue	1·40	6·00
32		3d. purple on yellow	3·00	50
34		5d. purple and green	3·75	7·50
35a		6d. purple	3·25	6·00
36		1s. black and green	1·75	65
37		2s. 6d. black and red on blue	9·50	25·00
38		5s. green and red on yellow	23·00	70·00
39		10s. green and red on green	42·00	45·00

1912.

40	5	½d. green	75	60
41		1d. red	75	60
42		2d. grey	3·00	4·50
43		3d. purple on yellow	2·25	1·25
44		4d. black and red on yellow	75	2·00
45		5d. purple and olive	4·00	5·50
46		6d. purple and violet	3·75	4·00
47		9d. purple and red	2·00	10·00
48		1s. black on green	3·50	2·00
49		2s. 6d. black and red on blue	7·00	30·00
50		5s. green and red on yellow	18·00	70·00
51		10s. green and red on green	38·00	45·00
52		£1 purple and black on red	£170	£110

NORTHERN RHODESIA

A British territory in central Africa, north of the Zambesi. From 1954 to 1963 part of the Central African Federation and using the stamps of Rhodesia and Nyasaland (q.v.). A new constitution was introduced on 3 January, 1964, with internal self-government and independence came on 24 October, 1964 when the country was renamed Zambia (q.v.).

12 pence = 1 shilling;
20 shillings = 1 pound

1

1925. The shilling values are larger and the view is in first colour.

1	1	½d. green	1·25	60
2		1d. brown	1·25	10
3		1½d. red	1·00	30
4		2d. orange	2·00	10
5		3d. blue	2·00	1·25
6		4d. violet	3·00	50
7		6d. grey	3·00	40
8		8d. purple	3·75	35·00
9		10d. olive	3·75	35·00
10		1s. orange and black	2·75	1·50
11		2s. brown and blue	13·00	20·00
12	1	2s. 6d. black and green	14·00	6·00
13		3s. violet and blue	22·00	14·00
14		5s. grey and violet	25·00	16·00
15		7s. 6d. purple and black	90·00	£140
16		10s. green and black	60·00	65·00
17		20s. red and purple	£140	£160

1935. Silver Jubilee. As T **13** of Antigua.

18		1d. blue and olive	60	1·00
19		2d. green and blue	60	1·00
20		3d. brown and blue	2·50	4·50
21		6d. grey and purple	2·50	1·25

1937. Coronation. As T **2** of Aden.

22		1½d. red	30	35
23		2d. brown	40	35
24		3d. blue	60	1·25

1938. As 1925, but with portrait of King George VI facing right and "POSTAGE & REVENUE" omitted.

25		½d. green	10	10
26		½d. brown	10	80
27		1d. brown	10	10
28		1d. green	60	90
29		1½d. red	45·00	40
30		1½d. orange	30	10
31		2d. brown	50·00	1·25
32		2d. red	30	30
33		2d. purple	45	90
34		3d. blue	30	10
35		3d. red	50	1·75
36		4d. violet	30	40
37		4½d. blue	40	4·25
38		6d. grey	30	10
39		9d. violet	40	2·25
40		1s. orange and black	2·00	40
41		2s. 6d. black and green	7·00	2·00
42		3s. violet and blue	13·00	4·00
43		5s. grey and violet	9·00	5·50
44		10s. green and black	12·00	12·00
45		20s. red and purple	38·00	45·00

1946. Victory. As T **9** of Aden.

46		1½d. orange	10	10
47		2d. red	10	40

1948. Silver Wedding. As T **10/11** of Aden.

48		1½d. orange	30	10
49		20s. red	42·00	45·00

1949. U.P.U. As T **20/23** of Antigua.

50		2d. red	30	30
51		3d. blue	1·90	1·25
52		6d. grey	1·00	1·25
53		1s. orange	1·00	1·00

5 Cecil Rhodes and Victoria Falls

1953. Birth Centenary of Cecil Rhodes.

54	5	½d. brown	50	50
55		1d. green	40	40
56		2d. mauve	40	15
57		4½d. blue	40	3·25
58		1s. orange and black	75	4·00

6 Arms of the Rhodesias and Nyasaland

9 Arms

1953. Rhodes Centenary Exhibition.

59	6	6d. violet	40	70

1953. Coronation. As T **13** of Antigua.

60		1½d. black and orange	40	10

1953. As 1938 but with portrait of Queen Elizabeth II facing left.

61		½d. brown	65	10
62		1d. green	65	10
63		1½d. orange	80	10
64		2d. purple	75	10
65		3d. red	60	10
66		4d. violet	1·25	1·25
67		4½d. blue	90	3·50
68		6d. grey	1·25	10
69		9d. violet	60	3·50
70		1s. orange and black	60	10
71		2s. 6d. black and green	6·50	2·75
72		5s. grey and purple	6·50	12·00
73		10s. green and black	6·00	22·00
74		20s. red and purple	20·00	26·00

1963. Arms black, gold and blue; portrait and inscriptions black; background colours given.

75	9	½d. violet	40	60
76		1d. blue	60	10
77		2d. brown	30	10
78		3d. yellow	20	10
79		4d. green	30	20
80		6d. green	30	10
81		9d. bistre	30	90
82		1s. purple	30	10
83		1s. 3d. purple	1·50	10
84		2s. orange	1·25	2·25
85		2s. 6d. purple	1·25	90
86		5s. mauve	5·00	5·00
87		10s. mauve	4·50	12·00
88		20s. blue	5·50	14·00

Nos. 84/88 are larger (27 × 23 mm).

POSTAGE DUE STAMPS

D 1

D 2

1929.

D1	D 1	1d. black	2·50	2·50
D2		2d. black	3·00	3·00
D3		3d. black	3·00	23·00
D4		4d. black	9·00	28·00

1963.

D 5	D 2	1d. orange	80	3·50
D 6		2d. blue	80	3·75
D 7		3d. lake	90	4·25
D 8		4d. blue	90	6·00
D 9		6d. purple	5·00	8·00
D10		1s. green	6·00	18·00

For later issues see **ZAMBIA**.

NOVA SCOTIA

An eastern province of the Dominion of Canada, whose stamps it now uses.

Currency: As Canada

1

2 Emblem of the United Kingdom

1953. Imperf.

1	1	1d. brown	£2000	£400
4	2	3d. blue	£750	£130
5		6d. green	£4000	£400
8		1s. purple	£14000	£2500

3

4

1860. Perf.

9	3	1 c. black	3·00	12·00
20		2 c. purple	3·25	14·00
13		5 c. blue	£300	16·00
26	4	8½ c. green	17·00	40·00
27		10 c. red	4·00	20·00
17		12½ c. black	26·00	26·00

NYASALAND PROTECTORATE

A British Protectorate in central Africa. Formerly known as British Central Africa. From 1954 to 1963 part of the Central African Federation using the stamps of Rhodesia and Nyasaland (q.v.). From July 1964 independent within the Commonwealth under its new name of Malawi.

12 pence = 1 shilling;
20 shillings = 1 pound

1891. Stamps of Rhodesia optd **B.C.A.**

1	1	1d. black	3·25	3·75
2		2d. green and red	3·25	3·75
3		4d. brown and black	3·50	4·75
5		6d. blue	5·00	8·00
6		8d. red and blue	12·00	28·00
7		1s. brown	12·00	11·00
8		2s. red	24·00	48·00
9		2s. 6d. purple	55·00	75·00
10		3s. brown and green	50·00	55·00
11		4s. black and red	55·00	80·00
12		5s. yellow	55·00	70·00
13		10s. green	£110	£170
14	–	£1 blue	£475	£500
15	–	£2 red	£800	
16	–	£5 olive	£1400	
17	–	£10 brown	£3250	

1892. Stamps of Rhodesia surch **B.C.A.** and value in words.

18	1	3s. on 4s. black and red	£300	£300
19		4s. on 5s. yellow	70·00	80·00

1895. No. 2 surch **ONE PENNY.** and bar.

20	1	1d. on 2d. green and red	6·00	25·00

5 Arms of the Protectorate 7

1895. The 2s. 6d. and higher values are larger.

32	5	1d. black	3·00	4·50
33		2d. black and green	13·00	5·00
34		4d. black and orange	19·00	17·00
35		6d. black and blue	19·00	10·00
36		1s. black and red	19·00	12·00
37		2s. 6d. black and mauve	£110	£110
38		3s. black and yellow	80·00	48·00
39		5s. black and olive	£110	£140
29		£1 black and orange	£850	£375
40		£1 black and blue	£750	£475
30		£10 black and orange	£3750	£3250
31		£25 black and green	£6500	

1897. The 2s. 6d. and higher values are larger.

43	7	1d. black and blue	2·25	70
57d		1d. purple and red	1·75	40
44		2d. black and yellow	1·60	1·25
45		4d. black and red	5·00	1·50
57e		4d. purple and olive	7·50	10·00
46		6d. black and green	40·00	4·25
58		6d. purple and brown	3·50	3·00
47		1s. black and purple	8·50	7·00
48		2s. 6d. black and blue	42·00	42·00
49		3s. black and green	£190	£225
50		4s. black and red	70·00	80·00
50a		10s. black and olive	£110	£120
51		£1 black and purple	£275	£160
52		£10 black and yellow	£3750	£1700

1897. No. 49 surch **ONE PENNY**.

53	7	1d. on 3s. black and green	5·00	8·50

10 11

1898.

56a	10	1d. red and blue (imperf)	£1700	£120
57		1d. red and blue (perf)	£1900	16·00

1903. The 2s. 6d. and higher values are larger.

59	11	1d. grey and red	4·00	2·00
60		2d. purple	3·25	1·00
61		4d. green and black	2·50	8·50
62		6d. grey and brown	2·50	2·00
62b		1s. grey and blue	2·50	9·00
63		2s. 6d. green	38·00	60·00
64		4s. purple	60·00	75·00
65		10s. green and black	85·00	£170
66		£1 grey and red	£200	£170
67		£10 grey and blue	£4250	£3250

13 14

1908.

73	13	½d. green	1·50	1·75
74		1d. red	3·00	90
75		3d. purple on yellow	1·25	3·50
76		4d. black & red on yellow	1·25	1·50
77		6d. purple	3·75	9·00
72		1s. black on green	2·50	7·00
78	14	2s. 6d. black & red on blue	42·00	75·00
79		4s. red and black	75·00	95·00
80		10s. green & red on green	£100	£170
81		£1 purple & black on red	£425	£500
82		£10 purple and blue	£7000	£4500

1913. As 1908, but portrait of King George V.

100	½d. green	90	30
101	1d. red	1·25	30
102	1½d. orange	3·25	17·00
103	2d. grey	90	30
89	2½d. blue	2·25	6·00
90	3d. purple on yellow	3·75	3·75
91	4d. black and red on yellow	2·00	2·25
107	6d. purple	3·00	3·25
93a	1s. black on green	4·50	1·50
109	2s. purple and blue on blue	13·00	10·00
94	2s. 6d. black & red on blue	11·00	10·00
111	4s. red and black	17·00	19·00
112	5s. green & red on yellow	32·00	70·00
96	10s. green and red on green	60·00	80·00
98	£1 purple and black on red	£150	£140
99a	£10 purple and blue	£2750	£1700

17 King George V and Symbol of the Protectorate

1934.

114	17	½d. green	75	95
115		1d. brown	75	75
116		1½d. red	75	2·25
117		2d. grey	80	1·25
118		3d. blue	2·25	1·50
119		4d. mauve	2·25	3·00
120		6d. violet	2·25	40
121		9d. olive	4·50	9·00
122		1s. black and orange	7·00	12·00

1935. Silver Jubilee. As T **13** of Antigua.

123	1d. blue and grey	1·00	1·50
124	2d. green and blue	1·00	60
125	3d. brown and blue	7·00	13·00
126	1s. grey and purple	16·00	30·00

1937. Coronation. As T **2** of Aden.

127	½d. green	30	50
128	1d. brown	50	40
129	2d. grey	50	1·25

1938. As T **17** but with head of King George VI and "POSTAGE REVENUE" omitted.

130	½d. green	30	85
130a	½d. brown	10	1·25
131	1d. brown	40	15
131a	1d. green	30	50
132	1½d. red	1·75	4·25
132a	1½d. grey	30	3·50
133	2d. grey	3·50	1·00
133a	2d. red	30	1·00
134	3d. blue	60	30
135	4d. mauve	1·75	1·00
136	6d. violet	2·00	1·00
137	9d. olive	2·50	2·25
138	1s. black and orange	2·75	90

1938. As T **14** but with head of King George VI facing right.

139	2s. purple and blue on blue	10·00	8·00
140	2s. 6d. black and red on blue	12·00	8·00
141	5s. green and red on yellow	40·00	18·00
142	10s. green and red on green	60·00	24·00
143	£1 purple and black on red	30·00	24·00

20 Lake Nyasa 21 King's African Rifles

1945.

144	20	½d. black and brown	30	10
145	21	1d. black and green	40	70
160	–	1d. brown and green	50	20
146	–	1½d. black and grey	20	50
147	–	2d. black and red	30	40
148	–	3d. black and blue	20	30
149	–	4d. black and red	1·00	45
150	–	6d. black and violet	1·25	40
151	20	9d. black and olive	1·50	2·50
152	–	1s. blue and green	1·25	20
153	–	2s. green and purple	3·75	4·25
154	–	2s. 6d. green and blue	7·50	4·25
155	–	5s. purple and blue	4·50	6·00
156	–	10s. red and green	12·00	12·00
157	–	20s. red and black	17·00	22·00

DESIGNS—HORIZ: 1½d., 6d. Tea estate; 2d., 1s., 10s. Map of Nyasaland; 4d., 2s. 6d. Tobacco; 5s., 20s. Badge of Nyasaland. VERT: 1d. (No. 160), Leopard and sunrise; 3d., 2s. Fishing village.

1946. Victory. As T **9** of Aden.

158	1d. green	10	10
159	2d. red	30	10

1948. Silver Wedding. As T **10/11** of Aden.

161	1d. green	15	10
162	10s. mauve	15·00	24·00

1949. U.P.U. As T **20/23** of Antigua.

163	1d. green	50	20
164	3d. blue	2·00	2·25
165	6d. purple	1·00	50
166	1s. blue	75	50

27 Arms in 1891 and 1951

1951. Diamond Jubilee of Protectorate.

167	27	2d. black and red	1·00	85
168		3d. black and blue	1·00	85
169		6d. black and violet	1·00	1·50
170		5s. black and blue	1·75	6·50

1953. Rhodes Centenary Exhibition. As T **6** of Northern Rhodesia.

171	6d. violet	20	30

1953. Coronation. As T **13** of Aden.

172	2d. black and orange	50	50

29 Grading Cotton

1953. As 1945 but with portrait of Queen Elizabeth II as in T **29**. Designs as for corresponding values except where stated.

173	20	½d. black and brown	10	85
174	–	1d. brown and green (as No. 160)	65	20
175	–	1½d. black and grey	20	1·90
176a	–	2d. black and orange	30	10
177	29	2½d. green and black	20	50
178	–	3d. black & red (as 4d.)	30	10
179	–	4½d. black & blue (as 3d.)	30	40
180a	–	6d. black and violet	90	50
181	20	9d. black and olive	70	2·50
182	–	1s. blue and green	1·75	50
183	–	2s. green and red	2·00	3·00
184	–	2s. 6d. green and blue	3·25	4·25
185	–	5s. purple and blue	7·00	4·50
186	–	10s. red and green	4·25	12·00
187	–	20s. red and black	13·00	16·00

30 32 Mother and Child

34 Tea Industry

1963. Revenue stamps optd **POSTAGE** as in T **30** or surch also.

188	30	½d. on 1d. blue	30	30
189		1d. green	30	10
190		2d. red	30	30
191		3d. blue	30	10
192		6d. purple	30	10
193		9d. on 1s. red	40	25
194		1s. purple	45	10
195		2s. 6d. black	60	2·00
196		5s. brown	1·50	1·50
197		10s. olive	2·75	4·25
198		£1 violet	3·75	4·25

1964.

199	32	½d. violet	10	30
200	–	1d. black and green	10	10
201	–	2d. brown	10	10
202	–	3d. brown, green & bistre	10	10
203	–	4d. blue and yellow	20	30
204	34	6d. purple, green and blue	60	30
205	–	1s. brown, blue and yellow	15	10
206	–	1s. 3d. bronze and brown	2·50	10
207	–	2s. 6d. brown and blue	2·50	50
208	–	5s. blue, green, yellow & blk	1·50	1·25
209	–	10s. green, salmon & black	2·00	3·00
210	–	£1 brown and yellow	7·00	4·75

DESIGNS—HORIZ (as Type **32**): 1d. Chambo (fish); 2d. Zebu bull; 3d. Groundnuts; 4d. Fishing. (As Type **34**): 1s. Timber; 1s. 3d. Turkish tobacco industry; 2s. 6d. Cotton industry; 5s. Monkey Bay, Lake Nyasa; 10s. Forestry, Afzelia. VERT (as Type **34**): £1 Nyala.

POSTAGE DUE STAMPS

1950. As Type D **1** of Gold Coast, but inscr "NYASALAND".

D1	1d. red	3·75	16·00
D2	2d. blue	8·50	22·00
D3	3d. green	9·00	6·00
D4	4d. purple	16·00	38·00
D5	6d. orange	23·00	90·00

For later issues see **MALAWI**.

ORANGE FREE STATE (ORANGE RIVER COLONY)

British possession 1848–54. Independent 1854–99. Annexed by Great Britain, 1900. Later a province of the Union of South Africa.

12 pence = 1 shilling;
20 shillings = 1 pound

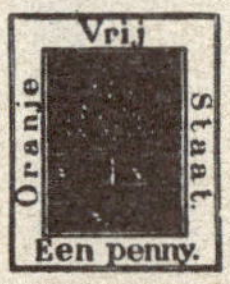

1 38 King Edward VII, Springbok and Gnu

1869.

48	1	½d. brown	1·25	50
84		½d. yellow	1·75	35
2		1d. brown	7·00	45
68		1d. purple	2·00	30
50		2d. mauve	7·50	30
51		3d. blue	2·00	2·00
19		4d. blue	4·00	2·50
7		6d. red	9·00	2·00
9		1s. orange	22·00	1·50
87		1s. brown	14·00	1·50
20		5s. green	9·00	11·00

1877. Surch in figures.

75	1	½d. on 3d. blue	3·75	2·75
36		½d. on 5s. green	8·50	3·75
54		1d. on 3d. blue	2·50	60
57		1d. on 4d. blue	19·00	3·75
22		1d. on 5s. green	42·00	13·00
53		2d. on 3d. blue	22·00	2·00
67		2½d. on 3d. blue	7·00	70
83		2½d. on 3d. blue	3·00	80
40		3d. on 4d. blue	26·00	16·00
12		4d. on 6d. red	£110	25·00

1896. Surch **Halve Penny**.

77	1	½d. on 3d. blue	35	50

1900. Surch **V.R.I.** and value in figures.

112	1	½d. on ½d. orange	30	20
113		1d. on 1d. purple	30	20
114		2d. on 2d. mauve	60	30
104		2½d. on 3d. blue (No. 83)	9·00	6·00
117		3d. on 3d. blue	30	30
118		4d. on 4d. blue	1·25	2·25
108		6d. on 6d. red	35·00	35·00
120		6d. on 6d. blue	70	40
121		1s. on 1s. brown	2·00	45
122		5s. on 5s. green	6·50	8·50

1900. Stamps of Cape of Good Hope optd **ORANGE RIVER COLONY.**

133	17	½d. green	20	10
134		1d. red	30	10
135	6	2½d. blue	40	35

1902. No. 120 surch **4d** bar.

136	1	4d. on 6d. blue	80	75

1902. Surch **E. R. I. 6d**.

137	1	6d. on 6d. blue	2·25	6·50

1902. No. 20 surch **One Shilling** and star.

138	1	1s. on 5s. green	6·50	8·00

1903.

139	38	½d. green	7·00	1·25
140		1d. red	3·50	10
141		2d. brown	4·00	80
142		2½d. blue	1·60	50
143		3d. mauve	6·50	90
150		4d. red and green	4·50	1·75
145		6d. red and mauve	6·50	90
146		1s. red and brown	25·00	1·75
147		5s. blue and brown	75·00	22·00

MILITARY FRANK STAMP

M 1

1899.

M1	M 1	(–) black/yellow	12·00	45·00

POLICE FRANK STAMPS

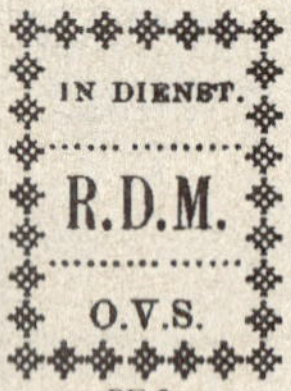

PF 1 PF 2

1896.

PF2	PF 1	(–) black	£130	£160

1899.

PF3	PF 2	(–) black on yellow	£120	£120

ORCHHA

A state of Central India. Now uses Indian stamps.

12 pies = 1 anna; 16 annas = 1 rupee

1 2

1913. Imperf.

1	1	¼ a. green	28·00	75·00
2		1 a. red	19·00	

1914. Imperf.

3a	**2**	$\frac{1}{4}$ a. blue	35	3·00
4		$\frac{1}{2}$ a. green	50	3·50
5c		1 a. red	2·50	3·75
6		2 a. brown	4·50	18·00
7b		4 a. yellow	8·00	23·00

3 Maharaja Vir Singh II

5 Maharaja Vir Singh II

1935.

8b	**3**	$\frac{1}{4}$ a. purple and grey	30	1·25
9		$\frac{1}{2}$ a. grey and green	50	75
10		$\frac{3}{4}$ a. mauve and green	50	85
11	–	1 a. green and brown	50	65
12	**3**	1$\frac{1}{4}$ a. grey and mauve	45	70
13		1$\frac{1}{2}$ a. brown and red	45	75
14		2 a. blue and orange	45	75
15		2$\frac{1}{2}$ a. brown and orange	65	80
16		3 a. blue and mauve	65	85
17		4 a. purple and green	65	2·50
18		6 a. black and buff	70	2·50
19		8 a. brown and purple	1·50	2·75
20		12 a. green and purple	1·00	3·00
21		12 a. blue and purple	23·00	45·00
22		1 r. brown and green	80	3·75
24		2 r. brown and yellow	2·75	9·00
25		3 r. black and blue	1·50	9·00
26		4 r. black and brown	2·50	10·00
27		5 r. blue and purple	3·00	11·00
28	–	10 r. green and red	7·00	17·00
29	–	15 r. black and green	12·00	40·00
30	–	25 r. orange and blue	16·00	45·00

DESIGN: 1 a., 10 r. to 25 r. As Type **3**, but inscr "POSTAGE & REVENUE". There are two different versions of the portrait for the 1 r. value.

1939.

31	**5**	$\frac{1}{4}$ a. brown	2·25	45·00
32		$\frac{1}{2}$ a. green	2·50	38·00
33		$\frac{3}{4}$ a. blue	2·50	60·00
34		1 a. red	2·50	12·00
35		1$\frac{1}{4}$ a. blue	2·50	60·00
36		1$\frac{1}{2}$ a. mauve	2·75	75·00
37		2 a. red	2·50	45·00
38		2$\frac{1}{2}$ a. green	2·50	£130
39		3 a. violet	3·75	70·00
40		4 a. slate	4·75	20·00
41		8 a. mauve	8·00	£130
42	–	1 r. green	14·00	
43	–	2 r. violet	30·00	£350
44	–	5 r. orange	85·00	
45	–	10 r. green	£325	
46	–	15 r. lilac	£2250	
47	–	25 r. purple	£2250	

The rupee values are larger (25 × 30 mm) and have different frame.

PAHANG

A state of the Federation of Malaya, incorporated in Malaysia in 1963.

100 cents = 1 dollar (Straits or Malayan)

1899. Nos. 52/3 and 63 of Straits Settlements optd **PAHANG**.

4	2 c. red	8·50	12·00
2	8 c. orange	£1600	£1400
3	10 c. grey	£225	£250

1891. No. 68 of Straits Settlements surch **PAHANG Two CENTS**.

7	2 c. on 24 c. green	95·00	£110

9 Tiger

10 Tiger

1891.

11	**9**	1 c. green	3·75	2·75
12		2 c. red	4·00	2·75
13		5 c. blue	9·00	30·00

1895.

14	**10**	3 c. purple and red	4·75	2·50
15		4 c. purple and red	15·00	10·00
16		5 c. purple and yellow	19·00	18·00

1897. No. 13 divided, and each half surch.

18	**9**	2 c. on half of 5 c. blue	£1000	£325
18d		3 c. on half of 5 c. blue	£1000	£325

1898. Stamps of Perak optd **Pahang.**

19	**44**	10 c. purple and orange	15·00	25·00
20		25 c. green and red	75·00	£120
21		50 c. purple and black	£225	£250
22		50 c. green and black	£160	£170
23	**45**	$1 green	£250	£275
24		$5 green and blue	£750	£900

1898. Stamp of Perak surch **Pahang Four cents**.

25	**44**	4 c. on 8 c. purple & blue	2·50	5·50

1899. No. 15 surch **Four cents.**

28	**10**	4 c. on 5 c. purple & yellow	8·50	40·00

15 Sultan Sir Abu Bakar

16 Sultan Sir Abu Bakar

1935.

29	**15**	1 c. black	15	40
30		2 c. green	60	50
31		3 c. green	11·00	12·00
32		4 c. orange	30	40
33		5 c. brown	60	10
34		6 c. red	8·50	2·25
35		8 c. grey	60	10
36		8 c. red	1·00	42·00
37		10 c. purple	30	10
38		12 c. blue	1·00	1·75
39		15 c. blue	7·00	48·00
40		25 c. purple and red	80	1·50
41		30 c. purple and orange	80	1·10
42		40 c. red and purple	75	2·25
43		50 c. black on green	2·75	1·75
44		$1 black and red on blue	1·75	7·00
45		$2 green and red	18·00	26·00
46		$5 green and red on green	7·00	50·00

1948. Silver Wedding. As T **10/11** of Aden.

47	10 c. violet	15	60
48	$5 green	22·00	40·00

1949. U.P.U. As T **20/23** of Antigua.

49	10 c. purple	30	20
50	15 c. blue	90	70
51	25 c. orange	35	1·10
52	50 c. black	70	2·00

1950.

53	**16**	1 c. black	10	10
54		2 c. orange	10	10
55		3 c. green	20	40
56		4 c. brown	30	10
57a		5 c. purple	25	15
58		6 c. grey	15	10
59		8 c. red	20	1·00
60		8 c. green	85	75
61		10 c. mauve	15	10
62		12 c. red	85	1·25
63		15 c. blue	30	10
64		20 c. black and green	25	2·50
65		20 c. blue	75	10
66		25 c. purple and orange	30	10
67		30 c. red and purple	1·25	35
68		35 c. red and purple	60	25
69		40 c. red and purple	90	7·50
70		50 c. black and blue	1·00	10
71		$1 blue and purple	2·50	2·50
72		$2 green and red	13·00	19·00
73		$5 green and brown	55·00	45·00

1953. Coronation. As T **13** of Aden.

74	10 c. black and purple	65	10

1957. As Nos. 92/102 of Kedah but inset portrait of Sultan Sir Abu Bakar.

75	1 c. black	10	10
76	2 c. red	10	10
77	4 c. sepia	10	10
78	5 c. lake	10	10
79	8 c. green	80	2·00
80	10 c. sepia	50	10
81	10 c. purple	2·00	20
82	20 c. blue	1·00	10
83	50 c. black and blue	20	30
84	$1 blue and purple	4·00	1·75
85	$2 green and red	3·00	8·50
86	$5 brown and green	8·50	11·00

17 "Vanda hookeriana"

1965. As Nos. 115/21 of Kedah but with inset portrait of Sultan Sir Abu Bakar as in T **17**.

87	**17**	1 c. multicoloured	10	50
88	–	2 c. multicoloured	10	50
89	–	5 c. multicoloured	15	10
90	–	6 c. multicoloured	30	50
91	–	10 c. multicoloured	20	10
92	–	15 c. multicoloured	1·00	10
93	–	20 c. multicoloured	1·60	30

The higher values used in Pahang were Nos. 20/7 of Malaysia (National Issue).

18 "Precis orithya"

19 Sultan Haji Ahmad Shah

1971. Butterflies. As Nos. 124/30 of Kedah, but with portrait of Sultan Sir Abu Bakar as in T **18**.

96	–	1 c. multicoloured	20	80
97	–	2 c. multicoloured	40	80
98	–	5 c. multicoloured	75	50
99	–	6 c. multicoloured	1·50	1·10
100	–	10 c. multicoloured	90	20
101	**18**	15 c. multicoloured	1·60	10
102	–	20 c. multicoloured	1·75	30

The higher values in use with this issue were Nos. 64/71 of Malaysia (National Issues).

1975. Installation of the Sultan.

103	**19**	10 c. green, lilac and gold	50	80
104		15 c. black, yellow & green	60	10
105		50 c. black, blue & green	1·75	3·50

1977. As Nos. 97/8, 100/102 but with portrait of Sultan Haji Ahmad Shah.

106	–	2 c. multicoloured	35·00	38·00
107	–	5 c. multicoloured	60	80
108	–	10 c. multicoloured	80	40
109	**18**	15 c. multicoloured	80	30
110	–	20 c. multicoloured	4·00	1·75

20 "Rhododendron scortechinii"

21 Rice

1979. Flowers. As Nos. 135/41 of Kedah but with portrait of Sultan Haji Ahmad Shah as in T **20**.

111	1 c. "Rafflesia hasseltii"	10	50
112	2 c. "Pterocarpus indicus"	10	50
113	5 c. "Lagerstroemia speciosa"	10	20
114	10 c. "Durio zibethinus"	15	10
115	15 c. "Hibiscus rosa-sinensis"	15	10
116	20 c. Type **20**	20	10
117	25 c. "Etlingera elatior" (inscr "Phaeomeria speciosa")	40	40

1986. As Nos. 152/8 of Kedah but with portrait of Sultan Ahmad Shah as in T **21**.

125	1 c. Coffee	10	10
126	2 c. Coconuts	10	10
127	5 c. Cocoa	10	10
128	10 c. Black pepper	10	10
129	15 c. Rubber	10	10
130	20 c. Oil palm	10	10
131	30 c. Type **21**	15	20

PAKISTAN

A Dominion created in 1947 from territory with predominantly Moslem population in Eastern and Western India. Became an independent Islamic Republic within the British Commonweath in 1956. The eastern provinces declared their independence in 1971 and are now known as Bangladesh.

On 30 January 1972 Pakistan left the Commonweath but rejoined on 1 October 1989.

1947. 12 pies = 1 anna;
16 annas = 1 rupee.
1961. 100 paisa = 1 rupee.

1947. King George VI stamps of India optd **PAKISTAN**.

1	**100a**	3 p. grey	10	10
2		½ a. purple	10	10
3		9 p. green	10	10
4		1 a. red	10	10
5	**101**	1½ a. violet	10	10
6		2 a. red	10	20
7		3 a. violet	10	20
8		3½ a. blue	65	2·25
9	**102**	4 a. brown	20	10
10		6 a. green	1·00	75
11		8 a. violet	30	60
12		12 a. red	1·00	20
13	–	14 a. purple (No. 277)	2·50	1·00
14	**93**	1 r. grey and brown	1·75	70
15		2 r. purple and brown	3·25	1·00
16		5 r. green and blue	4·00	3·50
17		10 r. purple and claret	4·00	2·25
18		15 r. brown and green	48·00	75·00
19		25 r. violet and purple	55·00	40·00

3 Constituent Assembly Building, Karachi

1948. Independence.

20	**3**	1½ a. blue	70	50
21	–	2½ a. green	70	10
22	–	3 a. brown	70	20
23	–	1 r. red	70	50

DESIGNS—HORIZ: 2½ a. Entrance to Karachi Airport; 3 a. Gateway to Lahore Fort. VERT: 1 r. Crescent and Stars in foliated frame.

7 Scales of Justice

9 Lloyds Barrage

12 Salimullah Hostel, Dacca University

13 Khyber Pass

1948. Designs with crescent moon pointing to right.

24	**7**	3 p. red	10	10
25		6 p. violet	80	10
26		9 p. green	50	10
27	–	1 a. blue	10	50
28	–	1½ a. green	10	10
29	–	2 a. red	40	50
30	**9**	2½ a. green	2·75	6·00
31	–	3 a. green	7·50	65
32	**9**	3½ a. blue	3·50	4·50
33		4 a. brown	50	10
34	–	6 a. blue	50	50
35	–	8 a. black	50	50
36	–	10 a. red	4·50	7·00
37	–	12 a. red	6·50	80
38	**12**	1 r. blue	5·50	10
39		2 r. brown	20·00	30
40a		5 r. red	9·00	20
41b	**13**	10 r. mauve	18·00	30
42		15 r. green	16·00	11·00
210b		25 r. violet	3·00	4·00

DESIGNS—VERT (as Type **7**): 1 a., 1½ a., 2 a. Star and Crescent; 6 a., 8 a., 12 a. Karachi Port Trust. HORIZ (as Type **12**): 3 a., 10 a. Karachi Airport.

1949. As 1948 but with crescent moon pointing to left.

44a	–	1 a. blue	3·50	10
45a	–	1½ a. green	3·00	10
46a	–	2 a. red	3·50	10
47	–	3 a. green	7·50	65
48	–	6 a. blue	8·50	45
49	–	8 a. black	4·50	1·00
50	–	10 a. red	14·00	1·50
51	–	12 a. red	18·00	30

16

1949. 1st Death Anniv of Mohammed Ali Jinnah.

52	**16**	1½ a. brown	1·25	90
53		3 a. green	1·25	90
54	–	10 a. black	4·00	6·50

DESIGN: 10 a. inscription reads "QUAID-I-AZAM MOHAMMAD ALI JINNAH" etc.

17 Pottery

1951. 4th Anniv of Independence.

55	**17**	2½ a. red	1·00	50
56	–	3 a. purple	50	10
57	**17**	3½ a. blue (A)	75	2·75
57a	–	3½ a. blue (B)	3·25	2·50
58	–	4 a. green	35	10
59	–	6 a. orange	45	10
60	–	8 a. sepia	4·00	10
61	–	10 a. violet	80	80
62	–	12 a. slate	90	10

DESIGNS—VERT: 3, 12 a. Airplane and hourglass; 4, 6 a. Saracenic leaf pattern. HORIZ: 8, 10 a. Archway and lamp.

(A) has Arabic fraction on left as in Type **17** (B) has it on right. For similar 3½ a. see No. 88.

21 "Scinde Dawk" Stamp and Ancient and Modern Transport

1952. Cent of "Scinde Dawk" Issue of India.

63	**21**	3 a. green on olive	75	85
64		12 a. brown on salmon	1·00	15

22 Kaghan Valley

24 Tea Plantation, East Pakistan

1954. 7th Anniv of Independence.

65	**22**	6 p. violet	10	10
66	–	9 p. blue	3·25	1·75
67	–	1 a. red	10	10
68	–	1½ a. red	10	10
69	**24**	14 a. myrtle	55	10
70	–	1 r. green	11·00	10
71	–	2 r. orange	2·75	10

DESIGNS—HORIZ (as Type **22**): 9 p. Mountains, Gilgit; 1 a. Badshahi Mosque, Lahore. (As Type **24**): 1 r. Cotton plants, West Pakistan; 2 r. Jute fields and river, East Pakistan. VERT (as Type **22**): 1½ a. Mausoleum of Emperor Jehangir, Lahore.

29 View of K2

30 Karnaphuli Paper Mill, East Bengal

1954. Conquest of K2 (Mount Godwin-Austen).

72	**29**	2 a. violet	30	30

1955. 8th Anniv of Independence.

73	**30**	2½ a. red (A)	50	85
73a	–	2½ a. red (B)	30	85
74	–	6 a. blue	1·00	10
75	–	8 a. violet	3·75	10
76	–	12 a. red and orange	4·00	10

DESIGNS: 6 a. Textile mill, W. Pakistan; 8 a. Jute mill, E. Pakistan; 12 a. Main Sui gas plant.

(A) has Arabic fraction on left as in Type **30**. (B) has it on right. For similar 2½ a. see No. 87.

1955. 10th Anniv of U.N. Nos. 68 and 76 optd **TENTH ANNIVERSARY UNITED NATIONS 24.10.55.**

77		1½ a. red	1·50	5·00
78		12 a. red and orange	50	3·50

35 Map of West Pakistan

1955. West Pakistan Unity.

79	**35**	1½ a. green	15	10
80		2 a. brown	15	10
81		12 a. red	75	15

36 Constituent Assembly Building, Karachi

1956. Republic Day.

82	**36**	2 a. green	80	10

37

38 Map of East Pakistan

1956. 9th Anniv of Independence.

83	**37**	2 a. red	65	10

1956. 1st Session of National Assembly of Pakistan at Dacca.

84	**38**	1½ a. green	30	1·00
85		2 a. brown	30	10
86		12 a. red	30	65

41 Orange Tree

42 Pakistani Flag

1957. 1st Anniv of Republic.

87	–	2½ a. red	20	10
88	–	3½ a. blue	30	10
89	**41**	10 r. green and orange	80	20

DESIGNS: 2½ a. as Type **30** without value in Arabic at right; 3½ a. as Type **17** without value in Arabic at right.

1957. Centenary of Struggle for Independence (Indian Mutiny).

90	**42**	1½ a. green	50	10
91		12 a. blue	1·25	10

43 Pakistani Industries

1957. 10th Anniv of Independence.

92	**43**	1½ a. blue	20	30
93		4 a. salmon	40	75
94		12 a. mauve	40	50

1958. 2nd Anniv of Republic. As T **41**.

209		15 r. red and purple	1·50	2·00

DESIGN: 15 r. Coconut tree.

45

46 U.N. Charter and Globe

1958. 20th Death Anniv of Mohammed Iqbal (poet).

96	**45**	1½ a. olive and black	55	10
97		2 a. brown and black	55	10
98		14 a. turquoise and black	90	10

1958. 10th Anniv of Declaration of Human Rights.

99	**46**	1½ a. turquoise	10	10
100		14 a. sepia	65	10

1958. Scout Jamboree. Optd **PAKISTAN BOY SCOUT 2nd NATIONAL JAMBOREE CHITTAGONG Dec. 58-Jan. 59**.

101	**22**	6 p. violet	30	10
102	–	8 a. violet (No. 75)	65	10

1959. Revolution Day. No. 74 optd **REVOLUTION DAY Oct. 27, 1959**.

103		6 a. blue	80	10

49 "Centenary of An Idea"

50 Armed Forces Badge

1959. Red Cross Commemoration.

104	**49**	2 a. red and green	30	10
105		10 a. red and blue	55	10

1960. Armed Forces Day.

106	**50**	2 a. red, blue and green	60	10
107		14 a. red and blue	1·50	10

51 Map of Pakistan

1960.

108	**51**	6 p. purple	40	10
109		2 a. red	60	10
110		8 a. green	1·25	10
111		1 r. blue	2·00	10

52 "Uprooted Tree"

53 Punjab Agricultural College

1960. World Refugee Year.

112	**52**	2 a. red	20	10
113		10 a. green	30	10

1960. Golden Jubilee of Punjab Agricultural College, Lyallpur.

114	**53**	2 a. blue and red	10	10
115	–	8 a. green and violet	20	10

DESIGN: 8 a. College arms.

55 "Land Reforms, Rehabilitation and Reconstruction"

56 Caduceus

1960. Revolution Day.

116	**55**	2 a. green, pink & brown	10	10
117		14 a. green, yellow & blue	50	50

1960. Centenary of King Edward Medical College, Lahore.

118	**56**	2 a. yellow, black & blue	50	10
119		14 a. green, black & red	1·75	50

57 "Economic Co-operation"

58 Zam-Zama Gun, Lahore ("Kim's Gun" after Rudyard Kipling)

1960. Int Chamber of Commerce C.A.F.E.A. Meeting, Karachi.

120	**57**	14 a. brown	30	10

1960. 3rd Pakistan Boy Scouts' National Jamboree, Lahore.

121	**58**	2 a. red, yellow & green	70	10

1961. Surch in "PAISA".
122 – 1 p. on 1½ a. red (No. 68) . 30 10
123 **7** 2 p. on 3 p. red . 10 10
124 **51** 3 p. on 6 p. purple . 10 10
125 – 7 p. on 1 a. red (No. 67) . 30 10
126 **51** 13 p. on 2 a. red . 30 10
127 **37** 13 p. on 2 a. red . 20 10
See also Nos. 262/4.

60 Khyber Pass

61 Shalimar Gardens, Lahore
62 Chota Sona Masjid (gateway)

1961.
170 **60** 1 p. violet . 10 10
132 2 p. red . 70 10
133 3 p. purple . 30 10
173 5 p. blue . 10 10
135 7 p. green . 1·25 10
175 **61** 10 p. brown . 10 10
176 13 p. violet . 10 10
176a 15 p. purple . 15 10
176b 20 p. green . 30 10
138 25 p. blue . 4·75 10
178 40 p. purple . 15 20
179 50 p. green . 15 10
141 75 p. red . 40 10
142 90 p. green . 50 10
204 **62** 1 r. red . 30 10
144 1 r. 25 violet . 75 55
206 2 r. orange . 55 15
207 5 r. green . 4·50 55

1961. Lahore Stamp Exn. No. 110 optd **LAHORE STAMP EXHIBITION 1961** and emblem.
145 **51** 8 a. green . 90 1·50

64 Warsak Dam and Power Station

1961. Completion of Warsak Hydro-Electric Project.
146 **64** 40 p. black and blue . 60 10

65 Narcissus

1961. Child Welfare Week.
147 **65** 13 p. turquoise . 40 10
148 90 p. mauve . 1·10 20

66 Ten Roses
67 Police Crest and "Traffic Control"

1961. Co-operative Day.
149 **66** 13 p. red and green . 50 10
150 90 p. red and blue . 1·25 40

1961. Police Centenary.
151 **67** 13 p. silver, black & blue . 50 10
152 40 p. silver, black & red . 1·00 20

RAILWAY CENTENARY 1861-1961
68 Locomotive "Eagle", 1861

1961. Railway Centenary.
153 **68** 13 p. green, black & yellow 1·00 80
154 – 50 p. yellow, black & green 1·25 1·00
DESIGN: 50 p. Diesel locomotive No. 20 and tracks forming "1961".

1962. First Karachi–Dacca Jet Flight. No. 87 surch with Boeing 720B airliner and **FIRST JET FLIGHT KARACHI-DACCA 13 Paisa**.
155 13 p. on 2½ a. red . 1·50 90

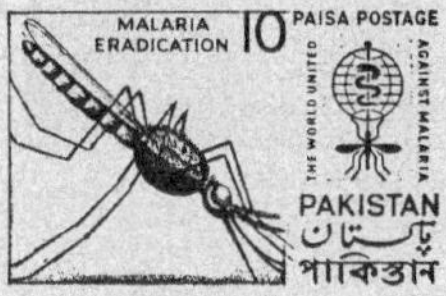
71 "Anopheles sp." (mosquito)

1962. Malaria Eradication.
156 **71** 10 p. black, yellow & red . 50 10
157 – 13 p. black, lemon & red . 50 10
DESIGN: 13 p. Mosquito pierced by blade.

73 Pakistan Map and Jasmine

1962. New Constitution.
158 **73** 40 p. green, turq & grey . 1·00 10

74 Football

1962. Sports.
159 **74** 7 p. black and blue . 10 10
160 – 13 p. black and green . 60 40
161 – 25 p. black and purple . 20 10
162 – 40 p. black and brown . 2·00 2·25
DESIGNS: 13 p. Hockey; 25 p. Squash; 40 p. Cricket.

78 Marble Fruit Dish and Bahawalpuri Clay Flask

1962. Small Industries.
163 **78** 7 p. lake . 10 10
164 – 13 p. green . 4·00 1·75
165 – 25 p. violet . 10 10
166 – 40 p. green . 10 10
167 – 50 p. red . 10 10
DESIGNS: 13 p. Sports equipment; 25 p. Camel-skin lamp and brassware; 40 p. Wooden powder-bowl and basket-work; 50 p. Inlaid cigarette-box and brassware.

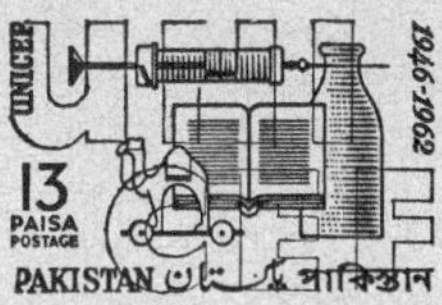
83 "Child Welfare"

1962. 16th Anniv of U.N.I.C.E.F.
168 **83** 13 p. black, blue & purple 35 10
169 40 p. black, yellow & blue 35 10

1963. Pakistan U.N. Force in West Irian. Optd **U.N. FORCE W. IRIAN**.
182 **61** 13 p. violet . 10 20

85 "Dancing" Horse, Camel and Bull

1963. National Horse and Cattle Show.
183 **85** 13 p. blue, sepia & pink . 10 10

86 Wheat and Tractor

1963. Freedom from Hunger.
184 **86** 13 p. brown . 2·00 10
185 – 50 p. bistre . 3·50 55
DESIGN: 50 p. Lifting rice.

1963. 2nd International Stamp Exhibition, Dacca. Surch **13 PAISA INTERNATIONAL DACCA STAMP EXHIBITION 1963**.
186 **51** 13 p. on 2 a. red . 75 10

89 Centenary Emblem
90 Paharpur

1963. Centenary of Red Cross.
187 **89** 40 p. red and olive . 2·00 15

1963. Archaeological Series.
188 **90** 7 p. blue . 45 10
189 – 13 p. sepia . 45 10
190 – 40 p. red . 80 10
191 – 50 p. violet . 85 10
DESIGNS—VERT: 13 p. Moenjodaro. HORIZ: 40 p. Taxila; 50 p. Mainamati.

1963. Cent of Pakistan Public Works Department. Surch **100 YEARS OF P.W.D. OCTOBER, 1963 13**.
192 **60** 13 p. on 3 p. purple . 10 10

95 Ataturk's Mausoleum

1963. 25th Death Anniv of Kemal Ataturk.
193 **95** 50 p. red . 80 10

96 Globe and U.N.E.S.C.O. Emblem

1963. 15th Anniv of Declaration of Human Rights.
194 **96** 50 p. brown, red and blue . 70 10

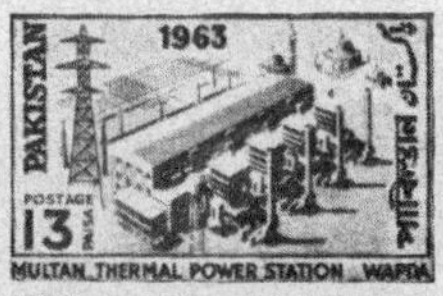
97 Thermal Power Installations

1963. Completion of Multan Thermal Power Station.
195 **97** 13 p. blue . 10 10

99 Temple of Thot, Queen Nefertari and Maids

1964. Nubian Monuments Preservation.
211 **99** 13 p. blue and red . 75 10
212 – 50 p. purple and black . 1·25 10
DESIGN: 50 p. Temple of Abu Simbel.

101 "Unisphere" and Pakistan Pavilion

1964. New York World's Fair.
213 **101** 13 p. blue . 10 10
214 – 1 r. 25 blue and orange . 40 20
DESIGN—VERT: 1 r. 25, Pakistan Pavilion on "Unisphere".

103 Shah Abdul Latif's Mausoleum

1964. Death Bicentenary of Shah Abdul Latif of Bhit.
215 **103** 50 p. blue and red . 80 10

104 Mausoleum of Quaid-i-Azam

1964. 16th Death Anniv of Mohammed Ali Jinnah (Quaid-i-Azam).
216 **104** 15 p. green . 75 10
217 – 50 p. green . 1·75 10
DESIGN: 50 p. As Type **104**, but 26½ × 31½ mm.

106 Bengali and Urdu Alphabets
108 "Help the Blind"

107 University Building

1964. Universal Children's Day.
218 **106** 15 p. brown . 10 10

1964. 1st Convocation of the West Pakistan University of Engineering and Technology, Lahore.
219 **107** 15 p. brown . 10 10

1965. Blind Welfare.
220 **108** 15 p. blue and yellow . 20 10

109 I.T.U. Emblem and Symbols

1965. Centenary of I.T.U.
221 **109** 15 p. purple . 1·50 30

110 I.C.Y. Emblem

1965. International Co-operation Year.
222 **110** 15 p. black and blue . 50 15
223 50 p. green and yellow . 1·00 40

111 "Co-operation"

1965. 1st Anniv of Regional Development Co-operation Pact. Multicoloured.
224 15 p. Type **111** . 20 10
225 50 p. Globe and flags of Turkey, Iran and Pakistan (54¾ × 30¾ mm) . 1·10 10

113 Soldier and Tanks

1965. Pakistan Armed Forces. Multicoloured.
226 7 p. Type **113** 75 30
227 15 p. Naval Officer and "Tughril" (destroyer) . . . 1·50 10
228 50 p. Pilot and Lockheed F-104C Starfighters . . . . 2·50 30

116 Army, Navy and Air Force Crests

1966. Armed Forces Day.
229 **116** 15 p. blue, green & buff . 65 10

117 Atomic Reactor, Islamabad
118 Bank Crest

1966. Inauguration of Pakistan's 1st Atomic Reactor.
230 **117** 15 p. black 10 10

1966. Silver Jubilee of Habib Bank.
231 **118** 15 p. green, orge & sepia . 10 10

119 Children
120 U.N.E.S.C.O. Emblem

1966. Universal Children's Day.
232 **119** 15 p. black, red & yellow . 10 10

1966. 20th Anniversary of U.N.E.S.C.O.
233 **120** 15 p. multicoloured . . . 2·75 30

121 Flag, Secretariat Building and President Ayub

1966. Islamabad (new capital).
234 **121** 15 p. multicoloured . . . 25 10
235 50 p. multicoloured . . . 60 10

122 Avicenna
123 Mohammed Ali Jinnah

1966. Foundation of Health and Tibbi Research Institute.
236 **122** 15 p. green and salmon . 40 10

1966. 90th Birth Anniv of Mohammed Ali Jinnah.
237 **123** 15 p. black, orange & blue 20 10
238 – 50 p. black, purple & blue 50 10
DESIGN: 50 p. Same portrait as 15 p. but different frame.

124 Tourist Year Emblem

1967. International Tourist Year.
239 **124** 15 p. black, blue & brown 10 10

125 Emblem of Pakistan T.B. Association
126 Scout Salute and Badge

1967. Tuberculosis Eradication Campaign.
240 **125** 15 p. red, sepia & brown 10 10

1967. 4th National Scout Jamboree.
241 **126** 15 p. brown and purple . 15 10

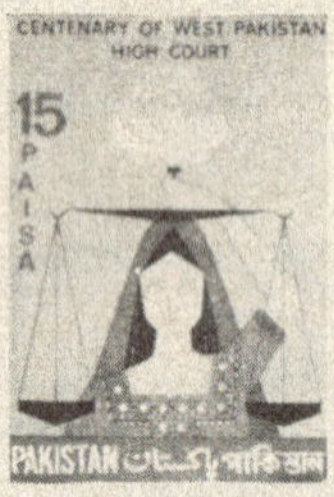

127 "Justice"

1967. Cent of West Pakistan High Court.
242 **127** 15 p. multicoloured . . . 10 10

128 Dr. Mohammed Iqbal (philosopher)

1967. Iqbal Commemoration.
243 **128** 15 p. sepia and red . . . 15 10
244 1 r. sepia and green . . . 60 10

129 Hilal-i-Isteqlal Flag

1967. Award of Hilal-i-Isteqlal (for Valour) to Lahore, Sialkot and Sargodha.
245 **129** 15 p. multicoloured . . . 10 10

130 "20th Anniversary"

1967. 20th Anniv of Independence.
246 **130** 15 p. red and green . . . 10 10

131 "Rice Exports"

1967. Pakistan Exports. Multicoloured.
247 10 p. Type **131** 10 15
248 15 p. Cotton plant, yarn and textiles 10 10
249 50 p. Raw jute, bale and bags . 20 15
Nos. 248/9 are vert, and larger 27 × 45 mm.

134 Clay Toys

1967. Universal Children's Day.
250 **134** 15 p. multicoloured . . . 10 10

135 Shah and Empress of Iran and Gulistan Palace, Teheran

1967. Coronation of Shah Mohammed Riza Pahlavi and Empress Farah of Iran.
251 **135** 50 p. purple, blue & ochre . 70 10

136 "Each For All–All for Each"

1967. Co-operative Day.
252 **136** 15 p. multicoloured . . . 10 10

137 Mangla Dam

1967. Indus Basin Project.
253 **137** 15 p. multicoloured . . . 10 10

138 Crab pierced by Sword
139 Human Rights Emblem

1967. The Fight Against Cancer.
254 **138** 15 p. red and black . . . 70 10

1968. Human Rights Year.
255 **139** 15 p. red and blue 10 15
256 50 p. red, yellow & grey . 10 15

140 Agricultural University, Mymensingh
141 W.H.O. Emblem

1968. First Convocation of East Pakistan Agricultural University.
257 **140** 15 p. multicoloured . . . 10 10

1968. 20th Anniv of W.H.O.
258 **141** 15 p. orange and red . . 10 15
259 50 p. orange and blue . . 10 15

142 Kazi Nazrul Islam (poet, composer and patriot)

1968. Nazrul Islam Commemoration.
260 **142** 15 p. sepia and yellow . . 30 15
261 50 p. sepia and red . . . 60 15

1968. Nos. 56, 74 and 61 surch.
262 4 p. on 3 a. purple . . . . 65 1·25
263 4 p. on 6 a. blue . . . . . . 1·00 1·25
264 60 p. on 10 a. violet 50 35

144 Children running with Hoops

1968. Universal Children's Day.
265 **144** 15 p. multicoloured 10 10

145 National Assembly

1968. "A Decade of Development".
266 **145** 10 p. multicoloured . . . 10 10
267 – 15 p. multicoloured . . . 15 10
268 – 50 p. multicoloured . . . 2·25 20
269 – 60 p. blue, purple & red . 1·00 35
DESIGNS: 15 p. Industry and Agriculture; 50 p. Army, Navy and Air Force; 60 p. Minaret and atomic reactor plant.

149 Chittagong Steel Mill

1969. Pakistan's First Steel Mill, Chittagong.
270 **149** 15 p. grey, blue and olive . 10 10

150 "Family"

1969. Family Planning.
271 **150** 15 p. purple and blue . . 10 10

151 Olympic Gold Medal and Hockey Player

1969. Olympic Hockey Champions.
272 **151** 15 p. multicoloured . . . 1·00 50
273 1 r. multicoloured . . . . 2·50 1·00

152 Mirza Ghalib and Lines of Verse

1969. Death Cent of Mirza Ghalib (poet).
274 **152** 15 p. multicoloured . . . 20 15
275 50 p. multicoloured . . . 50 15
The lines of verse on No. 275 are different from those in Type **152**.

153 Dacca Railway Station

1969. 1st Anniv of New Dacca Railway Station.
276 **153** 15 p. multicoloured . . . 30 10

154 I.L.O. Emblem and "1919–1969"

1969. 50th Anniv of I.L.O.
277 **154** 15 p. buff and green . . . 10 10
278 50 p. brown and red . . . 40 10

155 "Ladyon Balcony" (18th-cent Mogul)

1969. 5th Anniv of Regional Co-operation for Development. Miniatures. Multicoloured.
279 20 p. Type **155** 15 10
280 50 p. "Kneeling Servant" (17th-cent Persian) 15 10
281 1 r. "Suleiman the Magnificent holding Audience" (16th-cent Turkish) 20 10

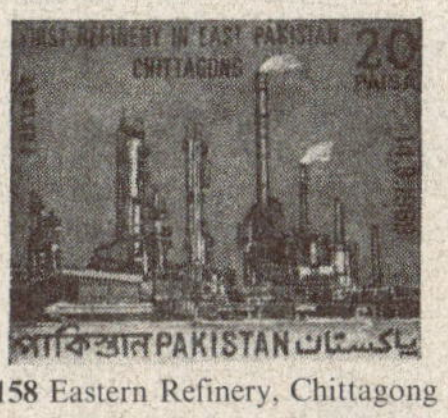

158 Eastern Refinery, Chittagong

1969. First East Pakistan Oil Refinery.
282 **158** 20 p. multicoloured . . . 10 10

159 Children playing outside "School"

1969. Universal Children's Day.
283 **159** 20 p. multicoloured . . . 10 10

160 Japanese Doll and P.I.A. Air Routes

1969. Inauguration of P.I.A. Pearl Route, Dacca–Tokyo.
284 **160** 20 p. multicoloured . . . 60 10
285 50 p. multicoloured . . . 90 40

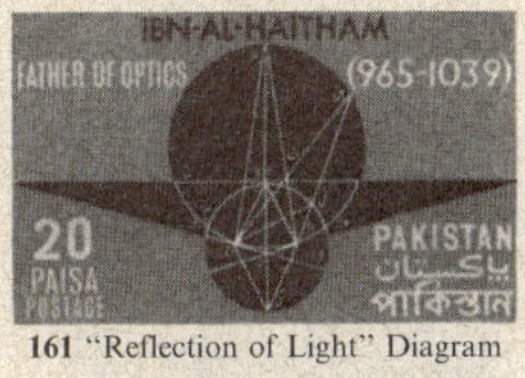

161 "Reflection of Light" Diagram

1969. Milenary Commemorative of Ibn-al-Haitham (physicist).
286 **161** 20 p. black, yellow & blue 10 10

162 Vickers Vimy and Karachi Airport

1969. 50th Anniv of 1st England–Australia Flight.
287 **162** 50 p. multicoloured . . . 1·00 35

163 Flags, Sun Tower and Expo Site Plan

1970. "Expo-70" World Fair, Osaka.
288 **163** 50 p. multicoloured . . . 20 30

164 New U.P.U. H.Q. Building

1970. New U.P.U. Headquarters Building.
289 **164** 20 p. multicoloured . . . 15 10
290 50 p. multicoloured . . . 25 25

165 U.N. H.Q. Building

1970. 25th Anniv of United Nations. Mult.
291 20 p. Type **165** 10 10
292 50 p. U.N. emblem 15 20

167 I.E.Y. Emblem, Book and Pen

1970. International Education Year.
293 **167** 20 p. multicoloured . . . 10 10
294 50 p. multicoloured . . . 20 20

168 Saiful Malook Lake (Pakistan)

1970. 6th Anniv of Regional Co-operation for Development. Multicoloured.
295 20 p. Type **168** 15 10
296 50 p. Seeyo-Se-Pol Bridge, Esfahan (Iran) 20 10
297 1 r. View from Fethiye (Turkey) 20 15

171 Asian Productivity Symbol

1970. Asian Productivity Year.
298 **171** 50 p. multicoloured . . . 20 20

172 Dr. Maria Montessori

1970. Birth Centenary of Dr. Maria Montessori (educationist).
299 **172** 20 p. multicoloured . . . 15 10
300 50 p. multicoloured . . . 15 30

173 Tractor and Fertilizer Factory

1970. 10th Near East F.A.O. Regional Conference, Islamabad.
301 **173** 20 p. green and brown . . 15 20

174 Children and Open Book

175 Pakistan Flag and Text

1970. Universal Children's Day.
302 **174** 20 p. multicoloured . . . 15 10

1970. Elections for National Assembly.
303 **175** 20 p. green and violet . . 15 10

1970. Elections for Provincial Assemblies. As No. 303 but inscr "PROVINCIAL ASSEMBLIES".
304 **175** 20 p. green and red . . . 15 10

176 Conference Crest and burning Al-Aqsa Mosque

1970. Conference of Islamic Foreign Ministers, Karachi.
305 **176** 20 p. multicoloured . . . 15 15

177 Coastal Embankments

1971. East Pakistan Coastal Embankments Project.
306 **177** 20 p. multicoloured . . . 15 15

178 Emblem and United Peoples of the World

180 Chaharbagh School (Iran)

179 Maple Leaf Cement Factory, Daudkhel

1971. Racial Equality Year.
307 **178** 20 p. multicoloured . . . 10 15
308 50 p. multicoloured . . . 20 45

1971. 20th Anniv of Colombo Plan.
309 **179** 20 p. brown, black & violet 10 10

1971. 7th Anniv of Regional Co-operation for Development. Multicoloured.
310 10 p. Selimiye Mosque (Turkey) (horiz) 10 15
311 20 p. Badshahi Mosque, Lahore (horiz) 20 25
312 50 p. Type **180** 30 35

181 Electric Train and Boy with Toy Train

1971. Universal Children's Day.
313 **181** 20 p. multicoloured . . . 1·75 50

182 Horseman and Symbols

1971. 2500th Anniv of Persian Monarchy.
314 **182** 10 p. multicoloured . . . 35 30
315 20 p. multicoloured . . . 45 40
316 50 p. multicoloured . . . 55 75

183 Hockey-player and Trophy

1971. World Cup Hockey Tournament, Barcelona.
317 **183** 20 p. multicoloured . . . 1·75 65

184 Great Bath, Moenjodaro

1971. 25th Anniv of U.N.E.S.C.O. and Campaign to save the Moenjodaro Excavations.
318 **184** 20 p. multicoloured . . . 20 30

185 U.N.I.C.E.F. Symbol

1971. 25th Anniv of U.N.I.C.E.F.
319 **185** 50 p. multicoloured . . . 30 60

186 King Hussein and Jordanian Flag

1971. 50th Anniv of Hashemite Kingdom of Jordan.
320 **186** 20 p. multicoloured . . . 15 20

187 Badge of Hockey Federation and Trophy

1971. Hockey Championships Victory.
321 **187** 20 p. multicoloured . . . 2·50 90

188 Reading Class

1972. International Book Year.
322 **188** 20 p. multicoloured . . . 20 30

189 View of Venice

1972. U.N.E.S.C.O. Campaign to Save Venice.
323 **189** 20 p. multicoloured . . . 30 30

190 E.C.A.F.E. Emblem and Discs

1972. 25th Anniv of E.C.A.F.E.
324 **190** 20 p. multicoloured . . . 15 30

191 Human Heart **192** "Only One Earth"

1972. World Health Day.
325 **191** 20 p. multicoloured . . . 20 30

1972. U.N. Conf on the Human Environment, Stockholm.
326 **192** 20 p. multicoloured . . . 20 30

193 "Fisherman" (Cevat Dereli) **194** Mohammed Ali Jinnah and Tower

1972. 8th Anniv of Regional Co-operation for Development. Multicoloured.
327 10 p. Type **193** . . . 20 20
328 20 p. "Iranian Woman" (Behzad) 35 25
329 50 p. "Will and Power" (A. R. Chughtai) . . . 55 70

1972. 25th Anniv of Independence. Mult.
330 10 p. Type **194** . . . 10 10
331 20 p. "Land Reform" . . . 15 25
332 20 p. "Labour Reform" . . . 15 25
333 20 p. "Education Policy" . . 15 25
334 20 p. "Health Policy" . . . 15 25
335 60 p. National Assembly Building . . . 25 35

The 60 p. is 46 × 28 mm; Nos. 331/4 are 74 × 23½ mm.

195 Donating Blood **196** People and Squares

1972. National Blood Transfusion Service.
336 **195** 20 p. multicoloured . . . 20 30

1972. Centenary of Population Census.
337 **196** 20 p. multicoloured . . . 20 20

197 Children from Slums

1972. Universal Children's Day.
338 **197** 20 p. multicoloured . . . 20 30

198 People and Open Book

1972. Education Week.
339 **198** 20 p. multicoloured . . . 20 30

199 Nuclear Power Plant

1972. Inauguration of Karachi Nuclear Power Plant.
340 **199** 20 p. multicoloured . . . 20 30

200 Copernicus in Observatory

1973. 500th Birth Anniv of Nicholas Copernicus (astronomer).
341 **200** 20 p. multicoloured . . . 20 30

201 Moenjodaro Excavations

1973. 50th Anniv of Moenjodaro Excavations.
342 **201** 20 p. multicoloured . . . 20 30

202 Elements of Meteorology

1973. Centenary of I.M.O./W.M.O.
343 **202** 10 p. multicoloured . . . 20 30

203 Prisoners-of-war

1973. Prisoners-of-war in India.
344 **203** 1 r. 25 multicoloured . . . 1·50 2·25

204 National Assembly Building and Constitution Book

1973. Constitution Week.
345 **204** 20 p. multicoloured . . . 40 40

205 Badge and State Bank Building

1973. 25th Anniv of Pakistan State Bank.
346 **205** 20 p. multicoloured . . . 15 30
347 1 r. multicoloured . . . 30 50

206 Lut Desert Excavations (Iran) **207** Constitution Book and Flag

1973. 9th Anniv of Regional Co-operation for Development. Multicoloured.
348 20 p. Type **206** . . . 30 20
349 60 p. Main Street, Moenjodaro (Pakistan) . . . 55 50
350 1 r. 25 Mausoleum of Antiochus I (Turkey) . . . 75 1·25

1973. Independence Day and Enforcement of the Constitution.
351 **207** 20 p. multicoloured . . . 15 30

208 Mohammed Ali Jinnah (Quaid-i-Azam) **209** Wallago

1973. 25th Death Anniv of Mohammed Ali Jinnah.
352 **208** 20 p. green, yellow & black 15 30

1973. Fishes. Multicoloured.
353 10 p. Type **209** . . . 1·10 1·10
354 20 p. Rohu . . . 1·25 1·25
355 60 p. Mozambique mouth-brooder . . . 1·40 1·40
356 1 r. Catla . . . 1·40 1·40

210 Children's Education

1973. Universal Children's Day.
357 **210** 20 p. multicoloured . . . 15 30

211 Harvesting

1973. 10th Anniv of World Food Programme.
358 **211** 20 p. multicoloured . . . 60 40

212 Ankara and Kemal Ataturk

1973. 50th Anniv of Turkish Republic.
359 **212** 50 p. multicoloured . . . 45 35

213 Boy Scout **214** "Basic Necessities"

1973. National Silver Jubilee Jamboree.
360 **213** 20 p. multicoloured . . . 1·75 50

1973. 25th Anniv of Declaration of Human Rights.
361 **214** 20 p. multicoloured . . . 30 30

215 Al-Biruni and Nandana Hill

1973. Al-Biruni Millennium Congress.
362 **215** 20 p. multicoloured . . . 40 20
363 1 r. 25 multicoloured . . . 1·10 75

216 Dr. Hansen, Microscope and Bacillus

218 Conference Emblem

217 Family and Emblem

1973. Centenary of Hansen's Discovery of Leprosy Bacillus.
364 **216** 20 p. multicoloured . . . 1·00 60

1974. World Population Year.
365 **217** 20 p. multicoloured . . . 10 10
366 1 r. 25 multicoloured . . . 30 40

1974. Islamic Summit Conference, Lahore. Multicoloured.
367 20 p. Type **218** 10 10
368 65 p. Emblem on "Sun" . . . 25 60
No. 368 is larger, 42 × 30 mm.

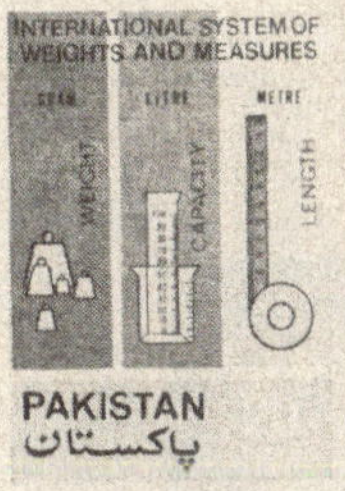

219 Units of Weight and Measurement

220 "Chand Chauthai" Carpet, Pakistan

1974. Adoption of Int Weights and Measures System.
370 **219** 20 p. multicoloured . . . 15 25

1974. 10th Anniversary of Regional Co-operation for Development. Multicoloured.
371 20 p. Type **220** 20 15
372 60 p. Persian carpet, 16th-century 40 55
373 1 r. 25 Anatolian carpet, 15th-century . . . . 65 1·25

221 Hands protecting Sapling

222 Torch and Map

1974. Tree Planting Day.
374 **221** 20 p. multicoloured . . . 50 50

1974. Namibia Day.
375 **222** 60 p. multicoloured . . . 35 60

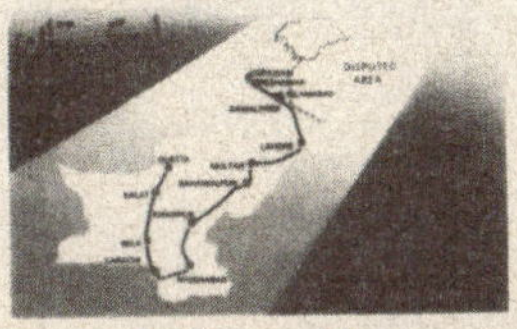
223 Highway Map

1974. Shahrah-e-Pakistan (Pakistan Highway).
376 **223** 20 p. multicoloured . . . 90 60

224 Boy at Desk

225 U.P.U. Emblem

1974. Universal Children's Day.
377 **224** 20 p. multicoloured . . . 30 30

1974. Centenary of U.P.U. Multicoloured.
378 20 p. Type **225** 20 20
379 2 r. 25 U.P.U. emblem, Boeing 707 and mail-wagon (30 × 41 mm) . . . . 55 1·40

226 Liaquat Ali Khan

227 Dr. Mohammed Iqbal (poet and philosopher)

1974. Liaquat Ali Khan (First Prime Minister of Pakistan).
381 **226** 20 p. black and red . . . 30 30

1974. Birth Centenary of Dr. Iqbal (1977) (1st issue).
382 **227** 20 p. multicoloured . . . 30 30
See also Nos. 399, 433 and 445/9.

228 Dr. Schweitzer and River Scene

1975. Birth Cent of Dr. Albert Schweitzer.
383 **228** 2 r. 25 multicoloured . . 2·75 3·25

229 Tourism Year Symbol

1975. South East Asia Tourism Year.
384 **229** 2 r. 25 multicoloured . . 55 80

230 Assembly Hall, Flags and Prime Minister Bhutto

1975. 1st Anniv of Islamic Summit Conference, Lahore.
385 **230** 20 p. multicoloured . . . 35 25
386 1 r. multicoloured . . . . 75 1·40

231 "Scientific Research"

1975. International Women's Year. Mult.
387 20 p. Type **231** 20 25
388 2 r. 25 Girl teaching woman ("Adult Education") . . . . 1·10 2·00

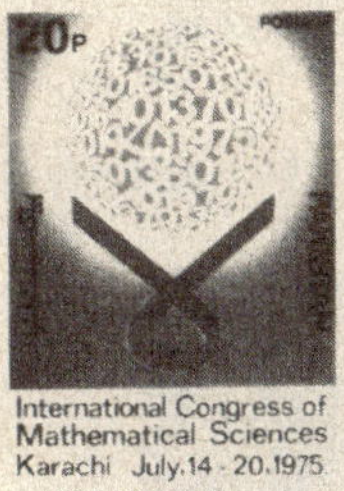

232 "Globe" and Algebraic Symbol

233 Pakistani Camel-skin Vase

1975. Int Congress of Mathematical Sciences, Karachi.
389 **232** 20 p. multicoloured . . . 50 50

1975. 11th Anniv of Regional Co-operation for Development. Multicoloured.
390 20 p. Type **233** 25 30
391 60 p. Iranian tile (horiz) . . . 50 1·00
392 1 r. 25 Turkish porcelain vase . 75 1·50

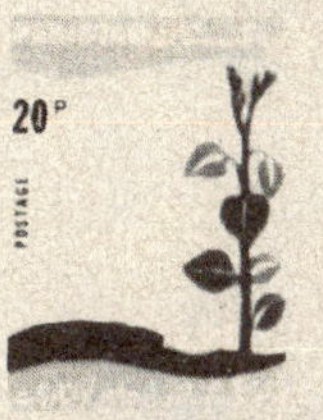

234 Sapling and Dead Trees

235 Black Partridge

1975. Tree Planting Year.
393 **234** 20 p. multicoloured . . . 35 40

1975. Wildlife Protection (1st series).
394 **235** 20 p. multicoloured . . . 1·25 35
395 2 r. 25 multicoloured . . . 4·00 4·75
See also Nos. 400/1, 411/12, 417/18, 493/6, 560, 572/3, 581/2, 599, 600, 605, 621/2, 691, 702, 752, 780/3, 853 and 1027.

236 "Today's Girls"

238 Dr. Mohammed Iqbal

237 Hazrat Amir Khusrau, Sitar and Tabla (½-size illustration)

1975. Universal Children's Day.
396 **236** 20 p. multicoloured . . . 30 30

1975. 700th Birth Anniv of Hazrat Amir Khusrau (poet and musician).
397 **237** 20 p. multicoloured . . . 20 45
398 2 r. 25 multicoloured . . . 75 1·60

1975. Birth Cent (1977) of Dr. Iqbal. (2nd issue).
399 **238** 20 p. multicoloured . . . 30 30

239 Urial (wild sheep)

241 Dome and Minaret of the Rauza-e-Mubarak

240 Moenjodaro Remains

1975. Wildlife Protection (2nd series).
400 **239** 20 p. multicoloured . . . 40 30
401 3 r. multicoloured . . . . 2·50 3·25

1976. "Save Moenjodaro" (1st issue). Multicoloured.
402 10 p. Type **240** 65 75
403 20 p. Remains of houses . . . 75 85
404 65 p. The Citadel 75 85
405 3 r. Well inside a house . . . 75 85
406 4 r. The "Great Bath" 85 95
See also Nos. 414 and 430.

1976. International Congress on Seerat.
407 **241** 20 p. multicoloured . . . 20 20
408 3 r. multicoloured 70 90

242 Alexander Graham Bell and Dial

1976. Telephone Centenary.
409 **242** 3 r. multicoloured . . . . 1·25 2·00

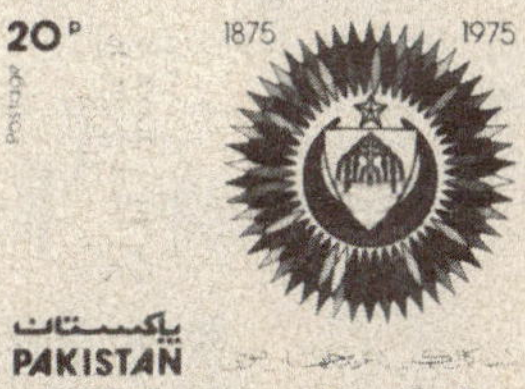

243 College Arms within "Sun"

1976. Cent of National College of Arts, Lahore.
410 **243** 20 p. multicoloured . . . 30 40

244 Common Peafowl

1976. Wildlife Protection (3rd series).
411 **244** 20 p. multicoloured . . . 1·00 35
412 3 r. multicoloured . . . . 3·50 4·50

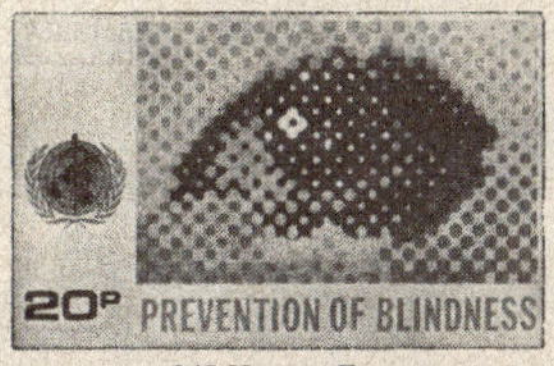

245 Human Eye

1976. Prevention of Blindness.
413 **245** 20 p. multicoloured . . . 70 70

246 Unicorn and Ruins

1976. "Save Moenjodaro" (2nd series).
414 246 20 p. multicoloured 30 35

247 Jefferson Memorial

1976. Bicent of American Revolution. Mult.
415 90 p. Type 247 . . . . 1·00 60
416 4 r. "Declaration of Independence" . . . . . . 3·75 5·00
No. 416 is larger, 47 × 36 mm.

248 Ibex

1976. Wildlife Protection (4th series).
417 248 20 p. multicoloured . . . 30 35
418 3 r. multicoloured . . . . 1·75 2·50

249 Mohammed Ali Jinnah

1976. 12th Anniv of Regional Co-operation for Development. Multicoloured.
419 20 p. Type 249 . . . . 80 80
420 65 p. Reza Shah the Great (Iran) 80 80
421 90 p. Kemal Ataturk (Turkey) . . 80 80

250 Urdu Text

251 Mohammed Ali Jinnah and Wazir Mansion

1976. Birth Cent of Mohammed Ali Jinnah (1st issue).
(a) Type 250.
422 250 5 p. black, blue & yellow . 20 25
423 10 p. black, yellow & pur . 20 25
424 15 p. black and blue . . . 20 25
425 1 r. black, yellow & blue . 30 30
(b) Type 251. Background Buildings given. Mult.
426 20 p. Type 251 . . . . 20 25
427 40 p. Sind Madressah 20 25
428 50 p. Minar Qarardad-e-Pakistan 20 25
429 3 r. Mausoleum 45 50
See also No. 436.

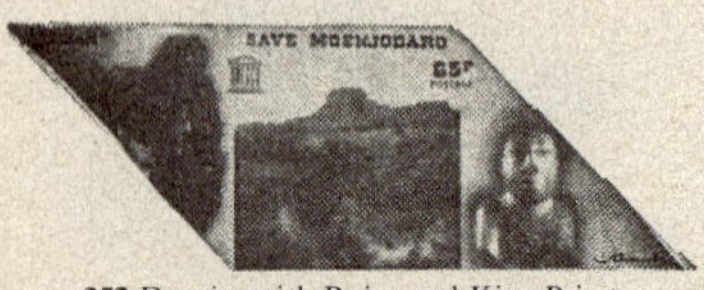

252 Dancing-girl, Ruins and King Priest

1976. "Save Moenjodaro" (3rd series).
430 252 65 p. multicoloured . . . 35 60

253 U.N. Racial Discrimination Emblem

1976. U.N. Decade to Combat Racial Discrimination.
431 253 65 p. multicoloured . . . 30 60

254 Child in Maze and Basic Services

1976. Universal Children's Day.
432 254 20 p. multicoloured . . . 30 30

255 Verse from "Allama Iqbal"

1976. Birth Centenary (1977) of Dr. Iqbal (3rd issue).
433 255 20 p. multicoloured . . . 15 30

256 Mohammed Ali Jinnah giving Scout Salute

257 Children Reading

1976. Quaid-i-Azam Centenary Jamboree.
434 256 20 p. multicoloured . . . 65 30

1976. Children's Literature.
435 257 20 p. multicoloured . . . 40 30

258 Mohammed Ali Jinnah

1976. Birth Centenary of Mohammed Ali Jinnah (2nd issue).
436 258 10 r. green and gold . . . 2·50 3·50

259 Rural Family

261 Forest

260 Turkish Vase, 1800 B.C.

1977. Social Welfare and Rural Development Year.
437 259 20 p. multicoloured . . . 15 10

1977. 13th Anniv of Regional Co-operation for Development.
438 260 20 p. orange, blue & black 35 10
439 – 65 p. multicoloured . . . 55 40
440 – 90 p. multicoloured . . . 80 1·50
DESIGNS: 60 p. Pakistani toy bullock cart from Moenjodaro; 90 p. Pitcher with spout from Sialk Hill, Iran.

1977. National Tree Plantation Campaign.
441 261 20 p. multicoloured . . . 20 30

262 Desert Scene

1977. U.N. Conference on Desertification, Nairobi.
442 262 65 p. multicoloured . . . 50 30

263 "Water for Children of the World"

265 Iqbal and Spirit of the Poet Roomi (from painting by Behzad)

264 Aga Khan III

1977. Universal Children's Day.
443 263 50 p. multicoloured . . . 40 30

1977. Birth Centenary of Aga Khan III.
444 264 2 r. multicoloured . . . 55 1·00

1977. Birth Centenary of Dr. Mohammed Iqbal (4th issue). Multicoloured.
445 20 p. Type 265 . . . . 40 50
446 65 p. Iqbal looking at Jamaluddin Afghani and Saeed Haleem Pasha at prayer (Behzad) 40 50
447 1 r. 25 Urdu verse 45 55
448 2 r. 25 Persian verse 50 65
449 3 r. Iqbal 55 75

266 The Holy "Khana-Kaaba" (House of God, Mecca)

267 Rheumatic Patient and Healthy Man

1977. Haj (pilgrimage to Mecca).
450 266 65 p. multicoloured . . . 30 30

1977. World Rheumatism Year.
451 267 65 p. blue, black & yellow 30 20

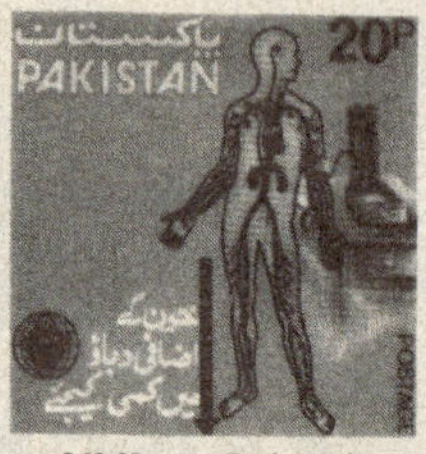

268 Woman in Costume of Rawalpindi-Islamabad

269 Human Body and Sphygmomanometer

1978. Indonesia-Pakistan Economic and Cultural Co-operation Organization.
452 268 75 p. multicoloured . . . 30 20

1978. World Hypertension Month.
453 269 20 p. multicoloured . . . 15 10
454 – 2 r. multicoloured . . . 60 90
The 2 r. value is as Type 269 but has the words "Down with high blood pressure" instead of the Urdu inscription at bottom left.

270 Henri Dunant

1978. 150th Birth Anniv of Henri Dunant (founder of the Red Cross).
455 270 1 r. multicoloured . . . 1·00 20

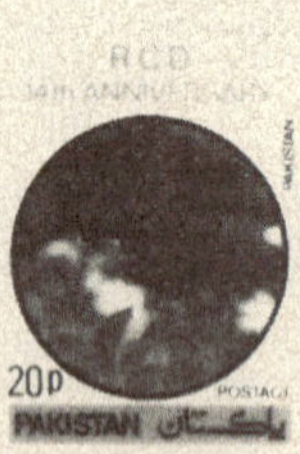

271 Red Roses (Pakistan)

272 "Pakistan, World Cup Hockey Champions"

1978. 14th Anniv of Regional Co-operation for Development. Roses. Multicoloured.
456 20 p. Type 271 . . . . . . 35 20
457 90 p. Pink roses (Iran) . . . 50 20
458 2 r. Yellow rose (Turkey) . . . 75 25

1978. "Riccione '78" International Stamp Fair. Multicoloured.
459 1 r. Type 272 . . . . 1·75 25
460 2 r. Fountain at Piazza Turismo 1·00 35

273 Cogwheels within Globe Symbol

1978. U.N. Technical Co-operation amongst Developing Countries Conference.
461 273 75 p. multicoloured . . . 15 10

274 St. Patrick's Cathedral, Karachi.

275 Minar-i-Qarardad-e-Pakistan

1978. Centenary of St. Patrick's Cathedral, Karachi. Multicoloured.
462 1 r. Type 274 . . . . 10 10
463 2 r. Stained glass window . . 25 25

1978.
464 275 2 p. green 10 10
465 3 p. black 10 10
466 5 p. blue 10 10
467 – 10 p. blue & turquoise . 10 10
468 – 20 p. green 50 10
469 – 25 p. green and mauve . 80 10
470 – 40 p. blue and mauve . . 10 10
471 – 50 p. lilac and green . . 30 10
472 – 60 p. black 10 10
473b – 75 p. red 55 10
474 – 90 p. mauve and blue . . 20 10
475 – 1 r. green 10 10
476 – 1 r. 50 orange 10 10
477 – 2 r. red 10 10
478 – 3 r. blue 15 10
479 – 4 r. black 15 10
480 – 5 r. brown 20 10
DESIGNS—HORIZ (25 × 20 mm): 10 p. to 90 p. Tractor. VERT (21 × 25 mm): 1 r. to 5 r. Mausoleum of Ibrahim Khan Makli, Thatta.

277 Emblem and "United Races" Symbol **278** Maulana Mohammad Ali Jauhar

1978. International Anti-Apartheid Year.
481 **277** 1 r. multicoloured 15 15

1978. Birth Centenary of Maulana Mohammad Ali Jauhar (patriot).
482 **278** 50 p. multicoloured . . . 40 20

279 Panavia MRCA Tornado, De Havilland Dragon Rapide and Wright Flyer I

1978. 75th Anniv of Powered Flight. Mult.
483 65 p. Type **279** . . . . 1·50 1·75
484 1 r. McDonnell Douglas Phantom II, Lockheed Tristar 500 and Wright Flyer I . . . 1·60 1·75
485 2 r. North American X-15, Tupolev Tu-104 and Wright Flyer I . . . . 1·75 2·00
486 2 r. 25 Mikoyan Gurevich Mig-15, Concorde and Wright Flyer I . . . . 2·00 2·25

280 "Holy Koran illuminating Globe" and Raudha-e-Mubarak (mausoleum)

1979. "12th Rabi-ul-Awwal" (Prophet Mohammed's birthday).
487 **280** 20 p. multicoloured . . . 30 15

281 "Aspects of A.P.W.A."

1979. 30th Anniv of A.P.W.A. (All Pakistan Women's Association).
488 **281** 50 p. multicoloured . . . 60 15

282 Tippu Sultan Shaheed of Mysore

1979. Pioneers of Freedom (1st series). Multicoloured.
490 10 r. Type **282** . . . . 75 1·25
491 15 r. Sir Syed Ahmad Khan . . 1·00 1·75
492 25 r. Altaf Hussain Hali . . . 1·50 2·00
See also Nos. 757, 801/27, 838/46, 870/2, 904/6, 921/8, 961/2 and 1007.

283 Himalayan Monal Pheasant

1979. Wildlife Protection (5th series). Pheasants. Multicoloured.
493 20 p. Type **283** . . . . 1·25 60
494 25 p. Kalij pheasant . . . . . 1·25 80
495 40 p. Koklass pheasant . . . 1·60 1·75
496 1 r. Cheer pheasant . . . . . 3·00 2·00

284 "Pakistan Village Scene" (Ustad Bakhsh)

1979. 15th Anniv of Regional Co-operation for Development. Multicoloured.
497 40 p. Type **284** 20 25
498 75 p. "Iranian Goldsmith" (Kamal al Molk) 20 25
499 1 r. 60 "Turkish Harvest" (Namik Ismail) 25 30

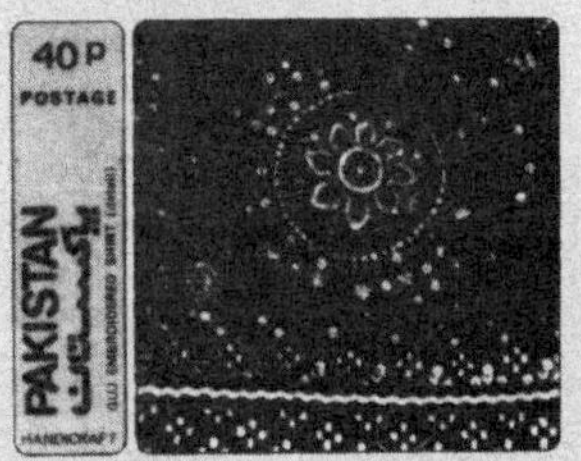

285 Guj Embroidered Shirt (detail)

1979. Handicrafts (1st series). Multicoloured.
500 40 p. Type **285** 20 20
501 1 r. Enamel inlaid brass plate 25 25
502 1 r. 50 Baskets 30 30
503 2 r. Chain-stitch embroidered rug (detail) 40 40
See also Nos. 578/9, 595/6 and 625/8.

286 Children playing on Climbing-frame

1979. S.O.S. Children's Village, Lahore.
504 **286** 50 p. multicoloured . . . 40 40

287 "Island" (Z. Maloof)

1979. International Year of the Child. Children's Paintings. Multicoloured.
505 40 p. Type **287** 15 15
506 75 p. "Playground" (R. Akbar) 25 25
507 1 r. "Fairground" (M. Azam) 25 25
508 1 r. 50 "Hockey Match" (M. Tayyab) 30 30

288 Warrior attacking Crab **289** Pakistan Customs Emblem

1979. "Fight Against Cancer".
510 **288** 40 p. black, yellow and purple 70 70

1979. Centenary of Pakistan Customs Service.
511 **289** 1 r. multicoloured 30 30

290 Boeing 747-200 and Douglas DC-3 Airliners **291** Islamic Pattern

1980. 25th Anniv of Pakistan International Air Lines.
512 **290** 1 r. multicoloured . . . . 1·75 90

1980.
513 **291** 10 p. green and yellow . . 10 10
514 15 p. deep green & green . 10 10
515 25 p. violet and red . . . 10 30
516 35 p. red and green . . . 10 30
517 – 40 p. red and brown . . . 15 10
518 – 50 p. violet and green . . 10 30
519 – 80 p. green and black . . . 15 40
The 40 to 80 p. values also show different Islamic patterns, the 40 p. being horizontal and the remainder vertical.

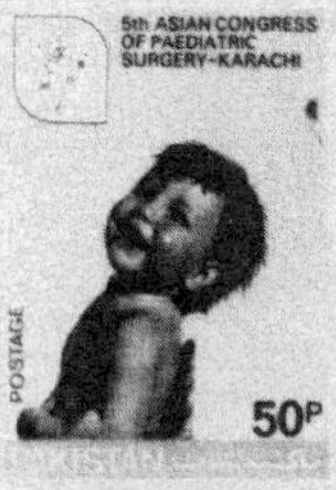

292 Young Child **293** Conference Emblem

1980. Fifth Asian Congress of Paediatric Surgery, Karachi.
530 **292** 50 p. multicoloured . . . 75 1·50

1980. 11th Islamic Conference of Foreign Ministers, Islamabad.
531 **293** 1 r. multicoloured 65 50

294 Karachi Port (½-size illustration)

1980. Centenary of Karachi Port Authority.
532 **294** 1 r. multicoloured . . . . 1·75 1·40

1980. "Riccione 80" International Stamp Exhibition. Nos. 505/8 optd **RICCIONE 80**.
533 **287** 40 p. multicoloured . . . 30 60
534 – 75 p. multicoloured . . . 40 70
535 – 1 r. multicoloured 45 70
536 – 1 r. 50 multicoloured . . . 60 90

296 College Emblem with Old and New Buildings

1980. 75th Anniv of Command and Staff College, Quetta.
537 **296** 1 r. multicoloured 10 15

1980. World Tourism Conference, Manila. No. 496 optd **WORLD TOURISM CONFERENCE MANILA 80.**
538 1 r. Cheer pheasant 75 30

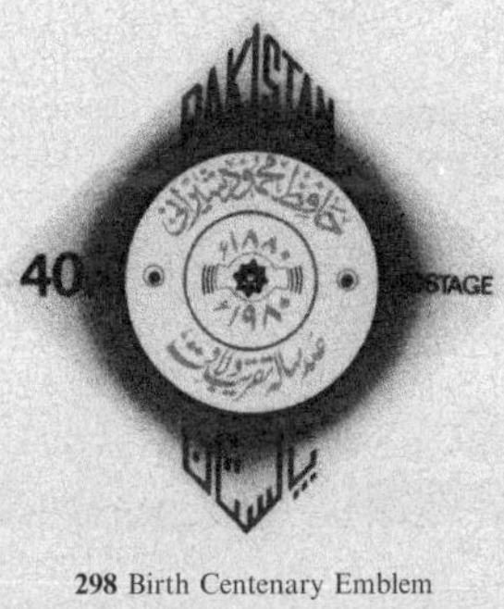

298 Birth Centenary Emblem

1980. Birth Cent of Hafiz Mahmood Shairani.
539 **298** 40 p. multicoloured . . . 30 75

299 Shalimar Gardens, Lahore

1980. Aga Khan Award for Architecture.
540 **299** 2 r. multicoloured 40 75

300 Rising Sun

1980. 1400th Anniv of Hegira (1st issue). Multicoloured.
541 40 p. Type **300** 10 10
542 2 r. Ka'aba and symbols of Moslem achievement (33 × 33 mm) 25 40
543 3 r. Holy Koran illuminating the World (30 × 54 mm) 30 60

301 Money Order Form **302** Postcards encircling Globe

1980. Centenary of Money Order Service.
545 **301** 40 p. multicoloured . . . 20 60

1980. Centenary of Postcard Service.
546 **302** 40 p. multicoloured . . . 20 60

303 Heinrich von Stephan and U.P.U. Emblem

1981. 150th Birth Anniv of Heinrich von Stephan (U.P.U. founder).
547 **303** 1 r. multicoloured 30 20

304 Aircraft and Airmail Letters

1981. 50th Anniv of Airmail Service.
548 **304** 1 r. multicoloured 60 20

305 Mecca

1981. 1400th Anniv of Hegira (2nd issue).
549 **305** 40 p. multicoloured . . . 20 60

306 Conference Emblem and Afghan Refugees

1981. Islamic Summit Conference (1st issue). Multicoloured.

550 40 p. Type **306** 30 10
551 40 p. Conference emblem encircled by flags and Afghan refugees (28 × 58 mm) . . . 30 10
552 1 r. Type **306** 50 10
553 1 r. As No. 551 . . . . 50 10
554 2 r. Conference emblem and map showing Afghanistan (48 × 32 mm) 65 50

307 Conference Emblem

1981. Islamic Summit Conference (2nd issue). Multicoloured.

555 40 p. Type **307** 10 10
556 40 p. Conference emblem and flags (28 × 46 mm) 10 10
557 85 p. Type **307** 20 40
558 85 p. As No. 556 . . . . . . 20 40

308 Kemal Ataturk **309** Green Turtle

1981. Birth Centenary of Kemal Ataturk (Turkish statesman).

559 **308** 1 r. multicoloured 50 15

1981. Wildlife Protection (6th series).

560 **309** 40 p. multicoloured . . . 1·25 40

310 Dome of the Rock **312** Pakistan Steel "Furnace No. 1"

311 Malubiting West

1981. Palestinian Welfare.

561 **310** 2 r. multicoloured 35 35

1981. Mountain Peaks (1st series). Karakoram Range. Multicoloured.

562 40 p. Type **311** 40 40
563 40 p. Malubiting West (24 × 31 mm) 40 40
564 1 r. Haramosh 75 75
565 1 r. Haramosh (24 × 31 mm) . 75 75
566 1 r. 50 K6 . . . . 90 1·00
567 1 r. 50 K6 (24 × 31 mm) . . . 90 1·00
568 2 r. K2, Broad Peak, Gasherbrum 4 and Gasherbrum 2 . . . . . 1·00 1·40
569 2 r. K2 (24 × 31 mm) . . . . 1·00 1·40
See also Nos. 674/5.

1981. 1st Firing of Pakistan Steel "Furnace No. 1", Karachi.

570 **312** 40 p. multicoloured . . . 25 10
571 2 r. multicoloured . . . . 65 1·25

313 Western Tragopan

1981. Wildlife Protection (7th series).

572 **313** 40 p. multicoloured . . . 1·50 75
573 – 2 r. multicoloured . . . 3·50 4·25
DESIGN: 2 r. As Type **313** but with background showing a winter view.

314 Disabled People and I.Y.D.P. Emblem

1981. International Year for Disabled Persons.

574 **314** 40 p. multicoloured . . . 40 50
575 2 r. multicoloured . . . . 1·40 1·75

315 World Hockey Cup below Flags of participating Countries

1982. Pakistan—World Cup Hockey Champions. Multicoloured.

576 1 r. Type **315** . . . . 2·00 1·50
577 1 r. World Hockey Cup above flags of participating countries 2·00 1·50

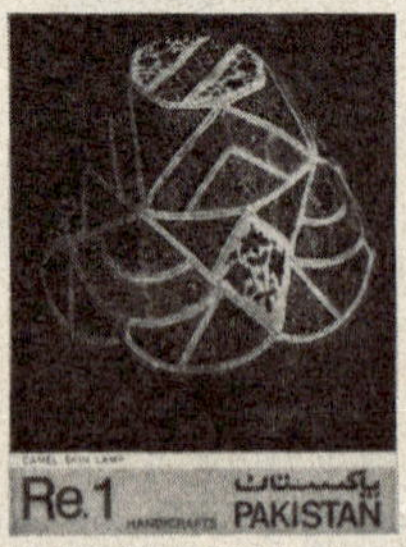

316 Camel Skin Lamp

1982. Handicrafts (2nd series). Multicoloured.

578 1 r. Type **316** 70 70
579 1 r. Hala pottery 70 70
See also Nos. 595/6.

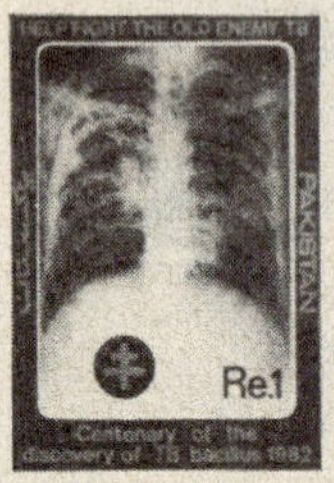

317 Chest X-Ray of Infected Person **318** Indus Dolphin

1982. Centenary of Robert Koch's Discovery of Tubercle Bacillus.

580 **317** 1 r. multicoloured . . . . 1·75 90

1982. Wildlife Protection (8th series).

581 **318** 40 p. multicoloured . . . . 1·50 1·00
582 – 1 r. multicoloured . . . . 3·00 2·25
DESIGN: 1 r. As Type **318** but with design reversed.

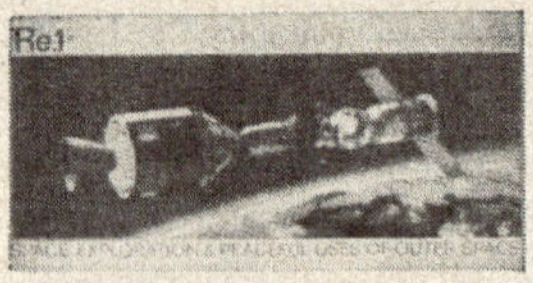

319 "Apollo–Soyuz" Link-up, 1975

1982. Peaceful Use of Outer Space.

583 **319** 1 r. multicoloured . . . . 2·50 1·25

320 Sukkur Barrage

1982. 50th Anniv of Sukkur Barrage.

584 **320** 1 r. multicoloured 30 30

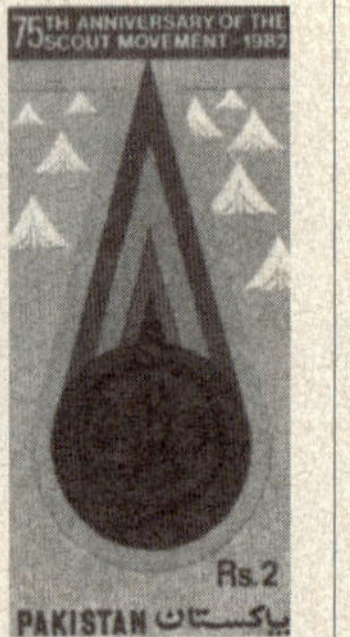

321 Pakistan National Flag and Stylised Sun **324** Scout Emblem and Tents

323 Arabic Inscription and University Emblem ($\frac{2}{3}$-size illustration)

1982. Independence Day. Multicoloured.

585 40 p. Type **321** 10 30
586 85 p. Map of Pakistan and stylised torch 20 50

1982. "Riccione '82" Stamp Exhibition. No. 584 optd **RICCIONE-82.**

587 **320** 1 r. multicoloured 20 20

1982. Centenary of the Punjab University.

588 **323** 40 p. multicoloured . . . 75 30

1983. 75th Anniv of Boy Scout Movement.

589 **324** 2 r. multicoloured 50 45

325 Laying Pipeline

1983. Inauguration of Quetta Natural Gas Pipeline Project.

590 **325** 1 r. multicoloured 30 20

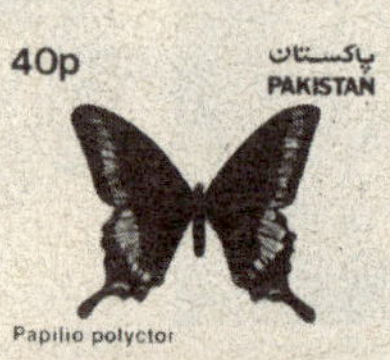

326 "Papilio polyctor"

1983. Butterflies. Multicoloured.

591 40 p. Type **326** . . . . 1·25 20
592 50 p. "Atrophaneura aristolochiae" . . . . 1·50 20
593 60 p. "Danaus chrysippus" . . 1·75 60
594 1 r. 50 "Papilio demoleus" . . 2·50 3·25

1983. Handicrafts (3rd series). As T **316**. Multicoloured.

595 1 r. Five flower motif needlework, Sind 15 15
596 1 r. Straw mats 15 15

327 School of Nursing and University Emblem

1983. Presentation of Charter to Aga Khan University, Karachi.

597 **327** 2 r. multicoloured 40 30

328 Yak Caravan crossing Zindiharam-Darkot Pass, Hindu Kush

1983. Trekking in Pakistan.

598 **328** 1 r. multicoloured . . . . 1·50 60

329 Marsh Crocodile **331** Floral Design

330 Goitred Gazelle

1983. Wildlife Protection (9th series).

599 **329** 3 r. multicoloured . . . . 3·50 2·00

1983. Wildlife Protection (10th series).

600 **330** 1 r. multicoloured . . . . 2·75 2·00

1983. 36th Anniv of Independence. Mult.

601 60 p. Type **331** 10 10
602 4 r. Hand holding flaming torch 40 45

332 Traditional Weaving, Pakistan

1983. Indonesian–Pakistan Economic and Cultural Co-operation Organization, 1969–1983. Mult.

603 2 r. Type **332** 20 25
604 2 r. Traditional weaving, Indonesia 20 25

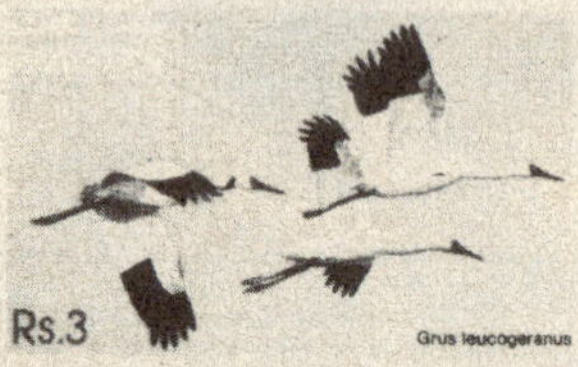

333 "Siberian Cranes" (Great White Cranes) (Sir Peter Scott)

1983. Wildlife Protection (11th series).

605	333	3 r. multicoloured	3·00	3·00

334 W.C.Y. Emblem

1983. World Communications Year. Multicoloured.

606		2 r. Type **334**	20	25
607		3 r. W.C.Y. emblem (different) (33 × 33 mm)	30	35

335 Farm Animals

1983. World Food Day. Multicoloured.

608		3 r. Type **335**	1·50	1·75
609		3 r. Fruit	1·50	1·75
610		3 r. Crops	1·50	1·75
611		3 r. Sea food	1·50	1·75

336 Agriculture Produce and Fertilizer Factory **337** Lahore, 1852

1983. National Fertilizer Corporation.

612	336	60 p. multicoloured	15	30

1983. National Stamp Exn, Lahore. Mult.

613		60 p. Musti Durwaza Dharmsala	60	70
614		60 p. Khabgha	60	70
615		60 p. Type **337**	60	70
616		60 p. Summan Burj Hazuri	60	70
617		60 p. Flower Garden, Samadhi Northern Gate	60	70
618		60 p. Budda Darya, Badshahi Masjid	60	70

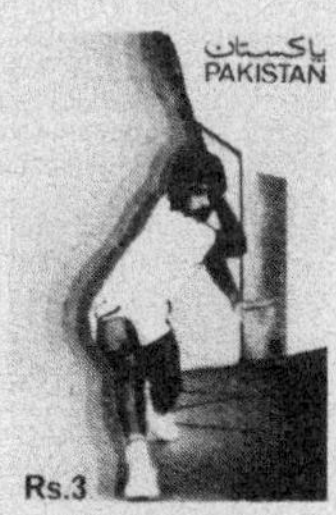

338 Winner of "Enterprise" Event **340** Jahangir Khan (World Squash Champion)

339 Snow Leopard

1983. Yachting Champions, Asian Games, Delhi. Multicoloured.

619		60 p. Type **338**	1·75	1·75
620		60 p. Winner of "OK" Dinghy event	1·75	1·75

1984. Wildlife Protection (12th series).

621	339	40 p. multicoloured	1·75	90
622		1 r. 60 multicoloured	4·75	6·00

1984. Squash.

623	340	3 r. multicoloured	2·25	1·75

341 P.I.A. Boeing 707 Airliner

1984. 20th Anniv of Pakistan International Airways Service to China.

624	341	3 r. multicoloured	5·00	5·00

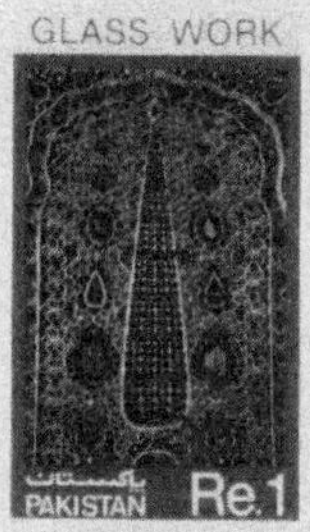

342 Glass-work **343** Attock Fort

1984. Handicrafts (4th series). Multicoloured, frame colours given.

625	342	1 r. blue	25	15
626	–	1 r. red	25	15
627	–	1 r. green	25	15
628	–	1 r. violet	25	15

DESIGNS: showing glass-work in Sheesh Mahal, Lahore Fort. Nos. 627/8 are horizontal designs.

1984. Forts.

629	–	5 p. black and purple	10	10
630	–	10 p. black and red	10	10
631	–	15 p. violet and brown	10	10
632	343	20 p. black and violet	10	10
633	–	50 p. brown and red	30	10
634	–	60 p. lt brown & brown	20	10
635	–	70 p. blue	20	10
636	–	80 p. brown and red	40	10

DESIGNS: 5 p. Kot Diji Fort; 10 p. Rohtas Fort; 15 p. Bala Hissar Fort; 50 p. Hyderabad Fort; 60 p. Lahore Fort; 70 p. Sibi Fort; 80 p. Ranikot Fort.

344 Shah Rukn i Alam's Tomb, Multan

1984. Aga Khan Award for Architecture.

647	344	60 p. multicoloured	1·75	1·75

345 Radio Mast and Map of World

1984. 20th Anniv of Asia–Pacific Broadcasting Union.

648	345	3 r. multicoloured	80	60

346 Wrestling

1984. Olympic Games, Los Angeles. Mult.

649		3 r. Type **346**	1·50	1·50
650		3 r. Boxing	1·50	1·50
651		3 r. Athletics	1·50	1·50
652		3 r. Hockey	1·50	1·50
653		3 r. Yachting	1·50	1·50

347 Jasmine (National flower) and Inscription

1984. Independence Day. Multicoloured.

654		60 p. Type **347**	10	10
655		4 r. Symbolic torch	45	50

348 Gearwheel Emblem and Flags of Participating Nations

1984. Pakistan International Trade Fair.

656	348	60 p. multicoloured	60	30

349 Interior of Main Dome

1984. Tourism Convention, Shahjahan Mosque, Thatta. Multicoloured.

657		1 r. Type **349**	50	60
658		1 r. Brick and glazed tile work	50	60
659		1 r. Gateway	50	60
660		1 r. Symmetrical archways	50	60
661		1 r. Interior of a dome	50	60

350 Bank Emblem in Floral Pattern

1984. 25th Anniv of United Bank Ltd.

662	350	60 p. multicoloured	70	70

351 Conference Emblem

1984. 20th United Nations Conference of Trade and Development.

663	351	60 p. multicoloured	70	40

352 Postal Life Insurance Emblem within Hands **353** Bull (wall painting)

1984. Centenary of Postal Life Insurance. Multicoloured.

664		60 p. Type **352**	45	15
665		1 r. "100" and Postal Life Insurance emblem	55	15

1984. U.N.E.S.C.O. Save Moenjadoro Campaign. Multicoloured.

666		2 r. Type **353**	1·40	1·00
667		2 r. Bull (seal)	1·40	1·00

354 International Youth Year Emblem and "75"

1985. 75th Anniv of Girl Guide Movement.

668	354	60 p. multicoloured	2·50	1·25

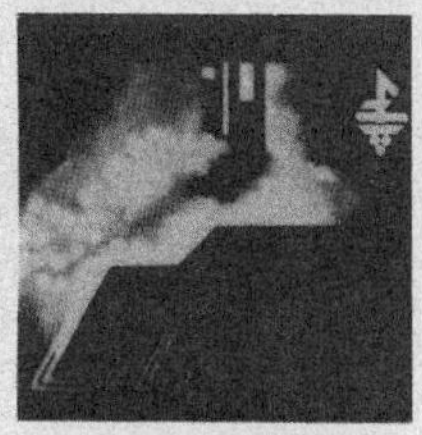
355 Smelting Ore

1985. Inauguration of Pakistan Steel Corporation. Multicoloured.

669		60 p. Type **355**	65	25
670		1 r. Pouring molten steel from ladle (28 × 46 mm)	1·10	25

356 Map of Pakistan and Rays of Sun

1985. Presidential Referendum of 19 December 1984.

671	356	60 p. multicoloured	1·00	55

357 Ballot Box and Voting Paper

1985. March Elections. Multicoloured.

672		1 r. Type **357**	65	15
673		1 r. Minar-e-Qarardad-e-Pakistan Tower, and word "Democracy" (31 × 43 mm)	65	15

1985. Mountain Peaks (2nd series). As T **311**. Multicoloured.

674		40 p. Rakaposhi (Karakoram Range)	1·75	75
675		2 r. Nangaparbat (Western Himalayas)	3·75	5·00

358 Trophy and Medals from Olympic Games 1984, Asia Cup 1985 and World Cup 1982

1985. Pakistan Hockey Team "Grand Slam" Success.

676	358	1 r. multicoloured	2·50	1·50

359 King Edward Medical College

1985. 125th Anniv of King Edward Medical College, Lahore.

677	359	3 r. multicoloured	1·75	65

360 Illuminated Inscription in Urdu

1985. Independence Day. Multicoloured.
678 60 p. Type **360** 40 50
679 60 p. Illuminated "XXXVIII" (inscr in English) 40 50

361 Sind Madressah-tul-Islam, Karachi

1985. Centenary of Sind Madressah-tul-Islam (theological college), Karachi.
680 **361** 2 r. multicoloured . . . . 1·75 70

362 Jamia Masjid Mosque by Day

1985. Inauguration of New Jamia Masjid Mosque, Karachi. Multicoloured.
681 1 r. Type **362** 90 35
682 1 r. Jamia Masjid illuminated at night 90 35

363 Lawrence College, Murree

1985. 125th Anniv of Lawrence College, Murree.
683 **363** 3 r. multicoloured . . . . 2·00 65

364 United Nations Building, New York

1985. 40th Anniv of United Nations Organization. Multicoloured.
684 1 r. Type **364** 30 15
685 2 r. U.N. Building and emblem 40 25

365 Tents and Jamboree Emblem

1985. 10th National Scout Jamboree.
686 **365** 60 p. multicoloured . . . 2·25 2·25

366 Islamabad

367 Map of S.A.A.R.C. Countries and National Flags

1985. 25th Anniv of Islamabad.
687 **366** 3 r. multicoloured . . . . 2·00 45

1985. 1st Summit Meeting of South Asian Association for Regional Co-operation, Dhaka, Bangladesh. Multicoloured.
688 1 r. Type **367** . . . . 2·25 4·50
689 2 r. National flags (39×39 mm) 1·75 2·25

368 Globe and Peace Dove

1985. 25th Anniv of U.N. General Assembly's Declaration on Independence for Colonial Territories.
690 **368** 60 p. multicoloured . . . 1·00 60

369 Peregrine Falcon

1986. Wildlife Protection (13th series). Peregrine Falcon.
691 **369** 1 r. 50 multicoloured . . 4·25 4·25

370 A.D.B.P. Building, Islamabad

1986. 25th Anniv of Agricultural Development Bank of Pakistan.
692 **370** 60 p. multicoloured . . . 90 50

371 Government S.E. College

1986. Centenary of Government Sadiq Egerton College, Bahawalpur.
693 **371** 1 r. multicoloured . . . . 1·50 40

372 Emblem and Bar Graph

373 "1947 1986"

1986. 25th Anniv of Asian Productivity Organization.
694 **372** 1 r. multicoloured . . . . 1·50 30

1986. 39th Anniv of Independence. Multicoloured.
695 80 p. Type **373** 50 15
696 1 r. Illuminated inscription in Urdu 50 15

374 Open Air Class

375 Mother and Child

1986. International Literacy Day.
697 **374** 1 r. multicoloured 75 30

1986. U.N.I.C.E.F. Child Survival Campaign.
698 **375** 80 p. multicoloured . . . 1·50 30

376 Aitchison College

1986. Centenary of Aitchison College, Lahore.
699 **376** 2 r. 50 multicoloured. . . 45 30

377 Two Doves carrying Olive Branches

378 Table Tennis Players

1986. International Peace Year.
700 **377** 4 r. multicoloured 50 50

1986. 4th Asian Cup Table Tennis Tournament, Karachi.
701 **378** 2 r. multicoloured . . . . 2·00 65

379 Argali

1986. Wildlife Protection (14th series). Argali.
702 **379** 2 r. multicoloured . . . . 3·00 3·00

380 Selimiye Mosque, Edirne, Turkey

382 Mistletoe Flowerpecker and Defence Symbols

381 St. Patrick's School

1986. "Ecophilex '86" International Stamp Exhibition, Islamabad. Multicoloured.
703 3 r. Type **380** . . . . 1·40 1·60
704 3 r. Gawhar Shad Mosque, Mashhad, Iran . . . . . . 1·40 1·60
705 3 r. Grand Mosque, Bhong, Pakistan . . . . 1·40 1·60

1987. 125th Anniv of St. Patrick's School, Karachi.
706 **381** 5 r. multicoloured . . . . 1·75 90

1987. Post Office Savings Bank Week. Multicoloured.
707 5 r. Type **382** . . . . 1·10 70
708 5 r. Spotted pardalote and laboratory apparatus . . . . 1·10 70
709 5 r. Black-throated blue warbler and agriculture symbols . . 1·10 70
710 5 r. Red-capped manakin and industrial skyline . . . . . . 1·10 70

383 New Parliament House, Islamabad

1987. Inauguration of New Parliament House, Islamabad.
711 **383** 3 r. multicoloured 30 30

384 Opium Poppies and Flames

1987. Campaign Against Drug Abuse.
712 **384** 1 r. multicoloured 45 20

385 Flag and National Anthem Score

1987. 40th Anniv of Independence. Mult.
713 80 p. Type **385** 25 10
714 3 r. Text of speech by Mohammed Ali Jinnah, Minar-e-Qardad-e-Pakistan Tower and arms 75 25

386 Hawker Tempest Mk II

1987. Air Force Day. Military Aircraft. Multicoloured.
715 3 r. Type **386** . . . . 1·25 1·25
716 3 r. Hawker Fury . . . . 1·25 1·25
717 3 r. Supermarine Attacker . . 1·25 1·25
718 3 r. North American F-86 Sabre 1·25 1·25
719 3 r. Lockheed F-104C Starfighter 1·25 1·25
720 3 r. Lockheed C-130 Hercules 1·25 1·25
721 3 r. Shenyang/Tianjin F-6 . . 1·25 1·25
722 3 r. Dassault Mirage III . . . 1·25 1·25
723 3 r. North American A-5A Vigilante . . . . 1·25 1·25
724 3 r. General Dynamics F-16 Fighting Falcon . . . . . . 1·25 1·25

387 Pasu Glacier

1987. Pakistan Tourism Convention. Views along Karakoram Highway. Multicoloured.
725 1 r. 50 Type **387** 60 40
726 1 r. 50 Apricot trees 60 40
727 1 r. 50 Karakoram Highway . . 60 40
728 1 r. 50 View from Khunjerab Pass 60 40

388 Shah Abdul Latif Bhitai Mausoleum

1987. Shah Abdul Latif Bhitai (poet) Commem.
729 **388** 80 p. multicoloured . . . 20 20

389 D. J. Sind Science College, Karachi

1987. Centenary of D. J. Sind Science College, Karachi.
730 **389** 80 p. multicoloured . . . 20 20

390 College Building

1987. 25th Anniv of College of Physicians and Surgeons.
731 **390** 1 r. multicoloured 30 20

391 Homeless People, Houses and Rising Sun

393 Honeycomb and Arms

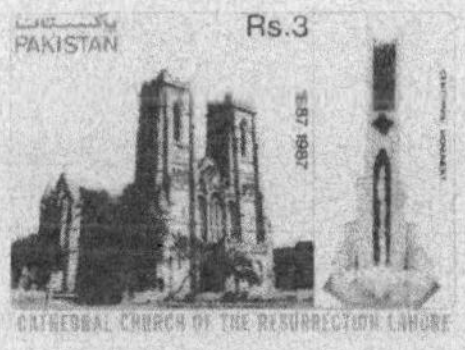

392 Cathedral Church of the Resurrection, Lahore

1987. International Year of Shelter for the Homeless.
732 **391** 3 r. multicoloured 30 30

1987. Centenary of Cathedral Church of the Resurrection, Lahore.
733 **392** 3 r. multicoloured 30 30

1987. 40th Anniv of Pakistan Post Office.
734 **393** 3 r. multicoloured 30 30

394 Corporation Emblem

1987. Radio Pakistan's New Programme Schedules.
735 **394** 80 p. multicoloured . . . 15 15

395 Jamshed Nusserwanjee Mehta and Karachi Municipal Corporation Building

1988. Birth Centenary (1986) of Jamshed Nusserwanjee Mehta (former President of Karachi Municipal Corporation).
736 **395** 3 r. multicoloured 30 30

396 Leprosy Symbols within Flower

398 Globe

397 W.H.O. Building, Geneva

1988. World Leprosy Day.
737 **396** 3 r. multicoloured 75 30

1988. 40th Anniv of W.H.O.
738 **397** 4 r. multicoloured 60 35

1988. 125th Anniv of Int Red Cross and Crescent.
739 **398** 3 r. multicoloured 30 30

399 Crescent, Leaf Pattern and Archway

1988. Independence Day.
740 **399** 80 p. multicoloured . . . 10 10
741 4 r. multicoloured 25 30

400 Field Events

1988. Olympic Games, Seoul. Multicoloured.
742 10 r. Type **400** . . . . 1·10 1·10
743 10 r. Track events . . . . . 1·10 1·10
744 10 r. Jumping and pole vaulting 1·10 1·10
745 10 r. Gymnastics . . . . . . 1·10 1·10
746 10 r. Table tennis, tennis, hockey and baseball . . . . 1·10 1·10
747 10 r. Volleyball, football, basketball and handball . . 1·10 1·10
748 10 r. Wrestling, judo, boxing and weightlifting . . . . 1·10 1·10
749 10 r. Shooting, fencing and archery . . . . 1·10 1·10
750 10 r. Water sports . . . . . 1·10 1·10
751 10 r. Equestrian events and cycling . . . . 1·10 1·10

401 Markhor

1988. Wildlife Protection (15th series).
752 **401** 2 r. multicoloured 40 40

402 Islamia College, Peshawar

1988. 75th Anniv of Islamia College, Peshawar.
753 **402** 3 r. multicoloured 30 30

403 Symbols of Agriculture, Industry and Education with National Flags

1988. South Asian Association for Regional Co-operation 4th Summit Meeting, Islamabad. Multicoloured.
754 25 r. Type **403** . . . . 1·50 1·50
755 50 r. National flags on globe and symbols of communications (33 × 33 mm) . . . . . . 3·25 3·25
756 75 r. Stamps from member countries (52 × 29 mm) . . . 4·50 4·50

1989. Pioneers of Freedom (2nd series). As T **282**. Multicoloured.
757 3 r. Maulana Hasrat Mohani . 15 20

404 Logo

1989. "Adasia 89" 16th Asian Advertising Congress, Lahore.
758 **404** 1 r. multicoloured ("Pakistan" in yellow) . 80 80
759 1 r. multicoloured ("Pakistan" in blue) . . 80 80
760 1 r. multicoloured ("Pakistan" in white) . . 80 80

405 Zulfikar Ali Bhutto

1989. 10th Death Anniv of Zulfikar Ali Bhutto (statesman). Multicoloured.
761 1 r. Type **405** 15 10
762 2 r. Zulfikar Ali Bhutto (different) 20 20

406 "Daphne" Class Submarine

1989. 25 Years of Pakistan Navy Submarine Operations. Multicoloured.
763 1 r. Type **406** . . . . 1·10 1·10
764 1 r. "Fleet Snorkel" class submarine . . . . 1·10 1·10
765 1 r. "Agosta" class submarine . 1·10 1·10

407 "The Oath of the Tennis Court" (David)

1989. Bicentenary of French Revolution.
766 **407** 7 r. multicoloured . . . . 1·75 90

408 Pitcher, c. 2200 B.C.

409 Satellites and Map of Asian Telecommunications Network

1989. Archaeological Artefacts. Terracotta pottery from Baluchistan Province. Mult.
767 1 r. Type **408** 15 15
768 1 r. Jar, c. 2300 B.C. 15 15
769 1 r. Vase, c. 3600 B.C. 15 15
770 1 r. Jar, c. 2600 B.C. 15 15

1989. 10th Anniv of Asia–Pacific Telecommunity.
771 **409** 3 r. multicoloured 30 30

410 Container Ship at Wharf

411 Mohammed Ali Jinnah

1989. Construction of Integrated Container Terminal, Port Qasim.
772 **410** 6 r. multicoloured . . . . 3·00 3·50

1989.
773 **411** 1 r. multicoloured 30 10
774 1 r. 50 multicoloured . . 35 20
775 2 r. multicoloured 45 30
776 3 r. multicoloured 60 40
777 4 r. multicoloured 70 45
778 5 r. multicoloured 75 60

412 Mausoleum of Shah Abdul Latif Bhitai

1989. 300th Birth Anniv of Shah Abdul Latif Bhitai (poet).
779 **412** 2 r. multicoloured 20 20

413 Asiatic Black Bear

414 Ear of Wheat encircling Globe

1989. Wildlife Protection (16th series). Asiatic Black Bear. Multicoloured.
780 4 r. Type **413** . . . . 90 1·10
781 4 r. Bear among boulders . . 90 1·10
782 4 r. Standing on rock . . . . 90 1·10
783 4 r. Sitting by trees . . . . . 90 1·10

1989. World Food Day.
784 **414** 1 r. multicoloured 35 35

415 Games Emblem and Flags of Member Countries

1989. 4th South Asian Sports Federation Games, Islamabad.
785 **415** 1 r. multicoloured 35 35

416 Patchwork Kamblee (cloth) entering Gate of Heaven

1989. 800th Birth Anniv of Baba Farid (Muslim spiritual leader).
786 **416** 3 r. multicoloured 30 30

417 Pakistan Television Logo

1989. 25th Anniv of Television Broadcasting in Pakistan.
787 **417** 3 r. multicoloured 30 30

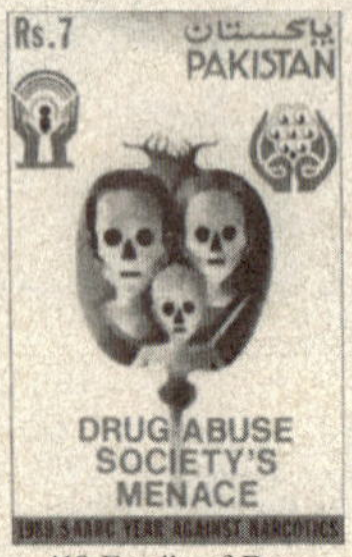

418 Family of Drug Addicts in Poppy Bud

1989. South Asian Association for Regional Co-operation Anti-Drugs Campaign.
788 **418** 7 r. multicoloured . . . . 1·40 85

419 Murray College, Sialkot

1989. Centenary of Murray College, Sialkot.
789 **419** 6 r. multicoloured 50 70

420 Government College, Lahore

1989. 125th Anniv of Government College, Lahore.
790 **420** 6 r. multicoloured 50 80

421 Fields, Electricity Pylons and Rural Buildings

1989. 10th Anniv of Centre for Asia and Pacific Integrated Rural Development.
791 **421** 3 r. multicoloured 55 65

422 Emblem and Islamic Patterns

1990. 20th Anniv of Organization of the Islamic Conference.
792 **422** 1 r. multicoloured 50 20

423 Hockey Match

1990. 7th World Hockey Cup, Lahore.
793 **423** 2 r. multicoloured . . . . 3·50 3·50

424 Mohammed Iqbal addressing Crowd and Liaquat Ali Khan taking Oath

1990. 50th Anniv of Passing of Pakistan Resolution. Multicoloured.
794 1 r. Type **424** 80 90
795 1 r. Maulana Mohammad Ali Jauhar and Mohammed Ali Jinnah with banner 80 90
796 1 r. Women with Pakistan flag, and Mohammed Ali Jinnah taking Governor-General's oath, 1947 . . . . 80 90
797 7 r. Minar-i-Qarardad-e-Pakistan Monument and Resolution in Urdu and English (86 × 42 mm) . . . . 1·75 2·25
Nos. 794/6 were printed together, se-tenant, forming a composite design.

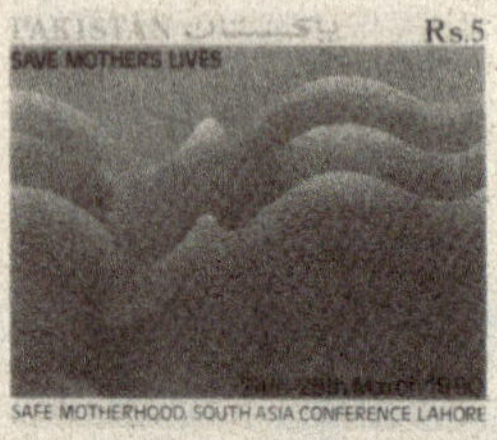

425 Pregnant Woman resting

1990. "Safe Motherhood" South Asia Conference, Lahore.
798 **425** 5 r. multicoloured 75 75

426 "Decorated Verse by Ghalib" (Shakir Ali)

1990. Painters of Pakistan (1st series). Shakir Ali.
799 **426** 1 r. multicoloured . . . . 1·00 75
See also Nos. 856/7.

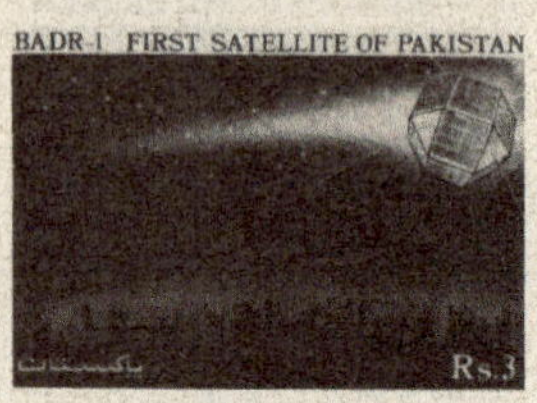

427 Satellite in Night Sky

1990. Launch of "Badr I" Satellite.
800 **427** 3 r. multicoloured . . . . 2·00 2·00

428 Allama Mohammed Iqbal

1990. Pioneers of Freedom (3rd series). Each brown and green.
801 1 r. Type **428** 25 25
802 1 r. Mohammed Ali Jinnah . . 25 25
803 1 r. Sir Syed Ahmad Khan . . 25 25
804 1 r. Nawab Salimullah 25 25
805 1 r. Mohtarma Fatima Jinnah . 25 25
806 1 r. Aga Khan III 25 25
807 1 r. Nawab Mohammad Ismail Khan 25 25
808 1 r. Hussain Shaheed Suhrawardy 25 25
809 1 r. Syed Ameer Ali 25 25
810 1 r. Nawab Bahadur Yar Jung 25 25
811 1 r. Khawaja Nazimuddin . . 25 25
812 1 r. Maulana Obaidullah Sindhi 25 25
813 1 r. Sahibzada Abdul Qaiyum Khan 25 25
814 1 r. Begum Jahanara Shah Nawaz 25 25
815 1 r. Sir Ghulam Hussain Hidayatullah 25 25
816 1 r. Qazi Mohammad Isa . . . 25 25
817 1 r. Sir M. Shahnawaz Khan Mamdot 25 25
818 1 r. Pir Sahib of Manki Sharif 25 25
819 1 r. Liaquat Ali Khan 25 25
820 1 r. Maulvi A. K. Fazl-ul-Haq 25 25
821 1 r. Allama Shabbir Ahmad Usmani 25 25
822 1 r. Sadar Abdur Rab Nishtar 25 25
823 1 r. Bi Amma 25 25
824 1 r. Sir Abdullah Haroon . . 25 25
825 1 r. Chaudhry Rahmat Ali . . 25 25
826 1 r. Raja Sahib of Mahmudabad 25 25
827 1 r. Hassanally Effendi 25 25
See also Nos. 838/46, 870/2, 904/6, 921/8, 961/2, 1007 and 1019/20.

429 Cultural Aspects of Indonesia and Pakistan

1990. Indonesia–Pakistan Economic and Cultural Co-operation Organization.
828 **429** 7 r. multicoloured 80 80

430 Globe, Open Book and Pen

1990. International Literacy Year.
829 **430** 3 r. multicoloured . . . . 90 1·00

431 College Crests **432** Children and Globe

1990. Joint Meeting between Royal College of Physicians, Edinburgh, and College of Physicians and Surgeons, Pakistan.
830 **431** 2 r. multicoloured 60 45

1990. U.N. World Summit for Children, New York.
831 **432** 7 r. multicoloured 55 65

433 Girl within Members' Flags

1990. South Asian Association for Regional Co-operation Year of Girl Child.
832 **433** 2 r. multicoloured 70 75

434 Paper passing over Rollers **435** Civil Defence Worker protecting Islamabad

1990. 25th Anniv of Security Papers Limited.
833 **434** 3 r. multicoloured . . . . 85 1·00

1991. International Civil Defence Day.
834 **435** 7 r. multicoloured . . . . 1·25 1·50

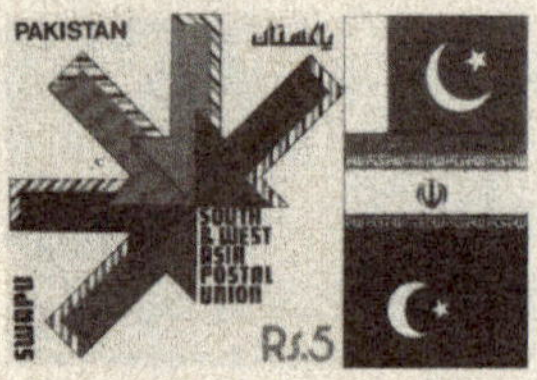

436 Logo and Flags of Member Countries

1991. South and West Asia Postal Union Commemoration.
835 **436** 5 r. multicoloured . . . . 1·60 1·60

437 Globe and Figures

1991. World Population Day.
836 **437** 10 r. multicoloured . . . 1·90 2·00

438 Mentally Handicapped Athlete **439** Habib Bank Headquarters and Emblem

1991. Pakistan Participation in Special Olympic Games.
837 **438** 7 r. multicoloured . . . . 1·75 2·00

1991. Pioneers of Freedom (4th series). As T **428**. Each brown and green.
838 1 r. Maulana Zafar Ali Khan 30 30
839 1 r. Maulana Mohamed Ali Jauhar 30 30
840 1 r. Chaudhry Khaliquzzaman 30 30
841 1 r. Hameed Nizami 30 30
842 1 r. Begum Ra'ana Liaquat Ali Khan 30 30
843 1 r. Mirza Abol Hassan Ispahani 30 30
844 1 r. Raja Ghazanfar Ali Khan 30 30
845 1 r. Malik Barkat Ali 30 30
846 1 r. Mir Jaffer Khan Jamali . 30 30

1991. 50th Anniv of Habib Bank.
847 **439** 1 r. multicoloured 40 10
848 5 r. multicoloured . . . . 2·00 2·50

440 St. Joesph's Convent School

1991. 130th Anniv (1992) of St. Joesph's Convent School, Karachi.
849 **440** 5 r. multicoloured . . . . 2·00 2·25

441 Emperor Sher Shah Suri
443 Houbara Bustard

442 Jinnah Antarctic Research Station

1991. Emperor Sher Shah Suri (founder of road network) Commemoration.
850 **441** 5 r. multicoloured . . . . 1·50 2·00

1991. Pakistan Scientific Expedition to Antarctica.
852 **442** 7 r. multicoloured . . . . 2·50 2·25

1991. Wildlife Protection (17th series).
853 **443** 7 r. multicoloured . . . . 2·00 2·00

444 Mosque

1991. 300th Death Anniv of Hazrat Sultan Bahoo.
854 **444** 7 r. multicoloured 70 80

445 Development Symbols and Map of Asia

1991. 25th Anniv of Asian Development Bank.
855 **445** 7 r. multicoloured . . . . 1·25 1·50

1991. Painters of Pakistan (2nd series). As T **426**. Multicoloured.
856 1 r. "Procession" (Haji Muhammad Sharif) . . . . 1·00 1·00
857 1 r. "Women harvesting" (Ustad Allah Bux) . . . . 1·00 1·00

446 American Express Travellers Cheques of 1891 and 1991
(⅔-size illustration)

1991. Centenary of American Express Travellers Cheques.
858 **446** 7 r. multicoloured . . . . 1·75 2·00

447 Flag, Banknote and Banking Equipment

1992. 1st Anniv of Muslim Commercial Bank Privatisation. Multicoloured.
859 1 r. Type **447** 10 10
860 7 r. Flag with industrial and commercial scenes 45 60

448 Imran Khan (team captain) and Trophy

1992. Pakistan's Victory in World Cricket Championship. Multicoloured.
861 2 r. Type **448** 70 70
862 5 r. Trophy and national flags (horiz) . . . . 1·50 1·50
863 7 r. Pakistani flag, trophy and symbolic cricket ball . . . 1·75 1·75

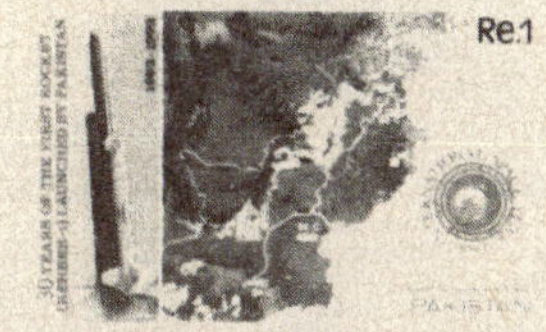

449 "Rehber-1" Rocket and Satellite View of Earth

1992. International Space Year. Mult.
864 1 r. Type **449** 15 10
865 2 r. Satellite orbiting Earth and logo 20 20

450 Surgical Instruments

1992. Industries. Multicoloured.
866 10 r. Type **450** 60 80
867 15 r. Leather goods . . . . . 75 1·00
868 25 r. Sports equipment . . . 1·25 1·50

451 Globe and Symbolic Family

1992. Population Day.
869 **451** 6 r. multicoloured 80 90

1992. Pioneers of Freedom (5th series). As T **428**. Each brown and green.
870 1 r. Syed Suleman Nadvi . . 60 60
871 1 r. Nawab Iftikhar Hussain Khan Mamdot 60 60
872 1 r. Maulana Muhammad Shibli Naumani 60 60

452 Scout Badge and Salute

1992. 6th Islamic Scout Jamboree and 4th Islamic Scouts Conference. Multicoloured.
873 6 r. Type **452** 50 75
874 6 r. Conference centre and scout salute 50 75

453 College Building

1992. Centenary of Islamia College, Lahore.
875 **453** 3 r. multicoloured 35 50

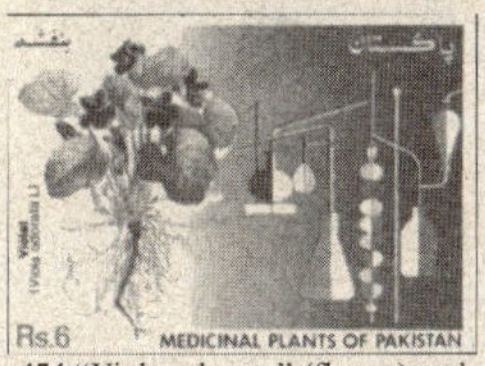

454 "Viola odorata" (flower) and Symbolic Drug Manufacture

1992. Medicinal Plants (1st series).
876 **454** 6 r. multicoloured . . . . 90 1·00
See also Nos. 903, 946, 1010, 1026 and 1037.

455 Emblem

1992. Extraordinary Ministerial Council Session of Economic Co-operation Organization, Islamabad.
877 **455** 7 r. multicoloured . . . . 85 1·00

456 Emblems and Field
457 Alhambra Palace, Granada, Spain

1992. International Conference on Nutrition, Rome.
878 **456** 7 r. multicoloured 70 90

1992. Cultural Heritage of Muslim Granada.
879 **457** 7 r. multicoloured 70 90

458 Mallard
459 Baluchistan Costume

Four different versions of designs as T **458**:
Type A. "Rs.5" at right with rainbow 8 mm beneath "P" of "PAKISTAN"
Type B. "Rs.5" at right with rainbow 2 mm beneath "P"
Type C. "Rs.5" at left with rainbow 2 mm beneath "N" of "PAKISTAN"
Type D. "Rs.5" at left with rainbow 8 mm beneath "N"

1992. Water Birds. Multicoloured.
880 5 r. Type **458** (A) 60 60
881 5 r. Type **458** (B) 60 60
882 5 r. Type **458** (C) 60 60
883 5 r. Type **458** (D) 60 60
884 5 r. Greylag goose (A) 60 60
885 5 r. As No. 884 (B) 60 60
886 5 r. As No. 884 (C) 60 60
887 5 r. As No. 884 (D) 60 60
888 5 r. Gadwall (A) 60 60
889 5 r. As No. 888 (B) 60 60
890 5 r. As No. 888 (C) 60 60
891 5 r. As No. 888 (D) 60 60
892 5 r. Common shelduck (A) . . . 60 60
893 5 r. As No. 892 (B) 60 60
894 5 r. As No. 892 (C) 60 60
895 5 r. As No. 892 (D) 60 60
Nos. 880/95 were printed together, se-tenant, each horizontal row having a composite design of a rainbow.

1993. Women's Traditional Costumes. Multicoloured.
896 6 r. Type **459** . . . . 1·25 1·25
897 6 r. Punjab . . . . 1·25 1·25
898 6 r. Sindh . . . . 1·25 1·25
899 6 r. North-west Frontier Province . . . . 1·25 1·25

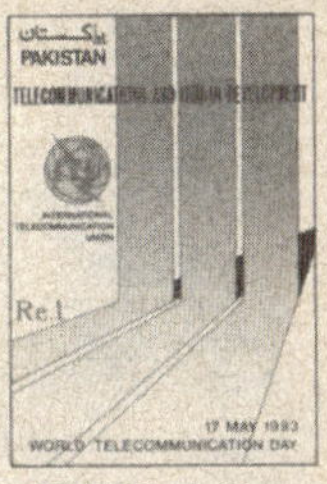

460 Clasped Hands and Islamic Symbols
461 I.T.U. Emblem

1993. 21st Conference of Islamic Foreign Ministers, Karachi.
900 **460** 1 r. multicoloured 30 10
901 6 r. multicoloured . . . . 95 1·25

1993. 25th Anniv of World Telecommunication Day.
902 **461** 1 r. multicoloured 55 30

1993. Medicinal Plants (2nd issue). As T **454**. Multicoloured.
903 6 r. Fennel and symbolic drug manufacture . . . . 1·40 1·40

1993. Pioneers of Freedom (6th series). As T **428**. Each brown and red.
904 1 r. Ghulam Mohammad Bhurgri 60 60
905 1 r. Ahmed Yar Khan 60 60
906 1 r. Mohammad Pir Sahib Zakori Sharif 60 60

462 College Building and Arms

1993. Centenary of Gordon College, Rawalpindi.
907 **462** 2 r. multicoloured 65 65

463 Juniper Forest

1993. Campaign to Save the Juniper Forest, Ziarat.
907a **463** 1 r. multicoloured . . . 40 20
908 7 r. multicoloured . . . 1·75 1·75

464 Globe, Produce and Emblem

1993. World Food Day.
909 **464** 6 r. multicoloured 70 80

465 Burn Hall Institution, Abbottabad
466 Peace Dove carrying Letter and National Flags

1993. 50th Anniv of Burn Hall Institutions.
910 **465** 7 r. multicoloured . . . . 1·00 1·25

1993. South and West Asia Postal Union Commemoration.
911 **466** 7 r. multicoloured . . . . 1·00 1·25

467 Congress Emblem

468 Wazir Mansion (birthplace)

1993. Pakistan College of Physicians and Surgeons International Medical Congress.
912 **467** 1 r. multicoloured 60 30

1993. 45th Death Anniv of Mohammed Ali Jinnah.
913 **468** 1 r. multicoloured 60 30

469 Emblem and National Flag

1994. 75th Anniv of I.L.O.
914 **469** 7 r. multicoloured 50 60

470 Ratan Jot (flower)

1994. Ratification of International Biological Diversity Convention. Multicoloured.
915 6 r. Type **470** 35 35
916 6 r. Wetlands habitat 35 35
917 6 r. Golden mahseer ("Tor putitora") (fish) 35 35
918 6 r. Brown bear 35 35

471 Silhouette of Family and Emblem

1994. International Year of the Family.
919 **471** 7 r. multicoloured 40 40

472 Symbolic Globe and Logo

1994. World Population Day.
920 **472** 7 r. multicoloured 40 40

1994. Pioneers of Freedom (7th series). As T **428**. Each brown and green.
921 1 r. Nawab Mohsin-Ul-Mulk . . 10 10
922 1 r. Sir Shahnawaz Bhutto . . 10 10
923 1 r. Nawab Viqar-Ul-Mulk . . 10 10
924 1 r. Pir Ilahi Bux 10 10
925 1 r. Sheikh Abdul Qadir . . . 10 10
926 1 r. Dr. Sir Ziauddin Ahmed . . 10 10
927 1 r. Jam Mir Ghulam Qadir Khan 10 10
928 1 r. Sardar Aurangzeb Khan . 10 10

473 Hala Pottery, Pakistan

474 Boy writing and Globe

1994. Indonesia–Pakistan Economic and Cultural Co-operation Organization. Multicoloured.
929 10 r. Type **473** 45 50
930 10 r. Lombok pottery, Indonesia 45 50

1994. International Literacy Day.
931 **474** 7 r. multicoloured 30 35

475 Mohammed Ali Jinnah and Floral Pattern

1994.
932 **475** 1 r. multicoloured 10 10
933 2 r. multicoloured 10 10
934 3 r. multicoloured 10 10
935 4 r. multicoloured 10 10
936 5 r. multicoloured 10 15
937 7 r. multicoloured 15 20
938 10 r. multicoloured . . . 25 30
939 12 r. multicoloured . . . 35 40
940 15 r. multicoloured . . . 40 45
941 20 r. multicoloured . . . 50 55
942 25 r. multicoloured . . . 60 65
943 30 r. multicoloured . . . 70 75

476 Gateway and Emblem

477 Engraver

1994. 2nd South Asian Association for Regional Co-operation and 12th National Scout Jamborees, Quetta.
944 **476** 7 r. multicoloured 30 35

1994. 1st Int Festival of Islamic Artisans at Work.
945 **477** 2 r. multicoloured 40 30

478 Henbane

479 Abu-I Kasim Firdausi (poet)

1994. Medicinal Plants (3rd issue).
946 **478** 6 r. multicoloured 55 60

1994. Millenary of "Shahnama" (poem).
947 **479** 1 r. multicoloured 15 15

480 Museum Building

1994. Centenary of Lahore Museum.
948 **480** 4 r. multicoloured 40 40

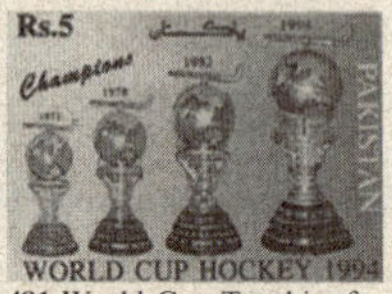

481 World Cup Trophies for 1971, 1978, 1982 and 1994

1994. Victory of Pakistan in World Cup Hockey Championship.
949 **481** 5 r. multicoloured 50 50

482 Tourist Attractions

1995. 20th Anniv of World Tourism Organization.
950 **482** 4 r. multicoloured 40 40

483 Khan Khushal of Khattak and Army

1995. Khan Khushal of Khattak (poet) Commemoration.
951 **483** 7 r. multicoloured 65 65

484 E.C.O. Emblem

1995. 3rd Economic Co-operation Organization Summit, Islamabad.
952 **484** 6 r. multicoloured 55 55

485 Common Indian Krait

1995. Snakes. Multicoloured.
953 6 r. Type **485** 70 70
954 6 r. Indian cobra 70 70
955 6 r. Indian python 70 70
956 6 r. Russell's viper 70 70

486 Globe and Environments

1995. Earth Day.
957 **486** 6 r. multicoloured 55 55

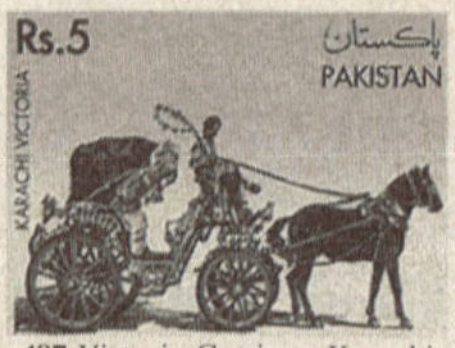

487 Victoria Carriage, Karachi

1995. Traditional Transport.
958 **487** 5 r. multicoloured 50 50

488 Prime Minister Tansu Ciller of Turkey and Rose

1995. 1st Muslim Women Parliamentarians' Conference, Islamabad. Multicoloured.
959 5 r. Type **488** 40 50
960 5 r. Prime Minister Benazir Bhutto and jasmine 40 50

1995. Pioneers of Freedom (8th series). As T **428**. Each brown and green.
961 1 r. Maulana Shaukat Ali . . 25 25
962 1 r. Chaudhry Ghulam Abbas 25 25

489 Oil Sardine

1995. Fishes. Multicoloured.
963 6 r. Type **489** 50 60
964 6 r. Mozambique mouthbrooder ("Tilapia") 50 60
965 6 r. Brown trout 50 60
966 6 r. Rohu 50 60

490 "Erasmia pulchella"

1995. Butterflies. Multicoloured.
967 6 r. Type **490** 50 60
968 6 r. "Callicore astarte" (inscr "Catogramme") 50 60
969 6 r. "Ixias pyrene" 50 60
970 6 r. "Heliconius" 50 60

491 Major Raja Aziz Bhatti Shaheed and Medal

1995. Defence Day.
971 **491** 1 r. 25 multicoloured . . 55 50

492 Presentation Convent School, Rawalpindi

1995. Centenary of Presentation Convent School, Rawalpindi.
972 **492** 1 r. 25 multicoloured . . 30 20

493 Women Soldiers, Golfer and Scientist

494 "Louis Pasteur in Laboratory" (Edelfelt)

1995. 4th World Conference on Women, Peking. Multicoloured.
973 1 r. 25 Type **493** 20 20
974 1 r. 25 Women graduates, journalist, computer operator and technicians 20 20
975 1 r. 25 Sewing machinist and women at traditional crafts 20 20
976 1 r. 25 Army officer and women at traditional tasks 20 20

1995. Death Centenary of Louis Pasteur (chemist).
977 **494** 5 r. multicoloured 50 60

495

496 Liaquat Ali Khan

1995.
978 **495** 5 p. blue, orange and brown 10 10
979 15 p. orange, violet and brown 10 10
980 25 p. blue, mauve and purple 10 10
981 75 p. green, brown and deep brown 10 10

1995. Birth Centenary (1995) of Liaquat Ali Khan (statesman).

987 **496** 1 r. 25 multicoloured . . 20 10

497 Village and Irrigated Fields

1995. 50th Anniv of F.A.O.

988 **497** 1 r. 25 multicoloured . . 20 10

498 Pakistani Soldier treating Somali Refugees

1995. 50th Anniv of United Nations.

989 **498** 7 r. multicoloured 50 50

499 Education Emblem

500 Hand holding Book, Eye and Pen Nib

1995. 80th Anniv (1993) of Kinnaird College for Women, Lahore.

990 **499** 1 r. 25 multicoloured . . 20 10

1995. International Conference of Writers and Intellectuals, Islamabad.

991 **500** 1 r. 25 multicoloured . . 20 10

501 Children holding Hands and S.A.A.R.C. Logo

502 Jet Skier

1995. 10th Anniv of South Asian Association for Regional Co-operation.

992 **501** 1 r. 25 multicoloured . . 20 10

1995. National Water Sports Gala, Karachi. Multicoloured.

993 1 r. 25 Type **502** 20 20

994 1 r. 25 Local punts 20 20

995 1 r. 25 Wind surfers 20 20

996 1 r. 25 Water skier 20 20

503 Mortar Board and Books

1995. 20th Anniv of Allama Iqbal Open University.

997 **503** 1 r. 25 multicoloured . . 20 10

504 Balochistan Quetta University Building

1995. 25th Anniv of Balochistan Quetta University.

998 **504** 1 r. 25 multicoloured . . 20 10

505 Zulfikar Ali Bhutto, Flag and Crowd

1996. 17th Death Anniv of Zulfikar Ali Bhutto (former Prime Minister). Multicoloured.

999 1 r. 25 Type **505** 30 10

1000 4 r. Zulfikar Ali Bhutto and flag (53 × 31 mm) . . . . . . 95 1·10

506 Wrestling

1996. Olympic Games, Atlanta. Multicoloured.

1002 5 r. Type **506** 40 40

1003 5 r. Boxing 40 40

1004 5 r. Pierre de Coubertin . . 40 40

1005 5 r. Hockey 40 40

1996. Pioneers of Freedom (9th series). Allama Abdullah Yousuf Ali. As T **428**.

1007 1 r. brown and green 10 10

507 G.P.O. Building, Lahore

1996. Restoration of G.P.O. Building, Lahore.

1008 **507** 5 r. multicoloured . . . 30 35

508 Symbolic Open Book and Text

1996. International Literacy Day.

1009 **508** 2 r. multicoloured . . . 20 15

509 Yarrow

510 Faiz Ahmed Faiz

1996. Medicinal Plants (4th series).

1010 **509** 3 r. multicoloured . . . 40 30

1997. 86th Birth Anniv of Faiz Ahmed Faiz (poet).

1011 **510** 3 r. multicoloured . . . 10 15

511 Golden Jubilee and O.I.C. Emblems

512 Amir Timur

1997. Special Summit Conference of Organisation of Islamic Countries commemorating 50th anniv of Pakistan.

1012 **511** 2 r. multicoloured . . . 10 10

1997. 660th Birth Anniv of Timur (founder of Timurid Empire).

1013 **512** 3 r. multicoloured . . . 10 15

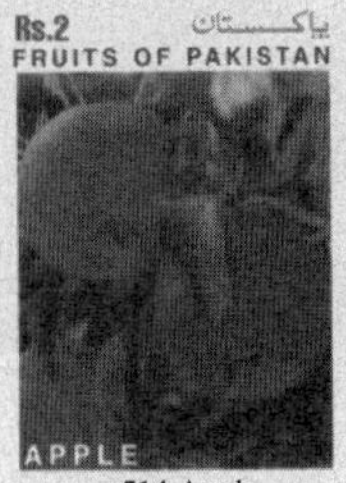

513 Jalal-al-din Moulana Rumi

514 Apple

1997. Pakistan–Iran Joint Issue.

1014 3 r. Type **513** 10 15

1015 3 r. Allama Mohammad Iqbal (poet) 10 15

1997. Fruit.

1016 **514** 2 r. multicoloured . . . 10 10

515 People on Globe

1997. World Population Day.

1017 **515** 2 r. multicoloured . . . 10 10

516 Stylised Dove of Peace

1997. 40th Anniv of Co-operation between International Atomic Energy Agency and Pakistan Atomic Energy Corporation.

1018 **516** 2 r. multicoloured . . . 10 10

1997. Pioneers of Freedom (10th series). As T **428**. Each brown and green.

1019 1 r. Mohammad Ayub Khuhro 10 10

1020 1 r. Begum Salma Tassaduq Hussain 10 10

517 Mohammed Ali Jinnah

1997. 50th Anniv of Independence. Multicoloured.

1021 3 r. Type **517** 10 10

1022 3 r. Allama Mohammad Iqbal 10 10

1023 3 r. Mohtarma Fatima Jinnah 10 10

1024 3 r. Liaquat Ali Khan 10 10

518 College Building

1997. 75th Anniv of Lahore College for Women.

1025 **518** 3 r. multicoloured . . . 10 10

519 Garlic

1997. Medicinal Plants (5th series).

1026 **519** 2 r. multicoloured . . . 10 10

520 Himalayan Monal Pheasant

521 Globe and Cracked Ozone Layer

1997. Wildlife Protection (18th series).

1027 **520** 2 r. multicoloured . . . 10 10

1997. Save Ozone Layer Campaign.

1028 **521** 3 r. multicoloured . . . 10 10

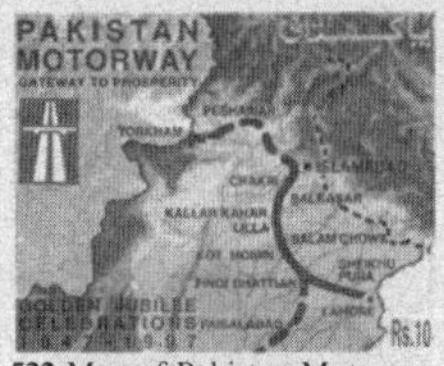

522 Map of Pakistan Motorway Project

1997. Pakistan Motorway Project.

1029 **522** 10 r. multicoloured . . 25 30

523 Emblem and Disabled People

1997. International Day for the Disabled.

1031 **523** 4 r. multicoloured . . . 10 10

524 Karachi Grammar School

1997. 150th Anniv of Karachi Grammar School.

1032 **524** 2 r. multicoloured . . . 10 10

525 Mirza Ghalib

1998. Birth Bicentenary (1997) of Mirza Ghalib (poet).

1033 **525** 2 r. multicoloured . . . 10 10

No. 1033 is inscr "DEATH ANNIVERSARY".

526 Servicemen, Pakistan Flag and "50"

1998. 50th Anniv (1997) of Armed Forces.

1034	526	7 r. multicoloured	15	20

527 Sir Syed Ahmed Khan

1998. Death Centenary of Sir Syed Ahmed Khan (social reformer).

1035	527	7 r. brown, green & stone	15	20

528 Olympic Torch and Sports

1998. 27th National Games, Peshawar.

1036	528	7 r. multicoloured	15	20

529 Thornapple

1998. Medicinal Plants (6th series).

1037	529	2 r. multicoloured	10	10

OFFICIAL STAMPS

1947. King George VI Official stamps of India optd **PAKISTAN**.

O 1	O 20	3 p. slate	80	10
O 2		½ a. purple	30	10
O 3		9 p. green	4·00	2·50
O 4		1 a. red	30	10
O 5		1½ a. violet	30	10
O 6		2 a. orange	30	10
O 7		2½ a. violet	6·00	7·50
O 8		4 a. brown	1·25	30
O 9		8 a. violet	1·50	1·25
O10	93	1 r. slate and brown (No. O138)	80	85
O11		2 r. purple and brown (No. O139)	3·50	2·75
O12		5 r. green and blue (No. O140)	15·00	26·00
O13		10 r. purple and red (No. O141)	38·00	85·00

1948. Optd **SERVICE**. Crescent moon pointing to right.

O14	7	3 p. red	10	10
O15		6 p. violet	10	10
O37		9 p. green	10	10
O17	–	1 a. blue	3·75	10
O18	–	1½ a. green	3·50	10
O19	–	2 a. red	1·50	10
O20	–	3 a. green	22·00	6·00
O21	9	4 a. brown	80	10
O22	–	8 a. black	1·50	6·00
O23	12	1 r. blue	1·00	10
O42		2 r. brown	3·50	10
O61		5 r. red	6·00	15
O26	13	10 r. mauve	13·00	40·00

1949. Optd **SERVICE**. Crescent moon pointing to left.

O38	–	1 a. blue	10	10
O39	–	1½ a. green	10	10
O40	–	2 a. red	15	10
O30	–	3 a. green	18·00	4·50
O31	–	8 a. black	27·00	14·00

1951. 4th Anniv of Independence. As Nos. 56, 58 and 60 but inscr "SERVICE" instead of "PAKISTAN POSTAGE".

O32		3 a. purple	6·00	8·00
O33		4 a. green	1·50	10
O34		8 a. sepia	7·00	2·50

1954. 7th Anniv of Independence. Nos. 65/71 optd **SERVICE**.

O53		6 p. violet	10	10
O54		9 p. blue	10	10
O55		1 a. red	10	10
O56		1½ a. red	10	10
O57		14 a. myrtle	40	3·50
O58		1 r. green	40	10
O51		2 r. orange	1·50	15

1955. 8th Anniv of Independence. Nos. 74/5 optd **SERVICE**.

O63		6 a. blue	15	10
O64		8 a. violet	15	10

1959. 9th Anniv of Independence. Optd **SERVICE**.

O65	37	2 a. red	10	10

1961. 1st Anniv of Republic. Optd **SERVICE**.

O62	41	10 r. green and orange	7·00	8·00

1961. Optd **SERVICE**.

O66	51	8 a. green	20	10
O67		1 r. blue	20	10

1961. New currency. Provisional stamps. Nos. 122 etc. optd **SERVICE**.

O68	–	1 p. on 1½ a. red	10	10
O69	7	2 p. on 3 p. red	10	10
O70	51	3 p. on 6 p. purple	10	10
O71	–	7 p. on 1 a. red	10	10
O72	51	13 p. on 2 a. red	10	10
O73	37	13 p. on 2 a. red	10	10

1961. Definitive issue optd **SERVICE**.

O 74	60	1 p. violet	10	10
O 75		2 p. red	10	10
O 79		3 p. purple	10	10
O 94		5 p. blue	10	10
O 81		7 p. green	10	10
O 82	61	10 p. brown	10	10
O 83		13 p. violet	10	10
O 98		15 p. purple	10	50
O 99		20 p. green	10	30
O100		25 p. blue	6·00	2·00
O 85		40 p. purple	10	10
O102		50 p. turquoise	10	15
O 87		75 p. red	20	10
O104		90 p. green	3·75	3·75
O 88	62	1 r. red	35	10
O 89		2 r. orange	1·50	20
O 90		5 r. green	4·25	6·50

1979. Optd **SERVICE**.

O109	275	2 p. green	10	10
O110	–	3 p. black	10	10
O111	–	5 p. blue	10	10
O112	275	10 p. blue and turquoise	10	10
O113	–	20 p. green (No. 468)	10	10
O114	–	25 p. green and mauve (No. 489)	10	10
O115	–	40 p. blue and mauve (No. 470)	30	10
O116	–	50 p. lilac and green (No. 471)	10	10
O117	–	60 p. black (No. 472)	1·00	10
O118	–	75 p. red (No. 473)	1·00	10
O119	–	1 r. green (No. 475)	2·25	10
O120	–	1 r. 50 orange (No. 476)	10	10
O121	–	2 r. red (No. 477)	15	10
O122	–	3 r. blue (No. 478)	20	20
O123	–	4 r. black (No. 479)	1·25	25
O124	–	5 r. brown (No. 480)	1·25	30

1980. As Nos. 513/19 but inscr "SERVICE".

O125	291	10 p. green and yellow	1·00	10
O126		15 p. dp green & green	1·00	10
O127		25 p. violet and red	15	10
O128		35 p. red and green	20	10
O129	–	40 p. red and brown	1·00	10
O130	–	50 p. red and green	20	10
O131	–	80 p. green and black	30	60

1984. Nos. 629/30 and 632/6 optd **SERVICE**.

O132	–	5 p. black and purple	10	10
O133	–	10 p. black and red	10	10
O135	343	20 p. black and violet	10	10
O136	–	50 p. brown and red	10	10
O137	–	60 p. lt brown & brown	10	10
O138	–	70 p. blue	10	10
O139	–	80 p. brown and red	10	10

1989. No. 773 optd **SERVICE**.

O140	411	1 r. multicoloured	1·75	60

O 7 State Bank of Pakistan Building, Islamabad

1990.

O141	O 7	1 r. red and green	10	10
O142		2 r. red and pink	10	10
O143		3 r. red and blue	10	10
O144		4 r. red and brown	10	10
O145		5 r. red and purple	20	25

PALESTINE

A territory at the extreme east of the Mediterranean Sea, captured from the Turks by Great Britain in 1917 and under Military Occupation till 1920. It was a British Mandate of the League of Nations from 1923 to May 1948 when the State of Israel was proclaimed.

1918. 10 milliemes = 1 piastre.
1927. 1,000 mills = £P1.

1

(2)

1918.

3	1	1 p. blue	2·25	2·25

1918. Surch with T 2.

4	1	5 m. on 1 p. blue	4·00	3·50

3 "E.E.F." = Egyptian Expeditionary Force

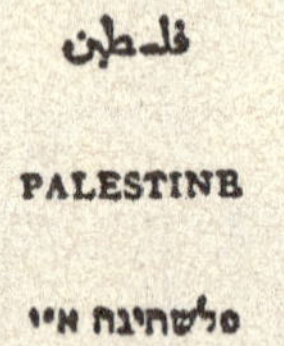

(4)

1918.

5	3	1 m. brown	30	40
6		2 m. green	30	45
7		3 m. brown	35	35
8		4 m. red	35	40
9		5 m. orange	80	30
10		1 p. blue	35	25
11		2 p. olive	60	60
12		5 p. purple	1·75	2·25
13		9 p. ochre	2·50	4·50
14		10 p. blue	2·25	3·00
15		20 p. grey	11·00	16·00

Nos. 1/15 were also valid in Transjordan, Cilicia, Lebanon and Syria.

1920. Optd with T 4.

71	3	1 m. brown	30	30
61		2 m. green	70	30
72		2 m. yellow	45	30
62		3 m. brown	90	30
73		3 m. blue	45	15
74		4 m. red	40	20
75		5 m. orange	55	50
76		6 m. green	80	30
77		7 m. brown	80	30
78		8 m. red	80	30
79		1 p. grey	80	30
65		1 p. blue	90	35
80		13 m. blue	75	15
66		2 p. olive	1·40	40
82		5 p. purple	4·75	1·25
87		9 p. ochre	9·00	9·00
88		10 p. blue	7·50	2·50
26		20 p. grey	18·00	42·00
89		20 p. violet	9·00	5·50

9 Rachel's Tomb

10 Dome of the Rock

11 Citadel, Jerusalem

12 Sea of Galilee

1927.

90	9	2 m. blue	30	10
91		3 m. green	40	10
92	10	4 m. red	3·25	1·25
104		4 m. purple	65	10
93	11	5 m. orange	65	10
94a	10	6 m. green	50	20
95	11	7 m. red	4·00	60
105		7 m. violet	45	10
96	10	8 m. brown	12·00	6·00
106		8 m. red	60	20
97b	9	10 m. grey	75	10
98	10	13 m. blue	4·00	30
107		13 m. brown	70	10
108a		15 m. blue	1·00	40
99	11	20 m. olive	1·00	15
100a	12	50 m. purple	1·25	30
101		90 m. bistre	55·00	60·00
102		100 m. blue	2·00	70
103b		200 m. violet	6·00	3·50
109		250 m. brown	3·75	1·75
110		500 m. red	4·50	3·00
111		£P1 black	5·00	3·50

POSTAGE DUE STAMPS

D 1

D 2

1920.

D1	D 1	1 m. brown	25·00	38·00
D2		2 m. green	18·00	27·00
D3		4 m. red	22·00	35·00
D4		8 m. mauve	15·00	26·00
D5		13 m. blue	15·00	26·00

1924.

D 6	D 2	1 m. brown	90	2·00
D 7		2 m. yellow	1·75	1·75
D 8		4 m. green	1·75	1·25
D 9		8 m. red	3·00	90
D10		13 m. blue	2·75	2·50
D11		5 p. violet	8·00	1·75

1928. As Type D 2, but inscr "MIL" instead of "MILLIEME".

D12	D 2	1 m. brown	45	85
D13		2 m. yellow	55	60
D14		4 m. green	80	1·60
D15		6 m. brown	11·00	8·50
D16		8 m. red	1·75	90
D17		10 m. grey	1·25	60
D18		13 m. blue	1·50	1·75
D19		20 m. olive	1·60	1·25
D20		50 m. violet	2·50	1·25

PAPUA

(Formerly **BRITISH NEW GUINEA**)

The eastern portion of the island of New Guinea, to the North of Australia, a territory of the Commonwealth of Australia, now combined with New Guinea. Australian stamps were used after the Japanese defeat in 1945 until the combined issue appeared in 1952.

12 pence = 1 shilling
20 shilling = 1 pound

1 Lakatoi (native canoe) with Hanuabada Village in Background

6

1901.

9	1	½d. black and green	5·00	3·75
10		1d. black and red	3·50	2·00
11		2d. black and violet	9·50	4·00
12		2½d. black and blue	9·50	12·00
13		4d. black and brown	32·00	48·00
6		6d. black and green	45·00	35·00
7		1s. black and orange	60·00	65·00
8		2s. 6d. black and brown	£600	£550

1906. Optd **Papua**.

38	1	½d. black and green	6·00	7·50
39		1d. black and red	3·50	5·00
40		2d. black and violet	4·50	2·25
24		2½d. black and blue	3·75	15·00
42		4d. black and brown	25·00	48·00
43		6d. black and green	24·00	38·00
19		1s. black and orange	20·00	38·00
37		2s. 6d. black and brown	32·00	48·00

1907.

66	6	½d. black and green	1·60	3·25
94a		1d. black and red	1·60	1·00
68		2d. black and purple	3·50	4·25
51a		2½d. black and blue	5·50	6·50
63		4d. black and brown	4·25	7·50
80		6d. black and green	7·50	7·50
81		1s. black and orange	5·50	17·00
82		2s. 6d. black and brown	35·00	45·00

1911.

84a	6	½d. green	40	2·25
85		1d. red	70	65
86		2d. mauve	70	75
87		2½d. blue	4·75	8·50
88		4d. olive	2·00	11·00
89		6d. brown	3·75	5·00
90		1s. yellow	9·00	15·00
91		2s. 6d. red	32·00	38·00

1916.

93	6	½d. green and olive	80	1·00
95		1½d. blue and brown	2·00	80
96		2d. purple and red	1·75	75
97		2½d. green and blue	4·75	12·00
98		3d. black and turquoise	1·25	1·75
99		4d. brown and orange	2·50	5·00
100		5d. grey and brown	4·25	16·00
101		6d. purple	3·25	9·50
127		9d. lilac and violet	4·50	27·00
102		1s. brown and olive	3·50	6·50
128		1s. 3d. lilac and blue	7·50	32·00
103		2s. 6d. red and pink	18·00	40·00
104		5s. black and green	40·00	48·00
105		10s. green and blue	£140	£180

1917. Surch **ONE PENNY**.

106a	6	1d. on ½d. green	50	1·25
107		1d. on 2d. mauve	12·00	15·00
108		1d. on 2½d. blue	1·25	3·75
109		1d. on 4d. green	1·75	4·00
110		1d. on 6d. brown	8·00	17·00
111		1d. on 2s. 6d. red	1·50	8·00

1929. Air. Optd **AIR MAIL**.

114	6	3d. black and turquoise	90	7·00

(11)

1930. Air. Optd with T **11**.

118	6	3d. black and turquoise	90	6·00
119		6d. purple	7·00	10·00
120		1s. brown and olive	4·25	15·00

1931. Surch in words or figs and words.

122	6	2d. on 1½d. blue & brown	1·00	2·00
125		5d. on 1s. brown & olive	75	1·75
126		9d. on 2s. 6d. red & pink	5·50	8·50
123		1s. 3d. on 5d. black & green	4·00	9·00

15 Motuan Girl

18 Raggiana Bird of Paradise

20 Native Mother and Child

1932.

130	15	½d. black and orange	1·00	3·25
131	–	1d. black and green	1·50	60
132	–	1½d. black and red	70	6·50
133	18	2d. red	8·50	30
134	–	3d. black and blue	2·75	6·00
135	20	4d. olive	4·50	8·00
136	–	5d. black and green	2·25	3·00
137	–	6d. brown	6·00	5·50
138	–	9d. black and violet	8·50	18·00
139	–	1s. green	3·50	8·50
140	–	1s. 3d. black and purple	13·00	23·00
141	–	2s. black and green	14·00	22·00
142	–	2s. 6d. black and mauve	25·00	38·00
143	–	5s. black and brown	55·00	50·00
144	–	10s. violet	80·00	80·00
145	–	£1 black and grey	£180	£140

DESIGNS—VERT (as T **15**): 1d. Chieftain's son; 1½d. Tree houses; 3d. Papuan dandy; 5d. Masked dancer; 9d. Shooting fish; 1s. Ceremonial platform; 1s. 3d. Lakatoi; 2s. Papuan art; 2s. 6d. Pottery-making; 5d. Native policeman; £1 Delta house. VERT (as T **18**): 6d. Papuan mother. HORIZ: (as T **20**): 10s. Lighting fire.

31 Hoisting the Union Jack

35 King George VI

1934. 50th Anniv of Declaration of British Protectorate. Inscr "1884 1834".

146	31	1d. green	1·00	3·00
147	–	2d. red	1·75	3·00
148	31	3d. blue	1·75	3·00
149	–	5d. purple	11·00	12·00

DESIGN: 2d., 5d. Scene on H.M.S. "Nelson".

1935. Silver Jubilee. Optd **HIS MAJESTY'S JUBILEE 1910 1935** (1910 – 1935 on 2d.).

150	–	1d. black & green (No. 131)	75	1·75
151	18	2d. red	2·00	1·75
152	–	3d. black & blue (No. 134)	1·75	2·50
153	–	5d. black & green (No. 136)	2·50	2·75

1937. Coronation.

154	35	1d. green	55	15
155		2d. red	55	40
156		3d. blue	55	55
157		5d. purple	55	1·25

36 Port Moresby

1938. Air. 50th Anniv of Declaration of British Possession.

158	36	2d. red	3·75	2·25
159		3d. blue	3·75	2·25
160		5d. green	3·75	3·25
161		8d. red	11·00	14·00
162		1s. mauve	30·00	15·00

37 Natives poling Rafts

1939. Air.

163	37	2d. red	4·50	3·75
164		3d. blue	4·50	6·50
165		5d. green	5·50	1·50
166		8d. red	10·00	2·50
167		1s. mauve	13·00	6·00
168		1s. 6d. olive	40·00	32·00

OFFICIAL STAMPS

1931. Optd **O S**.

O55	6	½d. green and olive	1·00	4·75
O56a		1d. black and red	3·75	7·50
O57		1½d. blue and brown	1·40	12·00
O58		2d. brown and purple	2·50	9·00
O59		3d. black and turquoise	2·50	18·00
O60		4d. brown and orange	2·50	16·00
O61		5d. grey and brown	6·00	38·00
O62		6d. purple and red	4·00	8·50
O63		9d. lilac and violet	40·00	55·00
O64		1s. brown and olive	9·00	28·00
O65		1s. 3d. lilac and blue	40·00	55·00
O66		2s. 6d. red and pink	40·00	85·00

PAPUA NEW GUINEA

Combined territory on the island of New Guinea administered by Australia under trusteeship. Self-government was established during 1973.

1952. 12 pence = 1 shilling;
20 shillings = 1 pound.
1966. 100 cents = $1 Australian.
1975. 100 toea = 1 kina.

1 Matschie's Tree Kangaroo

7 Kiriwina Chief House

1952.

1	1	½d. green	30	10
2	–	1d. brown	20	10
3	–	2d. blue	35	10
4	–	2½d. orange	2·00	40
5	–	3d. myrtle	80	10
6	–	3½d. red	60	10
6a	–	3½d. black	8·00	1·50
18	–	4d. red	1·00	10
19	–	5d. green	1·00	10
7	7	6½d. purple	2·00	10
20	–	7d. green	8·00	10
8	–	7½d. blue	3·50	1·50
21	–	8d. blue	1·00	1·50
9	–	9d. brown	4·50	60
10	–	1s. green	2·75	10
11	–	1s. 6d. myrtle	8·00	80
22	–	1s. 7d. brown	17·00	10·00
12	–	2s. blue	7·00	10
23	–	2s. 5d. red	4·75	2·25
13	–	2s. 6d. purple	6·50	40
24	–	5s. red and olive	12·00	1·50
14	–	10s. slate	40·00	13·00
15	–	£1 brown	40·00	13·00

DESIGNS—VERT (as T **1**): 1d. Buka head-dresses; 2d. Native youth; 2½d. Greater bird of paradise; 3d. Native policeman; 3½d. Papuan head-dress; 4d., 5d. Cacao plant. (As T **7**): 7½d. Kiriwina Yam house; 1s. 6d. Rubber tapping; 2s. Sepik dancing masks; 5s. Coffee beans; £1 Papuan shooting fish. HORIZ (as T **7**): 7, 8d. Klinki plymill; 9d. Copra making; 1s. Lakatoi; 1s. 7d., 2s. 5d. Cattle; 2s. 6d. Native shepherd and flock; 10s. Map of Papua and New Guinea.

1957. Nos. 4, 1 and 10 surch.

16	–	4d. on 2½d. orange	70	10
25	1	5d. on ½d. green	1·00	10
17	–	7d. on 1s. green	40	10

23 Council Chamber, Port Moresby

1961. Reconstitution of Legislative Council.

26	23	5d. green and yellow	1·50	25
27		2s. 3d. green and salmon	4·50	1·50

24 Female, Goroka, New Guinea

26 Female Dancer

39 Waterfront, Port Moresby

28 Traffic Policeman

1961.

28	24	1d. lake	1·25	10
29	–	3d. blue	30	10
47	39	8d. green	30	15
30	26	1s. green	4·00	15
31	–	2s. purple	45	15
48	–	2s. 3d. blue	50	30
32	28	3s. green	2·25	1·00

DESIGNS—As Type **24**: 3d. Tribal elder, Tari, Papua. As Type **39**: 2s. 3d. Piaggio P-166B Portofino aircraft landing at Tapini. As Type **26**: 2s. Male dancer.

29 Campaign Emblem

30 Map of South Pacific

1962. Malaria Eradication.

33	29	5d. lake and blue	40	15
34		1s. red and brown	75	25
35		2s. black and green	1·10	70

1962. 5th South Pacific Conf, Pago Pago.

36	30	5d. red and green	65	15
37		1s. 6d. violet and yellow	1·75	70
38		2s. 6d. green and blue	1·75	1·40

31 Throwing the Javelin

1962. 7th British Empire and Commonwealth Games, Perth.

39	31	5d. brown and blue	20	10
40	–	5d. brown and orange	20	10
41	–	2s. 3d. brown and green	1·25	75

SPORTS—As T **31**: No. 40, High jump. 32 × 23 mm: No. 41, Runners.

34 Raggiana Bird of Paradise

37 Queen Elizabeth II

36 Rabaul

40 Games Emblem

1963.

42	34	5d. yellow, brown and sepia	1·50	10
43	–	6d. red, brown and grey	75	90
44	36	10s. multicoloured	15·00	8·50
45	37	£1 brown, gold and green	4·00	2·50

DESIGN—As Type **34**: 6d. Common phalanger.

1963. Cent of Red Cross. As T **163** of Australia.

46	5d. red, grey and green	60	10

1963. 1st South Pacific Games, Suva.

49	40	5d. brown	10	10
50		1s. green	30	20

41 Watam Head

45 Casting Vote

1964. Native Artefacts. Multicoloured.

51	11d. Type **41**	45	10
52	2s. 5d. Watam head (different)	50	75
53	2s. 6d. Bosmun head	50	10
54	5s. Medina head	60	15

1964. Common Roll Elections.

55	45	5d. brown and drab	10	10
56		2s. 3d. brown and blue	20	25

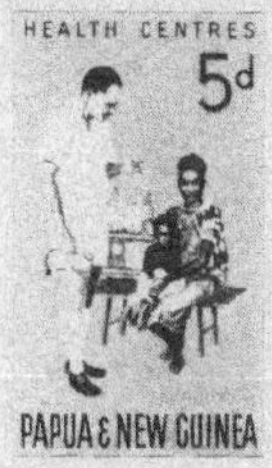

46 "Health Centres"

50 Striped Gardener Bowerbird

1964. Health Services.

57	46	5d. violet	10	10
58	–	8d. green	15	10
59	–	1s. blue	15	10
60	–	1s. 2d. red	35	35

DESIGNS: 8d. "School health"; 1s. "Infant child and maternal health"; 1s. 2d. "Medical training".

1964. Multicoloured.

61	1d. Type **50**	40	10
62	3d. Adelbert bowerbird	50	10
63	5d. Blue bird of paradise	55	10
64	6d. Lawes's parotia	75	10
65	8d. Black-billed sicklebill	1·50	20
66	1s. Emperor of Germany bird of paradise	1·50	10
67	2s. Brown sicklebill	75	30
68	2s. 3d. Lesser bird of paradise	75	85
69	3s. Magnificent bird of paradise	75	1·25
70	5s. Twelve-wired bird of paradise	12·00	2·50
71	10s. Magnificent riflebird	6·00	10·00

Nos. 66/71 are larger, 25½ × 36½ mm.

61 Canoe Prow

1965. Sepik Canoe Prows in Port Moresby Museum.

72	61	4d. multicoloured	50	10
73	–	1s. 2d. multicoloured	2·25	1·50
74	–	1s. 6d. multicoloured	50	10
75	–	4s. multicoloured	1·00	30

Each show different carved prows as Type **61**.

1965. 50th Anniv of Gallipoli Landing. As T **184** of Australia, but slightly larger 22 × 34½ mm.

76	2s. 3d. brown, black and green	20	10

65 Urban Plan and Native House

69 "Papilio ulysses"

66 Mother and Child

1965. 6th South Pacific Conf, Lae.

77	**65** 6d. multicoloured	10	10
78	– 1s. multicoloured	10	10

No. 78 is similar to Type **65** but with the plan on the right and the house on the left. Also "URBANISATION" reads downwards.

1965. 20th Anniv of U.N.O.

79	**66** 6d. sepia, blue and turquoise	10	10
80	– 1s. brown, blue and violet	10	10
81	– 2s. blue, green and olive	10	10

DESIGNS—VERT: 1s. Globe and U.N. emblem; 2s. U.N. emblem and globes.

1966. Decimal Currency. Butterflies. Mult.

82	1 c. Type **69**	40	70
83	3 c. "Cyrestis acilia"	40	70
84	4 c. "Graphium weiskei"	40	70
85	5 c. "Terinos alurgis"	40	10
86	10 c. "Ornithoptera priamus"	50	30
86a	12 c. "Euploea callithoe"	2·25	2·25
87	15 c. "Papilio euchenor"	2·00	80
88	20 c. "Parthenos sylvia"	75	25
89	25 c. "Delias aruna"	1·50	1·00
90	50 c. "Apaturina erminea"	12·00	1·25
91	$1 "Doleschallia dascylus"	4·00	1·50
92	$2 "Ornithoptera paradisea"	6·00	8·50

Nos. 86/92 are horiz.

80 "Molala Harai"

84 Throwing the Discus

1966. Folklore. Elema Art (1st series).

93	**80** 2 c. black and red	10	10
94	– 7 c. black, yellow and blue	10	10
95	– 30 c. black, red and green	15	15
96	– 60 c. black, red and yellow	40	50

DESIGNS: 7 c. "Marai"; 30 c. "Meavea Kivovia"; 60 c. "Toivita Tapaivita".

1966. South Pacific Games, Noumea. Mult.

97	5 c. Type **84**	10	10
98	10 c. Football	15	10
99	20 c. Tennis	20	30

87 "Mucuna novoguineensis"

91 "Fine Arts"

1966. Flowers. Multicoloured.

100	5 c. Type **87**	15	10
101	10 c. "Tecomanthe dendrophila"	15	10
102	20 c. "Rhododendron macgregoriae"	35	10
103	60 c. "Rhododendron konori"	1·00	2·00

1967. Higher Education. Multicoloured.

104	1 c. Type **91**	10	10
105	3 c. "Surveying"	10	10
106	4 c. "Civil Engineering"	10	10
107	5 c. "Science"	10	10
108	20 c. "Law"	10	10

96 "Sagra speciosa"

100 Laloki River

1967. Fauna Conservation (Beetles). Mult.

109	5 c. Type **96**	20	10
110	10 c. "Eupholus schoenherri"	30	10
111	20 c. "Sphingnotus albertisi"	50	10
112	25 c. "Cyphogastra albertisi"	55	10

1967. Laloki River Hydro-Electric Scheme, and "New Industries". Multicoloured.

113	5 c. Type **100**	10	10
114	10 c. Pyrethrum	10	10
115	20 c. Tea plant	15	10
116	25 c. Type **100**	15	10

103 Air Attack at Milne Bay

107 Papuan Lory

1967. 25th Anniv of Pacific War. Mult.

117	2 c. Type **103**	10	50
118	5 c. Kokoda Trail (vert)	10	10
119	20 c. The Coast watchers	25	10
120	50 c. Battle of the Coral Sea	80	70

1967. Christmas. Territory Parrots. Mult.

121	5 c. Type **107**	25	10
122	7 c. Pesquet's parrot	30	90
123	30 c. Dusky lory	70	10
124	25 c. Edward's fig parrot	70	10

111 Chimbu Head-dress

115 "Hyla thesaurensis"

1968. "National Heritage". Designs showing different Head-dresses. Multicoloured.

125	5 c. Type **111**	10	10
126	10 c. Southern Highlands (horiz)	15	10
127	20 c. Western Highlands (horiz)	20	10
128	60 c. Chimbu (different)	70	45

1968. Fauna Conservation (Frogs). Mult.

129	5 c. Type **115**	15	40
130	10 c. "Hyla iris"	15	10
131	15 c. "Ceratobatrachus guentheri"	15	10
132	20 c. "Nyctimystes narinosa"	20	40

119 Human Rights Emblem and Papuan Head-dress (abstract)

1968. Human Rights Year. Multicoloured.

133	5 c. Type **119**	10	20
134	10 c. Human Rights in the World (abstract)	10	10

121 Leadership (abstract)

1968. Universal Suffrage. Multicoloured.

135	20 c. Type **121**	15	20
136	25 c. Leadership of the Community (abstract)	15	20

123 Common Egg Cowrie

1968. Sea Shells. Multicoloured.

137	1 c. Type **123**	10	10
138	3 c. Laciniate conch	30	60
139	4 c. Lithograph cone	20	60
140	5 c. Marbled cone	25	10
141	7 c. Episcopal mitre	35	10
142	10 c. "Cymbiola rutila ruckeri"	45	10
143	12 c. Checkerboard bonnet	1·25	1·50
144	15 c. Scorpion conch	60	70
145	20 c. Fluted giant clam or scale tridacna	70	10
146	25 c. Camp pitar venus	70	40
147	30 c. Ramose murex	90	1·00
148	40 c. Chambered or pearly nautilus	75	1·00
149	60 c. Trumpet triton	80	45
150	$1 Manus green papuina	2·00	1·00
151	$2 Glory of the sea cone	18·00	7·00

138 Tito Myth

142 "Fireball" Class Yacht

1969. Folklore. Elema Art (2nd series).

152	**138** 5 c. black, yellow and red	10	50
153	– 5 c. black, yellow and red	10	50
154	– 10 c. black, grey and red	15	50
155	– 10 c. black, grey and red	15	50

DESIGNS: No. 153, Iko Myth; No. 154, Luvuapo Myth; No. 155, Miro Myth.

1969. 3rd South Pacific Games, Port Moresby.

156	**142** 5 c. black	10	10
157	– 10 c. violet	10	10
158	– 20 c. green	15	15

DESIGNS—HORIZ: 10 c. Swimming pool, Boroko; 20 c. Games arena, Konedobu.

145 "Dendrobium ostrinoglossum"

149 Bird of Paradise

1969. Flora Conservation (Orchids). Multicoloured.

159	5 c. Type **145**	25	10
160	10 c. "Dendrobium lawesii"	35	70
161	20 c. "Dendrobium pseudofrigidum"	45	90
162	30 c. "Dendrobium conanthum"	55	70

1969.

162a	**149** 2 c. blue, black and red	10	15
163	5 c. green, brown & orge	10	10

150 Native Potter

151 Tareko

1969. 50th Anniv of I.L.O.

164	**150** 5 c. multicoloured	10	10

1969. Musical Instruments.

165	**151** 5 c. multicoloured	10	10
166	– 10 c. black, green & yellow	10	10
167	– 25 c. black, yellow & brn	15	15
168	– 30 c. multicoloured	25	15

DESIGNS: 10 c. Garamut; 25 c. Iviliko; 30 c. Kundu.

155 Prehistoric Ambun Stone

159 King of Saxony Bird of Paradise

1970. "National Heritage". Multicoloured.

169	5 c. Type **155**	10	10
170	10 c. Masawa canoe of Kula Circuit	10	10
171	25 c. Torres' map, 1606	40	15
172	30 c. H.M.S. "Basilisk" (paddle-sloop), 1873	65	25

1970. Fauna Conservation. Birds of Paradise. Multicoloured.

173	5 c. Type **159**	1·00	15
174	10 c. King bird of paradise	1·00	60
175	15 c. Raggiana bird of paradise	1·50	1·00
176	25 c. Sickle-crested bird of paradise	1·75	70

163 Douglas DC-6B and Mt. Wilhelm

1970. Australian and New Guinea Air Services. Multicoloured.

177	5 c. Type **163**	30	10
178	5 c. Lockheed Electra and Mt. Yule	30	10
179	5 c. Boeing 727-100 and Mt. Giluwe	30	10
180	5 c. Fokker Friendship and Manam Island	30	10
181	25 c. Douglas DC-3 and Matupi Volcano	70	40
182	30 c. Boeing 707 and Hombrom's Bluff	70	60

169 N. Miklouho-Maclay (scientist) and Effigy

1970. 42nd A.N.Z.A.A.S. Congress, Port Moresby. Multicoloured.

183	5 c. Type **169**	10	10
184	10 c. B. Malinowski (anthropologist) and native hut	20	10
185	15 c. T. Salvadori (ornithologist) and double-wattled cassowary	90	25
186	20 c. F.R.R. Schlechter (botanist) and flower	60	25

A.N.Z.A.A.S. = Australian–New Zealand Association for the Advancement of Science.

170 Wogeo Island Food Bowl

171 Eastern Highlands Dwelling

1970. Native Artefacts. Multicoloured.

187	5 c. Type **170**	10	10
188	10 c. Lime pot	20	10
189	15 c. Albom sago storage pot	20	10
190	30 c. Manus island bowl (horiz)	25	30

1971. Native Dwellings. Multicoloured.

191	5 c. Type **171**	15	10
192	7 c. Milne Bay stilt dwelling	15	50
193	10 c. Purari Delta dwelling	15	10
194	40 c. Sepik dwelling	35	75

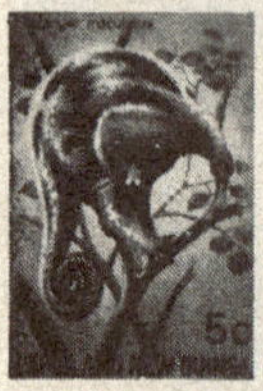

172 Spotted Phalanger

173 "Basketball"

1971. Fauna Conservation. Multicoloured.

195	5 c. Type **172**	30	10
196	10 c. Long-fingered possum	60	15
197	15 c. Feather-tailed possum	1·25	1·00
198	25 c. Long-tailed echidna	1·75	1·00
199	30 c. Ornate tree kangaroo (horiz)	1·75	70

1971. 4th South Pacific Games, Papeete. Multicoloured.

200	7 c. Type **173**	10	10
201	14 c. "Sailing"	15	20
202	21 c. "Boxing"	15	30
203	28 c. "Athletics"	15	40

174 Bartering Fish for Vegetables

175 Sia Dancer

1971. Primary Industries. Multicoloured.

204	7 c. Type **174**	10	10
205	9 c. Man stacking yams	15	30
206	14 c. Vegetable market	25	10
207	30 c. Highlanders cultivating garden	45	65

1971. Native Dancers. Multicoloured.

208	7 c. Type **175**	20	10
209	9 c. Urasena dancer	25	20
210	20 c. Siassi Tubuan dancers (horiz)	60	75
211	28 c. Sia dancers (horiz)	80	90

176 Papuan Flag over Australian Flag

1971. Constitutional Development.

212	**176** 7 c. multicoloured	30	10
213	– 7 c. multicoloured	30	10

DESIGN: No. 213, Crest of Papua New Guinea and Australian coat of arms.

177 Map of Papua New Guinea and Flag of South Pacific Commission

1972. 25th Anniv of South Pacific Commission.

214 **177**	15 c. multicoloured	45	55
215 –	15 c. multicoloured	45	55

DESIGN: No. 215, Man's face and flag of the Commission.

178 Turtle

1972. Fauna Conservation (Reptiles). Mult.

216	7 c. Type **178**	40	10
217	14 c. Rainforest dragon	1·00	1·25
218	21 c. Green python	1·00	1·50
219	30 c. Salvador's monitor	1·25	1·25

179 Curtiss MF-6 Seagull and "Eureka" (schooner)

1972. 50th Anniv of Aviation. Multicoloured.

220	7 c. Type **179**	50	10
221	14 c. De Havilland D.H.37 and native porters	1·00	1·25
222	20 c. Junkers G.31 and gold dredger	1·25	1·25
223	25 c. Junkers F-13 and mission church	1·25	1·25

180 New National Flag **181** Rev. Copland King

1972. National Day. Multicoloured.

224	7 c. Type **180**	20	10
225	10 c. Native drum	25	25
226	30 c. Trumpet triton	45	50

1972. Christmas. Missionaries. Mult.

227	7 c. Type **181**	25	40
228	7 c. Rev. Dr. Flierl	25	40
229	7 c. Bishop Verjus	25	40
230	7 c. Pastor Ruatoka	25	40

182 Mt. Tomavatur Station **183** Queen Carola's Parotia

1973. Completion of Telecommunications Project, 1968–72. Multicoloured.

231	7 c. Type **182**	25	20
232	7 c. Mt. Kerigomma Station	25	20
233	7 c. Sattelburg Station	25	20
234	7 c. Wideru Station	25	20
235	9 c. Teleprinter	25	35
236	30 c. Network map	80	1·00

Nos. 235/6 are larger, 36 × 26 mm

1973. Birds of Paradise. Multicoloured.

237	7 c. Type **183**	1·25	35
238	14 c. Goldie's bird of paradise	2·75	1·25
239	21 c. Ribbon-tailed bird of paradise	3·00	2·00
240	28 c. Princess Stephanie's bird of paradise	4·25	2·50

Nos. 239/40 are size 18 × 49 mm.

184 Wood Carver

1973. Multicoloured.

241	1 c. Type **184**	10	10
242	3 c. Wig-makers	40	10
243	5 c. Mt. Bagana	55	10
244	6 c. Pig exchange	70	90
245	7 c. Coastal village	30	10
246	8 c. Arawe mother	35	30
247	9 c. Fire dancers	30	20
248	10 c. Tifalmin hunter	55	10
249	14 c. Crocodile hunters	45	70
250	15 c. Mt. Elimbari	50	30
251	20 c. Canoe-racing, Manus	1·50	40
252	21 c. Making sago	50	80
253	25 c. Council House	50	45
254	28 c. Menyamya bowmen	50	75
255	30 c. Shark-snaring	50	50
256	40 c. Fishing canoes, Madang	50	40
257	60 c. Tapa cloth-making	55	50
258	$1 Asaro Mudmen	1·00	1·10
259	$2 Enga "Sing Sing"	3·50	6·00

185 Stamps of German New Guinea, 1897

1973. 75th Anniv of Papua New Guinea Stamps.

260 **185**	1 c. multicoloured	15	15
261 –	6 c. indigo, blue and silver	25	35
262 –	7 c. multicoloured	25	35
263 –	9 c. multicoloured	25	45
264 –	25 c. orange and gold	50	1·00
265 –	30 c. plum and silver	55	1·25

DESIGNS—As Type **185**: 6 c. 2 mark stamp of German New Guinea, 1900; 7 c. Surcharged registration label of New Guinea, 1914. 46 × 35 mm: 9 c. Papuan 1s. stamp, 1901. 45 × 38 mm: 25 c. ½d. stamp of New Guinea, 1925; 30 c. Papuan 10s. stamp, 1932.

186 Native Carved Heads **187** Queen Elizabeth II (from photo by Karsh)

1973. Self-Government.

266 **186**	7 c. multicoloured	30	15
267	10 c. multicoloured	50	65

1974. Royal Visit.

268 **187**	7 c. multicoloured	25	15
269	30 c. multicoloured	75	1·50

188 Blyth's Hornbill

1974. Birds' Heads. Multicoloured.

270	7 c. Type **188**	2·00	70
271	10 c. Double-wattled cassowary (33 × 49 mm)	3·00	3·25
272	30 c. New Guinea harpy eagle	7·00	8·50

189 "Dendrobium bracteosum" **191** 1-toea Coin

190 Motu Lakatoi

1974. Flora Conservation. Multicoloured.

273	7 c. Type **189**	50	10
274	10 c. "D. anosmum"	60	50
275	20 c. "D. smillieae"	75	1·25
276	30 c. "D. insigne"	1·00	1·75

1974. National Heritage. Canoes. Mult.

277	7 c. Type **190**	30	10
278	10 c. Tami two-master morobe	50	70
279	25 c. Aramia racing canoe	1·00	2·50
280	30 c. Buka Island canoe	1·00	1·25

1975. New Coinage. Multicoloured.

281	1 t. Type **191**	10	10
282	7 t. New 2 t. and 5 t. coins	50	10
283	10 t. New 10 t. coin	50	30
284	20 t. New 20 t. coin	90	80
285	1 k. New 1 k. coin	2·75	4·00

SIZES: 10, 20 t. As Type **191**; 7 t., 1 k. 45 × 26 mm.

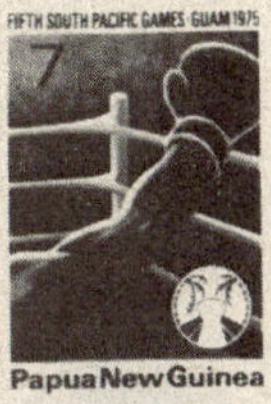

192 "Ornithoptera alexandrae" **193** Boxing

1975. Fauna Conservation (Birdwing Butterflies). Multicoloured.

286	7 t. Type **192**	50	10
287	10 t. "O. victoriae"	60	65
288	30 t. "O. allottei"	1·00	2·00
289	40 t. "O. chimaera"	1·25	3·25

1975. 5th South Pacific Games, Guam. Multicoloured.

290	7 t. Type **193**	15	10
291	20 t. Running	25	30
292	25 t. Basketball	30	45
293	30 t. Swimming	35	50

194 Map and National Flag

1975. Independence. Multicoloured.

294	7 t. Type **194**	20	10
295	30 t. Map and National emblem	40	65

195 M.V. "Bulolo"

1976. Ships of the 1930's. Multicoloured.

297	7 t. Type **195**	35	10
298	15 t. M.V. "Macdhui"	45	30
299	25 t. M.V. "Malaita"	60	65
300	60 t. S.S. "Montoro"	1·25	2·50

196 Rorovana Carvings

1976. Bougainville Art. Multicoloured.

301	7 t. Type **196**	15	10
302	20 t. Upe hats	30	50
303	25 t. Kapkaps	35	60
304	30 t. Canoe paddles	40	90

197 Rabaul House

1976. Native Dwellings. Multicoloured.

305	7 t. Type **197**	15	10
306	15 t. Aramia house	25	30
307	30 t. Telefomin house	50	75
308	40 t. Tapini house	55	1·25

198 Landscouts

1976. 50th Annivs of Survey Flight and Scouting in Papua New Guinea. Multicoloured.

309	7 t. Type **198**	30	10
310	10 t. De Havilland D.H.50A seaplane	30	30
311	15 t. Seascouts	40	65
312	60 t. De Havilland D.H.50A seaplane on water	1·00	2·50

199 Father Ross and New Guinea Highlands

1976. William Ross Commemoration.

313 **199**	7 t. multicoloured	40	15

200 Picture Wrasse

1976. Fauna Conservation (Tropical Fish). Multicoloured.

314	5 t. Type **200**	30	10
315	15 t. Emperor angelfish	60	45
316	30 t. Six-blotched hind	1·10	80
317	40 t. Thread-finned butterflyfish	1·40	1·10

201 Man from Kundiawa **202** Headdress, Wasara Tribe

1977. Headdresses. Multicoloured.

318	1 t. Type **201**	10	10
319	5 t. Masked dancer, Abelam area of Maprik	10	10
320	10 t. Headdress from Koiari	30	15
321	15 t. Woman with face paint, Hanuabada	30	20
322	20 t. Orokaiva dancer	50	30
323	25 t. Haus Tambaran dancer, Abelam area of Maprik	40	30
324	30 t. Asaro Valley headdress	45	35
325	35 t. Singsing costume, Garaina	70	45
326	40 t. Waghi Valley headdress	60	35
327	50 t. Trobriand Island dancer	1·00	60
328	1 k. Type **202**	1·00	1·50
329	2 k. Headdress, Meko tribe	1·75	3·00

SIZES: 1, 5, 20 t. 25 × 31 mm; 35, 40 t. 23 × 38 mm; 1 k. 28 × 35 mm; 2 k. 33 × 23 mm; Others 26 × 26 mm.

203 National Flag and Queen Elizabeth II

1977. Silver Jubilee. Multicoloured.

330	7 t. Type **203**	20	10
331	15 t. The Queen and national emblem	25	35
332	35 t. The Queen and map of P.N.G.	40	70

204 White-breasted Ground Pigeon

1977. Fauna Conservation (Birds). Mult.

333	5 t. Type **204**	35	10
334	7 t. Victoria crowned pigeon	35	10
335	15 t. Pheasant pigeon	65	65
336	30 t. Orange-fronted fruit dove	1·00	1·10
337	50 t. Banded imperial pigeon	1·60	3·50

205 Guides and Gold Badge

206 Kari Marupi Myth

1977. 50th Anniv of Guiding in Papua New Guinea. Multicoloured.

338 7 t. Type **205** 20 10
339 15 t. Guides mapping 35 20
340 30 t. Guides washing 55 50
341 35 t. Guides cooking 60 60

1977. Folklore. Elema Art (3rd series).

342 **206** 7 t. multicoloured 15 10
343 – 20 t. multicoloured 35 35
344 – 30 t. red, blue and black 40 75
345 – 35 t. red, yellow and black 40 75

DESIGNS: 20 t. Savoripi clan myth; 30 t. Oa-Laea myth; 35 t. Oa-Iriarapo myth.

207 Blue-tailed Skink

1978. Fauna Conservation (Skinks). Mult.

346 10 t. Type **207** 25 10
347 15 t. Green tree skink 30 25
348 35 t. Crocodile skink 45 70
349 40 t. New Guinea blue-tongued skink 60 85

208 "Roboastra arika"

1978. Sea Slugs. Multicoloured.

350 10 t. Type **208** 20 10
351 15 t. "Chromodoris fidelis" 25 30
352 35 t. "Flabellina macassarana" 45 85
353 40 t. "Chromodoris marginata" 50 1·00

209 Present Day Royal Papua New Guinea Constabulary

1978. History of Royal Papua New Guinea Constabulary. Uniformed Police and Constabulary Badges. Multicoloured.

354 10 t. Type **209** 20 10
355 15 t. Mandated New Guinea Constabulary, 1921–1941 30 15
356 20 t. British New Guinea Armed Constabulary, 1890–1906 35 40
357 25 t. German New Guinea Police, 1899–1914 35 45
358 30 t. Royal Papua and New Guinea Constabulary, 1906–1964 40 60

210 Ocarina

211 East New Britain Canoe Prow

1979. Musical Instruments. Multicoloured.

359 7 t. Type **210** 10 10
360 20 t. Musical bow (horiz) 20 20
361 28 t. Launut 25 30
362 35 t. Nose flute (horiz) 30 45

1979. Traditional Canoe Prows and Paddles. Multicoloured.

363 14 t. Type **211** 20 15
364 21 t. Sepik war canoe 30 25
365 25 t. Trobriand Island canoe 30 30
366 40 t. Milne Bay canoe 40 60

212 Katudababila (waist belt)

213 "Aenetus cyanochlora"

1979. Traditional Currency. Multicoloured.

367 7 t. Type **212** 10 10
368 15 t. Doga (chest ornament) 20 30
369 25 t. Mwali (armshell) 35 55
370 35 t. Soulava (necklace) 45 75

1979. Fauna Conservation. Moths. Multicoloured.

371 7 t. Type **213** 20 10
372 15 t. "Celerina vulgaris" 30 35
373 20 t. "Alcidis aurora" (vert) 40 65
374 25 t. "Phyllodes conspicillator" 45 80
375 30 t. "Lyssa patroclus" (vert) 55 90

214 "The Right to Affection and Love"

216 Detail from Betrothal Ceremony Mural, Minj District, Western Highlands Province

215 "Post Office Service"

1979. International Year of the Child. Multicoloured.

376 7 t. Type **214** 10 10
377 15 t. "The right to adequate nutrition and medical care" 15 15
378 30 t. "The right to play" 20 20
379 60 t. "The right to a free education" 45 60

1980. Admission to U.P.U. (1979). Multicoloured.

380 7 t. Type **215** 10 10
381 25 t. "Wartime mail" 25 25
382 35 t. "U.P.U. emblem 35 40
383 40 t. "Early postal services" 40 50

1980. South Pacific Festival of Arts.

384 **216** 20 t. yellow, orange & blk 25 35
385 – 20 t. mult (two figures, left-hand in black and yellow; right-hand in black, yellow and red) 25 35
386 – 20 t. mult (two figures, left-hand in black and orange; right-hand in black) 25 35
387 – 20 t. mult (two figures, one behind the other) 25 35
388 – 20 t. mult (one figure) 25 35

DESIGNS: Nos. 385/8, further details of Betrothal Ceremony. Nos. 384/8 were issued together in horizontal se-tenant strips of five within the sheet, forming a composite design.

217 Family being Interviewed

1980. National Census. Multicoloured.

389 7 t. Type **217** 10 10
390 15 t. Population symbol 15 15
391 40 t. Papua New Guinea map 30 40
392 50 t. Heads symbolising population growth 35 50

218 Donating Blood

219 Dugong

1980. Red Cross Blood Bank. Multicoloured.

393 7 t. Type **218** 15 10
394 15 t. Receiving transfusion 20 20
395 30 t. Map of Papua New Guinea showing blood transfusion centres 25 25
396 60 t. Blood and its components 40 60

1980. Mammals. Multicoloured.

397 7 t. Type **219** 10 10
398 30 t. New Guinea marsupial cat (vert) 30 45
399 35 t. Tube-nosed bat (vert) 30 45
400 45 t. Rufescent bandicoot 40 55

220 White-headed Kingfisher

221 Native Mask

1981. Kingfishers. Multicoloured.

401 3 t. Type **220** 30 60
402 7 t. Forest kingfisher 30 10
403 20 t. Sacred kingfisher 70 50
404 25 t. White-tailed kingfisher (26 × 46 mm) 70 85
405 60 t. Blue-winged kookaburra 1·40 3·00

1981.

406 **221** 2 t. violet and orange 10 20
407 – 5 t. red and green 10 20

DESIGN: 5 t. Hibiscus flower.

222 Mortar Team

1981. Defence Force. Multicoloured.

408 7 t. Type **222** 15 10
409 15 t. Douglas DC-3 and aircrew 25 25
410 40 t. "Aitape" (patrol boat) and seamen 45 65
411 50 t. Medical team examining children 50 75

223 M.A.F. (Missionary Aviation Fellowship) Cessna Super Skywagon

224 Scoop Net Fishing

1981. "Mission Aviation". Multicoloured.

412 10 t. Type **223** 20 10
413 15 t. Catholic mission British Aircraft Swallow "St. Paulus" 25 15
414 20 t. S.I.L. (Summer Institute of Linguistics) Hiller 12E helicopter 25 25
415 30 t. Lutheran mission Junkers F-13 35 40
416 35 t. S.D.A. (Seventh Day Adventist Church) Piper PA-23 Aztec 35 55

1981. Fishing. Multicoloured.

417 10 t. Type **224** 15 10
418 15 t. Kite fishing 20 30
419 30 t. Rod fishing 30 50
420 60 t. Scissor net fishing 55 85

225 Buhler's Papuina

1981. Land Snail Shells. Multicoloured.

421 5 t. Type **225** 10 10
422 15 t. Yellow naninia 20 25
423 20 t. Adonis papuina and Hermoine papuina 25 35
424 30 t. Hinde's papuina and New Pommeranian papuina 35 50
425 40 t. "Papuina strabo" 50 80

226 Lord Baden-Powell and Flag-raising Ceremony

227 Yangoru and Boiken Bowls, East Sepik

1981. 75th Anniv of Boy Scout Movement. Multicoloured.

426 15 t. Type **226** 20 15
427 25 t. Scout leader and camp 25 30
428 35 t. Scout and hut building 35 45
429 50 t. Percy Chaterton and Scouts administering first aid 50 75

1981. Native Pottery. Multicoloured.

430 10 t. Type **227** 10 10
431 20 t. Utu cooking pot and small Gumalu pot, Madang 20 30
432 40 t. Wanigela pots, Northern (37 × 23 mm) 40 55
433 50 t. Ramu Valley pots, Madang (37 × 23 mm) 45 80

228 "Eat Healthy Foods"

1982. Food and Nutrition. Multicoloured.

434 10 t. Type **228** 10 10
435 15 t. Protein foods 20 30
436 30 t. Protective foods 40 55
437 40 t. Energy foods 45 70

229 "Stylophora sp."

1982. Multicoloured.

438 1 t. Type **229** 10 20
439 3 t. "Dendrophyllia sp." (vert) 60 60
440 5 t. "Acropora humilis" 15 10
441 10 t. "Dendronephthya sp." (vert) 80 30
442 12 t. As 10 t. 4·00 4·75
443 15 t. "Distichopora sp.." 30 20
444 20 t. "Isis sp" (vert) 90 25
445 25 t. "Acropora sp." (vert) 40 50
446 30 t. "Dendronephthya sp" (different) (vert) 1·50 90
447 35 t. "Stylaster elegans" (vert) 1·40 50
448 40 t. "Antipathes sp." (vert) 2·00 75
449 45 t. "Turbinarea sp." (vert) 2·50 50
450 1 k. "Xenia sp." 1·25 85
451 3 k. "Distichopora sp." (vert) 3·75 3·50
452 5 k. Raggiana bird of paradise (33 × 33 mm) 7·00 8·00

230 Missionaries landing on Beach

231 Athletics

1982. Centenary of Catholic Church in Papua New Guinea. Mural on Wall of Nordup Catholic Church, East New Britain. Multicoloured.

457 10 t. Type **230** 20 30
458 10 t. Missionaries talking to natives 20 30
459 10 t. Natives with slings and spears ready to attack 20 30

Nos. 457/9 were issued together, se-tenant, forming a composite design.

1982. Commonwealth Games and "Anpex 82" Stamp Exhibition, Brisbane. Multicoloured.

460 10 t. Type **231** 15 10
461 15 t. Boxing 20 25
462 45 t. Rifle-shooting 40 70
463 50 t. Bowls 45 75

232 National Flag

1983. Commonwealth Day. Multicoloured.

464	10 t. Type **232**	15	10
465	15 t. Basket-weaving and cabbage-picking	20	30
466	20 t. Crane hoisting roll of material	25	35
467	50 t. Lorries and ships	60	75

233 Transport Communications

1983. World Communications Year. Multicoloured.

468	10 t. Type **233**	30	10
469	25 t. "Postal service"	50	25
470	30 t. "Telephone service"	55	30
471	60 t. "Transport service"	1·10	90

234 "Chelonia depressa"

1984. Turtles. Multicoloured.

472	5 t. Type **234**	20	10
473	10 t. "Chelonia mydas"	30	10
474	15 t. "Eretmochelys imbricata"	40	30
475	20 t. "Lepidochelys olivacea"	50	35
476	25 t. " Caretta caretta"	55	50
477	40 t. "Dermochelys coriacea"	80	75

235 Avro Type 618 Ten "Faith in Australia"

237 Ceremonial Shield and Club, Central Province

236 Parliament House

1984. 50th Anniv of First Airmail Australia–Papua New Guinea. Multicoloured.

478	20 t. Type **235**	40	30
479	25 t. De Havilland Dragon Express "Carmania"	40	45
480	40 t. Westland Widgeon	65	80
481	60 t. Consolidated PBY-5 Catalina flying boat	1·00	1·25

1984. Opening of New Parliament House.

482	**236** 10 t. multicoloured	30	30

1984. Ceremonial Shields. Multicoloured.

483	10 t. Type **237**	25	10
484	20 t. Ceremonial shield, West New Britain	40	50
485	30 t. Ceremonial shield, Madang Province	60	1·00
486	50 t. Ceremonial shield, East Sepik	1·00	2·75

See also Nos. 558/61.

238 H.M.S. "Nelson" at Port Moresby, 1884

239 Fergusson Island

1984. Centenary of Protectorate Proclamations for British New Guinea and German New Guinea. Multicoloured.

487	10 t. Type **238**	35	55
488	10 t. Papua New Guinea flag and Port Moresby, 1984	35	55
489	45 t. Papua New Guinea flag and Rabaul, 1984	75	1·90
490	45 t. German warship "Elizabeth" at Rabaul, 1884	75	1·90

Nos. 487/8 and 489/90 were issued in se-tenant pairs, each pair forming a composite picture.

1985. Tourist Scenes. Multicoloured.

491	10 t. Type **239**	25	10
492	25 t. Sepik River	50	60
493	40 t. Chimbu George (horiz)	75	1·25
494	60 t. Dali Beach, Vanimo (horiz)	1·25	1·75

1985. No. 408 surch **12t**.

495	**222** 12 t. on 7 t. multicoloured	60	75

241 Dubu Platform, Central Province

242 Head of New Britain Sparrow Hawk

1985. Ceremonial Structures. Multicoloured.

496	15 t. Type **241**	35	15
497	20 t. Tamuniai house, West New Britain	50	50
498	30 t. Traditional yam tower, Trobriand Island	65	80
499	60 t. Huli grave, Tari	1·00	1·75

1985. Birds of Prey. Multicoloured.

500	12 t. Type **242**	70	1·50
501	12 t. New Britain sparrow hawk in flight	70	1·50
502	30 t. Doria's goshawk	1·00	1·75
503	30 t. Doria's goshawk in flight	1·00	1·75
504	60 t. Long-tailed honey buzzard	1·50	2·25
505	60 t. Long-tailed honey buzzard in flight	1·50	2·25

243 National Flag and Parliament House

244 Early Postcard, Aerogramme, Inkwell and Spectacles

1985. 10th Anniv of Independence.

506	**243** 12 t. multicoloured	60	70

1985. Centenary of Papua New Guinea Post Office. Multicoloured.

507	12 t. Type **244**	45	10
508	30 t. Queensland 1897 1d. die with proof and modern press printing stamps	1·10	1·00
509	40 t. Newspaper of 1885 announcing shipping service and loading mail into aircraft	1·75	2·00
510	60 t. Friedrich-Wilhelmshafen postmark of 1892 and Port Moresby F.D.C postmark of 9 Oct 1985	2·00	3·50

245 Figure with Eagle

246 Valentine or Prince Cowrie

1985. Nombowai Wood Carvings. Mult.

512	12 t. Type **245**	50	10
513	30 t. Figure with clam shell	1·25	75
514	60 t. Figure with dolphin	2·00	2·75
515	80 t. Figure of woman with cockerel	2·50	4·75

1986. Sea Shells. Multicoloured.

516	15 t. Type **246**	75	15
517	35 t. Bulow's olive	1·60	1·40
518	45 t. Parkinson's olive	2·00	2·00
519	70 t. Golden cowrie	2·50	5·25

1986. 60th Birthday of Queen Elizabeth II. As T **110** of Ascension. Multicoloured.

520	15 t. Princess Elizabeth in A.T.S. uniform, 1945	20	15
521	35 t. Silver Wedding Anniversary photograph (by Patrick Lichfield), Balmoral, 1972	35	40
522	50 t. Queen inspecting guard of honour, Port Moresby, 1982	55	75
523	60 t. On board Royal Yacht "Britannia", Papua New Guinea, 1982	75	90
524	70 t. At Crown Agents' Head Office, London 1983	75	1·10

247 Rufous Fantail

248 Martin Luther nailing Theses to Cathedral Door, Wittenberg and Modern Lutheran Pastor

1986. "Ameripex '86" International Stamp Exhibition, Chicago. Small Birds (1st series). Multicoloured.

525	15 t. Type **247**	90	30
526	35 t. Streaked berry pecker	1·75	1·25
527	45 t. Red-breasted pitta	1·90	1·25
528	70 t. Olive-yellow robin (vert)	2·50	5·50

See also Nos. 597/601.

1986. Centenary of Lutheran Church in Papua New Guinea. Multicoloured.

529	15 t. Type **248**	75	15
530	70 t. Early church, Finschhafen, and modern Martin Luther Chapel, Lae Seminary	2·25	3·25

249 "Dendrobium vexillarius"

250 Maprik Dancer

1986. Orchids. Multicoloured.

531	15 t. Type **249**	95	20
532	35 t. "Dendrobium lineale"	2·00	75
533	45 t. "Dendrobium johnsoniae"	2·00	1·10
534	70 t. "Dendrobium cuthbertsonii"	2·75	4·00

1986. Papua New Guinea Dancers. Multicoloured.

535	15 t. Type **250**	65	15
536	35 t. Kiriwina	1·40	80
537	45 t. Kundiawa	1·50	95
538	70 t. Fasu	2·40	3·25

251 White-bonnet Anemonefish

1987. Anemonefish. Mult.

539	17 t. Type **251**	70	25
540	30 t. Orange-finned anemonefish	1·40	1·10
541	35 t. Fire anemonefish ("Tomato clownfish")	1·50	1·40
542	70 t. Spine-cheeked anemonefish	2·50	5·50

252 "Roebuck" (Dampier), 1700

1987. Ships. Multicoloured.

543	1 t. "La Boudeuse" (De Bougainville, 1768)	50	90
544	5 t. Type **252**	70	1·00
545	10 t. H.M.S. "Swallow" (Philip Carteret), 1767	1·00	1·00
546	15 t. H.M.S. "Fly" (Blackwood), 1845	1·00	80
547	17 t. As 15 t.	1·00	40
548	20 t. H.M.S. "Rattlesnake" (Owen Stanley), 1849	1·00	90
549	30 t. "Vitiaz" (Maclay), 1871	1·40	1·75
550	35 t. "San Pedrico" (Torres) and zabra, 1606	70	60
551	40 t. "L'Astrolabe" (D'Urville), 1827	1·75	2·00
552	45 t. "Neva" (D. Albertis), 1876	75	1·00
553	60 t. Spanish galleon (Jorge de Meneses), 1526	2·50	3·25
554	70 t. "Eendracht" (Schouten and Le Maire), 1616	1·75	2·25
555	1 k. H.M.S. "Blanche" (Simpson), 1872	2·50	2·75
556	2 k. "Merrie England" (steamer), 1889	3·25	2·75
557	3 k. "Samoa" (German colonial steamer), 1884	4·00	5·50

For some of these designs redrawn for "Australia '99" World Stamp Exhibition see Nos. 853/6.

1987. War Shields. As T **237**. Multicoloured.

558	15 t. Gulf Province	20	25
559	35 t. East Sepik	45	50
560	45 t. Madang Province	55	60
561	70 t. Telefomin	85	90

1987. No. 442 surch **15t**.

562	15 t. on 12 t. "Dendronephthya sp." (vert)	65	65

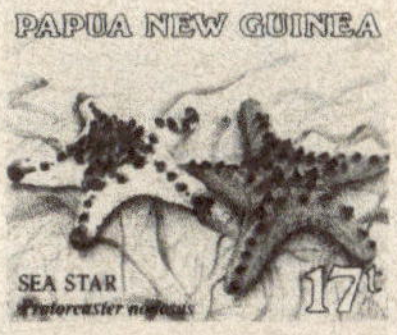

254 "Protoreaster nodosus"

1987. Starfish. Multicoloured.

563	17 t. Type **254**	55	25
564	35 t. "Gomophia egeriae"	1·10	70
565	45 t. "Choriaster granulatus"	1·25	80
566	70 t. "Neoferdina ocellata"	1·75	2·75

255 Cessna Stationair 6 taking off, Rabaraba

1987. Aircraft in Papua New Guinea. Multicoloured.

567	15 t. Type **255**	80	25
568	35 t. Britten Norman Islander over Hombrum Bluff	1·50	75
569	45 t. De Havilland Twin Otter 100 over Highlands	1·50	90
570	70 t. Fokker F.28 Fellowship over Madang	2·50	3·75

256 Pre-Independence Policeman on Traffic Duty and Present-day Motorcycle Patrol

1988. Centenary of Royal Papua New Guinea Constabulary. Multicoloured.

571	17 t. Type **256**	45	25
572	35 t. British New Guinea Armed Constabulary, 1890, and Governor W. MacGregor	80	50
573	45 t. Police badges	90	65
574	70 t. German New Guinea Police 1888, and Dr. A Hahl (founder)	1·50	1·75

257 Lakatoi (canoe) and Sydney Opera House

1988. "Sydpex '88" Nat Stamp Exn, Sydney.

575	**257** 35 t. multicoloured	80	65

258 Papua New Guinea Flag on Globe and Fireworks

1988. Bicent of Australian Settlement. Mult.

576	35 t. Type **258**	55	75
577	35 t. Australian flag on globe and fireworks	55	75

Nos. 576/7 were printed together, se-tenant, forming a composite design.

MINIMUM PRICE

The minimum price quoted is 10p which represents a handling charge rather than a basis for valuing common stamps. For further notes about prices see introductory pages.

259 Male and Female Butterflies in Courtship

1988. Endangered Species. "Ornithoptera alexandrae" (butterfly). Multicoloured.

579 5 t. Type **259** 85 50
580 17 t. Female laying eggs and mature larva (vert) . . . . 1·75 40
581 25 t. Male emerging from pupa (vert) . . . . 2·50 2·50
582 35 t. Male feeding . . . . . . 3·00 2·75

260 Athletics

1988. Olympic Games, Seoul. Multicoloured.

583 17 t. Type **260** 20 25
584 45 t. Weightlifting 60 65

261 "Rhododendron zoelleri"

263 Writing Letter

1989. Rhododendrons. Multicoloured.

585 3 t. Type **261** 10 10
586 20 t. "Rhododendron cruttwellii" 50 30
587 60 t. "Rhododendron superbum" 1·25 1·25
588 70 t. "Rhododendron christianae" . . . . 1·50 1·50

1989. Int Letter Writing Week. Mult.

589 20 t. Type **263** 30 30
590 35 t. Stamping letter 55 50
591 60 t. Posting letter . . . . . . 90 1·10
592 70 t. Reading letter . . . . . 1·10 1·40

264 Village House, Buka Island, North Solomons

1989. Traditional Dwellings. Multicoloured.

593 20 t. Type **264** 40 35
594 35 t. Tree house, Koiari, Central Province 70 60
595 60 t. Longhouse, Lauan, New Ireland . . . . 1·25 1·40
596 70 t. Decorated house, Basilaki, Milne Bay . . . . 1·50 1·60

265 Tit Berrypecker (female)

266 Motu Motu Dancer, Gulf Province

1989. Small Birds (2nd issue). Multicoloured.

597 20 t. Type **265** . . . . 1·00 1·00
598 20 t. Tit berrypecker (male) . . 1·00 1·00
599 35 t. Blue-capped babbler . . 1·50 80
600 45 t. Black-throated robin . . 1·50 1·00
601 70 t. Large mountain sericornis 2·25 2·50

1989. No. 539 surch **20t**.

602 20 t. on 17 t. Type **251** 60 70

1989. Traditional Dancers. Multicoloured.

603 20 t. Type **266** 65 35
604 35 t. Baining, East New Britain 1·10 90
605 60 t. Vailala River, Gulf Province 2·00 2·25
606 70 t. Timbunke, East Sepik Province . . . . 2·00 2·50

267 Hibiscus, People going to Church and Gope Board

268 Guni Falls

1989. Christmas. Designs showing flowers and carved panels. Multicoloured.

607 20 t. Type **267** 40 35
608 35 t. Rhododendron, Virgin and Child and mask 60 60
609 60 t. D'Albertis creeper, Christmas candle and war shield . . . . 1·25 1·60
610 70 t. Pacific frangipani, peace dove and flute mask . . . 1·40 1·90

1990. Waterfalls. Multicoloured.

611 20 t. Type **268** 60 35
612 35 t. Rouna Falls 85 75
613 60 t. Ambua Falls . . . . . 1·40 1·50
614 70 t. Wawoi Falls . . . . . . 1·60 1·75

269 Boys and Census Form

270 Gwa Pupi Dance Mask

1990. National Census. Multicoloured.

615 20 t. Type **269** 40 30
616 70 t. Family and census form . 1·50 2·00

1990. Gogodala Dance Masks. Multicoloured.

617 20 t. Type **270** 80 30
618 35 t. Tauga paiyale . . . . . 1·25 70
619 60 t. A: ga . . . . 2·00 3·00
620 70 t. Owala . . . . 2·00 3·25

271 Sepik and Maori Kororu Masks

272 Dwarf Cassowary and Great Spotted Kiwi

1990. "New Zealand 1990" International Stamp Exhibition, Auckland.

621 **271** 35 t. multicoloured . . . 75 75

1990. 150th Anniv of Treaty of Waitangi. Multicoloured.

622 20 t. Type **272** . . . . 1·25 50
623 35 t. Double-wattled cassowary and brown kiwi . . . . . 1·50 1·50

273 Whimbrel

1990. Migratory Birds. Multicoloured.

624 20 t. Type **273** 85 40
625 35 t. Sharp-tailed sandpiper . 1·25 80
626 60 t. Turnstone . . . . . . 2·25 3·00
627 70 t. Terek sandpiper . . . . 2·50 3·00

274 Jew's Harp

1990. Musical Instruments. Multicoloured.

628 20 t. Type **274** 60 30
629 35 t. Musical bow 90 50
630 60 t. Wantoat drum . . . . . 1·75 2·25
631 70 t. Gogodala rattle . . . . 1·75 2·50

275 Weigman's Papuina

276 Magnificent Riflebird

1991. Land Shells. Multicoloured.

632 21 t. Type **275** 65 30
633 40 t. "Papuina globula" and "Papuina azonata" . . . . . 1·00 85
634 50 t. "Planispira deaniana" . . 1·40 1·60
635 80 t. Chance's papuina and golden-mouth papuina . . . 2·00 2·75

1991. Birds of Paradise. Multicoloured. (a) Face values shown as "t" or "K".

636 1 t. Type **276** 15 40
637 5 t. Loria's bird of paradise . . 20 40
638 10 t. Sickle crested bird of paradise 20 40
639 20 t. Wahnes' parotia 50 30
640 21 t. Crinkle-collared manucode 70 30
641 30 t. Goldie's bird of paradise 30 40
642 40 t. Wattle-billed bird of paradise 40 50
643 45 t. King bird of paradise . . 2·75 80
644 50 t. Short-tailed paradigalla bird of paradise 50 55
645 60 t. Queen Carola's parotia 4·50 2·75
646 90 t. Emperor of Germany bird of paradise . . . . 5·00 4·00
647 1 k. Magnificent bird of paradise 1·75 1·75
648 2 k. Superb bird of paradise . . 1·90 2·00
649 5 k. Trumpet bird . . . . . . 7·00 9·00
650 10 k. Lesser bird of paradise (32 × 32 mm) . . . . 10·00 12·00

(b) Face values shown as "T".

650a 21 t. Crinkle-collared manucode 90 40
650b 45 t. King bird of paradise . . 2·00 1·00
650c 60 t. Queen Carola's parotia . 2·25 2·25
650d 90 t. Emperor of Germany bird of paradise . . . . 2·75 3·50

For designs as Nos. 642, 644 and 647/8 but without "1992 BIRD OF PARADISE" at foot, see Nos. 704/7.

277 Cricket

1991. 9th South Pacific Games. Multicoloured.

651 21 t. Type **277** . . . . 1·50 40
652 40 t. Athletics . . . . 1·50 1·00
653 50 t. Baseball . . . . 1·75 2·25
654 80 t. Rugby Union . . . . . 2·50 4·00

278 Cathedral of St. Peter and St. Paul, Dogura

279 Rambusto Headdress, Manus Province

1991. Cent of Anglican Church in Papua New Guinea. Multicoloured.

655 21 t. Type **278** 70 30
656 40 t. Missionaries landing, 1891, and Kaieta shrine . . . . . 1·40 1·40
657 80 t. First church and Modawa tree . . . . 2·25 3·50

1991. Tribal Headdresses. Multicoloured.

658 21 t. Type **279** 60 30
659 40 t. Marawaka, Eastern Highlands . . . . 1·10 1·40
660 50 t. Tufi, Oro Province . . . 1·25 1·60
661 80 t. Sina Sina, Simbu Province 2·00 3·25

280 "Nina"

281 Canow Prow Shield, Bamu

1992. 500th Anniv of Discovery of America by Columbus and "EXPO '92" World's Fair, Seville. Multicoloured.

662 21 t. Type **280** 60 30
663 45 t. "Pinta" . . . . 1·25 1·00
664 60 t. "Santa Maria" . . . . . 1·75 2·00
665 90 t. Christopher Columbus and ships . . . . 2·25 3·00

1992. Papuan Gulf Artifacts. Multicoloured.

667 21 t. Type **281** 40 30
668 45 t. Skull rack, Kerewa . . . 85 75
669 60 t. Ancestral figure, Era River 1·25 1·50
670 90 t. Gope (spirit) board, Urama 1·60 2·50

282 Papuan Infantryman

283 "Hibiscus tiliaceus"

1992. 50th Anniv of Second World War Campaigns in Papua New Guinea. Multicoloured.

671 21 t. Type **282** 60 30
672 45 t. Australian militiaman . . 1·25 90
673 60 t. Japanese infantryman . . 1·75 2·25
674 90 t. American infantryman . . 2·50 3·50

1992. Flowering Trees. Multicoloured.

675 21 t. Type **283** 65 30
676 45 t. "Castanospermum australe" . . . . 1·50 1·00
677 60 t. "Cordia subcordata" . . 2·50 2·75
678 90 t. "Acacia auriculiformis" . 2·75 4·00

284 Three-striped Dasyure

285 Rufous Wren Warbler

1993. Mammals. Multicoloured.

679 21 t. Type **284** 40 30
680 45 t. Striped bandicoot 90 80
681 60 t. Dusky black-eared giant rat 1·25 1·50
682 90 t. Painted ringtail possum . 1·75 2·50

1993. Small Birds. Multicoloured.

683 21 t. Type **285** 45 30
684 45 t. Superb pitta 90 80
685 60 t. Mottled whistler . . . . 1·25 1·50
686 90 t. Slaty-chinned longbill . . 1·60 2·50

1993. "Taipei '93" Asian Int Stamp Exn, Taiwan. Nos. 683/6 optd **TAIPEI'93** and emblem.

687 21 t. Type **285** 55 30
688 45 t. Superb pitta . . . . . . 1·00 80
689 60 t. Mottled whistler . . . . 1·40 2·00
690 90 t. Slaty-chinned longbill . . 2·00 2·75

287 Thread-finned Rainbowfish

1993. Freshwater Fishes. Multicoloured.

691 21 t. Type **287** 60 30
692 45 t. Peacock gudgeon . . . . 1·25 80
693 60 t. Northern rainbowfish . . 1·60 2·00
694 90 t. Popondetta blue-eye . . 2·25 3·25

289 Douglas DC-3

1993. 20th Anniv of Air Niugini. Multicoloured.

696 21 t. Type **289** 75 25
697 45 t. Fokker F.27 Friendship . . 1·75 70
698 60 t. De Havilland D.H.C.7 Dash Seven . . . . 2·00 2·25
699 90 t. Airbus Industrie A310 . . 2·75 3·75

MINIMUM PRICE

The minimum price quoted is 10p which represents a handling charge rather than a basis for valuing common stamps. For further notes about prices see introductory pages.

290 Girl holding Matschie's Tree Kangaroo

292 Hagen Axe, Western Highlands

1994. Matschie's (Huon Gulf) Tree Kangaroo. Multicoloured.

700	21 t. Type **290**	35	25
701	45 t. Adult male	90	60
702	60 t. Female with young in pouch	1·25	1·75
703	90 t. Adolescent on ground	1·90	2·75

1994. "Hong Kong '94 International Stamp Exhibition. Designs as Nos. 642, 644 and 647/8, but without "1992 BIRD OF PARADISE" at foot. Multicoloured.

704	40 t. Yellow-breasted bird of paradise	85	1·25
705	50 t. Short-tailed paradigalla bird of paradise	1·25	1·50
706	1 k. Magnificent bird of paradise	2·00	2·50
707	2 k. Superb bird of paradise	3·00	3·25

1994. Nos. 541 and 551 surch.

708	21 t. on 35 t. Fire anemonefish	9·00	50
709	1 k. 20 on 40 t. "L'Astrolabe" (D'Urville)	2·50	1·50

1994. Artifacts. Multicoloured.

710	1 t. Type **292**	10	30
711	2 t. Telefomin shield, West Sepik	10	10
712	20 t. Head mask, Gulf Province	35	30
713	21 t. Kanganaman stool, East Sepik	10	10
714	45 t. Trobriand lime gourd, Milne Bay	25	20
715	60 t. Yuat River flute stopper, East Sepik	35	25
716	90 t. Tami Island dish, Morobe	50	30
717	1 k. Kundu (drum), Ramu River estuary	1·75	1·60
723	5 k. Gogodala dance mask, Western Province	2·50	2·75
724	10 k. Malanggan mask, New Ireland	5·00	5·25

293 Ford Model "T", 1920

1994. Historical Cars. Multicoloured.

725	21 t. Type **293**	35	25
726	45 t. Chevrolet "490", 1915	90	60
727	60 t. Austin "7", 1931	1·25	1·75
728	90 t. Willys jeep, 1942	1·90	2·75

1994. Surch.

730	–	5 t. on 35 t. multicoloured (No. 604)	1·00	75
731	–	5 t. on 35 t. multicoloured (No. 629)	18·00	13·00
732	**271**	10 t. on 35 t. multicoloured	25·00	8·00
733	–	10 t. on 35 t. multicoloured (No. 623)	13·00	5·00
734	–	21 t. on 80 t. multicoloured (No. 635)	45·00	1·00
735	–	50 t. on 35 t. multicoloured (No. 612)	35·00	18·00
736	–	50 t. on 35 t. multicoloured (No. 618)	90·00	25·00
737	–	65 t. on 70 t. multicoloured (No. 542)	2·75	1·40
738	–	65 t. on 70 t. multicoloured (No. 616)	2·75	1·40
739	–	1 k. on 70 t. multicoloured (No. 614)	20·00	6·00
740	–	1 k. on 70 t. multicoloured (No. 620)	2·75	3·00

297 "Daphnis hypothous pallescens"

1994. Moths. Multicoloured.

741	21 t. Type **297**	35	25
742	45 t. "Tanaorhinus unipuncta"	80	65
743	60 t. "Neodiphthera sciron"	1·10	1·50
744	90 t. "Parotis marginata"	1·60	2·25

298 Peter To Rot

1995. Beatification of Peter To Rot (catechist) and Visit of Pope John Paul II. Multicoloured.

745	21 t. Type **298**	1·00	1·00
746	1 k. on 90 t. Pope John Paul II	1·75	2·00

No. 746 was not issued without surcharge.

299 Airliner over Holiday Village

1995. Tourism. Multicoloured.

747	21 t. "Melanesian Discoverer" (cruise ship) and launch	50	50
748	21 t. Tourist taking photo of traditional mask	50	50
749	50 t. on 45 t. Type **299**	1·25	1·25
750	50 t. on 45 t. Holiday homes	1·25	1·25
751	65 t. on 60 t. Tourists and guide crossing river	1·50	1·50
752	65 t. on 60 t. White water rafting	1·50	1·50
753	1 k. on 90 t. Scuba diver and launch	2·00	2·00
754	1 k. on 90 t. Divers and wreck of aircraft	2·00	2·00

Nos. 749/54 were not issued without surcharge.

1995. Nos. 643, 646, 650b, 650d and 692/4 surch **21t**.

755	21 t. on 45 t. King bird of paradise (643)	2·00	1·00
757	21 t. on 45 t. King bird of paradise (650b)	4·75	3·00
759	21 t. on 45 t. Peacock gudgeon	55	40
760	21 t. on 60 t. Northern rainbowfish	2·00	2·00
756	21 t. on 90 t. Emperor of Germany bird of paradise (646)	2·00	1·00
758	21 t. on 90 t. Emperor of Germany bird of paradise (650d)	6·00	1·00
761	21 t. on 90 t. Popondetta blue-eye	55	60

302 "Lentinus umbrinus"

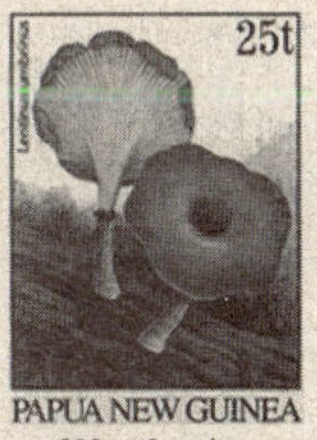

302a "Lentinus umbrinus"

1995. Fungi. Multicoloured.

762	25 t. Type **302**	35	30
765a	25 t. Type **302**a	35	35
763	50 t. "Amanita hemibapha"	70	80
764	65 t. "Boletellus emodensis"	85	1·00
765	1 k. "Ramaria zippellii"	1·40	1·75

On Type **302a** the fungi illustration is larger, 26 × 32 mm instead of 27 × 30½ mm, face value and inscriptions are in a different type and there is no imprint date at foot.

303 Anniversary Emblem and Map of Papua New Guinea

1995. 20th Anniv of Independence. Multicoloured.

766	21 t. Type **303**	30	25
767	50 t. Emblem and lines on graph	70	80
768	1 k. As 50 t.	1·40	2·00

306 Volcanic Eruption, Tavarvur

1995. 1st Anniv of Volcanic Eruption, Rabaul.

771	**306**	2 k. multicoloured	2·75	2·75

307 "Zosimus aeneus"

1995. Crabs. Multicoloured.

772	21 t. Type **307**	30	25
773	50 t. "Cardisoma carnifex"	60	60
774	65 t. "Uca tetragonon"	75	95
775	1 k. "Eriphia sebana"	1·10	1·50

308 Pesquet's Parrot

309 "Lagriomorpha indigacea"

1996. Parrots. Multicoloured.

776	25 t. Type **308**	50	30
777	50 t. Rainbow lory	85	65
778	65 t. Papuan king parrot	1·00	1·00
779	1 k. Red-winged parrot	1·40	2·00

1996. Beetles. Multicoloured.

780	25 t. Type **309**	45	25
781	50 t. "Eupholus geoffroyi"	80	65
782	65 t. "Promechus pulcher"	95	1·00
783	1 k. "Callistola pulchra"	1·10	1·90

311 Rifle-shooting

1996. Olympic Games, Atlanta. Multicoloured.

785	25 t. Type **311**	50	25
786	50 t. Athletics	1·00	70
787	65 t. Weightlifting	1·25	1·25
788	1 k. Boxing	1·50	2·25

312 Air Traffic Controller

1996. Centenary of Radio. Multicoloured.

789	25 t. Type **312**	35	25
790	50 t. Radio disc-jockey	70	65
791	65 t. Dish aerials	85	1·00
792	1 k. Early radio transmitter	1·25	1·60

314 "Hibiscus rosa-sinensis"

1996. Flowers. Multicoloured.

794	1 t. Type **314**	10	10
795	5 t. "Bougainvillea spectabilis"	10	10
796	10 t. "Thunbergia fragrans" (vert)	10	10
797	20 t. "Caesalpinia pulcherrima" (vert)	10	15
798	25 t. "Hoya sp." (vert)	15	20
799	30 t. "Heliconia spp." (vert)	15	20
800	50 t. "Amomum goliathensis" (vert)	30	35
801	65 t. "Plumeria rubra"	40	45
802	1 k. "Mucuna novo-guineensis"	55	60

316 Gogodala Canoe Prow

1997. Canoe Prows. Multicoloured.

809	25 t. Type **316**	25	25
810	50 t. East New Britain	50	60
811	65 t. Trobriand Island	70	80
812	1 k. Walomo	1·00	1·40

1997. Golden Wedding of Queen Elizabeth and Prince Philip. As T **87** of Kiribati. Multicoloured.

813	25 t. Prince Philip on polo pony, 1972	30	40
814	25 t. Queen Elizabeth at Windsor Polo Club	30	40
815	50 t. Prince Philip carriage-driving, 1995	55	65
816	50 t. Queen Elizabeth and Prince Edward on horseback	55	65
817	1 k. Prince Philip waving and Peter and Zara Phillips on horseback	1·10	1·25
818	1 k. Queen Elizabeth waving and Prince Harry on horseback	1·10	1·25

Nos. 813/14, 815/16 and 818/19 respectively were printed together, se-tenant, with the backgrounds forming composite designs.

318 "Pocillopora woodjonesi"

1997. Pacific Year of the Coral Reef. Corals. Multicoloured.

821	25 t. Type **318**	25	20
822	50 t. "Subergorgia mollis"	65	55
823	65 t. "Oxypora glabra"	85	85
824	1 k. "Turbinaria reinformis"	1·50	2·00

319 Sooty Owl

1998. Birds. Multicoloured.

825	25 t. Type **319**	30	20
826	50 t. Wattled brush turkey	50	40
827	65 t. New Guinea grey-headed goshawk	60	60
828	1 k. Forest bittern	90	1·10

320 Mother Teresa and Child

1998. Mother Teresa Commemoration. Mult.

830	65 t. Type **320**	45	50
831	1 k. Mother Teresa	55	60

1998. No. 774 surch **25t**.

832	25 t. on 65 t. "Uca tetragonon"	15	20

322 "Daphnis hypothous pallescens"

1998. Moths. Multicoloured.

833	25 t. Type **321**	25	20
834	50 t. "Theretra polistratus"	45	40
835	65 t. "Psilogramma casurina"	55	55
836	1 k. "Meganoton hyloicoides"	70	80

323 "Coelogyne fragrans"

324 Weightlifting

1998. Orchids. Multicoloured.

837	25 t. Type **323**	30	20
838	50 t. "Den cuthbertsonii"	60	50
839	65 t. "Den vexillarius "var" retroflexum"	70	70
840	1 k. "Den finisterrae"	1·25	1·40

1998. 16th Commonwealth Games, Kuala Lumpur, Malaysia. Multicoloured.

841	25 t. Type **324**	25	20
842	50 t. Lawn bowls	45	45
843	65 t. Rugby Union	60	60
844	1 k. Squash	80	90

325 Double Kayak

1998. Sea Kayaking World Cup, Manus Island. Multicoloured.

845	25 t. Type **325**	25	20
846	50 t. Running	45	45
847	65 t. Traditional canoe and modern kayak	60	60
848	1 k. Single kayak and stylised bird of paradise	80	90

326 The Holy Child

1998. Christmas. Multicoloured.

849	25 t. Type **326**	15	20
850	50 t. Mother breast-feeding baby	30	35
851	65 t. Holy Child and tribal elders	40	45
852	1 k. Map of Papua New Guinea and festive bell	55	60

1999. "Australia '99" World Stamp Exhibition, Melbourne. Designs as Nos. 543, 552 and 556/7, showing ships, redrawn to include exhibition emblem at top right and with some face values changed. Multicoloured.

853	25 t. "La Boudeuse" (De Bougainville) (as No. 543)	15	20
854	50 t. "Neva" (D'Albertis) (as No. 552)	30	35
855	65 t. "Merrie England" (steamer) (as No. 556)	40	45
856	1 k. "Samoa" (German colonial steamer) (as No. 557)	55	60

No. 855 is inscribed "Merrir England" in error.

POSTAGE DUE STAMPS

1960. Stamps of 1952 surch **POSTAL CHARGES** and value.

D2	1d. on 6½d. purple	6·00	6·00
D3	3d. on ½d. green	7·50	4·50
D1	6d. on 7½d. blue (A)	£800	£425
D4	6d. on 7½d. blue (B)	30·00	12·00
D5	1s. 3d. on 3½d. black	8·50	7·50
D6	3s. on 2½d. orange	25·00	14·00

In (A) value and "POSTAGE" is obliterated by a solid circle and a series of "IX's" but these are omitted in (B).

D 3

1960.

D 7 D 3	1d. orange	65	75
D 8	3d. brown	70	75
D 9	6d. blue	75	40
D10	9d. red	75	1·75
D11	1s. green	75	50
D12	1s. 3d. violet	1·00	2·00
D13	1s. 6d. blue	4·50	6·00
D14	3s. yellow	4·50	1·25

PATIALA

A "convention" state in the Punjab, India.

12 pies = 1 anna;
16 annas = 1 rupee

1884. Stamps of India (Queen Victoria) with curved opt **PUTTIALLA STATE** vert.

1 **23**	½ a. turquoise	1·90	2·00
2 –	1 a. purple	38·00	38·00
3 –	2 a. blue	8·50	8·50
4 –	4 a. green (No. 96)	48·00	48·00
5 –	8 a. mauve	£250	£600
6 –	1 r. grey (No. 101)	£110	£350

1885. Stamps of India (Queen Victoria) optd **PUTTIALLA STATE** horiz.

7 **23**	½ a. turquoise	1·25	20
11 –	1 a. purple	15	15
8 –	2 a. blue	2·75	1·10
9 –	4 a. green (No. 96)	2·00	1·75
12 –	8 a. mauve	11·00	24·00
10 –	1 r. grey (No. 101)	5·50	48·00

Stamps of India optd **PATIALA STATE**.

1891. Queen Victoria.

32 **40**	3 p. red	10	10
13 **23**	½ a. turquoise (No. 84)	10	10
33 –	½ a. green (No. 114)	55	30
14 –	9 p. red	35	80
15 –	1 a. purple	75	25
34 –	1 a. red	1·75	60
17 –	1 a. 6 p. brown	50	45
18 –	2 a. blue	75	20
20 –	3 a. orange	1·00	35
22 –	4 a. green (No. 96)	1·50	40
23 –	6 a. brown (No. 80)	1·25	7·00
26 –	8 a. mauve	1·00	7·00
27 –	12 a. purple on red	1·00	8·50
28 **37**	1 r. green and red	3·50	29·00
29 **38**	2 r. red and orange	90·00	£475
30	3 r. brown and green	£120	£500
31	5 r. blue and violet	£150	£550

1903. King Edward VII.

36	3 p. grey	10	10
37	½ a. green (No. 122)	85	10
38	1 a. red (No. 123)	10	10
39	2 a. lilac	80	65
40	3 a. orange	45	30
41	4 a. olive	2·25	65
42	6 a. bistre	2·25	5·00
43	8 a. mauve	2·00	1·10
44	12 a. purple on red	4·00	16·00
45	1 r. green and red	1·60	3·00

1912. King Edward VII. Inscr "INDIA POSTAGE & REVENUE".

46	½ a. green (No. 149)	10	15
47	1 a. red (No. 150)	70	40

1912. King George V. Optd in two lines.

48 **55**	3 p. grey	15	10
49 **56**	½ a. green	45	15
50 **57**	1 a. red	65	15
61	1 a. brown	1·75	30
51 **58**	1½d. brown (A)	30	55
52 **59**	2 a. lilac	45	35
53 **62**	3 a. orange	90	60
62	3 a. blue	1·40	4·50
54 **63**	4 a. olive	1·60	1·40
55a **64**	6 a. bistre	80	2·50
56 **65**	8 a. mauve	1·50	90
57 **66**	12 a. red	1·60	5·00
58 **67**	1 r. brown and green	3·00	9·00
59	2 r. red and orange	9·00	£100
60	5 r. blue and violet	21·00	£100

1928. King George V. Optd in one line.

63 **55**	3 p. grey	1·00	10
64 **56**	½ a. green	25	10
75 **79**	½ a. green	30	20
65 **80**	9 p. green	70	20
66 **57**	1 a. brown	70	20
76 **81**	1 a. brown	40	15
67 **82**	1 a. 3 p. mauve	2·50	15
77 **59**	2 a. red	30	60
68 **70**	2 a. lilac	80	30
69 **61**	2 a. 6 p. orange	2·75	1·25
70 **62**	3 a. blue	1·75	75
78	3 a. red	3·50	3·50
71 **71**	4 a. green	2·25	65
79 **63**	4 a. olive	85	1·25
72 **65**	8 a. mauve	3·50	1·50
73 **66**	1 r. brown and green	5·00	5·00
74w	2 r. red and orange	8·00	38·00

1937. King George VI. Optd in one line.

80 **91**	3 p. grey	25·00	30
81	½ a. brown	6·50	20
82	9 p. green	2·25	45
83	1 a. red	1·50	20
84 **92**	2 a. red	1·50	5·00
85 –	2 a. 6 p. violet	2·75	11·00
86 –	3 a. green	2·25	4·75
87 –	3 a. 6 p. blue	3·00	15·00
88 –	4 a. brown	16·00	9·00
89 –	6 a. green	18·00	30·00
90 –	8 a. violet	18·00	23·00
91 –	12 a. red	18·00	35·00
92 **93**	1 r. grey and brown	18·00	32·00
93	2 r. purple and brown	27·00	75·00
94	5 r. green and blue	38·00	£140
95	10 r. purple and red	55·00	£225
96	15 r. brown and green	£100	£375
97	25 r. grey and purple	£130	£450

1943. King George VI. Optd **PATIALA** only. (a) Issue of 1938.

98 **94**	3 p. grey	8·00	60
99	½ a. brown	6·50	25
100	9 p. green	£130	2·50
101	1 a. red	18·00	65
102 **93**	1 r. grey and brown	7·50	55·00

(b) Issue of 1940.

103 **92**	3 p. grey	1·40	15
104	½ a. mauve	1·75	15
105 **92**	9 p. green	1·00	15
106	1 a. red	80	10
107 **101**	1 a. 3 p. bistre	1·60	1·75
108	1½ a. violet	7·00	1·60
109	2 a. red	6·00	25
110	3 a. violet	4·00	75
111	3½ a. blue	14·00	21·00
112 **102**	4 a. brown	4·50	1·10
113	6 a. green	2·50	14·00
114	8 a. violet	3·00	7·00
115	12 a. purple	9·00	45·00

OFFICIAL STAMPS

Overprinted **SERVICE**.

1884. Nos. 1 to 3 (Queen Victoria).

O1 **23**	½ a. turquoise	9·00	20
O2 –	1 a. purple	35	10
O3 –	2 a. blue	£4000	95·00

1885. Nos. 7, 11 and 8 (Queen Victoria).

O4 **23**	½ a. turquoise	30	10
O5 –	1 a. purple	30	10
O7 –	2 a. blue	30	15

1891. Nos. 13 to 28 and No. 10 Q.V.

O 8 **23**	½ a. turquoise (No. 13)	10	10
O 9 –	1 a. purple	3·50	10
O20 –	1 a. red	15	10
O10a –	2 a. blue	3·00	1·50
O12 –	3 a. orange	45	1·50
O13a –	4 a. green	40	20
O15 –	6 a. brown	85	35
O16a –	8 a. mauve	80	75
O18 –	12 a. purple on red	50	50
O19 –	1 r. grey	65	55
O21 **37**	1 r. green and red	5·00	9·00

1903. Nos. 36 to 45 (King Edward VII).

O22	3 p. grey	10	10
O24	½ a. green	10	10
O25	1 a. red	10	10
O26a	2 a. lilac	20	10
O28	3 a. brown	1·60	1·60
O29	4 a. olive	50	20
O30	8 a. mauve	60	55
O32	1 r. green and red	70	70

1907. Nos. 46/7 (King Edward VII). Inscr "INDIA POSTAGE & REVENUE".

O33	½ a. green	10	10
O34	1 a. red	10	10

1913. Official stamps of India (King George V). Optd **PATIALA STATE** in two lines.

O35 **55**	3 p. grey	10	10
O36 **56**	½ a. green	10	10
O37 **57**	1 a. red	10	10
O38	1 a. brown	4·75	90
O39 **59**	2 a. mauve	50	20
O40 **63**	4 a. olive	40	30
O41 **64**	6 a. bistre	75	1·75
O42 **65**	8 a. purple	55	45
O43 **67**	1 r. brown and green	1·25	1·40
O44	2 r. red and brown	11·00	32·00
O45	5 r. blue and violet	9·00	19·00

1927. Postage stamps of India (King George V) optd **PATIALA STATE SERVICE** in two lines.

O47 **55**	3 p. grey	10	10
O48 **56**	½ a. green	35	55
O58 **79**	½ a. green	10	10
O49 **57**	1 a. brown	15	10
O59 **81**	1 a. brown	10	30
O50 **82**	1 a. 3 p. mauve	30	10
O51 **70**	2 a. purple	20	30
O52	2 a. red	30	35
O60 **59**	2 a. red	15	15
O53w **61**	2½ a. orange	50	75
O54 **71**	4 a. green	40	30
O62 **63**	4 a. olive	95	40
O55 **65**	8 a. purple	80	60
O56w **66**	1 r. brown and green	2·25	1·75
O57	2 r. red and orange	6·50	26·00

1938. Postage stamps of India (King George VI) optd **PATIALA STATE SERVICE**.

O63 **91**	½ a. brown	75	20
O64	9 p. green	13·00	50·00
O65	1 a. red	75	20
O66 **93**	1 r. grey and brown	1·00	3·75
O67	2 r. purple and green	6·00	5·00
O68	5 r. green and blue	15·00	50·00

1939. Surch **1A SERVICE 1A**.

O70 **82**	1 a. on 1¼ a. mauve	4·75	1·60

1940. Official stamps of India optd **PATIALA**.

O71 **O 20**	3 p. grey	45	10
O72	½ a. brown	3·25	10
O73	½ a. purple	45	10
O74	9 p. green	45	20
O75	1 a. red	85	10
O76	1 a. 3 p. bistre	85	25
O77	1½ a. violet	3·25	40
O78	2 a. orange	4·75	15
O79	2½ a. violet	95	65
O80	4 a. brown	85	1·25
O81	8 a. violet	1·50	4·00

1940. Postage stamps of India (King George VI) optd **PATIALA SERVICE**.

O82 **93**	1 r. slate and brown	7·00	7·00
O83	2 r. purple and brown	15·00	40·00
O84	5 r. green and blue	21·00	60·00

PENANG

A British Settlement which became a state of the Federation of Malaya, incorporated in Malaysia in 1963.

100 cents = 1 dollar (Straits or Malayan)

1948. Silver Wedding. As T **10/11** of Aden.

1	10 c. violet	30	20
2	$5 brown	30·00	27·00

1949. As T **58** of Straits Settlement.

3	1 c. black	10	10
4	2 c. orange	40	10
5	3 c. green	20	30
6	4 c. brown	20	10
7	5 c. purple	40	1·50
8	6 c. grey	20	20
9	8 c. red	30	2·75
10	8 c. green	80	1·00
11	10 c. mauve	15	10
12	12 c. red	80	3·00
13	15 c. blue	20	30
14	20 c. black and green	20	1·00
15	20 c. blue	55	40
16	25 c. purple and orange	85	10
17	35 c. red and purple	60	80
18	40 c. red and purple	85	7·50
19	50 c. black and blue	1·25	15
20	$1 blue and purple	12·00	1·75
21	$2 green and red	14·00	1·75
22	$3 green and brown	48·00	2·00

1949. U.P.U. As T **20/23** of Antigua.

23	10 c. purple	20	10
24	15 c. blue	1·50	1·50
25	25 c. orange	45	1·75
26	30 c. black	1·50	2·25

1953. Coronation. As T **13** of Aden.

27	10 c. black and purple	60	10

1954. As T **1** of Malacca, but inscr "PENANG".

28	1 c. black	10	50
29	2 c. orange	50	30
30	4 c. brown	70	10
31	5 c. mauve	2·00	2·25
32	6 c. grey	15	70
33	8 c. green	20	2·50
34	10 c. purple	20	10
35	12 c. red	30	2·50
36	20 c. blue	50	10
37	25 c. purple and orange	30	10
38	30 c. red and purple	30	10
39	35 c. red and purple	70	40
40	50 c. black and blue	40	10
41	$1 blue and purple	2·25	10
42	$2 green and red	6·50	3·00
43	$5 green and brown	40·00	3·25

1957. As Nos. 92/102 of Kedah, but inset portrait of Queen Elizabeth II.

44	1 c. black	10	60
45	2 c. red	10	60
46	4 c. sepia	10	10
47	5 c. lake	10	10
48	8 c. green	1·25	1·75
49	10 c. brown	30	10
50	20 c. blue	40	40
51	50 c. black and blue	30	40
52	$1 blue and purple	5·00	40
53	$2 green and red	10·00	8·00
54	$5 brown and green	16·00	8·50

1 Copra

1960. As Nos. 44/54, but with inset Arms of Penang as in T **1**.

55	1 c. black	10	75
56	2 c. red	10	75
57	4 c. brown	10	10
58	5 c. lake	10	10
59	8 c. green	2·75	3·50
60	10 c. purple	30	10
61	20 c. blue	40	10
62	50 c. black and blue	30	15
63	$1 blue and purple	4·00	1·00
64	$2 green and red	4·25	4·00
65	$5 brown and green	10·00	6·00

2 "Vanda hookeriana"

1965. As Nos. 115/21 of Kedah, but with Arms of Penang inset and inscr "PULAU PINANG" as in T **2**.

66 **2**	1 c. multicoloured	10	75
67 –	2 c. multicoloured	10	75
68 –	5 c. multicoloured	20	10
69 –	6 c. multicoloured	30	75
70 –	10 c. multicoloured	20	10
71 –	15 c. multicoloured	1·00	10
72 –	20 c. multicoloured	1·60	30

The higher values used in Penang were Nos. 20/7 of Malaysia (National Issues).

3 "Valeria valeria"

1971. Butterflies. As Nos. 124/30 of Kedah but with Arms of Penang inset and inscr "pulau pinang" as in T **3**.
75 – 1 c. multicoloured 30 75
76 – 2 c. multicoloured 60 75
77 – 5 c. multicoloured . . . . . 1·00 30
78 – 6 c. multicoloured . . . . . 1·10 1·00
79 – 10 c. multicoloured . . . . . 1·10 15
80 – 15 c. multicoloured . . . . . 1·10 10
81 **3** 20 c. multicoloured . . . . . 1·25 40
The higher values in use with this issue were Nos. 64/71 of Malaysia (National Issues).

4 "Etlingera elatior" (inscr "Phaeomeria speciosa")

5 Cocoa

1979. Flowers. As Nos. 135/41 of Kedah, but with Arms of Penang and inscr "pulau pinaug" as in T **4**.
86 1 c. "Rafflesia hasseltii" 10 50
87 2 c. "Pterocarpus indicus" . . . 10 50
88 5 c. "Lagerstroemia speciosa" . 10 10
89 10 c. "Durio zibethinus" . . . 15 10
90 15 c. "Hibiscus rosa-sinensis" . 15 10
91 20 c. "Rhododendron scortechinii" 20 10
92 25 c. Type **4** 40 20

1986. As Nos. 152/8 of Kedah but with Arms of Penang and inscr "PULAU PINANG" as in T **5**.
100 1 c. Coffee 10 10
101 2 c. Coconuts 10 10
102 5 c. Type **5** 10 10
103 10 c. Black pepper 10 10
104 15 c. Rubber 10 10
105 20 c. Oil palm 10 10
106 30 c. Rice 15 20

PENRHYN ISLAND

One of the Cook Islands in the South Pacific. A dependency of New Zealand. Used Cook Islands stamps until 1973 when further issues for use in the Northern group of the Cook Islands issues appeared.

A. NEW ZEALAND DEPENDENCY

1902. Stamps of New Zealand (Pictorials) surch **PENRHYN ISLAND.** and value in native language.
4 **23** ½d. green . . . . 80 4·25
10 **42** 1d. red . . . . 1·00 3·00
1 **26** 2½d. blue (No. 249) . . . . 2·50 6·50
14 **28** 3d. brown . . . . 10·00 20·00
15 **31** 6d. red . . . . 15·00 32·00
16a **34** 1s. orange . . . . 48·00 48·00

1914. Stamps of New Zealand (King Edward VII) surch **PENRHYN ISLAND.** and value in native language.
19c **51** ½d. green . . . . 80 6·50
22 6d. red . . . . 27·00 70·00
23 1s. orange . . . . 48·00 95·00

1917. Stamps of New Zealand (King George V) optd **PENRHYN ISLAND.**
28 **62** ½d. green . . . . 1·00 2·00
29 1½d. grey . . . . 6·50 14·00
30 1½d. brown . . . . 60 14·00
24a 2½d. blue . . . . 2·00 4·50
31 3d. brown . . . . 3·50 16·00
26a 6d. red . . . . 5·00 16·00
27a 1s. orange . . . . 12·00 30·00

1920. Pictorial types as Cook Islands (1920), but inscr "PENRHYN".
32 **9** ½d. black and green . . . . 1·00 12·00
33 – 1d. black and red . . . . . 1·50 12·00
34 – 1½d. black and violet . . . 6·50 17·00
40 – 2½d. brown and black . . . 2·75 22·00
35 – 3d. black and red . . . . . 2·50 8·00
36 – 6d. brown and red . . . . . 3·25 20·00
37 – 1s. black and blue . . . . . 10·00 23·00

B. PART OF COOK ISLANDS

1973. Nos. 228/9, 231, 233/6, 239/40 and 243/5 of Cook Is. optd **PENRHYN NORTHERN** or **PENRHYN** ($1, 2).
41B 1 c. multicoloured 10 10
42B 2 c. multicoloured 10 10
43B 3 c. multicoloured 20 10
44B 4 c. multicoloured 10 10
45B 5 c. multicoloured 10 10
46B 6 c. multicoloured 20 30
47B 8 c. multicoloured 30 40
48B 15 c. multicoloured 45 50
49B 20 c. multicoloured . . . . . 1·50 80
50B 50 c. multicoloured . . . . . 90 1·75
51B $1 multicoloured . . . . . 90 2·25
52B $2 multicoloured . . . . . 90 2·50

1973. Nos. 450/2 of Cook Is. optd **PENRHYN NORTHERN**.
53 **138** 25 c. multicoloured . . . 30 20
54 – 30 c. multicoloured . . . 30 20
55 – 50 c. multicoloured . . . 30 20

10 "Ostracion sp."

1974. Fishes. Multicoloured.
56 ½ c. Type **10** 50 50
57 1 c. "Monodactylus argenteus" 70 50
58 2 c. "Pomacanthus imperator" 80 50
59 3 c. "Chelmon rostratus" . . . 80 50
60 4 c. "Chaetodon ornatissimus" 80 50
61 5 c. "Chaetodon melanotus" . 80 50
62 8 c. "Chaetodon raffessi" . . . 80 50
63 10 c. "Chaetodon ephippium" 85 50
64 20 c. "Pygoplites diacanthus" . 1·75 50
65 25 c. "Heniochus acuminatus" 1·75 50
66 60 c. "Plectorhynchus chaetodonoides" . . . . . 2·50 90
67 $1 "Balistipus undulatus" . . 2·75 1·25
68 $2 Bird's-eye view of Penrhyn . 4·50 12·00
69 $5 Satellite view of Australasia 4·50 6·00
Nos. 68/9 are size 63 × 25 mm.

11 Penrhyn Stamps of 1902

13 Churchill giving "V" sign

12 "Adoration of the Kings" (Memling)

1974. Cent of Universal Postal Union. Mult.
70 25 c. Type **11** 20 30
71 50 c. Stamps of 1920 . . . . . 35 40

1974. Christmas. Multicoloured.
72 5 c. Type **12** 20 25
73 10 c. "Adoration of the Shepherds" (Hugo van der Goes) 25 25
74 25 c. "Adoration of the Magi" (Rubens) 40 35
75 30 c. "The Holy Family" (Borgianni) 45 50

1974. Birth Cent of Sir Winston Churchill.
76 **13** 30 c. brown and gold 35 85
77 – 50 c. green and gold 45 90
DESIGN: 50 c. Full-face portrait.

1975. "Apollo–Soyuz" Space Project. Optd **KIA ORANA ASTRONAUTS** and emblem.
78 $5 Satellite view of Australasia 1·75 2·50

15 "Virgin and Child" (Bouts)

16 "Pieta"

1975. Christmas. Paintings of the "Virgin and Child" by artists given below. Multicoloured.
79 7 c. Type **15** 40 10
80 15 c. Leonardo da Vinci 70 20
81 35 c. Raphael . . . . 1·10 35

1976. Easter. 500th Birth Anniv of Michelangelo.
82 **16** 15 c. brown and gold 25 15
83 – 20 c. lilac and gold 30 20
84 – 35 c. green and gold 40 45
DESIGNS: Nos. 83/4 show different views of the "Pieta".

17 "Washington crossing the Delaware" (E. Leutze)

18 Running

1976. Bicentenary of American Revolution.
86 **17** 30 c. multicoloured 30 15
87 – 30 c. multicoloured 30 15
88 – 30 c. multicoloured 30 15
89 – 50 c. multicoloured 40 20
90 – 50 c. multicoloured 40 20
91 – 50 c. multicoloured 40 20
DESIGNS: Nos. 86/88, "Washington crossing the Delaware" (E. Leutze); Nos. 89/91, "The Spirit of '76" (A. M. Willard).
Nos. 86/88 and 89/91 were each printed together, se-tenant, forming a composite design of the complete painting. Type **17** shows the left-hand stamp of the 30 c. design.

1976. Olympic Games, Montreal. Multicoloured.
93 25 c. Type **18** 25 15
94 30 c. Long jumping 30 15
95 75 c. Throwing the javelin . . . 55 25

19 "The Flight into Egypt"

20 The Queen in Coronation Robes

1976. Christmas. Durer Engravings.
97 **19** 7 c. black and silver 15 10
98 – 15 c. blue and silver 25 15
99 – 35 c. violet and silver 35 25
DESIGNS: 15 c. "Adoration of the Magi"; 35 c. "The Nativity".

1977. Silver Jubilee. Multicoloured.
100 50 c. Type **20** 25 60
101 $1 The Queen and Prince Philip 35 65
102 $2 Queen Elizabeth II 50 80

21 "The Annunciation"

1977. Christmas. Illustrations by J. S. von Carolsfeld.
104 **21** 7 c. brown, purple and gold 40 15
105 – 15 c. red, purple and gold . 60 15
106 – 35 c. deep green, green and gold . . . . 1·00 30
DESIGNS: 15 c. "The Announcement to the Shepherds"; 35 c. "The Nativity".

22 Iiwi

23 "The Road to Calvary"

1978. Bicentenary of Discovery of Hawaii. Birds and Artefacts. Multicoloured.
107 20 c. Type **22** 80 30
108 20 c. Elgin cloak 80 30
109 30 c. Apapane 90 40
110 30 c. Feather image of a god . 90 40
111 35 c. Moorhen 90 45
112 35 c. Feather cape, helmet and staff 90 45
113 75 c. Hawaii O-o . . . . . . 1·50 80
114 75 c. Feather image and cloak . 1·50 80

1978. Easter. 400th Birth Anniv of Rubens. Multicoloured.
116 10 c. Type **23** 20 10
117 15 c. "Christ on the Cross" . . 25 15
118 35 c. "Christ with Straw" . . 45 25

24 Royal Coat of Arms

25 "Madonna of the Pear"

1978. 25th Anniv of Coronation.
121 **24** 90 c. black, gold and mauve 30 60
122 – 90 c. multicoloured 30 60
123 – 90 c. black, gold and green 30 60
DESIGNS: No. 122, Queen Elizabeth II; No. 123, New Zealand coat of arms.

1978. Christmas. 450th Death Anniv of Albrecht Durer. Multicoloured.
125 30 c. Type **25** 65 30
126 35 c. "The Virgin and Child with St. Anne" (Durer) 65 30

26 Sir Rowland Hill and G.B. Penny Black Stamp

27 Max and Moritz

1979. Death Centenary of Sir Rowland Hill. Multicoloured.
128 75 c. Type **26** 50 55
129 75 c. 1974 U.P.U. Centenary 25 c. and 50 c. commemoratives 50 55
130 90 c. Sir Rowland Hill 60 70
131 90 c. 1978 Coronation Anniversary 90 c. commemorative 60 70

1979. Int Year of the Child. Illustrations from "Max and Moritz" stories by Wilhelm Busch. Multicoloured.
133 12 c. Type **27** 20 10
134 12 c. Max and Moritz looking down chimney 20 10
135 12 c. Max and Moritz making off with food 20 10
136 12 c. Cook about to beat dog . 20 10
137 15 c. Max sawing through bridge 25 10
138 15 c. Pursuer approaching bridge 25 10
139 15 c. Collapse of bridge . . . 25 10
140 15 c. Pursuer in river 25 10
141 20 c. Baker locking shop . . . 30 20

142 20 c. Max and Moritz emerge from hiding 30 20
143 20 c. Max and Moritz falling in dough 30 20
144 20 c. Max and Moritz made into buns 30 20

28 "Christ carrying Cross" (Book of Ferdinand II)

29 "Queen Elizabeth, 1937" (Sir Gerald Kelly)

1980. Easter. Scenes from 15th-cent Prayer Books. Multicoloured.
145 12 c. Type **28** 15 20
146 20 c. "The Crucifixion" (William Vrelant, Book of Duke of Burgundy) 20 25
147 35 c. "Descent from the Cross" (Book of Ferdinand II) 30 45

1980. 80th Birthday of The Queen Mother.
150 **29** $1 multicoloured 1·25 1·25

30 Falk Hoffman, East Germany. (platform diving) (gold)

31 "The Virgin of Counsellors" (Luis Dalmau)

1980. Olympic Medal Winners. Multicoloured.
152 10 c. Type **30** 10 10
153 10 c. Martina Jaschke, East Germany (platform diving) 10 10
154 20 c. Tomi Polkolainen, Finland (archery) 15 15
155 20 c. Kete Losaberidse, U.S.S.R. (archery) 15 15
156 30 c. Czechoslovakia (football) 20 20
157 30 c. East Germany (football) 20 20
158 50 c. Barbel Wockel, East Germany (200 metres) 30 30
159 50 c. Pietro Mennea, Italy (200 metres) 30 30

1980. Christmas. Multicoloured.
161 20 c. Type **31** 15 15
162 35 c. "Virgin and Child" (Serra brothers) 20 20
163 50 c. "The Virgin of Albocacer" (Master of the Porciuncula) 30 30

32 Amatasi

33 "Jesus at the Grove" (Veronese)

1981. Sailing Craft and Ships (1st series). Multicoloured.
166 1 c. Type **32** 20 15
167 1 c. Ndrua (canoe) 20 15
168 1 c. Waka (canoe) 20 15
169 1 c. Tongiaki (canoe) 20 15
170 3 c. Va'a Teu'ua (canoe) 40 15
171 3 c. "Vitoria" (Del Cano's ship) 40 15
172 3 c. "Golden Hind" (Drake's ship) 40 15
173 3 c. "La Boudeuse" (Bougainville's ship) 40 15
174 4 c. H.M.S. "Bounty" 50 15
175 4 c. "L'Astrolabe" (Dumont d'Urville's ship) 50 15
176 4 c. "Star of India" (full-rigged ship) 50 15
177 4 c. "Great Republic" (clipper) 50 15
178 6 c. "Balcutha" (clipper) 50 20
179 6 c. "Coonatto" (clipper) 50 20
180 6 c. "Antiope" (clipper) 50 20
181 6 c. "Teaping" (clipper) 50 20
182 10 c. "Preussen" (full-rigged ship) 50 75
183 10 c. "Pamir" (barque) 50 75
184 10 c. "Cap Hornier" (full-rigged ship) 50 75
185 10 c. "Patriarch" (clipper) 50 75
186 15 c. Type **32** 50 85
187 15 c. As No. 167 50 85
188 15 c. As No. 168 50 85
189 15 c. As No. 169 50 85
190 20 c. As No. 170 50 85
191 20 c. As No. 171 50 85
192 20 c. As No. 172 50 85
193 20 c. As No. 173 50 85
194 30 c. As No. 174 50 95
195 30 c. As No. 175 50 95
196 30 c. As No. 176 50 95
197 30 c. As No. 177 50 95
198 50 c. As No. 178 1·00 1·75
199 50 c. As No. 179 1·00 1·75
200 50 c. As No. 180 1·00 1·75
201 50 c. As No. 181 1·00 1·75
202 $1 As No. 182 2·00 1·50
203 $1 As No. 183 2·00 1·50
204 $1 As No. 184 2·00 1·50
205 $1 As No. 185 2·00 1·50
206 $2 "Cutty Sark" (clipper) 4·50 3·25
207 $4 "Mermerus" (clipper) 9·00 5·00
208 $6 H.M.S. "Resolution" and H.M.S. "Discovery" (Cook's ships) 15·00 12·00

Nos. 186/201 are 41 × 35 mm, Nos. 202/5 41 × 25 mm and Nos. 206/8 47 × 33 mm in size.
See also Nos. 337/55.

1981. Easter. Paintings. Multicoloured.
218 30 c. Type **33** 40 20
219 40 c. "Christ with Crown of Thorns" (Titian) 55 25
220 50 c. "Pieta" (Van Dyck) 60 30

34 Prince Charles as Young Child

35 Footballers

1981. Royal Wedding. Multicoloured.
223 40 c. Type **34** 20 35
224 50 c. Prince Charles as schoolboy 25 40
225 60 c. Prince Charles as young man 25 40
226 70 c. Prince Charles in ceremonial Naval uniform 25 45
227 80 c. Prince Charles as Colonel-in-Chief, Royal Regiment of Wales 25 45

1981. International Year for Disabled Persons. Nos. 223/7 surch **+5c**.
229 **34** 40 c. + 5 c. multicoloured 20 50
230 – 50 c. + 5 c. multicoloured 25 55
231 – 60 c. + 5 c. multicoloured 25 55
232 – 70 c. + 5 c. multicoloured 25 60
233 – 80 c. + 5 c. multicoloured 25 65

1981. World Cup Football Championships, Spain (1982). Multicoloured.
235 15 c. Type **35** 20 15
236 15 c. Footballer wearing orange jersey with black and mauve stripes 20 15
237 15 c. Player in blue jersey 20 15
238 35 c. Player in blue jersey 30 25
239 35 c. Player in red jersey 30 25
240 35 c. Player in yellow jersey with green stripes 30 25
241 50 c. Player in orange jersey 40 35
242 50 c. Player in mauve jersey 40 35
243 50 c. Player in black jersey 40 35

36 "The Virgin on a Crescent"

37 Lady Diana Spencer as Baby

1981. Christmas. Engravings by Durer.
245 **36** 30 c. violet, purple and stone 90 1·00
246 – 40 c. violet, purple and stone 1·25 1·40
247 – 50 c. violet, purple and stone 1·50 1·75
DESIGNS: 40 c. "The Virgin at the Fence"; 50 c. "The Holy Virgin and Child".

1982. 21st Birthday of Princess of Wales. Multicoloured.
250 30 c. Type **37** 30 30
251 50 c. As young child 40 45
252 70 c. As schoolgirl 60 60
253 80 c. As teenager 70 80
254 $1.40 As a young lady 1·10 1·25

1982. Birth of Prince William of Wales (1st issue). Nos. 223/7 optd **BIRTH OF PRINCE WILLIAM OF WALES 21 JUNE 1982**.
256 40 c. Type **34** 40 45
257 50 c. Prince Charles as schoolboy 50 60
258 60 c. Prince Charles as young man 55 65
259 70 c. Prince Charles in ceremonial Naval uniform 60 70
260 80 c. Prince Charles as Colonel-in-Chief, Royal Regiment of Wales 70 80

1982. Birth of Prince William of Wales (2nd issue). As Nos. 250/4 but with changed inscriptions. Multicoloured.
262 30 c. As Type **37** (A) 30 30
263 30 c. As Type **37** (B) 30 30
264 50 c. As No. 251 (A) 45 45
265 50 c. As No. 251 (B) 45 45
266 70 c. As No. 252 (A) 65 60
267 70 c. As No. 252 (B) 65 65
268 80 c. As No. 253 (A) 65 65
269 80 c. As No. 253 (B) 65 65
270 $1.40 As No. 254 (A) 1·25 1·25
271 $1.40 As No. 254 (B) 1·25 1·25
INSCR: A. "21 JUNE 1982. BIRTH OF PRINCE WILLIAM OF WALES"; B. "COMMEMORATING THE BIRTH OF PRINCE WILLIAM OF WALES".

39 "Virgin and Child" (detail, Joos Van Cleve)

40 Red Coral

1982. Christmas. Details from Renaissance Paintings of "Virgin and Child". Multicoloured.
273 25 c. Type **39** 30 40
274 48 c. "Virgin and Child" (Filippino Lippi) 45 55
275 60 c. "Virgin and Child" (Cima da Conegliano) 60 70

1983. Commonwealth Day. Multicoloured.
278 60 c. Type **40** 50 55
279 60 c. Aerial view of Penrhyn atoll 50 55
280 60 c. Eleanor Roosevelt on Penrhyn during Second World War 50 55
281 60 c. Map of South Pacific 50 55

41 Scout Emblem and Blue Tropical Flower

1983. 75th Anniv of Boy Scout Movement. Multicoloured.
282 36 c. Type **41** 1·50 65
283 48 c. Emblem and pink flower 1·75 75
284 60 c. Emblem and orange flower 1·75 1·00

1983. 15th World Scout Jamboree, Alberta, Canada. Nos. 282/4 optd **XV WORLD JAMBOREE CANADA 1983**.
286 36 c. Type **41** 1·25 40
287 48 c. Emblem and pink flower 1·50 55
288 60 c. Emblem and orange flower 1·60 75

43 School of Sperm Whales

1983. Whale Conservation. Multicoloured.
290 8 c. Type **43** 1·00 70
291 15 c. Harpooner preparing to strike 1·40 95
292 35 c. Whale attacking boat 2·00 1·40
293 60 c. Dead whales marked with flags 3·00 2·00
294 $1 Dead whales on slipway 3·75 3·00

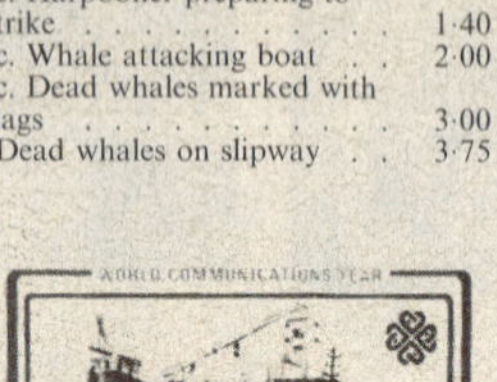

44 "Mercury" (cable ship)

1983. World Communications Year. Multicoloured.
295 36 c. Type **44** 80 35
296 48 c. Men watching cable being laid 85 45
297 60 c. "Mercury" (different) 1·10 60

1983. Various stamps surch. (a) Nos. 182/5, 190/7 and 206.
299 18 c. on 10 c. "Preussen" 20 20
300 18 c. on 10 c. "Pamir" 20 20
301 18 c. on 10 c. "Cap Hornier" 20 20
302 18 c. on 10 c. "Patriarch" 20 20
303 36 c. on 20 c. Va'a Teu'ua 35 35
304 36 c. on 20 c. "Vitoria" 35 35
305 36 c. on 20 c. "Golden Hind" 35 35
306 36 c. on 20 c. "La Boudeuse" 35 35
307 36 c. on 30 c. H.M.S. "Bounty" 35 35
308 36 c. on 30 c. "L'Astrolabe" 35 35
309 36 c. on 30 c. "Star of India" 35 35
310 36 c. on 30 c. "Great Republic" 35 35
311 $1.20 on $2 "Cutty Sark" 1·40 1·40

(b) Nos. 252/3.
312 72 c. on 70 c. Princess Diana as schoolgirl 2·00 1·50
313 96 c. on 80 c. Princess Diana as teenager 2·25 1·75

1983. Nos. 225/6, 268/9, 254 and 208 surch.
314 48 c. on 60 c. Prince Charles as young man 3·50 1·50
315 72 c. on 70 c. Prince Charles in ceremonial Naval uniform 4·00 1·75
316 96 c. on 80 c. As No. 253 (inscr "21 JUNE 1982") 2·75 1·00
317 96 c. on 80 c. As No. 253 (inscr "COMMEMORATING") 1·75 1·00
318 $1.20 on $4.40 As young lady 3·25 1·50
319 $5.60 on $6 H.M.S. "Resolution" and "Discovery" 15·00 6·50

45 George Cayley's Airship Design, 1837

1983. Bicentenary of Manned Flight. Mult
A. Inscr "NORTHERN COOK ISLANDS".
B. Corrected spelling optd in black on silver, over original inscription.

		A		B	
320	36 c. Type **45**	1·10	80	30	35
321	48 c. Dupuy de Lome's airship, 1872	1·25	90	40	45
322	60 c. Santos Dumont's "Airship" No. "6", 1901	1·50	1·25	45	50
323	96 c. Lebaudy-Juillot's pratical airship, No. 1 "La Jaune", 1902	2·25	1·75	75	80
324	$1.32 Airship, Graf Zeppelin, 1929	3·00	2·50	1·00	1·10

46 "Madonna in the Meadow"

47 Waka

1983. Christmas. 500th Birth Anniv of Raphael. Multicoloured.
326 36 c. Type **46** 60 40
327 42 c. "Tempi Madonna" 60 40
328 48 c. "The Smaller Cowper Madonna" 80 50
329 60 c. "Madonna della Tenda" 95 60

1983. Nos. 266/7, 227 and 270 surch.
331 72 c. on 70 c. As No. 252 (inscr "21 JUNE 1982 ...") 1·50 80
332 72 c. on 70 c. As No. 252 (inscr "COMMEMORATING ...") 80 60
333 96 c. on 80 c. Prince Charles as Colonel-in-Chief, Royal Regiment of Wales 1·50 65
334 $1.20 on $1.40 As No. 254 (inscr "21 JUNE 1982 ...") 1·75 70
335 $1.20 on $1.40 As No. 254 (inscr "COMMEMORATING ...") 1·25 65

1984. Sailing Craft and Ships (2nd series). Multicoloured.
337 2 c. Type **47** 20 50
338 4 c. Amatasi 30 50
339 5 c. Ndrua 30 50
340 8 c. Tongiaki 40 60
341 10 c. "Vitoria" 40 60
342 18 c. "Golden Hind" 50 70
343 20 c. "La Boudeuse" 50 70
344 30 c. H.M.S. "Bounty" 60 70
345 36 c. "L'Astrolabe" 60 70
346 48 c. "Great Republic" 60 70
347 50 c. "Star of India" 60 70
348 60 c. "Coonatto" 60 70
349 72 c. "Antiope" 60 70
350 80 c. "Balcutha" 70 70
351 96 c. "Cap Hornier" 85 85
352 $1.20 "Pamir" 2·50 1·40
353 $3 "Mermerus" (41 × 31 mm) 5·00 3·00
354 $5 "Cutty Sark" (41 × 31 mm) 5·50 5·00
355 $9.60 H.M.S. "Resolution" and H.M.S. "Discovery" (41 × 31 mm) 13·00 12·00

48 Olympic Flag

1984. Olympic Games, Los Angeles. Multi.

356	35 c. Type **48**	30	35
357	60 c. Olympic torch and flags	50	55
358	$1.80 Ancient athletes and Coliseum	1·50	1·60

49 Penrhyn Stamps of 1978, 1979 and 1981

1984. "Ausipex" International Stamp Exhibition, Melbourne. Multicoloured.

360	60 c. Type **49**	50	75
361	$1.20 Location map of Penrhyn	1·00	1·25

1984. Birth of Prince Henry. Nos. 223/4 and 250/1 surch **$2 Birth of Prince Henry 15 Sept. 1984**.

363	$2 on 30 c. Type **37**	1·40	1·50
364	$2 on 40 c. Type **34**	1·60	1·75
365	$2 on 50 c. Prince Charles as schoolboy	1·60	1·75
366	$2 on 50 c. Lady Diana as young child	1·40	1·50

51 "Virgin and Child" (Giovanni Bellini)

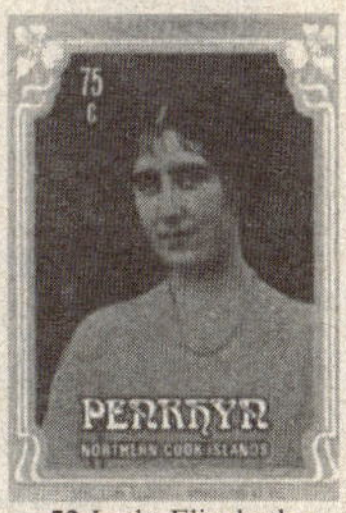
53 Lady Elizabeth Bowes-Lyon, 1921

52 Harlequin Duck

1984. Christmas. Paintings of the Virgin and Child by different artists. Multicoloured.

367	36 c. Type **51**	60	35
368	48 c. Lorenzo di Credi	75	45
369	60 c. Palma the Older	80	50
370	96 c. Raphael	1·00	80

1985. Birth Bicentenary of John J. Audubon (ornithologist). Multicoloured.

373	20 c. Type **52**	2·00	1·75
374	55 c. Sage grouse	2·75	2·75
375	65 c. Solitary sandpiper	3·00	3·00
376	75 c. Dunlin	3·25	3·50

Nos. 373/6 show original paintings.

1985. Life and Times of Queen Elizabeth the Queen Mother. Each violet, silver and yellow.

378	75 c. Type **53**	40	65
379	95 c. With baby Princess Elizabeth, 1926	50	80
380	$1.20 Coronation Day, 1937	65	1·00
381	$2.80 On her 70th birthday	1·25	2·00

54 "The House in the Wood"

1985. International Youth Year. Birth Centenary of Jacob Grimm (folklorist). Multicoloured.

383	75 c. Type **54**	2·00	2·00
384	95 c. "Snow-White and Rose-Red"	2·25	2·25
385	$1.15 "The Goose Girl"	2·50	2·50

55 "The Annunciation"

1985. Christmas. Paintings by Murillo. Mult.

386	75 c. Type **55**	1·25	1·25
387	$1.15 "Adoration of the Shepherds"	1·75	1·75
388	$1.80 "The Holy Family"	2·50	2·50

56 Halley's Comet

1986. Appearance of Halley's Comet. Design showing details of the painting "Fire and Ice" by Camille Rendal. Multicoloured.

391	$1.50 Type **56**	1·75	1·50
392	$1.50 Stylized "Giotto" spacecraft	1·75	1·50

Nos. 391/2 were printed together, forming a composite design of the complete painting.

57 Princess Elizabeth aged Three, 1929, and Bouquet

1986. 60th Birthday of Queen Elizabeth II. Multicoloured.

394	95 c. Type **57**	1·00	80
395	$1.45 Profile of Queen Elizabeth and St. Edward's Crown	1·50	1·25
396	$2.50 Queen Elizabeth aged three and in profile with Imperial State Crown (56 × 30 mm)	2·25	2·00

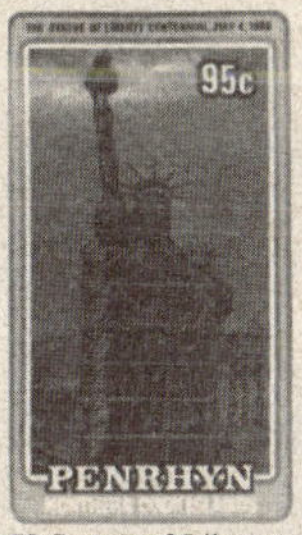
58 Statue of Liberty under Construction, Paris

59 Prince Andrew and Miss Sarah Ferguson

1986. Centenary of Statue of Liberty. Each black, gold and green.

397	95 c. Type **58**	65	70
398	$1.75 Erection of Statue, New York	1·10	1·25
399	$3 Artist's impression of Statue, 1876	2·10	2·25

1986. Royal Wedding. Multicoloured.

400	$2.50 Type **59**	3·50	3·50
401	$3.50 Profiles of Prince Andrew and Miss Sarah Ferguson	4·00	4·00

61 "Adoration of the Shepherds"

65 "The Garvagh Madonna"

1986. Christmas. Engravings by Rembrandt. Each brown, ochre and gold.

404	65 c. Type **61**	1·75	1·75
405	$1.75 "Virgin and Child"	3·00	3·00
406	$2.50 "The Holy Family"	4·25	4·25

1986. Visit of Pope John Paul II to South Pacific. Nos. 404/6 surch **SOUTH PACIFIC VISIT 21 TO 24 NOVEMBER 1986 +10c**.

408	65 c. + 10 c. Type **61**	2·25	2·00
409	$1.75 + 10 c. "Virgin and Child"	3·75	3·50
410	$2.50 + 10 c. "The Holy Family"	4·50	4·00

1987. Royal Ruby Wedding. Nos. 68/9 optd **Fortieth Royal Wedding Anniversary 1947–87**.

413	$2 Birds-eye view of Penrhyn	2·00	2·25
414	$5 Satellite view of Australasia	3·50	4·25

1987. Christmas. Religious Paintings by Raphael. Multicoloured.

415	95 c. Type **65**	1·50	1·50
416	$1.60 "The Alba Madonna"	2·00	2·00
417	$2.25 "The Madonna of the Fish"	3·00	3·00

66 Athletics

1988. Olympic Games, Seoul. Multicoloured.

420	55 c. Type **66**	65	65
421	95 c. Pole vaulting (vert)	1·00	1·00
422	$1.25 Shot putting	1·40	1·40
423	$1.50 Lawn tennis (vert)	2·25	1·75

1988. Olympic Gold Medal Winners, Seoul. Nos. 420/3 optd.

425	55 c. Type **66** (optd **CARL LEWIS UNITED STATES 100 METERS**)	70	60
426	95 c. Pole vaulting (optd **LOUISE RITTER UNITED STATES HIGH JUMP**)	1·00	90
427	$1.25 Shot putting (optd **ULF TIMMERMANN EAST GERMANY SHOT-PUT**)	1·50	1·25
428	$1.50 Lawn tennis (optd **STEFFI GRAF WEST GERMANY WOMEN'S TENNIS**)	2·75	1·40

67 "Virgin and Child"

69 Virgin Mary

68 Neil Armstrong stepping onto Moon

1988. Christmas. Designs showing different "Virgin and Child" paintings by Titian.

430 **67**	70 c. multicoloured	90	90
431 –	85 c. multicoloured	1·00	1·00
432 –	95 c. multicoloured	1·25	1·25
433 –	$1.25 multicoloured	1·50	1·50

1989. 20th Anniv of First Manned Moon Landing. Multicoloured.

435	55 c. Type **68**	70	60
436	75 c. Astronaut on Moon carrying equipment	85	75
437	95 c. Conducting experiment on Moon	1·10	95
438	$1.25 Crew of "Apollo 11"	1·40	1·25
439	$1.75 Crew inside "Apollo 11"	1·75	1·60

1989. Christmas. Details from "The Nativity" by Durer. Multicoloured.

440	55 c. Type **69**	80	80
441	70 c. Christ Child and cherubs	90	90
442	85 c. Joseph	1·25	1·25
443	$1.25 Three women	1·60	1·60

70 Queen Elizabeth the Queen Mother

1990. 90th Birthday of Queen Elizabeth the Queen Mother.

445 **70**	$2.25 multicoloured	2·50	2·50

71 "Adoration of the Magi" (Veronese)

1990. Christmas. Religious Paintings. Multicoloured.

447	55 c. Type **71**	1·00	1·00
448	70 c. "Virgin and Child" (Quentin Metsys)	1·40	1·40
449	85 c. "Virgin and Child Jesus" (Hugo van der Goes)	1·60	1·60
450	$1.50 "Adoration of the Kings" (Jan Gossaert)	2·50	2·50

1990. "Birdpex '90" Stamp Exhibition, Christchurch, New Zealand. Nos. 373/6 surch **Birdpex '90** and emblem.

452	$1.50 on 20 c. Type **52**	1·50	1·75
453	$1.50 on 55 c. Sage grouse	1·50	1·75
454	$1.50 on 65 c. Solitary sandpiper	1·50	1·75
455	$1.50 on 75 c. Dunlin	1·50	1·75

1991. 65th Birthday of Queen Elizabeth II. No. 208 optd **COMMEMORATING 65th BIRTHDAY OF H.M. QUEEN ELIZABETH II**.

456	$6 H.M.S. "Resolution" and "Discovery", 1776–80	9·00	10·00

74 "The Virgin and Child with Saints" (G. David)

1991. Christmas. Religious Paintings. Multicoloured.

457	55 c. Type **74**	1·00	1·00
458	85 c. "Nativity" (Tintoretto)	1·50	1·50
459	$1.15 "Mystic Nativity" (Botticelli)	1·75	1·75
460	$1.85 "Adoration of the Shepherds" (B. Murillo)	2·75	3·25

1992. Olympic Games, Barcelona. As T **94** of Aitutaki. Multicoloured.

462	75 c. Running	1·25	1·25
463	95 c. Boxing	1·50	1·50
464	$1.15 Swimming	1·60	1·60
465	$1.50 Wrestling	1·75	1·75

75 Marquesan Canoe

1992. 6th Festival of Pacific Arts, Rarotonga. Multicoloured.

466	$1.15 Type **75**	1·40	1·40
467	$1.75 Tangaroa statue from Rarotonga	1·90	1·90
468	$1.95 Manihiki canoe	2·00	2·00

1992. Royal Visit by Prince Edward. Nos. 466/8 optd **ROYAL VISIT**.

469	$1.15 Type **75**	1·75	1·75
470	$1.75 Tangaroa statue from Rarotonga	2·50	2·50
471	$1.95 Manihiki canoe	3·00	3·00

76 "Virgin with Child and Saints" (Borgognone)

77 Vicente Pinzon and "Nina"

1992. Christmas. Religious Paintings by Ambrogio Borgognone. Multicoloured.

472	55 c. Type **76**	75	75
473	85 c. "Virgin on Throne"	1·10	1·10
474	$1.05 "Virgin on Carpet"	1·40	1·40
475	$1.85 "Virgin of the Milk"	2·25	2·25

1992. 500th Anniv of Discovery of America by Columbus. Multicoloured.
477 $1.15 Type **77** . . . . 2·00 2·00
478 $1.35 Martin Pinzon and "Pinta" 2·25 2·25
479 $1.75 Christopher Columbus and "Santa Maria" . . . . . . 3·00 3·00

78 Queen Elizabeth II in 1953

80 "Virgin on Throne with Child" (detail) (Tura)

79 Bull-mouth Helmet

1993. 40th Anniv of Coronation.
480 **78** $6 multicoloured . . . . . 6·50 8·00

1993. Marine Life. Multicoloured.
481 5 c. Type **79** 10 10
482 10 c. Daisy coral 10 10
483 15 c. Hydroid coral 10 15
484 20 c. Feather-star 15 20
485 25 c. Sea star 15 20
486 30 c. Varicose nudibranch . . 20 25
487 50 c. Smooth sea star 30 35
488 70 c. Black-lip pearl oyster . . 45 50
489 80 c. Four-coloured nudibranch 50 55
490 85 c. Prickly sea cucumber . . 55 60
491 90 c. Organ pipe coral 55 60
492 $1 Blue sea lizard 65 70
493 $2 Textile cone shell . . . . . 1·25 1·40
494 $3 Starfish . . . . 1·40 2·00
495 $5 As $3 . . . . 3·25 3·50
496 $8 As $3 . . . . 5·00 5·25
497 $10 As $3 . . . . 6·25 6·50
Nos. 494/7 are larger, 47 × 34 mm, and include a portrait of Queen Elizabeth II at top right.

1993. Christmas.
499 **80** 55 c. multicoloured . . . . 1·00 1·00
500 – 85 c. multicoloured . . . . 1·50 1·50
501 – $1.05 multicoloured . . . . 1·75 1·75
502 – $1.95 multicoloured . . . . 2·75 3·00
503 – $4.50 mult (32 × 47 mm) . . 6·00 7·00
DESIGNS: 80 c. to $4.50, Different details from "Virgin on Throne with Child" (Cosme Tura).

81 Neil Armstrong stepping onto Moon

1994. 25th Anniv of First Manned Moon Landing.
504 **81** $3.25 multicoloured . . . . 5·50 6·00

82 "The Virgin and Child with Sts. Paul and Jerome" (Vivarini)

84 Queen Elizabeth the Queen Mother at Remembrance Day Ceremony

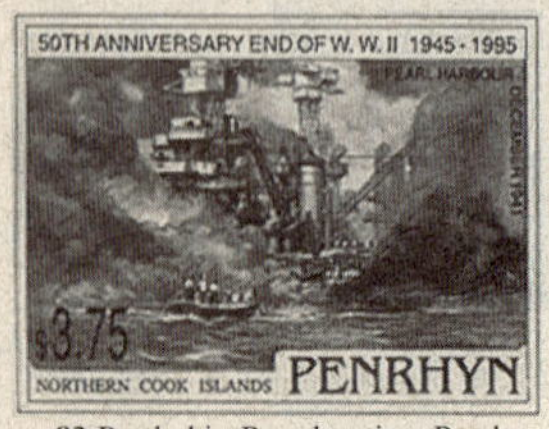

83 Battleship Row burning, Pearl Harbor

1994. Christmas. Religious Paintings. Multicoloured.
505 90 c. Type **82** . . . . 1·10 1·25
506 90 c. "The Virgin and Child with St. John" (Luini) . . . . . 1·10 1·25
507 90 c. "The Virgin and Child with Sts. Jerome and Dominic" (Lippi) . . . . 1·10 1·25
508 90 c. "Adoration of the Shepherds" (Murillo) . . . 1·10 1·25
509 $1 "Adoration of the Kings" (detail of angels) (Reni) . . 1·10 1·25
510 $1 "Madonna and Child with the Infant Baptist" (Raphael) . . 1·10 1·25
511 $1 "Adoration of the Kings" (detail of manger) (Reni) . . 1·10 1·25
512 $1 "Virgin and Child" (Borgognone) . . . . . . 1·10 1·25

1995. 50th Anniv of End of Second World War. Multicoloured.
513 $3.75 Type **83** . . . . 4·25 4·75
514 $3.75 Boeing B-25 Superfortress "Enola Gay" over Hiroshima 4·25 4·75

1995. 95th Birthday of Queen Elizabeth the Queen Mother.
515 **84** $4.50 multicoloured . . . . 6·00 7·00

85 Anniversary Emblem, United Nations Flag and Headquarters

1995. 50th Anniv of United Nations.
516 **85** $4 multicoloured . . . . . 4·00 5·00

86 Loggerhead Turtle

1995. Year of the Sea Turtle. Multicoloured.
517 $1.15 Type **86** . . . . 1·75 2·00
518 $1.15 Hawksbill turtle . . . . 1·75 2·00
519 $1.65 Olive ridley turtle . . . 2·25 2·50
520 $1.65 Green turtle . . . . . . 2·25 2·50

87 Queen Elizabeth II and Rose

1996. 70th Birthday of Queen Elizabeth.
521 **87** $4.25 multicoloured . . . 4·75 5·50

88 Olympic Flame, National Flags and Sports

1996. Centenary of Modern Olympic Games.
522 **88** $5 multicoloured . . . . 5·50 6·00

89 Royal Wedding, 1947

1997. Golden Wedding of Queen Elizabeth and Prince Philip.
523 **89** $3 multicoloured . . . . 2·50 2·75

90 Diana, Princess of Wales with Sons

1998. Diana, Princess of Wales Commemoration.
525 **90** $1.50 multicoloured . . . . 95 1·00

OFFICIAL STAMPS

1978. Optd or surch **O.H.M.S.**
O 1 1 c. multicoloured (No. 57) . 15 10
O 2 2 c. multicoloured (No. 58) . 15 10
O 3 3 c. multicoloured (No. 59) . 25 10
O 4 4 c. multicoloured (No. 60) . 25 10
O 5 5 c. multicoloured (No. 61) . 30 10
O 6 8 c. multicoloured (No. 62) . 35 15
O 7 10 c. multicoloured (No. 63) . 40 15
O 8 15 c. on 60 c. mult (No. 66) . 45 25
O 9 18 c. on 60 c. mult (No. 66) . 50 25
O10 20 c. multicoloured (No. 64) . 50 25
O11 25 c. multicoloured (No. 65) . 55 30
O12 30 c. on 60 c. mult (No. 66) . 55 35
O13 50 c. multicoloured (No. 89) . 90 55
O14 50 c. multicoloured (No. 90) . 90 55
O15 50 c. multicoloured (No. 91) . 90 55
O16 $1 multicoloured (No. 101) . . 2·25 65
O17 $2 multicoloured (No. 102) . . 4·00 80

1965. Nos. 206/8, 278/81, 337/47 and 349/55 optd **O.H.M.S.** or surch also.
O18 2 c. Type **47** 30 30
O19 4 c. Amatasi 30 30
O20 5 c. Ndrua 30 30
O21 8 c. Tongiaki 30 30
O22 10 c. "Vitoria" 30 30
O23 18 c. "Golden Hind" 50 50
O24 20 c. "La Boudeuse" 50 50
O25 30 c. H.M.S. "Bounty" . . . 50 50
O26 40 c. on 36 c. "L'Astrolabe" . 55 50
O27 50 c. "Star of India" 60 50
O28 55 c. on 48 c. "Great Republic" 60 50
O39 65 c. on 60 c. Type **40** 70 60
O40 65 c. on 60 c. Aerial view of Penrhyn atoll 70 60
O41 65 c. on 60 c. Eleanor Roosevelt on Penrhyn during Second World War 70 60
O42 65 c. on 60 c. Map of South Pacific 70 60
O29 75 c. on 72 c. "Antiope" . . . 1·00 70
O30 75 c. on 96 c. "Cap Hornier" . 1·00 70
O31 80 c. "Balcutha" . . . . . . 1·00 70
O32 $1.20 "Pamir" . . . . 1·25 1·00
O33 $2 "Cutty Sark" . . . . . . 2·00 1·60
O34 $3 "Mermerus" . . . . 3·00 2·40
O35 $4 "Mermerus" . . . . 4·00 3·25
O36 $5 "Cutty Sark" . . . . . . 5·00 4·00
O37 $6 H.M.S. "Resolution" and H.M.S. "Discovery" . . . . 6·00 5·00
O38 $9.60 H.M.S. "Resolution" and H.M.S. "Discovery" . . . . 9·50 7·25

1998. Nos. 481/93 optd **O.H.M.S.**
O43 5 c. Type **79** 10 10
O44 10 c. Daisy coral 10 10
O45 15 c. Hydroid coral 10 15
O46 20 c. Feather-star 15 20
O47 25 c. Sea star 15 20
O48 30 c. Varicose nudibranch . . 20 25
O49 50 c. Smooth sea star 30 35
O50 70 c. Black-lip pearl oyster . . 45 50
O51 80 c. Four-coloured nudibranch 50 55
O52 85 c. Prickly sea cucumber . . 55 60
O53 90 c. Organ pipe coral 55 60
O54 $1 Blue sea lizard 65 70
O55 $2 Textile cone shell . . . . . 1·25 1·40

PERAK

A state of the Federation of Malaya, incorporated in Malaysia in 1963.

100 cents = 1 dollar (Straits or Malayan)

Stamps of Straits Settlement optd or surch.

1878. No. 11 optd with crescent and star and **P** in oval.
1 2 c. brown £1300 £950

1880. Optd **PERAK**.
10 **9** 2 c. brown . . . . 19·00 35·00
17 2 c. red . . . . 1·25 1·10

1883. Surch **2 CENTS PERAK**.
16 2 c. on 4 c. red £475 £225

1886. No. 63a surch **ONE CENT PERAK**. (a) Without full point
30 1 c. on 2 c. red . . . . 28·00 40·00
(b) With final full point.
26 1 c. on 2 c. red . . . . 45·00 65·00

1886. No. 63a surch **1 CENT PERAK**.
28 1 c. on 2 c. red . . . . 85·00 95·00

1886. No. 63a surch **One CENT PERAK**.
33b 1 c. on 2 c. red . . . . 1·25 1·90

1889. No. 17 surch **ONE CENT** (with full point).
41 1 c. on 2 c. red £160 £120

1891. Surch **PERAK One CENT**.
57 1 c. on 2 c. red . . . . 55 3·50
43 1 c. on 6 c. lilac . . . . . . 40·00 25·00

1891. Surch **PERAK Two CENTS**.
48 2 c. on 24 c. green . . . . . . 9·00 9·00

42 Tiger **44** Tiger

45 Elephants

1892.
61 **42** 1 c. green . . . . 2·25 15
62 2 c. red . . . . 1·75 30
63 2 c. orange . . . . 35 3·25
64 5 c. blue . . . . 3·25 7·50

1895. Surch **3 CENTS**.
65 **42** 3 c. red . . . . 1·00 1·75

1895.
66 **44** 1 c. purple and green . . . 1·00 40
67 2 c. purple and brown . . . 75 40
68 3 c. purple and red . . . . 1·50 30
69 4 c. purple and red . . . . 7·50 4·75
70 5 c. purple and yellow . . . 2·75 55
71 8 c. purple and blue . . . . 38·00 65
72 10 c. purple and orange . . 8·00 45
73 25 c. green and red . . . . £110 12·00
74 50 c. purple and black . . . 35·00 29·00
75 50 c. green and black . . . £140 £140
76 **45** $1 green £100 £110
77 $2 green and red £170 £180
78 $3 green and yellow £200 £250
79 $5 green and blue £425 £400
80 $25 green and orange . . . £5500 £1800

1900. Surch in words.
81 **44** 1 c. on 2 c. purple and brown 40 2·00
82 1 c. on 4 c. purple and red . 65 7·50
83 1 c. on 5 c. purple & yellow . 90 8·50
84 3 c. on 8 c. purple and blue 2·50 6·00
85 3 c. on 50 c. green and black 1·50 5·00
86 **45** 3 c. on $1 green . . . . . . 55·00 £140
87 3 c. on $2 green and red . . 28·00 85·00

50 Sultan Iskandar **51** Sultan Iskandar

1935.
88 **50** 1 c. black 30 10
89 2 c. green 30 10
90 4 c. orange 30 10
91 5 c. brown 30 10
92 6 c. red . . . . 9·00 3·25
93 8 c. grey 50 10
94 10 c. purple 30 15
95 12 c. blue 70 90
96 25 c. purple and red 85 85
97 30 c. purple and orange . . 1·00 1·50
98 40 c. red and purple . . . . 2·75 4·25
99 50 c. black on green . . . . 3·50 90
100 $1 black and red on blue . 2·25 90
101 $2 green and red . . . . . 15·00 8·50
102 $5 green and red on green . 60·00 28·00

1938.

103	51	1 c. black	5·50	10
104		2 c. green	2·75	10
105		2 c. orange	2·00	6·00
106		3 c. green	1·75	4·25
107		4 c. orange	30·00	10
108		5 c. brown	4·25	10
109		6 c. red	26·00	10
110		8 c. grey	22·00	10
111		8 c. red	1·00	60·00
112		10 c. purple	22·00	10
113		12 c. blue	20·00	2·00
114		15 c. blue	1·75	13·00
115		25 c. purple and red	70·00	4·25
116		30 c. purple and orange	9·50	3·00
117		40 c. red and purple	50·00	2·00
118		50 c. black on green	26·00	75
119		$1 black and red on blue	£130	16·00
120		$2 green and red	£140	60·00
121		$5 green and red on green	£200	£275

1948. Silver Wedding. As T **10/11** of Aden.

122		10 c. violet	15	10
123		$5 green	20·00	25·00

1949. U.P.U. As T **20/23** of Antigua.

124		10 c. purple	15	10
125		15 c. blue	1·00	1·00
126		25 c. orange	45	45
127		50 c. black	1·75	2·75

52 Sultan Yussuf 'Izzuddin Shah — **53** Sultan Idris Shah

1950.

128	52	1 c. black	10	10
129		2 c. orange	10	10
130		3 c. green	1·75	10
131		4 c. brown	10	10
132		5 c. purple	50	90
133		6 c. grey	10	10
134		8 c. red	30	85
135		8 c. green	1·00	60
136		10 c. purple	10	10
137		12 c. red	1·00	2·75
138		15 c. blue	30	10
139		20 c. black and green	30	30
140		20 c. blue	75	10
141		25 c. purple and orange	30	10
142		30 c. red and purple	1·25	20
143		35 c. red and purple	70	25
144		40 c. red and purple	1·50	4·25
145		50 c. black and blue	80	10
146		$1 blue and purple	7·00	40
147		$2 green and red	13·00	4·50
148		$5 green and brown	38·00	11·00

1953. Coronation. As T **13** of Aden.

149		10 c. black and purple	70	10

1957. As Nos. 92/102 of Kedah, but portrait of Sultan Yussuf Izzuddin Shah.

150		1 c. black	10	20
151		2 c. orange	30	30
152		4 c. brown	10	10
153		5 c. lake	10	10
154		8 c. green	2·00	2·25
155		10 c. sepia	55	10
156		10 c. purple	1·25	10
157		20 c. blue	1·25	10
158a		50 c. black and blue	30	10
159		$1 blue and purple	5·00	30
160a		$2 green and red	3·25	1·50
161a		$5 brown and green	8·00	4·25

1963. Installation of Sultan of Perak.

162	53	10 c. multicoloured	10	10

54 "Vanda hookeriana"

1965. As Nos. 115/21 of Kedah, but with inset portrait of Sultan Idris as in T **54**.

163	54	1 c. multicoloured	10	30
164	–	2 c. multicoloured	10	30
165	–	5 c. multicoloured	10	10
166	–	6 c. multicoloured	15	30
167	–	10 c. multicoloured	15	10
168	–	15 c. multicoloured	80	10
169	–	20 c. multicoloured	1·25	10

The higher values used in Perak were Nos. 20/7 of Malaysia (National Issues).

55 "Delias ninus"

1971. Butterflies. As Nos. 124/30 of Kedah, but with portrait of Sultan Idris as In T **55**.

172	55	1 c. multicoloured	30	90
173	–	2 c. multicoloured	80	90
174	–	5 c. multicoloured	90	10
175	–	6 c. multicoloured	90	90
176	–	10 c. multicoloured	90	10
177	–	15 c. multicoloured	90	10
178	–	20 c. multicoloured	1·50	30

The higher values in use with this issue were Nos. 64/71 of Malaysia (National Issues).

56 "Rafflesia hasseltii" — **57** Coffee

1979. Flowers. As Nos. 135/41 of Kedah but with portrait of Sultan Idris as in T **56**.

184		1 c. Type **56**	10	30
185		2 c. "Pterocarpus indicus"	10	30
186		5 c. "Lagerstroemia speciosa"	10	10
187		10 c. "Durio zibethinus"	15	10
188		15 c. "Hibiscus rosa-sinensis"	15	10
189		20 c. "Rhododendron scortechinii"	20	10
190		25 c. "Etlingera elatior" (inscr"Phaeomeria speciosa")	40	10

1986. As Nos. 152/8 of Kedah but with portrait of Sultan Azlan Shah as in T **57**.

198		1 c. Type **57**	10	10
199		2 c. Coconuts	10	10
200		5 c. Cocoa	10	10
201		10 c. Black pepper	10	10
202		15 c. Rubber	10	10
203		20 c. Oil palm	10	10
204		30 c. Rice	15	20

OFFICIAL STAMPS

1889. Stamps of Straits Settlements optd **P.G.S.**

O1	30	2 c. red	2·50	3·25
O2		4 c. brown	8·00	16·00
O3		6 c. lilac	18·00	35·00
O4		8 c. orange	24·00	65·00
O5	38	10 c. grey	75·00	75·00
O6	30	12 c. blue	£170	£180
O7		12 c. purple	£200	£250
O9		24 c. green	£140	£160

1894. No. 64 optd **Service.**

O10	30	5 c. blue	45·00	80

1895. No. 70 optd **Service.**

O11	31	5 c. purple and yellow	1·50	35

PERLIS

A state of the Federation of Malaya, incorporated in Malaysia in 1963.

100 cents = 1 dollar (Straits or Malayan)

1948. Silver Wedding. As T **10/11** of Aden.

1		10 c. violet	30	2·00
2		$5 brown	28·00	42·00

1949. U.P.U. As T **20/23** of Antigua.

3		10 c. purple	30	60
4		15 c. blue	1·25	3·00
5		25 c. orange	65	2·00
6		50 c. black	1·40	3·75

1 Raja Syed Putra — **2** "Vanda hookeriana"

1951.

7	1	1 c. black	10	80
8		2 c. orange	15	40
9		3 c. green	60	2·75
10		4 c. brown	80	30
11		5 c. purple	30	2·50
12		6 c. grey	80	1·25
13		8 c. red	1·50	4·50
14		8 c. green	75	2·50
15		10 c. purple	30	20
16		12 c. red	75	2·50
17		15 c. blue	1·75	3·00
18		20 c. black and green	80	5·00
19		20 c. blue	85	65
20		25 c. purple and orange	1·00	1·25
21		30 c. red and purple	1·75	8·00
22		35 c. red and purple	75	3·25
23		40 c. red and purple	1·50	15·00
24		50 c. black and blue	2·50	4·00
25		$1 blue and purple	5·50	14·00
26		$2 green and red	12·00	22·00
27		$5 green and brown	50·00	60·00

1953. Coronation. As T **13** of Aden.

28		10 c. black and purple	50	2·25

1957. As Nos. 92/102 of Kedah, but inset portrait of Raja Syed Putra.

29		1 c. black	10	30
30		2 c. red	10	30
31		4 c. brown	10	10
32		5 c. lake	10	10
33		8 c. green	2·00	1·75
34		10 c. brown	50	1·25
35		10 c. purple	3·00	2·00
36		20 c. blue	1·25	2·00
37		50 c. black and blue	40	2·00
38		$1 blue and purple	4·25	6·50
39		$2 green and red	4·25	6·00
40		$5 brown and green	8·00	9·00

1965. As Nos. 115/21 of Kedah, but with inset portrait of Tunku Bendahara Abu Bakar as in T **2**.

41	2	1 c. multicoloured	10	60
42	–	2 c. multicoloured	10	70
43	–	5 c. multicoloured	15	15
44	–	6 c. multicoloured	65	45
45	–	10 c. multicoloured	65	15
46	–	15 c. multicoloured	1·00	35
47	–	20 c. multicoloured	1·00	95

The higher values used in Perlis were Nos. 20/7 of Malaysia (National Issues).

3 "Danaus melanippus" — **4** Raja Syed Putra

1971. Butterflies. As Nos. 124/30 of Kedah, but with portrait of Raja Syed Putra as in T **3**.

48	–	1 c. multicoloured	20	80
49	3	2 c. multicoloured	30	1·00
50	–	5 c. multicoloured	90	55
51	–	6 c. multicoloured	90	1·50
52	–	10 c. multicolored	90	65
53	–	15 c. multicoloured	90	30
54	–	20 c. multicoloured	90	1·25

The higher values in use with this issue were Nos. 64/71 of Malaysia (National Issues).

1971. 25th Anniv of Installation of Raja Syed Putra.

56	4	10 c. multicoloured	30	1·25
57		15 c. multicoloured	30	50
58		50 c. multicoloured	80	3·25

5 "Pterocarpus indicus" — **6** Coconuts

1979. Flowers. As Nos. 135/41 of Kedah, but with portrait of Raja Syed Putra as in T **5**.

59		1 c. "Rafflesia hasseltii"	10	60
60		2 c. Type **5**	10	60
61		5 c. "Lagerstroemia speciosa"	10	60
62		10 c. "Durio zibethinus"	15	10
63		15 c. "Hibiscus rosa-sinensis"	15	10
64		20 c. "Rhododendron scortechinii"	20	10
65		25 c. "Etlingera elatior" (inscr "Phaeomeria speciosa")	40	45

1986. As Nos. 152/8 of Kedah, but with portrait of Raja Syed Putra as in T **6**.

73		1 c. Coffee	10	10
74		2 c. Type **6**	10	10
75		5 c. Cocoa	10	10
76		10 c. Black pepper	10	10
77		15 c. Rubber	10	10
78		20 c. Oil palm	10	10
79		30 c. Rice	15	20

7 Raja Syed Putra and Aspects of Perlis

1995. 50th Anniv of Raja Syed Putra's Accession. Multicoloured.

80		30 c. Type **7**	20	30
81		$1 Raja Syed Putra and Palace	60	1·25

PITCAIRN ISLANDS

An island group in the Pacific Ocean, nearly midway between Australia and America.

1940. 12 pence = 1 shilling;
20 shillings = 1 pound.
1967. 100 cents = 1 New Zealand dollar.

4 Lt. Bligh and the "Bounty"

1940.

1	–	½d. orange and green	40	60
2	–	1d. mauve and magenta	55	70
3	–	1½d. grey and red	55	50
4	**4**	2d. green and brown	1·75	1·40
5	–	3d. green and blue	1·25	1·40
5b	–	4d. black and green	15·00	9·00
6	–	6d. brown and blue	5·00	2·00
6a	–	8d. green and mauve	16·00	7·00
7	–	1s. violet and grey	3·00	2·00
8	–	2s. 6d. green and brown	7·50	3·75

DESIGNS—HORIZ: ½d. Oranges; 1d. Fletcher Christian, crew and Pitcairn Is; 1½d. John Adams and house; 3d. Map of Pitcairn Is. and Pacific; 4d. Bounty Bible; 6d. H.M.S. "Bounty"; 8d. School, 1949; 1s. Christian and Pitcairn Is; 2s. 6d. Christian, crew and Pitcairn coast.

1946. Victory. As T **9** of Aden.

9	2d. brown	60	15
10	3d. blue	60	15

1949. Silver Wedding. As T **10/11** of Aden.

11	1½d. red	2·00	1·00
12	10s. mauve	48·00	50·00

1949. U.P.U. As T **20/23** of Antigua.

13	2½d. brown	1·50	3·50
14	3d. blue	12·00	4·00
15	6d. green	8·00	5·00
16	1s. purple	8·00	5·00

1953. Coronation. As T **13** of Aden.

17	4d. black and green	2·00	3·25

12 Handicrafts: Bird Model

1957.

33	–	½d. green and mauve	45	60
19	–	1d. black and green	2·75	1·00
20	–	2d. brown and blue	75	60
21	**12**	2½d. brown and pink	50	40
22	–	3d. green and blue	80	40
23	–	4d. red and blue (I)	90	40
23a	–	4d. red and blue (II)	5·00	1·50
24	**12**	6d. buff and blue	1·50	55
25	–	8d. green and red	60	40
26	–	1s. black and brown	1·50	40
27	–	2s. green and orange	19·00	10·00
28	–	2s. 6d. blue and red	19·00	9·00

DESIGNS—HORIZ: ½d. "Cordyline terminalis"; 3d. Bounty Bay; 4d. Pitcairn School; 6d. Map of Pacific; 8d. Inland scene; 1s. Model of the "Bounty"; 2s. 6d. Launching new whaleboat. VERT: 1d. Map of Pitcairn; 2d. John Adams and "Bounty" Bible; 2s. Island wheelbarrow.

The 4d. Type I is inscr "PITCAIRN SCHOOL"; Type II is inscr "SCHOOL TEACHER'S HOUSE".

20 Pitcairn Island and Simon Young

1961. Cent of Return of Pitcairn Islanders.

29	**20**	3d. black and yellow	50	40
30	–	6d. brown and blue	1·00	1·00
31	–	1s. orange and green	1·00	1·10

DESIGNS: 6d. Maps of Norfolk and Pitcairn Islands; 1s. Migrant brigantine "Mary Ann".

1963. Freedom from Hunger. As T **28** of Aden.

32	2s. 6d. blue	14·00	3·00

1963. Cent of Red Cross. As T **33** of Antigua.

34	2d. red and black	2·50	1·00
35	2s. 6d. red and blue	9·50	5·50

23 Pitcairn Is. Longboat

24 Queen Elizabeth II
(after Anthony Buckley)

1964. Multicoloured.

36	½d. Type **23**	10	30
37	1d. H.M.S. "Bounty"	30	30
38	2d. "Out from Bounty Bay"	30	30
39	3d. Great frigate bird	75	30
40	4d. White tern	75	30
41	6d. Pitcairn warbler	75	30
42	8d. Red-footed booby	75	30
43	10d. Red-tailed tropic birds	60	30
44	1s. Henderson Island crake	60	30
45	1s. 6d. Stephen's lory	5·50	1·25
46	2s. 6d. Murphy's petrel	5·00	1·50
47	4s. Henderson Island fruit dove	7·00	1·75
48	8s. Type **24**	2·75	1·75

1965. Cent of I.T.U. As T **36** of Antigua.

49	1d. mauve and brown	1·00	40
50	2s. 6d. turquoise and blue	14·00	3·50

1965. I.C.Y. As T **37** of Antigua.

51	1d. purple and turquoise	1·00	40
52	2s. 6d. green and lavender	12·00	4·50

1966. Churchill Commem. As T **38** of Antigua.

53	2d. blue	1·50	85
54	3d. green	4·50	1·00
55	6d. brown	5·50	2·00
56	1s. violet	7·50	3·25

1966. World Cup Football Championship. As T **40** of Antigua.

57	4d. multicoloured	1·75	1·00
58	2s. 6d. multicoloured	4·75	1·75

1966. Inauguration of W.H.O. Headquarters, Geneva. As T **41** of Antigua.

59	8d. black, green and blue	5·00	3·00
60	1s. 6d. black, purple and ochre	9·00	3·50

1966. 20th Anniv of U.N.E.S.C.O. As T **54/6** of Antigua.

61	½d. multicoloured	20	40
62	10d. yellow, violet and olive	4·50	2·25
63	2s. black, purple and orange	9·00	3·50

36 Mangarevan Canoe, c. 1325

1967. Bicentenary of Discovery of Pitcairn Islands'. Multicoloured.

64	½d. Type **36**	10	15
65	1d. P. F. de Quiros and "San Pedro y Pablo", 1606	20	15
66	8d. "San Pedro y Pablo" and "Los Tres Reyes", 1606	40	20
67	1s. Carteret and H.M.S. "Swallow", 1767	40	20
68	1s. 6d. "Hercules", 1819	40	20

1967. Decimal Currency. Nos. 36/48 surch with "Bounty" anchor and value.

69	**23**	½ c. on ½d. multicoloured	10	10
70	–	1 c. on 1d. multicoloured	30	50
71	–	2 c. on 2d. multicoloured	25	50
72	–	2½ c. on 3d. multicoloured	25	50
73	–	3 c. on 4d. multicoloured	25	20
74	–	5 c. on 6d. multicoloured	30	50
75	–	10 c. on 8d. multicoloured	30	30
76	–	15 c. on 10d. multicoloured	1·25	40
77	–	20 c. on 1s. multicoloured	1·25	55
78	–	25 c. on 1s. 6d. multicoloured	2·75	1·25
79	–	30 c. on 2s. 6d. multicoloured	3·25	1·25
80	–	40 c. on 4s. multicoloured	4·50	1·25
81	**24**	45 c. on 8s. multicoloured	4·25	1·50

42 Bligh and "Bounty's" "Launch"

1967. 150th Death Anniv of Admiral Bligh.

82	**42**	1 c. black, ultram & blue	10	10
83	–	8 c. black, yellow and mauve	40	65
84	–	20 c. black, brown and buff	45	70

DESIGNS: 8 c. Bligh and followers cast adrift; 20 c. Bligh's tomb.

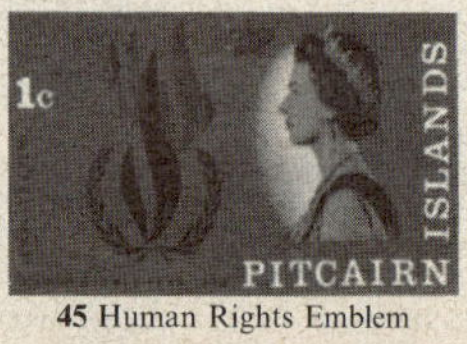

45 Human Rights Emblem

1968. International Human Rights Year.

85	**45**	1 c. multicoloured	10	10
86		2 c. multicoloured	10	10
87		25 c. multicoloured	35	35

46 Moro Wood and Flower

1968. Handicrafts (1st series).

88	**46**	5 c. multicoloured	25	30
89	–	10 c. green, brown & orange	30	40
90	–	15 c. violet, brown & salmon	35	40
91	–	20 c. multicoloured	40	45

DESIGNS—HORIZ: 10 c. flying fish model. VERT: 15 c. "Hand" vases; 20 c. Woven baskets.

See also Nos. 207/10.

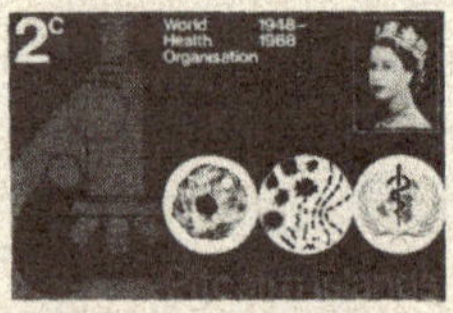

50 Microscope and Slides

1968. 20th Anniv of World Health Organization.

92	**50**	2 c. black, turquoise & blue	10	20
93	–	20 c. black, orange & purple	40	50

DESIGN: 20 c. Hypodermic syringe and jars of tablets.

52 Pitcairn Island

64b Queen Elizabeth II **65** Lantana

1969. Multicoloured.

94	1 c. Type **52**	75	30
95	2 c. Captain Bligh and "Bounty" chronometer	25	15
96	3 c. "Bounty" anchor	25	15
97	4 c. Plans and drawing of "Bounty"	60	15
98	5 c. Breadfruit containers and plant	30	15
99	6 c. Bounty Bay	30	20
100	8 c. Pitcairn longboat	50	20
101	10 c. Ship landing point	2·00	85
102	15 c. Fletcher Christian's Cave	60	50
103	20 c. Thursday October Christian's house	60	40
104	25 c. "Flying fox" cable system	70	40
105	30 c. Radio Station, Taro Ground	55	45
106	40 c. "Bounty" Bible	75	60
106a	50 c. Pitcairn Coat-of-Arms	7·00	11·00
106b	$1 Type **64b**	13·00	17·00

The 3 c. and 25 c. are vert.

1970. Flowers. Multicoloured.

107	1 c. Type **65**	20	50
108	2 c. "Indian Shot"	35	65
109	5 c. Pulau	60	75
110	25 c. Wild gladiolus	1·25	2·00

69 Band-tailed Hind

1970. Fishes. Multicoloured.

111	5 c. Type **69**	2·75	70
112	10 c. High-finned rudderfish	2·75	85
113	15 c. Elwyn's wrasse	3·25	1·00
114	20 c. Yellow wrasse ("Whistling daughter")	3·50	1·25

1971. Royal Visit. No. 101 optd **ROYAL VISIT 1971**.

115	10 c. multicoloured	1·75	2·50

71 Polynesian Rock Carvings

1971. Polynesian Pitcairn. Multicoloured.

116	5 c. Type **71**	2·00	1·00
117	10 c. Polynesian artefacts (horiz)	2·50	1·25
118	15 c. Polynesian stone fish-hook (horiz)	2·75	1·25
119	20 c. Polynesian stone deity	2·75	1·50

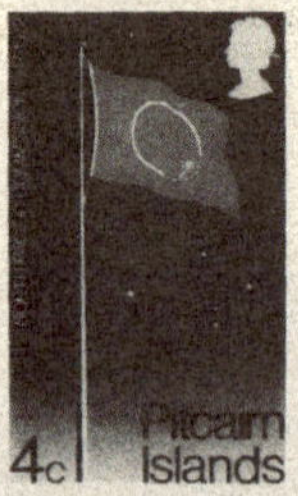

72 Commission Flag **74** Rose-apple

1972. 25th Anniv of South Pacific Commission. Multicoloured.

120	4 c. Type **72**	75	75
121	8 c. Young and elderly (Health)	75	75
122	18 c. Junior school (Education)	80	1·10
123	20 c. Goods store (Economy)	1·50	1·75

1972. Royal Silver Wedding. As T **52** of Ascension, but with red-tailed tropic birds and longboat in background.

124	4 c. green	30	60
125	20 c. blue	45	90

1973. Flowers. Multicoloured.

126	4 c. Type **74**	1·00	55
127	8 c. Mountain-apple	1·25	75
128	15 c. "Lata"	2·25	1·00
129	20 c. "Dorcas-flower"	2·25	1·25
130	35 c. Guava	2·75	1·75

1973. Royal Wedding. As T **47** of Anguilla. Multicoloured, background colours given.

131	10 c. mauve	20	15
132	25 c. green	25	30

75 Obelisk Vertagus and Episcopal Mitre Shells

1974. Shells. Multicoloured.

147	4 c. Type **75**	1·50	70
148	10 c. Turtle dove-shell	1·75	90
149	18 c. Indo-Pacific limpet, fringed false limpet and "Siphonaria normalis"	2·00	1·25
150	50 c. "Ctena divergen"	2·75	1·75

76 Island Post Office

1974. Centenary of U.P.U.

152	**76**	4 c. multicoloured	25	35
153	–	20 c. purple, brown & black	40	60
154	–	35 c. multicoloured	50	70

DESIGNS: 20 c. Pre-stamp letter, 1922; 35 c. Mailship and Pitcairn longboat.

77 Churchill and Text "Lift up your Hearts . . ."

1974. Birth Cent of Sir Winston Churchill.

155	**77**	20 c. olive, green and grey	40	85
156	–	35 c. brown, green & grey	60	90

DESIGN: 35 c. Text "Give us the tools . . .".

78 H.M.S. "Seringapatam" (frigate), 1830

1975. Mailboats. Multicoloured.

157	4 c. Type **78**	40	60
158	10 c. "Pitcairn" (missionary schooner), 1890	50	85
159	18 c. "Athenic" (liner), 1904	60	1·40
160	50 c. "Gothic" (liner), 1948	1·25	2·25

79 "Polistes jadwigae" (wasp)

1975. Pitcairn Insects. Multicoloured.

162	4 c. Type **79**	40	45
163	6 c. "Euconocephalus sp." (grasshopper)	50	55
164	10 c. "Anomis flavia" and "Chasmina tibialis" (moth)	60	70
165	15 c. "Pantala flavescens" (skimmer)	80	1·25
166	20 c. "Gnathothlibus erotus" (banana moth)	1·10	1·50

80 Fletcher Christian   81 Chair of Homage

1976. Bicent of American Revolution. Mult.

167	5 c. Type **80**	30	65
168	10 c. H.M.S. "Bounty"	40	80
169	30 c. George Washington	50	95
170	50 c. "Mayflower", 1620	70	1·50

1977. Silver Jubilee. Multicoloured.

171	8 c. Prince Philip's visit, 1971	10	15
172	20 c. Type **81**	20	25
173	50 c. Enthronement	40	50

82 The Island's Bell

1977. Multicoloured.

174	1 c. Type **82**	30	50
175	2 c. Building a longboat (horiz)	30	50
176	5 c. Landing cargo (horiz)	35	50
177	6 c. Sorting supplies (horiz)	35	50
178	9 c. Cleaning wahoo (fish)	30	50
179	10 c. Cultivation (horiz)	30	50
179a	15 c. Sugar Mill (horiz)	1·25	1·00
180	20 c. Grating coconut and bananas (horiz)	30	50
181	35 c. The Island church (horiz)	35	70
182	50 c. Fetching miro logs, Henderson Is. (horiz)	35	80
182b	70 c. Burning obsolete stamp issues	1·25	1·25
183	$1 Prince Philip, Bounty Bay and Royal Yacht "Britannia" (horiz)	50	1·10
184	$2 Queen Elizabeth II (photograph by Reginald Davis)	90	1·75

83 Building a "Bounty" Model

1978. "Bounty" Day. Multicoloured.

185	6 c. Type **83**	35	35
186	20 c. The model at sea	45	60
187	35 c. Burning the model	60	70

85 Harbour before Development

1978. "Operation Pallium" (Harbour Development Project). Multicoloured.

190	15 c. Type **85**	30	50
191	20 c. Unloading R.F.A. "Sir Geraint"	40	60
192	30 c. Work on the jetty	45	70
193	35 c. Harbour after development	50	80

86 John Adams and Diary Extract

1979. 150th Death Anniv of John Adams ("Bounty" mutineer). Multicoloured.

194	35 c. Type **86**	30	70
195	70 c. John Adams' grave and diary extract	45	90

87 Pitcairn's Island sketched from H.M.S. "Amphitrite"

1979. 19th-century Engravings.

196	**87**	6 c. black, brown and stone	15	20
197	–	9 c. black, violet & lt violet	15	25
198	–	20 c. black, green & yellow	15	40
199	–	70 c. black, scarlet and red	50	1·00

DESIGNS: 9 c. Bounty Bay and Village of Pitcairn; 20 c. Lookout Ridge; 70 c. Church and School House.

88 Taking Presents to the Square

1979. Christmas. Int Year of the Child. Mult.

200	6 c. Type **88**	10	20
201	9 c. Decorating trees with presents	10	25
202	20 c. Chosen men distributing gifts	20	40
203	35 c. Carrying presents home	25	50

90 Queen Elizabeth the Queen Mother at Henley Regatta

1980. 80th Birthday of The Queen Mother.

206	**90**	50 c. multicoloured	40	70

1980. Handicrafts (2nd series). As T **46**. Multicoloured.

207	9 c. Turtles (wood carvings)	10	10
208	20 c. Pitcairn wheelbarrow (wood carving)	10	15
209	35 c. Gannet (wood carving) (vert)	15	25
210	40 c. Woven bonnet and fan (vert)	15	25

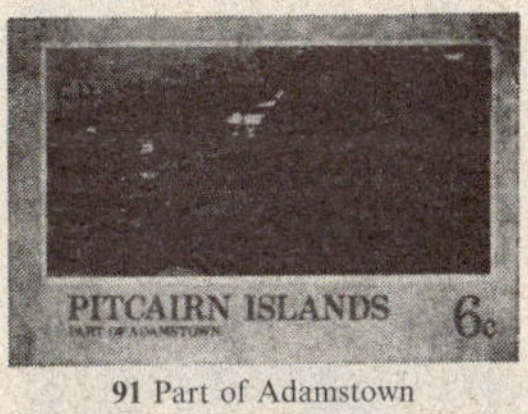

91 Part of Adamstown

1981. Landscapes. Multicoloured.

211	6 c. Type **91**	10	10
212	9 c. Big George	10	15
213	20 c. Christian's Cave, Gannets Ridge	15	20
214	35 c. Radio Station from Pawala Valley Ridge	20	30
215	70 c. Tatrimoa	30	45

92 Islanders preparing for Departure

1981. 125th Anniv of Pitcairn Islanders' Migration to Norfolk Island. Multicoloured.

216	9 c. Type **92**	30	35
217	35 c. View of Pitcairn Island from "Morayshire"	50	60
218	70 c. "Morayshire"	80	1·00

93 Prince Charles as Colonel-in-Chief, Cheshire Regiment   95 Pitcairn Islands Coat of Arms

94 Lemon

1981. Royal Wedding. Multicoloured.

219	20 c. Wedding bouquet from Pitcairn Islands	20	20
220	35 c. Type **93**	25	20
221	$1.20 Prince Charles and Lady Diana Spencer	75	60

1982. Fruit. Multicoloured.

222	9 c. Type **94**	10	10
223	20 c. Pomegranate	15	20
224	35 c. Avocado	25	30
225	70 c. Pawpaw	50	65

1982. 21st Birthday of Princess of Wales. Multicoloured.

226	6 c. Type **95**	10	20
227	9 c. Princess at Royal Opera House, Covent Garden, December 1981	30	20
228	70 c. Balcony Kiss	70	60
229	$1.20 Formal portrait	1·25	80

96 Raphael's Angels

1982. Christmas. Raphael's Angels.

230	**96**	15 c. black, silver and pink	15	15
231	–	20 c. black, silver and yellow	15	15
232	–	50 c. brown, silver and stone	30	30
233	–	$1 black, silver and blue	40	40

DESIGNS: 20 c. to $1 Different details, the 50 c. and $1 being vertical.

97 Radio Operator

1983. Commonwealth Day. Multicoloured.

234	6 c. Type **97**	10	10
235	9 c. Postal clerk	10	10
236	70 c. Fisherman	35	65
237	$1.20 Artist	60	1·10

98 "Topaz" sights Smoke on Pitcairn

1983. 175th Anniv of Folger's Discovery of the Settlers. Multicoloured.

238	6 c. Type **98**	30	20
239	20 c. Three islanders approach the "Topaz"	45	30
240	70 c. Capt. Mayhew Folger welcomed by John Adams	85	75
241	$1.20 Folger presented with "Bounty" chronometer	1·25	1·10

99 Hattie-Tree

1983. Trees of Pitcairn Islands (1st series). Multicoloured.

242	35 c. Type **99**	30	55
243	35 c. Leaves from Hattie-Tree	30	55
244	70 c. Pandanus	50	90
245	70 c. Pandanus and basket weaving	50	90

See also Nos. 304/7.

100 Atava wrasse

1984. Fishes. Multicoloured.

246	1 c. Type **100**	20	30
247	4 c. Black-eared wrasse	30	35
248	6 c. Long-finned parrotfish	30	35
249	9 c. Yellow-edged lyretail	30	35
250	10 c. Black-eared angelfish	30	40
251	15 c. Emery's damselfish	30	40
252	20 c. Smith's butterflyfish	40	50
253	35 c. Crosshatched triggerfish	50	60
254	50 c. Yellow damselfish	50	75
255	70 c. Pitcairn angelfish	70	95
312	90 c. As 9 c.	2·25	2·50
256	$1 Easter Island soldierfish	90	1·25
257	$1.20 Long-finned anthias	1·00	2·00
258	$2 White trevally	1·50	2·50
313	$3 Wakanoura moray	4·25	4·75

101 "Southern Cross"

1984. Night Sky.

259	**101**	15 c. blue, lilac and gold	20	20
260	–	20 c. blue, green and gold	30	30
261	–	70 c. blue, brown and gold	75	75
262	–	$1 blue, lt blue and gold	1·00	1·00

DESIGNS: 20 c. "Southern Fish"; 70 c. "Lesser Dog"; $1 "The Virgin".

103 "H.M.S. 'Portland' standing off Bounty Bay" (J. Linton Palmer)   104 The Queen Mother with the Queen and Princess Margaret, 1980

1985. 19th-Century Paintings (1st series). Mult.

264	6 c. Type **103**	30	20
265	9 c. "Christian's Look Out" (J. Linton Palmer)	30	20
266	35 c. "The Golden Age" (J. Linton Palmer)	65	50
267	$2 "A View of the Village, 1825" (William Smyth) (48 × 31 mm)	1·75	1·60

See also Nos. 308/11.

1985. Life and Times of Queen Elizabeth the Queen Mother. Multicoloured.

268	6 c. Receiving the Freedom of Dundee, 1964	10	20
269	35 c. Type **104**	30	55

270 70 c. The Queen Mother in 1983 . . . 50 80
271 $1.20 With Prince Henry at his christening (from photo by Lord Snowdon) . . . . . . 70 1·00

105 "Act 6" (container ship)

1985. Ships (1st issue). Multicoloured.
273 50 c. Type **105** . . . . . . 90 1·50
274 50 c. "Columbus Louisiana" (container ship) . . . . . . 90 1·50
275 50 c. "Essi Gina" (tanker) (48×35 mm) . . . . . . 90 1·50
276 50 c. "Stolt Spirit" tanker (48×35 mm) . . . . . . 90 1·50
See also Nos. 296/9.

106 "Madonna and Child" (Raphael)

108 John I. Tay (pioneer missionary) and First Church

107 Green Turtle

1985. Christmas. Designs showing "Madonna and Child" paintings. Multicoloured.
277 6 c. Type **106** 50 40
278 9 c. Krause (after Raphael) . . 50 40
279 35 c. Andreas Mayer 85 60
280 $2 Unknown Austrian master 2·50 3·25

1986. Turtles. Multicoloured.
281 9 c. Type **107** 85 75
282 20 c. Green turtle and Pitcairn Island . . . . . . 1·40 1·25
283 70 c. Hawksbill turtle . . . . 2·75 3·50
284 $1.20 Hawksbill turtle and Pitcairn Island . . . . . . 3·25 4·00

1986. 60th Birthday of Queen Elizabeth II. As T **110** of Ascension. Multicoloured.
285 6 c. Princess Elizabeth at Royal Lodge, Windsor, 1946 . . . 15 15
286 9 c. Wedding of Princess Anne, 1973 . . . . . . 15 15
287 20 c. At Order of St. Michael and St. George service, St. Paul's Cathedral, 1961 . . . . . . 25 30
288 $1.20 At Electrical Engineering Concert, Royal Festival Hall, 1971 . . . . . . 65 1·25
289 $2 At Crown Agents Head Office, London 1983 . . . 1·00 1·75

1986. Royal Wedding. As T **112** of Ascension. Multicoloured.
290 20 c. Prince Andrew and Miss Sarah Ferguson 50 50
291 $1.20 Prince Andrew aboard "Bluenose II" off Halifax, Canada, 1985 . . . . . . 1·40 2·00

1986. Centenary of Seventh-Day Adventist Church on Pitcairn. Multicoloured.
292 6 c. Type **108** 40 40
293 20 c. "Pitcairn" (missionary schooner) and second church (1907) . . . . . . 1·00 1·00
294 35 c. Baptism at Down Isaac and third church (1945) . . . . 1·50 1·50
295 $2 Islanders singing farewell hymn and present church (1954) . . . . . . 3·25 3·75

1987. Ships (2nd series). As T **105**. Multicoloured.
296 50 c. "Samoan Reefer" (freighter) . . . . . . 1·25 1·90
297 50 c. "Brussel" (container ship) 1·25 1·90
298 50 c. "Australian Exporter" (container ship) (48×35 mm) 1·25 1·90
299 50 c. "Taupo" (cargo liner) (48×35 mm) . . . . . . 1·25 1·90

109 Pitcairn Island Home

1987. Pitcairn Island Homes.
300 **109** 70 c. black, dp violet & vio 60 60
301 – 70 c. black, yell & brn . . 60 60
302 – 70 c. black, blue & dp blue 60 60
303 – 70 c. black, green & deep green 60 60
DESIGNS: Nos. 301/3, different houses.

1987. Trees of Pitcairn Islands (2nd series). As T **99**. Multicoloured.
304 40 c. Leaves and flowers from "Erythrina variegata" . . . 80 1·10
305 40 c. "Erythrina variegata" tree 80 1·10
306 $1.80 Leaves from "Aleurites moluccana" and nut torch 2·25 2·75
307 $1.80 "Aleurites moluccana" tree 2·25 2·75

1987. 19th-century Paintings (2nd series). Paintings by Lt. Conway Shipley in 1848. As T **103**. Multicoloured.
308 20 c. "House and Tomb of John Adams" 45 45
309 40 c. "Bounty Bay" 70 70
310 90 c. "School House and Chapel" . . . . . . 1·25 1·50
311 $1.80 "Pitcairn Island" (48×31 mm) . . . . . . 2·00 2·50

111 H.M.S. "Swallow" (survey ship), 1767

1988. Ships. Multicoloured.
315 5 c. Type **111** 40 60
316 10 c. H.M.S. "Pandora" (frigate), 1791 . . . . . . 40 60
317 15 c. H.M.S. "Briton" and H.M.S. "Tagus" (frigates), 1814 . . . . . . 55 70
318 20 c. H.M.S. "Blossom" (survey ship), 1825 . . . . . . 60 75
319 30 c. "Lucy Anne" (barque), 1831 . . . . . . 70 80
320 35 c. "Charles Doggett" (whaling brig), 1831 . . . . . . 70 80
321 40 c. H.M.S. "Fly" (sloop), 1838 75 85
322 60 c. "Camden" (missionary brig.), 1840 . . . . . . 1·00 1·25
323 90 c. H.M.S. "Virago" (paddle-sloop), 1853 . . . . . . 1·25 1·50
324 $1.20 "Rakaia" (screw-steamer), 1867 . . . . . . 1·50 1·75
325 $1.80 H.M.S. "Sappho" (screw-sloop), 1882 . . . . 1·75 2·25
326 $5 H.M.S. "Champion" (corvette), 1893 . . . . . . 4·50 5·00

112 Raising the Union Jack, 1838

113 Angel

1988. 150th Anniv of Pitcairn Island Constitution. Each showing different extract from original Constitution. Multicoloured.
327 20 c. Type **112** 15 20
328 40 c. Signing Constitution on board H.M.S. "Fly", 1838 . 30 35
329 $1.05 Voters at modern polling station 75 80
330 $1.80 Modern classroom . . 1·25 1·40

1988. Christmas. Multicoloured.
331 90 c. Type **113** 65 70
332 90 c. Holy Family 65 70
333 90 c. Two Polynesian Wise Men 65 70
334 90 c. Polynesian Wise Man and shepherd 65 70

114 Loading Stores, Deptford

1989. Bicentenary of Pitcairn Island Settlement (1st issue). Multicoloured.
335 20 c. Type **114** 70 70
336 20 c. H.M.S. "Bounty" leaving Spithead 70 70
337 20 c. H.M.S. "Bounty" at Cape Horn 70 70
338 20 c. Anchored in Adventure Bay, Tasmania 70 70
339 20 c. Crew collecting breadfruit 70 70
340 20 c. Breadfruit in cabin . . . 70 70
See also Nos. 341/7, 356/61 and 389/94.

1989. Bicentenary of Pitcairn Island Settlement (2nd issue). As T **114**. Multicoloured.
341 90 c. H.M.S. "Bounty' leaving Tahiti . . . . . . 1·75 2·00
342 90 c. Bligh awoken by mutineers 1·75 2·00
343 90 c. Bligh before Fletcher Christian . . . . . . 1·75 2·00
344 90 c. Provisioning "Bounty's" launch . . . . . . 1·75 2·00
345 90 c. "Mutineers casting Bligh adrift" (Robert Dodd) . . . 1·75 2·00
346 90 c. Mutineers discarding breadfruit plants . . . . . . 1·75 2·00

115 R.N.Z.A.F. Lockheed Orion making Mail Drop, 1985

1989. Aircraft. Multicoloured.
348 20 c. Type **115** 80 35
349 80 c. Beech 80 Queen Air on photo-mission, 1983 . . . . 1·75 95
350 $1.05 Boeing-Vertol Chinook helicopter landing diesel fuel from U.S.S. "Breton", 1969 . 2·00 1·25
351 $1.30 R.N.Z.A.F. Lockheed Hercules dropping bulldozer, 1983 . . . . . . 2·00 1·40

116 Ducie Island

1989. Islands of Pitcairn Group. Mult.
352 15 c. Type **116** 30 25
353 90 c. Henderson Island . . . . 1·40 90
354 $1.05 Oeno Island . . . . . . 1·50 1·25
355 $1.30 Pitcairn Island . . . . . 1·50 1·25

1990. Bicentenary of Pitcairn Island Settlement (3rd issue). As T **114**. Multicoloured.
356 40 c. Mutineers sighting Pitcairn Island 90 80
357 40 c. Ship's boat approaching landing 90 80
358 40 c. Exploring island 90 80
359 40 c. Ferrying goods ashore . . 90 80
360 40 c. Burning of H.M.S. "Bounty" 90 80
361 40 c. Pitcairn Island village . . 90 80

117 Ennerdale, Cumbria, and Peter Heywood

1990. "Stamp World London '90" International Stamp Exhibition, London. Designs showing English landmarks and "Bounty" crew members. Multicoloured.
362 80 c. Type **117** 75 80
363 90 c. St. Augustine's Tower, Hackney, and John Adams . 85 90
364 $1.05 Citadel Gateway, Plymouth, and William Bligh 1·00 1·25
365 $1.30 Moorland Close, Cockermouth, and Fletcher Christian . . . . . . 1·25 1·40

1990. 90th Birthday of Queen Elizabeth the Queen Mother. As T **134** of Ascension.
378 40 c. multicoloured 75 75
379 $3 black and red . . . . 3·00 3·50
DESIGNS—21×36 mm: 40 c. Queen Elizabeth, 1937. 29×37 mm: $3 King George VI and Queen Elizabeth on way to Silver Wedding Service, 1948.

118 "Bounty" Chronometer and 1940 1d. Definitive

1990. 50th Anniv of Pitcairn Islands Stamps. Multicoloured.
380 20 c. Type **118** 70 60
381 80 c. "Bounty" Bible and 1958 4d definitive . . . . . . 1·50 1·50
382 90 c. "Bounty" Bell and 1969 30 c. definitive . . . . . . 1·60 1·60
383 $1.05 Mutiny on the "Bounty" and 1977 $1 definitive . . . 1·75 2·00
384 $1.30 Penny Black and 1988 15 c. definitive . . . . . . 2·00 2·25

119 Stephen's Lory ("Redbreast")

1990. "Birdpex '90" International Stamp Exhibition, Christchurch, New Zealand. Multicoloured.
385 20 c. Type **119** 65 60
386 90 c. Henderson Island fruit dove ("Wood Pigeon") . . . . 1·50 1·60
387 $1.30 Pitcairn warbler ("Sparrow") . . . . . . 1·75 2·25
388 $1.80 Henderson Island crake ("Chicken Bird") . . . . 2·00 2·50

1991. Bicent of Pitcairn Island Settlement (4th issue). Celebrations. As T **114**. Multicoloured.
389 80 c. Re-enacting landing of mutineers . . . . . . 1·60 2·00
390 80 c. Commemorative plaque . 1·60 2·00
391 80 c. Memorial church service . 1·60 2·00
392 80 c. Cricket match . . . . 1·60 2·00
393 80 c. Burning model of "Bounty" 1·60 2·00
394 80 c. Firework display . . . . 1·60 2·00

120 "Europa"

1991. Cruise Liners. Multicoloured.
395 15 c. Type **120** . . . . . . 1·00 60
396 80 c. "Royal Viking Star" . . 2·00 1·75
397 $1.30 "World Discoverer" . . 2·50 2·75
398 $1.80 "Sagafjord" . . . . . . 3·00 3·50

1991. 65th Birthday of Queen Elizabeth II and 70th Birthday of Prince Philip. As T **280** of Antigua. Multicoloured.
399 20 c. Prince Philip (vert) . . . 40 30
400 $1.30 Queen in robes of the Order of St. Michael and St. George (vert) . . . . . . 1·60 1·25

121 Bulldozer

1991. Island Transport. Multicoloured.
401 20 c. Type **121** 40 30
402 80 c. Two-wheeled motorcycle 1·25 1·00
403 $1.30 Tractor . . . . . . 1·25 1·40
404 $1.80 Three-wheeled motorcycle 2·00 2·25

122 The Annunciation

1991. Christmas. Multicoloured.
405 20 c. Type **122** 30 30
406 80 c. Shepherds and lamb . . 90 90
407 $1.30 Holy Family . . . . 1·25 1·25
408 $1.80 Three Wise Men . . . 1·75 1·75

1992. 40th Anniv of Queen Elizabeth II's Accession. As T **143** of Ascension. Multicoloured.
409 20 c. Bounty Bay 25 25
410 60 c. Sunset over Pitcairn . . 70 70
411 90 c. Pitcairn coastline 90 90
412 $1 Three portraits of Queen Elizabeth 95 95
413 $1.80 Queen Elizabeth II . . . 1·60 1·60

123 Insular Shark

1992. Sharks. Multicoloured.

414	20 c. Type **123**	70	40
415	$1 Sand tiger	1·75	1·40
416	$1.50 Black-finned reef shark	2·00	1·90
417	$1.80 Grey reef shark	2·25	2·00

124 "Montastrea sp." and "Acropora spp." (corals)

1992. The Sir Peter Scott Memorial Expedition to Henderson Island. Multicoloured.

418	20 c. Type **124**	70	60
419	$1 Henderson sandalwood	1·75	1·50
420	$1.50 Murphy's petrel	2·75	2·75
421	$1.80 Henderson hawkmoth	2·75	3·00

125 Bligh's Birthplace at St. Tudy, Cornwall

1992. 175th Death Anniv of William Bligh. Multicoloured.

422	20 c. Type **125**	50	50
423	$1 Bligh on "Bounty"	1·50	1·50
424	$1.50 Voyage in "Bounty's" launch	2·00	2·50
425	$1.80 "William Bligh" (R. Combe) and epitaph	2·25	2·75

126 H.M.S. "Chichester" (frigate)

1993. Modern Royal Navy Vessels. Mult.

426	15 c. Type **126**	65	50
427	20 c. H.M.S. "Jaguar" (frigate)	65	50
428	$1.80 H.M.S. "Andrew" (submarine)	3·00	3·25
429	$3 H.M.S. "Warrior" (aircraft carrier) and Westland Dragonfly helicopter	5·00	5·50

127 Queen Elizabeth II in Coronation Robes

1993. 40th Anniv of Coronation.

430	**127** $5 multicoloured	6·00	6·50

128 Pawala Valley Ridge

1993. Island Views. Multicoloured.

431	10 c. Type **128**	20	20
432	90 c. St. Pauls	90	90
433	$1.20 Matt's Rocks from Water Valley	1·25	1·50
434	$1.50 Ridge Rope to St. Paul's Pool	1·50	1·75
435	$1.80 Ship Landing Point	1·75	2·25

129 Indo-Pacific Tree Gecko

1993. Lizards. Multicoloured.

436	20 c. Type **129**	70	50
437	45 c. Stump-toed gecko	90	1·00
438	45 c. Mourning gecko	90	1·00
439	$1 Moth skink	1·75	1·50
440	$1.50 Snake-eyed skink	2·25	2·50
441	$1.50 White-bellied skink	2·25	2·50

1994. "Hong Kong '94" International Stamp Exhibition. Nos. 437/8 and 440/1 optd **HONG KONG '94** and emblem.

442	45 c. Stump-toed gecko	80	90
443	45 c. Mourning gecko	80	90
444	$1.50 Snake-eyed skink	2·25	2·75
445	$1.50 White-bellied skink	2·25	2·75

130 Friday October Christian

131 Landing Stores from Wreck of "Wildwave", Oeno Island, 1858

1994. Early Pitcairners. Multicoloured.

446	5 c. Type **130**	20	30
447	20 c. Moses Young	50	40
448	$1.80 James Russell McCoy	2·25	2·75
449	$3 Rosalind Amelia Young	3·75	5·00

1994. Shipwrecks. Multicoloured.

450	20 c. Type **131**	65	60
451	90 c. Longboat trying to reach "Cornwallis", Pitcairn Island, 1875	1·75	1·75
452	$1.80 "Acadia" aground, Ducie Island, 1881	3·00	3·50
453	$3 Rescuing survivors from "Oregon", Oeno Island, 1883	4·25	4·50

132 Fire Coral

133 Angel and "Ipomoea acuminata"

1994. Corals. Multicoloured.

454	20 c. Type **132**	65	60
455	90 c. Cauliflower coral and arc-eyed hawkfish (horiz)	1·75	2·00
456	$1 Lobe coral and high-finned rudderfish	1·75	2·00

1994. Christmas. Flowers. Multicoloured.

458	20 c. Type **133**	35	25
459	90 c. Shepherds and "Hibiscus rosa-sinensis" (vert)	1·25	1·40
460	$1 Star and "Plumeria rubra"	1·25	1·40
461	$3 Holy Family and "Alpinia speciosa" (vert)	3·00	3·25

134 White ("Fairy") Tern on Egg

1995. Birds. Multicoloured.

462	5 c. Type **134**	10	10
463	10 c. Red-tailed tropic bird chick (vert)	10	10
464	15 c. Henderson Island crake with chick	15	20
465	20 c. Red-footed booby feeding chick (vert)	15	20
466	45 c. Blue-grey noddy	30	35
467	50 c. Pitcairn ("Henderson Reed") warbler in nest	30	35
468	90 c. Common noddy	55	60
469	$1 Blue-faced ("Masked") booby and chick (vert)	65	70
470	$1.80 Henderson Island fruit dove	1·10	1·25
471	$2 Murphy's petrel	1·25	1·40
472	$3 Christmas Island shearwater	1·90	2·00
473	$5 Red-tailed tropic bird juvenile	3·25	3·50

135 Islanders in Longboats

1995. Oeno Island Holiday. Multicoloured.

474	20 c. Type **135**	25	35
475	90 c. Playing volleyball on beach	1·00	1·10
476	$1.80 Preparing picnic	1·90	2·25
477	$3 Singsong	3·25	3·75

137 Guglielmo Marconi and Early Wireless, 1901

139 Chinese Junk

138 Early Morning at the Jetty

1995. Centenary of First Radio Transmission. Multicoloured.

479	20 c. Type **137**	25	35
480	$1 Pitcairn radio transmitter, c. 1938	1·10	1·25
481	$1.50 Satellite Earth Station equipment, 1994	1·75	2·25
482	$3 Communications satellite in orbit, 1992	3·25	3·75

1995. 50th Anniv of United Nations. As T **284** of Jamaica. Multicoloured.

483	20 c. United Nations float, Lord Mayor's Show	30	30
484	$1 R.F.A. "Brambleleaf" (tanker)	1·40	1·25
485	$1.50 U.N. Ambulance	2·00	2·25
486	$3 R.A.F. Lockheed L-1011 TriStar	3·50	3·75

1996. Supply Ship Day. Multicoloured.

487	20 c. Type **138**	25	30
488	40 c. Longboat meeting "America Star" (supply ship)	45	55
489	90 c. Loading supplies into longboats	1·00	1·10
490	$1 Landing supplies on jetty	1·10	1·25
491	$1.50 Sorting supplies at the Co-op	1·75	2·25
492	$1.80 Tractor towing supplies	1·90	2·25

1996. 70th Birthday of Queen Elizabeth II. As T **55** of Tokelau, each incorporating a different photograph of the Queen. Multicoloured.

493	20 c. Bounty Bay	45	45
494	90 c. Jetty and landing point, Bounty Bay	1·40	1·40
495	$1.80 Matt's Rocks	2·25	2·50
496	$3 St. Pauls	4·00	4·50

1996. "CHINA '96" 9th Asian International Stamp Exhibition, Peking. Multicoloured.

497	$1.80 Type **139**	1·90	2·25
498	$1.80 H.M.S. "Bounty"	1·90	2·25

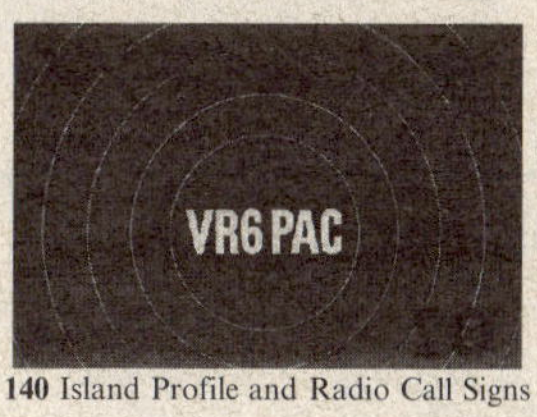

140 Island Profile and Radio Call Signs

1996. Amateur Radio Operations from Pitcairn Islands. Multicoloured.

500	20 c. Type **140**	45	45
501	$1.50 Radio operator calling for medical assistance	2·00	2·25
502	$1.50 Doctors giving medical advice by radio	2·00	2·25
503	$2.50 Andrew Young (first radio operator), 1938	2·75	3·00

MORE DETAILED LISTS
are given in the Stanley Gibbons Catalogues referred to in the country headings.
For lists of current volumes see Introduction.

141 Henderson Island Reed Warbler

1996. Endangered Species. Local Birds. Mult.

504	5 c. Type **141**	20	20
505	10 c. Stephen's lory	20	20
506	20 c. Henderson Island crake	35	35
507	90 c. Henderson Island fruit dove	1·10	1·10
508	$2 White tern (horiz)	2·00	2·25
509	$2 Blue-faced booby (inscr "Masked Booby") (horiz)	2·00	2·25

144 Health Centre

1997. Island Health Care. Multicoloured.

512	20 c. Type **144**	30	25
513	$1 Nurse treating patient	1·00	1·00
514	$1.70 Dentist treating woman	1·75	1·90
515	$3 Evacuating patient by ship	3·00	3·25

1997. Golden Wedding of Queen Elizabeth and Prince Philip. As T **87** of Kiribati. Multicoloured.

516	20 c. Prince Philip driving carriage	30	40
517	20 c. Queen Elizabeth	30	40
518	$1 Prince Philip at Royal Windsor Horse Show, 1996	1·00	1·25
519	$1 Queen Elizabeth with horse	1·00	1·25
520	$1.70 Queen Elizabeth and Prince Philip at the Derby, 1991	1·50	1·75
521	$1.70 Prince Charles hunting, 1995	1·50	1·75

Nos. 516/17, 518/19 and 520/21 respectively were printed together, se-tenant, with the backgrounds forming composite designs.

145 Island and Star

1997. Christmas. Multicoloured.

522	20 c. Type **145**	35	25
523	80 c. Hand ringing bell	1·00	80
524	$1.20 Presents in baskets	1·40	1·50
525	$3 Families outside church	2·75	3·00

146 Christian's Cave

1997. Christian's Cave. Multicoloured.

526	5 c. Type **146**	10	15
527	20 c. View from the beach	25	25
528	35 c. Cave entrance (vert)	35	35
529	$5 Pathway through forest (vert)	3·75	4·75

147 H.M.S. "Bounty" (Bligh), 1790

1998. Millennium Commemoration (1st issue). Sailing Ships. Multicoloured.

530	20 c. Type **147**	25	25
531	90 c. H.M.S. "Swallow" (Carteret), 1767	70	70
532	$1.80 H.M.S. "Briton" and H.M.S. "Tagus" (frigates), 1814	1·25	1·40
533	$3 H.M.S. "Fly" (sloop), 1838	2·25	2·50

See also Nos. 549/52.

148 "Bidens mathewsii"

1998. Flowers: Multicoloured.

535	20 c. Type **148**	25	30
536	90 c. "Hibiscus" sp.	70	75
537	$1.80 "Osteomeles anthyllidifolia"	1·40	1·50
538	$3 "Ipomoea littoralis"	2·25	2·50

149 Fishing

1998. International Year of the Ocean. Multicoloured.

539	20 c. Type **149**	25	30
540	90 c. Diver at wreck of "Cornwallis" (vert)	70	75
541	$1.80 Reef fish	1·40	1·50
542	$3 Murphy's petrel (vert)	2·25	2·50

150 George Nobbs and Class, 1838

1999. Development of Local Education. Mult.

544	20 c. Type **150**	15	20
545	90 c. Children outside thatched school, 1893	55	60
546	$1.80 Boy in wheelbarrow outside wooden school, 1932	1·10	1·25
547	$3 Modern classroom with computer	1·90	2·00

152 John Adams (survivor of "Bounty" crew) and Bounty Bay

1999. Millennium Commemoration (2nd issue). Multicoloured.

549	20 c. Type **152**	15	20
550	90 c. "Topaz" (sealer), 1808	55	60
551	$1.80 George Hunn Nobbs and Norfolk Island	1·10	1·25
552	$3 H.M.S "Champion" (corvette), 1893	1·90	2·00

153 Prince Edward and Miss Sophie Rhys-Jones

1999. Royal Wedding. Multicoloured.

553	$2.50 Type **153**	1·60	1·75
554	$2.50 Engagement photograph	1·60	1·75

POONCH

A state in Kashmir, India. Now uses Indian stamps.

12 pies = 1 anna;
16 annas = 1 rupee

1

4

1876. Imperf.

1	**1**	6 p. red	£3000	95·00
2		½ a. red	—	£1800

1880. Imperf.

32	**1**	1 p. red	1·40	1·90
12	**4**	½ a. red	1·60	2·25
50		1 a. red	1·10	2·00
52		2 a. red (22 × 22 mm)	1·25	2·00
31		4 a. red (28 × 27 mm)	2·25	2·75

These stamps were printed on various coloured papers.

OFFICIAL STAMPS

1888. Imperf.

O1	**1**	1 p. black	1·60	1·75
O2	**4**	½ a. black	1·60	2·50
O3		1 a. black	1·50	1·60
O4		2 a. black	2·50	2·50
O5		4 a. black	4·25	7·00

PRINCE EDWARD ISLAND

An island off the East coast of Canada, now a province of that Dominion, whose stamps it uses.

1861. 12 pence = 1 shilling.
1872. 100 cents = 1 dollar.

1

7

1861. Queen's portrait in various frames. Values in pence.

9	**1**	1d. orange	22·00	27·00
28		2d. red	5·50	8·00
30		3d. blue	8·00	9·00
31		4d. black	4·00	26·00
18		6d. green	65·00	70·00
20		9d. mauve	45·00	45·00

1870.

32	**7**	4½d. (3d. stg.) brown	35·00	42·00

8

1872. Queen's portrait in various frames. Values in cents.

35	**8**	1 c. orange	3·50	9·00
38		2 c. blue	10·00	30·00
37		3 c. red	13·00	17·00
40		4 c. green	4·50	13·00
41		6 c. black	3·50	14·00
42		12 c. mauve	3·50	25·00

QATAR

An independent Arab Shaikhdom with British postal administration until 23 May, 1963. The stamps of Muscat were formerly used at Doha and Umm Said.

100 naye paise = 1 rupee

Stamps of Great Britain surcharged **QATAR** and value in Indian currency.

1957. Queen Elizabeth II and pictorials.

1	**157**	1 n.p. on 5d. brown	10	10
2	**154**	3 n.p. on ½d. orange	15	15
3		6 n.p. on 1d. blue	15	15
4		9 n.p. on 1½d. green	15	10
5		12 n.p. on 2d. brown	20	60
6	**155**	15 n.p. on 2½d. red	15	10
7		20 n.p. on 3d. lilac	15	10
8		25 n.p. on 4d. blue	40	60
9	**157**	40 n.p. on 6d. purple	15	10
10	**158**	50 n.p. on 9d. olive	40	15
11	**159**	75 n.p. on 1s. 3d. green	50	70
12		1 r. on 1s. 6d. blue	6·00	10
13	**166**	2 r. on 2s. 6d. brown	3·50	2·25
14	–	5 r. on 5s. red	4·50	2·75
15	–	10 r. on 10s. blue	5·50	10·00

1957. World Scout Jubilee Jamboree.

16	**170**	15 n.p. on 2½d. red	25	35
17	**171**	25 n.p. on 4d. blue	25	35
18	–	75 n.p. on 1s. 3d. green	30	35

8 Shaikh Ahmad bin All al Thani

9 Peregrine Falcon

11 Oil Derrick

1961.

27	**8**	5 n.p. red	10	10
28		15 n.p. black	10	10
29		20 n.p. purple	10	10
30		30 n.p. green	10	10
31	**9**	40 n.p. red	85	10
32		50 n.p. brown	1·25	10
33	–	75 n.p. blue	60	1·50
34	**11**	1 r. red	70	10
35		2 r. blue	2·00	50
36	–	5 r. green	13·00	1·75
37	–	10 r. black	35·00	3·75

DESIGNS—As Type **9**: 75 n.p. Dhow. As Type **11**:- 5 r., 10 r. Mosque.

For later issues see Volume 2.

QUEENSLAND

The north eastern state of the Commonwealth of Australia whose stamps it now uses.

12 pence = 1 shilling;
20 shillings = 1 pound.

1

7

1860. Imperf.

1	**1**	1d. red	£2750	£800
2		2d. blue	£5500	£1500
3		6d. green	£4000	£800

1860. Perf.

94	**1**	1d. red	38·00	5·00
99		2d. blue	25·00	1·00
101		3d. brown	60·00	9·00
65		3d. green	80·00	6·00
53		4d. grey	£150	20·00
55		4d. lilac	£100	16·00
103		4d. yellow	£600	20·00
27		6d. green	80·00	12·00
108		1s. purple	45·00	9·00
29		1s. grey	£130	22·00
119		2s. blue	65·00	22·00
121		2s. 6d. red	£110	42·00
58		5s. red	£200	55·00
123		5s. yellow	£150	60·00
125		10s. brown	£350	£110
127		20s. red	£700	£130

1879.

134	**7**	1d. brown	35·00	5·00
135		1d. orange	17·00	3·00
136		1d. red	14·00	1·75
138		2d. blue	27·00	1·00
141		4d. yellow	£100	10·00
142		6d. green	60·00	4·50
145		1s. mauve	48·00	5·50

1880. Nos. 136 surch **Half-penny**.

151	**7**	½d. on 1d. brown	£160	90·00

9

13

12

14

1882.

152	**9**	2s. blue	60·00	17·00
158		2s. 6d. orange	38·00	22·00
159		5s. red	35·00	30·00
155		10s. brown	95·00	40·00
161		£1 green	£170	60·00

1882. Shaded background around head.

184	**13**	½d. green	3·00	50
206	**12**	1d. orange	2·00	15
204		2d. blue	3·25	20
191	**14**	2½d. red	10·00	70
192	**12**	3d. brown	8·50	1·60
193		4d. yellow	13·00	1·50
170		6d. green	9·00	1·00
173		1s. mauve	11·00	1·75
182		2s. brown	50·00	25·00

15

16

17

1895. Head on white background.

208	**15**	½d. green	1·00	60
211	**16**	1d. red	2·25	20
212		2d. blue	4·50	35
213	**17**	2½d. red	10·00	3·25
215		5d. brown	14·00	3·25

19

21

1896.

229	**19**	1d. red	9·00	40

1897. Same designs, but figures in all four corners, as T **21**.

286	½d. green	1·50	40
232	1d. red	1·75	15
234	2d. blue	1·75	15
236	2½d. red	16·00	11·00
238	2½d. purple on blue	8·50	85
241	3d. brown	8·00	1·00
244	4d. yellow	8·00	1·25
294	4d. black	13·00	1·60
246	5d. brown	7·50	1·00
250	6d. green	6·00	1·50
298	1s. mauve	11·00	1·60
300	2s. green	30·00	10·00

26

27

28

1899.

262	**26**	½d. green	1·50	50

1900. S. African War Charity. Inscr "PATRIOTIC FUND 1900".

264a	**27**	1d. (1s.) mauve	£100	£100
264b	–	2d. (2s.) violet (horiz)	£250	£250

1903.

265	**28**	9d. brown and blue	11·00	2·25

REGISTRATION STAMP

1861. Inscr "REGISTERED".

20	**1**	(No value) yellow	50·00	35·00

RAJASTHAN

Formed in 1948 from states in Rajputana, India, which included Bundi, Jaipur and Kishangarh whose separate posts functioned until 1 April 1950. Now uses Indian stamps.

12 pies = 1 anna;
16 annas = 1 rupee

BUNDI

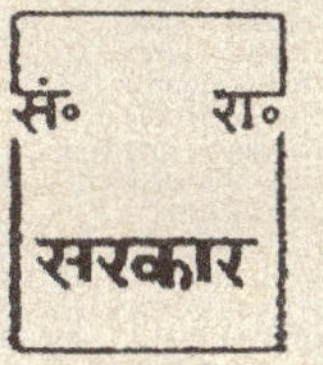

(1)

1949. Nos. 86/92 of Bundi or optd with T **1**.

1	**21**	¼ a. green	4·00	
2		½ a. violet	3·00	
3		1 a. green	4·00	
11	–	2 a. red	3·50	50·00
12	–	4 a. orange	2·00	50·00
6	–	8 a. blue	3·75	
14	–	1 r. brown	7·50	

Nos. 1, 2, 3 and 6 used are worth about six times the unused prices.

JAIPUR

राजस्थान

RAJASTHAN

(2)

1949. Stamps of Jaipur optd with T **2**.

15	**7**	¼ a. black and purple	3·50	13·00
16		½ a. black and violet	3·25	14·00
17		¾ a. black and orange	5·50	16·00
18		1 a. black and blue	4·00	27·00
19		2 a. black and orange	5·50	35·00
20		2½ a. black and red	6·50	17·00
21		3 a. black and green	7·00	40·00
22		4 a. black and green	7·00	45·00
23		6 a. black and blue	8·00	70·00
24		8 a. black and brown	11·00	90·00
25		1 r. black and bistre	12·00	£130

KISHANGARH

1949. Stamps of Kishangarh handstamped with T **1**.

(a) On stamps of 1899.

26a	**2**	¼ a. pink	—	£130
27		½ a. blue	£225	
29		1 a. lilac	14·00	38·00
30		4 a. brown	50·00	70·00
31		1 r. green	£160	£170
31a		2 r. red	£190	
32		5 r. mauve	£180	£180

(b) On stamps of 1904.

33	**13**	½ a. brown	—	90·00
33a		1 a. blue	—	£120
34		4 a. brown	13·00	
35	**2**	8 a. grey	70·00	£110
36	**13**	8 a. violet	11·00	
37		1 r. green	11·00	
38		2 r. yellow	18·00	
39		5 r. brown	23·00	

(c) On stamps of 1912.

40	**14**	½ a. green	—	£110
41		1 a. red	—	£110
43		2 a. purple	2·25	5·50
44		4 a. blue	—	£300
45		8 a. brown	5·00	
46		1 r. mauve	10·00	
47		2 r. green	10·00	
48		5 r. brown	£200	

(d) On stamps of 1928.

56	**16**	¼ a. blue	38·00	38·00
57		½ a. green	23·00	25·00
58	–	1 a. red	35·00	35·00
59	–	2 a. purple	£100	£100
61	**16**	4 a. brown	1·75	5·50
51		8 a. violet	6·00	50·00
63		1 r. green	6·00	
53		2 r. yellow	14·00	
54		5 r. red	15·00	

RAJPIPLA

A state of Bombay, India. Now uses Indian stamps.

12 pies = 1 anna;
12 annas = 1 rupee

1 (1 pice)

2 (2 a.)

1880.

1	**1**	1 p. blue	1·75	22·00
2	**2**	2 a. green	20·00	60·00
3		4 a. red	10·00	38·00

REDONDA

A dependency of Antigua.

The following stamps were issued in anticipation of commercial and tourist development, philatelic mail being handled by a bureau in Antigua. Since at the present time the island is uninhabited, we do not list or stock these items. It is understood that the stamps are valid for the prepayment of postage in Antigua. Miniature sheets, imperforate stamps etc, are excluded from this section.

1979.

Antigua 1976 definitive issue optd **REDONDA**. 3, 5, 10, 25, 35, 50, 75 c., $1, $2.50, $5, $10.

Antigua Coronation Anniversary issue optd **REDONDA**. 10, 30, 50, 90 c., $2.50.

Antigua World Cup Football Championship issue optd **REDONDA**. 10, 15 c., $3.

Death Centenary of Sir Rowland Hill. 50, 90 c., $2.50, $3.

International Year of the Child 25, 50 c., $1, $2.

Christmas. Paintings. 8, 50, 90 c., $3.

1980.

Marine Life. 8, 25, 50 c., $4.

75th Anniv of Rotary International. 25, 50 c., $1, $2.

Birds of Redonda. 8, 10, 15, 25, 30, 50 c., $1, $2, $5.

Olympic Medal Winners, Lake Placid and Moscow. 8, 25, 50 c., $3.

80th Birthday of Queen Elizabeth the Queen Mother. 10 c., $2.50.

Christmas Paintings. 8, 25, 50 c., $4.

1981.

Royal Wedding. 25, 55 c., $4.

Christmas. Walt Disney Cartoon Characters. ½, 1, 2, 3, 4, 5, 10 c., $2.50, $3.

World Cup Football Championship, Spain (1982). 30 c.×2, 50 c.×2, $1×2, $2×2.

1982.

Boy Scout Annivs. 8, 25, 50 c., $3, $5.

Butterflies. 8, 30, 50 c., $2.

21st Birthday of Princess of Wales. $2, $4.

Birth of Prince William of Wales. Optd on Princess of Wales 21st Birthday issue. $2, $4.

Christmas. Walt Disney's "One Hundred and One Dalmatians". ½, 1, 2, 3, 4, 5, 10 c., $2.50, $3.

1983.

Easter. 500th Birth Anniv. of Raphael. 10, 50, 90 c., $5.

Bicent of Manned Flight. 10, 50, 90 c., $2.50.

Christmas. Walt Disney Cartoon Characters. "Deck the Halls". ½, 1, 2, 3, 4, 5, 10 c., $2.50, $3.

1984.

Easter. Walt Disney Cartoon Characters. ½, 1, 2, 3, 4, 5, 10 c., $2, $4.

Olympic Games, Los Angeles. 10, 50, 90 c., $2.50.

Christmas. 50th Birthday of Donald Duck. 45, 60, 90 c., $2, $4.

1985.

Birth Bicentenary of John J. Audubon (ornithologist) (1st issue). 60, 90 c., $1, $3.

Life and Times of Queen Elizabeth the Queen Mother. $1, $1.50, $2.50.

Royal Visit. 45 c., $1, $4.

150th Birth Anniv of Mark Twain (author). 25, 50 c., $1.50, $3.

Birth Bicentenaries of Grimm Brothers (folklorists). Walt Disney cartoon characters. 30, 60, 70 c., $4.

1986.

Birth Bicentenary of John J. Audubon (ornithologist) (2nd issue). 90 c., $1, $1.50, $3.

Appearance of Halley's Comet. 5, 15, 55 c., $4.

Centenary of Statue of Liberty (1st issue). 20, 25, 30 c., $4.

60th Birthday of Queen Elizabeth II. 50, 60 c., $4.

Royal Wedding. 60 c., $1, $4.

Christmas (1st issue). Disney characters in Hans Andersen Stories. 30, 60, 70 c., $4.

Christmas (2nd issue). "Wind in the Willows" (by Kenneth Grahame). 25, 50 c., $1.50, $3.

1987.

"Capex '87" International Stamp Exhibition, Toronto. Disney characters illustrating Art of Animation. 25, 30, 50, 60, 70 c., $1.50, $3, $4.

Birth Centenary of Marc Chagall (artist). 10, 30, 40, 60, 90 c., $1, $3, $4.

Centenary of Statue of Liberty (2nd issue). 10, 15, 25, 30, 40, 60, 70, 90 c., $1, $2, $3, $4.

250th Death Anniv of Sir Isaac Newton (scientist). 20 c., $2.50.

750th Anniv of Berlin. $1, $4.

Bicentenary of U.S. Constitution. 30 c., $3.

16th World Scout Jamboree, Australia. 10 c., $4.

1988.

500th Anniv (1992) of Discovery of America by Columbus. 15, 30, 45, 60, 90 c., $1, $2, $3.

"Finlandia '88" International Stamp Exhibition, Helsinki. Disney characters in Finnish scenes. 1, 2, 3, 4, 5, 6 c., $5, $6.

Olympic Games, Seoul. 25, 60 c., $1.25, $3.

500th Birth Anniv of Titian. 10, 25, 40, 70, 90 c., $2, $3, $4.

1989.

20th Anniv of First Manned Landing on Moon. Disney characters on moon. ½, 1, 2, 3, 4, 5 c., $5, $6.

500th Anniv (1992) of Discovery of America by Columbus (2nd issue). Pre-Columbian Societies. 15, 45, 45, 50 c., $2, $2, $3, $3.

Christmas. Disney Characters and Cars of 1950's. 25, 35, 45, 60 c., $1, $2, $3, $4.

1990.

Christmas. Disney Characters and Hollywood cars. 25, 35, 40, 60 c., $2, $3, $4, $5.

1991.

Nobel Prize Winners. 5, 15, 25, 40, 50 c., $1, $2, $4.

RHODESIA

A British territory in central Africa, formerly administered by the British South Africa Co. In 1924 divided into the territories of Northern and Southern Rhodesia which issued their own stamps (q.v.). In 1964 Southern Rhodesia was renamed Rhodesia; on becoming independent in 1980 it was renamed Zimbabwe.

1890. 12 pence = 1 shilling;
20 shillings = 1 pound.
1970. 100 cents = 1 dollar.

1 Arms of the Company

1890. The pound values are larger.

18	**1**	½d. blue and red	2·50	1·75
1		1d. black	9·00	2·25
20		2d. green and red	16·00	1·75
21		3d. black and green	8·50	2·75
22		4d. brown and black	16·00	2·00
3		6d. blue	22·00	3·25
23		8d. red and blue	10·00	7·50
4		1s. brown	32·00	7·50
5		2s. red	40·00	25·00
6		2s. 6d. purple	27·00	28·00
25		3s. brown and green	£120	70·00
26		4s. black and red	30·00	45·00
8	**1**	5s. yellow	60·00	50·00
9		10s. green	70·00	95·00
10	–	£1 blue	£170	£130
11	–	£2 red	£400	£150
12	–	£5 green	£1600	£450
13	–	£10 brown	£2750	£700

1891. Surch in figures.

14	**1**	½d. on 6d. blue	80·00	£200
15		2d. on 6d. blue	80·00	£300
16		4d. on 6d. blue	£100	£375
17		8d. on 1s. brown	£100	£400

5

9

1896. The ends of ribbons containing motto cross the animals' legs.

41	**5**	½d. grey and mauve	2·00	2·75
42		1d. red and green	2·50	3·00
43		2d. brown and mauve	6·00	4·00
31		3d. brown and blue	3·25	1·25
44a		4d. blue and mauve	7·50	50
46		6d. mauve and red	6·00	50
34		8d. green and mauve on buff	4·50	60
35		1s. green and blue	15·00	2·25
47		2s. blue and green on buff	20·00	8·00
48		2s. 6d. brown & pur on yell	65·00	40·00
36		3s. green and mauve on blue	60·00	30·00
37		4s. red and blue on green	45·00	2·50
49		5s. brown and green	38·00	9·00
50		10s. grey and red on rose	85·00	60·00

1896. Surch in words.

51	**1**	1d. on 3d. black and green	£400	£400
52		1d. on 4s. black and red	£250	£250
53		3d. on 5s. yellow	£160	£200

1896. Cape of Good Hope stamps optd **BRITISH SOUTH AFRICA COMPANY.**

58	**6**	½d. black (No. 48)	8·50	14·00
59	**17**	1d. red (No. 58a)	9·50	14·00
60	**6**	2d. brown (No. 60)	10·00	8·50
61		3d. red (No. 40)	45·00	65·00
62		4d. blue (No. 51)	12·00	12·00
63	**4**	6d. violet (No. 52a)	48·00	60·00
64	**6**	1s. yellow (No. 65)	£110	£130

1897. The ends of motto ribbons do not cross the animals' legs.

66	**9**	½d. grey and mauve	1·60	3·50
67		1d. red and green	3·00	3·75
68		2d. brown and mauve	4·25	80
69		3d. brown and blue	2·50	30
70		4d. blue and mauve	6·50	1·25
71		6d. mauve and red	6·50	3·50
72		8d. green and mauve on buff	11·00	40
73		£1 black and brown on green	£350	£225

10

11

1898. Nos. 90/3 are larger (24 × 28½ mm).

75a	**10**	½d. green	1·50	40
77		1d. red	2·00	30
79		2d. brown	1·50	15
80		2½d. blue	3·75	60
81		3d. red	3·75	65
82		4d. olive	4·25	20
83		6d. purple	8·00	1·75
84	**11**	1s. brown	9·50	1·50
85		2s. 6d. grey	38·00	65
86		3s. violet	11·00	1·00
87		5s. orange	28·00	8·50
88		7s. 6d. black	60·00	14·00
89		10s. green	17·00	1·00
90		£1 purple	£170	70·00
91		£2 brown	70·00	6·50
92	–	£5 blue	£3000	£2250
93	–	£10 lilac	£3250	£2250
93a	–	£20 brown	£13000	

13 Victoria Falls

1905. Visit of British Assn. and Opening of Victoria Falls Bridge across Zambesi.

94	**13**	1d. red	2·75	4·00
95		2½d. blue	7·50	4·75
96		5d. red	21·00	48·00
97		1s. green	21·00	32·00
98		2s. 6d. black	£100	£150
99		5s. violet	85·00	40·00

1909. Optd **RHODESIA.** or surch also.

100	**10**	½d. green	1·50	60
101c		1d. red	1·50	40
102		2d. brown	1·60	3·25
103		2½d. blue	1·00	60
104		3d. red	1·60	30
105		4d. olive	2·75	70
114		5d. on 6d. purple	6·50	9·50
106		6d. purple	5·00	2·75
116	**11**	7½d. on 2s. 6d. grey	3·50	2·75
117a		10d. on 2s. violet	4·00	3·50
107c		1s. brown	8·50	2·25
118		2s. on 5s. orange	12·00	7·00
108		2s. 6d. grey	16·00	7·00
109		3s. violet	15·00	7·00
110		5s. orange	25·00	23·00
111		7s. 6d. black	70·00	11·00
112		10s. green	28·00	9·00
113	–	£1 purple	£100	65·00
113d	–	£2 brown	£3250	£275
113e	–	£5 blue	£6000	£3000

17

18

1910.

119	**17**	½d. green	7·50	1·00
123		1d. red	12·00	1·00
128		2d. black and grey	40·00	4·75
131a		2½d. blue	15·00	5·00
135		3d. purple and yellow	26·00	10·00
140		4d. black and orange	26·00	10·00
141		5d. purple and olive	20·00	35·00
145		6d. purple and mauve	24·00	9·50
148		8d. black and purple	£120	70·00
149		10d. red and purple	27·00	48·00
151		1s. black and green	28·00	15·00
153		2s. black and blue	65·00	50·00
157		2s. 6d. black and red	£275	£275
158		3s. green and violet	£140	£140
160a		5s. red and green	£225	£180
160b		7s. 6d. red and blue	£600	£425
164		10s. green and orange	£375	£300
165		£1 red and black	£950	£400

1913.

187	**18**	½d. green	4·00	75
192		1d. red	2·75	75
198		1½d. brown	2·25	60
291		2d. black and grey	3·00	1·75
200		2½d. blue	3·25	18·00
259		3d. black and yellow	5·00	1·40
225		4d. black and orange	8·00	5·00
212		5d. black and green	3·50	8·00
266		6d. black and mauve	4·00	3·25
230		8d. violet and green	9·50	42·00
247		10d. blue and red	4·75	23·00

272 18 1s. black and blue . . . . 5·50 3·75
273 2s. black and brown . . . 12·00 15·00
236 2s. 6d. blue and brown . . 42·00 22·00
304 3s. brown and blue . . . . 70·00 85·00
239 5s. blue and green . . . . 42·00 48·00
252 7s. 6d. mauve and grey . . 90·00 £140
309 10s. red and green £160 £190
242 £1 black and purple £350 £450

1917. Surch **Half Penny** (without hyphen or full stop).
280 18 ½d. on 1s. red . . . . 2·50 6·50

1917. Surch **Half- Penny.** (with hyphen and full stop).
281 18 ½d. on 1d. red . . . . . . 1·75 5·00

RHODESIA

The following stamps are for the former Southern Rhodesia, renamed Rhodesia.

59 "Telecommunications"

60 Bangala Dam

1965. Centenary of I.T.U.
351 59 6d. violet and olive . . . . 1·50 40
352 1s. 3d. violet and lilac . . . 1·50 40
353 2s. 6d. violet and brown . . 2·50 4·50

1965. Water Conservation. Multicoloured.
354 3d. Type **60** 30 10
355 4d. Irrigation canal . . . . . 1·00 1·00
356 2s. 6d. Cutting sugar cane . . 2·25 3·50

63 Sir Winston Churchill, Quill, Sword and Houses of Parliament

1965. Churchill Commemoration.
357 63 1s. 3d. black and blue . . . 60 35

64 Coat of Arms

67 Emeralds

1965. "Independence".
358 64 2s. 6d. multicoloured 15 15

1966. Optd **INDEPENDENCE. 11th November 1965.**
(a) On Nos. 92/105 of Southern Rhodesia.
359 45 ½d. yellow, green and blue . 10 10
360 – 1d. violet and ochre 10 10
361 – 2d. yellow and violet . . . 10 10
362 – 3d. brown and blue 10 10
363 – 4d. orange and green . . . 15 10
364 50 6d. red, yellow and green . . 15 10
365 – 9d. brown, yellow and green 30 10
366 – 1s. green and ochre 40 10
367 – 1s. 3d. red, violet and green 80 20
368 – 2s. blue and ochre . . . . 90 3·25
369 – 2s. 6d. blue and red . . . . 60 1·00
370 56 5s. multicoloured . . . . . 2·50 5·50
371 – 10s. multicoloured . . . . 3·00 2·25
372 – £1 multicoloured . . . . . 1·25 2·25
(b) Surch on No. 357.
373 63 5s. on 1s. 3d. black and blue 8·00 20·00

1966. As Nos. 92/105 of Southern Rhodesia, but inscr "RHODESIA" as in T **67**. Some designs and colours changed.
374 – 1d. violet and ochre 10 10
375 – 2d. orange and green (As No. 96) 10 10
376 – 3d. brown and blue 10 10
377 67 4d. green and brown 70 10
378 50 6d. red, yellow and green . . 15 10
379 – 9d. yellow and violet (As No. 94) 15 20
380 45 1s. yellow, green and blue . . 15 10
381 – 1s. 3d. blue and ochre (As No. 101) 25 15
382 – 1s. 6d. brown, yellow and green (As No. 98) . . . . 1·75 25
383 – 2s. red, violet and green (As No. 100) 40 80
384 – 2s. 6d. blue, red & turquoise 40 20
385 56 5s. multicoloured 40 90
386 – 10s. multicoloured . . . . 2·25 4·00
387 – £1 multicoloured . . . . . 8·00 8·00
Nos. 379/80 are in larger format as Type **50** of Southern Rhodesia.
Stamps in these designs were later printed locally. These vary only slightly from the above in details and shade.
For Nos. 376, 380 and 382/4 in dual currency see Nos. 408/12.

68 Zeederberg Coach, c. 1895

1966. 28th Congress of Southern Africa Philatelic Federation ("Rhopex").
388 68 3d. multicoloured 25 10
389 – 9d. multicoloured 30 40
390 – 1s. 6d. blue and black . . 50 50
391 – 2s. 6d. pink, green and black 55 80
DESIGNS: 9d. Sir Rowland Hill; 1s. 6d. The Penny Black; 2s. 6d. Rhodesian stamp of 1892 (No. 12).

69 De Havilland Dragon Rapide (1946)

70 Kudu

1966. 20th Anniv of Central African Airways.
393 69 6d. multicoloured . . . . 1·00 50
394 – 1s. 3d. multicoloured . . . 1·25 55
395 – 2s. 6d. multicoloured . . . 3·50 2·50
396 – 5s. black and blue . . . . 6·00 5·50
AIRCRAFT: 1s. 3d. Douglas DC-3 (1953); 2s. 6d. Vickers Viscount 748 "Matopos" (1956); 5s. B.A.C. One Eleven.

1967. Dual Currency Issue. As Nos. 376, 380 and 382/4. but value in dual currency as T **70**.
408 70 3d./2½ c. brown and blue . . 60 20
409 – 1s./10 c. yellow, green and blue (No. 380) 70 45
410 – 1s. 6d./15 c. brown, yellow and green (No. 382) . . 4·75 70
411 – 2s./20 c. red, violet and green (No. 383) . . . . 4·00 6·50
412 – 2s. 6d./25 c. ultramarine, red and blue (No. 384) . . . 35·00 48·00

71 Dr. Jameson (administrator)

1967. Famous Rhodesians (1st series). 50th Death Anniv of Dr. Jameson.
413 71 1s. 6d. multicoloured 30 35
See also Nos. 426, 430, 457, 458, 469, 480, 488 and 513.

72 Soapstone Sculpture (Joram Mariga)

1967. 10th Anniv of Opening of Rhodes National Gallery.
414 72 3d. brown, green and black 10 10
415 – 9d. blue, brown and black 20 20
416 – 1s. 3d. multicoloured . . . 20 25
417 – 2s. 6d. multicoloured . . . 25 35
DESIGNS: 9d. "The Burgher of Calais" (detail, Rodin); 1s. 3d. "The Knight" (stamp design wrongly inscr) (Roberto Crippa); 2s. 6d. "John the Baptist" (Mossini).

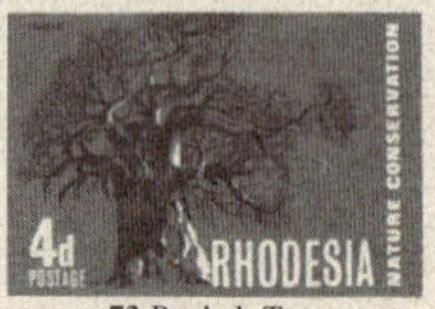
73 Baobab Tree

1967. Nature Conservation.
418 73 4d. brown and black . . . 25 25
419 – 4d. green and black . . . 25 25
420 – 4d. grey and black 25 25
421 – 4d. orange and black . . . 25 25
DESIGNS—HORIZ: No. 419, White rhinoceros; No. 420, African elephants. VERT: No. 421, Wild gladiolus.

74 Wooden Hand Plough

1968. 15th World Ploughing Contest, Norton, Rhodesia.
422 74 3d. orange, red and brown . 10 10
423 – 9d. multicoloured 20 25
424 – 1s. 6d. multicoloured . . . 25 65
425 – 2s. 6d. multicoloured . . . 30 95
DESIGNS: 9d. Early wheel plough; 1s. 6d. Steam powered tractor, and ploughs; 2s. 6d. Modern tractor, and plough.

75 Alfred Beit (national benefactor)

1968. Famous Rhodesians (2nd issue).
426 75 1s. 6d. orange, black & brn 30 30

76 Raising the Flag, Bulawayo, 1893

1968. 75th Anniv of Matabeleland.
427 76 3d. orange, red and black 15 10
428 – 9d. multicoloured 25 20
429 – 1s. 6d. green, emerald & blk 25 60
DESIGNS: 9d. View and coat of arms of Bulawayo; 1s. 6d. Allan Wilson (combatant in the Matabele War).

77 Sir William Henry Milton (administrator)

1969. Famous Rhodesians (3rd issue).
430 77 1s. 6d. multicoloured . . . 20 55

78 2 ft. Gauge Locomotive No. 15, 1897

1969. 70th Anniv of Opening of Beira–Salisbury Railway. Multicoloured.
431 3d. Type **78** . . . . 1·00 20
432 9d. 7th Class steam locomotive No. 43, 1903 . . . . . . 1·50 75
433 1s. 6d. Beyer, Peacock 15th Class steam locomotive No. 413, 1951 . . . . 4·50 3·25
434 2s. 6d. Class DE2 diesel-electric locomotive No. 1203, 1955 6·50 7·00

79 Low Level Bridge

1969. Bridges of Rhodesia. Multicoloured.
435 3d. Type **79** 75 20
436 9d. Mpudzi bridge . . . . . 1·00 30
437 1s. 6d. Umniati bridge . . . . 2·50 2·00
438 2s. 6d. Birchenough bridge . . 3·50 3·00

80 Harvesting Wheat

81 Devil's Cataract, Victoria Falls

1970. Decimal Currency.
439 80 1 c. multicoloured 10 10
440 – 2 c. multicoloured 10 10
441 – 2½ c. multicoloured . . . 10 10
441c – 3 c. multicoloured . . . . 1·25 10
442 – 3½ c. multicoloured 10 10
442b – 4 c. multicoloured . . . . 1·75 40
443 – 5 c. multicoloured 15 10
443b – 6 c. multicoloured . . . . 4·00 3·75
443c 81 7½ c. multicoloured . . . . 7·50 80
444 8 c. multicoloured . . . . 1·25 20
445 – 10 c. multicoloured . . . 60 10
446 – 12½ c. multicoloured . . . 1·00 10
446a – 14 c. multicoloured . . . 15·00 90
447 – 15 c. multicoloured . . . 2·50 15
448 – 20 c. multicoloured . . . 1·75 15
449 – 25 c. multicoloured . . . 4·50 90
450 – 50 c. turquoise and blue . 2·25 55
451 – $1 multicoloured . . . . 4·50 1·75
452 – $2 multicoloured . . . . 10·00 23·00
DESIGNS—As Type **80**: 2 c. Pouring molten metal; 2½ c. Zimbabwe Ruins; 3 c. Articulated lorry; 3½ c., 4 c. Statue of Cecil Rhodes; 5 c. Mine headgear; 6 c. Hydrofoil "Seaflight". As Type **81**: 10 c. Yachting on Lake McIlwaine; 12½ c. Hippopotamus in river; 14 c., 15 c. Kariba Dam; 20 c. Irrigation canal. 31×26 mm: 25 c. Bateleurs; 50 c. Radar antenna and Vickers Viscount 810; $1 "Air Rescue"; $2 Rhodesian flag.

82 Despatch Rider, c. 1890

1970. Inauguration of Posts and Telecommunications Corporation. Multicoloured.
453 2½ c. Type **82** 35 10
454 3½ c. Loading mail at Salisbury airport 75 50
455 15 c. Constructing telegraph line, c. 1890 . . . . 1·50 2·25
456 25 c. Telephone and modern telecommunications equipment 2·25 4·00

83 Mother Patrick (Dominican nurse and teacher)

1971. Famous Rhodesians (4th issue).
457 83 15 c. multicoloured 60 50

84 Fredrick Courteney Selous (big-game hunter, explorer and pioneer)

1971. Famous Rhodesians (5th issue).
458 84 15 c. multicoloured 40 70

85 Hoopoe

86 Porphyritic Granite

1971. Birds of Rhodesia (1st series). Multicoloured.
459 2 c. Type **85** . . . . 1·25 20
460 2½ c. Half-collared kingfisher (horiz) . . . . 1·25 20
461 5 c. Golden-breasted bunting . 3·50 70
462 7½ c. Carmine bee eater . . . 4·00 1·25
463 8 c. Red-eyed bulbul . . . . 4·00 1·50
464 25 c. Senegal wattled plover (horiz) . . . . 8·50 3·25
See also Nos. 537/42.

1971. "Granite 71" Geological Symposium. Multicoloured.
465 2½ c. Type **86** 85 10
466 7½ c. Muscovite mica seen through microscope . . . . 2·25 1·25
467 15 c. Granite seen through microscope . . . . 3·00 3·75
468 25 c. Geological map of Rhodesia . . . . 3·50 5·50

87 Dr. Robert Moffat (missionary)

1972. Famous Rhodesians (6th issue).

469	87	13 c. multicoloured	65	1·40

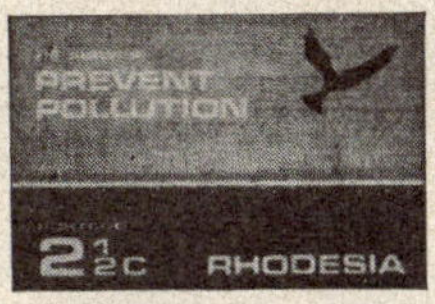

88 Bird ("Be Airwise")

1972. "Prevent Pollution". Multicoloured.

470		$2\frac{1}{2}$ c. Type **88**	20	10
471		$3\frac{1}{2}$ c. Antelope ("Be Countrywise")	20	20
472		7 c. Fish ("Be Waterwise")	30	45
473		13 c. City ("Be Citywise")	45	70

89 "The Three Kings" 91 W.M.O. Emblem

90 Dr. David Livingstone

1972. Christmas.

477	89	2 c. multicoloured	10	10
478		5 c. multicoloured	20	25
479		13 c. multicoloured	50	75

1973. Famous Rhodesians (7th issue).

480	90	14 c. multicoloured	70	1·00

1973. Centenary of I.M.O./W.M.O.

481	91	3 c. multicoloured	15	10
482		14 c. multicoloured	80	80
483		25 c. multicoloured	1·25	2·50

92 Arms of Rhodesia

1973. 50th Anniv of Responsible Government.

484	92	$2\frac{1}{2}$ c. multicoloured	15	10
485		4 c. multicoloured	25	20
486		$7\frac{1}{2}$ c. multicoloured	40	80
487		14 c. multicoloured	70	2·50

93 George Pauling (construction engineer)

1974. Famous Rhodesians (8th issue).

488	93	14 c. multicoloured	80	1·75

94 Greater Kudu 95 Thunbergia

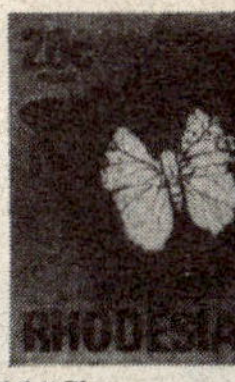

96 "Charaxes varanes"

1974. Multicoloured. (a) Antelopes.

489	1 c. Type **94**	10	10
490	$2\frac{1}{2}$ c. Eland	75	10
491	3 c. Roan antelope	10	10
492	4 c. Reedbuck	30	10
493	5 c. Bushbuck	40	10

(b) Wild Flowers.

494	6 c. Type **95**	40	10
495	$7\frac{1}{2}$ c. Flame lily	3·00	35
496	8 c. As $7\frac{1}{2}$ c.	40	10
497	10 c. Devil thorn	40	10
498	12 c. Hibiscus	70	2·50
499	$12\frac{1}{2}$ c. Pink sabi star	4·00	50
500	14 c. Wild pimpernel	4·00	50
501	15 c. As $12\frac{1}{2}$ c.	70	75
502	16 c. As 14 c.	70	45

(c) Butterflies.

503	20 c. Type **96**	2·50	35
504	24 c. "Precis hierta"	1·25	40
505	25 c. As 24 c.	6·00	3·50
506	50 c. "Colotis regina"	70	90
507	$1 "Graphium antheus"	70	1·50
508	$2 "Hamanumida daedalus"	80	2·25

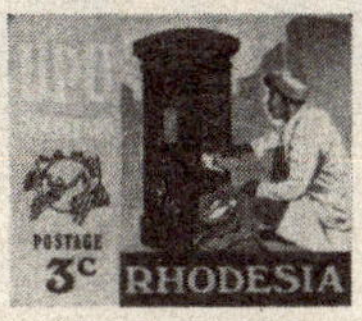

97 Collecting Mail

1974. Centenary of U.P.U. Multicoloured.

509	3 c. Type **97**	15	10
510	4 c. Sorting mail	15	10
511	$7\frac{1}{2}$ c. Mail delivery	50	75
512	14 c. Weighing parcel	1·10	2·25

98 Thomas Baines (artist)

1975. Famous Rhodesians (9th issue).

513	98	14 c. multicoloured	90	1·25

99 "Euphorbia confinalis" 100 Prevention of Head Injuries

1975. Int Succulent Congress, Salisbury ("Aloe '75"). Multicoloured.

514	$2\frac{1}{2}$ c. Type **99**	20	10
515	3 c. "Aloe excelsa"	20	10
516	4 c. "Hoodia lugardii"	25	10
517	$7\frac{1}{2}$ c. "Aloe ortholopha"	35	15
518	14 c. "Aloe musapana"	70	20
519	25 c. "Aloe saponaria"	1·00	3·00

1975. Occupational Safety. Multicoloured.

520	$2\frac{1}{2}$ c. Type **100**	15	10
521	4 c. Bandaged hand and gloved hand	25	10
522	$7\frac{1}{2}$ c. Broken glass and eye	45	30
523	14 c. Blind man and welder with protective mask	55	1·00

101 Telephones, 1876 and 1976 103 Roan Antelope

1976. Telephone Centenary.

524	101	3 c. grey and blue	10	10
525	–	14 c. black and brown	20	55

DESIGN: 14 c. Alexander Graham Bell.

1976. Nos. 495, 500 and 505 surch.

526	8 c. on $7\frac{1}{2}$ c. multicoloured	15	15
527	16 c. on 14 c. multicoloured	20	15
528	24 c. on 25 c. multicoloured	30	80

1976. Vulnerable Wildlife. Multicoloured.

529	4 c. Type **103**	15	10
530	6 c. Brown hyena	15	40
531	8 c. Hunting dog	25	20
532	16 c. Cheetah	35	45

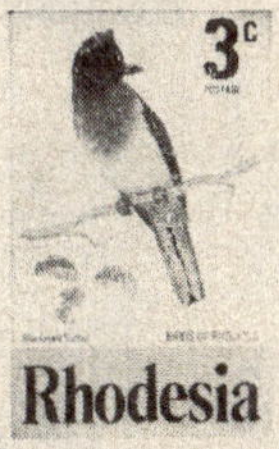

104 Msasa 105 Common Bulbul

1976. Trees of Rhodesia. Multicoloured.

533	4 c. Type **104**	15	10
534	6 c. Red mahogany	15	10
535	8 c. Mukwa	20	15
536	16 c. Rhodesian teak	25	65

1977. Birds of Rhodesia (2nd series). Mult.

537	3 c. Type **105**	20	10
538	4 c. Yellow-mantled whydah	20	10
539	6 c. Cape longclaw	25	35
540	8 c. Eastern long-tailed shrike	35	50
541	16 c. Lesser blue-eared glossy starling	55	1·10
542	24 c. Green wood hoopoe	70	1·50

106 "Lake Kyle" (Joan Evans) 107 Virgin and Child

1977. Landscape Paintings. Multicoloured.

543	3 c. Type **106**	10	10
544	4 c. "Chimanimani Mountains" (Joan Evans)	10	10
545	6 c. "Rocks near Bonsor Reef" (Alice Balfour)	15	40
546	8 c. "A Dwala near Devil's Pass" (Alice Balfour)	20	10
547	16 c. "Zimbabwe" (Alice Balfour)	25	40
548	24 c. "Victoria Falls" (Thomas Baines)	30	75

1977. Christmas.

549	107	3 c. multicoloured	10	10
550		6 c. multicoloured	10	20
551		8 c. multicoloured	15	10
552		16 c. multicoloured	30	75

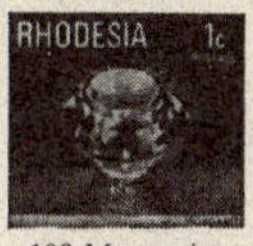

108 Fair Spire 109 Morganite

1978. Trade Fair Rhodesia, Bulawayo. Multicoloured.

553	4 c. Type **108**	15	10
554	8 c. Fair Spire (different)	20	25

1978. Gemstones, Wild Animals and Waterfalls. Multicoloured.

555	1 c. Type **109**	20	10
556	3 c. Amethyst	30	10
557	4 c. Garnet	30	10
558	5 c. Citrine	30	10
559	7 c. Blue topaz	30	10
560	9 c. White rhinoceros	20	10
561	11 c. Lion	20	30
562	13 c. Warthog	20	55
563	15 c. Giraffe	20	30
564	17 c. Common zebra	20	10
565	21 c. Odzani Falls	20	40
566	25 c. Goba Falls	20	40
567	30 c. Inyangombi Falls	25	30
568	$1 Bridal Veil Falls	35	80
569	$2 Victoria Falls	50	1·00

Nos. 560/4 are 26 × 23 mm, and Nos. 565/9 32 × 27 mm.

112 Wright Flyer I

1978. 75th Anniv of Powered Flight. Mult.

570	4 c. Type **112**	10	10
571	5 c. Bleriot XI	10	10
572	7 c. Vickers Vimy "Silver Queen II"	10	10
573	9 c. Armstrong Whitworth A.W.15 Atalanta	10	10
574	17 c. Vickers Viking 1B "Zambezi"	15	15
575	25 c. Boeing 720B	20	50

POSTAGE DUE STAMPS

D 2 D 3 Zimbabwe Bird (soapstone sculpture)

1965. Roul.

D 8	D 2	1d. red	70	12·00
D 9		2d. blue	50	8·00
D10		4d. green	60	8·00
D11		6d. plum	60	6·00

1966.

D12	D 3	1d. red	1·00	3·25
D13		2d. blue	1·25	2·50
D14		4d. green	1·25	4·25
D15		6d. violet	1·25	2·25
D16		1s. brown	1·25	2·25
D17		2s. black	1·50	5·00

1970. Decimal Currency. As Type D 3 but larger ($26 \times 22\frac{1}{2}$ mm).

D18	D 3	1 c. green	1·00	2·00
D19		2 c. blue	1·00	80
D20		5 c. violet	2·50	3·00
D21		6 c. yellow	4·25	4·00
D22		10 c. red	2·50	4·50

RHODESIA AND NYASALAND

Stamps for the Central African Federation of Northern and Southern Rhodesia and Nysaland Protectorate. The stamps of the Federation were withdrawn on 19 February 1964 when all three constituent territories had resumed issuing their own stamps.

12 pence = 1 shilling;
20 shillings = 1 pound

1 Queen Elizabeth II 2 Queen Elizabeth II

1954.

1	1	½d. red	15	10
2		1d. blue	15	10
3		2d. green	15	10
3a		$2\frac{1}{2}$d. ochre	3·00	10
4		3d. red	20	10
5		4d. brown	60	15
6		$4\frac{1}{2}$d. green	15	30
7		6d. purple	1·75	10
8		9d. violet	65	70
9		1s. grey	1·50	10
10	2	1s. 3d. red and blue	2·50	10
11		2s. blue and brown	7·00	1·00
12		2s. 6d. black and red	5·50	1·00
13		5s. violet and olive	15·00	3·50
14	–	10s. turquoise and orange	17·00	7·00
15	–	£1 olive and lake	27·00	24·00

The 10s. and £1 are as Type 2 but larger (31 × 17 mm) and have the name at top and foliage on either side of portrait.

4 De Havilland Comet 1 over Victoria Falls 5 Livingstone and Victoria Falls

1955. Cent of Discovery of Victoria Falls.

16	4	3d. blue and turquoise	55	30
17	5	1s. purple and blue	55	70

6 Tea Picking 11 Lake Bangweulu

17 Rhodes Statue

1959.

18	6	½d. black and green	60	30
19	–	1d. red and black	15	10
20	–	2d. violet and brown	1·00	40
21	–	2½d. purple and blue	40	40
22	–	3d. black and blue	15	10
23	11	4d. purple and green	1·25	10
24	–	6d. blue and green	60	10
24a	–	9d. brown and violet	8·00	2·50
25	–	1s. green and blue	80	10
26	–	1s. 3d. green and brown	3·00	10
27	–	2s. green and red	3·25	60
28	–	2s. 6d. blue and brown	4·25	30
29	17	5s. brown and green	8·00	2·25
30	–	10s. brown and red	25·00	13·00
31	–	£1 black and violet	45·00	38·00

DESIGNS—VERT (as Type **6**): 1d. V.H.F. mast; 2d. Copper mining; 2½d. Fairbridge Memorial. (As Type **11**): 6d. Eastern Cataract, Victoria Falls. HORIZ (as Type **6**): 3d. Rhodes's grave. (As Type **11**): 9d. Rhodesian railway trains; 1s. Tobacco; 1s. 3d. Lake Nyasa; 2s. Chirundu Bridge; 2s. 6d. Salisbury Airport. (As Type **17**): 10s. Mlanje; £1 Federal Coat of Arms.

20 Kariba Gorge, 1955

1960. Opening of Kariba Hydro-Electric Scheme.

32	20	3d. green and orange	60	10
33	–	6d. brown and bistre	70	20
34	–	1s. blue and green	2·50	2·50
35	–	1s. 3d. blue and brown	2·50	1·75
36	–	2s. 6d. purple and red	3·50	7·00
37	–	5s. violet and turquoise	8·00	11·00

DESIGNS: 6d. 330 k.V. power lines; 1s. Barrage wall; 1s. 3d. Barrage and lake; 2s. 6d. Interior of power station; 5s. Queen Mother and barrage wall (inscr "ROYAL OPENING").

26 Miner drilling

1961. 7th Commonwealth Mining and Metallurgical Congress.

38	26	6d. green and brown	50	15
39	–	1s. 3d. black and blue	50	60

DESIGN: 1s. 3d. Surface installations, Nchanga Mine.

28 De Havilland Hercules "City of Basra" on Rhodesian Airstrip

1962. 30th Anniv of 1st London–Rhodesian Airmail Service.

40	28	6d. green and red	35	25
41	–	1s. 3d. blue, black & yellow	1·50	50
42	–	2s. 6d. red and violet	6·50	4·25

DESIGNS: 1s. 3d. Short S.23 flying boat "Canopus" taking off from Zambesi; 2s. 6d. Hawker Siddeley Comet 4 at Salisbury Airport.

31 Tobacco Plant 35

1963. World Tobacco Congress, Salisbury.

43	31	3d. green and olive	30	10
44	–	6d. green, brown and blue	40	35
45	–	1s. 3d. brown and blue	60	45
46	–	2s. 6d. yellow and brown	1·00	2·75

DESIGNS: 6d. Tobacco field; 1s. 3d. Auction floor; 2s. 6d. Cured tobacco.

1963. Centenary of Red Cross.

47	35	3d. red	85	10

36 African "Round Table" Emblem

1963. World Council of Young Men's Service Clubs, Salisbury.

48	36	6d. black, gold and green	50	1·25
49		1s. 3d. multicoloured	50	1·00

POSTAGE DUE STAMPS

D 1

1961.

D1	D 1	1d. red	2·50	4·50
D2		2d. blue	2·25	3·00
D3		4d. green	2·25	8·50
D4		6d. purple	4·50	7·50

ROSS DEPENDENCY

A dependency of New Zealand in the Antarctic on the Ross Sea.

The post office closed on 30 September 1987, but re-opened in November 1994.

1957. 12 pence = 1 shilling;
20 shillings = 1 pound.
1967. 100 cents = 1 dollar.

3 Map of Ross Dependency and New Zealand 4 Queen Elizabeth II

1957.

1	–	3d. blue	2·00	1·00
2	–	4d. red	2·00	75
3	3	8d. red and blue	2·00	1·00
4	4	1s. 6d. purple	2·00	1·25

DESIGNS—HORIZ (As Type **3**): 3d. H.M.S. "Erebus"; 4d. Shackleton and Scott.

5 H.M.S. "Erebus"

1967. Nos. 1/4 with values inscr in decimal currency as T **5**.

5	5	2 c. blue	12·00	4·75
6	–	3 c. red	8·00	4·75
7	3	7 c. red and blue	11·00	7·50
8	4	15 c. purple	11·00	12·00

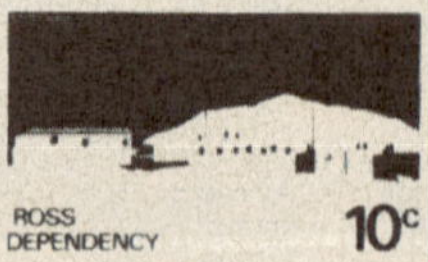

6 McCormick's Skua 7 Scott Base

1972.

9	6	3 c. black, grey and blue	1·50	1·40
10a	–	4 c. black, blue and violet	30	1·60
11a	–	5 c. black, grey and lilac	20	1·60
12a	–	8 c. black, grey and brown	20	1·60
13a	7	10 c. black, green and grey	30	1·60
14a	–	18 c. black, violet and bright violet	30	1·60

DESIGNS—As Type **6**: 4 c. Lockheed Hercules airplane at Williams Field; 5 c. Shackleton's Hut; 8 c. Supply ship H.M.N.Z.S. "Endeavour". As Type **7**: 18 c. Tabular ice flow.

8 Adelie Penguins

1982. Multicoloured.

15	5 c. Type **8**	1·00	1·00
16	10 c. Tracked vehicles	40	40
17	20 c. Scott Base	40	40
18	30 c. Field party	40	40
19	40 c. Vanda Station	40	40
20	50 c. Scott's hut, Cape Evans	40	40

9 McCormick's Skua

1994. Wildlife. Multicoloured.

21	5 c. Type **9**	10	10
22	10 c. Snow petrel chick	10	10
23	20 c. Black-browed albatross	15	20
24	40 c. Emperor penguins	25	30
25	45 c. As 40 c.	30	35
26	50 c. Chinstrap penguins	30	35
27	70 c. Adelie penguin	45	50
28	80 c. Elephant seals	50	55
29	$1 Leopard seal	65	70
30	$2 Weddell seal	1·25	1·40
31	$3 Crabeater seal pup	1·90	2·00

10 Capt. James Cook with H.M.S. "Resolution" and H.M.S. "Adventure"

1995. Antarctic Explorers. Multicoloured.

32	40 c. Type **10**	55	55
33	80 c. James Clark Ross with H.M.S. "Erebus" and H.M.S. "Terror"	95	95
34	$1 Roald Amundsen and "Fram"	1·10	1·10
35	$1.20 Robert Scott with "Terra Nova"	1·40	1·40
36	$1.50 Ernest Shackleton with "Endurance"	1·75	1·75
37	$1.80 Richard Byrd with Ford 4-AT-B Trimotor "Floyd Bennett" (airplane)	2·00	2·00

11 Inside Ice Cave 12 Snow Petrel

1996. Antarctic Landscapes. Multicoloured.

38	40 c. Type **11**	40	35
39	80 c. Base of glacier	70	65
40	$1 Glacier ice fall	85	80
41	$1.20 Climbers on crater rim (horiz)	1·00	95
42	$1.50 Pressure ridges (horiz)	1·25	1·25
43	$1.80 Fumarole ice tower (horiz)	1·40	1·40

1997. Antarctic Seabirds. Multicoloured. (a) With "WWF" panda emblem.

44	40 c. Type **12**	40	40
45	80 c. Cape petrel	70	70
46	$1.20 Antarctic fulmar	1·00	1·00
47	$1.50 Antarctic petrel	1·25	1·25

(b) Without "WWF" panda emblem.

48	40 c. Type **12**	40	40
49	80 c. Cape petrel	70	70
50	$1 Antarctic prion	90	90
51	$1.20 Antarctic fulmar	1·00	1·00
52	$1.50 Antarctic petrel	1·25	1·40
53	$1.80 Antarctic tern	1·25	1·50

Nos. 48/53 were printed together, se-tenant, with the backgrounds forming a composite design.

13 Sculptured Sea Ice

1997. Ice Formation. Multicoloured.

54	40 c. Type **13**	35	35
55	80 c. Glacial tongue	60	60
56	$1 Stranded tabular iceberg	80	80
57	$1.20 Autumn at Cape Evans	90	90
58	$1.50 Sea ice in summer thaw	1·10	1·10
59	$1.80 Sunset at tubular icebergs	1·25	1·40

SABAH

Formerly North Borneo, now part of Malaysia.

100 cents = 1 Malaysian dollar

1964. Nos. 391/406 of North Borneo optd **SABAH**.

408	1 c. green and red	10	10
409	4 c. olive and orange	15	50
410	5 c. sepia and violet	15	10
411	6 c. black and turquoise	10	10
412	10 c. green and red	15	10
413	12 c. brown and myrtle	15	10
414	20 c. turquoise and blue	3·50	10
415	25 c. black and red	45	90
416	30 c. sepia and olive	25	10
417	35 c. slate and brown	30	20
418	50 c. green and bistre	30	10
419	75 c. blue and purple	3·25	65
420	$1 brown and green	5·50	50
421	$2 brown and slate	9·00	2·00
422	$5 green and purple	9·00	12·00
423	$10 red and blue	13·00	25·00

138 "Vanda hookeriana"

1965. As No. 115/21 of Kedah, but with Arms of Sabah inset as T **138**.

424	138	1 c. multicoloured	10	70
425	–	2 c. multicoloured	10	80
426	–	5 c. multicoloured	10	10
427	–	6 c. multicoloured	30	80
428	–	10 c. multicoloured	30	10
429	–	15 c. multicoloured	2·00	10
430	–	20 c. multicoloured	2·75	50

The higher values used in Sabah were Nos. 20/7 of Malaysia.

139 "Hebomoia glaucippe"

1971. Butterflies. As Nos. 124/30 of Kedah, but with Sabah Arms inset as T **139**.

432	–	1 c. multicoloured	30	1·50
433	–	2 c. multicoloured	60	1·50
434	–	5 c. multicoloured	80	30
435	–	6 c. multicoloured	80	80
436	139	10 c. multicoloured	80	10
437	–	15 c. multicoloured	80	10
438	–	20 c. multicoloured	1·10	70

The higher values in use with this issue were Nos. 64/71 of Malaysia.

140 "Hibiscus rosa-sinensis" 141 Coffee

1979. As Nos. 135/41 of Kedah, but with Arms of Sabah as T **140**.

445	1 c. "Rafflesia hasseltii"	10	55
446	2 c. "Pterocarpus indicus"	10	55
447	5 c. "Lagerstroemia speciosa"	15	10
448	10 c. "Durio zibethinus"	30	10
449	15 c. Type **140**	50	10
450	20 c. "Rhododendron scortechinii"	30	10
451	25 c. "Etlingera elatior" (inscr "Phaeomeria speciosa")	65	10

The higher values in use with this issue were Nos. 190/7 of Malaysia.

1986. As Nos. 152/8 of Kedah but with Arms of Sabah as in T **141**.

459	1 c. Type **141**	10	10
460	2 c. Coconuts	10	10
461	5 c. Cocoa	10	10
462	10 c. Black pepper	10	10
463	15 c. Rubber	10	10
464	20 c. Oil palm	10	10
465	30 c. Rice	15	20

ST. CHRISTOPHER

One of the Leeward Is. Stamps superseded in 1890 by Leeward Islands general issue.

12 pence = 1 shilling

1

1870.

11	1	½d. green	70	1·25
2		1d. mauve	48·00	27·00
13		1d. red	1·00	1·75
14		2½d. brown	£170	55·00
16		2½d. blue	1·50	1·50
8		4d. blue	£150	15·00
18		4d. grey	1·25	80
9		6d. green	55·00	5·00
19		6d. olive	80·00	£300
20		1s. mauve	90·00	65·00

1885. Surch in words.

23	1	1d. on half of 1d. red	24·00	38·00
26		1d. on ½d. green	28·00	38·00
28		1d. on 2½d. blue	50·00	50·00
24		1d. on 6d. green	16·00	28·00
22		4d. on 6d. green	55·00	48·00

1886. Surch in figures.

25	1	4d. on 6d. green	48·00	90·00

ST. HELENA

An island in the South Atlantic Ocean, West of Africa.

1856. 12 pence = 1 shilling;
20 shillings = 1 pound.
1971. 100 pence = 1 pound.

1

11

The early stamps of St. Helena, other than the 6d. were formed by printing the 6d. in various colours and surcharging it with new values in words or (in case of the 2½d.) in figures.

1856. Imperf.

4	1	1d. on 6d. red	£120	£170
5		4d. on 6d. red	£500	£250
1		6d. blue	£500	£180

1861. Perf.

36	1	½d. on 6d. green	1·00	1·25
37		1d. on 6d. red	2·75	2·25
39		2d. on 6d. yellow	1·25	3·50
40		2½d. on 6d. blue	2·00	5·00
42		3d. on 6d. purple	2·50	3·25
14		4d. on 6d. red	90·00	48·00
43c		4d. on 6d. brown	17·00	8·50
25		6d. blue	£300	45·00
44		6d. grey	11·00	4·00
30		1s. on 6d. green	20·00	12·00
20		5s. on 6d. yellow	40·00	60·00

1890.

46	11	½d. green	2·75	4·50
47		1d. red	9·50	1·00
48		1½d. brown and green	4·50	7·00
49		2d. yellow	5·00	11·00
50		2½d. blue	7·50	11·00
51		5d. violet	11·00	27·00
52		10d. brown	18·00	48·00

12

13 Government House

14 The Wharf

1902. Inscr "POSTAGE POSTAGE".

53	12	½d. green	1·50	1·25
54		1d. red	4·75	70

1903.

55	13	½d. brown and green	2·00	3·00
56	14	1d. black and red	1·50	35
57	13	2d. black and green	6·00	1·25
58	14	8d. black and brown	20·00	32·00
59	13	1s. brown and orange	20·00	40·00
60	14	2s. black and violet	48·00	85·00

1908. Inscr "POSTAGE & REVENUE".

64	12	2½d. blue	1·25	1·40
66a		4d. black and red on yellow	1·25	9·00
67a		6d. purple	3·00	13·00
71		10s. green and red on green	£170	£250

1912. As T 13/14 but with medallion of King George V.

72	13	½d. black and green	1·50	9·00
73	14	1d. black and red	2·50	1·75
89		1d. green	1·00	24·00
74		1½d. black and orange	2·75	5·50
90		1½d. red	7·50	26·00
75	13	2d. black and grey	2·75	1·75
76	14	2½d. black and blue	2·75	5·50
77	13	3d. black & purple on yellow	2·25	5·00
91		3d. blue	17·00	48·00
78	14	8d. black and purple	5·50	50·00
79	13	1s. black on green	8·00	32·00
80	14	2s. black and blue on blue	35·00	80·00
81		3s. black and violet	48·00	£130

18

22 Badge of St. Helena

1912. Inscr "POSTAGE & REVENUE".

83	18	4d. black and red on yellow	8·00	20·00
84		6d. purple	3·00	5·00

1913. Inscr "POSTAGE POSTAGE".

85	18	4d. black and red on yellow	7·00	2·75
86		6d. purple	12·00	22·00

1916. Surch **WAR TAX ONE PENNY.**

87		1d. + 1d. black & red (No. 73)	1·00	2·75

1919. Surch **WAR TAX 1d.**

88		1d. + 1d. black & red (No. 73)	55	3·25

1922.

97	22	½d. grey and black	1·25	1·75
98		1d. grey and green	1·75	1·40
99		1½d. red	2·75	12·00
100		2d. grey and brown	2·75	2·00
101		3d. blue	2·00	4·00
92		4d. grey & black on yellow	8·50	6·00
103		5d. green and red on green	3·00	5·50
104		6d. grey and purple	3·50	8·00
105		8d. grey and violet	3·25	6·50
106		1s. grey and brown	6·00	9·00
107		1s. 6d. grey & green on grn	14·00	45·00
108		2s. purple and blue on blue	16·00	38·00
109		2s. 6d. grey & red on yellow	13·00	50·00
110		5s. grey & green on yellow	38·00	75·00
111		7s. 6d. grey and orange	75·00	£120
112		10s. grey and green	£110	£160
113		15s. grey and purple on blue	£800	£1400
96		£1 grey and purple on red	£350	£450

23 Lot and Lots wife

1934. Centenary of British Colonisation.

114	23	½d. black and purple	85	80
115	–	1d. black and green	65	85
116	–	1½d. black and red	2·50	3·25
117	–	2d. black and orange	2·00	1·25
118	–	3d. black and blue	1·40	4·50
119	–	6d. black and blue	3·25	3·00
120	–	1s. black and brown	6·00	18·00
121	–	2s. 6d. black and red	35·00	48·00
122	–	5s. black and brown	75·00	85·00
123	–	10s. black and purple	£200	£250

DESIGNS—HORIZ: 1d. The "Plantation"; 1½d. Map of St. Helena; 2d. Quay, Jamestown; 3d. James Valley; 6d. Jamestown; 1s. Munden's Promontory; 5s. High Knoll; 10s. Badge of St. Helena. VERT: 2s. 6d. St. Helena.

1935. Silver Jubilee. As T 13 of Antigua.

124		1½d. blue and red	75	5·00
125		2d. blue and grey	1·25	90
126		6d. green and blue	6·50	2·75
127		1s. grey and purple	9·00	11·00

1937. Coronation. As T 2 of Aden.

128		1d. green	40	30
129		2d. orange	55	30
130		3d. blue	80	30

33 Badge of St. Helena

1938.

131	33	½d. violet	10	40
132		1d. green	15·00	2·75
132a		1d. orange	20	30
149		1d. black and green	60	80
133		1½d. red	20	40
150		1½d. black and red	60	80
134		2d. orange	20	15
151		2d. black and red	60	80
135		3d. blue	90·00	18·00
135a		3d. grey	30	30
135b		4d. blue	2·00	45
136		6d. blue	2·00	30
136a		8d. green	3·25	90
137		1s. brown	90	30
138		2s. 6d. purple	17·00	4·00
139		5s. brown	18·00	10·00
140		10s. purple	18·00	18·00

1946. Victory. As T 9 of Aden.

141		2d. orange	10	10
142		10s. blue	10	10

1948. Silver Wedding. As T 10/11 of Aden.

143		3d. black	30	20
144		10s. blue	23·00	28·00

1949. U.P.U. As T 20/23 of Antigua.

145		3d. red	50	30
146		4d. blue	3·00	90
147		6d. green	90	90
148		1s. black	90	1·10

1953. Coronation. As T 13 of Aden.

152		3d. black and lilac	1·00	65

34 Badge of St. Helena

1953.

153	34	½d. black and green	30	30
154	–	1d. black and green	15	20
155	–	1½d. black and purple	1·75	70
156	–	2d. black and red	50	30
157	–	2½d. black and red	40	30
158	–	3d. black and brown	3·25	30
159	–	4d. black and blue	40	40
160	–	6d. black and violet	40	30
161	–	7d. black and grey	65	1·25
162	–	1s. black and red	40	40
163	–	2s. 6d. black and violet	13·00	7·00
164	–	5s. black and sepia	18·00	11·00
165	–	10s. black and yellow	40·00	22·00

DESIGNS—HORIZ: 1d. Flax plantation; 2d. Lace-making; 2½d. Drying flax; 3d. St. Helena sand plover; 4d. Flagstaff and The Barn (hills); 6d. Donkeys carrying flax; 7d. Map; 1s. The Castle; 2s. 6d. Cutting flax; 5s. Jamestown; 10s. Longwood House. VERT: 1½d. Heart-shaped Waterfall.

45 Stamp of 1856

47 East Indiaman "London" off James Bay

1956. Cent of First St. Helena Postage Stamp.

166	45	3d. blue and red	10	10
167		4d. blue and brown	10	20
168		6d. blue and purple	15	25

1959. Tercentenary of Settlement.

169	–	3d. black and red	10	15
170	47	6d. green and blue	40	75
171	–	1s. black and orange	40	75

DESIGNS—HORIZ: 3d. Arms of East India Company; 1s. Commemoration Stone.

1961. Tristan Relief Fund. Nos. 46 and 49/51 of Tristan da Cunha surch **ST. HELENA Tristan Relief** and premium.

172		2½ c. + 3d. black and red	—	£400
173		5 c. + 6d. black and blue	—	£425
174		7½ c. + 9d. black and red	—	£475
175		10 c. + 1s. black and brown	—	£550

50 St. Helena Butterflyfish

63 Queen Elizabeth II with Prince Andrew (after Cecil Beaton)

1961.

176	50	1d. multicoloured	30	20
177	–	1½d. multicoloured	50	20
178	–	2d. red and grey	15	20
179	–	3d. multicoloured	70	20
180	–	4½d. multicoloured	60	50
181	–	6d. red, sepia and olive	5·50	60
182	–	7d. brown, black and violet	35	60
183	–	10d. purple and blue	35	60
184	–	1s. yellow, green and brown	55	60
185	–	1s. 6d. grey and blue	13·00	4·00
186	–	2s. 6d. red, yellow & turq	2·50	2·25
187	–	5s. yellow, brown & green	14·00	4·00
188	–	10s. red, black and blue	17·00	11·00
189	63	£1 brown and blue	17·00	17·00

DESIGNS—VERT (as Type 50): 1½d. Yellow canary; 3d. Queen Elizabeth II; 4½d. Red-wood flower; 6d. Madagascar red fody; 1s. Gum-wood flower; 1s. 6d. White tern; 5s. Night-blooming Cereus. HORIZ (as T 50): 2d. Brittle starfish; 7d. Trumpetfish; 10d. Feather starfish; 2s. 6d. Orange starfish; 10s. Deep-water bullseye.

1963. Freedom from Hunger. As T 28 of Aden.

190		1s. 6d. blue	1·50	40

1963. Cent of Red Cross. As T 33 of Antigua.

191		3d. red and black	75	25
192		1s. 6d. red and blue	3·00	1·50

1965. First Local Post. Optd **FIRST LOCAL POST 4th JANUARY 1965.**

193	50	1d. multicoloured	10	10
194	–	3d. multicoloured (No. 179)	10	10
195	–	6d. red, sepia & olive (No. 181)	40	10
196	–	1s. 6d. grey & blue (No. 185)	60	15

1965. Cent of I.T.U. As T 36 of Antigua.

197		3d. blue and brown	35	15
198		6d. purple and green	55	15

1965. Cent of I.C.Y. As T 37 of Antigua.

199		1d. purple and turquoise	30	15
200		6d. green and lavender	80	15

1966. Churchill Commem. As T 38 of Antigua.

201		1d. blue	15	15
202		3d. green	35	15
203		6d. brown	50	20
204		1s. 6d. violet	70	60

1966. World Cup Football Championship. As T 40 of Antigua.

205		3d. multicoloured	50	25
206		6d. multicoloured	75	25

1966. Inauguration of W.H.O. Headquarters, Geneva. As T 41 of Antigua.

207		3d. black, green and blue	75	20
208		1s. 6d. black, purple and ochre	2·75	80

1966. 20th Anniv of U.N.E.S.C.O. As T 54/6 of Antigua.

209		3d. multicoloured	75	20
210		6d. yellow, violet and olive	1·25	40
211		1s. 6d. black, purple & orange	2·00	1·60

65 Badge of St. Helena

1967. New Constitution.

212	65	1s. multicoloured	10	10
213		2s. 6d. multicoloured	20	20

66 Fire of London

1967. 300th Anniv of Arrival of Settlers after Great Fire of London.

214	66	1d. red and black	15	10
215	–	3d. blue and black	20	10
216	–	6d. violet and black	20	10
217	–	1s. 6d. green and black	20	10

DESIGNS: 3d. East Indiaman "Charles"; 6d. Settlers landing at Jamestown; 1s. 6d. Settlers clearing scrub.

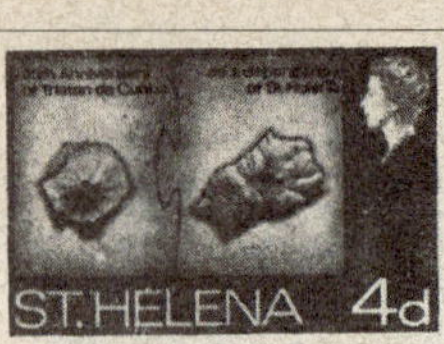

70 Interlocking Maps of Tristan and St. Helena

1968. 30th Anniv of Tristan da Cunha as a Dependency of St. Helena.
218 70 4d. purple and brown . . . 10 10
219 – 8d. olive and brown 10 25
220 70 1s. 9d. blue and brown . . 10 35
221 – 2s. 3d. blue and brown . . 15 35
DESIGNS: 8d. and 2s. 3d. Interlocking maps of Tristan and St. Helena (different).

72 Queen Elizabeth and Sir Hudson Lowe

1968. 150th Anniv of Abolition of Slavery in St. Helena.
222 72 3d. multicoloured 10 10
223 9d. multicoloured 10 15
224 – 1s. 6d. multicoloured . . . 15 20
225 – 2s. 6d. multicoloured . . . 25 25
DESIGN: Nos. 224 and 225, Queen Elizabeth and Sir George Bingham.

74 Blue Gum Eucalyptus and Road Construction

1968. Multicoloured.
226 ½d. Type 74 . . . . 10 10
227 1d. Electricity development . . 10 10
228 1½d. Dental unit 15 10
229 2d. Pest control 15 10
230 3d. Flats in Jamestown 30 10
231 4d. Livestock improvement . . 20 10
232 6d. Schools broadcasting . . . 50 10
233 8d. Country Cottages 30 10
234 10d. New school buildings . . 30 10
235 1s. Reafforestation 30 10
236 1s. 6d. Heavy lift crane . . . 70 2·00
237 2s. 6d. Lady Field Children's Home . . . . 80 2·75
238 5s. Agricultural training . . . 90 3·50
239 10s. New General Hospital . 2·50 3·75
240 £1 Lifeboat "John Dutton" . . 11·00 15·00
PLANTS SHOWN: ½d., 4d., 1s. 6d. Blue gum eucalyptus; 1d., 6d., 2s. 6d. Cabbage-tree; 1½d., 8d., 5s. St. Helena redwood; 2d., 10d., 10s. Scrubweed; 3d., 1s., £1 Tree-fern.

89 Brig "Perseverance"

1969. Mail Communications. Multicoloured.
241 4d. Type 89 . . . . 20 20
242 8d. "Phoebe" (screw steamer) 30 40
243 1s. 9d. "Llandovery Castle" (liner) 40 60
244 2s. 3d. "Good Hope Castle" (cargo liner) 45 75

93 W.O. and Drummer of the 53rd Foot, 1815

1969. Military Uniforms. Multicoloured.
245 6d. Type 93 . . . . 25 20
246 8d. Officer and Surgeon, 20th Foot, 1816 . . . . 35 20
247 1s. 8d. Drum Major, 66th Foot, 1816, and Royal Artillery Officer, 1920 . . . . 40 35
248 2s. 6d. Private, 91st Foot, and 2nd Corporal, Royal Sappers and Miners, 1832 . . . . . 45 40

97 Dickens, Mr. Pickwick and Job Trotter ("Pickwick Papers")

1970. Death Cent of Charles Dickens. Mult.
249 4d. Type 97 . . . . 60 15
250 8d. Mr. Bumble and Oliver ("Oliver Twist") 70 20
251 1s. 6d. Sairey Gamp and Mark Tapley ("Martin Chuzzlewit") 85 25
252 2s. 6d. Jo and Mr. Turveydrop ("Bleak House") . . . . . 1·00 35
All designs include a portrait of Dickens as Type 97.

98 "Kiss of Life"

1970. Centenary of British Red Cross.
253 98 6d. bistre, red and black . 15 15
254 – 9d. green, red and black . 20 15
255 – 1s. 9d. grey, red and black 30 20
256 – 2s. 3d. lilac, red and black 30 30
DESIGNS: 9d. Nurse with girl in wheelchair; 1s. 9d. Nurse bandaging child's knee; 2s. 3d. Red Cross emblem.

99 Officer's Shako Plate (20th Foot)

1970. Military Equipment (1st issue). Mult.
257 4d. Type 99 . . . . 35 20
258 9d. Officer's breast plate (66th Foot) 40 30
259 1s. 3d. Officer's Full Dress shako (91st Foot) 50 40
260 2s. 11d. Ensign's shako (53rd Foot) 70 60
See also Nos. 281/4, 285/8 and 291/4.

100 Electricity Development

1971. Decimal Currency. Designs as Nos. 227/39, inscr as T 100.
261 ½p. multicoloured 10 10
262 1p. multicoloured 10 10
263 1½p. multicoloured 10 10
264 2p. multicoloured . . . . . . 1·75 90
265 2½p. multicoloured 10 10
266 3½p. multicoloured 30 10
267 4½p. multicoloured 10 10
268 5p. multicoloured 10 10
269 7½p. multicoloured 40 35
270 10p. multicoloured 30 35
271 12½p. multicoloured 30 50
272 25p. multicoloured . . . . . 60 1·25
273 50p. multicoloured . . . . . 1·25 2·00

101 St. Helena holding the "True Cross"

102 Napoleon (after painting by J. L. David) and Tomb on St. Helena

1971. Easter.
275 101 2p. multicoloured 10 10
276 5p. multicoloured 15 15
277 7½p. multicoloured 25 20
278 12½p. multicoloured . . . 30 25

1971. 150th Death Anniv of Napoleon. Mult.
279 2p. Type 102 . . . . 30 40
280 34p. "Napoleon at St. Helena" (H. Delaroche) 60 85

1971. Military Equipment (2nd issue). As T 99. Multicoloured.
281 1½p. Artillery Private's hanger . 45 30
282 4p. Baker rifle and socket bayonet 60 60
283 6p. Infantry Officer's sword . . 60 80
284 22½p. Baker rifle and sword bayonet . . . . 1·00 1·25

1972. Military Equipment (3rd issue). As T 99. Multicoloured.
285 2p. multicoloured 30 20
286 5p. lilac, blue and black . . . 40 40
287 7½p. multicoloured 50 50
288 12½p. sepia, brown and black . 55 60
DESIGNS: 2p. Royal Sappers and Miners breast-plate, post 1823; 5p. Infantry sergeant's spontoon, c. 1830; 7½p. Royal Artillery officer's breast-plate, c. 1830; 12½p. English military pistol, c. 1800.

1972. Royal Silver Wedding. As T 52 of Ascension but with St. Helena sand plover and white tern in background.
289 2p. green 25 40
290 16p. brown 50 85

1973. Military Equipment (4th issue). As T 99. Multicoloured.
291 2p. Other Rank's shako, 53rd Foot, 1815 . . . . 55 55
292 5p. Band and Drums sword, 1830 60 1·00
293 7½p. Royal Sappers and Miners Officer's hat, 1830 . . . . 80 1·25
294 12½p. General's sword, 1831 . 1·00 1·50

1973. Royal Wedding. As T 47 of Anguilla. Multicoloured, background colours given.
295 2p. blue 15 10
296 18p. green 25 20

104 "Westminster" and "Claudine" beached, 1849

1973. Tercentenary of East India Company Charter. Multicoloured.
297 1½p. Type 104 . . . . 40 45
298 4p. "True Britton", 1790 . . . 50 70
299 6p. "General Goddard" in action, 1795 . . . . 50 70
300 22½p. "Kent" burning in the Bay of Biscay, 1825 . . . . . . 1·10 2·25

105 U.P.U. Emblem and Ships

1974. Centenary of U.P.U. Multicoloured.
301 5p. Type 105 . . . . 20 25
302 25p. U.P.U. emblem and letters 40 55

106 Churchill in Sailor Suit and Blenheim Palace

1974. Birth Cent of Sir Winston Churchill.
304 106 5p. multicoloured 20 20
305 – 25p. black, pink and purple 40 60
DESIGN: 25p. Churchill and River Thames.

107 Capt. Cook and H.M.S. "Resolution"

108 "Mellissia begonifolia" (tree)

1975. Bicentenary of Capt. Cook's Return to St. Helena.
307 5p. Type 107 . . . . 40 40
308 25p. Capt. Cook and Jamestown 70 1·00

1975. Centenary of Publication of "St. Helena" by J. C. Melliss. Multicoloured.
310 2p. Type 108 . . . . 20 30
311 5p. "Mellissius adumbratus" (beetle) 25 45
312 12p. St. Helena sand plover (bird) (horiz) . . . . . . 60 1·00
313 25p. Melliss's scorpionfish (horiz) . . . . 75 1·40

109 £1 Note

1976. First Issue of Currency Notes. Mult.
314 8p. Type 109 . . . . 30 30
315 33p. £5 Note 60 80

110 1d. Stamp of 1863

1976. Festival of Stamps, London.
316 110 5p. brown, black and pink 15 15
317 – 8p. black, green & lt green 20 30
318 – 25p. multicoloured . . . 35 45
DESIGNS—VERT: 8p. 1d. stamp of 1922. HORIZ: 25p. Mail carrier "Good Hope Castle".

111 "High Knoll, 1806" (Capt. Barnett)

1976. Aquatints and Lithographs of St. Helena. Multicoloured.
319B 1p. Type 111 . . . . 30 60
320A 3p. "The Friar Rock, 1815" (G. Bellasis) 40 90
321A 5p. "The Column Lot, 1815" (G. Bellasis) 30 90
322A 6p. "Sandy Bay Valley, 1809" (H. Salt) 30 90
323A 8p. "Scene from Castle Terrace, 1815" (G. Bellasis) 40 90
324A 9p. "The Briars, 1815" . . . 40 90
325A 10p. "Plantation House, 1821" (J. Wathen) 50 60
326A 15p. "Longwood House, 1821" (J. Wathen) 45 55
327A 18p. "St. Paul's Church" (V. Brooks) . . . . 45 1·25
328A 26p. "St. James's Valley, 1815" (Capt. Hastings) . . . . . 45 1·00
329A 40p. "St. Matthew's Church, 1860" (V. Brooks) . . . . 70 1·75
330A £1 "St. Helena, 1815" (G. Bellasis) . . . . 1·50 3·75
331B £2 "Sugar Loaf Hill, 1821" (J. Wathen) . . . . 3·75 5·00
Nos. 330A and 331B are larger, 47 × 34 mm.
The 1 and 10p. and the £2 come with or without date imprint.

112 Duke of Edinburgh paying Homage

1977. Silver Jubilee. Multicoloured.
332 8p. Royal Visit, 1947 . . . . 10 25
333 15p. Queen's sceptre with dove 20 35
334 26p. Type 112 . . . . 30 40

113 Halley's Comet (from Bayeux Tapestry)

114 Sea Lion

1977. Tercentenary of Halley's Visit. Mult.
335 5p. Type 113 . . . . 35 20
336 8p. Late 17th-century sextant . 50 20
337 27p. Halley and Halley's Mount, St. Helena . . . . 1·00 60

1978. 25th Anniv of Coronation.
338 – 25p. agate, red and silver . 30 50
339 – 25p. multicoloured 30 50
340 **114** 25p. agate, red and silver . 30 50
DESIGNS: No. 338, Black Dragon of Ulster; No. 339, Queen Elizabeth II.

115 Period Engraving of St. Helena

1978. Wreck of the "Witte Leeuw". Multicoloured.
341 3p. Type **115** 15 15
342 5p. Chinese porcelain 15 20
343 8p. Bronze cannon 20 30
344 9p. Chinese porcelain (different) 20 35
345 15p. Pewter mug and ceramic flasks 30 55
346 20p. Dutch East Indiaman . . 40 70

116 H.M.S. "Discovery" **117** Sir Rowland Hill

1979. Bicentenary of Captain Cook's Voyages, 1768–79. Multicoloured.
347 3p. Type **116** 20 15
348 8p. Cook's portable observatory 20 25
349 12p. "Pharnaceum acidum" (sketch by Joseph Banks) . . 25 35
350 25p. Flaxman/Wedgwood medallion of Capt. Cook . . 35 90

1979. Death Centenary of Sir Rowland Hill.
351 **117** 5p. multicoloured 10 15
352 – 8p. multicoloured 15 20
353 – 20p. multicoloured 30 40
354 – 32p. black, magenta & mve 40 55
DESIGNS—HORIZ: 8p. 1965 1d. "First Local Post" stamp; 20p. 1863 1d. on 6d. surcharged stamp; 32p. 1902 1d. stamp.

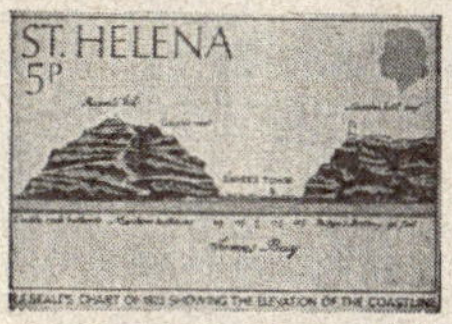

118 R. F. Seal's Chart of 1823 showing the Elevation of the Coastline

1979. 150th Anniv of Inclined Plane.
355 **118** 5p. black, grey and stone . 15 15
356 – 8p. black, grey and stone . 15 20
357 – 50p. multicoloured . . . 60 75
DESIGNS—HORIZ: 8p. The Inclined Plane in 1829; VERT: 50p. The Inclined Plane in 1979.

119 Napoleon's Tomb, 1848

1980. Centenary of Empress Eugenie's Visit.
358 **119** 5p. brown, pink and gold . 10 20
359 – 8p. brown, stone and gold 15 25
360 – 62p. brown, flesh and gold 65 80
DESIGNS: 8p. Landing at St. Helena; 62p. The Empress at Napoleon's Tomb.

120 East Indiaman

1980. "London 1980" Int Stamp Exhibition. Mult.
362 5p. Type **120** 10 15
363 8p. "Dolphin" postal stone . . 10 15
364 47p. Postal stone outside Castle entrance, Jamestown . . . 50 60

121 Queen Elizabeth the Queen Mother in 1974

1980. 80th Birthday of the Queen Mother.
366 **121** 24p. multicoloured . . . 35 50

122 The Briars, 1815

1980. 175th Anniv of Wellington's Visit. Multicoloured.
367 9p. Type **122** 15 15
368 30p. "Wellington" (Goya) (vert) 45 45

123 Redwood

1981. Endemic Plants. Multicoloured.
369 5p. Type **123** 15 15
370 8p. Old father live forever . . 15 20
371 15p. Gumwood 20 25
372 27p. Black cabbage 35 45

124 Detail from Reinel Portolan Chart, c. 1530

1981. Early Maps.
373 **124** 5p. multicoloured 15 15
374 – 8p. black, red and grey . 15 20
375 – 20p. multicoloured . . . 30 35
376 – 30p. multicoloured . . . 35 50
DESIGNS: 8p. John Thornton's Map of St. Helena, c. 1700; 20p. Map of St. Helena, 1815; 30p. Map of St. Helena, 1817.

125 Prince Charles as Royal Navy Commander **126** Atlantic Trumpet Triton

1981. Royal Wedding. Multicoloured.
378 14p. Wedding bouquet from St. Helena 15 20
379 29p. Type **125** 25 30
380 32p. Prince Charles and Lady Diana Spencer 30 35

1981. Sea Shells. Multicoloured.
381 7p. Type **126** 30 20
382 10p. St. Helena cowrie . . . 35 25
383 25p. Common purple janthina 60 60
384 53p. Rude pen shell . . . . . 1·00 1·25

127 Traffic Duty **129** Charles Darwin

128 "Sympetrum dilatatum" (dragonfly)

1981. 25th Anniv of Duke of Edinburgh Award Scheme. Multicoloured.
385 7p. Type **127** 10 10
386 11p. Signposting 15 15
387 25p. Animal care 30 30
388 50p. Duke of Edinburgh, in Guard's uniform, on horse back 60 60

1981. Insects (1st series). Multicoloured.
389 7p. Type **128** 20 20
390 10p. "Aplothorax burchelli" (beetle) 25 25
391 25p. "Ampulex compressa" (wasp) 45 45
392 32p. "Labidura herculeana" (earwig) 55 55
See also Nos. 411/14.

1982. 150th Anniv of Charles Darwin's Voyage. Multicoloured.
393 7p. Type **129** 25 25
394 14p. Flagstaff Hill and Darwin's hammer 35 50
395 25p. Ring-necked pheasant and Chukar partridge 60 85
396 29p. H.M.S. "Beagle" off St. Helena . . . . 75 1·00

130 Prince and Princess of Wales at Balmoral, Autumn, 1981 **132** Lord Baden-Powell

1982. 21st Birthday of Princess of Wales. Multicoloured.
397 7p. St. Helena coat of arms . . 15 20
398 11p. Type **130** 30 20
399 29p. Bride on Palace balcony 70 65
400 55p. Formal portrait . . . . . 1·60 1·10

1982. Commonwealth Games, Brisbane. Nos. 326 and 328 optd **1st PARTICIPATION COMMONWEALTH GAMES 1982.**
401 15p. "Longwood House, 1821" (J. Wathen) 25 25
402 26p. "St. James's Valley, 1815" (Capt. Hastings) 45 45

1982. 75th Anniv of Boy Scout Movement.
403 **132** 3p. brown, grey and yellow 15 15
404 – 11p. brown, grey and green 30 25
405 – 29p. brown, grey & orange 55 60
406 – 59p. brown, grey and green 90 1·25
DESIGNS—HORIZ: 11p. Boy Scout (drawing by Lord Baden-Powell); 59p. Camping at Thompsons Wood. VERT: 29p. Canon Walcott.

133 King and Queen Rocks **134** "Trametes versicolor" ("Coriolus versicolor")

1982. Views of St. Helena by Roland Svensson. Multicoloured.
407 7p. Type **133** 20 20
408 11p. "Turk's Cap" 25 25
409 29p. Coastline from Jamestown (horiz) 50 65
410 59p. "Mundens Point" (horiz) . 1·00 1·40

1983. Insects (2nd series). As T **128**. Mult.
411 11p. "Acherontia atropos" (hawk moth) 25 30
412 15p. "Helenasaldula aberrans" (shore-bug) 30 35
413 29p. "Anchastus compositarum" (click beetle) 40 55
414 59p. "Lamprochrus cossonoides" (weevil) . . . . 75 1·25

1983. Fungi. Multicoloured.
415 11p. Type **134** 25 25
416 15p. "Pluteus brunneisucus" . 35 40
417 29p. "Polyporus induratus" (horiz) 55 75
418 59p. "Coprinus angulatus" . . 80 1·60

135 Java Sparrow **136** Birth of St. Helena

1983. Birds. Multicoloured.
419 7p. Type **135** 30 20
420 15p. Madagascar red fody . . 45 35
421 33p. Common waxbill 80 70
422 59p. Yellow canary . . . . . 1·50 1·40

1983. Christmas. Life of St. Helena (1st series). Multicoloured.
423 10p. Type **136** 20 35
424 15p. St. Helena being taken to convent 20 35
See also Nos. 450/3 and 468/71.

137 1934 Centenary ½d. Stamp **139** "St. Helena" (schooner)

138 Prince Andrew and H.M.S. "Invincible" (aircraft carrier)

1984. 150th Anniv of St. Helena as a British Colony. Multicoloured.
425 1p. Type **137** 10 20
426 3p. 1934 1d. stamp 10 20
427 6p. 1934 1½d. stamp 10 30
428 7p. 1934 2d. stamp 15 30
429 11p. 1934 3d. stamp 20 40
430 15p. 1934 6d. stamp 25 45
431 29p. 1934 1s. stamp 50 95
432 33p. 1934 5s. stamp . . . . 55 1·25
433 59p. 1934 10s. stamp . . . . 80 2·00
434 £1 1934 2s. 6d. stamp . . . 1·50 3·25
435 £2 St. Helena Coat of Arms . 2·75 5·00

1984. Visit of Prince Andrew. Multicoloured.
436 11p. Type **138** 25 25
437 60p. Prince Andrew and H.M.S. "Herald" (survey ship) . . 75 1·40

1984. 250th Anniv of "Lloyd's List" (newspaper). Multicoloured.
438 10p. Type **139** 20 20
439 18p. Solomons Facade (local agent) 35 35
440 25p. Lloyd's Coffee House, London 50 55
441 50p. "Papanui" (freighter) . . 1·00 1·00

140 Twopenny Coin and Donkey

1984. New Coinage. Multicoloured.
442 10p. Type **140** 30 35
443 15p. Five pence coin and St. Helena sand plover 35 45
444 29p. Penny coin and yellow-finned tuna 55 75
445 50p. Ten pence coin and arum lily . . . . 90 1·25

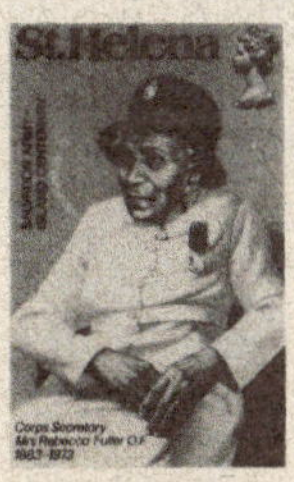

141 Mrs. Rebecca Fuller (former Corps Secretary) **142** Queen Elizabeth the Queen Mother aged Two

1984. Centenary of Salvation Army on St. Helena. Multicoloured.

446	7p. Type **141**	30	45
447	11p. Meals-on-wheels service (horiz)	40	55
448	25p. Salvation Army Citadel, Jamestown (horiz)	60	1·00
449	60p. Salvation Army band at Jamestown Clock Tower	90	2·25

1984. Christmas. Life of St. Helena (2nd series). As T **136**. Multicoloured.

450	6p. St. Helena visits prisoners	20	20
451	10p. Betrothal of St. Helena	30	30
452	15p. Marriage of St. Helena to Constantius	40	40
453	33p. Birth of Constantine	70	70

1985. Life and Times of Queen Elizabeth the Queen Mother. Multicoloured.

454	11p. Type **142**	20	25
455	15p. At Ascot with the Queen	20	35
456	29p. Attending Gala Ballet at Covent Garden	40	65
457	55p. With Prince Henry at his christening	60	1·00

143 Axillary Cardinalfish

144 John J. Audubon

1985. Marine Life. Multicoloured.

459	7p. Type **143**	25	25
460	11p. Chub mackerel	30	30
461	15p. Skipjack tuna	40	40
462	33p. Yellow-finned tuna	75	75
463	50p. Stump	1·25	1·25

1985. Birth Bicentenary of John J. Audubon (ornithologist).

464	**144**	11p. black and brown	45	25
465	–	15p. multicoloured	55	35
466	–	25p. multicoloured	75	55
467	–	60p. multicoloured	1·40	1·40

DESIGN—HORIZ (from original Audubon paintings): 15p. Moorhen ("Common Gallinule); 25p. White-tailed tropic bird; 68p. Common noddy.

1985. Christmas. Life of St. Helena (3rd series). As T **136**. Multicoloured.

468	7p. St. Helena jouneys to the Holy Land	25	25
469	10p. Zambres slays the bull	30	30
470	15p. The bull restored to life: conversion of St. Helena	40	40
471	60p. Resurrection of the corpse: the True Cross identified	1·00	1·50

145 Church Provident Society for Women Banner

1986. Friendly Societies' Banners. Mult.

472	10p. Type **145**	20	25
473	11p. Working Men's Christian Association	20	25
474	25p. Church Benefit Society for Children	40	55
475	29p. Mechanics and Friendly Benefit Society	45	65
476	33p. Ancient Order of Foresters	50	70

1986. 60th Birthday of Queen Elizabeth II. As T **110** of Ascension. Multicoloured.

477	10p. Princess Elizabeth making 21st birthday broadcast, South Africa, 1947	15	20
478	15p. Silver Jubilee photograph, 1977	25	30
479	20p. Princess Elizabeth on board H.M.S. "Vanguard", 1947	30	35
480	50p. In the U.S.A., 1976	65	75
481	65p. At Crown Agents Head Office, London, 1983	80	90

146 Plaque at Site of Halley's Observatory on St. Helena

1986. Appearance of Halley's Comet. Multicoloured.

482	9p. Type **146**	25	35
483	12p. Edmond Halley	30	35
484	20p. Halley's planisphere of the southern stars	55	60
485	65p. "Unity" on passage to St. Helena, 1676	1·75	2·00

1986. Royal Wedding. As T **112** of Ascension. Multicoloured.

486	10p. Prince Andrew and Miss Sarah Ferguson	20	25
487	40p. Prince Andrew with Governor J. Massingham on St. Helena	80	85

147 James Ross and H.M.S. "Erebus"

1986. Explorers.

488	**147**	1p. brown and pink	30	1·25
489	–	3p. deep blue and blue	30	1·25
490	–	5p. deep green and green	30	1·25
491	–	9p. brown and red	40	1·25
492	–	10p. deep brown & brown	40	1·25
493	–	12p. green and light green	50	1·25
494	–	15p. brown and pink	60	1·25
495	–	20p. blue and light blue	70	1·25
496	–	25p. sepia and pink	70	1·25
497	–	40p. deep green and green	1·10	1·75
498	–	60p. deep brown & brown	1·25	2·00
499	–	£1 deep blue and blue	2·00	3·00
500	–	£2 deep lilac and lilac	4·00	5·00

DESIGNS: 3p. Robert FitzRoy and H.M.S. "Beagle"; 5p. Adam Johann von Krusenstern and "Nadezhda"; 9p. William Bligh and H.M.S. "Resolution"; 10p. Otto von Kotzebue and "Rurik"; 12p. Philip Carteret and H.M.S. "Swallow"; 15p. Thomas Cavendish and "Desire"; 20p. Louis-Antoine de Bougainville and "La Boudeuse"; 25p. Fyedor Petrovich Lutke and "Senyavin"; 40p. Louis Isidore Duperrey and "La Coquille"; 60p. John Byron and H.M.S. "Dolphin"; £1 James Cook and H.M.S. "Endeavour"; £2 Jules Dumont d'Urville and "L'Astrolabe".

148 Prince Edward and H.M.S. "Repulse" (battle cruiser), 1925

1987. Royal Visits to St. Helena. Multicoloured.

501	9p. Type **148**	70	70
502	13p. King George VI and H.M.S. "Vanguard" (battleship), 1947	95	1·00
503	38p. Prince Philip and Royal Yacht "Britannia", 1957	2·00	2·75
504	45p. Prince Andrew and H.M.S. "Herald" (survey ship), 1984	2·25	3·00

149 St. Helena Tea Plant

151 "Defence" and Dampier's Signature. 1691

150 Lesser Rorqual

1987. Rare Plants (1st series). Multicoloured.

505	9p. Type **149**	65	55
506	13p. Baby's toes	80	75
507	38p. Salad plant	1·50	2·00
508	45p. Scrubwood	1·75	2·25

See also Nos. 531/4.

1987. Marine Mammals. Multicoloured.

509	9p. Type **150**	90	75
510	13p. Risso's dolphin	95	95
511	45p. Sperm whale	2·25	2·75
512	60p. Euphrosyne dolphin	2·50	3·25

1987. Royal Ruby Wedding. Nos. 477/81 optd **40TH WEDDING ANNIVERSARY**.

514	10p. Princess Elizabeth making 21st birthday broadcast, South Africa, 1947	15	30
515	15p. Silver Jubilee photograph, 1977	20	35
516	20p. Princess Elizabeth on board H.M.S. "Vanguard", 1947	35	45
517	50p. In the U.S.A., 1976	60	1·00
518	65p. At Crown Agents Head Office, London, 1983	70	1·40

1988. Bicentenary of Australian Settlement. Ships and Signatures. Multicoloured.

519	9p. Type **151**	1·50	90
520	13p. H.M.S. "Resolution" (Cook), 1775	2·00	2·00
521	45p. H.M.S. "Providence" (Bligh), 1792	3·25	4·00
522	60p. H.M.S. "Beagle" (Darwin), 1836	4·25	5·50

152 "The Holy Virgin with the Child"

153 Ebony

1988. Christmas. Religious Paintings. Mult.

523	5p. Type **152**	10	30
524	20p. "Madonna"	40	50
525	38p. "The Holy Family with St. John"	75	1·50
526	60p. "The Holy Virgin with the Child"	1·25	2·00

1988. 300th Anniv of Lloyd's of London. As T **123** of Ascension.

527	9p. deep brown and brown	25	30
528	20p. multicoloured	80	60
529	45p. multicoloured	1·40	1·40
530	60p. multicoloured	1·60	1·60

DESIGNS—VERT: 9p. Lloyd's Underwriting Room, 1886; 60p. "Spangereid" (full-rigged ship) on fire, St. Helena, 1920. HORIZ: 20p. "Edinburgh Castle" (liner); 45p. "Bosun Bird" (freighter).

1989. Rare Plants (2nd series). Multicoloured.

531	9p. Type **153**	40	40
532	20p. St. Helena lobelia	70	70
533	45p. Large bellflower	1·40	2·00
534	60p. She cabbage tree	1·60	2·50

154 Private, 53rd Foot

156 Agricultural Studies

1989. Military Uniforms of 1815. Multicoloured.

535	9p. Type **154**	65	80
536	13p. Officer, 53rd Foot	75	90
537	20p. Royal Marine	85	1·00
538	45p. Officer, 66th Foot	1·40	1·75
539	60p. Private, 66th Foot	1·60	2·00

1989. "Philexfrance 89" International Stamp Exhibition, Paris. Nos. 535/9 optd **PHILEXFRANCE 89** and emblem.

540	9p. Type **154**	65	80
541	13p. Officer, 53rd Foot	75	90
542	20p. Royal Marine	85	1·00
543	45p. Officer, 66th Foot	1·40	1·75
544	60p. Private, 66th Foot	1·60	2·00

1989. New Prince Andrew Central School. Multicoloured.

545	13p. Type **156**	55	55
546	20p. Geography lesson	85	85
547	25p. Walkway and classroom block	95	95
548	60p. Aerial view of School	2·25	3·00

157 "The Madonna with the Pear" (Durer)

159 Sheep

158 Chevrolet "6" 30 cwt Lorry, 1930

1989. Christmas. Religious Paintings. Multicoloured.

549	10p. Type **157**	60	40
550	20p. "The Holy Family under the Appletree" (Rubens)	85	80
551	45p. "The Virgin in the Meadow" (Raphael)	2·00	2·25
552	60p. "The Holy Family with St. John" (Raphael)	2·50	3·00

1989. Early Vehicles. Multicoloured.

553	9p. Type **158**	85	60
554	20p. Austin "Seven", 1929	1·25	90
555	45p. Morris "Cowley" 11.9 h.p., 1929	2·00	2·25
556	60p. Sunbeam 25 h.p., 1932	2·50	3·00

1990. Farm Animals. Multicoloured.

558	9p. Type **159**	50	50
559	13p. Pigs	60	60
560	45p. Cow and calf	1·50	2·00
561	60p. Geese	2·00	2·50

160 1840 Twopence Blue

1990. "Stamp World London 90" International Stamp Exhibition, London.

562	**160**	13p. black and blue	50	50
563	–	20p. multicoloured	75	85
564	–	38p. multicoloured	1·25	2·00
565	–	45p. multicoloured	1·60	2·25

DESIGNS: 20p. 1840 Penny Black and 19th-century St. Helena postmark; 38p. Delivering mail to sub-post office; 45p. Mail van and Post Office, Jamestown.

161 Satellite Dish

1990. Modern Telecommunications Links. Multicoloured.

566	20p. Type **161**	75	1·00
567	20p. Digital telephone exchange	75	1·00
568	20p. Public card phone	75	1·00
569	20p. Facsimile machine	75	1·00

1990. 90th Birthday of Queen Elizabeth the Queen Mother. As T **134** of Ascension.

570	25p. multicoloured	1·00	75
571	£1 black and brown	2·75	3·75

DESIGNS—21 × 36 mm: 25p. Lady Elizabeth Bowes-Lyon, April 1923. 29 × 37 mm: £1 Queen Elizabeth visiting communal kitchen, 1940.

1990. Maiden Voyage of "St. Helena II". As T **137** of Ascension. Multicoloured.

572	13p. "Dane" (mail ship), 1857	1·00	75
573	20p. "St. Helena I" off-loading at St. Helena	1·40	1·25
574	38p. Launch of "St. Helena II"	2·00	2·25
575	45p. The Duke of York launching "St. Helena II"	2·50	2·75

163 Baptist Chapel, Sandy Bay

1990. Christmas. Local Churches. Multicoloured.

577	10p. Type **163**	30	30
578	13p. St. Martin in the Hills Church	35	35
579	20p. St. Helena and the Cross Church	55	65
580	38p. St. James Church	1·00	2·00
581	45p. St. Paul's Cathedral	1·25	2·00

164 "Funeral Cortege, Jamestown Wharf" (detail V. Adam)

1990. 150th Anniv of Removal of Napoleon's Body.

582	**164**	13p. black, brown & green	75	60
583	–	20p. black, brown and blue	1·25	1·00

584 – 38p. black, brown & mve . 2·00 2·25
585 – 45p. multicoloured . . . . 2·00 2·50

DESIGNS: 20p. "Coffin being conveyed to the 'Belle Poule'" (detail, V. Adam); 38p. "Transfer of the Coffin to the 'Normandie', Cherbourg" (detail, V. Adam); 45p. "Napoleon's Tomb, St. Helena" (T. Sutherland).

165 Officer, Leicestershire Regiment

166 "Madonna and Child" (T. Vecellio)

1991. Military Uniforms of 1897. Multicoloured.
586 13p. Type **165** 80 80
587 15p. Officer, York & Lancaster Regiment 85 85
588 20p. Colour-sergeant, Leicestershire Regiment . . 1·25 1·25
589 38p. Bandsman, York and Lancaster Regiment . . . . 2·00 2·50
590 45p. Lance-corporal, York and Lancaster Regiment . . . . 2·50 3·00

1991. 65th Birthday of Queen Elizabeth II and 70th Birthday of Prince Philip. As T **139** of Ascension. Multicoloured.
591 25p. Queen Elizabeth II . . . 80 1·25
592 25p. Prince Philip in naval uniform . . . . 80 1·25

1991. Christmas. Religious Paintings. Multicoloured.
593 10p. Type **166** 70 55
594 13p. "The Holy Family" (A. Mengs) 80 65
595 20p. "Madonna and Child" (W. Dyce) . . . . 1·25 1·00
596 38p. "The Two Trinities" (B. Murillo) . . . . 2·00 2·50
597 45p. "The Virgin and Child" (G. Bellini) . . . . 2·25 3·00

167 Matchless (346cc) Motorcycle, 1947

169 H.M.S. "Ledbury" (minesweeper)

168 "Eye of the Wind" (cadet brig) and Compass Rose

1991. "Phila Nippon '91" International Stamp Exn, Tokyo. Motorcycles. Multicoloured.
598 13p. Type **167** 85 70
599 20p. Triumph "Tiger 100" (500cc), 1950 . . . . . . 1·25 1·00
600 38p. Honda "CD" (175cc), 1967 2·00 2·50
601 45p. Yamaha "DTE 400", 1976 2·25 2·75

1992. 500th Anniv of Discovery of America by Columbus and Re-enactment Voyages. Multicoloured.
603 15p. Type **168** . . . . 1·25 90
604 25p. "Soren Larsen" (cadet brigantine) and map of Re-enactment Voyages . . . . 1·75 1·75
605 35p. "Santa Maria", "Nina" and "Pinta" . . . . 2·25 2·50
606 50p. Columbus and "Santa Maria" . . . . 2·50 3·25

1992. 40th Anniv of Queen Elizabeth II's Accession. As T **143** of Ascension. Multicoloured.
607 11p. Prince Andrew Central School 40 40
608 15p. Plantation House 55 55
609 25p. Jamestown 85 95
610 35p. Three portraits of Queen Elizabeth . . . . 1·10 1·50
611 50p. Queen Elizabeth II . . . 1·40 1·90

1992. 10th Anniv of Liberation of Falkland Islands. Ships. Multicoloured.
612 13p. Type **169** 80 70
613 20p. H.M.S. "Brecon" (minesweeper) . . . . . . 1·10 90
614 38p. "St. Helena I" (mail ship) off South Georgia . . . . . 1·75 2·00
615 45p. Launch collecting first mail drop, 1982 . . . . 2·25 2·50

170 Shepherds and Angel Gabriel

1992. Christmas. Children's Nativity Plays. Multicoloured.
617 13p. Type **170** 80 75
618 15p. Shepherds and Three Kings 90 85
619 20p. Mary and Joseph . . . 1·25 1·00
620 45p. Nativity scene . . . . . 2·50 3·00

171 Disc Jockey, Radio St. Helena (25th anniv)

172 Moses in the Bulrush

1992. Local Anniversaries. Multicoloured.
621 13p. Type **171** 75 60
622 20p. Scout parade (75th anniv of Scouting on St. Helena) . . 1·25 1·00
623 38p. H.M.S. "Providence" (sloop) and breadfruit (bicent of Capt. Bligh's visit) . . . 2·25 2·50
624 45p. Governor Brooke and Plantation House (bicent) . . 2·25 2·50

1993. Flowers (1st series). Multicoloured.
625 9p. Type **172** 65 65
626 13p. Periwinkle 80 80
627 20p. Everlasting flower . . . 1·10 1·10
628 38p. Cigar plant . . . . . . 1·75 2·00
629 45p. "Lobelia erinus" . . . . 2·00 2·50
See also Nos. 676/80.

173 Adult St. Helena Sand Plover and Eggs

1993. Endangered Species. St. Helena Sand Plover ("Wirebird"). Multicoloured.
630 3p. Type **173** 50 40
631 5p. Male attending brooding female 50 40
632 12p. Adult with downy young . 90 70
633 25p. Two birds in immature plumage . . . . 1·25 1·00
634 40p. Adult in flight . . . . . 1·50 1·75
635 60p. Young bird on rocks . . 1·75 2·50
Nos. 634/5 are without the W.W.F. emblem.

174 Yellow Canary ("Swainson's Canary")

176 Arum Lily

175 Football and Teddy Bear

1993. Birds. Multicoloured.
636 1p. Type **174** 30 50
637 3p. Rock partridge 40 50
638 11p. Rock dove 55 55
639 12p. Common waxbill 55 55
640 15p. Common mynah 60 60
641 18p. Java sparrow 65 65
642 25p. Red-billed tropic bird (horiz) 80 80
643 35p. Madeiran storm petrel (horiz) . . . . 1·10 1·10
644 75p. Madagascar red fody . . 2·00 2·25
645 £1 White tern ("Common fairy tern") (horiz) . . . . . . 2·25 2·50
646 £2 Giant petrel (horiz) . . . 4·25 4·75
647 £5 St. Helena sand plover ("Wirebird") . . . . . . 10·00 11·00

1993. Christmas. Toys. Multicoloured.
648 12p. Type **175** 65 55
649 15p. Yacht and doll 70 60
650 18p. Palette and rocking horse . 75 65
651 25p. Model airplane and kite . 1·10 1·10
652 60p. Guitar and roller skates . 2·00 2·75

1994. Flowers and Children's Art. Multicoloured.
653 12p. Type **176** 40 65
654 12p. "Arum Lily" (Delphia Mittens) 40 65
655 25p. Ebony . . . . 75 1·00
656 25p. "Ebony" (Jason Rogers) . 75 1·00
657 35p. Shell ginger . . . . . . 95 1·10
658 35p. "Shell Ginger" (Jeremy Moyce) . . . . 95 1·10

177 Abyssinian Guinea Pig

1994. "Hong Kong '94" International Stamp Exhibition. Pets. Multicoloured.
659 12p. Type **177** 55 55
660 25p. Common tabby cat . . . 1·25 1·25
661 53p. Plain white and black rabbits . . . . 2·00 2·50
662 60p. Golden labrador . . . . 2·25 2·75

178 Springer's Blenny

1994. Fishes. Multicoloured.
663 12p. Type **178** 65 65
664 25p. St. Helena damselfish . . 1·25 1·25
665 53p. Melliss's scorpionfish . . 2·00 2·50
666 60p. St. Helena wrasse . . . . 2·50 2·75

179 "Lampides boeticus"

1994. Butterflies. Multicoloured.
667 12p. Type **179** 60 55
668 25p. "Cynthia cardui" . . . . 1·00 1·00
669 53p. "Hypolimnas bolina" . . 1·75 2·25
670 60p. "Danaus chrysippus" . . 2·25 2·75

180 "Silent Night!"

1994. Christmas. Carols. Multicoloured.
671 12p. Type **180** 55 45
672 15p. "While Shepherds watched their Flocks by Night" . . . 60 50
673 25p. "Away in a Manger" . . 1·00 90
674 38p. "We Three Kings" . . . 1·50 2·00
675 60p. "Angels from the Realms of Glory" . . . . 2·25 3·00

1994. Flowers (2nd series). As T **172**. Multicoloured.
676 12p. Honeysuckle 35 35
677 15p. Gobblegheer 40 40
678 25p. African lily 70 80
679 38p. Prince of Wales feathers . 1·00 1·60
680 60p. St. Johns lily . . . . . 1·75 2·75

181 Fire Engine

1995. Emergency Services. Multicoloured.
681 12p. Type **181** 70 60
682 25p. Lifeboat 95 80
683 53p. Police car . . . . . . 2·25 2·50
684 60p. Ambulance . . . . . . 2·50 2·75

182 Site Clearance

1995. Construction of Harpers Valley Earth Dam. Multicoloured.
685 25p. Type **182** . . . . 80 1·00
686 25p. Earthworks in progress . 80 1·00
687 25p. Laying outlet pipes . . . 80 1·00
688 25p. Revetment block protection 80 1·00
689 25p. Completed dam . . . . 80 1·00
Nos. 685/9 were printed together, se-tenant, forming a composite design.

1995. 50th Anniv of End of Second World War. As T **161** of Ascension. Multicoloured.
690 5p. "Lady Denison Pender" (cable ship) 40 50
691 5p. H.M.S. "Dragon" (cruiser) 40 50
692 12p. R.F.A. "Darkdale" (tanker) 65 75
693 12p. H.M.S. "Hermes" (aircraft carrier, launched 1919) . . 65 75
694 25p. Men of St. Helena Rifles 1·00 1·25
695 25p. Governor Major W. J. Bain Gray taking salute . . . . 1·00 1·25
696 53p. 6-inch coastal gun, Ladder Hill . . . . 1·75 1·75
697 53p. Flags signalling "VICTORY" . . . . 1·75 1·75
The two designs for each value were printed together, se-tenant, forming composite designs.

183 Blushing Snail

1995. Endemic Invertebrates. Multicoloured.
699 12p. Type **183** 65 65
700 25p. Golden sail spider . . . 1·25 1·25
701 53p. Spiky yellow woodlouse . 2·00 2·50
702 60p. St. Helena shore crab . . 2·25 2·75

185 "Santa Claus outside Market" (Jason Alex Rogers)

1995. Christmas. Children's Paintings. Multicoloured.
705 12p. Type **185** 35 35
706 15p. "Santa Claus and band" (Che David Yon) 45 45
707 25p. "Santa Claus outside Community Centre" (Leon Williams) 70 75
708 38p. "Santa Claus in decorated street" (Stacey McDaniel) . 1·00 1·25
709 60p. "Make a better World" (Kissha Karla Kacy Thomas) 1·75 2·50

186 "Walmer Castle", 1915

1996. Union Castle Mail Ships (1st series). Multicoloured.
710 12p. Type **186** 45 35
711 25p. "Llangibby Castle", 1934 75 65
712 53p. "Stirling Castle", 1940 . 1·40 2·00
713 60p. "Pendennis Castle", 1965 1·60 2·00
See also Nos. 757/60.

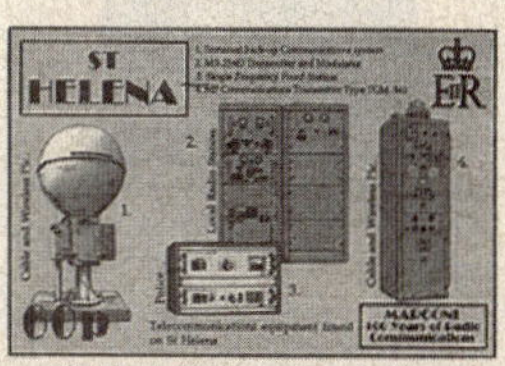

187 Early Telecommunications Equipment

1996. Centenary of Radio. Multicoloured.
714 60p. Type **187** . . . . 1·50 1·75
715 £1 Guglielmo Marconi and "Elettra" (yacht) . . . . . 2·25 2·75

1996. 70th Birthday of Queen Elizabeth II. As T **55** of Tokelau, each incorporating a different photograph of the Queen. Multicoloured.

716	15p. Jamestown	40	40
717	25p. Prince Andrew School	65	65
718	53p. Castle entrance	1·25	2·00
719	60p. Plantation House	1·50	2·00

188 Helicopter Mail to H.M.S. "Protector" (ice patrol ship), 1964

1996. "CAPEX '96" International Stamp Exhibition, Toronto. Mail Transport. Multicoloured.

721	12p. Type **188**	50	45
722	25p. Postman on motor scooter, 1965	75	65
723	53p. Loading mail plane, Wideawake Airfield, Ascension Island	1·40	2·00
724	60p. "St. Helena II" (mail ship) unloading at St. Helena	1·50	2·00

189 "Mr. Porteous's House"

1996. Napoleonic Sites. Multicoloured.

726	12p. Type **189**	35	35
727	25p. "The Briars' Pavilion"	65	65
728	53p. "Longwood House"	1·40	2·00
729	60p. "Napoleon's Tomb"	1·50	2·00

190 Frangipani and Sandy Bay from Diana's Peak

191 Black Cabbage Tree

1996. Christmas. Flowers and Views. Multicoloured.

730	12p. Type **190**	40	40
731	15p. Bougainvillaea and Upper Jamestown from Sampsons's Battery	50	50
732	25p. Jacaranda and Jacob's Ladder	75	75
733	£1 Pink periwinkle and Lot's Wife Ponds	2·75	4·00

1997. Endemic Plants from Diana's Peak National Park. Multicoloured.

734	25p. Type **191**	80	90
735	25p. Whitewood	80	90
736	25p. Tree fern	80	90
737	25p. Dwarf jellico	80	90
738	25p. Lobelia	80	90
739	25p. Dogwood	80	90

Nos. 734/9 were printed together, se-tenant, with the backgrounds forming a composite design.

192 Joao da Nova's Lookout sighting St. Helena, 1502

1997. 500th Anniv of the Discovery of St. Helena (1st issue). Multicoloured.

741	20p. Type **192**	70	60
742	25p. Don Fernando Lopez (first inhabitant) and cockerel, 1515	80	70
743	30p. Thomas Cavendish and "Desire", 1588	90	90
744	80p. "Royal Merchant", 1591	2·25	2·75

See also Nos. 762/5.

1997. Golden Wedding of Queen Elizabeth and Prince Philip. As T **87** of Kiribati. Multicoloured.

746	10p. Royal Family's Visit, 1947	35	40
747	10p. Wedding photograph of Princess Elizabeth and Prince Philip	35	40
748	15p. Princess Elizabeth and Prince Philip, 1947	50	65
749	15p. Presenting bouquets, Royal Visit, 1947	50	65
750	50p. Prince Philip on Royal Visit, 1957	1·40	1·75
751	50p. Wedding party on balcony, 1947	1·40	1·75

193 Flower Arrangement

1997. Christmas. 25th Anniv of the Duke of Edinburgh's Award in St. Helena. Multicoloured.

753	15p. Type **193**	40	35
754	20p. Calligraphy	50	45
755	40p. Camping	1·00	1·25
756	75p. Table laid for Christmas dinner	2·00	2·50

1998. Union Castle Mail Ships (2nd series). As T **186**. Multicoloured.

757	20p. "Avondale Castle", 1900	50	45
758	25p. "Dunnottar Castle", 1936	60	55
759	30p. "Llandovery Castle", 1943	75	75
760	80p. "Good Hope Castle", 1977	2·00	2·50

194 Settlers planting Crops, 1659

1998. 500th Anniv of the Discovery of St. Helena (2nd issue). Multicoloured.

762	20p. Type **194**	55	55
763	25p. Dutch invasion, 1672	60	60
764	30p. Recapture by the English, 1673	70	70
765	80p. Royal Charter of 1673	1·75	2·00

195 "Desire" (Cavendish), 1588

1998. Maritime Heritage. Multicoloured.

766	10p. Type **195**	20	25
767	15p. "Witte Leeuw" (Dutch East Indiaman), 1602	30	35
768	20p. H.M.S. "Swallow" (sloop) and H.M.S. "Dolphin" (frigate), 1751	40	45
769	25p. H.M.S. "Endeavour" (Cook), 1771	50	55
770	30p. H.M.S. "Providence" (sloop), 1792	60	65
771	35p. "St. Helena" (East India Company schooner), 1815	70	75
772	40p. H.M.S. "Northumberland" (ship of the line), 1815	80	85
773	50p. "Rurik" (Von Kotzebue), 1815	1·00	1·10
774	75p. H.M.S. "Erebus" (Ross), 1826	1·50	1·60
775	80p. "Keying" (junk), 1847	1·60	1·75
776	£2 "La Belle Poule" (French frigate), 1840	4·00	4·25
777	£5 H.M.S "Rattlesnake" (screw corvette), 1861	10·00	10·50

196 Metal Lanterns

1998. Christmas. Island Crafts. Multicoloured.

778	15p. Type **196**	40	40
779	20p. Wood-turned bowls	50	50
780	30p. Inlaid woodwork on jewellery box	70	70
781	85p. Hessian and seedwork bag and hat	2·00	2·25

1999. Royal Wedding. As T **153** of Pitcairn Islands. Multicoloured.

783	30p. Photographs of Prince Edward and Miss Sophie Rhys-Jones	60	65
784	£1.30 Engagement photograph	2·50	2·75

POSTAGE DUE STAMPS

D 1 Outline Map of St. Helena

1986.

D1	**D 1**	1p. deep brown & brown	10	10
D2		2p. brown and orange	10	10
D3		5p. brown and red	10	15
D4		7p. black and violet	10	10
D5		10p. black and blue	20	25
D6		25p. black and green	50	55

ST. KITTS

On 23 June 1980 separate postal administrations were formed for St. Kitts and for Nevis, although both islands remained part of the State of St. Kitts-Nevis.

100 cents = 1 West Indian dollar

1980. As Nos. 394/406 of St. Kitts-Nevis optd **St Kitts**.

29B	5 c. multicoloured	10	10
30B	10 c. multicoloured	10	10
31A	12 c. multicoloured	60	80
32B	15 c. multicoloured	10	10
33B	25 c. multicoloured	10	10
34B	30 c. multicoloured	10	10
35B	40 c. multicoloured	10	15
36A	45 c. multicoloured	50	15
37A	50 c. multicoloured	15	15
38A	55 c. multicoloured	15	15
39A	$1 multicoloured	15	25
40A	$5 multicoloured	45	1·00
41A	$10 multicoloured	55	1·75

9 H.M.S. "Vanguard", 1762

10 Queen Elizabeth the Queen Mother at Royal Variety Performance, 1978

1980. Ships. Multicoloured.

42	4 c. Type **9**	10	10
43	10 c. H.M.S. "Boreas", 1787	10	10
44	30 c. H.M.S. "Druid", 1827	15	10
45	55 c. H.M.S. "Winchester", 1831	20	15
46	$1.50 Harrison Line "Philosopher", 1857	40	30
47	$2 Harrison Line "Contractor", 1930	50	40

1980. 80th Birthday of The Queen Mother.

48	**10**	$2 multicoloured	25	60

11 The Three Wise Men

1980. Christmas. Multicoloured.

49	5 c. Type **11**	10	10
50	15 c. The Shepherds	10	10
51	30 c. Bethlehem	10	10
52	$4 Nativity scene	50	60

12 Purple-throated Carib

13 Bananaquit

1981. Birds. Multicoloured.

53A	1 c. Magnificent frigate bird	15	20
54A	4 c. Wied's crested flycatcher	25	20
55A	5 c. Type **12**	25	20
56A	6 c. Burrowing owl	35	30
57A	8 c. Caribbean martin	30	30
58A	10 c. Yellow-crowned night heron	25	20
59A	15 c. Type **13**	25	20
60A	20 c. Scaly-breasted thrasher	30	20
61A	25 c. Grey kingbird	30	20
62A	30 c. Green-throated carib	30	20
63A	40 c. Turnstone	35	30
64A	45 c. Black-faced grassquit	35	30
65A	50 c. Cattle egret	40	30
66A	55 c. Brown pelican	40	30
67A	$1 Lesser Antillean bullfinch	60	60
68A	$2.50 Zenaida dove	1·25	2·25
69A	$5 American kestrel	2·25	3·50
70A	$10 Antillean crested humming-bird	4·50	6·00

The 1 c. to 10 c. are vertical as Type **12**. The remainder are horizontal as Type **13**.

14 Battalion Company Sergeant 3rd Regt of Foot ("The Buffs"), c. 1801

15 Miriam Pickard (first Guide Commissioner)

1981. Military Uniforms. Multicoloured.
71 5 c. Type **14** 10 10
72 30 c. Battalion Company Officer, 45th Regt of Foot, 1796–97 15 10
73 55 c. Battalion Company Officer, 9th Regt of Foot, 1790 15 10
74 $2.50 Grenadier, 38th Regt of Foot, 1751 45 35

1981. Royal Wedding. Royal Yachts. As T **26/27** of Kiribati. Multicoloured.
75 55 c. "Saudadoes" 10 10
82 55 c. Prince Charles and Lady Diana Spencer 15 30
77 $2.50 "Royal George" 25 30
78 $2.50 As No.76 70 70
79 $4 "Britannia" 35 50
80 $4 As No. 76 75 1·00

1981. 50th Anniv of St. Kitts Girl Guide Movement. Multicoloured.
84 5 c. Type **15** 10 10
85 30 c. Lady Baden-Powell's visit, 1964 15 10
86 55 c. Visit of Princess Alice, 1960 30 10
87 $2 Thinking Day parade, 1980's 60 35

16 Stained-glass Windows

1981. Christmas.
88 **16** 5 c. multicoloured 10 10
89 – 30 c. multicoloured 10 10
90 – 55 c. multicoloured 15 10
91 – $3 multicoloured 50 50
DESIGNS: 30 c. to $3, Various designs showing stained-glass windows.

17 Admiral Samuel Hood

1982. Bicentenary of Brimstone Hill Siege.
92 **17** 15 c. multicoloured 10 10
93 – 55 c. multicoloured 20 10
DESIGNS: 55 c. Marquis De Bouille.

18 Alexandra, Princess of Wales, 1863
20 Naturalist Badge

1982. 21st Birthday of Princess of Wales. Multicoloured.
95 15 c. Type **18** 10 10
96 55 c. Coat of arms of Alexandra of Denmark 15 15
97 $6 Diana, Princess of Wales 55 80

1982. Birth of Prince William of Wales. Nos. 95/7 optd **ROYAL BABY**.
98 15 c. Type **18** 10 10
99 55 c. Coat of Arms of Alexandra of Denmark 15 15
100 $6 Diana, Princess of Wales 55 80

1982. 75th Anniv of Boy Scout Movement. Multicoloured.
101 5 c. Type **20** 10 10
102 55 c. Rescuer badge 30 15
103 $2 First Aid badge 80 80

21 Santa with Christmas Tree and Gifts

1982. Christmas. Children's Paintings. Multicoloured.
104 5 c. Type **21** 10 10
105 55 c. The Inn 15 10
106 $1.10 Three Kings 20 15
107 $3 Annunciation 40 40

22 Cruise Ship "Stella Oceanis" at Basseterre

1983. Commonwealth Day. Multicoloured.
108 55 c. Type **22** 15 10
109 $2 "Queen Elizabeth 2" at Basseterre 35 40

1983. Military Uniforms (2nd series). As T **14**. Multicoloured.
110 15 c. Light Company Private, 15th Regt. of Foot, c. 1814 20 10
111 30 c. Battalion Company Officer, 15th Regt. of Foot, c. 1780 30 15
112 55 c. Light Company Officer, 5th Regt. of Foot, c. 1822 30 20
113 $2.50 Battalion Company Officer, 11th Regt. of Foot, c. 1804 60 1·60

23 Sir William Smith (founder)
25 Montgolfier Balloon, 1783

1983. Centenary of Boys' Brigade. Multicoloured.
114 10 c. Type **23** 25 10
115 45 c. B.B. members on steps of Sandy Point Methodist Church 30 20
116 50 c. Brigade drummers 30 25
117 $3 Boys' Brigade badge 70 2·75

1983. Nos. 55, 59/63 and 66/70 optd **INDEPENDENCE 1983**.
118A 5 c. Type **12** 15 10
119B 15 c. Type **13** 30 10
120B 20 c. Scaly-breasted thrasher 35 10
121B 25 c. Grey kingbird 40 10
122B 30 c. Green-throated carib 45 15
123B 40 c. Turnstone 50 20
124B 55 c. Brown pelican 55 30
125B $1 Lesser Antillean bullfinch 1·00 50
126B $2.50 Zenaida dove 1·75 1·75
127A $5 American kestrel 2·75 2·75
128B $10 Antillean crested hummingbird 5·00 5·50

1983. Bicentenary of Manned Flight. Multicoloured.
129 10 c. Type **25** 10 10
130 45 c. Sikorsky "Russkiy Vityaz" biplane (horiz) 15 10
131 50 c. Lockhead Tristar 500 (horiz) 15 15
132 $2.50 Bell XS-1 (horiz) 50 90

26 Star over West Indian Town

1983. Christmas. Multicoloured.
134 15 c. Type **26** 10 10
135 30 c. Shepherds watching Star 10 10
136 55 c. Mary and Joseph 10 10
137 $2.50 The Nativity 30 40

27 Parrot in Tree

1984. Batik Designs (1st series).
139 **27** 45 c. multicoloured 10 10
140 – 50 c. multicoloured 10 10
141 – $1.50 blue, yellow & purple 35 60
142 – $3 multicoloured 55 1·50
DESIGNS: 50 c. Man under coconut tree; $1.50, Women with fruit; $3 Butterflies.
See also Nos. 169/72.

28 Cushion Star

1984. Marine Life. Multicoloured.
143 5 c. Type **28** 30 30
144 10 c. Rough file shell 35 30
145 15 c. Red-lined cleaning shrimp 35 15
146 20 c. Bristleworm 35 15
147 25 c. Flamingo tongue 40 15
148 30 c. Christmas tree worm 40 20
149 40 c. Pink-tipped anemone 55 25
150 50 c. Smallmouth grunt 55 30
151 60 c. Glass-eyed snapper 1·25 75
152 75 c. Reef squirrelfish 90 70
153 $1 Sea fans and flamefish (vert) 1·00 60
154 $2.50 Reef butterflyfish (vert) 2·25 3·50
205 $5 Black-barred soldierfish (vert) 7·50 10·00
156 $10 Cocoa damselfish (vert) 9·00 14·00
The 10 c., 60 c., $5 and $10 come with or without imprint date.

29 Agriculture

1984. 25th Anniv of The 4-H Organisation. Multicoloured.
157 30 c. Type **29** 20 10
158 55 c. Animal husbandry 30 15
159 $1.10 The 4-H Pledge 55 60
160 $3 On parade 90 1·25

30 Construction of Royal St. Kitts Hotel

1984. 1st Anniv of Independence of St. Kitts-Nevis. Multicoloured.
161 15 c. Type **30** 15 10
162 30 c. Independence celebrations 20 15
163 $1.10 National Anthem and aerial view (vert) 40 60
164 $3 "Dawn of a New Day" (vert) 1·00 1·40

31 Opening Presents

1984. Christmas. Multicoloured.
165 15 c. Type **31** 15 10
166 60 c. Singing carols 45 35
167 $1 Nativity play 75 60
168 $2 Leaving church on Christmas Day 1·40 1·10

1985. Batik Designs (2nd series). Horiz designs as T **27**.
169 15 c. black, green and light green 15 10
170 40 c. black, blue and light blue 30 15
171 60 c. black, orange and red 45 25
172 $3 black, brown and light brown 1·75 2·25
DESIGNS: 15 c. Country bus; 40 c. Donkey cart; 60 c. Rum shop and man on bicycle; $3 "Polynesia" (cruise schooner).

32 Container Ship "Tropic Jade"

1985. Ships. Multicoloured.
173 40 c. Type **32** 1·00 30
174 $1.20 "Atlantic Clipper" (schooner) 2·00 1·50
175 $2 "Mandalay" (schooner) 2·25 2·50
176 $2 "Cunard Countess" (liner) 2·25 2·50

33 James Derrick Cardin (leading Freemason)
34 Map of St. Kitts

1985. 150th Anniv of Mount Olive S. C. Masonic Lodge. Multicoloured.
177 15 c. Type **33** 40 20
178 75 c. Banner of Mount Olive Lodge 1·00 1·10
179 $1.20 Masonic symbols (horiz) 1·25 2·50
180 $3 Lodge Charter, 1835 1·75 4·50

1985. Christmas. 400th Anniv of Sir Francis Drake's Visit. Multicoloured.
181 10 c. Type **34** 25 15
182 40 c. "Golden Hind" 50 35
183 60 c. Sir Francis Drake 50 50
184 $3 Drake's heraldic shield 75 2·50

35 Queen Elizabeth and Prince Philip on St. Kitts
38 Adult Green Monkey with Young

36 Family on Smallholding

1986. 60th Birthday of Queen Elizabeth. Multicoloured.
185 10 c. Type **35** 15 10
186 20 c. Queen Elizabeth on St. Kitts 25 15
187 40 c. At Trooping the Colour 50 30
188 $3 In Sweden 2·00 3·00

1986. Royal Wedding. As T **112** of Ascension. Multicoloured.
189 15 c. Prince Andrew and Miss Sarah Ferguson 15 10
190 $2.50 Prince Andrew 1·00 2·00

1986. Agriculture Exhibition. Multicoloured.
191 15 c. Type **36** 20 10
192 $1.20 Hands holding people, computers and crops 1·25 1·60

1986. 40th Anniv of U.N. Week. Nos. 185/8 optd **40th ANNIVERSARY U.N. WEEK 19–26 OCT.**
207 10 c. Type **35** 20 15
208 20 c. Queen Elizabeth on St. Kitts 30 20
209 40 c. At Trooping the Colour 40 30
210 $3 In Sweden 1·25 3·25

1986. Green Monkeys on St. Kitts. Multicoloured.
211 15 c. Type **38** 1·75 40
212 20 c. Adult on ground 2·00 40
213 60 c. Young monkey in tree 4·50 2·25
214 $1 Adult grooming young monkey 5·50 4·50

39 Frederic Bartholdi (sculptor)
40 Officer, 9th Regt. (East Norfolk), 1792

1986. Centenary of Statue of Liberty. Multicoloured.
215 40 c. Type **39** 40 30
216 60 c. Torch (1876) and head (1878) on exhibition (horiz) 50 60
217 $1.50 "Isere" (French warship) carrying statue (horiz) 1·25 1·75
218 $3 Statue of Liberty, Paris 1884 1·50 2·75

1987. Military Uniforms (3rd series). Multicoloured.
220 15 c. Type **40** 40 30
221 15 c. Officer, Regt de Neustrie, 1779 . . . . 40 30
222 40 c. Sergeant, 3rd Regt of Foot ("The Buffs"), 1801 . . . . 65 45
223 40 c. Officer, French Artillery, 1812 . . . . 65 45
224 $2 Light Company Private, 5th Regt, 1778 . . . . 1·75 3·00
225 $2 Grenadier of the Line, 1796 1·75 3·00

41 Sugar Cane Warehouse

43 "Hygrocybe occidentalis"

42 B.W.I.A. L-1011 Tristar 500

1987. Sugar Cane Industry. Multicoloured (colour of panel behind "ST. KITTS" given).
227 **41** 15 c. yellow 20 30
228 – 15 c. brown 20 30
229 – 15 c. lilac 20 30
230 – 15 c. blue 20 30
231 – 15 c. turquoise 20 30
232 – 75 c. bright green 50 85
233 – 75 c. lilac 50 85
234 – 75 c. dull green 50 85
235 – 75 c. yellow 50 85
236 – 75 c. turquoise 50 85
DESIGNS: Nos. 227/31, Sugar cane factory; Nos. 232/6, Loading sugar train.
Nos. 227/31 and 232/6 were each printed together, se-tenant, forming composite designs.

1987. Aircraft visiting St. Kitts. Multicoloured.
237 40 c. Type **42** 75 30
238 60 c. L.I.A.T. Hawker Siddeley Super 748 . . . . 95 60
239 $1.20 W.I.A. De Havilland DHC-6 Twin Otter . . . . 1·50 2·50
240 $3 American Eagle Aerospatiale/ Aeritalia ATR-42 . . . . . 2·75 4·25

1987. Fungi. Multicoloured.
241 15 c. Type **43** 80 20
242 40 c. "Marasmius haematocephalus" . . . . . 1·25 40
243 $1.20 "Psilocybe cubensis" . . 2·75 2·75
244 $2 "Hygrocybe acutoconica" . . 3·50 3·50
245 $3 "Boletellus cubensis" . . . 4·00 4·50

44 Carnival Clown

45 Ixora

1987. Christmas. Designs showing different clowns.
246 **44** 15 c. multicoloured 25 15
247 – 40 c. multicoloured 55 30
248 – $1 multicoloured . . . . . 1·25 1·40
249 – $3 multicoloured . . . . . 2·50 4·00
See also Nos. 266/9.

1988. Flowers. Multicoloured.
250 15 c. Type **45** 30 15
251 40 c. Shrimp plant 55 30
252 $1 Poinsettia . . . . 1·00 1·40
253 $3 Honolulu rose . . . . . . 2·50 4·00

46 Fort Thomas Hotel

47 Ball, Wicket and Leeward Islands Cricket Association Emblem

1988. Tourism (1st series). Hotels. Multicoloured.
254 60 c. Type **46** 60 60
255 60 c. Fairview Inn 60 60
256 60 c. Frigate Bay Beach Hotel 60 60
257 60 c. Ocean Terrace Inn . . . 60 60
258 $3 The Golden Lemon . . . . 2·00 2·50
259 $3 Royal St. Kitts Casino and Jack Tar Village . . . . . . 2·00 2·50
260 $3 Rawlins Plantation Hotel and Restaurant . . . . 2·00 2·50
See also Nos. 270/5.

1988. 75th Anniv of Leeward Islands Cricket Tournament. Multicoloured.
261 40 c. Type **47** . . . . 1·50 30
262 $3 Cricket match at Warner Park 3·75 4·50

48 Flag of St. Kitts-Nevis

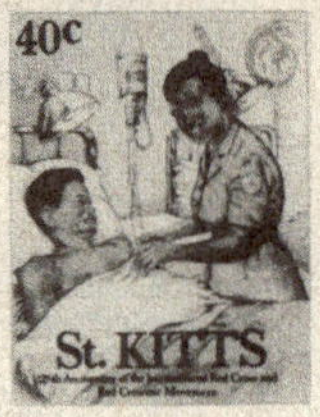

49 Red Cross Nurse with Hospital Patient

1988. 5th Anniv of Independence. Multicoloured.
263 15 c. Type **48** 25 10
264 60 c. Arms of St. Kitts . . . 75 60

1988. Christmas. As T **44** showing carnival masqueraders.
266 15 c. multicoloured 10 10
267 40 c. multicoloured 20 25
268 80 c. multicoloured 40 55
269 $3 multicoloured . . . . . 1·25 2·25

1989. Tourism (2nd series). Colonial Architecture. As T **46**. Multicoloured.
270 20 c. Georgian house 20 15
271 20 c. Colonial-style house . . 20 15
272 $1 Romney Manor 60 80
273 $1 Lavington Great House . . 60 80
274 $2 Government House . . . 90 1·60
275 $2 Treasury Building . . . . 90 1·60

1989. 125th Anniv of International Red Cross.
276 **49** 40 c. multicoloured . . . 30 30
277 – $1 multicoloured 65 75
278 – $3 red and black . . . . . 1·75 2·50
DESIGNS: $1 Loading patient into ambulance; $3 125th anniversary logo.

1989. 20th Anniv of First Manned Landing on Moon. As T **126** of Ascension. Multicoloured.
280 10 c. Lunar rover on Moon . . 10 10
281 20 c. Crew of "Apollo 13" (30×30 mm) 10 10
282 $1 "Apollo 13" emblem (30×30 mm) 45 60
283 $2 "Apollo 13" splashdown, South Pacific . . . . 95 1·25

51 Outline Map of St. Kitts

52 "Santa Mariagallante" passing St. Kitts, 1493

1989.
285 **51** 10 c. mauve and black . . 15 20
286 15 c. red and black 20 10
287 20 c. orange and black . . 20 10
288 40 c. yellow and black . . 30 20
289 60 c. blue and black . . . 50 40
290 $1 green and black . . . . 80 1·00

1989. 500th Anniv (1992) of Discovery of America by Columbus (1st issue). Multicoloured.
291 15 c. Type **52** . . . . 1·00 30
292 80 c. Arms of Columbus and map of fourth voyage, 1502–04 . 2·25 1·50
293 $1 Navigation instruments c, 1500 . . . . 2·25 1·60
294 $5 Columbus and map of second voyage, 1493–96 . . . . . 7·00 9·00
See also Nos. 359/60.

53 Poinciana Tree

1989. "World Stamp Expo '89" International Stamp Exhibition, Washington. Multicoloured.
295 15 c. Type **53** 30 10
296 40 c. Fort George Citadel, Brimstone Hill 65 30
297 $1 Private, Light Company, 5th Foot, 1778 . . . . 1·40 1·25
298 $3 St. George's Anglican Church 3·00 4·50

54 "Junonia evarete"

1990. Butterflies. Multicoloured.
299 15 c. Type **54** 80 30
300 40 c. "Anartia jatrophae" . . 1·25 30
301 60 c. "Heliconius charitonia" . 1·40 70
302 $3 "Biblis hyperia" . . . . . 3·25 5·00

1990. "Expo '90" International Garden and Greenery Exhibition, Osaka. Nos. 299/302 optd **EXPO 90** and logo.
303 15 c. Type **54** 80 30
304 40 c. "Anartia jatrophae" . . . 1·25 30
305 60 c. "Heliconius charitonia" . 1·40 70
306 $3 "Biblis hyperia" . . . . . 3·25 5·00

56 Brimstone Hill

1990. 300th Anniv of English Bombardment of Brimstone Hill. Multicoloured.
307 15 c. Type **56** 20 10
308 40 c. Restored Brimstone Hill fortifications 35 30
309 60 c. 17th-century English marine and Fort Charles under attack 50 1·00
310 $3 English sailors firing cannon 2·25 3·00
The 309 exists se-tenant, as a horizontal pair, with No. 310, each pair showing a composite design.

58 "Romney" (freighter)

1990. Ships. Multicoloured.
312 10 c. Type **58** 20 20
313 15 c. "Baralt" (freighter) . . . 20 20
314 20 c. "Wear" (mail steamer) . . 30 20
315 25 c. "Sunmount" (freighter) . . 30 20
316 40 c. "Inanda" (cargo liner) . . 40 25
317 50 c. "Alcoa Partner" (freighter) 40 30
318 60 c. "Dominica" (freighter) . . 40 30
319 80 c. "C.G.M Provence" (container ship) 55 40
320 $1 "Director" (freighter) . . . 65 50
321 $1.20 Barque 75 75
322 $2 "Chignecto" (packet steamer) 1·40 1·50
323 $3 "Berbice" (mail steamer) . . 1·90 2·25
324 $5 "Vamos" (freighter) . . . . 2·50 3·00
325 $10 "Federal Maple" (freighter) 4·75 6·00

59 Single Fork Game

1990. Christmas. Traditional Games. Multicoloured.
326 10 c. Type **59** 15 10
327 15 c. Boulder breaking 15 10
328 40 c. Double fork 30 30
329 $3 The run up . . . . 1·75 2·75

60 White Periwinkle

1991. Flowers. Multicoloured.
330 10 c. Type **60** 40 20
331 40 c. Pink oleander 75 30
332 60 c. Pink periwinkle (vert) . . 1·10 70
333 $2 White oleander (vert) . . . 2·25 3·25

61 Census Logo

1991. National Census.
334 **61** 15 c. multicoloured 25 15
335 $2.40 multicoloured . . . . 2·00 2·50
The $2.40 differs from Type **61** by showing "ST. KITTS" in a curved panel.

1991. 65th Birthday of Queen Elizabeth II and 70th Birthday of Prince Philip. As T **139** of Ascension. Multicoloured.
336 $1.20 Prince Philip . . . . . 75 1·00
337 $1.80 Queen holding bouquet of flowers . . . . 1·00 1·10

62 Nassau Grouper

1991. Fishes. Multicoloured.
338 10 c. Type **62** 50 20
339 60 c. Hogfish . . . . 1·25 50
340 $1 Red hind . . . . 2·00 1·50
341 $3 Porkfish . . . . 3·50 4·50

63 School of Continuing Studies, St. Kitts and Chancellor Sir Shridath Ramphal

1991. 40th Anniv of University of West Indies. Multicoloured.
342 15 c. Type **63** 40 15
343 50 c. Administration Building, Barbados 70 40
344 $1 Engineering Building, Trinidad and Tobago . . . 1·25 1·25
345 $3 Mona Campus, Jamaica and Sir Shridath Ramphal . . . 3·00 4·50

64 Whipping The Bull

1991. Christmas. "The Bull" (Carnival play). Multicoloured.
346 10 c. Type **64** 35 10
347 15 c. Death of The Bull . . . 35 10
348 60 c. Cast of characters and musicians . . . . 1·00 60
349 $3 The Bull in procession . . 2·75 4·00

1992. 40th Anniv of Queen Elizabeth II's Accession. As T **143** of Ascension. Multicoloured.
350 10 c. St. Kitts coastline . . . 20 10
351 40 c. Warner Park Pavilion . . 35 25
352 60 c. Brimstone Hill 50 40
353 $1 Three portraits of Queen Elizabeth 75 85
354 $3 Queen Elizabeth II . . . . 1·90 2·50

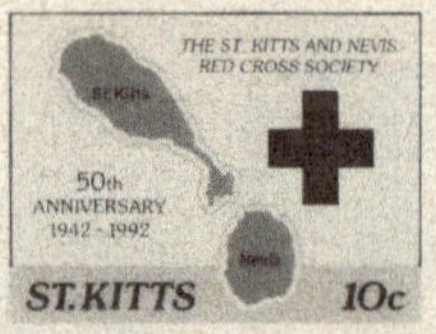

65 Map of St. Kitts-Nevis

1992. 50th Anniv of St. Kitts-Nevis Red Cross Society. Multicoloured.
355 10 c. Type **65** 55 25
356 20 c. St. Kitts-Nevis flag . . . 75 25
357 50 c. Red Cross House, St. Kitts 1·00 80
358 $2.40 Henri Dunant . . . . . 2·75 3·75

66 Columbus meeting Amerindians

1992. Organization of East Caribbean States. 500th Anniv of Discovery of America by Columbus (2nd issue). Multicoloured.
359 $1 Type **66** . . . . 1·50 1·00
360 $2 Ships approaching island . 2·25 3·00

67 Fountain, Independence Square

68 Joseph and Mary travelling to Bethlehem

1992. Local Monuments. Multicoloured.

361	25 c. Type **67**	25	20
362	50 c. Berkeley Memorial Drinking Fountain	35	35
363	80 c. Sir Thomas Warner's Tomb	55	65
364	$2 War Memorial	1·10	1·75

1992. Christmas. Multicoloured.

365	20 c. Type **68**	30	20
366	25 c. Shepherds and star	30	20
367	80 c. Wise Men with gifts	65	55
368	$3 Mary, Joseph and Holy Child	1·75	3·25

1993. 75th Anniv of Royal Air Force. Aircraft. As T **166** of Montserrat. Multicoloured.

369	25 c. Short Singapore III	55	20
370	50 c. Bristol Beaufort Mk II	80	30
371	80 c. Westland Whirlwind Series 3 H.A.R.10 helicopter	1·75	1·50
372	$1.60 English Electric Canberra	2·00	3·25

69 Members of Diocesan Conference, Basseterre, 1992

1993. 150th Anniv of Anglican Diocese of North-eastern Caribbean and Aruba. Multicoloured.

374	25 c. Type **69**	15	10
375	50 c. Cathedral of St. John the Divine (vert)	40	35
376	80 c. Coat of arms and motto	70	85
377	$2 The Right Revd. Daniel Davis (first bishop) (vert)	1·50	2·50

70 1953 Coronation 2 c. Stamp and Ampulla

1993. 40th Anniv of Coronation. Multicoloured.

378	10 c. Type **70**	40	20
379	25 c. 1977 Silver Jubilee $1.50 stamp and anointing spoon	50	20
380	80 c. 1977 Silver Jubilee 55 c. stamp and tassels	1·00	1·25
381	$2 1978 25th anniv of Coronation stamps and sceptre	2·00	3·50

71 Flags of Girls Brigade and St. Kitts-Nevis

1993. Centenary of Girls Brigade. Multicoloured.

382	80 c. Type **71**	1·25	1·00
383	$3 Girls Brigade badge and coat of arms	2·75	3·75

72 Aspects of St. Kitts on Flag

1993. 10th Anniv of Independence. Multicoloured.

384	20 c. Type **72**	30	10
385	80 c. Coat of arms and Independence anniversary logo	90	80
386	$3 Coat of arms and map	2·75	3·50

73 "Hibiscus sabdariffa"

1993. Christmas. Flowers. Multicoloured.

387	25 c. Type **73**	15	10
388	50 c. "Euphorbia pulcherrima"	45	45
389	$1.60 "Euphorbia leucocephala"	1·50	2·25

74 Mesosaurus

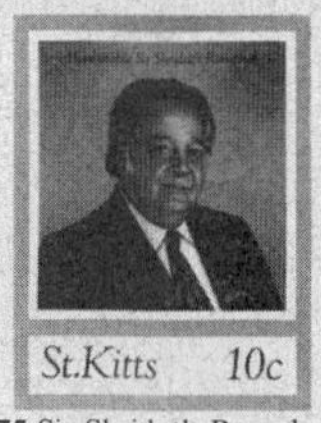

75 Sir Shridath Ramphal

1994. Prehistoric Aquatic Reptiles. Multicoloured.

390	$1.20 Type **74**	1·10	1·25
391	$1.20 Placodus	1·10	1·25
392	$1.20 Liopleurodon	1·10	1·25
393	$1.20 Hydrotherosaurus	1·10	1·25
394	$1.20 Caretta	1·10	1·25

Nos. 390/4 were printed together, se-tenant, with the background forming a composite design.

1994. "Hong Kong '94" International Stamp Exhibition. Nos. 390/4 optd **HONG KONG '94** and emblem.

395	$1.20 Type **74**	1·25	1·40
396	$1.20 Placodus	1·25	1·40
397	$1.20 Liopleurodon	1·25	1·40
398	$1.20 Hydrotherosaurus	1·25	1·40
399	$1.20 Caretta	1·25	1·40

1994. First Recipients of Order of the Caribbean Community. Multicoloured.

401	10 c. Type **75**	10	15
402	10 c. Star of Order	10	15
403	10 c. Derek Walcott	10	15
404	10 c. William Demas	10	15
405	$1 Type **75**	90	1·00
406	$1 As No. 402	90	1·00
407	$1 As No. 403	90	1·00
408	$1 As No. 404	90	1·00

76 Family singing Carols

1994. Christmas. Int Year of the Family. Mult.

409	25 c. Type **76**	15	10
410	25 c. Family unwrapping Christmas presents	15	10
411	80 c. Preparing for Christmas carnival	60	60
412	$2.50 Nativity	1·90	2·75

77 Green Turtle swimming

1995. Endangered Species. Green Turtle. Multicoloured.

427	10 c. Type **77**	40	50
428	40 c. Turtle crawling up beach	45	60
429	50 c. Burying eggs	45	60
430	$1 Young heading for sea	55	70

78 St. Christopher 1d. Stamps of 1870

1995. 125th Anniv of St. Kitts Postage Stamps. Each including the St. Christopher 1870 1d. Multicoloured.

431	25 c. Type **78**	15	15
432	80 c. St. Kitts-Nevis 1935 Silver Jubilee 1d.	45	50
433	$2.50 St. Kitts-Nevis 1946 Victory 1d.	1·75	2·25
434	$3 St. Christopher Nevis Anguilla 1953 Coronation 2 c.	2·00	2·50

1995. 50th Anniv of End of Second World War. As T **161** of Ascension. Multicoloured.

435	20 c. Caribbean Regiment patrol, North Africa	15	15
436	50 c. Grumman TBF Avengers (bombers)	35	35
437	$2 Supermarine Spitfire MK Vb (fighter)	1·25	1·50
438	$8 U. S. Navy destroyer escort	5·00	6·00

79 Telecommunication Links between Islands

1995. 10th Anniv of SKANTEL (telecommunications company). Multicoloured.

440	10 c. Type **79**	25	10
441	25 c. Payphone and computer link	30	15
442	$2 Telecommunications tower and dish aerial	2·25	2·50
443	$3 Silhouette of dish aerial at sunset	2·50	3·00

80 Water Treatment Works

1995. 50th Anniv of United Nations. Multicoloured.

444	40 c. Type **80**	30	25
445	50 c. Beach	35	30
446	$1.60 Dust cart	1·10	1·60
447	$2.50 Forest	1·90	2·75

81 F.A.O. Emblem and Vegetables

1995. 50th Anniv of F.A.O. Multicoloured.

448	25 c. Type **81**	20	10
449	50 c. Glazed carrots and West Indian peas with rice	35	30
450	80 c. Tania and cassava plants	50	60
451	$1.50 Waterfall, Green Hill Mountain	90	1·40

82 Flame Helmet

84 Athlete and National Flag

83 L.M.S. No. 45614 Steam Locomotive "Leeward Islands" in Green Livery

1996. Sea Shells. Multicoloured.

452	$1.50 Type **82**	95	1·00
453	$1.50 Triton's trumpet	95	1·00
454	$1.50 King helmet	95	1·00
455	$1.50 True tulip	95	1·00
456	$1.50 Queen conch	95	1·00

1996. "CAPEX '96" International Stamp Exhibition, Toronto.

457	**83** 10 c. multicoloured	40	30

1996. Centennial Olympic Games, Atlanta. Multicoloured.

459	10 c. Type **84**	15	15
460	25 c. High jumper and U.S.A. flag	20	20
461	80 c. Athlete and Olympic flag	50	55
462	$3 Poster for 1896 Olympic Games, Athens	1·75	2·50

85 Volunteer Rifleman, 1896

86 "Holy Virgin and Child" (A. Colin)

1996. Centenary of Defence Force. Multicoloured.

464	10 c. Type **85**	15	15
465	50 c. Mounted infantryman, 1911	35	35
466	$2 Drummer, 1940–60	1·25	1·75
467	$2.50 Ceremonial uniform, 1996	1·40	2·00

1996. Christmas. Religious Paintings. Multicoloured.

468	15 c. Type **86**	15	10
469	25 c. "Holy Family" (after Rubens)	20	10
470	50 c. "Madonna with the Goldfinch" (Krause after Raphael)	40	30
471	80 c. "Madonna on Throne with Angels" (17th-cent Spanish)	60	60

87 Princess Parrotfish

1997. Fishes. Multicoloured.

473	$1 Type **87**	60	65
474	$1 Yellow-bellied hamlet	60	65
475	$1 Coney	60	65
476	$1 Fin-spot wrasse	60	65
477	$1 Doctor fish	60	65
478	$1 Squirrelfish	60	65
479	$1 Queen angelfish	60	65
480	$1 Spanish hogfish	60	65
481	$1 Red hind	60	65
482	$1 Red grouper	60	65
483	$1 Yellow-tailed snapper	60	65
484	$1 Mutton hamlet	60	65

1997. Golden Wedding of Queen Elizabeth and Prince Philip. As T **87** of Kiribati. Multicoloured.

485	10 c. Queen Elizabeth in evening dress	20	30
486	10 c. Prince Philip and Duke of Kent at Trooping the Colour	20	30
487	25 c. Queen Elizabeth in phaeton at Trooping the Colour	35	40
488	25 c. Prince Philip in naval uniform	35	40
489	$3 Queen Elizabeth and Prince Philip	1·75	2·00
490	$3 Peter Phillips on horseback	1·75	2·00

Nos. 485/6, 487/8 and 489/90 respectively were printed together, se-tenant, with the backgrounds forming composite designs.

88 C. A. Paul Southwell (first Chief Minister)

1997. National Heroes Day. Multicoloured.

492	25 c. Type **88**	15	20
493	25 c. Sir Joseph France (trade union leader)	15	20
494	25 c. Robert Bradshaw (first Prime Minister)	15	20
495	$3 Sir Joseph France, Robert Bradshaw and C. A. Paul Southwell (horiz)	1·75	2·25

89 Wesley Methodist Church

1997. Christmas. Churches. Multicoloured.

496	10 c. Type **89**	10	10
497	10 c. Zion Moravian Church	10	10
498	$1.50 St. George's Anglican Church (vert)	1·00	1·00
499	$15 Co-Cathedral of the Immaculate Conception (vert)	8·50	10·00

90 Common Long-tail Skipper

1997. Butterflies. Multicoloured.

500	10 c. Type **90**	10	10
501	15 c. White peacock	10	10
502	25 c. Caribbean buckeye	10	15
503	30 c. The red rim	15	20
504	40 c. Cassius blue	15	20
505	50 c. The flambeau	20	25
506	60 c. Lucas's blue	25	30
507	90 c. Cloudless sulphur	40	45
508	$1 The monarch	45	50
509	$1.20 Fiery skipper	50	55
510	$1.60 The zebra	70	75
511	$3 Southern dagger tail	1·25	1·40
512	$5 Polydamus swallowtail	2·10	2·25
513	$10 Tropical chequered skipper	4·25	4·50

1998. Diana, Princess of Wales Commemoration. As T **91** of Kiribati, but vert. Multicoloured.

514	30 c. Wearing hat	20	30

91 University Arms on Book

1998. 50th Anniv of University of West Indies. Multicoloured.

516	80 c. Type **91**	35	40
517	$2 University arms and mortar-board	85	90

92 Santa at Carnival

1998. Christmas. Multicoloured.

518	80 c. Type **92**	35	40
519	$1.20 Santa with two carnival dancers	50	55

93 Launching Rowing Boat

1999. 125th Anniv of Universal Postal Union. Multicoloured.

520	30 c. Type **93**	15	20
521	90 c. Pictorial map of St. Kitts	40	45

94 Caribbean Martin

1999. Birds of the Eastern Caribbean. Multicoloured.

522	80 c. Type **94**	35	40
523	80 c. Spotted sandpiper	35	40
524	80 c. Sooty tern	35	40
525	80 c. Red-tailed hawk	35	40
526	80 c. Brown trembler	35	40
527	80 c. Belted kingfisher	35	40
528	80 c. Black-billed whistling duck	35	40
529	80 c. Yellow warbler	35	40
530	80 c. Blue-headed hummingbird	35	40
531	80 c. Blue-headed euphonia ("Antillean Euphonia")	35	40
532	80 c. Fulvous whistling duck	35	40
533	80 c. Mangrove cuckoo	35	40
534	80 c. Carib grackle	35	40
535	80 c. Caribbean elaenia	35	40
536	80 c. Scaly-breasted ground dove ("Common Ground Dove")	35	40
537	80 c. Forest thrush	35	40

OFFICIAL STAMPS

1980. Nos. 32/41 optd **OFFICIAL**.

O 1A	15 c. multicoloured	10	10
O 2A	25 c. multicoloured	10	10
O 3A	30 c. multicoloured	10	10
O 4A	40 c. multicoloured	10	15
O 5A	45 c. multicoloured	15	15
O 6A	50 c. multicoloured	15	15
O 7A	55 c. multicoloured	15	15
O 8A	$1 multicoloured	25	25
O 9A	$5 multicoloured	80	1·50
O10A	$10 multicoloured	1·00	2·50

1981. Nos. 59/70 optd **OFFICIAL**.

O11	15 c. Bananaquit	20	10
O12	20 c. Scaly-breasted thrasher	20	10
O13	25 c. Grey kingbird	25	10
O14	30 c. Green-throated carib	25	10
O15	40 c. Turnstone	35	15
O16	45 c. Black-faced grassquit	40	20
O17	50 c. Cattle egret	40	20
O18	55 c. Brown pelican	50	25
O19	$1 Lesser Antillean bullfinch	75	45
O20	$2.50 Zenaida dove	1·60	1·00
O21	$5 American kestrel	2·75	2·00
O22	$10 Antillean crested hummingbird	5·00	4·25

1983. Nos. 75/80 optd **OFFICIAL** or surch also.

O23	45 c. on $2.50 "Royal George"	15	15
O24	45 c. on $2.50 Prince Charles and Lady Diana Spencer	25	25
O25	55 c. "Saudadoes"	15	15
O26	55 c. Prince Charles and Lady Diana Spencer	30	30
O27	$1.10 on $4 "Britannia"	30	40
O28	$1.10 on $4 Prince Charles and Lady Diana Spencer	60	70

1984. Nos. 145/56 optd **OFFICIAL**.

O29	15 c. Red-lined cleaning shrimp	70	80
O30	20 c. Bristleworm	80	1·00
O31	25 c. Flamingo tongue	80	1·00
O32	30 c. Christmas tree worm	90	1·25
O33	40 c. Pink-tipped anemone	1·00	1·25
O34	50 c. Small-mouthed grunt	1·00	1·25
O35	60 c. Glass-eyed snapper	1·25	1·50
O36	75 c. Reef squirrelfish	1·50	2·25
O37	$1 Sea fans and flamefish (vert)	2·00	2·25
O38	$2.50 Reef butterflyfish (vert)	3·75	5·50
O39	$5 Black-barred soldierfish (vert)	5·50	5·50
O40	$10 Cocoa damselfish (vert)	8·50	8·50

ST. KITTS-NEVIS

Islands of the Leeward Is., Br. W. Indies. The general issues for Leeward Is, were in concurrent use until 1 July 1956. From 1952 the stamps are inscribed "St. Christopher, Nevis and Anguilla". Achieved Associated Statehood on 27 February 1967. St. Kitts and Nevis had separate postal administrations from 23 June 1980.

1903. 12 pence = 1 shilling;
20 shillings = 1 pound.
1951. 100 cents = 1 West Indian dollar.

1 Christopher Columbus

2 Medicinal Spring

1903.

1	**1**	½d. purple and green	1·50	70
12		½d. green	55	35
13	**2**	1d. grey and red	1·00	25
14a		1d. red	35	20
15a	**1**	2d. purple and brown	4·50	6·00
4		2½d. black and blue	16·00	4·00
17		2½d. blue	1·75	40
18a	**2**	3d. green and orange	2·00	2·50
6	**1**	6d. black and purple	3·25	28·00
7		1s. green and orange	6·00	11·00
8		2s. green and black	12·00	19·00
9	**1**	2s. 6d. black and violet	18·00	40·00
21	**2**	5s. purple and green	30·00	75·00

1916. Optd **WAR TAX**.

22	**1**	½d. green	40	40

1918. Optd **WAR STAMP**.

23	**1**	1½d. orange	30	40

4

5

1920.

37a	**4**	½d. green	1·25	80
38	**5**	1d. red	50	15
39		1d. violet	3·50	55
26	**4**	1½d. yellow	1·25	1·50
40		1½d. red	2·50	2·50
40a		1½d. brown	65	30
41	**5**	2d. grey	40	60
44	**4**	2½d. blue	1·50	3·50
43		2½d. brown	1·75	8·00
45a	**5**	3d. purple on yellow	60	3·50
45		3d. blue	70	3·50
46	**4**	6d. purple and mauve	3·75	5·50
31	**5**	1s. black on green	3·25	3·50
47	**4**	2s. purple and blue on blue	8·00	20·00
33	**5**	2s. 6d. black and red on blue	5·00	27·00
34	**4**	5s. green and red on yellow	5·00	38·00
35	**5**	10s. green and red on green	12·00	48·00
36	**4**	£1 purple and black on red	£225	£300

6 Old Road Bay and Mount Misery

1923. Tercentenary Commemoration.

48	**6**	½d. black and green	2·00	6·50
49		1d. black and violet	3·50	1·50
50		1½d. black and red	4·50	10·00
51		2d. black and grey	2·75	1·50
52		2½d. black and brown	4·50	28·00
53		3d. black and blue	3·75	14·00
54		6d. black and purple	8·50	30·00
55		1s. black and green	13·00	30·00
56		2s. black and blue on blue	35·00	50·00
57		2s. 6d. black and red on blue	45·00	70·00
59		5s. black and red on yellow	65·00	£160
58		10s. black and red on green	£250	£375
60		£1 black and purple on red	£700	£1300

1935. Silver Jubilee. As T **13** of Antigua.

61	1d. blue and red	1·00	70
62	1½d. blue and grey	75	75
63	2½d. brown and blue	1·00	80
64	1s. grey and purple	5·50	14·00

1937. Coronation. As T **2** of Aden.

65	1d. red	30	20
66	1½d. brown	40	10
67	2½d. blue	60	45

Nos. 61/7 are inscribed "ST. CHRISTOPHER AND NEVIS".

7 King George VI

8 King George VI and Medicinal Spring

10 King George VI and Anguilla Island

1938.

68a	**7**	½d. green	10	10
69a		1d. red	65	40
70		1½d. orange	20	30
71b	**8**	2d. red and grey	70	1·25
72a	**7**	2½d. blue	30	30
73g	**8**	3d. purple and red	3·50	4·00
74c	–	6d. green and purple	4·75	1·50
75c	**8**	1s. black and green	2·75	3·00
76ab		2s. 6d. black and red	12·00	3·75
77b	–	5s. green and red	24·00	11·00
77d	**10**	10s. black and blue	10·00	19·00
77e		£1 black and brown	10·00	23·00

The 6d. and 5s. are as Type **8**, but with the Christopher Columbus device as in Type **4**.

1946. Victory. As T **9** of Aden.

78	1½d. orange	10	10
79	3d. red	10	10

1949. Silver Wedding. As T **10/11** of Aden.

80	2½d. blue	10	10
81	5s. red	6·00	2·50

1949. U.P.U. As T **20/23** of Antigua.

82	2½d. blue	35	20
83	3d. red	1·00	60
84	6d. mauve	40	30
85	1s. green	40	30

1950. Tercent of British Settlement in Anguilla. Optd **ANGUILLA TERCENTENARY 1650–1950**.

86	**7**	1d. red	10	10
87		1½d. orange	10	10
88		2½d. blue	10	10
89	**8**	3d. purple and red	10	30
90	–	6d. green & purple (No. 74d)	10	10
91	**8**	1s. black and green	20	10

1951. Inauguration of B.W.I. University College. As T **24/25** of Antigua.

92	**22**	3 c. black and orange	30	15
93	**23**	12 c. green and mauve	30	70

ST. CHRISTOPHER, NEVIS AND ANGUILLA

13 Bath House and Spa

1952.

94	**13**	1 c. green and ochre	15	90
95	–	2 c. green	60	90
96	–	3 c. red and violet	30	80
97	–	4 c. red	20	20
98	–	5 c. blue and grey	30	10
99	–	6 c. blue	30	15
100	–	12 c. blue and brown	30	10
101	–	24 c. black and red	30	10
102	–	48 c. olive and brown	1·50	1·50
103	–	60 c. ochre and green	1·50	1·75
104	–	$1.20 green and blue	5·50	2·25
105	–	$4.80 green and red	12·00	18·00

DESIGNS—HORIZ: 2 c. Warner Park; 4 c. Brimstone Hill; 5 c. Nevis from the sea, North; 6 c. Pinney's Beach, Nevis; 24 c. Old Road Bay; 48 c. Sea Island cotton, Nevis; 60 c. The Treasury; $1.20, Salt pond, Anguilla; $4.80, Sugar factory. VERT: 3 c. Map of the islands; 12 c. Sir Thomas Warner's tomb.

1953. Coronation. As T **13** of Aden.

106	2 c. black and green	30	15

1954. As 1952 but with portrait of Queen Elizabeth II.

106a	½ c. olive (as $1.20)	30	10
107	1 c. green and ochre	20	10
108	2 c. green	45	10
109	3 c. red and violet	65	10
110	4 c. red	15	10
111	5 c. blue and grey	15	10
112	6 c. blue	50	10
112b	8 c. black	4·50	10
113	12 c. blue and brown	15	10
114	24 c. black and red	15	10
115	48 c. olive and brown	60	50
116	60 c. ochre and green	5·50	1·75
117	$1.20 green and blue	18·00	1·75
117b	$2.40 black and orange	10·00	11·00
118	$4.80 green and red	13·00	11·00

DESIGNS (new values)—VERT: 8 c. Sombrero Lighthouse. HORIZ: $2.40, Map of Anguilla and Dependencies.

27 Alexander Hamilton and View of Nevis

1956. Birth Bicent of Alexander Hamilton.

119	**27**	24 c. green and blue	30	15

1958. British Caribbean Federation. As T **28** of Antigua.

120	3 c. green	60	15
121	6 c. blue	1·00	2·00
122	12 c. red	1·50	30

28 1d. Stamp of 1861

1961. Centenary of Nevis Stamp.

123 **28**	2 c. red and green	15	20
124	8 c. red and blue	20	10
125	12 c. lilac and red	30	15
126	24 c. green and orange	35	15

The 8 c., 12 c. and 24 c. show the original 4d., 6d. and 1s. stamps of Nevis respectively.

1963. Cent of Red Cross. As T **33** of Antigua.

127	3 c. red and black	10	10
128	12 c. red and blue	20	40

33 Loading Sugar Cane, St. Kitts

1963. Multicoloured.

129	½ c. New Lighthouse, Sombrero	10	10
130	1 c. Type **33**	10	10
131	2 c. Pall Mall Square, Basseterre	10	10
132	3 c. Gateway, Brimstone Hill Fort, St. Kitts	10	10
133	4 c. Nelson's Spring, Nevis	10	10
134	5 c. Grammar School, St. Kitts	2·00	10
135	6 c. Crater, Mt. Misery, St. Kitts	10	10
136	10 c. Hibiscus	15	10
137	15 c. Sea Island cotton, Nevis	55	10
138	20 c. Boat-building, Anguilla	20	10
139	25 c. White-crowned pigeon	90	10
140	50 c. St. George's Church Tower, Basseterre	40	25
141	60 c. Alexander Hamilton	1·00	30
142	$1 Map of St. Kitts-Nevis	2·50	40
143	$2.50 Map of Anguilla	2·50	2·50
144	$5 Arms of St. Christopher, Nevis and Anguilla	5·00	3·50

The ½, 2, 3, 15, 25, 60 c., $1 and $5 are vert, the rest horiz

1964. Arts Festival. Optd **ARTS FESTIVAL ST KITTS 1964**.

145	3 c. multicoloured (No. 132)	10	15
146	25 c. multicoloured (No. 139)	20	15

1965. Cent of I.T.U. As T **36** of Antigua.

147	2 c. bistre and red	10	10
148	50 c. blue and olive	40	50

1965. I.C.Y. As T **37** of Antigua.

149	2 c. purple and green	10	20
150	25 c. green and violet	20	10

1966. Churchill Commem. As T **38** of Antigua.

151	½ c. blue	10	15
152	3 c. green	15	10
153	15 c. brown	30	20
154	25 c. violet	35	20

1966. Royal Visit. As T **39** of Antigua.

155	3 c. black and blue	25	15
156	25 c. black and mauve	45	15

1966. World Cup Football Championship. As T **40** of Antigua.

157	6 c. multicoloured	40	20
158	25 c. multicoloured	60	10

49 Festival Emblem

53 John Wesley and Cross

50 Government Headquarters, Basseterre

1966. Arts Festival.

159 **49**	3 c. multicoloured	10	10
160	25 c. multicoloured	20	10

1968. Inauguration of W.H.O. Headquarters, Geneva. As T **41** of Antigua.

161	3 c. black, green and blue	10	10
162	40 c. black, purple and brown	20	20

1966. 20th Anniv of U.N.E.S.C.O. As T **54/6** of Antigua.

163	3 c. multicoloured	10	10
164	6 c. yellow, violet and olive	10	10
165	40 c. black, purple and orange	30	35

1967. Statehood. Multicoloured.

182	3 c. Type **50**	10	10
183	10 c. National flag	10	10
184	25 c. Coat of arms	15	15

1967. West Indies Methodist Conference.

185 **53**	3 c. black, red and violet	10	10
186 –	25 c. black, turquoise & bl	15	10
187 –	40 c. black, yellow & orange	15	15

DESIGNS: 25 c. Charles Wesley and cross; 40 c. Thomas Coke and cross.

56 Handley Page Dart Herald over "Jamaica Producer" (freighter)

1968. Caribbean Free Trade Area.

188 **56**	25 c. multicoloured	40	10
189	50 c. multicoloured	40	20

57 Dr. Martin Luther King

58 "Mystical Nativity" (Botticelli)

1968. Martin Luther King Commemoration.

190 **57**	50 c. multicoloured	10	10

1968. Christmas.

191 **58**	12 c. multicoloured	10	10
192 –	25 c. multicoloured	10	10
193 **58**	40 c. multicoloured	15	10
194 –	50 c. multicoloured	15	10

DESIGN: 25 c., 50 c. "The Adoration of the Magi" (Rubens).

60 Tarpon Snook

1968. Fishes.

195 **60**	6 c. multicoloured	10	10
196 –	12 c. black, green and blue	15	10
197 –	40 c. multicoloured	25	10
198 –	50 c. multicoloured	30	15

FISHES: 12 c. Needlefish; 40 c. Horse-eyed jack; 50 c. Black-finned snapper.

64 The Warner Badge and Islands

1969. Sir Thomas Warner Commem. Multicoloured.

199	20 c. Type **64**	10	10
200	25 c. Sir Thomas Warner's tomb	10	10
201	40 c. Charles I's Commission	15	15

67 "The Adoration of the Kings" (Mostaert)

73 Portuguese Caravels (16th-cent)

1969. Christmas. Multicoloured.

202	10 c. Type **67**	10	10
203	25 c. As 10 c.	10	10
204	40 c. "The Adoration of the Kings" (Geertgen)	10	10
205	50 c. As 40 c.	10	10

1970. Multicoloured. (except ½ c.).

206	½ c. Pirates and treasure at Frigate Bay (black, orange and green)	10	10
207	1 c. English two-decker warship, 1650	30	10
208	2 c. Naval flags of colonising nations	15	10
209	3 c. Rapier hilt (17th-century)	15	10
210	4 c. Type **73**	20	10
211	5 c. Sir Henry Morgan and fireships, 1669	30	10
212	6 c. L'Ollonois and pirate carrack (16th-century)	30	10
213	10 c. 17th-century smugglers' ship	30	10
214a	15 c. "Piece of Eight"	50	10
215	20 c. Cannon (17th-century)	35	10
216	25 c. Humphrey Cole's astrolabe, 1574	40	10
217	50 c. Flintlock pistol (17th-cent)	85	80
218	60 c. Dutch flute (17th-cent)	2·25	70
219	$1 Capt. Bartholomew Roberts and his crew's death sentence	2·50	75
220	$2.50 Railing piece (gun) (16th-century)	2·00	3·25
221	$5 Drake, Hawkins and sea battle	2·50	4·50
280	$10 The Apprehension of Blackbeard (Edward Teach)	20·00	13·00

The ½ c. to 3 c., 15 c., 25 c., 60 c. and $1 are vert designs.

85 Graveyard Scene ("Great Expectations")

1970. Death Cent of Charles Dickens.

222 **85**	4 c. brown, gold and green	10	10
223 –	20 c. brown, gold & purple	10	15
224 –	25 c. brown, gold and green	10	15
225 –	40 c. brown, gold and blue	15	30

DESIGNS—HORIZ: 20 c. Miss Havisham and Pip ("Great Expectations"). VERT: 25 c. Dickens' birthplace; 40 c. Charles Dickens.

86 Local Steel Band

1970. Festival of Arts. Multicoloured.

226	20 c. Type **86**	10	10
227	25 c. Local string band	10	10
228	40 c. Scene from "A Midsummer Night's Dream"	15	15

87 1d. Stamp of 1870 and Post Office, 1970

1970. Stamp Centenary.

229 **87**	½ c. green and red	10	10
230 –	20 c. purple, green and red	10	10
231 –	25 c. purple, green and red	10	10
232 –	50 c. red, green and black	30	45

DESIGNS: 20 c., 25 c., 1d. and 6d. stamps of 1870; 50 c. 6d. stamp of 1870 and early postmark.

88 "Adoration of the Shepherds" (Frans van Floris)

1970. Christmas. Multicoloured.

233	3 c. Type **88**	10	10
234	20 c. "The Holy Family" (Van Dyck)	10	10
235	25 c. As 20 c.	10	10
236	40 c. Type **88**	15	40

89 Monkey Fiddle

1971. Flowers. Multicoloured.

237	½ c. Type **89**	10	10
238	20 c. Tropical mountain violet	15	10
239	30 c. Trailing morning glory	15	15
240	50 c. Fringed epidendrum	30	80

90 Royal Poinciana

1971. Philippe de Poincy Commem. Mult.

241	Type **90**	10	10
242	30 c. Chateau de Poincy	10	10
243	50 c. De Poincy's badge (vert)	20	15

91 The East Yorks

1971. Siege of Brimstone Hill, 1782. Multicoloured.

244	½ c. Type **91**	10	10
245	20 c. Royal Artillery	35	10
246	30 c. French infantry	45	10
247	50 c. The Royal Scots	60	20

92 "Crucifixion" (Massys)

93 "Virgin and Child" (Borgognone)

1972. Easter.

248 **92**	4 c. multicoloured	10	10
249	20 c. multicoloured	10	10
250	30 c. multicoloured	10	10
251	40 c. multicoloured	10	10

1972. Christmas. Multicoloured.

252	3 c. Type **93**	10	10
253	20 c. "Adoration of the Kings" (J. Bassano) (horiz)	15	10
254	25 c. "Adoration of the Shepherds" (Domenichino)	15	10
255	40 c. "Virgin and Child" (Fiorenzo di Lorenzo)	20	10

1972. Royal Silver Wedding. As T **52** of Ascension but with Brown Pelicans in background.

256	20 c. red	20	15
257	25 c. blue	20	15

95 Landing on St. Christopher, 1623

1973. 300th Anniv of Sir Thomas Warner's Landing on St. Christopher. Multicoloured.

258	4 c. Type **95**	15	10
259	25 c. Growing tobacco	15	10
260	40 c. Building fort at Old Road	20	10
261	$2.50 "Concepcion"	80	1·10

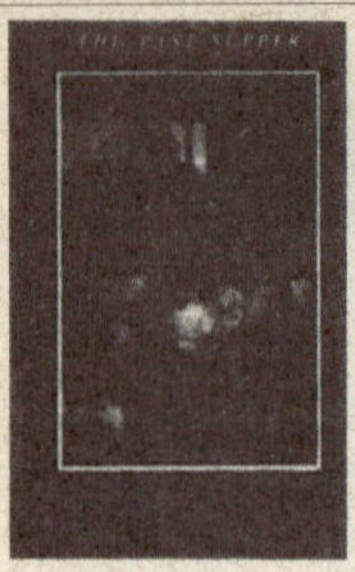

96 "The Last Supper" (Titian)

100 "Madonna and Child" (Murillo)

99 Harbour Scene and 2d. Stamp of 1903

1973. Easter. Paintings of "The Last Supper" by the artists listed. Multicoloured.

262	4 c. Type **96**	10	10
263	25 c. Ascribed to Roberti	10	10
264	$2.50 Juan de Juanes (horiz)	70	60

1973. Royal Visit. Nos. 258/61 optd **VISIT OF H. R. H. THE PRINCE OF WALES 1973.**

265	**95** 4 c. multicoloured	10	15
266	– 25 c. multicoloured	10	15
267	– 40 c. multicoloured	15	15
268	– $2.50 multicoloured	45	50

1973. 70th Anniv of First St. Kitts-Nevis Stamps. Multicoloured.

285	4 c. Type **99**	10	10
286	25 c. Sugar-mill and 1d. stamp of 1903	15	10
287	40 c. Unloading boat and ½d. stamp of 1903	35	10
288	$2.50 Rock-carvings and 3d. stamp of 1903	2·00	1·00

1973. Royal Wedding. As T **47** of Anguilla. Multicoloured, background colours given.

290	25 c. green	15	10
291	40 c. brown	15	10

1973. Christmas. Paintings of "The Holy Family" by the artists listed. Multicoloured.

292	4 c. Type **100**	10	10
293	40 c. Mengs	15	10
294	60 c. Sassoferrato	20	15
295	$1 Filippino Lippi (horiz)	25	30

101 "Christ carrying the Cross" (S. del Piombo)

103 Hands reaching for Globe

102 University Centre, St. Kitts

1974. Easter. Multicoloured.

296	4 c. Type **101**	10	10
297	25 c. "The Crucifixion" (Goya)	15	10
298	40 c. "Trinity" (Ribera)	15	10
299	$2.50 "The Deposition" (Fra Bartolomeo) (horiz)	1·00	75

1974. 25th Anniv of University of West Indies. Multicoloured.

300	10 c. Type **102**	10	10
301	$1 As Type **102** but showing different buildings	20	25

1974. Family Planning.

303	**103** 4 c. brown, blue and black	10	10
304	– 25 c. multicoloured	10	10
305	– 40 c. multicoloured	10	10
306	– $2.50 multicoloured	35	55

DESIGNS—HORIZ: 25 c. Instruction by nurse; $2.50, Emblem and globe on scales. VERT: 40 c. Family group.

104 Churchill as Army Lieutenant

106 "The Last Supper" (Dore)

1974. Birth Centenary of Sir Winston Churchill. Multicoloured.

307	4 c. Type **104**	10	10
308	25 c. Churchill as Prime Minister	15	10
309	40 c. Churchill as Knight of the Garter	15	10
310	60 c. Churchill's statue, London	50	15

1975. Easter. Paintings by Dore. Multicoloured.

314	4 c. Type **106**	10	10
315	25 c. "Christ Mocked"	10	10
316	40 c. "Jesus falling beneath the Cross"	10	10
317	$1 "The Erection of the Cross"	25	30

107 E.C.C.A. H.Q. Buildings, Basseterre

1975. Opening of East Caribbean Currency Authority's Headquarters.

318	**107** 12 c. multicoloured	10	10
319	– 25 c. multicoloured	10	10
320	– 40 c. red, silver and grey	15	10
321	– 45 c. multicoloured	15	15

DESIGNS: 25 c. Specimen one-dollar banknote; 40 c. Half-dollar of 1801 and current 4-dollar coin; 45 c. Coins of 1801 and 1960.

108 Evangeline Booth (Salvation Army General)

109 Golfer

1975. International Women's Year. Multicoloured.

338	4 c. Type **108**	30	10
339	25 c. Sylvia Pankhurst	35	10
340	40 c. Marie Curie	2·00	80
341	$2.50 Lady Annie Allen (teacher and guider)	1·50	4·00

1975. Opening of Frigate Bay Golf Course.

342	**109** 4 c. black and red	70	10
343	25 c. black and yellow	1·00	10
344	40 c. black and green	1·25	20
345	$1 black and blue	1·75	2·00

110 "St. Paul" (Pier Francesco Sacchi)

111 "Crucifixion" (detail)

1975. Christmas. Religious Paintings. Multicoloured.

346	25 c. Type **110**	25	10
347	40 c. "St. James" (Bonifazio di Pitati)	40	10
348	45 c. "St. John the Baptist" (Mola)	40	10
349	$1 "St. Mary" (Raphael)	1·25	1·40

1976. Easter. Stained Glass Window. Multicoloured.

350	4 c. Type **111**	10	20
351	4 c. Type **111**	10	20
352	4 c. Type **111**	10	20
353	25 c. "Last Supper"	35	10
354	40 c. "Last Supper" (different)	40	10
355	$1 "Baptism of Christ"	70	70

Nos. 350/2 were printed together, se-tenant, forming a composite design. No. 350 being the left-hand stamp.

Nos. 353/5 are size 27×35 mm.

1976. West Indian Victory in World Cricket Cup. As Nos. 559/60 of Barbados.

356	12 c. Map of the Caribbean	60	20
357	40 c. Prudential Cup	1·40	50

112 Crispus Attucks and the Boston Massacre

1976. Bicent of American Revolution. Multicoloured.

359	20 c. Type **112**	20	10
360	40 c. Alexander Hamilton and Battle of Yorktown	35	10
361	45 c. Jefferson and Declaration of Independence	35	10
362	$1 Washington and the Crossing of the Delaware	70	80

113 "The Nativity" (Sforza Book of Hours)

114 Royal Visit, 1966

1976. Christmas. Multicoloured.

363	20 c. Type **113**	10	10
364	40 c. "Virgin and Child with St. John" (Pintoricchio)	15	10
365	45 c. "Our Lady of Good Children" (Ford Maddox-Brown)	15	10
366	$1 "Little Hands Outstretched to Bless" (Margaret Tarrant)	35	50

1977. Silver Jubilee. Multicoloured.

367	50 c. Type **114**	10	10
368	55 c. The Sceptre	10	10
369	$1.50 Bishops paying homage	25	50

115 "Christ on the Cross" (Niccolo di Liberatore)

116 Estridge Mission

1977. Easter. Paintings from National Gallery, London. Multicoloured.

370	25 c. Type **115**	10	10
371	30 c. "The Resurrection" (imitator of Mantegna)	10	10
372	50 c. "The Resurrection" (Ugolino da Siena) (horiz)	15	10
373	$1 "Christ Rising from the Tomb" (Gaudenzio Ferrari)	25	30

1977. Bicentenary of Moravian Mission.

374	**116** 4 c. black, green and blue	10	10
375	– 20 c. black, mauve & violet	10	10
376	– 40 c. black, yellow & orge	15	15

DESIGNS: 20 c. Mission symbol; 40 c. Basseterre Mission.

117 Laboratory Instruments

118 "Nativity" (West Window)

1977. 75th Anniv of Pan-American Health Organization.

377	**117** 3 c. multicoloured	20	10
378	– 12 c. multicoloured	30	10
379	– 20 c. multicoloured	40	10
380	– $1 brown, orange & black	1·10	1·25

DESIGNS: 12 c. Fat cells, blood cells and nerve cells; 20 c. "Community participation in health"; $1 Inoculation.

1977. Christmas. Stained-glass windows from Chartres Cathedral. Multicoloured.

381	4 c. Type **118**	10	10
382	6 c. "Three Magi" (west window)	10	10
383	40 c. "La Belle Verriere"	35	10
384	$1 "Virgin and Child" (Rose window)	75	45

119 Savanna Monkey with Vervet

120 Falcon of Edward III

1978. The Savanna Monkey.

385	**119** 4 c. brown, red and black	10	10
386	– 5 c. multicoloured	10	10
387	**119** 55 c. brown, green & black	30	10
388	– $1.50 multicoloured	75	60

DESIGN: 5 c., $1.50, Savanna monkeys on branch.

1978. 25th Anniv of Coronation.

389	**120** $1 brown and red	15	20
390	– $1 multicoloured	15	20
391	– $1 brown and red	15	20

DESIGNS: No. 390, Queen Elizabeth II; No. 391, Brown pelican.

121 Tomatoes

1978. Multicoloured.

392	1 c. Type **121**	10	20
393	2 c. Defence Force band	10	20
394	5 c. Radio and T.V. station	10	10
395	10 c. Technical college	10	10
396	12 c. T.V. assembly plant	10	20
397	15 c. Sugar canoe harvesting	15	10
398	25 c. Crafthouse (craft centre)	15	10
399	30 c. "Europa" (liner)	80	70
400	40 c. Lobster and sea crab	30	10
401	45 c. Royal St. Kitts Hotel and golf course	2·75	75
402	50 c. Pinney's Beach, Nevis	30	10
403	55 c. New runway at Golden Rock	50	10
404	$1 Cotton picking	35	30
405	$5 Brewery	75	1·25
406	$10 Pineapples and peanuts	1·50	2·50

122 Investiture

123 Wise Man with Gift of Gold

1978. 50th Anniv of Boy Scout Movement on St. Kitts and Nevis. Multicoloured.

407	5 c. Type **122**	10	10
408	10 c. Map reading	10	10
409	25 c. Pitching tent	20	15
410	40 c. Cooking	35	25
411	50 c. First aid	40	35
412	55 c. Rev. W. A. Beckett (founder of scouting in St. Kitts)	45	45

1978. Christmas. Multicoloured.

413	5 c. Type **123**	10	10
414	15 c. Wise Man with gift of Frankincense	10	10
415	30 c. Wise Man with gift of Myrrh	10	10
416	$2.25 Wise Man paying homage to the Infant Jesus	35	50

124 "Canna coccinea"

126 "The Woodman's Daughter"

125 St. Christopher 1870 1d. Stamp and Sir Rowland Hill

1979. Local Flowers (1st series). Multicoloured.

417		5 c. Type **124**	10	10
418		30 c. "Heliconia bihai"	30	20
419		55 c. "Ruellia tuberosa"	50	30
420		$1.50 "Gesneria ventricosa"	1·10	1·60

See also Nos. 430/3.

1979. Death Centenary of Sir Rowland Hill. Multicoloured.

421		5 c. Type **125**	10	10
422		15 c. 1970 Stamp Centenary 50 c. commemorative	10	10
423		50 c. Great Britain 1841 2d. blue	30	35
424		$2.50 St. Kitts-Nevis 1923 300th Anniv of Colony £1 commemorative	70	1·10

1979. Christmas. International Year of the Child. Paintings by Sir John Millais. Multicoloured.

425		5 c. Type **126**	10	10
426		25 c. "Cherry Ripe"	25	25
427		30 c. "The Rescue"	25	25
428		55 c. "Bubbles"	30	30

1980. Local Flowers (2nd series). As T **124**. Multicoloured.

430		4 c. "Clerodendrum aculeatum"	30	10
431		55 c. "Inga laurina"	40	20
432		$1.50 "Epidendrum difforme"	1·25	1·40
433		$2 "Salvia serotina"	1·10	2·00

127 Nevis Lagoon

1980. "London 1980" International Stamp Exhibition. Multicoloured.

434		5 c. Type **127**	15	10
435		30 c. Fig Tree Church (vert)	25	10
436		55 c. Nisbet Plantation	45	25
437		$3 "Nelson" (Fuger) (vert)	1·25	1·60

OFFICIAL STAMPS

1980. Nos. 396, 398 and 400/6 optd **OFFICIAL**.

O1		12 c. multicoloured	80	1·00
O2		25 c. multicoloured	15	20
O3		40 c. multicoloured	40	50
O4		45 c. multicoloured	45	45
O5		50 c. multicoloured	30	40
O6		55 c. multicoloured	30	40
O7		$1 multicoloured	70	2·25
O8		$5 multicoloured	80	2·50
O9		$10 multicoloured	1·50	3·50

ST. LUCIA

One of the Windward Islands, British West Indies. Achieved Associated Statehood on 1 March 1967.

1860. 12 pence = 1 shilling;
20 shilllings = 1 pound.
1949. 100 cents = 1 West Indian dollar.

1

HALFPENNY
(3)

1860. No value on stamps.

5	**1**	(1d.) red	55·00	80·00
11a		(1d.) black	15·00	11·00
7		(4d.) blue	90·00	90·00
16		(4d.) yellow	70·00	18·00
8		(6d.) green	£150	£150
17a		(6d.) violet	70·00	18·00
14c		(1s.) orange	£150	25·00

1881. With value added by surch as T **3**.

25	**1**	½d. green	14·00	23·00
26		1d. black	20·00	8·50
24		2½d. red	25·00	19·00
27		4d. yellow	£180	17·00
28		6d. violet	23·00	26·00
29		1s. orange	£250	£160

5

9

1882.

43	**5**	½d. green	1·50	70
32		1d. red	30·00	8·00
46		2½d. blue	2·25	70
48		4d. brown	1·75	2·25
35		6d. lilac	£250	£200
36		1s. brown	£350	£140

1886.

44	**5**	1d. mauve	1·75	20
45		2d. blue and orange	1·00	1·00
47		3d. mauve and green	3·25	5·50
41		6d. mauve and blue	3·50	7·50
50		1s. mauve and red	3·25	5·00
51		5s. mauve and orange	38·00	£120
52		10s. mauve and black	75·00	£120

1891. Surch in words.

56	**5**	½d. on 3d. mauve and green	50·00	20·00
55		1d. on 4d. brown	3·00	3·25

1891. Surch **½d.**

54	**5**	½d. on half 6d. (No. 41)	15·00	3·25

1902.

64a	**9**	½d. purple and green	2·25	95
65		½d. green	1·75	90
66a		1d. purple and red	2·00	90
67		1d. red	3·50	30
68		2½d. purple and blue	8·50	1·25
69		2½d. blue	3·75	1·50
70		3d. purple and yellow	3·75	3·00
71		3d. purple on yellow	2·00	11·00
72ab		6d. purple and violet	5·50	18·00
73		6d. purple	26·00	48·00
62		1s. green and black	10·00	20·00
75		1s. black on green	4·00	7·50
76		5s. green and red	55·00	£130
77		5s. green and red on yellow	55·00	65·00

11 The Pitons

12

13

14

1902. 400th Anniv of Discovery by Columbus.

63	**11**	2d. green and brown	8·00	1·75

1912.

91	**12**	½d. green	30	30
79		1d. red	1·90	10
93		1d. brown	80	15
94	**14**	1½d. red	50	2·00
95	**13**	2d. grey	30	15
96	**12**	2½d. blue	3·00	2·75
97		2½d. orange	10·00	48·00
82		3d. purple on yellow	1·25	2·00
99a		3d. blue	1·50	11·00
83a	**14**	4d. black & red on yellow	70	1·50
102	**12**	6d. purple	1·75	4·75
85		1s. black on green	2·50	4·50
103		1s. brown	1·75	3·25
104	**13**	2s. 6d. black & red on blue	17·00	26·00
88	**12**	5s. green and red on yellow	22·00	75·00

1916. No. 79 optd **WAR TAX** in two lines.

89	**12**	1d. red	7·00	7·00

1916. No. 79 optd **WAR TAX** in one line.

90	**12**	1d. red	30	30

1935. Silver Jubilee. As T **13** of Antigua.

109		½d. black and green	15	30
110		2d. blue and grey	45	45
111		2½d. brown and blue	90	75
112		1s. grey and purple	3·75	7·00

19 Port Castries

1936. King George V.

113	**19**	½d. black and green	30	45
114	–	1d. black and brown	40	10
115	–	1½d. black and red	55	30
116	**19**	2d. black and grey	40	15
117	–	2½d. black and blue	40	15
118	–	3d. black and green	1·25	70
119	**19**	4d. black and brown	30	1·00
120	–	6d. black and orange	85	1·00
121	–	1s. black and blue	1·25	2·25
122	–	2s. 6d. black and blue	7·50	14·00
123	–	5s. black and violet	8·00	20·00
124	–	10s. black and red	42·00	65·00

DESIGNS—HORIZ: 1d., 2½d., 6d. Columbus Square, Castries (inscr "Colombus Square" in error); 1s. Fort Rodney, Pigeon Island; 5s. Government House; 10s. Badge of Colony. VERT: 1½d, 3d. Ventine Falls; 2s. 6d. Inniskilling Monument.

1937. Coronation. As T **2** of Aden.

125		1d. violet	30	30
126		1½d. red	55	20
127		2½d. blue	55	40

26 King George VI

27 Columbus Square

1938. King George VI.

128a	**26**	½d. green	10	10
129a		1d. violet	10	15
129b		1d. red	10	10
130a		1½d. red	15	45
131a		2d. grey	10	10
132a		2½d. blue	10	10
132b		2½d. violet	30	10
133a		3d. orange	10	10
133b		3½d. blue	30	15
134b	**27**	6d. red	1·00	45
134c	**26**	8d. brown	2·50	30
135a	–	1s. brown	40	20
136	–	2s. blue and red	3·50	1·25
136a	**26**	3s. purple	8·00	2·25
137	–	5s. black and purple	14·00	6·00
138	–	10s. black on yellow	4·50	9·00
141	**26**	£1 brown	11·00	8·00

DESIGNS—As Type **27**: 1s. Government House; 2s. The Pitons; 5s. "Lady Hawkins" loading bananas. VERT: 10s. Device of St. Lucia as Type **33**.

1946. Victory. As T **9** of Aden.

142		1d. violet	10	10
143		3½d. blue	10	10

1948. Silver Wedding. As T **10/11** of Aden.

144		1d. red	15	10
145		£1 purple	13·00	35·00

33 Device of St. Lucia

34 Phoenix rising from Burning Buildings

1949. New Currency.

146	**26**	1 c. green	10	10
147		2 c. mauve	10	10
148		3 c. red	10	75
149		4 c. grey	10	10
150		5 c. violet	10	10
151		6 c. orange	15	75
152		7 c. blue	1·00	1·50
153		12 c. red	4·00	80
154		16 c. brown	1·50	20
155	**33**	24 c. blue	30	10
156		48 c. olive	1·50	85
157		$1.20 purple	2·25	6·00
158		$2.40 green	3·00	17·00
159		$4.80 red	6·00	18·00

1949. U.P.U. As T **20/23** of Antigua.

160		5 c. violet	20	20
161		6 c. orange	1·10	75
162		12 c. mauve	30	20
163		24 c. green	65	20

1951. Inauguration of B.W.I. University College. As T **24/25** of Antigua.

164		3 c. black and red	45	50
165		12 c. black and red	45	50

1951. Reconstruction of Castries.

166	**34**	12 c. red and blue	15	70

1951. New Constitution. Optd **NEW CONSTITUTION 1951**.

167	**26**	2 c. mauve	15	50
168		4 c. grey	15	50
169		5 c. violet	15	30
170		12 c. red	15	50

1953. Coronation. As T **13** of Aden.

171		3 c. black and red	50	10

1953. As 1949 but portrait of Queen Elizabeth II facing left and new Royal Cypher.

172	**26**	1 c. green	10	10
173		2 c. purple	10	10
174		3 c. red	10	10
175		4 c. grey	10	10
176		5 c. violet	10	10
177		6 c. orange	15	10
178	**26**	8 c. red	20	10
179		10 c. blue	10	10
180		15 c. brown	30	10
181	**33**	25 c. blue	30	10
182		50 c. olive	4·50	50
183		$1 green	4·00	1·75
184		$2.50 red	5·00	4·25

1958. British Caribbean Federation. As T **28** of Antigua.

185		3 c. green	40	20
186		6 c. blue	65	1·50
187		12 c. red	90	75

38 Columbus's "Santa Maria" off the Pitons

39 Stamp of 1860

1960. New Constitution for the Windward and Leeward Islands.

188	**38**	8 c. red	40	35
189		10 c. orange	40	35
190		25 c. blue	60	40

1960. Stamp Centenary.

191	**39**	5 c. red and blue	15	10
192		16 c. blue and green	40	60
193		25 c. green and red	40	20

1963. Freedom from Hunger. As T **28** of Aden.

194		25 c. green	30	10

1963. Cent of Red Cross. As T **33** of Antigua.

195		4 c. red and black	20	35
196		25 c. red and blue	65	1·40

40 Queen Elizabeth II 41 (after A. C. Davidson-Houston)

42 Fishing Boats

1964.

197	**40**	1 c. red	10	10
198		2 c. violet	30	30
199		4 c. green	35	30
200		5 c. blue	30	10
201		6 c. brown	45	50
202	**41**	8 c. multicoloured	10	10
203		10 c. multicoloured	50	10
204	**42**	12 c. multicoloured	30	70
205	–	15 c. multicoloured	20	10
206	–	25 c. multicoloured	20	10
207	–	35 c. blue and buff	2·50	10
208	–	50 c. multicoloured	2·00	10
209	–	$1 multicoloured	1·25	65
210	–	$2.50 multicoloured	2·00	2·00

HORIZ (as Type **42**): 15 c. Pigeon Island; 25 c. Reduit Beach; 35 c. Castries Harbour; 50 c. The Pitons. VERT (as Type **42**): $1 Vigie Beach. (As Type **41**): $2.50, Head and shoulders portrait of Queen Elizabeth II.

The 35 c. and 50 c. show a royal Cypher in place of the portrait.

1964. 400th Birth Anniv of Shakespeare. As T **34** of Antigua.

211		10 c. green	10	10

1965. Cent of I.T.U. As T **36** of Antigua.

212		2 c. mauve and purple	10	10
213		50 c. lilac and green	70	75

1965. I.C.Y. As T **37** of Antigua.

214		1 c. purple and green	10	10
215		25 c. green and violet	20	20

1966. Churchill Commem. As T **38** of Antigua.

216		4 c. blue	10	10
217		6 c. green	20	60
218		25 c. brown	25	15
219		35 c. violet	30	20

1966. Royal Visit. As T **39** of Antigua.

220		4 c. black and blue	20	20
221		25 c. black and mauve	60	60

1966. World Cup Football Championship. As T **40** of Antigua.

222		4 c. multicoloured	25	10
223		25 c. multicoloured	65	30

1966. Inauguration of W.H.O. Headquarters, Geneva. As T **41** of Antigua.

224		4 c. black, green and blue	10	10
225		25 c. black, purple and brown	25	20

1966. 20th Anniv of U.N.E.S.C.O. As T **54/6** of Antigua.
226 4 c. multicoloured 10 10
227 12 c. yellow, violet and olive . . 20 30
228 25 c. black, purple and orange . . 35 35

51 Map of St. Lucia

52 "Madonna and Child with the Infant Baptist" (Raphael)

1967. Statehood. Nos. 198, 202/9 and 257 optd **STATEHOOD 1st MARCH 1967.**
229 **40** 2 c. violet (postage) 20 15
230 5 c. blue 10 10
231 6 c. brown 10 10
232 **41** 8 c. multicoloured 20 10
233 10 c. multicoloured 25 10
234 **42** 12 c. multicoloured 20 10
235 – 15 c. multicoloured 40 30
236 – 25 c. multicoloured 30 30
237 – 35 c. blue and buff 50 35
238 – 50 c. multicoloured 50 55
239 – $1 multicoloured 50 55
240 **51** 15 c. blue (air) 10 10

1967. Christmas.
241 **52** 4 c. multicoloured 10 10
242 25 c. multicoloured 30 10

53 Batsman and Sir Frederick Clarke (Governor)

54 "The Crucified Christ with the Virgin Mary Saints and the Angels" (Raphael)

1968. M.C.C.'s West Indies Tour.
243 **53** 10 c. multicoloured 20 30
244 35 c. multicoloured 45 55

1968. Easter Commemoration.
245 **54** 10 c. multicoloured 10 10
246 – 15 c. multicoloured 10 10
247 **54** 25 c. multicoloured 15 10
248 – 35 c. multicoloured 15 10
DESIGN: 15, 35 c. "Noli me tangere" (detail by Titian).

56 Dr. Martin Luther King

57 "Virgin and Child in Glory" (Murillo)

1968. Martin Luther King Commemoration.
250 **56** 25 c. blue, black and flesh . 15 15
251 35 c. blue, black and flesh . 15 15

1968. Christmas.
252 **57** 5 c. multicoloured 10 10
253 – 10 c. multicoloured 10 10
254 **57** 25 c. multicoloured 15 10
255 – 35 c. multicoloured 15 10
DESIGN: 10, 35 c. "Madonna with Child" (Murillo).

59 Purple-throated Carib

1969. Birds. Multicoloured.
256 10 c. Type **59** 55 35
257 15 c. St. Lucia amazon 70 40
258 25 c. Type **59** 90 45
259 35 c. As 15 c. . . . . 1·25 50

61 "Head of Christ Crowned with Thorns" (Reni)

1969. Easter. Multicoloured.
260 10 c. Type **61** 10 10
261 15 c. "Resurrection of Christ" (Sodoma) 10 10
262 25 c. Type **61** 15 15
263 35 c. As the 15 c. 15 15

63 Map showing CARIFTA Countries

1969. 1st Anniv of CARIFTA.
264 **63** 5 c. multicoloured 10 10
265 10 c. multicoloured 10 10
266 – 25 c. multicoloured . . . 15 15
267 – 35 c. multicoloured . . . 15 15
DESIGN: 25, 35 c. Handclasp and names of CARIFTA countries.

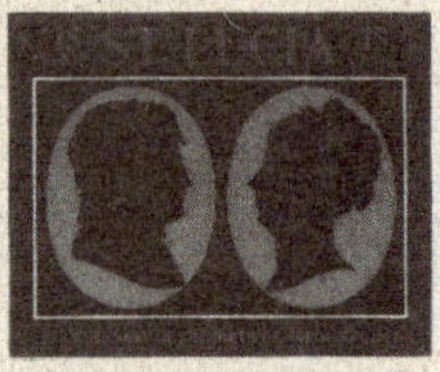

65 Emperor Napoleon and Empress Josephine

1969. Birth Bicent of Napoleon Bonaparte.
268 **65** 15 c. multicoloured . . . 10 10
269 25 c. multicoloured . . . 10 10
270 35 c. multicoloured . . . 10 10
271 50 c. multicoloured . . . 15 55

66 "Virgin and Child" (P. Delaroche)

69 "The Sealing of the Tomb" (Hogarth)

1969. Christmas. Paintings. Multicoloured, background colours given.
272 **66** 5 c. gold and purple . . . 10 10
273 – 10 c. gold and blue 10 10
274 **66** 25 c. gold and red 20 10
275 – 35 c. gold and green . . . 20 10
DESIGN: 10 c., 35 c. "Holy Family" (Rubens).

68 House of Assembly

1970. Multicoloured.
276 1 c. Type **68** 10 10
277 2 c. Roman Catholic Cathedral 15 10
278 4 c. The Boulevard, Castries . 90 10
279 5 c. Castries Harbour . . . 1·00 10
280 6 c. Sulphur springs 15 10
281 10 c. Vigie Airport 65 10
282 12 c. Reduit Beach 20 10
283 15 c. Pigeon Island 30 10
284 25 c. The Pitons and yacht . 80 10
285 35 c. Marigot Bay 40 10
286 50 c. Diamond Waterfall . . 70 80
287 $1 Flag of St. Lucia 60 70
288 £2.50 St. Lucia coat of arms 80 1·75
289 $5 Queen Elizabeth II . . . 2·00 4·00
289a $10 Map of St. Lucia . . . 6·00 9·00
Nos. 286/9a are vert.

1970. Easter. Multicoloured.
290 25 c. Type **69** 15 20
291 35 c. "The Three Marys at the Tomb" (Hogarth) 15 20
292 $1 "The Ascension" (Hogarth) 30 40
The $1 is larger 39 × 54 mm.
Nos. 290/2 were issued in a triptych, with the $1 value 10 mm higher than the other values.

72 Charles Dickens and Dickensian Characters

1970. Death Cent of Charles Dickens.
293 **72** 1 c. multicoloured 10 10
294 25 c. multicoloured 20 10
295 35 c. multicoloured 25 10
296 50 c. multicoloured . . . . 35 1·25

73 Nurse and Emblem

1970. Cent of British Red Cross. Multicoloured.
297 10 c. Type **73** 15 15
298 15 c. Flags of Great Britain, Red Cross and St. Lucia 25 25
299 25 c. Type **73** 35 40
300 35 c. As 15 c. 40 40

74 "Madonna with the Lilies" (Luca della Robbia)

75 "Christ on the Cross" (Rubens)

1970. Christmas.
301 **74** 5 c. multicoloured 10 10
302 10 c. multicoloured 15 10
303 35 c. multicoloured 30 10
304 40 c. multicoloured 30 30

1971. Easter. Multicoloured.
305 10 c. Type **75** 10 10
306 15 c. "Descent from the Cross" (Rubens) 15 10
307 35 c. Type **75** 30 10
308 40 c. As 15 c. 30 40

76 Moule a Chique Lighthouse

1971. Opening of Beane Field Airport. Mult.
309 5 c. Type **76** 30 15
310 25 c. Boeing 727-200 landing at Beane Field 45 15

77 Morne Fortune

78 Morne Fortune, Modern View

1971. Old and New Views of St. Lucia. Multicoloured.
311 5 c. Type **77** 10 15
312 5 c. Type **78** 10 15
313 10 c. Castries City (old view) . 10 15
314 10 c. Castries City (modern view) 10 15
315 25 c. Pigeon Island (old view) . 15 30
316 25 c. Pigeon Island (modern view) 15 30
317 50 c. Old view from grounds of Government House 25 65
318 50 c. Modern view from grounds of Government House . . . 25 65
The old views are taken from paintings by J. H. Caddy.

79 "Virgin and Child with two Angels" (Verrocchio)

81 "The Dead Christ Mourned" (Carracci)

80 "St. Lucia" (Dolci School) and Coat of Arms

1971. Christmas. Multicoloured.
319 5 c. Type **79** 10 10
320 10 c. "Virgin and Child, St. John the Baptist and an Angel" (Morando) 10 10
321 35 c. "Madonna and Child" (Battista) 15 10
322 40 c. Type **79** 20 25

1971. National Day.
323 **80** 5 c. multicoloured 10 10
324 10 c. multicoloured 15 10
325 25 c. multicoloured 25 10
326 50 c. multicoloured 45 40

1972. Easter. Multicoloured.
327 10 c. Type **81** 10 10
328 25 c. "Angels weeping over the dead Christ" (Guercino) . . 20 10
329 35 c. Type **81** 30 10
330 50 c. As 25 c. 40 40

82 Science Block and Teachers' College

1972. Morne Educational Complex. Mult.
331 5 c. Type **82** 10 10
332 15 c. University Centre 10 10
333 25 c. Secondary School . . . 10 10
334 35 c. Technical College . . . 15 10

83 Steamship Stamp and Map

1972. Centenary of First Postal Service by St. Lucia Steam Conveyance Co. Ltd.
335 **83** 5 c. multicoloured 15 10
336 – 10 c. blue, mauve and black 20 10
337 – 35 c. red, blue and black . 60 10
338 – 50 c. multicoloured . . . . 1·00 1·00
DESIGNS: 10 c. Steamship stamp and Castries Harbour; 35 c. Steamship stamp and Soufriere; 50 c. Steamship stamps.

84 "The Holy Family" (Sebastiano Ricci)

1972. Christmas.
339 **84** 5 c. multicoloured 10 10
340 10 c. multicoloured 10 10
341 35 c. multicoloured 20 10
342 40 c. multicoloured 25 15

1972. Royal Silver Wedding. As T **52** of Ascension but with Arms and St. Lucia Amazon.

343 **83**	15 c. red	20	20
344	35 c. green	20	20

86 Week-day Headdress **87** Coat of Arms

1973. Local Headdresses. Multicoloured.

345	5 c. Type **86**	10	10
346	10 c. Formal style	10	10
347	25 c. Unmarried girl's style	15	10
348	50 c. Ceremonial style	25	50

1973.

349A **87**	5 c. green	10	65
350A	10 c. blue	15	65
953	10 c. green	40	40
351A	25 c. brown	15	65

88 H.M.S. "St. Lucia", 1830

1973. Historic Ships. Multicoloured.

352	15 c. Type **88**	20	10
353	35 c. H.M.S. "Prince of Wales", 1765	25	10
354	50 c. "Oliph Blossom", 1605	40	20
355	$1 H.M.S. "Rose", 1757	55	65

89 Plantation and Flower

1973. Banana Industry. Multicoloured.

357	5 c. Type **89**	10	10
358	15 c. Aerial spraying	15	10
359	35 c. Boxing plant	20	10
360	50 c. Loading a boat	50	40

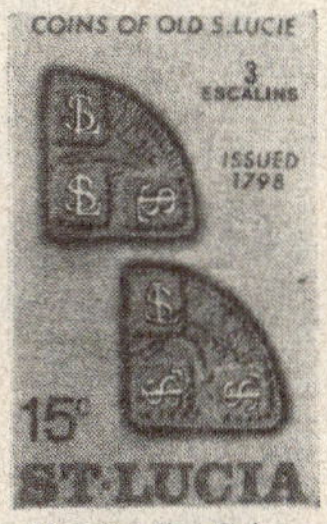

90 "The Virgin with Child" (Maratta) **92** 3-Escalins Coins, 1798

91 "The Betrayal"

1973. Christmas. Multicoloured.

361	5 c. Type **90**	10	10
362	15 c. "Madonna in the Meadow" (Raphael)	10	10
363	35 c. "The Holy Family" (Bronzino)	20	10
364	50 c. "Madonna of the Pear" (Durer)	30	35

1973. Royal Wedding. As T **47** of Anguilla. Multicoloured, background colours given.

365	40 c. green	10	10
366	50 c. lilac	10	10

1974. Easter. Paintings by Ugolino da Siena. Multicoloured.

369	5 c. Type **91**	10	10
370	35 c. "The Way to Calvary"	15	10
371	80 c. "The Deposition"	15	15
372	$1 "The Resurrection"	20	25

1974. Coins of Old St. Lucia. Multicoloured.

374	15 c. Type **92**	15	10
375	35 c. 6-esculins coins, 1798	15	10
376	40 c. 2-livres 5-sols coins, 1813	20	10
377	$1 6-livres 15-sols coins, 1813	35	65

93 Baron de Laborie **94** "Virgin and Child" (Andrea del Verrocchio)

1974. Past Governors of St. Lucia. Mult.

379	5 c. Type **93**	10	10
380	35 c. Sir John Moore	10	10
381	80 c. Sir Dudley Hill	15	10
382	$1 Sir Frederick Clarke	25	35

1974. Christmas. Multicoloured.

384	5 c. Type **94**	10	10
385	35 c. "Virgin and Child" (Andrea della Robbia)	10	10
386	80 c. "Madonna and Child" (Luca della Robbia)	15	15
387	$1 "Virgin and Child" (Rossellino)	20	25

95 Churchill and Montgomery

1974. Birth Centenary of Sir Winston Churchill.

389	5 c. Type **95**	10	10
390	$1 Churchill and Truman	30	35

96 "Christ on the Cross" (School of Van der Weyden) **97** "Nativity" (French Book of Hours)

1975. Easter. Multicoloured.

391	5 c. Type **96**	10	10
392	35 c. "Noli me tangere" (Romano)	10	10
393	80 c. "Calvary" (Gallego)	20	20
394	$1 "Noli me tangere" (Correggio)	30	35

1975. Christmas. Multicoloured.

399	5 c. Type **97**	10	10
400	10 c. "King" (stained glass window)	10	15
401	10 c. "Virgin and Child" (stained glass window)	10	15
402	10 c. "King and Cattle" (stained glass window)	10	15
403	40 c. "Nativity" (Hastings Book of Hours)	30	20
404	$1 "Virgin and Child with Saints" (Borgognone)	70	60

Nos. 400/2 were printed together, se-tenant, forming a composite design of the Epiphany.

98 America Schooner "Hanna"

1975. Bicent of American Revolution. Ships. Mult.

406	½ c. Type **98**	10	10
407	1 c. "Prince of Orange" (British sailing packet)	10	10
408	2 c. H.M.S. "Edward" (sloop)	10	10
409	5 c. "Millern" (British merchantman)	30	10
410	15 c. "Surprise" (American lugger)	60	10
411	35 c. H.M.S. "Serapis" (frigate)	80	20
412	50 c. "Randolph" (American frigate)	85	1·00
413	$1 "Alliance" (American frigate)	1·40	2·50

99 Laughing Gull **100** H.M.S. "Ceres"

1976. Birds. Multicoloured.

415	1 c. Type **99**	30	90
416	2 c. Little blue heron	30	90
417	4 c. Belted kingfisher	35	90
418	5 c. St. Lucia amazon	1·75	90
419	6 c. St. Lucia oriole	1·25	90
420	8 c. Brown trembler	1·50	1·50
421	10 c. American kestrel	1·25	35
422	12 c. Red-billed tropic bird	2·00	2·50
423	15 c. Moorhen	1·25	15
424a	25 c. Common noddy	1·00	30
425	35 c. Sooty tern	3·25	1·25
426	50 c. Osprey	6·00	3·50
427	$1 White-breasted trembler	4·00	3·50
428	$2.50 St. Lucia black finch	7·00	6·00
429	$5 Red-necked pigeon	7·00	4·50
430a	$10 Caribbean elaenia	4·00	7·50

1976. West Indies Victory in World Cricket Cup. As Nos. 599/60 of Barbados. Mult.

431	50 c. Caribbean map	1·00	1·00
432	$1 Prudential Cup	1·50	2·50

1976. Royal Navy Crests. Multicoloured.

434	10 c. Type **100**	35	10
435	20 c. H.M.S. "Pelican"	60	10
436	40 c. H.M.S. "Ganges"	85	10
437	$2 H.M.S. "Ariadne"	2·00	2·00

101 "Madonna and Child" (Murillo) **103** Scouts from Tapion School

102 Queen Elizabeth II

1976. Christmas. Multicoloured.

438	10 c. Type **101**	10	10
439	20 c. "Madonna and Child with Angels" (Costa)	10	10
440	50 c. "Madonna and Child Enthroned" (Isenbrandt)	15	10
441	$2 "Madonna and Child with St. John" (Murillo)	50	65

1977. Silver Jubilee.

443 **102**	10 c. multicoloured	10	10
444	20 c. multicoloured	10	10
445	40 c. multicoloured	10	15
446	$2 multicoloured	40	90

1977. Caribbean Boy Scout Jamboree. Multicoloured.

448	½ c. Type **103**	10	10
449	1 c. Sea scouts	10	10
450	2 c. Scout from Micoud	10	10
451	10 c. Two scouts from Tapion School	15	10
452	20 c. Venture scout	15	10
453	50 c. Scout from Gros Islet	30	45
454	$1 Sea scouts in motor boat	50	1·00

104 "Nativity" (Giotto) **105** "Susan Lunden"

1977. Christmas. Multicoloured.

456	½ c. Type **104**	10	10
457	1 c. "Perugia triptych" (Fra Angelico)	10	10
458	2 c. "Virgin and Child" (El Greco)	10	10
459	20 c. "Madonna of the Rosary" (Caravaggio)	15	10
460	50 c. "Adoration of the Magi" (Velazquez)	20	10
461	$1 "Madonna of Carmel" (Tiepolo)	30	35
462	$2.50 "Adoration of the Magi" (Tiepolo)	45	80

1977. 400th Birth Anniv of Rubens. Mult.

463	10 c. Type **105**	10	10
464	35 c. "The Rape of the Sabine Women" (detail)	15	10
465	50 c. "Ludovicus Nonnius"	30	10
466	$2.50 "Minerva protects Pax from Mars" (detail)	85	80

106 Yeoman of the Guard and Life Guard

1978. 25th Anniv of Coronation. Mult.

468	15 c. Type **106**	10	10
469	20 c. Groom and postillion	10	10
470	50 c. Footman and coachman	10	10
471	$3 State trumpeter and herald	35	80

107 Queen Angelfish

1978. Fish. Multicoloured.

473	10 c. Type **107**	15	10
474	20 c. Four-eyed butterflyfish	30	10
475	50 c. French angelfish	60	30
476	$2 Yellow-tailed damselfish	1·10	1·75

108 French Grenadier and Map of the Battle

1978. Bicent of Battle of Cul-de-Sac. Mult.

478	10 c. Type **108**	35	10
479	30 c. British Grenadier officer and Map of St. Lucia (Bellin), 1762	55	10
480	50 c. Coastline from Gros Islet to Cul-de-Sac and British Fleet opposing French landings	75	15
481	$2.50 General James Grant, 1798, and Light Infantrymen of 46th Regiment	1·75	1·25

109 The Annunciation

1978. Christmas. Multicoloured.

482	30 c. Type **109**	10	10
483	50 c. Type **109**	15	10
484	55 c. The Nativity	15	10
485	80 c. As 55 c.	20	20

110 Hewanorra International Air Terminal

1979. Independence. Multicoloured.

486	10 c. Type **110**	10	10
487	30 c. New coat of arms	10	10
488	50 c. Government House and Sir Allen Lewis (first Governor-General)	15	10
489	$2 French, St. Lucia and Union flags on map of St. Lucia	30	45

111 Popes Paul VI and John Paul I

1979. Pope Paul VI Commemoration. Mult.

491	10 c. Type **111**	10	10
492	30 c. Pres. Sadat of Egypt with Pope Paul	20	10
493	50 c. Pope Paul with Secretary-General U Thant	35	20
494	55 c. Pope Paul and Prince Minister Golda Meir of Israel	40	25
495	$2 Martin Luther King received in audience by Pope Paul	1·00	80

112 Dairy Farming

1979. Agricultural Diversification. Mult.

496	10 c. Type **112**	10	10
497	35 c. Fruit and vegetables	10	10
498	50 c. Water conservation	10	10
499	$3 Copra industry	35	70

113 Lindbergh and Sikorsky S-38A Flying Boat

1979. 50th Anniv of Lindbergh's Inaugural Airmail Flight via St. Lucia.

500	**113** 10 c. black, red & orange	30	10
501	– 30 c. multicoloured	40	10
502	– 50 c. multicoloured	40	10
503	– $2 multicoloured	60	40

DESIGNS: 30 c. Sikorsky S-38A flying boat and route map; 50 c. Arrival at La Toc, September, 1929; $2 Letters on first flight.

114 "A Prince of Saxony" (Cranach the Elder)

115 Notice of Introduction of Penny Post

1979. International Year of the Child. Famous Paintings. Multicoloured.

504	10 c. Type **114**	10	10
505	50 c. "The Infanta Margarita" (Velazquez)	15	10
506	$2 "Girl playing Badminton" (Chardin)	40	40
507	$2.50 "Mary and Francis Wilcox" (Stock)	45	45

1979. Death Cent of Sir Rowland Hill. Mult.

509	10 c. Type **115**	10	10
510	50 c. Wyon essay	15	10
511	$2 First St. Lucia stamp	35	50
512	$2.50 G.B. 1840 Penny Black	45	60

116 "Madonna and Child" (Bernardino Fungai)

118 Mickey Mouse astride Rocket

117 St. Lucia Steam Conveyance Co. Ltd. Cover, 1873

1979. Christmas. International Year of the Child. Paintings of the "Madonna and Child" by artists named. Multicoloured.

514	10 c. Type **116**	10	10
515	50 c. Carlo Dolci	25	10
516	$2 Titian	70	40
517	$2.50 Giovanni Bellini	75	50

1980. "London 1980" Int Stamp Exhibition. Mult.

519	10 c. Type **117**	10	10
520	30 c. S.S. "Assistance" 1d. postmark, 1879	10	10
521	50 c. Postage due handstamp, 1929	15	10
522	$2 Crowned-circle Paid stamp, 1844	40	55

1980. 10th Anniv (1979) of Moon Landing. Disney characters in Space Scenes. Multicoloured.

524	½ c. Type **118**	10	10
525	1 c. Donald Duck being towed by rocket (horiz)	10	10
526	2 c. Minnie Mouse on Moon	10	10
527	3 c. Goofy hitching lift to Mars	10	10
528	4 c. Goofy and Moondog (horiz)	10	10
529	5 c. Pluto burying bone on Moon (horiz)	10	10
530	10 c. Donald Duck and love-sick Martian (horiz)	10	10
531	$2 Donald Duck paddling spaceship (horiz)	1·75	1·00
532	$2.50 Mickey Mouse driving moonbuggy (horiz)	2·00	1·10

119 Queen Elizabeth the Queen Mother

1980. 80th Birthday of The Queen Mother.

534	**119** 10 c. multicoloured	15	10
535	$2.50 multicoloured	35	1·00

120 Hawker Siddeley H.S.748

1980. Transport. Multicoloured.

537	5 c. Type **120**	30	30
538	10 c. Douglas DC-10-30 airliner	65	20
539	15 c. Local bus	35	30
540	20 c. Refrigerated freighter	35	30
541	25 c. Britten Norman Islander aircraft	65	20
542	30 c. "Charles" (pilot boat)	40	40
543	50 c. Boeing 727-200 airliner	1·00	60
544	75 c. "Cunard Countess" (liner)	65	1·00
545	$1 Lockheed TriStar 500 airliner	85	1·10
546	$2 Cargo liner	1·25	2·00
547	$5 Boeing 707-420 airliner	4·50	6·00
548	$10 "Queen Elizabeth 2" (liner)	5·00	8·00

121 Shot-putting

122 Coastal Landscape within Cogwheel

1980. Olympic Games, Moscow. Mult.

549	10 c. Type **121**	10	10
550	50 c. Swimming	20	10
551	$2 Gymnastics	70	50
552	$2.50 Weightlifting	80	60

1980. 75th Anniv of Rotary International. Different coastal landscapes within cogwheel.

554	**122** 10 c. multicoloured	10	10
555	– 50 c. multicoloured	15	10
556	– $2 black, red and yellow	40	40
557	– $2.50 multicoloured	50	55

123 Sir Arthur Lewis

125 "The Nativity" (Giovanni Battista)

1980. Nobel Prize Winners. Multicoloured.

559	10 c. Type **123**	10	10
560	50 c. Martin Luther King Jnr.	20	15
561	$2 Ralph Bunche	50	60
562	$2.50 Albert Schweitzer	70	80

1980. Hurricane Relief. Nos. 538/9 and 542 surch **$1.50 1980 HURRICANE RELIEF.**

564	$1.50 on 15 c. multicoloured	30	40
565	$1.50 on 20 c. multicoloured	30	40
566	$1.50 on 50 c. multicoloured	30	40

1980. Christmas. Paintings. Multicoloured.

567	10 c. Type **125**	10	10
568	30 c. "Adoration of the Kings" (Pieter the Elder)	10	10
569	$2 "Adoration of the Shepherds" (ascribed to Murillo)	40	60

126 Brazilian Agouti

127 Prince Charles at Balmoral

1981. Wildlife. Multicoloured.

571	10 c. Type **126**	15	10
572	50 c. St. Lucia amazon	1·00	20
573	$2 Purple-throated carib	1·75	80
574	$2.50 Fiddler crab	1·25	1·00

1981. Royal Wedding. Multicoloured.

576	25 c. Prince Charles and Lady Diana Spencer	10	10
577	50 c. Clarence House	10	10
578	$4 Type **127**	40	55

128 Lady Diana Spencer

129 "The Cock"

1981. Royal Wedding. Mult. Self-adhesive.

580	50 c. Type **128**	15	30
581	$2 Prince Charles	30	60
582	$5 Prince Charles and Lady Diana Spencer	1·25	1·75

1981. Birth Bicentenary of Picasso. Mult.

583	30 c. Type **129**	25	10
584	50 c. "Man with an Ice-cream"	35	10
585	55 c. "Woman dressing her Hair"	35	10
586	$3 "Seated Woman"	95	85

130 "Industry"

131 Louis Braille

1981. 25th Anniv of Duke of Edinburgh Award Scheme. Multicoloured.

588	10 c. Type **130**	10	10
589	35 c. "Community service"	15	10
590	50 c. "Physical recreation"	15	10
591	$2.50 Duke of Edinburgh speaking at Caribbean Conference, 1975	45	70

1981. International Year for Disabled People. Famous Disabled People. Multicoloured.

592	10 c. Type **131**	10	10
593	50 c. Sarah Bernhardt	20	10
594	$2 Joseph Pulitzer	60	70
595	$2.50 Henri de Toulouse-Lautrec	65	85

132 "Portrait of Fanny Travis Cochran" (Cecilia Beaux)

133 "Adoration of the Magi" (Sfoza)

1981. Decade for Women. Paintings. Mult.

597	10 c. Type **132**	10	10
598	50 c. "Women with Dove" (Marie Laurencin)	20	10
599	$2 "Portrait of a Young Pupil of David" (Aimee Duvivier)	60	70
600	$2.50 "Self-portrait" (Rosalba Carriera)	65	85

1981. Christmas. Paintings. Multicoloured.

602	10 c. Type **133**	10	10
603	30 c. "The Adoration of the Kings" (Orcanga)	20	10
604	$1.50 "The Adoration of the Kings" (Gerard)	45	50
605	$2.50 "The Adoration of the Kings" (Foppa)	75	85

134 1860 1d. Stamp

1981. 1st Anniv of U.P.U. Membership. Mult.

606	10 c. Type **134**	20	10
607	30 c. 1969 First Anniversary of Caribbean Free Trade Area 25 c. commemorative	40	10
608	50 c. 1979 Independence $2 commemorative	45	50
609	$2 U.P.U. emblem with U.P.U. and St. Lucia flags	95	2·25

135 Scene from Football Match

1982. World Cup Football Championship, Spain.

611	**135** 10 c. multicoloured	35	10
612	– 50 c. multicoloured	90	15
613	– $2 multicoloured	1·50	90
614	– $2.50 multicoloured	1·75	1·00

DESIGNS: 50 c. to $2.50, Scenes from different matches.

136 Pigeon Island National Park

1982. Bicent of Battle of the Saints. Mult.

616	10 c. Type **136**	25	15
617	35 c. Battle scene	80	15
618	50 c. Rodney (English admiral) and De Grasse (French admiral)	1·10	65
619	$2.50 Map of the Saints, Martinique and St. Lucia	3·25	4·50

137 Map-reading

138 Leeds Castle

1982. 75th Anniv of Boy Scout Movement. Multicoloured.

621	10 c. Type **137**	10	10
622	50 c. First Aid practice	30	15
623	$1.50 Camping	75	80
624	$2.50 Campfire singsong	1·25	1·50

1982. 21st Birthday of Princess of Wales. Mult.

625	50 c. Type **138**	30	20
626	$2 Princess Diana boarding aircraft	1·75	75
627	$4 Wedding	2·00	1·40

139 "Adoration of the Kings" (detail, Jan Brueghel)

141 Crown Agents Headquarters, Millbank, London

140 The Pitons

1982. Christmas. Multicoloured.
629 10 c. Type **139** 10 10
630 30 c. "Nativity" (Lorenzo Costa) 15 10
631 50 c. "Virgin and Child" (Fra Filippo Lippi) 25 15
632 80 c. "Adoration of the Shepherds" (Nicolas Poussin) 40 55

1983. Commonwealth Day. Multicoloured.
633 10 c. Type **140** 10 10
634 30 c. Tourist beach 15 10
635 50 c. Banana harvesting . . . 20 15
636 $2 Flag of St. Lucia . . . . . 60 1·00

1983. 150th Anniv of Crown Agents. Mult.
637 10 c. Type **141** 10 10
638 15 c. Road construction . . . 10 10
639 50 c. Road network map . . . 20 25
640 $2 First St. Lucia stamp . . . 60 1·25

142 Communications at Sea

1983. World Communications Year. Mult.
641 10 c. Type **142** 15 10
642 50 c. Communications in the air 40 15
643 $1.50 T.V. transmission via satellite 90 75
644 $2.50 Computer communications 1·40 1·25

143 Long-jawed Squirrelfish

1983. Coral Reef Fishes. Multicoloured.
646 10 c. Type **143** 10 10
647 50 c. Banded butterflyfish . . 20 15
648 $1.50 Black-barred soldierfish . 60 85
649 $2.50 Yellow-tailed snapper . . 80 1·40

144 "Duke of Sutherland" (1930)

1983. Leaders of the World. Railway Locomotives (1st series).
651 **144** 35 c. multicoloured . . . 15 20
652 – 35 c. multicoloured . . . 15 20
653 – 35 c. multicoloured . . . 15 20
654 – 35 c. multicoloured . . . 15 20
655 – 50 c. multicoloured . . . 20 30
656 – 50 c. multicoloured . . . 20 30
657 – 50 c. multicoloured . . . 20 30
658 – 50 c. multicoloured . . . 20 30
659 – $1 multicoloured 30 50
660 – $1 multicoloured 30 50
661 – $1 multicoloured 30 50
662 – $1 multicoloured 30 50
663 – $2 multicoloured 40 70
664 – $2 multicoloured 40 70
665 – $2 multicoloured 40 70
666 – $2 multicoloured 40 70

DESIGNS—(The first in each pair shows technical drawings and the second the locomotive at work): Nos. 651/2, "Duke of Sutherland", Great Britain (1930); 653/4, "City of Glasgow", Great Britain (1940); 655/6, "Lord Nelson", Great Britain (1926); 657/8, "Leeds United", Great Britain (1928); 659/60, "Bodmin", Great Britain (1945); 661/2, "Eton", Great Britain (1930); 663/4, "Flying Scotsman", Great Britain (1923); 665/6, "Rocket", Great Britain (1829).

See also Nos. 715/26, 761/76, 824/31 and 858/73.

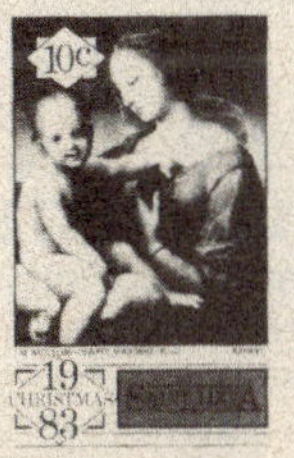

145 "The Niccolini-Cowper Madonna"

146 George III

1983. Christmas. 500th Birth Anniv of Raphael. Multicoloured.
667 10 c. Type **145** 10 10
668 30 c. "The Holy Family with a Palm Tree" 15 10
669 50 c. "The Sistine Madonna" 20 30
670 $5 "The Alba Madonna" . . 1·00 3·25

1984. Leaders of the World. British Monarchs. Multicoloured.
671 5 c. Battle of Waterloo . . . 10 10
672 5 c. Type **146** 10 10
673 10 c. George III at Kew . . . 10 10
674 10 c. Kew Palace 10 10
675 35 c. Coat of Arms of Elizabeth I 10 20
676 35 c. Elizabeth I 10 20
677 60 c. Coat of Arms of George III 15 30
678 60 c. George III (different) . 15 30
679 $1 Elizabeth I at Hatfield . . 15 35
680 $1 Hatfield Palace 15 35
681 $2.50 Spanish Armada . . . 30 60
682 $2.50 Elizabeth I (different) . 30 60

147 Clarke & Co's Drug Store

1984. Historic Buildings. Multicoloured.
683 10 c. Type **147** 10 10
684 45 c. Colonial architecture (horiz) 30 25
685 65 c. Colonial "chattel" house (horiz) 45 35
686 $2.50 Treasury after 1906 earthquake (horiz) . . . . 1·75 1·60

148 Logwood

1984. Forestry Resources. Multicoloured.
699 10 c. Type **148** 10 10
700 45 c. Calabash 30 30
701 65 c. Gommier (vert) 35 55
702 $2.50 Raintree . . . . 60 2·75

149 Bugatti Type "57SC Atlantic Coupe"

1984. Leaders of the World. Automobiles (1st series). The first in each pair showing technical drawings and the second paintings.
703 **149** 5 c. black, lilac & yellow 10 10
704 – 5 c. multicoloured . . . 10 10
705 – 10 c. black, blue and red 10 10
706 – 10 c. multicoloured . . . 10 10
707 – $1 black, green and brown 15 25
708 – $1 multicoloured 15 25
709 – $2.50 black, pink and blue 30 40
710 – $2.50 multicoloured . . . 30 40

DESIGNS: Nos. 703/4, Bugatti Type "57SC Atlantic Coupe"; 705/6, Chevrolet "Bel Air Convertible"; 707/8, Alfa Romeo "1750 GS (Zagato)"; 709/10, Duesenberg "SJ Roadster".

See also Nos. 745/60, 789/96 and 902/13.

150 Pygmy Gecko

1984. Endangered Wildlife. Multicoloured.
711 10 c. Type **150** 30 10
712 45 c. Maria Island ground lizard 70 50
713 65 c. Green iguana 75 85
714 $2.50 Couresse snake . . . . 1·60 3·50

1984. Leaders of the World. Railway Locomotives (2nd series). As T **144**, the first in each pair showing technical drawings and the second the locomotive at work.
715 1 c. multicoloured 10 10
716 1 c. multicoloured 10 10
717 15 c. multicoloured 10 15
718 15 c. multicoloured 10 15
719 50 c. multicoloured 15 20
720 50 c. multicoloured 15 20
721 75 c. multicoloured 15 25
722 75 c. multicoloured 15 25
723 $1 multicoloured 20 30
724 $1 multicoloured 20 30
725 $2 multicoloured 25 50
726 $2 multicoloured 25 50

DESIGNS: Nos. 715/16, "Taw", Great Britain (1897); 717/18, Class Be 6/8 "Crocodile" electric locomotive, Switzerland (1920); 719/20, "The Countess", Great Britain (1903); 721/2, Class GE 6/6 electric locomotive, Switzerland (1921); 723/4, Class P8, Germany (1906); 725/6, "Adler", Germany (1835).

151 Men's Volleyball

152 Glass of Wine and Flowers

1984. Leaders of the World. Olympic Games, Los Angeles. Multicoloured.
727 5 c. Type **151** 10 10
728 5 c. Women's volleyball . . . 10 10
729 10 c. Women's hurdles . . . 10 10
730 10 c. Men's hurdles 10 10
731 65 c. Show jumping 15 20
732 65 c. Dressage 15 20
733 $2.50 Women's gymnastics . . 40 50
734 $2.50 Men's gymnastics . . . 40 50

1984. Christmas. Multicoloured.
735 10 c. Type **152** 10 10
736 35 c. Priest and decorated altar 10 10
737 65 c. Nativity scene 15 25
738 $3 Holy Family . . . . 50 1·50

153 Slaves preparing Manioc

154 Girl Guide Badge in Shield and Crest of St. Lucia

1984. 150th Anniv of Abolition of Slavery. Each black and brown.
740 10 c. Type **153** 10 10
741 35 c. Sifting and cooking cassava flour 10 10
742 55 c. Cooking pot, and preparing tobacco 10 20
743 $5 Stripping tobacco leaves for twist tobacco . . . . . . 55 1·50

1984. Leaders of the World. Automobiles (2nd series). As T **149**, the first in each pair showing technical drawings and the second paintings.
745 10 c. black, green and brown . 10 10
746 10 c. multicoloured 10 10
747 30 c. black, blue and green . . 15 15
748 30 c. multicoloured 15 15
749 55 c. black, yellow and brown . 20 30
750 55 c. multicoloured 20 30
751 65 c. black, grey and lilac . . . 20 35
752 65 c. multicoloured 20 35
753 75 c. black, brown and red . . 20 35
754 75 c. multicoloured 20 35
755 $1 black, brown and blue . . . 20 40
756 $1 multicoloured 20 40
757 $2 black, green and red 25 50
758 $2 multicoloured 25 50
759 $3 black, brown and red . . . 30 60
760 $3 multicoloured 30 60

DESIGNS: Nos. 745/6, Panhard and Levassor; 747/8, N.S.U. "RO-80" Saloon; 749/50, Abarth "Bialbero"; 751/2, TVR "Vixen 2500M"; 753/4, Ford "Mustang" Convertible; 755/6, Ford "Model T"; 757/8, Aston Martin "DB3S"; 759/60, Chrysler "Imperial CG Dual Cowl" Phaeton.

1985. Leaders of the World. Railway Locomotives (3rd series). As T **144**, the first in each pair showing technical drawings and the second the locomotive at work.
761 5 c. multicoloured 10 10
762 5 c. multicoloured 10 10
763 15 c. multicoloured 10 15
764 15 c. multicoloured 10 15
765 35 c. multicoloured 15 15
766 35 c. multicoloured 15 15
767 60 c. multicoloured 15 15
768 60 c. multicoloured 15 15
769 75 c. multicoloured 15 20
770 75 c. multicoloured 15 20
771 $1 multicoloured 15 20
772 $1 multicoloured 15 20
773 $2 multicoloured 25 40
774 $2 multicoloured 25 40
775 $2.50 multicoloured 30 55
776 $2.50 multicoloured 30 55

DESIGNS: Nos. 761/2, Class C53, Japan (1928); 763/4, Class L No. 39, India (1885); 765/6, Class B18¼, Australia (1926); 767/8, "Owain Glyndwr", Great Britain (1923); 769/70, "Lion", Great Britain (1838); 771/2, LNWR locomotive, Great Britain (1873); 773/4, Class Q6 No. 2238, Great Britain (1921); 775/6, Class H No. 106, Great Britain (1920).

1985. 75th Anniv of Girl Guide Movement and 60th Anniv of Guiding in St. Lucia.
777 **154** 10 c. multicoloured . . . 30 10
778 35 c. multicoloured . . . 1·00 15
779 65 c. multicoloured . . . 1·50 65
780 $3 multicoloured . . . . 3·75 4·50

155 "Clossiana selene"

156 Grenadier, 70th Regiment, c. 1775

1985. Leaders of the World. Butterflies. Mult.
781 15 c. Type **155** 10 10
782 15 c. "Inachis io" 10 10
783 40 c. "Philaethria dido" . . . 10 15
784 40 c. "Callicore sorana" . . . 10 15
785 60 c. "Kallima inachus" . . . 15 15
786 60 c. "Hypanartia paullus" . . 15 15
787 $2.25 "Morpho helena" . . . 25 50
788 $2.25 "Ornithoptera meridionalis" 25 50

1985. Leaders of the World. Automobiles (3rd series). As T **149**, the first in each pair showing technical drawings and the second paintings.
789 15 c. black, blue and red . . . 10 10
790 15 c. multicoloured 10 10
791 50 c. black, orange and red . . 15 20
792 50 c. multicoloured 15 20
793 $1 black, green and orange . . 15 20
794 $1 multicoloured 15 20
795 $1.50 black, green and brown . 20 35
796 $1.50 multicoloured 20 35

DESIGNS: 789/90, Hudson "Eight" (1940); 791/2, KdF (1937); 793/4, Kissel "Goldbug" (1925); 795/6, Ferrari "246 GTS" (1973).

1985. Military Uniforms. Multicoloured.
928 5 c. Type **156** 20 30
798 10 c. Officer, Grenadier Company, 14th Regiment, 1780 . . . . 25 15
930 15 c. Private, Battalion Company, 2nd West India Regiment, 1803 . . . . . 35 35
799 20 c. Officer, Battalion Company, 46th Regiment, 1781 . . . . 40 30
800 25 c. Officer, Royal Artillery, c. 1782 . . . . 40 15
801 30 c. Officer, Royal Engineers, 1782 . . . . 60 30
802 35 c. Officer, Battalion Company, 54th Regiment, 1782 . . . . 50 20
935 45 c. Private, Grenadier Company, 14th Regiment, 1782 . . . . 50 50
936 50 c. Gunner, Royal Artillery, 1796 . . . . 60 60
937 60 c. Officer, Battalion Company, 5th Regiment, 1778 70 70
805 65 c. Private, Battalion Company, 85th Regiment, c. 1796 . . . . 70 55
806 75 c. Private, Battalion Company, 76th Regiment, c. 1796 . . . . 75 80
940 80 c. Officer, Battalion Company, 27th Regiment, c. 1780 . . . . 90 90
807 90 c. Private, Battalion Company, 81st Regiment, c. 1796 . . . . 85 90
808 $1 Sergeant, 74th (Highland) Regiment, 1796 . . . . . 90 90
943 $2.50 Private, Light Company, 93rd Regiment, 1803 . . 3·00 4·50
944 $5 Private, Battalion Company, 1st West India Regiment, 1803 3·75 9·00
811 $15 Officer, Royal Artillery, 1850 11·00 18·00
946 $20 Private, Grenadier Company, 46th Regiment, 1778 . . . . 17·00 24·00

157 Messerschmitt Bf 109E

1985. Leaders of the World. Military Aircraft. The first in each pair shows paintings and the second technical drawings.
812 **157** 5 c. multicoloured 10 15
813 – 5 c. black, blue and yellow 10 15
814 – 55 c. multicoloured . . . 25 40
815 – 55 c. black, blue & yellow 25 40
816 – 60 c. multicoloured . . . 25 40
817 – 60 c. black, blue & yellow 25 40
818 – $2 multicoloured 40 75
819 – $2 black, blue and yellow 40 75

DESIGNS: Nos. 812/13, Messerschmitt Bf 109E; 814/15, Avro Lancaster Type 683 Mk I; 816/17, North American P-51D Mustang; 818/19, Supermarine Spitfire Mk II.

158 Magnificent Frigate Birds, Frigate Island Bird Sanctuary

1985. Nature Reserves. Multicoloured.
820 10 c. Type **158** 35 20
821 35 c. Mangrove cuckoo, Scorpion Island, Savannes Bay 65 45
822 65 c. Lesser yellowlegs, Maria Island Reserve 75 85
823 $3 Audubon's shearwaters, Lapins Island Reserve . . . 1·00 5·00

1985. Leaders of the World Railway Locomotives (4th series). As T **144**. The first in each pair shows technical drawings and the second the locomotive at work.
824 10 c. multicoloured 10 10
825 10 c. multicoloured 10 10
826 30 c. multicoloured 15 15
827 30 c. multicoloured 15 15
828 75 c. multicoloured 20 20
829 75 c. multicoloured 20 20
830 $2.50 multicoloured 40 55
831 $2.50 multicoloured 40 55
DESIGNS: Nos. 824/5, Tank locomotive No. 28, Great Britain (1897); 826/7, Class M No. 1621, Great Britain (1893); 828/9, Class "Dunalastair", Great Britain (1896); 830/1, "Big Bertha" type No. 2290, Great Britain (1919).

159 Queen Elizabeth the Queen Mother

160 "Youth playing Banjo" (Wayne Whitfield)

1985. Leaders of the World. Life and Times of Queen Elizabeth the Queen Mother. Various portraits.
832 **159** 40 c. multicoloured . . . 10 20
833 – 40 c. multicoloured . . . 10 20
834 – 75 c. multicoloured . . . 10 25
835 – 75 c. multicoloured . . . 10 25
836 – $1.10 multicoloured . . . 15 35
837 – $1.10 multicoloured . . . 15 35
838 – $1.75 multicoloured . . . 20 55
839 – $1.75 multicoloured . . . 20 55
Each value was issued in pairs showing a floral pattern across the bottom of the portraits which stops short of the left-hand edge on the first stamp and of the right-hand edge on the second.

1985. International Youth Year. Paintings by Young St. Lucians.
841 **160** 10 c. black, blue & mauve 10 10
842 – 45 c. multicoloured . . . 30 25
843 – 75 c. multicoloured . . . 50 50
844 – $3.50 multicoloured . . . 2·00 3·00
DESIGNS—VERT (as T **160**): 45 c. "Motorcyclist" (Mark Maragh); 75 c. "Boy and Girl at Pitons" (Bartholomew Eugene); $3.50, "Abstract" (Lyndon Samuel). HORIZ (80 × 55 mm): $5 Young people and St. Lucia landscapes.

1985. Royal Visit. Nos. 649, 685/6, 702, 713, 778 and 836/7 optd **CARIBBEAN ROYAL VISIT 1985**.
846 **154** 35 c. multicoloured . . . 4·50 2·75
847 – 65 c. mult (No. 685) . . . 1·00 2·50
848 – 65 c. mult (No. 713) . . . 4·00 3·50
849 – $1.10 mult (No. 836) . . . 4·75 7·00
850 – $1.10 mult (No. 837) . . . 4·75 7·00
851 – $2.50 mult (No. 649) . . . 5·50 7·00
852 – $2.50 mult (No. 686) . . . 1·00 2·75
853 – $2.50 mult (No. 702) . . . 1·00 2·75

161 "Papa Jab"

1985. Christmas. Masqueraders. Mult.
854 10 c. Type **161** 15 10
855 45 c. "Paille Bananne" 25 25
856 65 c. "Cheval Bois" 30 75

1986. Leaders of the World. Railway Locomotives (5th series). As T **144**. The first in each pair shows technical drawings and the second the locomotive at work.
858 5 c. multicoloured 10 15
859 5 c. multicoloured 10 15
860 15 c. multicoloured 15 15
861 15 c. multicoloured 15 15
862 30 c. multicoloured 20 30
863 30 c. multicoloured 20 30
864 60 c. multicoloured 25 40
865 60 c. multicoloured 25 40
866 75 c. multicoloured 30 50
867 75 c. multicoloured 30 50
868 $1 multicoloured 35 60
869 $1 multicoloured 35 60
870 $2.25 multicoloured 45 80
871 $2.25 multicoloured 45 80
872 $3 multicoloured 45 80
873 $3 multicoloured 45 80
DESIGNS: Nos. 858/9, Cog locomotive "Tip Top", U.S.A. (1983); 860/1, Electric locomotive "Stephenson", Great Britain (1975); 862/3, Class D No. 737, Great Britain (1901); 864/5, No. 13 Class electric locomotive, Great Britain (1922); 866/7, Electric locomotive "Electra", Great Britain (1954); 868/9, "City of Newcastle", Great Britain (1922); 870/1, Von Kruckenburg propeller-driven railcar, Germany (1930); 872/3, No. 860, Japan (1893).

1986. 60th Birthday of Queen Elizabeth II (1st issue). As T **167** of British Virgin Islands. Multicoloured.
876 5 c. Queen Elizabeth II . . . 10 10
877 $1 Princess Elizabeth 15 30
878 $3.50 Queen Elizabeth II (different) 40 90
879 $6 In Canberra, 1982 (vert) . 55 1·40

163 Queen Elizabeth and Marian Home

1986. 60th Birthday of Queen Elizabeth II (2nd issue). Multicoloured.
881 10 c. Type **163** 25 15
882 45 c. Queen addressing rally, Mindoo Phillip Park, 1985 . 55 35
883 50 c. Queen opening Leon Hess Comprehensive School, 1985 65 50
884 $5 Queen Elizabeth and Government House, Castries 2·50 4·00

164 Pope John Paul II kissing Ground, Castries Airport

1986. Visit of Pope John Paul II. Multicoloured.
886 55 c. Type **164** 70 70
887 60 c. Pope and St. Joseph's Convent 70 80
888 80 c. Pope and Castries Catholic Cathedral (vert) . . . . . 1·10 1·60

1986. Royal Wedding (1st issue). As T **168** of British Virgin Islands. Multicoloured.
890 80 c. Miss Sarah Ferguson . . 45 65
891 80 c. Prince Andrew 45 65
892 $2 Prince Andrew and Miss Sarah Ferguson (horiz) . . 70 1·60
893 $2 Prince Andrew with Mrs. Nancy Reagan (horiz) . . . 70 1·60
See also Nos. 897/900.

165 Peace Corps Teacher with Students

1986. 25th Anniv of United States Peace Corps. Multicoloured.
894 80 c. Type **165** 35 40
895 $2 President John Kennedy (vert) 1·10 1·60
896 $3.50 Peace Corps emblem between arms of St. Lucia and U.S.A. . . . . 1·60 2·50

166 Prince Andrew in Carriage

167 Chak-Chak Band

1986. Royal Wedding (2nd issue). Mult.
897 50 c. Type **166** 40 30
898 80 c. Miss Sarah Ferguson in coach 50 50
899 $1 Duke and Duchess of York at altar 55 60
900 $3 Duke and Duchess of York in carriage . . . . 1·00 2·25

1986. Automobiles (4th series). As T **149**, the first in each pair showing technical drawings and the second paintings.
902 20 c. multicoloured 15 15
903 20 c. multicoloured 15 15
904 50 c. multicoloured 20 20
905 50 c. multicoloured 20 20
906 60 c. multicoloured 20 20
907 60 c. multicoloured 20 20
908 $1 multicoloured 20 20
909 $1 multicoloured 20 20
910 $1.50 multicoloured 20 20
911 $1.50 multicoloured 20 20
912 $3 multicoloured 30 45
913 $3 multicoloured 30 45
DESIGNS: Nos. 902/3, AMC "AMX" (1969); 904/5, Russo-Baltique (1912); 906/7, Lincoln "K.B" (1932); 908/9, Rolls-Royce "Phantom II Continental" (1933); 910/11, Buick "Century" (1939); 912/13, Chrysler "300 C" (1957).

1986. Tourism (1st series). Multicoloured.
914 15 c. Type **167** 10 10
915 45 c. Folk dancing 15 15
916 80 c. Steel band 30 50
917 $5 Limbo dancing . . . . . 75 2·25
See also Nos. 988/91.

168 St. Ann Catholic Church, Mon Repos

1986. Christmas. Multicoloured.
919 10 c. Type **168** 10 10
920 40 c. St. Joseph the Worker Catholic Church, Gros Islet . 25 15
921 80 c. Holy Trinity Anglican Church, Castries 35 60
922 $4 Our Lady of the Assumption Catholic Church, Soufriere (vert) . . . . 85 2·50

169 Outline Map of St. Lucia

170 Statue of Liberty and Flags of France and U.S.A.

1987.
924B **169** 5 c. black and brown . 20 20
925A 10 c. black and green . 20 20
926A 45 c. black and orange 50 50
927B 50 c. black and blue . 50 50
927cA $1 black and red . . . 75 75

1987. Cent of Statue of Liberty (1986). Mult.
947 15 c. Type **170** 15 10
948 80 c. Statue and "Mauretania I" (liner) 75 55
949 $1 Statue and Concorde . . . 1·75 1·00
950 $5 Statue and flying boat at sunset . . . . 2·25 4·25

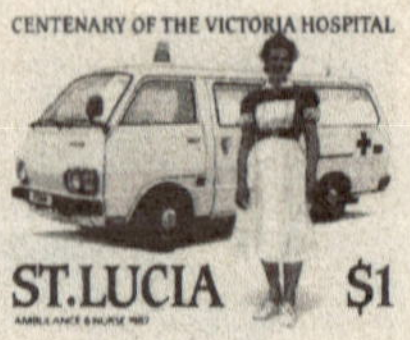

171 First Cadastral Survey Map and Surveying Instruments, 1775

172 Ambulance and Nurse, 1987

1987. New Cadastral Survey of St. Lucia. Multicoloured.
955 15 c. Type **171** 60 15
956 60 c. Map and surveying instruments, 1814 . . . . 1·25 85
957 $1 Map and surveying instruments, 1888 . . . . . 1·50 1·50
958 $2.50 Cadastral survey map and surveying instruments, 1987 . 2·75 4·00

1987. Cent of Victoria Hospital, Castries. Mult.
959 **172** $1 multicoloured . . . . . 1·75 2·00
960 – $1 blue . . . . 1·75 2·00
961 – $2 multicoloured . . . . . 2·25 2·50
962 – $2 blue . . . . 2·25 2·50
DESIGNS: No. 960, Nurse and carrying hammock, 1913; 961, $2 Victoria Hospital, 1987; 962, Victoria Hospital 1887.

173 "The Holy Family"

174 St. Lucia Amazon perched on Branch

1987. Christmas. Paintings. Multicoloured.
964 15 c. Type **173** 30 10
965 50 c. "Adoration of the Shepherds" 60 30
966 60 c. "Adoration of the Magi" 60 80
967 90 c. "Madonna and Child" . 85 2·00

1987. St. Lucia Amazon. Multicoloured.
969 15 c. Type **174** . . . . . . 1·75 40
970 35 c. Pair in flight . . . . . 2·75 55
971 50 c. Perched on branch (rear view) . . . . 3·75 2·25
972 $1 Emerging from tree . . . . 5·00 5·00

175 Carib Clay Zemi

1988. Amerindian Artifacts. Multicoloured.
973 25 c. Type **175** 15 10
974 30 c. Troumassee cylinder . . 20 15
975 80 c. Three pointer stone . . 45 45
976 $3.50 Dauphine petroglyph . 1·75 3·50

176 East Caribbean Currency

1988. 50th Anniv of St. Lucia Co-operative Bank. Multicoloured.
977 10 c. Type **176** 20 10
978 45 c. Castries branch 55 35
979 60 c. As 45 c. 75 95
980 80 c. Vieux Fort branch . . . 1·25 1·60

177 Rural Telephone Exchange

1988. 50th Anniv of Cable and Wireless (West Indies) Ltd. Multicoloured.
981 15 c. Type **177** 10 10
982 25 c. Early and modern telephones 15 15
983 80 c. St. Lucia Teleport dish aerial 40 45
984 $2.50 Map showing Eastern Caribbean Microwave System 1·00 1·60

178 Stained Glass Window

1988. Cent of Methodist Church in St. Lucia. Mult.
985 15 c. Type **178** 10 10
986 80 c. Church interior 40 45
987 $3.50 Methodist Church, Castries . . . . 1·50 2·25

MORE DETAILED LISTS
are given in the Stanley Gibbons Catalogues referred to in the country headings.
For lists of current volumes see Introduction.

179 Garnished Lobsters

1988. Tourism (2nd series). Designs showing local delicacies. Multicoloured.
988 10 c. Type **179** 55 65
989 30 c. Cocktail and tourists at buffet 65 75
990 80 c. Fresh fruits and roasted breadfruit . . . . 1·10 1·25
991 $2.50 Barbecued red snappers (fish) . . . . 2·25 2·50
Nos. 988/91 were printed together, se-tenant, forming a composite design of tourists at beach barbecue.

1988. 300th Anniv of Lloyd's of London. As T **123** of Ascension.
1004 10 c. black, lilac and brown . . 45 15
1005 60 c. multicoloured . . . . . 1·25 75
1006 80 c. multicoloured . . . . . 1·60 1·25
1007 $2.50 multicoloured . . . . . 3·00 4·50
DESIGNS—VERT: 10 c. San Francisco earthquake, 1906; $2.50, Castries fire, 1948. HORIZ: 60 c. Castries Harbour; 80 c. "Lady Nelson" (hospital ship), 1942.

180 Snow on the Mountain

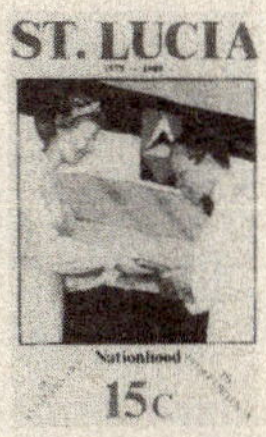

181 Princess Alexandra presenting Constitution.

1988. Christmas. Flowers. Multicoloured.
1008 15 c. Type **180** 30 10
1009 45 c. Christmas candle . . . 55 50
1010 60 c. Balisier 70 90
1011 80 c. Poinsettia . . . . 1·00 1·60

1989. 10th Anniv of Independence. Mult.
1013 15 c. Type **181** 30 10
1014 80 c. Geothermal well . . . . 1·00 60
1015 $1 Sir Arthur Lewis Community College 70 60
1016 $2.50 Pointe Seraphine shopping centre . . . . . 1·10 2·00

182 "Gerronema citrinum"

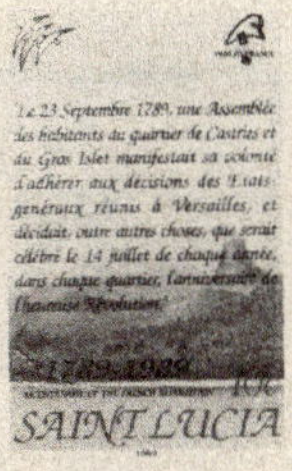

183 Local Revolutionary Declaration, 1789 and View of St. Lucia

1989. Fungi. Multicoloured.
1022 15 c. Type **182** . . . . . . 1·00 30
1023 25 c. "Lepiota spiculata" . . . 1·25 30
1024 50 c. "Calocybe cyanocephala" 2·00 1·10
1025 $5 "Russula puiggarii" . . . 7·00 9·50

1989. Bicentenary of the French Revolution. Designs include the "PHILEXFRANCE". International Stamp Exhibition logo. Mult.
1026 10 c. Type **183** 25 15
1027 60 c. Hoisting Revolutionary flag, Morne Fortune, 1791 (horiz) . . . . 1·50 80
1028 $1 Declaration of Rights of Man and view of St. Lucia 1·75 1·50
1029 $3.50 Arrival of Capt. La Crosse, Gros Islet, 1792 (horiz) . . . . 6·00 7·50

184 Red Cross Headquarters, St. Lucia

1989. 125th Anniv of Int Red Cross. Mult.
1030 50 c. Type **184** . . . . . . 1·25 1·25
1031 80 c. Red Cross seminar, Castries, 1987 . . . . . 1·75 2·00
1032 $1 Red Cross ambulance . . 2·00 2·25

185 Christmas Lantern

186 Gwi Gwi

1989. Christmas.
1033 **185** 10 c. multicoloured . . 25 10
1034 – 50 c. multicoloured . . 65 40
1035 – 90 c. multicoloured . . 1·00 1·25
1036 – $1 multicoloured . . . . 1·25 1·25
DESIGNS: 50 c. to $1 various decorative "building" lanterns.

1990. Endangered Trees. Multicoloured.
1081 10 c. Chinna 10 10
1082 15 c. Latanier 15 15
1039 20 c. Type **186** 45 45
1084 25 c. L'encens 20 20
1085 50 c. Bois lele 30 30
1042 80 c. Bois d'amande 70 40
1043 95 c. Mahot piman grand bois 75 65
1044 $1 Balata 75 65
1045 $1.50 Pencil cedar . . . . . 1·50 1·75
1046 $2.50 Bois cendre . . . . . 2·00 2·50
1047 $5 Lowye cannelle . . . . . 3·00 3·75
1048 $25 Chalantier grand bois . 13·00 16·00

187 Father Tapon and Original College Building

1990. International Literacy Year. Centenary of St. Mary's College, Castries. Multicoloured.
1049 30 c. Type **187** 15 15
1050 45 c. Brother M. C. Collins and St. Mary's College 25 25
1051 75 c. Literacy class 45 55
1052 $2 Children approaching "door to knowledge" . . . . . . 1·50 2·00

1990. 90th Birthday of Queen Elizabeth the Queen Mother. As T **134** of Ascension.
1053 50 c. multicoloured 35 35
1054 $5 black and blue . . . . 2·75 3·50
DESIGNS—(21 × 36 mm): 50 c. Crowning of Queen Consort, 1937. (29 × 37 mm): $5 Queen Elizabeth arriving at New Theatre, London 1949.

1990. "EXPO 90" International Garden and Greenery Exhibition, Osaka. No. 1047 optd **EXPO '90** and emblem.
1055 $5 Lowye cannelle . . . . . 2·75 3·50

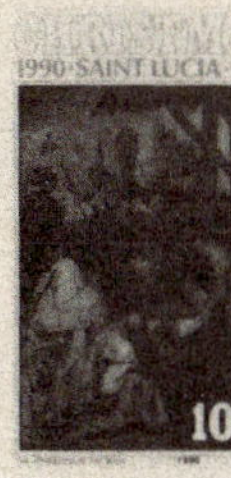

189 "Adoration of the Magi" (Rubens)

191 "Battus polydamas"

190 "Vistafjord" (liner)

1990. Christmas. Religious Paintings. Mult.
1056 10 c. Type **189** 30 10
1057 30 c. "Adoration of the Shepherds" (Murillo) . . 70 15
1058 80 c. "Adoration of the Magi" (Rubens) (different) . . . 1·75 75
1059 $5 "Adoration of the Shepherds" (Philippe de Champaigne) . . . . . . 5·00 6·50

1991. Cruise Ships. Multicoloured.
1060 50 c. Type **190** . . . . . . 1·25 30
1061 80 c. "Windstar" (schooner) 1·75 1·10
1062 $1 "Unicorn" (brig) . . . . 2·00 1·50
1063 $2.50 Game-fishing launch . 4·50 6·50

1991. Butterflies. Multicoloured.
1065 60 c. Type **191** . . . . . . 1·75 65
1066 80 c. "Strymon simaethis" . . 2·00 1·10
1067 $1 "Mestra cana" . . . . . 2·50 1·25
1068 $2.50 "Allosmaitia piplea" . . 5·00 6·50

192 Mural, Jacmel Church

1991. Christmas. Paintings by Duncan St. Omer. Multicoloured.
1069 10 c. Type **192** 30 10
1070 15 c. "Red Madonna" (vert) . 40 10
1071 80 c. Mural, Monchy Church 1·50 70
1072 $5 "Blue Madonna" (vert) . . 4·50 6·50

193 Yacht and Map

1991. Atlantic Rally for Cruising Yachts. Multicoloured.
1073 60 c. Type **193** . . . . . . 1·50 1·50
1074 80 c. Yachts off St. Lucia . . 1·75 1·75

1992. Organization of East Caribbean States. 500th Anniv of Discovery of America by Columbus. As T **66** of St. Kitts. Multicoloured.
1075 $1 Columbus meeting Amerindians . . . . . . 2·00 1·75
1076 $2 Ships approaching island . 2·75 3·25

194 Amerindian Village

1992. Discovery of St. Lucia. Multicoloured.
1077 15 c. Type **194** 40 20
1078 40 c. Ships of Juan de la Cosa and islands, 1499 . . . . 1·50 50
1079 50 c. Columbus sailing between Martinique and St. Lucia, 1502 . . . . 1·60 70
1080 $5 Legendary shipwreck of Gimie . . . . 6·00 8·00

195 "Virgin and Child" (Delaroche)

196 "Death" and Gravestone

1992. Christmas. Religious Paintings. Mult.
1092 10 c. Type **195** 40 20
1093 15 c. "The Holy Family" (Rubens) 40 20
1094 60 c. "Virgin and Child" (Luini) 1·75 1·75
1095 80 c. "Virgin and Child" (Sassoferrato) . . . . . . 2·00 2·00

1993. Anti-drugs Campaign.
1096 **196** $5 multicoloured . . . . 5·50 6·50

197 "Gros Piton from Delcer, Choiseul" (Dunstan St. Omer)

1993. Carib Art. Multicoloured.
1097 20 c. Type **197** 20 10
1098 75 c. "Reduit Bay" (Derek Walcott) 75 75
1099 $5 "Woman and Child at River" (Nancy Cole Auguste) 4·25 5·75

198 "The Madonna of the Rosary" (Murillo)

1993. Christmas. Religious Paintings. Mult.
1100 15 c. Type **198** 15 10
1101 60 c. "The Madonna and Child" (Van Dyck) 55 55
1102 95 c. "The Annunciation" (Champaigne) . . . . . . 80 1·25

199 The Pitons

200 "Euphorbia pulcherrima"

1994. Bicentenary of the Abolition of Slavery in St. Lucia.
1103 **199** 20 c. multicoloured . . . 65 45

1994. Christmas. Flowers. Multicoloured.
1105 20 c. Type **200** 15 10
1106 75 c. "Heliconia rostrata" . . 55 50
1107 95 c. "Alpinia purpurata" . . 75 75
1108 $5.50 "Anthurium andreanum" 3·75 5·50
See also Nos. 1122/5 and 1156/9.

201 18th-century Map of St. Lucia

1995. Bicentenary of Battle of Rabot. Multicoloured.
1109 20 c. Type **201** 15 15
1110 75 c. Insurgent slaves . . . 55 55
1111 95 c. 9th Foot (Royal Norfolk Regiment) attacking . . . 80 1·10

1995. 50th Anniv of End of Second World War. As T **161** of Ascension. Multicoloured.
1113 20 c. St. Lucian members of the A.T.S. 40 15
1114 75 c. German U-boat off St. Lucia . . . . 1·00 80
1115 95 c. Bren gun-carriers of the Caribbean Regiment, North Africa . . . . 1·25 1·25
1116 $1.10 Supermarine Spitfire Mk V "St. Lucia" . . . . . . 1·50 1·75

1995. 50th Anniv of United Nations. As T **284** of Jamaica. Multicoloured.
1118 10 c. Sud Aviation SE 330 Puma helicopter, Cambodia, 1991–93 . . . . 15 10
1119 65 c. Renault lorry, Bosnia, 1995 . . . . 50 50
1120 $1.35 Transall C-160 aircraft, Cambodia, 1991–93 . . . 95 1·40
1121 $5 Douglas DC-3 aircraft, Korea, 1950–54 . . . . . 3·75 5·00

1995. Christmas. Flowers. As T **200**, each including Madonna and Child. Multicoloured.
1122 15 c. "Eranthemum nervosum" 15 10
1123 70 c. Bougainvillea 45 45
1124 $1.10 "Allamanda cathartica" 70 90
1125 $3 "Rosa sinensis" . . . . . 1·75 2·75

202 Calypso King

203 Dry River Bed

1996. Carnival. Multicoloured.
1126 20 c. Type **202** 30 10
1127 65 c. Carnival dancers . . . 75 55
1128 95 c. King of the Band float 1·00 85
1129 $3 Carnival Queen . . . . . 2·50 3·50

1996. Inaug of New Irrigation Project. Mult.
1130 20 c. Type **203** 10 10
1131 65 c. People bathing in stream 40 45
1132 $5 New dam . . . . 3·00 4·00

204 Produce Market

1996. Tourism. Multicoloured.
1133 65 c. Type **204** 45 45
1134 75 c. Horse-riding on beach . 55 55
1135 95 c. Bride and groom . . . 70 75
1136 $5 Jazz band . . . . 2·75 4·00

205 Athlete of 1896

1996. Centenary of Modern Olympic Games. Multicoloured.
1137 15 c. Type **205** 25 35
1138 15 c. Athlete of 1996 . . . . 25 35
1139 75 c. Catamaran and yacht . 80 90
1140 75 c. Sailing dinghies 80 90

Nos. 1137/8 and 1139/40 respectively were printed together, se-tenant, forming composite designs.

206 Spanish Royal Standard, 1502, and Caravel

1996. Flags and Ships. Multicoloured.
1141 10 c. Type **206** 10 10
1142 15 c. Skull and crossbones, 1550, and pirate carrack . 10 10
1143 20 c. Dutch royal standard, 1650, and galleon 10 10
1144 25 c. Union Jack, 1739, and ship of the line 10 15
1145 40 c. French royal standard, 1750, and ship of the line . 15 20
1146 50 c. Martinique and St. Lucia flag, 1766, and French brig 20 25
1147 55 c. White Ensign, 1782, and frigate squadron 25 30
1148 65 c. Red Ensign, 1782, and frigates in action 30 35
1149 75 c. Blue Ensign, 1782, and brig 35 40
1150 95 c. The Tricolour, 1792, and French frigate 40 45
1151 $1 Union Jack, 1801, and West Indies Grand Fleet 45 50
1152 $2.50 Confederate States of America flag, 1861, and cruiser . . . . 1·10 1·25
1153 $5 Canadian flag, 1915–19, and "V & W" class destroyer . 2·10 2·25
1154 $10 United States flag, 1942–48, and "Fletcher" class destroyer . . . . 4·25 4·50
1155 $25 Flag of St. Lucia and cruise liner . . . . 10·50 11·00

1996. Christmas. Flowers. As T **200**, each including Madonna and Child. Multicoloured.
1156 20 c. "Cordia sebestena" . . 15 10
1157 75 c. "Cryptostegia grandiflora" 50 50
1158 95 c. "Hibiscus elatus" . . . 65 65
1159 $5 "Caularthron bicornutum" 3·50 4·25

1997. Golden Wedding of Queen Elizabeth and Prince Philip. As T **87** of Kiribati. Multicoloured.
1160 75 c. Queen Elizabeth at Warwick, 1996 . . . . . . 45 55
1161 75 c. Prince Philip with carriage horses 45 55
1162 95 c. Prince Philip 55 65
1163 95 c. Queen in phaeton at Trooping the Colour . . . 55 65
1164 $1 Queen Elizabeth and Prince Philip at Sandringham, 1982 65 75
1165 $1 Princess Anne show jumping 65 75

Nos. 1160/1, 1162/3 and 1164/5 respectively were printed together, se-tenant, with the backgrounds forming composite designs.

207 "St. George" capsized, 1935

1997. Marine Disasters. Multicoloured.
1167 20 c. Type **207** 30 10
1168 55 c. Wreak of "Belle of Bath" (freighter) 45 30
1169 $1 "Ethelgonda" (freighter) aground on rocks, 1897 . 80 75
1170 $2.50 Hurricane, 1817 . . . 1·75 2·25

208 Attack on Praslin

1997. Bicentenary of the Brigands' War. Mult.
1171 20 c. Type **208** 30 10
1172 55 c. British troops at Battle of Dennery 45 30
1173 70 c. Discussing peace agreement 65 50
1174 $3 Members of 1st West India Regiment . . . . 2·00 2·50

209 "Roseau Church" (detail, Dunstan St. Omer)

1997. Christmas. Paintings by Dunstan St. Omer. Multicoloured.
1175 20 c. Type **209** 20 10
1176 60 c. Altarpiece, Regional Seminary, Trinidad . . . 45 35
1177 95 c. "Our Lady of the Presentation", Trinidad . 60 60
1178 $5 "The Four Days of Creation" . . . . 2·75 3·50

210 Diana, Princess of Wales

212 St. Lucia Oriole

211 Signatories to CARICOM Treaty, 1973

1998. Diana, Princess of Wales Commemoration.
1179 **210** $1 multicoloured 60 65

1998. 25th Anniv of CARICOM. Multicoloured.
1180 20 c. Type **211** 15 10
1181 75 c. Flags of CARICOM and St. Lucia 45 50

1998. Birds. Multicoloured.
1197 70 c. Type **212** 30 35
1198 75 c. Lesser antillean pewee . 35 40
1199 95 c. Bridled quail dove . . 40 45
1200 $1.10 Semper's warbler . . . 50 55

213 "Siproeta stelenes" and Chain

1998. 50th Anniv of Universal Declaration of Human Rights. Butterflies. Multicoloured.
1201 20 c. Type **213** 20 10
1202 65 c. "Pseudolycaena marsyas" and chain 50 40
1203 70 c. "Heliconius melpomene" and rope 50 40
1204 $5 "Phoebis philea" and chain 3·00 3·50

214 "Tabebuia serratifolia"

1998. Christmas. Flowers. Multicoloured.
1205 20 c. Type **214** 10 10
1206 50 c. "Hibiscus sabdariffa" . 25 30
1207 95 c. "Euphorbia leucocephala" 40 45
1208 $2.50 "Calliandra slaneae" . . 1·10 1·25

215 "The Black Prometheus" (wall painting)

1998. 50th Anniv of University of West Indies. Multicoloured.
1209 15 c. Type **215** 10 10
1210 75 c. Sir Arthur Lewis College, St. Lucia 35 40
1211 $5 University arms and the Pitons, St. Lucia . . . . . 2·10 2·25

OFFICIAL STAMPS

1983. Nos. 537/48 optd **OFFICIAL**.
O 1 5 c. Type **120** 15 10
O 2 10 c. Douglas DC-10-30 . . 25 10
O 3 15 c. Local bus 30 15
O 4 20 c. Refrigerated freighter . 40 20
O 5 25 c. Britten Norman Islander aircraft 50 20
O 6 30 c. "Charles" (pilot boat) . 55 25
O 7 50 c. Boeing 727-200 . . . . 70 35
O 8 75 c. "Cunard Countess" (liner) 85 50
O 9 $1 Lockheed TriStar 500 . . 1·25 75
O10 $2 Cargo liner . . . . 1·75 1·75
O11 $5 Boeing 707-420 airliner . . 3·50 3·50
O12 $10 "Queen Elizabeth 2" (liner) 6·50 7·50

1985. Nos. 797/811 optd **OFFICIAL**.
O13 5 c. Type **156** 40 50
O14 10 c. Officer, Grenadier Company, 14th Regiment, 1780 . . . . 40 50
O15 20 c. Officer, Battalion Company, 46th Regiment, 1781 . . . . 40 50
O16 25 c. Officer, Royal Artillery, c. 1782 . . . . 40 50
O17 30 c. Officer, Royal Engineers, 1782 . . . . 50 60
O18 35 c. Officer, Battalion Company, 54th Regiment, 1782 . . . . 50 60
O19 45 c. Private, Grenadier Company, 14th Regiment, 1782 . . . . 60 75
O20 50 c. Gunner, Royal Artillery, 1796 . . . . 60 75
O21 65 c. Private, Battalion Company, 85th Regiment, c. 1796 . . . . 80 1·00
O22 75 c. Private, Battalion Company, 76th Regiment, 1796 . . . . 90 1·50
O23 90 c. Private, Battalion Company, 81st Regiment, c. 1796 . . . . 1·00 1·50
O24 $1 Sergeant 74th (Highland) Regiment, 1796 . . . . . 1·10 1·50
O25 $2.50 Private, Light Company, 93rd Regiment, 1803 . . . 2·50 3·50
O26 $5 Private, Battalion Company, 1st West India Regiment, 1803 . . . . 4·00 3·50
O27 $15 Officer, Royal Artillery, 1850 . . . . 9·00 11·00

1990. Nos. 1081/2, 1039/40, 1085 and 1042/48 optd **OFFICIAL**.
O28 10 c. Chinna 15 10
O29 15 c. Latanier 15 10
O30 20 c. Type **186** 15 10
O31 25 c. L'encens 15 10
O32 50 c. Bois lele 25 30
O33 80 c. Bois d'amande 35 40
O34 95 c. Mahot piman grand bois 45 50
O35 $1 Balata 45 50
O36 $1.50 Pencil cedar 85 90
O37 $2.50 Bois cendre . . . . . 1·40 1·50
O38 $5 Lowye cannelle . . . . . 2·50 2·75
O39 $25 Chalantier grand bois . . 12·00 13·00

POSTAGE DUE STAMPS

D 1

D 2

1930.
D1 D 1 1d. black on blue . . . . 3·75 14·00
D2 2d. black on yellow . . . 11·00 40·00

1933.
D3 D 2 1d. black . . . . 4·25 5·50
D4 2d. black . . . . 15·00 7·50
D5 4d. black . . . . 5·00 30·00
D6 8d. black . . . . 5·00 40·00

D 3

D 4 St. Lucia Coat of Arms

1949.
D 7a D 3 2 c. black . . . . 10 7·00
D 8a 4 c. black . . . . 40 8·50
D 9 8 c. black . . . . 3·25 20·00
D10a 16 c. black . . . . 3·75 45·00

1981.
D13 D 4 5 c. purple 10 45
D17 5 c. red 10 10
D18 15 c. green 10 10
D19 25 c. orange 10 10
D20 $1 blue 45 50

ST. VINCENT

One of the Windward Islands, British West Indies.

1861. 12 pence = 1 shilling; 20 shillings = 1 pound.
1949. 100 cents = 1 West Indian dollar.

7

1

3

1861.

36	**7**	½d. orange	7·00	3·00
47		½d. green	1·00	50
48b	**1**	1d. red	1·60	75
18		1d. black	40·00	7·50
29		1d. olive	£120	3·50
39		1d. drab	40·00	1·75
61		2½d. blue	2·75	1·75
43		4d. blue	£375	20·00
56		4d. yellow	1·60	6·00
51		4d. brown	48·00	75
62		5d. sepia	5·50	18·00
4		6d. green	55·00	18·00
57		6d. violet	2·25	8·50
11		1s. grey	£225	£120
13		1s. blue	£325	90·00
14		1s. brown	£450	£160
45		1s. red	£110	55·00
58		1s. orange	5·50	11·00
53	**3**	5s. red	27·00	50·00

1880. Surch in figures.

33	**1**	½d. on half 6d. green	£160	£160
28		1d. on half 6d. green	£425	£325

1881. Surch in words.

34	**1**	1d. on 6d. green	£400	£275
63		3d. on 1d. mauve	6·00	17·00
60a		5d. on 6d. red	1·00	1·75

1881. Surch in figures.

54	**1**	2½d. on 4d. brown	65·00	90·00
35		4d. on 1s. orange	£1300	£700

1882. Surch in figures and words.

40	**1**	2½d. on 1d. red	11·00	40
55a		2½d. on 1d. blue	1·25	35
59		5d. on 4d. brown	15·00	26·00

1885. No. 40 further surch **1d** and bars.

46	**1**	1d. on 2½d. on 1d. red	20·00	16·00

13

17 Seal of the Colony

1899.

67	**13**	½d. mauve and green	2·50	1·75
68		1d. mauve and red	4·00	90
69		2½d. mauve and blue	4·00	2·00
70		3d. mauve and green	4·00	10·00
71		4d. mauve and orange	4·00	14·00
72		5d. mauve and black	7·00	13·00
73		6d. mauve and brown	13·00	28·00
74		1s. green and red	13·00	48·00
75		5s. green and blue	75·00	£130

1902. As T **13**, but portait of King Edward VII.

85a	½d. purple and green	1·25	80
77	1d. purple and red	3·00	30
78	2d. purple and black	2·00	2·25
79	2½d. purple and blue	4·25	3·25
80	3d. purple and green	3·50	2·50
81	6d. purple and brown	11·00	30·00
90a	1s. green and red	10·00	45·00
83	2s. green and violet	25·00	55·00
91	2s. purple and blue on blue	22·00	42·00
84	5s. green and blue	70·00	£120
92	5s. green and red on yellow	17·00	48·00
93	£1 purple and black on red	£250	£300

1907.

94	**17**	½d. green	2·50	2·00
95		1d. red	3·00	15
96		2d. orange	1·50	6·50
97		2½d. blue	25·00	8·50
98		3d. violet	6·50	15·00

18 Seal of the Colony

19

1909.

102	**18**	½d. green	1·50	50
99		1d. red	1·25	30
104		2d. grey	4·00	8·50
105		2½d. blue	8·00	3·25
106		3d. purple on yellow	2·50	5·00
107		6d. purple	7·00	5·00
101		1s. black on green	3·75	8·50
139		2s. blue and purple	7·00	13·00
140		5s. red and green	17·00	32·00
141		£1 mauve and black	75·00	£120

1913.

108	**19**	½d. green	45	20
109		1d. red	60	25
132b		1½d. brown	2·00	15
133		2d. grey	2·00	60
111		2½d. blue	35	50
135		3d. purple on yellow	75	1·50
134		3d. blue	90	6·00
113		4d. red on yellow	80	2·00
136		5d. green	80	6·00
137		6d. purple	90	3·50
116		1s. black on green	1·50	3·50
138a		1s. brown	2·50	15·00

1915. Surch **ONE PENNY.**

121	**19**	1d. on 1s. black on green	7·50	24·00

1916. Optd **WAR STAMP.** in two lines.

122	**19**	1d. red	3·25	5·50

1916. Optd **WAR STAMP** in one line.

129	**19**	1d. red	30	80

1935. Silver Jubilee. As T **13** of Antigua.

142	1d. blue and red	40	1·25
143	1½d. blue and grey	1·00	2·75
144	2½d. brown and blue	1·90	3·00
145	1s. grey and purple	2·00	3·50

1937. Coronation. As T **2** of Aden.

146	1d. violet	35	40
147	1½d. red	40	30
148	2½d. blue	45	1·50

25

26 Young's Island and Fort Duvernette

1938.

149	**25**	½d. blue and green	10	10
150	**26**	1d. blue and brown	10	10
151	–	1½d. green and red	20	10
152	**25**	2d. green and black	40	35
153	–	2½d. black and green	20	40
153a	–	2½d. green and brown	20	20
154	**25**	3d. orange and purple	20	10
154a	–	3½d. blue and green	40	1·50
155	**25**	6d. black and red	1·00	40
156	–	1s. purple and green	1·00	70
157	**25**	2s. blue and purple	6·00	75
157a		2s. 6d. brown and blue	1·00	3·50
158		5s. red and green	10·00	2·50
158a		10s. violet and brown	3·75	8·00
159		£1 purple and black	16·00	15·00

DESIGNS—HORIZ: 1½d. Kingstown and Fort Charlotte; 2½d. (No. 153), 3½d. Bathing beach at Villa; 2½d. (No. 153a), 1s. Victoria Park, Kingstown.

1946. Victory. As T **9** of Aden.

160	1½d. red	10	10
161	3½d. blue	10	10

1948. Silver Wedding. As T **10/11** of Aden.

162	1½d. red	10	10
163	£1 mauve	15·00	17·00

1949. As 1938 issue, but values in cents and dollars.

164	**25**	1 c. blue and green	20	80
164a		1 c. green and black	30	1·75
165	**26**	2 c. blue and brown	15	30
166	–	3 c. green and red	40	40
166a	**25**	3 c. orange and purple	30	1·75
167		4 c. green and black	35	20
167a		4 c. blue and green	30	15
168	–	5 c. green and brown	15	10
169	**25**	6 c. orange and purple	40	60
169a	–	6 c. green and red	30	1·75
170	–	7 c. black and blue	3·50	65
170a	–	10 c. black and turquoise	50	20
171	**25**	12 c. black and red	35	15
172	–	24 c. purple and green	35	45
173	**25**	48 c. blue and purple	1·50	1·50
174		60 c. brown and blue	1·75	2·50
175		$1.20 red and green	4·25	4·00
176		$2.40 violet and brown	6·00	9·00
177		$4.80 purple and black	11·00	19·00

DESIGNS—HORIZ: 3 c. (No. 166), 6 c. (No. 169a) Kingstown and Fort Charlotte; 5, 24 c. Victoria Park, Kingstown; 7, 10 c. Bathing beach at Villa.

1949. U.P.U. As T **20/23** of Antigua.

178	5 c. blue	25	15
179	6 c. purple	55	1·10
180	12 c. mauve	30	1·10
181	24 c. green	50	25

1951. Inauguration of B.W.I. University College. As T **24/25** of Antigua.

182	**18**	3 c. green and red	30	30
183	**19**	12 c. black and purple	30	50

1951. New Constitution. Optd **NEW CONSTITUTION 1951.**

184	–	3 c. green and red (No. 166)	15	65
185	**25**	4 c. green and black	15	30
186	–	5 c. green & brn (No. 168)	15	30
187	**25**	12 c. black and red	40	30

1953. Coronation. As T **13** of Aden.

188		4 c. black and green	30	20

30

31

1955.

189	**30**	1 c. orange	10	10
190		2 c. blue	10	10
191		3 c. grey	30	10
192		4 c. brown	20	10
215		5 c. red	15	10
216		10 c. lilac	15	10
195		15 c. blue	65	30
218		20 c. green	45	10
197		25 c. sepia	50	10
198	**31**	50 c. brown	4·50	1·75
199		$1 green	8·00	1·00
200		$2.50 blue	14·00	7·00

1958. British Caribbean Federation. As T **28** of Antigua.

201	3 c. green	30	20
202	6 c. blue	35	1·00
203	12 c. red	45	45

1963. Freedom from Hunger. As T **28** of Aden.

204	8 c. violet	60	50

1963. Cent of Red Cross. As T **33** of Antigua.

205	4 c. red and black	15	20
206	8 c. red and blue	35	50

32 Scout Badge and Proficiency Badges

33 Tropical Fruits

1964. 50th Anniv of St. Vincent Boy Scouts Association.

221	**32**	1 c. green and brown	10	10
222		4 c. blue and purple	10	10
223		20 c. yellow and violet	30	10
224		50 c. red and green	45	50

1965. Bicentenary of Botanic Gardens. Mult.

225	1 c. Type **33**	10	10
226	4 c. Breadfruit and H.M.S. "Providence" (sloop), 1793	10	10
227	25 c. Doric Temple and pond (vert)	15	10
228	40 c. Talipot palm and Doric Temple (vert)	30	90

1965. Cent of I.T.U. As T **36** of Antigua.

229	4 c. blue and green	20	10
230	48 c. ochre and orange	55	45

37 Boat-building, Bequia

1965. Multicoloured.

231	1 c. Type **37** (inscr "BEOUIA")	10	85
231a	1 c. Type **37** (inscr "BEQUIA")	65	30
232	2 c. Friendship Beach, Bequia	10	10
233	3 c. Terminal Building, Arnos Vale Airport	30	10
261	4 c. Woman with bananas	30	30
235	5 c. Crater Lake	15	10
236	6 c. Carib stone	15	40
237	8 c. Arrowroot	30	10
238	10 c. Owia Salt Pond	30	10
239	12 c. Deep water wharf	70	10
240	20 c. Sea island cotton	30	10
241	25 c. Map of St. Vincent and islands	35	10
242	50 c. Breadfruit	50	30
243	$1 Baleine Falls	4·00	30
244	$2.50 St. Vincent amazon	18·00	5·50
245	$5 Arms of St. Vincent	5·00	8·50

Nos. 261, 236/7 and 240/5 are vert.

1966. Churchill Commem. As T **38** of Antigua.

246	1 c. blue	10	10
247	4 c. green	20	10
248	20 c. brown	35	30
249	40 c. violet	55	1·00

1966. Royal Visit. As T **39** of Antigua.

250	4 c. black, green and blue	75	20
251	25 c. black and mauve	2·00	80

1966. Inauguration of W.H.O. Headquarters, Geneva. As T **41** of Antigua.

252	4 c. black, green and blue	30	10
253	25 c. black, purple and ochre	70	80

1966. 20th Anniv of U.N.E.S.C.O. As T **54/6** of Antigua.

254	4 c. multicoloured	30	10
255	8 c. yellow, violet and olive	55	10
256	25 c. black, purple and orange	1·25	60

38 Coastal View of Mount Coke Area

1967. Autonomous Methodist Church. Mult.

257	2 c. Type **38**	10	10
258	8 c. Kingstown Methodist Church	10	10
259	25 c. First Licence to perform marriages	25	10
260	35 c. Conference Arms	25	10

39 Meteorological Institute

1968. World Meteorological Day.

262	**39**	4 c. multicoloured	10	10
263		25 c. multicoloured	10	10
264		35 c. multicoloured	15	15

40 Dr. Martin Luther King and Cotton Pickers

1968. Dr. Martin Luther King Commem.

265	**40**	5 c. multicoloured	10	10
266		25 c. multicoloured	10	10
267		35 c. multicoloured	15	15

41 Speaker addressing Demonstrators

1968. Human Rights Year.

268	**41**	3 c. multicoloured	10	10
269	–	35 c. blue	20	10

DESIGN—VERT: 35 c. Scales of Justice and Human Rights emblem.

43 Male Masquerader

1969. St. Vincent Carnival.

270	**43**	1 c. multicoloured	10	10
271	–	5 c. red and brown	10	10
272	–	8 c. multicoloured	10	10
273	–	25 c. multicoloured	15	20

DESIGNS—VERT: 5 c. Steel bandsman; 25 c. Queen of Bands. HORIZ: 8 c. Carnival revellers.

1969. Methodist Conference. Nos. 241, 257/8 and 260 optd **METHODIST CONFERENCE MAY 1969.**

274	**38**	2 c. multicoloured	10	15
275	–	8 c. multicoloured	15	25
276	–	25 c. multicoloured	15	25
277	–	35 c. multicoloured	1·00	2·75

48 "Strength in Unity"

1969. 1st Anniv of "C.A.R.I.F.T.A.".

278	**48**	2 c. black, buff and red	10	10
279	–	5 c. multicoloured	10	10
280	**48**	8 c. black, buff and green	10	10
281	–	25 c. multicoloured	35	15

DESIGN—VERT: 5, 25 c. Map.

50 Flag of St. Vincent

1969. Statehood.

282	50	4 c. multicoloured	10	10
283	–	10 c. multicoloured	10	10
284	–	50 c. grey, black and orange	35	20

DESIGNS: 10 c. Battle scene with insets of Petroglyph and Carib Chief Chatoyer; 50 c. Carib House with maces and scales.

51 Green Heron

1970. Multicoloured.

285	½ c. House wren	10	85
286a	1 c. Type **51**	30	1·50
287	2 c. Lesser Antillean bullfinches	15	40
288	3 c. St. Vincent amazon	15	30
289	4 c. Rufous-throated solitaire	20	30
364	5 c. Red-necked pigeon	50	20
291	6 c. Bananaquits	30	30
292	8 c. Purple-throated Carib	40	20
293	10 c. Mangrove cuckoo	30	10
294	12 c. Common black hawk	40	10
295	20 c. Bare-eyed thrush	60	15
296	25 c. Hooded tanager	70	20
297	50 c. Blue hooded euphonia	2·00	75
298	$1 Barn owl	7·50	4·00
299	$2.50 Yellow-bellied elaenia	7·00	4·75
300	$5 Ruddy quail dove	12·00	6·50

Nos. 285, 289, 364, 293/4 and 298/9 are vert.

52 De Havilland D.H.C.6 Twin Otter 100

1970. 20th Anniv of Regular Air Services. Multicoloured.

301	5 c. Type **52**	10	10
302	8 c. Grumman Goose	15	10
303	10 c. Hawker Siddeley H.S.748	20	10
304	25 c. Douglas DC-3	65	30

53 "Children's Nursery"

1970. Centenary of British Red Cross. Mult.

305	3 c. Type **53**	10	10
306	5 c. "First Aid"	15	10
307	12 c. "Voluntary Aid Detachment"	35	70
308	25 c. "Blood Transfusion"	55	50

54 "Angel and the Two Marys at the Tomb" (stained-glass window)

1970. 150th Anniv of St. George's Cathedral, Kingstown. Multicoloured.

309	½ c. Type **54**	10	10
310	5 c. St. George's Cathedral	10	10
311	25 c. Tower, St. George's Cathedral	10	10
312	35 c. Interior, St. George's Cathedral	15	10
313	50 c. Type **54**	20	30

Nos. 310 and 312 are horiz.

55 "The Adoration of the Shepherds" (Le Nain)

1970. Christmas. Multicoloured.

314	8 c. "The Virgin and Child" (Bellini) (vert)	10	10
315	25 c. Type **55**	10	10
316	35 c. As 8 c.	10	10
317	50 c. Type **55**	15	20

56 New Post Office and 6d. Stamp of 1861

1971. 110th Anniv of First St. Vincent Stamps. Multicoloured.

318	2 c. Type **56**	10	10
319	4 c. 1d. stamp of 1861 and new Post Office	10	10
320	25 c. Type **56**	10	10
321	$1 As 4 c.	35	45

57 Trust Seal and Wildlife

1971. St. Vincent's National Trust. Mult.

322	12 c. Type **57**	40	40
323	30 c. Old cannon, Fort Charlotte	35	20
324	40 c. Type **57**	55	35
325	45 c. As 30 c.	40	80

58 "Madonna appearing to St. Anthony" (Tiepolo)

59 Careening

1971. Christmas. Multicoloured.

326	5 c. Type **58**	10	10
327	10 c. "The Holy Family on the Flight into Egypt" (detail, Pietro da Cortona)	10	10
328	25 c. Type **58**	10	10
329	$1 As 10 c.	40	35

1971. The Grenadines of St. Vincent. Multicoloured.

330	1 c. Type **59**	10	10
331	5 c. Seine fishermen	10	10
332	6 c. Map of the Grenadines	10	10
333	15 c. Type **59**	20	10
334	20 c. As 5 c.	20	10
335	50 c. As 6 c.	65	80

60 Private, Grenadier Company, 32nd Foot (1764)

61 Breadnut Fruit

1972. Military Uniforms.

337	60	12 c. multicoloured	90	15
338	–	30 c. multicoloured	1·25	65
339	–	50 c. multicoloured	1·50	1·25

DESIGNS: 30 c. Officer, Battalion Company, 31st Foot (1772); 50 c. Private, Grenadier Company, 6th Foot (1772).

1972. Fruit. Multicoloured.

340	3 c. Type **61**	10	10
341	5 c. Pawpaw	10	10
342	12 c. Plumrose or roseapple	20	30
343	25 c. Mango	60	70

62 Candlestick Cassia

1972. Flowers. Multicoloured.

344	1 c. Type **62**	10	10
345	30 c. Lobster claw	20	10
346	40 c. White trumpet	25	15
347	$1 Soufriere tree	70	1·25

63 Sir Charles Brisbane and Coat of Arms

1972. Birth Bicentenary of Sir Charles Brisbane.

348	63	20 c. brown, gold and red	15	10
349	–	30 c. yellow, mauve & black	40	10
350	–	$1 multicoloured	1·40	70

DESIGNS: 30 c. H.M.S. "Arethusa", 1807; $1 H.M.S. "Blake", 1808.

1972. Royal Silver Wedding. As T **52** of Ascension, but with Arrowroot and Breadfruit in background.

352	30 c. brown	10	10
353	$1 green	20	20

65 Sighting of St. Vincent

1973. 475th Anniv of Columbus's Third Voyage to the West Indies. Multicoloured.

354	5 c. Type **65**	25	30
355	12 c. Caribs watching Columbus's fleet	45	30
356	30 c. Christopher Columbus	75	90
357	50 c. "Santa Maria"	1·25	2·25

66 "The Last Supper" (French stained-glass window)

1973. Easter.

358	66	15 c. multicoloured	10	10
359	–	60 c. multicoloured	20	20
360	–	$1 multicoloured	20	20

Nos. 358/60 are in the form of a triptych which make a composite design depicting "The Last Supper".

67 William Wilberforce and Poster

1973. 140th Death Anniv of William Wilberforce. Multicoloured.

369	30 c. Type **67**	15	10
370	40 c. Slaves cutting cane	20	15
371	50 c. Wilberforce and medallion	20	15

68 P.P.F. Symbol

71 "The Descent from the Cross" (Sansovino)

69 Administration Block, Mona

1973. 21st Anniv of International Planned Parenthood Federation. Multicoloured.

372	12 c. Type **68**	10	10
373	40 c. "IPPF" and symbol	20	20

1973. Royal Wedding. As T **47** of Anguilla. Multicoloured, background colours given.

374	50 c. blue	15	10
375	70 c. green	15	10

1973. 25th Anniv of West Indies University. Multicoloured.

376	5 c. Type **69**	10	10
377	10 c. University Centre, Kingstown	10	10
378	30 c. Aerial view, Mona University	15	10
379	$1 University coat of arms (vert)	35	60

1973. Nos. 297, 292 and 298 surch.

380	30 c. on 50 c. multicoloured	2·00	1·00
381	40 c. on 8 c. multicoloured	2·00	1·00
382	$10 on $1 multicoloured	10·00	8·00

1974. Easter. Multicoloured.

383	5 c. Type **71**	10	10
384	30 c. "The Deposition" (English, 14th-century)	10	10
385	40 c. "Pieta" (Fernandez)	10	10
386	$1 "The Resurrection" (French, 16th-century)	20	25

72 "Istra"

1974. Cruise Ships. Multicoloured.

387	15 c. Type **72**	20	10
388	20 c. "Oceanic"	25	10
389	30 c. "Aleksandr Pushkin"	25	10
390	$1 "Europa"	50	30

73 U.P.U. Emblem

1974. Centenary of U.P.U. Multicoloured.

392	5 c. Type **73**	10	10
393	12 c. Globe within posthorn	10	10
394	60 c. Map of St. Vincent and hand-cancelling	20	10
395	90 c. Map of the World	25	30

74 Royal Tern

1974. Multicoloured.

396	30 c. Type **74**	2·00	90
397	40 c. Brown pelican	2·00	90
398	$10 Magnificent frigate bird	18·00	11·00

75 Scout Badge and Emblems
76 Sir Winston Churchill

1974. Diamond Jubilee of Scout Movement in St. Vincent.

399	75	10 c. multicoloured	10	10
400		25 c. multicoloured	20	10
401		45 c. multicoloured	30	15
402		$1 multicoloured	55	90

1974. Birth Centenary of Sir Winston Churchill. Multicoloured.

403	25 c. Type **76**	15	10
404	35 c. Churchill in military uniform	15	10
405	45 c. Churchill in naval uniform	20	10
406	$1 Churchill in air force uniform	30	70

77 The Shepherds

1974. Christmas.

407	**77**	3 c. blue and black	10	10
408	–	3 c. blue and black	10	10
409	–	3 c. blue and black	10	10
410	–	3 c. blue and black	10	10
411	**77**	8 c. green and black	10	10
412	–	35 c. pink and black	15	10
413	–	45 c. brown and black	15	10
414	–	$1 mauve and black	30	50

DESIGNS: Nos. 408, 411, Mary and crib; Nos. 409, 413, Joseph, ox and ass; Nos. 410, 414, The Magi.

78 Faces

1975. Kingstown Carnival 75. Mult.

415	1 c. Type **78**	10	10
416	15 c. Pineapple women	15	15
417	25 c. King of the Bands	15	15
418	35 c. Carnival dancers	15	15
419	45 c. Queen of the Bands	15	20
420	$1.25 "African Splendour"	25	55

79 French Angelfish

1975. Marine Life. Multicoloured.

422	1 c. Type **79**	15	80
423	2 c. Spot-finned butterflyfish	15	95
424	3 c. Yellow jack	15	55
425	4 c. Spanish mackerel	20	10
426	5 c. French grunt	20	45
427	6 c. Spotted goatfish	20	90
428	8 c. Ballyhoo	20	1·75
429	10 c. Sperm whale	30	10
430	12 c. Humpback whale	40	1·60
431	15 c. Scribbled cowfish	1·25	1·60
432	15 c. Skipjack tuna	3·50	1·00
433	20 c. Queen angelfish	40	10
434	25 c. Princess parrotfish	45	20
435	35 c. Red hind	65	1·75
436	45 c. Atlantic flyingfish	80	90
437	50 c. Porkfish	65	1·75
438	70 c. Yellow-finned tuna	6·50	1·00
439	90 c. Pompano	6·50	70
440	$1 Queen triggerfish	90	20
441a	$2.50 Sailfish	2·00	1·50
442	$5 Dolphin (fish)	3·75	2·50
443	$10 Blue marlin	3·00	8·50

80 Cutting Bananas

1975. Banana Industry. Multicoloured.

447	25 c. Type **80**	15	10
448	35 c. Packaging Station, La Croix	15	10
449	45 c. Cleaning and boxing	20	10
450	70 c. Shipping bananas aboard "Geestide" (freighter)	40	30

81 Snorkel Diving

1975. Tourism. Multicoloured.

451	15 c. Type **81**	40	15
452	20 c. Aquaduct Golf Course	1·50	1·00
453	35 c. Steel band at Mariner's Inn	45	15
454	45 c. Sunbathing at Young Island	45	15
455	$1.25 Yachting marina	1·40	2·75

82 George Washington, John Adams, Thomas Jefferson and James Madison

1975. Bicentenary of American Revolution.

456	**82**	½ c. black and mauve	10	10
457	–	1 c. black and green	10	10
458	–	1½ c. black and mauve	10	10
459	–	5 c. black and green	10	10
460	–	10 c. black and blue	10	10
461	–	25 c. black and yellow	10	10
462	–	35 c. black and blue	15	10
463	–	45 c. black and red	15	10
464	–	$1 black and orange	30	40
465	–	$2 black and green	40	85

PRESIDENTS: 1 c. Monroe, Quincy Adams, Jackson, van Buren; 1½ c. W. Harrison, Tyler, Polk, Taylor; 5 c. Fillmore, Pierce, Buchanan, Lincoln; 10 c. Andrew Johnson, Grant, Hayes, Garfield; 25 c. Arthur, Cleveland, B. Harrison, McKinley; 35 c. Theodore Roosevelt, Taft, Wilson, Harding; 45 c. Coolidge, Hoover, Franklin Roosevelt, Truman; $1 Eisenhower, Kennedy, Lyndon Johnson, Nixon; $2 Pres. Ford and White House.

83/4 "Shepherds"

1975. Christmas.

467A	–	3 c. black and mauve	10	10
468A	–	3 c. black and mauve	10	10
469A	–	3 c. black and mauve	10	10
470A	–	3 c. black and mauve	10	10
471A	–	8 c. black and blue	10	10
472A	–	8 c. black and blue	10	10
473A	–	35 c. black and yellow	15	20
474A	–	35 c. black and yellow	15	20
475A	**83**	45 c. black and green	15	30
476A	**84**	45 c. black and green	15	30
477A	–	$1 black and purple	30	80
478A	–	$1 black and purple	30	80

DESIGNS: No. 467, "Star of Bethlehem"; No. 468, "Holy Trinity"; No. 469, As Type **83**; No. 470, "Three Kings"; Nos. 471/2, As No. 467; Nos. 473/4, As No. 468; Nos. 475/6, Types **83/4**; Nos. 477/8, As No. 470. The two designs of each value (Nos. 467/8) differ in that the longest side is at the foot or at the top as shown in Types **83/4**.

85 Carnival Dancers

1976. Kingstown "Carnival. Mult.

479	1 c. Type **85**	10	10
480	2 c. Humpty-Dumpty people	10	10
481	5 c. Smiling faces	10	10
482	35 c. Dragon worshippers	15	10
483	45 c. Carnival tableaux	20	10
484	$1.25 Bumble-bee dancers	30	50

1976. Nos. 424 and 437 surch.

485	70 c. on 3 c. Horse-eyed jack	55	1·00
486	90 c. on 50 c. Porkfish	55	1·25

87 Blue-headed Hummingbird and Yellow Hibiscus

1976. Hummingbirds and Hibiscuses. Mult.

487	5 c. Type **87**	35	10
488	10 c. Antillean crested hummingbird and pink hibiscus	60	15
489	35 c. Purple-throated carib and white hibiscus	1·00	30
490	45 c. Blue-headed hummingbird and red hibiscus	1·00	35
491	$1.25 Green-throated carib and peach hibiscus	7·00	5·00

1976. West Indian Victory in World Cricket Cup. As Nos. 431/2 of St. Lucia.

492	15 c. Map of the Caribbean	75	25
493	45 c. Prudential Cup	1·25	1·00

88 St. Mary Church, Kingstown

1976. Christmas. Multicoloured.

494	35 c. Type **88**	15	10
495	45 c. Anglican Church, Georgetown	15	10
496	50 c. Methodist Church, Georgetown	20	10
497	$1.25 St. George's Cathedral, Kingstown	40	60

89 Barrancoid Pot-stand

1977. National Trust. Multicoloured.

498	5 c. Type **89**	10	10
499	45 c. National Museum	15	10
500	70 c. Carib sculpture	20	20
501	$1 Ciboney petroglyph	30	50

90 William I, William II, Henry I and Stephen

1977. Silver Jubilee. Multicoloured.

502	½ c. Type **90**	10	10
503	1 c. Henry II, Richard I, John, Henry III	10	10
504	1½ c. Edward I, Edward II, Edward III, Richard II	10	10
505	2 c. Henry IV, Henry V, Henry VI, Edward IV	10	10
506	5 c. Edward V, Richard III, Henry VII, Henry VIII	10	10
507	10 c. Edward VI, Lady Jane Grey, Mary I, Elizabeth I	10	10
508	25 c. James I, Charles I, Charles II, James II	10	10
509	35 c. William III, Mary II, Anne, George I	10	10
510	45 c. George II, George III, George IV	10	10
511	75 c. William IV, Victoria, Edward VII	15	25
512	$1 George V, Edward VIII, George VI	20	40
513	$2 Elizabeth II leaving Westminster Abbey	30	60

91 Grant of Arms

1977. Centenary of Windward Islands Diocese. Multicoloured.

527	15 c. Type **91**	10	10
528	35 c. Bishop Berkeley and mitres	10	10
529	45 c. Map and arms of diocese	10	10
530	$1.25 St. George's Cathedral and Bishop Woodroffe	30	55

1977. Kingstown Carnival. Nos. 426, 429, 432/3 and 440 optd **CARNIVAL 1977 JUNE 25TH – JULY 5TH.**

531	5 c. French grunt	10	10
532	10 c. Sperm whale	10	10
533	15 c. Skipjack tuna	10	10
534	20 c. Queen angelfish	10	10
535	$1 Queen triggerfish	40	70

93 Guide and Emblem
95 Map of St. Vincent

1977. 50th Anniv of St. Vincent Girl Guides. Multicoloured.

536	5 c. Type **93**	10	10
537	15 c. Early uniform, ranger, guide and brownie	15	10
538	20 c. Early uniform and guide	15	10
539	$2 Lady Baden-Powell	50	90

1977. Royal Visit. No. 513 optd **CARIBBEAN VISIT 1977**

540	$2 Queen Elizabeth leaving Westminster Abbey	30	30

1977. Surch as in T **95**.

541	**95**	20 c. light blue and blue	15	15
542		40 c. light orange & orange	25	20
543		40 c. pink and mauve	20	15

Nos. 541/3 were originally printed without face values.

96 Opening Verse and Scene

1977. Christmas. Scenes and Verses from the carol "While Shepherds Watched their Flocks by Night". Multicoloured.

544	5 c. Type **96**	10	10
545	10 c. Angel consoling shepherds	10	10
546	15 c. View of Bethlehem	10	10
547	25 c. Nativity scene	10	10
548	50 c. Throng of angels	10	10
549	$1.25 Praising God	30	65

97 "Cynthia cardui" and "Bougainvillea glabra var alba"
99 "Co-operation in Education Leads to Mutual Understanding and Respect"

98 Rotary International Emblem and Motto

1978. Butterflies and Bougainvilleas. Multicoloured.

551 5 c. Type **97** 15 10
552 25 c. "Dione juno" and "Golden Glow" 20 10
553 40 c. "Anartia amathea" and "Mrs McLean" 30 10
554 50 c. "Hypolimnas misippus" and "Cyphen" 35 10
555 $1.25 "Pseudolycaena marsyas" and "Thomasii" 70 70

1978. 25th Anniv of Coronation. As Nos. 422/5 of Montserrat. Multicoloured.

556 40 c. Westminster Abbey 10 10
557 50 c. Gloucester Cathedral 10 10
558 $1.25 Durham Cathedral 15 15
559 $2.50 Exeter Cathedral 15 25

1978. International Service Clubs. Emblems and Mottoes. Multicoloured.

561 40 c. Type **98** 15 10
562 50 c. Lions International 15 10
563 $1 Jaycees 35 50

1978. 10th Anniv of Project School to School (St. Vincent–Canada school twinning project). Mult.

564 40 c. Type **99** 10 10
565 $2 "Co-operation in Education Leads to the Elimination of Racial Intolerance" (horiz) 40 50

100 Arnos Vale Airport

1978. 75th Anniv of Powered Flight. Mult.

566 10 c. Type **100** 10 10
567 40 c. Wilbur Wright landing Wright Flyer I 15 10
568 50 c. Orville Wright in Wright Flyer III 15 10
569 $1.25 Orville Wright and Wright Flyer I airborne 45 35

101 Young Child

1979. International Year of the Child.

570 **101** 8 c. black, gold and green 10 10
571 – 20 c. black, gold and lilac 10 10
572 – 50 c. black, gold and blue 15 10
573 – $2 black, gold and flesh 50 50

DESIGNS: 20, 50 c., $2 Different portraits of young children.

1979. Soufriere Eruption Relief Fund. As T **95** but surch **SOUFRIERE RELIEF FUND 1979** and premium.

574 **95** 10 c. + 5 c. blue and lilac 10 15
575 50 c. + 25 c. brown & buff 20 20
576 $1 + 50 c. brown and grey 25 30
577 $2 + $1 green and light green 40 50

103 Sir Rowland Hill

1979. Death Cent of Sir Rowland Hill. Mult.

578 40 c. Type **103** 15 10
579 50 c. Penny Black and Two Penny Blue stamps 15 15
580 $3 1861 1d. and 6d. stamps 40 1·10

104 First and Latest Buccament Postmarks and Map of St. Vincent

1979. Post Office of St. Vincent. Early and modern postmarks. Multicoloured.

582 1 c. Type **104** 10 10
583 2 c. Sion Hill 10 10
584 3 c. Cumberland 10 10
585 4 c. Questelles 10 10
586 5 c. Layou 10 10
587 6 c. New Ground 10 10
588 8 c. Mesopotamia 10 10
589 10 c. Troumaca 10 10
590 12 c. Arnos Vale 15 10
591 15 c. Stubbs 15 10
592 20 c. Orange Hill 15 10
593 25 c. Calliaqua 15 10
594 40 c. Edinboro 25 20
595 50 c. Colonarie 30 25
596 80 c. Biabou 40 35
597 $1 Chateaubelair 50 50
598 $2 Head P.O. Kingstown 60 80
599 $3 Barrouallie 60 1·25
600 $5 Georgetown 90 2·00
601 $10 Kingstown 1·75 4·00

1979. Opening of St. Vincent and the Grenadines Air Service. Optd **ST VINCENT AND THE GRENADINES AIR SERVICE 1979.**

602 10 c. Type **100** 10 10

106 National Flag and "Ixora occinea" (flower)

1979. Independence. Multicoloured.

603 20 c. Type **106** 15 10
604 50 c. House of Assembly and "Ixora stricta" (flower) 20 10
605 80 c. Prime Minister R. Milton Cato and "Ixora williamsii" (flower) 25 20

1979. Independence. Nos. 422, 425/30, 432, 437/41 and 443 optd **INDEPENDENCE 1979.**

606 1 c. Type **79** 10 10
607 4 c. Spanish mackerel 10 10
608 5 c. French grunt 10 10
609 6 c. Spotted goatfish 10 10
610 8 c. Ballyhoo 10 10
611 10 c. Sperm whale 15 15
612 12 c. Humpback whale 15 15
613 15 c. Skipjack tuna 15 15
614 25 c. Princess parrotfish 20 20
615 50 c. Porkfish 35 35
616 70 c. Yellow-finned tuna 45 45
617 90 c. Pompano 60 50
618 $1 Queen triggerfish 60 50
619 $2.50 Sailfish 90 1·00
620 $10 Blue marlin 1·75 4·25

108 Virgin and Child

1979. Christmas. Scenes and quotations from "Silent Night" (carol). Multicoloured.

621 10 c. Type **108** 10 10
622 20 c. Jesus sleeping 10 10
623 25 c. Shepherds 10 10
624 40 c. Angel 10 10
625 50 c. Angels holding Jesus 10 10
626 $2 Nativity 40 45

109 "Polistes cinctus" (wasp) and Oleander

1979. Flowers and Insects. Different varieties of oleander. Multicoloured.

628 5 c. Type **109** 10 10
629 10 c. "Pyrophorus noctiluca" (click beetle) 10 10
630 25 c. "Stagmomantis limbata" (mantid) 10 10
631 50 c. "Psiloptera lampetis" (beetle) 10 10
632 $2 "Diaprepies abbreviatus" (weevil) 30 30

110 Queen Elizabeth II

1980. "London 1980" International Stamp Exhibition. Multicoloured.

634 80 c. Type **110** 15 20
635 $1 Great Britain 1954 3d. and St. Vincent 1954 5 c. definitives 20 30
636 $2 Unadopted postage stamp design of 1971 35 60

111 Steel Band

1980. Kingstown Carnival. Multicoloured.

638 20 c. Type **111** 15 40
639 20 c. Steel band (different) 15 40

112 Football 114 Brazilian Agouti

1980. "Sport for All". Multicoloured.

640 10 c. Type **112** 10 10
641 60 c. Cycling 30 15
642 80 c. Basketball 40 40
643 $2.50 Boxing 40 1·25

1980. Hurricane Relief. Nos. 640/3 surch **HURRICANE RELIEF 50c.**

644 **112** 10 c. + 50 c. mult 15 15
645 – 60 c. + 50 c. mult 20 25
646 – 80 c. + 50 c. mult 35 40
647 – $2.50 + 50 c. mult 40 85

1980. Wildlife. Multicoloured.

648 25 c. Type **114** 10 10
649 50 c. Giant toad 15 10
650 $2 Small Indian mongoose 40 55

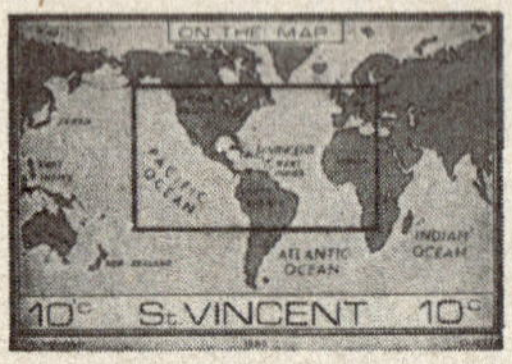

115 Map of World showing St. Vincent

1980. St. Vincent "On the Map". Maps showing St. Vincent. Multicoloured.

651 10 c. Type **115** 10 10
652 50 c. Western hemisphere 15 10
653 $1 Central America 30 15
654 $2 St. Vincent 50 30

116 "Ville de Paris" (French ship of the line), 1782

1981. Sailing Ships. Multicoloured.

656 50 c. Type **116** 55 20
657 60 c. H.M.S. "Ramillies" (ship of the line), 1782 60 40
658 $1.50 H.M.S. "Providence" (sloop), 1793 1·25 1·75
659 $2 "Dee" (paddle-steamer packet) 1·50 2·00

117 Arrowroot Cultivation

1981. Agriculture. Multicoloured.

660 25 c. Type **117** 10 15
661 25 c. Arrowroot processing 10 15
662 50 c. Banana cultivation 15 25
663 50 c. Banana export packaging station 15 25
664 60 c. Coconut plantation 15 30
665 60 c. Copra drying frames 15 30
666 $1 Cocoa cultivation 30 45
667 $1 Cocoa beans and sun drying frames 30 45

1981. Royal Wedding. Royal Yachts. As T **26/27** of Kiribati. Multicoloured.

668 60 c. "Isabella" 15 15
669 60 c. Prince Charles and Lady Diana Spencer 30 30
670 $2.50 "Alberta" (tender) 30 30
671 $2.50 As No. 669 70 70
672 $4 "Britannia" 35 40
673 $4 As No. 669 1·00 1·25

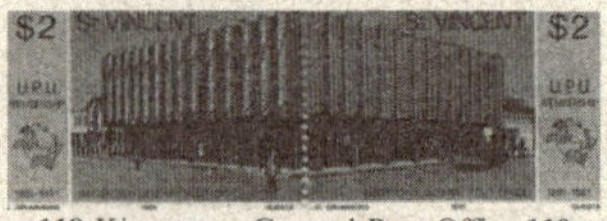

118 Kingstown General Post Office 119 (½-size illustration)

1981. U.P.U. Membership.

677 **118** $2 multicoloured 40 90
678 **119** $2 multicoloured 40 90

Nos. 677/8 were printed together, se-tenant, forming the composite design illustrated.

120 St. Vincent Flag with Flags of other U.N. Member Nations

1981. 1st Anniv of U.N. Membership. Mult.

679 $1.50 Type **120** 35 25
680 $2.50 Prime Minister Robert Milton Cato 55 50

Nos. 679/80 are inscribed "ST. VINCENT and the GRENADINES".

121 Silhouettes of Figures at Old Testament Reading and Bible Extract

1981. Christmas. Designs showing silhouettes of figures. Multicoloured.

681 50 c. Type **121** 15 10
682 60 c. Madonna and angel 15 10
683 $1 Madonna and Bible extract 25 25
684 $2 Joseph and Mary travelling to Bethlehem 50 50

122 Sugar Boilers

1982. 1st Anniv of Re-introduction of Sugar Industry. Multicoloured.

686 50 c. Type **122** 25 15
687 60 c. Sugar drying plant 25 20
688 $1.50 Sugar mill machinery 55 75
689 $2 Crane loading sugar cane 75 1·00

123 Butterfly Float

1982. Carnival 1982. Multicoloured.

690 50 c. Type **123** 20 15
691 60 c. Angel dancer (vert) 20 15
692 $1.50 Winged dancer (vert) 50 80
693 $2 Eagle float 70 1·50

124 Augusta of Saxe-Gotha, Princess of Wales, 1736

125 Scout Emblem

1982. 21st Birthday of Princess of Wales. Multicoloured.

694 50 c. Type **124** 15 20
695 60 c. Coat of arms of Augusta of Saxe-Gotha 15 25
696 $6 Diana, Princess of Wales . 70 1·25

1982. 75th Anniv of Boy Scout Movement. Multicoloured.

697 $1.50 Type **125** . . . . . . 70 1·00
698 $2.50 75th anniversary emblem 95 1·50

1982. Birth of Prince William of Wales. Nos. 694/6 optd **ROYAL BABY**.

699 50 c. Type **124** 15 20
700 60 c. Coat of arms of Augusta of Saxe-Gotha 15 25
701 $6 Diana, Princess of Wales . 70 1·50

126 De Havilland Gipsy Moth, 1932

1982. 50th Anniv of Airmail Service. Mult.

702 50 c. Type **126** 55 30
703 60 c. Grumman Goose, 1952 . 65 40
704 $1.50 Hawker Siddeley H.S.748, 1968 . . . . 1·25 1·50
705 $2 Britten Norman "long nose" Trislander, 1982 . . . . . . 1·40 2·00

127 "Geestport" (freighter)

1982. Ships. Multicoloured.

706 45 c. Type **127** 40 25
707 60 c. "Stella Oceanis" (liner) . 50 40
708 $1.50 "Victoria" (liner) . . . 95 1·50
709 $2 "Queen Elizabeth 2" (liner) 1·25 2·00

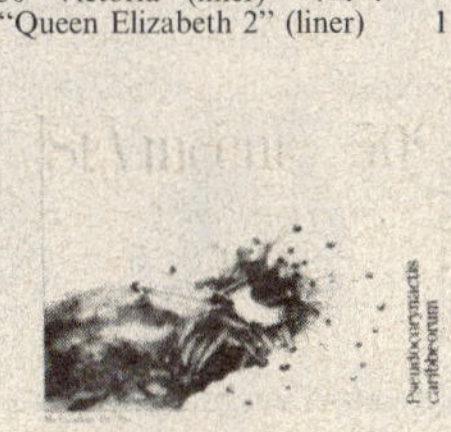

128 "Pseudocorynactis caribbeorum"

1983. Marine Life. Multicoloured.

710 50 c. Type **128** 65 25
711 60 c. "Actinoporus elegans" (vert) 75 40
712 $1.50 "Arachnanthus nocturnus" (vert) . . . . 1·40 1·75
713 $2 Reid's seahorse (vert) . . 1·60 2·00

129 Satellite View of St. Vincent

1983. Commonwealth Day. Multicoloured.

714 45 c. Type **129** 15 20
715 60 c. Flag of St. Vincent . . . 20 25
716 $1.50 Prime Minister R. Milton Cato 30 65
717 $2 Harvesting bananas . . . 45 90

Nos. 714/17 are inscribed "ST. VINCENT and the GRENADINES".

1983. No. 681 surch **45c**.

718 45 c. on 50 c. Type **121** . . . 40 30

131 Symbolic Handshake

132 William A. Smith (founder)

1983. 10th Anniv of Treaty of Chaguaramas. Multicoloured.

719 45 c. Type **131** 25 20
720 60 c. Commerce emblem . . 30 30
721 $1.50 Caribbean map . . . . 60 1·00
722 $2 Flags of member countries and map of St. Vincent . . 85 1·25

1983. Centenary of Boys' Brigade. Mult.

723 45 c. Type **132** 25 25
724 60 c. On parade 30 35
725 $1.50 Craftwork . . . . . . 70 1·10
726 $2 Community service . . . . 95 1·60

133 Ford "Model T" (1908)

1983. Leaders of the World. Automobiles (1st series).

727 **133** 10 c. multicoloured . . . 10 10
728 – 10 c. multicoloured . . . 10 10
729 – 60 c. multicoloured . . . 15 15
730 – 60 c. multicoloured . . . 15 15
731 – $1.50 multicoloured . . . 15 20
732 – $1.50 multicoloured . . . 15 20
733 – $1.50 multicoloured . . . 15 20
734 – $1.50 multicoloured . . . 15 20
735 – $2 multicoloured 20 30
736 – $2 multicoloured 20 30
737 – $2 multicoloured 20 30
738 – $2 multicoloured 20 30

DESIGNS: (the first in each pair shows technical drawings and the second paintings of the cars). Nos. 727/8, Ford "Model T" (1908); 729/30, Supercharged Cord "812" (1937); 731/2, Citroen "Open Tourer" (1937); 733/4, Mercedes Benz "300SL Gull-Wing" (1954); 735/6, Rolls-Royce "Phantom I" (1925); 737/8, Ferrari "Boxer 512BB" (1967).

See also Nos. 820/9, 862/7, 884/91 and 952/63.

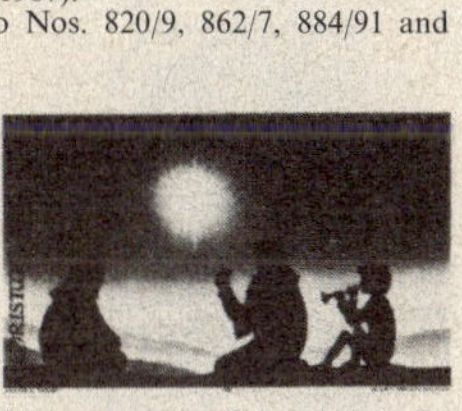

134 Appearance of the Nativity Star

1983. Christmas. Multicoloured

739 10 c. Type **134** 10 10
740 50 c. Message of the Angel . 20 10
741 $1.50 The Heavenly Host . . 50 65
742 $2.40 Worshipping Jesus . . 75 1·00

135 "King Henry VIII"

1983. Leaders of the World. Railway Locomotives (1st series). First in each pair shows technical drawings and the second the locomotive at work.

744 **135** 10 c. multicoloured . . . 10 10
745 – 10 c. multicoloured . . . 10 10
746 – 10 c. multicoloured . . . 10 10
747 – 10 c. multicoloured . . . 10 10
748 – 25 c. multicoloured . . . 10 10
749 – 25 c. multicoloured . . . 10 10
750 – 50 c. multicoloured . . . 15 20
751 – 50 c. multicoloured . . . 15 20
752 – 60 c. multicoloured . . . 15 20
753 – 60 c. multicoloured . . . 15 20
754 – 75 c. multicoloured . . . 15 25
755 – 75 c. multicoloured . . . 15 25
756 – $2.50 multicoloured . . . 30 55
757 – $2.50 multicoloured . . . 30 55
758 – $3 multicoloured 35 70
759 – $3 multicoloured 35 70

DESIGNS: Nos. 744/5, "King Henry VIII", Great Britain (1927); 746/7, Diesel locomotive "Royal Scots Greys", Great Britain (1961); 748/9, "Hagley Hall", Great Britain (1928); 750/1, "Sir Lancelot", Great Britain (1925 (dated 1926 in error)); 752/3, Class B12, Great Britain (1912); 754/5, Deeley "Compound type", Great Britain (1902); 756/7, "Cheshire", Great Britain (1927); 758/9, Bulleid "Austerity" Class QI, Great Britain (1942).

See also Nos. 792/807, 834/41, 872/83, 893/904 and 1001/8.

136 Fort Duvernette

1984. Fort Duvernette. Multicoloured.

760 35 c. Type **136** 20 30
761 45 c. Soldiers on fortifications . 25 30
762 $1 Cannon facing bay 40 60
763 $3 Map of St. Vincent and mortar . . . . 1·25 1·75

137 White Frangipani

1984. Flowering Trees and Shrubs. Mult.

764 5 c. Type **137** 20 10
765 10 c. Genip 25 10
766 15 c. Immortelle 30 10
767 20 c. Pink poui 40 10
768 25 c. Buttercup 50 10
769 35 c. Sandbox 65 20
770 45 c. Locust 70 25
771 60 c. Colville's glory 75 60
772 75 c. Lignum vitae . . . . . . 1·00 75
773 $1 Golden shower . . . . . . 1·00 1·00
774 $5 Angelin . . . . 2·75 8·00
775 $10 Roucou . . . . 3·75 13·00

138 Trench Warfare, First World War

1984. Leaders of the World. British Monarchs. Multicoloured.

776 1 c. Type **138** 10 10
777 1 c. George V and trenches . . 10 10
778 5 c. Battle of Bannockburn . . 10 10
779 5 c. Edward II and battle . . . 10 10
780 60 c. George V 20 20
781 60 c. York Cottage, Sandringham 20 20
782 75 c. Edward II 20 20
783 75 c. Berkeley Castle 20 20
784 $1 Coat of arms of Edward II 20 25
785 $1 Edward II (different) . . . 20 25
786 $4 Coat of arms of George V . 50 60
787 $4 George V and Battle of Jutland 50 60

Nos. 776/7, 778/9, 780/1, 782/3, 784/5 and 786/7 were printed together, se-tenant, each pair forming a composite design.

139 Musical Fantasy Costume

1984. Carnival 1984. Costumes. Multicoloured.

788 35 c. Type **139** 15 15
789 45 c. African princess 20 20
790 $1 Market woman 40 40
791 $3 Carib hieroglyph . . . . 1·25 1·75

1984. Leaders of the World. Railway Locomotives (2nd series). As T **135**, the first in each pair shows technical drawings and the second the locomotive at work.

792 1 c. multicoloured 10 10
793 1 c. multicoloured 10 10
794 2 c. multicoloured 10 10
795 2 c. multicoloured 10 10
796 3 c. multicoloured 10 10
797 3 c. multicoloured 10 10
798 50 c. multicoloured 20 30
799 50 c. multicoloured 20 30
800 75 c. multicoloured 25 35
801 75 c. multicoloured 25 35
802 $1 multicoloured 25 35
803 $1 multicoloured 25 35
804 $2 multicoloured 30 40
805 $2 multicoloured 30 40
806 $3 multicoloured 35 50
807 $3 multicoloured 35 50

DESIGNS: Nos. 792/3, Class 141-R Liberation, France (1945); 794/5, Diesel locomotive "Dreadnought", Great Britain (1967); 796/7, No. 242A1, France (1946); 798/9, Class "Dean Goods", Great Britain (1883); 800/1, Hetton Colliery No. 1, Great Britain (1822); 802/3, "Pen-y-Darren", Great Britain (1804); 804/5, "Novelty", Great Britain (1829); 806/7, Class 44, Germany (1925).

140 Slaves tilling Field

1984. 150th Anniv of Emancipation of Slaves on St. Vincent. Multicoloured.

808 35 c. Type **140** 20 20
809 45 c. Sugar-cane harvesting . . 25 25
810 $1 Cutting sugar-cane 45 60
811 $3 William Wilberforce and African slave caravan . . . 1·25 2·50

141 Weightlifting

142 Grenadier, 70th Regt of Foot, 1773

1984. Leaders of the World. Olympic Games, Los Angeles. Multicoloured.

812 1 c. Judo 10 10
813 1 c. Type **141** 10 10
814 3 c. Pursuit cycling 10 10
815 3 c. Cycle road-racing 10 10
816 60 c. Women's backstroke swimming 15 15
817 60 c. Men's butterfly swimming 15 15
818 $3 Sprint start 40 55
819 $3 Finish of long distance race 40 55

1984. Leaders of the World. Automobiles (2nd series). As T **133**, the first in each pair shows technical drawings and the second paintings.

820 5 c. black, drab and green . . 10 10
821 5 c. multicoloured 10 10
822 20 c. black, pink and blue . . 10 15
823 20 c. multicoloured 10 15
824 55 c. black, green and brown . 20 25
825 55 c. multicoloured 20 25
826 $1.50 black, light turquoise and turquoise 25 35
827 $1.50 multicoloured 25 35
828 $2.50 black, turquoise and lilac 30 40
829 $2.50 multicoloured 30 40

DESIGNS: Nos. 820/1, Austin-Healey "Sprite" (1958); 822/3, Maserati "Ghibli Coupe" (1971); 824/5, Pontiac "GTO" (1964); 826/7, Jaguar "D-Type" (1957); 828/9, Ferrari "365 GTB4 Daytona" (1970).

1984. Military Uniforms. Multicoloured.

830 45 c. Type **142** 50 30
831 60 c. Grenadier, 6th Regt of Foot, 1775 . . . . 60 35
832 $1.50 Grenadier, 3rd Regt of Foot, 1768 . . . . 1·00 1·10
833 $2 Battalion Company Officer, 14th Regt of Foot, 1780 . . 1·25 1·60

1984. Leaders of the World. Railway Locomotives (3rd series). As T **135**, the first in each pair shows technical drawings and the second the locomotive at work.

834 5 c. multicoloured 10 10
835 5 c. multicoloured 10 10
836 40 c. multicoloured 15 20
837 40 c. multicoloured 15 20
838 75 c. multicoloured 15 25
839 75 c. multicoloured 15 25
840 $2.50 multicoloured 50 80
841 $2.50 multicoloured 50 80

DESIGNS: Nos. 834/5, 20th Class, Rhodesia (1954); 836/7, "Southern Maid", Great Britain (1928); 838/9, "Prince of Wales", Great Britain (1911); 840/1, Class 05, Germany (1935).

143 N. S. Taylor

144 Eye Lash Orchid

1985. Leaders of the World. Cricketers. The first in each pair shows a head portrait and the second the cricketer in action.

842 **143** 5 c. multicoloured 10 10
843 – 5 c. multicoloured 10 10
844 – 35 c. multicoloured . . . 35 20
845 – 35 c. multicoloured . . . 35 20
846 – 50 c. multicoloured . . . 45 30
847 – 50 c. multicoloured . . . 45 30
848 – $3 multicoloured . . . . 75 1·25
849 – $3 multicoloured . . . . 75 1·25

DESIGNS: Nos. 842/3, N. S. Taylor; 844/5, T. W. Graveney; 846/7, R. G. D. Willis; 848/9, S. D. Fletcher.

1985. Orchids. Multicoloured.

850	35 c. Type **144**	20	30
851	45 c. "Ionopsis utricularioides"	20	30
852	$1 "Epidendrum secundum"	30	65
853	$3 "Oncidium altissimum"	40	2·00

145 Brown Pelican

146 Pepper

1985. Leaders of the World. Birth Bicentenary of John J. Audubon (ornithologist). Multicoloured.

854	15 c. Type **145**	15	10
855	15 c. Green heron	15	10
856	40 c. Pileated woodpecker	15	20
857	40 c. Common flicker	15	20
858	60 c. Painted bunting	15	30
859	60 c. White-winged crossbill	15	30
860	$2.25 Red-shouldered hawk	45	90
861	$2.25 Common caracara	45	90

1985. Leaders of the World. Automobiles (3rd series). As T **133**, the first in each pair shows technical drawings and the second paintings.

862	1 c. black, yellow and green	10	10
863	1 c. multicoloured	10	10
864	55 c. black, blue and grey	15	25
865	55 c. multicoloured	15	25
866	$2 black, yellow and purple	40	70
867	$2 multicoloured	40	70

DESIGNS: Nos. 862/3, Lancia "Aprilia", (1937); 864/5, Pontiac "Firebird Trans Am", (1973); 866/7, Cunningham "C-5R", (1953).

1985. Herbs and Spices. Multicoloured.

868	25 c. Type **146**	10	10
869	35 c. Sweet marjoram	10	15
870	$1 Nutmeg	20	50
871	$3 Ginger	55	2·25

1985. Leaders of the World. Railway Locomotives (4th series). As T **135**, the first in each pair shows technical drawings and the second the locomotive at work.

872	1 c. multicoloured	10	10
873	1 c. multicoloured	10	10
874	10 c. multicoloured	10	10
875	10 c. multicoloured	10	10
876	40 c. multicoloured	15	30
877	40 c. multicoloured	15	30
8'5	60 c. multicoloured	15	30
879	60 c. multicoloured	15	30
880	$1 multicoloured	25	40
881	$1 multicoloured	25	40
882	$2.50 multicoloured	40	60
883	$2.50 multicoloured	40	60

DESIGNS: Nos. 872/3, "Glen Douglas", Great Britain (1913); 874/5, "Fenchurch", Great Britain (1872); 876/7, No. 1 Stirling "single", Great Britain (1870); 878/9, No. 158A, Great Britain (1866); 880/1, Jones Goods locomotive No. 103, Great Britain (1893); 882/3, "The Great Bear", Great Britain (1908).

1985. Leaders of the World. Automobiles (4th series). As T **133**, the first in each pair shows technical drawings and the second paintings.

884	25 c. black, grey and red	10	10
885	25 c. multicoloured	10	10
886	60 c. black, pink and orange	15	20
887	60 c. multicoloured	15	20
888	$1 black, blue and violet	15	25
889	$1 multicoloured	15	25
890	$1.50 black, blue and red	20	30
891	$1.50 multicoloured	20	30

DESIGNS: Nos. 884/5, Essex "Coach" (1922); 886/7, Nash "Rambler" (1950); 888/9, Ferrari "Tipo 156" (1961); 890/1, Eagle-Weslake "Type 58" (1967).

1985. Leaders of the World. Railway Locomotives (5th series). As T **135**, the first in each pair shows technical drawings and the second the locomotive at work.

893	**151**	5 c. multicoloured	10	10
894	–	5 c. multicoloured	10	10
895	–	30 c. multicoloured	15	20
896	–	30 c. multicoloured	15	20
897	–	60 c. multicoloured	20	30
898	–	60 c. multicoloured	20	30
899	–	75 c. multicoloured	20	30
900	–	75 c. multicoloured	20	30
901	–	$1 multicoloured	25	40
902	–	$1 multicoloured	25	40
903	–	$2.50 multicoloured	30	60
904	–	$2.50 multicoloured	30	60

DESIGNS: Nos. 893/4, "Loch", Isle of Man (1874); 895/6, Class 47XX, Great Britain (1919); 897/8, Class 121, France (1876); 899/900, Class 24, Germany (1927); 901/2, Tank locomotive No. 1008, Great Britain (1889); 903/4, Class PS-4, U.S.A. (1926).

147 Bamboo Flute

1985. Traditional Musical Instruments. Mult.

905	25 c. Type **147**	10	15
906	35 c. Quatro (four-stringed guitar)	10	25
907	$1 Ba-ha (bamboo pipe) (vert)	25	55
908	$2 Goat-skin drum (vert)	35	1·10

148 Queen Elizabeth the Queen Mother

149 Elvis Presley

1985. Leaders of the World. Life and Times of Queen Elizabeth the Queen Mother. Various portraits.

910	**148**	35 c. multicoloured	10	20
911	–	35 c. multicoloured	10	20
912	–	85 c. multicoloured	10	25
913	–	85 c. multicoloured	10	25
914	–	$1.20 multicoloured	15	30
915	–	$1.20 multicoloured	15	30
916	–	$1.60 multicoloured	15	30
917	–	$1.60 multicoloured	15	35

Each value issued in pairs showing a floral pattern across the bottom of the portraits which stops short of the left-hand edge on the first stamp and of the right-hand edge on the second.

1985. Leaders of the World. Elvis Presley (entertainer). Various portraits. Multicoloured, background colours given.

919	**149**	10 c. multicoloured	30	15
920	–	10 c. mult (blue)	30	15
921	–	60 c. mult (brown)	40	35
922	–	60 c. mult (grey)	40	35
923	–	$1 mult (brown)	45	55
924	–	$1 mult (blue)	45	55
925	–	$5 mult (light blue)	70	1·75
926	–	$5 mult (blue)	70	1·75

150 Silos and Conveyor Belt

1985. St. Vincent Flour Milling Industry. Multicoloured.

928	20 c. Type **150**	10	15
929	30 c. Roller mills	10	20
930	75 c. Administration building	20	35
931	$3 Bran finishers	50	1·40

1985. Royal Visit. Nos. 672/3, 697/8, 711, 724 and 912/3 optd **CARIBBEAN ROYAL VISIT 1985** or surch also.

932	–	60 c. multicoloured (711)	1·50	2·00
933	–	60 c. multicoloured (724)	1·75	2·25
934	–	85 c. multicoloured (912)	2·50	4·00
935	–	85 c. multicoloured (913)	2·50	4·00
936	**125**	$1.50 multicoloured	1·75	2·75
937	–	$1.60 on $4 mult (672)	1·00	2·25
938	–	$1.60 on $4 mult (673)	10·00	15·00
939	–	$2.50 multicoloured (698)	2·00	3·50

No. 938 shows a new face value only.

151 Michael Jackson

152 "The Serenaders" (Kim de Freitas)

1985. Leaders of the World. Michael Jackson (entertainer). Various portraits. Multicoloured.

940	**151**	60 c. multicoloured	25	30
941	–	60 c. multicoloured	25	30
942	–	$1 multicoloured	30	45
943	–	$1 multicoloured	30	45
944	–	$2 multicoloured	45	80
945	–	$2 multicoloured	45	80
946	–	$5 multicoloured	70	1·75
947	–	$5 multicoloured	70	1·75

Each value issued in pairs, the left-hand design showing the face value at top left (as on Type **151**) and the right-hand design at top right.

1985. Christmas. Children's Paintings. Mult.

949	25 c. Type **152**	10	15
950	75 c. "Poinsettia" (Jackie Douglas)	20	40
951	$2.50 "Jesus our Master" (Bernadette Payne)	55	2·00

153 "Santa Maria"

155 Halley's Comet

1986. 500th Anniv (1992) of Discovery of America by Columbus (1st issue). Multicoloured.

952	60 c. Type **153**	40	55
953	60 c. Christopher Columbus	40	55
954	$1.50 Columbus at Spanish Court	55	1·25
955	$1.50 King Ferdinand and Queen Isabella of Spain	55	1·25
956	$2.75 "Santa Maria" and fruits	90	2·00
957	$2.75 Maize and fruits	90	2·00

See also Nos. 1125/31, 1305/24, 1639/56, 1677/84, 1895/1900 and 1981/2.

1986. Leaders of the World. Automobiles (5th series). As T **133**, the first in each pair shows technical drawings and the second paintings.

959	30 c. black, blue and orange	10	15
960	30 c. multicoloured	10	15
961	45 c. black, grey and blue	10	15
962	45 c. multicoloured	10	15
963	60 c. black, blue and red	15	20
964	60 c. multicoloured	15	20
965	90 c. black, yellow and blue	20	25
966	90 c. multicoloured	20	25
967	$1.50 black, lilac and mauve	25	40
968	$1.50 multicoloured	25	40
969	$2.50 black, blue and light blue	25	50
970	$2.50 multicoloured	25	50

DESIGNS: Nos. 959/60, Cadillac "Type 53" (1916); 961/2, Triumph "Dolomite" (1939); 963/4, Panther "J-72" (1972); 965/6, Ferrari "275 GTB/4" (1967); 967/8, Packard "Caribbean" (1953); 969/70, Bugatti "Type 41 Royale" (1931).

1986. Appearance of Halley's Comet. Multicoloured.

973	45 c. Type **155**	25	30
974	60 c. Edmond Halley	25	30
975	75 c. Newton's telescope and astronomers	30	55
976	$3 Amateur astronomer on St. Vincent	60	2·25

1986. 60th Birthday of Queen Elizabeth II (1st issue). As T **117a** of Montserrat. Multicoloured.

978	10 c. Queen Elizabeth II	10	10
979	90 c. Princess Elizabeth	20	30
980	$2.50 Queen gathering bouquets from crowd	35	75
981	$8 In Canberra, 1982 (vert)	1·00	2·25

See also Nos. 996/9.

156 Mexican Player

1986. World Cup Football Championship, Mexico. Multicoloured.

983	1 c. Football and world map (horiz)	10	10
984	2 c. Type **156**	10	10
985	5 c. Mexican player (different)	10	10
986	5 c. Hungary v Scotland	10	10
987	10 c. Spain v Scotland	10	10
988	30 c. England v U.S.S.R. (horiz)	20	20
989	45 c. Spain v France	30	30
990	75 c. Mexican team (56 × 36 mm)	45	45
991	$1 England v Italy	75	65
992	$2 Scottish team (56 × 36 mm)	1·10	1·50
993	$4 Spanish team (56 × 36 mm)	2·10	2·75
994	$5 English team (56 × 36 mm)	2·25	3·25

157 Queen Elizabeth at Victoria Park, Kingstown

1986. 60th Birthday of Queen Elizabeth II (2nd issue). Scenes from 1985 Royal Visit. Multicoloured.

996	45 c. Type **157**	45	30
997	60 c. Queen and Prime Minister James Mitchell, Bequia	55	55
998	75 c. Queen, Prince Philip and Mr. Mitchell, Port Elizabeth, Bequia	65	65
999	$2.50 Queen, Prince Philip and Mr. Mitchell watching Independence Day parade, Victoria Park	1·40	2·50

1986. Leaders of the World. Railway Locomotives (6th series). As T **135**. Multicoloured.

1001	30 c. multicoloured	10	10
1002	30 c. multicoloured	10	10
1003	50 c. multicoloured	20	20
1004	50 c. multicoloured	20	20
1005	$1 multicoloured	25	30
1006	$1 multicoloured	25	30
1007	$3 multicoloured	50	70
1008	$3 multicoloured	50	70

DESIGNS: Nos. 1001/2, Class ED41 BZZB electric rack and adhesion locomotive, Japan (1926); 1003/4, "The Judge", Chicago Railroad Exposition, U.S.A. (1883); 1005/6, Class E60C electric locomotive, U.S.A. (1973); 1007/8, Class SD40-2 diesel locomotive, U.S.A. (1972).

1986. Royal Wedding (1st issue). As T **168** of British Virgin Islands. Multicoloured.

1009	60 c. Profile of Prince Andrew	20	25
1010	60 c. Miss Sarah Ferguson	20	25
1011	$2 Prince Andrew with Mrs. Nancy Reagan (horiz)	45	75
1012	$2 Prince Andrew in naval uniform (horiz)	45	75

See also Nos. 1022/5.

158 "Acrocomia aculeata"

159 Cadet Force Emblem and Cadets of 1936 and 1986

1986. Timber Resources of St. Vincent. Mult.

1014	10 c. Type **158**	40	20
1015	60 c. "Pithecellobium saman"	1·25	80
1016	75 c. White cedar	1·60	95
1017	$3 "Andira inermis"	3·50	4·50

1986. 50th Anniv of St. Vincent Cadet Force (45 c., $2) and 75th Anniv of St. Vincent Girls' High School (others). Multicoloured.

1018	45 c. Type **159**	40	30
1019	60 c. Grimble Building, Girls' High School (horiz)	45	40
1020	$1.50 High School pupils (horiz)	1·25	1·75
1021	$2 Cadets on parade (horiz)	1·75	2·25

1986. Royal Wedding (2nd issue). Nos. 1009/12 optd **Congratulations to T.R.H. The Duke & Duchess of York.**

1022	60 c. Profile of Prince Andrew	40	65
1023	60 c. Miss Sarah Ferguson	40	65
1024	$2 Prince Andrew with Mrs. Nancy Reagan (horiz)	1·25	2·00
1025	$2 Prince Andrew in naval uniform (horiz)	1·25	2·00

160 King Arthur

1986. The Legend of King Arthur. Multicoloured.

1026	30 c. Type **160**	40	40
1027	45 c. Merlin taking baby Arthur	50	50
1028	60 c. Arthur pulling sword from stone	60	60
1029	75 c. Camelot	70	70
1030	$1 Arthur receiving Excalibur from the Lady of the Lake	80	80
1031	$1.50 Knights at the Round Table	1·00	1·25
1032	$2 The Holy Grail	1·25	1·50
1033	$5 Sir Lancelot jousting	2·00	2·75

161 Statue of Liberty Floodlit

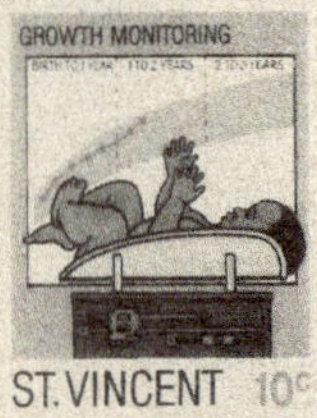

163 Baby on Scales

162 Fishing for Tri Tri

1986. Centenary of Statue of Liberty. Designs showing aspects of the Statue.

1034	161 15 c. multicoloured	10	10
1035	– 25 c. multicoloured	15	15
1036	– 40 c. multicoloured	20	25
1037	– 55 c. multicoloured	25	30
1038	– 75 c. multicoloured	35	45
1039	– 90 c. multicoloured	45	60
1040	– $1.75 multicoloured	75	1·10
1041	– $2 multicoloured	80	1·25
1042	– $2.50 multicoloured	85	1·60
1043	– $3 multicoloured	1·00	1·75

1986. Freshwater Fishing. Multicoloured.

1045	75 c. Type 162	25	40
1046	75 c. Plumier's goby ("Tri Tri")	25	40
1047	$1.50 Crayfishing	35	80
1048	$1.50 Crayfish	35	80

1987. Child Health Campaign. Multicoloured.

1049	10 c. Type 163	10	10
1050	50 c. Oral rehydration therapy	45	55
1051	75 c. Breast feeding	60	90
1052	$1 Nurse giving injection	85	1·25

1987. World Population Control. Nos. 1049/52 optd **WORLD POPULATION 5 BILLION 11TH JULY 1987.**

1053	10 c. Type 163	10	10
1054	50 c. Oral rehydration therapy	50	55
1055	75 c. Breast feeding	65	90
1056	$1 Nurse giving injection	90	1·25

165 Hanna Mandlikova

1987. International Lawn Tennis Players. Mult.

1057	40 c. Type 165	25	25
1058	60 c. Yannick Noah	25	35
1059	80 c. Ivan Lendl	25	40
1060	$1 Chris Evert	25	45
1061	$1.25 Steffi Graf	25	50
1062	$1.50 John McEnroe	25	55
1063	$1.75 Martina Navratilova with Wimbledon trophy	30	65
1064	$2 Boris Becker with Wimbledon trophy	30	75

166 Miss Prima Donna, Queen of the Bands, 1986

1987. 10th Anniv of Carnival. Multicoloured.

1066	20 c. Type 166	10	15
1067	45 c. Donna Young, Miss Carnival, 1985	15	15
1068	55 c. Miss St. Vincent and the Grenadines, 1986	15	15
1069	$3.70 "Spirit of Hope" costume, 1986	50	1·40

The 45 c. value is inscribed "Miss Carival" in error.

1987. 10th Death Anniv of Elvis Presley (entertainer). Nos. 919/26 optd **THE KING OF ROCK AND ROLL LIVES FOREVER AUGUST 16TH 1977-1987.**

1070	149 10 c. mult	10	10
1071	– 10 c. mult (blue)	10	10
1072	– 60 c. mult (brown)	25	30
1073	– 60 c. mult (grey)	25	30
1074	– $1 mult (brown)	30	45
1075	– $1 mult (blue)	30	45
1076	– $5 mult (light blue)	1·40	2·25
1078	– $5 mult (blue)	1·40	2·25

168 Queen Victoria, 1841

1987. Royal Ruby Wedding and 150th Anniv of Queen Victoria's Accession. Multicoloured.

1079	15 c. Type 168	10	10
1080	75 c. Queen Elizabeth and Prince Andrew, 1960	25	35
1081	$1 Coronation, 1953	30	40
1082	$2.50 Duke of Edinburgh, 1948	90	1·40
1083	$5 Queen Elizabeth II, c. 1980	1·40	1·90

169 Karl Benz and Benz Three-wheeler (1886)

1987. Century of Motoring. Multicoloured.

1085	$1 Type 169	40	60
1086	$2 Enzo Ferrari and Ferrari "Dino 206SP" (1966)	50	1·10
1087	$4 Charles Rolls and Rolls-Royce and Rolls-Royce "Silver Ghost" (1907)	65	1·50
1088	$5 Henry Ford and Ford "Model T" (1908)	65	1·75

170 Everton Football Team

1987. English Football Teams. Mult.

1090	$2 Type 170	1·25	1·25
1091	$2 Manchester United	1·25	1·25
1092	$2 Tottenham Hotspur	1·25	1·25
1093	$2 Arsenal	1·25	1·25
1094	$2 Liverpool	1·25	1·25
1095	$2 Derby County	1·25	1·25
1096	$2 Portsmouth	1·25	1·25
1097	$2 Leeds United	1·25	1·25

171 Five Cent Coins 172 Charles Dickens

1987. East Caribbean Currency. Mult.

1098	5 c. Type 171	20	10
1099	6 c. Two cent coins	20	10
1100	10 c. Ten cent coins	20	10
1101	12 c. Two and ten cent coins	30	10
1102	15 c. Five cent coins	30	10
1103	20 c. Ten cent coins	35	10
1115g	25 c. Twenty-five cent coins	30	15
1105	30 c. Five and twenty-five cent coins	40	15
1106	35 c. Twenty-five and ten cent coins	40	20
1107	45 c. Twenty-five and two ten cent coins	50	30
1108	50 c. Fifty cent coins	50	30
1109	65 c. Fifty, ten and five cent coins	60	45
1110	75 c. Fifty and twenty-five cent coins	60	50
1111	$1 One dollar note (horiz)	75	65
1112	$2 Two one dollar notes (horiz)	1·25	1·75
1113	$3 Three one dollar notes (horiz)	1·50	2·50
1115q	$5 Five dollar note (horiz)	3·25	4·00
1115	$10 Ten dollar note (horiz)	4·50	8·00
1115s	$20 Twenty dollar note (horiz)	10·00	14·00

1987. Christmas. 175th Birth Anniv of Charles Dickens. Multicoloured.

1116	6 c. Type 172	15	25
1117	6 c. "Mr. Fezziwig's Ball"	15	25
1118	25 c. Type 172	25	30
1119	25 c. "Scrooge's Third Visitor"	25	30
1120	50 c. Type 172	30	55
1121	50 c. "The Cratchits' Christmas"	30	55
1122	75 c. Type 172	35	75
1123	75 c. "A Christmas Carol"	35	75

Nos. 1116/17, 1118/19, 1120/1 and 1122/3 were printed together, se-tenant, each pair forming a composite design showing an open book. The first design in each pair shows Type 172 and the second a scene from "A Christmas Carol".

173 "Santa Maria"

1988. 500th Anniv (1992) of Discovery of America by Columbus (2nd issue). Multicoloured.

1125	15 c. Type 173	20	20
1126	75 c. "Nina" and "Pinta"	30	60
1127	$1 Compass and hourglass	30	60
1128	$1.50 Claiming the New World for Spain	40	1·00
1129	$3 Arawak village	60	1·50
1130	$4 Blue and yellow macaw, Cuban tody, pineapple and maize	70	2·00

174 Brown Pelican 175 Windsurfing

1988.

1132	174 45 c. multicoloured	30	30

1988. Tourism. Multicoloured.

1133	10 c. Type 175	10	10
1134	45 c. Scuba diving	20	25
1135	65 c. Aerial view of Young Island (horiz)	30	60
1136	$5 Cruising yacht (horiz)	2·10	3·50

176 "Nuestra Senora del Rosario" (Spanish galleon) and Spanish Knight's Cross

1988. 400th Anniv of Spanish Armada. Mult.

1137	15 c. Type 176	15	10
1138	75 c. "Ark Royal" (galleon) and English Armada medal	30	35
1139	$1.50 English fleet and Drake's dial	50	75
1140	$2 Dismasted Spanish galleon and 16th-century shot	55	85
1141	$3.50 Attack of English fireships at Calais and 16th-century grenade	70	1·75
1142	$5 "Revenge" (English galleon) and Drake's Drum	90	2·00

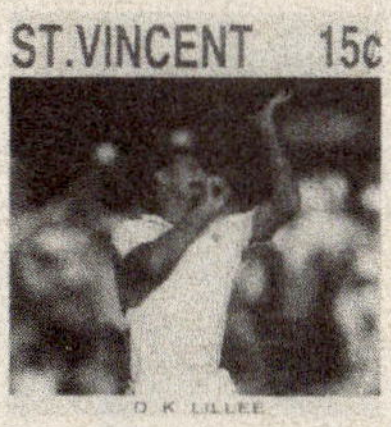

177 D. K. Lillee 179 Babe Ruth

178 Athletics

1988. Cricketers of 1988 International Season. Multicoloured.

1144	15 c. Type 177	30	30
1145	50 c. G. A. Gooch	50	50
1146	75 c. R. N. Kapil Dev	70	70
1147	$1 S. M. Gavaskar	85	85
1148	$1.50 M. W. Gatting	1·25	1·50
1149	$2.50 Imran Khan	1·50	2·00
1150	$3 I. T. Botham	1·50	2·25
1151	$4 I. V. A. Richards	1·75	2·50

1988. Olympic Games, Seoul. Multicoloured.

1153	10 c. Type 178	10	10
1154	50 c. Long jumping (vert)	20	25
1155	$1 Triple jumping	40	50
1156	$5 Boxing (vert)	2·10	2·75

1988. Famous Baseball Players (1st series).

1158	179 $2 multicoloured	1·40	1·40

See also Nos. 1264/75, 1407, 1408/88, 2152/4, 2155/6, 2426 and 3004/12.

1988. Christmas. "Mickey's Christmas Train". As T 246 of Antigua. Multicoloured.

1160	1 c. Minnie Mouse in railway van loaded with candy (horiz)	10	10
1161	2 c. Mordie and Ferdie in wagon with toys (horiz)	10	10
1162	3 c. Chip n' Dale in wagon with Christmas trees (horiz)	10	10
1163	4 c. Donald Duck's nephews riding with reindeer (horiz)	10	10
1164	5 c. Donald and Daisy Duck in restaurant car (horiz)	10	10
1165	10 c. Grandma Duck, Uncle Scrooge McDuck, Goofy and Clarabelle carol singing in carriage (horiz)	10	10
1166	$5 Mickey Mouse driving locomotive (horiz)	3·25	3·50
1167	$6 Father Christmas in guard's van (horiz)	4·00	4·50

181 Mickey Mouse as Snake Charmer

1989. "India-89" International Stamp Exhibition, New Delhi. Multicoloured.

1169	1 c. Type 181	10	10
1170	2 c. Goofy with chowsingha antelope	10	10
1171	3 c. Mickey and Minnie Mouse with common peafowl	10	10
1172	5 c. Goofy with Briolette Diamond and Mickey Mouse pushing mine truck	10	10
1173	10 c. Clarabelle with Orloff Diamond	10	10
1174	25 c. Mickey Mouse as tourist and Regent Diamond, Louvre, Paris	20	15
1175	$4 Minnie and Mickey Mouse with Kohinoor Diamond	3·50	4·00
1176	$5 Mickey Mouse and Goofy with Indian rhinoceros	3·50	4·00

182 Harry James

1989. Jazz Musicians. Multicoloured.

1178	10 c. Type 182	30	20
1179	15 c. Sidney Bechet	40	20
1180	25 c. Benny Goodman	50	20
1181	35 c. Django Reinhardt	55	20
1182	50 c. Lester Young	70	35
1183	90 c. Gene Krupa	85	85
1184	$3 Louis Armstrong	2·00	2·75
1185	$4 Duke Ellington	2·50	3·00

183 Birds in Flight

1989. Wildlife Conservation. Noah's Ark. Multicoloured.

1187	40 c. Type 183	30	30
1188	40 c. Rainbow (left side)	30	30
1189	40 c. Noah's Ark on mountain	30	30
1190	40 c. Rainbow (right side)	30	30
1191	40 c. Birds in flight (different)	30	30
1192	40 c. Cow elephant	30	30
1193	40 c. Bull elephant	30	30
1194	40 c. Top of eucalyptus tree	30	30
1195	40 c. Kangaroos	30	30
1196	40 c. Hummingbird	30	30
1197	40 c. Lions	30	30
1198	40 c. White-tailed deer	30	30
1199	40 c. Koala in fork of tree	30	30

1200 40 c. Koala on branch . . . 30 30
1201 40 c. Hummingbird approaching flower . . . 30 30
1202 40 c. Keel-billed toucan and flower . . . 30 30
1203 40 c. Keel-billed toucan facing right . . . 30 30
1204 40 c. Camels . . . 30 30
1205 40 c. Giraffes . . . 30 30
1206 40 c. Mountain sheep . . . 30 30
1207 40 c. Ladybirds on leaf . . . 30 30
1208 40 c. Swallowtail butterfly . . 30 30
1209 40 c. Swallowtail butterfly behind leaves . . . 30 30
1210 40 c. Pythons . . . 30 30
1211 40 c. Dragonflies . . . 30 30
Nos. 1187/1211 were printed together, se-tenant, forming a composite design showing Noah's Ark and animals released after the Flood.

1989. Easter. 500th Birth Anniv of Titian (artist). As T **238** of Antigua. Multicoloured.
1212 5 c. "Baptism of Christ" (detail) 10 10
1213 30 c. "Temptation of Christ" 25 15
1214 45 c. "Ecce Homo" . . . 40 25
1215 65 c. "Noli Me Tangere" (fragment) . . . 55 55
1216 75 c. "Christ carrying the Cross" (detail) . . . 60 65
1217 $1 "Christ crowned with Thorns" (detail) . . . 70 75
1218 $4 "Lamentation over Christ" (detail) . . . 2·75 3·25
1219 $5 "The Entombment" (detail) 3·25 3·75

184 "Ile de France"

1989. Ocean Liners. Multicoloured.
1221 10 c. Type **184** . . . 40 20
1222 40 c. "Liberte" . . . 75 30
1223 50 c. "Mauretania I" (launched 1906) . . . 80 40
1224 75 c. "France" . . . 1·25 1·00
1225 $1 "Aquitania" . . . 1·50 1·10
1226 $2 "United States" . . . 2·25 2·50
1227 $3 "Olympic" . . . 3·00 3·25
1228 $4 "Queen Elizabeth" . . . 3·00 3·50

185 Space Shuttle deploying West German Satellite, 1983

186 "Mercury 9" Capsule and Astronaut L. Gordon Cooper

1989. Int Co-operation in Space. Mult.
1230 40 c. Type **185** . . . 60 20
1231 60 c. Vladimir Remek (Czech cosmonaut) and "Soyuz 28", 1978 . . . 80 50
1232 $1 Projected "Hermes" space plane and "Columbus" Space Station . . . 1·00 90
1233 $4 Ulf Merbold (West German astronaut), 1983 and proposed European Spacelab 3·00 4·25

1989. 25th Anniv of Launching of "Telestar II" Communications Satellite (1988). Each showing satellite and T.V. screen. Multicoloured.
1235 15 c. Type **186** . . . 20 15
1236 35 c. Martin Luther King addressing crowd, 1963 . . 30 20
1237 50 c. Speed skater, Winter Olympic Games, Innsbruck, 1964 . . . 45 50
1238 $3 Pope John XXIII blessing crowd . . . 1·75 2·75

187 Head of St. Vincent Amazon

1989. Wildlife Conservation. St. Vincent Amazon ("St. Vincent Parrot"). Multicoloured.
1240 10 c. Type **187** . . . 55 30
1241 20 c. St. Vincent amazon in flight . . . 90 45
1242 40 c. Feeding (vert) . . . 1·75 65
1243 70 c. At entrance to nest (vert) 2·25 3·00

188 Blue-hooded Euphonia

1989. Birds of St. Vincent. Multicoloured.
1244 25 c. Type **188** . . . 45 20
1245 75 c. Common black hawk ("Crab hawk") . . . 1·00 65
1246 $2 Mangrove cuckoo ("Coucou") . . . 1·75 1·90
1247 $3 Hooded tanager ("Prince bird") . . . 2·00 2·25

1989. Japanese Arts. As T **250** of Antigua. Multicoloured.
1249 10 c. "Autumn Flowers in Front of the Full Moon" (Hiroshige) . . . 10 10
1250 40 c. "Hibiscus" (Hiroshige) 25 25
1251 50 c. "Iris" (Hiroshige) . . . 30 30
1252 75 c. "Morning Glories" (Hiroshige) . . . 50 50
1253 $1 "Dancing Swallows" (Hiroshige) . . . 1·00 75
1254 $2 "Sparrow and Bamboo" (Hiroshige) . . . 2·00 2·00
1255 $3 "Yellow Bird and Cotton Rose" (Hiroshige) . . . 2·25 2·25
1256 $4 "Judos Chrysanthemums in a Deep Ravine in China" (Hiroshige) . . . 2·25 2·50

189 Schooner

1989. "Philexfrance 89" International Stamp Exhibition, Paris and Bicentenary of French Revolution. 18th-century French Naval Vessels. Multicoloured.
1258 30 c. Type **189** . . . 60 30
1259 55 c. Corvette . . . 80 50
1260 75 c. Frigate . . . 1·10 1·00
1261 $1 Ship of the line . . . 1·40 1·40
1262 $3 "Ville de Paris" (ship of the line) . . . 3·50 5·00

190 Johnny Bench

191 Dante Bichette, 1989

1989. Famous Baseball Players (2nd series). Multicoloured.
1264 $2 Type **190** . . . 1·10 1·00
1265 $2 Red Schoendienst . . . 1·10 1·00
1266 $2 Carl Yastrzemski . . . 1·10 1·00
1267 $2 Ty Cobb . . . 1·10 1·00
1268 $2 Willie Mays . . . 1·10 1·00
1269 $2 Stan Musial . . . 1·10 1·00
1270 $2 Ernie Banks . . . 1·10 1·00
1271 $2 Lou Gehrig . . . 1·10 1·00
1272 $2 Jackie Robinson . . . 1·10 1·00
1273 $2 Bob Feller . . . 1·10 1·00
1274 $2 Ted Williams . . . 1·10 1·00
1275 $2 Al Kaline . . . 1·10 1·00

1989. Major League Baseball Rookies. Mult.
1276 60 c. Type **191** . . . 50 50
1277 60 c. Carl Yastrzemski, 1961 50 50
1278 60 c. Randy Johnson, 1989 . . 50 50
1279 60 c. Jerome Walton, 1989 . . 50 50
1280 60 c. Ramon Martinez, 1989 50 50
1281 60 c. Ken Hill, 1989 . . . 50 50
1282 60 c. Tom McCarthy, 1989 . . 50 50
1283 60 c. Gaylord Perry, 1963 . . 50 50
1284 60 c. John Smoltz, 1989 . . 50 50
1285 60 c. Bob Milacki, 1989 . . 50 50
1286 60 c. Babe Ruth, 1915 . . . 50 50
1287 60 c. Jim Abbott, 1989 . . 50 50
1288 60 c. Gary Sheffield, 1989 . . 50 50
1289 60 c. Gregg Jeffries, 1989 . . 50 50
1290 60 c. Kevin Brown, 1989 . . 50 50
1291 60 c. Cris Carpenter, 1989 . . 50 50
1292 60 c. Johnny Bench, 1968 . . 50 50
1293 60 c. Ken Griffey Jr. 1989 . . 50 50

MINIMUM PRICE

The minimum price quoted is 10p which represents a handling charge rather than a basis for valuing common stamps. For further notes about prices see introductory pages.

192 Chris Sabo

194 St. Vincent Amazon

1989. Major League Baseball Award Winners. Multicoloured.
1294 60 c. Type **192** . . . 50 50
1295 60 c. Walt Weiss . . . 50 50
1296 60 c. Willie Mays . . . 50 50
1297 60 c. Kirk Gibson . . . 50 50
1298 60 c. Ted Williams . . . 50 50
1299 60 c. Jose Canseco . . . 50 50
1300 60 c. Gaylord Perry . . . 50 50
1301 60 c. Orel Hershiser . . . 50 50
1302 60 c. Frank Viola . . . 50 50

1989.
1304 **194** 55 c. multicoloured . . . 45 35

195 Queen or Pink Conch and Wide-mouthed Purpura Shells

1989. 500th Anniv (1992) of Discovery of America by Columbus (3rd issue).
1305 **195** 50 c. multicoloured . . . 40 50
1306 – 50 c. multicoloured . . . 40 50
1307 – 50 c. ultramarine, blk & bl 40 50
1308 – 50 c. ultramarine, blk & bl 40 50
1309 – 50 c. multicoloured . . . 40 50
1310 – 50 c. multicoloured . . . 40 50
1311 – 50 c. multicoloured . . . 40 50
1312 – 50 c. black and blue . . . 40 50
1313 – 50 c. multicoloured . . . 40 50
1314 – 50 c. multicoloured . . . 40 50
1315 – 50 c. multicoloured . . . 40 50
1316 – 50 c. multicoloured . . . 40 50
1317 – 50 c. multicoloured . . . 40 50
1318 – 50 c. multicoloured . . . 40 50
1319 – 50 c. multicoloured . . . 40 50
1320 – 50 c. multicoloured . . . 40 50
1321 – 50 c. multicoloured . . . 40 50
1322 – 50 c. multicoloured . . . 40 50
1323 – 50 c. multicoloured . . . 40 50
1324 – 50 c. multicoloured . . . 40 50
DESIGNS: No. 1306, Caribbean reef fishes; 1307, Sperm whale; 1308, Fleet of Columbus; 1309, Sharksucker (fish); 1310, Columbus planting flag; 1311, Navigational instruments; 1312, Sea monster; 1313, Kemp's ridley turtle; 1314, Magnificent frigate bird; 1315, Caribbean manatee; 1316, Caribbean monk seal; 1317, Mayan chief, dugout canoe and caravel; 1318, Blue-footed boobies; 1319, Venezuelan pile village; 1320, Atlantic wing oyster and lion's-paw scallop; 1321, Great hammerhead and short-finned mako; 1322, Brown pelican and hyacinth macaw; 1323, Venezuelan bowmen; 1324, Capuchin and squirrel monkeys.
Nos. 1305/24 were printed together, se-tenant, forming a composite design of a map of the Caribbean showing the voyages of Columbus.

196 Command Module "Columbia" returning to Earth

1989. 20th Anniv of First Manned Landing on Moon. Multicoloured.
1325 35 c. Type **196** . . . 45 25
1326 75 c. Lunar module "Eagle" landing . . . 80 65
1327 $1 "Apollo 11" launch . . . 90 70
1328 $2 Buzz Aldrin on Moon . . 1·40 1·50
1329 $2 Lunar module "Eagle" . . 1·40 1·50
1330 $2 Earth rise from the Moon 1·40 1·50
1331 $2 Neil Armstrong . . . 1·40 1·50
1332 $3 "Eagle" and "Columbia" in Moon orbit . . . 1·75 2·00

197 Jay Howell and Alejandro Pena

1989. Centenary of the Los Angeles Dodgers (1st issue). Baseball Players. Multicoloured.
1334 60 c. Type **197** . . . 45 45
1335 60 c. Mike Davis and Kirk Gibson . . . 45 45
1336 60 c. Fernando Valenzuela and John Shelby . . . 45 45
1337 60 c. Jeff Hamilton and Franklin Stubbs . . . 45 45
1338 60 c. Aerial view of Dodger Stadium (no inscription) . 45 45
1339 60 c. Ray Searage and John Tudor . . . 45 45
1340 60 c. Mike Sharperson and Mickey Hatcher . . . 45 45
1341 60 c. Coaching staff . . . 45 45
1342 60 c. John Wetteland and Ramon Martinez . . . 45 45
1343 60 c. Tim Belcher and Tim Crews . . . 45 45
1344 60 c. Orel Hershiser and Mike Morgan . . . 45 45
1345 60 c. Mike Scioscia and Rick Dempsey . . . 45 45
1346 60 c. Dave Anderson and Alfredo Griffin . . . 45 45
1347 60 c. Dodgers' emblem . . . 45 45
1348 60 c. Kal Daniels and Mike Marshall . . . 45 45
1349 60 c. Eddie Murray and Willie Randolph . . . 45 45
1350 60 c. Tom Lasorda and Jose Gonzalez . . . 45 45
1351 60 c. Lenny Harris, Chris Gwynn and Billy Bean . . 45 45
See also Nos. 1541/58.

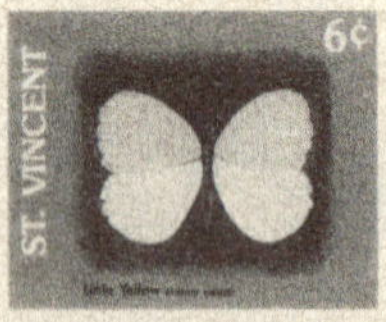

198 "Eurema venusta"

1989. Butterflies. Multicoloured.
1352 6 c. Type **198** . . . 25 15
1353 10 c. "Historis odius" . . . 30 15
1354 15 c. "Cynthia virginiensis" . . 40 15
1355 75 c. "Leptotes cassius" . . 80 65
1356 $1 "Battus polydamas" . . . 90 75
1357 $2 "Astraptes talus" . . . 2·00 2·25
1358 $3 "Danaus gilippus" . . . 2·50 2·75
1359 $5 "Myscelia antholia" . . . 3·50 4·00

199 Young Footballers

1989. World Cup Football Championship, Italy (1990) (1st issue). Multicoloured.
1361 10 c. Type **199** . . . 35 20
1362 55 c. Youth football teams . . 70 30
1363 $1 St. Vincent team in training 1·25 90
1364 $5 National team with trophies 3·00 4·50
See also Nos. 1559/62.

200 St. Vincent Amazon

1989. Wildlife. Multicoloured.
1366 65 c. Type **200** . . . 75 65
1367 75 c. Whistling warbler . . . 90 75
1368 $5 Black snake . . . 4·00 5·50

1989. California Earthquake Relief Fund. Nos. 1276/302 surch **+10c CALIF. EARTHQUAKE RELIEF.**
1370 60 c. + 10 c. Type **191** . . . 40 40
1371 60 c. + 10 c. Carl Yastrzemski 40 40
1372 60 c. + 10 c. Randy Johnson 40 40
1373 60 c. + 10 c. Jerome Walton 40 40
1374 60 c. + 10 c. Ramon Martinez 40 40
1375 60 c. + 10 c. Ken Hill . . . 40 40
1376 60 c. + 10 c. Tom McCarthy 40 40
1377 60 c. + 10 c. Gaylord Perry 40 40
1378 60 c. + 10 c. John Smoltz . 40 40
1379 60 c. + 10 c. Bob Milacki . 40 40
1380 60 c. + 10 c. Babe Ruth . . 40 40
1381 60 c. + 10 c. Jim Abbott . . 40 40
1382 60 c. + 10 c. Gary Sheffield . 40 40
1383 60 c. + 10 c. Gregg Jeffries . 40 40
1384 60 c. + 10 c. Kevin Brown . 40 40
1385 60 c. + 10 c. Cris Carpenter 40 40
1386 60 c. + 10 c. Johnny Bench . 40 40
1387 60 c. + 10 c. Ken Griffey Jr 40 40
1388 60 c. + 10 c. Type **192** . . 40 40
1389 60 c. + 10 c. Walt Weiss . . 40 40
1390 60 c. + 10 c. Willie Mays . 40 40
1391 60 c. + 10 c. Kirk Gibson . 40 40
1392 60 c. + 10 c. Ted Williams . 40 40
1393 60 c. + 10 c. Jose Canseco . 40 40
1394 60 c. + 10 c. Gaylord Perry . 40 40
1395 60 c. + 10 c. Orel Hershiser 40 40
1396 60 c. + 10 c. Frank Viola . 40 40

1989. "World Stamp Expo '89" International Stamp Exhibition, Washington (1st issue). As T **256** of Antigua showing Walt Disney cartoon characters and U.S. monuments. Multicoloured.

1397 1 c. Mickey and Minnie Mouse by Seagull Monument, Utah (vert) . . . 10 10
1398 2 c. Mickey Mouse and Goofy at Lincoln Memorial (vert) 10 10
1399 3 c. Mickey and Minnie Mouse at Crazy Horse Memorial, South Dakota (vert) . . . 10 10
1400 4 c. Mickey Mouse saluting "Uncle Sam" Wilson statue, New York (vert) . . . 10 10
1401 5 c. Goofy and Mickey Mouse at Benjamin Franklin Memorial, Philadelphia (vert) 10 10
1402 10 c. Goofy and Mickey Mouse at George Washington statue, New York (vert) . . . 10 10
1403 $3 Mickey Mouse at John F. Kennedy's birthplace, Massachusetts (vert) . . . 3·50 4·00
1404 $6 Mickey and Minnie Mouse at Mount Vernon, Virginia (vert) . . . 5·50 6·00

202 Nolan Ryan

204 Arms and 1979 Independence 50 c. Stamp

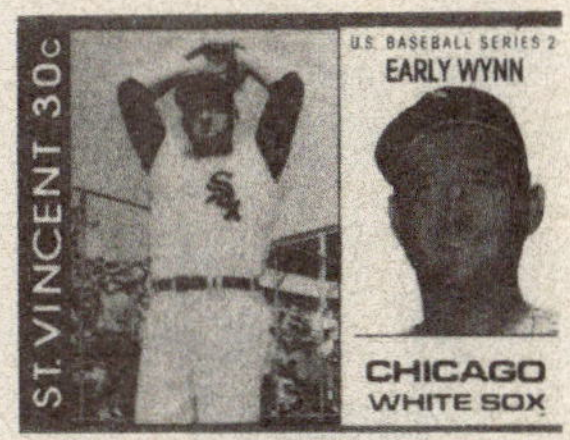

203 Early Wynn

1989. Famous Baseball Players (3rd series).

1407 **202** $2 multicoloured . . . . 85 1·00

1989. Famous Baseball Players (4th series). As T **203**

1408/88 30 c. × 81 multicoloured Set of 81 . . . 16·00 18·00

1989. 10th Anniv of Independence.

1489 **204** 65 c. multicoloured . . . 50 50

1989. Christmas. Paintings by Botticelli and Da Vinci. As T **259** of Antigua. Multicoloured.

1491 10 c. Holy Family (detail, "The Adoration of the Magi") (Botticelli) . . . 15 10
1492 25 c. Crowd (detail, "The Adoration of the Magi") (Botticelli) . . . 25 15
1493 30 c. "The Madonna of the Magnificat" (detail) (Botticelli) . . . 25 15
1494 40 c. "The Virgin and Child with St. Anne and St. John the Baptist" (detail) (Da Vinci) . . . 30 20
1495 55 c. Angel (detail, "The Annunciation") (Da Vinci) 40 30
1496 75 c. Virgin Mary (detail, "The Annunciation") (Da Vinci) 50 50
1497 $5 "Madonna of the Carnation" (detail) (Da Vinci) . . . 3·00 3·50
1498 $6 "The Annunciation" (detail) (Botticelli) . . . 3·50 4·00

205 Boy Scout, 1989

206 Man and Blind Girl

1989. 75th Anniv of Boy Scout and 60th Anniv of Girl Guide Movements in St. Vincent. Mult.

1500 35 c. Type **205** . . . 55 35
1501 35 c. Guide, ranger and brownie 55 35
1502 55 c. Boy scout in original uniform . . . 75 35
1503 55 c. Mrs. Jackson (founder of St. Vincent Girl Guides) . 75 35
1504 $2 Scouts' 75th Anniv logo . 2·00 3·00
1505 $2 Mrs. Russell (Girl Guide leader, 1989) . . . 2·00 3·00

1990. 25th Anniv (1989) of Lions Club of St. Vincent. Multicoloured.

1507 10 c. Type **206** . . . 40 20
1508 65 c. Handing out school books (horiz) . . . 70 50
1509 75 c. Teacher explaining diabetes (horiz) . . . 80 60
1510 $2 Blood sugar testing machine (horiz) . . . 1·75 2·00
1511 $4 Distributing book on drugs (horiz) . . . 2·75 3·50

1990. 50th Anniv of Second World War. As T **98** of Grenada Grenadines. Multicoloured.

1512 5 c. Scuttling of "Admiral Graf Spee" (German pocket battleship), 1939 . . . 10 10
1513 10 c. General de Gaulle and French resistance, 1940 . . 15 15
1514 15 c. British tank, North Africa, 1940 . . . 20 20
1515 25 c. U.S.S. "Reuben James" (destroyer) in periscope sight, 1941 . . . 30 30
1516 30 c. General MacArthur and map of S.W. Pacific, 1942 35 35
1517 40 c. American parachute drop on Corregidor, 1945 . . . 40 40
1518 55 c. H.M.S. "King George V" (battleship) engaging "Bismarck" (German battleship), 1941 . . . 55 55
1519 75 c. American battleships entering Tokyo Bay, 1945 70 70
1520 $5 Hoisting the Soviet flag on the Reichstag, Berlin, 1945 3·25 3·25
1521 $6 American aircraft carriers, Battle of Philippines Sea, 1944 . . . 3·75 3·75

207 Two Pence Blue

210 Maradona, Argentina

1990. 150th Anniv of the Penny Black.

1523 **207** $2 black, green & mauve 1·25 1·50
1524 – $4 black and mauve . . 2·50 3·25

DESIGN: $4 Penny Black.

1990. "Stamp World London '90" International Stamp Exhibition. British Uniforms. As T **193** of Gambia showing Walt Disney cartoon characters. Multicoloured.

1526 5 c. Scrooge McDuck as 18th-century Admiral . . . 20 15
1527 10 c. Huey as Light Infantry bugler, 1854 . . . 25 15
1528 15 c. Minnie Mouse as Irish Guards drummer, 1900 . . 35 20
1529 25 c. Goofy as Seaforth Highlanders lance-corporal, 1944 . . . 45 30
1530 $1 Mickey Mouse as 58th Regiment ensign, 1879 . . 1·25 1·00
1531 $2 Donald Duck as Royal Engineers officer, 1813 . . 1·90 2·00
1532 $4 Mickey Mouse as Duke of Edinburgh's Royal Regiment drum major . . . 3·00 3·50
1533 $5 Goofy as Cameronians sergeant piper, 1918 . . . 3·00 3·50

1990. Nolan Ryan—Sixth No-hitter. No. 1407 optd **Sixth No-Hitter 11 June 90 Oakland Athletics**.

1535 **202** $2 multicoloured . . . . 95 1·00

1990. 90th Birthday of Queen Elizabeth the Queen Mother. As T **99** of Grenada Grenadines.

1536 $2 black, green and mauve . 1·40 1·75
1537 $2 black, green and mauve . 1·40 1·75
1538 $2 black, green and mauve . 1·40 1·75

DESIGNS: No. 1536, Queen Elizabeth signing visitors' book; 1537, Queen Elizabeth in evening dress; 1538, Queen Elizabeth the Queen Mother in Coronation robes, 1953.

1990. Nolan Ryan—300th Win. No. 1407 optd **300th Win Milwaukee Brewers July 31, 1990**.

1540 **202** $2 multicoloured . . . . 95 1·00

1990. Cent of Los Angeles Dodgers (2nd issue). Baseball Players. As T **197**. Multicoloured.

1541 60 c. Mickey Hatcher and Jay Howell . . . 45 45
1542 60 c. Juan Samuel and Mike Scioscia . . . 45 45
1543 60 c. Lenny Harris and Mike Hartley . . . 45 45
1544 60 c. Ramon Martinez and Mike Morgan . . . 45 45
1545 60 c. Aerial view of Dodger Stadium (inscr "DODGER STADIUM") . . . 45 45
1546 60 c. Stan Javier and Don Aase 45 45
1547 60 c. Ray Searage and Mike Sharperson . . . 45 45
1548 60 c. Tim Belcher and Pat Perry 45 45
1549 60 c. Dave Walsh, Jose Vizcaino, Jim Neidlinger, Jose Offerman and Carlos Hernandez . . . 45 45
1550 60 c. Hubie Brooks and Orel Hershiser . . . 45 45
1551 60 c. Tom Lasorda and Tim Crews . . . 45 45
1552 60 c. Fernando Valenzuela and Eddie Murray . . . 45 45
1553 60 c. Kal Daniels and Jose Gonzalez . . . 45 45
1554 60 c. Dodgers emblem . . . 45 45
1555 60 c. Chris Gwynn and Jeff Hamilton . . . 45 45
1556 60 c. Kirk Gibson and Rick Dempsey . . . 45 45
1557 60 c. Jim Gott and Alfredo Griffin . . . 45 45
1558 60 c. Ron Perranoski, Bill Russell, Joe Ferguson, Joe Amalfitano, Mark Cresse, Ben Hines and Manny Mota 45 45

1990. World Cup Football Championship, Italy (2nd issue). Multicoloured.

1559 10 c. Type **210** . . . 35 15
1560 75 c. Valderrama, Colombia . 75 65
1561 $1 Francescoli, Uruguay . . . 95 85
1562 $5 Beulemans, Belgium . . . 4·00 5·00

1990. 95th Anniv of Rotary International. Nos. 1230/8 optd with Rotary emblem.

1564 10 c. Type **186** . . . 30 20
1565 40 c. "Liberte" . . . 50 40
1566 50 c. "Mauretania I" (launched 1906) . . . 55 45
1567 75 c. "France" . . . 80 60
1568 $1 "Aquitania" . . . 90 80
1569 $2 "United States" . . . 1·60 1·75
1570 $3 "Olympic" . . . 2·00 2·50
1571 $4 "Queen Elizabeth" . . . 2·25 2·75

1990. Olympic Medal Winners, Seoul. Nos. 1153/6 optd.

1573 10 c. Type **178** (optd **JOE DELOACH U.S.A. STEVE LEWIS U.S.A. PAUL ERANG KENYA**) . . . 20 20
1574 50 c. Long jumping (optd **CARL LEWIS U.S.A.**) . . 60 60
1575 $1 Triple jumping (optd **HRISTO MARKOV BULGARIA**) . . . 90 90
1576 $5 Boxing (optd **HENRY MASKE E. GERMANY**) . 3·25 3·75

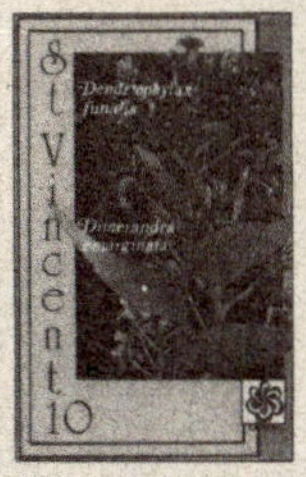

213 "Dendrophylax funalis" and "Dimerandra emarginata"

214 "Miraculous Draught of Fishes" (detail, Rubens)

1990. "EXPO 90" International Garden and Greenery Exposition, Osaka. Orchids. Mult.

1578 10 c. Type **213** . . . 35 20
1579 15 c. "Epidendrum elongatum" 40 25
1580 45 c. "Comparettia falcata" . 60 30
1581 60 c. "Brassia maculata" . . 75 60
1582 $1 "Encyclia cochleata" and "Encyclia cordigera" . . . 90 80
1583 $2 "Cyrtopodium punctatum" 1·50 1·75
1584 $4 "Cattleya labiata" . . . 2·50 2·75
1585 $5 "Bletia purpurea" . . . 2·75 3·25

1990. Christmas. 350th Death Anniv of Rubens. Multicoloured.

1587 10 c. Type **214** . . . 25 20
1588 45 c. "Crowning of Holy Katherine" (detail) . . . 45 25
1589 50 c. "St. Ives of Treguier" (detail) . . . 50 30
1590 65 c. "Allegory of Eternity" (detail) . . . 65 45
1591 $1 "St. Bavo receives Monastic Habit of Ghent" (detail) . . 90 80
1592 $2 "Crowning of Holy Katherine" (different detail) 1·50 1·50
1593 $4 "St. Bavo receives Monastic Habit of Ghent" (different detail) . . . 2·75 3·25
1594 $5 "Communion of St. Francis" (detail) . . . 3·00 3·25

215 Geoffrey Chaucer

1990. International Literacy Year (1st issue). Chaucer's "Canterbury Tales". Mult.

1596 40 c. Type **215** . . . 40 40
1597 40 c. "When April with his showers" . . . 40 40
1598 40 c. "When Zephyr also has..." 40 40
1599 40 c. "And many little birds ..." 40 40
1600 40 c. "And palmers to go seeking out ..." . . . 40 40
1601 40 c. Quill in ink well and open book . . . 40 40
1602 40 c. Green bird in tree . . . 40 40
1603 40 c. Brown bird in tree and franklin's head . . . 40 40
1604 40 c. Purple bird in tree and banner . . . 40 40
1605 40 c. Canterbury . . . 40 40
1606 40 c. Knight's head . . . 40 40
1607 40 c. Black bird in tree and squire's head . . . 40 40
1608 40 c. Friar . . . 40 40
1609 40 c. Franklin . . . 40 40
1610 40 c. Prioress and monk holding banner . . . 40 40
1611 40 c. Summoner, Oxford clerk and parson . . . 40 40
1612 40 c. Sergeant-at-Law and knight on horseback . . . 40 40
1613 40 c. Squire . . . 40 40
1614 40 c. "In fellowship ..." . . . 40 40
1615 40 c. Cockerel and horse's legs 40 40
1616 40 c. Hens . . . 40 40
1617 40 c. Hen and rabbit . . . 40 40
1618 40 c. Horses' legs and butterfly 40 40
1619 40 c. "And briefly, when the sun..." . . . 40 40

Nos. 1596/1619 were printed together, se-tenant, forming a composite design.

See also Nos. 1777/88 and 1790/1801.

1990. Death Centenary of Vincent van Gogh (artist). As T **278** of Antigua. Multicoloured.

1620 1 c. Self-portrait, 1889 . . . 30 30
1621 5 c. Self-portrait, 1886 . . . 30 30
1622 10 c. Self-portrait with hat and pipe, 1888 . . . 30 30
1623 15 c. Self-portrait at easel, 1888 30 30
1624 20 c. Self-portrait, 1887 . . . 75 75
1625 45 c. Self-portrait, 1889 (different) . . . 90 90
1626 $5 Self-portrait with pipe, 1889 2·75 3·00
1627 $6 Self-portrait wearing straw hat, 1887 . . . 3·00 3·25

1990. Hummel Figurines. As T **256** of Maldive Islands. Multicoloured.

1628 10 c. "The Photographer" . 15 15
1629 15 c. "Ladder and Rope" . . 15 15
1630 40 c. "Druggist" . . . 30 30
1631 60 c. "Hello" . . . 45 45
1632 $1 "Boots" . . . 80 80
1633 $2 "The Artist" . . . 1·40 1·40
1634 $4 "Waiter" . . . 2·50 2·50
1635 $5 "The Postman" . . . 2·75 2·75

218 U.S.A. 1893 1 c. Columbus Stamp

1991. 500th Anniv (1992) of Discovery of America by Columbus (4th issue). Designs showing U.S.A. 1893 Columbian Exposition, Chicago, stamps (Nos. 1639/54) or ships (others). Multicoloured.

1639 1 c. Type **218** . . . 10 10
1640 2 c. Columbus 2 c. . . . 10 10
1641 3 c. Columbus 3 c. . . . 10 10
1642 4 c. Columbus 4 c. . . . 10 10
1643 5 c. Columbus 5 c. . . . 10 10
1644 6 c. Columbus 6 c. . . . 10 10
1645 8 c. Columbus 8 c. . . . 10 10
1646 10 c. Columbus 10 c. . . . 10 10
1647 15 c. Columbus 15 c. . . . 10 10
1648 30 c. Columbus 30 c. . . . 15 20
1649 50 c. Columbus 50 c. . . . 25 30
1650 $1 Columbus $1 . . . 50 55
1651 $2 Columbus $2 . . . 95 1·00
1652 $3 Columbus $3 . . . 1·40 1·50
1653 $4 Columbus $4 . . . 2·00 2·10
1654 $5 Columbus $5 . . . 2·40 2·50
1655 $10 "Santa Maria", scarlet macaw and tropical flower 5·00 5·25
1656 $10 Logo, "Santa Maria" and Amerindian hut . . . 5·00 5·25

219 Pebbles and Hoppy boxing

1991. Sports. Characters from the "Flintstones" cartoons. Multicoloured.

1658 10 c. Type **219** . . . 20 10
1659 15 c. Fred Flintstone and Dino playing football . . . 30 15
1660 45 c. Fred losing rowing race to Barney Rubble . . . 50 30
1661 55 c. Betty Rubble, Wilma Flintstone and Pebbles in dressage competition . . . 70 50
1662 $1 Fred playing basketball . 1·00 1·00
1663 $2 Bamm Bamm wrestling Barney with Fred as referee 1·50 1·50
1664 $4 Fred and Barney playing tennis . . . 2·75 2·75
1665 $5 Fred, Barney and Dino cycling . . . 2·75 2·75

220 Board Meeting

1991. "The Jetsons" (cartoon film). Mult.

1667 5 c. Type **220** . . . 15 10
1668 20 c. Jetsons with Dog . . . 30 15
1669 45 c. Judy and Apollo Blue . . 50 25
1670 50 c. Cosmo Spacely and George Jetson 50 35
1671 60 c. George and Elroy catching cogs (horiz) 70 50
1672 $1 Judy, Apollo, Elroy and Teddy in cavern (horiz) . . 1·00 1·00
1673 $2 Drill destroying the cavern (horiz) . . . . 1·50 1·50
1674 $4 Jetsons celebrating with the Grungees . . . . . . 2·75 2·75
1675 $5 The Jetsons returning home 2·75 2·75

1991. 500th Anniv (1992) of Discovery of America by Columbus, (5th issue). History of Exploration. As T **64** of Nevis. Multicoloured.

1677 5 c. "Sanger 2" (projected space shuttle) 15 15
1678 10 c. "Magellan satellite, 1990" 15 15
1679 25 c. "Buran" space shuttle . . 25 25
1680 75 c. Projected "Freedom" space station 65 65
1681 $1 Projected Mars mission space craft 80 80
1682 $2 "Hubble" telescope, 1990 . 1·60 1·60
1683 $4 Projected Mars mission "sailship" . . . . . . 2·50 2·50
1684 $5 Projected "Craf" satellite . 2·50 2·50

1991. 65th Birthday of Queen Elizabeth II. As T **280** of Antigua. Multicoloured.

1686 5 c. Queen and Prince Philip during visit to Spain, 1988 15 15
1687 60 c. Queen and Prince Philip in landau 60 45
1688 $2 Queen at Caen Hill Waterway, 1990 . . . . . 1·75 1·75
1689 $4 Queen at Badminton, 1983 3·00 3·25

1991. 10th Wedding Anniv of the Prince and Princess of Wales. As T **280** of Antigua. Multicoloured.

1691 20 c. Prince and Princess in hard hats, 1987 . . . . . . 30 20
1692 25 c. Portraits of Prince and Princess and sons 30 20
1693 $1 Prince Henry and Prince William, both in 1988 . . . 90 90
1694 $5 Princess Diana in France and Prince Charles in 1987 . . 4·25 4·25

221 Class D51 Steam Locomotive

1991. "Phila Nippon '91" International Stamp Exhibition, Tokyo. Japanese Trains. Mult.

1696 75 c. Type **221** 50 50
1697 75 c. Class 9600 steam locomotive 50 50
1698 75 c. Goods wagons and chrysanthemum emblem . . 50 50
1699 75 c. Passenger coach . . . 50 50
1700 75 c. Decorated Class C57 steam locomotive 50 50
1701 75 c. Oil tanker wagon . . . 50 50
1702 75 c. Class C53 steam locomotive 50 50
1703 75 c. First Japanese steam locomotive 50 50
1704 75 c. Class C11 steam locomotive 50 50
1705 $1 Class 181 electric unit . . 60 60
1706 $1 Class EH10 electric locomotive 60 60
1707 $1 Passenger coaches and Special Express symbol . . 60 60
1708 $1 Class 1 electric tramcar, Sendai City 60 60
1709 $1 Class 485 electric unit . . 60 60
1710 $1 Street-cleaning tram, Sendai City 60 60
1711 $1 "Hikari" express train . . 60 60
1712 $1 Class ED11 electric locomotive 60 60
1713 $1 Class EF66 electric locomotive 60 60

222 Marcello Mastroianni (actor)

1991. Italian Entertainers. Multicoloured.

1715 $1 Type **222** 70 70
1716 $1 Sophia Loren (actress) . . 70 70
1717 $1 Mario Lanza (singer) . . 70 70
1718 $1 Federico Fellini (director) 70 70
1719 $1 Arturo Toscanini (conductor) 70 70
1720 $1 Anna Magnani (actress) . 70 70
1721 $1 Giancarlo Giannini (actor) 70 70
1722 $1 Gina Lollobrigida (actress) 70 70
1723 $1 Enrico Caruso (operatic tenor) 70 70

223 Madonna

1991. Madonna (American singer). Mult.

1725 $1 Type **223** 80 80
1726 $1 In strapless dress 80 80
1727 $1 Wearing necklaces, looking right 80 80
1728 $1 In green dress 80 80
1729 $1 Wearing necklaces, looking to front 80 80
1730 $1 With wrist bangles . . . 80 80
1731 $1 With hand to face . . . 80 80
1732 $1 In purple dress 80 80
1733 $1 With microphone 80 80

224 John Lennon

1991. John Lennon (British musician). Mult.

1735 $1 + 2 c. Type **224** . . . 90 90
1736 $1 + 2 c. With Beatle hair cut 90 90
1737 $1 + 2 c. In cap 90 90
1738 $1 + 2 c. In red polka-dot shirt 90 90
1739 $1 + 2 c. In green polo-neck jumper and jacket . . . 90 90
1740 $1 + 2 c. In glasses and magenta jacket 90 90
1741 $1 + 2 c. With long hair and glasses 90 90
1742 $1 + 2 c. In black jumper . . 90 90
1743 $1 + 2 c. In polo-neck jumper 90 90

225 Free French Resistance Fighters, 1944

1991. Anniversaries and Events. Multicoloured.

1744 10 c. Type **225** 20 15
1745 45 c. De Gaulle with Churchill, 1944 . . . . 60 40
1746 50 c. Protestor with banner . 45 45
1747 65 c. Tales around the camp fire (vert) 70 50
1748 75 c. Liberation of Paris, 1944 70 60
1749 75 c. Building Berlin Wall . 70 60
1750 90 c. German flag and protestors' shadows . . . 70 70
1751 $1 Presidents Bush and Gorbachev shaking hands 80 80
1752 $1 "Marriage of Figaro" . . 1·25 1·00
1753 $1.50 British trenches and Mafeking Siege 3d. stamp . 1·50 1·50
1754 $1.50 Class P-36 steam locomotive, Trans-Siberian Railway . . . . 1·50 1·50
1755 $1.50 Map of Switzerland and woman in traditional costume 1·50 1·50
1756 $1.65 Lilienthal's signature and "Flugzeug Nr. 13 Doppeldecker" . . . . . 1·75 1·75
1757 $2 Street fighting, Kiev . . 2·25 2·25
1758 $2 Gottfried Leibniz (mathematician) . . . . 2·25 2·25
1759 $3 "The Clemency of Titus" . 2·50 2·50
1760 $3.50 Angelfish and scout diver 2·50 2·50

ANNIVERSARIES AND EVENTS: Nos. 1744/5, 1748, Birth centenary of Charles de Gaulle (French statesman); Nos. 1746, 1749/51, Bicentenary of Brandenburg Gate, Berlin; Nos. 1747, 1753, 1760, 50th death anniv of Lord Baden-Powell and World Scout Jamboree, Korea; Nos. 1752, 1759, Death bicentenary of Mozart; No. 1754, Centenary of Trans-Siberian Railway; No. 1755, 700th anniv of Swiss Confederation; No. 1756, Centenary of Otto Lilienthal's gliding experiments; No. 1757, 50th anniv of capture of Kiev; No. 1758, 750th anniv of Hanover.

226 Myrvyn Bennion

1991. 50th Anniv of Japanese Attack on Pearl Harbour. Recipients of Congressional Medal of Honor. Multicoloured.

1762 $1 Type **226** 70 70
1763 $1 George Cannon 70 70
1763 $1 John Finn 70 70
1765 $1 Francis Flaherty 70 70
1766 $1 Samuel Fuqua 70 70
1767 $1 Edwin Hill 70 70
1768 $1 Herbert Jones 70 70
1769 $1 Isaac Kidd 70 70
1770 $1 Jackson Pharris 70 70
1771 $1 Thomas Reeves 70 70
1772 $1 Donald Ross 70 70
1773 $1 Robert Scott 70 70
1774 $1 Franklin van Valkenburgh 70 70
1775 $1 James Ward 70 70
1776 $1 Cassin Young 70 70

1991. International Literacy Year (1990) (2nd issue). As T **269** of Antigua but horiz, showing scenes from Disney cartoon films. Multicoloured.

(a) "The Prince and The Pauper".

1777 5 c. Mickey Mouse, Goofy and Pluto as pauper pals . . . 15 15
1778 10 c. Mickey as the bored prince 15 15
1779 15 c. Donald Duck as the valet 20 20
1780 25 c. Mickey as the prince and the pauper 25 25
1781 60 c. Exchanging clothes . . . 55 55
1782 75 c. Prince and pauper with suit of armour 65 65
1783 80 c. Throwing food from the battlements 70 70
1784 $1 Pete as Captain of the Guard 85 85
1785 $2 Mickey and Donald in the dungeon . . . . 1·50 1·50
1786 $3 Mickey and Donald at dungeon window . . . . . 1·75 1·75
1787 $4 Goofy rescuing Mickey and Donald . . . . 2·50 2·50
1788 $5 Crowning the real prince . 2·50 2·50

(b) "The Rescuers Down Under".

1790 5 c. Miss Bianca 15 15
1791 10 c. Bernard 15 15
1792 15 c. Matre d'Francoise . . . 20 20
1793 25 c. Wilbur the Albatross . . 25 25
1794 60 c. Jake the Kangaroo Mouse 55 55
1795 75 c. Bernard, Bianca and Jake in the outback 65 65
1796 80 c. Bianca and Bernard to the rescue 70 70
1797 $1 Marahute the Eagle . . . 85 85
1798 $2 Cody and Marahute with eggs . . . . 1·50 1·50
1799 $3 McLeach and his pet, Joanna the Goanna . . . . . . 1·75 1·75
1800 $4 Frank the Frill-necked Lizard . . . . 2·50 2·50
1801 $5 Red Kangaroo, Krebbs Koala and Polly Platypus . 2·50 2·75

227 Hans-Dietrich Genscher and "Winged Victory" Statue

1991. European History. Multicoloured.

1803 $1 Type **227** . . . . 1·00 1·00
1804 $1 Destruction of Berlin Wall 1·00 1·00
1805 $1 Churchill, De Gaulle and Appeal to the French, 1940 1·00 1·00
1809 $1 Eisenhower, De Gaulle and D-Day, 1944 . . . . 1·00 1·00
1807 $1 Brandenburg Gate, Berlin (bicentenary) . . . . 1·00 1·00
1808 $1 Chancellor Helmut Kohl and meeting of Berlin mayors, 1989 . . . . 1·00 1·00
1809 $1 De Gaulle with Chancellor Adenauer . . . . 1·00 1·00
1810 $1 Pres. Kennedy's visit to Europe, 1961, Washington and Lafayette . . . . . 1·00 1·00

1991. Famous Golfers. As T **227**. Mult.

1812 $1 Gary Player . . . . . . 1·10 1·10
1813 $1 Nick Faldo . . . . 1·10 1·10
1814 $1 Severiano Ballesteros . . 1·10 1·10
1815 $1 Ben Hogan . . . . 1·10 1·10
1816 $1 Jack Nicklaus . . . . . 1·10 1·10
1817 $1 Greg Norman . . . . . . 1·10 1·10
1818 $1 Jose-Maria Olazabal . . . 1·10 1·10
1819 $1 Bobby Jones . . . . . . 1·10 1·10

1991. Famous Entertainers. As T **277**. Mult.

1820 $2 Michael Jackson . . . . 1·75 1·75
1821 $2 Madonna . . . . 1·75 1·75
1822 $2 Elvis Presley . . . . . . 1·75 1·75
1823 $2 David Bowie . . . . . . 1·75 1·75
1824 $2 Prince . . . . 1·75 1·75
1825 $2 Frank Sinatra . . . . . 1·75 1·75
1826 $2 George Michael . . . . . 1·75 1·75
1827 $2 Mick Jagger . . . . . . 1·75 1·75

1991. Famous Chess Masters. As T **227**. Mult.

1829 $1 Francoise Philidor . . . . 1·00 1·00
1830 $1 Karl Anderssen . . . . . 1·00 1·00
1831 $1 Wilhelm Steinitz . . . . 1·00 1·00
1832 $1 Alexandrovich Alekhine . 1·00 1·00
1833 $1 Boris Spassky . . . . . . 1·00 1·00
1834 $1 Robert Fischer . . . . . 1·00 1·00
1835 $1 Anatoly Karpov . . . . . 1·00 1·00
1836 $1 Garry Kasparov . . . . 1·00 1·00

1991. Nobel Prize Winners. As T **227**. Mult.

1837 $1 Albert Einstein (mathematical physicist) . . 70 70
1838 $1 Wilhelm Rontgen (physicist) 70 70
1839 $1 William Shockley (chemist) 70 70
1840 $1 Charles Townes (physicist) 70 70
1841 $1 Lev Landau (physicist) . . 70 70
1842 $1 Guglielmo Marconi (applied physicist) 70 70
1843 $1 Willard Libby (chemist) . 70 70
1844 $1 Ernest Lawrence (nuclear physicist) 70 70

228 Walt Disney Characters decorating Christmas Tree, 1982

1991. Christmas. Walt Disney Christmas Cards. Multicoloured.

1845 10 c. Type **228** 15 15
1846 45 c. Mickey and Moose, 1980 40 30
1847 55 c. Mickey, Pluto and Donald carrying bauble, 1970 . . . 50 40
1848 75 c. Duckling and egg shell, 1943 . . . . 70 70
1849 $1.50 Walt Disney characters decorating globe, 1941 . . 1·25 1·25
1850 $2 The Lady and the Tramp by Christmas tree, 1986 . . . 1·50 1·50
1851 $4 Walt Disney characters carol singing, 1977 . . . . . 2·75 2·75
1852 $5 Mickey in fairy-tale castle, 1965 . . . . 2·75 3·00

229 Kings Hill

1992. Preserving the Environment. Mult.

1854 10 c. Type **229** 20 20
1855 55 c. Planting sapling . . . 50 45
1856 75 c. Doric Temple, Botanic Gardens 60 55
1857 $2 18th-century map of Kings Hill . . . . 1·40 1·75

1992. 40th Anniv of Queen Elizabeth II's Accession. As T **288** of Antigua. Multicoloured.

1858 10 c. Kingstown from the cliffs 15 15
1859 20 c. Deep water wharf, Kingstown 25 15
1860 $1 Residential suburb, Kingstown 60 60
1861 $5 Kingstown from the interior 2·50 3·00

230 Women's Luge

1992. Winter Olympic Games, Albertville (1st issue). Multicoloured.
1863 10 c. Type **230** 15 15
1864 15 c. Women's figure skating (vert) 20 20
1865 25 c. Two-man bobsleigh . . 25 25
1866 30 c. Mogul skiing (vert) . . 30 30
1867 45 c. Nordic combination . . 40 40
1868 55 c. Ski jumping 55 55
1869 75 c. Men's giant slalom . . 65 65
1870 $1.50 Women's slalom (vert) . 1·10 1·10
1871 $5 Ice hockey . . . . . . 3·25 3·50
1872 $8 Biathlon (vert) . . . . . 4·25 4·50
See also Nos. 1966/79.

231 Women's Synchronized Swimming

1992. Olympic Games, Barcelona. Multicoloured.
1874 10 c. Type **231** 10 10
1875 15 c. Men's high jump (vert) 10 10
1876 25 c. Men's small-bore rifle shooting 10 10
1877 30 c. Men's 200 metres (vert) 15 20
1878 45 c. Men's judo (vert) . . . 20 25
1879 55 c. Men's 200 metres freestyle swimming 25 30
1880 75 c. Men's javelin (vert) . . 35 40
1881 $1.50 Men's 4000 metre pursuit cycling (vert) . . . . . . 1·50 1·50
1882 $5 Boxing . . . . 2·50 3·00
1883 $8 Women's basketball (vert) 7·00 7·50

1992. International Stamp Exhibitions. As T **215** of Lesotho showing Walt Disney cartoon characters. Multicoloured. (a) "Granada '92", Spain. The Three Pigs in Spanish Uniforms.
1885 15 c. The wolf as general of Spanish Moors 20 10
1886 40 c. Pig as captain of infantry 40 25
1887 $2 Pig as halberdier . . . . 1·25 1·50
1888 $4 Pig as nobleman . . . . 2·25 2·75

(b) "World Columbian Stamp Expo '92", Chicago Landmarks.
1890 10 c. Mickey Mouse and Goofy looking at Picasso sculpture (horiz) 20 15
1891 50 c. Mickey and Donald Duck admiring Robie House (horiz) 45 35
1892 $1 Calder sculpture in Sears Tower (horiz) 80 60
1893 $5 Goofy in Buckingham Memorial Fountain (horiz) 2·50 2·75

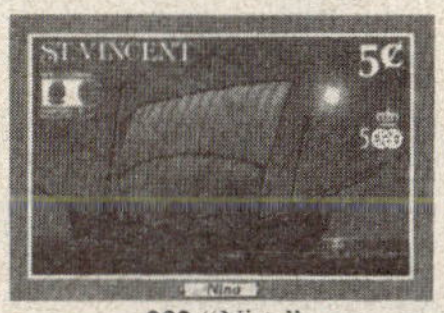

232 "Nina"

1992. 500th Anniv of Discovery of America by Columbus (6th issue). "World Columbian Stamp Expo '92", Chicago. Multicoloured.
1895 5 c. Type **232** 40 40
1896 10 c. "Pinta" 40 30
1897 45 c. "Santa Maria" 75 50
1898 55 c. Fleet leaving Palos, 1492 75 55
1899 $4 Christopher Columbus (vert) 3·00 3·50
1900 $5 Arms of Columbus (vert) . 3·00 3·50

1992. 15th Death Anniv of Elvis Presley (1st issue). As T **298** of Antigua. Multicoloured.
1902 $1 Elvis looking pensive . . . 90 90
1903 $1 Wearing black and yellow striped shirt 90 90
1904 $1 Singing into microphone . 90 90
1905 $1 Wearing wide-brimmed hat 90 90
1906 $1 With microphone in right hand 90 90
1907 $1 In Army uniform 90 90
1908 $1 Wearing pink shirt . . . 90 90
1909 $1 In yellow shirt 90 90
1910 $1 In jacket and bow tie . . 90 90
See also Nos. 2029/37, 2038/45 and 2047/9.

234 Bonnie Blair

235 "Astraptes anaphus"

1992. Bonnie Blair's Victories in 500 metres Speed Skating at Calgary and Albertville Olympic Games.
1912 **234** $3 multicoloured . . . . 2·25 2·50

1992. "Genova '92" International Thematic Stamp Exhibition (1st issue). Butterflies. Multicoloured.
1914 5 c. Type **235** 30 40
1915 10 c. "Anartia jatrophae" (horiz) 30 20
1916 35 c. "Danaus eresimus" . . 55 40
1917 45 c. "Battus polydamus" . . 60 45
1918 55 c. "Junonia evarete" (horiz) 70 50
1919 65 c. "Urbanus proteus" . . 80 60
1920 75 c. "Pyrgus oileus" (horiz) 90 65
1921 $1 "Biblis hyperia" . . . . 1·00 75
1922 $2 "Eurema daira" . . . . 1·50 1·50
1923 $3 "Leptotes cassius" (horiz) 1·75 2·00
1924 $4 "Ephyriades brunnea" (horiz) . . . . 2·25 2·50
1925 $5 "Victorina stelenes" . . . 2·50 2·75
See also Nos. 1940/51.

236 "Collybia subpruinosa"

237 Rufous-breasted Hermit

1992. Fungi. Multicoloured.
1927 10 c. Type **236** 30 20
1928 15 c. "Gerronema citrinum" 40 20
1929 20 c. "Amanita antillana" . 45 30
1930 45 c. "Dermoloma atrobrunneum" 60 35
1931 50 c. "Inopilus maculosus" . 70 40
1932 65 c. "Pulveroboletus brachyspermus" 80 55
1933 75 c. "Mycena violacella" . . 90 60
1934 $1 "Xerocomus brasiliensis" 1·00 70
1935 $2 "Amanita ingrata" . . . 1·50 1·75
1936 $3 "Leptonia caeruleocapitata" 1·75 2·25
1937 $4 "Limacella myochroa" . . 2·25 2·75
1938 $5 "Inopilus magnificus" . . 2·50 2·75
No. 1936 is inscribed "Leptonia caeruleocaptata" in error.

1992. "Genova '92" International Thematic Stamp Exhibition (2nd issue). Hummingbirds. Multicoloured.
1940 5 c. Type **237** 30 40
1941 15 c. Hispaniolan emerald . . 35 20
1942 45 c. Green-throated carib . 60 35
1943 55 c. Jamaican mango . . . 70 45
1944 65 c. Vervain hummingbird . 80 60
1945 75 c. Purple-throated carib . 90 70
1946 90 c. Green mango 90 75
1947 $1 Bee hummingbird . . . . 1·00 80
1948 $2 Cuban emerald . . . . . 1·75 1·75
1949 $3 Puerto Rican emerald . . 1·90 2·00
1950 $4 Antillean mango . . . . 2·40 2·75
1951 $5 Streamertail . . . . . . 2·75 2·75

238 Coral Vine

239 Kristi Yamaguchi (U.S.A.) (figure skating)

1992. Medicinal Plants. Multicoloured.
1953 75 c. Type **238** 70 70
1954 75 c. Cocoplum 70 70
1955 75 c. Angel's trumpet . . . 70 70
1956 75 c. Lime 70 70
1957 75 c. White ginger 70 70
1958 75 c. Pussley 70 70
1959 75 c. Sea grape 70 70
1960 75 c. Indian mulberry . . . 70 70
1961 75 c. Plantain 70 70
1962 75 c. Lignum vitae 70 70
1963 75 c. Periwinkle 70 70
1964 75 c. Guava 70 70

1992. Winter Olympic Games, Albertville (2nd issue). Gold Medal Winners. Multicoloured.
1966 $1 Type **239** 80 80
1967 $1 Pernilla Wiberg (Sweden) (giant slalom skiing) . . . 80 80
1968 $1 Lyubov Yegorova (C.I.S.) (10 kms cross-country skiing) 80 80
1969 $1 Josef Polig (Italy) (combined alpine skiing) 80 80
1970 $1 Fin Christian-Jagge (Norway) (slalom skiing) . 80 80
1971 $1 Kerrin Lee-Gartner (Canada) (downhill skiing) 80 80
1972 $1 Steffania Belmondo (Italy) (30 kms cross-country skiing) 80 80
1973 $1 Alberto Tomba (Italy) (giant slalom skiing) 80 80
1974 $1 Fabrice Guy (France) (nordic combined skiing) . 80 80
1975 $1 Patrick Ortlieb (Austria) (downhill skiing) 80 80
1976 $1 Vegard Ulvang (Norway) (nordic cross-country skiing) 80 80
1977 $1 Edgar Grospiron (France) (freestyle mogul skiing) . . 80 80
1978 $1 Andre Aamodt (Norway) (super giant slalom skiing) 80 80
1979 $1 Viktor Petrenko (C.I.S.) (figure skating) 80 80
No. 1968 is inscribed "LYUBOV EGOROVA" in error.

1992. 500th Anniv of Discovery of America by Columbus (7th issue). Organization of East Caribbean States. As Nos. 1670/1 of Antigua. Multicoloured.
1981 $1 Columbus meeting Amerindians . . . . 1·00 75
1982 $2 Ships approaching island . 1·75 2·00

240 "Pinocchio"

1992. Opening of Euro-Disney Resort, Paris. Multicoloured.
1983 $1 Type **240** . . . . 1·00 1·00
1984 $1 "Alice in Wonderland" . . 1·00 1·00
1985 $1 "Bambi" . . . . 1·00 1·00
1986 $1 "Cinderella" . . . . . . 1·00 1·00
1987 $1 "Snow White and the Seven Dwarfs" . . . . 1·00 1·00
1988 $1 "Peter Pan" . . . . . . 1·00 1·00

1992. Christmas. Religious Paintings. As T **218** of Lesotho. Multicoloured.
1992 10 c. "Hospitality refused to the Virgin Mary and Joseph" (detail) (Metsys) 20 20
1993 40 c. "The Nativity" (detail) (Durer) 40 30
1994 45 c. "The Nativity" (Geertgen Tot Sint Jans) 40 30
1995 50 c. "The Nativity" (Jacopo Tintoretto) 50 35
1996 55 c. "The Nativity" (detail) (Follower of Calcar) . . . 50 35
1997 65 c. "The Nativity" (Workshop of Fra Angelico) 60 50
1998 75 c. "The Nativity" (Master of the Louvre Nativity) . . . 65 50
1999 $1 "The Nativity" (detail) (Lippi) 80 75
2000 $2 "The Nativity" (Petrus Christus) . . . . 1·50 1·50
2001 $3 "The Nativity" (detail) (Edward Burne-Jones) . . . 2·00 2·25
2002 $4 "The Nativity" (detail) (Giotto) . . . . 2·50 2·75
2003 $5 "Birth of Christ" (detail) (Domenico Ghirlandaio) . . 2·75 3·00

242 Gaston

1992. Walt Disney's "Beauty and the Beast" (cartoon film). Multicoloured.
2005 2 c. Type **242** 15 15
2006 3 c. Belle and her father, Maurice 15 15
2007 5 c. Lumiere, Mrs. Potts and Cogsworth 20 20
2008 10 c. Philippe 20 20
2009 15 c. Beast and Lumiere . . . 20 20
2010 20 c. Lumiere and Feather Duster 20 20
2011 60 c. Belle and Gaston . . . 40 40
2012 60 c. Maurice 40 40
2013 60 c. The Beast 40 40
2014 60 c. Mrs. Potts 40 40
2015 60 c. Belle and enchanted vase 40 40
2016 60 c. Belle discovers enchanted rose 40 40
2017 60 c. Belle with wounded Beast 40 40
2018 60 c. Belle 40 40
2019 60 c. Household objects alarmed 40 40
2020 60 c. Belle and Chip (vert) . . 40 40
2021 60 c. Lumiere (vert) 40 40
2022 60 c. Cogsworth (vert) 40 40
2023 60 c. Armoire (vert) 40 40
2024 60 c. Belle and Beast (vert) . . 40 40
2025 60 c. Feather Duster (vert) . . 40 40
2026 60 c. Footstool (vert) 40 40
2027 60 c. Belle sitting on stone (vert) 40 40

1992. 15th Death Anniv of Elvis Presley (2nd issue). Nos. 1902/10 optd **15th Anniversary**.
2029 $1 Elvis looking pensive . . . 90 90
2030 $1 Wearing black and yellow striped shirt 90 90
2031 $1 Singing into microphone . 90 90
2032 $1 Wearing wide-brimmed hat 90 90
2033 $1 With microphone in right hand 90 90
2034 $1 In Army uniform 90 90
2035 $1 Wearing pink shirt 90 90
2036 $1 In yellow shirt 90 90
2037 $1 In jacket and bow tie . . . 90 90

1992. 15th Death Anniv of Elvis Presley (3rd issue). Nos. 1820/7 optd **15th Anniversary Elvis Presley's Death August 16, 1977**.
2038 $2 Michael Jackson . . . . . 1·75 1·75
2039 $2 Madonna . . . . 1·75 1·75
2040 $2 Elvis Presley . . . . . . 1·75 1·75
2041 $2 David Bowie . . . . . . 1·75 1·75
2042 $2 Prince . . . . 1·75 1·75
2043 $2 Frank Sinatra . . . . . . 1·75 1·75
2044 $2 George Michael . . . . . 1·75 1·75
2045 $2 Mick Jagger . . . . . . 1·75 1·75

1992. 15th Death Anniv of Elvis Presley (4th issue). As Nos. 1666/8 of Dominica. Mult.
2047 $1 Elvis Presley . . . . . . 1·75 1·75
2048 $1 Elvis with guitar . . . . 1·75 1·75
2049 $1 Elvis with microphone . . 1·75 1·75

245 Fifer Pig building House of Straw

1992. Walt Disney Cartoon Films. As T **245**.
2050/2138 60 c. × 89 multicoloured Set of 89 . . . . . . 24·00 28·00
Nos. 2050/2138 were printed as ten se-tenant sheetlets, each of nine different designs except for that for "Darkwing Duck" which contains eight vertical designs (Nos. 2131/8). The other nine sheetlets depict scenes from "The Three Little Pigs", "Thru the Mirror", "Clock Cleaners", "Orphans Benefit", "The Art of Skiing", "Symphony Hour", "How to Play Football", "The Small One" and "Chip N' Dale Rescue Rangers".
For Nos. 2050/8 ("The Three Little Pigs") with different face values see Nos. 2852/60.

246 Scottie Pippen

1992. Olympic Gold Medal Winners, Barcelona. Members of U.S.A. basketball team. Multicoloured.
2140 $2 Type **246** . . . . 1·25 1·25
2141 $2 Earvin "Magic" Johnson . 1·25 1·25
2142 $2 Larry Bird . . . . 1·25 1·25
2143 $2 Christian Laettner . . . . 1·25 1·25
2144 $2 Karl Malone . . . . . . 1·25 1·25
2145 $2 David Robinson . . . . . 1·25 1·25
2146 $2 Michael Jordan . . . . . 1·25 1·25
2147 $2 Charles Barkley . . . . . 1·25 1·25
2148 $2 John Stockton . . . . . . 1·25 1·25
2149 $2 Chris Mullin . . . . . . 1·25 1·25
2150 $2 Clyde Drexler . . . . . . 1·25 1·25
2151 $2 Patrick Ewing . . . . . . 1·25 1·25

247 Tom Seaver

248 Don Mattingly

1992. Famous Baseball Players (5th issue). Multicoloured.
2152 $2 Type **247** . . . . 1·40 1·40
2153 $2 Roberto Clemente . . . . 1·40 1·40
2154 $2 Hank Aaron . . . . . . 1·40 1·40

1992. Famous Baseball Players (6th issue). Multicoloured.
2155 $5 Type **248** . . . . 3·00 3·50
2156 $5 Howard Johnson . . . . . 3·00 3·50

249 Earth and U.N. Emblem

1992. Anniversaries and Events. Mult.
2157 10 c. Type **249** 30 20
2158 45 c. Airship LZ-11 "Viktoria Luise" over Kiel Regatta, 1912 (vert) 60 25
2159 75 c. Adenauer and German flag 60 50
2160 75 c. Trophy and Bill Koch (skipper) of "America III", 1992 . . . . 60 50
2161 $1 Konrad Adenauer 60 50
2162 $1 Snow leopard and emblem 80 50
2163 $1.50 Caribbean manatee . . 1·25 1·25
2164 $2 Humpback whale . . . . 2·00 2·00
2165 $3 Adenauer and Pres. Kennedy, 1962 . . . . . . 1·60 1·60
2166 $3 Doctor checking patient's eye 2·00 2·00
2167 $4 "Discovery" space shuttle (vert) . . . . 2·75 2·75
2168 $4 Adenauer and Pope John XXIII, 1960 . . . . 2·75 2·75

2169 $5 Schumacher and racing car 3·25 3·25
2170 $6 Zeppelin LZ-1 over Lake Constance, 1900 3·50 3·75

ANNIVERSARIES AND EVENTS: Nos. 2157, 2167, International Space Year; Nos. 2158, 2170, 75th death anniv of Count Ferdinand von Zeppelin; Nos. 2159, 2161, 2165, 2168, 25th death anniv of Konrad Adenauer (German statesman); No. 2160, Americas Cup Yachting Championship; Nos. 2162/4, Earth Summit '92, Rio; No. 2166, 75th anniv of International Association of Lions Clubs; No. 2169, Michael Schumacher's Victory in 1992 Belgium Grand Prix.

1992. Ecology. As T **71** of Nevis. Mult.
2172 75 c. Care Bear and American white pelican 55 45

250 Farmer, Fisherman and Emblem

1993. International Conference on Nutrition, Rome.
2174 **250** 65 c. multicoloured 70 70

251 Coastal Village

1993. "Uniting the Windward Islands". Mult.
2175 10 c. Type **251** 30 20
2176 40 c. Children from different islands 70 60
2177 45 c. Children and palm tree 70 60

252 Fisherman holding Catch

1993. Fishing. Multicoloured.
2178 5 c. Type **252** 15 15
2179 10 c. Fish market 15 15
2180 50 c. Fishermen landing catch 60 60
2181 $5 Fishing with nets 3·00 3·50

253 Brown Pelican

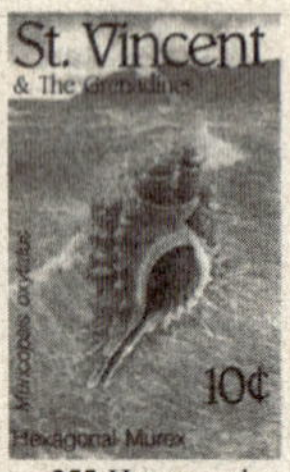

255 Hexagonal Muricop

254 Sergeant Major

1993. Migratory Birds. Multicoloured.
2182 10 c. Type **253** 30 20
2183 25 c. Red-necked grebe (horiz) 35 20
2184 45 c. Belted kingfisher (horiz) 45 30
2185 55 c. Yellow-bellied sapsucker 50 30
2186 $1 Great blue heron 75 60
2187 $2 Common black hawk ("Crab Hawk") (horiz) 1·40 1·40
2188 $4 Yellow warbler 2·25 2·50
2189 $5 Northern oriole (horiz) 2·25 2·50

1993. Fishes. Multicoloured.
2191 5 c. Type **254** 30 20
2192 10 c. Rainbow parrotfish 35 20
2193 55 c. Hogfish 45 30
2194 75 c. Porkfish 50 40
2195 $1 Spot-finned butterflyfish 75 60
2196 $2 Buffalo trunkfish 1·40 1·40
2197 $4 Queen triggerfish 2·25 2·50
2198 $5 Queen angelfish 2·25 2·50

1993. Bicentenary of the Louvre, Paris. As T **305** of Antigua.
2200/39 $1 × 40 multicoloured Set of 40 21·00 23·00

Nos. 2200/39 were printed as five se-tenant sheetlets showing paintings by Gericault, Ingres, Le Sueur and Poussin, Poussin, and Boucher, Brueghel, Dumont, Gainsborough, Goya and Van Eyck.

1993. Shells. Multicoloured.
2241 10 c. Type **255** 30 20
2242 15 c. Caribbean vase 30 20
2243 30 c. Measled cowrie 40 20
2244 45 c. Dyson's keyhole limpet 50 25
2245 50 c. Atlantic hairy triton 50 40
2246 65 c. Orange-banded marginella 60 45
2247 75 c. Bleeding tooth 70 50
2248 $1 Queen or pink conch 80 65
2249 $2 Hawk-wing conch 1·25 1·40
2250 $3 Musice volute 1·75 2·00
2251 $4 Alphabet cone 2·25 2·75
2252 $5 Antillean or incomparable cone 2·25 2·75

256 Ishihara holding Tennis Racket

257 "Erynnyis ello"

1993. 7th Death Anniv of Yujiro Ishihara (Japanese actor).
2254 **256** 55 c. black, grey & bl 80 80
2255 – 55 c. black, grey & bl 80 80
2256 – 55 c. black, grey & bl 80 80
2257 – 55 c. multicoloured 80 80
2258 – 55 c. multicoloured 80 80
2259 – $1 multicoloured 80 80
2260 – $1 multicoloured 80 80
2261 – $1 multicoloured 80 80
2262 – $1 multicoloured 80 80

DESIGNS: No. 2255, Ishihara holding camera; No. 2256, In striped shirt; No. 2257, Holding drink and cigarette; No. 2258, On board yacht; No. 2259, In naval uniform; No. 2260, In jacket and tie; No. 2261, Wearing sunglasses; No. 2262, Wearing pink shirt.

1993. 40th Anniv of Coronation. As T **307** of Antigua.
2264 45 c. multicoloured 45 55
2265 65 c. multicoloured 55 65
2266 $2 green and black 1·25 1·40
2267 $4 multicoloured 1·90 2·00

DESIGNS: 45 c. Queen Elizabeth II at Coronation (photograph by Cecil Beaton); 65 c. Queen Elizabeth opening Parliament; $2 Queen Elizabeth during Coronation; $4 Queen Elizabeth with corgi.

1993. Moths. Multicoloured.
2269 10 c. Type **257** 20 20
2270 50 c. "Aellopos tantalus" 55 30
2271 65 c. "Erynnyis alope" 60 40
2272 75 c. "Manduca rustica" 70 50
2273 $1 "Xylophanes pluto" 80 65
2274 $2 "Hyles lineata" 1·50 1·75
2275 $4 "Pseudosphinx tetrio" 2·50 2·75
2276 $5 "Protambulyx strigilis" 2·50 2·75

258 Early Astronomical Quadrant

260 First Ford Car, Model "T" and "V8"

259 Supermarine Spitfire

1993. Anniversaries and Events. Red and black (Nos. 2281, 2293) or multicoloured (others).
2278 45 c. Type **258** 40 25
2279 45 c. "Massacre in Korea" (Picasso) (horiz) 40 25
2280 45 c. Marc Girardelli (Luxembourg) (giant slalom) (horiz) 40 25
2281 45 c. Willy Brandt and Pres. Nixon, 1971 (horiz) 40 25
2282 45 c. Count Johannes and Countess Gloria of Thurn and Taxis 40 25
2283 65 c. Count and Countess of Thurn and Taxis with children (horiz) 60 40
2284 65 c. Masako Owada and engagement photographs (horiz) 60 40
2285 $1 "Family of Saltimbanques" (Picasso) (horiz) 60 50
2286 $1 Princess Stephanie of Monaco 60 60
2287 $1 "Deux Tetes" (left detail) (S. Witkiewicz) 80 80
2288 $2 Countess Gloria of Thurn & Taxis 1·25 1·25
2289 $3 "Deux Tetes" (right detail) (S. Witkiewicz) 1·50 1·50
2290 $4 Launch of American space shuttle 2·25 2·25
2291 $4 "La Joie de Vivre" (Picasso) (horiz) 2·25 2·25
2292 $5 Paul Accola (Switzerland) (downhill skiing) (horiz) 2·75 2·75
2293 $5 Willy Brandt and Robert F. Kennedy, 1967 (horiz) 2·75 2·75
2294 $5 Prince Naruhito in traditional dress and engagement photographs (horiz) 2·75 2·75
2295 $5 Pres. Clinton with school children (horiz) 2·75 2·75
2296 $6 Bogusz Church, Gozlin (horiz) 3·00 3·00

ANNIVERSARIES AND EVENTS: Nos. 2278, 2290, 450th death anniv of Copernicus (astronomer); Nos. 2279, 2285, 2291, 20th death anniv of Picasso (artist); Nos. 2280, 2292, Winter Olympic Games '94, Lillehammer; Nos. 2281, 2293, 80th birth anniv of Willy Brandt (German politician); Nos. 2282/3, 2288, 500th anniv (1990) of Thurn and Taxis postal service; Nos. 2284, 2294, Marriage of Crown Prince Naruhito of Japan; No. 2286, Marriage of Princess Stephanie of Monaco; Nos. 2287, 2289, 2296, "Polska '93" International Stamp Exhibition, Poznan; No. 2295, Inauguration of U.S. President William Clinton.

1993. Aviation Anniversaries. Multicoloured.
2298 50 c. Type **259** 45 30
2299 $1 Eckener and airship "Graf Zeppelin" over Egypt, 1931 80 65
2300 $1 Blanchard and Pres. Washington with balloon, 1793 80 65
2301 $2 De Havilland Mosquito Mk VI 1·40 1·50
2302 $2 Eckener and "Graf Zeppelin" over New York, 1928 1·40 1·50
2303 $3 Eckener and "Graf Zeppelin" over Tokyo, 1929 2·25 2·50
2304 $4 Blanchard's balloon ascending from Walnut St. Prison, Philadelphia 2·25 2·50

ANNIVERSARIES: Nos. 2298, 2301, 75th anniv of Royal Air Force; Nos. 2299, 2302/3, 125th birth anniv of Hugo Eckener (airship commander); Nos. 2300, 2304, Bicentenary of first airmail flight.

No. 2303 is inscr "Toyko" in error.

1993. Centenaries of Henry Ford's First Petrol Engine (Nos. 2306, 2309) and Karl Benz's First Four-wheeled car (others). Mult.
2306 $1 Type **260** 80 60
2307 $2 Benz racing car, 1908, "Stuttgart" and "540K" 1·50 1·50
2308 $3 Benz car, 1894, "Tourenwagen" and "Blitzen Benz" 2·00 2·25
2309 $4 Ford "Runabout", 1903, Model "T" Tourer and saloon, 1935 2·25 2·50

261 Pope John Paul II and Denver Skyline

1993. Papal Visit to Denver, Colorado, U.S.A.
2311 **261** $1 multicoloured 80 60

262 Corvette of 1953

1993. 40th Anniv of Corvette Range of Cars. Multicoloured.
2313 $1 Type **262** 80 80
2314 $1 1993 model 80 80
2315 $1 1958 model 80 80
2316 $1 1960 model 80 80
2317 $1 "40" and symbolic chequered flag emblem 80 80
2318 $1 1961 model 80 80
2319 $1 1963 model 80 80
2320 $1 1968 model 80 80
2321 $1 1973 model 80 80
2322 $1 1975 model 80 80
2323 $1 1982 model 80 80
2324 $1 1984 model 80 80

1993. Asian International Stamp Exhibitions. Multicoloured designs, as T **268** of Dominica.

(a) "Indopex '93", Surabaya, Indonesia. Horiz designs.
2325/54 5, 10, 20, 45, 55, 75 c., $1 × 2, $1.50 × 18, $2, $4, $5 × 2 Set of 30 23·00 24·00

Nos. 2325/32 and 2351/4 show Indonesian scenes, Nos. 2333/50 masks (Nos. 2333/8) or paintings (Nos 2339/50).

(b) "Taipei '93", Taiwan. Horiz designs.
2356/85 5, 10, 20, 45, 55, 75 c., $1 × 2, $1.50 × 18, $2, $4, $5 × 2 Set of 30 23·00 24·00

Nos. 2356/63 and 2382/5 show Chinese scenes, Nos. 2364/81 kites. (Nos. 2364/9) or paintings (Nos. 2370/81).

(c) "Bangkok '93", Thailand. Vert (5, 55 c., $2, 4) or horiz (others).
2387/2416 5, 10, 20, 45, 55, 75 c., $1 × 2, $1.50 × 18, $2, $4, $5 × 2 Set of 30 22·00 23·00

Nos. 2387/4 and 2413/16 show Thai scenes, Nos. 2395/2412 murals from Buddhaisawan Chapel (Nos. 2395/2400), paintings (Nos. 2401/6) or sculptures (Nos. 2407/12).

264 Players from St. Vincent and Mexico

1993. Qualifying Rounds for World Cup Football Championship, U.S.A. Multicoloured.
2418 5 c. Type **264** 15 20
2419 10 c. Honduras match 15 15
2420 65 c. Costa Rica match 55 35
2421 $5 St. Vincent goalkeeper 3·25 4·00

265 Fish Delivery Van

1993. Japanese Aid for Fishing Industry. Multicoloured.
2422 10 c. Type **265** 20 10
2423 50 c. Fish aggregation device (vert) 45 30
2424 75 c. Game fishing launch 60 50
2425 $5 Fish market 3·25 4·00

1993. Famous Baseball Players (7th issue). As T **247**. Multicoloured
2426 $2 Reggie Jackson 1·10 1·10

1993. Christmas. Religious Paintings. As T **270** of Dominica. Black, yellow and red (Nos. 2427/9, 2434) or multicoloured (others).
2427 10 c. "Adoration of the Magi" (detail) (Durer) 15 10
2428 35 c. "Adoration of the Magi" (different detail) (Durer) 30 20
2429 40 c. "Adoration of the Magi" (different detail) (Durer) 35 25
2430 50 c. "Holy Family with Saint Francis" (detail) (Rubens) 45 30
2431 55 c. "Adoration of the Shepherds" (detail) (Rubens) 45 30
2432 65 c. "Adoration of the Shepherds" (different detail) (Rubens) 55 40
2433 $1 "Holy Family" (Rubens) 75 60
2434 $5 "Adoration of the Magi" (different detail) (Durer) 2·25 3·25

267 Barbra Streisand

1993. Barbra Streisand's Grand Garden Concert.
2436 **267** $2 multicoloured 1·10 1·10

268 Roy Acuff

1994. Legends of Country Music. Multicoloured.
2437 $1 Type **268** 65 65
2438 $1 Patsy Cline in pink shirt 65 65
2439 $1 Jim Reeves in dinner jacket 65 65
2440 $1 Hank Williams in brown jacket 65 65
2441 $1 Hank Williams in purple jacket 65 65
2442 $1 Roy Acuff with microphone 65 65
2443 $1 Patsy Cline wearing white scarf 65 65
2444 $1 Jim Reeves with microphone 65 65
2445 $1 Jim Reeves in orange jacket 65 65
2446 $1 Patsy Cline with microphone 65 65
2447 $1 Hank Williams in grey jacket 65 65
2448 $1 Roy Acuff in grey jacket 65 65

269 Mobile Library

1994. Centenary of Library Service. Multicoloured.

2449	5 c. Type **269**	10	20
2450	10 c. Old Public Library building	10	10
2451	$1 Family reading	65	70
2452	$1 Line of books joining youth and old man	65	70

270 Woman planting Breadfruit

1994. Bicent of Introduction of Breadfruit. Mult.

2453	10 c. Type **270**	15	10
2454	45 c. Captain Bligh with breadfruit plant	30	25
2455	65 c. Slice of breadfruit	40	40
2456	$5 Breadfruit growing on branch	3·00	4·00

271 Family Picnic

1994. Int Year of the Family (1st issue). Mult.

2457	10 c. Type **271**	15	10
2458	50 c. Family in church	40	30
2459	65 c. Working in the garden	50	35
2460	75 c. Jogging	55	55
2461	$1 Family group (vert)	70	70
2462	$2 On the beach	1·40	1·75

See also No. 2836.

1994. "Hong Kong '94" International Stamp Exn (1st issue). As T 317 of Antigua. Mult.

2463	40 c. Hong Kong 1992 $2.30 Olympic Games stamp and "Hong Kong Harbour in 19th Century" (left detail)	25	30
2464	40 c. St. Vincent 1991 $3.50 Scouts Jamboree stamp and "Hong Kong Harbour in 19th Century" (right detail)	25	30

Nos. 2463/4 were printed together, se-tenant, forming the complete painting.

See also Nos. 2465/94 and 2495/500.

1994. "Hong Kong '94" International Stamp Exn (2nd issue). As T **318** of Antigua. Mult.

2465/94	40 c. × 12, 45 c. × 12, 50 c. × 6 Set of 30	7·50	8·50

Nos. 2465/94 were printed as five se-tenant sheetlets, each of six different designs, depicting Ching porcelain (40 c.), dragon boat races (40 c.), seed-stitch purses (45 c.), junks (45 c.) and Qing ceramic figures (vert designs) (50 c.).

272 Bird on a Flowering Spray Plate, Qianlong

1994. "Hong Kong '94" International Stamp Exhibition (3rd issue). Multicoloured.

2495	50 c. Type **272**	40	40
2496	50 c. Large decorated dish, Kangxi	40	40
2497	50 c. Cocks on rocky ground plate, Yongzheng	40	40
2498	50 c. Green decorated dish, Yuan	40	40
2499	50 c. Porcelain pug dog	40	40
2500	50 c. Dish decorated with Dutch ship, Qianlong	40	40

No. 2497 is incorrectly inscribed "Cocks on a Rocky Groung".

273 Blue Flasher

1994. Butterflies. Multicoloured.

2502	50 c. Type **273**	35	35
2503	50 c. Tiger swallowtail	35	35
2504	50 c. Lustrous copper	35	35
2505	50 c. Tailed copper	35	35
2506	50 c. Blue copper	35	35
2507	50 c. Ruddy copper	35	35
2508	50 c. Viceroy	35	35
2509	50 c. California sister	35	35
2510	50 c. Mourning cloak	35	35
2511	50 c. Red passion-flower	35	35
2512	50 c. Small flambeau	35	35
2513	50 c. Blue wave	35	35
2514	50 c. Chiricahua metalmark	35	35
2515	50 c. Monarch	35	35
2516	50 c. Anise swallowtail	35	35
2517	50 c. Buckeye	35	35

274 Antonio Cabrini

275 "Epidendrum ibaguense"

1994. Juventus Football Club (Italy) Commemoration. Past and present players. Multicoloured.

2518	$1 Type **274**	65	65
2519	$1 Michel Platini and Roberto Baggio	65	65
2520	$1 Roberto Bettega	65	65
2521	$1 Gaetano Scirea	65	65
2522	$1 Jurgen Kohler	65	65
2523	$1 Marco Tardelli	65	65
2524	$1 Paolo Rossi	65	65
2525	$1 Giuseppe Furino	65	65
2526	$1 Dino Zoff	65	65
2527	$1 Franco Causio	65	65
2528	$1 Claudio Gentile	65	65

1994. Orchids. Multicoloured.

2530	10 c. Type **275**	40	30
2531	25 c. "Ionopsis utricularioides"	50	30
2532	50 c. "Brassavola cucullata"	60	50
2533	65 c. "Enclyclia cochleata"	70	60
2534	$1 "Liparis nervosa"	85	75
2535	$2 "Vanilla phaeantha"	1·40	1·60
2536	$4 "Elleanthus cephalotus"	2·50	2·75
2537	$5 "Isochilus linearis"	2·50	2·75

276 Dimorphodon

1994. Prehistoric Animals (1st series). Multicoloured.

2539	75 c. Type **276**	60	60
2540	75 c. Camarasaurus	60	60
2541	75 c. Spinosaurus	60	60
2542	75 c. Allosaurus	60	60
2543	75 c. Rhamphorhynchus	60	60
2544	75 c. Pteranodon and body of Allosaurus	60	60
2545	75 c. Eudimorphodon	60	60
2546	75 c. Ornithomimus	60	60
2547	75 c. Protoavis	60	60
2548	75 c. Pteranodon	60	60
2549	75 c. Quetzalcoatlus	60	60
2550	75 c. Lesothosaurus	60	60
2551	75 c. Heterodontosaurus	60	60
2552	75 c. Archaeopteryx	60	60
2553	75 c. Cearadactylus	60	60
2554	75 c. Anchisaurus	60	60

Nos. 2539/46 and 2547/54 respectively were printed together, se-tenant, forming composite designs.

See also Nos. 2556/603.

278 Albertosaurus

1994. Prehistoric Animals (2nd series). As T **278**. Multicoloured.

2556/2603	75 c. × 48 Set of 48	20·00	22·00

Nos. 2556/2603 were printed together, se-tenant, as four sheetlets of 12 with Nos. 2556/79 being horizontal and Nos. 2580/2603 vertical. The species depicted are Albertosaurus, Chasmosaurus, Brachiosaurus, Coelophysis, Deinonychus, Anatosaurus, Iguanodon, Baryonyx, Steneosaurus, Nanotyrannus, Camptosaurus, Camarasaurus, Hesperonis, Mesosaurus, Plesiosaurus Dolichorhynchops, Squalicorax, Tylosaurus, Plesiosoar, Stenopterygius Ichthyosaurus, Steneosaurus, Eurhinosaurus Longirostris, Cryptocleidus Oxoniensis, Caturus, Protostega, Dimorphodon, Pterodactylus, Rhamphorhynchus, Pteranodon, Gallimimus, Stegosaurus, Acanthopholis, Trachodon, Thecodonts, Ankylosaurus, Compsognathus, Protoceratops, Quetzalcoatlus, Diplodocus, Spinosaurus, Apatosaurus, Ornitholestes, Lesothosaurus, Trachodon, Protoavis, Oviraptor, Coelophysis, Ornitholestes and Archaeopteryx.

279 Mickey Mouse as Pilot

1994. 65th Anniv (1993) of Mickey Mouse. Walt Disney cartoon characters. Multicoloured.

2605	5 c. Type **279**	30	30
2606	10 c. Mickey in Foreign Legion	30	30
2607	15 c. Mickey as frontiersman	40	40
2608	20 c. Mickey, Goofy and Donald Duck	40	40
2609	35 c. Horace Horsecollar and Clarabelle Cow	50	50
2610	50 c. Minnie Mouse, Frankie and Figuro	60	60
2611	75 c. Donald and Pluto	70	70
2612	80 c. Mickey holding balloons	75	75
2613	85 c. Daisy Duck and Minnie	75	75
2614	95 c. Minnie	80	80
2615	$1 Mickey in red trousers	80	80
2616	$1.50 Mickey raising hat	1·40	1·40
2617	$2 Mickey with hands in pockets	1·60	1·60
2618	$3 Mickey and Minnie	2·50	2·50
2619	$4 Mickey with birthday cake	2·75	2·75
2620	$5 Mickey as Uncle Sam	2·75	2·75

280 Argentine Team

1994. World Cup Football Championship, U.S.A. Competing teams. Multicoloured.

2622	50 c. Type **280**	35	35
2623	50 c. Belgium	35	35
2624	50 c. Bolivia	35	35
2625	50 c. Brazil	35	35
2626	50 c. Bulgaria	35	35
2627	50 c. Cameroun	35	35
2628	50 c. Colombia	35	35
2629	50 c. Germany	35	35
2630	50 c. Greece	35	35
2631	50 c. Netherlands	35	35
2632	50 c. Republic of Ireland	35	35
2633	50 c. Italy	35	35
2634	50 c. Mexico	35	35
2635	50 c. Morocco	35	35
2636	50 c. Nigeria	35	35
2637	50 c. Norway	35	35
2638	50 c. Rumania	35	35
2639	50 c. Russia	35	35
2640	50 c. Saudi Arabia	35	35
2641	50 c. South Korea	35	35
2642	50 c. Spain	35	35
2643	50 c. Sweden	35	35
2644	50 c. Switzerland	35	35
2645	50 c. U.S.A.	35	35

281 Marilyn Monroe

1994. Marilyn Monroe (American film star) Commemoration. Different portraits. Multicoloured.

2646	$1 Type **281**	75	75
2647	$1 Asleep	75	75
2648	$1 With long hair style and pendulum earrings	75	75
2649	$1 Wearing striped sweater	75	75
2650	$1 With gloved hand to face	75	75
2651	$1 With bare hand to face	75	75
2652	$1 In black and white dress	75	75
2653	$1 In sequined evening dress	75	75
2654	$1 With short hair and no earrings	75	75

282 Capt. Jean-Luc Picard

1994. "Star Trek – The Next Generation" (T.V. series). Multicoloured.

2655	$2 Type **282**	1·10	1·10
2656	$2 Commander William Riker	1·10	1·10
2657	$2 Lt.-Commander Data	1·10	1·10
2658	$2 Lt. Worf	1·10	1·10
2659	$2 Crew members	1·10	1·10
2660	$2 Dr. Beverley Crusher	1·10	1·10
2661	$2 Lt. Worf and female crew member	1·10	1·10
2662	$2 Q wearing hat	1·10	1·10
2663	$2 Counsellor Deanna Troi	1·10	1·10

283 Shigetatsu Matsunaga (Yokohama Marinos)

284 Jef United Team

1994. Japanese Professional Football League. (a) As T **283** showing individual players and league emblem. Multicoloured.

2665/76	55 c. × 8, $1.50 × 4 Set of 12	6·00	6·00

DESIGNS: 55 c. Masami Ihara (Yokohama Marinos); Shunzoh Ohno (Kashima Antlers); Luiz Carlos Pereira (Verdy Kawasaki); Tetsuji Hashiratani (Verdy Kawasaki); Carlos Alberto Souza dos Santos (Kashima Antlers); Yasuto Honda (Kashima Antlers); Kazuyoshi Miura (Verdy Kawasaki); $1.50, League emblem; Takumi Horiike (Shimizu S-Pulse); Rui Ramos (Verdy Kawasaki); Ramon Angel Diaz (Yokohama Marinos).

(b) As T **284** showing teams.

2677/88	55 c. × 8, $1.50 × 4 Set of 12	6·00	6·00

DESIGNS: 55 c. Verdy Yomiuri; Yokohama Marinos; A. S. Flugels; Bellmare; Shimizu S-Pulse; Jubilo Iwata; Panasonic Gamba Osaka; $1.50, Kashima Antlers; Red Diamonds; Nagoya Grampus Eight; Sanfrecce Hiroshima.

(c) As T **284** showing players and teams.

2689/94	55 c. × 3, $1.50 × 2, $3 A. S. Flugels	3·50	3·75
2695/700	55 c. × 3, $1.50 × 2, $3 Bellmare	3·50	3·75
2701/6	55 c. × 3, $1.50 × 2, $3 Panasonic Gamba Osaka	3·50	3·75
2707/12	55 c. × 3, $1.50 × 2, $3 Jef United	3·50	3·75
2713/18	55 c. × 3, $1.50 × 2, $3 Jubilo Iwata	3·50	3·75
2719/24	55 c. × 3, $1.50 × 2, $3 Kashima Antlers	3·50	3·75
2725/30	55 c. × 3, $1.50 × 2, $3 Nagoya Grampus Eight	3·50	3·75
2731/36	55 c. × 3, $1.50 × 2, $3 Sanfrecce Hiroshima	3·50	3·75
2737/42	55 c. × 3, $1.50 × 2, $3 Shimizu S-Pulse	3·50	3·75
2743/48	55 c. × 3, $1.50 × 2, $3 Red Diamonds	3·50	3·75

2749/54 55 c. × 3, $1.50 × 2, $3 Verdy Kawasaki . . . 3·50 3·75
2755/60 55 c. × 3, $1.50 × 2, $3 Yokohama Marinos . 3·50 3·75

Prices quoted are for se-tenant sheetlets of six stamps.

1994. 25th Anniv of First Manned Moon Landing. As T **326** of Antigua. Multicoloured.

2761 $1 Fred Whipple and Halley's Comet 75 75
2762 $1 Robert Gilruth and "Gemini 12" 75 75
2763 $1 George Mueller and space walk from "Gemini 4" . . 75 75
2764 $1 Charles Berry and Johnsville Centrifuge 75 75
2765 $1 Christopher Kraft and "Apollo 4" 75 75
2766 $1 James van Allen and "Explorer 1" 75 75
2767 $1 Robert Goddard and Goddard-liquid fuel rocket 75 75
2768 $1 James Webb and "Spirit of 76" flight 75 75
2769 $1 Rocco Patrone and "Apollo 8" 75 75
2770 $1 Walter Dornberger and German rocket 75 75
2771 $1 Alexander Lippisch and Messerschmitt ME 163B Komet (airplane) 75 75
2772 $1 Kurt Debus and "A4b" rocket 75 75
2773 $1 Hermann Oberth and projected spaceship 75 75
2774 $1 Hanna Reitsch and "Reichenberg" flying bomb 75 75
2775 $1 Ernst Stuhlinger and "Explorer 1" 75 75
2776 $1 Werner von Braun and rocket-powered Heinkel He 112 . . . . 75 75
2777 $1 Arthur Rudolph and rocket motor 75 75
2778 $1 Willy Ley and rocket airplane 75 75

1994. 50th Anniv of D-Day. As T **331** of Antigua. Multicoloured.

2780 40 c. Supply convoy 40 25
2781 $5 Unloading beached supply ship . . . . 2·75 3·00

285 Yorkshire Terrier Bitch

288 Sir Shridath Ramphal and Map of Guyana

287 St. Vincent Family

1994. Chinese New Year ("Year of the Dog"). Multicoloured.

2783 10 c. Type **285** 30 20
2784 25 c. Yorkshire terrier dog . . 35 20
2785 50 c. Golden retriever 45 45
2786 50 c. Pomeranian 45 45
2787 50 c. English springer spaniel 45 45
2788 50 c. Bearded collie 45 45
2789 50 c. Irish wolfhound 45 45
2790 50 c. Pekingese 45 45
2791 50 c. Irish setter 45 45
2792 50 c. Old English sheepdog . 45 45
2793 50 c. Basset hound 45 45
2794 50 c. Cavalier King Charles spaniel 45 45
2795 50 c. Kleiner Munsterlander . 45 45
2796 50 c. Shetland sheepdog . . . 45 45
2797 50 c. Dachshund 45 45
2798 65 c. Bernese mountain dog . 55 55
2799 $1 Vorstehhund 70 70
2800 $2 Tibetan terrier . . . . . 1·40 1·40
2801 $4 West Highland terrier . . 2·50 2·50
2802 $5 Shih tzu . . . . 2·75 2·75

1994. Centenary of International Olympic Committee. Gold Medal Winners. As T **327** of Antigua. Multicoloured.

2804 45 c. Peter Frennel (Germany) (20 km walk), 1972 (vert) . . 40 25
2805 50 c. Kijung Son (Japan) (marathon), 1936 (vert) . . 45 30
2806 75 c. Jesse Owens (U.S.A.) (100 and 200 metres), 1936 (vert) 65 50
2807 $1 Greg Louganis (U.S.A.) (diving), 1984 and 1988 (vert) 70 75

1994. Cent of First English Cricket Tour to the West Indies (1995). As T **329** of Antigua. Mult.

2809 10 c. Mark Ramprakash (England) and Wisden Trophy 30 20
2810 30 c. Phil Simmonds (West Indies) and Wisden Trophy 40 25
2811 $2 Garfield Sobers (West Indies) (vert) . . . . 1·40 1·75

1994. "Philakorea '94" International Stamp Exn, Seoul. As T **330** of Antigua. Mult.

2813 10 c. Oryon Waterfall (vert) 30 20
2814 45 c. Indoor sports stadium, Pyongyang 40 25
2815 50 c. Illuminated character with house at bottom right . . 40 40
2816 50 c. Illuminated character with red dots in centre 40 40
2817 50 c. Illuminated character with animal at right 40 40
2818 50 c. Illuminated character with flowers at bottom right . . 40 40
2819 50 c. Illuminated character with dragon at left 40 40
2820 50 c. Illuminated character with house at top 40 40
2821 50 c. Illuminated character with dragon at top 40 40
2822 50 c. Illuminated character with sun at top 40 40
2823 50 c. Fish and character . . 40 40
2824 50 c. Two pheasants and character 40 40
2825 50 c. Plant and cabinet . . . 40 40
2826 50 c. Vases and cabinet . . . 40 40
2827 50 c. Books on decorated cabinet 40 40
2828 50 c. Pheasant, decorated cabinet and vase 40 40
2829 50 c. Pheasant and lamp on table 40 40
2830 50 c. Cabinet, vase and table 40 40
2831 65 c. Pombong, Chonhwadae (vert) 50 50
2832 75 c. Uisangdae, Naksansa (vert) 55 55
2833 $1 Buddha of the Sokkuram Grotto, Kyangju 60 60
2834 $2 Moksogwon . . . . . . 1·10 1·10

Nos. 2825/6 and 2830 are inscr "Bookshlef" in error.

1994. International Year of the Family (2nd issue).

2836 **287** 75 c. multicoloured . . 50 50

1994. First Recipients of Order of the Caribbean Community. Multicoloured.

2837 $1 Type **288** 70 50
2838 $2 Derek Walcott and map of St. Lucia . . . . 1·75 1·75
2839 $5 William Demas and map of Trinidad (horiz) . . . . 3·00 3·50

No. 2838 is inscribed "Wilcott" in error.

289 Twin-engined Airliner, Bequia Airport

1994. 50th Anniv of I.C.A.O. Multicoloured.

2840 10 c. Type **289** 10 10
2841 65 c. Union Island Airport . . 30 35
2842 75 c. L.I.A.T. 8-100 at E. T. Joshua Airport 35 40
2843 $1 Aircraft and logo 45 50
2844 $1 Britten Norman Islander at J. F. Mitchell Airport, Bequia 45 50

290 "The Annunciation"

1994. Christmas. Religious Paintings from Jean de Berry's "Book of Hours". Multicoloured.

2845 10 c. Type **290** 15 10
2846 45 c. "The Visitation" . . . 40 25
2847 50 c. "The Nativity" 45 30
2848 65 c. "The Purification of the Virgin" (detail) 60 35
2849 75 c. "Presentation of Jesus in the Temple" 70 40
2850 $5 "Flight into Egypt" . . . 3·25 3·75

No. 2847 is inscribed "The Annunciation" in error.

1995. Chinese New Year ("Year of the Pig") (1st issue). Designs as Nos. 2050/8, but with different face values and with Year of the Pig logo.

2852 30 c. Type **245** 40 40
2853 30 c. Fiddler Pig building house of sticks 40 40
2854 30 c. Practical Pig building house of bricks 40 40
2855 30 c. The Big Bad Wolf . . . 40 40
2856 30 c. Wolf scaring Fiddler and Fifer Pig 40 40
2857 30 c. Wolf blowing down straw house 40 40
2858 30 c. Wolf in sheep costume 40 40
2859 30 c. Wolf blowing down stick house 40 40
2860 30 c. Wolf attempting to blow down brick house 40 40

See also Nos. 2900/2.

291 Mealy Amazon Parrot

1995. Parrots. Multicoloured.

2862 $1 Type **291** 70 70
2863 $1 Nanday conure 70 70
2864 $1 Black-headed caique . . . 70 70
2865 $1 Scarlet macaw 70 70
2866 $1 Red-masked conure . . . 70 70
2867 $1 Blue-headed parrot 70 70
2868 $1 Hyacinth macaw 70 70
2869 $1 Sun conure 70 70
2870 $1 Blue and yellow macaw . . 70 70

Nos. 2862/70 were printed together, se-tenant, forming a composite design.

292 Snowshoe

1995. Cats. Multicoloured.

2872 $1 Type **292** 70 70
2873 $1 Abyssinian 70 70
2874 $1 Ocicat 70 70
2875 $1 Tiffany 70 70
2876 $1 Russian blue 70 70
2877 $1 Siamese 70 70
2878 $1 Bi-colour 70 70
2879 $1 Malayan 70 70
2880 $1 Manx 70 70

Nos. 2872/80 were printed together, se-tenant, forming a composite design.

293 Blue-faced Booby ("Masked Booby")

1995. Birds. Multicoloured.

2882 75 c. Type **293** 35 40
2883 75 c. Pair of blue-faced boobies 35 40
2884 75 c. Blue-faced booby preening 35 40
2885 75 c. Blue-faced booby stretching 35 40
2886 75 c. Great egrets 35 40
2887 75 c. Roseate spoonbills . . . 35 40
2888 75 c. Ring-billed gull 35 40
2889 75 c. Ruddy quail dove . . . 35 40
2890 75 c. Royal terns 35 40
2891 75 c. Killdeers 35 40
2892 75 c. Osprey 35 40
2893 75 c. Magnificent frigate bird 35 40
2894 75 c. Blue-faced boobies ("Masked Booby") 35 40
2895 75 c. Green heron 35 40
2896 75 c. Double-crested cormorants 35 40
2897 75 c. Brown pelican 35 40

Nos. 2886/97 were printed together, se-tenant, forming a composite design.

294 Churchill, Roosevelt and Stalin at Yalta Conference

1995. 50th Anniv of V.E. Day.

2899 **294** $1 multicoloured 45 50

295 Pig

296 National Flag and Globe

1995. Chinese New Year ("Year of the Pig") (2nd issue). Multicoloured, central panel in colours indicated.

2900 75 c. Type **295** (green) . . . 35 40
2901 75 c. Pig (brown) 35 40
2902 75 c. Pig (red) 35 40

1995. 18th World Scout Jamboree, Netherlands. Multicoloured.

2904 $1 Type **296** 45 50
2905 $4 Lord Baden-Powell . . . 1·75 1·90
2906 $5 Handshake . . . . 2·10 2·25

1995. 50th Anniv of End of Second World War in Europe. As T **340** of Antigua. Multicoloured.

2858 $2 Tank of U.S. First Army 85 90
2909 $2 V2 rocket 85 90
2910 $2 Consolidated B-24 Liberator bombers 85 90
2911 $2 French troops advancing to Strasbourg 85 90
2912 $2 Gloster G.41 Meteor fighter 85 90
2913 $2 Berlin on fire 85 90
2914 $2 Soviet tanks in Berlin . . 85 90
2915 $2 "Chicago Daily Tribune" headline 85 90

No. 2909 is inscribed "Y2" in error.

297 Globe and Peace Dove

298 Women preparing Food

1995. 50th Anniv of United Nations. Multicoloured.

2917 $2 Type **297** 85 90
2918 $2 Liberty 85 90
2919 $2 U.N. Building, New York, and peace dove 85 90

Nos. 2917/19 were printed together, se-tenant, forming a composite design.

1995. 50th Anniv of F.A.O. Multicoloured.

2921 $2 Type **298** 85 90
2922 $2 Woman mixing food . . . 85 90
2923 $2 Harvesting grain 85 90

Nos. 2921/3 were printed together, se-tenant, forming a composite design.

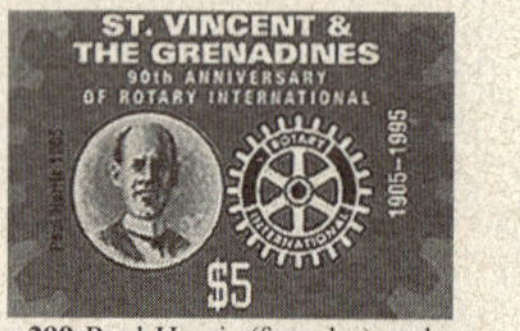

299 Paul Harris (founder) and Logo

1995. 90th Anniv of Rotary International.

2925 **299** $5 multicoloured . . . . 2·10 2·25

1995. 95th Birthday of Queen Elizabeth the Queen Mother. As T **344** of Antigua.

2927 $1.50 brown, light brown and black 65 70
2928 $1.50 multicoloured 65 70
2929 $1.50 multicoloured 65 70
2930 $1.50 multicoloured 65 70

DESIGNS: No. 2927, Queen Elizabeth the Queen Mother (pastel drawing); 2928, Wearing blue hat; 2929, At desk (oil painting); 2930, Wearing mauve dress.

1995. 50th Anniv of End of Second World War in the Pacific. As T **340** of Antigua. Multicoloured.

2932 $2 Douglas Devastator torpedo bomber 85 90
2933 $2 Doolittle's North American B-25 Mitchell "Ruptured Duck" 85 90
2934 $2 Curtiss SB2C Helldiver bomber 85 90
2935 $2 U.S.S. "Yorktown" (aircraft carrier) 85 90
2936 $2 U.S.S. "Wasp" (aircraft carrier) 85 90
2937 $2 U.S.S. "Lexington" (aircraft carrier) sinking 85 90

300 Head of Humpback Whale

1995. Marine Life. Multicoloured.

2939 90 c. Type **300** 40 45
2940 90 c. Green turtles 40 45

2941	90 c. Bottlenose dolphin	40	45
2942	90 c. Monk seals	40	45
2943	90 c. Krill	40	45
2944	90 c. Blue sharks	40	45
2945	90 c. Porkfish	40	45
2946	90 c. Reef butterflyfish	40	45
2947	90 c. Shipwreck	40	45
2948	$1 Beaugregory (fish) (horiz)	45	50
2949	$1 Grey angelfish (horiz)	45	50
2950	$1 Yellow-tailed damselfish (horiz)	45	50
2951	$1 Four-eyed butterflyfish (horiz)	45	50

Nos. 2939/47 were printed together, se-tenant, forming a composite design.

301 Symbolic Disabled Athlete

1995. Paralympic Games '95, Connecticut.

2953	**301** $1 yellow, blue and black	65	65

302 Ingrid Kristiansen

1995. World Athletic Championships, Gothenburg. Norwegian Athletes. Multicoloured.

2954	$1 Type **302**	45	50
2955	$1 Trine Hattestad	45	50
2956	$1 Grete Waitz	45	50
2957	$1 Vebjorn Rodal	45	50
2958	$1 Geir Moen	45	50
2959	$1 Steinar Hoen (horiz)	45	50

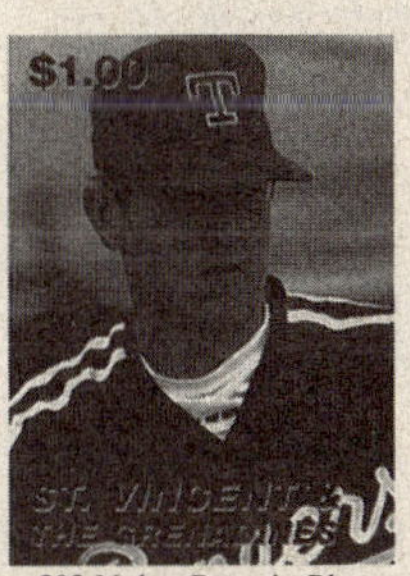

303 Nolan Ryan in Blue Jersey

1995. Retirement of Nolan Ryan (baseball player) (1993). Multicoloured.

2960	$1 Type **303**	45	50
2961	$1 With glove	45	50
2962	$1 In white jersey	45	50
2963	$1 Making pitch from left	45	50
2964	$1 Texas Rangers "All Star Game" emblem	45	50
2965	$1 Making pitch from right	45	50
2966	$1 Bleeding from blow to mouth	45	50
2967	$1 Preparing to pitch	45	50
2968	$1 Waving cap	45	50
2969	$1 Wearing "NY" cap	45	50
2970	$1 Wearing stetson with dog	45	50
2971	$1 Wearing "T" cap	45	50
2972	$1 Throwing American football	45	50
2973	$1 Nolan Ryan Foundation emblem	45	50
2974	$1 With son	45	50
2975	$1 Laughing	45	50
2976	$1 With family	45	50
2977	$1 Wearing "H" cap	45	50

304 Breast and Bowl of Baby Food

1995. "Baby Friendly" Campaign. Multicoloured.

2979	15 c. Type **304**	10	10
2980	20 c. Hands squeezing milk into bowl (vert)	10	10
2981	90 c. Breast feeding (vert)	40	45
2982	$5 Breast feeding emblem (vert)	2·10	2·25

305 Aerial View of Leeward Coastal Road

1995. 25th Anniv of Caribbean Development Bank. Multicoloured.

2983	10 c. Type **305**	10	10
2984	15 c. Feeder roads project	10	10
2985	25 c. "Anthurium andraeanum" (flower)	10	10
2986	50 c. Coconut palm tree (vert)	20	30
2987	65 c. Fairhall Housing Scheme	30	35

306 "The God of Fire" (woodcut) (Shunichi Kadowaki)

307 Jean Shiley (U.S.A.) (high jump)

1995. Japanese Art.

2988	**306** $1.40 multicoloured	65	70

1995. Olympic Games, Atlanta (1996) (1st issue). Multicoloured.

2989	$1 Type **307**	45	50
2990	$1 Ruth Fuchs (Germany) (javelin)	45	50
2991	$1 Alessandro Andrei (Italy) (shot put)	45	50
2992	$1 Dorando Pietri (Italy) (marathon)	45	50
2993	$1 Heide Rosendahl (Germany) (long jump)	45	50
2994	$1 Mitsuoki Watanabe (Japan) (gymnastics)	45	50
2995	$1 Yasuhiro Yamashita (Japan) (judo)	45	50
2996	$1 Dick Fosbury (U.S.A.) (high jump)	45	50
2997	$2 Long jumper and dove	85	90
2998	$2 Hurdler and deer	85	90
2999	$2 Sprinter and cheetah	85	90
3000	$2 Marathon runner and tiger	85	90
3001	$2 Gymnast and dove	85	90
3002	$2 Rower and duck	85	90

See also Nos. 3357/3400.

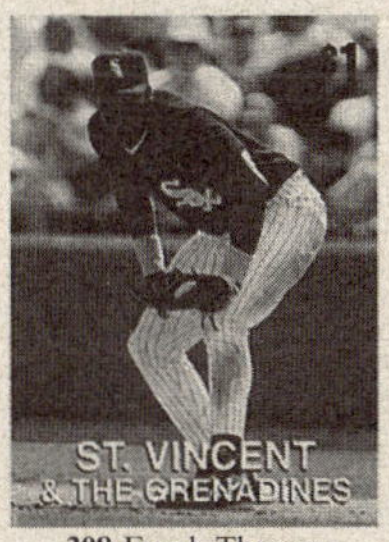

308 Frank Thomas

1995. Famous Baseball Players (8th series). Multicoloured.

3004	$1 Type **308**	45	50
3005	$1 Cal Ripken Jnr wearing "8" jersey and helmet	45	50
3006	$1 Ken Griffey Jnr wearing "S" cap	45	50
3007	$1 Ken Griffey Jnr wearing turquoise-blue jersey	45	50
3008	$1 Frank Thomas in "Sox" cap with bat on shoulder	45	50
3009	$1 Cal Ripken Jnr with ball and glove	45	50
3010	$1 Cal Ripkin Jnr wearing Orioles cap	45	50
3011	$1 Ken Griffey Jnr wearing "Seattle" jersey and helmet	45	50
3012	$1 Frank Thomas wearing "Chicago 35" jersey	45	50

309 John Lennon

1995. Centenary of Cinema. Entertainers. Mult.

3013/21	$1 × 9, John Lennon (as T **309**)		
3022/30	$1 × 9, Elvis Presley		
3031/6	$1 × 6, Elvis Presley		
3037/45	$1 × 9, Marilyn Monroe (with stairway in centre of sheetlet)		
3046/54	$1 × 9, Marilyn Monroe (with superimposed full length portrait)		
3055/63	$1 × 9, Marilyn Monroe (design with hand raised in centre of top row)		
3013/63	Set of 51	20·00	21·00

310 Heinrich Boll (1972 Literature)

1995. Centenary of Nobel Prize Trust Fund. Multicoloured.

3065/3112	$1 × 48 Set of 48	22·00	24·00

DESIGNS: No. 3065, Type **310**; 3066, Walther Bothe (1954 Physics); 3067, Richard Kuhn (1938 Chemistry); 3068, Hermann Hesse (1946 Literature); 3069, Knut Hamsun (1920 Literature); 3070, Konrad Lorenz (1973 Medicine); 3071, Thomas Mann (1929 Literature); 3072, Fridtjof Nansen (1922 Peace); 3073, Fritz Pregl (1923 Chemistry); 3074, Christian Lange (1921 Peace); 3075, Otto Loewi (1936 Medicine); 3076, Erwin Schrodinger (1933 Physics); 3077, Giosue Carducci (1906 Literature); 3078, Wladyslaw Reymont (1924 Literature); 3079, Ivan Bunin (1933 Literature); 3080, Pavel Cherenkov (1958 Physics); 3081, Ivan Pavlov (1904 Medicine); 3082, Pyotr Kapitza (1978 Physics); 3083, Lev Landau (1962 Physics); 3084, Daniel Bovet (1957 Medicine); 3085, Henryk Sienkiewicz (1905 Literature); 3086, Aleksandr Prokhorov (1964 Physics); 3087, Julius von Jauregg (1927 Medicine); 3088, Grazia Deledda (1926 Literature); 3089, Bjornstjerne Bjornson (1903 Literature); 3090, Frank Kellogg (1929 Peace); 3091, Gustav Hertz (1925 Physics); 3092, Har Khorana (1968 Medicine); 3093, Kenichi Fukui (1981 Chemistry); 3094, Henry Kissinger (1973 Peace); 3095, Martin Luther King Jr. (1964 Peace); 3096, Odd Hassel (1969 Chemistry); 3097, Polykarp Kusch (1955 Physics); 3098, Ragnar Frisch (1969 Economics); 3099, Willis Lamb Jr. (1955 Physics); 3100, Sigrid Undset (1928 Literature); 3101, Robert Barany (1914 Medicine); 3102, Ernest Walton (1951 Physics); 3103, Alfred Fried (1911 Peace); 3104, James Franck (1925 Physics); 3105, Werner Forssmann (1956 Medicine); 3106, Yasunari Kawabata (1968 Literature); 3107, Wolfgang Pauli (1945 Physics); 3108, Jean-Paul Sartre (1964 Literature); 3109, Aleksandr Solzhenitsyn (1970 Literature); 3110, Hermann Staudinger (1953 Chemistry); 3111, Igor Tamm (1958 Physics); 3112, Samuel Beckett (1969 Literature).

311 ET4-03 Electric Train, Germany

1995. History of Transport. Modern passenger trains (Nos. 3114/19) or classic cars (Nos. 3120/5). Multicoloured.

3114	$1.50 Type **311**	65	70
3115	$1.50 TGV express train, France	65	70
3116	$1.50 Class 87 electric locomotive, Great Britain	65	70
3117	$1.50 Class "Beijing" diesel locomotive, China	65	70
3118	$1.50 Amtrak turbotrain, U.S.A.	65	70
3119	$1.50 Class RC4 electric train, Sweden	65	70
3120	$1.50 Duesenberg Model "J", 1931	65	70
3121	$1.50 Sleeve-valve Minerva, 1913	65	70
3122	$1.50 Delage "D.8. SS", 1933	65	70
3123	$1.50 Bugatti "Royale Coupe' De Ville", 1931–32	65	70
3124	$1.50 Rolls Royce "Phantom I Landauette", 1926	65	70
3125	$1.50 Mercedes Benz "S236/120/180PS", 1927	65	70

Nos. 3120/5 also include the "Singapore '95" International Stamp Exhibition logo.

312 Grey Wolf

1995. Centenary (1992) of Sierra Club (environmental protection society). Multicoloured.

3127	$1 Type **312**	45	50
3128	$1 Grey wolf cub	45	50
3129	$1 Head of grey wolf	45	50
3130	$1 Hawaiian goose	45	50
3131	$1 Pair of Hawaiian geese	45	50
3132	$1 Head of jaguar	45	50
3133	$1 Liontail macaque	45	50
3134	$1 Sand cat kitten	45	50
3135	$1 Three sand cat kittens	45	50
3136	$1 Orang-utan in tree (horiz)	45	50
3137	$1 Orang-utan on ground (horiz)	45	50
3138	$1 Young orang-utan (horiz)	45	50
3139	$1 Jaguar lying down (horiz)	45	50
3140	$1 Head of jaguar (horiz)	45	50
3141	$1 Pair of sand cats (horiz)	45	50
3142	$1 Hawaiian goose (horiz)	45	50
3143	$1 Three liontail macaques (horiz)	45	50
3144	$1 Head of liontail macaque (horiz)	45	50

Nos. 3136/8 are inscribed "Orangutang" in error.

313 River Nile, Egypt

1995. Natural Landmarks. Multicoloured.

3145	$1.10 Type **313**	50	55
3146	$1.10 River Yangtze, China	50	55
3147	$1.10 Niagara Falls, U.S.A.–Canada border	50	55
3148	$1.10 Victoria Falls, Zambia–Zimbabwe border	50	55
3149	$1.10 Grand Canyon, U.S.A.	50	55
3150	$1.10 Sahara Desert, Algeria	50	55
3151	$1.10 Mt. Kilimanjaro, Tanzania	50	55
3152	$1.10 River Amazon, Brazil	50	55

314 Lionel Santa Handcar

1995. Christmas. Antique Disney Toys. Mult.

3154	1 c. Type **314**	10	10
3155	2 c. Mickey Mouse "choo-choo"	10	10
3156	3 c. Minnie Mouse pram	10	10
3157	5 c. Mickey Mouse acrobats pull-toy	10	10
3158	10 c. Mickey and Pluto clockwork cart	15	10
3159	25 c. Mickey Mouse motorcycle	35	10
3160	$3 Lionel Mickey Mouse handcar	2·75	2·75
3161	$5 Casey Jr. Disneyland train	4·25	4·50

315 Symbolic Rat

316 Spock giving Vulcan Salute

1996. Chinese New Year ("Year of the Rat").

3163	**315** 75 c. black, mauve and green	35	40
3164	– 75 c. black, red and green	35	40
3165	– 75 c. black, purple and green	35	40

DESIGNS: Nos. 3164/5, Different rats.

1996. 30th Anniv of "Star Trek" Television Series. Multicoloured.

3168	$1 Type **316**	45	50
3169	$1 Capt. Kirk and Spock dressed as gangsters	45	50
3170	$1 Kirk in front of computer	45	50
3171	$1 Kirk with Tribbles	45	50
3172	$1 Kirk, Spock and Lt. Uhura in front of Time Portal	45	50
3173	$1 Uhura and Lt. Sulu	45	50
3174	$1 Romulan commander and crew	45	50
3175	$1 City and planet	45	50
3176	$1 Khan	45	50
3177	$1 Spock with phaser	45	50
3178	$1 Capt. Kirk	45	50
3179	$1 Lt. Uhura	45	50
3180	$1 Lt. Sulu	45	50
3181	$1 Starship U.S.S. "Enterprise"	45	50
3182	$1 Dr. McCoy	45	50
3183	$1 Chief Engineer Scott	45	50
3184	$1 Kirk, Spock and McCoy	45	50
3185	$1 Chekov	45	50

317 Goofy the Stamp Dealer

1996. Occupations (1st series). Walt Disney Cartoon Characters at Work. Multicoloured.
3187/95 10 c. × 9 (Type **317**; Supermarket assistant; Car salesman; Florist; Fast food assistant; Street vendor; Gift shop assistant; Hobby shop assistant; Baker)
3196/3204 50 c. × 9 (Delivery man; Truck driver; Aircraft flight crew; Tour guide; Cycle messenger; Tram conductor; Air traffic controller)
3205/13 75 c. × 9 (Postal inspector; Traffic policeman; Private detectives; Highway Patrolman; Justice of the Peace; Security guard; Judge and lawyer; Sheriff; Court stenographer)
3214/22 90 c. × 9 (Basketball player; Referee; Athletic coach; Ice skater; Golfer and caddy; Sports commentator; Tennis players; Football coach; Racing car driver)
3223/31 95 c. × 9 (Paleontologist; Archaeologist; Inventor; Astronaut; Chemist; Engineer; Computer expert; Astronomer; Zoologist)
3232/9 $1.10 × 8 (Classroom teacher; Nursery school teacher; Music teacher; Electronic teacher; School psychologist; School principal; Professor; Graduate (all vert))
3240/8 $1.20 × 9 (Ship builders; Fisherman; Pearl diver; Underwater photographer; Bait and tackle shop owner; Swim suit models; Marine life painter; Life guard; Lighthouse keeper)
3187/3248 Set of 62 . . . . 27·00 29·00
See also Nos. 3510/56.

1996. 125th Anniv of Metropolitan Museum of Art, New York. As T **331** of Maldive Islands. Multicoloured.
3250/7 75 c. × 8 "Moses striking Rock" (Abraham Bloemaert); "The Last Communion" (Botticelli); "The Musicians" (Caravaggio); "Francesco Sassetti and Son" (Ghirlandaio); "Pepito Costa y Bunells" (Goya); "Saint Andrew" (Martini); "The Nativity" (The Dutch School); "Christ Blessing" (Solario))
3258/66 90 c. × 9 ("Madame Cezanne"; "Still Life with Apples and Pears"; "Man in a Straw Hat"; "Still Life with a Ginger Jar"; "Madame Cezanne in a Red Dress"; "Still Life with Crockery"; "Dominique Aubert"; "Still Life with Flowers"; "The Card Players" (all by Cezanne))
3267/75 $1 × 9 ("Bullfight" (Goya); "Portrait of a Man" (Hals); "Mother and Son" (Sully); "Portrait of a Young Man" (Memling); "Matilde Stoughton de Jaudenes" (Stuart); "Josef de Jaudenes y Nebot" (Stuart); "Mont Sainte-Victoire" (Cezanne); "Gardanne" (Cezanne); "Empress Eugenie" (Winterhalter))
3276/84 $1.10 × 9 ("The Dissolute Household" (Steen); "Gerard de Lairesse" (Rembrandt); "Juan de Pareja" (Velazquez); "Curiosity" (Ter Borch); "The Companions of Rinaldo" (Poussin); "Don Gaspar de Guzman" (Velazquez); "Merry Company on a Terrace" (Steen); "Pilate washing Hands" (Rembrandt); "Portrait of a Man" (Van Dyck))
3250/84 Set of 35 . . . . 15·00 16·00

318 Alien Band

319 Yoda

1996. "Star Wars" (film trilogy). Multicoloured. (a) As T **318**.

3286	35 c. Type **318**	70	70
3287	35 c. Darth Vader in battle	70	70
3288	35 c. Fighter ship	70	70
3289	35 c. Space craft orbiting planet	70	70
3290	35 c. Space craft and shuttle	70	70
3291	35 c. Luke Skywalker on space bike	70	70

(b) As T **319**. Self-adhesive.

3292	$1 Darth Vader	1·25	1·25
3293	$1 Type **319**	1·25	1·25
3294	$1 Storm trooper	1·25	1·25

320 "Anteos menippe"

321 Michael Jordan (basketball player)

1996. Butterflies. Multicoloured.

3296	70 c. Type **320**	30	35
3297	90 c. "Papilio lycophron"	40	45
3298	90 c. "Prepona buckleyana"	40	45
3299	90 c. "Parides agavus"	40	45
3300	90 c. "Papilio cacicus"	40	45
3301	90 c. "Euryades duponchelli"	40	45
3302	90 c. "Diaethria dymena"	40	45
3303	90 c. "Orimba jansoni"	40	45
3304	90 c. "Polystichtis siaka"	40	45
3305	90 c. "Papilio machaonides"	40	45
3306	$1 "Eunica alcmena"	45	50
3307	$1.10 "Doxocopa lavinia"	50	55
3308	$2 "Tithorea tarricina"	85	90

Nos. 3297/3305 were printed together, se-tenant, the backgrounds forming a composite design.

1996. Sports Legends. (a) As T **321**. Multicoloured. Perf.

3310	$2 Type **321**	90	1·00
3311	$2 Joe Montana (American footballer)	90	1·00

(b) Size 69 × 103 mm. Imperf.

3312	$6 Michael Jordan	4·50	5·50
3313	$10 Joe Montana	6·50	7·50

322 The Monkey King

1996. "CHINA '96" 9th Asian International Stamp Exhibition (1st issue). Chinese Animated Films – "Uproar in Heaven" (Nos. 3314/18) and "Nezha conquers the Dragon King" (Nos. 3319/23). Multicoloured.

3314	15 c. Type **322**	10	10
3315	15 c. Monkey King flying towards illuminated pole	10	10
3316	15 c. Monkey King and flying horses	10	10
3317	15 c. Monkey King picking fruit	10	10
3318	15 c. Monkey King drinking from flask	10	10
3319	15 c. Nezha waking up	10	10
3320	15 c. Nezha swimming with fish	10	10
3321	15 c. Nezha on back of sea serpent	10	10
3322	15 c. Nezha with sword	10	10
3323	15 c. Nezha in battle	10	10

1996. 70th Birthday of Queen Elizabeth II. As T **334** of Maldive Islands showing different photographs. Multicoloured.

3326	$2 As Type **334** of Maldive Islands	85	90
3327	$2 Wearing Garter robes	85	90
3328	$2 Wearing pink hat and coat	85	90

324 West Indian Boy

1996. 50th Anniv of U.N.I.C.E.F. Multicoloured.

3330	$1 Type **324**	45	50
3331	$1.10 European girl	50	55
3332	$2 South-east Asian girl	85	90

325 Menorah and The Knesset

1996. 3000th Anniv of Jerusalem. Multicoloured.

3334	$1 Type **325**	45	50
3335	$1.10 The Montefiore Windmill	50	55
3336	$2 Shrine of the Book	85	90

The captions on Nos. 3334 and 3336 were transposed in error.

326 Walter Winchell

1996. Centenary of Radio. Entertainers. Mult.

3338	90 c. Type **326**	40	45
3339	$1 Fred Allen	45	50
3340	$1.10 Hedda Hopper	50	55
3341	$2 Eve Arden	85	90

327 Bananaquit

328 Maurice King (St. Vincent) (weightlifting), Pan American Games, 1959

1996. Birds. Multicoloured.

3343	60 c. Type **327**	25	30
3344	$1 Rufous-throated solitare	45	50
3345	$1 Purple martin (horiz)	45	50
3346	$1 Broad-winged hawk (horiz)	45	50
3347	$1 White-tailed tropic bird (horiz)	45	50
3348	$1 Black-winged stilt (horiz)	45	50
3349	$1 Bridled tern (horiz)	45	50
3350	$1 Blue-hooded euphonia (horiz)	45	50
3351	$1 Turnstone (horiz)	45	50
3352	$1 Green-throated carib (horiz)	45	50
3353	$1 Yellow-crowned night heron (horiz)	45	50
3354	$1.10, Hooded tanager	50	55
3355	$2 Purple-throated carib	90	95

Nos. 3345/53 were printed together, se-tenant, with the backgrounds forming a composite design.

1996. Olympic Games, Atlanta (2nd issue). Multicoloured.

3357	20 c. Type **328**	10	10
3358	70 c. Eswort Coombs (St. Vincent) (400m sprint), World University Student Games)	30	35
3359	90 c. Pamenos Ballantyne (St. Vincent) (O.E.C.S. road-running) and Benedict Ballantyne (St. Vincent) (Guinness Half-marathon, 1994)	40	45
3360	90 c. Ancient Greek runners, Olympia (horiz)	40	45
3361	$1 London landmarks (horiz)	45	50
3362	$1 Women's archery (Korea), 1988, 1992	45	50
3363	$1 Gymnastics (Japan), 1960–76	45	50
3364	$1 Basketball (U.S.A.), 1936, 1948–68, 1976, 1984 and 1992	45	50
3365	$1 Soccer (Spain), 1992	45	50
3366	$1 Water polo (Hungary), 1956	45	50
3367	$1 Baseball (Cuba), 1992	45	50
3368	$1 Kayak (Germany), 1980	45	50
3369	$1 Fencing (France), 1980	45	50
3370	$1 Cycling (Germany), 1908, 1964, 1972–76 and 1992	45	50
3371	$1 Vitaly Shcherbo (Russia) (gymastics), 1992	45	50
3372	$1 Fu Mingxia (China) (diving), 1992	45	50
3373	$1 Wilma Rudolph (U.S.A.) (track and field), 1960	45	50
3374	$1 Rafer Johnson (U.S.A.) (decathlon), 1960	45	50
3375	$1 Teofilo Stevenson (Cuba) (boxing), 1972–80	45	50
3376	$1 Babe Didrikson (U.S.A.) (track and field), 1932	45	50
3377	$1 Kyoko Iwasaki (Japan) (swimming), 1992	45	50
3378	$1 Yoo Namkyu (Korea) (table tennis), 1988	45	50
3379	$1 Michael Gross (Germany) (swimming), 1984–88	45	50
3380	$1 Yasuhiro Yamashita (Japan) (judo), 1984 (horiz)	45	50
3381	$1 Peter Rono (Kenya) (1500m race), 1988 (horiz)	45	50
3382	$1 Aleksandr Kourlovitch (Russia) (weight-lifting), 1988 (horiz)	45	50
3383	$1 Juha Tiainen (Finland) (hammer throw), 1984 (horiz)	45	50
3384	$1 Sergei Bubka (Russia) (pole vault), 1988 (horiz)	45	50
3385	$1 Q.F. Newall (Great Britain) (archery), 1908 (horiz)	45	50
3386	$1 Nadia Comaneci (Rumania) (gymnastics), 1976 (horiz)	45	50
3387	$1 Carl Lewis (U.S.A.) (long jump), 1988 (horiz)	45	50
3388	$1 Bob Mathias (U.S.A.) (decathlon), 1948 (horiz)	45	50
3389	$1 Chuhei Nambu (Japan) (triple jump), 1932 (horiz)	45	50
3390	$1 Duncan McNaughton (Canada) (high jump), 1932 (horiz)	45	50
3391	$1 Jack Kelly (U.S.A.) (single sculls), 1920 (horiz)	45	50
3392	$1 Jackie Joyner-Kersee (U.S.A.) (heptathlon), 1988 (horiz)	45	50
3393	$1 Tyrell Biggs (U.S.A.) (super heavy-weight boxing), 1984 (horiz)	45	50
3394	$1 Larisa Latynina (Russia) (gymnastics), 1964 (horiz)	45	50
3395	$1 Bob Garrett (U.S.A.) (discus), 1896 (horiz)	45	50
3396	$1 Paavo Nurmi (Finland) (5000m), 1924 (horiz)	45	50
3397	$1 Eric Lemming (Sweden) (javelin), 1908 (horiz)	45	50
3398	$1.10 Rodney Jack (St. Vincent) (1995 Caribbean Nations Football Cup)	50	55
3399	$1.10 Dorando Pietri (Italy) (marathon), 1908	50	55
3400	$2 Yachting (horiz)	85	90

No. 3371 is inscribed "GYMNASTIECS" in error.

329 Notre Dame Cathedral, Paris

1996. "The Hunchback of Notre Dame". Scenes from the Disney cartoon film. Multicoloured.
3402/7 10 c. × 6 (Type **329**; People watching puppet show; Judge Frollo on black horse; Quasimodo and his parents captured; Gargoyles; Quasimodo)
3408/16 30 c. × 9 (Captain Phoebus meets Esmeralda; Captain Phoebus and Judge Frollo; Esmeralda dancing; Esmeralda and candidates for King of Fools; Quasimodo wearing crown; Quasimodo pelted; Quasimodo carrying Esmeralda; Phoebus on black horse; Quasimodo, Esmeralda and a wounded Phoebus (all horiz))
3417/25 $1 × 9 (Quasimodo chained to bell tower; Three gargoyles and Quasimodo; Quasimodo pulling down pillars; Quasimodo rescuing Esmeralda; Phoebus leading citizens; Quasimodo throwing wood; Quasimodo weeping over Esmeralda; Quasimodo and Frollo fighting; Quasimodo and Esmeralda on ledge (all horiz))
3426/33 $1 × 8 (Quasimodo; Phoebus; Laverne and Hugo; Clopin; Frollo; Esmeralda; Victor; Djali)
3402/33 Set of 32 . . . . 13·00 14·00
No. 3416 is inscribed "wonded phoebus" in error.

330 French Angelfish

1996. Fishes. Multicoloured.

3435	70 c. Type **330**	30	35
3436	90 c. Red-spotted hawkfish	40	45
3437	$1 Barred hamlet	45	50
3438	$1 Flamefish	45	50
3439	$1 Caribbean long-nosed butterflyfish	45	50
3440	$1 Royal gramma ("Fairy Basslet")	45	50
3441	$1 Red-tailed parrotfish	45	50
3442	$1 Black-barred soldierfish	45	50
3443	$1 Three-spotted damselfish	45	50
3444	$1 Candy basslet	45	50
3445	$1 Spot-finned hogfish	45	50
3446	$1 Jackknife fish	45	50
3447	$1 Surgeon fish	45	50
3448	$1 Muttonfish	45	50
3449	$1 Seahorse	45	50

3450 $1 Comber fish 45 50
3451 $1 Angel shark 45 50
3452 $1 Moray eel 45 50
3453 $1 Bicolour parrotfish . . . 45 50
3454 $1 "Tritonium nodiferum" (sea snail) 45 50
3455 $1.10 Balloonfish ("Spiny Puffer") 50 55
3456 $2 Grey triggerfish 85 90

Nos. 3446/54 were printed together, se-tenant, with the backgrounds forming a composite design.
No. 3445 is inscribed "HOFGFISH" in error.

331 "Beloperone guttata"

1996. Flowers. Multicoloured.
3458 70 c. Type **331** 30 35
3459 90 c. "Datura candida" . . . 40 45
3460 90 c. "Amherstia nobilis" . . 40 45
3461 90 c. "Ipomoea acuminata" . 40 45
3462 90 c. "Bougainvillea glabra" . 40 45
3463 90 c. "Cassia alata" 40 45
3464 90 c. "Cordia sebestena" . . 40 45
3465 90 c. "Opuntia dilenii" . . . 40 45
3466 90 c. "Cryptostegia grandiflora" 40 45
3467 90 c. "Rodriguezia lanceolata" 40 45
3468 $1 "Epidendrum elongatum" 45 50
3469 $1.10 "Petrea volubilis" . . . 50 55
3470 $2 "Oncidium altissimum" . 85 90

Nos. 3459/67 were printed together, se-tenant, with the backgrounds forming a composite design.

332 "Doric", 1923

1996. Passenger Ships. Multicoloured.
3472 $1.10 Type **332** 50 55
3473 $1.10 "Nerissa", 1926 . . . . 50 55
3474 $1.10 "Howick Hall", 1910 . 50 55
3475 $1.10 "Jervis Bay", 1922 . . 50 55
3476 $1.10 "Vauban", 1912 . . . 50 55
3477 $1.10 "Orinoco", 1928 . . . 50 55
3478 $1.10 "Lady Rodney", 1929 . 50 55
3479 $1.10 "Empress of Russia", 1913 . . . . 50 55
3480 $1.10 "Providence", 1914 . . 50 55
3481 $1.10 "Reina Victori-Eugenia", 1913 . . . . 50 55
3482 $1.10 "Balmoral Castle", 1910 50 55
3483 $1.10 "Tivives", 1911 . . . . 50 55

333 Elvis Presley

334 Sandy Koufax (baseball player)

1996. Elvis Presley (singer) Commemoration. Different portraits. Multicoloured.
3485 $2 Type **333** 85 90
3486 $2 Wearing checked shirt with guitar 85 90
3487 $2 Playing piano 85 90
3488 $2 Wearing black jacket and playing guitar 85 90
3489 $2 Wearing white shirt and black tie 85 90
3490 $2 Singing into studio microphone 85 90

1996. Sports Legends. Sandy Koufax. Multicoloured.
3491 $2 Type **334** 85 90
3492 $2 Pitching ball 85 90
3493 $2 Preparing to pitch with arm raised 85 90
3494 $6 Sandy Koufax (69 × 103 mm) . . . . . . 2·50 2·75

335 Richard Petty's 1990 Pontiac

1996. Richard Petty (stock car driver) Commemoration. Multicoloured.
3495 $2 Type **335** 85 90
3496 $2 Richard Petty 85 90
3497 $2 1972 Plymouth 85 90
3498 $2 1974 Dodge 85 90

336 D.S. Cozier (founder) and Cadet Force Emblem

1996. 60th Anniv of St. Vincent Army Cadet Force. Multicoloured.
3500 70 c. Type **336** 30 35
3501 90 c. Emblem and first cadets with Cozier 40 45

337 "Virgin and Child" (detail, Memling)

339 Symbolic Ox

1996. Christmas. Religious Paintings. Multicoloured.
3502 70 c. Type **337** 30 35
3503 90 c. "St. Anthony" (detail, Memling) 40 45
3504 $1 "Madonna and Child" (detail, D. Bouts) 45 50
3505 $1.10 "Virgin and Child" (detail, Lorenzo Lotto) . . 50 55
3506 $2 "St. Roch" (detail, Lotto) 85 90
3507 $5 "St. Sebastian" (detail, Lotto) . . . . 2·10 2·25

1996. Occupations (2nd series). Multicoloured. As Nos. 3196/3248, but all with face value of 10 c.
3510/17 10 c. × 8 As Nos. 3196/9 and 3201/4
3518/25 10 c. × 8 As Nos. 3205/8 and 3210/13
3526/33 10 c. × 8 As Nos. 3214/17 and 3519/22
3534/41 10 c. × 8 As Nos. 3523/6 and 3528/31
3542/8 10 c. × 7 As Nos. 3232/4 and 3236/9 (all vert)
3549/56 10 c. × 8 As Nos. 3240/3 and 3245/8
3510/56 Set of 47 . . . . 4·00 4·50

1997. Chinese New Year ("Year of the Ox").
3557 **339** 75 c. black, orange and pink 45 50
3558 – 75 c. black, green and lilac 45 50
3559 – 75 c. black, pink and red 45 50
DESIGNS: Nos. 3558/9, Different oxen.

340 Lieut. Tuvok

341 Mickey Mantle

1997. "Star Trek Voyager" (television series). Multicoloured.
3562 $2 Type **340** 85 90
3563 $2 Kes 85 90
3564 $2 Tom Paris 85 90
3565 $2 The Doctor 85 90
3566 $2 Captain Katherine Janeway 85 90
3567 $2 B'Elanna Torres 85 90
3568 $2 Neelix 85 90
3569 $2 Harry Kim 85 90
3570 $2 First Officer Chakotay . . 85 90

1997. Sports Legends. Mickey Mantle (baseball player). Multicoloured. Perf ($2) or imperf. ($6).
3572 $2 Type **341** 85 90
3573 $6 Mickey Mantle (67 × 100 mm) . . . . 2·50 2·75

342 Hong Kong Waterfront

1997. "Hong Kong '97" International Stamp Exhibition. Designs showing the Hong Kong waterfront by day (Nos. 3574/8) or night (Nos. 3579/83). Multicoloured.
3574 90 c. Type **342** 40 45
3575 90 c. Two ferries in foreground 40 45
3576 90 c. Construction site on waterfront 40 45
3577 90 c. One launch 40 45
3578 90 c. Hong Kong Bank and yellow building in centre . . 40 45
3579 90 c. Large building with spire on right 40 45
3580 90 c. Electronic billboards including HITACHI . . . 40 45
3581 90 c. Mansions on hillside at right 40 45
3582 90 c. Toshiba and NEC billboards in centre 40 45
3583 90 c. Hong Kong bank building under Union Jack 40 45

Nos. 3574/83 were printed together, se-tenant, forming two composite designs.

1997. 50th Anniv of U.N.E.S.C.O. As T **348** of Maldive Islands. Multicoloured.
3585 70 c. Lord Howe Island, Australia 30 35
3586 90 c. Uluru-kata Tjuta National Park, Australia 40 45
3587 $1 Cave paintings, Kakadu National Park, Australia . 45 50
3588 $1.10 Te Wahipounamu National Park, New Zealand 50 55
3589 $1.10 Castle, Himeji-jo, Japan 50 55
3590 $1.10 Temple, lake and gardens, Kyoto, Japan 50 55
3591 $1.10 Walkway, Kyoto, Japan 50 55
3592 $1.10 Buddha, Temple of Ninna, Japan 50 55
3593 $1.10 View from castle, Himeji-jo, Japan 50 55
3594 $1.10 Forest, Shirakami-sanchi, Japan 50 55
3595 $1.10 Forest and mountains, Yakushima, Japan 50 55
3596 $1.10 Forest, Yakushima, Japan 50 55
3597 $1.10 City of San Gimignano, Italy 50 55
3598 $1.10 Cathedral of Santa Maria Asunta, Pisa, Italy 50 55
3599 $1.10 Cathedral of Santa Maria Fiore, Florence, Italy . . . 50 55
3600 $1.10 Archaeological site, Valley of the Boyne, Ireland 50 55
3601 $1.10 Church of St. Savin-sur-Gartempe, France 50 55
3602 $1.10 Regency mansion, Bath, England 50 55
3603 $1.10 Rooftop view of Bath, England 50 55
3604 $1.10 Street in Bath, England 50 55
3605 $1.10 Monastery of Rossanou, Meteora, Greece 50 55
3606 $1.10 Ceiling painting, Mount Athos, Greece 50 55
3607 $1.10 Monastery Osios Varlaam, Meteora, Greece . 50 55
3608 $1.10 Ruins, Athens, Greece . 50 55
3609 $1.10 Carvings, Acropolis Museum, Athens, Greece . 50 55
3610 $1.10 Painted cloisters, Mount Athos, Greece 50 55
3611 $1.10 Lake, Mount Athos, Greece 50 55
3612 $1.10 Painting above door, Mount Athos, Greece . . . 50 55
3613 $1.50 Palace, Wudang Mountains, China (horiz) . 65 70
3614 $1.50 Caves, Mogao, China (horiz) 65 70
3615 $1.50 House, Taklamakan Desert, China (horiz) . . . 65 70
3616 $1.50 Section going through forest, Great Wall, China (horiz) 65 70
3617 $1.50 Section going through desert, Great Wall, China (horiz) 65 70
3618 $1.50 House and church, Quedlinburg, Germany (horiz) 65 70
3619 $1.50 Decorated house fronts, Quedlinburg (horiz) . . . 65 70
3620 $1.50 Decorative house windows, Quedlinburg, Germany (horiz) 65 70
3621 $1.50 House front, Quedlinburg, Germany (horiz) 65 70
3622 $1.50 Church spires, Quedlinburg (horiz) . . . 65 70
3623 $1.50 Valley of the Ingenios, Cuba (horiz) 65 70
3624 $1.50 City of Zacatecas, Mexico (horiz) 65 70
3625 $1.50 Lima, Peru (horiz) . . 65 70
3626 $1.50 Monastic ruins, Paraguay (horiz) 65 70
3627 $1.50 Mayan ruins, Copan, Honduras (horiz) 65 70
3628 $2 Tongariro National Park, New Zealand (horiz) . . . 85 90
3629 $5 Tongariro National Park, New Zealand . . . . . . 2·10 2·25

343 Microwave Radio Relay Tower, Dorsetshire Hill

1997. 125th Anniv of Telecommunications in St. Vincent. Multicoloured (except 70 c.).
3631 5 c. Type **343** 10 10
3632 10 c. Cable and Wireless headquarters, Kingstown . 10 10
3633 20 c. Microwave relay tower (vert) 10 10
3634 35 c. Cable and Wireless complex, Arnos Vale . . . 15 20
3635 50 c. Cable and Wireless tower, Mount St. Andrew 25 30
3636 70 c. Early cable ship (black and violet) 30 35
3637 90 c. Eastern telecommunications network map, 1872 40 45
3638 $1.10 World telegraph map, 1876 . . . . 50 55

344 Smooth-billed Ani

1997. Birds of the World. Multicoloured.
3639 60 c. Type **344** 25 30
3640 70 c. Belted kingfisher . . . 30 35
3641 90 c. Blackburnian warbler . 40 45
3642 $1 Blue grosbeak 45 50
3643 $1 Bananaquit 45 50
3644 $1 Cedar waxwing 45 50
3645 $1 Ovenbird 45 50
3646 $1 Hooded warbler 45 50
3647 $1 Flicker 45 50
3648 $1.10 Blue tit 50 55
3649 $2 Chaffinch 85 90
3650 $2 Song thrush 85 90
3651 $2 Robin 85 90
3652 $2 Blackbird 85 90
3653 $2 Great spotted woodpecker 85 90
3654 $2 Wren 85 90
3655 $2 Kingfisher 85 90
3656 $5 Ruddy turnstone . . . . 2·10 2·25

Nos. 3642/7 and 3650/5 respectively were printed together, se-tenant, with the backgrounds forming composite designs.

345 Mandarin Duck

1997. Sea Birds. Multicoloured.
3658 70 c. Type **345** 30 35
3659 90 c. Green heron 40 45
3660 $1 Ringed teal drake 45 50
3661 $1.10 Blue-footed booby and chick 50 55
3662 $1.10 Crested auklet (vert) . 50 55
3663 $1.10 Whiskered auklet (vert) 50 55
3664 $1.10 Pigeon guillemot (vert) 50 55
3665 $1.10 Adelie penguins (vert) . 50 55
3666 $1.10 Rockhopper penguin (vert) 50 55
3667 $1.10 Emperor penguin and chick (vert) 50 55
3668 $2 Australian jacana (vert) . 85 90
3669 $5 Reddish egret (vert) . . . 2·10 2·25

Nos. 3662/7 were printed together, se-tenant, with the backgrounds forming a composite design.

346 Frank Robinson

347 Child's Face and U.N.E.S.C.O. Emblem

1997. Baseball Legends. Multicoloured. Imperf ($6) or perf (others).

3671 $1 Type **346** 45 50
3672 $1 Satchel Paige 45 50
3673 $1 Billy Williams 45 50
3674 $1 Reggie Jackson 45 50
3675 $1 Roberto Clemente 45 50
3676 $1 Ernie Banks 45 50
3677 $1 Hank Aaron 45 50
3678 $1 Roy Campanella 45 50
3679 $1 Willie McCovey 45 50
3680 $1 Monte Irvin 45 50
3681 $1 Willie Stargell 45 50
3682 $1 Rod Carew 45 50
3683 $1 Ferguson Jenkins 45 50
3684 $1 Bob Gibson 45 50
3685 $1 Lou Brock 45 50
3686 $1 Joe Morgan 45 50
3687 $6 Jackie Robinson (67 × 101 mm) . . . . . . 2·50 2·75

1997. 10th Anniv of Chernobyl Nuclear Disaster. Multicoloured.

3690 $2 Type **347** 85 90
3691 $2 As Type **347** but inscribed "CHABAD'S CHILDREN OF CHERNOBYL" at foot 85 90

1997. 50th Death Anniv of Paul Harris (founder of Rotary International). As T **113** of Nevis. Mult.

3692 $2 Paul Harris and Thai children receiving blankets 85 90

1997. Golden Wedding of Queen Elizabeth and Prince Philip. As T **350** of Maldive Islands. Multicoloured.

3694 $1.10 Queen Elizabeth II . . . 50 55
3695 $1.10 Royal coat of arms . . 50 55
3696 $1.10 Queen Elizabeth and Prince Philip 50 55
3697 $1.10 Queen Elizabeth and Prince Philip on royal visit 50 55
3698 $1.10 Buckingham Palace . . 50 55
3699 $1.10 Prince Philip in naval uniform 50 55

1997. "Pacific '97" International Stamp Exhibition, San Francisco. Death Centenary of Heinrich von Stephan (founder of the U.P.U.). As T **351** of Maldive Islands.

3701 $2 violet and black 85 90
3702 $2 brown and black 85 90
3703 $2 blue and black 85 90

DESIGNS: No. 3701, Bicycle postman, India, 1800s; 3702, Von Stephan and Mercury; 3703, Ox-drawn postal cart, Indochina.

1996. Birth Bicentenary of Hiroshige (Japanese painter). "One Hundred Famous Views of Edo". As T **352** of Maldive Islands. Mult.

3705 $1.50 "Furukawa River, Hiroo" 65 70
3706 $1.50 "Chiyogaike Pond, Meguro" 65 70
3707 $1.50 "New Fuji, Meguro" . 65 70
3708 $1.50 "Moon-viewing Point" . 65 70
3709 $1.50 "Ushimachi, Takanawa" 65 70
3710 $1.50 "Original Fuji, Meguro" 65 70

348 Couple with Dog

349 Deng Xiaoping

1997. 175th Anniv of Brothers Grimm's Third Collection of Fairy Tales. "Old Sultan" (Nos. 3712/14) and "The Cobbler and the Elves" (Nos. 3715/17). Multicoloured.

3712 $2 Type **348** 85 90
3713 $2 Sheepdog on hillside . . . 85 90
3714 $2 Wolf and sheepdog . . . 85 90
3715 $2 The cobbler 85 90
3716 $2 The elves 85 90
3717 $2 Cobbler with elf 85 90

1997. Deng Xiaoping (Chinese statesman) Commemoration.

3719 **349** $2 brown 85 90
3720 – $2 brown 85 90
3721 – $2 brown 85 90
3722 – $2 brown 85 90
3723 – $2 blue and light blue . 85 90
3724 – $2 blue and light blue . 85 90
3725 – $2 blue and light blue . 85 90
3726 – $2 blue and light blue . 85 90
3727 – $2 black 85 90
3728 – $2 black 85 90
3729 – $2 black 85 90
3730 – $2 black 85 90

DESIGNS: No. 3720, Looking left; 3721, In military uniform; 3722, Full face; 3723, Looking right; 3724, Smiling; 3725, With head tilted to right; 3726, Looking down; 3727, Looking right; 3728, Looking left; 3729, Full face; 3730, Facing left and smiling.

350 Alphonso Theodore Roberts

1997. Inaugural Cricket Test Match at Arnos Vale. Multicoloured.

3732 90 c. Type **350** 40 45
3733 $5 Arnos Vale cricket ground (horiz) . . . . 2·10 2·25

351 "Cinemax" Mardi Gras Band

1997. 20th Anniv of Vincy Mas Carnival. Multicoloured.

3734 10 c. Type **351** 10 10
3735 20 c. Queen of the Bands "Jacintha Ballantyne" . . 10 10
3736 50 c. Queen of the Bands "Out of the Frying Pan and into the Fire" (vert) 25 30
3737 70 c. King of the Bands "Conquistodore" 30 35
3738 90 c. Starlift Steel Orchestra 40 45
3739 $2 Frankie McIntosh (musical arranger) (vert) 85 90

1997. World Cup Football Championship, France (1998). As T **246** of Lesotho.

3740 70 c. multicoloured . . . 30 35
3741 90 c. brown 40 45
3742 $1 multicoloured 45 50
3743/50 $1 × 8 (black; multicoloured; black; black; black; black; multicoloured; black)
3751/8 $1 × 8 (each multicoloured)
3759/66 $1 × 8 (multicoloured; black; multicoloured; black; black; multicoloured; black; multicoloured)
3767/74 $1 × 8 (blue; multicoloured; blue; multicoloured; blue; multicoloured; blue)
3775 $1.10 brown 50 55
3776 $2 multicoloured 85 90
3777 $10 black . . . . 4·25 4·50
3740/77 Set of 38 . . . . 22·00 23·00

DESIGNS—HORIZ: No. 3740, Beckenbauer, West Germany; 3741, Moore, England; 3742, Lato, Poland; 3759, Argentine and West German players, 1986; 3760 and 3769, English and West German players, 1966; 3761, Goal mouth melee, 1986; 3762, Italian and West German players, 1982; 3763 and 3770, English player heading ball, 1966; 3764, Argentine player with ball, 1978; 3765, Argentine player chasing ball, 1978; 3766, Dutch player with ball; 3767, Wembley Stadium, England, 1966; 3768, West German player with ball; 3771, English player in air heading ball; 3772, German player tackling English player; 3773, Celebrating English team; 3774, Celebrating German player; 3775, Pele, Brazil; 3776, Maier, West Germany; 3777, Eusebio, Portugal. VERT—No. 3743, Argentine player kicking ball; 3744, Argentine player holding trophy; 3745, Goal mouth melee; 3746, Dutch player; 3747, Celebrating Argentine player; 3748, Argentine player tackling Dutch player; 3749, Argentine and two Dutch players; 3750, Players attempting to head ball; 3751, Bergkamp, Netherlands; 3752, Seaman, England; 3753, Schmeichel, Denmark; 3754, Ince, England; 3755, Futre, Portugal; 3756, Ravanelli, Italy; 3757, Keane, Republic of Ireland; 3758, Gascoigne, England.

352 Hand above Globe of Flowers

353 "Rhyncholaelia digbyana"

1997. 10th Anniv of the Signing of the Montreal Protocol on Substances that Deplete the Ozone Layer.

3779 **352** 90 c. multicoloured . . . 40 45

1997. Orchids of the World. Multicoloured.

3780 90 c. Type **353** 40 45
3781 $1 "Laeliocattleya" "Chitchat Tangerine" 45 50
3782 $1 "Eulophia speciosa" . . . 45 50
3783 $1 "Aerangis rhodosticta" . . 45 50
3784 $1 "Angraecum infundibularea" 45 50
3785 $1 "Calanthe sylvatica" . . . 45 50
3786 $1 "Phalaenopsis mariae" . . 45 50
3787 $1 "Paphiopedilum insigne" . 45 50
3788 $1 "Dendrobium nobile" . . . 45 50
3789 $1 "Aerangis kotschyana" . . 45 50
3790 $1 "Cyrtorchis chailluana" . . 45 50
3791 $1.10 "Doritis pulcherrima" . 50 55
3792 $2 "Phalaenopsis" "Barbara Moler" 85 90

354 Snow Leopard

1997. Sierra Club Conservation. Multicoloured.

3794/3802 20 c. × 9 (Type **354**; Polar bear; Plants, Isle Royale National Park; Waterway, Isle Royale National Park; Denali National Park at night; Denali National Park; Plants, Joshua Tree National Park; Mountains, Joshua Tree National Park; Rock, Joshua Tree National Park)
3803/11 40 c. × 9 (Mountain gorilla showing teeth; Mountain gorilla; Young mountain gorilla; Snow leopard; Young snow leopard; Polar bear; Polar bear cub; Denali National Park; Isle Royale National Park (all vert))
3812/20 50 c. × 9 (Sifaka with young; Sifaka on branch; Head of sifaka; Peregrine falcon; Peregrine falcon with stretched wings; Galapagos tortoise; Waterfall, African rainforest; Tree, African rainforest; China's Yellow Mountains (all vert))
3821/9 60 c. × 9 (Head of red panda; Red panda on branch; Red panda on ground; Peregrine falcon with chicks; Head of Galapagos tortoise; Galapagos tortoise on grass; African rainforest; Tops of trees, China's Yellow Mountains; Gorge, China's Yellow Mountains)
3830/8 70 c. × 9 (Mountain lion; Siberian tiger; Head of Siberian tiger; Red wolf; Black bear; Lake, Wolong National Reserve; Belize rainforest; Base of tree, Belize rainforest; Mountains, Wolong National Reserve)
3839/47 90 c. × 9 (Siberian tiger; Head of mountain lion; Mountain lion cubs; Black bear on branch; Head of black bear; Red Wolf; Head of red wolf; Belize rainforest; Wolong National Reserve (all vert))
3848/56 $1 × 9 (Indri hanging from tree; Indri face on; Indri holding onto tree; Gopher tortoise inside shell; Gopher tortoise on ground; Black-footed ferret facing forward; Head of black-footed ferret; Haleakala National Park; Grand Teton National Park (all vert))
3857/65 $1.10 × 9 (Black-footed ferret; Gopher tortoise; River, Grand Teton National Park; Hillside, Grand Teton National Park; River, Haleakala National Park; Plants, Haleakala National Park; Misty view of Madagascar rainforest; Trees, Madagascar rainforest; Cleared forest, Madagascar rainforest)
3794/3865 Set of 72 . . . . 22·00 23·00

355 Raised Stern of "Titanic"

356 "Morrison Hotel" Album Cover, February 1970

1997. 85th Anniv of the Sinking of the "Titanic" (liner). Multicoloured.

3867 $1 Type **355** 75 75
3868 $1 Lifeboat rowing away . . 75 75
3869 $1 One funnel and lifeboat being lowered into water . 75 75
3870 $1 Two funnels 75 75
3871 $1 One funnel in water and lifeboat rowing away . . . 75 75

Nos. 3867/71 were printed together, se-tenant, forming a composite design.

1997. 30th Anniv of The Doors (rock group) and Rock and Roll Hall of Fame, Cleveland. Multicoloured.

3872 90 c. Type **356** 40 45
3873 95 c. "Waiting for the Sun" album cover, April 1968 . 40 45
3874 $1 Rock and Roll Hall of Fame and Museum, Cleveland, Ohio 45 50
3875 $1 "L.A. Women" album cover, April 1971 . . . . 45 50
3876 $1.10 "The Soft Parade" album cover, July 1969 . . . . 50 55
3877 $1.20 "Strange Days" album cover, October 1967 . . . 50 55
3878 $1.50 Rock and Roll Hall of Fame guitar logo 65 70
3879 $1.50 "The Doors" album cover, January 1967 . . . 65 70

357 Joe "King" Oliver

1997. New Orleans School of Jazz Commemoration. Multicoloured.

3880 $1 Type **357** 60 60
3881 $1 Louis Armstrong 60 60
3882 $1 Sidney Bechet 60 60
3883 $1 Nick Larocca 60 60
3884 $1 Louis Prima 60 60
3885 $1 "Buddy" Charles Bolden . 60 60

1997. Millennium Series. Famous People of the Twentieth Century. As T **139** of Nevis. Multicoloured. (a) Sculptors.

3886 $1.10 Constantin Brancusi . 50 55
3887 $1.10 "The New Born" (Brancusi) (56 × 42 mm) . 50 55
3888 $1.10 "Four Elements" (Calder) (56 × 42 mm) 50 55
3889 $1.10 Alexander Calder . . . 50 55
3890 $1.10 Isamu Noguchi 50 55
3891 $1.10 "Dodge Fountain" (Noguchi) (56 × 42 mm) . 50 55
3892 $1.10 "The Shuttlecock" (Oldenburg) (56 × 42 mm) . 50 55
3893 $1.10 Claes Oldenburg . . . 50 55

(b) Opera Singers.

3894 $1.10 Lily Pons 50 55
3895 $1.10 Lily Pons in Donizetti's "Lucia di Lammermoor" (56 × 42 mm) 50 55
3896 $1.10 Maria Callas in Bellini's "I Puritani" (56 × 42 mm) . 50 55
3897 $1.10 Maria Callas 50 55
3898 $1.10 Beverly Sills 50 55
3899 $1.10 Beverly Sills in Donizetti's "La Fille du Regiment" (56 × 42 mm) 50 55
3900 $1.10 Jessye Norman in Schoenberg's "Erwartung" (56 × 42 mm) 50 55
3901 $1.10 Jessye Norman 50 55

3902 $1.10 Enrico Caruso 50 55
3903 $1.10 Enrico Caruso in Verdi's "Rigoletto" (56×42 mm) 50 55
3904 $1.10 Mario Lanza in "The Seven Hills of Rome" (56×42 mm) 50 55
3905 $1.10 Mario Lanza 50 55
3906 $1.10 Luciano Pavarotti 50 55
3907 $1.10 Luciano Pavarotti in Donizetti's "L'Elisir d'Amore" (56×42 mm) 50 55
3908 $1.10 Placido Domingo in Puccini's "Tosca" (56×42 mm) 50 55
3909 $1.10 Placido Domingo 50 55

358 Diana, Princess of Wales

1997. Diana, Princess of Wales Commemoration. Multicoloured.
3910 $2 Type **358** 85 90
3911 $2 Wearing pearl-drop earrings 85 90
3912 $2 Wearing black jacket 85 90
3913 $2 Wearing blue jacket and pearl earrings 85 90
3914 $2 Wearing tiara 85 90
3915 $2 In black evening dress 85 90
3916 $2 Wearing blue jacket 85 90
3917 $2 Wearing beige blouse 85 90

359 "The Sistine Madonna" (detail, Raphael)

1997. Christmas. Paintings and Sculptures. Multicoloured.
3919 60 c. Type **359** 25 30
3920 70 c. "Angel" (Edward Burne-Jones) 30 35
3921 90 c. "Cupid" (sculpture, Etienne-Maurice Flaconet) 40 45
3922 $1 "Saint Michael" (sculpture, Hubert Gerhard) 45 50
3923 $1.10 "Apollo and the Hoare" (Giambattista Tiepolo) 50 55
3924 $2 "Madonna in a Garland of Flowers" (detail, Rubens and Brueghel the Elder) 85 90

360 Symbolic Tiger

361 Children and School Savings Bank

1998. Chinese New Year ("Year of the Tiger").
3926 **360** $1 black, grey and brown 45 50
3927 – $1 black, silver and brown 45 50
3928 – $1 black, lilac and pink 45 50
DESIGNS: Nos. 3927/8, Different tigers.

1998. Economic Development. Multicoloured.
3930 20 c. Type **361** 10 10
3931 90 c. Agricultural workers and Credit Union Office (vert) 40 45
3932 $1.10 Freighter at quay 50 55

362 Ice Hockey

1998. Winter Olympic Games, Nagano. Mult.
3933 70 c. Type **362** 30 35
3934 $1.10 Bobsleigh 50 55
3935 $1.10 Bjorn Dachlie (Norway) (Gold medal, Nordic skiing, 1994) 50 55
3936 $1.10 Gillis Grafstrom (Sweden) (Gold medal, figure skating, 1924, 1928) 50 55
3937 $1.10 Sonja Henie (Norway) (Gold medal, figure skating, 1928, 1932) 50 55
3938 $1.10 Ingemar Stenmark (Sweden) (Gold medal, slalom and giant slalom, 1980) 50 55
3939 $1.10 Christian Jagge (Norway) (Gold medal, slalom, 1992) 50 55
3940 $1.10 Tomas Gustafson (Sweden) (Gold medal, 5000m speed skating, 1992) 50 55
3941 $1.10 Johann Olav Koss (Norway) (Gold medal, 1500m speed skating, 1992, 1994) 50 55
3942 $1.10 Thomas Wassberg (Sweden) (Gold medal, 50km cross country skiing, 1984) 50 55
3943 $1.50 Downhill (red suit) (vert) 65 70
3944 $1.50 Two-man bobsleigh (vert) 65 70
3945 $1.50 Ski jump (red suit) (vert) 65 70
3946 $1.50 Downhill (red and white suit) (vert) 65 70
3947 $1.50 Luge (vert) 65 70
3948 $1.50 Biathlon (vert) 65 70
3949 $1.50 Downhill (yellow and red suit) (vert) 65 70
3950 $1.50 Figure skating (vert) 65 70
3951 $1.50 Ski jump (green suit) (vert) 65 70
3952 $1.50 Speed skating (vert) 65 70
3953 $1.50 Four-man bobsleigh (vert) 65 70
3954 $1.50 Cross-country skiing (vert) 65 70
3955 $2 Pairs figure skating 85 90
3956 $2 Ski jump (vert) 85 90
Nos. 3943/8 and 3949/54 respectively were printed together, se-tenant, with the backgrounds forming composite designs.

363 Rock-iguana (Anegada)

1998. Endangered Species of the Caribbean. Multicoloured.
3958 50 c. Type **363** 20 25
3959 70 c. "Papilio homerus" (butterfly) (Jamaica) 30 35
3960 90 c. Blossom-bat (Cuba) 40 45
3961 $1 Haitian solenodon (Dominican Republic) 45 50
3962 $1.10 Hawksbill turtle (Grenada) 50 55
3963 $1.10 Roseate spoonbill 50 55
3964 $1.10 Golden swallow 50 55
3965 $1.10 Short-snouted spinner dolphin 50 55
3966 $1.10 Queen or pink conch ("Strombus gigas") 50 55
3967 $1.10 American manatee 50 55
3968 $1.10 Loggerhead turtle 50 55
3969 $1.10 Magnificent frigate bird 50 55
3970 $1.10 Humpback whale 50 55
3971 $1.10 "Marpesia petreus" (butterfly) 50 55
3972 $1.10 St. Lucia whiptail 50 55
3973 $1.10 St. Lucia oriole 50 55
3974 $1.10 Green turtle 50 55
3975 $2 Black-billed whistling duck (Barbuda) 85 90
Nos. 3963/8 and 3964/74 respectively were printed together, se-tenant, forming composite background designs.

364 "Gymnopilus spectabilis" and "Atildes halesus" (butterfly)

1998. Fungi. Multicoloured.
3977 10 c. Type **364** 10 10
3978 20 c. "Entoloma lividium" 10 10
3979 70 c. "Pholiota flammans" 30 35
3980 90 c. "Panaeolus semiovatus" 40 45
3981 $1 "Stropharia rugosoannulata" 45 50
3982 $1 "Tricholoma sulphureum" 45 50
3983 $1 "Amanita caesarea" 45 50
3984 $1 "Amanita muscaria" 45 50
3985 $1 "Amanita ovoidea" 45 50
3986 $1 "Amanita phalloides" 45 50
3987 $1 "Amanitopsis inaurata" 45 50
3988 $1 "Amanitopsis vaginata" 45 50
3989 $1 "Psalliota campestris" 45 50
3990 $1 "Psalliota arvensis" 45 50
3991 $1 "Coprinus comatus" 45 50
3992 $1.10 "Coprinus picaceus" 50 55
3993 $1.10 "Stropharia umbonatescens" 50 55
3994 $1.10 "Hebeloma crustuliniforme" 50 55
3995 $1.10 "Cortinarius collinitus" 50 55
3996 $1.10 "Cortinarius violaceus" 50 55
3997 $1.10 "Cortinarius armillatus" 50 55
3998 $1.10 "Tricholoma aurantium" 50 55
3999 $1.10 "Russula virescens" 50 55
4000 $1.10 "Clitocybe infundibuliformis" 50 55

365 "Amarynthis meneria meneria"

1998. Butterflies. Multicoloured.
4002 20 c. Type **365** 10 10
4003 50 c. "Papilio polyxenes" 20 25
4004 70 c. "Emesis fatima fatima" (vert) 30 35
4005 $1 "Anartia amathea" 45 50
4006 $1 "Heliconius erato" (vert) 45 50
4007 $1 "Danaus plexippus" (vert) 45 50
4008 $1 "Papilio phorcas" (vert) 45 50
4009 $1 "Morpho peleides" (vert) 45 50
4010 $1 "Pandoriana pandora" (vert) 45 50
4011 $1 "Basilarchia astyanax" (vert) 45 50
4012 $1 "Vanessa cardui" (vert) 45 50
4013 $1 "Colobura dirce" (vert) 45 50
4014 $1 "Heraclides cresphontes" (vert) 45 50
Nos. 4006/14 were printed together, se-tenant, with the backgrounds forming a composite design.

366 Pluto waking Mickey

1998. 70th Birthday of Disney's Mickey Mouse (1st issue). Multicoloured.
4016 2 c. Type **366** 10 10
4017 3 c. Mickey and Pluto on morning run 10 10
4018 4 c. Singing in the bath 10 10
4019 5 c. Breakfast time 10 10
4020 10 c. Mickey going to school 10 10
4021 65 c. Mickey playing basketball 30 35
4022 $1.10 Mickey as drum major (vert) 50 55
4023 $1.10 Mickey with hat and cane (vert) 50 55
4024 $1.10 Mickey in bow tie and tails (vert) 50 55
4025 $1.10 Mickey the magician (vert) 50 55
4026 $1.10 Mickey as circus musician (vert) 50 55
4027 $1.10 Mickey as cowboy (vert) 50 55
4028 $3 Mickey in soup kitchen 1·25 1·40
4029 $4 Mickey and Minnie in restaurant 1·75 1·90
4030 $5 Mickey and Pluto praying 2·10 2·25
See also Nos. 4179/96.

367 Winnie the Pooh in Window

1998. Stories of Winnie the Pooh. Multicoloured.
4032 $1 Type **367** 45 50
4033 $1 Eeyore, Kanga and Roo 45 50
4034 $1 Winnie the Pooh with balloon 45 50
4035 $1 Pooh stuck in Rabbit's burrow 45 50
4036 $1 Christopher Robin pulling Pooh 45 50
4037 $1 Piglet sweeping leaves 45 50
4038 $1 Pooh asleep 45 50
4039 $1 Eeyore 45 50
4040 $1 Pooh and Tigger 45 50

368 Australian Terrier

371 Cock-of-the-Rock

370 L.M.S. No. 5596 "Bahamas"

1998. Dogs of the World. Multicoloured.
4042 70 c. Type **368** 30 35
4043 90 c. Bullmastiff 40 45
4044 $1.10 Pomeranian 50 55
4045 $1.10 Beagle (horiz) 50 55
4046 $1.10 German shepherd and cockerel (horiz) 50 55
4047 $1.10 Pointer (horiz) 50 55
4048 $1.10 Vizsla (horiz) 50 55
4049 $1.10 Bulldog (horiz) 50 55
4050 $1.10 Shetland sheepdogs (horiz) 50 55
4051 $1.10 Tyrolean hunting dog (horiz) 50 55
4052 $1.10 King Charles spaniel (horiz) 50 55
4053 $1.10 Fox terriers (horiz) 50 55
4054 $1.10 Bernese mountain dog (horiz) 50 55
4055 $1.10 Papillon (horiz) 50 55
4056 $1.10 German shepherd (horiz) 50 55
4057 $2 Dandie dinmont terrier 85 90
Nos. 4045/50 and 4051/6 respectively were printed together, se-tenant, with the backgrounds forming composite designs.
The captions on Nos. 4052 and 4055 are transposed in error.

1998. "Israel 98" International Stamp Exhibition, Tel-Aviv. Nos. 3334/6 optd **98** in emblem.
4059 $1 Type **325** 45 50
4060 $1.10 The Montefiore Windmill 50 55
4061 $2 Shrine of the Book 85 90

1998. Railway Steam Locomotives of the World. Multicoloured.
4063 10 c. Type **370** 10 10
4064 20 c. Ex.Mza 1400 10 10
4065 50 c. "Mallard" 20 25
4066 70 c. Tank locomotive "Monarch" 30 35
4067 90 c. "Big Chief" 40 45
4068 $1.10 L.M.S. No. 6228 "Duchess of Rutland" 50 55
4069 $1.10 Holmes J36 50 55
4070 $1.10 "Patentee" 50 55
4071 $1.10 "Kingfisher" 50 55
4072 $1.10 No. 23 "St Pierre" 50 55
4073 $1.10 South African Railways Class 19c 50 55
4074 $1.10 South African Railways Class 6J 50 55
4075 $1.10 No. 92220 "Evening Star" 50 55
4076 $1.10 No. 1 50 55
4077 $1.10 "The Hadrian Flyer" 50 55
4078 $1.10 Class "Highland Jones Goods" No. 103 50 55
4079 $1.10 No. 34023 "Blackmore Vale" 50 55
4080 $1.10 S.E.C.R. No. 27 50 55
4081 $1.10 Class "Brighton Terrier" "Stepney" 50 55
4082 $1.10 R.E.N.F.E. No. 2184 50 55
4083 $1.10 Southern Railway No. 24 "Calbourne" 50 55
4084 $1.10 "Clun Castle" 50 55

1998. Birds of the World. Multicoloured.
4086 50 c. Type **371** 20 25
4087 60 c. Resplendant quetzal 25 30
4088 70 c. American wood stork 30 35
4089 90 c. St. Vincent amazon (species inscr at right) 40 45
4090 90 c. Toucan (horiz) 40 45
4091 90 c. Racquet-tailed motmot 40 45
4092 90 c. Red-billed quelea 40 45
4093 90 c. Leadbeater's cockatoo 40 45
4094 90 c. Scarlet macaw 40 45
4095 90 c. Bare-throated bellbird 40 45
4096 90 c. Tucaman amazon 40 45
4097 90 c. Black-lored red tanager 40 45
4098 90 c. Fig parrot 40 45
4099 90 c. St. Vincent amazon (species inscr at top) 40 45
4100 90 c. Peach-faced love birds 40 45
4101 90 c. Blue-fronted amazon 40 45
4102 90 c. Yellow-billed amazon 40 45
4103 $1 Greater bird of paradise (horiz) 45 50
4104 $1.10 Sun-bittern (horiz) 50 55
4105 $2 Green honeycreeper (horiz) 85 90
Nos. 4091/4102 were printed together, se-tenant, with the backgrounds forming a composite design.

372 White Whale

1998. International Year of the Ocean. Multicoloured.
4107 70 c. Type **372** 30 35
4108 90 c. Atlantic manta 40 45
4109 $1 Harlequin wrasse and pelican (vert) 45 50
4110 $1 Blue surgeonfish (vert) 45 50
4111 $1 Spotted trunkfish and sailing ship (vert) 45 50
4112 $1 Regal angelfish (vert) 45 50
4113 $1 Porcupine fish (vert) 45 50
4114 $1 Clownfish (vert) 45 50
4115 $1 Lion fish (vert) 45 50
4116 $1 Moray eel (vert) 45 50

4117 $1 French angelfish (vert) . . 45 50
4118 $1 Lemonpeel angelfish, flying fish and gulls (vert) 45 50
4119 $1 Narwhal (vert) 45 50
4120 $1 Panther grouper, puffin and house (vert) 45 50
4121 $1 Fur seal and jellyfish (vert) 45 50
4122 $1 Spiny boxfish (vert) . . . 45 50
4123 $1 Loggerhead turtle (vert) . 45 50
4124 $1 Opah (vert) 45 50
4125 $1 Clown triggerfish (vert) . 45 50
4126 $1 Bighead searobin (vert) . . 45 50
4127 $1.10 Forceps butterflyfish, moorish idol and copperband butterflyfish 50 55
4128 $2 Octopus 85 90

Nos. 4109/17 and 4118/26 respectively were printed together, se-tenant, with the backgrounds forming composite designs.

No. 4108 is inscribed "Harlequin Warasse" in error.

1998. 25th Anniv of Caribbean Community. As T **293** of Jamaica showing flags of St. Vincent and CARICOM.
4130 $1 multicoloured 45 50

1998. 50th Anniv of Organization of American States. As T **128** of Nevis.
4131 $1 violet, green and black . . 45 50

373 "Landscape"

1998. 25th Death Anniv of Pablo Picasso (painter). Multicoloured.
4132 $1.10 Type **373** 50 55
4133 $2 "The Death of the Female Torero" 85 90
4134 $2 "The Kiss" 85 90

1998. Birth Centenary of Enzo Ferrari (car manufacturer). As T **129** of Nevis. Multicoloured.
4136 $2 365 GTS 85 90
4137 $2 Testarossa 85 90
4138 $2 365 GT4 B B 85 90

1998. 19th World Scout Jamboree, Chile. As T **130** of Nevis.
4140 $2 lilac, violet and black . . 85 90
4141 $2 brown, violet and black . 85 90
4142 $2 brown, violet and black . 85 90

DESIGNS: No. 4140, Presentation of Silver Buffalo award to John Glenn (U.S. astronaut); 4141, Herb Shriner learning knot-tying, 1960; 4142, Breaking camp, 1940s.

1998. 50th Death Anniv of Mahatma Gandhi. As T **131** of Nevis.
4144 $1 multicoloured 45 50

DESIGN: $1 Mahatma Gandhi.

1998. 80th Anniv of Royal Air Force. As T **132** of Nevis. Multicoloured.
4146 $2 AEW 1 (Airborne Early Warning) 85 90
4147 $2 Eurofighter EF-2000 . . . 85 90
4148 $2 Sepecat Jaguar GR1A . . 85 90
4149 $2 BAe Hawk T1A trainer . 85 90
4150 $2 Two Sepecat Jaguar GR1s 85 90
4151 $2 Panavia Tornado F3 . . . 85 90
4152 $2 Three BAe Harrier GR7s . 85 90
4153 $2 Panavia Tornado F3 IDV 85 90

1998. 1st Death Anniv of Diana, Princess of Wales. As T **365** of Maldive Islands. Multicoloured.
4155 $1.10 Diana, Princess of Wales 50 55

374 H. Daisley (64 years of service)

1998. 150th Anniv of Local Court of Ancient Order of Foresters. Multicoloured (except 70 c.).
4156 10 c. Type **374** 10 10
4157 20 c. R. Jack (71 years of service) 10 10
4158 50 c. Ancient Order of Foresters' arms 20 25
4159 70 c. Bow and arrow symbol (green and black) 30 35
4160 90 c. Court's headquarters . . 40 45

375 Bi-colour Longhair

376 Flautist

1998. Christmas. Cats. Multicoloured.
4161 20 c. Type **375** 10 10
4162 50 c. Korat 20 25
4163 60 c. Seal-point Siamese . . . 25 30
4164 70 c. Red self longhair . . . 30 35
4165 90 c. Black longhair 40 45
4166 $1.10 Red tabby exotic shorthair 50 55

1998. 900th Birth Anniv of St. Hildegard von Bingen (German mystic). Multicoloured.
4168 $1.10 Type **376** 50 55
4169 $1.10 St. Hildegard and abbey 50 55
4170 $1.10 Viola player 50 55
4171 $1.10 Pope Eugenius 50 55
4172 $1.10 Town of Bingen 50 55
4173 $1.10 St. Hildegard 50 55

377 Rabbit facing Right

1999. Chinese New Year ("Year of the Rabbit"). Designs showing stylised rabbits. Multicoloured.
4175 $1 Type **377** 45 50
4176 $1 Rabbit facing front . . . 45 50
4177 $1 Rabbit facing left 45 50

378 Mickey Mouse

1999. 70th Birthday of Mickey Mouse (2nd issue). Walt Disney characters playing Winter sports. Multicoloured.
4179 $1.10 Type **378** 50 55
4180 $1.10 Goofy on skis wearing goggles 50 55
4181 $1.10 Donald Duck skiing in yellow sweatshirt 50 55
4182 $1.10 Goofy and Mickey in red bobsleigh 50 55
4183 $1.10 Goofy on skis in yellow 50 55
4184 $1.10 Minnie on skis with yellow bow 50 55
4185 $1.10 Daisy Duck on skis wearing purple bow . . . 50 55
4186 $1.10 Mickey on skis wearing goggles 50 55
4187 $1.10 Goofy and Mickey in green bobsleigh 50 55
4188 $1.10 Goofy on skis in blue . 50 55
4189 $1.10 Minnie snowboarding 50 55
4190 $1.10 Donald on skis in blue sweatshirt 50 55
4191 $1.10 Minnie skiing with blue and purple bow 50 55
4192 $1.10 Mickey snowboarding 50 55
4193 $1.10 Goofy on skis in blue and purple vest 50 55
4194 $1.10 Donald skiing in blue and purple sweatshirt 50 55
4195 $1.10 Mickey snowboarding in yellow hat and goggles . . 50 55
4196 $1.10 Daisy skiing in blue and purple 50 55

381 Plateosaurus

1999. "Australia '99" World Stamp Exhibition, Melbourne. Prehistoric Animals. Mult.
4198 70 c. Type **381** 30 35
4199 70 c. Struthiomimus 30 35
4200 70 c. Indricotherium 30 35
4201 70 c. Giant moa 30 35
4202 70 c. Deinonychus 30 35
4203 70 c. Sabre tooth tiger 30 35
4204 70 c. Dawn horse 30 35
4205 70 c. Peittacosaurus 30 35
4206 70 c. Giant ground sloth . . . 30 35
4207 70 c. Woolly rhinoceros . . . 30 35
4208 70 c. Mosasaur 30 35
4209 70 c. Mastodon 30 35
4210 70 c. Syndyoceras 30 35
4211 90 c. Euoplacephalus 40 45
4212 90 c. Rhamphorhynchus . . . 40 45
4213 90 c. Pteranodon 40 45
4214 90 c. Archaeopterix 40 45
4215 90 c. Dimetrodon 40 45
4216 90 c. Stegasaurus 40 45
4217 90 c. Parasaurolophus 40 45
4218 90 c. Iguanadon 40 45
4219 90 c. Triceratops 40 45
4220 90 c. Tyrannosaurus 40 45
4221 90 c. Ichthyosaurus 40 45
4222 90 c. Plesiosaurus 40 45
4223 90 c. Hesperonis 40 45
4224 $1.10 Pachycephalosaurus . . 50 55
4225 $1.40 Dilophosaurus 60 65

OFFICIAL STAMPS

1982. Nos. 668/73 optd **OFFICIAL**.
O1 60 c. "Isabella" 15 15
O2 60 c. Prince Charles and Lady Diana Spencer 40 50
O3 $2.50 "Alberta" (tender) . . . 15 25
O4 $2.50 Prince Charles and Lady Diana Spencer 55 70
O5 $4 "Britannia" 25 30
O6 $4 Prince Charles and Lady Diana Spencer 80 90

SAMOA

Islands in the W. Pacific administered jointly from 1889–99 by Gt. Britain, Germany and the U.S.A. In 1889 the eastern islands were assigned to the U.S.A. and the western to Germany (for issues see Vol. 2). The latter were occupied by British forces in 1914 and were taken over by New Zealand, under mandate, in 1920. W. Samoa was under United Nations trusteeship until it became independent on 1 January 1962.

1877. 12 pence = 1 shilling;
20 shillings = 1 pound.
1967. 100 sene or cents = 1 tale or dollar.

INDEPENDENT KINGDOM

1

2 Palm Trees

3 King Malietoa Laupepa

8

1877.
15 **1** 1d. blue . . . . 24·00 40·00
16 3d. red . . . . 48·00 70·00
17 6d. violet . . . . 40·00 48·00
20 9d. brown . . . . 60·00 £120
7b 1s. yellow . . . . 80·00 95·00
18 2s. brown £150 £250
19a 5s. green £375 £550

The majority of the stamps of T **1** found in old collections are worthless reprints. A 2d. stamp exists but was never issued.

1886.
57a **2** ½d. brown . . . . 1·25 1·75
88 ½d. green . . . . 1·40 2·00
58 1d. green . . . . 4·25 1·75
89 1d. brown . . . . 1·40 2·00
59c 2d. orange . . . . 4·50 1·25
60 **3** 2½d. red . . . . 1·75 4·50
81 2½d. black . . . . 1·25 3·00
61 **2** 4d. blue . . . . 7·50 2·00
72a **8** 5d. red . . . . 2·00 15·00
62 **2** 6d. lake . . . . 7·50 3·00
63 1s. red . . . . 7·50 3·75
64b 2s. 6d. violet . . . . . . 4·75 9·50

1893. Surch **FIVE PENCE** and bar.
65 **2** 5d. on 4d. blue . . . . 50·00 45·00

1893. Surch **5d** and bar.
69 **2** 5d. on 4d. blue . . . . 22·00 29·00

1893. Surch **Surcharged** and value in figures.
75 **2** 1½d. on 2d. orange . . . . . 2·25 5·50
84 2½d. on 1d. green . . . . . 75 2·50
85 2½d. on 1s. red . . . . . . 6·00 12·00
87 2½d. on 2s. 6d. violet . . . 6·50 14·00

1895. Surch **R 3d.**
76 **2** 3d. on 2d. orange . . . . . 7·00 9·00

1899. Optd **PROVISIONAL GOVT.**
90 **2** ½d. green . . . . 90 2·50
91 1d. brown . . . . 2·00 5·00
92a 2d. orange . . . . 1·50 5·50
93 4d. blue . . . . 70 6·50
94a **8** 5d. red . . . . 2·00 6·50
95 **2** 6d. lake . . . . 1·25 6·00
96 1s. red . . . . 1·50 18·00
97 2s. 6d. violet . . . . 4·75 19·00

NEW ZEALAND DEPENDENCY
(under Mandate from League of Nations and United Nations).

1914. "Yacht" key-types as German Cameroons, but inscr "SAMOA", surch **G.R.I.** and value in British currency.
101 N ½d. on 3 pf. brown . . . 25·00 9·00
102 ½d. on 5 pf. green . . . 48·00 10·00
103 1d. on 10 pf. red . . . . 95·00 40·00
104 2½d. on 20 pf. blue . . . 32·00 10·00
105 3d. on 25 pf. black and red on yellow . . . . 55·00 40·00
106 4d. on 30 pf. black and orange on buff . . . £110 60·00
107 5d. on 40 pf. black and red £110 70·00
108 6d. on 50 pf. black and purple on buff . . . . 60·00 35·00
109 9d. on 80 pf. black and red on rose £200 £100
110 O 1s on 1 m. red £3250 £3250
112 2s. on 2 m. blue £3000 £2750
113 3s. on 3 m. black . . . £1400 £1200
114 5s. on 5 m. red and black £1100 £1000

1914. Stamps of New Zealand (King Edward VII) optd **SAMOA.**
115 **51** ½d. green 55 30
116 **50** 1d. red 55 10
117 **51** 2d. mauve 75 95
118 **26** 2½d. blue (B) . . . . 1·50 1·75
119 **51** 6d. red . . . . 1·50 1·75
121 1s. red . . . . 4·25 14·00

1914. Large stamps of New Zealand (Queen Victoria) optd **SAMOA.**

127	F 4	2s. blue	4·75	5·50
123		2s. 6d. brown	5·50	8·50
129		3s. violet	15·00	40·00
124		5s. green	12·00	11·00
125		10s. brown	21·00	28·00
126		£1 red	60·00	45·00

1916. Stamps of New Zealand (King George V) optd **SAMOA.**

134	62	½d. green	50	80
135		1½d. grey	40	25
136		1½d. brown	30	40
137		2d. yellow	1·00	20
139		2½d. blue	55	35
140a		3d. brown	35	90
141a		6d. red	1·50	90
142		1s. red	1·50	1·50

1920. Stamps of New Zealand (Victory issue. Nos. 453/8) optd **SAMOA.**

143	64	½d. green	2·75	5·00
144	65	1d. red	2·25	4·75
145	–	1½d. orange	1·50	7·00
146	–	3d. brown	7·00	8·50
147	–	6d. violet	4·00	6·50
148	–	1s. orange	13·00	11·00

16 Native Hut

1921.

153	16	½d. green	3·50	1·75
150		1d. lake	2·25	20
151		1½d. brown	70	8·50
152		2d. yellow	2·25	2·00
157		2½d. blue	1·75	6·00
158		3d. sepia	1·75	3·75
159		4d. violet	1·75	3·00
160		5d. blue	1·75	6·00
161		6d. red	1·75	5·00
162		8d. brown	1·75	9·00
163		9d. olive	2·00	20·00
164		1s. red	1·75	20·00

1926. Stamps of New Zealand (King George V) optd **SAMOA.**

167	71	2s.blue	4·50	15·00
168		3s. mauve	10·00	38·00

1932. Stamps of New Zealand (Arms type) optd **SAMOA.**

171	F 6	2s. 6d. brown	15·00	38·00
172		5s. green	24·00	40·00
173		10s. red	45·00	90·00
174		£1 pink	60·00	£120
175		£2 violet	£650	
176		£5 blue	£1700	

1935. Silver Jubilee. Stamps of 1921 optd **SILVER JUBILEE OF KING GEORGE V 1910-1935.**

177	16	1d. lake	30	30
178		2½d. blue	60	65
179		6d. red	2·75	2·50

18 Samoan Girl

19 Apia

1935.

180	18	½d. green	10	35
181	19	1d. black and red	10	10
182	–	2d. black and orange	3·50	3·00
183	–	2½d. black and blue	10	10
184	–	4d. grey and brown	60	15
205	–	5d. brown and blue	1·00	50
185	–	6d. mauve	40	10
186	–	1s. violet and brown	30	10
187	–	2s. green and purple	80	50
188	–	3s. blue and orange	1·50	3·50

DESIGNS—HORIZ: 2d. River scene; 4d. Samoan canoe and house; 5d. Apia post office; 6d. R. L. Stevenson's home, "Vailima"; 1s. Stevenson's tomb. VERT: 2½d. Samoan chief and wife; 2s. Lake Lanuto'o; 3s. Falefa Falls.

1935. Stamps of New Zealand (Arms types) optd **WESTERN SAMOA.**

207w	F 6	2s. 6d. brown	6·00	9·00
208		5s. green	11·00	11·00
209		10s. red	18·00	17·00
234		£1 pink	18·00	38·00
211		30s. brown	£150	£300
235		£2 violet	80·00	£150
213		£3 green	£275	£450
214		£5 blue	£300	£450

28 Coastal Scene

31 Robert Louis Stevenson

1939. 25th Anniv of New Zealand Control.

195	28	1d. olive and red	30	10
196	–	1½d. blue and brown	45	30
197	–	2½d. brown and blue	90	65
198	31	7d. violet and green	6·50	2·75

DESIGNS—HORIZ: 1½d. Map of Western Samoa; 2½d. Samoan dancing party.

32 Samoan Chief

1940. Surch.

199	32	3d. on 1½d. brown	10	10

1946. Peace stamps of New Zealand optd **WESTERN SAMOA.**

215	132	1d. green	10	10
216	–	2d. purple (No. 670)	10	10
217	–	6d. brown and red (No. 674)	20	10
218	139	8d. black and red	20	10

35 Making Siapo Cloth

36 Native Houses and Flags

1952.

219	35	½d. red and brown	10	1·50
220	36	1d. olive and green	10	15
221	–	2d. red	10	10
222	–	3d. blue and indigo	40	10
223	–	5d. brown and green	4·75	70
224	–	6d. blue and mauve	75	10
225	–	8d. red	30	30
226	–	1s. sepia and blue	15	10
227	–	2s. brown	1·00	40
228	–	3s. brown and olive	2·50	2·75

DESIGNS—VERT (as Type **35**); 2d. Seal of Samoa; 5d. Tooth-billed pigeon. (As Type **36**): 3 s. Samoan chieftainess. HORIZ (as Type **35**): 1s. Thatching native hut. (As Type **36**): 3d. Malifa Falls, wrongly inscr on stamp "Aleisa Falls"; 6d. Bonito fishing canoe; 8d. Cacao harvesting; 2s. Preparing copra.

1953. Coronation. As Types of New Zealand.

229	164	2d. brown	1·00	15
230	166	6d. grey	1·00	35

48 Map of Samoa, and the Mace

1958. Inaug of Samoan Parliament. Inscr "FONO FOU 1958".

236	–	4d. red (As T **36**)	15	15
237	–	6d. violet (As No. 221)	15	15
238	48	1s. blue	90	30

INDEPENDENT STATE

49 Samoan Fine Mat

1962. Independence.

239	49	1d. brown and red	10	10
240	–	2d. multicoloured	10	10
241	–	3d. brown, green and blue	10	10
242	–	4d. multicoloured	15	10
243	–	6d. yellow and blue	80	10
261	–	8d. turquoise, green & blue	30	10
245	–	1s. brown and green	20	10
246	–	1s. 3d. green and blue	1·25	45
247	–	2s. 6d. red and blue	2·75	2·00
248	–	5s. multicoloured	3·50	3·50

DESIGNS—HORIZ: 2d. Samoa College; 3d. Public library; 4d. Fono house; 6d. Map of Samoa; 8d. Airport; 1s. 3d. "Vailima"; 2s. 6d. Samoan flag; 5s. Samoan Seal. VERT: 1s. Samoan orator.

59 Seal and Joint Heads of State

1963. 1st Anniv of Independence.

249	59	1d. sepia and green	10	10
250		4d. sepia and blue	10	10
251		8d. sepia and pink	10	10
252		2s. sepia and orange	20	15

60 Signing the Treaty

1964. 2nd Anniv of New Zealand–Samoa Treaty of Friendship.

253	60	1d. multicoloured	10	10
254		8d. multicoloured	10	10
255		2s. multicoloured	20	10
256		3s. multicoloured	20	30

62 Red-tailed Tropic Bird

1965. Air.

263	62	8d. black, orange and blue	50	10
264	–	2s. black and blue	75	20

DESIGN: 2s. Flyingfish.

64 Aerial View of Deep Sea Wharf

1966. Opening of First Deep Sea Wharf, Apia. Multicoloured.

265		1d. Type **64**	10	10
266		8d. Aerial view of wharf and bay	15	10
267		2s. As 8d.	25	20
268		3s. Type **64**	30	30

66 W.H.O. Building

1966. Inaug of W.H.O. Headquarters, Geneva.

269	66	3d. ochre, blue and slate	35	10
270	–	4d. multicoloured	40	15
271	66	6d. lilac, green and olive	45	20
272	–	1s. multicoloured	80	25

DESIGN: 4d. and 1s. W.H.O. Building on flag.

1966. Hurricane Relief Fund. No. 244 surch **HURRICANE RELIEF 6d.**

273		8d. + 6d. turquoise, green & bl	10	10

69 Hon. Tuatagaloa L. S. (Minister of Justice)

1967. 5th Anniv of Independence.

274	69	3d. sepia and violet	10	10
275	–	8d. sepia and blue	10	10
276	–	2s. sepia and olive	10	10
277	–	3s. sepia and mauve	15	15

DESIGNS: 8d. Hon. F. C. F. Nelson (Minister of Works, Marine and Civil Aviation); 2s. Hon. To'omata T. L. (Minister of Lands); 3s. Hon. Fa'alava'au G. (Minister of Post Office, Radio and Broadcasting).

73 Samoan Fales (houses), 1890

1967. Centenary of Mulinu'u as Seat of Government. Multicoloured.

278		8d. Type **73**	15	10
279		1s. Fono (Parliament) House, 1967.	15	10

75 Caruncuated Honeyeater

1967. Decimal Currency. Birds. Multicoloured.

280		1 s. Type **75**	10	10
281		2 s. Pacific pigeon	10	10
282		3 s. Samoan starling	10	10
283		5 s. White-vented flycatcher	10	10
284		7 s. Red-headed parrot finch	10	10
285		10 s. Purple swamphen	15	10
286		20 s. Barn owl	2·00	40
287		25 s. Tooth-billed pigeon	70	15
288		50 s. Island thrush	70	30
289		$1 Samoan fantail	1·00	1·75
289a		$2 Black-breasted honeyeater	4·50	7·00
289b		$4 Savaii white eye	45·00	45·00

Nos. 289a/b are larger, 43 × 28 mm.

85 Nurse and Child

1967. South Pacific Health Service. Mult.

290		3 s. Type **85**	15	10
291		7 s. Leprosarium	20	10
292		20 s. Mobile x-ray unit	35	25
293		25 s. Apia Hospital	40	30

89 Thomas Trood

1968. 6th Anniv of Independence. Multicoloured.

294		2 s. Type **89**	10	10
295		7 s. Dr. Wilhelm Solf	10	10
296		20 s. J. C. Williams	10	10
297		25 s. Fritz Marquardt	15	10

93 Cocoa

1968. Agricultural Development.

298	93	3 s. brown, green and black	10	10
299	–	5 s. green, yellow and brown	10	10
300	–	10 s. red, brown and yellow	10	10
301	–	20 s. bistre, yellow and olive	15	15

DESIGNS: 5 s. Breadfruit; 10 s. Copra; 20 s. Bananas.

97 Women weaving Mats

1968. 21st Anniv of South Pacific Commission. Multicoloured.

302		7 s. Type **97**	10	10
303		20 s. Palm trees and bay	15	10
304		25 s. Sheltered cove	15	15

1968. 40th Anniv of Kingsford-Smith's Trans-Pacific Flight. No. 285 surch **1928-1968 KINGSFORD-SMITH TRANSPACIFIC FLIGHT 20 SENE.**

305		20 s. on 10 s. multicoloured	10	10

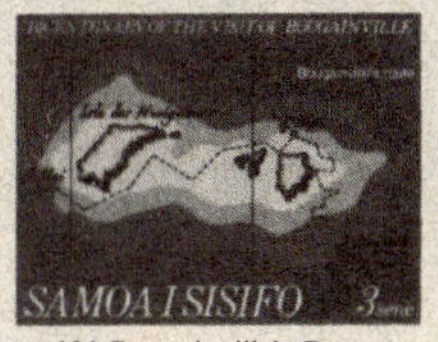

101 Bougainville's Route

1968. Bicent of Bougainville's Visit to Samoa.

306	101	3 s. blue and black	10	10
307	–	7 s. ochre and black	15	10
308	–	20 s. multicoloured	45	20
309	–	25 s. multicoloured	60	30

DESIGNS: 7 s. Louis de Bougainville; 20 s. Bougainvillea flower; 25 s. Ships "La Boudeuse" and "L'Etoile".

105 Globe and Human Rights Emblem

1968. Human Rights Year.

310	**105**	7 s. blue, brown and gold	10	10
311		20 s. orange, green & gold	10	15
312		25 s. violet, green and gold	15	15

106 Dr. Martin Luther King

107 Polynesian Version of Madonna and Child

1968. Martin Luther King.

313	**106**	7 s. black and green	15	10
314		20 s. black and purple	15	10

1968. Christmas.

315	**107**	1 s. multicoloured	10	10
316		3 s. multicoloured	10	10
317		20 s. multicoloured	10	10
318		30 s. multicoloured	15	15

108 Frangipani—"Plumeria acuminata"

1969. 7th Anniv of Independence. Multicoloured.

319	2 s. Type **108**	10	10
320	7 s. Hibiscus (vert)	15	10
321	20 s. Red-ginger (vert)	25	10
322	30 s. Moso'oi	35	80

109 R. L. Stevenson and "Treasure Island"

1969. 75th Death Anniv of Robert Louis Stevenson. Multicoloured.

323	3 s. Type **109**	15	10
324	7 s. R. L. Stevenson and "Kidnapped"	15	10
325	20 s. R. L. Stevenson and "Dr. Jekyll and Mr. Hyde"	25	50
326	22 s. R. L. Stevenson and "Weir of Hermiston"	25	50

110 Weightlifting

114 "Virgin with Child" (Murillo)

113 U.S. Astronaut on the Moon and the Splashdown near Samoan Islands

1969. 3rd South Pacific Games, Port Moresby.

327	**110**	3 s. black and green	10	10
328	–	20 s. black and blue	10	10
329	–	22 s. black and orange	15	15

DESIGNS: 20 s. Yachting; 22 s. Boxing.

1969. First Man on the Moon.

330	**113**	7 s. multicoloured	15	15
331		20 s. multicoloured	15	15

1969. Christmas. Multicoloured.

332	1 s. Type **114**	10	10
333	3 s. "The Holy Family" (El Greco)	10	10
334	20 s. "The Nativity" (El Greco)	35	10
335	30 s. "The Adoration of the Magi" (detail) (Velazquez)	40	15

115 Seventh Day Adventists Sanatorium, Apia

1970. 8th Anniv of Independence.

337	**115**	2 s. brown, slate and black	10	10
338	–	7 s. violet, buff and black	10	10
339	–	20 s. rose, lilac and black	15	10
340	–	22 s. green, buff and black	15	15

DESIGNS—HORIZ: 7 s. Rev. Father Violette and Roman Catholic Cathedral, Apia; 22 s. John Williams, 1797–1839, and London Missionary Society Church, Sapapali'i. VERT: 20 s. Mormon Church of Latter Day Saints, Tuasivi-on-Safotulafai.

119 Wreck of "Adler" (German steam gunboat)

1970. Great Apia Hurricane of 1889. Mult.

341	5 s. Type **119**	30	10
342	7 s. U.S.S. "Nipsic" (steam sloop)	30	10
343	10 s. H.M.S. "Calliope" (steam corvette)	40	25
344	20 s. Apia after the hurricane	1·10	75

120 Sir Gordon Taylor's Short S.25 Sandringham 7 Flying Boat "Frigate Bird III"

1970. Air. Multicoloured.

345	3 s. Type **120**	45	10
346	7 s. Polynesian Airlines Douglas DC-3	70	10
347	20 s. Pan-American Airways Sikorsky S-42A flying boat "Samoan Clipper"	2·00	60
348	30 s. Air Samoa Britten Norman Islander	2·25	1·75

121 Kendal's Chronometer and Cook's Sextant

122 "Peace for the World" (F. B. Eccles)

1970. Cook's Exploration of the Pacific.

349	**121**	1 s. red, silver and black	15	15
350	–	2 s. multicoloured	30	15
351	–	10 s. black, blue and gold	75	25
352	–	30 s. multicoloured	1·50	80

DESIGN—VERT: 2 s. Cook's statue, Whitby; 10 s. Cook's head. HORIZ (83×25 mm): 30 s. Cook, H.M.S. "Endeavour" and island.

1970. Christmas. Multicoloured.

353	2 s. Type **122**	10	10
354	3 s. "The Holy Family" (W. E. Jahnke)	10	10
355	20 s. "Mother and Child" (F. B. Eccles)	15	10
356	30 s. "Prince of Peace" (Meleane Fe'ao)	20	15

123 Pope Paul VI

124 Native and Tree

1970. Visit of Pope Paul to Samoa.

358	**123**	8 s. black and blue	15	15
359		20 s. black and red	35	15

1971. Timber Industry. Multicoloured.

360	3 s. Type **124**	10	10
361	8 s. Bulldozer in clearing	15	10
362	20 s. Log in sawmill	30	10
363	22 s. Floating logs and harbour	30	15

The 8 s. and 20 s. are horiz.

126 Siva Dance

1971. Tourism. Multicoloured.

365	5 s. Type **126**	40	10
366	7 s. Samoan cricket	1·00	60
367	8 s. Hideaway Hotel	1·00	35
368	10 s. Aggie Grey and her hotel	1·00	60

127 "Queen Salamasina"

128 "The Virgin and Child" (Bellini)

1971. Myths and Legends of Old Samoa (1st series). Multicoloured.

369	3 s. Type **127**	10	10
370	8 s. "Lu and his Sacred Hens"	15	10
371	10 s. "God Tagaloa fishes Samoa from the sea"	20	10
372	22 s. "Mount Vaea and the Pool of Tears"	35	40

1971. Christmas.

373	**128**	2 s. multicoloured	10	10
374		3 s. multicoloured	10	10
375	–	20 s. multicoloured	30	10
376	–	30 s. multicoloured	40	20

DESIGN: 20, 30 s. "The Virgin and Child with St. Anne and John the Baptist" (Leonardo da Vinci).

129 Map and Scales of Justice

1972. First South Pacific Judicial Conference.

377	**129**	10 s. multicoloured	15	15

130 Asau Wharf, Savaii

1972. 10th Anniv of Independence. Mult.

378	1 s. Type **130**	10	10
379	8 s. Parliament Building	10	10
380	10 s. Mothers' Centre	10	10
381	22 s. "Vailima" Residence and rulers	20	25

131 Flags of Member Countries

132 Expedition Ships

1972. 25th Anniv of South Pacific Commission. Multicoloured.

382	3 s. Type **131**	10	15
383	7 s. Flag and Afoafouvale Misimoa (Secretary-General)	10	15
384	8 s. H.Q. building, Noumea (horiz)	15	15
385	10 s. Flags and area map (horiz)	15	15

1972. 250th Anniv of Sighting of Western Samoa by Jacob Roggeveen. Multicoloured.

386	2 s. Type **132**	15	10
387	8 s. Ships in storm (horiz)	45	10
388	10 s. Ships passing island (horiz)	50	10
389	30 s. Route of voyage (85×25 mm)	1·75	1·50

133 Bull Conch

1972. Multicoloured.

390	1 s. Type **133**	30	30
391	2 s. "Oryctes rhinoceros" (beetle)	30	30
392	3 s. Skipjack tuna	30	65
393	4 s. Painted crab	30	30
394	5 s. Melon butterflyfish	35	30
395	7 s. "Danaus hamata" (butterfly)	2·00	70
396	10 s. Trumpet triton	2·50	70
397	20 s. "Chrysochroa abdominalis" (beetle)	1·25	30
398	50 s. Spiny lobster	2·00	2·75
399	$1 "Gnathothlibus erotus" (moth) (29×45 mm)	8·00	4·50
399a	$2 Green turtle (29×45 mm)	5·50	3·50
399b	$4 Black marlin (29×45 mm)	3·00	7·00
399c	$5 Green tree lizard (29×45 mm)	3·00	9·00

134 "The Ascension"

135 Erecting a Tent

1972. Christmas. Stained-glass windows. Multicoloured.

400	1 s. Type **134**	10	10
401	4 s. "The Blessed Virgin, and Infant Christ"	10	10
402	10 s. "St. Andrew blessing Samoan canoe"	10	10
403	30 s. "The Good Shepherd"	40	30

1973. Boy Scout Movement. Multicoloured.

405	2 s. Saluting the flag	10	10
406	3 s. First-aid	10	10
407	8 s. Type **135**	25	10
408	20 s. Samoan action-song	90	85

136 Hawker Siddeley H.S.748

1973. Air. Multicoloured.

409	8 s. Type **136**	55	15
410	10 s. Hawker Siddeley H.S.748 in flight	65	15
411	12 s. Hawker Siddeley H.S.748 on runway	75	35
412	22 s. B.A.C. One Eleven	1·10	60

137 Apia General Hospital

138 Mother and Child, and Map

1973. 25th Anniv of W.H.O. Multicoloured.

413	2 s. Type **137**	10	10
414	8 s. Baby clinic	20	10
415	20 s. Filariasis research	45	20
416	22 s. Family welfare	45	30

1973. Christmas. Multicoloured.

417	3 s. Type **138**	10	10
418	4 s. Mother and child, and village	10	10
419	10 s. Mother and child, and beach	10	10
420	30 s. Samoan stable	55	50

139 Boxing

1973. Commonwealth Games, Christchurch. Multicoloured.

422	8 s. Type **139**	10	10
423	10 s. Weightlifting	10	10
424	20 s. Bowls	20	10
425	30 s. Athletics stadium	35	45

1974. Myths and Legends of Old Samoa (2nd series). As T **127**. Multicoloured.

426	2 s. Tigilau and sacred dove	10	10
427	8 s. Pili, his sons and fishing net	10	10
428	20 s. Sina and the origin of the coconut	30	10
429	30 s. The warrior, Nafanua	45	55

140 Mail-van at Faleolo Airport

1974. Centenary of U.P.U. Multicoloured.

430	8 s. Type **140**	35	10
431	20 s. "Mariposa" (cargo liner) at Apia wharf	50	15
432	22 s. Early post office, Apia and letter	50	25
433	50 s. William Willis and "Age Unlimited" (sailing raft) (87 × 29 mm)	95	1·25

141 "Holy Family" (Sebastiano)

1974. Christmas. Multicoloured.

435	3 s. Type **141**	10	10
436	4 s. "Virgin and Child with Saints" (Lotto)	10	10
437	10 s. "Madonna and Child with St. John" (Titian)	20	10
438	30 s. "Adoration of the Shepherds" (Rubens)	55	45

142 Winged Passion Flower

1975. Tropical Flowers. Multicoloured.

440	8 s. Type **142**	15	10
441	20 s. Gardenia (vert)	30	25
442	22 s. "Barringtonia samoensis" (vert)	30	30
443	30 s. Malay apple	35	75

143 "Joyita" (inter-island coaster) loading at Apia

1975. "Interpex 1975" Stamp Exhibition, New York, and "Joyita" Mystery. Multicoloured.

444	1 s. Type **143**	10	10
445	8 s. "Joyita" sails for Tokelau Islands	15	10
446	20 s. Taking to rafts	20	25
447	25 s. "Joyita" abandoned	25	30
448	50 s. Discovery of "Joyita" north of Fiji	70	1·25

144 "Pate" Drum

145 "Mother and Child" (Meleane Fe'ao)

1975. Musical Instruments. Multicoloured.

450	8 s. Type **144**	10	10
451	20 s. "Lali" drum	20	10
452	22 s. "Logo" drum	20	10
453	30 s. "Pu" shell horn	35	30

1975. Christmas. Multicoloured.

454	3 s. Type **145**	10	10
455	4 s. "The Saviour" (Polataia Tuigamala)	10	10
456	10 s. "A Star is Born" (Iosua To'afa)	10	10
457	30 s. "Madonna and Child" (Ernesto Coter)	30	45

146 "The Boston Massacre, 1770" (Paul Revere)

1976. Bicent of American Revolution. Mult.

459	7 s. Type **146**	20	15
460	8 s. "The Declaration of Independence" (John Trumbull)	20	15
461	20 s. "The Ship that Sank in Victory, 1779" (J. L. G. Ferris)	60	20
462	22 s. "Pitt addressing the Commons, 1782" (R. A. Hickel)	60	20
463	50 s. "Battle of Princeton" (William Mercer)	1·25	1·50

147 Mullet Fishing

1976. Fishing. Multicoloured.

465	10 s. Type **147**	10	10
466	12 s. Fish traps	15	10
467	22 s. Samoan fisherman	30	10
468	50 s. Net fishing	85	70

149 Boxing

1976. Olympic Games, Montreal. Mult.

470	10 s. Type **149**	10	10
471	12 s. Wrestling	10	10
472	22 s. Javelin	15	10
473	50 s. Weightlifting	45	50

150 Mary and Joseph going to Bethlehem

1976. Christmas. Multicoloured.

474	3 s. Type **150**	10	10
475	5 s. The Shepherds	10	10
476	22 s. The Holy Family	15	10
477	50 s. The Magi	55	65

151 Queen Elizabeth and View of Apia

1977. Silver Jubilee and Royal Visit. Mult.

479	12 s. Type **151**	10	10
480	26 s. Presentation of Spurs of Chivalry	15	20
481	32 s. Queen and Royal Yacht "Britannia"	20	25
482	50 s. Queen leaving Abbey	20	60

152 Map of Flight Route

1977. 50th Anniv of Lindbergh's Transatlantic Flight. Multicoloured.

483	22 s. Type **152**	25	10
484	24 s. In flight	35	15
485	26 s. Landing	35	15
486	50 s. Col. Lindbergh	80	75

Designs show the "Spirit of St. Louis".

153 3d. Express Stamp and First Mail Notice

1977. Stamp Centenary.

488	**153**	12 s. yellow, red and brown	20	10
489	–	13 s. multicoloured	20	15
490	–	26 s. multicoloured	45	30
491	–	50 s. multicolored	80	1·50

DESIGNS: 13 s. Early cover and 6d. Express; 26 s. Apia P.O. and 1d. Express; 50 s. Schooner "Energy" (1877) and 6d. Express.

154 Apia Automatic Telephone Exchange

1977. Telecommunications Project. Mult.

492	12 s. Type **154**	15	10
493	13 s. Mulinuu radio terminal	15	10
494	26 s. Old and new telephones	30	20
495	50 s. Global communication	50	70

155 "Samoan Nativity" (P. Feata)

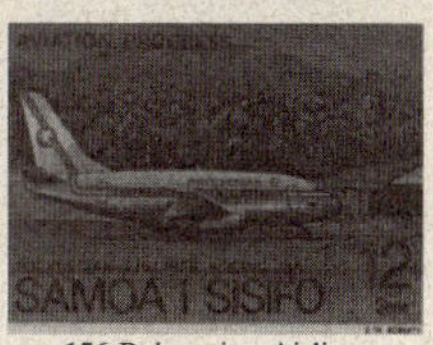

156 Polynesian Airlines Boeing 737

1977. Christmas. Multicoloured.

496	4 s. Type **155**	10	10
497	6 s. "The Offering" (E. Saofaiga)	10	10
498	25 s. "Madonna and Child" (F. Tupou)	20	10
499	50 s. "Emmanuel" (M. Sapa'u)	35	40

1978. Aviation Progress. Multicoloured.

501	12 s. Type **156**	20	10
502	24 s. Wright brothers' Flyer I	40	20
503	26 s. Kingsford Smith's Fokker F.VIIa/3m "Southern Cross"	40	20
504	50 s. Concorde	1·10	85

157 Hatchery, Aleipata

1978. Hawksbill Turtle Conservation Project. Multicoloured.

506	24 s. Type **157**	1·00	30
507	$1 Hawksbill turtle	3·75	1·60

158 Pacific Pigeon

160 Captain Cook

1978. 25th Anniv of Coronation.

508	–	26 s. black, brown & mve	20	30
509	–	26 s. multicoloured	20	30
510	**158**	26 s. black, brown & mve	20	30

DESIGNS: No. 508, King's Lion; 509, Queen Elizabeth II.

1978. 250th Birth Anniv of Captain Cook. Multicoloured.

512	12 s. Type **160**	30	15
513	24 s. Cook's Cottage, Gt. Ayton, Yorkshire	35	35
514	26 s. Old drawbridge over the river Esk, Whitby	35	35
515	50 s. H.M.S. "Resolution"	1·00	1·50

161 Thick-edged Cowrie

162 "Madonna on the Crescent"

1978. Shells. Multicoloured.

516	1 s. Type **161**	15	10
517	2 s. Controversial Isabelle cowrie	15	10
518	3 s. Money cowrie	25	10
519	4 s. Eroded cowrie	30	10
520	6 s. Honey cowrie	30	10
521	7 s. Asellus or banded cowrie	35	10
522	10 s. Globular or globe cowrie	40	10
523	11 s. Mole cowrie	40	10
524	12 s. Children's cowrie	40	10
525	13 s. Flag cone	40	10
526	14 s. Soldier cone	40	10
527	24 s. Textile or cloth-of-gold cone	40	10
528	26 s. Lettered cone	45	10
529	50 s. Tesselate or tiiled cone	50	15
530	$1 Black marble cone	80	60
530a	$2 Marlin-spike auger	85	70
530b	$3 Scorpion conch	1·00	1·25
530c	$5 Common or major harp	1·75	2·25

Nos. 530a/c are larger, 36 × 26 mm.

1978. Christmas. Woodcuts by Durer. Multicoloured.

531	**162**	4 s. black and brown	10	10
532	–	6 s. black and green	10	10
533	–	26 s. black and blue	15	10
534	–	50 s. black and violet	35	50

DESIGNS: 6 s. "Nativity"; 26 s. "Adoration of the Kings"; 50 s. "Annunciation".

163 Boy with Coconuts

1979. International Year of the Child. Multicoloured.

536	12 s. Type **163**	15	10
537	24 s. White Sunday	20	15
538	25 s. Children at pump	20	15
539	50 s. Girl with ukulele	60	80

164 "Charles W. Morgan"

165 Launch of "Apollo 11"

1979. Sailing Ships (1st series). Whaling Ships. Multicoloured.

540	12 s. Type **164**	30	10
541	14 s. "Lagoda"	30	10
542	24 s. "James T. Arnold"	40	20
543	50 s. "Splendid"	70	85

See also Nos. 561/4 and 584/7.

1979. 10th Anniv of Moon Landing.

544	**165**	12 s. brown and red	20	10
545	–	14 s. multicoloured	25	10
546	–	24 s. multicoloured	30	15
547	–	26 s. multicoloured	30	15
548	–	50 s. multicoloured	45	55
549	–	$1 multicoloured	1·00	1·50

DESIGNS—HORIZ: 14 s. Lunar module and astronaut on Moon; 26 s. Astronaut on Moon; $1 Command module after splashdown. VERT: 24 s. View of Earth from Moon; 50 s. Lunar and Command modules in Space.

166 Sir Rowland Hill (statue) and Penny Black

167 Anglican Church, Apia

1979. Death Cent of Sir Rowland Hill. Mult.

551 12 s. Type **166** 15 10
552 24 s. Two-penny Blue with "Maltese Cross" postmark 15 15
553 26 s. Sir Rowland Hill and Penny Black 15 15
554 $1 Two-penny Blue and Sir Rowland Hill 45 75

1979. Christmas. Churches.

556 **167** 4 s. black and blue 10 10
557 – 6 s. black and yellow 10 10
558 – 26 s. black and brown 15 10
559 – 50 s. black and lilac 30 30

DESIGNS: 6 s. Congregational Christian, Leulumoega; 26 s. Methodist, Piula; 50 s. Protestant, Apia.

1980. Sailing Ships (2nd series). Whaling Ships. As T **164**. Multicoloured

561 12 s. "William Hamilton" 35 10
562 14 s. "California" 35 15
563 24 s. "Liverpool II" 40 25
564 50 s. "Two Brothers" 60 1·10

168 "Equipment for a Hospital"

1980. Anniversaries. Multicoloured.

565 12 s. Type **168** 45 10
566 13 s. John Williams, dove with olive twig and commemorative inscription 45 20
567 14 s. Dr. Wilhelm Solf (instigator), flag and commemorative inscription 50 15
568 24 s. Cairn Monument 65 25
569 26 s. Williams Memorial, Savai'i 70 25
570 50 s. Paul P. Harris (founder) 1·25 2·50

COMMEMORATIONS: 12, 50 s. 75th anniv of Rotary International; 13, 26 s. 150th anniv of John Williams (missionary) arrival in Samoa; 14, 24 s. 80th anniv of raising of German flag.

170 Queen Elizabeth the Queen Mother in 1970

1980. 80th Birthday of The Queen Mother.

572 **170** 50 s. multicoloured 30 30

172 Afiamalu Satellite Earth Station

1980. Afiamalu Satellite Earth Station. Multicoloured.

574 12 s. Type **172** 15 10
575 14 s. Satellite station (different) 20 10
576 24 s. Satellite station and map of Savai'i and Upolu 30 15
577 50 s. Satellite and globe 60 60

174 "The Saviour" (J. Poynton)

176 Hotel Tusitala

175 President Franklin D. Roosevelt and Hyde Park (family home)

1980. Christmas. Paintings. Multicoloured.

579 8 s. Type **174** 10 10
580 14 s. "Madonna and Child" (Lealofi F. Siaopo) 10 10
581 27 s. "Nativity" (Pasila Feata) 15 10
582 50 s. "Yuletide" (R. P. Aiono) 25 40

1981. Sailing Ships (3rd series). As T **164**. Multicoloured.

584 12 s. "Ocean" (whaling ship) 30 10
585 18 s. "Horatio" (whaling ship) 40 15
586 27 s. H.M.S. "Calliope" (screw corvette) 55 25
587 32 s. H.M.S. "Calypso" (screw corvette) 60 50

1981. Int Year for Disabled Persons. President Franklin D. Roosevelt Commem. Mult.

588 12 s. Type **175** 15 10
589 18 s. Roosevelt's inauguration, 4 March 1933 15 10
590 27 s. Franklin and Eleanor Roosevelt 20 15
591 32 s. Roosevelt's Lend-lease Bill (Atlantic convoy, 1941) 25 20
592 38 s. Roosevelt the philatelist 25 25
593 $1 Campobello House (summer home) 50 90

1981. Tourism. Multicoloured.

594 12 s. Type **176** 15 10
595 18 s. Apia Harbour 25 15
596 27 s. Aggie Greys' Hotel 25 20
597 32 s. Preparation for Ceremonial Kava 30 30
598 54 s. Piula water pool 55 55

177 Wedding Bouquet from Samoa

178 Tattooing Instruments

1981. Royal Wedding. Multicoloured.

599 18 s. Type **177** 15 10
600 32 s. Prince Charles as Colonel-in-Chief, Gordon Highlanders 20 10
601 $1 Prince Charles and Lady Diana Spencer 30 50

1981. Tattooing. Multicoloured.

602 12 s. Type **178** 15 20
603 18 s. First stage of tattooing 20 25
604 27 s. Progessive stage 25 30
605 $1 Completed tattoo 50 70

180 "Thespesia populnea"

181 George Washington's Pistol

1981. Christmas. Flowers. Multicoloured.

607 11 s. Type **180** 15 10
608 15 s. Copper leaf 15 15
609 23 s. "Allamanda cathartica" 20 25
610 $1 Mango 60 1·00

1982. 250th Birth Anniv of George Washington.

612 **181** 23 s. black, brown & stone 25 30
613 – 25 s. black, brown & stone 25 30
614 – 34 s. black, brown & stone 30 40

DESIGNS: 25 s. Mount Vernon (Washington's home); 34 s. George Washington.

182 "Forum Samoa" (container ship)

184 Boxing

183 Scouts map-reading and "75"

1982. 20th Anniv of Independence. Mult.

616 18 s. Type **182** 30 20
617 23 s. "Air services" 40 30
618 25 s. N.P.F. (National Provident Fund) Building, Apia 40 30
619 $1 "Telecommunications" 1·10 1·00

1982. 75th Anniv of Boy Scout Movement. Multicoloured.

620 5 s. Type **183** 10 10
621 38 s. Scout salute and "75" 40 40
622 44 s. Scout crossing river by rope and "75" 50 50
623 $1 "Tower" of Scouts and "75" 1·00 1·00

1982. Commonwealth Games, Brisbane. Multicoloured.

625 23 s. Type **184** 20 20
626 23 s. Hurdling 20 20
627 34 s. Weightlifting 25 30
628 $1 Bowling 75 1·50

185 "Mary and Joseph" (Emma Dunlop)

1982. Christmas. Children's Pictures. Mult.

629 11 s. Type **185** 15 10
630 15 s. "Mary, Joseph and Baby Jesus" (Marie Tofaeono) 15 15
631 38 s. "Madonna and Child" (Ralph Laban and Fetalaiga Fareni) 40 30
632 $1 "Mother and Child" (Panapa Pouesi) 90 2·00

186 Satellite View of Australasia

1983. Commonwealth Day. Multicoloured.

634 14 s. Type **186** 10 10
635 29 s. Flag of Samoa 15 20
636 43 s. Harvesting copra 25 25
637 $1 Head of State Malietoa Tanumafili II 50 80

188 Pole vaulting

189 Lime

1983. South Pacific Games. Multicoloured.

639 8 s. Type **188** 35 10
640 15 s. Netball 45 20
641 25 s. Tennis 70 50
642 32 s. Weightlifting 70 50
643 35 s. Boxing 75 1·00
644 46 s. Football 90 1·40
645 48 s. Golf 1·40 1·50
646 56 s. Rugby 1·40 1·75

1983. Fruit. Multicoloured.

647 1 s. Type **189** 10 60
648 2 s. Starfruit 10 70
649 3 s. Mangosteen 10 70
650 4 s. Lychee 10 70
651 7 s. Passion fruit 15 70
652 8 s. Mango 15 70
653 11 s. Pawpaw 20 70
654 13 s. Pineapple 20 70
655 14 s. Breadfruit 20 70
656 15 s. Banana 30 70
657 21 s. Cashew nut 1·75 1·50
658 25 s. Guava 1·75 80
659 32 s. Water melon 1·75 1·50
660 48 s. Sasalapa 2·00 2·25
661 56 s. Avocado 2·00 2·25
662 $1 Coconut 2·00 2·00
663 $2 Vi apple 1·75 3·00
664 $4 Grapefruit 2·50 4·50
665 $5 Orange 3·00 4·75

Nos. 663/5 are larger, 25 × 35½ mm.

191 Togitogiga Falls, Upolu

1984. Scenic Views. Multicoloured.

669 25 s. Type **191** 40 15
670 32 s. Lano Beach, Savai'i 50 60
671 48 s. Mulinu'u Point, Upolu 70 1·10
672 56 s. Nu'utele Island 70 1·75

192 Apia Harbour

1984. 250th Anniv of "Lloyd's List" (newspaper). Multicoloured.

673 32 s. Type **192** 25 20
674 48 s. Apia hurricane, 1889 50 45
675 60 s. "Forum Samoa" (container ship) 45 50
676 $1 "Matua" (inter-island freighter) 75 80

1984. Universal Postal Union Congress, Hamburg. No. 662 optd **19th U.P.U. CONGRESS HAMBURG 1984**.

677 $1 Coconut 1·40 80

194 Olympic Stadium

1984. Olympic Games, Los Angeles. Multicoloured.

678 25 s. Type **194** 20 20
679 32 s. Weightlifting 20 25
680 48 s. Boxing 30 45
681 $1 Running 60 80

196 "Faith"

1984. Christmas. "The Three Virtues" (Raphael). Multicoloured.

684 25 s. Type **196** 30 15
685 35 s. "Hope" 40 40
686 $1 "Charity" 1·60 2·75

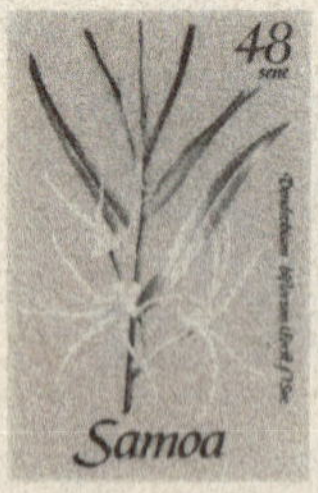

197 "Dendrobium biflorum"

199 "Dictyophora indusiata"

198 Ford "Model A", 1903

1985. Orchids (1st series). Multicoloured.

688 48 s. Type **197** 55 35
689 56 s. "Dendrobium vaupelianum Kraenzl" 65 45
690 67 s. "Glomera montana" 80 60
691 $1 "Spathoglottis plicata" 1·10 1·10

See also Nos. 818/21.

1985. Veteran and Vintage Cars. Multicoloured.

692 48 s. Type **198** 1·25 60
693 56 s. Chevrolet "Tourer", 1912 1·40 85
694 67 s. Morris "Oxford", 1913 1·50 1·50
695 $1 Austin "Seven", 1923 2·00 2·75

1985. Fungi. Multicoloured.
696 48 s. Type **199** 1·10 55
697 56 s. "Ganoderma tornatum" 1·25 85
698 67 s. "Mycena chlorophos" 1·60 1·75
699 $1 "Mycobonia flava" 2·25 3·25

200 The Queen Mother at Liverpool Street Station

202 I.Y.Y. Emblem and Map (Alaska–Arabian Gulf)

1985. Life and Times of Queen Elizabeth the Queen Mother. Multicoloured.
700 32 s. At Glamis Castle, aged 9 30 25
701 48 s. At Prince Henry's christening with other members of the Royal Family 40 35
702 56 s. Type **200** 45 45
703 $1 With Prince Henry at his christening (from photo by Lord Snowdon) 75 1·25

1985. International Youth Year. Designs showing background map and emblem (Nos. 706 and 710) or raised arms (others). Multicoloured.
706 60 s. Type **202** 40 45
707 60 s. Raised arms (Pakistan–Mexico) 40 45
708 60 s. Raised arms (Central America–China) 40 45
709 60 s. Raised arms (Japan–Greenland) 40 45
710 60 s. Type **202** (Iceland–Siberia) 40 45
Nos. 706/10 were printed together in horizontal strips of 5, the background forming a composite design of three continuous world maps.

203 "System"

204 "Hypolimnas bolina"

1985. Christmas. Designs showing illustrations by Millicent Sowerby for R. L. Stevenson's "A Child's Garden of Verses". Multicoloured.
711 32 s. Type **203** 20 25
712 48 s. "Time to Rise" 30 35
713 56 s. "Auntie's Skirts" 35 40
714 $1 "Good Children" 65 1·00

1986. Butterflies. Multicoloured.
716 25 s. Type **204** 35 30
717 32 s. "Belenois java" 40 30
718 48 s. "Deudorix epijarbas" 60 45
719 56 s. "Badamia exclamationis" 65 85
720 60 s. "Danaus hamata" 65 85
721 $1 "Catochrysops taitensis" 1·00 1·75

205 Halley's Comet over Apia

1986. Appearance of Halley's Comet. Mult.
722 32 s. Type **205** 40 20
723 48 s. Edmond Halley 50 35
724 60 s. Comet passing Earth 60 50
725 $2 Preparing "Giotto" spacecraft 1·25 1·75

1986. 60th Birthday of Queen Elizabeth II. As T **110** of Ascension. Multicoloured.
726 32 s. Engagement photograph, 1947 15 20
727 48 s. Queen with Liberty Bell, U.S.A., 1976 20 35
728 56 s. At Apia, 1977 25 40
729 67 s. At Badminton Horse Trials, 1978 30 45
730 $2 At Crown Agents Head Office, London, 1983 80 1·25

206 U.S.S. "Vincennes" (frigate)

1986. "Ameripex '86" International Stamp Exhibition, Chicago. Multicoloured.
731 48 s. Type **206** 50 35
732 56 s. Sikorsky S-42A flying boat 55 40
733 60 s. U.S.S. "Swan" (patrol boat) 55 40
734 $2 "Apollo 10" descending 1·25 2·00

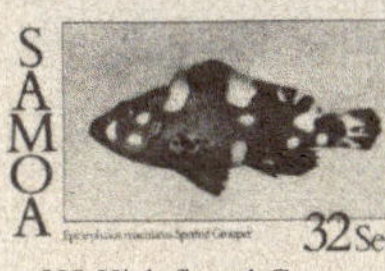

208 High-finned Grouper

1986. Fishes. Multicoloured.
736 32 s. Type **208** 50 30
737 48 s. Scarlet-finned squirrelfish 80 40
738 60 s. Yellow-edged lyretail ("Lunartail grouper") 90 80
739 67 s. Yellow-striped snapper 95 1·40
740 $1 Big-scaled soldierfish 1·25 2·00

209 Samoan Prime Ministers, American Presidents and Parliament House

1986. Christmas. 25th Anniv of United States Peace Corps. Multicoloured.
741 45 s. Type **209** 25 30
742 60 s. French and American Presidents, Samoan Prime Minister and Statue of Liberty 35 40

210 "Hibiscus rosa-sinensis" and Map of Samoa

1987. 25th Anniv of Independence. Mult.
744 15 s. Type **210** 25 10
745 45 s. Parliament Building, Apia 40 30
746 60 s. Longboat race at Independence celebration 45 40
747 70 s. Peace dove and laurel wreath 50 60
748 $2 Head of State Malietoa Tanumafili II and national flag (horiz) 1·25 2·00

211 Gulper ("Eurypharynx")

1987. Deep Ocean Fishes. Multicoloured.
749 45 s. Type **211** 45 30
750 60 s. Hatchetfish 60 60
751 70 s. Bearded angelfish 70 1·00
752 $2 Swallower ("Saccopharynx") 1·40 3·00

213 Lefaga Beach, Upolu

1987. Coastal Scenery. Multicoloured.
754 45 s. Type **213** 70 30
755 60 s. Vaisala Beach, Savaii 90 40
756 70 s. Solosolo Beach, Upolu 95 75
757 $2 Neiafu Beach, Savaii 1·75 2·50

214 Abel Tasman

216 Christmas Tree

1987. Bicentenary of Australian Settlement (1988) (1st issue). Explorers of the Pacific. Multicoloured.
758 40 s. Type **214** 50 25
759 45 s. Capt. James Cook 65 40
760 80 s. Comte Louis-Antoine de Bougainville 80 75
761 $2 Comte Jean de la Perouse 1·40 2·00
See also Nos. 768/72.

1987. Christmas. Multicoloured.
764 40 s. Type **216** 30 25
765 45 s. Family going to church 40 30
766 50 s. Bamboo fire-gun 45 35
767 80 s. Inter-island transport 1·10 1·00

217 Samoa Coat of Arms and Australia Post Logo

1988. Bicentenary of Australian Settlement (2nd issue). Postal Services. Multicoloured.
768 45 s. Type **217** 80 80
769 45 s. Samoan mail van and Boeing 727 airplane 80 80
770 45 s. Loading Boeing 727 mail plane 80 80
771 45 s. Australian mail van and Boeing 727 80 80
772 45 s. "Congratulations Australia" message on airmail letter 80 80
Nos. 768/72 were printed together, se-tenant, Nos. 769/71 forming a composite design.

218 Airport Terminal and Douglas DC-9 Airliner taking off

1988. Opening of Faleolo Airport. Mult.
773 40 s. Type **218** 60 25
774 45 s. Boeing 727 65 30
775 60 s. De Havilland D.H.C.6 Twin Otter 80 55
776 70 s. Boeing 737 90 1·00
777 80 s. Boeing 727 and control tower 1·00 1·25
778 $1 Douglas DC-9 over "fale" (house) 1·10 1·40

219 "Expo '88" Pacific Islands Village

221 Athletics

1988. "Expo '88" World Fair, Brisbane. Multicoloured.
779 45 s. Type **219** 30 30
780 70 s. Expo Complex and monorail 1·25 1·25
781 $2 Map of Australia showing Brisbane 2·00 2·50

1988. Olympic Games, Seoul. Multicoloured.
783 15 s. Type **221** 10 10
784 60 s. Weightlifting 30 35
785 80 s. Boxing 40 45
786 $2 Olympic stadium 1·10 1·25

222 Spotted Triller

223 Forest

1988. Birds. Multicoloured.
788 10 s. Type **222** 60 30
789 15 s. Samoan wood rail 70 35
790 20 s. Flat-billed kingfisher 90 45
791 25 s. Samoan fantail 90 45
797a 25 s. Many-coloured fruit dove (25 × 40 mm) 10 10
792 35 s. Scarlet robin 1·00 55
793 40 s. Black-breasted honeyeater ("Mao") 1·00 55
794 50 s. Cardinal honeyeater 1·00 40
795 65 s. Yellow-fronted whistler 1·50 50
796 75 s. Many-coloured fruit dove 1·75 60
798 75 s. Silver gull (45 × 28 mm) 1·75 80
797 85 s. White-throated pigeon 1·75 70
799 85 s. Great frigate bird (45 × 28 mm) 1·75 90
800 90 s. Eastern reef heron (45 × 28 mm) 2·00 1·25
801 $3 Short-tailed albatross (45 × 28 mm) 1·50 1·40
802 $10 White tern (45 × 28 mm) 4·00 4·25
803 $20 Shy albatross (45 × 28 mm) 8·25 8·50

1988. National Conservation Campaign. Mult.
807 15 s. Type **223** 50 15
808 40 s. Samoan handicrafts 55 30
809 45 s. Forest wildlife 90 35
810 50 s. Careful use of water (horiz) 80 40
811 60 s. Fishing (horiz) 1·10 60
812 $1 Coconut plantation (horiz) 1·25 1·00

224 Congregational Church of Jesus, Apia

225 "Phaius flavus"

1988. Christmas. Samoan Churches. Mult.
813 15 s. Type **224** 15 10
814 40 s. Roman Catholic Church, Leauva'a 35 25
815 45 s. Congregational Christian Church, Moataa 40 30
816 $2 Baha'i Temple, Vailima 1·50 2·25

1989. Orchids (2nd series). Multicoloured.
818 15 s. Type **225** 15 10
819 45 s. "Calanthe triplicata" 35 30
820 60 s. "Luisia teretifolia" 40 35
821 $3 "Dendrobium mohlianum" 1·75 2·00

226 "Eber" (German gunboat)

1989. Cent of Great Apia Hurricane. Mult.
822 50 s. Type **226** 90 55
823 65 s. "Olga" (German corvette) 1·00 65
824 85 s. H.M.S. "Calliope" (screw corvette) 1·25 75
825 $2 U.S.S. "Vandalia" (corvette) 1·50 1·40

227 Samoan Red Cross Youth Group on Parade

1989. 125th Anniv of Int Red Cross. Mult.
826 50 s. Type **227** 30 30
827 65 s. Blood donors 40 45
828 75 s. Practising first aid 45 55
829 $3 Red Cross volunteers carrying patient 1·60 2·25

1989. 20th Anniv of First Manned Landing on Moon. As T **126** of Ascension. Multicoloured.
830 18 s. Saturn rocket on mobile launcher 40 15
831 50 s. Crew of "Apollo 14" (30 × 30 mm) 60 35
832 65 s. "Apollo 14" emblem (30 × 30 mm) 75 45
833 $2 Tracks of lunar transporter 1·60 1·75

228 Virgin Mary and Joseph

1989. Christmas. Multicoloured.
835 18 s. Type **228** 30 10
836 50 s. Shepherds 75 30
837 55 s. Donkey and ox 80 35
838 $2 Three Wise Men 2·50 3·50

MINIMUM PRICE

The minimum price quoted is 10p which represents a handling charge rather than a basis for valuing common stamps. For further notes about prices see introductory pages.

229 Pao Pao Outrigger

1990. Local Transport. Multicoloured.

840		18 s. Type **229**	35	20
841		55 s. Fautasi (large canoe)	85	65
842		60 s. Polynesian Airlines De havilland Twin Otter aircraft	1·75	1·25
843		$3 "Lady Samoa" (ferry)	3·75	4·50

230 Bismarck and Brandenburg Gate, Berlin

1990. Treaty of Berlin, 1889 and Opening of Berlin Wall, 1989. Multicoloured.

844		75 s. Type **230**	1·50	2·00
845		$3 "Adler" (German steam gunboat)	4·75	5·50

Nos. 844/5 were printed together, se-tenant, forming a composite design showing Berliners on the Wall near the Brandenburg Gate.

231 Penny Black and Alexandra Palace, London (½ size illustration)

1990. "Stamp World London 90" Int Stamp Exn.

846	**231**	$3 multicoloured	2·50	3·00

232 Visitors' Bureau

1990. Tourism. Multicoloured.

847		18 s. Type **232**	30	10
848		50 s. Village resort	55	30
849		65 s. Aggie's Hotel	70	60
850		$3 Swimming pool, Tusitala Hotel	2·50	4·00

234 "Virgin and Child" (Bellini)

236 Black-capped Lory

235 William Draper III (administrator) and 40th Anniv Logo

1990. Christmas. Paintings. Multicoloured.

852		18 s. Type **234**	30	10
853		50 s. "Virgin and Child with St. Peter and St. Paul" (Bouts)	70	30
854		55 s. "School of Love" (Correggio)	75	35
855		$3 "Virgin and Child" (Cima)	3·25	4·25

The 55 s. value should have shown "The Madonna of the Basket" by the same artist and is so inscribed.

1990. 40th Anniv of United Nations Development Programme.

856	**235**	$3 multicoloured	2·50	3·25

1991. Parrots. Multicoloured.

857		18 s. Type **236**	60	40
858		50 s. Eclectus parrot	1·00	60
859		65 s. Scarlet macaw	1·25	85
860		$3 Palm cockatoo	2·75	4·00

1991. 65th Birthday of Queen Elizabeth II and 70th Birthday of Prince Philip. As T **139** of Ascension. Multicoloured.

861		75 s. Prince Philip in the countryside	90	1·25
862		$2 Queen wearing yellow lei	2·40	3·00

238 "O Come All Ye Faithful"

1991. Christmas. Carols (1st series). Mult.

864		20 s. Type **238**	45	10
865		60 s. "Joy to the World"	85	40
866		75 s. "Hark the Herald Angels Sing"	1·10	70
867		$4 "We wish you a Merry Christmas"	4·00	5·50

See also Nos. 886/9 and 907/11.

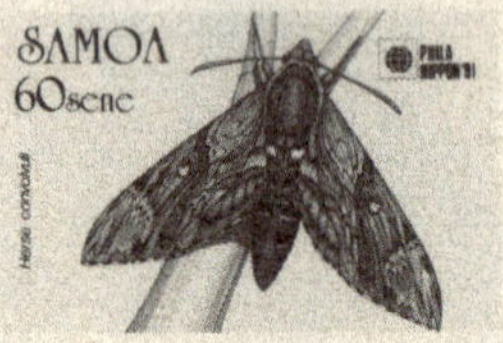

239 "Herse convolvuli"

1991. "Phila Nippon '91" International Stamp Exhibition, Tokyo. Samoan Hawkmoths. Mult.

868		60 s. Type **239**	1·00	70
869		75 s. "Gnathothlibus erotus"	1·10	80
870		85 s. "Deilephila celerio"	1·25	1·00
871		$3 "Cephonodes armatus"	4·00	4·75

240 Head of State inspecting Guard of Honour

1992. 30th Anniv of Independence. Mult.

872		50 s. Type **240**	70	30
873		65 s. Siva ceremony	75	50
874		$1 Commemorative float	1·25	1·25
875		$3 Raising Samoan flag	3·00	4·25

1992. 40th Anniv of Queen Elizabeth II's Accession. As T **143** of Ascension. Multicoloured.

876		20 s. Queen and Prince Philip with umbrellas	45	10
877		60 s. Queen and Prince Philip on Royal Yacht	1·25	70
878		75 s. Queen in multicoloured hat	85	75
879		85 s. Three portraits of Queen Elizabeth	95	85
880		$3 Queen Elizabeth II	2·25	3·25

242 Weightlifting

1992. Olympic Games, Barcelona. Mult.

882		60 s. Type **242**	80	70
883		75 s. Boxing	90	80
884		85 s. Running	1·00	1·00
885		$3 Montjuic Olympic Stadium, Barcelona	3·00	4·00

1992. Christmas. Carols (2nd series). As T **238**. Multicoloured.

886		50 s. "God rest you Merry Gentle-men"	55	30
887		60 s. "While Shepherds watched their Flocks by Night"	65	55
888		75 s. "Away in a Manger, no Crib for a Bed"	75	70
889		$4 "O Little Town of Bethlehem"	3·25	4·50

243 Narrow-banded Batfish

1993. Fishes. Multicoloured.

890		60 s. Type **243**	70	60
891		75 s. Clown surgeonfish	85	85
892		$1 Black-tailed snapper	1·25	1·50
893		$3 Long-nosed emperor	2·75	3·75

244 Samoan Players performing Traditional War Dance

1993. Rugby World Cup Seven-a-Side Championship, Edinburgh. Multicoloured.

894		60 s. Type **244**	85	65
895		75 s. Two players (vert)	95	75
896		85 s. Player running with ball and badge (vert)	1·10	1·10
897		$3 Edinburgh Castle	4·00	4·75

245 Flying Foxes hanging from Branch

1993. Endangered Species. Flying Foxes. Multicoloured.

898		20 s. Type **245**	80	30
899		50 s. Flying fox with young	1·25	70
900		60 s. Flying foxes hunting for food	1·40	1·00
901		75 s. Flying fox feeding from plant	1·60	1·60

247 Globe, Letter and Flowers

1993. World Post Day. Multicoloured.

903		60 s. Type **247**	55	45
904		75 s. Post Office counter	70	80
905		85 s. Hands exchanging letter	80	90
906		$4 Globe, national flags and letter	3·50	5·00

1993. Christmas Carols (3rd series). As T **238**. Multicoloured.

907		20 s. "Silent Night"	25	10
908		60 s. "As with Gladness Men of Old"	65	45
909		75 s. Mary had a Baby yes, Lord"	80	55
910		$1.50 "Once in Royal David's City"	1·40	2·25
911		$3 "Angels from the Realms of Glory"	3·50	4·50

248 "Alveopora allingi"

1994. Corals. Multicoloured.

912		20 s. Type **248**	30	10
913		60 s. "Acropora polystoma"	65	45
914		90 s. "Acropora listeri"	90	90
915		$4 "Acropora grandis"	2·75	3·75

1994. "Hong Kong '94" International Stamp Exhibition. Nos. 912/15 optd **HONG KONG '94** and emblem.

916		20 s. Type **248**	35	10
917		60 s. "Acropora polystoma"	65	45
918		90 s. "Acrophora listeri"	90	90
919		$4 "Acropora grandis"	2·75	3·75

249 Samoan Rugby Management Team

1994. Samoan National Rugby Team. Mult.

920		70 s. Type **249**	70	60
921		90 s. Test match against Wales	80	80
922		95 s. Test match against New Zealand	80	80
923		$4 Apia Park Stadium	3·50	5·00

251 Solo Singer and Choir

1994. Teuila Tourism Festival. Multicoloured.

925		70 s. Type **251**	65	45
926		90 s. Fire dancer	75	65
927		95 s. Festival float	75	65
928		$4 Band outside hotel	3·75	5·00

252 "Equator" (schooner)

253 Santa Claus on House

1994. Death Centenary of Robert Louis Stevenson (author). Multicoloured.

929		70 s. Type **252**	60	50
930		90 s. Robert Louis Stevenson	70	80
931		$1.20 Stevenson's tomb, Mt Vaea	95	1·25
932		$4 Vailima House (horiz)	3·25	4·00

1994. Christmas. Children's Paintings. Multicoloured.

933		70 s. Type **253**	60	50
934		95 s. Star over house and palm trees	70	70
935		$1.20 Family outing	95	1·25
936		$4 "Merry Christmas"	3·25	4·50

254 Lotofaga Beach, Aleipata

1995. Scenic Views. Multicoloured.

937		5 s. Type **254**	10	10
938		10 s. Nuutele Island	10	10
939		30 s. Satuiatua, Savaii	10	15
940		50 s. Sinalele, Aleipata	20	25
941		60 s. Paradise Beach, Lefaga	25	30
942		70 s. Houses at Piula Cave	30	35
943		80 s. Taga blowholes	35	40
944		90 s. View from East Coast road	35	40
945		95 s. Outrigger canoes, Leulumoega	40	45
946		$1 Parliament Building	40	45

255 Under-12s' Rugby Players

1995. World Cup Rugby Championship, South Africa. Multicoloured.

957		70 s. Type **255**	55	55
958		90 s. Secondary school players	70	70
959		$1 Samoan and New Zealand test match	75	75
960		$4 Ellis Park Stadium, Johannesburg	2·75	3·50

1995. 50th Anniv of End of Second World War. As T **161** of Ascension. Multicoloured.

961		70 s. Vought Sikorsky OS2U Kingfisher (seaplane)	65	55
962		90 s. Chance Vought F4U Corsair (fighter)	80	70
963		95 s. U.S. transport and landing craft	85	75
964		$3 U.S. Marines landing on Samoa	3·00	4·00

256 Leatherback Turtle — 258 Madonna and Child

1995. Year of the Sea Turtle. Multicoloured.
966 70 s. Type **256** 55 55
967 90 s. Loggerhead turtle . . . 70 70
968 $1 Green turtle 75 75
969 $4 Pacific ridley turtle . . . . 2·75 3·50

1995. 50th Anniv of United Nations. As T **284** of Jamaica. Multicoloured.
971 70 s. Hospital lorry, Bosnia, 1995 80 55
972 90 s. Bell Sioux helicopter and ambulance, Korea, 1952 . . 1·25 85
973 $1 Bell 212 helicopter, Bosnia, 1995 . . . . 1·40 95
974 $4 R.N.Z.A.F. Hawker Siddeley Andover, Somalia, 1995 . . 3·25 4·00

1995. Christmas. Multicoloured.
975 25 s. Type **258** 20 10
976 70 s. Wise Man wearing green turban 60 50
977 90 s. Wise Man with Child in manger 75 65
978 $5 Wise Man wearing red turban 3·50 5·00

259 Hands cupped under Waterfall and Bird — 262 Boxing

1996. Environment. Water Resources. Multicoloured.
979 70 s. Type **259** 50 50
980 90 s. Young girl and "WATER FOR LIFE" slogan 65 65
981 $2 Village and waterfall . . . 1·40 1·75
982 $4 Irrigation system . . . . . 2·75 3·50

1996. 70th Birthday of Queen Elizabeth II. As T **55** of Tokelau each incorporating a different photograph of the Queen. Multicoloured.
983 70 s. Main Street, Apia . . . 50 40
984 90 s. Beach scene, Neiafu . . 65 50
985 $1 Vailima House (Head of State's residence) 75 60
986 $3 Parliament Building . . . . 2·00 3·25

1996. Centenary of Modern Olympic Games. Multicoloured.
990 70 s. Type **262** 60 40
991 90 s. Running 70 55
992 $1 Weightlifting 80 60
993 $4 Throwing the javelin . . . 2·75 4·00

263 Festival Logo

1996. 7th Pacific Festival of Arts, Apia. Multicoloured.
994 60 s. Type **263** 40 35
995 70 s. Decorated pottery . . . 50 40
996 80 s. Textile pattern 55 55
997 90 s. Traditional dancing . . . 60 60
998 $1 Carved poles 70 70
999 $4 Man wearing traditional headdress and necklace . . 2·00 2·75

264 Young Children

1996. 50th Anniv of U.N.I.C.E.F. Multicoloured.
1000 70 s. Type **264** 45 40
1001 90 s. Children in hospital . . 60 60
1002 $1 Child receiving injection . . 70 70
1003 $4 Mothers and children . . 2·00 2·50

1997. Golden Wedding of Queen Elizabeth and Prince Philip. As T **87** of Kiribati. Multicoloured.
1007 70 s. Queen Elizabeth . . . 55 65
1008 70 s. Prince Philip carriage-driving at Royal Windsor Horse Show, 1996 . . . . 55 65
1009 90 s. Queen Elizabeth and horse 75 90
1010 90 s. Prince Philip laughing . 75 90
1011 $1 Prince Philip and Prince Edward with Zara Phillips on horseback, 1993 . . . . . 75 90
1012 $1 Queen Elizabeth and Prince William 75 90

Nos. 1007/8, 1009/10 and 1011/12 respectively were printed together, se-tenant, with the backgrounds forming composite designs.

267 Dolphin on Surface

1997. 26th Anniv of Greenpeace (environmental organisation). Multicoloured.
1014 50 s. Type **267** 30 25
1015 60 s. Two dolphins swimming underwater 40 35
1016 70 s. Heads of two dolphins underwater 45 50
1017 $1 Dolphin "laughing" . . . 55 75

268 Christmas Bells

1997. Christmas. Multicoloured.
1019 70 s. Type **268** 45 35
1020 80 s. Christmas bauble . . . 50 40
1021 $2 Candle . . . . 1·40 1·75
1022 $3 Christmas star . . . . . 1·60 2·00

269 Mangrove Fruit

1998. Mangroves. Multicoloured.
1023 70 s. Type **269** 30 35
1024 80 s. Mangrove seedlings . . 35 40
1025 $2 Mangrove roots . . . . 1·00 1·25
1026 $4 Mangrove tree on seashore 2·00 2·50

1998. Diana, Princess of Wales Commemoration. As T **91** of Kiribati. Multicoloured.
1027 50 s. Wearing red jacket, 1990 20 25

270 Westland Wallace

1998. 80th Anniv of the Royal Air Force. Multicoloured.
1029 70 s. Type **270** 45 35
1030 80 s. Hawker Fury Mk I . . 45 40
1031 $2 Vickers Varsity . . . . . 1·10 1·40
1032 $5 BAC Jet Provost . . . . 2·50 2·75

271 Christmas Star

1998. Christmas. Multicoloured.
1034 70 s. Type **271** 40 35
1035 $1.05 Bell 60 50
1036 $1.40 Bauble 75 70
1037 $5 Cross . . . . 2·75 3·00

HAVE YOU READ THE NOTES AT THE BEGINNING OF THIS CATALOGUE?
These often provide answers to the enquiries we receive.

272 Outrigger Canoe

1999. "Australia '99" World Stamp Exhibition, Melbourne. Maritime Heritage. Multicoloured.
1038 70 s. Type **272** 40 35
1039 90 s."Heemskerk" and "Zeehan" (Tasman), 1642 . 50 45
1040 $1.05 H.M.S. "Resolution" and H.M.S. "Adventure" (Cook), 1773 . . . . 60 50
1041 $6 New Zealand scow schooner, 1880 . . . . 3·50 3·75

1999. Royal Wedding. Vert designs as T **153** of Pitcairn Islands. Multicoloured.
1042 $1.50 Photographs of Prince Edward and Miss Sophie Rhys-Jones 75 70
1043 $6 Engagement photograph . 3·50 3·75

SARAWAK

Formerly an independent state on the north coast of Borneo under British protection. Under Japanese occupation from 1941 until 1945. A Crown Colony from 1946 until September 1963, when it became a state of the Federation of Malaysia.

100 cents = 1 dollar (Malayan or Malaysian)

1 Sir James Brooke — 2 Sir Charles Brooke

1869.
1 **1** 3 c. brown on yellow . . . . 42·00 £225

1871.
3 **2** 2 c. mauve on lilac . . . . . 3·25 15·00
2 3 c. brown on yellow . . . . 1·50 3·00
4 4 c. brown on yellow . . . . 3·25 3·00
5 6 c. green on green . . . . . 2·75 3·50
6 8 c. blue on blue . . . . . . 2·75 3·50
7 12 c. red on red . . . . 6·50 6·50

4 Sir Charles Brooke 11

1888.
8 **4** 1 c. purple and black . . . . 1·00 50
9 2 c. purple and red . . . . . 85 1·10
10 3 c. purple and blue . . . . 1·75 1·75
11 4 c. purple and yellow . . . 11·00 38·00
12 5 c. purple and green . . . . 8·00 1·75
13 6 c. purple and brown . . . 9·50 48·00
14 8 c. green and red . . . . . 5·50 2·50
15 10 c. green and purple . . . 29·00 14·00
16 12 c. green and blue . . . . 5·50 7·50
17 16 c. green and orange . . . 38·00 60·00
18 25 c. green and brown . . . 35·00 35·00
19 32 c. green and black . . . . 25·00 45·00
20 50 c. green . . . . 25·00 75·00
21 $1 green and black . . . . . 50·00 70·00

1889. Surch in words (1 c.) or figures (others).
27 **2** 1 c. on 3 c. brown on yellow (surch **ONE CENT**) . . . 75 1·50
22 **4** 1 c. on 3 c. purple and blue (surch **One Cent.**) . . . . 26·00 24·00
23 1 c. on 3 c. purple and blue (surch **one cent.**) . . . . . 2·75 2·75
24 2 c. on 8 c. green and red . . 2·75 5·00
25a 5 c. on 12 c. green and blue 20·00 38·00

1895. Various frames.
28c **11** 2 c. red . . . . 6·50 4·50
29 4 c. black . . . . 6·00 2·50
30 6 c. violet . . . . 6·00 9·00
31 8 c. green . . . . 20·00 6·00

1889. Surch in figures and words.
32 **2** 2 c. on 3 c. brown on yellow 1·00 1·25
33 2 c. on 12 c. red on red . . . 2·50 3·00
34 4 c. on 6 c. green on green 20·00 48·00
35 4 c. on 8 c. blue on blue . . 3·25 6·00

1899. As T **4**, but inscr "POSTAGE POSTAGE".
36 1 c. blue and red . . . . . . 1·00 1·00
37 2 c. green . . . . 1·25 90
38 3 c. purple . . . . 4·00 50
39a 4 c. red . . . . 1·75 15
40 8 c. yellow and black . . . . 1·75 80
41 10 c. blue . . . . 1·75 80
42 12 c. mauve . . . . 3·75 3·75
43 16 c. brown and green . . . 1·75 1·50
44 20 c. brown and mauve . . . 4·00 3·00
45 25 c. brown and blue . . . . 2·75 4·25
46 50 c. green and red . . . . . 16·00 21·00
47 $1 red and green . . . . . . 40·00 85·00

17 Sir Charles Vyner Brooke 19

1918.
76 **17** 1 c. blue and red 80 35
51 2 c. green . . . . 1·75 1·25
77 2 c. purple . . . . 70 1·00
52 3 c. purple . . . . 3·25 2·50
64 3 c. green . . . . 1·00 1·25
53 4 c. red . . . . 3·50 2·25
65 4 c. purple . . . . 1·00 60
66 5 c. orange . . . . 1·25 90
81 6 c. purple . . . . 1·00 30
54 8 c. yellow and black . . . 10·00 50·00
82 8 c. red . . . . 2·25 11·00
55 10 c. blue . . . . 2·75 2·75
83 10 c. black . . . . 1·75 1·25
56 12 c. purple . . . . 8·50 20·00
84 12 c. blue . . . . 2·25 17·00
85 16 c. brown and green . . . 2·25 3·50
86 20 c. bistre and violet . . . 2·25 4·50
87 25 c. brown and blue . . . 4·25 7·00
71 30 c. brown and grey . . . 3·75 4·25
89 50 c. green and red . . . . 4·25 8·50
90 $1 pink and green . . . . . 13·00 22·00

1923. Surch in words.

72	**17**	1 c. on 10 c. blue	9·00	48·00
73		2 c. on 12 c. purple	6·00	32·00

1932.

91	**19**	1 c. blue	70	80
92		2 c. green	70	80
93		3 c. violet	2·25	80
94		4 c. orange	1·25	55
95		5 c. red	4·00	1·00
96		6 c. red	6·00	7·00
97		8 c. yellow	3·50	7·00
98		10 c. black	2·25	3·00
99		12 c. blue	3·50	6·50
100		15 c. brown	5·00	6·50
101		20 c. orange and violet	4·25	7·00
102		25 c. yellow and brown	9·00	17·00
103		30 c. brown and red	6·50	17·00
104		50 c. red and olive	8·00	10·00
105		$1 green and red	13·00	25·00

21 Sir Charles Vyner Brooke

23 Sir James Brooke, Sir Charles Vyner Brooke and Sir Charles Brooke

1934.

106	**21**	1 c. purple	15	10
107		2 c. green	15	10
107a		2 c. black	1·25	1·60
108		3 c. black	15	10
108a		3 c. green	3·00	4·00
109		4 c. purple	20	15
110		5 c. violet	50	10
111		6 c. red	85	60
111a		6 c. brown	4·00	8·00
112		8 c. brown	90	10
112a		8 c. red	3·00	10
113		10 c. red	1·25	40
114		12 c. blue	1·75	25
114a		12 c. orange	2·00	4·75
115		15 c. orange	2·00	5·50
115a		15 c. blue	3·75	13·00
116		20 c. green and red	2·00	70
117		25 c. violet and orange	2·00	1·25
118		30 c. brown and violet	2·00	2·25
119		50 c. violet and red	2·00	75
120		$1 red and brown	60	65
121		$2 purple and violet	8·00	8·00
122		$3 red and green	24·00	25·00
123		$4 blue and red	24·00	30·00
124		$5 red and brown	24·00	30·00
125		$10 black and yellow	18·00	40·00

1945. Optd **B M A**.

126	**21**	1 c. purple	40	50
127		2 c. black	40	50
128		3 c. green	40	30
129		4 c. purple	40	30
130		5 c. violet	50	90
131		6 c. brown	80	75
132		8 c. red	11·00	9·00
133		10 c. red	60	70
134		12 c. orange	90	3·75
135		15 c. blue	1·50	40
136		20 c. green and red	2·25	1·40
137		25 c. violet and orange	2·25	2·75
138		30 c. brown and violet	4·75	2·75
139		50 c. violet and red	1·25	35
140		$1 red and brown	2·50	1·25
141		$2 purple and violet	9·00	7·00
142		$3 red and green	17·00	35·00
143		$4 blue and red	25·00	30·00
144		$5 red and brown	£110	£130
145		$10 black and yellow	£110	£150

1946. Centenary Issue.

146	**23**	8 c. red	80	30
147		15 c. blue	80	1·75
148		50 c. black and red	90	1·75
149		$1 black and brown	1·25	13·00

1947. Optd with the Royal Cypher.

150	**21**	1 c. purple	15	30
151		2 c. black	15	15
152		3 c. green	15	15
153		4 c. purple	15	15
154		6 c. brown	20	90
155		8 c. red	40	10
156		10 c. red	20	20
157		12 c. orange	20	90
158		15 c. blue	20	40
159		20 c. green and red	75	50
160		25 c. violet and orange	40	30
161		50 c. violet and red	40	40
162		$1 red and brown	75	90
163		$2 purple and violet	1·40	3·25
164		$5 red and brown	3·00	3·25

1948. Silver Wedding. As T **10/11** of Aden.

165	8 c. red	30	30
166	$5 brown	28·00	28·00

1949. U.P.U. As T **20/23** of Antigua.

167	8 c. red	1·25	50
168	15 c. blue	2·50	2·25
169	25 c. green	2·00	1·50
170	50 c. violet	2·00	4·00

25 "Trogonoptera brookiana"

26 Western Tarsier

27 Kayan Tomb

1950.

171	**25**	1 c. black	30	30
172	**26**	2 c. orange	20	40
173	**27**	3 c. green	10	60
174	–	4 c. brown	10	20
175	–	6 c. blue	10	15
176	–	8 c. red	10	30
177	–	10 c. orange	50	3·25
186	–	10 c. orange	75	40
178	–	12 c. violet	1·75	1·50
179	–	15 c. blue	1·00	15
180	–	20 c. brown and orange	60	30
181	–	25 c. green and red	1·00	30
182	–	50 c. brown and violet	1·25	15
183	–	$1 green and brown	11·00	2·50
184	–	$2 blue and red	22·00	11·00
185	–	$5 multicoloured	19·00	11·00

DESIGNS—VERT: 4 c. Kayan boy and girl; 6 c. Beadwork; 50 c. Iban woman. HORIZ: 8 c. Dayak dancer; 10 c. (No. 177) Malayan Pangolin; 10 c. (No. 186) Map of Sarawak; 12 c. Kenyah boys; 15 c. Fire-making; 20 c. Kelemantan rice barn; 25 c. Pepper vines; $1 Kelabit smithy; $2 Map of Sarawak; $5 Arms of Sarawak.

1953. Coronation. As T **13** of Aden.

187	10 c. black and blue	1·00	1·25

47 Barong Panau (sailing prau)

51 Queen Elizabeth II

52 Queen Elizabeth II (after Annigoni)

1955.

188	–	1 c. green	10	30
189	–	2 c. orange	30	55
190	–	4 c. brown	45	60
191	–	6 c. blue	3·00	1·50
192	–	8 c. red	30	30
193	–	10 c. green	20	10
194	**47**	12 c. plum	3·75	55
195	–	15 c. blue	1·00	30
196	–	20 c. olive and brown	1·00	10
197	–	25 c. sepia and green	6·50	20
198	**51**	30 c. brown and lilac	3·00	30
199		50 c. black and red	2·00	30
200	**52**	$1 green and brown	4·50	60
201		$2 violet and green	12·00	2·75
202	–	$5 multicoloured	16·00	8·50

DESIGNS—VERT (as Type **47**): 1 c. Logging; 2 c. Young orang-utan; 4 c. Kayan dancing. HORIZ: 6 c. Malabar pied hornbill; 8 c. Shield with spears; 10 c. Kenyah ceremonial carving; 15 c. Turtles; 20 c. Melanau basket-making; 25 c. Astana, Kuching; $5 Arms of Sarawak.

1963. Freedom from Hunger. As T **28** of Aden.

203	12 c. sepia	1·50	85

53 "Vanda hookeriana"

1965. As Nos. 155/21, of Kedah but with Arms of Sarawak inset as in T **53**.

212	**53**	1 c. multicoloured	10	60
213	–	2 c. multicoloured	20	70
214	–	5 c. multicoloured	45	10
215	–	6 c. multicoloured	60	85
216	–	10 c. multicoloued	80	10
217	–	15 c. multicoloured	1·50	10
218	–	20 c. multicoloured	2·00	50

The higher values used in Sarawak were Nos. 20/7 of Malaysia (National issues).

54 "Precis orithya"

1971. Butterflies. As Nos. 124/30 of Kedah, but with Sarawak Arms as in T **54**.

219	–	1 c. multicoloured	30	90
220	–	2 c. multicoloured	50	90
221	–	5 c. multicoloured	1·00	10
222	–	6 c. multicoloured	1·25	1·50
223	–	10 c. multicoloured	1·25	10
224	**54**	15 c. multicoloured	1·75	10
225	–	20 c. multicoloured	1·75	1·00

The higher values in use with this issue were Nos. 64/71 of Malaysia (National issues).

55 "Precis orithya" (different crest at right)

1977. As Nos. 219/21 and 223/5, but showing new State Crest.

226	–	1 c. multicoloured	6·50	10·00
227	–	2 c. multicoloured	7·00	6·50
228	–	5 c. multicoloured	80	70
230	–	10 c. multicoloured	50	30
231	**55**	15 c. multicoloured	1·25	20
232	–	20 c. multicoloured	3·00	2·25

56 "Rhododendron scortechinii"

57 Coffee

1979. As Nos. 135/41 of Kedah, but with Arms of Sarawak as in T **56**.

233	1 c. "Rafflesia hasseltii"	10	40
234	2 c. "Pterocarpus indicus"	10	40
235	5 c. "Lagerstroemia speciosa"	20	20
236	10 c. "Durio zibethinus"	20	10
237	15 c. "Hibiscus rosa-sinensis"	20	10
238	20 c. Type **56**	30	10
239	25 c. "Etlingera elatior" (inscr "Phaeomeria speciosa")	50	20

1986. As Nos. 152/8 of Kedah, but with Arms of Sarawak as in T **57**.

247	1 c. Type **57**	10	10
248	2 c. Coconuts	10	10
249	5 c. Cocoa	10	10
250	10 c. Black pepper	10	10
251	15 c. Rubber	10	10
252	20 c. Oil palm	10	10
253	30 c. Rice	15	20

Nos. 247/53 exist with slightly different versions to state arms at right.

JAPANESE OCCUPATION

(**1**) "Imperial Japanese Government"

1942. Stamps of Sarawak optd with T **1**.

J 1	**21**	1 c. purple	32·00	55·00
J 2		2 c. green	75·00	£130
J 3		2 c. black	70·00	80·00
J 4		3 c. black	£225	£225
J 5		3 c. green	42·00	65·00
J 6		4 c. purple	45·00	65·00
J 7		5 c. violet	55·00	65·00
J 8		6 c. red	85·00	90·00
J 9		6 c. brown	55·00	65·00
J10		8 c. brown	£180	£190
J11		8 c. red	75·00	£110
J12		10 c. red	50·00	70·00
J13		12 c. blue	£110	£120
J14		12 c. orange	£110	£130
J15		15 c. orange	£225	£225
J16		15 c. blue	75·00	80·00
J17		20 c. green and red	42·00	70·00
J18		25 c. violet and orange	70·00	70·00
J19		30 c. brown and violet	45·00	75·00
J20		50 c. violet and red	55·00	75·00
J21		$1 red and brown	70·00	90·00
J22		$2 purple and violet	£150	£180
J23		$3 red and green	£800	£900
J24		$4 blue and red	£170	£225
J25		$5 red and brown	£170	£225
J26		$10 black and yellow	£170	£225

SELANGOR

A state of the Federation of Malaya, incorporated in Malaysia in 1963.

100 cents = 1 dollar (Straits or Malayan)

1881. Stamps of Straits Settlements optd **SELANGOR**.

3	**5**	2 c. brown	80·00	85·00
35		2 c. red	5·50	2·25

1882. Straits Settlements stamp optd **S.**

8	**5**	2 c. brown	—	£2000

1891. Stamp of Straits Settlements surch **SELANGOR Two CENTS**.

44	**5**	2 c. on 24 c. green	18·00	55·00

40

42

43

1891.

49	**40**	1 c. green	70	25
50		2 c. red	3·50	1·00
51		2 c. orange	1·75	60
52		5 c. blue	18·00	4·50

1894. Surch **3 CENTS**.

53	**40**	3 c. on 5 c. red	1·50	40

1895.

54	**42**	3 c. purple and red	5·50	30
55		5 c. purple and yellow	2·00	30
56		8 c. purple and blue	60·00	7·00
57		10 c. purple and orange	8·50	1·50
58		25 c. green and red	80·00	48·00
60		50 c. green and black	£275	£110
59		50 c. purple and black	40·00	22·00
61	**43**	$1 green	45·00	90·00
62		$2 green and red	£150	£150
63		$3 green and yellow	£375	£250
64		$5 green and blue	£140	£190
65		$10 green and purple	£425	£500
66		$25 green and orange	£1800	

1900. Surch in words.

66a	**42**	1 c. on 5 c. purple & yellow	60·00	£100
66b		1 c. on 50 c. green and black	1·00	17·00
67		3 c. on 50 c. green and black	4·00	17·00

46 Mosque at Palace, Klang

47 Sultan Suleiman

1935.

68	**46**	1 c. black	30	10
69		2 c. green	70	10
70		2 c. orange	3·25	75
71a		3 c. green	1·00	7·00
72		4 c. orange	30	10
73		5 c. brown	60	10
74		6 c. red	4·75	10
75		8 c. grey	50	10
76		10 c. purple	50	10
77		12 c. blue	1·00	10
78		15 c. blue	9·50	32·00
79		25 c. purple and red	1·00	60
80		30 c. purple and orange	1·00	85
81		40 c. red and purple	1·25	1·25
82		50 c. black on green	1·00	15
83	**47**	$1 black and red on blue	6·00	65
84		$2 green and red	20·00	8·00
85		$5 green and red on green	48·00	23·00

48 Sultan Hisamud-din Alam Shah **49**

1941.

86	**48**	$1 black and red on blue	11·00	6·00
87		$2 green and red	48·00	27·00

1948. Silver Wedding. As T **10/11** of Aden.

88	10 c. violet	20	10
89	$5 green	23·00	14·00

1949.

90	**49**	1 c. black	10	20
91		2 c. orange	10	20
92		3 c. green	30	1·50
93		4 c. brown	10	10
94a		5 c. purple	30	10
95		6 c. grey	10	10
96		8 c. red	25	65
97		8 c. green	65	80
98		10 c. purple	10	10
99		12 c. red	80	2·50
100		15 c. blue	1·75	10
101		20 c. black and green	45	10
102		20 c. blue	80	10
103		25 c. purple and orange	85	10
104		30 c. red and purple	1·25	80
105		35 c. red and purple	70	1·00
106		40 c. red and purple	3·50	3·50
107		50 c. black and blue	70	10
108		$1 blue and purple	2·75	30
109		$2 green and red	8·50	30
110		$5 green and brown	45·00	1·75

1949. U.P.U. As T **20/23** of Antigua.

111	10 c. purple	30	10
112	15 c. blue	1·50	1·00
113	25 c. orange	50	2·25
114	50 c. black	1·25	2·25

1953. Coronation. As T **13** of Aden.

115	10 c. black and purple	70	10

1957. As Nos. 92/102 of Kedah but inset portrait of Sultan Hisamud-din Alam Shah.

116	1 c. black	10	1·25
117	2 c. red	10	50
118	4 c. sepia	10	10
119	5 c. lake	10	10
120	8 c. green	1·10	1·75
121	10 c. sepia	40	10
122	10 c. purple	3·00	10
123	20 c. blue	1·00	10
124a	50 c. black and blue	30	10
125	$1 blue and purple	2·00	10
126	$2 green and red	2·50	1·00
127a	$5 brown and green	4·75	1·00

50 Sultan Salahuddin Abdul Aziz Shah

51 Sultan Salahuddin Abdul Aziz Shah

1961. Coronation of the Sultan.

128	**50**	10 c. multicoloured	20	10

1961. As Nos. 116 etc but with inset portrait of Sultan Salahuddin Abdul Aziz as in T **51**.

129	1 c. black	10	1·00
130	2 c. red	10	1·00
131	4 c. sepia	10	10
132	5 c. lake	10	10
133	8 c. green	1·75	2·75
134	10 c. purple	30	10
135	20 c. blue	2·75	30

52 "Vanda hookeriana"

1965. As Nos. 115/21 of Kedah but with inset portrait of Sultan Salahuddin Abdul Aziz Shah as in T **52**.

136	**52**	1 c. multicoloured	10	10
137	–	2 c. multicoloured	10	80
138	–	5 c. multicoloured	15	10
139	–	6 c. multicoloured	15	10
140	–	10 c. multicoloured	15	10
141	–	15 c. multicoloured	1·25	10
142	–	20 c. multicoloured	1·90	40

The higher values used in Selangor were Nos. 20/7 of Malaysia (National issues).

53 "Parthenos sylvia"

1971. Butterflies. As Nos. 124/30 of Kedah, but with portrait of Sultan Salahuddin Abdul Aziz Shah as in T **53**.

146	–	1 c. multicoloured	30	90
147	–	2 c. multicoloured	85	90
148	**53**	5 c. multicoloured	85	10
149	–	6 c. multicoloured	85	90
150	–	10 c. multicoloured	85	10
151	–	15 c. multicoloured	85	10
152	–	20 c. multicoloured	1·00	30

The higher values in use with this issue were Nos. 64/71 of Malaysia (National issues).

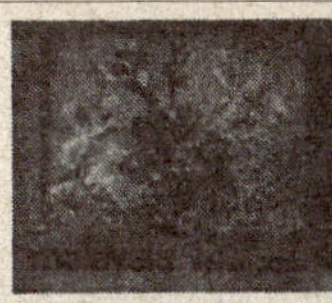
54 "Lagerstroemia speciosa"

1979. Flowers. As Nos. 135/41 of Kedah but with portrait of Sultan Salahuddin Abdul Aziz Shah as in T **54**.

158	1 c. "Rafflesia hasseltii"	10	50
159	2 c. "Pterocarpus indicus"	10	50
160	5 c. Type **54**	10	10
161	10 c. "Durio zibethinus"	15	10
162	15 c. "Hibiscus rosa sinensis"	15	10
163	20 c. "Rhododendron scortechinii"	20	10
164	25 c. "Etlingera elatior" (inscr "Phaeomeria speciosa")	40	10

55 Sultan Salahuddin Abdul Aziz Shah and Royal Crest

56 Black Pepper

1985. Silver Jubilee of Sultan.

173	**55**	15 c. multicoloured	1·00	10
174		20 c. multicoloured	1·00	15
175		$1 multicoloured	4·50	6·00

1986. As Nos. 152/8 of Kedah but with portrait of Sultan Salahuddin Abdul Aziz Shah as in T **56**.

176	1 c. Coffee	10	10
177	2 c. Coconuts	10	10
178	5 c. Cocoa	10	10
179	10 c. Type **56**	10	10
180	15 c. Rubber	10	10
181	20 c. Oil palm	10	10
182	30 c. Rice	15	20

SEYCHELLES

A group of islands in the Indian Ocean, east of Africa.

100 cents = 1 rupee

1

6

1890.

9	**1**	2 c. green and red	2·00	70
28		2 c. brown and green	1·75	60
22		3 c. purple and orange	1·25	30
10		4 c. red and green	2·00	1·00
29		6 c. red	3·00	40
11		8 c. purple and blue	4·75	1·75
12		10 c. blue and brown	6·50	3·25
23		12 c. brown and green	1·75	50
13		13 c. grey and black	2·50	1·75
24		15 c. olive and lilac	4·25	2·00
30		15 c. blue	3·25	3·25
6		16 c. brown and blue	3·75	3·75
31		18 c. blue	3·25	90
32		36 c. brown and red	18·00	4·00
25		45 c. brown and red	23·00	32·00
7		48 c. bistre and green	19·00	16·00
33		75 c. yellow and violet	48·00	70·00
8		96 c. mauve and red	50·00	48·00
34		1 r. mauve and red	11·00	3·75
35		1 r. 50 grey and red	60·00	85·00
36		2 r. 25 mauve and green	85·00	85·00

1893. Surch in figures and words in two lines.

15	**1**	3 c. on 4 c. red and green	1·10	1·50
16		12 c. on 16 c. brown and blue	1·50	3·75
19		15 c. on 16 c. brown and blue	8·00	2·50
20		45 c. on 48 c. brown and green	17·00	5·00
21		90 c. on 96 c. mauve and red	38·00	30·00

1896. Surch in figures and words in one line.

26	**1**	18 c. on 45 c. brown and red	7·00	2·75
27		36 c. on 45 c. brown and red	8·00	45·00

1901. Surch in figures and words.

41	**1**	2 c. on 4 c. red and green	1·60	2·75
37		3 c. on 10 c. blue and brown	75	60
38		3 c. on 16 c. brown and blue	1·50	2·75
39		3 c. on 36 c. brown and red	50	60
40		6 c. on 8 c. purple and blue	75	2·25
42		30 c. on 75 c. yellow & violet	1·50	4·00
43		30 c. on 1 r. mauve and red	4·50	23·00
44		45 c. on 1 r. mauve and red	3·50	23·00
45		45 c. on 2 r. mauve and green	35·00	65·00

1903.

46	**6**	2 c. brown and green	1·75	1·25
61		3 c. green	1·25	1·00
62		6 c. red	1·50	70
49		12 c. brown and green	2·25	2·00
64		15 c. blue	3·00	2·00
65		18 c. olive and red	3·00	6·50
66		30 c. violet and green	6·00	8·00
67		45 c. brown and red	3·00	6·50
54		75 c. yellow and violet	9·50	26·00
69		1 r. 50 black and red	50·00	55·00
70		2 r. 25 purple and green	32·00	55·00

1903. Surch **3 cents**.

57	**6**	3 c. on 15 c. blue	75	2·75
58		3 c. on 18 c. olive and red	2·25	28·00
59		3 c. on 45 c. brown and red	2·25	2·50

9

11

1912. Inscr "POSTAGE POSTAGE".

71	**9**	2 c. brown and green	50	3·75
72		3 c. green	1·00	50
73a		6 c. red	3·25	45
74		12 c. brown and green	1·25	3·50
75		15 c. blue	2·50	40
76		18 c. olive and red	2·00	3·50
77		30 c. violet and green	5·00	1·25
78		45 c. brown and red	2·50	30·00
79		75 c. yellow and violet	2·50	5·50
80		1 r. 50 black and red	5·50	85
81		2 r. 25 purple and green	40·00	2·50

1917. Inscr "POSTAGE & REVENUE".

98	**11**	2 c. brown and green	15	15
99		3 c. green	1·00	15
100		3 c. black	80	30
101		4 c. green	80	2·00
102		4 c. olive and red	4·75	14·00
103		5 c. brown	75	5·00
85		6 c. red	1·00	1·25
105		6 c. mauve	50	10
106		9 c. red	2·50	3·75
86		12 c. grey	65	1·00
108		12 c. red	45	20
87		15 c. blue	1·25	1·25
111		15 c. yellow	60	2·50
112		18 c. purple on yellow	2·25	10·00
113		20 c. blue	1·25	35
89b		25 c. black & red on yell	1·50	8·50
90		30 c. purple and olive	1·50	7·50
116		45 c. purple and orange	1·00	5·00
117		50 c. purple and black	2·00	2·25
93		75 c. black on green	1·40	13·00
119		1 r. purple and red	12·00	18·00
121		1 r. 50 purple & blue on bl	12·00	20·00
122		2 r. 25 green and violet	9·00	13·00
123		5 r. green and blue	50·00	£130

1935. Silver Jubilee. As T **13** of Antigua.

128	6 c. blue and black	80	1·50
129	12 c. green and blue	2·25	80
130	20 c. brown and blue	2·00	80
131	1 r. grey and purple	4·25	10·00

1937. Coronation. As T **2** of Aden.

132	6 c. green	35	15
133	12 c. orange	50	30
134	20 c. blue	70	65

14 Coco-de-mer Palm

1938.

135a	**14**	2 c. brown	20	75
136	–	3 c. green	6·50	1·25
136a	–	3 c. orange	1·25	50
137	–	6 c. orange	6·50	2·50
137ab	–	6 c. green	55	1·00
138	**14**	9 c. red	10·00	2·00
138a	–	9 c. blue	4·00	40
139	–	12 c. mauve	38·00	1·25
139ab	–	15 c. red	3·75	1·50
139ca	**14**	18 c. red	3·25	1·50
140	–	20 c. blue	42·00	5·00
140ab	–	20 c. yellow	2·50	1·50
141	**14**	25 c. brown	60·00	14·00
142	–	30 c. red	60·00	9·00
142ab	–	30 c. blue	1·75	2·50
143a	–	45 c. brown	1·75	1·75
144b	**14**	50 c. violet	60	1·50
145	–	75 c. blue	85·00	38·00
145ab	–	75 c. mauve	1·25	2·00
146	–	1 r. green	£100	48·00
146ab	–	1 r. black	1·25	2·25
147a	**14**	1 r. 50 blue	4·50	4·50
148a	–	2 r. 25 olive	10·00	11·00
149	–	5 r. red	8·00	3·25

DESIGNS—VERT: 3, 12, 15, 30, 75 c., 2 r. 25, Giant tortoise. HORIZ: 6, 20, 45 c., 1, 5 r. Fishing pirogue.

1946. Victory. As T **9** of Aden.

150	9 c. blue	10	10
151	30 c. blue	10	10

1948. Silver Wedding. As T **10/11** of Aden.

152	9 c. blue	15	25
153	5 r. red	11·00	22·00

1949. U.P.U. As T **20/23** of Antigua.

154	18 c. mauve	30	15
155	50 c. purple	1·25	50
156	1 r. grey	40	15
157	2 r. 25 olive	50	60

17 Sailfish

21 "La Pierre de Possession"

1952. Full face portrait.

158	**17**	2 c. lilac	50	70
159	–	3 c. orange	50	30
160	–	9 c. blue	50	1·25
161	–	15 c. green	40	75
162	–	18 c. lake	65	20
163	–	20 c. yellow	90	60
164	–	25 c. red	70	70
165	**17**	40 c. blue	70	90
166	–	45 c. brown	70	30
167	–	50 c. violet	1·25	60
168	–	1 r. black	2·50	1·75
169	–	1 r. 50 blue	5·50	10·00
170	–	2 r. 25 olive	7·50	10·00
171	–	5 r. red	7·50	12·00
172	**17**	10 r. green	15·00	24·00

DESIGNS—VERT: 2, 25 c., 2 r. 25, Giant tortoise; 9, 50 c., 1 r. 50, Coco-de-mer palm. HORIZ: 15, 20, 45 c. Fishing pirogue; 18 c., 1, 5 r. Map of Indian Ocean.

1953. Coronation. As T **13** of Aden.

173	9 c. black and blue	50	50

1954. Designs as 1952 but with portrait of Queen Elizabeth II.

174	2 c. lilac	10	10
175	3 c. orange	10	10
175a	5 c. violet	30	30
176	9 c. blue	10	10
176a	10 c. blue (as 9 c.)	40	60
177	15 c. green	20	15
178	18 c. lake	10	10
179	20 c. yellow	30	20
180	25 c. red	60	85
180a	35 c. lake (as 18 c.)	2·75	90
181	40 c. blue	30	25
182	45 c. brown	20	15
183	50 c. violet	30	20
183a	70 c. brown (as 45 c.)	4·50	1·25
184	1 r. black	50	40
185	1 r. 50 blue	3·50	3·75
186	2 r. 25 olive	3·50	7·00
187	5 r. red	18·00	8·00
188	10 r. green	28·00	18·00

NEW DESIGN: 5 c. Seychelles flying fox.

1956. Bicent of "La Pierre de Possession".

189	21	40 c. blue	15	15
190		1 r. black	15	15

1957. No. 182 surch **5 cents** and bars.

191	5 c. on 45 c. brown	15	10

23 Mauritius 6d. Stamp with Seychelles "B 64" Cancellation

1961. Cent of First Seychelles Post Office.

193	23	10 c. blue, black and purple	30	10
194		35 c. blue, black and green	60	10
195		2 r. 25 blue, black & brown	1·10	45

24 Black Parrot

40 Colony's Badge

1962. Multicoloured.

196	5 c. Type **24**	2·00	10
234	10 c. Vanilla vine	30	15
198	15 c. Fisherman	30	10
199	20 c. Denis Is. Lighthouse	30	10
200	25 c. Clock Tower, Victoria	30	10
200a	30 c. Anse Royale Bay	4·00	3·50
201	35 c. Anse Royale Bay	1·75	2·00
202	40 c. Government House	20	85
203	45 c. Fishing pirogue	3·50	3·75
204	50 c. Cascade Church	40	25
236	60 c. red, blue and brown (Flying fox)	1·75	45
205	70 c. ultramarine and blue (Sailfish)	6·00	3·00
206	75 c. Coco-de-mer palm	2·25	3·50
237	85 c. ultramarine and blue (Sailfish)	90	40
207	1 r. Cinnamon	30	10
208	1 r. 50 Copra	5·50	6·00
209	2 r. 25 Map	5·50	4·50
210	3 r. 50 Land settlement	2·25	5·50
211	5 r. Regina Mundi Convent	3·50	2·50
212	10 r. Type **40**	12·00	4·50

The 30, 35, 40, 85 c., 1, 1 r. 50, 2 r. 25, 3 r. 50 and 5 r. are horiz.

No. 236 is 23 × 25 mm.

1963. Freedom from Hunger. As T **28** of Aden.

213	70 c. violet	60	25

1963. Cent of Red Cross. As T **33** of Antigua.

214	10 c. red and black	25	10
215	75 c. red and blue	75	40

1965. Surch.

216	45 c. on 35 c. (No. 201)	10	15
217	75 c. on 70 c. (No. 205)	20	15

1965. Cent of I.T.U. As T **36** of Antigua.

218	5 c. orange and blue	10	10
219	1 r. 50 mauve and green	50	25

1965. I.C.Y. As T **37** of Antigua.

220	5 c. purple and turquoise	10	10
221	40 c. green and lavender	20	20

1966. Churchill Commem. As T **38** of Antigua.

222	5 c. blue	15	10
223	15 c. green	35	10
224	75 c. brown	60	10
225	1 r. 50 violet	90	60

1966. World Cup Football Championship. As T **40** of Antigua.

226	15 c. multicoloured	20	10
227	1 r. multicoloured	35	20

1966. Inauguration of W.H.O. Headquarters, Geneva. As T **41** of Antigua.

228	20 c. black, green and blue	15	10
229	30 c. black, purple and ochre	25	20

1966. 20th Anniv of U.N.E.S.C.O. As T **54/6** of Antigua.

230	15 c. multicoloured	20	10
231	1 r. yellow, violet and olive	35	10
232	5 r. black, purple and orange	80	1·00

1967. Universal Adult Suffrage. Nos. 198, 203, 206 and 210 optd **UNIVERSAL ADULT SUFFRAGE 1967**.

238	15 c. multicoloured	10	10
239	45 c. multicoloured	10	10
240	75 c. multicoloured	10	10
241	3 r. 50 multicoloured	20	15

44 Money Cowrie, Mole Cowrie and Tiger Cowrie

1967. International Tourist Year. Mult.

242	15 c. Type **44**	20	10
243	40 c. Beech cone, textile or cloth of gold cone and Virgin cone	25	10
244	1 r. Arthritic spider conch	35	10
245	2 r. 25 Subulate auger and trumpet triton shells	60	90

1968. Nos. 202/3 and 206 surch.

246	30 c. on 40 c. multicoloured	10	10
247	60 c. on 45 c. multicoloured	15	10
248	85 c. on 75 c. multicoloured	20	15

49 Farmer with Wife and Children at Sunset

1968. Human Rights Year.

249	49	20 c. multicoloured	10	10
250		50 c. multicoloured	10	10
251		85 c. multicoloured	10	10
252		2 r. 25 multicoloured	20	75

50 Expedition landing at Anse Possession

54 Apollo Launch

1968. Bicent of First Landing on Praslin. Mult.

253	20 c. Type **50**	30	10
254	50 c. French warships at anchor (vert)	35	15
255	85 c. Coco-de-mer and Black parrot (vert)	70	20
256	2 r. 25 French warships under sail	70	1·50

1969. First Man on the Moon. Multicoloured.

257	5 c. Type **54**	10	30
258	20 c. Module leaving mother ship for the Moon	15	10
259	50 c. Astronauts and Space Module on the Moon	20	15
260	65 c. Tracking station	25	15
261	2 r. 25 Moon craters with Earth on the "Horizon"	45	1·50

59 Picault's Landing, 1742

1969. Multicoloured.

262	5 c. Type **59**	10	10
263	10 c. U.S. satellite-tracking station	10	10
264	15 c. "Konigsberg I" (German cruiser) at Aldabra, 1914	2·25	2·00
265	20 c. Fleet re-fuelling off St. Anne, 1939-45	70	10
266	25 c. Exiled Ashanti King, Prempeh	20	10
267	30 c. Laying Stone of Possession, 1756	1·00	3·25
268	40 c. As 30 c.	1·50	1·25
269	50 c. Pirates and treasures	30	15
270	60 c. Corsairs attacking merchantman	1·00	1·50
271	65 c. As 60 c.	5·00	6·00
272	85 c. Impression of proposed airport	1·75	1·75
273a	95 c. As 85 c.	4·50	3·25
274	1 r. French Governor capitulating to British naval officer, 1794	35	15
275	1 r. 50 H.M.S. "Sybille" (frigate) and "Chiffone" (French frigate) in battle, 1801	1·75	2·00
276	3 r. 50 Visit of the Duke of Edinburgh, 1956	1·50	2·00
277	5 r. Chevalier Queau de Quincy	1·50	2·75
278	10 r. Indian Ocean chart, 1574	3·25	6·00
279	15 r. Badge of Seychelles	4·00	11·00

NOTE: The design of No. 264 incorrectly shows the vessel "Konigsberg II" and date "1915".

74 White Terns, French Warship and Island

1970. Bicentenary of First Settlement, St Anne Island. Multicoloured.

280	20 c. Type **74**	60	10
281	50 c. Spot-finned flyingfish, ship and island	40	10
282	85 c. Compass and chart	40	10
283	3 r. 50 Anchor on sea-bed	60	80

78 Girl and Optician's Chart

1970. Centenary of British Red Cross. Mult.

284	20 c. Type **78**	40	10
285	50 c. Baby, scales and milk bottles	40	10
286	85 c. Woman with child and umbrella (vert)	40	10
287	3 r. 50 Red Cross local headquarters building	1·50	2·50

79 Pitcher Plant

81 Piper Navajo

1970. Flowers. Multicoloured.

288	20 c. Type **79**	35	15
289	50 c. Wild vanilla	45	15
290	85 c. Tropic-bird orchid	1·40	30
291	3 r. 50 Vare hibiscus	2·00	1·50

1971. Airport Completion. Multicoloured.

294	5 c. Type **81**	20	10
295	20 c. Westland Wessex HAS-1 helicopter	45	10
296	50 c. Consolidated Catalina amphibian (horiz)	60	10
297	60 c. Grumman Albatross	65	10
298	85 c. Short "G" Class flying boat "Golden Hind" (horiz)	85	10
299	3 r. 50 Vickers Supermarine Walrus Mk I amphibian (horiz)	4·50	3·00

82 Santa Claus delivering Gifts (Jean-Claude Waye Hive)

1971. Christmas. Multicoloured.

300	10 c. Type **82**	10	10
301	15 c. Santa Claus seated on turtle (Edison Theresine)	10	10
302	3 r. 50 Santa Claus landing on island (Isabelle Tirant)	40	70

1971. Nos. 267, 270 and 272 surch.

303	40 c. on 30 c. multicoloured	30	55
304	65 c. on 60 c. multicoloured	40	75
305	95 c. on 85 c. multicoloured	45	1·00

1972. Royal Visit. Nos. 265 and 277 optd **ROYAL VISIT 1972**.

306	20 c. multicoloured	15	20
307	5 r. multicoloured	1·50	2·50

85 Seychelles Brush Warbler

86 Fireworks Display

1972. Rare Seychelles Birds. Multicoloured.

308	5 c. Type **85**	55	50
309	20 c. Bare-legged scops owl	1·75	50
310	50 c. Seychelles blue pigeon	1·75	65
311	65 c. Seychelles magpie robin	2·25	75
312	95 c. Seychelles paradise flycatcher	2·50	2·50
313	3 r. 50 Seychelles kestrel	7·00	11·00

1972. "Festival '72". Multicoloured.

315	10 c. Type **86**	10	10
316	15 c. Pirogue race (horiz)	10	10
317	25 c. Floats and costumes	10	10
318	5 r. Water skiing (horiz)	60	80

1972. Royal Silver Wedding. As T **52** of Ascension, but with Giant Tortoise and Sailfish in background.

319	95 c. blue	15	10
320	1 r. 50 brown	15	10

1973. Royal Wedding. As T **47** of Anguilla. Multicoloured, background colours given.

321	95 c. brown	10	10
322	1 r. 50 blue	10	10

88 Seychelles Squirrelfish

1974. Fishes. Multicoloured.

323	20 c. Type **88**	25	15
324	50 c. Harlequin filefish	35	15
325	95 c. Pennant coralfish ("Papillon")	40	40
326	1 r. 50 Oriental sweetlips ("Peau d'ane canal")	85	1·50

89 Globe and Letter

1974. Centenary of U.P.U. Multicoloured.

327	20 c. Type **89**	10	10
328	50 c. Globe and radio beacon	20	10
329	95 c. Globe and postmark	35	40
330	1 r. 50 Emblems within "UPU"	50	70

90 Sir Winston Churchill

1974. Birth Centenary of Sir Winston Churchill. Multicoloured.

331	95 c. Type **90**	20	15
332	1 r. 50 Profile portrait	35	40

1975. Visit of Liner "Queen Elizabeth II". Nos. 265, 269, 273a and 275 optd **VISIT OF Q.E. II** and silhouette of liner.

334	20 c. multicoloured	15	15
335	50 c. multicoloured	20	20
336	95 c. multicoloured	25	40
337	1 r. 50 multicoloured	35	80

1975. Internal Self-Government. Nos. 265, 271, 274 and 276 optd **INTERNAL SELF-GOVERNMENT OCTOBER 1975**.

338	20 c. multicoloured	15	15
339	65 c. multicoloured	25	30
340	1 r. multicoloured	30	35
341	3 r. 50 multicoloured	75	1·50

93 Queen Elizabeth I

94 Map of Praslin and Postmark

1975. International Women's Year. Mult.

342	10 c. Type **93**	10	10
343	15 c. Gladys Aylward	10	10
344	20 c. Elizabeth Fry	10	10
345	25 c. Emmeline Pankhurst	10	10
346	65 c. Florence Nightingale	25	20
347	1 r. Amy Johnson	40	35
348	1 r. 50 Joan of Arc	50	80
349	3 r. 50 Eleanor Roosevelt	1·50	2·75

1976. Rural Posts. Multicoloured.

350	20 c. Type **94**	20	10
351	65 c. La Digue	30	20
352	1 r. Mahe with Victoria postmark	35	25
353	1 r. 50 Mahe with Anse Royale postmark	55	1·25

Nos. 350/53 show maps and postmarks.

95 First Landing, 1609 (inset portrait of Premier James Mancham)

1976. Independence. Multicoloured.

355	20 c. Type **95**	15	10
356	25 c. The Possession Stone	15	10
357	40 c. First settlers, 1770	20	15
358	75 c. Chevalier Queau de Quincy	25	20
359	1 r. Sir Bickham Sweet-Escott	25	20
360	1 r. 25 Legislative Building	40	50
361	1 r. 50 Seychelles badge	45	60
362	3 r. 50 Seychelles flag	90	1·60

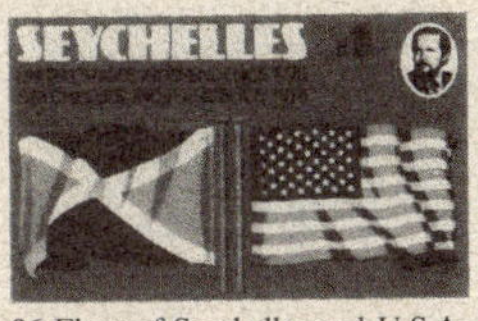

96 Flags of Seychelles and U.S.A.

1976. Seychelles Independence and American Bicent of Independence. Multicoloured.

363	1 r. Type **96**	25	15
364	10 r. Statehouses of Seychelles and Philadelphia	1·50	2·50

97 Swimming

1976. Olympic Games, Montreal.

365	**97**	20 c. blue, lt blue & brown	10	10
366	–	65 c. lt green, green & grey	35	10
367	–	1 r. brown, blue and grey	35	10
368	–	3 r. 50 light red, red & grey	50	2·25

DESIGNS: 65 c. Hockey; 1 r. Basketball; 3 r. 50, Football.

98 Seychelles Paradise Flycatcher

1976. 4th Pan-African Ornithological Congress, Seychelles. Multicoloured.

369	20 c. Type **98**	40	20
370	1 r. 25 Seychelles sunbird (horiz)	1·10	1·00
371	1 r. 50 Seychelles brown white eye (horiz)	1·50	1·25
372	5 r. Black parrot	2·50	4·00

1976. Independence. Nos. 265, 269, 271, 273a, 274 and 276/9 optd **Independence 1976** or surch also.

374	20 c. Fleet re-fuelling off St. Anne, 1939–45	70	1·50
375	50 c. Pirates and treasure	60	1·75
376	95 c. Impression of proposed airport	1·25	1·75
377	1 r. French Governor capitulating to British naval officer, 1794	55	1·75
378	3 r. 50 Visit of Duke of Edinburgh, 1956	2·75	3·50
379	5 r. Chevalier Queau de Quincy	2·75	5·00
380	10 r. Indian Ocean chart, 1574	4·50	10·00
381	15 r. Badge of Seychelles	6·00	10·00
382	25 r. on 65 c. Corsairs attacking merchantman	8·00	16·00

100 Inauguration of George Washington

1976. Bicentenary of American Revolution.

383	**100**	1 c. deep red and red	10	10
384	–	2 c. violet and lilac	10	10
385	–	3 c. light blue and blue	10	10
386	–	4 c. brown and yellow	10	10
387	–	5 c. green and yellow	10	10
388	–	1 r. 50 brown & lt brown	60	35
389	–	3 r. 50 blue and green	70	70
390	–	5 r. brown and yellow	80	80
391	–	10 r. blue and light blue	1·25	1·50

DESIGNS: 2 c. Jefferson and Louisiana Purchase; 3 c. William Seward and Alaska Purchase; 4 c. Pony Express, 1860; 5 c. Lincoln's Emancipation Proclamation; 1 r. 50, Transcontinental Railroad, 1869; 3 r. 50, Wright Brothers flight, 1903; 5 r. Henry Ford's assembly-line, 1913; 10 r. J. F. Kennedy and 1969 Moon-landing.

101 Silhouette of the Islands

1977. Silver Jubilee. Multicoloured.

393	20 c. Type **101**	10	10
394	40 c. Silhouette (different)	10	10
395	50 c. The Orb	10	10
396	1 r. St. Edward's Crown	10	10
397	1 r. 25 Ampulla and Spoon	10	15
398	1 r. 50 Sceptre with Cross	10	15
399	5 r. Silhouette (different)	25	30
400	10 r. Silhouette (different)	45	60

The 50 c. to 1 r. 50 are vertical designs.

102 Cruiser "Aurora" and Flag

1977. 60th Anniv of Russian Revolution.

402	**102**	1 r. 50 multicoloured	55	30

103 Coral Scene

1977. Marine Life. Rupee face value shown as "Re" or "Rs". Multicoloured.

404A	5 c. Reef fish	30	90
405B	10 c. Hawksbill turtle	10	10
406B	15 c. Coco-de-mer	15	15
407A	20 c. Wild vanilla orchid	1·50	20
408A	25 c. "Hypolimnas misippus" (butterfly)	1·50	75
409B	40 c. Type **103**	15	10
410A	50 c. Giant tortoise	20	10
411A	75 c. Crayfish	20	10
412A	1 r. Madagascar red fody	1·25	10
413A	1 r. 25 White tern	1·25	20
414A	1 r. 50 Seychelles flying fox	1·50	20
736	3 r. Green gecko	2·50	3·00
415A	3 r. 50 As 3 r.	75	2·50
416A	5 r. Octopus	2·00	40
417A	10 r. Tiger cowrie	2·25	2·50
418A	15 r. Pitcher plant	2·25	2·50
419A	20 r. Coat of arms	2·50	2·50

The 40 c., 1 r., 1 r. 25 and 1 r. 50 values are horizontal, 31 × 27 mm. The 5, 10, 15 and 20 r. are vertical, 28 × 36 mm. The others are horizontal, 29 × 25 mm.

Nos. 405/12 and 414 exist with or without imprint date at foot.

For similar designs with rupee face values shown as "R" see Nos. 487a/94.

104 St. Roch Roman Catholic Church, Bel Ombre

1977. Christmas. Multicoloured.

420	20 c. Type **104**	10	10
421	1 r. Anglican cathedral, Victoria	10	10
422	1 r. 50 Roman Catholic cathedral, Victoria	15	10
423	5 r. St. Mark's Anglican church, Praslin	30	45

105 Liberation Day ringed on Calendar

106 Stamp Portraits of Edward VII, George V and George VI

1978. Liberation Day. Multicoloured.

424	40 c. Type **105**	10	10
425	1 r. 25 Hands holding bayonet, torch and flag	15	10
426	1 r. 50 Fisherman and farmer	15	15
427	5 r. Soldiers and rejoicing people	35	40

1978. 25th Anniv of Coronation. Mult.

428	40 c. Type **106**	10	10
429	1 r. 50 Queen Victoria and Elizabeth II	10	10
430	3 r. Queen Victoria Monument	20	25
431	5 r. Queen's Building, Victoria	30	35

107 Gardenia

1978. Wildlife. Multicoloured.

433	40 c. Type **107**	15	10
434	1 r. 25 Seychelles magpie robin	1·10	50
435	1 r. 50 Seychelles paradise flycatcher	1·10	50
436	5 r. Green turtle	1·10	1·25

108 Possession Stone

1978. Bicentenary of Victoria. Multicoloured.

437	20 c. Type **108**	10	10
438	1 r. 25 Plan of 1782 "L' Etablissement"	15	15
439	1 r. 50 Clock Tower	15	15
440	5 r. Bust of Pierre Poivre	40	50

109 Seychelles Fody

110 Patrice Lumumba

1979. Birds (1st series). Multicoloured.

441	2 r. Type **109**	55	50
442	2 r. Green heron	55	50
443	2 r. Thick-billed Bulbul	55	50
444	2 r. Seychelles cave swiftlet	55	50
445	2 r. Grey-headed lovebird	55	50

See also Nos. 463/7, 500/4 and 523/7.

1979. Africa Liberation Heroes.

446	**110**	40 c. black, violet and lilac	10	10
447	–	2 r. black, blue & lt blue	20	25
448	–	2 r. 25 black, brn & orge	20	30
449	–	5 r. black, olive and green	45	80

DESIGNS: 2 r. Kwame Nkrumah; 2 r. 25, Dr. Eduardo Mondlane; 5 r. Hamilcar Cabral.

111 1978 5 r. Liberation Day Commemorative and Sir Rowland Hill

113 The Herald Angel

112 Child with Book

1979. Death Cent of Sir Rowland Hill. Mult.

450	40 c. Type **111**	10	10
451	2 r. 25 1972 50 c. Seychelles blue pigeon commemorative	35	40
452	3 r. 1962 50 c. definitive	45	55

1979. International Year of the Child. Multicoloured.

454	40 c. Type **112**	10	10
455	2 r. 25 Children of different races	15	30
456	3 r. Young child with ball (vert)	20	45
457	5 r. Girl with glove puppet (vert)	35	65

1979. Christmas. Multicoloured.

458	20 c. Type **113**	10	10
459	2 r. 25 The Virgin and Child	30	40
460	3 r. The Three Kings (horiz)	40	55

1980. No. 415 surch **R.1.10**.

462	1 r. 10 on 3 r. 50 Green gecko	30	30

115 Seychelles Kestrel

117 Sprinting

116 10 Rupees Banknote

1980. Birds (2nd series). Seychelles Kestrel. Multicoloured.

463	2 r. Type **115**	70	50
464	2 r. Pair of Seychelles kestrels	70	50
465	2 r. Seychelles kestrel with eggs	70	50
466	2 r. Seychelles kestrel on nest with chick	70	50
467	2 r. Seychelles kestrel chicks in nest	70	50

1980. "London 1980" International Stamp Exhibition. Currency Notes. Multicoloured.

468	40 c. Type **116**	15	10
469	1 r. 50 25 rupees	30	15
470	2 r. 25 50 rupees (vert)	40	25
471	5 r. 100 rupees (vert)	80	75

1980. Olympic Games, Moscow. Mult

473	40 c. Type **117**	10	10
474	2 r. 25 Weightlifting	20	20
475	3 r. Boxing	30	30
476	5 r. Yachting	60	40

118 Boeing 747-200 Airliner

1980. Int Tourism Conference, Manila. Mult.

478	40 c. Type **118**	10	10
479	2 r. 25 Bus	25	30
480	3 r. Cruise liner	35	40
481	5 r. "La Belle Coralline" (tourist launch)	55	65

119 Female Palm

121 Male White Tern

120 Vasco da Gama's "Sao Gabriel", 1497

1980. Coco-de-Mer (palms). Multicoloured.

482	40 c. Type **119**	10	10
483	2 r. 25 Male palm	25	20
484	3 r. Artefacts	40	35
485	5 r. Fisherman's gourd	55	55

1981. As Nos. 412/14, 415 (with new value), and 416/19 but face values redrawn as "R" instead of "Re" or "Rs".

487a	1 r. Madagascar red fody	50	50
488	1 r. 10 Green gecko	40	50
489	1 r. 25 White tern	2·50	1·00
490	1 r. 50 Seychelles flying fox	45	60
491	5 r. Octopus	1·25	1·40
492	10 r. Tiger cowrie	2·75	3·25
493	15 r. Pitcher plant	3·75	4·50
494	20 r. Seychelles coat of arms	5·00	6·00

1981. Ships. Multicoloured.

495	40 c. Type **120**	15	10
496	2 r. 25 Mascarenhas' caravel, 1505	50	55
497	3 r. 50 Darwin's H.M.S. "Beagle", 1831	70	1·00
498	5 r. "Queen Elizabeth 2" (liner), 1968	85	1·40

1981. Birds (3rd series). White Tern. Multicoloured.

500	2 r. Type **121**	90	65
501	2 r. Pair of white terns	90	65
502	2 r. Female white tern	90	65
503	2 r. Female white tern on nest and egg	90	65
504	2 r. White tern and chick	90	65

1981. Royal Wedding. Royal Yachts. As T **26/27** of Kiribati. Multicoloured.

505	1 r. 50 "Victoria and Albert I"	15	25
506	1 r. 50 Prince Charles and Lady Diana Spencer	50	75
507	5 r. "Cleveland"	40	60
513	5 r. As No. 506	80	1·75
509	10 r. "Britannia"	80	1·50
510	10 r. As No. 506	2·00	2·75

122 Britten Norman Islander

1981. 10th Anniv of Opening of Seychelles International Airport. Aircraft. Multicoloured.

514	40 c. Type **122**	15	10
515	2 r. 25 Britten Norman "long nose" Trislander	55	45
516	3 r. 50 Vickers Super VC-10 airliner	80	70
517	5 r. Boeing 747-100 airliner	1·00	1·00

123 Seychelles Flying Foxes in Flight

124 Chinese Little Bittern (male)

1981. Seychelles Flying Fox (Roussette). Multicoloured.

518	40 c. Type **123**	10	10
519	2 r. 25 Flying fox eating	30	45
520	3 r. Flying fox climbing across tree branch	45	70
521	5 r. Flying fox hanging from tree branch	55	1·00

1982. Birds (4th series). Chinese Little Bittern. Multicoloured.

523	3 r. Type **124**	2·00	1·00
524	3 r. Chinese little bittern (female)	2·00	1·00
525	3 r. Hen on nest	2·00	1·00
526	3 r. Nest and eggs	2·00	1·00
527	3 r. Hen with chicks	2·00	1·00

125 Silhouette Island and La Digue

1982. Modern Maps. Multicoloured.

528	40 c. Type **125**	15	10
529	1 r. 50 Denis and Bird Islands	30	25
530	2 r. 75 Praslin	55	65
531	7 r. Mahe	1·00	2·00

126 "Education"

1982. 5th Anniv of Liberation. Mult.

533	40 c. Type **126**	10	10
534	1 r. 75 "Health"	25	25
535	2 r. 75 "Agriculture"	30	45
536	7 r. "Construction"	80	1·40

127 Tourist Board Emblem

1982. Tourism. Multicoloured.

538	1 r. 75 Type **127**	25	35
539	1 r. 75 Northolme Hotel	25	35
540	1 r. 75 Reef Hotel	25	35
541	1 r. 75 Barbarous Beach Hotel	25	35
542	1 r. 75 Coral Strand Hotel	25	35
543	1 r. 75 Beau Vallon Bay Hotel	25	35
544	1 r. 75 Fisherman's Cove Hotel	25	35
545	1 r. 75 Mahe Beach Hotel	25	35

128 Tata Bus

1982. Land Transport. Multicoloured.

546	20 c. Type **128**	10	10
547	1 r. 75 Mini-moke	25	25
548	2 r. 75 Ox-cart	40	55
549	7 r. Truck	1·10	1·75

129 Radio Seychelles Control Room

1983. World Communications Year. Mult.

550	40 c. Type **129**	10	10
551	2 r. 75 Satellite Earth station	35	50
552	3 r. 50 Radio Seychelles television control room	60	75
553	5 r. Postal services sorting office	80	1·25

130 Agricultural Experimental Station

1983. Commonwealth Day. Multicoloured.

554	40 c. Type **130**	10	10
555	2 r. 75 Food processing plant	25	40
556	3 r. 50 Unloading fish catch	40	60
557	7 r. Seychelles flag	65	1·40

131 Denis Island Lighthouse

1983. Famous Landmarks. Multicoloured.

558	40 c. Type **131**	10	10
559	2 r. 75 Victoria Hospital	30	45
560	3 r. 50 Supreme Court	35	65
561	7 r. State House	55	1·40

132 "Royal Vauxhall" Balloon, 1836

1983. Bicentenary of Manned Flight. Mult.

563	40 c. Type **132**	15	10
564	1 r. 75 De Havilland D.H.50J	50	30
565	2 r. 75 Grumman Albatros flying boat	75	55
566	7 r. Swearingen Merlin IIIA	1·60	1·75

133 Douglas DC-10-30

1983. 1st International Flight of Air Seychelles.

567	**133** 2 r. multicoloured	1·75	1·75

134 Swamp Plant and Moorhen

137 Victoria Port

136 Coconut Vessel

1983. Centenary Visit to Seychelles by Marianne North (botanic artist). Multicoloured.

568	40 c. Type **134**	15	10
569	1 r. 75 "Wormia flagellaria"	50	30
570	2 r. 75 Asiatic pancratium	65	60
571	7 r. Pitcher plant	1·25	1·60

1983. Nos. 505/7, 509/10 and 513 surch.

573	50 c. on 1 r. 50 "Victoria and Albert I"	15	20
574	50 c. on 1 r. 50 Prince Charles and Lady Diana Spencer	40	70
575	2 r. 25 on 5 r. "Clevland"	45	50
576	2 r. 25 on 5 r. As No. 574	1·25	2·25
577	3 r. 75 on 10 r. "Britannia"	75	80
578	3 r. 75 on 10 r. As No. 574	1·60	2·75

1984. Traditional Handicrafts. Multicoloured.

579	50 c. Type **136**	15	10
580	2 r. Scarf and doll	40	70
581	3 r. Coconut-fibre roses	45	1·00
582	10 r. Carved fishing boat and doll	1·25	3·50

1984. 250th Anniv of "Lloyd's List" (newspaper). Multicoloured.

583	50 c. Type **137**	25	10
584	2 r. Cargo liner	65	55
585	3 r. "Sun Viking" (liner)	90	80
586	10 r. Loss of R.F.A. "Ennerdale II" (tanker)	2·40	2·75

138 Old S.P.U.P. Office

1984. 20th Anniv of Seychelles People's United Party. Multicoloured.

587	50 c. Type **138**	10	10
588	2 r. Liberation statue (vert)	30	50
589	3 r. New S.P.U.D. office	40	80
590	10 r. President Rene (vert)	1·25	3·25

140 Long Jumping

1984. Olympic Games, Los Angeles. Mult.

592	50 c. Type **140**	10	10
593	2 r. Boxing	40	45
594	3 r. Swimming	60	75
595	10 r. Weightlifting	1·75	2·50

141 Sub-aqua Diving

1984. Water Sports. Multicoloured.

597	50 c. Type **141**	20	10
598	2 r. Paraskiing	80	45
599	3 r. Sailing	1·00	75
600	10 r. Water-skiing	2·40	2·50

142 Humpback Whale

1984. Whale Conservation. Multicoloured.

601	50 c. Type **142**	1·50	20
602	2 r. Sperm whale	2·75	1·75
603	3 r. Black right whale	3·00	2·50
604	10 r. Blue whale	6·00	8·00

143 Two Bare-legged Scops Owls in Tree

144 Giant Tortoises

1985. Birth Bicentenary of John J. Audubon (ornithologist). Bare-legged Scops Owl. Mult.

605	50 c. Type **143**	1·75	50
606	2 r. Owl on branch	2·50	2·25
607	3 r. Owl in flight	2·75	2·75
608	10 r. Owl on ground	5·50	8·50

1985. "Expo '85" World Fair, Japan. Multicoloured.

609	50 c. Type **144**	70	30
610	2 r. White terns	1·75	1·75
611	3 r. Windsurfing	1·75	2·25
612	5 r. Coco-de-mer	1·75	3·00

145 The Queen Mother with Princess Anne and Prince Andrew, 1970

147 Agriculture Students

146 Boxing

1985. Life and Times of Queen Elizabeth the Queen Mother. Multicoloured.

614	50 c. The Queen Mother in 1930	10	10
615	2 r. Type **145**	35	50
616	3 r. On her 75th Birthday . .	50	70
617	5 r. With Prince Henry at his christening (from photo by Lord Snowdon)	80	1·25

1985. 2nd Indian Ocean Islands Games. Multicoloured.

619	50 c. Type **146**	15	10
620	2 r. Football	55	50
621	3 r. Swimming	75	75
622	10 r. Windsurfing	2·40	2·75

1985. Acquisition of First Air Seychelles "Airbus". As No. 735, but additionally inscribed "AIR SEYCHELLES FIRST AIRBUS".

623	1 r. 25 White tern	1·75	1·75

1985. International Youth Year. Mult.

624	50 c. Type **147**	10	10
625	2 r. Construction students building wall	55	50
626	3 r. Carpentry students . . .	70	80
627	10 r. Science students	2·25	3·00

148 Ford "Model T" (1919)

1985. Vintage Cars. Multicoloured.

628	50 c. Type **148**	50	20
629	2 r. Austin "Seven" (1922) . .	1·50	1·00
630	3 r. Morris "Oxford" (1924) .	1·60	1·40
631	10 r. Humber "Coupe" (1929)	3·00	4·50

149 Five Foot Transit Instrument

150 Ballerina

1986. Appearance of Halley's Comet. Mult.

632	50 c. Type **149**	30	10
633	2 r. Eight foot quadrant . . .	1·00	50
634	3 r. Comet's orbit	1·25	75
635	10 r. Edmond Halley	2·25	2·40

1986. Visit of Ballet du Louvre Company, "Giselle". Multicoloured.

636	2 r. Type **150**	50	60
637	3 r. Male dancer	60	90

1986. 60th Birthday of Queen Elizabeth II. As T **110** of Ascension. Multicoloured.

639	50 c. Wedding photograph, 1947	10	10
640	1 r. 25 At State Opening of Parliament, 1982	25	35
641	2 r. Queen accepting bouquet, Seychelles, 1972	30	50
642	3 r. On board Royal Yacht "Britannia", Qatar, 1979 . .	40	75
643	5 r. At Crown Agents Head Office, London, 1983 . . .	60	1·25

151 Ferry to La Digue

1986. "Ameripex '86" Int Stamp Exhibition, Chicago. Inter-island Communications. Multicoloured.

644	50 c. Type **151**	60	10
645	2 r. Telephone kiosk (vert) . .	1·25	60
646	3 r. Post Office counter, Victoria (vert)	1·40	85
647	7 r. Air Seychelles Britten Norman "short nose" Trislander aircraft	4·00	2·00

152 Crests of Seychelles and Knights of Malta

154 Pope John Paul at Seychelles Airport

1986. Seychelles Knights of Malta Day.

648	**152**	5 r. multicoloured	1·10	1·40

1986. Royal Wedding. As T **112** of Ascension. Multicoloured.

651	2 r. Prince Andrew and Miss Sarah Ferguson	35	50
652	10 r. Prince Andrew boarding Wessex helicopter, 1983 . .	1·25	2·40

1986. International Creole Day. No. 487 optd **LAZOURNEN ENTERNASYONAL KREOL**.

653	1 r. Madagascar red fody . .	1·50	1·00

1986. Visit of Pope John Paul II. Designs showing Pope and Seychelles scenes. Multicoloured.

654	50 c. Type **154**	75	30
655	2 r. Catholic Cathedral, Victoria	2·00	1·25
656	3 r. Baie Lazare Parish Church	2·50	2·00
657	10 r. Aerial view of People's Stadium	4·25	6·00

155 "Melanitis leda"

1987. Butterflies. Multicoloured.

659	1 r. Type **155**	1·00	30
660	2 r. "Phalanta philiberti" . .	1·60	85
661	3 r. "Danaus chrysippus" . .	1·90	1·60
662	10 r. "Euploea mitra"	5·00	6·00

156 Royal Oak Scallop

157 Statue of Liberation

1987. Sea Shells. Multicoloured.

663	1 r. Type **156**	1·25	30
664	2 r. Golden thorny oyster . .	2·00	85
665	3 r. Ventral or single harp and ornate pitar venus	2·25	1·60
666	10 r. Silver conch	5·50	6·00

1987. 10th Anniv of Liberation. Mult.

667	1 r. Type **157**	20	25
668	2 r. Seychelles hospital (horiz)	35	50
669	3 r. Orphanage village (horiz)	55	75
670	10 r. Proposed Sail-fish Monument	1·40	2·50

158 Seychelles Savings Bank, Praslin

1987. Centenary of Banking in Seychelles.

671	**158**	1 r. deep green and green	20	25
672	–	2 r. brown and orange .	35	50
673	–	10 r. deep blue and blue .	1·40	2·50

DESIGNS: 2 r. Development Bank; 10 r. Central Bank.

1987. Royal Ruby Wedding. Nos. 639/43 optd **40TH WEDDING ANNIVERSARY**.

674	50 c. Wedding photograph, 1947	15	15
675	1 r. 25 At State Opening of Parliament, 1982	25	40
676	2 r. Queen accepting bouquet, Seychelles, 1972	30	60
677	3 r. On board Royal Yacht "Britannia", Qatar, 1979 .	40	85
678	5 r. At Crown Agents Head Office, London, 1983 . . .	60	1·40

159 Tuna-canning Factory

1987. Seychelles Fishing Industry. Mult.

679	50 c. Type **159**	15	15
680	2 r. Trawler	45	50
681	3 r. Weighing catch	70	75
682	10 r. Unloading net	2·25	2·40

160 Water Sports

1988. Tourism. Multicoloured.

683	1 r. Type **160**	40	25
684	2 r. Speedboat and yachts . .	75	65
685	3 r. Yacht at anchor	1·10	1·25
686	10 r. Hotel at night	3·00	4·50

161 Young Turtles making for Sea

162 Shot Put

1988. The Green Turtle. Multicoloured.

687	2 r. Type **161**	1·50	2·00
688	2 r. Young turtles hatching . .	1·50	2·00
689	3 r. Female turtle leaving sea .	1·75	2·25
690	3 r. Female laying eggs	1·75	2·25

Nos. 687/8 and 689/90 were printed together, se-tenant, each pair forming a composite design.

•

1988. Olympic Games, Seoul. Multicoloured.

691	1 r. Type **162**	30	25
692	2 r. Type **162**	55	60
693	2 r. High jump	55	60
694	2 r. Gold medal winner on podium	55	60
695	2 r. Athletics	55	60
696	2 r. Javelin	55	60
697	3 r. As No. 694	60	65
698	4 r. As No. 695	80	85
699	5 r. As No. 696	1·00	1·10

1988. 300th Anniv of Lloyd's of London. As T **123** of Ascension. Multicoloured.

701	1 r. Leadenhall Street, 1928 . .	60	25
702	2 r. "Cinq Juin" (travelling post office) (horiz)	1·25	65
703	3 r. "Queen Elizabeth 2" (liner) (horiz)	1·75	1·10
704	10 r. Loss of "Hindenburg" (airship), 1937	4·50	4·00

163 Police Motorcyclists

1988. 1st Anniv of Defence Forces Day. Mult.

705	1 r. Type **163**	1·75	40
706	2 r. Hindustan Aircraft Chetak helicopter	3·00	2·25
707	3 r. "Andromanche" (patrol boat)	3·00	2·75
708	10 r. BRDM armoured car . .	6·75	8·50

164 Father Christmas with Basket of Presents

165 "Dendrobium sp"

1988. Christmas. Multicoloured.

709	50 c. Type **164**	15	10
710	2 r. Bird and gourd filled with presents	70	70
711	3 r. Father Christmas basket weaving	90	90
712	10 r. Christmas bauble and palm tree	2·50	3·00

1988. Orchids (1st series). Multicoloured.

713	1 r. Type **165**	45	25
714	2 r. Arachnis" hybrid (horiz) .	75	65
715	3 r. "Vanda caerulea"	95	95
716	10 r. "Dendrobium phalaenopsis" (horiz)	2·75	4·25

See also Nos. 767/70 and 795/8.

166 India 1976 25 p. Nehru Stamp

1989. Birth Centenary of Jawaharlal Nehru (Indian statesman). Each showing flags of Seychelles and India. Multicoloured.

724	2 r. Type **166**	75	50
725	10 r. Jawaharlal Nehru . . .	2·75	3·50

167 Pres. Rene addressing Rally at Old Party Office

169 Black Parrot and Map of Praslin

168 British Red Cross Ambulance, Franco-Prussian War, 1870

1989. 25th Anniv of Seychelles People's United Party. Multicoloured.

742	1 r. Type **167**	20	25
743	2 r. Women with Party flags and Maison du Peuple	40	45
744	3 r. President Rene making speech and Torch of Freedom	60	65
745	10 r. President Rene, Party flag and Torch of Freedom . .	2·00	2·50

1989. 20th Anniv of First Manned Landing on Moon. As T **126** of Ascension. Multicoloured.

746	1 r. Lift off of "Saturn 5" rocket	35	25
747	2 r. Crew of "Apollo 15" (30 × 30 mm)	65	65
748	3 r. "Apollo 15" emblem (30 × 30 mm)	80	90
749	5 r. James Irwin saluting U.S. flag on Moon	1·50	1·75

1989. 125th Anniv of International Red Cross.

751	**168**	1 r. black and red	1·50	35
752	–	2 r. black, green and red .	2·00	1·50
753	–	3 r. black and red	2·50	2·50
754	–	10 r. black and red . . .	7·50	9·00

DESIGNS: 2 r. "Liberty" (hospital ship), 1914–18; 3 r. Sunbeam "Standard" army ambulance, 1914–18; 10 r. "White Train" (hospital train), South Africa, 1899–1902.

1989. Island Birds. Multicoloured.

755	50 c. Type **169**	1·00	35
756	2 r. Sooty tern and Ile aux vaches	2·00	1·75
757	3 r. Seychelles magpie robin and Fregate	2·25	2·25
758	5 r. Roseate tern and Aride .	2·75	4·25

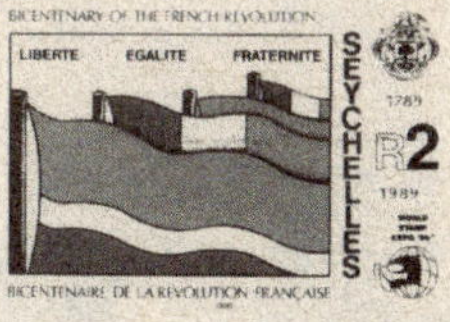

170 Flags of Seychelles and France

1989. Bicentenary of French Revolution and "World Stamp Expo '89". International Stamp Exhibition, Washington.

760	**170**	2 r. multicoloured	2·00	1·50
761	–	5 r. black, blue and red .	3·25	4·25

DESIGN: 5 r. Storming the Bastille, Paris, 1789.

171 Beau Vallon School

1989. 25th Anniv of African Development Bank. Multicoloured.

763	1 r. Type **171**	45	25
764	2 r. Seychelles Fishing Authority Headquarters	80	90
765	3 r. "Variola" (fishing boat) (vert)	2·25	2·25
766	10 r. "Deneb" (fishing boat) (vert)	6·00	8·00

172 "Disperis tripetaloides"

174 Fumiyo Sako

173 Seychelles 1903 2 c. and Great Britain 1880 1½d. Stamps

1990. Orchids (2nd series). Multicoloured.
767 1 r. Type **172** . . . . 1·50 40
768 2 r. "Vanilla phalaenopsis" . . 2·00 1·50
769 3 r. "Angraecum eburneum" subsp. "superbum" . . . . 2·25 2·25
770 10 r. "Polystachya concreta" . 5·50 7·00

1990. "Stamp World London '90" International Stamp Exhibition. Each showing stamps. Mult.
771 1 r. Type **173** 75 25
772 2 r. Seychelles 1917 25 c. and G.B. 1873 1s. . . . . 1·25 1·25
773 3 r. Seychelles 1917 2 c. and G.B. 1874 6d. . . . . 1·75 2·25
774 5 r. Seychelles 1890 2 c. and G.B. 1841 1d. red . . . . 2·50 3·50

1990. "EXPO 90" International Garden and Greenery Exhibition, Osaka. Multicoloured.
776 2 r. Type **174** . . . . 1·00 1·00
777 3 r. Male and female coco-de-mer palms . . . . 1·25 1·25
778 5 r. Pitcher plant and Aldabra lily 1·75 2·25
779 7 r. Arms of Seychelles and gardenia . . . . 2·50 3·00

175 Air Seychelles Boeing 767-200ER over Island

1990. Air Seychelles "Boeing 767-200ER" World Record-breaking Flight (1989).
781 **175** 3 r. multicoloured . . . . 2·25 2·50

1990. 90th Birthday of Queen Elizabeth the Queen Mother. As T **134** of Ascension.
782 2 r. multicoloured . . . . . . 1·25 75
783 10 r. black and violet . . . . 3·25 4·25
DESIGNS—(21 × 36 mm): 2 r. Queen Elizabeth in Coronation robes, 1937. (29 × 37 mm): 10 r. Queen Elizabeth visiting Lord Roberts Workshops, 1947.

176 Adult Class

177 Sega Dancers

1990. International Literacy Year. Mult.
784 1 r. Type **176** 75 25
785 2 r. Reading a letter . . . . 1·50 1·25
786 3 r. Following written instructions . . . . 2·00 2·00
787 10 r. Typewriter, calculator and crossword . . . . 4·50 7·00

1990. Kreol Festival. Sega Dancing. Mult.
788 2 r. Type **177** . . . . 1·50 1·60
789 2 r. Dancing couple (girl in yellow dress) . . . . 1·50 1·60
790 2 r. Female Sega dancer . . . 1·50 1·60
791 2 r. Dancing couple (girl in floral pattern skirt) . . . . 1·50 1·60
792 2 r. Dancing couple (girl in red patterned skirt) . . . . . . 1·50 1·60

178 Beach

1990. 1st Indian Ocean Regional Seminar on Petroleum Exploration. Multicoloured.
793 3 r. Type **178** . . . . 1·75 1·50
794 10 r. Geological map . . . . 5·25 6·50

1991. Orchids (3rd series). As T **172**. Mult.
795 1 r. "Bullbophyllum intertextum" . . . . 1·40 45
796 2 r. "Agrostophyllum occidentale" . . . . 2·00 1·75
797 3 r. "Vanilla planifolia" . . . 2·25 2·25
798 10 r. "Malaxis seychellarum" 5·50 6·50

1991. 65th Birthday of Queen Elizabeth II and 70th Birthday of Prince Philip. As T **139** of Ascension. Multicoloured.
799 4 r. Queen in evening dress . 1·60 2·00
800 4 r. Prince Philip in academic robes . . . . 1·60 2·00

179 "Precis rhadama"

1991. "Phila Nippon '91" International Stamp Exhibition, Tokyo. Butterflies. Mult.
801 1 r. 50 Type **179** . . . . . . 1·75 85
802 3 r. "Lampides boeticus" . . 2·25 2·25
803 3 r. 50 "Zizeeria knysna" . . 2·50 2·50
804 10 r. "Phalanta phalantha" . 6·75 7·50

180 "The Holy Virgin, Joseph, The Holy Child and St. John" (S. Vouillemont after Raphael)

181 Seychelles Brush Warbler

1991. Christmas. Woodcuts.
806 **180** 50 c. black, brown and red 50 15
807 – 1 r. black, brown and green 90 25
808 – 2 r. black, brown and blue 1·75 1·10
809 – 7 r. black, brown and blue 4·50 6·50
DESIGNS: 1 r. "Holy Virgin, the Child and Angel" (A. Blooting after Van Dyck); 2 r. "The Holy Family, St. John and St. Anna" (L. Vorsterman after Rubens); 7 r. "The Holy Family, Angel and St. Cathrin" (C. Bloemaert).

1992. 40th Anniv of Queen Elizabeth II's Accession. As T **143** of Ascension. Mult.
810 1 r. Seychelles coastline . . . 55 25
811 1 r. 50 Clock Tower, Victoria 70 40
812 3 r. Victoria harbour . . . . 1·40 1·50
813 3 r. 50 Three portraits of Queen Elizabeth . . . . 1·50 1·75
814 5 r. Queen Elizabeth II . . . 1·60 2·50

1993. Flora and Fauna. Multicoloured.
815 10 c. Type **181** 10 10
816 25 c. Bronze gecko (vert) . . 10 10
817 50 c. Seychelles tree frog . . 10 15
818 1 r. Seychelles splendid palm (vert) 25 30
819 1 r. 50 Seychelles skink (vert) 35 40
820 2 r. Giant tenebrionid beetle . 50 55
821 3 r. Seychelles sunbird . . . 70 75
822 3 r. 50 Seychelles killifish . . 85 90
823 4 r. Seychelles magpie robin . 95 1·00
824 5 r. Seychelles vanilla (plant) (vert) . . . . 1·25 1·40
825 10 r. Tiger chameleon . . . . 2·40 2·50
826 15 r. Coco-de-mer (vert) . . . 3·50 3·75
827 25 r. Seychelles paradise flycatcher (vert) . . . . . . 6·00 6·25
828 50 r. Giant tortoise . . . . . 12·00 12·50

182 Archbishop George Carey and Anglican Cathedral, Victoria

1993. First Visit of an Archbishop of Canterbury to Seychelles. Multicoloured.
834 3 r. Type **182** . . . . 2·00 1·50
835 10 r. Archbishop Carey with Air France Boeing 747-400 and Air Seychelles Boeing 737-200 airliners . . . . 4·50 6·00

183 Athletics

184 "Scotia" (cable ship) off Victoria, 1893

1993. 4th Indian Ocean Island Games. Mult.
836 1 r. 50 Type **183** 55 55
837 3 r. Football . . . . 1·00 1·00
838 3 r. 50 Cycling . . . . 1·75 1·75
839 10 r. Yachting . . . . 3·25 4·50

1993. Century of Telecommunications. Mult.
840 1 r. Type **184** . . . . 1·25 50
841 3 r. Eastern Telegraph Co office, Victoria, 1904 . . . . 2·00 1·75
842 4 r. HF Transmitting Station, 1971 . . . . 2·25 2·25
843 10 r. New Telecoms House, Victoria, 1993 . . . . . . 4·50 6·00

1994. "Hong Kong '94" Int Stamp Exhibition. Nos. 62, 64 and 66/7 of Zil Elwannyen Sesel surch **HONG KONG '94**, emblem and value.
844 1 r. on 2 r. 10 Souimanga sunbird 40 30
845 1 r. 50 on 2 r. 75 Sacred ibis . 55 60
846 3 r. 50 on 7 r. Seychelles kestrel (vert) . . . . 1·40 1·60
847 10 r. on 15 r. Comoro blue pigeon (vert) . . . . 3·00 3·75

186 "Eurema floricola"

187 Lady Elizabeth Bowes-Lyon

1994. Butterflies. Multicoloured.
848 1 r. 50 Type **186** . . . . . . 1·50 75
849 3 r. "Coeliades forestan" . . . 2·25 2·00
850 3 r. 50 "Borbo borbonica" . . 2·50 2·50
851 10 r. "Zizula hylax" . . . . . 5·00 6·50

1995. 95th Birthday of Queen Elizabeth the Queen Mother. Multicoloured.
852 1 r. 50 Type **187** 50 40
853 3 r. Duchess of York on wedding day, 1923 . . . . 1·00 1·00
854 3 r. 50 Queen Elizabeth . . . 1·10 1·40
855 10 r. Queen Elizabeth the Queen Mother . . . . 3·25 5·00

188 Female Seychelles Paradise Flycatcher feeding Chick

189 Swimming

1996. Endangered Species. Seychelles Paradise Flycatcher. Multicoloured.
856 1 r. Type **188** 55 65
857 1 r. Male bird in flight 55 65
858 1 r. Female bird on branch . . 55 65
859 1 r. Male bird on branch . . . 55 65

1996. Centenary of Modern Olympic Games. Multicoloured.
861 50 c. Type **189** 40 20
862 1 r. 50 Running 60 45
863 3 r. Sailing . . . . 1·25 1·25
864 5 r. Boxing . . . . 1·90 2·50

190 Archbishop Makarios at Table

191 Comoro Blue Pigeon

1996. 40th Anniv of Exile of Archbishop Makarios of Cyprus to Seychelles. Multicoloured.
865 3 r. Type **190** . . . . 1·25 1·00
866 10 r. Archbishop Makarios in priest's robes . . . . 3·25 4·00

1996. Birds. Multicoloured.
867 3 r. Type **191** . . . . 1·25 1·25
868 3 r. Seychelles blue pigeon . . 1·25 1·25
869 3 r. Souimanga sunbird . . . 1·25 1·25
870 3 r. Seychelles sunbird . . . . 1·25 1·25
871 3 r. Red-headed fody . . . . 1·25 1·25
872 3 r. Seychelles fody . . . . . 1·25 1·25
873 3 r. Madagascar white eye . . 1·25 1·25
874 3 r. Seychelles white eye . . . 1·25 1·25
Nos. 867/8, 869/70, 871/2 and 873/4 respectively were printed together, se-tenant, with the background of each pair forming a composite design showing a regional map.

1997. "HONG KONG '97" International Stamp Exhibition. No. 226 of Zil Elwannyen Sesel surch **R1.50** and emblem.
875 1 r. 50 on 2 r. Western reef heron ("Dimorphic Little Egret") . 60 60

1997. Golden Wedding of Queen Elizabeth and Prince Philip. As T **87** of Kiribati. Multicoloured.
876 1 r. Queen Elizabeth wearing red and white suit 35 45
877 1 r. Prince Philip driving carriage 35 45
878 1 r. 50 Prince Philip 45 65
879 1 r. 50 Queen Elizabeth with horse 45 65
880 3 r. Prince Charles and Princess Anne on horseback . . . . 90 1·00
881 3 r. Prince Philip and Queen Elizabeth . . . . 90 1·00
Nos. 876/7, 878/9 and 880/1 respectively were printed together, se-tenant, with the backgrounds forming composite designs.

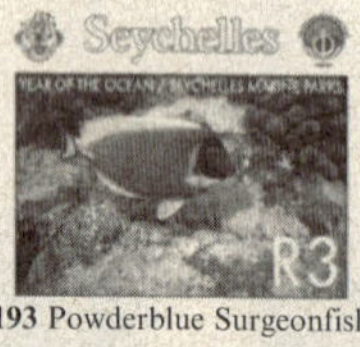
193 Powderblue Surgeonfish

1998. International Year of the Ocean. Multicoloured.
884 3 r. Type **193** 70 75
885 3 r. Shoal of soldierfish . . . 70 75
886 3 r. Lionfish 70 75
887 3 r. School of fish 70 75
888 3 r. Coral 70 75
889 3 r. Turtle 70 75

194 "Vierge du Cap" (galleon), 1721

1999. 18th-century Ships. Multicoloured.
890 1 r. 50 Type **194** 25 30
891 3 r. "L'Elizabeth" (corvette), 1741 . . . . 70 75
892 3 r. 50 "Curieuse" (sloop), 1768 85 90
893 10 r. "La Fleche" (frigate), 1801 2·40 2·50

POSTAGE DUE STAMPS

D 1

1951. Value in red.
D1 D 1 2 c. red and carmine . . 80 1·50
D2 3 c. red and green . . . . 2·00 1·50
D3 6 c. red and bistre . . . 2·00 1·25
D4 9 c. red and orange . . . 2·00 1·25
D5 15 c. red and violet . . . 1·75 11·00
D6 18 c. red and blue . . . 1·75 11·00
D7 20 c. red and brown . . 1·75 11·00
D8 30 c. red and claret . . . 1·75 7·50

1980. As D 1 but 18 × 22 mm.
D11 D 1 5 c. red and mauve . . . 15 80
D12 10 c. red and green . . . 15 80
D13 15 c. red and bistre . . . 20 80
D14 20 c. red and brown . . 20 80
D15 25 c. red and violet . . 20 80
D16 75 c. red and maroon . . 30 80
D17 80 c. red and blue . . . 30 90
D18 1 r. red and purple . . . 30 90

SHAHPURA

One of the Indian Feudatory States. Now uses Indian stamps.

12 pies = 1 anna; 16 annas = 1 rupee

RAJ
SHAHPURA
Postage 1 pice

1

1914. Perf (No. 1) or imperf (No. 2).

1	1	1 p. red on grey	—	£250
2		1 p. red on brown	—	£375

1920. As T 1 but "Postage" omitted. Imperf.

3		1 p. red on brown	—	£425
4		1 a. black on pink	—	£425

SIERRA LEONE

A British colony on the west coast of Africa. Achieved independence within the British Commonwealth in 1961. By vote of the Assembly on 19 April, 1971, Sierra Leone was proclaimed a Republic.

1859. 12 pence = 1 shilling;
20 shillings = 1 pound.
1964. 100 cents = 1 leone.

1

2

1859.

16	2	½d. brown	2·00	6·00
27		½d. green	60	70
28		1d. red	2·00	70
29		1½d. lilac	2·25	6·00
25		2d. mauve	45·00	8·00
30		2d. grey	25·00	2·25
31		2½d. blue	7·00	85
32		3d. yellow	2·25	8·00
21		4d. blue	£120	6·50
33		4d. brown	1·50	1·25
37	1	6d. purple	2·00	6·50
22	2	1s. green	55·00	6·50
34		1s. brown	16·00	10·00

1893. Surch **HALF PENNY.**

39	2	½d. on 1½d. lilac	2·75	3·00

4

6

1896.

41	4	¼d. mauve and green	1·00	2·25
42		1d. mauve and red	1·00	1·50
43		1½d. mauve and black	3·25	13·00
44		2d. mauve and orange	2·25	5·00
45		2½d. mauve and blue	1·40	1·25
46		3d. mauve and grey	7·00	7·00
47		4d. mauve and red	8·50	13·00
48		5d. mauve and black	9·00	11·00
49		6d. mauve	7·00	17·00
50		1s. green and black	6·00	17·00
51		2s. green and blue	24·00	40·00
52		5s. green and red	55·00	£130
53		£1 purple on red	£140	£350

1897. T 6 optd **POSTAGE AND REVENUE.**

54	6	1d. purple and green	1·75	2·00

1897. T 6 optd **POSTAGE AND REVENUE** and surch **2½d.** and bars.

55	6	2½d. on 3d. purple and green	11·00	13·00
59		2½d. on 6d. purple and green	8·50	13·00
63		2½d. on 1s. lilac	80·00	60·00
67		2½d. on 2s. lilac	£1600	£1700

15

1903.

73	15	½d. purple and green	3·00	4·00
87		1d. purple and red	80	80
75	15	1½d. purple and black	1·25	8·50
89		2d. purple and orange	4·25	3·75
90		2½d. purple and blue	4·50	2·00
78		3d. purple and grey	8·00	12·00
92		4d. purple and red	6·50	6·50
93		5d. purple and black	12·00	23·00
94		6d. purple	4·00	3·25
95		1s. green and black	7·50	9·00
96		2s. green and blue	17·00	26·00
97		5s. green and red	28·00	48·00
85		£1 purple on red	£200	£225

1907.

99	15	½d. green	35	30
100a		1d. red	4·00	50
101		1½d. orange	60	2·00
102		2d. grey	80	1·50
103		2½d. blue	2·50	2·50
104		3d. purple on yellow	7·50	2·75
105		4d. black and red on yellow	2·25	1·10
106		5d. purple and green	5·50	5·00
107		6d. purple and light purple	5·50	7·00
108		1s. black on green	5·50	5·00
109		2s. purple and blue on blue	15·00	18·00
110		5s. green and red on yellow	35·00	50·00
111		£1 purple and black on red	£200	£180

17

20

1912.

131	17	½d. green	1·00	15
113		1d. red	1·25	10
132a		1d. violet	2·75	10
114		1½d. orange	1·50	1·75
133		1½d. red	1·00	80
134		2d. grey	80	10
116a		2½d. blue	1·00	65
116b	20	3d. purple on yellow	3·00	3·00
136	17	3d. blue	75	60
137		4d. black & red on yellow	1·75	3·00
138		5d. purple and green	75	75
139		6d. purple and light purple	1·25	2·25
120		7d. purple and orange	2·25	8·00
141		9d. purple and black	2·75	12·00
122		10d. purple and red	3·00	17·00
124a	20	1s. black on green	4·50	3·00
125		2s. blue & purple on blue	13·00	5·00
126		5s. red & green on yellow	13·00	24·00
127		10s. red & green on green	60·00	£100
128		£1 black & purple on red	£130	£170
147		£2 blue and purple	£425	£650
148		£5 orange and green	£1100	£1500

21 Rice Field

22 Palms and Cola Tree

1932.

155	21	½d. green	15	30
156		1d. violet	20	20
157		1½d. red	30	1·25
158		2d. brown	30	20
159		3d. blue	60	1·50
160		4d. orange	60	4·50
161		5d. green	75	2·00
162		6d. blue	50	2·00
163		1s. red	1·40	4·00
164	22	2s. brown	4·25	4·50
165		5s. blue	11·00	16·00
166		10s. green	55·00	£110
167		£1 purple	85·00	£170

23 Arms of Sierra Leone

1933. Cent of Abolition of Slavery and of Death of William Wilberforce. Dated "1833 1933".

168	23	½d. green	45	1·25
169	–	1d. black and brown	40	10
170	–	1½d. brown	4·50	4·50
171	–	2d. purple	2·75	20
172	–	3d. blue	2·75	1·75
173	–	4d. brown	6·50	10·00
174	–	5d. green and brown	7·00	16·00
175	–	6d. black and orange	7·00	8·00
176	–	1s. violet	4·75	17·00
177	–	2s. brown and blue	22·00	40·00
178	–	5s. black and purple	£140	£160
179	–	10s. black and olive	£160	£225
180	–	£1 violet and orange	£300	£375

DESIGNS—VERT: 1d. "Freedom"; 1½d. Map of Sierra Leone; 4d. Government sanatorium; 5s. African elephant. HORIZ: 2d. Old Slave Market, Freetown; 3d. Native fruit seller; 5d. Bullom canoe; 6d. Punting near Banana Is; 1s. Government. buildings, Freetown; 2s. Bunce Is; 10s. King George V; £1 Freetown Harbour.

1935. Silver Jubilee. As T 13 of Antigua.

181		1d. blue and black	80	1·75
182		3d. brown and blue	1·00	8·00
183		5d. green and blue	1·40	8·00
184		1s. grey and purple	5·50	4·25

1937. Coronation. As T 2 of Aden.

185		1d. orange	70	50
186		2d. purple	90	50
187		3d. blue	1·50	3·25

30 Freetown from the Harbour

1938. King George VI.

188	30	½d. black and green	15	30
189		1d. black and red	40	40
190	–	1½d. red	20·00	70
190a	–	1½d. mauve	30	60
191	–	2d. mauve	40·00	1·75
191a	–	2d. red	30	80
192	30	3d. black and blue	40	40
193		4d. black and brown	80	2·25
194	–	5d. green	5·00	3·50
195	–	6d. grey	75	40
196	30	1s. black and green	1·50	50
196a	–	1s. 3d. orange	40	40
197	30	2s. black and brown	4·50	1·75
198	–	5s. brown	10·00	5·00
199	–	10s. green	16·00	7·50
200	30	£1 blue	17·00	18·00

DESIGNS: 1½, 2, 5, 6d., 1s. 3d., 5s., 10s. Rice harvesting.

1946. Victory. As T 9 of Aden.

201		1½d. lilac	15	10
202		3d. blue	15	10

1948. Silver Wedding. As T 10/11 of Aden.

203		1½d. mauve	15	15
204		£1 blue	16·00	16·00

1949. 75th Anniv of U.P.U. As T 20/23 of Antigua.

205		1½d. purple	20	40
206		3d. blue	90	2·25
207		6d. grey	35	2·50
208		1s. green	35	1·00

1953. Coronation. As T 13 of Aden.

209		1½d. black and lilac	30	30

32 Cape Lighthouse

1956. Centres in black.

210	32	½d. lilac	90	1·75
211	–	1d. olive	90	30
212	–	1½d. blue	1·60	3·50
213	–	2d. brown	70	10
214	–	3d. blue	1·25	10
215	–	4d. slate	2·50	95
216	–	6d. violet	1·00	30
217	–	1s. red	1·25	20
218	–	1s. 3d. sepia	11·00	10
219	–	2s. 6d. brown	14·00	6·00
220	–	5s. green	2·25	1·75
221	–	10s. mauve	3·50	2·50
222	–	£1 orange	12·00	16·00

DESIGNS—HORIZ: 1d. Queen Elizabeth II Quay; 1½d. Piassava workers; 4d. Iron ore production, Marampa; 6d. Whale Bay, York Village; 1s. 3d. Bristol 170 Freighter Mk 31 airplane and map; 10s. Law Courts, Freetown; £1 Government House. VERT: 2d. Cotton tree, Freetown; 3d. Rice harvesting; 1s. Bullom canoe; 2s. 6d. Orugu railway bridge; 5s. Kuranko chief.

46 Licensed Diamond Miner

1961. Independence.

223	–	½d. brown and turquoise	20	10
224	46	1d. brown and green	1·25	10
225	–	1½d. black and green	20	10
226	–	2d. black and blue	20	10
227	–	3d. brown and blue	20	10
228	–	4d. blue and red	20	10
229	–	6d. black and purple	20	10
230	–	1s. brown and orange	20	10
231	–	1s. 3d. blue and violet	20	10
232	46	2s. 6d. green and black	2·75	20
233	–	5s. black and red	1·00	1·25
234	–	10s. black and green	1·00	1·25
235	–	£1 red and yellow	8·00	5·00

DESIGNS—VERT: ½d., 1s. Palm fruit gathering; 1½d., 5s. Bundu mask; 2d., 10s. Bishop Crowther and Old Fourah Bay College; £1 Forces bugler. HORIZ: 3d., 6d. Sir Milton Margai; 4d., 1s. 3d. Lumley Beach, Freetown.

53 Royal Charter, 1799

55 Old House of Representatives, Freetown, 1924

1961. Royal Visit.

236	53	3d. black and red	15	10
237	–	4d. black and violet	15	90
238	55	6d. black and orange	20	10
239	–	1s. 3d. black and blue	2·50	90

DESIGNS—VERT: 4d. King's Yard Gate, Freetown, 1817. HORIZ: 1s. 3d. Royal Yacht "Britannia" at Freetown.

57 Campaign Emblem

58 Fireball Lily

1962. Malaria Eradication.

240	57	3d. red	10	10
241		1s. 3d. green	20	10

1963. Flowers in natural colours; background colours given below.

242	58	½d. bistre	10	10
243	–	1d. red	10	10
244	–	1½d. green	20	10
245	–	2d. olive	20	10
246	–	3d. green	20	10
247	–	4d. blue	20	10
248	–	6d. blue	30	10
249	–	1s. green	40	10
250	–	1s. 3d. green	1·50	20
251	–	2s. 6d. purple	1·25	30
252	–	5s. violet	1·25	80
253	–	10s. purple	2·50	1·50
254	–	£1 blue	8·00	7·00

FLOWERS—VERT: 1½d. Stereospermum; 3d. Beniseed; 4d. Blushing hibiscus; 1s. Beautiful crinum; 2s. 6d. Broken hearts; 5s. Ra-ponthi; 10s. Blue plumbago. HORIZ: 1d. Jina-gbo; 2d. Black-eyed Susan; 6d. Climbing lily; 1s. 3d. Blue bells; £1 African tulip tree.

71 Threshing Machine and Corn Bins

75 Centenary Emblem

1963. Freedom from Hunger.

255	71	3d. black and ochre	15	10
256	–	1s. 3d. sepia and green	35	10

DESIGN: 1s. 3d. Girl with onion crop.

1963. 2nd Anniv of Independence. Stamps of 1956 surch **2ND YEAR OF INDEPENDENCE PROGRESS DEVELOPMENT 1963** and value (except 2s. 6d.). Centres in black. (a) Postage.

257		3d. on ½d. lilac	40	10
258		4d. on 1½d. blue	15	10
259		6d. on ½d. lilac	30	10
260		10d. on 3d. blue	50	10
261		1s. 6d. on 3d. blue	30	20
262		3s. 6d. on 3d. blue	40	20

(b) Air. Optd **AIR MAIL** in additon.

263		7d. on 1½d. blue	20	10
264		1s. 3d. on 1½d. blue	20	10
265		2s. 6d. brown	70	20
266		3s. on 3d. blue	40	20
267		6s. on 3d. blue	1·00	20
268		11s. on 10s. mauve	1·40	85
269		11s. on £1 orange	£500	£180

1963. Centenary of Red Cross.

270	75	3d. red and violet	30	10
271	–	6d. red and black	45	15
272	–	1s. 3d. red and green	65	20

DESIGNS: 6d. Red Cross emblem; 1s. 3d. As T 75 but with lined background and value on left.

1963. Postal Commemorations. (a) Postage. Optd or surch **1853-1859-1963 Oldest Postal Service Newest G.P.O. in West Africa** and value.

273	–	3d. (No. 214)	10	10
274	–	4d. on 1½d. (No. 212)	10	10
275	–	9d. on 1½d. (No. 212)	10	10
276	–	1s. on 1s. 3d. (No. 231)	10	10
277	32	1s. 6d. on ½d.	15	10
278	–	2s. on 3d. (No. 214)	15	10

(b) Air. Optd or surch as above but **Postage Stamp** instead of **Postal Service** and **AIRMAIL** in addition.

279	**53**	7d. on 3d.	20	50
280	–	1s. 3d. (No. 239)	2·00	1·25
281	–	2s. 6d. on 4d. (No. 228)	1·25	20
282	**52**	3s. on 3d.	2·50	1·75
283	**55**	6s. on 6d.	1·00	70
284	–	£1 (No. 222)	17·00	15·00

Commemoration dates:—
1853—"First Post Office".
1859—"First Postage Stamps".
1963—"Newest G.P.O. in West Africa".

80 Lion Emblem and Map

81 Globe and Map

1964. World's Fair, New York. Imperf. Self-adhesive.

285	**80**	1d. multicoloured (postage)	10	10
286		3d. multicoloured	10	10
287		4d. multicoloured	10	10
288		6d. multicoloured	10	10
289		1s. multicoloured	10	10
290		2s. multicoloured	20	10
291		5s. multicoloured	40	25
292	**81**	7d. multicoloured (air)	10	10
293		9d. multicoloured	10	10
294		1s. 3d. multicoloured	15	10
295		2s. 6d. multicoloured	20	10
296		3s. 6d. multicoloured	20	10
297		6s. multicoloured	40	30
298		11s. multicoloured	55	80

WARNING:—These self-adhesive stamps should be kept mint on their backing paper and used on cover or piece.

82 Inscription and Map

83 Pres. Kennedy and Map

1964. President Kennedy Memorial Issue. Imperf. Self-adhesive.

299	**82**	1d. multicoloured (postage)	10	10
300		3d. multicoloured	10	10
301		4d. multicoloured	10	10
302		6d. multicoloured	10	10
303		1s. multicoloured	10	10
304		2s. multicoloured	15	15
305		5s. multicoloured	35	25
306	**83**	7d. multicoloured (air)	10	10
307		9d. multicoloured	10	10
308		1s. 3d. multicoloured	15	10
309		2s. 6d. multicoloured	25	20
310		3s. 6d. multicoloured	25	20
311		6s. multicoloured	45	45
312		11s. multicoloured	70	80

The note below No. 298 applies also to the above issue.

1964. Decimal Currency. Various stamps surch. (i) First issue. Surch in figures. (a) Postage.

313	–	1 c. on 6d. (No. 248)	10	10
314	**53**	2 c. on 3d. (No. 236)	10	10
315	–	3 c. on 3d. (No. 246)	10	10
316	–	5 c. on $\frac{1}{2}$d. (No. 223)	10	10
317	**71**	8 c. on 3d. (No. 255)	10	10
318	–	10 c. on 1s. 3d. (No. 250)	10	10
319	–	15 c. on 1s. (No. 249)	15	10
320	**55**	25 c. on 6d. (No. 238)	30	25
321	**46**	50 c. on 2s. 6d. (No. 232)	1·50	65

(b) Air. Nos. 322/5 additonally optd **AIRMAIL**.

322	–	7 c. on 1s. 3d. (No. 256)	10	10
323	–	20 c. on 4d. (No. 228)	25	15
324	–	30 c. on 10s. (No. 234)	40	30
325	–	40 c. on 5s. (No. 233)	50	40
326	**83**	1 l. on 1s. 3d. (No. 308)	75	90
327		2 l. on 11s. (No. 312)	1·25	1·60

(ii) Second issue. Surch in figures or figures and words (Nos. 332/3).

328	–	1 c. on 3d. (No. 227) (postage)	10	10
329	**82**	2 c. on 1d. (No. 299)	10	10
330		4 c. on 3d. (No. 300)	10	10
331	–	5 c. on 2d. (No. 245)	10	10
332	–	1 l. on 5s. (No. 252)	1·25	1·25
333	–	2 l. on £1 (No. 235)	2·25	2·25
334	**83**	7 c. on 7d. (No. 306) (air)	10	10
335		60 c. on 9d. (Nos. 307)	50	45

(iii) Third issue. Surch in figures.

336	–	1 c. on $1\frac{1}{2}$d. (No. 225) (postage)	10	10
337	**82**	2 c. on 3d. (No. 300)	10	10
338	**80**	2 c. on 4d. (No. 287)	10	10
339	–	3 c. on 1d. (No. 243)	10	10
340	–	3 c. on 2d. (No. 226)	10	10
341	–	5 c. on 1s. 3d. (No. 231)	10	10
342	**82**	15 c. on 6d. (No. 302)	80	50
343		15 c. on 1s. (No. 303)	1·25	90
344	–	20 c. on 6d. (No. 229)	30	15
345	–	25 c. on 6d. (No. 248)	35	20
346	–	50 c. on 3d. (No. 227)	80	55
347	**80**	60 c. on 5s. (No. 291)	3·25	2·00
348	**82**	1 l. on 4d. (No. 301)	3·75	3·50
349	–	2 l. on £1 (No. 235)	7·00	5·00
350	**81**	7 c. on 9d. (air)	15	10

(iv) Fourth issue. Surch in figures.

351	**80**	1 c. on 6d. (postage)	2·25	7·00
352		1 c. on 2s.	2·25	7·00
353	**82**	1 c. on 2s.	2·25	7·00
354		1 c. on 5s.	2·25	7·00
355	**81**	2 c. on 1s. 3d. (air)	2·25	7·00
356	**83**	2 c. on 1s. 3d.	2·25	7·00
357		2 c. on 3s. 6d.	2·25	7·00
358	**81**	3 c. on 7d.	2·25	7·00
359	**83**	3 c. on 9d.	2·25	7·00
360	**81**	5 c. on 2s. 6d.	2·25	7·00
361	**83**	5 c. on 2s. 6d.	2·25	7·00
362	**81**	5 c. on 3s. 6d.	2·25	7·00
363		5 c. on 6s.	2·25	7·00
364	**83**	5 c. on 6s.	2·25	7·00

(v) Fifth issue. No. 374 further surch **TWO Leones**.

365	–	2 l. on 30 c. on 6d. (air)	1·50	1·50

(**91** Margai and Churchill)

1965. Sir Milton Margai and Sir Winston Churchill Commem. Flower stamps of 1963 surch as T **91** on horiz designs or with individual portraits on vert designs as indicated. Mult. (a) Postage.

366	–	2 c. on 1d.	10	10
367	–	3 c. on 3d. Margai	10	10
368	–	10 c. on 1s. Churchill	20	10
369	–	20 c. on 1s. 3d.	40	10
370	–	50 c. on 4d. Margai	90	35
371	–	75 c. on 5s. Churchill	2·25	90

(b) Air. Additionally optd **AIRMAIL**.

372	–	7 c. on 2d.	20	10
373	**58**	15 c. on $\frac{1}{2}$d. Margai	35	10
374	–	30 c. on 6d.	1·25	25
375	–	1 l. on £1	4·00	1·00
376	–	2 l. on 10s. Churchill	11·00	5·00

92 Cola Plant and Nut

1965. Various shapes, backed with paper bearing advertisements. Imperf. Self-adhesive.

A. Printed in green, yellow and red on silver foil. Values in colours given.

377	**92**	1 c. green (postage)	25	10
378		2 c. red	25	10
379		3 c. yellow	25	10
380		4 c. silver on green	30	10
381		5 c. silver on red	30	10

B. Designs 45 × 49 mm showing Arms of Sierra Leone.

382	–	20 c. mult on cream (postage)	1·75	50
383	–	50 c. mult on cream	3·50	3·50
384	–	40 c. mult on cream (air)	3·25	3·50

C. Designs 48 × $44\frac{1}{2}$ mm showing inscription and necklace.

385	–	7 c. multicoloured (air)	70	15
386	–	15 c. multicoloured	1·00	70

1966. 5th Anniv of Independence. Surch **FIVE YEARS INDEPENDENCE 1961-1966** and value. (a) Postage.

387	–	1 c. on 6d. (No. 248)	10	10
388	–	2 c. on 4d. (No. 247)	10	10
389	–	3 c. on $1\frac{1}{2}$d. (No. 212)	10	10
390	–	8 c. on 1s. (No. 249)	15	10
391	–	10 c. on 2s. 6d. (No. 251)	15	10
392	–	20 c. on 2d. (No. 213)	20	10

(b) Air. Surch **AIRMAIL** also.

393	**75**	7 c. on 3d.	10	10
394	–	15 c. on 1s. (No. 249)	20	10
395	–	25 c. on 2s. 6d. (No. 251)	65	60
396	–	50 c. on $1\frac{1}{2}$d. (No. 244)	1·00	80
397	–	1 l. on 4d. (No. 247)	1·60	1·60

97 Lion's Head

1966. First Sierra Leone Gold Coinage Commem. Circular designs, embossed on gold foil, backed with paper bearing advertisements. Imperf. (a) Postage.

(i) $\frac{1}{4}$ golde coin. Diameter $1\frac{1}{2}$ in.

398	**97**	2 c. mauve and orange	10	10
399	–	3 c. green and purple	10	10

(ii) $\frac{1}{2}$ golde coin. Diameter $2\frac{1}{8}$ in.

400	**97**	5 c. red and blue	10	10
401	–	8 c. turquoise and black	15	15

(iii) 1 golde coin. Diameter $3\frac{1}{4}$ in.

402	**97**	25 c. violet and green	35	35
403	–	1 l. orange and red	2·50	2·75

(b) Air. (i) $\frac{1}{4}$ golde coin. Diameter $1\frac{1}{2}$ in.

404	**97**	7 c. orange and red	10	10
405	–	30 c. purple and black	15	15

(ii) $\frac{1}{2}$ golde coin. Diameter $2\frac{1}{8}$ in.

406	**97**	15 c. orange and red	25	25
407	–	30 c. purple and black	40	45

(iii) 1 golde coin. Diameter $3\frac{1}{4}$ in.

408	**97**	50 c. green and purple	75	75
409	–	2 l. black and green	3·75	4·00

DESIGNS: Nos. 399, 401, 403, 405, 407 and 409, Map of Sierra Leone.

1967. Decimal Currency Provisionals. Nos. 347/8, 369/71 and 383/4 surch.

410	$6\frac{1}{2}$ c. on 75 c. on 5s. (postage)	15	15
411	$7\frac{1}{2}$ c. on 75 c. on 5s.	15	15
412	$9\frac{1}{2}$ c. on 50 c. on 4d.	20	20
413	$12\frac{1}{2}$ c. on 20 c. on 1s. 3d.	25	25
414	$17\frac{1}{2}$ c. on 50 c.	1·40	1·40
415	$17\frac{1}{2}$ c. on 1 l. on 4d.	1·40	1·40
416	$18\frac{1}{2}$ c. on 1 l. on 4d.	1·40	1·40
417	$18\frac{1}{2}$ c. on 60 c. on 5s.	4·00	4·50
418	25 c. on 50 c.	60	70
419	$11\frac{1}{2}$ c. on 40 c. (air)	20	20
420	25 c. on 40 c.	60	70

1967. Decimal Currency. Imperf. Self-adhesive. As T **92**, but embossed on white paper, backed with paper bearing advertisements. Background colours given first, and value tablet colours in brackets.

421	**92**	$\frac{1}{2}$ c. red (red on white)	10	10
422		1 c. red (red on white)	15	10
423		$1\frac{1}{2}$ c. yellow (green on white)	20	15
424		2 c. red (green on white)	35	10
425		$2\frac{1}{2}$ c. green (yellow on white)	50	40
426		3 c. red (white on red)	30	10
427		$3\frac{1}{2}$ c. purple (white on grn)	50	40
428		4 c. red (white on green)	50	15
429		$4\frac{1}{2}$ c. green (green on white)	50	40
430		5 c. red (yellow and white)	50	15
431		$5\frac{1}{2}$ c. red (green on white)	50	50

102 Eagle
($\frac{2}{3}$-size illustration)

1967. T **102** embossed on black paper, backed with paper bearing advertisements; or, as No. 382 also with advertisements (No. 433/b)

432	**102**	$9\frac{1}{2}$ c. red & gold on black	60	60
432a		$9\frac{1}{2}$ c. blue & gold on black	5·00	5·00
433	–	10 c. mult (red frame)	65	65
433b	–	10 c. mult (black frame)	5·50	5·50
434	**102**	15 c. green & gold on blk	85	85
434a		15 c. red and gold on black	6·00	6·00

See also Nos. 538/44.

1968. No advertisements on back and colours in value tablet reversed. Background coloures given first, and value tablet colours in brackets.

435	**92**	$\frac{1}{2}$ c. red (white on green)	10	10
436		1 c. red (white on red)	15	10
437		2 c. red (white on green)	4·25	4·50
438		$2\frac{1}{2}$ c. green (white on yellow)	4·75	5·00
439		3 c. red (red on white)	1·75	65

On Nos. 435 and 438 the figure "$\frac{1}{2}$" is larger than on Nos. 421 and 425.

1968. No advertisements on back, colours changed and new value (7 c.). Background colours given.

440	**92**	2 c. pink (postage)	1·75	1·50
441		$2\frac{1}{2}$ c. green	1·75	1·50
442		$3\frac{1}{2}$ c. yellow	2·25	1·60
442a		7 c. yellow (air)	6·50	3·50

On Nos. 441/2 the fraction "$\frac{1}{2}$" is larger than on Nos. 425 and 427.

103 Outline Map of Africa

1968. Human Rights Year. Each value comes in six types showing the following territories: Portuguese Guinea; South Africa; Mozambique: Rhodesia: South West Africa and Angola. Imperf. Self-adhesive.

443	**103**	$\frac{1}{2}$ c. multicoloured (postage)	10	10
444		2 c. multicoloured	10	10
445		$2\frac{1}{2}$ c. multicoloured	10	10
446		$3\frac{1}{2}$ c. multicoloured	10	10
447		10 c. multicoloured	15	15
448		$11\frac{1}{2}$ c. multicoloured	20	20
449		15 c. multicoloured	25	25
450	**103**	$7\frac{1}{2}$ c. multicoloured (air)	15	15
451		$9\frac{1}{2}$ c. multicoloured	20	20
452		$14\frac{1}{2}$ c. multicoloured	25	25
453		$18\frac{1}{2}$ c. multicoloured	30	30
454		25 c. multicoloured	40	40
455		1 l. multicoloured	4·00	5·50
456		2 l. multicoloured	10·00	12·00
		Set of 84 (6 different territories)	75·00	£100

Nos. 443/56 were issued in sheets of 30 (6 × 5) on backing paper depicting diamonds or the coat-of-arms on the reverse. The six types occur once in each horiz row.

1968. Mexico Olympics Participation. Nos. 383/4 surch or optd (Nos. 461 and 466) **OLYMPIC PARTICIPATION 1968 MEXICO** etc.

457	$6\frac{1}{2}$ c. on 50 c. mult (postage)	20	15
458	$17\frac{1}{2}$ c. on 50 c. multicoloured	25	20
459	$22\frac{1}{2}$ c. on 50 c. multicoloured	40	35
460	$28\frac{1}{2}$ c. on 50 c. multicoloured	50	60
461	50 c. multicoloured	80	90
462	$6\frac{1}{2}$ c. on 40 c. mult (air)	20	15
463	$17\frac{1}{2}$ c. on 40 c. multicoloured	25	20
464	$22\frac{1}{2}$ c. on 40 c. multicoloured	40	35
465	$28\frac{1}{2}$ c. on 40 c. multicoloured	50	60
466	40 c. multicoloured	80	90

105 1859 6d. Stamp

111 1965 15 c. Self-adhesive

1969. 5th Anniv of World's First Self-adhesive Postage Stamps. Multicoloured. Self-adhesive. Imperf.

467	1 c. Type **105** (postage)	10	10
468	2 c. 1965 2 c. self-adhesive	10	10
469	$3\frac{1}{2}$ c. 1961 Independence £1	10	10
470	5 c. 1965 20 c. self-adhesive	10	10
471	$12\frac{1}{2}$ c. 1948 Royal Silver Wedding £1	30	15
472	1 l. 1923 £2	3·00	2·00
473	$7\frac{1}{2}$ c. Type **111** (air)	20	10
474	$9\frac{1}{2}$ c. 1967 $9\frac{1}{2}$ c. self-adhesive	20	10
475	20 c. 1964 1s. 3d. self-adhesive	40	25
476	30 c. 1964 President Kennedy Memorial 6s. self-adhesive	55	35
477	50 c. 1933 Centenary of Abolition of Slavery £1	1·50	75
478	2 l. 1963 2nd Anniv of Independence 11s.	11·00	9·00

DESIGNS—As Type **105**, Nos. 468/72; As Type **111**, Nos. 474/8.

All values are on white backing paper with advertisement printed on the reverse.

117 Ore Carrier, Globe and Flags of Sierra Leone and Japan

118 Ore Carrier, Map of Europe and Africa and Flags of Sierra Leone and Netherlands

1969. Pepel Port Improvements. Imperf. Self-adhesive, backed with paper bearing advertisements.

479	**117**	1 c. mult (postage)	10	10
480	**118**	2 c. multicoloured	10	10
481	–	$3\frac{1}{2}$ c. multicoloured	10	10
482	–	10 c. multicoloured . . .	10	10
483	**118**	$18\frac{1}{2}$ c. multicoloured . . .	20	25
484	–	50 c. multicoloured . . .	80	85
485	**117**	$7\frac{1}{2}$ c. multicoloured (air) .	10	10
486	–	$9\frac{1}{2}$ c. multicoloured	15	10
487	**117**	15 c. multicoloured . . .	20	25
488	**118**	25 c. multicoloured . . .	30	35
489	–	1 l. multicoloured	1·75	1·75
490	–	2 l. multicoloured	2·50	4·00

The $3\frac{1}{2}$, $9\frac{1}{2}$ c., 2 l. and 10, 50 c., 1 l. show respectively the flags of Great Britain and West Germany instead of the Netherlands.

119 African Development Bank Emblem

1969. 5th Anniv of African Development Bank. Imperf. Self-adhesive, backed with paper bearing advertisements.

491	**119**	$3\frac{1}{2}$ c. green, gold and black (postage)	25	40
492		$9\frac{1}{2}$ c. violet, gold and green (air)	30	70

120 Boy Scouts Emblem in "Diamond"

1969. Boy Scouts Diamond Jubilee. Imperf. Self-adhesive.

493	**120**	1 c. multicoloured (postage)	10	10
494		2 c. multicoloured	10	10
495		$3\frac{1}{2}$ c. multicoloured	15	10
496		$4\frac{1}{2}$ c. multicoloured	15	15
497		5 c. multicoloured	15	15
498		75 c. multicoloured . . .	5·50	2·75
499	–	$7\frac{1}{2}$ c. multicoloured (air) .	35	20
500	–	$9\frac{1}{2}$ c. multicoloured	45	25
501	–	15 c. multicoloured . . .	70	50
502	–	22 c. multicoloured . . .	90	70
503	–	55 c. multicoloured . . .	4·00	2·00
504	–	3 l. multicoloured	50·00	35·00

DESIGNS—OCTAGONAL (65 × 51 mm): Nos. 499/504, Scout saluting, Baden-Powell and badge.

1970. Air. No. 443 surch **AIRMAIL** twice and new value.

505	**103**	$7\frac{1}{2}$ c. on $\frac{1}{2}$ c. multicoloured	20	10
506		$9\frac{1}{2}$ c. on $\frac{1}{2}$ c. multicoloured	20	10
507		15 c. on $\frac{1}{2}$ c. multicoloured	40	25
508		28 c. on $\frac{1}{2}$ c. multicoloured	70	55
509		40 c. on $\frac{1}{2}$ c. multicoloured	1·25	1·40
510		2 l. on $\frac{1}{2}$ c. multicoloured .	6·00	10·00
		Set of 36 (6 different territories)	45·00	60·00

122 Expo Symbol and Maps of Sierra Leone and Japan

1970. World Fair, Osaka. Imperf. Self-adhesive.

511	**122**	2 c. mult (postage) . . .	10	10
512		$3\frac{1}{2}$ c. multicoloured . . .	10	10
513		10 c. multicoloured . . .	15	10
514		$12\frac{1}{2}$ c. multicoloured . . .	15	10
515		20 c. multicoloured . . .	20	10
516		45 c. multicoloured . . .	45	45
517	–	$7\frac{1}{2}$ c. multicoloured (air) .	10	10
518	–	$9\frac{1}{2}$ c. multicoloured . . .	15	10
519	–	15 c. multicoloured . . .	20	10
520	–	25 c. multicoloured . . .	40	20
521	–	50 c. multicoloured . . .	55	50
522	–	3 l. multicoloured . . .	2·50	5·50

DESIGN—CHRYSANTHEMUM (43 × 42 mm): Nos. 517/22, Maps of Sierra Leone and Japan.

123 Diamond

124 Palm Nut

1970. Imperf. Self-adhesive.

523	**123**	1 c. multicoloured	10	10
524		$1\frac{1}{2}$ c. multicoloured . . .	10	10
525		2 c. multicoloured	10	10
526		$2\frac{1}{2}$ c. multicoloured . . .	10	10
527		3 c. multicoloured	15	10
528		$3\frac{1}{2}$ c. multicoloured . . .	15	10
529		4 c. multicoloured	15	10
530		5 c. multicoloured	20	10
531	**124**	6 c. multicoloured	25	10
532		7 c. multicoloured	30	15
533		$8\frac{1}{2}$ c. multicoloured . . .	40	15
534		9 c. multicoloured	40	15
535		10 c. multicoloured . . .	45	15
536		$11\frac{1}{2}$ c. multicoloured . . .	55	20
537		$18\frac{1}{2}$ c. multicoloured . . .	85	45

1970. Air. As T **102**, but on white paper.

538	**102**	$7\frac{1}{2}$ c. gold and red	35	10
539		$9\frac{1}{2}$ c. silver and green . .	40	10
540		15 c. silver and blue . . .	70	20
541		25 c. gold and purple . .	1·25	50
542		50 c. green and orange .	2·50	1·75
543		1 l. blue and silver . . .	6·00	8·00
544		2 l. blue and gold	11·00	17·00

126 Jewellery Box and Sewa Diadem

1970. Diamond Industry. Imperf. Self-adhesive.

545	**126**	2 c. mult (postage) . . .	30	10
546		$3\frac{1}{2}$ c. multicoloured . . .	30	10
547		10 c. multicoloured . . .	55	15
548		$12\frac{1}{2}$ c. multicoloured . . .	75	25
549		40 c. multicoloured . . .	1·75	1·00
550		1 l. multicoloured	10·00	8·50
551	–	$7\frac{1}{2}$ c. multicoloured (air) .	50	10
552	–	$9\frac{1}{2}$ c. multicoloured . . .	60	10
553	**126**	15 c. multicoloured	95	30
554	–	25 c. multicoloured	1·40	60
555	–	75 c. multicoloured	5·50	4·50
556	–	2 l. multicoloured	24·00	20·00

DESIGN—HORIZ (63 × 61 mm): Nos. 551/6, Diamond and curtain.

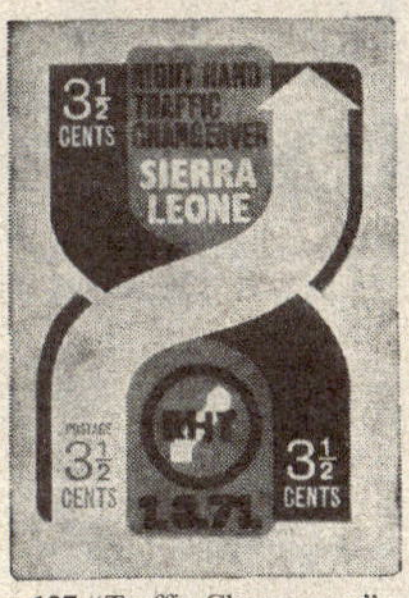

127 "Traffic Changeover"

1971. Changeover to Driving on the Right of the Road. Imperf. Self-adhesive.

557	**127**	$3\frac{1}{2}$ c. orange, blue and black (postage)	1·50	1·00
558		$9\frac{1}{2}$ c. blue, orange and black (air)	2·00	2·50

1971. Air. Various stamps surch **AIRMAIL** and value (Nos. 559/61) or value only (Nos. 562/3).

559		10 c. on 2d. (No. 226) . . .	40	20
560		20 c. on 1s. (No. 230) . . .	70	45
561		50 c. on 1d. (No. 243) . . .	1·25	1·25
562		70 c. on 30 c. (No. 476) . . .	2·00	3·50
563		1 l. on 30 c. (No. 476) . . .	3·00	4·50

129 Flag and Lion's Head

1971. 10th Anniv of Independence. Imperf. Self-adhesive.

564	**129**	2 c. mult (postage)	10	10
565		$3\frac{1}{2}$ c. multicoloured	10	10
566		10 c. multicoloured	15	10
567		$12\frac{1}{2}$ c. multicoloured . . .	20	10
568		40 c. multicoloured	70	40
569		1 l. multicoloured	1·50	2·50
570	–	$7\frac{1}{2}$ c. multicoloured (air) .	15	10
571	–	$9\frac{1}{2}$ c. multicoloured	15	10
572	–	15 c. multicoloured	25	10
573	–	25 c. multicoloured	35	35
574	–	75 c. multicoloured	1·10	1·50
575	–	2 l. multicoloured	3·00	6·50

DESIGN—"Map" shaped as Type **129**: Nos. 570/5, Bugles and lion's head.

130 Pres. Siaka Stevens

1972. Multicoloured. Background colour given.

576	**130**	1 c. lilac	10	10
577		2 c. lavender	10	10
578		4 c. blue	10	10
579		5 c. brown	10	10
580		7 c. pink	15	10
581		10 c. brown	15	10
582		15 c. green	25	15
583		18 c. yellow	25	15
584		20 c. blue	30	15
585		25 c. orange	35	15
586		50 c. green	1·00	55
587		1 l. mauve	1·50	1·00
588		2 l. pink	2·75	3·50
589		5 l. cream	5·50	8·50

131 Guma Valley Dam and Bank Emblem

1975. 10th Anniv of African Development Bank.

590	**131**	4 c. multicoloured (postage)	45·00	28·00
591		15 c. multicoloured (air) .	1·00	80

132 Opening Ceremony

1975. New Congo Bridge Opening and 70th Birthday of President Stevens.

592	**132**	5 c. multicoloured (postage)	3·00	1·50
593		20 c. multicoloured (air) .	50	25

133 Presidents Tolbert and Stevens, and Handclasp

1975. 1st Anniv of Mano River Union.

594	**133**	4 c. multicoloured (postage)	30	40
595		15 c. multicoloured (air) .	20	20

134 "Quaid-i-Azam" (Mohammed Ali Jinnah)

135 Queen Elizabeth II

1977. Birth Centenary of Mohammed Ali Jinnah (Quaid-i-Azam).

596	**134**	30 c. multicoloured . . .	75	30

1977. Silver Jubilee.

597	**135**	5 c. multicoloured	10	10
598		1 l. multicoloured	65	80

136 College Buildings

1977. 150th Anniv of Fourah Bay College. Multicoloured.

599	5 c. Type **136**	10	10
600	20 c. The old college (vert) . .	35	30

137 St. Edward's Crown and Sceptres

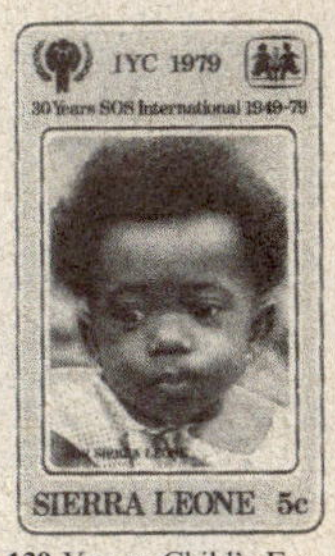

139 Young Child's Face

138 "Myrina silenus"

1978. 25th Anniv of Coronation. Mult.

601	5 c. Type **137**	10	10
602	50 c. Queen Elizabeth II in Coronation Coach	20	40
603	1 l. Queen Elizabeth II and Prince Philip	35	60

1979. Butterflies (1st series). Multicoloured.

604	5 c. Type **138**	10	10
605	15 c. "Papilio nireus"	25	15
606	25 c. "Catacroptera cloanthe"	40	15
607	1 l. "Druryia antimachus" . .	1·50	1·50

See also Nos. 646/9.

1979. International Year of the Child. 30th Anniv of S.O.S. International. Multicoloured.

608 5 c. Type **139** 10 10
609 27 c. Young child with baby . . 20 25
610 1 l. Mother with young child . . 50 1·10

140 Presidents Stevens (Sierra Leone) and Tolbert (Liberia), Dove with Letter and Bridge

1979. 5th Anniv of Mano River Union and 1st Anniv of Postal Union.

612 **140** 5 c. brown, orange & yell . . 10 10
613 22 c. brown, yellow & violet 10 15
614 27 c. brown, blue & orange 10 15
615 35 c. brown, green and red 15 20
616 1 l. brown, violet and blue 50 1·00

141 Great Britain 1848 10d. Stamp

1979. Death Centenary of Sir Rowland Hill.

618 **141** 10 c. black, brown & blue 15 10
619 – 15 c. black, brown & blue 25 15
620 – 50 c. black, red and yellow 60 70

DESIGNS: 15 c. 1872 4d. stamp; 50 c. 1961 £1 Independence commemorative.

142 Knysna Turaco

1980. Birds. Multicoloured.

622A 1 c. Type **142** . . . . 50 1·00
623A 2 c. Olive-bellied sunbird . . 50 1·00
624B 3 c. Western black-headed oriole . . . . 40 1·25
625B 5 c. Spur-winged goose . . . 40 65
626A 7 c. Didric cuckoo 80 40
627B 10 c. Grey parrot (vert) . . 40 70
628B 15 c. Blue quail (vert) . . . 50 1·75
629B 20 c. African wood owl (vert) 50 2·00
630B 30 c. Greater blue turaco (vert) 50 2·25
631B 40 c. Blue-breasted kingfisher (vert) . . . . 60 2·25
632B 50 c. Black crake (vert) . . . 60 2·25
633A 1 l. Hartlaub's duck . . . . 1·40 2·50
634A 2 l. Black bee eater . . . . 2·00 4·00
635B 5 l. Barrow's bustard . . . . 1·40 11·00

143 Paul P. Harris (founder), President Stevens of Sierra Leone and Rotary Emblem

1980. 75th Anniv of Rotary International.

636 **143** 5 c. multicoloured 10 10
637 27 c. multicoloured . . . 10 10
638 50 c. multicoloured . . . 20 25
639 1 l. multicoloured 40 55

144 "Maria", 1844

1980. "London 1980" Int Stamp Exhibition. Mult.

640 6 c. Type **144** 30 10
641 31 c. "Tarquah", 1902 . . . 40 35
642 50 c. "Aureol", 1951 . . . . 50 70
643 1 l. "Africa Palm", 1974 . . . 60 1·60

145 Organization for African Unity Emblem

146 "Graphium policenes"

1980. African Summit Conference, Freetown.

644 **145** 20 c. black, blue & purple 10 10
645 1 l. black, purple and blue 45 45

1980. Butterflies (2nd series). Multicoloured.

646 5 c. Type **146** 10 10
647 27 c. "Charaxes varanes" . . 30 15
648 35 c. "Charaxes brutus" . . . 35 25
649 1 l. "Euphaedra zaddachi" . . 1·10 1·40

147 Arrival at Freetown Airport

149 Soldiers (Defence)

148 Servals

1980. Tourism. Multicoloured.

650 6 c. Type **147** 10 10
651 26 c. Welcome to tourists . . 15 20
652 31 c. Freetown cotton tree . . 15 25
653 40 c. Beinkongo Falls 25 30
654 50 c. Sports facilities 30 40
655 1 l. African elephant . . . . 1·25 95

1981. Wild Cats. Multicoloured.

656 6 c. Type **148** 20 10
657 6 c. Servals cubs 20 10
658 31 c. African golden cats . . 50 30
659 31 c. African golden cat cubs 50 30
660 50 c. Leopards 70 45
661 50 c. Leopard cubs 70 45
662 1 l. Lions . . . . 1·00 80
663 1 l. Lion cubs . . . . 1·00 80

The two designs of each value were printed together, se-tenant, in horizontal pairs, forming composite designs.

1981. 20th Anniv of Independence and 10th Anniv of Republic. National Services. Multicoloured.

664 6 c. Type **149** 40 10
665 31 c. Nurses administering first aid, and ambulance (Health) (horiz) . . . . 1·25 20
666 40 c. Traffic (Police Force) . 2·25 60
667 1 l. Patrol boat (Coastguard) (horiz) . . . . 2·75 2·50

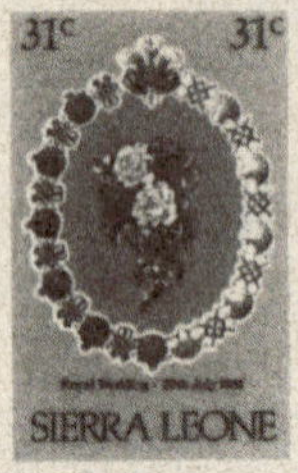

150 Wedding Bouquet from Sierra Leone

151 Sandringham

1981. Royal Wedding (1st issue). Mult.

668 31 c. Type **150** 15 20
669 45 c. Prince Charles as helicopter pilot 15 30
670 1 l. Prince Charles and Lady Diana Spencer . . . . . . 35 1·10

1981. Royal Wedding (2nd issue). Mult.

671 35 c. Type **151** 15 25
672 60 c. Prince Charles in outdoor clothes 20 40
675 70 c. Type **151** 75 90
676 1 l. 30 As 60 c. 75 90
673 1 l. 50 Prince Charles and Lady Diana Spencer 40 90
677 2 l. As 1 l. 50 . . . . 1·50 2·00

152 "Physical Recreation"

153 Pineapples

1981. 25th Anniv of Duke of Edinburgh Award Scheme and President's Award Scheme Publicity. Multicoloured.

678 6 c. Type **152** 10 10
679 31 c. "Community service" . . 15 10
680 1 l. Duke of Edinburgh 30 40
681 1 l. President Siaka Stevens . . 30 40

1981. World Food Day. Multicoloured.

682 6 c. Type **153** 10 10
683 31 c. Ground nuts 15 10
684 50 c. Cassava fruits 20 15
685 1 l. Rice plants 50 50

154 Groundnut

1981. World Food Day (2nd issue). Agricultural Industry. Multicoloured.

686 6 c. Type **154** 10 10
687 31 c. Cassava 25 10
688 50 c. Rice 40 25
689 1 l. Pineapples 65 70

155 Scouts with Cattle

1982. 75th Anniv of Boy Scout Movement. Multicoloured.

690 20 c. Type **155** 25 10
691 50 c. Scouts picking flowers . . 50 40
692 1 l. Lord Baden-Powell . . . . 90 1·00
693 2 l. Scouts fishing . . . . . . 1·90 2·00

1982. Nos. 668/74 surch.

695 50 c. on 31 c. Type **150** . . . 40 40
696 50 c. on 35 c. Type **151** . . . 40 40
697 50 c. on 45 c. Prince Charles as helicopter pilot 40 40
698 50 c. on 60 c. Prince Charles in outdoor clothes 40 40
699 90 c. on 1 l. Prince Charles and Lady Diana Spencer . . . 75 75
699a 1 l. 30 on 60 c. Prince Charles in outdoor clothes . . . . . . 1·75 2·00
699b 2 l. on 35 c. Type **151** . . . . 2·75 3·00
700 2 l. on 1 l. 50 Prince Charles and Lady Diana Spencer . . . 1·50 1·75
700a 8 l. on 1 l. 50 Prince Charles and Lady Diana Spencer . . . 8·75 9·50

157 Heading

158 Prince and Princess of Wales

1982. World Cup Football Championship, Spain. Multicoloured.

702 20 c. Type **157** 45 15
703 30 c. Dribbling 70 20
704 1 l. Tackling . . . . 2·25 2·25
705 2 l. Goalkeeping . . . . . . 3·50 3·75

1982. 21st Birthday of Princess of Wales. Multicoloured.

707 31 c. Caernarvon Castle . . . 20 15
708 50 c. Type **158** 40 15
709 2 l. Princess of Wales . . . . 1·75 75

1982. Birth of Prince William of Wales. Nos. 707/9 optd **ROYAL BABY 21.6.82.**

711 31 c. Caernarvon Castle . . . 15 15
712 50 c. Type **158** 30 15
713 2 l. Princess of Wales . . . . 1·00 75

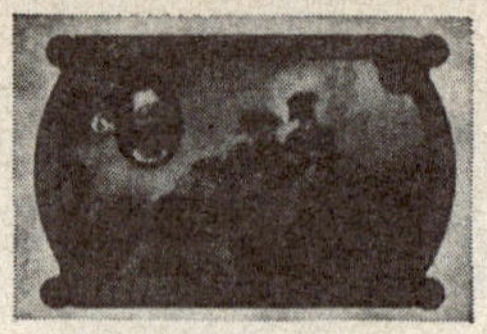

159 Washington with Troops

1982. 250th Birth Anniv of George Washington. Multicoloured.

715 6 c. Type **159** 10 10
716 31 c. Portrait of Washington (vert) 20 20
717 50 c. Washington with horse . 35 35
718 1 l. Washington standing on battlefield (vert) 65 80

160 Temptation of Christ

162 Long Snouted Crocodile

1982. Christmas. Stained-glass Windows. Multicoloured.

720 6 c. Type **160** 10 10
721 31 c. Baptism of Christ . . . 15 20
722 50 c. Annunciation 20 40
723 1 l. Nativity 55 90

1982. World Cup Football Championship Winners. Nos. 702/5 optd **WORLD CUP WINNERS ITALY (3) vs. W. GERMANY (1).**

725 20 c. Type **157** 20 20
726 30 c. Dribbling 25 30
727 1 l. Tackling 65 75
728 2 l. Goalkeeping . . . . . . 1·25 1·75

1982. Death Cent of Charles Darwin. Mult.

730 6 c. Type **162** 60 20
731 31 c. Rainbow lizard . . . . 1·50 75
732 50 c. River turtle . . . . . . 2·00 2·00
733 1 l. Chameleon . . . . 3·25 4·50

163 Diogenes

1983. 500th Birth Anniv of Raphael. Details from painting "The School of Athens". Multicoloured.

735 6 c. Type **163** 15 10
736 31 c. Euclid, Ptolemy, Zoroaster, Raphael and Sodoma . . . 30 30
737 50 c. Euclid and his pupils . . 45 45
738 2 l. Pythagoras, Francesco Maria della Rovere and Heraclitus 1·40 1·40

164 Agricultural Training

1983. Commonwealth Day. Multicoloured.

740 6 c. Type **164** 10 10
741 10 c. Tourism development . . 10 10
742 50 c. Broadcasting training . . 45 45
743 1 l. Airport services . . . . . 1·50 1·25

165 Map of Africa and Flag of Sierra Leone

1983. 25th Anniv of Economic Commission for Africa.

744	**165** 1 l. multicoloured	80	1·10

166 Chimpanzees in Tree

1983. Endangered Species. Multicoloured.

745	6 c. Type **166**	1·50	20
746	10 c. Three chimpanzees (vert)	1·75	30
747	31 c. Chimpanzees swinging in tree (vert)	3·25	90
748	60 c. Group of chimpanzees	5·50	7·50

167 Traditional Communications

1983. World Communications Year. Mult.

750	6 c. Type **167**	10	10
751	10 c. Mail via Mano River	15	10
752	20 c. Satellite ground station	15	10
753	1 l. British packet, circa 1805	90	65

168 Montgolfier Balloon, Paris, 1783

1983. Bicentenary of Manned Flight. Mult.

755	6 c. Type **168**	30	10
756	20 c. Wolfert's "Deutschland" airship, Berlin, 1879 (horiz)	70	20
757	50 c. Amundsen's airship N.1 "Norge", North Pole, 1926 (horiz)	1·75	1·75
758	1 l. "Cap Sierra" sport balloon, Freetown, 1983	1·75	2·25

169 Mickey Mouse

1983. Space Ark Fantasy. Walt Disney Cartoon Characters. Multicoloured.

774	1 c. Type **169**	10	10
775	1 c. Huey, Dewey and Louie	10	10
776	3 c. Goofy in spaceship	10	10
777	3 c. Donald Duck	10	10
778	10 c. Ludwig von Drake	10	10
779	10 c. Goofy	10	10
780	2 l. Mickey Mouse and Giraffe in spaceship	1·25	1·60
781	3 l. Donald Duck floating in space	1·75	2·00

170 Graduates from Union Training Programme

1984. 10th Anniv of Mano River Union. Mult.

783	6 c. Type **170**	10	10
784	25 c. Intra-Union trade	10	10
785	31 c. Member Presidents on map	10	10
786	41 c. Signing ceremony marking Guinea's accession	15	15

171 Gymnastics

1984. Olympic Games, Los Angeles. Mult.

788	90 c. Type **171**	30	40
789	1 l. Hurdling	30	40
790	3 l. Javelin-throwing	75	1·25

172 "Apollo 11" Liftoff

1984. 15th Anniv of First Moonwalk. Mult.

792	50 c. Type **172**	20	20
793	75 c. Lunar module	30	30
794	1 l. 25 First Moonwalk	45	45
795	2 l. 50 Lunar exploration	85	85

173 Concorde

1984. Universal Postal Union Congress, Hamburg.

797	**173** 4 l. multicoloured	2·75	1·75

174 Citroen "Traction Avante"

1984. United Nations Decade of African Transport. Multicoloured.

799	12 c. Type **174**	30	10
800	60 c. Locomotive	50	35
801	90 c. A.C. "Ace"	65	45
802	1 l. Vauxhall "Prince Henry"	65	45
803	1 l. 50 Delahaye "135"	80	70
804	2 l. Mazda "1105"	90	90

1984. Nos. 625, 627 and 634 surch.

811	25 c. on 10 c. Grey parrot (vert)	75	85
812	40 c. on 10 c. Grey parrot (vert)	50	70
813	50 c. on 2 l. Black bee eater	50	70
814	70 c. on 5 c. Spur-winged goose	50	70
815	10 l. on 5 c. Spur-winged goose	3·00	3·50

1984. "Ausipex" International Stamp Exhibition, Melbourne. Nos. 632 and 635 optd **AUSIPEX 84**.

818	50 c. Black crake (vert)	1·00	75
819	5 l. Barrow's bustard	2·75	2·00

177 Portuguese Caravel

1984. History of Shipping. Multicoloured.

820B	2 c. Type **177**	55	1·25
821B	5 c. "Merlin" of Bistol	55	70
822B	10 c. "Golden Hind"	75	70
823A	15 c. "Mordaunt"	1·25	90
824B	20 c. "Atlantic" (sail transport)	80	60
825B	25 c. H.M.S. "Lapwing" (frigate), 1785	80	60
826B	30 c. "Traveller" (brig)	80	60
827B	40 c. "Amistad" (schooner)	90	60
828B	50 c. H.M.S. "Teazer" (gun vessel), 1868	1·00	60
829B	70 c. "Scotia" (cable ship)	1·75	1·75
830B	1 l. H.M.S. "Alecto" (paddle-steamer), 1882	1·75	1·75
831B	2 l. H.M.S. "Blonde" (cruiser), 1889	2·00	2·50
832B	5 l. H.M.S. "Fox" (cruiser), 1895	2·75	4·00
833B	10 l. "Accra" (liner)	3·25	5·00
833cA	15 l. H.M.S. "Favourite" (sloop), 1829	2·50	3·00
833dA	25 l. H.M.S. "Euryalus" (screw frigate), 1883	2·75	3·50

Nos. 820/2 and 824/33 come both with and without imprint dates.

178 Mail Runner approaching Mano River Depot, c. 1843

1984. 125th Anniv of First Postage Stamps. Multicoloured.

834	50 c. Type **178**	35	15
835	2 l. Isaac Fitzjohn, first Postmaster, receiving letters, 1855	1·25	85
836	3 l. 1859 packet franked with four 6d. stamps	1·75	1·50

179 "Madonna and Child" (Pisanello)

1984. Christmas. Madonna and Child Paintings by artists named. Multicoloured.

838	20 c. Type **179**	10	10
839	1 l. Memling	40	40
840	2 l. Raphael	75	90
841	3 l. Van der Werff	1·10	1·40

180 Donald Duck in "The Wise Little Hen"

1984. 50th Birthday of Donald Duck. Walt Disney Cartoon Characters. Multicoloured.

843	1 c. Type **180**	10	10
844	2 c. Mickey Mouse and Donald Duck in "Boat Builders"	10	10
845	3 c. Panchito, Donald Duck and Jose Carioca in "The Three Caballeros"	10	10
846	4 c. Donald Duck meeting Pythagoras in "Mathmagic Land"	10	10
847	5 c. Donald Duck and nephew in "The Mickey Mouse Club"	10	10
848	10 c. Mickey Mouse, Goofy and Donald Duck in "Donald on Parade"	10	10
849	1 l. Donald Duck riding donkey in "Don Donald"	1·00	1·00
850	2 l. Donald Duck in "Donald Gets Drafted"	2·00	2·00
851	4 l. Donald Duck meeting children in Tokyo Disneyland	3·25	3·25

181 Fischer's Whydah

1985. Birth Bicentenary of John J. Audubon (ornithologist). Songbirds of Sierra Leone. Multicoloured.

853	40 c. Type **181**	1·75	55
854	90 c. Spotted flycatcher	3·00	1·75
855	1 l. 30 Garden warbler	3·25	3·50
856	3 l. Speke's weaver	5·50	7·50

182 Fishing

1985. International Youth Year. Mult.

858	1 l. 15 Type **182**	45	55
859	1 l. 50 Sawing timber	60	75
860	2 l. 15 Rice farming	75	95

183 Eddie Rickenbacker and Spad "XIII", 1918

1985. 40th Anniv of I. C. A. O. Multicoloured.

862	70 c. Type **183**	1·50	75
863	1 l. 25 Samuel P. Langley and "Aerodrome A", 1903	2·00	1·75
864	1 l. 30 Orville and Wilbur Wright with Wright Flyer I, 1903	2·00	1·75
865	2 l. Charles Lindbergh and "Spirit of St. Louis", 1927	2·25	2·75

184 "Temptation of Christ' (Botticelli)

1985. Easter. Religious Paintings. Mult.

867	45 c. Type **184**	30	15
868	70 c. "Christ at the Column" (Velasquez)	55	35
869	1 l. 55 "Pieta" (Botticelli) (vert)	90	75
870	10 l. "Christ on the Cross" (Velasquez) (vert)	4·75	5·00

185 The Queen Mother at St. Paul's Cathedral

190 "Madonna and Child" (Crivelli)

188 Chater-Lea (1905) at Hill Station House

1985. Life and Times of Queen Elizabeth the Queen Mother. Multicoloured.

872	1 l. Type **185**	20	25
873	1 l. 70 With her racehorse, "Double Star", at Sandown (horiz)	30	40
874	10 l. At Covent Garden, 1971	1·75	2·50

1985. 75th Anniv of Girl Guide Movement. Nos. 690/3 surch **75th ANNIVERSARY OF GIRL GUIDES**.

876	70 c. on 20 c. Type **155**	30	30
877	1 l. 30 on 50 c. Scouts picking flowers	55	55
878	5 l. on 1 l. Lord Baden-Powell	1·60	1·60
879	7 l. on 2 l. Scouts fishing	2·25	2·25

1985. Olympic Gold Medal Winners, Los Angeles. Nos. 788/90 surch.

881	2 l. on 90 c. Type **171** (surch **Le2 MA YANHONJG CHINA GOLD MEDAL**)	50	55
882	4 l. on 1 l. Hurdling (surch **Le4 E. MOSES U.S.A. GOLD MEDAL**)	1·00	1·25
883	8 l. on 3 l. Javelin-throwing (surch **Le8 A. HAERKOENEN FINLAND GOLD MEDAL**)	2·00	2·10

1985. Centenary of Motor Cycle and Decade for African Transport. Multicoloured.

885	1 l. 40 Type **188**	1·00	1·00
886	2 l. Honda "XR 350 R" at Queen Elizabeth II Quay, Freetown	1·40	1·40
887	4 l. Kawasaki "Vulcan" at Bo Clock Tower	2·50	2·50
888	5 l. Harley-Davidson "Electra-Glide" in Makeni village	2·75	2·75

1985. 300th Birth Anniv of Johann Sebastian Bach (composer). As T **206** of Antigua. Mult.

890	70 c. Viola pomposa	85	25
891	3 l. Spinet	2·00	80
892	4 l. Lute	2·10	1·10
893	5 l. Oboe	2·25	1·40

1985. Nos. 707/9 and 711/13 surch.

895	70 c. on 3 l. Caernarvon Castle (707)	30	30
899	1 l. 30 on 3l c. Caernarvon Castle (711)	1·25	1·25
896	4 l. on 50 c. Type **158** (708)	2·00	2·50
897	5 l. on 2 l. Princess of Wales (709)	2·50	3·00
900	5 l. on 50 c. Type **158** (712)	3·00	3·50
901	7 l. on 2 l. Princess of Wales (713)	4·00	4·50

1985. Christmas. "Madonna and Child" Paintings by artists named. Multicoloured.

903	70 c. Type **190**	25	10
904	3 l. Bouts	80	40
905	4 l. Da Messina	95	55
906	5 l. Lochner	1·10	65

1985. 150th Birth Anniv of Mark Twain (author). As T **118** of Anguilla showing Walt Disney cartoon characters illustrating Mark Twain quotations. Multicoloured.

908	1 l. 50 Snow White and Bashful	40	40
909	3 l. Three Little Pigs	60	90
910	4 l. Donald Duck and nephew	70	1·10
911	5 l. Pinocchio and Figaro the cat	85	1·25

1985. Birth Bicentenaries of Grimm Brothers (folklorists). Walt Disney cartoon characters in scenes from "Rumpelstiltskin". As T **119** of Anguilla. Multicoloured.

913	70 c. The Miller (Donald Duck) and his daughter (Daisy Duck) meet the King (Uncle Scrooge)	20	25
914	1 l. The King puts the Miller's daughter to work	35	40
915	2 l. Rumpelstiltskin demands payment	50	55
916	10 l. The King with gold spun from straw	2·75	3·50

1985. 40th Anniv of U.N.O. As T **208** of Antigua showing United Nations (New York) stamps. Multicoloured.

918	2 l. John Kennedy and 1954 Human Rights 8 c. stamp	70	70
919	4 l. Albert Einstein (scientist) and 1958 Atomic Energy 3 c.	1·40	1·60
920	7 l. Maimonides (physician) and 1956 W.H.O. 8 c.	3·75	4·25

191 Player kicking Ball

193 "Monodora myristica"

192 Chicago-Milwaukee "Hiawatha Express"

1986. World Cup Football Championship, Mexico. Multicoloured.

922	70 c. Type **191**	45	10
923	3 l. Player controlling ball	90	50
924	4 l. Player chasing ball	1·10	70
925	5 l. Player kicking ball (different)	1·50	80

1986. Centenary of Statue of Liberty. As T **163b** of Lesotho. Multicoloured.

927	40 c. Times Square, 1905 (vert)	10	10
928	70 c. Times Square, 1986 (vert)	15	10
929	1 l. "Tally Ho" coach, c. 1880	25	15
930	10 l. Express bus, 1986	1·75	1·90

1986. Appearance of Halley's Comet (1st issue). As T **123** of Anguilla. Multicoloured.

932	15 c. Johannes Kepler (astronomer) and Paris Observatory	30	10
933	50 c. N.A.S.A. Space Shuttle landing, 1985	40	10
934	70 c. Halley's Comet (from Bayeux Tapestry)	40	15
935	10 l. Comet of 530 A.D. and Merlin predicting coming of King Arthur	2·00	1·60

See also Nos. 988/91.

1986. 60th Birthday of Queen Elizabeth II. As T **125** of Anguilla.

937	10 c. black and yellow	20	10
938	1 l. 70 multicoloured	45	35
939	10 l. multicoloured	2·00	2·50

DESIGNS: 10 c. Princess Elizabeth inspecting guard of honour, Cranwell, 1951; 1 l. 70, In Garter robes; 10 l. Braemar Games, 1970.

1986. "Ameripex" International Stamp Exhibition, Chicago. American Trains. Multicoloured.

941	50 c. Type **192**	80	40
942	2 l. Rock Island Line "The Rocket"	1·60	1·75
943	4 l. Rio Grande "Prospector"	2·50	3·00
944	7 l. Southern Pacific "Daylight Express"	3·00	4·50

1986. Royal Wedding. As T **213** of Antigua. Multicoloured.

946	10 c. Prince Andrew and Miss Sarah Ferguson	10	10
947	1 l. 70 Prince Andrew at clay pigeon shoot	30	35
948	10 l. Prince Andrew in naval uniform	1·40	1·75

1986. Flowers of Sierra Leone. Multicoloured.

950	70 c. Type **193**	15	10
951	1 l. 50 "Gloriosa simplex"	20	15
952	4 l. "Mussaenda erythrophylla"	35	25
953	6 l. "Crinum ornatum"	50	40
954	8 l. "Bauhinia purpurea"	60	60
955	10 l. "Bombax costatum"	70	70
956	20 l. "Hibiscus rosasinensis"	1·25	1·50
957	30 l. "Cassia fistula"	1·75	2·00

194 Handshake and Flags of Sierra Leone and U.S.A.

1986. 25th Anniv of United States Peace Corps.

959	**194** 4 l. multicoloured	70	70

195 Transporting Goods by Canoe

1986. International Peace Year. Mult.

960	1 l. Type **195**	30	15
961	2 l. Teacher and class	40	25
962	5 l. Rural post office	80	50
963	10 l. Fishermen in longboat	1·60	1·25

1986. Various stamps surch.

968	70 c. on 10 c. Princess Elizabeth inspecting guard of honour, Cranwell (No. 937)	40	10
971	70 c. on 10 c. Prince Andrew and Miss Sarah Ferguson (No. 946)	10	10
964	30 l. on 2 c. Type **177** (No. 820)	2·00	2·50
965	40 l. on 30 c. "Traveller" (brig) (No. 826)	2·50	3·00
969	45 l. on 10 l. Queen at Braemar Games, 1970 (No. 934)	3·50	2·50
972	45 l. on 10 l. Prince Andrew in naval uniform (No. 948)	2·40	2·50
966	45 l. on 40 c. "Amistad" (schooner) (No. 827)	2·75	3·25
967	50 l. on 70 c. "Scotia" (cable ship) (No. 829)	3·00	3·25

1986. World Cup Football Championship Winners, Mexico. Nos. 922/5 optd **WINNERS Argentina 3 W.Germany 2** or surch also.

974	70 c. Type **191**	35	10
975	3 l. Player controlling ball	65	30
976	4 l. Player chasing ball	70	40
977	40 l. on 5 l. Player kicking ball (different)	6·00	4·50

198 Mickey and Minnie Mouse as Jack and Jill

1986. "Stockholmia '86" International Stamp Exn, Sweden. Walt Disney cartoon characters in scenes from nursery rhymes. Mult.

979	70 c. Type **198**	10	10
980	1 l. Donald Duck as Wee Willie Winkie	15	15
981	2 l. Minnie Mouse as Little Miss Muffet	20	20
982	4 l. Goofy as Old King Cole	40	40
983	5 l. Clarabelle as Mary Quite Contrary	50	50
984	10 l. Daisy Duck as Little Bo Peep	90	1·00
985	25 l. Daisy Duck and Minnie Mouse in "Polly put the Kettle on"	2·00	2·75
986	35 l. Goofy, Mickey Mouse and Donald Duck as the Three Men in a Tub	2·50	3·25

1986. Appearance of Halley's Comet (2nd issue). Nos. 932/5 optd as T **218** of Antigua.

988	50 c. N.A.S.A. Space Shuttle landing, 1985	20	10
989	70 c. Halley's Comet (from Bayeux Tapestry)	20	10
990	1 l. 50 on 15 c. Johannes Kepler (astronomer) and Paris Observatory	20	10
991	45 l. on 10 l. Comet of 530 A.D. and Merlin predicting coming of King Arthur	4·00	3·75

199 "Virgin and Child with St. Dorothy"

1986. Christmas. Paintings by Titian. Mult.

993	70 c. Type **199**	10	10
994	1 l. 50 "The Gypsy Madonna" (vert)	15	10
995	20 l. "The Holy Family"	2·25	2·50
996	30 l. "Virgin and Child in an Evening Landscape" (vert)	2·75	3·25

200 Nomoli (soapstone figure)

201 Removing Top of Statue's Torch

1987. Bicentenary of Sierra Leone. Mult.

998	2 l. Type **200**	15	15
999	5 l. King's Yard Gate, Royal Hospital, 1817	30	40

1987. Centenary of Statue of Liberty (1986) (2nd issue). Multicoloured.

1001	70 c. Type **201**	10	10
1002	1 l. 50 View of Statue's torch and New York harbour (horiz)	10	10
1003	2 l. Crane lifting torch	10	10
1004	3 l. Workman steadying torch	10	15
1005	4 l. Statue's crown (horiz)	15	20
1006	5 l. Statue of Liberty (side view) and fireworks	20	25
1007	10 l. Statue of Liberty and fireworks	40	45
1008	25 l. Bedloe Island, statue and fireworks (horiz)	1·00	1·40
1009	30 l. Statue's face	1·25	1·75

202 Emblem, Mother and Child and Syringe

1987. 40th Anniv of U.N.I.C.E.F.

1010	**202** 10 l. multicoloured	40	55

203 "U.S.A.", 1987

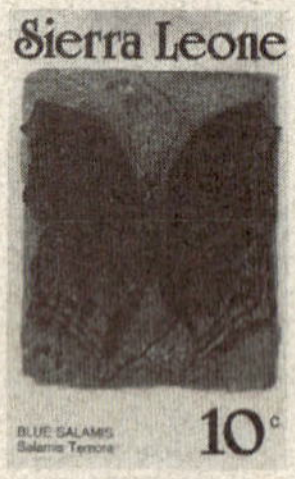

205 "Salamis temora"

204 Mickey Mouse as Mountie and Parliament Building, Ottawa

1987. America's Cup Yachting Championship. Multicoloured.

1011	1 l. Type **203**	10	10
1012	1 l. 50 "New Zealand II", 1987 (horiz)	10	10
1013	2 l. 50 "French Kiss", 1987	10	10
1014	10 l. "Stars and Stripes", 1987 (horiz)	65	45
1015	15 l. "Australia II", 1983	90	75
1016	25 l. "Freedom", 1980	1·60	1·40
1017	30 l. "Kookaburra", 1987 (horiz)	1·75	1·60

1987. "Capex '87" International Stamp Exhibition, Toronto. Walt Disney cartoon characters in Canada. Multicoloured.

1019	2 l. Type **204**	20	20
1020	5 l. Goofy dressed as Mountie and totem poles	35	35
1021	10 l. Goofy windsurfing and Donald Duck fishing off Perce Rock	60	45
1022	20 l. Goofy with mountain goat in Rocky Mountains	1·00	1·25
1023	25 l. Donald Duck and Mickey Mouse in Old Quebec	1·25	1·40
1024	45 l. Goofy emerging from igloo and "Aurora Borealis"	1·75	2·50
1025	50 l. Goofy as gold prospector and post office, Yukon	2·00	3·00
1026	75 l. Dumbo flying over Niagara Falls	3·25	4·50

1987. Butterflies. Multicoloured, "Sierra Leone" in black.

1028B	10 c. Type **205**	40	40
1029B	20 c. "Stugeta marmorea"	40	40
1030B	40 c. "Graphium ridleyanus"	40	40
1031B	1 l. "Papilio bromius"	60	60
1032B	2 l. "Iterus zalmoxis"	75	75
1033B	3 l. "Cymothoe sangaris"	90	90
1033cB	3 l. As 40 c.	3·00	2·00
1034Ac	5 l. "Graphium tynderaeus"	1·25	30
1034cB	9 l. As 3 l. (No. 1033)	4·00	2·75
1035Ac	10 l. "Graphium policenes"	1·25	30
1035cB	12 l. Type **205**	4·50	3·00
1035dB	16 l. As 20 c.	4·50	3·00
1036Ac	20 l. "Tanuetheira timon"	1·50	60
1037Ac	25 l. "Danaus limniace"	1·50	30
1038Ac	30 l. "Papilio hesperus"	1·75	65
1039Ac	45 l. "Charaxes smaragdalis"	1·75	30
1040Ac	60 l. "Charaxes lucretius"	2·00	2·25
1041Ac	75 l. "Antanartia delius"	2·25	2·75
1042A	100 l. "Abisara talantus"	3·25	6·00

For similar stamps but with "Sierra Leone" in blue, see Nos. 1658/72.

206 Cycling

1987. Olympic Games, Seoul (1988) (1st series). Multicoloured.

1043	5 l. Type **206**	20	25
1044	10 l. Three-day eventing	40	50
1045	45 l. Athletics	1·75	2·00
1046	50 l. Tennis	2·00	2·40

See also Nos. 1137/41.

1987. Birth Centenary of Marc Chagall (artist). As T **225** of Antigua. Multicoloured.

1048	3 l. "The Quarrel"	15	15
1049	5 l. "Rebecca giving Abraham's Servant a Drink"	20	25
1050	10 l. "The Village"	40	45
1051	20 l. "Ida at the Window"	60	65
1052	25 l. "Promenade"	1·00	1·10
1053	45 l. "Peasants"	2·00	2·25
1054	50 l. "Turquoise Plate" (ceramic)	2·25	2·25
1055	75 l. "Cemetery Gate"	3·25	3·75

1987. Milestones of Transportation. As T **226** of Antigua. Multicoloured.

1057	3 l. "Apollo 8" spacecraft (first manned Moon orbit), 1968	15	15
1058	5 l. Blanchard's balloon (first U.S. balloon flight), 1793	20	20
1059	10 l. Amelia Earhart's Lockheed Vega 5B (first solo transatlantic flight by woman), 1932	40	40
1060	15 l. Vicker's Vimy (first non-stop transatlantic flight), 1919	60	70
1061	20 l. British "Mk 1" tank (first combat tank), 1916	80	90
1062	25 l. Vought-Sikorsky VS-300 (first U.S. helicopter flight), 1939	90	1·00
1063	30 l. Wright brothers Flyer I (first powered flight), 1903	1·10	1·25
1064	35 l. Bleriot XI (first cross Channel flight), 1909	1·25	1·40
1065	40 l. Paraplane (first flexible-wing ultralight), 1983	1·50	1·75
1066	50 l. Daimler's first motorcycle, 1885	1·75	2·00

Nos. 1058/64 are horiz.

207 Evonne Goolagong

1987. Wimbledon Tennis Champions. Mult.

1068	2 l. Type **207**	35	35
1069	5 l. Martina Navratilova	55	55
1070	10 l. Jimmy Connors	85	85
1071	15 l. Bjorn Borg	1·25	1·25
1072	30 l. Boris Becker	2·25	2·25
1073	40 l. John McEnroe	2·50	2·50
1074	50 l. Chris Evert Lloyd	2·75	2·75
1075	75 l. Virginia Wade	3·50	3·50

208 Ducats, "Santa Maria" and Isaac Abravanel (financier)

1987. 500th Anniv (1992) of Discovery of America by Columbus. Multicoloured.

1077	5 l. Type **208**	70	20
1078	10 l. Astrolabe, "Pinta" and Abraham Zacuto (astronomer)	80	35
1079	45 l. Maravedis (coins), "Nina" and Luis de Santangel (financier)	2·50	3·00
1080	50 l. Carib and Spaniard with tobacco plant and Luis de Torres (translator)	2·75	3·25

209 Cotton Tree

1987. Flora and Fauna. Multicoloured.

1082	3 l. Type **209**	15	15
1083	5 l. Dwarf crocodile	35	25
1084	10 l. Kudu	40	35
1085	20 l. Yellowbells	65	65
1086	25 l. Hippopotamus and calf	1·75	1·25
1087	45 l. Comet orchid	3·25	2·50
1088	50 l. Baobab tree	2·25	2·50
1089	75 l. Elephant and calf	4·25	5·00

210 Scouts at Ayers Rock

1987. World Scout Jamboree, Australia. Mult.

1091	5 l. Type **210**	30	20
1092	15 l. Scouts sailing yacht	65	65
1093	40 l. Scouts and Sydney skyline	1·50	2·50
1094	50 l. Scout, Sydney Harbour Bridge and Opera House	2·50	2·75

1987. Bicentenary of U.S. Constitution. As T **232** of Antigua. Multicoloured.

1096	5 l. White House	15	20
1097	10 l. George Washington (Virginia delegate) (vert)	30	35
1098	30 l. Patrick Henry (statesman) (vert)	90	95
1099	65 l. State Seal, New Hampshire	1·90	2·40

1987. 60th Anniv of Mickey Mouse (Walt Disney cartoon character). Cartoon characters at Tokyo Disneyland. As T **220** of Dominica. Mult.

1101	20 c. Mickey and Minnie Mouse on Space Mountain	10	10
1102	40 c. Mickey Mouse at Country Bear Jamboree	10	10
1103	80 c. Mickey Mouse as bandleader and Minnie Mouse, Goofy and Pluto as musicians	10	10
1104	1 l. Goofy, Mickey Mouse and children in canoe and Mark Twain's river boat	10	10
1105	2 l. Mickey Mouse, Goofy and Chip n'Dale on Western River Railroad	10	10
1106	3 l. Goofy and Mickey Mouse as Pirates of the Caribbean	15	15
1107	10 l. Mickey Mouse, Goofy and children aboard Big Thunder Mountain train	55	55
1108	20 l. Mickey Mouse, Morty and Ferdie in boat and Goofy on flying carpet	1·25	1·50
1109	30 l. Mickey and Minnie Mouse in kimonos at Disneyland entrance	1·75	2·00

211 "The Annunciation" (detail) (Titian)

1987. Christmas. Religious Paintings by Titian. Multicoloured.

1111	2 l. Type **211**	20	10
1112	10 l. "Madonna and Child with Saints"	60	35
1113	20 l. "Madonna and Child with Saints Ulfus and Brigid"	1·10	1·25
1114	35 l. "The Madonna of the Cherries"	1·90	2·75

1988. Royal Ruby Wedding. As T **234** of Antigua.

1116	2 l. brown, black and grey	10	10
1117	3 l. multicoloured	10	10
1118	10 l. brown, black and orange	30	35
1119	50 l. multicoloured	2·00	2·50

DESIGNS: 2 l. Wedding of Princess Elizabeth and Duke of Edinburgh, 1947; 3 l. Prince Charles's christening photograph, 1949; 10 l. Queen Elizabeth II with Prince Charles and Princess Anne, c. 1951; 50 l. Queen Elizabeth, c. 1960.

212 "Russula cyanoxantha"

213 Golden Pheasant Panchax

1988. Fungi. Multicoloured.

1121	3 l. Type **212**	45	30
1122	10 l. "Lycoperdon perlatum"	1·10	70
1123	20 l. "Lactarius deliciosus"	1·90	2·00
1124	30 l. "Boletus edulis"	2·25	2·75

1988. Fishes of Sierra Leone. Multicoloured.

1126	3 l. Type **213**	15	15
1127	10 l. Banded panchax	30	30
1128	20 l. Jewel cichlid	50	75
1129	35 l. Freshwater butterflyfish	75	1·40

1988. Stamp Exhibitions. Nos. 1016, 1072 and 1079 optd.

1131	25 l. "Freedom", 1980 (optd **INDEPENDENCE 40**, Israel)	1·10	1·40
1132	30 l. Boris Becker (optd **OLYMPHILEX '88** Seoul)	1·25	1·75
1133	45 l. Maravedis (coins), "Nina" and Luis de Santangel (financier) (optd **PRAGA 88**, Prague)	1·75	2·25

214 Hands holding Coffee Beans and Woman with Cocoa

1988. International Fund for Agricultural Development. Multicoloured.

1134	3 l. Type **214**	20	20
1135	15 l. Tropical fruits and man climbing palm tree	70	80
1136	25 l. Sheaf of rice and harvesters	1·25	1·50

215 Basketball

216 Swallow-tailed Bee Eater

1988. Olympic Games, Seoul (2nd issue). Mult.

1137	3 l. Type **215**	10	10
1138	10 l. Judo	30	35
1139	15 l. Gymnastics	45	55
1140	40 l. Synchronized swimming	1·25	1·75

1988. Birds. Multicoloured.

1142	3 l. Type **216**	75	75
1143	5 l. Double-toothed barbet	1·00	1·00
1144	8 l. African golden oriole	1·25	1·25
1145	10 l. Red bishop	1·25	1·25
1146	12 l. Red-billed shrike	1·25	1·25
1147	20 l. European bee eater	1·40	1·40
1148	35 l. Common gonolek ("Barbary Shrike")	2·00	2·00
1149	40 l. Western black-headed oriole	2·25	2·25

217 "Aureol" (liner)

1988. Ships. Multicoloured.

1151	3 l. Type **217**	60	30
1152	10 l. "Dunkwa" (freighter)	1·50	80
1153	15 l. "Melampus" (container ship)	2·00	1·60
1154	30 l. "Dumbaia" (freighter)	2·75	3·00

1988. 500th Birth Anniv of Titian (artist). As T **238** of Antigua. Multicoloured.

1156	1 l. "The Concert" (detail)	10	10
1157	2 l. "Philip II of Spain"	15	15
1158	3 l. "Saint Sebastian" (detail)	20	20
1159	5 l. "Martyrdom of St. Peter Martyr"	30	30
1160	15 l. "St. Jerome"	75	85
1161	20 l. "St. Mark enthroned with Saints"	90	1·10
1162	25 l. "Portrait of a Young Man"	1·10	1·40
1163	30 l. "St. Jerome in Penitence"	1·25	1·50

218 Sikorsky S-58 Helicopter lowering "Mercury" Capsule to Flight Deck

1988. 25th Death Anniv of John F. Kennedy (American statesman). U.S. Space Achievements. Multicoloured.

1165	3 l. Type **218**	55	15
1166	5 l. "Liberty Bell 7" capsule descending (vert)	55	20
1167	15 l. Launch of first manned American capsule (vert)	80	70
1168	40 l. "Freedom 7" orbiting Earth	1·50	2·00

219 Famine Relief Convoy crossing Desert

220 "Adoration of the Magi" (detail)

1988. 125th Anniv of Int Red Cross. Mult.

1170	3 l. Type **219**	50	40
1171	10 l. Rifle and map of Battle of Solferino, 1859	1·75	90
1172	20 l. World War II hospital ship in Pacific	2·25	2·00
1173	40 l. Red Cross tent and World War I German biplanes	3·25	3·25

1988. Christmas. "Mickey's Christmas Dance". As T **228** of Dominica showing Walt Disney cartoon characters. Multicoloured.

1175	10 l. Donald Duck's nephews playing as band	70	80
1176	10 l. Clarabelle	70	80
1177	10 l. Goofy	70	80
1178	10 l. Scrooge McDuck and Grandma Duck	70	80
1179	10 l. Donald Duck	70	80
1180	10 l. Daisy Duck	70	80
1181	10 l. Minnie Mouse	70	80
1182	10 l. Mickey Mouse	70	80

Nos. 1175/82 were printed together, se-tenant, forming a composite design.

1988. Christmas. Religious Paintings by Rubens. Multicoloured.

1184	3 l. Type **220**	15	15
1185	3 l. 60 "Adoration of the Shepherds" (detail)	15	15
1186	5 l. "Adoration of the Magi" (detail)	25	25
1187	10 l. "Adoration of the Shepherds" (different detail)	40	40
1188	20 l. "Virgin and Child surrounded by Flowers"	75	75
1189	40 l. "St. Gregory the Great and Other Saints" (detail)	1·60	1·75
1190	60 l. "Adoration of the Magi" (detail)	2·25	2·75
1191	80 l. "Madonna and Child with Saints" (detail)	2·75	3·25

222 Brazil v. Sweden, 1958

1989. World Cup Football Championship, Italy (1st issue). Designs showing action from previous World Cup finals. Multicoloured.

1194	3 l. Type **222**	40	30
1195	6 l. West Germany v. Hungary, 1954	50	40
1196	8 l. England v. West Germany, 1966	60	45
1197	10 l. Argentina v. Netherlands, 1978	70	50
1198	12 l. Brazil v. Czechoslovakia, 1962	75	75
1199	20 l. West Germany v. Netherlands, 1974	1·00	1·00
1200	30 l. Italy v. West Germany, 1982	1·40	1·60
1201	40 l. Brazil v. Italy, 1970	1·75	1·90

See also Nos. 1455/74.

223 Decathlon (Gold, C. Schenk, East Germany)

1989. Olympic Medal Winners, Seoul (1988). Multicoloured.

1203	3 l. Type **223**	60	30
1204	6 l. Men's heavyweight judo (Gold, H. Saito, Japan)	70	40
1205	10 l. Women's cycle road race (Silver, J. Niehaus, West Germany)	90	50
1206	15 l. Men's single sculls (Gold, T. Lange, East Germany)	1·10	80
1207	20 l. Men's 50 metres freestyle swimming (Gold, M. Biondi, U.S.A.)	1·25	1·00
1208	30 l. Men's 100 metres (Gold, C. Lewis, U.S.A.)	1·50	1·50
1209	40 l. Dressage (Gold, West Germany)	1·60	1·75
1210	50 l. Greco-Roman wrestling (57 kg) (Gold, A. Sike, Hungary)	1·75	1·90

224 Map of Union States, Mail Lorry and Post Office

1989. 15th Anniv of Mano River Union. Mult.

1212	1 l. Type **224**	30	20
1213	3 l. Map of West Africa and Presidents Momoh, Conte and Doe	60	20
1214	10 l. Construction of Freetown-Monrovia Highway	1·25	80

225 "Richard III"

1989. 425th Birth Anniv of Shakespeare. Mult.

1216	15 l. Type **225**	60	60
1217	15 l. "Othello" (Iago)	60	60
1218	15 l. "Two Gentlemen of Verona"	60	60
1219	15 l. "Macbeth" (Lady Macbeth)	60	60
1220	15 l. "Hamlet"	60	60
1221	15 l. "The Taming of the Shrew"	60	60
1222	15 l. "The Merry Wives of Windsor"	60	60
1223	15 l. "Henry IV" (Sir John Falstaff)	60	60
1224	15 l. "Macbeth" (The Witches)	60	60
1225	15 l. "Romeo and Juliet"	60	60
1226	15 l. "Merchant of Venice"	60	60
1227	15 l. "As You Like It"	60	60
1228	15 l. "The Taming of the Shrew" (banquet scene)	60	60
1229	15 l. "King Lear"	60	60
1230	15 l. "Othello" (Othello and Desdemona)	60	60
1231	15 l. "Henry IV" (Justice Shallow)	60	60

226 Centenary Logo

1989. Cent of Ahmadiyya Muslim Society.

1233	**226** 3 l. black and blue	30	30

1989. Japanese Art (1st series). Paintings by Seiho. As T **250** of Antigua. Multicoloured.

1234	3 l. "Lapping Waves"	35	35
1235	6 l. "Hazy Moon" (vert)	45	45
1236	8 l. "Passing Spring" (vert)	45	45
1237	10 l. "Mackerels"	45	45
1238	12 l. "Calico Cat"	45	45
1239	30 l. "The First Time to be a Model" (vert)	80	80
1240	40 l. "Kingly Lion"	1·10	1·10
1241	75 l. "After a Shower" (vert)	1·75	1·75

See also Nos. 1321/50.

227 Robespierre and Bastille

1989. "Philexfrance '89" International Stamp Exhibition, Paris and Bicentenary of French Revolution. Multicoloured.

1243 6 l. Type **227** 45 35
1244 20 l. Danton and Louvre 90 80
1245 45 l. Queen Marie Antoinette and Notre Dame 1·40 1·25
1246 80 l. Louis XVI and Palace of Versailles 2·00 2·75

228 "Sputnik" Satellite in Orbit, 1957

1989. History of Space Exploration. As T **228** multicoloured

1248/1301 10 l. × 27, 15 l. × 27
Set of 54 22·00 23·00

229 "Bulbophyllum barbigerum"

1989. Orchids of Sierra Leone. Multicoloured.

1303 3 l. Type **229** 55 40
1304 6 l. "Bulbophyllum falcatum" 85 60
1305 12 l. "Habenaria macrara" 1·25 90
1306 20 l. "Eurychone rothchildiana" 1·60 1·40
1307 50 l. "Calyptrochilum christyanum" 2·25 2·25
1308 60 l. "Bulbophyllum distans" 2·50 2·75
1309 70 l. "Eulophia guineensis" 2·50 2·75
1310 80 l. "Diaphananthe pellucida" 2·75 3·25

230 "Salamis temora"

1989. Butterflies. Multicoloured.

1312 6 l. Type **230** 75 75
1313 12 l. "Pseudacraea lucretia" 1·10 1·10
1314 18 l. "Charaxes boueti" (vert) 1·40 1·40
1315 30 l. "Graphium antheus" (vert) 2·00 2·00
1316 40 l. "Colotis protomedia" 2·25 2·25
1317 60 l. "Asterope pechueli" (vert) 2·75 2·75
1318 72 l. "Coenyra aurantiaca" 3·00 3·00
1319 80 l. "Precis octavia" (vert) 3·00 3·00

1989. Japanese Art (2nd series). Paintings by Hiroshige of "The Fifty-three Stations on the Tokaido Road". As T **250** of Antigua. Mult.

1321 25 l. "Ferry-boat to Kawasaki" 80 80
1322 25 l. "The Hilly Town of Hodogaya" 80 80
1323 25 l. "Lute Players at Fujisawa" 80 80
1324 25 l. "Mild Rainstorm at Oiso" 80 80
1325 25 l. "Lake Ashi and Mountains of Hakone" 80 80
1326 25 l. "Twilight at Numazu" 80 80
1327 25 l. "Mount Fuji from Hara" 80 80
1328 25 l. "Samurai Children riding through Yoshiwara" 80 80
1329 25 l. "Mountain Pass at Yui" 80 80
1330 25 l. "Harbour at Ejiri" 80 80
1331 25 l. "Halt at Fujieda" 80 80
1332 25 l. "Misty Kanaya on the Oi River" 80 80
1333 25 l. "The Bridge to Kakegawa" 80 80
1334 25 l. "Teahouse at Fukuroi" 80 80
1335 25 l. "The Ford at Mistuke" 80 80
1336 25 l. "Coolies warming themselves at Hamamatsu" 80 80
1337 25 l. "Imakiri Ford at Maisaka" 80 80
1338 25 l. "Pacific Ocean from Shirasuka" 80 80
1339 25 l. "Futakawa Street-singers" 80 80
1340 25 l. "Repairing Yoshida Castle" 80 80
1341 25 l. "The Inn at Akasaka" 80 80
1342 25 l. "The Bridge to Okazaki" 80 80
1343 25 l. "Samurai's Wife entering Narumi" 80 80
1344 25 l. "Harbour at Kuwana" 80 80
1345 25 l. "Autumn in Ishiyakushi" 80 80
1346 25 l. "Snowfall at Kameyama" 80 80
1347 25 l. "The Frontier-station of Seki" 80 80
1348 25 l. "Teahouse at Sakanoshita" 80 80
1349 25 l. "Kansai Houses at Minakushi" 80 80
1350 25 l. "Kusatsu Station" 80 80

231 Formosan Sika Deer

1989. "World Stamp Expo '89" International Stamp Exhibition, Washington (2nd issue). Endangered Fauna. Multicoloured.

1353 6 l. Humpback whale 50 40
1354 9 l. Type **231** 40 40
1355 16 l. Spanish lynx 65 60
1356 20 l. Goitred gazelle 60 60
1357 30 l. Japanese sea lion 65 65
1558 50 l. Long-eared owl 1·50 1·25
1559 70 l. Lady Amherst's ("Chinese Copper") pheasant 1·50 1·50
1360 100 l. Siberian tiger 2·25 2·50

1989. Christmas. Walt Disney cartoon characters with cars. As T **183** of Gambia. Multicoloured.

1362 3 l. Mickey Mouse and Goofy in Rolls-Royce "Phantom II Roadstar", 1934 50 30
1363 6 l. Mickey and Minnie Mouse in Mercedes-Benz "500K", 1935 70 40
1364 10 l. Mickey and Minnie Mouse with Jaguar "SS-100", 1938 80 45
1365 12 l. Mickey Mouse and Goofy with U.S. army jeep, 1941 90 55
1366 20 l. Mickey and Minnie Mouse with Buick Roadmaster Sedan "Model 91", 1937 1·25 90
1367 30 l. Mickey Mouse driving 1948 Tucker 1·50 1·25
1368 40 l. Mickey and Minnie Mouse in Alfa Romeo, 1933 1·60 1·40
1369 50 l. Mickey and Minnie Mouse with 1937 Cord 1·75 1·60

1989. Christmas. Paintings by Rembrandt. As T **259** of Antigua. Multicoloured.

1371 3 l. "The Adoration of the Magi" 40 30
1372 6 l. "The Holy Family with a Cat" 50 40
1373 10 l. "The Holy Family with Angels" 60 45
1374 15 l. "Simeon in the Temple" 75 55
1375 30 l. "The Circumcision" 1·25 1·10
1376 90 l. "The Holy Family" 2·25 2·50
1377 100 l. "The Visitation" 2·25 2·50
1378 120 l. "The Flight into Egypt" 2·50 2·75

232 Johann Kepler (astronomer)

1990. Exploration of Mars. Designs as T **232** showing astronomers, spacecraft and Martian landscapes.

1380/1415 175 l. × 36 multicoloured
Set of 36 60·00 70·00

1990. 50th Anniv of Second World War. American Aircraft. As T **188** of Gambia. Multicoloured.

1417 1 l. Dolittle's North American B-25 Mitchell "Ruptured Duck", 1942 20 10
1418 2 l. Consolidated B-24 Liberator 30 10
1419 3 l. Douglas A20J Boston attacking Japanese convoy, Bismark Sea, 1943 30 10
1420 9 l. Lockheed P-38 Lightning 50 35
1421 12 l. Martin B-26 Marauder 60 40
1422 16 l. Boeing B-17F Flying Fortress bombers 75 55
1423 50 l. North American B-25D Mitchell bomber 1·75 1·75
1424 80 l. Boeing B-29 Superfortress 2·25 2·50
1425 90 l. Boeing B-17G Flying Fortress bomber 2·25 2·50
1426 100 l. Boeing B-29 Superfortress "Enola Gay" 2·25 2·75

233 Mickey Mouse at Bauxite Mine

1990. Sierra Leone Sites and Scenes. Walt Disney cartoon characters. Multicoloured.

1428 3 l. Type **233** 20 15
1429 6 l. Scrooge McDuck panning for gold 20 15
1430 10 l. Minnie Mouse at Lungi Airport 25 20
1431 12 l. Mickey Mouse at Old Fourah Bay College 35 20
1432 16 l. Mickey Mouse mining bauxite 45 25
1433 20 l. Huey, Dewey and Louie harvesting rice 50 30
1434 30 l. Mickey and Minnie Mouse admire the Freetown Cotton Tree 60 40
1435 100 l. Mickey Mouse flying over Rutile Mine 2·00 2·25
1436 200 l. Mickey Mouse fishing at Goderich 2·75 3·25
1437 225 l. Mickey and Minnie Mouse at Bintumani Hotel 2·75 3·25

234 Olivier as Antony in "Antony and Cleopatra", 1951

235 Penny Black

1990. Sir Laurence Olivier (actor) Commemoration. Multicoloured.

1439 3 l. Type **234** 30 20
1440 9 l. As King Henry V in "Henry V", 1943 40 30
1441 16 l. As Oedipus in "Oedipus", 1945 55 35
1442 20 l. As Heathcliffe in "Wuthering Heights", 1939 60 40
1443 30 l. As Szell in "Marathon Man", 1976 70 55
1444 70 l. As Othello in "Othello", 1964 1·25 1·40
1445 175 l. As Michael in "Beau Geste", 1929 2·25 2·50
1446 200 l. As King Richard III in "Richard III", 1956 2·50 2·75

1990. 150th Anniv of the Penny Black.

1448 **235** 50 l. blue 1·50 1·50
1449 100 l. brown 2·25 2·25

236 Cameroons World Cup Team

1990. World Cup Football Championship, Italy (2nd issue). Finalists. Multicoloured.

1451/74 15 l. × 8 (Type **236**, Colombia, Costa Rica, Egypt, Rumania, South Korea, U.A.E., Yugoslavia).
30 l. × 8 (Austria, Belgium, Czechoslovakia, Netherlands, Scotland, Sweden, Uruguay, U.S.S.R.).
45 l. × 8 (Argentina, Brazil, England, Ireland, Italy, Spain, U.S.A., West Germany)
Set of 24 14·00 15·00

No. 1452 is inscr "COLUMBIA" in error.

237 Great Crested Grebe

1990. Birds. Multicoloured.

1475 3 l. Type **237** 20 20
1476 6 l. Green wood hoopoe 25 25
1477 10 l. African jacana 30 30
1478 12 l. Avocet 35 35
1479 20 l. Peter's finfoot 40 40
1480 80 l. Glossy ibis 1·25 1·50
1481 150 l. Hammerkop 1·75 2·00
1482 200 l. Black-throated honeyguide 2·00 2·50

1990. "Stamp World London '90" International Stamp Exhibition. British Costumes. As T **193** of Gambia showing Walt Disney cartoon characters. Multicoloured.

1484 3 l. Mickey Mouse as a Yeoman Warder 15 15
1485 6 l. Scrooge McDuck as a lamplighter 15 15
1486 12 l. Goofy as a medieval knight 20 20
1487 15 l. Clarabelle as Ann Boleyn 20 20
1488 75 l. Minnie Mouse as Queen Elizabeth I 1·75 1·75
1489 100 l. Donald Duck as a chimney sweep 2·00 2·00
1490 125 l. Pete as King Henry VIII 2·25 2·25
1491 150 l. Clarabell, Minnie Mouse and Daisy Duck as May dancers 2·25 2·25

1990. 90th Birthday of Queen Elizabeth the Queen Mother. As T **99** of Grenada Grenadines. Multicoloured.

1493 75 l. Queen Mother on Remembrance Sunday 85 1·00
1494 75 l. Queen Mother in yellow hat 85 1·00
1495 75 l. Waving to crowds on 85th birthday 85 1·00

238 Golden Cat

1990. Wildlife. Multicoloured.

1497 25 l. Type **238** 50 50
1498 25 l. White-backed night heron 50 50
1499 25 l. Bateleur 50 50
1500 25 l. Marabou stork 50 50
1501 25 l. White-faced whistling duck 50 50
1502 25 l. Aardvark 50 50
1503 25 l. Royal antelope 50 50
1504 25 l. Pygmy hippopotamus 50 50
1505 25 l. Leopard 50 50
1506 25 l. Sacred ibis 50 50
1507 25 l. Mona monkey 50 50
1508 25 l. African darter 50 50
1509 25 l. Chimpanzee 50 50
1510 25 l. African elephant 50 50
1511 25 l. Potto 50 50
1512 25 l. African manatee 50 50
1513 25 l. African fish eagle 50 50
1514 25 l. African spoonbill 50 50

239 Rabbit

240 Morty assembling Bicycle by Christmas Tree

1990. Fairground Carousel Animals. Mult.

1516 5 l. Type **239** 15 15
1517 10 l. Horse with panther saddle 20 20
1518 20 l. Ostrich 30 30
1519 30 l. Zebra 40 40
1520 50 l. Horse 55 55
1521 80 l. Sea monster 80 80
1522 100 l. Giraffe 1·00 1·00
1523 150 l. Armoured horse 1·40 1·40
1524 200 l. Camel 1·75 1·75

1990. Olympic Games, Barcelona (1992). As T **268** of Antigua.

1526 5 l. Start of Men's 100 metres 20 15
1527 10 l. Men's 4 × 400 metres relay 25 20
1528 20 l. Men's 100 metres in progress 40 30
1529 30 l. Weightlifting 50 40
1530 40 l. Freestyle wrestling 55 45
1531 80 l. Water polo 80 90
1532 150 l. Women's gymnastics 1·40 1·50
1533 200 l. Cycling 2·25 2·25

1990. Christmas. "The Night before Christmas". As T **240** showing Walt Disney cartoon characters in scenes from Clement Moore's poem. Multicoloured.

1535/58 50 l. × 8, 75 l. × 8, 100 l. × 8
Set of 24 16·00 18·00

241 "Holy Family with St. Elizabeth" (Mantegna)

242 "Chlorophyllum molybdites"

1990. Christmas. Paintings. Multicoloured.

1560 10 l. "Holy Family resting" (Rembrandt) 25 15
1561 20 l. Type **241** 35 20
1562 30 l. "Virgin and Child with an Angel" (Correggio) 45 30
1563 50 l. "Annunciation" (Bernardo Strozzi) 50 45
1564 100 l. "Madonna and Child appearing to St. Anthony" (Lippi) 1·25 80

1565 175 l. "Virgin and Child" (Giovanni Boltraffio) 1·90 2·00
1566 200 l. "Esterhazy Madonna" (Raphael) 2·00 2·25
1567 300 l. "Coronation of Mary" (Andrea Orcagna) 2·50 2·75

1990. 350th Death Anniv of Rubens (1st issue). As T **273** of Antigua but vert. Mult.
1569 5 l. "Helena Fourment as Hagar in the Wilderness" (detail) 15 10
1570 10 l. "Isabella Brant" 20 15
1571 20 l. "Countess of Arundel and her Party" (detail) 30 20
1572 60 l. "Countess of Arundel and her Party" (different detail) 70 70
1573 80 l. "Nicolaas Rockox" 90 90
1574 100 l. "Adriana Perez" 1·00 1·00
1575 150 l. "George Villiers, Duke of Buckingham" (detail) 1·75 2·00
1576 300 l. "Countess of Buckingham" 2·50 2·75
See also Nos. 1595/602.

1990. Fungi. Multicoloured.
1578 3 l. Type **242** 30 15
1579 5 l. "Lepista nuda" 30 15
1580 10 l. "Clitocybe nebularis" 40 20
1581 15 l. "Cyathus striatus" 50 30
1582 20 l. "Bolbitius vitellinus" 55 35
1583 25 l. "Leucoagaricus naucinus" 55 40
1584 30 l. "Suillus luteus" 60 45
1585 40 l. "Podaxis pistillaris" 70 55
1586 50 l. "Oudemansiella radicata" 80 60
1587 60 l. "Phallus indusiatus" 90 70
1588 80 l. "Macrolepiota rhacodes" 1·00 1·10
1589 100 l. "Mycena pura" 1·25 1·25
1590 150 l. "Volvariella volvacea" 1·60 1·75
1591 175 l. "Omphalotus olearius" 1·90 2·25
1592 200 l. "Sphaerobolus stellatus" 2·00 2·50
1593 250 l. "Schizophyllum commune" 2·25 2·75

243 "The Flight of St. Barbara" (detail) (Rubens)

1991. Easter. 350th Death Anniv (1990) of Rubens (2nd issue). Multicoloured.
1595 10 l. Type **243** 30 15
1596 20 l. "The Last Judgement" (detail) 40 20
1597 30 l. "St. Gregory of Nazianzus" 50 30
1598 50 l. "Doubting Thomas" 65 45
1599 80 l. "The Way to Calvary" (detail) 1·10 1·10
1600 100 l. "St. Gregory with Sts. Domitilla, Maurus and Papianus" 1·25 1·25
1601 175 l. "Sts. Gregory, Maurus and Papianus" 2·00 2·25
1602 300 l. "Christ and the Penitent Sinners" 2·75 4·00

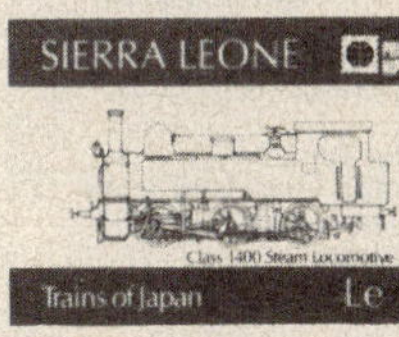

244 Krauss Class 1400 Steam Locomotive, 1895

1991. "Phila Nippon '91" International Stamp Exhibition, Tokyo. Japanese Trains. Mult.
1604 10 l. Type **244** 35 20
1605 20 l. Class C55 streamline steam locomotive, 1935 50 25
1606 30 l. Class ED17 electric locomotive, 1931 70 40
1607 60 l. Class EF13 electric locomotive, 1944 1·00 85
1608 100 l. Baldwin Mikado steam locomotive, 1897 1·25 1·25
1609 150 l. Class C62 steam locomotive, 1948 1·75 2·00
1610 200 l. Class Kiha 81 diesel multiple unit, 1960 2·00 2·25
1611 300 l. Schenectady Class 8550 steam locomotive, 1899 2·25 2·75

245 Turquoise Killifish

1991. Fishes. Multicoloured.
1613 10 l. Type **245** 45 20
1614 20 l. Red-chinned panchax 65 25
1615 30 l. Peters' killifish 80 40
1616 60 l. Micro-walkeri killifish 1·40 90
1617 100 l. Freshwater butterflyfish 1·60 1·25
1618 150 l. Green panchax 2·00 2·25
1619 200 l. Six-banded lyretail 2·25 2·50
1620 300 l. Nile pufferfish 2·25 2·50

1991. Death Centenary of Vincent van Gogh (artist). As T **278** of Antigua. Multicoloured.
1622 10 c. "The Langlois Bridge at Arles" (horiz) 10 10
1623 50 c. "Tree in Garden at Saint-Paul Hospital" 10 10
1624 1 l. "Wild Flowers and Thistles in a Vase" 10 10
1625 2 l. "Still Life: Vase with Oleanders and Books" (horiz) 10 10
1626 5 l. "Farmhouses in a Wheatfield near Arles" (horiz) 15 10
1627 10 l. "Self-portrait, September 1889" 25 15
1628 20 l. "Patience Escalier" 35 20
1629 30 l. "Doctor Felix Rey" 45 30
1630 50 l. "The Iris" 70 45
1631 60 l. "The Shepherdess" 80 65
1632 80 l. "Vincent's House in Arles" (horiz) 1·00 1·00
1633 100 l. "The Road Menders" (horiz) 1·10 1·10
1634 150 l. "The Garden of Saint-Paul Hospital" 1·75 2·00
1635 200 l. "View of the Church, Saint-Paul-de-Mausole" (horiz) 2·00 2·25
1636 250 l. "Seascape at Saintes-Maries" (horiz) 2·25 2·50
1637 300 l. "Pieta" 2·25 2·50

1991. 65th Birthday of Queen Elizabeth II. As T **280** of Antigua. Multicoloured.
1639 10 l. The Queen and Prince Charles at polo match 15 10
1640 30 l. The Queen at Windsor, 1989 20 20
1641 200 l. The Queen and Princess Diana in Nigeria, 1989 1·75 2·00
1642 250 l. The Queen and Prince Philip 2·00 2·25

1991. 10th Wedding Anniv of Prince and Princess of Wales. As T **280** of Antigua. Multicoloured.
1644 20 l. Prince and Princess of Wales in August 1987 30 15
1645 80 l. Separate photographs of Prince, Princess and sons 85 85
1646 100 l. Prince Henry in Majorca and Prince William on his first day at school 90 95
1647 300 l. Prince Charles at Caister, April 1988 and Princess Diana in Hyde Park, May 1989 2·50 2·75

246 "Graphium latreillianus" and "Ancistrochilus rothschildianus"

1991. Butterflies and Flowers. Multicoloured.
1649 10 l. Type **246** 55 30
1650 30 l. "Euphraedra eleus" and "Clitoria ternatea" 85 45
1651 50 l. "Graphium antheus" and "Gloriosa simplex" 1·25 60
1652 60 l. "Salamis cacta" and "Stenandriopsis guineensis" 1·40 85
1653 80 l. "Kallima rumia" and "Cassia fistula" 1·75 1·25
1654 100 l. "Hypolimnas salmacis" and "Amorphophallus abyssinicus" 2·00 1·50
1655 200 l. "Danaus formosa" and "Nephthytis afzelii" 2·75 3·00
1656 300 l. "Graphium leonidas" and "Clappertonia ficifolia" 3·00 3·50

1991. Butterflies. As Nos. 1028/42 but "Sierra Leone" in blue. Multicoloured.
1658 10 c. "Danaus limniace" 7·50 40
1660 50 c. "Graphium ridleyanus" 7·50 30
1661 1 l. "Papilio bromius" 7·50 30
1662 2 l. "Iterus ("Papilio") zalmoxis" 7·50 30
1663 5 l. "Graphium tynderaeus" — 30
1665 10 l. "Graphium policenes" 7·50 30
1666 20 l. "Tanuetheira ("Iolaus") timon" — 40
1667 30 l. "Cymothoe sangaris" — 50
1668 50 l. Type **205** 7·50 55
1669 60 l. "Charaxes lucretius" 7·50 70
1670 80 l. "Stugeta ("Iolaus") marmorea" 14·00 1·00
1671 100 l. "Abisara talantus" — 1·00
1672 300 l. "Papilio hesperus" 14·00 2·50

247 Audie Murphy in "To Hell and Back"

1991. Films of Second World War. Mult.
1675 2 l. Type **247** 10 10
1676 5 l. Jack Palance in "Attack" 15 15
1677 10 l. Greer Garson and Walter Pidgeon in "Mrs. Miniver" 20 20
1678 20 l. Heavy artillery from "The Guns of Navarone" 30 30
1679 30 l. Charlie Chaplin and Paulette Goddard in "The Great Dictator" 40 40
1680 50 l. Steam locomotive from "The Train" 60 60
1681 60 l. Diary and fountain pen from "The Diary of Anne Frank" 70 70
1682 80 l. William Holden in "The Bridge on the River Kwai" 90 90
1683 100 l. Tallulah Bankhead in "Lifeboat" and Alfred Hitchcock (director) 1·00 1·00
1684 200 l. John Wayne in "Sands of Iwo Jima" 1·90 1·90
1685 300 l. Van Johnson and Spencer Tracy in "Thirty Seconds over Tokyo" 2·75 2·75
1686 350 l. Humphrey Bogart and Ingrid Bergman in "Casablanca" 3·00 3·00

248 Meissen China Parrot Ornament, Munich Botanic Garden

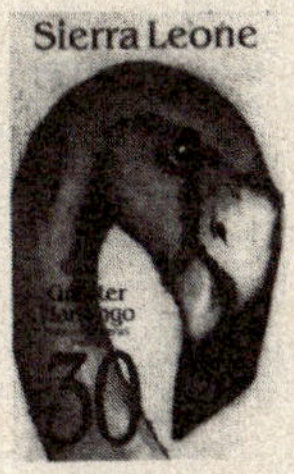

251 Greater Flamingo

250 Aichi D3A "Val" Dive Bomber

1991. Botanical Gardens of the World. As T **248** Multicoloured
1688/1735 60 l. × 48 Set of 48 18·00 19·00
Issued in 3 sheetlets of 16 stamps, depicting features and plants from Munich (Nos. 1688/1703), Kyoto (Nos. 1704/19) and Brooklyn (Nos. 1720/35).

1991. Christmas. Drawings and Paintings by Albrecht Durer. As T **291** of Antigua.
1737 6 l. black and mauve 15 10
1738 60 l. black and blue 35 30
1739 80 l. multicoloured 45 40
1740 100 l. multicoloured 65 65
1741 200 l. multicoloured 1·60 1·60
1742 300 l. multicoloured 2·00 2·00
1743 700 l. multicoloured 4·75 5·00
DESIGNS: 6 l. "Mary being Crowned by Two Angels"; 60 l. "St. Christopher"; 80 l. "Virgin and Child with St. Anne" (detail); 100 l. "Virgin with the Pear" (detail); 200 l. "Madonna and Child" (detail); 300 l. "The Virgin in Half-Length" (detail); "The Madonna with the Siskin" (detail).

1991. Anniversaries and Events. As T **285** of Antigua. Multicoloured.
1745 50 l. National Theatre, Prague 15 15
1746 100 l. St. Peter's Abbey, Salzburg 30 30
1747 250 l. Sea Scouts learning sailing 1·00 1·00
1748 300 l. Sierra Leone scouts emblem and Lord Baden-Powell 1·00 1·00
1749 400 l. Scouts playing baseball at Mt. Sorak Jamboree 1·40 1·40
1750 500 l. Scene from "Idomeneo" 2·25 2·25
ANNIVERSARIES AND EVENTS: Nos. 1745/6, 1750, Death bicentenary of Mozart; Nos. 1747/9, 50th death anniv of Lord Baden-Powell and World Scout Jamboree, Korea.

1991. 50th Anniv of Japanese Attack on Pearl Harbor. Multicoloured.
1752 75 l. Type **250** 55 55
1753 75 l. Japanese Aichi D3A "Val" dive bomber and smoke 55 55
1754 75 l. Battleship Row burning 55 55
1755 75 l. Planes and burning dockyard 55 55
1756 75 l. Burning installations 55 55
1757 75 l. Two Japanese Aichi D3A "Val" dive bombers 55 55
1758 75 l. Burning ships and hangars 55 55
1759 75 l. Airfield under attack 55 55
1760 75 l. American Curtiss P-40C fighter 55 55
1761 75 l. Japanese Mitsubishi A6M Zero-Sen fighter-bombers 55 55
1762 75 l. Japanese Mitsubishi A6M Zero-Sen fighter-bombers over suburb 55 55
1763 75 l. Japanese Nakajima B5N "Kate" bombers attacking ships 55 55
1764 75 l. Japanese Nakajima B5N "Kate" aircraft on fire 55 55
1765 75 l. Japanese Nakajima B5N "Kate" bombers over jungle 55 55
1766 75 l. Mitsubishi A6M Zero-Sen fighters 55 55

1991. Christmas. Walt Disney Christmas Cards. As T **228** of St. Vincent. Multicoloured.
1767 12 l. Mickey Mouse, Donald Duck and characters from "Peter Pan", 1952 (horiz) 20 10
1768 30 l. Disney characters reading "Alice in Wonderland", 1950 (horiz) 30 10
1769 60 l. Sleepy and animals, 1938 (horiz) 45 25
1770 75 l. Mickey, Minnie, Donald and Pluto posting card, 1936 (horiz) 55 30
1771 100 l. Disney cartoon characters, 1984 (horiz) 70 45
1772 125 l. Mickey and Donald singing carols with Donald's nephews and Pluto reading, 1954 (horiz) 90 90
1773 150 l. "101 Dalmatians", 1960 (horiz) 1·10 1·10
1774 200 l. Mickey and Donald opening presents, 1948 (horiz) 1·40 1·40
1775 300 l. Mickey, Minnie, Morte and Ferdie decorating tree, 1983 (horiz) 1·75 2·00
1776 400 l. Donald decorating tree and nephews watching television, 1956 (horiz) 2·00 2·25
1777 500 l. Characters from Disney films, 1972 (horiz) 2·00 2·25
1778 600 l. Mickey, Donald, Pluto and friends singing, 1964 (horiz) 2·00 2·50

1992. Mickey's World Tour. As T **270** of Maldive Islands showing Walt Disney cartoon characters in different countries. Multicoloured.
1780 6 l. Minnie Mouse as Chiquita with Pluto, Cuba 20 10
1781 10 l. Goofy as Olympic discus champion, Greece 20 10
1782 20 l. Donald and Daisy Duck as flamenco dancers, Spain 30 15
1783 30 l. Goofy and Donald as guardsman, England 40 15
1784 50 l. Mickey and Minnie at Paris fashion show, France 50 25
1785 100 l. Goofy in the Alps, Switzerland 80 50
1786 200 l. Daisy and Minnie in grass skirts, Hawaii 1·50 1·75
1787 350 l. Mickey, Donald and Goofy as ancient Egyptians (horiz) 2·00 2·25
1788 500 l. Daisy and Minnie as cancan dancers, France (horiz) 2·25 2·50

1992. 40th Anniv of Queen Elizabeth II's Accession. As T **288** of Antigua. Multicoloured.
1790 60 l. State House 45 20
1791 100 l. Beach 70 40
1792 300 l. Parliament Building 2·00 2·25
1793 400 l. Canoe on beach 2·25 2·50

1992. "Granada '92" International Stamp Exhibition, Spain. Paintings by Francisco Zurbaran. As T **292** of Antigua. Multicoloured.
1795 1 l. "Visit of St. Thomas Aquinas to St. Bonaventure" 10 10
1796 10 l. "St. Gregory" 10 10
1797 30 l. "St. Andrew" 20 20
1798 50 l. "St. Gabriel the Archangel" 30 30
1799 60 l. "The Blessed Henry Suso" 30 30
1800 100 l. "St. Lucy" 40 40
1801 300 l. "St. Casilda" 95 95
1802 400 l. "St. Margaret of Antioch" 1·40 1·40
1803 500 l. "St. Apollonia" 1·60 1·60
1804 600 l. "St. Bonaventure at Council of Lyons" 1·75 1·75
1805 700 l. "St. Bonaventure on his Bier" 2·00 2·00
1806 800 l. "The Martyrdom of St. James" (detail) 2·25 2·25

1992. Prehistoric Animals. As T **290** of Antigua. Multicoloured.
1808 50 l. Rhamphorhynchus 50 50
1809 50 l. Pteranodon 50 50
1810 50 l. Dimorphodon 50 50
1811 50 l. Pterodactyl 50 50
1812 50 l. Archaeopteryx 50 50
1813 50 l. Iguanodon 50 50
1814 50 l. Hypsilophodon 50 50
1815 50 l. Nothosaurus 50 50
1816 50 l. Brachiosaurus 50 50
1817 50 l. Kentrosaurus 50 50
1818 50 l. Plesiosaurus 50 50
1819 50 l. Trachodon 50 50
1820 50 l. Hesperornis 50 50
1821 50 l. Henodus 50 50
1822 50 l. Steneosaurus 50 50
1823 50 l. Stenopterygius 50 50
1824 50 l. Eurhinosaurus 50 50
1825 50 l. Placodus 50 50
1826 50 l. Mosasaurus 50 50
1827 50 l. Mixosaurus 50 50
Nos. 1808/27 were printed together, se-tenant, forming a composite design.

1992. Birds. Multicoloured.
1829 30 l. Type **251** 30 30
1830 50 l. African white-crested hornbill 35 35
1831 100 l. Crested touraco 55 55
1832 170 l. Yellow-spotted barbet 95 95
1833 200 l. African spoonbill 1·10 1·10
1834 250 l. Saddle-bill stork 1·25 1·25
1835 300 l. Red-faced lovebird ("Red Headed Lovebird") 1·50 1·50
1836 600 l. Yellow-billed barbet 3·75 3·75

1992. Olympic Games, Albertville and Barcelona. As T **216** of Lesotho. Multicoloured.

1838	10 l. Marathon	20	20
1839	20 l. Men's parallel bars	25	25
1840	30 l. Men's discus	25	25
1841	50 l. Men's 110 metres hurdles (horiz)	30	30
1842	60 l. Women's long jump	30	30
1843	100 l. Men's floor exercise (horiz)	45	45
1844	200 l. Windsurfing	80	80
1845	250 l. Women's biathlon	1·00	1·00
1846	300 l. Cycle road race	1·75	1·75
1847	400 l. Weightlifting	2·00	2·00
1848	500 l. Men's speed skating	2·50	2·50
1849	600 l. Men's downhill skiing (horiz)	3·50	3·50

252 Minnie Mouse and Chip decorating Christmas Tree

1992. Christmas. Walt Disney cartoon characters. Multicoloured.

1851	10 l. Type **252**	20	10
1852	20 l. Goofy as Father Christmas	30	10
1853	30 l. Daisy Duck and Minnie decorating Christmas tree	30	10
1854	50 l. Mickey Mouse, and Goofy lighting candle	45	20
1855	80 l. Big Pete as Father Christmas	60	40
1856	100 l. Donald Duck as Father Christmas	60	40
1857	150 l. Morty and Ferdie decorating cake	1·00	1·00
1858	200 l. Mickey and bauble	1·10	1·10
1859	300 l. Goofy and toy Father Christmas	1·40	1·50
1860	500 l. Chip and Dale with sledge	1·90	2·00
1861	600 l. Donald and Dale with musical instruments	2·00	2·50
1862	800 l. Huey, Dewey and Louie making patterns in snow	2·50	3·00

253 Toy Pennsylvania Railroad GG-1 Electric Locomotive No. 6-18306, 1992

254 African Pygmy Goose

1992. "Genova '92" International Thematic Stamp Exhibition. Toy Trains. Designs showing electric locomotives and rolling stock manufactured by Lionel. Multicoloured.

1864	150 l. Type **253**	95	95
1865	150 l. Wabash Railroad Hudson locomotive No. 8610, 1985	95	95
1866	150 l. Locomotive No. 1911, 1911	95	95
1867	150 l. Chesapeake & Ohio locomotive No. 6-18627, 1992	95	95
1868	150 l. Gang car No. 50, 1954	95	95
1869	150 l. Rock Island & Peoria locomotive No. 8004, 1980	95	95
1870	150 l. Western Maryland Railroad Shay locomotive No. 6-18023, 1992	95	95
1871	150 l. Boston & Albany Railroad Hudson locomotive No. 784, 1986	95	95
1872	150 l. Locomotive No. 6, 1906	95	95
1873	170 l. Special F-3 diesel locomotive, 1947	95	95
1874	170 l. Pennsylvania Railroad diesel switcher locomotive No, 6-18905, 1992	95	95
1875	170 l. No. 1 Trolley, 1913	95	95
1876	170 l. Seaboard Railroad diesel freight locomotive No. 602, 1958	95	95
1877	170 l. Pennsylvania Railroad S-2 turbine locomotive, 1991	95	95
1878	170 l. Western Pacific GP-9 diesel locomotive No. 6-18822, 1992	95	95
1879	170 l. Locomotive No. 10, 1929	95	95
1880	170 l. Locomotive No. 400E, 1931	95	95
1881	170 l. Locomotive No. 384E, 1928	95	95
1882	170 l. Pennsylvania Railroad "Torpedo" locomotive No. 238EW, 1936	95	95
1883	170 l. Denver & Rio Grande Western Type PA diesel locomotive, 1992	95	95
1884	170 l. Locomotive No. 408E, 1930	95	95
1885	170 l. Mickey Mouse 60th Birthday boxcar No. 19241, 1991	95	95
1886	170 l. Polished brass locomotive No. 54, 1913	95	95
1887	170 l. Pennsylvania Railroad "Broadway Limited" locomotive No. 392E, 1936	95	95
1888	170 l. Great Northern Railroad EP-5 electric locomotive No. 18302, 1988	95	95
1889	170 l. Locomotive No. 6, 1918	95	95
1890	170 l. Locomotive No. 400E, 1933	95	95

Nos. 1874 and 1877 are inscribed "Pennsylvannia" in error.

1992. Birds. Multicoloured.

1892A	50 c. Type **254**	10	10
1893A	1 l. Spotted eagle owl	10	10
1894A	2 l. Crested touraco	10	10
1895A	5 l. Saddle-bill stork	10	10
1896A	10 l. African golden oriole	10	10
1897A	20 l. Malachite kingfisher	10	10
1898A	30 l. Red-crowned bishop ("Fire-crowned Bishop")	10	10
1899A	40 l. Fire-bellied woodpecker	10	10
1900B	50 l. Red-billed fire finch	10	10
1901A	80 l. Blue flycatcher	10	10
1902B	100 l. Crested malimbe	10	10
1903B	150 l. Vitelline masked weaver	10	15
1904A	170 l. Great blue turaco ("Blue Plantain-eater")	10	10
1905B	200 l. Superb sunbird	15	20
1906B	250 l. Swallow-tailed bee eater	20	25
1907B	300 l. Cabanis's yellow bunting	25	30
1908B	500 l. Egyptian plover ("Crocodile Bird")	40	45
1909A	750 l. White-faced scops owl	60	65
1910B	1000 l. African blue cuckoo shrike	80	85
1911A	2000 l. White-necked bald crow ("Bare-headed rock fowl")	1·60	1·75
1912B	3000 l. African red-tailed buzzard	2·40	2·50

1992. Christmas. Religious Paintings. As T **218** of Lesotho. Multicoloured.

1916	1 l. "Virgin and Child" (Fiorenzo di Lorenzo)	10	10
1917	10 l. "Madonna and Child on a Wall" (School of Bouts)	15	15
1918	20 l. "Virgin and Child with the Flight into Egypt" (Master of Hoogstraeten)	20	20
1919	30 l. "Madonna and Child before Firescreen" (Robert Campin)	25	20
1920	50 l. "Mary in a Rosegarden" (detail) (Hans Memling)	30	25
1921	100 l. "Virgin Mary and Child" (Lucas Cranach the Elder)	55	45
1922	170 l. "Virgin and Child" (Rogier van der Weyden)	1·00	1·00
1923	200 l. "Madonna and Saints" (detail) (Perugino)	1·10	1·10
1924	250 l. "Madonna Enthroned with Sts. Catherine and Barbara" (Master of Hoogstraeten)	1·25	1·25
1925	300 l. "The Virgin in a Rose Arbour" (Stefan Lochner)	1·50	1·50
1926	500 l. "Madonna with Child and Angels" (Botticelli)	2·50	2·75
1927	1000 l. "Madonna and Child with young St. John the Baptist" (Fra Bartolommeo)	4·50	5·00

255 Mickey Mouse and Sousaphone (magazine cover, 1936)

1992. Mickey Mouse in Literature. Designs showing Walt Disney cartoon characters on magazine or book covers. Multicoloured.

1929	10 l. Type **255**	15	10
1930	20 l. Mickey and Minnie Mouse, 1936	20	10
1931	30 l. Mickey and Donald Duck, 1936	20	10
1932	40 l. Mickey, Minnie and Goofy in car, 1936	20	15
1933	50 l. Mickey as Ringmaster, 1937	20	15
1934	60 l. Mickey as Father Christmas, 1937	25	25
1935	70 l. Donald and Goofy representing 1937 and 1938	25	25
1936	150 l. Mickey and Minnie steering ship, 1935	70	70
1937	170 l. Mickey and Tanglefoot the horse, 1936	75	75
1938	200 l. Mickey tied up	85	85
1939	300 l. Mickey and Goofy in Jungle	1·00	1·00
1940	400 l. Mickey and Goofy on submarine	1·40	1·60
1941	500 l. Mickey and Minnie singing and dancing, 1931	1·50	1·75

256 Emblems

1993. Anniversaries and Events. Multicoloured.

1943	150 l. Type **256**	70	70
1944	170 l. Cow and cereal with emblems	80	80
1945	170 l. Airship LZ-127 "Graf Zeppelin"	80	80
1946	200 l. Starving child with W.H.O. emblem	95	95
1947	250 l. Summit emblem and cottonwood tree	1·25	1·25
1948	250 l. Lions Club emblem and World map	1·25	1·25
1949	300 l. Emblem and African elephant	1·40	1·40
1950	300 l. Columbus, King Ferdinand and Queen Isabella	1·40	1·40
1951	500 l. Landing in the New World	2·25	2·25
1952	600 l. American space shuttle	2·40	2·40
1953	700 l. Construction drawings of "Graf Zeppelin"	2·75	2·75

ANNIVERSARIES AND EVENTS: Nos. 1943/4, International Conference on Nutrition, Rome; Nos. 1945, 1953, 75th death anniv of Count Ferdinand von Zeppelin (airship pioneer); No. 1946, United Nations World Health Organization Projects; Nos. 1947, 1949, Earth Summit '92, Rio; No. 1948, 75th anniv of International Association of Lions Clubs; Nos. 1950/1, 500th anniv of discovery of America by Columbus; No. 1952, International Space Year.

257 Joe Louis

1993. Centenary of Modern Boxing (1st issue). World Champions. Multicoloured.

1955	200 l. Type **257**	80	80
1956	200 l. Archie Moore	80	80
1957	200 l. Muhammad Ali	80	80
1958	200 l. George Foreman	80	80
1959	200 l. Joe Frazier	80	80
1960	200 l. Marvin Hagler	80	80
1961	200 l. Sugar Ray Leonard	80	80
1962	200 l. Evander Holyfield	80	80

1993. Centenary of Modern Boxing (2nd issue). Boxing Films. As T **257**. Multicoloured.

1964	200 l. Wallace Beery ("The Champ")	80	80
1965	200 l. William Holden ("Golden Boy")	80	80
1966	200 l. John Garfield ("Body and Soul")	80	80
1967	200 l. Kirk Douglas ("Champion")	80	80
1968	200 l. Robert Ryan ("The Set-Up")	80	80
1969	200 l. Anthony Quinn ("Requiem for a Heavyweight")	80	80
1970	200 l. Elvis Presley ("Kid Galahad")	80	80
1971	200 l. Jeff Bridges ("Fat City")	80	80

1993. Bicentenary of the Louvre, Paris. Paintings by Delacroix. As T **305** of Antigua. Multicoloured.

1973	70 l. "Young Orphan at a Cemetery"	40	40
1974	70 l. "Algerian Women in their Apartment" (left detail)	40	40
1975	70 l. "Algerian Women in their Apartment" (right detail)	40	40
1976	70 l. "Dante and Virgil"	40	40
1977	70 l. "Self-portrait"	40	40
1978	70 l. "Massacre of Chios" (left detail)	40	40
1979	70 l. "Massacre of Chios" (right detail)	40	40
1980	70 l. "Frederic Chopin"	40	40
1981	70 l. "Entry of the Crusaders into Constantinople" (left detail)	40	40
1982	70 l. "Entry of the Crusaders into Constantinople" (right detail)	40	40
1983	70 l. "Jewish Wedding, Morocco" (left detail)	40	40
1984	70 l. "Jewish Wedding, Morocco" (right detail)	40	40
1985	70 l. "Death of Sardanopoulous" (left detail)	40	40
1986	70 l. "Death of Sardanopoulous" (right detail)	40	40
1987	70 l. "Liberty leading the People" (left detail)	40	40
1988	70 l. "Liberty leading the People" (right detail)	40	40

258 "Amanita flammeola"

259 "Pseudacraea boisduvali"

1993. Mushrooms. Multicoloured.

1990	30 l. Type **258**	30	20
1991	50 l. "Cantharellus pseudocibarius"	35	20
1992	100 l. "Volvariella volvacea"	50	40
1993	200 l. "Termitomyces microcarpus"	90	90
1994	300 l. "Auricularia auricula-judae"	1·40	1·40
1995	400 l. "Lentinus tuber-regium" ("Pleurotus tuberregium")	1·75	1·75
1996	500 l. "Schizophyllum commune"	1·90	1·90
1997	600 l. "Termitomyces robustus"	2·00	2·00

1993. Butterflies. Multicoloured.

1999	20 l. Type **259**	35	20
2000	30 l. "Salamis temora"	40	25
2001	50 l. "Charaxes jasius"	40	30
2002	100 l. "Amblypodia anita"	50	40
2003	150 l. "Papilio nireus"	60	60
2004	170 l. "Danaus chrysippus"	65	65
2005	200 l. "Meneris tulbaghia"	70	70
2006	250 l. "Precis octavia"	75	75
2007	300 l. "Palla usseri"	80	80
2008	500 l. "Catacroptera cloanthe"	1·25	1·25
2009	600 l. "Cynthia cardui"	1·40	1·40
2010	700 l. "Euphaedra neophron"	1·50	1·50

260 Black Persian

1993. Cats. Multicoloured.

2012	150 l. Type **260**	65	65
2013	150 l. Blue-point Siamese	65	65
2014	150 l. American wirehair	65	65
2015	150 l. Birman	65	65
2016	150 l. Scottish fold	65	65
2017	150 l. American shorthair red tabby	65	65
2018	150 l. Blue and white Persian bicolour	65	65
2019	150 l. Havana brown	65	65
2020	150 l. Norwegian forest cat	65	65
2021	150 l. Brown tortie Burmese	65	65
2022	150 l. Angora	65	65
2023	150 l. Exotic shorthair	65	65
2024	150 l. Somali	65	65
2025	150 l. Egyptian mau smoke	65	65
2026	150 l. Chocolate-point Siamese	65	65
2027	150 l. Mi-Ke Japanese bobtail	65	65
2028	150 l. Chinchilla	65	65
2029	150 l. Red Burmese	65	65
2030	150 l. British shorthair brown tabby	65	65
2031	150 l. Blue Persian	65	65
2032	150 l. British silver classic tabby	65	65
2033	150 l. Oriental ebony	65	65
2034	150 l. Red Persian	65	65
2035	150 l. British calico shorthair	65	65

261 Gorilla

1993. Wildlife. Multicoloured.

2037	30 l. Type **261**	40	30
2038	100 l. Bongo	50	35
2039	150 l. Potto	60	60
2040	170 l. Chimpanzee	80	80
2041	200 l. Dwarf galago	90	90
2042	300 l. African linsang	1·10	1·25
2043	500 l. Banded duiker	1·50	1·60
2044	750 l. Diana monkey	2·00	2·50

262 "Clerodendrum thomsonae"

1993. Flowers. Multicoloured.

2046	30 l. Type **262**	30	20
2047	40 l. "Passiflora quadrangularis"	35	25
2048	50 l. "Hydrangea macrophylla"	35	25

2049 60 l. "Begonia semperflorens" 40 30
2050 100 l. "Hibiscus rosa-sinensis" 50 40
2051 150 l. "Lagerstroemia indica" 75 75
2052 170 l. "Bougainvillea glabra" 85 85
2053 200 l. "Plumbago capensis" 1·00 1·00
2054 250 l. "Gerbera jamesonae" 1·25 1·25
2055 300 l. "Thunbergia alata" 1·40 1·50
2056 500 l. "Gloriosa superba" 1·75 2·00
2057 900 l. "Viola odorata" 2·75 3·25

263 Royal Family

1993. Anniversaries and Events. Black (No. 2061) or multicoloured (others).
2059 100 l. Type **263** 40 30
2060 170 l. "Woman with Hat" (Picasso) 65 65
2061 200 l. Coronation procession 80 80
2062 200 l. "Buste de Femme" (Picasso) 80 80
2063 250 l. Early telescope 90 90
2064 600 l. Queen Elizabeth II in Coronation robes (from photograph by Cecil Beaton) 1·60 1·60
2065 800 l. "Maya with a Doll" (Picasso) 2·00 2·00
2066 800 l. Craters on Moon 2·00 2·00
ANNIVERSARIES AND EVENTS: Nos. 2059, 2061, 2064, 40th anniv of Coronation; Nos. 2060, 2062, 2065, 20th death anniv of Picasso (artist); Nos. 2063, 2066, 450th death anniv of Copernicus (astronomer).

1993. Christmas. Religious Paintings. As T **270** of Dominca. Black, yellow and red (Nos. 2071/4) or multicoloured (others).
2068 50 l. "Madonna of the Fish" (detail) (Raphael) 20 10
2069 100 l. "Madonna of the Fish" (different detail) (Raphael) 35 20
2070 150 l. "Madonna and Child enthroned with Five Saints" (detail) (Raphael) 60 30
2071 200 l. "The Circumcision" (detail) (Durer) 70 50
2072 250 l. "The Circumcision" (different detail) (Durer) 80 70
2073 300 l. "The Circumcision" (different detail) (Durer) 85 90
2074 500 l. "Holy Family with Saints and Two Angels playing Music" (detail) (Durer) 1·60 2·00
2075 800 l. "The Holy Family with the Lamb" (detail) (Raphael) 2·25 2·75

265 Donald Duck and Toy Train

1993. Christmas. Walt Disney cartoon characters in Christmas scenes. Mult.
2077 50 l. Type **265** 30 10
2078 100 l. Disney carol singers 40 20
2079 170 l. Mickey drinking punch 75 70
2080 200 l. Pluto with cream-covered bones 90 85
2081 250 l. Goofy eating angel cakes 1·25 1·25
2082 500 l. Donald's nephews decorating Christmas tree 2·00 2·25
2083 600 l. Donald dropping Christmas cake on foot 2·25 2·75
2084 800 l. Uncle Scrooge and Daisy under mistletoe 2·50 2·75

1993. World Cup Football Championship, U.S.A. (1994) (1st issue). As T **278** of Maldive Islands. Multicoloured.
2086 30 l. Jose Brown with goalkeeper (Argentina) 35 20
2087 50 l. Gary Lineker (England) 50 25
2088 100 l. Carlos Valderrama (Colombia) 60 35
2089 250 l. Tomas Skuhravy (Czechoslovakia) and Hector Marchena (Costa Rica) 1·25 1·25
2090 300 l. Butragueno (Spain) 1·50 1·50
2091 400 l. Roger Milla (Cameroun) 1·75 2·00
2092 500 l. Roberto Donadoni (Italy) 2·00 2·25
2093 700 l. Enzo Scifo (Belgium) 2·25 2·50
See also Nos. 2130/5.

1994. "Hong Kong '94" International Stamp Exhibition (1st issue). As T **317** of Antigua. Multicoloured.
2095 200 l. Hong Kong 1985 $1.70 Bauhinia stamp and Pagoda, Tiger Baum Garden 40 50
2096 200 l. Sierra Leone 1989 70 l. Orchid stamp and Aw Par Gardens 80 1·00
See also Nos. 2097/2102 and 2103/4.

1994. "Hong Kong '94" International Stamp Exhibition (2nd issue). Ching Dynasty Carved Lacquerware. As T **318** of Antigua. Mult.
2097 100 l. Bowl 30 30
2098 100 l. Four-wheeled box 30 30
2099 100 l. Flower container 30 30
2100 100 l. Box with human figure design 30 30
2101 100 l. Shishi dog 30 30
2102 100 l. Box with persimmon design 30 30

1994. "Hong Kong '94" International Stamp Exhibition (3rd issue). Nos. 2013 and 2025 optd **HONG KONG '94** and emblem.
2103 150 l. Blue-point Siamese 40 40
2104 150 l. Egyptian mau smoke 40 40

267 Pekingese

1994. Chinese New Year ("Year of the Dog"). Multicoloured.
2106 100 l. Type **267** 50 55
2107 150 l. Dobermann pinscher 60 65
2108 200 l. Tibetan terrier 70 75
2109 250 l. Weimaraner 70 75
2110 400 l. Rottweiler 1·00 1·10
2111 500 l. Akita 1·10 1·25
2112 600 l. Schnauzer 1·25 1·50
2113 1000 l. Tibetan spaniel 1·50 1·60

1994. 50th Anniv of D-Day. As T **331** of Antigua. Multicoloured.
2115 500 l. British paratroop drop 1·25 1·25
2116 750 l. U.S. paratrooper jumping from aircraft 1·75 1·75

1994. "Philakorea '94" International Stamp Exn, Seoul. As T **330** of Antigua. Multicoloured.
2118 100 l. Traditional wedding 40 25
2119 200 l. Tiger and cubs 60 60
2120 200 l. Munsa-pasal 60 60
2121 200 l. Extinct Korean tiger 60 60
2122 200 l. Tiger and bamboo 60 60
2123 200 l. Tiger, three cubs and magpies 60 60
2124 200 l. Tiger, two cubs and magpies 60 60
2125 200 l. Mountain spirit 60 60
2126 200 l. Tiger and magpie 60 60
2127 400 l. Royal tombs, Kaesong 1·00 1·00
2128 600 l. Terraced fields, Chungmu 1·50 1·75

268 Kim Ho (South Korea)

1994. World Cup Football Championship, U.S.A. (2nd issue). Multicoloured.
2130 250 l. Type **268** 75 75
2131 250 l. Cobi Jones (U.S.A.) ("No. 13") 75 75
2132 250 l. Claudio Suarez (Mexico) ("No. 2") 75 75
2133 250 l. Tomas Brolin (Sweden) ("No. 11") 75 75
2134 250 l. Ruud Gullit (Holland) (red shirt without number) 75 75
2135 250 l. Andreas Herzog (Austria) (white shirt without number) 75 75

1994. 25th Anniv of First Manned Moon Landing. As T **326** of Antigua. Multicoloured.
2137 200 l. Buzz Aldrin gathering Moon samples 50 50
2138 200 l. Lunar Module "Eagle" on Moon's surface 50 50
2139 200 l. Tranquility Base 50 50
2140 200 l. Aldrin with U.S. flag 50 50
2141 200 l. Plaque 50 50
2142 200 l. "Apollo 11" crew with stamps 50 50
2143 200 l. Edwin Aldrin 50 50
2144 200 l. Michael Collins 50 50
2145 200 l. Neil Armstrong 50 50
2146 200 l. "Apollo 11" lift off 50 50
2147 200 l. Aldrin descending to Moon's surface 50 50
2148 200 l. Reflection in Aldrin's face shield 50 50

269 White-necked Bald Crow ("Picathartes") feeding Chicks

1994. Birds. Multicoloured.
2150 50 l. Type **269** 50 50
2151 100 l. Adult white-necked bald crow 60 60
2152 150 l. Pair of white-necked bald crows 75 75
2153 200 l. Young white-necked bald crow 80 80
2154 250 l. Black kite 85 85
2155 300 l. Superb sunbird 95 95
2156 500 l. Martial eagle 1·60 1·75
2157 800 l. Red bishop 2·00 2·50

270 "Aerangis kotschyana"

1994. Orchids. Multicoloured.
2159 50 l. Type **270** 30 20
2160 100 l. "Brachycorythis kalbreyeri" 40 30
2161 150 l. "Diaphananthe pellucida" 55 55
2162 200 l. "Eulophia guineensis" 65 65
2163 300 l. "Eurychone rothschildiana" 85 85
2164 500 l. "Tridactyle tridactylites" 1·40 1·40
2165 750 l. "Cyrtorchis arcuata" 2·00 2·50
2166 900 l. "Ancistrochilus rothschildianus" 2·25 2·75

1994. Christmas. Religious Paintings. As T **290** of St. Vincent. Multicoloured.
2168 50 l. "The Birth of the Virgin" (Murillo) 25 10
2169 100 l. "Education of the Virgin" (Murillo) 35 20
2170 150 l. "Annunciation" (detail) (Filippino Lippi) 60 55
2171 200 l. "Marriage of the Virgin" (Bernard van Orley) 75 70
2172 250 l. "The Visitation" (Nicolas Vleughels) 90 90
2173 300 l. "Castelfranco Altarpiece" (detail) (Giorgione) 1·10 1·10
2174 400 l. "Adoration of the Magi" (workshop of Bartholome Zeitblom) 1·40 1·60
2175 600 l. "Presentation of Infant Jesus in the Temple" (Master of the Prado) 1·75 2·25

271 Family working in Field

1994. International Year of the Family. Mult.
2177 300 l. Type **271** 25 30
2178 350 l. Family on beach 25 30

272 Mickey Mouse stroking Cat

1995. Christmas. Walt Disney cartoon characters. Multicoloured.
2179 50 l. Type **272** 25 10
2180 100 l. Goofy with Christmas tree and axe (vert) 30 20
2181 150 l. Donald Duck giving Daisy Duck a plant 55 45
2182 200 l. Donald finding Chipmunk in stocking (vert) 70 60
2183 250 l. Minnie Mouse in airplane 85 85
2184 300 l. Goofy in snowball (vert) 1·00 1·00
2185 400 l. Goofy with Chip N' Dale at mail box 1·25 1·40
2186 500 l. Mickey and Donald on sledge (vert) 1·50 1·60
2187 600 l. Mickey and Minnie making snowmouse 1·75 2·25
2188 800 l. Mickey and Pluto with cake (vert) 2·00 2·50

273 "Madonna Duck" (after Da Vinci)

274 Ragnar Lundberg (Sweden) (1952 pole vault bronze medal)

1995. Donald's Gallery of Old Masters. Donald and Daisy Duck in portraits inspired by famous paintings. Multicoloured.
2190 50 l. Type **273** 25 15
2191 100 l. "Portrait of a Venetian Duck" (after Tintoretto) 35 25
2192 150 l. "Duck with a Glove" (after Frans Hals) 50 50
2193 200 l. "Donald with a Pink" (after Massys) 60 60
2194 250 l. "Pinkie Daisy" (after Lawrence) 70 70
2195 300 l. "Donald's Whistling Mother" (after Whistler) 80 80
2196 400 l. "El Quacko" (after El Greco) 90 90
2197 500 l. "The Noble Snob" (after Rembrandt) 1·00 1·00
2198 600 l. "The Blue Duck" (after Gainsborough) 1·25 1·50
2199 800 l. "Modern Quack" (after Picasso) 1·40 1·60

1995. Centenary of International Olympic Committee. Medal Winners. Multicoloured.
2201 75 l. Type **274** 10 10
2202 75 l. Karin Janz (Germany) (1972 gymnastics silver) 10 10
2203 75 l. Matthias Volz (Germany) (1936 gymnastics bronze) 10 10
2204 75 l. Carl Lewis (U.S.A.) (1988 long jump gold) 10 10
2205 75 l. Sara Simeoni (Italy) (1976 high jump silver) 10 10
2206 75 l. Daley Thompson (Great Britain) (1980 decathlon gold) 10 10
2207 75 l. Japan and Britain (1964 football) 10 10
2208 75 l. Gabriella Dorio (Italy) (1984 1500 metres gold) 10 10
2209 75 l. Daniela Hunger (Germany) (1988 swimming gold) 10 10
2210 75 l. Kyoko Iwasaki (Japan) (1992 swimming bronze) 10 10
2211 75 l. Italian team (1960 water polo gold) 10 10
2212 75 l. David Wilkie (Great Britain) (1976 swimming gold) 10 10
2213 200 l. Katja Seizinger (Germany) (1994 alpine skiing gold) 15 20
2214 200 l. Hot air balloon showing Olympic Rings 15 20
2215 200 l. Elvis Stojko (Canada) (1994 figure skating silver) 15 20
2216 200 l. Jans Weissflog (Germany) (1994 ski jumping gold) 15 20
2217 200 l. Bjorn Daehlie (Norway) (1994 cross-country skiing gold) 15 20
2218 200 l. German team (1994 four-man bobsled gold) 15 20
2219 200 l. Markus Wasmeier (Germany) (1994 alpine skiing gold) 15 20
2220 200 l. Georg Hacki (Germany) (1994 luge gold) 15 20
2221 200 l. Jayne Torvill and Christopher Dean (Great Britain) (1994 ice dancing bronze) 15 20
2222 200 l. Bonnie Blair (U.S.A.) (1994 speed skating gold) 15 20
2223 200 l. Nancy Kerrigan (U.S.A.) (1994 figure skating silver) 15 20
2224 200 l. Sweden team (1994 ice hockey gold) 15 20

275 Ceratosaurus

1995. Prehistoric Animals. Multicoloured.
2226 200 l. Type **275** 15 20
2227 200 l. Brachiosaurus 15 20
2228 200 l. Pteranodon 15 20
2229 200 l. Stegoceras 15 20
2230 200 l. Saurolophus 15 20
2231 200 l. Ornithomumus 15 20
2232 200 l. Compsognathus 15 20
2233 200 l. Deinonychus 15 20
2234 200 l. Ornitholestes 15 20
2235 200 l. Archaeopteryx 15 20
2236 200 l. Heterodontosaurus 15 20
2237 200 l. Lesothosaurus 15 20
Nos. 2226/37 were printed together, se-tenant, forming a composite design.

276 Pig (on red panel)

1995. Chinese New Year ("Year of the Pig"). Multicoloured.

2240	100 l. Type **276**	10	10
2241	100 l. Pig facing right (on green panel)	10	10
2242	100 l. Pig facing left (on green panel)	10	10
2243	100 l. Pig facing right (on red panel)	10	10

1995. Centenary (1992) of Sierra Club (environmental protection society). Endangered Species. As T **320** of Antigua. Multicoloured.

2245	150 l. Black-faced impalas	10	15
2246	150 l. Herd of black-faced impalas	10	15
2247	150 l. Black-faced impalas drinking	10	15
2248	150 l. Bonobo with young	10	15
2249	150 l. Black-footed cat in foliage	10	15
2250	150 l. Close-up of black-footed cat	10	15
2251	150 l. L'Hoest's monkey on all fours	10	15
2252	150 l. L'Hoest's monkey squatting	10	15
2253	150 l. Pair of mandrills	10	15
2254	150 l. L'Hoest's monkey (vert)	10	15
2255	150 l. Black-footed cat (vert)	10	15
2256	150 l. Head of colobus monkey (vert)	10	15
2257	150 l. Colobus monkey in tree fork (vert)	10	15
2258	150 l. Head of mandrill (vert)	10	15
2259	150 l. Bonobo with young (vert)	10	15
2260	150 l. Bonobo asleep on log (vert)	10	15
2261	150 l. Mandrill facing right (vert)	10	15
2262	150 l. Colobus monkey on log (vert)	10	15

277 Denver and Rio Grande Western Railroad

1995. Railways of the World. Multicoloured.

2263/74 200 l. × 12 (Type **277**; Central of Georgia; Seaboard Air Line; Missouri Pacific Lines; Atchison, Topeka and Santa Fe; Chicago, Milwaukee, St. Paul and Pacific; Texas and Pacific; Minneapolis, St. Paul and Sault Ste. Marie; Western Pacific; Great Northern; Baltimore and Ohio; Chicago, Rock Island and Pacific)

2275/86 200 l. × 12 (Southern Pacific; Belgian National; Indian; Southern Australian; Union Pacific; British Railways; German Federal; Japanese National; Pennsylvania; East African; Milwaukee; Paris-Orleans)

2287/98 250 l. × 12 (Eurostar; E.T.R. 401 Pendolino express; British Rail Intercity 125; Talgo "Virgen" express, Spain; French National TGV; Amtrak "Southwest Chief" express; French National TGV "Atlantique" express; Greek "Peloponnese Express"; Japanese "Hikari" express train; Canadian National Turbotrain; Australian XPT high-speed train; Chinese SS1 electric locomotive)

2299/2310 300 l. × 12 (Canadian National U1-f locomotive; Union Pacific steam locomotive No. 119; LNER Class A4 No. 4468 "Mallard"; New York Central Class J3a steam locomotive; Canadian National Class U4 locomotive; Australian Class 38 locomotive; Canadian Pacific Class G3c locomotive; Southern Railway Class "West Country" locomotive; Norfolk & Western Class J locomotive; China Class RM locomotive; Russia Class P-36 locomotive; GWR Class "King" locomotive)

2263/2310	Set of 48	9·00	9·50

No. 2290 is inscribed "VIRGIN", No. 2300 "CENTRAL PACIFIC RAILWAY" and No. 2302 "J-32", all in error.

278 National Flag and Scout Emblems

1995. 18th World Scout Jamboree, Netherlands. Multicoloured.

2312	400 l. Type **278**	30	35
2313	500 l. Lord Baden-Powell	40	45
2314	600 l. Scout sign	45	50

1995. 50th Anniv of End of Second World War in Europe. As T **340** of Antigua, showing warships. Multicoloured.

2316	250 l. U.S.S. "Idaho" (battleship)	20	25
2317	250 l. H.M.S. "Ark Royal" (aircraft carrier)	20	25
2318	250 l. Admiral "Graf Spee" (German pocket battleship)	20	25
2319	250 l. American destroyer	20	25
2320	250 l. H.M.S. "Nelson" (battleship)	20	25
2321	250 l U.S.S. "PT 109" (motor torpedo boat)	20	25
2322	250 l. U.S.S. "Iowa" (battleship)	20	25
2323	250 l. "Bismark" (German battleship)	20	25

1995. 50th Anniv of the United Nations. As T **341** of Antigua. Multicoloured.

2325	300 l. U.N. emblem above podium	25	30
2326	400 l. U Thant (Secretary-General, 1961–71)	30	35
2327	500 l. Peace dove and U.N. Building, New York	40	45

Nos. 2325/7 were printed together, se-tenant, forming a composite design.

1995. 50th Anniv of F.A.O. As T **298** of St. Vincent. Multicoloured.

2329	300 l. Fisherman in boat (horiz)	25	30
2330	400 l. Boy carrying wood (horiz)	30	35
2331	500 l. Woman with fruit (horiz)	40	45

1995. 90th Anniv of Rotary International. As T **299** of St. Vincent. Multicoloured.

2333	500 l. National flag and Rotary logo	40	45

1995. 95th Birthday of Queen Elizabeth the Queen Mother. As T **344** of Antigua.

2335	400 l. brown, light brown and black	30	35
2336	400 l. multicoloured	30	35
2337	400 l. multicoloured	30	35
2338	400 l. multicoloured	30	35

DESIGNS: No. 2335, Queen Elizabeth the Queen Mother (pastel drawing); 2336, Holding bouquet of flowers; 2337, At desk (oil painting); No. 2338, Wearing pink evening dress.

1995. 50th Anniv of End of Second World War in the Pacific. As T **340** of Antigua. Multicoloured.

2340	300 l. American B-179 bomber	25	30
2341	300 l. American B-25 bomber	25	30
2342	300 l. American Consolidated B-24 Liberator bomber	25	30
2343	300 l. U.S.S. "Missouri" (battleship)	25	30
2344	300 l. American Douglas A-20 Boston bomber	25	30
2345	300 l. American battle fleet in Lingayen Gulf	25	30

279 Black-spotted Pufferfish

1995. "Singapore '95" International Stamp Exhibition (1st issue). Marine Life. Multicoloured.

2347	300 l. Type **279**	25	30
2348	300 l. Coral hind	25	30
2349	300 l. Hawksbill turtle	25	30
2350	300 l. Hogfish	25	30
2351	300 l. Emperor angelfish	25	30
2352	300 l. Red-tailed butterflyfish	25	30
2353	300 l. Lemon butterflyfish	25	30
2354	300 l. Green-beaked parrotfish	25	30
2355	300 l. Spotted reef moray	25	30
2356	300 l. Cape pigeons	25	30
2357	300 l. Pelican	25	30
2358	300 l. Puffin	25	30
2359	300 l. Humpback whale	25	30
2360	300 l. Greater shearwater	25	30
2361	300 l. Bottlenose dolphin	25	30
2362	300 l. Gurnards	25	30
2363	300 l. Atlantic salmon	25	30
2364	300 l. John Dory	25	30

Nos. 2347/55 and 2356/64 were printed together, se-tenant, forming composite designs.

280 Flame Lily

1995. "Singapore '95" International Stamp Exhibition (2nd issue). African Flora and Fauna. Mult.

2366	300 l. Type **280**	25	30
2367	300 l. Grant's gazelle	25	30
2368	300 l. Dogbane	25	30
2369	300 l. Gold-banded forester	25	30
2370	300 l. Horned chameleon	25	30
2371	300 l. Malachite kingfisher	25	30
2372	300 l. Leaf beetle	25	30
2373	300 l. Acanthus	25	30
2374	300 l. African tulip tree	25	30
2375	300 l. Senegal bush locust	25	30
2376	300 l. Killfish	25	30
2377	300 l. Bird of paradise (flower)	25	30
2378	300 l. Mandrill	25	30
2379	300 l. Painted reed frog	25	30
2380	300 l. Large spotted acraea	25	30
2381	300 l. Carmine bee eater	25	30

281 School Building and Emblem

1995. 150th Anniv of Sierra Leone Grammar School.

2383 **281**	300 l. brown, mauve and black	25	30

1995. Christmas. Religious Paintings. As T **100** of Nevis. Multicoloured.

2384	50 l. "Holy Family" (detail) (Beccafumi)	10	10
2385	100 l. "The Rest on the Flight into Egypt" (detail) (Federico Barocci)	10	10
2386	150 l. "The Virgin" (Jacopo Bellini)	10	15
2387	200 l. "The Flight" (Cavaliere d'Arpino)	15	20
2388	600 l. "Adoration of the Magi" (detail) (Francken)	45	50
2389	800 l. "The Annunciation" (Cima de Conegliano)	60	65

282 Mickey Mouse Doll

1995. Christmas. Disney Toys. Multicoloured.

2391	5 l. Type **282**	10	10
2392	10 l. Donald Duck drum-major doll	10	10
2393	15 l. Donald Duck wind-up toy	10	10
2394	20 l. Donald Duck toothbrush holder	10	10
2395	25 l. Mickey Mouse telephone	10	10
2396	30 l. Mickey Mouse walking toy	10	10
2397	800 l. Toy film projector	2·25	2·25
2398	1000 l. Goofy tricycle toy	2·50	2·50

283 Andrew Huxley (1963 Medicine)

1995. Cent of Nobel Prize Trust Fund. Mult.

2400/8 250 l. × 9 (Type **283**; Nelson Mandela (1993 Peace); Gabriela Mistral (1945 Literature); Otto Diels (1950 Chemistry); Hannes Alfven (1970 Physics); Wole Soyinka (1986 Literature); Hans Dehmelt (1989 Physics); Desmond Tutu (1984 Peace); Leo Esaki (1973 Physics))

2409/17 250 l. × 9 (Tobias Asser (1911 Peace); Andrei Sakharov (1975 Peace); Frederic Passy (1901 Peace); Dag Hammarskjold (1961 Peace); Aung San Suu Kyi (1991 Peace); Ludwig Quidde (1927 Peace); Elie Wiesel (1986 Peace); Bertha von Suttner (1905 Peace); The Dalai Lama (1989 Peace))

2418/26 50 l. × 9 (Richard Zsigmondy (1925 Chemistry); Robert Huber (1988 Chemistry); Wilhelm Ostwald (1909 Chemistry); Johann Deisenhofer (1988 Chemistry); Heinrich Wieland (1922 Chemistry); Gerhard Herzberg (1971 Chemistry); Hans von Euler-Chelpin (1929 Chemistry); Richard Willsatter (1915 Chemistry); Fritz Haber (1918 Chemistry))

2427/35 250 l. × 9 (Maria Goeppert Mayer (1963 Physics); Irene Joliot-Curie (1935 Chemistry); Mother Teresa (1979 Peace); Selma Lagerlof (1909 Literature); Rosalyn Yalow (1977 Medicine); Dorothy Hodgkin (1964 Chemistry); Rita Levi-Montalcini (1986 Medicine); Mairead Corrigan (1976 Peace); Betty Williams (1976 Peace))

2400/35	Set of 36	7·00	8·00

284 Rat

1996. Chinese New Year ("Year of the Rat"). Background colour given.

2437 **284**	200 l. mult (brown background)	15	20
2438 –	200 l. mult (pink background)	15	20
2439 –	200 l. mult (orange background)	15	20
2440 –	200 l. mult (blue background)	15	20

285 Mickey Mouse as Magician

1996. Disney Circus Performers. Cartoon Characters. Multicoloured.

2443	100 l. Type **285**	30	20
2444	200 l. Clarabelle Cow walking tightrope	50	50
2445	250 l. Donald Duck and nephews as clowns	60	60
2446	300 l. Donald as lion tamer	75	75
2447	800 l. Minnie Mouse riding bareback	2·00	2·00
2448	1000 l. Goofy on trapeze	2·25	2·25

286 Lumiere Brothers (cine camera inventors) and Train

1996. Centenary of Cinema. Multicoloured.

2450	250 l. Type **286**	20	25
2451	250 l. Georges Melies (director)	20	25
2452	250 l. Toshiro Mefune (director)	20	25
2453	250 l. David O. Selznick (director)	20	25
2454	250 l. Character from "Metropolis"	20	25
2455	250 l. Akira Kurosawa (director)	20	25
2456	250 l. Charlie Chaplin (actor)	20	25
2457	250 l. Marlene Dietrich (actress)	20	25
2458	250 l. Steven Spielberg (director)	20	25
2459	250 l. Film camera	20	25
2460	250 l. Pete (dog)	20	25
2461	250 l. Silver (horse)	20	25
2462	250 l. Rin-Tin-Tin (dog)	20	25
2463	250 l. King Kong (gorilla)	20	25
2464	250 l. Flipper (dolphin)	20	25
2465	250 l. Great White Shark from "Jaws"	20	25
2466	250 l. Elsa (lioness)	20	25
2467	250 l. Whale from "Moby Dick"	20	25

Nos. 2450/8 and 2459/67 respectively were printed together, se-tenant, forming composite designs.

1996. 125th Anniv of Metropolitan Museum of Art, New York. As T **331** of Maldive Islands. Multicoloured.

2469/76 200 l. × 8 ("Honfleur" (detail) (Jongkind); "A Boat on the Shore" (detail) (Courbet); "Barges at Pontoise" (detail) (Pissarro); "The Dead Christ with Angels" (Manet); "Salisbury Cathedral" (detail) (Constable); "Lady with a Setter Dog" (detail) (Eakins); "Tahitian Women Bathing" (detail) (Gauguin); "Majas on a Balcony" (detail) (Goya))

2477/84 200 l. × 8 ("In the Meadow"; "By the Seashore" (detail); "Still Life with Peaches and Grapes" (detail); "Marguerite Berard"; "Young Girl in Pink and Black Hat"; "Waitress at Duval's Restaurant" (detail); "A Road in Louveciennes" (detail); "Two Young Girls at the Piano" (detail) (all by Renoir))

2485/92 200 l. × 8 ("Morning, An Overcast Day, Rouen" (detail) (Pissarro); "The Horse Fair" (detail) (Bonheur); "High Tide: The Bathers" (detail) (Homer); "The Dance Class" (Degas); "The Brioche" (detail) (Manet); "The Grand Canal, Venice" (detail) (Turner); "St. Tecia interceding for plague-stricken Este" (detail) (G. B. Tiepolo); "Bridge at Villeneuve" (detail) (Sisley))

2493/2500 200 l. × 8 ("Madame Charpentier" (detail) (Renoir); "Head of Christ" (detail) (Rembrandt); "The Standard-bearer" (detail) (Rembrandt); "Girl Asleep" (Vermeer); "Lady with a Lute" (Vermeer); "Portrait of a Woman" (detail) (Rembrandt); "La Grenouillere" (detail) (Monet); "Woman with Chrysanthemums" (detail) (Degas))

2469/2500 Set of 32 . . . . . . 4·25 5·00

287 Olympic Stadium, Los Angeles, 1932

1996. Olympic Games, Atlanta. Multicoloured.

2502 100 l. Type **287** 10 10
2503 150 l. Archery 10 15
2504 300 l. Hockey 25 30
2505 300 l. Swimming 25 30
2506 300 l. Equestrian 25 30
2507 300 l. Boxing 25 30
2508 300 l. Pommel horse exercises . . 25 30
2509 300 l. 100m running 25 30
2510 500 l. Rings exercises 40 45
2511 600 l. Pole vault 45 50

288 "Cantharellus cinnabarinus"

289 Abyssinian Cat

1996. Fungi. Multicoloured.

2513 50 l. Type **288** 10 10
2514 250 l. "Poronidulus conchifer" and "Aphyllophorales polyporaceae" 20 25
2515 250 l. "Ceratiomyxa fruticulosa" 20 25
2516 250 l. "Cortinarius semisanguineus" and "Cortinariaceae agaricales" 20 25
2517 250 l. "Volvamella surrecta" and "Pluteaceae agricales" 20 25
2518 250 l. "Lepiota cepaestipes" . 20 25
2519 250 l. "Amanita rubescans" . 20 25
2520 250 l. "Phyllotopsis nidulans" and "Tricholomataceas agaricales" 20 25
2521 250 l. "Lysyrus gardneri" and "Clathraceae phallales" . . 20 25
2522 250 l. "Lactarius indigo" . . 20 25
2523 250 l. "Coprinus quadrifidus" 20 25
2524 250 l. "Geopyxis carbonaria" 20 25
2525 250 l. "Astraeus hygrometricus" 20 25
2526 250 l. "Agaicaceae agaricales" 20 25
2527 250 l. "Mycena maculata" . . 20 25
2528 250 l. "Lactarius delciosus" . . 20 25
2529 250 l. "Amanita fulva" . . . 20 25
2530 300 l. "Suillus grevillci" . . . 20 25
2531 400 l. "Morchella esculenta" . 30 35
2532 500 l. "Cortinamaceae agaricales" 40 45

1996. Cats. Multicoloured.

2534 200 l. Type **289** 15 20
2535 200 l. British tabby 15 20
2536 200 l. Norwegian forest cat . 15 20
2537 200 l. Maine coon 15 20
2538 200 l. Bengal 15 20
2539 200 l. Asian 15 20
2540 200 l. American curl 15 20
2541 200 l. Devon rex 15 20
2542 200 l. Tonkinese 15 20
2543 200 l. Egyptian mau 15 20
2544 200 l. Burmese 15 20
2545 200 l. Siamese 15 20
2546 200 l. British shorthair . . . 15 20
2547 200 l. Tiffany 15 20
2548 200 l. Birman 15 20
2549 200 l. Somali 15 20
2550 200 l. Malayan 15 20
2551 200 l. Japanese bobtail . . . 15 20
2552 200 l. Himalayan 15 20
2553 200 l. Tortoiseshell 15 20
2554 200 l. Oriental 15 20
2555 200 l. Ocicat 15 20
2556 200 l. Chartreux 15 20
2557 200 l. Ragdoll 15 20

1996. 70th Birthday of Queen Elizabeth II. As T **363** of Antigua. Different photographs. Multicoloured.

2559 600 l. As Type **363** of Antigua 45 50
2560 600 l. Receiving posy . . . 45 50
2561 600 l. Carrying bouquets . . 45 50

290 Three Asian Girls reading

1996. 50th Anniv of U.N.I.C.E.F. Multicoloured.

2563 300 l. Type **290** 25 30
2564 400 l. African children reading 30 35
2565 500 l. Children in class . . . 40 45

291 "Pioneer" Spacecraft in Venus Orbit, 1986–1992

1996. Space Exploration. Multicoloured.

2567 300 l. Type **291** 25 30
2568 300 l. Hubble space telescope 25 30
2569 300 l. "Voyager" space probe 25 30
2570 300 l. Space Shuttle "Challenger" 25 30
2571 300 l. "Pioneer II" space probe 25 30
2572 300 l. "Viking I" Mars lander 25 30

Nos. 2567/72 were printed together, se-tenant, the background forming a composite design.

292 Rat

1996. Chinese Lunar Calendar. Multicoloured.

2574 150 l. Type **292** 10 15
2575 150 l. Ox 10 15
2576 150 l. Tiger 10 15
2577 150 l. Hare 10 15
2578 150 l. Dragon 10 15
2579 150 l. Snake 10 15
2580 150 l. Horse 10 15
2581 150 l. Sheep 10 15
2582 150 l. Monkey 10 15
2583 150 l. Cockerel 10 15
2584 150 l. Dog 10 15
2585 150 l. Pig 10 15

293 "Charaxes pleione"

1996. Butterflies. Multicoloured.

2586 150 l. Type **293** 10 15
2587 200 l. "Eurema brigitta" . . 15 20
2588 250 l. "Precis orithya" . . . 20 25
2589 250 l. "Palla ussheri" . . . 20 25
2590 250 l. "Junonia orithya" . . 20 25
2591 250 l. "Cymothoe sangaris" . 20 25
2592 250 l. "Cyrestis camillus" . . 20 25
2593 250 l. "Precis rhadama" . . 20 25
2594 250 l. "Precis cebrene" . . . 20 25
2595 250 l. "Hypolimnas misippus" 20 25
2596 250 l. "Colotis danae" . . . 20 25
2597 300 l. "Charaxes ameliae" . . 25 30
2598 500 l. "Kallimoides rumia" . 40 45

294 "Begonia multiflora" "Rambouillet"

1996. Flowers. Multicoloured.

2600 150 l. "Tulipa" "Georgette" . 10 15
2601 200 l. "Helichrysum bracteatum" "Monstrosum" 15 20
2602 200 l. Fountain 15 20
2603 200 l. Type **294** 15 20
2604 200 l. Narcissus "Trumpet Daffodil" 15 20
2605 200 l. "Crocus speciosus" . . 15 20
2606 200 l. "Chrysanthemum frutescens" "Marguerite" . 15 20
2607 200 l. Petunia "Polaris" and "Danaus gilippus" (butterfly) 15 20
2608 200 l. "Cosmos pipinnatus" "Sensation" and "Papilio calguanabus" (butterfly) . . 15 20
2609 200 l. "Anemone coronaris" . 15 20
2610 200 l. "Convolvulus minor" . 15 20
2611 300 l. "Paphiopedilum" "Claire de Lune" 25 30
2612 300 l. "Cymbidium" "Peach Bloom" 25 30
2613 300 l. Yacht 25 30
2614 300 l. "Mitonia" "Peach Blossom" 25 30
2615 300 l. "Parides gundalachianus" (butterfly) 25 30
2616 300 l. "Laeliocattleya" "Grand Gate" 25 30
2617 300 l. "Lycaste aromatica" . 25 30
2618 300 l. "Brassolaeliocattleya" "Golden Land" 25 30
2619 300 l. "Cymbidium" "Southern Lace" and "Catastica teutila" (butterfly) 25 30
2620 400 l. Vida "Pansy" 30 35
2621 500 l. "Phalaenopsis" "Pink Beauty" 40 45

Nos. 2602/10 and 2611/19 respectively were printed together, se-tenant, with the backgrounds forming composite designs.

295 Greek War Galley (4th-century B.C.)

1996. History of Ships. Multicoloured.

2623 300 l. Type **295** 25 30
2624 300 l. Roman war galley (A.D. 50) 25 30
2625 300 l. Viking longship (9th-century) 25 30
2626 300 l. Flemish carrack (15th-century) 25 30
2627 300 l. Merchantman (16th-century) 25 30
2628 300 l. Tudor galleon (16th-century) 25 30
2629 300 l. Elizabethan galleon (17th-century) 25 30
2630 300 l. Dutch warship (17th-century) 25 30
2631 300 l. "Maestrale" (18th-century Maltese galley) . . 25 30
2632 300 l. "Cutty Sark" (19th-century clipper) 25 30
2633 300 l. "Great Britain", 1846 (steam/sail liner) 25 30
2634 300 l. H.M.S. "Dreadnought", 1906 (battleship) 25 30
2635 300 l. "Queen Elizabeth", 1940 (liner) 25 30
2636 300 l. Ocean-going yacht, 1962 25 30
2637 300 l. "United States", 1952 (liner) 25 30
2638 300 l. Nuclear-powered submarine, 1950s 25 30
2639 300 l. Super tanker, 1960s . . 25 30
2640 300 l. U.S.S. "Enterprise", 1961 (aircraft carrier) 25 30

No. 2634 is inscribed "Dreadnaught" in error.

1996. Christmas. Religious Paintings. As T **337** of St. Vincent. Multicoloured.

2642 200 l. "Madonna of Humility" (Filippo Lippi) 15 20
2643 250 l. "Coronation of the Virgin" (Lippi) 20 25
2644 400 l. "The Annunciation" (Lippi) 30 35
2645 500 l. "Annunciation" (different) (Lippi) 40 45
2646 600 l. "Barbadori Altarpiece" (Lippi) 45 50
2647 800 l. "Coronation of the Virgin" (different) (Lippi) . 60 65

No. 2646 is inscribed "Alterpiece" in error.

297 Ox

1997. Chinese New Year ("Year of the Ox"). Multicoloured.

2650 250 l. Type **297** (on purple panel) 20 25
2651 250 l. Ox (on green panel) . . 20 25
2652 250 l. Ox (on blue panel) . . 20 25
2653 250 l. Ox (on brown panel) . . 20 25

298 Aladdin and Jasmine

1997. Christmas. Aladdin. Disney Cartoon Characters. Multicoloured.

2656 10 l. Type **298** 10 10
2657 15 l. Genie and Santa Claus . 10 10
2658 20 l. Aladdin and Jasmine on magic carpet 10 10
2659 25 l. Genie as a Christmas tree 10 10
2660 30 l. Genie as Santa Claus and Aladdin 10 10
2661 100 l. Aladdin, Jasmine and Genie on magic carpet . . 15 20
2662 800 l. Genie writing letter to Santa Claus . . . . . 1·10 1·25
2663 1000 l. Genie with four heads . 1·50 1·60

1997. 50th Anniv of U.N.E.S.C.O. As T **348** of Maldive Islands. Multicoloured.

2666 60 l. Church, Kizhi Pogost, Russia 10 10
2667 200 l. Durmitor National Park, Yugoslavia 15 20
2668 250 l. Nessebar, Bulgaria . . 20 25
2669 300 l. Roros, Norway . . . 25 30
2670 300 l. Varsovia city gate, Poland 25 30
2671 300 l. Nuestra Senora Cathedral, Luxembourg . 25 30
2672 300 l. Tower, Vilnius, Lithuania 25 30
2673 300 l. Jelling, Denmark . . . 25 30
2674 300 l. Petajavesi Church, Finland 25 30
2675 300 l. Round house, Sweden . 25 30
2676 300 l. Berne Cathedral, Switzerland 25 30
2677 300 l. Slopes of Mount Kilimanjaro, Tanzania . . 25 30
2678 300 l. Tombs, Fasil Ghebbi, Ethiopia 25 30
2679 300 l. Mount Ruwenzori National Park, Uganda . . 25 30
2680 300 l. Nubia Monument, Abu Simbel, Egypt 25 30
2681 300 l. Tsingy of Bemaraha Nature Reserve, Madagascar 25 30
2682 300 l. House, Djenne, Mali . . 25 30
2683 300 l. Traditional house, Ghana 25 30
2684 300 l. House, Abomey, Benin 25 30
2685 400 l. Gateway, Bukhara, Uzbekistan 30 35
2686 500 l. Monastery, Petchersk, Ukraine 40 45
2687 500 l. Tower, Himeji-jo, Japan (horiz) 40 45
2688 500 l. Gateway, Himeji-jo, Japan (horiz) 40 45
2689 500 l. Outer wall and turrets, Himeji-jo, Japan (horiz) . 40 45
2690 500 l. Village, Himeji-jo, Japan (horiz) 40 45
2691 500 l. Ornate gables, Himeji-jo, Japan (horiz) 40 45
2692 800 l. Mountains, Slovakia . . 60 65

No. 2676 is inscribed "BERNA", No. 2677 "KILIMANDJARO" and No. 2686 "MONESTRY", all in error.

1997. 10th Anniv of Chernobyl Nuclear Disaster. As T **347** of St. Vincent. Multicoloured.

2695 1000 l. Child's face and U.N.E.S.C.O. emblem . . 85 85
2696 1500 l. As 1000 l., but inscribed "CHABAD'S CHILDREN OF CHERNOBYL" at foot 1·10 1·25

1997. Golden Wedding of Queen Elizabeth and Prince Philip. As T **350** of Maldive Islands. Multicoloured (except Nos. 2699/2700).

2697 400 l. Queen Elizabeth II . . 30 35
2698 400 l. Royal coat of arms . . 30 35
2699 400 l. Queen Elizabeth with Prince Philip in military uniform (black) 30 35
2700 400 l. Queen Elizabeth with Prince Philip in naval mess dress (black) 30 35
2701 400 l. St. James's Palace . . 30 35
2702 400 l. Prince Philip 30 35

1997. Birth Bicentenary of Hiroshige (Japanese painter). "One Hundred Famous Views of Edo". As T **352** of Maldive Islands. Multicoloured.

2704 400 l. "Hatsune Riding Grounds, Bakuro-cho" 30 35
2705 400 l. "Mannen Bridge, Fukagawa" 30 35
2706 400 l. "Ryogoku Bridge and the Great Riverbank" 30 35
2707 400 l. "Asakusa River, Great Riverbank, Miyato River" 30 35
2708 400 l. "Silk-goods Lane, Odenma-cho" 30 35
2709 400 l. "Mokuboji Temple, Uchigawa Inlet, Gozensaihata" 30 35

300 Hong Kong Skyline

1997. Return of Hong Kong to China.

2711 **300** 400 l. multicoloured 30 35
2712 – 500 l. multicoloured 40 45
2713 – 550 l. multicoloured 45 50
2714 – 600 l. multicoloured 45 50
2715 – 650 l. multicoloured 55 60
2716 – 800 l. multicoloured 60 65

DESIGNS: 500 l. to 800 l. Different views of modern Hong Kong; 800 l. Deng Xiaoping.

301 Calgary Stadium, 1988

1997. Winter Olympic Games, Nagano, Japan (1998). Multicoloured.

2717 250 l. Type **301** 20 25
2718 300 l. Freestyle Skiing Aerials, 1994 (vert) 25 30
2719 300 l. Peggy Fleming (U.S.A.) (figure skating, 1968) (vert) 25 30
2720 300 l. Japanese competitor (Nordic combined–ski jump, 1992/4) (vert) 25 30
2721 300 l. German team (two-man luge, 1968 to 1992) (vert) 25 30
2722 300 l. Frank-Peter Roetsch (East Germany) (biathlon, 1988) (vert) 25 30
2723 500 l. Ice Hockey (vert) 40 45
2724 800 l. Dan Jansen (U.S.A.) (speed skating, 1994) (vert) 60 65

1997. World Cup Football Championship, France (1998). As T **246** of Lesotho.

2726 100 l. black 10 10
2727 150 l. black 10 15
2728 200 l. black 15 20
2729 250 l. black 20 25
2730 300 l. multicoloured 25 30
2731 300 l. multicoloured 25 30
2732 300 l. multicoloured 25 30
2733 300 l. multicoloured 25 30
2734 300 l. multicoloured 25 30
2735 300 l. multicoloured 25 30
2736 300 l. multicoloured 25 30
2737 300 l. multicoloured 25 30
2738 500 l. black 40 45
2739 600 l. black 45 50

DESIGNS: No. 2726, Stabile, Uruguay; 2727, Schavio, Italy; 2728, Kocsis, Hungary; 2729, Nejedly, Czechoslovakia; 2730, Dwight Yorke, Trinidad and Tobago; 2731, Dennis Bergkamp, Netherlands; 2732, Steve McManaman, England; 2733, Ryan Giggs, Wales; 2734, Romario, Brazil; 2735, Faustino Asprilla, Colombia; 2736, Roy Keane, Republic of Ireland; 2737, Peter Schmeichel, Denmark; 2738, Leonidas, Brazil; 2739, Ademir, Brazil.

302 "Vindula erota"

1997. Butterflies of the World. Multicoloured.

2741 150 l. Type **302** 10 15
2742 200 l. "Pereute leucodrosime" 15 20
2743 250 l. "Dynastor napolean" 20 25
2744 300 l. "Thauria aliris" 25 30
2745 500 l. "Lycaena dispar" 40 45
2746 500 l. "Graphium sarpedon" 40 45
2747 500 l. "Euploe core" 40 45
2748 500 l. "Papilio cresphontes" 40 45
2749 500 l. "Colotis danae" 40 45
2750 500 l. "Battus philenor" 40 45
2751 600 l. "Papilio aegeus" 45 50
2752 600 l. "Mylothris chloris" 45 50
2753 600 l. "Argynnis lathonia" 45 50
2754 600 l. "Elymnias agondas" 45 50
2755 600 l. "Palla ussheri" 45 50
2756 600 l. "Papilio glaucus" 45 50
2757 600 l. "Cercyonis pegala" 45 50
2758 800 l. "Amblypodia anita" 60 65
2759 1500 l. "Kallimoides rumia" 1·10 1·25
2760 2000 l. "Papilio dardanas" 1·60 1·75

Nos. 2745/50 and 2752/7 respectively were printed together, se-tenant, with the backgrounds forming composite designs.

303 Lon Chaney in "Phantom of the Opera", 1925

1997. Famous Films. Horror classics (Nos. 2762/70) or the films of Alfred Hitchcock (Nos. 2771/9). Multicoloured.

2762 300 l. Type **303** 25 30
2763 300 l. Boris Karloff in "The Mummy", 1932 25 30
2764 300 l. Fredric March in "Dr. Jekyll and Mr Hyde", 1932 25 30
2765 300 l. Lon Chaney Jr. in "The Wolf Man", 1941 25 30
2766 300 l. Charles Laughton in "Island of Lost Souls", 1933 25 30
2767 300 l. Lionel Atwill in "Mystery of the Wax Museum", 1933 25 30
2768 300 l. Bela Lugosi in "Dracula", 1931 25 30
2769 300 l. Vincent Price in "The Haunted Palace", 1963 25 30
2770 300 l. Elsa Lanchester in "Bride of Frankenstein", 1935 25 30
2771 350 l. Ray Milland in "Dial M for Murder", 1954 25 30
2772 350 l. James Stewart and Kim Novak in "Vertigo", 1958 25 30
2773 350 l. Cary Grant, Ingrid Bergman and Claude Rains in "Notorious", 1946 25 30
2774 350 l. Farley Granger and John Dall in "Rope", 1948 25 30
2775 350 l. Cary Grant in "North by Northwest", 1959 25 30
2776 350 l. James Stewart and Grace Kelly in "Rear Window", 1954 25 30
2777 350 l. Joan Fontaine and Laurence Olivier in "Rebecca", 1940 25 30
2778 350 l. Tippi Hedren in "The Birds", 1963 25 30
2779 350 l. Janet Leigh in "Psycho", 1960 25 30

Nos. 2762/70 and 2771/9 respectively were printed together, se-tenant, with the backgrounds forming composite designs.

304 Shetland Sheepdog

305 "Ansellia africana"

1997. Dogs and Cats. Multicoloured.

2781 100 l. Type **304** 10 10
2782 150 l. American shorthair tabby cat 10 15
2783 200 l. British shorthair cat 15 20
2784 250 l. Alaskan husky 20 25
2785 400 l. Basset hound 30 35
2786 400 l. Irish setter 30 35
2787 400 l. St. Bernard 30 35
2788 400 l. German shepherd 30 35
2789 400 l. Dalmatian 30 35
2790 400 l. Cocker spaniel 30 35
2791 400 l. Chartreux cat 30 35
2792 400 l. Abyssinian cat 30 35
2793 400 l. Burmese cat 30 35
2794 400 l. White angora cat 30 35
2795 400 l. Japanese bobtail cat 30 35
2796 400 l. Cymric cat 30 35
2797 500 l. Turkish angora cat 40 45
2798 600 l. Jack Russell terrier 45 60

1997. Orchids of the World. Multicoloured.

2800 150 l. Type **305** 10 15
2801 200 l. "Maxillaria praestans" 15 20
2802 250 l. "Cymbidium mimi" 20 25
2803 300 l. "Dendrobium bigibbum" 25 30
2804 400 l. "Laelia anceps" 30 35
2805 400 l. "Paphiopedilum fairrieanum" 30 35
2806 400 l. "Restrepia lansbergii" 30 35
2807 400 l. "Yamadara cattleya" 30 35
2808 400 l. "Cleistes divaricata" 30 35
2809 400 l. "Calypso bulbosa" 30 35
2810 500 l. "Encyclia vitellina" 40 45
2811 800 l. "Epidendrum prismatocarpum" 60 65

306 Daisy Duck

1997. Christmas. Disney Holidays. Multicoloured.

2813 50 l. Type **306** 10 10
2814 50 l. Huey, Dewey and Louie 10 10
2815 50 l. Donald Duck 10 10
2816 50 l. Minnie Mouse 10 10
2817 50 l. Morty and Ferdie 10 10
2818 50 l. Mickey Mouse 10 10
2819 150 l. As No. 2814 20 25
2820 200 l. As No. 2817 30 35
2821 250 l. Type **306** 35 40
2822 300 l. As No. 2816 45 50
2823 400 l. As No. 2818 60 65
2824 500 l. As No. 2815 75 80
2825 600 l. Pluto 85 90
2826 800 l. Goofy 1·10 1·25

307 Benoist Type XIV

1997. Development of the Civil Airliner. Multicoloured.

2828 600 l. Type **307** 45 50
2829 600 l. Douglas DC-3 45 50
2830 600 l. Junkers JU52/3m sea plane 45 50
2831 600 l. Sikorsky S-42 flying boat 45 50
2832 600 l. Sud Caravelle 6 45 50
2833 600 l. Boeing 707 45 50
2834 600 l. De Havilland Comet 45 50
2835 600 l. Airbus Industrie A300 45 50

308 "The Annunciation" (Titian)

1997. Christmas. Religious Paintings. Multicoloured.

2837 100 l. Type **308** 10 10
2838 150 l. "The Annunciation" (Titian) (different) 10 15
2839 200 l. "Madonna of Foligno" (Raphael) 15 20
2840 250 l. "The Annunciation" (Michelino) 20 25
2841 500 l. "The Prophet Isaiah" (Michelangelo) 40 45
2842 600 l. "Three Angels" (Master of the Rhenish Housebook) 45 50

1998. Diana, Princess of Wales Commemoration. As T **249** of Lesotho. Multicoloured (except Nos. 2844, 2849, 2854 and 2856).

2844 400 l. With daffodils (violet and black) 30 35
2845 400 l. Carrying bouquet 30 35
2846 400 l. With Mother Teresa 30 35
2847 400 l. Wearing green and black jacket 30 35
2848 400 l. With shawl over head 30 35
2849 400 l. In evening dress (red and black) 30 35
2850 400 l. Wearing choker and earrings 30 35
2851 400 l. With Prince William 30 35
2852 400 l. Wearing blue jacket and hat 30 35
2853 400 l. Wearing white jacket 30 35
2854 400 l. Wearing hat (brown and black) 30 35
2855 400 l. Wearing black evening dress 30 35
2856 400 l. Laughing (blue and black) 30 35
2857 400 l. Wearing blue and white jacket and hat 30 35
2858 400 l. Wearing green jacket with arms folded 30 35
2859 400 l. Wearing black and white hat 30 35
2860 400 l. Wearing open white shirt 30 35
2861 400 l. Getting out of car 30 35

309 Tiger

1998. Chinese New Year ("Year of the Tiger"). Designs with the tiger in the colour given.

2863 **309** 250 l. multicoloured (mauve) 20 25
2864 – 250 l. multicoloured (lake) 20 25
2865 – 250 l. multicoloured (purple) 20 25
2866 – 250 l. multicoloured (red) 20 25

310 "Metagyrphus nitens"

311 Hypsilophodon

1998. Fauna and Flora. Multicoloured.

2868 200 l. Type **310** 15 20
2869 250 l. Lord Derby's parakeet 20 25
2870 300 l. Narcissus 25 30
2871 400 l. "Barbus tetrazona" (fish) (horiz) 30 35
2872 450 l. Japanese white-eyes (bird) (horiz) 40 45
2873 450 l. Rhododendron (horiz) 40 45
2874 450 l. Slow loris (horiz) 40 45
2875 450 l. Gentiana (flower) (horiz) 40 45
2876 450 l. "Orthetrum albistylum" (dragonfly) (horiz) 40 45
2877 450 l. "Coluber jugularis" (snake) (horiz) 40 45
2878 450 l. Cheetah (horiz) 40 45
2879 450 l. "Ornithogalum thyrsoides" (plant) (horiz) 40 45
2880 450 l. Ostrich (horiz) 40 45
2881 450 l. Common chameleon (horiz) 40 45
2882 450 l. Fennec fox (horiz) 40 45
2883 450 l. "Junonia hierta cebrene" (butterfly) (horiz) 40 45
2884 500 l. "Agalychnis callidryas" (frog) (horiz) 40 45
2885 600 l. Wolverine (horiz) 45 50

Nos. 2872/7 and 2878/83 respectively were printed together, se-tenant, with the backgrounds forming composite designs.

1998. Prehistoric Animals. Multicoloured.

2887 200 l. Type **311** 15 20
2888 400 l. Lambeosaurus 30 35
2889 500 l. Corythosaurus 40 45
2890 500 l. Tyrannosaurus (horiz) 40 45
2891 500 l. Tenontosaurus (horiz) 40 45
2892 500 l. Deinonychus (horiz) 40 45
2893 500 l. Triceratops (horiz) 40 45
2894 500 l. Maiasaura with eggs (horiz) 40 45
2895 500 l. Struthiomimus (horiz) 40 45
2896 500 l. Plateosaurus 40 45
2897 500 l. Tyrannosaurus 40 45
2898 500 l. Brachiosaurus 40 45
2899 500 l. Iguanodon 40 45
2900 500 l. Styracosaurus 40 45
2901 500 l. Hadrosaurus 40 45
2902 600 l. Stegosaurus 45 50
2903 800 l. Antrodemus (horiz) 60 65

Nos. 2890/5 and 2896/2901 respectively were printed together, se-tenant, with the backgrounds forming composite designs.

312 Phoenician Galley

1998. Ships of the World. Multicoloured.

2905 300 l. Type **312** 25 30
2906 300 l. Viking longship 25 30
2907 300 l. Carrack 25 30
2908 300 l. Venetian galley 25 30
2909 300 l. Galeasse 25 30
2910 300 l. Chebeck 25 30
2911 300 l. Junk 25 30
2912 300 l. H.M.S. "Victory" (ship of the line, 1765) 25 30
2913 300 l. "Savannah" (paddle-steamer) 25 30
2914 300 l. Gaissa (sailing canoe) 25 30
2915 300 l. H.M.S. "Warrior" (ironclad) 25 30
2916 300 l. "Preussen" (full-rigged ship) 25 30

1998. 70th Birthday of Mickey Mouse. Nos. 2813/18 optd with Mickey Mouse and **HAPPY BIRTHDAY** 1998.

o2918 50 l. Type **306** 10 10
2919 50 l. Huey, Duey and Louie 10 10
2920 50 l. Donald Duck 10 10

2921	50 l. Minnie Mouse	10	10
2922	50 l. Morty and Ferdie	10	10
2923	50 l. Mickey Mouse	10	10

314 Kiara and Butterfly

1998. Disney's "Lion King" (cartoon film). Multicoloured.

2925	500 l. Type **314**	40	45
2926	500 l. Timon and Pumbaa	40	45
2927	500 l. Kiara	40	45
2928	500 l. Kiara and Kovu lying down	40	45
2929	500 l. Kovu with bird	40	45
2930	500 l. Kiara sitting with Kovu	40	45
2931	500 l. Kiara and bird	40	45
2932	500 l. Pumbaa	40	45
2933	500 l. Kiara and Kovu side by side	40	45
2934	500 l. Kovu	40	45
2935	500 l. Kiara and Kovu back to back	40	45
2936	500 l. Timon	40	45

315 "Mary Magdalen Penitent" (Titian)

1998. Christmas. Religious Paintings. Multicoloured.

2938	200 l. Type **315**	15	20
2939	500 l. "Lamentation of Christ" (Veronese)	40	45
2940	1500 l. "Building of Noah's Ark" (Guido Reni)	1·10	1·25
2941	2000 l. "Abraham and Isaac" (Rembrandt)	1·60	1·75

1998. 25th Death Anniv of Pablo Picasso (painter). As T **373** of St. Vincent. Multicoloured.

2943	400 l. "Man with Straw Hat and Ice Cream Cone" (vert)	30	35
2944	600 l. "Woman in a Red Armchair" (vert)	45	50
2945	800 l. "Nude in a Garden"	60	65

1998. 19th World Scout Jamboree, Chile. As T **364** of Maldive Islands. Multicoloured (except No. 2950).

2947	1500 l. Dan Beard and Lord Baden-Powell, 1937	1·10	1·25
2948	1500 l. Kuwaiti Scouts	1·10	1·25
2949	1500 l. Scout leader feeding bear cub	1·10	1·25
2950	1500 l. William D. Boyce (founder of Lone Scouts) (purple, brown and black) (vert)	1·10	1·25
2951	1500 l. Guion S. Bluford (astronaut and former Eagle scout) (vert)	1·10	1·25
2952	1500 l. Ellison S. Onizuka (astronaut and former Eagle scout) (vert)	1·10	1·25

316 Mahatma Gandhi

1998. 50th Death Anniv of Mahatma Gandhi.

2954	**316**	600 l. multicoloured	45	50

1998. 80th Anniv of Royal Air Force. As T **132** of Nevis. Multicoloured.

2956	800 l. McDonnell Douglas FRG2 Phantom	60	65
2957	800 l. Pair of Panavia Tornado GR1s	60	65
2958	800 l. Sepecat Jaguar GR1A	60	65
2959	800 l. Lockheed C-130 Hercules	60	65

317 "Rocks and a Small Valley"

1998. Birth Bicentenary of Eugene Delacroix (painter). Multicoloured.

2961	400 l. Type **317**	30	35
2962	400 l. "Jewish Musicians from Magador"	30	35
2963	400 l. "Moroccans travelling"	30	35
2964	400 l. "Women of Algiers in their Apartment"	30	35
2965	400 l. "Moroccan Military Training"	30	35
2966	400 l. "Arabs skirmishing in the Mountains"	30	35
2967	400 l. "Arab Chieftain reclining on a Carpet"	30	35
2968	400 l. "Procession in Tangier"	30	35

1998. 1st Death Anniv of Diana, Princess of Wales. As T **365** of Maldive Islands. Multicoloured.

2970	600 l. Diana, Princess of Wales	45	50

318 Rabbit

1998. Chinese New Year ("Year of the Rabbit"). Designs with the rabbit in the colour given.

2971	**318**	700 l. multicoloured (red)	55	60
2972	–	700 l. multicoloured (purple)	55	60
2973	–	700 l. multicoloured (blue)	55	60
2974	–	700 l. multicoloured (violet)	55	60

319 Powder-blue Surgeonfish

1999. International Year of the Ocean. Multicoloured.

2976	150 l. Type **319**	10	15
2977	250 l. Frilled anemone	20	25
2978	400 l. Eastern reef heron	30	35
2979	400 l. Dolphins	30	35
2980	400 l. Humpback whale and ship	30	35
2981	400 l. Green-winged Macaw ("Red and Green Macaw")	30	35
2982	400 l. Blue tangs	30	35
2983	400 l. Guitarfish and blue-striped pipefish	30	35
2984	400 l. Manatees	30	35
2985	400 l. Hammerhead shark	30	35
2986	400 l. Blue shark	30	35
2987	400 l. Lemon goby and moorish idol	30	35
2988	400 l. Ribbon moray ("Ribbon Eels")	30	35
2989	400 l. Loggerhead turtle	30	35
2990	500 l. Blue shark	40	45
2991	500 l. Tiger shark	40	45
2992	500 l. Bull shark	40	45
2993	500 l. Great white shark	40	45
2994	500 l. Scalloped hammerhead shark	40	45
2995	500 l. Oceanic white-tipped shark	40	45
2996	500 l. Zebra shark	40	45
2997	500 l. Leopard shark	40	45
2998	500 l. Horn shark	40	45
2999	600 l. Red beard sponge	45	50
3000	800 l. Dusky batfish ("Red-finned Batfish")	60	65

Nos. 2978/89 and 2990/8 respectively were printed together, se-tenant, with the backgrounds forming composite designs.

320 Grumman X-29

1999. Aircraft. Multicoloured.

3002	200 l. Type **320**	15	20
3003	300 l. Bell XS-1 rocket aircraft	25	30
3004	400 l. Mikoyan Gurevich MiG-21	30	35
3005	600 l. Bleriot XI	45	50
3006	600 l. Nieuport 11 "Bebe"	45	50
3007	600 l. D.H.100 Vampire	45	50
3008	600 l. Aerospatiale/Aeritalia ATR 72	45	50
3009	600 l. Fiat CR-32	45	50
3010	600 l. Curtiss P-6E Hawk	45	50
3011	600 l. SAAB JA 37 Viggen	45	50
3012	600 l. Piper PA-46 Malibu	45	50
3013	600 l. Grumman F-14 Tomcat	45	50
3014	600 l. Grumman F3F-1	45	50
3015	600 l. North American F-86A Sabre	45	50
3016	600 l. Cessna 377 Super Skymaster	45	50
3017	600 l. General Dynamics F-16 Fighting Falcon	45	50
3018	600 l. "Voyager" experimental aircraft	45	50
3019	600 l. Fairchild A10A Thunderbolt II	45	50
3020	600 l. Wiley Post's Lockheed Vega, 1933	45	50
3021	600 l. Amelia Earhart's Lockheed Vega, 1930	45	50
3022	800 l. Fokker F.VIIa/3m "Southern Cross"	60	65
3023	1500 l. Supermarine S6B (seaplane)	1·10	1·25

Nos. 3014 and 3021 are inscribed "GUMMAN F3F-1" or "Amella Earhart" both in error.

321 "Geranium wallichianum"

1999. "Australia '99" World Stamp Exhibition, Melbourne. Flowers. Multicoloured.

3025	150 l. Type **321**	10	15
3026	200 l. "Osmanthus x burkwoodii"	15	20
3027	250 l. "Iris pallida dalmatica" (vert)	20	25
3028	500 l. Rhododendron (vert)	40	45
3029	600 l. Rose (vert)	45	50
3030	600 l. "Clematis hybrida" (vert)	45	50
3031	600 l. "Cardiospermum halicacabum" (vert)	45	50
3032	600 l. "Fritillaria imperialis" (vert)	45	50
3033	600 l. "Iris foetidiissima" (vert)	45	50
3034	600 l. Pyracantha (vert)	45	50
3035	600 l. "Hepatica transsilvanica" (vert)	45	50
3036	800 l. Papoose (vert)	60	65
3037	1500 l. "Viola labradorica" (vert)	1·10	1·25
3038	2000 l. "Rosa banksiae lutea" (vert)	1·60	1·75

Nos. 3030/5 were printed together, se-tenant, with the backgrounds forming a composite design.

Only Nos. 3025/9 and 3036/8 show the "Australia '99" emblem actually printed on the stamp.

SINGAPORE

An island to the south of the Malay peninsula, formerly part of the Straits Settlement but became a separate Crown Colony on 1 April, 1946. From 1 August, 1958, an internally self-governing territory designated the State of Singapore. From 16 September, 1963 part of the Malaysian Federation until 9 August, 1965, when it became an independent republic within the Commonwealth.

100 cents = 1 dollar

1948. As T **58** of Straits Settlements, but inscr "MALAYA SINGAPORE".

1	1 c. black	15	40
2	2 c. orange	15	10
3	3 c. green	50	30
4	4 c. brown	20	65
19a	5 c. purple	2·50	90
5	6 c. grey	40	40
6	8 c. red	30	40
21a	8 c. green	4·00	3·00
7	10 c. mauve	20	10
22a	12 c. red	4·00	6·00
8	15 c. blue	7·50	10
9	20 c. black and green	3·50	20
24a	20 c. blue	4·00	10
25	25 c. purple and orange	80	10
25a	35 c. red and purple	4·00	90
11	40 c. red and purple	8·00	5·00
12	50 c. black and blue	3·25	10
13	$1 blue and purple	10·00	1·75
14	$2 green and red	48·00	3·25
15	$5 green and brown	£120	4·25

1948. Silver Wedding. As T **10/11** of Aden.

31	10 c. violet	75	30
32	$5 brown	£110	29·00

1949. 75th Anniv of U.P.U. As T **20/23** of Antigua.

33	10 c. purple	75	30
34	15 c. blue	6·00	2·25
35	25 c. orange	6·00	2·25
36	50 c. black	6·00	3·00

1953. Coronation. As T **13** of Aden.

37	10 c. black and purple	1·75	10

1 Chinese Sampan

16 The Singapore Lion

3 Singapore River

1955.

38	**1**	1 c. black	10	50
39	–	2 c. orange	1·50	1·00
40	–	4 c. brown	90	15
41	–	5 c. purple	65	15
42	–	6 c. grey	65	40
43	–	8 c. turquoise	1·25	70
44	–	10 c. lilac	3·00	10
45	–	12 c. red	3·00	2·75
46	–	20 c. blue	2·25	10
47	–	25 c. orange and violet	3·00	80
48	–	30 c. violet and lake	3·75	10
49	–	50 c. blue and black	2·25	10
50	–	$1 blue and purple	30·00	20
51	**3**	$2 green and red	42·00	1·50
52	–	$5 multicoloured	42·00	4·50

DESIGNS—HORIZ (as Type **1**) (2 c. to 20 c. are sailing craft): 2 c. Malay kolek; 4 c. Twa-kow lighter; 5 c. Lombok sloop; 6 c. Trengganu pinas; 8 c. Palari schooner; 10 c. Timber tongkong; 12 c. Hainan junk; 20 c. Cocos-Keeling schooner; 25 c. Douglas DC-4M2 "Argonaut" aircraft; 30 c. Oil tanker; 50 c. "Chusan III" (liner). VERT (as Type **3**): $1 Raffles statue; $5 Arms of Singapore.

1959. New Constitution. Lion in yellow and sepia.

53	**16**	4 c. red	65	60
54		10 c. purple	1·00	30
55		20 c. blue	2·25	2·75
56		25 c. green	2·50	2·00
57		30 c. violet	2·50	3·00
58		50 c. slate	3·25	3·00

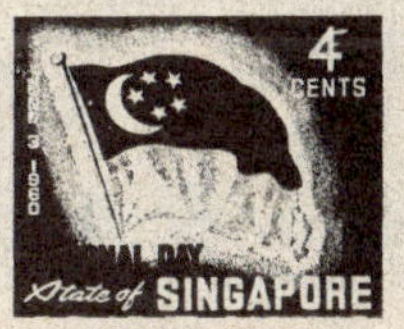

17 State Flag

1960. National Day.

59	**17**	4 c. red, yellow and blue	75	90
60		10 c. red, yellow and grey	2·25	30

18 Clasped Hands

1961. National Day.

61	18	4 c. black, brown and yellow	1·00	85
62		10 c. black, green and yellow	1·25	10

19 "Arachnis" "Maggie Oei" (orchid)

20 Yellow Seahorse

1962. Orchids, Fishes and Birds.

63	19	1 c. multicoloured	30	75
64	20	2 c. brown and green	30	1·50
65	–	4 c. black and red	30	30
66	–	5 c. red and black	20	10
67	–	6 c. black and yellow	55	70
68	–	8 c. multicoloured	1·25	3·50
69	–	10 c. orange and black	40	10
70	–	12 c. multicoloured	1·25	3·50
70a	–	15 c. multicoloured	1·75	10
71	–	20 c. orange and blue	40	10
72	–	25 c. black and orange	75	10
73	–	30 c. multicoloured	1·25	10
74	–	50 c. multicoloured	1·25	10
75	–	$1 multicolorued	20·00	60
76	–	$2 multicoloured	14·00	75
77	–	$5 multicoloured	27·00	4·00

DESIGNS—HORIZ (as Type 20): 4 c. Tiger barb; 5 c. Orange clownfish; 10 c. Harlequinfish; 25 c. Three-spotted goramy. (As Type 19): 50 c. White-rumped shama; $1 White-breasted kingfisher.VERT (as Type 20): 6 c. Archerfish; 20 c. Copper-banded butterflyfish. (As Type 19): 8 c. "Vanda" "Tan Chay Yan" (orchid); 12 c. "Grammatophyllum speciosum" (orchid); 15 c. Black-naped tern; 30 c. "Vanda" "Miss Joaquim" (orchid); $2 Yellow-bellied sunbird; $5 White-bellied sea eagle.

34 "The Role of Labour in Nation-Building"

1962. National Day.

78	34	4 c. yellow, red and black	90	1·50
79		10 c. yellow, blue and black	1·00	60

35 Blocks of Flats, Singapore

1963. National Day.

80	35	4 c. multicoloured	40	65
81		10 c. multicoloured	85	15

36 Dancers in National Costume

1963. South East Asia Cultural Festival.

82	36	5 c. multicoloured	40	40

37 Workers

1966. 1st Anniv of Republic.

89	37	15 c. multicoloured	75	30
90		20 c. multicoloured	1·00	1·25
91		30 c. multicoloured	1·25	2·00

38 Flag Procession

1967. National Day.

92	38	6 c. red, brown and slate	50	75
93		15 c. purple, brown and slate	80	10
94		50 c. blue, brown and slate	1·50	1·60

Nos. 92/4 are respectively inscr "Build a Vigorous Singapore" in Chinese, Malay and Tamil, in additon to the English inscr.

39 Skyscrapers and Afro-Asian Map

1967. 2nd Afro-Asian Housing Congress.

95	39	10 c. multicoloured	30	10
96		25 c. multicoloured	75	1·00
97		50 c. multicoloured	1·40	1·60

40 Symbolical Figure wielding Hammer and Industrial Outline of Singapore

45 Sword Dance

43 Mirudhangam

1968. National Day. Inscription at top in Chinese (6 c.), Malay (15 c.) or Tamil (50 c.).

98	40	6 c. red, black and gold	35	65
99		15 c. green, black and gold	45	15
100		50 c. blue, black and gold	1·00	1·25

1968.

101	43	1 c. multicoloured	15	2·25
102	–	4 c. multicoloured	60	2·75
103	45	5 c. multicoloured	60	80
104	–	6 c. black, lemon & orange	1·25	1·75
105	–	10 c. multicoloured	20	10
106	–	15 c. multicoloured	60	10
107	–	20 c. multicoloured	1·00	85
108	–	25 c. multicoloured	1·00	70
109	–	30 c. multicoloured	40	70
110	–	50 c. black, red and brown	50	50
111	–	75 c. multicoloured	3·00	2·25
112	–	$1 multicoloured	4·00	80
113	–	$2 multicoloured	3·50	1·00
114	–	$5 multicoloured	13·00	2·00
115	–	$10 multicoloured	38·00	15·00

DESIGNS—VERT (as Type 43): 4 c. Pi Pa; $2 Rebab; $10 Ta Ku. (As Type 45): 6 c. Lion Dance; 10 c. Bharatha Natyam; 15 c. Tari Payong; 20 c. Kathak Kali; 25 c. Lu Chih Shen and Lin Chung; 50 c. Tari Lilin; 75 c. Tarian Kuda Kepang; $1 Yao Chi. HORIZ (as Type 43): $5 Vine. (As Type 45): 30 c. Dragon dance.

58 E.C.A.F.E. Emblem

1969. Plenary Session of Economic Commission for Asia and the Far East.

116	58	15 c. black, silver and blue	40	20
117		30 c. black, silver and red	85	1·25
118		75 c. black, silver and violet	1·40	2·50

MINIMUM PRICE

The minimum price quoted is 10p which represents a handling charge rather than a basis for valuing common stamps. For further notes about prices see introductory pages.

59 "100000" and Slogan as Block of Flats

60 Aircraft over Silhouette of Singapore Docks

1969. Completion of "100000 Homes for the People" Project.

119	59	25 c. black and green	1·00	50
120		50 c. black and blue	1·25	1·25

1969. 150th Anniv of Founding of Singapore.

121	60	15 c. black, red and yellow	2·50	70
122	–	30 c. black and blue	2·50	1·75
123	–	75 c. multicoloured	4·50	2·00
124	–	$1 black and red	10·00	10·00
125	–	$5 red and black	35·00	55·00
126	–	$10 black and green	48·00	55·00

DESIGNS: 30 c. U.N. emblem and outline of Singapore; 75 c. Flags and outline of Malaysian Federation; $1 Uplifted hands holding crescent and stars; $5 Tail of Japanese aircraft and searchlight beams; $10 Bust from statue of Sir Stamford Raffles.

61 Sea Shells

1970. World Fair, Osaka. Multicoloured.

128		15 c. Type 61	1·50	15
129		30 c. Veil-tailed guppys	2·75	90
130		75 c. Greater flamingo and helmeted hornbill	7·50	3·75
131		$1 Orchid	7·50	6·00

62 "Kindergarten"

63 Soldier charging

1970. 10th Anniv of People's Association.

133	62	15 c. brown and orange	85	20
134	–	50 c. blue and orange	2·25	2·75
135	–	75 c. purple and black	3·50	4·50

DESIGNS: 50 c. "Sport"; 75 c. "Culture".

1970. National Day. Multicoloured.

136		15 c. Type 63	1·25	20
137		50 c. Soldier on assault course	3·75	3·50
138		$1 Soldier jumping	5·00	8·50

64 Sprinters

1970. Festival of Sports.

139	64	10 c. mauve, black and blue	2·00	3·00
140	–	15 c. black and orange	2·50	3·25
141	–	25 c. black, orange & green	2·75	3·50
142	–	50 c. black, green & mauve	3·00	3·50

DESIGNS: 15 c. Swimmers; 25 c. Tennis-players; 50 c. Racing-cars.

65 "Neptune Aquamarine" (freighter)

1970. Singapore Shipping.

143	65	15 c. multicoloured	2·75	65
144	–	30 c. yellow and blue	6·00	5·50
145	–	75 c. yellow and red	10·00	8·50

DESIGNS: 30 c. Container berth; 75 c. Ship-building.

66 Country Names in Circle

1971. Commonwealth Heads of Government Meeting, Singapore. Multicoloured.

146		15 c. Type 66	90	20
147		30 c. Flags in circle	1·75	80
148		75 c. Commonwealth flags	3·25	3·75
149		$1 Commonwealth flags linked to Singapore (63 × 61 mm)	4·25	6·50

67 Bicycle Rickshaws

1971. Tourism. ASEAN Year. (ASEAN = Association of South East Asian Nations).

150	67	15 c. black, violet & orange	80	25
151	–	20 c. indigo, orange, & blue	1·10	1·00
152	–	30 c. red and purple	1·40	1·75
153	–	50 c. multicoloured	4·75	7·50
154	–	75 c. multicoloured	6·50	9·50

DESIGNS—SQUARE: 20 c. Houseboat "village" and boats; 30 c. Bazaar. HORIZ (68 × 18 mm): 50 c. Modern harbour skyline; 75 c. Religious buildings.

68 Chinese New Year

69 "Dish" Aerial

1971. Singapore Festivals. Multicoloured.

155		15 c. Type 68	1·25	15
156		30 c. Hari Raya	3·00	2·50
157		50 c. Deepavali	4·00	6·50
158		75 c. Christmas	5·00	7·50

1971. Opening of Satellite Earth Station.

160	69	15 c. multicoloured	3·00	1·50
161	–	30 c. multicoloured	13·00	11·00
162	–	30 c. multicoloured	13·00	11·00
163	–	30 c. multicoloured	13·00	11·00
164	–	30 c. multicoloured	13·00	11·00

DESIGNS: Nos. 161/4 were printed in se-tenant blocks of four throughout the sheet, the four stamps forming a composite design similar to Type 69. They can be identified by the colour of the face values which are: yellow (No. 161), green (No. 162), red (No. 163) or orange (No. 164).

70 "Singapore River and Fort Canning, 1843–7" (Lieut. E. A. Porcher)

1971. Art. Multicoloured.

165		10 c. Type 70	2·50	2·50
166		15 c. "The Padang, 1851" (J. T. Thomson)	3·50	4·00
167		20 c. "Singapore Waterfront, 1848–9"	4·50	4·50
168		35 c. "View from Fort Canning 1846" (J. T. Thomson)	9·00	9·00
169		50 c. "View from Mt. Wallich, 1857" (P. Carpenter)	13·00	14·00
170		$1 "Singapore Waterfront, 1861" (W. Gray)	16·00	19·00

The 50 c. and $1 are larger, 69 × 47 mm.

71 One Dollar of 1969

1972. Coins.
171 – 15 c. orange, black & green . . 1·25 35
172 71 35 c. black and red . . . . 2·75 3·00
173 – $1 yellow, black and blue . 5·00 8·00
DESIGNS: 15 c. One-cent coin of George V; $1 One hundred and fifty dollar gold coin of 1969.

72 "Moon Festival" (Seah Kim Joo)

1972. Contemporary Art. Multicoloured.
174 15 c. Type **72** 80 30
175 35 c. "Complimentary Forces" (Thomas Yeo) . . . . 2·00 3·00
176 50 c. "Rhythm in Blue" (Yusman Aman) . . . . 3·00 4·50
177 $1 "Gibbons" (Chen Wen Hsi) 5·50 7·50
Nos. 175/6 are 36 × 54 mm.

73 Lanterns and Fish

75 "Maria Rickmers" (barque)

74 Student Welding

1972. National Day. Designs symbolising Festivals. Multicoloured.
178 15 c. Type **73** 75 20
179 35 c. Altar and candles . . . . 1·40 2·75
180 50 c. Jug, bowl and gifts . . . 2·00 4·00
181 75 c. Candle . . . . 3·00 5·50

1972. Youth.
182 **74** 15 c. multicoloured 80 30
183 – 35 c. multicoloured . . . . 2·50 3·50
184 – $1 orange, violet and green 4·50 8·00
DESIGNS: 35 c. Sport; $1 Dancing.

1972. Shipping. Multicoloured.
185 15 c. "Neptune Ruby" (container ship) (42 × 29 mm) . . . . . 2·25 80
186 75 c. Type **75** . . . . 7·50 8·00
187 $1 Chinese junk . . . . 8·00 9·00

76 P.Q.R. Slogan

77 Jurong Bird Park

1973. "Prosperity Through Quality and Reliability" Campaign. Multicoloured.
189 15 c. Type **76** 60 15
190 25 c. Badge . . . . 2·00 3·25
191 75 c. Text (different) . . . . . 2·25 3·75
192 $1 Seal . . . . 2·25 5·00

1973. Singapore Landmarks.
193 **77** 15 c. black and orange . . 1·00 15
194 – 35 c. black and green . . . 2·50 3·25
195 – 50 c. black and brown . . . 3·25 4·25
196 – $1 black and purple . . . . 5·00 6·50
DESIGNS: 35 c. National Theatre; 50 c. City Hall; $1 Fullerton Building and Singapore River.

78 Aircraft Tail-fins

1973. Aviation. Multicoloured.
197 10 c. Type **78** 50 10
198 35 c. Emblems of Singapore Airlines and destinations . . 1·75 2·00
199 75 c. Emblem on tail-fin . . . 2·25 2·50
200 $1 Emblems encircling the globe 2·75 3·50

79 "Culture"

80 Athletics, Judo and Boxing

1973. National Day.
201 **79** 10 c. orange and black . . 2·00 2·25
202 – 35 c. orange and black . . 2·25 2·75
203 – 50 c. orange and black . . 2·50 3·00
204 – 75 c. orange and black . . 2·75 3·50
Nos. 201/4 were printed in se-tenant blocks of four within the sheet, and form a composite design representing Singapore's culture.

1973. 7th S.E.A.P.* Games.
205 **80** 10 c. gold, silver and blue . 55 20
206 – 15 c. gold and black . . . 1·75 1·50
207 – 25 c. gold, silver and black 1·50 1·75
208 – 35 c. gold, silver and blue . 3·00 3·25
209 – 50 c. multicoloured . . . 2·00 4·00
210 – $1 silver, blue and green . 3·25 7·00
DESIGNS—SQUARE (as Type **80**): 15 c. Cycling, weight-lifting, pistol-shooting and sailing; 25 c. Footballs; 35 c. Table-tennis bat, shuttlecock, tennis ball and hockey stick. HORIZ (41 × 25 mm): 50 c. Swimmers; $1 Stadium.
*S.E.A.P. = South East Asian Peninsula.

81 Agave

82 Mangosteen

1973. Multicoloured. (a) Flowers and plants as T **81**.
212 1 c. Type **81** 90 65
213 5 c. "Coleus blumei" 10 45
214 10 c. "Vinca rosea" 15 10
215 15 c. "Helianthus angustifolius" 1·25 10
216 20 c. "Licuala grandis" . . . 45 60
217 25 c. "Wedelia trilobata" . . 3·00 55
218 35 c. "Chrysanthemum frutescens" 90 90
219 50 c. "Costus malorticanus" . 1·00 55
220 75 c. "Gerbera jamesonii" . . 2·50 90

(b) Fruits as T **82**.
221 $1 Type **82** . . . . 1·50 40
222 $2 Jackfruit . . . . 3·25 1·25
223 $5 Coconut . . . . 6·00 9·00
224 $10 Pineapple . . . . . . 11·00 16·00

83 Tiger and Orang-Utans

84 Delta Guppy

1973. Singapore Zoo. Multicoloured.
225 5 c. Type **83** 85 85
226 10 c. Leopard and waterbuck . 1·00 45
227 35 c. Leopard and thamin . . 4·50 5·50
228 75 c. Horse and lion . . . . 6·00 7·50

1974. Tropical Fish. Multicoloured.
229 5 c. Type **84** 60 50
230 10 c. Half-black delta guppy . 60 15
231 35 c. Delta guppy (different) . 2·50 3·50
232 $1 Black delta guppy . . . . 4·50 7·00

85 Scout Badge within "9"

86 U.P.U. Emblem and Multiple "Centenary"

1974. 9th Asian-Pacific Scout Conference.
233 **85** 10 c. multicoloured . . . 40 10
234 75 c. multicoloured . . . 1·60 2·00

1974. Centenary of U.P.U.
235 **86** 10 c. brown, purple & gold 20 10
236 – 35 c. blue, deep blue & gold 55 1·60
237 – 75 c. multicoloured . . . 1·25 2·75
DESIGNS: 35 c. U.P.U. emblem and multiple U.N. symbols; 75 c. U.P.U. emblem and multiple peace doves.

87 Family Emblem

88 "Tree and Sun" (Chia Keng San)

1974. World Population Year. Multicoloured.
238 10 c. Type **87** 30 10
239 35 c. Male and female symbols 80 1·60
240 75 c. World population map . 1·75 3·25

1974. Universal Children's Day. Mult.
241 5 c. Type **88** 40 50
242 10 c. "My Daddy and Mummy" (Angeline Ang) 40 20
243 35 c. "A Dump Truck" (Si-Hoe Yeen Joong) . . . . 2·50 3·50
244 50 c. "My Aunt" (Raymond Teo) 2·75 4·25

89 Street Scene

1975. Singapore Views. Multicoloured.
246 15 c. Type **89** 80 20
247 20 c. Singapore River . . . . 1·50 1·50
248 $1 "Kelong" (fish-trap) . . . . 5·00 7·50

90 Emblem and Lighters' Prows

1975. 9th Biennial Conference of Int Association of Ports and Harbours, Singapore. Multicoloured.
249 5 c. Type **90** 30 15
250 25 c. Freighter and ship's wheel 1·75 1·50
251 50 c. Oil-tanker and flags . . . 2·25 3·00
252 $1 Container-ship and propellers 3·50 6·00

91 Satellite Earth Station, Sentosa

92 "Homes and Gardens"

1975. "Science and Industry". Mult.
253 10 c. Type **91** 35 10
254 35 c. Oil refineries (vert) . . . 2·50 2·75
255 75 c. "Medical Sciences" . . . 2·75 4·00

1975. 10th National Day. Multicoloured.
256 10 c. Type **92** 20 10
257 35 c. "Shipping and Ship-building" . . . . 1·75 2·00
258 75 c. "Communications and Technology" . . . . 2·25 3·50
259 $1 "Trade, Commerce and Industry" . . . . 2·50 4·00

93 South African Crowned Cranes

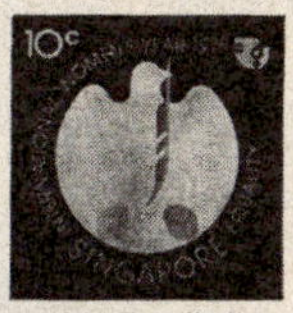

94 "Equality"

1975. Birds. Multicoloured.
260 5 c. Type **93** . . . . 1·75 80
261 10 c. Great Indian hornbill . . 1·75 30
262 35 c. White-breasted kingfishers and White-collared kingfisher 9·50 9·50
263 $1 Sulphur-crested cockatoo and blue and yellow macaw . . . 14·00 16·00

1975. International Women's Year. Mult.
264 10 c. Type **94** 25 10
265 35 c. "Development" . . . . . 2·00 3·00
266 75 c. "Peace" . . . . 2·75 6·00

95 Yellow Flame

96 "Arachnis hookeriana × Vanda" Hilo Blue

1976. Wayside Trees. Multicoloured.
268 10 c. Type **95** 60 10
269 35 c. Cabbage tree . . . . . 2·50 3·50
270 50 c. Rose of India . . . . . 2·75 3·50
271 75 c. Variegated coral tree . . 3·25 6·25

1976. Singapore Orchids. Multicoloured.
272 10 c. Type **96** . . . . 1·50 10
273 35 c. "Arachnis Maggie Oei × Vanda insignis" . . . . 4·00 4·00
274 50 c. "Arachnis Maggie Oei × Vanda" Rodman . . 4·75 4·50
275 75 c. "Arachnis hookeriana × Vanda" Dawn Nishimura . . . . 6·00 8·00

97 Festival Symbol and Band

1976. 10th Anniv of Singapore Youth Festival. Multicoloured.
276 10 c. Type **97** 20 10
277 35 c. Athletes . . . . 1·25 1·25
278 75 c. Dancers . . . . 1·40 2·00

98 "Queen Elizabeth Walk"

1976. Paintings of Old Singapore. Mult.
279 10 c. Type **98** 50 20
280 50 c. "The Padang" . . . . . 3·75 4·00
281 $1 "Raffles Place" . . . . . 4·50 5·50

99 Chinese Costume

100 Radar, Missile and Soldiers

1976. Bridal Costumes. Multicoloured.
283 10 c. Type **99** 65 10
284 35 c. Indian costume . . . . 2·25 2·50
285 75 c. Malay costume . . . . 3·75 5·75

1977. 10th Anniv of National Service. Multicoloured.
286 10 c. Type **100** 65 10
287 50 c. Tank and soldiers . . . 2·50 2·50
288 75 c. Soldiers, wireless operators, pilot and Douglas A-4 Skyhawk aircraft . . . . 3·50 3·50

101 Lyrate Cockle

102 Spotted Hermit Crab

1977. Multicoloured. (a) Shells as T **101**.
289 1 c. Type **101** . . . . 50 1·25
290 5 c. Folded or plicate scallop . 20 10
291 10 c. Marble cone 20 10
292 15 c. Scorpion conch . . . . 1·00 40
293 20 c. Amplustre or royal paper bubble 90 10
294 25 c. Spiral babylon . . . . . 1·25 1·50
295 35 c. Royal thorny or spiny oyster . . . . 1·50 1·50
296 50 c. Maple-leaf triton or winged frog shell . . . . 2·00 10
297 75 c. Troschel's murex . . . . 3·00 20

(b) Fish and Crustaceans as T **102**.
298 $1 Type **102** . . . . 2·25 15
299 $2 Zuge's stingray . . . . . 2·25 75
300 $5 Cuttlefish . . . . 4·00 2·25
301 $10 Lionfish . . . . 7·50 5·50

103 Shipbuidling

104 Keyhole and Banknotes

1977. Labour Day. Multicoloured.

302	10 c. Type **103**	30	10
303	50 c. Building construction	1·25	1·00
304	75 c. Road construction	1·75	1·25

1977. Cent of Post Office Savings Bank. Mult.

305	10 c. Type **104**	30	10
306	35 c. On-line banking service	1·00	50
307	75 c. GIRO service	2·25	1·50

105 Flags of Member Nations

106 "Chingay Procession" (Liang Yik Yin)

1977. 10th Anniv of ASEAN (Association of South-East Asian Nations). Multicoloured.

308	10 c. Type **105**	30	10
309	35 c. "Agriculture"	1·00	50
310	75 c. "Industry"	2·00	1·10

1977. Children's Art. Multicoloured.

311	10 c. Type **106**	30	10
312	35 c. "At the Bus Stop" (Chong Khing Ann) (horiz)	1·00	50
313	75 c. "Playground" (Yap Li Hwa) (horiz)	2·25	2·75

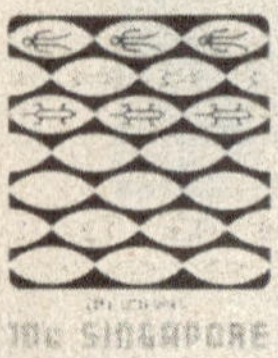
107 "Life Sciences"

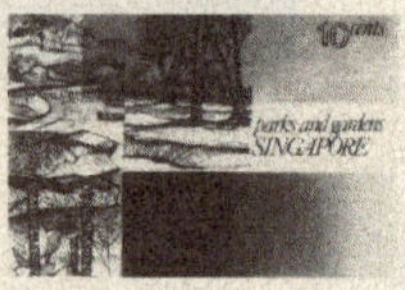
108 Botanical Gardens and Esplanade, Jurong Bird Park

1977. Singapore Science Centre. Mult.

315	10 c. Type **107**	10	10
316	35 c. "Physical sciences"	45	30
317	75 c. "Science and technology"	1·25	1·75
318	$1 Singapore Science Centre	1·50	1·75

1978. Park and Gardens. Multicoloured.

319	10 c. Type **108**	20	10
320	35 c. Lagoon, East Coast Park (vert)	80	70
321	75 c. Botanical Gardens (vert)	1·50	2·00

109 Red-whiskered Bulbul

111 Map of South East Asia showing Cable Network

110 Thian Hock Keng Temple

1978. Singing Birds. Multicoloured.

322	10 c. Type **109**	60	20
323	35 c. Oriental white eye	1·75	1·25
324	50 c. White-rumped shama	2·00	2·00
325	75 c. White-crested laughing thrush and hwamei	2·25	3·25

1978. National Monuments. Multicoloured.

326	10 c. Type **110**	45	55
327	10 c. Hajjah Fatimah Mosque	45	55
328	10 c. Armenian Church	45	55
329	10 c. Sri Mariamman Temple	45	55

1978. A.S.E.A.N. Submarine Cable (1st issue). Philippines–Singapore Section.

331	**111** 10 c. multicoloured	15	10
332	35 c. multicoloured	60	55
333	50 c. multicoloured	80	85
334	75 c. multicoloured	90	1·25

See also Nos. 385/8 and 458/61.

112 "Neptune Spinel" (bulk carrier)

1978. 10th Anniv of Neptune Orient Shipping Lines. Multicoloured.

335	10 c. Type **112**	70	15
336	35 c. "Neptune Aries" (tanker)	1·75	1·00
337	50 c. "Anro Temasek" (container ship)	2·00	2·00
338	75 c. "Neptune Pearl" (container ship)	2·50	3·00

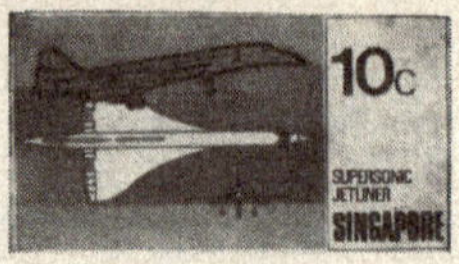
113 Concorde

1978. Aviation. Multicoloured.

339	10 c. Type **113**	1·00	30
340	35 c. Boeing 747-200	1·25	1·00
341	50 c. Vickers Vimy	1·50	1·75
342	75 c. Wright Brothers' Flyer I	1·75	3·00

114 10-Kilometre Marker

115 Vanda Hybrid

1979. Metrication. Multicoloured.

343	10 c. Type **114**	15	10
344	35 c. Tape measure	30	50
345	75 c. Weighing scales	60	1·25

1979. Orchids.

346	**115** 10 c. multicoloured	30	10
347	– 35 c. multicoloured	75	75
348	– 50 c. multicoloured	90	1·00
349	– 75 c. multicoloured	1·25	1·40

DESIGNS—HORIZ: 35 c. VERT: 50, 75 c. Different varieties of vanda hybrid.

116 Envelope with new Singapore Postcode

1979. Postal Code Publicity.

350	**116** 10 c. multicoloured	10	10
351	– 50 c. multicoloured	60	80

The 50 c. design is as Type **116**, but the envelope is addressed to the Philatelic Bureau, General Post Office and has the postcode "Singapore 0104".

117 Early Telephone and Overhead Cables

1979. Centenary of Telephone Service.

352	**117** 10 c. brown and blue	15	10
353	– 35 c. orange and violet	30	40
354	– 50 c. blue, turquoise & grn	45	70
355	– 75 c. green and orange	65	1·25

DESIGNS: 35 c. Telephone dial and world map; 50 c. Modern telephone and city scene; 75 c. Latest computerised telephone and circuit diagram.

118 "Lantern Festival" (Eng Chun-Ngan)

1979. International Year of the Child. Children's Drawings. Multicoloured.

356	10 c. Type **118**	10	10
357	35 c. "Singapore Harbour" (Wong Chien Chien)	30	40
358	50 c. "Use Your Hands" (Leong Choy Yeen)	40	70
359	75 c. "Soccer" (Tan Cheong Hin)	60	1·25

119 View of Gardens

1979. 120th Anniv of Botanic Gardens.

361	**119** 10 c. multicoloured	30	10
362	– 50 c. multicoloured	1·00	1·50
363	– $1 multicoloured	1·50	2·50

DESIGNS: 50 c., $1 Different views of Botanic Gardens.

120 Hainan Junk

1980. Ships. Multicoloured.

364	1 c. Type **120**	50	90
365	5 c. Full-rigged clipper	30	55
366	10 c. Fujian junk	30	10
367	15 c. Golekkan (sailing craft)	40	15
368	20 c. Palari (sailing craft)	70	40
369	25 c. East Indiaman	80	50
370	35 c. Galleon	90	50
371	50 c. Caravel	60	70
372	75 c. Jiangsu trading junk	1·25	1·50
373	$1 "Kedah" (coaster)	70	55
374	$2 "Murex" (tanker)	1·25	90
375	$5 "Chusan" (screw steamer)	3·00	3·00
376	$10 "Braganza" (paddle-steamer)	6·00	6·00

Nos. 373/6 are 42 × 25 mm.

121 Straits Settlements 1867 1½ c. Stamp and Map of Singapore, 1843

1980. "London 1980" International Stamp Exn. Mult.

377	10 c. Type **121**	20	10
378	35 c. Straits Settlements 1906 $500 stamp and treaty between Johore and British Colony of Singapore	35	25
379	$1 1948 $2 stamp and map of Malaysia	70	1·10
380	$2 1969 150th Anniv of Singapore $10 commemorative and letter to Col. Addenbrooke from Sir Stamford Raffles	1·25	2·25

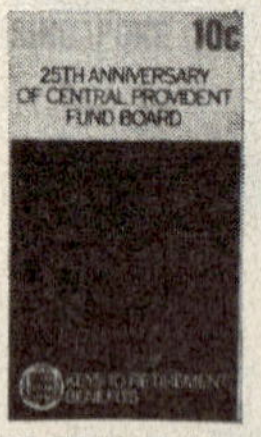
122 C.P.F. Emblem and "Keys to Retirement Benefits"

123 Map of South East Asia showing Cable Network

1980. 25th Anniv of Central Provident Fund Board. Multicoloured.

382	10 c. Type **122**	10	10
383	50 c. "C.P.F. savings for home ownership"	40	40
384	$1 "C.P.F. savings for old-age"	75	1·25

1980. A.S.E.A.N. (Association of South-East Asian Nations) Submarine Cable Network (2nd issue). Completion of Indonesia—Singapore Section.

385	**123** 10 c. multicoloured	10	10
386	35 c. multicoloured	40	30
387	50 c. multicoloured	50	75
388	75 c. multicoloured	65	1·25

124 A.S.E.A.N. Trade Fair Emblem

1980. A.S.E.A.N. (Association of South-East Asian Nations) Trade Fair.

389	**124** 10 c. multicoloured	10	10
390	35 c. multicoloured	30	30
391	75 c. multicoloured	60	1·00

125 Ixora

1980. National Tree Planting Day. Flowers. Multicoloured.

392	10 c. Type **125**	10	10
393	35 c. Allamanda	40	45
394	50 c. Sky vine	50	70
395	75 c. Bougainvillea	60	1·10

126 International Currency Symbols

128 Woodwork

1981. 10th Anniv of Singapore Monetary Authority.

396	**126** 10 c. black, red and yellow	10	10
397	35 c. multicoloured	30	30
398	75 c. multicoloured	55	1·25

1981. No. 65 surch **10 CENTS**.

399	10 c. on 4 c. black and red	30	40

1981. Technical Training. Multicoloured.

400	10 c. Type **128**	10	10
401	35 c. Building construction	25	25
402	50 c. Electronics	40	60
403	75 c. Precision machining	50	1·10

129 Figures representing various Sports

130 "The Right to Environmental Aids"

1981. "Sports for All".

404	**129** 10 c. multicoloured	30	10
405	– 75 c. multicoloured	2·00	2·25
406	– $1 multicoloured	2·50	3·00

DESIGNS: 75 c. and $1 Figures representing different sports.

1981. International Year for Disabled Persons. Multicoloured.

407	10 c. Type **130**	10	10
408	35 c. "The right to social integration"	40	25
409	50 c. "The right to education"	60	50
410	75 c. "The right to work"	80	90

131 Control Tower and Passenger Terminal Building, Changi Airport

132 "Parthenos sylvia"

1981. Opening of Changi Airport.

411	**131** 10 c. multicoloured	10	10
412	35 c. multicoloured	30	20
413	50 c. multicoloured	40	60
414	75 c. multicoloured	50	1·10
415	$1 multicoloured	55	1·40

The background emblem differs for each value.

1982. Butterflies. Multicoloured.

417	10 c. Type **132**	40	15
418	50 c. "Danaus vulgaris"	1·25	75
419	$1 "Trogonoptera brookiana"	1·75	1·75

133 A.S.E.A.N. Emblem

134 Football and Stylised Player

1982. 15th Anniv of A.S.E.A.N. (Association of South-East Asian Nations).

420	133	10 c. multicoloured	10	10
421		35 c. multicoloured	30	35
422	–	50 c. multicoloured	40	65
423	–	75 c. multicoloured	60	1·00

The 50 and 75 c. values are as Type **133** but are inscribed "15th ASEAN Ministerial Meeting".

1982. World Cup Football Championship, Spain.

424	134	10 c. black, light blue & bl	20	10
425	–	75 c. multicoloured	75	1·50
426	–	$1 multicoloured	95	1·50

DESIGNS: 75 c. Football and World Cup, Asian Four emblem; $1 Football and globe.

135 Sultan Shoal Lighthouse, 1896

1982. Lighthouses of Singapore. Mult.

427	10 c. Type **135**	50	15
428	75 c. Horsburgh Lighthouse, 1855	1·40	1·75
429	$1 Raffles Lighthouse, 1855	1·50	2·00

136 Yard Gantry Cranes

1982. 10th Anniv of Container Terminal. Multicoloured.

431	10 c. Type **136**	10	10
432	35 c. Computer	25	30
433	50 c. Freightlifter	35	50
434	75 c. Straddle carrier	65	70

137 Scouts on Parade

138 Productivity Movement Slogans

1982. 75th Anniv of Boy Scout Movement. Multicoloured.

435	10 c. Type **137**	15	10
436	35 c. Scouts hiking	45	25
437	50 c. Scouts building tower	65	35
438	75 c. Scouts canoeing	95	80

1983. Productivity Movement.

439	138	10 c. orange and green	10	10
440	–	35 c. brown and blue	35	40
441	–	50 c. red, yellow and grey	55	80
442	–	75 c. red and yellow	75	1·10

DESIGNS: 35 c. Family and housing ("Benefits of Productivity"); 50 c. Works meeting ("Quality Control Circles"); 75 c. Aspects of Singapore business ("Everybody's Business").

139 Commonwealth Logo and Country Names

140 Soccer

1983. Commonwealth Day.

443	139	10 c. multicoloured	10	10
444		35 c. multicoloured	20	25
445		75 c. multicoloured	45	85
446		$1 multicoloured	65	1·00

1983. 12th South-East Asia Games. Mult.

447	10 c. Type **140**	10	10
448	35 c. Racket games	20	25
449	75 c. Athletics	45	50
450	$1 Swimming	65	70

141 Policeman and Family

142 1977 A.S.E.A.N. Stamps and Statue of King Chulalongkorn

1983. Neighbourhood Watch Scheme. Mult.

451	10 c. Type **141**	15	10
452	35 c. Policeman and children	55	35
453	75 c. Policeman and inhabitants with linked arms	1·00	1·00

1983. Bangkok Int Stamp Exhibition. Mult.

454	10 c. Type **142**	15	10
455	35 c. 1980 A.S.E.A.N. stamps and map of South-east Asia	45	50
456	$1 1982 A.S.E.A.N. stamps and signatures of Heads of State	1·10	1·60

143 Map of South-East Asia showing Cable Network

145 Blue-breasted Banded Rail

144 Teletex Service (½-size illustration)

1983. A.S.E.A.N. (Association of South-East Asian Nations) Submarine Cable Network (3rd issue). Completion of Malaysia–Singapore–Thailand section.

458	143	10 c. multicoloured	15	10
459		35 c. multicoloured	55	75
460		50 c. multicoloured	80	1·25
461		75 c. multicoloured	1·25	1·75

1983. World Communications Year.

463	144	10 c. yellow, green & black	20	15
464	–	35 c. yellow, red and brown	55	65
465	–	75 c. green, blue & dp blue	1·00	1·40
466	–	$1 yellow, brown and black	1·25	2·00

DESIGNS: 35 c. World telephone numbering plan; 75 c. Satellite transmission; $1 Sea communications.

1984. Coastal Birds. Multicoloured.

467	10 c. Type **145**	60	15
468	35 c. Black bittern	1·50	1·40
469	50 c. Brahminy kite	1·75	1·90
470	75 c. Moorhen	2·00	2·75

146 House of Tan Yeok Nee

147 1970 $1 National Day Stamp

1984. National Monuments. Multicoloured.

471	10 c. Type **146**	15	10
472	35 c. Thong Chai building	55	60
473	50 c. Telok Ayer market	75	90
474	$1 Nagore Durgha shrine	1·25	2·00

1984. "25 Years of Nation Building". Multicoloured.

475	10 c. Type **147**	15	10
476	35 c. 1981 $1 "Sports for All" stamp	60	60
477	50 c. 1969 25 c. "100, 000 Homes for the People" stamp	75	90
478	75 c. 1976 10 c. Wayside Trees stamp	90	1·25
479	$1 1981 $1 Opening of Changi Airport stamp	1·00	1·75
480	$2 1981 10 c. Monetary Authority stamp	1·90	3·50

148 Schoolchildren

150 "Ceriagrion cerinorubellum" (damselfly)

149 Coleman Bridge

1984. "Total Defence".

482	148	10 c. brown and red	15	20
483	–	10 c. brown, olive and blue	15	20
484	–	10 c. brown, violet and salmon	15	20
485	–	10 c. brown, light brown and mauve	15	20
486	–	10 c. brown, yellow & olive	15	20

DESIGNS: No. 483, People of Singapore; 484, Industrial workers; 485, Civil Defence first aid worker; 486, Anti-aircraft gun crew.

1985. Bridges of Singapore.

487	10 c. black (Type **149**)	15	10
488	35 c. black (Cavenagh Bridge)	30	30
489	75 c. black (Elgin Bridge)	55	55
490	$1 black (Benjamin Sheares Bridge)	70	70

1985. Insects. Multicoloured.

491	5 c. Type **150**	1·00	30
492	10 c. "Apis javana" (bee)	1·00	30
493	15 c. "Delta arcuata" (wasp)	1·25	50
494	20 c. "Xylocopa caerulea" (bee)	1·00	70
495	25 c. "Donacia javana" (water beetle)	1·00	80
496	35 c. "Heteroneda reticulata" (ladybird)	1·25	30
497	50 c. "Catacanthus nigripes" (bug)	1·50	55
498	75 c. "Chremistica pontianaka" (cicadu)	1·50	1·50
499	$1 "Homoexipha lycoides" (cricket)	1·75	60
500	$2 "Traulia azureipennis" (grasshopper)	1·50	1·25
501	$5 "Trithemis aurora" (dragonfly)	2·75	3·50
502	$10 "Scambophyllum sanguinolentum" (grasshopper)	5·75	7·50

Nos. 499/502 are larger, 35×30 mm.

151 Tennis, Canoeing, Judo and Children Playing

1985. 25th Anniv of People's Assn. Mult.

503	10 c. Type **151**	25	10
504	35 c. Lion dance, martial arts and athletes with flags	30	30
505	50 c. Tae-kwon-do, Indian dance and Dragon dance	40	40
506	75 c. Boxing, table tennis, basketball and dancing	75	75

152 Modern Housing Estate and Squatter Settlement

1985. 25th Anniv of Housing and Development Board. Designs show different aspects of housing at left. Multicoloured.

507	10 c. Type **152**	15	10
508	35 c. Singapore family (home-ownership)	30	30
509	50 c. Group of residents (community development)	40	40
510	75 c. Construction workers (building technology)	55	55

153 Brownies

154 Badges and Emblems of Singapore Youth Organizations

1985. 75th Anniv of Girl Guide Movement. Multicoloured.

512	10 c. Type **153**	15	10
513	35 c. Guides practising first aid	35	30
514	50 c. Senior Branch	45	45
515	75 c. Adult leaders and guides	65	75

1985. International Youth Year. Multicoloured.

516	10 c. Type **154**	10	10
517	75 c. Hand protecting sapling	70	55
518	$1 Stylised figures and dove	90	70

155 Guava

156 Laboratory Technician and Salesmen with Bar Graph

1986. Singapore Fruits. Multicoloured.

519	10 c. Type **155**	30	10
520	35 c. Jambu air	85	45
521	50 c. Rambutan	1·10	70
522	75 c. Ciku	1·40	1·10

1986. 25th Anniv of National Trades Union Congress. Multicoloured.

523	10 c. Type **156**	25	40
524	10 c. Computer operator and welder	25	40
525	10 c. Draughtsmen and surveyors	25	40
526	10 c. Group of workers	25	40

157 Calligraphy

158 Industrial Automation

1986. "Expo '86" World Fair, Vancouver. Multicoloured.

528	50 c. Type **157**	45	75
529	75 c. Garland maker	60	95
530	$1 Batik printer	75	1·25

1986. 25th Anniv of Economic Development Board. Multicoloured.

531	10 c. Type **158**	10	10
532	35 c. Manufacture of aircraft components	25	30
533	50 c. Electronics industry	30	50
534	75 c. Biotechnology industry	50	90

159 Map showing Route of Cable and "Vercors" (cable ship)

1986. SEA-ME-WE Submarine Cable Project.

535	159	10 c. multicoloured	40	10
536		35 c. multicoloured	85	45
537		50 c. multicoloured	1·10	80
538		75 c. multicoloured	1·40	1·40

160 Stylized Citizens

161 Peace Doves and People of Different Races

1986. 21st Anniv of Citizens' Consultative Committees.

539	160	10 c. multicoloured	30	35
540	–	35 c. multicoloured	45	50
541	–	50 c. multicoloured	55	60
542	–	75 c. multicoloured	75	80

DESIGN: 35 c. to 75 c. Citizens.

Nos. 539/42 were printed together, se-tenant, forming a composite design.

1986. International Peace Year. Multicoloured.

543	10 c. Type **161**	15	10
544	35 c. Doves and map of A.S.E.A.N. countries	40	45
545	$1 Doves and globe	95	1·75

162 Orchard Road

1987. Singapore Skyline. Multicoloured.

546	10 c. Type **162**	15	10
547	50 c. Central Business District	50	65
548	75 c. Marina Centre and Raffles City	75	1·25

163 Flags of Members Nations and Logo

164 Soldier with Rocket Launcher and Tank

1987. 20th Anniv of Association of South-east Asian Nations.

549 **163**	10 c. multicoloured	10	10
550	35 c. multicoloured	30	30
551	50 c. multicoloured	45	45
552	75 c. multicoloured	55	55

1987. 20th Anniv of National Service. Multicoloured.

553	10 c. Type **164**	55	70
554	10 c. Radar operator and patrol boat	55	70
555	10 c. Fighter pilot and General Dynamics Fighting Falcon and Douglas A-4 Skyhawk aircraft	55	70
556	10 c. Servicemen pledging allegiance	55	70

165 Singapore River and Dragon Boats

1987. River Conservation. Multicoloured.

558	10 c. Type **165**	30	10
559	50 c. Kallang Basin, canoe and fishing punt	80	90
560	$1 Kranji Reservoir, athletes and cyclist	2·00	2·50

166 Majapahit Gold Bracelet and Museum

1987. Centenary of National Museum. Each showing different drawings of Museum. Multicoloured.

561	10 c. Type **166**	30	10
562	75 c. Ming fluted kendi (water vessel)	1·25	1·50
563	$1 Patani hulu pekakak keris (sword)	1·40	1·75

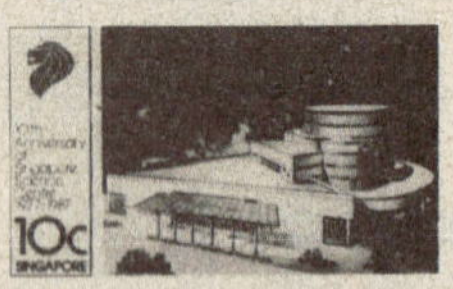

167 Omni-theatre

1987. 10th Anniv of Singapore Science Centre. Multicoloured.

564	10 c. Type **167**	15	10
565	35 c. Omni planetarium	1·50	60
566	75 c. Model of body cell	1·50	1·50
567	$1 Physical sciences exhibits	1·50	2·00

168 Modern Anti-aircraft Gun

1988. Centenary of Singapore Artillery. Mult.

568	10 c. Type **168**	55	15
569	35 c. 25-pounder field gun firing salute	1·40	80
570	50 c. Gunner and 12-pounder gun, c. 1920	1·50	1·75
571	$1 Gunner and Maxim gun, 1889	2·25	3·00

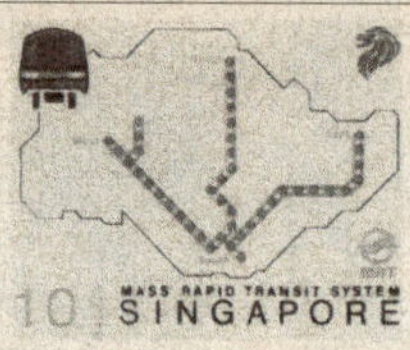

169 Route Map

1988. Singapore Mass Rapid Transit System. Multicoloured.

572	10 c. Type **169**	50	15
573	50 c. Train on elevated section	1·75	1·75
574	$1 Train in tunnel	2·75	3·00

170 Camera, Film and Outside Broadcast Van

171 Water Droplet and Blocks of Flats

1988. 25th Anniv of Television in Singapore. Multicoloured.

575	10 c. Type **170**	40	10
576	35 c. Camera, studio lights and microphone	70	50
577	75 c. Television set and transmitter	1·00	1·25
578	$1 Globe on TV screen and dish aerial	1·25	1·50

1988. 25th Anniv of Public Utilities Board. Multicoloured.

579	10 c. Type **171**	20	10
580	50 c. Electric light bulb and city centre	1·00	1·00
581	$1 Gas flame and factories	1·90	2·25

172 Greeting Neighbours

1988. 10th Anniv of National Courtesy Campaign. Each showing campaign mascot "Singa". Multicoloured.

583	10 c. Type **172**	15	10
584	30 c. Queueing at checkout	40	35
585	$1 Helping the elderly	1·25	1·50

173 Modern 30 Metre Turntable Fire Appliance

1988. Centenary of Fire Service. Multicoloured.

586	10 c. Type **173**	75	25
587	$1 Steam fire engine, c. 1890	2·75	2·00

174 Container Ships and Warehouses

175 "Sago Street"

1989. 25th Anniv of Singapore Port Authority. Multicoloured.

588	10 c. Type **174**	40	10
589	30 c. Shipping and oil storage depot	75	40
590	75 c. Container ships and Singapore skyline	1·40	1·25
591	$1 Container port at night	1·50	1·50

1989. Paintings of Chinatown by Choo Keng Kwang. Multicoloured.

592	10 c. Type **175**	40	15
593	35 c. "Pagoda Street"	1·00	60
594	75 c. "Trengganu Street"	1·75	1·75
595	$1 "Temple Street"	2·00	2·00

176 North-west Singapore City, 1920

1989. Maps of Singapore. Multicoloured.

596	15 c. Type **176** (top left)	90	90
597	15 c. North-east Singapore (top right)	90	90
598	15 c. South-west Singapore (bottom left)	90	90
599	15 c. South-east Singapore (bottom right)	90	90
600	50 c. Singapore Island and Dependencies, 1860s	1·75	1·75
601	$1 British Settlement of Singapore, 1820s	2·50	2·50

Nos. 596/9 were printed together, se-tenant, forming a composite design. Individual stamps can be identifed by the position of the lion emblem which is quoted in brackets.

177 Clown Triggerfish

178 "Hari Raya Puasa" (Loke Yoke Yum)

1989. Fishes. Multicoloured.

602	15 c. Type **177**	85	20
603	30 c. Blue-girdled angelfish	1·50	90
604	75 c. Emperor angelfish	2·75	3·00
605	$1 Regal angelfish	3·00	3·75

1989. Festivals of Singapore Children's Drawings. Multicoloured.

606	15 c. Type **178**	40	10
607	35. "Chinese New Year" (Simon Koh)	70	55
608	75 c. "Thaipusam" (Henry Setiono)	1·40	1·00
609	$1 "Christmas" (Wendy Ang Lin Min)	1·75	1·50

179 North Entrance of Stadium

1989. Opening of Singapore Indoor Stadium. Multicoloured.

611	30 c. Type **179**	85	30
612	75 c. Arena	1·75	1·50
613	$1 East entrance	2·00	1·75

180 "Singapore River, 1839" (Louis le Breton)

1990. Lithographs of 19th-century Singapore. Multicoloured.

615	15 c. Type **180**	40	15
616	30 c. "Chinatown, 1837" (Barthelemy Lauvergne)	85	55
617	75 c. "Singapore Harbour, 1837" (Barthelemy Lauvergne)	1·50	1·50
618	$1 "View from the French Resident's House, 1824" (Deroy)	1·75	1·75

181 1969 150th Anniv of Singapore Stamp Issue

1990. 150th Anniv of the Penny Black. Mult.

619	50 c. Type **181**	1·00	60
620	75 c. Indian stamps, including bisect, used from Singapore in 1859	1·25	1·25
621	$1 Indian stamps used from Singapore in 1854	1·90	1·75
622	$2 Penny Black and Two Pence Blue	3·00	4·00

182 Zoological Gardens

183 Chinese Opera Singer and Siong Lim Temple

1990. Tourism. Multicoloured. (a) As T **182**.

624	5 c. Type **182**	30	40
625	15 c. Sentosa Island	30	10
626	20 c. Singapore River	30	20
627	25 c. Dragon Boat Festival	55	25
628	30 c. Raffles Hotel	70	30
629	35 c. Coffee shop bird singing contest	1·25	35
630	40 c. Jurong Bird Park	1·50	40
631	50 c. Chinese New Year boat float	1·25	45
632	75 c. Peranakan Place	1·75	70

(b) As T **183**.

633	$1 Type **183**	2·50	90
634	$2 Malay dancer and Sultan Mosque	3·25	1·75
635	$5 Indian dancer and Sri Mariamman Temple	6·00	5·50
636	$10 Ballet dancer and Victoria Memorial Hall	10·00	10·00

184 Armed Forces Personnel

1990. 25th Anniv of Indpendence. Mult.

637	15 c. Type **184**	40	15
638	35 c. Inhabitants of Singapore	90	75
639	75 c. Workers and technological achievements	1·60	1·75
640	$1 Cultural activities	1·75	2·50

185 Stag's Horn Fern

1990. Ferns. Multicoloured.

641	15 c. Type **185**	25	10
642	35 c. Maiden hair fern	60	55
643	75 c. Bird's nest fern	1·25	1·25
644	$1 Rabbit's foot fern	1·60	1·75

186 Carved Dragon Pillar, Hong San See Temple

1991. National Monuments. Multicoloured.

645	20 c. Type **186**	30	50
646	20 c. Hong San See Temple (40 × 25 mm)	30	50
647	50 c. Interior of dome, Abdul Gaffoor Mosque	55	75
648	50 c. Abdul Gaffoor Mosque (40 × 25 mm)	55	75
649	75 c. Statue of Vishnu, Sri Perumal Hindu Temple	80	1·00
650	75 c. Sri Perumal Temple (40 × 25 mm)	80	1·00
651	$1 Stained glass window, St. Andrew's Cathedral	90	1·40
652	$1 St. Andrew's Cathedral (40 × 25 mm)	90	1·40

187 "Vanda Miss Joaquim"

188 Changi Airport Terminal II, 1991, and Boeing 747-400

1991. "Singapore '95" International Stamp Exhibition. Orchids (1st issue). Mult.
653 $2 Type **187** . . . . 3·25 3·50
654 $2 "Dendrobium anocha" . . 3·25 3·50
See also Nos. 674/5, 725/6, 755/6 and 795/6.

1991. Singapore Civil Aviation. Mult.
656 20 c. Type **188** 85 20
657 75 c. Changi Airport Terminal I, 1981, and Boeing 747-200 . 2·00 1·50
658 $1 Paya Lebar Airport, 1955–1981, and Concorde . 2·25 1·75
659 $2 Kallang Airport, 1937–1955, and Douglas DC-2 . . . . 3·50 5·00

189 "Arachnopsis Eric Holttum"

190 Long-tailed Tailor Bird

1991. Orchid Dress Motifs. Multicoloured.
660 20 c. Type **189** . . . . 1·00 20
661 30 c. "Cattleya meadii" . . . 1·25 1·10
662 $1 "Calanthe vestita" . . . . 3·00 3·75

1991. Garden Birds. Multicoloured.
663 20 c. Type **190** 45 20
664 35 c. Scarlet-backed flowerpecker 1·50 90
665 75 c. Black-naped oriole . . . 2·25 2·25
666 $1 Common iora . . . . . . 2·50 3·00

191 Productivity Discussion

192 Railway Creeper

1991. 10th Anniv of Productivity Movement. Multicoloured.
667 20 c. Type **191** 30 30
668 $1 Construction workers . . . 95 1·60

1992. "Phila Nippon '91" International Stamp Exhibition, Tokyo. Wild Flowers. Mult.
669 30 c. Type **192** 75 25
670 75 c. Asystasia . . . . 1·25 85
671 $1 Singapore rhododendron . 1·50 1·40
672 $2 Coat buttons . . . . . . 2·50 3·50

1992. "Singapore '95" International Stamp Exn. Orchids (2nd issue). As T **187**. Mult.
674 $2 "Dendrobium Sharifah Fatimah" . . . . 2·75 3·50
675 $2 "Phalaenopsis Shim Beauty" 2·75 3·50

193 "Singapore Waterfront" (Georgette Chen Liying)

1992. Local Artists (1st series). Multicoloured.
677 20 c. Type **193** 40 20
678 75 c. "Kampung Hut" (Lim Cheng Hoe) . . . . 85 1·00
679 $1 "The Bridge" (Poh Siew Wah) 1·10 1·25
680 $2 "Singapore River" (Lee Boon Wang) . . . . 2·25 3·25
See also Nos. 818/21.

194 Football

1992. Olympic Games, Barcelona. Mult.
681 20 c. Type **194** 25 20
682 35 c. Athletics 35 30
683 50 c. Swimming 55 65
684 75 c. Basketball . . . . . . 1·25 1·25
685 $1 Tennis . . . . 1·50 1·50
686 $2 Sailing . . . . 2·00 2·75

195 Chinese Family and Samfu Pattern

1992. Singapore Costumes of 1910. Mult.
688 20 c. Type **195** 40 20
689 35 c. Malay family and sarong pattern 50 45
690 75 c. Indian family and sari pattern . . . . 1·00 1·25
691 $2 Straits Chinese family and belt pattern . . . . 2·00 3·00

196 Infantryman, Air Force Pilot and Navy Gunner

1992. 25th Anniv of National Service. Mult.
692 20 c. Type **196** 60 30
693 35 c. Navy diver, General Dynamics F-16 Fighting Falcon and FH-88 155 mm howitzer 85 75
694 $1 General Dynamics F-16 Fighting Falcon in flight, corvette and AMX-13SM1 tank . . . . 2·50 3·50

197 Crafts from A.S.E.A.N. Countries

1992. 25th Anniv of A.S.E.A.N. (Association of South-East Asian Nations). Multicoloured.
695 20 c. Type **197** 40 20
696 35 c. National dances 90 70
697 $1 National landmarks . . . 2·00 3·25

198 Mosaic Crab

1992. Crabs. Multicoloured.
698 20 c. Type **198** 35 25
699 50 c. Johnson's freshwater crab 1·00 1·25
700 75 c. Singapore freshwater crab 1·50 1·75
701 $1 Swamp forest crab . . . . 1·75 2·50

199 Coins

1992. 25th Anniv of Singapore Currency. Mult.
702 20 c. Type **199** . . . . 75 1·00
703 75 c. Currency note from "orchid" series . . . . . 1·50 2·00
704 $1 Currency note from "ship" series . . . . 1·75 2·25
705 $2 Currency note from "bird" series . . . . 2·25 2·50
Nos. 702/5 were printed together, se-tenant, forming a composite design.

INDEX

Countries can be quickly located by referring to the index at the end of this volume.

200 Sun Bear

1993. South-East Asian Mammals. Mult.
706 20 c. Type **200** 30 20
707 30 c. Orang-utan 60 55
708 75 c. Slow loris . . . . 1·10 1·25
709 $2 Greater Malay chevrotain ("Large Mouse Deer") . . . 2·25 3·25

201 "Thank You"

203 "Cranes" (painting) (Chen Wen Hsi)

202 Shophouses

1993. Greetings Stamps. Multicoloured.
710 20 c. Type **201** 55 80
711 20 c. "Congratulations" . . . 55 80
712 20 c. "Best Wishes" 55 80
713 20 c. "Happy Birthday" . . . 55 80
714 20 c. "Get Well Soon" 55 80

1993. Conservation of Tanjong Pagar District. Multicoloured.
715 20 c. Type **202** 35 20
716 30 c. Jinrikisha Station 75 60
717 $2 View of Tanjong Pagar . . 3·25 4·00

1993. Indopex '93" International Stamp Exhibition, Surabaya.
718 **203** $2 multicoloured . . . . . 2·00 3·00

204 Football

205 "Danaus chrysippus"

1993. 17th South-East Asian Games, Singapore. Mult.
719 20 c. Type **204** 30 20
720 35 c. Basketball 70 60
721 50 c. Badminton . . . . 90 1·00
722 75 c. Athletics . . . . 1·00 1·25
723 $1 Water polo . . . . 1·40 1·75
724 $2 Yachting . . . . 2·25 3·50

1993. "Singapore '95" International Stamp Exhibition. Orchids (3rd issue). As T **187** but 25 × 35 mm. Multicoloured.
725 $2 "Phalaenopsis amabilis" . . 3·00 3·50
726 $2 "Vanda sumatrana" . . . . 3·00 3·50

1993. Butterflies. Multicoloured.
728 20 c. Type **205** 30 30
729 50 c. "Cethosia hypsea" . . . 65 60
730 75 c. "Amathusia phidippus" . 90 1·10
731 $1 "Papilio demolion" . . . . 1·25 1·60

206 Papaya

207 Egrets drinking

1993. "Bangkok '93" International Stamp Exhibition. Local Fruits. Multicoloured.
732 20 c. Type **206** 40 20
733 35 c. Pomegranate 60 50
734 75 c. Starfruit . . . . 1·25 1·25
735 $2 Durian . . . . 2·25 3·25

1993. Endangered Species. Swinhoe's Egret ("Chinese Egret"). Multicoloured.
737 20 c. Type **207** 40 60
738 25 c. Egrets eating 45 65
739 30 c. Egrets searching for fish 55 75
740 35 c. Egrets in flight 55 75
Nos. 737/40 were printed together, se-tenant, with the background forming a composite design.

208 Palm Tree

209 Tiger Cowrie

1993. Self-adhesive. Imperf.
741 **208** (20 c.) multicoloured . . 30 30
No. 741 was only valid for use on mail to local addresses and was initially sold at 20 c..

1994. Reef Life (1st series). Multicoloured.
742 5 c. Type **209** 30 30
743 20 c. Sea-fan 30 20
744 25 c. Tunicate 40 25
745 30 c. Clown anemonefish . . 40 30
746 35 c. Ruppell's nudibranch . . 50 40
747 40 c. Sea-urchin 60 50
748 50 c. Soft coral 70 50
749 75 c. Pin cushion star . . . . 1·00 70
750 $1 Knob coral (31 × 27 mm) . 1·40 90
751 $2 Mushroom coral (31 × 27 mm) 2·25 2·25
752 $5 Bubble coral (31 × 27 mm) 5·00 5·50
753 $10 Octopus coral (31 × 27 mm) 9·00 10·00
See also No. 784.

1994. "Singapore '95" International Stamp Exhibition. Orchids (4th issue). As T **187** but each 25 × 35 mm. Multicoloured.
755 $2 "Paphiopedilum victoriaregina" . . . . . . 3·50 3·75
756 $2 "Dendrobium smillieae" . . 3·50 3·75

210 Dancers

1994. Singapore Festival of Arts. Mult.
758 20 c. Type **210** 35 20
759 30 c. Actors and puppet . . . 55 55
760 50 c. Musicians . . . . 75 1·00
761 $1 Artists . . . . 1·40 2·25

211 Civilian taking Pledge, National Day Parade and Soldier with Anti-tank Missile

1994. 25th Anniv of Operationally-ready National Servicemen. Multicoloured.
762 20 c. Type **211** 60 30
763 30 c. Serviceman on beach with family and on jungle patrol 70 70
764 35 c. Serviceman relaxing at home and with machine gun 85 85
765 75 c. National Service officer at work and commanding patrol 1·75 2·25

212 Black-crowned Night Heron

214 Balloons

213 Traditional and Modern Education

1994. Herons. Multicoloured.
766 20 c. Type **212** 50 60
767 50 c. Green heron ("Little Heron") 70 85
768 75 c. Purple heron . . . . . 85 1·00
769 $1 Grey heron . . . . 95 1·25
Nos. 766/9 were printed together, se-tenant, forming a composite design.

1994. 175th Anniv of Modern Singapore. Mult.
770 20 c. Type **213** 25 25
771 50 c. Rickshaws and Mass Rapid Transit train 70 75
772 75 c. Sampans and modern container port . . . . . . 1·00 1·40
773 $1 Victorian buildings and modern skyline . . . . . . 1·25 2·00

1994. Self-adhesive Greetings Stamps. Multicoloured.

775	(20 c.) Type **214**	40	55
776	(20 c.) Fireworks	40	55
777	(20 c.) Gift-wrapped parcel	40	55
778	(20 c.) Bouquet of flowers	40	55
779	(20 c.) Birthday cake	40	55

215 Logo and Globe

1994. 50th Anniv of I.C.A.O. Multicoloured.

780	20 c. Type **215**	20	20
781	35 c. Boeing 747 and Changi Airport control tower	60	50
782	75 c. Projected hypersonic aircraft over airport	85	1·00
783	$2 Control tower, satellite and Boeing 747	2·00	3·00

1994. Reef Life (2nd series). Multicoloured design as T **209**, but inscr "FOR LOCAL ADDRESSES ONLY".

784	(20 c.) Blue-spotted stingray	20	25

No. 784 exists with either ordinary or self-adhesive gum.

216 Singapore International Convention and Exhibition Centre, Suntec City

217 "Love, LOVE, Love"

1995. Opening of Singapore International Convention and Exhibition Centre. Multicoloured.

786	(20 c.) Type **216**	20	20
787	75 c. Suntec City skyline	75	85
788	$1 Temasek Boulevard	90	1·25
789	$2 Fountain Terrace	1·75	2·50

No. 786 is inscr "FOR LOCAL ADDRESSES ONLY".

1995. Self-adhesive Greetings Stamps.

790	**217**	(20 c.) multicoloured	30	40
791	–	(20 c.) red and black	30	40
792	–	(20 c.) multicoloured	30	40
793	–	(20 c.) multicoloured	30	40
794	–	(20 c.) multicoloured	30	40

DESIGNS: No. 791, "LOVE" forming spiral around heart; No. 792, "LOVE, LOVE"; No. 793, "Love" in four different languages; No. 794, Geometric symbols.

1995. "Singapore '95" International Stamp Exhibition. Orchids (5th issue). As T **187**. Multicoloured.

795	$2 Vanda "Marlie Dolera"	2·00	2·75
796	$2 "Vanda limbata"	2·00	2·75

218 Ribbons and "My Singapore, My Country, Happy Birthday"

219 Rejoicing Crowd and 1945 B.M.A. $5 Stamp

1995. 30th Anniv of Independence. Multicoloured.

798	(22 c.) Type **218**	20	20
799	50 c. Chinese inscr and 1985 Housing and Development 50 c. stamp (horiz)	65	70
800	75 c. National anthem, Civil Aviation 20 c. and inscr in Malay (horiz)	90	1·00
801	$1 National flag, 1986 Economic Development Board and inscr in Tamil	1·25	1·75

No. 798 is inscribed "For Local Addresses Only".

1995. 50th Anniv of End of Second World War. Multicoloured.

803	(22 c.) Type **219**	30	20
804	60 c. Lord Mountbatten accepting Japanese surrender at Singapore and 1945 B.M.A. 15 c. stamp	1·00	80
805	70 c. Emergency food kitchen (horiz)	80	1·00
806	$2 Police road block during State of Emergency (horiz)	2·75	3·50

No. 803 is inscribed "For Local Addresses Only".

220 Yellow-faced Angelfish

1995. Marine Fishes. Multicoloured.

807	(22 c.) Type **220**	35	25
808	60 c. Harlequin sweetlips	80	80
809	70 c. Lionfish	90	1·00
810	$1 Pennant coralfish ("Longfin bannerfish")	1·25	1·75

No. 807 is inscribed "For Local Addresses Only".

221 Envelope, Stamps and Museum

1995. Opening of Singapore Philatelic Museum. Each showing Museum. Multicoloured.

811	(22 c.) Type **221**	30	25
812	50 c. Stamps and stamp booklet	70	55
813	60 c. Stamps and philatelic equipment	80	80
814	$2 Museum displays	2·25	3·00

No. 811 is inscribed "FOR LOCAL ADDRESSES ONLY".

222 Two, Four and Six Digit Post Codes

1995. Introduction of Six Digit Postal Codes. Multicoloured.

815	(22 c.) Type **222**	30	25
816	$2 Six empty post code boxes	2·25	2·75

No. 815 is inscribed "For local addresses only".

223 "Tropical Fruits" (Georgette Chen Liying)

1995. Local Artists (2nd series). Multicoloured.

818	(22 c.) Type **223**	30	25
819	30 c. "Bali Beach" (Cheong Soo Pieng)	40	40
820	70 c. "Gibbons" (Chen Wen Hsi)	80	90
821	$2 "Shi (Lion)" (Pan Shou) ($22\frac{1}{2} \times 38\frac{1}{2}$ mm)	2·25	3·00

No. 818 is inscribed "FOR LOCAL ADDRESSES ONLY".

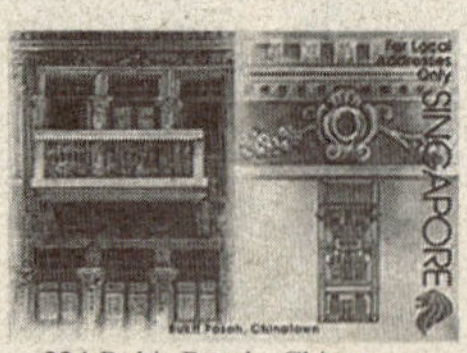

224 Bukit Pasoh, Chinatown

1996. Architectural Conservation. Multicoloured.

822	(22 c.) Type **224**	35	25
823	35 c. Jalan Sultan, Kampong Glam	50	45
824	70 c. Dalhousie Lane, Little India	80	90
825	$1 Supreme Court, Civic District	1·10	1·40

No. 822 is inscribed "FOR LOCAL ADDRESSES ONLY".

225 Pair of Rats

1996. Chinese New Year ("Year of the Rat"). Multicoloured.

826	(22 c.) Type **225**	30	25
827	$2 Rat holding orange	2·25	2·75

No. 826 is inscribed "FOR LOCAL ADDRESSES ONLY".

226 The Straits of Singapore, 1794 (Thomas Jefferys)

1996. Old Maps. Multicoloured.

828	(22 c.) Type **226**	35	25
829	60 c. Singapore (19th-century)	65	75
830	$1 Singapore by James Duncan, 1835	1·00	1·25
831	$2 Singapore by J. B. Tassin, 1839	2·00	2·75

No. 828 is inscribed "FOR LOCAL ADDRESSES ONLY" and was sold for 22 c.

227 17th-century Chinese Calligraphy by Zhang Ruitu and Museum Building

1996. Inauguration of Asian Civilizations Museum. Each including museum building. Multicoloured.

834	(22 c.) Type **227**	35	25
835	60 c. Javanese divination manuscript, 1842	70	70
836	70 c. 19th-century temple hanging, South India	80	80
837	$2 17th to 19th-century calligraphic implements, Iran and Turkey	2·00	3·00

No. 834 is inscribed "FOR LOCAL ADDRESSES ONLY" and was sold for 22 c.

228 "Children in Library" (Ivan Chang)

229 Wind Surfing and Dinghy Sailing

1996. Self-adhesive Greetings Stamps. "Courtesy". Children's Drawings. Multicoloured.

839	(22 c.) Type **228**	20	25
840	35 c. "Children crossing Road" (Cheong Kah Yin)	40	45
841	50 c. "Waiting for Bus" (Jeannie Fong)	55	65
842	60 c. "In the Rain" (Liew Cai Yun)	60	70
843	$1 "On the Train" (Yong Wan Quan)	1·00	1·25

No. 839 is inscribed "For Local Addresses Only".

1996. Olympic Games, Atlanta. Multicoloured.

845	(22 c.) Type **229**	35	25
846	60 c. Tennis and football	90	80
847	70 c. Pole vaulting and hurdling	90	90
848	$2 Diving and swimming	2·25	2·75

No. 845 is inscribed "For Local Addresses Only".

230 "Cinnamomum iners"

1996. Singapore Trees. Multicoloured.

850	(22 c.) Type **230**	30	25
851	60 c. "Hibiscus tiliaceus"	70	80
852	70 c. "Parkia speciosa"	80	90
853	$1 "Terminalia catappa"	1·25	1·50

No. 850 is inscribed "FOR LOCAL ADDRESSES ONLY".

231 Panmen Gate, Suzhou, China

1996. Singapore–China Joint Issue. Multicoloured.

854	(22 c.) Type **231**	30	25
855	60 c. Singapore waterfront	80	1·00

No. 854 is inscribed "FOR LOCAL ADDRESSES ONLY".

232 Conference Logo

1996. Inaugural Ministerial Conference of World Trade Organization.

857	**232**	(22 c.) multicoloured	30	25
858		60 c. multicoloured	70	80
859		$1 multicoloured	1·25	1·50
860		$2 multicoloured	2·25	3·00

No. 857 is inscribed "For local addresses Only".

233 Ox

1997. Chinese New Year ("Year of the Ox").

861	**233**	(22 c.) multicoloured	30	25
862	–	$2 multicoloured	2·25	2·75

DESIGN: $2 Stylized ox.

No. 861 is inscribed "FOR LOCAL ADDRESSES ONLY" and was sold for 22 c.

234 Shuttlecock

1997. "SINGPEX '97" International Stamp Exhibition. Traditional Games. Multicoloured.

864	(22 c.) Type **234**	30	30
865	35 c. Marbles	50	35
866	60 c. Tops	70	75
867	$7 Fivestones	1·10	1·25

No. 864 is inscribed "For Local Addresses Only" and was sold for 22 c.

235 Bullock Cart

236 Taxi

1997. Transportation. Multicoloured. Ordinary or self-adhesive gum (No. 871), ordinary gum (others). (a) As T **235**.

869	5 c. Type **235**	10	10
870	20 c. Bicycle (vert)	15	20
871	(22 c.) Jinrickshaw (vert)	15	20
872	30 c. Electric tram	20	25
873	35 c. Trolley bus	25	30
874	40 c. Trishaw (vert)	30	35
875	50 c. Vintage car (vert)	35	40
876	60 c. Horse-drawn carriage	40	45
877	70 c. Fire engine	50	55

(b) As T **236**.

879	$1 Type **236**	70	75
880	$2 Bus (43 × 24 mm)	1·40	1·50
881	$5 Mass Rapid Transit train	3·50	3·75
882	$10 Light Rapid Transit carriages (43 × 24 mm)	7·00	7·25

No. 871 is inscribed "For Local Addresses Only".

237 Man's Head

238 Family with Car

1997. Self-adhesive Greeting Stamps. "Friends". Multicoloured.

885	(22 c.) Type **237**	25	30
886	(22 c.) Hands holding umbrella	25	30
887	(22 c.) Two penguins	25	30
888	(22 c.) Two butterflies	25	30
889	(22 c.) Cup and saucer	25	30
890	(22 c.) Large flower	25	30
891	(22 c.) Candle	25	30
892	(22 c.) Tree	25	30
893	(22 c.) Jar with stars	25	30
894	(22 c.) Simple telephone	25	30

Nos. 885/94 are inscribed "FOR LOCAL ADDRESSES ONLY".

1997. Renovation of Housing and Development Board Estates. Multicoloured.

896	(22 c.) Type **238**	30	30
897	30 c. Family at playground	40	40
898	70 c. Couple walking through garden	80	80
899	$1 Family on balcony	1·10	1·25

No. 896 is inscribed "FOR LOCAL ADDRESSES ONLY" and was sold for 22 c.

239 Globe and Hand Clasp

240 Flower and Tree ("Clean Environment")

1997. 30th Anniv of A.S.E.A.N. (Association of Southeast Asian Nations). Multicoloured.

900	(22 c.) Type **239**	25	20
901	35 c. Dancers, kite flying and decorated truck	45	45
902	60 c. Dish aerial and map	70	85
903	$1 National landmarks	1·25	1·60

No. 900 is inscribed "FOR LOCAL ADDRESSES ONLY" and was sold for 22 c.

1997. 25th Anniv of the Ministry of the Environment. Multicoloured.

904	(22 c.) Type **240**	20	20
905	60 c. Fish and river ("Clean Waters")	65	65
906	70 c. Bird and sky ("Clean Air")	75	75
907	$1 Dustbin and block of flats ("Clean Homes")	1·00	1·00

No. 904 is inscribed "FOR LOCAL ADDRESSES ONLY" and was sold for 22 c.

241 "Drupa morum"

1997. Singapore–Thailand Joint Issue. Sea Shells. Multicoloured.

908	(22 c.) Type **241**	30	20
909	35 c. "Nerita chamaeleon"	40	40
910	60 c. "Littoraria melanostoma"	65	65
911	$1 "Cryptospira elegans"	1·10	1·25

No. 908 is inscribed "FOR LOCAL ADDRESSES ONLY" and was sold for 22 c.

242 Tiger

243 Pentaceratops

1998. Chinese New Year ("Year of the Tiger").

914	**242**	(22 c.) multicoloured	30	20
915	–	$2 multicoloured	1·75	2·00

DESIGN: $2 Stylized tigers.

No. 914 is inscribed "FOR LOCAL ADDRESSES ONLY" and was sold for 22 c.

1998. Dinosaurs. Multicoloured. Self-adhesive. Imperf.

916	(22 c.) Type **243**	30	30
917	(22 c.) Apatosaurus	30	30
918	(22 c.) Albertosaurus	30	30

Nos. 916/18 are inscribed "For Local Addresses Only" and were sold at 22 c.

244 Lesser Green Leafbird

1998. Songbirds. Multicoloured.

919	(22 c.) Type **244**	30	20
920	60 c. Magpie robin	65	65
921	70 c. Straw-crowned bulbul	75	75
922	$2 Yellow-bellied prinia	1·75	1·90

No. 919 is inscribed "For Local Addresses Only" and was sold for 22 c.

245 "Hello" in Yellow and Orange Bubble

246 Rhino Beetle

1998. Self-adhesive Greetings Stamps. Multicoloured.

924	(22 c.) Type **245**	15	20
925	(22 c.) "hello" in red and yellow bubble	15	20
926	(22 c.) "hello" in yellow and green bubble	15	20
927	(22 c.) "Hello" in violet and blue bubble	15	20
928	(22 c.) "Hello" in black, red and yellow bubble	15	20

Nos. 924/8 are inscribed "FOR LOCAL ADDRESSES ONLY".

1998. 25th Anniv of Singapore Zoological Gardens and Launch of New "Fragile Forest" Display. Multicoloured. Self-adhesive.

929	(22 c.) Type **246**	15	20
930	(22 c.) Surinam horned frog	15	20
931	(22 c.) Green iguana	15	20
932	(22 c.) Atlas moth	15	20
933	(22 c.) Giant scorpion	15	20
934	(22 c.) Hissing cockroach	15	20
935	(22 c.) Two-toed sloth	15	20
936	(22 c.) Cobalt blue tarantula	15	20
937	(22 c.) Archer fish	15	20
938	(22 c.) Greater mousedeer	15	20

Nos. 929/38 are inscribed "FOR LOCAL ADDRESSES ONLY".

247 Students and Workers Demonstrating, 1955–59

1998. "The Singapore Story" Exhibition. Mult.

939	(22 c.) Type **247**	15	20
940	60 c. Self-government, 1959–63	45	50
941	$1 Creation of Malaysian Federation, 1961–65	70	75
942	$2 Celebrating Independence, 1965	1·40	1·50

No. 939 is inscribed "FOR LOCAL ADDRESSES ONLY" and was sold for 22 c.

248 "Phalaenopsis rosenstromii"

249 "Canna" Hybrid

1998. Singapore–Australia Joint Issue. Orchids. Multicoloured.

944	(22 c.) Type **248**	15	20
945	70 c. "Arundina graminifolia"	50	55
946	$1 "Grammatophyllum speciosum"	70	75
947	$2 "Dendrobium phalaenopsis"	1·40	1·50

No. 944 is inscribed "For Local Addresses Only" and was sold for 22 c.

1998. Flowers of Singapore. Multicoloured.

949	(22 c.) Type **249**	15	20
950	(22 c.) "Caesalpinia pulcherrima"	15	20
951	(22 c.) "Wedilia trilobata"	15	20
952	(22 c.) "Dillenia suffruticosa"	15	20
953	35 c. "Zephyranthes rosea"	25	30
954	35 c. "Cassia alata"	25	30
955	60 c. "Heliconia rostrata"	40	45
956	60 c. "Allamanda cathartica"	40	45

Nos. 949/52 are inscribed "FOR LOCAL ADDRESSES ONLY" and were sold for 22 c.

250 Hari Raya Aidilfitri (Muslim)

1998. Festivals. Multicoloured.

958	(22 c.) Type **250**	15	20
959	(22 c.) Christmas	15	20
960	(22 c.) Chinese New Year	15	20
961	(22 c.) Deepavali (Hindu)	15	20
962	30 c. Boy and decorations (Hari Raya Aidilfitri) (20 × 39 mm)	20	25
963	30 c. Girl with holly (Christmas) (20 × 39 mm)	20	25
964	30 c. Boy with lanterns (Chinese New Year) (20 × 39 mm)	20	25
965	30 c. Girl with oil lamps (Deepavali) (20 × 39 mm)	20	25

Nos. 958/61 are inscribed "For Local Addresses Only" and come with either ordinary or self-adhesive gum.

Nos. 958/61 were printed together, se-tenant, forming a composite design.

251 Parliament House

1998. Historical Buildings. Multicoloured.

971	(22 c.) Type **251**	15	20
972	70 c. Chapel of former Convent of the Holy Infant Jesus	50	55
973	$1 Hill Street Building	70	75
974	$2 Sun Yat Sen Nanyang Memorial Hall	1·40	1·50

No. 971 is inscribed "For Local Addresses Only" and was sold for 22 c.

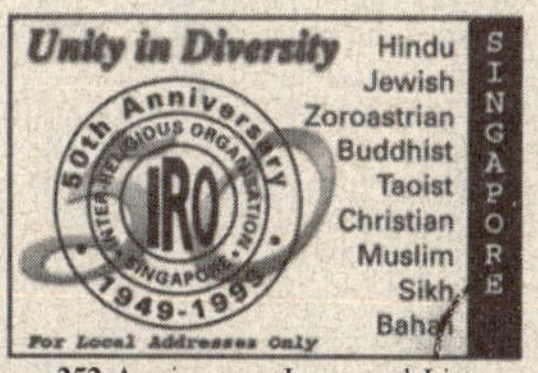

252 Anniversary Logo and List of Religions

1999. 50th Anniv of Inter-Religious Organization.

975	**252**	(22 c.) multicoloured	15	20
976		60 c. multicoloured	40	45
977		$1 multicoloured	70	75

No. 975 is inscribed "For Local Addresses Only" and was sold for 22 c.

253 Rabbit

1999. Chinese New Year ("Year of the Rabbit").

978	**253**	(22 c.) multicoloured	15	20
979	–	$2 multicoloured	1·40	1·50

DESIGN: $2 Stylized rabbits.

No. 978 is inscribed "FOR LOCAL ADDRESSES ONLY" and was sold for 22 c.

254 Clipper, Tank Locomotive and Tongkang Junk

1999. Maritime Heritage. Multicoloured.

980	(22 c.) Type **254**	15	20
981	70 c. Twakow (barge) and Sampan Kotek (vert)	50	55
982	$1 Fujian junk (vert)	70	75
983	$2 Maduran golekkan (sailing vessel)	1·40	1·50

No. 980 is inscribed "For Local Addresses Only" and was sold for 22 c.

POSTAGE DUE STAMPS

The postage due stamps of Malayan Postal Union were in use in Singapore from 1948 until replaced by the following issue.

D 1

D 2

1968.

D1	D **1**	1 c. green	60	1·75
D2		2 c. red	60	2·25
D3		4 c. orange	1·10	5·00
D4		8 c. brown	50	1·00
D5		10 c. mauve	50	90
D6		12 c. violet	1·50	1·75
D7		20 c. blue	2·00	3·25
D8		50 c. green	8·50	5·00

1978.

D16a	D **2**	1 c. green	15	2·25
D17a		4 c. orange	20	3·75
D18a		10 c. blue	50	1·50
D19a		20 c. blue	65	2·00
D20a		50 c. green	90	2·50

D 3

1989.

D21	D **3**	1 c. green		
D22		4 c. brown		
D23		5 c. mauve	20	50
D24		10 c. red	20	40
D25		20 c. blue	30	60
D26		50 c. green	60	1·00
D27		$1 brown	1·50	2·00

SIRMOOR

A state of the Punjab, India. Now uses Indian stamps.

12 pies = 1 anna; 16 annas = 1 rupee

1

2

1876.

1	1	1 pice green	8·00	£200
2		1 pice blue	4·00	£130

1892.

3b	2	1 pice green	50	55
4		1 pice blue	60	60

3 Raja Shamsher Parkash

4

1885.

5a	3	3 p. brown	30	35
6a		3 p. orange	30	20
7c		6 p. green	40	25
8d		1 a. blue	50	1·75
9a		2 a. red	3·50	3·00

1895.

22	4	3 p. orange	1·50	30
23		6 p. green	75	30
24		1 a. blue	2·50	70
25		2 a. red	1·10	1·00
26		3 a. green	14·00	27·00
27		4 a. green	7·00	13·00
28		8 a. blue	10·00	18·00
29		1 r. red	24·00	42·00

5 Raja Shamsher Parkash

1899.

30	5	3 a. green	1·60	18·00
31		4 a. green	2·25	12·00
32		8 a. blue	4·25	12·00
33		1 r. red	8·00	30·00

OFFICIAL STAMPS

1890. Optd **On S. S. S.**

60	3	3 p. orange	50	40
79		6 p. green	40	45
80		1 a. blue	35	50
63a		2 a. red	7·00	7·00

SOLOMON ISLANDS

A group of islands in the west Pacific, east of New Guinea.

1907. 12 pence = 1 shilling;
20 shillings = 1 pound.
1966. 100 cents = $1 Australian.

1

2

1907.

1	1	½d. blue	8·50	14·00
2		1d. red	22·00	25·00
3		2d. blue	26·00	30·00
4		2½d. yellow	32·00	38·00
5		5d. green	50·00	65·00
6		6d. brown	55·00	60·00
7		1s. purple	75·00	75·00

1908.

8	2	½d. green	1·50	80
9		1d. red	1·25	50
10		2d. grey	1·25	1·00
11		2½d. blue	3·75	2·00
11a		4d. red on yellow	3·25	11·00
12		5d. olive	8·50	7·00
13		6d. red	10·00	6·50
14		1s. black on green	8·50	8·00
15		2s. purple on blue	38·00	50·00
16		2s. 6d. red on blue	48·00	70·00
17		5s. green on yellow	75·00	£100

3

5 Spears and Shield

1913. Inscr "POSTAGE POSTAGE".

18	3	½d. green	80	3·50
19		1d. red	80	13·00
42		1½d. red	2·00	30
20		3d. purple on yellow	80	4·00
21		11d. purple and red	3·00	12·00

1914. Inscr "POSTAGE REVENUE".

39	3	½d. green	30	2·75
24		1d. red	1·50	1·00
41		1d. violet	1·00	6·50
26		2d. grey	2·75	9·00
27		2½d. blue	2·00	5·00
28		3d. purple on yellow	19·00	80·00
44		3d. blue	70	3·50
29		4d. black and red on yellow	2·00	2·50
45a		4½d. brown	3·00	18·00
46		5d. purple and green	2·75	24·00
47		6d. purple	3·75	24·00
33		1s. black on green	4·75	7·00
34		2s. purple and blue on blue	7·00	10·00
35		2s. 6d. black and red on blue	8·50	20·00
36		5s. green and red on yellow	27·00	45·00
37		10s. green and red on green	75·00	80·00
38		£1 purple and black on red	£200	£120

1935. Silver Jubilee. As T **13** of Antigua.

53	1½d. blue and red	1·00	70
54	3d. brown and blue	3·00	5·50
55	6d. blue and green	7·50	12·00
56	1s. grey and purple	7·50	9·00

1937. Coronation. As T **2** of Aden.

57	1d. violet	30	50
58	1½d. red	30	60
59	3d. blue	50	50

1939. Portrait of King George VI.

60	5	½d. blue and green	15	80
61	–	1d. brown and violet	30	80
62	–	1½d. green and red	70	1·25
63a	–	2d. brown and black	30	1·50
64	–	2½d. mauve and olive	1·50	1·00
65	–	3d. black and blue	1·00	1·00
66	–	4½d. green and brown	5·00	13·00
67	–	6d. violet and purple	75	1·00
68	–	1s. green and black	1·25	65
69	–	2s. black and orange	6·00	4·50
70	–	2s. 6d. black and violet	26·00	4·50
71	–	5s. green and red	32·00	9·00
72	–	10s. green and mauve	6·00	8·50

DESIGNS—VERT: 1d. Native constable and chief; 4½d., 10s. Native house, Reef Islands; 6d. Coconut plantation. HORIZ: 1½d. Artificial Island., Malaita; 2½d. Roviana canoe; 1s. Breadfruit; 5s. Malaita canoe. LARGER (35½ × 22 mm): 2d. Canoe house; 3d. Roviana canoes; 2s. Tinakula volcano; 2s. 6d. Common scrub hen.

1946. Victory. As T **9** of Aden.

73	1½d. red	15	70
74	3d. blue	15	10

1949. Silver Wedding. As T **10/11** of Aden.

75	2d. grey	50	40
76	10s. mauve	13·00	11·00

1949. 75th Anniv of U.P.U. As T **20/23** of Antiga.

77	2d. brown	1·00	1·00
78	3d. blue	2·25	1·00
79	5d. green	1·00	1·40
80	1s. black	1·00	1·00

1953. Coronation. As T **13** of Aden.

81	2d. black and grey	50	1·00

17 Ysabel Canoe

1956. Portrait of Queen Elizabeth II.

82	17	½d. orange and purple	15	50
83	–	1d. green & brn (as No. 65)	15	15
84	–	1½d. slate and red (No. 62)	15	60
105	–	2d. sepia and green (No. 63)	20	20
86	–	2½d. black and blue	60	50
106	–	3d. green and red (No. 71)	55	15
88	–	5d. black and blue	30	55
89	–	6d. black and green	50	25
90	–	8d. blue and black	25	15
108	–	9d. green and black	20	35
91	–	1s. slate and brown	50	50
109	–	1s. 3d. black and blue	60	70
110	–	2s. black and red (No. 69)	1·00	5·50
93	–	2s. 6d. green & pur (No. 66)	7·50	45
94	–	5s. brown	15·00	3·25
95	–	10s. sepia (No. 61)	19·00	4·25
96	–	£1 black and blue	42·00	35·00

DESIGNS—VERT: 2½d. Prow of Roviana canoe. 10s. Similar to No. 61, but constable in different uniform, without rifle; HORIZ: 5d., 1s. 3d. Map; 6d. "Miena" (schooner); 8d., 9d. Henderson Airfield, Guadalcanal; 1s. Chart showing voyage of H.M.S. "Swallow" in 1767; 5s. Mendana and "Todos los Santos"; £1 Arms of the Protectorate.

32 Great Frigate Bird

1961. New Constitution, 1960.

97	32	2d. black and turquoise	10	30
98		3d. black and red	10	10
99		9d. black and purple	15	30

1963. Freedom from Hunger. As T **28** of Aden.

100	1s. 3d. blue	1·50	35

1963. Cent of Red Cross. As T **33** of Antigua.

101	2d. red and black	50	20
102	9d. red and blue	1·00	1·00

33 Makira Food Bowl

1965. Central design in black; background colours given.

112	33	½d. blue and light blue	10	70
113	–	1d. orange and yellow	70	30
114	–	1½d. blue and green	35	50
115	–	2d. ultramarine and blue	60	60
116	–	2½d. brown and light brown	10	45
117	–	3d. green and light green	10	10
118	–	6d. mauve and orange	35	70
119	–	9d. green and yellow	40	15
120	–	1s. brown and mauve	90	15
121	–	1s. 3d. red	3·50	2·25
122	–	2s. purple and lilac	7·00	3·00
123	–	2s. 6d. brown and light brown	1·00	70
124	–	5s. blue and violet	12·00	5·00
125	–	10s. green and yellow	14·00	4·00
126	–	£1 violet and pink	12·00	5·00

DESIGNS: 1d. "Dendrobium veratrifolium" (orchid); 1½d. Chiragra spider conch; 2d. Blyth's hornbill; 2½d. Ysabel shield; 3d. Rennellese club; 6d. Moorish idol (fish); 9d. Lesser frigate bird; 1s. "Dendrobium macrophyllum" (orchid); 1s. 3d. "Dendrobium spectabilis" (orchid); 2s. Sanford's sea eagle; 2s. 6d. Malaita belt; 5s. "Ornithoptera victoreae" (butterfly); 10s. Ducorp's cockatoo; £1 Western canoe figurehead.

1965. Cent of I.T.U. As T **36** of Antigua.

127	2d. red and turquoise	20	10
128	3d. turquoise and drab	20	10

1965. I.C.Y. As T **37** of Antigua.

129	1d. purple and turquoise	10	10
130	2s. 6d. green and lavender	45	15

1966. Churchill Commem. As T **38** of Antigua.

131	2d. blue	15	10
132	9d. green	25	10
133	1s. 3d. brown	35	10
134	2s. 6d. violet	40	25

1966. Decimal Currency. Nos. 112/26 surch.

135A	1 c. on ½d.	10	10
136A	2 c. on 1d.	10	10
137A	3 c. on 1½d.	10	10
138A	4 c. on 2d.	15	10
139A	5 c. on 6d.	15	10
140B	6 c. on 2½d.	10	10
141B	7 c. on 3d.	10	10
142B	8 c. on 9d.	15	10
143A	10 c. on 1s.	30	10
144B	12 c. on 1s. 3d.	65	10
145A	13 c. on 1s. 3d.	1·50	15
146B	14 c. on 3d.	40	10
147A	20 c. on 2s.	2·50	25
148A	25 c. on 2s. 6d.	60	40
149B	35 c. on 2d.	1·75	25
150A	50 c. on 5s.	5·50	2·75
151A	$1 on 10s.	3·00	3·00
152B	$2 on £1	5·00	3·00

1966. World Cup Football Championship. As T **40** of Antigua.

153	8 c. multicoloured	15	10
154	35 c. multicoloured	30	10

1966. Inauguration of W.H.O. Headquarters. Geneva. As T **41** of Antigua.

155	3 c. black, green and blue	20	10
156	50 c. black, purple and ochre	60	20

1966. 20th Anniv of U.N.E.S.C.O. As T **54/6** of Antigua.

157	3 c. multicoloured	15	10
158	25 c. yellow, violet and olive	30	15
159	$1 black, purple and orange	75	70

49 Henderson Field

1967. 25th Anniv of Guadalcanal Campaign (Pacific War). Multicoloured.

160	8 c. Type **49**	15	10
161	35 c. Red Beach landings	15	10

51 Mendana's "Todos los Santos" off Point Cruz

1968. 400th Anniv of Discovery of the Solomon Is. Multicoloured.

162	3 c. Type **51**	20	10
163	8 c. Arrival of missionaries	20	10
164	35 c. Pacific Campaign, World War II	40	10
165	$1 Proclamation of the Protectorate	60	1·50

55 Vine Fishing

1968.

166	55	1 c. blue, black and brown	10	10
167	–	2 c. green, black and brown	10	10
168	–	3 c. green, myrtle and black	10	10
169	–	4 c. purple, black and brown	15	10
170	–	6 c. multicoloured	30	10
171	–	8 c. multicoloured	25	10
172	–	12 c. ochre, red and black	65	40
173	–	14 c. red, brown and black	2·00	2·25
174	–	15 c. multicoloured	80	70
175	–	20 c. blue, red and black	3·75	2·75
176	–	24 c. red, black and yellow	2·00	2·50
177	–	35 c. multicoloured	2·00	50
178	–	45 c. multicoloured	1·50	50
179	–	$1 blue, green and black	2·50	2·00
180	–	$2 multicoloured	6·00	5·00

DESIGNS: 2 c. Kite fishing; 3 c. Platform fishing; 4 c. Net fishing; 6 c. Gold lip shell diving; 8 c. Night fishing; 12 c. Boat building; 14 c. Cocoa; 15 c. Road building; 20 c. Geological survey; 24 c. Hauling timber; 35 c. Copra; 45 c. Harvesting rice; $1 Honiara Port; $2 Internal air service.

70 Map of Australasia and Diagram

1969. Inaugural Year of South Pacific University.

181	70	3 c. multicoloured	10	10
182		12 c. multicoloured	10	10
183		35 c. multicoloured	15	10

71 Basketball Player

75 South Sea Island with Star of Bethlehem

1969. 3rd South Pacific Games, Port Moresby. Multicoloured.

184	3 c. Type **71**	10	10
185	8 c. Footballer	10	10
186	14 c. Sprinter	10	10
187	45 c. Rugby player	20	15

1969. Christmas.

189	75	8 c. black, violet and green	10	10
190	–	35 c. multicoloured	20	20

DESIGN; 35 c. Southern Cross, "PAX" and frigate bird (stained glass window).

77 "Paid" Stamp, New South Wales 1896–1906 2d. Stamp and 1906-07 Tulagi Postmark

1970. New G.P.O., Honiara.

191	77	7 c. mauve, blue and black	20	15
192	–	14 c. green, blue and black	25	15
193	–	18 c. multicoloured	25	15
194	–	23 c. multicoloured	30	20

DESIGNS: 14 c. 1906–07 2d. stamp and C. M. Woodford; 18 c. 1910–14 5s. stamp and Tulagi postmark, 1913; 23 c. New G.P.O., Honiara.

81 Coat of Arms

1970. New Constitution.

195 **81** 18 c. multicoloured 15 10
196 – 35 c. green, blue and ochre 30 20
DESIGN—HORIZ: 35 c. Map.

83 British Red Cross H.Q., Honiara

1970. Centenary of British Red Cross.

197 **83** 3 c. multicoloured 10 10
198 – 35 c. blue, red and black . 25 20
DESIGN—VERT: 35 c. Wheelchair and map.

86 Reredos (Altar Screen)

1970. Christmas.

199 – 8 c. ochre and violet . . . 10 10
200 **86** 45 c. chestnut, orange and brown 25 20
DESIGN—HORIZ: 8 c. Carved angel.

87 La Perouse and "La Boussole"

1971. Ships and Navigators (1st series). Mult.

201 3 c. Type **87** 45 20
202 4 c. Astrolabe and Polynesian reed map 45 20
203 12 c. Abel Tasman and "Heemskerk" 70 30
204 35 c. Te puki canoe, Santa Cruz 80 50
See also Nos. 215/18, 236/9, 254/7 and 272/5.

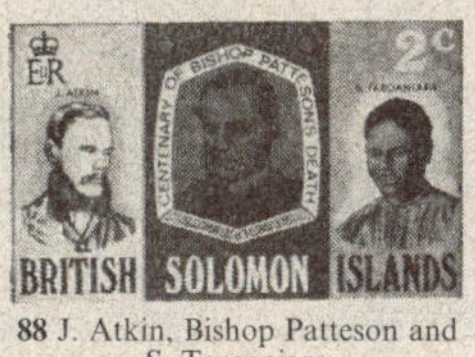

88 J. Atkin, Bishop Patteson and S. Taroaniara

1971. Death Cent of Bishop Patteson. Mult.

205 2 c. Type **88** 10 10
206 4 c. Last landing at Nukapu . 10 10
207 14 c. Memorial Cross and Nukapu (vert) 10 10
208 45 c. Knotted leaf and canoe (vert) 20 10

89 Torch Emblem and Boxers

1971. South Pacific Games, Tahiti. Mult.

209 3 c. Type **89** 10 10
210 8 c. Emblem and footballers . 10 10
211 12 c. Emblem and runner . . 10 10
212 35 c. Emblem and skin-diver . 15 15

90 Melanesian Lectern

1971. Christmas. Multicoloured.

213 9 c. Type **90** 10 10
214 45 c. "United we Stand" (Margarita Bara) 20 20

1972. Ships and Navigators (2nd series). As T **87**. Multicoloured.

215 4 c. Bougainville and "La Boudeuse" 30 10
216 9 c. Horizontal planisphere and ivory backstaff 50 10
217 15 c. Philip Carteret and H.M.S. "Swallow" 60 15
218 45 c. Malaita canoe . . . . . 2·25 90

91 "Cupha woodfordi"

1972. Multicoloured.

219 1 c. Type **91** 15 30
220 2 c. "Ornithoptera priamus" 25 40
221 3 c. "Vindula sapor" 25 40
222 4 c. "Papilio ulysses" . . . 25 40
223 5 c. Big-eyed trevally 25 30
224 8 c. Australian bonito . . . 40 50
225 9 c. Blue demoiselle 50 55
226 12 c. "Costus speciosus" . . 1·25 80
227 15 c. Clown anemonefish ("Orange anenome fish") . 1·25 1·00
228 20 c. "Spathoglottis plicata" 3·00 1·75
229 25 c. "Ephemerantha comata" 3·00 1·50
230 35 c. "Dendrobium cuthbertsonii" . . . . . . 3·00 2·25
231 45 c. "Heliconia salomonica" 2·50 3·00
232 $1 Dotty triggerfish . . . . 3·00 4·50
233 $2 "Ornithoptera alottei" . . 9·00 15·00
233a $5 Great frigate bird . . . . 14·00 15·00
The 2, 3, 4 c. and $2 are butterflies; the 5, 8, 9, 15 c. and $1 are fishes, and the 12, 20, 25, 35, 45 c. are flowers.

1972. Royal Silver Wedding. As T **52** of Ascension, but with Greetings and Message Drum in background.

234 8 c. red 10 10
235 45 c. green 20 20

1973. Ships and Navigators (3rd series). As T **87**. Multicoloured.

236 4 c. D'Entrecasteaux and "La Recherche" 30 15
237 9 c. Ship's hour-glass and chronometer 60 15
238 15 c. Lt. Shortland and H.M.S. "Alexander" 75 20
239 35 c. Tomoko (war canoe) . . 1·50 1·00

93 Pan Pipes

1973. Musical Instruments. Multicoloured.

240 4 c. Type **93** 10 10
241 9 c. Castanets 10 10
242 15 c. Bamboo flute 15 10
243 35 c. Bauro gongs 35 25
244 45 c. Bamboo band 35 30

1973. Royal Wedding. As T **47** of Anguilla.

245 4 c. blue 10 10
246 35 c. blue 15 10

94 "Adoration of the Kings" (Jan Brueghel)

1973. Christmas. "Adoration of the Kings" by the artists listed. Multicoloured.

247 8 c. Type **94** 10 10
248 22 c. Pieter Brueghel (vert) . 30 25
249 45 c. Botticelli (48 × 35 mm) . 60 50

95 Queen Elizabeth II and Map

1974. Royal Visit.

250 **95** 4 c. multicoloured 25 10
251 9 c. multicoloured 30 10
252 15 c. multicoloured 40 20
253 35 c. multicoloured . . . . 60 1·25

1974. Ships and Navigators (4th series). As T **87**. Multicoloured.

254 4 c. Commissioner landing from "S.S. Titus" 20 10
255 9 c. Radar scanner 20 10
256 15 c. Natives being transported to a "Blackbirder" brig . . . 35 15
257 45 c. Lieut. John F. Kennedy's "P.T. 109" . . . . 1·50 90

96 "Postman"

1974. Centenary of U.P.U.

258 **96** 4 c. green, dp green & black 10 10
259 – 9 c. lt brown, brown & blk 10 10
260 – 15 c. mauve, purple & black 15 10
261 – 45 c. blue, dp blue & black 35 80
DESIGNS (Origami figures)—HORIZ: 9 c. Carrier-pigeon; 45 c. Pegasus. VERT: 15 c. St. Gabriel.

97 "New Constitution" Stamp of 1970

1974. New Constitution.

262 **97** 4 c. multicoloured 10 10
263 – 9 c. red, black and brown . 15 10
264 – 15 c. red, black and brown . 20 10
265 **97** 35 c. multicoloured 45 50
DESIGNS: 9 c, 15 c. "New Constitution" stamp of 1961 (inscr "1960").

98 Golden Whistler

1975. Birds. Multicoloured.

267 1 c. Type **98** 45 65
268 2 c. Common kingfisher . . . 50 80
269 3 c. Red-bibbed fruit dove . . 55 85
270 4 c. Little button quail 55 85
271 $2 Duchess lorikeet . . . . . 9·50 10·50
See also Nos. 305/20.

1975. Ships and Navigators (5th series). As T **87**. Multicoloured.

272 4 c. "Walande" (coaster) . . . 45 10
273 9 c. "Melanesian" (coaster) . . 60 10
274 15 c. "Marsina" (container ship) 80 15
275 45 c. "Himalaya" (liner) . . . 1·50 1·50

99 800 Metres Race

1975. 5th South Pacific Games. Multicoloured.

276 4 c. Type **99** 10 10
277 9 c. Long jump 10 10
278 15 c. Javelin-throwing 15 10
279 45 c. Football 45 45

100 Nativity Scene and Candles

1975. Christmas. Multicoloured.

281 15 c. Type **100** 20 10
282 35 c. Shepherds, angels and candles 40 15
283 45 c. The Magi and candles . 50 40

1975. Nos. 267/70, 223/32, 271 and 233a with obliterating bar over "BRITISH". Mult.

285 1 c. Type **98** 60 55
286 2 c. Common kingfisher . . . 90 55
287 3 c. Red-bibbed fruit dove . . 70 55
288 4 c. Little button quail . . . 95 55
289 5 c. Big-eyed trevally 45 55
290 8 c. Australian bonito 50 60
291 9 c. Blue demoiselle 50 60
292 12 c. "Costus speciosus" . . . 1·50 1·00
293 15 c. Clown anemonefish ("Orange anemone fish") . 1·75 1·25
294 20 c. "Spathoglottis plicata" . 2·75 1·50
295 25 c. "Ephemerantha comata" 2·75 1·75
296 35 c. "Dendrobium cuthbertsonii" . . . . . . 3·50 1·75
297 45 c. "Heliconia salomonica" 3·50 3·00
298 $1 Dotty triggerfish . . . . . 3·00 2·00
299 $2 Duchess lorikeet . . . . . 8·00 10·00
300 $5 Great frigate bird . . . . 6·00 13·00

102 Ceremonial Food-bowl

1975. Artefacts (1st series). Multicoloured.

301 4 c. Type **102** 10 10
302 15 c. Chieftains' money . . . 10 10
303 35 c. Nguzu-nguzu (canoe protector spirit) (vert) . . . 25 20
304 45 c. Nguzu-nguzu canoe prow 30 25
See also Nos. 337/40, 353/6 and 376/9.

103 Golden Whistler

1976. Multicoloured.

305 1 c. Type **103** 30 50
306 2 c. Common kingfisher . . . 70 80
307 3 c. Red-bibbed fruit dove . . 50 50
308 4 c. Little button quail . . . 50 50
309 5 c. Willie wagtail 70 80
310 6 c. Golden cowrie 60 50
311 10 c. Glory of the sea cone . . 60 60
312 12 c. Rainbow lory 60 80
313 15 c. Chambered or pearly nautilus 65 40
314 20 c. Venus comb murex . . . 1·25 45
315 25 c. Commercial trochus . . 85 50
316 35 c. Blood-red volute . . . . 1·00 70
317 45 c. Orange spider conch . . 1·00 1·25
318 $1 Trumpet triton . . . . . . 2·75 3·00
319 $2 Duchess lorikeet . . . . . 5·50 4·75
320 $5 Great frigate bird . . . . 5·50 6·00

104 Coastwatchers, 1942

1976. Bicent of American Revolution. Mult.

321 6 c. Type **104** 25 10
322 20 c. "Amagiri" (Japanese destroyer) ramming U.S.S. "PT109" and Lt. J. F. Kennedy 75 30
323 35 c. Henderson Airfield . . . 1·25 40
324 45 c. Map of Guadalcanal . . 1·25 70

105 Alexander Graham Bell

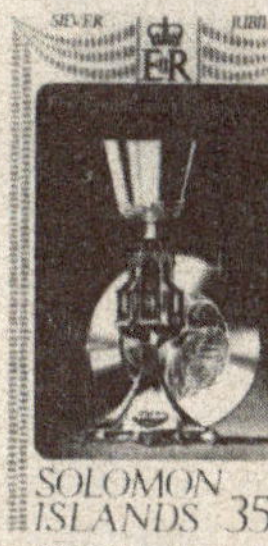

107 The Communion Plate

106 B.A.C. One Eleven 200/400

1976. Centenary of Telephone.
326 **105** 6 c. multicoloured 10 10
327 – 20 c. multicoloured 15 10
328 – 35 c. brown, orange & red 30 15
329 – 45 c. multicoloured . . . 40 35
DESIGNS: 20 c. Radio telephone via satellite; 35 c. Ericson's magneto telephone; 45 c. Stick telephone and first telephone.

1976. 50th Anniv of First Flight to Solomon Is. Multicoloured.
330 6 c. Type **106** 35 10
331 20 c. Britten Norman Islander 65 15
332 35 c. Douglas DC-3 . . . . . 90 20
333 45 c. De Havilland D.H.50A Seaplane A8-1 . . . . . . 95 55

1977. Silver Jubilee. Multicoloured.
334 6 c. Queen's visit, 1974 . . . . 10 10
335 35 c. Type **107** 15 20
336 45 c. The Communion 25 45

108 Carving from New Georgia

110 The Shepherds

109 Spraying Roof and Mosquito

1977. Artefacts (2nd series). Carvings.
337 **108** 6 c. multicoloured 10 10
338 – 20 c. multicoloured 10 10
339 – 35 c. black, grey and red . 20 15
340 – 45 c. multicoloured . . . 25 30
DESIGNS: 20 c. Sea adaro (spirit); 35 c. Shark-headed man; 45 c. Man from Ulawa or Malaita.

1977. Malaria Eradication. Multicoloured.
341 6 c. Type **109** 10 10
342 20 c. Taking blood samples . . 15 10
343 35 c. Microscope and map . . 20 15
344 45 c. Delivering drugs 30 40

1977. Christmas. Multicoloured.
345 6 c. Type **110** 10 10
346 20 c. Mary and Jesus in stable 10 10
347 35 c. The Three Kings 20 15
348 45 c. "The Flight into Egypt" 25 25

111 Feather Money

1977. Introduction of Solomon Islands Coins and Bank-notes. Multicoloured.
349 6 c. Type **111** 10 10
350 6 c. New currency coins . . . 10 10
351 45 c. New currency notes . . . 25 25
352 45 c. Shell money 25 25

112 Figure from Shortland Island

113 Sanford's Sea Eagle

1977. Artefacts (3rd series).
353 **112** 6 c. multicoloured 10 10
354 – 20 c. multicoloured 10 10
355 – 35 c. brown, black & orge 20 15
356 – 45 c. multicoloured . . . 25 30
DESIGNS: 20 c. Ceremonial shield; 35 c. Santa Cruz ritual figure; 45 c. Decorative combs.

1978. 25th Anniv of Coronation. Multicoloured.
357 – 45 c. black, red and silver 15 25
358 – 45 c. multicoloured . . . 15 25
359 **113** 45 c. black, red and silver 15 25
DESIGNS: No. 357, King's Dragon; 358, Queen Elizabeth II.

114 National Flag

115 John

1978. Independence. Multicoloured.
360 6 c. Type **114** 10 10
361 15 c. Governor-General's flag 20 10
362 35 c. The Cenotaph, Honiara 35 30
363 45 c. National coat of arms . 40 50

1978. 450th Death Anniv of Durer. Detail's from "Four Apostles". Multicoloured.
364 6 c. Type **115** 10 10
365 20 c. Peter 15 10
366 35 c. Paul 20 15
367 45 c. Mark 30 30

116 Firelighting

1978. 50th Anniv of Scouting in Solomon Islands. Multicoloured.
368 6 c. Type **116** 15 10
369 20 c. Camping 20 20
370 35 c. Solomon Islands scouts 40 40
371 45 c. Canoeing 50 70

117 H.M.S. "Discovery"

1979. Bicentenary of Captain Cook's Voyages, 1768–79.
372 **117** 8 c. multicoloured 30 10
373 – 18 c. multicoloured 30 15
374 – 35 c. black, green and grey 40 25
375 – 45 c. multicoloured . . . 40 40
DESIGNS: 18 c. Portrait of Captain Cook by Nathaniel Dance; 35 c. Sextant; 45 c. Flaxman/Wedgwood medallion of Captain Cook.

118 Fish Net Float

1979. Artefacts (4th series).
376 **118** 8 c. multicoloured 10 10
377 – 20 c. multicoloured 10 10
378 – 35 c. black, grey and red 15 15
379 – 45 c. black, brown & grn 20 30
DESIGNS—VERT: 20 c. Armband of shell money; 45 c. Forehead ornament. HORIZ: 35 c. Ceremonial food bowl.

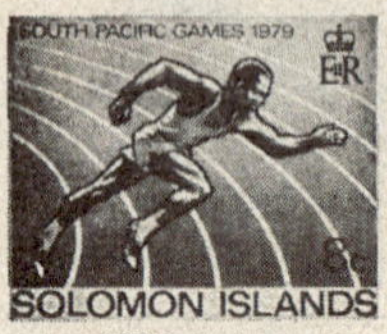

119 Running

120 1908 6d. Stamp

1979. South Pacific Games, Fiji. Multicoloured.
380 8 c. Type **119** 10 10
381 20 c. Hurdling 10 10
382 35 c. Football 15 15
383 45 c. Swimming 25 35

1979. Death Centenary of Sir Rowland Hill.
384 **120** 8 c. red and pink 10 10
385 – 20 c. mauve & pale mauve 15 30
386 – 35 c. multicoloured . . . 25 45
DESIGNS: 20 c. Great Britian 1856 6d.; 35 c. 1978 45 c. Independence commemorative.

121 Sea Snake

122 "Madonna and Child" (Morando)

1979. Reptiles. Multicoloured.
388A 1 c. Type **121** 10 60
389A 3 c. Red-banded tree snake 10 60
390A 4 c. Whip snake 10 60
391A 6 c. Pacific boa 10 60
392A 8 c. Skink 10 40
393A 10 c. Gecko 10 40
394Bw 12 c. Monitor 30 80
395A 15 c. Anglehead 30 50
396A 20 c. Giant toad 30 50
397Bw 25 c. Marsh frog 30 90
398A 30 c. Horned frog . . . . . 1·50 1·00
399A 35 c. Tree frog 30 70
399cB 40 c. Burrowing snake . . . 45 1·75
400A 45 c. Guppy's snake . . . . 30 1·25
400cB 50 c. Tree gecko 50 75
401B $1 Large skink . . . . . . 1·50 90
402A $2 Guppy's frog . . . . . 75 2·75
403B $5 Estuarine crocodile . . . 3·00 3·00
403cB $10 Hawksbill turtle . . . 5·00 5·00

1979. Int Year of the Child. "Madonna and Child" paintings by various artists. Mult.
404 4 c. Type **122** 10 10
405 20 c. Luini 15 15
406 35 c. Bellini 20 15
407 50 c. Raphael 30 70

123 H.M.S. "Curacoa" (frigate), 1839

1980. Ships and Crests (1st series). Mult.
409 8 c. Type **123** 30 10
410 20 c. H.M.S. "Herald" (survey ship), 1854 . . . . 45 30
411 35 c. H.M.S. "Royalist" (screw corvette), 1889 . . . . . . 65 80
412 45 c. H.M.S. "Beagle" (survey schooner), 1878 . . . . . . 70 1·40
See also Nos. 430/3.

124 "Solomon Fisher" (fishery training vessel)

1980. Fishing. Ancillary Craft. Multicoloured.
413 8 c. Type **124** 15 10
414 20 c. "Solomon Hunter" (fishery training vessel) 20 20
415 45 c. "Ufi Na Tasi" (refrigerated fish transport) 35 40
416 80 c. Research vessel . . . . 60 1·50

125 "Comliebank" (cargo-liner) and 1935 Tulagi Registered Letter Postmark

1980. "London 1980" International Stamp Exhibition. Mail-carrying Transport. Multicoloured.
417 45 c. Type **125** 30 45
418 45 c. Douglas C-47 Skytrain (U.S. Army Postal Service, 1943) 30 45
419 45 c. B.A.C. One Eleven airliner and 1979 Honiara postmark 30 45
420 45 c. "Corabank" (container ship) and 1979 Auki postmark 30 45

126 Queen Elizabeth the Queen Mother

1980. 80th Birthday of The Queen Mother.
421 **126** 45 c. multicoloured . . . 30 35

127 Angel with Trumpet

129 Francisco Antonio Maurelle

128 "Parthenos sylvia"

1980. Christmas. Multicoloured.
422 8 c. Type **127** 10 10
423 20 c. Angel with fiddle . . . 10 10
424 45 c. Angel with trumpet (different) 25 25
425 80 c. Angel with lute 40 45

1980. Butterflies (1st series). Multicoloured.
426 8 c. Type **128** 25 10
427 20 c. "Delias schoenbergi" . . 45 20
428 45 c. "Jamides cephion" . . . 70 40
429 80 c. "Ornithoptera victoriae" 1·25 1·40
See also Nos. 456/9 and 610/13.

1981. Ships and Crests (2nd series). As T **123**. Multicoloured.
430 8 c. H.M.S. "Mounts Bay" (frigate), 1959 . . . . 15 10
431 20 c. H.M.S. "Charybdis" (frigate), 1970 . . . . 25 20
432 45 c. H.M.S. "Hydra" (survey ship), 1972 . . . . 50 40
433 $1 Royal Yacht "Britannia", 1974 . . . . 1·40 1·75

1981. Bicentenary of Maurelle's Visit and Production of Bauche's Chart, 1791.
434 **129** 8 c. black, brown and yellow 15 10
435 – 10 c. black, red and yellow 20 10
436 – 45 c. multicoloured . . . 60 65
437 – $1 multicoloured . . . . 1·00 1·10
DESIGNS—VERT: $1 Spanish compass cards, 1745. HORIZ: 10 c. Bellin's map of 1742 showing route of "La Princesa"; 45 c. "La Princesa".

130 Netball

131 Prince Charles as Colonel-in-Chief, Royal Regiment of Wales

1981. Mini South Pacific Games. Multicoloured.
439 8 c. Type **130** 10 10
440 10 c. Tennis 15 15
441 25 c. Running 25 25
442 30 c. Football 25 25
443 45 c. Boxing 40 40

1981. Royal Wedding. Multicoloured.
445 8 c. Wedding bouquet from Solomon Islands 10 10
446 45 c. Type **131** 15 15
447 $1 Prince Charles and Lady Diana Spencer 45 70

132 "Music"

135 Pair of Sanford's Sea Eagles constructing Nest

133 Primitive Church

1981. 25th Anniv of Duke of Edinburgh Award Scheme. Multicoloured.

448	8 c. Type **132**	10	10
449	25 c. "Handicrafts"	10	10
450	45 c. "Canoeing"	15	10
451	$1 Duke of Edinburgh	35	60

1981. Christmas. Churches.

452	**133** 8 c. black, buff and blue	10	10
453	– 10 c. multicoloured	10	10
454	– 25 c. black, buff and green	15	10
455	– $2 multicoloured	70	1·25

DESIGNS: 10 c. St. Barnabas Anglican Cathedral, Honiara; 25 c. Early church; $2 Holy Cross Cathedral, Honiara.

1982. Butterflies (2nd series). As T **128**. Mult.

456	10 c. "Doleschallia bisaltide"	15	10
457	25 c. "Papilio bridgei"	35	25
458	35 c. "Taenaris phorcas"	40	30
459	$1 "Graphium sarpedon"	1·50	1·50

1982. Cyclone Relief Fund. No. 447 surch **50 CENTS SURCHARGE CYCLONE RELIEF FUND 1982**.

460	$1 + 50 c. Prince Charles and Lady Diana Spencer	1·00	2·50

1982. Sanford's Sea Eagle. Multicoloured.

461	12 c. Type **135**	35	50
462	12 c. Egg and chick	35	50
463	12 c. Hen feeding chicks	35	50
464	12 c. Fledgelings	35	50
465	12 c. Young bird in flight	35	50
466	12 c. Pair of birds and village dwellings	35	50

136 Wedding Portrait

137 Flags of Solomon Islands and United Kingdom

1982. 21st Birthday of Princess of Wales. Multicoloured.

467	12 c. Solomon Islands coat of arms	10	10
468	40 c. Lady Diana Spencer at Broadlands, May 1981	15	40
469	50 c. Type **136**	70	50
470	$1 Formal portrait	1·50	1·50

1982. Royal Visit (Nos. 471/2) and Commonwealth Games, Brisbane (Nos. 473/4). Multicoloured.

471	12 c. Type **137**	15	20
472	12 c. Queen and Prince Philip	15	20
473	25 c. Running	30	45
474	25 c. Boxing	30	45

138 Boy Scouts

1982. 75th Anniv of Boy Scout Movement (Nos. 477, 479, 481, 483) and Centenary of Boys' Brigade (others). Multicoloured.

477	12 c. Type **138**	15	15
478	12 c. Boys' Brigade cadets	15	15
479	25 c. Lord Baden-Powell	20	40
480	25 c. Sir William Smith	20	40
481	35 c. Type **138**	20	50
482	35 c. As No. 478	20	50
483	50 c. As No. 479	30	1·10
484	50 c. As No. 480	30	1·10

139 Leatherback Turtle

1983. Turtles. Multicoloured.

485	18 c. Type **139**	25	25
486	35 c. Loggerhead turtle	45	45
487	45 c. Pacific ridley turtle	60	60
488	50 c. Green turtle	65	65

140 Black Olive, General Cone and Troschell's Murex

1983. Commonwealth Day. Shells. Mult.

489	12 c. Type **140**	15	15
490	35 c. Romu, Kurila, Kakadu and money belt	35	40
491	45 c. Shells from "Bride-price" necklaces	50	60
492	50 c. Commercial trochus polished and in its natural state	55	65

141 Montgolfier Balloon

1983. Bicentenary of Manned Flight. Mult.

493	30 c. Type **141**	40	40
494	35 c. R.A.A.F. Lockheed Hercules	45	45
495	40 c. Wright Brothers' Type A	55	55
496	45 c. Space shuttle "Columbia"	60	60
497	50 c. Beech C55 Baron	65	65

142 Weto Dancers

1983. Christmas. Multicoloured.

498	12 c. Type **142**	10	10
499	15 c. Custom wrestling	10	20
500	18 c. Girl dancers	15	20
501	20 c. Devil dancers	15	20
502	25 c. Bamboo band	20	35
503	35 c. Gilbertese dancers	25	45
504	40 c. Pan pipers	25	55
505	45 c. Girl dancers	30	65
506	50 c. Cross surrounded by flowers	30	70

143 Earth Satellite Station

1983. World Communications Year. Mult.

508	12 c. Type **143**	20	15
509	18 c. Ham radio operator	25	20
510	25 c. 1908 2½d. Canoe stamp	35	30
511	$1 1908 6d. Canoe stamp	75	2·75

144 "Calvatia gardneri"

146 "Olivebank" (barque), 1882

145 Cross surrounded by Flowers

1984. Fungi. Multicoloured.

513	6 c. Type **144**	10	10
514	18 c. "Marasmiellus inoderma"	20	25
515	35 c. "Pycnoporus sanguineus"	35	45
516	$2 "Filoboletus manipularis"	2·25	3·00

1984. Visit of Pope John Paul II.

517	**145** 12 c. multicoloured	20	15
518	50 c. multicoloured	65	1·10

1984. 250th Anniv of "Lloyds List" (newspaper). Multicoloured.

519	12 c. Type **146**	70	15
520	15 c. "Tinhow" (freighter), 1906	75	40
521	18 c. "Oriana" (liner) at Point Cruz, Honiara	85	60
522	$1 "Silwyn Range" (container ship), Point Cruz, Honiara	1·40	3·25

147 Village Drums

1984. 20th Anniv of Asia-Pacific Broadcasting Union. Multicoloured.

524	12 c. Type **147**	15	15
525	45 c. Radio City, Guadalcanal	45	60
526	60 c. S.I.B.C. studios, Honiara	80	80
527	$1 S.I.B.C. Broadcasting House	80	1·40

148 Solomon Islands Flag and Torch-bearer

149 Little Pied Cormorant

1984. Olympic Games, Los Angeles. Multicoloured.

528	12 c. Type **148**	15	10
529	25 c. Lawson Tama Stadium, Honiara (horiz)	30	65
530	50 c. Honiara Community Centre (horiz)	40	50
531	95 c. Alick Wickham inventing crawl stroke, Bronte Baths, New South Wales, 1898 (horiz)	5·50	7·50
532	$1 Olympic Stadium, Los Angeles (horiz)	50	1·10

1984. "Ausipex" International Stamp Exhibition, Melbourne. Birds. Multicoloured.

533	12 c. Type **149**	40	40
534	18 c. Spotbill duck	55	40
535	35 c. Rufous night heron	80	50
536	$1 Eastern broad-billed roller	1·60	3·00

150 The Queen Mother with Princess Margaret at Badminton Horse Trials

1985. Life and Times of Queen Elizabeth the Queen Mother. Multicoloured.

538	12 c. With Winston Churchill at Buckingham Palace, VE Day 1945	10	10
539	25 c. Type **150**	20	30
540	35 c. At St. Patrick's Day parade	25	35
541	$1 With Prince Henry at his christening (from photo by Lord Snowdon)	75	95

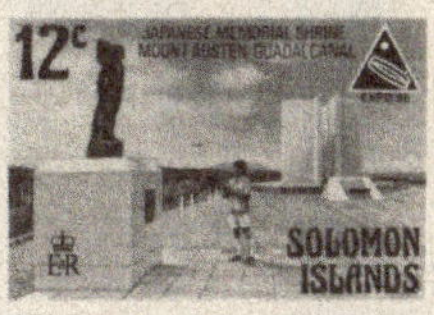

151 Japanese Memorial Shrine, Mount Austen, Guadalcanal

1985. "Expo '85" World Fair, Japan. Multicoloured.

543	12 c. Type **151**	10	10
544	25 c. Digital telephone exchange equipment	25	30
545	45 c. Fishing vessel "Soltai No. 7"	50	55
546	85 c. Coastal village scene	90	1·40

152 Titiana Village

1985. Christmas. "Going Home for the Holiday". Multicoloured.

547	12 c. Type **152**	10	10
548	25 c. Sigana, Santa Isabel	25	30
549	35 c. Artificial Island and Langa Lagoon	30	35

153 Girl Guide Activities

1985. 75th Anniv of Girl Guide Movement (12, 45 c.) and International Youth Year (others). Mult.

550	12 c. Type **153**	60	10
551	15 c. Boys playing and child in wheelchair (Stop Polio)	65	40
552	25 c. Runners and Solomon Island scenes	90	70
553	35 c. Runners and Australian scenes ("Run Round Australia")	1·10	80
554	45 c. Guide colour party and badges	1·25	90

156 Building Red Cross Centre, Gizo

158 "Freedom" (winner, 1980)

1986. Operation Raleigh (volunteer project). Multicoloured.

558	18 c. Type **156**	80	20
559	30 c. Exploring rainforest	1·50	45
560	60 c. Observing Halley's Comet	2·25	1·40
561	$1 "Sir Walter Raleigh" (support ship) and "Zebu" (brigantine)	2·75	2·00

1986. 60th Birthday of Queen Elizabeth II. As T **110** of Ascension. Multicoloured.

562	5 c. Princess Elizabeth and Duke of Edinburgh at Clydebank Town Hall, 1947	10	10
563	18 c. At St. Paul's Cathedral for Queen Mother's 80th birthday service, 1980	15	20
564	22 c. With children, Solomon Islands, 1982	20	25
565	55 c. At Windsor Castle on her 50th birthday, 1976	40	45
566	$2 At Crown Agents Head Office, London, 1983	1·40	1·50

1986. Royal Wedding. As T **112** of Ascension. Multicoloured.

568	55 c. Prince Andrew and Miss Sarah Ferguson	40	55
569	60 c. Prince Andrew at helm of yacht "Bluenose II" off Nova Scotia, 1985	45	70

1986. America's Cup Yachting Championship (1987).

570	**158** 18 c. multicoloured	15	25
571	– 30 c. multicoloured	75	1·25
572	– $1 multicoloured	75	1·25

Nos. 570/2 were issued as a sheet of 50, each horizontal strip of 5 being separated by gutter margins. The sheet contains 20 different designs at 18 c., 10 at 30 c. and 20 at $1. Individual stamps depict yachts, charts, the America's Cup or the emblem of the Royal Perth Yacht Club.

1986. Cyclone Relief Fund. No. 541 surch **+ 50c Cyclone Relief Fund 1986**.

573	$1 + 50 c. Queen Mother with Prince Henry at his christening	75	1·25

160 "Dendrophyllia gracilis"

161 "Cassia fistula"

1987. Corals. Multicoloured.

576	18 c. Type **160**	20	15
577	45 c. "Dendronephthya sp."	60	50
578	60 c. "Clavularia sp."	80	1·40
579	$1.50 "Melithaea squamata"	1·60	3·50

1987. Flowers. Multicoloured.

580	1 c. Type **161**	10	30
581	5 c. "Allamanda cathartica"	20	40
582	10 c. "Catharanthus roseus"	30	40
583	18 c. "Mimosa pudica"	50	10
584	20 c. "Hibiscus rosa-sinensis"	50	15
585	22 c. "Clerodendrum thomsonae"	50	20
586	25 c. "Bauhinia variegata"	50	30
587	28 c. "Gloriosa rothschildiana"	50	20
588	30 c. "Heliconia solomonensis"	55	20
589	40 c. "Episcia" hybrid	60	20
590	45 c. "Bougainvillea" hybrid	70	25
591	50 c. "Alpinia purpurata"	70	25
592	55 c. "Plumeria rubra"	70	35
593	60 c. "Acacia farnesiana"	85	60
594	$1 "Ipomea purpurea"	2·00	80
595	$2 "Dianella ensifolia"	3·00	4·25
596	$5 "Passiflora foetida"	4·50	8·00
597	$10 "Hemigraphis sp"	7·00	12·00

162 Mangrove Kingfisher on Branch

163 "Dendrobium conanthum"

1987. Mangrove Kingfisher. Multicoloured.

598	60 c. Type **162**	2·25	2·75
599	60 c. Kingfisher diving	2·25	2·75
600	60 c. Entering water	2·25	2·75
601	60 c. Kingfisher with prey	2·25	2·75

Nos. 598/601 were printed together, se-tenant, forming a composite design.

1987. Christmas. Orchids (1st series). Mult.

602	18 c. Type **163**	85	10
603	30 c. "Spathoglottis plicata"	1·50	20
604	55 c. "Dendrobium gouldii"	1·75	50
605	$1.50 "Dendrobium goldfinchii"	3·75	3·00

See also Nos. 640/3 and 748/51.

164 Telecommunications Control Room and Satellite

1987. Asia-Pacific Transport and Communications Decade. Multicoloured.

606	18 c. Type **164**	20	15
607	30 c. De Havilland Twin Otter 300 mail plane	45	20
608	60 c. Guadalcanal road improvement project	50	60
609	$2 Beech 80 Queen Air and Henderson Control Tower	2·00	2·50

165 Pupa of "Ornithoptera victoriae"

166 Student and National Agriculture Training Institute

1987. Butterflies (3rd series). "Ornithoptera victoriae" (Queen Victoria's Birdwing). Mult.

610	45 c. Type **165**	3·00	3·00
611	45 c. Larva	3·00	3·00
612	45 c. Female butterfly	3·00	3·00
613	45 c. Male butterfly	3·00	3·00

1988. 10th Anniv of International Fund for Agricultural Development. Multicoloured.

614	50 c. Type **166**	40	55
615	50 c. Students working in fields	40	55
616	$1 Transport by lorry	65	1·00
617	$1 Canoe transport	65	1·00

Nos. 614/15 and 616/17 were printed together, se-tenant, each pair forming a composite design.

167 Building Fishing Boat

1988. "Expo '88" World Fair, Brisbane. Mult.

618	22 c. Type **167**	20	15
619	80 c. War canoe	50	45
620	$1.50 Traditional village	95	85

168 "Todos los Santos" in Estrella Bay, 1568

1988. 10th Anniv of Independence. Mult.

622	22 c. Type **168**	65	15
623	55 c. Raising the Union Jack, 1893	90	45
624	80 c. High Court Building	1·25	1·10
625	$1 Dancers at traditional celebration	1·40	1·40

169 "Papuan Chief" (container ship)

1988. "Sydpex '88" National Stamp Exhibition, Sydney and Bicentenary of Australian Settlement. Multicoloured.

626	35 c. Type **169**	80	25
627	60 c. "Nimos" (container ship)	95	40
628	70 c. "Malaita" (liner)	1·10	65
629	$1.30 "Makambo" (inter-island freighter)	1·40	1·50

170 Archery

171 "Bulbophyllum dennisii"

1988. Olympic Games, Seoul. Multicoloured.

631	22 c. Type **170**	50	20
632	55 c. Weightlifting	70	45
633	70 c. Athletics	80	65
634	80 c. Boxing	95	70

1988. 300th Anniv of Lloyd's of London. As T **123** of Ascension.

636	22 c. black and brown	30	15
637	50 c. multicoloured	1·10	30
638	65 c. multicoloured	1·25	55
639	$2 multicoloured	2·75	1·75

DESIGNS—VERT: 22 c. King George V and Queen Mary laying foundation stone of Leadenhall Street Building, 1925; $2 "Empress of China" (liner), 1911. HORIZ: 50 c. "Forthbank" (container ship); 65 c. Soltel satellite communications station.

1989. Orchids (2nd series). Multicoloured.

640	22 c. Type **171**	65	15
641	35 c. "Calanthe langei"	80	30
642	55 c. "Bulbophyllum blumei"	1·00	55
643	$2 "Grammatophyllum speciosum"	2·00	2·00

172 Red Cross Workers with Handicapped Children

1989. 125th Anniv of Int Red Cross. Mult.

644	35 c. Type **172**	35	35
645	35 c. Handicapped Children Centre minibus	35	35
646	$1.50 Blood donor	1·25	1·25
647	$1.50 Balance test	1·25	1·25

Nos. 644/5 and 646/7 were each printed together, se-tenant, each pair forming a composite design.

173 Varicose Nudibranch

1989. Nudibranchs (Sea Slugs). Multicoloured.

648	22 c. Type **173**	70	20
649	70 c. Bullock's nudibranch	1·75	1·50
650	80 c. "Chromodoris leopardus"	1·75	1·60
651	$1.50 "Phidiana indica"	2·50	3·50

1989. 20th Anniv of First Manned Landing on Moon. As T **126** of Ascension. Multicoloured.

652	22 c. "Apollo 16" descending by parachute	45	20
653	35 c. Launch of "Apollo 16" (30 × 30 mm)	70	45
654	70 c. "Apollo 16" emblem (30 × 30 mm)	1·25	1·60
655	80 c. Ultra-violet colour photograph of Earth	1·40	1·75

174 Five Stones Catch

176 Man wearing Headband, Necklace and Sash

175 Fishermen and Butterfly

1989. "World Stamp Expo '89". International Stamp Exhibition, Washington. Children's Games. Multicoloured.

657	5 c. Type **174**	15	40
658	67 c. Blowing soap bubbles (horiz)	1·25	1·40
659	73 c. Coconut shell game (horiz)	1·25	1·40
660	$1 Seed wind sound	1·75	2·00

1989. Christmas. Multicoloured.

662	18 c. Type **175**	40	10
663	25 c. The Nativity	55	20
664	45 c. Hospital ward at Christmas	1·00	30
665	$1.50 Village tug-of-war	2·50	3·50

1990. Personal Ornaments. Multicoloured.

666	5 c. Type **176**	20	40
667	12 c. Pendant	35	20
668	18 c. Man wearing medallion, nose ring and earrings	35	20
669	$2 Forehead ornament	3·75	4·50

177 Spindle Cowrie or Tokio's Volva

1990. Cowrie Shells. Multicoloured.

670	4 c. Type **177**	25	40
671	20 c. All-red map cowrie	65	30
672	35 c. Sieve cowrie	85	35
673	50 c. Umbilical ovula or little egg cowrie	1·25	1·50
674	$1 Valentine or prince cowrie	2·00	2·50

1990. 90th Birthday of Queen Elizabeth the Queen Mother. As T **134** of Ascension.

675	25 c. multicoloured	75	25
676	$5 black and red	3·75	4·75

DESIGNS—21 × 36 mm: 25 c. Queen Mother, 1987. 29 × 37 mm: $5 King George VI and Queen Elizabeth inspecting bomb damage to Buckingham Palace, 1940.

178 Postman with Mail Van

1990. 150th Anniv of the Penny Black. Mult.

677	35 c. Type **178**	80	35
678	45 c. General Post Office	90	40
679	50 c. 1907 ½d. stamp	1·00	1·00
680	55 c. Child collecting stamps	1·25	1·40
681	60 c. Penny Black and Solomon Islands 1913 1d. stamp	1·25	1·75

179 Purple Swamphen

1990. "Birdpex '90" Stamp Exhibition, Christchurch, New Zealand. Multicoloured.

682	10 c. Type **179**	55	45
683	25 c. Mackinlay's cuckoo dove ("Rufous Brown Pheasant Dove")	85	45
684	30 c. Superb fruit dove	1·00	50
685	45 c. Cardinal honeyeater	1·25	55
686	$2 Finsch's pygmy parrot	2·25	3·50

180 "Cylas formicarius" (weevil)

182 Volleyball

181 Child drinking from Coconut

1991. Crop Pests. Multicoloured.

687	7 c. Type **180**	50	30
688	25 c. "Dacus cucurbitae" (fruit-fly)	75	30
689	40 c. "Papuana uninodis" (beetle)	1·00	45
690	90 c. "Pantorhytes biplagiastus" (weevil)	1·75	2·00
691	$1.50 "Scapanes australis" (beetle)	2·25	3·25

1991. 65th Birthday of Queen Elizabeth II and 70th Birthday of Prince Philip. As T **139** of Ascension. Multicoloured.

692	90 c. Prince Philip in evening dress	1·00	1·25
693	$2 Queen Elizabeth II	2·40	3·00

1991. Health Campaign. Multicoloured.

694	5 c. Type **181**	15	40
695	75 c. Mother feeding child	1·10	1·10
696	80 c. Breast feeding	1·25	1·40
697	90 c. Local produce	1·40	1·60

1991. 9th South Pacific Games. Multicoloured.

698	25 c. Type **182**	80	25
699	40 c. Judo	1·10	45
700	65 c. Squash	1·50	1·75
701	90 c. Bowling	2·00	2·75

183 Preparing Food for Christmas

1991. Christmas. Multicoloured.

703	10 c. Type **183**	30	10
704	25 c. Christmas Day church service	60	15
705	65 c. Christmas Day feast	1·50	85
706	$2 Cricket match	3·75	4·50

184 Yellow-finned Tuna

1991. "Phila Nippon '91" International Stamp Exhibition, Tokyo. Tuna Fishing. Mult.

708	5 c. Type **184**	10	20
709	30 c. Pole and line tuna fishing boat	60	25
710	80 c. Pole and line fishing	1·50	1·75
711	$2 Processing "arabushi" (smoked tuna)	2·75	3·50

1992. 40th Anniv of Queen Elizabeth II's Accession. As T **143** of Ascension. Multicoloured.

713	5 c. Aerial view of Honiara	15	40
714	20 c. Sunset across lagoon	40	20
715	40 c. Honiara harbour	75	40
716	60 c. Three portraits of Queen Elizabeth	80	1·00
717	$5 Queen Elizabeth II	3·25	4·00

185 Mendana's Fleet in Thousand Ships Bay, 1568

1992. "Granada '92" International Stamp Exhibition, Spain. Mendana's Discovery of Solomon Islands. Multicoloured.
718 10 c. Type **185** 35 15
719 65 c. Map of voyage 80 60
720 80 c. Alvaro Mendana de Niera 1·10 1·25
721 $1 Settlement at Graciosa Bay 1·40 1·75
722 $5 Mendana's fleet at sea . . 3·50 4·75

186 Sgt-major Jacob Vouza

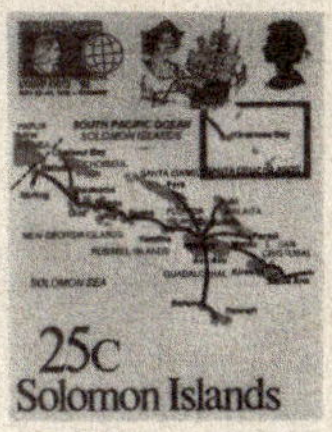

187 Solomon Airlines Domestic Routes

1992. Birth Centenary of Sgt-major Jacob Vouza (war hero). Multicoloured.
723 25 c. Type **186** 50 30
724 70 c. Vouza in U.S. Marine Corps battle dress . . . . . 1·00 1·25
725 90 c. Vouza in U.S. Marine Corps uniform . . . . . . 1·00 1·40
726 $2 Statue of Vouza . . . . . 1·25 2·25

1992. 500th Anniv of Discovery of America by Columbus and "World Columbian Stamp Expo '92" Exhibition, Chicago. Multicoloured.
728 25 c. Type **187** 60 20
729 80 c. Solomon Airlines Boeing 737-400 "Guadalcanal" . . 1·40 1·25
730 $1.50 Solomon Airlines international routes . . . . 2·00 2·25
731 $5 Columbus and "Santa Maria" 4·75 6·00

188 Japanese Troops landing at Esperance

1992. 50th Anniv of Battle of Guadalcanal. Multicoloured.
733 30 c. Type **188** 80 80
734 30 c. American troops in landing craft 80 80
735 30 c. Australian cruiser . . . 80 80
736 30 c. U.S. Navy post office . . 80 80
737 30 c. R.N.Z.A.F. Consolidated PBY-5A Catalina flying boat 80 80
738 80 c. U.S. Marine Corps Grumman F4F Wildcat fighters . . . . 1·00 1·00
739 80 c. Henderson Field . . . . 1·00 1·00
740 80 c. U.S.S. "Quincy" (heavy cruiser) . . . . 1·00 1·00
741 80 c. H.M.A.S. "Canberra" (heavy cruiser) . . . . . . 1·00 1·00
742 80 c. U.S. Marine Corps landing craft . . . . 1·00 1·00
743 80 c. "Ryujo" (Japanese aircraft carrier) . . . . 1·00 1·00
744 80 c. Japanese Mitsubishi A6M Zero-Sen fighters . . . . 1·00 1·00
745 80 c. Japanese Mitsubishi G4M "Betty" bombers . . . . 1·00 1·00
746 80 c. Japanese destroyer . . . 1·00 1·00
747 80 c. "Chockai" (Japanese heavy cruiser) . . . . 1·00 1·00
No. 745 is inscribed "BEACHEAD" in error.

189 "Dendrobium" hybrid

1992. Orchids (3rd series). Multicoloured.
748 15 c. Type **189** 50 20
749 70 c. "Vanda Amy Laycock" . 1·00 90
750 95 c. "Dendrobium mirbelianum" . . . . 1·25 1·25
751 $2.50 "Dendrobium macrophyllum" . . . . . . 2·00 3·00

190 Stalk-eyed Ghost Crab

1993. Crabs. Multicoloured.
752 5 c. Type **190** 10 10
753 10 c. Red-spotted crab 10 10
754 25 c. Flat crab 10 10
755 30 c. Land hermit crab 10 10
756 40 c. Grapsid crab 10 10
757 45 c. Red and white painted crab 10 15
758 55 c. Swift-footed crab 15 20
759 60 c. Spanner crab 15 20
760 70 c. Red hermit crab 20 25
761 80 c. Red-eyed crab 20 25
762 90 c. Rathbun red crab . . . 25 30
763 $1 Coconut crab 25 30
764 $1.10 Red-spotted white crab 30 35
765 $4 Ghost crab . . . . 1·10 1·25
766 $10 Mangrove fiddler crab . 2·75 3·00

191 U.S. War Memorial, Skyline Ridge

1993. 50th Anniv of Second World War. Multicoloured.
767 30 c. Type **191** 35 20
768 80 c. National flags at half mast 1·00 1·10
769 95 c. Major-general Alexander Vandegrift and map . . . 1·10 1·25
770 $4 Aerial dogfight, U.S. carrier and Solomon Islands scouts 4·00 5·00

1993. 14th World Orchid Conference, Glasgow. As Nos. 748 and 751, but different face values, additionally inscr "World Orchid Conference". Multicoloured.
771 20 c. Type **189** 40 25
772 $3 "Dendrobium macrophyllum" . . . . . . 2·00 2·75

1993. "Indopex '93" International Stamp Exhibition, Surabaya. As Nos. 749/50, but different face values, additionally inscr "Indopex '93" Exhibition". Multicoloured.
773 85 c. "Vanda Amy Laycock" 90 1·00
774 $1.15 "Dendrobium mirbelianum" . . . . . . 1·00 1·25

192 U.S.S. "PT 109" being rammed by "Amagiri" (Japanese destroyer)

1993. 50th Anniv of Sinking of U.S.S. "PT 109" (motor torpedo-boat commanded by John F. Kennedy). Multicoloured.
775 30 c. Type **192** 30 20
776 50 c. Kennedy thanking islander 45 45
777 95 c. Message in coconut shell and islanders in canoe . . . 75 1·00
778 $1.10 Pres. Kennedy and medal 1·00 1·40

193 Nicobar Pigeon

1993. Endangered Species. Nicobar Pigeon. Multicoloured.
781 30 c. Type **193** 35 20
782 50 c. Pigeon on ground . . . 50 35
783 65 c. Pair of pigeons perched on branches 60 50
784 70 c. Pigeon on branch looking left 65 60
785 $1.10 Pigeon on branch looking right . . . . 1·00 1·10
786 $3 Pigeons in flight . . . . . 2·25 2·75

194 Pair of Dachshunds

1994. "Hong Kong '94" Int Stamp Exn. Chinese New Year ("Year of the Dog"). Mult.
787 30 c. Type **194** 25 20
788 80 c. German shepherd dog . 65 75
789 95 c. Pair of Dobermann pinschers 70 90
790 $1.10 Australian cattle dog . 80 1·25

195 Striped Dolphin

1994. Dolphins. Multicoloured.
792 75 c. Type **195** 70 65
793 85 c. Risso's dolphin 80 80
794 $1.15 Common dolphin . . . 1·10 1·25
795 $2.50 Spinner dolphin . . . 2·25 2·50
796 $3 Bottlenose dolphin . . . 2·50 3·00

196 "Vindula sapor"

1994. "Philakorea '94" International Stamp Exhibition, Seoul. Butterflies. Multicoloured.
797 70 c. Type **196** 50 55
798 70 c. "Papilio aegeus" 50 55
799 70 c. "Graphium hicetaon" . . 50 55
800 70 c. "Graphium mendana" . . 50 55
801 70 c. Exhibition logo 50 55
802 70 c. "Graphium meeki" . . . 50 55
803 70 c. "Danaus schenkii" . . . 50 55
804 70 c. "Papilio ptolychus" . . . 50 55
805 70 c. "Phaedyma fissizonata vella" 50 55

197 Girl in Brisbane writing letter to Family in Santa Islabel

1994. Int Year of the Family. Mult.
806 $1.10 Type **197** 75 85
807 $1.10 Boeing 737-400 leaving Brisbane 75 85
808 $1.10 Boeing 737-400 at Henderson Airfield and De Havilland D.H.C.6 Twin Otter leaving for Santa Isabel . . 75 85
809 $1.10 De Havilland D.H.C.6 Twin Otter at Fera Airfield, Santa Isabe 75 85
810 $1.10 Family reunited 75 85

198 Cook Island Volcano, 1967

1994. Volcanoes. Multicoloured.
812 30 c. Type **198** 30 15
813 70 c. Kavachi underwater eruption, 1977 . . . . 50 60
814 80 c. Kavachi volcano forming temporary island, 1978 . . . 60 70
815 90 c. Tinakula volcanic island . 80 1·00

199 La Perouse with King Louis XVI and Map

1994. Loss of the La Perouse Expedition, Santa Cruz Islands, 1788. Multicoloured.
817 30 c. Type **199** 40 20
818 80 c. Map of Ile de La Perouse 80 70
819 95 c. "L'Astrolabe" 85 85
820 $1.10 "La Boussole" . . . . . 1·00 1·10
821 $3 "L'Astrolabe" foundering on reef . . . . 2·00 3·00

200 Hermit Crab, Shells and Dancers

1995. Visit South Pacific Year. Multicoloured.
822 30 c. Type **200** 20 20
823 50 c. "Dendrobium rennellii" (orchid) and "Danaus plexippus" (butterfly) . . . 50 40
824 95 c. Scuba diver and fish . . 60 90
825 $1.15 Grapsid crab, canoes, rusty Second World War gun and catamaran . . . . 65 1·00

201 Emblem and Bananas

1995. 50th Anniv of F.A.O. Fruits. Multicoloured.
827 70 c. Type **201** 60 60
828 75 c. Paw paws 60 60
829 95 c. Pomelos 75 85
830 $2 Star fruits . . . . 1·75 2·50

1995. 50th Anniv of End of Second World War. As T **161** of Ascension. Multicoloured.
832 95 c. Vice-Admiral Nagumo and "Akagi" (Japanese aircraft carrier) 80 80
833 $1 Rear-Admiral Fletcher and U.S.S "Yorktown" (aircraft carrier) 80 80
834 $2 Vice-Admiral Ghormley and U.S.S. "Wasp" (aircraft carrier) . . . . 1·50 1·75
835 $3 Vice-Admiral Halsey and U.S.S. "Enterprise" (aircraft carrier) . . . . 2·25 2·50

202 "Calanthe triplicata"

204 Marconi demonstrating Radio Transmitter, Salisbury Plain, 1896

203 Start of Canoe Race

1995. Orchids. Mutlicoloured.
837 45 c. Type **202** 55 30
838 75 c. "Dendrobium mohlianum" 60 70
839 85 c. "Flickingeria comata" . 90 90
840 $1.15 "Dendrobium spectabile" 1·25 1·75

1995. Christmas. Local Festivities. Multicoloured.
842 90 c. Type **203** 60 60
843 $1.05 Pan-pipe players and Christmas Tree 60 70
844 $1.25 Picnic on the beach . . 70 75
845 $1.45 Church service and infant Jesus 80 90

1996. Centenary of Radio. Multicoloured.
846 $1.05 Type **204** 60 60
847 $1.20 Ship's radio room, 1900 70 70
848 $1.35 Wireless transmitter, Croydon Aerodrome, 1920 . 80 1·00
849 $1.45 Marconi in Japan, 1933 90 1·25

205 Palm Lorikeet

1996. Birds. Multicoloured.
850 75 c. Type **205** 60 45
851 $1.05 Duchess lorikeet 75 75
852 $1.20 Yellow-bibbed lory . . 80 80
853 $1.35 Cardinal lory . . . . . 1·00 1·25
854 $1.45 Meek's lorikeet . . . . 1·00 1·25

206 Dug-out Canoe on Beach and Canoe with Outboard Motor

1996. "CAPEX '96" International Stamp Exhibition, Toronto. Mail Transport. Multicoloured.
856 40 c. Type **206** 35 20
857 90 c. Postman with bicycle . . 75 60
858 $1.20 Post van 80 85
859 $1.45 "Tulagi Express" (cruise launch) . . . . 1·40 1·75

207 Tokyo 1964 Poster

1996. Centenary of Modern Olympic Games. Promotional Posters from Previous Games.

861	90 c. Type **207**	50	40
862	$1.20 Los Angeles, 1932	60	70
863	$1.35 Paris, 1924	65	80
864	$2.50 London, 1908	1·10	1·50

208 Suiesi and Map of Makira Bay

1996. 150th Anniv of First Christian Mission. Multicoloured.

865	40 c. Type **208**	30	20
866	65 c. Surimahe and sketches of artefacts by Revd. L. Verguet	45	35
867	$1.35 Bishop Espalle and grave, Isabel	60	90
868	$1.45 John Claude Colin and Makira Mission	65	1·00

210 Children eating Fruit

1996. 50th Anniv of U.N.I.C.E.F. Multicoloured.

870	40 c. Type **210**	25	20
871	$1.05 Children in canoes	50	50
872	$1.35 Doctor and child	60	75
873	$2.50 Teacher and child	1·00	1·75

1997. "Singpex '97" International Stamp Exhibition. No. 797 optd **"SINGPEX '97 FEBRUARY 21-23 SINGAPORE"** and logo within "perforation" frame across the entire sheetlet.

875	70 c. Type **196**	35	40
876	70 c. "Papilio aegeus"	35	40
877	70 c. "Graphium hicetaon"	35	40
878	70 c. "Graphium mendana"	35	40
879	70 c. "Exhibition logo"	35	40
880	70 c. "Graphium meeki"	35	40
881	70 c. "Danaus schenkii"	35	40
882	70 c. "Papilio ptolychus"	35	40
883	70 c. "Phaedyma fissizonata vella"	35	40

Individual stamps show parts of the overprint only.

211 Common Phalanger

1997. Common Phalanger ("Northern Common Cuscus"). Multicoloured.

884	15 c. Type **211**	20	15
885	60 c. Common phalanger eating fruit	25	30
886	$2.50 Common phalanger hanging on branch	75	1·00
887	$3 Two common phalangers	85	1·10

1997. Golden Wedding of Queen Elizabeth and Prince Philip. As T **87** of Kiribati. Multicoloured.

889	$3 Prince Philip playing polo	1·50	1·75
890	$3 Queen Elizabeth	1·50	1·75
891	$3 Queen Elizabeth leading two horses	1·50	1·75
892	$3 Prince Philip	1·50	1·75

Nos. 889/90 and 891/2 respectively were printed together, se-tenant, with the backgrounds forming composite designs.

213 Turtle laying Eggs

1997. 50th Anniv of the South Pacific Commission. Common Green Turtle. Multicoloured.

894	50 c. Type **213**	30	20
895	90 c. Young turtles heading towards sea	50	40
896	$1.50 Four turtles swimming under water	70	90
897	$2 Pair of turtles swimming	85	1·10

214 Oni Mako Player

1997. Christmas. Multicoloured.

898	$1.10 Type **214**	50	35
899	$1.40 Ysabel dancing women	60	50
900	$1.50 Pan pipers from Small Malaita	60	60
901	$1.70 Western bamboo band	75	90

216 Black Marlin

1998. Billfishes. Multicoloured.

903	50 c. Type **216**	25	20
904	$1.20 Shortbill swordfish	50	50
905	$1.40 Swordfish	60	60
906	$2 Indo-Pacific sailfish	85	90

1998. Diana, Princess of Wales Commemoration. As T **91** of Kiribati. Multicoloured.

907	$2 Wearing pearl earrings	50	55

217 Water Melon Cultivation

1998. Technical Co-operation between Solomon Islands and Republic of China (Taiwan). Multicoloured.

909	50 c. Type **217**	20	20
910	$1.50 Harvesting rice	55	55

218 War Dance

1998. Melanesian Trade and Culture Show. Multicoloured.

912	50 c. Type **218**	25	30
913	50 c. Islanders with bows and arrows	25	30
914	50 c. Man on beach	25	30
915	$1.20 War dance (different)	35	40
916	$1.20 Warrior in mask	35	40
917	$1.20 Woman wearing shell necklace and headband	35	40
918	$1.50 Dance with poles	40	45
919	$1.50 Hunter with spear, shield and axe	40	45
920	$1.50 Man with nose and ear ornaments	40	45

POSTAGE DUE STAMPS

D 1

1940.

D1	D 1	1d. green	6·50	7·00
D2		2d. red	7·00	7·00
D3		3d. brown	7·00	11·00
D4		4d. blue	11·00	11·00
D5		5d. olive	12·00	20·00
D6		6d. purple	12·00	15·00
D7		1s. violet	16·00	26·00
D8		1s. 6d. green	26·00	48·00

SOMALILAND PROTECTORATE

A British protectorate in north-east Africa on the Gulf of Aden. Amalgamated with the Somalia Republic on 1 July, 1960, whose stamps it now uses (see volume 2).

1903. 16 annas = 1 rupee.
1951. 100 cents = 1 shilling.

1903. Stamps of India (Queen Victoria) optd **BRITISH SOMALILAND**.

1	**23**	½ a. green	2·75	3·50
2	–	1 a. red	2·75	3·00
3	–	2 a. lilac	2·00	1·25
4	–	2½ a. blue	2·00	1·75
5	–	3 a. orange	3·00	2·25
6	–	4 a. green (No. 96)	3·25	2·75
19	–	6 a. brown (No. 80)	4·50	4·50
8	–	8 a. mauve	3·25	5·00
9	–	12 a. purple on red	2·75	7·00
21	**37**	1 r. green and red	2·25	11·00
11	**38**	2 r. red and orange	23·00	40·00
12		3 r. brown and green	18·00	45·00
13		5 r. blue and violet	28·00	50·00

1903. Stamps of India of 1902 (King Edward VII) optd **BRITISH SOMALILAND**.

25	½ a. green (No. 122)	1·75	55
26	1 a. red (No. 123)	1·00	30
27	2 a. lilac	1·50	2·50
28	3 a. orange	2·00	2·50
29	4 a. olive	1·50	4·00
30	8 a. mauve	1·50	2·25

2

1904.

32	**2**	½ a. green	60	3·50
33		1 a. black and red	5·00	2·75
59		1 a. red	2·50	1·50
34		2 a. purple	1·50	1·75
35		2½ a. blue	1·75	3·25
36		3 a. brown and green	1·00	2·25
37		4 a. green and black	1·50	3·00
38		6 a. green and violet	3·00	14·00
39		8 a. black and blue	3·25	5·50
53		12 a. black and orange	6·50	10·00
41		1 r. green	12·00	38·00
42		2 r. purple	35·00	65·00
43		3 r. green and black	35·00	75·00
44		5 r. black and red	35·00	75·00

The rupee values are larger, 26 × 31 mm.

1912. As 1904, but portrait of King George V.

60	½ a. green	40	7·00
61	1 a. red	1·75	50
75	2 a. purple	3·50	1·00
76	2½ a. blue	1·00	3·50
64	3 a. brown and green	1·75	5·50
78	4 a. green and black	2·50	6·00
66	6 a. green and violet	2·00	4·50
80	8 a. black and blue	2·00	5·00
68	12 a. black and orange	2·00	17·00
69	1 r. green	9·00	13·00
83	2 r. purple	22·00	45·00
84	3 r. green and black	32·00	£100
72	5 r. black and red	50·00	£150

1935. Silver Jubilee. As T **13** of Antigua.

86	1 a. blue and red	2·25	2·00
87	2 a. blue and grey	2·25	1·75
88	3 a. brown and blue	2·25	8·50
89	1 r. grey and purple	6·00	8·50

1937. Coronation. As T **2** of Aden.

90	1 a. red	15	10
91	2 a. grey	55	1·25
92	3 a. blue	70	55

6 Berbera Blackhead Sheep 9

8 Somaliland Protectorate

1938. Portrait faces left.

93	**6**	½ a. green	20	3·50
94		1 a. red	20	70
95		2 a. purple	45	70
96		3 a. blue	6·50	8·00
97	–	4 a. brown	3·50	5·00
98	–	6 a. violet	4·25	9·50
99	–	8 a. grey	85	9·50
100	–	12 a. orange	3·25	10·00
101	**8**	1 r. green	8·50	35·00
102		2 r. purple	12·00	35·00
103		3 r. blue	17·00	24·00
104		5 r. black	17·00	24·00

DESIGN—As T **6**: 4 a. to 12 a. Lesser kudu antelope.

1942. As Nos. 93/104 but with full-face portraits as in T **9**.

105	**9**	$\frac{1}{2}$ a. green	20	20
106		1 a. red	20	10
107		2 a. purple	40	10
108		3 a. blue	1·25	20
109	–	4 a. brown	1·75	20
110	–	6 a. violet	2·25	20
111	–	8 a. grey	1·25	20
112	–	12 a. orange	2·75	20
113	–	1 r. green	1·25	40
114	–	2 r. purple	1·25	3·50
115	–	3 r. blue	1·50	6·50
116	–	5 r. black	5·50	4·00

1946. Victory. As T **9** of Aden.

117	1 a. red	10	10
118	3 a. blue	10	10

1949. Silver Wedding. As T **10/11** of Aden.

119	1 a. red	10	10
120	5 r. black	3·50	3·25

1949. 75th Anniv of U.P.U. As T **20/23** of Antigua.

121	1 a. on 10 c. red	30	15
122	3 a. on 30 c. blue	75	40
123	6 a. on 50 c. purple	40	40
124	12 a. on 1 s. orange	55	40

1951. 1942 issue surch with figures and **Cents** or **Shillings**.

125	5 c. on $\frac{1}{2}$ a. green	10	40
126	10 c. on 2 a. purple	10	20
127	15 c. on 3 a. blue	45	30
128	20 c. on 4 a. brown	60	20
129	30 c. on 6 a. violet	80	20
130	50 c. on 8 a. grey	70	20
131	70 c. on 2 a. orange	1·25	2·75
132	1 s. on 1 r. green	50	20
133	2 s. on 2 r. purple	3·00	8·00
134	2 s. on 3 r. blue	3·25	2·50
135	5 s. on 5 r. black	4·00	4·00

1953. Coronation. As T **13** of Aden.

136	15 c. black and green	30	20

12 Camel and Gurgi

13 Askari

1953.

137	**12**	5 c. black	15	50
138	**13**	10 c. orange	1·75	60
139	**12**	15 c. green	50	60
140		20 c. red	50	40
141	**13**	30 c. brown	2·00	40
142	–	35 c. blue	2·00	1·50
143	–	50 c. brown and red	2·50	55
144	–	1 s. blue	50	30
145	–	1 s. 30 blue and black	7·50	3·25
146	–	2 s. brown and violet	20·00	3·50
147	–	5 s. brown and green	20·00	6·00
148	–	10 s. brown and violet	15·00	14·00

DESIGNS—HORIZ: 35 c., 2 s. Somali stock dove; 50 c., 5 s. Martial eagle; 1 s. Berbera blackhead sheep; 1 s. 30, Sheikh Isaaq's Tomb; 10 s. Taleh Fort.

1957. Opening of Legislative Council. Optd **OPENING OF THE LEGISLATIVE COUNCIL 1957**.

149	**12**	20 c. red	10	15
150	–	1 s. blue (No. 144)	30	15

1960. Legislative Council's Unofficial Majority. Optd **LEGISLATIVE COUNCIL UNOFFICIAL MAJORITY. 1960**.

151	**12**	20 c. red	10	15
152	–	1 s. blue (No. 144)	50	15

OFFICIAL STAMPS

1903. Official stamps of India (Queen Victoria) (optd **O.H.M.S.**) further optd **BRITISH SOMALILAND**.

O1	**23**	$\frac{1}{2}$ a. turquoise	5·50	48·00
O2	–	1 a. red	13·00	8·00
O3	–	2 a. lilac	8·00	48·00
O4	–	8 a. mauve	10·00	£375
O5	**37**	1 r. green and red	10·00	£550

1904. Stamps of 1904 optd **O.H.M.S**.

O10	**2**	$\frac{1}{2}$ a. green	3·25	48·00
O11		1 a. black and red	3·25	7·00
O12		2 a. purple	£140	50·00
O13		8 a. black and blue	60·00	£130
O15	–	1 r. green (No. 41)	£160	£475

SORUTH

A state of India. In 1948 the Saurashtra Union was formed which included Jasdan, Morvi, Nawanagar and Wadhwan as well as Soruth. Now uses Indian stamps.

12 pies = 1 anna; 16 annas = 1 rupee

JUNAGADH

1

2 (1 a.)

1864. On paper of various colours. Imperf.

2	**1**	1 a. black	£650	50·00

1867. (Nos. 11 and 13 are on paper of various colours). Imperf.

11	**2**	1 a. black	70·00	8·00
13		1 a. red	15·00	17·00
14		4 a. black	£110	£180

6

7

1877. Imperf or perf.

40	**7**	3 p. green	35	35
24	**6**	1 a. green	15	15
41		1 a. red	60	95
26	**7**	4 a. red	1·25	60

1913. Surch in words in English and in native characters.

34	**6**	3 p. on 1 a. green	15	20
39	**7**	1 a. on 4 a. red	1·40	3·75

ત્રણ પાઇ
(14)

13 Nawab Mahabat Khan III

1923. Surch as T **14**.

43	**13**	3 p. on 1 a. red	3·00	7·00

1924. Imperf or perf.

44	**13**	3 p. mauve	35	40
46b		1 a. red	2·25	2·75

The 1 a. is smaller.

15 Junagadh City

17 Nawab Mahabat Khan III

1929. Inscr "POSTAGE".

49	**15**	3 p. black and green	60	10
50	–	$\frac{1}{2}$ a. black and blue	4·75	10
51	**17**	1 a. black and red	3·25	85
52	–	2 a. black and orange	8·50	1·75
53	**15**	3 a. black and red	3·00	6·00
54	–	4 a. black and purple	12·00	18·00
55	–	8 a. black and green	10·00	18·00
56	**17**	1 r. black and blue	3·75	18·00

DESIGNS—HORIZ: $\frac{1}{2}$ a., 4 a. Lion; 2 a., 8 a. Kathi horse.

1936. Inscr "POSTAGE AND REVENUE".

57	**17**	1 a. black and red	4·25	90

OFFICIAL STAMPS

1929. Nos. 49/56 optd **SARKARI**.

O1a	**15**	3 p. black and green	70	10
O2	–	$\frac{1}{2}$ a. black and blue	1·60	10
O3a	**17**	1 a. black and red	1·40	15
O4	–	2 a. black and orange	2·50	60
O5	**15**	3 a. black and red	60	30
O6	–	4 a. black and purple	1·75	40
O7	–	8 a. black and green	1·90	1·25
O8	**17**	1 r. black and blue	2·25	13·00

1938. No. 57 optd **SARKARI**.

O13a	**17**	1 a. black and red	8·50	1·40

UNITED STATE OF SAURASHTRA

1949. Surch **POSTAGE & REVENUE ONE ANNA**.

61	**15**	1 a. on 3 p. black and green	45·00	48·00
58	–	1 a. on $\frac{1}{2}$ a. black & bl (No. 50)	8·50	4·25

1949. Surch **Postage & Revenue ONE ANNA**.

59	1 a. on 2 a. grey & yell (No. 52)	9·00	19·00

21

1949.

60	**21**	1s. purple	7·50	8·00

OFFICIAL STAMPS

1948. Official stamps of 1929 surch **ONE ANNA**.

O14	1 a. on 2 a. grey and yellow	£4000	19·00
O15	1 a. on 3 a. black and red	£1700	42·00
O16	1 a. on 4 a. black and purple	£275	38·00
O17	1 a. on 8 a. black and green	£250	29·00
O19	1 a. on 1 r. black and blue	£325	32·00

1949. No. 59 optd **SARKARI**.

O22	1 a. on 2 a. grey and yellow	55·00	18·00

SOUTH AFRICA

The Union of South Africa consisted of the Provinces of the Cape of Good Hope, Natal, the Orange Free State and the Transvaal. It became an independent republic outside the Commonwealth on 31 May 1961. Rejoined the Commonwealth on 1 June 1994.

1910. 12 pence = 1 shilling;
20 shillings = 1 pound.
1961. 100 cents = 1 rand.

1

2

1910.

2	**1**	$2\frac{1}{2}$d. blue	1·75	1·40

1913.

3	**2**	$\frac{1}{2}$d. green	1·00	20
4		1d. red	85	10
5		$1\frac{1}{2}$d. brown	45	10
6		2d. purple	1·50	10
7		$2\frac{1}{2}$d. blue	3·50	1·25
8		3d. black and red	8·00	30
9		3d. blue	3·50	1·75
10a		4d. orange and green	5·50	45
11		6d. black and violet	5·50	60
12		1s. orange	15·00	80
13		1s. 3d. violet	12·00	7·00
14		2s. 6d. purple and green	50·00	1·50
15		5s. purple and blue	£110	7·50
16		10s. blue and olive	£180	5·50
17		£1 green and red	£600	£350

5 De Havilland D.H.9 Biplane

1925. Air.

26	**5**	1d. red	4·50	9·50
27		3d. blue	8·50	9·50
28		6d. mauve	12·00	14·00
29		9d. green	23·00	48·00

NOTE—"Bilingual" in heading indicates that the stamps are inscribed alternately in English and Afrikaans throughout the sheet.

Our prices for such issues are for mint bilingual pairs and used single stamps of either inscription.

6 Springbok

7 "Dromedaris" (Van Riebeeck's ship)

8 Orange Tree

10 "Hope"

11 Union Buildings, Pretoria

12 Groot Schuur

1926. Bilingual pairs ("SUIDAFRIKA" in one word on Afrikaans stamps). No. 33 is imperf.

42w	**6**	$\frac{1}{2}$d. black and green	2·00	10
31	**7**	1d. black and red	2·00	10
34	**11**	2d. grey and purple	12·00	60
44cw		2d. grey and lilac	16·00	20
44d		2d. blue and violet	£250	2·50
35	**12**	3d. black and red	20·00	60
45cw	**12**	3d. blue	8·50	10
33	**10**	4d. blue	1·50	85
46c	–	4d. brown	3·25	10
47	**8**	6d. green and orange	17·00	10
36	–	1s. brown and blue	35·00	1·00
49	–	2s. 6d. green and brown	95·00	3·25
49b	–	2s. 6d. blue and brown	22·00	20
38	–	5s. black and green	£225	35·00
39	–	10s. blue and brown	£150	10·00

DESIGNS—As Type **11**: 4d. (No. 118) A native kraal; 1s. Black and blue wildebeest; 2s. 6d. Ox-wagon inspanned; 5s. Ox-wagon outspanned; 10s. Cape Town and Table Bay.

On No. 33 the English and Afrikaans inscriptions are on separate sheets and our price is for a single stamp of either language.

For these designs with Afrikaans stamps inscr "SUID-AFRIKA", see Nos. 114 etc (issued 1933). For $\frac{1}{2}$d., 1d., 2d., 3d. and 10s. in similar designs see Nos. 105/6, 107a, 116/17 and 64ba respectively.

17 De Havilland D.H.60 Cirrus Moth

18 Church of the Vow

1929. Air.

40	**17**	4d. green	5·50	2·50
41		1s. orange	15·00	12·00

1933. Voortrekker Memorial Fund. Inscr as in T **18**. Bilingual pairs.

50	**18**	$\frac{1}{2}$d. + $\frac{1}{2}$d. green	3·75	50
51	–	1d. + $\frac{1}{2}$d. black and pink	3·25	25
52	–	2d. + 1d. green and purple	4·00	55
53	–	3d. + $1\frac{1}{2}$d. green and blue	7·00	70

DESIGNS: 1d. The "Great Trek" (C. Michell); 2d. Voortrekker man; 3d. Voortrekker woman.

22 Gold Mine

1933. As Nos. 42 etc but with Afrikaans stamps inscr "SUID-AFRIKA" (with hyphen) and new design. Bilingual pairs.

114	**6**	$\frac{1}{2}$d. grey and green	80	10
56	**7**	1d. grey and red	50	10
57	**22**	$1\frac{1}{2}$d. green and gold	2·00	10
58	**11**	2d. blue and violet	65·00	75
58a		2d. grey and purple	40·00	1·25
118	–	4d. brown	1·25	10
119a	**8**	6d. green and red	1·50	10
120	–	1s. brown and blue	10·00	10
121	–	2s. 6d. green and brown	10·00	70
64b	–	5s. black and green	35·00	35

24

1935. Silver Jubilee. Bilingual pairs.

65	**24**	$\frac{1}{2}$d. black and green	2·25	10
66		1d. black and red	2·25	10
67		3d. blue	17·00	2·25
68		6d. green and orange	30·00	3·25

The positions of Afrikaans and English inscriptions are transposed on alternate stamps.

25 King George VI

1937. Coronation. Bilingual pairs.

71	**25**	$\frac{1}{2}$d. grey and green	30	10
72		1d. grey and red	35	10
73		$1\frac{1}{2}$d. orange and green	50	10
74		3d. blue	2·00	10
75		1s. brown and blue	3·50	15

27 Wagon crossing Drakensberg

28 Signing of Dingaan-Retief Treaty

1938. Voortrekker Centenary Memorial Fund. Dated "1838 1938". Bilingual pairs.
76 – ½d. + ½d. blue and green . . 10·00 30
77 **27** 1d. + 1d. blue and red . . . 11·00 40
78 **28** 1½d. + 1½d. brown and green 15·00 80
79 – 3d. + 3d. blue . . . . . . 17·00 1·00
DESIGNS—As T **27**: ½d. Voortrekker ploughing. As T **28**: 3d. Voortrekker Monument.

31 Voortrekker Family

1938. Voortrekker Commem. Bilingual pairs.
80 – 1d. blue and red . . . . . . 4·00 30
81 **31** 1½d. blue and brown . . . . 6·00 30
DESIGN: 1d. Wagon wheel.

22a Groot Schuur **23** Groot Constantia

1939. Bilingual pairs.
117 **22a** 3d. blue . . . . 2·00 10
64ca **23** 10s. blue and brown . . 42·00 30

32 Old Vicarage, Paarl, now a Museum **33** Symbol of the Reformation

34 Huguenot Dwelling, Drakenstein Mountain Valley **34a** Gold Mine

1939. 250th Anniv of Landing of Huguenots in S Africa. Bilingual pairs.
82 **32** ½d. + ½d. brown and green . . 4·75 30
83 **33** 1d. + 1d. green and red . . 11·00 30
84 **34** 1½d. + 1½d. green and purple 26·00 1·00

1941. Bilingual pair.
87 **34a** 1½d. green and buff 65 10

35 Infantry **38** Sailor, Destroyer and Lifebelts

39 Women's Auxiliary Services

1941. War Effort. Bilingual pairs except the 2d. and 1s. which are inscr in both languages on each stamp.
88 **35** ½d. green . . . . 1·50 10
89 – 1d. red . . . . 2·00 10
90 – 1½d. green . . . . 1·50 10
95 **38** 2d. violet 90 30
91 **39** 3d. blue . . . . 20·00 50
92 – 4d. brown . . . . 18·00 15
93 – 6d. orange . . . . 12·00 15
96 – 1s. brown . . . . 3·25 50
94a – 1s. 3d. brown . . . . . . 4·00 20
DESIGNS—As Type **35**: 1d. Nurse and ambulance; 1½d. Airman; 1s. 3d. Signaller. As Type **38**: 4d. Artillery; 6d. Welding. As Type **39**: 1s. Tank corps.

43 Infantry **54** Union Buildings, Pretoria

1942. War Effort. Reduced size. Bilingual except 4d. and 1s. which are inscr in both languages on each stamp.
97 **43** ½d. green 70 10
98a – 1d. red . . . . 1·00 10
99 – 1½d. brown 65 10
100 – 2d. violet 90 10
101 – 3d. blue . . . . 7·00 10
103 – 4d. green . . . . 18·00 10
102 – 6d. orange . . . . 2·00 10
104 – 1s. brown . . . . 15·00 10
DESIGNS—VERT: 1d. Nurse; 1½d. Airman; 2d. Sailor; 6d. Welder. HORIZ: 3d. Women's Auxiliary Services; 6d. Heavy gun; 1s. Tanks.
Our unused prices for Nos. 97, 98, 101 and 103 are for units of three. The other stamps are in units of two.

1943. As 1926, but in single colours and with plain background to central oval. Bilingual pairs.
105 **6** ½d. green 75 20
106 **7** 1d. red . . . . 2·00 15

1945. Type **11** redrawn. Bilingual pairs.
107a **54** 2d. slate and violet . . . 2·50 15
116 2d. blue and purple . . . 90 10

55 "Victory" **58** King George VI

59 King George VI and Queen Elizabeth

1945. Victory. Bilingual pairs.
108 **55** 1d. brown and red 20 10
109 – 2d. blue and violet 20 10
110 – 3d. blue 20 10
DESIGNS: 2d. Man and oxen ploughing ("Peace"); 3d. Man and woman gazing at a star ("Hope").

1947. Royal Visit. Bilingual pairs.
111 **58** 1d. black and red 10 10
112 **59** 2d. violet 15 10
113 – 3d. blue 15 10
DESIGN—As Type **59**: 3d. Queen Elizabeth II when Princess and Princess Margaret.

61 Gold Mine **62** King George VI and Queen Elizabeth

1948. Bilingual.
124 **61** 1½d. green and buff . . . 1·75 10
The price for No. 124 is for a unit of four stamps.

1948. Royal Silver Wedding. Bilingual pair.
125 **62** 3d. blue and silver 50 10

63 "Wanderer" (emigrant ship) entering Durban **64** Hermes

1949. Centenary of Arrival of British Settlers in Natal. Bilingual pair.
127 **63** 1½d. brown 30 10

1949. 75th Anniv of U.P.U. Bilingual pairs.
128 **64** ½d. green 60 10
129 1½d. red 60 10
130 3d. blue . . . . 1·00 10

65 Wagons approaching Bingham's Berg **68** Union Buildings, Pretoria

1949. Inauguration of Voortrekker Monument, Pretoria.
131 **65** 1d. mauve 10 10
132 – 1½d. green 10 10
133 – 3d. blue 10 10
DESIGNS: 1½d. Voortrekker Monument, Pretoria; 3d. Bible, candle and Voortrekkers.

1950. Bilingual pair.
134 **68** 2d. blue and violet 30 10

INSCRIPTIONS. In all later issues except Nos. 167 and 262/5, the stamps are inscribed in both Afrikaans and English. Our prices are for single examples, unused and used.

70 "Maria de la Quellerie" (D. Craey) **76** Queen Elizabeth II

1952. Tercentenary of Landing of Van Riebeeck. Dated "1652–1952".
136 – ½d. purple and sepia 10 10
137 **70** 1d. green 10 10
138 – 2d. violet 50 10
139 – 4½d. blue 10 10
140 – 1s. brown 40 10
DESIGNS—HORIZ: ½d. Seal and monogram; 2d. Arrival of Van Riebeeck's ships; 1s. Landing at the Cape (D. Craey). VERT: 4½d. "Jan van Riebeeck" (D. Craey).

1952. South African Tercentenary Stamp Exn, Cape Town. No. 137 optd **SATISE** and No. 138 optd **SADIPU**.
141 **70** 1d. green . . . . 20 1·75
142 – 2d. violet . . . . 50 1·25

1953. Coronation.
143 **76** 2d. blue 30 10

77 1d. Cape Triangular Stamp

1953. Stamp Cent of Cape of Good Hope.
144 **77** 1d. sepia and red 10 10
145 – 4d. indigo and blue 30 20
DESIGN: 4d. as Type **77** but reproducing 4d. "Triangular".

79 Merino Ram

1953.
146 **79** 4½d. purple and yellow . . . 20 10
147 – 1s. 3d. brown . . . . . . 1·50 10
148 – 1s. 6d. red and green . . . 80 45
DESIGNS: 1s. 3d. Springbok; 1s. 6d. Aloes.

82 Arms of Orange Free State and Scroll

1954. Centenary of Orange Free State.
149 **82** 2d. sepia and red 10 10
150 4½d. purple and grey 20 50

83 Warthog **87** White Rhinoceros

1954. Wild Animals.
151 **83** ½d. turquoise 10 10
152 – 1d. lake 10 10
153 – 1½d. sepia 10 10
154 – 2d. plum 10 10
155 **87** 3d. brown and blue 15 10
156 – 4d. blue and green 50 10
157 – 4½d. indigo and blue . . . . 60 1·50
158 – 6d. sepia and orange 50 10
159 – 1s. brown and red 80 10
160 – 1s. 3d. brown and green . . 1·75 10
161 – 1s. 6d. brown and pink . . 1·75 60
162 – 2s. 6d. sepia and green . . 3·50 20
163 – 5s. sepia and buff . . . . 10·00 1·40
164 – 10s. black and blue . . . . 17·00 4·50
DESIGNS—VERT (as Type **83**): 1d. Black wildebeest; 1½d. Leopard; 2d. Mountain zebra. (As Type **87**): 4d. African elephant; 4½d. Hippopotamus; 1s. Greater kudu; 1s. 6d. Gemsbok; 2s. 6d. Nyala; 5s. Giraffe; 10s. Sable antelope. HORIZ (as Type **87**): 6d. Lion; 1s. 3d. Springbok.

97 President Kruger **99** A. Pretorius, Church of the Vow and Flag

1955. Centenary of Pretoria.
165 **97** 3d. green 10 10
166 – 6d. purple (Pres. M. Pretorius) 10 20

1955. Voortrekker Covenant Celebrations Pietermaritzburg. Bilingual pair.
167 **99** 2d. blue and red 45 10

100 Settlers' Block-wagon and House

1958. Centenary of Arrival of German Settlers in South Africa.
168 **100** 2d. brown and purple . . 10 10

101 Arms of the Academy

1959. 50th Anniv of South African Academy of Science and Art. Pretoria.
169 **101** 3d. blue and turquoise . . 10 10

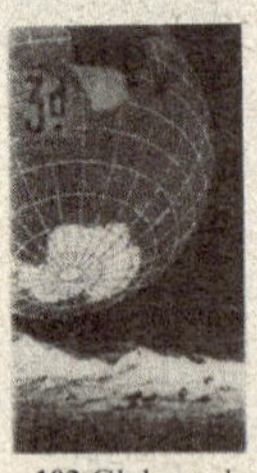

103 Globe and Antarctic Scene **104** Union Flag

1959. South African National Antarctic Expedition.
178 **103** 3d. turquoise and orange . . 20 10

1960. 50th Anniv of Union of South Africa.
179 **104** 4d. orange and blue . . . 30 10
180 – 6d. red, brown and green . . 30 10
181 – 1s. blue and yellow . . . 30 10
182 – 1s. 6d. black and blue . . 1·10 2·00
DESIGNS—VERT: 6d. Union arms. HORIZ: 1s. "Wheel of Progress"; 1s. 6d. Union Festival emblem.
See also Nos. 190 and 192/3.

108 Steam Locomotives "Natal" (1860) and Class 25 (1950s)

1960. Centenary of South African Railways.
183 **108** 1s. 3d. blue . . . . . . 2·00 30

109 Prime Ministers Botha, Smuts, Hertzog, Malan, Strijdom and Verwoerd

1960. Union Day.
184 **109** 3d. brown and light brown 10 10

1961. Types as before but new currency.
185 **83** ½ c. turquoise 10 10
186 – 1 c. lake (as No. 152) . . 10 10
187 – 1½ c. sepia (as No. 153) . . 10 10
188 – 2 c. plum (as No. 154) . . 20 10
189 **109** 2½ c. brown 20 10
190 **104** 3½ c. orange and blue . . 15 1·25
191 – 5 c. sepia & orge (as No. 158) 20 10
192 – 7½ c. red, brown and green (as No. 180) . . . . . 20 1·50
193 – 10 c. blue & yellow (as No. 181) 30 30
194 – 12½ c. brown & green (as No. 160) . . . . 1·00 1·75

195 – 20 c. brown & pink (as No. 161) . . . . 2·25 3·25
196 – 50 c. sepia & buff (as No. 163) . . . . 6·00 10·00
197 – 1 r. black & blue (as No. 164) 18·00 26·00

110 African Pygmy Kingfisher

115 Burchell's Gonolek

1961. Republic Issue.
238 **110** ½ c. blue, red and brown . 10 10
199 – 1 c. red and grey 10 10
200 – 1½ c. lake and purple . . 10 10
229 – 2 c. blue and yellow . . . 15 20
230 – 2½ c. violet and green . . 10 10
243 **115** 3 c. red and blue 30 10
243b – 4 c. violet and green . . 75 30
204 – 5 c. yellow and turquoise 30 10
290 – 6 c. brown and green . . 1·00 30
205 – 7½ c. brown and green . . 60 10
292 – 9 c. red, yellow and green 1·50 30
233 – 10 c. sepia and green . . 40 10
247 – 12½ c. red, yell & green 1·75 40
248 – 15 c. black, olive & orge 1·75 25
234 – 20 c. turq, red & salmon 1·50 70
250 – 50 c. black and blue . . 3·00 40
251 – 1 r. orange, green & blue 3·00 1·00
DESIGNS—VERT (as Type **110**): 1 c. Kafferboom flower (As Type **115**): 2½, 4 c. Groot Constantia; 5 c. Baobab tree; 6, 7½ c. Maize; 9, 12½ c. Protea (flower); 10 c. Cape Town Castle entrance; 15 c. Industry; 20 c. Secretary bird. HORIZ (as Type **110**): 1½ c. Afrikander bull. (As Type **115**) 2 c. Pouring gold; 50 c. Cape Town harbour; 1 r. Strelitzia (flower).

Most values exist in two forms showing differences in the size of the inscriptions and figures of value.

See also Nos. 276/7.

123 Bleriot XI Monoplane and Boeing 707 Airliner over Table Mountain

124 Folk-dancers

1962. 50th Anniv of First South African Aerial Post.
220 **123** 3 c. blue and red 40 10

1962. 50th Anniv of Volkspele (folk-dancing) in South Africa.
221 **124** 2½ c. red and brown . . . 15 10

125 "The Chapman" (emigrant ship)

1962. Unveiling of Precinct Stone, British Settlers Monument, Grahamstown.
222 **125** 2½ c. green and purple . . 40 10
223 12½ c. blue and brown . . 3·00 1·75

126 Red Disa (orchid), Castle Rock and Gardens

128 Centenary Emblem and Nurse

1963. 50th Anniv of Kirstenbosch Botanic Gardens, Cape Town.
224 **126** 2½ c. multicoloured 20 10

1963. Cent of Red Cross. Inscr "1863–1963".
225 **128** 2½ c. red, black and purple 20 10
226 – 12½ c. red and blue . . . . 3·25 1·00
DESIGN—HORIZ: 12½ c. Centenary emblem and globe.

MORE DETAILED LISTS
are given in the Stanley Gibbons Catalogues referred to in the country headings.
For lists of current volumes see Introduction.

130 Assembly Building, Umtata

145 "Springbok" Badge of Rugby Board

1963. First Meeting of Transkei Legislative Assembly.
237 **130** 2½ c. sepia and green . . 10 10

1964. 75th Anniv of South African Rugby Board.
252 **145** 2½ c. brown and green . . 15 10
253 – 12½ c. black and green . . 4·50 4·25
DESIGN—HORIZ: 12½ c. Rugby footballer.

147 Calvin

148 Nurse's Lamp

1964. 400th Death Anniv of Calvin (Protestant reformer).
254 **147** 2½ c. cerise, violet & brown 10 10

1964. 50th Anniv of South African Nursing Association.
255 **148** 2½ c. blue and gold . . . 10 10
257 – 12½ c. blue and gold . . . 3·25 2·25
DESIGN—HORIZ: 12½ c. Nurse holding lamp.

150 I.T.U. Emblem and Satellites

152 Pulpit in Groote Kerk, Cape Town

1965. Centenary of I.T.U.
258 **150** 2½ c. orange and blue . . 25 10
259 – 12½ c. purple and green . 3·00 1·75
DESIGN: 12½ c. I.T.U. emblem and symbols.

1965. Tercentenary of Nederduites Gereformeerde Kerk (Dutch Reformed Church) in South Africa.
260 **152** 2½ c. brown and yellow . 15 10
261 – 12½ c. black, orange & bl 1·75 1·25
DESIGN—HORIZ: 12½ c. Church emblem.

155 Bird in Flight

1965. 5th Anniv of Republic. Bilingual pairs.
262 – 1 c. black, green & yellow 45 10
263 **155** 2½ c. blue, indigo & green 1·25 10
264 – 3 c. red, yellow and brown 4·75 10
265 – 7½ c. blue, ultram & yell . 5·50 20
DESIGNS—VERT: 1 c. Diamond; 3 c. Maize plants. HORIZ: 7½ c. Mountain landscape.

158 Verwoerd and Union Buildings, Pretoria

161 "Martin Luther" (Cranach the Elder)

1966. Verwoerd Commemoration.
266 **158** 2½ c. brown and turquoise 10 10
267 – 3 c. brown and green . . 10 10
268 – 12½ c. brown and blue . . 80 60
DESIGNS: 3 c. "Dr. H. F. Verwoerd" (I. Henkel); 12½ c. Verwoerd and map of South Africa.

1967. 450th Anniv of Reformation.
269 **161** 2½ c. black and red 10 10
270 – 12½ c. black and orange . . 1·75 2·50
DESIGN: 12½ c. Wittenberg Church door.

163 "Profile of Pres. Fouche" (I. Henkel)

165 Hertzog in 1902

1968. Inauguration of President Fouche.
271 **163** 2½ c. brown 10 10
272 – 12½ c. blue . . . . 80 1·25
DESIGN: 12½ c. Portrait of Pres. Fouche.

1968. Inauguration of General Hertzog Monument, Bloemfontein.
273 **165** 2½ c. black, brown & yell . 10 10
274 – 3 c. multicoloured 15 10
275 – 12½ c. black, red & orge . 2·00 1·50
DESIGNS—HORIZ: 3 c. Hertzog in 1924. VERT; 12½ c. Hertzog Monument.

168 African Pygmy Kingfisher

170 Springbok and Olympic Torch

1969.
276 **168** ½ c. blue, red and ochre . . 10 30
277 – 1 c. red and brown 10 10
DESIGN—VERT: 1 c. Kafferboom flower.

1969. South African Games, Bloemfontein.
278 **170** 2½ c. black, red and green . 15 10
279 12½ c. black, red and brown 1·00 1·75

171 Professor Barnard and Groote Schuur Hospital

1969. World's First Heart Transplant and 47th South African Medical Association Congress.
280 **171** 2½ c. purple and red . . . 15 10
281 – 12½ c. red and blue . . . . 2·00 2·25
DESIGN: 12½ c. Hands holding heart.

173 Mail Coach

1969. Centenary of First Stamps of the South African Republic (Transvaal).
297 **173** 2½ c. yellow, blue & brown 15 10
298 – 12½ c. green, gold & brn . 3·25 3·25
DESIGN—VERT: 12½ c. Transvaal stamp of 1869.

175 "Water 70" Emblem

177 "The Sower"

1970. Water 70 Campaign.
299 **175** 2½ c. green, blue & brown . 30 10
300 – 3 c. blue and buff 30 20
DESIGN—HORIZ: 3 c. Symbolic waves.

1970. 150th Anniv of Bible Society of South Africa.
301 **177** 2½ c. multicoloured 15 10
302 – 12½ c. gold, black and blue 2·00 2·75
DESIGN—HORIZ: 12½ c. "Biblia" and open book.

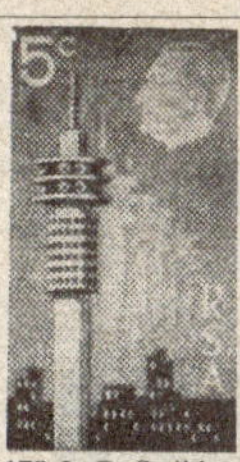

178 J. G. Strijdom and Strijdom Tower

179 Map and Antarctic Landscape

1971. "Interstex" Stamp Exhibition, Cape Town.
303A **178** 5 c. blue, black and yellow 20 10

1971. 10th Anniv of Antarctic Treaty.
304 **179** 12½ c. black, blue and red 2·50 5·00

180 "Landing of British Settlers, 1820" (T. Baines)

1971. 10th Anniv of Republic of South Africa.
305 **180** 2 c. flesh and red 15 20
306 – 4 c. green and black . . . 15 10
DESIGN—VERT: 4 c. Presidents Steyn and Kruger and Treaty of Vereeniging Monument.

181 View of Dam

1972. Opening of Hendrik Verwoerd Dam. Multicoloured.
307 4 c. Type **181** 20 10
308 5 c. Aerial view of dam . . . 25 10
309 10 c. Dam and surrounding country (58 × 21 mm) . . . 1·50 2·50

182 Sheep

183 Black and Siamese Cats

1972. Sheep and Wood Industry.
310 **182** 4 c. multicoloured 30 10
311 – 15 c. stone, dp blue & blue 3·25 20
DESIGN: 15 c. Lamb.

1972. Centenary of Societies for the Prevention of Cruelty to Animals.
312 **183** 5 c. multicoloured . . . . 1·75 10

184 Transport and Industry

185 University Coat of Arms

1973. 50th Anniv of ESCOM (Electricity Supply Commission). Multicoloured.
326 4 c. Type **184** 20 10
327 5 c. Pylon (21 × 28 mm) . . . 30 10
328 15 c. Cooling towers (21 × 28 mm) . . . . 3·00 3·50

1973. Centenary of University of South Africa.
329 **185** 4 c. multicoloured 20 10
330 – 5 c. multicoloured 30 15
331 – 15 c. black and gold . . . 3·00 3·50
DESIGNS—HORIZ (38 × 21 mm): 5 c. University Complex, Pretoria. VERT (as Type **185**): 15 c. Old University Building, Cape Town.

186 Rescuing Sailors

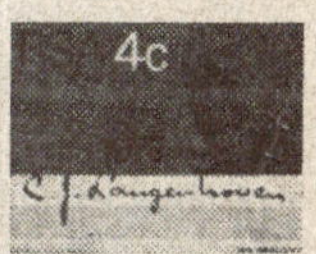

187 C. J. Langenhoven

1973. Bicentenary of Rescue by Wolraad Woltemade.
332 **186** 4 c. brown, green & black 20 10
333 – 5 c. olive, green and black 40 10
334 – 15 c. brown, green & black 5·00 6·00
DESIGNS: 5 c. "De Jonge Thomas" foundering; 15 c. "De Jonge Thomas" breaking up and sailors drowning.

1973. Birth Cent of C. J. Langenhoven (politician and composer of national anthem).
335 **187** 4 c. multicoloured 25 10
336 – 5 c. multicoloured 35 10
337 – 15 c. multicoloured . . . 5·00 6·00
Nos. 336/7 are as Type **187** but with motifs re-arranged. The 5 c. is vert, 21 × 38 mm, and the 15 c. is horiz, 38 × 21 mm.

188 Communications Map

1973. World Communications Day.
338 **188** 15 c. multicoloured . . . . 80 1·40

189 Restored Buildings

190 Burgerspond (obverse and reverse)

1974. Restoration of Tulbagh. Multicoloured.
340 4 c. Type **189** 15 10
341 5 c. Restored Church Street (58 × 21 mm) 40 60

1974. Centenary of Burgerspond (coin).
342 **190** 9 c. brown, red and olive . . 60 95

191 Dr. Malan

192 Congress Emblem

1974. Birth Centenary of Dr. D. F. Malan (Prime Minister).
343 **191** 4 c. blue and light blue . . 20 10

1974. 15th World Sugar Congress, Durban.
344 **192** 15 c. blue and silver . . . 75 1·25

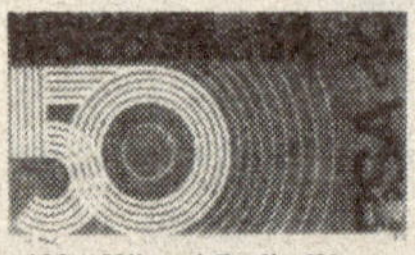

193 "50" and Radio Waves

1974. 50th Anniv of Broadcasting in South Africa.
345 **193** 4 c. red and black 10 10

194 Monument Building

1974. Inauguration of British Settlers' Monument, Grahamstown.
346 **194** 5 c. red and black 10 10

195 Stamps of the South African Provinces

1974. Centenary of Universal Postal Union.
347 **195** 15 c. multicoloured . . . 70 80

196 Iris

197 Bokmakierie Shrikes

1974. Multicoloured. (a) As Type **196**.
348 1 c. Type **196** 10 10
349a 2 c. Wild heath 10 10
350a 3 c. Geranium 10 10
351a 4 c. Arum lily 10 10
352 5 c. Cape gannet (horiz) . . 20 10
353 6 c. Galjoen (fish) (horiz) . . 25 10
354 7 c. Bontrok seabream (horiz) 25 10
355 9 c. Dusky batfish (horiz) . 30 10
356 10 c. Moorish idol (horiz) . 30 10
357 14 c. Roman seabream (horiz) 30 10
358 15 c. Greater double-collared sunbird (horiz) 30 10
359 20 c. Yellow-billed hornbill (horiz) 45 10
360 25 c. Barberton daisy . . . 45 10

(b) As Type **197**.
361 30 c. Type **197** . . . . . . 8·50 70
362 50 c. Stanley cranes . . . . . 2·00 35
363 1 r. Bateleurs . . . . 8·50 3·00

1974. Coil Stamps. As Nos. 348/9a, 352 and 356. Colours changed.
370a **196** 1 c. violet and pink . . 55 60
371 – 2 c. green and yellow . . 80 60
372 – 5 c. black and blue . . . 2·25 80
373a – 10 c. violet and blue . . 4·75 5·25

198 Voortrekker Monument and Encampment

1974. 25th Anniv of Voortrekker Monument, Pretoria.
374 **198** 4 c. multicoloured 20 30

199 SASOL Complex

1975. 25th Anniv of South African Coal, Oil and Gas Corporation Ltd (SASOL).
375 **199** 15 c. multicoloured . . . 75 1·50

200 President Diederichs

201 Jan Smuts

1975. Inauguration of State President.
376 **200** 4 c. brown and gold . . . 10 10
377 15 c. blue and gold . . . 50 1·25

1975. Smuts Commemoration.
378 **201** 4 c. black and grey . . . 10 10

202 "Dutch East Indiaman, Table Bay"

1975. Death Centenary of Thomas Baines (painter). Multicoloured.
379 5 c. Type **202** 15 10
380 9 c. "Cradock, 1848" 30 20
381 15 c. "Thirsty Flat, 1848" . . 50 50
382 30 c. "Pretoria, 1874" . . . . 80 1·75

203 Gideon Malherbe's House, Paarl

1975. Cent of Genootskap van Regte Afrikaners (Afrikaner Language Movement).
384 **203** 4 c. multicoloured 10 10

204 "Automatic Sorting"

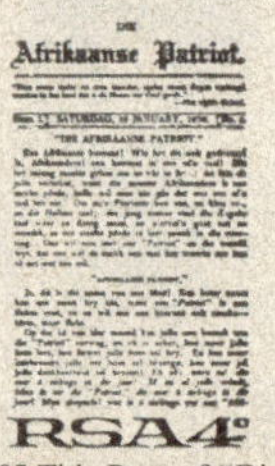

205 Title Page of "Die Afrikaanse Patriot"

1975. Postal Mechanisation.
385 **204** 4 c. multicoloured 10 10

1975. Inaug of Language Monument, Paarl.
386 **205** 4 c. black, brown & orge . 10 10
387 – 5 c. multicoloured 10 10
DESIGN: 5 c. "Afrikaanse Taalmonument".

206 Table Mountain

1975. Tourism. Multicoloured.
388 15 c. Type **206** . . . . 3·50 4·25
389 15 c. Johannesburg . . . . . 3·50 4·25
390 15 c. Cape vineyards . . . . 3·50 4·25
391 15 c. Lions in Kruger National Park . . . . 3·50 4·25

207 Globe and Satellites

1975. Satellite Communication.
392 **207** 15 c. multicoloured 30 30

208 Bowls

210 "Picnic under a Baobab Tree"

1976. Sporting Commemorations.
393 **208** 15 c. black and green . . . 30 70
394 – 15 c. black and green . . . 75 1·40
395 – 15 c. black and green . . . 40 60
396 – 15 c. black and green . . . 60 55
DESIGNS AND EVENTS: No. 393, Type **208** (World Bowls Championships, Johannesburg); 394, Batsman (Centenary of organised cricket in South Africa); 395, Polo player; 396, Gary Player (golfer).

1976. South Africa's Victory in World Bowls Championships. Optd **WERELDKAMPIOENE WORLD CHAMPIONS**.
398 **208** 15 c. black and green . . . 30 80

1976. Birth Cent of Erich Mayer (painter). Mult.
399 4 c. Type **210** 15 10
400 10 c. "Foot of the Blaauwberg" 35 25
401 15 c. "Harteespoort Dam" . . 50 1·25
402 20 c. "Street scene, Doornfontein" . . . . . . 70 1·50

211 Cheetah

1976. World Environment Day. Multicoloured.
404 3 c. Type **211** 15 10
405 10 c. Black rhinoceros 70 40
406 15 c. Blesbok . . . . 85 1·25
407 20 c. Mountain zebra . . . . 1·25 2·00

212 "Emily Hobhouse" (H. Naude)

214 Family with Globe

213 Steam Packet, 1876

1976. 50th Death Anniv of Emily Hobhouse (welfare worker).
408 **212** 4 c. multicoloured 10 10

1976. Centenary of Ocean Mail Service.
409 **213** 10 c. multicoloured . . . 60 85

1976. Family Planning and Child Welfare.
410 **214** 4 c. brown and orange . . 10 10

215 Glasses of Wine

216 Dr. Jacob du Toit

1977. International Wine Symposium, Cape Town.
411 **215** 15 c. multicoloured . . . 40 85

1977. Birth Centenary of J. D. du Toit (theologian and poet).
412 **216** 4 c. multicoloured 10 10

217 Palace of Justice

1977. Centenary of Transvaal Supreme Court.
413 **217** 4 c. brown 10 10

218 "Protea repens"

219 Gymnast

1977. Succulents. Multicoloured.
414 1 c. Type **218** 10 10
431 1 c. "Leucadendron argenteum" 35 70
415 2 c. "P. punctata" 15 40
432 2 c. "Mimetes cucullatus" . . 35 70
416 3 c. "P. neriifolia" 10 10
417 4 c. "P. longifolia" 10 10
418 5 c. "P. cynaroides" 10 10
433 5 c. "Serruria florida" . . . 35 70
419b 6 c. "P. canaliculata" 30 70
420b 7 c. "P. lorea" 20 70
421a 8 c. "P. mundii" 15 10
422 9 c. "P. roupelliae" 20 70
423 10 c. "P. aristata" 30 10
434 10 c. "Leucadendron sessile" . 35 70
424 15 c. "P. eximia" 25 10
425 20 c. "P. magnifica" 30 10
426c 25 c. "P. grandiceps" 40 60
427 30 c. "P. amplexicaulis" . . . 45 10
428a 50 c. "Leucospermum cordifolium" 45 15
429a 1 r. "Paranomus reflexus" . 60 75
430a 2 r. "Orothamnus zeyheri" . 80 1·00

1977. 8th Congress of Int Assn of Physical Education and Sports for Girls and Women.
435 **219** 15 c. black, red and yellow 30 30

220 Metrication Symbol on Globe

1977. Metrication.
436 **220** 15 c. multicoloured . . . 30 30

221 Atomic Diagram

1977. Uranium Development.
437 **221** 15 c. multicoloured . . . 30 30

222 National Flag

224 Dr. Andrew Murray

223 Walvis Bay, 1878

1977. 50th Anniv of National Flag.
438 **222** 5 c. multicoloured 10 10

1977. Centenary of Annexation of Walvis Bay.
439 **223** 15 c. multicoloured . . . 60 60

1978. 150th Birth Anniv of Dr. Andrew Murray (church statesman).
440 **224** 4 c. multicoloured 10 10

225 Steel Rail

1978. 50th Anniv of I. S. C. O. R. (South African Iron and Steel Industrial Corporation).
441 **225** 15 c. multicoloured . . . 30 30

226 Richards Bay

1978. Harbours. Multicoloured.
442 15 c. Type **226** . . . . 50 1·00
443 15 c. Saldanhabaai . . . . . 50 1·00

227 "Shepherd's Lonely Dwelling, Riversdale"

1978. 125th Birth Anniv of J. E. A. Volschenk (painter). Multicoloured.
444 10 c. Type **227** 20 20
445 15 c. "Clouds and Sunshine, Laneberg Range, Riversdale" 40 35
446 20 c. "At the Foot of the Mountain" . . . . 60 1·00
447 25 c. "Evening on the Veldt" . 70 1·75

228 Pres. B. J. Vorster

1978. Inauguration of President Vorster.
449a **228** 4 c. brown and gold . . 10 10
450 15 c. violet and gold . . 25 60

229 Golden Gate

1978. Tourism. Multicoloured.
451 10 c. Type **229** 15 10
452 15 c. Blyde River Canyon . . 25 35
453 20 c. Amphitheatre, Drakensberg 40 1·00
454 25 c. Cango Caves . . . . . . 55 1·40

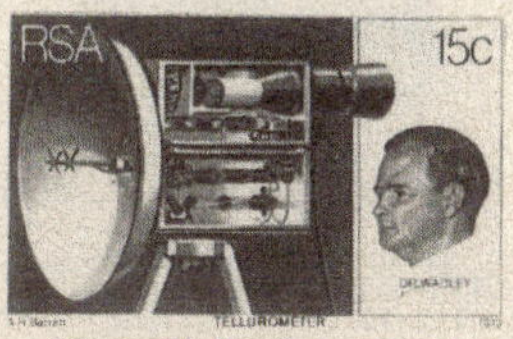

230 Dr. Wadley (inventor) and Tellurometer

1979. 25th Anniv of Tellurometer (radio distance measurer).
455 **230** 15 c. multicoloured . . . 20 20

231 1929 4d. Airmail Stamp

1979. 50th Anniv of Stamp Production in South Africa.
456 **231** 15 c. green, cream and grey 30 20

232 "Save Fuel"

1979. Fuel Conservation.
457 **232** 4 c. black and red 25 50
458 – 4 c. black and red 25 50
No. 458 is as Type **232** but with face value and country initials in bottom left-hand corner, and Afrikaans inscription above English.

233 Isandlwana

1979. Centenary of Zulu War.
459 **233** 4 c. black and red 15 10
460 – 15 c. black and red . . . 45 45
461 – 20 c. black and red . . . 60 75
DESIGNS: 15 c. Ulundi; 20 c. Rorke's Drift.

234 "Health Care"

1979. Health Year.
463 **234** 4 c. multicoloured 10 10

235 Children looking at Candle

1979. 50th Anniv of Christmas Stamp Fund.
464 **235** 4 c. multicoloured 10 10

236 University of Cape Town

237 "Gary Player"

1979. 50th Anniv of University of Cape Town.
465a **236** 4 c. multicoloured . . . 15 15

1979. "Rosafari 1979" World Rose Convention, Pretoria. Multicoloured.
466 4 c. Type **237** 15 10
467 15 c. "Prof. Chris Barnard" . 40 40
468 20 c. "Southern Sun" . . . 50 60
469 25 c. "Soaring Wings" . . . 55 70

238 University of Stellenbosch

1979. 300th Anniv of Stellenbosch (oldest town in South Africa). Multicoloured.
471 4 c. Type **238** 10 10
472 15 c. Rhenish Church on the Braak 20 40

239 F.A.K. Emblem

240 "Still-life with Sweet Peas"

1979. 50th Anniv of F.A.K. (Federation of Afrikaans Cultural Societies).
473 **239** 4 c. multicoloured 10 15

1980. Paintings by Pieter Wenning. Multicoloured.
474 5 c. Type **240** 10 10
475 25 c. "House in the Suburbs, Cape Town" ($44\frac{1}{2} \times 37$ mm) . 40 60

241 "Cullinan II"

242 C. L. Leipoldt

1980. World Diamond Congresses, Johannesburg. Multicoloured.
477 15 c. Type **241** 60 60
478 20 c. "Cullinan I (Great Star of Africa)" 65 65

1980. Birth Centenary of C. L. Leipoldt (poet).
479 **242** 5 c. multicoloured 10 10

243 University of Pretoria

1980. 50th Anniv of University of Pretoria.
480 **243** 5 c. multicoloured 10 10

244 "Marine with Shipping" (Willem van de Velde)

1980. Paintings from South African National Gallery, Cape Town. Multicoloured.
481 5 c. Type **244** 15 10
482 10 c. "Firetail and his Trainer" (George Stubbs) 20 20
483 15 c. "Lavinia" (Thomas Gainsborough) (vert) 25 45
484 20 c. "Classical Landscape" (Pieter Post) 30 65

245 Joubert, Kruger and M. Pretorius (Triumvirate Government)

1980. Centenary of Paardekraal Monument (cairn commemorating formation of Boer Triumvirate Government). Multicoloured.
486 5 c. Type **245** 10 10
487 10 c. Paardekraal Monument (vert) 20 40

246 Boers advancing up Amajuba Mountain

1981. Centenary of Battle of Amajuba. Mult.
488 5 c. Type **246** 20 10
489 15 c. British troops defending hill (horiz) 40 65

247 Ballet "Raka"

1981. Opening of State Theatre, Pretoria. Multicoloured.
490 20 c. Type **247** 25 30
491 25 c. Opera "Aida" 40 35

248 Former Presidents C. R. Swart, J. J. Fouche, N. Diederichs and B. J. Vorster

1981. 20th Anniv of Republic.
493 **248** 5 c. black, green & brown 15 10
494 – 15 c. multicoloured . . . 30 30
DESIGN—28 × 22 mm: 15 c. President Marais Viljoen.

249 Girl with Hearing Aid

250 Microscope

1981. Centenary of Institutes for Deaf and Blind, Worcester. Multicoloured.
495 5 c. Type **249** 10 10
496 15 c. Boy reading braille . . . 20 25

1981. 50th Anniv of National Cancer Association.
497 **250** 5 c. multicoloured 10 10

251 "Calanthe natalensis"

252 Voortrekkers in Uniform

1981. 10th World Orchid Conference, Durban. Multicoloured.
498 5 c. Type **251** 15 10
499 15 c. "Eulophia speciosa" . . 30 35
500 20 c. "Disperis fanniniae" . . 40 65
501 25 c. "Disa uniflora" 50 90

1981. 50th Anniv of Voortrekker Movement (Afrikaans cultural youth organization).
503 **252** 5 c. multicoloured 10 10

INDEX

Countries can be quickly located by referring to the index at the end of this volume.

253 Lord Baden-Powell

254 Dr Robert Koch

1982. 75th Anniv of Boy Scout Movement.
504 253 15 c. multicoloured . . . 15 15

1981. Cent of Discovery of Tubercle Bacillus.
505 254 20 c. multicoloured . . . 15 30

255 "Maria van Riebeck" submarine

1982. 25th Anniv of Simonstown as South African Naval Base. Multicoloured.
506 8 c. Type **255** . . . 10 10
507 15 c. Missile patrol vessel . . 15 30
508 20 c. Minesweeper . . 25 50
509 25 c. Harbour patrol boats . . 30 70

256 Old Provost, Grahamstown

257 Bradysaurus

1982. South African Architecture.
511 256 1 c. brown . . . 15 20
512b – 2 c. green . . . 10 20
513 – 3 c. violet . . . 30 30
514 – 4 c. green . . . 20 15
515 – 5 c. red . . . 30 30
515a – 5 c. purple . . . 10 10
516 – 6 c. green . . . 45 40
517 – 7 c. green . . . 30 50
518a – 8 c. blue . . . 40 10
519 – 9 c. mauve . . . 40 20
520 – 10 c. red . . . 40 40
520a – 10 c. brown . . . 35 10
520b – 11 c. mauve . . . 40 15
520c – 12 c. blue . . . 70 10
520d – 14 c. brown . . . 1·25 10
521 – 15 c. blue . . . 30 15
521a – 16 c. red . . . 1·00 50
522 – 20 c. red . . . 65 30
522a – 20 c. black . . . 80 10
523 – 25 c. brown . . . 50 30
524 – 30 c. brown . . . 65 30
525 – 50 c. blue . . . 80 30
526 – 1 r. violet . . . 1·00 15
527a – 2 r. red . . . 1·25 50
DESIGNS—(28 × 20 mm): 2 c. Tuynhuys, Cape Town; 3 c. Appelhof, Bloemfontein; 4 c. Raadsaal, Pretoria; 5 c. Cape Town Castle; 6 c. Goewermentsgebou, Bloemfontein; 7 c. Drostdy, Graaff-Reinet; 8 c. Leeuwenhof, Cape Town; 9 c. Libertas, Pretoria; 10 c. City Hall, Pietermaritzburg; 11 c. City Hall, Kimberley; 12 c. City Hall, Port Elizabeth;
14 c. City Hall, Johannesburg; 15 c. Matjesfontein; 16 c. City Hall, Durban; 20 c. Post Office, Durban; 25 c. Melrose House, Pretoria. (45 × 28 mm): 30 c. Old Legislative Asembly Building, Pietermaritzburg; 50 c. Raadsaal, Bloemfontein; 1 r. Houses of Parliament, Cape Town; 2 r. Uniegebou, Pretoria.

1982. Coil Stamps. As T **256**.
528 1 c. brown . . . 30 60
529 2 c. green . . . 30 65
530 5 c. brown . . . 30 65
531 10 c. brown . . . 30 70
DESIGNS: 1 c. Drostdy, Swellendam; 2 c. City Hall, East London; 5 c. Head Post Office, Johannesburg; 10 c. Morgenster, Somerset West.

1982. Karoo Fossils. Multicoloured.
532 8 c. Type **257** . . . 40 10
533 15 c. Lystrosaurus . . . 55 75
534 20 c. Euparkeria . . . 70 85
535 25 c. Thrinaxodon . . . 80 1·10

258 Gough Island Base

1983. Weather Stations. Multicoloured.
537 8 c. Type **258** . . . 20 10
538 20 c. Marion Island base . . 45 45
539 25 c. Taking meteorological readings . . . 45 50
540 40 c. Launching weather balloon, Sanae . . . 70 90

259 Class S2 Krupp Locomotive, 1952

260 Rugby

1983. Steam Railway Locomotives. Multicoloured.
541 10 c. Type **259** . . . 35 10
542 20 c. Class 16E Henschel express locomotive, 1935 . . . 70 75
543 25 c. Class 6H locomotive, 1901 80 1·00
544 40 c. Class 15F locomotive, 1939 1·25 1·75

1983. Sport in South Africa. Multicoloured.
545 10 c. Type **260** . . . 15 10
546 20 c. Soccer (horiz) . . . 35 40
547 25 c. Yachting . . . 45 50
548 40 c. Horse-racing (horiz) . . 75 95

261 Plettenberg Bay

1983. Tourism Beaches. Multicoloured.
549 10 c. Type **261** . . . 10 10
550 20 c. Durban . . . 25 30
551 25 c. West coast . . . 30 35
552 40 c. Clifton . . . 50 65

262 Thomas Pringle

263 Manganese

1984. South African English Authors.
554 262 10 c. brown, lt brn & grey 10 10
555 – 20 c. brown, green & grey 25 40
556 – 25 c. brown, pink and grey 30 50
557 – 40 c. brown, lt brn & grey 50 85
DESIGNS: 20 c. Pauline Smith; 25 c. Olive Schreiner; 40 c. Sir Percy Fitzpatrick.

1984. Strategic Minerals. Multicoloured.
558 11 c. Type **263** . . . 40 10
559 20 c. Chromium . . . 75 75
560 25 c. Vanadium . . . 90 1·00
561 30 c. Titanium . . . 1·00 1·25

264 Bloukrans River Bridge

1984. South African Bridges. Multicoloured.
562 11 c. Type **264** . . . 40 10
563 25 c. Durban four level interchange . . . 80 75
564 30 c. Mfolozi railway bridge . 85 95
565 45 c. Gouritz River bridge . . 1·10 1·75

265 Preamble to the Constitution in Afrikaans

266 Pres. P. W. Botha

1984. New Constitution.
566 – 11 c. stone, black & bistre 90 1·25
567 265 11 c. stone, black & bistre 90 1·25
568 – 25 c. stone, purple & bistre 60 65
569 – 30 c. multicoloured . . . 60 65
DESIGNS: No. 566, Preamble to the Constitution in English; 568, Last two lines of National Anthem; 569, South African coat of arms.

1984. Inauguration of President Botha.
570 266 11 c. multicoloured . . . 30 10
571 25 c. multicoloured . . . 55 40

267 Pro Patria Medal

268 "Reflections" (Frans Oerder)

1984. Military Decorations. Multicoloured.
572 11 c. Type **267** . . . 25 10
573 25 c. De Wet decoration . . 40 45
574 30 c. John Chard decoration . 45 65
575 45 c. Honoris Crux (Diamond) decoration . . . 55 1·10

1985. Paintings by Frans Oerder. Multicoloured.
577 11 c. Type **268** . . . 30 15
578 25 c. "Ladies in a Garden" . . 45 35
579 30 c. "Still-life with Lobster" . 50 45
580 50 c. "Still-life with Marigolds" 80 70

269 Cape Parliament Building

270 Freesia

1985. Centenary of Cape Parliament Building. Multicoloured.
582 12 c. Type **269** . . . 30 10
583 25 c. Speaker's Chair . . . 55 55
584 30 c. "National Convention 1908–9" (Edward Roworth) 70 80
585 50 c. Republic Parliamentary emblem . . . 1·10 1·50

1985. Floral Emigrants. Multicoloured.
586 12 c. Type **270** . . . 35 10
587 25 c. Nerine . . . 65 75
588 30 c. Ixia . . . 75 85
589 50 c. Gladiolus . . . 1·10 1·60

271 Sugar Bowl

1985. Cape Silverware. Multicoloured.
590 12 c. Type **271** . . . 35 10
591 25 c. Teapot . . . 70 60
592 30 c. Loving cup (vert) . . . 70 80
593 50 c. Coffee pot (vert) . . . 1·00 2·00

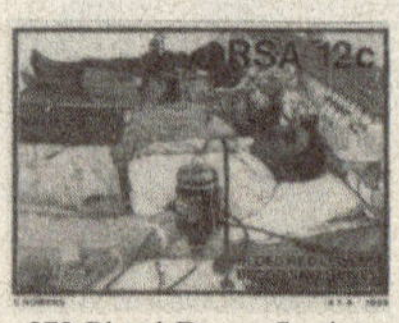

272 Blood Donor Session

1986. Blood Donor Campaign. Multicoloured.
594 12 c. Type **272** . . . 45 10
595 20 c. Baby receiving blood transfusion . . . 75 80
596 25 c. Operation in progress . . 80 95
597 30 c. Ambulanceman and accident victim . . . 95 1·60

273 National Flag

1986. 25th Anniv of Republic of South Africa.
598 14 c. Type **273** . . . 75 1·00
599 14 c. As Type **273**, but inscr "UNITY IS STRENGTH" . 75 1·00

274 Drostdyhof, Graaff-Reinet

1986. Restoration of Historic Buildings. Multicoloured.
600 14 c. Type **274** . . . 30 10
601 20 c. Pilgrim's Rest mining village . . . 55 70
602 25 c. Strapp's Store, Bethlehem 60 90
603 30 c. Palmdene, Pietermaritzburg 75 1·40

275 Von Brandis Square, Johannesburg, c. 1900

1986. Centenary of Johannesburg. Multicoloured.
604 14 c. Type **275** . . . 35 10
605 20 c. Gold mine (26 × 20 mm) 1·00 1·25
606 25 c. Johannesburg skyline, 1986 1·00 1·40
607 30 c. Gold bars (26 × 20 mm) . 1·50 2·25

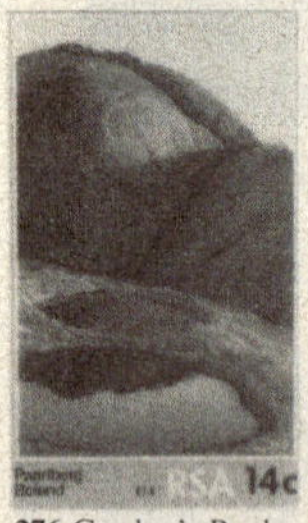

276 Gordon's Rock, Paarlberg

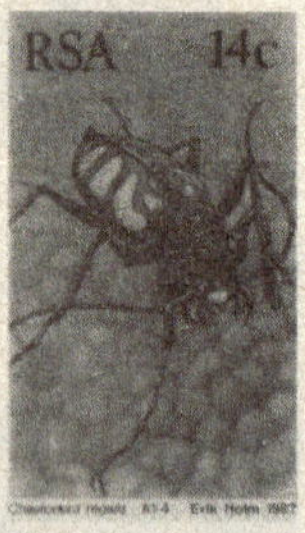

277 "Cicindela regalis"

1986. Rock Formations. Multicoloured.
608 14 c. Type **276** . . . 60 10
609 20 c. The Column, Drakensberg 85 90
610 25 c. Maltese Cross, Sederberge 95 1·25
611 30 c. Bourke's Luck Potholes, Blyde River Gorge . . . 1·25 1·60

1987. South African Beetles. Multicoloured.
612 14 c. Type **277** . . . 50 10
613 20 c. "Trichostetha fascicularis" 70 75
614 25 c. "Julodis viridipes" . . 85 1·00
615 30 c. "Ceroplesis militaris" . . 1·10 1·75

278 Eland, Sebaaieni Cave

1987. Rock Paintings. Multicoloured.
616 16 c. Type **278** . . . 50 10
617 20 c. Leaping lion, Clocolan . 75 75
618 25 c. Black wildebeest, uMhlwazini Valley . . . 90 1·00
619 30 c. Bushman dance, Floukraal 1·10 1·75

279 Oude Pastorie, Paarl

1987. 300th Anniv of Paarl. Multicoloured.
620 16 c. Type **279** . . . 30 10
621 20 c. Grapevines . . . 50 70
622 25 c. Wagon-building . . . 55 85
623 30 c. KWV Cathedral Wine Cellar . . . 75 1·50

1987. Natal Flood Relief Fund (1st issue). No. 521a surch.
624 16 c. + 10 c. red (surch **VLOEDRAMP NATAL +10c**) . . . 45 70
625 16 c. + 10 c. (surch **NATAL FLOOD DISASTER +10c**) 45 70
See also Nos. 629/30 and 635/6.

281 "Belshazzar's Feast" (Rembrandt)

1987. The Bible Society of South Africa. Multicoloured.
626 16 c. "The Bible" in 75 languages (54 × 34 mm) . . . 40 10
627 30 c. Type **281** . . . 70 85
628 50 c. "St. Matthew and the Angel" (Rembrandt) (vert) 90 1·25

1987. Natal Flood Relief Fund (2nd issue). No. 626 surch.

629	16 c. + 10 c. multicoloured (surch as No. 625)	45	70
630	16 c. + 10 c. multicoloured (surch as No. 624)	45	70

282 Bartolomeu Dias and Cape of Good Hope

1988. 500th Anniv of Discovery of Cape of Good Hope by Bartolomeu Dias. Multicoloured.

631	16 c. Type **282**	55	10
632	30 c. Kwaaihoek Monument	80	85
633	40 c. Caravels	90	1·25
634	50 c. Martellus map, c. 1489	1·25	1·75

1988. Natal Flood Relief Fund (3rd issue). No. 631 surch.

635	16 c. + 10 c. multicoloured (surch as No. 624)	45	70
636	16 c. + 10 c. multicoloured (surch as No. 625)	45	70

283 Huguenot Monument, Franschhoek

1988. 300th Anniv of Arrival of First French Huguenots at the Cape. Multicoloured.

637	16 c. Type **283**	30	10
638	30 c. Map of France showing Huguenot areas	70	80
639	40 c. Title page of French/Dutch New Testament of 1672	80	1·25
640	50 c. St. Bartholomew's Day Massacre, Paris, 1572	1·00	1·50

1988. National Flood Relief Fund Nos. 637/40 surch in English (**National Flood Disaster +10c**) (E) or in Afrikaans (**Nasionale Vloedramp +10c**) (A).

641	16 c. + 10 c. mult (E)	40	65
642	16 c. + 10 c. mult (A)	40	65
643	30 c. + 10 c. mult (A)	55	75
644	30 c. + 10 c. mult (E)	55	75
645	40 c. + 10 c. mult (A)	70	90
646	40 c. + 10 c. mult (E)	70	90
647	50 c. + 10 c. mult (E)	90	1·25
648	50 c. + 10 c. mult (A)	90	1·25

285 Pelican Point Lighthouse, Walvis Bay

1988. Lighthouses. Multicoloured.

649	16 c. Type **285**	50	10
650	30 c. Green Point, Cape Town	70	70
651	40 c. Cape Agulhas	90	1·10
652	50 c. Umhlanga Rocks, Durban	1·25	1·60

286 "Huernia zebrina"

287 Map of Great Trek Routes

1988. Succulents. Multicoloured.

654	1 c. Type **286**	10	10
655	2 c. "Euphorbia symmetrica"	10	10
656	5 c. "Lithops dorotheae"	10	10
657	7 c. "Gibbaeum nebrownii"	15	10
658	10 c. "Didymaotus lapidiformis"	15	10
659	16 c. "Vanheerdea divergens"	40	10
659a	18 c. "Faucaria tigrina"	50	10
660	20 c. "Conophytum mundum"	40	10
660a	21 c. "Gasteria armstrongii"	40	10
661	25 c. "Cheiridopsis peculiaris"	40	10
662	30 c. "Tavaresia barklyi"	40	20
663	35 c. "Dinteranthus wilmotianus"	50	20
664	40 c. "Frithia pulchra"	55	25
665	50 c. "Lapidaria margaretae"	60	25
666	90 c. "Dioscorea elephantipes"	85	45
667	1 r. "Trichocaulon cactiforme"	75	50
668	2 r. "Crassula columnaris"	1·25	90
668a	5 r. "Anacampseros albissima"	3·00	2·40

See also No. 778.

1988. Coil stamps. As T **286**. Multicoloured.

669	1 c. "Adromischus marianiae"	1·00	1·50
670	2 c. "Titanopsis calcarea"	50	60
671	5 c. "Dactylopsis digitata"	50	60
672	10 c. "Pleiospilos bolusii"	55	70

1988. 150th Anniv of Great Trek. Multicoloured.

673	16 c. Type **287**	60	10
674	30 c. "Exodus" (tapestry by W. Coetzer) (56 × 20 mm)	90	90
675	40 c. "Crossing the Drakensberg" (tapestry by W. Coetzer) (77 × 20 mm)	1·10	1·10
676	50 c. "After the Service, Church of the Vow" (J. H. Pierneef) (horiz)	1·40	1·75

288 Coelacanth

1989. 50th Anniv of Discovery of Coelacanth. Multicoloured.

677	16 c. Type **288**	65	15
678	30 c. Prof. J. L. B. Smith and Dr. M. Courtenay-Latimer examining Coelacanth	1·00	1·25
679	40 c. J. L. B. Smith Institute of Ichthyology, Grahamstown	1·25	1·50
680	50 c. Coelacanth and "GEO" midget submarine	1·50	2·00

289 Man-made Desert

1989. National Grazing Strategy. Multicoloured.

681	18 c. Type **289**	40	15
682	30 c. Formation of erosion gully	65	75
683	40 c. Concrete barrage in gully	70	1·00
684	50 c. Reclaimed veldt	80	1·40

290 South Africa v. France Match, 1980

1989. Cent of South African Rugby Board. Mult.

685	18 c. Type **290**	50	15
686	30 c. South Africa v. Australia, 1963	85	90
687	40 c. South Africa v. New Zealand, 1937	1·00	1·40
688	50 c. South Africa v. British Isles, 1896	1·10	1·60

291 "Composition in Blue"

292 Pres. F. W. de Klerk

1989. Paintings by Jacob Hendrik Pierneef. Multicoloured.

689	18 c. Type **291**	30	15
690	30 c. "Zanzibar"	50	60
691	40 c. "The Bushveld"	65	90
692	50 c. "Cape Homestead"	75	1·10

1989. Inaug of President F. W. de Klerk. Mult.

694	18 c. Type **292**	40	15
695	45 c. F. W. de Klerk (different)	70	1·10

293 Gas-drilling Rig, Mossel Bay

1989. Energy Sources. Multicoloured.

696	18 c. Type **293**	40	10
697	30 c. Coal to oil conversion plant	70	70
698	40 c. Nuclear power station	80	85
699	50 c. Thermal electric power station	90	1·25

294 Electric Goods Train and Map of Railway Routes

1990. Co-operation in Southern Africa. Mult.

700	18 c. Cahora Bassa Hydro-electric Scheme, Mozambique, and map of transmission lines (68 × 26 mm)	50	25
701	30 c. Type **294**	70	70
702	40 c. Projected dam on upper Orange River, Lesotho, and map of Highlands Water Project (68 × 26 mm)	85	90
703	50 c. Cow, syringe and outline map of Africa	95	1·10

295 Great Britain 1840 Penny Black

296 Knysna Turaco

1990. National Stamp Day. Multicoloured.

705	21 c. Type **295**	40	50
706	21 c. Cape of Good Hope 1853 4d. triangular pair	40	50
707	21 c. Natal 1857 1s.	40	50
708	21 c. Orange Free State 1868 1s.	40	50
709	21 c. Transvaal 1869 1s.	40	50

1990. Birds. Multicoloured.

710	21 c. Type **296**	50	20
711	35 c. Red-capped robin chat	70	80
712	40 c. Rufous-naped bush lark	70	90
713	50 c. Bokmakierie shrike	90	1·40

297 Karoo Landscape near Britstown

298 Woltemade Cross for Bravery

1990. Tourism. Multicoloured.

714	50 c. Type **297**	85	1·10
715	50 c. Camps Bay, Cape of Good Hope	85	1·10
716	50 c. Giraffes in Kruger National Park	85	1·10
717	50 c. Boschendal Vineyard, Drakenstein Mts	85	1·10

1990. National Orders. Multicoloured.

718	21 c. Type **298**	30	40
719	21 c. Order of the Southern Cross	30	40
720	21 c. Order of the Star of South Africa	30	40
721	21 c. Order for Meritorious Service	30	40
722	21 c. Order of Good Hope	30	40

299 Boer Horses

300 Diagram of Human Heart and Transplant Operation

1991. Animal Breeding in South Africa. Mult.

724	21 c. Type **299**	50	55
725	21 c. Bonsmara bull	50	55
726	21 c. Dorper sheep	50	55
727	21 c. Ridgeback dogs	50	55
728	21 c. Putterie racing pigeons	50	55

1991. 30th Anniv of Republic. Scientific and Technological Achievements. Multicoloured.

729	25 c. Type **300**	20	10
730	40 c. Matimba Power Station (horiz)	35	35
731	50 c. Dolos design breakwater (horiz)	45	45
732	60 c. Western Deep Levels gold mine	60	60

301 State Registration of Nurses Act, 1891

302 South Africa Post Office Ltd Emblem

1991. Centenary of State Registration for Nurses and Midwives.

733	**301** 60 c. multicoloured	60	60

1991. Establishment of Post Office Ltd and Telekom Ltd. Multicoloured.

734	27 c. Type **302**	25	25
735	27 c. Telekom SA Ltd emblem	25	25

303 Sir Arnold Theiler (veterinarian)

1991. South African Scientists. Multicoloured.

736	27 c. Type **303**	30	15
737	45 c. Sir Basil Schonland (physicist)	60	60
738	65 c. Dr. Robert Broom (palaeontologist)	80	90
739	85 c. Dr. Alex du Toit (geologist)	1·00	1·50

304 "Agulhas" (Antarctic research ship)

1991. 30th Anniv of Antarctic Treaty. Mult.

740	27 c. Type **304**	50	10
741	65 c. Chart showing South African National Antarctic Expedition base	1·25	80

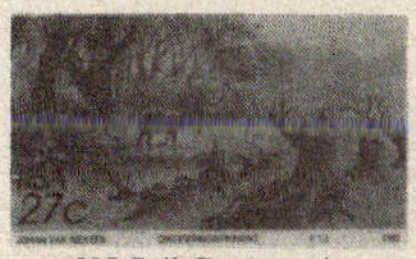

305 Soil Conservation

306 Dutch Fleet approaching Table Bay

1992. Environmental Conservation. Mult.

742	27 c. Type **305**	35	15
743	65 c. Water pollution	85	65
744	85 c. Air pollution	1·10	85

1992. National Stamp Day. Cape of Good Hope Postal Stones. Multicoloured.

745	35 c. Type **306**	45	35
746	35 c. Landing for water and provisions	45	35
747	35 c. Discovering a postal stone	45	35
748	35 c. Leaving letters under a stone	45	35
749	35 c. Reading letters	45	35

307 Queen Anne Settee, c 1750

1992. Antique Cape Furniture. Multicoloured.

750	35 c. Type **307**	35	35
751	35 c. Stinkwood settee, c 1800	35	35
752	35 c. Canopy bed, c 1800 (vert)	35	35
753	35 c. 19th-century rocking cradle	35	35
754	35 c. Waterbutt, c 1800 (vert)	35	35
755	35 c. Flemish style cabinet, c 1700 (vert)	35	35
756	35 c. Armoire, c 1780 (vert)	35	35
757	35 c. Late 17th-century church chair (vert)	35	35
758	35 c. Tub chair, c 1770 (vert)	35	35
759	35 c. Bible desk, c 1750 (vert)	35	35

308 Grand Prix Motor Racing

309 "Women's Monument" (Van Wouw)

1992. Sports. Multicoloured.

760 35 c. Type **308** 25 25
761 35 c. Football 25 25
762 55 c. Total Paris–Cape Motor Rally 35 35
763 70 c. Athletics 50 50
764 90 c. Rugby 65 65
765 1 r. 05 Cricket 1·00 1·00

1992. 130th Birth Anniv of Anton van Wouw (sculptor). Multicoloured.

767 35 c. Type **309** 30 20
768 70 c. "Sekupu Player" 60 60
769 90 c. "The Hunter" 80 80
770 1 r. 05 "Postman Lehman" 85 1·00

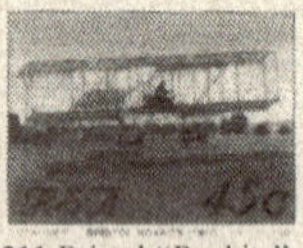

310 Walvis Bay Harbour

311 Bristol "Boxkite", 1907

1993. South African Harbours. Multicoloured.

772 35 c. Type **310** 30 20
773 55 c. East London 40 35
774 70 c. Port Elizabeth 60 50
775 90 c. Cape Town 80 75
776 1 r. 05 Durban 85 95

1993. Succulents. As T **286**, but inscr "Standardised mail" in English and Afrikaans.

778 (–) "Stapelia grandiflora" 40 25

No. 778 was sold at 45 c.

1993. Aviation in South Africa. Multicoloured.

779 45 c. Type **311** 55 30
780 45 c. Voisin "Boxkite", 1909 55 30
781 45 c. Bleriot XI, 1911 55 30
782 45 c. Paterson No. 2 biplane, 1913 55 30
783 45 c. Henri Farman H.F.27, 1915 55 30
784 45 c. Royal Aircraft Factory B.E.2.E, 1918 55 30
785 45 c. Vickers Vimy "Silver Queen II", 1920 55 30
786 45 c. Royal Aircraft Factory S.E.5A, 1921 55 30
787 45 c. Avro 504k, 1921 55 30
788 45 c. Armstrong Whitworth Atalanta, 1930 55 30
789 45 c. De Havilland D.H.66 Hercules, 1931 55 30
790 45 c. Westland Wapiti, 1931 55 30
791 45 c. Junkers F-13, 1932 55 30
792 45 c. Handley Page H.P.42, 1933 55 30
793 45 c. Junkers Ju 52/3m, 1934 55 30
794 45 c. Junkers Ju 86, 1936 55 30
795 45 c. Hawker Hartbees, 1936 55 30
796 45 c. Short Empire "C" Class flying boat "Canopus", 1937 55 30
797 45 c. Miles Master II and Airspeed A.S.10 Oxford, 1940 55 30
798 45 c. North American Harvard Mk IIa, 1942 55 30
799 45 c. Short Sunderland flying boat, 1945 55 30
800 45 c. Avro Type 685 York, 1946 55 30
801 45 c. Douglas DC-7B, 1955 55 30
802 45 c. Sikorsky S-55c helicopter, 1956 55 30
803 45 c. Boeing 707-344, 1959 55 30

312 Table Mountain Ghost Frog

313 Dragoons carrying Mail between Cape Town and False Bay, 1803

1993. Endangered Fauna. Multicoloured. (a) Face values as T **312**.

804 1 c. Type **312** (I) 10 10
804c 1 c. Type **312** (II) 20 20
805 2 c. Smith's dwarf chameleon (I) 10 10
805c 2 c. Smith's dwarf chameleon (II) 20 20
806 5 c. Giant girdle-tailed lizard (I) 10 10
807 10 c. Geometric tortoise (I) 10 10
807c 10 c. Geometric tortoise (II) 30 30
808 20 c. Southern African hedgehog (I) 10 10
913 20 c. Southern African hedgehog (II) 10 10
809 40 c. Riverine rabbit (I) 20 10
809c 40 c. Riverine rabbit (II) 10 10
810 50 c. Samango monkey (I) 25 20
914 50 c. Samango monkey (II) 10 10
811 55 c. Aardwolf (I) 10 10
811c 55 c. Aardwolf (II) 30 30
812 60 c. Cape hunting dog (I) 30 20
915 60 c. Cape hunting dog (II) 10 10
813 70 c. Roan antelope (I) 30 25
813c 70 c. Roan antelope (II) 15 20
814 75 c. African striped weasel (I) 15 20
815 80 c. Kori bustard (I) 20 25
815a 85 c. Lemon-breasted seedeater (I) 20 25
816 90 c. Jackass penguin (I) 60 30
816c 90 c. Jackass penguin (II) 25 30
817 1 r. Wattled crane (I) 45 30
916 1 r. Wattled crane (II) 20 25
818 2 r. Blue swallow (I) 70 55
818c 2 r. Blue swallow (II) 50 55
819 5 r. Martial eagle (I) 1·75 1·40
819c 5 r. Martial eagle (II) 1·25 1·40
820 10 r. Bateleur (I) 2·00 2·10
917 20 r. Fish eagle (II) 4·00 4·25

(b) Inscr "Standardised mail" in Afrikaans and English (Nos. 821 and 918b) or "Airmail postcard rate" (others).

821 (–) Black rhinoceros (III) 30 25
821b (–) Black rhinoceros (IV) 30 25
821c (1 r.) White rhinoceros (II) 35 30
821d (1 r.) Buffalo (II) 35 30
821e (1 r.) Lion (II) 35 30
821f (1 r.) Leopard (II) 35 30
821g (1 r.) African elephant (II) 35 30

I and III. Species name in Latin. II and IV. Species name in English. No. 821 has a small rhinoceros and No. 821b a larger rhinoceros; they were sold at 45 c. at first but this was later increased to the prevailing rates.

For redrawn designs without frame and inscribed "South Africa" only, see Nos. 1029/44.

1993. National Stamp Day. Early 19th-century Postal Services. Multicoloured.

822 45 c. Type **313** 30 25
823 65 c. Ox wagon carrying Stellenbosch to Cape Town mail, 1803 45 50
824 85 c. Khoi-Khoin mail runners from Stellenbosch, 1803 65 70
825 1 r. 05 Mounted postmen, 1804 80 90

314 Flowers from Namaqualand

1993. Tourism. Multicoloured.

826 85 c. Type **314** (Afrikaans inscr) 65 55
827 85 c. North Beach, Durban (English inscr) 65 55
828 85 c. Lion (German inscr) 65 55
829 85 c. "Appel Express" on Van Staden's Bridge (Dutch inscr) 65 55
830 85 c. Gemsbok (antelope) (French inscr) 65 55

315 Grapes and Packing Bench

1994. Export Fruits. Multicoloured.

831 85 c. Type **315** 50 50
832 90 c. Apple and picker 50 50
833 1 r. 05 Plum and fork-lift truck 60 60
834 1 r. 25 Orange and tractor with trailer 70 70
835 1 r. 40 Avocado and loading freighter 80 80

316 "Children of Different Races" (Nicole Davies)

1994. Peace Campaign. Children's Paintings. Multicoloured.

836 45 c. Type **316** 25 20
837 70 c. "Dove and Tree" (Robynne Lawrie) 40 40
838 95 c. "Children and Dove" (Batami Nothmann) 55 55
839 1 r. 15 "Multi-racial Crowd" (Karen Uys) 75 80

317 Pres. Mandela

1994. Inaug of President Nelson Mandela. Mult.

840 45 c. Type **317** 35 20
841 70 c. South African national anthems 55 50
842 95 c. New national flag 75 75
843 1 r. 15 Union Buildings, Pretoria 95 1·10

318 Tug "McEwen" towing "Winchester Castle" (liner), 1935

1994. Tugboats. Multicoloured.

844 45 c. Type **318** 30 20
845 70 c. "Sir William Hoy" with "Karanja" (liner), 1970 50 40
846 95 c. "Sir Charles Elliott" and wreck of "Dunedin Star" (liner), 1942 65 55
847 1 r. 15 "Eland" and freighter at wharf, 1955 85 75
848 1 r. 35 "Pioneer" (paddle tug) and sailing ships, 1870 95 90

319 "Mother hands out Work" (Emile du Toit)

1994. International Year of the Family. Children's Paintings. Multicoloured.

850 45 c. Type **319** 30 30
851 45 c. "My Friends and I at Play" (Patrick Mackenzie) 30 30
852 45 c. "Family Life" (Michelle du Pisani) 30 30
853 45 c. "Sunday in Church" (Elizabeth Nel) 30 30
854 45 c. "I visit my Brother in Hospital" (Zwelinzema Sam) 30 30

320 Hands holding Invoice and Bulk Mail Envelope

1994. National Stamp Day. Multicoloured.

855 50 c. Type **320** 30 25
856 70 c. Certified mail 40 40
857 95 c. Registered mail 50 55
858 1 r. 15 Express Delivery mail 60 65

321 "Erica tenuifolia"

1994. Heathers. Multicoloured.

859 95 c. Type **321** 55 55
860 95 c. "Erica urna-viridis" 55 55
861 95 c. "Erica decora" 55 55
862 95 c. "Erica aristata" 55 55
863 95 c. "Erica dichrus" 55 55

322 Warthogs (Eastern Transvaal) and Map (⅔-size illustration)

1995. Tourism. Multicoloured. (a) With face value.

864 50 c. Type **322** 40 25
865 50 c. Lost City resort (North-West Province) 40 25

(b) Inscr "Standardised mail" in English and Afrikaans

866 (60 c.) White rhinoceros and calf (KwaZulu/Natal) 40 25
867 (60 c.) Cape Town waterfront (Western Cape) 40 25
868 (60 c.) Baobab tree (Northern Transvaal) 40 40
869 (60 c.) Highland Route (Free State) 40 40
870 (60 c.) Augrabies Falls (Northern Cape) 40 40
871 (60 c.) Herd of elephants, Addo National Park (Eastern Cape) 40 40
872 (60 c.) Union Buildings, Pretoria (Gauteng) 40 40

323 De Havilland D.H.9 Biplane and Cheetah D Jet Fighter

1995. Aviation Anniversaries. Multicoloured.

873 50 c. Type **323** (75th anniv of South African Air Force) 45 30
874 95 c. Vickers Vimy "Silver Queen II" (75th anniv of first Trans-African flight) 60 60

324 Player running with Ball and Silhouettes

1995. World Cup Rugby Championship, South Africa. Multicoloured.

875 (60 c.) Type **324** 20 25
876 (60 c.) Player running with ball and silhouettes (vert) 20 25
877 1 r. 15 Player taking ball from scrum (68 × 26½ mm) 40 45

Nos. 875/6 are inscribed "STANDARD POSTAGE" in English and Afrikaans.

325 Rural Water Purification System

1995. 50th Anniv of C.S.I.R. (technological research organization).

879 **325** (60 c.) multicoloured 30 30

No. 879 is inscribed "Standardised mail" in English and Afrikaans.

326 Player with Ball

1995. South Africa's Victory in Rugby World Cup. Multicoloured.

880 (60 c.) Type **326** 30 30
881 (60 c.) South African player holding trophy aloft (vert) 30 30

Nos. 880/1 are inscribed "STANDARD POSTAGE" in English and Afrikaans.

327 Dr. John Gilchrist, South African Pilchards and "Africana" (oceanographic research ship)

1995. Centenary of Marine Science in South Africa.

882 **327** (60 c.) multicoloured 30 30

No. 882 is inscribed "Standard Postage" in English and Afrikaans.

329 People building Flag Wall

330 Papal Arms

1995. Masakhane Campaign.
884 **329** (60 c.) multicoloured (34 × 24 mm) 20 20
884b (60 c.) multicoloured (26 × 20 mm) 20 20
Nos. 884 and 884b are inscribed "STANDARD POSTAGE" in English and Afrikaans.

1995. Visit of Pope John Paul II.
885 **330** (60 c.) multicoloured . . . 40 30
No. 885 is inscribed "STANDARD POSTAGE" in English and Afrikaans.

331 Gandhi wearing Suit

332 Traditional African Postman

1995. 125th Birth Anniv (1994) of Mahatma Gandhi.
886 **331** (60 c.) violet 50 25
887 – 1 r. 40 brown 75 85
DESIGN: 1 r. 40, Gandhi wearing dhoti.
No. 886 is inscribed "STANDARD POSTAGE" in English and Afrikaans.

1995. World Post Day.
889 **332** (60 c.) multicoloured . . . 30 30
No. 889 is inscribed "STANDARD POSTAGE" in English and Afrikaans.

333 "50" and U.N. Emblem

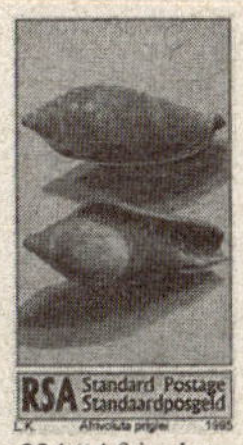

334 "Afrivoluta pringlei"

1995. 50th Annivs of United Nations and U.N.E.S.C.O. Multicoloured.
891 **333** (60 c.) multicoloured . . . 30 30
No. 891 is inscribed "STANDARD POSTAGE" in English and Afrikaans.

1995. Sea Shells. Multicoloured.
893 (60 c.) Type **334** 35 35
894 (60 c.) "Lyria africana" 35 35
895 (60 c.) "Marginella mosaica" . . 35 35
896 (60 c.) "Conus pictus" 35 35
897 (60 c.) "Gypreaea fultoni" . . 35 35
Nos. 893/7 are inscribed "STANDARD POSTAGE" in English and Afrikaans.
No. 893 is inscribed "priglei" in error.

335 Map of Africa and Player

336 South African Player, Map and Trophy

1996. African Nations Football Championship, South Africa. Map and Players.
898 **335** (60 c.) multicoloured ("RSA" in blue) . . . 35 35
899 – (60 c.) multicoloured ("RSA" in brown) . . . 35 35
900 – (60 c.) multicoloured ("RSA" in red) 35 35
901 – (60 c.) multicoloured ("RSA" in grey) 35 35
902 – (60 c.) multicoloured ("RSA" in green) 35 35
Nos. 898/903 are inscribed "STANDARD POSTAGE" in English and Afrikaans.

1996. South Africa's Victory in African Nations Football Championship.
904 **336** (60 c.) multicoloured . . . 30 20
No. 904 is inscribed "STANDARD POSTAGE" in English and Afrikaans.

MORE DETAILED LISTS
are given in the Stanley Gibbons Catalogues referred to in the country headings. For lists of current volumes see Introduction.

337 Historical Buildings, Bloemfontein

1996. 150th Anniv of City of Bloemfontein.
905 **337** (60 c.) multicoloured . . 40 20
No. 905 is inscribed "Standard Postage" in English and Afrikaans.

339 "Man in a Donkey Cart" (Gerard Sekoto)

1996. Gerard Sekoto (artist) Commemoration. Multicoloured.
907 1 r. Type **339** 30 30
908 2 r. "Song of the Pick" . . . 80 80

341 Children playing

1996. Youth Day.
911 **341** (60 c.) multicoloured . . . 30 20
No. 911 is inscribed "STANDARD POSTAGE" in English and Afrikaans.

342 Marathon Runners

1996. 75th Anniv of Comrades Marathon.
912 **342** (60 c.) multicoloured . . . 30 20
No. 912 is inscribed "Standard postage" in English and Afrikaans.

343 Cycling

344 Constitutional Assembly Logo

1996. Olympic Games, Atlanta. Multicoloured.
919 (70 c.) Type **343** 30 30
920 (70 c.) Swimming 30 30
921 (70 c.) Boxing 30 30
922 (70 c.) Running 30 30
923 (70 c.) Pole vaulting 30 30
924 1 r. 40 South African Olympic emblem 55 55
Nos. 919/24 are inscribed "STANDARD POSTAGE" in English and Afrikaans.

1996. New Democratic Constitution.
925 **344** (70 c.) green, red and black 30 30
926 (70 c.) blue, violet, and black 30 30
927 (70 c.) violet, yellow and black 30 30
928 (70 c.) blue, red and black 30 30
929 (70 c.) red, yellow and black 30 30
Nos. 925/9 are inscribed "Standard Postage" in English and Afrikaans.

345 "Sea Pioneer" (bulk carrier)

1996. 50th Anniv of South African Merchant Marine. Multicoloured.
930 (70 c.) Type **345** 40 40
931 (70 c.) "Winterberg" (container ship) 40 40
932 $1.40 "Langkloof" (freighter) . 80 80
933 $1.40 "Vaal" (liner) 80 80
Nos. 930/1 are inscribed "Standard Postage" in English and Afrikaans.

346 "Xhosa Woman" (G. Pemba)

347 Postman delivering Letters

1996. National Women's Day.
935 **346** 70 c. multicoloured . . . 30 25

1996. World Post Day.
936 **347** 70 c. multicoloured . . . 30 25

348 Candles and Holly

350 Max Theiler (Medicine, 1951)

1996. Christmas.
937 **348** 70 c. multicoloured . . . 25 25

1996. South African Nobel Laureates.
939 **350** (70 c.) violet and purple . 30 30
940 – (70 c.) green, purple and violet 30 30
941 – (70 c.) purple and violet . 30 30
942 – (70 c.) green, purple and violet 30 30
943 – (70 c.) violet and purple . 30 30
944 – (70 c.) violet and purple . 30 30
945 – (70 c.) green, purple and violet 30 30
946 – (70 c.) purple and violet . 30 30
947 – (70 c.) green, purple and violet 30 30
948 – (70 c.) violet and purple . 30 30
DESIGNS: No. 940, Albert Luthuli (Peace, 1961); 941, Alfred Nobel; 942, Allan Cormack (Medicine, 1979); 943, Aaron Klug (Chemistry, 1982); 944, Desmond Tutu (Peace, 1984); 945, Nadine Gordimer (Literature, 1991); 946, Nobel Prizes symbol; 947, Nelson Mandela (Peace, 1993); 948, F. W. de Klerk (Peace, 1993).
Nos. 939/48 are inscribed "Standard Postage" in English and Afrikaans.

351 Early Motor Car

1997. Centenary of Motoring in South Africa.
949 **351** (70 c.) multicoloured . . . 30 25
No. 949 is inscribed "STANDARD POSTAGE" in English and Afrikaans.

353 Vegetables and Water Pump

355 Election Day Poster

354 S.A.S. "Umkomaas" (minesweeper)

1997. National Water Conservation. Multicoloured.
951 (70 c.) Type **353** 25 30
952 (70 c.) Flowers and watering can 25 30
953 (70 c.) Child in bath 25 30
954 (70 c.) Building tools 25 30
955 (70 c.) Water cart and stand pipe 25 30
Nos. 951/5 are inscribed "STANDARD POSTAGE".

1997. 75th Anniv of South African Navy. Multicoloured.
956 (70 c.) Type **354** 15 20
957 (70 c.) S.A.S. "Emily Hobhouse" (submarine) and S.A.S. "President Steyn" (frigate) . 15 20
958 (70 c.) S.A.S. "Kobie Coetsee" (fast attack craft) 15 20
959 (70 c.) S.A.S. "Protea" (hydrographic survey ship) . 15 20
Nos. 956/9 are inscribed "Standard Postage" in English and Afrikaans.

1997. Freedom Day. Each black and red.
960 (1 r.) Type **355** 20 25
961 (1 r.) People queueing 20 25
962 (1 r.) People registering . . . 20 25
963 (1 r.) Voting booth 20 25
964 (1 r.) Woman placing vote in ballot box 20 25
Nos. 960/4, which are inscribed "STANDARD POSTAGE", were printed together, se-tenant, forming a composite design.

357 Zulu Baskets

359 White-breasted Cormorant

1997. Year of Cultural Experiences. Multicoloured.
966 (1 r.) Type **357** 20 25
967 (1 r.) Southern Sotho figure . 20 25
968 (1 r.) South Ndebele figure . . 20 25
969 (1 r.) Venda door 20 25
970 (1 r.) Tsonga medicine gourd . 20 25
971 (1 r.) Wooden pot, Northern Cape 20 25
972 (1 r.) Khoi walking stick . . . 20 25
973 (1 r.) Tswana knife handle . . 20 25
974 (1 r.) Xhosa pipe 20 25
975 (1 r.) Swazi vessel 20 25
Nos. 966/75 are inscribed "Standard Postage".

1997. World Environment Day. Waterbirds. Multicoloured.
977 (1 r.) Type **359** 20 25
978 (1 r.) Hamerkop 20 25
979 (1 r.) Pied kingfisher 20 25
980 (1 r.) Purple heron 20 25
981 (1 r.) Black-headed heron . . 20 25
982 (1 r.) Darter 20 25
983 (1 r.) Green-backed heron . . 20 25
984 (1 r.) White-faced duck . . . 20 25
985 (1 r.) Saddle-billed stork . . . 20 25
986 (1 r.) Water dikkop 20 25
Nos. 977/86 are inscribed "STANDARD POSTAGE".

360 Double-headed Class 6E 1 Electric Locomotives

1997. Inaurguration of Revived Blue Train Service. Multicoloured.
987 (1 r. 20) Type **360** 25 30
988 (1 r. 20) Double-headed Class 6E 1 electric locomotives (different) 25 30
989 (1 r. 20) Double-headed Class 25NC steam locomotives, 1960s 25 30
990 (1 r. 20) Double-headed Class 34,900 diesel locomotives on Modder River bridge . . . 25 30
991 (1 r. 20) Double-headed Class 34 diesel locomotives and baobab tree 25 30
Nos. 987/91 are inscribed "AIRMAIL POSTAGE RATE".

361 Nguni Breed

1997. Cattle Breeds. Multicoloured.
992 (1 r.) Type **361** 20 25
993 (1 r.) Bonsmara 20 25
994 (1 r.) Afrikander 20 25
995 (1 r.) Drakensberger 20 25
Nos. 992/5 are inscribed "Standard Postage" in English and Afrikaans.

362 Leopard Seal

1997. Antarctic Fauna. Multicoloured.
996 (1 r.) Type **362** 20 25
997 1 r. 20 Antarctic skua 25 30
998 1 r. 70 King penguin 35 40
No. 996 is inscribed "Standard Postage" in English and Afrikaans.

363 Enoch Sontonga and Verse from "Nkosi Sikelel'i Afrika"

1997. Heritage Day. Centenary of "Nkosi Sikele'i Afrika" (National Anthem). Multicoloured.
999 (1 r.) Type **363** 20 25
1000 (1 r.) As Type **363** but portrait at right 20 25
Nos. 999/1000 are inscribed "Standard Postage".

366 Bethlehem

367 Black Rhinoceros

1997. Christmas. 50th Anniv of S.A.N.T.A. (South African National Tuberculosis Association). Charity Labels. Multicoloured.
1003 (1 r.) Type **366** 20 25
1004 (1 r.) Cross of Lorraine and candles 20 25
1005 (1 r.) Cross of Lorraine, angels and candles 20 25
1006 (1 r.) Angel kneeling before Cross of Lorraine 20 25
1007 (1 r.) Father Christmas carrying sack 20 25
1008 (1 r.) Mary and Jesus 20 25
1009 (1 r.) Christmas trees 20 25
1010 (1 r.) Wise men on camels . . 20 25
1011 (1 r.) Christmas bell 20 25
1012 (1 r.) Child kneeling 20 25
Nos. 1003/12 are inscribed "STANDARD POSTAGE".

1998. Endangered Fauna (3rd series). Redrawn values as 1993–97 issue and new designs (Nos. 1030/4), all without frame and inscr "South Africa" only as T **367**. Multicoloured.

(c) Inscr "Standard Postage" (No. 1029) or "standard postage" (others).
1029 (1 r.) Type **367** 20 25
1030 (1 r.) Eland (vert) 20 25
1031 (1 r.) Greater kudu (vert) . . 20 25
1032 (1 r.) Impala (vert) 20 25
1033 (1 r.) Waterbuck (vert) . . . 20 25
1034 (1 r.) Blue wildebeest (vert) . . 20 25

(d) Inscr "Airmail Postcard".
1040 (1 r. 20) White rhinoceros . . 30 35
1041 (1 r. 20) Buffalo 30 35
1042 (1 r. 20) Lion 30 35
1043 (1 r. 20) Leopard 30 35
1044 (1 r. 20) African elephant . . 30 35

369 "Rescue 8" (lifeboat)

1998. 30th Anniv (1997) of National Sea Rescue Institute.
1052 **369** (1 r.) multicoloured . . . 20 25

OFFICIAL STAMPS

Prices for bilingual pairs are for the pair mint, for single stamps used.

1926. Optd **OFFICIAL. OFFISIEEL.** (with full points). (a) On stamp of 1913.
O1 **3** 2d. purple . . . . 18·00 1·75

(b) On pictorial issues.
O2 **6** ½d. black and green . . . . 5·50 1·50
O3 **7** 1d. black and red . . . . . 3·00 50
O4 **8** 6d. green and orange . . . . £550 10·00

1928. Optd **OFFICIAL OFFISIEEL** (without full points).
O 7 **6** ½d. black and green (No. 42) . . . . 2·25 35
O39 ½d. black and green (No. 114) 70 15
O 8 **7** 1d. black and red (No. 31) . . . . 3·00 45
O21aw 1d. grey and red (No. 56) 1·75 20
O22 **22** 1½d. green and gold . . 26·00 1·75
O44 **34a** 1½d. green and buff . . . 1·40 30
O 5a **11** 2d. grey and purple (No. 34) . . . . 4·00 1·50
O14 2d. grey and lilac (No. 44) 6·00 1·50
O15 2d. blue and violet (No. 44d) . . . . . . £100 9·00
O45 2d. blue and violet (No. 58) . . . . 1·00 20
O30 2d. grey and purple (No. 58a) . . . . 7·00 2·25
O36 **54** 2d. slate and violet . . 2·50 1·75
O45 **68** 2d. blue and violet . . 1·00 20
O16 **8** 6d. green and orange (No. 47) . . . . 7·00 85
O46 6d. green and red (No. 119a) . . . . 1·00 35
O10 – 1s. brown and blue (No. 36) . . . . 32·00 9·50
O47 – 1s. brown & blue (No. 120) . . . . 5·50 2·00
O18 – 2s. 6d. green and brown (No. 49) . . . . . . 48·00 8·50
O48 – 2s. 6d. green and brown (No. 121) . . . . . 8·50 3·50
O19 – 2s. 6d. blue and brown (No. 49a) . . . . . 30·00 6·50
O50 – 5s. black and green (No. 64a) . . . . . 60·00 6·50
O51 – 10s. blue and brown (No. 39) . . . . 70·00 22·00

POSTAGE DUE STAMPS

D 1

D 2

1914. Perf or roul.
D11 **D 1** ½d. black and green . . 70 1·75
D12 1d. black and red . . . 80 15
D13 1½d. black and brown . . 90 1·25
D14 2d. black and violet . . 80 70
D 4 3d. black and blue . . 2·25 40
D 5 5d. black and brown . . 4·00 23·00
D16 6d. black and grey . . 11·00 6·00
D 7 1s. red and black . . . 60·00 £140

1927.
D17 **D 2** ½d. black and green . . 70 3·25
D18 1d. black and red . . . 1·25 30
D19 2d. black and mauve . . 1·25 30
D23 2d. black and purple . 7·00 1·75
D20 3d. black and blue . . 8·00 19·00
D28 3d. indigo and blue . . 6·50 30
D21 6d. black and grey . . 19·00 6·00
D29 6d. green and brown . 24·00 8·50
D29a 6d. green and orange . 10·00 4·00

D 3

D 5

1943.
D30 **D 3** ½d. green . . . . 10·00 30
D31 1d. red . . . . 9·50 10
D32 2d. violet . . . . 6·50 15
D33 3d. blue . . . . 48·00 1·25
The above mint prices are for horiz units of three.

1948. Frame as Type D **2**, but with bolder figures of value and capital "D".
D34 ½d. black and green . . . . 6·00 10·00
D39 1d. black and red 70 30
D40 2d. black and violet 50 20
D41 3d. indigo and blue . . . . 4·50 2·00
D42 4d. turquoise and green . . 12·00 14·00
D43 6d. green and orange . . . 7·00 9·00
D44 1s. brown and purple . . . 12·00 14·00

1961.
D45 **D 5** 1 c. black and red . . . 20 3·50
D46 2 c. black and violet . . 35 3·50
D47 4 c. turquoise and green 80 8·00
D48 5 c. indigo and blue . . 1·75 8·00
D49 6 c. green and orange . 8·50 8·50
D50 10 c. sepia and brown . 9·00 10·00

D 6

D 8

1961. (A) Inscr as in Type D **6**; (B) English at top and left, Afrikans at bottom and right.
D59 **D 6** 1 c. black and red (A) 20 55
D60 1 c. black and red (B) . 20 30
D61 2 c. black and violet (A) 30 1·25
D53 2 c. black and violet (B) 40 55
D54 4 c. myrtle and green (A) 3·25 2·25
D54a 4 c. myrtle and green (B) 15·00 20·00
D63 4 c. black and green (A) 27·00 27·00
D64 4 c. black and green (B) 27·00 27·00
D55 5 c. indigo and blue (B) 2·75 4·00
D65 5 c. black and blue (A) 50 50
D66 5 c. black and blue (B) 50 50
D67 **D 6** 6 c. green & salmon (A) 5·00 8·50
D68 6 c. green & salmon (B) 5·00 8·50
D58 10 c. sepia and brown (B) 3·50 1·75
D69 10 c. black and brown (A) 1·00 2·75
D70 10 c. black and brown (B) 1·00 2·75

1972.
D75 **D 8** 1 c. green . . . . 50 2·00
D76 2 c. orange . . . . . . 70 2·75
D77 4 c. plum . . . . 1·75 3·25
D78 6 c. yellow . . . . . . 1·75 4·50
D79 8 c. blue . . . . 2·00 5·00
D80 10 c. red . . . . 6·00 7·00

SOUTH ARABIAN FEDERATION

Comprising Aden and most of the territories of the former Western Aden Protectorate plus one from the Eastern Aden Protectorate. The South Arabian Federation became fully independent on 30 November 1967.

1963. 100 cents = 1 shilling.
1965. 1000 fils = 1 dinar.

1963. Cent of Red Cross. As T **33** of Antigua, but without portrait. Value in English and Arabic.
1 15 c. red and black 40 30
2 1 s. 25 red and blue 85 95

2 Federal Crest

3 Federal Flag

1965.
3 **2** 5 f. blue 20 10
4 10 f. lavender 20 10
5 15 f. green 20 10
6 20 f. green 20 10
7 25 f. brown 20 10
8 30 f. bistre 20 10
9 35 f. brown 20 10
10 50 f. red 20 10
11 65 f. green 30 30
12 75 f. red 30 10
13 **3** 100 f. multicoloured 30 10
14 250 f. multicoloured . . . . 4·00 45
15 500 f. multicoloured . . . . 8·00 50
16 1 d. multicoloured . . . . . 15·00 8·00

4 I.C.Y. Emblem

1965. International Co-operation Year.
17 **4** 5 f. purple and turquoise . . 20 10
18 65 f. green and lavender . . 70 20

5 Sir Winston Churchill and St. Paul's Cathedral in Wartime

1966. Churchill Commem. Designs in black, cerise and gold with background in colours given.
19 **5** 5 f. blue 10 10
20 10 f. green 30 10
21 65 f. brown 80 20
22 125 f. violet . . . . 1·25 1·75

6 Footballer's Legs, Ball and Jules Rimet Cup

1966. World Cup Football Championships, England.
23 **6** 10 f. multicoloured 50 10
24 50 f. multicoloured . . . . . 1·50 20

7 W.H.O. Building

1966. Inaug of W.H.O. Headquarters, Geneva.
25 **7** 10 f. black, green and blue . 50 10
26 75 f. black, purple and brown 1·25 45

8 "Education"

1966. 20th Anniv of U.N.E.S.C.O.

27	8	10 f. multicoloured	30	20
28	–	65 f. yellow, violet and olive	1·25	1·40
29	–	125 f. black, purple & orange	3·25	4·75

DESIGNS: 65 f. "Science"; 125 f. "Culture".

For later issues see **SOUTHERN YEMEN** and **YEMEN PEOPLE'S DEMOCRATIC REPUBLIC** in Volume 2.

SOUTH AUSTRALIA

A state of the Australian Commonwealth whose stamps it now uses.

12 pence = 1 shilling;
20 shillings = 1 pound

1

1855. Imperf.

1	1	1d. green	£2500	£350
9		2d. red	£650	40·00
3		6d. blue	£2000	£150
12		1s. orange	£3750	£325

3

4

1858. Roul or perf.

20	1	1d. green	42·00	23·00
26		2d. red	42·00	2·75
112	3	3d. on 4d. blue	60·00	15·00
138		4d. purple	38·00	2·00
141	1	6d. blue	40·00	1·75
118	4	8d. on 9d. brown	60·00	5·00
124		9d. purple	10·00	3·25
35		10d. on 9d. orange	£130	24·00
38	1	1s. yellow	£450	28·00
130		1s. brown	24·00	3·00
151	3	2s. red	22·00	9·00

The 3d., 8d. and 10d. are formed by surcharges: **3-PENCE**, **8 PENCE** and **TEN PENCE** (curved).

15

11

12

1868. Various frames.

191	15	½d. brown	2·50	30
173	11	1d. green	4·50	20
176		1d. red	2·75	10
177	12	2d. orange	4·25	10
178		2d. violet	2·50	10
229b	–	2½d. on 4d. green	8·00	1·75
192a	–	3d. green	5·00	90
193	–	4d. violet	6·00	40
230a	–	5d. on 6d. brown	16·00	3·75
194	–	6d. blue	7·00	65

Nos. 230 and 231 are surch in figures over straight or curved line.

1882. Surch **HALF - PENNY** in two lines.

181	11	½d. on 1d. green	11·00	3·25

19

24 G.P.O., Adelaide

22 Red Kangaroo

23

1886.

195a	19	2s. 6d. mauve	27·00	6·00
196a		5s. pink	35·00	12·00
197a		10s. green	80·00	35·00
198a		15s. brown	£300	£120
199a		£1 blue	£150	80·00

1894.

242	24	½d. green	1·50	40
236	22	2½d. violet	12·00	70
237		2½d. blue	4·50	30
238a	23	5d. purple	6·50	45

1902. Inscr "POSTAGE" at top.

268	19	3d. green	3·50	1·00
269		4d. orange	5·00	1·50
270		6d. green	6·00	1·50
285		8d. blue	7·00	3·25
273		9d. red	8·00	2·25
274		10d. orange	11·00	4·50
303b		1s. brown	10·00	2·50
276a		2s. 6d. violet	22·00	7·00
290		5s. red	40·00	26·00
278		10s. green	£100	60·00
292a		£1 blue	£130	80·00

OFFICIAL STAMPS

1874. Various postage issues optd **O.S.** A. Issue of 1858.

O 6	1	1d. green	£1000	16·00
O 7	3	3d. on 4d. blue	£1200	£475
O17		4d. mauve	26·00	2·50
O19	1	6d. blue	40·00	4·00
O26	4	8d. on 9d. brown	£900	£375
O11		9d. purple	£600	£250
O33	1	1s. brown	27·00	4·50
O35	3	2s. red	60·00	9·00

B. Issues of 1868–82.

O60	15	½d. brown	9·00	3·50
O48	11	½d. on 1d. green	55·00	14·00
O56		1d. green	8·50	40
O81		1d. red	9·00	85
O44	12	2d. orange	7·50	40
O82		2d. violet	9·00	50
O71	–	2½d. on 4d. green	32·00	4·50
O84	–	4d. violet	48·00	2·25
O72	–	5d. on 6d. brown	38·00	12·00
O67	–	6d. blue	15·00	1·25

C. Issue of 1886.

O86	19	2s. 6d. violet	£2000	£1600
O87		5s. pink	£2000	£1600

D. Issue of 1894.

O80	24	½d. green	8·50	4·25
O75	22	2½d. blue	42·00	4·00
O74	23	5d. purple	55·00	6·00

SOUTH GEORGIA

An island in the Antarctic. From May 1980 to 1985 used stamps inscribed FALKLAND ISLANDS DEPENDENCIES and thereafter those of South Georgia and the South Sandwich Islands (q.v.).

1963. 12 pence = 1 shilling;
20 shillings = 1 pound.
1971. 100 pence = 1 pound.

1 Reindeer

1963.

1	1	½d. red	50	75
2	–	1d. blue	70	50
3	–	2d. blue	1·00	60
4	–	2½d. black	4·50	2·00
5	–	3d. bistre	2·50	30
6	–	4d. green	4·50	80
7	–	5½d. violet	2·00	30
8	–	6d. orange	75	30
9	–	9d. blue	4·00	1·50
10	–	1s. purple	75	30
11	–	2s. olive and blue	18·00	4·50
12	–	2s. 6d. blue	21·00	4·00
13	–	5s. brown	21·00	4·00
14	–	10s. mauve	42·00	10·00
15	–	£1 blue	85·00	48·00
16	–	£1 black	10·00	16·00

DESIGNS—HORIZ: 2½d. King penguins and chinstrap penguin; 4d. Fin whale; 5½d. Southern elephant-seal; 9d. Whale-catcher; 1s. Leopard seal; 2s. Shackleton's Cross; 2s. 6d. Wandering albatross; 5s. Southern elephant seal and South American fur seal; £1 (No. 15) Blue whale. VERT: 1d. South Sandwich Islands map; 2d. Sperm whale; 3d. South American fur seal; 6d. Light-mantled sooty albatross; 10s. Plankton and krill; £1 (No. 16) King penguins.

1971. Decimal Currency. Nos. 1/14 surch.

18a	½p. on ½d. red	1·00	90
19	1p. on 1d. blue	1·50	55
55	1½p. on 5½d. violet	90	1·75
21	2p. on 2d. blue	70	50
22	2½p. on 2½d. black	1·50	40
23	3p. on 3d. bistre	1·00	50
24	4p. on 4d. green	90	50
25	5p. on 6d. orange	90	50
26	6p. on 9d. blue	1·50	70
27	7½p. on 1s. purple	2·00	70
63w	10p. on 2s. olive and blue	1·75	8·00
64w	15p. on 2s. 6d. blue	2·00	8·00
65w	25p. on 5s. brown	1·75	8·00
66	50p. on 10s. mauve	1·75	7·50

6 "Endurance" beset in Weddell Sea

1972. 50th Death Anniv of Sir Ernest Shackleton. Multicoloured.

32	1½p. Type 6	1·00	1·25
33	5p. Launching of the longboat "James Caird"	1·25	1·75
34	10p. Route of the "James Caird"	1·75	2·00
35	20p. Sir Ernest Shackleton and the "Quest"	2·00	2·25

1972. Royal Silver Wedding. As T **52** of Ascension, but with Elephant Seal and King Penguins in background.

36	5p. green	75	35
37	10p. violet	75	35

1973. Royal Wedding. As T **47** of Anguilla. Background colours given. Multicoloured.

38	5p. brown	25	10
39	15p. lilac	35	20

8 Churchill and Westminster Skyline

1974. Birth Cent of Sir Winston Churchill. Mult.

40	15p. Type 8	1·50	1·25
41	25p. Churchill and warship	1·50	1·25

9 Captain Cook

10 "Discovery" and Biological Laboratory

1975. Bicentenary of Possession by Captain Cook.

43	2p. Type 9	2·25	1·25
44	8p. H.M.S. "Resolution"	3·50	2·00
45	16p. Possession Bay	3·75	2·25

Nos. 44/5 are horiz.

1976. 50th Anniv of "Discovery" Investigations. Multicoloured.

46	2p. Type 10	1·50	45
47	8p. "William Scoresby" and water-sampling bottles	1·75	60
48	11p. "Discovery II" and plankton net	2·00	65
49	25p. Biological station and krill	2·50	95

11 The Queen and Retinue after Coronation

1977. Silver Jubilee. Multicoloured.

50	6p. Visit by Prince Philip, 1957	50	30
51	11p. Queen Elizabeth and Westminster Abbey	70	35
52	33p. Type 11	80	50

12 Fur Seal

13 H.M.S. "Resolution"

1978. 25th Anniv of Coronation.

67	–	25p. deep blue, blue and silver	35	1·10
68	–	25p. multicoloured	35	1·10
69	12	25p. deep blue, blue and silver	35	1·10

DESIGNS: No. 67, Panther of Henry VI; No. 68, Queen Elizabeth II.

1979. Bicentenary of Captain Cook's Voyages, 1768–79. Multicoloured.

70	3p. Type 13	1·50	1·25
71	6p. "Resolution" and Map of South Georgia and S. Sandwich Isles showing route	1·50	1·00
72	11p. King penguin (from drawing by George Forster)	2·50	2·25
73	25p. Flaxman/Wedgwood medallion of Capt. Cook	2·75	2·75

SOUTH GEORGIA AND THE SOUTH SANDWICH ISLANDS

Under the new constitution, effective 3 October 1985, South Georgia and the South Sandwich Islands ceased to be dependencies of the Falkland Islands.

100 pence = 1 pound

1986. 60th Birthday of Queen Elizabeth II. As T **110** of Ascension. Multicoloured.

153	10p. Four generations of Royal Family at Prince Charles's christening, 1948	35	35
154	24p. With Prince Charles and Lady Diana Spencer, Buckingham Palace, 1981	60	65
155	29p. In robes of Order of the British Empire, St. Paul's Cathedral, London	60	70
156	45p. At banquet, Canada, 1976	80	95
157	58p. At Crown Agents Head Office London, 1983	1·00	1·25

1986. Royal Wedding. As T **153** of Falkland Islands. Multicoloured.

158	17p. Prince Andrew and Miss Sarah Ferguson at Ascot	75	1·00
159	22p. Wedding photograph	85	1·25
160	29p. Prince Andrew with Westland Lynx helicopter on board H.M.S. "Brazen"	1·50	1·50

26 Southern Black-backed Gull

1987. Birds. Multicoloured.

161	1p. Type 26	55	70
162	2p. Blue-eyed cormorant	65	80
163	3p. Snowy sheathbill (vert)	80	90
164	4p. Great skua (vert)	65	90
165	5p. Pintado petrel	65	90
166	6p. Georgian diving petrel	65	90
167	7p. South Georgia pipit (vert)	75	1·10
168	8p. Georgian teal ("South Georgian Pintail") (vert)	75	1·10
169	9p. Fairy prion	75	1·40
170	10p. Chinstrap penguin	1·00	1·40
171	20p. Macaroni penguin (vert)	1·25	1·75
172	25p. Light-mantled sooty albatross (vert)	1·25	1·75
173	50p. Giant petrel (vert)	1·75	2·25
174	£1 Wandering albatross	2·25	3·50
175	£3 King penguin (vert)	6·00	7·50

1987. 30th Anniv of International Geophysical Year. As T **39** of British Antarctic Territory.

176	24p. black and blue	70	55
177	29p. multicoloured	75	60
178	58p. multicoloured	1·40	1·25

DESIGNS: 24p. I.G.Y. logo; 29p. Grytviken; 58p. Glaciologist using hand-drill to take core sample.

27 "Gaimardia trapesina"

1988. Sea Shells. Multicoloured.

179	10p. Type 27	55	30
180	24p. "Margarella tropidophoroides"	85	60
181	29p. "Trophon geversianus"	90	65
182	58p. "Chlanidota densesculpta"	1·40	1·25

1988. 300th Anniv of Lloyd's of London. As T **123** of Ascension.

183	10p. black and brown	40	40
184	24p. multicoloured	75	75
185	29p. black and green	80	80
186	58p. black and red	1·40	1·40

DESIGNS—VERT: 10p. Queen Mother at opening of new Lloyd's building, 1957; 58p. "Horatio" (tanker) on fire, 1916. HORIZ: 24p. "Lindblad Explorer" (cruise liner); 29p. Whaling station, Leith Harbour.

28 Glacier Headwall

1989. Glacier Formations. Multicoloured.

187	10p. Type **28**	40	35
188	24p. Accumulation area	80	70
189	29p. Ablation area	90	80
190	58p. Calving front	1·60	1·40

29 Retracing Shackleton's Trek

30 "Brutus", Prince Olav Harbour

1989. 25th Anniv of Combined Services Expedition to South Georgia. Multicoloured.

191	10p. Type **29**	40	35
192	24p. Surveying at Royal Bay	90	70
193	29p. H.M.S. "Protector" (ice patrol ship)	1·00	80
194	58p. Raising Union Jack on Mount Paget	1·60	1·40

1990. 90th Birthday of Queen Elizabeth the Queen Mother. As T **134** of Ascension.

195	26p. multicoloured	1·00	1·25
196	£1 black and blue	2·75	3·25

DESIGNS—(21×36 mm): 26p. Queen Mother. (29×37 mm): King George VI and Queen Elizabeth with A.R.P. wardens, 1940.

1990. Wrecks and Hulks. Multicoloured.

197	12p. Type **30**	55	40
198	26p. "Bayard", Ocean Harbour	1·00	80
199	31p. "Karrakatta", Husvik	1·10	95
200	62p. "Louise", Grytviken	1·90	1·75

1991. 65th Birthday of Queen Elizabeth II and 70th Birthday of Prince Philip. As T **139** of Ascension. Multicoloured.

201	31p. Queen Elizabeth II	1·00	1·40
202	31p. Prince Philip in Grenadier Guards uniform	1·00	1·40

31 Contest between two Bull Elephant Seals

1991. Elephant Seals. Multicoloured.

203	12p. Type **31**	50	50
204	26p. Adult elephant seal	1·00	1·00
205	29p. Seal throwing sand	1·10	1·10
206	31p. Head of elephant seal	1·10	1·10
207	34p. Seals on beach	1·25	1·25
208	62p. Cow seal with pup	2·00	2·00

1992. 40th Anniv of Queen Elizabeth II's Accession. As T **143** of Ascension. Multicoloured.

209	7p. Ice-covered mountains	30	30
210	14p. Zavodovski Island	45	55
211	29p. Gulbrandsen Lake	80	95
212	34p. Three portraits of Queen Elizabeth	90	1·10
213	68p. Queen Elizabeth II	1·40	1·50

32 Adult Teal and Young Bird

1992. Endangered Species. Georgian Teal ("South Georgia Teal"). Multicoloured.

214	2p. Type **32**	40	20
215	6p. Adult with eggs	50	30
216	12p. Teals swimming	70	50
217	20p. Adult and two chicks	90	90

1992. 10th Anniv of Liberation. As T **169** of St. Helena. Multicoloured.

218	14p. + 6p. King Edward Point	70	70
219	29p. + 11p. "Queen Elizabeth 2" (liner) in Cumberland Bay	1·25	1·25
220	34p. + 16p. Royal Marines hoisting Union Jack on South Sandwich Islands	1·60	1·60
221	68p. + 32p. H.M.S. "Endurance" (ice patrol ship) and Westland Wasp helicopter	3·00	3·00

33 Disused Whale Factory, Grytviken

1993. Opening of South Georgia Whaling Museum. Multicoloured.

223	15p. Type **33**	55	55
224	31p. Whaler's lighter and whale bones	1·00	1·00
225	36p. Aerial view of King Edward Cove	1·25	1·25
226	72p. Museum building	2·25	2·50

34 Pair of Swimming Penguins

1993. Macaroni Penguin. Multicoloured.

227	16p. Type **34**	60	45
228	34p. Group of penguins	1·25	1·00
229	39p. Two juvenile penguins	1·40	1·25
230	78p. Two adult penguins	2·25	2·25

35 Hourglass Dolphin

1994. Whales and Dolphins. Multicoloured.

231	1p. Type **35**	10	10
232	2p. Southern right whale dolphin	10	10
233	5p. Long-finned pilot whale	10	10
234	8p. Southern bottlenose whale	15	20
235	9p. Killer whale	20	25
236	10p. Minke whale	20	25
237	20p. Sei whale	40	45
238	25p. Humpback whale	50	55
239	50p. Southern right whale	1·00	1·10
240	£1 Sperm whale	2·00	2·10
241	£3 Fin whale	6·00	6·25
242	£5 Blue whale	10·00	10·50

1994. "Hong Kong '94" International Stamp Exhibition. Nos. 227/30 optd **HONG KONG '94** and emblem.

243	16p. Type **34**	60	60
244	34p. Group of penguins	1·25	1·25
245	39p. Two juvenile penguins	1·40	1·40
246	78p. Two adult penguins	2·25	2·25

36 Bull Elephant Seals

1994. "Life in the Freezer". Scenes from the B.B.C. Natural History Unit series. Multicoloured.

247	17p. Type **36**	50	50
248	35p. Young fur seal (vert)	90	90
249	40p. Pair of grey-headed albatrosses	1·60	1·60
250	65p. King penguins in courtship display (vert)	2·50	2·50

37 Map of Jason Harbour

1994. Centenary of C. A. Larsen's First Voyage to South Georgia. Multicoloured.

251	17p. Type **37**	60	60
252	35p. "Castor" (whaling ship), 1886	1·10	1·10
253	40p. "Hertha" (whaling ship), 1886	1·25	1·25
254	65p. "Jason" (whaling ship), 1881	2·25	2·50

1994. 50th Anniv of Second World War. As T **161** of Ascension. Multicoloured.

255	50p. H.M.S. "Queen of Bermuda" (armed merchant cruiser), Leith Harbour	1·50	1·75
256	50p. 4-inch coastal gun, Hansen Point	1·50	1·75

Nos. 255/6 were printed together, se-tenant, forming a composite design

38 "Damien II" (research schooner)

1995. Sailing Ships. Multicoloured.

258	35p. Type **38**	1·25	1·50
259	40p. "Curlew" (cutter)	1·40	1·60
260	76p. "Mischief" (yacht)	2·25	2·50

39 Sir Ernest Shackleton and Ridge 2493

1996. 80th Anniv of Sir Ernest Shackleton's Trek across South Georgia. Multicoloured.

261	15p. Type **39**	65	65
262	20p. Frank Worsley and King Haakon Bay	70	70
263	30p. Map of route	85	85
264	65p. Tom Crean and Manager's villa, Stromness whaling station	1·40	1·40

40 Chinstrap Penguin swimming

1996. Chinstrap Penguins. Multicoloured.

265	17p. Type **40**	55	55
266	35p. Mutual display	90	90
267	40p. Adult feeding chicks	1·10	1·10
268	76p. Feeding on krill	1·90	1·90

1997. Golden Wedding of Queen Elizabeth and Prince Philip. As T **87** of Kiribati. Multicoloured.

270	15p. Queen Elizabeth wearing red hat, 1996	40	40
271	15p. Prince Philip in carriage-driving at Royal Windsor Horse Show	40	40
272	17p. Queen Elizabeth with show jumping team, 1993	45	45
273	17p. Prince Philip smiling	45	45
274	40p. Princess Anne on horseback and Queen Elizabeth	1·25	1·25
275	40p. Zara Phillips horse riding and Prince Philip	1·25	1·25

Nos. 270/1, 272/3 and 274/5 respectively were printed together, se-tenant, with the backgrounds forming composite designs.

42 "Explorer" (cruise ship)

1998. Tourism. Multicoloured.

279	30p. Type **42**	80	90
280	35p. Wandering albatross	90	90
281	40p. Elephant seal	1·00	1·00
282	65p. Post Office at King Edward Point	1·75	1·75

43 Grytviken and Sugartop Mountain

1999. Island Views. Multicoloured.

283	9p. Type **43**	30	30
284	17p. Abandoned sealing ships, Grytviken	50	50
285	35p. King Edward Point	90	90
286	40p. South Georgia from the sea	1·00	1·00
287	65p. Grytviken Church	1·50	1·50

SOUTH WEST AFRICA

A territory in S.W. Africa formerly the German Colony of German South West Africa (q.v. in Volume 1). Administered by South Africa until 1990 when it became independent as Namibia.

1923. 12 pence = 1 shilling;
20 shillings = 1 pound.
1961. 100 cents = 1 rand.

NOTE. Stamps overprinted for South West Africa are always of South Africa, except where otherwise indicated.

"Bilingual" in heading indicates that the stamps are inscribed alternately in English and Afrikaans throughout the sheet, "Bilingual" is not repeated in the heading where bilingual stamps of South Africa are overprinted.

Our prices for surch issues are for mint bilingual pairs and used single stamps of either inscription.

1923. Optd **South West Africa.** or **Zuid-West Afrika.** alternately

1	**2**	½d. green	2·25	1·00
2		1d. red	2·75	1·00
3		2d. purple	3·75	1·50
4		3d. blue	7·50	2·75
5		4d. orange and green	13·00	4·00
6		6d. black and violet	8·00	4·00
7		1s. yellow	23·00	5·00
8		1s. 3d. violet	30·00	5·50
9		2s. 6d. purple and green	70·00	18·00
10		5s. purple and blue	£160	50·00
11		10s. blue and green	£1600	£400
12		£1 green and red	£900	£250

1923. Optd **Zuidwest Afrika.** or **South West Africa.*** alternately.

16	**2**	½d. green	5·00	3·50
30		1d. red	3·25	1·40
18		2d. purple	5·00	1·25
19		3d. blue	5·00	1·25
20		4d. yellow and green	6·00	2·75
34		6d. black and violet	8·00	5·00
35		1s. yellow	11·00	5·00
36		1s. 3d. violet	15·00	5·00
37		2s. 6d. purple and green	35·00	10·00
38		5s. purple and blue	55·00	14·00
39		10s. blue and green	85·00	20·00
40a		£1 green and red	£250	90·00

*The English overprint is the same, for the purposes of this catalogue, as that on Nos. 1/12.

1926. Optd **South West Africa.** (on stamps inscr in English) or **Suidwes Afrika.** (on stamps inscr in Afrikaans) alternately.

41	**6**	½d. black and green	3·75	1·00
42	**7**	1d. black and red	3·00	80
49	**11**	2d. grey and purple	4·50	1·75
50	–	3d. black and red	4·50	2·50
43	**8**	6d. green and orange	29·00	7·00
51	–	1s. brown and blue	15·00	4·00
52	–	2s. 6d. green and brown	45·00	13·00
53	–	5s. black and green	75·00	20·00
54	–	10s. blue and brown	85·00	20·00

1926. Optd **SOUTH WEST AFRICA** in two lines or **SUIDWES-AFRIKA** in one line. Imperf or perf.

44A	**10**	4d. blue	65	2·75

1927. Optd as Nos. 41/2 and 43 but with Afrikaans opt on stamp inscr in English and vice versa.

45	**6**	½d. black and green	1·60	80
46	**7**	1d. black and red	1·60	50
47	**8**	6d. green and orange	14·00	3·00

1927. Optd **SOUTH WEST AFRICA** in one line. Imperf.

48	**10**	4d. blue	7·50	19·00

1927. Optd **S.W.A.**

56	**2**	1s. 3d. violet	1·25	6·00
57		£1 olive and red	£120	£180

1927. Optd **S.W.A.**

58	**6**	½d. black and green	2·00	75
59	**7**	1d. black and red	1·25	55
60	**11**	2d. grey and purple	7·00	1·50
61	–	3d. black and red	6·00	3·25
62	–	4d. brown	18·00	7·00
63	**8**	6d. green and orange	13·00	2·75
64	–	1s. brown and blue	24·00	5·00
65	–	2s. 6d. green and brown	45·00	11·00
66	–	5s. black and green	65·00	18·00
67	–	10s. blue and brown	£120	28·00

1930. Air. Optd **S.W.A.**

72	**17**	4d. green	1·25	6·00
73		1s. orange	3·50	15·00

12 Kori Bustard

1931. Bilingual pairs.

74	**12**	½d. black and green	2·00	10
75	–	1d. blue and red	1·90	10
76	–	2d. blue and brown	60	15
77	–	3d. dull blue and blue	60	15
78	–	4d. green and purple	1·50	20
79	–	6d. blue and brown	1·00	20
80	–	1s. brown and blue	1·25	25
81	–	1s. 3d. violet and yellow	9·50	50
82	–	2s. 6d. red and grey	23·00	1·75
83	–	5s. green and brown	20·00	2·75
84	–	10s. brown and green	55·00	7·00
85	–	£1 red and green	£110	12·00

DESIGNS: 1d. Cape Cross; 2d. Bogenfels; 3d. Windhoek; 4d. Waterberg; 6d. Luderitz Bay; 1s. Bush scene; 1s. 3d. Elands; 2s. 6d. Mountain zebra and wildebeests; 5s. Herero huts; 10s. Welwitschia plant; £1 Okuwahaken Falls.

24 Fokker Monoplane over Windhoek

1931. Air. Bilingual pairs.

86	**24**	3d. brown and blue	32·00	3·50
87	–	10d. black and brown	55·00	9·00

DESIGN: 10d. Handley Page H.P.25 Hendon biplane over Windhoek.

26

1935. Silver Jubilee.

88	**26**	1d. black and red	1·00	25
89		2d. black and brown	1·00	25
90		3d. black and blue	13·00	17·00
91		6d. black and purple	6·00	9·00

1935. Voortrekker Memorial. Nos. 50/3 of South Africa optd **S.W.A.**

92	½d. + ½d. black and green	1·00	75
93	1d. + ½d. black and pink	1·50	40
94	2d. + 1d. green and purple	5·50	80
95	3d. + 1½d. green and blue	16·00	4·00

27 Mail Transport

28

1937. Bilingual pair.

96	**27**	1½d. brown	18·00	25

1937. Coronation. Bilingual pairs.

97	**28**	½d. black and green	50	15
98		1d. black and red	50	15
99		1½d. black and orange	50	15
100		2d. black and brown	50	15
101		3d. black and blue	50	15
102		4d. black and purple	50	20
103		6d. black and yellow	60	20
104		1s. black and grey	80	25

1938. Voortrekker Centenary Fund. Nos. 76/9 of South Africa optd **S.W.A.**

105	½d. + ½d. blue and green	8·00	1·75
106	1d. + 1d. blue and red	18·00	1·00
107	1½d. + 1½d. brown & green	22·00	2·75
108	3d. + 3d. blue	42·00	6·50

1938. Voortrekker Commem. Nos. 80/1 of South Africa optd **S.W.A.**

109	1d. blue and red	10·00	1·50
110	1½d. blue and brown	12·00	1·75

1939. 250th Anniv of Landing of Huguenots in South Africa. Nos. 82/4 of South Africa optd **S.W.A.**

111	½d. + ½d. brown and green	11·00	1·10
112	1d. + 1d. green and red	15·00	1·25
113	1½d. + 1½d. green & purple	20·00	1·25

1941. War Effort. Nos. 88/94a of South Africa optd **SWA**.

114a	½d. green	65	15
115	1d. red	55	15
116	1½d. green	55	15
121	2d. violet	50	40
117	3d. blue	22·00	1·00
118	4d. brown	6·50	1·00
119	6d. orange	2·50	50
122	1s. brown	60	40
120	1s. 3d. brown	11·00	1·25

1943. War Effort. Nos. 97/104 of South Africa optd **SWA**.

123	½d. green (T)	40	10
124	1d. red (T)	1·25	10
125	1½d. brown (P)	45	10
126	2d. violet (P)	5·00	10
127	3d. blue (T)	3·25	45
129	4d. green (T)	2·00	45
128	6d. orange (P)	5·00	30
130b	1s. brown (P)	4·00	30

The units refered to above consist of pairs (P) or triplets (T).

1945. Victory. Nos. 108/10 of South Africa optd **SWA**.

131	1d. brown and red	25	10
132	2d. blue and violet	30	10
133	3d. blue	1·25	10

1947. Royal Visit. Nos. 111/13 of South Africa optd **SWA**.

134	1d. black and red	10	10
135	2d. violet	10	10
136	3d. blue	15	10

1948. Silver Wedding. No. 125 of South Africa optd **SWA**.

137	3d. blue and silver	1·50	10

1949. 75th Anniv of U.P.U. Nos 128/30 of South Africa optd **SWA**.

138	½d. mauve	1·00	25
139	1½d. red	1·00	15
140	3d. blue	1·50	25

1949. Inauguration of Voortrekker Monument Pretoria. Nos. 131/3 of South Africa optd **S W A**.

141	1d. mauve	10	10
142	1½d. green	10	10
143	3d. blue	15	25

1952. Tercentenary of Landing of Van Riebeeck. Nos. 136/40 of South Africa optd **SWA**.

144	½d. purple and sepia	10	40
145	1d. green	10	10
146	2d. violet	50	10
147	4½d. blue	30	2·50
148	1s. brown	1·25	20

33 Queen Elizabeth II and "Catophracies alexandri"

34 "Two Bucks" (rock painting)

1953. Coronation. Native Flowers.

149	**33**	1d. red	60	10
150	–	2d. green ("Bauhinia macrantha")	60	10
151	–	4d. mauve ("Caralluma nebrownii")	80	55
152	–	6d. blue ("Gloriosa virescens")	80	1·25
153	–	1s. brown ("Rhigozum tricholotum")	80	40

1954.

154	**34**	1d. red	30	10
155	–	2d. brown	35	10
156	–	3d. purple	2·25	10
157	–	4d. black	2·50	10
158	–	4½d blue	1·25	20
159	–	6d. green	1·25	50
160	–	1s. mauve	1·25	50
161	–	1s. 3d. red	5·00	1·00
162	–	1s. 6d. purple	5·00	50
163	–	2s. 6d. brown	8·00	70
164	–	5s. blue	12·00	2·75
165	–	10s. green	42·00	15·00

DESIGNS—VERT: 2d. "White Lady" (rock painting); 4½d. Karakul lamb; 6d. Ovambo woman blowing horn; 1s. Ovambo woman; 1s. 3d. Herero woman; 1s. 6d. Ovambo girl; 2s. 6d. Lioness; 5s. Gemsbok; 10s. African elephant. HORIZ: 3d. "Rhinoceros Hunt" (rock painting); 4d. "White Elephant and Giraffe" (rock painting).

46 G.P.O., Windhoek

59 "Agricultural Development"

1961.

171	**46**	½ c. brown and blue	60	10
172	–	1 c. brown and lilac	15	10
173	–	1½ c. violet and orange	20	10
174	–	2 c. green and yellow	75	75
175	–	2½ c. brown and blue	35	10
176	–	3 c. blue and red	4·25	40
177	–	3½ c. blue and green	85	15
209	–	4 c. brown and blue	1·50	2·50
178	–	5 c. red and blue	6·50	10
211	–	6 c. sepia and yellow	8·50	11·00
179	–	7½ c. brown and lemon	70	15
213	–	9 c. blue and yellow	8·50	11·00
180	–	10 c. blue and yellow	1·75	15
181	–	12½ c. blue and yellow	85	30
182	–	15 c. brown and blue	14·00	3·25
183	–	20 c. brown and orange	8·00	30
184	–	50 c. green and orange	11·00	1·50
185	–	1 r. yellow, purple and blue	22·00	15·00

DESIGNS—VERT: 1 c. Finger Rock; 1½ c. Mounted Soldier Monument; 2 c. Quivertree; 3 c. Greater flamingoes and Swakopmund Lighthouse; 3½ c. Fishing industry; 5 c. Greater flamingo; 6 c., 7½ c. German Lutheran Church, Windhoek; 10 c. Diamond; 20 c. Topaz; 50 c. Tourmaline; 1 r. Heliodor. HORIZ: 2½ c., 4 c. S.W.A. House, Windhoek; 9 c., 12½ c. Fort Namutoni; 15 c. Hardap Dam.

See also Nos. 224/26.

1963. Opening of Hardap Dam.

192	**59**	3 c. brown and green	30	15

61 Centenary Emblem and part of Globe

62 Interior of Assembly Hall

1963. Centenary of Red Cross.

193	–	7½ c. red, black and blue	7·00	6·00
194	**61**	15 c. red, black and brown	11·00	9·00

DESIGN: 7½ c. Centenary emblem and map.

1964. Opening of Legislative Assembly Hall, Windhoek.

195	**62**	3 c. blue and orange	50	30

63 Calvin

64 Mail Runner of 1890

1965. 400th Death Anniv of Calvin (Protestant reformer).

196	**63**	2½ c. purple and gold	50	15
197		15 c. green and gold	2·75	3·25

1965. 75th Anniv of Windhoek.

198	**64**	3 c. sepia and red	50	15
199	–	15 c. brown and green	1·25	2·25

DESIGN: 15 c. Kurt von Francois (founder).

66 Dr. H. Vedder

70 Pres. Swart

67 Camelthorn Tree

1966. 90th Birth Anniv of Dr. H. Vedder (philosopher and writer).

200	**66**	3 c. green and orange	50	15
201		15 c. brown and blue	1·25	65

1967. Verwoerd Commemoration.

217	**67**	2½ c. black and green	20	10
218	–	3 c. brown and blue	30	10
219	–	15 c. brown and purple	1·10	45

DESIGNS—VERT: 3 c. Waves breaking against rock; 15 c. Dr. H. F. Verwoerd.

1968. Swart Commemoration. Inscr in German, Afrikaans or English.

220	**70**	3 c. red, blue and black	45	15
221	–	15 c. red, green and olive	1·50	1·75

DESIGN: 15 c. Pres. and Mrs. Swart.

1970. Water 70 Campaign. As Nos. 299/300 of South Africa, but inscr "SWA".

222	2½ c. green, blue and brown	75	30
223	3 c. blue and buff	75	30

1970. As Nos. 171 etc, but with "POSGELD" "INKOMSTE" omitted and larger figure of value.

224	**46**	½ c. brown and blue	1·50	30
225	–	1½ c. violet and orange	13·00	16·00
226	–	2 c. green and yellow	5·00	40

1970. 150th Anniv of Bible Society of South Africa. As Nos. 301/2 of South Africa. Inscr "SWA"

228	2½ c. multicoloured	1·50	10
229	12½ c. gold, black and blue	8·00	8·00

1971. "Interstex" Stamp Exhibition, Cape Town. As No. 303 of South Africa. Inscr "SWA".

230	5 c. blue, black and yellow	4·75	1·50

1971. 10th Anniv of Antarctic Treaty. As No. 401 of South Africa. Inscr "SWA".

231	12½ c. black, blue and red	32·00	21·00

1971. 10th Anniv of South African Republic. As Nos. 305/6 of South Africa. Inscr "SWA".

232	2 c. flesh and red	3·25	75
233	4 c. green and black	3·25	75

1972. Centenary of S.P.C.A. As No. 312 of South Africa. Inscr "SWA".

234	5 c. multicoloured	3·50	55

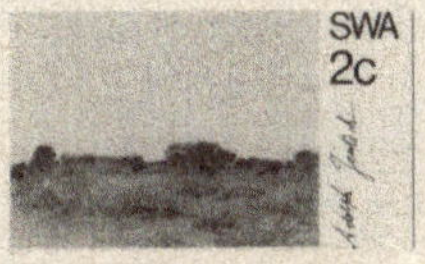

73 "Red Sand-dunes, Eastern South-West Africa"

1973. Scenery. Paintings by Adolph Jentsch. Multicoloured.

235	2 c. Type **73**	75	75
236	4 c. "After the Rain"	1·10	1·25
237	5 c. "Barren Country"	1·40	1·50
238	10 c. "Schaap River" (vert)	2·25	2·75
239	15 c. "Namib Desert" (vert)	3·50	4·00

74 "Sarcocaulon rigidum" **75** "Euphorbia virosa"

1973. Succulents. Multicoloured. (a) As T **74**.

241	1 c. Type **74**	15	10
242a	2 c. "Lapidaria margaretae"	20	10
243	3 c. "Titanopsis schwantesii"	20	10
244	4 c. "Lithops karasmontana"	25	10
245b	5 c. "Caralluma lugardii"	50	20
246	6 c. "Dinteranthus mircospermus"	1·25	1·50
247	7 c. "Conophytum gratum"	70	1·50
248	9 c. "Huernia oculata"	65	1·75
249b	10 c. "Gasteria pillansii"	40	30
250	14 c. "Stapelia pedunculata"	1·50	2·25
251	15 c. "Fenestraria aurantiaca"	65	30
252	20 c. "Decabelone grandiflora"	4·50	2·50
253	25 c. "Hoodia bainii"	3·00	2·00

(b) As T **75**.

254	30 c. Type **75**	1·00	80
255a	50 c. "Pachypodium namaquanum" (vert)	1·25	1·25
256	1 r. "Welwitschia bainesii"	2·00	5·00

1973. As Nos. 241/2a and 245. Colours changed.

257	**18**	1 c. black and mauve	70	60
258	–	2 c. black and yellow	50	50
259	–	5 c. black and red	1·25	60

76 Chat-shrikes **77** Giraffe, Antelope and Spoor

1974. Rare Bird. Multicoloured.

260	4 c. Type **76**	3·25	1·00
261	5 c. Peach-faced lovebirds	4·25	1·50
262	10 c. Damaraland rock jumper	11·00	5·50
263	15 c. Ruppell's parrots	15·00	9·50

1974. Twyfelfontein Rock-engravings. Mult.

264	4 c. Type **77**	1·50	50
265	5 c. Elephant, hyena, antelope and spoor	1·50	80
266	15 c. Kudu cow	7·00	7·50

No. 266 is horizontal, size 38×21 mm.

78 Cut Diamond **79** Wagons and Map of the Trek

1974. Diamond Mining. Multicoloured.

267	10 c. Type **78**	6·00	6·00
268	15 c. Diagram of shore workings	6·00	6·00

1974. Centenary of Thirstland Trek.

269	**79**	4 c. multicoloured	1·00	1·00

80 Peregrine Falcon **81** Kolmannskop (ghost town)

1975. Protected Birds of Prey. Mult.

270	4 c. Type **80**	2·00	1·25
271	5 c. Verreaux's eagle	2·25	1·75
272	10 c. Martial eagle	6·00	5·50
273	15 c. Egyptian vulture	7·50	8·00

1975. Historic Monuments. Multicoloured.

274	5 c. Type **81**	30	15
275	9 c. "Martin Luther" (steam tractor)	50	60
276	15 c. Kurt von Francois and Old Fort, Windhoek	1·00	1·00

82 "View of Luderitz"

1975. Otto Schroder (painter). Multicoloured.

277	15 c. Type **82**	60	60
278	15 c. "View of Swakopmund"	60	60
279	15 c. "Harbour Scene"	60	60
280	15 c. "Quayside, Walvis Bay"	60	60

83 Elephants

1976. Prehistoric Rock Paintings. Mult.

282	4 c. Type **83**	50	15
283	10 c. Rhinoceros	75	70
284	15 c. Antelope	90	85
285	20 c. Man with bow and arrow	1·25	1·40

84 Schwerinsburg

1976. Castles. Multicoloured.

287	10 c. Type **84**	40	30
288	15 c. Schloss Duwisib	55	60
289	20 c. Heynitzburg	75	90

85 Large-toothed Rock Hyrax

1976. Fauna Conservation. Multicoloured.

290	4 c. Type **85**	50	20
291	10 c. Kirk's dik-dik	1·25	90
292	15 c. Kuhl's tree squirrel	2·00	2·25

86 The Augustineum, Windhoek

1976. Modern Buildings.

293	**86**	15 c. black and yellow	50	65
294	–	20 c. black and yellow	60	75

DESIGN: 20 c. Katutura Hospital, Windhoek.

87 Ovambo Water Canal System

1976. Water and Electricity Supply. Mult.

295	15 c. Type **87**	40	40
296	20 c. Ruacana Falls Power Station	50	50

88 Coastline, near Pomona

1977. Namib Desert. Multicoloured.

297	4 c. Type **88**	20	15
298	10 c. Bush and dunes, Sossusvlei	30	30
299	15 c. Plain near Brandberg	50	50
300	20 c. Dunes, Sperr Gebiet	60	60

89 Kraal

1977. The Ovambo People.

301	**89**	4 c. multicoloured	10	10
302	–	10 c. black, orange & brown	30	20
303	–	15 c. multicoloured	30	25
304	–	20 c. multicoloured	35	45

DESIGNS: 10 c. Grain baskets; 15 c. Pounding grain; 20 c. Women in tribal dress.

90 Terminal Buildings

1977. J. G. Strijdom Airport, Windhoek.

305	**90**	20 c. multicoloured	40	30

91 Drostdy, Luderitz

1977. Historic Houses. Multicoloured.

306	5 c. Type **91**	15	10
307	10 c. Woermannhaus, Swakopmund	30	30
308	15 c. Neu-Heusis, Windhoek	35	35
309	20 c. Schmelenhaus, Bethanie	55	40

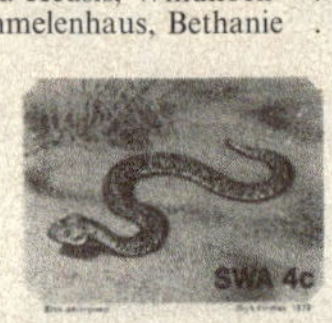

92 Side-winding Adder

1978. Small Animals. Multicoloured.

311	4 c. Type **92**	15	10
312	10 c. Grant's desert golden mole	35	30
313	15 c. Palmato gecko	50	30
314	20 c. Namaqua chameleon	65	40

93 Ostrich Hunting

1978. The Bushmen. Each brown, stone and black.

315	4 c. Type **93**	30	10
316	10 c. Woman carrying ostrich eggs	30	20
317	15 c. Hunters kindling fire	45	30
318	20 c. Woman with musical instrument	55	40

94 Lutheran Church, Windhoek

1978. Historic Churches.

319	**94**	4 c. black and brown	10	10
320	–	10 c. black and brown	15	20
321	–	15 c. black and pink	20	25
322	–	20 c. black and blue	30	35

DESIGNS: 10 c. Lutheran Church, Swakopmund; 15 c. Rhenish Mission Church, Otjimbingwe; 20 c. Rhenish Missionary Church, Keetmanshoop.

1978. Universal Suffrage. Nos. 244/5, 249b and 251/3 optd **ALGEMENE STEMREG** (Afrikaans), **UNIVERSAL SUFFRAGE** (English) or **ALLGEMEINES WAHLRECHT** (German).

324	4 c. "Lithops karasmontana"	10	10
325	5 c. "Caralluma lugardii"	10	10
326	10 c. "Gasteria pillansii"	10	10
327	15 c. "Fenestraria aurantiaca"	15	15
328	20 c. "Decabelone grandiflora"	15	15
329	25 c. "Hoodia bainii"	15	15

Nos. 324/9 were issued in se-tenant strips of three, each stamp in the strip being optd in either Afrikaans, English or German. The same prices apply for any of the three languages.

96 Greater Flamingo **98** Killer Whale

97 Silver Topaz

1979. Water Birds. Multicoloured.

330	4 c. Type **96**	20	10
331	15 c. White-breasted cormorant	45	25
332	20 c. Chestnut-banded sand plover	50	35
333	25 c. Eastern white pelican	55	40

1979. Gemstones. Multicoloured.

334	4 c. Type **97**	30	10
335	15 c. Aquamarine	65	20
336	20 c. Malachite	70	25
337	25 c. Amethyst	70	30

1980. Whales. Multicoloured.

338	4 c. Type **98**	35	20
339	5 c. Humpback whale (38×22 mm)	40	20
340	10 c. Black right whale (38×22 mm)	55	30
341	15 c. Sperm whale (58×22 mm)	1·00	75
342	20 c. Fin whale (58×22 mm)	1·25	90
343	25 c. Blue whale (88×22 mm)	1·60	1·25

99 Impala

1980. 25th Anniv of Division of Nature Conservation and Tourism. Antelopes. Multicoloured.

345	5 c. Type **99**	15	10
346	10 c. Topi	20	10
347	15 c. Roan antelope	40	15
348	20 c. Sable antelope	50	20

100 Black-backed Jackal **101** Meerkat

1980. Wildlife. Multicoloured.

349	1 c. Type **100**	15	10
350	2 c. Hunting dog	30	10
351	3 c. Brown hyena	20	10
352	4 c. Springbok	20	10
353	5 c. Gemsbok	20	10
354	6 c. Greater kudu	20	10
355	7 c. Mountain zebra (horiz)	40	20
356	8 c. Cape porcupine (horiz)	30	10
357	9 c. Ratel (horiz)	30	10
358	10 c. Cheetah (horiz)	30	10
358a	11 c. Blue wildebeest	40	30
358b	12 c. African buffalo (horiz)	70	1·25
358c	14 c. Caracal (horiz)	3·00	2·25
359	15 c. Hippopotamus (horiz)	30	10
359ba	16 c. Warthog (horiz)	1·75	1·75
360	20 c. Eland (horiz)	30	10
361	25 c. Black rhinoceros (horiz)	50	20
362	30 c. Lion (horiz)	80	20
363	50 c. Giraffe	50	30
364	1 r. Leopard	1·00	55
365	2 r. African elephant	1·00	90

1980. Wildlife.

366	**101**	1 c. brown	20	20
367	–	2 c. blue	20	20
368	–	5 c. green	30	30

DESIGNS: 2 c. Savanna monkey; 5 c. Chacma baboon.

102 Von Bach

1980. Water Conservation. Dams. Mult.

369	5 c. Type **102**	10	10
370	10 c. Swakoppoort	15	10
371	15 c. Naute	20	20
372	20 c. Hardap	25	25

103 View of Fish River Canyon

1981. Fish River Canyon.

373	–	5 c. multicoloured	10	10
374	–	15 c. multicoloured	20	20
375	–	20 c. multicoloured	25	25
376	**103**	25 c. multicoloured	30	30

DESIGNS: 5 c. to 20 c. Various views of Canyon.

104 "Aloe erinacea"

1981. Aloes. Multicoloured.

377	5 c. Type **104**	15	10
378	15 c. "Aloe viridiflora"	35	25
379	20 c. "Aloe pearsonii"	40	25
380	25 c. "Aloe littoralis"	50	30

105 Paul Weiss-Haus

1981. Historic Buildings of Luderitz.

381	5 c. Type **105**	10	10
382	15 c. Deutsche Afrika Bank	20	20
383	20 c. Schroederhaus	30	30
384	25 c. Altes Postamt	30	35

106 Salt Pan

1981. Salt Industry. Multicoloured.

386	5 c. Type **106**	10	10
387	15 c. Dumping and washing	20	20
388	20 c. Loading by conveyor	25	30
389	25 c. Dispatch to refinery	30	35

107 Kalahari Starred Tortoise ("Psammobates oculifer")

1982. Tortoises. Multicoloured.

390	5 c. Type **107**	15	10
391	15 c. Leopard tortoise ("Geochelone pardalis")	25	25
392	20 c. Angulate tortoise ("Chersina angulata")	30	35
393	25 c. Speckled padloper ("Homopus signatus")	40	45

108 Mythical Sea-monster

1982. Discoveries of South West Africa (1st series). Multicoloured.

394	15 c. Type **108**	20	20
395	20 c. Bartolomeu Dias and map of Africa showing voyage	40	30
396	25 c. Dias' caravel	65	40
397	30 c. Dias erecting commemorative cross, Angra das Voltas, 25 July 1488	70	45

See also Nos. 455/8.

109 Brandberg

1982. Mountains of South West Africa. Mult.

398	6 c. Type **109**	10	10
399	15 c. Omatako	20	20
400	20 c. Die Nadel	25	30
401	25 c. Spitzkuppe	30	35

110 Otjikaeva Headdress of Herero Woman

1982. Traditional Headdresses of South West Africa (1st series). Multicoloured.

402	6 c. Type **110**	10	10
403	15 c. Ekori headdress of Himba	25	35
404	20 c. Oshikoma hair-piece and iipanda plaits of Ngandjera	35	45
405	25 c. Omhatela headdress of Kwanyama	35	60

See also Nos. 427/30.

111 Fort Vogelsang

1983. Centenary of Luderitz.

406	**111** 6 c. black and red	10	10
407	– 20 c. black and brown	25	30
408	– 25 c. black and brown	30	35
409	– 30 c. black and purple	35	40
410	– 40 c. black and green	50	55

DESIGNS—VERT (23 × 29 mm): 20 c. Chief Joseph Fredericks; 30 c. Heinrich Vogelsang (founder); 40 c. Adolf Luderitz (colonial promoter). HORIZ (as T **111**): 25 c. Angra Pequena.

112 Searching for Diamonds, Kolmanskop, 1908

1983. 75th Anniv of Discovery of Diamonds.

411	**112** 10 c. dp brown & brown	15	15
412	– 20 c. red and brown	30	40
413	– 25 c. blue and brown	35	40
414	– 40 c. black and brown	55	70

DESIGNS—HORIZ (34 × 19 mm): 20 c. Digging for diamonds, Kolmanskop, 1908. VERT (19 × 26 mm): 25 c. Sir Ernest Oppenheimer (industrialist); 40 c. August Stauch (prospector).

113 "Common Zebras drinking" (J. van Ellinckhuijzen)

1983. Painters of South West Africa. Mult.

415	10 c. Type **113**	15	15
416	20 c. "Rossing Mountain" (H. Henckert)	25	30
417	25 c. "Stampeding African Buffalo" (F. Krampe)	30	35
418	40 c. "Erongo Mountains" (J. Blatt)	50	55

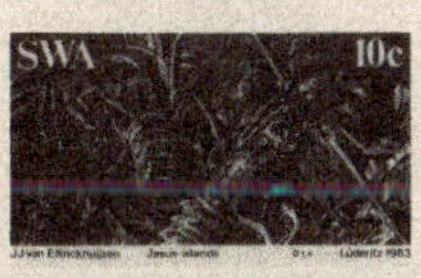

114 The Rock Lobster

1983. The Lobster Industry. Multicoloured.

419	10 c. Type **114**	15	15
420	20 c. Mother ship and fishing dinghies	25	30
421	25 c. Netting lobsters from a dinghy	30	35
422	40 c. Packing lobsters	50	55

115 Hohenzollern House

1984. Historic Buildings of Swakopmund.

423	**115** 10 c. black and brown	15	15
424	– 20 c. black and blue	30	25
425	– 25 c. black and green	30	30
426	– 30 c. black and brown	35	30

DESIGNS: 20 c. Railway Station; 25 c. Imperial District Bureau; 30 c. Ritterburg.

1984. Traditional Headdresses of South West Africa (2nd series). As T **110**. Multicoloured.

427	11 c. Eendjushi headdress of Kwambi	25	15
428	20 c. Bushman woman	40	25
429	25 c. Omulenda headdress of Kwaluudhi	45	30
430	30 c. Mbukushu women	45	30

116 Map and German Flag

1984. Cent of German Colonisation. Mult.

431	11 c. Type **116**	25	15
432	25 c. Raising the German flag, 1884	50	50
433	30 c. German Protectorate boundary marker	50	60
434	45 c. "Elizabeth" and "Leipzig" (German corvettes)	1·25	1·75

117 Sweet Thorn **118** Head of Ostrich

1984. Spring in South West Africa. Mult.

435	11 c. Type **117**	25	15
436	25 c. Camel thorn	50	35
437	30 c. Hook thorn	55	45
438	45 c. Candle-pod acacia	70	70

1985. Ostriches. Multicoloured.

439	11 c. Type **118**	40	10
440	25 c. Ostrich on eggs	70	30
441	30 c. Newly-hatched chick and eggs	80	50
442	50 c. Mating dance	1·10	75

119 Kaiserstrasse

1985. Historic Buildings of Windhoek.

443	**119** 12 c. black and brown	25	10
444	– 25 c. black and green	45	25
445	– 30 c. black and brown	45	30
446	– 50 c. black and brown	90	70

DESIGNS: 25 c. Turnhalle; 30 c. Old Supreme Court Building; 50 c. Railway Station.

120 Zwilling Locomotive

1985. Narrow-gauge Railway Locomotives. Multicoloured.

447	12 c. Type **120**	30	10
448	25 c. Feldspur side-tank locomotive	60	25
449	30 c. Jung and Henschel side-tank locomotive	70	35
450	50 c. Henschel Hd locomotive	90	60

121 Lidumu-dumu (keyboard instrument)

1985. Traditional Musical Instruments. Mult.

451	12 c. Type **121**	10	10
452	25 c. Ngoma (drum)	20	20
453	30 c. Okambulumbumbwa (stringed instrument)	25	25
454	50 c. //Gwashi (stringed instrument)	35	35

122 Erecting Commemorative Pillar at Cape Cross, 1486

1986. Discoverers of South West Africa (2nd series). Diogo Cao.

455	**122** 12 c. black, grey and green	35	10
456	– 20 c. black, grey and brown	55	25
457	– 25 c. black, grey and blue	70	35
458	– 30 c. black, grey & purple	85	60

DESIGNS: 20 c. Diogo Cao's coat of arms; 25 c. Caravel; 30 c. Diogo Cao.

123 Ameib, Erongo Mountains

1986. Rock Formations. Multicoloured.

459	14 c. Type **123**	60	15
460	20 c. Vingerklip, near Outjo	70	25
461	25 c. Petrified sand dunes, Kuiseb River	85	40
462	30 c. Orgelpfeifen, Twyfelfontein	95	55

124 Model wearing Swakara Coat **125** Pirogue, Lake Liambezi

1986. Karakul Industry. Multicoloured.

463	14 c. Type **124**	35	15
464	20 c. Weaving karakul wool carpet	55	30
465	25 c. Flock of karakul ewes in veld	55	45
466	30 c. Karakul rams	75	60

1986. Life in the Caprivi Strip. Mult.

467	14 c. Type **125**	50	15
468	20 c. Ploughing with oxen	80	80
469	25 c. Settlement in Eastern Caprivi	1·00	1·25
470	30 c. Map of Caprivi Strip	1·25	2·00

126 "Gobabis Mission Station", 1863

1987. Paintings by Thomas Baines. Multicoloured.

471	14 c. Type **126**	50	15
472	20 c. "Outspan at Koobie", 1861	90	90
473	25 c. "Outspan under Oomahaama Tree", 1862	1·25	1·50
474	30 c. "Swakop River", 1861	1·50	2·50

127 "Garreta nitens" (beetle)

1987. Useful Insects. Multicoloured.

475	16 c. Type **127**	60	15
476	20 c. "Alcimus stenurus" (fly)	95	95
477	25 c. "Anthophora caerulea" (bee)	1·25	1·75
478	30 c. "Hemiempusa capensis" (mantid)	1·60	2·50

128 Okaukuejo

1987. Tourist Camps. Multicoloured.

479	16 c. Type **128**	55	15
480	20 c. Daan Viljoen	70	75
481	25 c. Ai-Ais	80	1·40
482	30 c. Hardap	85	1·60

129 Wreck of "Hope" (Dutch whaling schooner, 1804) **130** Bartolomeu Dias

1987. Shipwrecks. Multicoloured.

483	16 c. Type **129**	60	15
484	30 c. "Tilly" (brig), 1885	1·00	1·00
485	40 c. "Eduard Bohlen" (steamer), 1909	1·25	2·25
486	50 c. "Dunedin Star" (liner), 1942	1·50	2·75

1988. 500th Anniv of Discovery of Cape of Good Hope by Bartolomeu Dias. Multicoloured.

487	16 c. Type **130**	45	15
488	30 c. Caravel	85	55
489	40 c. Map of South West Africa, c. 1502	1·00	70
490	50 c. King Joao II of Portugal	1·00	75

131 Sossusvlei

1988. Landmarks of South West Africa. Multicoloured.

491	16 c. Type **131**	45	15
492	30 c. Sesriem Canyon	80	65
493	40 c. Hoaruseb "clay castles"	95	1·00
494	50 c. Hoba meteorite	1·00	1·25

132 First Postal Agency, Otyimbingue, 1888

1988. Centenary of Postal Service in South West Africa. Multicoloured.

495	16 c. Type **132**	45	15
496	30 c. Post Office, Windhoek, 1904	80	55
497	40 c. Mail-runner and map	90	75
498	50 c. Camel mail, 1904	1·00	1·00

133 Herero Chat

134 Dr. C. H. Hahn and Gross-Barmen Mission

1988. Birds of South West Africa. Mult.

499	16 c. Type **133**	60	15
500	30 c. Gray's lark	90	65
501	40 c. Ruppell's bustard	1·25	90
502	50 c. Monteiro's hornbill	1·25	95

1989. Missionaries. Multicoloured.

503	16 c. Type **134**	30	10
504	30 c. Revd. J. G. Kronlein and Berseba Mission	60	60
505	40 c. Revd. F. H. Kleinschmidt and Rehoboth Mission	70	70
506	50 c. Revd. J. H. Schmelen and Bethanien Mission	70	85

135 Beech Commuter 1900

1989. 75th Anniv of Aviation in South West Africa. Multicoloured.

507	18 c. Type **135**	40	15
508	30 c. Ryan Navion	70	50
509	40 c. Junkers F-13	80	55
510	50 c. Pfalz Otto biplane	90	70

136 Barchan Dunes

1989. Namib Desert Sand Dunes. Mult.

511	18 c. Type **136**	35	15
512	30 c. Star dunes (36 × 20 mm)	65	40
513	40 c. Transverse dunes	75	60
514	50 c. Crescentic dunes (36 × 20 mm)	1·00	80

137 Ballot Box and Outline Map of South West Africa

1989. South West Africa Constitutional Election.

515	**137**	18 c. brown and orange	30	15
516		35 c. blue and green	50	40
517		45 c. purple and yellow	70	60
518		60 c. green and ochre	80	80

138 Gypsum

140 Arrow Poison

139 Oranjemund Alluvial Diamond Field

1989. Minerals. Multicoloured.

519	1 c. Type **138**	10	10
520	2 c. Fluorite	15	10
521	5 c. Mimetite	20	10
522	7 c. Cuprite	20	10
523	10 c. Azurite	25	10
524	18 c. Boltwoodite	25	10
525	20 c. Dioptase	40	15
526	25 c. Type **139**	50	15
527	30 c. Tsumeb lead and copper complex	65	20
528	35 c. Rosh Pinah zinc mine	65	20
529	40 c. Diamonds	85	30
530	45 c. Wulfenite	85	30
531	50 c. Uis tin mine	1·00	40
532	1 r. Rossing uranium mine	1·75	1·00
533	2 r. Gold	2·75	2·00

The 1, 2, 5, 7, 10, 18, 20, 40, 45 c. and 2 r. are vert as T **138**, and the 25, 30, 35, 50 c. and 1 r. horiz as T **139**.

1990. Flora. Multicoloured.

534	18 c. Type **140**	45	10
535	35 c. Baobab flower	85	40
536	45 c. Sausage tree flowers	95	50
537	60 c. Devil's claw	1·10	90

OFFICIAL STAMPS

Prices are for pairs mint and for single stamps used.

1927. Pictorial and portrait (2d.) stamps alternately optd **OFFICIAL South West Africa.** or **OFFISIEEL Suidwes Afrika.**

O1	**6**	½d. black and green	70·00	30·00
O2	**7**	1d. black and red	70·00	30·00
O3	**2**	2d. purple	£160	45·00
O4	**8**	6d. green and orange	90·00	30·00

1929. Pictorial stamps alternately optd **OFFICIAL S.W.A.** or **OFFISIEEL S.W.A.** horizontally or vertically.

O 9	**6**	½d. black and green	65	2·75
O10		1d. black and red	75	2·75
O11	**11**	2d. grey and purple	90	3·25
O 8	**8**	6d. green and orange	3·00	3·75

1931. Optd alternately **OFFICIAL** or **OFFISIEEL**.

O13	**12**	½d. black and green	10·00	3·50
O14	–	1d. blue and red (No. 75)	75	3·50
O25	**27**	1½d. brown	24·00	5·00
O15	–	2d. blue and brown (No. 76)	1·60	2·25
O16	–	6d. blue and brown (No. 79)	2·25	3·25

POSTAGE DUE STAMPS

Prices for Nos. D1/46 are for pairs mint and for single stamps used.

1923. Optd **South West Africa.** or **Zuid-West Afrika.** alternately. (i) On Postage Due stamps of Transvaal.

D1	D **1**	5d. black and violet	4·00	10·00
D2		6d. black and brown	17·00	11·00

(ii) On Postage Due stamps of South Africa.

D 6	D **1**	½d. black and green	5·50	5·50
D 7		1d. black and pink	7·00	6·00
D 8		1½d. black and brown	1·00	2·75
D 9		2d. black and violet	3·50	5·00
D12		3d. black and blue	7·50	5·50
D 5		6d. black and grey	25·00	13·00

1923. Optd **South West Africa.*** or **Zuidwest Afrika.** (i) on Postage Due stamps of Transvaal.

D25	D **1**	5d. black and violet	2·50	3·50
D14		6d. black and brown	20·00	20·00

(ii) On Postage Due stamps of South Africa.

D23	D **1**	½d. black and green	2·50	6·50
D28		1d. black and pink	2·00	1·60
D29		1½d. black and brown	4·00	6·00
D30		2d. black and violet	2·50	3·25
D31		3d. black and blue	4·25	3·50
D20		6d. black and grey	2·25	9·00

*The English overprint is the same, for the purposes of this catalogue, as that on the previous set.

1927. Optd **South West Africa.*** or **Suidwes Afrika.** (a) On Postage Due stamps of Transvaal.

D33	D **1**	5d. black and violet	19·00	23·00

(b) On Postage Due stamps of South Africa.

D39	D **2**	1d. black and red	1·00	2·25
D34	D **1**	1½d. black and brown	80	3·25
D35		2d. black and violet	4·00	3·25
D37		3d. black and blue	13·00	11·00
D38		6d. black and grey	7·50	8·50

*The English overprint is the same, for the purposes of this catalogue, as that on Nos. D33 and D34/8 of the previous sets.

1928. Postage Due stamps of South Africa optd **S.W.A.** (a) On Nos. D4 and D16.

D40	D **1**	3d. black and blue	1·50	12·00
D41		6d. black and grey	6·00	25·00

(b) On Nos. D17 etc.

D42	D **2**	½d. black and green	40	7·00
D43		1d. black and red	40	3·25
D44		2d. black and mauve	40	4·25
D45		3d. black and blue	2·25	23·00
D46		6d. black and grey	1·50	18·00

D 3

1931. Size 19 × 23½ mm.

D47	D **3**	½d. black and green	70	8·50
D48		1d. black and red	70	1·25
D49		2d. black and violet	70	2·75
D50		3d. black and blue	3·25	16·00
D51		6d. black and slate	13·00	26·00

1959. As Type D **3** but smaller 17½ × 21 mm.

D55	1d. black and red	2·50	4·50
D53	2d. black and violet	1·50	14·00
D56	3d. black and blue	2·50	6·50

1961. As Nos. D55, etc, but values in cents.

D57	1 c. black and turquoise	70	3·50
D58	2 c. black and red	70	3·50
D59	4 c. black and violet	70	3·50
D60	5 c. black and blue	1·00	4·00
D61	6 c. black and green	1·25	6·00
D62	10 c. black and yellow	3·25	7·50

1972. As Type D **8** of South Africa. Inscr "S.W.A."

D63	1 c. green	75	4·50
D64	8 c. blue	3·00	8·50

For subsequent issues see **NAMIBIA**.

SOUTHERN NIGERIA

A British possession on the west coast of Africa. In 1914 joined with Northern Nigeria to form Nigeria (q.v.).

12 pence = 1 shilling;
20 shillings = 1 pound

1

1901.

1	**1**	½d. black and green	1·60	2·00
2		1d. brown and red	1·40	1·25
3		2d. black and brown	2·75	3·50
4		4d. black and green	2·25	11·00
5		6d. black and purple	2·25	6·00
6		1s. green and black	7·00	23·00
7		2s. 6d. black and brown	40·00	75·00
8		5s. black and yellow	45·00	90·00
9		10s. black & purple on yellow	80·00	£130

2

3

1903.

21	**2**	½d. black and green	50	10
11		1d. black and red	1·25	50
23		2d. black and brown	2·50	45
24		2½d. black and blue	1·00	95
25		3d. brown and purple	9·00	1·25
14		4d. black and green	2·00	5·00
27		6d. black and purple	9·00	2·50
28		1s. green and black	3·00	3·00
29		2s. 6d. black and brown	18·00	14·00
30		5s. black and yellow	35·00	70·00
19		10s. black & purple on yell	26·00	80·00
32ab		£1 green and violet	£130	£170

1907.

33	**2**	½d. green	80	20
34ab		1d. red	50	10
35		2d. grey	1·75	70
36		2½d. blue	1·25	3·75
37		3d. purple on yellow	1·25	30
38		4d. black and red on yellow	1·40	80
39		6d. purple	19·00	3·25
40		1s. black on green	7·00	40
41		2s. 6d. black & red on blue	4·50	90
42		5s. green and red on yellow	32·00	48·00
43		10s. green and red on green	60·00	90·00
44		£1 purple and black on red	£170	£180

1912.

45	**3**	½d. green	1·25	10
46		1d. red	80	10
47		2d. grey	60	85
48		2½d. blue	2·50	2·75
49		3d. purple on yellow	75	30
50		4d. black and red on yellow	70	2·00
51	**3**	6d. purple	75	1·25
52		1s. black on green	2·75	75
53		2s. 6d. black and red on blue	7·50	24·00
54		5s. green and red on yellow	17·00	60·00
55		10s. green and red on green	42·00	80·00
56		£1 purple and black on red	£160	£170

SOUTHERN RHODESIA

A Br. territory in the N. part of S. Africa, S. of the Zambesi. In 1954 became part of the Central African Federation which issued its own stamps inscribed "Rhodesia and Nyasaland" (q.v.), until 1964 when it resumed issuing after the break-up of the Federation. In October, 1964, Southern Rhodesia was renamed Rhodesia.

12 pence = 1 shilling;
20 shillings = 1 pound

1

1924.

1	**1**	½d. green	1·25	10
2		1d. pink	1·60	10
3		1½d. brown	1·00	55
4		2d. black and grey	2·00	50
5		3d. blue	2·25	2·25
6		4d. black and red	2·25	2·75
7		6d. black and mauve	2·00	3·00
8		8d. purple and green	11·00	42·00
9		10d. blue and pink	11·00	42·00
10		1s. black and blue	5·00	4·00
11		1s. 6d. black and yellow	19·00	30·00
12		2s. black and brown	17·00	17·00
13		2s. 6d. black and brown	35·00	60·00
14		5s. blue and green	60·00	£110

2 King George V

3 Victoria Falls

1931.

15a	**2**	½d. green	65	20
16b		1d. red	50	20
16d		1½d. brown	2·50	65
17	**3**	2d. black and brown	3·75	1·25
18		3d. blue	10·00	11·00
19	**2**	4d. black and red	1·25	1·25
20		6d. black and mauve	2·25	2·00
21		8d. violet and green	1·75	3·25
21b		9d. red and green	6·00	9·00
22		10d. blue and red	7·00	3·00
23		1s. black and blue	2·00	2·25
24		1s. 6d. black and yellow	10·00	16·00
25		2s. black and brown	21·00	5·50
26a		2s. 6d. blue and brown	28·00	30·00
27		5s. blue and green	48·00	48·00

4

1932.

29	**4**	2d. green and brown	3·50	60
30		3d. blue	3·75	1·75

5 Victoria Falls

1935. Silver Jubilee.

31	**5**	1d. green and red	3·25	1·75
32		2d. green and brown	5·50	5·00
33		3d. violet and blue	5·50	10·00
34		6d. black and purple	8·00	13·00

1935. As Nos. 29/30, but inscr "POSTAGE AND REVENUE".

35a	**4**	2d. green and brown	1·25	10
35b		3d. blue	3·00	10

6 Victoria Falls and Railway Bridge

1937. Coronation.
36 **6** 1d. olive and red 80 60
37 2d. green and brown . . . . 80 1·50
38 3d. violet and blue . . . . 3·75 7·00
39 6d. black and purple . . . . 2·25 3·25

7 King George VI

10 Cecil John Rhodes (after S. P. Kendrick)

8 British South Africa Co's Arms

1937.
40 **7** ½d. green 50 10
41 1d. red 40 10
42 1½d. brown . . . . 1·00 10
43 4d. orange . . . . 1·50 10
44 6d. black . . . . 1·50 30
45 8d. green . . . . 2·00 1·25
46 9d. blue . . . . 1·50 30
47 10d. purple . . . . 2·25 1·75
48 1s. black and green . . . . . 1·75 10
49 1s. 6d. black and yellow . . . 9·50 2·00
50 2s. black and brown . . . . 13·00 55
51 2s. 6d. blue and purple . . . 8·50 4·50
52 5s. blue and green . . . . . 26·00 2·00

1940. Golden Jubilee of British South Africa Company.
53 **8** ½d. violet and green 10 55
54 – 1d. blue and red 10 10
55 **10** 1½d. black and brown . . . 15 70
56 – 2d. green and violet 30 60
57 – 3d. black and blue . . . . . 30 1·25
58 – 4d. green and brown . . . . 1·75 2·25
59 – 6d. brown and green . . . . 30 1·75
60 – 1s. blue and green . . . . . 45 1·75
DESIGNS—HORIZ: 1d. Fort Salisbury, 1890; 2d. Fort Victoria; 3d. Rhodes makes peace, 1896; 1s. Queen Victoria, King George VI, Lobengula's kraal and Govt. House, Salisbury. VERT: 4d. Victoria Falls Bridge; 6d. Statue of Sir Charles Coghlan.

16 Mounted Pioneer

20 King George VI

17 Queen Elizabeth II when Princess, and Princess Margaret

1943. 50th Anniv of Occupation of Matabeleland.
61 **16** 2d. brown and green 20 50

1947. Royal Visit.
62 **17** ½d. black and green 15 60
63 – 1d. black and red 15 60
DESIGN: 1d. King George VI and Queen Elizabeth.

1947. Victory.
64 – 1d. red 10 10
65 **20** 2d. slate 10 10
66 – 3d. blue 55 40
67 – 6d. orange 30 65
PORTRAITS: 1d. Queen Elizabeth; 3d. Queen Elizabeth II when Princess; 6d. Princess Margaret.

1949. 75th Anniv of U.P.U. As T **19/20** of Antigua.
68 2d. green 80 20
69 3d. blue . . . . 1·10 3·00

23 Queen Victoria, Arms and King George VI

1950. Diamond Jubilee of S. Rhodesia.
70 **23** 2d. green and brown . . . 30 70

24 "Medical Services"

27 "Water Supplies"

1953. Birth Cent of Cecil Rhodes. Inscr "RHODES CENTENARY".
71 **24** ½d. blue and sepia . . . . 15 1·75
72 – 1d. chestnut and green . . . 15 10
73 – 2d. green and violet 15 10
74 **27** 4½d. green and blue . . . 75 2·50
75 – 1s. black and brown . . . . 3·00 80
DESIGNS: 1d. "Agriculture"; 2d. "Building"; 4½d. "Water Supplies"; 1s. "Transport".
No. 74 also commemorates the Diamond Jubilee of Matabeleland.

1953. Rhodes Centenary Exhibition, Bulawayo. As No. 59 of Northern Rhodesia.
76 6d. violet 30 50

30 Queen Elizabeth II

1953. Coronation.
77 **30** 2s. 6d. red . . . . 4·50 6·00

31 Sable Antelope

33 Rhodes's Grave

43 Balancing Rocks

1953.
78 **31** ½d. grey and claret 30 40
79 – 1d. green and brown 30 10
80 **33** 2d. brown and violet 30 10
81 – 3d. brown and red 55 70
82 – 4d. red, green and blue . . . 3·25 10
83 – 4½d. black and blue . . . . 2·00 2·75
84 – 6d. olive and turquoise . . . 3·00 60
85 – 9d. blue and brown . . . . 3·50 2·75
86 – 1s. violet and blue . . . . 1·25 10
87 – 2s. purple and red . . . . 11·00 3·50
88 – 2s. 6d. olive and brown . . . 6·50 3·75
89 – 5s. brown and green . . . . 14·00 8·50
90 **43** 10s. brown and olive . . . 17·00 35·00
91 – £1 red and black . . . . . 27·00 35·00
DESIGNS—VERT (as Type **31**): 1d Tobacco planter. (As Type **33**): 6d. Baobab tree; 5s. Basket maker. HORIZ (as Type **33**): 3d. Farm worker; 4d. Flame lily; 4½d. Victoria Falls; 9d. Lion; 1s. Zimbabwe ruins; 2s. Birchenough Bridge; 2s. 6d. Kariba Gorge. (As Type **43**): £1 Coat of arms.

45 Maize

50 Flame Lily

56 Cattle

1964.
92 **45** ½d. yellow, green and blue . 20 1·50
93 – 1d. violet and ochre 15 10
94 – 2d. yellow and violet . . . 60 10
95 – 3d. brown and blue 20 10
96 – 4d. orange and green . . . 30 10
97 **50** 6d. red, yellow and green . . 40 10
98 – 9d. brown, yellow and green 2·50 80
99 – 1s. green and ochre . . . . 4·00 10
100 – 1s. 3d. red, violet and green 3·75 10
101 – 2s. blue and ochre . . . . 3·00 1·25
102 – 2s. 6d. blue and red . . . . 5·00 70
103 **56** 5s. multicoloured . . . . 5·00 2·25
104 – 10s. multicoloured . . . . 13·00 6·50
105 – £1 multicoloured . . . . . 7·00 16·00
DESIGNS—As Type **45**: 1d. African buffalo; 2d. Tobacco; 3d. Greater kudu; 4d. Citrus. As Type **50**: 9d. Ansellia orchid; 1s. Emeralds; 1s. 3d. Aloe; 2s. Lake Kyle; 2s. 6d. Tigerfish. As Type **56**: 10s. Helmet guineafowl; £1 Coat of arms.
Similar designs inscribed "RHODESIA" are listed under that heading.

POSTAGE DUE STAMPS

1951. Postage due stamps of Great Britain optd **SOUTHERN RHODESIA**.
D1 **D 1** ½d. green . . . . 3·25 14·00
D2 1d. blue . . . . 3·00 2·75
D3 2d. black . . . . 4·00 1·75
D4 3d. violet . . . . 2·75 2·00
D5 4d. blue . . . . 1·75 3·25
D6 4d. green £170 £550
D7 1s. blue . . . . 3·00 2·50

For later issues see **RHODESIA**.

SRI LANKA

Ceylon became a republic within the British Commonwealth on 22 May 1972 and changed its name to Sri Lanka (= "Resplendent Island").

100 cents = 1 rupee

208 National Flower and Mountain of the Illustrious Foot

209 Map of World with Buddhist Flag

1972. Inaug of Republic of Sri Lanka.
591 **208** 15 c. multicoloured 30 30

1972. 10th World Fellowship of Buddhists Conference.
592 **209** 5 c. multicoloured 30 60

210 Book Year Emblem

211 Emperor Angelfish

1972. International Book Year.
593 **210** 20 c. orange and brown . . . 20 30

1972. Fishes. Multicoloured.
594 2 c. Type **211** 10 80
595 5 c. Green chromide 10 80
596 30 c. Skipjack tuna . . . . . 1·25 30
597 2 r. Black ruby barb . . . . . 3·50 5·25

212 Memorial Hall

1973. Opening of Bandaranaike Memorial Hall.
598 **212** 15 c. cobalt and blue . . . 30 30

213 King Vessantara giving away his Children

1973. Rock and Temple Paintings. Mult.
599 35 c. Type **213** 30 10
600 50 c. The Prince and the grave-digger 35 10
601 90 c. Bearded old man 50 75
602 1 r. 55 Two female figures . . 65 1·50

214 Bandaranaike Memorial Conference Hall

215 Prime Minster Bandaranaike

1974. 20th Commonwealth Parliamentary Conference, Colombo.
604 **214** 85 c. multicoloured . . . 30 30

1974.
605 **215** 15 c. multicoloured . . . 15 10

216 "U.P.U." and "100"

1974. Centenary of U.P.U.
606 **216** 50 c. multicoloured . . . 75 75

217 Sri Lanka Parliament Building

1975. Inter-Parliamentary Meeting.
607 **217** 1 r. multicoloured 30 50

218 Sir Ponnambalam Ramanathan (politician)

219 D. J. Wimalasurendra (engineer)

1975. Ramanathan Commemoration.
608 **218** 75 c. multicoloured . . . 30 70

1975. Wimalasurendra Commemoration.
609 **219** 75 c. black and blue . . . 30 70

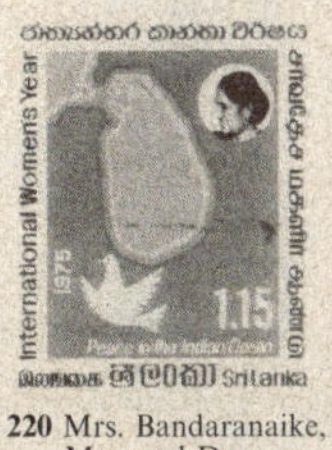

220 Mrs. Bandaranaike, Map and Dove

221 Ma-ratmal

1975. International Women's Year.
610 **220** 1 r. 15 multicoloured . . 2·25 1·25

1976. Indigenous Flora. Multicoloured.
611 25 c. Type **221** 10 10
612 50 c. Binara 10 10
613 75 c. Daffodil orchid 15 15
614 10 r. Diyapara . . . . 3·00 4·25

222 Mahaweli Dam

1976. Mahaweli River Diversion.
616 222 85 c. turquoise, bl & azure . . 30 80

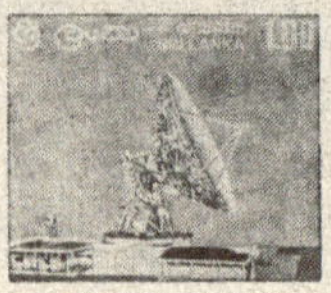
223 Dish Aerial

1976. Opening of Satellite Earth Station, Padukka.
617 223 1 r. multicoloured 65 85

224 Conception of the Buddha

1976. Vesak. Multicoloured.
618 5 c. Type 224 . . . . 10 60
619 10 c. King Suddhodana and the astrologers 10 60
620 1 r. 50 The astrologers being entertained 80 70
621 2 r. The Queen in a palanquin . . 85 75
622 2 r. 25 Royal procession . . . 95 1·60
623 5 r. Birth of the Buddha . . . 1·25 2·75
Nos. 618/23 show paintings from the Dambava Temple.

225 Blue Sapphire

1976. Gems of Sri Lanka. Multicoloured.
625 60 c. Type 225 . . . . 3·75 30
626 1 r. 15 Cat's eye . . . . . . 5·50 1·50
627 2 r. Star sapphire . . . . . . 6·00 3·25
628 5 r. Ruby . . . . 8·50 9·50

226 Prime Minister Mrs. S. Bandaranaike

227 Statue of Liberty

1976. Non-aligned Summit Conf, Colombo.
630 226 1 r. 15 multicoloured . . . 25 25
631 2 r. multicoloured 40 45

1976. Bicent of American Revolution.
632 227 2 r. 25 blue and indigo . . 65 1·25

228 Bell, Early Telephone and Telephone Lines

229 Maitreya (pre-carnate Buddha)

1976. Centenary of Telephone.
633 228 1 r. multicoloured 60 20

1976. Centenary of Colombo Museum. Mult.
634 50 c. Type 229 . . . . 25 15
635 1 r. Sundara Murti Swami (Tamil psalmist) 30 30
636 5 r. Tara (goddess) . . . . . 2·25 4·00

230 Kandyan Crown

231 Sri Rahula Thero (poet)

1977. Regalia of the Kings of Kandy. Multicoloured.
637 1 r. Type 230 . . . . 35 40
638 2 r. Throne and footstool . . 75 2·40

1977. Sri Rahula Commemoration.
639 231 1 r. multicoloured 75 75

232 Sir Ponnambalam Arunachalam

233 Brass Lamps

1977. Sir Ponnambalam Arunachalam (social reformer) Commemoration.
640 232 1 r. multicoloured 50 65

1977. Handicrafts. Multicoloured.
641 20 c. Type 233 . . . . 15 15
642 25 c. Jewellery box 15 15
643 50 c. Caparisoned elephant . . 30 20
644 5 r. Mask . . . . 1·60 3·00

234 Siddi Lebbe (author and educationist)

235 Girl Guide

1977. Siddi Lebbe Commemoration.
646 234 1 r. multicoloured 30 60

1977. 60th Anniv of Sri Lanka Girl Guides Association.
647 235 75 c. multicoloured . . . 85 30

236 Parliament Building and "Wheel of Life"

237 Youths Running

1978. Election of New President.
648 236 15 c. gold, green & emer . . 20 10
For similar design in a smaller format, see Nos. 680/c.

1978. National Youth Service Council.
649 237 15 c. multicoloured . . . 30 50

238 Prince Siddhartha's Renunciation

1978. Vesak. Rock Carvings from Borobudur Temple.
650 238 15 c. buff, brown and blue 75 30
651 – 50 c. buff, brown and blue 1·00 1·50
DESIGN: 50 c. Prince Siddhartha shaving his hair.

1978. Surch.
652 5 c. on 90 c. Bearded old man (No. 601) . . . . 1·25 2·50
653 10 c. on 35 c. Type 213 . . . 50 50
654 25 c. on 15 c. Type 215 . . . 3·50 3·50
655 25 c. on 15 c. Type 236 . . . 3·50 3·50
656 25 c. on 15 c. Type 237 . . . 3·50 3·50
657 1 r. on 1 r. 55 Two female figures (No. 602) . . . . 1·25 45

240 Veera Puran Appu

241 "Troides helena"

1978. 130th Death Anniv of Veera Puran Appu (revolutionary).
658 240 15 c. multicoloured 15 20

1978. Butterflies. Multicoloured.
659 25 c. Type 241 . . . . 55 10
660 50 c. "Cethosia nietneri" . . . 1·00 10
661 5 r. "Kallima horsfieldi" . . . 1·50 1·25
662 10 r. "Papilio polymnestor" . . 1·75 1·75

1979. No. 486 of Ceylon surch **SRI LANKA 15**.
664 15 c. on 10 c. green . . . . . 1·75 1·40

243 Prince Danta and Princess Hema Mala bringing the Sacred Tooth Relic from Kalinga

244 Piyadasa Sirisena

1979. Vesak. Kelaniya Temple Paintings. Multicoloured.
665 25 c. Type 243 . . . . 10 10
666 1 r. Theri Sanghamitta bringing the Bodhi Tree branch to Sri Lanka 15 15
667 10 r. King Kirti Sri Rajasinghe offering fan of authority to the Sangha Raja . . . . . . 1·50 2·50

1979. Piyadasa Sirisena (writer) Commem.
669 244 1 r. 25 multicoloured . . . 40 40

245 Wrestlers

246 Dudley Senanayake

1979. Wood Carvings from Embekke Temple.
670 245 20 r. brown, ochre & green 1·25 1·50
671 – 50 r. agate, yellow & green 2·00 3·25
DESIGN: 50 r. Dancer.

1979. Dudley Senanayake (former Prime Minister) Commemoration.
672 246 1 r. 25 green 15 20

247 Mother with Child

1979. International Year of the Child. Multicoloured.
673 5 c. Type 247 . . . . 10 10
674 3 r. Superimposed heads of children of different races . . 40 1·00
675 5 r. Children playing . . . . . 50 1·10

248 Ceylon 1857 6d. Stamp and Sir Rowland Hill

1979. Death Centenary of Sir Rowland Hill.
676 248 3 r. multicoloured 30 55

249 Conference Emblem and Parliament Building

1979. International Conference of Parliamentarians on Population and Development, Colombo.
677 249 2 r. multicoloured . . . . 70 1·00

250 Airline Emblem on Aircraft Tail-fin

251 Coconut Tree

1979. Inauguration of "Airlanka" Airline.
678 250 3 r. black, blue and red . 70 1·00

1979. 10th Anniv of Asian and Pacific Coconut Community.
679 251 2 r. multicoloured . . . . 70 1·00

1979. As No. 648, but 20 × 24 mm.
680 236 25 c. gold, green and emerald 20 20
680a 50 c. gold, green and emerald . . . . 2·50 10
680b 60 c. gold, green and emerald . . . . 5·50 1·25
680c 75 c. gold, green and emerald 10 10

252 Swami Vipulananda

253 Inscription and Crescent

1979. Swami Vipulananda (philosopher) Commemoration.
681 252 1 r. 25 multicoloured . . . 20 30

1979. 1500th Anniv of Hegira (Mohammedan religion).
682 253 3 r. 75 black, deep green and green . . . . 35 1·25

254 "The Great Teacher" (Institute emblem)

255 Ceylon Blue Magpie

1979. 50th Anniv of Institute of Ayurveda (school of medicine).
683 254 15 c. multicoloured . . . 30 50

1979. Birds (1st series). Multicoloured.
684 10 c. Type 255 . . . . 10 75
685 15 c. Ceylon hanging parrot . . 75 10
686 75 c. Ceylon whistling thrush . . 15 15
687 1 r. Ceylon spurfowl 15 15
688 5 r. Yellow-fronted barbet . . 60 1·75
689 10 r. Yellow-tufted bulbul . . . 75 1·75
See also Nos. 827/30, 985/8 and 1242/5.

256 Rotary International Emblem and Map of Sri Lanka

257 A. Ratnayake

1980. 75th Anniv of Rotary International and 50th Anniv of Sri Lanka Rotary Movement.
691 256 1 r. 50 multicoloured . . 70 1·25

1980. 80th Birth Anniv of A. Ratnayake (politician).
692 257 1 r. 25 green 20 30

1980. No. 680 surch **.35**.
693 236 35 c. on 25 c. gold, green and emerald 15 15

259 Tank and Stupa (symbols of Buddhist culture)
260 Colonel Olcott

1980. 60th Anniv of All Ceylon Buddhist Congress. Multicoloured.
694 10 c. Type **259** 20 90
695 35 c. Bo-leaf wheel and fan . . 20 20

1980. Centenary of Arrival of Colonel Olcott (campaigner for Buddhism).
696 **260** 2 r. multicoloured . . . . 80 1·50

261 Patachara's Journey through Forest
262 George E. de Silva

1980. Vesak. Details from Temple Paintings, Purvaramaya, Kataluwa. Multicoloured.
697 35 c. Type **261** 30 15
698 1 r. 60 Patachara crossing river 1·25 2·00

1980. George E. de Silva (politician) Commemoration.
699 **262** 1 r. 60 multicoloured . . . 20 30

263 Dalada Maligawa

1980. U.N.E.S.C.O. —Sir Lanka Cultural Triangle Project.
700 **263** 35 c. claret 10 30
701 – 35 c. grey 10 30
702 – 35 c. red 10 30
703 – 1 r. 60 olive 40 90
704 – 1 r. 60 green 40 90
705 – 1 r. 60 brown 40 90
DESIGNS: No. 701, Dambulla; 702, Alahana Pirivena; 703, Jetavanarama; 704, Abhayagiri; 705, Sigiri.

264 Co-operation Symbols
266 The Holy Family

265 Lanka Mahila Samiti Emblem

1980. 50th Anniv of Co-operative Department.
707 **264** 20 c. multicoloured 10 30

1980. 50th Anniv of Lanka Mahila Samiti (Rural Women's Movement).
708 **265** 35 c. violet, red and yellow 10 45

1980. Christmas. Multicoloured.
709 35 c. Type **266** 10 10
710 3 r. 75 The Three Wise Men . 60 1·25

267 Colombo Public Library

1980. Opening of Colombo Public Library.
712 **267** 35 c. multicoloured . . . 10 10

268 Flag of Walapane Disawa
269 Fishing Cat

1980. Ancient Flags.
713 **268** 10 c. black, green & pur . 10 10
714 – 25 c. black, yellow & pur 10 10
715 – 1 r. 60 black, yellow & pur 15 20
716 – 20 r. black, yellow & pur 1·25 2·50
DESIGNS: 25 c. Flag of the Gajanayaka Huduhumpola, Kandy; 1 r. 60, Sinhala royal flag; 20 r. Sinhala royal flag, Ratnapura.

1981. Animals. Multicoloured.
718 2 r. 50 on 1 r. 60 Type **269** . 15 15
719 3 r. on 1 r. 50 Golden palm civet 15 20
720 4 r. on 2 r. Indian-spotted chevrotain 25 30
721 5 r. on 3 r. 75 Rusty-spotted cat 35 45
Nos. 718/21 are previously unissued stamps surcharged as in T **269**.
For stamps with revised face values see Nos. 780/3.

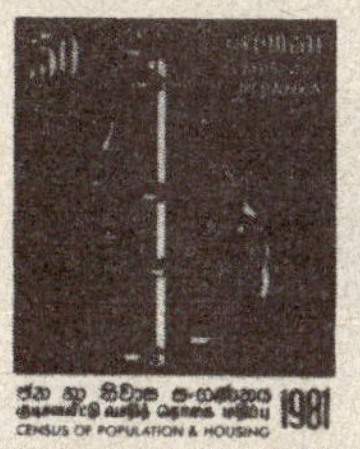

270 Heads and Houses on Map of Sri Lanka
271 Sri Lanka Light Infantry Regimental Badge

1981. Population and Housing Census.
723 **270** 50 c. multicoloured . . . 60 90

1981. Centenary of Sri Lanka Light Infantry.
724 **271** 2 r. multicoloured . . . . 1·00 75

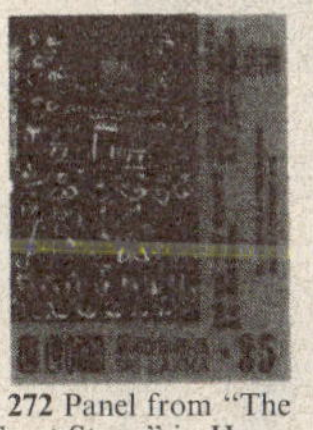

272 Panel from "The Great Stupa" in Honour of the Buddha, Sanci, India, 1st-century A.D.
274 Rev. Polwatte Sri Buddadatta

273 St. John Baptist de la Salle

1981. Vesak.
725 **272** 35 c. black, dp grn & grn 10 10
726 – 50 c. multicoloured . . . 10 10
727 – 7 r. black and pink . . . 1·25 3·00
DESIGNS: 50 c. Silk banner representing a Bodhisattva from "Thousand Buddhas", Tun-Huang, Central Asia; 7 r. Bodhisattva from Fondukistan, Afghanistan.

1981. 300th Anniv of De La Salle Brothers (Religious Order of the Brothers of the Christian Schools).
729 **273** 2 r. pink, light blue & blue 80 1·00

1981. National Heroes.
730 **274** 50 c. brown 50 80
731 – 50 c. pink 50 80
732 – 50 c. mauve 50 80
DESIGNS: No. 731, Rev. Mohottiwatte Gunananda; 732, Dr. Gnanaprakasar. (each a scholar, writer and Buddhist campaigner).

275 Dr. Al-Haj T. B. Jayah
276 Dr. N. M. Perera

1981. Dr. Al-Haj T. B. Jayah (statesman) Commemoration.
733 **275** 50 c. green 50 70

1981. Dr. N. M. Perera (campaigner for social reform) Commemoration.
734 **276** 50 c. red 50 70

277 Stylised Disabled Person and Globe

1981. International Year for Disabled Persons.
735 **277** 2 r. red, black and grey . . 85 1·50

278 Hand placing Vote into Ballot Box

1981. 50th Anniv of Universal Franchise. Multicoloured.
736 50 c. Type **278** 25 15
737 7 r. Ballot box and people forming map of Sri Lanka (vert) . . . . 1·50 2·00

279 T. W. Rhys Davids (founder)

1981. Centenary of Pali Text Society.
738 **279** 35 c. stone, dp brn & brn . 50 20

280 Federation Emblem and "25"

1981. 25th Anniv of All-Ceylon Buddhist Students' Federation.
739 **280** 2 r. black, yellow and red . 60 40

281 "Plan for Happiness"
282 Dove Symbol with Acupuncture Needle and "Yin-Yang" (Chinese universe duality emblem)

1981. Population and Family Planning.
740 **281** 50 c. multicoloured 60 80

1981. World Acupuncture Congress.
741 **282** 2 r. black, yellow & orange 2·50 2·75

283 Union and Sri Lanka Flags

1981. Royal Visit.
742 **283** 50 c. multicoloured 50 25
743 5 r. multicoloured . . . . 1·75 3·25

284 "Conserve our Forests"
285 Sir James Peiris

1981. Forest Conservation.
745 **284** 35 c. multicoloured . . . 15 10
746 – 50 c. brown and stone . . 20 20
747 – 5 r. multicoloured . . . 1·90 3·75
DESIGNS: 50 c. "Plant a tree"; 5 r. Jak (tree).

1981. Birth Centenary of Sir James Peiris (politician).
749 **285** 50 c. brown 60 80

286 F. R. Senanayaka
287 Philip Gunawardhane

1982. Birth Centenary of F. R. Senanayaka (national hero).
750 **286** 50 c. brown 60 85

1982. 10th Death Anniv of Philip Gunawardhane (politician).
751 **287** 50 c. red 60 85

288 Department of Inland Revenue Building, Colombo
289 Rupavahini Emblem

1982. 50th Anniv of Department of Inland Revenue.
752 **288** 50 c. black, blue & orange 60 85

1982. Inauguration of Rupavahini (national television service).
753 **289** 2 r. 50 yellow, brn and grey 2·25 3·00

290 Cricketer and Ball
292 Mother breast-feeding Child

291 "Obsbeckia wightiana"

1982. 1st Sri Lanka–England Test Match, Colombo.
754 **290** 2 r. 50 multicoloured . . 4·00 4·00

1982. Flowers. Multicoloured.
755 3 c. Type **291** 10 10
756 2 r. "Mesua nagassarium" . . 20 20
757 7 r. "Rhodomyrtus tomentosa" 50 1·00
758 20 r. "Phaius tancarvilleae" . 1·40 3·00

1982. Food and Nutrition Policy Planning.
760 **292** 50 c. multicoloured . . . 95 95

293 Conference Emblem

1982. World Hindu Conference.
761 **293** 50 c. multicoloured . . . 85 85

294 King Vessantara giving away Magical, Rain-making White Elephant

1982. Vesak. Legend of Vessantara Jataka. Details of Cloth Painting from Arattana Rajamaha Vihara (temple), Hanguranketa, District of Nuwara Eliya. Multicoloured.
762 35 c. Type **294** 45 10
763 40 c. King Vessantara with family in Vankagiri Forest . 55 15
764 2 r. 50 Vessantara giving away his children as slaves . . . . 2·00 2·25
765 5 r. Vessantara and family returning to Jetuttara in royal chariot . . . . 2·75 3·50

295 Parliament Buildings, Sri Jayawardanapura

1982. Opening of Parliament Building Complex, Sri Jayawardanapura, Kotte.
767 **295** 50 c. multicoloured . . . 85 85

296 Dr. C. W. W. Kannangara **298** Dr. G. P. Malalasekara

297 Lord Baden-Powell

1982. Dr. C. W. W. Kannangara ("Father of Free Education") Commemoration.
768 **296** 50 c. green 85 85

1982. 125th Birth Anniv of Lord Baden-Powell.
769 **297** 50 c. multicoloured . . . 1·75 85

1982. Dr. G. P. Malalasekara (founder of World Fellowship of Buddhists) Commem.
770 **298** 50 c. green 85 85

299 Wheel encircling Globe

1982. World Buddhist Leaders Conference.
771 **299** 50 c. multicoloured . . . 95 95

300 Wildlife

1982. World Environment Day.
772 **300** 50 c. multicoloured . . . 1·60 1·10

301 Sir Waitialingam Duraiswamy **303** Rev. Weliwita Sri Saranankara Sangharaja

302 Y.M.C.A. Emblem

1982. Sir Waitialingam Duraiswamy (statesman and educationalist) Commemoration.
773 **301** 50 c. deep brown and brown 85 85

1982. Centenary of Colombo Y.M.C.A.
774 **302** 2 r. 50 multicoloured . . 3·00 3·50

1982. Rev. Weliwita Sri Saranankara Sangharaja (Buddhist leader) Commemoration.
775 **303** 50 c. brown and orange . . 85 85

304 Maharagama Sasana Sevaka Samithiya Emblem

1982. 25th Anniv of Maharagama Sasana Sevaka Samithiya (Buddhist Social Reform Movement).
776 **304** 50 c. multicoloured . . . 85 85

305 Dr. Robert Koch

1982. Centenary of Robert Koch's Discovery of Tubercle Bacillus.
777 **305** 50 c. multicoloured . . . 1·75 1·00

306 Sir John Kotelawala **307** Eye Donation Society and Lions Club Emblems

1982. 2nd Death Anniv of Sir John Kotelawala.
778 **306** 50 c. green 85 85

1982. World-Wide Sight Conservation Project.
779 **307** 2 r. 50 multicoloured . . 3·00 3·50

1982. As Nos. 718/21 but without surcharges and showing revised face values.
780 2 r. 50 Type **269** 20 15
781 3 r. Golden palm civet* . . . 2·00 2·00
1081 3 r. Golden palm civet* . . . 75 30
782 4 r. Indian-spotted chevrotain 25 30
783 5 r. Rusty-spotted cat 25 30
*No. 781 has the face value and inscriptions in brown, No. 1081 in black.

308 1859 4d. Rose and 1948 15 c. Independence Commemorative

1982. 125th Anniv of First Postage Stamps. Multicoloured.
784 50 c. Type **308** 50 50
785 2 r. 50 1859 1s. 9d. green and 1981 50 c. "Just Society" stamps . . . . 1·50 2·50

309 Goonetilleke

1983. 4th Death Anniv of Sir Oliver Goonetilleke (statesman).
787 **309** 50 c. grey, brown & black 60 75

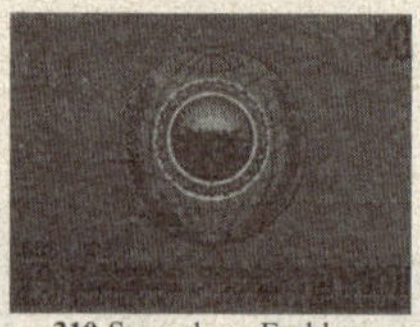

310 Sarvodaya Emblem

1983. 25th Anniv of Sarvodaya Movement.
788 **310** 50 c. multicoloured 90 90

311 Morse Key, Radio Aerial and Amateur Radio Society Emblem

1983. Amateur Radio Society.
789 **311** 2 r. 50 multicoloured . . . 2·75 3·50

312 Customs Co-operation Council Emblem and Sri Lanka Flag

1983. 30th Anniv of International Customs Day.
790 **312** 50 c. multicoloured 40 40
791 5 r. multicoloured . . . . 3·00 4·25

313 Bottle-nosed Dolphin

1983. Marine Mammals.
792 **313** 50 c. black, blue and green 40 15
793 – 2 r. multicoloured 80 80
794 – 2 r. 50 black, blue and grey 1·75 1·75
795 – 10 r. multicoloured . . . . 4·50 5·50
DESIGNS: 2 r. Dugongs; 2 r. 50, Humpback whale; 10 r. Sperm whale.

314 "Lanka Athula" (container ship)

1983. Ships of the Ceylon Shipping Corporation. Multicoloured.
796 50 c. Type **314** 20 15
797 2 r. 50 Map of routes 60 60
798 5 r. "Lanka Kalyani" (freighter) 1·00 1·50
799 20 r. "Tammanna" (tanker) . 2·00 4·25

315 Woman with I.W.D. Emblem and Sri Lanka Flag

1983. International Women's Day. Mult.
800 50 c. Type **315** 15 25
801 5 r. Woman, emblem, map and symbols of progress . . . . 70 2·00

316 Waterfall

1983. Commonwealth Day. Multicoloured.
802 50 c. Type **316** 10 10
803 2 r. 50 Tea plucking 15 25
804 5 r. Harvesting rice 25 40
805 20 r. Decorated elephants . . 80 2·00

317 Lions Club International Badge

1983. 25th Anniv of Lions Club International in Sri Lanka.
806 **317** 2 r. 50 multicoloured . . 2·50 2·50

318 "The Dream of Queen Mahamaya"

1983. Vesak. Life of Prince Siddhartha at Gotami Vihara. Multicoloured.
807 35 c. Type **318** 10 10
808 50 c. "Prince Siddhartha given to Maha Brahma" 10 10
809 5 r. "Prince Siddhartha and the Sleeping Dancers" . . . 55 1·25
810 10 r. "The Meeting with Mara" 90 2·25

319 First Telegraph Transmission, Colombo to Galle, 1858 **320** Henry Woodward Amarasuriya (philanthropist)

1983. 125th Anniv of Telecommunications in Sri Lanka (2 r.) and World Communications Year (10 r.). Multicoloured.
812 2 r. Type **319** 40 50
813 10 r. World Communications Year emblem . . . . . . 2·00 3·50

1983. National Heroes.
814 **320** 50 c. green 30 80
815 – 50 c. blue 30 80
816 – 50 c. mauve 30 80
817 – 50 c. green 30 80
DESIGNS: No. 815, Father Simon Perera (historian); 816, Charles Lorenz (lawyer and newspaper editor); 817, Noordeen Abdul Cader (first President of All-Ceylon Muslim League).

321 Family and Village

1983. Gam Udawa (Village Re-awakening Movement). Multicoloured.
818 50 c. Type **321** 10 25
819 5 r. Village view . . . . 40 1·50

322 Caravan of Bulls

1983. Transport. Multicoloured.
820 35 c. Type **322** 10 10
821 2 r. Steam train . . . . 1·25 1·25
822 2 r. 50 Ox and cart . . . . . 90 1·40
823 5 r. Ford motor car . . . . . 1·75 3·25

323 Sir Tikiri Banda Panabokke
324 C. W. Thamotheram Pillai

1983. 20th Death Anniv of Adigar Sir Tikiri Banda Panabokke.
824 **323** 50 c. red 85 85

1983. C. W. Thamotheram Pillai (Tamil scholar) Commemoration.
825 **324** 50 c. brown 85 85

325 Arabi Pasha
326 Sri Lanka Wood Pigeon

1983. Centenary of Banishment of Arabi Pasha (Egyptian nationalist).
826 **325** 50 c. green . . . . 1·00 1·00

1983. Birds (2nd series). Multicoloured.
827 25 c. Type **326** 30 30
828 35 c. Large Sri Lanka white eye 30 30
829 2 r. Sri Lanka dusky blue flycatcher 30 10
829a 7 r. As 35 c. 30 25
830 20 r. Ceylon coucal . . . . . 80 1·75

327 Pelene Siri Vajiragnana
328 Mary praying over Jesus and St. Joseph welcoming Shepherds

1983. Pelene Siri Vajiragnana (scholar) Commem.
832 **327** 50 c. brown 90 90

1983. Christmas.
833 **328** 50 c. multicoloured . . . 10 15
834 5 r. multicoloured 25 60

1983. No. 680a surch **.60**.
836 **236** 60 c. on 50 c. gold, green and emerald . . . . 1·75 1·25

331 Paddy Field, Globe and F.A.O. Emblem

1984. World Food Day.
838 **331** 3 r. multicoloured . . . . 40 1·25

332 Modern Tea Factory
333 Students and University

1984. Centenary of Colombo Tea Auctions. Multicoloured.
839 1 r. Type **332** 15 15
840 2 r. Logo 30 45
841 5 r. Girl picking tea . . . . . 75 1·75
842 10 r. Auction in progress . . 1·50 2·75

1984. 4th Anniv of Mahapola Scheme for Development and Education. Multicoloured.
843 60 c. Type **333** 10 15
844 1 r. Teacher with Gnana Darsana class 10 15
845 5 r. 50 Student with books and microscope . . . . 35 1·25
846 6 r. Mahapola lamp symbol . 40 1·25

334 King Daham Sonda instructing Angels

1984. Vesak. The Story of King Daham Sonda from Ancient Casket Paintings. Multicoloured.
847 35 c. Type **334** 15 10
848 60 c. Elephant paraded with gift of gold 30 25
849 5 r. King Daham Sonda leaps into mouth of God Sakra . 1·00 2·25
850 10 r. God Sakra carrying King Daham Sonda . . . . . . 1·40 3·25

335 Development Programme Logo
336 Dodanduwe Siri Piyaratana Tissa Mahanayake Thero (Buddhist scholar)

1984. Sri Lanka Lions Clubs' Development Programme.
852 **335** 60 c. multicoloured . . . 1·40 90

1984. National Heroes.
853 **336** 60 c. bistre 30 75
854 – 60 c. green 30 75
855 – 60 c. green 30 75
856 – 60 c. red 30 75
857 – 60 c. brown 30 75
DESIGNS: No. 854, G. P. Wickremarachchi (physician); 855, Sir Mohamed Macan Markar (politician); 856, Dr. W. Arthur de Silva (philanthropist); 857, K. Balasingham (lawyer).

337 Association Emblem

1984. Centenary of Public Service Mutual Provident Association.
858 **337** 4 r. 60 multicoloured . . . 45 1·75

338 Sri Lanka Village

1984. 6th Anniv of "Gam Udawa" (Village Re-awakening Movement).
859 **338** 60 c. multicoloured 30 65

339 World Map showing A.P.B.U. Countries

1984. 20th Anniv of Asia-Pacific Broadcasting Union.
860 **339** 7 r. multicoloured . . . . 2·00 3·00

340 Drummers and Elephant carrying Royal Instructions

1984. Esala Perahera (Procession of the Tooth), Kandy. Multicoloured.
861 4 r. 60 Type **340** . . . . . . 90 1·75
862 4 r. 60 Dancers and elephants 90 1·75
863 4 r. 60 Elephant carrying Tooth Relic . . . . 90 1·75
864 4 r. 60 Custodian of the Sacred Tooth and attendants . . . 90 1·75
Nos. 861/4 were printed together, se-tenant, forming a composite design.

341 "Vanda memoria Ernest Soysa" (orchid)
342 Symbolic Athletes and Stadium

1984. 50th Anniv of Ceylon Orchid Circle. Multicoloured.
866a 60 c. Type **341** . . . . 60 1·25
867a 4 r. 60 "Acanthephippium bicolor" . . . . 1·50 3·50
868a 5 r. "Vanda tessellata var. rufescens" . . . . 1·00 3·50
869 10 r. "Anoectochilus setaceus" 3·75 5·50

1984. 1st National School Games.
871 **342** 60 c. black, grey & blue . 1·50 1·50

343 D. S. Senanayake, Temple and Fields

1984. Birth Centenary of D. S. Senanayake (former Prime Minister). Multicoloured.
872 35 c. Type **343** 10 10
873 60 c. Senanayake and statue . 10 10
874 4 r. 60 Senanayake and irrigation project 35 50
875 6 r. Senanayake and House of Representatives 40 60

344 Lake House
345 Agricultural Workers and Globe

1984. 150th Anniv of "Observer" Newspaper.
876 **344** 4 r. 60 multicoloured . . 1·75 3·00

1984. 20th Anniv of World Food Programme.
877 **345** 7 r. multicoloured . . . . 1·50 1·25

346 College Emblem
347 Dove and Stylized Figures

1984. Centenary of Baari Arabic College, Weligama.
878 **346** 4 r. 60 green, turq & bl . 1·25 2·50

1985. International Youth Year. Mult.
879 4 r. 60 Type **347** 50 60
880 20 r. Dove, stylized figures and flower . . . . 2·00 3·00

348 Religious Symbols
349 College Crest

1985. World Religion Day.
881 **348** 4 r. 60 multicoloured . . 1·25 1·50

1985. 150th Anniv of Royal College, Colombo.
882 **349** 60 c. yellow and blue . . 10 25
883 – 7 r. multicoloured . . . . 70 2·25
DESIGN: 7 r. Royal College.

350 Banknotes, Buildings, Ship and "Wheel of Life"
351 Wariyapola Sri Sumangala Thero

1985. 5th Anniv of Mahapola Scheme.
884 **350** 60 c. multicoloured . . . 90 1·00

1985. Wariyapola Sri Sumangala Thero (Buddhist priest and patriot) Commemoration.
885 **351** 60 c. brown, yellow & blk . 70 1·00

352 Victoria Dam

1985. Inaug of Victoria Hydro-electric Project. Mult.
886 60 c. Type **352** 75 50
887 7 r. Map of Sri Lanka enclosing dam and power station (vert) 3·50 4·50

353 Cover of 50th Edition of International Buddhist Annual, "Vesak Sirisara"

354 Ven. Waskaduwe Sri Subhuthi (priest and scholar)

1985. Centenary of Vesak Poya Holiday. Mult.

888 35 c. Type **353** 10 10
889 60 c. Buddhists worshipping at temple 10 10
890 6 r. Buddhist Theosophical Society Headquarters, Colombo 50 75
891 9 r. Buddhist flag . . . . . . 80 1·25

1985. Personalities.

893 **354** 60 c. black, orange & brown 20 40
894 – 60 c. black, orange & mauve 20 40
895 – 60 c. black, orange & brown 20 40
896 – 60 c. black, orange & green 20 40

DESIGNS: 894, Revd. Fr. Peter A. Pillai (educationist and social reformer); 895, Dr. Senarath Paranavitane (scholar); 896, A. M. Wapche Marikar (architect and educationist).

355 Stylised Village and People

356 Emblem

1985. Gam Udawa '85 (Village Re-awakening Movement).

897 **355** 60 c. multicoloured . . . 1·00 1·00

1985. 50th Anniv of Colombo Young Poets' Association.

898 **356** 60 c. multicoloured . . . 30 75

357 Kothmale Dam and Reservoir

1985. Inauguration of Kothmale Hydro-electric Project. Multicoloured.

899 60 c. Type **357** 60 25
900 6 r. Kothmale Power Station . 1·40 2·50

358 Federation Logo

359 Breast feeding

1985. 10th Asian and Oceanic Congress of Obstetrics and Gynaecology.

901 **358** 7 r. multicoloured . . . . 3·25 2·50

1985. U.N.I.C.E.F. Child Survival and Development Programme. Multicoloured.

902 35 c. Type **359** 30 10
903 60 c. Child and oral rehydration salts 45 30
904 6 r. Weighing child (growth monitoring) . . . . 2·25 3·00
905 9 r. Immunization . . . . . . 2·75 4·00

360 Blowing Indian Chank Shell

1985. 10th Anniv of World Tourism Organization. Multicoloured.

907 1 r. Type **360** 20 10
908 6 r. Parliamentary Complex, Jayawardhanapura, Kotte . 70 80
909 7 r. Tea plantation 80 90
910 10 r. Ruwanveliseya (Buddhist shrine), Anuradhapura . . . 1·25 1·40

361 Casket containing Land Grant Deed

362 Koran and Map of Sri Lanka

1985. 50th Anniv of Land Development Ordinance.

912 **361** 4 r. 60 multicoloured . . 2·00 2·50

1985. Translation of The Koran into Sinhala.

913 **362** 60 c. violet and gold . . 1·00 1·00

363 "Our Lady of Matara" Statue

365 Linked Arms and Map of S.A.A.R.C. Countries

1985. Christmas. Multicoloured.

914 60 c. Type **363** 30 15
915 9 r. "Our Lady of Madhu" Statue . . . . 1·50 2·25

1985. Nos. 680b, 780, 828, 860 and 879 surch.

917 **236** 75 c. on 60 c. gold, green and emerald 10 10
918 **347** 1 r. on 4 r. 60 mult . . . 2·00 1·50
919 **339** 1 r. on 7 r. multicoloured 2·50 1·50
920 **269** 5 r. 75 on 2 r. 50 mult . . 2·75 1·00
921 – 7 r. on 35 c. multicoloured (No. 828) . . . . 2·75 1·25

1985. 1st Summit Meeting of South Asian Association for Regional Co-operation, Dhaka, Bangladesh. Multicoloured.

922 60 c. Type **365** . . . . 2·25 4·25
923 5 r. 50 Logo and flags of member countries . . . . 2·25 4·25

366 "Viceroy Special" Train

368 Wijewardena

367 Girl and Boy Students

1986. Inaugural Run of "Viceroy Special" Train from Colombo to Kandy.

924 **366** 1 r. multicoloured . . . . 1·50 1·50

1986. 6th Anniv of Mahapola Scheme.

925 **367** 75 c. multicoloured . . . 40 60

1986. Birth Centenary of D. R. Wijewardena (newspaper publisher).

926 **368** 75 c. brown and green . . 30 60

369 Ven. Welitara Gnanatillake Maha Nayake Thero

370 Red Cross Flag and Personnel

1986. Ven. Welitara Gnanatillake Maha Nayake Thero (scholar) Commemoration.

927 **369** 75 c. multicoloured 70 80

1986. 50th Anniv of Sri Lanka Red Cross Society.

928 **370** 75 c. multicoloured . . . . 2·00 1·75

371 Comet depicted as Goddess visiting Sun-god

372 Woman lighting Lamp

1986. Appearance of Halley's Comet. Multicoloured.

929 50 c. Type **371** 10 20
930 75 c. Comet and constellations of Scorpius and Sagittarius . . 10 20
931 6 r. 50 Comet's orbit . . . . . 30 1·25
932 8 r. 50 Edmond Halley . . . . 55 1·75

1986. Sinhalese and Tamil New Year. Multicoloured.

934 50 c. Type **372** 10 20
935 75 c. Woman and festive foods 10 20
936 6 r. 50 Women playing drum . 30 1·60
937 8 r. 50 Anointing and making offerings at temple . . . . . 55 2·00

373 The King donating Elephant to the Brahmin

1986. Vesak. Wall paintings from Samudragiri Temple, Mirissa. Multicoloured.

939 50 c. Type **373** 15 20
940 75 c. The Bodhisattva in the Vasavarthi heaven 15 20
941 5 r. The offering of milk rice by Sujatha . . . . 40 1·75
942 10 r. The offering of parched corn and honey by Thapassu and Bhalluka . . . . 60 2·25

374 Ven. Kalukondayave Sri Prajnasekhara Maha Nayake Thero (Buddhist leader and social refomer)

375 Stylized Village and People

1986. National Heroes. Multicoloured.

943 75 c. Type **374** 20 60
944 75 c. Brahmachari Walisinghe Harischandra (social reformer) (birth centenary) 20 60
945 75 c. Martin Wickramasinghe (author and scholar) 20 60
946 75 c. G. G. Ponnambalam (politician) 20 60
947 75 c. A. M. A. Azeez (Islamic scholar) (75th birth anniv) . . 20 60

1986. Gam Udawa '86 (Village Re-awakening Movement).

948 **375** 75 c. multicoloured . . . . 1·50 1·50

376 Co-op Flag and Emblem

377 Arthur V. Dias

1986. 75th Anniv of Sri Lanka Co-operative Movement.

949 **376** 1 r. multicoloured . . . . 1·50 1·50

1986. Birth Centenary of Arthur V. Dias (philanthropist).

950 **377** 1 r. brown and blue . . . 1·50 1·50

378 Bull Elephant

1986. Sri Lanka Wild Elephant. Mult.

951 5 r. Type **378** . . . . 4·50 4·50
952 5 r. Cow elephant and calf . . 4·50 4·50
953 5 r. Cow elephant . . . . . . 4·50 4·50
954 5 r. Elephants bathing . . . . 4·50 4·50

379 Congress Logo

381 Anniversary Logo

380 Map showing Route of Cable and Telephone Receiver

1986. 2nd Indo-Pacific Congress on Legal Medicine and Forensic Sciences.

955 **379** 8 r. 50 multicoloured . . 2·25 1·75

1986. SEA-ME-WE Submarine Cable Project.

956 **380** 5 r. 75 multicoloured . . 2·50 1·50

1986. 25th Anniv of Dag Hammarskjold Award.

957 **381** 2 r. multicoloured 75 65

382 Logo on Flag

383 Logo

1986. 2nd National School Games.

958 **382** 1 r. multicoloured . . . . 2·75 1·90

1986. 60th Anniv of Surveyors' Institute of Sri Lanka.

959 **383** 75 c. brown & light brown 60 85

384 College Building and Crest

1986. Centenary of Ananda College, Colombo.

960 **384** 75 c. multicoloured . . . 10 10
961 – 5 r. multicoloured 30 50
962 – 5 r. 75 multicoloured . . 30 50
963 – 6 r. red, gold and lilac . . 35 60

DESIGNS: 5 r. Sports field and college crest; 5 r. 75, Col. H. S. Olcott (founder), Ven. Migettuwatte Gunananda, Ven. Hikkaduwe Sri Sumangala (Buddhist leaders) and Buddhist flag; 6 r. College flag.

385 Mangrove Swamp

1986. Mangrove Conservation. Multicoloured.

964	35 c. Type **385**	40	20
965	50 c. Mangrove tree	50	30
966	75 c. Germinating mangrove flower	60	30
967	6 r. Fiddler crab	4·00	5·00

386 Family and Housing Estate

1987. International Year of Shelter for the Homeless.

968 **386** 75 c. multicoloured . . . 1·75 40

387 Ven. Ambagahawatte Indasabhawaragnanasamy Thero

388 Proctor John de Silva

1987. Ven. Ambagahawatte Indasabhawaragnanasamy Thero (Buddhist monk) Commem.

969 **387** 5 r. 75 multicoloured . . . 2·25 1·00

1987. Proctor John de Silva (playwright) Commemoration.

970 **388** 5 r. 75 multicoloured . . . 70 70

389 Mahapola Logo and Aspects of Communication

1987. 7th Anniv of Mahapola Scheme.

971 **389** 75 c. multicoloured . . . 75 75

390 Dr. R. L. Brohier

1987. Dr Richard L. Brohier (historian amd surveyor) Commemoration.

972 **390** 5 r. 75 multicoloured . . . 1·75 75

391 Tyre Corporation Building, Kelaniya, and Logo

1987. 25th Anniv of Sri Lanka Tyre Corporation.

973 **391** 5 r. 75 black, red and orange 45 45

392 Logo

1987. Centenary of Sri Lanka Medical Association.

974 **392** 5 r. 75 brown, yellow and black . . . 1·75 1·75

393 Clasped Hands, Farmer and Paddy Field

394 Exhibition Logo

1987. Inauguration of Farmers' Pension and Social Security Benefit Scheme.

975 **393** 75 c. multicoloured . . . 55 65

1987. Mahaweli Maha Goviya Contest and Agro Mahaweli Exhibition.

976 **394** 75 c. multicoloured . . . 30 30

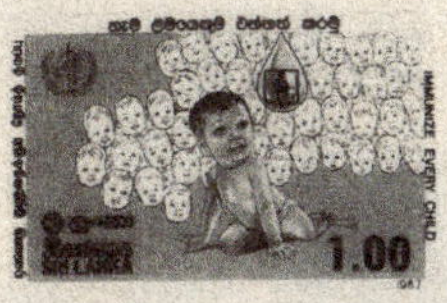

395 Young Children with W.H.O. and Immunization Logos

1987. World Health Day.

977 **395** 1 r. multicoloured . . . 2·50 40

396 Girls playing on Swing

397 Lotus Lanterns

1987. Sinhalese and Tamil New Year. Multicoloured.

978	75 c. Type **396**	10	10
979	5 r. Girls with oil lamp and sun symbol	50	50

1987. Vesak. Multicoloured.

980	50 c. Type 397	10	10
981	75 c. Octagonal lanterns	10	10
982	5 r. Star lanterns	30	30
983	10 r. Gok lanterns	45	55

398 Emerald-collared Parakeet

1987. Birds (3rd series). Multicoloured.

985A	50 c. Type **398**	40	10
986A	1 r. Legge's flowerpecker	60	10
987A	5 r. Ceylon white-headed starling	1·25	1·25
988A	10 r. Ceylon jungle babbler	1·75	2·00

399 Ven. Heenatiyana Sri Dhammaloka Maha Nayake Thero (Buddhist monk)

1987. National Heroes. Multicoloured.

990	75 c. Type **399**	40	35
991	75 c. P. de S. Kularatne (educationist)	40	35
992	75 c. M. C. Abdul Rahuman (legislator)	40	35

400 Peasant Family and Village

1987. Gam Udawa '87 (Village Re-awakening Movement).

993 **400** 75 c. multicoloured . . . 30 30

401 "Mesua nagassarium"

1987. Forest Conservation. Multicoloured.

994	75 c. Type **401**	10	10
995	5 r. Elephants in forest	1·00	70

402 Dharmaraja College, Crest and Col. Olcott (founder)

1987. Centenary of Dharmaraja College, Kandy.

996 **402** 75 c. multicoloured . . . 1·50 30

403 Youth Sevices Logo

1987. 20th Anniv of National Youth Services.

997 **403** 75 c. multicoloured . . . 20 20

404 Arm holding Torch and Mahaweli Logo

405 Open Bible and Logo

1987. Mahaweli Games.

998 **404** 75 c. multicoloured . . . 2·50 2·00

1987. 175th Anniv of Ceylon Bible Society.

999 **405** 5 r. 75 multicoloured . . . 40 40

406 Hurdler and Committee Symbol

1987. 50th Anniv of National Olympic Committee.

1000 **406** 10 r. multicoloured . . . 2·50 1·25

407 Madonna and Child, Flowers and Oil Lamp

408 Sir Ernest de Silva

1987. Christmas. Multicoloured.

1001	75 c. Type **407**	10	10
1002	10 r. Christ Child in manger, star and dove	35	40

1987. Birth Centenary of Sir Ernest de Silva (philanthropist and philatelist).

1004 **408** 75 c. multicoloured . . . 30 30

409 Society Logo

410 University Flag and Graduates

1987. 150th Anniv of Kandy Friend-in-Need Society.

1005 **409** 75 c. multicoloured . . . 30 30

1987. 1st Convocation of Buddhist and Pali University.

1006 **410** 75 c. multicoloured . . . 30 30

411 Father Joseph Vaz

412 Wheel of Dhamma, Dagaba and Bo Leaf

1987. 300th Anniv of Arrival of Father Joseph Vaz in Kandy.

1007 **411** 75 c. multicoloured . . . 30 30

1988. 30th Anniv of Buddhist Publication Society, Kandy.

1008 **412** 75 c. multicoloured . . . 30 30

413 Dharmayatra Lorry

414 Society Logo

1988. 5th Anniv of Mahapola Dharmayatra Service.

1009 **413** 75 c. multicoloured . . . 30 30

1988. Centenary of Ceylon Society of Arts.

1010 **414** 75 c. multicoloured . . . 30 30

415 National Youth Centre, Maharagama

416 Citizens with National Flag and Map of Sri Lanka

1988. Opening of National Youth Centre, Maharagama.

1011 **415** 1 r. multicoloured . . . 2·25 30

1988. 40th Anniv of Independence. Mult.

1012	75 c. Type **416**	10	10
1013	8 r. 50 "40" in figures and lion emblem	70	70

417 Graduates, Clay Lamp and Open Book

419 Ven. Weligama Sri Sumangala Maha Nayake Thero

418 Bus and Logo

1988. 8th Anniv of Mahapola Scheme.
1014 **417** 75 c. multicoloured . . . 20 20

1988. 30th Anniv of Sri Lanka Transport Board.
1015 **418** 5 r. 75 multicoloured . . 55 55

1988. Ven. Weligama Sri Sumangala Maha Nayake Thero (Buddhist monk) Commemoration.
1016 **419** 75 c. multicoloured . . . 20 20

420 Regimental Colour

421 Chevalier I. X. Pereira

1988. Centenary of Regiment of Artillery.
1017 **420** 5 r. 75 multicoloured . . 2·25 80

1986. Birth Centenary of Chevalier I. X. Pereira (politician).
1018 **421** 5 r. 75 multicoloured . . 30 30

422 Invitation to the Deities and Brahmas

423 Father Ferdinand Bonnel (educationist)

1988. Vesak. Paintings from Narendrarama Rajamaha Temple, Suriyagoda. Multicoloured.
1019 50 c. Type **422** 15 15
1020 75 c. Bodhisathva at the Seventh Step 15 15

1988. National Heroes. Multicoloured.
1022 75 c. Type **423** 15 15
1023 75 c. Sir Razik Fareed (politician) 15 15
1024 75 c. W. F. Gunawardhana (scholar) 15 15
1025 75 c. Edward Nugawela (politician) 15 15
1026 75 c. Chief Justice Sir Arthur Wijeyewardene 15 15

424 Stylized Figures and Re-awakened Village

1988. 10th Anniv of Gam Udawa (Village Re-awakening Movement).
1027 **424** 75 c. multicoloured . . . 20 20

425 Maliyadeva College, Kurunegala, and Crest

1988. Centenary of Maliyadeva College, Kurunegala.
1028 **425** 75 c. multicoloured . . . 20 20

426 M. J. M. Lafir, Billiard Game and Trophy

1988. Mohamed Junaid Mohamed Lafir (World Amateur Billiards Champion, 1973) Commem.
1029 **426** 5 r. 75 multicoloured . . 30 30

427 Flags of Australia and Sri Lanka, Handclasp and Map of Australia

1988. Bicentenary of Australian Settlement.
1030 **427** 8 r. 50 multicoloured . . 40 40

428 Ven. Kataluwe Sri Gunaratana Maha Nayake Thero

429 Athlete, Rice and Hydro-electric Dam

1988. Ven. Kataluwe Sri Gunaratana Maha Nayake Thero (Buddhist monk) Commem.
1031 **428** 75 c. multicoloured . . 20 20

1988. Mahaweli Games.
1032 **429** 75 c. multicoloured . . 20 20

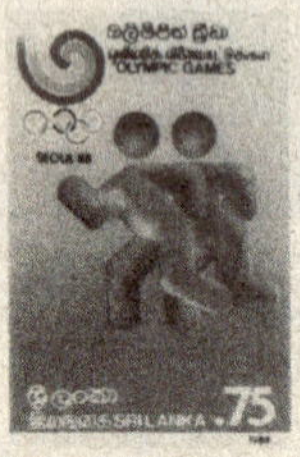

430 Athletics

431 Outline Map of Sri Lanka and Anniversary Logo

1988. Olympic Games, Seoul. Multicoloured.
1033 75 c. Type **430** 10 10
1034 1 r. Swimming 10 10
1035 5 r. 75 Boxing 40 40
1036 8 r. 50 Map of Sri Lanka and logos of Olympic Committee and Seoul Games 70 70

1988. 40th Anniv of W.H.O.
1038 **431** 75 c. multicoloured . . 20 20

432 Games Logo

433 Mahatma Gandhi

1988. 3rd National School Games.
1039 **432** 1 r. black, gold & mauve 1·40 20

1988. 40th Death Anniv of Mahatma Gandhi.
1040 **433** 75 c. multicoloured . . 50 20

434 Globe with Forms of Transport and Communications

1988. Asia-Pacific Transport and Communications Decade.
1041 **434** 75 c. multicoloured . . 20 10
1042 – 5 r. 75 mauve, blue & blk 80 50
DESIGN: 5 r. 75, Antenna tower with dish aerials and forms of transport.

435 Woman with Rice Sheaf and Hydro-electric Project

1988. Commissioning of Randenigala Project. Multicoloured.
1043 75 c. Type **435** 10 10
1044 5 r. 75 Randenigala Dam and reservoir 45 45

436 Handicrafts and Centre Logo in Cupped Hands

437 Angel, Dove, Olive Branch and Globe

1988. Opening of Gramodaya Folk Art Centre, Colombo.
1045 **436** 75 c. multicoloured . . . 20 20

1988. Christmas. Multicoloured.
1046 75 c. Type **437** 10 10
1047 8 r. 50 Shepherds and Star of Bethlehem 50 60

438 Dr. E. W. Adikaram

439 Open Book in Tree and Children reading

1988. Dr. E. W. Adikaram (educationist) Commemoration.
1049 **438** 75 c. multicoloured . . . 20 20

1989. 10th Anniv of Free Distribution of School Text Books.
1050 **439** 75 c. multicoloured . . . 20 20

440 Wimalaratne Kumaragama

441 Logo and New Chamber of Commerce Building

1989. Poets of Sri Lanka. Multicoloured.
1051 75 c. Type **440** 15 15
1052 75 c. G. H. Perera 15 15
1053 75 c. Sagara Palansuriya . . . 15 15
1054 75 c. P. B. Alwis Perera . . . 15 15

1989. 150th Anniv of Ceylon Chamber of Commerce.
1055 **441** 75 c. multicoloured . . . 20 20

442 Bodhisatva at Lunch and Funeral Pyre

1989. Vesak. Wall Paintings from Medawala Monastery, Harispattuwa. Multicoloured.
1056 50 c. Type **442** 10 10
1057 75 c. Rescue of King Vessantara's childen by god Sakra 10 10
1058 5 r. Bodhisatva ploughing and his son attacked by snake . 30 35
1059 5 r. 75 King Vessantara giving away his children 30 35

443 Parawahera Vajiragnana Thero (Buddhist monk)

444 College Crest

1989. National Heroes. Multicoloured.
1061 75 c. Type **443** 15 15
1062 75 c. Fr. Maurice Jacques Le Goc (educationist) 15 15
1063 75 c. Hemapala Munidasa (author) 15 15
1064 75 c. Ananda Samarakoon (composer) 15 15
1065 75 c. Simon Casie Chitty (scholar) (horiz) 15 15

1989. 150th Anniv of Harley College, Point-Pedro (1988).
1066 **444** 75 c. multicoloured . . . 20 20

445 Dramachakra, Lamp, Buddhist Flag and Map

1989. Establishment of Ministry of Buddha Sasana.
1067 **445** 75 c. multicoloured . . . 20 20

446 Hands holding Brick and Trowel, House and Family

1989. Gam Udawa '89 (Village Re-awakening Movement).
1068 **446** 75 c. multicoloured . . . 20 20

447 Two Families and Hand turning Cogwheel

448 Dunhinda Falls

1989. Janasaviya Development Programme.
1069 **447** 75 c. multicoloured . . . 20 20
1070a 1 r. multicoloured . . . 10 10

1989. Waterfalls. Multicoloured.
1071 75 c. Type **448** 10 10
1072 1 r. Rawana Falls 10 10
1073 5 r. 75 Laxapana Falls . . . 45 45
1074 8 r. 50 Diyaluma Falls . . . 60 60

449 Rev. James Chater (missionary) and Baptist Church

1989. 177th Anniv of Baptist Church in Sri Lanka.
1075 **449** 5 r. 75 multicoloured . . 30 30

450 Bicentenary Logo

1989. Bicentenary of French Revolution.
1076 **450** 8 r. 50 black, blue & red 70 70

451 Old and New Bank Buildings and Logo

452 Water Lily, Dharma Chakra and Books

1989. 50th Anniv of Bank of Ceylon. Mult.
1077 75 c. Type **451** 10 10
1078 5 r. "Bank of Ceylon orchid and logo" 45 45

1989. State Literary Festival.
1079 **452** 75 c. multicoloured 20 20

453 Wilhelm Geiger **454** H. V. Perera, Q.C.

1989. Wilhelm Geiger (linguistic scholar) Commemoration.
1080 **453** 75 c. multicoloured 20 20

1989. Constitutional Pioneers. Multicoloured.
1082 75 c. Type **454** 20 20
1083 75 c. Prof. Ivor Jennings 20 20

455 Sir Cyril de Zoysa **456** Map of South-east Asia and Telecommunications Equipment

1989. Sir Cyril de Zoysa (Buddhist philanthropist) Commemoration.
1084 **455** 75 c. multicoloured 20 20

1989. 10th Anniv of Asia-Pacific Telecommunity.
1085 **456** 5 r. 75 multicoloured 45 45

457 Members with Offerings and Water Lily on Map of Sri Lanka **458** "Apollo 11" Blast-off and Astronauts

1989. 50th Anniv of Sri Sucharitha Welfare Movement.
1086 **457** 75 c. multicoloured 20 20

1989. 20th Anniv of First Manned Landing on Moon. Multicoloured.
1087 75 c. Type **458** 15 10
1088 1 r. Armstrong leaving lunar module "Eagle" 20 10
1089 2 r. Astronaut on Moon 35 30
1090 5 r. 75 Lunar surface and Earth from Moon 60 70

459 Shepherds **460** Ven. Sri Devananda Nayake Thero

1989. Christmas. Multicoloured.
1092 75 c. Type **459** 10 10
1093 8 r. 50 Magi with gifts 45 1·25

1989. Ven. Sri Devananda Nayake Thero (Buddhist monk) Commemoration.
1095 **460** 75 c. multicoloured 20 20

461 College Building, Crest and Revd. William Ault (founder)

1989. 175th Anniv of Methodist Central College, Batticaloa.
1096 **461** 75 c. multicoloured 20 20

462 Golf Ball, Clubs and Logo

1989. Cent of Nuwara Eliya Golf Club. Mult.
1097 75 c. Type **462** 1·00 25
1098 8 r. 50 Course and club house 3·00 1·25

463 "Raja" **464** College Building and G. Wickremarachchi (founder)

1989. "Raja" Royal Ceremonial Elephant, Kandy Commemoration.
1099 **463** 75 c. multicoloured 2·50 65

1989. 60th Anniv of Gampaha Wickremarachchi Institute of Ayurveda Medicine.
1100 **464** 75 c. multicoloured 20 20

465 Ven. Udunuwara Sri Sarananda Thero **466** Diesel Train on Viaduct, Ella-Demodara Line

1989. Ven. Udunuwara Sri Sarananda Thero (Buddhist monk) Commemoration.
1101 **465** 75 c. multicoloured 20 20

1989. 125 Years of Sir Lanka Railways. Mult.
1102 75 c. Type **466** 30 20
1103 2 r. Diesel train at Maradana Station 40 25
1104 3 r. Steam train and semaphore signal 45 30
1105 7 r. Steam train leaving station, 1864 75 50

467 Cardinal Thomas Cooray **468** Farmer and Wife with Dagaba and Dam

1989. Cardinal Thomas Cooray Commem.
1106 **467** 75 c. multicoloured 75 30

1989. Agro Mahaweli Development Programme.
1107 **468** 75 c. multicoloured 20 20

469 Justin Wijayawardena **470** Ven. Induruwe Uttarananda Mahanayake Thero

1990. Justin Wijayawardena (scholar) Commem.
1108 **469** 1 r. multicoloured 1·25 20

1990. Surch.
1108a 25 c. on 5 r. 75 King Vessantara giving away his children (No. 1059) 30 20
1109a 1 r. on 75 c. Type **447** 40 30

1990. 4th Death Anniv of Ven. Induruwe Uttarananda Mahanayake Thero (Buddhist theologian).
1109 **470** 1 r. multicoloured 90 90

471 Two Graduates, Lamp and Open Book

1990. 9th Anniv of Mahapola Scheme.
1110 **471** 75 c. multicoloured 20 20

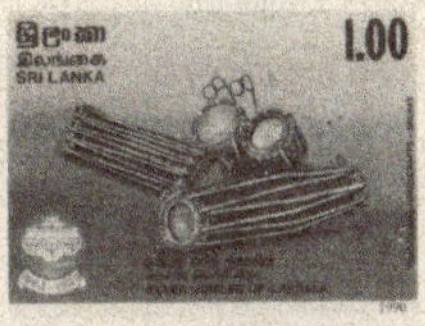

472 Traditional Drums

1990. 25th Anniv of Laksala Traditional Handicrafts Organization. Multicoloured.
1111 1 r. Type **472** 10 10
1112 2 r. Silverware 15 15
1113 3 r. Lacquerware 20 20
1114 8 r. Dumbara mats 40 40

473 King Maha Prathapa visiting Queen Chandra

1990. Vesak. Wall Paintings from Buduraja Maha Viharaya, Wewurukannala. Mult.
1115 75 c. Type **473** 10 10
1116 1 r. Execution of Prince Dharmapala 10 10
1117 2 r. Prince Mahinsasaka with the Water Demon 15 15
1118 8 r. King Dahamsonda with the God Sakra disguised as a demon 35 35

474 Father T. Long (educationist) **476** Gold Reliquary

475 Janasaviya Workers

1990. National Heroes. Multicoloured.
1120 1 r. Type **474** 20 20
1121 1 r. Prof. M. Ratnasuriya (37×25 mm) 20 20
1122 1 r. D. Wijewardene (patriot) (37×25 mm) 20 20
1123 1 r. L. Manjusri (artist) (37×25 mm) 20 20

1990. 12th Anniv of Gam Udawa and Opening of Janasaviya Centre, Pallekele.
1124 **475** 1 r. multicoloured 90 30

1990. Cent of Department of Archaeology.
1125 **476** 1 r. black and yellow 10 10
1126 – 2 r. black and grey 15 15
1127 – 3 r. black, green & brown 20 20
1128 – 8 r. black and brown 45 35

DESIGNS: 2 r. Statuette of Ganesh; 3 r. Terrace of the Bodhi-tree, Isurumuniya Vihara; 8 r. Inscription of King Nissankamalla.

477 Male Tennis Player at Left

1990. 75th Anniv of Sri Lanka Tennis Association. Multicoloured.
1129 1 r. Type **477** 65 65
1130 1 r. Male tennis player at right 65 65
1131 8 r. Male tennis players 1·75 2·00
1132 8 r. Female tennis players 1·75 2·00

Nos. 1129/30 and 1131/2 were each printed together, se-tenant, each pair forming a composite design of a singles (1 r.) or doubles (8 r.) match.

478 Spotted Loach **479** Rukmani Devi

1990. Endemic Fishes. Multicoloured.
1133 25 c. Type **478** 10 10
1134 2 r. Spotted gourami ("Ornate paradise fish") 30 10
1135 8 r. Mountain labeo 75 80
1136 20 r. Cherry barb 1·50 2·00

1990. 12th Death Anniv of Rukmani Devi (actress and singer).
1138 **479** 1 r. multicoloured 1·75 1·00

480 Innkeeper turning away Mary and Joseph

1990. Christmas. Multicoloured.
1139 1 r. Type **480** 30 10
1140 10 r. Adoration of the Magi 1·75 2·50

481 Health Worker talking to Villagers

1990. World Aids Day. Multicoloured.
1142 1 r. Type **481** 50 15
1143 8 r. Emblem and Aids virus 2·00 2·50

482 Main College Building and Flag **483** Peri Sundaram

1990. 50th Anniv of Dharmapala College, Pannipitiya.
1144 **482** 1 r. multicoloured 1·00 90

1990. Birth Centenary of Peri Sundaram (lawyer and politician).
1145 **483** 1 r. brown and green 1·00 90

484 Letter Box, Galle, 1904

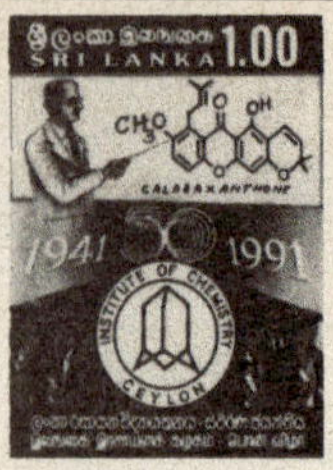

485 Chemical Structure Diagram, Graduating Students and Emblem

1990. 175th Anniv of Sri Lanka Postal Service. Multicoloured.
1146 1 r. Type **484** 40 10
1147 2 r. Mail runner, 1815 . . . . 75 30
1148 5 r. Mail coach, 1832 . . . . 1·25 1·50
1149 10 r. Nuwara-Eliya Post Office, 1894 . . . . 2·00 2·50

1991. 50th Anniv of Institute of Chemistry.
1150 **485** 1 r. multicoloured . . . 1·75 90

486 Kastavahana on Royal Elephant

1991. Vesak. Temple Paintings from Karagampitiya Subodarama. Mult.
1151 75 c. Type **486** 20 10
1152 1 r. Polo Janaka in prison . . 25 10
1153 2 r. Two merchants offering food to Buddha 45 35
1154 11 r. Escape of Queen . . . 2·00 3·00

487 Narada Thero (Buddhist missionary)

488 Society Building

1991. National Heroes. Multicoloured.
1156 1 r. Type **487** 30 35
1157 1 r. Wallewatta Silva (novelist) 30 35
1158 1 r. Sir Muttu Coomaraswamy (lawyer and politician) . . 30 35
1159 1 r. Dr. Andreas Nell (ophthalmic surgeon) . . . 30 35

1991. Centenary of Maha Bodhi Society.
1160 **488** 1 r. multicoloured . . . 1·00 80

489 Women working at Home

1991. 13th Anniv of Gam Udawa Movement.
1161 **489** 1 r. multicoloured . . . 1·25 80

490 Globe and Plan Symbol

492 Ven. Henpitagedera Gnanaseeha Nayake Thero

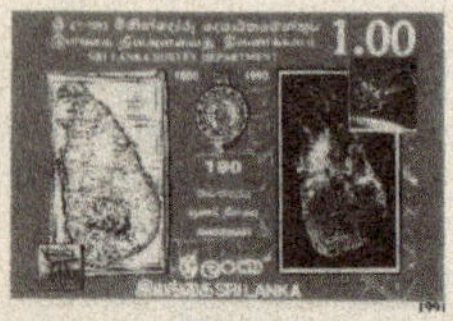

491 17th-century Map and Modern Satellite Photo of Sri Lanka

1991. 40th Anniv of Colombo Plan.
1162 **490** 1 r. violet and blue . . . 1·25 80

1991. 190th Anniv of Sri Lanka Survey Department.
1163 **491** 1 r. multicoloured . . . 1·25 80

1991. 10th Death Anniv of Ven. Nayak Henpitagedera Gnanaseeha Nayake Thero (Buddhist theologian).
1164 **492** 1 r. multicoloured . . . 1·25 80

493 Police Officers of 1866 and 1991 with Badge

1991. 125th Anniv of Sri Lanka Police Force.
1165 **493** 1 r. multicoloured . . . 90 60

494 Kingswood College

1991. Centenary of Kingswood College, Kandy.
1166 **494** 1 r. multicoloured . . . 30 30

495 The Annunciation

496 Early Magneto Telephone

1991. Christmas. Multicoloured.
1167 1 r. Type **495** 20 20
1168 10 r. The Presentation of Jesus in the Temple . . . . . . 75 1·00

1991. Inauguration of Sri Lankan Telecom Corporation. Multicoloured.
1170 1 r. Type **496** 15 10
1171 2 r. Manual switchboard and telephonist 20 15
1172 8 r. Satellite communications system 40 70
1173 10 r. Fibre optics cable and mobile phone 50 80

497 S.A.A.R.C. Logo and Bandaranaike Memorial Hall

1991. 6th South Asian Association for Regional Co-operation Summit, Colombo. Multicoloured.
1174 1 r. Type **497** 15 10
1175 8 r. Logo and hall surrounded by national flags 45 60

498 "Pancha" (Games mascot)

1991. 5th South Asian Federation Games. Multicoloured.
1176 1 r. Type **498** 30 10
1177 2 r. Games logo 35 20
1178 4 r. Sugathadasa Stadium . . . 70 80
1179 11 r. Asia map on globe and national flags . . . . . . 1·75 2·25

499 Crate, Boeing 747-300/400 Airliner and Container Ship

1992. Exports Year.
1180 **499** 1 r. multicoloured . . . . 1·00 80

500 Plucking Tea

501 General Ranjan Wijeratne

1992. 125th Anniv of Tea Industry. Mult.
1181 1 r. Type **500** 35 10
1182 2 r. Healthy family, tea and tea estate 65 20
1183 5 r. Ceylon tea symbol . . . 1·50 1·75
1184 10 r. James Taylor (founder) . 2·00 2·50

1992. 1st Death Anniv of General Ranjan Wijeratne.
1185 **501** 1 r. multicoloured 20 20

502 Olcott Hall, Mahinda College

1992. Centenary of Mahinda College, Galle.
1186 **502** 1 r. multicoloured 20 20

503 Newstead College and Logo

1992. 175th Anniv (1991) of Newstead Girls' College, Negombo.
1187 **503** 1 r. multicoloured 20 20

504 Student and Oil Lamp

506 Ven. Devamottawe Amarawansa (Buddhist missionary)

505 Sama's Parents leaving for Forest

1992. 11th Anniv of Mahapola Scholarship Fund.
1188 **504** 1 r. multicoloured 20 20

1992. Vesak Festival. Sama Jataka Paintings from Kottimbulwala Cave Temple. Multicoloured.
1189 75 c. Type **505** 15 10
1190 1 r. Sama and parents in forest 15 10
1191 8 r. Sama leading blind parents 75 95
1192 11 r. Sama's parents grieving for wounded son . . . . . . 1·25 1·75

1992. National Heroes. Multicoloured.
1194 1 r. Type **506** 10 15
1195 1 r. Richard Mirando (Buddhist philanthropist) . 10 15
1196 1 r. Gate Mudaliyar N. Canaganayagam (Buddhist social reformer) 10 15
1197 1 r. Abdul Azeez (Moorish social reformer) 10 15

MINIMUM PRICE

The minimum price quoted is 10p which represents a handling charge rather than a basis for valuing common stamps. For further notes about prices see introductory pages.

507 Map of Sri Lanka, Flag and Symbol

508 Family in House

1992. 2300th Anniv of Arrival of Buddhism in Sri Lanka.
1198 **507** 1 r. multicoloured . . . 20 20

1992. 14th Anniv of Gam Udawa Movement.
1199 **508** 1 r. multicoloured . . . 20 20

509 Postal Activities and Award

510 Narilata Mask

1992. Postal Service Awards. Multicoloured.
1200 1 r. Type **509** 30 10
1201 10 r. Medals and commemorative cachet . . 1·75 2·00

1992. Kolam Dance Masks. Multicoloured.
1202 1 r. Type **510** 10 10
1203 2 r. Mudali mask 15 10
1204 5 r. Queen mask 35 45
1205 10 r. King mask 55 75

511 19th and 20th-century Players and Match of 1838

512 Running

1992. 160th Anniv of Cricket in Sri Lanka.
1207 **511** 5 r. multicoloured . . . 1·75 1·75

1992. Olympic Games, Barcelona. Mult.
1208 1 r. Type **512** 15 10
1209 11 r. Shooting . . . . 1·00 1·25
1210 13 r. Swimming . . . . . . 1·25 1·50
1211 15 r. Weightlifting . . . . . 1·40 1·75

513 Vijaya Kumaratunga

514 College Building and Crest

1992. Vijaya Kumaratunga (actor) Commem.
1213 **513** 1 r. multicoloured . . . 30 20

1992. Centenary of Al-Bahjathhul Ibraheemiyyah Arabic College.
1214 **514** 1 r. multicoloured . . . 30 20

515 Official Church Seal

516 Nativity

1992. 350th Anniv of Dutch Reformed Church in Sri Lanka.
1215 **515** 1 r. black, green & yellow 60 40

1992. Christmas. Multicoloured.
1216 1 r. Type **516** 10 10
1217 9 r. Family going to church . 70 90

517 Fleet of Columbus

1992. 500th Anniv of Discovery of America by Columbus. Multicoloured.
1219 1 r. Type 517 . . . . 40 10
1220 11 r. Columbus landing in New World . . . . 1·00 1·10
1221 13 r. Wreck of "Santa Maria" 1·25 1·50
1222 15 r. Columbus reporting to Queen Isabella and King Ferdinand . . . . 1·40 1·75

1992. No. 684 surch **2.00.**
1224 **255** 2 r. on 10 c. mult 60 50

519 Ven. Sumedhankara Thero and Dagoba

1992. Birth Centenary of Ven. Dambagasare Sumedhankara Nayake Thero.
1225 **519** 1 r. multicoloured . . . 20 20

520 University Logo, Students and Building

1992. 50th Anniv of University Education in Sri Lanka (1st issue).
1226 **520** 1 r. multicoloured . . . 20 20
See also No. 1227.

521 University of Colombo Building and Logo

1993. 50th Anniv of University Education in Sri Lanka (2nd issue).
1227 **521** 1 r. multicoloured . . . 20 20

522 College Building and Crest

1993. Centenary of Zahira College, Colombo.
1228 **522** 1 r. multicoloured . . . 30 30

523 Magandiya being presented to Buddha

524 Girl Guide, Badge and Camp

1993. Vesak Festival. Verses from the "Dhammapada". Multicoloured.
1229 75 c. Type 523 . . . . 15 10
1230 1 r. Kisa Gotami carrying her dead baby 15 10
1231 3 r. Patachara and her dying family 35 40
1232 10 r. Angulimala praying . . 75 1·00

1993. 75th Anniv of Sri Lanka Girl Guides Association. Multicoloured.
1234 1 r. Type 524 . . . . 30 10
1235 5 r. Girl Guide activities . . 1·00 1·25

525 Ven. Yagirala Pagnananda Maha Nayaka Thero (scholar)

526 Family arriving at New Home

1993. National Heroes. Multicoloured.
1236 1 r. Type 525 . . . . 15 15
1237 1 r. Charles de Silva (politician) 15 15
1238 1 r. Wilmot A. Perera (politician) 15 15
1239 1 r. Abdul Caffoor (philanthropist) 15 15

1993. "Gam Udawa '93".
1240 **526** 1 r. multicoloured . . . 50 30

527 Consumer Movement Flag and Logo

1993. 50th Anniv (1992) of Co-operative Consumer Movement.
1241 **527** 1 r. multicoloured . . . 50 30

528 Ashy-headed Laughing Thrush

1993. Birds (4th series). Multicoloured.
1242 3 r. Type 528 . . . . 10 10
1243 4 r. Brown-capped jungle babbler 10 10
1244 5 r. Red-faced malkoha . . 10 10
1245 10 r. Ceylon grackle ("Ceylon Hill-Mynah") 20 25

529 Talawila Church

1993. 150th Anniv of Talawila Church.
1247 **529** 1 r. multicoloured . . . 50 30

530 Rosette and Mail Delivery

531 College and Flag

1993. Sri Lanka Post Excellent Service Awards.
1248 **530** 1 r. multicoloured . . . 30 20

1993. Centenary of Musaeus College.
1249 **531** 1 r. multicoloured . . . 60 30

532 Presentation of Jesus in the Temple

1993. Christmas. Multicoloured.
1250 1 r. Type 532 . . . . 10 10
1251 17 r. Boy Jesus with the Jewish teachers . . . . 70 1·25

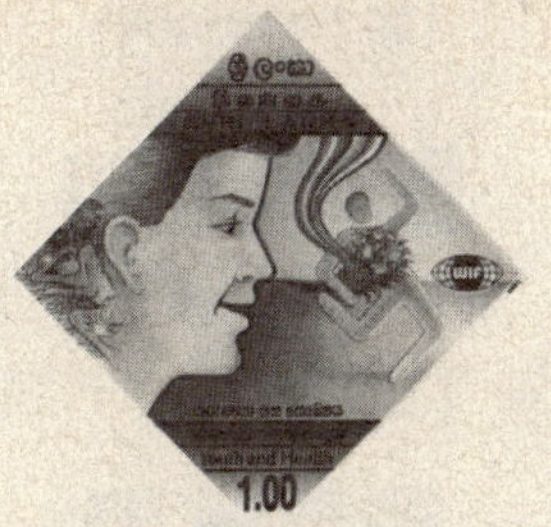
533 Healthy Youth and Drug Addict

1993. Youth and Health Campaign.
1253 **533** 1 r. multicoloured 30 30

534 Maradana Technical College Building and Emblems

535 Trinity College Logo

1993. Centenary of Technical Education.
1254 **534** 1 r. multicoloured 45 30

1994. Centenary of Trinity College, Kandy, Old Boys' Association.
1255 **535** 1 r. multicoloured 20 20

536 College Flag

1994. 150th Anniv of St. Thomas' College, Matara.
1256 **536** 1 r. brown and blue . . . 20 20

537 Ven. Siyambalangamuwe Sri Gunaratana Thero

1994. Ven. Siyambalangamuwe Sri Gunaratana Thero (educationist) Commemoration.
1257 **537** 1 r. multicoloured 40 30

538 College Building and Arms

1994. 125th Anniv of St. Joseph's College, Trincomalee.
1258 **538** 1 r. multicoloured 20 20

539 Man distributing Water

1994. Vesak Festival. Dasa Paramita (Ten Virtues). Multicoloured.
1259 1 r. Type 539 . . . . 10 10
1260 2 r. Man and elephant 50 30
1261 5 r. Man surrounded by women 65 75
1262 17 r. Ruler with snake charmer 1·50 2·00

INDEX

Countries can be quickly located by referring to the index at the end of this volume.

540 I.L.O. Monument, Geneva, Logo and Workers

1994. 75th Anniv of I.L.O.
1264 **540** 1 r. multicoloured . . . 20 20

541 Mahakavindra Dhammaratana Thero (Buddhist theologian)

1994. National Heroes. Multicoloured.
1265 1 r. Type 541 . . . . 10 10
1266 1 r. Ranasinghe Premadasa (former President) 10 10
1267 1 r. Dr. Colvin de Silva (trade union leader) 10 10
1268 1 r. E. Periyathambipillai (Tamil poet) 10 10

542 Conference Logo

1994. 13th International Federation of Social Workers World Conference, Colombo.
1269 **542** 8 r. multicoloured . . . 50 70

543 Ven. Sri Somaratana Thero and Temple

1994. 10th Death Anniv of Ven. Sri Somaratana Thero (Buddhist religious leader).
1270 **543** 1 r. multicoloured . . . 40 30

544 Communication Technology and Logo

1994. "INFOTEL LANKA '94" International Computers and Telecommunications Exhibition.
1271 **544** 10 r. multicoloured . . . 60 80

545 Veddah Tribesman stringing Bow

546 Luca Pacioli (pioneer), Logo and Equipment inside "500"

1994. Year of Indigenous People (1993). Multicoloured.
1272 1 r. Type 545 . . . . 20 10
1273 17 r. Veddah artist and rock paintings . . . . 1·50 1·75

1994. 500th Anniv of Accountancy.
1274 **546** 1 r. multicoloured . . . 40 30

547 Society Emblem

1994. Centenary of Wildlife and Nature Society of Sri Lanka.

1275	547	1 r. green and black . . .	15	10
1276	–	2 r. multicoloured . . .	30	20
1277	–	10 r. multicoloured . . .	1·00	1·10
1278	–	17 r. multicoloured . . .	1·50	2·00

DESIGNS: 2 r. Horned lizard; 10 r. Giant squirrel; 17 r. Sloth bear.

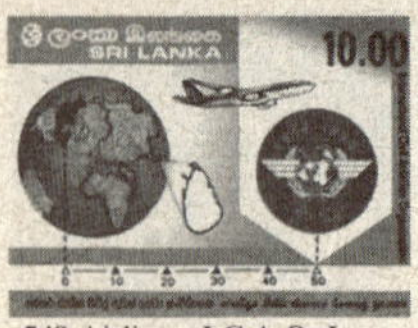

548 Airliner, I.C.A.O. Logo and Globe

1994. 50th Anniv of I.C.A.O.

1280	548	10 r. multicoloured . . .	90	1·00

549 Christmas Crib

1994. Christmas. Multicoloured.

1281	1 r. Type 549	10	10
1282	17 r. St. Joseph's carpentry workshop, Nazareth . . .	75	1·00

550 Map of Sri Lanka and Aspects of Science

1994. 50th Anniv of Sri Lankan Association for the Advancement of Science.

1284	550	1 r. multicoloured . . .	45	30

551 College Building and Arms

552 "Dendrobium maccarthiae"

1994. Cent of Richmond College Old Boys' Assn.

1285	551	1 r. black, red and blue . .	20	20

1994. 60th Anniv of Orchid Circle of Ceylon. Multicoloured.

1286	50 c. Type 552	10	10
1287	1 r. "Cottonia peduncularis" .	15	10
1288	5 r. "Bulbophyllum wightii" .	35	45
1289	17 r. "Habenaria crinifera" .	80	1·25

553 Father Joseph Vaz and Pope John Paul II

554 Blue Water Lily

1995. Papal Visit and Beatification of Father Joseph Vaz.

1291	553	1 r. multicoloured . . .	70	30

1995.

1292	554	1 r. multicoloured . . .	20	10

555 College Building and Arms

1995. Centenary of St. Joseph's College, Colombo.

1293	555	1 r. multicoloured . . .	15	10

556 Sirimavo Bandaranaike and National Flag

1995. Election of Sirimavo Banadaranaike as Prime Minister.

1294	556	2 r. multicoloured . . .	40	30

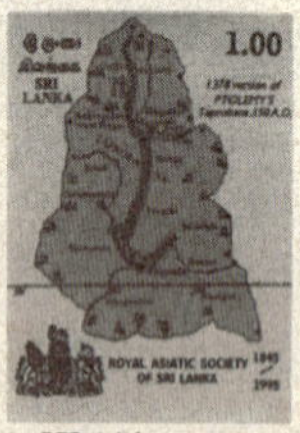

557 Man offering Water to Crew of Outrigger Canoe

558 14th-century Map of Sri Lanka and Society Arms

1995. Vesak Festival. Dasa Paramita (Ten Virtues). Multicoloured.

1295	1 r. Type 557	10	10
1296	2 r. Catching falling man . .	10	15
1297	10 r. Teacher with students .	35	50
1298	17 r. Stopping man digging .	65	80

1995. 150th Anniv of Royal Asiatic Society of Sri Lanka.

1300	558	1 r. multicoloured . . .	30	20

559 Abdul Cader

1995. 120th Birth Anniv of Abdul Cader (lawyer).

1301	559	2 r. multicoloured . . .	30	20

560 College Building

1995. Centenary of St. Aloysius's College, Galle.

1302	560	2 r. multicoloured . . .	40	30

561 Tikiri Ilangaratna

1995. Tikiri Bandara Ilangaratna (politician and author) Commemoration.

1303	561	2 r. multicoloured . . .	40	30

562 Lamps and Schools Flag

1995. Centenary of Dhamma Schools Movement.

1304	562	2 r. multicoloured . . .	40	30

563 G.P.O. Building

1995. Centenary of General Post Office, Colombo.

1305	563	1 r. multicoloured	20	15

564 Young Hands surrounding Old Hand

1995. International Day for the Elderly.

1306	564	2 r. multicoloured	40	30

565 Sri Lankan Parliament Building and C.P.A. Logo

1995. 41st Commonwealth Parliamentary Conference, Colombo.

1307	565	2 r. multicoloured	40	30

566 Anniversary Emblem and Map of Sri Lanka

567 Money falling into Globe Money Box

1995. 50th Anniv of United Nations.

1308	566	2 r. multicoloured	40	30

1995. 71st Anniv of World Thrift Day and 110th Anniv of National Savings Bank.

1309	567	2 r. multicoloured	30	20

568 Diocesan Arms of Colombo and Kurunegala

1995. Christmas. 150th Anniv of Anglican Diocese of Colombo. Multicoloured.

1310	2 r. Type 568	10	10
1311	20 r. Nativity scene and hands surrounding map	80	1·10

569 Flags of Member Countries

570 School Emblem

1995. 10th Anniv of South Asian Association for Regional Co-operation.

1313	569	2 r. multicoloured	40	30

1996.. 175th Anniv of Vincent Girls' High School, Batticaloa.

1314	570	2 r. multicoloured	40	30

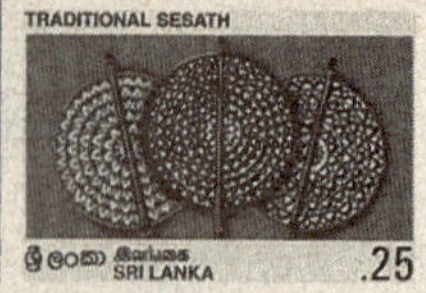

571 Little Basses Lighthouse

572 Traditional Sesath (umbrellas)

1996. Lighthouses. Multicoloured.

1315	50 c. Type 571	10	10
1316	75 c. Great Basses	10	10
1317	2 r. Devinuwara	10	10
1317a	2 r. 50 As 2 r.	10	10
1318	20 r. Galle	40	45

1996. Traditional Handicrafts. Multicoloured.

1320	25 c. Type 572	10	10
1321	8 r. 50 Pottery	15	20
1322	10 r. 50 Mats	20	25
1323	17 r. Lace	30	35

573 School Emblem and Trees

1996. Centenary of Chundikuli Girls' College, Jaffna.

1325	573	2 r. multicoloured . . .	30	20

574 Upaka and Capa

575 Diving

1996. Vesak Festival. Multicoloured.

1326	1 r. Type 574	10	10
1327	2 r. Dantika and elephant . .	15	15
1328	5 r. Subha removing her eye	20	25
1329	10 r. Punna and the Brahmin	25	40

1996. Olympic Games, Atlanta. Multicoloured.

1331	1 r. Type 575	15	10
1332	2 r. Tennis	30	10
1333	5 r. Rifle shooting (horiz) . .	50	50
1334	17 r. Running (horiz)	1·00	1·25

576 Bowler

1996. Sri Lanka's Victory in World Cup Cricket Tournament. Multicoloured.

1335	2 r. Type 576	25	15
1336	10 r. 50 Wicket-keeper . . .	55	65
1337	17 r. Batsman	90	1·25
1338	20 r. World Cup Trophy . .	1·10	1·40

577 Main Building, Jaffna Central College

1996. 180th Anniv of Jaffna Central College.

1340	577	2 r. multicoloured . . .	40	30

578 Globe in Flowers and White Dove

579 Jesus washing the Disciples' Feet

1996. 50th Anniv of U.N.E.S.C.O.

1341	578	2 r. multicoloured	40	30

1996. Christmas. Murals by David Paynter from Trinity College Chapel, Kandy. Multicoloured.

1342	2 r. Type **579**	10	10
1343	17 r. Parable of the Good Samaritan	55	70

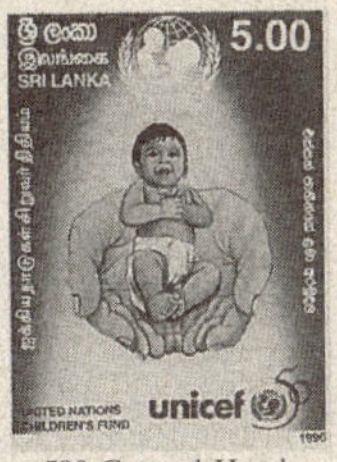

580 Cupped Hands holding Child

581 Swami Vivekananda and Globe

1996. 50th Anniv of U.N.I.C.E.F.

1345	580	5 r. multicoloured	30	35

1997. Centenary of Swami Vivekananda's Visit to Sri Lanka.

1346	581	2 r. 50 multicoloured	30	30

1997. No. 1317 surch **2.50.**

1347	2 r. 50 on 2 r. multicoloured	10	10

586 Venerable Welivitiye Sorata Thero (scholar)

589 Thuparama Stupa, 3rd-century B.C.

1997. National Heroes (1st series). Multicoloured.

1351	2 r. Type **586**	15	15
1352	2 r. Mahagama Sekera (writer and artist)	15	15
1353	2 r. Dr. S. A. Wickremasinghe (physician)	15	15
1354	2 r. Lt. Gen. Denzil Kobbekaduwa	15	15

See also Nos. 1373/6.

1997. No. 1322 surch **11.00.**

1355	11 r. on 10 r. 50 multicoloured	20	25

1997. Vesak Festival. Anauradhapura Sites. Multicoloured.

1357	1 r. Type **589**	10	10
1358	2 r. 50 Ruwanvalisaya stupa, 61–137 B.C.	10	10
1359	3 r. Abhayagiri Dagaba, 103–102 B.C	10	10
1360	17 r. Jethavana Dagaba, 276–303 A.D.	45	50

590 Don Johannes Kumarage

1997. Birth Centenary of D. J. Kumarage (Buddhist teacher).

1362	590	2 r. 50 multicoloured	30	20

HAVE YOU READ THE NOTES AT THE BEGINNING OF THIS CATALOGUE?
These often provide answers to the enquiries we receive.

591 "Munronia pinnata"

1997. Medicinal Herbs. Multicoloured.

1363	2 r. 50 Type **591**	20	10
1364	14 r. "Rauvolfia serpentina"	50	65

592 Tourist Board Logo, Airliner and Holiday Resorts

1997. Visit Sri Lanka.

1365	592	20 r. multicoloured	70	80

1997. No. 1321 surch **1.00.**

1366	1 r. on 8 r. 50 Pottery	10	15

594 Lyre Head Lizard

1997. Reptiles. Multicoloured.

1367	2 r. 50 Type **594**	10	10
1368	5 r. Boie's roughside (snake)	20	20
1369	7 r. Common Lanka skink	55	60
1370	20 r. Great forest gecko	60	70

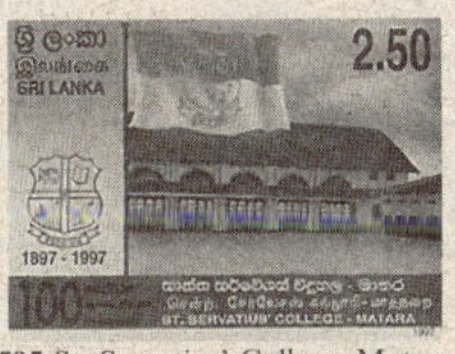

595 St. Servatius' College, Matara

1997. Centenary of St. Servatius' College, Matara.

1372	595	2 r. 50 multicoloured	20	15

1997. National Heroes (2nd series). As T **586**. Multicoloured.

1373	2 r. 50 Sri Indasara Nayake Thero (Buddhist leader)	10	15
1374	2 r. 50 Abdul Aziz (trade union leader)	10	15
1375	2 r. 50 Prof. Subramaniam Vithiananthan	10	15
1376	2 r. 50 Vivienne Goonewardene (politician)	10	15

596 The Nativity

1997. Christmas. Multicoloured.

1377	2 r. 50 Type **596**	10	10
1378	20 r. Visit of the Three Kings	60	75

597 Young Men's Buddhist Association Building, Colombo

1998. Centenary of Young Men's Buddhist Association, Colombo.

1380	597	2 r. 50 multicoloured	20	15

598 Sri Jayawardenapura Vidyalaya School

1998. 175th Anniv of Sri Jayawardenapura Vidyalaya School, Kotte.

1381	598	2 r. 50 multicoloured	20	15

599 Children and Mathematical Symbols

1998. 50th Anniv of Independence. Multicoloured.

1382	2 r. Type **599**	10	10
1383	2 r. 50 Flag and 1949 4 c. Independence stamp (38 × 28 mm)	15	15
1384	2 r. 50 People with technological and industrial symbols	15	15
1385	5 r. Dancers with arts and music symbols	20	25
1386	10 r. Women with cultural and historical symbols	25	35

600 Scouts raising Flag and Jamboree Logo

601 W.H.O. Emblem in "50" and Flag of Sri Lanka

1998. 5th National Scout Jamboree, Kandy. Multicoloured.

1387	2 r. 50 Type **600**	20	10
1388	17 r. Scout saluting and Jamboree emblem	70	75

1998. 50th Anniv of W.H.O.

1389	601	2 r. 50 multicoloured	20	15

602 Chunam Box

603 Kelani River and Stupa

1998. Traditional Jewellery and Crafts. Mult.

1390	2 r. 50 Type **602**	15	10
1391	5 r. Agate necklace	25	20
1392	10 r. Bangle and hairpin	40	40
1393	17 r. Sigiri ear-ring	60	75

1998. Vesak Festival. Wall Paintings from Kelaniya Temple. Multicoloured.

1395	1 r. Type **603**	10	10
1396	2 r. 50 Crown Prince Mahanaga and his court on way to Magampura	15	10
1397	4 r. Mahanaga and wife with baby Yatala Tissa	20	20
1398	17 r. Prince Mahanaga with King's minister	50	60

604 School Building and Emblem

1998. 175th Anniv of St. John's College, Jaffna.

1400	604	2 r. 50 multicoloured	20	15

605 Elephants in River

1998. Elephants. Multicoloured.

1401	2 r. 50 Type **605**	20	10
1402	10 r. Cow and calf	35	35
1403	17 r. Family group	50	50
1404	50 r. Bull elephant	1·25	1·50

606 S.A.A.R.C. Flags and Logo

1998. 10th Anniv of South Asian Association for Regional Co-operation.

1406	606	2 r. 50 multicoloured	20	15

607 William Gopallawa

1998. William Gopallawa (first President of Sri Lanka) Commemoration.

1407	607	2 r. 50 multicoloured	20	15

608 Satellite and Computer

1998. Year of Information Technology.

1408	608	2 r. 50 multicoloured	10	10

609 Ven. Kotahene Pannakitti Nayaka Thero (Buddhist scholar)

610 Flag of Sri Lanka and Lions Club Emblem

1998. Distinguished Personalities. Multicoloured.

1409	2 r. 50 Type **609**	10	10
1410	2 r. 50 Prof. Ediriweera Sarachchandra (scholar)	10	10
1411	2 r. 50 Sir Nicholas Attygalle (medical pioneer)	10	10
1412	2 r. 50 Dr. Samuel Fisk Green (Tamil scholar)	10	10

1998. Lions Clubs International 26th South Asia, Africa and Middle East Forum, Colombo.

1413	610	2 r. 50 multicoloured	10	10

611 "50" and Meteorological Symbols

1998. 50th Anniv of Department of Meteorology.

1414	611	2 r. 50 multicoloured	10	10

612 Virgin Mary and the Infant Jesus

1998. Christmas. Multicoloured.

1415	2 r. 50 Type **612**	10	10
1416	20 r. The Annunciation	40	45

STELLALAND

A temporary Boer republic annexed by the British in 1885 and later incorporated in Br. Bechuanaland.

12 pence = 1 shilling;
20 shillings = 1 pound

1 Arms of the Republic

1884.

1	**1**	1d. red	£170	£275
2		3d. orange	20·00	£275
3		4d. blue	20·00	£300
4		6d. mauve	20·00	£300
5		1s. green	40·00	

1885. Surch **Twee.**

6	**1**	2d. on 4d. blue	£3500	

STRAITS SETTLEMENTS

A British Crown colony which included portions of the mainland of the Malay Peninsula and islands off its coasts, and the island of Labuan off the N. coast of Borneo.

100 cents = 1 dollar (Straits)

1867. Stamps of India surch with crown and value.

1	**11**	1½ c. on ½ a. blue	75·00	£180
2		2 c. on 1 a. brown	85·00	65·00
3		3 c. on 1 a. brown	95·00	70·00
4		4 c. on 1 a. brown	£180	£200
5		6 c. on 2 a. orange	£425	£180
6		8 c. on 2 a. orange	£130	38·00
7		12 c. on 4 a. green	£700	£250
8		24 c. on 8 a. red	£275	70·00
9		32 c. on 2 a. orange	£250	75·00

1869. No. 1 with "THREE HALF" deleted and "2" written above in manuscript.

10	**11**	2 on 1½ c. on ½ c. blue	£6500	£3500

5

8

9

1867.

11	**5**	2 c. brown	19·00	3·00
98		4 c. red	3·75	1·25
66a		6 c. lilac	1·60	2·25
52		8 c. orange	2·50	75
15		12 c. blue	75·00	5·50
68a		24 c. green	3·25	3·75
69	**8**	30 c. red	7·00	6·50
70	**9**	32 c. red	6·50	2·00
71		96 c. grey	75·00	38·00

1879. Surch in words.

20	**5**	5 c. on 8 c. orange	70·00	£100
21	**9**	7 c. on 32 c. red	75·00	95·00

1880. Surch in figures and words.

47	**5**	5 c. on 4 c. red	£225	£250
42		5 c. on 8 c. orange	80·00	£100
44		10 c. on 6 c. lilac	45·00	6·00
45a		10 c. on 12 c. blue	35·00	9·00
23	**8**	10 c. on 30 c. red	£190	48·00

1880. Surch in figures only.

33	**8**	"10" on 30 c. red	£110	42·00

18

19

1882.

63a	**5**	2 c. pink	4·00	50
64		4 c. brown	18·00	1·25
65	**18**	5 c. blue	8·50	80
99		5 c. brown	2·75	1·00
100		5 c. mauve	1·75	2·00
101	**5**	8 c. blue	4·50	50
53	**19**	10 c. grey	3·25	90
102	**5**	12 c. purple	8·00	8·50

1883. Surch in words in one line horiz (No. 109) or vert.

57	**5**	2 c. on 8 c. orange	80·00	50·00
59	**9**	2 c. on 32 c. orange	£425	£130
109	**18**	4 c. on 5 c. red	60	30

1883. Surch with figures over words in two lines.

61	**5**	2 c. on 4 c. red	65·00	75·00
62		2 c. on 12 c. blue	£160	85·00
82	**18**	3 c. on 5 c. blue	90·00	£200
84		3 c. on 5 c. purple	£150	£160
106		4 c. on 5 c. brown	2·00	4·75
73		4 c. on 5 c. blue (A)*	90·00	80·00
107		4 c. on 5 c. blue (B)*	1·75	9·00
108b	**5**	4 c. on 8 c. blue	80	90
74		8 c. on 12 c. blue	£225	95·00
75		8 c. on 12 c. purple	£190	£120

*(A) "Cents" in italics. (B) "cents" (with small "c") in roman type.

1884. Surch **TWO CENTS** vert.

76	**18**	2 c. on 5 c. blue	95·00	£100

1884. No. 75 additionally surch with large figure **8**.

80	**5**	8 on 8 c. on 12 c. purple	£190	£190

1885. Surch with words in one line and thick bar.

93	**5**	1 c. on 8 c. green	90	1·50
83a	**9**	3 c. on 32 c. purple	1·25	90
94		3 c. on 32 c. red	2·25	70

1887. Surch **2 Cents** in one line.

85	**18**	2 c. on 5 c. blue	18·00	45·00

1891. Surch **10 CENTS** in one line and thin bar.

86	**5**	10 c. on 24 c. green	2·00	1·25

1891. Surch with words in two lines and thin bar.

88	**5**	1 c. on 2 c. red	1·75	3·00
89		1 c. on 4 c. brown	4·00	4·25
90		1 c. on 6 c. lilac	1·25	4·00
91		1 c. on 8 c. orange	1·00	90
92		1 c. on 12 c. purple	4·25	9·00
87	**9**	30 c. on 32 c. orange	5·50	3·50

33

37

1892.

95	**33**	1 c. green	1·50	50
96		3 c. red	10·00	40
97		3 c. brown	3·75	60
103c		25 c. purple and green	16·00	4·25
104		50 c. olive and red	18·00	2·50
105		$5 orange and red	£300	£250

1902.

110	**37**	1 c. green	2·00	2·50
111		3 c. purple and orange	3·00	15
112		4 c. purple on red	4·25	30
113		5 c. purple	4·00	85
157		5 c. orange	2·75	80
114		8 c. purple on blue	3·25	20
132		10 c. purple & blk on yell	4·50	60
159		10 c. purple on yellow	4·25	80
116		25 c. purple and green	10·00	4·50
161		25 c. purple	9·50	4·25
117		30 c. grey and red	15·00	8·00
162		30 c. purple and yellow	28·00	2·75
118		50 c. green and red	20·00	20·00
164		50 c. black on green	4·75	3·50
136a		$1 green and black	38·00	15·00
165		$1 black and red on blue	11·00	4·00
120		$2 purple and black	55·00	55·00
166		$2 green and red on yellow	23·00	21·00
138a		$5 green and orange	£140	£140
167		$5 green and red on green	95·00	65·00
139		$25 green and black	£1100	£1100

39

42

46

47

1903.

127	**39**	1 c. green	2·25	10
128		3 c. purple	1·75	30
153		3 c. red	1·50	10
125		4 c. purple on red	3·00	30
154		4 c. red	5·50	2·50
155		4 c. purple	4·50	10
131a	**42**	8 c. purple on blue	15·00	2·00
158		8 c. blue	3·50	50
160	**46**	21 c. purple	6·50	27·00
163		45 c. black on green	2·50	3·75
168	**47**	$25 purple and blue	£1000	£800

1907. Stamps of Labuan (Crown type) optd **Straits Settlements.** (10 c.) or **STRAITS SETTLEMENTS** (others) or surch in words also.

141	**18**	1 c. black and purple	50·00	£140
142a		2 c. black and green	£150	£250
143		3 c. black and brown	17·00	85·00
144		4 c. on 12 c. black & yellow	1·75	6·00
145		4 c. on 16 c. green & brown	2·75	7·50
146		4 c. on 18 c. black & brown	2·25	6·00
147		8 c. black and orange	2·00	8·00
148		10 c. brown and blue	5·00	6·00
149		25 c. green and blue	7·00	30·00
150		50 c. purple and lilac	11·00	65·00
151		$1 red and orange	42·00	£100

48

54

52

53

1912.

193	**48**	1 c. green	4·50	1·00
196a		3 c. red	1·75	10
197		4 c. purple	1·00	50
225	**54**	5 c. orange	1·00	15
227	**52**	6 c. purple	2·00	15
201		8 c. blue	80	60
202	**54**	10 c. purple on yellow	1·00	70
204	**53**	21 c. purple	4·25	9·00
234b	**54**	25 c. purple and mauve	4·50	1·75
235a		30 c. purple and orange	2·00	1·25
208b	**53**	45 c. black on green	3·25	13·00
238	**54**	50 c. black on green	1·75	40
239		$1 black and red on blue	6·00	65
240		$2 green and red on yellow	10·00	8·00
240a		$5 green and red on green	75·00	32·00
240b	–	$25 purple & blue on blue	£475	95·00

No. 240b is as Type **47** but with head of King George V.

1917. Surch **RED CROSS 2c.**

216	**48**	2 c. on 3 c. red	1·75	22·00
217		2 c. on 4 c. purple	1·75	22·00

1919.

218	**48**	1 c. black	30	10
219	**52**	2 c. green	30	10
220		2 c. brown	7·00	2·25
221	**48**	3 c. green	1·50	70
222		4 c. red	2·00	3·75
223		4 c. violet	50	10
224		4 c. orange	1·00	10
226	**54**	5 c. brown	1·75	10
227	**52**	6 c. red	2·00	15
230	**54**	10 c. blue	1·75	1·25
232	**52**	12 c. blue	1·00	10
236a	**53**	35 c. purple and orange	3·50	5·50
237		35 c. red and purple	10·00	7·00

1922. Optd **MALAYA- BORNEO EXHIBITION.**

250	**48**	1 c. black	2·00	9·50
251	**52**	2 c. green	1·40	12·00
252	**48**	4 c. red	2·00	21·00
243	**54**	5 c. orange	4·25	17·00
244	**52**	8 c. blue	1·75	6·50
254	**54**	10 c. blue	2·25	22·00
245		25 c. purple and mauve	3·00	25·00
246	**53**	45 c. black on green	3·00	22·00
255	**54**	$1 black and red on blue	15·00	95·00
248		$2 green and red on yellow	25·00	£100
249		$5 green and red on green	£200	£375

1935. Silver Jubilee. As T **13** of Antigua.

256	5 c. blue and grey	2·50	30
257	8 c. green and blue	2·75	2·50
258	12 c. brown and blue	2·75	2·75
259	25 c. grey and purple	3·00	4·50

57

58

1936.

260	**57**	1 c. black	70	20
261		2 c. green	70	50
262		4 c. orange	1·50	50
263		5 c. brown	40	30
264		8 c. red	90	85
265		8 c. grey	75	50
266		10 c. purple	1·25	30
267		12 c. blue	2·00	2·00
268		25 c. purple and red	1·00	30
269		30 c. purple and orange	1·25	3·00
270		40 c. red and purple	1·25	2·50
271		50 c. black and green	3·50	80
272		$1 black and red on blue	16·00	90
273		$2 green and red	30·00	10·00
274		$5 green and red on green	60·00	10·00

1937. Coronation. As T **2** of Aden.

275	4 c. orange	30	10
276	8 c. grey	70	10
277	12 c. blue	1·25	60

1937.

278	58	1 c. black	4·00	10
279		2 c. green	18·00	10
294		2 c. orange	1·75	8·00
295		3 c. green	3·25	4·00
280		4 c. orange	13·00	20
281		5 c. brown	20·00	30
282		6 c. red	10·00	50
283		8 c. grey	40·00	10
284		10 c. purple	7·50	10
285		12 c. blue	8·00	30
298		15 c. blue	4·75	10·00
286		25 c. purple and red	42·00	1·10
287		30 c. purple and orange	30·00	2·00
288		40 c. red and purple	10·00	2·25
289		50 c. black on green	10·00	10
290		$1 black and red on blue	15·00	20
291		$2 green and red	30·00	4·00
292		$5 green and red on green	25·00	3·25

For Japanese issues see **JAPANESE OCCUPATION OF MALAYA** and for British military administration see **MALAYA**.

POSTAGE DUE STAMPS

D 1

1924.

D1	D 1	1 c. violet	4·50	5·50
D2		2 c. black	3·00	1·25
D3		4 c. green	2·00	4·75
D4		8 c. red	4·50	55
D5		10 c. orange	6·00	85
D6		12 c. blue	7·00	65

For later issues see **MALAYAN POSTAL UNION**.

SUDAN

A territory in Africa, extending south from Egypt towards the Equator, jointly administered by Gt. Britain and Egypt until 1954 when the territory was granted a large measure of self-government. Became independent on 1 January 1956.

1000 milliemes = 100 piastres = £1 Sudanese

1897. Stamps of Egypt optd **SOUDAN** in English and Arabic.

1	18	1 m. brown	1 50	2·00
3		2 m. green	1·25	1·75
4		3 m. yellow	1·40	1·50
5		5 m. red	2·00	70
6	10	1 p. blue	7·00	2·00
7	–	2 p. orange	50·00	13·00
8	–	5 p. grey	42·00	14·00
9	18	10 p. mauve	30·00	42·00

2 Arab Postman 6

1898.

18	2	1 m. brown and red	1·25	10
19		2 m. green and brown	1·75	10
20		3 m. mauve and green	2·25	25
21		4 m. blue and brown	1·50	2·50
22		4 m. red and brown	1·50	75
23		5 m. red and black	2·00	10
24		1 p. blue and brown	2·25	30
25		2 p. black and blue	24·00	1·75
44		2 p. purple and orange	80	10
44b		3 p. brown and blue	2·75	10
44c		4 p. blue and black	3·50	10
45		5 p. brown and green	1·00	10
45b		6 p. blue and black	4·25	20
45c		8 p. green and black	5·50	2·00
46		10 p. black and mauve	2·00	10
46b		20 p. blue	2·00	10

1903. Surch **5 Milliemes.**

29	2	5 m. on 5 p. brown and green	6·50	9·00

1921.

37	6	1 m. black and orange	50	10
38		2 m. yellow and brown	40	10
39		3 m. mauve and green	40	10
40		4 m. green and brown	30	10
41		5 m. brown and black	30	10
42		10 m. red and black	1·00	10
43		15 m. blue and brown	80	10

For stamps as Type **2** and **6** with different Arabic inscriptions see issue of 1948.

1931. Air. Nos. 41/2 and 44 optd **AIR MAIL.**

47	6	5 m. brown and black	35	70
48		10 m. red and black	85	7·50
49	2	2 p. purple and yellow	85	6·00

10 Statue of General Gordon

1931. Air.

49b	10	3 m. green and brown	2·50	5·50
50		5 m. black and green	1·00	10
51		10 m. black and red	1·00	20
52		15 m. brown	40	10
53		2 p. black and orange	30	10
53c		2½ p. mauve and blue	3·00	10
54		3 p. black and grey	60	15
55		3½ p. black and violet	1·50	80
56		4½ p. brown and grey	10·00	15·00
57		5 p. black and blue	1·00	30
57c		7½ p. green	4·00	9·00
57d		10 p. brown and blue	8·50	75

1932. Air. Surch 2½ 2½ **AIR MAIL** and value in Arabic figures.

58	2	2½ p. on 2 p. purple & orge	1·40	3·50

12 General Gordon (after C. Ouless) 13 Gordon Memorial College, Khartoum

1935. 50th Death Anniv of Gen. Gordon.

59	12	5 m. green	35	10
60		10 m. brown	85	25
61		13 m. blue	85	8·00
62		15 m. red	1·75	25
63		2 p. blue	1·25	20
64		5 p. orange	1·25	40
65	13	10 p. purple	7·50	8·50
66	–	20 p. black	22·00	48·00
67	–	50 p. brown	75·00	95·00

DESIGN—(44 × 20 mm): 20, 50 p. Gordon Memorial Service, Khartoum.

1935. Air. Stamps of 1931 surch in English and Arabic.

74	10	5 m. on 2½ p. mauve & blue	3·50	10
68		15 m. on 10 m. black and red	40	10
69		2½ p. on 3 m. green & brown	85	5·50
70		2½ p. on 5 m. black & green	40	1·50
75		3 p. on 3½ p. black & violet	35·00	48·00
71		3 p. on 4½ p. brown & grey	1·75	13·00
76		3 p. on 7½ p. green	7·00	6·50
77		5 p. on 10 p. brown & blue	1·75	4·75
72		7½ p. on 4½ p. brown and grey	6·00	42·00
73		10 p. on 4½ p. brown and grey	6·00	42·00

1940. No. 42 surch **5 Mills.** and in Arabic.

78	6	5 m. on 10 m. red and black	50	30

1940. Nos. 41 surch **4½ PIASTRES** and No. 45c surch **4½ Piastres** in English and Arabic.

79	6	4½ p. on 5 m. brown and black	48·00	3·50
80	2	4½ p. on 8 p. green and black	38·00	8·50

20 Tuti Island, R. Nile near Khartoum

1941.

81	20	1 m. black and orange	80	3·00
82		2 m. orange and brown	80	3·00
83		3 m. mauve and green	80	20
84		4 m. green and brown	80	30
85		5 m. brown and black	30	10
86		10 m. red and black	7·00	1·75
87		15 m. blue and brown	70	10
88		2 p. purple and yellow	3·50	60
89		3 p. brown and blue	70	10
90		4 p. blue and black	80	10
91		5 p. brown and green	4·50	8·00
92		6 p. blue and black	18·00	40
93		8 p. green and black	14·00	45
94		10 p. black and violet	50·00	75
95		20 p. blue	50·00	28·00

The piastre values are larger, 30 × 25 mm.

22 Arab Postman 23

1948.

96	22	1 m. black and orange	35	3·00
97		2 m. orange and brown	80	3·25
98		3 m. mauve and green	30	3·00
99		4 m. green and brown	30	10
100		5 m. brown and black	4·00	1·25
101		10 m. red and black	5·00	10
102		15 m. blue and brown	4·00	10
103	23	2 p. purple and yellow	6·50	1·00
104		3 p. brown and blue	6·00	20
105		4 p. blue and black	4·00	1·50
106		5 p. orange and green	4·00	1·50
107	23	6 p. blue and black	4·50	3·00
108		8 p. green and black	4·50	3·00
109		10 p. black and mauve	11·00	3·00
110		20 p. blue	4·50	30
111		50 p. red and blue	6·50	1·75

In this issue the Arabic inscriptions below the camel differ from those in Types **2** and **6**.

24 Arab Postman 25

1948. Golden Jubilee of "Camel Postman" design.

112	24	2 p. black and blue	10	10

1948. Opening of Legislative Assembly.

113	25	10 m. red and black	20	10
114		5 p. orange and green	30	50

26 Blue Nile Bridge, Khartoum

1950. Air.

115	26	2 p. black and green	4·50	80
116	–	2½ p. blue and orange	75	1·00
117	–	3 p. purple and blue	3·00	50
118	–	3½ p. sepia and brown	1·00	2·50
119	–	4 p. brown and blue	1·00	1·75
120	–	4½ p. black and blue	2·50	3·50
121	–	6 p. black and red	1·00	2·25
122	–	20 p. black and purple	1·75	4·25

DESIGNS: 2½ p. Kassala Jebel; 3 p. Sagia (water wheel); 3½ p. Port Sudan; 4 p. Gordon Memorial College; 4½ p. "Gordon Pasha" (Nile mail boat); 6 p. Suakin; 20 p. G.P.O. Khartoum.

34 Ibex 35 Cotton Picking

1951.

123	34	1 m. black and orange	55	1·00
124	–	2 m. black and blue	1·50	45
125	–	3 m. black and green	4·00	2·00
126	–	4 m. black and green	75	2·25
127	–	5 m. black and purple	1·00	10
128	–	10 m. black and blue	20	10
129	–	15 m. black and brown	2·50	10
130	35	2 p. blue	20	10
131	–	3 p. brown and blue	4·50	10
132	–	3½ p. green and brown	1·00	10
133	–	4 p. blue and black	50	10
134	–	5 p. brown and green	30	10
135	–	6 p. blue and black	6·00	2·50
136	–	8 p. blue and brown	10·00	2·00
137	–	10 p. black and green	1·25	10
138	–	20 p. turquoise and black	4·50	1·10
139	–	50 p. red and black	12·00	1·00

DESIGNS—VERT (As Type **34**): 2 m. Whale headed stork; 3 m. Giraffe; 4 m. Baggara girl; 5 m. Shilluk warrior; 10 m. Hadendowa; 15 m. Policeman. (As Type **35**): 50 p. Camel postman. HORIZ (As Type **35**): 3 p. Ambatch reed canoe; 3½ p. Nuba wrestlers; 4 p. Weaving; 5 p. Saluka farming; 6 p. Gum tapping; 8 p. Darfur chief; 10 p. Stack Laboratory; 20 p. Nile lechwe (antelope).

51 Camel Postman

1954. Self-Government.

140	51	15 m. brown and green	50	90
141		3 p. blue and indigo	50	1·40
142		5 p. black and purple	50	1·00

Stamps as Type **51** but dated "1953" were released in error at the Sudan Agency in London. They had no postal validity.

For later issues see Volume 2.

ARMY SERVICE STAMPS

1905. Optd **ARMY OFFICIAL.**

A 1	2	1 m. brown and red	2·50	2·00

1906. Optd **ARMY SERVICE.**

A 6	2	1 m. brown and red	1·50	20
A 7		2 m. green and brown	7·50	1·00
A 8		3 m. mauve and green	17·00	40
A 9		5 m. red and black	1·50	10
A10		1 p. blue and brown	13·00	15
A11		2 p. black and blue	45·00	13·00
A12		5 p. brown and green	95·00	60·00
A16		10 p. black and mauve	£120	£225

OFFICIAL STAMPS

1902. Optd **O.S.G.S.**

O 5	2	1 m. brown and red	50	10
O 6		3 m. mauve and green	2·50	15
O 7		5 m. red and black	2·50	10
O 8		1 p. blue and brown	2·50	10
O 9		2 p. black and blue	22·00	20
O10		5 p. brown and green	2·00	30
O 4		10 p. black and mauve	13·00	22·00

1936. Optd **S.G.**

O32	6	1 m. black and orange	1·40	9·00
O33		2 m. yellow and brown	40	3·25
O34		3 m. mauve and green	2·25	10
O35		4 m. green and brown	2·75	2·50
O36		5 m. brown and black	80	10
O37		10 m. red and black	70	10
O38		15 m. blue and brown	6·00	20
O39		2 p. purple and orange	10·00	10
O39b		3 p. brown and blue	5·00	1·50
O39c		4 p. blue and black	22·00	3·00
O40		5 p. brown and green	12·00	10
O40b		6 p. blue and black	7·00	6·50
O40c	2	8 p. green and black	5·00	24·00
O41		10 p. black and mauve	25·00	7·50
O42		20 p. blue	23·00	19·00

1948. Optd **S.G.**

O43	22	1 m. black and orange	30	3·25
O44		2 m. orange and brown	1·25	10
O45		3 m. mauve and green	2·25	5·00
O46		4 m. green and brown	2·25	2·75
O47		5 m. brown and black	2·25	10
O48		10 m. red and black	2·00	90
O49		15 m. blue and brown	2·25	10
O50	23	2 p. purple and yellow	2·25	10
O51		3 p. brown and blue	2·25	10
O52		4 p. blue and black	2·25	10
O53		5 p. orange and green	2·50	10
O54		6 p. blue and black	2·00	10
O55		8 p. green and black	2·00	2·25
O56		10 p. black and mauve	3·00	20
O57		20 p. blue	3·75	25
O58		50 p. red and blue	55·00	45·00

1950. Air. Nos. 115/22 optd **S.G.**

O59	2 p. black and green	14·00	3·00
O60	2½ p. blue and orange	1·50	1·75
O61	3 p. purple and blue	80	1·00
O62	3½ p. sepia and brown	80	6·50
O63	4 p. brown and blue	80	6·00
O64	4½ p. black and blue	3·75	15·00
O65	6 p. black and red	1·00	4·25
O66	20 p. black and purple	5·00	12·00

1951. Nos. 123/39 optd **S.G.**

O67	1 m. black and orange	40	3·75
O68	2 m. black and blue	40	60
O69	3 m. black and green	3·00	14·00
O70	4 m. black and green	10	5·00
O71	5 m. black and purple	10	10
O72	10 m. black and blue	10	10
O73	15 m. black and brown	10	10
O74	2 p. blue	10	10
O75	3 p. brown and blue	4·00	10
O76	3½ p. green and brown	25	10
O77	4 p. blue and black	30	10
O78	5 p. brown and green	25	10
O79	6 p. blue and black	30	2·75
O80	8 p. blue and brown	45	10
O81	10 p. black and green	50	10
O82	20 p. turquoise and black	1·25	30
O83	50 p. red and black	3·50	1·25

POSTAGE DUE STAMPS

1897. Postage Due Stamps of Egypt optd **SOUDAN** in English and Arabic.

D1	D 23	2 m. green	1·75	8·00
D2		4 m. purple	1·75	8·00
D3		1 p. blue	10·00	5·00
D4		2 p. orange	10·00	11·00

D 1 Gunboat "Zafir" D 2

1901.

D 5	D 1	2 m. black and brown	55	60
D10		4 m. brown and green	90	80
D11		10 m. green and mauve	1·25	1·60
D 8		20 m. blue and red	3·25	3·25

1948.

D 12	D 2	2 m. black and brown	80	28·00
D 13		4 m. brown and green	2·00	26·00
D394		10 m. green and mauve	15	15
D395		20 m. blue and red	15	15

The Arabic inscription in Type D 2 differs from that in Type D 1.

SUNGEI UJONG

A native state of the Malay Peninsula, later incorporated in Negri Sembilan.

100 cents = 1 dollar (Straits)

1878. Stamp of Straits Settlements optd with Crescent, Star and **SU** in an oval.

1	**5**	2 c. brown	£1800	£2000

1881. Stamps of Straits Settlements optd **SUNGEI UJONG**.

28	**5**	2 c. brown	38·00	90·00
43		2 c. red	4·75	8·00
22		4 c. red	£950	£1000
34		4 c. brown	£180	£225
24		8 c. orange	£1100	£850
26	**19**	10 c. grey	£425	£425

1882. Stamps of Straits Settlements optd **S.U.** (2 c. with or without stops).

13	**5**	2 c. brown	£225	£275
14		4 c. red	£2000	£2000

1891. Stamp of Straits Settlements surch **SUNGEI UJONG Two CENTS**.

49	**5**	2 c. on 24 c. green	£100	£120

35 Tiger

37 Tiger

1891.

50	**35**	2 c. red	24·00	27·00
51		2 c. orange	1·40	4·25
55	**37**	3 c. purple and red	6·50	1·75
52	**35**	5 c. blue	4·50	5·50

1894. Surch in figures and words.

53	**35**	1 c. on 5 c. green	65	70
54		3 c. on 5 c. red	2·00	4·75

SWAZILAND

A kingdom in the eastern part of S. Africa. Its early stamps were issued under joint control of Gt. Britain and the S. Africa Republic. Incorporated into the latter state in 1895 it was transferred in 1906 to the High Commissioner for S. Africa. Again issued stamps in 1933.

Achieved Independence in 1968.

1961. 100 cents = 1 rand.
1974. 100 cents = 1 lilangeni (plural-emalangeni).

1889. Stamps of Transvaal optd **Swazieland**.

10	**18**	$\frac{1}{2}$d. grey	7·50	16·00
1		1d. red	17·00	16·00
5		2d. bistre	14·00	15·00
6		6d. blue	17·00	30·00
3		1s. green	10·00	13·00
7		2s. 6d. yellow	£200	£225
8		5s. blue	£140	£170
9		10s. brown	£4500	£3000

2 King George V

7 Swazi Married Woman

1933.

11	**2**	$\frac{1}{2}$d. green	30	30
12		1d. red	30	20
13		2d. brown	30	45
14		3d. blue	45	1·50
15		4d. red	2·25	2·50
16		6d. mauve	1·00	80
17		1s. olive	1·50	2·75
18		2s. 6d. violet	15·00	22·00
19		5s. grey	30·00	45·00
20		10s. brown	80·00	£100

1935. Silver Jubilee. As T **13** of Antigua.

21	1d. blue and red	40	60
22	2d. blue and black	40	60
23	3d. brown and blue	55	3·50
24	6d. grey and purple	65	1·25

1937. Coronation. As T **2** of Aden.

25	1d. red	50	1·25
26	2d. brown	50	20
27	3d. blue	50	50

1938. As T **2**, but with portraits of King George VI and inscr "SWAZILAND" only below portrait.

28	$\frac{1}{2}$d. green	1·25	70
29	1d. red	1·00	60
30b	$1\frac{1}{2}$d. blue	30	75
31a	2d. brown	30	50
32b	3d. blue	2·00	3·75
33a	4d. orange	45	1·40
34b	6d. purple	3·50	1·25
35a	1s. olive	1·25	65
36a	2s. 6d. violet	8·00	2·50
37b	5s. grey	24·00	13·00
38a	10s. brown	6·50	6·00

1945. Victory stamps of South Africa (inscr alternately in English or Afrikaans) optd **Swaziland**.

39	**55**	1d. brown and red	55	10
40	–	2d. blue and violet (No. 109)	55	10
41	–	3d. blue (No. 110)	55	20

Unused prices are for bilingual pairs, used prices for single stamps in either language.

1947. Royal Visit. As Nos. 32/5 of Basutoland.

42	1d. red	10	10
43	2d. green	10	10
44	3d. blue	10	10
45	1s. mauve	10	10

1948. Silver Wedding. As T **10/11** of Aden.

46	$1\frac{1}{2}$d. blue	50	10
47	10s. purple	23·00	25·00

1949. 75th Anniv of U.P.U. As T **20/23** of Antigua.

48	$1\frac{1}{2}$d. blue	10	10
49	3d. blue	1·40	60
50	6d. mauve	60	60
51	1s. olive	60	60

1953. Coronation. As T **13** of Aden.

52	2d. black and brown	20	20

1956.

53	–	$\frac{1}{2}$d. black and orange	10	10
54	–	1d. black and green	10	10
55	**7**	2d. black and brown	30	10
56	–	3d. black and red	20	10
57	–	$4\frac{1}{2}$d. black and blue	60	10
58	–	6d. black and mauve	45	10
59	–	1s. black and olive	20	10
60	–	1s. 3d. black and sepia	1·00	1·75
61	–	2s. 6d. green and red	1·00	1·50
62	–	5s. violet and grey	7·50	2·00
63	**7**	10s. black and violet	15·00	7·00
64	–	£1 black and turquoise	38·00	26·00

DESIGNS—HORIZ: $\frac{1}{2}$d., 1s. Havelock asbestos mine; 1d., 2s. 6d. Highveld view. VERT: 3d., 1s. 3d. Swazi courting couple; $4\frac{1}{2}$d., 5s. Swazi warrior; 6d., £1 Greater kudu.

1961. Stamps of 1956 surch in new currency.

65	$\frac{1}{2}$ c. on $\frac{1}{2}$d. black and orange	3·25	3·50
66	1 c. on 1d. black and green	10	50
67	2 c. on 2d. black and brown	10	70
68	$2\frac{1}{2}$ c. on 2d. black and brown	10	20
69	$2\frac{1}{2}$ c. on 3d. black and red	10	10
70	$3\frac{1}{2}$ c. on 2d. black and brown	10	20
71	4 c. on $4\frac{1}{2}$d. black and blue	10	10
72	5 c. on 6d. black and mauve	10	10
73	10 c. on 1s. black and olive	25·00	3·00
74	25 c. on 2s. 6d. green and red	30	65
75	50 c. on 5s. violet and grey	30	60
76	1 r. on 10s. black and violet	1·50	60
77a	2 r. on £1 black and turquoise	4·50	6·00

1961. As 1956 but values in new currency.

78	$\frac{1}{2}$ c. black and orange (as $\frac{1}{2}$d.)	10	30
79	1 c. black and green (as 1d.)	10	10
80	2 c. black and brown (as 2d.)	10	1·50
81	$2\frac{1}{2}$ c. black and red (as 3d.)	15	10
82	4 c. black and blue (as $4\frac{1}{2}$d.)	15	60
83	5 c. black and mauve (as 6d.)	30	15
84	10 c. black and olive (as 1s.)	15	10
85	$12\frac{1}{2}$ c. black & sepia (as 1s. 3d.)	1·25	40
86	25 c. green and red (as 2d. 6d.)	1·75	2·50
87	50 c. violet and grey (as 5s.)	2·00	1·40
88	1 r. black and violet (as 10s.)	4·00	7·50
89	2 r. black and turquoise (as £1)	9·00	11·00

15 Swazi Shields

31 Goods Train and Map of Swaziland Railway

1962.

90	**15**	$\frac{1}{2}$ c. black, brown and buff	10	10
91	–	1 c. orange and black	10	10
92	–	2 c. green, black and olive	10	50
93	–	$2\frac{1}{2}$ c. black and red	10	10
94	–	$3\frac{1}{2}$ c. green and grey	10	40
95	–	4 c. black and turquoise	10	10
96	–	5 c. black, red and deep red	40	10
97	–	$7\frac{1}{2}$ c. brown and buff	70	30
98	–	10 c. black and blue	2·00	10
99	–	$12\frac{1}{2}$ c. red and olive	1·25	2·25
100	–	15 c. black and mauve	1·50	70
101	–	20 c. black and green	40	90
102	–	25 c. black and blue	50	70
103	–	50 c. black and red	9·00	3·75
104	–	1 r. green and ochre	3·00	2·25
105	–	2 r. red and blue	14·00	8·00

DESIGNS—VERT: 1 c. Battle axe; 2 c. Forestry; $2\frac{1}{2}$ c. Ceremonial headdress; $3\frac{1}{2}$ c. Musical instrument; 4 c. Irrigation; 5 c. Long-tailed whydah; $7\frac{1}{2}$ c. Rock paintings; 10 c. Secretary bird; $12\frac{1}{2}$ c. Pink arum; 15 c. Swazi married woman; 20 c. Malaria control; 25 c. Swazi warrior; 1 r. Aloes. HORIZ: 50 c. Southern ground hornbill; 2 r. Msinsi in flower.

1963. Freedom from Hunger. As T **28** of Aden.

106	15 c. violet	40	15

1963. Cent of Red Cross. As T **33** of Antigua.

107	$2\frac{1}{2}$ c. red and black	30	10
108	15 c. red and blue	95	70

1964. Opening of Swaziland Railway.

109	**31**	$2\frac{1}{2}$ c. green and purple	55	10
110		$3\frac{1}{2}$ c. blue and olive	55	70
111		15 c. orange and brown	70	70
112		25 c. yellow and blue	85	80

1965. Cent of I.T.U. As T **36** of Antigua.

113	$2\frac{1}{2}$ c. blue and bistre	10	10
114	15 c. purple and red	25	20

1965. I.C.Y. As T **37** of Antigua.

115	$\frac{1}{2}$ c. purple and turquoise	10	10
116	15 c. green and lavender	40	20

1966. Churchill Commem. As T **38** of Antigua.

117	$\frac{1}{2}$ c. blue	10	90
118	$2\frac{1}{2}$ c. green	20	10
119	15 c. brown	35	25
120	25 c. violet	50	70

1966. 20th Anniv of U.N.E.S.C.O. As T **54/6** of Antigua.

121	$2\frac{1}{2}$ c. multicoloured	10	10
122	$7\frac{1}{2}$ c. yellow, violet and olive	25	40
123	15 c. black, purple and orange	45	95

32 King Sobhuza II and Map

1967. Protected State.

124	**32**	$2\frac{1}{2}$ c. multicoloured	10	10
125	–	$7\frac{1}{2}$ c. multicoloured	15	15
126	**32**	15 c. multicoloured	20	25
127	–	25 c. multicoloured	25	35

DESIGN—VERT: $7\frac{1}{2}$, 25 c. King Sobhuza II.

1967. First Conferment of University Degrees. As T **66** of Botswana.

128	$2\frac{1}{2}$ c. sepia, blue and orange	10	10
129	$7\frac{1}{2}$ c. sepia, blue and turquoise	10	10
130	15 c. sepia, blue and red	20	25
131	25 c. sepia, blue and violet	25	30

35 Incwala Ceremony

1968. Traditional Customs.

132	**35**	3 c. silver, red and black	10	10
133	–	10 c. multicoloured	10	10
134	**35**	15 c. gold, red and black	15	20
135	–	25 c. multicoloured	15	20

DESIGN—VERT: 10, 25 c. Reed dance.

1968. No. 96 surch **3c.**

136	3 c. on 5 c. black, red and deep red	20	10

38 Cattle Ploughing

1968. Independence.

137	**38**	3 c. multicoloured	10	10
138	–	$4\frac{1}{2}$ c. multicoloured	10	15
139	–	$17\frac{1}{2}$ c. multicoloured	15	20
140	–	25 c. slate, black and gold	45	80

DESIGNS: $4\frac{1}{2}$ c. Overhead cable carrying asbestos; $17\frac{1}{2}$ c. Cutting sugar cane; 25 c. Iron ore mining and railway map.

1968. Nos. 90/105 optd **INDEPENDENCE 1968** and No. 93 additionally surch **3 c**.

142	**15**	$\frac{1}{2}$ c. black, brown & buff	10	10
143	–	1 c. orange and black	10	10
144	–	2 c. green, black and olive	10	10
145a	–	$2\frac{1}{2}$ c. black and red	90	10
146	–	3 c. on $2\frac{1}{2}$ c. black and red	10	10
147	–	$3\frac{1}{2}$ c. green and grey	15	10
148	–	4 c. black and turquoise	10	10
149	–	5 c. black, red & deep red	1·75	10
150	–	$7\frac{1}{2}$ c. brown and buff	50	10
151	–	10 c. black and blue	2·00	10
152	–	$12\frac{1}{2}$ c. red and olive	25	45
153	–	15 c. black and mauve	25	45
154	–	20 c. black and green	75	1·50
155	–	25 c. black and blue	35	40
159	–	50 c. black and red	4·50	3·25
157	–	1 r. green and ochre	2·50	3·75
160	–	2 r. red and blue	6·00	5·00

43 Porcupine

1969. Multicoloured.

161	$\frac{1}{2}$ c. Caracal	10	10
162	1 c. Type **43**	10	10
163	2 c. Crocodile	20	10
164	3 c. Lion	60	10
165	3 c. African elephant	60	10
166	5 c. Bush pig	30	10
167	$7\frac{1}{2}$ c. Impala	35	10
168	10 c. Chacma baboon	45	10
169	$12\frac{1}{2}$ c. Ratel	70	2·50
170	15 c. Leopard	1·25	70
171	20 c. Blue wildebeest	95	60
172	25 c. White rhinoceros	1·40	1·75
173	50 c. Common zebra	1·50	3·25
174	1 r. Waterbuck	3·00	6·50
175	2 r. Giraffe	8·00	11·00

Nos. 174/5 are vert. Nos. 164/5 are larger, $35 \times 24\frac{1}{2}$ mm.

For designs as Nos. 174/5, but in new currency, see Nos. 219/20.

44 King Sobhuza II and Flags

1969. Swaziland's Admission to the U.N. Multicoloured.

176	3 c. Type **44**	10	10
177	$7\frac{1}{2}$ c. King Sobhuza II, U.N. Building and emblem	15	10
178	$12\frac{1}{2}$ c. As Type **44**	25	10
179	25 c. As $7\frac{1}{2}$ c.	40	40

46 Athlete, Shield and Spears

47 "Bauhinia galpinii"

1970. 9th Commonweath Games. Multicoloured.

180	3 c. Type **46**	10	10
181	$7\frac{1}{2}$ c. Runner	20	10
182	$12\frac{1}{2}$ c. Hurdler	25	10
183	25 c. Procession of Swaziland competitors	35	40

1971. Flowers. Multicoloured.

184	3 c. Type **47**	20	10
185	10 c. "Crocosmia aurea"	25	10
186	15 c. "Gloriosa superba"	40	15
187	25 c. "Watsonia densiflora"	55	35

48 King Sobhuza II in Ceremonial Dress

49 U.N.I.C.E.F. Emblem

1971. Golden Jubilee of King Sobhuza II's Accession. Multicoloured.

188	3 c. Type **48**	10	10
189	$3\frac{1}{2}$ c. Sobhuza II in medallion	10	10
190	$7\frac{1}{2}$ c. Sobhuza II attending Incwala ceremony	15	10
191	25 c. Sobhuza II and aides at opening of Parliament	30	35

1972. 25th Anniv of U.N.I.C.E.F.

192	**49**	15 c. black and lilac	15	10
193	–	25 c. black and green	20	35

DESIGN: 25 c. As Type **49**, but inscription rearranged.

50 Local Dancers

1972. Tourism. Multicoloured.

194	$3\frac{1}{2}$ c. Type **50**	10	10
195	$7\frac{1}{2}$ c. Swazi beehive hut	15	15
196	15 c. Ezulwini Valley	20	50
197	25 c. Fishing, Usutu River	65	1·25

51 Spraying Mosquitoes

1973. 25th Anniv of W.H.O. Multicoloured.

198	3½ c. Type **51**	35	10
199	7½ c. Anti-malaria vaccination	55	70

52 Mining

1973. Natural Resources. Multicoloured.

200	3½ c. Type **52**	55	10
201	7½ c. Cattle	25	15
202	15 c. Water	30	20
203	25 c. Rice	35	50

53 Coat of Arms

1973. 5th Anniv of Independence.

204	**53** 3 c. pink and black	10	10
205	– 10 c. multicoloured	20	10
206	– 15 c. multicoloured	45	65
207	– 25 c. multicoloured	55	1·25

DESIGNS: 10 c. King Sobhuza II saluting; 15 c. Parliament buildings; 25 c. National Somhlolo stadium.

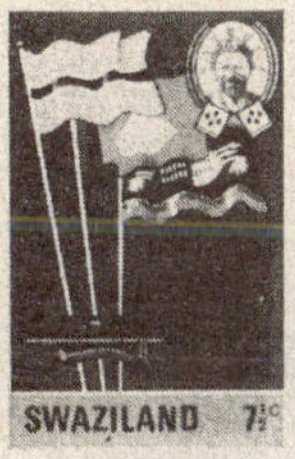

54 Flags and Mortar-board

55 King Sobhuza as College Student

1973. 10th Anniv of University of Botswana, Lesotho and Swaziland. Multicoloured.

208	7½ c. Type **54**	20	10
209	12½ c. University campus	25	10
210	15 c. Map of Southern Africa	30	20
211	25 c. University badge	40	35

1974. 75th Birth Anniv of King Sobhuza II. Multicoloured.

212	3 c. Type **55**	10	10
213	9 c. King Sobhuza in middle-age	10	10
214	50 c. King Sobhuza at 75 years of age	70	60

56 New Post Office, Lobamba

1974. Centenary of U.P.U. Multicoloured.

215	4 c. Type **56**	10	10
216	10 c. Mbabane Temporary Post Office, 1902	15	15
217	15 c. Carrying mail by cableway	30	50
218	25 c. Mule-drawn mail-coach	40	70

1975. As Nos. 174/5, but in new currency.

219	1 e. Waterbuck	1·00	2·00
220	2 e. Giraffe	2·00	4·00

MINIMUM PRICE

The minimum price quoted is 10p which represents a handling charge rather than a basis for valuing common stamps. For further notes about prices see introductory pages.

57 Umcwasho Ceremony

1975. Swazi Youth. Multicoloured.

221	3 c. Type **57**	10	10
222	10 c. Butimba (hunting party)	15	10
223	15 c. Lusekwane (sacred shrub) (horiz)	40	40
224	25 c. Goina Regiment	60	70

58 Control Tower, Matsapa Airport

1975. 10th Anniv of Internal Air Service. Multicoloured.

225	4 c. Type **58**	30	10
226	5 c. Fire engine	70	20
227	15 c. Douglas DC-3	1·75	1·40
228	25 c. Hawker Siddeley H.S.748	2·50	2·00

1975. Nos. 167 and 169 surch.

230	3 c. on 7½ c. Impala	1·00	1·25
231	6 c. on 12½ c. Ratel	1·50	1·50

60 Elephant Symbol

1975 International Women's Year.

232	**60** 4 c. grey, black and blue	10	10
233	– 5 c. multicoloured	10	10
234	– 15 c. multicoloured	30	50
235	– 25 c. multicoloured	50	80

DESIGNS—HORIZ: 5 c. Queen Labotsibeni. VERT: 15 c. Craftswoman; 25 c. "Women in Service".

61 African Black-headed Oriole

1976. Birds. Multicoloured.

236	1 c. Type **61**	75	1·25
237	2 c. African green pigeon (vert)	80	1·25
238	3 c. Green-winged pytilia	1·00	1·00
239	4 c. Violet starling (vert)	80	15
240	5 c. Black-headed heron (vert)	90	70
241	6 c. Stonechat (vert)	1·50	1·25
242	7 c. Chorister robin chat (vert)	1·40	1·50
243	10 c. Four-coloured bush-shrike (vert)	1·50	70
244	15 c. Black-collared barbet (vert)	2·25	55
245	20 c. Grey heron (vert)	3·25	2·00
246	25 c. Giant kingfisher (vert)	3·50	2·00
247	30 c. Verreaux's eagle (vert)	3·50	2·50
248a	50 c. Red bishop (vert)	90	1·00
249a	1 e. Pin-tailed whydah (vert)	1·75	2·50
250a	2 e. Lilac-breasted roller	2·50	5·00

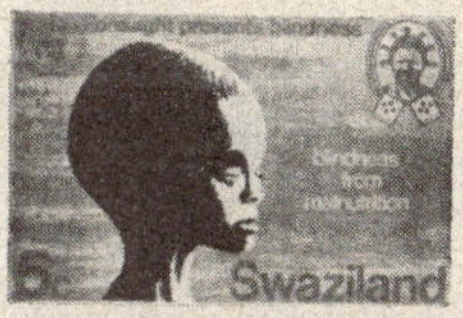

62 Blindness from Malnutrition

1976. Prevention of Blindness. Mult.

251	5 c. Type **62**	25	10
252	10 c. Infected retina	30	10
253	20 c. Blindness from trachoma	60	35
254	25 c. Medicines	65	40

63 Marathon

64 Footballer Shooting

1976. Olympic Games, Montreal. Mult.

255	5 c. Type **63**	15	10
256	6 c. Boxing	20	10
257	20 c. Football	45	25
258	25 c. Olympic torch and flame	55	35

1976. F.I.F.A. Membership. Multicoloured.

259	4 c. Type **64**	20	10
260	6 c. Heading	20	10
261	20 c. Goalkeeping	50	25
262	25 c. Player about to shoot	50	30

65 Alexander Graham Bell and Telephone

1976. Centenary of Telephone.

263	**65** 4 c. multicoloured	10	10
264	– 5 c. multicoloured	10	10
265	– 10 c. multicoloured	10	10
266	– 15 c. multicoloured	30	20
267	– 20 c. multicoloured	40	30

Nos. 264/7 as Type **65**, but showing different telephones.

66 Queen Elizabeth II and King Sobhuza II

1977. Silver Jubilee. Multicoloured.

268	20 c. Type **66**	15	15
269	25 c. Coronation Coach at Admiralty Arch	15	15
270	50 c. Queen in coach	20	40

67 Matsapa College

1977. 50th Anniv of Police Training. Mult.

271	5 c. Type **67**	10	10
272	10 c. Policemen and women on parade	50	20
273	20 c. Royal Swaziland Police badge (vert)	70	85
274	25 c. Dog handling	80	95

68 Animals and Hunters

1977. Rock Paintings. Multicoloured.

275	5 c. Type **68**	25	10
276	10 c. Four dancers in a procession	30	10
277	15 c. Man with cattle	40	20
278	20 c. Four dancers	45	30

69 Timber, Highveld Region

1977. Maps of the Regions. Multicoloured.

280	5 c. Type **69**	30	10
281	10 c. Pineapple, Middleveld	35	10
282	15 c. Orange and lemon, Lowveld	55	65
283	20 c. Cattle, Lubombo region	75	95

71 Cabbage Tree

1978. Trees of Swaziland.

285	**71** 5 c. green, brown and black	15	10
286	– 10 c. multicoloured	20	10
287	– 20 c. multicoloured	45	95
288	– 25 c. multicoloured	55	1·10

DESIGNS: 10 c. Marula; 20 c. Kiaat; 25 c. Lucky bean-tree.

72 Rural Electrification at Lobamba

1978. Hydro-electric Power.

289	**72** 5 c. black and brown	10	10
290	– 10 c. black and green	15	10
291	– 20 c. black and blue	25	30
292	– 25 c. black and purple	30	35

DESIGNS: 10 c. Edwaleni Power Station; 20 c. Switchgear, Magudza Power Station; 25 c. Turbine Hall, Edwaleni.

73 Elephant

75 Defence Force

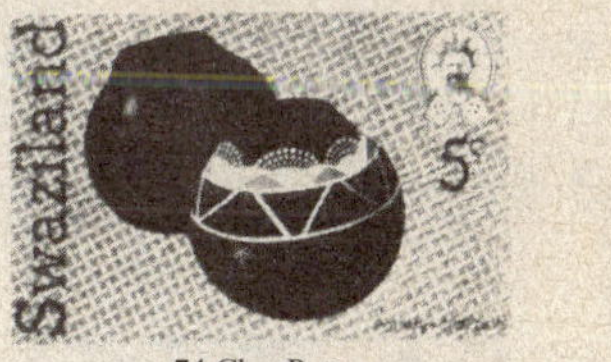

74 Clay Pots

1978. 25th Anniv of Coronation.

293	– 25 c. blue, black and green	15	25
294	– 25 c. multicoloured	15	25
295	**73** 25 c. blue, black and green	15	25

DESIGNS: No. 293, Queen's Lion; No. 294, Queen Elizabeth II.

1978. Handicrafts (1st series). Multicoloured.

296	5 c. Type **74**	10	10
297	10 c. Basketwork	10	10
298	20 c. Wooden utensils	15	15
299	30 c. Wooden pot	25	30

See also Nos. 310/13.

1978. 10th Anniv of Independence. Mult.

300	4 c. Type **75**	15	10
301	6 c. The King's Regiment	15	10
302	10 c. Tinkabi tractor (agricultural development)	15	10
303	15 c. Water-pipe laying (self-help scheme)	25	10
304	25 c. Sebenta adult literacy scheme	30	25
305	50 c. Fire emergency service	1·25	50

76 Archangel Gabriel appearing before Shepherds

1978. Christmas. Multicoloured.

306	5 c. Type **76**	10	10
307	10 c. Wise men paying homage to infant Jesus	10	10
308	15 c. Archangel Gabriel warning Joseph	10	10
309	25 c. Flight into Egypt	20	20

1979. Handicrafts (2nd series). As T **74**. Multicoloured.

310	5 c. Sisal bowls	10	10
311	15 c. Pottery	15	10
312	20 c. Basket work	20	15
313	30 c. Hide shield	30	20

77 Prospecting at Phophonyane

1979. Centenary of Discovery of Gold in Swaziland.

314	**77**	5 c. gold and blue	25	10
315	–	15 c. gold and brown	45	20
316	–	25 c. gold and green	65	30
317	–	50 c. gold and red	90	90

DESIGNS: 15 c. Early 3-stamp battery mill; 25 c. Cyanide tanks at Piggs Peak; 50 c. Pouring off molten gold.

78 "Girls at the Piano"

1979. International Year of the Child. Paintings by Renoir. Multicoloured.

318	5 c. Type **78**	10	10
319	15 c. "Madame Charpentier and her Children"	25	10
320	25 c. "Girls picking Flowers"	35	15
321	50 c. "Girl with Watering Can"	70	55

79 1933 1d. Carmine Stamp and Sir Rowland Hill

1979. Death Centenary of Sir Rowland Hill. Multicoloured.

323	10 c. 1945 3d. Victory commemorative	15	10
324	20 c. Type **79**	25	25
325	25 c. 1968 25 c. Independence commemorative	25	30

80 Obverse and Reverse of 5 Cents

1979. Coins.

327	**80**	5 c. black and brown	15	10
328	–	10 c. black and blue	20	10
329	–	20 c. black and green	35	20
330	–	50 c. black and orange	50	45
331	–	1 e. black and cerise	75	80

DESIGNS: 10 c. Obverse and reverse of 10 cents; 20 c. Obverse and reverse of 20 cents; 50 c. Reverse of 50 cents; 1 e. Reverse of 1 lilangeni.

81 Big Bend Post Office

1979. Post Office Anniversaries.

332	**81**	5 c. multicoloured	10	10
333	–	15 c. multicoloured	15	10
334	–	20 c. black, green and red	20	15
335	–	50 c. multicoloured	40	60

DESIGNS AND COMMEMORATIONS—HORIZ: 5 c. Type **81** (25th anniv of Posts and Telecommunications Services); 20 c. 1949 75th anniv of U.P.U. 1 s. stamp (10th anniv of U.P.U. membership); 50 c. 1974 Centenary of U.P.U. 25 c. stamp (10th anniv of U.P.U membership). VERT: 15 c. Microwave antenna, Mount Ntondozi (25th anniv of Posts and Telecommunications Services).

82 Map of Swaziland

83 "Brunsvigia radulosa"

1980. 75th Anniv of Rotary International.

336	**82**	5 c. blue and gold	25	10
337	–	15 c. blue and gold	45	10
338	–	50 c. blue and gold	50	55
339	–	1 e. blue and gold	85	1·25

DESIGNS: 15 c. Vitreous cutter and optical illuminator; 50 c. Scroll; 1 e. Rotary Headquarters, Evanston, U.S.A.

1980. Flowers. Multicoloured.

340A	1 c. Type **83**	15	10
341A	2 c. "Aloe suprafoliata"	15	10
342A	3 c. "Haemanthus magnificus"	15	10
343A	4 c. "Aloe marlothii"	20	10
344A	5 c. "Dicoma zeyheri"	15	10
345A	6 c. "Aloe kniphofioides"	20	30
346A	7 c. "Cyrtanthus bicolor"	15	10
347A	10 c. "Eucomis autumnalis" (horiz)	25	10
348A	15 c. "Leucospermum gerrardii" (horiz)	15	10
349A	20 c. "Haemanthus multiflorus" (horiz)	40	25
350A	30 c. "Acridocarpus natalitius" (horiz)	20	20
351A	50 c. "Adenium swazicum" (horiz)	30	30
352A	1 e. "Protea simplex"	55	60
353A	2 e. "Calodendrum capense"	1·10	1·25
354A	5 e. "Gladiolus ecklonii"	2·25	3·00

Nos. 347A/51A are 42 × 45 mm and Nos. 352A/4A 28 × 38 mm.

Nos. 340A/1A, 343A, 345A, 347A and 349A come with and without date imprint.

84 Mail Runner

1980. "London 1980" International Stamp Exhibition. Multicoloured.

355	10 c. Type **84**	15	10
356	20 c. Post Office mail truck	25	15
357	25 c. Mail sorting office	30	20
358	50 c. Ropeway conveying mail at Bulembu	70	70

85 Scaly

1980. River Fishes. Multicoloured.

359	5 c. Type **85**	30	10
360	10 c. Silver catfish ("Silver barbel")	30	10
361	15 c. Tiger fish	55	15
362	30 c. Brown squeaker	85	30
363	1 e. Red-breasted tilapia ("Bream")	1·10	1·40

86 Oribi

1980. Wildlife Conservation. Multicoloured.

364	5 c. Type **86**	15	10
365	10 c. Nile crocodile (vert)	30	10
366	50 c. Temminck's ground pangolin	75	70
367	1 e. Leopard (vert)	1·60	1·50

87 Public Bus Service

1981. Transport. Multicoloured.

368	5 c. Type **87**	10	10
369	25 c. Royal Swazi National Airways	25	15
370	30 c. Swaziland United Transport	30	20
371	1 e. Swaziland Railway	1·25	1·75

88 Mantenga Falls

1981. Tourism. Multicoloured.

372	5 c. Type **88**	10	10
373	15 c. Mananga Yacht Club	15	10
374	30 c. White rhinoceros in Mlilwane Game Sanctuary	40	30
375	1 e. Gambling equipment (casinos)	1·10	1·60

89 Prince Charles on Hike

91 "Physical Recreation"

90 Installation of King Sobhuza II, 22 December 1921

1981. Royal Wedding. Multicoloured.

376	10 c. Wedding bouquet from Swaziland	10	10
377	25 c. Type **89**	15	10
378	1 e. Prince Charles and Lady Diana Spencer	40	70

1981. Diamond Jubilee of King Sobhuza II. Multicoloured.

379	5 c. Type **90**	10	10
380	10 c. Royal Visit, 1947	10	10
381	15 c. King Sobhuza II and Coronation of Queen Elizabeth II, 1953	15	15
382	25 c. King Sobhuza taking Royal Salute, Independence, 1968	15	15
383	30 c. King Sobhuza in youth	20	20
384	1 e. King Sobhuza and Parliament Buildings	50	90

1981. 25th Anniv of Duke of Edinburgh Award Scheme. Multicoloured.

385	5 c. Type **91**	10	10
386	20 c. "Expeditions"	10	10
387	50 c. "Skills"	25	25
388	1 e. Duke of Edinburgh in ceremonial dress	50	80

92 Disabled Person in Wheelchair

1981. International Year of Disabled Persons. Multicoloured.

389	5 c. Type **92**	30	10
390	15 c. Teacher with disabled child (vert)	50	15
391	25 c. Disabled craftsman (vert)	75	20
392	1 e. Disabled driver in invalid carriage	2·25	1·75

93 "Papilio demodocus"

1981. Butterflies. Multicoloured.

393	5 c. Type **93**	50	10
394	10 c. "Charaxes candiope"	60	10
395	50 c. "Papilio nireus"	2·00	85
396	1 e. "Terias desjardinsii"	2·50	2·00

94 Man holding a Flower after discarding Cigarettes

95 Male Pel's Fishing Owl

1982. Pan-African Conference on Smoking and Health. Multicoloured.

397	5 c. Type **94**	50	85
398	10 c. Smoker and non-smoker	60	90

1982. Wildlife Conservation (1st series). Pel's Fishing Owl. Multicoloured.

399	35 c. Type **95**	6·00	4·00
400	35 c. Female Pel's fishing owl at nest	6·00	4·00
401	35 c. Pair of Pel's fishing owls	6·00	4·00
402	35 c. Pel's fishing owl, nest and eggs	6·00	4·00
403	35 c. Adult Pel's fishing owl with youngster	6·00	4·00

See also Nos. 425/29 and 448/52.

96 Swaziland Coat of Arms

97 Irrigation

1982. 21st Birthday of Princess of Wales. Multicoloured.

404	5 c. Type **96**	10	10
405	20 c. Princess leaving Eastleigh Airport, Southampton	70	10
406	50 c. Bride at Buckingham Palace	80	25
407	1 e. Formal portrait	1·75	65

1982. Sugar Industry. Multicoloured.

408	5 c. Type **97**	10	10
409	20 c. Harvesting	25	15
410	30 c. Mhlume mills	35	25
411	1 e. Sugar transportation by train	1·00	1·40

98 Doctor with Child

1982. Swaziland Red Cross Society (Baphaladi). Multicoloured.

412	5 c. Type **98**	10	10
413	20 c. Juniors carrying stretcher	25	15
414	50 c. Disaster relief	55	60
415	1 e. Henri Dunant (founder of Red Cross)	1·25	1·40

99 Taking the Oath

1982. 75th Anniv of Boy Scout Movement. Multicoloured.

416	5 c. Type **99**	10	10
417	10 c. Hiking and exploration	15	10
418	25 c. Community development	30	30
419	75 c. Lord Baden-Powell	1·00	1·25

100 Satellite View of Earth

102 Montgolfier Balloon

1982. Commonwealth Day. Multicoloured.

421 6 c. Type **100** 10 10
422 10 c. King Sobhuza II 10 10
423 50 c. Swazi woman and beehive huts (horiz) 35 55
424 1 e. Spraying sugar crops (horiz) 70 1·00

1983. Wildlife Conservation (2nd series). Lammergeier. As T **95**. Multicoloured.

425 35 c. Adult male . . . . . . 2·25 2·25
426 35 c. Pair . . . . 2·25 2·25
427 35 c. Nest and egg . . . . . . 2·25 2·25
428 35 c. Female at nest . . . . . 2·25 2·25
429 35 c. Adult bird with fledgling 2·25 2·25

1983. Bicentenary of Manned Flight. Mult.

431 5 c. Type **102** 10 10
432 10 c. Wright brothers' Flyer I (horiz) 15 10
433 25 c. Fokker Fellowship (horiz) 30 35
434 50 c. Bell XS-1 (horiz) 60 65

103 Dr. Albert Schweitzer (Peace Prize, 1952)

1983. 150th Birth Anniv of Alfred Nobel. Multicoloured.

436 6 c. Type **103** 90 20
437 10 c. Dag Hammarskjold (Peace Prize, 1961) 70 15
438 50 c. Albert Einstein (Physics Prize, 1921) . . . . 3·00 1·75
439 1 e. Alfred Nobel . . . . . . 3·25 3·50

104 Maize

1983. World Food Day. Multicoloured.

440 6 c. Type **104** 10 10
441 10 c. Rice 10 10
442 50 c. Cattle herding 70 80
443 1 e. Ploughing . . . . 1·25 1·60

105 Women's College

1984. Education. Multicoloured.

444 5 c. Type **105** 10 10
445 15 c. Technical training school 15 15
446 50 c. University 35 60
447 1 e. Primary school . . . . . 65 1·10

106 Male on Ledge

1984. Wildlife Conservation (3rd series). Bald Ibis. Multicoloured.

448 35 c. Type **106** . . . . 3·00 3·00
449 35 c. Male and female . . . . 3·00 3·00
450 35 c. Bird and egg . . . . . . 3·00 3·00
451 35 c. Female on nest of eggs . 3·00 3·00
452 35 c. Adult and fledgling . . . 3·00 3·00

107 Mule-drawn Passenger Coach

1984. Universal Postal Union Congress, Hamburg. Multicoloured.

453 7 c. Type **107** 30 10
454 15 c. Ox-drawn post wagon . 45 15
455 50 c. Mule-drawn mail coach . 90 60
456 1 e. Bristol to London mail coach 1·40 1·10

108 Running

1984. Olympic Games, Los Angeles. Multicoloured.

457 7 c. Type **108** 10 10
458 10 c. Swimming 10 10
459 50 c. Shooting 45 75
460 1 e. Boxing . . . . 90 1·60

109 "Suillus bovinus"

1984. Fungi. Multicoloured.

462 10 c. Type **109** . . . . 1·50 30
463 15 c. "Langermannia gigantea" (vert) . . . . 2·50 55
464 50 c. "Trametes versicolor" ("Coriolus versicolor") (vert) 2·75 2·50
465 1 e. "Boletus edulis" . . . . 3·25 4·50

110 King Sobhuza opening Railway, 1964

1984. 20th Anniv of Swaziland Railways. Multicoloured.

466 10 c. Type **110** 30 15
467 25 c. Type 15A locomotive at Siweni Yard 65 40
468 30 c. Container loading, Matsapha Station 65 40
469 1 e. Locomotive No. 268 leaving Alto Tunnel . . . . 1·50 2·00

1985. Nos. 340, 342, 343, 345 and 346 surch.

471a 10 c. on 4 c. "Aloe marlothii" 50 10
472 15 c. on 7 c. "Cyrtanthus bicolor" 60 20
473 20 c. on 3 c. "Haemanthus magnificus" 50 15
474 25 c. on 6 c. "Aloe kniphofioides" 60 20
475 30 c. on 1 c. Type **83** 70 20
476 30 c. on 2 c. "Aloe suprafoliata" 2·50 3·00

112 Rotary International Logo and Map of World

1985. 80th Anniv of Rotary International. Multicoloured.

477 10 c. Type **112** 30 10
478 15 c. Teacher and handicapped children 70 20
479 50 c. Youth exchange . . . . 1·00 55
480 1 e. Nurse and children . . . 2·00 1·10

113 Male Southern Ground Hornbill

114 The Queen Mother in 1975

1985. Birth Bicentenary of John J. Audubon (ornithologist). Southern Ground Hornbills. Multicoloured.

481 25 c. Type **113** . . . . 2·00 3·00
482 25 c. Male and female ground hornbills . . . . 2·00 3·00
483 25 c. Female at nest . . . . . 2·00 3·00
484 25 c. Ground hornbill in nest, and egg . . . . 2·00 3·00
485 25 c. Adult and fledgling . . . 2·00 3·00

1985. Life and Times of Queen Elizabeth the Queen Mother. Multicoloured.

486 10 c. The Queen Mother in South Africa, 1947 . . . . 10 10
487 15 c. With the Queen and Princess Margaret, 1985 (from photo by Norman Parkinson) 10 10
488 50 c. Type **114** 25 40
489 1 e. With Prince Henry at his christening (from photo by Lord Snowdon) 50 90

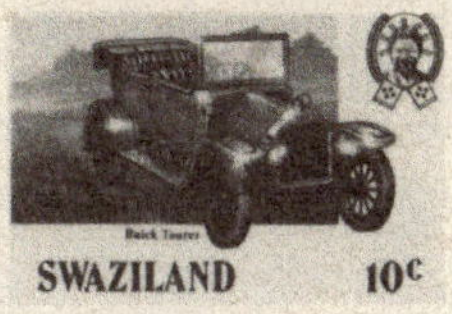

115 Buick "Tourer"

1985. Century of Motoring. Multicoloured.

491 10 c. Type **115** 50 10
492 15 c. Four cylinder Rover . . 70 20
493 50 c. De Dion Bouton . . . . 1·75 2·00
494 1 e. "Model T" Ford . . . . . 2·25 3·75

116 Youths building Bridge over Ravine

1985. International Youth Year (10, 50 c.) and 75th Anniv of Girl Guide Movement (others). Multicoloured.

495 10 c. Type **116** 15 10
496 20 c. Girl Guides in camp . . 20 15
497 50 c. Youth making model from sticks 45 75
498 1 e. Guides collecting brushwood 80 1·50

117 Halley's Comet over Swaziland

1986. Appearance of Halley's Comet.

499 **117** 1 e. 50 multicoloured . . 2·75 3·50

1986. 60th Birthday of Queen Elizabeth II. As T **110** of Ascension. Multicoloured.

500 10 c. Christening of Princess Anne, 1950 . . . . 10 10
501 30 c. On Palace balcony after wedding of Prince and Princess of Wales, 1981 . . . . 15 25
502 45 c. Royal visit to Swaziland, 1947 . . . . 15 30
503 1 e. At Windsor Polo Ground, 1984 . . . . 30 60
504 2 e. At Crown Agents Head Office, London 1983 . . . . 60 1·25

118 King Mswati III

119 Emblems of Round Table and Project Orbis (eye disease campaign)

1986. Coronation of King Mswati III.

505 **118** 10 c. black and gold . . . 35 10
506 – 20 c. multicoloured 70 30
507 – 25 c. multicoloured 80 35
508 – 30 c. multicoloured 90 50
509 – 40 c. multicoloured . . . . 2·00 1·75
510 – 2 e. multicoloured . . . . 3·50 6·00

DESIGNS—HORIZ: 20 c. Prince with King Sobhuza II at Incwala ceremony; 25 c. At primary school; 30 c. At school in England; 40 c. Inspecting guard of honour at Matsapha Airport; 2 e. Dancing the Simemo.

1986. 50th Anniv of Round Table Organization. Designs showing branch emblems. Multicoloured.

511 15 c. Type **119** 20 10
512 25 c. Ehlanzeni 51 . . . . . . 30 20
513 55 c. Mbabane 30 . . . . . . 65 60
514 70 c. Bulembu 54 . . . . . . 75 85
515 2 e. Manzini 44 . . . . 1·75 2·50

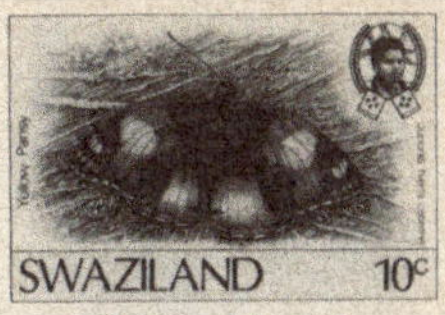

120 "Precis hierta"

1987. Butterflies (1st series). Multicoloured.

516 10 c. Type **120** 55 70
517 15 c. "Hamanumida daedalus" 65 40
518 20 c. "Charaxes boueti" . . . 65 90
519 25 c. "Abantis paradisea" . . 65 65
520 30 c. "Acraea anemosa" . . . 65 70
521 35 c. "Graphium leonidas" . . 65 75
522 45 c. "Graphium antheus" . . 70 85
523 50 c. "Precis orithya" 70 85
524 55 c. "Pinacopteryx eriphia" . 70 85
525 70 c. "Precis octavia" . . . . 80 1·40
526 1 e. "Mylothris chloris" . . . 1·00 2·25
527 5 e. "Colotis regina" . . . . 1·00 1·10
528 10 e. "Spindasis natalensis" . . 2·00 2·10

For these designs and similar 5 c. with different portrait of King Mswati III, see Nos. 606/17.

121 Two White Rhinoceroses

122 Hybrid Tea Rose "Blue Moon"

1987. White Rhinoceros. Multicoloured.

529 15 c. Type **121** . . . . 2·00 45
530 25 c. Female and calf . . . . 2·75 1·00
531 45 c. Rhinoceros charging . . 4·25 3·25
532 70 c. Rhinoceros wallowing . 6·50 7·00

1987. Garden Flowers. Multicoloured.

533 15 c. Type **122** 90 20
534 35 c. Rambler rose "Danse du feu" . . . . 1·75 80
535 55 c. Pompon dahlia "Odin" . 2·25 1·50
536 2 e. "Lilium davidii var. willmottiae" . . . . 5·75 9·00

1987. Royal Ruby Wedding. Nos. 501/4 optd **40TH WEDDING ANNIVERSARY**.

537 30 c. On Palace balcony after wedding of Prince and Princess of Wales, 1981 . . . . 20 20
538 45 c. Royal visit to Swaziland, 1947 . . . . 30 30
539 1 e. At Windsor Polo Ground, 1984 . . . . 50 1·25
540 2 e. At Crown Agents Head Office, London, 1983 . . . 75 2·25

123 "Zabalius aridus" (grasshopper)

1988. Insects. Multicoloured.

541 15 c. Type **123** 80 15
542 55 c. "Callidea bohemani" (shieldbug) . . . . 2·00 85
543 1 e. "Phymateus viridipes" (grasshopper) . . . . 3·25 3·75
544 2 e. "Nomadacris septemfasciata" (locust) . . 5·00 7·00

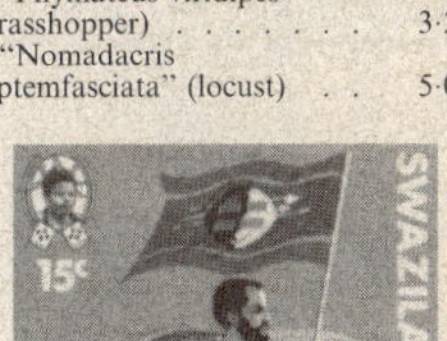

124 Athlete with Swazi Flag and Olympic Stadium

1988. Olympic Games, Seoul. Multicoloured.

545 15 c. Type **124** 25 10
546 35 c. Taekwondo 80 45
547 1 e. Boxing . . . . 1·25 2·00
548 2 e. Tennis . . . . 2·75 4·25

125 Savanna Monkey

1989. Small Mammals. Multicoloured.

549 35 c. Type **125** . . . . 1·25 30
550 55 c. Large-toothed rock hyrax 1·60 75
551 1 e. Zorilla . . . . 2·75 3·50
552 2 e. African wild cat . . . . . 4·50 6·00

126 Dr. David Hynd (founder of Swazi Red Cross)

1989. 125th Anniv of Int Red Cross. Mult.

553	15 c. Type **126**	20	15
554	60 c. First aid training	55	40
555	1 e. Sigombeni Clinic	90	80
556	2 e. Refugee camp	1·40	1·40

127 King Mswati III with Prince of Wales, 1987

1989. 21st Birthday of King Mswati III. Mult.

557	15 c. Type **127**	10	10
558	60 c. King with Pope John Paul II, 1988	30	35
559	1 e. Introduction of Crown Prince to people, 1983	50	55
560	2 e. King Mswati III and Queen Mother	95	1·00

128 Manzini to Mahamba Road

1989. 25th Anniv of African Development Bank. Multicoloured.

561	15 c. Type **128**	10	10
562	60 c. Microwave Radio Receiver, Mbabane	30	40
563	1 e. Mbabane Government Hospital	50	85
564	2 e. Ezulwini Power Station switchyard	95	1·75

129 International Priority Mail Van

1990. "Stamp World London 90" International Stamp Exhibition. Multicoloured.

565	15 c. Type **129**	15	10
566	60 c. Facsimile service operators	40	40
567	1 e. Rural post office	75	1·00
568	2 e. Ezulwini Earth Station	1·40	1·90

1990. 90th Birthday of Queen Elizabeth the Queen Mother. As T **134** of Ascension.

570	75 c. multicoloured	50	50
571	4 e. black and green	2·25	3·00

DESIGNS—21 × 36 mm: 75 c. Queen Mother. 29 × 37 mm: 4 e. King George VI and Queen Elizabeth visiting Civil Resettlement Unit, Hatfield House.

130 Pictorial Teaching

1990. International Literacy Year. Mult.

572	15 c. Type **130**	10	10
573	75 c. Rural class	45	45
574	1 e. Modern teaching methods	60	95
575	2 e. Presentation of certificates	1·10	1·60

131 Rural Water Supply

133 Lobamba Hot Spring

1990. 40th Anniv of United Nations Development Programme. "Helping People to Help Themselves". Multicoloured.

576	60 c. Type **131**	35	35
577	1 e. Seed multiplication project	60	95
578	2 e. Low-cost housing project	1·25	1·75

1990. Nos. 519/20, 522 and 524 surch.

579	10 c. on 25 c. "Abantis paradisea"	30	30
580	15 c. on 30 c. "Acraea anemosa"	40	40
580a	15 c. on 45 c. "Graphium antheus"	12·00	12·00
581	20 c. on 45 c. "Graphium antheus"	40	40
582	40 c. on 55 c. "Pinacopteryx eriphia"	55	55

1991. National Heritage. Multicoloured.

583	15 c. Type **133**	15	10
584	60 c. Sibebe Rock	40	45
585	1 e. Jolobela Falls	70	80
586	2 e. Mantjolo Sacred Pool	1·25	1·60

134 King Mswati III making Speech

1991. 5th Anniv of King Mswati III's Coronation. Multicoloured.

588	15 c. Type **134**	15	10
589	75 c. Butimba Royal Hunt	50	60
590	1 e. King and visiting school friends, 1986	70	1·00
591	2 e. King opening Parliament	1·25	2·00

1991. 65th Birthday of Queen Elizabeth II and 70th Birthday of Prince Philip. As T **139** of Ascension. Multicoloured.

592	1 e. Prince Philip	70	1·00
593	2 e. Queen Elizabeth II	1·25	1·40

135 "Xerophyta retinervis"

136 Father Christmas arriving with Gifts

1991. Indigenous Flowers. Multicoloured.

594	15 c. Type **135**	15	10
595	75 c. "Bauhinia galpinii"	60	70
596	1 e. "Dombeya rotundifolia"	80	1·25
597	2 e. "Kigelia africana"	1·75	2·25

1991. Christmas. Multicoloured.

598	20 c. Type **136**	15	10
599	70 c. Singing carols	65	50
600	1 e. Priest reading from Bible	80	1·25
601	2 e. The Nativity	1·50	2·50

137 Lubombo Flat Lizard

1992. Reptiles (1st series). Multicoloured.

602	20 c. Type **137**	75	20
603	70 c. Natal hinged tortoise	1·75	1·25
604	1 e. Swazi thick-toed gecko	2·25	2·25
605	2 e. Nile monitor	3·00	4·00

See also Nos. 658/61.

138 "Precis hierta"

1992. Butterflies (2nd series). Nos. 516/26 and new value (5 c.) showing different portrait of King Mswati III. Multicoloured.

606	5 c. "Colotis antevippe"	10	10
607	10 c. Type **138**	10	10
608	15 c. "Hamanumida daedalus"	10	10
609	20 c. "Charaxes boueti"	10	10
610	25 c. "Abantis paradisea"	10	10
611	30 c. "Acraea anemosa"	10	10
612	35 c. "Graphium leonidas"	10	10
613	45 c. "Graphium antheus"	10	10
614	50 c. "Precis orithya"	10	10
615	55 c. "Pinacopteryx eriphia"	10	10
616	70 c. "Precis octavia"	15	20
617	1 e. "Mylothris chloris"	20	25

139 Missionaries visiting King Sobhuza II and Queen Lomawa

140 Calabashes

1992. Centenary of Evangelical Alliance Missions. Multicoloured.

620	20 c. Type **139**	25	10
621	1 e. Pioneer missionaries	1·25	1·75

1993. Archaeological and Contemporary Artifacts. Multicoloured.

622	20 c. Type **140**	35	10
623	70 c. Contemporary cooking pot	85	85
624	1 e. Wooden bowl and containers	1·25	1·50
625	2 e. Quern for grinding seeds	2·00	2·75

141 King Mswati III as Baby

142 Male and Female Common Waxbills

1993. 25th Birthday of King Mswati III and 25th Anniv of Independence. Mult.

626	25 c. Type **141**	15	10
627	40 c. King Mswati III addressing meeting	20	20
628	1 e. King Sobhuza II receiving Instrument of Independence	65	90
629	2 e. King Mswati III delivering Coronation speech	1·25	1·90

1993. Common Waxbill. Multicoloured.

630	25 c. Type **142**	40	20
631	40 c. Waxbill and eggs in nest	55	25
632	1 e. Waxbill on nest	1·25	1·50
633	2 e. Waxbill feeding chicks	2·00	2·75

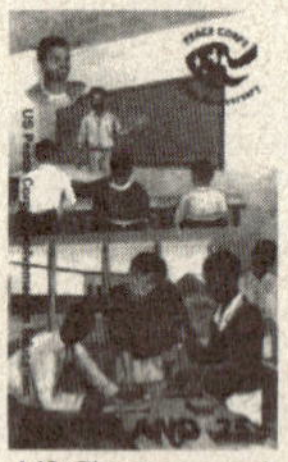

143 Classroom and Practical Training

144 "Agaricus arvensis"

1994. 25th Anniv of U.S. Peace Corps in Swaziland. Multicoloured.

634	25 c. Type **143**	15	10
635	40 c. Rural water supply	25	20
636	1 e. Americans and Swazis in traditional costumes	70	1·00
637	2 e. Swazi–American co-operation	1·10	2·00

1994. Fungi. Multicoloured.

638	30 c. Type **144**	55	30
639	40 c. "Boletus edulis"	60	30
640	1 e. "Russula virescens"	1·25	1·50
641	2 e. "Armillaria mellea"	2·00	2·50

145 Emblem and Airliner on Runway

1994. 50th Anniv of I.C.A.O. Multicoloured.

642	30 c. Type **145**	30	10
643	40 c. Control tower and dish aerial	35	20
644	1 e. Crash tenders	75	1·00
645	2 e. Air traffic controllers	1·25	2·00

146 Wooden Bowls

147 Harvesting Maize

1995. Handicrafts. Multicoloured.

646	35 c. Type **146**	20	20
647	50 c. Chicken nests	30	35
648	1 e. Leather crafts	50	70
649	2 e. Wood carvings	90	1·50

1995. 50th Anniv of F.A.O. Multicoloured.

650	35 c. Type **147**	20	20
651	50 c. Planting vegetables	30	35
652	1 e. Herd of cattle	50	70
653	2 e. Harvesting sorghum	90	1·50

148 Knysna Turaco

1995. Turacos ("Louries"). Multicoloured.

654	35 c. Type **148**	30	30
655	50 c. Knysna turaco in flight	45	40
656	1 e. Violet-crested turaco	70	90
657	2 e. Livingstone's turaco	1·10	1·75

1996. Reptiles (2nd series). As T **137** with King's portrait at right. Multicoloured.

658	35 c. Chameleon	25	20
659	50 c. Rock monitor	35	35
660	1 e. African python	60	75
661	2 e. Tree agama	90	1·50

149 Waterberry

1996. Trees. Multicoloured.

662	40 c. Type **149**	15	15
663	60 c. Sycamore fig	20	20
664	1 e. Stem fruit	40	60
665	2 e. Wild medlar	80	1·25

150 Mahamba Methodist Church

1996. Historic Monuments. Multicoloured.

666	40 c. Type **150**	15	15
667	60 c. Colonial Secretariat, Mbabane	20	20
668	1 e. King Sobhuza II Monument, Lobamba	40	60
669	2 e. First High Court Building, Hlatikulu	80	1·25

151 Children in Class

1996. 50th Anniv of U.N.I.C.E.F. Multicoloured.

670	40 c. Type **151**	15	15
671	60 c. Child being inoculated (vert)	20	20
672	1 e. Child on crutches (vert)	40	60
673	2 e. Mother and children (vert)	80	1·25

152 Klipspringer

153 Umgaco Costume

1997. Mammals. Multicoloured.

674	50 c. Type **152**	25	20
675	70 c. Grey duiker	30	30
676	1 e. Antbear (horiz)	40	55
677	2 e. Cape clawless otter (horiz)	70	1·00

1997. Traditional Costumes. Multicoloured.

678	50 c. Type **153**	15	15
679	70 c. Sigeja cloak	25	25
680	1 e. Umdada kilt	35	35
681	2 e. Ligcebesha costume	65	65

154 Olive Toad

1998. Amphibians. Multicoloured.

682	55 c. Type **154**	15	15
683	75 c. African bullfrog	25	25
684	1 e. Water lily frog	35	35
685	2 e. Bushveld rain frog	65	65

155 Aerial View of King Sobhuza II Memorial Park

1998. 30th Anniv of Independence and 30th Birthday of King Mswati III. Multicoloured.

686	55 c. Type **155**	15	15
687	75 c. King Mswati III taking oath (vert)	25	25
688	1 e. King Mswati delivering speech	35	35
689	2 e. King Sobhuza II receiving Instrument of Independence	65	65

156 Grinding Stone

1999. Local Culinary Utensils. Multicoloured.

690	60 c. Type **156**	10	10
691	75 c. Stirring sticks	15	20
692	80 c. Clay pot	20	25
693	95 c. Swazi spoons	20	25
694	1 e. 75 Beer cups	40	45
695	2 e. 40 Mortar and pestle	50	55

POSTAGE DUE STAMPS

D 1

D 6

1933.

D1	D **1**	1d. red	30	7·50
D2		2d. violet	1·75	20·00

1961. Surch **Postage Due 2d.**

D3	**7**	2d. on 2d. black and brown	1·75	3·25

These prices apply to stamps with large figure measuring 4½ mm high.

1961. As Type D **1** but with value in cents.

D4	1 c. red	15	75
D5	2 c. violet	15	1·10
D6	5 c. green	20	1·10

1961. Surch **Postage Due** and value in cents.

D10	**7**	1 c. on 2d. black and brown	90	2·75
D11		2 c. on 2d. black and brown	65	2·75
D12		5 c. on 2d. black and brown	1·25	2·75

1971.

D19	D **6**	1 c. red	30	1·00
D23		2 c. purple	10	10
D24		5 c. green	10	10
D25		10 c. blue	10	10
D26		25 c. brown	10	10

TANGANYIKA

Formerly the German colony of German East Africa. After the 1914–18 War it was under British mandate until 1946 and then administered by Britain under United Nations trusteeship until 1961 when it became independent within the British Commonwealth. It had a common postal service with Kenya and Uganda from 1935 to 1961 (for these issues see under Kenya, Uganda and Tanganyika). Renamed Tanzania in 1965.

1915. 16 annas = 1 rupee.
1917. 100 cents = 1 rupee.
1922. 100 cents = 1 shilling.

1915. Stamps of the Indian Expeditionary Forces optd **G. R. POST MAFIA.**

M33	**55**	3 p. grey	24·00	55·00
M34	**56**	½ a. green	42·00	60·00
M35	**57**	1 a. red	45·00	60·00
M36	**59**	2 a. lilac	65·00	95·00
M37	**61**	2½ a. blue	85·00	£120
M38	**62**	3 a. orange	90·00	£130
M39	**63**	4 a. olive	£110	£150
M40	**65**	8 a. mauve	£180	£275
M41	**66**	12 a. red	£275	£375
M42	**67**	1 r. brown and green	£325	£400

1916. Stamps of Nyasaland (King George V) optd **N.F.**

N1	½d. green	1·50	7·50
N2	1d. red	1·50	3·25
N3	3d. purple on yellow	6·00	15·00
N4	4d. black and red on yellow	28·00	35·00
N5	1s. black on green	28·00	38·00

1917. Stamps of Kenya and Uganda (King George V, 1912) optd **G.E.A.**

45	1 c. black	15	80
47	3 c. green	15	15
48	6 c. red	15	10
49	10 c. orange	40	50
50	12 c. grey	40	1·75
51	15 c. blue	70	1·75
52	25 c. black and red on yellow	80	2·75
53	50 c. black and lilac	80	3·25
54	75 c. black on green	1·00	4·50
55	1 r. black on green	2·50	7·00
56	2 r. red and black on blue	7·00	35·00
57	3 r. violet and green	13·00	60·00
58	4 r. red and green on yellow	17·00	75·00
59	5 r. blue and purple	30·00	75·00
60	10 r. red and green on green	55·00	£225
61	20 r. black and purple on red	£190	£325
62	50 r. red and green	£475	£750

4 Giraffe 5

1922.

74	**4**	5 c. black and purple	2·00	20
89		5 c. black and green	75	1·50
75		10 c. black and green	2·00	70
90		10 c. black and yellow	3·00	1·50
76		15 c. black and red	2·00	10
77		20 c. black and orange	1·75	10
78		25 c. black	5·50	6·00
91		25 c. black and blue	3·50	16·00
79		30 c. black and blue	5·00	4·50
92		30 c. black and purple	3·50	8·50
80		40 c. black and brown	2·50	4·50
81		50 c. black and grey	2·00	1·50
82		75 c. black and yellow	3·25	17·00
83a	**5**	1 s. black and green	2·25	11·00
84		2 s. black and purple	4·50	13·00
85		3 s. black	9·00	28·00
86a		5 s. black and red	12·00	65·00
87a		10 s. black and blue	45·00	85·00
88a		£1 black and orange	£130	£225

6

7

1927.

93	**6**	5 c. black and green	80	10
94		10 c. black and yellow	1·75	10
95		15 c. black and red	80	10
96		20 c. black and orange	2·00	10
97		25 c. black and blue	2·25	2·00
98		30 c. black and purple	2·50	2·50
98a		30 c. black and blue	21·00	30
99		40 c. black and brown	2·00	4·00
100		50 c. black and grey	2·00	1·00
101		75 c. black and olive	2·00	9·00
102	**7**	1 s. black and green	3·00	2·25
103		2 s. black and purple	11·00	3·75
104		3 s. black	11·00	42·00
105		5 s. black and red	11·00	15·00
106		10 s. black and blue	48·00	80·00
107		£1 black and orange	£110	£180

8 Teacher and Pupils

15 Freedom Torch over Mt. Kilimanjaro

1961. Independence. Inscr "UHURU 1961".

108	**8**	5 c. sepia and green	10	10
109	–	10 c. turquoise	10	10
110	–	15 c. sepia and blue	10	10
111	–	20 c. brown	10	10
112	–	30 c. black, green & yellow	10	10
113	–	50 c. black and yellow	10	10
114	–	1 s. brown, blue and yellow	15	10
115	**15**	1 s. 30 multicoloured	1·75	10
116	–	2 s. multicoloured	50	10
117	–	5 s. turquoise and red	50	40
118	–	10 s. black, purple and blue	12·00	4·75
119	**15**	20 s. multicoloured	3·25	7·50

DESIGNS—VERT (as Type **8**): 10 c. District nurse and child; 15 c. Coffee picking; 20 c. Harvesting maize; 50 c. Serengeti lions. HORIZ (as Type **8**): 30 c. Tanganyikan flag. (As Type **15**): 1 s. "Maternity" (mother with nurse holding baby); 2 s. Dar-es-Salaam waterfront; 5 s. Land tillage; 10 s. Diamond mine.

19 Pres. Nyerere inaugurating Self-help Project

23 Map of Republic

1962. Inauguration of Republic.

120	**19**	30 c. green	10	10
121	–	50 c. multicoloured	10	10
122	–	1 s. 30 multicoloured	10	10
123	–	2 s. 30 black, red and blue	30	40

DESIGNS: 50 c. Hoisting flag on Mt. Kilimanjaro; 1 s. 30, Presidential emblem; 2 s. 50, Independence monument.

1964. United Republic of Tanganyika and Zanzibar Commemoration.

124	**23**	20 c. green and blue	10	10
125	–	30 c. blue and sepia	10	10
126	–	1 s. 50 purple and blue	10	10
127	**23**	2 s. 50 purple and blue	80	40

DESIGN: 30 c., 1 s. 30, Torch and spear emblem.

Despite the inscription on the stamps the above issue was only on sale in Tanganyika and had no validity in Zanzibar.

OFFICIAL STAMPS

1961. Independence stamps of 1961 optd **OFFICIAL.**

O1	5 c. brown and green	10	10
O2	10 c. turquoise	10	10
O3	15 c. brown and blue	10	10
O4	20 c. brown	10	10
O5	30 c. black, green and yellow	10	10
O6	50 c. black and yellow	10	10
O7	1 s. brown, blue and yellow	10	10
O8	5 s. turquoise and red	65	75

For later issues see **TANZANIA**.

TANZANIA

A republic within the British Commonwealth formerly known as Tanganyika and incorporating Zanzibar.

100 cents = 1 shilling

NOTE—Stamps inscribed "UGANDA KENYA TANGANYIKA & ZANZIBAR" (or "TANZANIA UGANDA KENYA") will be found listed under Kenya, Uganda and Tanganyika (Tanzania).

A. For use in Tanzania. Issues to No. 176 were also valid for use in Kenya and Uganda.

25 Hale Hydro-Electric Scheme

39 Black-footed Cardinalfish

33 Dar-es-Salaam Harbour

1965.

128	**25**	5 c. blue and orange	10	10
129	–	10 c. multicoloured	10	10
130	–	15 c. multicoloured	10	10
131	–	20 c. sepia, green and blue	10	10
132	–	30 c. black and brown	10	10
133	–	40 c. multicoloured	65	20
134	–	50 c. multicoloured	30	10
135	–	65 c. green, brown and blue	2·50	1·75
136	**33**	1 s. multicoloured	80	10
137	–	1 s. 30 multicoloured	5·50	85
138	–	2 s. 50 blue and brown	5·50	90
139	–	5 s. brown, green and blue	80	20
140	–	10 s. yellow, green and blue	1·00	2·50
141	–	20 s. multicoloured	5·50	15·00

DESIGNS—HORIZ (as Type **25**): 10 c. Tanzania flag; 20 c. Road-building; 50 c. Common zebras, Manyara National Park; 65 c. Mt. Kilimanjaro. (As Type **33**): 1 s. 30, Skull of "Zinjanthropus" and excavations, Olduvai Gorge; 2 s. 50, Fishing; 5 s. Sisal industry; 10 s. State House, Dar-es-Salaam. VERT (as Type **25**): 15 c. National servicemen; 30 c. Drum, spear, shield and stool; 40 c. Giraffes, Mikumi National Park. (As Type **33**): 20 s. Arms of Tanzania.

1967. Fishes. Multicoloured.

142	**39**	5 c. mauve, green & black	10	1·00
143	–	10 c. brown and bistre	10	10
144	–	15 c. grey, blue and black	10	50
145	–	20 c. brown and green	10	10
146	–	30 c. green and black	20	10
147	–	40 c. yellow, brown & grn	70	10
148	–	50 c. multicoloured	20	10
149	–	65 c. yellow, green & black	2·75	4·25
150	–	70 c. multicoloured	1·00	2·50
151	–	1 s. brown, blue & purple	30	10
152	–	1 s. 30 multicoloured	5·00	10
153a	–	1 s. 50 multicoloured	2·25	10
154	–	2 s. 50 multicoloured	3·25	2·50
155a	–	5 s. yellow, black & green	3·25	10
156a	–	10 s. multicoloured	1·75	10
157a	–	20 s. mutlicoloured	8·00	15

DESIGNS—As Type **39**: 10 c. Sobrinus mud-skipper; 15 c. White-spotted puffer; 20 c. Thorny seahorse; 30 c. Dusky batfish; 40 c. Black-spotted sweetlips; 50 c. Blue birdwrasse; 65 c. Bennett's butterflyfish; 70 c. Black-tipped grouper. 42 × 25 mm: 1 s. Lionfish; 1 s. 30, Powder-blue surgeonfish; 1 s. 50, Yellow-finned fusilier; 2 s. 50, Emperor snapper; 5 s. Moorish idol; 10 s. Painted triggerfish; 20 s. Horned squirrelfish.

53 "Papilio hornimani"

54 "Euphaedra neophron"

1973. (a) As T **53**.

158	**53**	5 c. green, blue and black	60	30
159	–	10 c. multicoloured	60	15
160	–	15 c. lavender and black	60	30
161	–	20 c. brown, yellow & black	70	15
162	–	30 c. yellow, orange & black	70	10
163	–	40 c. multicoloured	70	15
164	–	50 c. multicoloured	1·00	15
165	–	60 c. brown, yellow & lake	1·50	20
166	–	70 c. green, orange & black	1·50	20

(b) As T **54**.

167	**54**	1 s. multicoloured	1·50	15
168	–	1 s. 50 multicoloured	3·00	45
169	–	2 s. 50 multicoloured	3·25	80
170a	–	5 s. multicoloured	3·50	60
171	–	10 s. multicoloured	3·75	6·00
172	–	20 s. multicoloured	5·50	13·00

BUTTERFLIES: 10 c. "Colotis ione"; 15 c. "Amauris hyalites" (s sp. "makuyuenis"); 20 c. "Libythea labdrea (s sp. "laius"; 30 c. "Danaus chrysippus"; 40 c. "Asterope rosa"; 50 c. "Axiocerses styx"; 60 c. "Terias hecabe"; 70 c. "Acraea insignis"; 1 s. "Euphaedra neophron"; 1 s. 50, "Precis octavia"; 2 s. 50, "Charaxes eupale"; 5 s. "Charaxes pollux"; 10 s. "Salamis parhassus"; 20 s. "Papilio ophidicephalus".

1975. Nos. 165, 168/9 and 172 surch.

173	80 c. on 60 c. "Terias hecabe"	2·00	2·00
174	2 s. on 1 s. 50 "Precis octavia"	3·75	6·00
175	3 s. on 2 s. 50 "Charaxes eupale"	14·00	27·00
176	40 s on 20 s. "Papilio ophidicephalus"	6·50	12·00

1976. Telecommunications Development. As Nos. 56/9 of Kenya.

177	50 c. Microwave tower	10	10
178	1 s. Cordless switchboard	15	10
179	2 s. Telephones	25	30
180	3 s. Message switching centre	30	40

1976. Olympic Games, Montreal. As Nos. 61/4 of Kenya.

182	50 c. Akii Bua, Ugandan hurdler	10	10
183	1 s. Filbert Bayi, Tanzanian runner	15	10
184	2 s. Steve Muchoki, Kenyan boxer	25	40
185	3 s. Olympic flame and East African flags	30	40

1976. Railway Transport. As Nos. 66/9 of Kenya.
187 50 c. Diesel-hydraulic train, Tanzania–Zambia Railway . 20 10
188 1 s. Nile Bridge, Uganda . . . 30 10
189 2 s. Nakuru Station, Kenya . . 60 30
190 3 s. Uganda Railway Class A locomotive, 1896 . . . . . 70 75

1977. Game Fish of East Africa. As Nos. 71/4 of Kenya.
192 50 c. Nile perch 30 10
193 1 s. Nile mouthbrooder . . . 35 10
194 3 s. Sailfish . . . . 1·25 40
195 5 s. Black marlin . . . . . . 1·50 60

1977. Second World Black and African Festival of Arts and Culture. As No. 76/9 of Kenya.
197 50 c. Maasai manyatta (village), Kenya 15 10
198 1 s. "Heartbeat of Africa" (Ugandan dancers) 20 10
199 2 s. Makonde sculpture . . . 45 70
200 3 s. "Early Man and Technology" (skinning hippopotamus) . . . . . . 55 1·00

1977. 25th Anniv of Safari Rally. As Nos. 81/4 of Kenya. Multicoloured.
202 50 c. Rally-car and villagers . 15 10
203 1 s. Starting line 15 10
204 2 s. Car fording river 30 40
205 5 s. Car and elephants . . . . 1·00 1·10

1977. Centenary of Ugandan Church. As Nos. 86/9 of Kenya. Multicoloured.
207 50 c. Canon Kivebulaya . . . 10 10
208 1 s. Modern Namirembe Cathedral 15 10
209 2 s. The first Cathedral . . . 30 40
210 5 s. Early congregation Kigezi 60 1·10

1977. Endangered Species. As Nos. 96/100 of Kenya. Multicoloured.
212 50 c. Pancake tortoise 40 10
213 1 s. Nile crocodile 45 10
214 2 s. Hunter's hartebeest . . . 1·40 55
215 3 s. Red colobus monkey . . . 2·00 75
216 5 s. Dugong . . . . 2·50 1·50

56 Prince Philip and President Nyerere

1977. Silver Jubilee. Multicoloured.
218 50 c. Type **56** 10 10
219 5 s. Pres. Nyerere with Queen and Prince Philip 15 25
220 10 s. Jubilee emblem and Commonwealth flags . . . 25 40
221 20 s. The Crowning 40 60

57 Improvements in Rural Living Standards

1978. 1st Anniv of Chama Cha Mapinduzi (New Revolutionary Party).
223 **57** 50 c. multicoloured 10 10
224 – 1 s. multicoloured 10 10
225 – 3 s. multicoloured 35 60
226 – 5 s. black, green and yellow 55 85
DESIGNS: 1 s. Flag-raising ceremony, Zanzibar; 3 s. Handing over of TANU headquarters, Dodoma; 5 s. Chairman Julius Nyerere.

1978. World Cup Football Championships. As Nos. 122/5 of Kenya. Multicoloured.
228 50 c. Joe Kadenge and forwards 10 10
229 1 s. Mohamed Chuma and cup presentation 10 10
230 2 s. Omari Kidevu and goal mouth scene 30 60
231 3 s. Polly Ouma and forwards 40 75

1979. 25th Anniv of Coronation. Nos. 218/21 optd **25th ANNIVERSARY CORONATION 2nd JUNE 1953**.
233A 50 c. Type **56** 10 10
234A 5 s. Pres. Nyerere with Queen and Prince Philip 20 30
235A 10 s. Jubilee emblem and Commonwealth flags . . . 25 40
236A 20 s. The Crowning 40 70

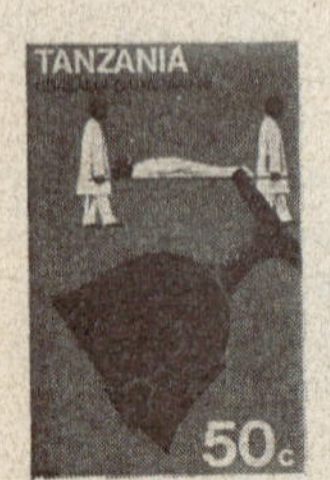

60 "Do not Drink and Drive"

61 Lake Manyara Hotel

1978. Road Safety.
238 **60** 50 c. multicoloured . . . 15 10
239 – 1 s. multicoloured 20 10
240 – 3 s. orange, black & brown 70 60
241 – 5 s. multicoloured . . . . 1·00 90
DESIGNS: 1 s. "Show courtesy to young, old and crippled"; 3 s. "Observe the Highway Code"; 5 s. "Do not drive a faulty vehicle.

1978. Game Lodges. Multicoloured.
243 50 c. Type **61** 10 10
244 1 s. Lobo Wildlife Lodge . . 15 10
245 3 s. Ngorongoro Crater Lodge 25 35
246 5 s. Ngorongoro Wildlife Lodge 35 55
247 10 s. Mafia Island Lodge . . 50 90
248 20 s. Mikumi Wildlife Lodge 1·00 2·50

62 "Racial Suppression"

1978. International Anti-Apartheid Year.
250 **62** 50 c. multicoloured . . . 10 10
251 – 1 s. black, green and yellow 10 10
252 – 2 s. 50 multicoloured . . . 30 75
253 – 5 s. multicoloured . . . . 60 1·10
DESIGNS: 1 s. "Racial division"; 2 s. 50, "Racial harmony"; 5 s. "Fall of suppression and rise of freedom".

63 Fokker F.27 Friendship

1978. 75th Anniv of Powered Flight. Mult.
255 50 c. Type **63** 20 10
256 1 s. De Havilland Dragon Mk 1 on Zanzibar Island, 1930's . 25 10
257 2 s. Concorde . . . . 1·00 45
258 5 s. Wright brothers' Flyer I, 1903 . . . . 1·25 85

64 Corporation Emblem

1979. 1st Anniv of Tanzania Posts and Telecommunications Corporation. Mult.
260 50 c. Type **64** 10 10
261 5 s. Headquarters buildings . 50 70

65 Pres. Nyerere (patron of National I.Y.C. Committee) with Children

1979. Int Year of the Child. Mult.
263 50 c. Type **65** 10 10
264 1 s. Day care centre 15 10
265 2 s. "Immunisation" (child being vaccinated) 25 45
266 5 s. National I.Y.C. Committee emblem 40 80

1979. Nos. 159 and 166 surch.
268 10 c. + 30 c. multicoloured . 1·50 1·00
269 50 c. on 70 c. green, orange and black . . . . 2·50 2·25
No. 268 was used as a 40 c. value.

67 Planting Young Trees

1979. Forest Preservation. Multicoloured.
270 50 c. Type **67** 15 10
271 1 s. Replacing dead trees with saplings 15 10
272 2 s. Rainfall cycle 55 65
273 5 s. Forest fire warning . . . 90 1·75

68 Mwenge Earth Satellite Station

1979. Inauguration of Mwenge Earth Satellite Station.
274 **68** 10 c. multicoloured 10 10
275 40 c. multicoloured 15 10
276 50 c. multicoloured 15 10
277 1 s. multicoloured 25 20

69 Tabata Dispensary, Dar-es-Salaam

1980. 75th Anniv of Rotary International. Multicoloured.
278 50 c. Type **69** 10 10
279 1 s. Ngomvu Village water project 15 10
280 5 s. Flying Doctor service (plane donation) 55 70
281 20 s. Torch and 75th anniversary emblem . . . . 1·25 2·50

70 Zanzibar 1896 2 r. Stamp and 1964 25 c. Definitive

1980. Death Cent of Sir Rowland Hill. Mult.
283 40 c. Type **70** 10 10
284 50 c. Tanganyika 1962 Independence 50 c. commemorative and man attaching stamp to letter (vert) 10 10
285 10 s. Tanganyika 1922 25 c. stamp and 1961 1 s. 30 definitive . . . . 50 1·00
286 20 s. Penny Black and Sir Rowland Hill (vert) . . . . 80 1·60

1980. "London 1980" International Stamp Exhibition. Nos. 283/6 optd **'LONDON 1980' PHILATELIC EXHIBITION.**
288 **70** 40 c. multicoloured 10 10
289 – 50 c. multicoloured 10 10
290 – 10 s. multicoloured . . . . 50 1·00
291 – 20 s. multicoloured . . . . 80 1·60

1980. Annual Conference of District 920. Rotary International, Arusha. Nos. 278/81 optd **District 920–55th Annual Conference, Arusha. Tanzania.**
293 **69** 50 c. multicoloured 20 10
294 – 1 s. multicoloured 20 10
295 – 5 s. multicoloured 45 70
296 – 20 s. multicoloured . . . . 1·00 2·50

73 Conference, Tanzanian Posts and Telecommunications Corporation and U.P.U. Emblems

1980. P.A.P.U. (Pan-African Postal Union) Plenipotentiary Conference, Arusha.
298 **73** 50 c. black and violet . . . 10 10
299 1 s. black and blue . . . 10 10
300 5 s. black and red . . . 50 70
301 10 s. black and green . . . 1·00 1·60

74 Gidamis Shahanga (marathon)

75 Spring Hare

1980. Olympic Games, Moscow. Multicoloured.
302 50 c. Type **74** 10 15
303 1 s. Nzael Kyomo (sprints) . . 15 15
304 10 s. Zakayo Malekwa (javelin) 60 1·00
305 20 s. William Lyimo (boxing) . 1·00 1·75

1980. Wildlife. Multicoloured.
307 10 c. Type **75** 10 15
308 20 c. Large-spotted genet . . 15 15
309 40 c. Banded mongoose . . . 20 10
310 50 c. Ratel 20 10
311 75 c. Large-toothed rock hyrax 20 15
312 80 c. Leopard 30 15
313 1 s. Impala 20 10
314 1 s. 50 Giraffe 30 20
315 2 s. Common zebra 30 20
316 3 s. Buffalo 30 20
317 5 s. Lion 40 30
318 10 s. Black rhinoceros . . . . 75 1·25
319 20 s. African elephant . . . 1·25 1·75
320 40 s. Cheetah . . . . 1·50 4·00
Nos. 313/20 are larger, 40 × 24 mm.

77 Ngorongoro Conservation Area Authority Emblem

1981. 60th Anniv of Ngorongoro and Serengeti National Parks.
321 **77** 50 c. multicoloured 10 10
322 – 1 s. black, gold and green . 10 10
323 – 5 s. multicoloured 35 60
324 – 20 s. multicoloured . . . . 1·10 2·25
DESIGNS: 1 s. Tanzania National Parks emblem; 5 s. Friends of the Serengeti emblem; 20 s. Friends of Ngorongoro emblem.

1981. Royal Wedding. Nos. 220/1 optd **ROYAL WEDDING H.R.H. PRINCE CHARLES 29th JULY 1981.**
325 10 s. Jubilee emblem and Commonwealth flags . . . 35 60
326 20 s. The Crowning 55 80

79 Mail Runner

1981. Commonwealth Postal Administrations Conference, Arusha. Multicoloured.
328 50 c. Type **79** 10 10
329 1 s. Letter sorting 15 15
330 5 s. Letter Post symbols . . . 40 1·00
331 10 s. Flags of Commonwealth nations . . . . 75 2·00

80 Morris Nyunyusa (blind drummer)

1981. International Year of Disabled Persons. Multicoloured.
333 50 c. Type **80** 25 10
334 1 s. Mgulani Rehabilitation Centre, Dar-es-Salaam . . . 30 10
335 5 s. Aids for disabled persons 2·00 2·25
336 10 s. Disabled children cleaning school compound . . . . . 2·75 3·75

81 Pres. Mwalimu Julius K. Nyerere

1981. 20th Anniv of Independence. Mult.
337 50 c. Type **81** 10 10
338 1 s. Electricity plant, Mtoni . . 10 10
339 3 s. Sisal industry 35 90
340 10 s. "Universal primary education" . . . . 80 2·25

82 Ostrich

83 Jella Mtaga

1982. Birds. Multicoloured.
342 50 c. Type **82** 70 10
343 1 s. Secretary bird 80 10
344 5 s. Kori bustard . . . . . 2·75 2·75
345 10 s. Saddle-bill stork . . . . 3·50 5·50

1982. World Cup Football Championship, Spain. Multicoloured.

No.	Description	Mint	Used
346	50 c. Type **83**	30	10
347	1 s. Football stadium	35	10
348	10 s. Diego Maradona	3·00	3·00
349	20 s. FIFA emblem	4·75	5·00

84 "Jade" of Seronera (cheetah) with Cubs

1982. Animal Personalities. Multicoloured.

No.	Description	Mint	Used
351	50 c. Type **84**	20	10
352	1 s. Female golden jackal and cubs	30	10
353	5 s. "Fiji" and two sons of "Gombe" (chimpanzees)	75	2·00
354	10 s. "Bahati" of Lake Manyara with twins, "Rashidi" and "Ramadhani" (elephants)	1·50	3·00

85 Brick-laying

1982. 75th Anniv of Boy Scout Movement. Multicoloured.

No.	Description	Mint	Used
356	50 c. Type **85**	15	10
357	1 s. Camping	20	10
358	10 s. Tracing signs	1·50	2·25
359	20 s. Lord Baden-Powell	2·50	3·75

86 Ploughing Field

1982. World Food Day. Multicoloured.

No.	Description	Mint	Used
361	50 c. Type **86**	10	10
362	1 s. Dairy farming	10	10
363	5 s. Maize farming	45	60
364	10 s. Grain storage	75	1·25

87 Immunization

1982. Centenary of Robert Koch's Discovery of Tubercle Bacillus. Multicoloured.

No.	Description	Mint	Used
366	50 c. Type **87**	15	10
367	1 s. Dr. Robert Koch	20	10
368	5 s. International Union against TB emblem	65	1·25
369	10 s. World Health Organization emblem	1·25	2·50

88 Letter Post

1982. 5th Anniv of Posts and Telecommunications Corporation. Multicoloured.

No.	Description	Mint	Used
370	50 c. Type **88**	10	10
371	1 s. Training institute	10	10
372	5 s. Satellite communications	55	90
373	10 s. U.P.U., I.T.U. and T.P.T.C.C. (Tanzania Post and Telecommunications Corporation) emblems	90	2·00

89 Pres. Mwalimu Julius Nyerere

1982. Commonwealth Day. Multicoloured.

No.	Description	Mint	Used
375	50 c. Type **89**	10	10
376	1 s. Athletics and boxing	15	10
377	5 s. Flags of Commonwealth countries	40	90
378	10 s. Pres. Nyerere and members of British Royal Family	70	1·90

90 Eastern and Southern African Management Institute, Arusha, Tanzania

1983. 25th Anniv of Economic Commission for Africa. Multicoloured.

No.	Description	Mint	Used
380	50 c. Type **90**	15	10
381	1 s. 25th Anniversary inscription and U.N. logo	20	10
382	5 s. Mineral collections	2·75	2·75
383	10 s. E.C.A. Silver Jubilee logo and O.A.U. flag	2·75	3·50

91 Telephone Cables

1983. World Communications Year. Mult.

No.	Description	Mint	Used
385	50 c. Type **91**	15	10
386	1 s. W.C.Y. logo	15	10
387	5 s. Postal service	60	1·50
388	10 s. Microwave tower	80	2·50

92 Bagamoyo Boma

1983. Historical Buildings of Tanzania. Multicoloured.

No.	Description	Mint	Used
390	1 s. Type **92**	10	10
391	1 s. 50 Beit el Ajaib, Zanzibar	15	25
392	5 s. Anglican Cathedral, Zanzibar	40	1·00
393	10 s. Original German Government House and present State House, Dar-es-Salaam	75	2·00

93 Sheikh Abeid Amani Karume (founder of Afro-Shirazi Party)

1984. 20th Anniv of Zanzibar Revolution. Multicoloured.

No.	Description	Mint	Used
395	1 s. Type **93**	10	10
396	1 s. 50 Clove farming	15	25
397	5 s. Symbol of Industrial Development	40	1·00
398	10 s. New housing schemes	75	2·00

94 Boxing

1984. Olympic Games, Los Angeles. Multicoloured.

No.	Description	Mint	Used
400	1 s. Type **94**	10	10
401	1 s. 50 Running	15	10
402	5 s. Basketball	45	60
403	20 s. Football	1·50	2·25

95 Icarus in Flight

1984. 40th Anniv of I.C.A.O. Mult.

No.	Description	Mint	Used
405	1 s. Type **95**	10	10
406	1 s. 50 Douglas DC-10, Boeing 737 aircraft and air traffic controller	15	20
407	5 s. Boeing 737 undergoing maintenance	55	1·25
408	10 s. I.C.A.O. badge	1·10	2·00

96 Sochi Conical House

1984. Traditional Houses. Multicoloured.

No.	Description	Mint	Used
410	1 s. Type **96**	10	10
411	1 s. 50 Isyenga circular type	15	20
412	5 s. Tembe flatroofed type	40	1·25
413	10 s. Banda coastal type	70	2·00

97 Production of Cotton Textiles

1985. 5th Anniv of Southern African Development Co-ordination Conference. Multicoloured.

No.	Description	Mint	Used
415	1 s. 50 Type **97**	30	15
416	4 s. Diamond mining	2·00	1·50
417	5 s. Map of member countries and means of communication	2·00	1·50
418	20 s. Flags and signatures of member countries	2·75	4·00

98 Tortoise

1985. Rare Animals of Zanzibar. Mult.

No.	Description	Mint	Used
420	1 s. Type **98**	50	10
421	4 s. Leopard	2·25	1·50
422	10 s. Civet cat	2·75	3·75
423	17 s. 50 Red colobus monkey (vert)	3·50	5·50

99 The Queen Mother

1985. Life and Times of Queen Elizabeth the Queen Mother. Multicoloured.

No.	Description	Mint	Used
425	20 s. Type **99**	10	15
426	20 s. Queen Mother waving to crowd	10	15
427	100 s. Oval portrait with flowers	30	75
428	100 s. Head and shoulders portrait	30	75

100 Steam Locomotive No. 3022

1985. Tanzanian Railway Steam Locomotives (1st series). Multicoloured.

No.	Description	Mint	Used
430	5 s. Type **100**	10	15
431	10 s. Locomotive No. 3107	15	30
432	20 s. Locomotive No. 6004	25	60
433	30 s. Locomotive No. 3129	40	90

See also Nos. 445/9.

1985. Olympic Games Gold Medal Winners, Los Angeles. Nos. 400/3 optd.

No.	Description	Mint	Used
435	1 s. Type **94** (optd **GOLD MEDAL HENRY TILLMAN USA**)	10	10
436	1 s. 50 Running (optd **GOLD MEDAL USA**)	15	20
437	5 s. Baketball (optd **GOLD MEDAL USA**)	75	1·00
438	20 s. Football (optd **GOLD MEDAL FRANCE**)	1·75	3·00

102 Cooking and Water Pots

1985. Pottery. Multicoloured.

No.	Description	Mint	Used
440	1 s. 50 Type **102**	20	10
441	2 s. Large pot and frying pot with cover	25	15
442	5 s. Trader selling pots	60	35
443	40 s. Beer pot	2·25	4·25

103 Class 64 Diesel Locomotive

1985. Tanzanian Railway Locomotives (2nd series).

No.	Type	Description	Mint	Used
445	**103**	1 s. 50 multicoloured	40	20
446	–	2 s. multicoloured	40	30
447	–	5 s. multicoloured	55	75
448	–	10 s. multicoloured	80	1·60
449	–	30 s. black, brown and red	2·00	3·25

DESIGNS: 2 s. Class 36 diesel locomotive; 5 s. DFH1013 diesel shunter; 10 s. DE1001 diesel-electric locomotive; 30 s. Steam locomotive, Zanzibar, 1906.

104 Young Pioneers

1986. International Youth Year.

No.	Type	Description	Mint	Used
451	**104**	1 s. 50 multicoloured	15	15
452	–	4 s. brown, light brown and black	30	50
453	–	10 s. multicoloured	70	1·25
454	–	20 s. brown, light brown and black	1·40	2·50

DESIGNS: 4 s. Child health care; 10 s. Uhuru Torch Race; 20 s. Young workers and globe.

105 Rolls-Royce "20/25" (1936)

1986. Centenary of Motoring. Multicoloured.

No.	Description	Mint	Used
456	1 s. 50 Type **105**	10	10
457	5 s. Rolls-Royce "Phantom II" (1933)	15	25
458	10 s. Rolls-Royce "Phantom I" (1926)	25	60
459	30 s. Rolls-Royce "Silver Ghost" (1907)	40	1·50

106 Rotary Logo and Staunton Queen Chess Piece

1986. World Chess Championships, London and Leningrad.

No.	Type	Description	Mint	Used
461	**106**	20 s. blue and mauve	35	50
462	–	100 s. multicoloured	50	2·50

DESIGN: 100 s. Hand moving rook on board.

No. 461 also commemorates Rotary International.

107 Mallard

1986. Birth Bicentenary (1985) of John J. Audubon (ornithologist). Multicoloured.

No.	Description	Mint	Used
464	5 s. Type **107**	15	35
465	10 s. Eider	25	50
466	20 s. Scarlet ibis	30	1·10
467	30 s. Roseate spoonbill	40	1·25

108 Pearls

1986. Tanzanian Minerals. Multicoloured.

No.	Description	Mint	Used
469	1 s. 50 Type **108**	80	15
470	2 s. Sapphire	1·10	65
471	5 s. Tanzanite	2·00	1·25
472	40 s. Diamonds	7·25	10·00

110 "Hibiscus calyphyllus"

111 Oryx

1986. Flowers of Tanzania. Multicoloured.

474	1 s. 50 Type **110**	10	10
475	5 s. "Aloe graminicola"	15	25
476	10 s. "Nersium oleander"	20	35
477	30 s. "Nymphaea caerulea"	40	1·50

1986. Endangered Animals of Tanzania. Multicoloured.

479	5 s. Type **111**	15	15
480	10 s. Giraffe	20	35
481	20 s. Rhinoceros	25	75
482	30 s. Cheetah	25	1·25

112 Immunization

1986. U.N.I.C.E.F. Child Survival Campaign. Multicoloured.

484	1 s. 50 Type **112**	20	10
485	2 s. Growth monitoring	30	15
486	5 s. Oral rehydration therapy	50	40
487	40 s. Breast feeding	2·25	3·50

113 Angelfish

1986. Marine Life. Multicoloured.

489	1 s. 50 Type **113**	70	10
490	4 s. Parrotfish	1·50	85
491	10 s. Turtle	2·25	2·50
492	20 s. Octopus	3·50	4·25

114 Team Captains shaking Hands

1986. World Cup Football Championship, Mexico. Multicoloured.

494	1 s. 50 Type **114**	15	10
495	2 s. Referee sending player off	15	10
496	10 s. Goalkeeper and ball in net	60	90
497	20 s. Goalkeeper saving ball	1·00	2·00

115 Pres. Nyerere receiving Beyond War Award

1986. International Peace Year. Mult.

499	1 s. 50 Type **115**	30	10
500	2 s. Children of many races	50	20
501	10 s. African cosmonaut and rocket launch	1·25	1·75
502	20 s. United Nations Headquarters, New York	1·75	3·00

116 Mobile Bank Service

1987. 20th Anniv of National Bank of Commerce. Multicoloured.

504	1 s. 50 Type **116**	30	10
505	2 s. National Bank of Commerce Head Office	50	20
506	5 s. Pres. Mwinyi laying foundation stone	80	90
507	20 s. Cotton harvesting	2·00	3·25

117 Parade of Young Party Members

1987. 10th Anniv of Chama Cha Mapinduzi Party and 20th Anniv of Arusha Declaration. Mult.

508	2 s. Type **117**	15	10
509	3 s. Harvesting coffee	20	10
510	10 s. Pres. Nyerere addressing Second Peace Initiative Reunion	30	30
511	30 s. Presidents Julius Nyerere and Ali Hassan Mwinyi	50	1·25

118 Nungu Nungu Hair Style

121 "Apis mellifera" (bee)

120 Royal Family on Buckingham Palace Balcony after Trooping the Colour

1987. Traditional Hair Styles. Multicoloured.

512	1 s. 50 Type **118**	30	10
513	2 s. Upanga wa jogoo style	45	20
514	10 s. Morani style	80	1·25
515	20 s. Twende kilioni style	1·50	2·50

1987. 60th Birthday (1986) of Queen Elizabeth II. Multicoloured.

517	5 s. Type **120**	10	10
518	10 s. Queen and Prince Philip at Royal Ascot	15	20
519	40 s. Queen Elizabeth II	50	80
520	60 s. Queen Elizabeth with crowd	70	1·25

1987. Insects. Multicoloured.

522	1 s. 50 Type **121**	60	15
523	2 s. "Prostephanus truncatus" (grain borer)	80	25
524	10 s. "Glossina palpalis" (tsetse fly)	1·50	2·00
525	20 s. "Polistes sp." (wasp)	2·25	3·75

122 Crocodile

1987. Reptiles. Multicoloured.

527	2 s. Type **122**	55	25
528	3 s. Black-striped grass-snake	60	30
529	10 s. Adder	1·00	1·40
530	20 s. Green mamba	1·75	2·50

123 Emblems of Posts/Telecommunications and Railways

1987. 10th Anniv of Tanzania Communications and Transport Corporations. Multicoloured.

532	2 s. Type **123**	20	10
533	8 s. Emblems of Air Tanzania and Harbours Authority	30	20

124 Basketry

1987. Traditional Handicrafts. Multicoloured.

535	2 s. Type **124**	15	10
536	3 s. Decorated gourds	15	15
537	10 s. Stools	25	20
538	20 s. Makonde carvings	40	45

1987. 10th Anniv of Tanzania–Zambia Railway (1986). Nos. 445/9 optd **10th Anniversary of TANZANIA ZAMBIA RAILWAY AUTHORITY 1976–1986.**

540	**103** 1 s. 50 multicoloured	40	15
541	– 2 s. multicoloured	45	25
542	– 5 s. multicoloured	70	70
543	– 10 s. multicoloured	1·10	1·40
544	– 30 s. black, brown and red	1·75	3·00

126 Mdako (pebble game)

1988. Traditional Pastimes. Multicoloured.

545	2 s. Type **126**	10	10
546	3 s. Wrestling	10	10
547	8 s. Bull fighting, Zanzibar	15	15
548	20 s. Bao (board game)	35	35

127 Plateosaurus

1988. Prehistoric and Modern Animals. Mult.

550	2 s. Type **127**	20	30
551	3 s. Pteranodon	20	30
552	5 s. Apatosaurus ("Brontosaurus")	20	35
553	7 s. Lion	30	50
554	8 s. Tiger	30	50
555	12 s. Orang-utan	35	65
556	20 s. Elephant	70	1·25
557	100 s. Stegosaurus	1·75	2·50

128 Marchers with Party Flag

1988. National Solidarity Walk. Mult.

558	2 s. + 1 s. Type **128**	15	15
559	3 s. + 1 s. Pres. Mwinyi leading Walk	15	15

129 Population Symbols on Map

1988. 3rd National Population Census. Mult.

561	2 s. Type **129**	10	10
562	3 s. Census official at work	10	10
563	10 s. Community health care	15	15
564	20 s. Population growth 1967–1988	30	30

130 Javelin

1988. Olympic Games, Seoul (1st issue). Mult.

566	2 s. Type **130**	40	10
567	3 s. Hurdling	40	10
568	7 s. Long distance running	75	30
569	12 s. Relay racing	1·00	45

131 Football

132 Goat

1988. Olympic Games, Seoul (2nd issue). Mult.

571	10 s. Type **131**	10	10
572	20 s. Cycling	20	25
573	50 s. Fencing	45	50
574	70 s. Volleyball	60	65

1988. Winter Olympic Games, Calgary. As T **131**. Multicoloured.

576	5 s. Cross-country skiing	35	10
577	25 s. Figure skating	75	25
578	50 s. Downhill skiing	1·25	50
579	75 s. Bobsleighing	1·40	70

1988. Domestic Animals. Multicoloured.

581	4 s. Type **132**	20	20
582	5 s. Rabbit (horiz)	20	20
583	8 s. Cows (horiz)	30	30
584	10 s. Kitten (horiz)	40	40
585	12 s. Pony	45	45
586	20 s. Puppy	70	70

133 "Love You, Dad" (Pinocchio)

1988. Greetings Stamps. Walt Disney cartoon characters. Multicoloured.

588	4 s. Type **133**	10	10
589	5 s. "Happy Birthday" (Brer Rabbit and Chip n' Dale)	10	10
590	10 s. "Trick or Treat" (Daisy and Donald Duck)	15	15
591	12 s. "Be Kind to Animals" (Ferdie and Mordie with Pluto)	15	15
592	15 s. "Love" (Daisy and Donald Duck)	20	20
593	20 s. "Let's Celebrate" (Mickey Mouse and Goofy)	30	30
594	30 s. "Keep in Touch" (Daisy and Donald Duck)	65	65
595	50 s. "Love you, Mom" (Minnie Mouse with Ferdie and Mordie)	1·25	1·25

134 "Charaxes varanes"

135 Independence Torch and Mt. Kilimanjaro

1988. Butterflies. Multicoloured.

597	8 s. Type **134**	30	10
598	30 s. "Neptis melicerta"	65	30
599	40 s. "Mylothris chloris"	75	40
600	50 s. "Charaxes bohemani"	90	50
601	60 s. "Myrina silenus"	1·00	70
602	75 s. "Papilio phorcas"	1·50	90
603	90 s. "Cyrestis camillus"	1·75	1·10
604	100 s. "Salamis temora"	2·00	1·25

1988. National Monuments. Multicoloured.

606	5 s. Type **135**	10	10
607	12 s. Arusha Declaration Monument	10	10
608	30 s. Askari Monument	25	30
609	60 s. Independence Monument	55	60

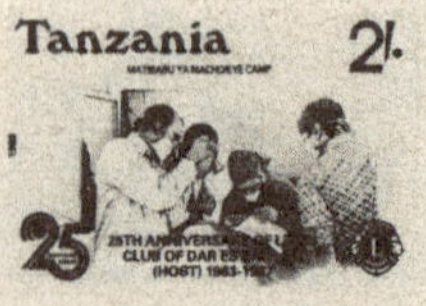

136 Eye Clinic

1988. 25th Anniv of Dar-es-Salaam Lions Club. Multicoloured.

611	2 s. Type **136**	20	15
612	3 s. Family at shallow water well	20	15
613	7 s. Rhinoceros and outline map of Tanzania	50	20
614	12 s. Club presenting school desks	30	25

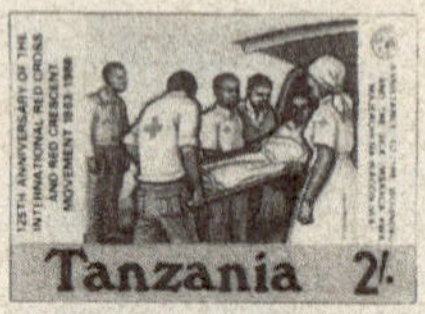

137 Loading Patient into Ambulance

1988. 125th Anniv of International Red Cross and Red Crescent. Multicoloured.

616	2 s. Type **137**	20	15
617	3 s. Mother and baby health clinic	20	15
618	7 s. Red Cross flag	40	20
619	12 s. Henri Dunant (founder)	45	30

138 Paradise Whydah

139 Bushbaby

1989. Birds. Multicoloured.
621 20 s. Type **138** 75 75
622 20 s. Black-collared barbet . . 75 75
623 20 s. Bateleur 75 75
624 20 s. Lilac-breasted roller and African open-bill storks in flight 75 75
625 20 s. Red-tufted malachite sunbird and African open-bill stork in flight 75 75
626 20 s. Dark chanting goshawk 75 75
627 20 s. White-fronted bee eater, carmine bee eater and little bee eaters 75 75
628 20 s. Narina trogon and marabou stork in flight 75 75
629 20 s. Grey parrot 75 75
630 20 s. Hoopoe 75 75
631 20 s. Masked lovebird ("Yellow-collared lovebird") 75 75
632 20 s. Yellow-billed hornbill . . 75 75
633 20 s. Hammerkop 75 75
634 20 s. Violet-crested turaco and flamingos in flight 75 75
635 20 s. Malachite kingfisher . . 75 75
636 20 s. Greater flamingos . . . 75 75
637 20 s. Yellow-billed storks . . . 75 75
638 20 s. Whale-headed stork ("Shoebill stork") 75 75
639 20 s. Saddle-bill stork and blacksmith plover 75 75
640 20 s. South African crowned crane 75 75
Nos. 622/40 were printed together, se-tenant, forming a composite design of birds at a waterhole.

1989. Fauna and Flora. Multicoloured.
642 5 s. Type **139** 10 10
643 10 s. Bushbaby holding insect (horiz) 15 15
644 20 s. Bushbaby on forked branch 25 25
645 30 s. Black cobra on umbrella acacia 50 50
646 45 s. Bushbaby at night (horiz) 50 50
647 70 s. Red-billed tropic bird and tree ferns . . . . 2·25 2·25
648 100 s. African tree frog on cocoa tree . . . . 2·25 2·25
649 150 s. Black-headed heron and Egyptian papyrus . . . . . 4·00 4·00
Nos. 646 and 648/49 are without the World Wildlife Fund logo.

140 Juma Ikangaa (marathon runner)

142 Chama Cha Mapinduzi Party Flag

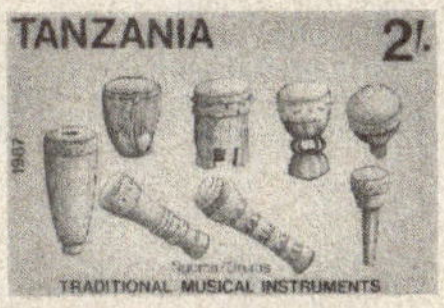

141 Drums

1989. Int Sporting Personalities. Mult.
651 4 s. Type **140** 15 15
652 8 s. 50 Steffi Graf (tennis player) 80 30
653 12 s. Yannick Noah (tennis player) 80 40
654 40 s. Pele (footballer) 90 65
655 100 s. Erhard Keller (speed skater) . . . . 1·00 80
656 125 s. Sadanoyama (sumo wrestler) . . . . 1·25 1·00
657 200 s. Taino (sumo wrestler) . 1·75 1·75
658 250 s. T. Nakajima (golfer) . . 4·00 2·75
No. 658 is inscribed "I. Aoki" in error.

1989. Musical Instruments. Multicoloured.
660 2 s. Type **141** 40 20
661 3 s. Xylophones 40 20
662 10 s. Thumbpiano 75 70
663 20 s. Fiddles . . . . 1·25 1·50

1989. National Solidarity Walk. Mult.
665 5 s. + 1 s. Type **142** 15 20
666 10 s. + 1 s. Marchers with party flag and President Mwinyi . 15 20

143 Class P36 Locomotive, Russia, 1953

1989. Steam Locomotives. Multicoloured.
668 10 s. Type **143** 35 35
669 25 s. Class 12 streamlined locomotive, Belgium, 1939 . 45 45
670 60 s. Class C62 locomotive, Japan, 1948 . . . . 75 75
671 75 s. Pennsylvania Railroad Class T1 streamlined locomotive, U.S.A., 1942 . 85 85
672 80 s. Class WP locomotive, India, 1946 . . . . 90 90
673 90 s. East African Railways Class 59 Garratt locomotive No. 5919 . . . . 1·00 1·00
674 150 s. Class "People" locomotive No. 1206, China . . . . . 1·60 1·60
675 200 s. Southern Pacific "Daylight" express, U.S.A. . 1·60 1·60

144 "Luna 3" Satellite orbiting Moon, 1959

1989. History of Space Exploration and 20th Anniv of First Manned Landing on Moon. Multicoloured.
678 20 s. Type **144** 35 35
679 30 s. "Gemini 6" and "7", 1965 45 45
680 40 s. Astronaut Edward White in space, 1965 . . . . 55 55
681 60 s. Astronaut Aldrin on Moon, 1969 . . . . 75 75
682 70 s. Aldrin performing experiment, 1969 . . . . . 80 80
683 100 s. "Apollo 15" astronaut and lunar rover, 1971 . . . . 1·00 1·00
684 150 s. "Apollo 18" and "Soyuz 19" docking in space, 1975 1·25 1·25
685 200 s. Spacelab, 1983 . . . . 1·50 1·50

1989. Olympic Medal Winners, Calgary and Seoul. Various stamps optd. (a) Nos. 571/4.
687 10 s. Type **131** (optd **Gold-USSR Silver-Brazil Bronze-W. Germany**) 40 40
688 20 s. Cycling (optd **Men's Match Sprint, Lutz Hesslich, DDR**) 1·00 80
689 50 s. Fencing (optd **Epee, Schmitt, W. Germany**) . . . 1·25 1·25
690 70 s. Volleyball (optd **Men's Team, USA**) . . . . 1·75 2·00

(b) Nos. 576/9.
692 5 s. Cross-country skiing (optd **Biathlon, Peter-Roetsch, DDR**) 30 30
693 25 s. Figure skating (optd **Pairs, Gordeeva & Grinkov, USSR**) 65 65
694 50 s. Downhill skiing (optd **Zurbriggen, Switzerland**) . . 1·10 1·10
695 75 s. Bobsleighing (optd **Gold-USSR Silver-DDR Bronze-DDR**) . . . . 1·40 1·40

146 Spotted Tilapia

1989. Reef and Freshwater Fishes of Tanzania. Multicoloured.
697 9 s. Type **146** 55 40
698 13 s. Painted triggerfish . . . 55 40
699 20 s. Powder-blue surgeonfish 70 50
700 40 s. Red-tailed butterflyfish . 1·00 75
701 70 s. Red-tailed notho . . . . 1·25 1·25
702 100 s. Ansorge's neolebias . . 1·50 1·75
703 150 s. Blue panchax . . . . . 2·00 2·25
704 200 s. Regal angelfish . . . . 2·00 2·25

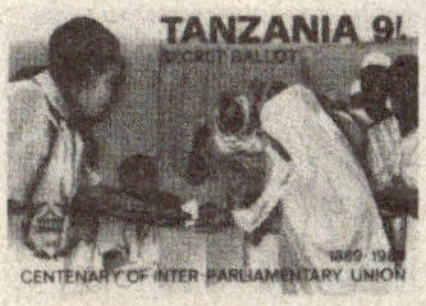

147 Rural Polling Station

1989. Cent of Inter-Parliamentary Union.
706 **147** 9 s. multicoloured 10 10
707 – 13 s. multicoloured . . . 10 10
708 – 80 s. multicoloured . . . 40 55
709 – 100 s. black, ultram & bl 50 75
DESIGNS: 13 s. Parliament Building, Dar-es-Salaam; 40 s. Sir William Randal Cremer and Frederic Passy (founders); 80 s. Tanzania Parliament in session; 100 s. Logo.

148 Logo

1990. 10th Anniv of Pan-African Postal Union.
711 **148** 9 s. yellow, green and black 15 15
712 – 13 s. multicoloured 15 15
713 – 70 s. multicoloured 70 80
714 – 100 s. multicoloured . . . 1·25 1·50
DESIGNS: 13 s. Collecting mail from post office box; 40 s. Logos of Tanzania Posts and Telecommunications Corporation, P.A.P.U. and U.P.U.; 70 s. Taking mail to post office; 100 s. Mail transport.

149 Admiral's Flag and "Nina"

1990. 500th Anniv (1992) of Discovery of America by Columbus (50, 60, 75, 200 s.) and Modern Scientific Discoveries (others). Multicoloured.
716 9 s. Bell XS-1 aircraft (first supersonic flight, 1947) . . . 40 40
717 13 s. "Trieste" (bathyscaphe) (first dive to depth of 35,000 ft, 1960) 40 40
718 50 s. Type **149** 70 70
719 60 s. Fleet flag and "Pinta" . . 80 80
720 75 s. Standard of Castile and Leon and "Santa Maria" . . 90 90
721 150 s. Transistor technology . 1·25 1·25
722 200 s. Arms of Columbus and map of First Voyage . . . . 1·90 1·90
723 250 s. DNA molecule . . . . 1·90 1·90

150 Tecopa Pupfish

1990. Extinct Species. Multicoloured.
725 25 s. Type **150** 60 60
726 40 s. Thylacine 90 90
727 50 s. Quagga . . . . 1·10 1·10
728 60 s. Passenger pigeon . . . . 1·75 1·75
729 75 s. Rodriguez saddleback tortoise . . . . 1·75 1·75
730 100 s. Toolache wallaby . . . 1·75 1·75
731 150 s. Texas red wolf . . . . 1·90 1·90
732 200 s. Utah lake sculpin . . . 1·90 1·90

151 Camping

1990. 60th Anniv of Girl Guides Movement in Tanzania. Multicoloured.
734 9 s. Type **151** 15 15
735 13 s. Guides planting sapling . 15 15
736 50 s. Guide teaching woman to write 40 60
737 100 s. Guide helping at child-care clinic 65 95

152 Fishing

1990. 25th Anniv of Union of Tanganyika and Zanzibar. Multicoloured.
739 9 s. Type **152** 20 20
740 13 s. Vineyard 20 20
741 50 s. Cloves 85 95
742 100 s. Presidents Nyerere and Karume exchanging Union instruments (vert) . . . . . 1·75 2·25

153 Footballer

154 Miriam Makeba

1990. World Cup Football Championship, Italy (1st issue). Multicoloured.
744 25 s. Type **153** 75 30
745 60 s. Player passing ball . . . 1·25 90
746 75 s. Player turning . . . . . 1·50 1·00
747 200 s. Player kicking ball . . . 3·25 3·25
See also Nos. 789/92 and 794/7.

1990. Famous Black Entertainers. Mult.
749 9 s. Type **154** 15 10
750 13 s. Manu Dibango 15 10
751 25 s. Fela 20 15
752 70 s. Smokey Robinson . . . 60 40
753 100 s. Gladys Knight 75 55
754 150 s. Eddie Murphy . . . . 1·50 1·50
755 200 s. Sammy Davis Jnr. . . . 1·75 2·00
756 250 s. Stevie Wonder . . . . 2·00 2·25

155 Ring of People round Party Flag

1990. Solidarity Walk, 1990. Multicoloured.
758 9 s. + 1 s. Type **155** 55 65
759 13 s. + 1 s. President Mwinyi . 55 65

156 Diesel Train

157 Pope John Paul II

1990. 10th Anniv of Southern African Development Co-ordination Conference. Multicoloured.
761 8 s. Type **156** 65 20
762 11 s. 50 Paper-making plant . 25 20
763 25 s. Tractor factory and ploughing 30 20
764 100 s. Map and national flags . 1·75 2·25

1990. Papal Visit to Tanzania. Multicoloured.
766 10 s. Type **157** 20 15
767 15 s. Pope in ceremonial robes 25 15
768 20 s. Pope giving blessing . . 30 15
769 100 s. Papal coat of arms . . . 80 1·10

158 Mickey and Minnie Mouse in Herby the Love Bug

1990. Motor Cars from Disney Films. Mult.
771 20 s. Type **158** 30 30
772 30 s. The Absent-minded Professor's car 35 35
773 45 s. Chitty-Chitty Bang-Bang 45 45
774 60 s. Mr. Toad's car 65 65
775 75 s. Scrooge's limousine . . 75 75
776 100 s. The Shaggy Dog's car . 1·00 1·00
777 150 s. Donald Duck's nephews cleaning car . . . . 1·60 1·60
778 200 s. Fire engine from "Dumbo" . . . . 1·75 1·75

159 "St. Mary Magdalen in Penitence" (detail)

160 Klinsmann of West Germany

1990. Paintings by Titian. Multicoloured.

780 5 s. Type **159** . . . 10 10
781 10 s. "Averoldi Polyptych" (detail) . . . 10 10
782 15 s. "Saint Margaret" (detail) 15 15
783 50 s. "Venus and Adonis" (detail) . . . 40 40
784 75 s. "Venus and the Lutenist" (detail) . . . 55 55
785 100 s. "Tarquin and Lucretia" (detail) . . . 70 70
786 125 s. "Saint Jerome" (detail) 90 90
787 150 s. "Madonna and Child in Glory with Saints" (detail) . 1·00 1·00

1990. World Cup Football Championship, Italy (2nd issue). Multicoloured.

789 10 s. Type **160** . . . 40 20
790 60 s. Serena of Italy . . . 85 60
791 100 s. Nicol of Scotland . . 1·50 1·50
792 300 s. Susic of Yugoslavia . . 3·00 3·75

161 Throw-in

1990. World Cup Football Championship, Italy (3rd issue). Multicoloured.

794 9 s. Type **161** . . . 30 20
795 13 s. Penalty kick . . . 30 20
796 25 s. Dribbling . . . 40 25
797 100 s. Corner kick . . . 1·40 2·00

162 Canoe

163 Lesser Masked Weaver

164 Lesser Flamingo

1990. Marine Transport. Multicoloured.

799 9 s. Type **162** . . . 15 15
800 13 s. Sailing canoe . . . 20 15
801 25 s. Dhow . . . 30 15
802 100 s. Freighter . . . 1·50 2·00

1990. Birds. Designs as T **163** (5 s. to 30 s.) or T **164** (40 s. to 500 s.). Multicoloured.

804 5 s. Type **163** . . . 10 10
805 9 s. African emerald cuckoo . 15 10
806 13 s. Little bee eater . . . 15 10
807 15 s. Red bishop . . . 15 10
808 20 s. Bateleur . . . 20 10
809 25 s. Scarlet-chested sunbird . 20 10
809a 30 s. African wood pigeon . . 20 10
810 40 s. Type **164** . . . 20 10
811 70 s. Helmet guineafowl . . 30 20
812 100 s. Eastern white pelican . 40 25
813 170 s. Saddle-bill stork . . 55 50
814 200 s. South African crowned crane . . . 65 55
814a 300 s. Pied crow . . . 85 85
814b 400 s. White-headed vulture . 1·00 1·10
815 500 s. Ostrich . . . 1·10 1·25

165 Athletics

1990. 14th Commonwealth Games, Auckland, New Zealand. Multicoloured.

817 9 s. Type **165** . . . 25 15
818 13 s. Netball (vert) . . . 45 15
819 25 s. Pole vaulting . . . 60 20
820 100 s. Long jumping (vert) . . 1·50 2·25

166 Former German Post Office, Dar-es-Salaam

1991. 150th Anniv of the Penny Black and "Stamp World London 90" International Stamp Exhibition. Multicoloured.

822 50 s. Type **166** . . . 55 55
823 50 s. "Reichstag" (German mail steamer), 1890 . . . 55 55
824 75 s. Dhows, Zanzibar . . . 75 75
825 75 s. Cobham's Short S.5 Singapore I flying boat, Mwanza, Lake Victoria, 1928 75 75
826 100 s. Air Tanzania Fokker F.27 Friendship over Livingstone's house, Zanzibar . . . 1·00 1·00
827 100 s. Mail train at Moshi station 1·00 1·00
828 100 s. English mail coach, 1840 1·00 1·00
829 150 s. Stephenson's "Rocket" and mail coach, 1838 . . . 1·75 1·75
830 200 s. Imperial Airways Handley Page H.P.42 at Croydon . 1·90 1·90

167 Petersberg Railway, Konigswinter, Germany

1991. Cog Railways. Multicoloured.

832 8 s. Type **167** . . . 40 30
833 25 s. "Waumbek" (locomotive), Mt. Washington Railway, U.S.A. . . . 60 60
834 50 s. Sarajevo–Dubrovnik line, Yugoslavia . . . 75 75
835 100 s. Budapest Rack Railway, Hungary . . . 1·00 1·00
836 150 s. Steam locomotive No. 97218, Vordenberg–Eisenerz line, Austria . . . 1·50 1·50
837 200 s. Last train on Rimutaka Incline, New Zealand, 1955 1·60 1·60
838 250 s. "John Stevens" rack and pinion drive locomotive, U.S.A., 1825 . . . 1·60 1·75
839 300 s. Mt. Pilatus Rack Railway steam railcar, Switzerland . 1·75 1·75

1991. International Literacy Year (1st issue). As T **269** of Antigua, but horiz, showing Walt Disney cartoon characters illustrating the Alphabet. Multicoloured.

841/67 1, 2, 3, 5, 10, 15, 18, 20, 25, 30, 35, 40, 45, 50, 55, 60, 75, 80, 90, 100, 120, 125, 145, 150, 160, 175, 200 s. Set of 27 . . . 11·00 13·00

See also Nos. 905/8.

1991. Olympic Games, Barcelona (1st issue). As T **268** of Antigua. Multicoloured.

869 5 s. Archery . . . 30 20
870 10 s. Women's gymnastics . . 30 20
871 25 s. Boxing . . . 40 30
872 50 s. Canoeing . . . 60 50
873 100 s. Volleyball . . . 1·25 1·25
874 150 s. Men's gymnastics . . 1·40 1·50
875 200 s. 4 × 100 metres relay . 1·75 2·00
876 300 s. Judo . . . 2·00 2·25

See also Nos. 1309/12 and 1404/11.

1991. "EXPO 90" International Garden and Greenery Exhibition, Osaka. Orchids. As T **198** of Lesotho. Multicoloured.

878 10 s. "Phalaenopsis Lipperose" (vert) . . . 20 15
879 25 s. "Lycoste Aquila" (vert) 30 20
880 30 s. "Vuylstekeara Cambria Plush" (vert) . . . 30 20
881 50 s. "Vuylstekeara Monica Burnham" (vert) . . . 45 35
882 90 s. "Odontocidium Crowborough Plush" (vert) 85 85
883 100 s. "Oncidioda Crowborough Chelsea" (vert) . . . 85 85
884 250 s. "Sophrolaeliocattleya Phena Saturn" (vert) . . 1·40 1·60
885 300 s. "Laeliocattleya Lykas" (vert) . . . 1·50 1·75

168 Olympic "Sailing" Class Yacht Racing

1991. Record-breaking Sports Events. Mult.

887 5 s. Type **168** . . . 20 20
888 20 s. Olympic downhill skiing 50 35
889 30 s. "Tour de France" cycle race 75 50
890 40 s. Le Mans 24-hour endurance motor race . . . 80 60
891 75 s. Olympic two man bob-sleighing . . . 90 90
892 100 s. Belgian Grand Prix motor cycle race . . . 1·40 1·50
893 250 s. Indianapolis 500 motor race . . . 2·00 2·25
894 300 s. Gold Cup power boat championship . . . 2·00 2·50

169 Mickey Mouse as Cowboy

1991. Mickey Mouse in Hollywood. Walt Disney cartoon characters as actors. Mult.

896 5 s. Type **169** . . . 30 30
897 10 s. Mickey as boxer . . . 30 30
898 15 s. Mickey as astronaut . . 30 30
899 20 s. Mickey and Minnie as lovers . . . 30 30
900 100 s. Mickey as pirate rescuing Minnie . . . 1·25 1·25
901 200 s. Mickey and Donald Duck as policemen arresting Big Pete 2·50 2·50
902 350 s. Mickey and Donald with Goofy in historical drama . 2·75 2·75
903 450 s. Mickey, Donald and Goofy as sailors . . . 2·75 2·75

170 Women learning to Read

1991. International Literacy Year (2nd issue). Multicoloured.

905 9 s. Type **170** . . . 20 15
906 13 s. Teacher with blackboard 25 15
907 25 s. Literacy aids . . . 35 20
908 100 s. Reading newspaper . . 1·40 2·00

171 Ngorongoro Crater

1991. Historical Craters and Caves. Mult.

910 3 s. Type **171** . . . 85 85
911 5 s. Prehistoric rock painting, Kondoa Caves . . . 85 85
912 9 s. Inner crater, Mt. Kilimanjaro 1·00 1·00
913 12 s. Olduvai Gorge . . . 1·50 1·50

1991. 350th Death Anniv of Rubens. Cartoons for Decius Mus Tapestries. As T **273** of Antigua. Multicoloured.

915 85 s. "Proclamation of the Vision" . . . 1·25 1·25
916 85 s. "Divining of the Entrails" 1·25 1·25
917 85 s. "Dispatch of the Lictors" 1·25 1·25
918 85 s. "Dedication to Death" . 1·25 1·25
919 85 s. "Victory and Death of Decius Mus" . . . 1·25 1·25
920 85 s. "Funeral Rites" . . . 1·25 1·25

172 Stegosaurus

173 Dairy Farming

1991. Prehistoric Creatures. Multicoloured.

922 10 s. Type **172** . . . 25 25
923 15 s. Triceratops . . . 25 25
924 25 s. Edmontosaurus . . . 40 40
925 30 s. Plateosaurus . . . 40 40
926 35 s. Diplodocus . . . 45 45
927 100 s. Iguanodon . . . 1·40 1·40
928 200 s. Silviasaurus . . . 2·00 2·00

1991. 20th Anniv of Tanzania Investment Bank. Multicoloured.

930 10 s. Type **173** . . . 20 15
931 13 s. Industrial development . 25 15
932 25 s. Engineering . . . 30 15
933 100 s. Tea picking . . . 1·50 2·00

174 Pres. Mwinyi leading Walk

1991. National Solidarity Walk. Multicoloured.

935 4 s. + 1 s. Type **174** . . . 40 55
936 30 s. + 1 s. Pres. Mwinyi planting sapling . . . 40 55

1991. "Phila Nippon '91" International Stamp Exhibition, Tokyo. Japanese Railway Locomotives. As T **257** of Maldive Islands but horiz. Multicoloured.

938 10 s. Class 150 steam locomotive, 1872 (first locomotive in Japan) . . . 50 50
939 25 s. Class 4500 steam locomotive, 1902 . . . 75 75
940 35 s. Class C 62 steam locomotive, 1948 . . . 85 85
941 50 s. Mikado steam locomotive 1·00 1·00
942 75 s. Class 6250 steam locomotive, 1915 . . . 1·25 1·25
943 100 s. Class C 11 steam locomotive, 1932 . . . 1·50 1·50
944 200 s. Class E 10 steam locomotive, 1948 . . . 1·75 1·75
945 300 s. Class 8550 steam locomotive, 1899 . . . 2·00 2·00

175 Zebra and Golden-winged Sunbird, Ngorongoro Crater

1991. National Game Parks. Multicoloured.

947 10 s. Type **175** . . . 70 70
948 25 s. Greater kudu and elephant, Ruaha Park . . . 1·00 1·00
949 30 s. Sable antelope and red and yellow barbet, Mikumi Park 1·00 1·00
950 50 s. Leopard and wildebeest, Serengeti Park . . . 1·25 1·25
951 90 s. Giraffe and starred robin, Ngurdoto Park . . . 2·00 2·00
952 100 s. Eland and Abbot's duiker, Kilimanjaro Park . . . 1·75 1·75
953 250 s. Lion and impala, Lake Manyara Park . . . 3·00 3·00
954 300 s. Black rhinoceros and ostrich, Tarangire Park . . 3·75 3·75

176 "Eronia cleodora"

1991. Butterflies. Multicoloured.

956 10 s. Type **176** . . . 45 45
957 15 s. "Precis westermanni" . . 60 60
958 35 s. "Antanartia delius" . . 90 90
959 75 s. "Bematistes aganice" . . 1·60 1·60
960 100 s. "Kallima jacksoni" . . 1·75 1·75
961 150 s. "Apaturopsis cleocharis" . 2·50 2·50
962 200 s. "Colotis aurigineus" . . 2·75 2·75
963 300 s. "Iolaus crawshayi" . . 3·00 3·00

177 Microwave Tower and Dish Aerial

1991. 25th Anniv of Intelsat Satellite System. Multicoloured.

965 10 s. Type **177** . . . 40 20
966 25 s. Satellite picture of Earth 55 30
967 100 s. Mwenge "B" Earth station 1·50 1·50
968 500 s. Mwenge "A" Earth station 4·00 5·00

178 Rice Cultivation

1991. 40th Anniv of United Nations Development Programme. Multicoloured.
970 10 s. Type **178** 10 10
971 15 s. Vocational and Civil Service training 15 10
972 100 s. Terrace farming . . . . 1·25 1·40
973 500 s. Renovated Arab door (vert) . . . . 3·75 5·00

179 Netball

180 "TELECOM 91" Logo

1991. All-Africa Games, Cairo. Mult.
975 10 s. Type **179** 30 20
976 15 s. Football (horiz) 30 20
977 100 s. Tennis . . . . 1·50 1·50
978 200 s. Athletics . . . . 1·75 1·75
979 500 s. Baseball (horiz) . . . . 5·00 6·00

1991. "TELECOM 91" International Telecommunication Exhibition, Geneva (10, 15 s.) and World Telecommunications Day (others). Mult.
981 10 s. Type **180** 10 10
982 15 s. "TELECOM '91" logo and address on envelope (horiz) . 15 10
983 35 s. Symbolic telecommunication signals 25 20
984 100 s. Symbolic telecommunication signals (horiz) . 70 1·00

181 Japanese Bobtail Cat

1991. Cats. Multicoloured.
985 50 s. Type **181** 60 60
986 50 s. Cornish rex 60 60
987 50 s. Malayan 60 60
988 50 s. Tonkinese 60 60
989 50 s. Abyssinian 60 60
990 50 s. Russian blue 60 60
991 50 s. Cymric 60 60
992 50 s. Somali 60 60
993 50 s. Siamese 60 60
994 50 s. Himalayan 60 60
995 50 s. Singapura 60 60
996 50 s. Manx 60 60
997 50 s. Oriental shorthair . . . 60 60
998 50 s. Maine coon 60 60
999 50 s. Persian 60 60
1000 50 s. Birman 60 60

182 Shire Horse

1991. Horses and Ponies. Multicoloured.
1001 50 s. Type **182** 65 65
1002 50 s. Thoroughbred 65 65
1003 50 s. Kladruber 65 65
1004 50 s. Appaloosa 65 65
1005 50 s. Hanoverian 65 65
1006 50 s. Arab 65 65
1007 50 s. Breton 65 65
1008 50 s. Exmoor 65 65
1009 50 s. Connemara 65 65
1010 50 s. Lipizzaner 65 65
1011 50 s. Shetland 65 65
1012 50 s. Percheron 65 65
1013 50 s. Pinto 65 65
1014 50 s. Orlov 65 65
1015 50 s. Palomino 65 65
1016 50 s. Welsh cob 65 65
Nos. 1001/16 were printed together, se-tenant, as a sheetlet of 16 with the backgrounds of each horizontal strip of 4 forming a composite design.

183 Yellow Tetra

1991. Aquarium Fish. Multicoloured.
1017 75 s. Type **183** 65 65
1018 75 s. Five-banded barb . . . 65 65
1019 75 s. Simpson platy 65 65
1020 75 s. Guppy 65 65
1021 75 s. Zebra danio 65 65
1022 75 s. Neon tetra 65 65
1023 75 s. Siamese fighting fish 65 65
1024 75 s. Tiger barb 65 65
1025 75 s. Two-striped lyretail . . 65 65
1026 75 s. Fan-tailed goldfish . . 65 65
1027 75 s. Pearl gourami 65 65
1028 75 s. Freshwater angelfish . 65 65
1029 75 s. Clown loach 65 65
1030 75 s. Red swordtail 65 65
1031 75 s. Blue discus 65 65
1032 75 s. Rosy barb 65 65
Nos. 1017/32 were printed together, se-tenant, with the backgrounds of each stamp forming a composite design.

184 African Elephant

186 Indian Elephant

185 Budgerigar

1991. African Elephants. Multicoloured.
1033 75 s. Type **184** 85 85
1034 75 s. Two elephants fighting . 85 85
1035 75 s. Elephant facing forward and tree 85 85
1036 75 s. Elephant facing left and tree 85 85
1037 75 s. Cow elephant and calf facing right standing in water 85 85
1038 75 s. Cow watching over calf in water 85 85
1039 75 s. Two adults and calf in water 85 85
1040 75 s. Cow and calf facing left standing in water 85 85
1041 75 s. Elephant facing right . . 85 85
1042 75 s. Elephants feeding . . . 85 85
1043 75 s. Elephant feeding . . . 85 85
1044 75 s. Elephant and zebra . . 85 85
1045 75 s. Cow and calf drinking 85 85
1046 75 s. Calf suckling 85 85
1047 75 s. Bull elephant 85 85
1048 75 s. Cow with small calf . . 85 85
Nos. 1033/48 were printed together, se-tenant, as a sheetlet of 16 with each horizontal strip of 4 forming a composite design.

1991. Pet Birds. Multicoloured.
1049 75 s. Type **185** 65 65
1050 75 s. Orange-breasted bunting ("Rainbow Bunting") . . 65 65
1051 75 s. Golden-fronted leafbird 65 65
1052 75 s. Black-headed caique . 65 65
1053 75 s. Java sparrow 65 65
1054 75 s. Diamond firetail finch . 65 65
1055 75 s. Peach-faced lovebird . 65 65
1056 75 s. Golden conure 65 65
1057 75 s. Military macaw 65 65
1058 75 s. Yellow-faced parrotlet . 65 65
1059 75 s. Sulphur-crested cockatoo 65 65
1060 75 s. White-fronted amazon ("Spectacled Amazon Parrot") 65 65
1061 75 s. Paradise tanager . . . 65 65
1062 75 s. Gouldian finch 65 65
1063 75 s. Masked lovebird . . . 65 65
1064 75 s. Hill mynah 65 65
Nos. 1049/64 were printed together, se-tenant, forming a composite design.

1991. Death Centenary (1990) of Vincent van Gogh (artist). As T **278** of Antigua. Multicoloured.
1065 10 s. "Peasant Woman Sewing" 25 25
1066 15 s. "Head of Peasant Woman with Greenish Lace Cap" . 35 35
1067 35 s. "Flowering Orchard" . 60 60
1068 75 s. "Portrait of a Girl" . . 1·00 1·00
1069 100 s. "Portrait of a Woman with Red Ribbon" . . . . 1·25 1·25
1070 150 s. "Vase with Flowers" . 1·75 1·75
1071 200 s. "Houses in Antwerp" 2·00 2·00
1072 400 s. "Seated Peasant Woman with White Cap" . . . . 4·00 4·00

1991. Elephants. Multicoloured.
1074 10 s. Type **186** 50 50
1075 15 s. Indian elephant uprooting tree 65 65
1076 25 s. Indian elephant with calf 80 80
1077 30 s. African elephant . . . 80 80
1078 35 s. Head of African elephant (horiz) 85 85
1079 100 s. African elephant and calf bathing (horiz) . . . . . 1·75 1·75
1080 200 s. Two African elephants (horiz) . . . . 3·00 3·00

187 Class Em Steam Locomotive, Russia, 1930

1991. Locomotives of the World. Mult.
1082 10 s. Type **187** 25 25
1083 15 s. "Hikari" express train, Japan, 1964 . . . . 35 35
1084 25 s. Russian steam locomotive, 1834 (vert) 45 45
1085 35 s. TGV express train, France, 1979 . . . . 55 55
1086 60 s. Diesel railcar No. R16-01, France, 1972 . . . . . . 80 80
1987 100 s. High Speed Train 125, Great Britain, 1972 . . . . 1·40 1·40
1088 300 s. Russian steam locomotive, 1833 (vert) . . 3·00 3·00
No. 1088 is inscribed "1837" in error.

1991. Christmas. Walt Disney Christmas Cards. As T **228** of St. Vincent. Multicoloured.
1090 10 s. Disney characters in "JOY", 1968 (horiz) . . . 20 20
1091 25 s. Mickey, Donald, Pluto and Goofy hanging up stockings, 1981 (horiz) 40 40
1092 35 s. Characters from Disney film "Robin Hood", 1973 (horiz) 45 45
1093 75 s. Mickey looking at Christmas tree, 1967 (horiz) 90 90
1094 100 s. Goofy, Mickey, Donald, Chip 'n' Dale on film set, 1969 . . . . 1·25 1·25
1095 150 s. Mickey on giant bubble, 1976 . . . . 1·60 1·60
1096 200 s. Clarabelle Cow with electric cow bell, 1935 . . 2·00 2·00
1097 300 s. Mickey's nephews with book, 1935 . . . . 2·75 2·75

188 Bruce Lee

1992. Entertainers.
1099/1134 75 s. × 36 multicoloured Set of 36 . . . . . . 20·00 22·00
Nos. 1099/1134 were issued as four sheetlets each of nine different designs, as Type **188**, depicting Bruce Lee, Marilyn Monroe, Elvis Presley and black entertainers (Scott Joplin, Sammy Davis Jnr, Joan Armatrading, Louis Armstrong, Miriam Makeba, Lionel Ritchie, Whitney Houston, Bob Marley, Tina Turner).

189 Sand Tilefish

1992. Fishes. Multicoloured.
1136 10 s. Type **189** 40 40
1137 15 s. Five-banded cichlid . . . 45 45
1138 25 s. Pearly lamprologus . . 60 60
1139 35 s. Jewel cichlid 70 70
1140 60 s. Two-striped lyretail . . 1·00 1·00
1141 100 s. Reef stonefish . . . . 1·50 1·50
1142 300 s. Ahl's lyretail . . . . . 3·75 3·75

190 Chimpanzee in Tree

191 Pope John Paul II in Dominican Republic, 1979

1992. Common Chimpanzee. Multicoloured.
1144 10 s. Type **190** 50 50
1145 15 s. Feeding 55 55
1146 35 s. Two chimpanzees . . . 85 85
1147 75 s. Adult male with arms folded . . . . 1·25 1·25
1148 100 s. Breaking branch . . . . 1·50 1·50
1149 150 s. Young chimpanzee in tree 2·00 2·00
1150 200 s. Female holding young . 2·50 2·50
1151 300 s. Chimpanzee sitting in tree 3·00 3·00

1992. Papal Visits.
1153/1272 100 s. × 120 multicoloured Set of 120 . . . . . 70·00 70·00
DESIGNS: Nos. 1154/1272 Various scenes on Papal visits as Type **191**.

192 Balcony

193 Gogo Costume

1992. Zanzibar Stone Town. Multicoloured.
1273 10 s. Type **192** 30 20
1274 20 s. Bahlnara Mosque . . . 55 35
1275 30 s. High Court Building . . 65 40
1276 200 s. National Museum (horiz) 3·00 4·00

1992. Traditional Costumes. Multicoloured.
1278 3 s. Type **193** 40 40
1279 5 s. Swahili 40 40
1280 9 s. Hehe and Makonde . . 50 50
1281 12 s. Maasai 65 65

194 Melisa and Mike (chimpanzees)

1992. Chimpanzees of the Gombe. Multicoloured. (a) Horiz designs as T **194**.
1283 10 s. Type **194** 30 30
1284 15 s. Leakey and David Greybeard 40 40
1285 30 s. Fifi termiting 55 55
1286 35 s. Galahad 60 60
(b) Vert design showing individual chimpanzees.
1288 10 s. Leakey 65 65
1289 15 s. Fifi 65 65
1290 20 s. Faben 65 65
1291 30 s. David Greybeard . . . 65 65
1292 35 s. Mike 65 65
1293 65 s. Galahad 65 65
1294 100 s. Melisa 70 70
1295 200 s. Flo 90 90

195 Sorghum Farming, Serena

1992. 25th Anniv of National Bank of Commerce. Multicoloured.
1296 10 s. Type **195** 30 15
1297 15 s. Samora Avenue branch and computer operator (vert) 35 25
1298 35 s. Training centre 55 55
1299 40 s. Women dyeing textiles . 60 70

196 Giant Spider Conch

197 Basketball

1992. Shells. Multicoloured.
1301 10 s. Type **196** 30 30
1302 15 s. Bull-mouth helmet . . 35 35
1303 25 s. Rugose mitre 50 50
1304 30 s. Lettered cone 50 50
1305 35 s. True heart cockle . . . 50 50
1306 50 s. Ramose murex 70 70
1307 250 s. Indian volute . . . . 2·75 3·25

1992. Olympic Games, Barcelona (2nd issue). Multicoloured.
1309 40 s. Type **197** 45 30
1310 100 s. Billiards 75 60
1311 200 s. Table tennis . . . . . 1·25 1·40
1312 400 s. Darts . . . . 2·75 3·25

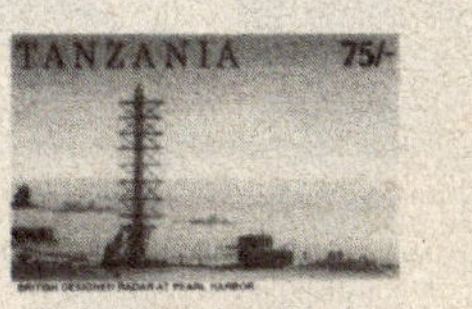

198 British-designed Radar, Pearl Harbor

1992. 50th Anniv of Japanese Attack on Pearl Harbor. Multicoloured.
1314 75 s. Type **198** . . . . 1·10 1·10
1315 75 s. Winston Churchill . . . 1·10 1·10
1316 75 s. Sinking of H.M.S. "Repulse" (battle cruiser) . 1·10 1·10

1317 75 s. Sinking of H.M.S. "Prince of Wales" (battleship) . . . 1·10 1·10
1318 75 s. Surrender of Singapore . 1·10 1·10
1319 75 s. Sinking of H.M.S. "Hermes" (aircraft carrier) . 1·10 1·10
1320 75 s. Japanese attack on Malayan airfield . . . . . 1·10 1·10
1321 75 s. Japanese gun crew, Hong Kong . . . . 1·10 1·10
1322 75 s. Japanese landing craft . 1·10 1·10
1323 75 s. "Haguro" (Japanese cruiser) . . . . 1·10 1·10

199 French Resistance Monument and Medal

1992. Birth Centenary (1990) of Charles de Gaulle (French statesman). Multicoloured.
1324 25 s. Type **199** 50 40
1325 30 s. Free French tank on Omaha beach, D-Day . . . 50 40
1326 150 s. Concorde at Charles de Gaulle Airport . . . . . . 4·00 4·50

200 Scout Bridge, Giraffe and Elephant

1992. 50th Death Anniv (1991) of Lord Baden-Powell (founder of Boy Scout movement). Multicoloured.
1328 10 s. Type **200** 50 30
1329 15 s. Scouts in boat 50 30
1330 400 s. John Glenn's space capsule . . . . 4·50 5·00

201 Marcella Sembrich as Zerlina in "Don Giovanni"

1992. Death Bicentenary of Mozart.
1332 **201** 10 s. black and mauve . . 65 40
1333 – 50 s. multicoloured . . . 1·50 1·10
1334 – 300 s. black and mauve . 4·00 4·75
DESIGNS: 50 s. Planet Jupiter (Symphony No. 41); 300 s. Luciano Pavarotti as Idamente in "Idomeneo".

1992. "Granada '92" International Stamp Exhibition, Spain. Paintings. As T **292** of Antigua.
1336 25 s. red and black 40 40
1337 35 s. multicoloured 50 50
1338 50 s. multicoloured 60 60
1339 75 s. multicoloured 85 85
1340 100 s. black, brown & pink . 1·25 1·25
1341 150 s. red and black . . . . 1·75 1·75
1342 200 s. red and black . . . . 2·00 2·00
1343 300 s. multicoloured . . . . 2·50 2·50
DESIGNS—HORIZ: 25 s. "A Picador, mounted on a Chulo's Shoulders, spears a Bull" (Goya); 150 s. "Another Madness (of Martincho) in the Plaza de Zaragoza" (Goya); 200 s. "Recklessness of Martincho in the Plaza de Zaragoza" (Goya). VERT: 35 s. "Philip IV at Fraga" (Velazquez); 50 s. "Head of a Stag" (Velazquez); 75 s. "The Cardinal-Infante Ferdinand as a Hunter" (Velazquez); 100 s. "The Dream of Reason brings forth Monsters" (Goya); 300 s. "Pablo de Valladolid" (Velazquez)

202 Lucky Omens

203 Superb Starling

1992. 500th Anniv of Discovery of America by Columbus. Multicoloured.
1345 10 s. Type **202** 20 20
1346 15 s. Map and compass . . . 25 25
1347 25 s. Look-out in crow's nest 35 35
1348 30 s. Amerindians sighting ships (horiz) 40 40
1349 35 s. "Pinta" and "Nina" (horiz) 45 45
1350 75 s. "Santa Maria" (horiz) . 70 70
1351 250 s. Wreck of "Santa Maria" 1·50 2·00

1992. Birds. Multicoloured.
1353 5 s. Type **203** 25 25
1354 10 s. Golden Bishop ("Canary") 30 30
1355 15 s. Four-coloured bush shrike 40 40
1356 25 s. Grey-headed kingfisher 45 45
1357 30 s. Common kingfisher . . 45 45
1358 35 s. Yellow-billed oxpecker 45 45
1359 150 s. Black-throated honeyguide . . . . 1·40 1·40

1992. 15th Death Anniv of Elvis Presley. Nos. 1117/25 optd **15th Anniversary**.
1361 75 s. Looking pensive . . . 75 75
1362 75 s. Wearing black and yellow striped shirt 75 75
1363 75 s. Singing into microphone 75 75
1364 75 s. Wearing wide-brimmed hat 75 75
1365 75 s. With microphone in right hand 75 75
1366 75 s. In Army uniform . . . 75 75
1367 75 s. Wearing pink shirt . . 75 75
1368 75 s. In yellow shirt 75 75
1369 75 s. In jacket and bow tie . 75 75

205 Iguanodon

1992. African Dinosaurs. Multicoloured.
1370 100 s. Type **205** 70 70
1371 100 s. Saltasaurus 70 70
1372 100 s. Cetiosaurus 70 70
1373 100 s. Camarasaurus 70 70
1374 100 s. Spinosaurus 70 70
1375 100 s. Stegosaurus 70 70
1376 100 s. Allosaurus 70 70
1377 100 s. Ceratosaurus 70 70
1378 100 s. Lesothosaurus 70 70
1379 100 s. Anchisaurus 70 70
1380 100 s. Ornithomimus 70 70
1381 100 s. Baronyx 70 70
1382 100 s. Pachycephalosaurus . 70 70
1383 100 s. Heterodontosaurus . . 70 70
1384 100 s. Dryosaurus 70 70
1385 100 s. Coelophysis 70 70
Nos. 1370/85 were printed together, se-tenant, forming a composite design.

206 Spotted Tilapia

1992. Fishes. Multicoloured.
1386 100 s. Type **206** 80 80
1387 100 s. Butterfly barb 80 80
1388 100 s. Blunthead Molino cichlid 80 80
1389 100 s. Angel squeaker 80 80
1390 100 s. Dickfield's Julie . . . 80 80
1391 100 s. Nile mouthbrooder . . 80 80
1392 100 s. Blue-finned notho . . 80 80
1393 100 s. Crabro mbuna 80 80
1394 100 s. Pearl-scaled lamprologus 80 80
1395 100 s. Zebra mbuna 80 80
1396 100 s. Marlier's Julie 80 80
1397 100 s. Brichard's chalinochromis 80 80
Nos. 1386/97 were printed together, se-tenant, forming a composite design.

207 Hunting Birds with Catapults

1992. Traditional Hunting. Multicoloured.
1399 20 s. Type **207** 40 30
1400 70 s. Hunting antelope with bow and arrow 65 55
1401 100 s. Hunting antelopes with dogs 90 90
1402 150 s. Hunting lion with spears and shields . . . . . . 1·75 2·00

1992. Olympic Games, Albertville and Barcelona (3rd issue). As T **216** of Lesotho. Multicoloured.
1404 20 s. Men's 4000 metre pursuit cycling 15 15
1405 40 s. Men's double sculls rowing (horiz) 20 20
1406 50 s. Waterpolo (horiz) . . . 20 20
1407 70 s. Women's single luge (horiz) 30 30
1408 100 s. Marathon (horiz) . . 50 50
1409 150 s. Women's asymmetrical bars gymnastics (horiz) . . 90 90
1410 200 s. Ice hockey . . . . . 1·25 1·25
1411 400 s. Men's rings gymnastics 2·50 2·50

1992. Mickey's Portrait Gallery. As T **70** of Nevis, showing Walt Disney cartoon characters. Multicoloured.
1413 25 s. Donald Duck in "Sea Scouts", 1939 . . . . . . 20 20
1414 25 s. Minnie Mouse in "Hawaiian Holiday", 1937 20 20
1415 25 s. Pluto in "Society Dog Show", 1939 . . . . . . 20 20
1416 35 s. Donald in "Fire Chief", 1940 . . . . 30 30
1417 50 s. Donald in "Truant Officer Donald", 1941 . . . . . 40 40
1418 75 s. Goofy in "Clock Cleaners", 1937 . . . . . . 45 45
1419 100 s. Goofy in "Goofy and Wilbur", 1939 . . . . . . 55 55
1420 100 s. Mickey Mouse in "Magician Mickey", 1937 . 55 55
1421 200 s. Minnie in "The Nifty Nineties", 1941 . . . . . . 90 90
1422 300 s. Mickey and Pluto in "Society Dog Show", 1939 1·25 1·25
1423 400 s. Pluto and pups in "Pluto's Quin-Puplets", 1937 1·40 1·40
1424 500 s. Daisy and Donald in "Mr. Duck Steps Out", 1940 1·60 1·60

208 "Couroupita guianensis"

209 Abyssinian Cat

1993. Botanical Gardens of the World. Rio de Janeiro. African Plants. Vert designs as T **208**.
1426/45 70 s. × 20 multicoloured
Set of 20 . . . . 11·00 13·00

1992. Cats. Multicoloured.
1447 20 s. Type **209** 45 45
1448 30 s. Havana cat 45 45
1449 50 s. Persian black cat . . . 55 55
1450 70 s. Persian blue cat 65 65
1451 100 s. European silver tabby cat 85 85
1452 150 s. Persian silver tabby cat 1·00 1·00
1453 200 s. Maine coon cat . . . . 1·25 1·25

1992. "Genova '92" International Stamp Exhibition. Toy Trains manufactured by Lionel. As T **257** of Dominica. Multicoloured.
1455 10 s. Baltimore & Ohio tunnel locomotive No. 5, 1904 . . 25 25
1456 20 s. "Liberty Bell" locomotive No. 385E, 1930 . . . . . 35 35
1457 30 s. Armoured rail car No. 203, 1917 . . . . 40 40
1458 50 s. Open trolley No. 202, 1910–14 . . . . 60 60
1459 70 s. "Macy Special" electric locomotive No. 405 . . . . 70 70
1460 100 s. "Milwaukee Road" bi-polar electric locomotive, 1929 . . . . 80 80
1461 200 s. New York Central Type S locomotive, 1912 . . . . 1·25 1·25
1462 300 s. Locomotive No. 7, 1914 1·50 1·50

210 Count Ferdinand von Zeppelin

1992. Anniversaries and Events. Mult.
1464 30 s. Type **210** 30 30
1465 70 s. "Santa Maria" 55 55
1466 70 s. "Apollo–Soyuz" link-up, 1975 . . . . 55 55
1467 150 s. African elephant . . . 1·00 1·00
1468 150 s. Child being offered apple 1·00 1·00
1469 200 s. Zebra . . . . 1·10 1·10
1470 200 s. Trying on glasses . . 1·10 1·10
1471 300 s. Airship "Graf Zeppelin", 1929 . . . . 1·60 1·60
1472 300 s. Christopher Columbus 1·60 1·60
1473 400 s. Space shuttle . . . . 2·25 2·25
1474 400 s. Wolfgang Amadeus Mozart (vert) . . . . . . 2·25 2·25
ANNIVERSARIES AND EVENTS: Nos. 1464, 1471, 75th death anniv of Count Ferdinand von Zeppelin; Nos. 1465, 1472, 500th anniv of discovery of America by Columbus; Nos. 1466, 1473, International Space Year; Nos. 1467, 1469, Earth Summit '92, Rio; No. 1468, International Conference on Nutrition, Rome; No. 1470, 75th anniv of International Association of Lions Clubs; No. 1474, Death bicentenary of Mozart.

1992. Bicentenary of the Louvre, Paris. Paintings by Jean Chardin. As T **305** of Antigua. Mult.
1476 100 s. "Young Draughtsman sharpening Pencil" 70 70
1477 100 s. "The Buffet" 70 70
1478 100 s. "Return from the Market" 70 70
1479 100 s. "The Hard-working Mother" 70 70
1480 100 s. "Grace" 70 70
1481 100 s. "The Copper Water Urn" 70 70
1482 100 s. "The House of Cards" 70 70
1483 100 s. "Boy with a Top" . . 70 70

211 Carved Head

1992. Makonde Art.
1485 **211** 20 s. multicoloured . . . 15 15
1486 – 30 s. multicoloured . . . 15 15
1487 – 50 s. multicoloured . . . 20 20
1488 – 70 s. multicoloured . . . 30 30
1489 – 100 s. multicoloured . . 40 40
1490 – 150 s. multicoloured . . 70 70
1491 – 200 s. multicoloured . . 80 80
DESIGNS: 30 s. to 200 s. Various carvings.

212 Russian Cycle, 1813

1992. Bicycles of the World. Multicoloured.
1493 20 s. Type **212** 20 20
1494 30 s. German, 1840 . . . . 20 20
1495 50 s. German, 1818 . . . . 30 30
1496 70 s. German, 1850 . . . . 40 40
1497 100 s. Italian, 1988 . . . . 50 50
1498 150 s. Swedish, 1982 . . . . 80 80
1499 300 s. Italian, 1989 . . . . 1·25 1·25

213 Seal

1993. Large Sea Creatures. Multicoloured.
1501 20 s. Type **213** 50 50
1502 30 s. Whale 75 75
1503 70 s. Shark 90 90
1504 100 s. Walrus . . . . 1·00 1·00

214 Boxing

215 "Macrolepiota rhacodes"

1993. Sports. Multicoloured.
1506 20 s. Type **214** 15 15
1507 50 s. Hockey 50 20
1508 70 s. Show jumping 40 40
1509 100 s. Marathon running . . 45 45
1510 150 s. Football 60 60
1511 200 s. Diving 70 70
1512 400 s. Basketball . . . . . 1·50 1·75

1993. 40th Anniv of Coronation. As T **307** of Antigua.
1514 100 s. multicoloured 50 50
1515 150 s. multicoloured 75 75
1516 200 s. lilac and black . . . 1·00 1·00
1517 300 s. multicoloured . . . . 1·25 1·25
DESIGNS: 100 s. Queen Elizabeth II at Coronation (photograph by Cecil Beaton); 150 s. Gold salt-cellar; 200 s. Prince Philip at Coronation; 300 s. Queen Elizabeth II and Prince Andrew.

1993. Fungi. Multicoloured.
1519 20 s. Type **215** 35 35
1520 40 s. "Mycena pura" 50 50
1521 50 s. "Chlorophyllum molybdites" 50 50
1522 70 s. "Agaricus campestris" . 60 60
1523 100 s. "Volvariella volvacea" 70 70
1524 150 s. "Leucoagaricus naucinus" 90 90
1525 200 s. "Oudemansiella radicata" 1·00 1·00
1526 300 s. "Clitocybe nebularis" . 1·25 1·25

216 "Geochelone elephantopus" (tortoise)

217 Pancake Tortoise on Rock

1993. Reptiles. Multicoloured.

1528	20 s. Type **216**	20	20
1529	50 s. "Iguana iguana"	30	30
1530	70 s. "Varanus salvator" (lizard) (horiz)	70	70
1531	100 s. "Naja oxiana" (cobra)	45	45
1532	150 s. "Chamaeleo jacksoni" (horiz)	70	70
1533	200 s. "Eunectes murinus" (snake) (horiz)	80	80
1534	250 s. "Alligator mississippensis" (horiz)	90	90

1993. Endangered Species. Pancake Tortoise. Multicoloured.

1536	20 s. Type **217**	30	30
1537	30 s. Drinking	35	35
1538	50 s. Under rock	50	50
1539	70 s. Tortoise hatching	65	65

218 Elephant

1993. Wildlife.

1540/87	100 s. × 48 multicoloured Set of 48	18·00	20·00

Nos. 1540/87 were issued together, se-tenant, as four sheetlets each of twelve different vertical designs. The species depicted are, in addition to Type **218**, Gazelle, Hartebeest, Duiker, Genet, Civet, Eastern white pelican, Waterbuck, Blacksmith plover, Lesser pied kingfisher, Black-winged stilt, Bush pig, Brown-hooded kingfisher, Sable antelope, Impala, Buffalo, Leopard, Aardvark, Hippopotamus, Spotted hyena, South African crowned crane, Crocodile, Greater flamingo, Baboon, Potto, Lesser flamingo, Grey-headed kingfisher, Red colobus monkey, Dik-dik, Aardwolf (incorrectly inscribed "ARDWOLF"), Black-backed jackal, Tree pangolin, Serval, Yellow-billed hornbill, Pygmy mongoose, Bat-eared fox, Bushbaby, Egyptian vulture, Ostrich, Greater kudu, Diana monkey, Giraffe, Cheetah, Wildebeest, Chimpanzee, Warthog, Zebra and Rhinoceros.

219 Grant's Zebra galloping

1992. Wild Animals. Multicoloured.

1589	100 s. Type **219**	70	70
1590	100 s. Grant's zebra standing	70	70
1591	100 s. Grant's gazelle doe	70	70
1592	100 s. Grant's gazelle buck	70	70
1593	100 s. Thomson's gazelle	70	70
1594	100 s. White-bearded gnu with calf	70	70
1595	100 s. Female cheetah with cubs	70	70
1596	100 s. Young cheetah drinking	70	70
1597	100 s. Lioness carring cub in mouth	70	70
1598	100 s. Pair of hunting dogs	70	70
1599	100 s. Three hunting dogs	70	70
1600	100 s. Four hunting dogs	70	70

220 Valentina Tereshkova (first woman in space)

222 Arthur Ashe (tennis)

221 "Iolaus aphnaeoides"

1993. Famous 20th-century Women. Mult.

1602	20 s. Type **220**	40	40
1603	40 s. Marie Curie (physicist)	60	60
1604	50 s. Indira Gandhi (Prime Minister of India)	60	60
1605	70 s. Wilma Rudolph (Olympic athlete)	60	60
1606	100 s. Margaret Mead (anthropologist)	60	60
1607	150 s. Golda Meir (Prime Minister of Israel)	80	80
1608	200 s. Dr. Elizabeth Blackwell (first female medical doctor)	90	90
1609	400 s. Margaret Thatcher (Prime Minister of Great Britain)	1·75	1·75

1993. Butterflies.

1611/54	100 s. × 44 multicoloured Set of 44	30·00	30·00

Nos. 1611/54 were printed se-tenant in two sheetlets of 12 (Nos. 1611/34) and one of 20 (Nos. 1635/54). The species depicted, in addition to Type **221**, are "Charaxes eupale", "Danaus formosa", "Antanartia hippomene", "Mylothris sagala", "Charaxes anticlea", "Salamis temora", "Nepheronia argia", "Acraea pseudolycia", "Hypolimnas antevorta", "Colotis hildebrandti", "Acraea bonasia", "Eurema desjardinsi", "Myrina silenus", "Iolaus ismenias", "Charaxes candiope", "Precis artaxia", "Danaus chrysippus", "Axiocerses bambana", "Precis orithya", "Pinacopteryx eriphia", "Iolaus coecolus", "Precis hierta", "Colotis regina", "Euphaedra neophron", "Mylothris poppea", "Aphaneus flavescens", "Eronia leda", "Charaxes zoolina", "Papilio bromius", "Cyrestis camillus", "Hypolycaena buxtoni", "Charaxes achaemenes", "Asterope rosa", "Graphium antheus", "Charaxes acuminatus", "Kallima rumia", "Leptosia alcesta", "Pseudacraea boisduvali", "Iolaus sidus", "Salamis parhassus", "Charaxes protoclea azota", "Charaxes bohemani" and "Papilio ophidicephalus".

1993. Black Sporting Personalities. Multicoloured.

1656	20 s. Type **222**	40	40
1657	40 s. Michael Jordan (basketball)	40	40
1658	50 s. Daley Thompson (decathlon)	40	40
1659	70 s. Jackie Robinson (baseball)	40	40
1660	100 s. Kareem Abdul-Jabbar (basketball)	50	50
1661	150 s. Florence Joyner (athletics)	60	60
1662	200 s. Jesse Owens (athletics)	70	70
1663	400 s. Jack Johnson (boxing)	1·50	1·50

223 Short-finned Mako

1993. Sharks. Multicoloured.

1665	20 s. Type **223**	15	15
1666	30 s. Lantern shark	20	20
1667	50 s. Tiger shark	25	25
1668	70 s. African angelshark	35	35
1669	100 s. "Pristiophorus cirratus"	45	45
1670	150 s. White-tipped reef shark	65	65
1671	200 s. Scalloped hammerhead	75	75

224 Alpha Jet

225 Gordon Setter

1993. Military Aircraft. Multicoloured.

1673	20 s. Type **224**	20	20
1674	30 s. Northrop F-5E	25	25
1675	50 s. Dassault Mirage 3NG	30	30
1676	70 s. MB 339C	45	45
1677	100 s. MiG-31	50	50
1678	150 s. C-101 Aviojet	70	70
1679	200 s. General Dynamics F-16 Fighting Falcon	80	80

1993. Dogs. Multicoloured.

1681	20 s. Type **225**	20	20
1682	30 s. Zwergschnauzer	25	25
1683	50 s. Labrador retriever	30	30
1684	70 s. Wire fox terrier	45	45
1685	100 s. English springer spaniel	50	50
1686	150 s. Newfoundlander	70	70
1687	200 s. Moscow toy terrier	80	80

226 Rhinoceros, Ngorongoro Crater

227 "Ansellia africana"

1993. National Parks. Multicoloured.

1689	20 s. Type **226**	20	20
1690	50 s. Buffalo, Ngurdoto Crater	20	20
1691	70 s. Leopard, Kilimanjaro	30	30
1692	100 s. Baboon, Gombe	35	35
1693	150 s. Lion, Selous	45	45
1694	200 s. Giraffe, Mikumi	65	65
1695	250 s. Zebra, Serengeti	70	70

1993. Flowers. Multicoloured.

1697	20 s. Type **227**	20	20
1698	30 s. "Saintpaulia ionantha"	25	25
1699	40 s. "Stapelia semota lutea"	30	30
1700	50 s. "Impatiens walleriana"	30	30
1701	60 s. "Senecio petraeus"	35	35
1702	70 s. "Kalanchoe velutina"	40	40
1703	100 s. "Kaempferia brachystemon"	50	50
1704	150 s. "Nymphaea colorata"	70	70
1705	200 s. "Thunbergia battiscombei"	80	80
1706	250 s. "Crossandra nilotica"	90	90
1707	300 s. "Spathodea campanulata"	1·00	1·00
1708	350 s. "Ruttya fruticosa"	1·00	1·00

228 Norman-Arab

229 Berts Warrior

1993. Horses. Multicoloured.

1710	20 s. Type **228**	30	30
1711	40 s. Nonius	40	40
1712	50 s. Boulonnais	40	40
1713	70 s. Arab	50	50
1714	100 s. Anglo-Arab	55	55
1715	150 s. Tarpon	70	70
1716	200 s. Thoroughbred	80	80

No. 1716 is inscribed "THOROUGBLED" in error.

1993. Traditional African Costumes. Multicoloured.

1718	20 s. Type **229**	10	10
1719	40 s. Galla	15	15
1720	50 s. Guinean	15	15
1721	70 s. Goloff	20	25
1722	100 s. Peul	30	30
1723	150 s. Abyssinian	45	45
1724	200 s. Pahuin	55	55

1994. Hummel Figurines. As T **302** of Antigua. Multicoloured.

1726	20 s. Boy playing accordion	25	25
1727	40 s. Girl with guitar and boy with lute	30	30
1728	50 s. Boy playing euphonium	30	30
1729	70 s. Boy playing mouth organ	35	35
1730	100 s. Boy with trumpet on fence	45	45
1731	150 s. Boy playing recorder	70	70
1732	200 s. Boy with trumpet and bird on feet	80	80
1733	300 s. Girl playing banjo	1·10	1·25
1734	350 s. Boy carrying double bass on back	1·25	1·50
1735	400 s. Girls with banjo and song sheet	1·25	1·50

230 Downhill Skiing

231 Ruud Gullit (Netherlands)

1994. Winter Olympic Games, Lillehammer, Norway. Multicoloured.

1737	40 s. Type **230**	20	20
1738	50 s. Ice hockey	20	20
1739	70 s. Speed skating	30	30
1740	100 s. Bobsleighing	35	35
1741	120 s. Figure skating	40	40
1742	170 s. Free style skiing	55	55
1743	250 s. Biathlon	75	75

1994. World Cup Football Championship, U.S.A. (1st issue). Multicoloured.

1745	20 s. Type **231**	30	30
1746	30 s. Kevin Sheedy (Ireland)	30	30
1747	50 s. Giuseppe Giannini (Italy)	40	40
1748	70 s. Julio Cesar (Brazil)	45	45
1749	250 s. John Barnes (England) and Grun (Belgium)	1·25	1·25
1750	300 s. Chendo (Spain)	1·25	1·25
1751	350 s. Frank Rijkaard (Netherlands)	1·40	1·40
1752	400 s. Lothar Matthaeus (Germany)	1·40	1·40

See also Nos. 1838/45 and 1892/8.

1994. "Hong Kong '94" International Stamp Exhibition. As T **317** of Antigua. Mult.

1754	350 s. Blue-barred orange parrotfish and red cap white pearl-scale goldfish at right	1·25	1·25
1755	350 s. Regal angelfish and red cap white pearl-scale goldfish at left	1·25	1·25

Nos. 1754/5 were printed together, se-tenant, forming a composite design.

232 Mickey Mouse, Goofy, Pluto and Donald Duck boarding Airliner

1994. 65th Anniv of Mickey Mouse. Walt Disney Cartoon Characters on World Tour. Mult.

1756	10 s. Type **232**	25	25
1757	20 s. Daisy Duck and Minnie Mouse dancing, Tonga	30	30
1758	30 s. Mickey and Goofy playing bowls, Australia	35	35
1759	40 s. Mickey, Donald and Goofy building igloo, Arctic Circle	40	40
1760	50 s. Pluto, Goofy, Mickey and Donald on guard at Buckingham Palace, London	40	40
1761	60 s. Pluto at Esna Bazaar, Egypt	45	45
1762	70 s. Donald being chased by Zsambox herders, Hungary (vert)	45	45
1763	100 s. Donald and Daisy on Grand Canal, Venice (vert)	60	60
1764	150 s. Goofy dancing, Bali (vert)	90	90
1765	200 s. Donald with monks, Thailand (vert)	1·00	1·00
1766	300 s. Goofy water skiing at Taj Mahal, India (vert)	1·25	1·25
1767	400 s. Mickey, Minnie, Goofy and Donald being carried by Sherpas, Nepal	1·25	1·25

233 Bonelli's Eagle ("African Hawk Eagle")

1994. Birds. Multicoloured.

1769	20 s. Type **233**	40	40
1770	30 s. Whale-headed stork ("Shoe-bill stork")	40	40
1771	50 s. Brown harrier eagle	50	50
1772	70 s. Black-casqued hornbill	60	60
1773	100 s. Crowned cranes	70	70
1774	150 s. Greater flamingos	80	80
1775	200 s. Pair of eastern white pelicans (horiz)	80	80
1776	250 s. African jacana and black crake (horiz)	90	90
1777	300 s. Pair of ostriches (horiz)	1·00	1·00
1778	350 s. Pair of helmet guineafowl (horiz)	1·00	1·00
1779	400 s. Malachite kingfisher (horiz)	1·00	1·00
1780	500 s. Pair of saddle-bill storks (horiz)	1·00	1·10

234 Henry Ford and Model "T"

1994. Centenaries of Henry Ford's First Petrol Engine (Nos. 1781 and 1783) and Karl Benz's First Four-wheeled Car (others). Multicoloured.

1781	200 s. Type **234**	90	90
1782	200 s. Benz, 1893, and "500 SEL", 1993	90	90
1783	400 s. Ford, 1893, Mustang Cobra and emblem	1·40	1·40
1784	400 s. Karl Benz and emblem	1·40	1·40

235 Sopwith Pup Biplane

1994. Aviation Anniversaries. Multicoloured.

1786	200 s. Type **235**	80	80
1787	200 s. Inflating hot-air balloons	80	80
1788	400 s. Hawker Siddeley Harrier and design drawing	1·25	1·25
1789	400 s. Jean-Pierre Blanchard and his balloon	1·25	1·25

ANNIVERSARIES: Nos. 1786, 1788, 75th anniv of Royal Air Force; Nos. 1787, 1789, Bicentenary of first balloon flight in the U.S.A.

236 Jahazi (sailing canoe)

237 Diatryma

1994. Sailing Ships. Multicoloured.

1791	40 s. Type **236**	15	15
1792	50 s. Caravel	15	15
1793	70 s. Pirate carrack	25	25
1794	100 s. Baltic galeass	30	30
1795	170 s. Frigate (inscr "Battle-ship")	55	55
1796	200 s. British ship of the line (inscr "Frigate")	65	65
1797	250 s. Brig	75	75

1994. Prehistoric Animals. Multicoloured.

1799	40 s. Type **237**	20	20
1800	50 s. Tyrannosaurus rex	20	20
1801	100 s. Uintaterius	35	35
1802	120 s. Stiracosaurus	45	45
1803	170 s. Diplodocus	60	60
1804	250 s. Archaeopteryx	80	80
1805	300 s. Sordes	90	90

No. 1799 is inscribed "DIATRUMA" in error.

238 Koala Bear with Cub

1994. Endangered Species. Multicoloured.

1807	40 s. Type **238**	25	25
1808	70 s. Giant panda with cub	40	40
1809	100 s. Eagles	55	55
1810	120 s. African elephant with calf	70	70
1811	250 s. Carribean monk seals	90	90
1812	400 s. Dolphins	1·00	1·00
1813	500 s. Whales	1·50	1·50

239 Pres. Salmin Amour of Zanzibar

241 Tanzanian Family

240 Lorry at Customs Post

1994. 30th Anniv of Zanzibar Revolution. Multicoloured.

1815	40 s. Type **239**	20	10
1816	70 s. Amani Karume (first President of Zanzibar)	30	20
1817	120 s. Harvesting cloves (horiz)	55	55
1818	250 s. Carved door	1·00	1·50

1994. 81st/82nd Customs Co-Operation Council Meeting, Arusha. Multicoloured.

1820	20 s. Type **240**	20	10
1821	50 s. Container ship	30	15
1822	100 s. Passengers and airliner	50	40
1823	150 s. Customs and U.P.U. logos	60	75

1994. Int Year of the Family. Mult.

1825	40 s. Type **241**	15	10
1826	120 s. Father playing with children	35	35
1827	170 s. Family clinic (horiz)	50	55
1828	250 s. Woman harvesting tobacco	70	80

242 "Trombidium sp"

1994. Arachnids. Multicoloured.

1830	40 s. Type **242**	20	20
1831	50 s. "Eurypelma sp"	20	20
1832	100 s. "Salticus sp"	30	30
1833	120 s. "Micrommata rosea" (vert)	35	35
1834	170 s. "Araneus sp" (vert)	50	50
1835	250 s. "Micrathena sp" (vert)	70	70
1836	300 s. "Araneus diadematus" (vert)	80	80

243 Giuseppe Signori (Italy)

244 Bateleur

1994. World Cup Football Championship, U.S.A. (2nd issue). Multicoloured.

1838	300 s. Type **243**	90	90
1839	300 s. Ruud Gullit (Netherlands)	90	90
1840	300 s. Roberto Mancini (Italy)	90	90
1841	300 s. Marco van Basten (Netherlands)	90	90
1842	300 s. Dennis Bergkamp (Netherlands)	90	90
1843	300 s. Oscar Ruggeri (Argentina)	90	90
1844	300 s. Frank Rijkaard (Netherlands)	90	90
1845	300 s. Peter Schmeichel (Denmark)	90	90

See also Nos. 1892/8.

1994. Birds of Prey. Multicoloured.

1847	40 s. Type **244**	40	40
1848	50 s. Ornate hawk eagle	40	40
1849	100 s. Osprey	60	60
1850	120 s. Andean condor	60	60
1851	170 s. African fish eagle (horiz)	70	70
1852	250 s. King vulture	80	80
1853	400 s. Peregrine falcon (horiz)	1·25	1·25

245 Afghan Hound

1994. Dogs of the World. Multicoloured.

1855/63	120 s. × 9 (Type **245**; Basenji; Siberian husky; Irish setter; Norwegian elkhound; Bracco Italiano; Australian cattle dog; German short-haired pointer; Rhodesian ridgeback)		
1864/72	120 s. × 9 (Alsatian; Japanese chin; Shetland sheepdog; Italian spinone; Great dane; English setter; Welsh corgi; St. Bernard; Irish wolfhound)		
1873/81	120 s. × 9 (Doberman pinscher; Chihuahua; Bloodhound; Keeshond; Tibetan spaniel; Japanese akita; Tervueren; Chow; Pharaoh hound)		
1882/90	120 s. × 9 (Alaskan malamute; Scottish cairn terrier; American foxhound; British bulldog; Boston terrier; Borzoi; Shar pei; Saluki; Bernese mountain dog)		
1855/90	Set of 36	12·00	14·00

246 Players and Flags from Group B

1994. World Cup Football Championship, U.S.A. (3rd issue). Multicoloured.

1892	40 s. Type **246**	45	45
1893	50 s. Players and flags from Group C	50	50
1894	70 s. Players and flags from Group D	60	60
1895	100 s. Players and flags from Group E	65	65
1896	170 s. Players and flags from Group A	90	90
1897	200 s. Players and World Cup	1·10	1·10
1898	250 s. Players and flags from Group F	1·40	1·40

247 "Rangaeris amaniensis"

248 "Dicentra spectabilis"

1994. Orchids. Multicoloured.

1900	200 s. Type **247**	60	60
1901	200 s. "Eulophia macowanii"	60	60
1902	200 s. "Cytorchis arcuata"	60	60
1903	200 s. "Centrostigma occultans"	60	60
1904	200 s. "Cirrhopetalum umbellatum"	60	60
1905	200 s. "Ansellia gigantea"	60	60
1906	200 s. "Angraecum ramosum"	60	60
1907	200 s. "Disa englerana"	60	60
1908	200 s. "Nervilia stolziana"	60	60
1909	200 s. "Satyrium orbiculare"	60	60
1910	200 s. "Schizochilus sulphureus"	60	60
1911	200 s. "Disa stolzii"	60	60
1912	200 s. "Platycorne mediocris"	60	60
1913	200 s. "Satyrium breve"	60	60
1914	200 s. "Eulophia nuttii"	60	60
1915	200 s. "Disa ornithantha"	60	60

1994. Flowers. Multicoloured.

1917	40 s. Type **248**	30	30
1918	100 s. "Thunbergia alata"	45	45
1919	120 s. "Cyrtanthus minimiflorus"	50	50
1920	170 s. "Nepenthes hybrida"	70	70
1921	250 s. "Allamanda cathartica"	80	80
1922	300 s. "Encyclia pentotis"	85	85
1923	400 s. "Protea lacticolor"	90	90

249 "Limenitis sydyi"

1994. Butterflies. Multicoloured.

1925	120 s. Type **249**	50	50
1926	120 s. "Agraulis vanillae"	50	50
1927	120 s. "Danaus chrysippus"	50	50
1928	120 s. "Eurytides marcellus"	50	50
1929	120 s. "Artopoetes pryeri"	50	50
1930	120 s. "Heliconius charitonius"	50	50
1931	120 s. "Limenitis weidemeyerii"	50	50
1932	120 s. "Phoebis sennae"	50	50
1933	120 s. "Timelaea albescens"	50	50
1934	120 s. "Papilio glaucus"	50	50
1935	120 s. "Danaus plexippus"	50	50
1936	120 s. "Papilio troilus"	50	50
1937	120 s. "Hypolimnas antevorta"	50	50
1938	120 s. "Cirrochroa imperatrix"	50	50
1939	120 s. "Vanessa atalanta"	50	50
1940	120 s. "Limenitis archippus"	50	50
1941	120 s. "Hypolimnas pandarus"	50	50
1942	120 s. "Anthocharis belia"	50	50

250 Donald Duck and Goofy with Safari Equipment

1994. Mickey Mouse Safari Club. Walt Disney Cartoon Characters on Safari. Multicoloured.

1944	70 s. Type **250**	35	35
1945	70 s. Donald and Mickey Mouse with leopard cubs	35	35
1946	100 s. Donald photographing antelope	40	40
1947	100 s. Donald between elephant's legs	40	40
1948	120 s. Mickey with monkeys	50	50
1949	120 s. Donald with hippopotamuses	50	50
1950	150 s. Goofy carrying equipment	60	60
1951	150 s. Mickey, Donald and Goofy sheltering under elephant's ears	60	60
1952	200 s. Goofy with zebras	70	70
1953	200 s. Donald, Goofy and Mickey with lion	70	70
1954	250 s. Donald filming monkeys	80	80
1955	250 s. Giraffe licking Mickey	80	80

HAVE YOU READ THE NOTES AT THE BEGINNING OF THIS CATALOGUE?

These often provide answers to the enquiries we receive.

251 Plan indicating Moon Landing Point

1994. 25th Anniv of First Moon Landing. Multicoloured.

1957	150 s. Type **251**	65	65
1958	150 s. Photograph showing Sea of Tranquility	65	65
1959	150 s. Lunar surface	65	65
1960	150 s. Lift-off	65	65
1961	150 s. Jettisoning first stage rocket	65	65
1962	150 s. Jettisoning second stage rocket	65	65
1963	150 s. Lunar module "Eagle" leaving command module	65	65
1964	150 s. "Eagle" descending towards lunar surface	65	65
1965	150 s. Armstrong and Aldrin (astronauts) inside "Eagle"	65	65
1966	150 s. "Apollo 11" crew in space suits	65	65
1967	150 s. "Eagle" on lunar surface	65	65
1968	150 s. Armstrong descending to lunar surface	65	65
1969	150 s. Astronaut, "Eagle" and experiment	65	65
1970	150 s. Astronaut setting-up equipment	65	65
1971	150 s. Reflection in astronaut's visor	65	65
1972	150 s. Astronaut and U.S.A. flag	65	65
1973	150 s. Astronaut carrying equipment	65	65
1974	150 s. "Eagle" blasting off from Moon	65	65
1975	150 s. Command module	65	65
1976	150 s. "Eagle" leaving Moon	65	65
1977	150 s. Capsule leaving Moon orbit	65	65
1978	150 s. Capsule heading for Earth	65	65
1979	150 s. Capsule re-entering Earth's atmosphere	65	65
1980	150 s. Capsule in sea	65	65
1981	150 s. Recovery crew opening hatch	65	65
1982	150 s. Transferring astronauts by helicopter	65	65
1983	150 s. Armstrong, Collins and Aldrin (astronauts) after recovery	65	65

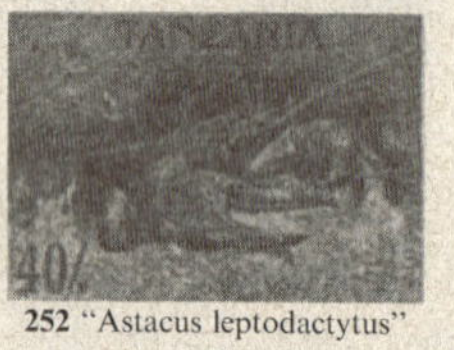
252 "Astacus leptodactylus"

1994. Crabs. Multicoloured.

1984	40 s. Type **252**	30	30
1985	100 s. "Eriocheir sinensis" (vert)	50	50
1986	120 s. "Caneer opillo" (vert)	55	55
1987	170 s. "Cardisoma quanhumi"	70	70
1988	250 s. "Birgus latro" (vert)	85	85
1989	300 s. "Menippe mercenaria"	90	90
1990	400 s. "Dromia vulgaris" (vert)	95	95

1994. Centenary of International Olympic Committee. Gold Medal Winners. As T **327** of Antigua. Multicoloured.

1992	350 s. Kristin Otto (Germany) (50 metres freestyle swimming), 1988	1·00	1·00
1993	500 s. Carl Lewis (U.S.A.) (various track and field events), 1984 and 1988	1·40	1·40

1994. 50th Anniv of D-Day (1st issue). As T **331** of Antigua. Multicoloured.

1995	350 s. Troops leaving landing craft	1·25	1·25
1996	600 s. Amphibious tank and troops, Omaha Beach	1·75	1·75

See also Nos. 1998/2015.

253 Supermarine Spitfire over Beaches

1994. 50th Anniv of D-Day (2nd issue). Multicoloured.

1998	200 s. Type **253**	70	70
1999	200 s. D.U.K.W.s landing on Gold Beach	70	70
2000	200 s. Canadian troops landing on Juno Beach	70	70
2001	200 s. Canadian cyclists disembarking, Juno Beach	70	70
2002	200 s. Amphibious Sherman tank on beach	70	70

2003	200 s. German gun emplacement	70	70
2004	200 s. General Montgomery and British troops on beach	70	70
2005	200 s. British engineers with AVRE Churchill tank, Gold Beach	70	70
2006	200 s. U.S.S. "Thompson" (destroyer) being refuelled	70	70
2007	200 s. H.M.S. "Warspite" (battleship)	70	70
2008	200 s. Royal Marines on Juno Beach	70	70
2009	200 s. Sherman Mark 1 flail tank leaving landing craft	70	70
2010	200 s. General Eisenhower and U.S. troops on Omaha Beach	70	70
2011	200 s. North American P-51 Mustang escorting ships	70	70
2012	200 s. U.S. coastguard cutter alongside landing craft	70	70
2013	200 s. U.S. troops in landing craft	70	70
2014	200 s. U.S. troops landing on Omaha Beach	70	70
2015	200 s. U.S. troops on Omaha Beach	70	70

No. 2004 is inscribed "COMMANDER-IN-CHEIF" and No. 2010 "OPERATION OVERLOAD", both in error.

254 "Deinonychus"

1994. Prehistoric Animals.

2017/48	120 s. × 32 multicoloured	15·00	16·00

DESIGNS—VERT: No. 2018, Styracosaurus; 2019, Anatosaurus; 2020, Plateosaurus; 2021, Iguanodon; 2022, Oviraptor; 2023, Dimorphodons; 2024, Ornithomimus; 2025, Lambeosaurus; 2026, Megalosaurus; 2027, Cetiosaurus; 2028, Hypsilophodon; 2029, Rhamphorynchus; 2030, Scelidosaurus; 2031, Antrodemus; 2032, Dimetrodon. HORIZ: No. 2033, Brontosaurus; 2034, Albertosaurus; 2035, Parasaurolophus; 2036, Pteranodons; 2037, Stegosaurus; 2038, Tyrannosaurus rex; 2039, Triceratops; 2040, Ornitholestes; 2041, Camarasaurus; 2042, Ankylosaurus; 2043, Trachodon; 2044, Allosaurus; 2045, Corythosaurus; 2046, Struthiomimus; 2047, Camptosaurus; 2048, Heterodontosaurus.

Nos. 2017/32 and 2033/48 respectively were printed together, se-tenant, Nos. 2033/48 forming a composite design.

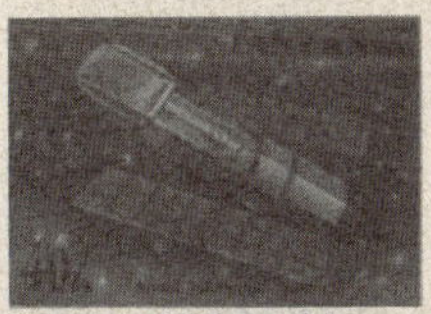
255 "Hubble" Space Telescope

1994. Space Research. Multicoloured.

2050	40 s. Type **255**	30	30
2051	100 s. "Mariner"	50	50
2052	120 s. "Voyager 2"	55	55
2053	170 s. "Work Package-03"	70	70
2054	250 s. Orbiting solar observer	85	85
2055	300 s. "Magellan"	90	90
2056	400 s. "Galilei"	95	95

OFFICIAL STAMPS

1965. Nos. 128 etc, optd **OFFICIAL**.

O 9	**25**	5 c. blue and orange	10	50
O10	–	10 c. multicoloured	10	50
O11	–	15 c. multicoloured	10	50
O12	–	20 c. sepia, green and blue	10	50
O13	–	30 c. black and brown	10	30
O14	–	50 c. multicoloured	15	50
O15	**33**	1 s. multicoloured	30	30
O16	–	5 s. brown, green and blue	1·75	5·50

1967. Nos. 142, etc, optd **OFFICIAL**.

O20	5 c. mauve, green and black	10	1·50
O21	10 c. brown and bistre	10	50
O22	15 c. grey, blue and black	10	1·50
O23	20 c. brown and green	10	30
O24	30 c. green and black	10	30
O36	40 c. yellow, brown and green	–	2·50
O25	50 c. multicoloured	15	80
O26	1 s. brown, blue and purple	30	1·75
O27	5 s. yellow, black and green	2·50	9·00

1973. Nos. 158 etc, optd **OFFICIAL**.

O40	**53**	5 c. green, blue and black	50	1·50
O41	–	10 c. multicoloured	65	30
O42	–	20 c. brown, yellow & blk	80	30
O43	–	40 c. multicoloured	1·25	30
O44	–	50 c. multicoloured	1·25	30
O45	–	70 c. green, orange & black	1·50	65
O46	**54**	1 s. multicoloured	1·50	30
O47	–	1 s. 50 multicoloured	3·50	2·75
O48	–	2 s. 50 multicoloured	4·00	6·00
O49	–	5 s. multicoloured	4·50	7·50

1980. Nos. 307/13 and 315/17 optd **OFFICIAL**.

O54	10 c. Type **75**	20	50
O55	20 c. Large-spotted genet	25	50
O56	40 c. Banded mongoose	30	50
O57	50 c. Ratel	30	30
O58	75 c. Large-toothed rock hyrax	40	50
O59	80 c. Leopard	55	80
O60	1 s. Impala	55	30
O66	1 s. 50 Giraffe	3·75	4·00
O61	2 s. Common zebra	85	1·75
O62	3 s. African buffalo	1·00	2·00
O63	5 s. Lion	1·50	2·75

1990. Nos. 804/12 optd **OFFICIAL**.

O70	5 s. Type **163**	10	10
O71	9 s. African emerald cuckoo	10	10
O72	13 s. Little bee eater	10	10
O73	15 s. Red bishop	10	10
O74	20 s. Bateleur	10	10
O75	25 s. Scarlet-chested sunbird	10	10
O76	30 s. African wood pigeon	10	10
O77	40 s. Type **164**	10	10
O78	70 s. Helmet guineafowl	15	20
O79	100 s. Eastern white pelican	20	25

B. For use in Zanzibar only.

Z 39 Pres. Nyerere and First Vice-Pres. Karume within Bowl of Flame

1966. 2nd Anniv of United Republic. Mult.

Z142	30 c. Type Z **39**	30	45
Z143	50 c. Hands supporting Bowl of Flame	30	45
Z144	1 s. 30 As 50 c.	30	45
Z145	2 s. 50 Type Z **39**	45	1·25

POSTAGE DUE STAMPS

The Postage Due stamps of Kenya, Uganda and Tanganyika were used in Tanganyika until 2 January, 1967.

D 1

D 2

1967.

D19	D **1**	5 c. red	15	2·00
D20		10 c. green	20	2·00
D21		20 c. blue	30	2·25
D22		30 c. brown	45	3·00
D23		40 c. purple	50	4·25
D24		1 s. orange	70	4·75

1990.

D30	D **2**	50 c. green	10	10
D31		80 c. blue	10	10
D32		1 s. brown	10	10
D33		2 s. green	10	10
D34		3 s. purple	10	10
D35		5 s. brown	10	10
D36		10 s. brown	10	10
D37		20 s. brown	10	10

APPENDIX

The following stamps have either been issued in excess of postal needs, or have not been made available to the public in reasonable quantities at face value.

1986.

Caribbean Royal Visit. Optd on previous issues. (a) On Nos. 425/8 20 s. × 2, 100 s. × 2. (b) On Nos. 430/3, 5, 10, 20, 30 s.

"Ameripex" International Stamp Exhibition, Chicago. Optd on Nos. 425/8, 20 s. × 2, 100 s. × 2.

1988.

Cent of Statue of Liberty (1986). 1, 2, 3, 4, 5, 6, 7, 8, 10, 12, 15, 18, 20, 25, 30, 35, 40, 45, 50, 60 s.

Royal Ruby Wedding. Optd on No. 378. 10 s.

125th Anniv of Red Cross. Optd on Nos. 486/7, 5, 40 s.

63rd Anniv of Rotary International in Africa. Optd on Nos. 422/3, 10 s., 17 s. 50.

TASMANIA

An island south of Australia, one of the States of the Australian Commonwealth, whose stamps it now uses.

12 pence = 1 shilling;
20 shillings = 1 pound

1

2

1853. Imperf.

3	**1**	1d. blue	£3000	£700
8	**2**	4d. orange	£1800	£350

3

7

8

1855. Imperf.

28	**3**	1d. red	80·00	15·00
34		2d. green	£120	45·00
36		4d. blue	£100	11·00
46	**7**	6d. purple	£130	50·00
41	**8**	1s. orange	£500	65·00

1864. Perf.

82	**3**	1d. red	27·00	7·00
71		2d. green	£110	38·00
72		4d. blue	70·00	11·00
143	**7**	6d. purple	24·00	12·00
141	**8**	1s. orange	75·00	38·00

11

20

1870.

159	**11**	½d. orange	2·25	1·90
156		1d. red	2·75	50
157		2d. green	3·00	50
165		3d. brown	8·00	3·00
130		4d. blue	£700	£400
226		4d. yellow	12·00	5·50
158		8d. purple	14·00	4·00
256		9d. blue	7·00	2·75
131		10d. black	23·00	17·00
149b		5s. mauve	£120	40·00

1889. Surch **Halfpenny**.

167	**11**	2½d. on 9d. blue	8·00	9·00

1889. Surch **d. 2½**.

169	**11**	2½d. on 9d. blue	5·00	3·00

1892. Various frames.

216	**20**	½d. orange and mauve	1·25	50
217		2½d. purple	2·50	1·00
218		5d. blue and brown	4·50	1·60
219		6d. violet and black	5·50	2·00
220		10d. lake and green	9·00	7·00
221		1s. red and green	6·00	1·75
222		2s. 6d. brown and blue	22·00	9·00
223		5s. purple and red	38·00	18·00
224		10s. mauve and brown	75·00	50·00
225		£1 green and yellow	£225	£150

22 Lake Marion

23 Mount Wellington

1899.

249	**22**	½d. green	1·25	20
250	**23**	1d. red	1·50	10
251b	–	2d. violet	2·50	10
232	–	2½d. blue	10·00	3·75
253	–	3d. brown	6·50	2·50
247	–	4d. orange	12·00	3·00
235	–	5d. blue	14·00	6·50
236	–	6d. lake	18·00	10·00

DESIGNS—HORIZ: 2d. Hobart; 3d. Spring River, Port Davey; 5d. Mt. Gould, Lake St. Clair; 6d. Dilston Falls. VERT: 2½d. Tasman's Arch; 4d. Russell Falls.

1904. No. 218 surch **1½d.**

244	**20**	1½d. on 5d. blue and brown	1·25	60

1912. No. 251b surch **ONE PENNY**.

260	1d. on 2d. violet	90	30

TOBAGO

An island in the British West Indies, north-east of Trinidad. From 1896 to 1913 it used the stamps of Trinidad; from 1913 there were combined issues for Trinidad and Tobago.

12 pence = 1 shilling;
20 shillings = 1 pound

1

2

1879.

1	**1**	1d. red	75·00	60·00
2		3d. blue	70·00	42·00
3		6d. orange	32·00	45·00
4		1s. green	£350	60·00
5		5s. grey	£550	£500
6		£1 mauve	£4000	

In the above issue only stamps watermarked Crown CC were issued for postal use and our prices are for stamps bearing this watermark. Stamps with watermark Crown CA are fiscals and were never admitted to postal use.

1880. No. 3 divided vertically down the centre and surch with pen and ink.

7	**1**	1d. on half of 6d. orange	£4500	£750

1880. "POSTAGE" added in design.

14	**2**	½d. lilac	1·00	12·00
20		½d. green	90	30
21		1d. red	1·50	20
16a		2½d. blue	3·75	75
10		4d. green	£180	26·00
22		4d. grey	1·00	55
11		6d. buff	£250	90·00
23		6d. brown	85	3·00
24		1s. yellow	1·25	12·00

1883. Surch in figures and words.

26	**2**	½d. on 2½d. blue	3·50	9·00
30		½d. on 4d. grey	11·00	38·00
27		½d. on 6d. buff	2·25	17·00
28		½d. on 6d. brown	85·00	£110
29		1d. on 2½d. blue	40·00	15·00
31		2½d. on 4d. grey	3·75	6·50
13		2½d. on 6d. buff	35·00	35·00

1896. Surch **½d POSTAGE**.

33	**1**	½d. on 4d. lilac and red	42·00	26·00

TOGO

A territory in west Africa, formerly a German Colony. Divided between France and Gt. Britain in 1919, the British portion being attached to the Gold Coast for administration and using the stamps of that country.

1914. Nos. 7/19 (German Colonial Types) optd **TOGO Anglo-French Occupation**.

H 1	N	3 pf. brown	£110	95·00
H 2		5 pf. green	£100	90·00
H 3		10 pf. red	£120	£100
H17		20 pf. blue	16·00	12·00
H18		25 pf. blk & red on yell	19·00	29·00
H19		30 pf. blk & orge on buff	19·00	29·00
H 7		40 pf. black and red	£225	£250
H 8		50 pf. black and purple on buff	£9000	£7000
H 9		80 pf. black & red on rose	£225	£275
H10	O	1 m. red	£5000	£2500
H11		2 m. blue	£8000	£8500
H25		3 m. black		† £38000
H26		5 m. lake and black		† £38000

1914. Nos. 1/2 surch in words.

H27	N	½d on 3 pf. brown	30·00	26·00
H28		1d. on 5 pf. green	4·00	4·25

1915. Stamps of Gold Coast (King George V) optd **TOGO ANGLO-FRENCH OCCUPATION**.

H34	½d. green	30	60
H35	1d. red	30	30
H49	2d. grey	35	45
H50	2½d. blue	45	1·50
H38	3d. purple on yellow	65	80
H52	6d. purple	55	1·00
H53	1s. black on green	1·75	3·00
H54	2s. purple and blue on blue	4·50	8·50
H55	2s. 6d. black and red on blue	4·50	7·00
H44	5s. green and red on yellow	8·00	15·00
H57a	10s. green and red on green	16·00	50·00
H58	20s. purple and black on red	£130	£140

For other Togo issues see Volume 2.

TOKELAU

Three islands situated north of Samoa. Formerly known as the Union Islands, they were administered as part of the Gilbert and Ellice Islands until transferred to New Zealand in 1925. Administered by Western Samoa (using stamps of Samoa) until they became a dependency of New Zealand in 1949. Adopted name of Tokelau in 1946.

1948. 12 pence = 1 shilling;
20 shillings = 1 pound.
1967. 100 cents or sene = 1 New Zealand dollar.

1 Atafu Village and Map

8 British Protectorate (1877)

1948.

1	1	½d. brown and purple	15	40
2	–	1d. red and green	15	30
3	–	2d. green and blue	15	30

DESIGNS: 1d. Nukunonu hut and map; 2d. Fakaofo village and map.

1953. Coronation. As T **164** of New Zealand.

4		3d. brown	2·00	2·00

1956. Surch **ONE SHILLING**.

5	1	1s. on ½d. brown and purple	1·50	2·00

1966. Arms types of New Zealand without value, surch **TOKELAU ISLANDS** and value in sterling.

6	F 6	6d. blue	40	80
7		8d. green	50	80
8		2s. pink	50	80

1967. Decimal currency. Nos. 1/3 surch.

9	–	1 c. on 1d. (No. 2)	50	60
10	–	2 c. on 2d. (No. 3)	75	1·00
11	1	10 c. on ½d. (No. 1)	1·50	2·00

1968. Arms types of New Zealand without value, surch **TOKELAU ISLANDS** and value in decimal currency.

12	F 6	3 c. lilac	30	30
13		5 c. blue	30	30
14		7 c. green	30	30
15		20 c. pink	30	40

1969. History of Tokelau Islands.

16	8	5 c. blue, yellow and black	30	10
17	–	10 c. red, yellow and black	35	10
18	–	15 c. green, yellow and black	40	15
19	–	20 c. brown, yellow and black	60	15

DESIGNS: 10 c. Annexed to Gilbert and Ellice Islands (1916); 15 c. New Zealand Administration (1925); 20 c. New Zealand Territory (1948).

1969. Christmas. As T **301** of New Zealand.

20	2 c. multicoloured	10	15

1970. Christmas. As T **314** of New Zealand.

21	2 c. multicoloured	10	20

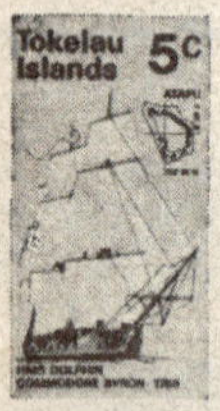

12 H.M.S. "Dolphin", 1765

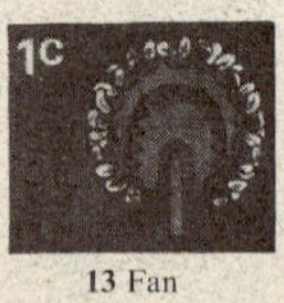

13 Fan

1970. Discovery of Tokelau Islands. Mult.

22		5 c. Type **12**	1·00	35
23		10 c. H.M.S. "Pandora", 1791	1·00	35
24		25 c. "General Jackson" (American whaling ship), 1835 (horiz)	2·50	70

1971. Handicrafts. Multicoloured.

25	1 c. Type **13**	20	20
26	2 c. Hand-bag	30	30
27	3 c. Basket	30	40
28	5 c. Hand-bag	35	65
29	10 c. Shopping-bag	35	80
30	15 c. Hand-bag	50	1·50
31	20 c. Canoe	50	1·75
32	25 c. Fishing hooks	50	1·75

14 Windmill Pump

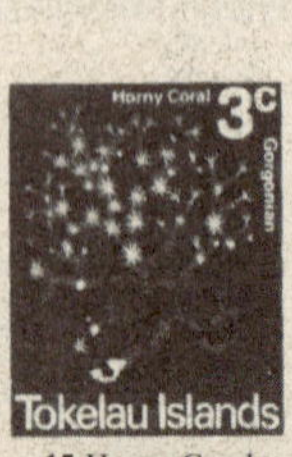

15 Horny Coral

1972. 25th Anniv of South Pacific Commission. Multicoloured.

33	5 c. Type **14**	40	60
34	10 c. Community well	50	75
35	15 c. Pest eradication	70	1·25
36	20 c. Flags of member nations	75	1·25

On No. 35 "PACIFIC" is spelt "PACFIC".

1973. Coral. Multicoloured.

37	3 c. Type **15**	80	80
38	5 c. Soft coral	80	90
39	15 c. Mushroom coral	1·25	1·50
40	25 c. Staghorn coral	1·50	1·75

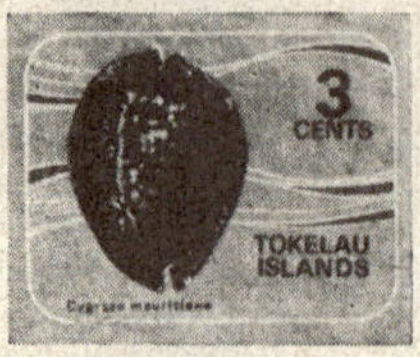

16 Hump-back Cowrie

17 Moorish Idol

1975. "Shells of the Coral Reef". Mult.

41	3 c. Type **16**	1·00	1·25
42	5 c. Tiger cowrie	1·10	1·50
43	15 c. Mole cowrie	1·75	3·00
44	25 c. Eyed cowrie	2·25	3·25

1975. Fishes. Multicoloured.

45	5 c. Type **17**	40	1·00
46	10 c. Long-nosed butterflyfish	60	1·25
47	15 c. Lined butterflyfish	70	1·50
48	25 c. Lionfish ("Red-Fire Fish")	80	1·75

18 Canoe Building

1976. Multicoloured.

49a	1 c. Type **18**	10	15
50	2 c. Reef fishing	30	1·60
51a	3 c. Weaving preparation	10	15
52a	5 c. Uma (kitchen)	10	15
53a	9 c. Carving (vert)	10	15
54a	20 c. Husking coconuts (vert)	15	20
55a	50 c. Wash day (vert)	20	20
56a	$1 Meal time (vert)	30	30

19 White Tern

20 Westminster Abbey

1977. Birds of Tokelau. Multicoloured.

57	8 c. Type **19**	40	50
58	10 c. Turnstone	45	55
59	15 c. White-capped noddy	70	1·00
60	30 c. Common noddy	90	1·60

1978. 25th Anniv of Coronation. Mult.

61	8 c. Type **20**	20	20
62	10 c. King Edward's Chair	20	20
63	15 c. Coronation regalia	30	35
64	30 c. Queen Elizabeth II	50	60

21 Canoe Race

1978. Canoe Racing.

65	21	8 c. multicoloured	20	30
66	–	12 c. multicoloured	25	35
67	–	15 c. multicoloured	30	40
68	–	30 c. multicoloured	50	70

DESIGNS: 12 c. to 30 c. Different scenes of canoe racing.

22 Rugby

1979. Local Sports. Multicoloured.

69	10 c. Type **22**	20	25
70	15 c. Cricket	55	75
71	20 c. Rugby (different)	55	80
72	30 c. Cricket (different)	70	1·00

23 Surfing

24 Pole Vaulting

1980. Water Sports. Multicoloured.

73	10 c. Type **23**	10	15
74	20 c. Surfing (different)	15	20
75	30 c. Swimming	20	25
76	50 c. Swimming (different)	25	35

1981. Sports. Multicoloured.

77	10 c. Type **24**	10	10
78	20 c. Volleyball	20	20
79	30 c. Athletics (different)	25	30
80	50 c. Volleyball (different)	30	35

25 Wood Carving

26 Octopus Lure

1982. Handicrafts. Multicoloured.

81	10 s. Type **25**	10	15
82	22 s. Bow drilling sea shell	15	30
83	34 s. Bowl finishing	20	40
84	60 s. Basket weaving	35	70

1982. Fishing Methods. Multicoloured.

85	5 s. Type **26**	15	10
86	18 s. Multiple-hook fishing	35	20
87	23 s. Ruvettus fishing	40	25
88	34 s. Netting flying fish	45	30
89	63 s. Noose fishing	55	40
90	75 s. Bonito fishing	60	45

27 Outrigger Canoe

1983. Transport. Multicoloured.

91	5 s. Type **27**	10	10
92	18 s. Wooden whaleboat	15	15
93	23 s. Aluminium whaleboat	15	20
94	34 s. "Alia" (fishing catamaran)	25	25
95	63 s. "Frysna" (freighter)	35	40
96	75 s. Grumman MacKinnon Goose flying boat	45	50

28 Javelin Throwing

1983. Traditional Pastimes. Multicoloured.

97	5 s. Type **28**	10	10
98	18 s. String game	15	15
99	23 s. Fire making	15	20
100	34 s. Shell throwing	25	25
101	63 s. Hand-ball game	35	40
102	75 s. Mass wrestling	45	50

29 Planting and Harvesting

30 Convict Tang ("Manini")

1984. Copra Industry. Multicoloured.

103	48 s. Type **29**	30	40
104	48 s. Husking and splitting	30	40
105	48 s. Drying	30	40
106	48 s. Bagging	30	40
107	48 s. Shipping	30	40

1984. Fishes. Multicoloured.

108	1 s. Type **30**	15	10
109	2 s. Flyingfish ("Hahave")	15	10
110	5 s. Surge wrasse ("Uloulo")	15	10
111	9 s. Unicornfish ("Ume ihu")	20	10
112	23 s. Wrasse ("Lafilafi")	40	20
113	34 s. Red snapper ("Fagamea")	50	25
114	50 s. Yellow-finned tuna ("Kakahi")	70	40
115	75 s. Oilfish ("Palu po")	1·00	55
116	$1 Grey shark ("Mokoha")	1·50	70
117	$2 Black marlin ("Hakula")	2·00	1·40

31 "Ficus tinctoria" ("Mati")

1985. Native Trees. Multicoloured.

118	5 c. Type **31**	10	10
119	18 c. "Morinda citrifolia" ("Nonu")	15	15
120	32 c. Breadfruit tree ("Ulu")	20	25
121	48 c. "Pandanus tectorius" ("Fala")	35	40
122	60 c. "Cordia subcordata" ("Kanava")	40	45
123	75 s. Coconut palm ("Niu")	50	55

32 Administration Centre, Atafu

1985. Tokelau Architecture (1st series). Public Buildings. Multicoloured.

124	5 c. Type **32**	10	10
125	18 c. Administration Centre, Nukunonu	15	15
126	32 c. Administration Centre, Fakaofo	20	25
127	48 c. Congregational Church, Atafu	35	40
128	60 c. Catholic Church, Nukunonu	40	45
129	75 c. Congregational Church, Fakaofo	50	55

See also Nos. 130/5.

33 Atafu Hospital

1986. Tokelau Architecture (2nd series). Hospitals and Schools. Multicoloured.

130	5 c. Type **33**	20	15
131	18 c. St. Joseph's Hospital, Nukunonu	20	15
132	32 c. Fenuafala Hospital, Fakaofo	30	30
133	48 c. Matauala School, Atafu	45	45
134	60 c. Matiti School, Nukunonu	50	60
135	75 c. Fenuafala School, Fakaofo	80	90

34 Coconut Crab

1986. Agricultural Livestock. Multicoloured.

136	5 c. Type **34**	10	10
137	18 c. Pigs	15	15
138	32 c. Chickens	25	25
139	48 c. Reef hawksbill turtle	40	40
140	60 c. Goats	45	45
141	75 c. Ducks	60	60

35 "Scaevola taccada" ("Gahu")

1987. Tokelau Flora. Multicoloured.

142	5 c. Type **35**	45	50
143	18 c. "Hernandia nymphaeifolia" ("Puka")	70	80
144	32 c. "Pandanus tectorius" ("Higano")	1·00	1·10
145	48 c. "Gardenia taitensis" (Tialetiale")	1·25	1·40
146	60 c. "Pemphis acidula" ("Gagie")	1·60	1·75
147	75 c. "Guettarda speciosa" ("Puapua")	1·75	1·90

36 Javelin Throwing

1987. Tokelau Olympic Sports. Multicoloured.

148	5 c. Type **36**	25	30
149	18 c. Shot-putting	45	50
150	32 c. Long jumping	70	80
151	48 c. Hurdling	85	1·10
152	60 c. Sprinting	1·25	1·75
153	75 c. Wrestling	1·50	1·90

37 Small Boat Flotilla in Sydney Harbour

1988. Bicentenary of Australian Settlement and "Sydpex '88" National Stamp Exhibition, Sydney. Multicoloured.

154	50 c. Type **37**	1·75	1·90
155	50 c. Sailing ships and liners	1·75	1·90
156	50 c. Sydney skyline and Opera House	1·75	1·90
157	50 c. Sydney Harbour Bridge	1·75	1·90
158	50 c. Sydney waterfront	1·75	1·90

Nos. 154/8 were printed together, se-tenant, forming a composite aerial view of the re-enactment of First Fleet's arrival.

38 Island Maps and Ministerial Representatives

1988. Political Development. Multicoloured.

159	5 c. Type **38** (administration transferred to N.Z. Foreign Affairs Ministry, 1975)	25	35
160	18 c. General Fono (island assembly) meeting, 1977	35	40
161	32 c. Arms of New Zealand (first visit by New Zealand Prime Minister, 1985)	60	70
162	48 c. U.N. logo (first visit by U.N. representative, 1976)	75	85
163	60 c. Canoe and U.N. logo (first Tokelau delegation to U.N., 1987)	90	1·00
164	75 c. Secretary and N.Z. flag (first islander appointed as Official Secretary, 1987)	1·00	1·10

39 Three Wise Men in Canoe and Star

1988. Christmas. Designs showing Christmas in Tokelau. Multicoloured.

165	5 c. Type **39**	25	25
166	20 c. Tokelau Nativity	30	30
167	40 c. Flight to Egypt by canoe	60	60
168	60 c. Children's presents	80	90
169	70 c. Christ Child in Tokelauan basket	90	1·00
170	$1 Christmas parade	1·10	1·25

40 Launching Outrigger Canoe

1989. Food Gathering. Multicoloured.

171	50 c. Type **40**	1·25	1·40
172	50 c. Paddling canoe away from shore	1·25	1·40
173	50 c. Fishing punt and sailing canoe	1·25	1·40
174	50 c. Canoe on beach	1·25	1·40
175	50 c. Loading coconuts into canoe	1·25	1·40
176	50 c. Tokelauans with produce	1·25	1·40

Nos. 171/3 and 174/6 were each printed together, se-tenant, forming composite designs.

41 Basketwork

1990. Women's Handicrafts. Multicoloured.

177	5 c. Type **41**	45	45
178	20 c. Preparing cloth	85	85
179	40 c. Tokelau fabrics	1·25	1·25
180	60 c. Mat weaving	1·75	2·00
181	80 c. Weaving palm fronds	2·50	2·75
182	$1 Basket making	2·75	3·25

42 Man with Adze and Wood Blocks

1990. Men's Handicrafts. Multicoloured.

183	50 c. Type **42**	1·50	1·75
184	50 c. Making fishing boxes	1·50	1·75
185	50 c. Fixing handles to fishing boxes	1·50	1·75
186	50 c. Two men decorating fishing boxes	1·50	1·75
187	50 c. Canoe building (two men)	1·50	1·75
188	50 c. Canoe building (three men)	1·50	1·75

43 Swimming

44 "Santa Maria"

1992. Olympic Games, Barcelona. Mult.

189	40 c. Type **43**	60	60
190	60 c. Long jumping	80	90
191	$1 Volleyball	1·60	1·75
192	$1.80 Running	2·25	2·75

1992. 500th Anniv of Discovery of America by Columbus. Multicoloured.

193	40 c. Type **44**	70	70
194	60 c. Christopher Columbus	1·00	1·10
195	$1.20 Fleet of Columbus	2·25	2·50
196	$1.80 Columbus landing in the New World	3·25	3·50

45 Queen Elizabeth II in 1953

1993. 40th Anniv of Coronation. Mult.

197	25 c. Type **45**	60	60
198	40 c. Prince Philip	80	80
199	$1 Queen Elizabeth II in 1993	1·40	1·60
200	$2 Queen Elizabeth II and Prince Philip	2·50	2·75

46 Bristle-thighed Curlew

1993. Birds of Tokelau. Multicoloured.

201	25 c. Type **46**	60	60
202	40 c. Red-tailed tropic bird	90	90
203	$1 Eastern reef heron	1·60	1·60
204	$2 American golden plover	2·25	3·00

47 Great Egret ("White Heron")

1994. "Philakorea '94" International Stamp Exhibition, Seoul.

206	**47** $2 multicoloured	2·50	2·75

48 Model Outrigger Canoe

1994. Handicrafts. Multicoloured.

208	5 c. Type **48**	10	10
209	25 c. Plaited fan	15	20
210	40 c. Plaited baskets	25	30
211	50 c. Fishing box	30	35
212	80 c. Water bottle	50	55
213	$1 Fishing hook	65	70
214	$2 Coconut gourds	1·25	1·40
215	$5 Shell necklace	3·25	3·50

50 Pacific Pigeon on Branch

1995. Endangered Species. Pacific Pigeon. Multicoloured.

220	25 c. Type **50**	45	45
221	40 c. On branch (different)	70	70
222	$1 On branch with berries	1·40	1·40
223	$2 Chick in nest	2·40	2·75

51 Long Nosed Butterfly-fish

52 "Danaus plexippus"

1995. Reef Fishes. Multicoloured.

224	25 c. Type **51**	45	45
225	40 c. Emperor angelfish	70	70
226	$1 Moorish idol	1·40	1·60
227	$2 Lined butterflyfish	2·40	2·75

1995. Butterflies and Moths. Multicoloured.

230	25 c. Type **52**	55	55
231	40 c. "Precis villida samoensis"	80	80
232	$1 "Hypolimnas bolina"	1·75	2·00
233	$2 "Euploea lewenii"	3·00	3·25

53 Hawksbill Turtle

1995. Year of the Sea Turtle. Multicoloured.

234	25 c. Type **53**	55	55
235	40 c. Leatherback turtle	80	80
236	$1 Green turtle	1·75	2·00
237	$2 Loggerhead turtle	3·00	3·25

55 Queen Elizabeth II and Nukunonu

1996. 70th Birthday of Queen Elizabeth II. Each incorporating a different photograph of the Queen. Multicoloured.

240	40 c. Type **55**	50	50
241	$1 Atafu at night	1·40	1·50
242	$1.25 Atafu	1·60	1·75
243	$2 Atafu village	2·00	2·50

56 Fraser's Dolphin

1996. Dolphins. Multicoloured.

246	40 c. Type **56**	85	85
247	$1 Common dolphin	2·25	2·25
248	$1.25 Striped dolphin	2·50	2·50
249	$2 Spotted dolphin	3·50	3·50

57 Mole Cowrie

1996. Sea Shells. Multicoloured.

250	40 c. Type **57**	60	60
251	$1 Humpback cowrie	1·50	1·50
252	$1.25 Eyed cowrie	1·60	1·75
253	$2 Tiger cowrie	2·25	2·75

59 Humpback Whale

1997. Humpback Whales. Multicoloured.

259	40 c. Type **59**	50	45
260	$1 Family of humpback whales	1·00	1·00
261	$1.25 Humpback whale feeding	1·40	1·50
262	$2 Humpback whale and calf	2·00	2·25

60 Church by Lagoon

1997. 50th Anniv of South Pacific Commission. Multicoloured.

264	40 c. Type **60**	45	45
265	$1 Boy looking across lagoon	90	90
266	$1.25 Bungalow on small island	1·25	1·50
267	$2 Tokelau from the air	1·90	2·25

61 Gorgonian Coral and Emperor Angelfish

1997. Pacific Year of the Coral Reef. Multicoloured.

268	$1 Type **61**	90	1·00
269	$1 Soft coral	90	1·00
270	$1 Mushroom coral	90	1·00
271	$1 Staghorn coral	90	1·00
272	$1 Staghorn coral and moorish idols	90	1·00

Nos. 268/72 were printed together, se-tenant, with the backgrounds forming a composite design.

1998. Diana, Princess of Wales Commemoration. As T **91** of Kiribati. Multicoloured.

275	$1 Carrying yellow bouquet	80	85

64 "Oryctes rhinoceros"

1998. Beetles. Multicoloured.

278	40 c. Type **64**	35	35
279	$1 "Tribolium castaneum"	80	80
280	$1.25 "Coccinella repanda"	95	95
281	$2 "Amarygmus hydrophiloides"	1·50	1·50

65 "Ipomoea pes-caprae"

1998. Tropical Flowers. Multicoloured.

283	40 c. Type **65**	25	30
284	$1 "Ipomoea littoralis"	65	70
285	$1.25 "Scaevola taccada"	80	85
286	$2 "Thespesia populnea"	1·25	1·40

TONGA

(Or Friendly Is.). A group of islands in the S. Pacific Ocean. An independent Polynesian kingdom formerly under British protection, Tonga became a member of the Commonwealth in June 1970.

1886. 12 pence = 1 shilling;
20 shillings = 1 pound.
1967. 100 seniti = 1 pa'anga.

1 King George I

1886.

1b	**1**	1d. red	10·00	3·25
2b		2d. violet	28·00	2·75
3ab		6d. blue	26·00	2·25
9		6d. orange	15·00	26·00
4ba		1s. green	55·00	3·25

1891. Surch with value in words.

5	**1**	4d. on 1d. red	2·75	11·00
6		8d. on 2d. violet	35·00	90·00

1891. Optd with stars in upper right and lower left corners.

7	**1**	1d. red	40·00	48·00
8		2d. violet	65·00	38·00

5 Arms of Tonga

6 King George I

1892.

10	**5**	1d. red	12·00	17·00
11	**6**	2d. olive	14·00	15·00
12	**5**	4d. brown	48·00	70·00
13	**6**	8d. mauve	55·00	£140
14		1s. brown	75·00	£110

1893. Surch in figures.

15	**5**	½d. on 1d. blue	23·00	25·00
16	**6**	2½d. on 2d. green	14·00	12·00
18		7½d. on 6d. red	24·00	75·00

1893. Surch **FIVE PENCE.**

17	**5**	5d. on 4d. orange	4·00	6·50

1894. Surch vert **SURCHARGE.** and value in words.

21	**5**	½d. on 4d. brown	1·75	7·00
22	**6**	½d. on 1s. brown	2·00	11·00
25		1d. on 2d. blue	42·00	22·00

1894. Surch vert **SURCHARGE.** and value in figures.

26b	**6**	1½d. on 2d. blue	42·00	27·00
27		2½d. on 2d. blue	40·00	45·00
23		2½d. on 8d. mauve	5·00	8·00
24b	**1**	2½d. on 1s. green	15·00	35·00
28b	**6**	7½d. on 2d. blue	60·00	45·00

13 King George II

15 Arms

16 Ovava Tree, Kana-Kubolu

21 View of Haapai

1895. Surch **SURCHARGE** and new value.

29	**13**	½d. on 2½d. red	30·00	32·00
30		1d. on 2½d. red	50·00	32·00
31		7½d. on 2½d. red	50·00	50·00

1895.

32	**13**	1d. green	16·00	26·00
33		2½d. red	20·00	20·00
34		5d. blue	20·00	48·00
35		7½d. yellow	27·00	42·00

1896. Nos. 26a and 28a surch with typewritten **Half-Penny-** and Tongan inscription.

36Aa	**6**	½d. on 1½d. on 2d. blue	£400	£400
37A		½d. on 7½d. on 2d. blue	80·00	£100

1897.

38a	**15**	½d. blue	70	2·50
55		½d. green	90	1·25
39	**16**	1d. black and red	80	80
40a	–	2d. sepia and bistre	13·00	3·50
43b	–	2½d. black and blue	3·50	1·60
78	–	3d. black and green	40	2·00
45	–	4d. green and purple	3·75	4·00
46	–	5d. black and orange	32·00	13·00
79	–	6d. red	2·00	2·00
48	–	7½d. black and green	15·00	23·00
49	–	10d. black and red	42·00	42·00
50	–	1s. black and brown	14·00	7·50
51a	**21**	2s. black and blue	19·00	27·00
81	–	2s. 6d. purple	25·00	20·00
82	–	5s. black and red	16·00	42·00

DESIGNS—VERT (as Type **26**): 2, 2½, 5, 7½, 10d., 1s. King George II. (As Type **16**): 6d. Coral. (As Type **21**): 2s. 6d. Red shining parrot. HORIZ (as Type **16**): 3d. Prehistoric trilith at Haamonga; 4d. Breadfruit. (As Type **21**): 5s. Vavau Harbour.

1899. Royal Wedding. Optd **T – L 1 June, 1899.**

54	**16**	1d. black and red	27·00	55·00

26 Queen Salote **29**

1920.

56	**26**	1½d. black	30	2·75
57		2d. purple and violet	7·00	13·00
76		2d. black and purple	3·00	1·75
58		2½d. black and blue	4·50	32·00
77		2½d. blue	1·00	1·25
60		5d. black and orange	3·25	4·50
61		7½d. black and green	1·75	1·75
62		10d. black and red	2·50	4·75
63		1s. black and brown	1·25	2·25

1923. Nos. 46 and 48/82 surch **TWO PENCE PENI-E-UA.**

64	2d. on 5d. black and orange	1·00	85
65	2d. on 7½d. black and green	13·00	23·00
66	2d. on 10d. black and red	7·00	45·00
67	2d. on 1s. black and brown	40·00	22·00
68a	2d. on 2s. black and blue	8·50	4·50
69	2d. on 2s. 6d. purple	27·00	6·50
70a	2d. on 5s. black and red	3·00	2·50

1938. 20th Anniv of Queen Salote's Accession. Dated "1918–1938" at foot.

71	**29**	1d. black and red	60	3·00
72		2d. black and purple	6·50	2·25
73		2½d. black and blue	6·50	3·00

1944. Silver Jubilee of Queen Salote's Accession. Tablet at foot dated "1918–1943".

83	**29**	1d. black and red	15	70
84		2d. black and violet	15	70
85		3d. black and green	15	70
86		6d. black and orange	65	1·40
87		1s. black and brown	55	1·40

1949. 75th Anniv of U.P.U. As T **20/23** of Antigua.

88	2½d. blue	40	50
89	3d. olive	1·60	2·50
90	6d. red	50	30
91	1s. brown	50	35

31 Queen Salote **32**

1950. 50th Birthday of Queen Salote.

92	**31**	1d. red	40	1·50
93	**32**	5d. green	40	1·75
94	–	1s. violet	40	2·00

DESIGN—VERT: 1s. Half-length portrait of Queen.

34 Map **35** Palace, Nuku'alofa

1951. 50th Anniv of Treaty of Friendship with Great Britain.

95	**34**	½d. green	15	2·00
96	**35**	1d. black and red	15	1·50
97	–	2½d. green and brown	30	2·00
98	–	3d. yellow and blue	1·25	2·00
99	–	5d. red and green	75	70
100	–	1s. orange and violet	75	70

DESIGNS—HORIZ: 2½d. Beach scene; 5d. Flag and island; 1s. Arms of Tonga and Great Britain. VERT: 3d. H.M.N.Z.S. "Bellona".

40 Royal Palace, Nuku'alofa

1953.

101	**40**	1d. black and brown	10	10
102	–	1½d. blue and green	10	10
103	–	2d. turquoise and black	75	20
104	–	3d. blue and green	50	20
105	–	3½d. yellow and red	50	70
106	–	4d. yellow and red	1·00	10
107	–	5d. blue and brown	50	10
108	–	6d. black and blue	50	30
109	–	8d. green and violet	1·00	40
110	–	1s. blue and black	70	10
111	–	2s. olive and brown	4·00	60
112	–	5s. yellow and lilac	24·00	6·50
113	–	10s. yellow and black	6·00	6·50
114	–	£1 yellow, red and blue	8·00	6·50

DESIGNS HORIZ: 1½d. Shore fishing with throw-net; 2d. "Hifofua" and "Aoniu" (ketches); 3½d. Map of Tongatapu; 4d. Vava'u Harbour; 5d. Post Office Nuku'alofa; 6d. Aerodrome, Fua'amotu; 8d. "Matua" (inter-island freighter) at Nuku'alofa Wharf; 2s. Lifuka, Ha'apai; 5s. Mutiny on the "Bounty". VERT: 3d. Swallows' Cave, Vava'u; 1s. Map of Tonga Islands; 10s. Queen Salote; £1 Arms of Tonga.

54 Stamp of 1886

1961. 75th Anniv of Tongan Postal Service.

115	**54**	1d. red and orange	10	10
116	–	2d. blue	75	35
117	–	4d. turquoise	15	35
118	–	5d. violet	75	35
119	–	1s. brown	75	35

DESIGNS: 2d. Whaling ship and whaleboat; 4d. Queen Salote and Post Office, Nuku'alofa; 5d. "Aoniu II" (inter-island freighter); 1s. Douglas DC-4 mail plane over Tongatapu.

1962. Centenary of Emancipation. Stamps of 1953 and No. 117 optd **1862 TAU'ATAINA EMANCIPATION 1962** or surch also.

120	1d. black and brown	10	40
121	4d. turquoise (No. 117)	10	50
122	5d. blue and brown	15	50
123	6d. black and blue	20	60
124	8d. green and violet	40	1·00
125	1s. blue and black	20	60
126	2s. on 3d. blue and green	40	2·75
127	5s. yellow and lilac	5·50	2·75

60 "Protein Foods"

1963. Freedom from Hunger.

128	**60**	11d. blue	50	15

61 Coat of Arms

1963. First Polynesian Gold Coinage Commem. Circular designs backed with paper, inscr overall "TONGA THE FRIENDLY ISLANDS". Imperf. (a) Postage ¼ koula coin. Diameter $1\frac{5}{8}$ in.

129	**61**	1d. red on gold	10	10
130	A	2d blue on gold	10	10
131	**61**	6d. green on gold	15	15
132	A	9d purple on gold	15	15
133	**61**	1s. 6d. violet on gold	25	25
134	A	2s green on gold	30	30

(b) Air (i) ½ koula coin. Diameter $2\frac{1}{8}$ in.

135	B	10d. red on gold	20	20
136	**61**	2s. 4d. green on gold	20	20
137	B	1s. 1d. blue on gold	20	20

(ii) 1 koula coin. Diameter $3\frac{1}{8}$ in.

138	B	2s 1d. purple on gold	35	30
139	**61**	2s. 4d. green on gold	40	35
140	B	2s. 9d. violet on gold	40	40

DESIGNS: A, Queen Salote (head); B. Queen Salote (full length).

64 Red Cross Emblem

1963. Centenary of Red Cross.
141 **64** 2d. red and black 25 10
142 11d. red and blue 50 1·25

65 Queen Salote

66 Map of Tongatapu
(⅔-size illustration)

1964. Pan-Pacific South-East Asia Women's Assn Meeting, Nuku'alofa. T **65/66** backed with paper inscr overall "TONGA THE FRIENDLY ISLANDS". Imperf.
143 **65** 3d. pink (postage) 15 15
144 9d. blue 20 20
145 2s. green 35 35
146 3s. lilac 65 70
147 **66** 10d. turquoise (air) 20 15
148 1s. 2d. black 30 25
149 3s. 6d. red 50 55
150 6s. 6d. violet 85 1·25

1965. "Gold Coin" stamps of 1963 surch and with star over old value.
151 **61** 1s. 3d. on 1s. 6d. (postage) 15 15
152 A 1s. 9d. on 9d. 15 20
153 **61** 2s. 6d. on 6d. 20 35
154 5s. on 1d. 14·00 17·00
155 A 5s. on 2d. 2·50 3·25
156 5s. on 2s. 60 75
157 B 2s. 3d. on 10d. (air) 15 25
158 **61** 2s. 9d. on 11d. 20 35
159 B 4s 6d. on 2s. 1d. 10·00 13·00
160 **61** 4s. 6d. on 2s. 4d. 10·00 13·00
161 B 4s 6d. on 2s. 9d. 7·00 8·00

1966. Centenary of Tupou College and Secondary Education. Nos. 115/6 and 118/9 optd or surch **1866–1966 TUPOU COLLEGE & SECONDARY EDUCATION.**
162 **54** 1d. red & orange (postage) 10 10
163 3d. on 1d. red and orange 10 10
164 – 6d. on 2d. blue 10 10
165 – 1s. 2d. on 2d. blue 20 10
166 – 2s. on 2d. blue 40 10
167 – 3s. on 2d. blue 40 15

As above opt but with additional **AIRMAIL** and **CENTENARY.**
168 – 5d. violet (air) 10 10
169 **54** 10d. on 1d. red and brown 10 10
170 – 1s. brown 10 10
171 – 2s. 9d. on 2d. blue 40 15
172 – 3s. 6d. on 5d. violet 45 15
173 – 4s. 6d. on 1s. brown 50 15

1966. Queen Salote Commemoration. Nos. 143/4 and 147/8 optd. (a) **IN MEMORIAM QUEEN SALOTE 1900 + 1965.** (b) **1900 1965** + and laurel spray or surch also. Inscr and new figures of value in first colour and obliterating shapes in second colour given.
174 **65** 3d. (silver and blue) (post) 10 10
175 5d. on 9d. (silver and black) 15 10
176 9d. (silver and black) 20 10
177 1s. 7d. on 3d. (silver and blue) 50 40
178 3s. 6d. on 9d. (silver and black) 70 60
179 6s. 6d. on 3d. (silver and blue) 1·25 1·40
180 **66** 10d. (silver and black) (air) 20 10
181 1s. 2d. (black and gold) 25 20
182 4s. on 10d. (silver and black) 80 60
183 5s. 6d. on 1s. 2d. (black and gold) 1·10 1·25
184 10s. 6d. on 1s. 2d. (gold and black) 1·50 1·75

1967. Various stamps surch **SENITI** or **Seniti** and value. (a) Postage.
185 1 s. on 1d. (No. 101) 10 10
229 2 s. on 4d. (No. 106) 10 10
230 3 s. on 3d. (No. 104) 10 10
187 3 s. on 5d. (No. 107) 10 10
231 4 s. on 5d. (No. 107) 10 10
232 5 s. on 2d. (No. 108) 10 10
189 5 s. on 3½d. (No. 105) 10 10
233 6 s. on 6d. (No. 108) 10 10
190 6 s. on 8d. (No. 109) 30 10
191 7 s. on 1½d. (No. 102) 10 10
192 8 s. on 6d. (No. 108) 30 10
235 8 s. on 8d. (No. 109) 10 15
193 9 s. on 3d. (No. 104) 15 15
236 9 s. on 3½d. (No. 105) 20 20
194 10 s. on 1s. (No. 110) 15 15
195 11 s. on 3d. on 1d. (No. 163) 30 20
238 20 s. on 5s. (No. 112) 90 40
196 21 s. on 3s. on 2d. (No. 167) 25 35
197 23 s. on 1d. (No. 101) 25 35
198 30 s. on 2s. (No. 111) 2·25 2·50
199 30 s. on 2s. (No. 111) 2·50 3·00
200 50 s. on 6d. (No. 108) 1·25 1·75
201 60 s. on 2d. (No. 103) 1·50 2·00
239 2 p. on 2s. (No. 111) 1·50 2·25

(b) Air. Surch with **AIRMAIL** added.
240 11 s. on 10s. (No. 113) 25 25
241 21 s. on 10s. (No. 113) 40 40
242 23 s. on 10s. (No. 113) 40 40

74 Coat of Arms (reverse)

1967. Coronation of King Taufa'ahau IV. Circular designs backed with paper inscr overall "TONGA, THE FRIENDLY ISLANDS" etc. Imperf.

Sizes:
(a) Diameter $1\frac{1}{2}$ in. (d) Diameter $2\frac{3}{10}$ in.
(b) Diameter $1\frac{7}{10}$ in. (e) Diameter $2\frac{7}{10}$ in.
(c) Diameter 2 in. (f) Diameter $2\frac{6}{10}$ in.

202 **74** 1 s. orange & bl (b) (post) 10 10
203 A 2 s. blue and mauve (c) 10 10
204 **74** 4 s. green and purple (d) 10 10
205 A 15 s. turquoise & violet (e) 30 25
206 **74** 28 s. black and purple (a) 70 60
207 A 50 s. red and blue (c) 1·00 1·00
208 **74** 1 p. blue and red (f) 1·75 2·00
209 A 7 s. red & black (b) (air) 15 10
210 **74** 9 s. purple and green (c) 15 10
211 A 11 s. blue and orange (d) 20 15
212 **74** 21 s. black and green (e) 40 30
213 A 23 s. purple & green (a) 55 45
214 **74** 29 s. blue and green (c) 70 60
215 A 2 p. purple and orange (f) 2·50 2·75
DESIGN: A King Taufa'ahau IV (obverse).
The commemorative coins depicted in reverse (Type **74**) are inscribed in various denominations as follows: 1 s. —"20 SENITI"; 4 s. —"PA'ANGA"; 9 s. —"50 SENITI"; 21 s. —"TWO PA'ANGA"; 28 s. —"QUARTER HAU"; 29 s. —"HALF HAU"; 1 p. —"HAU".

1967. Arrival of U.S. Peace Corps in Tonga. As Nos. 101/13 but imperf in different colours and surch **The Friendly Islands welcome the United States Peace Corps** and new value (or $ only).
216 1 s. on 1d. black & yellow (postage) 10 10
217 2 s. on 2d. blue and red 10 10
218 3 s. on 3d. brown and yellow 10 10
219 4 s. on 4d. violet and yellow 10 10
220 5 s. on 5d. green and yellow 10 10
221 10 s. on 1s. red and yellow 10 10
222 20 s. on 2s. red and blue 30 15
223 50 s. on 5s. sepia and yellow 1·00 35
224 1 p. on 10s. yellow 70 55
225 11 s. on 3½d. blue (air) 15 10
226 21 s. on 1½d. green 30 20
227 23 s. on 3½d. blue 30 20

1968. 50th Birthday of King Taufa'ahua IV. Nos. 202/15 optd **H.M'S BIRTHDAY 4 JULY 1968.**
243 **74** 1 s. orange and blue (post) 10 10
244 A 2 s. blue and mauve 10 10
245 **74** 4 s. green and purple 15 10
246 A 15 s. turquoise and violet 40 15
247 **74** 28 s. black and purple 80 30
248 A 50 s. red and blue 1·60 80
249 **74** 1 p. blue and red 3·00 2·50
250 A 7 s. red and black (air) 20 10
251 **74** 9 s. purple and green 25 10
252 A 11 s. blue and orange 30 10
253 **74** 21 s. black and green 65 25
254 A 23 s. purple and green 65 25
255 **74** 29 s. blue and green 85 35
256 A 2 p. purple and orange 5·50 4·25

1968. South Pacific Games Field and Track Trials. Port Moresby, New Guinea. As Nos. 101/13 surch **Friendly Islands Field & Track Trials South Pacific Games Port Moresby 1969** and value.
257 5 s. on 5d. green & yell (post) 10 10
258 10 s. on 1s. red and yellow 10 10
259 15 s. on 2s. red and blue 15 15
260 25 s. on 2d. blue and red 20 15
261 50 s. on 1d. black and yellow 35 35
262 75 s. on 10 s. orange & yellow 60 50
263 6 s. on 6d. black & yellow (air) 10 10
264 7 s. on 4d. violet and yellow 10 10
265 8 s. on 8d. black and yellow 10 10
266 9 s. on 1½d. green 10 10
267 11 s. on 3d. brown and yellow 15 10
268 21 s. on 3½d. blue 20 15
269 38 s. on 5s. sepia and yellow 1·00 50
270 1 p. on 10s. yellow 70 70

1969. Emergency Provisionals. Various stamps (Nos. 273/6 are imperf and in different colours) surch. (a) Postage.
271 1 s. on 1s. 2d. blue (No. 165) 1·50 2·00
272 1 s. on 2s. on 3d. blue (No. 166) 1·50 2·00
273 1 s. on 6d. black and yellow (No. 108) 50 50
274 2 s. on 3½d. blue (No. 105) 55 50
275 3 s. on 1½d. green (No. 102) 55 50
276 4 s. on 8d. black and yellow (No. 109) 80 80

(b) Air. Nos. 171/3 surch.
277 1 s. on 2s. 9d. on 2d. blue 1·50 2·00
278 1 s. on 3s. 6d. on 5d. violet 1·50 2·00
279 1 s. on 4s. 6d. on 1s. brown 1·50 2·00

83 Banana

1969. Coil stamps. Self-adhesive.
280 **83** 1 s. red, black and yellow 60 70
281 2 s. green, black and yellow 70 80
282 3 s. violet, black and yellow 80 90
283 4 s. blue, black and yellow 90 1·00
284 5 s. green, black and yellow 1·00 1·25
See also Nos. 325/9, 413/17, 657/89, O45/9, O82/6 and O169/83.

84 Putting the Shot

1969. 3rd South Pacific Games, Port Moresby. Imperf. Self-adhesive.
285 **84** 1 s. black, red & buff (post) 10 10
286 3 s. green, red and buff 10 10
287 6 s. blue, red and buff 10 10
288 10 s. violet, red and buff 10 10
289 30 s. blue, red and buff 15 20
290 – 9 s. black, violet and orange (air) 10 10
291 – 11 s. black, blue and orange 10 10
292 – 20 s. black, green & orange 15 15
293 – 60 s. black, red and orange 50 65
294 – 1 p. black, green & orange 80 1·25
DESIGN: Nos. 290/4, Boxing.

86 Oil Derrick and Map

1969. First Oil Search in Tonga. Imperf. Self-adhesive.
295 **86** 3 s. multicoloured (postage) 15 10
296 7 s. multicoloured 20 15
297 20 s. multicoloured 50 40
298 25 s. multicoloured 55 45
299 35 s. multicoloured 80 80
300 – 9 s. multicoloured (air) 30 20
301 – 10 s. multicoloured 30 20
302 – 24 s. multicoloured 60 45
303 – 29 s. multicoloured 70 70
304 – 38 s. multicoloured 80 80
DESIGN: Nos. 300/4, Oil derrick and island of Tongatapu.

87 Members of the British and Tongan Royal Families

1970. Royal Visit. Imperf. Self-adhesive.
305 **87** 3 s. multicoloured (postage) 20 15
306 5 s. multicoloured 25 15
307 10 s. multicoloured 40 30
308 25 s. multicoloured 1·00 65
309 50 s. multicoloured 2·00 1·75
310 – 7 s. multicoloured (air) 35 20
311 – 9 s. multicoloured 40 30
312 – 24 s. multicoloured 1·00 65
313 – 29 s. multicoloured 1·25 70
314 – 38 s. multicoloured 1·50 90
DESIGN: Nos. 310/14, Queen Elizabeth II and King Taufu'aha Tupou IV.

89 Book, Tongan Rulers and Flag
(⅗-size illustration)

1970. Entry into British Commonwealth. Imperf. Self-adhesive.
315 **89** 3 s. multicoloured (postage) 10 15
316 7 s. multicoloured 15 20
317 15 s. multicoloured 35 20
318 25 s. multicoloured 45 25
319 50 s. multicoloured 75 85
320 – 9 s. blue, gold and red (air) 15 20
321 – 10 s. purple, gold and blue 15 20
322 – 24 s. yellow, gold and green 45 30
323 – 29 s. blue, gold and red 50 30
324 – 38 s. yellow, gold and green 60 40
DESIGN—"Star" shaped (size 44 × 51 mm): Nos. 320/24, Star and King Taufa'ahua Tupou IV.

90 Coconut

1970. Coil stamps. Imperf. Self-adhesive. (a) As T **83** but colours changed.
325 **83** 1 s. yellow, purple & black 45 50
326 2 s. yellow, blue and black 55 60
327 3 s. yellow, brown & black 55 60
328 4 s. yellow, green and black 55 60
329 5 s. yellow, red and black 60 65

(b) Multicoloured; colour of face values given.
330 **90** 6 s. red 70 80
331 7 s. purple 75 85
332 8 s. violet 85 95
333 9 s. green 95 1·10
334 10 s. orange 95 1·10

91 "Red Cross"

1970. Centenary of British Red Cross. Imperf. Self-adhesive.
335 **91** 3 s. red, black and green (postage) 10 10
336 7 s. red, black and blue 15 15
337 15 s. red, black and purple 40 40
338 25 s. red, black and blue 70 70
339 75 s. red, black and brown 4·50 4·50
340 – 9 s. red and turquoise (air) 20 20
341 – 10 s. red and purple 20 20
342 – 18 s. red and green 50 50
343 – 38 s. red and blue 2·25 2·25
344 – 1 p. red and silver 5·50 5·50
DESIGN—As Type **91**: Nos. 340/4. As Nos. 335/9 but with inscription rearranged and coat of arms omitted.

1971. 5th Death Anniv of Queen Salote. Nos. 174/80, 182/4 with part of old surch obliterated and further surch **1965 1970** and value. On air values the surch includes two laurel leaves.
345 **65** 2 s. on 5d. on 9d. (postage) 20 20
346 3 s. on 9d. 20 20
347 5 s. on 3d. 30 20
348 15 s. on 3s. 6d. on 9d. 1·00 35
349 25 s. on 6s. 6d. on 3d. 1·75 80
350 50 s. on 1s. 7d. on 3d. 2·75 2·00
351 **66** 9 s. on 10d. (air) 75 20
352 24 s. on 4s. on 10d. 1·75 75
353 29 s. on 5s. 6d. on 1s. 2d. 2·00 1·00
354 38 s. on 10 s. 6d. on 1s. 2d. 2·50 1·50

1971. "Philatokyo '71" Stamp Exhibition, Japan. As Nos. 101 etc but imperf with colours changed and surch **PHILATOKYO '71**, emblem and value or **HONOURING JAPANESE POSTAL CENTENARY 1871–1971** (Nos. 357, 362, 364). Nos. 360/4 also surch **AIRMAIL.**
355 3 s. on 8d. blk & yell (postage) 10 10
356 7 s. on 4d. violet and yellow 15 10
357 15 s. on 1s. red and yellow 30 20
358 25 s. on 1d. black and yellow 40 30
359 75 s. on 2s. red and blue 1·75 1·50

360		9 s. on $1\frac{1}{2}$d. green (air)	15	10
361		10 s. on 4d. violet and yellow	15	10
362		18 s. on 1s. red and yellow	35	25
363		38 s. on 1d. black and yellow	70	50
364		1 p. on 2s. red and blue	1·75	1·75

96 Wristwatch

1971. Air. Imperf. Self-adhesive.

365	**96**	14 s. multicolorued	1·50	1·50
365a		17 s. multicoloured	1·75	1·75
366		21 s. multicoloured	1·75	1·75
366a		38 s. multicoloured	2·75	2·75

See also Nos. O65/6a.

97 Pole-vaulter

98 Medal of Merit (reverse)

1971. 4th South Pacific Games, Tahiti. Imperf. Self-adhesive.

367	**97**	3 s. multicoloured (postage)	10	10
368		7 s. multicoloured	10	10
369		15 s. multicoloured	20	20
370		25 s. multicoloured	30	35
371		50 s. multicoloured	60	90
372	–	9 s. multicoloured (air)	10	10
373	–	10 s. multicoloured	10	10
374	–	24 s. multicoloured	30	35
375	–	29 s. multicoloured	40	50
376	–	38 s. multicoloured	55	70

DESIGN—HORIZ: Nos. 372/6, High-jumper.

1971. Investiture of Royal Tongan Medal of Merit. Multicoloured colour of medal given. Imperf. Self-adhesive.

377	**98**	3 s. gold (postage)	10	10
378		24 s. silver	25	25
379	–	38 s. brown	50	50
380	–	10 s. gold (air)	15	15
381	–	75 s. silver	90	1·00
382	**98**	1 p. brown	1·10	1·40

DESIGN—As Type **98**: Nos. 379/81, Obverse of the Medal of Merit.

99 Child

1971. 25th Anniv of U.N.I.C.E.F. Imperf. Self-adhesive.

383	**99**	2 s. multicoloured (postage)	10	10
384		4 s. multicoloured	10	10
385		8 s. multicoloured	10	10
386		16 s. multicoloured	25	25
387		30 s. multicoloured	45	45
388	–	10 s. multicoloured (air)	15	15
389	–	15 s. multicoloured	25	25
390	–	25 s. multicoloured	40	40
391	–	50 s. multicoloured	85	1·00
392	–	1 p. multicoloured	1·75	2·00

DESIGN—VERT (21×42 mm): Nos. 388/92, Woman.

100 Map of South Pacific, and "Olovaha"

1972. Merchant Marine Routes. Imperf. Self-adhesive.

393	**100**	2 s. mult (postage)	30	30
394		10 s. multicoloured	60	20
395		17 s. multicoloured	90	30
396		21 s. multicoloured	1·00	40
397		60 s. multicoloured	4·25	3·25
398	–	9 s. multicoloured (air)	60	25
399	–	12 s. multicoloured	75	25
400	–	14 s. multicoloured	85	25
401	–	75 s. multicoloured	4·50	3·50
402	–	90 s. multicoloured	4·75	4·75

DESIGN: Nos. 398/402, Map of South Pacific, and "Niuvakai".

101 $\frac{1}{4}$ Hau Coronation Coin

1972. 5th Anniv of Coronation. Imperf. Self-adhesive.

403	**101**	5 s. mult (postage)	10	10
404		7 s. multicoloured	10	10
405		10 s. multicoloured	15	15
406		17 s. multicoloured	30	20
407		60 s. multicoloured	1·00	85
408	–	9 s. multicoloured (air)	15	15
409	–	12 s. multicoloured	20	15
410	–	14 s. multicoloured	25	20
411	–	21 s. multicoloured	35	20
412	–	75 s. multicoloured	1·25	85

DESIGNS—(47×41 mm): Nos. 408/12, As T **101** but with coins above inscription instead of beneath it.

102 Water Melon

1972. Imperf. Self-adhesive. (a) As T **83** but inscription altered omitting "Best in the Pacific", and colours changed.

413	**83**	1 s. yellow, red and black	25	10
414		2 s. yellow, blue and black	30	15
415		3 s. yellow, green and black	35	20
416		4 s. yellow, blue and black	35	20
417		5 s. yellow, brown & black	35	20

(b) As T **90** but colours changed. Multicoloured. Colour of face value given.

418	**90**	6 s. orange	40	20
419		7 s. blue	45	25
420		8 s. purple	45	25
421		9 s. orange	45	25
422		10 s. blue	55	30

(c) Type **102**. Multicoloured. Colour of face value given.

423	**102**	15 s. blue	1·00	45
424		20 s. orange	1·25	60
425		25 s. brown	1·40	70
426		40 s. orange	2·50	1·50
427		50 s. lemon	2·50	1·75

1972. Inaug of Internal Airmail. No. 398 surch **NOVEMBER 1972 INAUGURAL Internal Airmail Nuku'alofa — Vava'u 7s**.

428		7 s. on 9 s. multicoloured	1·25	2·25

104 Hoisting Tongan Flag

1972. Proclamation of Sovereignty over Minerva Reefs. Imperf. Self-adhesive.

429	**104**	5 s. mult (postage)	10	10
430		7 s. multicoloured	10	10
431		10 s. multicoloured	15	15
432		15 s. multicoloured	25	20
433		40 s. multicoloured	80	55
434	–	9 s. multicoloured (air)	15	15
435	–	12 s. multicoloured	20	15
436	–	14 s. multicoloured	25	15
437	–	38 s. multicoloured	75	55
438	–	1 p. multicoloured	2·00	2·50

DESIGN—SPHERICAL (52 mm diameter): Nos. 434/8, Proclamation in Govt Gazette.

105 Coins around Bank

1973. Foundation of Bank of Tonga. Imperf. Self-adhesive.

439	**105**	5 s. mult (postage)	10	10
440		7 s. multicoloured	10	10
441		10 s. multicoloured	15	10
442		20 s. multicoloured	40	20
443		30 s. multicoloured	60	30
444	–	9 s. multicoloured (air)	20	10
445	–	12 s. multicoloured	20	10
446	–	17 s. multicoloured	35	15
447	–	50 s. multicoloured	1·25	90
448	–	90 s. multicoloured	2·50	2·25

DESIGN—HORIZ—(64×52 mm): Nos. 444/8, Bank and banknotes.

106 Handshake and Scout in Outrigger Canoe

1973. Silver Jubilee of Scouting in Tonga. Imperf. Self-adhesive.

449	**106**	5 s. mult (postage)	20	10
450		7 s. multicoloured	30	15
451		15 s. multicoloured	95	40
452		21 s. multicoloured	1·25	50
453		50 s. multicoloured	4·50	2·25
454	–	9 s. multicoloured (air)	50	20
455	–	12 s. multicoloured	60	30
456	–	14 s. multicoloured	85	50
457	–	17 s. multicoloured	95	60
458	–	1 p. multicoloured	12·00	6·50

DESIGN—SQUARE (53×53 mm): Nos. 454/8, Scout badge.

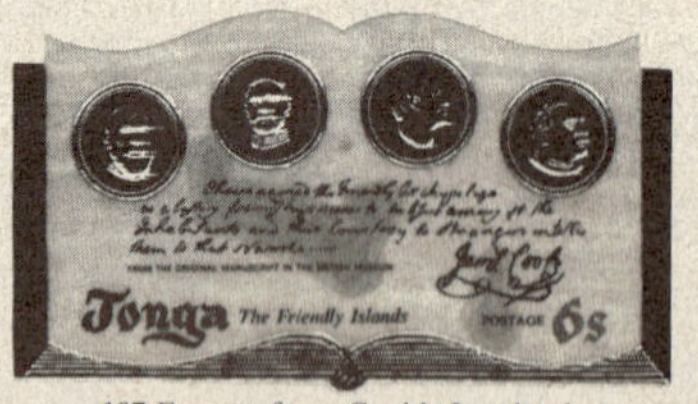

107 Excerpt from Cook's Log-book ($\frac{3}{5}$-size illustration)

1973. Bicentenary of Capt. Cook's Visit to Tonga. Imperf. Self-adhesive.

459	**107**	6 s. mult (postage)	40	30
460		8 s. multicoloured	40	35
461		11 s. multicoloured	60	40
462		35 s. multicoloured	4·00	2·25
463		40 s. multicoloured	4·00	2·50
464	–	9 s. multicoloured (air)	70	30
465	–	14 s. multicoloured	1·25	50
466	–	29 s. multicoloured	4·00	2·00
467	–	38 s. multicoloured	4·50	2·50
468	–	75 s. multicoloured	8·50	4·50

DESIGN—VERT: Nos. 464/8, H.M.S. "Resolution".

1973. Commonwealth Games, Christchurch. Various stamps surch **Commonwealth Games CHRISTCHURCH 1974** and No. 474 optd **AIRMAIL** in addition.

469	**97**	5 s. on 50 s. multicoloured (No. 371) (postage)	15	10
470	–	12 s. on 38 s. multicoloured (No. 379)	30	15
471	–	14 s. on 75 s. multicoloured (No. 381)	30	15
472	**98**	20 s. on 1 p. multicoloured (No. 382)	50	30
473		50 s. on 24 s. multicoloured (No. 378)	1·25	1·00
474	**97**	7 s. on 25 s. multicoloured (No. 370) (air)	15	10
475	–	9 s. on 38 s. multicoloured (No. 376)	20	10
476	–	24 s. multicoloured (No. 374)	60	30
477	–	29 s. on 9 s. multicoloured (No. 374)	70	40
478	–	40 s. on 14 s. multicoloured (No. 456)	1·00	90

109 Red Shining Parrot

1974. Air. Imperf. Self-adhesive.

479	**109**	7 s. multicoloured	70	45
480		9 s. multicoloured	75	50
481		12 s. multicoloured	80	60
482		14 s. multicoloured	85	60
483		17 s. multicoloured	95	85
484		29 s. multicoloured	1·75	1·25
485		38 s. multicoloured	2·25	1·40
486		50 s. multicoloured	2·75	3·50
487		75 s. multicoloured	4·00	5·00

For 25 s. value in smaller design, 27×36 mm, see No. 1284.

110 "Stamped Letter"

1974. Centenary of U.P.U. Imperf. Self-adhesive.

488	**110**	5 s. mult (postage)	10	15
489		10 s. multicoloured	15	15
490		15 s. multicoloured	25	25
491		20 s. multicoloured	30	30
492		50 s. multicoloured	1·00	1·50
493	–	14 s. multicoloured (air)	25	25
494	–	21 s. multicoloured	35	35
495	–	60 s. multicoloured	1·10	1·60
496	–	75 s. multicoloured	1·25	1·75
497	–	1 p. multicoloured	1·50	2·00

DESIGN—HORIZ: Nos. 493/7, Carrier pigeon scattering letters over Tonga.

111 Girl Guides Badges

1974. Tongan Girl Guides. Imperf. Self-adhesive.

498	**111**	5 s. mult (postage)	40	30
499		10 s. multicoloured	60	30
500		20 s. multicoloured	1·50	65
501		40 s. multicoloured	3·25	1·75
502		60 s. multicoloured	4·00	2·75
503	–	14 s. multicoloured (air)	1·00	45
504	–	16 s. multicoloured	1·00	45
505	–	29 s. multicoloured	2·00	1·00
506	–	31 s. multicoloured	2·25	1·25
507	–	75 s. multicoloured	5·50	3·50

DESIGN—VERT: Nos. 503/7, Girl Guide leaders.

112 H.M.S. "Resolution"

1974. Establishment of Royal Marine Institute. Imperf. Self-adhesive.

508	112	5 s. mult (postage)	1·25	50
509		10 s. multicoloured	1·40	50
510		25 s. multicoloured	2·75	80
511		50 s. multicoloured	4·00	3·00
512		75 s. multicoloured	5·50	4·50
513	–	9 s. multicoloured (air)	1·25	30
514	–	14 s. multicoloured	1·75	55
515	–	17 s. multicoloured	2·00	60
516	–	60 s. multicoloured	4·25	3·75
517	–	90 s. multicoloured	6·00	5·50

DESIGN—HORIZ (53×47 mm): Nos. 513/17, "James Cook" (bulk carrier).

113 Dateline Hotel, Nuku'alofa

1975. South Pacific Forum and Tourism. Imperf. Self-adhesive.

518	113	5 s. multicoloured (postage)	10	10
519		10 s. multicoloured	10	10
520		15 s. multicoloured	20	20
521		30 s. multicoloured	45	45
522		1 p. multicoloured	1·60	2·00
523	113	9 s. multicoloured (air)	10	10
524	–	12 s. multicoloured	15	15
525	–	14 s. multicoloured	20	20
526	–	17 s. multicoloured	20	20
527	–	38 s. multicoloured	55	65

DESIGNS—(46×60 mm): 9, 12, 14 s. Beach; 17, 38 s. Surf and sea.

114 Boxing

1975. 5th South Pacific Games, Guam. Imperf. Self-adhesive.

528	114	5 s. mult (postage)	15	10
529		10 s. multicoloured	20	10
530		20 s. multicoloured	30	25
531		25 s. multicoloured	35	35
532		65 s. multicoloured	80	1·00
533	–	9 s. multicoloured (air)	20	10
534	–	12 s. multicoloured	25	15
535	–	14 s. multicoloured	25	15
536	–	17 s. multicoloured	30	20
537	–	90 s. multicoloured	1·10	1·40

DESIGN—(37×43 mm): Nos. 533/7, Throwing the discus.

115 Commemorative Coin

1975. F.A.O. Commemoration. Imperf. Self-adhesive.

538	115	5 s. mult (postage)	15	10
539	–	20 s. multicoloured	35	15
540	–	50 s. blue, black and silver	75	35
541	–	1 p. blue, black and silver	1·50	1·25
542	–	2 p. black and silver	2·50	2·25
543	–	12 s. multicoloured (air)	30	15
544	–	14 s. multicoloured	30	15
545	–	25 s. red, black and silver	45	20
546	–	50 s. purple, black & silver	70	50
547	–	1 p. black and silver	1·50	1·25

DESIGNS: Nos. 539/47 are as T 52 but showing different coins. Nos. 542 and 544 are horiz, size 75×42 mm.

116 Commemorative Coin

1975. Centenary of Tongan Constitution. Multicoloured. Imperf. Self-adhesive.

548	5 s. Type 116 (postage)	15	15
549	10 s. King George I	25	20
550	20 s. King Taufa'ahau IV	40	25
551	50 s. King George II	90	75
552	75 s. Tongan arms	1·50	1·60
553	9 s. King Taufa'ahau IV (air)	25	20
554	12 s. Queen Salote	30	25
555	14 s. Tongan arms	30	25
556	38 s. King Taufa'ahau IV	70	40
557	1 p. Four monarchs	1·75	2·00

SIZES: 60×40 mm, Nos. 549 and 551; 76×76 mm, Nos. 552 and 557; 57×56 mm, others.

117 Montreal Logo

1976. First Participation in Olympic Games. Imperf. Self-adhesive. (a) Type **117**.

558		5 s. red, black & blue (postage)	30	15
559		10 s. red, black and green	35	15
560		25 s. red, black and brown	1·00	35
561		35 s. red, black and mauve	1·25	45
562		70 s. red, black and green	2·75	1·75

(b) Montreal logo optd on Nos. 500/1, 504, 507.

563	111	12 s. on 20 s. multicoloured (air)	50	15
564	–	14 s. on 16 s. mult	50	15
565	–	16 s. multicoloured	55	15
566	111	38 s. on 40 s. mult	1·75	45
567	–	75 s. multicoloured	3·00	1·75

118 Signatories of Declaration of Independence

1976. Bicentenary of American Revolution. Imperf. Self-adhesive.

568	118	9 s. multicoloured (postage)	30	15
569	–	10 s. multicoloured	30	15
570	–	15 s. multicoloured	50	45
571	–	25 s. multicoloured	80	70
572	–	75 s. multicoloured	2·50	2·50
573	–	12 s. multicoloured (air)	40	15
574	–	14 s. multicoloured	50	20
575	–	17 s. multicoloured	60	35
576	–	38 s. multicoloured	1·10	75
577	–	1 p. multicoloured	3·00	3·50

DESIGNS: Nos. 569/77 show the signatories to the Declaration of Independence.

119 Nathaniel Turner and John Thomas (Methodist missionaries)

1976. 150th Anniv of Christianity in Tonga. Imperf. Self-adhesive.

578	119	5 s. mult (postage)	20	25
579		10 s. multicoloured	30	25
580		20 s. multicoloured	50	40
581		25 s. multicoloured	55	45
582		85 s. multicoloured	2·25	2·50
583	–	9 s. multicoloured (air)	30	25
584	–	12 s. multicoloured	35	30
585	–	14 s. multicoloured	40	35
586	–	17 s. multicoloured	50	40
587	–	38 s. multicoloured	1·25	1·00

DESIGN: Nos. 583/7 show missionary ship "Triton".

120 Emperor Wilhelm I and King George Tupou I

1976. Centenary of Treaty of Friendship with Germany. Imperf. Self-adhesive.

588	120	9 s. mult (postage)	20	20
589		15 s. multicoloured	30	30
590		22 s. multicoloured	40	45
591		50 s. multicoloured	90	1·25
592		73 s. multicoloured	1·40	1·90
593	–	11 s. multicoloured (air)	25	25
594	–	17 s. multicoloured	40	45
595	–	18 s. multicoloured	40	45
596	–	31 s. multicoloured	60	80
597	–	39 s. multicoloured	70	90

DESIGNS—CIRCULAR (52 mm diameter): Nos. 593/7, Treaty signing.

121 Queen Salote and Coronation Procession

1977. Silver Jubilee. Imperf. Self-adhesive.

598	121	11 s. mult (postage)	50	30
599		20 s. multicoloured	40	30
600		30 s. multicoloured	40	30
601		50 s. multicoloured	60	65
602		75 s. multicoloured	75	85
603	–	15 s. multicoloured (air)	40	25
604	–	17 s. multicoloured	40	30
605	–	22 s. multicoloured	3·50	1·25
606	–	31 s. multicoloured	40	40
607	–	39 s. multicoloured	40	40

DESIGN—SQUARE (59×59 mm): Nos. 603/7, Queen Elizabeth and King Taufa'ahau.

122 Tongan Coins

1977. 10th Anniv of King's Coronation. Imperf. Self-adhesive.

608	122	10 s. mult (postage)	20	20
609		15 s. multicoloured	25	25
610		25 s. multicoloured	35	45
611		50 s. multicoloured	75	90
612		75 s. multicoloured	1·00	1·50
613	–	11 s. multicoloured (air)	25	20
614	–	17 s. multicoloured	30	30
615	–	18 s. multicoloured	30	30
616	–	39 s. multicoloured	45	60
617	–	1 p. multicoloured	1·50	2·25

DESIGN—OVAL (64×46 mm): Nos. 613/17 1967 Coronation coin.

123 H.M.S. "Resolution"

1977. Bicentenary of Capt. Cook's Last Voyage. Imperf. Self-adhesive.

618	123	10 s. mult (postage)	1·75	75
619		17 s. multicoloured	2·25	1·10
620		25 s. multicoloured	3·75	2·00
621		30 s. multicoloured	3·75	2·75
622		40 s. multicoloured	4·50	4·50
623	–	15 s. multicoloured (air)	1·75	1·25
624	–	22 s. multicoloured	2·75	2·25
625	–	31 s. multicoloured	3·25	2·75
626	–	50 s. multicoloured	4·50	4·50
627	–	1 p. multicoloured	8·00	8·50

DESIGN—52×46 mm: Nos. 623/7, Medal and extract from Cook's journal.

124 Humpback Whale

1977. Whale Conservation. Imperf. Self-adhesive.

628	124	15 s. black, grey and blue (postage)	2·50	70
629		22 s. black, grey and green	2·75	1·00
630		31 s. black, grey & orange	3·25	1·50
631		38 s. black, grey and lilac	3·50	2·00
632		64 s. black, grey and brown	5·50	4·50
633	–	11 s. multicoloured (air)	2·50	60
634	–	17 s. multicoloured	2·75	80
635	–	18 s. multicoloured	2·75	90
636	–	39 s. multicoloured	3·75	2·00
637	–	50 s. multicoloured	4·75	2·75

DESIGN—HEXAGONAL (66×51 mm): Nos. 633/7, Sei and fin whales.

For 60 s. value as Type **124**, see No. 1282.

1978. Various stamps surch.

638	115	15 s. on 5 s. mult (postage)	1·50	1·75
639	119	15 s. on 5 s. mult	1·50	1·75
640	117	15 s. on 10 s. red, black and green	1·50	1·75
641	119	15 s. on 10 s. mult	1·50	1·75
642	121	15 s. on 11 s. mult	1·50	2·75
643	114	15 s. on 20 s. mult	1·50	1·75
644	–	15 s. on 38 s. mult (No. O133)	1·50	1·75
645	–	17 s. on 9 s. mult (No. 533) (air)	1·75	2·00
646	–	17 s. on 9 s. mult (No. 583)	1·75	2·00
647	–	17 s. on 12 s. mult (No. 534)	1·75	2·00
648	–	17 s. on 12 s. mult (No. 573)	1·75	2·00
649	–	17 s. on 18 s. mult (No. 595)	1·75	2·00
650	–	17 s. on 38 s. mult (No. 527)	1·75	2·00
651	–	17 s. on 38 s. mult (No. 556)	1·75	2·00
652	–	1 p. on 35 s. mult (No. O151)	20·00	27·00
653	–	1 p. on 38 s. mult (No. 576)	8·50	9·00
654	–	1 p. on 75 s. mult (No. 572)	8·50	9·00

The surcharges on Nos. 638/9 are formed by adding a "1" to the existing face value.

126 Flags of Canada and Tonga

1978. 11th Commonwealth Games, Edmonton. Imperf. Self-adhesive.

655	126	10 s. blue, red and black (postage)	15	15
656		15 s. multicoloured	25	25
657		20 s. green, black and red	35	35
658		25 s. red, blue and black	40	40
659		45 s. black and red	90	1·00
660	–	17 s. black and red (air)	30	30
661	–	35 s. black, red and blue	60	65
662	–	38 s. black, red and green	75	85
663	–	40 s. black, red and green	80	90
664	–	65 s. black, red and brown	1·40	1·60

DESIGN—LEAF-SHAPED (39×40 mm): Nos 660/4, Maple leaf.

127 King Taufa'ahau Tupou IV

1978. 60th Birthday of King Taufa'ahau Tupou IV. Imperf. Self-adhesive.
665 **127** 2 s. black, deep blue and blue (postage) 10 20
666 5 s. black, blue and pink . 10 20
667 10 s. black, blue & mauve 20 20
668 25 s. black, blue and grey 45 35
669 75 s. black, blue & yellow 1·10 1·25
670 – 11 s. black, blue and yellow (air) 20 20
671 – 15 s. black, blue & brown 30 25
672 – 17 s. black, blue and lilac . 35 25
673 – 39 s. black, blue and green 60 55
674 – 1 p. black, blue and pink . 1·75 1·75
DESIGN—STAR SHAPED (44×51 mm): Nos. 670/4, Portrait of King.

128 Banana

1978. Coil stamps. Imperf. Self-adhesive.
675 **128** 1 s. black and yellow . . 20 30
676 – 2 s. blue and yellow . . . 20 30
677 – 3 s. brown and yellow . . 30 30
678 – 4 s. blue and yellow . . . 30 30
679 – 5 s. red and yellow . . . 30 30
680 – 6 s. purple, green & brn 40 40
681 – 7 s. blue, green & brown 40 40
682 – 8 s. red, green and brown 40 40
683 – 9 s. mauve, green & brn . 40 40
684 – 10 s. green and brown . . 40 40
684a – 13 s. mauve, green & brn 7·00 5·00
685 – 15 s. green and brown . . 1·25 1·25
686 – 20 s. brown and green . . 1·40 1·40
687 – 30 s. mauve, brown & grn 1·60 1·60
688 – 50 s. black, brown & grn 2·00 2·00
689 – 1 p. purple, brown & grn 2·50 3·00
689a – 2 p. multicoloured . . . 9·50 9·00
689b – 3 p. multicoloured . . . 10·00 11·00
DESIGNS—As Type **128**: 2 s. to 5 s. Bananas, the number shown coinciding with the face value; 18×26 mm, 6 s. to 10 s. Coconuts; 17×30 mm, 13 s. to 1 p. Pineapple; 55×29 mm, 2, 3 p. Mixed fruit.
For 10 s. value as Type **128** but in smaller size (21×9 mm), see No. 1281.

129 Humpback Whale

1978. Endangered Wildlife. Multicoloured. Self-adhesive
690 15 s. Type **129** (postage) . . . 2·25 1·00
691 18 s. Insular flying fox . . . . 2·25 1·00
692 25 s. Turtle . . . . 2·25 1·25
693 28 s. Red shining parrot . . . 3·50 1·75
694 60 s. Type **129** . . . . 6·00 4·50
695 17 s. Type **129** (air) . . . . . 2·25 1·00
696 22 s. As 18 s. . . . . 2·25 1·00
697 31 s. As 25 s. . . . . 2·25 1·75
698 39 s. As 28 s. . . . . 4·50 2·75
699 45 s. As Type **129** . . . . . . 5·00 3·25

130 Metrication Symbol

1979. Decade of Progress. Self-adhesive.
700 **130** 5 s. multicoloured (postage) 10 10
701 – 11 s. multicoloured . . . 15 15
702 – 18 s. multicoloured . . . 25 20
703 – 22 s. multicoloured . . . 35 25
704 – 50 s. multicoloured . . . 80 50
705 – 15 s. multicoloured (air) . 20 20
706 – 17 s. multicoloured . . . 25 20
707 – 31 s. gold and blue . . . 45 35
708 – 39 s. multicoloured . . . 60 40
709 – 1 p. multicoloured . . . 1·60 1·25
DESIGNS—VERT (58×55 mm): 11, 17 s. Map of South Pacific Islands; 22 s. New churches; 50, 15 s. Air routes; 39 s. Government offices; 1 p. Communications. TEAR DROP (35×52 mm): 18 s. Building wall of progress with the assistance of United States Peace Corps. As Type **130**: 31 s. Rotary International emblem.

131 Various Envelopes bearing Self-adhesive Stamps

1979. Death Centenary of Sir Rowland Hill and 10th Anniv of Tongan Self-adhesive Stamps. Self-adhesive.
710 **131** 5 s. multicoloured (postage) 20 10
711 10 s. multicoloured . . . 30 15
712 25 s. multicoloured . . . 65 35
713 50 s. multicoloured . . . 1·25 60
714 1 p. multicoloured . . . 2·00 1·25
715 – 15 s. multicoloured (air) . 40 20
716 – 17 s. multicoloured . . . 45 25
717 – 18 s. multicoloured . . . 45 25
718 – 31 s. multicoloured . . . 75 40
719 – 39 s. multicoloured . . . 90 45
DESIGN—MULTI-ANGULAR (53×53 mm): 15 s. to 39 s. Self-adhesive stamps.

132

1979. Air. Coil stamps. Self-adhesive.
720 **132** 5 s. black and blue . . . 40 50
721 11 s. black and blue . . 50 50
722 14 s. black and violet . . 50 50
723 15 s. black and mauve . 55 50
724 17 s. black and mauve . 55 50
725 18 s. black and red . . . 55 50
726 22 s. black and red . . . 65 50
726a 29 s. black and red . . . 8·00 5·00
727 31 s. black and yellow . 85 1·00
727a 32 s. black and brown . 9·00 5·50
728 39 s. black and green . . 1·00 1·00
728a 47 s. black and brown . 9·00 6·50
729 75 s. black and green . . 1·50 2·50
730 1 p. black and green . . 2·00 3·25

133 Rain Forest, Island of 'Eua

1979. Views as seen through the Lens of a Camera. Self-adhesive.
731 **133** 10 s. mult (postage) . . . 25 30
732 18 s. multicoloured . . . 30 40
733 31 s. multicolorued . . . 40 40
734 50 s. multicoloured . . . 70 95
735 60 s. multicoloured . . . 80 1·50
736 – 5 s. multicoloured (air) . 15 30
737 – 15 s. multicoloured . . . 30 30
738 – 17 s. multicoloured . . . 30 30
739 – 39 s. multicoloured . . . 60 60
740 – 75 s. multicoloured . . . 90 1·50
DESIGN: 5 s. to 75 s. Isle of Kao.

134 King Tupou I, Admiral Du Bouzet and Map of Tonga

1979. 125th Anniv of France–Tonga Treaty of Friendship. Self-adhesive.
741 **134** 7 s. mult (postage) 15 15
742 10 s. multicoloured 20 20
743 14 s. multicoloured 30 30
744 50 s. multicoloured . . . . 1·25 1·25
745 75 s. multicoloured . . . . 1·75 2·00
746 – 15 s. multicoloured (air) . 30 30
747 – 17 s. multicoloured . . . 35 35
748 – 22 s. multicoloured . . . 55 55
749 – 31 s. multicoloured . . . 90 90
750 – 39 s. multicoloured . . . 1·00 1·00
DESIGN: 15 s. to 39 s. King Tupou II, Napoleon III and "L'Aventure" (French warship).

1980. Olympic Games, Moscow. Nos. 710/19 surch or optd only (Nos. 753 and 755) **1980 OLYMPIC GAMES**, Olympic mascot and symbol.
751 **131** 13 s. on 5 s. multicoloured (postage) 35 35
752 – 20 s. on 10 s. multicoloured 55 55
753 – 25 s. multicoloured 70 70
754 – 33 s. on 50 s. multicoloured 85 85
755 – 1 p. multicoloured . . . . 3·25 3·50
756 – 9 s. on 15 s. multicoloured (air) 30 30
757 – 16 s. on 17 s. multicoloured 50 50
758 – 29 s. on 18 s. multicoloured 80 80
759 – 32 s. on 31 s. multicoloured 90 90
760 – 47 s. on 39 s. multicoloured 1·50 1·75

136 Scout at Campfire

1980. South Pacific Scout Jamboree, Tonga and 75th Anniv of Rotary International. Self-adhesive.
761 **136** 9 s. multicoloured (postage) 30 20
762 13 s. multicoloured 40 20
763 15 s. multicoloured 40 20
764 30 s. multicoloured 75 50
765 – 29 s. multicoloured (air) . 75 45
766 – 32 s. multicoloured 80 45
767 – 47 s. multicoloured . . . . 1·10 70
768 – 1 p. multicoloured . . . . 2·00 2·00
DESIGN: 29 s. to 1 p. Scout activities and Rotary emblem.

1980. Various stamps surch.
769 **117** 9 s. on 35 s. red, black and mauve (postage) . . . 40 40
770 **119** 13 s. on 20 s. multicoloured 55 55
771 13 s. on 25 s. multicoloured 55 55
772 – 19 s. on 25 s. multicoloured (No. 571) 75 75
773 **114** 1 p. on 65 s. multicoloured 3·00 3·75
773a – 5 p. on 25 s. multicoloured (No. O214) . . . . . 12·00 14·00
773b – 5 p. on 2 p. multicoloured (No. O215) . . . . . 12·00 14·00
774 – 29 s. on 14 s. multicoloured (No. 585) (air) 90 90
775 – 29 s. on 39 s. multicoloured (No. 597) 90 90
776 – 32 s. on 12 s. multicoloured (No. 554) . . . . 1·10 1·10
777 – 32 s. on 14 s. multicoloured (No. 574) . . . . 1·10 1·10
778 – 47 s. on 12 s. multicoloured (No. 524) . . . . 1·60 1·60
779 – 47 s. on 12 s. multicoloured (No. 584) . . . . 1·60 1·60

138 Red Cross and Tongan Flags, with Map of Tonga

1981. International Year of Disabled Persons. Self-adhesive.
780 **138** 2 p. multicoloured (postage) 2·00 1·25
781 3 p. multicoloured . . . . 2·25 1·50
782 – 29 s. multicoloured (air) . 50 20
783 – 32 s. multicoloured 60 25
784 – 47 s. multicoloured 70 30
DESIGN: Nos. 782/4, Red Cross flag and map depicting Tongatapu and Eua.

MINIMUM PRICE

The minimum price quoted is 10p which represents a handling charge rather than a basis for valuing common stamps. For further notes about prices see introductory pages.

139 Prince Charles and King Taufa'ahau Tupou IV

141 Landing Scene

140 Report of Printing in "Missionary Notices"

1981. Royal Wedding and Centenary of Treaty of Friendship between Tonga and Great Britain. Multicoloured. Self-adhesive.
785 13 s. Type **139** 30 20
786 47 s. Prince Charles and Lady Diana Spencer 60 30
787 1 p. 50 Prince Charles and Lady Diana (different) . . . . . 1·00 90
788 3 p. Prince and Princess of Wales after wedding ceremony . . . 1·40 1·40

1981. Christmas. 150th Anniv of First Books Printed in Tonga. Multicoloured. Self-adhesive.
789 9 s. Type **140** 25 25
790 13 s. "Missionary Notice" report (different) 30 30
791 32 s. Type in chase 85 85
792 47 s. Bible class . . . . 1·40 1·40

1981. Bicentenary of Maurelle's Discovery of Vava'u. Multicoloured. Self-adhesive.
793 9 s. Type **141** 40 40
794 13 s. Map of Vava'u 60 50
795 47 s. "La Princesa" . . . . . 2·75 1·50
796 1 p. "La Princesa" (different) . 5·00 6·50

142 Battle Scene

1981. 175th Anniv of Capture of "Port au Prince" (ship). Each black and blue. Self-adhesive.
798 29 s. Type **142** . . . . 1·00 45
799 32 s. Battle scene (different) . . 1·00 55
800 47 s. Map of the Ha'apali Group 1·50 1·25
801 47 s. Native canoes preparing to attack . . . . 1·50 1·25
802 1 p. "Port au Prince" . . . . 2·25 2·00

143 Baden-Powell at Brownsea Island, 1907

145 Ball Control

1982. 75th Anniv of Boy Scout Movement and 125th Birth Anniv of Lord Baden-Powell (founder). Multicoloured. Self-adhesive.
803 29 s. Type **143** 80 30
804 32 s. Baden-Powell on his charger "Black Prince" 90 35
805 47 s. Baden-Powell at Imperial Jamboree, 1924 . . . . . . 1·25 45
806 1 p. 50 Cover of first "Scouting for Boys" journal . . . . . 3·00 1·75
807 2 p. 50 Newsboy, 1900 and Mafeking Siege 3d. stamp . . 5·25 4·00

1982. Cyclone Relief. No. 788 optd **CYCLONE RELIEF T$1+50s POSTAGE & RELIEF.**
808 1 p. + 50 s. on 3 p. Prince and Princess of Wales after wedding ceremony . . . . 1·25 2·50

1982. World Cup Football Championship, Spain. Multicoloured. Self-adhesive.
809 32 s. Type **145** 65 45
810 47 s. Goalkeeping 85 60
811 75 s. Heading . . . . 1·25 95
812 1 p. 50 Shooting . . . . . . 2·25 1·75

146 "Olovaha II" (inter-island freighter)

147 Mail Canoe

1982. Inter-Island Transport. Multicoloured. Self-adhesive.

813 9 s. Type **146** 45 15
814 13 s. Type **146** 50 25
815 47 s. SPIA De Havilland Twin Otter 300 . . . . 1·25 1·00
816 1 p. As 47 s. . . . . 2·25 3·00

1982. Centenary of Tin Can Mail. Self-adhesive.

817 **147** 13 s. multicoloured . . . 15 15
818 – 32 s. multicoloured . . . 25 25
819 – 47 s. mutlicoloured . . . 35 35
820 – 2 p. black and green . . . 1·40 1·40

DESIGNS: 32 s. Mail canoe and ship; 47 s. Collecting Tin Can mail; 2 p. Map of Niuafo'ou.

148 Decathlon

1982. Commonwealth Games, Brisbane. Multicoloured. Self-adhesive.

823 32 s. Type **148** 50 50
824 $1.50 Tongan Police band at opening ceremony (horiz) . 4·50 5·00

149 Pupils

1982. Cent of Tonga College. Mult. Self-adhesive.

825 5 s. Type **149** (Tongan inscription) 50 80
826 5 s. Type **149** (English inscription) 50 80
827 29 s. School crest and monument (Tongan inscr) (29 × 22 mm) 2·00 2·50
828 29 s. As No. 827 but inscr in English . . . . 2·00 2·50
829 29 s. King George Tupou I (founder) and school (Tongan inscr) (29 × 22 mm) . . . 2·00 2·50
830 29 s. As No. 829 but inscr in English . . . . 2·00 2·50

1982. Christmas. Nos. 817/9 optd **Christmas Greetings 1982**.

831 13 s. Type **147** 15 40
832 32 s. Mail boat and ship . . . 45 65
833 47 s. Collecting Tin Can mail . 55 75

151 H.M.S. "Resolution" and S.S. "Canberra"

1983. Sea and Air Transport. Mult. Self-adhesive.

834 29 s. Type **151** . . . . . . 3·00 1·75
835 32 s. Type **151** . . . . . . 3·00 1·75
836 47 s. Montgolfier's balloon and Concorde . . . . 4·25 3·00
837 1 p. 50 As No. 836 . . . . . 6·50 9·00

152 Globe and Inset of Tonga

1983. Commonwealth Day. Multicoloured. Self-adhesive.

839 29 s. Type **152** 35 45
840 32 s. Tongan dancers . . . . 6·00 4·00
841 47 s. Trawler 50 80
842 1 p. 50 King Taufa'ahau Tupou IV and flag . . . . 1·75 4·00

153 SPIA De Havilland Twin Otter 300

154 "Intelsat IV" Satellite

1983. Inauguration of Niuafo'ou Airport. Multicoloured. Self-adhesive.

843 32 s. Type **153** 90 30
844 47 s. Type **153** 95 35
845 1 p. SPIA Boeing 707 . . . . 1·75 1·25
846 1 p. 50 As No. 845 . . . . . 2·50 1·75

1983. World Communications Year. Multicoloured. Self-adhesive.

847 29 s. Type **154** 40 20
848 32 s. "Intelsat IVA" satellite . 50 25
849 75 s. "Intelsat V" satellite . . 1·00 70
850 2 p. Moon post cover (45 × 32 mm) . . . . 2·00 2·00

155 Obverse and Reverse of Pa'anga Banknote

1983. 10th Anniv of Bank of Tonga. Self-adhesive.

851 **155** 1 p. multicoloured . . . 1·25 1·50
852 2 p. multicoloured . . . 2·25 2·50

156 Early Printing Press

157 Yacht off Coast

1983. Printing in Tonga. Multicoloured. Self-adhesive.

853 13 s. Type **156** 20 15
854 32 s. Arrival of W. Woon . . 40 30
855 1 p. Early Tongan print . . . 95 95
856 2 p. "The Tonga Chronicle" . 1·50 2·00

1983. Christmas. Yachting off Vava'u. Multicoloured. Self-adhesive.

857 29 s. Type **157** 60 35
858 32 s. View of yacht from cave . 60 35
859 1 p. 50 Anchored yacht . . . 2·00 2·25
860 2 p. 50 Yacht off coast (different) 2·75 3·50

158 Abel Tasman and "Zeehan"

1984. Navigators and Explorers of the Pacific (1st series). Self-adhesive.

861 **158** 32 s. green and black . . 1·50 1·50
862 – 47 s. violet and black . . 2·00 2·00
863 – 90 s. brown and black . . 3·75 3·75
864 – 1 p. 50 blue and black . . 5·00 5·00

DESIGNS: 47 s. Capt. Samuel Wallis and H.M.S. "Dolphin"; 90 s. Capt. William Bligh and H.M.S. "Bounty"; 1 p. 50, Capt. James Cook and H.M.S. "Resolution".

See also Nos. 896/9.

159 Chaste Mitre

160 Printer checking Newspaper

1984. Marine Life. Multicoloured. Self-adhesive.

865 1 s. Type **159** 30 70
866 2 s. "Porites sp" 60 70
867 3 s. Red squirrelfish 60 80
868 5 s. Green map cowrie 40 70
869 6 s. "Dardanus megistos" (crab) 75 80
870 9 s. Variegated shark 75 55
871 10 s. Bubble cone 70 75
872 13 s. Lionfish . . . . 1·00 65
873 15 s. Textile or cloth of gold cone 90 90
874 20 s. White-tailed damselfish . 1·75 1·00
875 29 s. Princely cone . . . . . 1·75 80
876 32 s. Powder-blue surgeonfish . 2·50 90
877 47 s. Giant spider conch . . . 2·50 1·60
878 1 p. "Millepora dichotama" . 7·00 7·00
879 2 p. "Birgus latro" (crab) . . . 10·00 11·00
880 3 p. Rose-branch murex . . . . 9·00 12·00
881 5 p. Yellow-finned tuna . . . 11·00 14·00

Nos. 865/77 are 25 × 28 mm in size and Nos. 878/81 38 × 23 mm.

For these designs with normal gum but redrawn see Nos. 999/1017a and 1087/95. For similar designs but with face value at foot see Nos. 1218/34 and 1346/7.

1984. 20th Anniv of "Tonga Chronicle" (newspaper). Self-adhesive.

882 **160** 3 s. brown and blue . . . 15 20
883 32 s. brown and red . . . 60 65

161 U.S.A. Flag and Running

1984. Olympic Games, Los Angeles. Each in black, red and blue. Self-adhesive.

884 29 s. Type **161** 25 25
885 47 s. Javelin-throwing 30 30
886 1 p. 50 Shot-putting . . . . . 1·00 1·00
887 3 p. Olympic torch . . . . . . 1·90 1·90

162 Sir George Airy and Dateline on World Map

1984. Centenary of International Dateline. Multicoloured. Self-adhesive.

888 47 s. Type **162** . . . . 1·25 1·00
889 2 p. Sir Sandford Fleming and Map of Pacific time zones . 4·25 4·50

163 Australia 1914 Laughing Kookaburra 6d. Stamp

164 Beach at Sunset ("Silent Night")

1984. "Ausipex" International Stamp Exhibition, Melbourne. Multicoloured. Self-adhesive.

890 32 s. Type **163** . . . . 1·25 75
891 1 p. 50 Tonga 1897 Red shining parrot 2s. 6d. . . . . 3·25 3·00

1984. Christmas. Carols. Mult. Self-adhesive.

892 32 s. Type **164** 60 45
894 47 s. Hut and palm trees ("Away in a Manger") 85 65
895 1 p. Sailing boats ("I Saw Three Ships") . . . . 1·75 2·75

1985. Navigators and Explorers of the Pacific (2nd series). As T **158**. Self-adhesive.

896 32 s. black and blue . . . . . 2·75 1·25
897 47 s. black and green . . . . 3·00 1·50
898 90 s. black and red . . . . . . 6·50 4·00
899 1 p. 50 black and brown . . . 7·00 6·50

DESIGNS: 32 s. Willem Schouten and "Eendracht"; 47 s. Jacob Le Maire and "Hoorn"; 90 s. Fletcher Christian and "Bounty"; 1 p. 50, Francisco Maurelle and "La Princessa".

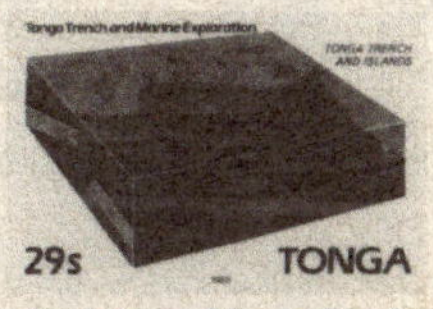

165 Section of Tonga Trench

1985. Geological Survey of the Tonga Trench. Multicoloured. Self-adhesive.

900 29 s. Type **165** . . . . 1·25 1·00
901 32 s. Diagram of marine seismic survey . . . . 1·25 1·00
902 47 s. Diagram of aerial oil survey (vert) . . . . 1·50 1·50
903 1 p. 50 Diagram of sea bed survey (vert) . . . . 4·75 6·00

166 "Port au Prince" at Gravesend, 1805

1985. 175th Anniv of Will Mariner's Departure for England. Multicoloured. Self-adhesive.

905B 29 s. Type **166** 60 50
906B 32 s. Capture of "Port au Prince", Tonga, 1806 . . 60 50
907B 47 s. Will Mariner on Tongan canoe, 1807 . . . . 80 70
908B 1 p. 50 Mariner boarding brig "Favourite", 1810 . . . . 2·25 2·75
909B 2 p. 50 "Cuffnells" in English Channel, 1811 . . . . . 3·50 4·25

167 Quintal (Byron Russell) and Captain Bligh (Charles Laughton)

1985. 50th Anniv of Film "Mutiny on the Bounty". Multicoloured. Self-adhesive.

910 47 s. Type **167** . . . . 6·50 6·50
911 47 s. Captain Bligh and prisoners 6·50 6·50
912 47 s. Fletcher Christian (Clark Gable) . . . . 6·50 6·50
913 47 s. Mutineers threatening Bligh 6·50 6·50
914 47 s. Bligh and Roger Byam (Franchot Tone) in boat . . 6·50 6·50

168 Lady Elizabeth Bowes-Lyon, 1910

169 Mary and Joseph arriving at Inn

1985. Life and Times of Queen Elizabeth the Queen Mother and 75th Anniv of Girl Guide Movement. Self-adhesive.

915A **168** 32 s. black, pink and brown 90 90
916A – 47 s. black, lilac and brown . . . . 1·25 1·25
917A – 1 p. 50 black, yellow and brown . . . . 3·50 4·00
918A – 2 p. 50 multicoloured . . 5·50 6·50

DESIGNS: 47 s. Duchess of York at Hadfield Girl Guides' Rally, 1931; 1 p. 50, Duchess of York in Girl Guide uniform; 2 p. 50, Queen Mother in 1985 (from photo by Norman Parkinson).

1985. Christmas. Mult. Self-adhesive.

919 32 s. Type **169** 55 30
920 42 s. The Shepherds 60 40
921 1 p. 50 The Three Wise Men . 2·25 3·00
922 2 p. 50 The Holy Family . . 3·25 4·00

170 Comet and Slogan "Maybe Twice in a Lifetime"

1986. Appearance of Halley's Comet. Multicoloured.

923 42 s. Type **170** . . . . 2·50 2·50
924 42 s. Edmond Halley . . . . 2·50 2·50
925 42 s. Solar System . . . . . . 2·50 2·50
926 42 s. Telescope . . . . 2·50 2·50
927 42 s. "Giotto" spacecraft . . 2·50 2·50
928 57 s. Type **170** . . . . 2·75 2·75
929 57 s. As No. 924 . . . . 2·75 2·75
930 57 s. As No. 925 . . . . 2·75 2·75
931 57 s. As No. 926 . . . . 2·75 2·75
932 57 s. As No. 927 . . . . 2·75 2·75

Nos. 923/7 and 928/32 were each printed together, se-tenant, forming composite designs.

1986. Nos. 866/7, 869/70, 872, 874, 879 and 881 surch.

933 4 s. on 2 s. "Porites sp" . . . 70 80
934 4 s. on 13 s. Lionfish 70 80
935 42 s. on 3 s. Red squirrelfish . 1·25 80
936 42 s. on 9 s. Variegated shark . 1·25 80
937 57 s. on 6 s. "Dardanus megistos" . . . . 1·75 1·25
938 57 s. on 20 s. White-tailed damselfish . . . . 1·75 1·25
939 2 p. 50 on 2 p. "Birgus latro" 4·75 6·00
940 2 p. 50 on 5 p. Yellow-finned tuna . . . . 4·75 6·00

172 King Taufa'ahau Tupou IV of Tonga

1986. Royal Links with Great Britain and 60th Birthday of Queen Elizabeth II.
941 **172** 57 s. multicoloured . . . 75 1·00
942 – 57 s. multicoloured . . . 75 1·00
943 – 2 p. 50 brown, black and blue . . . . 3·25 3·75
DESIGNS—HORIZ (as Type **172**): No. 942, Queen Elizabeth II. SQUARE (40 × 40 mm): No. 943, Queen Elizabeth II and King Taufa'ahau Tupou IV, Tonga, 1970.

173 Peace Corps Nurse giving Injection

1986. "Ameripex '86" International Stamp Exhibition, Chicago. 25th Anniv of United States Peace Corps. Multicoloured.
944 57 s. Type **173** . . . . 1·25 1·00
945 1 p. 50 Peace Corps teacher and pupil . . . . 2·25 2·75

174 Hockey

1986. Sporting Events. Multicoloured.
947 42 s. Type **174** (World Hockey Cup for Men, London) . . 1·50 85
948 57 s. Handball (13th Commonwealth Games, Edinburgh) . . . . 1·25 85
949 1 p. Boxing (13th Commonwealth Games, Edinburgh) . . . . 1·75 2·50
950 2 p. 50 Football (World Cup Football Championship, Mexico) . . . . 4·25 5·50

175 1886 1d. King George I Definitive

1986. Cent of First Tonga Stamps. Mult.
951 32 s. Type **175** . . . . 1·25 95
952 42 s. 1897 7½d. King George II inverted centre error . . . . 1·50 1·00
953 57 s. 1950 Queen Salote's 50th Birthday 1d. . . . . 2·00 1·25
954 2 p. 50 1986 Royal Links with Great Britain 2 p. 50 . . . 4·00 5·50

176 Girls wearing Shell Jewellery

1986. Christmas. Multicoloured.
956 32 s. Type **176** . . . . 1·25 70
957 42 s. Boy with wood carvings (vert) . . . . 1·50 75
958 57 s. Children performing traditional dance (vert) . . . 1·75 1·10
959 2 p. Children in dugout canoe 4·50 7·00

1986. Scout Jamboree, Tongatapu. Nos. 957/8 optd **BOY SCOUT JAMBOREE 5TH-10TH DEC'86.**
960 42 s. Boy with wood carvings (vert) . . . . 1·75 1·75
961 57 s. Children performing traditional dance (vert) . . . 2·25 2·25

178 Dumont D'Urville and "L'Astrolabe"

1987. 150th Anniv of Dumont D'Urville's Second Voyage. Multicoloured.
962 32 s. Type **178** . . . . 3·00 1·75
963 42 s. Tongan girls (from "Voyage au Pole et dans l'Oceanie") . 3·00 1·75
964 1 p. Contemporary chart . . 6·50 6·00
965 2 p. 50 Wreck of "L'Astrolabe" 12·00 13·00

180 Two Paddlers in Canoe

181 King Taufa'ahau Tupou IV

1987. "Siv'a'alo (Tonga-Fiji-Samoa) Canoe Race. Multicoloured.
967 32 s. Type **180** 55 40
968 42 s. Five paddlers 65 50
969 57 s. Paddlers and canoe bow 80 65
970 1 p. 50 Two paddlers (different) 2·10 2·75

1987. 20th Anniv of Coronation of King Taufa'ahau Tupou IV. Self-adhesive.
972 **181** 1 s. black and green . . 15 40
972d 2 s. black and orange . . 1·75 2·00
973 5 s. black and mauve . . 15 40
974 10 s. black and lilac . . 20 40
975 15 s. black and red . . . 25 50
976 32 s. black and blue . . 45 70

182 Arms and Tongan Citizens

1987. 125th Anniv of First Parliament.
977 **182** 32 s. multicoloured . . . 40 30
978 42 s. multicoloured . . . 50 40
979 75 s. multicoloured . . . 90 1·00
980 2 p. multicoloured . . . 2·25 2·75

183 Father Christmas Octopus and Rat with Sack of Presents

1987. Christmas. Cartoons. Multicoloured.
981 42 s. Type **183** 70 45
982 57 s. Delivering presents by outrigger canoe 90 65
983 1 p. Delivering presents by motorized tricycle . . . . . 1·75 2·00
984 3 p. Drinking cocktails . . . . 4·50 5·50

184 King Taufa'ahau Tupou IV, "Olovaha II" (inter-island freighter), Oil Rig and Pole Vaulting

1988. 70th Birthday of King Taufa'ahau Tupou IV. Designs each show portrait. Multicoloured.
985 32 s. Type **184** . . . . 1·25 80
986 42 s. Banknote, coins, Ha'amonga Trilithon and woodcarver . . . . 1·25 80
987 57 s. Rowing, communications satellite and Red Cross worker 1·40 90
988 2 p. 50 Scout emblem, 1982 47 s. Scout stamp and Friendly Islands Airways De Havilland Twin Otter 200/300 aircraft 5·50 7·00
See also Nos. 1082/5.

186 Athletics

1988. Olympic Games, Seoul. Multicoloured.
990 57 s. Type **186** 65 65
991 75 s. Yachting 95 95
992 2 p. Cycling . . . . 3·25 3·50
993 3 p. Tennis . . . . 4·50 4·75

187 Traditional Tongan Fale

1988. Music in Tonga. Multicoloured.
994 32 s. Type **187** 30 35
995 42 s. Church choir 40 45
996 57 s. Tonga Police Band outside Royal Palace 75 80
997 2 p. 50 "The Jets" pop group . 2·40 3·25

1988. Redrawn designs (each showing wider gap between upper and lower lines) as Nos. 865/6, 868/9, 871/6 and 879/81 and new values, all normal gum. Multicoloured.
999 1 s. Type **159** 30 55
1000 2 s. "Porites sp" 40 70
1001 4 s. Lionfish 70 90
1002 5 s. Green map cowrie . . . 50 70
1003 6 s. "Dardanus megistos" (crab) . . . . 70 1·25
1004 7 s. Wandering albatross . . 2·00 1·50
1005 10 s. Bubble cone 60 50
1006 15 s. Textile or cloth of gold cone 60 60
1007 20 s. White-tailed damselfish 90 90
1008 32 s. Powder-blue surgeonfish 1·00 60
1009 35 s. Seahorse . . . . 1·75 1·75
1010 42 s. Lesser frigate bird . . . 2·00 70
1011 50 s. Princely cone . . . . . 1·75 90
1012 57 s. Brown booby . . . . . 2·50 90
1013 1 p. "Chelonia mydas" (turtle) 3·00 3·00
1014 1 p. 50 Humpback whale . . 7·00 5·00
1015 2 p. "Birgus latro" (crab) . . 4·50 5·00
1016 3 p. Rose-branch murex . . 2·75 5·00
1017 5 p. Yellow-finned tuna . . 10·00 12·00
1017a 10 p. Variegated shark . . . 14·00 17·00
Nos. 1013/17 are 41 × 22 mm and No. 1017a 26 × 41.
For smaller designs, 19 × 22 mm, see Nos. 1087/95.

189 Capt. Cook's H.M.S. "Resolution"

1988. Centenary of Tonga–U.S.A. Treaty of Friendship. Multicoloured.
1018 42 s. Type **189** 80 70
1019 57 s. "Santa Maria" . . . . 1·00 80
1020 2 p. Capt. Cook and Christopher Columbus . . 3·25 4·00

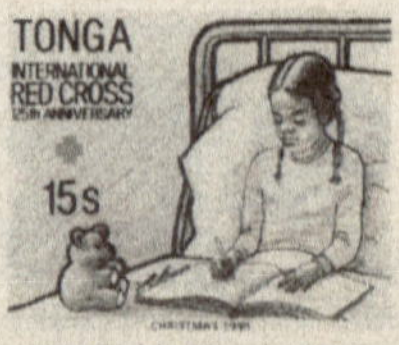

190 Girl in Hospital Bed

1988. Christmas. 125th Anniv of International Red Cross and 25th Anniv of Tongan Red Cross. Multicoloured.
1022 15 s. Type **190** (A) 15 20
1023 15 s. Type **190** (B) 15 20
1024 32 s. Red Cross nurse reading to young boy (A) 30 35
1025 32 s. Red Cross nurse reading to young boy (B) 30 35
1026 42 s. Red Cross nurse taking pulse (A) 40 45
1027 42 s. Red Cross nurse taking pulse (B) 40 45
1028 57 s. Red Cross nurse with sleeping child (A) 55 60
1029 57 s. Red Cross nurse with sleeping child (B) 55 60
1030 1 p. 50 Boy in wheelchair (A) 1·40 2·00
1031 1 p. 50 Boy in wheelchair (B) 1·40 2·00
Nos. 1022/3, 1024/5, 1026/7, 1028/9 and 1030/1 were printed together, se-tenant, in horizontal pairs throughout the sheets with the first stamp in each pair inscribed "INTERNATIONAL RED CROSS 125TH ANNIVERSARY" (A) and the second "SILVER JUBILEE OF TONGAN RED CROSS" (B).

191 Map of Tofua Island and Breadfruit

1989. Bicentenary of Mutiny on the "Bounty". Multicoloured.
1032 32 s. Type **191** . . . . . . 2·25 1·50
1033 42 s. H.M.S. "Bounty" and chronometer . . . . 3·50 1·75
1034 57 s. Captain Bligh and "Bounty's" launch cast adrift 4·50 2·75

192 "Hypolimnas bolina"

1989. Butterflies. Multicoloured.
1036 42 s. Type **192** . . . . . . 1·00 80
1037 57 s. "Jamides bochus" . . . 1·25 90
1038 1 p. 20 "Melanitis leda" . . . 2·25 2·75
1039 2 p. 50 "Danaus plexippus" . . 3·75 5·50

193 Football at Rugby School, 1870

1989. Inauguration of National Sports Stadium and South Pacific Mini Games, Tonga. Designs showing development of rugby, tennis and cricket. Multicoloured.
1040 32 s. Type **193** 65 65
1041 32 s. D. Gallaher (All Black's captain, 1905) and Springboks rugby match, 1906 . . . . 65 65
1042 32 s. King George V with Cambridge team, 1922 and W. Wakefield (England captain, 1926) 65 65
1043 32 s. E. Crawford (Ireland captain, 1926) and players on cigarette cards 65 65
1044 32 s. S. Mafi (Tonga captain, 1970s) and modern rugby match 65 65
1045 42 s. Royal tennis, 1659 . . 1·00 1·00
1046 42 s. Major Wingfield and lawn tennis, 1873 . . . . 1·00 1·00
1047 42 s. Oxford and Cambridge tennis teams, 1884 . . . . 1·00 1·00
1048 42 s. Bunny Ryan, 1910 and players on cigarette cards . 1·00 1·00
1049 42 s. Boris Becker and modern tennis match . . . . 1·00 1·00
1050 57 s. Cricket match, 1743, and F. Pilch memorial . . . . 1·50 1·50
1051 57 s. W. G. Grace (19th-century cricketer) . . . . 1·50 1·50
1052 57 s. "Boys Own Paper" cricket article, 1909 . . . . 1·50 1·50
1053 57 s. Australian cricket team, 1909 and players on cigarette cards . . . . 1·50 1·50
1054 57 s. The Ashes urn, and modern cricket match . . 1·50 1·50

194 Short S.30 Modified "G" Class Flying Boat "Aotearoa", 1939 (50th anniv of first flight)

195 CASA C-212 Aviocar landing

1989. Aviation in Tonga. Multicoloured.
1055 42 s. Type **194** . . . . 2·00 1·10
1056 57 s. Chance Vought F4U Corsair, 1943 . . . . 2·50 1·50
1057 90 s. Boeing 737 at Fua'amotu Airport . . . . 4·50 4·50
1058 3 p. Montgolfier balloon, Wright Flyer I biplane . . Concorde and space shuttle (97 × 26 mm) . . . . . . 9·50 11·00

1989. Christmas. "Flying Home".
1059 **195** 32 s. green, brown & orge 1·25 80
1060 – 42 s. green, brn & lt grn . 1·40 80
1061 – 57 s. green, brn & red . . 1·60 90
1062 – 3 p. green, brown & mve 5·50 7·00
DESIGNS: 42 s. Villagers waving to CASA C-212 Aviocar aircraft; 57 s. Outrigger canoe and CASA C-212 Aviocar aircraft; 3 p. CASA C-212 Aviocar over headland.

197 1989 U.P.U. Congress Stamps

1989. "World Stamp Expo '89" International Stamp Exhibition, Washington.
1064 **197** 57 s. multicoloured . . . 1·75 1·50

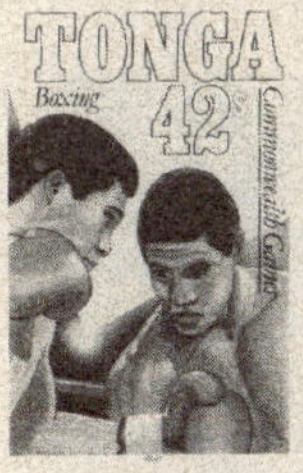

198 Boxing 199 Wave Power Installation

1990. 14th Commonwealth Games, Auckland. Multicoloured.
1065 42 s. Type **198** 90 70
1066 57 s. Archery . . . . . . 1·50 1·10
1067 1 p. Bowls . . . . 2·00 2·50
1068 2 p. Swimming . . . . . . 3·50 4·50

1990. Alternative Sources of Electricity. Multicoloured.
1069 32 s. Type **199** . . . . 1·00 65
1070 57 s. Wind farm . . . . . . 1·50 1·10
1071 1 p. 20 Experimental solar cell vehicle . . . . 3·00 4·25

200 Penny Black 201 Departure of Canoe

1990. 150th Anniv of the Penny Black.
1073 **200** 42 s. multicoloured . . . 1·25 1·25
1074 – 42 s. multicoloured . . . 1·25 1·25
1075 – 57 s. red and black . . . 1·50 1·25
1076 – 1 p. 50 multicoloured . . 3·50 4·00
1077 – 2 p. 50 multicoloured . . 5·00 5·50
DESIGNS: 42 s. (1074) Great Britain 1840 Twopence Blue; 57 s. Tonga 1886 1d.; 1 p. 50, 1980 South Pacific Scout Jamboree and Rotary 75th anniv 2 p. official stamp; 2 p. 50, 1990 Alternative Sources of Electricity 57 s.

1990. Polynesian Voyages of Discovery.
1078 **201** 32 s. green 75 65
1079 – 42 s. blue . . . . 1·00 80
1080 – 1 p. 20 brown . . . . . 2·75 3·00
1081 – 3 p. violet . . . . . . 5·50 8·00
DESIGNS: 42 s. Navigating by night; 1 p. 20, Canoe and sea birds; 3 p. Landfall.

1990. Silver Jubilee of King Taufa'ahau Tupou IV. As Nos. 985/8 but inscr "Silver Jubilee of His Majesty King Taufa'ahau Tupou IV. 1965–1990" and with "TONGA" and values in silver.
1082 32 s. Type **184** . . . . . . 1·10 75
1083 42 s. Banknote, coins Ha'amonga Trilithon and woodcarver . . . . 1·10 75
1084 57 s. Rowing, communications satellite and Red Cross worker . . . . 1·40 85
1085 2 p. 50 Scout emblem, 1982 47 s. Scout stamp and Friendly Island Airways De Havilland Twin Otter aircraft . . . . 5·00 6·50

1990. As Nos. 1000, 1002, 1003 (value changed), 1005 and 1008 redrawn smaller, 19 × 22 mm. Multicoloured.
1087 2 s. "Porites sp." 40 50
1089 5 s. Green map cowrie 40 50
1092 10 s. Bubble cone 40 50
1093 15 s. "Dardanus megistos" (crab) 80 80
1095 32 s. Powder-blue surgeonfish 40 50

202 Iguana searching for Food

1990. Endangered Species. Banded Iguana. Multicoloured.
1105 32 s. Type **202** . . . . . . 1·50 75
1106 42 s. Head of male . . . . . 1·75 85
1107 57 s. Pair of iguanas during courtship . . . . 2·25 1·25
1108 1 p. 20 Iguana basking . . . 5·00 6·00

203 Tourism

1990. 40th Anniv of United Nations Development Programme. Multicoloured.
1109 57 s. Type **203** . . . . 1·25 1·25
1110 57 s. Agriculture and Fisheries 1·25 1·25
1111 3 p. Education . . . . . . 6·00 7·00
1112 3 p. Healthcare . . . . . . 6·00 7·00

204 Boy 205 Safety at Work

1990. Christmas. Rotary International Interact Project. Multicoloured.
1113 32 s. Type **204** 70 40
1114 42 s. Young boys 90 55
1115 2 p. Girls in western clothes . 3·50 4·00
1116 3 p. Girls in traditional costumes . . . . 4·50 5·00

1991. Accident Prevention. Multicoloured.
1117 32 s. Type **205** (English inscription) 80 80
1118 32 s. Safety at home (English inscription) 80 80
1119 32 s. As No. 1118 (Tongan inscription) 80 80
1120 32 s. As Type **205** (incorrectly inscr "Ngauo tokanga") 80 80
1120a 32 s. As Type **205** (inscr corrected to "Ngaue tokanga") . . . . . . 18·00 18·00
1121 42 s. Safety in cars (English inscription) . . . . . . 1·25 1·25
1122 42 s. Safety on bikes (English inscription) . . . . . . 1·25 1·25
1123 42 s. As No. 1122 (Tongan inscription) . . . . . . 1·25 1·25
1124 42 s. As No. 1121 (Tongan inscription) . . . . . . 1·25 1·25
1125 57 s. Safety at sea (English inscription) . . . . . . 1·50 1·50
1126 57 s. Safety on the beach (English inscription) . . 1·50 1·50
1127 57 s. As No. 1126 (Tongan inscription) . . . . . . 1·50 1·50
1128 57 s. As No. 1125 (Tongan inscription) . . . . . . 1·50 1·50

207 Fishes in the Sea 208 Tonga Temple

1991. Heilala Week. Multicoloured.
1130 42 s. Type **207** 70 55
1131 57 s. Island and yacht . . . 90 65
1132 2 p. Pile of fruit . . . . . 2·75 3·50
1133 3 p. Turtle on beach . . . . 3·50 4·00

1991. Centenary of Church of Latter Day Saints in Tonga. Multicoloured.
1134 42 s. Type **208** . . . . . . 1·10 1·10
1135 57 s. Temple at night . . . 1·40 1·40

209 Making T.V. Childcare Programme

1991. Telecommunications in Tonga. Mult.
1136 15 s. Type **209** 35 35
1137 15 s. T.V. satellite 35 35
1138 15 s. Mothers watching programme 35 35
1139 32 s. Man on telephone and woman with computer . . . 65 65
1140 32 s. Telecommunications satellite 65 65
1141 32 s. Overseas customer on telephone 65 65
1142 42 s. Sinking coaster 90 90
1143 42 s. Coastguard controller . 90 90
1144 42 s. Maritime rescue 90 90
1145 57 s. Weather satellite above Southern Hemisphere . . . 1·10 1·10
1146 57 s. Meteorologists collecting data . . . . 1·10 1·10
1147 57 s. T.V. weather map and storm . . . . 1·10 1·10

210 Women's Rowing Eight

1991. "Siu'a'alo" Rowing Festival. Mult.
1148 42 s. Type **210** 85 45
1149 57 s. Longboat . . . . . . 1·00 55
1150 1 p. Outrigger canoe . . . . 2·00 2·00
1151 2 p. Stern of fautasi (large canoe) . . . . 3·25 4·00
1152 2 p. Bow of fautasi . . . . 3·25 4·00
Nos. 1151/2 were printed together, se-tenant, forming a composite design.

211 Turtles pulling Santa's Sledge

1991. Christmas. Multicoloured.
1153 32 s. Type **211** 85 35
1154 42 s. Santa Claus on roof of fala (Tongan house) 95 45
1155 57 s. Family opening presents 1·10 60
1156 3 p. 50 Family waving goodbye to Santa . . . . 6·50 8·00

212 "Pangai" (patrol boat)

1991. Royal Tongan Defence Force. Mult.
1157 42 s. Type **212** . . . . . . 1·00 1·00
1158 42 s. Marine in battle dress . 1·00 1·00
1159 57 s. Tonga Royal Guards . . 1·25 1·25
1160 57 s. Raising the ensign on "Neiafu" (patrol boat) . . 1·25 1·25
1161 2 p. "Savea" (patrol boat) (horiz) . . . . 3·00 3·50
1162 2 p. King Taufa'ahau Tupou IV inspecting parade (horiz) . 3·00 3·50

1992. No. 1007 surch **1s**.
1163 1 s. on 20 s. White-tailed damselfish 55 55

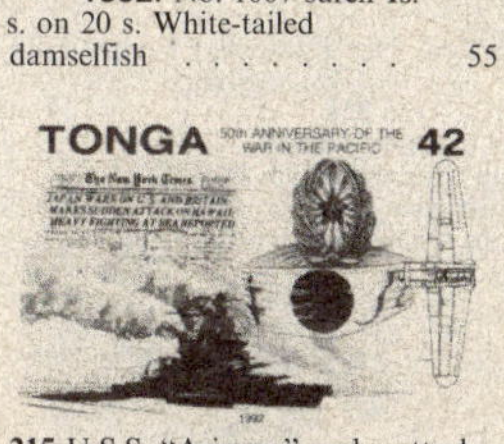

215 U.S.S. "Arizona" under attack, Pearl Harbor, 1441

1992. 50th Anniv of Outbreak of Pacific War. Multicoloured.
1165 42 s. Type **215** . . . . . . 1·25 1·25
1166 42 s. Japanese invasion of the Philippines . . . . . . 1·25 1·25
1167 42 s. U.S. landings in the Gilbert Islands . . . . . 1·25 1·25
1168 42 s. Landing on Iwo Jima . 1·25 1·25
1169 42 s. Admiral Nimitz and Battle of Midway map . . . . 1·25 1·25
1170 42 s. General MacArthur and liberation of Philippines map 1·25 1·25
1171 42 s. Lt-Gen. Holland Smith and map of landings on Saipan and Tinian . . . . 1·25 1·25
1172 42 s. Major-Gen. Curtis Lemay and bombing of Japan map 1·25 1·25
1173 42 s. Japanese Mitsubishi A6M Zero-Sen . . . . 1·25 1·25
1174 42 s. Douglas SBD Dauntless 1·25 1·25
1175 42 s. Grumman FM-2 Wildcat 1·25 1·25
1176 42 s. Supermarine Seafire Mk III . . . . 1·25 1·25
Nos. 1165/76 were printed togther, se-tenant, forming a composite design.

216 Boxing 217 King Taufa'ahau Taupou IV and Queen Halaevalu

1992. Olympic Games, Barcelona. Mult.
1177 42 s. Type **216** 75 50
1178 57 s. Diving 95 55
1179 1 p. 50 Tennis . . . . . . 4·00 4·25
1180 3 p. Cycling . . . . 6·00 6·50

1992. 25th Anniv of the Coronation of King Tupou IV.
1181 **217** 45 s. multicoloured . . . 75 45
1182 – 80 s. multicoloured . . . 1·50 1·75
1183 – 80 s. black and brown . . 1·50 1·75
1184 – 80 s. multicoloured . . . 1·50 1·75
1185 – 2 p. multicoloured . . . 3·50 4·00
DESIGNS—48 × 35 mm: No. 1182, King Tupou IV and Crown; No. 1183, Extract from Investiture ceremony; No. 1184, King Tupou IV and 1967 Coronation 2 p. commemorative; No. 1185, As Type **217** but larger.
Nos. 1181/5 show the King's first name incorrectly spelt as "Tauf'ahau".

1992. No. 1095 surch **45s 45s**.
1186 45 s. on 32 s. Powder-blue surgeonfish . . . . . . 2·50 1·50

1992. Nos. 1121/4 surch **60**.
1187 60 s. on 42 s. Safety in cars (English inscr) . . . . . 2·25 2·25
1188 60 s. on 42 s. Safety on bikes (English inscr) . . . . . 2·25 2·25
1189 60 s. on 42 s. As No. 1187 (Tongan inscr) . . . . . 2·25 2·25
1190 60 s. on 42 s. As No. 1188 (Tongan inscr) . . . . . 2·25 2·25

220 Bats flying Home 222 Tonga Flag and Rotary Emblem (25th anniv of Rotary International in Tonga)

221 Tongan Pearls

1992. Sacred Bats of Kolovai. Multicoloured.
1191 60 s. Type **220** . . . . . . 1·60 1·60
1192 60 s. Tongan fruit bat . . . 1·60 1·60
1193 60 s. Bats alighting on branches 1·60 1·60
1194 60 s. Bats hanging from tree . 1·60 1·60
1195 60 s. Tongan fruit bat in tree 1·60 1·60
Nos. 1191/5 were printed together, se-tenant, forming a composite design.

1992. Christmas. Multicoloured.
1197 60 s. Type **221** 70 65
1198 80 s. Reef fish 90 80
1199 2 p. Pacific orchids . . . . 4·25 4·75
1200 3 p. Red shining parrots from Eua . . . . 5·50 6·50

1992. Anniversaries and Events.
1201 **222** 60 s. multicoloured . . . 1·00 65
1202 – 80 s. multicoloured . . . 1·25 90
1203 – 1 p. 50 violet, lilac & black 2·75 3·50
1204 – 3 p. 50 multicoloured . . 5·50 6·50
DESIGNS: 80 s. Pres. Kennedy and Peace Corps emblem (25th anniv of Peace Corps in Tonga); 1 p. 50, F.A.O. and W.H.O. emblems (International Conference); 3 p. 50, Globe and Rotary Foundation emblem (75th anniv of Rotary Foundation).

223 Mother and Child

226 Chaste Mitre

224 Anti-smoking and Anti-drugs Symbols with Healthy Food (½-size illustration)

1993. Family Planning.
1205 **223** 15 s. black, blue and mauve (English inscr) 40 40
1206 – 15 s. black, blue and mauve (Tongan inscr) 40 40
1207 – 45 s. black, yellow and green (English inscr) . 90 90
1208 – 45 s. black, yellow and green (Tongan inscr) . 90 90
1209 – 60 s. black, red and yellow (English inscr) . . 1·90 1·90
1210 – 60 s. black, red and yellow (Tongan inscr) . . 1·90 1·90
1211 – 2 p. black, yellow & orange (English inscr) . . . . 4·00 4·00
1212 – 2 p. black, yellow & orange (Tongan inscr) . . . . 4·00 4·00
DESIGNS: 45 s. Child on bike; 60 s. Girl with cats; 2 p. Old man and boy playing chess.

1993. Health and Fitness Campaign. Mult.
1213 60 s. Type **224** . . . . 1·25 90
1214 80 s. Anti-smoking symbol and weight training . . . . . . 1·60 1·10
1215 1 p. 50 Anti-drugs symbol and water sports . . . . . . 2·75 3·50
1216 2 p. 50 Healthy food with cyclist and jogger . . . . 5·00 6·00

1993. Nos. 1001 and 1087 surch.
1217 10 s. on 2 s. "Porites sp." . 50·00 15·00
1217a 20 s. on 4 s. Lionfish £400

1993. As Nos. 867, 872, 875, 877, 999, 1002, 1005, 1007, 1013/16 and 1017a, some with new face values, redrawn as in T **226** with species inscr at foot. Multicoloured.
1218 1 s. Type **226** 10 10
1219 3 s. Red squirrelfish 10 10
1220 5 s. Green map cowrie . . . 10 10
1221a 10 s. Bubble cone 10 10
1223a 20 s. White-tailed damselfish 15 20
1225a 45 s. Giant spider conch (as No. 877) 35 40
1227a 60 s. Princely cone (as No. 875) 45 50
1229a 80 s. Lionfish (as No. 872) . 60 65
1230 1 p. "Chelonia mydas" (turtle) 75 80
1231 2 p. "Birgus latro" (crab) . 1·50 1·60
1232 3 p. Rose-branch murex . . 2·25 2·40
1233 5 p. Humpback whale (as No. 1014) . . . . 3·75 4·00
1234 10 p. Variegated shark . . . 7·50 7·75
Nos. 1218/29 are 19 × 22 mm, Nos. 1230/3 are 40 × 28 mm and No. 1234, 28 × 40 mm.
For 1 to 10 p. with species inscription at top left, see Nos. 1345/9.

227 Fire Brigade Badge

1993. 25th Annivs of Police Training College and Fire Service. Multicoloured.
1235 45 s. Type **227** . . . . 1·50 1·50
1236 45 s. Police badge and van . . 1·50 1·50
1237 60 s. Police band . . . . . . 1·75 1·75
1238 60 s. Fire engine at fire . . . 1·75 1·75
1239 2 p. Fire engine at station . . 4·00 4·50
1240 2 p. Policeman and dog handler 4·00 4·50

228 Old Map of Islands

229 King Taufa'ahau Tupou IV and Musical Instruments

1993. 300th Anniv of Abel Tasman's Discovery of Eua. Multicoloured.
1241 30 s. Type **228** 80 55
1242 60 s. "Heemskirk" and "Zeehaan" at sea . . . . 1·25 85
1243 80 s. Tongan canoes welcoming ships . . . . 1·60 1·25
1244 3 p. 50 Tasman landing on Eua 6·00 8·00

1993. 75th Birthday of King Taufa'ahau Tupou IV. Multicoloured.
1245 45 s. Type **229** 60 45
1246 80 s. King Tupou IV and sporting events . . . . . 1·00 1·40
1247 80 s. King Tupou IV and ancient landmarks . . . . 1·00 1·40
1248 80 s. King Tupou IV and Royal Palace . . . . 1·00 1·40
1249 2 p. As Type **229** but larger . 2·50 3·25
Nos. 1246/9 are larger, 38½ × 51 mm.

230 Christmas Feast

231 "Land of Sun, Sea and Sand" (Kiley and Peter Moala)

1993. Christmas. Multicoloured.
1250 60 s. Type **230** 90 60
1251 80 s. Firing home-made cannon 1·25 80
1252 1 p. 50 Band playing carols . 2·50 3·25
1253 3 p. Going to church . . . . 5·00 6·00

1993. Winners of Children's Painting Competition.
1254 **231** 10 s. multicoloured . . . 30 50
1255 – 10 s. multicoloured . . . 30 50
1256 – 10 s. multicoloured . . . 30 50
1257 – 10 s. multicoloured . . . 30 50
1258 – 10 s. black and grey . . . 30 50
1259 – 10 s. black and grey . . . 30 50
1260 **231** 80 s. multicoloured . . . 1·40 1·60
1261 – 80 s. multicoloured . . . 1·40 1·60
1262 – 80 s. multicoloured . . . 1·40 1·60
1263 – 80 s. multicoloured . . . 1·40 1·60
1264 – 80 s. multicoloured . . . 1·40 1·60
1265 – 80 s. multicoloured . . . 1·40 1·60
DESIGNS: Nos. 1255 and 1261, "Maui, Fisher God of Tonga" (Kiley and Peter Moala); Nos. 1256 and 1262, "Traditional Island Transport" (Kiley and Peter Moala); Nos. 1257 and 1263, "Young Girl making Kava" (Pulotu Pole'o); Nos. 1258 and 1264, "Maui and his Hook" (Salome Tapou); Nos. 1259 and 1265, "Communications in the South Pacific" (Fe'ofa'aki Taufa).

233 Tiger Shark

1994. Game Fishing. Multicoloured.
1267 60 s. Type **233** . . . . . . 1·10 85
1268 80 s. Dolphin (fish) . . . . 1·50 1·10
1269 1 p. 50 Yellow-finned tuna . 2·75 3·25
1270 2 p. 50 Blue marlin . . . . 3·50 4·00

234 Hands holding World Cup

1994. World Cup Football Championship, U.S.A. Multicoloured.
1271 80 s. Type **234** . . . . . . 1·50 1·50
1272 80 s. Player's legs . . . . . 1·50 1·50
1273 2 p. German player (black shorts) . . . . 3·25 4·00
1274 2 p. American player . . . . 3·25 4·00

235 Policewoman

1994. Pan Pacific and South East Asia Women's Association Conference, Tonga. Multicoloured.
1275 45 s. Type **235** . . . . 1·50 1·50
1276 45 s. Woman barrister . . . . 1·50 1·50
1277 2 p. 50 Nurse . . . . 4·25 4·75
1278 2 p. 50 Woman doctor . . . 4·25 4·75

1994. Visit South Pacific Year '95 (1st issue). No. 1204 surch **VISIT SOUTH PACIFC YEAR '95 60** and emblem.
1280 60 s. on 3 p. 50 multicoloured 1·25 1·25
See also Nos. 1297/1308.

1994. 25th Anniv of Tongan Self-adhesive Stamps. (a) Various previous self-adhesive designs, some in smaller size, with new values.
1281 **128** 10 s. black and yellow (21 × 9 mm) (postage) . 20 30
1282 **124** 60 s. black, grey and brown 1·40 1·75
1283 – 60 s. multicoloured (as Nos. O214/15) . . . . 1·40 1·75
1284 **109** 25 s. multicoloured (27 × 36 mm) (air) . . . . . . 1·00 1·25
(b) As Nos. 915/18, but new face value and inscr "SELF-ADHESIVE ANNIVERSARY 1969–1994".
1285 **168** 45 s. black, pink and brown 75 85
1286 – 45 s. black, lilac and brown (as No. 916) 75 85
1287 – 45 s. black, yellow and brown (as No. 917) . . 1·25 1·50
1288 – 45 s. mult (as No. 918) . 2·75 3·25
(c) Hologram design, 39 × 29 mm, showing "Tongastar 1" satellite.
1289 – 2 p. multicoloured . . . . 5·00 6·00

238 Farmer, Produce and Emblem

1995. 50th Anniv of F.A.O.
1290 **238** 5 p. multicoloured . . . 7·00 8·00

239 Polynesian Girl with Bicycle on Beach

1995. 25th Anniv of Tonga's Entry into Commonwealth. Children with Bicycles. Mult.
1291 45 s. Type **239** 75 55
1292 60 s. Children and skyscrapers, Hong Kong 90 60
1293 80 s. Boy in African village . 1·25 80
1294 2 p. Indian boy and palace . 2·75 3·50
1295 2 p. 50 English children and village church . . . . . . 3·25 3·75

1995. Visit South Pacific Year '95 (2nd issue). (a) Nos. 1149/52, but inscr "VISIT SOUTH PACIFIC YEAR '95", optd or surch **WHERE TIME BEGINS** and emblem.
1297 60 s. on 57 s. Longboat . . . 75 60
1298 80 s. on 2 p. Stern of fautasi (large canoe) . . . . . . 1·00 1·25
1299 80 s. on 2 p. Bow of fautasi . 1·00 1·25
1300 1 p. Outrigger canoe . . . . 1·40 1·60
(b) Nos. 1197/1200 inscr either (A) "WHERE TIME BEGINS" or (B) "THE 21st CENTURY STARTS HERE" and surch **WHERE TIME BEGINS 60** and emblem.
1301 60 s. on 60 s. Type **221** (A) . 75 75
1302 60 s. on 60 s. Type **221** (B) . 75 75
1303 60 s. on 80 s. Reef fish (A) . 75 75
1304 60 s. on 80 s. Reef fish (B) . . 75 75
1305 60 s. on 2 p. Pacific orchids (A) 75 75
1306 60 s. on 2 p. Pacific orchids (B) 75 75
1307 60 s. on 3 p. Red shining parrots from Eua (A) 75 75
1308 60 s. on 3 p. Red shining parrots from Eua (B) 75 75

242 Soldier on Scrambling Net

1995. 50th Anniv of End of Second World War in the Pacific.
1309 **242** 60 s. yellow, blk & blue . 1·25 1·25
1310 – 60 s. yellow, blk & blue . 1·25 1·25
1311 – 60 s. yellow, blk & blue . 1·25 1·25
1312 – 60 s. multicoloured . . . 1·25 1·25
1313 – 60 s. multicoloured . . . 1·25 1·25
1314 **242** 80 s. yellow, black and red 1·25 1·25
1315 – 80 s. yellow, black and red 1·25 1·25
1316 – 80 s. yellow, black and red 1·25 1·25
1317 – 80 s. multicoloured . . . 1·25 1·25
1318 – 80 s. multicoloured . . . 1·25 1·25
DESIGNS: Nos. 1310 and 1315, U.S.S. "Nevada" (battleship) with troops in foreground; 1311 and 1316, U.S.S. "West Virginia" (battleship) and rear of landing craft; 1312 and 1317, U.S.S. "Idaho" (battleship) and front of landing craft; 1313 and 1318, Map of South-east Asia and Pacific.
Nos. 1309/18 were printed together, se-tenant, in sheetlets of 10 with the horizontal strips of 5 forming the same composite design.

243 1995 Commonwealth 45 s. Stamp and Exhibition Emblem

1995. "Singapore '95" International Stamp Exhibition. Multicoloured.
1319 45 s. Type **243** . . . . 1·00 1·25
1320 60 s. 1995 Commonwealth 60 s. stamp and emblem . . . . 1·00 1·25

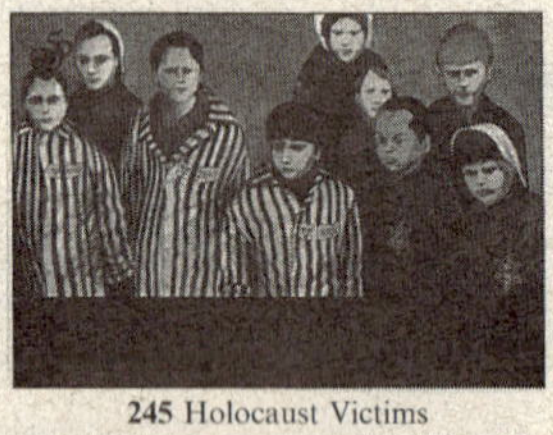
245 Holocaust Victims

1995. 50th Anniv of United Nations and End of Second World War. Multicoloured.
1323 **245** 60 s. multicoloured . . . 75 85
1324 – 60 s. black and blue . . 75 85
1325 – 60 s. multicoloured . . . 75 85
1326 – 80 s. multicoloured . . . 1·00 1·25
1327 – 80 s. blue and black . . 1·00 1·25
1328 – 80 s. multicoloured . . . 1·00 1·25
DESIGNS—As T **245**: No. 1325, Children of Holocaust survivors with balloons; 1326, Atomic explosion, Hiroshima; 1328, U.S. Space Shuttle. 23 × 35 mm: Nos. 1324 and 1327, U.N. anniversary emblem.

246 "Calanthe triplicata"

249 Running

247 Humpback Whale

1995. Greetings Stamps. Orchids. Inscribed either "MERRY CHRISTMAS" (A) or "A HAPPY 1996" (B). Multicoloured.
1329 20 s. Type **246** (A) 50 50
1330 45 s. "Spathoglottis plicata" (A) 75 75
1331 45 s. As No. 1330 (B) . . . 75 75
1332 60 s. "Dendrobium platygastrium" (A) 90 90
1333 60 s. As No. 1332 (B) . . . 90 90
1334 80 s. "Goodyera rubicunda" (B) . . . . 1·25 1·25
1335 2 p. "Dendrobium toki" (B) . 2·75 3·00
1336 2 p. 50 "Phaius tankervillae" (A) . . . . 3·50 3·75

1996. Endangered Species. Humpback Whale. Multicoloured.
1337 45 s. Type **247** . . . . 1·10 75
1338 60 s. Whale and calf . . . . . 1·50 80
1339 1 p. 50 Whale's tail and herald petrels . . . . 3·00 3·50
1340 2 p. 50 Whale breaking surface 4·50 5·50

1996. Multicoloured designs as Nos. 1230/4, but redrawn with species inscriptions at top left.
1345 1 p. "Chelonia mydas" (turtle) 75 80
1346 2 p. "Birgus latro" (crab) . . 1·50 1·60
1347 3 p. Rose branch murex . . 2·25 2·40
1348 5 p. Humpback whale . . . 3·75 4·00
1349 10 p. Variegated shark (vert) 7·50 7·75

1996. Centennial Olympic Games, Atlanta. Ancient Greek and Modern Athletes. Multicoloured.
1350 45 s. Type **249** 90 65
1351 80 s. Throwing the discus . . 1·50 1·10
1352 2 p. Throwing the javelin . . 4·00 4·25
1353 3 p. Equestrian dressage . . 5·50 6·00

250 Aspects of Prehistoric Life

1996. 13th Congress of International Union of Prehistoric and Protohistoric Sciences, Forli, Italy. Multicoloured.
1354 1 p. Type **250** . . . . 1·75 1·75
1355 1 p. Aspects of Egyptian, Greek and Roman civilisations . . 1·75 1·75

251 "Virgin and Child" (Sassoferrato)

1996. Christmas. Religious Paintings. Multicoloured.
1356 20 s. Type **251** 45 40
1357 60 s. "Adoration of the Shepherds" (Murillo) . . . 1·10 75
1358 80 s. "Virgin and Child" (Delaroche) . . . . 1·40 1·00
1359 3 p. "Adoration of the Shepherds" (Champaigne) . 4·50 5·50

252 Athletics and Rugby

1996. 50th Anniv of U.N.I.C.E.F. Children's Sports. Multicoloured.
1360 80 s. Type **252** . . . . 1·40 1·60
1361 80 s. Tennis . . . . 1·40 1·60
1362 80 s. Cycling . . . . 1·40 1·60
Nos. 1360/2 were printed together, se-tenant, forming a composite design.

253 Queen Halaevalu Mata'aho and Flag

1996. 70th Birthday of Queen Halaevalu Mata'aho. Multicoloured.
1363 60 s. Type **253** . . . . 1·00 65
1364 2 p. Queen and obverse (portrait) of commemorative coin . . . . 3·25 3·75
1365 2 p. Queen and reverse (arms) of commemorative coin . . . 3·25 3·75

254 Globe, the Ha'amonga and Kao Island

1996. "Towards the Millennium". Multicoloured.
1366 80 s. Type **254** . . . . 1·50 1·50
1367 80 s. Mount Talau, Royal Palace and satellite . . . . 1·50 1·50
1368 2 p. Type **254** . . . . 3·25 3·75
1369 2 p. As No. 1367 . . . . 3·25 3·75

1997. Nos. 1235/40 surch.
1371 10 s. on 45 s. Type **227** . . . . 1·75 1·75
1372 10 s. on 45 s. Police badge and van . . . . 1·75 1·75
1373 10 s. on 60 s. Police band . . 1·75 1·75
1374 10 s. on 60 s. Fire engine at fire . . . . 1·75 1·75
1375 20 s. on 2 p. Fire engine at station . . . . 2·00 2·00
1376 20 s. on 2 p. Policeman and dog handler . . . . 2·00 2·00

1997. Tongan Medal Winner at Atlanta Olympic Games. Nos. 1350/3 surch **A SILVER FOR TONGA**.
1378 10 s. on 45 s. Type **249** . . . 40 40
1379 10 s. on 80 s. Throwing the discus 40 40
1380 10 s. on 2 p. Throwing the javelin 40 40
1381 3 p. Equestrian dressage . . 3·50 4·00

258 Captain James Wilson and "Duff"

1997. Birth Bicentenary of King George I and Bicentenary of Christianity in Tonga (1st issue). Multicoloured.
1382 10 s. Type **258** 70 70
1383 10 s. King George Tupou I . 70 70
1384 10 s. Missionaries landing at Tongatapu 70 70
1385 10 s. Missionaries and Tongans 70 70
1386 60 s. Type **258** 90 90
1387 60 s. As No. 1384 . . . . . 90 90
1388 60 s. As No. 1385 . . . . . 90 90
1389 80 s. Type **258** 90 90
1390 80 s. As No. 1384 . . . . . 90 90
1391 80 s. As No. 1385 . . . . . 90 90
For 10 s. (value as Nos. 1382/5, but smaller, 28 × 18 mm), see Nos. 1405/8.

260 Children and School Building

1997. 50th Anniv of Tonga High School. Multicoloured.
1393 20 s. Type **260** 45 45
1394 60 s. Athletic team . . . . . 1·00 75
1395 80 s. School band . . . . . . 1·25 1·00
1396 3 p. 50 Athletics meeting . . 4·00 5·00

261 King and Queen of Tonga during Coronation
262 "Lenzites elegans"

1997. King and Queen of Tonga's Golden Wedding and 30th Anniv of the Coronation. Multicoloured. (a) Size 23 × 34 mm.
1397 10 s. Type **261** 40 40
1398 10 s. Moment of Crowning and procession 40 40
1399 10 s. King and Queen of Tonga 40 40
1400 45 s. Royal Crown 75 75

(b) Size 50 × 37 mm.
1401 60 s. As T **261** . . . . 90 1·00
1402 60 s. As No. 1398 . . . . . 90 1·00
1403 60 s. As No. 1399 . . . . . 90 1·00
1404 2 p. As No. 1400 . . . . . 2·50 3·00

1997. Birth Bicentenary of King George I and Bicentenary of Christianity in Tonga (2nd issue). As Nos. 1382/5, but smaller, 28 × 18 mm.
1405 10 s. Type **258** 30 30
1406 10 s. As No. 1384 . . . . . 30 30
1407 10 s. As No. 1385 . . . . . 30 30
1408 10 s. As No. 1383 . . . . . 30 30

1997. Fungi. Multicoloured. (a) Size 18 × 28 mm.
1409 10 s. Type **262** 40 40
1410 10 s. "Marasmiellus semiustus" 40 40
1411 10 s. "Aseroe rubra" 40 40
1412 10 s. "Podoscypha involuta" . 40 40
1413 10 s. "Microporus xanthopus" 40 40
1414 10 s. "Lentinus tuber-regium" 40 40

(b) Size 28 × 42 mm
1415 20 s. Type **262** 70 70
1416 20 s. As No. 1410 . . . . . 70 70
1417 60 s. As No. 1411 . . . . . 1·25 1·25
1418 60 s. As No. 1412 . . . . . 1·25 1·25
1419 2 p. As No. 1413 . . . . . 2·50 2·50
1420 2 p. As No. 1414 . . . . . 2·50 2·50
Nos. 1409/14 were printed together, se-tenant, with the backgrounds forming a composite design.

263 King Taufa'ahua Tupou IV
264 White Tern ("Fairy tern")

1998. 80th Birthday of King Taufa'ahua Tupou IV.
1422 **263** $2.70 multicoloured . . 2·00 2·10

1998. Birds. Multicoloured.
1425 5 s. Type **264** 10 10
1426 10 s. Tongan whistler 10 10
1427 15 s. Common barn owl . . . 15 20
1428 20 s. Purple swamphen . . . 15 20
1429 30 s. Red-footed booby . . . 25 30
1430 40 s. Banded rail (horiz) . . . 30 35
1431 50 s. Swamp harrier (horiz) . . 40 45
1432 55 s. Blue-crowned lorikeet . . 40 45
1433 60 s. Great frigate bird . . . 45 50
1434 70 s. Friendly ground dove (horiz) 55 60
1435 80 s. Red-tailed tropic bird . . 60 65
1436 1 p. Red shining parrot . . . 75 80
1437 2 p. Pacific pigeon . . . . . 1·50 1·60
1438 3 p. Pacific golden plover (horiz) 2·25 2·40
1439 5 p. Tongan megapode (horiz) 3·75 4·00

265 "Chaetodon pelewensis"

1998. International Year of the Ocean. Multicoloured.
1440 10 s. Type **265** 10 15
1441 55 s. "Chaetodon lunula" . . 40 45
1442 1 p. "Chaetodon ephippium" 75 80

266 Angel (inscr in Tongan)

1998. Christmas. Multicoloured.
1443 10 s. Type **266** 10 15
1444 80 s. Angel (inscr in English) . 60 65
1445 1 p. Boy with candle (inscr in Tongan) 75 80
1446 1 p. 60 Girl holding candle (inscr in English) . . . . . 1·10 1·25

268 "Heemskerk" (Tasman), 1643

1999. Early Explorers. Multicoloured.
1448 55 s. Type **268** 40 45
1449 80 s. "L'Astrolabe" (La Perouse), 1788 . . . . . . 60 65
1450 1 p. H.M.S. "Bounty" (Bligh), 1789 . . . . 75 80
1451 2 p. 50 H.M.S. "Resolution" (Cook), 1777 . . . . . . 1·90 2·00

269 Neiafu

1999. Scenic Views of Vava'u. Multicoloured.
1453 10 s. Type **269** 10 15
1454 55 s. Yachts at Port of Refuge 40 45
1455 80 s. Port of Refuge from the air 60 65
1456 1 p. Sunset at Neiafu 75 80
1457 2 p. 50 Mounu Island . . . . 1·90 2·00

EXPRESS STAMPS

E **1** Short-eared Owl in Flight

1990. Air.
E1 E **1** 10 p. black, red and blue . 7·50 7·75

OFFICIAL STAMPS

1893. Optd **G.F.B.**
O1 **5** 1d. blue . . . . 10·00 42·00
O2 **6** 2d. blue . . . . 27·00 48·00
O3 **5** 4d. blue . . . . 45·00 90·00
O4 **6** 8d. blue . . . . 85·00 £160
O5 1s. blue . . . . 95·00 £180

1893. Nos. O1/5 variously surch.
O 6 **5** ½d. on 1d. blue . . . . . 16·00 48·00
O 7 **6** 2½d. on 2d. blue . . . . . 22·00 40·00
O 8 **5** 5d. on 4d. blue . . . . . 22·00 40·00
O 9 **6** 7½d. on 8d. blue . . . . . 22·00 70·00
O10 10d. on 1s. blue . . . . . 26·00 75·00

1962. Air. Stamps of 1953 and 1961 optd as Nos. 120/7 but with **OFFICIAL AIRMAIL** in addition.
O11 2d. blue . . . . 11·00 6·00
O12 5d. violet . . . . 12·00 6·50
O13 1s. brown . . . . 7·50 3·75
O14 5s. yellow and lilac . . . . 90·00 55·00
O15 10s. yellow and black . . . 42·00 22·00
O16 £1 yellow, red and blue . . 70·00 35·00

1963. Air. First Polynesian Gold Coinage Commemoration. As No. 138 but additionally inscr "OFFICIAL". 1 koula coin. Diameter 3⅛ in. Imperf.
O17 B 15 s. black on gold . . . . 5·50 6·50

1965. Air. Surch as Nos. 151/61.
O18 B 30 s. on 15 s. (No. O17) . . 3·00 3·75

1966. Air. Tupou College and Secondary Education Centenary. No. 117 surch **OFFICIAL AIRMAIL** and new value, with commemoration inscr as Nos. 168/73.
O19 10 s. on 4d. green 80 35
O20 20 s. on 4d. green . . . . . 1·00 50

1967. Air. No. 112 surch **OFFICIAL AIRMAIL ONE PA'ANGA.**
O21 1 p. on 5 s. yellow and lilac . 4·50 2·25

1967. Air. No. 114 surch **OFFICIAL AIRMAIL** and new value
O22 40 s. on £1 yellow, red & blue 50 60
O23 60 s. on £1 yellow, red & blue 70 80
O24 1 p. on £1 yellow, red & blue 90 1·50
O25 2 p. on £1 yellow, red & blue 1·50 2·00

1967. Air. Arrival of U.S. Peace Corps in Tonga. As No. 114, but imperf and background colour changed, surch as Nos. 216/27 but with **Official Airmail** in addition.
O26 30 s. on £1 multicoloured . . 50 25
O27 70 s. on £1 multicoloured . . 70 45
O28 1 p. 50 on £1 multicoloured . 1·00 85

1968. Air. 50th Birthday of King Taufa'ahua IV. No. 207 surch **HIS MAJESTY'S 50th BIRTHDAY OFFICIAL AIRMAIL** and new value.
O29 40 s. on 50 s. red and blue . 1·50 70
O30 60 s. on 50 s. red and blue . 2·00 1·25
O31 1 p. on 50 s. red and blue . . 2·75 2·75
O32 2 p. on 50 s. red and blue . . 5·00 5·00

1968. Air. South Pacific Games Field and Track Trials, Port Moresby, New Guinea. As No. 114 but imperf, background colour changed, surch **Friendly Islands Trials Field & Track South Pacific Games Port Moresby 1969 OFFICIAL AIRMAIL** and value.
O33 20 s. on £1 multicoloured . . 20 15
O34 1 p. on £1 multicoloured . . 70 70

1969. Air. 3rd South Pacific Games, Port Moresby. As Nos. 290/4 surch **OFFICIAL AIRMAIL.**
O35 70 s. red, green and turquoise 55 80
O36 80 s. red, orange & turquoise 65 90

1969. Air. Oil Search. As No. 114 but imperf, background colour changed and optd **1969 OIL SEARCH** and new value.
O37 90 s. on £1 multicoloured . . 3·50 3·50
O38 1 p. 10 on £1 multicoloured . 3·50 3·50
No. O37 is additionally optd **OFFICIAL AIRMAIL.**

1969. Air. Royal Visit. As No. 110, but imperf, colour changed, and surch **Royal Visit MARCH 1970 OFFICIAL AIRMAIL** and new value.
O39 75 s. on 1s. red and yellow . 3·50 3·25
O40 1 p. on 1s. red and yellow . . 4·00 3·75
O41 1 p. 25 on 1s. red and yellow 4·75 5·00

1970. Air. Entry into British Commonwealth. As No. 112, but imperf and surch **Commonwealth Member JUNE 1970 OFFICIAL AIRMAIL** and value.
O42 50 s. on 5s. yellow and brown 1·00 1·00
O43 90 s. on 5s. yellow and brown 1·40 1·60
O44 1 p. 50 on 5s. yellow & brown 2·25 2·75

1970. Imperf. Self-adhesive. Colour of "TONGA" given for 6 s. to 10 s.
O45 **83** 1 s. yellow, purple & black 45 50
O46 2 s. yellow, blue and black 55 60
O47 3 s. yellow, brown & black 55 60
O48 4 s. yellow, green and black 55 60
O49 5 s. yellow, red and black . 60 65
O50 **90** 6 s. blue 70 80
O51 7 s. mauve 75 85
O52 8 s. gold 85 95
O53 9 s. red . . . . 95 1·10
O54 10 s. silver . . . . 95 1·10

On the official issues Nos. O45 to O54, the value tablet is black (banana issue) or green (coconut issue). On the postage issues the colour is white.
See also Nos. O82/91.

1970. Air. Centenary of British Red Cross. As No. 102 and 112 but imperf in different colours and surch **Centenary British Red Cross 1870–1970 OFFICIAL AIRMAIL** and value.
O55 30 s. on 1½d. green . . . . . 1·75 1·75
O56 80 s. on 5s. yellow and brown 4·25 4·25
O57 90 s. on 5s. yellow and brown 4·25 4·25

1971. Air. 5th Death Anniv of Queen Salote. As No. 113, but imperf and colour changed surch **OFFICIAL AIRMAIL 1965 IN MEMORIAM 1970** and value.
O58 20 s. on 10s. orange . . . . . 1·25 80
O59 30 s. on 10s. orange . . . . . 1·50 1·00
O60 50 s. on 10s. orange . . . . . 2·75 2·00
O61 2 p. on 10s. orange . . . . . 9·00 8·00

1971. Air. Philatokyo '71 Stamp Exhibition, Japan. Nos. O55/7 optd **PHILATOKYO '71** and emblem.
O62 30 s. on 5d. green and yellow 90 65
O63 80 s. on 5d. green and yellow 1·75 1·75
O64 90 s. on 5d. green and yellow 2·00 2·00

1971. Air. As T **96** but inscr "OFFICIAL AIRMAIL".
O65 14 s. multicoloured . . . . 1·50 1·50
O65a 17 s. multicoloured . . . . 1·75 1·75
O66 21 s. multicoloured . . . . 1·75 1·75
O66a 38 s. multicoloured . . . . 2·75 2·75

O 13

1971. Air. 4th South Pacific Games, Tahiti. Imperf. Self-adhesive.
O67 O **13** 50 s. multicoloured . . 60 90
O68 90 s. multicoloured . . 85 1·50
O69 1 p. 50 multicoloured . 1·25 1·75

1971. Air. Investiture of Royal Tongan Medal of Merit surch **INVESTITURE 1971 OFFICIAL AIRMAIL.**
O70 **89** 60 s. on 3 s. multicoloured 70 90
O71 80 s. on 25 s. multicoloured 90 1·25
O72 1 p. 10 on 7 s. multicoloured 1·00 1·50

O **15** "U.N.I.C.E.F." and Emblem

1971. Air. 25th Anniv of U.N.I.C.E.F. Imperf Self-adhesive.
O73 O **15** 70 s. multicoloured . . 1·40 1·60
O74 80 s. multicoloured . . 1·50 1·75
O75 90 s. multicoloured . . 1·60 1·90

1972. Air. Merchant Marine Routes. As T **100** but inscr "OFFICIAL AIRMAIL". Imperf. Self-adhesive.
O76 20 s. multicoloured . . . . . 1·25 80
O77 50 s. multicoloured . . . . . 2·75 2·50
O78 1 p. 20 multicoloured . . . . 5·50 6·50
DESIGN: Nos. O76/8, Map of South Pacific and "Aoniu".

1972. Air. 5th Anniv of Coronation. Design similar to T **101**, but inscr "OFFICIAL AIRMAIL".
O79 50 s. multicoloured . . . . . 1·00 85
O80 70 s. multicoloured . . . . . 1·40 1·25
O81 1 p. 50 multicoloured . . . . 2·75 2·50
DESIGN—(47 × 57 mm): Nos. O79/81, As Type **101** but with different background.

1972. As Nos. 413/27 but inscr "OFFICIAL POST".
(a) As Nos. 413/17.
O82 **83** 1 s. yellow, red and black . 20 10
O83 2 s. yellow, green and black 25 15
O84 3 s. yellow, green and black 30 20
O85 4 s. yellow and black . . . 30 20
O86 5 s. yellow and black . . . 30 20

(b) As Nos. O50/4 but colours changed. Mult. Colour of "TONGA" given.
O87 **90** 6 s. green 35 20
O88 7 s. green 40 25
O89 8 s. green 40 25
O90 9 s. green 40 25
O91 10 s. green 50 30

(c) As Nos. 423/7. Multicoloured. Colour of face value given.
O92 **102** 15 s. blue 85 45
O93 20 s. orange . . . . . . 1·00 60
O94 25 s. brown . . . . . . 1·10 70
O95 40 s. orange . . . . . . 2·25 1·50
O96 50 s. blue . . . . 2·50 1·75

1972. Air. Proclamation of Sovereignty over Minerva Reefs. As T **104**, but inscr "OFFICIAL AIRMAIL".
O97 25 s. multicoloured 40 35
O98 75 s. multicoloured . . . . . 1·25 1·50
O99 1 p. 50 multicoloured . . . . 2·50 3·00

1973. Air. Foundation of Bank of Tonga. No. 396 surch **TONGA 1973 ESTABLISHMENT BANK OF TONGA OFFICIAL AIRMAIL**, star and value.
O100 **100** 40 s. on 21 s. mult . . 1·50 1·25
O101 85 s. on 21 s. mult . . 2·75 2·50
O102 1 p. 25 on 21 s. mult . 3·50 3·50

1973. Silver Jubilee of Scouting in Tonga. Nos. O76, O74 and 319 surch or optd.
O103 – 30 s. on 20 s. mult . 12·00 2·75
O104 O **15** 80 s. multicoloured 28·00 10·00
O105 **89** 1 p. 40 on 50 s. mult 42·00 25·00
OVERPRINT AND SURCHARGES: 30 s. **SILVER JUBILEE TONGAN SCOUTING 1948–1973**, scout badge and value; 80 c. **SILVER JUBILEE 1948–1973** and scout badge; 1 p. 40, **OFFICIAL AIRMAIL 1948–1973 SILVER JUBILEE TONGAN SCOUTING** and value.

1973. Air. Bicentenary of Capt. Cook's Visit. Design similar to T **107** but inscr "OFFICIAL AIRMAIL".
O106 25 s. multicoloured . . . . 3·25 1·50
O107 80 s. multicoloured . . . . 8·50 4·50
O108 1 p. 30 multicoloured . . . 10·00 7·50
DESIGN—HORIZ (52 × 45 mm): Nos. O106/108, "James Cook" (bulk carrier).

1973. Air. Commonwealth Games, Christchurch Nos. O67/9 optd **1974 Commonwealth Games Christchurch OFFICIAL AIRMAIL.**
O109 O **13** 50 s. multicoloured . 1·00 1·10
O110 90 s. multicoloured . 1·75 1·75
O111 1 p. 50 multicoloured 2·50 2·50

O **19** Dove of Peace

1974. Air.
O112 O **19** 7 s. green, violet & red 60 20
O113 9 s. green, violet & brn 65 25
O114 12 s. green, violet & brn 70 75
O115 14 s. green, violet & yell 75 40
O116 17 s. multicoloured . 85 60
O117 29 s. multicoloured . 1·50 1·00
O118 38 s. multicoloured . 2·00 1·25
O119 50 s. multicoloured . 2·50 2·75
O120 75 s. multicoloured . 3·75 4·25

1974. Air. Centenary of U.P.U. As Nos. 488/97 but inscr "OFFICIAL AIRMAIL".
O121 25 s. orange, green and black 50 60
O122 35 s. yellow, red and black . 60 75
O123 70 s. orange, blue and black 1·25 2·00
DESIGNS—HORIZ (43 × 40 mm): Nos. O121/3, Letters "UPU".

1974. Air. Tongan Girl Guides. As Nos. 498/507 inscr "OFFICIAL AIRMAIL".
O124 45 s. multicoloured . . . . 4·00 2·00
O125 55 s. multicoloured . . . . 4·25 2·25
O126 1 p. multicoloured . . . . 7·50 5·50
DESIGNS—OVAL (36 × 52 mm): Nos. O124/6, Lady Baden-Powell.

1974. Air. Establishment of Royal Marine Institute. No. 446 surch **OFFICIAL AIRMAIL 80s** and RMI emblem and No. 451 surch **Establishment Royal Marine Institute Official Airmail TONGA TONGA**, RMI emblem and value.
O127 **106** 30 s. on 15 s. multicoloured 2·50 1·75
O128 – 35 s. on 15 s. multicoloured 2·75 2·00
O129 – 80 s. on 17 s. multicoloured 4·25 4·50

1975. Air. South Pacific Forum and Tourism. As T **113**. Imperf. Self-adhesive.
O130 50 s. multicoloured . . . . 1·10 1·00
O131 75 s. multicoloured . . . . 1·75 1·50
O132 1 p. 25 multicoloured . . . 2·50 2·25
DESIGNS—(49 × 43 mm): 50 s. Jungle arch; 75 s., 1 p. 25, Sunset scene.

1975. Air. 5th South Pacific Games. As T **114**. Imperf. Self-adhesive.
O133 38 s. multicoloured 55 50
O134 75 s. multicoloured . . . . 90 1·25
O135 1 p. 20 multicoloured . . . 1·60 2·25
DESIGN—OVAL (51 × 27 mm): Nos. O133/5, Runners on track.

O **21** Tongan Monarchs
(⅔-size illustration)

1975. Air. Centenary of Tongan Constitution. Imperf. Self-adhesive.
O136 O **21** 17 s. multicoloured . . 55 40
O137 60 s. multicoloured . . 1·25 1·50
O138 90 s. multicoloured . . 1·75 2·00

1976. Air. First Participation in Olympic Games. As Nos. 558/67 but inscr "OFFICIAL AIRMAIL".
O139 45 s. multicoloured . . . . . 2·75 1·00
O140 55 s. multicoloured . . . . . 3·00 1·25
O141 1 p. multicoloured . . . . . 5·00 3·50
DESIGN—OVAL (36 × 53 mm): Montreal logo.

1976. Air. Bicentenary of American Revolution. As Nos. 568/77 but inscr "OFFICIAL AIRMAIL".
O142 20 s. multicoloured 90 50
O143 50 s. multicoloured . . . . . 1·50 1·50
O144 1 p. 15 multicoloured . . . . 3·25 3·50

1976. Air. 150th Anniv of Christianity in Tonga.
O145 65 s. multicoloured . . . . . 1·75 1·75
O146 85 s. multicoloured . . . . . 2·00 2·25
O147 1 p. 15 multicoloured . . . . 2·75 3·25
DESIGN—HEXAGONAL (65 × 52 mm): Lifuka Chapel.

1976. Air. Centenary of Treaty of Friendship with Germany.
O148 30 s. multicoloured 60 70
O149 60 s. multicoloured . . . . . 1·40 1·75
O150 1 p. 25 multicoloured . . . . 2·75 3·50
DESIGN—RECTANGULAR (51 × 47 mm): Text.

1977. Air. Silver Jubilee.
O151 35 s. multicoloured 90 40
O152 45 s. multicoloured 40 30
O153 1 p. 10 multicoloured 55 50
DESIGN—57 × 66 mm: Flags of Tonga and the U.K.

1977. Air. 10th Anniv of King's Coronation.
O154 20 s. multicoloured 40 45
O155 40 s. multicoloured . . . . . 80 1·00
O156 80 s. multicoloured . . . . . 1·75 2·25
DESIGN—SQUARE (50 × 50 mm): 1967 Coronation coin.

1977. Air. Bicent of Capt. Cook's Last Voyage.
O157 20 s. multicoloured . . . . . 2·75 2·50
O158 55 s. on 20 s. multicoloured . 6·00 6·50
O159 85 s. on 20 s. multicoloured . 8·50 9·00
DESIGN—RECTANGULAR (52 × 46 mm): Text.

1977. Air. Whale Conservation.
O160 45 s. multicoloured . . . . . 4·50 2·75
O161 65 s. multicoloured . . . . . 6·00 4·50
O162 85 s. multicoloured . . . . . 7·50 5·50
DESIGN—HEXAGONAL (66 × 51 mm): Blue whale.

1978. Air. Commonwealth Games, Edmonton.
O163 30 s. black, blue and red . . 45 50
O164 60 s. black, red and blue . . 1·00 1·25
O165 1 p. black, red and blue . . . 1·60 1·75
DESIGN—TEAR-DROP (35 × 52 mm): Games emblem.

1978. Air. 60th Birthday of King Taufa'ahau Tupou IV.
O166 26 s. black, red and yellow . 35 30
O167 85 s. black, brown and yell . 1·10 1·25
O168 90 s. black, violet and yellow 1·25 1·25
DESIGN—MEDAL-SHAPED (21 × 45mm): Portrait of King.

1978. Coil stamps. As Nos. 675/89 but inscr "OFFICIAL POST".
O169 1 s. purple and yellow . . . 20 20
O170 2 s. brown and yellow . . . 20 20
O171 3 s. red and yellow 30 30
O172 4 s. brown and yellow . . . 30 30
O173 5 s. green and yellow 30 30
O174 6 s. brown and green 40 40
O175 7 s. black, green and brown . 40 40
O176 8 s. red, green and brown . . 40 40
O177 9 s. brown and green 40 40
O178 10 s. green and brown . . . 40 40
O179 15 s. black, brown and green 1·00 1·00
O180 20 s. red, brown and green . 1·10 1·10
O181 30 s. green and brown . . . 1·25 1·50
O182 50 s. blue, brown and green . 1·50 1·75
O183 1 p. violet, brown and green 2·25 2·75

1978. Air. Endangered Wildlife. Multicoloured.
O184 40 s. Type **129** . . . . 4·00 3·00
O185 50 s. Insular flying fox . . . 4·00 3·00
O186 1 p. 10 Turtle . . . . 6·00 6·00

1979. Air. Decade of Progress. As Nos. 700/9, but inscr "OFFICIAL AIRMAIL".
O187 G 38 s. multicoloured . . 65 40
O188 E 74 s. multicoloured . . 1·25 75
O189 A 80 s. multicoloured . . 1·40 80

1979. Air. Death Centenary of Sir Rowland Hill and 10th Anniv of Tongan Self-adhesive Stamps.
O190 45 s. multicoloured . . . . . 1·00 60
O191 65 s. multicoloured . . . . . 1·40 85
O192 80 s. multicoloured . . . . . 1·75 1·10
DESIGN—HAND SHAPED (45 × 53 mm): 45 s. to 80 s. Removing self-adhesive stamp from backing paper.

O **22** Blue-crowned Lory (with foliage)

O **23** Blue-crowned Lory (without foliage)

1979. Air. Coil Stamps.
O193 O **22** 5 s. multicoloured . . 50 40
O194 11 s. multicoloured . . 55 40
O195 14 s. multicoloured . . 55 40
O196 15 s. multicoloured . . 60 40
O197 17 s. multicoloured . . 60 40
O198 18 s. multicoloured . . 60 40
O199 22 s. multicoloured . . 70 45
O200 31 s. multicoloured . . 75 65
O201 39 s. multicoloured . . 90 80
O202 75 s. multicoloured . . 1·75 2·50
O203 1 p. multicoloured . . 2·25 3·25

1979. Air. Views as seen through the Lens of a Camera.
O204 35 s. multicoloured 55 55
O205 45 s. multicoloured 65 65
O206 1 p. multicoloured . . . . . 1·40 2·25
DESIGN: 35 s. to 1 p. Niuatoputapu and Tafahi.

1980. Air. 125th Anniv of France–Tonga Friendship Treaty.
O207 40 s. multicoloured . . . . 1·00 1·00
O208 55 s. multicoloured . . . . 1·25 1·25
O209 1 p. 25 multicoloured . . . 2·50 2·75
DESIGN: 40 s. to 1 p. 25, Establishment of the Principle of Religious Freedom in the Pacific Islands.

1980. Air. Olympic Games, Moscow. Nos. O190/2 surch mascot, **1980 OLYMPIC GAMES**, value and emblem.
O210 26 s. on 45 s. multicoloured 85 85
O211 40 s. on 65 s. multicoloured 1·40 1·40
O212 1 p. 10 on 1 p. multicoloured 3·50 3·75

1980. No. O193 redrawn without foliage as Type O **23**.
O213 O **23** 5 s. multicoloured . . £100

1980. Air. South Pacific Scout Jamboree, Tonga and 75th Anniv of Rotary International.
O214 25 s. multicoloured 70 50
O215 2 p. multicoloured . . . . . 3·50 4·00
DESIGN: 25 s., 2 p. Scout camp and Rotary emblem.
Nos. O214/15 show maps of Tonga on the reverse.

1980. Air. Nos. O145 surch **T.$2**.
O216 2 p. on 65 s. multicoloured . 4·50 5·50

1983. Nos. 834/6 optd **OFFICIAL**.
O217 29 s. Type **151** . . . . . . 3·25 3·50
O218 32 s. Type **151** . . . . . . 3·75 4·00
O219 47 s. Montgolfier's balloon and Concorde . . . . 6·50 7·00

1984. Nos. 865/79 and 881 optd **OFFICIAL**.
O220 1 s. Type **159** 30 40
O221 2 s. "Porites sp" 30 40
O222 3 s. Red squirrelfish 30 40
O223 5 s. Green map cowrie . . . 30 30
O224 6 s. "Dardanus megistos" . 30 40
O225 9 s. Variegated shark . . . 40 40
O226 10 s. Bubble cone 40 30
O227 13 s. Lionfish 55 40
O228 15 s. Textile or cloth of gold cone 65 65
O229 20 s. White-tailed damselfish 70 70
O230 29 s. Princely cone 80 60
O231 32 s. Powder-blue surgeonfish 80 60
O232 47 s. Giant spider conch . . 1·00 80
O233 1 p. "Millepora dichotama" 2·50 2·50
O234 2 p. "Birgus latro" . . . . 4·00 4·00
O235 5 p. Yellow-finned tuna . . 8·00 9·00

1986. Nos. 933/9 optd **OFFICIAL**.
O236 4 s. on 2 s. "Porites sp" . . 70 80
O237 4 s. on 13 s. Lionfish . . . 70 80
O238 42 s. on 3 s. Red squirrelfish 1·75 1·75
O239 42 s. on 9 s. Variegated shark 1·75 1·75
O240 57 s. on 6 s. "Dardanus megistos" . . . . 2·00 2·00
O241 57 s. on 20 s. White-tailed damselfish . . . . 2·00 2·00
O242 2 p. 50 on 2 p. "Birgus latro" 7·00 8·00

1994. Air. 25th Anniv of Tongan Self-adhesive Stamps. Design as No. O192, but inscr "25th ANNIVERSARY OF THE INTRODUCTION OF SELFADHESIVE STAMPS 1969–1994 BERNARD MECHANICK: 1915–80 INVENTOR FREEFORM SELFADHESIVE STAMPS" at centre foot.
O243 80 s. multicoloured . . . . 3·00 3·50

O **30** Bubble Cone

1995. Designs as Nos. 1221a, 1223a, 1225a, 1227a and 1229a, but inscr as Type O **30**.
O247 10 s. Bubble cone 10 10
O249 20 s. White-tailed dascyllus . 15 20
O251 45 s. Giant spider conch . . 35 40
O253 60 s. Princely cone 45 50
O255 80 s. Lionfish 60 65
O256 1 p. "Chelonia mydas" (turtle) 75 80
O257 2 p. "Birgus latro" (crab) . 1·50 1·60
O258 3 p. Rose branch murex . . 2·25 2·40
O259 5 p. Humpback whale . . . 3·75 4·00
O260 10 p. Variegated shark (vert) 7·50 7·75

TRANSKEI

The Republic of Transkei was established on 26 October 1976, as the first of the independent "black homelands" constructed from the territory of the Republic of South Africa.

This independence did not receive international political recognition, but the stamps were accepted as valid on international mail.

Transkei was reincorporated with the Republic of South Africa on 27 April 1994.

100 cents = 1 rand

1 Lubisi Dam

1976. Transkei Scenes and Occupations. Multicoloured.

1	1 c. Type 1	10	10
2	2 c. Soil cultivation	10	10
3	3 c. Threshing sorghum	15	10
4a	4 c. Transkei matron	15	10
5a	5 c. Grinding maize	15	10
6	6 c. Cutting "Phormium tenax"	15	10
7	7 c. Herd-boy	40	10
8	8 c. Felling timber	20	10
9	9 c. Agricultural schooling	15	15
10a	10 c. Tea picking	20	15
11a	15 c. Carrying wood	30	15
12a	20 c. Weaving industry	35	15
13	25 c. Cattle	45	25
14a	30 c. Sledge transportation	75	45
15	50 c. Coat of arms and map	85	50
16	1 r. Administration building, Umtata	1·00	1·25
17	2 r. The Bunga (Parliamentary building), Umtata	1·75	2·25

2 K. D. Matanzima

4 "Artemisia afra"

3 Beech 100 King Air of Transkei Airways

1976. Independence. Multicoloured.

18	4 c. Type 2	25	20
19	10 c. Flag and mace	45	45
20	15 c. K. D. Matanzima, Paramount Chief (different)	85	85
21	20 c. Coat of arms	95	1·00

1977. Transkei Airways' Inaugural Flight. Multicoloured.

22	4 c. Type 3	30	25
23	15 c. Beech King Air landing at Matanzima Airport	1·25	1·50

1977. Medicinal Plants (1st series). Mult.

24	4 c. Type 4	20	10
25	10 c. "Bulbine natalensis"	70	75
26	15 c. "Melianthus major"	80	95
27	20 c. "Cotyledon orbiculata"	1·25	1·75

See also Nos. 88/91.

5 Disc Jockey

6 Blind Basket Weaver

1977. 1st Anniv of Transkei Radio. Mult.

28	4 c. Type 5	15	10
29	15 c. Announcer	60	60

1977. Help for the Blind.

30	6 4 c. black, lilac and gold	15	10
31	– 15 c. black, drab and gold	35	35
32	– 20 c. black, brown and gold	75	80

DESIGNS: 15 c. Hands reading braille; 20 c. Blind woman spinning.

7 Men's Carved Pipes

1978. Carved Pipes. Multicoloured.

33	4 c. Type 7	10	10
34	10 c. Two men's pipes	15	15
35	15 c. Multi-bowled men's pipes	45	55
36	20 c. Woman's and witch-doctor's pipes	60	70

8 Angora Goat

9 "Carissa bispinosa"

1978. Weaving Industry. Multicoloured.

37	4 c. Type 8	15	10
38	10 c. Spinning mohair	15	15
39	15 c. Dyeing mohair	30	35
40	20 c. Weaving a mohair rug	45	55

1978. Edible Wild Fruits. Multicoloured.

41	4 c. Type 9	15	10
42	10 c. "Dovyalis caffra"	30	25
43	15 c. "Harpephyllum caffrum"	55	55
44	20 c. "Syzygium cordatum"	60	70

10 Calipers

12 President K. D. Matanzima

11 Chi Cha Youth

1978. Care of Cripples.

45	10 4 c. black, brown and gold	15	10
46	– 10 c. black, grey and gold	40	40
47	– 15 c. black, yellow and gold	50	55

DESIGNS: 10 c. Child in wheelchair; 15 c. Nurse examining child's leg.

1979. Abakwetha (coming-of-age ceremony of Xhosa males). Multicoloured.

48	4 c. Type 11	15	10
49	10 c. Youths in three-month seclusion	30	25
50	15 c. Umtshilo dance	55	55
51	20 c. Burning of seclusion hut at end of final ceremony	60	70

1979. Inaug of Second State President.

52	12 4 c. red and gold	15	10
53	15 c. green and gold	50	45

13 Windpump

14 Magwa Falls

1979. Water Resources. Multicoloured.

54	4 c. Type 13	15	10
55	10 c. Woman ladling water into jar	30	25
56	15 c. Indwe River Dam (horiz)	55	55
57	20 c. Ncora Dam (horiz)	60	70

1979. Waterfalls. Multicoloured.

58	4 c. Type 14	15	10
59	10 c. Bawa Falls	30	25
60	15 c. Waterfall Bluff (horiz)	55	55
61	20 c. Tsitsa Falls (horiz)	60	70

15 Expectant Mother pouring Milk

16 Black Gnat (dry fly)

1979. Child Health. Multicoloured.

62	5 c. Type 15	15	10
63	15 c. Mother breast-feeding baby	45	45
64	20 c. Immunising child	60	65

1980. Fishing Flies (1st series). Multicoloured.

65	5 c. Type 16	35	35
66	5 c. Zug Bug (nymph)	35	35
67	5 c. March Brown (wet fly)	35	35
68	5 c. Durham Ranger (salmon fly)	35	35
69	5 c. Colonel Bates (streamer)	35	35

See also Nos. 83/7, 99/103, 116/20 and 133/7.

17 Rotary Emblem

18 "Encephalartos altensteinii"

1980. 75th Anniv of Rotary International.

70	17 15 c. blue and gold	35	30

1980. Cycads. Multicoloured.

71	5 c. Type 18	15	10
72	10 c. "Encephalartos princeps"	25	25
73	15 c. "Encephalartos villosus"	40	40
74	20 c. "Encephalartos friderici-guilielmi"	50	55

19 Red-chested Cuckoo

1980. Birds. Multicoloured.

75	5 c. Type 19	20	10
76	10 c. Cape puff-back fly-catcher	45	25
77	15 c. South African crowned crane	65	60
78	20 c. Spectacled Weaver	70	70

20 Hole in the Wall

1980. Tourism. Multicoloured.

79	5 c. Type 20	15	10
80	10 c. Port St. Johns	25	25
81	15 c. The Citadel (rock)	40	40
82	20 c. The Archway (rock)	50	55

1981. Fishing Flies (2nd series). As T 16. Multicoloured.

83	10 c. Kent's Lightning (streamer)	25	25
84	10 c. Wickham's Fancy (dry fly)	25	25
85	10 c. Jock Scott (wet fly)	25	25
86	10 c. Green Highlander (salmon fly)	25	25
87	10 c. Tan Nymph	25	25

1981. Medicinal Plants (2nd series). As T 4. Multicoloured.

88	5 c. "Leonotis leonurus"	15	10
89	15 c. "Euphorbia bupleurifolia"	35	35
90	20 c. "Pelargonium reniforme"	45	45
91	25 c. "Hibiscus trionum"	50	55

21 Eyamakhwenkwe

1981. Xhosa Women's Headdresses. Multicoloured.

92	5 c. Type 21	10	10
93	15 c. Eyabafana	30	35
94	20 c. Umfazana	35	45
95	25 c. Ixhegokazi	40	55

22 State House, Umtata

1981. 5th Anniv of Independence.

97	22 5 c. black, brown & green	15	10
98	– 15 c. black, brown & green	45	30

DESIGN: 15 c. University of Transkei.

1982. Fishing Flies (3rd series). As T 16. Multicoloured.

99	10 c. Blue Charm	25	25
100	10 c. Royal Coachman	25	25
101	10 c. Light Spruce	25	25
102	10 c. Montana Nymph	25	25
103	10 c. Butcher	25	25

23 Cub Scout

24 Hippocrates

1982. 75th Anniv of Boy Scout Movement. Multicoloured.

104	8 c. Type 23	15	10
105	10 c. Scout planting tree	15	10
106	20 c. Scout on raft	35	30
107	25 c. Scout with dog	35	30

1982. Celebrities of Medicine (1st series). Multicoloured.

108	15 c. Type 24	25	20
109	20 c. Antonie van Leeuwenhoek	35	30
110	25 c. William Harvey	45	40
111	30 c. Joseph Lister	50	45

See also Nos. 125/8, 160/3, 176/9, 249/52, 273/6, 281/4 and 305/8.

25 City Hall

1982. Centenary of Umtata. Multicoloured.

112	8 c. Type 25	10	10
113	15 c. The Bunga	15	15
114	20 c. Botha Sigcau Building	20	20
115	25 c. Palace of Justice and K. D. Matanzima Building	25	30

1983. Fishing Flies (4th series). As T 16. Multicoloured.

116	20 c. Alexandra	25	25
117	20 c. Kent's Marbled Sedge	25	25
118	20 c. White Marabou	25	25
119	20 c. Mayfly Nymph	25	25
120	20 c. Silver Wilkinson	25	25

26 Hotel Complex, Mzamba

1983. Wildcoast Holiday Complex, Mzamba. Multicoloured.

121	10 c. Type 26	15	15
122	20 c. Beach scene	25	25
123	25 c. Casino	35	35
124	40 c. Carousel	50	50

1983. Celebrities of Medicine (2nd series). As T 24. Multicoloured.

125	10 c. Edward Jenner	15	15
126	20 c. Gregor Mendel	30	30
127	25 c. Louis Pasteur	35	35
128	40 c. Florence Nightingale	55	55

27 Lady Frere Post Office

1983. Transkei Post Offices (1st series). Multicoloured.

129	10 c. Type 27	15	15
130	20 c. Idutywa	25	30
131	25 c. Lusikisiki	30	35
132	40 c. Cala	40	55

See also Nos. 156/9.

1984. Fishing Flies (5th series). As T 16. Multicoloured.

133	20 c. Silver Grey	45	45
134	20 c. Ginger Quill	45	45
135	20 c. Hardy's Favourite	45	45
136	20 c. March Brown	45	45
137	20 c. Kent's Spectrum Mohawk	45	45

28 Amagqira

1984. Xhosa Culture. Multicoloured.

138	1 c. Type **28**	20	10
139	2 c. Horseman	20	10
140	3 c. Mat making	20	10
141	4 c. Xhosa dancers	20	10
142	5 c. Shopping with donkeys	20	10
143	6 c. Young musicians	30	15
144	7 c. Fingo brides	30	20
145	8 c. Tasting the beer	30	20
146	9 c. Thinning the maize	30	30
147	10 c. Dancing demonstration	30	15
148	11 c. Water from the river	30	15
148a	12 c. Preparing a meal	30	15
148b	14 c. Weeding mealies	30	20
149	15 c. National sport: stick fighting	20	20
149a	16 c. Morning pasture	30	20
150	20 c. Abakhwetha dance	30	25
150a	21 c. Building of initiation hut	75	20
151	25 c. Tribesman singing	30	25
152	30 c. Jovial matrons	70	35
153	50 c. Pipe making	70	60
154	1 r. Intonjane	80	1·10
155	2 r. Abakhwetha	1·50	2·00

1984. Transkei Post Offices (2nd series). As T **27**. Multicoloured.

156	11 c. Umzimkulu	15	15
157	20 c. Mount Fletcher	25	25
158	25 c. Qumbu	25	25
159	50 c. Umtata	45	50

1984. Celebrities of Medicine (3rd series). As T **24**. Multicoloured.

160	11 c. Nicholas of Cusa	20	15
161	25 c. William Morton	30	25
162	30 c. Wilhelm Rontgen	40	40
163	45 c. Karl Landsteiner	60	60

29 Soil Erosion by Overgrazing

1985. Soil Conservation. Multicoloured.

164	11 c. Type **29**	20	15
165	25 c. Removal of stock and construction of walls as sediment collectors	30	25
166	30 c. Regeneration of vegetation	40	40
167	50 c. Cattle grazing in lush landscape	60	60

30 Tsitsa Bridge

1985. Bridges. Multicoloured.

168	12 c. Type **30**	20	15
169	25 c. White Kei Railway Bridge	25	25
170	30 c. Mitchell Bridge	35	35
171	50 c. Umzimvubu Bridge	55	60

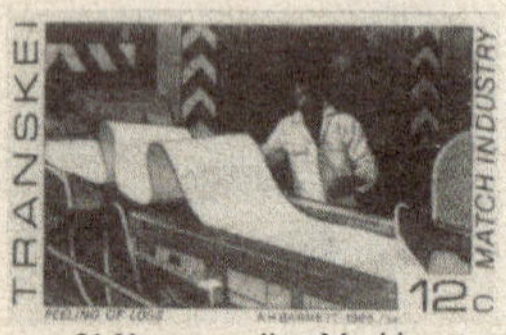

31 Veneer-peeling Machine

1985. Match Industry, Butterworth. Mult.

172	12 c. Type **31**	20	15
173	25 c. Cutting wood to match-size	25	25
174	30 c. Dipping splints in chemical to form match heads	35	35
175	50 c. Boxing matches	60	65

1985. Celebrities of Medicine (4th series). As T **24**. Multicoloured.

176	12 c. Andreas Vesalius	20	15
177	25 c. Marcello Malpighi	40	40
178	30 c. Francois Magendie	45	45
179	50 c. William Stewart Halsted	65	70

32 Early Street Scene

1986. Historic Port St. Johns. Multicoloured.

180	12 c. Type **32**	20	15
181	20 c. "Umzimvubu" (coaster) anchored at old jetty	35	35
182	25 c. Wagons off-loading maize at jetty	40	40
183	30 c. View of town at end of 19th century	45	45

33 "Aloe ferox"

34 First Falls Station, Umtata River

1986. Aloes. Multicoloured.

185	14 c. Type **33**	20	15
186	20 c. "Aloe arborescens"	30	30
187	25 c. "Aloe maculata"	35	35
188	30 c. "Aloe ecklonis"	45	45

1986. Hydro-electric Power Stations. Mult.

189	14 c. Type **34**	20	15
190	20 c. Second Falls, Umtata River	25	25
191	25 c. Ncora, Qumanco River	40	40
192	30 c. Collywobbles, Mbashe River	50	50

35 Prime Minister George Matanzima

1986. 10th Anniv of Independence. Mult.

193	14 c. Type **35**	20	15
194	20 c. Technical College, Umtata	30	30
195	25 c. University of Transkei, Umtata	40	40
196	30 c. Palace of Justice, Umtata	50	50

36 Piper Apache 235 "Ulundi" flying through Clouds

1987. 10th Anniv of Transkei Airways Corporation. Multicoloured.

197	14 c. Type **36**	20	15
198	20 c. Tail fin of "Ulundi"	30	30
199	25 c. Beech 100 King Air	40	40
200	30 c. Control tower, K. D. Matanzima Airport	55	60

37 Pondo Girl

38 "Latrodectus indistinctus"

1987. Transkei Beadwork. Multicoloured.

201	16 c. Type **37**	20	15
202	20 c. Bomvana woman	30	30
203	25 c. Xessibe woman	40	40
204	30 c. Xhosa man	55	60

1987. Spiders. Multicoloured.

205	16 c. Type **38**	20	15
206	20 c. "Naephila pilipes"	30	30
207	25 c. "Lycosidue sp"	40	40
208	30 c. "Argiope nigrovittata"	50	55

39 Common Black Pigs

40 "Plocamium corallorhiza"

1987. Domestic Animals. Multicoloured.

209	16 c. Type **39**	20	15
210	30 c. Goats	30	30
211	40 c. Merino sheep	45	45
212	50 c. Cattle	55	55

1988. Seaweed. Multicoloured.

213	16 c. Type **40**	20	15
214	30 c. "Gelidium amanzii"	30	30
215	40 c. "Ecklonia biruncinata"	40	40
216	50 c. "Halimeda cuneata"	50	55

41 Spinning

1988. Blanket Factory, Butterworth. Mult.

217	16 c. Type **41**	20	15
218	30 c. Warping	30	30
219	40 c. Weaving	40	40
220	50 c. Raising the nap	50	55

42 Map showing Wreck Site

1988. 206th Anniv of Shipwreck of "Grosvenor" (East Indiaman). Multicoloured.

221	16 c. Type **42**	40	20
222	30 c. "The Wreck of the 'Grosvenor'" (R. Smirke)	50	50
223	40 c. Dirk hilt, dividers and coins from wreck	55	55
224	50 c. "African Hospitality" (G. Morland)	60	70

43 Small-spotted Cat

1988. Endangered Animals. Multicoloured.

225	16 c. Type **43**	40	20
226	30 c. Blue duiker	60	50
227	40 c. Oribi	75	65
228	50 c. Hunting dog	90	90

44 Class 14 CRB Steam Locomotives

1989. Trains. Multicoloured.

229	16 c. Type **44**	20	15
230	30 c. Class 14 CRB locomotive and passenger train at Toleni Halt	40	40
231	40 c. Double-headed steam train on Great Kei River Bridge (vert)	60	60
232	50 c. Double-headed steam train in Kei Valley (vert)	65	65

45 Mat, Baskets and Jar

1989. Basketry. Multicoloured.

233	18 c. Type **45**	20	15
234	30 c. Basket and jar	30	30
235	40 c. Jars and bag	40	40
236	50 c. Dish and jars	55	60

46 Chub Mackerel

1989. Seafood. Multicoloured.

237	18 c. Type **46**	40	15
238	30 c. Squid	55	45
239	40 c. Perna or brown mussels	65	55
240	50 c. Rock lobster	80	85

47 Broom Cluster Fig

1989. Trees. Multicoloured.

241	18 c. Type **47**	35	15
242	30 c. Natal fig	55	45
243	40 c. Broad-leaved coral	65	55
244	50 c. Cabbage tree	80	85

48 "Ginkgo koningensis"

49 Aretaeus (discoverer of diabetes)

1990. Plant Fossils. Multicoloured.

245	18 c. Type **48**	45	25
246	30 c. "Pseudoctenis spatulata"	70	70
247	40 c. "Rissikia media"	80	85
248	50 c. "Taeniopteris anavolans"	90	1·10

1990. Celebrities of Medicine (5th series). Diabetes Research. Multicoloured.

249	18 c. Type **49**	50	20
250	30 c. Claude Bernard (discovered sugar formation by liver)	70	60
251	40 c. Oscar Minkowski (discovered pancreas removal caused diabetes)	80	80
252	50 c. Frederick Banting (discoverer of insulin)	1·00	1·10

50 Diviner dancing to Drum

51 Soldier Lily

1990. Diviners. Multicoloured.

253	21 c. Type **50**	45	20
254	35 c. Lecturing Imichetywa (novitiates)	70	60
255	40 c. Neophyte initiation	80	80
256	50 c. Diviner's induction ceremony	1·00	1·10

1990. Flowers. Multicoloured.

257	21 c. Type **51**	30	20
258	35 c. "Disa crassicornis"	50	50
259	40 c. Christmas bells	60	60
260	50 c. Port St. John's creeper	80	90

52 Pink Ink Plant

53 Common Dolphin

1991. Parasitic Plants. Multicoloured.

261	21 c. Type **52**	40	20
262	35 c. White harveya	60	60
263	40 c. "Alectra sessiliflora"	70	80
264	50 c. "Hydnora africana"	90	1·00

1991. Dolphins. Multicoloured.

265	25 c. Type **53**	55	25
266	40 c. Bottle-nosed dolphin	80	70
267	50 c. Humpbacked dolphin	1·00	1·00
268	60 c. Risso's dolphin	1·10	1·10

54 South African Crowned Crane

55 Emil von Behring and Shibasaburo Kitasao (diphtheria)

1991. Endangered Birds. Multicoloured.

269	25 c. Type **54**	55	30
270	40 c. Cape vulture	80	70
271	50 c. Wattled crane	1·00	90
272	60 c. Egyptian vulture	1·25	1·25

1991. Celebrities of Medicine (6th series). Vaccine Development. Multicoloured.

273	25 c. Type **55**	55	25
274	40 c. Camile Guerin and Albert Calmette (tuberculosis)	90	80
275	50 c. Jonas Salk (poliomyelitis)	1·10	1·10
276	60 c. John Enders (measles)	1·25	1·25

56 "Eulophia speciosa"

57 Thomas Weller (researcher into infectious viruses)

1992. Orchids. Multicoloured.

277		27 c. Type **56**	25	15
278		45 c. "Satyrium sphaerocarpum"	40	·40
279		65 c. "Disa scullyi"	60	65
280		85 c. "Disa tysonii"	80	85

1992. Celebrities of Medicine (7th series). Mult.

281		27 c. Type **57**	50	25
282		45 c. Ignaz Semmelweis	75	70
283		65 c. Sir James Simpson	1·00	1·00
284		85 c. Rene Laennec	1·25	1·40

58 Red-billed Pintail

59 "Pseudomelania sutherlandi" (gastropod)

1992. Waterfowl. Multicoloured.

285		35 c. Type **58**	50	50
286		35 c. Hottentot teal	50	50
287		70 c. Maccoa duck	80	80
288		70 c. White-backed duck	80	80
289		90 c. African black duck	1·00	1·00
290		90 c. Egyptian goose	1·00	1·00
291		1 r. 05 Cape shoveler	1·25	1·25
292		1 r. 05 Cape teal	1·25	1·25

1992. Marine Fossils. Multicoloured.

293		35 c. Type **59**	75	35
294		70 c. "Gaudryceras denseplicatum" (ammonite)	1·10	95
295		90 c. "Neithea quinquecostata" (bivalve)	1·25	1·40
296		1 r. 05 "Pugilina acuticarinatus" (gastropod)	1·40	1·50

60 Papillon

1993. Dogs. Multicoloured.

297		35 c. Type **60**	50	30
298		70 c. Pekingese	80	80
299		90 c. Chihuahua	1·00	1·10
300		1 r. 05 Dachshund	1·25	1·40

61 Fabrosaurus

1993. Prehistoric Animals. Multicoloured.

301		45 c. Type **61**	75	35
302		65 c. Diictodon	1·10	95
303		85 c. Chasmatosaurus	1·40	1·50
304		1 r. 05 Rubidgea	1·50	1·60

62 Sir Alexander Fleming and Howard Florey (discoverer and refiner of penicillin)

63 Laughing Doves

1993. Celebrities of Medicine (8th series). Multicoloured.

305		45 c. Type **62**	70	35
306		65 c. Alexis Carrel	1·10	95
307		85 c. James Lind	1·25	1·40
308		1 r. 05 Santiago Ramon y Cajal	1·40	1·50

1993. Doves. Multicoloured.

309		45 c. Type **63**	50	30
310		65 c. Tambourine doves	80	80
311		85 c. Emerald-spotted wood doves	1·00	1·10
312		1 r. 05 Namaqua doves	1·25	1·40

64 "Clan Lindsay" (steamer) on Rocks, Mazeppa Bay, 1898

1994. Shipwrecks. Multicoloured.

314		45 c. Type **64**	75	45
315		65 c. "Horizon" (freighter) on rocks near River Mngazi, 1967	1·10	1·00
316		85 c. "Oceanos" (pleasure cruiser) sinking near Coffee Bay, 1991	1·25	1·40
317		1 r. 05 "Forresbank" (freighter) on fire near River Mtakatye, 1958	1·40	1·60

TRANSVAAL

Formerly South African Republic under Boer rule, annexed by Gt. Britain in 1877, restored to the Boers in 1881 and again annexed in 1900 and since 1919 a province of the Union of S. Africa.

12 pence = 1 shilling;
20 shillings = 1 pound

1

1870. Imperf or roul.

61	**1**	1d. red	20·00	14·00
22		1d. black	15·00	25·00
53		3d. lilac	45·00	38·00
54a		6d. blue	45·00	38·00
32		1s. green	70·00	38·00

1874. Perf.

38a	**1**	1d. red	75·00	35·00
171		1d. grey	3·75	1·25
172		3d. black on red	18·00	3·75
173		3d. red	7·00	1·75
173b		3d. brown	22·00	3·50
41		6d. blue	£100	45·00
174		1s. green	38·00	2·75

1877. Optd **V. R. TRANSVAAL.** Imperf or roul.

101	**1**	1d. red	20·00	20·00
102		3d. lilac	70·00	35·00
103		6d. blue	85·00	30·00
113		6d. blue on red	70·00	45·00
104		1s. green	85·00	40·00

1877. Optd **V. R. Transvaal**. Imperf or roul.

116	**1**	1d. red on blue	45·00	24·00
117		1d. red on orange	15·00	16·00
118		3d. lilac on brown	38·00	24·00
119d		3d. lilac on green	95·00	32·00
149		3d. lilac on blue	40·00	25·00
126		6d. blue on green	70·00	22·00
121		6d. blue on blue	48·00	22·00

9

18

1878. Perf.

133	**9**	$\frac{1}{2}$d. red	17·00	60·00
134a		1d. brown	7·50	2·50
135		3d. red	9·50	3·25
136		4d. olive	14·00	4·25
137		6d. black	7·00	3·25
138		1s. green	£100	32·00
139		2s. blue	£140	65·00

1879. Surch **1 Penny**.

145	**9**	1d. on 6d. black	35·00	22·00

1882. Surch **EEN PENNY.**

170	**9**	1d. on 4d. green	8·00	3·75

1885.

175	**18**	$\frac{1}{2}$d. grey	30	10
176		1d. red	30	10
177		2d. purple	1·40	1·40
178		2d. brown	40	10
179		2$\frac{1}{2}$d. mauve	1·25	40
180		3d. mauve	1·50	70
181		4d. olive	2·25	50
182		6d. blue	3·75	2·25
183		1s. green	2·50	35
184		2s. 6d. yellow	3·50	1·60
185		5s. grey	5·50	2·75
186		10s. brown	27·00	5·50
187		£5 green	£3250	£180

1885. Surch **HALVE PENNY** vert, reading up or down.

188	**1**	$\frac{1}{2}$d. on 3d. red (No. 173)	3·50	7·00
192	**18**	$\frac{1}{2}$d. on 3d. mauve	2·25	2·25
189	**1**	$\frac{1}{2}$d. on 1s. green (No. 174)	13·00	35·00

1885. Surch with value in words and **Z. A. R.** both vert.

190	**9**	$\frac{1}{2}$d. on 6d. black	32·00	55·00
191		2d. on 6d. black	3·00	5·00

1887. Surch **2d** and thick bar.

194	**18**	2d. on 3d. mauve	75	1·60

1893. Surch **Halve Penny** and bars

196	**18**	$\frac{1}{2}$d. on 2d. pale brown	75	60

1893. Surch in figures and words between bars. (A) in one line, (B) in two.

197	**18**	1d. on 6d. blue (A)	45	30
198		2$\frac{1}{2}$d. on 1s. green (A)	80	1·60
199		2$\frac{1}{2}$d. on 1s. green (B)	2·75	2·75

29 (Wagon with shafts)

30 (Wagon with pole)

1894.

200	**29**	$\frac{1}{2}$d. grey	40	10
201		1d. red	40	10
202		2d. brown	40	10
203		6d. blue	1·00	40
204		1s. green	6·50	8·50

1895.

205	**30**	$\frac{1}{2}$d. grey	30	10
206		1d. red	30	10
207		2d. brown	30	10
208		3d. mauve	65	10
209		4d. black	1·25	70
210		6d. blue	1·25	40
211		1s. green	1·75	75
212		5s. grey	10·00	17·00
212a		10s. brown	10·00	3·50

1895. Surch **Halve Penny** and bar.

213	**30**	$\frac{1}{2}$d. on 1s. green	30	10

1895. Surch **1d.** and thick bar.

214	**18**	1d. on 2$\frac{1}{2}$d. mauve	30	10

33

34

1895. Fiscal stamp optd **POSTZEGEL.**

215	**33**	6d. red	50	1·40

1895. Penny Postage Commem.

215b	**34**	1d. red	1·25	1·40

1896.

216	**30**	$\frac{1}{2}$d. green	20	10
217		1d. red and green	20	10
218		2d. brown and green	20	10
219		2$\frac{1}{2}$d. blue and green	30	10
220		3d. purple and green	70	70
221		4d. olive and green	70	70
222		6d. lilac and green	40	70
223		1s. pale brown and green	50	15
224		2s. 6d. violet and green	1·25	1·25

1900. Optd **V.R.I.**

226	**30**	$\frac{1}{2}$d. green	15	15
227		1d. red and green	15	15
228		2d. brown and green	1·60	60
229		2$\frac{1}{2}$d. blue and green	60	70
230		3d. purple and green	60	65
231		4d. olive and green	1·25	30
232		6d. lilac and green	1·25	60
233		1s. brown and green	1·25	1·40
234		2s. 6d. violet and green	2·00	4·50
235		5s. grey	4·25	6·50
236		10s. brown	6·50	8·50
237	**18**	£5 green	£1800	£750

The majority of the £5 stamps, No. 237 on the market, are forgeries.

1901. Optd **E.R.I.**

238	**30**	$\frac{1}{2}$d. green	30	30
239		1d. red and green	30	10
240		3d. purple and green	1·75	2·00
241		4d. olive and green	1·75	2·00
242		2s. 6d. violet and green	5·50	8·50

1901. Surch **E.R.I. Half Penny.**

243	**30**	$\frac{1}{2}$d. on 2d. brown and green	40	40

38

1902.

244	**38**	$\frac{1}{2}$d. black and green	1·25	20
273		$\frac{1}{2}$d. green	1·50	10
245		1d. black and red	1·25	15
274		1d. red	1·25	10
246		2d. black and purple	2·25	40
275		2d. purple	3·25	40
247		2$\frac{1}{2}$d. black and blue	3·25	1·25
276		2$\frac{1}{2}$d. blue	9·50	2·75
264		3d. black and green	3·50	30
265		4d. black and brown	3·50	40
266a		6d. black and orange	2·00	40
251		1s. black and green	9·00	4·75
267		1s. grey and brown	4·00	40
252		2s. black and brown	24·00	28·00
268		2s. grey and yellow	15·00	4·25
253	**38**	2s. 6d. mauve and black	13·00	7·50
270		5s. black & pur on yell	13·00	1·50
271		10s. black & pur on red	28·00	2·50
272		£1 green and violet	£130	20·00
259		£5 brown and violet	£1200	£450

Nos. 267, 268 and all values of 2s. 6d. and above have the inscription "POSTAGE" on both sides. The rest are inscribed "POSTAGE" at left and "REVENUE" at right.

POSTAGE DUE STAMPS

D 1

1907.

D1	**D 1**	$\frac{1}{2}$d. black and green	3·00	1·25
D2		1d. black and red	3·75	85
D3		2d. brown	3·75	1·25
D4		3d. black and blue	7·00	4·00
D5		5d. black and violet	2·00	12·00
D6		6d. black and brown	4·25	12·00
D7		1s. red and black	8·00	7·00

TRAVANCORE

A state of south-east India. In 1949 formed part of Travancore-Cochin.

16 cash = 1 chuckram;
28 chuckrams = 1 rupee

1 Conch or Chank Shell 3

1888. Various frames.

9	**3**	4 cash pink	20	10
24	–	5 cash olive	50	10
34	–	5 cash brown	2·25	20
10	**1**	6 cash brown	30	10
11a		$\frac{1}{2}$ ch. purple	65	10
27	–	10 cash pink	35	10
13	–	$\frac{3}{4}$ ch. black	1·10	20
39	–	$\frac{3}{4}$ ch. mauve	35	10
14c	**1**	1 ch. blue	65	10
15		1$\frac{1}{4}$ ch. purple	45	45
42		1$\frac{1}{2}$ ch. red	2·25	10
16a		2 ch. red	50	10
17	–	3 ch. violet	2·25	20
18a	**1**	4 ch. green	1·10	35
19	–	7 ch. purple	1·60	45
20	–	14 ch. orange	2·40	1·25

1906. Surch in figures.

21a	**1**	$\frac{1}{4}$ on $\frac{1}{2}$ ch. purple	20	20
22		$\frac{3}{8}$ on $\frac{1}{2}$ ch. purple	20	35

1921. Surch in figures.

31	**3**	1 c. on 4 cash pink	15	15
57	–	1 c. on 5 cash brown	15	15
58	–	1 c. on 5 cash purple	90	15
50	**1**	1 c. on 1$\frac{1}{4}$ ch. purple	15	45
59	–	2 c. on 10 cash pink	15	15
51	**1**	2 c. on 1$\frac{1}{4}$ ch. purple	15	15
32		5 c. on 1 ch. blue	80	10

11 Sri Padmanabha Shrine

13 Maharaja Bala Rama Varma

1931. Coronation.

47	**11**	6 cash black and green	85	85
48	–	10 cash black and blue	75	35
49	**13**	3 ch. black and purple	1·75	1·60

DESIGN—As Type **11**: 10 cash, State chariot.

16 Maharaja Bala Rama Varma and Subramania Shrine

1937. Temple Entry Proclamation.

60	**16**	6 cash red	50	65
61	–	12 cash blue	1·25	20
62	–	1$\frac{1}{2}$ ch. green	85	60
63	–	3 ch. violet	2·50	1·25

DESIGNS: Portraits of the Maharaja and the temples of Sri Padmanabha (12 cash), Mahadeva (1$\frac{1}{2}$ ch.) and Kanyakumari (3 ch.).

17 Lake Ashtamudi

18 Maharaja Vala Rama Varma

1939. 27th Birthday of Maharaja.

64	**17**	1 ch. green	3·00	10
65	–	1½ ch. red	1·40	1·60
66	**18**	2 ch. orange	3·50	60
67	–	3 ch. brown	4·50	10
68	–	4 ch. red	3·50	40
69	–	7 ch. blue	5·50	11·00
70	–	14 ch. green	5·50	35·00

DESIGNS—As Type **18**: 1½, 3 ch. Portraits of Maharaja. As Type **17**: 4 ch. Sri Padmanabha Shrine; 7 ch. Cape Comorin; 14 ch. Pachipari Reservoir.

19 Maharaja and Aruvikara Falls

21 Maharaja Bala Rama Varma

1941. 29th Birthday of Maharaja.

71	**19**	6 cash violet	4·25	10
72	–	¾ ch. brown	4·50	15

DESIGN: ¾ ch. Maharaja and Marthanda Varma Bridge, Alwaye.

1943. Stamps of 1939 and 1941 surch in figures and capital letters.

73c	–	2 cash on 1½ ch. red (No. 65)	30	20
74a	–	4 cash on ¾ ch. brown (No. 72)	2·75	20
75a	**19**	8 cash on 6 cash red (as No. 7)	2·00	10

1946. 34th Birthday of Maharaja.

76a	**21**	8 cash red	65	85

1946. No. O103 optd **SPECIAL.**

77	**19**	6 cash violet	6·00	2·00

OFFICIAL STAMPS

1911. Optd **On S S.**

O 1	**3**	4 cash pink	20	10
O14	–	5 cash olive	50	10
O29	–	5 cash brown	25	35
O15	**1**	6 cash brown	30	10
O54		½ ch. purple	20	10
O18	–	10 cash pink	55	10
O39	–	¾ ch. black	35	15
O56	–	¾ ch. mauve	30	15
O 5	**1**	1 ch. blue	55	10
O21		1¼ ch. purple	40	10
O59		1½ ch. red	40	10
O 6		2 ch. red	35	10
O 8	–	3 ch. violet	35	10
O10	**1**	4 ch. green	55	10
O64	–	7 ch. purple	1·10	30
O65	–	14 ch. orange	1·60	40

1932. Official stamps surch in figures.

O74	–	6 c. on 5 cash olive	1·40	85
O75	–	6 c. on 5 cash brown	20	25
O83	–	12 c. on 10 cash pink	20	15
O84	**1**	1 ch. 8 ch. on 1¼ ch. red	35	25

1939. Optd **SERVICE.**

O 85	**1**	6 cash brown	70	20
O 94	–	¾ ch. mauve (No. 39)	9·50	20
O 96	**17**	1 ch. green	70	10
O 97b	–	1½ ch. red (No. 65)	1·00	15
O 95a	**1**	1½ c. red	4·50	1·00
O 98	**17**	2 ch. orange	1·00	30
O 99	–	3 ch. brown (No. 67)	60	10
O100	–	4 ch. red (No. 68)	1·40	60
O101	–	7 ch. blue (No. 69)	4·75	35
O102	–	14 ch. green (No. 70)	9·00	70

1942. Optd **SERVICE.**

O103	**19**	6 cash violet	40	30
O104	–	¾ ch. brown (No. 72)	2·75	10

1942. Nos. 73/5 optd **SERVICE.**

O106a	–	2 cash on 1½ ch. red	45	15
O107a	–	4 cash on ¾ ch. brown	1·25	20
O105a	**19**	8 cash on 6 cash red	1·25	10

1947. Optd **SERVICE.**

O108	**21**	8 cash red	1·50	70

TRAVANCORE-COCHIN

In 1949 the states of Cochin and Travancore in south-east India were united under the name of the United States of Travancore and Cochin. Now uses stamps of India.

12 pies = 1 anna; 16 annas = 1 rupee

1949. Stamps of Travancore surch in **PIES** or **ANNAS** in English and native characters.

1e	**19**	2 p. on 6 cash violet	40	20
2d	**21**	2 p. on 8 cash red	45	30
3e	**17**	½ a. on 1 ch. green	65	40
4a	**18**	1 a. on 2 ch. orange	55	20
5d	**11**	2 a. on 4 ch. brown	1·60	55
6a	–	3 a. on 7 ch. blue (No. 69)	4·50	2·00
7b	–	6 a. on 14 ch. green (No. 70)	8·00	14·00

1949. No. 106 of Cochin optd **U.S.T.C.**

8	**21**	1 a. orange	4·50	50·00

1950. No. 106 of Cochin optd **T.-C.**

9	**21**	1 a. orange	5·50	48·00

1950. No. 9 surch with new value.

10	**21**	6 p. on 1 a. orange	2·50	30·00
11		9 p. on 1 a. orange	1·75	28·00

5 Conch or Chank Shell

6 Palm Trees

1950.

12	**5**	2 p. red	1·25	1·25
13	**6**	4 p. blue	2·00	10·00

OFFICIAL STAMPS

1949. Stamps of Travancore surch **SERVICE** and value in **PIES** or **ANNAS** in English and native characters.

O 1f	**19**	2 p. on 6 cash (No. 71)	35	20
O10	**21**	4 p. on 8 cash (No. 76a)	30	20
O11b	**17**	½ a. on 1 ch. (No. 64)	30	20
O12c	**18**	1 a. on 2 ch. (No. 66)	40	20
O 9a	–	2 a. on 4 ch. (No. 68)	60	65
O14e	–	3 a. on 7 ch. (No. 69)	1·50	1·10
O15	–	6 a. on 14 ch. (No. 70)	1·50	3·25

TRENGGANU

A state of the Federation of Malaya, incorporated in Malaysia in 1963.

100 cents = 1 dollar (Straits or Malayan)

1 Sultan Zain ul ab din 2

1910.

1	**1**	1 c. green	60	1·00
2		2 c. brown and purple	50	90
3		3 c. red	2·25	2·25
4		4 c. orange	3·50	5·50
5		4 c. brown and green	2·00	3·75
5a		4 c. red	60	1·75
6		5 c. grey	1·25	3·00
7		5 c. grey and brown	2·25	2·00
8		8 c. blue	1·25	8·50
9a		10 c. purple on yellow	3·00	4·00
10		10 c. green and red on yellow	1·00	2·25
11		20 c. mauve and purple	2·50	4·00
12		25 c. green and purple	5·00	26·00
13		30 c. purple and black	6·50	45·00
14		50 c. black on green	4·50	6·50
15		$1 black and red on blue	15·00	17·00
16		$3 green and red on green	£110	£200
17	**2**	$5 green and purple	£120	£350
18		$25 red and green	£750	

1917. Surch **RED CROSS 2c.**

19	**1**	2 c. on 3 c. red	30	4·50
20		2 c. on 4 c. orange	1·00	11·00
21		2 c. on 4 c. brown and green	1·75	27·00
22		2 c. on 8 c. blue	50	25·00

4 Sultan Suleiman

7 Sultan Ismail

1921. (a) T **4**.

26	**4**	1 c. black	1·25	90
27		2 c. green	1·25	1·00
28		3 c. green	1·50	85
29		3 c. brown	20·00	11·00
30		4 c. red	1·25	30
31		5 c. grey and brown	2·00	4·00
32		5 c. purple on yellow	1·75	70
33		6 c. orange	3·00	30
34		8 c. grey	20·00	4·00
35		10 c. blue	2·00	70
36		12 c. blue	4·25	4·00
37		20 c. purple and orange	2·00	1·50
38		25 c. green and purple	2·25	2·50
39		30 c. purple and black	3·25	2·00
40		35 c. red on yellow	4·50	8·00
41		50 c. green and red	5·00	2·00
42		$1 purple and blue on blue	9·00	3·50
43		$3 green and red on green	60·00	£110

(b) Larger type, as T **2**, but portrait of Sultan Suleiman.

25	$5 green and red on yellow	80·00	£225
45	$25 purple and blue	£600	£900
46	$50 green and yellow	£1500	£2500
47	$100 green and red	£4750	£5500

1922. Optd **MALAYA-BORNEO EXHIBITION.**

48	**4**	2 c. green	2·25	25·00
49		4 c. red	4·75	25·00
50		5 c. grey and brown	2·50	27·00
51	**1**	10 c. green and red on yellow	3·00	30·00
52		20 c. mauve and purple	2·75	35·00
53		25 c. green and purple	2·75	35·00
54		30 c. purple and black	2·75	35·00
55		50 c. black on green	2·75	35·00
56		$1 black and red on blue	10·00	65·00
57		$3 green and red on green	£110	£350
58	**2**	$5 green and purple	£200	£600

1941. Surch.

59	**4**	2 c. on 5 c. purple on yellow	6·50	3·50
60		8 c. on 10 c. blue	7·00	3·50

1948. Silver Wedding. As T **10/11** of Aden.

61	10 c. violet	15	70
62	$5 red	20·00	32·00

1949. 75th Anniv of U.P.U. As T **20/23** of Antigua.

63	10 c. purple	30	35
64	15 c. blue	1·10	1·90
65	25 c. orange	55	2·25
66	50 c. black	1·40	2·75

1949.

67	**7**	1 c. black	10	30
68		2 c. orange	10	30
69		3 c. green	30	2·25
70		4 c. brown	10	30
71		5 c. purple	30	90
72		6 c. grey	30	30
73		8 c. red	20	1·75
74		8 c. green	65	1·00
75		10 c. purple	15	10
76		12 c. red	65	1·75
77		15 c. blue	45	30
78		20 c. black and green	45	2·25
79		20 c. blue	80	30
80		25 c. purple and orange	60	75
81		30 c. red and purple	1·25	1·25
82		35 c. red and purple	70	1·60
83		40 c. red and purple	2·75	12·00
84		50 c. black and blue	60	1·25
85		$1 blue and green	3·50	5·00
86		$2 green and red	20·00	16·00
87		$3 green and brown	50·00	45·00

1953. Coronation. As T **13** of Aden.

88	10 c. black and purple	65	65

1957. As Nos. 92/102 of Kedah but inset portrait of Sultan Ismail.

89	1 c. black	10	20
90	2 c. red	80	30
91	4 c. brown	10	10
92	5 c. red	10	10
93	8 c. green	4·00	60
94	10 c. brown	30	10
94a	10 c. purple	3·00	10
95	20 c. blue	60	70
96a	50 c. black and blue	30	75
97	$1 blue and purple	5·00	4·00
98	$2 green and red	10·00	6·00
99	$5 brown and green	15·00	13·00

8 "Vanda hookeriana"

9 Sultan of Trengganu

1965. As Nos. 115/21 of Kedah, but inset portrait of Sultan Ismail as in T **8**.

100	**8**	1 c. multicoloured	10	90
101	–	2 c. multicoloured	10	90
102	–	5 c. multicoloured	15	20
103	–	6 c. multicoloured	15	70
104	–	10 c. multicoloured	20	10
105	–	15 c. multicoloured	1·50	10
106	–	20 c. multicoloured	1·50	60

The higher values used in Trengganu were Nos. 20/7 of Malaysia (National Issues).

1970. 25th Anniv of Installation of H.R.H. Tuanku Ismail Nasiruddin Shah as Sultan of Trengganu.

107	**9**	10 c. multicoloured	40	1·00
108		15 c. multicoloured	40	80
109		50 c. multicoloured	1·00	2·00

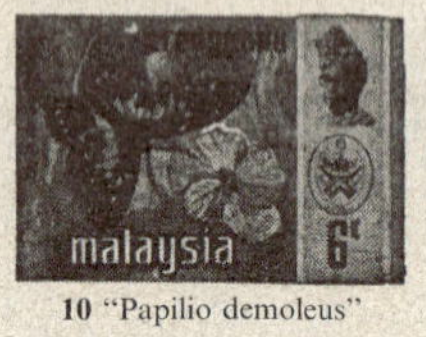

10 "Papilio demoleus"

1971. Butterflies. As Nos. 124/30 of Kedah but with portrait of Sultan Ismail Nasiruddin Shah as in T **10**.

110	–	1 c. multicoloured	30	1·25
111	–	2 c. multicoloured	70	1·25
112	–	5 c. multicoloured	1·00	50
113	**10**	6 c. multicoloured	1·00	1·50
114	–	10 c. multicoloured	1·00	40
115	–	15 c. multicoloured	1·10	20
116	–	20 c. multicoloured	1·25	80

The high values in use with this issue were Nos. 64/71 of Malaysia (National Issues).

11 "Durio zibethinus"

1979. Flowers. As Nos. 135/41 of Kedah, but with portrait of Sultan Ismail Nasiruddin Shah as in T **11**.

118	1 c. "Rafflesia hasseltii"	10	60
119	2 c. "Pterocarpus indicus"	10	60
120	5 c. "Largerstoemia speciosa"	10	30
121	10 c. Type **11**	15	10
122	15 c. "Hibiscus rosa-sinensis"	15	10
123	20 c. "Rhododendron scortechinii"	20	10
124	25 c. "Etlingera elatior" (inscr "Phaeomeria speciosa")	40	40

12 Sultan Mahmud

13 Rubber

1981. Installation of Sultan Mahmud.

125	**12**	10 c. black, blue and gold	25	80
126		15 c. black, yellow and gold	30	35
127		50 c. black, purple and gold	65	2·50

1986. As Nos. 152/8 of Kedah but with portrait of Sultan Mahmud and inscr "TERENGGANU" as in T **13**.

135	1 c. Coffee	10	10
136	2 c. Coconuts	10	10
137	5 c. Cocoa	10	10
138	10 c. Black pepper	10	10
139	15 c. Type **13**	10	10
140	20 c. Oil palm	10	10
141	30 c. Rice	15	20

POSTAGE DUE STAMPS

D 1

1937.

D1	**D 1**	1 c. red	7·50	55·00
D2		4 c. green	8·50	60·00
D3		8 c. yellow	55·00	£275
D4		10 c. brown	£110	95·00

TRINIDAD

An island in the Pterocarpus West Indies off the coast of Venezuela. Now uses stamps of Trinidad and Tobago.

12 pence = 1 shilling;
20 shillings = 1 pound

2 Britannia 4

1851. Imperf.

2	2	(1d.) purple	7·50	55·00
3		(1d.) blue	7·50	38·00
5		(1d.) grey	42·00	50·00
8		(1d.) red	£120	50·00
25	4	4d. lilac	60·00	£275
28		6d. green	—	£425
29		1s. blue	60·00	£275

3

1852.

18	3	(1d.) blue	£4000	£650
19		(1d.) grey	£4000	£400
20		(1d.) red	12·00	£450

1859. Perf.

75	2	(1d.) red	17·00	80
70	4	4d. lilac	85·00	8·00
76		4d. grey	80·00	70
72b		6d. green	48·00	3·00
63		1s. blue	£700	65·00
73b		1s. purple	75·00	4·25
78		1s. yellow	85·00	2·50

5 10

1869.

113	5	5s. red	45·00	70·00

1879. Surch in words.

98	2	$\frac{1}{2}$d. lilac	9·50	6·00
101		1d. red	18·00	60

1882. No. 95 surch **1d** with pen.

104	4	1d. on 6d. green	4·75	3·75

1883.

106	10	$\frac{1}{2}$d. green	2·00	90
107		1d. red	7·00	40
108		$2\frac{1}{2}$d. blue	9·00	40
110		4d. grey	2·25	40
111		6d. black	3·00	3·50
112		1s. orange	3·00	1·75

11 Britannia 12

1896.

114	11	$\frac{1}{2}$d. purple and green	3·00	30
126		$\frac{1}{2}$d. green	55	1·75
115		1d. purple and red	3·25	10
127		1d. black on red	1·00	10
135		1d. red	1·00	10
117		$2\frac{1}{2}$d. purple and blue	4·50	20
128		$2\frac{1}{2}$d. purple and blue on blue	13·00	25
137		$2\frac{1}{2}$d. blue	1·75	15
118		4d. purple and orange	5·00	13·00
129		4d. green and blue on buff	1·75	10·00
138		4d. grey and red on yellow	1·00	6·50
119		5d. purple and mauve	5·50	12·00
120		6d. purple and black	7·00	5·00
140		6d. purple and mauve	6·50	7·00
121		1s. green and brown	7·00	6·00
130		1s. black & blue on yellow	18·00	5·00
142		1s. purple & blue on yellow	10·00	11·00
143		1s. black on green	1·50	1·25
122	12	5s. green and brown	38·00	65·00
131		5s. purple and mauve	40·00	60·00
123		10s. green and blue	£120	£170
124		£1 green and red	£100	£150

13 Landing Columbus **14**

1898. 400th Anniv of Discovery of Trinidad.

125	13	2d. brown and violet	2·25	1·00

1909. Figures in corners.

146	14	$\frac{1}{2}$d. green	2·00	10
147	–	1d. red	1·25	10
148	–	$2\frac{1}{2}$d. blue	8·00	3·00

On the 1d. figures are in lower corners only.

POSTAGE DUE STAMPS

D 1

1885.

D 1	D 1	$\frac{1}{2}$d. black	15·00	42·00
D18		1d. black	70	1·25
D19		2d. black	70	1·25
D20		3d. black	70	2·00
D21		4d. black	2·25	16·00
D14		5d. black	11·00	9·00
D15		6d. black	6·00	9·50
D16		8d. black	12·00	14·00
D17		1s. black	12·00	26·00

For stamps in Type D **1** but with value in cents see under Trinidad and Tobago.

OFFICIAL STAMPS

1894. Optd **O S.**

O1	10	$\frac{1}{2}$d. green	30·00	50·00
O2		1d. red	32·00	55·00
O3		$2\frac{1}{2}$d. blue	42·00	80·00
O4		4d. grey	42·00	85·00
O5		6d. black	42·00	85·00
O6		1s. orange	60·00	£110
O7	5	5s. red	£140	£300

1909. Optd **OFFICIAL**.

O8	11	$\frac{1}{2}$d. green	40	4·25
O9		1d. red	50	4·25

1910. Optd **OFFICIAL**.

O10	14	$\frac{1}{2}$d. green	2·75	4·25

TRINIDAD AND TOBAGO

Combined issues for Trinidad and Tobago, administratively one colony. Part of the British Caribbean Federation from 1958 until 31 August 1962, when it became independent within the British Commonwealth.

1913. 12 pence = 1 shilling;
20 shillings = 1 pound.
1935. 100 cents = 1 West Indian dollar.

17 18

1913.

149	17	$\frac{1}{2}$d. green	3·00	10
207		1d. red	30	30
208		1d. brown	30	1·00
209		2d. grey	1·00	1·25
151		$2\frac{1}{2}$d. blue	4·50	40
211		3d. blue	2·25	2·50
152a		4d. black and red on yellow	70	5·00
153a		6d. purple and mauve	6·50	3·75
154c		1s. black on green	1·50	2·50
155d	18	5s. purple and mauve	40·00	90·00
156		£1 green and red	£100	£140

1915. Optd cross over **21. 10. 15**.

174	17	1d. red	1·25	1·50

1916. Optd **19.10.16** over cross.

175	17	1d. red	40	1·10

1917. Optd **WAR TAX** in one line (No. 176) or two lines (others).

177	17	$\frac{1}{2}$d. green	10	10
176		1d. red	1·25	2·50
180		1d. red	10	65

1918. Optd **War Tax** in two lines.

187	17	$\frac{1}{2}$d. green	10	1·50
188b		1d. red	10	50

27 **28** First Boca

1922.

218	27	$\frac{1}{2}$d. green	30	10
219		1d. brown	30	10
220b		$1\frac{1}{2}$d. red	1·25	30
222		2d. grey	40	1·00
223		3d. blue	40	1·00
224		4d. black and red on yellow	3·00	3·00
225		6d. purple and mauve	2·00	23·00
226		6d. green and red on green	1·00	30
227		1s. black on green	5·00	1·50
228		5s. purple and mauve	19·00	32·00
229		£1 green and red	85·00	£190

1935.

230a	28	1 c. blue and green	20	10
231a	–	2 c. blue and brown	50	10
232	–	3 c. black and red	60	10
233	–	6 c. brown and blue	3·75	1·75
234	–	8 c. green and orange	3·00	3·00
235	–	12 c. black and violet	3·00	1·25
236	–	24 c. black and green	2·00	1·25
237	–	48 c. green	7·00	13·00
238	–	72 c. green and red	28·00	27·00

DESIGNS: 2 c. Imperial College of Tropical Agriculture; 3 c. Mt. Irvine Bay, Tobago; 6 c. Discovery of Lake Asphalt; 8 c. Queen's Park, Savannah; 12 c. Town Hall, San Fernando; 24 c. Govt. House; 48 c. Memorial Park; 72 c. Blue Basin.

1935. Silver Jubilee. As T **13** of Antigua.

239	2 c. blue and black	30	50
240	3 c. blue and red	30	85
241	6 c. brown and blue	1·50	2·00
242	24 c. grey and purple	4·50	13·00

1937. Coronation. As T **2** of Aden.

243	1 c. green	15	10
244	2 c. brown	35	10
245	8 c. orange	90	1·25

37 First Boca **47** King George VI

1938. Designs as 1935 issue but with portrait of King George VI as in T **37** and without "POSTAGE & REVENUE", and T **47**.

246	37	1 c. blue and green	45	20
247	–	2 c. blue and brown	45	20
248	–	3 c. black and red	11·00	90
248a	–	3 c. green and purple	30	20
249	–	4 c. brown	29·00	1·00
249a	–	4 c. red	40	60
249b	–	5 c. mauve	30	15
250	–	6 c. brown and blue	1·75	60
251	–	8 c. olive and red	1·75	75
252a	–	12 c. black and purple	2·50	10
253	–	24 c. black and olive	75	10
254	–	60 c. green and red	8·50	1·25
255	47	$1.20 green	10·00	1·00
256		$4.80 red	20·00	25·00

NEW DESIGNS: 4 c. Memorial Park; 5 c. G.P.O. and Treasury; 60 c. As No. 238.

1946. Victory. As T **9** of Aden.

257	3 c. brown	10	10
258	6 c. blue	10	90

1948. Silver Wedding. As T **10/11** of Aden.

259	3 c. brown	10	10
260	$4.80 red	17·00	23·00

1949. 75th Anniv of U.P.U. As T **20/23** of Antigua.

261	5 c. purple	40	50
262	6 c. blue	1·00	65
263	12 c. violet	40	75
264	24 c. green	40	60

1951. B.W.I. University College. As T **24/25** of Antigua.

265	3 c. green and brown	20	50
266	12 c. black and violet	20	50

48 First Boca **51** Cipriani Memorial

53 Copper-rumped Hummingbird

1953. Designs as 1938 and 1940 issues but with portrait of Queen Elizabeth in place of King George VI as in T **48** (1 c., 2 c., 12 c.) or facing left (others).

267	48	1 c. blue and green	20	30
268	–	2 c. blue and brown	20	30
269	–	3 c. green and purple	20	10
270	–	4 c. red	20	30
271	–	5 c. mauve	30	30
272	–	6 c. brown and blue	30	30
273	–	8 c. olive and red	90	30
274	–	12 c. black and purple	30	10
275	–	24 c. black and olive	1·00	30
276	–	60 c. green and red	18·00	1·00
277a	–	$1.20 green	1·25	30
278a	–	$4.80 red	8·50	12·00

1953. Coronation. As T **13** of Aden.

279	3 c. black and green	20	10

1956. No. 268 surch **ONE CENT**.

280	1 c. on 2 c. blue and brown	80	1·10

1958. Inaug of British Caribbean Federation. As T **28** of Antigua.

281	5 c. green	20	10
282	6 c. blue	25	1·25
283	12 c. red	25	10

1960.

284	51	1 c. stone and black	10	10
285	–	2 c. blue	10	10
286	–	5 c. blue	10	10
287	–	6 c. brown	10	10
288	–	8 c. green	10	30
289	–	10 c. lilac	10	10
290	–	12 c. red	10	10
291	–	15 c. orange (A)	90	45
291a	–	15 c. orange (B)	2·50	10
292	–	25 c. red and blue	70	10
293	–	35 c. green and black	2·50	10
294	–	50 c. yellow, grey and blue	35	40
295	–	60 c. red, green and blue	55	30
296	53	$1.20 multicoloured	14·00	2·25
297	–	$4.80 green and blue	7·50	8·00

DESIGNS—HORIZ (as Type **51**): 2 c. Queen's Hall; 5 c. Whitehall; 6 c. Treasury Building; 8 c. Governor-General's House; 10 c. General Hospital, San Fernando; 12 c. Oil refinery; 15 c. (A) Crest, (B) Coat of arms; 25 c. Scarlet ibis; 35 c. Pitch Lake; 50 c. Mohammed Jinnah Mosque. VERT (as Type **51**): 60 c. Anthurium lilies. (As Type **53**): $4.80, Map of Trinidad and Tobago.

65 Scouts and Gold Wolf Badge

1961. 2nd Caribbean Scout Jamboree. Design multicoloured. Background colours given.

298	65	8 c. green	15	10
299		25 c. blue	15	10

66 "Buccoo Reef"
(painting by Carlisle Chang)

1962. Independence.

300	66	5 c. turquoise	10	10
301	–	8 c. grey	20	20
302	–	25 c. violet	15	10
303	–	35 c. multicoloured	2·25	15
304	–	60 c. red, black and blue	2·50	3·00

DESIGNS: 8 c. Piarco Air Terminal; 25 c. Hilton Hotel, Port-of-Spain; 35 c. Greater bird of paradise and map; 60 c. Scarlet ibis and map.

71 "Protein Foods" **72** Jubilee Emblem

1963. Freedom from Hunger.

305	71	5 c. red	10	10
306		8 c. bistre	10	30
307		25 c. blue	20	20

1964. Golden Jubilee of Trinidad and Tobago Girl Guides' Association.

308	72	6 c. yellow, blue and red	10	20
309		25 c. yellow, ultram & blue	15	20
310		35 c. yellow, blue and green	15	20

73 I.C.Y. Emblem

1965. International Co-operation Year.

311	73	35 c. brown, green & yellow	50	20

74 Eleanor Roosevelt, Flag and U.N. Emblem

1965. Eleanor Roosevelt Memorial Foundation.
312 **74** 25 c. black, red and blue . . 15 10

75 Parliament Building

1966. Royal Visit. Multicoloured.
313 5 c. Type **75** 15 10
314 8 c. Map, Royal Yacht "Britannia" and arms . . . 2·25 70
315 25 c. Map and flag . . . . 2·25 55
316 35 c. Flag and panorama . . . 2·25 70

1967. 5th Year of Independence. Nos. 289, 291a and 295 optd **FIFTH YEAR OF INDEPENDENCE 31st AUGUST 1967**.
318 8 c. green 10 10
319 10 c. lilac 10 10
320 15 c. orange 10 10
321 60 c. blue, green and red . . . 25 10

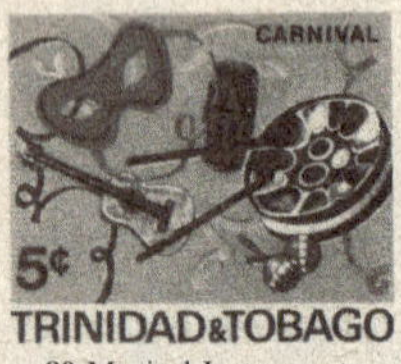

80 Musical Instruments

1968. Trinidad Carnival. Multicoloured.
322 5 c. Type **80** 10 10
323 10 c. Calypso King (vert) . . . 10 10
324 15 c. Steel band 10 10
325 25 c. Carnival procession . . . 20 10
326 35 c. Carnival King (vert) . . 20 10
327 60 c. Carnival Queen (vert) . . 35 1·25

86 Doctor giving Eye-test
87 Peoples of the World and Emblem

1968. 20th Anniv of World Health Organization.
328 **86** 5 c. red, brown and gold . . 15 10
329 25 c. orange, brown and gold . 35 10
330 35 c. blue, black and gold . . 40 15

1968. Human Rights Year.
331 **87** 5 c. red, black and yellow . . 10 10
332 10 c. blue, black and yellow . 15 10
333 25 c. green, black & yellow . 30 15

88 Cycling

1968. Olympic Games, Mexico. Mult.
334 5 c. Type **88** 20 10
335 15 c. Weightlifting 20 10
336 25 c. Relay-racing 20 10
337 35 c. Sprinting 20 10
338 $1.20 Maps of Mexico and Trinidad 70 30

93 Cocoa Beans

1969. Multicoloured.
339c 1 c. Type **93** 10 10
340 3 c. Sugar refinery 10 10
341a 5 c. Rufous-vented chachalaca 1·50 10
342 6 c. Oil refinery 10 10
343 8 c. Fertiliser plant . . . . 1·50 1·25
344 10 c. Green hermit . . . . 2·00 10
345 12 c. Citrus fruit . . . . 15 1·25
346 15 c. Arms of Trinidad and Tobago 10 10
347 20 c. Flag and outline of Trinidad and Tobago . . 15 10
348 25 c. As 20 c. 15 15
349 30 c. Chaconia plant . . . 30 10
350 40 c. Scarlet ibis . . . . 5·00 10
351 50 c. Maracas Bay . . . . 30 1·25
352 $1 Poui tree 60 15
353 $2.50 Fishing . . . . 1·00 3·50
354 $5 Red house . . . . 1·50 3·75
Nos. 344/9 and 352 are vert.

108 Captain A. A. Cipriani (labour leader) and Entrance to Woodford Square

1969. 50th Anniv of Int Labour Organization.
355 **108** 6 c. black, gold and red . . 15 15
356 – 15 c. black, gold and blue . 15 15
DESIGN: 15 c. Arms of Industrial Court and entrance to Woodford Square.

110 Cornucopia and Fruit
117 Parliamentary Chamber, Flags and Emblem

114 Space Module landing on Moon

1969. 1st Anniv of C.A.R.I.F.T.A. Mult.
357 6 c. Type **110** 10 10
358 10 c. Flags of Britain and member nations . . . 10 10
359 30 c. Map showing C.A.R.I.F.T.A. countries . . 30 20
360 40 c. Boeing 727-100 "Sunjet" in flight 55 70
The 10 c. and 40 c. are horiz.

1969. First Man on the Moon. Multicoloured.
361 6 c. Type **114** 10 10
362 40 c. Space module and astronauts on Moon . . 15 10
363 $1 Astronauts seen from inside space module . . . 45 20
The 40 c. is vert.

1969. 15th Commonwealth Parliamentary Association Conference, Port-of-Spain. Multicoloured.
364 10 c. Type **117** 10 10
365 15 c. J.F. Kennedy College . . 10 10
366 30 c. Parliamentary maces . . 25 40
367 40 c. Cannon and emblem . . 25 40

121 Congress Emblem
124 "Man in the Moon"

1969. Int Congress of the Junior Chamber of Commerce.
368 **121** 6 c. black, red and gold . . 10 10
369 – 30 c. gold, lake and blue . . 25 40
370 – 40 c. black, gold and blue . 25 40
DESIGNS: (both incorporating the Congress emblem). HORIZ: 30 c. Islands at daybreak. VERT: 40 c. Palm trees and ruin.

1970. Carnival Winners. Multicoloured.
371 5 c. Type **124** 10 10
372 6 c. "City beneath the Sea" . . 10 10
373 15 c. "Antelope" God Bamibara . 15 10
374 30 c. "Chanticleer" Pheasant Queen of Malaya 25 10
375 40 c. Steel Band of the Year . 25 20

129 Statue of Gandhi
131 Symbols of Culture, Science, Arts and Technology

1970. Gandhi Centenary Year (1969). Multicoloured.
376 10 c. Type **129** 25 10
377 30 c. Head of Gandhi and flag of India (horiz) 45 20

1970. 25th Anniv of U.N.
378 **131** 5 c. multicoloured . . . 10 10
379 – 10 c. multicoloured . . . 25 10
380 – 20 c. multicoloured . . . 35 30
381 – 30 c. multicoloured . . . 35 30
DESIGNS AND SIZES: 10 c. Children of different races, map and flag (34×25 mm); 20 c. Noah's Ark, rainbow and dove (34×23 mm); 30 c. New U.P.U. H.Q. Building (46×27½ mm).

1970. Inaug of National Commercial Bank. No. 341 optd **NATIONAL COMMERCIAL BANK ESTABLISHED 1.7.70.**
382 5 c. multicolured 30 10

134 "East Indian Immigrants" (J. Cazabon)
135 "The Adoration of the Shepherds" (detail, School of Seville)

1970. 125th Anniv of San Fernando. Paintings by Cazabon.
383 **134** 3 c. multicoloured . . . 10 65
384 – 5 c. black, blue and ochre . 10 10
385 – 40 c. black, blue and ochre 60 20
DESIGNS—HORIZ: 5 c. "San Fernando Town Hall"; 40 c. "San Fernando Harbour, 1860".

1970. Christmas. Multicoloured.
386 3 c. Type **135** 10 10
387 5 c. "Madonna and Child with Saints" (detail, Titian) . . . 10 10
388 30 c. "The Adoration of the Shepherds" (detail, Le Nain) 20 20
389 40 c. "The Virgin and Child, St. John and an Angel" (Morando) 20 10
390 $1 "The Adoration of the Kings" (detail, Veronese) . . . 70 1·75

136 Red Brocket

1971. Trinidad Wildlife. Multicoloured.
392 3 c. Type **136** 20 30
393 5 c. Collared peccary . . . 25 15
394 6 c. Paca 30 50
395 30 c. Brazilian agouti . . . 1·25 3·50
396 40 c. Ocelot . . . . 1·25 2·75

137 A. A. Cipriani
138 "Virgin and Child with St. John" (detail, Bartolommeo)

1971. 9th Anniv of Independence. Mult.
397 5 c. Type **137** 10 10
398 30 c. Chaconia medal . . . 30 60

1971. Christmas.
399 **138** 3 c. multicoloured . . . 15 15
400 – 5 c. multicoloured . . . 20 10
401 – 10 c. multicoloured . . . 25 10
402 – 15 c. multicoloured . . . 30 20
DESIGNS: 5 c. Local creche; 10 c. "Virgin and Child with Saints Jerome and Dominic" (detail, Lippi); 15 c. "Virgin and Child with St. Anne" (detail, Gerolamo dai Libri).

139 Satellite Earth Station, Matura

1971. Satellite Earth Station. Mult.
403 10 c. Type **139** 10 10
404 30 c. Dish antennae 25 50
405 40 c. Satellite and the Earth . 35 50

140 "Morpho peleides x achilleana"

1972. Butterflies. Multicoloured.
407 3 c. Type **140** 75 30
408 5 c. "Eryphanis polyxena" . . 80 10
409 6 c. "Phoebis philea" . . . 85 30
410 10 c. "Prepona laertes" . . . 1·00 15
411 20 c. "Eurytides telesilaus" . . 1·75 1·60
412 30 c. "Eurema proterpia" . . 2·00 2·50

141 "Lady McLeod" (paddle-steamer) and McLeod Stamp

1972. 125th Anniv of First Trinidad Postage Stamp.
413 **141** 5 c. multicoloured . . . 15 10
414 – 10 c. multicoloured . . . 25 10
415 – 30 c. blue, brown and black 70 45
DESIGNS: 10 c. Lady McLeod stamp and map; 30 c. Lady McLeod and inscription.

142 Trinity Cross
144 "Adoration of the Kings" (detail, Dosso)

143 Bronze Medal, 1964 Relay

1972. 10th Anniv of Independence. Mult.
417 5 c. Type **142** 10 10
418 10 c. Chaconia Medal . . . 10 10
419 20 c. Humming-bird Medal . . 15 15
420 30 c. Medal of Merit . . . 15 20
See also Nos. 440/3.

1972. Olympic Games, Munich. Multicoloured.
422 10 c. Type **143** 15 10
423 20 c. Bronze, 1964 200 metres . 25 25
424 30 c. Silver, 1952 weightlifting . 35 25
425 40 c. Silver, 1964 400 metres . 35 25
426 50 c. Silver, 1948 weightlifting . 35 1·75

1972. Christmas. Multicoloured.
431 3 c. Type **144** 10 10
432 5 c. "The Holy Family and a Shepherd" (Titian) . . . 10 10
433 30 c. As 5 c. 70 55

145 E.C.L.A. Building, Chile

1973. Anniversaries. Events described on stamps. Multicoloured.

435	10 c. Type **145**	10	10
436	20 c. Interpol emblem	45	30
437	30 c. W.M.O. emblem	45	30
438	40 c. University of the West Indies	45	80

1973. 11th Anniv of Independence. Medals as T **142**. Multicoloured.

440	10 c. Trinity Cross	10	10
441	20 c. Medal of Merit	20	35
442	30 c. Chaconia Medal	20	40
443	40 c. Hummingbird Medal	30	40

146 G.P.O., Port-of-Spain

1973. 2nd Commonwealth Conference of Postal Administrations, Trinidad. Mult.

445	30 c. Type **146**	20	50
446	40 c. Conference Hall, Chaguaramas (wrongly inscr "Chagaramas")	30	50

147 "Madonna with Child" (Murillo)

1973. Christmas.

448	**147** 5 c. multicoloured	10	10
449	$1 multicoloured	75	1·25

148 Berne H.Q within U.P.U. Emblem

1974. Centenary of U.P.U. Multicoloured.

451	40 c. Type **148**	45	15
452	50 c. Map within emblem	45	85

149 "Humming Bird I" (ketch) crossing Atlantic Ocean (1960)

1974. 1st Anniv of World Voyage by H. and K. La Borde. Multicoloured.

454	40 c. Type **149**	50	15
455	50 c. "Humming Bird II" (ketch) crossing globe	60	75

150 "Sex Equality"

1975. International Women's Year.

457	**150** 15 c. multicoloured	15	20
458	30 c. multicoloured	35	70

151 Common Vampire Bat, Microscope and Syringe

1975. Isolation of Rabies Virus. Mult.

459	25 c. Type **151**	40	40
460	30 c. Dr. Pawan, instruments and book	50	50

152 Route-map and Tail of Boeing 707

1975. 35th Anniv of British West Indian Airways. Multicoloured.

461	20 c. Type **152**	40	20
462	30 c. 707 on ground	60	85
463	40 c. 707 in flight	70	1·00

153 "From the Land of the Humming Bird"

1975. Carnival. 1974 Prize-winning Costumes. Multicoloured.

465	30 c. Type **153**	10	10
466	$1 "The Little Carib"	40	50

154 Angostura Building, Port-of-Spain

1976. 150th Anniv of Angostura Bitters. Multicoloured.

468	5 c. Type **154**	10	10
469	35 c. Medal, New Orleans 1885/6	20	35
470	45 c. Medal, Sydney 1879	25	40
471	50 c. Medal, Brussels 1897	25	80

1976. West Indian Victory in World Cricket Cup. As T **126** of Barbados.

474	35 c. Caribbean map	45	30
475	45 c. Prudential Cup	55	40

155 "Columbus sailing Through the Bocas" (Campins)

1976. Paintings, Hotels and Orchids. Mult.

479	5 c. Type **155**	1·25	10
480	6 c. Robinson Crusoe Hotel, Tobago	20	1·50
482	10 c. "San Fernando Hill" (J. Cazabon)	20	10
483	12 c. "Paphinia cristata"	2·00	2·50
484	15 c. Turtle Beach Hotel	50	1·50
485	20 c. "East Indians in a Landscape" (J. Cazabon)	70	10
486	25 c. Mt. Irvine Hotel	60	10
487	30 c. "Caularthron bicornutum"	2·00	1·25
488	35 c. "Los Gallos Point" (J. Cazabon)	1·00	10
489	40 c. "Miltassia"	2·00	10
490	45 c. "Corbeaux Town" (J. Cazabon)	1·00	10
491	50 c. "Oncidium ampliatum"	2·00	20
492	70 c. Beach facilities, Mt. Irvine Hotel	70	1·00
494	$2.50 "Oncidium papilio"	2·25	1·00
495	$5 Trinidad Holiday Inn	1·50	6·00

156 Hasely Crawford and Olympic Gold Medal

1977. Hasely Crawford Commemoration.

501	**156** 25 c. mulicoloured	30	50

157 Lindbergh's Sikorsky S-38, 1929

1977. 50th Anniv of Airmail Service. Mult.

503	20 c. Type **157**	45	20
504	35 c. Arrival of Charles and Anne Lindbergh	55	35
505	45 c. Boeing 707, c. 1960	70	60
506	50 c. Boeing 747-200, 1969	1·40	3·25

158 National Flag **159** White Poinsettia

1977. Inauguration of Republic. Mult.

508	20 c. Type **158**	40	15
509	35 c. Coat of arms	60	65
510	45 c. Government House	70	85

1977. Christmas. Multicoloured.

512	10 c. Type **159**	20	10
513	35 c. Type **159**	35	10
514	45 c. Red poinsettia	45	30
515	50 c. As 45 c.	55	1·75

160 Miss Janelle (Penny) Commissiong with Trophy **162** "Burst of Beauty"

161 Tayra

1978. "Miss Universe 1977" Commemoration. Multicoloured.

517	10 c. Type **160**	25	10
518	35 c. Portrait	50	60
519	45 c. In evening dress	60	75

1978. Wildlife. Multicoloured.

521	15 c. Type **161**	20	20
522	25 c. Ocelot	30	30
523	40 c. Brazilian tree porcupine	50	30
524	70 c. Tamandua	65	2·25

1979. Carnival 1978.

526	**162** 5 c. multicoloured	10	10
527	– 10 c. multicoloured	10	10
528	– 35 c. multicoloured	10	10
529	– 45 c. multicoloured	10	10
530	– 50 c. brown, red and lilac	10	15
531	– $1 multicoloured	20	65

DESIGNS: 10 c. Rain worshipper; 35 c. "Zodiac"; 45 c. Praying mantis; 50 c. "Eye of the Hurricane"; $1 Steel orchestra.

163 Day Care **164** Geothermal Exploration

1979. International Year of the Child. Multicoloured.

532	5 c. Type **163**	10	10
533	10 c. School feeding programme	10	10
534	35 c. Dental care	30	15
535	45 c. Nursery school	30	20
536	50 c. Free bus transport	30	40
537	$1 Medical care	65	1·50

1979. 4th Latin American Geological Congress. Multicoloured.

539	10 c. Type **164**	20	10
540	35 c. Hydrogeology	35	40
541	45 c. Petroleum exploration	40	40
542	70 c. Environmental preservation	55	1·60

165 1879 1d. Stamp and Map of Tobago

1979. Tobago Stamp Centenary.

544	**165** 10 c. multicoloured	10	10
545	– 15 c. multicoloured	15	10
546	– 35 c. multicoloured	25	20
547	– 45 c. multicoloured	25	20
548	– 70 c. multicoloured	30	1·50
549	– $1 black, lilac and orange	40	1·75

DESIGNS: 15 c. 1879 3d. and 1880 ½d. surcharged on half of 6d; 35 c. 1879 6d. and 1886 ½d. surcharged on 6d; 45 c. 1879 1s. and 1886 ½d. surcharged on 2½d; 70 c. 1879 5s. and Great Britain 1856 1s. with "A14" (Scarborough, Tobago) postmark; $1 1879 £1 and General Post Office, Scarborough, Tobago.

166 1962 60 c. Independence Commemorative Stamp and Sir Rowland Hill

1979. Death Cent of Sir Rowland Hill. Mult.

551	25 c. Type **166**	30	15
552	45 c. 1977 35 c. Inauguration of Republic commemorative	40	20
553	$1 1879 Trinidad ½d. surcharge and Tobago 1880 4d.	65	1·25

167 Poui Tree in Churchyard

1980. Centenary of Princes Town. Mult.

555	5 c. Type **167**	10	10
556	10 c. Princes Town Court House	10	10
557	50 c. Locomotive of the Royal Train, 1880	60	90
558	$1.50 H.M.S. "Bacchante" (screw corvette)	1·00	2·00

1980. Population Census. Nos. 479/80 and 482 optd **1844– 1980 POPULATION CENSUS 12th MAY 1980.**

560	5 c. Type **155**	20	20
561	6 c. Robinson Crusoe Hotel, Tobago	20	80
562	10 c. "San Fernando Hill" (J. Cazabon)	20	20

169 Scarlet Ibis (male)

1980. Scarlet Ibis. Multicoloured.

563	50 c. Type **169**	1·10	1·40
564	50 c. Male and female	1·10	1·40
565	50 c. Hen and nest	1·10	1·40
566	50 c. Nest and eggs	1·10	1·40
567	50 c. Chick in nest	1·10	1·40

170 Silver and Bronze Medals for Weightlifting, 1948 and 1952

1980. Olympic Games, Moscow. Multicoloured.

568	10 c. Type **170**	10	10
569	15 c. Hasely Crawford (100 metres sprint winner, 1976) and gold medal	10	10
570	70 c. Silver medal for 400 metres and bronze medals for 4 × 400 metres relay, 1964	45	65

171 Charcoal Production

1980. 11th Commonwealth Forestry Conf. Mult.

572	10 c. Type **171**	10	10
573	55 c. Logging	25	25
574	70 c. Teak plantation	35	60
575	$2.50 Watershed management	85	2·25

172 Beryl McBurnie (dance and culture) and Audrey Jeffers (social worker)

1980. Decade for Women (1st issue). Mult.

577 $1 Type **172** 45 55
578 $1 Elizabeth Bourne (judiciary) and Isabella Teshier (government) 45 55
579 $1 Dr. Stella Abidh (public health) and Louise Horne (nutrition) 45 55

See also Nos. 680/2.

173 Netball Stadium

1980. World Netball Tournament

580 **173** 70 c. multicoloured . . . 30 45

174 I.Y.D.P. Emblem, Athlete and Disabled Person

1981. International Year of Disabled Persons.

581 **174** 10 c. green, black and red 15 10
582 – 70 c. orange, black and red 40 70
583 – $1.50 blue, black and red . 60 1·40
584 – $2 flesh, black and red . . 60 1·75

DESIGNS: 70 c. I.Y.D.P. emblem and doctor with disabled person; $1.50, Emblem and blind man and woman; $2, Emblem and inscription.

175 "Our Land Must Live"

1981. Environmental Preservation. Mult.

585 10 c. Type **175** 15 10
586 55 c. "Our seas must live" . . 45 30
587 $3 "Our skies must live" . . . 1·60 1·60

176 "Food For Famine"

1981. World Food Day. Multicoloured.

589 10 c. Type **176** 10 10
590 15 c. "Produce more" (threshing and milling rice) 10 10
591 45 c. "Fish for food" (Bigeye) 30 20
592 55 c. "Prevent hunger" 35 25
593 $1.50 "Fight malnutrition" . . 85 90
594 $2 "Fish for food" (Small-mouthed grunt) . . . . . . 1·10 1·25

177 "First Aid Skills" **178** Pharmacist at Work

1981. President's Award Scheme. Mult.

596 10 c. Type **177** 20 10
597 70 c. "Motor mechanics" . . . 40 45
598 $1 "Expedition" 50 55
599 $2 Presenting an award . . . 90 1·40

1982. Commonwealth Pharmaceutical Conference. Multicoloured.

600 10 c. Type **178** 15 10
601 $1 Gerritoute (plant) . . . . . 1·75 2·25
602 $2 Rachette (plant) . . . . . 2·75 4·25

179 "Production" **180** Charlotteville

1982. 75th Anniv of Boy Scout Movement. Multicoloured.

603 15 c. Type **179** 60 10
604 55 c. "Tolerance" . . . . . . 1·50 30
605 $5 "Discipline" . . . . 5·50 7·00

1982. 25th Anniv of Tourist Board. Mult.

606 55 c. Type **180** 30 25
607 $1 Boating 40 55
608 $3 Fort George . . . . 1·25 2·25

181 "Pa Pa Bois"

1982. Folklore. Local Spirits and Demons. Multicoloured.

609 10 c. Type **181** 10 10
610 15 c. "La Diablesse" 10 10
611 65 c. "Lugarhoo", "Phantom" and "Soucouyant" 35 30
612 $5 "Bois de Soleil", "Davens" and "Mamma de l'Eau" . . 2·50 3·25

182 Cane Harvesting

1982. Cent of Canefarmers' Association. Mult.

614 30 c. Type **182** 30 15
615 70 c. Farmers loading bullock cart 60 85
616 $1.50 Cane field in bloom . . 1·10 1·75

183 National Stadium

1982. 20th Anniv of Independence. Mult.

618 10 c. Type **183** 15 10
619 35 c. Caroni water treatment plant 30 15
620 50 c. Mount Hope Maternity Hospital 60 25
621 $2 National Insurance Board Mall, Tobago . . . . . . 90 2·00

184 Commonwealth Flags

1983. Commonwealth Day. Multicoloured.

622 10 c. Type **184** 10 10
623 55 c. Satellite view of Trinidad and Tobago 25 20
624 $1 "Nodding donkey" oil pump (vert) 40 60
625 $2 Map of Trinidad and Tobago (vert) . . . . 85 1·25

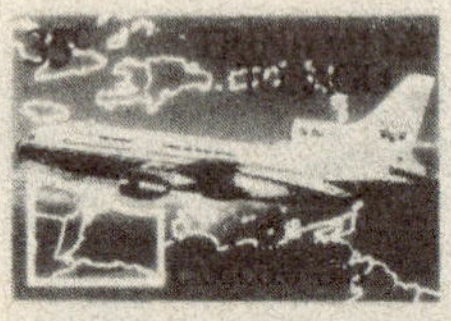

185 Lockheed Tristar 500 "Flamingo"

1983. 10th Anniv of CARICOM.

626 **185** 35 c. multicoloured . . . 80 1·25

186 V.D.U. Operator

1983. World Communications Year. Mult.

627 15 c. Type **186** 20 10
628 55 c. Scarborough Post Office, Tobago 40 20
629 $1 Textel building 70 70
630 $3 Morne Blue E.C.M.S. station 1·50 2·50

187 Financial Complex

1983. Conference of Commonwealth Finance Ministers.

631 **187** $2 multicoloured . . . . . 80 1·25

188 King Mackerel

1983. World Food Day. Multicoloured.

632 10 c. Type **188** 20 10
633 55 c. Four-winged flyingfish . 1·00 40
634 70 c. Queen or pink conch . . 1·25 1·40
635 $4 Red shrimp . . . . 4·50 7·00

189 Bois Pois **190** Rooks in Staunton and 17th-century Styles

1983. Flowers. Multicoloured.

636A 5 c. Type **189** . . . . 80 1·00
687 10 c. Maraval lily 30 30
638A 15 c. Star grass 60 30
639A 20 c. Bois caco 30 15
690 25 c. Strangling fig . . . . . 60 1·25
641A 30 c. "Cassia moschata" . . 40 15
642A 50 c. Chalice flower 30 30
643A 65 c. Black stick 55 30
644A 80 c. "Columnea scandens" . 65 85
695 95 c. Cat's claw 50 60
696 $1 Bois l'agli 65 30
647A $1.50 "Eustoma exaltatum" . 1·25 1·25
648A $2 Chaconia (39 × 29 mm) . 1·50 1·75
649A $2.50 "Chrysothemis pulchella" (39 × 29 mm) . 1·25 2·75
700 $5 "Centratherum punctatum" (39 × 29 mm) . . . . . . 1·75 1·75
701 $10 Savanna flower (39 × 29 mm) 3·50 4·25

1984. 60th Anniv of Int Chess Federation. Mult.

652 50 c. Type **190** . . . . 2·75 50
653 70 c. Bishops in Staunton and 12th-century Lewis styles . . 3·00 2·00
654 $1.50 Queens in Staunton and 13th-century Swedish styles . 4·00 5·00
655 $2 Kings in Staunton and 19th-century Chinese styles . . . 5·00 6·50

191 Swimming **192** Slave Schooner and Shackles

1984. Olympic Games, Los Angeles. Multicoloured.

656 15 c. Type **191** 10 10
657 55 c. Track and field events . . 30 20
658 $1.50 Sailing . . . . 1·00 1·50
659 $4 Cycling . . . . 3·50 4·25

1984. 150th Anniv of Abolition of Slavery. Multicoloured.

661 35 c. Type **192** 85 30
662 55 c. Slave and "Slave Triangle" map . . . . 1·25 50
663 41 "Capitalism and Slavery" (book by Dr. Eric Williams) . 2·00 1·75
664 $2 Toussaint l'Ouverture (Haitian revolutionary) . . 2·50 4·00

193 Children's Band

1984. 125th Anniv of St. Mary's Children's Home. Multicoloured.

666 10 c. Type **193** 15 10
667 70 c. St. Mary's Children's Home 50 50
668 $3 Group of children . . . . 2·25 2·75

194 Parang Band

1984. Parang Festival. Multicoloured.

669 10 c. Type **194** 20 10
670 30 c. Music and poinsettia . . 50 15
671 $1 Bandola, bandolin and cuatro (musical instruments) . . . 1·25 90
672 $3 Double bass, fiddle and guitar (musical instruments) . . . 2·50 3·50

195 Capt. A. A. Cipriani and T. U. B. Butler

1985. Labour Day. Labour Leaders.

673 **195** 55 c. black and red . . . 80 80
674 – 55 c. black and yellow . . 80 80
675 – 55 c. black and green . . 80 80

DESIGNS: No. 674, C. P. Alexander and Q. O'Connor; 675, A. Cola Rienzi and C. T. W. E. Worrell.

196 "Lady Nelson" (1928)

1985. Ships. Multicoloured.

676 30 c. Type **196** 70 25
677 95 c. "Lady Drake", (1928) . 1·50 1·75
678 $1.50 "Federal Palm" (1961) . 2·00 3·00
679 $2 "Federal Maple" (1961) . . 2·50 3·50

197 Marjorie Padmore (music) and Sybil Atteck (art)

1985. Decade for Women (2nd issue). Multicoloured.

680 $1.50 Type **197** . . . . 1·40 1·75
681 $1.50 May Cherrie (medical social worker) and Evelyn Tracey (social worker) . . . 1·40 1·75
682 $1.50 Umilta McShine (education) and Jessica Smith-Phillips (public service) . . 1·40 1·75

198 Badge of Trinidad and Tobago Cadet Force (75th Anniv) **199** Anne-Marie Javouhey (foundress)

1985. International Youth Year. Mult.

683 10 c. Type **198** 45 10
684 65 c. Guide badges (75th anniv of Girl Guide movement) . . . 2·00 2·25
685 95 c. Young people of Trinidad 2·50 2·75

1986. 150th Anniv of Arrival of Sisters of St. Joseph de Cluny. Multicoloured.
702 10 c. Type **199** 10 10
703 65 c. St. Joseph's Convent, Port-of-Spain 45 90
704 95 c. Children and statue of Anne-Marie Javouhey 65 1·25

200 Tank Locomotive "Arima"

1986. "Ameripex 86" International Stamp Exhibition, Chicago. Trinidad Railway Locomotives. Multicoloured.
705 65 c. Type **200** 25 35
706 95 c. Canadian-built steam locomotive No. 22 35 60
707 $1.10 Steam tender engine 40 95
708 $1.50 Saddle tank locomotive 60 1·25

201 Scout Camp

1986. 75th Anniv of Trinidad and Tobago Boy Scouts. Multicoloured.
710 $1.70 Type **201** 1·00 1·60
711 $2 Scouts of 1911 and 1986 1·25 1·90

202 Queen and Duke of Edinburgh laying Wreath at War Memorial
203 Eric Williams at Graduation, 1935

1986. 60th Birthday of Queen Elizabeth II. Multicoloured.
712 10 c. Type **202** 30 10
713 15 c. Queen with Trinidadian dignitaries aboard "Britannia" 75 20
714 30 c. With President Ellis Clarke 65 25
715 $5 Receiving bouquet 3·00 6·00

1986. 75th Birth Anniv of Dr. Eric Williams. Multicoloured.
716 10 c. Type **203** 30 10
717 30 c. Premier Eric Williams (wearing red tie) 55 20
718 30 c. As No. 717 but wearing black and orange tie 55 20
719 95 c. Arms of University of West Indies and Dr. Williams as Pro-Chancellor (horiz) 1·00 1·25
720 $5 Prime Minister Williams and Whitehall (horiz) 2·25 4·25

204 "PEACE" Slogan and Outline map of Trinidad and Tobago
205 Miss Giselle La Ronde and BWIA Airliner

1986. International Peace Year. Mult.
722 95 c. Type **204** 40 50
723 $3 Peace dove with olive branch 1·25 2·25

1987. Miss World 1986. Multicoloured.
724 10 c. Type **205** 50 10
725 30 c. In swimsuit on beach 1·00 30
726 95 c. Miss Giselle La Ronde 2·25 2·50
727 $1.65 Wearing Miss World sash 3·50 4·25

206 Colonial Bank, Port-of-Spain

1987. 150th Anniv of Republic Bank. Mult.
728 10 c. Type **206** 10 10
729 65 c. Cocoa plantation 50 70
730 95 c. Oil field 1·00 1·50
731 $1.10 Belmont Tramway Company tramcar 1·25 2·00

207 Sergeant in Parade Order and Soldiers in Work Dress and Battle Dress
208 Uriah Butler (labour leader)

1988. 25th Anniv of Defence Force. Mult.
732 10 c. Type **207** 65 15
733 30 c. Women soldiers 1·50 30
734 $1.10 Defence Force officers 2·75 2·75
735 $1.50 Naval ratings and patrol boat 3·50 3·50

1988. West Indian Cricket. As T **186** of Barbados, each showing portrait, cricket equipment and early belt buckle. Multicoloured.
736 30 c. George John 1·25 40
737 65 c. Learie Constantine 2·25 1·00
738 95 c. Sonny Ramadhin 2·50 1·75
739 $1.50 Gerry Gomez 3·00 3·50
740 $2.50 Jeffrey Stollmeyer 4·00 5·50

1988. 50th Anniv (1987) of Oilfield Workers Trade Union. Multicoloured.
741 10 c. Type **208** 10 10
742 30 c. Adrian Rienzi (O.W.T.U. president, 1937–42) 10 10
743 65 c. John Rojas (O.W.T.U. president, 1943–62) 15 25
744 $5 George Weekes (O.W.T.U. president, 1962–87) 1·25 2·25

209 Mary Werges and Santa Rosa Church

1988. Centenary of Borough of Arima. Mult.
745 20 c. Type **209** 15 10
746 30 c. Governor W. Robinson and Royal Charter 15 10
747 $1.10 Arrival of Governor Robinson at railway station 60 95
748 $1.50 Mayor J. F. Wallen and Centenary logo 90 1·50

1988. 300th Anniv of Lloyd's of London. As T **123** of Ascension. Multicoloured.
749 30 c. Queen Mother at topping out of new building, 1984 60 20
750 $1.10 BWIA Lockheed Tristar 500 airliner "Flamingo" (horiz) 2·00 1·40
751 $1.55 Steel works, Trinidad (horiz) 1·75 1·75
752 $2 "Atlantic Empress" (tanker) on fire off Tobago, 1979 3·50 2·75

210 Colonial Arms of Trinidad & Tobago and 1913 1d. Stamp

1989. Centenary of Union of Trinidad and Tobago. Multicoloured.
753 40 c. Type **210** 60 10
754 $1 Pre-1889 Tobago emblem and Tobago 1896 ½d. on 4d. stamp 1·50 1·00
755 $1.50 Pre-1889 Trinidad emblem and Trinidad 1883 4d. stamp 2·00 2·75
756 $2.25 Current Arms of Trinidad and Tobago and 1977 45 c. Republic commemorative 2·50 3·50

211 Common Piping Guan

1989. Rare Fauna of Trinidad and Tobago. Multicoloured.
757 $1 Type **211** 3·00 3·25
758 $1 "Phyllodytes auratus" (frog) 3·00 3·25
759 $1 "Cebus albifrons trinitatis" (monkey) 3·00 3·25
760 $1 Tamandua 3·00 3·25
761 $1 "Lutra longicaudis" (otter) 3·00 3·25
Nos. 757/61 were printed together, se-tenant, forming a composite background design.

212 Blind Welfare
213 Tenor Pan

1989. Anniveraries. Multicoloured.
762 10 c. Type **212** (75th anniv) 50 15
763 40 c. Port-of-Spain City Hall (75th anniv) 40 20
764 $1 Guides and Brownies (75th anniv) 1·75 60
765 $2.25 Red Cross members (50th anniv) 2·50 2·50

1989. Steel Pans (1st series). Multicoloured.
766 10 c. Type **213** 10 10
767 40 c. Guitar pans 15 15
768 $1 Cello pans 45 60
769 $2.25 Bass pans 85 1·75
See also Nos. 828/31.

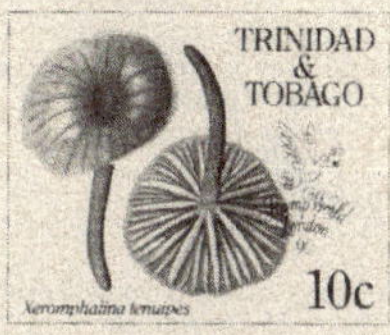

214 "Xeromphalina tenuipes"

1990. "Stamp World London 90" International Stamp Exhibition. Fungi. Mult.
770 10 c. Type **214** 35 20
771 40 c. "Phallus indusiatus" ("Dictyophora indusiata") 65 25
772 $1 "Leucocoprinus birnbaumii" 1·25 1·00
773 $2.25 "Crinipellis perniciosa" 2·00 3·75

215 Scarlet Ibis in Immature Plumage

1990. Scarlet Ibis. Multicoloured.
774 40 c. Type **215** 1·25 30
775 80 c. Pair in pre-nuptial display 1·50 1·25
776 $1 Male in breeding plumage 1·75 1·25
777 $2.25 Adult on nest with chick 2·75 3·75

216 Princess Alice and Administration Building

1990. 40th Anniv of University of West Indies. Multicoloured.
778 40 c. Type **216** 40 15
779 80 c. Sir Hugh Wooding and Library 70 70
780 $1 Sir Allen Lewis and Faculty of Engineering 90 90
781 $2.25 Sir Shridath Ramphal and Faculty of Medical Sciences 2·25 3·25

217 Lockheed Lodestar

1990. 50th Anniv of British West Indies Airways. Multicoloured.
782 40 c. Type **217** 1·00 30
783 80 c. Vickers Viking 1A 1·50 1·25
784 $1 Vickers Viscount 702 1·75 1·25
785 $2.25 Boeing 707 3·00 4·00

218 Yellow Oriole
219 "Lygodium volubile"

1990. Birds. Multicoloured.
787 20 c. Type **218** 10 10
837 25 c. Green-rumped parrotlet 10 10
789 40 c. Fork-tailed flycatcher 10 10
839 50 c. Copper-rumped hummingbird 10 10
840 $1 Bananaquit 20 25
841 $2 Violaceous euphonia 40 45
793 $2.25 Channel-billed toucan 45 50
794 $2.50 Bay-headed tanager 50 55
844 $5 Green honeycreeper 1·00 1·10
845 $10 Cattle egret 2·00 2·10
797 $20 Golden-olive woodpecker 4·00 4·25
798 $50 Peregrine falcon 10·00 10·50

1991. Ferns. Multicoloured.
799 40 c. Type **219** 40 15
800 80 c. "Blechnum occidentale" 75 70
801 $1 "Gleichenia bifida" 85 85
802 $2.25 "Polypodium lycopodioides" 2·00 3·50

220 Trinidad and Tobago Regiment Anti-aircraft Battery

1991. 50th Anniv of Second World War. Multicoloured.
803 40 c. Type **220** 85 30
804 80 c. Fairey Barracuda Mk III attacking U-boat 1·25 90
805 $1 Avro Type 683 Lancaster 1·50 1·00
806 $2.25 H.M.S. "Wye" (frigate) escorting convoy 2·50 3·75

221 H. E. Rapsey (founder)
222 Baptism (Baptist)

1992. Anniversaries. Multicoloured.
808 40 c. Type **221** (centenary of Trinidad Building and Loan Assoc.) 30 15
809 80 c. "Inca clathrata quesneli" (beetle) (Trinidad & Tobago Field Naturalists' Club) 90 90
810 $1 Holy Name Convent (centenary) 90 1·00

1992. Religions of Trinidad and Tobago. Mult.
811 40 c. Type **222** 55 55
812 40 c. Minaret with star and crescent (Islam) 55 55
813 40 c. Logo (Hinduism) 55 55
814 40 c. Cross (Christian) 55 55
815 40 c. Logo (Baha'i) 55 55

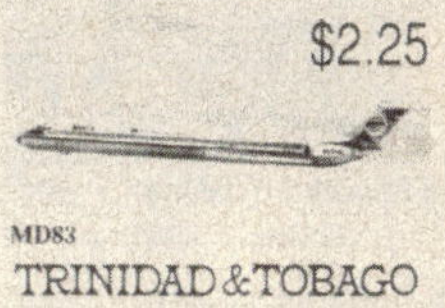

223 McDonnell Douglas MD-83

1992. Aircraft. Multicoloured.
816 $2.25 Type **223** 2·00 2·25
817 $2.25 Lockheed L-1011 TriStar aircraft 2·00 2·25

224 "Trinidad Guardian" Title (75th anniv of newspaper)

1992. Anniversaries. Multicoloured.
818 40 c. Type **224** 10 10
819 40 c. Nativity scene (Christmas) (vert) 10 10
820 $1 National Museum and Art Gallery (centenary) 35 40
821 $2.25 Cover to St. James Internment Camp, 1942 (50th anniv of Trinidad and Tobago Philatelic Society) . . . . . 80 1·25

225 Derek Walcott, Sir Shridath Ramphal and William Demas with Caribbean Maps (⅔-size illustration)

1994. 20th Anniv of CARICOM (Caribbean Economic Community). Recipients of Order of the Caribbean Community.
822 **225** 50 c. multicoloured . . . 20 20
823 $1.50 multicoloured . . . 45 60
824 $2.75 multicoloured . . . 85 1·10
825 $3 multicoloured . . . . 1·00 1·40

226 Aldwyn Roberts Kitchener (bass player)

1994. "Land of Calypso".
827 **226** 50 c. multicoloured . . . 70 70

227 Quadrophonic Pans

1994. Steel Pans (2nd series). Multicoloured.
828 50 c. Type **227** 20 20
829 $1 Tenor base pans 35 30
830 $2.25 Six pans . . . . . . 80 1·25
831 $2.50 Rocket pans . . . . . . 90 1·25

1994. "Hong Kong '94" International Stamp Exhibition. Nos. 837, 789, 841 and 796 optd **HONG KONG '94** and emblem.
832 25 c. Green-rumped parrotlet . . 30 20
833 40 c. Fork-tailed flycatcher . . 35 20
834 $2 Violaceous euphonia . . . 95 1·25
835 $10 Cattle egret . . . . 3·25 4·00

228 Trinidad Hilton

230 "Snowballman" (painting, Mahmoud Alladin)

229 Boa Constrictor

1994. Hotels and Lodgings. Multicoloured.
848 $3 Type **228** . . . . 90 1·25
849 $3 Sandy Point Village, Tobago 90 1·25
850 $3 Asa Wright Nature Centre and Lodge . . . . 90 1·25
851 $3 M.L.'s Bed and Breakfast . . 90 1·25

1994. Snakes. Multicoloured.
852 50 c. Type **229** 20 20
853 $1.25 Vine snake 45 55
854 $2.50 Bushmaster . . . . . . 80 1·10
855 $3 Large coral snake . . . . . 95 1·25

1995. 50th Anniv of Trinidad Art Society. Multicoloured.
856 50 c. Type **230** 35 45
857 50 c. "Fishermen" (painting, Sybil Atteck) 35 45
858 50 c. Copper sculpture (Ken Morris) 35 45

231 Loggerhead Turtle

1995. Conservation. Multicoloured.
859 $1.25 Type **231** 40 50
860 $2.50 Port-of-Spain Lighthouse (vert) . . . . 80 1·00
861 $3 "Knowsley" (location of Ministry of Foreign Affairs) 1·00 1·25

232 Brian Lara

234 Wendy Fitzwilliam

233 Red Cross Economy Label on Envelope

1996. Brian Lara (cricketer) Commemoration.
862 **232** 50 c. multicoloured . . . 20 10
863 – $1.25 multicoloured . . . 45 35
864 – $2.50 multicoloured . . . 75 1·25
865 – $3 multicoloured . . . . 90 1·40
DESIGNS: $1.25 to $3, Cricket scenes.

1996. 50th Anniv of End of Second World War (1995). Multicoloured.
867 50 c. Type **233** 20 10
868 $1.25 U.S.S. "Missouri" (battleship), 1944 . . . . . 45 35
869 $2.50 U.S. servicemen playing baseball, 1942 . . . . . . 75 1·25
870 $3 Fleet Air Arm Fulmar I (fighter) . . . . 90 1·40

1999. Wendy Fitzwilliam ("Miss Universe 1998"). Multicoloured.
873 50 c. Type **234** 10 15
874 $1.25 Lying on beach 25 30
875 $2.50 In national costume . . . 50 55
876 $3 In white evening gown . . . 60 65

OFFICIAL STAMP

1913. Optd **OFFICIAL**.
O14 **17** ½d. green . . . . 70 1·50

POSTAGE DUE STAMPS

1947. As Type D **1** of Trinidad but value in cents.
D26 2 c. black . . . . 1·25 2·25
D27 4 c. black . . . . 85 3·00
D28 6 c. black . . . . 95 6·00
D29a 8 c. black . . . . 35 15·00
D30 10 c. black . . . . 85 2·75
D31a 12 c. black . . . . 40 15·00
D32 16 c. black . . . . 2·00 35·00
D33 24 c. black . . . . 6·50 7·50

D 2

1969. Size 19 × 24 mm.
D34 D 2 2 c. green . . . . 15 2·50
D35 4 c. red . . . . 25 3·25
D36 6 c. brown . . . . 50 4·50
D37 8 c. violet . . . . 65 4·75
D38 10 c. red . . . . 65 4·75
D39 12 c. yellow . . . . 80 4·75
D40 16 c. green . . . . 80 3·25
D41 24 c. grey . . . . 80 3·50
D42 50 c. blue . . . . 85 4·00
D43 60 c. green . . . . 85 4·00

1976. Smaller design, 17 × 21 mm.
D44 D 2 2 c. green . . . . 20 1·00
D45 4 c. red . . . . 25 1·00
D46 6 c. brown . . . . 25 1·25
D47 8 c. lilac . . . . 30 1·25
D48 10 c. red . . . . 30 1·25
D49 12 c. orange . . . . . . 50 1·75

INDEX
Countries can be quickly located by referring to the index at the end of this volume.

TRISTAN DA CUNHA

An island in the south Atlantic Ocean west of S. Africa. Following a volcanic eruption the island was evacuated on 10 October 1961, but resettled in 1963.

1952. 12 pence = 1 shilling;
20 shilling = 1 pound.
1961. 100 cents = 1 rand.
1963. Reverted to sterling currency.

1952. Stamps of St. Helena optd **TRISTAN DA CUNHA**.
1 **33** ½d. violet 15 85
2 1d. black and green . . . . 50 1·25
3 1½d. black and red . . . . . 50 1·25
4 2d. black and red . . . . . 50 1·50
5 3d. grey . . . . 70 1·25
6 4d. blue . . . . 3·00 2·00
7 6d. blue . . . . 4·00 2·50
8 8d. green . . . . 3·00 3·00
9 1s. brown . . . . 4·00 2·00
10 2s. 6d. purple . . . . 17·00 14·00
11 5s. brown . . . . 21·00 23·00
12 10s. purple . . . . 35·00 38·00

1953. Coronation. As T **13** of Aden.
13 3d. black and green . . . . . . 50 1·25

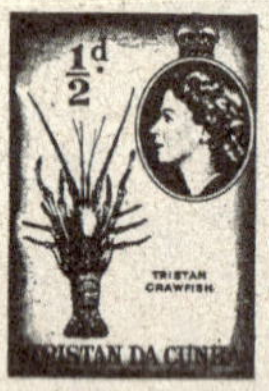
2 Tristan Crawfish

16 Starfish

1954.
14 **2** ½d. red and brown 10 10
15 – 1d. sepia and green 10 40
16 – 1½d. black and purple . . . . 1·75 90
17 – 2d. violet and orange 30 20
18 – 2½d. black and red . . . . . 1·50 60
19 – 3d. blue and olive 80 85
20 – 4d. turquoise and blue 90 90
21 – 5d. green and black 90 70
22 – 6d. green and violet 90 75
23 – 9d. lilac and red 90 45
24 – 1s. green and sepia 90 45
25 – 2s. 6d. sepia and blue . . . . 21·00 10·00
26 – 5s. black and red . . . . . . 48·00 16·00
27 – 10s. orange and purple . . . 22·00 20·00
DESIGNS—HORIZ: 1d. Carting flax; 2d. Big Beach factory; 2½d. Yellow-nosed albatross (sea birds); 4d. Tristan from S.W.; 5d. Girls on donkeys; 6d. Inaccessible Is. from Tristan; 9d. Nightingale Is; 1s. St. Mary's Church; 2s. 6d. Southern elephant seal at Gough Is; 5s. Inaccessible Island rail (bird); 10s. Spinning wheel. VERT: 1½d. Rockhopper penguin; 3d. Island longboat.

1960. Marine Life. Value, fish and inscriptions in black.
28 **16** ½d. orange 15 40
29 – 1d. purple 15 20
30 – 1½d. turquoise 15 50
31 – 2d. green 20 60
32 – 2½d. sepia 30 40
33 – 3d. red 55 20
34 – 4d. olive 55 40
35 – 5d. yellow 70 40
36 – 6d. blue 80 40
37 – 9d. red 90 40
38 – 1s. brown . . . . 1·00 30
39 – 2s. 6d. blue . . . . 10·00 15·00
40 – 5s. green . . . . 11·00 20·00
41 – 10s. violet . . . . 35·00 40·00
FISH: 1d. Concha wrasse; 1½d. Two-spined thornfish; 2d. Atlantic saury; 2½d. Bristle snipefish; 3d. Tristan crawfish; 4d. False jacopever; 5d. Five-fingered morwong; 6d. Long-finned scad; 9d. Christophersen's medusafish; 1s. Blue medusafish; 2s. 6d. Snoek; 5s. Blue shark; 10s. Black right whale.

1961. As 1960 issue but values in new currency. Value, fish and inscriptions in black.
42 **16** ½ c. orange 10 90
43 – 1 c. purple (as 1d.) 15 90
44 – 1½ c. turquoise (as 1½d.) . . . 35 90
45 – 2 c. sepia (as 2½d.) 40 90
46 – 2½ c. red (as 3d.) 50 90
47 – 3 c. olive (as 4d.) 65 90
48 – 4 c. yellow (as 5d.) 80 90
49 – 5 c. blue (as 6d.) 85 90
50 – 7½ c. red (as 9d.) 90 90
51 – 10 c. brown (as 1s.) . . . . . 1·75 90
52 – 25 c. blue (as 2s. 6d.) . . . . 6·00 11·00
53 – 50 c. green (as 5s.) . . . . . 13·00 24·00
54 – 1 r. violet (as 10s.) . . . . . 38·00 42·00

1963. Tristan Resettlement. Nos. 176/88 of St. Helena optd **TRISTAN DA CUNHA RESETTLEMENT 1963**.
55 **50** 1d. multicoloured 15 60
56 – 1½d. multicoloured 20 30
57 – 2d. red and grey 25 60
58 – 3d. multicoloured 30 50
59 – 4½d. multicoloured 50 50
60 – 6d. red, sepia and olive . . . 85 30
61 – 7d. brown, black and violet . 50 30
62 – 10d. purple and blue 50 30
63 – 1s. yellow, green and brown . 50 30
64 – 1s. 6d. grey, black and blue . 3·50 60
65 – 2s. 6d. red, yellow & turq . . 1·00 45
66 – 5s. yellow, brown and green . 6·00 1·25
67 – 10s. red, black and blue . . . 6·50 1·25

1963. Freedom from Hunger. As T **28** of Aden.
68 1s. 6d. red 50 30

1964. Cent of Red Cross. As T **33** of Antigua.
69 3d. red and black 25 15
70 1s. 6d. red and blue 50 20

31 South Atlantic Map

1965.
71 **31** ½d. black and blue 15 15
72 – 1d. black and green . . . 30 15
73 – 1½d. black and blue 30 15
74 – 2d. black and purple . . . 30 15
75 – 3d. black and turquoise . . 30 15
75a – 4d. black and orange . . . 5·50 4·00
76 – 4½d. black and brown . . . 30 15
77 – 6d. black and green . . . 30 15
78 – 7d. black and red 30 30
79 – 10d. black and brown . . 30 55
80 – 1s. black and red 30 30
81 – 1s. 6d. black and olive . . 3·50 2·50
82 – 2s. 6d. black and brown . 2·75 2·75
83 – 5s. black and violet . . . . 5·00 3·50
84 – 10s. blue and red . . . . . 1·75 1·25
84a – 10s. black and blue . . . . 17·00 15·00
84b – £1 blue and brown . . . . 17·00 19·00
DESIGNS—HORIZ: 1d. Flagship of Tristao da Cunha, 1506; 1½d. "Heemstede" (Dutch East Indiaman), 1643; 2d. "Edward" (American whaling ship), 1864; 3d. "Shenandoah" (Confederate warship), 1862; 4d. H.M.S. "Challenger" (survey ship), 1873; 4½d. H.M.S. "Galatea" (screw frigate), 1867; 6d. H.M.S. "Cilicia" (transport), 1942; 7d. Royal Yacht "Britannia"; 10d. H.M.S. "Leopard" (frigate); 1s. "Tjisadane" (liner); 1s. 6d. "Tristania" (crayfish trawler); 2s. 6d. "Boissevain" (cargo liner); 5s. "Bornholm" (liner); 10s. (No. 84a), "R.S.A." (research vessel). VERT: 10s. (No. 84), £1 Queen Elizabeth II (portrait as in T **31** but larger).

1965. Cent of I.T.U. As T **36** of Antigua.
85 3d. red and grey 30 15
86 6d. violet and orange 40 15

1965. I.C.Y. As T **37** of Antigua.
87 1d. purple and turquoise . . . 20 15
88 6d. green and lavender 75 25

1966. Churchill Commem. As T **38** of Antigua.
89 1d. blue 35 40
90 3d. green . . . . 1·25 50
91 6d. brown . . . . 1·50 65
92 1s. 6d. violet . . . . 2·00 70

45 H.M.S. "Falmouth" (frigate) at Tristan and Soldier of 1816

1966. 150th Anniv of Tristan Garrison.
93 **45** 3d. multicoloured 20 10
94 6d. multicoloured 20 15
95 1s. 6d. multicoloured . . . 30 25
96 2s. 6d. multicoloured . . . 30 25

1966. World Cup Football Championship. As T **40** of Antigua.
97 3d. multicoloured 20 10
98 2s. 6d. multicoloured 50 20

1966. Inauguration of W.H.O. Headquarters, Geneva. As T **41** of Antigua.
99 6d. black, green and blue . . 50 30
100 5s. black, purple and ochre . . 75 70

1966. 20th Anniv of U.N.E.S.C.O. As T **54/6** of Antigua.
101 10d. multicoloured 40 15
102 1s. 6d. yellow, violet and olive 45 20
103 2s. 6d. black, purple & orange 55 25

46 Calshot Harbour

1967. Opening of Calshot Harbour.
104 **46** 6d. multicoloured 10 10
105 10d. multicoloured 10 10
106 1s. 6d. multicoloured . . . 10 15
107 2s. 6d. multicoloured . . . 15 20

1967. No. 76 surch **4d** and bars.
108 4d. on 4½d. black and brown . 10 10

48 Prince Alfred, First Duke of Edinburgh

1967. Centenary of First Duke of Edinburgh's Visit to Tristan.

109	48	3d. multicoloured	10	10
110		6d. multicoloured	10	10
111		1s. 6d. multicoloured	10	10
112		2s. 6d. multicoloured	15	15

49 Wandering Albatross

1968. Birds. Multicoloured.

113		4d. Type 49	40	25
114		1s. Wilkin's finch	45	25
115		1s. 6d. Tristan thrush	50	45
116		2s. 6d. Greater shearwater	90	55

53 Union Jack and Dependency Flag

1968. 30th Anniv of Tristan da Cunha as a Dependency of St. Helena.

117	53	6d. multicoloured	10	20
118	–	9d. sepia and blue	10	25
119	53	1s. 6d. multicoloured	15	30
120	–	2s. 6d. red and blue	20	30

DESIGN: 9d. and 2s. 6d. St. Helena and Tristan on chart.

55 Frigate

1969. Clipper Ships.

121	55	4d. blue	40	25
122	–	1s. red	40	30
123	–	1s. 6d. green	45	60
124	–	2s. 6d. brown	50	65

DESIGNS: 1s. Full-rigged ship; 1s. 6d. Barque; 2s. 6d. Full-rigged clipper.

59 Sailing Ship off Tristan da Cunha

1969. United Society for the Propagation of the Gospel. Multicoloured.

125		4d. Type 59	30	25
126		9d. Islanders going to first gospel service	15	25
127		1s. 6d. Landing of the first minister	15	30
128		2s. 6d. Procession outside St. Mary's Church	20	30

63 Globe and Red Cross Emblem

1970. Centenary of British Red Cross.

129	63	4d. deep green, red and green	10	20
130		9d. bistre, red and green	15	25
131	–	1s. 9d. drab, red and blue	25	40
132	–	2s. 6d. purple, red and blue	30	50

DESIGN—VERT: Nos. 131/2, "Union Jack" and Red Cross flag.

64 Crawfish and Longboat

1970. Crawfish Industry. Multicoloured.

133		4d. Type 64	20	25
134		10d. Packing and storing crawfish	25	30
135		1s. 6d. Type 64	35	50
136		2s. 6d. As 10d.	40	60

1971. Decimal Currency. Nos. 72, etc surch.

137	31	½p. on 1d. black and green	15	15
138	–	1p. on 2d. black and purple	15	15
139	–	1½p. on 4d. black & orange	30	15
140	–	2½p. on 6d. black and green	30	15
141	–	3p. on 7d. black and red	30	15
142	–	4p. on 10d. black & brown	30	20
143	–	5p. on 1s. black and red	30	20
144	–	7½p. on 1s. 6d. black & olive	1·75	1·75
145	–	12½p. on 2s. 6d. black & brn	2·50	2·50
146	–	15p. on 1½d. black and blue	2·50	3·00
147	–	25p. on 5s. black and violet	2·50	5·50
148	–	50p. on 10s. black and blue (No. 84a)	3·50	11·00

66 "Quest"

1971. 50th Anniv of Shackleton-Rowett Expedition.

149	66	1½p. multicoloured	70	30
150	–	4p. brown, green and light green	70	40
151	–	7½p. black, purple and green	70	40
152	–	12½p. multicoloured	75	45

DESIGNS—HORIZ: 4p. Presentation of Scout Troop flag; 7½p. Cachet on pair of 6d. G.B. stamps; 12½p. Shackleton, postmarks and longboat taking mail to the "Quest".

67 H.M.S. "Victory" at Trafalgar and Thomas Swain catching Nelson

1971. Island Families. Multicoloured.

153		1½p. Type 67	20	40
154		2½p. "Emily of Stonington" (American schooner) (P. W. Green)	25	50
155		4p. "Italia" (barque) (Lavarello and Repetto)	30	60
156		7½p. H.M.S. "Falmouth" (frigate) (William Glass)	40	70
157		12½p. American whaling ship (Rogers and Hagan)	40	85

68 Cow Pudding

1972. Flowering Plants. Multicoloured.

158		½p. Type 68	20	15
159		1p. Peak berry	40	15
160		1½p. Sand flower (horiz)	40	20
161		2½p. N.Z. flax (horiz)	40	20
162		3p. Island tree	40	20
163		4p. Bog fern	40	25
164		5p. Dog catcher	85	25
165		7½p. Celery	3·00	70
166		12½p. Pepper tree	1·75	60
167		25p. Foul Berry (horiz)	1·75	1·50
168		50p. Tussock	7·00	2·25
169		£1 Tussac (horiz)	3·50	2·50

69 Launching

1972. Tristan Longboats. Multicoloured.

170		2½p. Type 69	20	15
171		4p. Under oars	25	15
172		7½p. Coxswain Arthur Repetto (vert)	25	20
173		12½p. Under sail for Nightingale Island (vert)	30	25

1972. Royal Silver Wedding. As T **52** of Ascension, but with Tristan thrushes and wandering albatrosses in background.

174		2½p. brown	25	30
175		7½p. blue	10	30

71 Church Altar

1973. Golden Jubilee of St. Mary's Church.

176	71	25p. multicoloured	40	40

72 H.M.S. "Challenger's" Laboratory

1973. Cent of H.M.S. "Challenger's" Visit. Mult.

177		4p. Type 72	20	25
178		5p. H.M.S. "Challenger" off Tristan	20	25
179		7½p. "Challenger's pinnace off Nightingale Is.	20	30
180		12½p. Survey route	30	40

73 Approaching English Port

1973. 10th Anniv of Return to Tristan da Cunha.

182	73	4p. brown, yellow and gold	20	25
183	–	5p. multicoloured	20	25
184	–	7½p. multicoloured	20	35
185	–	12½p. multicoloured	30	45

DESIGNS: 5p. Survey party; 7½p. Embarking on "Bornholm"; 12½p. Approaching Tristan.

1973. Royal Wedding. As T **47** of Anguilla. Multicoloured, background colours given.

186		7½p. blue	15	10
187		12½p. green	15	10

74 Rockhopper Penguin and Egg

1974. Rockhopper Penguins. Multicoloured.

188		2½p. Type 74	3·00	1·00
189		5p. Rockhopper colony, Inaccessible Island	3·50	1·40
190		7½p. Penguin fishing	4·00	1·60
191		25p. Adult and fledgling	4·50	2·00

76 Blenheim Palace

1974. Birth Centenary of Sir Winston Churchill.

193	76	7½p. yellow and black	10	10
194	–	25p. black, brown and grey	30	25

DESIGN: 25p. Churchill with Queen Elizabeth II.

77 "Plocamium fuscorubrum"

1975. Sea Plants.

196	77	4p. red, lilac and black	15	10
197	–	5p. green, blue & turquoise	15	15
198	–	10p. orge, brown & purple	20	15
199	–	20p. multicoloured	30	25

DESIGNS: 5p. "Ulva lactua"; 10p. "Epymenia flabellata"; 20p. "Macrocystis pyrifera".

78 Killer Whale

1975. Whales. Multicoloured.

200		2p. Type 78	65	35
201		3p. Rough-toothed dolphin	65	35
202		5p. Black right whale	80	40
203		20p. Fin whale	1·60	85

79 ½d. Stamp of 1952

1976. Festival of Stamps, London.

204	79	5p. black, violet and lilac	20	15
205	–	9p. black, green and blue	25	15
206	–	25p. multicoloured	40	40

DESIGNS—VERT: 9p. 1953 Coronation stamp. HORIZ: 25p. Mail carrier "Tristania II".

80 Island Cottage

1976. Paintings by Roland Svensson (1st series). Multicoloured.

207		3p. Type 80	15	15
208		5p. The potato patches (horiz)	15	15
209		10p. Edinburgh from the sea (horiz)	20	20
210		20p. Huts, Nightingale Is.	30	35

See also Nos. 234/7 and 272/5.

81 The Royal Standard

1977. Silver Jubilee. Multicoloured.

212		10p. Royal Yacht "Britannia"	15	20
213		15p. Type 81	15	20
214		25p. Royal family	20	20

82 H.M.S. "Eskimo" (frigate)

1977. Ships' Crests. Multicoloured.

215		5p. Type 82	15	15
216		10p. H.M.S. "Naiad" (frigate)	20	15
217		15p. H.M.S. "Jaguar" (frigate)	25	25
218		20p. H.M.S. "London" (destroyer)	30	30

83 Great-winged Petrel

1977. Birds. Multicoloured.

220 1p. Type **83** 15 60
221 2p. White-faced storm petrel 20 75
222 3p. Hall's giant petrel 20 75
223 4p. Soft-plumaged petrel 60 90
224 5p. Wandering albatross 60 90
225 10p. Kerguelen petrel 60 90
226 15p. Swallow-tailed tern 60 1·25
227 20p. Greater shearwater 1·00 1·25
228 25p. Broad-billed prion 1·25 1·25
229 50p. Great skua 1·50 1·25
230 £1 Common diving petrel 2·00 2·25
231 £2 Yellow-nosed albatross 4·50 3·50

The 3p. to £2 designs are vertical.

1978. Nos. 213/14 surch.

232 4p. on 15p. Type **81** 1·50 4·00
233 7½p. on 25p. Royal family 1·50 4·00

1978. Paintings by Roland Svensson (2nd series). As T **80**. Multicoloured.

234 5p. St. Mary's Church 15 15
235 10p. Longboats 15 15
236 15p. A Tristan home 20 25
237 20p. The harbour, 1970 20 25

85 King's Bull

1978. 25th Anniv of Coronation.

239 **85** 25p. brown, violet and silver 25 30
240 – 25p. multicoloured 25 30
241 – 25p. brown, violet and silver 25 30

DESIGNS: No. 240, Queen Elizabeth II; No. 241, Tristan crawfish.

86 Sodalite

1978. Local Minerals.

242 3p. Type **86** 25 25
243 5p. Aragonite 30 30
244 10p. Sulphur 45 40
245 20p. Lava containing pyroxene crystal 65 45

87 Two-spined Thornfish

1978. Fishes.

246 **87** 5p. black, brown and green 10 10
247 – 10p. black, brown & green 15 15
248 – 15p. multicoloured 20 20
249 – 20p. multicoloured 30 25

DESIGNS: 10p. Five-fingered morwong; 15p. Concha wrasse; 20p. Tristan jacopever.

88 R.A.F. "Orangeleaf" (tanker)

89 Southern Elephant Seal

1978. Royal Fleet Auxiliary Vessels. Multicoloured.

250 5p. Type **88** 15 10
251 10p. R.F.A. "Tarbatness" (store carrier) 20 10
252 20p. R.F.A. "Tidereach" (tanker) 30 25
253 25p. R.F.A. "Reliant" (store carrier) 35 30

1978. Wildlife Conservation. Multicoloured.

255 5p. Type **89** 10 10
256 10p. Afro-Australian fur seal 15 15
257 15p. Tristan thrush 25 20
258 20p. Nightingale finch 35 25

90 Tristan Longboat

1978. Visit of "Queen Elizabeth 2". Mult.

259 5p. Type **90** 15 20
260 10p. "Queen Mary" (liner) 15 20
261 15p. "Queen Elizabeth" (liner) 20 30
262 20p. "Queen Elizabeth 2" (liner) 20 30

91 1952 "TRISTAN DA CUNHA" overprint on St. Helena 10s. Definitive

1979. Death Centenary of Sir Rowland Hill.

264 **91** 5p. black, lilac and yellow 10 15
265 – 10p. black, red and green 15 20
266 – 25p. multicoloured 30 30

DESIGNS—HORIZ: 10p. 1954 5s. definitive. VERT: 25p. "TRISTAN DA CUNHA RESETTLEMENT 1963" overprint on St. Helena 3d. definitive.

92 "The Padre's House"

1979. International Year of the Child. Children's Drawings. Multicoloured.

268 5p. Type **92** 10 10
269 10p. "Houses in the Village" 15 15
270 15p. "St. Mary's Church" 15 15
271 20p. "Rockhopper Penguins" 20 25

1980. Paintings by Roland Svensson (3rd series). As T **80**. Multicoloured.

272 5p. "Stoltenhoff Island" (horiz) 10 10
273 10p. "Nightingale from the East" (horiz) 15 20
274 15p. "The Administrator's Abode" 15 25
275 20p. "Ridge where the Goat jump off" 20 30

93 "Tristania II" (crayfish trawler)

95 "Golden Hind"

94 Queen Elizabeth the Queen Mother at Royal Opera House, 1976

1980. "London 1980" Int Stamp Exhibition. Mult.

277 5p. Type **93** 10 10
278 10p. Mail being unloaded at Calshot Harbour 15 15
279 15p. Tractor transporting mail to Post Office 15 20
280 20p. Ringing the "dong" to summon people to Post Office 20 20
281 25p. Distributing mail 25 25

1980. 80th Birthday of The Queen Mother.

282 **94** 14p. multicoloured 25 25

1980. 400th Anniv of Sir Francis Drake's Circumnavigation of the World. Multicoloured.

283 5p. Type **95** 10 10
284 10p. Drake's route 15 15
285 20p. Sir Francis Drake 20 20
286 25p. Queen Elizabeth I 25 25

96 "Humpty Dumpty"

1980. Christmas. Scenes from Nursery Rhymes. Multicoloured.

287 15p. Type **96** 15 25
288 15p. "Mary had a little Lamb" 15 25
289 15p. "Little Jack Horner" 15 25
290 15p. "Hey Diddle Diddle" 15 25
291 15p. "London Bridge" 15 25
292 15p. "Old King Cole" 15 25
293 15p. "Sing a Song of Sixpence" 15 25
294 15p. "Tom, Tom the Piper's Son" 15 25
295 15p. "The Owl and the Pussy Cat" 15 25

97 South Atlantic Ocean showing Islands on Mid-Atlantic Ridge

98 Revd. Dodgson as Young Man

1980. 150th Anniv of Royal Geographical Society. Maps. Multicoloured.

296 5p. Type **97** 15 20
297 10p. Tristan da Cunha group (Beauforts Survey, 1806) 15 25
298 15p. Tristan Island (Crawford, 1937–38) 20 30
299 20p. Gough Island (1955–56) 25 40

1981. Centenary of Revd. Edwin Dodgson's Arrival on Tristan da Cunha. Multicoloured.

300 10p. Type **98** 15 15
301 20p. Dodgson and view of Tristan da Cunha (horiz) 25 30
302 30p. Dodgson with people of Tristan da Cunha 35 45

99 Detail from Captain Denham's Plan, 1853

1981. Early Maps. Multicoloured.

304 5p. Type **99** 15 10
305 14p. Detail from map by A. Dalrymple, 17 March 1781 30 20
306 21p. Detail from Captain Denham's plan, 1853 (different) 40 30

100 Wedding Bouquet from Tristan da Cunha

101 Explorer with Rucksack

1981. Royal Wedding. Multicoloured.

308 5p. Type **100** 10 10
309 20p. Investiture of Prince of Wales 15 15
310 50p. Prince Charles and Lady Diana Spencer 45 45

1981. 25th Anniv of Duke of Edinburgh Award Scheme. Multicoloured.

311 5p. Type **101** 10 10
312 10p. Explorer at campsite 10 10
313 20p. Explorer map reading 20 20
314 25p. Duke of Edinburgh 25 25

102 Inaccessible Island Rail on Nest

1981. Inaccessible Island Rail. Multicoloured.

315 10p. Type **102** 25 30
316 10p. Inaccessible Island rail eggs 25 20
317 10p. Rail chicks 25 30
318 10p. Adult rail 25 30

103 Six-gilled Shark

1982. Sharks. Multicoloured.

319 5p. Type **103** 30 10
320 14p. Porbeagle 40 20
321 21p. Blue shark 45 35
322 35p. Golden hammerhead 55 50

104 "Marcella" (barque)

1982. Sailing Ships (1st series). Multicoloured.

323 5p. Type **104** 25 35
324 15p. "Eliza Adams" (full-rigged ship) 30 50
325 30p. "Corinthian" (American whaling ship) 45 80
326 50p. "Samuel and Thomas" (American whaling ship) 70 1·10

See also Nos. 341/4.

105 Lady Diana Spencer at Windsor, July 1981 **106** Lord Baden-Powell

1982. 21st Birthday of Princess of Wales. Multicoloured.

327 5p. Tristan da Cunha coat of arms 10 10
328 15p. Type **105** 40 20
329 30p. Prince and Princess of Wales in wedding portrait 45 40
330 50p. Formal portrait 1·25 60

1982. 75th Anniv of Boy Scout Movement. Multicoloured.

331 5p. Type **106** 15 15
332 20p. First Scout camp, Brownsea, 1907 30 35
333 50p. Local Scouts on parade (horiz) 65 75

1982. Commonwealth Games, Brisbane. Nos. 224 and 228 optd **1ST PARTICIPATION COMMONWEALTH GAMES 1982**.

335 5p. Wandering albatross 15 10
336 25p. Broad-billed prion 40 30

108 Formation of Island

1982. Volcanoes. Multicoloured.

337 5p. Type **108** 15 15
338 15p. Plan showing surface cinder cones and cross-section of volcano showing feeders 30 35
339 25p. Eruption 45 50
340 35p. 1961 Tristan eruption 65 70

1983. Sailing Ships (2nd series). As T **104**. Multicoloured.

341 5p. "Islander" (barque) (vert) 25 15
342 20p. "Roscoe" (full-rigged ship) 45 35
343 35p. "Columbia" (whaling ship) 60 55
344 50p. "Emeline" (schooner) (vert) 80 80

109 Tractor pulling Trailer

1983. Land Transport. Multicoloured.

345	5p. Type **109**	10	15
346	15p. Pack donkeys	15	25
347	30p. Bullock cart	30	40
348	50p. Landrover	50	60

110 Early Chart of South Atlantic

1983. Island History. Multicoloured.

349	1p. Type **110**	30	30
350	3p. Tristao da Cunha's caravel	40	30
351	4p. Notice left by Dutch on first landing, 1643	40	30
352	5p. 17th-century views of the island	40	30
353	10p. British army landing party, 1815	45	40
354	15p. 19th-century view of the settlement	55	50
355	18p. Governor Glass's house	55	50
356	20p. The Revd. W. F. Taylor and Peter Green	65	65
357	25p. "John and Elizabeth" (American whaling ship)	85	75
358	50p. Letters Patent declaring Tristan da Cunha a dependency of St. Helena	1·40	1·25
359	£1 Commissioning of H.M.S. "Atlantic Isle", 1944	2·00	2·50
360	£2 Evacuation, 1961	2·75	4·00

111 "Christ's Charge to St. Peter" (detail)

113 "Agrocybe praecox var. cutefracta"

112 1952 6d. Stamp

1983. 500th Birth Anniv of Raphael.

361	**111**	10p. multicoloured	15	20
362	–	25p. multicoloured	25	35
363	–	40p. multicoloured	45	60

DESIGNS: 25, 40p. Different details of "Christ's Charge to St. Peter" (Raphael).

1984. 150th Anniv of St. Helena as British Colony. Multicoloured.

365	10p. Type **112**	25	35
366	15p. 1952 1s. stamp	35	45
367	25p. 1952 2s. 6d. stamp	40	70
368	60p. 1952 10s. stamp	85	1·25

1984. Fungi. Multicoloured.

369	10p. Type **113**	65	85
370	20p. "Laccaria tetraspora"	95	1·25
371	30p. "Agrocybe cylindracea" (horiz)	1·10	1·40
372	50p. "Sacoscypha coccinea" (horiz)	1·40	1·75

114 Constellation of "Orion"

115 Sheep-shearing

1984. The Night Sky. Multicoloured.

373	10p. Type **114**	45	80
374	20p. "Scorpius"	65	1·00
375	25p. "Canis Major"	75	1·10
376	50p. "Crux"	1·10	1·40

1984. Tristan Woollens Industry. Mult.

377	9p. Type **115**	20	45
378	17p. Carding wool	30	60
379	29p. Spinning	50	90
380	45p. Knitting	75	1·10

116 "Christmas Dinner-table"

1984. Christmas. Children's Drawings. Multicoloured.

382	10p. Type **116**	20	35
383	20p. "Santa Claus in ox cart"	30	50
384	30p. "Santa Claus in longboat"	40	80
385	50p. "The Nativity"	75	1·10

117 "H.M.S. 'Julia' Ashore, 1817" (Midshipman C. W. Browne)

118 The Queen Mother at Ascot with Princess Margaret

1985. Shipwrecks (1st series).

386	**117**	10p. blue and light blue	70	80
387	–	25p. brown and green	1·25	1·40
388	–	35p. brown and yellow	1·40	1·60

DESIGNS—VERT: 25p. Bell from "Mabel Clark", St. Mary's Church. HORIZ: 35p. "Barque 'Glenhuntley' foundering 1898" (John Hagan).

See also Nos. 411/14 and 426/8.

1985. Life and Times of Queen Elizabeth the Queen Mother. Multicoloured.

390	10p. The Queen Mother and Prince Charles, 1954	20	30
391	20p. Type **118**	30	60
392	30p. Queen Elizabeth the Queen Mother	40	85
393	50p. With Prince Henry at his christening	70	1·25

119 Jonathan Lambert and "Isles of Refreshment" Flag, 1811

1985. Flags. Multicoloured.

395	10p. Type **119**	80	80
396	15p. 21st Light Dragoons guidon and cannon from Fort Malcolm (1816–17) (vert)	1·00	1·00
397	25p. White Ensign and H.M.S. "Falmouth" (frigate) offshore, 1816 (vert)	1·40	1·60
398	60p. Union Jack and Tristan da Cunha (vert)	2·75	3·00

120 Lifeboat heading for Barque "West Riding"

1985. Cent of Loss of Island Lifeboat. Mult.

399	10p. Type **120**	25	60
400	30p. Map of Tristan da Cunha	55	1·25
401	50p. Memorial plaque to lifeboat crew	85	1·75

121 Halley's Comet, 1066, from Bayeux Tapestry

1986. Appearance of Halley's Comet. Mult.

402	10p. Type **121**	40	65
403	20p. Path of Comet	65	1·00
404	30p. Comet over Inaccessible Island	85	1·40
405	50p. H.M.S. "Paramour" (pink) and map of South Atlantic	1·40	1·75

1986. 60th Birthday of Queen Elizabeth II. As T **110** of Ascension. Multicoloured.

406	10p. With Prince Charles, 1950	15	30
407	15p. Queen at Trooping the Colour	20	40
408	25p. In robes of Order of the Bath, Westminster Abbey, 1972	35	60
409	45p. In Canada, 1977	55	1·00
410	65p. At Crown Agents Head Office, London 1983	75	1·50

122 "'Allanshaw' wrecked on East Beach, 1893" (drawing by John Hagan)

1986. Shipwrecks (2nd series).

411	**122**	9p. blue, deep blue and black	30	80
412	–	20p. green, yellow and black	60	1·40
413	–	40p. blue, violet and black	1·10	1·90

DESIGNS: 20p. Church font from wreck of "Edward Vittery", 1881; 40p. Ship's figurehead.

1986. Royal Wedding. As T **112** of Ascension. Multicoloured.

415	10p. Prince Andrew and Miss Sarah Ferguson	20	50
416	40p. Prince Andrew piloting helicopter, Digby, Canada, 1985	80	1·50

123 Wandering Albatross

124 "Dimorphinoctua cunhaensis" (flightless moth) and Edinburgh

1986. Flora and Fauna of Inaccessible Island. Multicoloured.

417	5p. Type **123**	40	60
418	10p. "Lagenophora nudicaulis" (daisy)	40	70
419	20p. "Cynthia virginiensis" (butterfly)	90	1·40
420	25p. Wilkin's finch	95	1·50
421	50p. White-chinned petrel	1·40	1·75

1987. Island Flightless Insects and Birds. Multicoloured.

422	10p. Type **124**	25	60
423	25p. "Tristanomyia frustilifera" (fly) and Crater Lake	55	1·25
424	35p. Inaccessible Island rail and Inaccessible Island	1·25	2·00
425	50p. Gough Island moorhen and Gough Island	1·75	2·25

125 Castaways from "Blenden Hall" attacking Sea Elephant, 1821

1987. Shipwrecks (3rd series).

426	**125**	11p. black and brown	70	1·00
427	–	17p. black and lilac	90	1·50
428	–	45p. black and green	1·40	2·00

DESIGNS—HORIZ: 17p. Barquentine "Henry A. Paull" stranded at Sandy Point, 1879. VERT: 45p. Gustav Stoltenhoff, 1871, and Stoltenhoff Island.

126 Rockhopper Penguin swimming

1987. Rockhopper Penguins. Multicoloured.

430	10p. Type **126**	75	85
431	20p. Adult with egg	1·10	1·40
432	30p. Adult with juvenile	1·40	1·75
433	50p. Head of rockhopper penguin	1·75	2·00

127 Microscope and Published Report

128 Nightingale Finch ("Tristan Bunting")

1987. 50th Anniv of Norwegian Scientific Expedition. Multicoloured.

434	10p. Type **127**	90	1·00
435	20p. Scientists ringing yellow-nosed albatross	1·90	2·00
436	30p. Expedition hut, Little Beach Point	2·25	2·50
437	50p. S.S. "Thorshammer" (whale factory ship)	3·25	3·50

1988. Royal Ruby Wedding. Nos. 406/10 optd **40TH WEDDING ANNIVERSARY**.

438	10p. Princess Elizabeth with Prince Charles, 1950	20	25
439	15p. Queen Elizabeth II at Trooping the Colour	30	35
440	25p. In robes of Order of the Bath, Westminster Abbey, 1972	50	55
441	45p. In Canada, 1977	95	95
442	65p. At Crown Agents Head Office, London 1983	1·00	1·40

1988. Fauna of Nightingale Island. Mult.

443	5p. Type **128**	50	50
444	10p. Tristan thrush (immature)	65	65
445	20p. Yellow-nosed albatross (chick)	85	90
446	25p. Greater shearwater	85	1·00
447	50p. Elephant seal	1·40	2·00

129 Painted Penguin Eggs

1988. Tristan da Cunha Handicrafts. Mult.

448	10p. Type **129**	25	35
449	15p. Moccasins	35	50
450	35p. Knitwear	75	1·00
451	50p. Model longboat	1·10	1·40

130 Processing Blubber

1988. 19th-century Whaling. Multicoloured.

452	10p. Type **130**	65	65
453	20p. Harpoon guns	85	85
454	30p. Scrimshaw (carved whale bone)	1·00	1·00
455	50p. Whaling ships	1·75	2·00

1988. 300th Anniv of Lloyd's of London. As T **123** of Ascension.

457	10p. multicoloured	30	40
458	25p. multicoloured	1·10	1·10
459	35p. black and green	1·50	1·50
460	50p. black and red	1·90	1·90

DESIGNS—VERT: 10p. New Lloyd's Building, 1988; 50p. "Kobenhavn" (cadet barque). HORIZ: 25p. "Tristania II" (crayfish trawler); 35p. "St. Helena" (mail ship).

131 "Government House"

1988. Augustus Earle's Paintings, 1824. Mult.

461	1p. Type **131**	20	40
462	3p. "Squall off Tristan"	30	50
463	4p. "Rafting Blubber"	35	50
464	5p. "View near Little Beach"	35	50
465	10p. "Man killing Albatross"	45	60
466	15p. "View on The Summit"	70	80
467	20p. "Nightingale Island"	85	95
468	25p. "Earle on Tristan"	1·00	1·10
469	35p. "Solitude-Watching the Horizon"	1·25	1·40
470	50p. "Northeaster"	1·50	1·75
471	£1 "Tristan Village"	2·75	2·75
472	£2 "Governor Glass at Dinner"	4·25	4·25

132 Hall's Giant Petrel

133 "Eriosorus cheilanthoides"

1989. Fauna of Gough Island. Multicoloured.

473 5p. Type **132** 60 60
474 10p. Gough Island moorhen . 70 70
475 20p. Gough Island finch ("Gough bunting") 90 90
476 25p. Sooty albatross . . . . . 1·00 1·00
477 50p. Amsterdam fur seal . . . 1·60 1·75

1989. Ferns. Multicoloured.

478 10p. Type **133** 50 50
479 25p. "Asplenium alvarezense" 90 90
480 35p. "Elaphoglossum hybridum" 1·10 1·10
481 50p. "Ophioglossum opacum" 1·50 1·50

134 Surgeon's Mortar

1989. Nautical Museum Exhibits. Mult.

482 10p. Type **134** 50 50
483 20p. Parts of darting-gun harpoon 90 90
484 30p. Ship's compass with binnacle-hood . . . . . . 1·10 1·10
485 60p. Rope-twisting device . . 1·75 1·75

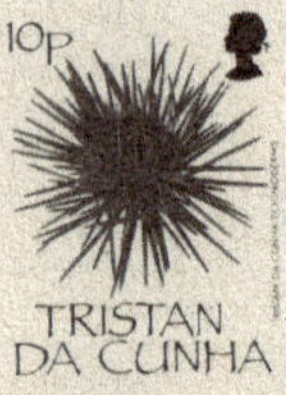

135 Cattle Egret

137 Sea Urchin

136 "Peridroma saucia"

1989. Vagrant Birds. Multicoloured.

486 10p. Type **135** . . . . 1·25 1·00
487 25p. Spotted sandpiper . . . . 2·00 2·00
488 35p. Purple gallinule . . . . . 2·25 2·25
489 50p. Barn swallow . . . . . . 2·50 2·75

1990. Moths. Multicoloured.

490 10p. Type **136** 80 70
491 15p. "Ascalapha odorata" . . 1·10 1·10
492 35p. "Agrius cingulata" . . . 1·75 1·75
493 60p. "Eumorpha labruscae" . 2·25 2·50

1990. Echinoderms.

494 **137** 10p. multicoloured 80 70
495 – 20p. multicoloured . . . . 1·25 1·25
496 – 30p. multicoloured . . . . 1·60 1·60
497 – 60p. multicoloured . . . . 2·25 2·50

DESIGNS: 20p. to 60p. Different starfish.

1990. 90th Birthday of Queen Elizabeth the Queen Mother. As T **134** of Ascension.

498 25p. multicoloured . . . . . 1·00 1·00
499 £1 brown and blue . . . . . 2·75 3·25

DESIGNS—21 × 36 mm: 25p. Queen Mother at the London Coliseum. 29 × 37 mm: £1 Queen Elizabeth broadcasting to women of the Empire, 1939.

1990. Maiden Voyage of "St. Helena II". As T **137** of Ascension. Multicoloured.

500 10p. "Dunnottar Castle" (liner), 1942 . . . . 90 90
501 15p. "St. Helena I" (mail ship) at Tristan . . . . 1·40 1·40
502 35p. Launch of "St. Helena II" (mail ship) . . . . 2·00 2·25
503 60p. Duke of York launching "St. Helena II" . . . . . . 2·75 3·25

138 H.M.S. "Pyramus" (frigate), 1829

1990. Ships of the Royal Navy (1st series). Multicoloured.

505 10p. Type **138** . . . . 1·25 1·00
506 25p. H.M.S. "Penguin" (sloop), 1815 . . . . 2·25 2·25
507 35p. H.M.S. "Thalia" (screw corvette), 1886 . . . . . 2·50 2·50
508 50p. H.M.S. "Sidon" (paddle frigate), 1858 . . . . . . 3·00 3·50

See also Nos. 509/12 and 565/8.

1991. Ships of the Royal Navy (2nd series). As T **138**. Multicoloured.

509 10p. H.M.S. "Milford" (sloop), 1938 . . . . 1·25 1·00
510 25p. H.M.S. "Dublin" (cruiser), 1923 . . . . 2·25 2·25
511 35p. H.M.S. "Yarmouth" (cruiser), 1919 . . . . . . 2·50 2·50
512 50p. H.M.S. "Carlisle" (cruiser), 1938 . . . . 3·00 3·50

140 Prince Alfred and H.M.S. "Galatea" (screw frigate), 1867

1991. 70th Birthday of Prince Philip, Duke of Edinburgh.

514 **140** 10p. black, lt blue & blue 1·50 1·50
515 – 25p. black, lt green & green 2·00 2·25
516 – 30p. black, brown & yellow 2·75 3·00
517 – 50p. multicoloured . . . 3·00 3·25

DESIGNS: 25p. Prince Philip meeting local inhabitants, 1957; 30p. Prince Philip and Royal Yacht "Britannia", 1957; 50p. Prince Philip and Edinburgh settlement.

141 Pair of Gough Island Moorhens

1991. Endangered Species. Birds. Mult.

518 8p. Type **141** . . . . 1·50 1·50
519 10p. Gough Island finch . . . 1·60 1·60
520 12p. Gough Island moorhen on nest . . . . 1·75 1·75
521 15p. Gough Island finch feeding chicks . . . . 1·90 1·90

1992. 500th Anniv of Discovery of America by Columbus and Re-enactment Voyages. As T **168** of St. Helena. Multicoloured.

522 10p. Map of re-enactment voyages and "Eye of the Wind" (cadet brig) 90 90
523 15p. Compass rose and "Soren Larsen" (cadet brigantine) . 1·25 1·25
524 35p. Ships of Columbus . . . 2·25 2·50
525 60p. Columbus and "Santa Maria" . . . . 2·50 2·75

1992. 40th Anniv of Queen Elizabeth II's Accession. As T **143** of Ascension. Mult.

526 10p. Tristan from the sea . . 50 50
527 20p. Longboat under sail . . 80 80
528 25p. Aerial view of Edinburgh 90 90
529 35p. Three portraits of Queen Elizabeth . . . . 1·10 1·10
530 65p. Queen Elizabeth II . . . 1·75 2·00

142 Coats' Perch

1992. Fishes. Multicoloured.

531 10p. Type **142** 80 80
532 15p. Lined trumpeter . . . . 1·25 1·25
533 35p. Karrer's morid cod . . . 2·25 2·50
534 60p. Long-finned scad . . . . 2·75 3·00

143 "Italia" leaving Greenock

1992. Cent of the Wreck of Barque "Italia". Mult.

535 10p. Type **143** . . . . 1·00 1·00
536 45p. In mid-Atlantic . . . . . 2·50 2·75
537 65p. Driving ashore on Stony Beach . . . . 3·00 3·25

144 "Stenoscelis hylastoides"

1993. Insects. Multicoloured.

539 15p. Type **144** . . . . 1·00 1·00
540 45p. "Trogloscaptomyza brevilamellata" . . . . . . 2·25 2·50
541 60p. "Senilites tristanicola" . . 2·75 3·00

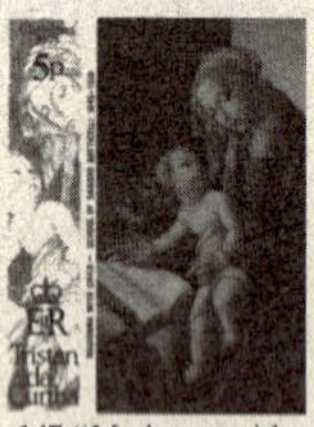

145 Ampulla and Anointing Spoon

147 "Madonna with Child" (School of Botticelli)

146 "Tristania" and "Frances Repetto" (crayfish trawlers)

1993. 40th Anniv of Coronation.

542 **145** 10p. green and black . . . 80 80
543 – 15p. mauve and black . . 1·10 1·25
544 – 35p. violet and black . . . 1·60 2·00
545 – 60p. blue and black . . . 2·25 2·75

DESIGNS: 15p. Orb; 35p. Imperial State Crown; 60p. St. Edward's Crown.

1993. 30th Anniv of Resettlement of Tristan. Multicoloured.

546 35p. Type **146** . . . . 2·00 2·25
547 35p. "Boissevain" (cargo liner) 2·00 2·25
548 50p. "Bornholm" (liner) and longboat . . . . 2·50 3·25

1993. Christmas. Religious Paintings. Mult.

549 5p. Type **147** 70 70
550 15p. "The Holy Family" (Daniel Gran) . . . . 1·50 1·50
551 35p. "The Holy Virgin and Child" (Rubens) . . . . . . 2·50 2·25
552 65p. "The Mystical Marriage of St. Catherine with the Holy Child" (Jan van Balen) . . . 3·00 3·75

148 "Duchess of Atholl" (liner)

1994. Ships. Multicoloured.

553 1p. Type **148** 10 10
554 3p. "Empress of Australia" (liner) 10 10
555 5p. "Anatolia" (freighter) . . . 10 10
556 8p. "Viceroy of India" (liner) . 15 20
557 10p. "Rangitata" (transport) . 20 25
558 15p. "Caronia" (liner) 30 35
559 20p. "Rotterdam" (liner) . . . 40 45
560 25p. "Leonardo da Vinci" (liner) 50 55
561 35p. "Vistafjord" (liner) . . . 70 75
562 £1 "World Discoverer" (liner) . 2·00 2·10
563 £2 "Astor" (liner) . . . . . . 4·00 4·25
564 £5 "St. Helena II" (mail ship) . 10·00 10·50

1994. Ships of the Royal Navy (3rd series). As T **138**. Multicoloured.

565 10p. H.M.S. "Nigeria" (cruiser), 1948 . . . . 90 90
566 25p. H.M.S. "Phoebe" (cruiser), 1949 . . . . 1·75 1·75
567 35p. H.M.S. "Liverpool" (cruiser), 1949 . . . . . . 2·00 2·00
568 50p. H.M.S. "Magpie" (frigate), 1955 . . . . 2·50 2·50

149 Blue Shark

1994. Sharks. Multicoloured.

569 10p. Type **149** 90 90
570 45p. Seven-gilled shark . . . 2·50 2·75
571 65p. Short-finned mako . . . 3·25 3·50

150 Pair of Donkeys

1994. Island Livestock (1st series). Multicoloured.

572 10p. Type **150** 70 70
573 20p. Cattle . . . . 1·10 1·10
574 35p. Ducks and geese . . . . 2·00 2·25
575 60p. Girl bottle-feeding lamb . 2·75 3·25

See also Nos. 620/3.

151 Pick-up Truck

1995. Local Transport. Multicoloured.

576 15p. Type **151** 90 90
577 20p. Sherpa van . . . . 1·25 1·25
578 45p. Scooter and Yamaha motorcycle . . . . 2·00 2·25
579 60p. Administrator's landrover 2·50 2·75

1995. 50th Anniv of End of Second World War. As T **161** of Ascension. Multicoloured.

580 15p. Sailors training on Lewis guns . . . . 1·00 1·00
581 20p. Tristan Defence Volunteers 1·25 1·25
582 45p. Wireless and meteorological station . . . . 2·00 2·25
583 60p. H.M.S. "Birmingham" (cruiser) . . . . 2·50 2·75

153 Sub-Antarctic Fur Seal on Rock

1995. Seals. Multicoloured.

586 10p. Type **153** 75 75
587 35p. Sub-Antarctic fur seals with pups . . . . 1·75 1·75
588 45p. Southern elephant seal asleep with pups . . . . . 2·00 2·00
589 50p. Southern elephant seals in water . . . . 2·00 2·00

1996. 50th Anniv of United Nations. As T **284** of Jamaica. Multicoloured.

590 20p. Bedford 4-ton lorry . . . 1·00 1·00
591 30p. Saxon armoured personnel carrier . . . . 1·40 1·40
592 45p. Mi26 heavy lift helicopter 2·25 2·25
593 50p. R.F.A. "Sir Tristram" (landing ship) . . . . 2·50 2·50

1996. 70th Birthday of Queen Elizabeth II. As T **55** of Tokelau, each incorporating a different photograph of the Queen.

594 15p. Tristan from the sea . . 65 70
595 20p. Traditional cottage . . . 75 80
596 45p. The Residency . . . . . 1·50 1·75
597 60p. The Queen and Prince Philip 2·00 2·25

154 Old Harbour and "St. Helena I" (mail ship)

1996. Construction of New Harbour. Multicoloured.

598 15p. Type **154** 80 80
599 20p. Excavator and dump truck (44 × 27 mm) 90 90
600 45p. Construction of new mole (44 × 27 mm) . . . . 1·75 2·00
601 60p. New harbour and "St. Helena II" (mail ship) . . . 2·50 2·75

155 Gough Island Moorhen

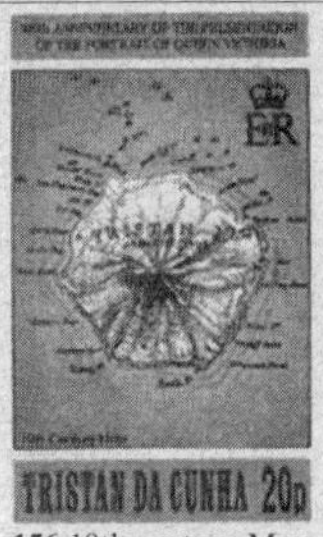

156 19th-century Map

1996. Declaration of Gough Island as World Heritage Site. Birds. Multicoloured.

602	15p. Type **155**	85	85
603	20p. Wandering albatross	95	95
604	45p. Sooty albatross	1·75	2·00
605	60p. Gough Island finch ("Gough Bunting")	2·25	2·75

1996. Centenary of the Presentation of the Queen Victoria Portrait to Tristan. Multicoloured.

606	20p. Type **156**	90	90
607	30p. H.M.S. "Magpie" (Gunboat)	1·40	1·40
608	45p. Governor Peter Green	1·60	1·75
609	50p. "Queen Victoria" (H. von Angeli) (detail)	1·75	2·00

158 Smoke Signals

1997. Visual Communications. Multicoloured.

611	10p. Type **158**	30	40
612	10p. H.M.S. "Eurydice" (frigate)	30	40
613	15p. H.M.S. "Challenger" (survey ship)	50	70
614	15p. Flag hoists	50	70
615	20p. Semaphore	65	80
616	20p. H.M.S. "Carlisle" (cruiser)	65	80
617	35p. Aldis lamp	80	90
618	35p. H.M.S. "Cilicia" (transport)	80	90

Nos. 611/12, 613/14, 615/16 and 617/18 respectively were printed together, se-tenant, forming composite designs.

1997. Island Livestock (2nd series). As T **150.** Multicoloured.

620	20p. Chickens	70	70
621	30p. Bull	90	90
622	45p. Sheep	1·40	1·40
623	50p. Collie dogs	1·75	1·75

1997. Golden Wedding of Queen Elizabeth and Prince Philip. As T **87** of Kiribati. Multicoloured.

624	15p. Queen Elizabeth	45	55
625	15p. Prince Philip playing polo	45	55
626	20p. Queen Elizabeth with horse	55	65
627	20p. Prince Philip	55	65
628	45p. Queen Elizabeth with Prince Philip in R.A.F. uniform	1·25	1·40
629	45p. Princess Anne on horseback	1·25	1·40

Nos. 624/5, 626/7 and 628/9 respectively were printed together, se-tenant, with the backgrounds forming composite designs.

159 "Hilary" and "Melodie"

1998. 50th Anniv of First Lobster Survey. Lobster Trawlers. Multicoloured.

631	15p. Type **159**	55	55
632	20p. "Tristania II" and "Hekla"	65	65
633	30p. "Pequena" and "Frances Repetto"	85	85
634	45p. "Tristania" and "Gillian Gaggins"	1·40	1·40
635	50p. "Kelso" and "Edinburgh"	1·40	1·40

160 "Livonia"

1998. Cruise Ships. Multicoloured.

639	15p. Type **160**	50	50
640	20p. "Professor Molchanov"	60	60
641	45p. "Explorer"	1·25	1·25
642	60p. "Hanseatic"	1·50	1·50

161 "H. G. Johnson" (barque)

1998. Maritime Heritage (1st series). Multicoloured.

643	15p. Type **161**	50	50
644	35p. "Theodore" (full-rigged ship)	1·00	1·00
645	45p. "Hesperides" (full-rigged ship)	1·25	1·25
646	50p. "Bessfield" (barque)	1·25	1·25

1999. Maritime Heritage (2nd series). As T **161**. Multicoloured.

647	20p. "Derwent" (full-rigged ship)	60	60
648	30p. "Strathgryfe" (full-rigged ship)	85	85
649	50p. "Celestial Empire" (full-rigged ship)	1·25	1·25
650	60p. "Lamorna" (full-rigged ship)	1·50	1·50

162 Wandering Albatross Courtship Dance

1999. Endangered Species. Wandering Albatross. Multicoloured.

651	5p. Type **162**	10	10
652	8p. Adult and chick	15	20
653	12p. Adult with spread wings	25	30
654	15p. Two adults in flight	30	35

1999. Royal Wedding. As T **153** of Pitcairn Islands. Multicoloured.

655	45p. Photographs of Prince Edward and Miss Sophie Rhys-Jones	90	95
656	£1.20 Engagement photograph	2·40	2·50

POSTAGE DUE STAMPS

1957. As Type D **1** of Barbados.

D1	1d. red	1·75	10·00
D2	2d. yellow	3·00	4·75
D3	3d. green	3·50	5·50
D4	4d. blue	7·00	7·00
D5	5d. lake	5·00	23·00

D 2

D 3 Outline Map of Tristan da Cunha

1976.

D11	D 2	1p. purple	10	40
D12		2p. green	15	40
D13		4p. violet	20	45
D14		5p. blue	20	50
D15		10p. brown	20	65

1986.

D16	D 3	1p. brown and light brown	10	10
D17		2p. brown and orange	10	10
D18		5p. brown and red	10	15
D19		7p. black and violet	15	20
D20		10p. black and blue	20	25
D21		25p. black and green	50	55

TRUCIAL STATES

Seven Arab shaikhdoms on the Persian Gulf and Gulf of Oman, in treaty relations with Great Britain. The following stamps were issued at the British Postal Agency at Dubai until it closed on 14 June 1963.

Individual issues were later made by Abu Dhabi, Ajman, Dubai, Fujeira, Ras al Khaima, Sharjah and Umm al Qiwain.

100 naye paise = 1 rupee

1 Palms

2 Dhow

1961.

1	1	5 n.p. green	50	10
2		15 n.p. brown	30	10
3		20 n.p. blue	40	10
4		30 n.p. orange	40	10
5		40 n.p. violet	40	10
6		50 n.p. bistre	40	10
7		75 n.p. grey	60	10
8	2	1 r. green	3·50	1·50
9		2 r. black	3·00	11·00
10		5 r. red	4·50	16·00
11		10 r. blue	12·00	21·00

TURKS ISLANDS

A group of islands in the Br. W. Indies, S.E. of the Bahamas, now grouped with the Caicos Islands and using the stamps of Turks and Caicos Islands. A dependency of Jamaica until August, 1962, when it became a Crown Colony.

12 pence = 1 shilling

1

1867.

55	1	1d. brown	50·00	30·00
63		1d. red	2·00	2·25
2		6d. black	80·00	£100
59		6d. brown	2·50	2·75
3		1s. blue	75·00	60·00
6		1s. lilac	£5000	£2000
60		1s. brown	4·00	2·75
52		1s. green	£110	£110

1881. Surch with large figures.

17	1	½ on 1d. red	50·00	90·00
7		½ on 6d. black	65·00	95·00
9		½ on 1s. blue	80·00	£130
19		½ on 1s. lilac	80·00	£140
34		2½ on 1d. red	£600	
28		2½ on 6d. black	£140	£225
29		2½ on 1s. lilac	£550	£850
38		2½ on 1s. blue	£700	
47		4 on 1d. red	£700	£475
43		4 on 6d. black	65·00	85·00
45		4 on 1s. lilac	£375	

31

34

1881.

70	31	½d. green	1·75	1·75
56		2½d. brown	14·00	10·00
65		2½d. blue	2·25	1·50
50		4d. blue	90·00	60·00
57		4d. grey	11·00	2·00
71		4d. purple and blue	8·00	12·00
72	34	5d. olive and red	3·25	11·00

1889. Surch **One Penny**.

61	31	1d. on 2½d. brown	6·50	9·50

1893. Surch **½d.** and bar.

68	31	½d. on 4d. grey	£120	£120

INDEX

Countries can be quickly located by referring to the index at the end of this volume.

TURKS AND CAICOS ISLANDS

(See TURKS ISLANDS)

1900. 12 pence = 1 shilling;
20 shillings = 1 pound.
1969. 100 cents = 1 dollar.

35 Badge of the Islands 36

1900.

110	35	½d. green	3·50	15
102		1d. red	3·50	75
103		2d. brown	75	1·25
104a		2½d. blue	1·75	1·00
112		3d. purple on yellow	1·50	6·00
105		4d. orange	3·50	7·00
106		6d. mauve	1·75	6·50
107		1s. brown	2·50	15·00
108	36	2s. purple	40·00	55·00
109		3s. red	50·00	70·00

37 Turk's-head Cactus

38

1909.

115	37	¼d. mauve	1·25	1·00
116		¼d. red	30	30
162		¼d. black	70	90
117	38	½d. green	55	30
118		1d. red	70	30
119		2d. grey	1·10	1·40
120		2½d. blue	1·25	3·75
121		3d. purple on yellow	1·75	2·00
122		4d. red on yellow	3·25	7·00
123		6d. purple	6·00	7·00
124		1s. black on green	6·00	8·50
125		2s. red and green	26·00	48·00
126		3s. black on red	26·00	35·00

39

1913.

129	39	½d. green	40	1·75
130		1d. red	1·00	2·25
131		2d. grey	1·40	3·00
132		2½d. blue	2·25	2·50
133d		3d. purple on yellow	2·00	7·50
134a		4d. red on yellow	1·60	7·00
135		5d. green	6·50	18·00
136		6d. purple	2·25	3·25
137		1s. orange	1·50	4·00
138		2s. red on green	7·50	25·00
139		3s. black on red	15·00	25·00

1917. Optd **WAR TAX** in one line.

143	39	1d. red	10	90
144		3d. purple on yellow	60	1·50

1918. Optd **WAR TAX** in two lines.

150	39	1d. red	10	90
148		3d. purple on yellow	10	1·75

44

45

1922. Inscr "POSTAGE".

163a	44	½d. green	1·25	1·75
164		1d. brown	50	3·00
165		1½d. red	5·50	12·00
166		2d. grey	50	4·25
167		2½d. purple on yellow	50	1·50
168		3d. blue	50	4·25
169		4d. red on yellow	85	11·00
170		5d. green	75	18·00
171		6d. purple	60	3·75
172		1s. orange	70	13·00
173		2s. red on green	2·00	7·50
175		3s. black on red	5·00	20·00

1928. Inscr "POSTAGE & REVENUE".

176	45	½d. green	60	50
177		1d. brown	60	70
178		1½d. red	60	2·75
179		2d. grey	60	40
180		2½d. purple on yellow	60	3·75
181		3d. blue	60	4·50
182		6d. purple	60	6·50
183		1s. orange	3·75	6·50
184		2s. red on green	6·00	35·00
185		5s. green on yellow	11·00	35·00
186		10s. purple on blue	45·00	95·00

1935. Silver Jubilee. As T **13** of Antigua.

187		½d. black and green	20	60
188		3d. brown and blue	2·25	4·00
189		5d. blue and green	1·75	4·25
190		1s. grey and purple	1·75	3·25

1937. Coronation. As T **2** of Aden.

191		½d. green	10	10
192		2d. grey	50	40
193		3d. blue	60	40

46 Raking Salt

47 Salt Industry

1938.

194	46	¼d. black	10	10
195a		½d. green	70	70
196		1d. brown	60	10
197		1½d. red	60	15
198		2d. grey	60	30
199a		2½d. orange	2·00	1·50
200		3d. blue	50	30
201		6d. mauve	8·50	1·25
201a		6d. brown	20	20
202		1s. brown	3·25	7·50
202a		1s. olive	20	20
203a	47	2s. red	17·00	15·00
204a		5s. green	35·00	19·00
205		10s. violet	12·00	5·50

1946. Victory. As T **9** of Aden.

206		2d. grey	10	10
207		3d. blue	15	10

1948. Silver Wedding. As T **10/11** of Aden.

208		1d. brown	15	10
209		10s. violet	6·50	10·00

50 Badge of the Islands

51 Blue Ensign bearing Dependency Badge

1948. Centenary of Dependency's Separation from the Bahamas.

210	50	½d. green	55	15
211		2d. red	1·00	15
212	51	3d. blue	1·25	15
213	–	6d. violet	50	30
214	–	2s. black and blue	65	55
215	–	5s. black and green	90	2·00
216	–	10s. black and brown	90	3·25

DESIGNS—HORIZ: 6d. Map of Turks and Caicos Is; 2, 5, 10s. Queen Victoria and King George VI.

1949. 75th Anniv of U.P.U. As T **20/23** of Antigua.

217		2½d. orange	40	55
218		3d. blue	1·40	50
219		6d. brown	50	50
220		1s. olive	50	35

65 Bulk Salt Loading

66 Dependency's Badge

1950.

221	65	½d. green	40	40
222	–	1d. brown	40	75
223	–	1½d. red	75	55
224	–	2d. orange	30	40
225	–	2½d. olive	60	50
226	–	3d. blue	30	40
227	–	4d. black and pink	2·50	70
228	–	6d. black and blue	2·00	50
229	–	1s. black and turquoise	80	40
230	–	1s. 6d. black and red	6·00	3·25
231	–	2s. green and blue	2·50	3·50
232	–	5s. blue and black	15·00	6·50
233	66	10s. black and violet	15·00	16·00

DESIGNS—As Type **65**: 1d. Salt Cay; 1½d. Caicos mail; 2d. Grand Turk; 2½d. Diving for sponges; 3d. South Creek; 4d. Map; 6d. Grand Turk Light; 1s. Government House; 1s. 6d. Cockburn Harbour; 2s. Govt Offices; 5s. Loading salt.

1953. Coronation. As T **13** of Aden.

234		2d. black and orange	30	80

1955. As 1950 but with portrait of Queen Elizabeth II.

235		5d. black and green	30	30
236		8d. black and brown	2·25	30

DESIGNS—HORIZ—As Type **65**: 5d. M.V. "Kirksons"; 8d. Greater flamingoes in flight.

69 Queen Elizabeth II (after Annigoni)

70 Bonefish

1957.

237	69	1d. blue and red	15	20
238	70	1½d. grey and orange	15	30
239	–	2d. brown and olive	15	15
240	–	2½d. red and green	15	15
241	–	3d. turquoise and purple	15	15
242	–	4d. lake and black	20	15
243	–	5d. green and brown	40	40
244	–	6d. red and blue	2·00	55
245	–	8d. red and black	3·00	20
246	–	1s. blue and black	40	10
247	–	1s. 6d. sepia and blue	7·00	70
248	–	2s. blue and brown	8·50	2·50
249	–	5s. black and red	1·25	2·00
250	–	10s. black and purple	12·00	8·00

DESIGNS—As Type **70**: 2d. Red grouper; 2½d. Spiny lobster; 3d. Albacore; 4d. Mutton snapper; 5d. Permit; 6d. Queen or pink conch; 8d. Greater flamingoes; 1s. Spanish mackerel; 1s. 6d. Salt Cay; 2s. "Uakon" (Caicos sloop); 5s. Cable Office. As Type **84**: 10s. Dependency's badge.

83 Map of the Turks and Caicos Is

1959. New Constitution.

251	83	6d. olive and orange	45	40
252		8d. violet and orange	45	40

84 Brown Pelican

1960.

253	84	£1 brown and red	40·00	16·00

1963. Freedom from Hunger. As T **28** of Aden.

254		8d. red	30	15

1963. Cent of Red Cross. As T **33** of Antigua.

255		2d. red and black	15	30
256		8d. red and blue	30	30

1964. 400th Birth Anniv of Shakespeare. As T **34** of Antigua.

257		8d. green	20	10

1965. Cent of I.T.U. As T **36** of Antigua.

258		1d. red and brown	10	10
259		2s. green and blue	20	20

1965. I.C.Y. As T **37** of Antigua.

260		1d. purple and turquoise	10	15
261		8d. green and blue	20	15

1966. Churchill Commem. As T **38** of Antigua.

262		1d. blue	10	10
263		2d. green	20	10
264		8d. brown	25	10
265		1s. 6d. violet	30	55

1966. Royal Visit. As T **39** of Antigua.

266		8d. black and blue	25	10
267		1s. 6d. black and mauve	45	20

86 Andrew Symmer and Royal Warrant

1966. Bicent of "Ties with Britain".

268	–	1d. blue and orange	10	10
269	86	8d. red, blue and yellow	20	15
270	–	1s. 6d. multicoloured	25	20

DESIGNS: 1d. Andrew Symmer going ashore; 1s. 6d. Arms and Royal Cypher.

1966. 20th Anniv of U.N.E.S.C.O. As T **54/6** of Antigua.

271		1d. multicoloured	10	10
272		8d. yellow, violet and olive	15	10
273		1s. 6d. black, purple & orange	20	40

88 Turk's-head Cactus

1967.

274	88	1d. yellow, red and violet	10	10
275	–	1½d. brown and yellow	30	10
276	–	2d. grey and yellow	20	10
277	–	3d. agate and green	20	10
278	–	4d. mauve, black & turq	1·25	10
279	–	6d. brown and blue	40	10
280	–	8d. yellow, turquoise & blue	20	10
281	–	1s. purple and turquoise	20	10
282	–	1s. 6d. yellow, brown & blue	50	20
283	–	2s. multicoloured	60	1·50
284	–	3s. mauve and blue	55	40
285	–	5s. ochre, blue and light blue	1·25	2·50
286	–	10s. multicoloured	1·75	3·00
287	–	£1 blue, silver and red	3·50	6·00

DESIGNS—HORIZ: 1½d. Boat-building; 4d. Conch industry; 1s. Fishing; 2s. Crawfish industry; 3s. Maps of Turks and Caicos Islands and West Indies; 5s. Fishing industry; 10s. Arms of Turks and Caicos Islands. VERT: 2d. Donkey; 3d. Sisal industry; 6d. Salt industry; 8d. Skin-diving; 1s. 6d. Water-skiing; £1 Queen Elizabeth II..

102 Turks Islands 1d. Stamp of 1867

1967. Stamp Centenary.

288	102	1d. black and mauve	15	10
289	–	6d. black and grey	25	15
290	–	1s. black and blue	25	15

DESIGNS: 6d. Queen Elizabeth "stamp" and Turks Islands 6d. stamp of 1867; 1s. Turks Islands 1s. of 1867.

104 Human Rights Emblem and Charter

1968. Human Rights Year.

291	104	1d. multicoloured	10	10
292		8d. multicoloured	15	15
293		1s. 6d. multicoloured	15	15

105 Dr. Martin Luther King and "Freedom March"

1968. Martin Luther King. Commem.

294	105	2d. brown and blue	10	10
295		8d. brown and lake	15	15
296		1s. 6d. brown and violet	15	15

1969. Decimal Currency. Nos. 274/87 surch. and new value in old design (¼ c.).

297		¼ c. mult (as No. 286)	10	10
298		1 c. on 1d. yellow, red & vio	10	10
299		2 c. on 2d. grey and yellow	10	10
300		3 c. on 3d. agate and green	10	10
301		4 c. on 4d. mauve, blk & turq	90	10
302		5 c. on 6d. brown and blue	10	10
303		7 c. on 8d. yellow, turq & bl	10	10
304		8 c. on 1½d. brown and yellow	10	10
305		10 c. on 1s. purple & turquoise	20	10
306		15 c. on 1s. 6d. yell, brn & blue	25	10
307		20 c. on 2s. multicoloured	30	25
308		30 c. on 3s. mauve and blue	55	35
309		50 c. on 5s. ochre, blue and light blue	1·25	45
310		$1 on 10s. multicoloured	2·50	1·00
311a		$2 on £1 blue, silver and red	2·00	3·00

MINIMUM PRICE

The minimum price quoted is 10p which represents a handling charge rather than a basis for valuing common stamps. For further notes about prices see introductory pages.

107 "The Nativity with John the Baptist"

109 Coat of Arms

1969. Christmas. Scenes from 16th-century "Book of Hours". Multicoloured.

312		1 c. Type **107**	10	10
313		3 c. "The Flight into Egypt"	10	10
314		15 c. Type **107**	15	10
315		30 c. As 3 c.	25	20

1970. New Constitution.

316	109	7 c. multicoloured	20	15
317		35 c. multicoloured	35	25

For similar $10 design but without commemorative inscription, see No. 946.

110 "Christ bearing the Cross"

1970. Easter. Details from the "Small Engraved Passion" by Durer.

318	110	5 c. grey and blue	10	10
319	–	7 c. grey and red	10	10
320	–	50 c. grey and brown	50	75

DESIGNS: 7 c. "Christ on the Cross" ; 50 c. "The Lamentation of Christ".

113 Dickens and Scene from "Oliver Twist"

1970. Death Cent of Charles Dickens.

321	113	1 c. black & blue on yellow	10	20
322	–	3 c. black & blue on flesh	10	20
323	–	15 c. black & blue on flesh	20	20
324	–	30 c. black & drab on blue	40	40

DESIGNS (showing Dickens and scene): 3 c. "A Christmas Carol"; 15 c. "Pickwick Papers"; 30 c. "The Old Curiosity Shop".

114 Ambulance—1870

1970. Cent of British Red Cross. Mult.

325		1 c. Type **114**	10	10
326		5 c. Ambulance—1970	20	10
327		15 c. Type **114**	40	15
328		30 c. As 5 c.	50	20

115 Duke of Albemarle and Coat-of-Arms

1970. Tercentenary of Issue of Letters Patent. Multicoloured.

329	1 c. Type **115**	10	15
330	8 c. Arms of Charles II and Elizabeth II	20	30
331	10 c. Type **115**	20	15
332	35 c. As 8 c.	40	75

116 Boat-building

1971. Designs as Nos. 274/87 but values in decimal currency as T **116**.

333	**88**	1 c. yellow, red and violet	10	10
334	–	2 c. grey and yellow (as No. 276)	10	10
335	–	3 c. agate and green (as No. 277)	15	10
336	–	4 c. mauve, black and turquoise (as No. 278)	1·25	10
337	–	5 c. brown and blue (as No. 279)	40	10
338	–	7 c. yellow, turquoise and blue (as No. 280)	30	10
339	**116**	8 c. brown and yellow	1·25	10
340	–	10 c. purple and turquoise (as No. 281)	75	10
341	–	15 c. yellow, brown and blue (as No. 282)	1·00	65
342	–	20 c. mult (as No. 283)	1·50	2·25
343	–	30 c. purple and blue (as No. 284)	2·00	1·00
344	–	50 c. ochre, blue and light blue (as No. 285)	3·00	2·00
345	–	$1 mult (as No. 286)	3·00	3·00
346	–	$2 blue, silver and red (as No. 287)	4·00	7·50

117 Lined Seahorse

119 The Wilton Diptych (Left Wing)

118 Pirate Sloop

1971. Tourist Development. Multicoloured.

347	1 c. Type **117**	10	10
348	3 c. Queen or pink conch shell	15	10
349	15 c. Oystercatcher (horiz)	80	20
350	30 c. Sailfish ("Blue marlin") (horiz)	65	25

1971. Pirates. Multicoloured.

351	2 c. Type **118**	10	10
352	3 c. Pirate treasure	10	10
353	15 c. Marooned sailor	45	15
354	30 c. Buccaneers	70	45

1971. Christmas. Multicoloured.

355	2 c. Type **119**	10	10
356	2 c. The Wilton Diptych (Right Wing)	10	10
357	8 c. Type **119**	10	10
358	8 c. As No. 356	10	10
359	15 c. Type **119**	20	10
360	15 c. As No. 356	20	10

120 Cape Kennedy Launching Area

1972. 10th Anniv of Colonel Glenn's Splashdown. Multicoloured.

361	5 c. Type **120**	10	10
362	10 c. "Friendship 7" space capsule	10	10
363	15 c. Map of Islands and splashdown	15	10
364	20 c. N.A.S.A. space medal (vert)	15	10

121 "Christ before Pilate" (Rembrandt)

122 Christopher Columbus

1972. Easter.

365	**121**	2 c. black and lilac	10	10
366	–	15 c. black and pink	20	10
367	–	30 c. black and yellow	30	15

DESIGNS—HORIZ: 15 c. "The Three Crosses" (Rembrandt). VERT: 30 c. "The Descent from the Cross" (Rembrandt).

1972. Discoverers and Explorers. Mult.

368	¼ c. Type **122**	15	10
369	8 c. Sir Richard Grenville (horiz)	70	10
370	10 c. Capt. John Smith	80	10
371	30 c. Juan Ponce de Leon (horiz)	1·50	90

1972. Royal Silver Wedding. As T **52** of Ascension but with Turk's-head cactus and spiny lobster in background.

372	10 c. blue	15	10
373	20 c. green	15	10

124 Treasure Hunting, c. 1700

126 Sooty Tern

125 Arms of Jamaica and Turks and Caicos Islands

1973. Treasure.

374	**124**	3 c. multicoloured	10	10
375	–	5 c. purple, silver & black	10	10
376	–	10 c. purple, silver & black	20	10
377	–	30 c. multicoloured	60	30

DESIGNS: 5 c. Silver Bank medallion (obverse); 10 c. Silver Bank medallion (reverse); 30 c. Treasure hunting, 1973.

1973. Centenary of Annexation by Jamaica.

379	**125**	15 c. multicoloured	25	10
380		35 c. multicoloured	45	20

1973.

381	¼ c. Type **126**	10	40
382	1 c. Magnificent frigate bird	30	60
383	2 c. Common noddy	30	60
384	3 c. Blue-grey gnatcatcher	85	50
385	4 c. Little blue heron	35	1·25
386	5 c. Catbird	30	30
387	7 c. Black-whiskered vireo	4·50	30
388	8 c. Osprey	5·00	2·50
389	10 c. Greater flamingo	70	90
390	15 c. Brown pelican	1·25	50
459	20 c. Parula warbler	1·50	75
392	30 c. Northern mockingbird	1·75	90
461	50 c. Ruby-throated hummingbird	1·50	2·25
462	$1 Bananaquit	2·25	2·75
463	$2 Cedar waxwing	5·00	4·50
464	$5 Painted bunting	2·25	2·75

127 Bermuda Sloop

1973. Vessels. Multicoloured.

396	2 c. Type **127**	20	40
397	5 c. H.M.S. "Blanche" (screw sloop)	35	10
398	8 c. "Grand Turk" (American privateer) and "Hinchinbrook II" (British packet), 1813	40	50
399	10 c. H.M.S. "Endymion" (frigate), 1790	40	15
400	15 c. "Medina" (paddle-steamer)	45	70
401	20 c. H.M.S. "Daring" (brig), 1804	50	1·25

1973. Royal Wedding. As T **47** of Anguilla.

403	12 c. blue	10	10
404	18 c. blue	10	10

128 Duho (stool)

1974. Lucayan Remains. Multicoloured.

405	6 c. Type **128**	10	10
406	10 c. Broken wood bowl	15	10
407	12 c. Greenstone axe	15	10
408	18 c. Wood bowl	15	10
409	35 c. Fragment of duho	20	20

129 G.P.O., Grand Turk

1974. Centenary of U.P.U. Multicoloured.

426	4 c. Type **129**	10	10
427	12 c. Sloop and island map	20	10
428	18 c. "U.P.U." and globe	20	10
429	55 c. Posthorn and emblem	35	35

130 Churchill and Roosevelt

1974. Birth Cent of Sir Winston Churchill. Mult.

430	12 c. Type **130**	15	15
431	18 c. Churchill and vapour-trails	15	15

131 Spanish Captain circa 1492

132 Ancient Windmill Salt Cay

1975. Military Uniforms. Multicoloured.

433	5 c. Type **131**	10	10
434	20 c. Officer, Royal Artillery, 1783	30	15
435	25 c. Officer, 67th Foot, 1798	35	15
436	35 c. Private, 1st West India Regiment, 1833	45	25

1975. Salt-raking Industry. Multicoloured.

438	6 c. Type **132**	15	10
439	10 c. Salt pans drying in sun (horiz)	15	10
440	20 c. Salt-raking (horiz)	25	25
441	25 c. Unprocessed salt heaps	30	30

133 Star Coral

1975. Island Coral. Multicoloured.

442	6 c. Type **133**	15	10
443	10 c. Elkhorn coral	20	10
444	20 c. Brain coral	35	15
445	25 c. Staghorn coral	40	20

134 American Schooner

136 "The Virgin and Child with Flowers" (C. Dolci)

135 1s. 6d. Royal Visit Stamp of 1966

1976. Bicent of American Revolution. Mult.

446	6 c. Type **134**	25	15
447	20 c. British ship of the line	30	20
448	25 c. American privateer "Grand Turk"	30	25
449	55 c. British ketch	40	65

1976. 10th Anniv of Royal Visit. Mult.

466	20 c. Type **135**	30	30
467	25 c. 8d. Royal Visit stamp	40	30

1976. Christmas. Multicoloured.

468	6 c. Type **136**	10	10
469	10 c. "Virgin and Child" with St. John and an Angel" (Studio of Botticelli)	10	10
470	20 c. "Adoration of the Magi" (Master of Paraiso)	30	15
471	25 c. "Adoration of the Magi" (French miniature)	30	20

137 Balcony Scene, Buckingham Palace

139 "Flight of the Holy Family" (Rubens)

138 Col. Glenn's "Mercury" Capsule

1977. Silver Jubilee. Multicoloured.

472	6 c. Queen presenting O.B.E. to E. T. Wood	10	10
473	25 c. Queen with regalia	15	20
474	55 c. Type **137**	30	45

1977. 25th Anniv of U.S. Tracking Station. Multicoloured.

476	1 c. Type **138**	10	10
477	3 c. Moon buggy "Rover" (vert)	10	10
478	6 c. Tracking Station, Grand Turk	10	10
479	20 c. Moon landing craft (vert)	15	15
480	25 c. Col. Glenn's rocket launch (vert)	20	20
481	50 c. "Telstar 1" satellite	30	40

1977. Christmas. 400th Birth Anniv of Rubens. Multicoloured.

482	¼ c. Type **139**	10	10
483	½ c. "Adoration of the Magi" (1634)	10	10
484	1 c. "Adoration of the Magi" (1624)	10	10
485	6 c. "Virgin within Garland"	10	10
486	20 c. "Madonna and Child Adored by Angels"	15	10
487	$2 "Adoration of the Magi" (1618)	1·25	1·25

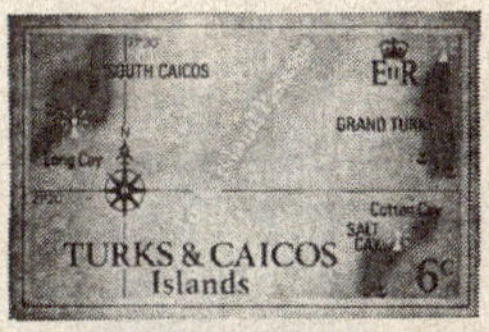

140 Map of Passage

1978. Turks Islands Passage. Multicoloured.

489A	6 c. Type **140**	15	15
490A	20 c. Caicos sloop passing Grand Turk Lighthouse	45	65
491A	25 c. Motor cruiser	45	75
492A	55 c. "Jamaica Planter" (freighter)	95	2·00

141 "Queen Victoria" (Sir George Hayter)

142 Ampulla and Anointing Spoon

1978. 25th Anniv of Coronation. Multicoloured.

(a) Monarchs in Coronation robes.

494 6 c. Type **141** 10 10
495 10 c. "King Edward VII" (Sir Samuel Fildes) 10 10
496 25 c. King George V 20 10
497 $2 King George VI 50 70

(b) Coronation regalia. Self-adhesive.

499 15 c. Type **142** 15 30
500 25 c. St. Edward's Crown . . . 15 30
501 $2 Queen Elizabeth II in Coronation robes . . . . . . 1·00 2·25

143 Wilbur Wright and Wright Type A

1978. 75th Anniv of Powered Flight. Mult.

502 1 c. Type **143** 10 10
503 6 c. Wright brothers and Cessna 337 Super Skymaster . . . 10 10
504 10 c. Orville Wright and Lockheed L.188 Electra . . 10 10
505 15 c. Wilbur Wright and Douglas C-47 Skytrain 15 15
506 35 c. Wilbur Wright and Britten Norman Islander 35 35
507 $2 Wilbur Wright and Wright Type A . . . . 1·00 1·75

No. 502 is inscr "FLYER III" in error.

144 Hurdling

1978. 11th Commonwealth Games, Edmonton. Multicoloured.

509 6 c. Type **144** 10 10
510 20 c. Weightlifting 15 15
511 55 c. Boxing 20 30
512 $2 Cycling . . . . 50 1·25

145 Indigo Hamlet

1978. Fishes. Multicoloured.

514A 1 c. Type **145** 15 50
515A 2 c. Tobacco fish 75 50
516A 3 c. Bar jack 30 30
517A 4 c. Porkfish 75 50
518A 5 c. Spanish grunt 30 40
519A 7 c. Yellow-tailed snapper . 1·00 80
520A 8 c. Four-eyed butterflyfish . 1·00 15
521A 10 c. Yellow-finned grouper . 30 15
522A 15 c. Beau Gregory 75 30
523A 20 c. Queen angelfish 30 30
524A 30 c. Hogfish . . . . 1·75 40
525A 50 c. Royal gramma ("Fairy basslet") . . . . 1·00 65
526A $1 Fin-spot wrasse . . . . . 1·75 1·60
527A $2 Stoplight parrotfish . . . 3·25 2·50
528A $5 Queen triggerfish . . . . 3·25 6·50

Some values exist both with or without imprint date at foot.

146 "Madonna of the Siskin"

1978. Christmas. Paintings by Durer. Mult.

529 6 c. Type **146** 15 10
530 20 c. "The Virgin and Child with St. Anne" 20 15
531 35 c. "Paumgartner Nativity" (horiz) 35 15
532 $2 "Praying Hands" . . . . 85 1·25

147 Osprey

1979. Endangered Wildlife. Multicoloured.

534 6 c. Type **147** 75 20
535 20 c. Green turtle 65 20
536 25 c. Queen or pink conch . . 75 25
537 55 c. Rough-toothed dolphin 90 50
538 $1 Humpback whale . . . . 2·00 2·00

148 "The Beloved" (painting by D. G. Rossetti)

1979. International Year of the Child. Multicoloured.

540 6 c. Type **148** 10 10
541 25 c. "Tahitian Girl" (P. Gauguin) 15 10
542 55 c. "Calmady Children" (Sir Thomas Lawrence) 25 20
543 $1 "Mother and Daughter" (detail, P. Gauguin) 45 45

149 "Medina" (paddle-steamer) and Handstamped Cover

150 Cuneiform Script

1979. Death Centenary of Sir Rowland Hill. (a) As T **149**. Multicoloured.

545 6 c. Type **149** 10 10
546 20 c. Sir Rowland Hill and map of Caribbean 15 15
547 45 c. "Orinoco I" (mail paddle-steamer) and cover bearing Penny Black stamp 20 20
548 75 c. "Shannon" (screw steamer) and letter to Grand Turk . 30 30
549 $1 "Trent I" (paddle-steamer) and map of Caribbean . . 35 35
550 $2 Turks Islands 1867 and Turks and Caicos Islands 1900 1d. stamps . . . . 2·50 2·25

(b) As T **150**. Self-adhesive.

552 **150** 5 c. black and green . . . 10 10
553 – 5 c. black and green . . . 10 10
554 – 5 c. black and green . . . 10 10
555 – 15 c. black and blue . . . 20 20
556 – 15 c. black and blue . . . 20 20
557 – 15 c. black and blue . . . 20 20
558 – 25 c. black and blue . . . 30 30
559 – 25 c. black and blue . . . 60 45
560 – 25 c. black and blue . . . 30 30
561 – 40 c. black and red . . . 45 45
562 – 40 c. black and red . . . 45 45
563 – 40 c. black and red . . . 45 45
564 – $1 black and yellow . . . 70 1·25

DESIGNS—HORIZ: No. 533, Egyptian papyrus; No. 554, Chinese paper; No. 555, Greek runner; No. 556, Roman post horse; No. 557, Roman post ship; No. 558, Pigeon post; No. 559, Railway post; No. 560, Packet paddle-steamer; No. 561, Balloon post; No. 562, First airmail; No. 563, Supersonic airmail. VERT: No. 564, Original stamp press.

152 "St. Nicholas", Prikra, Ukraine

153 Pluto and Starfish

1979. Christmas. Religious Art. Multicoloured.

566 1 c. Type **152** 10 10
567 3 c. "Emperor Otto II with Symbols of Empire" (Master of the Registrum Gregorii) . 10 10
568 6 c. "Portrait of St. John" (Book of Lindisfarne) 10 10
569 15 c. "Adoration of the Majestas Domini" (prayer book of Otto II) 10 10
570 20 c. "Christ attended by Angels" (Book of Kells) . . 15 15
571 25 c. "St. John the Evangelist" (Gospels of St. Medard of Soissons), Charlemagne . . 20 15
572 65 c. "Christ Pantocrator", Trocany, Ukraine 30 25
573 $1 "Portrait of St. John" (Canterbury Codex Aureus) . 45 45

1979. International Year of the Child. Walt Disney cartoon characters. At the Seaside. Multicoloured.

575 ¼ c. Type **153** 10 10
576 ½ c. Minnie Mouse in summer outfit 10 10
577 1 c. Mickey Mouse underwater 10 10
578 2 c. Goofy and turtle 10 10
579 3 c. Donald Duck and dolphin 10 10
580 4 c. Mickey Mouse fishing . . 10 10
581 5 c. Goofy surfing 10 10
582 25 c. Pluto and crab 45 20
583 $1 Daisy water-skiing . . . . 1·50 2·25

154 "Christina's World" (painting by Andrew Wyeth)

1979. Works of Art. Multicoloured.

585 6 c. Type **154** 10 10
586 10 c. Ivory leopards, Benin (19th-cent) 10 10
587 20 c. "The Kiss" (painting by Gustav Klimt) (vert) 15 15
588 25 c. "Portrait of a Lady" (painting by R. van der Weyden) (vert) 15 15
589 80 c. Bull's head harp Sumer c. 2600 B.C. (vert) 30 30
590 $1 "The Wave" (painting by Hokusai) 45 45

155 Pied-billed Grebe

1980. Birds. Multicoloured.

592 20 c. Type **155** 70 30
593 25 c. Ovenbirds at nest 75 30
594 35 c. Hen harrier . . . . . . 1·00 45
595 55 c. Yellow-bellied sapsucker . 1·25 50
596 $1 Blue-winged teal . . . . . 1·50 1·75

156 Stamp, Magnifying Glass and Perforation Gauge

1980. "London 1980" Int Stamp Exhibition. Mult.

598 **156** 25 c. black and yellow . . 15 15
599 – 40 c. black and green . . 15 25

DESIGN: 40 c. Tweezers, stamp and perforation gauge.

157 Atlantic Trumpet Triton

1980. Shells. Multicoloured.

601 14 c. Type **157** 20 20
602 20 c. Measled cowrie 25 25
603 30 c. True tulip 35 35
604 45 c. Lion's-paw scallop . . . 45 45
605 55 c. Sunrise tellin 55 55
606 70 c. Crown cone 70 70

158 Queen Elizabeth the Queen Mother

1980. 80th Birthday of The Queen Mother.

607 **158** 80 c. multicoloured . . . 50 1·25

159 Doctor examining Child and Lions International Emblem

1980. "Serving the Community". Mult.

609 10 c. Type **159** 15 10
610 15 c. Students receiving scholarships and Kiwanis International emblem . . . 20 10
611 45 c. Teacher with students and Soroptimist emblem 40 35
612 $1 Lobster trawler and Rotary International emblem . . . 75 80

1980. Christmas. Scenes from Walt Disney's "Pinocchio". As T **153**. Multicoloured.

614 ¼ c. Scene from "Pinocchio" . 10 10
615 ½ c. As puppet 10 10
616 1 c. Pinocchio changed into a boy 10 10
617 2 c. Captured by fox 10 10
618 3 c. Pinocchio and puppeteer . 10 10
619 4 c. Pinocchio and bird's nest nose 10 10
620 5 c. Pinocchio eating 10 10
621 75 c. Pinocchio with ass ears . 1·00 90
622 $1 Pinocchio underwater . . . 1·25 1·00

160 Martin Luther King Jr

1980. Human Rights. Personalities. Mult.

624 20 c. Type **160** 15 10
625 30 c. John F. Kennedy . . . 30 25
626 45 c. Roberto Clemente (baseball player) 45 35
627 70 c. Sir Frank Worrel (cricketer) 90 90
628 $1 Harriet Tubman . . . . . 1·10 1·25

161 Yachts

1980. South Caicos Regatta. Multicoloured.

630 6 c. Type **161** 10 10
631 15 c. Trophy and yachts . . . 15 15
632 35 c. Spectators watching speedboat race 25 20
633 $1 Caicos sloops 60 60

162 Night Queen Cactus

163 "Woman with Fan"

1981. Flowering Cacti. Multicoloured.

635	25 c. Type **162**	25	25
636	35 c. Ripsaw cactus	35	35
637	55 c. Royal strawberry cactus	40	60
638	80 c. Caicos cactus	60	1·00

1981. 50th Anniv of Walt Disney's Pluto (cartoon character). As T **153**. Multicoloured.

640	10 c. Pluto listening to queen or pink conch shell	10	10
641	75 c. Pluto on raft and porpoise	75	90

1981. Easter. Walt Disney Cartoon Characters. As T **153**. Multicoloured.

643	10 c. Donald Duck and Louie	20	20
644	25 c. Goofy and Donald Duck	40	40
645	60 c. Chip and Dale	70	1·00
646	80 c. Scrooge McDuck and Huey	90	1·40

1981. Birth Centenary of Picasso. Mult.

648	20 c. Type **163**	20	15
649	45 c. "Woman with Pears"	25	30
650	80 c. "The Accordionist"	45	50
651	$1 "The Aficionado"	60	80

164 Kensington Palace

165 Lady Diana Spencer

1981. Royal Wedding. Multicoloured.

653	35 c. Prince Charles and Lady Diana Spencer	15	10
654	65 c. Type **164**	20	20
655	90 c. Prince Charles as Colonel of the Welsh Guards	25	30

1981. Royal Wedding. Multicoloured. Self-adhesive.

657	20 c. Type **165**	25	30
658	$1 Prince Charles	35	70
659	$2 Prince Charles and Lady Diana Spencer	1·10	2·25

166 Marine Biology Observation

1981. Diving. Multicoloured.

660	15 c. Type **166**	20	15
661	40 c. Underwater photography	50	35
662	75 c. Wreck diving	90	70
663	$1 Diving with dolphins	1·25	1·00

1981. Christmas. As T **153** showing scenes from Walt Disney's cartoon film "Uncle Remus".

665	¼ c. multicoloured	10	10
666	½ c. multicoloured	10	10
667	1 c. multicoloured	10	10
668	2 c. multicoloured	10	10
669	3 c. multicoloured	10	10
670	4 c. multicoloured	10	10
671	5 c. multicoloured	10	10
672	75 c. multicoloured	1·00	80
673	$1 multicoloured	1·25	1·00

167 Map of Grand Turk, and Lighthouse

1981. Tourism. Multicoloured.

675	20 c. Type **167**	40	45
676	20 c. Map of Salt Cay, and "industrial archaeology"	40	45
677	20 c. Map of South Caicos, and "island flying"	40	45
678	20 c. Map of East Caicos, and "beach combing"	40	45
679	20 c. Map of Central Grand Caicos, and cave exploring	40	45
680	20 c. Map of North Caicos and camping and hiking	40	45
681	20 c. Map of North Caicos, Parrot Cay, Dellis Cay, Fort George Cay, Pine Cay and Water Cay, and "environmental studies"	40	45
682	20 c. Map of Providenciales, and scuba diving	40	45
683	20 c. Map of West Caicos, and "cruising and bird sanctuary"	40	45
684	20 c. Turks and Caicos Islands flag	40	45

168 "Junonia evarete"

169 Flag Salute on Queen's Birthday

1982. Butterflies. Multicoloured.

685	20 c. Type **168**	30	30
686	35 c. "Strymon maesites"	50	55
687	65 c. "Agraulis vanillae"	90	1·25
688	$1 "Eurema dina"	1·40	2·00

1982. 75th Anniv of Boy Scout Movement. Multicoloured.

690	40 c. Type **169**	50	50
691	50 c. Raft building	60	60
692	75 c. Sea scout cricket match	1·10	1·60
693	$1 Nature study	1·50	1·75

170 Footballer

171 Washington crossing the Delaware and Phillis Wheatley (poetess)

1982. World Cup Football Championship, Spain.

695	**170**	10 c. multicoloured	15	15
696	–	25 c. multicoloured	20	20
697	–	45 c. multicoloured	25	25
698	–	$1 multicoloured	80	80

DESIGNS: 25 c. to $1, Various footballers.

1982. 250th Birth Anniv of George Washington and Birth Centenary of Franklin D. Roosevelt.

700	20 c. Type **171**	30	30
701	35 c. George Washington and Benjamin Banneker (surveyor)	45	45
702	65 c. Franklin D. Roosevelt meeting George Washington Carver (agricultural researcher)	65	80
703	80 c. Roosevelt as stamp collector	80	1·00

172 "Second Thoughts"

173 Princess of Wales

1982. Norman Rockwell (painter) Commemoration. Multicoloured.

705	8 c. Type **172**	15	10
706	15 c. "The Proper Gratuity"	20	20
707	20 c. "Doctor's Office" (inscr "Before the Shot")	25	30
708	25 c. "Bottom of the Sixth" (inscr "The Three Umpires")	25	30

1982. 21st Birthday of Princess of Wales. Multicoloured.

713	8 c. Sandringham	15	35
714	35 c. Prince and Princess of Wales	55	1·00
709	55 c. As 8 c.	35	45
710	70 c. As 35 c.	60	55
711	$1 Type **173**	90	80
715	$1.10 Type **173**	80	2·00

174 Cessna 337 Super Skymaster over Caicos Cays

1982. Aircraft. Multicoloured.

716	8 c. Type **174**	15	15
717	15 c. Lockheed JetStar II over Grand Turk	20	25
718	65 c. Sikorsky S.58 helicopter over South Caicos	65	80
719	$1.10 Cessna 182 Skylan over Providenciales	1·10	1·25

1982. Christmas. Scenes from Walt Disney's Cartoon film "Mickey's Christmas Carol". As T **153**. Multicoloured.

721	1 c. Donald Duck, Mickey Mouse and Scrooge	10	10
722	1 c. Goofy (Marley's ghost) and Scrooge	10	10
723	2 c. Jiminy Cricket and Scrooge	10	10
724	2 c. Huey, Dewey and Louie	10	10
725	3 c. Daisy Duck and youthful Scrooge	10	10
726	3 c. Giant and Scrooge	10	10
727	4 c. Two bad wolves, a wise pig and a reformed Scrooge	10	10
728	65 c. Donald Duck and Scrooge	1·00	75
729	$1.10 Mortie and Scrooge	1·60	1·25

175 West Caicos Mule-drawn Wagon

1983. Trams and Locomotives. Mult.

731	15 c. Type **175**	20	25
732	55 c. West Caicos steam locomotive	65	70
733	90 c. East Caicos mule-drawn sisal train	90	1·00
734	$1.60 East Caicos steam locomotive	1·75	1·90

176 Policewoman on Traffic Duty

1983. Commonwealth Day. Multicoloured.

736	1 c. Type **176**	15	20
737	8 c. Stylized sun and weather vane	15	20
738	65 c. Yacht	85	90
739	$1 Cricket	1·50	1·60

177 "St. John and the Virgin Mary" (detail)

179 First Hydrogen Balloon "The Globe", 1783

178 Minke Whale

1983. Easter. Designs showing details from the "Mond Crucifixion" by Raphael. Multicoloured.

740	35 c. Type **177**	25	25
741	50 c. "Two Women"	35	35
742	95 c. "Angel with two jars"	55	60
743	$1.10 "Angel with one jar"	75	80

1983. Whales. Multicoloured.

745	50 c. Type **178**	2·00	2·00
746	65 c. Black right whale	2·25	2·25
747	70 c. Killer whale	2·50	2·50
748	95 c. Sperm whale	2·75	2·75
749	$1.10 Cuvier's beaked whale	3·00	3·00
750	$2 Blue whale	5·00	5·00
751	$2.20 Humpback whale	5·50	5·50
752	$3 Long-finned pilot whale	6·25	6·25

1983. Bicentenary of Manned Flight. Mult.

754	25 c. Type **179**	25	25
755	35 c. "Friendship 7"	35	35
756	70 c. First hot air balloon "Le Martial", 1783	70	70
757	95 c. Space shuttle "Columbia"	90	90

180 Fiddler Pig

1983. Christmas. Walt Disney Cartoon Characters. Multicoloured.

759	1 c. Type **180**	10	10
760	1 c. Fifer Pig	10	10
761	2 c. Practical Pig	10	10
762	2 c. Pluto	10	10
763	3 c. Goofy	10	10
764	3 c. Mickey Mouse	10	10
765	35 c. Gyro Gearloose	35	35
766	50 c. Ludwig von Drake	50	60
767	$1.10 Huey, Dewey and Louie	1·00	1·25

181 Bermudan Sloop

1983. Ships. Multicoloured.

769	4 c. Arawak dug-out canoe	40	1·25
770a	5 c. "Santa Maria"	70	1·00
771	8 c. British and Spanish ships in battle	2·00	1·25
772	10 c. Type **181**	2·00	90
773a	20 c. U.S. privateer "Grand Turk"	50	70
774a	25 c. H.M.S. "Boreas" (frigate)	50	70
775a	30 c. H.M.S. "Endymion" (frigate) attacking French ship, 1790s	3·00	80
776a	35 c. "Caesar" (barque)	60	70
777a	50 c. "Grapeshot" (American schooner)	60	80
778a	65 c. H.M.S. "Invincible" (battle cruiser)	2·50	2·50
779a	95 c. H.M.S. "Magicienne" (cruiser)	2·50	2·50
780	$1.10 H.M.S. "Durban" (cruiser)	5·50	3·75
781a	$2 "Sentinel" (cable ship)	2·50	3·50
782	$3 H.M.S. "Minerva" (frigate)	7·50	7·50
783	$5 Caicos sloop	7·50	11·00

182 Pres. Kennedy and Signing of Civil Rights Legislation

1983. 20th Death Anniv of J. F. Kennedy (U.S. President).

784	**182**	20 c. multicoloured	20	15
785		$1 multicoloured	1·10	1·25

183 Clarabelle Cow Diving

1984. Olympic Games, Los Angeles. Multicoloured.
A. Inscr "1984 LOS ANGELES".
B. Inscr "1984 OLYMPICS LOS ANGELES" and Olympic emblem.

		A		B	
786	1 c. Type **183**	10	10	10	10
787	1 c. Donald Duck in 500 m kayak race	10	10	10	10
788	2 c. Huey, Dewey and Louie in 1000m kayak race	10	10	10	10
789	2 c. Mickey Mouse in single kayak	10	10	10	10
790	3 c. Donald Duck highboard diving	10	10	10	10
791	3 c. Minnie Mouse in kayak slalom	10	10	10	10
792	25 c. Mickey Mouse freestyle swimming	60	45	60	45
793	75 c. Donald Duck playing water-polo	1·75	1·75	1·75	1·75
794	$1 Uncle Scrooge and Donald Duck yachting	1·90	2·00	2·00	2·00

184 "Cadillac V-16", 1933

1984. Classic Cars and 125th Anniv of first Commercial Oil Well. Multicoloured.

796	4 c. Type **184**	20	10
797	8 c. Rolls-Royce "Phanton III", 1937	30	15
798	10 c. Saab "99", 1969	30	15
799	25 c. Maserati "Bora", 1973	70	40
800	40 c. Datsun "260Z", 1970	1·00	65
801	55 c. Porsche "917", 1971	1·25	80
802	80 c. Lincoln "Continental", 1939	1·40	90
803	$1 Triumph "TR3A", 1957	1·50	1·25

185 "Rest during the Flight to Egypt, with St. Francis"

1984. Easter. 450th Death Anniv of Correggio (painter). Multicoloured.

805 15 c. Type **185** 20 15
806 40 c. "St. Luke and St. Ambrose" 45 40
807 60 c. "Diana and her Chariot" 65 65
808 95 c. "The Deposition of Christ" 80 80

1984. Universal Postal Union Congress, Hamburg. Nos. 748/9 optd **19TH UPU CONGRESS, HAMBURG, WEST GERMANY. 1874–1984** and emblem. Multicoloured.

810 95 c. Sperm whale . . . . . . 2·50 2·00
811 $1.10 Goosebeak whale . . . 2·50 2·00

187 "The Adventure of the Second Stain"

1984. 125th Birth Anniv of Sir Arthur Conan Doyle (author). Multicoloured.

813 25 c. Type **187** . . . . . . 2·25 1·50
814 45 c. "The Adventure of the Final Problem" . . . . . . 3·00 2·25
815 70 c. "The Adventure of the Empty House" . . . . . . 4·50 3·50
816 85 c. "The Adventure of the Greek Interpreter" . . . . . 5·50 4·00

188 Orange Clownfish

190 Magnolia Warbler

189 Donald Duck cutting down Christmas Tree

1984. "Ausipex" International Stamp Exhibition, Melbourne. 175th Birth Anniv of Charles Darwin. Multicoloured.

818 5 c. Type **188** 55 40
819 35 c. Monitor lizard . . . . . 2·00 1·75
820 50 c. Rainbow lory . . . . . 2·75 2·75
821 $1.10 Koalas . . . . 3·50 3·75

1984. Christmas. Walt Disney Cartoon Characters. Designs showing scenes form "Toy Tinkers". Multicoloured.

823 20 c. Type **189** 85 45
824 35 c. Donald Duck and Chip n' Dale playing with train set . 1·10 75
825 50 c. Donald Duck and Chip n' Dale playing with catapult . 1·60 1·10
826 75 c. Donald Duck, Chip n' Dale and Christmas tree . . . 2·25 1·75
827 $1.10 Donald Duck, toy soldier and Chip 'n' Dale . . . . 2·50 2·50

1985. Birth Bicentenary of John J. Audubon (ornithologist). Multicoloured.

829 25 c. Type **190** . . . . . . 2·00 75
830 45 c. Short-eared owl . . . . 3·00 1·50
831 70 c. Mourning dove and eggs 3·50 2·75
832 85 c. Caribbean martin . . . 3·50 3·00

191 Leonardo da Vinci and Illustration of Glider Wing (15th century)

1985. 40th Anniv of International Civil Aviation Organization. Pioneers. Multicoloured.

834 8 c. Type **191** 50 30
835 25 c. Sir Alliott Verdon Roe and Avro (Canada) CF-102 jetliner (1949) . . . . 1·50 40
836 65 c. Robert H. Goddard and first liquid fuel rocket (1926) 2·50 1·50
837 $1 Igor Sikorsky and Vought-Sikorsky VS-300 helicopter prototype (1939) . . . . . 4·00 3·00

192 Benjamin Franklin and Marquis de Lafayette

1985. Centenary of Statue of Liberty's Arrival in New York. Multicoloured.

839 20 c. Type **192** 80 50
840 30 c. Frederic Bartholdi (designer) and Gustave Eiffel (engineer) . . . . 1·10 80
841 65 c. "Isere" (French screw warship) arriving in New York with statue, 1885 . . . . . 2·50 1·75
842 $1.10 United States fund raisers Louis Agassiz, Charles Sumner, H. W. Longfellow and Joseph Pulitzer . . . . 2·50 2·00

193 Sir Edward Hawke and H.M.S. "Royal George" (ship of the line), 1782

1985. Salute to Royal Navy. Multicoloured.

844 20 c. Type **193** . . . . . . 2·25 1·75
845 30 c. Lord Nelson and H.M.S. "Victory" (ship of the line), 1805 . . . . 2·75 2·25
846 65 c. Admiral Sir George Cockburn and H.M.S. "Albion" (ship of the line), 1802 . . . . 3·75 3·00
847 95 c. Admiral Sir David Beatty and H.M.S. "Indefatigable" (battle cruiser), 1916 . . . 4·75 4·25

194 Mark Twain riding on Halley's Comet

1985. International Youth Year. Birth Annivs of Mark Twain (150th) and Jakob Grimm (Bicentenary). Multicoloured.

849 25 c. Type **194** . . . . . . 1·00 40
850 35 c. "Grand Turk" (Mississippi river steamer) . . . . . . 1·50 55
851 50 c. Hansel and Gretel and gingerbread house (vert) . . 1·75 85
852 95 c. Rumpelstiltskin (vert) . . 2·50 2·00

195 The Queen Mother outside Clarence House

196 King George II and Score of "Zadok the Priest" (1727)

1985. Life and Times of Queen Elizabeth the Queen Mother. Multicoloured.

854 30 c. Type **195** 45 45
855 50 c. Visiting Biggin Hill airfield (horiz) . . . . 1·25 75
856 $1.10 80th birthday portrait . 1·75 1·90

1985. 300th Birth Anniv of George Frederick Handel (composer). Multicoloured.

858 4 c. Type **196** 65 50
859 10 c. Queen Caroline and score of "Funeral Anthem" (1737) . 1·00 50
860 50 c. King George I and score of "Water Music" (1714) . . 2·75 2·50
861 $1.10 Queen Anne and score of "Or la Tromba" from "Rinaldo" (1711) . . . . . 4·75 5·50

1985. 300th Birth Anniv of Johann Sebastian Bach (composer). As T **206** of Antigua. Mult.

863 15 c. Bassoon . . . . 1·00 40
864 40 c. Natural horn . . . . . . 2·00 85
865 60 c. Viola d'amore . . . . . 2·50 1·25
866 95 c. Clavichord . . . . 3·00 2·25

197 Harley-Davidson Dual Cylinder (1915) on Middle Caicos

1985. Centenary of the Motor Cycle. Mult.

868 8 c. Type **197** 75 30
869 25 c. Triumph "Thunderbird" (1950) on Grand Turk . . . 1·50 70
870 55 c. BMW "K.100RS" (1985) on North Caicos . . . . . . 2·50 1·75
871 $1.20 Honda "1100 Shadow" (1985) on South Caicos . . . 3·50 6·00

198 Pirates in Prison

1985. 30th Anniv of Disneyland, U.S.A. Designs showing scenes from "Pirates of the Caribbean" exhibition. Multicoloured.

873 1 c. Type **198** 10 10
874 1 c. The fate of Captain William Kidd 10 10
875 2 c. Bartholomew Roberts . . 10 10
876 2 c. Two buccaneers 10 10
877 3 c. Privateers looting 10 10
878 3 c. Auction of captives . . . 10 10
879 35 c. Singing pirates . . . . . 1·50 80
880 75 c. Edward Teach—"Blackbeard" . . . . 3·00 3·25
881 $1.10 Sir Henry Morgan . . . 3·50 4·00

199 Brownies from China, Turks and Caicos and Papua New Guinea

1985. 75th Anniv of Girl Guide Movement and 35th Anniv of Grand Turk Company. Multicoloured.

883 10 c. Type **199** 75 40
884 40 c. Brownies from Surinam, Turks and Caicos and Korea 1·75 1·25
885 70 c. Guides from Australia, Turks and Caicos and Canada 2·50 3·00
886 80 c. Guides from West Germany, Turks and Caicos and Israel . . . . 2·75 3·00

200 Iguana and Log

1986. Turks and Caicos Ground Iguana. Multicoloured.

888 8 c. Type **200** . . . . 2·25 1·25
889 10 c. Iguana on beach . . . . 2·25 1·25
890 20 c. Iguana at nest . . . . . 3·50 2·50
891 35 c. Iguana eating flowers . . 6·50 4·50

201 Duke and Duchess of York after Wedding

202 "Prophecy of Birth of Christ to King Achaz"

1986. Royal Wedding. Multicoloured.

893 35 c. Type **201** 85 55
894 65 c. Miss Sarah Ferguson in wedding carriage . . . . . . 1·40 1·40
895 $1.10 Duke and Duchess of York on Palace balcony after wedding . . . . 2·00 2·75

1987. Christmas. Illuminated illustrations by Giorgio Clovio from "Farnese Book of Hours". Multicoloured.

897 35 c. Type **202** . . . . 1·25 85
898 50 c. "The Annunciation" . . 1·75 1·75
899 65 c. "The Circumcision" . . 2·25 2·25
900 95 c. "Adoration of the Kings" 3·25 4·00

203 H.M.S. "Victoria" (ship of the line), 1859, and Victoria Cross

1987. 150th Anniv of Accession of Queen Victoria. Multicoloured.

902 8 c. Type **203** . . . . 1·75 1·00
903 35 c. "Victoria" (paddle-steamer) and gold sovereign . . . . 2·75 2·25
904 55 c. Royal Yacht "Victoria and Albert I" and 1840 Penny Black stamp . . . . 3·00 2·75
905 95 c. Royal Yacht "Victoria and Albert II" and Victoria Public Library . . . . 4·00 5·00

1987. Bicentenary of U.S. Constitution. As T **232** of Antigua. Multicoloured.

907 10 c. State Seal, New Jersey . 25 35
908 35 c. 18th-century family going to church ("Freedom of Worship") (vert) 75 75
909 65 c. U.S. Supreme Court, Judicial Branch, Washington (vert) . . . . 1·40 1·75
910 80 c. John Adams (statesman) (vert) . . . . 1·60 2·25

204 "Santa Maria"

1988. 500th Anniv (1992) of Discovery of America by Columbus (1st issue). Multicoloured.

912 4 c. Type **204** 45 30
913 25 c. Columbus meeting Tainos Indians 95 60
914 70 c. "Santa Maria" anchored off Indian village . . . . 2·75 3·25
915 $1 Columbus in field of grain 2·75 3·25
See also Nos. 947/50, 1028/35, 1072/9 and 1166/75.

205 Arawak Artifact and Scouts in Cave, Middle Caicos

207 Football

1988. World Scout Jamboree, Australia. Mult.

917 8 c. Type **205** 20 15
918 35 c. "Santa Maria" scouts and Hawks Nest Island (horiz) . 55 55
919 65 c. Scouts diving to wreck of galleon . . . . 95 1·25
920 95 c. Visiting ruins of 19th-century sisal plantation (horiz) 1·40 1·75

1988. Royal Ruby Wedding. Nos. 772, 774 and 781 optd **40TH WEDDING ANNIVERSARY H.M. QUEEN ELIZABETH II H.R.H. THE DUKE OF EDINBURGH**.

922 10 c. Type **181** 40 40
923 25 c. H.M.S. "Boreas" (frigate) 70 55
924 $2 "Sentinel" (cable ship) . . 3·25 4·25

1988. Olympic Games, Seoul. Multicoloured.

925 8 c. Type **207** 40 15
926 30 c. Yachting 70 50
927 70 c. Cycling . . . . 2·00 2·00
928 $1 Athletics . . . . 1·75 2·25

208 Game-fishing Launch and Swordfish

210 Coat of Arms

209 Princess Alexandra and Government House

1988. Billfish Tournament. Multicoloured.
930 8 c. Type **208** 55 30
931 10 c. Competitors with swordfish catch 55 30
932 70 c. Game-fishing launch 2·25 3·00
933 $1 Atlantic blue marlin 2·75 3·50

1988. Christmas. 500th Birth Anniv of Titian (artist). As T **238** of Antigua inscr "CHRISTMAS 1988" and with royal cypher at top right. Multicoloured.
935 15 c. "Madonna and Child with Saint Catherine" 40 30
936 25 c. "Madonna with a Rabbit" 50 40
937 35 c. "Virgin and Child with Saints" 60 50
938 40 c. "The Gypsy Madonna" 70 60
939 50 c. "The Holy Family and a Shepherd" 80 70
940 65 c. "Madonna and Child" 95 85
941 $3 "Madonna and Child with Saints" 4·25 6·00

1988. Visit of Princess Alexandra. Mult.
943 70 c. Type **209** 1·50 1·50
944 $1.40 Princess Alexandra and map of islands 3·50 3·75

1988.
946 **210** $10 multicoloured 11·00 13·00

1989. 500th Anniv (1992) of Discovery of America by Columbus (2nd issue). Pre-Columbian Carib Society. As T **247** of Antigua. Multicoloured.
947 10 c. Cutting tree bark for canoe (vert) 15 15
948 50 c. Body painting 80 80
949 65 c. Religious ceremony 95 1·10
950 $1 Canoeing (vert) 1·50 1·75

1989. "World Stamp Expo '89" International Stamp Exhibition, Washington. Bicentenary of the U.S. Presidency. As T **238** of Dominica. Multicoloured.
953 50 c. Andrew Jackson and railway locomotive "DeWitt Clinton" 90 90
954 50 c. Martin van Buren, Moses Walker and early baseball game 90 90
955 50 c. William H. Harrison and campaign parade 90 90
956 50 c. John Tyler, Davy Crockett and the Alamo, Texas 90 90
957 50 c. James K. Polk, California gold miner and first U.S. postage stamp 90 90
958 50 c. Zachary Taylor and Battle of Buena Vista, 1846 90 90
959 50 c. Rutherford B. Hayes and end of Confederate Reconstruction 90 90
960 50 c. James A. Garfield and Battle of Shiloh 90 90
961 50 c. Chester A. Arthur and opening of Brooklyn Bridge, 1883 90 90
962 50 c. Grover Cleveland, Columbian Exposition, Chicago, 1893, and commemorative stamp 90 90
963 50 c. Benjamin Harrison, Pan-American Union Building and map of Americas 90 90
964 50 c. William McKinley and Rough Rider Monument 90 90
965 50 c. Hebert Hoover, Sonya Heine (skater) and Ralph Metcalf (athlete) 90 90
966 50 c. Franklin D. Roosevelt with dog and in wheelchair 90 90
967 50 c. Statue of Washington by Frazer and New York World's, 1939 90 90
968 50 c. Harry S. Truman, Veterans Memorial Building, San Francisco, and U.N. emblem 90 90
969 50 c. Dwight D. Eisenhower and U.S. troops landing in Normandy, 1944 90 90
970 50 c. John F. Kennedy and "Apollo 11" astronauts on Moon, 1969 90 90

1989. Christmas. Paintings by Bellini. As T **259** of Antigua. Multicoloured.
971 15 c. "Madonna and Child" 50 50
972 25 c. "The Madonna of the Shrubs" 60 50
973 35 c. "The Virgin and Child" 70 60
974 40 c. "The Virgin and Child with a Greek Inscription" 80 70
975 50 c. "The Madonna of the Meadow" 90 80
976 65 c. "The Madonna of the Pear" 1·75 1·75
977 70 c. "The Virgin and Child" (different) 2·00 2·00
978 $1 "Madonna and Child" (different) 2·75 2·75

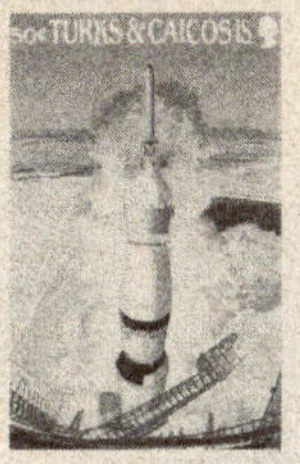

211 Lift-off "Apollo 11"

212 "Zephyranthes rosea"

1990. 20th Anniv of First Manned Landing on Moon. Multicoloured.
980 50 c. Type **211** 60 80
981 50 c. Lunar module "Eagle" on Moon 60 80
982 50 c. Aldrin gathering dust sample 60 80
983 50 c. Neil Armstrong with camera 60 80
984 50 c. "Eagle" re-united with command module "Columbia" 60 80
Nos. 980/4 were printed together, se-tenant, with Nos. 981/3 forming a composite design.

1990. Island Flowers. Multicoloured.
985 8 c. Type **212** 30 20
986 10 c. "Sophora tomentosa" 30 20
987 15 c. "Coccoloba uvifera" 40 25
988 20 c. "Encyclia gracilis" 40 30
989 25 c. "Tillandsia streptophylla" 50 35
990a 30 c. "Maurandella antirrhiniflora" 70 60
991 35 c. "Tillandsia balbisiana" 60 50
992a 50 c. "Encyclia rufa" 1·00 1·00
993a 65 c. "Aechmea lingulata" 1·25 1·25
994 80 c. "Asclepias curassavica" 1·40 1·50
995 $1 "Caesalpinia bahamensis" 1·50 1·60
996 $1.10 "Capparis cynophallophora" 2·00 2·75
997 $1.25 "Stachytarpheta jamaicensis" 2·50 3·00
998 $2 "Cassia biflora" 3·00 4·00
999 $5 "Clusia rosea" 7·00 9·00
1000 $10 "Opuntia bahamana" 14·00 17·00

213 Queen Parrotfish

1990. Fishes. Multicoloured.
1001 8 c. Type **213** 25 20
1002 10 c. Queen triggerfish 25 20
1003 25 c. Sergeant major 60 45
1004 40 c. Spotted goatfish 85 75
1005 50 c. Neon goby 1·00 85
1006 75 c. Nassau grouper 1·50 1·50
1007 80 c. Yellow-headed jawfish 1·75 2·00
1008 $1 Blue tang 1·75 2·00

214 Yellow-billed Cuckoo

1990. Birds (1st series). Multicoloured.
1010 10 c. Type **214** 60 50
1011 15 c. White-tailed tropic bird 75 50
1012 20 c. Kirtland's warbler 1·00 75
1013 30 c. Yellow-crowned night heron 1·10 75
1014 50 c. Black-billed whistling duck ("West Indian tree duck") 1·75 1·00
1015 80 c. Yellow-bellied sapsucker 2·25 2·25
1016 $1 American kestrel 2·25 2·25
1017 $1.40 Northern mockingbird 3·00 3·75
See also Nos. 1050/7.

215 "Anartia jatrophae"

216 Penny "Rainbow Trial" in Blue

1990. Butterflies (1st series). Multicoloured.
1019 15 c. Type **215** 70 45
1020 25 c. "Phoebis sennae" (horiz) 90 60
1021 35 c. "Euptoieta hegesia" (horiz) 1·10 75
1022 40 c. "Hylephila phylaeus" (horiz) 1·25 80
1023 50 c. "Eurema chamberlaini" (horiz) 1·25 1·00
1024 60 c. "Brephidium exilis" 1·50 1·40
1025 90 c. "Papilio aristodemus" (horiz) 2·50 3·00
1026 $1 "Marpesia eleuchea" 2·50 3·00
See also Nos. 1081/8.

1990. 500th Anniv (1992) of Discovery of America by Columbus (3rd issue). New World Natural History–Fishes. As T **260** of Antigua. Mult.
1028 10 c. Rock beauty 50 30
1029 15 c. Coney 60 40
1030 25 c. Red hind 85 60
1031 50 c. Banded butterflyfish 1·40 1·25
1032 60 c. French angelfish 1·75 1·50
1033 75 c. Black-barred soldierfish 1·90 1·90
1034 90 c. Stoplight parrotfish 2·00 2·25
1035 $1 French grunt 2·25 2·40

1990. 150th Anniv of the Penny Black.
1037 **216** 25 c. blue 85 60
1038 – 75 c. brown 2·00 2·00
1039 – $1 blue 2·50 2·75
DESIGNS: 75 c. 1d. red-brown colour trial of December, 1840; $1 2d. blue of 1840.

217 Pillar Box No. 1, 1855

219 Stripe-headed Tanager

1990. "Stamp World London 90" Int Stamp Exhibition. British Pillar Boxes.
1041 **217** 35 c. brown and grey 65 65
1042 – 50 c. blue and grey 90 1·00
1043 – $1.25 blue and grey 2·25 3·00
DESIGNS: 50 c. Penfold box, 1866; $1.25, Air mail box, 1935.

1990. 90th Birthday of Queen Elizabeth the Queen Mother. As T **266** of Antigua.
1045 10 c. multicoloured 25 15
1046 25 c. multicoloured 60 50
1047 75 c. multicoloured 1·40 1·60
1048 $1.25 multicoloured 2·00 2·50
DESIGNS: 10, 25, 75 c., $1.25, Recent photographs of the Queen Mother.

1990. Birds (2nd series). Multicoloured.
1050 8 c. Type **219** 60 50
1051 10 c. Black-whiskered vireo (horiz) 60 50
1052 25 c. Blue-grey gnatcatcher (horiz) 90 60
1053 40 c. Lesser scaup (horiz) 1·50 90
1054 50 c. Bahama pintail (horiz) 1·50 1·00
1055 75 c. Black-necked stilt (horiz) 2·00 2·00
1056 80 c. Oystercatcher 2·00 2·25
1057 $1 Louisiana heron (horiz) 2·50 2·75

220 "Triumph of Christ over Sin and Death" (detail, Rubens)

221 Canoeing

1990. Christmas. 350th Death Anniv of Rubens. Multicoloured.
1059 10 c. Type **220** 30 20
1060 35 c. "St. Theresa Praying" (detail) 60 45
1061 45 c. "St. Theresa Praying" (different detail) 70 60
1062 50 c. "Triumph of Christ over Sin and Death" (different detail) 80 65
1063 65 c. "St. Theresa Praying" (different detail) 1·00 1·00
1064 75 c. "Triumph of Christ over Sin and Death" (different detail) 1·25 1·25
1065 $1.25 "St. Theresa Praying" (different detail) 1·75 2·00

1991. Olympic Games, Barcelona (1992). Mult.
1067 10 c. Type **221** 20 20
1068 25 c. 100 metre sprint 50 50
1069 75 c. Pole vaulting 1·25 1·50
1070 $1.25 Javelin 1·90 2·50

1991. 500th Anniv (1992) of Discovery of America by Columbus (4th issue). History of Exploration. As T **64** of Nevis. Multicoloured.
1072 5 c. Henry Hudson in Hudson's Bay, 1611 20 20
1073 10 c. Roald Amundsen's airship N.1 "Norge", 1926 20 20
1074 15 c. Amundsen's "Gjoa" in the Northwest Passage, 1906 45 35
1075 50 c. Submarine U.S.S. "Nautilus" under North Pole, 1958 80 65
1076 75 c. Robert Scott's "Terra Nova", 1911 1·25 1·10
1077 $1 Byrd and Bennett's Fokker F.VIIa/3m "Josephine Ford" aircraft over North Pole, 1926 1·50 1·50
1078 $1.25 Lincoln Ellsworth's Northrop Gamma "Polar Star" on trans-Antarctic flight, 1935 2·00 2·50
1079 $1.50 Capt. James Cook in the Antarctic, 1772–75 2·25 2·75

222 "Anartia jatrophae"

1991. Butterflies (2nd series). Multicoloured.
1081 5 c. Type **222** 30 30
1082 25 c. "Historis osius" 70 50
1083 35 c. "Agraulis vanillae" 80 65
1084 45 c. "Junonia evarete" 95 80
1085 55 c. "Dryas julia" 1·10 1·00
1086 65 c. "Siproeta stelenes" 1·40 1·40
1087 70 c. "Appias drusilla" 1·50 1·50
1088 $1 "Ascia monuste" 1·75 1·90

223 Protohydrochoerus

1991. Extinct Species of Fauna. Mult.
1090 5 c. Type **223** 30 30
1091 10 c. Phororhacos 30 30
1092 15 c. Prothylacynus 45 35
1093 50 c. Borhyaena 1·00 75
1094 75 c. Smilodon 1·40 1·10
1095 $1 Thoatherium 1·50 1·40
1096 $1.25 Cuvieronius 1·75 2·00
1097 $1.50 Toxodon 2·00 2·25

1991. 65th Birthday of Queen Elizabeth II. As T **280** of Antigua. Multicoloured.
1099 25 c. Queen and Prince Philip at St. Paul's Cathedral, 1988 65 45
1100 35 c. Queen and Prince Philip 80 60
1101 65 c. Queen and Prince Philip at Garter Ceremony, 1988 1·40 1·40
1102 80 c. Queen at Windsor, May 1988 1·75 2·00

224 "Pluteus chrysophlebius"

1991. Fungi. Multicoloured.
1104 10 c. Type **224** 30 30
1105 15 c. "Leucopaxillus gracillimus 45 30
1106 20 c. "Marasmius haematocephalus" 55 40
1107 35 c. "Collybia subpruinosa" 70 45
1108 50 c. "Marasmius atrorubens" (vert) 90 75
1109 65 c. "Leucocoprinus birnbaumii" (vert) 1·25 1·10
1110 $1.10 "Trogia cantharelloides" (vert) 1·75 2·00
1111 $1.25 "Boletellus cubensis" (vert) 1·90 2·25

1991. 10th Wedding Anniv of the Prince and Princess of Wales. As T **280** of Antigua. Multicoloured.
1113 10 c. Prince and Princess of Wales, 1987 40 25
1114 45 c. Separate photographs of Prince, Princess and sons 1·50 90
1115 50 c. Prince Henry in fire engine and Prince William applauding 1·75 1·25
1116 $1 Princess Diana in Derbyshire, 1990, and Prince Charles 2·25 2·50

1991. Death Centenary (1990) of Vincent van Gogh (artist). As T **278** of Antigua. Multicoloured.
1118 15 c. "Weaver with Spinning Wheel" 35 30
1119 25 c. "Head of a Young Peasant with Pipe" (vert) 45 35
1120 35 c. "Old Cemetery Tower at Nuenen" (vert) 60 45
1121 45 c. "Cottage at Nightfall" 75 60
1122 50 c. "Still Life with Open Bible" 80 65
1123 65 c. "Lane, Jardin du Luxembourg" 1·00 1·00
1124 80 c. "Pont du Carrousel and Louvre, Paris" 1·25 1·50
1125 $1 "Vase with Poppies, Cornflowers, Peonies and Chrysanthemums" (vert) 1·40 1·50

225 Series "8550" Steam Locomotive, 1899

1991. "Phila Nippon '91" International Stamp Exhibition, Tokyo. Japanese Steam Locomotives. Multicoloured.

1127 8 c. Type **225** 20 20
1128 10 c. Class C57, 1937 20 20
1129 45 c. Series 4110, 1913 75 60
1130 50 c. Class C55, 1935 80 65
1131 65 c. Series 6250, 1915 1·00 1·00
1132 80 c. Class E10, 1948 1·25 1·40
1133 $1 Series 4500, 1902 1·40 1·50
1134 $1.25 Class C11, 1932 1·75 2·00

1991. Christmas. Religious Paintings by Gerard David. As T **211** of Lesotho. Multicoloured.

1136 8 c. "Adoration of the Shepherds" (detail) 20 15
1137 15 c. "Virgin and Child Enthroned with Two Angels" 35 25
1138 35 c. "The Annunciation" (outer wings) 65 50
1139 45 c. "The Rest on the Flight to Egypt" (different) 80 65
1140 50 c. "The Rest on the Flight to Egypt" (different) 90 90
1141 65 c. "Virgin and Child with Angels" 1·25 1·25
1142 80 c. "Adoration of the Shepherds" 1·50 1·75
1143 $1.25 "Perussis Altarpiece" (detail) 2·25 2·50

1992. 40th Anniv of Queen Elizabeth II's Accession. As T **288** of Antigua. Multicoloured.

1145 10 c. Garden overlooking sea 40 40
1146 20 c. Jetty 70 55
1147 25 c. Small bay 80 60
1148 35 c. Island road 85 75
1149 50 c. Grand Turk 1·25 1·00
1150 65 c. Beach 1·40 1·40
1151 80 c. Marina 1·50 1·75
1152 $1.10 Grand Turk (different) 1·60 1·90

1992. "Granada '92" Int Stamp Exn, Spain. Religious Paintings. As T **292** of Antigua. Mult.

1154 8 c. "St. Monica" (Luis Tristan) 20 20
1155 20 c. "The Vision of Ezekiel: The Resurrection of the Flesh" (detail) (Francisco Collantes) 40 30
1156 45 c. "The Vision of Ezekiel: The Resurrection of the Flesh" (different detail) (Collantes) 70 60
1157 50 c. "The Martyrdom of St. Phillip" (Jose de Ribera) 80 65
1158 65 c. "St. John the Evangelist" (Juan Ribalta) 1·00 1·00
1159 80 c. "Archimedes" (De Ribera) 1·25 1·40
1160 $1 "St. John the Baptist in the Desert" (De Ribera) 1·40 1·50
1161 $1.25 "The Martyrdom of St. Phillip" (detail) (De Ribera) 1·75 2·00

226 Boy Scout on Duty at New York World's Fair, 1964

1992. 17th World Scout Jamboree, Korea. Multicoloured.

1163 $1 Type **226** 2·00 2·25
1164 $1 Lord Baden-Powell (vert) 2·00 2·25

227 "Nina" and Commemorative Coin

1992. 500th Anniv of Discovery of America by Columbus (5th issue). Multicoloured.

1166 10 c. Type **227** 20 20
1167 15 c. Departure from Palos 35 25
1168 20 c. Coat of arms of Columbus 35 30
1169 25 c. Ships of Columbus 50 35
1170 30 c. "Pinta" 50 40
1171 35 c. Landfall in the New World 60 45
1172 50 c. Christopher Columbus 70 65
1173 65 c. "Santa Maria" 1·10 1·10
1174 80 c. Erecting commemorative cross 1·25 1·40
1175 $1.10 Columbus meeting Amerindian 1·40 1·50

1992. Christmas. Religious Paintings. As T **218** of Lesotho. Multicoloured.

1177 8 c. "Nativity" (detail) (Simon Bening) 20 15
1178 15 c. "Circumcision" (detail) (Bening) 40 30
1179 35 c. "Flight to Egypt" (detail) (Bening) 75 60
1180 50 c. "Massacre of the Innocents" (detail) (Bening) 90 80
1181 65 c. "The Annunciation" (Dieric Bouts) 1·25 1·25
1182 80 c. "The Visitation" (Bouts) 1·50 1·50
1183 $1.10 "Adoration of the Angels" (Bouts) 1·60 1·75
1184 $1.25 "Adoration of the Wise Men" (Bouts) 1·75 2·00

228 American Astronaut repairing Satellite

1993. Anniversaries and Events. Mult.

1186 25 c. Type **228** 75 50
1187 50 c. Dead and flourishing trees 1·10 80
1188 65 c. Food and World map 1·40 1·25
1189 80 c. Polluted and clean seas 2·00 2·00
1190 $1 Lions Club emblem 2·25 2·25
1191 $1.25 Projected orbiting quarantine modules 2·50 2·75

ANNIVERSARIES AND EVENTS: Nos. 1186, 1191, International Space Year; Nos. 1187, 1189, Earth Summit '92, Rio; No. 1188, International Conference on Nutrition, Rome; No. 1190, 75th anniv of International Association of Lions Clubs.

1993. Visit of the Duke of Edinburgh. Nos. 1100/1 optd **Royal Visit HRH Duke of Edinburgh 20th March 1993**.

1193 35 c. Queen and Prince Philip 75 60
1194 65 c. Queen and Prince Philip at Garter Ceremony, 1988 1·25 1·25

1993. 40th Anniv of Coronation. As T **307** of Antigua.

1196 15 c. multicoloured 20 25
1197 50 c. multicoloured 60 65
1198 $1 green and black 1·25 1·40
1199 $1.25 multicoloured 1·50 1·60

DESIGNS: 15 c. Communion Chalice and Plate; 50 c. Queen Elizabeth II at Coronation (photograph by Cecil Beaton); $1 Queen Elizabeth during Coronation ceremony; $1.25, Queen Elizabeth and Prince Philip.

230 Omphalosaurus

1993. Prehistoric Animals. Multicoloured.

1201 8 c. Type **230** 30 30
1202 15 c. Coelophysis 40 30
1203 20 c. Triceratops 45 30
1204 35 c. Dilophosaurus 65 50
1205 50 c. Pterodactylus 80 65
1206 65 c. Elasmosaurus 1·10 1·00
1207 80 c. Stegosaurus 1·25 1·40
1208 $1.25 Euoplocephalus 1·60 2·00

1993. Christmas. Religious Paintings. As T **270** of Dominica. Black, yellow and red (Nos. 1210/12, 1217) or multicoloured (others).

1210 8 c. "Mary, Queen of the Angels" (detail) (Durer) 25 10
1211 20 c. "Mary, Queen of the Angels" (different detail) (Durer) 50 30
1212 35 c. "Mary, Queen of the Angels" (different detail) (Durer) 75 50
1213 50 c. "Virgin and Child with St. John the Baptist" (Raphael) 90 70
1214 65 c. "The Canagiani Holy Family" (detail) (Raphael) 1·25 1·10
1215 80 c. "The Holy Family with the Lamb" (detail) (Raphael) 1·40 1·50
1216 $1 "Virgin and Child with St. John the Baptist" (different detail) (Raphael) 1·75 1·75
1217 $1.25 "Mary, Queen of the Angels" (different detail) (Durer) 2·00 2·50

231 Blue-headed Wrasse

1993. Fishes. Multicoloured.

1219 10 c. Type **231** 30 20
1220 20 c. Honeycomb cowfish 50 40
1221 25 c. Glass-eyed snapper 50 40
1222 35 c. Spotted drum 65 50
1223 50 c. Jolt-headed porgy 90 70
1224 65 c. Small-mouthed grunt 1·10 1·00
1225 80 c. Candy basslet ("Peppermint bass") 1·25 1·50
1226 $1.10 Indigo hamlet 1·75 2·25

232 Killdeer

1993. Birds. Multicoloured.

1228 10 c. Type **232** 40 40
1229 15 c. Yellow-crowned night heron (vert) 60 40
1230 35 c. Northern mockingbird 90 55
1231 50 c. Eastern kingbird (vert) 1·00 75
1232 65 c. Magnolia warbler 1·50 1·25
1233 80 c. Cedar waxwing (vert) 1·75 1·75
1234 $1.10 Ruby-throated hummingbird 2·00 2·00
1235 $1.25 Painted bunting (vert) 2·25 2·50

233 Sergio Goycoechea (Argentina)

1994. World Cup Football Championship, U.S.A. Multicoloured.

1237 8 c. Type **233** 30 20
1238 10 c. Bodo Illgner (Germany) 30 20
1239 50 c. Nico Claesen (Belgium), Bossis and Amoros (France) 1·00 70
1240 65 c. German players celebrating 1·25 1·10
1241 80 c. Cameroun players celebrating 1·60 1·60
1242 $1 Cuciuffo (Argentina), Santin and Francescoli (Uruguay) 1·75 1·75
1243 $1.10 Hugo Sanchez (Mexico) 1·75 2·00

No. 1237 is inscribed "Segio" and No. 1238 "Bado", both in error.

234 "Xerocomus guadelupae"

1994. Fungi. Multicoloured.

1245 5 c. Type **234** 10 10
1246 10 c. "Volvariella volvacea" 10 10
1247 35 c. "Hygrocybe atrosquamosa" (horiz) 40 45
1248 50 c. "Pleurotus ostreatus" (horiz) 60 65
1249 65 c. "Marasmius pallescens" (horiz) 80 85
1250 80 c. "Coprinus plicatilis" 1·00 1·10
1251 $1.10 "Bolbitius vitellinus" (horiz) 1·40 1·50
1252 $1.50 "Pyrrhoglossum lilaceipes" 1·75 1·90

235 "The Annunciation"

1994. Christmas. Illustrations from 15th-century French Book of Hours. Multicoloured.

1254 25 c. Type **235** 60 35
1255 50 c. "The Visitation" 1·00 75
1256 65 c. "Annunciation to the Shepherds" 1·25 1·25
1257 80 c. "The Nativity" 1·50 1·50
1258 $1 "Flight into Egypt" 1·75 1·75

236 "Dryas julia"

1994. Butterflies. Multicoloured.

1260 15 c. Type **236** 20 25
1261 20 c. "Urbanus proteus" 25 30
1262 25 c. "Colobura dirce" 30 35
1263 50 c. "Papilio homerus" 60 65
1264 65 c. "Chiodes catillus" 80 85
1265 80 c. "Eurytides zonaria" 1·00 1·10
1266 $1 "Hypolymnas misippus" 1·25 1·40
1267 $1.25 "Phoebis avellaneda" 1·50 1·60

INDEX

Countries can be quickly located by referring to the index at the end of this volume.

237 General Montgomery and British Troops landing on Juno Beach

1994. 50th Anniv of D-Day. Multicoloured.

1269 10 c. Type **237** 10 10
1270 15 c. Admiral Ramsay and British commandos at Sword Beach 20 25
1271 35 c. Gun crew on H.M.S. "Belfast" (cruiser) 40 45
1272 50 c. Montgomery and Eisenhower with Air Chief Marshal Tedder 60 65
1273 65 c. General Eisenhower and men of U.S. 101st Airborne Division 80 85
1274 80 c. Lt-Gen. Bradley and U.S. troops landing on Omaha Beach 1·00 1·10
1275 $1.10 Arrival of U.S. reinforcements 1·40 1·50
1276 $1.25 Eisenhower at briefing 1·50 1·60

238 "Cattleya deckeri"

1995. Orchids. Multicoloured.

1278 8 c. Type **238** 40 20
1279 20 c. "Epidendrum carpophorum" 60 30
1280 25 c. "Epidendrum ciliare" 60 35
1281 50 c. "Encyclia phoenicea" 85 70
1282 65 c. "Bletia patula" 1·10 1·10
1283 80 c. "Brassia caudata" 1·25 1·25
1284 $1 "Brassavola nodosa" 1·50 1·50
1285 $1.25 "Bletia purpurea" 1·75 2·00

1995. 25th Anniv of First Manned Moon Landing. As T **326** of Antigua. Multicoloured.

1287 10 c. "Apollo 11" 10 10
1288 20 c. Moon landing simulation 25 30
1289 25 c. "Astronauts on the Moon" (detail) (Kovales) 30 35
1290 35 c. First human foot on Moon 40 45
1291 50 c. Astronaut Aldrin conducting solar wind experiment 60 65
1292 65 c. Astronauts planting U.S.A. flag 80 85
1293 80 c. Space module "Columbia" over lunar surface 1·00 1·10
1294 $1.10 "Apollo 11" after splashdown 1·40 1·50

239 Elasmosaurus

1995. Jurassic Marine Reptiles. Multicoloured.

1296 35 c. Type **239** 60 60
1297 35 c. Plesiosaurus 60 60
1298 35 c. Ichthyosaurus 60 60
1299 35 c. Archelon 60 60
1300 35 c. Askeptosaurus 60 60
1301 35 c. Macroplata 60 60
1302 35 c. Ceresiosaurus 60 60
1303 35 c. Lipoleurodon 60 60
1304 35 c. Henodus 60 60
1305 35 c. Muraenosaurus 60 60
1306 35 c. Placodus 60 60
1307 35 c. Kronosaurus 60 60

Nos. 1296/1307 were printed together, se-tenant, forming a composite design.

240 Fencing

1995. Centenary of Int Olympic Committee. Mult.

1308 8 c. Type **240** 20 15
1309 10 c. Speed skating 20 15
1310 15 c. Diving 30 25
1311 20 c. Cycling 70 30
1312 25 c. Ice hockey 70 35
1313 35 c. Figure skating 65 50
1314 50 c. Football 80 70
1315 65 c. Bobsleighing 1·10 1·10
1316 80 c. Supergiant slalom 1·25 1·40
1317 $1.25 Show jumping 1·75 2·00

241 Cat and Kitten

242 Belted Kingfisher

1995. Cats. Multicoloured.
1319 15 c. Type **241** 20 25
1320 20 c. Tabby on branch 25 30
1321 35 c. Cat and ladybird 40 45
1322 50 c. Black and white cat 60 65
1323 65 c. Red cat with flower in paw 80 85
1324 80 c. White cat on pink pillow 1·00 1·10
1325 $1 Siamese with flower in paws 1·25 1·40
1326 $1.25 Cats preening 1·50 1·60

1995. Birds. Multicoloured.
1328 10 c. Type **242** 10 10
1329 15 c. Clapper rail 20 25
1330 20 c. American redstart 25 30
1331 25 c. Roseate tern 30 35
1332 35 c. Purple gallinule 40 45
1333 45 c. Turnstone 55 60
1334 50 c. Barn owl 60 65
1335 60 c. Brown booby 70 75
1336 80 c. Great blue heron 1·00 1·10
1337 $1 Antillean nighthawk 1·25 1·40
1338 $1.25 Thick-billed vireo 1·50 1·60
1339 $1.40 American flamingo 1·75 1·90
1340 $2 Wilson's plover 2·40 2·50
1341 $5 Blue-winged teal 6·00 6·25
1342 $10 Pair of reddish egrets (50 × 28 mm) 12·00 12·50

1995. 95th Birthday of Queen Elizabeth the Queen Mother. As T **344** of Antigua.
1344 50 c. brown, light brown and black 60 65
1345 50 c. multicoloured 60 65
1346 50 c. multicoloured 60 65
1347 50 c. multicoloured 60 65
DESIGNS: No. 1344, Queen Elizabeth the Queen Mother (pastel drawing); 1345, Wearing tiara; 1346, At desk (oil painting); 1347, Wearing blue dress.

1995. 50th Anniv of End of Second World War in Europe. As T **340** of Antigua. Multicoloured.
1349 10 c. Churchill, Roosevelt and Stalin at Yalta Conference 10 10
1350 15 c. Liberated Allied prisoners of war 20 25
1351 20 c. Meeting of American and Soviet soldiers at River Elbe 25 30
1352 25 c. Pres. Roosevelt's funeral cortege 30 35
1353 60 c. U.S. bugler sounding cease-fire 70 75
1354 80 c. U.S. sailor kissing nurse, New York 1·00 1·10
1355 $1 Nuremburg Trials 1·25 1·40

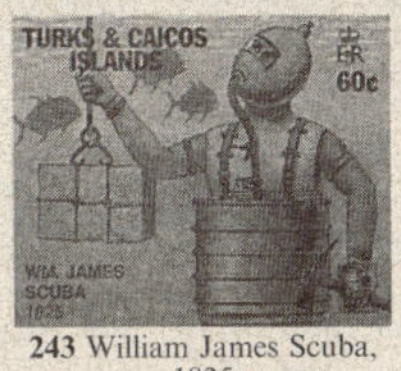

243 William James Scuba, 1825

1995. "Singapore '95" International Stamp Exhibition. Deep Sea Diving. Multicoloured.
1357 60 c. Type **243** 70 75
1358 60 c. Rouquayrol apparatus, 1864 70 75
1359 60 c. Fluess oxygen-rebreathing apparatus, 1878 70 75
1360 60 c. Armoured diving suit, 1900 70 75
1361 60 c. Diving on the "Lusitania" in Peress armoured diving suit, 1935 70 75
1362 60 c. Cousteau Gagnan aqualung, 1943 70 75
1363 60 c. Underwater camera, 1955 70 75
1364 60 c. Sylvia Earle's record dive, 1979 70 75
1365 60 c. Spider propeller-driven rigid suit, 1984 70 75

1995. Christmas. Religious Paintings by Piero di Cosimo. As T **98** of Nevis. Multicoloured.
1367 20 c. "Madonna and Child with St. Giovannino" 25 30
1368 25 c. "Adoration of the Child" 30 35
1369 60 c. "Madonna and Child with St. Giovannino, St. Margherita and Angel" 70 75
1370 $1 "Madonna and Child with Angel" 1·25 1·40

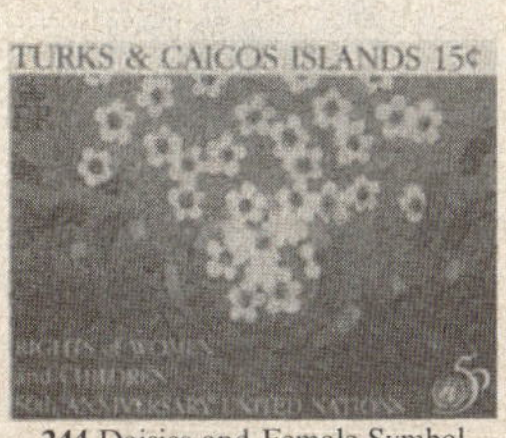

244 Daisies and Female Symbol ("Rights of Women and Children")

1996. 50th Anniv of the United Nations. Multicoloured.
1372 15 c. Type **244** 20 25
1373 60 c. Peace dove escaping from prison 70 75
1374 80 c. Symbolic candles ("Human Rights") 1·00 1·10
1375 $1 People on open book 1·25 1·40

1996. 70th Birthday of Queen Elizabeth II. As T **363** of Antigua. Multicoloured.
1378 80 c. As Type **363** of Antigua 1·00 1·10
1379 80 c. In blue coat and hat 1·00 1·10
1380 80 c. At Trooping the Colour 1·00 1·10

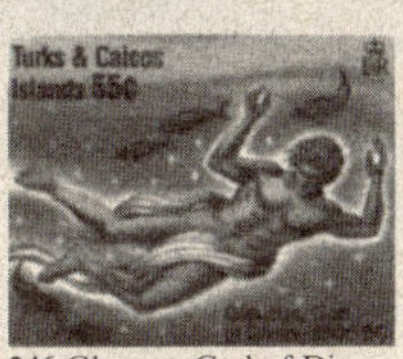

246 Glaucus, God of Divers, 2500 B.C.

1996. "China '96" Asian International Philatelic Exhibition, Beijing. Underwater Exploration (1st series). Multicoloured.
1382 55 c. Type **246** 65 70
1383 55 c. Alexander the Great, 332 B.C. 65 70
1384 55 c. Salvage diver, 1430 65 70
1385 55 c. Borelli's rebreathing device, 1680 65 70
1386 55 c. Edmund Halley's diving bell, 1690 65 70
1387 55 c. John Lethbridge's diving machine, 1715 65 70
1388 55 c. Klingert's diving apparatus, 1789 65 70
1389 55 c. Drieberg's triton, 1808 65 70
1390 55 c. Seibe's diving helmet, 1819 65 70
See also Nos. 1392/1400 and 1460/8.

1996. "Capex '96" World Stamp Exhibition, Toronto. Underwater Exploration (2nd series). As T **246**. Multicoloured.
1392 60 c. Jim Jarrat exploring "Lusitania", 1935 70 75
1393 60 c. Cousteau's first use of scuba gear for exploration, 1952 70 75
1394 60 c. Discovery of oldest shipwreck, 1959 70 75
1395 60 c. Raising of the "Vasa", 1961 70 75
1396 60 c. Mel Fisher discovering "Atocha", 1971 70 75
1397 60 c. Barry Clifford discovering "Whydah", 1984 70 75
1398 60 c. Argo robot over the "Bismarck", 1989 70 75
1399 60 c. Discovery of "Land Tortoise" in Lake George, New York, 1991 70 75
1400 60 c. Nuclear submarine recovering artefacts from Roman shipwreck, 1994 70 75

247 Show Jumping

1996. Olympic Games, Atlanta. Sports on Medals. Multicoloured.
1402 55 c. Type **247** 65 70
1403 55 c. Cycling 65 70
1404 55 c. Fencing 65 70
1405 55 c. Gymnastics 65 70
1406 55 c. Pole vaulting 65 70
1407 55 c. Sprinting 65 70
1408 55 c. Swimming 65 70
1409 55 c. Diving 65 70
1410 55 c. Hurdling 65 70
1411 55 c. Long-distance running 65 70

248 James McCartney (First Chief Minister)

249 Space Dog

1996. 20th Anniv of Ministerial Government.
1412 **248** 60 c. multicoloured 70 75

1996. Working Dogs. Multicoloured.
1413 25 c. Type **249** 30 35
1414 25 c. Greyhound 30 35
1415 25 c. St. Bernard 30 35
1416 25 c. Dog with medals 30 35
1417 25 c. Retriever 30 35
1418 25 c. Dog with bone 30 35
1419 25 c. "Hearing ear" dog 30 35
1420 25 c. Husky 30 35
1421 25 c. Police alsatian 30 35
1422 25 c. Guard dog 30 35
1423 25 c. Boxer 30 35
1424 25 c. Sniffer dog 30 35

250 Winnie the Pooh asleep in Chair

1996. Christmas. "Winnie the Pooh". Multicoloured.
1426 15 c. Type **250** 30 30
1427 20 c. Piglet holding star decoration 35 35
1428 35 c. Tigger carrying presents 55 55
1429 50 c. Pooh, Tigger and Piglet singing carols 75 75
1430 60 c. Winnie and Rabbit 90 90
1431 80 c. Tigger and Roo 1·25 1·25
1432 $1 Santa Pooh filling stockings 1·40 1·60
1433 $1.25 Christopher Robin and Winnie the Pooh 1·60 2·00

251 Giant Milkweed

253 White Dove (face value at right)

1997. Flowers. Multicoloured.
1435 20 c. Type **251** 25 30
1436 20 c. Geiger tree 25 30
1437 20 c. Passion flower 25 30
1438 20 c. Hibiscus 25 30
1439 60 c. Yellow elder 70 75
1440 60 c. Prickly poppy 70 75
1441 60 c. Frangipani 70 75
1442 60 c. Seaside mahoe 70 75

1997. 50th Anniv of U.N.I.C.E.F. Multicoloured.
1445 60 c. Type **253** 70 75
1446 60 c. White dove (with face value at left) 70 75
1447 60 c. Three children 70 75
1448 60 c. Two children with pets 70 75

1997. Golden Wedding of Queen Elizabeth and Prince Philip. As T **350** of Maldive Islands. Multicoloured.
1449 60 c. Queen Elizabeth II 70 75
1450 60 c. Royal coat of arms 70 75
1451 60 c. Queen Elizabeth and Prince Philip in carriage 70 75
1452 60 c. Queen Elizabeth and Prince Philip on royal visit 70 75
1453 60 c. Windsor Castle 70 75
1454 60 c. Prince Philip 70 75

1997. "Pacific '97" International Stamp Exhibition, San Francisco. Death Centenary of Heinrich von Stephan (founder of the U.P.U.). As T **351** of Maldive Islands.
1456 50 c. mauve 60 65
1457 50 c. brown 60 65
1458 50 c. blue 60 65
DESIGNS: No. 1456, British mail coach, 1700s; 1457, Von Stephan and Mercury; 1458, Space Shuttle.

1997. "STAMPSHOW '97" 111th Annual A.P.S. Convention, Milwaukee. Underwater Exploration (3rd series). As T **246**. Multicoloured.
1460 20 c. Edgerton underwater camera, 1954 25 30
1461 20 c. Conshelf habitat, 1963 25 30
1462 20 c. "Sealab II", 1965 25 30
1463 20 c. Research habitat Tektite, 1970 25 30
1464 20 c. Galapagos volcanic rift, 1974 25 30
1465 20 c. Epaulard robot survey craft, 1979 25 30
1466 20 c. Underwater sealife, 1995 25 30
1467 20 c. One-man research vessel, 1996 25 30
1468 20 c. Okhotsk Tower, Japan, 1996 25 30

254 "Adoration of an Angel" (detail) (Studio of Fra Angelico)

1997. Christmas. Religious Paintings. Multicoloured.
1470 15 c. Type **254** 20 25
1471 20 c. "Scenes from the life of St. John the Baptist" (detail) (Master of Saint Severin) 25 30
1472 35 c. "Archangel Gabriel" (Masolino de Panicale) 40 45
1473 50 c. "Jeremiah with two Angels" (detail) (Gherardo Starnina) 60 65
1474 60 c. "Jeremiah with Two Angels" (different detail) (Starnina) 70 75
1475 80 c. "The Annunciation" (detail) (Giovanni di Palo di Grazia) 1·00 1·10
1476 $1 "The Annunciation" (detail) (Carlo di Braccesco) 1·25 1·40
1477 $1.25 "The Nativity" (detail) (Benvenuto di Giovanni Guasta) 1·50 1·60

255 Black-finned Snapper

1998. Endangered Species. International Year of the Reef. Fishes. Multicoloured.
1479 25 c. Type **255** 30 35
1480 25 c. Dog snapper 30 35
1481 25 c. Cubera snapper 30 35
1482 25 c. Mahogany snapper 30 35

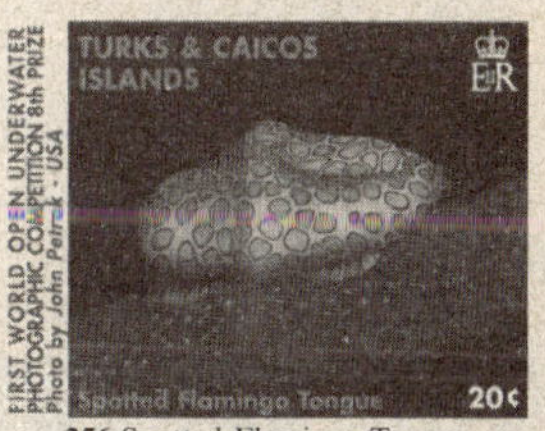

256 Spotted Flamingo Tongue (John Petrak)

1998. 1st World Open Underwater Photographic Competition Prizewinners (1997). Multicoloured.
1483 20 c. Type **256** 25 30
1484 50 c. Feather duster (Dave Bothwell) 60 65
1485 60 c. Squirrel fish (Waldemar Seifert) 70 75
1486 80 c. Queen angelfish (Ralph Oberlander) 1·00 1·10
1487 $1 Barracuda (Steve Rosenburg) 1·25 1·40
1488 $1.25 Royal gramma ("Fairy Basslet") (John Petrak) 1·50 1·60

257 Bird and Logo

258 University Arms on Banner (50th anniv of University of West Indies)

1998. International Year of the Ocean. Multicoloured.
1490 50 c. Type **257** 60 65
1491 50 c. Stylised crab 60 65
1492 50 c. Fish 60 65
1493 50 c. Logo in cloverleaf 60 65

1998. Anniversaries and Events. Multicoloured.
1495 20 c. Type **258** 25 30
1496 60 c. Global logo (U.N.E.S.C.O. World Solar Energy Programme Summit) 70 75
1497 80 c. Flame (50th anniv of Universal Declaration of Human Rights) 1·00 1·10
1498 $1 John Glenn (astronaut) (second space flight) 1·25 1·40

259 S.E. 5A Aircraft

1998. 80th Anniv of Royal Air Force. Multicoloured.

1500	20 c. Type **259**	25	30
1501	50 c. Sopwith Camel	60	65
1502	60 c. Supermarine Spitfire . .	70	75
1503	80 c. Avro Lancaster	1·00	1·10
1504	$1 Panavia Tornado	1·25	1·40
1505	$1.25 Hawker Hurricane . .	1·50	1·60

260 Diana, Princess of Wales

261 "Magi's Visit"

1998. 1st Death Anniv of Diana, Princess of Wales.

1507	**260**	60 c. multicoloured . .	70	75

1998. Christmas. Paintings by Thomasita Fessler. Multicoloured.

1508	50 c. Type **261**	60	65
1509	50 c. "Flight into Egypt" . .	60	65
1510	50 c. "Wedding Feast" . . .	60	65
1511	50 c. "Maria"	60	65
1512	50 c. "Annunciation and Visitation" (57 × 46 mm) .	60	65
1513	50 c. "Nativity" (57 × 46 mm)	60	65

TUVALU

Formerly known as the Ellice Islands and sharing a joint administration with the Gilbert group. On 1 January 1976 the two island groups separated and the Ellice Is. were renamed Tuvalu.

100 cents = $1 Australian

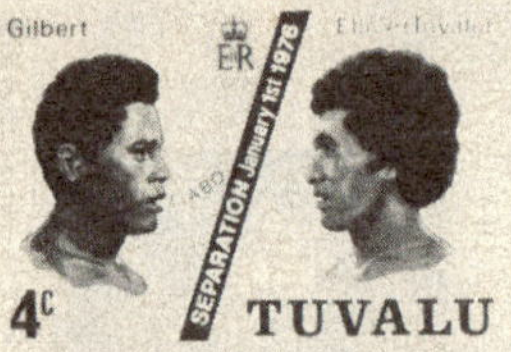

1 Tuvaluan and Gilbertese

1976. Separation. Multicoloured.

1	4 c. Type **1**	35	80
2	10 c. Map of the islands (vert) .	50	1·00
3	35 c. Gilbert and Ellice canoes .	70	1·50

1976. Nos. 173/87 of Gilbert and Ellice Islands optd **TUVALU**.

14	1 c. Cutting toddy	30	30
20	2 c. Lagoon fishing	60	40
21	3 c. Cleaning pandanus leaves	60	40
22	4 c. Casting nets	60	45
5	5 c. Gilbertese canoe	60	60
15	6 c. De-husking coconuts . . .	60	40
6	8 c. Weaving pandanus fronds	60	60
7	10 c. Weaving a basket	60	80
16	15 c. Tiger shark	60	50
23	20 c. Beating a rolled pandanus leaf	60	60
24	25 c. Loading copra	60	60
25	35 c. Fishing at night	75	70
17	50 c. Local handicrafts	60	65
18	$1 Weaving coconut screen . .	60	85
19	$2 Coat of arms	75	85

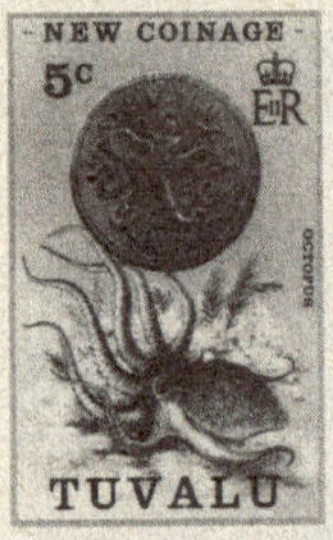

3 50 c. Coin and Octopus

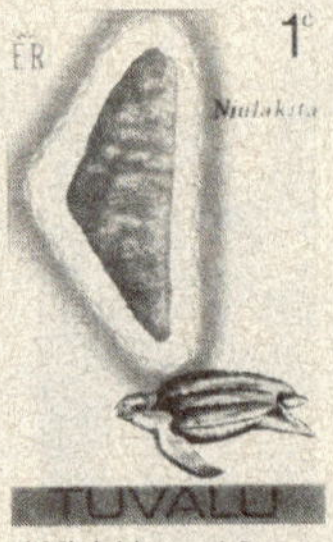

4 Niulakita and Seven-ridged Leathery Turtle

1976. New Coinage. Multicoloured.

26	5 c. Type **3**	30	15
27	10 c. Red-eyed crab	40	20
28	15 c. Flying fish	55	25
29	35 c. Green turtle	70	45

1976. Multicoloured.

58	1 c. Type **4**	50	15
59	2 c. Nukulaelae and sleeping mat	20	25
60	4 c. Nui and talo (vegetable) .	20	15
61	5 c. Nanumanga and grass skirt	25	15
62	6 c. Nukufetau and coconut crab	20	35
63	8 c. Funafuti and banana tree .	20	25
64	10 c. Map of Tuvalu	20	20
37	15 c. Niutao and flying fish . .	1·00	20
38	20 c. Vaitupu and maneapa (meeting hall)	70	50
39	25 c. Nanumea and fish-hook .	1·00	90
67	30 c. Fatele (local dancing) . .	30	20
40	35 c. Te Ano (game)	45	20
68	40 c. Screw pine	30	15
41	50 c. Canoe pole fishing . . .	55	30
42	$1 Reef fishing by flare . . .	60	30
43	$2 Living house	60	30
69	$5 M.V. "Nivanga"	2·00	3·00

5 Title Page of New Testament

1976. Christmas. Multicoloured.

45	5 c. Type **5**	20	25
46	20 c. Lotolelei Church	20	25
47	25 c. Kelupi Church	20	25
48	30 c. Mataloa o Tuvalu Church	20	25
49	35 c. Palataise o Keliso Church	20	25

6 The Queen and Duke of Edinburgh after Coronation

1977. Silver Jubilee. Multicoloured.

50	15 c. Type **6**	15	10
51	35 c. Prince Philip carried ashore at Vaitupu	20	15
52	50 c. The Queen and attendants	30	20

7 "Health"

1977. 30th Anniv of South Pacific Commission. Multicoloured.

54	5 c. Type **7**	15	20
55	20 c. "Education"	15	20
56	30 c. "Fruit-growing"	15	20
57	35 c. Map of S.P.C. area . . .	20	25

8 Scout Promise

1977. 50th Anniv of Scouting in the Central Pacific. Multicoloured.

73	5 c. Type **8**	15	20
74	20 c. Canoeing	15	20
75	30 c. Scout shelter	20	25
76	35 c. Lord Baden-Powell . . .	20	25

9 Hurricane Beach (Expedition photo)

1977. Royal Society Expeditions, 1896-97.

77	**9**	5 c. multicoloured	15	15
78	–	20 c. black and blue	15	20
79	–	30 c. black and blue	20	20
80	–	35 c. multicoloured	20	20

DESIGNS—VERT: 20 c. Boring apparatus on H.M.S. "Porpoise"; 30 c. Dredging chart. HORIZ: 35 c. Charles Darwin and H.M.S. "Beagle".

10 Pacific Pigeon

13 White Frangipani

11 "Lawedua" (inter-island coaster)

1978. Wild Birds. Multicoloured.

81	8 c. Type **10**	40	25
82	20 c. Eastern reef heron	55	40
83	30 c. White tern	65	50
84	40 c. Lesser frigate bird	65	55

1978. Ships. Multicoloured.

85	8 c. Type **11**	25	15
86	20 c. "Wallacia" (tug)	25	15
87	30 c. "Cenpac Rounder" (freighter)	25	20
88	40 c. "Pacific Explorer" (freighter)	30	20

1978. 25th Anniv of Coronation. As Nos. 422/5 of Montserrat. Multicoloured.

89	8 c. Canterbury Cathedral . . .	10	10
90	30 c. Salisbury Cathedral . . .	10	10
91	40 c. Wells Cathedral	10	10
92	$1 Hereford Cathedral	30	30

1978. Independence. Nos. 63/4, 37/8, 67/40 and 68 optd **INDEPENDENCE 1ST OCTOBER 1978**.

94	8 c. Funafuti and banana tree .	10	10
95	10 c. Map of Tuvalu	10	10
96	15 c. Niutao and four-winged flyingfish	10	10
97	20 c. Vaitupu and maneapa (house)	15	15
98	30 c. Fatele (local dancing) . .	15	15
99	35 c. Te Ano (game)	20	20
100	40 c. Screw pine	20	20

1978. Wild Flowers. Multicoloured.

101	8 c. Type **13**	10	10
102	20 c. Susana	10	10
103	30 c. Tiale	15	15
104	40 c. Inato	20	25

14 Squirrelfish

1979. Fishes (1st series). Multicoloured.

105	1 c. Type **14**	10	10
106	2 c. Band-tailed goatfish . .	10	10
107	4 c. Regal angelfish	10	10
108	5 c. Melon butterflyfish . . .	15	10
109	6 c. Semi-circle angelfish . .	15	10
110	8 c. Blue-striped snapper . .	15	10
111	10 c. Clown anemonefish . .	25	10
112	15 c. Chevron butterflyfish .	25	10
113	20 c. Yellow-edged lyretail ("Fairy cod")	35	15
114	25 c. Clown triggerfish . . .	35	20
115	30 c. Long-nosed butterflyfish	35	10
116	35 c. Yellow-finned tuna . .	40	20
117	40 c. Spotted eagle ray . . .	40	10
117a	45 c. Black-tipped grouper .	1·50	2·00
118	50 c. Hammerhead	40	20
119	70 c. Lionfish (vert)	40	30
120	$1 Painted triggerfish (vert) .	40	40
121	$2 Copper-banded butterflyfish ("Beaked coralfish") (vert)	70	40
122	$5 Tiger shark (vert)	90	55

See also Nos. 770/81.

15 "Explorer of the Pacific"

1979. Death Bicent of Capt. James Cook. Mult.

123	8 c. Type **15**	15	20
124	30 c. "A new island is discovered"	20	20
125	40 c. "Transit of Venus, Tahiti, 3 June, 1769"	20	20
126	$1 Cook's death	30	30

16 Grumman Mackinnon Goose Flying Boat and Nukulaelae Island

1979. Internal Air Service. Multicoloured.

127	8 c. Type **16**	15	15
128	20 c. Goose and Vaitupu . .	15	20
129	30 c. Goose and Nui	20	30
130	40 c. Goose and Funafuti . .	25	35

17 Sir Rowland Hill, 1976 4 c. Separation Commemorative and London's First Pillar Box, 1855

1979. Death Cent of Sir Rowland Hill. Mult.

131	30 c. Type **17**	15	15
132	40 c. Sir Rowland Hill, 1976 10 c. Separation commemorative and Penny Black	15	15
133	$1 Sir Rowland Hill, 1976 35 c. Separation commemorative and mail coach	35	30

18 Child's Face

1979. International Year of the Child.

135	18	8 c. multicoloured	10	10
136	–	20 c. multicoloured	10	10
137	–	30 c. multicoloured	10	15
138	–	40 c. multicoloured	15	25

DESIGN: 20 c. to 40 c. Children's faces.

19 Eyed Cowrie

1980. Cowrie Shells. Multicoloured.

139	8 c. Type **19**	10	10
140	20 c. Jester cowrie	10	10
141	30 c. Closely-related carnelian cowrie	15	15
142	40 c. Golden cowrie	25	20

20 Philatelic Bureau, Funafuti, and 1976 8 c. Definitive

1980. "London 1980" Int Stamp Exhibition. Mult.

143	10 c. Type **20**	10	10
144	20 c. Nukulaelae postmark and 1976 2 c. definitive	15	15
145	30 c. Fleet Post Office, U.S. Navy, airmail cover, 1943	15	20
146	$1 Map and arms of Tuvalu	35	40

21 Queen Elizabeth the Queen Mother at Royal Variety Performance, 1978

1980. 80th Birthday of The Queen Mother.

148	**21**	15 c. multicoloured	25	20

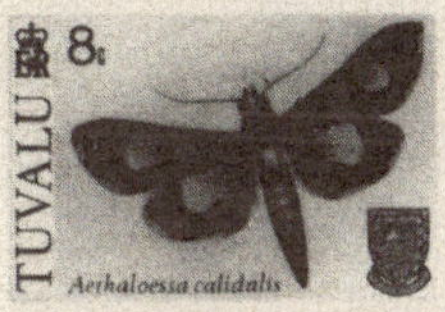

22 "Aethaloessa calidalis"

1980. Moths. Multicoloured.

149	8 c. Type **22**	10	10
150	20 c. "Parotis suralis"	15	10
151	30 c. "Dudua aprobola"	20	15
152	40 c. "Decadarchis simulans"	20	15

23 Air Pacific De Havilland Heron 2

1980. Aviation Commemorations. Mult.

153	8 c. Type **23**	10	10
154	20 c. Hawker Siddeley H.S.748	15	10
155	30 c. Short S.25 Sunderland flying boat	15	15
156	40 c. Orville Wright and Wright Flyer III	20	15

COMMEMORATIONS: 8 c. 1st regular air service to Tuvalu, 1964; 20 c. Air service to Tuvalu; 30 c. War time R.N.Z.A.F. flying boat service to Funafuti, 1945; 40 c. Wright Brothers' 1st flight, 17 December, 1903.

1981. No. 118 surch **45 CENTS**.

157	45 c. on 50 c. Hammerhead	25	40

25 "Hypolimnas bolina" (male)

27 U.P.U. Emblem

26 "Elizabeth" (brig), 1809

1981. Butterflies. Multicoloured.

158	8 c. Type **25**	15	10
159	20 c. "Hypolimnas bolina" (female)	20	15
160	30 c. "Hypolimnas bolina" (female) (different)	20	20
161	40 c. "Precis villida" (male)	25	20

1981. Ships (1st series). Multicoloured.

162	10 c. Type **26**	20	20
163	25 c. "Rebecca" (brigantine), 1819	20	25
164	35 c. "Independence II" (whaling ship), 1821	25	30
165	40 c. H.M.S. "Basilisk" (paddle-sloop), 1872	30	35
166	45 c. H.M.S. "Royalist" (screw-corvette), 1890	35	40
167	50 c. "Olivebank" (barque), 1920	35	40

See also Nos. 235/40, 377/80, 442/5, 809/12 and 832/5.

1981. Royal Wedding. Royal Yachts. As T **26/27** of Kiribati. Multicoloured.

168	10 c. "Carolina"	10	15
169	10 c. Prince Charles and Lady Diana Spencer	35	50
170	45 c. "Victoria and Albert III"	10	15
171	45 c. As No. 169	40	65
172	$2 "Britannia"	35	50
173	$2 As No. 169	1·00	1·50

1981. U.P.U. Membership.

177	**27**	70 c. blue	20	30
178		$1 brown	30	45

28 Map of Funafuti, and Anchor

1982. Amatuku Maritime School. Mult.

180	10 c. Type **28**	10	10
181	25 c. Motor launch	20	20
182	35 c. School buildings and jetty	25	30
183	45 c. School flag and freighter	30	35

29 Caroline of Brandenburg-Ansbach, Princess of Wales, 1714

1982. 21st Birthday of Princess of Wales. Multicoloured.

184	10 c. Type **29**	10	10
185	45 c. Coat of arms of Caroline of Brandenburg-Ansbach	10	10
186	$1.50 Diana, Princess of Wales	50	30

1982. Tonga Cyclone Relief. Nos. 170/1 optd **TONGA CYCLONE RELIEF 1982 +20c**.

187	45 c. + 20 c. "Victoria and Albert III"	15	30
188	45 c. + 20 c. Prince Charles and Lady Diana Spencer	45	95

1982. Birth of Prince William of Wales. Nos. 184/6 optd **ROYAL BABY**.

189	10 c. Type **29**	10	10
190	45 c. Coat of arms of Caroline of Brandenburg-Ansbach	10	10
191	$1.50 Diana, Princess of Wales	30	30

31 Tuvalu and World Scout Badge

1982. 75th Anniv of Boy Scout Movement. Multicoloured.

192	10 c. Type **31**	15	15
193	25 c. Campfire	40	40
194	35 c. Parade	45	45
195	45 c. Boy scout	55	55

32 Tuvalu Crest and Duke of Edinburgh's Standard

1982. Royal Visit. Multicoloured.

196	25 c. Type **32**	15	20
197	45 c. Tuvalu flag and Queen's Royal Standard	25	30
198	50 c. Portrait of Queen Elizabeth II	25	30

33 Fisherman's Hat and Equipment

1983. Handicrafts. Multicoloured.

200	1 c. Type **33**	30	10
201	2 c. Cowrie shell handbags	30	10
202	5 c. Wedding and baby food baskets	30	10
203	10 c. Model canoe	30	10
203a	15 c. Ladies' sun hats	2·25	1·75
204	20 c. Palm climbing rope and platform with toddy pot	30	20
205	25 c. Pandanus baskets	30	20
205a	30 c. Basket tray and coconut stand	2·00	1·40
206	35 c. Pandanus pillows and shell necklaces	40	30
207	40 c. Round baskets and fans	30	35
208	45 c. Reef sandals and fish trap	35	40
209	50 c. Rat trap (vert)	40	45
209a	60 c. Fisherman's waterproof boxes (vert)	2·75	1·40
210	$1 Pump drill and adze (vert)	45	45
211	$2 Fisherman's hat and canoe bailers (vert)	60	55
212	$5 Fishing rod, lures and scoop nets (vert)	1·00	75

34 "Te Tautai" (trawler)

1983. Commonwealth Day. Multicoloured.

213	20 c. Type **34**	15	15
214	35 c. Traditional dancing, Motufoua School	15	25
215	45 c. Satellite view of Pacific	20	30
216	50 c. "Morning Star" (container ship)	25	40

35 "Pantala flavescens"

1983. Dragonflies. Multicoloured.

217	10 c. Type **35**	15	10
218	35 c. "Anax guttatus"	35	35
219	40 c. "Tholymis tillarga"	35	40
220	50 c. "Diplacodes bipunctata"	40	50

36 Brigade Members Racing

1983. Centenary of Boys' Brigade. Mult.

221	10 c. Type **36**	10	10
222	35 c. B.B. members in outrigger canoe	25	30
223	$1 On parade	65	1·00

1983. No. 210 surch **60c**.

224	60 c. on $1 Pump drill and adze	70	70

38 Montgolfier Balloon, 1783

1983. Bicentenary of Manned Flight. Mult.

225	25 c. Type **38**	15	20
226	35 c. Grumman Mackinnon Turbo Goose (horiz)	20	25
227	45 c. Beech 200 Super King Air (horiz)	20	30
228	50 c. "Double Eagle II" balloon	25	35

39 Early Communications

1983. World Communications Year. Mult.

230	25 c. Type **39**	20	20
231	35 c. Radio operator	25	25
232	45 c. Modern teleprinter	25	25
233	50 c. Funafuti transmitting station	30	30

1984. No. 208 surch **30c**.

234	30 c. on 45 c. Reef sandals and fish trap	35	40

1984. Ships (2nd series). As T **26**. Mult.

235	10 c. "Titus" (freighter), 1897	25	15
236	20 c. "Malaita" (freighter), 1905	25	15
237	25 c. "Aymeric" (freighter), 1906	25	15
238	35 c. "Anshun" (freighter), 1965	30	25
239	45 c. "Beaverbank" (freighter), 1970	30	30
240	50 c. "Benjamin Bowring" (freighter), 1981	30	30

41 Southern Pacific Railroad Class GS-4

1984. Leaders of the World. Railway Locomotives (1st series). As T **41**. The first in each pair shows technical drawings and the second the locomotive at work.

241	1 c. multicoloured	10	10
242	1 c. multicoloured	10	10
243	15 c. multicoloured	20	25
244	15 c. multicoloured	20	25
245	40 c. multicoloured	25	35
246	40 c. multicoloured	25	35
247	60 c. multicoloured	35	45
248	60 c. multicoloured	35	45

DESIGNS: Nos. 241/2, Southern Pacific Railroad Class GS-4, U.S.A. (1941); 243/4, New South Wales Govt Class AD 60, Australia (1952); 245/6, New South Wales Govt Class C38, Australia (1943); 247/8, Class "Achilles" "Lord of the Isles", Great Britain (1892).

See also Nos. 253/68, 273/80, 313/20 and 348/55.

42 "Ipomoea pes-caprae"

1984. Beach Flowers. Multicoloured.

249	25 c. Type **42**	25	25
250	45 c. "Ipomoea macrantha"	40	40
251	50 c. "Triumfetta procumbens"	45	45
252	60 c. "Portulaca quadrifida"	50	50

1984. Leaders of the World. Railway Locomotives (2nd series). As T **41**. The first design in each pair shows technical drawings and the second the locomotive at work.

253	10 c. multicoloured	10	10
254	10 c. multicoloured	10	10
255	15 c. multicoloured	10	15
256	15 c. multicoloured	10	15
257	20 c. multicoloured	10	15
258	20 c. multicoloured	10	15
259	25 c. multicoloured	10	15
260	25 c. multicoloured	10	15
261	40 c. multicoloured	15	20
262	40 c. multicoloured	15	20
263	50 c. multicoloured	15	20
264	50 c. multicoloured	15	20
265	60 c. multicoloured	15	25
266	60 c. multicoloured	15	25
267	$1 multicoloured	20	30
268	$1 multicoloured	20	30

DESIGNS: Nos. 253/4, Illinois Central Railroad "Casey Jones" type locomotive No. 382, U.S.A. (1896); 255/6, Erie Railroad Triplex type, U.S.A. (1914); 257/8, Class 370 Advanced Passenger Train, Great Britain (1981); 259/60, LMS Class 4F, Great Britain (1924); 261/2, GWR Class "Tornado Rover", Great Britain (1888); 263/4, Class 73 electric locomotive "Broadlands", Great Britain (1967); 265/6, "Locomotion", Great Britain (1825); 267/8, Class C57, Japan (1937).

43 Exhibition Emblem

1984. "Ausipex" International Stamp Exhibition, Melbourne. Multicoloured.
269 60 c. Type **43** 20 30
270 60 c. Arms of Tuvalu 20 30
271 60 c. Tuvalu flag 20 30
272 60 c. Royal Exhibition Building, Melbourne 20 30

1984. Leaders of the World. Railway Locomotives (3rd series). As T **41**. The first in each pair shows technical drawings and the second the locomotive at work.
273 1 c. multicoloured 10 10
274 1 c. multicoloured 10 10
275 15 c. multicoloured 15 20
276 15 c. multicoloured 15 20
277 30 c. multicoloured 20 30
278 30 c. multicoloured 20 30
279 $1 multicoloured 40 80
280 $1 multicoloured 40 80
DESIGNS: Nos. 273/4, Class 9700, Japan (1897); 275/6, Paris–Lyon–Mediterranee Class 231C/K, France (1909); 277/8, Class 640, Italy (1907); 279/80, Paris–Orleans Class 4500, France (1906).

44 A. Shrewsbury

1984. Leaders of the World. Cricketers. As T **44**. The first in each pair shows the cricketer in action and the second a head portrait.
281 5 c. multicoloured 10 10
282 5 c. multicoloured 10 10
283 30 c. multicoloured 25 35
284 30 c. multicoloured 25 35
285 50 c. multicoloured 30 40
286 50 c. multicoloured 30 40
287 60 c. multicoloured 40 45
288 60 c. multicoloured 40 45
DESIGNS: 281/2, A. Shrewsbury; 283/4, H. Verity; 285/6, E. H. Hendren; 287/8, J. Briggs.

45 Trees and Stars

1984. Christmas. Children's Drawings. Multicoloured.
289 15 c. Type **45** 10 10
290 40 c. Fishing from outrigger canoes 20 20
291 50 c. Three Wise Men bearing gifts 25 25
292 60 c. The Holy Family 35 35

46 Morris Minor

1984. Leaders of the World. Automobiles (1st series). As T **46**. The first in each pair shows technical drawings and the second paintings.
293 1 c. black, brown and yellow . 10 10
294 1 c. multicoloured 10 10
295 15 c. black, pink and lilac . . 10 15
296 15 c. multicoloured 10 15
297 50 c. black, brown and mauve 20 20
298 50 c. multicoloured 20 20
299 $1 black, green and blue . . 30 40
300 $1 multicoloured 30 40
DESIGNS: Nos. 293/4, "Morris Minor"; 295/6, Studebaker "Avanti"; 297/8, Chevrolet "International Six"; 299/300, Allard "J2".
See also Nos. 321/8, 356/71, 421/32 and 446/69.

47 Common Flicker

1985. Leaders of the World. Birth Bicentenary of John J. Audubon (ornithologist). Multicoloured.
301 1 c. Type **47** 10 10
302 1 c. Say's phoebe 10 10
303 25 c. Townsend's warbler . . 30 30
304 25 c. Bohemian waxwing . . 30 30
305 50 c. Prothonotary warbler . . 40 50
306 50 c. Worm-eating warbler . . 40 50
307 70 c. Broad-winged hawk . . 50 75
308 70 c. Hen harrier 50 75

48 Black-naped Tern

1985. Birds and their Eggs. Multicoloured.
309 15 c. Type **48** 50 20
310 40 c. White-capped noddy . . 85 50
311 50 c. White-tailed tropicbird . 95 60
312 60 c. Sooty tern . . . . . . 1·00 70

1985. Leaders of the World. Railway Locomotives (4th series). As T **41**. The first in each pair shows technical drawings and the second the locomotive at work.
313 5 c. multicoloured 10 10
314 5 c. multicoloured 10 10
315 10 c. multicoloured 10 10
316 10 c. multicoloured 10 10
317 30 c. multicoloured 30 35
318 30 c. multicoloured 30 35
319 $1 multicoloured . . . . . . 75 1·00
320 $1 multicoloured . . . . . . 75 1·00
DESIGNS: Nos. 313/14, GWR "Churchward 28XX", Great Britain (1905); 315/16, Class KF No. 605, China (1935); 317/18, Class 99.77 No. 99773, Germany (1952); 319/20, Pearson type, Great Britain (1853).

1985. Leaders of the World. Automobiles (2nd series). As T **46**. The first in each pair shows technical drawings and the second paintings.
321 1 c. black, green and deep green 10 10
322 1 c. multicoloured 10 10
323 20 c. black, pink and red . . 15 20
324 20 c. multicoloured 15 20
325 50 c. black, blue and violet . 20 30
326 50 c. multicoloured 20 30
327 70 c. black, pink and brown . 20 35
328 70 c. multicoloured 20 35
DESIGNS: No. 321/2, Rickenbacker (1923); 323/4, Detroit-Electric two door brougham (1914); 325/6, Packard "Clipper" (1941); 327/8, Audi "Quattro" (1982).

49 Curtiss P-40N Warhawk

1985. World War II Aircraft. Multicoloured.
329 15 c. Type **49** . . . . 1·50 60
330 40 c. Consolidated B-24 Liberator . . . . 2·00 1·25
331 50 c. Lockhead PV-1 Ventura . 2·00 1·50
332 60 c. Douglas C-54 . . . . . 2·00 1·75

50 Queen Elizabeth the Queen Mother

51 Guide playing Guitar

1985. Leaders of the World. Life and Times of Queen Elizabeth the Queen Mother. Various portraits.
334 **50** 5 c. multicoloured 10 10
335 – 5 c. multicoloured 10 10
336 – 30 c. multicoloured . . . 10 15
337 – 30 c. multicoloured . . . 10 15
338 – 60 c. multicoloured . . . 15 20
339 – 60 c. multicoloured . . . 15 20
340 – $1 multicoloured 15 35
341 – $1 multicoloured 15 35
Each value issued in pairs showing a floral pattern across the bottom of the portraits which stops short of the left-hand edge on the first stamp and of the right-hand edge on the second.

1985. 75th Anniv of Girl Guide Movement. Multicoloured.
343 15 c. Type **51** 15 20
344 40 c. Building camp-fire . . . 40 45
345 50 c. Patrol leader with Guide flag 50 55
346 60 c. Guide saluting 60 65

1985. Leaders of the World. Railway Locomotives (5th series). As T **41**. The first in each pair shows technical drawings and the second the locomotive at work.
348 10 c. multicoloured 10 15
349 10 c. multicoloured 10 15
350 40 c. multicoloured 20 30
351 40 c. multicoloured 20 30
352 65 c. multicoloured 30 45
353 65 c. multicoloured 30 45
354 $1 multicoloured 40 70
355 $1 multicoloured 40 70
DESIGNS: Nos. 348/49, LNER "Green Arrow", Great Britain (1936); 350/1, Conrail Class SD-50 diesel locomotive No. 6729, U.S.A. (1982); 352/3, "Flying Hamburger", Germany (1932); 354/5, Class 1070, Japan (1925. Dated "1908" in error).

1985. Leaders of the World. Automobiles (3rd series). As T **46**. The first in each pair shows technical drawings and the second paintings.
356 5 c. black, grey and mauve . . 10 10
357 5 c. multicoloured 10 10
358 10 c. black, pink and red . . . 10 15
359 10 c. multicoloured 10 15
360 15 c. black, brown and red . . 10 15
361 15 c. multicoloured 10 15
362 35 c. black, red and blue . . 15 30
363 35 c. multicoloured 15 30
364 40 c. black, light green & green 15 30
365 40 c. multicoloured 15 30
366 55 c. black, stone and green . . 15 30
367 55 c. multicoloured 15 30
368 $1 black, deep brown & brown 25 45
369 $1 multicoloured 25 45
370 $1.50 black, pink and red . . 30 60
371 $1.50 multicoloured 30 60
DESIGNS: Nos. 356/7, Cord "L-29" (1929); 358/9, Horch "670 V-12" (1932); 360/1, Lanchester (1901); 362/3, Citroen "2 CV" (1950); 364/5, MGA (1957); 366/7, Ferrari "250 GTO" (1962); 368/9, Ford "V-8" (1932); 370/1, Aston Martin "Lagonda" (1977).

52 Stalk-eyed Ghost Crab

1986. Crabs. Multicoloured.
372 15 c. Type **52** 60 60
373 40 c. Red and white painted crab 80 85
374 50 c. Red-spotted crab . . . . 85 1·25
375 60 c. Red hermit crab . . . . 85 1·60

1986. Ships (3rd series). Missionary Vessels. As T **26**. Multicoloured.
377 15 c. "Messenger of Peace" (schooner) 50 50
378 40 c. "John Wesley" (brig) . . 75 80
379 50 c. "Duff" (full-rigged ship) . 80 90
380 60 c. "Triton" (brigantine) . . 90 1·25

1986. 60th Birthday of Queen Elizabeth II. As T **167** of British Virgin Islands. Mult.
381 10 c. Queen wearing ceremonial cloak, New Zealand, 1977 . . 10 10
382 90 c. Before visit to France, 1957 25 35
383 $1.50 Queen in 1982 . . . . . 45 65
384 $3 In Canberra, 1982 (vert) . . 80 1·25

54 Peace Dove carrying Wreath and Rainbow

1986. 25th Anniv of United States Peace Corps.
386 **54** 50 c. multicoloured 80 90

55 Island and Flags of Tuvalu and U.S.A.

56 South Korean Player

1986. "Ameripex" Int Stamp Exhibition, Chicago.
387 **55** 60 c. multicoloured 85 95

1986. World Cup Football Championship, Mexico. Multicoloured.
388 1 c. Type **56** 10 10
389 5 c. French player 10 10
390 10 c. West German captain with World Cup trophy, 1974 . . 10 10
391 40 c. Italian player 50 50
392 60 c. World Cup final, 1974 (59 × 39 mm) 65 65
393 $1 Canadian team (59 × 39 mm) 80 1·00
394 $2 Northern Irish team (59 × 39 mm) . . . . 1·50 2·00
395 $3 English team (59 × 39 mm) 2·50 3·00

1986. Royal Wedding (1st issue). As T **168** of British Virgin Islands. Multicoloured.
397 60 c. Prince Andrew and Miss Sarah Ferguson 25 35
398 60 c. Prince Andrew with prize-winning bull 25 35
399 $1 Prince Andrew at horse trials (horiz) 30 65
400 $1 Miss Sarah Ferguson and Princess Diana (horiz) . . . 30 65
See also Nos. 433/6.

57 Mourning Gecko

1986. Lizards. Multicoloured.
402 15 c. Type **57** 55 55
403 40 c. Oceanic stump-toed gecko 1·00 1·00
404 50 c. Azure-tailed skink . . . 1·25 1·50
405 60 c. Moth skink . . . . . . 1·50 2·00

1986. "Stampex '86" Stamp Exhibition, Adelaide. No. 386 optd **STAMPEX 86 ADELAIDE** and kangaroo.
406 **54** 50 c. multicoloured 55 60

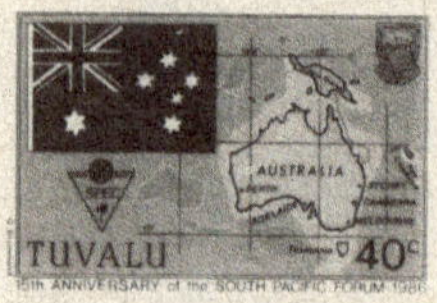

59 Map and Flag of Australia

1986. 15th Anniv of South Pacific Forum. Maps and national flags. Multicoloured.
407 40 c. Type **59** 55 60
408 40 c. Cook Islands 55 60
409 40 c. Micronesia 55 60
410 40 c. Fiji 55 60
411 40 c. Kiribati 55 60
412 40 c. Western Samoa 55 60
413 40 c. Nauru 55 60
414 40 c. Vanuatu 55 60
415 40 c. New Zealand 55 60
416 40 c. Tuvalu 55 60
417 40 c. Tonga 55 60
418 40 c. Solomon Islands 55 60
419 40 c. Papua New Guinea . . 55 60
420 40 c. Niue 55 60

1986. Automobiles (4th series). As T **46**. The first in each pair show technical drawings and the second paintings.
421 15 c. multicoloured 15 15
422 15 c. multicoloured 15 15
423 40 c. multicoloured 20 25
424 40 c. multicoloured 20 25
425 50 c. multicoloured 25 30
426 50 c. multicoloured 25 30
427 60 c. multicoloured 30 35
428 60 c. multicoloured 30 35
429 90 c. multicoloured 30 40
430 90 c. multicoloured 30 40
431 $1.50 multicoloured 45 65
432 $1.50 multicoloured 45 65
DESIGNS: Nos. 421/2, Copper "500" (1953); 423/4, Rover "2000" (1964); 425/6, Ruxton (1930); 427/8, Jowett "Jupiter" (1950); 429/30, Cobra "Daytona Coupe" (1964); 431/2, Packard Model F "Old Pacific" (1903).

1986. Royal Wedding (2nd issue). Nos. 397/400 optd **Congratulations to T.R.H. The Duke & Duchess of York.**
433 60 c. Prince Andrew and Miss Sarah Ferguson . . . . . . 70 1·00
434 60 c. Prince Andrew with prize-winning bull . . . . 70 1·00
435 $1 Prince Andrew at horse trials (horiz) . . . . 1·25 1·40
436 $1 Miss Sarah Ferguson and Princess Diana (horiz) . . . 1·25 1·40

60 Sea Star

1986. Coral Reef Life (1st series). Mult.

437	15 c. Type **60**	70	70
438	40 c. Pencil urchin	1·40	1·75
439	50 c. Fragile coral	1·60	1·90
440	60 c. Pink coral	1·75	2·00

See also Nos. 498/501, 558/62 and 826/9.

1987. Ships (4th series). Missionary Steamers. As T **26**. Multicoloured.

442	15 c. "Southern Cross IV"	85	85
443	40 c. "John Williams VI"	1·75	2·00
444	50 c. "John Williams IV"	2·00	2·25
445	60 c. M.S. "Southern Cross"	2·00	2·25

1987. Automobiles (5th series). As T **46**. The first in each pair shows technical drawings and the second paintings.

446	1 c. multicoloured	10	10
447	1 c. multicoloured	10	10
448	2 c. multicoloured	10	10
449	2 c. multicoloured	10	10
450	5 c. multicoloured	10	10
451	5 c. multicoloured	10	10
452	10 c. multicoloured	15	20
453	10 c. multicoloured	15	20
454	20 c. multicoloured	20	25
455	20 c. multicoloured	20	25
456	30 c. multicoloured	25	30
457	30 c. multicoloured	25	30
458	40 c. multicoloured	30	35
459	40 c. multicoloured	30	35
460	50 c. multicoloured	30	40
461	50 c. multicoloured	30	40
462	60 c. multicoloured	30	40
463	60 c. multicoloured	30	40
464	70 c. multicoloured	30	45
465	70 c. multicoloured	30	45
466	75 c. multicoloured	30	45
467	75 c. multicoloured	30	45
468	$1 multicoloured	40	70
469	$1 multicoloured	40	70

DESIGNS: Nos. 446/7, Talbot-Lago (1938); 448/9, Du Pont "Model G" (1930); 450/1, Riley "RM" (1950); 452/3, Chevrolet "Baby Grand" (1915); 454/5, Shelby "Mustang GT 500 KR" (1968); 456/7, Ferrari "212 Export Barchetta" (1952); 458/9, Peerless "Model 48-Six" (1912); 460/1, Sunbeam "Alpine" (1954); 462/3, Matra-Ford "MS 80" (1969); 464/5, Squire 1½ Litre (1934); 466/7, Talbot "105" (1931); 468/9, Plymouth "Model Q" (1928).

61 "Nephrolepis saligna"

62 Floral Arrangement

1987. Ferns. Multicoloured.

471	15 c. Type **61**	40	45
472	40 c. "Asplenium nidus"	70	80
473	50 c. "Microsorum scolopendria"	85	1·10
474	60 c. "Pteris tripartita"	95	1·25

1987. Flowers and "Fous". Designs showing either floral arrangements or "fous" (women's headdresses). Multicoloured.

476	15 c. Type **62**	25	25
477	15 c. "Fou"	25	25
478	40 c. "Fou"	55	65
479	40 c. Floral arrangement	55	65
480	50 c. Floral arrangement	65	80
481	50 c. "Fou"	65	80
482	60 c. "Fou"	75	90
483	60 c. Floral arrangement	75	90

63 Queen Victoria, 1897 (photo by Downey)

1987. Royal Ruby Wedding and 150th Anniv of Queen Victoria's Accession.

484	**63**	40 c. brown, black and green	45	50
485	–	60 c. purple, black and green	65	75
486	–	80 c. brown, black and blue	85	1·00
487	–	$1 brown, black and purple	1·10	1·25
488	–	$2 multicoloured	1·90	2·50

DESIGNS: 60 c. Wedding of Princess Elizabeth and Duke of Edinburgh, 1947; 80 c. Queen, Duke of Edinburgh and Prince Charles, 1950; $1 Queen with Princess Anne, 1950; $2 Queen Elizabeth II, 1970.

64 Coconut Crab

1987. Crustaceans. Multicoloured.

490	40 c. Type **64**	1·00	1·00
491	50 c. Painted crayfish	1·25	1·25
492	60 c. Ocean crayfish	1·40	1·75

65 Aborigine and Ayers Rock

1987. World Scout Jamboree, Australia, and Bicent of Australian Settlement. Multicoloured.

493	40 c. Type **65**	30	45
494	60 c. Capt. Cook and H.M.S. "Endeavour"	90	1·00
495	$1 Scout saluting and Scout Park entrance	95	1·25
496	$1.50 Koala and kangaroo	1·00	1·50

1988. Coral Reef Life (2nd series). As T **60**. Multicoloured.

498	15 c. Spanish dancer	60	60
499	40 c. Hard corals	1·00	1·25
500	50 c. Feather stars	1·00	1·50
501	60 c. Staghorn corals	1·00	1·50

66 Red Junglefowl

1988. Birds. Multicoloured.

502	5 c. Type **66**	15	15
503	10 c. White tern	20	20
504	15 c. Common noddy	30	20
505	20 c. Phoenix petrel	40	40
506	25 c. American golden plover	45	45
507	30 c. Crested tern	50	45
508	35 c. Sooty tern	50	50
509	40 c. Bristle-thighed curlew	50	40
510	45 c. Bar-tailed godwit	60	45
511	50 c. Eastern reef heron	60	50
512	55 c. Great frigate bird	70	70
513	60 c. Red-footed booby	70	75
514	70 c. Rufous-necked sandpiper	70	1·00
515	$1 Long-tailed koel	70	1·50
516	$2 Red-tailed tropic bird	80	3·00
517	$5 Banded rail	1·25	6·00

67 Henri Dunant (founder)

69 "Ganoderma applanatum"

68 H.M.S. "Endeavour"

1988. 125th Anniv of International Red Cross.

518	**67**	15 c. red and brown	10	20
519	–	40 c. red and blue	20	40
520	–	50 c. red and green	25	50
521	–	60 c. red and purple	35	70

DESIGNS: 40 c. Junior Red Cross members on parade; 50 c. Red Cross worker with boy in wheelchair; 60 c. First aid training.

1988. Voyages of Captain Cook. Multicoloured.

523	20 c. Type **68**	75	80
524	40 c. Stern of H.M.S. "Endeavour"	90	1·10
525	50 c. Cook preparing to land at Tahiti (vert)	1·00	1·25
526	60 c. Maori chief (vert)	1·00	1·40
527	80 c. H.M.S. "Resolution" and Hawaiian canoe	1·25	1·75
528	$1 "Captain Cook" (after Nathaniel Dance) (vert)	1·40	1·90

1988. Fungi (1st series). Multicoloured.

530	40 c. Type **69**	1·25	1·40
531	50 c. "Pseudoepicoccum cocos" (brown leaf spot)	1·40	1·50
532	60 c. "Rigidoporus lineatus" ("Rigidoporus zonalis")	1·60	1·75
533	90 c. "Rigidoporus microporus"	1·75	2·00

See also Nos. 554/7.

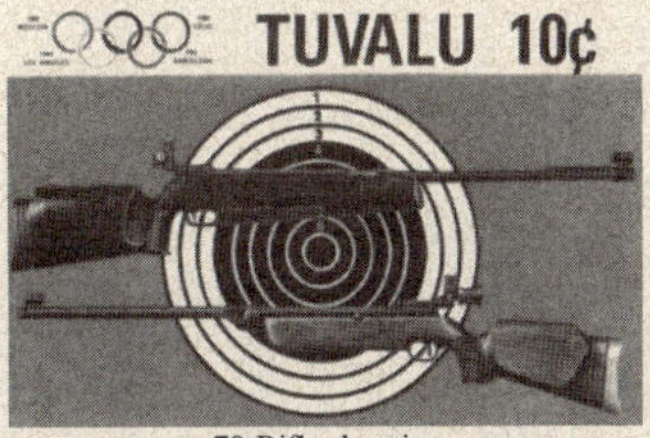

70 Rifle-shooting

1988. Olympic Games, Seoul. Multicoloured.

534	10 c. Type **70**	25	45
535	20 c. Judo	35	55
536	40 c. Canoeing	60	75
537	60 c. Swimming	80	1·10
538	80 c. Yachting	1·00	1·60
539	$1 Gymnastics	1·25	1·60

71 Queen Elizabeth II in Ceremonial Canoe

1988. 10th Anniv of Independence.

540	**71**	60 c. multicoloured	60	70
541	–	90 c. multicoloured	90	1·10
542	–	$1 multicoloured (horiz)	1·00	1·40
543	–	$1.20 multicoloured	1·25	1·75

DESIGNS: 90 c. to $1.20, Scenes from Royal Visit of 1982.

72 Virgin Mary

1988. Christmas. Multicoloured.

545	15 c. Type **72**	45	40
546	40 c. Christ Child	80	75
547	60 c. Joseph	95	1·50

73 Dancing Skirt and Dancer

1989. Traditional Dancing Skirts. Designs showing skirts and dancer silhouettes.

549	**73**	40 c. multicoloured	70	90
550	–	50 c. multicoloured	80	1·00
551	–	60 c. multicoloured	90	1·25
552	–	90 c. multicoloured	1·40	1·75

1989. Fungi (2nd series). As T **69**. Multicoloured.

554	40 c. "Trametes marianna" ("Trametes muelleri")	1·75	1·75
555	50 c. "Pestalotiopsis palmarum" (grey leaf spot)	1·90	1·90
556	60 c. "Trametes cingulata"	2·00	2·00
557	90 c. "Schizophyllum commune"	2·75	2·75

1989. Coral Reef Life (3rd series). As T **60**. Multicoloured.

558	40 c. Pennant coralfish	1·50	1·50
559	50 c. Orange-finned anemonefish	1·75	1·75
560	60 c. Narrow-banned batfish	2·00	2·00
561	90 c. Thread-finned butterflyfish	2·50	2·50

75 Trumpet Triton Shell

76 "Cocus nucifera"

1989. Christmas. Multicoloured.

564	40 c. Type **75**	75	75
565	50 c. Posy of flowers	90	90
566	60 c. Germinating coconut	1·10	1·10
567	90 c. Jewellery	2·00	2·40

1990. Tropical Trees. Multicoloured.

568	15 c. Type **76**	70	70
569	30 c. "Rhizophora samoensis"	1·00	1·00
570	40 c. "Messerschmidia argentea"	1·25	1·25
571	50 c. "Pandanus tectorius"	1·40	1·60
572	60 c. "Hernandia nymphaeifolia"	1·60	1·75
573	90 c. "Pisonia grandis"	2·00	2·50

77 Penny Black with "Stamp World London 90" Emblem

1990. 150th Anniv of the Penny Black, and "Stamp World London 90" International Stamp Exhibition.

574	**77**	15 c. multicoloured	1·25	1·25
575		40 c. multicoloured	2·50	2·50
576		90 c. multicoloured	4·00	4·50

78 Japanese Camouflaged Freighter

1990. Second World War Ships (1st series). Multicoloured.

578	15 c. Type **78**	1·00	1·00
579	30 c. U.S.S. "Unimack" (seaplane tender)	1·50	1·50
580	40 c. "Amagiri" (Japanese destroyer)	1·60	1·60
581	50 c. U.S.S. "Platte" (attack transport)	1·75	1·75
582	60 c. Japanese "Shumushu" Class escort	1·90	1·90
583	90 c. U.S.S. "Independence" (aircraft carrier)	2·75	2·75

See also Nos. 613/16.

79 "Erythrina fusca"

81 Mary and Joseph travelling to Bethlehem

80 Land Resources Survey

1990. Flowers. Multicoloured.

584	15 c. Type **79**	30	40
585	30 c. "Capparis cordifolia"	50	60
586	40 c. "Portulaca pilosa"	60	70
587	50 c. "Cordia subcordata"	75	85
588	60 c. "Scaevola taccada"	80	1·00
589	90 c. "Suriana maritima"	1·25	2·00

1990. 40th Anniv of United Nations Development Programme. Multicoloured.

590	40 c. Type **80**	80	80
591	60 c. Satellite earth station	1·50	1·50
592	$1.20 "Te Tautai" (trawler)	3·25	4·00

1990. Christmas. Multicoloured.

593	15 c. Type **81**	55	55
594	40 c. The Nativity	1·00	1·00
595	60 c. Shepherds with flock	1·50	1·50
596	90 c. Wise Men bearing gifts	2·00	2·25

82 Ramose Murex

84 Green Turtle

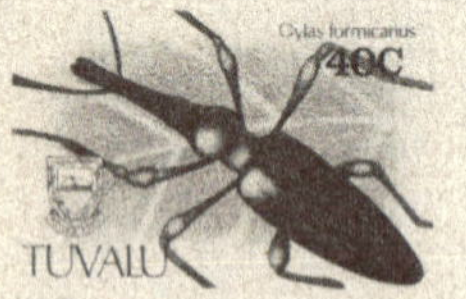

83 "Cylas formicarius" (beetle)

1991. Sea Shells. Multicoloured.

597	40 c. Type **82**	1·25	1·25
598	50 c. Marble cone	1·40	1·40
599	60 c. Commercial trochus	1·60	1·60
600	$1.50 Green map cowrie	3·25	3·75

1991. Insects. Multicoloured.

601	40 c. Type **83**	1·60	1·40
602	50 c. "Heliothis armiger" (moth)	1·75	1·50
603	60 c. "Spodoptera litura" (moth)	2·00	2·00
604	$1.50 "Agrius convolvuli" (moth)	4·75	6·00

1991. Endangered Marine Life. Multicoloured.

605	40 c. Type **84**	1·00	90
606	50 c. Humpback whale	1·50	1·00
607	60 c. Hawksbill turtle	1·50	1·40
608	$1.50 Sperm whale	3·25	5·00

85 Football

87 Traditional Dancers

86 U.S.S. "Tennessee" (battleship)

1991. 9th South Pacific Games. Multicoloured.

609	40 c. Type **85**	1·25	1·00
610	50 c. Volleyball	1·75	1·60
611	60 c. Lawn tennis	2·50	2·50
612	$1.50 Cricket	5·00	5·50

1991. Second World War Ships (2nd series). Multicoloured.

613	40 c. Type **86**	2·00	1·50
614	50 c. "Haguro" (Japanese cruiser)	2·25	1·75
615	60 c. H.M.N.Z.S. "Achilles" (cruiser)	2·50	2·25
616	$1.50 U.S.S. "North Carolina" (battleship)	5·50	6·50

1991. Christmas. Multicoloured.

617	40 c. Type **87**	1·60	1·25
618	50 c. Solo dancer	1·75	1·50
619	60 c. Dancers in green costumes	2·25	1·75
620	$1.50 Dancers in multicoloured costumes	4·50	6·00

88 Southern Fish Constellation

1992. Pacific Star Constellations. Mult.

621	40 c. Type **88**	1·75	1·50
622	50 c. Scorpion	2·00	1·75
623	60 c. Archer	2·50	2·25
624	$1.50 Southern Cross	5·50	6·50

89 King George VI and Cargo Liner

1992. Cent of British Occupation of Tuvalu. Mult.

625	40 c. Type **89**	1·75	1·50
626	50 c. King George V and freighter with barges at wharf	2·00	1·50
627	60 c. King Edward VII and freighter	2·25	1·75
628	$1.50 Queen Victoria and warship	4·00	5·50

90 Columbus with King Ferdinand and Queen Isabella of Spain

1992. 500th Anniv of Discovery of America by Columbus.

629	**90**	40 c. blue and black	70	70
630	–	50 c. purple and black	80	80
631	–	60 c. green and black	90	1·00
632	–	$1.50 purple and black	2·25	3·00

DESIGNS: 50 c. Columbus and Polynesians; 60 c. Columbus and South American Indians; $1.50, Columbus and North American Indians.

91 Blue-spotted Butterflyfish

1992. Fishes. Multicoloured.

633	15 c. Type **91**	40	30
634	20 c. Bridled parrotfish	45	30
635	25 c. Clown surgeonfish	45	40
636	30 c. Moon wrasse	55	40
637	35 c. Harlequin filefish	60	40
638	40 c. Bird wrasse	70	45
639	45 c. Black-finned pigfish	75	50
640	50 c. Blue damselfish	80	60
641	60 c. Hump-headed wrasse	90	70
642	70 c. Ornate butterflyfish (vert)	1·00	1·00
643	90 c. Saddle butterflyfish (vert)	1·25	1·25
644	$1 Vagabond butterflyfish (vert)	1·40	1·40
645	$2 Pennant coralfish (vert)	2·25	2·75
646	$3 Moorish idol (vert)	3·00	3·75

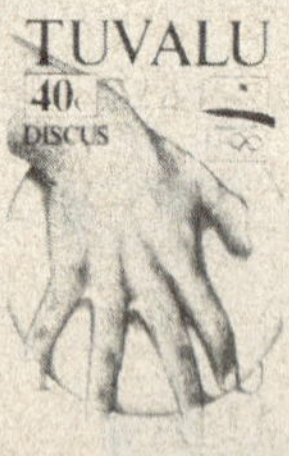

92 Discus Throwing

95 Fishermen and Angel

93 Blue Coral

1992. Olympic Games, Barcelona. Mult.

647	40 c. Type **92**	1·00	90
648	50 c. Javelin throwing	1·25	1·00
649	60 c. Shotput	1·50	1·25
650	$1.50 Competitor's foot	3·00	4·00

1992. Endangered Species. Blue Coral.

652	**93**	10 c. multicoloured	85	85
653	–	25 c. multicoloured	1·75	1·75
654	–	30 c. multicoloured	1·90	1·90
655	–	35 c. multicoloured	2·00	2·00

DESIGNS: 25 c. to 35 c. Different coral formations.

1992. "Kuala Lumpur '92" International Philatelic Exhibition. Nos. 636, 638 and 640/1 optd **KL92 KUALA LUMPUR '92** and emblem.

656	30 c. Moon wrasse	1·40	1·40
657	40 c. Bird wrasse	1·60	1·60
658	50 c. Blue damselfish	1·75	1·75
659	60 c. Hump-headed wrasse	1·75	1·75

1992. Christmas. Multicoloured.

660	40 c. Type **95**	80	60
661	50 c. Fishing canoes following star	90	70
662	60 c. Nativity scene	1·00	90
663	$1.50 Christmas gifts	2·00	3·00

96 "Calophyllum inophyllum"

1993. Flowers. Multicoloured.

664	40 c. Type **96**	90	80
665	50 c. "Hibiscus tiliaceus"	1·10	95
666	60 c. "Lantana camara"	1·25	1·10
667	$1.50 "Plumeria rubra"	2·75	3·75

97 Japanese Nakajima B5N "Kate" Bombers attacking Island

1993. 50th Anniv of War in the Pacific. Mult.

668	40 c. Type **97**	1·50	1·25
669	50 c. Japanese anti-aircraft gun (vert)	1·75	1·25
670	60 c. American troops storming beach	1·75	1·50
671	$1.50 Map of Funafuti Atoll (vert)	3·75	4·50

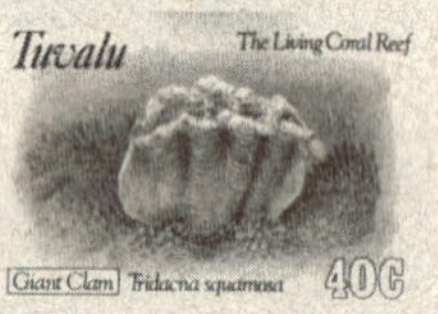

99 Fluted Giant Clam

1993. Marine Life. Multicoloured.

673	40 c. Type **99**	75	75
674	50 c. Anemone crab	85	85
675	60 c. Octopus	95	95
676	$1.50 Green turtle	2·25	2·75

100 Queen Elizabeth II and Prince Philip in Land Rover

1993. 40th Anniv of Coronation. Mult.

677	40 c. Type **100**	85	75
678	50 c. Queen Elizabeth drinking kava	95	90
679	60 c. Queen Elizabeth with parasol	1·10	1·10
680	$1.50 Ceremonial welcome	2·50	3·00

101 Hermit Crab and Shells on Beach

102 Virgin and Child with Christmas Tree

1993. Environmental Protection. Mult.

684	40 c. Type **101**	75	65
685	50 c. Conch shell and starfish	85	80
686	60 c. Crab, seaweed and shells	95	95
687	$1.50 Herring gull and human footprint on beach	2·25	3·00

1993. Christmas. Multicoloured.

689	40 c. Type **102**	80	70
690	50 c. Candle	90	80
691	60 c. Angel	1·00	1·00
692	$1.50 Decorated palm tree	2·25	3·50

103 Beach

1994. Island Scenery. Multicoloured.

694	40 c. Type **103**	80	70
695	50 c. Lagoon	90	80
696	60 c. Distant island	1·00	1·00
697	$1.50 Launch and outrigger canoes on beach	2·25	3·50

104 Irish Red Setter

105 World Cup, Australian Player and Sydney Opera House

1994. Chinese New Year ("Year of the Dog"). Multicoloured.

698	40 c. Type **104**	80	90
699	50 c. Golden retriever	90	1·00
700	60 c. West highland terrier	1·00	1·10
701	$1.50 German shepherd	2·50	3·75

1994. World Cup Football Championship, U.S.A. Multicoloured.

702	40 c. Type **105**	50	50
703	50 c. English player and Big Ben, London	60	60
704	60 c. Argentinian player and House of Assembly, Buenos Aires	70	75
705	$1.50 German player and Brandenburg Gate, Berlin	2·00	2·50

106 Giant Button Top

109 "Saturn V" Launch

1994. Sea Snails. Multicoloured.

707	40 c. Type **106**	90	75
708	50 c. Tapestry turban	1·00	85
709	60 c. "Planaxis savignyi"	1·25	1·00
710	$1.50 Green-lined paper bubble	2·75	3·50

1994. "Singpex '94" Stamp Exhibition. Nos. 502/3 and 509/10 optd **SINGPEX '94 AUG 31-SEP 5 SINGAPORE** and emblem.

712	5 c. Type **66**	30	40
713	10 c. White tern	30	40
714	40 c. Bristle-thighed curlew	60	65
715	45 c. Bar-tailed godwit	65	70

1994. 25th Anniv of First Manned Moon Landing. Multicoloured.

716	40 c. Type **109**	1·00	1·00
717	50 c. "Apollo 11" capsule	1·10	1·10
718	60 c. Neil Armstrong and American flag	1·25	1·25
719	$1.50 Capsule re-entry	2·00	2·00

110 Boys swimming with Log

1994. Christmas. Local Customs. Multicoloured.

720	40 c. Type **110**	85	60
721	50 c. Fishermen landing catch	95	75
722	60 c. Christmas dinner	1·10	95
723	$1.50 Traditional dancers	2·25	3·00

111 Pig asleep

1995. Chinese New Year ("Year of the Pig"). Multicoloured.

724 40 c. Type **111** . . . 65 60
725 50 c. Two pigs and vegetation 75 70
726 60 c. Three pigs . . . 85 85
727 $1.50 Sow suckling piglets . . 1·75 2·75

112 Emblem and Man with Produce in Wheelbarrow

1995. 50th Anniv of F.A.O. Multicoloured.

728 40 c. Type **112** . . . 80 70
729 50 c. Man holding basket of food 90 80
730 60 c. Woman slicing produce . 1·00 1·00
731 $1.50 Woman mixing food . . 2·25 3·00

113 Beach and Lagoon

1995. Visit South Pacific Year. Multicoloured.

732 40 c. Type **113** . . . 70 60
733 50 c. Catamaran . . . 80 70
734 60 c. Traditional hut . . . 90 90
735 $1.50 Village on beach . . . 2·00 2·75

114 "Dendrobium comptonii"

1995. Pacific Coastal Orchids. Multicoloured.

736 40 c. Type **114** . . . 80 70
737 50 c. "Dendrobium involutum" 90 80
738 60 c. "Dendrobium rarum" . . 1·00 1·00
739 $1.50 "Grammatophyllum scriptum" . . . 2·25 3·00

115 Japanese Soldier and Maps of Tuvalu and Japan

1995. 50th Anniv of End of Second World War. Multicoloured.

740 40 c. Type **115** . . . 1·25 90
741 50 c. American soldier and beach landing . . . 1·40 1·00
742 60 c. American marine and tree 1·50 1·25
743 $1.50 American soldier and atomic explosion . . . 3·00 3·50

119 "Silent Night" and Aerial View of Airfield

1995. Christmas. Christmas Carols. Multicoloured.

747 40 c. Type **119** . . . 70 60
748 50 c. "O Come all ye Faithful" and choir boys . . . 85 75
749 60 c. "The First Nowell" and choir girls . . . 1·00 1·00
750 $1.50 "Hark the Herald Angels sing" and angel . . . 2·50 3·25

123 Volleyball

1996. Olympic Games, Atlanta. Multicoloured.

756 40 c. Type **123** . . . 50 50
757 50 c. Swimming . . . 60 55
758 60 c. Weightlifting . . . 70 70
759 $1.50 Boxing . . . 1·75 2·25

1996. "TAIPEI '96" 10th Asian International Stamp Exhibition, Taiwan. No. 639 surch **$1.00 TAIPEI '96 21-27 OCTOBER** and emblem.

760 $1 on 45 c. Black-finned pigfish 1·25 1·50

125 Children being Immunised

1996. 50th Anniv of U.N.I.C.E.F. Multicoloured.

761 40 c. Type **125** . . . 55 55
762 50 c. Teacher and children . . 65 65
763 60 c. Domestic water tanks and child . . . 75 75
764 $1.50 Children in hydroponic greenhouse . . . 1·90 2·50

126 Wise Men following Star

1996. Christmas. Multicoloured.

765 40 c. Type **126** . . . 55 45
766 50 c. Shepherds and star . . 65 55
767 60 c. Wise men presenting gifts 75 75
768 $1.50 The Nativity . . . 1·90 2·75

1997. Fishes (2nd series). As T **14**. Multicoloured.

770 25 c. Sehel's grey mullet . . 20 25
771 30 c. Leatherback . . . 25 30
772 40 c. Hump-backed snapper ("Paddletail") . . . 30 35
773 45 c. Long-nosed emperor . . 35 40
774 50 c. Blue-spined unicornfish 40 45
775 55 c. Oblique-banded snapper 40 45
776 60 c. Twin-spotted snapper ("Red bass") . . . 45 50
777 70 c. Rusty jobfish . . . 55 60
778 90 c. Leopard flounder . . 70 75
779 $1 Ruby snapper . . . 75 80
780 $2 Yellow-striped snapper . . 1·50 1·60
781 $3 Black jack . . . 2·25 2·50

128 White Pekin Ducks

1997. "Pacific '97" International Stamp Exhibition, San Francisco. Ducks. Multicoloured.

782 40 c. Type **128** . . . 65 55
783 50 c. Muscovy ducks . . . 75 65
784 60 c. Pacific black ducks . . 85 85
785 $1.50 Mandarin ducks . . . 2·00 2·50

129 Korat King Cat

1997. Cats. Multicoloured.

786 40 c. Type **129** . . . 60 50
787 50 c. Long-haired ginger kitten 70 60
788 60 c. Shaded cameo . . . 80 80
789 $1.50 Maine coon . . . 2·00 2·50

1997. Golden Wedding of Queen Elizabeth and Prince Philip. As T **87** of Kiribati. Multicoloured.

791 40 c. Queen Elizabeth and Prince Philip in Land Rover . . . 40 55
792 40 c. Queen Elizabeth . . . 40 55
793 50 c. Queen Elizabeth accepting ceremonial gift . . . 50 65
794 50 c. Prince Philip . . . 50 65
795 60 c. Three portraits of Queen Elizabeth . . . 65 75
796 60 c. Queen Elizabeth and Prince Philip leaving Philatelic Bureau 65 75

Nos. 791/2, 793/4 and 795/6 respectively were printed together, se-tenant, with the backgrounds forming composite designs.

HAVE YOU READ THE NOTES AT THE BEGINNING OF THIS CATALOGUE?
These often provide answers to the enquiries we receive.

130 Turtle Hunting

1997. Christmas. Multicoloured.

798 40 c. Type **130** . . . 45 40
799 50 c. Pole fishing . . . 55 50
800 60 c. Canoe racing . . . 65 55
801 $1.50 Traditional dancing . . 1·40 2·00

1998. 80th Anniv of the Royal Air Force. As T **270** of Samoa. Multicoloured.

804 40 c. Hawker Woodcock . . . 50 50
805 50 c. Vickers Victoria . . . 60 60
806 60 c. Bristol Brigand . . . 70 70
807 $1.50 De Havilland D.H.C.1 Chipmunk . . . 1·50 2·00

132 "Los Reyes" and "Santiago" (Alvare Mendana)

1998. Ships (5th series). Multicoloured.

809 40 c. Type **132** . . . 45 40
810 50 c. "Morning Star II" (missionary schooner) . . . 55 50
811 60 c. "The Light" (missionary brigantine) . . . 65 60
812 $1.50 New Zealand missionary schooner . . . 1·40 1·75

133 Bottlenose Dolphin

1998. Dolphins and Porpoises. Multicoloured.

813 40 c. Type **133** . . . 45 40
814 50 c. Dall's porpoise . . . 55 50
815 60 c. Harbour porpoise . . . 65 60
816 $1.50 Common dolphin . . . 1·40 1·75

134 Prime Minister Bikenibeu Paeniu, Teacher and Class

1999. 20th Anniv of Independence. Multicoloured.

817 40 c. Type **134** . . . 30 35
818 60 c. Prime Minister Kamuta Latasi and diagram of communications network . . 45 50
819 90 c. Sir Tomasi Puapua and emblem of Trust Fund . . . 70 75
820 $1.50 Sir Toaripi Lauti and emblem of Maritime School 1·10 1·25

135 Mary and Joseph travelling to Bethlehem

1998. Christmas. Multicoloured.

822 40 c. Type **135** . . . 30 35
823 50 c. Shepherds and angel . . 40 45
824 60 c. The Nativity . . . 45 50
825 $1.50 Visit of Wise Men . . . 1·10 1·25

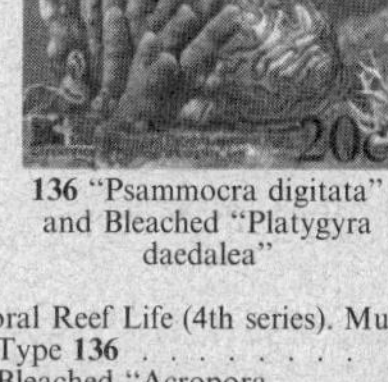

136 "Psammocra digitata" and Bleached "Platygyra daedalea"

1998. Coral Reef Life (4th series). Multicoloured.

826 20 c. Type **136** . . . 15 20
827 30 c. Bleached "Acropora robusta" . . . 25 30
828 50 c. Bleached "Acropora hyacinthus" . . . 40 45
829 $1 Bleached "Acropora danai" and "Montastrea curta" . . 75 80

138 "Heemskerk" (Tasman), 1642

1999. "Australia '99" World Stamp Exhibition, Melbourne. Ships (6th series). Multicoloured.

832 40 c. Type **138** . . . 30 35
833 50 c. H.M.S. "Endeavour" (Cook), 1769 . . . 40 45
834 90 c. "Sophia Jane" (paddle-steamer), 1831 . . . 70 75
835 $1.50 "Chusan I" (screw steamer), 1852 . . . 1·10 1·25

OFFICIAL STAMPS

1981. Nos. 105/22 optd **OFFICIAL**.

O 1	**14**	1 c. multicoloured	10	10
O 2	–	2 c. multicoloured	10	10
O 3	–	4 c. multicoloured	10	10
O 4	–	5 c. multicoloured	10	10
O 5	–	6 c. multicoloured	10	10
O 6	–	8 c. multicoloured	10	10
O 7	–	10 c. multicoloured . . .	15	15
O 8	–	15 c. multicoloured . . .	20	20
O 9	–	20 c. multicoloured . . .	25	25
O10a	–	25 c. multicoloured . . .	30	30
O11	–	30 c. multicoloured . . .	30	30
O12	–	35 c. multicoloured . . .	30	30
O13	–	40 c. multicoloured . . .	30	30
O14	–	45 c. multicoloured . . .	35	35
O15	–	50 c. multicoloured . . .	40	40
O16	–	70 c. multicoloured . . .	50	50
O17	–	$1 multicoloured	50	50
O18a	–	$2 multicoloured	1·10	1·00
O19	–	$5 multicoloured	1·40	1·00

1983. Nos. 202/3a, 205/12, 224 and 234 optd **OFFICIAL**.

O20	5 c. Wedding and baby food baskets	10	40
O21	10 c. Hand-carved model of canoe	10	40
O22	15 c. Ladies sun hats	15	70
O23	25 c. Pandanus baskets . . .	25	60
O24	30 c. on 45 c. Reef sandals and fish trap	50	70
O25	30 c. Basket tray and coconut stand	30	70
O26	35 c. Pandanus pillows and shell necklaces	40	75
O27	40 c. Round baskets and fans	45	75
O28	45 c. Reef sandals and fish trap	45	75
O29	50 c. Rat trap	50	75
O30	60 c. on $1 Pump drill and adze	75	75
O31	60 c. Fisherman's waterproof boxes	60	1·00
O32	$1 Pump drill and adze . . .	75	1·00
O33	$2 Fisherman's hat and canoe bailers	1·25	1·00
O34	$5 Fishing rod, lures and scoop nets	3·00	2·50

1989. Nos. 502/17 optd **OFFICIAL**.

O35	5 c. Type **66**	15	45
O36	10 c. White tern	15	45
O37	15 c. Common noddy	30	45
O38	20 c. Phoenix petrel	30	45
O39	25 c. American golden plover	40	65
O40	30 c. Crested tern	40	65
O41	35 c. Sooty tern	45	70
O42	40 c. Bristle-thighed curlew .	45	70
O43	45 c. Bar-tailed godwit . . .	55	75
O44	50 c. Eastern reef heron . . .	60	80
O45	55 c. Great frigate bird . . .	60	80
O46	60 c. Red-footed booby . . .	70	80
O47	70 c. Rufous-necked sandpiper	80	90
O48	$1 Long-tailed koel	1·10	1·10
O49	$2 Red-tailed tropic bird . .	2·00	1·90
O50	$5 Banded rail	4·25	4·50

POSTAGE DUE STAMPS

D **1** Tuvalu Crest

1981.

D 1	D **1**	1 c. black and purple . .	10	10
D 2		2 c. black and blue . . .	10	10
D 3		5 c. black and brown . .	10	10
D13		10 c. black and green . .	10	10
D14		20 c. black and brown .	15	20
D 6		30 c. black and orange .	20	30
D 7		40 c. black and blue . .	25	40
D 8		50 c. black and green . .	30	45
D 9		$1 black and mauve . .	50	80

Some values exist with or without the imprint date at foot.

APPENDIX

The following stamps for individual islands of Tuvalu have either been issued in excess of postal needs, or have not been made available to the public in reasonable quantities at face value.

FUNAFUTI

1984.

Leaders of the World. Railway Locomotives (1st series). Two designs for each value, the first showing technical drawings and the second the locomotive at work. 15, 20, 30, 40, 50, 60 c. each × 2.

Leaders of the World. Automobiles (1st series). Two designs for each value, the first showing technical drawings and the second the car in action. 1, 10, 40 c., $1 each × 2.

Leaders of the World. Railway Locomotives (2nd series). Two designs for each value, the first showing technical drawings and the second the locomotive at work. 5, 15, 25, 35, 40, 55, 60 c., $1 each × 2.

1985.

Leaders of the World. Automobiles (2nd series). Two designs for each value, the first showing technical drawings and the second the car in action. 1, 30, 55, 60 c. each × 2.

Leaders of the World. Railway Locomotives (3rd series). Two designs for each value, the first showing technical drawings and the second the locomotive at work. 5, 15, 35, 40, 50 c., $1 each × 2.

Leaders of the World. Life and Times of Queen Elizabeth the Queen Mother. Two designs for each value, showing different portraits. 5, 25, 80 c., $1.05 each × 2.

1986.

60th Birthday of Queen Elizabeth II. 10, 50 c., $1.50, $3.50.

Royal Wedding (1st issue). 60 c., $1 each × 2.

Royal Wedding (2nd issue). Previous Royal Wedding stamps optd **Congratulations T.R.H. The Duke & Duchess of York**. 60 c., $1 each × 2.

Railway Locomotives (4th series). Two designs for each value, the first showing technical drawings and the second the locomotive at work. 20, 40, 60 c., $1.50 each × 2.

1987.

Automobiles (3rd series). Two designs for each value, the first showing technical drawings and the second the car in action. 10, 20, 40, 60, 75, 80 c., $1.50 each × 2.

Royal Ruby Wedding. 20, 50, 75 c., $1.20, $1.75.

1988.

Olympic Games, Seoul. 10, 20, 40, 50, 80, 90 c.

NANUMAGA

1984.

Leaders of the World. Automobiles (1st series). Two designs for each value, the first showing technical drawings and the second the car in action. 5, 10, 25, 30, 40 c., $1 each × 2.

Leaders of the World. British Monarchs. Two designs for each value, forming a composite picture. 10, 20, 30, 40, 50 c., $1 each × 2.

Leaders of the World. Automobiles (2nd series). Two designs for each value, the first showing technical drawings and the second the car in action. 5, 10, 50 c., $1 each × 2.

1985.

Leaders of the World. Railway Locomotives. Two designs for each value, the first showing technical drawings and the second the locomotive at work. 10, 25, 50, 60 c. each × 2.

Leaders of the World. Flowers. 25, 30, 40, 50 c. each × 2.

Leaders of the World. Automobiles (3rd series). Two designs for each value, the first showing technical drawings and the second the car in action. 10, 25, 75 c., $1 each × 2.

Leaders of the World. Life and Times of Queen Elizabeth the Queen Mother. Two designs for each value, showing different portraits. 15, 55, 65, 90 c. each × 2.

1986.

60th Birthday of Queen Elizabeth II. 5 c., $1, $1.75, $2.50.

World Cup Football Championship, Mexico. 1, 2, 5, 5, 10, 20, 35, 50, 60, 75 c., $1, $2, $4.

Royal Wedding (1st issue). 60 c., $1 each × 2.

Royal Wedding (2nd issue). Previous Royal Wedding stamps optd as for Funafuti. 60 c., $1 each × 2.

1987.

Automobiles (4th series). Two designs for each value, the first showing technical drawings and the second the car in action. 5, 10, 15, 20, 25, 40, 60 c., $1 each × 2.

Royal Ruby Wedding. 15, 35, 60 c., $1.50, $1.75.

NANUMEA

1984.

Leaders of the World. Railway Locomotives (1st series). Two designs for each value, the first showing technical drawings and the second the locomotive at work. 15, 20, 30, 40, 50, 60 c. each × 2.

Leaders of the World. Famous Cricketers. Two designs for each value, the first showing a portrait and the second the cricketer in action. 1, 10, 40 c., $1 each × 2.

1985.

Leaders of the World. Automobiles (1st series). Two designs for each value, the first showing technical drawings and the second the car in action. 5, 40, 50, 60 c. each × 2.

Leaders of the World. Railway Locomotives (2nd series). Two designs for each value, the first showing technical drawings and the second the locomotive at work. 1, 35, 50, 60 c. each × 2.

Leaders of the World. Automobiles (2nd series). Two designs for each value, the first showing technical drawings and the second the car in action. 15, 20, 50, 60 c. each × 2.

Leaders of the World. Cats. 5, 30, 50 c., $1 each × 2.

Leaders of the World. Life and Times of Queen Elizabeth the Queen Mother. Two designs for each value, showing different portraits. 5, 30, 75 c., $1.05 each × 2.

1986.

60th Birthday of Queen Elizabeth II. 10, 80 c., $1.75, $3.

World Cup Football Championship, Mexico. 1, 2, 5, 10, 25, 40, 50, 75, 90 c., $1, $2.50, $4.

Royal Wedding (1st issue). 60 c., $1 each × 2.

Royal Wedding (2nd issue). Previous Royal Wedding stamps optd as for Funafuti. 60 c., $1 each × 2.

Automobiles (3rd series). Two designs for each value, the first showing technical drawings and the second the car in action. 10, 20, 35, 50, 75 c., $2 each × 2.

1987.

Royal Ruby Wedding. 40, 60, 80 c., $1, $2.

NIUTAO

1984.

Leaders of the World. Automobiles (1st series). Two designs for each value, the first showing technical drawings and the second the car in action. 15, 30, 40, 50 c. each × 2.

Leaders of the World. Railway Locomotives (1st series). Two designs for each value, the first showing technical drawings and the second the locomotive at work. 5, 10, 20, 40, 50 c., $1 each × 2.

1985.

Leaders of the World. Famous Cricketers. Two designs for each value, the first showing a portrait and the second the cricketer in action. 1, 15, 50 c., $1 each × 2.

Leaders of the World. Birth Bicent of John J. Audubon (ornithologist). Birds. 5, 15, 25 c., $1 each × 2.

Leaders of the World. Automobiles (2nd series). Two designs for each value, the first showing technical drawings and the second the car in action. 20, 25, 40, 60 c. each × 2.

Leaders of the World. Railway Locomotives (2nd series). Two designs for each value, the first showing technical drawings and the second the locomotive at work. 10, 30, 45, 60, 75 c., $1.20 each × 2.

Leaders of the World. Life and Times of Queen Elizabeth the Queen Mother. Two designs for each value, showing different portraits. 15, 35, 70, 95 c. each × 2.

1986.

60th Birthday of Queen Elizabeth II. 5, 60 c., $1.50, $3.50.

Royal Wedding (1st series). 60 c., $1 each × 2.

Royal Wedding (2nd series). Previous Royal Wedding stamps optd as for Funafuti. 60 c., $1 each × 2.

1987.

Royal Ruby Wedding. 60th Birthday of Queen Elizabeth II issue of 1986 optd **40th WEDDING ANNIVERSARY OF H.M. QUEEN ELIZABETH II**. 5, 60 c., $1.50, $3.50.

NUI

1984.

Leaders of the World. Railway Locomotives (1st series). Two designs for each value, the first showing technical drawings and the second the locomotive at work. 15, 25, 30, 50 c. each × 2.

Leaders of the World. British Monarchs. Two designs for each value, forming a composite picture. 1, 5, 15, 40, 50 c., $1 each × 2.

1985.

Leaders of the World. Railway Locomotives (2nd series). Two designs for each value, the first showing technical drawings and the second the locomotive at work. 5, 15, 25 c., $1 each × 2.

Leaders of the World. Automobiles (1st series). Two designs for each value, the first showing technical drawings and the second the car in action. 25, 30, 40, 50 c. each × 2.

Leaders of the World. Famous Cricketers. Two designs for each value, the first showing a portrait and the second the cricketer in action. 1, 40, 60, 70 c. each × 2.

Leaders of the World. Life and Times of Queen Elizabeth the Queen Mother. Two designs for each value, showing different portraits. 5, 50, 75, 85 c. each × 2.

Leaders of the World. Automobiles (2nd series). Two designs for each value, the first showing technical drawings and the second the car in action. 5, 15, 40, 60, 90 c., $1.10 each × 2.

1986.

60th Birthday of Queen Elizabeth II. 10, 80 c., $1.75, $3.

Royal Wedding (1st issue). 60 c., $1 each × 2.

Royal Wedding (2nd issue). Previous Royal Wedding stamps optd as for Funafuti. 60 c., $1 each × 2.

1987.

Railway Locomotives (3rd series). Two designs for each value, the first showing technical drawings and the second the locomotive at work. 10, 25, 35, 40, 60, 75 c., $1, $1.25 each × 2.

Royal Ruby Wedding. 20, 50, 75 c., $1.20, $1.75.

1988.

Railway Locomotives (4th series). Two designs for each value, the first showing technical drawings and the second the locomotive at work. 5, 10, 20, 25, 40, 50, 60, 75 c. each × 2.

NUKUFETAU

1984.

Leaders of the World. Automobiles (1st series). Two designs for each value, the first showing technical drawings and the second the car in action. 10, 25, 30, 50, 60 c. each × 2.

Leaders of the World. British Monarchs. Two designs for each value, forming a composite picture. 1, 10, 30, 50, 60 c., $1 each × 2.

1985.

Leaders of the World. Famous Cricketers. Two designs for each value, the first showing a portrait and the second the cricketer in action. 1, 10, 55 c., $1 each × 2.

Leaders of the World. Railway Locomotives (1st series). Two designs for each value, the first showing technical drawings and the second the locomotive at work. 1, 10, 60, 70 c. each × 2.

Leaders of the World. Automobiles (2nd series). Two designs for each value, the first showing technical drawings and the second the car in action. 5, 10, 15, 20, 50, 60, 75 c., $1.50 each × 2.

Leaders of the World. Life and Times of Queen Elizabeth the Queen Mother. Two designs for each value, showing different portraits. 10, 45, 65 c., $1 each × 2.

1986.

Leaders of the World. Railway Locomotives (2nd series). Two designs for each value, the first showing technical drawings and the second the locomotive at work. 20, 40, 60 c., $1.50 each × 2.

60th Birthday of Queen Elizabeth II. 5, 40 c., $2, $4.

Royal Wedding (1st issue). 60 c., $1 each × 2.

Royal Wedding (2nd issue). Previous Royal Wedding stamps optd as for Funafuti. 60 c., $1 each × 2.

1987.

Railway Locomotives (3rd series). Two designs for each value, the first showing technical drawings and the second the locomotive at work. 5, 10, 15, 25, 30, 50, 60 c., $1 each × 2.

Royal Ruby Wedding. 60th Birthday of Queen Elizabeth II issue of 1986 optd as for Niutao. 5, 40 c., $2, $4.

NUKULAELAE

1984.

Leaders of the World. Railway Locomotives (1st series). Two designs for each value, the first showing technical drawings and the second the locomotive at work. 5, 15, 40 c., $1 each × 2.

Leaders of the World. Famous Cricketers. Two designs for each value, the first showing a portrait and the second the cricketer in action. 5, 15, 30 c., $1 each × 2.

Leaders of the World. Railway Locomotives (2nd series). Two designs for each value, the first showing technical drawings and the second the locomotive at work. 5, 20, 40 c., $1 each × 2.

1985.

Leaders of the World. Automobiles (1st series). Two designs for each value, the first showing technical drawings and the second the car in action. 5, 35, 50, 70 c. each × 2.

Leaders of the World. Dogs. 5, 20, 50, 70 c. each × 2.

Leaders of the World. Railway Locomotives (3rd series). Two designs for each value, the first showing technical drawings and the second the locomotive at work. 10, 25, 50 c., $1 each × 2.

Leaders of the World. Automobiles (2nd series). Two designs for each value, the first showing technical drawings and the second the car in action. 10, 25, 35, 50, 75 c., $1 each × 2.

Leaders of the World. Life and Times of Queen Elizabeth the Queen Mother. Two designs for each value, showing different portraits. 5, 25, 85 c., $1 each × 2.

1986.

60th Birthday of Queen Elizabeth II. 10 c., $1, $1.50, $3.

Railway Locomotives (4th series). Two designs for each value, the first showing technical drawings and the second the locomotive at work. 10, 15, 25, 40, 50, 80 c., $1, $1.50 each × 2.

Royal Wedding (1st issue). 60 c., $1 each × 2.

Royal Wedding (2nd issue). Previous Royal Wedding stamps optd as for Funafuti. 60 c., $1 each × 2.

1987.

Royal Ruby Wedding. 15, 35, 60 c., $1.50, $1.75.

VAITUPU

1984.

Leaders of the World. Automobiles (1st series). Two designs for each value, the first showing technical drawings and the second the car in action. 15, 25, 30, 50 c. each × 2.

Leaders of the World. British Monarchs. Two designs for each value, forming a composite picture. 1, 5, 15, 40, 50 c., $1 each × 2.

Leaders of the World. Automobiles (2nd series). Two designs for each value, the first showing technical drawings and the second the car in action. 5, 15, 25, 30, 40, 50, 60 c. $1 each × 2.

1985.

Leaders of the World. Railway Locomotives (1st series). Two designs for each value, the first showing technical drawings and the second the locomotive at work. 10, 25, 50, 60 c. each × 2.

Leaders of the World. Butterflies. 5, 15, 50, 75 c. each × 2.

Leaders of the World. Automobiles (3rd series). Two designs for each value, the first showing technical drawings and the second the car in action. 15, 30, 40, 60 c. each × 2.

Leaders of the World. Life and Times of Queen Elizabeth the Queen Mother. Two designs for each value, showing different portraits. 15, 40, 65, 90 c. each × 2.

1986.

Leaders of the World. Railway Locomotives (2nd series). Two designs for each value, the first showing technical drawings and the second the locomotives at work. 5, 25, 80 c., $1 each × 2.

60th Birthday of Queen Elizabeth II. 5, 60 c., $2, $3.50.

Royal Wedding (1st issue). 60 c., $1 each × 2.

Royal Wedding (2nd issue). Previous Royal Wedding stamps optd as for Funafuti. 60 c., $1 each × 2.

1987.

Railway Locomotives (3rd series). Two designs for each value, the first showing technical drawings and the second the locomotive at work. 10, 15, 25, 35, 45, 65, 85 c., $1 each × 2.

Royal Ruby Wedding. 60th Birthday of Queen Elizabeth II issue of 1986 optd as for Niutao. 5, 60 c., $2, $3.50.

UGANDA

A Br. Protectorate in Central Africa until it attained independence within the British Commonwealth in 1962. From 1903 to 1962 used the stamps listed under "Kenya, Uganda and Tanganyika".

1895. 200 cowries = 1 rupee.
1896. 16 annas = 1 rupee.
1962. 100 cents = 1 shilling.

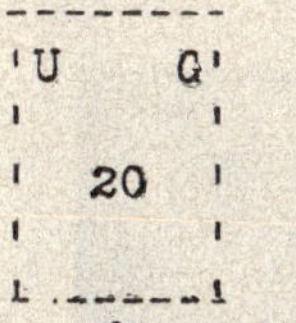

2

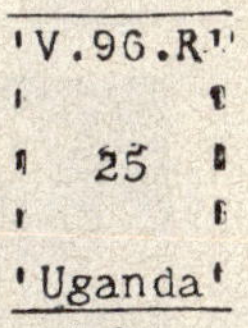

3

1895. Typewritten in black.

17	2	5 (c.) black	£1300	£950
18		10 (c.) black	£1400	£1000
19		15 (c.) black	£950	£1000
20		20 (c.) black	£1100	£650
21		25 (c.) black	£900	£950
6		30 (c.) black	£1400	£1200
7		40 (c.) black	£2250	£1200
8		50 (c.) black	£1200	£1000
9		60 (c.) black	£1600	£1600

1895. Typewritten in violet.

35	2	5 (c.) violet	£450	£475
36		10 (c.) violet	£425	£425
37		15 (c.) violet	£475	£400
38		20 (c.) violet	£350	£275
39		25 (c.) violet	£600	£600
40		30 (c.) violet	£850	£650
41		40 (c.) violet	£700	£700
42		50 (c.) violet	£700	£750
43		100 (c.) violet	£2500	£2500

1896. Typewritten in violet.

44	3	5 (c.) violet	£425	£450
45		10 (c.) violet	£375	£375
46		15 (c.) violet	£425	£450
47		20 (c.) violet	£275	£200
48		25 (c.) violet	£425	
49		30 (c.) violet	£475	£550
50		40 (c.) violet	£475	£550
51		50 (c.) violet	£600	£650
52		60 (c.) violet	£1400	
53		100 (c.) violet	£1200	£1300

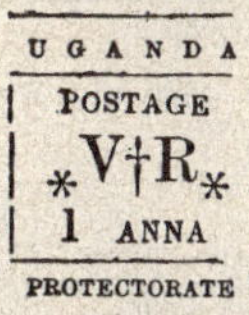

4

8

1896.

55	4	1 a. black	13·00	17·00
56		2 a. black	20·00	21·00
57		3 a. black	19·00	22·00
58		4 a. black	19·00	22·00
59		8 a. black	22·00	23·00
60		1 r. black	65·00	75·00
61		5 r. black	£170	£225

1896. Optd with large **L.**

70	4	1 a. black	£140	£110
71		2 a. black	65·00	85·00
72		3 a. black	£160	£180
73		4 a. black	75·00	£120
74		8 a. black	£130	£170
75		1 r. black	£250	£300
76		5 r. black	£7500	£7500

1898.

84a	8	1 a. red	1·75	1·00
86		2 a. brown	1·50	4·50
87a		3 a. grey	6·50	12·00
88		4 a. green	2·50	6·50
89		8 a. green	6·00	24·00

Larger type with lions at either side of portrait.

90	–	1 r. blue	27·00	35·00
91	–	5 r. brown	60·00	90·00

1902. Stamps of British East Africa optd **UGANDA.**

92	11	½ a. green	2·00	1·40
93		2½ a. blue	2·00	3·00

11 Ripon Falls and Speke Memorial

1962. Centenary of Speke's Discovery of Source of Nile.

95	11	30 c. black and red	15	10
96		50 c. black and violet	15	10
97		1 s. 30 black and green	30	10
98		2 s. 50 black and blue	1·60	1·40

12 Murchison Falls

14 Mulago Hospital

1962. Independence.

99	12	5 c. turquoise	10	10
100	–	10 c. brown	10	10
101	–	15 c. black, red and green	10	10
102	–	20 c. plum and buff	10	10
103	–	30 c. blue	10	10
104	–	50 c. black and turquoise	10	10
105	14	1 s. sepia, red and turquoise	15	10
106	–	1 s. 30 orange and violet	20	10
107	–	2 s. black, red and blue	40	40
108	–	5 s. red and deep green	4·00	1·00
109	–	10 s. slate and brown	1·75	2·00
110	–	20 s. brown and blue	4·50	11·00

DESIGNS—As Type **12**: 10 c. Tobacco growing; 15 c. Coffee growing; 20 c. Ankole cattle; 30 c. Cotton; 50 c. Mountains of the Moon. As Type **14**: 1 s. 30, Cathedrals and mosque; 2 s. Makerere College; 5 s. Copper mining; 10 s. Cement industry; 20 s. Parliament Buildings.

15 South African Crowned Crane

16 Black BeeEater

18 Ruwenzori Turaco

1965. International Trade Fair, Kampala.

111	15	30 c. multicoloured	10	10
112		1 s. 30 multicoloured	20	10

1965. Birds.

113	16	5 c. multicoloured	10	10
114	–	10 c. brown, black and blue	10	10
115	–	15 c. yellow and brown	20	10
116	–	20 c. multicoloured	20	10
117	–	30 c. black and brown	1·50	10
118	–	40 c. multicoloured	90	60
119	–	50 c. blue and violet	25	10
120	–	65 c. red, black and grey	2·50	2·00
121	18	1 s. multicoloured	50	10
122	–	1 s. 30 brown, black & yell	5·50	30
123	–	2 s. 50 multicoloured	4·25	65
124	–	5 s. multicoloured	7·00	3·75
125	–	10 s. multicoloured	11·00	10·00
126	–	20 s. multicoloured	21·00	35·00

DESIGNS—HORIZ (as Type **16**): 10 c. African jacana; 30 c. Sacred ibis; 65 c. Red-crowned bishop. (As Type **18**): 2 s. 50, Great blue turaco; 10 s. Black-collared lovebird. 20 s. South African crowned crane. VERT (as Type **16**): 15 c. Orange weaver; 20 c. Narina trogon; 40 c. Blue-breasted kingfisher; 50 c. Whale-headed stork. (As Type **18**): 1 s. 30, African fish eagle; 5 s. Lilac-breasted roller.

19 Carved Screen

1967. 13th Commonwealth Parliamentary Association Conference. Multicoloured.

127		30 c. Type **19**	10	10
128		50 c. Arms of Uganda	10	10
129		1 s. 30 Parliamentary Building	10	10
130		2 s. 50 Conference Chamber	15	1·25

20 "Cordia abyssinica"

21 "Acacia drepanolobium"

1969. Flowers.

131a	20	5 c. brown, green & yellow	40	10
132	–	10 c. multicoloured	10	10
133	–	15 c. multicoloured	40	10
134	–	20 c. violet, olive and green	15	10
135	–	30 c. multicoloured	20	10
136	–	40 c. violet, green and grey	20	10
137	–	50 c. multicoloured	20	10
138	–	60 c. multicoloured	45	90
139	–	70 c. multicoloured	35	30
140	21	1 s. multicoloured	20	10
141	–	1 s. 50 multicoloured	35	10
142a	–	2 s. 50 multicoloured	1·25	10
143a	–	5 s. multicoloured	1·75	10
144a	–	10 s. multicoloured	3·75	10
145	–	20 s. multicoloured	1·50	5·00

DESIGNS—As Type **20**: 10 c. "Grewia similis"; 15 c. "Cassia didymobotrya"; 20 c. "Coleus barbatus"; 30 c. "Ochna ovata"; 40 c. "Ipomoea spathulata"; 50 c. "Spathodea nilotica"; 60 c. "Oncoba spinosa"; 70 c. "Carissa edulis". As Type **21**: 1 s. 50, "Clerodendrum myricoides"; 2 s. 50, "Acanthus arboreus"; 5 s. "Kigelia aethiopium"; 10 s. "Erythrina abyssinica"; 20 s. "Monodora myristica".

1975. Nos. 140, 142a and 145 surch.

146	2 s. on 1 s. multicoloured	2·00	1·50
147	3 s. on 2 s. 50 multicoloured	20·00	40·00
148	40 s. on 20 s. multicoloured	5·50	3·50

23 Millet

24 Maize

1975. Ugandan Crops.

149	23	10 c. black, green and brown	10	10
150	–	20 c. multicoloured	10	10
151	–	30 c. multicoloured	10	10
152	–	40 c. multicoloured	10	10
153	–	50 c. multicoloured	10	10
154	–	70 c. black, green & turq	10	15
155	–	80 c. multicoloured	10	15
156	24	1 s. multicoloured	10	10
157	–	2 s. multicoloured	30	30
158	–	3 s. multicoloured	50	45
159	–	5 s. multicoloured	50	75
160	–	10 s. multicoloured	50	1·25
161	–	20 s. green, black & purple	70	2·50
162	–	40 s. green, blue and orange	1·10	5·50

DESIGNS—As Type **23**: 20 c. Sugar; 30 c. Tobacco; 40 c. Onions; 50 c. Tomatoes; 70 c. Tea; 80 c. Bananas. As Type **24**: 2 s. Pineapples; 3 s. Coffee; 5 s. Oranges; 10 s. Groundnuts; 20 s. Cotton; 40 s. Runner beans.

Face value colours: 5 s. green; 10 s. brown; 20 s. mauve; 40 s. orange.

For these values with colours changed, see Nos. 220/3.

1976. Telecommunications Development. As Nos. 56/60 of Kenya.

163	50 c. Microwave tower	10	10
164	1 s. Cordless switchboard	10	10
165	2 s. Telephone	20	25
166	3 s. Message Switching Centre	30	45

1976. Olympic Games, Montreal. As Nos. 61/5 of Kenya.

168	50 c. Akii Bua, hurdler	10	10
169	1 s. Filbert Bayi, runner	10	10
170	2 s. Steve Muchoki, boxer	30	30
171	3 s. East African flags	40	45

1976. Railway Transport. As Nos. 66/70 of Kenya.

173	50 c. Diesel-hydraulic train, Tanzania–Zambia railway	15	10
174	1 s. Nile Bridge, Uganda	15	10
175	2 s. Nakuru Station, Kenya	50	45
176	3 s. Uganda Railway Class A locomotive, 1896	55	55

1977. Game Fish of East Africa. As Nos. 71/5 of Kenya. Multicoloured.

178	50 c. Nile perch	15	10
179	1 s. Nile mouthbrooder	20	10
180	3 s. Sailfish	70	40
181	5 s. Black marlin	1·00	60

1977. Second World Black and African Festival of Arts and Culture. As Nos. 76/80 of Kenya. Multicoloured.

183	50 c. Maasai manyatta (village), Kenya	10	10
184	1 s. "Heartbeat of Africa" (Ugandan dancers)	10	10
185	2 s. Makonde sculpture, Tanzania	25	55
186	3 s. "Early man and technology" (skinning hippopotamus)	35	85

1977. 25th Anniv of Safari Rally. As Nos. 81/5 of Kenya. Multicoloured.

188	50 c. Rally-car and villagers	10	10
189	1 s. Starting-line	10	10
190	2 s. Car fording river	25	35
191	5 s. Car and elephants	80	1·00

1977. Centenary of Ugandan Church. As Nos. 86/90 of Kenya. Multicoloured.

193	50 c. Canon Kivebulaya	10	10
194	1 s. Modern Namirembe Cathedral	10	10
195	2 s. Old Namirembe Cathedral	20	40
196	5 s. Early congregation, Kigezi	45	90

1977. Design as No. 155 surch **80c.**

198	80 c. on 60 c. multicoloured	30	20

1977. Endangered Species. As Nos. 96/101 of Kenya. Multicoloured.

199	50 c. Pancake tortoise	30	10
200	1 s. Nile crocodile	45	10
201	2 s. Hunter's hartebeest	2·00	40
202	3 s. Red colobus monkey	2·50	75
203	5 s. Dugong	2·50	1·00

1978. World Cup Football Championship, Argentina (1st issue). As Nos. 122/6 of Kenya. Multicoloured.

205	50 c. Joe Kadenge and forwards	15	10
206	1 s. Mohamed Chuma and cup presentation	15	10
207	2 s. Omari Kidevu and goalmouth scene	30	35
208	5 s. Polly Ouma and forwards	50	85

26 Shot Putting

1978. Commonwealth Games, Edmonton. Multicoloured.

210	50 c. Type **26**	10	10
211	1 s. Long jumping	15	10
212	2 s. Running	20	30
213	5 s. Boxing	40	70

1978. World Cup Football Championship, Argentina (2nd issue). As Nos. 205/8, but additionally inscr "WORLD CUP 1978".

215	50 c. Polly Ouma and forwards	15	10
216	2 s. Omari Kidevu and goalmouth scene	30	10
217	5 s. Joe Kadenge and forwards	60	90
218	10 s. Mohamed Chuma and cup presentation	90	1·60

1978. As Nos. 159/62, but colours changed.

220	5 s. mult (face value in blue)	55	70
221	10 s. mult (face value in mauve)	60	1·00
222	20 s. mult (face value in brown)	70	1·00
223	40 s. mult (face value in red)	1·00	1·40

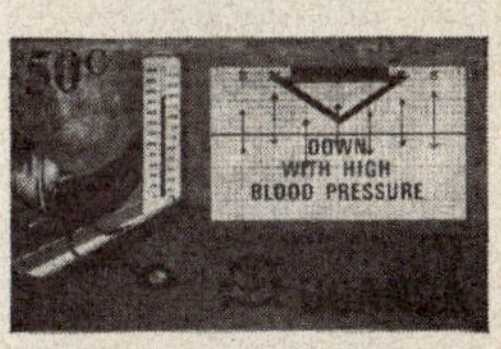

27 Measurements of High Blood Pressure

1978. "Down with High Blood Pressure". Multicoloured.

224	50 c. Type **27**	15	10
225	1 s. Hypertension and the heart	15	10
226	2 s. Fundus of the eye in hypertension	40	35
227	5 s. Kidney and high blood pressure	75	1·00

28 Off Loading Cattle

1978. 75th Anniv of Powered Flight. Multicoloured.

229	1 s. Type **28**	20	10
230	1 s. 50 "Domestic services" (passengers boarding Britten Norman Islander)	30	15
231	2 s. 70 Export of Uganda coffee	30	35
232	10 s. "Time machines in the air" (Wright Flyer III and Concorde)	1·00	1·25

29 Queen Elizabeth II leaving Owen Falls Dam

1979. 25th Anniv of Coronation (1978). Multicoloured.

234 1 s. Type **29** 15 10
235 1 s. 50 Regalia 20 10
236 2 s. 70 Coronation ceremony . 45 20
237 10 s. Royal family on balcony of Buckingham Palace 80 80

30 Dr. Joseph Kiwanuka (first Ugandan bishop)

1979. Centenary of Catholic Church in Uganda. Multicoloured.

239 1 s. Type **30** 10 10
240 1 s. 50 Lubaga Cathedral . . 10 10
241 2 s. 70 Ugandan pilgrimage to Rome, Holy Year, 1975 . . 15 25
242 10 s. Friar Lourdel-Mapeera (early missionary) 50 80

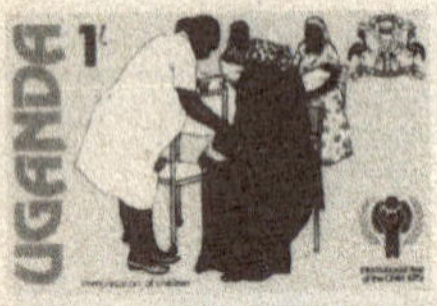

31 Immunisation of Children

1979. International Year of the Child. Multicoloured.

244 1 s. Type **31** 10 10
245 1 s. 50 Handicapped children at play 15 20
246 2 s. 70 Ugandan I.Y.C. emblem 20 35
247 10 s. Children in class 60 90

1979. Liberation. Optd **UGANDA LIBERATED 1979**. (a) Nos. 149/62.

249 **23** 10 c. black, green and brown 10 10
250 – 20 c. multicoloured 10 10
251 – 30 c. multicoloured 10 10
252 – 40 c. multicoloured 10 10
253 – 50 c. multicoloured 10 10
254 – 70 c. black, green & turq . . 10 10
255 – 80 c. multicoloured 10 10
256 **24** 1 s. multicoloured 15 15
257 – 2 s. multicoloured 20 25
258 – 3 s. multicoloured 35 40
259 – 5 s. multicoloured 55 60
260 – 10 s. multicoloured . . . . 80 1·25
261 – 20 s. green, black and purple 1·50 2·40
262 – 40 s. green, black & orange 3·00 4·75

(b) Nos. 210/13.

263 50 c. Type **26** 10 10
264 1 s. Long jumping 15 20
265 2 s. Running 25 30
266 5 s. Boxing 60 65

(c) Nos. 207, 215, 217/18.

267 50 c. Polly Ouma and forwards 10 10
268 2 s. Omari Kidevu and goalmouth scene 20 30
269 5 s. Joe Kadenge and forwards 55 65
270 10 s. Mohamed Chuma and cup presentation . . . . . . 1·00 1·40

(d) Nos. 220/3.

271 5 s. multicoloured 55 60
272 10 s. multicoloured . . . . . 80 1·25
273 20 s. multicoloured . . . . . 1·00 2·40
274 40 s. multicoloured . . . . . 1·50 4·75

(e) Nos. 229/32.

275 1 s. Type **28** 15 20
276 1 s. 50 "Domestic services" . . 40 25
277 2 s. 70 Export of Uganda coffee 50 55
278 10 s. "Time machines in the air" 2·25 2·00

(f) Nos. 234/7.

279 1 s. Type **29** 10 20
280 1 s. 50 Regalia 15 20
281 2 s. 70 Coronation ceremony . 20 30
282 10 s. Royal family on balcony of Buckingham Palace . . . . 85 1·50

(g) Nos. 239/42.

284 1 s. Type **30** 10 20
285 1 s. 50 Lubaga Cathedral . . 15 25
286 2 s. 70 Ugandan pilgrimage to Rome, Holy Year, 1975 . . 30 45
287 10 s. Friar Lourdel-Mapeera (early missionary) . . . . . 90 1·60

(h) Nos. 244/8.

289 1 s. Type **31** 15 20
290 1 s. 50 Handicapped children at play 20 25
291 2 s. 70 Ugandan I.Y.C. emblem 40 45
292 10 s. Children in class . . . . 1·25 1·40

35 Radio Wave Symbol

1979. 50th Anniv of International Consultative Radio Committee and International Telecommunications Union.

294 **35** 1 s. multicoloured 10 10
295 1 s. 50 multicoloured . . . 15 10
296 2 s. 70 multicoloured . . . 20 35
297 10 s. multicoloured . . . . 60 1·10

36 20 s. Definitive Stamp of 1965 and Sir Rowland Hill

1979. Death Cent of Sir Rowland Hill. Mult.

298 1 s. Type **36** 10 10
299 1 s. 50 1967 13th Commonwealth Parliamentary Association Conference 50 c. commemorative 15 10
300 2 s. 70 1962 Independence 20 s. commemorative 20 30
301 10 s. Uganda Protectorate 1898 1 a. . . . . 60 1·25

37 Impala

38 Lions with Cub

1979. Wildlife.

303A 10 c. Type **37** 10 20
304A 20 c. Large-spotted genet . 10 20
305A 30 c. Thomson's gazelle . . 15 20
306A 50 c. Lesser bushbaby . . . 15 10
307A 80 c. Hunting dog 20 10
308B 1 s. Type **38** 20 10
309A 1 s. 50 Gorilla 45 10
310B 2 s. Common zebra 30 20
311A 2 s. 70 Leopard with cub . 60 20
312A 3 s. 50 Black rhinoceros . . 70 55
313A 5 s. Waterbuck 70 55
314A 10 s. African buffalo . . . 70 1·00
315A 20 s. Hippopotamus . . . . 1·00 2·00
316A 40 s. African elephant . . . 1·75 3·50

SIZES—As Type **37**: 10 c. to 80 c. As Type **38**: 1 s. to 40 s.

See also Nos. 433/9.

1980. "London 1980" International Stamp Exhibition. Nos. 298/301 optd **LONDON 1980.**

317 **36** 1 s. multicoloured 15 10
318 – 1 s. 50 multicoloured . . . 20 10
319 – 2 s. 70 multicoloured . . . 35 25
320 – 10 s. multicoloured 80 80

40 Rotary Emblem

1980. 75th Anniv of Rotary International. Multicoloured.

322 1 s. Type **40** 10 10
323 20 s. Paul P. Harris (founder) with wheel-barrow containing "Rotary projects" (horiz) . . 1·50 1·75

41 Football

1980. Olympic Games, Moscow. Multicoloured.

325 1 s. Type **41** 10 10
326 2 s. Relay 10 10
327 10 s. Hurdles 35 65
328 20 s. Boxing . . . . 60 1·75

1981. Olympic Medal Winners. Nos. 325/8 optd.

330 **41** 1 s. multicoloured 10 10
331 – 2 s. multicoloured 10 15
332 – 10 s. multicoloured 35 60
333 – 20 s. multicoloured . . . . 60 1·25

OVERPRINTS: 1 s. **FOOTBALL GOLD MEDALISTS, C.S.S.R.**; 2 s. **RELAY GOLD MEDALIST U.S.S.R.**; 10 s. **HURDLES 110 m. GOLD MEDALIST THOMAS MUNKLET, D.D.R.**; 20 s. **BOXING WELTERWEIGHT SILVER MEDALIST JOHN MUGABI, UGANDA.**

44 Heinrich von Stephan and U.P.U. Emblem

1981. 150th Birth Anniv of Heinrich von Stephan (founder of U.P.U.). Multicoloured.

336 1 s. Type **44** 10 10
337 2 s. U.P.U. Headquarters . . . 15 15
338 2 s. 70 Air mail, 1935 . . . . 40 20
339 10 s. Mail transport by train, 1927 . . . . 1·10 80

45 Tower of London

1981. Royal Wedding. Multicoloured. (a) Previously unissued stamps surch.

341e 10 s. on 1 s. Prince Charles and Lady Diana Spencer 15 20
342e 50 s. on 5 s. Type **45** 20 30
343e 200 s. on 20 s. Prince Charles at Balmoral 45 80

(b) Stamps reissued with new face values.

345 10 s. As No. 341 . . . . . . 10 15
346 50 s. Type **45** 15 20
347 200 s. As No. 343 . . . . . . 30 40

48 "Sleeping Woman before Green Shutters"

1981. Birth Centenary of Picasso. Mult.

349 10 s. Type **48** 10 10
350 20 s. "Bullfight" 20 20
351 30 s. "Detail of a Nude asleep in a Landscape" 25 30
352 200 s. "Interior with a Girl Drawing" . . . . 2·25 3·25

49 Deaf People using Sign Language

1981. Int Year of Disabled Persons. Mult.

354 1 s. Type **49** 10 10
355 10 s. Disabled teacher in classroom 15 10
356 50 s. Teacher and disabled children 70 50
357 200 s. Blind person with guide dog . . . . 2·00 2·00

50 Footballers

1981. World Cup Football Championship, Spain (1982).

359 **50** 1 s. multicoloured 10 10
360 – 10 s. multicoloured 15 10
361 – 50 s. multicoloured 70 50
362 – 200 s. multicoloured . . . 2·00 2·00

DESIGNS: Nos. 360/62, various football scenes.

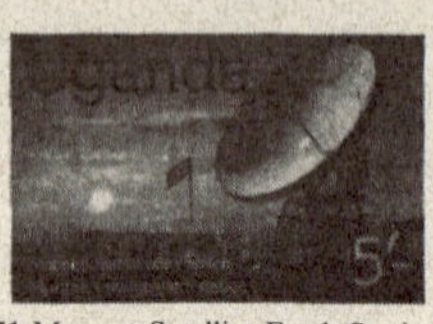

51 Mpoma Satellite Earth Station

1982. "Peaceful Use of Outer Space". Multicoloured.

364 5 s. Type **51** 25 15
365 10 s. "Pioneer II" (satellite) . . 35 35
366 50 s. Space Shuttle . . . . . 1·75 2·00
367 100 s. "Voyager 2" (satellite) . 2·75 4·00

MINIMUM PRICE

The minimum price quoted is 10p which represents a handling charge rather than a basis for valuing common stamps. For further notes about prices see introductory pages.

52 Dr. Robert Koch

54 Yellow-billed Hornbill

1982. Centenary of Robert Koch's Discovery of Tubercle Bacillus. Multicoloured.

369 1 s. Type **52** 30 10
370 10 s. Microscope . . . . . . 1·25 40
371 50 s. Ugandans receiving vaccinations . . . . 3·00 2·50
372 100 s. Tubercle virus . . . . . 4·50 4·25

1982. 21st Birthday of Princess of Wales. Nos. 345/7 optd **21st BIRTHDAY HRH Princess of Wales JULY 1 1982.**

374 10 s. Prince Charles and Lady Diana Spencer 20 10
375 50 s. Type **45** 50 40
376 200 s. Prince Charles at Balmoral 1·50 1·25

1982. Birds. Multicoloured.

378 1 s. Type **54** 15 10
379 20 s. Superb starling 60 35
380 50 s. Bateleur . . . . 1·25 1·75
381 100 s. Saddle-bill stork . . . 2·00 2·50

55 Scout Band

1982. 75th Anniv of Boy Scout Movement. Multicoloured.

383 5 s. Type **55** 40 10
384 20 s. Scout receiving Bata Shoe trophy . . . . 1·10 45
385 50 s. Scouts with wheelchair patient . . . . 2·25 2·25
386 100 s. First aid instruction . . 3·00 3·50

56 Swearing-in of Roosevelt

1982. 250th Birth Anniv of George Washington and Birth Centenary of Franklin D. Roosevelt. Multicoloured.

388 50 s. Type **56** 30 30
389 200 s. Swearing-in of Washington 75 1·25

57 Italy v West Germany

1982. World Cup Football Championship Winners. Multicoloured.

392 10 s. Type **57** 30 25
393 200 s. Victorious Italian team 1·50 3·50

58 Dancers

1983. Commonwealth Day. Cultural Art. Multicoloured.

395 5 s. Type **58** 10 10
396 20 s. Traditional currency . . 15 20
397 50 s. Homestead 35 55
398 100 s. Drums . . . . 70 1·10

59 "St. George and the Dragon" (Raphael)

1983. 500th Birth Anniv of Raphael (painter). Multicoloured.
399 5 s. Type **59** 10 10
400 20 s. "St. George and the Dragon" (different) 40 30
401 50 s. "Crossing the Red Sea" (detail) 80 80
402 200 s. "The Expulsion of Heliodorus" (detail) . . . . 1·50 3·25

60 Map showing Namibia and U.N. Flag

1983. Commemorations. Multicoloured.
404 5 s. Type **60** 10 10
405 200 s. 7th Non-aligned Summit Conference logo . . . . . . 80 2·50

61 Elephants in Grassland

1983. Endangered Species (1st series). Mult.
406 5 s. Elephants in "Elephants' Graveyard" . . . . 1·25 40
407 10 s. Type **61** . . . . 1·60 40
408 30 s. Elephants at waterhole . . 3·50 2·50
409 70 s. Elephants having dust bath 5·50 6·00
See also No. 642 for the 10 s. redrawn and Nos. 988/91 for these designs with different face values.

1983. Centenary of Boys' Brigade. Nos. 383/6 optd **BOYS BRIGADE CENTENARY 1883–1983** or surch also.
411 5 s. Type **55** 10 10
412 20 s. Scout receiving Bata Shoe trophy 15 15
413 50 s. Scouts with wheelchair patient 25 30
414 400 s. on 100 s. First aid instruction . . . . 2·40 2·75

63 Mpoma Satellite Earth Station

1983. World Communications Year. Mult.
416 20 s. Type **63** 25 15
417 50 s. Railroad computer and operator 65 85
418 70 s. Cameraman filming lions 75 1·50
419 100 s. Aircraft cockpit . . . . 95 2·00

1983. Nos. 303, 305/9 and 313 surch.
421 100 s. on 10 c. Type **37** 65 55
422 135 s. on 1 s. Type **38** 80 70
423 175 s. on 30 c. Thomson's gazelle 95 1·00
424 200 s. on 50 c. Lesser bushbaby 1·10 1·25
425 400 s. on 80 c. Hunting dog . . 2·00 2·25
426 700 s. on 5 s. Waterbuck . . . 3·25 4·50
427 1000 s. on 1 s. 50 Gorilla . . . 5·50 7·50

65 The Nativity

1983. Christmas. Multicoloured.
428 10 s. Type **65** 10 10
429 50 s. Shepherds and Angels . . 25 30
430 175 s. Flight into Egypt . . . 80 1·25
431 400 s. Angels blowing trumpets 1·60 2·75

1983. As Nos. 308/12 and 315/16, but with face values in revalued currency.
433 100 s. Type **38** 90 35
434 135 s. Gorilla . . . . 1·25 50
435 175 s. Common zebra . . . . . 1·40 80
436 200 s. Leopard with cub . . . 1·75 90
437 400 s. Black rhinoceros . . . . 3·00 3·25
438 700 s. African elephant . . . . 5·00 6·50
439 1000 s. Hippopotamus . . . . 5·50 7·50

66 Ploughing with Oxen

1984. World Food Day. Multicoloured.
440 10 s. Type **66** 15 10
441 300 s. Harvesting bananas . . 4·25 5·50

67 Ruth Kyalisiima, Sportsman of the Year 1983

1984. Olympic Games, Los Angeles. Mult.
442 5 s. Type **67** 10 10
443 115 s. Javelin-throwing . . . 65 90
444 155 s. Wrestling . . . . . . 70 1·00
445 175 s. Rowing . . . . 70 1·10

68 Entebbe Airport

1984. 40th Anniv of I.C.A.O. Mult.
447 5 s. Type **68** 15 10
448 115 s. Loading cargo plane . . 1·50 1·75
449 155 s. Uganda police helicopter 2·50 2·75
450 175 s. East African Civil Flying School, Soroti . . . . . . 2·75 3·25

69 "Charaxes druceanus"

1984. Butterflies. Multicoloured.
452 5 s. Type **69** 30 10
453 115 s. "Papilio lormieri" . . . 2·50 2·00
454 155 s. "Druryia antimachus" . . 3·00 2·50
455 175 s. "Salamis temora" . . . 4·25 3·25

70 Blue-finned notho

1985. Lake Fishes. Multicoloured.
457 5 s. Type **70** 30 40
458 10 s. Semutundu 40 40
459 50 s. Grey bichir 75 30
460 100 s. Walking catfish 85 30
461 135 s. Elephant-snout fish . . 1·25 1·00
462 175 s. Lake Victoria squeaker 1·40 1·60
463 205 s. Brown's haplochromis . . 1·40 2·00
464 400 s. Nile perch . . . . . . 1·50 2·25
465 700 s. African lungfish . . . 1·75 2·75
466 1000 s. Radcliffe's barb . . . 1·75 3·00
467 2500 s. Electric catfish . . . 1·75 3·75

71 The Last Supper

1985. Easter. Multicoloured.
468 5 s. Type **71** 10 10
469 115 s. Christ showing the nail marks to Thomas . . . . . 1·25 1·25
470 155 s. The raising of the Cross 1·40 2·00
471 175 s. Pentecost . . . . 1·75 2·50

72 Breast Feeding

1985. U.N.I.C.E.F. Child Survival Campaign. Multicoloured.
473 5 s. Type **72** 10 10
474 115 s. Growth monitoring . . 1·75 1·75
475 155 s. Immunisation . . . . 2·25 2·25
476 175 s. Oral re-hydration therapy 2·50 2·50

73 Queen Elizabeth the Queen Mother

74 Sedge Warbler

1985. Life and Times of Queen Elizabeth the Queen Mother and Decade for Women.
478 **73** 1000 s. multicoloured . . . 1·40 2·10

1985. Birth Bicentenary of John J. Audubon (ornithologist) (1st issue). Multicoloured.
480 115 s. Type **74** . . . . 2·00 1·50
481 155 s. Cattle egret . . . . . . 2·25 1·75
482 175 s. Crested lark . . . . . . 2·50 2·25
483 500 s. Tufted duck . . . . . . 3·25 4·50
See also Nos. 494/7.

1985. Olympic Gold Medal Winners, Los Angeles. Nos. 442/5 optd or surch also.
485 5 s. Type **67** (optd **GOLD MEDALIST BENITA BROWN-FITZGERALD USA**) 10 10
486 115 s. Javelin-throwing (optd **GOLD MEDALIST ARTO HAERKOENEN FINLAND**) 40 30
487 155 s. Wrestling (optd **GOLD MEDALIST ATSUJI MIYAHARA JAPAN**) . . . 50 40
488 1000 s. on 175 s. Rowing (surch **GOLD MEDALIST WEST GERMANY**) . . . . 2·00 2·00

76 Women carrying National Women's Day Banner

77 Man beneath Tree laden with Produce (F.A.O.)

1985. Decade for Women. Multicoloured.
490 5 s. Type **76** 10 10
491 115 s. Girl Guides (horiz) . . . 1·75 2·00
492 155 s. Mother Teresa (Nobel Peace Prize winner, 1979) . . 3·00 3·25
No. 491 also commemorates the 75th anniversary of Girl Guide movement.

1985. Birth Bicentenary of John J. Audubon (ornithologist) (2nd issue). As T **198** of Antigua. Multicoloured.
494 5 s. Rock ptarmigan 55 10
495 155 s. Sage grouse . . . . . . 2·00 1·75
496 175 s. Lesser yellowlegs . . . . 2·00 2·25
497 500 s. Brown-headed cowbird . 3·25 4·50

1986. 40th Anniv of U.N.O.
499 **77** 10 s. multicoloured 10 10
500 – 180 s. multicoloured 50 30
501 – 200 s. blue, brown and green 55 35
502 – 250 s. blue, black and red . . 55 40
503 – 2000 s. multicoloured . . . 1·75 5·00
DESIGNS—HORIZ: 180 s. Soldier of U.N. Peace-keeping Force; 250 s. Hands releasing peace dove. VERT: 200 s. U.N. emblem; 2000 s. Flags of U.N. and Uganda.

78 Goalkeeper catching Ball

1986. World Cup Football Championship, Mexico. Multicoloured.
505 10 s. Type **78** 10 10
506 180 s. Player with ball 85 55
507 250 s. Two players competing for ball . . . . 1·00 65
508 2500 s. Player running with ball 5·50 6·00

1986. Liberation by National Resistance Army. Nos. 462 and 464/7 optd **NRA LIBERATION 1986.**
510 175 s. Lake Victoria squeaker . 70 70
511 400 s. Nile perch . . . . 1·25 1·25
512 700 s. African lungfish . . . 2·00 2·50
513 1000 s. Radcliffe's barb . . . 2·25 3·00
514 2500 s. Electric catfish . . . 4·25 6·00

1986. Appearance of Halley's Comet (1st issue). As T **123** of Anguilla. Multicoloured.
515 50 s. Tycho Brahe and Arecibo Radio Telescope, Puerto Rico 20 10
516 100 s. Recovery of astronaut John Glenn from sea, 1962 . 35 15
517 140 s. "The Star in the East" (painting by Giotto) . . . 50 30
518 2500 s. Death of Davy Crockett at the Alamo, 1835 . . . . 3·75 6·00
See also Nos. 544/7.

80 Niagara Falls

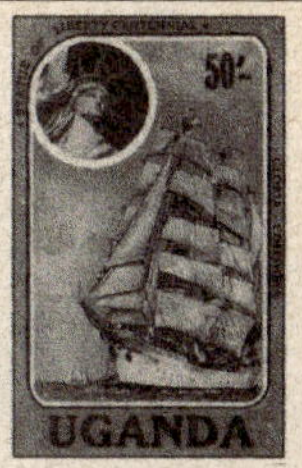

81 "Gloria" (Colombia)

1986. "Ameripex '86" International Stamp Exn, Chicago. American Landmarks. Mult.
520 50 s. Type **80** 15 10
521 100 s. Jefferson Memorial, Washington D.C. 25 15
522 250 s. Liberty Bell, Philadelphia 50 35
523 1000 s. The Alamo, San Antonio, Texas . . . . 1·50 2·25
524 2500 s. George Washington Bridge, New York–New Jersey 2·25 5·00

1986. 60th Birthday of Queen Elizabeth II. As T **125** of Anguilla.
526 100 s. black and yellow . . . 50 15
527 140 s. multicoloured 50 20
528 2500 s. multicoloured . . . . 3·25 4·00
DESIGNS: 100 s. Princess Elizabeth at London Zoo; 140 s. Queen Elizabeth at race meeting, 1970; 2500 s. With Prince Philip at Sandringham, 1982.

1986. Centenary of Statue of Liberty. Cadet Sailing Ships. Multicoloured.
530 50 s. Type **81** 60 20
531 100 s. "Mircea" (Rumania) . 95 30
532 140 s. "Sagres II" (Portugal) (horiz) . . . . 1·60 1·00
533 2500 s. "Gazela Primiero" (U.S.A.) (horiz) . . . . . . 7·00 10·00
No. 533 is inscribed "Primero" in error.

1986. Royal Wedding. As T **213** of Antigua. Multicoloured.
535 50 s. Prince Andrew and Miss Sarah Ferguson (horiz) . . 10 10
536 140 s. Prince Andrew with Princess Anne at shooting match (horiz) 20 20
537 2500 s. Prince Andrew and Miss Sarah Ferguson at Ascot (horiz) . . . . 2·75 3·75

1986. World Cup Football Championship Winners, Mexico. Nos. 505/8 optd **WINNERS Argentina 3 W.Germany 2** or surch also.
539 50 s. on 10 s. Type **78** 10 10
540 180 s. Player with ball 25 25
541 250 s. Two players competing for ball 35 35
542 2500 s. Player running with ball 2·75 4·00

1986. Appearance of Halley's Comet (2nd issue). Nos. 515/18 optd as T **218** of Antigua.
544 50 s. Tycho Brahe and Arecibo Radio Telescope, Puerto Rico 20 15
545 100 s. Recovery of astronaut John Glenn from sea, 1962 . 35 20
546 140 s. "The Star in the East" (painting by Giotto) . . . 55 40
547 2500 s. Death of Davy Crockett at the Alamo, 1835 . . . . 5·50 7·50

83 St. Kizito

1986. Christian Martyrs of Uganda. Mult.
549 50 s. Type **83** 10 10
550 150 s. St. Kizito instructing converts 25 25
551 200 s. Martyrdom of Bishop James Hannington, 1885 . . 30 30
552 1000 s. Burning of Bugandan Christians, 1886 . . . . . 1·50 2·75

84 "Madonna of the Cherries" (Titian)

1986. Christmas. Religious Paintings. Mult.
554 50 s. Type **84** 25 15
555 150 s. "Madonna and Child" (Durer) (vert) 60 30
556 200 s. "Assumption of the Virgin" (Titian) (vert) . . . 70 40
557 2500 s. "Praying Hands" (Durer) (vert) . . . . 5·50 8·00

85 Red-billed Fire Finch and Glory Lily

1987. Flora and Fauna. Multicoloured.

559	2 s. Type **85**	30	30
560	5 s. African pygmy kingfisher and nandi flame	45	30
561	10 s. Scarlet-chested sunbird and crown of thorns	55	30
562	25 s. White rhinoceros and yellow-billed oxpecker	1·00	80
563	35 s. Lion and elephant grass	1·00	1·10
564	45 s. Cheetahs and doum palm	1·25	1·50
565	50 s. Red-cheeked cordon bleu and desert rose	1·40	2·00
566	100 s. Giant eland and acacia	2·25	3·50

86 Tremml's "Eagle" (longest man-powered flight), 1987

1987. Milestones of Transportation. Mult.

568	2 s. Type **86**	20	20
569	3 s. Junkers W.33 "Bremen" (first east-west transatlantic flight), 1928	20	20
570	5 s. Lockheed Vega 5 "Winnie Mae" (Post's first solo round-the-world flight), 1933	30	30
571	10 s. "Voyager" (first non-stop round-the-world flight), 1986	40	40
572	15 s. Chanute biplane glider, 1896	60	60
573	25 s. Airship N.1 "Norge" and polar bear (first transpolar flight), 1926	90	90
574	35 s. Curtiss Golden Flyer biplane and U.S.S. "Pennsylvania" (battleship) (first take-off and landing from ship), 1911	1·25	1·25
575	45 s. Shepard and "Freedom 7" spacecraft (first American in space), 1961	1·40	1·50
576	100 s. Concorde (first supersonic passenger flight), 1976	4·25	4·50

87 Olympic Torch-bearer

1987. Olympic Games, Seoul (1988) (1st issue). Multicoloured.

577	5 s. Type **87**	10	10
578	10 s. Swimming	20	25
579	50 s. Cycling	1·00	1·25
580	100 s. Gymnastics	2·00	2·50

See also Nos. 628/31.

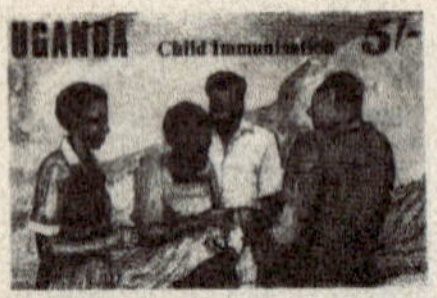

88 Child Immunization

1987. 25th Anniv of Independence. Mult.

582	5 s. Type **88**	15	10
583	10 s. Mulago Hospital, Kampala	30	25
584	25 s. Independence Monument, Kampala City Park	70	70
585	50 s. High Court, Kampala	1·25	1·50

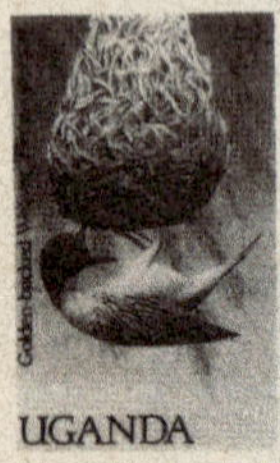

89 Golden-backed Weaver

90 Hippocrates (physician) and Surgeons performing Operation

1987. Birds of Uganda. Multicoloured.

587	5 s. Type **89**	75	70
588	10 s. Hoopoe	1·50	1·00
589	15 s. Red-throated bee eater	1·60	1·00
590	25 s. Lilac-breasted roller	2·00	1·60
591	35 s. African pygmy goose	2·25	1·75
592	45 s. Scarlet-chested sunbird	2·25	2·50
593	50 s. South African crowned crane	2·25	2·50
594	100 s. Long-tailed fiscal	3·75	4·50

1987. Great Scientific Discoveries. Mult.

596	5 s. Type **90**	50	30
597	25 s. Einstein and deep space (Theory of Relativity)	1·75	1·75
598	35 s. Isaac Newton and diagram from "Opticks" (Theory of Colour and Light)	2·00	2·50
599	45 s. Karl Benz and early Benz and modern Mercedes car	2·50	3·00

91 Scout with Stamp Album and Uganda Stamps

1987. World Scout Jamboree, Australia. Multicoloured.

601	5 s. Type **91**	20	10
602	25 s. Scouts planting tree	70	70
603	35 s. Canoeing, Lake Victoria	1·00	85
604	45 s. Hiking	1·75	1·10

92 "The Annunciation"

1987. Christmas. Scenes from French diptych, c. 1250. Multicoloured.

606	5 s. Type **92**	10	10
607	10 s. "The Nativity"	20	25
608	50 s. "Flight into Egypt"	1·00	1·25
609	100 s. "The Adoration of the Magi"	2·00	2·50

93 Class 12 Light Shunter Locomotive

94 Columbite-Tantalite

1988. Locomotives of East Africa Railways. Multicoloured.

611	5 s. Type **93**	35	35
612	10 s. Class 92 diesel-electric	45	45
613	15 s. Steam locomotive No. 2506	60	60
614	25 s. Class 11 tank locomotive	85	85
615	35 s. Class 24 steam locomotive	1·10	1·10
616	45 s. Class 21 steam locomotive	1·40	1·40
617	50 s. Class 59 Garratt steam locomotive, 1955	1·60	1·60
618	100 s. Class 87 diesel-electric locomotive	2·40	2·40

1988. Minerals. Multicoloured.

620	1 s. Type **94**	15	15
621	2 s. Galena	20	20
622	5 s. Malachite	35	35
623	10 s. Cassiterite	55	55
624	35 s. Ferberite	1·50	1·50
625	50 s. Emerald	2·00	2·00
626	100 s. Monazite	3·00	3·00
627	150 s. Microcline	4·00	4·00

95 Hurdling

1988. Olympic Games, Seoul (2nd issue). Mult.

628	5 s. Type **95**	10	10
629	25 s. High jumping	40	50
630	35 s. Javelin throwing	45	55
631	45 s. Long jumping	55	70

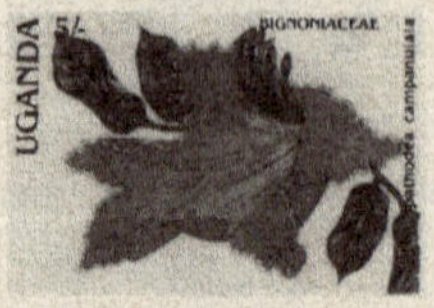

96 "Spathodea campanulata"

1988. Flowers. Multicoloured.

633	5 s. Type **96**	15	15
634	10 s. "Gloriosa simplex"	15	15
635	20 s. "Thevetica peruviana" (vert)	20	20
636	25 s. "Hibiscus schizopetalus"	20	25
637	35 s. "Aframomum sceptrum"	20	30
638	45 s. "Adenium obesum"	20	35
639	50 s. "Kigelia africana" (vert)	25	40
640	100 s. "Clappertonia ficifolia"	35	75

HAVE YOU READ THE NOTES AT THE BEGINNING OF THIS CATALOGUE?
These often provide answers to the enquiries we receive.

97 Elephants in Grassland (Type **61** redrawn)

1988. Endangered Species (2nd series).

642	**97**	10 s. multicoloured		

98 Red Cross Worker vaccinating Baby

1988. 125th Anniv of International Red Cross.

643	**98** 10 s. red, yellow and black	25	15
644	– 40 s. multicoloured	70	70
645	– 70 s. multicoloured	1·50	2·00
646	– 90 s. multicoloured	2·00	2·25

DESIGNS: 10 s. "AIDS" with test tube as "I"; 70 s. Distributing food to refugees; 90 s. Red Cross volunteers with accident victim.

1988. 500th Birth Anniv of Titian (artist). As T **238** of Antigua. Multicoloured.

648	10 s. "Portrait of a Lady"	15	15
649	20 s. "Portrait of a Man"	20	20
650	40 s. "Isabella d'Este"	35	35
651	50 s. "Vincenzo Mosti"	45	45
652	70 s. "Pope Paul III Farnese"	60	60
653	90 s. "Violante"	75	75
654	100 s. "Titian's Daughter Lavinia"	85	85
655	250 s. "Dr. Parma"	1·90	1·90

99 Giraffes, Kidepo Valley National Park

1988. National Parks of Uganda. Mult.

657	10 s. Type **99**	50	20
658	25 s. Zebras, Lake Mburo National Park	1·00	30
659	100 s. African buffalo, Murchison Falls National Park	2·00	2·50
660	250 s. Eastern white pelicans, Queen Elizabeth National Park	5·00	6·50

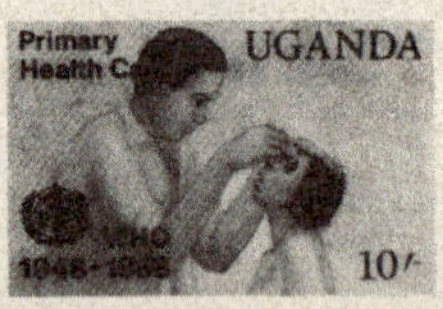

100 Doctor examining Child's Eyes

1988. 40th Anniv of W.H.O. Multicoloured.

662	10 s. Type **100**	20	15
663	25 s. Mental health therapist with patient	40	30
664	45 s. Surgeon performing operation	60	60
665	100 s. Dentist treating girl	1·25	1·50
666	200 s. Doctor examining child	2·00	2·50

1988. Christmas. "Santa's Helpers". As T **228** of Dominica showing Walt Disney cartoon characters. Multicoloured.

668	50 s. Father Christmas with list	85	1·00
669	50 s. Goofy carrying presents	85	1·00
670	50 s. Mickey Mouse on toy train	85	1·00
671	50 s. Reindeer at window	85	1·00
672	50 s. Donald Duck's nephew with building blocks	85	1·00
673	50 s. Donald Duck holding sack	85	1·00
674	50 s. Chip n' Dale on conveyor belt	85	1·00
675	50 s. Donald Duck's nephew operating conveyor belt	85	1·00

Nos. 668/75 were printed together, se-tenant, as a composite design.

1989. Olympic Gold Medal Winners, Seoul. Nos. 628/31 optd or surch.

677	5 s. Type **95** (**110 M HURDLES R. KINGDOM USA**)	10	10
678	25 s. High jumping (optd **HIGH JUMP G. AVDEENKO USSR**)	20	25
679	35 s. Javelin throwing (optd **JAVELIN T. KORJUS FINLAND**)	25	30
680	300 s. on 45 s. Long jumping (optd **LONG JUMP C. LEWIS USA**)	2·25	2·75

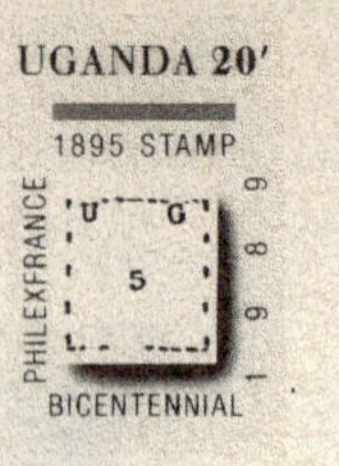

102 Goalkeeper with Ball

103 1895 5 Cowries Stamp

1989. World Cup Football Championship, Italy (1990) (1st issue). Multicoloured.

682	10 s. Type **102**	25	15
683	25 s. Player kicking ball (horiz)	55	40
684	75 s. Heading ball towards net (horiz)	1·25	1·10
685	200 s. Tackling	2·25	2·75

See also Nos. 849/52.

1989. Japanese Art. Paintings by Hokusai. As T **250** of Antigua. Multicoloured.

687	10 s. "Fuji and the Great Wave off Kanagawa"	20	20
688	15 s. "Fuji from Lake Suwa"	30	30
689	20 s. "Fuji from Kajikazawa"	30	30
690	60 s. "Fuji from Shichirigahama"	70	70
691	90 s. "Fuji from Ejiri in Sunshu"	90	90
692	120 s. "Fuji above Lightning"	1·10	1·10
693	200 s. "Fuji from Lower Meguro in Edo"	1·90	1·90
694	250 s. "Fuji from Edo"	2·10	2·10

1989. "Philexfrance 89" International Stamp Exhibition, Paris.

696	**103** 20 s. black, red and brown	40	35
697	– 70 s. black, green and blue	1·00	1·00
698	– 100 s. black, violet & pink	1·25	1·50
699	– 250 s. black, yell & lt yell	2·25	2·75

DESIGNS: 70 s. 1895 10 on 50 cowries stamp; 100 s. 1896 25 cowries stamp; 250 s. 1896 1 rupee stamp.

104 Scout advising on Immunization

1989. 2nd All African Scout Jamboree, Uganda, and 75th Anniv of Uganda Scout Movement. Multicoloured.

701	10 s. Type **104**	30	15
702	70 s. Poultry keeping	90	80
703	90 s. Scout on crutches leading family to immunization centre	1·40	1·25
704	100 s. Scouts making bricks	1·40	1·75

105 "Suillus granulatus"

106 Saddle-bill Stork

1989. Fungi. Multicoloured.

706	10 s. Type **105**	30	30
707	15 s. "Omphalotus olearius"	40	40
708	45 s. "Oudemansiella radicata"	1·00	1·00
709	50 s. "Clitocybe nebularis"	1·10	1·10
710	60 s. "Macrolepiota rhacodes"	1·25	1·25
711	75 s. "Lepista nuda"	1·40	1·40
712	150 s. "Suillus luteus"	2·50	2·50
713	200 s. "Agaricus campestris"	2·75	2·75

1989. Wildlife at Waterhole. Multicoloured.

715	30 s. Type **106**	60	60
716	30 s. Eastern white pelican	60	60
717	30 s. Marabou stork	60	60
718	30 s. Egyptian vulture	60	60
719	30 s. Bateleur	60	60
720	30 s. African elephant	60	60
721	30 s. Giraffe	60	60
722	30 s. Goliath heron	60	60
723	30 s. Black rhinoceros	60	60
724	30 s. Common zebra and oribi	60	60
725	30 s. African fish eagle	60	60
726	30 s. Hippopotamus	60	60
727	30 s. Black-backed jackal and eastern white pelican	60	60
728	30 s. African buffalo	60	60
729	30 s. Olive baboon	60	60
730	30 s. Bohar reedbuck	60	60
731	30 s. Lesser flamingo and serval	60	60
732	30 s. Whale-headed stork ("Shoebill Stork")	60	60
733	30 s. South African crowned crane	60	60
734	30 s. Impala	60	60

Nos. 715/34 were printed together, se-tenant, forming a composite design showing wildlife at a waterhole.

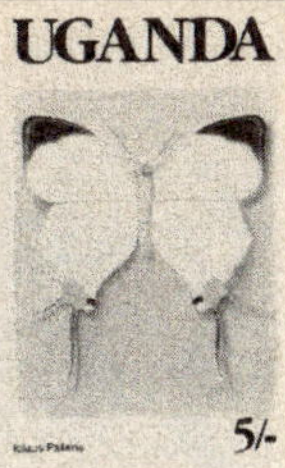

107 Rocket on Launch Pad

108 "Aphniolaus pallene"

1989. 20th Anniv of First Manned Landing on Moon. Multicoloured.

736 10 s. Type **107** . . . 20 20
737 20 s. Lunar module "Eagle" on Moon . . . 30 30
738 30 s. "Apollo 11" command module . . . 40 40
739 50 s. "Eagle" landing on Moon . . . 60 60
740 70 s. Astronaut Aldrin on Moon . . . 85 85
741 250 s. Neil Armstrong alighting from "Eagle" (vert) . . . 2·50 2·50
742 300 s. "Eagle" over Moon . . . 2·50 2·50
743 350 s. Astronaut Aldrin on Moon (vert) . . . 2·75 2·75

1989. Butterflies. T **108** and similar vert designs showing "UGANDA" in black. Multicoloured.

745 5 s. Type **108** . . . 25 20
746 10 s. "Hewitsonia boisduvali" . . . 35 25
747 20 s. "Euxanthe wakefieldi" . . . 45 30
748 30 s. "Papilio echerioides" . . . 50 30
749 40 s. "Acraea semivitrea" . . . 60 40
750 50 s. "Colotis antevippe" . . . 60 40
751 70 s. "Acraea perenna" . . . 70 70
752 90 s. "Charaxes cynthia" . . . 70 70
753 100 s. "Euphaedra neophron" . . . 70 70
754 150 s. "Cymothoe beckeri" . . . 1·00 1·00
755 200 s. "Vanessula milca" . . . 1·10 1·25
756 400 s. "Mimacraea marshalli" . . . 1·75 2·25
757 500 s. "Axiocerses amanga" . . . 2·00 2·50
758 1000 s. "Precis hierta" . . . 2·50 3·50

For these, and similar designs showing "UGANDA" in blue, see Nos. 864/80.

109 John Hanning Speke and Map of Lake Victoria

1989. Exploration of Africa. Multicoloured.

760 10 s. Type **109** . . . 45 35
761 25 s. Sir Richard Burton and map of Lake Tanganyika . . . 60 50
762 40 s. Richard Lander and Bakota bronze . . . 70 65
763 90 s. Rene Caillie and mosque, Timbuktu . . . 1·00 1·00
764 125 s. Sir Samuel Baker and dorcas gazelle . . . 1·25 1·25
765 150 s. Pharaoh Necho and ancient Phoenician merchant ship . . . 1·50 1·50
766 250 s. Vasco da Gama and 15th-century caravel . . . 2·25 2·50
767 300 s. Sir Henry Morton Stanley and "Lady Alice" (sectional boat) . . . 2·50 2·75

110 Logo (25th anniv of African Development Bank)

1989. Anniversaries. Multicoloured.

769 10 s. Type **110** . . . 15 15
770 20 s. Arrows and dish aerials (World Telecommunication Day) . . . 20 20
771 75 s. Two portraits of Nehru (birth centenary) . . . 1·50 1·50
772 90 s. Pan Am Boeing 314A flying boat "Dixie Clipper" (50th anniv of first scheduled trans-Atlantic airmail flight) . . . 1·50 1·50
773 100 s. George Stephenson and "Locomotion", 1825 (175th anniv of first practical steam locomotive) . . . 1·60 1·60
774 150 s. Concorde cockpit (20th anniv of first test flight) . . . 2·75 2·75
775 250 s. "Wapen von Hamburg" and "Leopoldus Primus" (galleons) (800th anniv of Port of Hamburg) . . . 2·75 2·75
776 300 s. Concorde and cockpit interior (20th anniv of first test flight) . . . 3·00 3·00

111 "Aerangis kotschyana"

112 "Thevetia peruviana"

1989. Orchids. Multicoloured.

778 10 s. Type **111** . . . 25 25
779 15 s. "Angraecum infundibulare" . . . 30 30
780 45 s. "Cyrtorchis chailluana" . . . 70 70
781 50 s. "Aerangis rhodosticta" . . . 75 75
782 100 s. "Eulophia speciosa" . . . 1·50 1·50
783 200 s. "Calanthe sylvatica" . . . 2·25 2·25
784 250 s. "Vanilla imperialis" . . . 2·40 2·40
785 350 s. "Polystachya vulcanica" . . . 2·75 2·75

1989. Christmas. Paintings by Fra Angelico. As T **259** of Antigua. Multicoloured.

787 10 s. "Madonna and Child" . . . 15 10
788 20 s. "Adoration of the Magi" . . . 20 15
789 40 s. "Virgin and Child enthroned with Saints" . . . 40 30
790 75 s. "The Annunciation" . . . 70 60
791 100 s. "Virgin and Child" (detail, "St. Peter Martyr" triptych) . . . 85 75
792 150 s. "Virgin and Child enthroned with Saints" (different) . . . 1·25 1·25
793 250 s. "Virgin and Child enthroned" . . . 1·75 2·00
794 350 s. "Virgin and Child" (from Annalena altarpiece) . . . 2·00 2·75

1990. "Expo '90" International Garden and Greenery Exhibition, Osaka (1st issue). Flowering Trees. Multicoloured.

796 10 s. Type **112** . . . 15 15
797 20 s. "Acanthus eminens" . . . 20 20
798 90 s. "Gnidia glauca" . . . 50 50
799 150 s. "Oncoba spinosa" . . . 70 70
800 175 s. "Hibiscus rosa-sinensis" . . . 75 75
801 400 s. "Jacaranda mimosifolia" . . . 1·25 1·50
802 500 s. "Erythrina abyssinica" . . . 1·40 1·75
803 700 s. "Bauhinia purpurea" . . . 1·60 2·00

See also Nos. 820/7.

1990. 50th Anniv of Second World War. As T **98** of Grenada Grenadines. Multicoloured.

805 5 s. Allied penetration of German West Wall, 1944 . . . 25 25
806 10 s. Flags of the Allies, VE Day, 1945 . . . 35 35
807 20 s. Capture of Okinawa, 1945 . . . 45 45
808 75 s. Appointment of Gen. De Gaulle to command all Free French forces, 1944 . . . 60 60
809 100 s. Invasion of Saipan, 1944 . . . 75 75
810 150 s. Airborne landing, Operation Market Garden, 1944 . . . 1·25 1·25
811 200 s. MacArthur's return to Philippines, 1944 . . . 1·40 1·40
812 300 s. Japanese attack on U.S. carrier, Coral Sea, 1942 . . . 1·50 1·50
813 350 s. First Battle of El Alamein, 1942 . . . 1·60 1·60
814 500 s. Naval Battle of Guadalcanal, 1942 . . . 2·00 2·00

1990. 90th Birthday of Queen Elizabeth the Queen Mother. As T **99** of Grenada Grenadines.

816 250 s. black, mauve and blue . . . 80 1·00
817 250 s. black, mauve and blue . . . 80 1·00
818 250 s. black, mauve and blue . . . 80 1·00

DESIGNS: No. 816, Queen Elizabeth with corgi; 817, Queen Elizabeth wearing feathered hat; 818, Queen Elizabeth at wartime inspection.

1990. "EXPO 90". International Garden and Greenery Exhibition, Osaka (2nd issue). Nos. 778/85 optd **EXPO '90** and emblem.

820 10 s. Type **111** . . . 40 30
821 15 s. "Angraecum infundibulare" . . . 40 30
822 45 s. "Cyrtorchis chailluana" . . . 65 45
823 50 s. "Aerangis rhodosticta" . . . 65 45
824 100 s. "Eulophia speciosa" . . . 80 70
825 200 s. "Calanthe sylvatica" . . . 1·25 1·25
826 250 s. "Vanilla imperialis" . . . 1·25 1·75
827 350 s. "Polystachya vulcanica" . . . 1·40 2·00

114 P.A.P.U. Emblem

1990. 10th Anniv of Pan-African Postal Union.

829 **114** 80 s. multicoloured . . . 50 50

MINIMUM PRICE

The minimum price quoted is 10p which represents a handling charge rather than a basis for valuing common stamps. For further notes about prices see introductory pages.

115 Unissued G. B. "V R" Penny Black

1990. 150th Anniv of the Penny Black.

831 **115** 25 s. multicoloured . . . 15 15
832 – 50 s. red, black and green . . . 25 25
833 – 100 s. multicoloured . . . 45 45
834 – 150 s. multicoloured . . . 65 75
835 – 200 s. multicoloured . . . 75 85
836 – 300 s. multicoloured . . . 1·00 1·10
837 – 500 s. multicoloured . . . 1·25 1·50
838 – 600 s. multicoloured . . . 1·25 1·50

DESIGNS: 50 s. Canada 1858–59 3d. Beaver; 100 s. Baden 1851 9 k. on green error; 150 s. Basel 1845 2½ r. Dove; 200 s. U.S.A. 1918 24 c. Inverted "Jenny" error; 300 s. Western Australia 1854 1d. Black Swan; 500 s. Uganda 1895 20 c. "narrow" typewritten stamp; 600 s. G. B. Twopenny blue.

116 African Jacana

1990. Wild Birds of Uganda. Multicoloured.

840 10 s. Type **116** . . . 50 35
841 15 s. Southern ground hornbill . . . 55 35
842 45 s. Kori bustard (vert) . . . 70 50
843 50 s. Secretary bird . . . 70 50
844 100 s. Egyptian geese . . . 95 85
845 300 s. Goliath heron (vert) . . . 2·00 2·50
846 500 s. Ostrich with chicks (vert) . . . 2·50 3·00
847 650 s. Saddle-bill stork (vert) . . . 2·75 3·25

117 Roger Milla of Cameroon

1990. World Cup Football Championship, Italy (2nd issue). Multicoloured.

849 50 s. Type **117** . . . 35 25
850 100 s. Ramzy of Egypt . . . 55 45
851 250 s. David O'Leary of Ireland . . . 1·25 1·25
852 600 s. Littbarsky of West Germany . . . 1·75 2·00

118 Mickey and Minnie Mouse at Breakfast

1990. Health and Safety Campaign. Designs showing Walt Disney cartoon characters. Multicoloured.

854 10 s. Type **118** . . . 20 10
855 20 s. Donald Duck's nephews doing kerb drill . . . 25 15
856 50 s. Donald and Mickey stopping Big Pete smoking . . . 55 35
857 90 s. Mickey stopping Donald choking . . . 70 40
858 100 s. Mickey and Goofy using seat belts . . . 75 45
859 250 s. Mickey and Minnie dancing . . . 1·50 1·50
860 500 s. Donald Duck's fitness class . . . 2·50 3·25
861 600 s. Mickey's nephews showing lights at night . . . 2·75 3·50

1990. As Nos. 746/55 and new values, showing butterflies, as T **108** with "UGANDA" in blue. Multicoloured.

864A 10 s. "Hewitsonia boisduvali" . . . 15 15
865A 20 s. "Euxanthe wakefieldi" . . . 20 20
866A 30 s. "Papilio echerioides" . . . 20 20
867A 40 s. "Acraea semivitrea" . . . 20 20
868B 50 s. "Colotis antevippe" . . . 30 30
869A 70 s. "Acraea perenna" . . . 30 30
870A 90 s. "Charaxes cynthia" . . . 30 30
871A 100 s. "Euphaedra neophron" . . . 40 40
872A 150 s. "Cymothoe beckeri" . . . 40 40
873A 200 s. "Vanessula milca" . . . 60 60
874B 400 s. "Mimacraea marshalli" . . . 1·00 1·00
875B 500 s. "Axiocerses amanga" . . . 1·00 1·00
876B 1000 s. "Precis hierta" . . . 2·00 2·50
877B 2000 s. "Precis hierta" . . . 3·25 4·25
878A 3000 s. "Euphaedra eusemoides" . . . 6·50 7·00
879A 4000 s. "Acraea natalica" . . . 8·00 8·50
880A 5000 s. "Euphaedra themis" . . . 8·00 9·50

1990. Christmas. 350th Death Anniv of Rubens. As T **273** of Antigua, but inscr "CHRISTMAS 1990". Multicoloured.

881 10 s. "Baptism of Christ" (detail) (vert) . . . 10 10
882 20 s. "St. Gregory the Great and other Saints" (detail) (vert) . . . 15 10
883 100 s. "Saints Nereus, Domitilla and Achilleus" (detail) (vert) . . . 45 35
884 150 s. "St. Gregory the Great and other Saints" (different detail) (vert) . . . 60 60
885 300 s. "Saint Augustine" (detail) (vert) . . . 1·00 1·40
886 400 s. "St. Gregory the Great and other Saints" (different detail) (vert) . . . 1·25 1·60
887 500 s. "Baptism of Christ" (different detail) (vert) . . . 1·40 1·75
888 600 s. "St. Gregory the Great and other Saints" (different detail) (vert) . . . 1·50 2·00

119 Census Emblem

1990. National Population and Housing Census.

890 **119** 20 s. multicoloured . . . 30 30

120 Damselfly

1991. Fauna of Uganda's Wetlands. Mult.

892 70 s. Type **120** . . . 50 50
893 70 s. Purple swamphen ("Gallinule") . . . 50 50
894 70 s. Sitatunga . . . 50 50
895 70 s. Western reef heron ("Purple heron") . . . 50 50
896 70 s. Bushpig . . . 50 50
897 70 s. Vervet monkey . . . 50 50
898 70 s. Long reed frog . . . 50 50
899 70 s. Malachite kingfisher . . . 50 50
900 70 s. Marsh mongoose . . . 50 50
901 70 s. Painted reed frog . . . 50 50
902 70 s. African jacana . . . 50 50
903 70 s. Charaxes butterfly . . . 50 50
904 70 s. Nile crocodile . . . 50 50
905 70 s. Herald snake . . . 50 50
906 70 s. Dragonfly . . . 50 50
907 70 s. Lungfish . . . 50 50

Nos. 892/907 were printed together, se-tenant, forming a composite design.

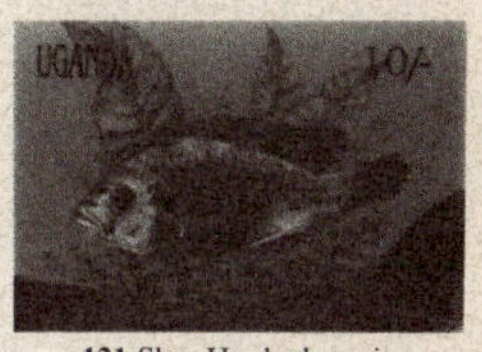

121 Slug Haplochromis

1991. Fishes of Uganda. Multicoloured.

909 10 s. Type **121** . . . 10 10
910 20 s. Palmquist's notho . . . 15 15
911 40 s. Silver distichodus . . . 20 20
912 90 s. Sauvege's haplochromis . . . 40 40
913 100 s. Blue calliurum . . . 45 45
914 350 s. Johnston's haplochromis . . . 1·10 1·10
915 600 s. Colour-tailed haplochromis . . . 2·25 2·25
916 800 s. Jewel cichlid . . . 2·50 2·50

1991. Olympic Games, Barcelona (1992). As T **268** of Antigua. Multicoloured.

918 20 s. Women's 100 metres hurdles . . . 30 15
919 40 s. Long jump . . . 40 20
920 125 s. Table tennis . . . 90 80
921 250 s. Football . . . 1·25 1·50
922 500 s. Men's 800 metres . . . 1·75 2·50

122 Rhodesian Railways 10th Class Steam Locomotive, 1930

1991. African Railway Locomotives. Mult.

924 10 s. Type **122** 30 30
925 20 s. Rhodesian Railways 12th Class steam locomotive, 1900s 45 45
926 80 s. Class "Tribal" steam locomotive, Tanzam Railway, 1951–56 . . . . 80 80
927 200 s. Steam locomotive, Egypt, 1905 . . . . 1·50 1·50
928 300 s. Mikado steam locomotive, Sudan, 1930 . . . . 1·60 1·60
929 400 s. East African Railways Class 59 Garratt steam locomotive, 1955 . . . . . 1·60 1·60
930 500 s. East African Railways Mallet steam locomotive, 1900 1·75 1·75
931 1000 s. Type 5 F 1 electric locomotive, South Africa, 1970 2·25 2·25

123 Lord Baden-Powell and Scout Emblem

1991. World Scout Jamboree, Mount Sorak, Korea.

933 **123** 20 s. multicoloured . . . 30 30
934 – 80 s. multicoloured . . . 65 65
935 – 100 s. multicoloured . . . 75 75
936 – 150 s. black and green . . 1·00 1·00
937 – 300 s. multicoloured . . . 1·50 1·50
938 – 400 s. multicoloured . . . 1·60 1·60
939 – 500 s. multicoloured . . . 1·75 1·75
940 – 1000 s. multicoloured . . 2·50 2·50

DESIGNS: 80 s. Scouts and Uganda 1982 100 s. anniversary stamp; 100 s. Scout encampment, New York World's Fair, 1939; 150 s. Cover and illustration from "Scouting for Boys"; 300 s. Cooking on campfire; 400 s. Aldrin and Armstrong on Moon; 500 s. Scout salutes; 1000 s. Statue to the Unknown Scout, Gillwell Park.

1991. "Phila Nippon '91" International Stamp Exhibition, Tokyo. As T **204** of Lesotho showing Walt Disney cartoon characters and Japanese traditions. Multicoloured.

942 10 s. Uncle Scrooge celebrating Ga-No-Iwai 15 15
943 20 s. Mickey Mouse removing shoes 25 20
944 70 s. Goofy leading cart-horse 60 50
945 80 s. Daisy Duck and Minnie Mouse exchanging gifts . . 70 60
946 300 s. Minnie kneeling at doorway . . . . 1·75 1·75
947 400 s. Donald Duck and Mickey taking a hot volcanic sand bath 1·90 1·90
948 500 s. Clarabelle Cow burning incense . . . . 2·00 2·00
949 1000 s. Mickey and Minnie writing New Year cards . . 2·75 3·00

1991. Death Cent (1990) of Vincent van Gogh (artist). As T **195** of British Virgin Islands. Multicoloured.

951 10 s. "Snowy Landscape with Arles" 20 20
952 20 s. "Peasant Woman binding Sheaves" (vert) 30 30
953 60 s. "The Drinkers" 50 50
954 80 s. "View of Auvers" . . . 65 65
955 200 s. "Mourning Man" (vert) 1·25 1·25
956 400 s. "Still Life: Vase with Roses" . . . . 1·75 1·75
957 800 s. "The Raising of Lazarus" 2·50 2·50
958 1000 s. "The Good Samaritan" (vert) . . . . 2·50 2·50

1991. 65th Birthday of Queen Elizabeth II. As T **280** of Antigua. Multicoloured.

960 70 s. Queen and Prince Charles after polo match 45 45
961 90 s. Queen at Balmoral, 1976 55 55
962 500 s. Queen with Princess Margaret, August 1980 . . 2·00 2·00
963 600 s. Queen and Queen Mother leaving St. George's Chapel, Windsor . . . . 2·00 2·00

1991. 10th Wedding Anniv of Prince and Princess of Wales. As T **280** of Antigua. Multicoloured.

965 20 s. Prince and Princess of Wales in July 1986 . . . . 30 15
966 100 s. Separate photographs of Prince, Princess and sons . . 70 45
967 200 s. Prince Henry and Prince William . . . . 1·00 1·00
968 1000 s. Separate photographs of Prince and Princess in 1988 . 3·75 3·75

124 General Charles de Gaulle

125 "Volvariella bingensis"

1991. Birth Centenary (1990) of Charles de Gaulle (French statesman). Multicoloured.

970 20 s. Type **124** 20 20
971 70 s. Liberation of Paris, 1944 45 45
972 90 s. De Gaulle with King George VI, 1940 . . . . . 55 55
973 100 s. Reviewing Free French troops, 1940 (horiz) 60 60
974 200 s. Broadcasting to France, 1940 (horiz) . . . . 1·00 1·00
975 500 s. De Gaulle in Normandy, 1944 (horiz) . . . . 1·75 1·75
976 600 s. De Gaulle at Albert Hall, 1940 (horiz) . . . . 1·75 1·75
977 1000 s. Inauguration as President, 1959 . . . . 2·50 2·50

1991. Fungi. Multicoloured.

979 20 s. Type **125** 30 30
980 70 s. "Agrocybe broadwayi" . 55 55
981 90 s. "Camarophyllus olidus" 65 65
982 140 s. "Marasmius arborescens" 90 90
983 180 s. "Marasmiellus subcinereus" . . . . 1·00 1·00
984 200 s. "Agaricus campestris" 1·25 1·25
985 500 s. "Chlorophyllum molybdites" . . . . 2·25 2·25
986 1000 s. "Agaricus bingensis" . 3·50 3·50

1991. Endangered Species (3rd series). As Nos. 406/9, but with changed face values, and additional horiz designs as T **61**. Multicoloured.

988 100 s. Elephants in "Elephants' Graveyard" 65 45
989 140 s. Type **61** 85 75
990 200 s. Elephants at waterhole 1·25 1·10
991 600 s. Elephants having dust bath 2·50 3·50

126 "Anigozanthos manglesii'

128 Boy Scout Monument, New York, and Ernest Thompson (first Chief Scout of U.S.A.)

1991. Botanical Gardens of the World. Mult.

993/1032 90 s. × 20, 100 s. × 20 Set of 40 . . . . 14·00 16·00

Nos. 993/1032 were issued together, se-tenant, as two sheetlets of 20 containing designs as Type **126**. The 90 s values show "Anigozanthos manglesii", "Banksia grandis", "Clianthus formosus", "Gossypium sturtianum", "Callistemon lanceolatus", "Saintpaulia ionantha", "Calodendrum capense", "Aloe ferox × arborescens", "Bolusanthus speciousus", "Lithops schwantesii", "Protea repens", "Plumbago capensis", "Clerodendrum thomsoniae", "Thunbergia alata", "Schotia latifolia", "Epacris impressa", "Acacia pycnantha", "Telopea speciosissima", "Wahlenbergia gloriosa", "Eucalyptus globulus" from Melbourne, and the 100 s. "Cypripedium calceolus", "Rhododendron thomsonii", "Ginkgo biloba", "Magnolia campbellii", "Wisteria sinensis", "Clerodendrum ugandense", "Eulophia horsfallii", "Aerangis rhodosticta", "Abelmoschus moschatus", "Gloriosa superba", "Carissa edulis", "Ochna kirkii", "Canarina abyssinica", "Nymphaea caerulea", "Ceropegia succulenta", "Strelitzia reginae", "Strongylodon macrobotrys", "Victoria amazonica", "Orchis militaris" and "Sophora microphylla" from Kew.

1991. Nos. 573, 597 and 614 surch **20/-**.

1034 20 s. on 25 s. Airship N.1 "Norge" and polar bear (first transpolar flight), 1926 . . . .
1035 20 s. on 25 s. Einstein and deep space (Theory of Relativity)
1035a 20 s. on 25 s. Tank locomotive No. 126 . . . .

1991. Christmas. Paintings by Piero della Francesca. As T **291** of Antigua. Multicoloured.

1036 20 s. "Madonna with Child and Angels" 30 15
1037 50 s. "The Baptism of Christ" 45 15
1038 80 s. "Polyptych of Mercy" . 60 40
1039 100 s. "Polyptych of Mercy" (detail) 60 40
1040 200 s. "The Annunciation" from "The Legend of the True Cross" . . . . 1·00 80
1041 500 s. "Pregnant Madonna" 2·00 2·00
1042 1000 s. "The Annunciation" from "Polyptych of St. Anthony" . . . . 3·00 3·50
1043 1500 s. "The Nativity" . . . 4·00 5·00

1992. Anniversaries and Events. Multicoloured.

1045 20 s. Type **128** 60 30
1046 50 s. Treehouse design and Daniel Beard (vert) . . . 75 40
1047 400 s. Lilienthal's signature and "Flugzeug Nr. 8" . . . . 1·50 1·60
1048 500 s. Demonstator demolishing Berlin Wall . . . . 1·60 2·25
1049 700 s. "The Magic Flute" . 2·50 2·75

ANNIVERSARIES AND EVENTS: Nos. 1045/6, 50th death anniv of Lord Baden-Powell and World Scout Jamboree, Korea; No. 1047, Centenary of Otto Lilienthal's first gliding experiments; No. 1048, Bicentenary of Brandenburg Gate, Berlin; No. 1049, Death bicentenary of Mozart.

129 U.S.S. "Vestal" (repair ship) under Attack

1992. 50th Anniv of Japanese Attack on Pearl Harbor. Multicoloured.

1051 200 s. Type **129** 75 75
1052 200 s. Japanese Mitsubishi A6M Zero-Sen 75 75
1053 200 s. U.S.S. "Arizona" (battleship) on fire 75 75
1054 200 s. U.S.S. "Nevada" (battleship) passing burning ships 75 75
1055 200 s. Japanese Aichi D3A "Val" bomber attacking . . 75 75
1056 200 s. Douglas SBD Dauntless bombers attacking "Hiryu" (carrier) at Midway 75 75
1057 200 s. Japanese Mitsubishi A6M Zero-Sen aircraft attacking Midway Island 75 75
1058 200 s. U.S. Marine Brewster F2A Buffalo (fighter) defending Midway 75 75
1059 200 s. American Grumman F6F Hellcat aircraft and carrier . 75 75
1060 200 s. U.S.S. "Yorktown" (carrier) torpedoed 75 75

130 Three Modern Hot Air Balloons

1992. 120th Anniv (1990) of Paris Balloon Post. Multicoloured.

1061 200 s. Type **130** 70 70
1062 200 s. Sport balloons and top of "Double Eagle II" 70 70
1063 200 s. Pro Juventute balloon and top of Branson's "Virgin Otsuka Pacific Flyer" . . . 70 70
1064 200 s. Blanchard and Jeffries' balloon 70 70
1065 200 s. Nadar's "Le Geant" and centre of "Double Eagle II" 70 70
1066 200 s. Branson's "Virgin Otsuka Pacific Flyer" 70 70
1067 200 s. Montgolfier balloon . . 70 70
1068 200 s. "Double Eagle II" basket and Paris balloon of 1870 . 70 70
1069 200 s. Henri Giffard's balloon "Le Grand Ballon Captif' . 70 70

Nos. 1061/9 were printed together, se-tenant, forming a composite design.

1992. Mickey's World Tour. As T **264** of Maldive Islands showing Walt Disney cartoon characters in different countries. Multicoloured.

1070 20 s. Mickey Mouse and Goofy on African safari (horiz) . . 25 15
1071 50 s. Mickey charming Pluto's tail, India (horiz) 40 15
1072 80 s. Minnie Mouse, Donald and Daisy Duck as Caribbean calypso band (horiz) . . . 60 25
1073 200 s. Goofy pulling Donald and Daisy in rickshaw, China (horiz) . . . . 1·00 60
1074 500 s. Mickey and Minnie on camel, Egypt (horiz) . . . 1·50 1·50
1075 800 s. Donald and Pete sumo wrestling, Japan (horiz) . . 1·75 2·00
1076 1000 s. Goofy bullfighting, Spain (horiz) . . . . 1·90 2·25
1077 1500 s. Mickey playing football, Italy (horiz) . . . . 2·50 3·25

1992. 40th Anniv of Queen Elizabeth II's Accession. As T **280** of Antigua. Multicoloured.

1079 100 s. Lake Victoria 55 25
1080 200 s. Lake and mountains . 85 60
1081 500 s. Lakeside fields . . . . 1·75 1·90
1082 1000 s. River Nile . . . . . . 2·75 3·00

1992. Prehistoric Animals. As T **290** of Antigua but horiz. Multicoloured.

1084 50 s. Kentrosaurus 45 30
1085 200 s. Iguanodon 90 80
1086 250 s. Hypsilophodon 95 90
1087 300 s. Brachiosaurus . . . . 1·10 1·10
1088 400 s. Peloneustes . . . . . . 1·25 1·25
1089 500 s. Pteranodon . . . . . . 1·40 1·40
1090 800 s. Tetralophodon . . . . 1·90 2·00
1091 1000 s. Megalosaurus . . . . 1·90 2·00

EASTER 1992

131 "The Entry into Jerusalem" (detail) (Giotto)

132 Adungu

1992. Easter. Religious Paintings. Mult.

1093 50 s. Type **131** 35 15
1094 100 s. "Pilate and the Watch" (Psalter of Robert de Lisle) 45 20
1095 200 s. "The Kiss of Judas" (detail) (Giotto) 75 55
1096 250 s. "Christ washing the Feet of the Disciples" (Vita Christi manuscript) 85 75
1097 300 s. "Christ seized in the Garden" (Melissende Psalter) 95 85
1098 500 s. "Doubting Thomas" (Vita Christi manuscript) . 1·40 1·60
1099 1000 s. "The Marys at the Tomb" (detail) (anon) . . 2·25 3·00
1100 2000 s. "The Ascension" (Florentine manuscript) . . 3·75 5·00

1992. Traditional Musical Instruments. Mult.

1102 50 s. Type **132** 20 20
1103 100 s. Endingidi 35 35
1104 200 s. Akogo 60 60
1105 250 s. Nanga 65 65
1106 300 s. Engoma 75 75
1107 400 s. Amakondere 80 80
1108 500 s. Akakyenkye . . . . . 1·10 1·25
1109 1000 s. Ennanga . . . . . . 2·25 2·75

133 Map of Known World, 1486

1992. 500th Anniv of Discovery of America by Columbus and "World Columbian Stamp Expo '92" Exhibition, Chicago. Multicoloured.

1110 50 s. Type **133** 20 20
1111 100 s. Map of Africa, 1508 . 30 30
1112 150 s. Map of West Indies, 1500 50 50
1113 200 s. "Nina" and astrolabe . 60 60
1114 600 s. "Pinta" and quadrant 1·50 1·50
1115 800 s. Sand glass . . . . . . 1·60 1·60
1116 900 s. 15th-century compass . 1·75 1·75
1117 2000 s. Map of World, 1492 3·50 3·50

1992. Hummel Figurines. As T **256** of Maldive Islands. Multicoloured.

1119 50 s. Girl with washing . . . 25 20
1120 200 s. Girl scrubbing floor . 60 50
1121 250 s. Girl sweeping floor . . 70 60
1122 300 s. Girl with baby 80 70
1123 600 s. Boy mountaineer . . . 1·75 1·75
1124 900 s. Girl knitting . . . . . 2·25 2·50
1125 1000 s. Boy on stool . . . . 2·50 2·75
1126 1500 s. Boy with telescope . 2·75 3·00

134 Spotted Hyena

1992. Wildlife. Multicoloured.

1128 50 s. Type **134** 15 15
1129 100 s. Impala 25 25
1130 200 s. Giant forest hog . . . 35 35
1131 250 s. Pangolin 45 45
1132 300 s. Golden monkey . . . 50 50
1133 800 s. Serval . . . . 1·40 1·40
1134 1000 s. Small-spotted genet ("Bush genet") . . . . . . 1·60 1·60
1135 3000 s. Waterbuck . . . . . 4·25 4·50

1992. Olympic Games, Barcelona. As T **216** of Lesotho. Multicoloured.

1137 50 s. Men's javelin 25 20
1138 100 s. Men's high jump (horiz) 35 30
1139 200 s. Fencing (pentathlon) . 50 45
1140 250 s. Men's volleyball . . . 60 60
1141 300 s. Women's platform diving 60 60
1142 500 s. Men's team cycling . . 1·75 1·75
1143 1000 s. Women's tennis . . . 2·50 2·50
1144 2000 s. Boxing (horiz) . . . 3·25 3·75

135 Red-headed Falcon   **136** Goofy in "Hawaiian Holiday", 1937

1992. Birds. Multicoloured.

1146 20 s. Type **135** 10 10
1147 30 s. Yellow-billed hornbill 15 10
1148 50 s. Purple heron 15 10
1149 100 s. Regal sunbird 20 20
1150 150 s. White-browed robin chat 25 25
1151 200 s. Shining-blue kingfisher 30 30
1152 250 s. Great blue turaco 45 40
1153 300 s. African emerald cuckoo 55 45
1154 500 s. Abyssinian roller 90 90
1155 800 s. South African crowned crane 1·40 1·50
1156 1000 s. Doherty's bush shrike 1·75 1·90
1157 2000 s. Splendid glossy starling 3·00 3·50
1158 3000 s. Little bee eater 4·50 5·50
1159 4000 s. Red-faced lovebird ("Red-headed Lovebird") 6·00 7·00

1992. 60th Anniv of Goofy. Multicoloured.

1162 50 s. Type **136** 25 20
1163 100 s. Riding pennyfarthing cycle, 1941 30 20
1164 200 s. Goofy and Mickey Mouse as firemen, 1935 50 35
1165 250 s. Skiing, 1941 (horiz) 55 40
1166 300 s. One man band, 1937 (horiz) 60 60
1167 1000 s. Asleep against boat, 1938 (horiz) 2·00 2·25
1168 1500 s. Ancient Olympic champion, 1942 3·00 3·25
1169 2000 s. Pole vaulting, 1942 3·25 3·75

137 "The Annunciation" (Zurbaran)

1992. Christmas. Religious Paintings by Francisco Zurbaran. Multicoloured.

1171 50 s. Type **137** 20 15
1172 200 s. "The Annunciation" (different) 50 35
1173 250 s. "The Virgin of the Immaculate Conception" 60 45
1174 300 s. "The Virgin of the Immaculate Conception" (detail) 65 50
1175 800 s. "Holy Family with Saints Anne, Joachim and John the Baptist" 1·75 2·00
1176 900 s. "Holy Family with Saints Anne, Joachim and John the Baptist" (detail) 1·90 2·25
1177 1000 s. "Adoration of the Magi" 2·00 2·25
1178 2000 s. "Adoration of the Magi" (detail) 3·50 4·25

138 Man cleaning Granary

1992. Anniversaries and Events. Multicoloured.

1180 50 s. Type **138** 15 15
1181 200 s. Mother breast feeding 40 40
1182 250 s. Mother feeding baby 50 50
1183 300 s. Boy collecting water from pump 60 60
1184 300 s. "Voyager 2" passing Jupiter 1·00 1·00
1185 800 s. Mother and baby 1·40 1·40
1186 800 s. Impala 1·40 1·40
1187 1000 s. Mountain zebra 2·25 2·25
1188 1000 s. Count Ferdinand von Zeppelin and airship 2·25 2·25
1189 2000 s. "Voyager 2" passing Neptune 4·50 4·50
1190 3000 s. Count Ferdinand von Zeppelin and Clement-Bayard airship "Fleurus" 5·50 5·50

ANNIVERSARIES AND EVENTS: Nos. 1180/3, 1185, United Nations World Health Organization Projects; Nos. 1184, 1189, International Space Year; Nos. 1186/7, Earth Summit '92, Rio; Nos. 1188, 1190, 75th death anniv of Count Ferdinand von Zeppelin (airship pioneer).

139 Hands releasing Dove with Lubaga and Kampala Catholic Cathedrals

1993. Visit of Pope John Paul II. Mult.

1192 50 s. Type **139** 25 10
1193 200 s. Pope and Kampala Cathedral 45 30
1194 250 s. Pope and Catholic worshipper 50 35
1195 300 s. Ugandan bishops and Pope 55 40
1196 800 s. Pope John Paul II waving 1·50 1·60
1197 900 s. Pope and Kampala Cathedral (different) 1·50 1·60
1198 1000 s. Pope, national flag and Kampala Cathedral 1·60 1·75
1199 2000 s. Pope and national flag 3·00 3·50

1993. Bicentenary of the Louvre, Paris. Paintings by Rembrandt. As T **305** of Antigua. Multicoloured.

1201 500 s. "Self Portrait at Easel" 80 85
1202 500 s. "Birds of Paradise" 80 85
1203 500 s. "The Carcass of Beef" 80 85
1204 500 s. "The Supper at Emmaus" 80 85
1205 500 s. "Hendrickje Stoffels" 80 85
1206 500 s. "The Artist's Son, Titus" 80 85
1207 500 s. "The Holy Family" (left detail) 80 85
1208 500 s. "The Holy Family" (right detail) 80 85

140 Afghan Hound

1993. Dogs of the World. Multicoloured.

1210 50 s. Type **140** 30 20
1211 100 s. Newfoundland 40 20
1212 200 s. Siberian huskies 65 40
1213 250 s. Briard 70 45
1214 300 s. Saluki 75 55
1215 800 s. Labrador guide-dog (vert) 1·50 1·75
1216 1000 s. Greyhound 1·75 2·00
1217 1500 s. Pointer 2·25 2·75

1993. 40th Anniv of Coronation. As T **307** of Antigua. Multicoloured.

1219 50 s. Queen Elizabeth II at Coronation (photograph by Cecil Beaton) 10 10
1220 200 s. Orb and Sceptre 25 30
1221 500 s. Queen Elizabeth during Coronation 60 65
1222 1500 s. Queen Elizabeth II and Princess Margaret 1·75 1·90

1993. Asian International Stamp Exhibitions. As T **268** of Dominica, but vert. Multicoloured. (a) "Indopex '93", Surabaya, Indonesia. Javanese Wayang Puppets

1224 600 s. Bupati karma, Prince of Wangga 90 1·00
1225 600 s. Rahwana 90 1·00
1226 600 s. Sondjeng Sandjata 90 1·00
1227 600 s. Raden Damar Wulan 90 1·00
1228 600 s. Unidentified puppet 90 1·00
1229 600 s. Hanaman 90 1·00

(b) "Taipei '93", Taiwan. Funerary Pottery Figures

1231 600 s. Tomb guardian god in green armour 90 1·00
1232 600 s. Civil official and shrine 90 1·00
1233 600 s. Tomb guardian god in green and gold armour 90 1·00
1234 600 s. Civil official in red robe 90 1·00
1235 600 s. Chimera (tomb guardian) 90 1·00
1236 600 s. Civil official in red and green robe 90 1·00

(c) "Bangkok '93", Thailand. Sculptured Figures

1238 600 s. Standing Buddha in gilded red sandstone, 13th–15th century 90 1·00
1239 600 s. Crowned Buddha in bronze, 13th century 90 1·00
1240 600 s. Thepanom in stone, 15th century 90 1·00
1241 600 s. Crowned Buddha in bronze, 12th century 90 1·00
1242 600 s. Avalokitesvara in bronze, 9th century 90 1·00
1243 600 s. Lop Buri standing Buddha in bronze, 13th-century 90 1·00

141 Gutierrez (Uruguay) and Voeller (Germany)   **142** York Minster, England

1993. World Cup Football Championship, U.S.A. (1994) (1st issue). Multicoloured.

1245 50 s. Type **141** 25 15
1246 200 s. Tomas Brolin (Sweden) 60 40
1247 250 s. Gary Lineker (England) 70 45
1248 300 s. Munoz and Butragueno (Spain) 75 55
1249 800 s. Carlos Valderrama (Colombia) 1·50 1·75
1250 900 s. Diego Maradona (Argentina) 1·60 1·90
1251 1000 s. Pedro Troglio (Argentina) 1·75 2·00
1252 2000 s. Enzo Scifo (Belgium) 3·00 3·50

See also Nos. 1322/8.

1993. Cathedrals of the World. Multicoloured.

1254 50 s. Type **142** 20 15
1255 100 s. Notre Dame, Paris 30 20
1256 200 s. Little Metropolis, Athens 55 40
1257 250 s. St. Patrick's, New York 60 45
1258 300 s. Ulm, Germany 65 50
1259 800 s. St. Basil's, Moscow 1·50 1·75
1260 1000 s. Roskilde, Denmark 1·75 2·00
1261 2000 s. Seville, Spain 3·25 3·75

1993. Christmas. Religious Paintings. As T **270** of Dominica. Black, yellow and red (Nos. 1263, 1265, 1267 and 1270) or multicoloured (others).

1263 50 s. "Virgin with Carthusian Monks" (detail) (Durer) 20 10
1264 100 s. "Sacred Family" (detail) (Raphael) 30 10
1265 200 s. "Virgin with Carthusian Monks" (different detail) (Durer) 45 30
1266 250 s. "The Virgin of the Rose" (Raphael) 55 35
1267 300 s. "Virgin with Carthusian Monks" (different detail) (Durer) 60 40
1268 800 s. "Sacred Family" (different detail) (Raphael) 1·50 1·75
1269 1000 s. "Virgin with Beardless Joseph" (Raphael) 1·75 2·00
1270 2000 s. "Virgin with Carthusian Monks" (different detail) (Durer) 3·00 3·75

143 Mickey Mouse asleep on Stegosaurus

1993. Prehistoric Animals and Walt Disney Cartoon Characters. Multicoloured.

1272 50 s. Type **143** 30 20
1273 100 s. Minnie Mouse on pterandon 40 20
1274 200 s. Mickey being licked by mamenchisaurus 60 40
1275 250 s. Mickey doing cave painting 70 45
1276 300 s. Mickey wind-surfing on dinosaur 75 55
1277 500 s. Mickey and Donald Duck sliding on diplodocus 1·00 1·00
1278 800 s. Mamenchisaurus carrying Mickey 1·50 1·75
1279 1000 s. Pluto on triceratops 1·75 2·00

No. 1273 is inscribed "PTERANDOM" and No. 1278 "MAMENSHISAURUS", both in error.

144 "Woman in Yellow" (Picasso)   **145** Passion Fruit

1993. Anniversaries and Events. Multicoloured.

1281 100 s. Type **144** 20 15
1282 200 s. Head of cow and syringe 40 30
1283 250 s. "Gertrude Stein" (Picasso) 50 35
1284 500 s. Early telescope 1·00 1·00
1285 800 s. "Creation" (S. Witkiewicz after J. Glogowski) 1·50 1·50
1286 1000 s. Modern telescope 1·75 2·00
1287 1000 s. "For the Right to Work" (A. Strumillo) 1·75 2·00

ANNIVERSARIES AND EVENTS: Nos. 1281, 1283, 20th death anniv of Picasso (artist); No. 1282, Pan African Rinderpest Campaign; Nos. 1284, 1286, 450th death anniv of Copernicus (astronomer); Nos. 1285, 1287, "Polska '93" International Stamp Exhibition, Poznan.

1994. Fruits and Crops. Multicoloured.

1289 50 s. Type **145** 20 10
1290 100 s. Sunflower 25 10
1291 150 s. Bananas 35 25
1292 200 s. Runner beans 45 30
1293 250 s. Pineapple 50 45
1294 300 s. Jackfruit 60 55
1295 500 s. Sorghum 1·00 1·10
1296 800 s. Maize 1·50 2·00

146 Ford Model "A", 1903

1994. Centenaries of Henry Ford's First Petrol Engine (Nos. 1298/1301) and Karl Benz's First Four-wheeled Car (others). Multicoloured.

1298 700 s. Type **146** 1·10 1·25
1299 700 s. Ford Model "T" snowmobile, 1932 1·10 1·25
1300 700 s. Ford "Mustang" 1·10 1·25
1301 700 s. Lotus-Ford racing car, 1965 1·10 1·25
1302 800 s. Mercedes-Benz "S600" coupe, 1994 1·10 1·25
1303 800 s. Mercedes-Benz "W196" racing car, 1955 1·10 1·25
1304 800 s. Mercedes-Benz "W125" road speed record car, 1938 1·10 1·25
1305 800 s. Benz "Viktoria", 1893 1·10 1·25

1994. "Hong Kong '94" International Stamp Exhibition (1st issue). As T **317** of Antigua. Multicoloured.

1307 500 s. Hong Kong 1988 60 c. Catholic Cathedral stamp and religious shrines, Repulse Bay 70 80
1308 500 s. Uganda 1993 2500 s. Namirembe Cathedral stamp and religious shrines, Repulse Bay (different) 70 80

Nos. 1307/8 were printed together, se-tenant, forming a composite design.

1994. "Hong Kong '94" International Stamp Exhibition (2nd issue). Ching Dynasty Snuff Boxes. As T **318** of Antigua, but vert. Multicoloured.

1309 200 s. Glass box with pavilion design 35 40
1310 200 s. Porcelain box with quail design 35 40
1311 200 s. Porcelain box with floral design 35 40
1312 200 s. Porcelain box with openwork design 35 40
1313 200 s. Agate box with carved Lion-dogs 35 40
1314 200 s. Agate box with man on donkey design 35 40

Captions for Nos. 1310/11 are transposed.

147 Meteorological Weather Station

1994. World Meteorological Day. Multicoloured.

1315 50 s. Type **147** 25 15
1316 200 s. Weather observatory at training school, Entebbe (vert) 65 40
1317 250 s. Satellite link 75 50
1318 300 s. Recording temperatures 80 55
1319 400 s. Automatic weather station (vert) 1·00 1·00
1320 800 s. Crops damaged by hailstones 1·75 2·25

1994. World Cup Football Championship, U.S.A. (2nd issue). As T **268** of Sierra Leone. Multicoloured.

1322 500 s. Georges Grun (Belgium) 1·00 1·10
1323 500 s. Oscar Ruggeri (Argentina) 1·00 1·10
1324 500 s. Frank Rijkaard (Netherlands) 1·00 1·10
1325 500 s. Magid "Tyson" Musisi (Uganda) 1·00 1·10
1326 500 s. Ronald Koeman (Netherlands) 1·00 1·10
1327 500 s. Igor Shalimov (Russia) 1·00 1·10

No. 1326 is inscribed "DONALD KOEMAN" in error.

148 Milking Cow

1994. 50th Anniv of Heifer Project International.
1329 148 100 s. multicoloured . . 45 30

149 "Lobobunaea goodii"

150 Wooden Stool

1994. Moths. Multicoloured.
1330 100 s. Type 149 30 20
1331 200 s. "Bunaeopsis hersilia" 55 40
1332 300 s. "Rufoglanis rosea" 70 60
1333 350 s. "Acherontia atropos" 75 75
1334 400 s. "Rohaniella pygmaea" 85 85
1335 450 s. "Euchloron megaera" 90 90
1336 500 s. "Epiphora rectifascia" 1·00 1·00
1337 1000 s. "Polyphychus coryndoni" 1·75 2·00

1994. Crafts. Multicoloured.
1339 100 s. Type 150 20 10
1340 200 s. Wood and banana fibre chair 40 30
1341 250 s. Raffia and palm leaves basket 45 35
1342 300 s. Wool tapestry showing tree planting 50 45
1343 450 s. Wool tapestry showing hair grooming 75 75
1344 500 s. Wood sculpture of a drummer 85 85
1345 800 s. Gourds 1·50 1·75
1346 1000 s. Bark cloth handbag 1·75 2·00

151 Turkish Angora Cat and Blue Mosque

1994. Cats. Multicoloured.
1348 50 s. Type 151 20 15
1349 100 s. Japanese bobtail and Mt Fuji 30 15
1350 200 s. Norwegian forest cat and windmill, Holland 45 35
1351 300 s. Egyptian mau and pyramids (vert) 55 55
1352 450 s. Rex and Stonehenge, England (vert) 70 70
1353 500 s. Chartreux and Eiffel Tower, France 75 75
1354 1000 s. Burmese and Shwe Dagon Pagoda (vert) 1·50 1·75
1355 1500 s. Maine coon and Pemaquid Point Lighthouse (vert) 2·00 2·50

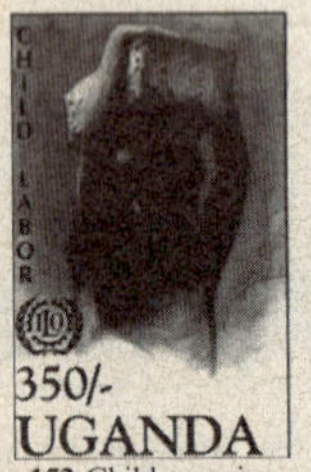

152 Child carrying Building Block

1994. 75th Anniv of I.L.O.
1357 152 350 s. multicoloured . . 75 75

1994. 25th Anniv of First Manned Moon Landing. Astronauts. As T 326 of Antigua. Multicoloured.
1358 50 s. Alan Shepard Jnr 25 25
1359 100 s. M. Scott Carpenter 30 35
1360 200 s. Virgil Grissom 50 55
1361 300 s. L. Gordon Cooper Jnr 60 65
1362 400 s. Walter Schirra Jnr 70 75
1363 500 s. Donald Slayton 75 80
1364 600 s. John Glenn Jnr 80 85

1994. Centenary of International Olympic Committee. Gold Medal Winners. As T 330 of Antigua. Multicoloured.
1366 350 s. John Akii-Bua (Uganda) (400 metres hurdles), 1972 (horiz) 60 45
1367 900 s. Heike Herkel (Germany) (high jump), 1992 (horiz) 1·25 1·50

1994. 50th Anniv of D-Day. As T 331 of Antigua. Multicoloured.
1369 300 s. Mulberry Harbour pier 50 40
1370 1000 s. Mulberry Harbour floating bridge 1·50 2·00

1994. "Philakorea '94" International Stamp Exhibition, Seoul. As T 279 of Dominica, but vert. Multicoloured.
1372 100 s. Sari Pagoda, Paekyangsa 10 10
1373 350 s. Ch'omsongdae 40 45
1374 1000 s. Pulguksa Temple 1·25 1·40

153 Ugandan family

1994. International Year of the Family.
1376 153 100 s. multicoloured . . 30 20

154 Baby Simba

1994. "The Lion King". Characters from Walt Disney's cartoon film. Multicoloured.
1377 100 s. Type 154 30 30
1378 100 s. Mufasa, Simba and Sarabi 30 30
1379 100 s. Young Simba and Nala 30 30
1380 100 s. Timon 30 30
1381 100 s. Rafiki 30 30
1382 100 s. Pumbaa 30 30
1383 100 s. The Hyenas 30 30
1384 100 s. Scar 30 30
1385 100 s. Zazu 30 30
1386 200 s. Rafiki and Mufasa 35 35
1387 200 s. Rafiki holding Simba with Mufasa and Sarabi 35 35
1388 200 s. Rafiki holding Simba aloft 35 35
1389 200 s. Scar and Zazu 35 35
1390 200 s. Rafiki having vision 35 35
1391 200 s. Simba and Scar 35 35
1392 200 s. Simba and Nala 35 35
1393 200 s. Simba with mane of leaves 35 35
1394 200 s. Simba, Nala and Zazu 35 35
1395 250 s. Scar and Simba 40 40
1396 250 s. Mufasa rescues Simba 40 40
1397 250 s. Scar killing Mufasa 40 40
1398 250 s. Simba falling off cliff 40 40
1399 250 s. Timon, Pumbaa and Simba at pool 40 40
1400 250 s. Simba, Timon and Pumbaa 40 40
1401 250 s. Rafiki with staff 40 40
1402 250 s. Simba and Nala 40 40
1403 250 s. Simba looking into pool 40 40

1994. Centenary (1992) of Sierra Club (environmental protection society). Endangered Species. As T 320 of Antigua. Multicoloured.

(a) Vert designs.
1405 100 s. Chimpanzee with arms folded 30 30
1406 200 s. Head of chimpanzee 40 45
1407 250 s. Head of African wild dog 40 45
1408 300 s. Head of cheetah 50 55
1409 500 s. Geleda baboon 70 75
1410 600 s. Geleda baboon from back 80 85
1411 800 s. Head of Grevy's zebra 95 1·00
1412 1000 s. Geleda baboon sitting on rock 1·25 1·40

(b) Horiz designs.
1413 200 s. Pair of cheetahs 40 45
1414 250 s. Cheetah cubs 40 45
1415 300 s. African wild dog at rest 50 55
1416 500 s. Head of African wild dog 70 75
1417 600 s. Grevy's zebra 80 85
1418 800 s. Chimpanzee lying down 95 1·00
1419 1000 s. Grevy's zebra feeding 1·25 1·40

155 Terminal Building, Entebbe International Airport

1994. 50th Anniv of I.C.A.O. Mult.
1420 100 s. Type 155 35 20
1421 250 s. Control tower, Entebbe International Airport 75 80

156 Game Poachers

157 "Adoration of the Christ Child" (Filippino Lippi)

1994. Ecology. Multicoloured.
1422 100 s. Type 156 20 10
1423 250 s. Villagers at rubbish dump 55 40
1424 350 s. Fishermen 70 70
1425 500 s. Deforestation 1·25 1·40

1994. Christmas. Religious Paintings. Multicoloured.
1426 100 s. Type 157 25 10
1427 200 s. "The Holy Family rests on the Flight into Egypt" (Annibale Carracci) 45 30
1428 300 s. "Madonna with Christ Child and St. John" (Piero di Cosimo) 60 40
1429 350 s. "The Conestabile Madonna" (Raphael) 70 55
1430 450 s. "Madonna and Child with Angels" (after Antonio Rossellino) 80 80
1431 500 s. "Madonna and Child with St. John" (Raphael) 90 90
1432 900 s. "Madonna and Child" (Luca Signorelli) 1·75 2·00
1433 1000 s. "Madonna with the Child Jesus, St. John and an Angel" (pseudo Pier Francesco Fiorentino) 1·90 2·00

No. 1426 is inscribed "Fillipino" in error.

158 "Self-portrait" (Tintoretto)

1995. 400th Death Anniv (1994) of Jacopo Tintoretto (painter). Multicoloured.
1435 100 s. Type 158 20 10
1436 300 s. "A Philosopher" 55 45
1437 400 s. "The Creation of the Animals" (detail) (horiz) 70 70
1438 450 s. "The Feast of Belshazzar" (detail) (horiz) 75 75
1439 500 s. "The Raising of the Brazen Serpent" 85 85
1440 1000 s. "Elijah fed by the Angel" 1·75 2·00

159 White-faced Whistling Duck ("White-faced Tree-duck")

1995. Waterfowl and Wetland Birds of Uganda. Multicoloured.
1442 200 s. Type 159 15 20
1443 200 s. Common shoveler ("European Shoveler") 15 20
1444 200 s. Hartlaub's duck 15 20
1445 200 s. Verreaux's eagle owl ("Milky Eagle-owl") 15 20
1446 200 s. Avocet 15 20
1447 200 s. African fish eagle 15 20
1448 200 s. Spectacled weaver 15 20
1449 200 s. Black-headed gonolek 15 20
1450 200 s. Great crested grebe 15 20
1451 200 s. Red-knobbed coot 15 20
1452 200 s. Woodland kingfisher 15 20
1453 200 s. Pintail 15 20
1454 200 s. Squacco heron 15 20
1455 200 s. Purple gallinule 15 20
1456 200 s. African darter 15 20
1457 200 s. African jacana 15 20

Nos. 1442/57 were printed together, se-tenant, forming a composite design.

1995. 18th World Scout Jamboree, Netherlands. Nos. 701/4 optd or surch **18th World Scout Jamboree Mondial, Holland, August 1995.**
1459 100 s. Scouts making bricks 10 10
1460 450 s. on 70 s. Poultry keeping 40 45
1461 800 s. on 90 s. Scout on crutches leading family to immunization centre 70 75
1462 1500 s. on 10 s. Type 104 1·10 1·25

1995. 50th Anniv of End of Second World War in Europe. As T 340 of Antigua. Multicoloured.
1464 500 s. Soviet artillery in action 45 50
1465 500 s. Soviet tanks on the Moltke Bridge 45 50
1466 500 s. Kaiser Wilhelm Memorial Church, Berlin 45 50
1467 500 s. Soviet tanks and Brandenburg Gate 45 50
1468 500 s. U.S. Boeing B-17 Flying Fortress 45 50
1469 500 s. Soviet tanks enter Berlin 45 50
1470 500 s. Ruins of the Chancellery 45 50
1471 500 s. The Reichstag on fire 45 50

161 Dove, Child, Dish Aerial, Food and Emblem

1995. 50th Anniv of United Nations. Multicoloured.
1473 450 s. Type 161 40 45
1474 1000 s. Hands releasing bird and insects 90 95

1995. 50th Anniv of F.A.O. As T 320 of Maldive Islands. Multicoloured.
1476 350 s. Woman peeling maize 30 35
1477 350 s. Woman and child with maize 30 35
1478 350 s. Woman and baby with maize 30 35

Nos. 1476/8 were printed together, se-tenant, forming a composite design.

1995. 90th Anniv of Rotary International. As T 299 of St. Vincent, but vert. Multicoloured.
1480 2000 s. Paul Harris (founder) and logo 1·75 1·90

1995. 95th Birthday of Queen Elizabeth the Queen Mother. As T 344 of Antigua. Multicoloured.
1482 500 s. brown, light brown and black 45 50
1483 500 s. multicoloured 45 50
1484 500 s. multicoloured 45 50
1485 500 s. multicoloured 45 50

DESIGNS: No. 1482, Queen Elizabeth the Queen Mother (pastel drawing); 1483, With bouquet of flowers; 1484, At desk (oil painting); 1485, Wearing turquoise-blue dress.

162 Australian Flag in Form of "VJ"

1995. 50th Anniv of End of Second World War in the Pacific. Designs showing national flags as "VJ".
1487 162 600 s. red, violet and black 55 60
1488 – 600 s. red, violet and black 55 60
1489 – 600 s. red, violet and black 55 60
1490 – 600 s. multicoloured 55 60
1491 – 600 s. red, orange and black 55 60
1492 – 600 s. red and black 55 60

DESIGNS: No. 1488, Great Britain; 1489, New Zealand; 1490, United States of America; 1491, People's Republic of China; 1492, Canada.

163 Velociraptor

1995. Prehistoric Animals. Multicoloured.
1494 150 s. Type 163 15 20
1495 200 s. Head of psittacosaurus 15 20
1496 300 s. Archaeopteryx (vert) 25 30
1497 300 s. Quetzalcoatlus and volcano (vert) 25 30
1498 300 s. Pteranodon and volcano (vert) 25 30
1499 300 s. Brachiosaurus (vert) 25 30
1500 300 s. Tsintaosaur (vert) 25 30
1501 300 s. Allosaur (vert) 25 30
1502 300 s. Tyrannosaurus (vert) 25 30
1503 300 s. Apatosaur (vert) 25 30
1504 300 s. Giant dragonfly (vert) 25 30
1505 300 s. Dimorphodon (vert) 25 30
1506 300 s. Triceratops (vert) 25 30
1507 300 s. Compsognathus (vert) 25 30
1508 350 s. Head of dilophosaurus 30 35
1509 400 s. Kentrosaurus 35 40
1510 500 s. Stegosaurus 45 50
1511 1500 s. Pterodaustro 1·10 1·25

Nos. 1496/1507 were printed together, se-tenant, forming a composite design.

No. 1502 is inscribed "Tyranosaur" and No. 1506 "Tricreatops", both in error.

164 Rough-scaled Bush Viper

165 Bell's Hinged Tortoise

1995. Reptiles. Multicoloured.
1513 50 s. Type 164 10 10
1514 100 s. Pygmy python 10 10
1515 150 s. Three-horned chameleon 15 20
1516 200 s. African rock python 15 20
1516a 300 s. Armadillo girdled lizard 25 30

1517 350 s. Nile monitor 30 35
1518 400 s. Savannah monitor . . 35 40
1519 450 s. Bush viper 40 45
1520 500 s. Nile crocodile 45 50
1520a 600 s. Spotted sandveld lizard 55 60
1521 700 s. Type **165** 60 65
1521a 700 s. Bell's hinged tortoise . 60 65
1522 900 s. Rhinoceros viper . . 80 85
1523 1000 s. Gabon viper 90 95
1524 2000 s. Spitting cobra . . . 1·75 1·90
1525 3000 s. Leopard tortoise . . 2·50 2·75
1526 4000 s. Puff adder . . . . 3·50 3·75
1527 5000 s. Common house gecko 4·50 4·75
1528 6000 s. Dwarf chameleon . . 5·25 5·50
1529 10000 s. Boemslang (snake) . 8·75 9·00

SIZES—21×21 mm: 50, 100, 150, 200, 350, 400, 450, 500 s.; 18×20 mm; 300, 600, 700 s. (No. 1521a); 38½×24½ mm: 700 s. (No. 1521), 900 s. to 10000 s.

166 Nsambya Church

1995. Local Anniversaries. Multicoloured.

1530 150 s. Type **166** 15 20
1531 450 s. Namilyango College . . 40 45
1532 500 s. Figures with symbolic wheel 45 50
1533 1000 s. Volunteers with food sacks 90 95

ANNIVERSARIES: Nos. 1530/1, Centenary of Mill Hill Missionaries in Uganda; 1532, Centenary of International Co-operative Alliance; 1533, 25th anniv of U.N. volunteers.

167 Bwindi Forest

1995. Landscapes. Multicoloured.

1534 50 s. Type **167** 10 10
1535 100 s. Karamoja 10 10
1536 450 s. Sunset, Lake Mburo National Park 40 45
1537 500 s. Sunset, Gulu District . 45 50
1538 900 s. Mist, Kabale District . 80 85
1539 1000 s. Ruwenzori Mountains 90 95

1995. Waterfalls. As T **167**. Multicoloured.

1540 50 s. Sipi Falls (vert) . . . 10 10
1541 100 s. Murchison Falls . . . 10 10
1542 450 s. Bujagali Falls 40 45
1543 500 s. The Two Falls at Murchison 45 50
1544 900 s. Falls, Ruwenzori Mountains (vert) 80 85
1545 1000 s. Falls, Ruwenzori Mountains (different) (vert) 90 95

168 Peter Rono (1500 metres), 1988

1995. Olympic Games, Atlanta (1996). Multicoloured.

1546 50 s. Type **168** 10 10
1547 350 s. Reiner Klimke (dressage), 1984 . . . . 30 35
1548 450 s. German team (cycling time trials), 1988 . . . . 40 45
1549 500 s. Grace Birungi (athlete) 45 50
1550 900 s. Francis Ogola (athlete) 80 85
1551 1000 s. Nyakana Godfrey (boxer) 90 95

169 Peacock

1995. Domestic Animals. Multicoloured.

1553 200 s. Type **169** 15 20
1554 200 s. Pouter pigeon 15 20
1555 200 s. Rock doves 15 20
1556 200 s. Rouen duck 15 20
1557 200 s. Guineafowl 15 20
1558 200 s. Donkey 15 20
1559 200 s. Shetland ponies . . . 15 20
1560 200 s. Palomino horse . . . 15 20
1561 200 s. Pigs 15 20
1562 200 s. Border collie 15 20
1563 200 s. Merino sheep 15 20
1564 200 s. Milch goat 15 20
1565 200 s. Black dutch rabbit . . 15 20
1566 200 s. Lop rabbit 15 20
1567 200 s. Somali cat 15 20
1568 200 s. Asian cat 15 20

Nos. 1553/68 were printed together, se-tenant, forming a composite design.

170 Scouts putting Child on Scales

171 Hermann Staudinger (1953 Chemistry)

1995. Uganda Boy Scouts in the Community. Multicoloured.

1570 150 s. Type **170** 15 20
1571 350 s. Scouts carrying children 30 35
1572 450 s. Checking health cards (horiz) 40 45
1573 800 s. Holding child for immunization (horiz) . . . 70 75
1574 1000 s. Weighing child before immunization 90 95

1995. Centenary of Nobel Prize Trust Fund. Multicoloured.

1575 300 s. Type **171** 25 30
1576 300 s. Fritz Haber (1918 Chemistry) 25 30
1577 300 s. Bert Sakmann (1991 Medicine) 25 30
1578 300 s. Adolf Windaus (1926 Chemistry) 25 30
1579 300 s. Wilhelm Wien (1911 Physics) 25 30
1580 300 s. Ernest Hemingway (1954 Literature) 25 30
1581 300 s. Richard Willstatter (1915 Chemistry) 25 30
1582 300 s. Stanley Cohen (1986 Medicine) 25 30
1583 300 s. Hans Jensen (1963 Physics) 25 30
1584 300 s. Otto Warburg (1931 Medicine) 25 30
1585 300 s. Heinrich Wieland (1927 Chemistry) 25 30
1586 300 s. Albrecht Kossel (1910 Medicine) 25 30
1587 300 s. Hideki Yukawa (1949 Physics) 25 30
1588 300 s. F. W. de Klerk (1993 Peace) 25 30
1589 300 s. Nelson Mandela (1993 Peace) 25 30
1590 300 s. Odysseus Elytis (1979 Literature) 25 30
1591 300 s. Ferdinand Buisson (1927 Peace) 25 30
1592 300 s. Lev Landau (1962 Physics) 25 30
1593 300 s. Halldor Laxness (1955 Literature) 25 30
1594 300 s. Wole Soyinka (1986 Literature) 25 30
1595 300 s. Desmond Tutu (1984 Peace) 25 30
1596 300 s. Susumu Tonegawa (1987 Medicine) 25 30
1597 300 s. Louis de Broglie (1929 Physics) 25 30
1598 300 s. George Seferis (1963 Literature) 25 30

Nos. 1575/86 and 1587/98 respectively were printed together, se-tenant, forming composite designs.

1995. Christmas. Religious Paintings. As T **98** of Nevis. Multicoloured.

1600 150 s. "The Virgin and Child" (Holbein the Younger) . . 15 20
1601 350 s. "Madonna" (Procaccini) 30 35
1602 500 s. "The Virgin and Child" (Pisanello) 45 50
1603 1000 s. "Madonna and Child" (Crivelli) 90 95
1604 1500 s. "The Nativity of the Virgin" (Le Nain) . . . . 1·10 1·25

172 "Ansellia africana"

1995. Orchids. Multicoloured.

1606 150 s. Type **172** 15 20
1607 350 s. "Aerangis iuteoalba" . 30 35
1608 350 s. "Satyrium sacculatum" 30 35
1609 350 s. "Bolusiella maudiae" . 30 35
1610 350 s. "Habenaria attenuata" 30 35
1611 350 s. "Cyrtorchis arcuata" . 30 35
1612 350 s. "Eulophia angolensis" 30 35
1613 350 s. "Tridactyle bicaudata" 30 35
1614 350 s. "Eulophia horsfallii" . 30 35
1615 350 s. "Diaphananthe fragrantissima" 30 35
1616 450 s. "Satyricum crassicaule" 40 45
1617 500 s. "Polystachya cultriformis" 45 50
1618 800 s. "Disa erubescens" . . 70 75

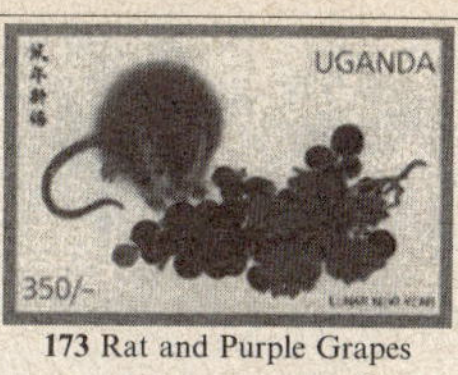

173 Rat and Purple Grapes

1996. Chinese New Year ("Year of the Rat"). Multicoloured.

1620 350 s. Type **173** 30 35
1621 350 s. Rat and radishes . . . 30 35
1622 350 s. Rat eating corn 30 35
1623 350 s. Rat eating cucumber . 30 35

174 Wild Dog and Pup

1996. Wildlife of Uganda. Multicoloured. (a) Horiz designs.

1626 150 s. Type **174** 15 20
1627 200 s. African fish eagle . . . 15 20
1628 250 s. Hippopotamus 20 25
1629 350 s. Leopard 30 35
1630 400 s. Lion 35 40
1631 450 s. Lioness 40 45
1632 500 s. Meerkats 45 50
1633 550 s. Pair of black rhinoceroses 50 55

(b) Vert designs.

1634 150 s. Gorilla 15 20
1635 200 s. Cheetah 15 20
1636 250 s. African elephant . . . 20 25
1637 350 s. Thomson's gazelle . . 30 35
1638 400 s. Crowned crane 35 40
1639 450 s. Saddlebill 40 45
1640 500 s. Vulture 45 50
1641 550 s. Zebra 50 55

175 Mickey Mouse and Goofy on Platform at Calais

1996. Mickey's Orient Express. Walt Disney Cartoon Characters. Multicoloured.

1643 50 s. Type **175** 15 15
1644 100 s. Mickey and Goofy at Athens 20 15
1645 150 s. Mickey showing Donald Duck his Pullman ticket . . 30 25
1646 200 s. Daisy and Donald Duck in Pullman car 40 30
1647 250 s. Mickey and Minnie Mouse in dining car . . . 50 35
1648 300 s. Goofy as guard assisting Mickey and Minnie . . . 35 40
1649 600 s. Mickey and Donald preparing for bed . . . . . 1·00 1·25
1650 700 s. Mickey and Minnie at Orient Express accident, Frankfurt, 1901 . . . . . 1·25 1·50
1651 800 s. Mickey and Goofy building snowman and Orient Express in snowdrift, 1929 . 1·40 1·50
1652 900 s. Disney characters filming "Murder on the Orient Express" . . . . 1·40 1·50

176 "Autumn Pond"

178 "Coprinus disseminatus"

1996. "CHINA '96" 9th Asian International Stamp Exhibition, Peking. Paintings by Qi Baishi. Multicoloured.

1654 50 s. Type **176** 10 10
1655 100 s. "Partridge and Smartweed" 10 10
1656 150 s. "Begonias and Mynah" 15 20
1657 200 s. "Chrysanthemums, Cocks and Hens" 15 20
1658 250 s. "Crabs" 20 25
1659 300 s. "Wisterias and Bee" . 25 30
1660 350 s. "Smartweed and Ink-drawn Butterflies" 30 35
1661 400 s. "Lotus and Mandarin Ducks" 35 40
1662 450 s. "Lichees and Locust" 40 45
1663 500 s. "Millet and Praying Mantis" 45 50

The painting titles on 150 s. and 200 s. are transposed in error with "CHRYSANTHEMUMS" shown as "RYSANTHEMUMS".

1996. African Fungi. Multicoloured.

1665 150 s. Type **178** 15 20
1666 300 s. "Coprinus radians" . 25 30
1667 350 s. "Hygrophorus coccineus" 30 35
1668 400 s. "Marasmius siccus" . 35 40
1669 450 s. "Cortinarius collinitus" 55 45
1670 500 s. "Cortinarius cinnabarinus" 45 50
1671 550 s. "Coltricia cinnamomea" 50 55
1672 1000 s. "Mutinus elegans" . 90 95

179 "Catopsilia philea"

1996. Butterflies. Multicoloured.

1674 50 s. Type **179** 10 10
1675 100 s. "Dione vanillae" . . . 10 10
1676 150 s. "Metamorpha dido" . . 15 20
1677 200 s. "Papilio sesostris" . . 15 20
1678 250 s. "Papilio neophilus" . 20 25
1679 300 s. "Papilio thoas" . . . 25 30
1680 350 s. "Diorina periander" . . 30 35
1681 400 s. "Morpho cipris" . . . 35 40
1682 450 s. "Catonephele numilia" 40 45
1683 500 s. "Heliconius doris" . . 45 50
1684 550 s. "Prepona antimache" . 50 55
1685 600 s. "Eunica alcmena" . . 55 60

1996. 70th Birthday of Queen Elizabeth II. As T **363** of Antigua. Different photographs. Multicoloured.

1687 500 s. As Type **363** of Antigua 45 50
1688 500 s. In evening dress . . . 45 50
1689 500 s. Wearing red coat and hat 45 50

1996. 50th Anniv of U.N.I.C.E.F. As T **335** of Maldive Islands. Multicoloured.

1691 450 s. Asian children (horiz) 40 45
1692 500 s. South American children (horiz) 45 50
1693 550 s. Boy holding pencil (horiz) 50 55

1996. 50th Anniv of U.N.E.S.C.O. As T **104** of Nevis. Multicoloured.

1695 450 s. Darien National Park, Panama 40 45
1696 500 s. Los Glaciares National Park, Argentina 45 50
1697 550 s. Tubbatha Reef Marine Park, Philippines 50 55

1996. Centenary of Radio. Entertainers. As T **326** of St. Vincent. Multicoloured.

1701 200 s. Ella Fitzgerald 15 20
1702 300 s. Bob Hope 25 30
1703 500 s. Nat "King" Cole . . 45 50
1704 800 s. George Burns and Gracie Allen 70 75

181 Electric Locomotive, 1968 (Japan)

1996. Railway Locomotives. Multicoloured.

1706 450 s. Type **181** 40 45
1707 450 s. Stephenson's "Rocket", 1829 . . . . 40 45
1708 450 s. William Norris's "Austria", 1843 . . . . . 40 45
1709 450 s. Early American steam locomotive 40 45
1710 450 s. Steam locomotive, 1947 (India) 40 45
1711 450 s. Class 103 electric locomotive (Germany) . . 40 45
1712 550 s. GWR steam locomotive "Lady of Lynn" (England) 50 55
1713 550 s. Steam locomotive, 1930 (China) 50 55
1714 550 s. Meyer-Kitson steam locomotive (Chile) 50 55

1715	550 s. Union Pacific "Centennial" diesel locomotive No. 6900 (U.S.A.)	50	55
1716	550 s. Type 581 diesel locomotive (Japan)	50	55
1717	550 s. Class 120 electric locomotive (Germany)	50	55

182 Postal and Telecommunications Corporation Emblem

1996. Centenary of Postal Services. Multicoloured.

1719	150 s. Type **182**	15	20
1720	450 s. Loading postbus	40	45
1721	500 s. Modern postal transportation	45	50
1722	550 s. 1896 25 c. violet and 1 r. black stamps	50	55

183 Two American River Steamers and 1904 Games, St. Louis

1996. Olympic Games, Atlanta (1st issue). Multicoloured.

1723	350 s. Type **183**	30	35
1724	450 s. George Finnegan (U.S.A.) (boxing), 1904	40	45
1725	500 s. Chariot racing	45	50
1726	800 s. John Flanagan (U.S.A.) (hammer), 1904 (vert)	70	75

See also Nos. 1764/81.

184 Mango

185 Traditional Costumes from Western Uganda

1996. Fruit. Multicoloured.

1727	150 s. Type **184**	15	20
1728	350 s. Orange	30	35
1729	450 s. Pawpaw	40	45
1730	500 s. Avocado	45	50
1731	550 s. Watermelon (horiz)	50	55

1996. Christmas. Religious Paintings. As T **337** of St. Vincent. Multicoloured.

1732	150 s. "Annunciation" (Lorenzo di Credi)	15	20
1733	350 s. "Madonna of the Loggia" (detail) (Botticelli)	30	35
1734	400 s. "Virgin in Glory with Child and Angels" (Lorenzetti)	35	40
1735	450 s. "Adoration of the Child" (Lippi)	40	45
1736	500 s. "Madonna of the Loggia" (Botticelli)	45	50
1737	550 s. "The Strength" (Botticelli)	50	55

1997. Traditional Costumes. Multicoloured.

1740	150 s. Type **185**	15	20
1741	300 s. Acholi headdress	25	30
1742	300 s. Alur headdress	25	30
1743	300 s. Bwola dance headdress	25	30
1744	300 s. Madi headdress	25	30
1745	300 s. Karimojong headdress with plume	25	30
1746	300 s. Karimojong headdress with two feathers	25	30
1747	350 s. Karimojong women	30	35
1748	450 s. Ganda traditional dress (horiz)	40	45
1749	500 s. Acholi traditional dress (horiz)	45	50

186 Ox

1997. Chinese New Year ("Year of the Ox"). Multicoloured.

1750	350 s. Type **186**	30	35
1751	350 s. Cow suckling calf	30	35
1752	350 s. Cow and calf lying down	30	35
1753	350 s. Ox lying down	30	35

187 Giraffe running

1997. Endangered Species. Rothschild's Giraffe. Multicoloured.

1756	300 s. Type **187**	25	30
1757	300 s. Two adult giraffes	25	30
1758	300 s. Head of giraffe	25	30
1759	300 s. Giraffe with calf	25	30

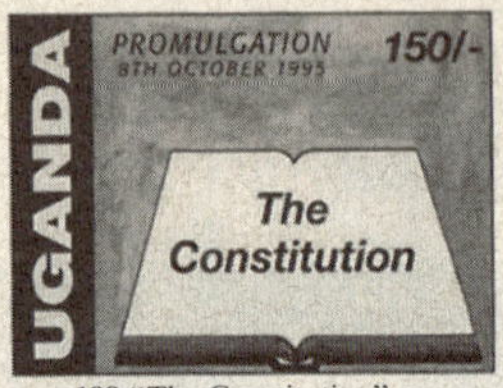

188 "The Constitution" on Open Book

1997. Promulgation of New Constitution (8 Oct 1995). Multicoloured.

1761	150 s. Type **188**	15	20
1762	350 s. "The Constitution" on scroll	30	35
1763	550 s. "THE CONSTITUTION" on closed book (vert)	50	55

189 Kitel Son (Japan) (marathon), 1936

190 "Red Plum Blossom and Daffodil"

1997. Olympic Games, Atlanta (2nd issue). Previous Gold Medal Winners. Multicoloured.

1764	150 s. Type **189**	15	20
1765	150 s. Bob Hayes (U.S.A.) (100m), 1964	15	20
1766	200 s. Walter Davis (U.S.A.) (high jump), 1952	15	20
1767	200 s. Rod Milburn (110m hurdles), 1972	15	20
1768	250 s. Matthes (swimming), 1968	20	25
1769	250 s. Filbert Bayi (Tanzania) (athletics), 1976	20	25
1770	300 s. Akii Bua (Uganda) (400m hurdles), 1972	25	30
1771	300 s. H. Kipchoge Keino (Kenya) (steeplechase), 1972	25	30
1772	350 s. Nordwig (Germany) (pole vault), 1972	30	35
1773	350 s. Ron Ray (U.S.A.) (athletics), 1976	30	35
1774	400 s. Wilma Rudolph (U.S.A.) (100m relay), 1960	35	40
1775	400 s. Joe Frazer (U.S.A.) (boxing), 1976	35	40
1776	450 s. Abebe Bikila (Ethiopia) (marathon), 1964	40	45
1777	450 s. Carl Lewis (U.S.A.) (100m), 1984	40	45
1778	500 s. Edwin Moses (U.S.A.) (400m hurdles), 1984	45	50
1779	500 s. Gisela Mauermayer (Germany) (discus), 1936	45	50
1780	550 s. Rady Williams (U.S.A.) (long jump), 1972	50	55
1781	550 s. Dietmar Mogenburg (Germany) (high jump), 1984	50	55

Nos. 1764, 1766, 1768, 1770, 1772, 1774, 1776, 1778 and 1780 and 1765, 1767, 1769, 1771, 1773, 1775, 1777, 1779 and 1781 respectively were printed together, se-tenant, with the backgrounds forming composite designs.

No. 1769 is incorrectly inscribed "Eiilbert" and is dated "1976"; Filbert Bayi did not participate in the 1976 Games. No. 1779 is incorrectly inscribed "Mauemayer" and wrongly identifies the event as the shotput.

1997. "HONG KONG '97" International Stamp Exhibition. Paintings by Wu Changshuo. Mult.

1782	50 s. Type **190**	10	10
1783	100 s. "Peony"	10	15
1784	150 s. "Rosaceae"	15	20
1785	200 s. "Pomegranate"	15	20
1786	250 s. "Peach, Peony and Plum Blossom"	20	25
1787	300 s. "Calyx Canthus"	25	30
1788	350 s. "Chrysanthemum"	30	35
1789	400 s. "Calabash"	35	40
1790	450 s. "Chrysanthemum" (different)	40	45
1791	500 s. "Cypress Tree"	45	50

191 Woody

1997. Disney's "Toy Story" (cartoon film). Multicoloured.

1793	100 s. Type **191**	20	20
1794	100 s. Buzz Lightyear	20	20
1795	100 s. Bo Peep	20	20
1796	100 s. Hamm	20	20
1797	100 s. Slinky	20	20
1798	100 s. Rex	20	20
1799	150 s. Woody on bed (horiz)	30	30
1800	150 s. Woody at microphone (horiz)	30	30
1801	150 s. Bo Peep (horiz)	30	30
1802	150 s. Buzz Lightyear (horiz)	30	30
1803	150 s. Slinky and Rex (horiz)	30	30
1804	150 s. Woody hiding (horiz)	30	30
1805	150 s. "Halt! Who goes there" (horiz)	30	30
1806	150 s. Rex, Slinky and Buzz Lightyear (horiz)	30	30
1807	150 s. "You're just an action figure!" (horiz)	30	30
1808	200 s. "I'm the only sheriff in these parts" (horiz)	35	35
1809	200 s. Green toy soldiers (horiz)	35	35
1810	200 s. Woody and Buzz (horiz)	35	35
1811	200 s. Woody pointing (horiz)	35	35
1812	200 s. Buzz Lightyear (horiz)	35	35
1813	200 s. Green aliens (horiz)	35	35
1814	200 s. "This is an intergalactic emergency" (horiz)	35	35
1815	200 s. Buzz and Woody argue (horiz)	35	35
1816	200 s. Buzz and Woody in buggy (horiz)	35	35

192 "Pioneer 10"

1997. Space Exploration. Multicoloured.

1818	250 s. Type **192**	20	25
1819	250 s. "Voyager 1"	20	25
1820	250 s. "Viking Orbiter"	20	25
1821	250 s. "Pioneer - Venus 1"	20	25
1822	250 s. "Mariner 9"	20	25
1823	250 s. "Galileo" Entry Probe	20	25
1824	250 s. "Mariner 10"	20	25
1825	250 s. "Voyager 2"	20	25
1826	300 s. "Sputnik 1"	25	30
1827	300 s. "Apollo" spacecraft	25	30
1828	300 s. "Soyuz" spacecraft	25	30
1829	300 s. "Intelsat 1"	25	30
1830	300 s. Manned manoeuvring Unit	25	30
1831	300 s. "Skylab"	25	30
1832	300 s. "Telstar 1"	25	30
1833	300 s. Hubble Telescope	25	30

Nos. 1818/25 and 1826/33 respectively were printed together, se-tenant, with the backgrounds forming composite designs.

193 Deng Xiaoping and Port

1997. Deng Xiaoping (Chinese statesman) Commemoration.

1835	**193**	500 s. multicoloured	45	50
1836		550 s. multicoloured	50	55
1837		1000 s. multicoloured	90	95

194 Water Hyacinth and Pebbles

195 Men's Slalom

1997. Environmental Protection. Multicoloured.

1839	500 s. Water hyacinth and Lake Victoria (inscr at top left)	45	50
1840	500 s. Water hyacinth and Lake Victoria (inscr at top right)	45	50
1841	500 s. Type **194**	45	50
1842	500 s. Larger clump of water hyacinth and pebbles	45	50
1843	550 s. Buffalo	50	55
1844	550 s. Uganda kob	50	55
1845	550 s. Guinea fowl	50	55
1846	550 s. Marabou stork	50	55

Nos. 1839/42 and 1843/6 respectively were printed together, se-tenant, with the backgrounds forming composite designs.

No. 1845 is inscribed "GUINEA FOWEL" and No. 1846 "MALIBU STORK", both in error.

1997. 10th Anniv of Chernobyl Nuclear Disaster. As T **347** of St. Vincent.

1848	500 s. As Type **347** of St. Vincent	45	50
1849	700 s. As No. 1848 but inscribed "CHABAD'S CHILDREN OF CHERNOBYL" at foot	60	65

1997. 50th Death Anniv of Paul Harris (founder of Rotary International). As T **113** of Nevis. Multicoloured.

1850	1000 s. Paul Harris and child drinking	90	95

1997. Golden Wedding of Queen Elizabeth and Prince Philip. As T **350** of Maldive Islands. Multicoloured.

1852	200 s. Queen Elizabeth II	15	20
1853	200 s. Royal coat of arms	15	20
1854	200 s. Queen Elizabeth and Prince Philip at reception	15	20
1855	200 s. Queen Elizabeth and Prince Philip on royal visit	15	20
1856	200 s. Buckingham Palace	15	30
1857	200 s. Prince Philip in military uniform	15	20

1997. "Pacific '97" International Stamp Exhibition, San Francisco. Death Centenary of Heinrich von Stephan (founder of the U.P.U.). As T **351** of Maldive Islands.

1859	800 s. blue	70	75
1860	800 s. brown	70	75
1861	800 s. green	70	75

DESIGNS: No. 1859, Chinese post boat; 1860, Von Stephan and Mercury; 1861, Russian post cart.

1997. Winter Olympic Games, Nagano, Japan (1998). Multicoloured.

1863	350 s. Type **195**	30	35
1864	450 s. Two-man bobsled	40	45
1865	500 s. Ski jumping (horiz)	45	50
1866	500 s. Giant slalom (horiz)	45	50
1867	500 s. Cross-country skiing (horiz)	45	50
1868	500 s. Ice hockey (horiz)	45	50
1869	500 s. Pairs figure skating (man) (horiz)	45	50
1870	500 s. Pairs figure skating (woman) (horiz)	45	50
1871	800 s. Women's slalom (horiz)	70	75
1872	2000 s. Men's speed skating (horiz)	1·75	1·90

Nos. 1865/70 were printed together, se-tenant, with the backgrounds forming a composite design.

196 Main Building, Makerere University

1997. 75th Anniv of Makerere University. Multicoloured.
1874 150 s. Type **196** 15 20
1875 450 s. East African School of Librarianship building (vert) 40 45
1876 500 s. Buyana Stock Farm, Makerere University 45 50
1877 550 s. Ceramic dish from School of Architecture and Fine Arts 50 55

1997. World Cup Football Championship, France (1998). As T **246** of Lesotho. Multicoloured (except Nos. 1878, 1880, 1883 and 1886).
1878 200 s. Fritz Walter, Germany (brown) 15 20
1879 250 s. Paulo Rossi (horiz) 20 25
1880 250 s. Mario Kempes (black) (horiz) 20 25
1881 250 s. Gerd Muller (horiz) 20 25
1882 250 s. Grzegorz Lato (horiz) 20 25
1883 250 s. Joseph Gaetjens (black) (horiz) 20 25
1884 250 s. Eusebio Ferreica da Silva (horiz) 20 25
1885 250 s. Salvatore Schillaci (horiz) 20 25
1886 250 s. Leonidas da Silva (black) (horiz) 20 25
1887 250 s. Gary Lineker (horiz) 20 25
1888 250 s. Argentine and West German player chasing ball (horiz) 20 25
1889 250 s. Azteca Stadium (horiz) 20 25
1890 250 s. Maradona holding World Cup (horiz) 20 25
1891 250 s. Argentine and West German players with goalkeeper (horiz) 20 25
1892 250 s. West German player tackling Argentine player (horiz) 20 25
1893 250 s. Ball in back of net (horiz) 20 25
1894 250 s. Argentine team (horiz) 20 25
1895 250 s. Players competing to head ball (horiz) 20 25
1896 300 s. Daniel Pasarella, Argentina 25 30
1897 450 s. Dino Zoff, Italy 40 45
1898 500 s. Bobby Moore, England 45 50
1899 550 s. Franz Beckenbaur, West Germany 50 55
1900 600 s. Diego Maradona, Argentina 55 60
No. 1883 is inscribed "ADEMIR" in error.

197 Mahatma Gandhi

1997. 50th Death Anniv of Mahatma Gandhi (1998) (1st issue).
1902 **197** 600 s. brown and black 55 60
1903 – 700 s. brown and black 60 65
DESIGN: 700 s. Different portait.
See also No. 2021.

198 "Cupid and Dolphin" (Andrea del Verrocchio)

1997. Christmas. Paintings and Sculptures. Multicoloured.
1905 200 s. Type **198** 15 20
1906 300 s. "The Fall of the Rebel Angels" (Pieter Brueghel the Elder) 25 30
1907 400 s. "The Immaculate Conception" (Bartolome Murillo) 35 40
1908 500 s. "Music-making Angel" (Rosso Fiorentino) 45 50
1909 600 s. "Cupid and Psyche" (Adolphe-William Bouguereau) 55 60
1910 700 s. "Cupid and Psyche" (Antonio Canova) 60 65

199 Diana, Princess of Wales

1997. Diana, Princess of Wales Commemoration.
1912 **199** 600 s. multicoloured 55 60

200 Tiger

1998. Chinese New Year ("Year of the Tiger"). Multicoloured.
1913 350 s. Type **200** 30 35
1914 350 s. Tiger leaping 30 35
1915 350 s. Tiger resting 30 35
1916 350 s. Tiger yawning 30 35

201 Mountain Gorilla

202 Namugongo Martyrs Shrine, Kampala

1998. 18th Anniv of Pan African Postal Union.
1918 **201** 300 s. + 150 s. mult 40 45

1998. Tourist Attractions. Multicoloured.
1919 300 s. Type **202** 25 30
1920 400 s. Kasubi Tombs, Kampala (horiz) 35 40
1921 500 s. Tourist launch in Kazinga Channel, Queen Elizabeth Park (horiz) 45 50
1922 600 s. Elephant, Queen Elizabeth Park (horiz) 55 60
1923 700 s. Bujagali Falls, River Nile at Jinja (horiz) 60 65

203 Mother Teresa, 1928

204 Child in Wheelchair

1998. Mother Teresa Commemoration. Multicoloured.
1924 300 s. Type **203** 25 30
1925 300 s. Holding child (56×42 mm) 25 30
1926 300 s. Mother Teresa at United Nations, 1975 (56×42 mm) 25 30
1927 300 s. Facing left 25 30
1928 300 s. Full face portrait 25 30
1929 300 s. With children (56×42 mm) 25 30
1930 300 s. Mother Teresa rescuing child (56×42 mm) 25 30
1931 300 s. Smiling 25 30

1998. 30th Anniv of U.N.I.C.E.F. Multicoloured.
1933 300 s. Type **204** 25 30
1934 400 s. Child receiving oral vaccination against polio 35 40
1935 600 s. Children outside toilet 55 60
1936 700 s. Children in class 60 65

205 Pteranodon

1998. Prehistoric Animals. Multicoloured.
1937 300 s. Type **205** 25 30
1938 400 s. Diplodocus 35 40
1939 500 s. Lambeosaurus 45 50
1940 600 s. Centrosaurus 55 60
1941 600 s. Cetiosaurus (vert) 55 60
1942 600 s. Brontosaurus (vert) 55 60
1943 600 s. Brachiosaurus (vert) 55 60
1944 600 s. Deinonychus (vert) 55 60
1945 600 s. Dimetrodon (vert) 55 60
1946 600 s. Megalosaurus (vert) 55 60
1947 700 s. Parasaurolophus 60 65
Nos. 1941/6 were printed together, se-tenant, with the backgrounds forming a composite design.

206 Rita Dove

1998. U.N.E.S.C.O. World Literacy Campaign. 20th-century Afro-American Writers. Multicoloured.
1949 300 s. Type **206** 25 30
1950 300 s. Mari Evans 25 30
1951 300 s. Sterling A. Brown 25 30
1952 300 s. June Jordan 25 30
1953 300 s. Stephen Henderson 25 30
1954 300 s. Zora Neale Hurston 25 30

207 Mickey Mouse and Monster

1998. 70th Birthday of Mickey Mouse. Scenes from cartoon film "Runaway Brain". Multicoloured.
1955 400 s. Type **207** 35 40
1956 400 s. Mickey and Pluto with newspaper 35 40
1957 400 s. Mickey and Pluto in front of television 35 40
1958 400 s. Mickey and Minnie fleeing 35 40
1959 400 s. Mickey on television screen 35 40
1960 400 s. Monster and hostage Minnie Mouse clinging to skyscraper 35 40
1961 400 s. Mickey Mouse throwing lasso 35 40
1962 400 s. Mickey circling Monster on lasso 35 40
1963 400 s. Mickey and Minnie on rope 35 40

209 "Santa Maria" (Columbus)

1998. Ships of the World. Multicoloured.
1967 1000 s. Type **209** 90 95
1968 1000 s. "Mayflower" (Pilgrim Fathers) 90 95
1969 1000 s. Barque 90 95
1970 1000 s. Fishing schooner 90 95
1971 1000 s. Chesapeake oyster boat 90 95
1972 1000 s. Java Sea schooner 90 95

210 Grumman F4F Wildcat (U.S.A.)

1998. Aircraft. Multicoloured.
1974 500 s. Type **210** 45 50
1975 500 s. Mitsubishi A6M Zero-Sen (Japan) 45 50
1976 500 s. Supermarine Seafire ("Spitfire") (Great Britain) 45 50
1977 500 s. Hawker Siddeley Harrier (Great Britain) 45 50
1978 500 s. S3A Viking (U.S.A.) 45 50
1979 500 s. Corsair (U.S.A.) 45 50
1980 600 s. Dornier Do-X (flying boat) (1929) 55 60
1981 600 s. German Zucker mail rocket (1930) 55 60
1982 600 s. North American X-15 rocket plane (1959) 55 60
1983 600 s. Goddard's rocket (1930s) 55 60
1984 600 s. Wright Brothers' "Flyer I" (1903) 55 60
1985 600 s. 160R Sikorsky (first helicopter) (1939) 55 60
Nos. 1974/9 and 1980/5 respectively were printed together, se-tenant, forming composite designs.

211 "Onosma" sp.

213 Diana, Princess of Wales

212 Bohemian Waxwing

1998. Flowers of the Mediterranean. Multicoloured.
1987 300 s. Type **211** 25 30
1988 300 s. "Rhododendron luteum" 25 30
1989 300 s. "Paeonia mascula" 25 30
1990 300 s. "Geranium macrorrhizum" 25 30
1991 300 s. "Cyclamen graecum" 25 30
1992 300 s. "Lilium rhodopaedum" 25 30
1993 300 s. "Narcissus pseudonarcissus" 25 30
1994 300 s. "Paeonia rhodia" 25 30
1995 300 s. "Aquilegia amaliae" 25 30
1996 600 s. "Paeonia peregrina" (horiz) 55 60
1997 600 s. "Muscari comutatum" (horiz) 55 60
1998 600 s. "Sternbergia" sp. (horiz) 55 60
1999 600 s. "Dianthus" sp. (horiz) 55 60
2000 600 s. "Verbascum" sp. (horiz) 55 60
2001 600 s. "Aubrieta gracilis" (horiz) 55 60
2002 600 s. "Galanthus nivalis" (horiz) 55 60
2003 600 s. "Campanula incurva" (horiz) 55 60
2004 600 s. "Crocus sieberi" (horiz) 55 60

1998. Christmas. Birds. Multicoloured.
2006 300 s. Type **212** 25 30
2007 400 s. House sparrow 35 40
2008 500 s. Black-capped chickadee 45 50
2009 600 s. Eurasian bullfinch 55 60
2010 700 s. Painted bunting 60 65
2011 1000 s. Common cardinal ("Northern Cardinal") 90 95

1998. 25th Death Anniv of Pablo Picasso (painter). As T **373** of St. Vincent. Multicoloured.
2013 500 s. "Woman Reading" (vert) 45 50
2014 600 s. "Portrait of Dora Maar" (vert) 55 60
2015 700 s. "Les Demoiselles d'Avignon" 60 65
No. 2015 is inscribed "Des Moiselles D'Avignon" in error.

1998. 19th World Scout Jamboree, Chile. As T **130** of Nevis. Multicoloured.
2017 700 s. Cub Scouts greeting President Eisenhower, 1956 60 65
2018 700 s. Scout with "Uncle Dan" Beard, 1940 60 65
2019 700 s. Vice-President Hubert Humphrey as Scout leader, 1934 60 65

1998. 50th Death Anniv of Mahatma Gandhi (2nd issue). As T **131** of Nevis.
2021 600 s. multicoloured 55 60
DESIGN: 600 s. Gandhi as a young man.

1998. 1st Death Anniv of Diana, Princess of Wales.
2023 **213** 700 s. multicoloured 60 65

214 Rabbit

1999. Chinese New Year ("Year of the Rabbit"). Multicoloured.
2024 350 s. White rabbit 30 35
2025 350 s. Rabbit with carrot 30 35
2026 350 s. Brown and white rabbit 30 35
2027 350 s. Type **214** 30 35

215 Post Office Emblem and Slogan

1999. Uganda Post Limited Commemoration.

2029	215 300 s. multicoloured	25	30

216 Iru Hairstyle

1999. Hairstyles. Multicoloured.

2030	300 s. Type **216**	25	30
2031	500 s. Enshunju hairstyle	45	50
2032	550 s. Elemungole hairstyle	50	55
2033	600 s. Lango hairstyle	55	60
2034	700 s. Ekikuura hairstyle	60	65

217 Blue Marlin

1999. International Year of the Ocean. Multicoloured.

2035	500 s. Type **217**	45	50
2036	500 s. Arctic tern	45	50
2037	500 s. Common dolphin	45	50
2038	500 s. Blacktip shark	45	50
2039	500 s. Manta ray	45	50
2040	500 s. Blackedge moray	45	50
2041	500 s. Loggerhead turtle	45	50
2042	500 s. Sail-finned tang	45	50
2043	500 s. Two-spotted octopus	45	50
2044	500 s. Atlantic wolffish	45	50
2045	500 s. Equal sea star	45	50
2046	500 s. Purple sea urchin	45	50
2047	500 s. Mountain crab	45	50

Nos. 2035/43 and Nos. 2044/7 respectively were printed together, se-tenant, with the backgrounds forming a composite design.

No. 2036 is inscribed "ARTIC TERN" in error.

POSTAGE DUE STAMPS

The Postage Due stamps of Kenya, Uganda and Tanganyika were used in Uganda until 2 January, 1967.

D 1

D 3 Lion

1967.

D 7	D 1 5 c. red	15	2·25
D 8	10 c. green	15	2·25
D 9	20 c. blue	25	2·75
D10	30 c. brown	35	3·75
D11	40 c. purple	55	4·25
D17	1 s. orange	2·75	10·00

These stamps exist in limited quantities overprinted **UGANDA LIBERATED 1979.**

1979. Liberation. As Nos. D7/11 and D17 optd **LIBERATED 1979.**

D18	D 1 5 c. red	20	40
D19	10 c. green	20	40
D20	20 c. blue	25	40
D21	30 c. brown	25	60
D22	40 c. purple	30	60
D23	1 s. orange	30	60

1985. Animals.

D24	D 3 5 s. black and turquoise	15	20
D25	– 10 s. black and lilac	15	20
D26	– 20 s. black and orange	30	40
D27	– 40 s. black and lilac	60	75
D28	– 50 s. black and blue	60	75
D29	– 100 s. black and mauve	1·00	1·25

DESIGNS: 10 s. African buffalo; 20 s. Kob; 40 s. African elephant; 50 s. Common zebra; 100 s. Black rhinoceros.

VANUATU

The New Hebrides became the Republic of Vanuatu on 30 July 1980.

1980. 100 centimes = 1 franc (Vanuatu).
1981. Vatus.

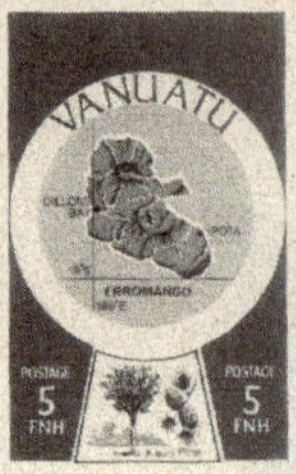

99 Island of Erromango and Kauri Pine

100 Rotary International

1980. As Nos. 242/54 of New Hebrides but inscr "VANUATU" and without royal and republican cyphers. (a) Inscr in English.

287E	5 f. Type **99**	15	15
288E	10 f. Territory map and copra making	15	15
289E	15 f. Espiritu Santo and cattle	25	25
290E	20 f. Efate and Vila P.O.	30	30
291E	25 f. Malakula and headdresses	35	35
292E	30 f. Aoba, Maewo and pigs' tusks	45	45
293E	35 f. Pentecost and land diver	50	50
294E	40 f. Tanna and John Frum cross	50	60
295E	50 f. Shepherd Is. and outrigger canoe	55	70
296E	70 f. Banks Is. and custom dancers	1·00	1·00
297E	100 f. Ambrym and idols	1·00	80
298E	200 f. Aneityum and baskets	1·10	1·40
299E	500 f. Torres Is. and archer fisherman	2·00	3·00

(b) Inscr in French.

287F	5 f. Type **99**	35	15
288F	10 f. Territory map and copra making	40	15
289F	15 f. Espiritu Santo and cattle	45	25
290F	20 f. Efate and Vila P.O.	50	30
291F	25 f. Malakula and headdresses	55	35
292F	30 f. Aoba, Maewo and pigs' tusks	55	45
293F	35 f. Pentecost and land diver	60	50
294F	40 f. Tanna and John Frum cross	90	60
295F	50 f. Shepherd Is. and outrigger canoe	1·00	70
296F	70 f. Banks Is. and custom dancers	1·40	1·00
297F	100 f. Ambrym and idols	1·50	1·10
298F	200 f. Aneityum and baskets	1·75	1·75
299F	500 f. Torres Is. and archer fisherman	4·00	3·50

1980. 75th Anniv of Rotary International. Multicoloured. (a) Inscr in English.

300E	10 f. Type **100**	10	10
301E	40 f. Rotary emblem (vert)	30	30

(b) Inscr in French.

300F	10 f. Type **100**	15	15
301F	40 f. Rotary emblem (vert)	45	45

101 Kiwanis Emblem and Globe

102 "The Virgin and Child enthroned with Saints and Angels" (Umkreis Michael Pacher)

1980. Kiwanis International (service club), New Zealand District Convention, Port Vila. (a) Inscr in English.

302E	**101** 10 f. gold, blue and brown	10	10
303E	– 40 f. green and blue	30	40

(b) Inscr in French.

302F	**101** 10 f. gold, blue and brown	40	15
303F	– 40 f. green and blue	85	70

DESIGN: 40 f. Kiwanis and Convention emblems.

1980. Christmas. Details from Paintings. Multicoloured.

304	10 f. Type **102**	10	10
305	15 f. "The Virgin and Child with Saints, Angels and Donors" (Hans Memling)	10	10
306	30 f. "The Rest on the Flight to Egypt" (Adriaen van der Werff)	20	20

103 Blue-faced Parrot Finch

104 Tribesman with Portrait of Prince Philip

1981. Birds (1st series). Multicoloured.

307	10 f. Type **103**	60	25
308	20 f. Emerald dove	80	45
309	30 f. Golden whistler	1·00	80
310	40 f. Silver-shouldered fruit dove	1·10	1·00

See also Nos. 327/30.

1981. 60th Birthday of Prince Philip, Duke of Edinburgh. Multicoloured.

311	15 v. Type **104**	10	15
312	25 v. Prince Philip in casual dress	15	20
313	35 v. Queen and Prince Philip with Princess Anne and Master Peter Phillips	15	25
314	45 v. Prince Philip in ceremonial dress	20	35

105 Prince Charles with his Dog, Harvey

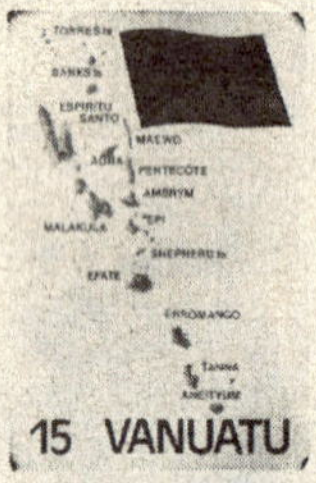

106 National Flag and Map of Vanuatu

1981. Royal Wedding. Multicoloured.

315	15 v. Wedding bouquet from Vanuatu	10	10
316	45 v. Type **105**	20	15
317	75 v. Prince Charles and Lady Diana Spencer	35	45

1981. 1st Anniv of Independence.

318	**106** 15 v. multicoloured	15	15
319	– 25 v. multicoloured	15	15
320	– 45 v. yellow and brown	20	20
321	– 75 v. multicoloured	35	70

DESIGNS—HORIZ: 25 v. Vanuatu emblem; 45 v. Vanuatu national anthem. VERT: 75 v. Vanuatu coat of arms.

107 Three Shepherds

1981. Christmas. Children's Paintings. Mult.

322	15 v. Type **107**	10	10
323	25 v. Vanuatu girl with lamb (vert)	15	15
324	35 v. Angel as butterfly	15	20
325	45 v. Boy carrying torch and gifts (vert)	25	30

108 New Caledonian Myiagra Flycatchers

109 "Flickingeria comata"

1982. Birds (2nd series). Multicoloured.

327	15 v. Type **108**	45	20
328	20 v. Rainbow lorys	50	30
329	25 v. Buff-bellied flycatchers	55	35
330	45 v. Collared grey fantails	80	65

1982. Orchids. Multicoloured.

331	1 v. Type **109**	10	50
332	2 v. "Calanthe triplicata"	10	50
333	10 v. "Dendrobium sladei"	15	30
334	15 v. "Dendrobium mohlianum"	20	20
335	20 v. "Dendrobium macrophyllum"	25	30
336	25 v. "Dendrobium purpureum"	30	35
337	30 v. "Robiquetia mimus"	35	40
338	35 v. "Dendrobium mooreanum" (horiz)	50	50
339	45 v. "Spathoglottis plicata" (horiz)	55	70
340	50 v. "Dendrobium seemannii" (horiz)	60	80
341	75 v. "Dendrobium conanthum" (horiz)	95	1·50
342	100 v. "Dendrobium macranthum"	1·25	1·50
343	200 v. "Coelogyne lamellata"	2·25	2·75
344	500 v. "Bulbophyllum longioscapum"	5·00	6·50

110 Scouts round Campfire

1982. 75th Anniv of Boy Scout Movement. Multicoloured.

345	15 v. Type **110**	45	20
346	20 v. First aid	50	25
347	25 v. Constructing tower	55	40
348	45 v. Constructing raft	80	70
349	57 v. Scout saluting	1·25	1·25

111 Baby Jesus

1982. Christmas. Nativity Scenes. Mult.

350	15 v. Type **111**	40	35
351	25 v. Mary and Joseph	60	45
352	35 v. Shepherds (vert)	75	1·00
353	45 v. Kings bearing gifts (vert)	80	1·40

112 "Euploea sylvester"

1983. Butterflies. Multicoloured.

355	15 v. Type **112**	75	50
356	15 v. "Hypolimnas octocula"	75	50
357	20 v. "Papilio canopus"	90	70
358	20 v. "Polyura sacco"	90	70
359	25 v. "Luthrodes cleotas"	1·00	80
360	25 v. "Danaus pumila"	1·00	80

113 President Afi George Sokomanu

1983. Commonwealth Day. Multicoloured.

361	15 v. Type **113**	15	10
362	20 v. Fisherman and liner "Oriana"	20	15
363	25 v. Herdsman and cattle	25	15
364	75 v. World map showing position of Vanuatu with Commonwealth and Vanuatu flags	50	70

115 Montgolfier Balloon of De Rozier and D'Arlandes, 1783

117 "Cymatoderma elegans var. lamellatum"

116 Mail at Bauerfield Airport

1983. Bicentenary of Manned Flight. Mult.

366 15 v. Type **115** — 15 15
367 20 v. J. A. C. Charles hydrogen balloon (first use of hydrogen, 1783) — 25 25
368 25 v. Blanchard and Jeffries crossing English Channel, 1785 — 30 30
369 35 v. Giffard's steam-powered dirigible airship, 1852 (horiz) — 40 40
370 40 v. "La France" (airship of Renard and Krebs), 1884 (horiz) — 45 45
371 45 v. "Graf Zeppelin" (first aerial circumnavigation, 1929) (horiz) — 55 55

1983. World Communications Year. Mult.

372 15 v. Type **116** — 20 25
373 20 v. Switchboard operator — 30 35
374 25 v. Telex operator — 35 40
375 45 v. Satellite earth station — 65 70

1984. Fungi. Multicoloured.

377 15 v. Type **117** — 70 45
378 25 v. "Lignosus rhinocerus" — 90 85
379 35 v. "Stereum ostrea" (horiz) — 1·25 1·25
380 45 v. "Ganoderma boninense" — 1·60 1·90

118 Port Vila

1984. 250th Anniv of "Lloyd's List" (newspaper). Multicoloured.

381 15 v. Type **118** — 20 25
382 20 v. "Induna" (container ship) — 30 35
383 25 v. Air Vanuatu Boeing 737 aircraft — 35 40
384 45 v. "Brahman Express" (container ship) — 65 70

1984. Universal Postal Union Congress, Hamburg. As No. 371 but inscr "UPU CONGRESS HAMBURG" and U.P.U. logo.

385 45 v. multicoloured — 80 80

119 Charolais

1984. Cattle. Multicoloured.

386 15 v. Type **119** — 20 25
387 25 v. Charolais-afrikander — 35 40
388 45 v. Friesian — 65 70
389 75 v. Charolais-brahman — 1·10 1·25

120 "Makambo"

1984. "Ausipex" International Stamp Exn, Melbourne. Inter-island Freighters. Multicoloured.

390 25 v. Type **120** — 70 50
391 45 v. "Rockton" — 1·10 90
392 100 v. "Waroonga" — 2·00 3·50

121 Father Christmas in Children's Ward

1984. Christmas. Multicoloured.

394 25 v. Type **121** — 45 40
395 45 v. Nativity play — 80 70
396 75 v. Father Christmas distributing presents — 1·40 1·25

1985. No. 331 surch.

397 5 v. on 1 v. Type **109** — 65 50

123 Ambrym Island Ceremonial Dance

124 Peregrine Falcon diving

1985. Traditional Costumes. Multicoloured.

398 20 v. Type **123** — 35 35
399 25 v. Pentecost Island marriage ceremony — 40 40
400 45 v. Women's grade ceremony, South West Malakula — 75 70
401 75 v. Ceremonial dance, South West Malakula — 1·10 1·25

1985. Birth Bicentenary of John J. Audubon (ornithologist). Peregrine Falcon. Mult.

402 20 v. Type **124** — 60 35
403 35 v. Peregrine falcon in flight — 75 50
404 45 v. Peregrine falcon perched on branch — 90 80
405 100 v. "Peregrine Falcon" (John J. Audubon) — 1·60 1·75

125 The Queen Mother with the Queen on her 80th Birthday

1985. Life and Times of Queen Elizabeth the Queen Mother. Multicoloured.

406 5 v. Duke and Duchess of York on wedding day, 1923 — 15 30
407 20 v. Type **125** — 40 40
408 35 v. At Ancona, Italy — 60 60
409 55 v. With Prince Henry at his christening (from photo by Lord Snowdon) — 85 90

126 "Mala" (patrol boat)

1985. 5th Anniv of Independence and "Expo '85" World Fair, Japan. Multicoloured.

411 35 v. Type **126** — 45 50
412 45 v. Japanese fishing fleet — 65 70
413 55 v. Vanuatu Mobile Force Band — 75 85
414 100 v. Prime Minister Fr. Walter H. Lini — 1·00 1·75

127 "Youth Activities" (Alain Lagaliu)

1985. Int Youth Year. Children's Paintings. Mult.

416 20 v. Type **127** — 55 35
417 30 v. "Village" (Peter Obed) — 65 45
418 50 v. "Beach and 'PEACE' Slogan" (Mary Estelle) — 1·10 75
419 100 v. "Youth Activities" (different) (Abel Merani) — 1·75 1·50

128 Map of Vanuatu with National and U.N. Flags

1985. 4th Anniv of United Nations Membership.

420 **128** 45 v. multicoloured — 70 70

129 Elizabeth's Nudibranch

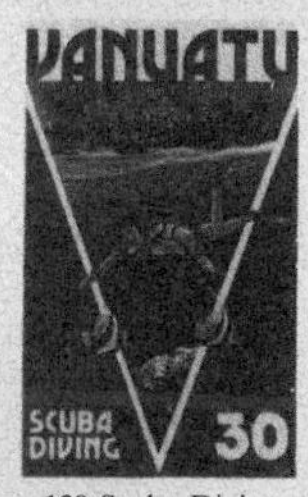

130 Scuba Diving

1985. Marine Life (1st series). Sea Slugs. Multicoloured.

421 20 v. Type **129** — 30 35
422 35 v. Tessellated nudibranch (horiz) — 45 50
423 55 v. "Chromodoris kuniei" (horiz) — 75 80
424 100 v. "Notodoris minor" — 1·40 1·50

See also Nos. 442/5 and 519/22.

1986. Tourism. Multicoloured.

425 30 v. Type **130** — 85 40
426 35 v. Yasur volcano, Tanna — 1·00 45
427 55 v. Land diving, Pentecost Island — 1·40 70
428 100 v. Windsurfing — 1·50 1·50

1986. 60th Birthday of Queen Elizabeth II. As T **110** of Ascension. Multicoloured.

429 20 v. With Prince Charles and Princess Anne, 1951 — 15 30
430 35 v. Prince William's Christening, 1982 — 20 45
431 45 v. In New Hebrides, 1974 — 25 60
432 55 v. On board Royal Yacht "Britannia", Mexico, 1974 — 30 70
433 100 v. At Crown Agents Head Office, London, 1983 — 40 1·25

131 Liner S.S. "President Coolidge" leaving San Francisco

1986. "Ameripex '86" International Stamp Exhibition, Chicago. Sinking of S.S. "President Coolidge". Multicoloured.

434 45 v. Type **131** — 1·00 60
435 55 v. S.S. "President Coolidge" as troopship, 1942 — 1·10 70
436 135 v. Map of Espiritu Santo showing site of sinking, 1942 — 2·00 1·75

132 Halley's Comet and Vanuatu Statue

1986. Appearance of Halley's Comet. Multicoloured.

438 30 v. Type **132** — 90 50
439 45 v. Family watching Comet — 1·25 1·00
440 55 v. Comet passing Earth — 1·40 1·25
441 100 v. Edmond Halley — 2·00 3·25

133 Daisy Coral

1986. Marine Life (2nd series). Corals. Multicoloured.

442 20 v. Type **133** — 60 40
443 45 v. Organ pipe coral — 90 75
444 55 v. Sea fan — 1·00 1·00
445 135 v. Soft coral — 2·25 3·50

134 Children of Different Races

1986. Christmas. Int Peace Year. Mult.

446 30 v. Type **134** — 90 50
447 45 v. Church and boy praying — 1·25 85
448 55 v. U.N. discussion and Headquarters Building, New York — 1·40 1·40
449 135 v. People of different races at work — 2·75 5·00

135 Datsun "240Z" (1969)

1987. Motor Vehicles. Multicoloured.

450 20 v. Type **135** — 30 30
451 45 v. Ford "Model A" (1927) — 60 60
452 55 v. Unic lorry (1924–5) — 70 70
453 135 v. Citroen "DS19" (1975) — 1·60 2·25

1987. Hurricane Relief Fund. No. 332, already surch, and Nos. 429/33 all surch **Hurricane Relief Fund** and premium.

454 20 v. + 10 v. on 2 v. "Calanthe triplicata" — 45 70
455 20 v. + 10 v. Princess Elizabeth with Prince Charles and Princess Anne, 1951 — 45 70
456 35 v. + 15 v. Prince William's Christening, 1982 — 75 1·00
457 45 v. + 20 v. Queen in New Hebrides, 1974 — 90 1·25
458 55 v. + 25 v. Queen on board Royal Yacht "Britannia", Mexico, 1974 — 1·50 1·60
459 100 v. + 50 v. Queen at Crown Agents Head Office, London, 1983 — 1·75 2·75

The surcharge on No. 454 also includes the word "Surcharge".

137 Young Coconut Plants

1987. 25th Anniv of I.R.H.O. Coconut Research Station. Multicoloured.

460 35 v. Type **137** — 40 45
461 45 v. Coconut flower and fronds — 55 60
462 100 v. Coconuts — 1·10 1·40
463 135 v. Research station — 1·60 2·00

The inscriptions on Nos. 462/3 are in French.

138 Spotted Hawkfish

1987. Fishes. Multicoloured.

464 1 v. Type **138** — 10 10
465 5 v. Moorish idol — 15 10
466 10 v. Black-saddled pufferfish — 15 10
467 15 v. Dusky anemonefish — 20 20
468 20 v. Striped surgeonfish — 30 25
469 30 v. Six-barred wrasse — 40 35
470 35 v. Yellow-striped anthias ("Purple queenfish") — 45 40
471 40 v. Squirrelfish — 50 45
472 45 v. Clown triggerfish — 60 55
473 50 v. Dragon wrasse — 65 65
474 55 v. Regal angelfish — 70 70
475 65 v. Lionfish — 80 80
476 100 v. Freckled hawkfish — 1·40 1·40
477 300 v. Undulate triggerfish — 3·50 4·00
478 500 v. Saddled butterflyfish — 5·50 6·00

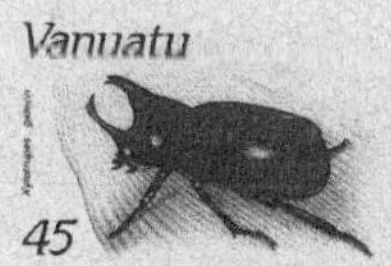

139 "Xylotrupes gideon" (beetle)

140 "Away in a Manger"

1987. Insects. Multicoloured.

479 45 v. Type **139** — 55 60
480 55 v. "Phyllodes imperialis" (moth) — 65 70
481 65 v. "Cyphogastra sp." (beetle) — 75 85
482 100 v. "Othreis fullonia" (moth) — 1·10 1·75

1987. Christmas. Christmas Carols. Mult.

483 20 v. Type **140** — 45 30
484 45 v. "Once in Royal David's City" — 80 65
485 55 v. "While Shepherds watched their Flocks" — 90 90
486 65 v. "We Three Kings of Orient Are" — 1·00 1·00

1987. Royal Ruby Wedding. Nos. 429/33 optd **40TH WEDDING ANNIVERSARY.**

487 20 v. Princess Elizabeth with Prince Charles and Princess Anne, 1951 — 30 30
488 35 v. Prince William's Christening, 1982 — 45 45
489 45 v. Queen Elizabeth II in New Hebrides, 1974 — 60 60
490 55 v. On board Royal Yacht "Britannia", Mexico, 1974 — 70 70
491 100 v. At Crown Agents Head Office, London, 1983 — 1·25 1·25

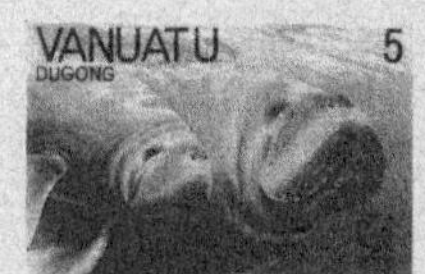

141 Dugong Cow and Calf

1988. Endangered Species. Dugong. Multicoloured.

492 5 v. Type **141** — 90 35
493 10 v. Dugong underwater — 1·40 35
494 20 v. Two dugongs surfacing to breathe — 1·90 1·00
495 45 v. Four dugongs swimming — 2·75 2·50

142 "Tambo"

1988. Bicentenary of Australian Settlement. Freighters. Multicoloured.

496 20 v. Type **142** 20 25
497 45 v. "Induna" 50 55
498 55 v. "Morinda" 60 65
499 65 v. "Marsina" 55 60

143 Captain James Cook

144 Boxer in training

1988. "Sydpex '88" National Stamp Exhibition, Sydney.

500 **143** 45 v. black and red . . . 75 75

1988. Olympic Games, Seoul. Multicoloured.

502 20 v. Type **144** 20 25
503 45 v. Athletics 50 55
504 55 v. Signing Olympic agreement 60 65
505 65 v. Soccer 70 75

1988. 300th Anniv of Lloyd's of London. As T **123** of Ascension. Multicoloured.

507 20 v. Interior of new Lloyd's Building, 1988 . . . . . . 30 25
508 55 v. "Shirrabank" (freighter) (horiz) . . . . 1·25 65
509 65 v. "Adela" (ferry) (horiz) . 1·40 75
510 145 v. "General Slocum" (excursion paddle-steamer) on fire, New York, 1904 . . . 2·25 1·75

145 Agricultural Crops

1988. F.A.O. Multicoloured.

511 45 v. Type **145** 45 55
512 55 v. Fisherman with catch (vert) 50 65
513 65 v. Livestock on smallholding (vert) 55 75
514 120 v. Market women with produce . . . . 80 1·40

146 Virgin and Child ("Silent Night")

1988. Christmas. Carols. Multicoloured.

515 20 v. Type **146** 25 25
516 45 v. Angels ("Angels from the Realms of Glory") 45 55
517 65 v. Shepherd boy with lamb ("O Come all ye Faithful") . 55 75
518 155 v. Baby ("In that Poor Stable how Charming Jesus Lies") . 1·50 1·90

147 "Periclimenes brevicarpalis"

1989. Marine Life (3rd series). Shrimps. Mult.

519 20 v. Type **147** 50 25
520 45 v. "Lysmata grabhami" . . 80 55
521 65 v. "Rhynchocinetes sp." . . 95 75
522 150 v. "Stenopus hispidus" . . 2·25 2·50

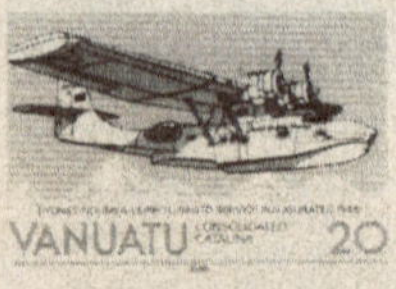

148 Consolidated Catalina Flying Boat

1989. Economic and Social Commission for Asia and the Pacific. Aircraft.

523 **148** 20 v. black and blue . . 75 30
524 – 45 v. black and green . . 1·10 65
525 – 55 v. black and yellow . . 1·50 80
526 – 200 v. black and red . . 4·00 3·00

DESIGNS: 45 v. Douglas DC-3; 55 v. Embraer EMB-110 Bandeirante; 200 v. Boeing 737-300.

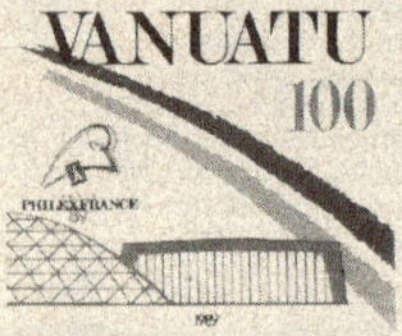

149 Porte de Versailles Hall No. 1

1989. "Philexfrance '89" International Stamp Exhibition, Paris. Multicoloured.

527 100 v. Type **149** . . . . . . 2·00 1·40
528 100 v. Eiffel Tower . . . . . 2·00 1·40

Nos. 527/8 were printed together, se-tenant, forming a composite design.

1989. 20th Anniv of First Manned Landing on Moon. As T **126** of Ascension. Multicoloured.

530 45 v. Command module seen from lunar module . . . . 1·10 80
531 55 v. Crew of "Apollo 17" (30 × 30 mm) . . . . 1·25 90
532 65 v. "Apollo 17" emblem (30 × 30 mm) . . . . 1·40 1·00
533 120 v. Launch of "Apollo 17" 2·00 2·00

1989. "Melbourne Stampshow '89". No. 332 surch **100** and Stampshow emblem.

535 100 v. on 2 v. "Calanthe triplicata" . . . . 3·50 4·00

151 New Hebrides 1978 "Concorde" 30 f. (French inscr) Stamp

1989. "World Stamp Expo '89" International Stamp Exhibition, Washington.

536 **151** 65 v. multicoloured . . . 2·50 2·50

152 "Alocasia macrorrhiza"

153 Kava (national plant)

1990. Flora. Multicoloured.

538 45 v. Type **152** 60 55
539 55 v. "Acacia spirorbis" . . . 70 70
540 65 v. "Metrosideros collina" . 80 80
541 145 v. "Hoya australis" . . . 1·75 2·50

1990. "Stamp World London 90" International Stamp Exhibition. Multicoloured.

542 45 v. Type **153** 80 55
543 65 v. Luganville Post Office . 1·00 95
544 100 v. Embraer EMB-110 Bandeirante mail plane and sailing packet . . . . 1·90 2·00
545 200 v. Penny Black and Vanuatu 1980 10 f. definitive . . . . 3·00 3·75

154 National Council of Women Logo

1990. 10th Anniv of Independence.

547 **154** 25 v. black and blue . . . 35 30
548 – 50 v. multicoloured . . . 60 70
549 – 55 v. purple, black & buff 65 70
550 – 65 v. multicoloured . . . 70 90
551 – 80 v. multicoloured . . . 85 1·25

DESIGNS: 50 v. President Frederick Kalomuana Timakata; 55 v. Preamble to the Constitution; 65 v. Vanuaaku Pati party flag; 80 v. Reserve Bank of Vanuatu.

155 General De Gaulle at Bayeux, 1944

1990. Birth Centenary of General Charles de Gaulle (French statesman). Multicoloured.

553 20 v. Type **155** . . . . 1·75 2·00
554 25 v. Generals De Lattre de Tassigny, De Gaulle, Devers and Patch in Alsace, 1945 . 1·75 2·00
555 30 v. De Gaulle as President of the French Republic . . . 75 80
556 45 v. De Gaulle at Biggin Hill, 1942 . . . . 80 90
557 55 v. Roosevelt, De Gaulle and Churchill, Casablanca, 1943 . 85 95
558 65 v. General De Gaulle and Liberation of Paris, 1944 . . 90 1·00

156 Angel facing Right

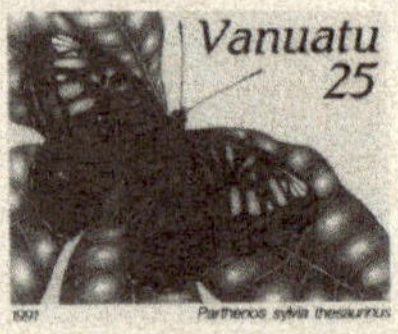

157 "Parthenos sylvia"

1990. Christmas. Multicoloured.

559 25 v. Type **156** 45 55
560 50 v. Shepherds 70 90
561 65 v. Nativity . . . . 80 1·00
562 70 v. Three Kings . . . . . 85 1·10
563 80 v. Angel facing left . . . . 85 1·25

Nos. 559/63 were printed together, se-tenant, forming a composite design.

1991. Butterflies. Multicoloured.

564 25 v. Type **157** 45 30
565 55 v. "Euploea leucostictus" . . 80 60
566 80 v. "Lampides boeticus" . . 1·25 1·25
567 150 v. "Danaus plexippus" . . 2·00 2·75

158 Dance Troupe from South-west Malakula

160 White-collared Kingfisher

1991. 2nd National Art Festival, Luganville. Multicoloured.

568 25 v. Type **158** 35 30
569 65 v. Women weavers and baskets 85 85
570 80 v. Woodcarver and carved animals, masks, dish and ceremonial figures . . . . . 1·10 1·25
571 150 v. Musicians playing bamboo flute, youtatau and pan pipes 1·90 2·25

1991. Nos. 332/4 and 337 surch.

572 20 v. on 2 v. "Calanthe triplicata" 50 50
573 60 v. on 10 v. "Dendrobium sladei" . . . . 1·25 1·60
574 70 v. on 15 v. "Dendrobium mohlianum" . . . . 1·40 1·75
575 80 v. on 30 v. "Robiquetia mimus" . . . . 1·40 1·75

See also No. 622.

1991. 65th Birthday of Queen Elizabeth II and 70th Birthday of Prince Philip. As T **139** of Ascension. Multicoloured.

576 65 v. Queen Elizabeth II . . . 90 1·25
577 70 v. Prince Philip . . . . . 90 1·25

1991. "Phila Nippon '91" International Stamp Exhibition, Tokyo. Birds. Multicoloured.

578 50 v. Type **160** 65 70
579 55 v. Palm lorikeet 70 75
580 80 v. Scarlet robin . . . . . 95 1·10
581 100 v. Pacific swallow . . . . 1·10 1·75

161 Group of Islanders

1991. World AIDS Day. Multicoloured.

583 25 v. Type **161** 55 30
584 65 v. Caring for AIDS victim . 1·00 85
585 80 v. AIDS shark . . . . . . 1·25 1·50
586 150 v. Children's playground . 2·00 2·50

1992. 40th Anniv of Queen Elizabeth II's Accession. As T **143** of Ascension. Multicoloured.

587 20 v. Reserve Bank of Vanuatu Building, Port Vila 25 30
588 25 v. Port Vila 30 30
589 60 v. Mural, Parliament House 75 75
590 65 v. Three portraits of Queen Elizabeth 80 80
591 70 v. Queen Elizabeth II . . . 85 1·25

162 Grumman F4F Wildcat

1992. 50th Anniv of Outbreak of the Pacific War (1st issue). Multicoloured.

592 50 v. Type **162** . . . . . . 1·50 1·00
593 55 v. Douglas SBD-3 Dauntless 1·50 1·10
594 65 v. Consolidated PBY-5A Catalina . . . . 1·75 1·50
595 80 v. U.S.S. "Hornet" (aircraft carrier) . . . . 2·50 2·50

See also Nos. 623/6.

163 Meteorological Station, Port Vila

165 Breast Feeding

164 Vanuatu National Football Team

1992. 10th Anniv of Vanuatu's Membership of World Meteorological Organization. Mult.

597 25 v. Type **163** 40 30
598 60 v. Satellite picture of tropical cyclone 80 80
599 80 v. Weather chart of Pacific showing cyclone . . . . . 1·00 1·25
600 105 v. Radio Vanuatu broadcasting cyclone warning 1·25 1·75

1992. Vanuatu's Participation in Melanesian Football Cup and Olympic Games, Barcelona. Multicoloured.

601 20 v. Type **164** 45 40
602 65 v. Melanesian Cup Final, 1990 1·25 1·25
603 70 v. Baptiste Firiam (800 metres) . . . . 1·40 1·25
604 80 v. Mary Estelle Kapalu (400, 400 hurdles, and 800 metres) 1·50 1·75

1992. World Food Day. Each brown and green.

605 20 v. Type **165** 25 25
606 70 v. Central Hospital, Port Vila 85 90
607 80 v. Children eating . . . . 95 1·00
608 150 v. Nutritious food . . . . 1·60 2·25

166 Leatherback Turtle

167 "Hibiscus rosa-sinensis" "Agnes Goult"

1992. Turtles. Multicoloured.

609 55 v. Type **166** . . . . . . 1·25 1·10
610 65 v. Loggerhead turtle laying eggs . . . . 1·40 1·25
611 70 v. Hawksbill turtle swimming 1·60 1·40
612 80 v. Green turtle under water 2·25 2·00

1993. Hibiscus Flowers (1st series). Multicoloured.

614 25 v. Type **167** 30 30
615 55 v. "Hibiscus tiliaceus" . . 70 70
616 80 v. "Hibiscus rosa-sinensis linnaeus" . . . . 95 1·00
617 150 v. "Hibiscus rosa-sinensis" "Rose of China" . . . . . 1·60 2·25

See also Nos. 682/5 and 736/9.

1993. 14th World Orchid Conference, Glasgow. Nos. 339 and 341/3 surch **WORLD ORCHID CONFERENCE 1993** and value.

618 40 v. on 45 v. "Spathoglottis plicata" (horiz) 50 50
619 55 v. on 75 v. "Dendrobium conanthum" (horiz) 70 75

620 65 v. on 100 v. "Dendrobium macranthum" 75 80
621 150 v. on 200 v. "Coelogyne lamellata" 1·60 2·25

1993. No. 338 surch **20**.
622 20 v. on 35 v. "Dendrobium mooreanum" 3·50 50

1993. 50th Anniv of Outbreak of the Pacific War (2nd issue). As T **162**. Multicoloured.
623 20 v. Grumman F6F Hellcat 80 50
624 55 v. Lockheed P-38F Lightning 1·50 1·25
625 65 v. Grumman TBF Avenger 1·60 1·50
626 80 v. U.S.S. "Essex" (aircraft carrier) 1·75 2·25

170 Port Vila and Iririki Island

1993. Local Scenery. Multicoloured.
628 5 v. Type **170** 10 10
629 10 v. Yachts and Iririki Island 10 10
630 15 v. Court House, Port Vila 15 20
631 20 v. Two girls, Pentecost Island 20 25
632 25 v. Women dancers, Tanna Island 25 30
633 30 v. Market, Port Vila 30 35
634 45 v. Man in canoe, Erakor Island (vert) 40 45
635 50 v. Coconut trees, Champagne Beach 45 50
636 55 v. Coconut trees, North Efate Islands 50 55
637 60 v. Underwater shoal of fishes, Banks Group 55 60
638 70 v. Sea fan, Tongoa Island (vert) 65 70
639 75 v. Santo Island 70 75
640 80 v. Sunset, Port Vila harbour (vert) 75 80
641 100 v. Mele Waterfall (vert) 95 1·00
642 300 v. Yasur Volcano, Tanna Island (vert) 2·75 3·00
643 500 v. Aerial view of Erakor Island 4·75 5·00

171 Commercial Trochus

1993. Shells (1st series). Multicoloured.
644 55 v. Type **171** 1·00 85
645 65 v. Camp pitar venus 1·10 95
646 80 v. Tapestry turban 1·40 1·60
647 150 v. Trapezium horse conch 2·25 3·25
See also Nos. 665/8 and 692/5.

172 "St. Joseph the Carpenter" (detail) (De la Tour)

1993. Christmas. Bicentenary of the Louvre, Paris. Religious Paintings by Georges de la Tour. Multicoloured.
648 25 v. Type **172** 35 30
649 55 v. "Holy Child" (detail) 70 65
650 80 v. "Adoration of the Shepherds" (detail) 90 1·00
651 150 v. "Adoration of the Shepherds" (different detail) 1·60 2·25

1993. South Pacific Mini Games, Port Vila. Nos. 602, 604, 631 and 633 surch **SOUTH PACIFIC MINI GAMES PORT VILA DECEMBER 1993** and value.
652 15 v. on 20 v. Two girls, Pentecost Island 25 25
653 25 v. on 30 v. Market, Port Vila 35 35
654 55 v. on 65 v. Melanesian Cup Final, 1990 75 75
655 70 v. on 80 v. Mary Estelle Kapalu (400, 400 hurdles and 800 metres) 80 1·10

174 Charity Horse Race and Kiwanis Emblem

175 Silhouetted Family

1994. "Hong Kong '94" International Stamp Exhibition. Charitable Organizations. Mult.
656 25 v. Type **174** 35 30
657 60 v. Twin Otter airplane and Lions Club emblem (horiz) 70 75
658 75 v. Mosquito and Rotary International emblem 90 1·00
659 150 v. Blood donor service ambulance and Red Cross emblem (horiz) 1·60 2·25

1994. International Year of the Family.
661 **175** 25 v. brown and violet 35 30
662 60 v. green and red 70 75
663 90 v. brown and green 1·00 1·10
664 150 v. violet and brown 1·60 2·00

1994. Shells (2nd series). As T **171**. Multicoloured.
665 60 v. Eyed cowrie 1·50 1·00
666 70 v. Marble cone 1·50 1·10
667 85 v. Chiragra spider conch 1·60 1·75
668 155 v. Adusta murex 2·50 3·25

176 Traditional Sculpture and Hut

178 Consolidated PBY-5 Catalina Flying Boat

177 Pink Anemonefish

1994. Tourism. Multicoloured.
669 25 v. Type **176** 70 80
670 75 v. Outrigger canoe and inflatable dinghy 1·40 1·50
671 90 v. Yachts, airliner and parrot 1·75 1·90
672 200 v. Helicopter and local woman with fruit 2·75 3·00
Nos. 669/72 were printed together, se-tenant, forming a composite design.

1994 Anemonefish. Multicoloured.
674 55 v. Type **177** 1·25 80
675 70 v. Yellow-tailed anemonefish 1·50 1·00
676 80 v. Fire anemonefish 1·75 1·75
677 140 v. Orange-finned anemonefish 3·00 4·00

1994. 50th Anniv of I.C.A.O. Multicoloured.
679 25 v. Type **178** 65 45
680 60 v. Douglas DC-3 1·10 90
681 75 v. De Havilland D.H.A.3 Drover 1·25 1·40
682 90 v. Boeing 737 on runway 1·50 2·00

179 "Hibiscus rosa-sinensis" "The Path"

1995. Hibiscus Flowers (2nd issue). Multicoloured.
683 25 v. Type **179** 60 45
684 60 v. "Hibiscus rosa-sinensis" "Old Frankie" 1·10 1·00
685 90 v. "Hibiscus sinensis" "Fijian White" 1·60 1·75
686 200 v. "Hibiscus rosa-sinensis" "Surfrider" 3·25 4·00

180 "Emoia nigromarginata"

1995. Lizards. Multicoloured.
687 25 v. Type **180** 50 45
688 55 v. "Nactus multicarinatus" 1·00 1·00
689 70 v. "Lepidodactylus" 1·25 1·25
690 80 v. "Emoia caeruleocauda" 1·40 1·40
691 140 v. "Emoia sanfordi" 2·25 2·75

1995. Shells (3rd series). As T **171**. Multicoloured.
692 25 v. "Epitonium scalare" 60 50
693 55 v. "Strombus latissimus" 1·25 1·25
694 90 v. "Conus bullatus" 1·75 1·75
695 200 v. "Pterynotus pinnatus" 3·50 4·00

181 "Tanna Girls" (A. Toni)

1995. 15th Anniv of Independence. Multicoloured.
696 25 v. Type **181** 45 40
697 55 v. "Black Coral Dancers" (sculpture, E. Watt) (vert) 90 90
698 75 v. Erromango tapestry by Juliet Peta (vert) 1·25 1·25
699 90 v. "Parade Day" (H. Di-Donna) 1·40 1·60
700 140 v. "Banks Dancers" (J. John) 2·00 2·75

182 Children with Doves and Flags

183 Rambaramp (effigy), Malakula

1995. 50th Anniv of United Nations.
702 **182** 60 v. multicoloured 1·25 1·00

1995. 50th Anniv of End of Second World War in the Pacific. As T **162** showing aircraft. Mult.
703 60 v. Curtiss SB2C Helldiver 1·50 1·25
704 70 v. Supermarine Spitfire Mk VIII 1·60 1·40
705 75 v. Chance Vought F4U-1A Corsair 1·75 1·60
706 80 v. Lockheed PV-1 Ventura 1·75 1·60

1995. Vanuatu Culture (1st series). Opening of New National Museum. Artefacts. Multicoloured.
708 25 v. Type **183** 35 30
709 60 v. Pot from Wusi, Espiritu Santo 75 75
710 75 v. Slit gong from Mele, Efate 90 1·00
711 90 v. Tapa cloth, Erromango 1·25 1·60
See also Nos. 772/6.

184 Boy throwing Cast Net

1996. Fishing. Multicoloured.
712 55 v. Type **184** 75 65
713 75 v. Fishing canoes 1·00 90
714 80 v. "Etelis" (fishing boat) and deep water fish (vert) 1·10 1·10
715 140 v. Game fisherman catching sailfish (vert) 2·25 2·75

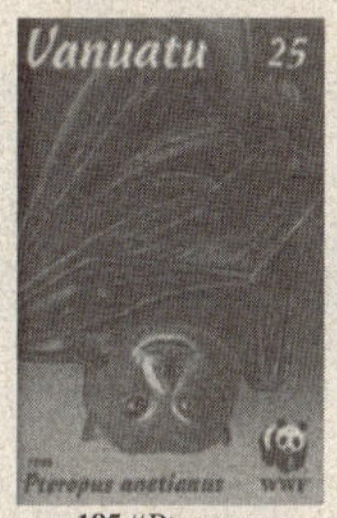

185 "Pteropus anetianus"

1996. Endangered Species. Flying Foxes. Mult.
716 25 v. Type **185** 40 50
717 25 v. "Notopteris macdonaldi" upside down eating fruit (horiz) 40 50
718 25 v. "Pteropus anetianus" hanging on branch 40 50
719 25 v. "Notopteris macdonaldi" on branch (horiz) 40 50

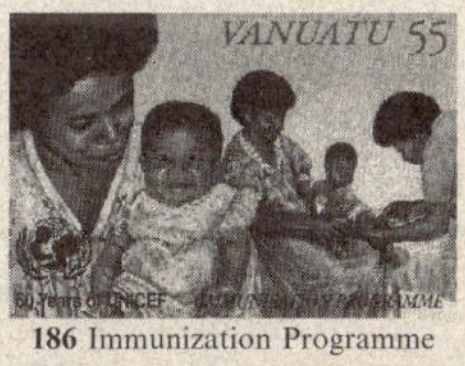

186 Immunization Programme

1996. 50th Anniv of U.N.I.C.E.F. Multicoloured.
722 55 v. Type **186** 90 90
723 60 v. Breast-feeding programme 90 90

187 Airliner and Radio Waves

1996. Centenary of Radio. Multicoloured.
724 60 v. Type **187** 80 90
725 75 v. Radio Vanuatu broadcaster 95 1·10
726 80 v. Guglielmo Marconi 1·00 1·25
727 90 v. Cruise liner and radio waves 1·10 1·40
Nos. 724/7 were issued together, se-tenant, forming a composite aerial view of Port Vila.

188 Marie Kapalu, Tawai Keiruan, Baptiste Firiam and Tava Kalo

1996. Centenary of Modern Olympics Games. Multicoloured.
728 25 v. Type **188** 35 30
729 70 v. Athletes training 95 95
730 75 v. Athletes from 1950s 1·00 1·00
731 200 v. Athletes in 1896 2·75 3·25

189 Children in Front of Presbyterian Church and Roman Catholic Cathedral

1996. Christmas. Religious Buildings. Multicoloured.
732 25 v. Type **189** 35 30
733 60 v. Children and Church of Christ 80 80
734 75 v. Children and Seventh Day Adventist and Apostolic churches 95 1·00
735 90 v. Children and Anglican church 1·25 1·60

190 "Hibiscus rosa-sinensis" "Lady Cilento"

1996. Hibiscus Flowers (3rd issue). Multicoloured.
736 25 v. Type **190** 40 30
737 60 v. "Hibiscus rosa-sinensis" "Kinchen's Yellow" 90 70
738 90 v. "Hibiscus rosa-sinensis" "D. J. O'Brien" 1·25 1·25
739 200 v. "Hibiscus rosa-sinensis" "Cuban Variety" 3·00 3·75

191 Coral Garden

1997. Diving. Multicoloured.
740 70 v. Type **191** 90 80
741 75 v. Carving on the "President Coolidge" 95 85
742 90 v. "Boris" (Giant grouper) 1·25 1·25
743 140 v. Wreck of the "President Coolidge" 2·25 2·75

192 View from Cockpit

1997. 10th Anniv of Air Vanuatu. Multicoloured.
746 25 v. Type **192** 40 30
747 60 v. 737-400 airliner being serviced, Bauerfield International Airport, Port Vila (81 × 31 mm) 80 70
748 90 v. Air stewardess serving drinks 1·25 1·25
749 200 v. Passengers disembarking 2·25 3·00

193 Sharp-tailed Sandpiper

1997. Birds (1st issue). Coastal Birds. Multicoloured.
751 25 v. Type **193** 35 30
752 55 v. Crested tern 70 70
753 60 v. Little pied cormorant 75 75
754 75 v. Brown booby 90 90
755 80 v. Reef heron (vert) 95 1·10
756 90 v. Red-tailed tropic bird (vert) 1·10 1·40
See also Nos. 799/802.

194 Thomas Edison and Light Bulb

1997. 150th Birth Anniv of Thomas Edison (inventor). Multicoloured.
757 60 v. Type **194** 90 1·00
758 70 v. Hydro-electric dam, Espiritu Santo 90 1·00
759 200 v. Port Vila at dusk (80 × 29 mm) 2·40 2·75

195 Yellow-faced Angelfish

1997. Angelfish. Multicoloured.
760 25 v. Type **195** 30 30
761 55 v. Flame angelfish 70 70
762 60 v. Lemonpeel angelfish 75 75
763 70 v. Emperor angelfish 85 85
764 140 v. Multi-barred angelfish 1·75 2·00

1998. No. 638 surch **5**.
765 5 v. on 70 v. Sea fan, Tongoa Island (vert) 10 10

197 Fale, Espiritu Santo

1998. Local Architecture. Multicoloured.
766 30 v. Type **197** 35 35
767 65 v. National Cultural Centre 80 80
768 80 v. University of South Pacific 95 95
769 200 v. Chiefs' Nakamal 1·90 2·25

1998. Diana, Princess of Wales Commemoration. As T **91** of Kiribati. Multicoloured.
770 95 v. Wearing black jacket, 1997 1·00 1·10

198 Nalawan Headdresses from South West Bay, Malakula

1998. Vanuatu Culture (2nd series). Masks. Mult.
772 30 v. Type **198** 30 35
773 65 v. Rom mask from North Ambrym 60 65
774 75 v. Tamate mask from Gaua Island 70 75
775 85 v. Banglulu headdress from Uripiv Island, north-east Malakula 80 85
776 95 v. Chubwan masks from Vao Island, Malakula, and from Pentecost 95 1·00

199 "Danaus plexippus"

1998. Butterflies. Self-adhesive. Multicoloured.
777 30 v. Type **199** 30 35
778 60 v. "Hypolimnas bolina" 55 60
779 65 v. "Eurema hecabe" 60 65
780 75 v. "Nymphalidae" sp. 70 75
781 95 v. "Precis villida" 95 1·00
782 205 v. "Tirumala hamata" 2·00 2·10

200 Yasur, Tanna

1998. Volcanoes in Vanuatu. Multicoloured.
784 30 v. Type **200** 30 35
785 60 v. Marum and Benbow, Ambrym 55 60
786 75 v. Mount Garet, Gaua 70 75
787 80 v. Lopevi 75 80
788 145 v. Lake Manaro Voui, Ambae 1·40 1·50

202 De Quiros and "San Pedro y Paulo"

1999. Early Explorers. Multicoloured.
793 34 v. Type **202** 35 40
794 73 v. De Bougainville and "La Boudeuse" 65 70
795 84 v. Cook and H.M.S. "Resolution" 80 85
796 90 v. La Perouse and "L'Astrolabe" 85 90
797 96 v. Dumont d'Urville and "L'Astrolabe" 1·00 1·10
No. 797 is inscribed "1788" in error.

203 Vanuatu Kingfisher

1999. Birds (2nd series). Bush and Lowland Birds. Multicoloured.
799 34 v. Type **203** 35 40
800 67 v. Shining cuckoo 60 65
801 73 v. Peregrine falcon 65 70
802 107 v. Rainbow lorikeet 1·00 1·10

VENDA

The Republic of Venda was established on 13 September, 1979, being constructed from tribal areas formerly part of the Republic of South Africa. This independence did not receive international political recognition, but the stamps were accepted as valid on international mail.
Venda was reincorporated into South Africa on 27 April 1994.

100 cents = 1 rand

1 Flag and Mace

2 "Tecomaria capensis"

1979. Independence. Multicoloured.
1 4 c. Type **1** 25 25
2 15 c. Government Buildings, Thohoyandou 60 80
3 20 c. Chief Minister P. R. Mphephu 85 1·10
4 25 c. Coat of arms 1·25 1·50

1979. Flowers. Multicoloured.
5 1 c. Type **2** 10 10
6a 2 c. "Catophractes alexandri" 20 15
7 3 c. "Tricliceras longipedunculatum" 30 10
8 4 c. "Dissotis princeps" 30 10
9a 5 c. "Gerbera jamesonii" 30 10
10 6 c. "Hibiscus mastersianus" 15 10
11 7 c. "Nymphaea caerulea" 20 10
12a 8 c. "Crinum lugardiae" 30 15
13 9 c. "Xerophyta retinervis" 20 15
14a 10 c. "Hypoxis angustifolia" 40 15
14b 11 c. "Combretum microphyllum" 30 15
14c 12 c. "Clivia caulescens" 30 15
15 15 c. "Pycnostachys urticifolia" 30 15
16 20 c. "Zantedeschia jucunda" 55 15
17a 25 c. "Leonotis mollis" 50 40
18 30 c. "Littonia modesta" 40 25
19 50 c. "Protea caffra" 40 30
20 1 r. "Adenium multiflorum" 1·00 65
21 2 r. "Strelitzia caudata" 1·75 2·00

3 Man drinking Beer

4 Tea Plants in Nursery

1980. Wood Carving. Multicoloured.
22 5 c. Type **3** 15 15
23 10 c. Frying mealies in gourd 25 25
24 15 c. King Nebuchadnezzar (horiz) 40 40
25 20 c. Python squeezing woman to death (horiz) 50 60

1980. Tea Cultivation. Multicoloured.
26 5 c. Type **4** 15 10
27 10 c. Tea pluckers 20 20
28 15 c. Withering in the factory 35 35
29 20 c. Cut, twist, curl unit 40 45

5 Young Banana Plants

6 "Precis tugela"

1980. Banana Cultivation. Multicoloured.
30 5 c. Type **5** 15 10
31 10 c. Cutting "hands" 25 25
32 15 c. Sorting and dividing into clusters 30 30
33 20 c. Packing 40 45

1980. Butterflies. Multicoloured.
34 5 c. Type **6** 20 15
35 10 c. "Charaxes bohemani" 40 40
36 15 c. "Catacroptera cloanthe" 55 55
37 20 c. "Papilio dardanus" 65 70

7 Collared Sunbird — 8 Nwandei Dam

1981. Sunbirds. Multicoloured.

38	5 c. Type **7**	20	15
39	15 c. Mariqua sunbird	55	55
40	20 c. Southern white-bellied sunbird	60	60
41	25 c. Scarlet-chested sunbird	75	80

1981. Lakes and Waterfalls. Multicoloured.

42	5 c. Type **8**	15	10
43	15 c. Mahovhohovho Falls	30	30
44	20 c. Phiphidi Falls	35	35
45	25 c. Lake Fundudzi	35	40

9 "Cynorkis kassnerana" — 10 Mbila

1981. Orchids. Multicoloured.

46	5 c. Type **9**	15	10
47	15 c. "Eulophia fridericii"	35	35
48	20 c. "Bonatea densiflora"	45	45
49	25 c. "Mystacidium brayboniae"	50	55

1981. Musical Instruments.

51	**10**	5 c. orange and black	10	10
52	–	15 c. orange and black	25	25
53	–	20 c. brown and black	30	35
54	–	25 c. brown and black	30	35

DESIGNS: 15 c. Phalaphala; 20 c. Tshizambi; 25 c. Ngoma.

11 Gathering Sisal

1982. Sisal Cultivation. Multicoloured.

55	5 c. Type **11**	10	10
56	10 c. Drying	20	20
57	20 c. Grading	30	35
58	25 c. Baling	30	40

12 Bison Petrograph, Altamira, Spain

1982. History of Writing (1st series). Multicoloured.

59	8 c. Type **12**	15	10
60	15 c. Petroglyph, Eastern California	30	30
61	20 c. Pictograph script (Sumerian tablet)	40	40
62	25 c. Bushman burial stone, Humansdorp	45	45

No. 59 is inscr "AHAMIRA" in error.
See also Nos. 75/8, 87/90, 107/10, 139/42, 171/4 and 203/6.

13 "Euphorbia ingens"

1982. Indigenous Trees (1st series). Multicoloured.

63	8 c. Type **13**	15	10
64	15 c. "Pterocarpus angolensis"	30	30
65	20 c. "Ficus ingens"	40	40
66	25 c. "Andansonia digitata"	50	55

See also Nos. 79/82, 95/8 and 227/30.

14 "Rana angolensis"

1982. Frogs. Multicoloured.

67	8 c. Type **14**	15	10
68	15 c. "Chiromantis xerampelina"	30	30
69	20 c. "Leptopelis sp"	40	40
70	25 c. "Ptychadena anchietae"	50	55

15 European Bee Eater

1983. Migratory Birds (1st series). Multicoloured.

71	8 c. Type **15**	25	15
72	20 c. Tawny eagle	65	65
73	25 c. Violet starling	75	75
74	40 c. Abdim's stork	1·40	1·50

See also Nos. 91/4.

1983. History of Writing (2nd series). As T **12**. Multicoloured.

75	10 c. Indus Valley script	15	10
76	20 c. Sumerian cuneiform	25	25
77	25 c. Egyptian hieroglyphics	30	30
78	40 c. Chinese handscroll	65	70

1983. Indigenous Trees (2nd series). As T **13**. Multicoloured.

79	10 c. "Gardenia spatulifolia"	15	10
80	20 c. "Hyphaene natalensis"	30	30
81	25 c. "Albizia adianthifolia"	40	40
82	40 c. "Sesamothamnus lugardii"	55	60

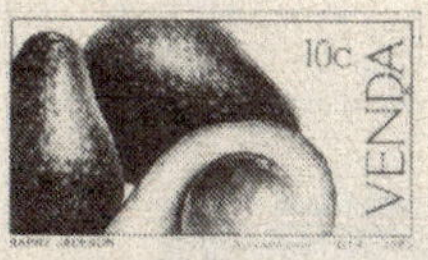

16 Avocado — 17 African Paradise Flycatcher

1983. Subtropical Fruit. Multicoloured.

83	10 c. Type **16**	15	10
84	20 c. Mango	30	30
85	25 c. Papaya	40	40
86	40 c. Litchi	55	60

1983. History of Writing (3rd series). As T **12**. Mult.

87	10 c. Evolution of cuneiform sign	15	10
88	20 c. Evolution of Chinese character	30	30
89	25 c. Development of Cretan hieroglyphics	40	40
90	40 c. Development of Egyptian hieroglyphics	55	60

1984. Migratory Birds (2nd series). Multicoloured.

91	11 c. White stork	30	20
92	20 c. Type **17**	50	50
93	25 c. Black kite	60	60
94	30 c. Wood sandpiper	70	85

1984. Indigenous Trees (3rd series). As T **13**. Mult.

95	11 c. "Afzelia quanzensis"	15	10
96	20 c. "Peltophorum africanum"	30	30
97	25 c. "Gyrocarpus americanus"	40	40
98	30 c. "Acacia sieberana"	50	55

18 Dzata Ruins, Nzhelele Valley — 19 White-browed Robin Chat

1984. 5th Anniv of Independence. Multicoloured.

99	11 c. Type **18**	15	10
100	25 c. Traditional hut	25	30
101	30 c. Sub-economical house	30	35
102	45 c. Modern home	45	65

1985. Songbirds. Multicoloured.

103	11 c. Type **19** (inscr "Heuglin's Robin")	35	20
104	25 c. Black-collared barbet	50	45
105	30 c. African black-headed oriole	65	55
106	50 c. Kurrichane thrush	1·00	1·00

1985. History of Writing (4th series). As T **12**. Mult.

107	11 c. Southern Arabic characters	15	10
108	25 c. Phoenician characters	30	30
109	30 c. Aramaic characters	40	40
110	50 c. Canaanite characters	75	75

20 Transvaal Red Milkwood — 21 "Pellaea dura"

1985. Food from the Veld (1st series). Multicoloured.

111	12 c. Type **20**	15	10
112	25 c. Buffalo thorn	30	30
113	30 c. Wild water melon	35	35
114	50 c. Brown ivory	55	60

See also Nos. 163/6.

1985. Ferns. Multicoloured.

115	12 c. Type **21**	15	10
116	25 c. "Actiniopteris radiata"	30	30
117	30 c. "Adiantum hispidulum"	40	40
118	50 c. "Polypodium polypodioides"	65	70

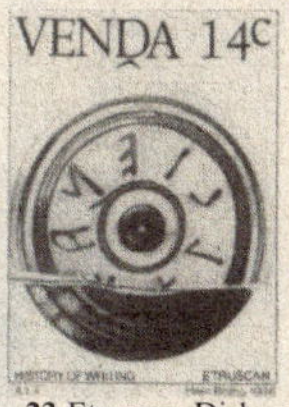

22 Three-lined Grass Snake — 23 Etruscan Dish

1986. Reptiles. Multicoloured.

119	1 c. Type **22**	10	10
120	2 c. Mole snake	10	10
121	3 c. Ornate scrub lizard	10	10
122	4 c. Puff adder	10	10
123	5 c. Three-lined skink	10	10
124	6 c. Egyptian cobra	15	10
125	7 c. Blue-tailed kopje skink	15	10
126	8 c. Spotted bush snake	20	20
127	9 c. Yellow-throated plated lizard	20	20
128	10 c. Northern lined shovelsnout	20	20
129	14 c. Transvaal flat lizard	90	20
130	15 c. Soutpansberg lizard	30	20
131	16 c. Iguana water leguan	60	20
132	18 c. Black mamba	75	20
133	20 c. Transvaal flat gecko	30	20
133b	21 c. Flap-necked chameleon	75	20
134	25 c. Longtailed garter snake	40	30
135	30 c. Tigroid thick-toed gecko	45	35
136	50 c. Cape file snake	70	50
137	1 r. Soutpansberg girdled lizard	1·25	1·00
138	2 r. African python	2·00	2·25

1986. History of Writing (5th series). Multicoloured.

139	14 c. Type **23**	15	10
140	20 c. Greek inscription, AD 70	30	30
141	25 c. Roman inscription	40	40
142	30 c. Cyrllic inscription (Byzantine mosaic)	55	60

24 Planting Pine Seedlings — 26 Comb Duck

25 Maxwell, 1910

1986. Forestry. Multicoloured.

143	14 c. Type **24**	20	15
144	20 c. Mule hauling logs	30	30
145	25 c. Off-loading logs at sawmill	40	40
146	30 c. Using timber in construction	55	60

1986. FIVA International Veteran Car Rally. Multicoloured.

147	14 c. Type **25**	20	15
148	20 c. Bentley 4½ l., 1929	30	30
149	25 c. Plymouth Coupe, 1933	40	40
150	30 c. Mercedes Benz 220, 1958	55	60

1987. Waterfowl. Multicoloured.

151	14 c. Type **26**	75	40
152	20 c. White-faced whistling duck	85	70
153	25 c. Spur-winged goose (horiz)	1·00	90
154	30 c. Egyptian goose (horiz)	1·25	1·25

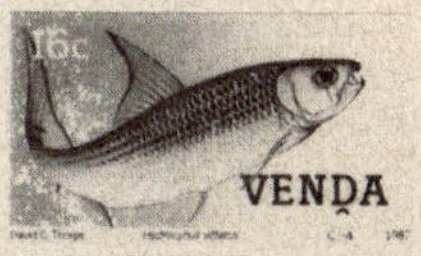

27 "Iron Master" — 28 Tigerfish

1987. Wood Sculptures by Meshack Matamela Raphalalani. Multicoloured.

155	16 c. Type **27**	15	15
156	20 c. "Distant Drums"	25	25
157	25 c. "Sunrise"	30	30
158	30 c. "Obedience"	40	40

1987. Freshwater Fishes. Multicoloured.

159	16 c. Type **28**	25	20
160	20 c. Barred minnow	35	35
161	25 c. Mozambique mouthbrooder	45	45
162	30 c. Sharp-toothed catfish	55	60

29 Cross-berry — 30 Picking Berries

1987. Food from the Veld (2nd series). Multicoloured.

163	16 c. Type **29**	20	15
164	30 c. Wild date palm	30	30
165	40 c. Tree fuchsia	40	40
166	50 c. Wild cucumber	50	55

1988. Coffee Industry. Multicoloured.

167	16 c. Type **30**	20	20
168	30 c. Weighing bags of berries	30	30
169	40 c. Drying beans in sun	35	35
170	50 c. Roasting graded beans	45	45

31 "Universal Love" in Chinese

1988. History of Writing (6th series).

171	**31**	16 c. stone, black & red	25	20
172	–	30 c. stone, black & red	35	35
173	–	40 c. stone, black & red	45	45
174	–	50 c. black and gold	55	60

DESIGNS: 30 c. "Picture of a lion on a stone" in Devanagari (Indian script); 40 c. "Information" in Russian; 50 c. "Peace be upon you" in Thuluth (Arabic script).

32 College

1988. 5th Anniv of Shayandima Nurses' Training College. Multicoloured.

175	16 c. Type **32**	25	20
176	30 c. Students using microscope	40	40
177	40 c. Anatomy class	50	50
178	50 c. Clinical training	55	60

33 "Fetching Water"

1988. Watercolours by Kenneth Thabo. Mult.

179	16 c. Type **33**	25	20
180	30 c. "Grinding Maize"	40	40
181	40 c. "Offering Food"	50	50
182	50 c. "Kindling the Fire"	55	60

34 Ndongwana (clay bowls)

1989. Traditional Kitchenware. Multicoloured.

183	16 c. Type **34**	20	20
184	30 c. Ndilo (wooden porridge bowls)	30	30
185	40 c. Mufaro (basket with lid)	40	40
186	50 c. Muthatha (dish woven from ilala palm)	45	45

35 Domba

36 Southern Ground Hornbill

1989. Traditional Dances. Multicoloured.

187	18 c. Type **35**	20	20
188	30 c. Tshinzerere	30	30
189	40 c. Malende	40	40
190	50 c. Malombo	45	45

1989. Endangered Birds. Multicoloured.

191	18 c. Type **36**	60	30
192	30 c. Lappet-faced vulture	90	70
193	40 c. Bateleur	1·10	90
194	50 c. Martial eagle	1·40	1·25

37 Pres. Gota F. N. Ravele

38 Lion

1989. 10th Anniv of Independence. Multicoloured.

195	18 c. Type **37**	20	20
196	30 c. Presidential offices	30	30
197	40 c. President's residence	40	40
198	50 c. Thohoyandou Sports Stadium	45	45

1990. Nwanedi National Park. Multicoloured.

199	18 c. Type **38**	30	25
200	30 c. Common zebra	55	55
201	40 c. Cheetah	65	65
202	50 c. White rhinoceros	75	80

39 Calligraphy

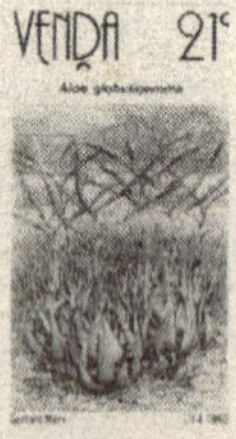

40 "Aloe globuligemma"

1990. History of Writing (7th series).

203	**39**	21 c. black and grey	20	15
204	–	30 c. black and brown	40	40
205	–	40 c. black and green	50	50
206	–	50 c. dp blue, blue & black	60	65

DESIGNS: 30 c. Part of score for Beethoven's "Moonlight Sonata"; 40 c. Characters from personal computer; 50 c. Television picture of message transmitted into outer space from Arecibo 1000 radio telescope.

1990. Aloes. Multicoloured.

207	21 c. Type **40**	30	25
208	35 c. "Aloe aculeata"	50	50
209	40 c. "Aloe lutescens"	60	60
210	50 c. "Aloe angelica"	70	75

41 "Pseudacraea boisduvalii"

42 Cape Puff-back Flycatchers

1990. Butterflies. Multicoloured.

211	21 c. Type **41**	60	40
212	35 c. "Papilio nireus"	90	70
213	40 c. "Charaxes jasius"	1·00	90
214	50 c. "Aeropetes tulbaghia"	1·10	1·10

1991. Birds. Paintings by Claude Finch-Davies. Multicoloured.

215	21 c. Type **42**	50	40
216	35 c. Red-capped robin chat	75	75
217	40 c. Collared sunbirds	85	85
218	50 c. Yellow-streaked greenbul	1·10	1·25

43 Paper made from Pulp

44 Venda Sun Hotel Complex, Thohoyandou

1991. Inventions (1st series). Multicoloured.

219	25 c. Type **43**	50	35
220	40 c. Magnetic compass	90	70
221	50 c. Abacus	1·00	85
222	60 c. Gunpowder	1·40	1·00

See also Nos. 239/42 and 260/3.

1991. Tourism. Multicoloured.

223	25 c. Type **44**	50	30
224	40 c. Mphephu resort	80	70
225	50 c. Sagole Spa	90	80
226	60 c. Luphephe-Nwanedi resort	95	1·10

1991. Indigenous Trees (4th series). As T **13**. Multicoloured.

227	27 c. Fever tree	55	30
228	45 c. Transvaal beech	90	70
229	65 c. Transvaal wild banana	1·00	90
230	85 c. Sausage tree	1·25	1·40

45 Setting the Web

1992. Clothing Factory. Multicoloured.

231	27 c. Type **45**	40	25
232	45 c. Knitting	55	50
233	65 c. Making up garment	80	80
234	85 c. Inspection of finished product	1·10	1·10

46 "Apis mellifera"

1992. Bees. Multicoloured.

235	35 c. Type **46**	55	40
236	70 c. "Anthidium cordiforme"	95	90
237	90 c. "Megachile frontalis"	1·25	1·25
238	1 r. 05 "Xylocopa caffia"	1·40	1·40

47 Egyptian Plough

1992. Inventions (2nd series). Multicoloured.

239	35 c. Type **47**	55	40
240	70 c. Early wheel, Mesopotamia	95	90
241	90 c. Making bricks, Egypt	1·25	1·25
242	1 r. 05 Early Egyptian sailing ship	1·40	1·40

48 Nile Crocodile

1992. Crocodile Farming. Multicoloured.

243	35 c. Type **48**	55	40
244	70 c. Egg laying	95	90
245	90 c. Eggs hatching	1·40	1·40
246	1 r. 05 Mother carrying young	1·50	1·60

49 Burmese

1993. Domestic Cats. Multicoloured.

247	45 c. Type **49**	75	45
248	65 c. Tabby	1·00	90
249	85 c. Siamese	1·40	1·25
250	1 r. 05 Persian	1·50	1·60

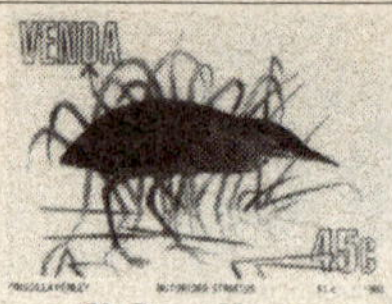

50 Green Heron

51 Punching-out Sole Lining

1993. Herons. Multicoloured.

251	45 c. Type **50**	70	50
252	65 c. Black-crowned night heron	95	95
253	85 c. Purple heron	1·25	1·25
254	1 r. 05 Black-headed heron	1·50	1·75

1993. Shoe Factory. Multicoloured.

256	45 c. Type **51**	30	25
257	65 c. Shaping heel	55	60
258	85 c. Joining the upper to inner sole	75	85
259	1 r. 05 Forming sole	90	1·10

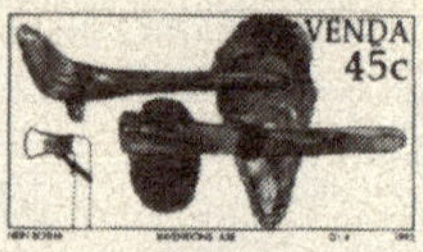

52 Axes

1993. Inventions (3rd series). Multicoloured.

260	45 c. Type **52**	40	35
261	65 c. Armour	75	65
262	85 c. Arches	95	85
263	1 r. 05 Pont du Gard aqueduct	1·10	1·25

53 Cocker Spaniel

1994. Dogs. Multicoloured.

264	45 c. Type **53**	65	40
265	65 c. Maltese	95	90
266	85 c. Scottish terrier	1·25	1·40
267	1 r. 05 Miniature schnauzer	1·60	1·75

54 Savanna Monkey

1994. Monkeys. Multicoloured.

268	45 c. Type **54**	65	45
269	65 c. Lesser bushbaby	90	90
270	85 c. Diademed monkey	1·25	1·40
271	1 r. 05 Thick-tailed bushbaby	1·50	1·75

55 Red-shouldered Glossy Starlings

1994. Starlings. Multicoloured.

273	45 c. Type **55**	75	55
274	70 c. Violet starlings	1·00	1·00
275	95 c. African red-winged starlings	1·25	1·40
276	1 r. 15 Wattled starlings	1·50	1·75

VICTORIA

The south-eastern state of the Australian Commonwealth, whose stamps it now uses.

12 pence = 1 shilling;
20 shillings = 1 pound

1 Queen Victoria ("half length")

2 Queen on Throne

1850. Imperf.

28	**1**	1d. red to brown	£375	32·00
6		2d. lilac to grey	£1100	£100
17		2d. brown	£500	95·00
31a		3d. blue	£350	30·00

1852. Imperf.

38	**2**	2d. brown to lilac	£170	22·00

3

4

1854. Imperf.

25	**3**	1s. blue	£650	22·00

1854. Imperf.

32a	**4**	6d. orange	£180	18·00
35		2s. green on yellow	£1100	£120

7 Queen on Throne

8 Emblems in Corners

1856. Imperf.

40	**7**	1d. green	£120	19·00

1857. Imperf.

41	**8**	1d. green	95·00	13·00
45		2d. lilac	£170	10·00
43		4d. red	£160	7·50

1857. Rouletted.

72	**8**	1d. green	£275	23·00
69		2d. lilac	£120	5·50
49	**1**	3d. blue	—	£190
71c	**8**	4d. red	£120	3·50
53a	**4**	6d. orange	—	35·00
54	**3**	1s. blue	—	80·00
56	**4**	2s. green on yellow	£3500	£350

1858. Rouletted.

73	**7**	6d. blue	£120	12·00

1859. Perf.

98	**8**	1d. green	65·00	4·50
100		2d. grey	£100	4·75
101		2d. lilac	£160	5·50
78	**1**	3d. blue	£750	£110
87		4d. red	£120	7·50
102	**4**	6d. black	£160	38·00
81	**3**	1s. blue	£130	15·00
82	**4**	2s. green on yellow	£250	30·00
129b		2s. blue on green	£140	4·75

9

12

1860. Perf.

90	**9**	3d. blue	£120	7·00
91		3d. purple	£100	25·00
92a		4d. red	80·00	3·25
93		6d. orange	£3000	£200
94		6d. black	£110	5·50

1861.

104	**12**	1d. green	60·00	6·00

13

14

15

16

17

18

1862.

107	**13**	6d. black	70·00	4·50

1863.

131d	**14**	1d. green	60·00	2·10
132b		2d. lilac	50·00	3·25
118	**15**	3d. lilac	£110	22·00

378 **15** 3d. orange . . . . 15·00 1·25
135d **14** 4d. pink . . . . 70·00 3·00
136c **16** 6d. blue . . . . 19·00 1·25
380 6d. green . . . . 9·00 5·50
112 **14** 8d. orange . . . . £300 50·00
137c 8d. brown on pink . . . . 75·00 5·00
119 **16** 10d. grey £450 £100
123 10d. brown on pink . . . 85·00 5·00
124 **17** 1s. blue on blue . . . . 55·00 2·50
139 **18** 5s. blue on yellow . . . £1600 £300
148 5s. blue and red . . . . £130 13·00
383 5s. red and blue . . . . 45·00 30·00
For designs additionally inscribed "POSTAGE", see Nos. 399 etc.

20

1870.
169a **20** 2d. lilac . . . . 50·00 1·00

1871. Surch in figures and words.
174 **14** ½d. on 1d. green . . . . . 45·00 12·00
171 **16** 9d. on 10d. brown on pink . £300 10·00

22 23

24 25

26 27

1873.
176b **22** ½d. red . . . . 6·00 70
195 ½d. red on pink . . . . . 23·00 11·00
376 ½d. green . . . . 2·00 85
177b **23** 1d. green . . . . 16·00 65
196 1d. green on yellow . . . 75·00 12·00
197 1d. green on grey . . . . £100 42·00
179 **24** 2d. mauve . . . . 20·00 55
198 2d. mauve on lilac . . . . — £400
199 2d. mauve on green . . . £130 12·00
200 2d. mauve on brown . . . £120 12·00
172a **25** 9d. brown on pink . . . . 60·00 8·50
319 9d. green . . . . 20·00 9·00
366 9d. red . . . . 11·00 1·75
180 **26** 1s. blue on blue . . . . 50·00 3·00
381 1s. yellow . . . . 35·00 30·00
190 **27** 2s. blue on green . . . . £120 18·00
382 2s. blue on pink . . . . 42·00 15·00
For design additionally inscribed "POSTAGE" see Nos. 399 etc.

1876. Surch **8d.. 8d.. EIGHTPENCE.**
191 **25** 8d. on 9d. brown on pink . £160 15·00

30 31

1880. Frame differs in 4d.
209b **30** 1d. green . . . . 14·00 1·25
210 **31** 2d. brown . . . . 18·00 75
377 2d. mauve . . . . 5·50 75
213 4d. red . . . . 42·00 5·50
379 4d. yellow . . . . 25·00 12·00
For designs additionally inscribed "POSTAGE" see Nos. 416 etc.

34 35

36

37

1884. Inscr "STAMP STATUTE". Frames differ.
220 – 1d. green . . . . 16·00 16·00
221 **34** 3d. mauve . . . . £110 75·00
222 – 4d. pink . . . . £100 55·00
223a – 6d. blue . . . . 42·00 11·00
224 – 1s. blue on blue . . . . 42·00 16·00
225 **35** 2s. blue on green . . . . 55·00 38·00
232 **36** 2s. 6d. yellow . . . . . £110 50·00
227 – 5s. blue on yellow . . . £130 42·00
228 – 10s. brown on pink . . . £500 £100
229 – £1 violet on yellow . . . £275 85·00
230 **37** £5 black and green . . . £2000 £425
DESIGNS—As T **34**/**36**: 1d., 6d., 1s., 5s. to £1, Uncrowned portrait of Queen Victoria in centre; 4d. Obverse and reverse of fourpenny coin.

1884. No. 220 surch **½d HALF.**
234 ½d. on 1d. green . . . . . 35·00 30·00

39 40

44 52

56 58

61

1884. Inscr "STAMP DUTY". Frames differ.
253 **39** 1d. green . . . . 28·00 8·00
254 **40** 1d. bistre . . . . 8·00 1·25
255 – 6d. blue . . . . 35·00 5·50
256 – 1s. blue on blue . . . . 55·00 4·50
257 – 1s. blue on yellow . . . 75·00 22·00
236 – 1s. 6d. red . . . . . . £120 17·00
258c **44** 2s. blue on green . . . . 80·00 17·00
259 – 3s. purple on blue . . . £160 24·00
345a – 3s. drab . . . . 55·00 16·00
371 – 3s. green . . . . £130 18·00
238 – 4s. red to orange . . . . 70·00 16·00
260 – 5s. purple on yellow . . . 50·00 4·50
347 – 5s. red . . . . 80·00 8·00
348 – 6s. green . . . . 80·00 23·00
240 – 10s. brown on pink . . . £300 55·00
349 – 10s. green . . . . £100 16·00
241 – 15s. mauve £800 £120
350 – 15s. brown . . . . . . £325 40·00
242 – £1 orange . . . . £350 60·00
243 **52** £1 5s. pink £750 £130
275 – £1 10s. green . . . . . £600 70·00
245 – 35s. violet £3000
276a – £2 blue . . . . £750 75·00
247 **44** 45s. lilac £1400 £100
248 **56** £5 red £1100 £225
249 **58** £6 blue on pink . . . . — £475
250 £7 violet on blue . . . . — £475
251 – £8 red on yellow . . . . — £600
252 – £9 green on green . . . . — £600
264a **61** £10 mauve . . . . £1500 95·00
DESIGNS—As T **39**/**52**: 6d. to 1s. 6d., 4s. to £1, £1 10s., £2, Various arms; 35s. "V R STAMP DUTY". As T **56**/**8**: £8, Crown; £9, Arms.

62

1884.
289 **62** £25 green . . . . — 90·00
352 £50 mauve . . . . — £140
291 £100 red . . . . — £190

63

1884.
292a **63** 2s. 6d. yellow . . . . . 80·00 11·00

64 65

66 67

68

1884. Inscr "STAMP DUTY".
296 **64** ½d. red . . . . 6·50 65
297 **65** 1d. green . . . . 7·50 50
298 **66** 2d. mauve . . . . 6·00 30
361 **65** 3d. buff . . . . 7·00 90
362 3d. green . . . . 21·00 7·00
300 **67** 4d. mauve . . . . 35·00 3·00
301a **65** 6d. blue . . . . 30·00 2·10
293 **68** 8d. red on pink . . . . . 20·00 5·50
294 **66** 1s. blue on yellow . . . . 50·00 7·00
303 **68** 2s. green on green . . . . 25·00 3·75
369 2s. green on white . . . . 17·00 5·50

1885. Optd **STAMP DUTY.**
308 **15** 3d. orange . . . . 60·00 22·00
309 **31** 4d. red . . . . 55·00 23·00
306 **26** 1s. blue on blue . . . . 95·00 20·00
307 **27** 2s. blue on green . . . . 85·00 18·00

70 71

72 73

74 75

76 77

78 79

80 81

1886. Inscr "STAMP DUTY".
310 **70** ½d. grey . . . . 18·00 3·00
330 ½d. red . . . . 3·00 15
356 ½d. green . . . . 4·75 40
312 **71** 1d. green . . . . 5·25 40
329 **72** 1d. brown on pink . . . 4·50 1·75
332 1d. brown . . . . 4·25 10
357a 1d. red . . . . 4·25 10
358 1d. green . . . . 5·00 4·00
333 **81** 1½d. green . . . . 4·00 1·50
355 1½d. red on yellow . . . 3·00 1·75
314d **73** 2d. purple . . . . 3·25 20
315b **74** 2½d. red on yellow . . . 6·00 70
360 2½d. blue . . . . 7·00 1·50
363 **75** 4d. red . . . . 4·75 95
317a **76** 5d. brown . . . . 6·50 80
365 **77** 6d. blue . . . . 7·00 65
341 **78** 1s. red . . . . 11·00 1·75
322 **79** 1s. 6d. blue . . . . . . £120 65·00
323 1s. 6d. orange . . . . . 15·00 4·50
324 **80** £5 blue and purple . . . £1000 80·00
325 £6 yellow and blue . . . £1200 £100
326 £7 red and black £1400 £120
327 £8 mauve and orange . . £1500 £150
328 £9 green and red £1800 £160
For designs additionally inscribed "POSTAGE" see Nos. 416 etc.

83 84

1897. Hospital Charity Fund.
353 **83** 1d. (1s.) blue . . . . . . 18·00 18·00
354 **84** 2½d. (2s. 6d.) brown . . . 85·00 70·00

86 87

1900. Empire Patriotic Fund.
374 **86** 1d. (1s.) brown . . . . . 55·00 35·00
375 **87** 2d. (2s.) green £110 £110

93

101

1901. As previous types but inscr "POSTAGE" instead of "STAMP DUTY" or with "POSTAGE" added to design, and new designs.

416	**22**	½d. green	1·60	15
417	**30**	1d. red	1·25	10
386a	**81**	1½d. purple on yellow	2·10	55
418c	**31**	2d. mauve	4·75	55
419	**74**	2½d. blue	3·00	40
389a	**93**	3d. brown	6·50	55
390	**31**	4d. yellow	5·50	55
391a	**76**	5d. brown	6·50	40
423	**16**	6d. green	12·00	80
424d	**25**	9d. red	9·50	1·25
425	**26**	1s. orange	8·00	2·00
395	**27**	2s. blue on pink	22·00	2·00
398a	**18**	5s. red and blue	70·00	10·00
399	**101**	£1 pink	£225	£100
400	–	£2 blue	£500	£250

DESIGN: £2, as Type **101** but different frame.

1912. Surch **ONE PENNY**.

456	**31**	1d. on 2d. mauve (No. 387)	70	45

POSTAGE DUE STAMPS

D 1

1890.

D 1	**D 1**	½d. blue and red	3·00	2·00
D 2		1d. blue and red	4·50	1·40
D 3		2d. blue and red	8·00	1·10
D 4		4d. blue and red	9·00	2·00
D 5		5d. blue and red	8·50	2·00
D 6		6d. blue and red	9·50	1·75
D 7		10d. blue and red	70·00	38·00
D 8		1s. blue and red	48·00	6·50
D 9		2s. blue and red	£110	48·00
D10		5s. blue and red	£160	90·00

1895.

D11	**D 1**	½d. red and green	3·00	1·60
D12		1d. red and green	2·75	50
D13		2d. red and green	4·25	60
D14		4d. red and green	8·00	1·50
D15a		5d. red and green	8·50	4·25
D25		6d. red and green	7·50	2·75
D17		10d. red and green	14·00	10·00
D18		1s. red and green	10·00	3·25
D19		2s. red and green	60·00	20·00
D20		5s. red and green	£100	40·00

REGISTRATION STAMP

6

1854. Imperf.

34	**6**	1s. red and blue	£800	£100

1857. Roul.

55	**6**	1s. red and blue	£3500	£180

TOO LATE STAMP

1855. As Type **6** but inscr "TOO LATE". Imperf.

33	6d. lilac and green	£650	£130

VICTORIA LAND

Stamps issued in connection with Capt. Scott's Antarctic Expedition.

12 pence = 1 shilling

1911. Scott Expedition. Stamps of New Zealand optd **VICTORIA LAND**.

A2	**51**	½d. green	£550	£650
A3	**53**	1d. red	45·00	85·00

WADHWAN

A state of Kathiawar, India. Now uses Indian stamps.

4 pice = 1 anna

1

1888.

5	**1**	½ pice black	5·50	6·50

WESTERN AUSTRALIA

The western state of the Australian Commonwealth, whose stamps it now uses.

12 pence = 1 shilling;
20 shillings = 1 pound

1

2

3

1854. Imperf or roul.

1	**1**	1d. black	£800	£180
25		2d. orange	65·00	50·00
3	**2**	4d. blue	£225	£150
26	**1**	4d. blue	£190	£1400
28		6d. green	£1100	£400
4c	**3**	1s. brown	£325	£275

5

7

1857. Imperf or roul.

15	**5**	2d. brown on red	£1700	£500
18		6d. bronze	£1900	£600

1861. Perf.

103	**1**	1d. red	13·00	1·75
76		1d. yellow	16·00	50
39		2d. blue	65·00	27·00
77		2d. yellow	20·00	50
104		2d. grey	35·00	1·00
56		4d. red	55·00	4·00
105		4d. brown	70·00	18·00
42		6d. brown	£180	35·00
57		6d. violet	65·00	6·00
61		1s. green	90·00	12·00

1871.

141	**7**	3d. brown	11·00	50

1874. Surch **ONE PENNY**.

67	**1**	1d. on 2d. yellow	£160	45·00

1884. Surch in figures.

90	**1**	½d. on 1d. yellow	9·00	14·00
91a	**7**	1d. on 3d. brown	38·00	8·00

12

13

14

15

1885.

94	**12**	½d. green	3·25	30
112	**13**	1d. red	4·00	10
96a	**14**	2d. grey	17·00	40
113		2d. yellow	10·00	1·25
97a	**15**	2½d. blue	7·50	35
98		4d. brown	7·50	40
99		5d. yellow	8·00	2·50
100		6d. violet	14·00	1·00
102		1s. green	17·00	3·00

1893. Surch in words.

110a	**7**	½d. on 3d. brown	5·50	17·00
107		1d. on 3d. brown	11·00	2·75

23

19

24

21

28

29

30

31

32

1901.

140	**23**	2d. yellow	5·00	1·25
114	**19**	2½d. blue	7·00	30
119	**24**	4d. brown	8·50	90
143	**15**	5d. olive	12·00	2·75
168	**19**	6d. violet	10·00	3·25
121	**12**	8d. green	18·00	2·50
145	**24**	9d. orange	22·00	3·50
146	**19**	10d. red	22·00	12·00
116	**21**	1s. green	22·00	3·50
124b	**28**	2s. red on yellow	40·00	8·50
125	**29**	2s. 6d. blue on red	40·00	8·00
126	**30**	5s. green	60·00	19·00
127	**31**	10s. mauve	£140	55·00
128	**32**	£1 orange	£275	£150

1906. Surch **ONE PENNY**.

172	**23**	1d. on 2d. yellow	80	30

ZAMBIA

Formerly Northern Rhodesia, attained independence on 24 October 1964, and changed its name to Zambia.

1964. 12 pence = 1 shilling;
20 shillings = 1 pound.
1968. 100 ngwee = 1 kwacha.

11 Pres. Kaunda and Victoria Falls

1964. Independence.

91	**11**	3d. sepia, green and blue	10	10
92	–	6d. violet and yellow	15	10
93	–	1s. 3d. multicoloured	20	15

DESIGNS—HORIZ: 6d. College of Further Education, Lusaka. VERT: 1s. 3d. Barotse dancer.

14 Maize – Farmer and Silo

22 Tobacco Worker

1964.

94	**14**	½d. red, black and green	10	20
95	–	1d. brown, black and blue	10	10
96	–	2d. red, brown and orange	10	10
97	–	3d. black and red	10	10
98	–	4d. black, brown and orange	15	10
99	–	6d. orange, brown and turquoise	15	10
100	–	9d. red, black and blue	15	10
101	–	1s. black, bistre and blue	15	10
102	**22**	1s. 3d. multicoloured	20	10
103	–	2s. multicoloured	25	10
104	–	2s. 6d. black and yellow	60	35
105	–	5s. black, yellow and green	1·00	45
106	–	10s. black and orange	3·50	3·50
107	–	£1 multicoloured	2·50	4·25

DESIGNS—VERT (as Type **14**): 1d. Health — radiographer; 2d. Chinyau dancer; 3d. Cotton-picking. (As Type **22**): 2s. Tonga basket-making; £1 Makishi dancer. HORIZ (as Type **14**): 4d. Angoni bull. (As Type **22**): 6d. Communications, old and new; 9d. Zambezi sawmills and redwood flower; 1s. Fishing at Mpulungu; 2s. 6d. Luangwa Game Reserve; 5s. Education — student; 10s. Copper mining.

28 I.T.U. Emblem and Symbols

1965. Centenary of I.T.U.

108	**28**	6d. violet and gold	15	10
109		2s. 6d. grey and gold	85	1·50

29 I.C.Y. Emblem

1965. Int Co-operation Year.

110	**29**	3d. turquoise and gold	10	10
111		1s. 3d. blue and gold	35	45

30 State House, Lusaka

35 University Building

34 W.H.O. Building and U.N. Flag

1965. 1st Anniv of Independence. Mult.

112	3d. Type **30**	10	10
113	6d. Fireworks, Independence Stadium	10	10
114	1s. 3d. Clematopsis (vert)	15	10
115	2s. 6d. "Tithonia diversifolia" (vert)	30	90

1966. Inauguration of W.H.O. Headquarters, Geneva.

116	**34**	3d. brown, gold and blue	20	10
117		1s. 3d. violet, gold and blue	80	80

1966. Opening of Zambia University.

118	**35**	3d. green and bronze	10	10
119		1s. 3d. violet and bronze	20	10

36 National Assembly Building

1967. Inaug of National Assembly Building.

120	**36**	3d. black and gold	10	10
121		6d. green and gold	10	10

37 Airport Scene

1967. Opening of Lusaka International Airport.

122	**37**	6d. blue and bronze	15	10
123		2s. 6d. brown and bronze	60	80

38 Youth Service Badge **43** Lusaka Cathedral

1967. National Development.

124	**38**	4d. black, red and gold	10	10
125	–	6d. black, gold and blue	10	10
126	–	9d. black, blue and silver	15	30
127	–	1s. multicoloured	50	10
128	–	1s. 6d. multicoloured	70	1·75

DESIGNS—HORIZ: 6d. "Co-operative Farming"; 1s. 6d. Road link with Tanzania. VERT: 9d. "Communications"; 1s. Coalfields.

1968. Decimal Currency.

129	**43**	1 n. multicoloured	10	10
130	–	2 n. multicoloured	10	10
131	–	3 n. multicoloured	10	10
132	–	5 n. brown and bronze	10	10
133	–	8 n. multicoloured	15	10
134	–	10 n. multicoloured	25	10
135	–	15 n. multicoloured	2·75	10
136	–	20 n. multicoloured	4·50	10
137	–	25 n. multicoloured	25	10
138	–	50 n. brown, orange and bronze	30	15
139	–	1 k. blue and bronze	4·00	20
140	–	2 k. black and bronze	2·25	1·25

DESIGNS—VERT (as Type **43**): 2 n. Baobab tree; 5 n. National Museum, Livingstone; 8 n. Vimbuza dancer; 10 n. Tobacco picking. (26 × 32 mm); 20 n. South African crowned cranes; 25 n. Angoni warrior; 50 n. Chokwe dancer. HORIZ (as Type **43**): 3 n. Zambia Airways Vickers VC-10 jetliner. (32 × 26 mm): 15 n. "Imbrasia zambesina" (moth); 1 k. Kafue Railway Bridge; 2 k. Eland.

55 Ndola on Outline of Zambia **56** Human Rights Emblem and Heads

1968. Trade Fair, Ndola.

141	**55**	15 n. green and gold	10	10

1968. Human Rights Year.

142	**56**	3 n. blue, violet and gold	10	10

57 W.H.O. Emblem **58** Group of Children

1968. 20th Anniv of World Health Organization.

143	**57**	10 n. gold and violet	10	10

1968. 22nd Anniv of U.N.I.C.E.F.

144	**58**	25 n. black, gold and blue	15	70

59 Copper Miner **61** Zambia outlined on Map of Africa

1969. 50th Anniv of Int Labour Organization.

145	**59**	3 n. copper and violet	25	10
146	–	25 n. yellow, copper & brown	1·00	1·00

DESIGN—HORIZ: 25 n. Poling a furnace.

1969. International African Tourist Year. Mult.

147	5 n. Type **61**	10	10
148	10 n. Waterbuck (horiz)	15	10
149	15 n. Kasaba Bay golden perch (horiz)	35	40
150	25 n. Carmine bee eater	1·00	1·50

PREVENTIVE MEDICINE

65 Satellite "Nimbus 3" orbiting the Earth **66** Woman collecting Water from Well

1970. World Meteorological Day.

151	**65**	15 n. multicoloured	20	50

1970. Preventive Medicine.

152	**66**	3 n. multicoloured	15	10
153	–	15 n. multicoloured	40	20
154	–	25 n. blue, red and sepia	80	35

DESIGNS: 15 n. Child on scales; 25 n. Child being immunized.

67 "Masks" (mural by Gabriel Ellison)

1970. Conference of Non-Aligned Nations.

155	**67**	15 n. multicoloured	30	30

68 Ceremonial Axe

1970. Traditional Crafts. Multicoloured.

156	3 n. Type **68**	10	10
157	5 n. Clay smoking-pipe bowl	15	10
158	15 n. Makishi mask	45	45
159	25 n. Kuomboka Ceremony	85	1·25

SIZES—HORIZ: 5 n. as T **68**; 25 n. 72 × 19 mm. VERT: 15 n. 30 × 47 mm.

69 Dag Hammarskjold and U.N. General Assembly

1971. 10th Death Anniv of Dag Hammarskjold. Multicoloured.

161	4 n. Type **69**	10	10
162	10 n. Tail of aircraft	20	10
163	15 n. Dove of Peace	25	25
164	25 n. Memorial tablet	45	1·50

70 Red-breasted Tilapia

1971. Fish. Multicoloured.

165	4 n. Type **70**	60	10
166	10 n. Long-finned tilapia ("Green-headed bream")	1·00	40
167	15 n. Tigerfish	1·25	2·50

71 North African Crested Porcupine

1972. Conservation Year (1st issue). Mult.

168	4 n. Cheetah (horiz)	20	25
169	10 n. Lechwe (horiz)	50	60
170	15 n. Type **71**	80	85
171	25 n. African elephant	2·00	3·00

Nos. 168/9 are size 58 × 21 mm.

1972. Conservation Year (2nd issue). As T **71**. Multicoloured.

172	4 n. Soil conservation	20	20
173	10 n. Forestry	30	45
174	15 n. Water	50	80
175	25 n. Maize	90	1·60

Nos. 174/5 are size 58 × 21 mm.

73 Zambian Flowers

1972. Conservation Year (3rd issue). Mult.

177	4 n. Type **73**	30	30
178	10 n. "Papilio demodocus" (butterfly)	90	80
179	15 n. "Apis mellifera" (bees)	1·40	1·40
180	25 n. "Nomadacris septemfasciata" (locusts)	2·25	2·25

74 Mary and Joseph

1972. Christmas. Multicoloured.

181	4 n. Type **74**	10	10
182	9 n. Mary, Joseph and Jesus	10	10
183	15 n. Mary, Jesus and the shepherds	10	10
184	25 n. The Three Wise Men	20	40

75 Oudenodon and Rubidgea

1973. Zambian Prehistoric Animals. Mult.

185	4 n. Type **75**	85	85
186	9 n. Broken Hill Man	90	90
187	10 n. Zambiasaurus	1·00	1·50
188	15 n. "Luangwa drysdalli"	1·10	2·00
189	25 n. Glossopteris	1·25	3·00

Nos. 186/9 are smaller, 38 × 21 mm.

76 "Dr. Livingstone, I Presume"

1973. Death Cent of Dr. Livingstone. Mult.

190	3 n. Type **76**	30	15
191	4 n. Scripture lesson	30	15
192	9 n. Victoria Falls	60	40
193	10 n. Scattering slavers	60	45
194	15 n. Healing the sick	60	1·60
195	25 n. Burial place of Livingstone's heart	70	2·75

77 Parliamentary Mace

1973. 3rd Commonwealth Conference of Speakers and Presiding Officers, Lusaka.

196	**77**	9 n. multicoloured	60	65
197		15 n. multicoloured	75	1·50
198		25 n. multicoloured	85	2·00

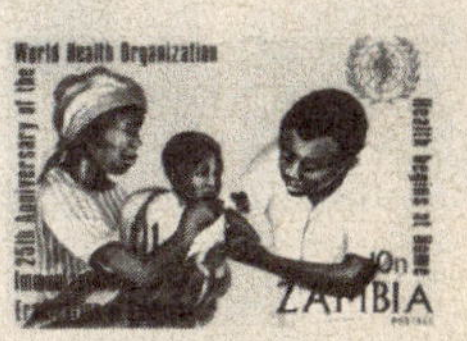

78 Inoculation

1973. 25th Anniv of W.H.O. Multicoloured.

199	4 n. Mother washing baby (vert)	48·00	23·00
200	9 n. Nurse weighing baby (vert)	45	2·25
201	10 n. Type **78**	50	3·00
202	15 n. Child eating meal	90	5·00

79 U.N.I.P. Flag **80** President Kaunda at Mulungushi

1974. 1st Anniv of Second Republic. Mult.

203	4 n. Type **79**	7·00	7·00
204	9 n. Freedom House	30	1·50
205	10 n. Army band	30	2·00
206	15 n. "Celebrations" (dancers)	50	3·25
207	25 n. Presidential chair	75	5·00

1974. 50th Birthday of President Kaunda. Multicoloured.

208	4 n. Type **80**	55	55
209	9 n. President's former residence	30	30
210	15 n. President holding Independence flame	70	1·75

81 Nakambala Sugar Estate

1974. 10th Anniv of Independence. Mult.

211	3 n. Type **81**	15	10
212	4 n. Local market	15	10
213	9 n. Kapiri glass factory	20	10
214	10 n. Kafue hydro-electric scheme	25	10
215	15 n. Kafue Railway Bridge	50	95
216	25 n. Non-aligned Conference, Lusaka, 1970	60	1·25

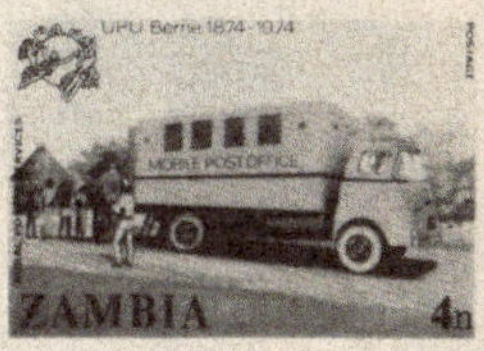

82 Mobile Post-van

1974. Centenary of U.P.U. Multicoloured.

218	4 n. Type **82**	20	15
219	9 n. Hawker Siddeley H.S.748 airplane on tarmac	30	30
220	10 n. Chipata Post Office	30	40
221	15 n. Modern training centre	45	1·75

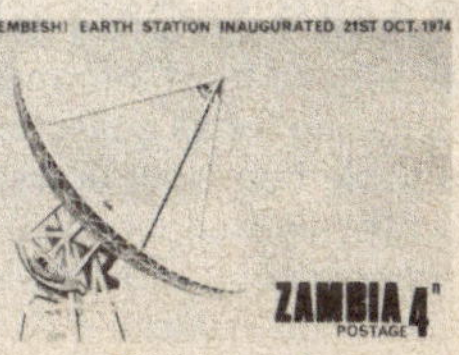

83 Dish Aerial

1974. Opening of Mwembeshi Earth Station. Multicoloured.

222		4 n. Type 83	25	20
223		9 n. View at dawn	35	30
224		15 n. View at dusk	40	70
225		25 n. Aerial view	50	1·50

84 Black Rhinoceros and Calf

86 Map of Namibia

85 Independence Monument

1975. Multicoloured.

226		1 n. Type 84	50	30
227		2 n. Helmet guineafowl	30	30
228		3 n. National Dancing Troupe	15	30
229		4 n. African fish eagle	40	10
230		5 n. Knife-edge Bridge	85	50
231		8 n. Sitatunga (antelope)	75	50
232		9 n. African elephant, Kasaba Bay	85	20
233		10 n. Temminck's ground pangolin	20	10
234		15 n. Type 85	30	10
235		20 n. Harvesting groundnuts	85	95
236		25 n. Tobacco growing	1·25	30
237		50 n. Flying Doctor service	1·75	1·75
238		1 k. Lady Ross's turaco	3·50	1·75
239		2 k. Village scene	3·00	5·50

Nos. 234/9 are as Type **85**.

1975. Namibia Day.

240	86	4 n. green and yellow	20	20
241		9 n. blue and green	25	30
242		15 n. orange and yellow	40	75
243		25 n. red and orange	50	1·25

87 Erection of Sprinkler Irrigation

1975. Silver Jubilee of International Commission on Irrigation and Drainage. Multicoloured.

244		4 n. Type 87	15	15
245		9 n. Sprinkler irrigation	30	40
246		15 n. Furrow irrigation	65	1·25

88 Mutondo

1976. World Forestry Day. Multicoloured.

247		3 n. Type 88	25	10
248		4 n. Mukunyu	25	10
249		9 n. Mukusi	45	25
250		10 n. Mopane	45	25
251		15 n. Musuku	70	1·40
252		25 n. Mukwa	85	1·75

89 Passenger Train

1976. Opening of Tanzania–Zambia Railway. Multicoloured.

253		4 n. Type 89	30	30
254		9 n. Copper exports	55	55
255		15 n. Machinery imports	90	95
256		25 n. Goods train	1·40	1·75

90 Kayowe Dance

1977. 2nd World Black and African Festival of Arts and Culture, Nigeria. Multicoloured.

258		4 n. Type 90	15	10
259		9 n. Lilombola dance	15	15
260		15 n. Initiation ceremony	30	40
261		25 n. Munkhwele dance	55	1·00

91 Grimwood's Longclaw

1977. Birds of Zambia. Multicoloured.

262		4 n. Type 91	40	10
263		9 n. Shelley's sunbird	55	60
264		10 n. Black-cheeked lovebird	55	60
265		15 n. Locust finch	1·25	2·00
266		20 n. Black-chinned tinkerbird	1·40	2·25
267		25 n. Chaplin's barbet	1·50	2·75

92 Girls with Building Blocks

1977. Decade for Action to Combat Racism and Racial Discrimination. Multicoloured.

268		4 n. Type 92	10	10
269		9 n. Women dancing	15	20
270		15 n. Girls with dove	25	70

93 Angels and Shepherds

1977. Christmas. Multicoloured.

271		4 n. Type 93	10	10
272		9 n. The Holy Family	10	10
273		10 n. The Magi	10	15
274		15 n. Jesus presented to Simeon	20	60

94 African Elephant and Road Check

1978. Anti-poaching Campaign. Multicoloured.

275		8 n. Type 94	45	20
276		18 n. Lechwe and canoe patrol	40	65
277		28 n. Warthog and Bell 206 JetRanger helicopter	1·00	1·10
278		32 n. Cheetah and game guard patrol	1·00	1·50

1979. Various stamps surch.

279	–	8 n. on 9 n. multicoloured (No. 232)	60	10
280	–	10 n. on 3 n. multicoloured (No. 228)	10	10
281	–	18 n. on 25 n. multicoloured (No. 236)	15	15
282	85	28 n. on 15 n. multicoloured	20	25

96 Kayowe Dance

1979. Commonwealth Summit Conference, Lusaka. Multicoloured.

283		18 n. Type 96	15	25
284		32 n. Kutambala dance	20	40
285		42 n. Chitwansombo drummers	20	60
286		58 n. Lilombola dance	25	80

97 "Kalulu and the Tug of War"

1979. International Year of the Child. Mult.

287		18 n. Type 97	20	30
288		32 n. "Why the Zebra has no Horns"	30	55
289		42 n. "How the Tortoise got his Shell"	40	85
290		58 n. "Kalulu and the Lion"	50	1·00

98 Children of Different Races holding Anti-Apartheid Emblem

1979. Int Anti-Apartheid Year. Mult.

292		18 n. Type 98	15	25
293		32 n. Children with toy car	25	40
294		42 n. Young children with butterfly	35	60
295		58 n. Children with microscope	50	80

99 Sir Rowland Hill and 2s. Definitive Stamp of 1964

1979. Death Cent of Sir Rowland Hill. Mult.

296		18 n. Type 99	20	25
297		32 n. Sir Rowland Hill and mailman	30	55
298		42 n. Sir Rowland Hill and Northern Rhodesia 1963 ½d. definitive stamp	40	70
299		58 n. Sir Rowland Hill and mail-carrying oxwaggon	50	1·10

1980. "London 1980" International Stamp Exhibition. Nos. 296/9 optd **LONDON 1980**.

301	99	18 n. multicoloured	25	40
302	–	32 n. multicoloured	30	60
303	–	42 n. multicoloured	40	75
304	–	58 n. multicoloured	60	90

101 Rotary Anniversary Emblem

1980. 75th Anniv of Rotary International.

306	101	8 n. multicoloured	10	10
307		32 n. multicoloured	40	55
308		42 n. multicoloured	45	80
309		58 n. multicoloured	70	1·00

102 Running

1980. Olympic Games, Moscow. Multicoloured.

311		18 n. Type 102	25	25
312		32 n. Boxing	40	45
313		42 n. Football	50	80
314		58 n. Swimming	80	1·25

103 "Euphaedra zaddachi"

1980. Butterflies. Multicoloured.

316		18 n. Type 103	15	15
317		32 n. "Aphnaeus questiauxi"	25	40
318		42 n. "Abantis zambesiaca"	40	80
319		58 n. "Spindasis modesta"	60	1·60

104 Zambia Coat of Arms

105 Nativity and St. Francis of Assisi (stained glass window, Ndola Church)

1980. 26th Commonwealth Parliamentary Association Conference, Lusaka.

321	104	18 n. multicoloured	15	25
322		32 n. multicoloured	25	45
323		42 n. multicoloured	30	65
324		58 n. multicoloured	40	1·25

1980. 50th Anniv of Catholic Church on the Copperbelt.

325	105	8 n. multicoloured	10	10
326		28 n. multicoloured	40	70
327		32 n. multicoloured	40	70
328		42 n. multicoloured	60	95

106 Musikili

1981. World Forestry Day. Seedpods. Mult.

329		8 n. Type 106	10	10
330		18 n. Mupapa	20	45
331		28 n. Mulunguti	25	80
332		32 n. Mulama	25	1·25

107 I.T.U. Emblem

108 Mask Maker

1981. World Telecommunications and Health Day. Multicoloured.

333		8 n. Type 107	20	10
334		18 n. W.H.O. emblems	35	35
335		28 n. Type 107	50	60
336		32 n. As 18 n.	60	75

1981. Native Crafts. Multicoloured.

337		1 n. Type 108	10	10
338		2 n. Blacksmith	10	10
339		5 n. Pottery making	10	10
340		8 n. Straw-basket fishing	10	10
341		10 n. Thatching	10	10
342		12 n. Mushroom picking	3·00	1·75
343		18 n. Millet grinding on stone	30	10
344		28 n. Royal Barge paddler	50	10
345		30 n. Makishi tightrope dancer	50	10
346		35 n. Tonga Ila granary and house	55	10

347 42 n. Cattle herding 55 80
348 50 n. Traditional healer (38 × 26 mm) 55 10
349 75 n. Women carrying water (38 × 26 mm) 55 60
350 1 k. Pounding maize (38 × 26 mm) 55 60
351 2 k. Pipe smoking, Gwembe Valley belle (38 × 26 mm) . . 55 60

109 Kankobele

110 Banded Ironstone

1981. Traditional Musical Instruments. Mult.
356 8 n. Type **109** 30 10
357 18 n. Inshingili 40 55
358 28 n. Ilimba . . . . 50 1·50
359 32 n. Bango . . . . 60 1·75

1982. Minerals (1st series). Multicoloured.
360 8 n. Type **110** 80 10
361 18 n. Cobaltocalcite . . . . . 1·75 80
362 28 n. Amazonite . . . . 2·25 1·90
363 32 n. Tourmaline . . . . . . 2·50 2·25
364 42 n. Uranium ore . . . . . . 2·75 3·25
See also Nos. 370/4.

111 Zambian Scouts

1982. 75th Anniv of Boy Scout Movement. Multicoloured.
365 8 n. Type **111** 30 10
366 18 n. Lord Baden-Powell and Victoria Falls 70 40
367 28 n. African buffalo and Zambian scout patrol pennant 70 50
368 1 k. African fish eagle and Zambian conservation badge 2·25 4·50

1982. Minerals (2nd series). As T **110**. Mult.
370 8 n. Bornite 95 10
371 18 n. Chalcopyrite . . . . . . 2·25 90
372 28 n. Malachite . . . . 2·75 3·00
373 32 n. Azurite . . . . 2·75 3·00
374 42 n. Vanadinite . . . . . . 3·25 4·25

112 Drilling Rig, 1926

1983. Early Steam Engines. Multicoloured.
375 8 n. Type **112** 60 10
376 18 n. Fowler road locomotive, 1900 . . . . 80 70
377 28 n. Borsig ploughing engine, 1925 . . . . 1·25 2·25
378 32 n. Rhodesian Railways 7th Class steam locomotive, 1900 1·60 2·50

113 Cotton Picking

1983. Commonwealth Day. Multicoloured.
379 12 n. Type **113** 20 10
380 18 n. Mining 40 30
381 28 n. Ritual pot and traditional dances 30 50
382 1 k. Violet-crested turaco and Victoria Falls . . . . . . 2·75 5·00

114 "Eulophia cucullata"

115 Giraffe

1983. Wild Flowers. Multicoloured.
383 12 n. Type **114** 25 10
384 28 n. "Kigelia africana" . . . 35 40
385 35 n. "Protea gaguedi" . . . 40 80
386 50 n. "Leonotis nepetifolia" . 60 2·00

1983. Wildlife of Zambia. Multicoloured.
388 12 n. Type **115** 70 10
389 28 n. Blue wildebeest 90 70
390 35 n. Lechwe . . . . 1·25 90
391 1 k. Yellow-backed duiker . . 2·50 4·25

116 Tigerfish

1983. Fishes of Zambia. Multicoloured.
392 12 n. Type **116** 40 15
393 28 n. Silver catfish 70 65
394 35 n. Large-spotted squeaker 80 1·50
395 38 n. Red-breasted tilapia . . 90 1·50

117 The Annunciation

1983. Christmas. Multicoloured.
396 12 n. Type **117** 15 10
397 28 n. The Shepherds 30 40
398 35 n. Three Kings . . . . . 40 1·00
399 38 n. Flight into Egypt . . . 45 1·50

118 Boeing 737

1984. Air Transport. Multicoloured.
400 12 n. Type **118** 25 10
401 28 n. De Havilland D.H.C.2 Beaver 45 40
402 35 n. Short S-45A Solent 3 flying boat 55 70
403 1 k. De Havilland D.H.66 Hercules "City of Basra" . 1·00 2·50

119 Receiving Flowers

120 Football

1984. 60th Birthday of President Kaunda. Multicoloured.
404 12 n. Type **119** 30 10
405 28 n. Swearing-in ceremony (vert) 45 40
406 60 n. Planting cherry tree . . 90 2·00
407 1 k. Opening of 5th National Assembly (vert) . . . . . . 1·25 3·00

1984. Olympic Games, Los Angeles. Multicoloured.
408 12 n. Type **120** 25 10
409 28 n. Running 30 50
410 35 n. Hurdling 40 80
411 60 n. Boxing . . . . 45 1·40

121 Gaboon Viper

1984. Reptiles. Multicoloured.
412 12 n. Type **121** 20 10
413 28 n. Chameleon 40 50
414 35 n. Nile crocodile 50 70
415 1 k. Blue-headed agama . . . 1·00 2·75

122 Pres. Kaunda and Mulungushi Rock

1984. 26th Anniv of United National Independence Party and 20th Anniv of Independence (1st issue). Multicoloured.
417 12 n. Type **122** 25 10
418 28 n. Freedom Statue 35 50
419 1 k. Pres. Kaunda and agricultural produce ("Lima Programme") . . . . 1·00 3·00

123 "Amanita flammeola"

1984. Fungi. Multicoloured.
420 12 n. Type **123** . . . . 1·10 30
421 28 n. "Amanita zambiana" . . 1·50 1·25
422 32 n. "Termitomyces letestui" . 2·00 2·25
423 75 n. "Cantharellus miniatescens" . . . . 3·25 4·50

1985. No. 237 surch **K5**.
424 5 k. on 50 n. Flying Doctor service . . . . 1·75 2·00

125 Chacma Baboon

1985. Zambian Primates. Multicoloured.
425 12 n. Type **125** 55 10
426 20 n. Diademed monkey . . . 75 40
427 45 n. Diademed monkey (different) . . . . 1·50 1·25
428 1 k. Savanna monkey . . . . 2·50 4·25

126 Map showing S.A.D.C.C. Member States

1985. 5th Anniv of Southern African Development Co-ordination Conference.
429 **126** 20 n. multicoloured . . . 75 15
430 – 45 n. black, blue and light blue . . . . 1·75 1·10
431 – 1 k. multicoloured . . . 2·00 3·25
DESIGNS: 45 n. Mining; 1 k. Flags of member states and Mulungushi Hall.

127 The Queen Mother in 1980

130 Boy in Maize Field

129 Postman and Lusaka Post Office, 1958

1985. Life and Times of Queen Elizabeth the Queen Mother.
432 **127** 25 n. multicoloured . . . 10 10
433 – 45 n. blue and gold . . . 10 15
434 – 55 n. blue and gold . . . 15 25
435 – 5 k. multicoloured . . . . 1·25 2·25
DESIGNS—VERT: 45 n. The Queen Mother at Clarence House, 1963. HORIZ: 55 n. With the Queen and Princess Margaret, 1980; 5 k. At Prince Henry's Christening, 1984.

1985. Nos. 340 and 342 surch.
436 20 n. on 12 n. Mushroom picking 2·75 30
437 25 n. on 8 n. Straw-basket fishing 1·00 65

1985. 26th Anniv of United National Independence Party (No. 438) and 20th Anniv of Independence (others) (2nd issue). As Nos. 417/19 but larger, 55 × 34 mm. On gold foil.
438 5 k. As Type **122** . . . . . . 75 2·00
439 5 k. Freedom Statue . . . . 75 2·00
440 5 k. Pres. Kaunda and agricultural produce ("Lima Programme") . . . . 75 2·00

1985. 10th Anniv of Posts and Telecommunication Corporation. Multicoloured.
441 20 n. Type **129** 55 10
442 45 n. Postman and Livingstone Post Office, 1950 . . . . . 85 25
443 55 n. Postman and Kalomo Post Office, 1902 . . . . 1·00 70
444 5 k. Africa Trans-Continental Telegraph Line under construction, 1900 . . . . . 3·25 5·50

1985. 40th Anniv of United Nations Organization.
445 **130** 20 n. multicoloured . . . 40 10
446 – 45 n. black, blue & brown 65 20
447 – 1 k. multicoloured . . . . 1·25 2·00
448 – 2 k. multicoloured . . . . 1·75 3·00
DESIGNS: 45 n. Logo and "40"; 1 k. President Kaunda addressing U.N. General Assembly, 1970; 2 k. Signing of U.N. Charter, San Francisco, 1945.

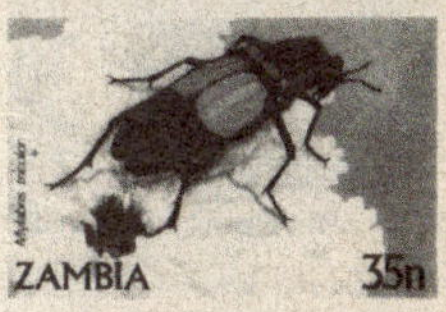

131 "Mylabris tricolor"

1986. Beetles. Multicoloured.
449 35 n. Type **131** 15 10
450 1 k. "Phasgonocnema melanianthe" 20 20
451 1 k. 70 "Amaurodes passerinii" 30 50
452 5 k. "Ranzania petersiana" . 85 2·00

1986. 60th Birthday of Queen Elizabeth II. As T **110** of Ascension. Multicoloured.
453 35 n. Princess Elizabeth at Flower Ball, Savoy Hotel, 1951 10 10
454 1 k. 25 With Prince Andrew, Lusaka Airport, 1979 . . . 15 20
455 1 k. 70 With President Kaunda 15 25
456 1 k. 95 In Luxembourg, 1976 . 15 30
457 5 k. At Crown Agents Head Office, London, 1983 . . . 40 85

1986. Royal Wedding. As T **112** of Ascension. Multicoloured.
458 1 k. 70 Prince Andrew and Miss Sarah Ferguson 30 35
459 5 k. Prince Andrew in Zambia, 1979 . . . . 80 1·40

132 Goalkeeper saving Goal

1986. World Cup Football Championship, Mexico. Multicoloured.
460 35 n. Type **132** 85 15
461 1 k. 25 Player kicking ball . . 2·00 1·40
462 1 k. 70 Two players competing for ball . . . . 2·25 1·90
463 5 k. Player scoring goal . . . 3·25 6·00

133 Sculpture of Edmond Halley by Henry Pegram

1986. Appearance of Halley's Comet.
464 **133** 1 k. 25 multicoloured . . 1·00 55
465 – 1 k. 70 multicoloured . . 1·25 85
466 – 2 k. multicoloured . . . . 1·75 1·75
467 – 5 k. blue and black . . . 3·50 6·00
DESIGNS: 1 k. 70, "Giotto" spacecraft approaching nucleus of Comet; 2 k. Studying Halley's Comet in 1682 and 1986; 5 k. Part of Halley's chart of southern sky.

134 The Nativity

1986. Christmas. Children's Paintings. Mult.
468 35 n. Type **134** 40 10
469 1 k. 25 Visit of the Three Kings 1·50 75
470 1 k. 60 The Holy Family with Shepherd and King 1·75 1·50
471 5 k. Angel and Christmas tree 3·75 6·00

135 Diesel Train in Kasama Cutting

1986. 10th Anniv of Tanzania–Zambia Railway. Multicoloured.
472 35 n. Type **135** 25 10
473 1 k. 25 Passenger train leaving Tunnel No. 21 45 50
474 1 k. 70 Train between Tunnels Nos. 6 and 7 50 70
475 5 k. Trains near Mpika Station 1·00 2·50

136 President Kaunda and Graduate

1987. 20th Anniv of University of Zambia. Multicoloured.
476 35 n. Type **136** 25 10
477 1 k. 25 University badge (vert) 65 60
478 1 k. 60 University statue 70 1·00
479 5 k. President Kaunda laying foundation stone (vert) 2·50 5·50

137 Arms of Kitwe

138 Chestnut-headed Crake

1987. Arms of Zambian Towns. Mult.
480 35 n. Type **137** 10 10
481 1 k. 25 Ndola 15 10
482 1 k. 70 Lusaka 20 25
483 20 k. Livingstone 2·75 5·00

1987. Birds (1st series). Multicoloured.
484 5 n. Cloud-scraping cisticola 10 10
485 10 n. White-winged starling 10 10
486a 20 n. on 1 n. Yellow swamp warbler 20 20
487 25 n. Type **138** 1·75 1·00
488 30 n. Red-fronted barbet ("Miombo pied barbet") 10 10
489 35 n. Black and rufous swallow 2·00 1·25
490 40 n. Wattled crane 10 10
491 50 n. Red-throated heron ("Slaty egret") 10 10
492 75 n. on 2 n. Olive-flanked robin chat 30 50
493 1 k. Bradfield's hornbill 2·00 40
494 1 k. 25 Boulton's puff-back flycatcher ("Margaret's Batis") 2·00 1·75
495 1 k. 60 Anchieta's sunbird 2·00 1·50
496 1 k. 65 on 30 n. Red-fronted barbet 30 85
497 1 k. 70 Boehm's bee eater 2·25 2·00
498 1 k. 95 Perrin's bush shrike 2·25 2·00
499 2 k. Whale-headed stork ("Shoebill") 35 35
500 5 k. Taita falcon 2·75 80
501 10 k. on 50 n. Red-throated heron 1·10 2·00
502 20 k. on 2 k. Whale-headed stork 2·10 3·50

Nos. 491, 493/5 and 497/502 are larger, size 24 × 39 mm.

No. 502 is surcharged "K20". For No. 499 surcharged "K20.00" see No. 594.

See also Nos. 587/95 and 625/38.

139 Look-out Tree, Livingstone

1987. Tourism. Multicoloured.
503 35 n. Type **139** 30 15
504 1 k. 25 Rafting on Zambezi 30 25
505 1 k. 70 Tourists photographing lions, Luangwa Valley 1·75 90
506 10 k. Eastern white pelicans 6·50 7·00

1987. Various stamps surch. (a) Nos. 432/5.
507 **127** 3 k. on 25 n. mult 55 55
508 – 6 k. on 45 n. blue and gold 1·00 1·00
509 – 10 k. on 55 n. blue and gold 1·60 1·60
510 – 20 k. on 5 k. mult 3·25 3·75

(b) Nos. 453/7.
511 3 k. on 35 n. Princess Elizabeth at Flower Ball, Savoy Hotel, 1951 55 55
512 4 k. on 1 k. 25 With Prince Andrew, Lusaka Airport, 1979 65 65
513 6 k. on 1 k. 70 With President Kaunda 1·00 1·00
514 10 k. on 1 k. 95 In Luxembourg, 1976 1·60 1·60
515 20 k. on 5 k. At Crown Agents Head Office, London, 1983 3·25 3·75

(c) Nos. 460/3.
516 3 k. on 35 n. Type **132** 55 55
517 6 k. on 1 k. 25 Player kicking ball 1·00 1·00
518 10 k. on 1 k. 70 Two players competing for ball 1·60 1·60
519 20 k. on 5 k. Player scoring goal 3·25 3·75

(d) Nos. 464/7.
520 **133** 3 k. on 1 k. 25 mult 90 70
521 – 6 k. on 1 k. 70 mult 1·50 1·25
522 – 10 k. on 2 k. mult 2·50 2·50
523 – 20 k. on 5 k. blue and black 4·50 5·00

141 De Havilland D.H.C.2 Beaver

1987. 20th Anniv of Zambia Airways. Aircraft. Multicoloured.
524 35 n. Type **141** 65 10
525 1 k. 70 Douglas DC-10 1·50 70
526 5 k. Douglas DC-3 3·50 3·50
527 10 k. Boeing 707 5·50 6·50

142 Friesian/Holstein Cow

1987. 40th Anniv of F.A.O. Multicoloured.
528 35 n. Type **142** 10 10
529 1 k. 25 Simmental bull 20 25
530 1 k. 70 Sussex bull 25 30
531 20 k. Brahman bull 1·50 3·00

143 Mpoloto Ne Mikobango

144 Black Lechwe at Waterhole

1987. People of Zambia. Multicoloured.
532 35 n. Type **143** 10 10
533 1 k. 25 Zintaka 20 25
534 1 k. 70 Mufuluhi 25 30
535 10 k. Ntebwe 1·00 1·50
536 20 k. Kubangwa Aa Mbulunga 1·75 3·00

1987. Black Lechwe. Multicoloured.
537 50 n. Type **144** 65 10
538 2 k. Black lechwe resting by pool (horiz) 1·75 40
539 2 k. 50 Running through water (horiz) 1·75 80
540 10 k. Watching for danger 4·50 5·50

145 Cassava Roots

1988. International Fund for Agricultural Development. Multicoloured.
542 50 n. Type **145** 10 10
543 2 k. 50 Fishing 60 50
544 2 k. 85 Farmer and cattle 65 55
545 10 k. Picking coffee beans 1·25 1·40

146 Breastfeeding

147 Asbestos Cement

1988. U.N.I.C.E.F. Child Survival Campaign. Multicoloured.
546 50 n. Type **146** 20 10
547 2 k. Growth monitoring 50 30
548 2 k. 85 Immunization 60 60
549 10 k. Oral rehydration 1·25 3·00

1988. Preferential Trade Area Fair. Mult.
550 50 n. Type **147** 10 10
551 2 k. 35 Textiles 20 30
552 2 k. 50 Tea 20 40
553 10 k. Poultry 75 2·50

148 Emergency Food Distribution

1988. 125th Anniv of Int Red Cross. Mult.
554 50 n. Type **148** 20 10
555 2 k. 50 Giving first aid 50 60
556 2 k. 85 Practising bandaging 55 70
557 10 k. Henri Dunant (founder) 1·75 3·00

149 Aardvark

1988. Endangered Species of Zambia. Mult.
558 50 n. Type **149** 25 10
559 2 k. Temminck's ground pangolin 50 40
560 2 k. 85 Hunting dog 60 75
561 20 k. Black rhinoceros and calf 6·00 7·00

150 Boxing

1988. Olympic Games, Seoul. Multicoloured.
562 50 n. Type **150** 15 10
563 2 k. Athletics 35 40
564 2 k. 50 Hurdling 40 65
565 20 k. Football 3·50 6·00

151 Red Toad

1989. Frogs and Toads. Multicoloured.
567 50 n. Type **151** 15 10
568 2 k. 50 Puddle frog 50 50
569 2 k. 85 Marbled reed frog 55 65
570 10 k. Young reed frogs 1·60 3·00

152 Common Slit-faced Bat

153 Pope John Paul II and Map of Zambia

1989. Bats. Multicoloured.
571 50 n. Type **152** 15 10
572 2 k. 50 Little free-tailed bat 45 55
573 2 k. 85 Hildebrandt's horseshoe bat 55 75
574 10 k. Peters' epauletted fruit bat 1·50 3·00

1989. Visit of Pope John Paul II. Designs each with inset portrait. Multicoloured.
575 50 n. Type **153** 75 20
576 6 k. 85 Peace dove with olive branch 2·75 2·75
577 7 k. 85 Papal arms 3·00 3·25
578 10 k. Victoria Falls 4·50 4·50

1989. Various stamp surch. (a) On Nos. 339, 341/3, 345/6, 349 and 351.
579 1 k. 20 on 35 n. Tonga Ila granary and house 15 15
580 3 k. 75 on 5 n. Pottery making 20 20
581 8 k. 11 on 10 n. Thatching 40 50
582 9 k. on 30 n. Makishi tightrope dancer 40 50
583 10 k. on 75 n. Women carrying water (38 × 26 mm) 40 50
584 18 k. 50 on 2 k. Pipe-smoking Gwembe Valley belle (38 × 26 mm) 1·00 1·25
585 19 k. 50 on 12 n. Mushroom picking 2·25 2·25
586 20 k. 50 on 18 n. Millet grinding on stone 1·00 1·50

(b) On Nos. 484, 489, 493/5 and 497/500.
587 70 n. on 35 n. Black and rufous swallow 50 15
588 3 k. on 5 n. Cloud-scraping cisticola 60 30
589 8 k. on 1 k. 25 Boulton's puff-back flycatcher 80 60
590 9 k. 90 on 1 k. 70 Boehm's bee eater 90 80
591 10 k. 40 on 1 k. 60 Anchieta's sunbird 90 80
592 12 k. 50 on 1 k. Bradfield's hornbill 1·00 1·00
593 15 k. on 1 k. 95 Perrin's bush strike 1·10 1·10
594 20 k. on 2 k. Whale-headed stork 1·75 2·00
595 20 k. 35 on 5 k. Taita falcon 1·75 2·00

No. 594 shows the surcharge as "K20.00". The previously listed 20 k. on 2 k., No. 499, is surcharged "K20" only.

156 "Parinari curatellifolia"

157 "Lamarckiana sp."

1989. Edible Fruits. Multicoloured.
596 50 n. Type **156** 15 10
597 6 k. 50 "Uapaca kirkiana" 1·25 1·50
598 6 k. 85 Wild fig 1·25 1·75
599 10 k. Bottle palm 2·25 2·75

1989. Grasshoppers. Multicoloured.
600 70 n. Type **157** 15 10
601 10 k. 40 "Dictyophorus sp." 1·25 1·50
602 12 k. 50 "Cymatomera sp." 1·50 2·25
603 15 k. "Phymateus iris" 2·00 2·75

158 Fireball

160 Footballer and Ball

159 Postvan, Postman on Bicycle and Main Post Office, Lusaka

1989. Christmas. Flowers. Multicoloured.
604 70 n. Type **158** 15 10
605 10 k. 40 Flame lily 1·00 1·25
606 12 k. 50 Foxglove lily 1·40 1·75
607 20 k. Vlei lily 2·40 3·50

1990. "Stamp World London 90" International Stamp Exhibition. Multicoloured.
608 1 k. 20 Type **159** 10 10
609 19 k. 50 Zambia 1980 18 n. butterflies stamp 2·00 2·50
610 20 k. 50 Rhodesia and Nyasaland 1962 9d. and Northern Rhodesia 1925 ½d. stamps 2·00 2·50
611 50 k. 1840 Penny Black and Maltese Cross cancellation 4·25 5·00

1990. World Cup Football Championship, Italy.
612 **160** 1 k. 20 multicoloured 10 10
613 – 18 k. 50 multicoloured 2·00 2·50
614 – 19 k. 50 multicoloured 2·00 2·50
615 – 20 k. 50 multicoloured 2·00 2·50

DESIGNS: 18 k. 50 to 20 k. 50, Different football scenes.

161 Road Tanker

1990. 10th Anniv of Southern African Development Co-ordination Conference. Each showing map of Southern Africa. Multicoloured.
617 1 k. 20 Type **161** 15 10
618 19 k. 50 Telecommunications 1·50 2·00
619 20 k. 50 "Regional Co-operation" 1·50 2·00
620 50 k. Transporting coal by cable 5·50 6·50

162 Irrigation

1990. 26th Anniv of Independence. Mult.
621 1 k. 20 Type **162** 10 10
622 19 k. 50 Shoe factory 1·10 1·40
623 20 k. 50 Mwembeshi II satellite earth station 1·25 1·60
624 50 k. "Mother and Child" (statue) 2·50 3·75

1990. Birds (2nd series). As T **138**. Mult.
625 10 n. Livingstone's flycatcher 10 10
626 15 n. Bar-winged weaver 10 10
627 30 n. Purple-throated cuckoo shrike 20 10
628 50 n. Retz's red-billed helmet shrike 20 10
629 50 n. As 10 n. 90 30
630 1 k. As 15 n. 90 40
631 1 k. 20 Bronze-naped pigeon 30 10
632 2 k. As 30 n. 90 50
633 3 k. As 50 n. 90 50
634 5 k. As 1 k. 20 1·00 60
635 15 k. Corncrake 30 30
636 20 k. Dickinson's kestrel 1·25 1·00
637 20 k. 50 As 20 k. 30 30
638 50 k. Barrow's bustard ("Denham's bustard") 45 60
Nos. 635/8 are larger, size 23 × 39 mm.

163 The Bird and the Snake **166** Woman cooking

164 Genet

1991. Int Literacy Year. Folklore. Mult.
639 1 k. 20 Type **163** 20 10
640 18 k. 50 Kalulu and the Leopard 2·00 2·25
641 19 k. 50 The Mouse and the Lion 2·00 2·25
642 20 k. 50 Kalulu and the Hippopotamus 2·00 2·25

1991. Small Carnivores. Multicoloured.
643 1 k. 20 Type **164** 20 10
644 18 k. 50 Civet 2·50 2·75
645 19 k. 50 Serval 2·50 2·75
646 20 k. 50 African wild cat 2·50 2·75

1991. Nos. 441/4 surch **K2**.
647 2 k. on 20 n. Type **129** 2·25 2·75
648 2 k. on 45 n. Postman and Livingstone Post Office, 1950 2·25 2·75
649 2 k. on 55 n. Postman and Kalomo Post Office, 1902 2·25 2·75
650 2 k. on 5 k. African Trans-Continental Telegraph Line under construction, 1900 2·25 2·75

1991. Soya Promotion Campaign. Mult.
651 1 k. Type **166** 10 10
652 2 k. Soya bean and field 10 10
653 5 k. Mother feeding child 20 15
654 20 k. Healthy and malnourished children 1·25 1·75
655 50 k. President Kaunda holding child 2·25 3·00

1991. Various stamps surch **K2**.
656 **130** 2 k. on 20 n. mult
657 **127** 2 k. on 25 n. mult
658 – 2 k. on 28 n. mult (No. 344)
659 – 2 k. on 28 n. mult (No. 393)
660 – 2 k. on 28 n. mult (No. 401)
661 – 2 k. on 28 n. mult (No. 418)
662 – 2 k. on 32 n. mult (No. 422)
663 – 2 k. on 35 n. mult (No. 453)
664 **134** 2 k. on 35 n. mult
665 **137** 2 k. on 35 n. mult
666 – 2 k. on 45 n. mult (No. 427)
667 – 2 k. on 45 n. black, blue and light blue (No. 430)
668 – 2 k. on 45 n. blue and gold (No. 433)
669 – 2 k. on 45 n. black, blue and brown (No. 446)
670 – 2 k. on 1 k. 60 mult (No. 470)
671 – 2 k. on 1 k. 70 mult (No. 451)
672 – 2 k. on 1 k. 70 mult (No. 482)
673 – 2 k. on 5 k. mult (No. 435)
674 – 2 k. on 5 k. mult (No. 452)
675 – 2 k. on 6 k. 50 mult (No. 597)
676 – 2 k. on 6 k. 85 mult (No. 576)
677 – 2 k. on 6 k. 85 mult (No. 598)
678 – 2 k. on 7 k. 85 mult (No. 577)

167 Chilubula Church near Kasama **169** "Disa hamatopetala"

168 "Adansonia digitata"

1991. 500th Birth Anniv of St. Ignatius Loyola. Multicoloured.
679 1 k. Type **167** 10 10
680 2 k. Chikuni Church near Monze 15 15
681 20 k. Bishop Joseph du Pont 2·00 2·25
682 50 k. Saint Ignatius Loyola 2·50 4·25

1991. Flowering Trees. Multicoloured.
683 1 k. Type **168** 10 10
684 2 k."Dichrostachys cinerea" 15 15
685 10 k. "Stereospermum kunthianum" 1·25 1·40
686 30 k. "Azana garckeana" 2·75 3·25
No. 685 is inscribed "Sterospermum" in error.

1992. 40th Anniv of Queen Elizabeth II's Accession. As T **143** of Ascension. Mult.
687 4 k. Queen's House 10 10
688 32 k.Traditional village 90 60
689 35 k. Fisherman hauling nets 90 80
690 38 k. Three portraits of Queen Elizabeth 1·10 1·10
691 50 k. Queen Elizabeth II 1·40 2·50

1992. Orchids. Multicoloured.
692 1 k. Type **169** 40 15
693 2 k."Eulophia paivaeana" 40 20
694 5 k. "Eulophia quartiniana" 70 40
695 20 k. "Aerangis verdickii" 3·00 4·00

170 Kasinja Mask

1992. Tribal Masks. Multicoloured.
696 1 k. Type **170** 10 10
697 2 k. Chizaluke 15 10
698 10 k. Mwanapweu 50 50
699 30 k. Maliya 1·75 2·25

171 Bushbuck

1992. Antelopes. Multicoloured.
700 4 k. Type **171** 10 10
701 40 k. Eland 40 40
702 45 k. Roan antelope 45 45
703 100 k. Sable antelope 1·10 1·75

172 De Havilland D.H.66 Hercules "City of Basra" **174** Hurdling

173 Wise Men with Gifts

1992. 60th Anniv of Airmail Service. Mult.
704 4 k. Type **172** 40 20
705 40 k. Vickers Super VC-10 1·50 75
706 45 k. Short S.45A Solent 3 flying boat "Severn" 1·50 75
707 100 k. Douglas DC-10 2·50 3·75

1992. Christmas. Multicoloured.
708 10 k. Type **173** 15 10
709 80 k. Nativity 1·40 1·50
710 90 k. Angelic choir 1·50 1·60
711 100 k. Angel and shepherds 1·60 1·75

1992. Olympic Games, Barcelona. Mult.
713 10 k. Type **174** 15 10
714 40 k. Boxing 50 40
715 80 k. Judo 1·00 1·40
716 100 k. Cycling 2·00 2·25

175 Nkundalila Falls

1993. Waterfalls. Multicoloured.
717 50 k. Type **175** 10 10
718 200 k. Chishimba Falls 20 25
719 250 k. Chipoma Falls 25 30
720 300 k. Lumangwe Falls 30 35

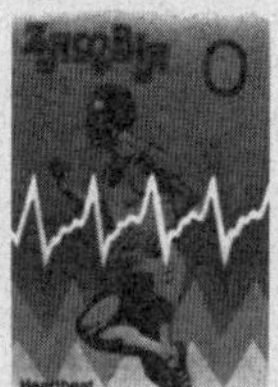

176 Athlete and Cardiograph

1993. Heartbeat Campaign. Multicoloured.
721 (O) Type **176** 50 55
722 (P) Heart and cardiograph 50 55
These stamps were initially sold at 50 k. (No. 721) for ordinary post and 80 k. (No. 722) for priority mail. These face values were increased to reflect postage rate increases.

177 Bronze Sunbird **178** Tiger Snake

1994. Sunbirds. Mult. (a) Face values as T **177**.
723 20 k. Type **177** 10 10
724 50 k. Violet-backed sunbird 10 10
725 100 k. Scarlet-chested sunbird 10 10
726 150 k. Bannerman's sunbird 15 20
727 200 k. Oustalet's white-bellied sunbird 20 25
728 250 k. Anchieta's sunbird ("Red and blue sunbird") 25 30
729 300 k. Olive sunbird 30 35
730 350 k. Green-headed sunbird 35 40
731 400 k. Red-tufted malachite sunbird 40 45
732 500 k. Variable sunbird 50 55
733 800 k. Coppery sunbird 75 80
734 1000 k. Orange-tufted sunbird 95 1·00
735 1500 k. Amethyst sunbird ("Black Sunbird") 1·40 1·50
736 2000 k. Green-throated sunbird 1·90 2·00

(b) Face values shown as capital letters.
737 (O) Mariqua sunbird ("Marico Sunbird") 50 55
738 (P) Eastern double-collared sunbird 50 55
Nos. 737/8 were initially sold at 50 k. for ordinary post (No. 737) and 80 k. for priority mail (No. 738). These rates were increased to 100 k. for ordinary post and 150 k. for priority mail on 20th June 1994. On 1st March 1995 the difference between the two rates was abolished and both "O" and "P" stamps were sold at 500 k. This was reduced to 400 k. each on 1 April 1995, but the rate reverted to 500 k. on 8 February 1996.

1994. Snakes. Multicoloured.
739 50 k. Type **178** 10 10
740 200 k. Egyptian cobra 20 25
741 300 k. African python 30 35
742 500 k. Green mamba 50 55

179 Women working on Road

1995. 75th Anniv of I.L.O. Multicoloured.
743 100 k. Type **179** 10 10
744 450 k. Women making cement blocks 45 50

180 Angel playing Kalimba and Flowers

1995. Christmas (1994). Multicoloured.
745 100 k. Type **180** 10 10
746 300 k. Angel at prayer and animals 30 35
747 450 k. Angel with flute and birds 45 50
748 500 k. Angel with drum and Baobab trees 50 55

181 Anniversary Emblem, Rainbow and Map **182** David Livingstone (missionary) and Memorial

1995. 50th Anniv of United Nations.
749 **181** 700 k. multicoloured 70 75

1995. Monuments. Multicoloured.
750 100 k. Type **182** 10 10
751 300 k. Mbereshi Mission 30 35
752 450 k. Von Lettow-Vorbeck Monument 45 50
753 500 k. Niamkolo Church 50 55

183 Saddle-bill Stork

1996. Endangered Species. Birds. Multicoloured.
754 200 k. Type **183** 20 25
755 300 k. Black-cheeked lovebird 30 35
756 500 k. Pair of black-cheeked lovebirds 50 55
757 900 k. Saddle-bill stork and chicks 90 95

1996. Christmas. Nos. 709/10 surch.
759 (O) on 90 k. Angelic choir 50 55
760 900 k. on 80 k. Nativity 85 90
No. 759 was sold at 500 k., which was the minimum local postage rate for ordinary post.

185 "Precis octavia sesamus"

187 Verreaux's Eagle Owl

1997. Butterflies and Moths. Multicoloured.

761	300 k. Type **185**	30	35
762	500 k. "Argema mimosae"	50	55
763	700 k. "Imbrasia dione"	70	75
764	900 k. "Papilio ophidicephalus cotterell"	90	95

1997. Nos. 688/90 surch.

766	(O) on 32 k. Traditional village	50	55
767	500 k. on 35 k. Fishermen hauling nets	50	55
768	900 k. on 38 k. Three portraits of Queen Elizabeth	90	95

No. 766 was sold at 500 k. which was the minimum local postage rate for ordinary post.

1997. Owls of Zambia. Multicoloured.

769	300 k. Type **187**	30	35
770	500 k. Pel's fishing owl	50	55
771	700 k. Barn owl	70	75
772	900 k. Spotted eagle owl	90	95

188 Gandhi as Law Student, London, 1888

1998. 50th Death Anniv of Mahatma Gandhi. Multicoloured.

774	250 k. Type **188**	25	30
775	(O) Gandhi at Red Fort, Delhi	50	55
776	500 k. Gandhi with Nehru, 1946 (horiz)	50	55
777	900 k. Gandhi at prayer	90	95

No. 775 was sold at 500 k. which was the minimum local postage rate for ordinary post.

189 Dove and Map of Zambia

1998. 18th Anniv of Pan African Postal Union.

779	**189**	(O) multicoloured	50	55
780	–	500 k. multicoloured	50	55
781	–	900 k. black, red and orange	90	95

DESIGNS: 500 k. Lechwe at Kafue Flats; 900 k. Dove with "18th" note in beak.

No. 779 was sold at 500 k. which was the minimum local postage rate for ordinary post.

POSTAGE DUE STAMPS

D 3

1964.

D11	D 3	1d. orange	30	1·00
D12		2d. blue	35	1·40
D13		3d. lake	45	1·60
D14		4d. blue	45	2·00
D15		6d. purple	45	2·25
D16		1s. green	55	4·25

APPENDIX

The following stamps have either been issued in excess of postal needs, or have not been made available to the public in reasonable quantities at face value.

1984.

Olympic Games, Los Angeles. 90 n. ×5, each embossed on gold foil.

1986.

Classic Cars 1 k. 50×25, each embossed on gold foil.

The follwing issues are reported by the Zimbia Postal Services Corporation as being available from Philatelic Counters only.

1997.

Disney's Chinese New Year. 250 k., 400 k., 500 k. ×7, 600 k., 750 k., 1000 k.

Endangered Species. 500 k.×6, 1000 k.×6

Trains of the World. 200 k., 300 k., 500 k.×7, 900 k., 1000 k., 1500 k.

Golden Wedding of Queen Elizabeth II and Prince Philip. 500 k.×6

50th Death Anniv of Paul P. Harris (founder of Rotary International). 1000 k.

"Pacific '97" International Stamp Exhibition, San Francisco. Death Centenary of Heinrich von Stephan (founder of the U.P.U.). 1000 k.×3

Christmas. Religious Paintings. 50 k.×2, 100 k.×2, 500 k., 1000 k.

1998.

Diana, Princess of Wales Commemoration. 500 k. ×6, 700 k.×6

Flowers. 500 k.×13

Chinese New Year ("Year of the Tiger"). 700 k.×4

Indian landmarks. 900 k.×3

Indian art. 700 k.×4

World Cup Football Championship, France. 450 k. ×8, 500 k.×16

ZANZIBAR

A Br. Protectorate consisting of several islands off the coast of Tanganyika, E. Africa. Independent in 1963 and a republic within the Br. Commonwealth in 1964. The "United Republic of Tanganyika and Zanzibar" was proclaimed in July 1964, and the country was later renamed Tanzania. Separate issues for Zanzibar ceased on 1 Jan. 1968 and Tanzania stamps became valid for the whole country.

1895. 16 annas = 1 rupee.
1908. 100 cents = 1 rupee.
1936. 100 cents = 1 shilling.

1895. Stamps of India (Queen Victoria) optd **Zanzibar**.

3	**23**	½ a. turquoise	3·00	3·00
4		1 a. purple	3·25	3·00
5		1½ a. brown	4·00	3·00
6	–	2 a. blue	4·25	4·00
8	–	2½ a. green	6·00	4·25
10	–	3 a. orange	9·00	8·50
12	–	4 a. green (No. 96)	8·50	11·00
13	–	6 a. brown (No. 80)	16·00	11·00
15	–	8 a. mauve	11·00	19·00
16	–	12 a. purple on red	14·00	10·00
17	–	1 r. grey	70·00	70·00
18	**37**	1 r. green and red	10·00	24·00
19	**38**	2 r. red and orange	42·00	65·00
20		3 r. brown and green	42·00	60·00
21		5 r. blue and violet	45·00	65·00

1895. Nos. 4/6 surch **2½**.

23	**23**	2½ on 1 a. purple	£130	£100
22		2½ on 1½ a. brown	42·00	35·00
26	–	2½ on 2 a. blue	48·00	25·00

1896. Stamps of British East Africa (Queen Victoria) optd **Zanzibar**.

41	**11**	½ a. green	28·00	16·00
42		1 a. red	24·00	15·00
43		2½ a. blue	75·00	42·00
44		4½ a. yellow	42·00	48·00
45		5 a. brown	48·00	28·00
46		7½ a. mauve	35·00	48·00

13 Sultan Seyyid Hamed-bin-Thwain

19 Sultan Seyyid Hamoud-bin-Mahommed bin Said

1896. The Rupee values are larger.

178	**13**	½ a. green and red	1·50	35
179		1 a. blue and red	1·50	55
159		2 a. brown and red	2·00	65
181		2½ a. blue and red	1·60	30
182		3 a. grey and red	4·50	60
183		4 a. green and red	2·50	1·00
184		4½ a. orange and red	5·50	70
166		5 a. brown and red	3·00	2·25
167		7½ a. mauve and red	2·50	2·25
187		8 a. olive and red	8·50	2·25
169	–	1 r. blue and red	9·50	9·00
171	–	2 r. green and red	22·00	9·50
172	–	3 r. purple and red	20·00	9·50
173	–	4 r. red	16·00	13·00
174	–	5 r. brown and red	21·00	13·00

1896. Surch **2½**.

175	**13**	2½ on 4 a. green and red	55·00	38·00

1899. The Rupee values are larger.

188	**19**	½ a. green and red	1·60	50
189		1 a. blue and red	3·50	20
190		1 a. red	1·40	10
191		2 a. brown and red	2·00	45
192		2½ a. blue and red	1·50	55
193		3 a. grey and red	1·50	2·00
194		4 a. green and red	2·50	1·00
195		4½ a. orange and red	7·00	2·25
196		4½ a. black and red	11·00	11·00
197		5 a. brown and red	2·50	1·25
198		7½ a. mauve and red	2·50	3·50
199		8 a. olive and red	2·75	4·50
200	–	1 r. blue and red	16·00	13·00
201	–	2 r. green and red	16·00	17·00
202	–	3 r. purple and red	28·00	32·00
203	–	4 r. red	40·00	48·00
204	–	5 r. brown and red	48·00	55·00

1904. Surch in words.

205	**19**	1 on 4½ a. orange and red	3·25	3·25
206		1 on 4½ a. black and red	4·25	15·00
207		2 on 4 a. green and red	13·00	16·00
208		2½ on 7½ a. mauve and red	12·00	18·00
209		2½ on 8 a. olive and red	14·00	28·00

23 Monogram of Sultan Seyyid Ali bin Hamoud bin Naherud

1904. The Rupee values are larger.

210	**23**	½ a. green	1·10	80
211		1 a. red	1·10	10
212		2 a. brown	1·25	45
213		2½ a. blue	2·25	35
214		3 a. grey	2·25	1·75
215		4 a. green	2·25	1·40
216		4½ a. black	3·00	2·50
217		5 a. brown	3·25	1·25
218	**23**	7½ a. mauve	4·00	6·50
219		8 a. olive	3·75	2·50
220	–	1 r. blue and red	20·00	10·00
221	–	2 r. green and red	19·00	32·00
222	–	3 r. violet and red	40·00	75·00
223	–	4 r. deep red and red	45·00	90·00
224	–	5 r. brown and red	48·00	95·00

25

27 Sultan Ali bin Hamoud

26

28 View of Port

1908.

225	**25**	1 c. grey	1·50	30
226		3 c. green	3·25	10
227		6 c. red	6·00	10
228		10 c. brown	1·75	1·75
229a		12 c. violet	8·00	90
230	**26**	15 c. blue	7·00	40
231		25 c. brown	2·75	80
232		50 c. green	4·75	3·50
233		75 c. black	8·00	11·00
234	**27**	1 r. green	22·00	11·00
235		2 r. violet	17·00	14·00
236		3 r. brown	22·00	45·00
237		4 r. red	40·00	75·00
238		5 r. blue	40·00	55·00
239	**28**	10 r. green and brown	90·00	£190
240		20 r. black and green	£180	£375
241		30 r. black and brown	£275	£500
242		40 r. black and orange	£425	
243		50 r. black and mauve	£375	
244		100 r. black and blue	£650	
245		200 r. black and blue	£1000	

29 Sultan Kalif bin Harub

30 Sailing Canoe

31 Dhow

1913.

246	**29**	1 c. grey	30	20
247		3 c. green	50	20
278		3 c. orange	30	10
279		4 c. green	50	60
280		6 c. red	30	50
281		6 c. purple on blue	35	10
264		8 c. purple on yellow	75	3·00
249		10 c. brown	1·10	1·40
265		10 c. green on yellow	75	30
283		12 c. violet	40	30
284		12 c. red	40	35
251		15 c. blue	1·25	30
286		20 c. blue	1·00	30
252		25 c. brown	90	45
288		50 c. green	1·25	3·00
254		75 c. black	2·00	2·50
290	**30**	1 r. green	3·50	2·75
291		2 r. violet	3·00	6·00
292		3 r. brown	4·25	7·00
293		4 r. red	11·00	32·00
259		5 r. blue	30·00	32·00
260	**31**	10 r. green and brown	80·00	£140
260a		20 r. black and green	£110	£250
260b		30 r. black and brown	£120	£325
260c		40 r. black and orange	£275	£450
260d		50 r. black and purple	£250	£450
260e		100 r. black and blue	£325	
260f		200 r. brown and black	£600	

32 Sultan Kalif bin Harub 33

1926.

299	32	1 c. brown	30	10
300		3 c. orange	20	15
301		4 c. green	20	30
302		6 c. violet	20	10
303		8 c. grey	90	4·50
304		10 c. olive	85	40
305		12 c. red	1·50	10
306		20 c. blue	40	30
307		25 c. purple on yellow	4·00	2·50
308		50 c. red	1·50	35
309		75 c. brown	12·00	15·00

1936.

310	33	5 c. green	10	10
311		10 c. black	10	10
312		15 c. red	10	60
313		20 c. orange	10	10
314		25 c. purple on yellow	10	10
315		30 c. blue	10	10
316		40 c. brown	15	10
317		50 c. red	30	10
318	30	1 s. green	45	10
319		2 s. violet	55	90
320		5 s. red	7·50	5·00
321		7 s. 50 c. blue	18·00	18·00
322	31	10 s. green and brown	18·00	18·00

In Type **33** the letters of the word "CENTS" are without serifs. In Type **32** they have serifs.

36 Sultan Kalif bin Harub

37 "Sham Alam" (Sultan's dhow)

1936. Silver Jubilee of Sultan.

323	36	10 c. black and olive	70	30
324		20 c. black and purple	2·25	30
325		30 c. black and blue	5·50	35
326		50 c. black and red	6·00	2·40

1944. Bicentenary of Al Busaid Dynasty.

327	37	10 c. blue	60	1·50
328		20 c. red	60	2·00
329		50 c. green	60	30
330		1 s. purple	60	45

1946. Victory. Optd **VICTORY ISSUE 8TH JUNE 1946**.

331	33	10 c. black	20	20
332		30 c. blue	20	40

1945. Silver Wedding. As T **10/11** of Aden.

333	20 c. orange	30	1·00
334	10 s. brown	17·00	27·00

1949. 75th Anniv of U.P.U. As T **20/23** of Antigua.

335	20 c. orange	40	1·75
336	30 c. blue	1·40	80
337	50 c. mauve	1·50	1·75
338	1 s. green	1·50	3·00

39 Sultan Kalif bin Harub

40 Seyyid Khalifa Schools, Beit-el-Ras

1952.

339	39	5 c. black	10	10
340		10 c. orange	10	10
341		15 c. green	40	1·75
342		20 c. red	40	50
343		25 c. purple	60	10
344		30 c. green	40	10
345		35 c. blue	30	2·50
346		40 c. brown	30	1·25
347		50 c. violet	1·50	10
348	40	1 s. green and brown	30	10
349		2 s. blue and purple	1·75	1·75
350		5 s. black and red	1·75	2·75
351		7 s. 50 black and green	18·00	23·00
352		10 s. red and black	9·50	8·00

41 Sultan Kalif bin Harub

42 Cloves

43 "Ummoja Wema" (dhow)

47 Dimbani Mosque

1954. 75th Birthday of Sultan.

353	41	15 c. green	10	10
354		20 c. red	10	10
355		30 c. blue	10	10
356		50 c. purple	15	10
357		1 s. 25 red	15	60

1957.

358	42	5 c. orange and green	10	30
359		10 c. green and red	10	10
360	43	15 c. green and sepia	10	1·75
361	–	20 c. blue	10	10
362	–	25 c. brown and black	10	30
363	43	30 c. red and black	15	30
364	–	35 c. slate and green	15	20
365	–	40 c. brown and black	15	10
366	–	50 c. blue and myrtle	15	10
367	47	1 s. red and black	20	10
368	43	1 s. 25 slate and red	3·00	10
369	47	2 s. orange and green	3·00	1·50
370	–	5 s. blue	4·75	2·00
371	–	7 s. 50 green	5·50	4·00
372	–	10 s. red	5·50	4·75

DESIGNS—HORIZ (as Type **47**): 20 c. Sultan's Barge; 25, 35, 50 c. Map of East African coast. VERT (as Type **47**): 40 c. Minaret Mosque. (As Type **43**) 5, 7 s. 50 c., 10 s. Kibweni Palace.

49 Sultan Seyyid Sir Abdulla bin Khalifa

50 "Protein Foods"

1961. As 1957 issue but with portrait of Sultan Sir Abdulla as in T **49**.

373	5 c. orange and green	10	40
374	10 c. green and red	10	10
375	15 c. green and sepia	50	1·75
376	20 c. blue	20	20
377	25 c. brown and black	30	20
378	30 c. red and black	1·50	30
379	35 c. slate and green	1·50	1·50
380	40 c. brown and black	30	10
381	50 c. blue and myrtle	50	10
382	1 s. red and black	40	50
383	1 s. 25 slate and red	2·00	1·50
384	2 s. orange and green	50	1·50
385	5 s. blue	2·75	6·00
386	7 s. 50 green	2·75	14·00
387	10 s. red	2·75	8·50
388	20 s. sepia (Kibweni Palace)	17·00	28·00

1963. Freedom from Hunger.

389	50	1 s. 30 sepia	80	40

51 Zanzibar Clove

58 Axe, Spear and Dagger

1963. Independence. Inscr "UHURU 1963". Multicoloured.

390	30 c. Type **51**	10	30
391	50 c. "To Prosperity" (Zanzibar doorway)	10	30
392	1 s. "Religious Tolerance" (mosques and churches)	10	3·50
393	2 s. 50 "Towards the Light" (Mangapwani Cave)	15	4·25

No. 392 is horiz.

1964. Optd **JAMHURI 1964**. (a) Nos. 373/88.

414	5 c. orange and green	10	10
415	10 c. green and red	10	10
416	15 c. green and sepia	10	10
417	20 c. blue	10	10
418	25 c. brown and black	10	10
419	30 c. red and black	10	10
420	35 c. slate and green	10	10
421	40 c. brown and black	10	10
422	50 c. blue and myrtle	10	10
423	1 s. red and black	10	10
424	1 s. 25 slate and red	1·25	20
425	2 s. orange and green	50	20
426	5 s. blue	50	35
407	7 s. 50 green	2·00	1·50
408	10 s. red	2·00	1·50
429	20 s. sepia	2·00	4·50

(b) Nos. 390/3.

430	30 c. multicoloured	10	10
431	50 c. multicoloured	10	10
432	1 s. 30 multicoloured	10	10
433	2 s. 50 multicoloured	15	30

The opt is in two lines on Nos. 421, 423, 425/429, 430, 431, 433.

NOTE. For the set inscribed "UNITED REPUBLIC OF TANGANYIKA & ZANZIBAR" see Nos. 124/7 of Tanganyika.

1964. Multicoloured.

434	5 c. Type **58**	10	10
435	10 c. Bow and arrow breaking chains	10	10
436	15 c. Type **58**	10	10
437	20 c. As 10 c.	30	10
438	25 c. Zanzibari with rifle	30	10
439	30 c. Zanzibari breaking manacles	20	10
440	40 c. As 25 c.	30	10
441	50 c. As 30 c.	20	10
442	1 s. Zanzibari, flag and sun	20	10
443	1 s. 30 Hands breaking chains (horiz)	30	30
444	2 s. Hand waving flag (horiz)	30	20
445	5 s. Map of Zanzibar and Pemba on flag (horiz)	55	90
446	10 s. Flag on map	3·00	2·25
447	20 s. National flag (horiz)	3·00	16·00

68 Soldier and Maps

1965. 1st Anniv of Revolution.

448	68	20 c. light green and green	10	10
449	–	30 c. brown and orange	10	10
450	68	1 s. 30 blue and deep blue	10	10
451	–	2 s. 50 violet and red	10	15

DESIGN—VERT: 30 c., 2 s. 50, Building construction.

70 Planting Rice

1965. Agricultural Development.

452	70	20 c. sepia and blue	10	90
453	–	30 c. sepia and mauve	10	90
454	–	1 s. 30 sepia and orange	30	1·75
455	70	2 s. 50 sepia and green	50	3·75

DESIGN: 30 c, 1 s. 30, Hands holding rice.

72 Freighter, Tractor, Factory and Open Book and Torch

74 Tree-felling

1966. 2nd Anniv of Revolution. Mult.

456	20 c. Type **72**	20	10
457	50 c. Soldier	15	10
458	1 s. 30 Type **72**	15	10
459	2 s. 50 As 50 c.	25	55

1966.

460	74	5 c. purple and olive	30	80
461	–	10 c. purple and green	30	80
462	–	15 c. purple and blue	30	80
463	–	20 c. blue and orange	20	20
464	–	25 c. purple and yellow	20	30
465	–	30 c. purple and yellow	30	20
466	–	40 c. brown and red	50	20
467	–	50 c. green and yellow	50	20
468	–	1 s. purple and blue	50	20
469	–	1 s. 30 purple and turquoise	50	1·75
470	–	2 s. purple and green	50	30
471	–	5 s. red and blue	80	4·25
472	–	10 s. red and yellow	2·25	16·00
473	74	20 s. brown and mauve	4·25	25·00

DESIGNS—HORIZ: 10 c., 1 s. Clove cultivation; 15 c., 40 c. Chair-making; 20 c., 5 s. Lumumba College; 25 c., 1 s. 30, Agriculture; 30 c., 2 s. Agricultural workers. VERT: 50 c., 10 s. Zanzibar street.

81 "Education"

1966. Introduction of Free Education.

474	81	50 c. black, blue and orange	10	90
475		1 s. 30 black, blue and green	15	1·40
476		2 s. 50 black, blue and pink	40	4·25

82 A.S.P. Flag

1967. 10th Anniv of Afro-Shirazi Party.

477	82	30 c. multicoloured	10	1·00
478	–	50 c. multicoloured	10	1·00
479	–	1 s. 30 multicoloured	10	2·00
480	82	2 s. 50 multicoloured	30	3·25

DESIGN—VERT: 50 c., 1 s. 30, Vice-President M. A. Karume of Tanzania, flag and crowd.

84 Voluntary Workers

1967. Voluntary Workers Brigade.

481	84	1 s. 30 multicoloured	15	2·25
482		2 s. 50 multicoloured	40	5·50

POSTAGE DUE STAMPS

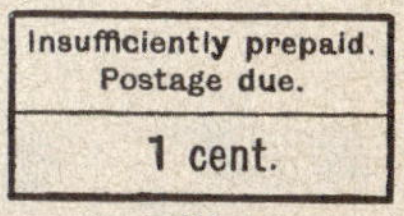

D 1

1930. Roul or roul × imperf.

D 1	D 1	1 c. black on orange	11·00	90·00
D18		2 c. black on orange	10·00	22·00
D 3		3 c. black on orange	5·00	35·00
D19		3 c. black on red	3·00	42·00
D21		6 c. black on yellow	3·00	26·00
D 5		9 c. black on orange	2·75	18·00
D 6		12 c. black on orange	£8000	£8000
D 7		12 c. black on green	£1400	£600
D22		12 c. black on blue	4·00	20·00
D 8		15 c. black on orange	2·75	19·00
D 9		18 c. black on orange	4·00	30·00
D11		20 c. black on orange	4·00	42·00
D12		21 c. black on orange	3·50	24·00
D13		25 c. black on purple	£2500	£1300
D14		25 c. black on orange	£9500	£9500
D23		25 c. black on red	9·00	55·00
D24		25 c. black on lilac	11·00	40·00
D15		31 c. black on orange	9·50	60·00
D16		50 c. black on orange	21·00	£120
D17		75 c. black on orange	65·00	£250

D 3

1936.

D25	D 3	5 c. violet	2·00	6·00
D26		10 c. red	2·00	2·50
D27		20 c. green	1·50	4·00
D28a		30 c. brown	30	9·00
D29a		40 c. blue	40	20·00
D30a		1 s. grey	1·00	16·00

ZIL ELWANNYEN SESEL

Beginning in June 1980 stamps were issued for use in Zil Elwannyen Sesel (Seychelles Outer Islands), including Aldabra, Coetivy, Farquhar and the Amirante Islands.

100 cents = 1 rupee

A. Inscr "ZIL ELOIGNE SESEL"

1980. As Nos. 404/19 of Seychelles but inscr "ZIL ELOIGNE SESEL".

1	–	5 c. multicoloured	15	40
2	–	10 c. multicoloured	15	40
3	–	15 c. multicoloured	15	40
4	–	20 c. multicoloured	20	40
5	–	25 c. multicoloured	80	40
6	103	40 c. multicoloured	30	40
7	–	50 c. multicoloured	30	40
8	–	75 c. multicoloured	35	40
9	–	1 r. multicoloured	1·00	50
10	–	1 r. 10 multicoloured	40	50
11	–	1 r. 25 multicoloured	1·25	55
12	–	1 r. 50 multicoloured	45	45
13	–	5 r. multicoloured	70	1·00
14	–	10 r. multicoloured	80	1·50
15a	–	15 r. multicoloured	1·00	2·50
16	–	20 r. multicoloured	1·00	3·25

2 "Cinq Juin"

1980. Establishment of Travelling Post Office. Multicoloured.

17	1 r. 50 Type **2**	20	15
18	2 r. 10 Hand-stamping covers	25	20
19	5 r. Map of Zil Eloigne Sesel	40	40

3 Yellow-finned Tuna

1980. Marine Life. Multicoloured.

20	1 r. 50 Type **3**	20	15
21	2 r. 10 Blue marlin	35	20
22	5 r. Sperm whale	70	50

1981. Royal Wedding. As T **26/27** of Kiribati. Multicoloured.

23	40 c. "Royal Escape"	10	10
24	40 c. Prince Charles and Lady Diana Spencer	40	55
25	5 r. "Victoria and Albert"	40	40
31	5 r. As No. 24	1·00	1·75
27	10 r. "Britannia"	85	85
28	10 r. As No. 24	2·00	3·25

4 Wright's Skink

1981. Wildlife. (1st series). Multicoloured.

32	1 r. 40 Type **4**	15	15
33	2 r. 25 Tree frog	20	20
34	5 r. Robber crab	40	40

See also Nos. 45/7.

5 "Cinq Juin" ("Communications")

1982. Island Development. Ships.

35 **5**	1 r. 75 black and orange	50	20
36 –	2 r. 10 black and blue	60	30
37 –	5 r. black and red	70	50

DESIGNS: 2 r. 10, "Junon" (fisheries protection); 5 r. "Diamond M. Dragon" (drilling ship).

B. Inscr "ZIL ELWAGNE SESEL"

6 "Paulette"

1982. Local Mail Vessels. Multicoloured.

38	40 c. Type **6**	45	35
39	1 r. 75 "Janette"	60	70
40	2 r. 75 "Lady Esme"	70	85
41	3 r. 50 "Cinq Juin"	70	95

7 Birds flying over Island

1982. Aldabra, World Heritage Site. Mult.

42	40 c. Type **7**	30	15
43	2 r. 75 Map of the atoll	60	35
44	7 r. Giant tortoises	80	75

8 Red Land Crab

1983. Wildlife (2nd series). Multicoloured.

45	1 r. 75 Type **8**	25	25
46	2 r. 75 Black terrapin	35	35
47	7 r. Madagascar green gecko	80	80

9 Map of Poivre Island and Ile du Sud

10 Aldabra Warbler

1983. Island Maps. Multicoloured.

48	40 c. Type **9**	25	20
49	1 r. 50 Ile des Roches	40	25
50	2 r. 75 Astove Island	50	40
51	7 r. Coetivy Island	80	1·10

1983. Birds. Multicoloured.

53	5 c. Type **10**	40	40
54	10 c. Zebra dove ("Barred Ground Dove")	90	40
55	15 c. Madagascar nightjar	30	10
56	20 c. Madagascar cisticola ("Malagasy Grass Warbler")	30	10
57	25 c. Madagascar white eye	60	30
58	40 c. Mascarene fody	30	10
59	50 c. White-throated rail	2·00	30
60	75 c. Black bulbul	40	25
61	2 r. Western reef heron ("Dimorphic little egret")	2·00	85
62	2 r. 10 Souimanga sunbird	50	55
63	2 r. 50 Madagascar turtle dove	1·00	65
64	2 r. 75 Sacred ibis	70	75
65	3 r. 50 Black coucal (vert)	90	95
66	7 r. Seychelles kestrel (vert)	1·75	1·90
67	15 r. Comoro blue pigeon (vert)	4·00	4·25
68	20 r. Greater flamingo (vert)	5·25	5·50

See also Nos. 165 etc. (1985).

11 Windsurfing

1983. Tourism. Multicoloured.

69	50 c. Type **11**	10	10
70	2 r. Hotel	25	25
71	3 r. View of beach	35	35
72	10 r. Islands at sunset	1·40	1·75

1983. Nos. 23/8 surch.

73	30 c. on 40 c. "Royal Escape"	25	25
74	30 c. on 40 c. Prince Charles and Lady Diana Spencer	50	60
75	2 r. on 5 r. "Victoria and Albert II"	70	70
76	2 r. on 5 r. As No. 74	1·25	1·75
77	3 r. on 10 r. "Britannia"	85	85
78	3 r. on 10 r. As No. 74	1·60	2·50

12 Map of Aldabra and Commemorative Postmark

1984. Re-opening of Aldabra Post Office. Multicoloured.

79	50 c. Type **12**	15	25
80	2 r. 75 White-throated rail	60	95
81	3 r. Giant tortoise	60	1·10
82	10 r. Red-footed booby	2·25	3·25

13 Fishing from Launch

1984. Game Fishing. Multicoloured.

83	50 c. Type **13**	15	25
84	2 r. Hooked fish (vert)	45	65
85	3 r. Weighing catch (vert)	60	85
86	10 r. Fishing from boat (different)	2·00	2·75

14 Giant Hermit Crab

15 Constellation of "Orion"

1984. Crabs. Multicoloured.

87	50 c. Type **14**	25	40
88	2 r. Fiddler crabs	65	1·10
89	3 r. Sand crab	80	1·50
90	10 r. Spotted pebble crab	2·50	4·25

1984. The Night Sky. Multicoloured.

91	50 c. Type **15**	25	15
92	2 r. "Cygnus"	60	55
93	3 r. "Virgo"	80	80
94	10 r. "Scorpio"	2·00	2·25

C. Inscr "ZIL ELWANNYEN SESEL"

16 "Lenzites elegans"

17 The Queen Mother attending Royal Opera House, Covent Garden

1985. Fungi. Multicoloured.

95	50 c. Type **16**	85	85
96	2 r. "Xylaria telfairei"	2·00	2·00
97	3 r. "Lentinus sajor-caju"	2·00	2·00
98	10 r. "Hexagonia tenuis"	3·50	3·50

1985. As Nos. 53/4, 57 and 61 but inscr "Zil Elwannyen Sesel".

165	5 c. Type **10**	1·40	1·40
166	10 c. Zebra dove ("Barred Ground Dove")	1·40	1·40
103	25 c. Madagascar white eye	1·50	1·25
105	50 c. White-throated rail	2·25	1·40
226	2 r. Western reef heron ("Diomorphic Little Egret")	2·75	2·75

1985. Life and Times of Queen Elizabeth the Queen Mother. Multicoloured.

115	1 r. The Queen Mother, 1936 (from photo by Dorothy Wilding)	20	25
116	2 r. With Princess Anne at Ascot, 1974	35	50
117	3 r. Type **17**	45	70
118	5 r. With Prince Henry at his christening (from photo by Lord Snowdon)	60	1·25

18 Giant Tortoise

1985. Giant Tortoises of Aldabra (1st series). Multicoloured.

120	50 c. Type **18**	2·25	60
121	75 c. Giant tortoises at stream	2·50	80
122	1 r. Giant tortoises on grassland	2·75	90
123	2 r. Giant tortoise (side view)	3·50	1·25

For stamps as Nos. 120/3 but without circular inscription around W.W.F. emblem see Nos. 153/6.

19 Phoenician Trading Ship (600 B.C.)

1985. Famous Visitors. Multicoloured.

125	50 c. Type **19**	80	80
126	2 r. Sir Hugh Scott and H.M.S. "Sealark", 1908	1·75	2·00
127	10 r. Vasco da Gama and "Sao Gabriel", 1502	3·50	4·50

1986. 60th Birthday of Queen Elizabeth II. As T **110** of Ascension. Multicoloured.

128	75 c. Princess Elizabeth at Chester, 1951	15	25
129	1 r. Queen and Duke of Edinburgh at Falklands Service, St. Paul's Cathedral, 1985	15	25
130	1 r. 50 At Order of St. Michael and St. George service, St. Paul's Cathedral, 1968	25	40
131	3 r. 75 In Mexico, 1975	40	90
132	5 r. At Crown Agents Head Office, London, 1983	40	1·25

1986. Royal Wedding. As T **112** of Ascension. Multicoloured.

133	3 r. Prince Andrew and Miss Sarah Ferguson on Buckingham Palace balcony	45	75
134	7 r. Prince Andrew in naval uniform	65	1·75

20 "Acropora palifera" and "Tubastraea coccinea"

21 "Hibiscus tiliaceus"

1986. Coral Formations. Multicoloured.

135	2 r. Type **20**	1·75	1·75
136	2 r. "Echinopora lamellosa" and "Favia pallida"	1·75	1·75
137	2 r. "Sarcophyton sp." and "Porites lutea"	1·75	1·75
138	2 r. "Goniopora sp." and "Goniastrea retiformis"	1·75	1·75
139	2 r. "Tubipora musica" and "Fungia fungites"	1·75	1·75

Nos. 135/9 were printed together, se-tenant, forming a composite design.

1986. Flora. Multicoloured.

140	50 c. Type **21**	35	30
141	2 r. "Crinum angustum"	1·60	1·50
142	3 r. "Phaius tetragonus"	2·25	2·00
143	10 r. "Rothmannia annae"	3·75	4·00

22 Teardrop Butterflyfish and Lined Butterflyfish

23 Coconut

1987. Coral Reef Fishes. Multicoloured.

144	2 r. Type **22**	1·10	1·40
145	2 r. Knifejaw	1·10	1·40
146	2 r. Narrow-banded batfish	1·10	1·40
147	2 r. Ringed-sergeant	1·10	1·40
148	2 r. Lined butterflyfish and Meyer's butterflyfish	1·10	1·40

Nos. 144/8 were printed together, se-tenant, forming a composite design.

1987. Trees. Multicoloured.

149	1 r. Type **23**	80	80
150	2 r. Mangrove	1·40	1·75
151	3 r. Pandanus palm	2·00	2·50
152	5 r. Indian almond	3·00	3·25

1987. Giant Tortoises of Aldabra (2nd series). Designs as Nos. 120/3 but without circular inscr around W.W.F. emblem. Multicoloured.

153	50 c. As Type **18**	1·75	1·75
154	75 c. Giant tortoises at pool	2·50	2·50
155	1 r. Giant tortoises on grassland	3·50	3·50
156	2 r. Giant tortoise (side view)	4·50	4·50

1987. Royal Ruby Wedding. Nos. 128/32 optd **40TH WEDDING ANNIVERSARY**.

157	75 c. Princess Elizabeth at Chester, 1951	20	20
158	1 r. Queen and Duke of Edinburgh at Falklands Service, St. Paul's Cathedral, 1985	25	25
159	1 r. 50 At Order of St. Michael and St. George service, St. Paul's Cathedral, 1968	35	40
160	3 r. 75 In Mexico, 1975	50	90
161	5 r. At Crown Agents Head Office, London, 1983	60	1·25

24 "Vallee de Mai" (Christine Harter)

1987. Tourism. Multicoloured.
162 3 r. Type **24** . . . . 2·00 1·60
163 3 r. Ferns . . . . 2·00 1·60
164 3 r. Bamboo . . . . 2·00 1·60
Nos. 162/4 were printed together, se-tenant, forming a composite picture.

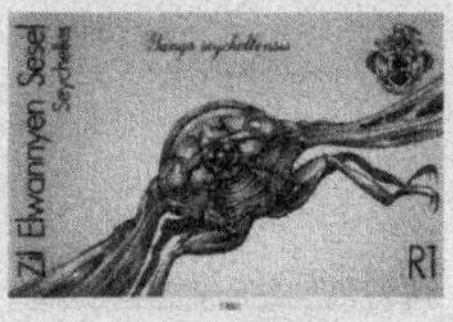

25 "Yanga seychellensis" (beetle)

1988. Insects. Multicoloured.
180 1 r. Type **25** . . . . 1·00 80
181 2 r. "Belenois aldabraensis" (butterfly) . . . . 1·75 1·40
182 3 r. "Polyspilota seychelliana" (mantid) . . . . 2·00 2·00
183 5 r. "Polposipus herculeanus" (beetle) . . . . 2·50 2·75

1988. 300th Anniv of Lloyd's of London. As T **123** of Ascension. Multicoloured.
185 1 r. Modern Lloyd's Building, London 70 55
186 2 r. "Retriever" (cable ship) (horiz) . . . . 1·00 90
187 3 r. "Chantel" (fishing boat) (horiz) . . . . 1·75 1·40
188 5 r. Wreck of "Torrey Canyon" (tanker), Cornwall, 1967 . . 2·25 1·75

27 "Father Christmas landing with Presents" (Jean-Claude Boniface)

1988. Christmas. Children's Paintings. Mult.
189 1 r. Type **27** 35 35
190 2 r. "Church" (Francois Barra) (vert) 60 60
191 3 r. "Father Christmas flying on Bird" (Wizy Ernesta) (vert) . 85 85
192 5 r. "Father Christmas in Sleigh over Island" (Federic Lang) 1·40 1·40

1989. 20th Anniv of First Manned Landing on Moon. As T **126** of Ascension. Multicoloured.
193 1 r. Firing Room, Launch Control Centre 80 80
194 2 r. Crews of "Apollo–Soyuz" mission (30 × 30 mm) . . . 1·25 1·25
195 3 r. "Apollo–Soyuz" emblem (30 × 30 mm) . . . . . . 1·60 1·75
196 5 r. "Apollo" and "Soyuz" docking in space . . . . . 2·25 2·50

28 Dumb Cane **29** Tec-Tec Broth

1989. Poisonous Plants (1st series). Mult.
198 1 r. Type **28** . . . . 1·50 1·50
199 2 r. Star of Bethlehem . . . . 2·00 2·00
200 3 r. Indian liquorice . . . . . 2·25 2·25
201 5 r. Black nightshade . . . . 3·25 3·25
See also Nos. 214/17.

1989. Creole Cooking. Multicoloured.
202 1 r. Type **29** . . . . 1·50 1·50
203 2 r. Pilaff a la Seychelloise . . 2·00 2·00
204 3 r. Mullet grilled in banana leaves . . . . 2·25 2·25
205 5 r. Daube . . . . 3·25 3·25

30 1980 Marine Life 5 r. Stamp

1990. "Stamp World London 90" International Stamp Exhibition. Showing stamps. Mult.
207 1 r. Type **30** . . . . 1·50 1·50
208 2 r. 1980 5 r. definitive . . . . 2·00 2·00
209 3 r. 1983 2 r. 75 definitive . . . 2·25 2·25
210 5 r. 1981 Wildlife 5 r. . . . . . 3·25 3·25

1990. 90th Birthday of Queen Elizabeth the Queen Mother. As T **134** of Ascension.
212 2 r. multicoloured . . . . . 1·75 1·75
213 10 r. black and brown . . . . 3·50 4·25
DESIGNS—21 × 36 mm: 2 r. Duchess of York with baby Princess Elizabeth, 1926. 29 × 37 mm: 10 r. King George VI and Queen Elizabeth visiting bombed district, London, 1940.

1990. Poisonous Plants (2nd series). As T **28**. Multicoloured.
214 1 r. Ordeal plant . . . . . . 1·50 1·50
215 2 r. Thorn apple . . . . . . 2·00 2·00
216 3 r. Strychnine tree . . . . . 2·25 2·25
217 5 r. Bwa zasmen . . . . . . 3·25 3·25

1991. 65th Birthday of Queen Elizabeth II and 70th Birthday of Prince Philip. As T **139** of Ascension. Multicoloured.
234 4 r. Queen Elizabeth II . . . 1·60 1·75
235 4 r. Prince Philip . . . . . . 1·60 1·75

31 "St. Abbs" (full-rigged ship), 1860

1991. Shipwrecks. Multicoloured.
236 1 r. 50 Type **31** . . . . 1·75 1·75
237 3 r. "Norden" (barque), 1862 2·25 2·25
238 3 r. 50 "Clan Mackay" (freighter), 1894 . . . . . 2·50 2·50
239 10 r. "Glenlyon" (freighter), 1905 6·00 7·00

1992. 40th Anniv of Queen Elizabeth II's Accession. As T **143** of Ascension. Mult.
240 1 r. Beach 75 75
241 1 r. 50 Aerial view of Desroches 1·10 1·25
242 3 r. Tree-covered coastline . . 1·50 1·75
243 3 r. 50 Three portraits of Queen Elizabeth II . . . . 1·60 1·90
244 5 r. Queen Elizabeth II . . . 1·75 2·25

32 "Lomatopyllum aldabrense" (plant)

1992. 10th Anniv of Aldabra as a World Heritage Site. Multicoloured.
245 1 r. 50 Type **32** . . . . . . 1·25 1·25
246 3 r. White-throated rail . . . 2·75 2·75
247 3 r. 50 Robber crab . . . . . 2·50 2·50
248 10 r. Aldabra drongo . . . . 7·00 8·00

ZIMBABWE

Rhodesia became independent on 18 April 1980 and was renamed Zimbabwe.

100 cents = 1 dollar

113 Morganite **114** Rotary Anniversary Emblem

1980. As Nos. 555/69 of Rhodesia and new value inscr "ZIMBABWE".
576 1 c. Type **113** 20 30
577 3 c. Amethyst 30 30
578 4 c. Garnet 30 10
579 5 c. Citrine 35 10
580 7 c. Blue topaz 35 10
581 9 c. White rhinoceros . . . 15 10
582 11 c. Lion 15 15
583 13 c. Warthog 15 15
584 15 c. Giraffe 15 20
585 17 c. Common zebra 15 20
586 21 c. Odzani Falls 20 25
587 25 c. Goba Falls 25 30
588 30 c. Inyangombi Falls . . . 30 50
588a 40 c. Bundi Falls . . . . . 6·00 4·50
589 $1 Bridal Veil Falls . . . . 50 2·00
590 $2 Victoria Falls . . . . . . 75 3·75

1980. 75th Anniv of Rotary International.
591 **114** 4 c. multicoloured 10 10
592 13 c. multicoloured 15 30
593 21 c. multicoloured 20 55
594 25 c. multicoloured . . . 20 80

115 Olympic Rings

1980. Olympic Games, Moscow.
596 **115** 17 c. multicoloured 30 40

116 Gatooma Post Office, 1912

1980. 75th Anniv of Post Office Savings Bank.
597 **116** 5 c. black and brown . . . 10 10
598 – 7 c. black and orange . . . 10 10
599 – 9 c. black and yellow . . . 10 10
600 – 17 c. black and white . . . 25 25
DESIGNS: 7 c. Salisbury Post Office, 1912; 9 c. Umtali Post Office, 1901; 17 c. Bulawayo Post Office, 1895.

117 Stylised Blind Person **118** Msasa

1981. Int Year of Disabled Persons. Mult.
602 5 c. Type **117** 15 10
603 7 c. Deaf person 15 10
604 11 c. Person with one leg . . . 20 15
605 17 c. Person with one arm . . 25 35

1981. National Tree Day. Multicoloured.
606 5 c. Type **118** 10 10
607 7 c. Mopane 15 15
608 21 c. Flat-crowned acacia . . . 45 85
609 30 c. Pod mahogany . . . . . 60 1·40

119 Painting from Gwamgwadza Cave, Mtoko Area **120** Scout Emblem

1982. Rock Paintings. Multicoloured.
610 9 c. Type **119** 75 20
611 11 c. Epworth Mission, near Harare . . . . 1·00 20
612 17 c. Diana's Vow, near Harare 1·00 65
613 21 c. Gwamgwadza Cave, Mtoko Area (different) . . . . . 1·40 1·25
614 25 c. Mucheka Cave, Msana Communal Land . . . . . 1·75 2·00
615 30 c. Chinzwini Shelter, Chiredzi Area . . . . 2·00 2·25

1982. 75th Anniv of Boy Scout Movement. Multicoloured.
616 9 c. Type **120** 35 15
617 11 c. Scouts around campfire . 35 15
618 21 c. Scouts map-reading . . . 55 1·25
619 30 c. Lord Baden-Powell . . . 65 2·00

121 Dr. Robert Koch **122** "Wing Woman" (Henry Mudzengerere)

1982. Centenary of Dr. Robert Koch's Discovery of Tubercle Bacillus.
620 **121** 11 c. orange, black and grey 85 25
621 – 30 c. multicoloured . . . . 1·40 3·25
DESIGN: 30 c. Man looking through microscope.

1983. Commonwealth Day. Sculptures. Multicoloured.
622 9 c. Type **122** 10 10
623 11 c. "Telling Secrets" (Joseph Ndandarika) (horiz) . . . 10 10
624 30 c. "Hornbill Man" (John Takawira) (horiz) 20 45
625 $1 "The Child" (Nicholas Mukomberanwa) . . . . . 55 1·75

123 Traditional Ploughing Team (moving right)

1983. World Ploughing Contest. Mult.
626 21 c. Type **123** 25 35
627 21 c. Traditional ploughing team (moving left) 25 35
628 30 c. Tractor ploughing . . . 40 65
629 30 c. Modern plough 40 65
The two designs of each value were issued in horizontal se-tenant pairs, forming composite designs.

124 Postman on Cycle **125** Map of Africa showing Zimbabwe

1983. World Communications Year. Mult.
630 9 c. Type **124** 20 10
631 11 c. Aircraft controller directing airliner 25 10
632 15 c. Switchboard operator . . 30 30
633 17 c. Printing works 35 30
634 21 c. Road transport (horiz) . . 50 60
635 30 c. Rail transport (horiz) . . 75 1·25

1984. Zimbabwe Int Trade Fair, 1984. Mult.
636 9 c. Type **125** 10 10
637 11 c. Globe 15 10
638 30 c. Zimbabwe flag and Trade Fair logo 45 50

126 Cycling

1984. Olympic Games, Los Angeles. Children's Pictures. Multicoloured.
639 11 c. Type **126** 35 15
640 21 c. Swimming 45 50
641 30 c. Running 65 85
642 40 c. Hurdling . . . . 80 1·75

127 Liberation Heroes **128** African Fish Eagle

1984. Heroes' Day. Multicoloured.
643 9 c. Type **127** 25 10
644 11 c. Symbolic tower and flame (vert) 25 10
645 17 c. Bronze sculpture (vert) . 40 60
646 30 c. Section of bronze mural . 55 95
DESIGNS: 9 c. to 30 c. Various aspects of Heroes' Acre.

1984. Birds of Prey. Multicoloured.
647 9 c. Type **128** 50 20
648 11 c. Long-crested eagle . . . 50 20
649 13 c. Bateleur 65 55
650 17 c. Verreaux's eagle 80 55
651 21 c. Martial eagle . . . . . 90 1·40
652 30 c. Bonelli's eagle . . . . . 1·25 2·25

INDEX

Countries can be quickly located by referring to the index at the end of this volume.

129 9th Class Locomotive No. 86

1985. "Zimbabwe Steam Safaris". Railway Locomotives. Multicoloured.

653	9 c. Type **129**	85	20
654	11 c. 12th Class locomotive No. 190	85	20
655	17 c. 15th Class Beyer-Garratt locomotive No. 424 "Isilwane"	1·50	1·00
656	30 c. 20th Class Garratt locomotive No. 726 "Gwaai"	2·50	3·00

130 "Intelsat V" Telecommunications Satellite

131 Tobacco

1985. Earth Satellite Station, Mazowe. Multicoloured.

657	26 c. Type **130**	1·50	60
658	57 c. Earth Satellite Station, Mazowe (65 × 25 mm)	3·00	6·00

1985. National Infrastructure. Multicoloured.

659	1 c. Type **131**	10	10
660	3 c. Maize	10	10
661	4 c. Cotton	15	10
662	5 c. Tea	30	10
663	10 c. Cattle	20	10
664	11 c. Birchenough Bridge	75	10
665	12 c. Ore stamp mill	1·25	10
666	13 c. Gold pouring	2·00	15
667	15 c. Dragline coal mining	1·50	15
668	17 c. Uncut amethyst	2·25	40
669	18 c. Electric locomotive	2·25	30
670	20 c. Kariba Dam	1·50	15
671	23 c. Elephants at water hole	2·00	45
672	25 c. Sunset over Zambezi	65	30
673	26 c. Baobab tree	65	20
674	30 c. Ruins of Great Zimbabwe	75	50
675	35 c. Traditional dancing	60	30
676	45 c. Village women crushing maize	75	40
677	57 c. Woodcarving	75	70
678	$1 Playing Mbira (musical instrument)	1·25	90
679	$2 Mule-drawn Scotch cart	2·00	3·00
680	$5 Zimbabwe coat-of-arms	3·75	5·50

132 Chief Mutapa Gatsi Rusere and 17th-century Seal

1985. 50th Anniv of National Archives. Multicoloured.

681	12 c. Type **132**	20	15
682	18 c. Chief Lobengula, seal and 1888 Treaty	25	40
683	26 c. Exhibition gallery	35	45
684	35 c. National Archives building	45	75

133 Computer Operator

1985. U.N. Decade for Women. Mult.

685	10 c. Type **133**	40	10
686	17 c. Nurse giving injection	75	70
687	26 c. Woman student	1·25	2·50

134 Harare Conference Centre

1986. Harare Int Conference Centre. Mult.

688	26 c. Type **134**	60	30
689	35 c. Interior of conference hall	1·00	1·40

135 Grain Storage Silo

1986. 6th Anniv of Southern African Development Co-ordination Conference. Multicoloured.

690	12 c. Type **135**	55	20
691	18 c. Rhinoceros and hawk at sunset	2·50	1·50
692	26 c. Map showing S.A.D.C.C. member states and Boeing 737	2·50	2·00
693	35 c. Map and national flags of S.A.D.C.C. members	2·75	2·25

136 "Bunaeopsis jacksoni"

1986. Moths of Zimbabwe. Multicoloured.

694	12 c. Type **136**	1·10	20
695	18 c. "Deilephila nerii"	1·60	1·10
696	26 c. "Bunaeopsis zaddachi"	2·00	1·50
697	35 c. "Heniocha apollonia"	2·40	4·25

137 Victoria Falls

1986. 8th Non-Aligned Summit Conference. Multicoloured.

698	26 c. Type **137**	1·75	30
699	$1 Ruins of Great Zimbabwe (62 × 24 mm)	4·25	5·50

138 Sopwith Motorcycle (1921)

1986. Centenary of Motoring. Multicoloured.

700	10 c. Type **138**	65	10
701	12 c. Gladiator motor car (1902)	65	30
702	17 c. Douglas motorcycle (1920)	1·00	40
703	26 c. Ford "Model A" (1930)	1·40	70
704	35 c. Schacht motor car (1909)	1·75	2·25
705	40 c. Benz three-wheeled car (1886)	1·75	2·25

139 Growth Monitoring

140 Barred Owlet

1987. Child Survival Campaign. Mult.

706	12 c. Type **139**	1·50	1·75
707	12 c. Breast-feeding	1·50	1·75
708	12 c. Oral rehydration therapy	1·50	1·75
709	12 c. Immunization	1·50	1·75

1987. Owls (1st series). Multicoloured.

710	12 c. Type **140**	2·00	30
711	18 c. Pearl-spotted owlet	2·50	1·25
712	26 c. White-faced scops owl	3·00	1·75
713	35 c. African scops owl	4·00	4·50

See also Nos. 850/3.

141 Brownie, Guide and Ranger saluting ("Commitment")

1987. 75th Anniv of Girl Guides Association of Zimbabwe. Multicoloured.

714	15 c. Type **141**	55	15
715	23 c. Guides preparing meal over campfire ("Adventure")	75	30
716	35 c. Guide teaching villagers to read ("Service")	85	45
717	$1 Handshake and globe ("International Friendship")	2·00	3·00

142 Common Grey Duiker

144 "Cockerel" (Arthur Azevedo)

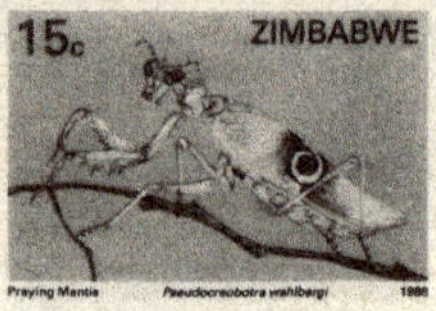

143 "Pseudocreobotra wahlberghi" (mantid)

1987. Duikers of Africa Survey. Mult.

718	15 c. Type **142**	70	15
719	23 c. Zebra duiker	80	25
720	25 c. Yellow-backed duiker	80	90
721	30 c. Blue duiker	95	1·10
722	35 c. Jentink's duiker	95	1·25
723	38 c. Red duiker	1·00	1·75

1988. Insects. Multicoloured.

724	15 c. Type **143**	70	15
725	23 c. "Dicranorrhia derbyana" (beetle)	85	30
726	35 c. "Dictyophorus spumans" (grasshopper)	1·10	85
727	45 c. "Chalcocoris rutilus" (bug)	1·40	2·00

1988. 30th Anniv of National Gallery of Zimbabwe. Designs showing painting (38 c.) or sculptures (others). Multicoloured.

728	15 c. Type **144**	20	10
729	23 c. "Man into Hippo" (Bernard Matemera)	30	20
730	30 c. "Spirit Python" (Henry Munyaradzi)	35	30
731	35 c. "Spirit Bird carrying People" (Thomas Mukarobgwa) (horiz)	35	30
732	38 c. "The Song of the Herd Boy" (George Nene) (horiz)	35	40
733	45 c. "War Victim" (Joseph Muzondo) (horiz)	40	50

145 "Aloe cameronii var. bondana"

146 White-faced Whistling Duck

1988. Aloes. Multicoloured.

734	15 c. Type **145**	20	10
735	23 c. "Orbeopsis caudata"	35	20
736	25 c. "Euphorbia wildii"	35	35
737	30 c. "Euphorbia fortissima"	40	45
738	35 c. "Aloe aculeata"	40	55
739	38 c. "Huernia zebrina"	45	70

1988. Wild Ducks and Geese of Zimbabwe. Multicoloured.

740	15 c. Type **146**	65	20
741	23 c. African pygmy goose	75	20
742	30 c. Hottentot teal	85	85
743	35 c. Comb duck ("Knob-billed duck")	95	95
744	38 c. White-backed duck	95	1·00
745	45 c. Maccoa duck	1·40	2·00

147 O'Shaughnessy's Banded Gecko

148 Spotted Leaved Arum-Lily

1989. Geckos. Multicoloured.

746	15 c. Type **147**	70	15
747	23 c. Tiger rock gecko	85	40
748	35 c. Tasman's gecko	1·25	1·25
749	45 c. Bibron's gecko	1·50	2·00

1989. Wild Flowers. Multicoloured.

750	15 c. Type **148**	35	10
751	23 c. Grassland vlei-lily	45	25
752	30 c. Manica protea	45	40
753	35 c. Flame lily	50	40
754	38 c. Poppy hibiscus	55	55
755	45 c. Blue sesbania	65	65

149 Red-breasted Tilapia

1989. Fishes (1st series). Multicoloured.

756	15 c. Type **149**	60	15
757	25 c. Chessa	80	25
758	30 c. Eastern bottlenose	90	70
759	35 c. Vundu	90	70
760	38 c. Large-mouthed black bass	1·00	1·00
761	45 c. Lesser tigerfish	1·40	1·75

See also Nos. 864/9.

150 Black Rhinoceros

1989. Endangered Species. Multicoloured.

762	15 c. Type **150**	1·25	40
763	23 c. Cheetah	1·25	45
764	30 c. Wild dog	1·40	90
765	35 c. Pangolin	1·40	1·25
766	38 c. Brown hyena	1·50	2·00
767	45 c. Roan antelope	1·60	2·25

151 Giant Tigerfish

152 Headrest

153 Bicycles

1990. Multicoloured. (a) Wildlife. As T **151**.

768	1 c. Type **151**	15	10
769	2 c. Helmet guineafowl	20	10
770	3 c. Scrub hare	20	10
771	4 c. Temminck's ground pangolin	20	10
772	5 c. Greater kudu	30	10
773	9 c. Black rhinoceros	50	30

(b) Cultural Artifacts. As T **152**.

774	15 c. Type **152**	20	20
775	20 c. Hand axe and adze	20	20
776	23 c. Gourd and water pot	20	20
777	25 c. Snuff container	20	20
778	26 c. Winnowing tray and basket	20	20
779	30 c. Grinding stone	30	30

(c) Transport. As T **153**.

780	33 c. Type **153**	40	30
781	35 c. Buses	70	40
782	38 c. Diesel train	70	40
783	45 c. Mail motorcycle and trailer	70	40
784	$1 Air Zimbabwe Boeing 737 airliner	1·50	90
785	$2 Lorry	1·50	1·60

154 Pres. Mugabe and Joshua Nkomo at Signing of Unity Accord, 1987

1990. 10th Anniv of Independence. Mult.

786	15 c. Type **154**	40	10
787	23 c. Conference Centre, Harare	45	20
788	30 c. Children in class	50	40
789	35 c. Intelsat aerial, Mazowe Earth Satellite Station	60	70
790	38 c. National Sports Stadium	60	80
791	45 c. Maize field	90	1·40

155 Runhare House, 1986

1990. Cent of the City of Harare. Mult.

792	15 c. Type **155**	30	10
793	23 c. Market Hall, 1894	50	20
794	30 c. Charter House, 1959	55	35
795	35 c. Supreme Court, 1927	60	80
796	38 c. Standard Chartered Bank, 1911	60	90
797	45 c. The Town House, 1933	80	1·40

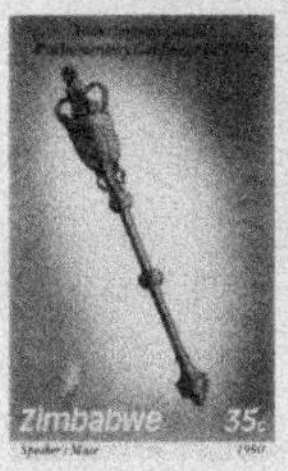
156 Speaker's Mace

157 Small-spotted Genet

1990. 36th Commonwealth Parliamentary Conference, Harare. Multicoloured.

798	35 c. Type **156**	50	25
799	$1 Speaker's chair	1·25	2·00

1991. Small Mammals. Multicoloured.

800	15 c. Type **157**	80	20
801	23 c. Red squirrel	85	30
802	35 c. Night-ape	1·25	1·25
803	45 c. Bat-eared fox	1·75	2·25

158 Hosho (rattles)

159 Snot-apple

1991. Traditional Musical Instruments. Mult.

804	15 c. Type **158**	45	10
805	23 c. Mbira (thumb piano)	50	15
806	30 c. Ngororombe (pan pipes)	55	40
807	35 c. Chipendani (mouth bow)	65	70
808	38 c. Marimba (xylophone)	65	80
809	45 c. Ngoma (drum)	75	1·10

1991. Wild Fruits. Multicoloured.

810	20 c. Type **159**	50	10
811	39 c. Marula	50	30
812	51 c. Mobola plum	60	80
813	60 c. Water berry	70	85
814	65 c. Northern dwaba berry	75	85
815	77 c. Mahobohobo	85	1·10

160 Bridal Veil Falls

162 "Amanita zambiana"

161 Lion

1991. Commonwealth Heads of Government Meeting, Harare. Multicoloured.

816	20 c. Type **160**	55	15
817	39 c. Meeting logo	55	35
818	51 c. Chinhoyi Caves	70	75
819	60 c. Kariba Dam	80	1·00
820	65 c. Victoria Falls	90	1·25
821	77 c. Balancing rocks	95	1·50

1992. Wildlife Conservation. Big Cats. Mult.

822	20 c. Type **161**	65	15
823	39 c. Leopard	95	40
824	60 c. Cheetah	1·40	1·75
825	77 c. Serval	1·75	2·00

1992. Edible Mushrooms. Multicoloured.

826	20 c. Type **162**	50	20
827	39 c. "Boletus edulis"	70	40
828	51 c. "Termitomyces sp."	75	75
829	60 c. "Cantharellus densifolius"	90	1·00
830	65 c. "Cantharellus longisporus"	1·00	1·25
831	77 c. "Cantharellus cibarius"	1·25	1·50

163 Common Bulbul

164 "Charaxes jasius"

1992. Birds. Multicoloured.

832	25 c. Type **163**	45	15
833	59 c. Fiscal shrike	65	45
834	77 c. Forktailed drongo	75	80
835	90 c. Cardinal woodpecker	80	95
836	98 c. Yellow-billed hornbill	80	95
837	$1.16 Crested francolin	95	1·40

1992. Butterflies. Multicoloured.

838	25 c. Type **164**	75	20
839	59 c. "Eronia leda"	1·25	75
840	77 c. "Princeps ophidicephalus"	1·50	1·25
841	90 c. "Junonia oenone"	1·75	1·75
842	98 c. "Danaus chrysippus"	1·90	1·90
843	$1.16 "Junonia octavia"	2·00	2·25

165 Uranium

1993. Minerals. Multicoloured.

844	25 c. Type **165**	60	20
845	59 c. Chrome	90	55
846	77 c. Copper	1·25	1·00
847	90 c. Coal	1·50	1·50
848	98 c. Gold	1·75	1·75
849	$1.16 Emerald	1·90	2·25

1993. Owls (2nd series). As T **140**. Mult.

850	25 c. African wood owl	1·00	30
851	59 c. Pel's fishing owl	1·75	65
852	90 c. Spotted eagle owl	2·50	2·50
853	$1.16 Verreaux's eagle owl ("Giant Eagle Owl")	2·75	3·25

166 Hadyana (relish pot)

167 "Polystachya dendrobiflora"

1993. Household Pottery. Multicoloured.

854	25 c. Type **166**	40	10
855	59 c. Chirongo (water jar)	55	30
856	77 c. Mbiya (relish bowl)	65	60
857	90 c. Pfuko (water jar)	75	85
858	98 c. Tsaya (cooking pot)	75	85
859	$1.16 Gate (beer pot)	85	1·00

1993. Orchids. Multicoloured.

860	35 c. Type **167**	65	20
861	$1 "Diaphananthe subsimplex"	1·25	75
862	$1.50 "Ansellia gigantea"	1·75	1·90
863	$1.95 "Vanilla polyepis"	2·00	2·50

1994. Fishes (2nd series). As T **149**. Mult.

864	35 c. Manyame labeo ("Hunyani salmon")	30	10
865	$1 Sharp-toothed catfish ("Barbel")	55	30
866	$1.30 Rainbow trout	65	65
867	$1.50 African mottled eel	70	70
868	$1.65 Common carp	75	85
869	$1.95 Nembwe ("Robustus bream")	85	1·00

168 City Hall, 1940

1994. Centenary of Bulawayo. Multicoloured.

870	35 c. Type **168**	15	10
871	80 c. Cresta Churchill Hotel, 1974	30	20
872	$1.15 High Court, 1938	40	40
873	$1.75 Douslin House, 1902	50	70
874	$1.95 Goldfields Building, 1895	60	90
875	$2.30 Parkade Centre, 1975	85	1·25

169 Strelitzia

170 The Annunciation

1994. Export Flowers. Multicoloured.

876	35 c. Type **169**	30	10
877	80 c. Protea	55	25
878	$1.15 Phlox	70	50
879	$1.75 Chrysanthemum	80	90
880	$1.95 Ullum	1·00	1·25
881	$2.30 Rose	1·25	1·75

1994. Christmas. Multicoloured.

882	35 c. Type **170**	25	10
883	80 c. Journey to Bethlehem	40	15
884	$1.15 The Nativity	55	40
885	$1.75 Shepherds	75	90
886	$1.95 Wise Men	85	1·10
887	$2.30 Mary and Jesus	95	1·40

171 Harvesting Maize

173 Football

172 Spider-hunting Wasp

1995. Zimbabwe Culture. Multicoloured.

888	1 c. Type **171**	10	10
889	2 c. Loading sugar cane	10	10
890	3 c. Sunflowers	10	10
891	4 c. Sorghum	10	10
892	5 c. Miners	10	10
893	10 c. Drilling for gold	10	10
894	20 c. Opencast coal mining, Wankie	10	10
895	30 c. Chrome smelting, Kwekwe	10	10
896	40 c. Opencast iron extraction, Redcliff	10	10
896a	45 c. Underground mining team	10	10
897	50 c. Gold smelting	10	10
898	70 c. Bogie Clock Tower, Gweru	10	10
899	80 c. Masvingo Watchtower	10	10
900	$1 Hanging Tree, Harare	10	10
901	$2 Cecil House, Harare	10	10
902	$5 The Toposcope, Harare	15	20
903	$10 Paper House, Kwekwe	30	35

1995. Insects. Multicoloured.

904	35 c. Type **172**	30	10
905	$1.15 European dragonfly	70	45
906	$1.75 Foxy charaxes (butterfly)	90	1·00
907	$2.30 Antlion	1·25	1·75

1995. 6th All-Africa Games, Harare. Each showing sport within map of Africa. Multicoloured.

908	35 c. Type **173**	20	10
909	80 c. Running	30	20
910	$1.15 Boxing	35	30
911	$1.75 Swimming	50	50
912	$1.95 Hockey	1·00	1·00
913	$2.30 Volleyball	1·00	1·40

174 Weighing Baby (Health)

175 Fernandoa Tree

1995. 50th Anniv of United Nations. Multicoloured.

914	35 c. Type **174**	15	10
915	$1.15 Women at pump (Environment)	30	30
916	$1.75 Workers on lorry (Food distribution)	50	55
917	$2.30 Teacher and children (Education)	60	75

1996. Indigenous Flowering Trees. Multicoloured.

918	45 c. Type **175**	15	10
919	$1 Round leaf mukwa	30	20
920	$1.50 Luckybean ree	45	45
921	$2.20 Winter cassia	60	65
922	$2.50 Sausage tree	65	70
923	$3 Sweet thorn	75	85

176 Mazvikadei Dam

1996. Dams of Zimbabwe. Multicoloured.

924	45 c. Type **176**	15	10
925	$1.50 Mutirikwi Dam	45	35
926	$2.20 Ncema Dam	65	70
927	$3 Odzani Dam	75	90

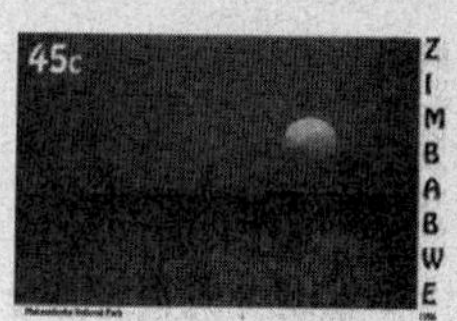
177 Matusadonha National Park at Sunset

1996. Scenic Views. Multicoloured.

928	45 c. Type **177**	15	10
929	$1.50 Juliasdale rocky outcrop	45	35
930	$2.20 Honde Valley	75	85
931	$3 Finger Rocks at Morgenster Mission	85	1·25

178 Carved Frog

1996. Animal Wood Carvings. Multicoloured.

932	45 c. Type **178**	15	10
933	$1.50 Tortoise	30	20
934	$1.70 Kudu	35	35
935	$2.20 Chimpanzee	50	55
936	$2.50 Porcupine	55	60
937	$3 Rhinoceros	60	70

179 Mashona Cow

1997. Cattle Breeds. Multicoloured.

938	45 c. Type **179**	15	10
939	$1.50 Tuli cow	30	15
940	$2.20 Nkoni bull	45	45
941	$3 Brahman bull	60	70

180 Cycad

1997. 10th Meeting of Convention on International Trade in Endangered Species Members, Harare. Multicoloured.

942	45 c. Type **180**	10	10
943	$1.50 Peregrine falcon	40	30
944	$1.70 Temminck's ground pangolin	30	30
945	$2.20 Black rhinoceros	50	50
946	$2.50 African elephant	50	50
947	$3 Python	50	60

181 Wood Carving

1997. Rural Life. Multicoloured.

948	65 c. Type **181**	15	10
949	$1 Winnowing	15	10
950	$2.40 Dancing	25	25
951	$2.50 Ploughing	25	25
952	$3.10 Stamping cereals	30	35
953	$4.20 Fetching water	40	45

ZIMBABWE

182 Passenger Coach No. 1826

1997. Centenary of Zimbabwe Railways. Mult.

954	65 c. Type **182**	15	15
955	$1 Class 12 steam locomotive No. 257	15	15
956	$2.40 Class 16A steam locomotive No. 605	20	20
957	$2.50 Class EL 1 electric locomotive No. 4107	20	20
958	$3.10 Steam locomotive No. 7 "Jack Tar"	25	25
959	$4.20 Class DE 2 diesel-electric locomotive No. 1211	30	40

183 Aardwolf

1998. Lesser Known Animals of Zimbabwe. Multicoloured.

960	65 c. Type **183**	15	10
961	$2.40 Large grey mongoose	20	20
962	$3.10 Clawless otter	20	20
963	$4.20 Antbear	25	30

184 Honeybee on Flower

186 Yellow-bellied Sunbird

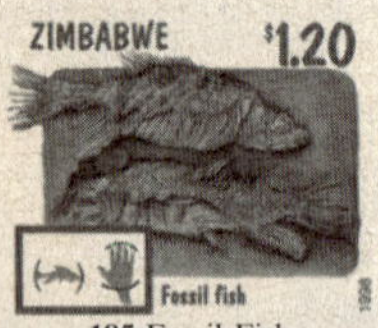

185 Fossil Fish

1998. Bees and Bee-keeping. Multicoloured.

964	$1.20 Type **184**	15	10
965	$4.10 Queen, worker and drone	20	20
966	$4.70 Queen and retinue	20	20
967	$5.60 Rural bee-keeper	25	25
968	$7.40 Commercial bee-keepers	35	40
969	$9.90 Products of the hive	45	50

1998. Fossils. Multicoloured.

970	$1.20 Type **185**	15	10
971	$5.60 Allosaurus footprints	35	35
972	$7.40 Left foot of Massospondylus	40	40
973	$9.90 Fossil wood	50	55

1998. Birds. Multicoloured.

974	$1.20 Type **186**	15	15
975	$4.10 Lesser blue-eared starling	20	20
976	$4.70 Grey-headed kingfisher ("Grey-hooded Kingfisher")	20	20
977	$5.60 Miombo grey tit	25	25
978	$7.40 Chirinda apalis	35	35
979	$9.90 Swynnerton's robin	45	45

187 Philatelic Counter

1999. 125th Anniv of U.P.U. Multicoloured.

980	$1.20 Type **187**	10	10
981	$5.60 Postman delivering letters	15	20
982	$7.40 19th-century runner, motorcycle and truck	25	30
983	$9.90 Harare Central Sorting Office	30	35

MORE DETAILED LISTS
are given in the Stanley Gibbons Catalogues referred to in the country headings.
For lists of current volumes see Introduction.

POSTAGE DUE STAMPS

D **4** Zimbabwe Bird (soapstone sculpture)

D 5

1980.

D23	D **4**	1 c. green	25	80
D24		2 c. blue	30	90
D25		5 c. violet	40	90
D26		6 c. yellow	50	1·60
D27		10 c. red	65	2·00

1985.

D28	D **5**	1 c. orange	15	40
D29		2 c. mauve	20	40
D30		6 c. green	35	55
D31		10 c. brown	40	55
D32		13 c. blue	40	55

1990. No. D27 surch **25**.

D33	D **4**	25 c. on 10 c. red	6·00	6·00

D 7

1995.

D34	D **7**	1 c. yellow	10	10
D35		2 c. orange	10	10
D36		5 c. mauve	10	10
D37		10 c. blue	10	10
D38		25 c. violet	10	10
D39		40 c. green	10	10
D40		60 c. orange	10	10
D41		$1 brown	10	10

ZULULAND

A territory of south-eastern Africa, annexed by Great Britain in 1887, and incorporated in Natal in 1897.

12 pence = 1 shilling;
20 shillings = 1 pound

1888. Stamps of Gt. Britain (Queen Victoria) optd **ZULULAND**.

1	**71**	½d. red	2·25	2·50
2	**57**	1d. lilac	24·00	3·75
3	**73**	2d. green and red	11·00	22·00
4	**74**	2½d. purple on blue	17·00	20·00
5	**75**	3d. purple on yellow	24·00	22·00
6	**76**	4d. green and brown	40·00	55·00
7	**78**	5d. purple and blue	90·00	£120
8	**79**	6d. purple on red	11·00	17·00
9	**80**	9d. purple and blue	85·00	85·00
10	**82**	1s. green	£110	£120
11	–	5s. red (No. 181)	£500	£600

1888. Natal stamps optd **ZULULAND**.

13	**23**	½d. green	22·00	35·00
16	–	6d. lilac (No. 103)	55·00	55·00

3

1894.

20	**3**	½d. mauve and green	2·50	4·25
21		1d. mauve and red	5·00	1·50
22		2½d. mauve and blue	14·00	8·00
23		3d. mauve and brown	8·00	3·00
24		6d. mauve and black	20·00	20·00
25		1s. green	35·00	38·00
26		2s. 6d. green and black	75·00	85·00
27		4s. green and red	£110	£150
28		£1 purple on red	£450	£475
29		£5 purple and black on red	£4250	£1500

ADDENDA AND CORRIGENDA

ANGUILLA

187 Saturn 5 Rocket and "Apollo 11" Command Module

1999. 30th Anniv of First Manned Landing on Moon. Multicoloured.

1031	30 c. Type **187**	15	20
1032	$1 Astronaut Edwin Aldrin, Lunar Module "Eagle" and first footprint on Moon	45	50
1033	$1.50 Lunar Module leaving Moon's surface	65	70
1034	$1.90 Recovery of Command Module	80	85

CAYMAN ISLANDS

200 "Cayman House" (Jessica Cranston)

1999. Vision 2008 Project. Children's Paintings. Multicoloured.

876	10 c. Type **200**	15	20
877	30 c. "Coral Reef" (Sarah Hetley)	40	45
878	40 c. "Fisherman on North Sound" (Sarah Cuff)	60	65
879	$2 "Three Fish and a Turtle" (Ryan Martinez)	3·00	2·25

1999. Royal Wedding. As T **185** of Ascension. Multicoloured.

880	10 c. Photographs of Prince Edward and Miss Sophie Rhys-Jones	15	20
881	$2 Engagement photograph	3·00	3·25

CYPRUS

TURKISH CYPRIOT POSTS

167 "Malpolon monspessulanus insignitus" (Montepellier)

1999. Snakes. Multicoloured.

488	50000 l. Type **167**	20	25
489	75000 l. "Hierophis jugularis"	30	35
490	195000 l. "Vipera lebetina lebetina" (levantine viper)	80	85
491	220000 l. "Natrix natrix" (grass snake)	85	90

NOTE. The first supplement containing new issues not in this catalogue or Addenda appeared in the October 1999 issue of *Gibbons Stamp Monthly*.

INDEX

Notes